THE BASEBALL ENCYCLOPEDIA

THE BASEBALL ENCYCLOPEDIA

EDITED BY **PETE PALMER** AND **GARY GILLETTE**

ASSOCIATE EDITORS **STUART SHEA, MATTHEW SILVERMAN, GREG SPIRA**
CONTRIBUTORS **BILL DEANE, SEAN LAHMAN, DOUG WHITE**

BARNES & NOBLE BOOKS
NEW YORK

A BARNES & NOBLE BOOK

Typesetting by Scribe, Inc. (www.scribenet.com)
Published by Barnes & Noble Publishing, Inc.

ISBN 0-7607-5349-0

Printed in U.S.A. by Von Hoffmann

1 3 5 7 9 10 8 6 4 2

Dedication

Dedicated to the hundreds of good people—many unsung and the large majority of them amateurs—whose selfless efforts have given our National Game the richest patrimony of all: a vibrant and gloriously detailed historical tapestry woven with thread spun from painstakingly scrupulous research.

—Gary Gillette

Dedicated to two friends, now gone, who showed me when I was young that there was nothing wrong with maintaining my fascination with baseball as an adult—my English teacher from Mount Hermon, Jack Baldwin, and my fellow engineer at Raytheon, Mason Huse.

—Pete Palmer

Acknowledgments

No baseball encyclopedia could be prepared without the assistance of many others in the field. The editors hereby extend their appreciation for many different favors—some small, some large—to the honor roll of kind people listed below:

Jim Albright, David Avins, Stephen Bannen, Evelyn Begley, Greg Beston, Cliff Blau, Arnie Braunstein, Jeffrey Burk, Bill Carle, Jim Callis, Andy Clarke, Clem Comly, Clay Davenport, Merl DeMoll, Dan Dischley, Beth Dowd, Jeff Elijah, Sean Forman, Jim Furtado, Steve Geitscher, Ray Gonzalez, Gary Hailey, Layton Hall, Hank Hammer, Chris Hand, Ed Hartig, Bill Hickman, Howard Hilton, Bob Hoie, Dan Holmes, Sean Holtz, David Horwich, Frederick Ivor-Campbell, Jonathan Jacobs, Jay Jaffe, Bill James, Mark Jareb, Chris Kahrl, Jonah Keri, Dave Kirsch, Herm Krabbenhoft, David Kronheim, Leonte Landino, Fred Lenger, Rich Malatzky, Steve Mann, Kenneth Matinale, Bob McConnell, Trent McCotter, Wayne McElreavy, Bill McNeil, Andrew Milner, Bill Moose, Peter Morris, Rod Nelson, Rob Neyer, David Nemec, Bill Nowlin, John O'Malley, Marc Okkonen, Mat Olkin, Phyllis Otto, Doug Pappas, Paul Parker, David Pease, Fred Percival, Bob Richardson, Tom Ruane, Mike Sandler, Michael Schell, David Schoenfield, John Schwartz, Alan Schwarz, Ron Shandler, Joseph Sheehan, Tom Shieber, Nate Silver, Joe Simenic, Dave Smith, Lyle Spatz, Ted Spencer, Dave Statz, Mike Statz, Marc Stephenson, Chuck Stevens, John Thorn, Bob Tiemann, Tom Tippett, Stephen Tomlinson, Wayne Townsend, Neal Traven, Jules Tygiel, Dixie Tourangeau, Frank Vaccaro, John Vaughan, David Vincent, Bill Way, Joe Wayman, Royce Webb, Jim Weigand, Dave Weiner, Paul Wendt, Frank Williams, Walt Wilson, Michael Wolverton, Keith Woolner, John Zajc, Larry Zuckerman. Special thanks go to David Pietrusza and Peter Bird for their assistance and advice.

Every baseball encyclopedia involves a huge amount of complicated design, typesetting, and editorial work. In our case, we are truly blessed to have collaborated with Andy Brown, Heath Missimer, and David Rech of Scribe in Philadelphia. We are indebted to Nathaniel Marunas, our editor at Barnes & Noble, and also very grateful for the support of B&N President and CEO Steve Riggio and B&N Publishing President Alan Kahn. Kudos to creative director Jeff Batzli; art director Kevin Ullrich; designer Kevin Baier; designer Christine Heun; photo researcher Lori Epstein; and production manager Michael Vagnetti. As Yogi might say, we look forward with great anticipation to working with all of them on future editions.

Finally, as anyone who has ever worked on a book of this scope knows, it never seems to get done without interfering with life outside the project. To call spouses "baseball widows" would do them a serious disservice, since they have often made valuable contributions quite aside from attending to family during the stretch drive. Vicki Gillette, Beth Palmer, Cecilia Garibay, Debbie Silverman, and Anita White deserve our love and gratitude for their support and their patience.

Table of Contents

INTRODUCTION

The past is never dead. It's not even past. —*William Faulkner*

Faulkner penned that memorable line in 1951. Though the titan of American letters was not talking about the National Pastime, his apt turn of phrase would serve well as a requiem for thousands big league ballplayers. Most of them are long past playing, but their exploits live on in the pages of this book as well as in the hearts and memories of uncounted millions of baseball fans worldwide.

Baseball in 1951 was in the midst of a postwar boom, though troubling signs had already started to appear. Even then, fifty-three years ago, the Grand Old Game had more than a century of history to brag about, including eighty years of professional play. Other professional team sports in the United States were still in their infancy, though pro football was soon to explode into a formidable rival to the National Game.

Now baseball boasts more than a century and a quarter of carefully documented history. A major part of that documentation is the voluminous amount of baseball statistics that have been compiled or calculated. These statistics record the successes and failures of the more than 16,000 big league players who have worn the uniforms of almost 150 different clubs in half a dozen major leagues.

The value of baseball statistics lies primarily in their completeness and accuracy. Because they are so well designed and so comprehensive, baseball statistics have a magical quality that most mere numbers lack. Because they are so accurate, baseball statistics can be relied upon to form opinions and to make judgments over many decades of play.

Nevertheless, there is a paradox inherent in the historical accuracy of baseball statistics. Too many people mistakenly believe that baseball stats are graven in stone, like birth and death dates on a granite tombstone. If the Macmillan *Baseball Encyclopedia* showed that Babe Ruth hit 714 career home runs, or that Ty Cobb finished with 4,191 hits and a career batting average of .367, most people believe that these are immutable facts.

Not so. At least four mistakes have been found in the past twenty-five years in the official batting records for Cobb. The net result in correcting these errors in pre-computer record keeping is that "The Georgia Peach" has 4,189 hits and a career .366 average *to the best of our knowledge.* So, when the nation watched as Pete Rose broke the all-time hits record on September 11, 1985 with his 4,192nd base hit, few knew that Rose already had broken Cobb's record three days earlier. By the way, the first edition of the Macmillan encyclopedia showed Ty Cobb with 4,192 official career hits, though that was changed without explanation to 4,191 in subsequent editions.

As for "The Sultan of Swat," how many people are aware that he used to have 715 home runs? His current career total of 714 home runs is accurate *to the best of our knowledge*—provided that one accepts a curious decision of the Special Baseball Records Committee on May 5, 1969. As part of the massive effort to computerize and clean up the game's official statistics and records, this committee was formed and charged with deciding how best to handle certain anomalies and inconsistencies.

In 1968 the Special Records Committee had voted to change the thirty-seven instances prior to 1920 where game-ending home runs were counted only as singles, doubles, or triples (whatever was needed to drive home the winning run). These over-the-fence hits were not home runs according to the scoring practices of their day, but became so with the 1968 ruling. The Special Records Committee also made other changes in previous scoring practices, many of them quite significant: e.g., counting stats in all tie games of five or more innings; not counting walks, wild pitches, passed balls, balks, and hit batsmen as errors at any time; and neither counting walks as outs (as was done in 1876) nor as hits (as was done in 1887).

The committee was logically prepared to count those hits as home runs until a controversy arose because doing so changed Ruth's official career total to 715. Fear of changing one of the game's most important records caused the committee to retract its earlier—and more enlightened—decision. Thus, "The Bambino" lost a home run, and his career total remained at the apparently sacrosanct number of 714.

Regardless of such high-profile examples of historical mistakes or inconsistencies, the level of accuracy of baseball statistics is exceedingly high—so high that it exceeds the standards of accuracy in virtually every other field of endeavor. Twenty-first century Americans make life-changing decisions every day based on evidence supported by underlying statistics not nearly as accurate as baseball stats.

This superlative accuracy is the reason that fans, researchers, and historians can argue about the number of hits compiled by a Hall of Fame player who started his career in 1871 and finished in 1897, more than a century ago. Cap Anson has been dead since 1922, yet his career is still under the contemporary microscope. Good history depends on truly accurate research, not on false allegiance to previously published numbers.

History is process, not perfection. We trust that our effort has contributed to the process of recording and understanding the history of our National Pastime.

—*Gary Gillette*

BASEBALL ENCYCLOPEDIA ON THE WEB

For the latest news and updates about *The Baseball Encyclopedia*, including extra statistical content that we couldn't squeeze into the book, information on upcoming author appearances, and new articles about baseball history, visit us on the web at http://www.247baseball.com.

To subscribe to our monthly *Baseball Encyclopedia* newsletter, which will include updates, Q&As, and other features, send an e-mail with "Subscribe Newsletter" as the subject to subscribe@247baseball.com and you will be registered to receive the newsletter.

If you have any corrections or suggestions for future editions of the Baseball Encyclopedia please e-mail us at feedback@247baseball.com or send a letter to:

The Baseball Encyclopedia
c/o Barnes & Noble Publishing, Inc.
122 Fifth Avenue, 5th floor
New York, NY 10011

Process. Like every reference work that is not created from whole cloth, this new encyclopedia builds on the foundation of its predecessors, most importantly the groundbreaking work done by John Thorn and Pete Palmer in *Total Baseball.* When *Total Baseball* made its debut in 1989, all previous baseball encyclopedias were instantly obsolete, including the beloved official *Baseball Encyclopedia* that had been published by Macmillan since 1969.

All of the editors who worked on this book have worked previously on, or contributed to, one or more editions of *Total Baseball.* Furthermore, Palmer, the co-editor of every previous edition of *Total Baseball,* has edited, co-edited, or contributed in one way or another to every complete baseball encyclopedia (i.e., encyclopedias that include year-by-year career registers) published since 1965.

Most of the data underlying the statistics in this encyclopedia comes from a new database compiled by Palmer in the past three years. Much of the remaining data comes from various databases compiled by Gary Gillette in the past four years. Other information has been generously provided by Retrosheet or by members of the Society for American Baseball Research (SABR).

In compiling his new database, Palmer—like everyone before him—has relied on the standard sources of official and unofficial statistics. He has also done new research into historical areas that have heretofore been neglected. After forty years of indefatigable work in the field, there are very few sources of information that Palmer has not examined carefully. Moreover, he has kept detailed records of the mistakes and omissions in each source, so that he can avoid repeating the mistakes of earlier reference books.

While these standard sources are generally accurate, Palmer has made tens of thousands of corrections to the original source material. Many mistakes were simply found by adding up the stats for all players on a team and comparing those totals to the reported team totals. Others were made from the input of various researchers who compared box scores or play-by-play records to the official data. Many of the hardest-to-find mistakes were corrected by comparing statistics in multiple reliable sources and looking for telltale differences. Thousands of hours have been spent in compiling, checking, verifying, and correcting this new database.

National Association Statistics. One of the decisions made by the Special Records Committee was to exclude the National Association from major league status. The editors respectfully disagree with that decision and, therefore, have included complete NA records in this encyclopedia. The National Association certainly had its problems—as the Special Records Committee indicated—but it was indisputably the Major League Baseball of its day. To use current standards of reliability as a reason for excluding the NA doesn't make sense.

Despite this, however, we have *not* included NA stats in the totals of the many players who played in both the NA and the NL. Instead, a separate totals line is shown for the NA if a player also later played in the NL. The reason? If the NA and NL totals were combined, they would not match what is in the official records. For most players, that wouldn't be a problem. For some players—like Cap Anson—it would further confuse the picture.

Sources. The primary sources for most of the statistics contained herein are the official National and American League records, starting in 1903 for the NL and 1905 for the AL. The source data for most of the earlier years come from computer printouts at the Hall of Fame originally compiled by Information Concepts, Incorporated, (ICI) for the 1969 *Baseball Encyclopedia.* These ICI printouts were turned over to the Hall in return for access to Lee Allen's biographical data. The primary source for 1876–90 NL statistics are the records compiled by historian John Tattersall and held by SABR. For the National Association (1871–75), records compiled from box scores by Bob Tiemann and Bob Richardson are the primary sources.

Tattersall used the figures from the annual official guides for basic batting and pitching stats for most players, though it should be noted that official pitching stats in those days consisted simply of games, wins, and losses. Tattersall obtained extra-base hits, batter walks, and strikeouts from figures compiled in *The Boston Globe* by Clarence Dow for some years of the 1876–90 period. The unheralded Dow was one of the great early statisticians, though he unfortunately died at the age of 38 in 1893. Dow actually played one game for the Boston Unions in 1884.

Since runs batted in were not officially defined from 1876–90, Tattersall determined RBIs as best he could from newspaper accounts of games. He also retroactively compiled "official" stats from box scores for all players appearing in less than 15 games; those reserve players were not shown in the stats printed in the annual official guides. Tattersall was forced to use box scores for the years when the *Globe* did not publish statistics.

In addition to filling in these gaps in the record, Tattersall counted stats from tie games for 1878–84, which had been excluded at that time. He also counted stats from various other games that had previously been excluded from the official records—for example, for 1877 Cincinnati games, where the team dropped out of the league after 58 games (almost a complete season). Tattersall also wisely standardized the handling of walks, which were counted as outs in 1876 and as hits in 1887 in the NL; ICI had done this for the 1887 American Association.

For the most part, Tattersall did not make other changes in the official stats as found in the guides. One notable exception was in 1879, when Tattersall was sure that, due to a clerical error, Cap Anson really had only 72 hits (not 90) and batted .317 (not .407). To our knowledge, Tattersall never changed any other official stats from 1871–90 unless he found a clerical or arithmetical error. All of his decisions were endorsed by the Special Records Committee in 1968.

Filling the gaps. Certain other stats were found in box scores. For batters hit-by-pitch, the work was done by John Tattersall, Pete Palmer, John Schwartz, Alex Haas, and others through 1917 in the NL and 1920 in the AL (when the statistic was first kept officially). Likewise, box scores were used for pitcher hit-batsmen before 1903 in the NL and 1908 in the AL.

Runs batted in for years where the totals were not previously complete (1885–87 and 1890 AA) were obtained mostly from incomplete data on the ICI printouts and from newspaper game accounts. Approximately 10 percent of RBIs had to be estimated from other player batting stats, including data on some players for the 1882–84 AA. David Neft supplied some additional RBI data for 1880–84 NL.

Many corrections to home run totals were made by Tattersall and by SABR stalwart Bob McConnell. Over the years, other SABR members also took it upon themselves to research different areas. Frank Williams carefully went over the 1901–19 AL pitching stats and corrected many errors. Joe Wayman did the same for shutouts throughout major league history. Walt Wilson checked games started, which were not kept officially in the AL until 1926 and in the NL until 1938.

Biographical data came originally from research done by Hy Turkin and S.C. Thompson in the 1950s, with additional help later from Bill Haber. Biographical information for current players is collected by the editors and exchanged with the SABR Biographical Committee, which was founded by Cliff Kachline. Richard Topp and the current chairmen, Bill Carle and David Vincent, later made valuable contributions, with yeoman help from Rich Malatsky and Peter Morris.

Manager data was originally compiled by Richard Topp and Bob Tiemann, who made many changes in the previous listings for early managers. They determined that the captain was really what we call the manager today, and that the listed manager was really the club's business manager.

New in this encyclopedia. Pitcher run support was obtained from Retrosheet game logs, which were compiled by Tom Ruane from various sources. This data originated with Bob Tiemann's notebook data, which was computerized by Arnie Braunstein.

Play-by-plays compiled by Retrosheet, Project Scoresheet, The Baseball Workshop, and by the editors from 1969–2003 were used to calculate blown saves, defensive innings, range, opponents' stolen base and caught stealing stats for catchers, plus throwing for outfielders and DP rates for infielders. Extensive examination and testing of the 1969–2003 play-by-plays provided the information needed to refine Palmer's previous estimates of defensive innings before 1969, as well as improve Palmer's defensive evaluations.

In the past three years, Retrosheet has released play-by-plays for the 1969 season and for most of the 1970s. President David Smith was also kind enough to allow us access to their 1970–72 archives. There are now thirty-five years of play-by-play records available, completely covering the era of divisional play and the careers of more than 5,600 players: 41 percent of everyone who has played since 1901 and 35 percent of all players in major league history.

Caught stealing for the 1913 NL came from newly discovered data compiled by Ernie Lanigan. Lanigan compiled caught stealing stats from 1912–19 and sold the data to different newspapers, though only about half of it has been found. Since Lanigan sold various features to papers across the country, it is certainly possible that there is more data out there that has not yet been found. We have checked *The Sporting News* and *Sporting Life*, but not individual city papers. If anyone knows of a newspaper that contains caught stealing stats for 1912–19 that is not shown in this book, please contact the editors.

SABR and Retrosheet. Any reader who pays careful attention to the explanations and introductions in this work will come across multiple references to both of these eminent non-profit organizations. For information on the Society for American Baseball Research, please see their page at the very end of the encyclopedia.

Some of the information in this encyclopedia came from the files of Retrosheet, an organization founded for the collection, computerization, and free public distribution of detailed play-by-play information of as many major league games as possible. Much of the information is currently available at (www.Retrosheet.org) and more is added regularly as additional data files are proofed and readied for release.

Retrosheet has become a standard source of information for many teams, writers, and announcers. It also provides box scores and play-by-play accounts for fans interested in specific games, such as the first one they ever attended. Dozens of ballplayers have received detailed analyses of their careers.

Jayson Stark of ESPN wrote, "Do we even remember life before Retrosheet? I am eternally grateful that Retrosheet pasted every one of them [box scores] into its notebook out there in cyberspace."

Not all the box scores are there yet, but more are on the way all the time as this epic effort continues. The website also includes a "most wanted" list of games for which Retrosheet still needs a scoresheet. If you have scoresheets of any games from 1947–73, or if you think there might still be some scoresheets or an old scorebook in your attic or in your parent's attic, please check out this list!

Slip-Sliding Away: The Ever-Changing Hit Total of Cap Anson. Tattersall's painstaking research was invaluable in creating official records for many players and in supplementing the skimpy official records for those included in the annual guides. Everyone has heretofore accepted Tattersall's numbers without questioning them. However, Pete Palmer has discovered that in 1889, Tattersall—for unknown reasons—changed the official hits totals for most of the White Stockings regulars. In this case, Tattersall apparently believed that the Chicago club (now the Cubs) had erroneously been given an extra 67 hits by either a generous scorer or by a league error, since his box scores did not agree with the league figures published in the official guide.

After poring over the surviving records and after careful reflection, we have decided to undo the changes Tattersall made to the official NL stats for the 1889 Chicago batters. We believe that there is not nearly enough evidence to prove any error that justified those changes. In those days, the teams, not the leagues, employed the official scorers. As one might imagine, there was a lot of favoritism in the selection of official scorers, whose names were kept secret to prevent players or fans from assailing them for controversial decisions.

Since the official scorer's decisions were unknown, virtually every nineteenth century newspaper box score was different. As a consequence, there was no way during the season to tell what the official statistics would later say (i.e., what would be published in the postseason compilations for the annual guides). Even if the official scorer in Chicago in 1889 awarded a somewhat higher number of hits rather than errors for some players—which is pure speculation at this point—it was the duty of those scorers to make judgments based on what they saw.

In 1897 public accusations were made that Baltimore official scorers unfairly aided Orioles outfielder Willie Keeler, who finished the season with a .432 average. One of those casting aspersions on the integrity of the Baltimore scorers was John Heydler, who would later become NL president. (Keeler's average was later revised to .424, based on ICI research.) Corrections due to obvious clerical or arithmetic mistakes were frequently made in the ICI process and in the decades since. In no other case, however, has the judgment of an historian decades later been substituted for the judgment of the scorer of the day about whether a batted ball should have been scored a hit or an error. The White Stockings' anonymous official scorer in the 1890s was later found to have been a female friend of team owner Al Spalding, yet her presumably non-objective decisions have never been overturned.

Why did Tattersall decide to make these changes? We cannot know for sure, as no documentation of Tattersall's reasoning—if, indeed, he recorded any—has survived. It appears that his changes to the White Stockings hit totals in 1889 were an attempt to reconcile the new league pitching stats that Tattersall was compiling with the existing official league batting stats. While that is understandable, the fact remains that there are thousands of differences between the batting and pitching stats in those years, most of which will never be reconciled because the source material (i.e., the official scoresheets) have been lost and only the final totals survive. Attempts to match the official totals for seasons in the 1880s by compiling stats from newspaper box scores have produced large and irreconcilable discrepancies.

Aside from the changes in scoring practices endorsed by the Special Records Committee, no one has ever changed any other official statistic without clear evidence that it was wrong. In fact, in many cases, "official" statistics continue to be published by reputable sources even though it has been documented that they are wrong. For example, there is overwhelming evidence of skullduggery in the final two games played by the St. Louis Browns in 1910, when well-regarded Nap Lajoie was in a tight race for the AL batting title with unpopular Ty Cobb. That malfeasance almost certainly resulted in a number of extra hits for Lajoie—

it's theoretically possible, though not very likely, that Lajoie would have gone 8-for-8 had the Browns not played deep at third base and allowed him to lay down seven uncontested bunt hits—yet no one has ever adjusted his hit totals.

If you're still reading at this point, you may enjoy this comparison of the differing career hit totals for Cap Anson in various reference sources. The first entry shows what *The Sporting News* (longtime publisher of the official annual guides and record books) and Elias Sports Bureau list for Anson. The other entries show the wandering totals for Anson in various encyclopedias—most of them official—in the past half-century.

Cap Anson's Hits, by the Books

***The Sporting News* and Elias Sports Bureau (official statisticians for MLB)**

3,081 Matches official guide data for 1876–97, Anson's entire NL career.

Barnes *Official Encyclopedia of Baseball,* 1951–79 (1st–10th editions)

3,516 Includes 435 hits in the National Association, 1871–75.

Macmillan *Baseball Encyclopedia,* 1969 (1st edition, official)

2,995 Sources Tattersall 1876–90; 72 instead of 90 in 1879 (correcting league error); ICI printouts 1891–97; 86 not 67 in 1877 (includes games vs. Cincinnati that had been thrown out); includes 6 hits in tie games 1878–84 which originally were not counted in the official averages); does not include 60 walks that were counted as hits in 1887; has 161 instead of official 177 in 1889 due to Tattersall change in official stats; has 17 fewer hits from ICI printouts 1891–97.

Macmillan *Baseball Encyclopedia,* 1974–88 (2nd–7th editions, official)

3,041 Restored the 18 hits in 1879 which everyone else had concluded was a league error or an intentional mistake to help his average; also restored the 16 in 1889 that Tattersall had changed; then used official guide figures in 1894 (+5) and 1897 (+7) for a total of +46. They used the ICI figures for 1891–93 and 1895–96 and also used Tattersall's tie games for 1878–84.

Macmillan *Baseball Encyclopedia,* 1990–96 (8th–10th editions; 8th edition official)

3,000 Apparently reverted to 1st edition number, then arbitrarily added 5 hits in 1894 without explanation.

***Total Baseball,* 1989–99 (1st–6th editions; 4th–6th editions official)**

2,995 Same sources and corrections as Macmillan, 1st edition.

***Total Baseball,* 2001 (7th edition, official)**

3,056 Per edict from Major League Baseball, reversing Special Records Committee decision to count bases on balls as walks for all seasons. Therefore, counts 60 walks in 1887 as hits; it also includes 1 hit in a protested game in 1894 that was not counted by ICI, though it should have been.

Barnes & Noble *Baseball Encyclopedia,* 2004 (1st edition)

3,012 ICI total with restoration of 16 hits subtracted without explanation by Tattersall in 1889; also counts 1 hit in 1894 protested game.

Without any further ado, let's go on to "The Show!"

THE SCIENCE OF HITTING: THE BATTER REGISTER

The two most commonly repeated things about hitting are both, not coincidentally, attributed to the late Ted Williams. The first statement was a trifle whose significance is overblown almost as often as it is paraphrased:

"Baseball is the only field of endeavor where a man can succeed three times out of ten and be considered a good performer."—sourced as "widely quoted" in *Baseball's Greatest Quotations.*

It should not have to be said that Williams was obviously indulging in hyperbole to make a point and not being literal here. After all, it is inconceivable that a player with a lifetime on-base percentage of .482 would think that the success of a batter was measured solely by his batting average.

On the very next page of that same book, the caption next to Williams' picture reads: "Ted Williams, who once termed his 2,019 career bases on balls (the equivalent of four seasons of walking) as my 'proudest record.' " (Williams was second to Babe Ruth in career walks when he retired; that figure has since been corrected to 2,021 walks and has been surpassed by both Rickey Henderson and Barry Bonds.)

No one ever accused "The Splendid Splinter" of being indecisive, so how does one reconcile these two seemingly divergent attitudes? The best way to view Williams' attitude about hitting is to understand that it wasn't reducible to the kind of catchy phrase so loved by the pundits.

The other oft-repeated Williams' comment on hitting—as quoted in Joe Falls' *Sporting News* column of February 8, 1969—is much more substantial and deserves much more scrutiny:

"First of all, the hardest single thing to do in sports is to hit a baseball. If this is true and it is, then it takes more hours of practice, more hours of dedication, more hours of desire to hit a baseball than it does to do anything else."

One reason that Teddy Ballgame is considered by many as the greatest hitter of all time was that he *studied* hitting. He turned it inside out, tested it, and thought constantly about how to improve his approach. For him, hitting *was* baseball. The study of hitting was serious science. Williams honed his bats to perfection, refined his ideas of the strike zone, thought about whether to swing down or up on the ball, and studied pitchers as if they were helpless butterflies he was about to pin to black paper.

Heeding the advice of Rogers Hornsby—often called the best right-handed batter of all time—Williams elected simply not to swing at bad pitches, either taking his walk or forcing the pitcher to come in to him and give him something truly good to swing at. The details are spelled out in *The Science of Hitting,* Williams' classic text (co-authored with John Underwood), which was first published in 1970 and remains in-print today.

Williams' scientific view of batting had little to do with that of the early part of the twentieth century, the era of great hitters like Ty Cobb and Joe Jackson. Players of that time used the term "scientific baseball" to describe things that *managers* told *players* to do. Called "little ball" today, it used stratagems such as sacrifice bunting, squeeze bunting, drag bunting, hitting-and-running, stealing, hitting behind the runner, and the like. Being *scientific* in those days meant employing the right *plays*, rather than how a batter approached his turn at bat.

F.C. Lane's classic work *Batting* was first published in 1925. It was reprinted by SABR in 2001 and is now available from the University of Nebraska Press (www.unp.unl.edu). The book is a treasure trove of insight into attitudes about hitting in the early twentieth century; all of the following quotations come from its pages.

Feared slugger Joe Jackson typified the view of the day, opining that hitters had little choice but to step up to the plate and whale away. "I don't care whether the ball is over the plate or not, so long as it looks good," he said, "Batters can't be choosers. They have to take what the pitcher gives them. And pitchers are not very accommodating."

The greatest hitter of his day, Ty Cobb, disagreed. Cobb believed that hitters controlled their destiny, and that they didn't have to take advantage of their first offering. "Many batters have the mistaken idea that the pitcher is working on them and that there is nothing they can do in self-defense . . . [T]hey reason, 'We have to hit what he gives us.' That's only partially true, however. The batter is seldom compelled to hit any particular ball. He has a choice."

Despite that clear-eyed assessment, Cobb didn't take many more free passes than Jackson on a year-by-year basis. Both of them, though, were smart enough to take a walk when they weren't offered anything to hit.

One of the most patient hitters of the era was Eddie Collins, the great second baseman who, according to Walter Johnson, would "never bite at a bad ball." However, most of the most patient hitters of the day were not stars.

Jack Graney, who twice led the AL in walks, knew what he was trying to accomplish. "Not only does waiting a pitcher out impair his confidence and his control," he said, "But it also makes him work harder . . . I believe the waiting game is the most effective batting system that could possibly be devised."

Another Dead Ball Era player who might be applying for a job as an Oakland or Boston hitting instructor if he were around today was Burt Shotton, who twice topped the AL in walks and later was a successful manager. "The very name baseball is almost the same as base on balls," Shotton noted. "The spectator at the game is likely to look upon the base on balls as a mere incident; a momentary wildness on the part of the pitcher, or a gift to a dangerous batter. This opinion is often justified, but just as often the base on balls is a real tribute to the batter's skill in working the pitcher."

Ted Williams' idea of science was to treat his precious at bats as lab experiments performed under controlled conditions. If he had good equipment, a good idea of the pitcher's strengths and weaknesses, and an eye for the strike zone, Williams believed he could hit anyone at any time. His approach had very little to do with the intricacies of what was—and still is—thought of as "strategic" baseball. Williams himself was the one who made the difference while in the batter's box.

Williams became a truly great hitter by combining a tremendously strong uppercut swing—which he practiced for hours and hours—with discerning strike-zone judgment. Power and plate discipline are still an unbeatable combination. Just ask Barry Bonds, the best player in the world today.

The science of hitting has certainly changed over time—like everything else in the game—though thoughtful and analytical hitters have followed similar approaches in different eras. When circumstances change dramatically in baseball, failure to make the appropriate adjustments is usually followed by a quick ticket out of the league.

Failure to adjust is a cardinal sin when analyzing baseball statistics. Baseball stats are certainly comparable over time, but they are not *directly* comparable. To take stats from twenty-five years ago and compare them directly to today's numbers is risky; to take stats from 1904 and compare them directly to today's stats is silly. To make judgments based simply on comparing raw stats is sheer folly.

The numbers in this Batter Register provide one with the opportunity to examine the raw stats, the ability to put them into the proper context, and a chance to make informed judgments. Barry Bonds can be compared to Willie Mays, Ted Williams to Joe DiMaggio, Babe Ruth to Ty Cobb. Context is not everything, but it is essential to understanding most things—including the game of baseball and the stats it produces.

BIOGRAPHICAL INFORMATION

There is a wealth of biographical information in a single line atop each player entry—in a handful of cases the information trickles to a second line. The biographical information answers questions about a player's life away from the batter's box: When was he born? Did he live to a ripe old age? How tall was he? Was he ever a manager, and for how long? Did he miss time to the military? And was he one of rare few to reach the Hall of Fame? The biographical line is a reminder that a player is more than just a collection of numbers.

Every player in this register has (at least) a last name and a debut date. If a player has a matronymic name, it is placed in parentheses—for example, Roberto Clemente (Walker). Nicknames are included in the biographical line; if a nickname is what the player is known by during his career, it will be part of his listed name—such as, McInnis, Stuffy. Other features and abbreviations for biographical information follow.

B (mm. dd. yyyy) is the date and place of birth.

D (mm. dd. yyyy) is the date and place of death, if death has occurred.

The side of the plate a player bats from is expressed *BR* (bats right), *BL* (bats left), or *BB* (bats both sides). The arm the player throws with is expressed *TR* (throws right), or *TL* (throws left). In rare cases when a pitcher throws with both hands during a season, *TB* (throws both) is used and the season is included in parentheses. Likewise, if a player changes from switch-hitting to hitting from one side during his career, the side of the plate he bats from exclusively and the length of that change are presented in parentheses.

Height is shown by feet followed by inches. Weight is expressed in pounds using **#**.

Debuts are marked *d*, followed by the date the player made his first major league appearance. The debut year is the first year listed in the register, so it is not included in the biographical line.

Besides these basic pieces of information available in the biographical line, there are several other designations for players whose career, family, or duty took them beyond the norm.

If a player on a major league roster missed significant parts of any season serving the United States during wartime, the following abbreviations are used to identify how the player served:

Mil indicates military service in the army, navy, air force, or marines;

Mer indicates the merchant marine;

Def indicates defense plant work.

The seasons the player missed at least a part of are listed after the abbreviation for duty. At least one major leaguer missed time during the seasons below as a result of the following wars (dates include post-war service by some veterans):

Spanish-American War, 1898;

World War I, 1917–19;

World War II, 1941–46;

Korean War 1951–59;

Vietnam War 1962–72.

If the player spent time as a coach, manager, or umpire, that is indicated by the following symbols which are followed by the number of seasons during which he performed those jobs. Abbreviations are:

C: Coach;

M: Manager;

U: Umpire.

HF indicates that the player is an inductee of the Hall of Fame; the year of election follows *HF*.

If the player had a close family member in the major leagues, the relative's relationship is identified by the codes listed below followed by the relative's first name (and, if it is different, the last name):

b: brother;

twb: twin brother;

f: father;

s: son;

gf: grandfather;

gs: grandson;

ggf: great grandfather;

ggs: great grandson.

Defensive games in outfield positions (*LF-CF-RF*) are included at the end of the biographical data if there is not enough room to place it in the position career line.

▲ at the end of the biographical information indicates that the player is also listed in the pitcher register. A player whose primary position was not pitcher must have pitched at least 9 innings to appear in the Pitching Register.

STATISTICAL INFORMATION

Symbols in the first two columns:

† before the team name means he participated in Postseason Play that year;

★ after team name means he participated in All-Star game;

☆ after team name means he was selected to All-Star team but did not play;

✳ after team name means he was selected to All-Star team but replaced due to injury.

Boldface statistics in any category indicates a league-leading total or average.

The columns that appear in the player register after **Year**:

TM: Team. Each team is identified by a three-letter code that is usually the first three letters of the city, state, or area where the team is located.

L: League. The leagues in this book include the National League (N), the American League (A), the Federal League (F), the Players League (P), the Union Association (U), the National Association (NA), and the American Association (AA).

G: Games. The number of games are boldfaced if the player appeared in all of his team's games for a given year.

AB: At Bats

R: Runs

H: Hits

2B: Doubles

3B: Triples

HR: Home Runs

RBI: Runs Batted In. RBI information is unavailable for 1882–84 American Association and 1884 Union Association. Since 1939, runs scoring on a groundball double play have not been counted as RBIs.

BB: Bases on Balls Generally referred to today as walks.

IB: Intentional Base on Balls. Walking an opponent on purpose was first counted as a distinct category in 1955.

HBP: Hit-by-Pitch. The rule awarding first base to batters hit by pitches was instituted in 1884 by the American Association. It was adopted in 1887 by the National League.

SO: Strikeouts Strikeouts are available for batters in all years except for 1884 in the Union Association, from 1882–88 and 1890 in the American Association, from 1897–1909 in the National League, and 1901–12 in the American League.

AVG: Batting Average. Hits divided by at bats.

OBP: On-Base Percentage. The official definition of on-base percentage, which was established when OBP was made an official statistic in 1984, is: (hits plus walks plus hit-by-pitches) divided by (at bats plus walks plus hit-by-pitches plus sacrifice flies). This definition is used for 1954 and all later seasons. In the years prior to 1954, the definition depends on the data available.

SLG: Slugging Percentage. Total bases divided by at bats.

AOPS: Adjusted On-Base plus Slugging. On-base percentage and slugging average are added and normalized for the context of the offensive level of the league and the player's home park(s) and then converted to a scale in which 100 is average.

ABR: Adjusted Batting Runs The linear weights values of the offensive events that the player's plate appearances precipitated are added and then normalized for the context of the offensive level of the league and the player's home park(s). It is then converted to a scale in which 0 is average and the output is the number of runs the player's batting added to or subtracted from his team compared what an average player would have done.

SB: Stolen Bases. Totals are available for all seasons in all leagues from 1886 on, as well as for all the seasons of the National Association.

CS: Caught Stealing. Totals are available for all American League players in 1914–15 and from 1920 on; caught stealing totals are available for all National League players in 1913, 1915, from 1920–26, and from 1951 on. Caught Stealing totals are also available for 1916 for all players who stole at least 20 bases.

FA: Fielding Average. Determined by the formula: (Assists plus Putouts) divided by (Assists plus Putouts plus Errors).

FR: Fielding Runs. This measures how many runs the player saves or loses for his team in the field compared to an average fielder. The formula takes into account assists, putouts, errors, and double plays, as well as passed balls for catchers. All of these defensive statistics are adjusted for context in several different ways. Defensive innings are based on play-by-play from 1969 forward and were estimated for previous years.

Rng: Range. This is calculated different ways for different positions. For infielders, range is based on assists per inning. For outfielders, range is based on putouts per inning. For catchers, range is based on stolen bases allowed per inning. The data is then adjusted in comparison to the league average, with 100 equaling league average—higher is always better. (Thus a 110 rating for a catcher means 10 percent fewer stolen bases allowed than average.) All statistics are adjusted for context, including the number of balls put into play and what direction the balls in play were likely to go in. Innings played data was calculated from play-by-play accounts from 1969 forward and is estimated for previous seasons. Outfielders are rated for their play at all outfield (weighted) positions, while infielders are only rated for their play at their primary position.

Thr: Throwing Throwing is calculated different ways for different positions. For infielders, throwing is based on double plays per inning. For outfielders, throwing is based on assists per inning. For catchers, throwing is based on caught stealing rates per inning. The data is then adjusted in comparison to league average, with 100 equaling league average. All statistics are adjusted for context by various methods. Innings played data was calculated from play-by-play accounts from 1969 forward and is estimated for previous seasons. Outfielders are rated for their play at all outfield positions, while infielders are only rated for their play at their primary position.

Stolen bases and caught stealing off catchers are italicized for both *range and throwing* for years prior to 1969 to indicate data was estimated from player and team data.

G/Pos: Games at Position. Positions are listed left to right by decreasing number of games. There are several different variations in this category.

A * before the position indicates that the player fielded the position in the great majority (100 since 1901) of his team's games during the season or for at least 1,000 games during his career

/: Any positions listed after the slash indicate that it was fielded by the player in less than 10 games that season or 100 games during his career.

Positions are identified by easily recognizable one-letter abbreviations:

P: Pitcher

1: First Base

2: Second Base

3: Third Base

S: Shortstop

O: Outfield

D: Designated Hitter.

Positions are followed by a dash and the number of games the player played at that position during the season or career. The positions are separated by commas except when there is a slash. If the player spent only one game at that position, the one-letter abbreviation is used without a dash or number. If the player spent only one game at multiple positions, no comma is placed between the abbreviations for those positions.

Outfield is officially counted as only position, but if the player spent time playing at least two of the three outfield positions, a breakdown of the games in left, center, and right is presented in that order, separated by dashes, in parentheses. If the outfielder only played one outfield position, that position will be identified (**LF**, **CF**, or **RF**) after the number of outfield games played. If a breakdown of the games in left, center, and right is needed in the career line, but there is not enough room, that information will be added to the end of the biographical data and the primary outfield position played will be identified by **L**, **C**, or **R** following the number of games played in the outfield.

BFW: Batter Fielder Base Stealer Wins. The sum of a player's batting wins, basestealing wins, and fielding wins, this figure indicates how many games the player won or lost for his team compared to an average player.

For any missing data, such as CS, RBI or SO, the career total is underlined if it is a partial figure.

More details on many of the statistics and formulas shown in this register can be found in the glossary at the end of the encylopedia.

Year	Tm Lg	G	AB	R	H	2B	3B	HR	RBI	BB-IB	HP	SO	AVG	OBP	SLG	AOPS	ABR	SB-CS	FA	FR	Rng	Thr	G at Pos	BFW
AARON, HANK Henry Louis "Hammerin' Hank" B 2.5.1934 Mobile, AL BR/TR 6/180# d4.13 HF1982 b-Tommie OF Total (313-LF 293-CF 2184-RF)																								
1954	Mil N	122	468	58	131	27	6	13	69	28	i3	39	.280	.322	.447	105	1	2-2	.970	-6	93	64	*O-116(105-0-11)	-1.2
1955	Mil N★	153	602	105	189	**37**	9	27	106	49-5	3	61	.314	.366	.540	144	37	3-1	.967	1	99	82	*O-126(26-0-105),2-27	3.4
1956	Mil N★	153	609	106	**200**	**34**	14	26	92	37-6	2	54	**.328**	.365	.558	154	43	2-4	.962	4	105	119	*O-152(RF)	**4.1**
1957	†Mil N★	151	615	**118**	198	27	6	**44**	**132**	57-15	0	58	.322	.378	.600	170	58	1-1	.983	-8	94	74	*O-150(1-69-83)	4.3
1958	†Mil N★	153	601	109	196	34	4	30	95	59-16	1	49	.326	.386	.546	157	48	4-1	.984	-6	94	91	*O-153(0-39-120)	3.6
1959	Mil N★	154	629	116	**223**	46	7	39	123	51-17	4	54	**.355**	.401	**.636**	**188**	**77**	8-0	.982	-4	91	105	*O-152(0-13-144)/3-5	**6.8**
1960	Mil N★	153	590	102	172	20	11	40	**126**	60-13	2	63	.292	.352	.566	160	46	16-7	.982	4	108	88	*O-153(0-3-151)/2-2	4.5
1961	Mil N★	**155**	603	115	197	**39**	10	34	120	56-20	2	64	.327	.381	.594	**165**	**55**	21-9	.982	-1	102	87	*O-154(0-71-88)/3-2	4.6
1962	Mil N★	156	592	127	191	28	6	45	128	66-14	3	73	.323	.390	.618	171	58	15-7	.980	-2	100	90	*O-153(0-83-71)/1	4.8
1963	Mil N★	161	631	**121**	201	29	4	**44**	**130**	78-18	0	94	.319	.391	**.586**	**180**	**66**	31-5	.979	-7	93	80	*O-161(RF)	5.6
1964	Mil N★	145	570	103	187	30	2	24	95	62-9	0	46	.328	.393	.514	152	41	22-4	.983	7	113	130	*O-139(RF),2-11	4.5
1965	Mil N★	150	570	109	181	**40**	1	32	89	60-10	1	81	.318	.379	.560	161	47	24-4	.987	6	110	88	*O-148(RF)	4.8
1966	Atl N★	158	603	117	168	23	1	**44**	**127**	76-15	1	96	.279	.356	.539	144	36	21-3	.988	8	**114**	109	*O-158(0-4-158)/2-2	3.8
1967	Atl N★	155	600	**113**	184	37	3	**39**	109	63-19	0	97	.307	.369	**.573**	169	**53**	17-6	.979	5	106	103	*O-152(0-11-141)/2	5.2
1968	Atl N★	160	606	84	174	33	4	29	86	64-23	1	62	.287	.354	.498	154	40	28-5	.991	9	115	98	*O-151(RF),1-14	4.7
1969	†Atl N★	147	547	100	164	30	3	44	97	87-19	2	47	.300	.396	.607	177	57	9-10	.982	2	105	100	*O-144(RF)/1-4	5.2
1970	Atl N★	150	516	103	154	26	1	38	118	74-15	2	63	.298	.385	.574	146	34	9-0	.977	2	110	74	*O-125(RF),1-11	3.0
1971	Atl N★	139	495	95	162	22	3	47	118	71-**21**	2	58	.327	.410	**.669**	**190**	59	1-1	.996	-9	77	92	1-71,O-60(1-0-59)	4.3
1972	Atl N★	129	449	75	119	10	0	34	77	92-15	1	55	.265	.390	.514	142	28	4-0	.987	1	101	88	*1-109,O-15(RF)	2.1
1973	Atl N★	120	392	84	118	12	1	40	96	68-13	1	51	.301	.402	.643	173	39	1-1	.977	1	91	63	*O-105(87-0-18)	3.5
1974	Atl N★	112	340	47	91	16	0	20	69	39-6	0	29	.268	.341	.491	126	11	1-0	.986	-3	89	54	O-89(LF)	0.4
1975	Mil A★	137	465	45	109	16	2	12	60	70-3	1	51	.234	.332	.355	95	-2	0-1	1.000	-1	38	0	*D-128/O-3(LF)	-0.6
1976	Mil A	85	271	22	62	8	0	10	35	35-1	0	38	.229	.315	.369	102	1	0-1	1.000	0	207	0	D-74/O(LF)	-0.1
Total	23	3298	12364	2174	3771	624	98	755	2297	1402-293	32	1383	.305	.374	.555	156	933	240-73	.980	4	102	92	*O-2760R,1-210,D-202/2-43,3-7	81.3
AARON, TOMMIE Tommie Lee B 8.5.1939 Mobile, AL D 8.16.1984 Atlanta, GA BR/TR 6-1/200# d4.10 C5 b-Hank																								
1962	Mil N	141	334	54	77	20	2	8	38	41-0	0	58	.231	.312	.374	86	-6	6-0	.989	3	**126**	**127**	*1-110,O-42(LF)/23	-0.7
1963	Mil N	72	135	6	27	6	1	1	15	11-1	0	27	.200	.257	.281	57	-8	0-3	1.000	-3	68	169	1-45,O-14(14-1-0)/2-6,3	-1.4
1965	Mil N	8	16	1	3	0	0	0	1	1-0	0	2	.188	.235	.188	21	-2	0-0	.961	0	138	85	/1-6	-0.2
1968	Atl N	98	283	21	69	10	3	1	25	21-1	0	37	.244	.295	.311	82	-6	3-4	.942	-1	96	96	O-62(LF),1-28/3	-1.4
1969	†Atl N	49	60	13	15	2	0	1	5	6-0	0	6	.250	.318	.333	82	-1	0-1	1.000	0	50	113	1-16/O-8(LF)	-0.2
1970	Atl N	44	63	3	13	2	0	2	7	3-0	0	10	.206	.242	.333	50	-5	0-0	.955	-2	48	22	1-16,O-12(10-0-2)	-0.7
1971	Atl N	25	53	4	12	2	0	0	3	3-1	0	5	.226	.268	.264	48	-4	0-0	.974	1	103	222	1-11/3-7	-0.3
Total	7	437	944	102	216	42	6	13	94	86-3	0	145	.229	.292	.327	75	-32	9-8	.990	-1	104	123	1-232,O-138(136-1-2)/3-10,2-7	-4.9
ABAD, ANDY Fausto Andres B 8.25.1972 Palm Beach, FL BL/TL 6-1/184# d9.10																								
2001	Oak A	1	1	0	0	0	0	0	0	0-0	0	0	.000	.000	.000	-99	0	0-0	1.000	0	0	1175	/1	0.0
2003	Bos A	9	17	1	2	0	0	0	0	2-0	0	5	.118	.211	.118	-10	-3	0-1	.973	-1	32	55	/1-7,O(RF)	-0.5
Total	2	10	18	1	2	0	0	0	0	2-0	0	5	.111	.200	.111	-14	-3	0-1	.974	-1	31	84	/1-8,O(RF)	-0.5
ABADIE, JOHN John B 11.4.1854 Philadelphia, PA D 5.17.1905 Pemberton, NJ BR/TR 6/192# d4.26																								
1875	Cen NA	11	45	3	10	0	0	0	4	0		3	.222	.222	.222	60	-2	1-0	.912	-0	141	18	1-11	-0.1
	Atl NA	1	4	1	1	0	0	0	1	0		0	.250	.250	.250	85	0	0-0	.875	-0	0	0	/1	0.0
	Year	12	49	4	11	0	0	0	5	0		3	.224	.224	.224	62	-2	1-0	.910	-1	132	17	1-12	-0.1
ABBATICCHIO, ED Edward James "Batty" B 4.15.1877 Latrobe, PA D 1.6.1957 Ft.Lauderdale, FL BR/TR 5-11/170# d9.4																								
1897	Phi N	3	10	0	3	0	0	0	0	1	0		.300	.364	.300	78	0	0	.875	-1	106	0	/2-3	-0.1
1898	Phi N	25	92	9	21	4	0	0	14	7	1		.228	.290	.272	64	-4	4	.818	-10	50	0	3-20/2-4,O(RF)	-1.3
1903	Bos N	136	489	61	111	18	5	1	46	52	4		.227	.306	.290	73	-16	23	.934	3	96	86	*2-116,S-17	-1.1
1904	Bos N	154	579	76	148	18	10	3	54	40	5		.256	.309	.337	103	1	24	.915	4	99	77	*S-154	1.0
1905	Bos N	153	610	70	170	25	12	3	41	35	8		.279	.326	.374	111	7	30	.919	-13	93	84	*S-152/O(CF)	-0.2
1907	Pit N	147	496	63	130	14	7	2	82	65	8		.262	.357	.331	114	11	35	.951	-22	90	76	*2-147	-1.1
1908	Pit N	146	500	43	125	16	7	1	61	58	7		.250	.336	.316	108	7	22	**.969**	-17	98	108	*2-144	-1.0
1909	†Pit N	36	87	13	20	0	0	1	16	19	0		.230	.368	.264	89	0	2	.966	0	113	101	S-18/2-4,O(CF)	0.1
1910	Pit N	3	3	0	0	0	0	0	0	0	0	0	.000	.000	.000	-95	-1	0	.500	-0	96	0	/S	-0.1
	Bos N	52	178	20	44	4	2	0	10	12	0	16	.247	.295	.292	68	-8	2	.910	-2	107	97	S-46/2	-0.8
	Year	55	181	20	44	4	2	0	10	12	0	16	.243	.290	.287	66	-8	2	.907	-2	107	96	S-47/2	-0.9
Total	9	855	3044	355	772	99	43	11	324	289	33	16	.254	.325	.325	98	-3	142	.949	-59	94	88	2-419,S-388/3-20,O-3(0-2-1)	-4.6
ABBEY, CHARLIE Charles S. B 10.14.1866 Falls City, NE D 4.27.1926 San Francisco, CA BL/TL 5-8.5/169# d8.16																								
1893	Was N	31	116	11	30	1	4	0	12	12	1	6	.259	.333	.336	80	-4	9	.937	3	113	76	O-31(LF)	-0.3
1894	Was N	129	523	95	164	26	18	7	101	58	7	38	.314	.389	.472	110	8	31	.909	8	113	99	*O-129(54-74-0)	0.5
1895	Was N	**133**	516	102	142	14	10	8	84	43	7	43	.275	.339	.388	88	-11	28	.902	7	166	152	*O-133(3-99-31)	-1.0
1896	Was N	79	301	47	79	12	6	1	49	27	4	20	.262	.331	.352	80	-9	16	.879	-3	123	110	O-78(2-11-65)/P	-1.3
1897	Was N	80	300	52	78	14	8	3	34	27	4		.260	.329	.390	90	-5	9	.946	1	120	42	O-80(2-1-77)	-0.7
Total	5	452	1756	307	493	67	46	19	280	167	23	107	.281	.351	.404	93	-21	93	.910	15	132	105	O-451(92-185-173)/P	-2.8
ABBOTT, FRED Harry Frederick (born Harry Frederick Winbigler) B 10.22.1874 Versailles, OH D 6.11.1935 Los Angeles, CA BR/TR 5-10/180# d4.25																								
1903	Cle A	77	255	25	60	11	3	1	25	7	5		.235	.270	.314	76	-8	8	.958	5	*113*	*111*	C-71/1-3	0.5
1904	Cle A	41	130	14	22	4	2	0	12	6	0		.169	.206	.231	38	-9	2	.953	-1	*115*	*109*	C-33/1-7	-0.8
1905	Phi N	42	128	9	25	6	1	0	12	6	3		.195	.248	.258	53	-7	4	.954	2	*119*	*88*	C-34/1-5	-0.3
Total	3	160	513	48	107	21	6	1	49	19	8		.209	.248	.279	61	-24	14	.956	6	*115*	*105*	C-138/1-15	-0.6
ABBOTT, JEFF Jeffrey William B 8.17.1972 Atlanta, GA BR/TL 6-2/190# d6.10																								
1997	Chi A	19	38	8	10	1	0	1	2	0-0	0	6	.263	.263	.368	65	-2	0-0	1.000	1	136	0	O-10(5-1-4)/D-3	-0.2
1998	Chi A	89	244	33	68	14	1	12	41	9-1	0	28	.279	.298	.492	105	1	3-3	.971	-4	96	0	O-76(20-38-27)/D-2	-0.5
1999	Chi A	17	57	5	9	0	0	2	6	5-0	0	12	.158	.222	.263	24	-7	1-1	.962	-2	81	0	O-17(LF)	-0.9
2000	†Chi A	80	215	31	59	15	1	3	29	21-1	2	38	.274	.343	.395	85	-4	2-1	.981	-5	85	67	O-65(20-33-16)/D-7	-0.9
2001	Fla N	28	42	5	11	3	0	0	5	3-0	1	7	.262	.326	.333	74	-2	0-0	.963	0	116	0	O-17(1-9-8)	-0.1
Total	5	233	596	82	157	33	2	18	83	38-2	3	91	.263	.307	.416	85	-14	6-5	.974	-10	93	25	O-185(63-81-55)/D-12	-2.6
ABBOTT, KURT Kurt Thomas B 6.2.1969 Zanesville, OH BR/TR 6/185# d9.8 OF Total (32-LF 4-CF 8-RF)																								
1993	Oak A	20	61	11	15	1	0	3	9	3-0	0	20	.246	.281	.410	89	-1	2-0	.971	1	129	136	O-13(LF)/S-6,2-2	-0.1
1994	Fla N	101	345	41	86	17	3	9	33	16-1	5	98	.249	.291	.394	75	-14	3-0	.966	-4	95	99	S-99	-1.0
1995	Fla N	120	420	60	107	18	7	17	60	36-4	5	110	.255	.318	.452	101	-1	4-3	.959	-16	89	96	*S-115	-0.8
1996	Fla N	109	320	37	81	18	7	8	33	22-1	3	99	.253	.307	.428	94	-4	3-3	.969	-3	99	130	S-44,3-33,2-20	-0.4
1997	†Fla N	94	252	35	69	18	2	6	30	14-3	1	68	.274	.315	.433	98	-2	3-1	.969	0	95	78	2-54,O-10(LF)/S-7,3-4,D-2	0.1
1998	Oak A	35	123	17	33	7	1	2	9	10-0	1	34	.268	.326	.390	88	-2	2-1	.909	-7	90	92	S-28/O-5(5-0-1),3D	-0.6
	Col N	42	71	9	18	6	0	3	15	2-0	1	19	.254	.276	.465	76	-2	0-0	.929	1	122	0	/O-9(4-0-5),2-7,S-7,3-3,D	-0.2
1999	Col N	96	286	41	78	17	2	8	41	16-0	0	69	.273	.310	.430	67	-14	3-2	.989	-5	94	81	2-66/1-8,O-4(0-2-2),S-3	-1.6
2000	†NY N	79	157	22	34	7	1	6	12	14-2	1	51	.217	.283	.389	71	-8	1-1	.953	-6	89	59	S-39,2-23/3-2,O-2(CF)	-1.1
2001	Atl N	6	9	0	2	0	0	0	0	0-0	0	3	.222	.222	.222	15	-1	1-0	1.000	2	245	0	/2S	0.1
Total	9	702	2044	273	523	109	23	62	242	133-11	17	571	.256	.305	.423	85	-49	22-11	.958	-38	93	99	S-349,2-173/3-43,O-43L,1-8,D-6	-5.6
ABBOTT, ODY Ody Cleon B 9.5.1888 New Eagle, PA D 4.13.1933 Washington, DC BR/TR 6-2/180# d9.10																								
1910	StL N	22	70	2	13	2	1	0	6	6	0	20	.186	.250	.243	46	-5	3	.982	1	109	70	O-21(CF)	-0.6
ABERCROMBIE, FRANCIS Francis Patterson B 1851 Fort Towson, MD D 11.11.1939 Philadelphia, PA d10.21																								
1871	Tro NA	1	4	0	0	0	0	0	0	0		0	.000	.000	.000	-99	-1	0-0	.667	-0	88	0	/S	-0.1
ABERNATHY, BRENT Michael Brent B 9.23.1977 Atlanta, GA BR/TR 6-1/185# d6.25																								
2001	TB A	79	304	43	82	17	1	5	33	27-1	0	35	.270	.328	.382	88	-5	8-3	.981	-2	93	108	2-79	-0.2
2002	TB A	117	463	46	112	18	4	2	40	25-0	6	46	.242	.288	.311	61	-27	10-4	.979	-4	96	103	*2-116/D	-2.4
2003	TB A	2	7	1	0	0	0	0	0	0-0	0	0	.000	.000	.000	-99	-2	1-0	.900	0	156	0	/2-2	-0.2
	KC A	10	27	2	2	0	0	0	0	1-0	0	3	.074	.107	.074	-45	-6	0-0	1.000	-1	102	82	/2-9	-0.6
	Year	12	34	3	2	0	0	0	0	1-0	0	3	.059	.086	.059	-55	-8	1-0	.976	-0	113	66	2-11	-0.8

Year	Tm Lg	G	AB	R	H	2B	3B	HR	RBI	BB-IB	HP	SO	AVG	OBP	SLG	AOPS	ABR	SB-CS	FA	FR	Rng	Thr	G at Pos	BFW
Total	3	208	801	92	196	35	5	7	73	53-1	6	84	.245	.295	.327	66	-40	19-7	.980	-6	96	103	2-206/D	-3.4
ABERSON, CLIFF Clifford Alexander "Kif" B 8.28.1921 Chicago, IL D 6.23.1973 Vallejo, CA BR/TR 6/200# d7.18																								
1947	Chi N	47	140	24	39	6	3	4	20	20	0	32	.279	.369	.450	121	4	0	.920	-1	78	255	O-40(LF)	0.1
1948	Chi N	12	32	1	6	1	0	1	6	5	0	10	.188	.297	.313	68	-1	0	.867	-1	76	168	/O-8(LF)	-0.3
1949	Chi N	4	7	0	0	0	0	0	0	0	0	2	.000	.000	.000	-99	-2	0	1.000	-0	97	0	/O(RF)	-0.2
Total	3	63	179	25	45	7	3	5	26	25	0	44	.251	.343	.408	103	1	0	.913	-1	78	235	/O-49(48-0-1)	-0.4
ABNER, SHAWN Shawn Wesley B 6.17.1966 Hamilton, OH BR/TR 6-1/190# d9.8																								
1987	SD N	16	47	5	13	3	1	2	7	2-0	0	8	.277	.306	.511	116	1	1-0	.926	1	101	257	O-14(6-2-6)	0.1
1988	SD N	37	83	6	15	3	0	2	5	4-1	1	19	.181	.225	.289	48	-6	0-1	.982	-0	98	78	O-35(10-11-17)	-0.8
1989	SD N	57	102	13	18	4	0	2	14	5-2	0	20	.176	.213	.275	39	-8	1-0	1.000	-0	101	0	O-51(23-23-6)	-1.0
1990	SD N	91	184	17	45	9	0	1	15	9-1	2	28	.245	.286	.310	64	-9	2-3	.991	-2	99	36	O-62(23-35-6)	-1.3
1991	SD N	53	115	15	19	4	1	1	5	7-4	1	25	.165	.218	.243	29	-11	0-0	1.000	2	117	58	O-39(0-36-3)	-1.1
	Cal A	41	101	12	23	6	1	2	9	4-0	0	18	.228	.257	.366	71	-4	1-2	1.000	2	101	205	O-38(0-31-7)/D-3	-0.4
1992	Chi A	97	208	21	58	10	1	1	16	12-2	3	35	.279	.323	.351	91	-3	1-2	1.000	3	115	49	O-94(12-14-75)/D	-0.2
Total	6	392	840	89	191	39	4	11	71	43-10	7	153	.227	.269	.323	65	-40	6-8	.993	5	106	75	O-333(74-152-120)/D-4	-4.7
ABRAMS, CAL Calvin Ross B 3.2.1924 Philadelphia, PA D 2.25.1997 Ft.Lauderdale, FL BL/TL 6/185# d4.20																								
1949	Bro N	8	24	6	2	1	0	0	0	7	0	6	.083	.290	.125	15	-3	1	.833	-1	67	197	/O-7(LF)	-0.4
1950	Bro N	38	44	5	9	1	0	0	4	9	0	13	.205	.340	.227	51	-3	0	1.000	0	114	0	O-15(9-1-5)	-0.3
1951	Bro N	67	150	27	42	8	0	3	19	36	0	26	.280	.419	.393	118	6	3-2	.944	-2	89	101	O-34(LF)	0.2
1952	Bro N	10	10	1	2	0	0	0	0	2	0	4	.200	.333	.200	51	-1	0-0	—	-0	0	0	/O(LF)	-0.1
	Cin N	71	158	23	44	9	2	2	13	19	0	25	.278	.356	.399	109	2	1-0	1.000	1	110	33	O-46(31-18-0)	0.1
	Year	81	168	24	46	9	2	2	13	21	0	29	.274	.354	.387	106	2	1-0	1.000	0	110	33	O-47(32-18-0)	0.0
1953	Pit N	119	448	66	128	10	6	15	43	58	0	70	.286	.368	.435	109	6	4-4	.973	3	97	158	*O-112(RF)	0.5
1954	Pit N	17	42	6	6	1	1	0	2	10	0	9	.143	.308	.214	39	-4	0-0	1.000	1	97	237	O-13(5-3-5)	-0.3
	Bal A	115	423	67	124	22	7	6	25	72	4	67	.293	.400	.421	135	24	1-4	.977	1	109	68	*O-115(0-14-101)	2.0
1955	Bal A	118	309	56	75	12	3	6	32	89-2	3	69	.243	.413	.359	118	15	2-8	.985	-2	94	114	O-96(13-58-46)/1-4	0.7
1956	Chi A	4	3	0	1	0	0	0	0	2-0	0	1	.333	.600	.333	150	1	0-0	1.000	0	123	0	/O-2(1-0-1)	0.1
Total	8	567	1611	257	433	64	19	32	138	304-2	7	290	.269	.386	.392	113	43	12-18	.977	1	100	107	O-441(101-94-270)/1-4	2.5
ABREU, BOBBY Bob Kelly B 3.11.1974 Aragua, Venezuela BL/TR 6/160# d9.1																								
1996	Hou N	15	22	1	5	1	0	0	1	2-0	0	3	.227	.292	.273	54	-1	0-0	1.000	-0	85	0	/O-7(6-0-1)	-0.2
1997	†Hou N	59	188	22	47	10	2	3	26	21-0	1	48	.250	.329	.372	86	-4	7-2	.978	-1	91	111	O-53(10-1-43)	-0.6
1998	Phi N	151	497	68	155	29	6	17	74	84-14	0	133	.312	.409	.497	136	29	19-10	.973	6	101	177	*O-146(RF)	2.7
1999	Phi N	152	546	118	183	35	**11**	20	93	109-8	3	113	.335	.446	.549	146	45	27-9	.989	-7	90	82	*O-146(RF)/D-5	3.0
2000	Phi N	154	576	103	182	42	10	25	79	100-9	1	116	.316	.416	.554	142	40	28-8	.989	11	111	136	*O-152(RF)	4.3
2001	Phi N	**162**	588	118	170	48	4	31	110	106-11	1	137	.289	.393	.543	144	42	36-14	.976	-3	93	101	*O-162(RF)	3.3
2002	Phi N	157	572	102	176	**50**	6	20	85	104-9	3	117	.308	.413	.521	156	49	31-12	.983	-6	90	97	*O-154(0-18-148)	3.8
2003	Phi N	158	577	99	173	35	1	20	101	109-13	2	126	.300	.409	.468	138	38	22-9	.981	-4	100	58	*O-158(RF)	2.7
Total	8	1008	3566	631	1091	250	40	136	569	635-64	11	793	.306	.409	.513	140	238	170-64	.982	-6	97	107	O-978(16-19-956)/D-5	19.0
ABREU, JOE Joseph Lawrence B 5.24.1913 Oakland, CA D 3.17.1993 Hayward, CA BR/TR 5-8/160# d4.23																								
1942	Cin N	9	28	4	6	1	0	1	3	4	0	4	.214	.313	.357	96	0	0	.941	-1	85	97	/3-6,2-2	0.0
ABSTEIN, BILL William Henry "Big Bill" B 2.2.1883 St.Louis, MO D 4.8.1940 St.Louis, MO BR/TR 6/185# d9.25																								
1906	Pit N	8	20	2	4	0	0	0	3	0	0		.200	.200	.200	24	-2	2	.769	-1	91	0	/2-3,O-2(RF)	-0.3
1909	†Pit N	137	512	51	133	20	10	1	70	27	4		.260	.302	.344	93	-6	16	.982	-6	86	**118**	*1-135	-1.7
1910	StL A	25	87	1	13	2	0	0	3	2	0		.149	.169	.172	7	-10	3	.963	1	148	104	1-23	-1.0
Total	3	170	619	54	150	22	10	1	76	29	4		.242	.281	.315	80	-18	21	.979	-6	95	116	1-158/2-3,O-2(RF)	-3.0
ACOSTA, MERITO Baldomero Pedro (Fernandez) B 5.19.1896 Bauta, Cuba D 11.17.1963 Miami, FL BL/TL 5-7/140# d6.15 b-Jose																								
1913	Was A	12	20	3	6	0	1	0	1	4	0	2	.300	.417	.400	136	1	2	.714	-1	62	0	/O-9(6-2-1)	-0.1
1914	Was A	39	74	10	19	2	2	0	4	11	0	18	.257	.353	.338	104	1	3-4	.857	1	79	268	O-25(15-5-5)	0.0
1915	Was A	72	163	20	34	4	1	0	18	28	4	15	.209	.338	.245	73	-4	8-4	.963	0	106	78	O-53(22-2-29)	-0.6
1916	Was A	5	8	0	1	0	0	0	0	2	0	0	.125	.300	.125	28	-1	0	1.000	1	148	231	/O-4(LF)	0.0
1918	Was A	3	2	0	0	0	0	0	0	0	0	1	.000	.000	.000	-99	0	0	—	0			H	-0.1
	Phi A	49	169	23	51	3	3	0	14	18	0	10	.302	.369	.355	117	4	4	.944	-2	87	117	O-45(5-20-21)	-0.1
	Year	52	171	23	51	3	3	0	14	18	0	11	.298	.365	.351	115	3	4	.944	-2	87	117	O-45(5-20-21)	-0.2
Total	5	180	436	56	111	9	7	0	37	63	4	46	.255	.354	.307	97	1	17-8	.933	-1	94	124	O-136(52-29-56)	-0.9
ADAIR, JIMMY James Aubrey "Choppy" B 1.25.1907 Waxahachie, TX D 12.9.1982 Dallas, TX BR/TR 5-10.5/154# d8.24 C11																								
1931	Chi N	18	76	9	21	3	1	0	3	1	0	8	.276	.286	.342	67	-4	1	.948	-1	97	76	S-18	-0.4
ADAIR, JERRY Kenneth Jerry B 12.17.1936 Sand Springs, OK D 5.31.1987 Tulsa, OK BR/TR 6/175# d9.2 C4																								
1958	Bal A	11	19	1	2	0	0	0	0	1-0	0	7	.105	.150	.105	-30	-3	0-0	.967	0	102	80	S-10/2	-0.3
1959	Bal A	12	35	3	11	0	1	0	2	1-0	0	5	.314	.333	.371	95	0	0-0	.932	-3	75	75	2-11/S	-0.3
1960	Bal A	3	5	1	1	0	0	1	1	0-0	0	0	.200	.200	.800	159	0	0-0	1.000	0	112	224	/2-3	0.1
1961	Bal A	133	386	41	102	21	1	9	37	35-4	2	51	.264	.326	.394	95	-3	5-2	.987	0	97	98	*2-107,S-27/3-2	0.7
1962	Bal A	139	538	67	153	29	4	11	48	27-1	2	77	.284	.319	.414	103	0	7-7	.969	-8	92	112	*S-113,2-34/3	0.3
1963	Bal A	109	382	34	87	21	3	6	30	9-2	2	51	.228	.246	.346	67	-18	3-3	.985	3	99	109	*2-103	-0.7
1964	Bal A	155	569	56	141	20	3	9	47	28-10	1	72	.248	.283	.341	73	-22	3-2	**.994**	9	99	115	*2-153	0.0
1965	Bal A	157	582	51	151	26	3	7	66	35-7	2	65	.259	.303	.351	84	-13	6-4	**.986**	9	106	104	*2-157	1.0
1966	Bal A	17	52	3	15	1	0	0	3	4-0	0	8	.288	.333	.308	89	-1	0-0	.969	-1	93	87	2-13	-0.1
	Chi A	105	370	27	90	18	2	4	36	17-0	1	44	.243	.275	.335	81	-10	3-2	.975	3	111	91	S-75,2-50	0.2
	Year	122	422	30	105	19	2	4	39	21-0	1	52	.249	.282	.332	82	-11	3-2	.975	2	111	91	S-75,2-63	0.1
1967	Chi A	28	98	6	20	4	0	0	9	4-0	1	17	.204	.240	.245	46	-7	0-1	.985	1	96	156	2-27	-0.5
	†Bos A	89	316	41	92	13	1	3	26	13-0	2	35	.291	.321	.367	96	-2	1-4	.952	-6	102	153	3-35,S-30,2-23	-0.6
	Year	117	414	47	112	17	1	3	35	17-0	3	52	.271	.302	.338	85	-8	1-5	.976	-6	89	129	2-50,3-35,S-30	-1.1
1968	Bos A	74	208	18	45	1	0	2	12	9-2	1	28	.216	.252	.250	49	-13	0-0	.976	-5	92	71	S-46,2-12/3-7,1	-1.6
1969	KC A	126	432	29	108	9	1	5	48	20-4	3	36	.250	.285	.310	67	-21	1-3	.984	-21	91	62	*2-109/S-8,3	-3.7
1970	KC A	7	27	0	4	0	0	0	1	5-1	0	3	.148	.281	.148	22	-3	0-1	1.000	-0	85	109	/2-7	-0.3
Total	13	1165	4019	378	1022	163	19	57	366	208-31	17	499	.254	.292	.347	80	-116	29-29	.985	-19	98	101	2-810,S-310/3-46,1	-5.8
ADAMS, SPARKY Earl John B 8.26.1894 Zerbe, PA D 2.24.1989 Pottsville, PA BR/TR 5-5.5/151# d9.18																								
1922	Chi N	11	44	5	11	0	1	0	3	4	0	3	.250	.313	.295	56	-3	1-2	.914	-2	98	89	2-11	-0.5
1923	Chi N	95	311	40	90	12	0	4	35	26	1	10	.289	.346	.367	88	-5	20-19	.935	-6	95	103	S-79/O(RF)	-0.5
1924	Chi N	117	418	66	117	11	5	1	27	40	1	20	.280	.344	.337	83	-9	15-17	.941	-5	97	117	S-88,2-19	-0.8
1925	Chi N	149	627	95	180	29	8	2	48	44	7	15	.287	.341	.368	80	-19	26-12	**.983**	**27**	109	105	*2-144/S-5	1.3
1926	Chi N	154	624	95	193	35	3	0	39	52	5	27	.309	.367	.375	99	1	27	.965	20	105	120	*2-136,3-19/S-2	2.6
1927	Chi N	146	647	100	189	17	7	0	49	42	0	26	.292	.335	.340	81	-18	26	.994	4	95	97	2-60,3-53,S-40	-0.5
1928	Pit N	135	539	91	149	14	6	0	38	64	4	18	.276	.357	.325	76	-17	8	.971	-7	97	79	*2-107,S-27/O(RF)	-1.7
1929	Pit N	74	196	37	51	8	1	0	11	15	1	5	.260	.316	.311	55	-14	3	.901	-10	85	66	S-30,2-20,3-15/O-2(LF)	-1.9
1930	†StL N	137	570	98	179	36	9	0	55	45	1	27	.314	.365	.409	84	-14	7	**.966**	-12	84	101	*3-104,2-25/S-7	-1.6
1931	†StL N	143	608	97	178	**46**	5	1	40	42	2	24	.293	.340	.390	92	-5	16	**.963**	-13	87	**122**	*3-138/S-6	-1.3
1932	StL N	31	127	22	35	3	1	0	13	14	1	5	.276	.352	.315	79	-3	0	.931	-2	81	215	3-30	-0.4
1933	StL N	8	30	1	5	1	0	0	0	1	1	3	.167	.219	.200	19	-3	0	.955	-1	101	66	/S-5,3-3	-0.4
	Cin N	137	538	59	141	21	1	1	22	44	2	30	.262	.320	.310	82	-11	3	.963	1	107	83	*3-132/S-8	-0.5
	Year	145	568	60	146	22	1	1	22	45	3	33	.257	.315	.305	78	-15	3	**.959**	0	**107**	87	*3-135,S-13	-0.9
1934	Cin N	87	278	38	70	16	1	0	14	20	2	10	.252	.307	.317	69	-12	2	.955	-1	102	175	3-38,2-29	-1.0
Total	13	1424	5557	844	1588	249	48	9	394	453	28	223	.286	.343	.353	82	-132	154-50	.974	-7	102	102	2-551,3-532,S-297/O-4(2-0-2)	-7.2
ADAMS, BUSTER Elvin Clark B 6.24.1915 Trinidad, CO D 9.1.1990 Rancho Mirage, CA BR/TR 6/180# d4.27																								
1939	StL N	2	1	1	0	0	0	0	0	0	0	0	.000	.000	.000	-94	0	0	—	0			H	0.0
1943	StL N	8	11	1	1	1	0	0	1	4	0	4	.091	.333	.182	48	0	0	1.000	0	111	0	/O-6(CF)	-0.1
	Phi N	111	418	48	107	14	7	4	38	39	0	67	.256	.319	.352	98	-2	2	.984	0	106	59	*O-107(1-107-0)	-0.6

Year	Tm Lg	G	AB	R	H	2B	3B	HR	RBI	BB-IB	HP	SO	AVG	OBP	SLG	AOPS	ABR	SB-CS	FA	FR	Rng	Thr	G at Pos	BFW
	Year	119	429	49	108	15	7	4	39	43	0	71	.252	.320	.347	96	-3	2	.984	0	106	57	*O-113(1-113-0)	-0.7
1944	Phi N	151	584	86	165	35	3	17	64	74	7	74	.283	.370	.440	132	27	2	.979	3	105	98	*O-151(CF)	2.5
1945	Phi N	14	56	6	13	3	1	2	8	5	0	5	.232	.295	.429	103	0	0	1.000	-1	93	0	O-14(LF)	-0.2
	StL N	140	578	98	169	26	0	20	101	57	3	75	.292	.359	.441	119	14	3	.978	-6	96	74	*O-140(14-126-0)	0.3
	Year	154	634	104	182	29	1	22	109	62	3	80	.287	.353	.440	117	14	3	.979	-7	96	68	*O-154(27-126-0)	0.1
1946	StL N	81	173	21	32	6	0	5	22	29	3	27	.185	.312	.306	73	-6	3	.990	-2	97	27	O-58(24-35-0)	-1.1
1947	Phi N	69	182	21	45	11	1	2	15	26	0	29	.247	.341	.352	88	-3	2	.954	-1	90	139	O-51(6-1-44)	-0.5
Total	6	576	2003	282	532	96	12	50	249	234	13	281	.266	.346	.400	110	30	12	.979	-7	100	77	O-527(58-426-44)	0.3
ADAMS, GEORGE George B Grafton, MA BR/TR 5-6/175# d6.14																								
1879	Syr N	4	13	0	3	0	0	0	0	1		1	.231	.286	.231	82	0		1.000	-1	0	0	/O-2(CF),1-2	-0.1
ADAMS, GLENN Glenn Charles B 10.4.1947 Northbridge, MA BL/TR 6/185# d5.4																								
1975	SF N	61	90	10	27	2	1	4	15	11-0	1	25	.300	.379	.478	132	4	1-0	.941	-1	92	77	O-25(16-0-9)	0.2
1976	SF N	69	74	2	18	4	0	0	3	1-0	0	12	.243	.253	.297	54	-5	1-0	1.000	-1	44	0	/O-6(4-0-2)	-0.6
1977	Min A	95	269	32	91	17	0	6	49	18-3	0	30	.338	.376	.468	132	12	0-2	.969	0	96	131	D-47,O-44(16-0-28)	0.9
1978	Min A	116	310	27	80	18	1	7	35	17-0	0	32	.258	.297	.390	90	-5	0-1	1.000	1	289	0	*D-101/O-5(2-0-3)	-0.8
1979	Min A	119	326	34	98	13	1	8	50	25-0	3	27	.301	.350	.420	104	2	2-2	.958	-4	81	67	D-55,O-53(45-0-8)	-0.6
1980	Min A	99	262	32	75	11	2	6	38	15-1	0	26	.286	.320	.412	94	-3	2-4	.947	-1	86	0	D-81,O-12(LF)	-0.8
1981	Min A	72	220	13	46	10	0	2	24	20-4	0	26	.209	.273	.282	57	-12	0-1	—	0	0	0	D-62	-1.5
1982	Tor A	30	66	2	17	4	0	1	11	4-0	0	5	.258	.288	.364	74	-2	0-0	—	0	0	0	D-27	-0.3
Total	8	661	1617	152	452	79	5	34	225	111-8	4	183	.280	.324	.398	96	-9	6-10	.959	-7	88	79	D-373,O-145(95-0-50)	-3.5
ADAMS, DOUG Harold Douglas B 1.27.1943 Blue River, WI BL/TR 6-3/185# d9.8																								
1969	Chi A	8	14	1	3	0	0	0	1	1-0	0	3	.214	.267	.214	34	-1	0-0	1.000	-1	0	0	/C-4	-0.2
ADAMS, HERB Herbert Loren B 4.14.1928 Hollywood, CA BL/TL 5-9/160# d9.17 Mil 1951-52																								
1948	Chi A	5	11	1	3	1	0	0	0	1	0	1	.273	.333	.364	88	0	0-0	1.000	2	111	706	/O-4(0-2-2)	0.1
1949	Chi A	56	208	26	61	5	3	0	16	9	0	16	.293	.323	.346	79	-8	1-2	.975	-1	93	120	O-48(14-33-1)	-1.1
1950	Chi A	34	118	12	24	2	3	0	2	12	2	7	.203	.288	.271	45	-10	3-0	.978	-1	104	37	O-33(CF)	-1.1
Total	3	95	337	39	88	8	6	0	18	22	2	24	.261	.310	.320	67	-18	4-2	.978	-1	98	113	/O-85(14-68-3)	-2.1
ADAMS, JIM James J. B 1868 E.St.Louis, IL TR d4.21																								
1890	StL AA	1	4	0	1	0	0	0	0	0	0		.250	.250	.250	42	0	0	1.000	-0	*99*	*84*	/C	0.0
ADAMS, BERT John Bertram B 6.21.1891 Wharton, TX D 6.24.1940 Los Angeles, CA BB/TR 6-1/185# d8.30																								
1910	Cle A	5	13	1	3	0	0	0	0	0	0		.231	.231	.231	44	-1	0	.964	2	*99*	*250*	/C-5	0.1
1911	Cle A	2	5	0	1	0	0	0	0	1	0		.200	.333	.200	50	0	0	.900	-1	*74*	*111*	/C-2	-0.1
1912	Cle A	20	54	5	11	2	1	0	6	4	0		.204	.259	.278	52	-4	0	.942	1	*97*	*102*	C-20	-0.1
1915	Phi N	24	27	1	3	0	0	0	2	2	0	3	.111	.172	.111	-13	-4	0	.974	-2	*99*	*70*	C-23/1	-0.6
1916	Phi N	11	13	2	3	0	0	0	1	0	0	3	.231	.231	.231	40	-1	0	.929	0	111	116	C-11	-0.1
1917	Phi N	43	107	4	22	4	1	1	7	0	0	20	.206	.206	.290	49	-7	0	.994	2	*112*	*111*	C-38/1	-0.3
1918	Phi N	84	227	10	40	4	0	0	12	10	1	26	.176	.214	.194	23	-21	5	.976	-3	*102*	*83*	C-76	-2.0
1919	Phi N	78	232	14	54	7	2	1	17	6	0	27	.233	.252	.293	59	-12	4	.966	-7	*82*	*112*	C-73/1	-1.5
Total	8	267	678	37	137	17	4	2	45	23	1	79	.202	.229	.248	42	-50	9	.970	-9	*96*	*102*	C-248/1-3	-4.6
ADAMS, DICK Richard Leroy B 4.8.1920 Tuolumne, CA BR/TL 6/185# d5.20 b-Bobby																								
1947	Phi A	37	89	9	18	2	3	2	11	2	0	18	.202	.220	.360	58	-6	0-0	.995	1	119	114	1-24/O-3(1-0-2)	-0.6
ADAMS, RICKY Ricky Lee B 1.21.1959 Upland, CA BR/TR 6-2/180# d9.15																								
1982	Cal A	8	14	1	2	0	0	0	0	0-0	1	2	.143	.200	.143	-4	-2	1-0	.947	-2	81	143	/S-8	-0.3
1983	Cal A	58	112	22	28	2	0	2	6	5-0	3	12	.250	.300	.321	72	-5	1-1	.960	13	127	135	S-38,3-16/2-4	1.1
1985	SF N	54	121	12	23	3	1	2	10	5-3	1	23	.190	.228	.281	44	-10	1-1	.964	2	98	83	S-25,3-16/2-6	-0.7
Total	3	120	247	35	53	5	1	4	16	10-3	5	37	.215	.260	.291	54	-17	3-2	.961	13	111	116	/S-71,3-32,2-10	0.1
ADAMS, BOBBY Robert Henry B 12.14.1921 Tuolumne, CA D 2.13.1997 Gig Harbor, WA BR/TR 5-10/170# d4.16 C6 b-Dick s-Mike																								
1946	Cin N	94	311	35	76	13	3	4	24	18	3	32	.244	.292	.344	83	-8	16	.967	22	123	177	2-74/O-2(RF),3	1.8
1947	Cin N	81	217	39	59	11	2	4	20	25	4	23	.272	.358	.396	101	1	9	.967	6	103	110	2-69	1.0
1948	Cin N	87	262	33	78	20	3	1	21	25	1	23	.298	.361	.408	112	5	6	.965	-7	86	88	2-64/3-7	0.1
1949	Cin N	107	277	32	70	16	2	0	25	26	0	36	.253	.317	.325	72	-11	4	.984	-9	90	74	2-63,3-14	-1.6
1950	Cin N	115	348	57	98	21	8	3	25	43	0	29	.282	.361	.414	103	2	7	.981	-5	98	80	2-53,3-42	0.0
1951	Cin N	125	403	57	107	12	5	5	24	43	1	40	.266	.338	.357	86	-8	4-10	.956	-7	98	59	3-60,2-42/O(RF)	-1.6
1952	Cin N	**154**	637	85	180	25	4	6	48	49	0	67	.283	.334	.363	93	-6	11-9	.962	7	**105**	105	*3-154	0.0
1953	Cin N	150	607	99	167	14	6	8	49	58	0	67	.275	.338	.357	81	-17	3-2	.951	2	104	121	*3-150	-1.5
1954	Cin N	110	390	69	105	25	6	3	23	55	3	46	.269	.362	.387	93	-2	2-5	.951	1	95	132	3-93/2-2	-0.3
1955	Cin N	64	150	23	41	11	2	2	20	20-1	3	21	.273	.368	.413	102	1	2-0	.969	4	113	158	3-42/2-5	0.5
	Chi A	28	21	8	2	0	1	0	3	4-0	0	4	.095	.240	.190	16	-3	0-0	.933	2	126	0	/3-9,2	-0.1
1956	Bal A	41	111	19	25	6	1	0	7	25-0	0	15	.225	.362	.297	84	-1	1-1	.984	-5	94	119	3-24,2-18	-0.5
1957	Chi N	60	187	21	47	10	2	1	10	17-0	2	28	.251	.320	.342	79	-5	0-3	.949	-5	84	58	3-47/2	-1.2
1958	Chi N	62	96	14	27	4	4	0	4	6-0	0	15	.281	.324	.406	93	-1	2-0	.961	-1	118	17	1-11/3-9,2-7	-0.2
1959	Chi N	3	2	0	0	0	0	0	0	0-0	0	1	.000	.000	.000	-99	-1	0-0	.667	-0	0	0	/1	-0.1
Total	14	1281	4019	591	1082	188	49	37	303	414-1	17	447	.269	.340	.368	90	-54	67-30	.955	4	100	103	3-652,2-399/1-12,O-3(RF)	-3.7
ADAMS, BOB Robert Melvin B 1.6.1952 Pittsburgh, PA BR/TR 6-2/200# d7.10																								
1977	Det A	15	24	2	6	1	0	2	2	0-0	0	5	.250	.250	.542	103	0	0-0	1.000	-0	71	59	/1-2,C	0.0
ADAMS, MIKE Robert Michael B 7.24.1948 Cincinnati, OH BR/TR 5-9/180# d9.10 f-Bobby																								
1972	Min A	3	6	0	2	0	0	0	0	0-0	0	1	.333	.333	.333	94	0	0-0	1.000	-0	45	0	/O(LF)	0.0
1973	Min A	55	66	21	14	2	0	3	6	17-0	1	18	.212	.381	.379	110	2	2-1	.978	-0	109	0	O-24(23-1-0)/D-2	0.0
1976	Chi N	25	29	1	4	2	0	0	2	8-0	1	7	.138	.342	.207	54	-1	0-0	1.000	-1	60	0	/O-4(2-0-2),3-3,2	-0.3
1977	Chi N	2	2	0	0	0	0	0	0	0-0	0	1	.000	.000	.000	-90	-1	0-0	—	-0	0	0	/O-2(1-1-0)	-0.1
1978	Oak A	15	15	5	3	1	0	0	1	7-0	0	2	.200	.455	.267	113	1	0-0	1.000	-0	58	134	/2-6,3-3,D-3	0.1
Total	5	100	118	27	23	5	0	3	9	32-0	2	29	.195	.375	.314	93	1	2-1	.980	-2	100	0	/O-31(27-2-2),2-7,3-6,D-5	-0.3
ADAMS, SPENCER Spencer Dewey B 6.21.1898 Layton, UT D 11.24.1970 Salt Lake City, UT BL/TR 5-9/158# d5.8																								
1923	Pit N	25	56	11	14	0	1	0	4	6	0	6	.250	.323	.286	60	-3	2-1	.879	-5	85	110	2-11/S-6	-0.7
1925	†Was A	39	55	11	15	4	1	0	4	5	0	4	.273	.333	.382	83	-2	1-1	.941	-3	89	85	2-15/S-8,3-3	-0.3
1926	†NY A	28	25	7	3	1	0	0	1	3	0	7	.120	.214	.160	-1	-4	1-0	1.000	2	109	163	/2-4,3	-0.2
1927	StL A	88	259	32	69	11	3	0	29	24	2	33	.266	.333	.332	71	-11	1-8	.948	2	97	99	2-54,3-28	-0.9
Total	4	180	395	61	101	16	5	0	38	38	2	50	.256	.324	.322	66	-20	5-10	.944	-3	95	101	/2-84,3-32,S-14	-2.1
ADCOCK, JOE Joseph Wilbur B 10.30.1927 Coushatta, LA D 5.3.1999 Coushatta, LA BR/TR 6-4/220# d4.23 M1																								
1950	Cin N	102	372	46	109	16	1	8	55	24	0	24	.293	.336	.406	94	-4	2	.968	2	107	106	O-75(LF),1-24	-0.8
1951	Cin N	113	395	40	96	16	4	10	47	24	1	29	.243	.288	.380	77	-14	1-2	.983	3	107	94	*O-107(LF)	-1.9
1952	Cin N	117	378	43	105	22	4	13	52	23	1	38	.278	.321	.460	115	6	1-4	.985	5	122	84	O-85(LF),1-17	0.3
1953	Mil N	**157**	590	71	168	33	6	18	80	42	2	82	.285	.334	.453	110	7	3-2	.991	-3	90	111	*1-157	-0.5
1954	Mil N	133	500	73	154	27	5	23	87	44	3	58	.308	.365	.520	137	26	1-4	.995	-11	68	108	*1-133	0.5
1955	Mil N	84	288	40	76	14	0	15	45	31-3	2	44	.264	.339	.469	118	7	0-2	.990	-5	80	96	1-78	-0.3
1956	Mil N	137	454	76	132	23	1	38	103	32-6	1	86	.291	.337	.597	**154**	32	1-0	**.995**	-4	87	118	*1-129	2.1
1957	†Mil N	65	209	31	60	13	2	12	38	20-3	1	51	.287	.351	.541	146	13	0-0	.996	-3	81	142	1-56	0.7
1958	†Mil N	105	320	40	88	15	1	19	54	21-1	1	63	.275	.317	.506	125	10	0-0	.989	-2	93	118	1-71,O-22(LF)	0.4
1959	Mil N	115	404	53	118	19	2	25	76	32-6	0	77	.292	.339	.535	141	22	0-0	.998	9	138	102	1-89,O-21(LF)	2.4
1960	Mil N★	138	514	55	153	21	4	25	91	46-7	1	86	.298	.354	.500	142	28	2-2	**.993**	3	107	96	*1-136	2.3
1961	Mil N	152	562	77	160	20	0	35	108	59-4	2	94	.285	.354	.507	133	26	2-1	**.993**	-6	92	106	*1-148	1.1
1962	Mil N	121	391	48	97	12	1	29	78	50-8	1	91	.248	.333	.506	126	13	2-0	**.997**	-2	88	92	*1-112	0.5
1963	Cle A	97	283	28	71	7	1	13	49	30-4	0	53	.251	.320	.420	107	2	1-2	.995	-4	72	86	1-78	-0.7
1964	LA A	118	366	39	98	13	0	21	64	48-4	0	61	.268	.352	.475	142	20	0-2	.993	-6	78	117	*1-105	0.8
1965	Cal A	122	349	30	84	14	0	14	47	37-3	1	74	.241	.315	.401	104	2	2-2	.996	-3	84	102	1-97	-0.7

Year	Tm Lg	G	AB	R	H	2B	3B	HR	RBI	BB-IB	HP	SO	AVG	OBP	SLG	AOPS	ABR	SB-CS	FA	FR	Rng	Thr	G at Pos	BFW
1966	Cal A	83	231	33	63	10	3	18	48	31-6	0	48	.273	.355	.576	168	20	2-2	.997	-0	98	124	1-71	1.7
Total	17	1959	6606	823	1832	295	35	336	1122	594-55	17	1059	.277	.337	.485	125	216	20-25	.994	-27	89	106	*1-1501,O-310(LF)	7.9
ADDIS, BOB Robert Gordon B 11.6.1925 Mineral, OH BL/TR 6/175# d9.1																								
1950	Bos N	16	28	7	7	1	0	0	2	3	0	5	.250	.323	.286	66	-1	1	1.000	-1	82	0	/O-7(2-1-4)	-0.2
1951	Bos N	85	199	23	55	7	0	1	24	9	0	10	.276	.308	.327	76	-7	3-2	.982	-1	108	25	O-46(31-10-5)	-1.1
1952	Chi N	93	292	38	86	13	2	1	20	23	0	30	.295	.346	.363	96	-1	4-4	.988	2	103	122	O-79(3-42-37)	-0.2
1953	Chi N	10	12	2	2	1	0	0	1	2	0	0	.167	.286	.250	40	-1	0-0	1.000	1	122	475	/O-3(0-1-2)	0.0
	Pit N	4	3	0	0	0	0	0	0	0	0	2	.000	.000	.000	-99	-1	0-0	—	0			H	-0.1
	Year	14	15	2	2	1	0	0	1	2	0	2	.133	.235	.200	15	-2	0-0	1.000	1	122	475	/O-3(0-1-2)	-0.1
Total	4	208	534	70	150	22	2	2	47	37	0	47	.281	.327	.341	84	-11	8-6	.986	2	105	90	O-135(36-54-48)	-1.6
ADDUCI, JIM James David B 8.9.1959 Chicago, IL BL/TL 6-5/200# d9.12																								
1983	StL N	10	20	0	1	0	0	0	0	1-0	0	6	.050	.095	.050	-59	-4	0-0	1.000	0	105	71	/1-6,O(LF)	-0.5
1986	Mil A	3	11	2	1	1	0	0	0	1-0	0	2	.091	.167	.182	-5	-2	0-0	1.000	0	142	42	/1-3	-0.1
1988	Mil A	44	94	8	25	6	1	1	15	0-0	0	15	.266	.258	.383	79	-3	0-1	.969	1	100	117	O-24(16-0-9),D-10/1-3	-0.4
1989	Phi N	13	19	1	7	1	0	0	0	0-0	0	4	.368	.368	.421	125	1	0-0	1.000	1	170	49	/1-4,O(LF)	0.1
Total	4	70	144	11	34	8	1	1	15	2-0	0	27	.236	.242	.326	58	-8	0-1	.969	1	98	115	/O-26(18-0-9),1-16,D-10	-0.9
ADDY, BOB Robert Edward "Magnet" B 2.1845 Rochester, NY D 4.9.1910 Pocatello, ID BL/TL 5-8/160# d5.6 M2																								
1871	Rok NA	**25**	118	30	32	6	0	0	13	4		0	.271	.295	.322	81	-2	8-1	.768	-1	**115**	65	*2-22/S-3	-0.2
1873	Phi NA	10	51	12	16	1	0	0	10	2		0	.314	.340	.333	97	0	1-1	.855	-2	87	54	2-10	-0.2
	Bos NA	31	152	37	54	6	3	1	32	2		1	.355	.364	.454	131	4	6-5	.702	-3	68	0	O-31(RF)	0.2
	Year	41	203	49	70	7	3	1	42	4		1	.345	.357	.424	122	4	7-6	.702	-5	68	0	O-31(RF),2-10	0.0
1874	Har NA	50	213	25	51	9	2	0	22	1		1	.239	.243	.300	70	-8	4-2	.846	2	113	44	*2-45/3-5,S	-0.7
1875	Phi NA	69	310	60	80	8	4	0	43	0		2	.258	.258	.310	93	-3	16-8	.761	-1	127	101	*O-68(0-1-67)/2-2,M	0.0
1876	Chi N	32	142	36	40	4	1	0	16	5		0	.282	.306	.324	98	-1		.800	-1	108	0	O-32(3-0-29)	-0.2
1877	Cin N	57	245	27	68	2	3	0	31	6		5	.278	.295	.310	102	1		.805	5	165	**229**	*O-57(0-1-56)/,M	0.6
Total	4 NA	185	844	164	233	30	9	1	120	9		4	.276	.284	.336	93	-9	35-17	.000	-5	108	69	/O-99(0-1-98),2-79,3-5,S-4	-0.9
Total	2	89	387	63	108	6	4	0	47	11		5	.279	.299	.315	100	0		.803	4	143	142	/O-89(3-1-85)	0.4
ADERHOLT, MORRIE Morris Woodroe B 9.13.1915 Mt.Olive, NC D 3.18.1955 Sarasota, FL BL/TR 6-1/188# d9.13																								
1939	Was A	7	25	5	5	0	0	1	4	2	0	6	.200	.259	.320	51	-2	0-1	.872	-1	92	64	/2-7	-0.3
1940	Was A	1	2	0	0	0	0	0	0	0	0	0	.000	.000	.000	-99	-1	0-0	1.000	0	59	237	/2	-0.1
1941	Was A	11	14	3	2	0	0	0	1	1	0	3	.143	.200	.143	-8	-2	0-0	.818	-1	45	97	/2-2,3	-0.3
1944	Bro N	17	59	9	16	2	3	0	10	4	0	4	.271	.317	.407	105	0	0	.871	-1	92	94	O-13(11-0-2)	-0.2
1945	Bro N	39	60	4	13	1	0	0	6	3	0	10	.217	.254	.233	36	-5	0	1.000	-1	66	0	/O-8(7-0-1)	-0.7
	Bos N	31	102	15	34	4	0	2	11	9	0	6	.333	.387	.431	127	4	3	.984	-0	108	0	O-24(LF)/2	0.2
	Year	70	162	19	47	5	0	2	17	12	0	16	.290	.339	.358	94	-1	3	.985	-1	101	0	O-32(31-0-1)/2	-0.5
Total	5	106	262	36	70	7	3	3	32	19	0	29	.267	.317	.351	85	-6	3-1	.949	-5	98	29	/O-45(42-0-3),2-11,3	-1.4
ADKINS, DICK Richard Earl B 3.3.1920 Electra, TX D 9.12.1955 Electra, TX BR/TR 5-10/165# d9.19																								
1942	Phi A	3	7	2	1	0	0	0	0	2	0	2	.143	.333	.143	37	0	0-0	.875	-1	91	81	/S-3	-0.1
ADKINSON, HENRY Henry Magee B 9.1.1874 Chicago, IL D 5.1.1923 Salt Lake City, UT d9.25																								
1895	StL N	1	5	1	2	0	0	0	0	0	0	2	.400	.400	.400	108	0	0	.667	-0	0	0	/O(LF)	0.0
ADLESH, DAVE David George B 7.15.1943 Long Beach, CA BR/TR 6/187# d5.12																								
1963	Hou N	6	8	0	0	0	0	0	0	0-0	0	4	.000	.000	.000	-99	-2	0-0	.889	-1	*74*	*0*	/C-6	-0.4
1964	Hou N	3	10	0	2	0	0	0	0	0-0	0	5	.200	.200	.200	14	-1	0-0	1.000	-0	*48*	*168*	/C-3	-0.2
1965	Hou N	15	34	2	5	1	0	0	3	2-0	1	12	.147	.216	.176	13	-4	0-0	1.000	-1	*95*	*88*	C-13	-0.4
1966	Hou N	3	6	0	0	0	0	0	0	0-0	0	4	.000	.000	.000	-99	-2	0-0	1.000	0	*0*	*0*	/C	-0.1
1967	Hou N	39	94	4	17	1	0	1	4	11-3	0	28	.181	.264	.223	43	-7	0-0	.995	-2	*83*	*56*	C-31	-0.9
1968	Hou N	40	104	3	19	1	1	0	4	5-2	1	27	.183	.227	.212	33	-9	0-0	.990	-3	*65*	*52*	C-36	-1.2
Total	6	106	256	9	43	3	1	1	11	18-5	2	80	.168	.227	.199	26	-25	0-0	.992	-7	*74*	*60*	/C-90	-3.2
AFENIR, TROY Michael Troy B 9.21.1963 Escondido, CA BR/TR 6-4/185# d9.14																								
1987	Hou N	10	20	1	6	1	0	0	1	0-0	0	12	.300	.300	.350	74	-1	0-0	.974	-3	49	44	C-10	-0.4
1990	Oak A	14	14	0	2	0	0	0	2	0-0	0	6	.143	.133	.143	-21	-2	0-0	1.000	-2	0	78	C-12/D	-0.4
1991	Oak A	5	11	0	1	0	0	0	0	0-0	0	2	.091	.091	.091	-53	-2	0-0	1.000	0	188	0	/C-4,D	-0.2
1992	Cin N	16	34	3	6	1	2	0	4	5-0	0	12	.176	.282	.324	69	-2	0-0	1.000	-3	166	26	C-15	-0.5
Total	4	45	79	4	15	2	2	0	7	5-0	0	32	.190	.235	.266	40	-7	0-0	.992	-8	113	35	/C-41,D-2	-1.5
AGBAYANI, BENNY Benny Peter B 12.28.1971 Honolulu, HI BR/TR 6/225# d6.17																								
1998	NY N	11	15	1	2	0	0	0	0	1-0	0	5	.133	.188	.133	-14	-3	0-2	1.000	-0	80	0	/O-9(1-2-6)	-0.4
1999	†NY N	101	276	42	79	18	3	14	42	32-4	3	60	.286	.363	.525	126	11	6-4	.984	-4	91	47	O-80(47-4-45)/D-2	0.4
2000	†NY N	119	350	59	101	19	1	15	60	54-2	7	68	.289	.391	.477	124	15	5-5	.975	-3	98	56	*O-110(102-2-12)/D	0.7
2001	NY N	91	296	28	82	14	2	6	27	36-0	5	73	.277	.364	.399	103	2	4-5	.954	-4	97	21	O-84(LF)	-0.6
2002	Col N	48	117	10	24	5	0	4	19	10-0	0	35	.205	.266	.350	55	-8	1-0	1.000	0	105	58	O-37(LF)/D	-0.9
	Bos A	13	37	5	11	1	0	0	8	6-1	0	5	.297	.395	.324	93	0	0-0	.962	1	109	157	O-13(11-1-3)	0.0
Total	5	383	1091	145	299	57	6	39	156	139-7	15	246	.274	.362	.445	108	17	16-16	.974	-11	97	48	O-333(282-9-66)/D-4	-0.8
AGEE, TOMMIE Tommie Lee B 8.9.1942 Magnolia, AL D 1.22.2001 New York, NY BR/TR 5-11/195# d9.14																								
1962	Cle A	5	14	0	3	0	0	0	2	0-0	0	4	.214	.214	.214	16	-2	0-0	1.000	-0	73	0	/O-3(2-1-0)	-0.2
1963	Cle A	13	27	3	4	1	0	1	3	2-0	0	9	.148	.207	.296	39	-2	0-0	1.000	0	64	384	O-13(4-3-6)	-0.3
1964	Cle A	13	12	0	2	0	0	0	0	0-0	0	3	.167	.167	.167	-7	-2	0-0	1.000	-0	93	0	O-12(0-3-10)	-0.2
1965	Chi A	10	19	2	3	1	0	0	3	2-1	0	6	.158	.238	.211	30	-2	0-1	1.000	0	112	0	/O-9(0-5-6)	-0.3
1966	Chi A★	160	629	98	172	27	8	22	86	41-3	10	127	.273	.326	.447	129	21	44-18	.982	-6	94	113	*O-159(8-156-0)	1.4
1967	Chi A★	158	529	73	124	26	2	14	52	44-5	8	129	.234	.302	.371	102	1	28-10	.969	-6	101	65	*O-152(10-136-9)	-0.8
1968	NY N	132	368	30	80	12	3	5	17	15-3	4	103	.217	.255	.307	68	-15	13-8	.978	2	104	100	*O-127(0-116-13)	-2.0
1969	†NY N	149	565	97	153	23	4	26	76	59-2	3	137	.271	.342	.464	121	15	12-9	.986	-1	104	78	*O-146(0-143-7)	1.1
1970	NY N	153	636	107	182	30	7	24	75	55-3	2	156	.286	.344	.469	115	12	31-15	.967	3	**115**	48	*O-150(0-149-2)	1.3
1971	NY N	113	425	58	121	19	0	14	50	50-2	2	84	.285	.362	.428	125	15	28-6	.978	6	114	118	*O-107(0-94-32)	2.3
1972	NY N	114	422	52	96	23	0	13	47	53-6	4	92	.227	.317	.374	99	0	8-9	.962	4	113	93	*O-109(6-91-20)	-0.1
1973	Hou N	83	204	30	48	5	2	8	15	16-1	1	55	.235	.294	.397	90	-4	2-5	.983	2	112	56	O-67(34-18-17)	-0.6
	StL N	26	62	8	11	3	1	3	7	5-0	0	13	.177	.239	.403	75	-3	1-0	.981	3	147	111	O-19(0-19-2)	0.0
	Year	109	266	38	59	8	3	11	22	21-1	1	68	.222	.281	.398	87	-6	3-5	.982	5	120	68	O-86(34-37-19)	-0.6
Total	12	1129	3912	558	999	170	27	130	433	342-26	34	918	.255	.320	.412	108	34	167-81	.975	8	106	86	*O-1073(64-934-124)	1.6
AGGANIS, HARRY Harry "The Golden Greek" B 4.20.1929 Lynn, MA D 6.27.1955 Cambridge, MA BL/TL 6-2/200# d4.13																								
1954	Bos A	132	434	54	109	13	8	11	57	47	0	57	.251	.321	.394	86	-9	6-3	.990	5	**118**	96	*1-119	-1.0
1955	Bos A	25	83	11	26	10	1	0	10	10-0	0	10	.313	.383	.458	116	2	2-0	.987	-1	95	78	1-20	0.1
Total	2	157	517	65	135	23	9	11	67	57-0	0	67	.261	.331	.404	91	-7	8-3	.989	5	114	93	1-139	-0.9
AGLER, JOE Joseph Abram B 6.12.1887 Coshocton, OH D 4.26.1971 Massillon, OH BL/TL 5-11/165# d10.1																								
1912	Was A	2	1	0	0	0	0	0	0	0	0		.000	.000	.000	-99	0	0	—	0	0	0	/1	0.0
1914	Buf F	135	463	82	126	17	6	0	20	77	0	78	.272	.376	.335	93	-8	21	.985	3	123	114	1-76,O-54(44-5-6)	-1.0
1915	Buf F	25	73	11	13	1	2	0	2	20	0	14	.178	.355	.247	69	-3	2	.973	-2	102	0	O-20(6-3-11)/1	-0.7
	Bal F	72	214	28	46	4	2	0	14	34	1	38	.215	.325	.252	62	-13	15	.981	4	141	124	1-58/O-4(2-1-1),2-3	-1.1
	Year	97	287	39	59	5	4	0	16	54	1	52	.206	.333	.251	64	-16	17	.981	2	140	123	1-59,O-24(8-4-12)/2-3	-1.8
Total	3	234	751	121	185	22	10	0	36	131	1	130	.246	.359	.302	81	-24	38	.983	5	130	118	1-136/O-78(52-9-18),2-3	-2.8
AGNEW, SAM Samuel Lester "Slam" B 4.12.1887 Farmington, MO D 7.19.1951 Sonoma, CA BR/TR 5-11/185# d4.10																								
1913	StL A	105	307	27	64	9	5	2	24	20	7	49	.208	.272	.290	66	-14	11	.952	5	*111*	*107*	*C-103	0.0
1914	StL A	115	311	22	66	5	4	0	16	24	5	63	.212	.279	.254	63	-15	10-8	.961	0	*98*	*108*	*C-115	-0.7
1915	StL A	104	295	18	60	4	2	0	19	12	5	36	.203	.247	.231	45	-21	5-2	.934	1	*94*	***127***	*C-102	-1.3
1916	Bos A	40	67	4	14	2	1	0	7	6	2	4	.209	.293	.269	69	-3	0	.952	5	155	150	C-38	0.5
1917	Bos A	85	260	17	54	6	2	0	16	19	2	30	.208	.267	.246	57	-14	2	.965	-4	*118*	*89*	C-85	-1.2

Year	Tm Lg	G	AB	R	H	2B	3B	HR	RBI	BB-IB	HP	SO	AVG	OBP	SLG	AOPS	ABR	SB-CS	FA	FR	Rng	Thr	G at Pos	BFW
1918	†Bos A	72	199	11	33	8	0	0	6	11	3	26	.166	.221	.206	29	-17	0	.965	8	113	115	C-72	-0.4
1919	Was A	42	98	6	23	7	0	0	10	10	1	8	.235	.312	.306	74	-3	1	.974	6	97	133	C-36	0.6
Total	7	563	1537	105	314	41	14	2	98	102	25	216	.204	.265	.253	56	-87	29-10	.955	21	108	113	C-551	-2.5
AGUAYO, LUIS Luis (Muriel) B 3.13.1959 Vega Baja, P.R. BR/TR 5-9/185# d4.19																								
1980	Phi N	20	47	7	13	1	2	1	8	2-0	0	3	.277	.300	.447	102	0	1-1	.962	3	101	121	2-14/S-5	0.3
1981	†Phi N	45	84	11	18	4	0	1	7	6-0	2	15	.214	.283	.298	62	-4	1-0	.938	-6	79	93	2-21,S-21/3-3	-0.9
1982	Phi N	50	56	11	15	1	2	3	7	5-1	1	7	.268	.339	.518	133	2	1-1	.966	-3	98	42	2-21,S-15/3-5	0.0
1983	Phi N	2	4	1	1	0	0	0	0	1-0	0	2	.250	.400	.250	85	0	0-0	1.000	-2	0	0	/S-2	-0.2
1984	Phi N	58	72	15	20	4	0	3	11	8-2	0	16	.278	.350	.458	123	2	0-0	.909	4	149	104	3-14,2-12,S-10	0.7
1985	Phi N	91	165	27	46	7	3	6	21	22-5	6	26	.279	.378	.467	133	8	1-0	.957	1	92	82	S-60,2-17/3-7	1.5
1986	Phi N	62	133	17	28	6	1	4	13	8-0	3	26	.211	.267	.361	70	-6	1-1	.967	-9	99	81	2-31,S-20/3	-1.3
1987	Phi N	94	209	25	43	9	1	12	21	15-1	5	56	.206	.273	.431	81	-7	0-0	.971	-2	96	94	S-78/2-6,3-2	-0.3
1988	Phi N	49	97	9	24	3	0	3	5	13-2	0	17	.247	.336	.371	101	0	2-0	.967	4	104	110	S-27,3-13/2-2	0.6
	NY A	50	140	12	35	4	0	3	8	7-1	1	33	.250	.289	.343	77	-5	0-2	.961	-7	97	83	3-33,2-13/S-6	-1.2
1989	Cle A	47	97	7	17	4	1	1	8	7-0	2	19	.175	.239	.268	44	-7	0-0	.950	1	99	42	3-19,S-15,2-10/D-2	-0.6
Total	10	568	1104	142	260	43	10	37	109	94-12	20	220	.236	.304	.393	91	-17	7-5	.960	-16	92	90	S-259,2-147/3-97,D-2	-1.4
AHEARN, CHARLIE Charles B Troy, NY d6.19																								
1880	Tro N	1	4	1	1	0	0	0	0	0		0	.250	.250	.250	67	0		.778	-0			/C	-0.1
AIKENS, WILLIE Willie Mays B 10.14.1954 Seneca, SC BL/TR 6-3/220# d5.17																								
1977	Cal A	42	91	5	18	4	0	0	6	10-2	0	23	.198	.277	.242	45	-7	1-2	.971	-0	104	105	1-13,D-13	-0.9
1979	Cal A	116	379	59	106	18	0	21	81	61-8	1	79	.280	.376	.493	138	22	1-3	.996	-4	73	94	1-55,D-51	1.2
1980	†KC A	151	543	70	151	24	0	20	98	64-3	7	88	.278	.356	.433	116	13	1-0	.990	-8	81	85	*1-138,D-13	-0.3
1981	†KC A	101	349	45	93	16	0	17	53	62-**12**	3	47	.266	.377	.458	142	22	0-0	.992	-4	89	95	1-99	1.2
1982	KC A	134	466	50	131	29	1	17	74	45-7	3	70	.281	.345	.457	119	13	0-1	.994	1	105	96	*1-128	0.6
1983	KC A	125	410	49	124	26	1	23	72	45-9	2	75	.302	.373	.539	148	27	0-0	.989	-1	100	111	*1-112/D-6	1.9
1984	Tor A	93	234	21	48	7	0	11	26	29-1	2	56	.205	.298	.376	82	-6	0-0	1.000	0	98	95	D-81/1-2	-0.8
1985	Tor A	12	20	2	4	1	0	1	5	3-0	0	6	.200	.292	.400	89	0	0-0	—	0	0	0	D-11	-0.1
Total	8	774	2492	301	675	125	2	110	415	319-42	18	444	.271	.354	.455	123	84	3-6	.991	-15	92	96	1-547,D-175	2.8
AINGE, DANNY Daniel Ray B 3.17.1959 Eugene, OR BR/TR (BB 1979 (part), 1981 (1 game)) 6-4/175# d5.21																								
1979	Tor A	87	308	26	73	7	1	2	19	12-1	2	58	.237	.269	.286	50	-23	1-0	.977	1	102	103	2-86/D	-1.7
1980	Tor A	38	111	11	27	6	1	0	4	2-0	1	29	.243	.263	.315	55	-7	3-0	.986	0	92	152	O-29(6-22-1)/3-3,2D	-0.6
1981	Tor A	86	246	20	46	6	2	0	14	23-1	1	41	.187	.258	.228	39	-19	8-5	.949	2	103	148	3-77/S-6,O-4(0-3-1),2-2,D	-1.9
Total	3	211	665	57	146	19	4	2	37	37-2	4	128	.220	.264	.269	47	-49	12-5	.977	3	102	101	/2-89,3-80,O-33(6-25-2),S-6,D-4	-4.2
AINSMITH, EDDIE Edward Wilbur "Dorf" B 2.4.1892 Cambridge, MA D 9.6.1981 Ft.Lauderdale, FL BR/TR 5-11/180# d8.9 Mil 1918																								
1910	Was A	33	104	4	20	1	2	0	9	6	0		.192	.236	.240	52	-6	0	.963	-2	98	110	C-30	-0.6
1911	Was A	61	149	12	33	2	3	0	14	10	1		.221	.275	.275	55	-10	5	.952	2	105	104	C-47	-0.4
1912	Was A	61	186	22	42	7	2	0	22	14	0		.226	.280	.285	61	-10	4	.958	15	145	83	C-59	1.0
1913	Was A	84	229	26	49	4	4	2	20	12	3	41	.214	.262	.293	61	-13	17	.967	6	120	83	C-79/P	-0.1
1914	Was A	62	151	11	34	7	0	0	13	9	1	28	.225	.273	.272	61	-7	8-5	.969	5	112	82	C-51	0.2
1915	Was A	47	120	13	24	4	2	0	6	10	1	18	.200	.267	.267	59	-6	7-4	.988	6	118	88	C-42	0.3
1916	Was A	51	100	11	17	4	0	0	8	8	0	14	.170	.231	.210	33	-8	3	.959	6	113	123	C-46	0.1
1917	Was A	125	350	38	67	17	4	0	42	40	3	48	.191	.280	.263	66	-13	16	.971	8	90	116	*C-119	0.4
1918	Was A	96	292	22	62	10	9	0	20	29	0	44	.212	.283	.308	80	-8	6	.975	3	102	109	C-89	0.3
1919	Det A	114	364	42	99	17	12	3	32	45	1	30	.272	.354	.409	117	8	9	.962	-11	88	80	*C-106	0.6
1920	Det A	69	186	19	43	5	3	1	19	14	0	19	.231	.285	.306	58	-12	4-3	.955	-6	92	95	C-61/1	-1.3
1921	Det A	35	98	6	27	5	2	0	12	13	0	7	.276	.360	.367	87	-2	1-0	.947	-4	87	109	C-34	-0.3
	StL N	27	62	5	18	0	1	0	5	3	0	4	.290	.323	.323	73	-3	0-0	.956	0	109	87	C-23/1	-0.1
1922	StL N	119	379	46	111	14	4	13	59	28	1	43	.293	.343	.454	109	4	2-3	.963	-2	108	98	*C-116	0.8
1923	StL N	82	263	22	56	11	6	3	34	22	1	19	.213	.276	.335	62	-16	4-0	.980	-7	93	83	C-80	-1.6
	Bro N	2	10	0	2	0	0	0	2	0	0	0	.200	.200	.200	6	-1	0-1	1.000	1	94	66	/C-2	-0.1
	Year	84	273	22	58	11	6	3	36	22	1	19	.212	.274	.330	60	-17	4-1	.981	-7	93	82	C-82	-1.7
1924	NY N	10	5	0	3	0	0	0	0	0	0	0	.600	.600	.600	229	1	0-0	1.000	-0	70	0	/C-9	0.1
Total	15	1078	3048	299	707	108	54	22	317	263	12	315	.232	.296	.324	76	-102	86-16	.966	20	104	96	C-993/1-2,P	-0.7
AITON, GEORGE George Wilson B 12.29.1890 Kingman, KS D 8.16.1976 Van Nuys, CA BB/TR 5-11.5/175# d6.29																								
1912	StL A	10	17	1	4	0	0	0	1	4	0		.235	.381	.235	80	0	0	.917	0	109	166	/O-7(5-2-0)	0.0
AKE, JOHN John Leckie B 8.29.1861 Altoona, PA D 5.11.1887 LaCrosse, WI BR/TR 6-1/180# d5.12																								
1884	Bal AA	13	52	1	10	0	1	0	2	0	1		.192	.208	.231	41	-4		.677	-3	86	195	/3-9,O-3(2-0-1),S	-0.6
AKERS, BILL William G. "Bump" B 12.25.1904 Chattanooga, TN D 4.13.1962 Chattanooga, TN BR/TR 5-11/178# d9.8																								
1929	Det A	24	83	15	22	4	1	1	9	10	1	9	.265	.351	.373	86	-2	2-0	.935	-6	83	83	S-24	-0.5
1930	Det A	85	233	36	65	8	5	9	40	36	0	34	.279	.375	.472	111	4	5-5	.944	6	104	123	S-49,3-26	1.4
1931	Det A	29	66	5	13	2	2	0	3	7	0	6	.197	.274	.288	46	-5	0-1	.935	-4	82	79	S-21/2-2	-0.8
1932	Bos N	36	93	8	24	3	1	1	17	10	0	15	.258	.330	.344	85	-2	0	.927	-5	95	30	3-20/2-5,S-5	-0.5
Total	4	174	475	64	124	17	9	11	69	63	1	64	.261	.349	.404	93	-5	7-6	.936	-9	94	106	/S-99,3-46,2-7	-0.4
ALBERTS, GUS Augustus Peter B 1861 Reading, PA D 5.7.1912 Idaho Springs, CO BR/TR 5-6.5/180# d5.1																								
1884	Pit AA	2	5	1	1	0	0	0		0	0		.200	.200	.200	31	0		.500	-1	76	0	/S-2	-0.1
	Was U	4	16	4	4	0	0	0		4			.250	.400	.250	105	0		.870	1	113	132	/S-4	0.1
1888	Cle AA	102	364	51	75	10	6	1	48	41	7		.206	.299	.275	87	-3	26	.862	8	107	111	S-53,3-49	0.6
1891	Mil AA	12	41	6	4	0	0	0	2	7	2	5	.098	.260	.098	2	-5	1	.814	-3	76	106	3-12	-0.8
Total	3	120	426	62	84	10	6	1	50	52	9	5	.197	.298	.256	76	-8	27	.880	5	97	119	/3-61,S-59	-0.2
ALBERTS, BUTCH Francis Burt B 5.4.1950 Williamsport, PA BR/TR 6-2/205# d9.7																								
1978	Tor A	6	18	1	5	1	0	0	0	0-0	0	2	.278	.278	.333	70	-1	0-0	—	0			/D-4	-0.1
ALBRIGHT, JACK Harold John B 6.30.1921 St.Petersburg, FL D 7.22.1991 San Diego, CA BR/TR 5-9/175# d5.19																								
1947	Phi N	41	99	9	23	4	0	2	5	10	0	11	.232	.303	.333	71	-4	1	.943	1	106	96	S-33	-0.2
ALCANTARA, ISRAEL Israel (Cristosomo) B 5.6.1973 Bani, D.R. BR/TR 6-2/180# d6.25																								
2000	Bos A	21	45	9	13	1	0	4	7	3-0	0	7	.289	.333	.578	121	1	0-0	.889	-1	94	0	/O-7(1-0-7),1-5,D-8	0.0
2001	Bos A	14	38	3	10	1	0	0	3	3-0	0	13	.263	.317	.289	61	-2	1-0	.900	-1	64	262	/O-8(6-0-2),1-4,D	-0.3
2002	Mil N	16	32	3	8	1	0	2	5	0-0	0	6	.250	.250	.469	88	-1	0-1	1.000	-1	76	0	/O-7(2-0-5),1-2	-0.3
Total	3	51	115	15	31	3	0	6	15	6-0	0	26	.270	.306	.452	93	-2	1-1	.923	-2	76	108	/O-22(9-0-14),1-11,D-9	-0.6
ALCARAZ, LUIS Angel Luis (Acosta) B 6.20.1941 Humacao, P.R. BR/TR 5-9/165# d9.13																								
1967	LA N	17	60	1	14	1	0	0	3	1-0	0	13	.233	.242	.250	46	-4	1-1	.990	5	113	176	2-17	0.2
1968	LA N	41	106	4	16	1	0	2	5	9-2	0	23	.151	.217	.217	33	-9	1-1	.979	1	99	80	2-20,3-13/S	-0.8
1969	KC A	22	79	15	20	2	1	1	7	7-0	0	9	.253	.314	.342	83	-2	0-0	.988	-4	91	44	2-19/3-2,S	-0.5
1970	KC A	35	120	10	20	5	1	1	14	4-0	0	13	.167	.192	.250	21	-13	0-0	.993	-12	76	58	2-31	-2.5
Total	4	115	365	30	70	9	2	4	29	21-2	0	58	.192	.235	.260	43	-28	2-2	.988	-10	91	83	/2-87,3-15,S-2	-3.6
ALCOCK, SCOTTY John Forbes B 11.29.1885 Wooster, OH D 1.30.1973 Wooster, OH BR/TR 5-9.5/160# d4.19																								
1914	Chi A	54	156	12	27	4	2	0	7	7	1	14	.173	.213	.224	32	-14	4-2	.905	1	104	169	3-48/2	-1.2
ALDRETE, MIKE Michael Peter B 1.29.1961 Carmel, CA BL/TL 5-11/185# d5.28																								
1986	SF N	84	216	27	54	18	3	2	25	33-4	2	34	.250	.353	.389	110	4	1-3	1.000	3	148	149	1-37,O-31(30-0-2)	0.4
1987	†SF N	126	357	50	116	18	2	9	51	43-5	0	50	.325	.396	.462	133	18	6-0	.986	1	107	67	O-79(43-13-30),1-33	1.7
1988	SF N	139	389	44	104	15	0	3	50	56-13	0	65	.267	.357	.329	103	4	6-5	.982	3	108	89	*O-115(83-7-40),1-10	0.3
1989	Mon N	76	136	12	30	8	1	1	12	19-0	1	30	.221	.316	.316	81	-3	1-3	.980	1	95	148	O-37(16-3-19),1-10	-0.4
1990	Mon N	96	161	22	39	7	1	1	18	37-2	1	31	.242	.385	.317	100	2	1-2	.982	1	91	207	O-38(26-0-14),1-18	0.1
1991	SD N	12	15	2	0	0	0	0	1	3-0	0	4	.000	.167	.000	-48	-3	0-1	1.000	1	118	593	/O-5(LF)	-0.3

Year	Tm Lg	G	AB	R	H	2B	3B	HR	RBI	BB-IB	HP	SO	AVG	OBP	SLG	AOPS	ABR	SB-CS	FA	FR	Rng	Thr	G at Pos	BFW
	Cle A	85	183	22	48	6	1	1	19	36-1	0	37	.262	.380	.322	97	1	1-2	.994	-1	92	102	1-47,O-16(LF)/D-7	-0.4
1993	Oak A	95	255	40	68	13	1	10	33	34-2	0	45	.267	.353	.443	120	7	1-1	.995	-4	74	84	1-59,O-20(17-0-3)/D-6	-0.2
1994	Oak A	76	178	23	43	5	0	4	18	20-1	0	35	.242	.313	.337	76	-7	2-0	1.000	-2	85	0	O-35(21-0-15),1-27/D	-1.1
1995	Oak A	60	125	18	34	8	0	4	21	19-1	1	23	.272	.367	.432	115	3	0-0	.989	-3	62	84	1-35,O-16(9-1-6)	-0.2
	Cal A	18	24	1	6	0	0	0	3	0-0	0	8	.250	.240	.250	31	-3	0-0	1.000	1	390	0	/O-2(LF),1D	-0.2
	Year	78	149	19	40	8	0	4	24	19-1	1	31	.268	.349	.403	101	1	0-0	.989	-2	61	83	1-36,O-18(11-1-6)/D-2	-0.4
1996	Cal A	31	40	5	6	1	0	3	8	5-0	0	4	.150	.239	.400	59	-3	0-0	.750	-1	46	0	/O-6(4-0-2),1D	-0.4
	†NY A	32	68	11	17	5	0	3	12	9-0	0	15	.250	.338	.456	98	0	0-1	1.000	-2	70	0	/O-9(6-0-4),1-8,PD	-0.3
	Year	63	108	16	23	6	0	6	20	14-0	0	19	.213	.301	.435	84	-3	0-1	.909	-3	61	0	O-15(10-0-6),D-15/1-9,P	-0.7
Total	10	930	2147	277	565	104	9	41	271	314-29	5	381	.263	.356	.377	104	20	19-18	.983	-3	100	87	O-409(278-24-135),1-286/D-31,P	-1.0
ALDRIDGE, CORY Cory Jerome B 6.13.1979 San Angelo, TX BL/TR 6/210# d9.5																								
2001	Atl N	8	5	1	0	0	0	0	0	0-0	0	4	.000	.000	.000	-98	-1	0-0	1.000	-0	64	0	/O-4(1-1-2)	-0.2
ALENO, CHUCK Charles B 2.19.1917 St.Louis, MO D 2.10.2003 DeLand, FL BR/TR 6-1.5/215# d5.15																								
1941	Cin N	54	169	23	41	7	3	1	18	11	0	16	.243	.289	.337	76	-6	3	.975	-1	96	89	3-40/1-2	-0.6
1942	Cin N	7	14	1	2	1	0	0	0	3	0	3	.143	.294	.214	50	-1	0	.727	0	99	0	/3-2,2	-0.1
1943	Cin N	7	10	0	3	0	0	0	1	2	0	1	.300	.417	.300	110	0	0	1.000	-0	69	0	/O-2(LF)	0.0
1944	Cin N	50	127	10	21	3	0	1	15	15	1	15	.165	.259	.213	35	-11	0	.952	-4	85	102	3-42/1-3,S-3	-1.5
Total	4	118	320	34	67	11	3	2	34	31	1	35	.209	.281	.281	60	-18	3	.954	-5	91	91	/3-84,1-5,S-3,O-2(LF),2	-2.2
ALEXANDER, DALE David Dale "Moose" B 4.26.1903 Greeneville, TN D 3.2.1979 Greeneville, TN BR/TR 6-3/210# d4.16																								
1929	Det A	**155**	626	110	**215**	43	15	25	137	56	0	63	.343	.397	.580	148	42	5-9	.988	-4	92	87	*1-155	2.4
1930	Det A	**154**	602	86	196	33	8	20	135	42	2	56	.326	.372	.507	118	15	6-5	.985	-6	83	106	*1-154	-0.1
1931	Det A	135	517	75	168	47	3	3	87	64	2	35	.325	.401	.445	118	17	5-8	.987	-8	75	92	*1-126/O-4(LF)	-0.4
1932	Det A	23	16	0	4	0	0	0	4	6	0	2	.250	.455	.250	84	0	0-0	1.000	-0	0	0	/1-2	0.0
	Bos A	101	376	58	140	27	3	8	56	55	1	19	.372	.454	.524	157	35	4-5	.992	2	107	101	*1-101	2.4
	Year	124	392	58	144	27	3	8	60	61	1	21	**.367**	.454	.513	152	34	4-5	.992	2	107	101	*1-103	2.4
1933	Bos A	94	313	40	88	14	1	5	40	25	1	22	.281	.336	.380	90	-5	0-1	.992	3	118	84	1-79	-0.8
Total	5	662	2450	369	811	164	30	61	459	248	6	197	.331	.394	.497	128	104	20-28	.988	-13	92	95	1-617/O-4(LF)	3.5
ALEXANDER, GARY Gary Wayne B 3.27.1953 Los Angeles, CA BR/TR 6-2/200# d9.12																								
1975	SF N	3	3	1	0	0	0	0	0	1-0	0	2	.000	.250	.000	-25	0	0-0	1.000	-2	13	0	/C-2	-0.2
1976	SF N	23	73	12	13	1	1	2	7	10-1	0	16	.178	.274	.301	62	-4	1-0	.964	-6	52	78	C-23	-0.9
1977	SF N	51	119	17	36	4	2	5	20	20-2	2	33	.303	.406	.496	143	8	3-1	.968	-10	53	53	C-33/O(RF)	0.0
1978	Oak A	58	174	18	36	6	1	10	22	22-2	1	66	.207	.298	.425	107	1	0-3	1.000	1	167	0	D-45/O-6(3-0-3),C1	-0.1
	Cle A	90	324	39	76	14	3	17	62	35-3	1	100	.235	.308	.454	114	5	0-2	.983	-3	89	114	C-66,D-25	0.3
	Year	148	498	57	112	20	4	27	84	57-5	2	166	.225	.304	.444	112	6	0-5	.983	-2	89	114	D-70,C-67/O-6(3-0-3),1	0.2
1979	Cle A	110	358	54	82	9	2	15	54	46-3	1	100	.229	.313	.391	90	-6	4-2	.961	-22	70	82	C-91,D-13/O-2(1-0-1)	-2.4
1980	Cle A	76	178	22	40	7	1	5	31	17-1	0	52	.225	.288	.360	77	-6	0-4	.971	-2	53	101	D-40,C-13/O-2(1-0-1)	-1.0
1981	Pit N	21	47	6	10	4	1	1	6	3-0	0	12	.213	.255	.404	84	-1	0-0	.964	2	49	86	/1-9,O-8(7-0-2)	0.0
Total	7	432	1276	169	293	45	11	55	202	154-12	5	381	.230	.311	.411	99	-3	8-12	.969	-42	70	87	C-229,D-123/O-19(12-0-8),1-10	-4.3
ALEXANDER, HUGH Hugh B 7.10.1917 Buffalo, MO D 11.25.2000 Oklahoma City, OK BR/TR 6/190# d8.15																								
1937	Cle A	7	11	0	1	0	0	0	0	0	0	5	.091	.091	.091	-54	-3	1-0	.667	-1	65	0	/O-3(1-0-3)	-0.3
ALEXANDER, MANNY Manuel De Jesus (born (Alexander)) B 3.20.1971 San Pedro De Macoris, D.R. BR/TR 5-10/165# d9.18 OF Total (4-LF 2-RF)																								
1992	Bal A	4	5	1	1	0	0	0	0	0-0	0	3	.200	.200	.200	12	-1	0-0	1.000	-0	68	109	/S-3	-0.1
1993	Bal A	3	0	1	0	0	0	0	0	0-0	0	0	—	—	—	—	0	0-0	—	0			/R	0.0
1995	Bal A	94	242	35	57	9	1	3	23	20-0	2	30	.236	.299	.318	60	-15	11-4	.971	-5	86	122	2-81/S-7,3-2,D	-1.4
1996	†Bal A	54	68	6	7	0	0	0	4	3-0	0	27	.103	.141	.103	-37	-15	3-3	.940	-2	111	89	S-21/2-7,3-7,O-3(LF),PD	-1.4
1997	NY N	54	149	26	37	9	3	2	15	9-1	1	38	.248	.294	.389	80	-5	11-0	.979	2	112	146	2-31,S-26/3	0.2
	Chi N	33	99	11	29	3	1	1	7	8-2	2	16	.293	.358	.374	90	-1	2-1	.942	-2	110	71	S-28/2-4	-0.1
	Year	87	248	37	66	12	4	3	22	17-3	3	54	.266	.320	.383	84	-6	13-1	.959	0	113	80	S-54,2-35/3	0.1
1998	†Chi N	108	264	34	60	10	1	5	25	18-1	1	66	.227	.278	.330	57	-17	4-1	.964	-12	81	80	S-50,2-27,3-19/O(LF)D	-2.5
1999	Chi N	90	177	17	48	11	2	0	15	10-0	0	38	.271	.309	.356	69	-9	4-0	.988	1	114	86	S-30,3-22,2-17/O-2(RF)	-0.4
2000	Bos A	101	194	30	41	4	3	4	19	13-0	0	41	.211	.261	.325	46	-17	2-0	.944	0	95	69	3-63,S-20/2-7,D-2	-1.4
Total	8	541	1198	161	280	46	11	15	108	81-4	6	259	.234	.285	.328	58	-80	37-9	.968	-17	103	84	S-185,2-174,3-114/O-6L,D-6,P	-7.1
ALEXANDER, MATT Matthew B 1.30.1947 Shreveport, LA BB/TR 5-11/169# d8.23 OF Total (25-LF 40-CF 31-RF)																								
1973	Chi N	12	5	4	1	0	0	0	1	1-0	0	1	.200	.333	.200	48	0	2-0	1.000	-0	57	0	/O-3(CF)	0.0
1974	Chi N	45	54	15	11	2	1	0	0	12-1	1	12	.204	.358	.278	76	-1	8-4	.921	-3	79	97	3-19/O-4(0-2-1),2-2	-0.4
1975	Oak A	63	10	16	1	0	0	0	0	1-0	0	1	.100	.182	.100	-19	-2	17-10	1.000	-1	102	0	D-17,O-11(1-3-7)/2-3,3-2	-0.3
1976	Oak A	61	30	16	1	0	0	0	0	0-0	0	5	.033	.033	.033	-84	-7	20-7	1.000	0	116	0	O-23(7-7-11),D-19	-0.6
1977	Oak A	90	42	24	10	1	0	0	2	4-0	0	6	.238	.304	.262	57	-2	26-14	1.000	-2	93	0	O-31(7-17-8),S-12,D-12/2-4,3	-0.4
1978	Pit N	7	0	2	0	0	0	0	0	0-0	0	0	—	—	—	—	0	4-1	—	0			R	0.0
1979	†Pit N	44	13	16	7	0	1	0	1	0-0	0	0	.538	.538	.692	223	2	13-1	1.000	0	99	359	O-11(6-3-3)/S	0.5
1980	Pit N	37	3	13	1	1	0	0	0	0-0	0	0	.333	.333	.667	170	0	10-3	1.000	0	189	0	/O-4(2-2-0),2	0.2
1981	Pit N	15	11	5	4	0	0	0	0	0-0	0	1	.364	.364	.364	104	0	3-2	1.000	0	125	0	/O-6(2-3-1)	0.0
Total	9	374	168	111	36	4	2	0	4	18-1	1	26	.214	.294	.262	56	-10	103-42	1.000	-5	105	41	/O-93C,D-48,3-22,S-13,2-10	-1.0
ALEXANDER, WALT Walter Ernest B 3.5.1891 Atlanta, GA D 12.29.1978 Fort Worth, TX BR/TR 5-10.5/165# d6.21																								
1912	StL A	37	97	5	17	4	0	0	5	8	1		.175	.245	.216	34	-8	1	.969	-3	84	96	C-37	-0.9
1913	StL A	43	110	5	15	2	1	0	7	4	1	36	.136	.174	.173	2	-14	1	.947	3	112	127	C-43	-0.9
1915	StL A	1	1	0	0	0	0	0	0	0	0	0	.000	.000	.000	-99	0	0	—	-0	0	0	/C	0.0
	NY A	25	68	7	17	4	0	1	5	13	0	16	.250	.370	.353	117	2	2-1	.967	5	105	118	C-24	1.0
	Year	26	69	7	17	4	0	1	5	13	0	16	.246	.366	.348	114	2	2-1	.967	5	105	117	C-25	1.0
1916	NY A	36	78	8	20	6	1	0	3	13	2	20	.256	.376	.359	118	3	0	.960	2	133	134	C-27	0.7
1917	NY A	20	51	1	7	2	1	0	4	4	0	11	.137	.200	.216	27	-5	1	.951	0	140	74	C-20	-0.3
Total	5	162	405	26	76	18	3	1	24	42	4	83	.188	.271	.254	56	-22	5-1	.959	7	111	112	C-152	-0.4
ALEXANDER, NIN William Henry B 11.24.1858 Pana, IL D 12.22.1933 Pana, IL BR/TR 5-4.5/163# d6.7																								
1884	KC U	19	65	2	9	0	0	0		1			.138	.152	.138	-13	-11		.907	-1			C-17/S-2,O-2(CF)	-0.9
	StL AA	1	4	0	0	0	0	0		0	0		.000	.000	.000	-97	-1		.667	-0			/CO(CF)	-0.1
Total	1	20	69	2	9	0	0	0		1	0		.130	.143	.130	-19	-12		.895	-1			/C-18,O-3(CF),S-2	-1.0
ALFONZO, EDGARDO Edgardo Antonio B 8.11.1973 Santa Teresa, Venezuela BR/TR 5-11/185# d4.26																								
1995	NY N	101	335	26	93	13	5	4	41	12-1	1	37	.278	.301	.382	82	-10	1-1	.962	-9	100	103	3-58,2-29/S-6	-1.7
1996	NY N	123	368	36	96	15	2	4	40	25-2	0	56	.261	.304	.345	75	-14	2-0	.974	-5	99	108	2-66,3-36,S-15	-1.4
1997	NY N	151	518	84	163	27	2	10	72	63-0	5	56	.315	.391	.432	121	18	11-6	.967	8	113	**137**	*3-143,S-12/2-3	2.8
1998	NY N	144	557	94	155	28	2	17	78	65-1	3	77	.278	.355	.427	107	6	8-3	.976	-7	90	83	*3-144/S	0.2
1999	†NY N	158	628	123	191	41	1	27	108	85-2	3	85	.304	.385	.502	127	28	9-2	**.993**	-9	95	102	*2-158	2.7
2000	†NY N★	150	544	109	176	40	2	25	94	95-1	5	70	.324	.425	.542	149	46	3-2	.985	6	101	96	*2-146/D-2	5.5
2001	NY N	124	457	64	111	22	0	17	49	51-0	5	62	.243	.322	.403	91	-6	5-0	.987	-6	98	93	*2-122	-0.5
2002	NY N	135	490	78	151	26	0	16	56	62-8	7	55	.308	.391	.459	133	23	6-0	.969	7	106	85	*3-134	3.2
2003	†SF N	142	514	56	133	25	2	13	81	58-4	4	41	.259	.334	.391	92	-6	5-2	.966	-17	89	74	*3-133/2-6	-2.0
Total	9	1228	4411	670	1269	237	16	133	619	516-19	33	539	.288	.363	.439	112	85	50-16	.968	-30	100	96	3-648,2-530/S-34,D-2	8.8
ALICEA, LUIS Luis Rene (De Jesus) B 7.29.1965 Santurce, P.R. BB/TR 5-9/177# d4.23 OF Total (LF)																								
1988	StL N	93	297	20	63	10	4	1	24	25-4	2	32	.212	.276	.283	61	-15	1-1	.970	0	99	105	2-91	-1.4
1991	StL N	56	68	5	13	3	0	0	0	8-0	0	19	.191	.276	.235	45	-5	0-1	1.000	1	103	83	2-11/3-2,S	-0.4
1992	StL N	85	265	26	65	9	11	2	32	27-1	4	40	.245	.320	.385	103	0	2-5	.989	-7	105	90	2-75/S-4	-0.7
1993	StL N	115	362	50	101	19	3	3	46	47-2	4	54	.279	.362	.373	101	3	11-1	.978	8	114	114	2-96/O-4(LF),3	1.7
1994	StL N	88	205	32	57	12	5	5	29	30-4	3	38	.278	.373	.459	119	6	4-5	.986	8	108	120	2-53/O-2(LF)	1.5
1995	†Bos A	132	419	64	113	20	3	6	44	63-0	7	61	.270	.367	.375	93	-2	13-10	.977	15	**109**	117	*2-132	1.7
1996	†StL N	129	380	54	98	26	3	5	42	52-10	5	78	.258	.350	.382	95	-1	11-3	.957	-11	93	108	*2-125	-0.4
1997	Ana A	128	388	59	98	16	7	5	37	69-3	8	65	.253	.375	.369	96	0	22-8	.978	-5	96	89	*2-105,3-12/D-6	0.3

Year	Tm Lg	G	AB	R	H	2B	3B	HR	RBI	BB-IB	HP	SO	AVG	OBP	SLG	AOPS	ABR	SB-CS	FA	FR	Rng	Thr	G at Pos	BFW
1998	†Tex A	101	259	51	71	15	3	6	33	37-0	5	40	.274	.372	.425	103	2	4-3	.970	1	97	101	2-45,3-26,D-17/O-2(LF)	0.4
1999	Tex A	68	164	33	33	10	0	3	17	28-0	0	32	.201	.316	.317	60	-10	2-1	.980	-4	89	87	2-37,3-10/O(LF)D	-1.1
2000	Tex A	139	540	85	159	25	8	6	63	59-1	5	75	.294	.365	.404	94	-4	1-3	.978	-13	95	91	*2-130/3-8,S-2,D-4	-1.0
2001	KC A	113	387	44	106	16	4	4	32	23-0	4	56	.274	.320	.367	74	-15	8-6	.958	1	109	120	2-67,D-22,3-18	-1.2
2002	KC A	94	237	28	54	8	2	1	23	32-1	1	34	.228	.322	.291	58	-14	2-3	.986	8	135	131	2-32,3-32,D-16/1-2,SO(LF)	-0.6
Total	13	1341	3971	551	1031	189	53	47	422	500-26	48	624	.260	.346	.369	88	-55	81-50	.975	2	102	105	2-999,3-109/D-72,O-10L,S-8,1-2	-1.2

ALLANSON, ANDY Andrew Neal B 12.22.1961 Richmond, VA BR/TR 6-5/225# d4.7

Year	Tm Lg	G	AB	R	H	2B	3B	HR	RBI	BB-IB	HP	SO	AVG	OBP	SLG	AOPS	ABR	SB-CS	FA	FR	Rng	Thr	G at Pos	BFW
1986	Cle A	101	293	30	66	7	3	1	29	14-0	1	36	.225	.260	.280	49	-22	10-1	.960	-12	88	73	C-99	-2.7
1987	Cle A	50	154	17	41	6	0	3	16	9-0	0	30	.266	.298	.364	76	-5	1-1	.986	-3	146	57	C-50	-0.6
1988	Cle A	133	434	44	114	11	0	5	50	25-2	3	63	.263	.305	.323	75	-15	5-9	.986	4	114	104	*C-133	-0.5
1989	Cle A	111	323	30	75	9	1	3	17	23-2	4	47	.232	.289	.294	64	-15	4-4	.986	5	96	92	*C-111	-0.5
1991	Det A	60	151	10	35	10	0	1	16	7-0	0	31	.232	.266	.318	60	-8	0-1	.979	-2	143	107	C-56/1-2,D	-0.8
1992	Mil A	9	25	6	8	1	0	0	0	1-0	0	2	.320	.346	.360	100	0	3-1	.943	-3	72	0	/C-9	-0.2
1993	SF N	13	24	3	4	1	0	0	2	1-0	0	2	.167	.200	.208	10	-3	0-0	1.000	-1	195	57	/C-8,1-2	-0.4
1995	Cal A	35	82	5	14	3	0	3	10	7-0	1	12	.171	.244	.317	45	-7	0-1	.994	2	73	139	C-35	-0.4
Total	8	512	1486	145	357	48	4	16	140	87-4	9	223	.240	.283	.310	64	-75	23-18	.980	-8	109	90	C-501/1-4,D	-6.1

ALLEN, NICK Artemus Ward B 9.14.1888 Norton, KS D 10.16.1939 Hines, IL BR/TR 6/180# d5.1 Mil 1918

Year	Tm Lg	G	AB	R	H	2B	3B	HR	RBI	BB-IB	HP	SO	AVG	OBP	SLG	AOPS	ABR	SB-CS	FA	FR	Rng	Thr	G at Pos	BFW
1914	Buf F	32	63	3	15	1	0	0	4	3	0	12	.238	.273	.254	43	-6	4	.969	2	*117*	*105*	C-26	-0.3
1915	Buf F	84	215	14	44	7	1	0	17	18	1	34	.205	.269	.247	45	-19	4	.956	-2	*80*	*110*	C-80	-1.7
1916	Chi N	5	16	1	1	0	0	0	1	0	0	3	.063	.063	.063	-56	-3	0	.958	-0	107	60	/C-4	-0.4
1918	Cin N	37	96	6	25	2	2	0	5	4	1	7	.260	.297	.323	91	-1	0	.950	5	*122*	*133*	C-31	0.6
1919	Cin N	15	25	7	8	0	1	0	5	2	1	6	.320	.393	.400	142	1	0	.958	2	*134*	*94*	C-12	0.4
1920	Cin N	43	85	10	23	3	1	0	4	6	3	11	.271	.340	.329	94	0	0-0	.961	3	*118*	*127*	C-36	0.6
Total	6	216	500	41	116	13	5	0	36	33	6	73	.232	.288	.278	62	-28	8-0	.958	9	*102*	*115*	C-189	-0.8

ALLEN, BERNIE Bernard Keith B 4.16.1939 E.Liverpool, OH BL/TR 6/185# d4.10

Year	Tm Lg	G	AB	R	H	2B	3B	HR	RBI	BB-IB	HP	SO	AVG	OBP	SLG	AOPS	ABR	SB-CS	FA	FR	Rng	Thr	G at Pos	BFW
1962	Min A	159	573	79	154	27	7	12	64	62-10	0	82	.269	.338	.403	96	-3	0-1	.983	-9	94	110	*2-158	0.1
1963	Min A	139	421	52	101	20	1	9	43	38-8	1	52	.240	.302	.356	83	-9	0-0	.976	-24	84	97	*2-128	-2.5
1964	Min A	74	243	28	52	8	1	6	20	33-7	1	30	.214	.309	.329	78	-7	1-2	.979	-7	92	88	2-71	-0.9
1965	Min A	19	39	2	9	2	0	0	6	6-2	0	8	.231	.326	.282	73	-1	0-0	1.000	-0	93	126	2-10/3	-0.1
1966	Min A	101	319	34	76	18	1	5	30	26-5	2	40	.238	.299	.348	80	-7	2-3	.974	-4	93	94	2-89/3-2	-0.5
1967	Was A	87	254	13	49	5	1	3	18	18-1	0	43	.193	.244	.256	51	-16	1-2	.990	14	117	148	2-75	0.3
1968	Was A	120	373	31	90	12	4	6	40	28-5	4	35	.241	.301	.343	98	-2	2-0	**.991**	6	103	104	*2-110/3-2	1.4
1969	Was A	122	365	33	90	17	4	9	45	50-3	0	35	.247	.337	.389	108	4	5-4	.974	9	106	112	*2-110/3-6	1.9
1970	Was A	104	261	31	61	7	1	8	29	43-4	0	21	.234	.342	.360	99	0	0-2	.969	8	103	119	2-80,3-12	1.2
1971	Was A	97	229	18	61	11	1	4	22	33-1	0	27	.266	.359	.376	115	5	2-1	.961	-6	100	58	2-41,3-34	0.1
1972	NY A	84	220	26	50	9	0	9	21	23-4	0	42	.227	.296	.391	108	2	0-1	.940	0	104	122	3-44,2-20	0.3
1973	NY A	17	57	5	13	3	0	0	4	5-1	0	5	.228	.290	.281	64	-3	0-0	.985	0	102	87	2-13/D-2	-0.2
	Mon N	16	50	5	9	1	0	2	9	5-1	0	4	.180	.255	.320	56	-3	0-0	.970	-3	80	41	/2-9,3-8	-0.6
Total	12	1139	3404	357	815	140	21	73	351	370-52	8	424	.239	.314	.357	91	-40	13-16	.980	-16	98	106	2-914,3-109/D-2	0.5

ALLEN, JACK Cyrus Alban B 10.2.1855 Woodstock, IL D 4.21.1915 Girard, PA BR/TR ?/160# d5.1

Year	Tm Lg	G	AB	R	H	2B	3B	HR	RBI	BB-IB	HP	SO	AVG	OBP	SLG	AOPS	ABR	SB-CS	FA	FR	Rng	Thr	G at Pos	BFW
1879	Syr N	11	48	7	9	2	1	0	3	1		5	.188	.204	.271	62	-2		.655	-5	30	0	/3-8,O-3(RF)	-0.6
	Cle N	16	60	7	7	1	1	0	4	1		9	.117	.131	.167	-3	-6		.845	2	96	101	3-14/O-2(CF)	-0.3
	Year	27	108	14	16	3	2	0	7	2		14	.148	.164	.213	24	-8		.790	-3	73	66	3-22/O-5(0-2-3)	-0.9

ALLEN, DUSTY Dustin R. B 8.9.1972 Oklahoma City, OK BR/TR 6-4/215# d7.1

Year	Tm Lg	G	AB	R	H	2B	3B	HR	RBI	BB-IB	HP	SO	AVG	OBP	SLG	AOPS	ABR	SB-CS	FA	FR	Rng	Thr	G at Pos	BFW
2000	SD N	9	12	0	0	0	0	0	0	2-0	0	5	.000	.143	.000	-64	-3	0-0	1.000	-0	64	0	/O-2(LF),1D	-0.3
	Det A	18	16	5	7	2	0	2	2	2-0	0	7	.438	.500	.938	260	4	0-0	1.000	-1	28	111	1-17/3O(LF)	0.2
Total	1	27	28	5	7	2	0	2	2	4-0	0	12	.250	.344	.536	123	1	0-0	1.000	-1	27	109	/1-18,O-3(LF),3D	-0.1

ALLEN, ETHAN Ethan Nathan B 1.1.1904 Cincinnati, OH D 9.15.1993 Brookings, OR BR/TR 6-1/180# d6.21

Year	Tm Lg	G	AB	R	H	2B	3B	HR	RBI	BB-IB	HP	SO	AVG	OBP	SLG	AOPS	ABR	SB-CS	FA	FR	Rng	Thr	G at Pos	BFW
1926	Cin N	18	13	3	4	1	0	0	0	0	0	3	.308	.308	.385	88	0	0	1.000	1	172	0	/O-9(5-0-4)	0.0
1927	Cin N	111	359	54	106	26	4	2	20	14	2	23	.295	.325	.407	98	-2	12	.988	-3	100	58	O-98(14-72-13)	-0.9
1928	Cin N	129	485	55	148	30	7	1	62	27	1	29	.305	.343	.402	96	-4	6	.981	-1	99	103	*O-129(1-128-0)	-1.0
1929	Cin N	143	538	69	157	27	11	6	64	20	0	21	.292	.317	.416	84	-17	21	**.988**	5	107	91	*O-137(24-134-10)	-1.7
1930	Cin N	21	46	10	10	1	0	3	7	5	0	2	.217	.294	.435	77	-2	1	.969	-0	109	0	O-15(1-13-1)	-0.3
	NY N	76	238	48	73	9	2	7	31	12	0	23	.307	.340	.450	91	-4	5	.985	-2	87	130	O-62(1-54-7)	-0.8
	Year	97	284	58	83	10	2	10	38	17	0	25	.292	.332	.447	89	-7	6	.981	-3	91	108	O-77(2-67-8)	-1.1
1931	NY N	94	298	58	98	18	2	5	43	15	1	15	.329	.363	.453	121	8	6	.975	-3	98	40	O-77(40-23-14)	0.2
1932	NY N	54	103	13	18	6	2	1	7	1	2	12	.175	.198	.301	33	-10	0	.957	-1	97	71	O-24(11-13-0)	-1.2
1933	StL N	91	261	25	63	7	3	0	36	13	1	22	.241	.280	.291	60	-14	3	.984	7	114	163	O-67(0-46-21)	-1.0
1934	Phi N	145	581	87	192	**42**	4	10	85	33	3	47	.330	.370	.468	108	8	6	.978	11	105	183	*O-145(87-47-16)	1.1
1935	Phi N	**156**	645	90	198	46	1	8	63	43	1	54	.307	.351	.419	96	-2	5	.980	13	102	**205**	*O-156(19-136-1)	0.6
1936	Phi N	30	125	21	37	3	1	1	9	4	0	8	.296	.318	.360	75	-5	4	.954	-1	108	39	O-30(11-16-6)	-0.7
	Chi N	91	373	47	110	18	6	3	39	13	2	30	.295	.322	.399	91	-6	12	.980	-3	99	31	O-89(73-16-0)	-1.3
	Year	121	498	68	147	21	7	4	48	17	2	38	.295	.321	.390	87	-11	16	.972	-4	101	33	*O-119(84-32-6)	-2.0
1937	StL A	103	320	39	101	18	1	0	31	21	1	17	.316	.360	.378	86	-7	3-4	.980	2	101	118	O-78(12-54-14)	-0.8
1938	StL A	19	33	4	10	3	1	0	4	2	0	4	.303	.343	.455	98	0	0-0	1.000	-0	99	0	/O-7(2-5-0)	-0.1
Total	13	1281	4418	623	1325	255	45	47	501	223	14	310	.300	.336	.410	92	-57	84-4	.981	22	102	115	*O-1123(301-757-107)	-7.9

ALLEN, SLED Fletcher Manson B 8.23.1886 West Plains, MO D 10.16.1959 Lubbock, TX BR/TR 6-1/180# d5.4

Year	Tm Lg	G	AB	R	H	2B	3B	HR	RBI	BB-IB	HP	SO	AVG	OBP	SLG	AOPS	ABR	SB-CS	FA	FR	Rng	Thr	G at Pos	BFW
1910	StL A	14	23	3	3	1	0	0	1	1	2		.130	.231	.174	29	-2	0	.903	-4	*67*	*77*	C-12/1	-0.6

ALLEN, HAM Frank Erwin B 4.20.1846 Augusta, ME D 2.6.1881 Natick, MA d4.27

Year	Tm Lg	G	AB	R	H	2B	3B	HR	RBI	BB-IB	HP	SO	AVG	OBP	SLG	AOPS	ABR	SB-CS	FA	FR	Rng	Thr	G at Pos	BFW
1872	Man NA	17	70	9	19	3	0	0	11	0		1	.271	.271	.314	84	-1	0-0	.778	6	136	110	/S-9,O-9(4-3-2),3-5	0.3

ALLEN, HANK Harold Andrew B 7.23.1940 Wampum, PA BR/TR 6/190# d9.9 b-Dick b-Ron OF Total (137-LF 95-CF 72-RF)

Year	Tm Lg	G	AB	R	H	2B	3B	HR	RBI	BB-IB	HP	SO	AVG	OBP	SLG	AOPS	ABR	SB-CS	FA	FR	Rng	Thr	G at Pos	BFW
1966	Was A	9	31	2	12	0	0	1	6	3-0	0	6	.387	.441	.484	167	3	0-0	.917	-0	118	0	/O-9(8-0-3)	0.2
1967	Was A	116	292	34	68	8	4	3	17	13-2	0	53	.233	.264	.318	75	-11	3-4	.980	-6	92	20	O-99(59-65-1)	-2.3
1968	Was A	68	128	16	28	2	2	1	9	7-1	1	16	.219	.265	.289	70	-5	0-0	.895	-1	60	0	O-25(12-0-13),3-16,2-11	-0.8
1969	Was A	109	271	42	75	9	3	1	17	13-1	1	28	.277	.311	.343	88	-6	12-3	.933	0	102	133	O-91(48-16-42)/3-6,2-3	-0.7
1970	Was A	22	38	3	8	2	0	0	4	5-1	0	9	.211	.295	.263	60	-2	0-0	1.000	-1	79	134	O-17(5-3-10)	-0.3
	Mil A	28	61	4	14	4	0	0	4	7-0	0	5	.230	.309	.295	67	-3	0-1	1.000	2	82	318	O-14(1-11-2)/2-5,1-4	-0.1
	Year	50	99	7	22	6	0	0	8	12-1	0	14	.222	.304	.283	65	-4	0-1	1.000	2	80	220	O-31(6-14-12)/2-5,1-4	-0.4
1972	Chi A	9	21	1	3	0	0	0	0	0-0	0	2	.143	.143	.143	-15	-3	0-0	.905	2	120	443	/3-6	-0.2
1973	Chi A	28	39	2	4	2	0	0	0	1-0	0	9	.103	.125	.154	-21	-6	0-1	1.000	-1	112	0	/3-9,1-8,O-5(4-0-1),C2	-0.8
Total	7	389	881	104	212	27	9	6	57	49-5	2	128	.241	.281	.312	74	-33	15-9	.957	-5	92	76	O-260L/3-37,2-20,1-12,C	-5.0

ALLEN, HEZEKIAH Hezekiah "Ki" B 2.25.1863 Westport, CT D 9.21.1916 Saugatuck, CT 5-11/160# d5.16

Year	Tm Lg	G	AB	R	H	2B	3B	HR	RBI	BB-IB	HP	SO	AVG	OBP	SLG	AOPS	ABR	SB-CS	FA	FR	Rng	Thr	G at Pos	BFW
1884	Phi N	1	3	0	2	0	0	0	0	0		0	.667	.667	.667	337	1		1.000	-0			/C	0.0

ALLEN, HORACE Horace Tanner "Pug" B 6.11.1899 DeLand, FL D 7.5.1981 Canton, NC BL/TR 6/187# d6.15

Year	Tm Lg	G	AB	R	H	2B	3B	HR	RBI	BB-IB	HP	SO	AVG	OBP	SLG	AOPS	ABR	SB-CS	FA	FR	Rng	Thr	G at Pos	BFW
1919	Bro N	4	7	0	0	0	0	0	0	0	0	2	.000	.000	.000	-98	-2	0	1.000	0	62	538	/O-2(1-1-0)	-0.2

ALLEN, JAMIE James Bradley B 5.29.1958 Yakima, WA BR/TR 6/205# d5.1

Year	Tm Lg	G	AB	R	H	2B	3B	HR	RBI	BB-IB	HP	SO	AVG	OBP	SLG	AOPS	ABR	SB-CS	FA	FR	Rng	Thr	G at Pos	BFW
1983	Sea A	86	273	23	61	10	0	4	21	33-0	1	52	.223	.309	.304	67	-12	6-5	.959	-2	92	90	3-82/D-2	-1.5

ALLEN, PETE Jesse Hall B 5.1.1868 Columbiana, OH D 4.16.1946 Philadelphia, PA BR/TR 5-8.5/185# d8.4

Year	Tm Lg	G	AB	R	H	2B	3B	HR	RBI	BB-IB	HP	SO	AVG	OBP	SLG	AOPS	ABR	SB-CS	FA	FR	Rng	Thr	G at Pos	BFW
1893	Cle N	1	4	0	0	0	0	0	0	0	0	0	.000	.000	.000	-94	-1	0	1.000	-1	*98*	*0*	/C	-0.1

ALLEN, CHAD John Chad B 2.6.1975 Dallas, TX BR/TR 6-1/195# d4.6

Year	Tm Lg	G	AB	R	H	2B	3B	HR	RBI	BB-IB	HP	SO	AVG	OBP	SLG	AOPS	ABR	SB-CS	FA	FR	Rng	Thr	G at Pos	BFW
1999	Min A	137	481	69	133	21	3	10	46	37-1	2	89	.277	.330	.395	81	-14	14-7	.975	2	105	108	*O-133(133-0-1)/D-2	-1.5
2000	Min A	15	50	2	15	3	0	0	7	3-0	1	14	.300	.345	.360	78	-2	0-2	1.000	1	90	207	O-15(2-0-13)	-0.2
2001	Min A	57	175	20	46	13	2	4	20	19-1	0	37	.263	.333	.429	97	-1	1-2	.968	2	107	176	O-27(16-0-15),D-23	-0.2
2002	Cle A	5	10	0	1	1	0	0	0	0-0	0	2	.100	.100	.200	-23	-2	0-0	1.000	-1	61	0	/O-4(3-0-1)	-0.3

Year	Tm Lg	G	AB	R	H	2B	3B	HR	RBI	BB-IB	HP	SO	AVG	OBP	SLG	AOPS	ABR	SB-CS	FA	FR	Rng	Thr	G at Pos	BFW
2003	Fla N	12	24	2	5	1	1	0	0	0-0	1	5	.208	.240	.333	49	-2	0-0	1.000	1	141	323	/O-8(6-1-2),D	-0.1
Total	5	226	740	93	200	39	6	14	73	59-2	4	147	.270	.326	.396	83	-21	15-11	.977	6	104	130	O-187(160-1-32)/D-26	-2.3
ALLEN, KIM Kim Bryant B 4.5.1953 Fontana, CA BR/TR 5-11/175# d9.2																								
1980	Sea A	23	51	9	12	3	0	0	3	8-2	1	3	.235	.350	.294	78	-1	10-3	.970	-1	115	88	2-15/O-4(3-0-2),S	0.0
1981	Sea A	19	3	1	0	0	0	0	0	0-0	0	2	.000	.000	.000	-96	-1	2-1	—	-1	0	0	/2-2,O-2(CF),D-2	-0.2
Total	2	42	54	10	12	3	0	0	3	8-2	1	5	.222	.333	.278	69	-2	12-4	.970	-1	111	85	/2-17,O-6(3-2-2),D-2,S	-0.2
ALLEN, LUKE Lucas G. B 8.4.1978 Covington, GA BL/TR 6-2/208# d9.10																								
2002	LA N	6	7	2	1	1	0	0	0	2-0	0	3	.143	.333	.286	73	0	0-0	1.000	0	110	0	/O-3(RF)	0.0
2003	Col N	2	2	0	0	0	0	0	0	0-0	0	0	.000	.000	.000	-88	-1	0-0	—	0			/H	-0.1
Total	2	8	9	2	1	1	0	0	0	2-0	0	3	.111	.273	.222	35	-1	0-0	1.000	0	110	0	/O-3(RF)	-0.1
ALLEN, MYRON Myron Smith "Zeke" B 3.22.1854 Kingston, NY D 3.8.1924 Kingston, NY BR/TR 5-8/150# d7.19 ▲																								
1883	NY N	1	4	0	0	0	0	0	1	0		2	.000	.000	.000	-99	-1		1.000	-0	64	0	/P	0.0
1886	Bos N	1	3	0	0	0	0	0	0	0		1	.000	.000	.000	-99	-1	0	1.000	-0	82	0	/2	-0.1
1887	Cle AA	117	463	66	128	22	10	4	77	36	5		.276	.335	.393	106	3	26	.894	6	113	119	*O-115(73-1-41)/3-3,S-2,P-2	0.6
1888	KC AA	37	136	23	29	6	4	0	10	9	1		.213	.267	.316	81	-3	4	.931	6	144	62	O-35(33-2-0)/P-2	0.1
Total	4	156	606	89	157	28	14	4	88	45	6	3	.259	.317	.371	98	-2	30	.903	12	121	105	O-150(106-3-41)/P-5,3-3,S-2,2	0.6
ALLEN, DICK Richard Anthony B 3.8.1942 Wampum, PA BR/TR 5-11/190# d9.3 b-Hank b-Ron OF Total (256-LF 1-CF)																								
1963	Phi N	10	24	6	7	2	1	0	2	0-0	0	5	.292	.280	.458	114	0	0-0	.833	-1	98	0	/O-7(LF),3	-0.1
1964	Phi N	**162**	632	**125**	201	38	**13**	29	91	67-13	0	138	.318	.382	.557	163	53	3-4	.921	6	103	**118**	*3-162	5.9
1965	Phi N★	161	619	93	187	31	14	20	85	74-6	2	150	.302	.375	.494	146	39	15-2	.943	-3	97	105	*3-160/S-2	4.0
1966	Phi N★	141	524	112	166	25	10	40	110	68-13	3	136	.317	.396	**.632**	**181**	**57**	10-6	.967	-4	97	86	3-91,O-47(LF)	5.2
1967	Phi N★	122	463	89	142	31	10	23	77	75-18	1	117	.307	**.404**	.566	**173**	46	20-5	.908	-6	98	113	*3-121/2S	4.5
1968	Phi N	152	521	87	137	17	9	33	90	74-15	1	161	.263	.352	.520	160	38	7-7	.973	-4	103	62	*O-139(139-1-0),3-10	3.0
1969	Phi N	118	438	79	126	23	3	32	89	64-10	0	144	.288	.375	.573	168	39	9-3	.985	-8	77	99	*1-117	2.4
1970	StL N★	122	459	88	128	17	5	34	101	71-16	2	118	.279	.377	.560	145	29	5-4	.993	-12	77	98	1-79,3-38/O-3(LF)	0.9
1971	LA N	155	549	82	162	24	1	23	90	93-13	1	113	.295	.395	.468	154	43	8-1	.918	-6	101	120	3-67,O-60(LF),1-28	3.4
1972	Chi A★	148	506	90	156	28	5	**37**	**113**	**99**-16	1	126	.308	**.420**	**.603**	**199**	**65**	19-8	.995	-4	86	83	*1-143/3-2	**5.8**
1973	Chi A✱	72	250	39	79	20	3	16	41	33-3	1	51	.316	.394	.612	175	25	7-2	.994	2	111	95	1-67/2-2,D	2.3
1974	Chi A★	128	462	84	139	23	1	**32**	88	57-9	1	89	.301	.375	**.563**	164	38	7-1	.986	-7	78	**106**	*1-125/2D	2.4
1975	Phi N	119	416	54	97	21	3	12	62	58-4	2	109	.233	.327	.385	94	-3	11-2	.982	2	110	96	*1-113	-0.8
1976	†Phi N	85	298	52	80	16	1	15	49	37-2	0	63	.268	.346	.480	130	11	11-4	.989	-1	93	124	1-85	0.6
1977	Oak A	54	171	19	41	4	0	5	31	24-0	1	36	.240	.330	.351	89	-2	1-3	.984	2	124	94	1-50/D	-0.3
Total	15	1749	6332	1099	1848	320	79	351	1119	894-138	16	1556	.292	.378	.534	156	478	133-52	.989	-44	90	100	1-807,3-652,O-256L/2-4,D-3,S-3	39.2
ALLEN, BOB Robert (born Alvah Charles Elliott) B 10.13.1894 Muscoda, WI D 12.18.1975 Naperville, IL BR/TR 5-10/180# d8.20																								
1919	Phi A	9	22	3	3	1	0	0	0	3	1	7	.136	.269	.182	27	-2	0	.889	-1	76	0	/O-6(CF)	-0.4
ALLEN, BOB Robert Gilman B 7.10.1867 Marion, OH D 5.14.1943 Little Rock, AR BR/TR 5-11/175# d4.19 M2																								
1890	Phi N	**133**	456	69	103	15	11	2	57	87	5	54	.226	.356	.320	95	0	13	.924	**32**	**108**	**138**	*S-133/,M	3.2
1891	Phi N	118	438	46	97	7	4	1	51	43	0	44	.221	.291	.263	60	-23	12	.896	8	106	117	*S-118	-1.0
1892	Phi N	152	563	77	128	20	14	2	64	61	1	60	.227	.304	.323	90	-8	15	.919	15	104	129	*S-152	1.4
1893	Phi N	124	471	86	126	19	12	8	90	71	5	40	.268	.369	.410	107	5	8	.919	15	103	126	*S-124	2.2
1894	Phi N	41	154	27	40	10	4	0	19	17	1	11	.260	.337	.377	73	-7	4	.917	-3	95	85	S-41	-0.6
1897	Bos N	34	119	33	38	5	0	1	24	18	0		.319	.409	.387	104	2	1	.924	5	111	113	S-32/O(CF)2	0.7
1900	Cin N	5	15	0	2	1	0	0	1	0	1		.133	.188	.200	7	-2	0	.864	-1	100	71	/S-5,M	-0.2
Total	7	607	2216	338	534	77	45	14	306	297	13	209	.241	.334	.335	88	-33	53	.915	72	105	124	S-605/2O(CF)	5.7
ALLEN, ROD Roderick Bernet B 10.5.1959 Los Angeles, CA BR/TR 6-1/185# d4.7																								
1983	Sea A	11	12	1	2	0	0	0	0	0-0	0	1	.167	.167	.167	-8	-2	0-0	1.000	0	133	0	/O-2(RF),D-3	-0.2
1984	Det A	15	27	6	8	1	0	0	3	2-0	1	8	.296	.367	.333	96	0	1-0	1.000	0	391	0	D-11/O-2(LF)	0.0
1988	Cle A	5	11	1	1	1	0	0	0	0-0	0	2	.091	.091	.182	-25	-2	0-0	—	0			/D-4	-0.2
Total	3	31	50	8	11	2	0	0	3	2-0	1	11	.220	.264	.260	45	-4	1-0	1.000	0	160	0	/D-18,O-4(2-0-2)	-0.4
ALLEN, RON Ronald Frederick B 12.23.1943 Wampum, PA BB/TR 6-3/205# d8.11 b-Hank b-Dick																								
1972	StL N	7	11	2	1	0	0	1	1	3-0	0	5	.091	.286	.364	84	0	0-0	.968	-1	52	42	/1-5	-0.1
ALLENSON, GARY Gary Martin B 2.4.1955 Culver City, CA BR/TR 5-11/185# d4.8 C6																								
1979	Bos A	108	241	27	49	10	2	3	22	20-0	1	42	.203	.264	.299	50	-17	1-1	.980	3	100	93	*C-104/3-3	-1.1
1980	Bos A	36	70	9	25	6	0	0	10	13-0	0	11	.357	.452	.443	141	5	2-2	.981	1	111	62	C-24/3-5,D-6	0.7
1981	Bos A	47	139	23	31	8	0	5	25	23-0	1	33	.223	.335	.388	102	1	0-0	.969	-3	73	63	C-47	0.0
1982	Bos A	92	264	25	54	11	0	6	33	38-1	1	39	.205	.306	.314	67	-11	0-3	.992	6	130	107	C-91	-0.2
1983	Bos A	84	230	19	53	11	0	3	30	27-0	2	43	.230	.311	.317	70	-9	0-1	.984	-2	83	98	C-84	-0.8
1984	Bos A	35	83	9	19	2	0	2	8	9-2	0	14	.229	.304	.325	71	-3	0-0	.987	-5	70	103	C-35	-0.8
1985	Tor A	14	34	2	4	1	0	0	3	0-0	0	10	.118	.118	.147	-27	-6	0-0	1.000	-3	211	65	C-14	-0.8
Total	7	416	1061	114	235	49	2	19	131	130-3	5	192	.221	.307	.325	71	-40	3-7	.984	-3	102	92	C-399/3-8,D-6	-3.0
ALLENSWORTH, JERMAINE Jermaine Lamont B 1.11.1972 Anderson, IN BR/TR 6/189# d7.23																								
1996	Pit N	61	229	32	60	9	3	4	31	23-0	4	50	.262	.337	.380	87	-4	11-6	.979	1	101	133	O-61(CF)	-0.3
1997	Pit N	108	369	55	94	18	2	3	43	44-1	7	79	.255	.340	.339	79	-10	14-7	.980	-7	87	109	*O-104(CF)	-1.6
1998	Pit N	69	233	30	72	13	3	3	24	17-0	7	43	.309	.372	.429	109	4	8-4	.980	-1	98	102	O-66(CF)	0.3
	KC A	30	73	15	15	5	0	0	3	9-0	4	17	.205	.326	.274	57	-4	7-0	.982	-1	105	0	O-27(1-24-2)	-0.3
	NY N	34	54	9	11	2	0	2	4	2-0	1	16	.204	.246	.352	56	-4	0-2	1.000	-2	73	0	O-31(4-4-25)	-0.7
1999	NY N	40	73	14	16	2	0	3	9	9-0	1	23	.219	.310	.370	74	-3	2-1	1.000	2	117	87	O-33(10-14-15)	-0.2
Total	4	342	1031	155	268	49	8	15	114	104-1	24	228	.260	.339	.367	84	-21	42-20	.982	-9	95	97	O-322(15-273-42)	-2.8
ALLEY, GENE Leonard Eugene B 7.10.1940 Richmond, VA BR/TR 6/165# d9.4																								
1963	Pit N	17	51	3	11	1	0	0	0	2-0	0	12	.216	.245	.235	39	-4	0-1	.947	1	111	214	/3-7,2-4,S-4	-0.3
1964	Pit N	81	209	30	44	3	1	6	13	21-2	2	56	.211	.286	.321	72	-8	0-1	.966	18	122	125	S-61/3-3,2	1.5
1965	Pit N	153	500	47	126	21	6	5	47	32-9	4	82	.252	.302	.348	82	-12	7-2	.968	25	**116**	**128**	*S-110,2-40/3	2.7
1966	Pit N	147	579	88	173	28	10	7	43	27-0	5	83	.299	.334	.418	108	5	8-8	.979	14	105	**148**	*S-143	3.1
1967	Pit N★	152	550	59	158	25	7	6	55	36-5	7	70	.287	.337	.391	108	5	10-5	.967	7	105	112	*S-146	2.7
1968	Pit N✱	133	474	48	116	20	2	4	39	39-6	5	78	.245	.307	.321	91	-5	13-5	.974	21	**115**	**142**	*S-109,2-24	3.2
1969	Pit N	82	285	28	70	3	2	8	32	19-1	1	48	.246	.293	.354	83	-8	4-0	.977	16	113	128	2-53,S-25/3-5	1.5
1970	†Pit N	121	426	46	104	16	5	8	41	31-9	3	70	.244	.297	.362	78	-15	7-3	.975	**31**	113	128	*S-108/2-8,3-2	3.0
1971	†Pit N	114	348	38	79	8	7	6	28	35-14	0	43	.227	.296	.342	81	-10	9-2	.958	-8	98	86	*S-108/3	-0.5
1972	†Pit N	119	347	30	86	12	2	3	36	38-10	0	52	.248	.321	.320	85	-6	4-3	.970	11	107	**153**	*S-114/3-4	1.8
1973	Pit N	76	158	25	32	3	2	2	8	20-6	0	28	.203	.292	.285	62	-8	1-0	.981	5	106	80	S-49/3-8	0.1
Total	11	1195	3927	442	999	140	44	55	342	300-62	27	622	.254	.310	.354	88	-66	63-30	.970	140	109	127	S-977,2-130/3-31	18.8
ALLIE, GAIR Gair Roosevelt B 10.28.1931 Statesville, NC BR/TR 6-1/190# d4.13																								
1954	Pit N	121	418	38	83	8	6	3	30	56	2	84	.199	.294	.268	49	-32	1-1	.952	-13	91	86	S-95,3-19	-3.7
ALLIETTA, BOB Robert George B 5.1.1952 New Bedford, MA BR/TR 6/190# d5.6																								
1975	Cal A	21	45	4	8	1	0	1	2	1-1	0	6	.178	.196	.267	32	-4	0-0	1.000	-1	72	73	C-21	-0.5
ALLISON, ANDY Andrew K. B 1848 New York, NY 5-10/150# d5.7 M1																								
1872	Eck NA	22	92	9	15	2	0	0	10	1		2	.163	.172	.185	11	-8	0-0	.930	-1	80	53	1-22/O(RF)M	-0.6
ALLISON, ART Arthur Algernon B 1.29.1849 Philadelphia, PA D 2.25.1916 Washington, DC 5-8/150# d5.4 b-Doug																								
1871	Cle NA	**29**	137	28	40	4	5	0	19	2		5	.292	.302	.394	104	1	3-1	.885	1	94	172	*O-29(CF)/2-2	0.2
1872	Cle NA	19	87	13	23	4	0	0	8	0		2	.264	.264	.310	80	-1	0-0	.804	-1	90	200	O-19(0-17-2)	-0.1
1873	Res NA	**23**	100	12	32	2	0	0	11	0		2	.320	.320	.340	104	1	0-0	.816	-2	64	142	O-21(8-9-4)/1-3,C	0.0
1875	Was NA	26	112	18	24	3	1	0	3	1		2	.214	.221	.259	69	-3	6-0	.924	-3	44	47	1-23/O-3(0-1-2),C	-0.4
	Har NA	40	175	26	42	4	1	1	19	0		3	.240	.240	.291	80	-4	1-2	.785	3	268	212	O-37(RF)/2-2,C1	0.1

Year	Tm Lg	G	AB	R	H	2B	3B	HR	RBI	BB-IB	HP	SO	AVG	OBP	SLG	AOPS	ABR	SB-CS	FA	FR	Rng	Thr	G at Pos	BFW
	Year	66	287	44	66	7	2	1	22	1		5	.230	.233	.279	76	-7	7-2	.800	-0	255	202	O-40(0-1-39),1-24/C-2,2-2	-0.3
1876	Lou N	31	130	9	27	2	1	0	10	2		6	.208	.220	.238	45	-8		.789	3	230	115	O-23(RF)/1-8	-0.5
Total	4 NA	137	611	97	161	17	7	1	60	3		14	.264	.267	.319	88	-6	10-3	.000	-2	146	182	O-109(8-56-45)/1-27,2-4,C-3	-0.2
ALLISON, DOUG Douglas L. B 7.1845 Philadelphia, PA D 12.19.1916 Washington, DC BR/TR 5-10.5/160# d5.5 M1 b-Art																								
1871	Oly NA	27	133	28	44	10	2	2	27	0		2	.331	.331	.481	137	7	1-1	.806	-3			*C-27	0.3
1872	Tro NA	23	114	23	35	4	2	0	20	1		3	.307	.313	.377	110	1	1-1	.897	6			C-22/S	0.5
	Eck NA	18	83	18	28	2	1	0	4	1		5	.337	.345	.386	146	6	0-0	.863	-7			C-18	-0.1
	Year	41	197	41	63	6	3	0	24	2		8	.320	.327	.381	124	6	1-1	.883	-1			C-40/S	0.4
1873	Res NA	19	80	11	24	6	0	0	8	2		1	.300	.317	.375	114	2	0-0	.800	0			C-18/O-4(0-1-3),M	0.2
	Mut NA	11	48	6	10	0	0	0	3	1		0	.208	.224	.208	30	-4	0-0	.868	2			C-11/O(RF)	-0.1
	Year	30	128	17	34	6	0	0	11	3		1	.266	.282	.313	81	-2	0-0	.831	3			C-29/O-5(0-1-4)	0.1
1874	Mut NA	**65**	318	68	90	7	5	0	28	6		5	.283	.296	.336	99	-1	1-0	.800	1	81	0	*O-47(0-3-44),C-34/2	0.2
1875	Har NA	61	269	38	67	7	0	0	21	6		3	.249	.265	.275	84	-5	2-0	**.896**	17			*C-59/1-2,O-2(RF)	1.1
1876	Har N	44	163	19	43	4	0	0	15	3		9	.264	.277	.288	82	-4		**.881**	10			C-40/O-6(0-1-5)	0.7
1877	Har N	29	115	14	17	2	0	0	6	3		7	.148	.169	.165	7	-11		.896	1			C-29	-0.8
1878	Pro N	19	76	9	22	2	0	0	7	1		8	.289	.299	.316	102	0		.911	0			C-19/P	0.1
1879	Pro N	1	5	0	0	0	0	0	0	0		1	.000	.000	.000	-99	-1		.833	-0			/C	-0.1
1883	Bal AA	1	3	2	2	0	0	0		0			.667	.667	.667	321	1		—	-0	0	0	/O(CF)C	0.1
Total	5 NA	224	1045	192	298	36	10	2	111	17		19	.285	.297	.344	102	6	5-2	.000	18			C-189/O-54(0-4-50),1-2,2S	2.1
Total	5	94	362	44	84	8	0	0	28	7		25	.232	.247	.254	63	-15		.892	11			/C-90,O-7(0-2-5),P	-0.0
ALLISON, MILO Milo Henry B 10.16.1889 Elk Rapids, MI D 6.18.1957 Kenosha, WI BL/TR 5-10/155# d9.26																								
1913	Chi N	2	6	1	2	0	0	0	0	0	0	1	.333	.333	.333	91	0	1	1.000	-0	92	0	/O(CF)	0.0
1914	Chi N	1	1	0	1	0	0	0	0	0	0	0	1.000	1.000	1.000	497	0	0	—	0			H	0.0
1916	Cle A	14	18	10	5	0	0	0	0	6	0	1	.278	.458	.278	115	1	0	1.000	-0	88	0	/O-5(1-0-4)	0.0
1917	Cle A	32	35	4	5	0	0	0	0	9	0	7	.143	.318	.143	38	-2	3	1.000	-1	76	96	O-11(4-5-2)	-0.4
Total	4	49	60	15	13	0	0	0	0	15	0	9	.217	.373	.217	74	-1	4	1.000	-1	81	58	/O-17(5-6-6)	-0.4
ALLISON, BILL William Andrew B 9.18.1848 Philadelphia, PA D 6.12.1923 d5.21																								
1872	Eck NA	5	19	5	3	0	0	0	1	0		1	.158	.158	.158	-3	-2	0-0	.500	-2	0	0	/O-2(0-1-1),1-2,2	-0.2
ALLISON, BOB William Robert B 7.11.1934 Raytown, MO D 4.9.1995 Rio Verde, AZ BR/TR 6-4/220# d9.16																								
1958	Was A	11	35	1	7	1	0	0	0	2-0	0	5	.200	.243	.229	31	-3	0-2	1.000	-0	109	0	O-11(1-10-0)	-0.5
1959	Was A☆	150	570	83	149	18	**9**	30	85	60-1	2	92	.261	.333	.482	122	15	13-8	.974	-10	90	79	*O-149(7-134-9)	-0.3
1960	Was A	144	501	79	126	30	3	15	69	92-4	2	94	.251	.367	.413	113	12	11-9	.965	6	112	113	*O-140(0-4-139)/1-4	1.2
1961	Min A	159	556	83	136	21	3	29	105	103-1	5	100	.245	.363	.450	111	11	2-7	.975	2	101	124	*O-150(RF),1-18	-0.1
1962	Min A	149	519	102	138	24	8	29	102	84-0	4	115	.266	.370	.511	130	23	8-5	.977	1	102	116	*O-147(2-0-146)	1.4
1963	Min A★	148	527	**99**	143	25	4	35	91	90-2	3	109	.271	.378	.533	**150**	38	6-1	.971	8	115	113	*O-147(0-8-146)	3.8
1964	Min A★	149	492	90	141	27	4	32	86	92-4	7	99	.287	.404	.553	163	46	10-1	.986	3	100	90	1-93,O-61(27-28-16)	4.4
1965	†Min A	135	438	71	102	14	5	23	78	73-4	2	114	.233	.342	.445	118	11	10-2	.972	8	107	150	*O-122(LF)/1-3	1.5
1966	Min A	70	168	34	37	6	1	8	19	30-2	3	34	.220	.345	.411	110	3	6-0	.967	1	105	107	O-56(44-1-11)	0.3
1967	Min A	153	496	73	128	21	6	24	75	74-2	2	114	.258	.356	.470	132	21	6-4	.978	-1	96	68	*O-145(138-0-9)	1.3
1968	Min A	145	469	63	116	16	8	22	52	52-5	2	98	.247	.324	.456	128	15	9-7	.966	-3	93	61	*O-117(116-1-1),1-17	0.5
1969	†Min A	81	189	18	43	8	2	8	27	29-5	1	39	.228	.333	.418	107	2	2-4	1.000	-1	94	49	O-58(LF)/1-3	-0.4
1970	†Min A	47	72	15	15	5	0	1	7	14-0	1	20	.208	.345	.319	83	-1	1-0	1.000	-0	100	0	O-17(12-1-4)/1-7	-0.2
Total	13	1541	5032	811	1281	216	53	256	796	795-30	34	1033	.255	.358	.471	126	193	84-50	.975	13	103	100	*O-1320(527-187-631),1-145	12.9
ALLRED, BEAU Dale Le Beau B 6.4.1965 Mesa, AZ BL/TL 6/190# d9.7																								
1989	Cle A	13	24	0	6	3	0	0	1	2-0	0	10	.250	.308	.375	90	0	0-0	1.000	1	122	343	/O-5(3-0-2),D-2	0.1
1990	Cle A	4	16	2	3	1	0	1	2	2-0	0	3	.188	.278	.438	98	0	0-0	.833	-1	64	0	/O-4(0-3-1)	-0.1
1991	Cle A	48	125	17	29	3	0	3	12	25-2	1	35	.232	.359	.328	92	0	2-2	.972	4	134	39	O-42(20-0-27)/D	0.2
Total	3	65	165	19	38	7	0	4	15	29-2	1	48	.230	.345	.345	93	0	2-2	.969	4	128	65	/O-51(23-3-30),D-3	0.2
ALMADA, MEL Baldomero Melo (Quiros) B 2.7.1913 Huatabampo, Mexico D 8.13.1988 Caborca, Mexico BL/TL 6/170# d9.8																								
1933	Bos A	14	44	11	15	0	0	1	3	11	0	3	.341	.473	.409	137	3	3-1	1.000	0	98	98	O-13(7-6-0)	0.3
1934	Bos A	23	90	7	21	2	1	0	10	6	0	8	.233	.281	.278	42	-8	3-2	.985	2	103	207	O-23(0-16-7)	-0.7
1935	Bos A	151	607	85	176	27	9	3	59	55	1	34	.290	.350	.379	83	-16	20-9	.968	-1	88	190	*O-149(0-126-25)/1-3	-1.9
1936	Bos A	96	320	40	81	16	4	1	21	24	0	15	.253	.305	.338	55	-24	2-4	.987	1	96	134	O-81(11-3-69)	-2.5
1937	Bos A	32	110	17	26	6	2	1	9	15	0	6	.236	.328	.355	69	-5	0-1	.927	-3	88	53	O-27(4-2-21)/1-4	-1.0
	Was A	100	433	74	134	21	4	4	33	38	0	21	.309	.365	.404	98	-1	12-4	.964	10	109	162	*O-100(0-97-3)	0.6
	Year	132	543	91	160	27	6	5	42	53	0	27	.295	.357	.394	91	-7	12-5	.960	6	105	143	*O-127(4-99-24)/1-4	-0.4
1938	Was A	47	197	24	48	7	4	1	15	8	1	16	.244	.277	.335	56	-15	4-1	.968	1	105	102	O-47(CF)	-1.3
	StL A	102	436	77	149	22	2	3	37	38	3	22	.342	.398	.422	106	5	9-5	.966	-3	96	99	*O-101(CF)	0.0
	Year	149	633	101	197	29	6	4	52	46	4	38	.311	.362	.395	92	-9	13-6	.967	-1	99	100	*O-148(CF)	-1.3
1939	StL A	42	134	17	32	2	1	1	7	10	0	8	.239	.292	.291	48	-11	1-0	.987	-1	93	80	O-34(3-31-0)	-1.2
	Bro N	39	112	11	24	4	0	0	3	9	0	17	.214	.273	.250	40	-9	2	.977	1	111	82	O-32(CF)	-0.9
Total	7	646	2483	363	706	107	27	15	197	214	5	150	.284	.342	.367	79	-81	56-27	.970	8	98	138	O-607(25-461-125)/1-7	-8.6
ALMEIDA, RAFAEL Rafael D. "Mike" B 6.30.1887 Havana, Cuba D 5.18.1969 Havana, Cuba BR/TR 5-9/164# d7.4																								
1911	Cin N	36	96	9	30	5	1	0	15	9	2	16	.313	.383	.385	120	3	3	.890	-3	94	27	3-27/2S	0.0
1912	Cin N	16	59	9	13	4	3	0	10	5	0	8	.220	.281	.390	85	-2	0	.891	-1	101	101	3-15	-0.2
1913	Cin N	50	130	14	34	4	2	3	21	11	1	16	.262	.324	.392	104	0	4-5	.919	3	113	130	3-37/O-3(CF),S-2,2	0.4
Total	3	102	285	32	77	13	6	3	46	25	3	40	.270	.335	.389	106	1	7-5	.904	-1	104	88	/3-79,O-3(CF),S-3,2-2	0.2
ALMON, BILL William Francis B 11.21.1952 Providence, RI BR/TR 6-3/190# d9.2 OF Total (123-LF 8-CF 35-RF)																								
1974	SD N	16	38	4	12	1	0	0	3	2-0	0	9	.316	.350	.342	98	0	1-0	.915	-4	86	53	S-14	-0.3
1975	SD N	6	10	0	4	0	0	0	0	0-0	0	1	.400	.400	.400	131	0	0-0	1.000	-1	67	0	/S-2	0.0
1976	SD N	14	57	6	14	3	0	1	6	2-0	0	9	.246	.271	.351	82	-2	3-1	.962	4	124	103	S-14	0.4
1977	SD N	155	613	75	160	18	11	2	43	37-1	0	114	.261	.303	.336	79	-21	20-9	.954	15	107	89	*S-155	1.1
1978	SD N	138	405	39	102	19	2	0	21	33-10	0	74	.252	.308	.309	79	-12	17-5	.933	-5	99	118	*3-114,S-15/2-7	-1.6
1979	SD N	100	198	20	45	3	0	1	8	21-7	0	48	.227	.299	.258	57	-12	6-5	.985	5	108	116	2-61,S-25/O(CF)	-0.3
1980	Mon N	18	38	2	10	1	1	0	3	1-0	0	5	.263	.275	.342	73	-2	0-0	.911	-3	84	19	S-12/2	-0.3
	NY N	48	112	13	19	3	2	0	4	8-1	0	27	.170	.225	.232	29	-11	2-0	.967	5	100	131	S-22,2-18/3-9	-0.4
	Year	66	150	15	29	4	3	0	7	9-1	0	32	.193	.237	.260	40	-13	2-0	.948	2	95	94	S-34,2-19/3-9	-0.7
1981	Chi A	103	349	46	105	10	2	4	41	21-0	2	60	.301	.341	.375	109	4	16-6	.969	15	102	117	*S-103	3.2
1982	Chi A	111	308	40	79	10	4	4	26	25-0	1	49	.256	.313	.354	83	-8	10-8	.949	20	**113**	**130**	*S-108/D	2.1
1983	Oak A	143	451	45	120	29	1	4	63	26-3	2	67	.266	.302	.361	89	-7	26-8	.941	-17	88	63	S-52,3-40,1-38,O-23(9-0-15)/2-5,D-4	-2.0
1984	Oak A	106	211	24	47	11	0	7	16	10-0	0	42	.223	.253	.374	78	-7	5-7	1.000	-4	96	43	O-48(33-1-17),1-44,D-12/3-4,CS	-1.6
1985	Pit N	88	244	33	66	17	0	6	29	22-0	1	61	.270	.330	.414	109	3	10-7	.987	-7	93	86	S-43,O-32(26-6-0)/1-7,3-7	-0.1
1986	Pit N	102	196	29	43	7	2	7	27	30-2	0	38	.219	.319	.383	92	-2	11-4	.983	-1	89	238	O-54(53-0-2),3-28,S-19/1-4	-0.3
1987	Pit N	19	20	5	4	1	0	0	1	1-0	0	5	.200	.238	.250	29	-2	0-0	.944	0	92	180	/S-4,O-2(LF),3	-0.1
	NY N	49	54	8	13	3	0	0	4	8-0	0	16	.241	.339	.296	74	-2	1-0	.972	-2	112	65	S-22,2-10/1-2,O(RF)	-0.3
	Year	68	74	13	17	4	0	0	5	9-0	0	21	.230	.313	.284	62	-4	1-0	.963	-2	107	96	S-26,2-10/O-3(2-0-1),1-2,3	-0.4
1988	Phi N	20	26	1	3	2	0	0	1	3-0	0	11	.115	.207	.192	15	-3	0-0	.944	1	142	0	/3-9,S-5,1	-0.2
Total	15	1236	3330	390	846	138	25	36	296	250-24	6	636	.254	.305	.343	83	-84	128-60	.956	22	104	101	S-616,3-212,O-161L,2-102/1-96,DC	-0.7
ALMONTE, ERICK Erick R. B 2.1.1978 Santo Domingo, D.R. BR/TR 6-2/180# d9.4																								
2001	NY A	8	4	0	2	1	0	0	0	0-0	0	1	.500	.500	.750	220	1	2-0	.875	0	93	150	/S-4,D-3	0.2
2003	NY A	31	100	17	26	6	0	1	11	8-0	1	24	.260	.321	.350	78	-3	1-0	.906	-7	81	74	S-31	-0.7
Total	2	39	104	17	28	7	0	1	11	8-0	1	25	.269	.327	.365	84	-2	3-0	.904	-6	81	77	/S-35,D-3	-0.5
ALOMAR, ROBERTO Roberto (Velazquez) B 2.5.1968 Ponce, P.R. BB/TR 6/185# d4.22 f-Sandy b-Sandy																								
1988	SD N	143	545	84	145	24	6	9	41	47-5	3	83	.266	.328	.382	105	3	24-6	.980	16	106	111	*2-143	2.7
1989	SD N	158	623	82	184	27	1	7	56	53-4	1	76	.295	.347	.376	108	7	42-17	.967	6	104	104	*2-157	2.1
1990	SD N★	147	586	80	168	27	5	6	60	48-1	2	72	.287	.340	.381	98	-1	24-7	.976	-0	100	99	*2-137/S-5	0.5

Year	Tm Lg	G	AB	R	H	2B	3B	HR	RBI	BB-IB	HP	SO	AVG	OBP	SLG	AOPS	ABR	SB-CS	FA	FR	Rng	Thr	G at Pos	BFW
1991	†Tor A★	161	637	88	188	41	11	9	69	57-3	4	86	.295	.354	.436	114	12	53-11	.981	-16	93	78	*2-160	0.9
1992	†Tor A★	152	571	105	177	27	8	8	76	87-5	5	52	.310	.405	.427	128	25	49-9	.993	-22	88	70	*2-150/D	1.5
1993	†Tor A★	153	589	109	192	35	6	17	93	80-5	5	67	.326	.408	.492	141	37	55-15	.980	-9	97	91	*2-150	4.1
1994	Tor A★	107	392	78	120	25	4	8	38	51-2	2	41	.306	.386	.452	115	11	19-8	.991	-2	91	107	*2-106	1.3
1995	Tor A★	130	517	71	155	24	7	13	66	47-3	0	45	.300	.354	.449	109	6	30-3	**.994**	-6	94	90	*2-128	1.1
1996	†Bal A★	153	588	132	193	43	4	22	94	90-10	1	65	.328	.411	.527	138	38	17-6	.985	22	**113**	111	*2-141,D-10	**6.1**
1997	†Bal A★	112	412	64	137	23	2	14	60	40-2	3	43	.333	.390	.500	136	22	9-3	.988	10	104	**108**	*2-109/D-2	3.6
1998	Bal A★	147	588	86	166	36	1	14	56	59-3	2	70	.282	.347	.418	100	1	18-5	.985	21	111	99	*2-144/D-3	2.9
1999	†Cle A★	159	563	**138**	182	40	3	24	120	99-3	7	96	.323	.422	.533	138	37	37-6	**.992**	7	102	100	*2-156/D-2	**5.2**
2000	Cle A★	155	610	111	189	40	2	19	89	64-4	6	82	.310	.378	.475	113	13	39-4	.980	14	99	103	*2-155	3.8
2001	†Cle A★	157	575	113	193	34	12	20	100	80-5	4	71	.336	.415	.541	149	43	30-6	**.993**	8	99	88	*2-157	5.9
2002	NY N	149	590	73	157	24	4	11	53	57-4	1	83	.266	.331	.376	93	-10	16-4	.983	-22	89	99	*2-147	-2.3
2003	NY N	73	263	34	69	17	1	2	22	29-2	2	40	.262	.336	.357	85	-5	6-0	.981	-10	92	104	2-72	-1.0
	Chi A	67	253	42	64	11	1	3	17	30-1	1	37	.253	.330	.340	78	-8	6-2	.990	-2	93	94	2-67	-0.6
Total	16	2323	8902	1490	2679	498	78	206	1110	1018-62	49	1109	.301	.372	.444	117	231	474-112	.984	14	99	97	*2-2279/D-18,S-5	37.8

ALOMAR, SANDY Santos Jr. (Velazquez) B 6.18.1966 Salinas, P.R. BR/TR 6-5/215# d9.30 f-Sandy b-Roberto

1988	SD N	1	1	0	0	0	0	0	0	0-0	0	1	.000	.000	.000	-99	0	0-0	—	0			H	0.0
1989	SD N	7	19	1	4	1	0	1	6	3-1	0	3	.211	.318	.421	110	0	0-0	1.000	1	178	0	/C-6	0.2
1990	Cle A★	132	445	60	129	26	2	9	66	25-2	2	46	.290	.326	.418	109	4	4-1	.981	-5	102	98	*C-129	0.7
1991	Cle A★	51	184	10	40	9	0	0	7	8-1	4	24	.217	.264	.266	47	-13	0-4	.987	7	138	82	C-46/D-4	-0.5
1992	Cle A★	89	299	22	75	16	0	2	26	13-3	5	32	.251	.293	.324	74	-11	3-3	.996	3	140	114	C-88/D	-0.3
1993	Cle A	64	215	24	58	7	1	6	32	11-0	6	28	.270	.318	.395	92	-3	3-1	.984	-4	94	71	C-64	-0.2
1994	Cle A	80	292	44	84	15	1	14	43	25-2	2	31	.288	.347	.490	113	5	8-4	.996	3	119	93	C-78	1.2
1995	†Cle A	66	203	32	61	6	0	10	35	7-0	3	26	.300	.332	.478	106	1	3-1	.995	7	93	94	C-61	1.1
1996	†Cle A★	127	418	53	110	23	0	11	50	19-0	3	42	.263	.299	.397	75	-17	1-0	.988	1	90	114	*C-124/1	-0.8
1997	†Cle A★	125	451	63	146	37	0	21	83	19-2	3	48	.324	.354	.545	126	16	0-2	.985	-10	90	104	*C-119/D	1.3
1998	†Cle A★	117	409	45	96	26	2	6	44	18-0	3	45	.235	.270	.352	59	-26	0-3	.992	5	111	82	*C-111/D-3	-1.3
1999	†Cle A	37	137	19	42	13	0	6	25	4-0	0	23	.307	.322	.533	109	2	0-1	.974	-1	77	38	C-35/D	0.2
2000	Cle A	97	356	44	103	16	2	7	42	16-1	4	41	.289	.324	.404	82	-10	2-2	.989	-12	71	96	C-95/D	-1.6
2001	Chi A	70	220	17	54	8	1	4	21	12-1	2	17	.245	.288	.345	65	-12	1-2	.990	-0	143	77	C-69	-0.8
2002	Chi A	51	167	21	48	10	1	7	25	5-0	1	14	.287	.309	.485	106	1	0-0	.994	-2	70	84	C-50	0.2
	Col N	38	116	8	31	4	0	0	12	4-0	0	19	.267	.292	.302	51	-8	0-0	1.000	-2	136	61	C-38	-0.9
2003	Chi A	75	194	22	52	12	0	5	26	4-0	0	17	.268	.281	.407	78	-7	0-0	.997	-3	162	43	C-75	-0.5
Total	16	1227	4126	485	1133	229	10	109	543	193-13	38	457	.275	.311	.414	88	-78	25-24	.989	-12	107	89	*C-1188/D-11,1	-2.0

ALOMAR, SANDY Santos Sr. (Conde) B 10.19.1943 Salinas, P.R. BB/TR (BR 1964 (part), 65-66) 5-9/155# d9.15 C9 s-Roberto s-Sandy OF Total (5-LF 3-RF)

1964	Mil N	19	53	3	13	1	0	0	6	0-0	0	11	.245	.245	.264	43	-4	1-0	.967	5	128	93	S-19	0.3
1965	Mil N	67	108	16	26	1	1	0	8	4-1	0	12	.241	.268	.269	51	-7	12-5	.964	6	109	88	S-39,2-19	0.3
1966	Atl N	31	44	4	4	1	0	0	2	1-1	0	10	.091	.111	.114	-37	-8	0-0	.981	1	103	179	2-21/S-5	-0.6
1967	NY N	15	22	1	0	0	0	0	0	0-0	0	6	.000	.000	.000	-99	-6	0-0	1.000	1	98	62	S-10/3-3,2-2	-0.5
	Chi A	12	15	4	3	0	0	0	0	2-0	0	0	.200	.294	.200	50	-1	2-0	.952	1	106	279	/S-8,2-2	0.1
1968	Chi A	133	363	41	92	8	2	0	12	20-1	1	42	.253	.292	.287	76	-11	21-8	.958	-14	96	96	2-99,3-27/S-9,O(LF)	-1.8
1969	Chi A	22	58	8	13	2	0	0	4	4-0	0	6	.224	.274	.259	47	-4	2-0	.980	3	105	129	2-22	0.0
	Cal A	134	559	60	140	10	2	1	30	36-2	0	48	.250	.296	.281	65	-28	18-3	.969	-6	95	113	*2-134	-2.3
	Year	156	617	68	153	12	2	1	34	40-2	0	54	.248	.294	.279	63	-32	20-3	.970	-3	96	115	*2-156	-2.3
1970	Cal A★	**162**	672	82	169	18	2	2	36	49-2	1	65	.251	.302	.293	68	-31	35-12	.979	12	107	**125**	*2-153,S-10/3	-0.4
1971	Cal A	**162**	689	77	179	24	3	4	42	41-4	0	60	.260	.301	.321	82	-19	39-10	.989	23	**115**	110	*2-137,S-28	2.3
1972	Cal A	**155**	610	65	146	20	3	1	25	47-5	0	55	.239	.292	.287	78	-18	20-12	.977	7	98	95	*2-154/S-4	-0.1
1973	Cal A	136	470	45	112	7	1	0	28	34-1	0	44	.238	.288	.257	60	-26	25-10	.979	5	96	97	*2-110,S-31	-0.9
1974	Cal A	46	54	12	12	0	1	0	1	2-0	0	8	.222	.250	.259	49	-4	2-0	.977	1	85	135	S-19,2-15/3-5,O(RF)D	-0.1
	NY A	76	279	35	75	8	0	1	27	14-0	0	25	.269	.302	.308	78	-8	6-4	.977	-11	89	79	2-76	-1.5
	Year	122	333	47	87	8	1	1	28	16-0	0	33	.261	.293	.300	74	-12	8-4	.976	-10	92	78	2-91,S-19/3-5,O(RF)D	-1.6
1975	NY A	151	489	61	117	18	4	2	39	26-0	0	58	.239	.277	.305	66	-24	28-6	**.985**	-4	93	104	*2-150/S	-1.5
1976	†NY A	67	163	20	39	4	0	1	10	13-0	0	12	.239	.295	.282	70	-6	12-7	.970	-3	103	83	2-38/S-6,3-3,1O(RF)D	-0.7
1977	Tex A	69	83	21	22	3	0	1	11	8-0	1	13	.265	.333	.337	84	-2	4-3	.973	-4	83	107	D-26,2-18/S-6,O-5(4-0-1),1-4,3	-0.5
1978	Tex A	24	29	3	6	1	0	0	1	1-0	0	7	.207	.233	.241	34	-3	0-0	.975	1	146	128	/1-9,2-6,3-3,S-2,D-3	-0.2
Total	15	1481	4760	558	1168	126	19	13	282	302-17	3	482	.245	.290	.288	68	-210	227-80	.977	25	100	105	*2-1156,S-197/3-43,D-39,1-14,OL	-8.1

ALOU, FELIPE Felipe Rojas (born Felipe Rojas (Alou)) B 5.12.1935 Haina, D.R. BR/TR 6/195# d6.8 M11 C5 b-Jesus b-Matty s-Moises OF Total (434-LF 484-CF 736-RF)

1958	SF N	75	182	21	46	9	2	4	16	19-2	1	34	.253	.325	.390	91	-2	4-2	.985	2	118	45	O-70(28-3-44)	-0.3
1959	SF N	95	247	38	68	13	2	10	33	17-1	0	38	.275	.318	.466	109	2	5-3	.974	-2	102	48	O-69(0-10-64)	-0.1
1960	SF N	106	322	48	85	17	3	8	44	16-1	2	42	.264	.299	.410	99	-2	10-2	.958	-1	103	74	O-95(68-7-24)	-0.6
1961	SF N	132	415	59	120	19	0	18	52	26-2	2	41	.289	.333	.465	113	7	11-4	.990	1	100	108	*O-122(42-6-87)	0.2
1962	†SF N★	154	561	96	177	30	3	25	98	33-2	5	66	.316	.356	.513	133	25	10-7	.971	-2	104	59	*O-150(11-2-141)	1.2
1963	SF N	157	565	75	159	31	9	20	82	27-3	6	87	.281	.319	.474	127	18	11-2	.986	2	107	81	*O-153(6-13-144)	1.2
1964	Mil N	121	415	60	105	26	3	9	51	30-5	4	41	.253	.306	.395	96	-2	5-2	.975	-1	109	35	O-92(14-60-27),1-18	-0.7
1965	Mil N	143	555	80	165	29	2	23	78	31-4	5	63	.297	.338	.481	128	19	8-4	.980	-0	102	44	O-91(66-24-9),1-69/3-2,S	1.2
1966	Atl N☆	154	666	**122**	**218**	32	6	31	74	24-6	12	51	.327	.361	.533	143	36	5-7	.988	1	95	88	1-90,O-79(47-40-4)/3-3,S	2.9
1967	Atl N	140	574	76	157	26	3	15	43	32-7	7	50	.274	.318	.408	108	5	6-5	.993	-10	55	105	1-85,O-56(24-30-5)	-1.4
1968	Atl N★	160	662	72	**210**	37	5	11	57	48-14	4	56	.317	.365	.438	140	33	12-11	.980	-2	100	78	*O-158(CF)	2.8
1969	†Atl N	123	476	54	134	13	1	5	32	23-4	4	23	.282	.319	.345	86	-10	4-6	.989	-0	106	56	*O-116(3-102-13)	-1.6
1970	Oak A	154	575	70	156	25	3	8	55	32-6	1	31	.271	.308	.367	89	-10	10-5	.977	8	109	119	*O-145(101-5-81)/1	-1.0
1971	Oak A	2	8	0	2	1	0	0	0	0-0	0	1	.250	.250	.375	77	0	0-0	1.000	1	195	0	/O-2(LF)	0.0
	NY A	131	461	52	133	20	6	8	69	32-3	2	24	.289	.334	.410	118	9	5-5	.985	-11	79	57	O-80(7-20-56),1-42	-1.1
	Year	133	469	52	135	21	6	8	69	32-3	2	25	.288	.333	.409	117	9	5-5	.986	-11	82	56	O-82(9-20-56),1-42	-1.1
1972	NY A	120	324	33	90	18	1	6	37	22-1	2	27	.278	.326	.395	118	7	1-0	.990	5	146	120	1-95,O-15(RF)	0.6
1973	NY A	93	280	25	66	12	0	4	27	9-5	0	25	.236	.256	.321	65	-14	0-1	.988	-2	90	100	1-67,O-22(1-1-21)	-2.3
	Mon N	19	48	4	10	1	0	1	4	2-1	0	4	.208	.240	.292	45	-4	0-1	1.000	3	123	275	O-15(14-3-0)/1	-0.2
1974	Mil A	3	3	0	0	0	0	0	0	0-0	0	2	.000	.000	.000	-99	-1	0-0	.000	-0	0	0	/O(RF)	-0.1
Total	17	2082	7339	985	2101	359	49	206	852	423-67	57	706	.286	.328	.433	114	116	107-67	.979	-10	103	81	*O-1531R,1-468/3-5,S-2	0.7

ALOU, JESUS Jesus Maria Rojas (born Jesus Maria Rojas (Alou)) B 3.24.1942 Haina, D.R. BR/TR 6-2/195# d9.10 C1 b-Felipe b-Matty

1963	SF N	16	24	3	6	1	0	0	5	0-0	1	3	.250	.280	.292	66	-1	0-1	.875	-1	88	0	O-12(11-0-3)	-0.2
1964	SF N	115	376	42	103	11	0	3	28	13-2	4	35	.274	.305	.327	77	-12	6-6	.973	2	102	115	*O-108(9-4-99)	-1.9
1965	SF N	143	543	76	162	19	4	9	52	13-0	3	40	.298	.317	.398	98	-3	8-5	.980	0	102	79	*O-136(6-0-133)	-1.3
1966	SF N	110	370	41	96	13	1	1	20	9-1	2	22	.259	.279	.308	62	-19	5-5	.967	-6	87	63	*O-100(59-0-42)	-3.4
1967	SF N	129	510	55	149	15	4	5	30	14-2	4	39	.292	.316	.367	96	-4	1-7	.948	-10	86	57	*O-123(79-0-50)	-2.7
1968	SF N	120	419	26	110	15	4	0	39	9-3	1	23	.263	.278	.317	79	-12	1-4	.989	1	96	126	*O-105(49-0-65)	-2.2
1969	Hou N	115	452	49	112	19	4	5	34	15-6	4	30	.248	.276	.341	74	-18	4-6	.928	0	100	124	*O-112(65-0-58)	-2.6
1970	Hou N	117	458	59	140	27	3	1	44	21-4	1	15	.306	.335	.384	97	-3	3-2	.962	-5	89	84	*O-108(30-0-88)	-1.3
1971	Hou N	122	433	41	121	21	4	2	40	13-3	4	17	.279	.305	.360	91	-7	3-7	.983	8	105	87	*O-109(52-0-63)	-0.7
1972	Hou N	52	93	8	29	4	1	0	11	7-4	1	5	.312	.366	.376	114	2	0-2	.970	-1	108	0	O-23(10-0-14)	0.0
1973	Hou N	28	55	7	13	2	0	1	8	1-1	2	6	.236	.276	.327	67	-3	0-0	.941	-1	91	0	O-14(1-0-13)	-0.4
	†Oak A	36	108	10	33	3	0	1	11	2-1	0	6	.306	.318	.361	96	-1	0-0	1.000	1	109	75	O-21(18-1-4)/D-6	-0.2
1974	†Oak A	96	220	13	59	8	0	2	15	5-1	2	9	.268	.288	.332	84	-5	0-0	1.000	4	132	301	D-41,O-25(9-0-16)	-0.4
1975	NY N	62	102	8	27	3	0	0	11	4-2	1	5	.265	.299	.294	68	-5	0-1	.963	1	82	279	O-20(15-0-5)	-0.6
1978	Hou N	77	139	7	45	5	1	2	19	6-1	0	5	.324	.345	.417	123	4	0-0	.976	-1	88	52	O-28(27-0-1)	0.1
1979	Hou N	42	43	3	11	4	0	0	10	6-1	0	7	.256	.347	.349	96	0	0-0	1.000	0	147	0	/O-6(5-0-1),1	0.0
Total	15	1380	4345	448	1216	170	26	32	377	138-32	30	267	.280	.305	.353	87	-87	31-46	.968	-9	96	92	*O-1050(445-5-655)/D-47,1	-17.8

ALOU, MATTY Mateo Rojas (born Mateo Rojas (Alou)) B 12.22.1938 Haina, D.R. BL/TL 5-9/160# d9.26 b-Felipe b-Jesus

1960	SF N	4	3	1	1	0	0	0	0	0-0	0	0	.333	.333	.333	88	0	0-0	1.000	0	159	0	/O(LF)	0.0
1961	SF N	81	200	38	62	7	2	6	24	15-2	0	18	.310	.356	.455	118	5	3-2	.978	-2	99	49	O-58(16-3-40)	0.0
1962	†SF N	78	195	28	57	8	1	3	14	14-0	3	17	.292	.349	.390	100	0	3-1	.976	0	102	95	O-57(35-9-21)	-0.2

Year	Tm Lg	G	AB	R	H	2B	3B	HR	RBI	BB-IB	HP	SO	AVG	OBP	SLG	AOPS	ABR	SB-CS	FA	FR	Rng	Thr	G at Pos	BFW
1963	SF N	63	76	4	11	1	0	0	2	2-0	1	13	.145	.177	.158	-3	-10	0-1	.952	1	109	151	O-20(13-2-7)	-1.2
1964	SF N	110	250	28	66	4	2	1	14	11-3	3	25	.264	.302	.308	71	-10	5-3	.976	1	108	49	O-80(42-18-35)	-1.4
1965	SF N	117	324	37	75	12	2	2	18	17-2	2	28	.231	.274	.299	60	-17	10-2	.986	1	98	130	*O-103(72-11-23)/P	-2.1
1966	Pit N	141	535	86	183	18	9	2	27	24-4	4	44	**.342**	.373	.421	121	14	23-15	.972	-5	90	123	*O-136(1-135-0)	0.6
1967	Pit N	139	550	87	186	21	7	2	28	24-1	6	42	.338	.372	.413	124	16	16-10	.989	-5	87	127	*O-134(CF)/1	0.8
1968	Pit N★	146	558	59	185	28	4	0	52	27-6	2	26	.332	.362	.396	130	20	18-10	.984	-8	90	88	*O-144(CF)	1.0
1969	Pit N★	**162**	698	105	**231**	**41**	6	1	48	42-9	2	35	.331	.369	.411	121	20	22-8	.977	-4	96	106	*O-162(1-162-0)	1.4
1970	†Pit N	155	677	97	201	21	8	1	47	30-3	4	18	.297	.329	.356	86	-15	19-11	.975	-7	86	172	*O-153(0-152-1)	-2.6
1971	StL N	149	609	85	192	28	6	7	74	34-3	4	27	.315	.352	.415	113	10	19-10	.981	-2	101	158	O-94(0-73-21),1-57	0.2
1972	StL N	108	404	46	127	17	2	3	31	24-2	1	23	.314	.353	.389	112	6	11-4	.988	-1	101	106	1-66,O-39(1-0-38)	0.0
	†Oak A	32	121	11	34	5	0	1	16	11-1	1	12	.281	.341	.347	112	2	2-1	1.000	-3	78	87	O-32(2-0-31)/1	-0.2
1973	NY A	123	497	59	147	22	1	2	28	30-0	3	43	.296	.338	.356	100	0	5-2	.974	-6	91	109	O-85(RF),1-40/D	-1.4
	StL N	11	11	1	3	0	0	0	1	1-1	0	0	.273	.333	.273	70	0	0-0	1.000	1	0	0	/1O(CF)	0.0
1974	SD N	48	81	8	16	3	0	0	3	5-1	0	6	.198	.241	.235	36	-7	0-0	.947	-2	83	0	O-13(LF)/1-2	-1.0
Total	15	1667	5789	780	1777	236	50	31	427	311-38	36	377	.307	.345	.381	105	34	156-80	.979	-39	93	117	*O-1312(197-844-302),1-168/DP	-6.1
ALOU, MOISES Moises Rojas (born B 7.3.1966 Atlanta, GA BR/TR 6-3/190# d7.26 f-Felipe																								
1990	Pit N	2	5	0	1	0	0	0	0	0-0	0	0	.200	.200	.200	11	-1	0-0	1.000	-0	102	0	/O-2(LF)	-0.1
	Mon N	14	15	4	3	0	1	0	0	0-0	0	3	.200	.200	.333	46	-1	0-0	1.000	1	106	548	/O-5(1-2-2)	-0.1
	Year	16	20	4	4	0	1	0	0	0-0	0	3	.200	.200	.300	37	-2	0-0	1.000	1	105	360	/O-7(3-2-2)	-0.2
1992	Mon N	115	341	53	96	28	2	9	56	25-0	1	46	.282	.328	.455	122	9	16-2	.978	-0	96	138	*O-100(79-13-15)	1.0
1993	Mon N	136	482	70	138	29	6	18	85	38-9	5	53	.286	.340	.483	114	9	17-6	.985	1	99	116	*O-136(102-12-34)	0.7
1994	Mon N★	107	422	81	143	31	5	22	78	42-10	2	63	.339	.397	.592	153	33	7-6	.986	-2	100	57	*O-106(63-0-45)	2.5
1995	Mon N	93	344	48	94	22	0	14	58	29-6	9	56	.273	.342	.459	106	3	4-3	.981	-3	92	88	O-92(61-4-30)	-0.3
1996	Mon N	143	540	87	152	28	2	21	96	49-7	2	83	.281	.339	.457	106	4	9-4	.989	2	102	93	*O-142(33-7-123)	0.0
1997	†Fla N★	150	538	88	157	29	5	23	115	70-9	4	85	.292	.373	.493	131	25	9-5	.988	-11	87	47	*O-150(89-55-22)	1.1
1998	†Hou N★	159	584	104	182	34	5	38	124	84-11	5	87	.312	.399	.582	159	52	11-3	.980	-8	83	109	*O-154(152-6-0)/D	3.9
2000	Hou N	126	454	82	161	28	2	30	114	52-4	2	45	.355	.416	.623	152	37	3-3	.970	-8	84	69	*O-121(59-0-64)/D	2.1
2001	†Hou N★	136	513	79	170	31	1	27	108	57-14	3	57	.331	.396	.554	136	29	5-1	.991	-6	83	121	*O-130(RF)/D-4	1.7
2002	Chi N	132	484	50	133	23	1	15	61	47-4	0	61	.275	.337	.419	104	0	8-0	.991	1	98	88	*O-124(122-1-4)/D-2	-0.3
2003	†Chi N	151	565	83	158	35	1	22	91	63-7	7	67	.280	.357	.462	114	12	3-1	.972	-8	87	52	*O-142(LF)/D-9	-0.1
Total	12	1464	5287	829	1588	318	31	239	986	556-81	40	706	.300	.367	.508	128	211	92-34	.983	-41	91	88	*O-1404(905-100-469)/D-17	12.1
ALPERMAN, WHITEY Charles Augustus B 11.11.1879 Etna, PA D 12.25.1942 Pittsburgh, PA BR/TR 5-10/180# d4.13																								
1906	Bro N	128	441	38	111	15	7	3	46	6	14		.252	.284	.338	102	-2	13	.940	-3	102	72	*2-103,S-24/3	-0.4
1907	Bro N	141	558	44	130	23	**16**	2	39	13	12		.233	.266	.342	98	-6	5	.953	12	112	100	*2-115,3-14,S-12	0.9
1908	Bro N	70	213	17	42	3	1	1	15	9	7		.197	.253	.235	58	-10	2	.934	-3	102	77	2-42/3-9,O-5(RF),S-2	-1.5
1909	Bro N	111	420	35	104	19	12	1	41	2	6		.248	.262	.357	95	-7	7	.931	9	100	84	*2-108	0.4
Total	4	450	1632	134	387	60	36	7	141	30	39		.237	.268	.331	93	-25	27	.941	16	105	85	2-368/S-38,3-24,O-5(RF)	-0.6
ALSTON, TOM Thomas Edison B 1.31.1926 Greensboro, NC D 12.30.1993 Winston-Salem, NC BL/TR 6-5/210# d4.13																								
1954	StL N	66	244	28	60	14	2	4	34	24	2	41	.246	.317	.369	78	-8	3-5	.989	10	154	97	1-65	-0.3
1955	StL N	13	8	0	1	0	0	0	0	0-0	0	0	.125	.125	.125	-33	-2	0-0	1.000	0	141	109	/1-7	-0.1
1956	StL N	3	2	0	0	0	0	0	0	0-0	0	0	.000	.000	.000	-99	-1	0-0	1.000	0	294	264	/1-3	0.0
1957	StL N	9	17	2	5	1	0	0	2	1-0	0	5	.294	.333	.353	83	0	0-0	.947	-1	36	135	/1-6	-0.2
Total	4	91	271	30	66	15	2	4	36	25-0	2	46	.244	.311	.358	74	-11	3-5	.987	9	148	100	/1-81	-0.6
ALSTON, WALTER Walter Emmons "Smokey" B 12.1.1911 Venice, OH D 10.1.1984 Oxford, OH BR/TR 6-2/195# d9.27 M23 HF1983																								
1936	StL N	1	1	0	0	0	0	0	0	0	0	1	.000	.000	.000	-99	0	0	.500	-0	0	0	/1	-0.1
ALSTON, DELL Wendell B 9.22.1952 Valhalla, NY BL/TR 6/180# d5.17																								
1977	NY A	22	40	10	13	4	0	1	4	3-0	0	4	.325	.364	.500	137	2	3-3	1.000	0	58	806	D-10/O-2(RF)	0.2
1978	NY A	3	3	0	0	0	0	0	0	0-0	0	2	.000	.000	.000	-99	-1	0-0	—	0			H	-0.1
	Oak A	58	173	17	36	2	0	1	10	10-0	0	21	.208	.250	.237	40	-14	11-10	.956	-3	99	0	O-50(22-0-29)/1-9,D-3	-2.2
	Year	61	176	17	36	2	0	1	10	10-0	0	23	.205	.246	.233	38	-15	11-10	.956	-3	99	0	O-50(22-0-29)/1-9,D-3	-2.3
1979	Cle A	54	62	10	18	0	2	1	12	10-1	0	10	.290	.384	.403	114	1	4-4	.969	0	94	178	O-30(18-0-12)/D-7	0.0
1980	Cle A	52	54	11	12	1	2	0	9	5-2	2	7	.222	.302	.315	72	-2	2-4	.947	0	104	89	O-26(12-4-11)/D-6	-0.4
Total	4	189	332	48	79	7	4	3	35	28-3	2	44	.238	.297	.310	71	-14	20-21	.957	-3	98	74	O-108(52-4-54)/D-26,1-9	-2.5
ALTENBURG, JESSE Jesse Howard B 1.2.1893 Ashley, MI D 3.12.1973 Lansing, MI BL/TR 5-9/158# d9.19																								
1916	Pit N	8	14	2	6	1	1	0	0	1	0	1	.429	.467	.643	237	2	0	1.000	-0	85	0	/O-8(4-2-0)	0.2
1917	Pit N	11	17	1	3	0	0	0	3	0	0	4	.176	.176	.176	8	-2	0	1.000	-0	99	0	/O-4(1-0-3)	-0.3
Total	2	19	31	3	9	1	1	0	3	1	0	5	.290	.313	.387	112	0	0	1.000	-1	91	0	/O-12(5-2-3)	-0.1
ALTIZER, DAVE David Tilden "Filipino" B 11.6.1876 Pearl, IL D 5.14.1964 Pleasant Hill, IL BL/TR 5-10.5/160# d5.29 OF Total (4-LF 53-CF 52-RF)																								
1906	Was A	115	433	56	111	9	5	1	27	35	8		.256	.324	.307	103	2	37	.931	-15	87	78	*S-113/O-2(RF)	-1.1
1907	Was A	147	540	60	145	15	5	2	42	34	6		.269	.319	.326	115	8	38	.923	-3	99	83	S-80,1-50,O-17(CF)	0.8
1908	Was A	67	205	19	46	1	1	0	18	13	1		.224	.274	.239	73	-6	8	.959	-2	105	105	2-38,3-16/1-4,S	-0.9
	Cle A	29	89	11	19	1	2	0	5	7	1		.213	.278	.270	78	-2	7	.952	0	165	266	O-24(0-20-4)/S-3	-0.4
	Year	96	294	30	65	2	3	0	23	20	2		.221	.275	.248	75	-8	15	.959	-2	105	105	2-38,O-24(0-20-4),3-16/1-4,S-4	-1.3
1909	Chi A	116	382	47	89	6	7	1	20	39	**16**		.233	.330	.293	101	2	27	.949	4	130	53	O-61(4-14-45),1-46	0.2
1910	Cin N	3	10	3	6	0	0	0	0	3	0	0	.600	.692	.600	290	3	0	.933	-1	75	77	/S-3	0.2
1911	Cin N	37	75	8	17	4	1	0	4	9	1	5	.227	.318	.307	78	-2	2	.907	-0	106	55	S-23/12O(RF)	-0.1
Total	6	514	1734	204	433	36	21	4	116	140	33	5	.250	.318	.302	101	5	119	.925	-17	93	76	S-223,O-105C,1-101/2-39,3-16	-1.3
ALTMAN, GEORGE George Lee B 3.20.1933 Goldsboro, NC BL/TR 6-4/200# d4.11																								
1959	Chi N	135	420	54	103	14	4	12	47	34-4	7	80	.245	.312	.383	85	-10	1-0	.990	-1	99	105	*O-121(CF)	-1.6
1960	Chi N	119	334	50	89	16	4	13	51	32-6	1	67	.266	.330	.455	114	6	4-3	.993	-1	105	37	O-79(26-32-23),1-21	0.1
1961	Chi N★	138	518	77	157	28	**12**	27	96	40-3	4	92	.303	.353	.560	137	26	6-2	.978	-2	99	92	*O-130(1-25-115)/1-3	1.6
1962	Chi N★	147	534	74	170	27	5	22	74	62-14	5	89	.318	.393	.511	136	29	19-7	.972	-3	99	72	*O-129(0-6-125),1-16	1.7
1963	StL N	135	464	62	127	18	7	9	47	47-2	2	93	.274	.339	.401	104	3	13-4	.979	-1	101	85	*O-124(12-0-116)	-0.5
1964	NY N	124	422	48	97	14	1	9	47	18-4	1	70	.230	.262	.332	68	-19	4-2	.968	9	110	**173**	*O-109(95-0-14)	-1.7
1965	Chi N	90	196	24	46	7	1	4	23	19-2	0	36	.235	.302	.342	79	-5	3-2	.943	-2	101	0	O-45(44-0-1)/1-2	-1.0
1966	Chi N	88	185	19	41	6	0	5	17	14-3	0	37	.222	.276	.335	68	-8	2-2	.958	-0	79	185	O-42(41-0-1)/1-4	-1.1
1967	Chi N	15	18	1	2	2	0	0	1	2-0	0	8	.111	.200	.222	20	-2	0-0	1.000	-0	59	0	/O-4(3-0-1),1	-0.3
Total	9	991	3091	409	832	132	34	101	403	268-38	20	572	.269	.329	.432	105	20	52-22	.977	-1	101	95	O-783(222-184-396)/1-47	-2.8
ALTOBELLI, JOE Joseph Salvatore B 5.26.1932 Detroit, MI BL/TL 6/185# d4.14 M7 C7																								
1955	Cle A	42	75	8	15	3	0	2	5	5-0	1	14	.200	.259	.320	53	-5	0-1	.992	-1	72	72	1-40	-0.9
1957	Cle A	83	87	9	18	3	2	0	9	5-0	1	14	.207	.253	.287	49	-6	3-2	.994	0	90	99	1-56/O-7(1-4-2)	-0.8
1961	Min A	41	95	10	21	2	1	3	14	13-0	0	14	.221	.312	.358	75	-3	0-0	.951	-0	111	0	O-25(LF)/1-2	-0.5
Total	3	166	257	27	54	8	3	5	28	23-0	2	42	.210	.277	.323	60	-14	3-3	.993	-2	79	79	/1-98,O-32(26-4-2)	-2.2
ALUSIK, GEORGE George Joseph B 2.11.1935 Ashley, PA BR/TR 6-3.5/175# d9.11																								
1958	Det A	2	2	0	0	0	0	0	0	0-0	0	1	.000	.000	.000	-93	-1	0-0	1.000	0	146	0	/O(LF)	-0.1
1961	Det A	15	14	0	2	0	0	0	2	1-0	0	4	.143	.188	.143	-6	-2	0-0	—	-0	0	0	/O(RF)	-0.2
1962	Det A	2	2	0	0	0	0	0	0	0-0	0	0	.000	.000	.000	-97	-1	0-0	—	0			H	-0.1
	KC A	90	209	29	57	10	1	11	35	16-1	1	29	.273	.326	.488	111	3	1-1	.968	-1	93	109	O-50(35-0-22)/1	-0.1
	Year	92	211	29	57	10	1	11	35	16-1	1	29	.270	.323	.483	109	2	1-1	.968	-1	93	109	O-50(35-0-22)/1	-0.2
1963	KC A	87	221	28	59	11	0	9	37	26-0	1	33	.267	.345	.439	112	4	0-1	1.000	1	93	133	O-63(30-1-36)	0.1
1964	KC A	102	204	18	49	10	1	3	19	30-2	2	36	.240	.342	.343	89	-2	0-0	.984	-1	102	58	O-44(43-0-3),1-12	-0.6
Total	5	298	652	75	167	31	2	23	93	73-3	4	103	.256	.333	.416	101	1	1-2	.985	-1	95	106	O-159(109-1-62)/1-13	-1.0
ALVARADO, LUIS Luis Cesar (Martinez) B 1.15.1949 Lajas, P.R. D 3.20.2001 Lajas, P.R. BR/TR 5-9/162# d9.13																								
1968	Bos A	11	46	3	6	2	0	0	1	1-0	1	11	.130	.167	.174	3	-5	0-0	.976	-4	75	92	S-11	-1.1
1969	Bos A	6	5	0	0	0	0	0	0	0-0	0	2	.000	.000	.000	-95	-1	0-1	1.000	1	125	199	/S-5	-0.1
1970	Bos A	59	183	19	41	11	0	1	10	9-2	0	30	.224	.258	.301	51	-12	1-2	.929	-0	101	34	3-29,S-27	-1.1

Year	Tm Lg	G	AB	R	H	2B	3B	HR	RBI	BB-IB	HP	SO	AVG	OBP	SLG	AOPS	ABR	SB-CS	FA	FR	Rng	Thr	G at Pos	BFW
1971	Chi A	99	264	22	57	14	1	0	8	11-2	0	34	.216	.246	.277	47	-19	1-2	.959	7	99	96	S-71,2-16	-0.5
1972	Chi A	103	254	30	54	4	1	4	29	13-5	1	36	.213	.254	.283	58	-14	2-2	.957	-3	98	70	S-81,2-16/3-2	-1.0
1973	Chi A	80	203	21	47	7	2	0	20	4-0	1	20	.232	.250	.286	49	-14	6-2	.980	-1	99	83	2-45,S-18,3-10/D	-1.2
1974	Chi A	8	10	1	1	0	0	0	0	0-0	0	1	.100	.100	.100	-41	-2	0-0	.667	-1	66	0	/S-4,23	-0.3
	StL N	17	36	3	5	2	0	0	1	2-0	0	6	.139	.179	.194	6	-5	0-0	.980	-3	86	112	S-17	-0.7
	Cle A	61	114	12	25	2	0	0	12	6-0	0	14	.219	.256	.237	44	-8	1-1	.972	-0	102	101	2-46/S-7,D-3	-0.6
1976	StL N	16	42	5	12	1	0	0	3	3-1	0	6	.286	.333	.310	82	-1	0-0	.936	-8	65	38	2-16	-0.9
1977	NY N	1	2	0	0	0	0	0	0	0-0	0	0	.000	.000	.000	-99	-1	0-0	1.000	0	156	0	/2	0.0
	Det A	2	1	0	0	0	0	0	0	0-0	0	0	.000	.000	.000	-95	0	0-0	—	-1	0	0	/3-2	-0.1
Total	9	463	1160	116	248	43	4	5	84	49-10	3	160	.214	.247	.271	47	-82	11-10	.957	-13	98	88	S-241,2-141/3-44,D-4	-7.6

ALVAREZ, TONY Antonio Enrique B 5.10.1979 Caracas, Venezuela BR/TR 6-1/202# d9.4

Year	Tm Lg	G	AB	R	H	2B	3B	HR	RBI	BB-IB	HP	SO	AVG	OBP	SLG	AOPS	ABR	SB-CS	FA	FR	Rng	Thr	G at Pos	BFW
2002	Pit N	14	26	6	8	2	0	1	2	3-0	0	5	.308	.379	.500	132	1	1-0	1.000	-2	63	0	/O-8(2-6-1)	0.0

ALVAREZ, CLEMENTE Clemente Rafael B 5.18.1968 Anzoategui, Venezuela BR/TR 5-11/180# d9.19

Year	Tm Lg	G	AB	R	H	2B	3B	HR	RBI	BB-IB	HP	SO	AVG	OBP	SLG	AOPS	ABR	SB-CS	FA	FR	Rng	Thr	G at Pos	BFW
2000	Phi N	2	5	1	1	0	0	0	0	0-0	0	1	.200	.200	.200	1	-1	0-0	1.000	0	28	0	/C-2	0.0

ALVAREZ, GABE Gabriel De Jesus B 3.6.1974 Navojoa, Mexico BR/TR 6-1/205# d6.22

Year	Tm Lg	G	AB	R	H	2B	3B	HR	RBI	BB-IB	HP	SO	AVG	OBP	SLG	AOPS	ABR	SB-CS	FA	FR	Rng	Thr	G at Pos	BFW
1998	Det A	58	199	16	46	11	0	5	29	18-1	2	65	.231	.299	.362	71	-9	1-3	.873	-3	102	74	3-55/D-2	-1.2
1999	Det A	22	53	5	11	3	0	2	4	3-0	0	9	.208	.250	.377	57	-4	0-0	1.000	-1	53	0	D-12/O-5(RF),3-2	-0.5
2000	Det A	1	1	0	0	0	0	0	0	2-0	0	1	.000	.667	.000	92	0	0-1	—	0			/D	0.0
	SD N	11	13	1	2	1	0	0	0	1-0	0	1	.154	.214	.231	13	-2	0-0	1.000	-1	69	0	/3-3,O-2(LF)	-0.2
Total	3	92	266	22	59	15	0	7	33	24-1	2	76	.222	.289	.357	66	-15	1-4	.875	-5	101	72	/3-60,D-15,O-7(2-0-5)	-1.9

ALVAREZ, ORLANDO Jesus Manuel Orlando (Monge) B 2.28.1952 Rio Grande, P.R. BR/TR 6/165# d9.1

Year	Tm Lg	G	AB	R	H	2B	3B	HR	RBI	BB-IB	HP	SO	AVG	OBP	SLG	AOPS	ABR	SB-CS	FA	FR	Rng	Thr	G at Pos	BFW
1973	LA N	4	4	0	1	1	0	0	0	0-0	0	1	.250	.250	.500	108	0	0-0	—	0			H	0.0
1974	LA N	2	1	0	0	0	0	0	0	0-0	0	0	.000	.000	.000	-99	0	0-0	1.000	0	230	0	/O(LF)	0.0
1975	LA N	4	4	0	0	0	0	0	0	0-0	0	1	.000	.000	.000	-99	-1	0-0	—	0			H	-0.1
1976	Cal A	15	42	4	7	1	0	2	8	0-0	0	3	.167	.167	.333	47	-3	0-0	1.000	-1	67	160	O-11(10-1-0)/D-2	-0.5
Total	4	25	51	4	8	2	0	2	8	0-0	0	5	.157	.157	.314	36	-4	0-0	1.000	-1	71	156	/O-12(11-1-0),D-2	-0.6

ALVAREZ, OSSIE Oswaldo (Gonzalez) B 10.19.1933 Bolondron, Cuba BR/TR 5-10/165# d4.19

Year	Tm Lg	G	AB	R	H	2B	3B	HR	RBI	BB-IB	HP	SO	AVG	OBP	SLG	AOPS	ABR	SB-CS	FA	FR	Rng	Thr	G at Pos	BFW
1958	Was A	87	196	20	41	3	0	0	5	16-0	0	26	.209	.269	.224	38	-17	1-1	.968	8	103	90	S-64,2-14/3-3	-0.4
1959	Det A	8	2	0	1	0	0	0	0	0-0	0	1	.500	.500	.500	166	0	0-0	—	0			H	0.0
Total	2	95	198	20	42	3	0	0	5	16-0	0	27	.212	.271	.227	39	-17	1-1	.968	8	103	90	/S-64,2-14,3-3	-0.4

ALVAREZ, ROGELIO Rogelio (Hernandez) B 4.18.1938 Pinar Del Rio, Cuba BR/TR 5-11/183# d9.18

Year	Tm Lg	G	AB	R	H	2B	3B	HR	RBI	BB-IB	HP	SO	AVG	OBP	SLG	AOPS	ABR	SB-CS	FA	FR	Rng	Thr	G at Pos	BFW
1960	Cin N	3	9	1	1	0	0	0	0	0-0	0	3	.111	.111	.111	-38	-2	0-0	1.000	-1	0	58	/1-2	-0.3
1962	Cin N	14	28	1	6	0	0	0	2	1-0	0	10	.214	.241	.214	23	-3	0-0	.973	-1	76	126	1-13	-0.4
Total	2	17	37	2	7	0	0	0	2	1-0	0	13	.189	.211	.189	8	-5	0-0	.979	-1	59	111	/1-15	-0.7

ALVIS, MAX Roy Maxwell B 2.2.1938 Jasper, TX BR/TR 5-11/187# d9.11

Year	Tm Lg	G	AB	R	H	2B	3B	HR	RBI	BB-IB	HP	SO	AVG	OBP	SLG	AOPS	ABR	SB-CS	FA	FR	Rng	Thr	G at Pos	BFW
1962	Cle A	12	51	1	11	2	0	0	3	2-0	0	13	.216	.245	.255	36	-5	3-1	.935	-3	74	48	3-12	-0.7
1963	Cle A	158	602	81	165	32	7	22	67	36-2	**10**	109	.274	.324	.460	118	13	9-7	.942	-6	91	111	*3-158	0.6
1964	Cle A	107	381	51	96	14	3	18	53	29-5	6	77	.252	.313	.446	110	4	5-5	.955	-6	92	95	*3-105	-0.3
1965	Cle A★	159	604	88	149	24	2	21	61	47-4	**9**	121	.247	.308	.397	99	-2	12-8	.958	-18	79	57	*3-156	-2.2
1966	Cle A	157	596	67	146	22	3	17	55	50-6	2	98	.245	.304	.378	95	-4	4-7	.958	-6	86	88	*3-157	-1.4
1967	Cle A★	161	637	66	163	23	4	21	70	38-1	4	107	.256	.301	.403	106	2	3-10	.965	-10	86	74	*3-161	-1.2
1968	Cle A	131	452	38	101	17	3	8	37	41-5	4	91	.223	.292	.327	89	-6	5-5	.960	-15	80	86	*3-128	-2.6
1969	Cle A	66	191	13	43	6	0	1	15	14-1	0	26	.225	.275	.272	53	-12	1-1	.973	-4	84	88	3-58/S	-1.8
1970	Mil A	62	115	16	21	2	0	3	12	5-1	0	20	.183	.217	.278	35	-11	1-2	.909	-0	111	75	3-36	-1.2
Total	9	1013	3629	421	895	142	22	111	373	262-25	35	662	.247	.302	.390	97	-21	43-46	.956	-69	86	84	3-971/S	-10.8

ALVORD, BILLY William Charles "Uncle Bill" B 8.1863 St.Louis, MO 5-10/187# d4.30

Year	Tm Lg	G	AB	R	H	2B	3B	HR	RBI	BB-IB	HP	SO	AVG	OBP	SLG	AOPS	ABR	SB-CS	FA	FR	Rng	Thr	G at Pos	BFW
1885	StL N	2	5	0	0	0	0	0	0	1		2	.000	.167	.000	-45	-1		.714	-1	27	0	/3-2	-0.2
1889	KC AA	50	186	23	43	8	9	0	18	10	0	35	.231	.270	.371	77	-8	3	.877	3	132	122	3-34/S-8,2-8	-0.3
1890	Tol AA	116	495	69	135	13	16	2	52	22	0		.273	.304	.376	97	-7	21	.872	4	98	76	*3-116	0.0
1891	Cle N	13	59	7	17	2	2	1	7	0	1	7	.288	.300	.441	110	0	0	.814	-2	95	50	3-13	-0.1
	Was AA	81	312	28	73	8	3	0	30	11	0	38	.234	.260	.279	57	-19	3	.862	17	117	63	3-81	-0.1
1893	Cle N	3	12	2	2	0	0	0	2	0	0	1	.167	.167	.167	-11	-2	0	.875	-1	38	0	/3-3	-0.3
Total	5	265	1069	129	270	31	30	3	109	44	1	83	.253	.283	.346	81	-37	27	.865	20	108	75	3-249/2-8,S-8	-1.0

ALYEA, BRANT Garrabrant Ryerson B 12.8.1940 Passaic, NJ BR/TR 6-3/215# d9.11

Year	Tm Lg	G	AB	R	H	2B	3B	HR	RBI	BB-IB	HP	SO	AVG	OBP	SLG	AOPS	ABR	SB-CS	FA	FR	Rng	Thr	G at Pos	BFW
1965	Was A	8	13	3	3	0	0	2	6	1-0	0	4	.231	.286	.692	171	1	0-0	1.000	-1	0	0	/1-3,O(LF)	0.0
1968	Was A	53	150	18	40	11	1	6	23	10-0	1	39	.267	.317	.473	141	7	0-0	1.000	1	120	0	O-39(16-0-24)	0.6
1969	Was A	104	237	29	59	4	0	11	40	34-4	1	67	.249	.341	.405	115	5	1-3	.938	-3	82	138	O-69(36-0-36)/1-3	-0.2
1970	†Min A	94	258	34	75	12	1	16	61	28-0	3	51	.291	.366	.531	143	15	3-3	.980	-1	90	110	O-75(73-0-2)	1.0
1971	Min A	79	158	13	28	4	0	2	15	24-3	1	38	.177	.282	.241	50	-10	1-1	.962	-3	74	144	O-48(47-0-1)	-1.6
1972	Oak A	20	31	3	6	1	0	1	2	3-0	0	5	.194	.265	.323	78	-1	0-0	1.000	4	160	618	/O-8(2-0-6)	0.3
	StL N	13	19	0	3	1	0	0	1	0-0	0	6	.158	.158	.211	4	-2	0-0	1.000	1	152	769	/O-3(1-0-2)	-0.1
Total	6	371	866	100	214	33	2	38	148	100-7	6	210	.247	.326	.421	113	15	5-7	.972	-1	93	127	O-243(176-0-71)/1-6	0.0

AMALFITANO, JOEY John Joseph B 1.23.1934 San Pedro, CA BR/TR 5-11/180# d5.3 M3 C31

Year	Tm Lg	G	AB	R	H	2B	3B	HR	RBI	BB-IB	HP	SO	AVG	OBP	SLG	AOPS	ABR	SB-CS	FA	FR	Rng	Thr	G at Pos	BFW
1954	NY N	9	5	2	0	0	0	0	0	0	0	4	.000	.000	.000	-99	-1	0-0	1.000	1	192	440	/3-4,2	-0.1
1955	NY N	36	22	8	5	1	1	0	1	2-0	0	2	.227	.292	.364	72	-1	0-0	.957	4	194	129	/S-5,3-2	0.3
1960	SF N	106	328	47	91	15	3	1	27	26-1	3	31	.277	.335	.351	94	-3	2-3	.935	1	105	86	3-63,2-33/S-3,O(LF)	0.0
1961	SF N	109	384	64	98	11	4	2	23	44-2	0	59	.255	.331	.320	77	-12	7-4	.970	-21	83	76	2-95/3-6	-2.5
1962	Hou N	117	380	44	90	12	5	1	27	45-5	1	43	.237	.317	.303	73	-14	4-4	.967	-4	92	110	*2-110/3-5	-1.0
1963	SF N	54	137	11	24	3	0	1	7	12-0	1	18	.175	.245	.219	36	-11	2-6	.980	-3	102	66	2-37/3-7	-1.5
1964	Chi N	100	324	51	78	19	6	4	27	40-1	5	42	.241	.333	.373	95	-1	2-7	.964	3	108	95	2-86/1S	0.7
1965	Chi N	67	96	13	26	4	0	0	8	12-0	2	14	.271	.364	.313	90	0	2-2	.989	3	133	85	2-24/S-4	0.4
1966	Chi N	41	38	8	6	2	0	0	3	4-0	0	10	.158	.227	.211	26	-4	0-0	.977	-0	94	100	2-12/3-3,S-2	-0.4
1967	Chi N	4	1	0	0	0	0	0	0	0-0	0	1	.000	.000	.000	-96	0	0-0	—	0			H	0.0
Total	10	643	1715	248	418	67	19	9	123	185-9	12	224	.244	.320	.321	78	-47	19-26	.970	-17	97	92	2-398/3-90,S-15,1O(LF)	-4.1

AMARAL, RICH Richard Louis B 4.1.1962 Visalia, CA BR/TR 6/175# d5.27 OF Total (232-LF 101-CF 52-RF)

Year	Tm Lg	G	AB	R	H	2B	3B	HR	RBI	BB-IB	HP	SO	AVG	OBP	SLG	AOPS	ABR	SB-CS	FA	FR	Rng	Thr	G at Pos	BFW
1991	Sea A	14	16	2	1	0	0	0	0	1-0	1	5	.063	.167	.063	-34	-3	0-0	1.000	1	164	256	/2-5,3-2,S-2,1D	-0.2
1992	Sea A	35	100	9	24	3	0	1	7	5-0	0	16	.240	.276	.300	61	-5	4-2	.955	1	115	121	3-17,S-17/O-3(3-1-1),1-2,2	-0.4
1993	Sea A	110	373	53	108	24	1	1	44	33-0	3	54	.290	.348	.367	92	-3	19-11	.975	15	104	102	2-77,3-19,S-14/1-3,D-9	1.6
1994	Sea A	77	228	37	60	10	2	4	18	24-1	1	28	.263	.333	.377	82	-6	5-1	.943	2	103	79	2-42,O-16(14-2-0)/S-7,1-2,D-6	-0.2
1995	†Sea A	90	238	45	67	14	2	2	19	21-0	1	33	.282	.342	.382	87	-4	21-2	.992	3	102	187	O-73(53-29-8)/D	0.1
1996	Sea A	118	312	69	91	11	3	1	29	47-0	5	55	.292	.392	.356	91	-2	25-6	1.000	-5	106	62	O-91(63-26-5),2-15,1-10/3D	-0.4
1997	†Sea A	89	190	34	54	5	0	1	21	10-0	3	34	.284	.327	.326	73	-8	12-8	1.000	-3	94	0	O-52(39-9-6),1-14,2-11/3SD	-1.1
1998	Sea A	73	134	25	37	6	0	1	4	13-0	1	24	.276	.342	.343	80	-4	11-1	1.000	-3	104	113	O-52(43-4-9),2-11/1-7,3D	-0.5
1999	Bal A	91	137	21	38	8	1	0	11	15-0	1	20	.277	.348	.350	83	-3	9-6	1.000	1	112	0	O-50(14-18-19),D-18/1-2,2-2,3	-0.4
2000	Bal A	30	60	10	13	1	1	0	6	7-0	0	8	.217	.299	.267	47	-5	6-2	1.000	4	130	133	O-19(3-12-4)/1D	-0.1
Total	10	727	1788	305	493	82	10	11	159	176-1	16	277	.276	.344	.351	82	-43	112-39	.996	16	104	89	O-356L,2-164/D-55,1-42,3-42,S-41	-1.6

AMARO, RUBEN Ruben Jr. B 2.12.1965 Philadelphia, PA BB/TR 5-10/175# d6.8 f-Ruben

Year	Tm Lg	G	AB	R	H	2B	3B	HR	RBI	BB-IB	HP	SO	AVG	OBP	SLG	AOPS	ABR	SB-CS	FA	FR	Rng	Thr	G at Pos	BFW
1991	Cal A	10	23	0	5	1	0	0	2	3-1	0	3	.217	.308	.261	59	-1	0-0	1.000	-1	51	578	/O-5(3-0-2),2-4,D	-0.2
1992	Phi N	126	374	43	82	15	6	7	34	37-1	9	54	.219	.303	.348	85	-8	11-5	.992	5	111	85	*O-113(27-27-68)	-0.5
1993	Phi N	25	48	7	16	2	2	1	6	6-0	0	5	.333	.400	.521	149	3	0-0	.963	1	107	140	O-16(3-8-6)	0.4
1994	Cle A	26	23	5	5	1	0	2	5	2-0	0	3	.217	.280	.522	100	0	2-1	.909	0	146	0	O-12(1-10-1)/D-3	0.0
1995	†Cle A	28	60	5	12	3	0	1	7	4-0	2	6	.200	.273	.300	48	-5	1-3	1.000	-0	103	0	O-22(5-14-6)/D-3	-0.6
1996	Phi N	61	117	14	37	10	0	2	15	9-0	3	18	.316	.380	.453	117	3	0-0	1.000	-0	108	0	O-35(0-7-28)/1	0.2
1997	Phi N	117	175	18	41	6	1	2	21	21-0	2	24	.234	.320	.314	68	-8	1-1	.987	2	112	107	O-72(26-37-15)/1	-0.7
1998	Phi N	92	107	7	20	5	0	1	10	6-0	0	15	.187	.224	.262	29	-11	0-0	1.000	0	76	258	O-51(43-3-6)	-1.2

Year	Tm Lg	G	AB	R	H	2B	3B	HR	RBI	BB-IB	HP	SO	AVG	OBP	SLG	AOPS	ABR	SB-CS	FA	FR	Rng	Thr	G at Pos	BFW
Total	8	485	927	99	218	43	9	16	100	88-2	16	128	.235	.310	.353	80	-27	15-10	.989	6	106	98	O-326(108-106-132)/D-7,2-4,1-2	-2.6
AMARO, RUBEN Ruben Sr. (Mora) B 1.6.1936 Veracruz, Mexico BR/TR 5-11/170# d7.15 C6 s-Ruben																								
1958	StL N	40	76	8	17	2	1	0	0	5-1	0	8	.224	.272	.276	44	-6	0-1	.948	-1	95	111	S-36/2	-0.6
1960	Phi N	92	264	25	61	9	1	0	16	21-2	2	32	.231	.292	.273	56	-16	0-1	.965	-7	96	95	S-92	-1.7
1961	Phi N	135	381	34	98	14	9	1	32	53-2	2	59	.257	.351	.349	88	-5	1-0	.970	13	106	112	*S-132/1-3,2	1.8
1962	Phi N	79	226	24	55	10	0	0	19	30-4	1	28	.243	.330	.288	71	-8	5-2	.968	5	102	106	S-78/1	0.4
1963	Phi N	115	217	25	47	9	2	2	19	19-6	0	31	.217	.276	.304	69	-9	0-1	.950	2	91	92	S-63,3-45/1-5	-0.3
1964	Phi N	129	299	31	79	11	0	4	34	16-2	3	37	.264	.307	.341	84	-7	1-6	.971	-5	89	109	S-79,1-58/2-3,3-3,O(LF)	-0.9
1965	Phi N	118	184	26	39	7	0	0	15	27-3	1	22	.212	.312	.250	63	-8	1-1	.990	-1	174	109	1-60,S-60/2-6	-0.6
1966	NY A	14	23	0	5	0	0	0	3	0-0	0	2	.217	.217	.217	26	-2	0-0	.977	3	113	185	S-14	0.1
1967	NY A	130	417	31	93	12	0	1	17	43-4	1	49	.223	.297	.259	68	-16	3-2	.973	8	107	109	*S-123/3-3,1-2	0.2
1968	NY A	47	41	3	5	1	0	0	0	9-0	0	6	.122	.280	.146	33	-3	0-0	.962	-4	85	113	S-23,1-22	-0.7
1969	Cal A	41	27	4	6	0	0	0	1	4-0	0	6	.222	.323	.222	58	-1	0-0	1.000	-2	0	37	1-18/2-9,S-5,3-2	-0.3
Total	11	940	2155	211	505	75	13	8	156	227-24	10	280	.234	.309	.292	70	-81	11-14	.967	10	99	106	S-705,1-169/3-53,2-20,O(LF)	-2.6
AMBLER, WAYNE Wayne Harper B 11.8.1915 Abington, PA D 1.3.1998 Ponte Vedra Beach, FL BR/TR 5-8.5/165# d6.4																								
1937	Phi A	56	162	3	35	5	0	0	11	13	0	8	.216	.274	.247	33	-17	1-0	.955	-1	102	102	2-56	-1.4
1938	Phi A	120	393	42	92	21	2	0	38	48	0	31	.234	.317	.298	56	-26	2-1	.942	-16	94	69	*S-116/2-4	-3.1
1939	Phi A	95	227	15	48	13	0	0	24	22	0	25	.211	.281	.269	42	-20	1-0	.954	-2	104	80	S-77,2-19	-1.6
Total	3	271	782	60	175	39	2	0	73	83	0	64	.224	.298	.279	47	-63	4-1	.946	-20	97	73	S-193/2-79	-6.1
AMELUNG, ED Edward Allen B 4.13.1959 Fullerton, CA BL/TL 5-11/180# d7.28																								
1984	LA N	34	46	7	10	0	0	0	4	2-0	0	4	.217	.250	.217	33	-4	3-2	1.000	1	136	0	O-23(9-4-11)	-0.4
1986	LA N	8	11	0	1	0	0	0	0	0-0	0	4	.091	.091	.091	-53	-2	0-0	1.000	0	140	0	/O-4(0-2-2)	-0.2
Total	2	42	57	7	11	0	0	0	4	2-0	0	8	.193	.220	.193	17	-6	3-2	1.000	1	137	0	/O-27(9-6-13)	-0.6
AMEZAGA, ALFREDO Alfredo (Delgado) B 1.16.1978 Obregon, Mexico BR/TR 5-10/165# d5.24																								
2002	Ana A	12	13	3	7	2	0	0	2	0-0	0	1	.538	.538	.692	224	2	1-0	1.000	-0	100	44	/S-5	0.3
2003	Ana A	37	105	15	22	3	2	2	7	9-0	1	23	.210	.278	.333	63	-6	2-2	.970	-0	93	79	S-24,3-13	-0.5
Total	2	49	118	18	29	5	2	2	9	9-0	1	24	.246	.305	.373	80	-4	3-2	.974	-0	94	74	/S-29,3-13	-0.2
AMOROS, SANDY Edmundo (Isasi) B 1.30.1930 Havana, Cuba D 6.27.1992 Miami, FL BL/TL 5-7.5/170# d8.22																								
1952	†Bro N	20	44	10	11	3	1	0	3	5	0	14	.250	.327	.364	90	-1	1-0	1.000	-1	95	0	O-10(3-4-7)	-0.2
1954	Bro N	79	263	44	72	18	6	9	34	31	1	24	.274	.353	.490	113	5	1-4	.987	1	99	128	O-70(68-1-2)	0.1
1955	†Bro N	119	388	59	96	16	7	10	51	55-5	6	45	.247	.347	.402	96	-1	10-5	.972	-1	93	127	*O-109(102-8-5)	-0.8
1956	†Bro N	114	292	53	76	11	8	16	58	59-6	1	51	.260	.385	.517	130	14	3-4	.955	-9	83	60	O-86(79-5-10)	0.0
1957	Bro N	106	238	40	66	7	1	7	26	46-3	3	42	.277	.399	.403	107	5	3-2	.984	-1	102	48	O-66(65-1-2)	0.0
1959	LA N	5	5	1	1	0	0	0	1	0-0	0	1	.200	.200	.200	6	-1	0-0	—	0			H	-0.1
1960	LA N	9	14	1	2	0	0	0	0	3-1	0	2	.143	.294	.143	23	-1	0-0	1.000	0	82	371	/O-3(0-1-3)	-0.1
	Det A	65	67	7	10	0	0	1	7	12-1	0	10	.149	.275	.194	29	-7	0-0	1.000	-0	106	0	O-10(1-9-0)	-0.7
Total	7	517	1311	215	334	55	23	43	180	211-16	11	189	.255	.361	.430	105	13	18-15	.976	-9	94	94	O-354(318-29-29)	-1.8
ANDERSON, ALF Alfred Walton B 1.28.1914 Gainesville, GA D 6.23.1985 Albany, GA BR/TR 5-11/165# d4.20 Mil 1944-45																								
1941	Pit N	70	223	32	48	7	2	1	10	14	1	30	.215	.265	.278	53	-15	2	.931	-6	100	94	S-58	-1.7
1942	Pit N	54	166	24	45	4	1	0	7	18	0	19	.271	.342	.307	89	-2	4	.942	-11	85	73	S-48	-1.1
1946	Pit N	2	1	0	0	0	0	0	0	1	0	0	.000	.500	.000	47	0	0	—	0			H	0.0
Total	3	126	390	56	93	11	3	1	17	33	1	49	.238	.300	.290	68	-17	6	.936	-17	94	85	S-106	-2.8
ANDERSON, ANDY Andy Holm B 11.13.1922 Bremerton, WA D 7.18.1982 Seattle, WA BR/TR 5-11/172# d5.10																								
1948	StL A	51	87	13	24	5	1	1	12	8	0	15	.276	.337	.391	91	-1	0-0	.917	-1	118	95	2-21,S-10/1-2	-0.1
1949	StL A	71	136	10	17	3	0	1	5	14	0	21	.125	.207	.169	-0	-20	0-1	.957	-3	93	89	S-44/2-8,3-8	-2.2
Total	2	122	223	23	41	8	1	2	17	22	0	36	.184	.257	.256	35	-21	0-1	.946	-4	90	93	/S-54,2-29,3-8,1-2	-2.3
ANDERSON, BRADY Brady Kevin B 1.18.1964 Silver Spring, MD BL/TL 6-1/185# d4.4																								
1988	Bos A	41	148	14	34	5	3	0	12	15-0	4	35	.230	.315	.304	72	-5	4-2	.989	0	95	141	O-41(0-17-25)	-0.6
	Bal A	53	177	17	35	8	1	1	9	8-0	0	40	.198	.232	.271	42	-14	6-4	.981	4	121	46	O-49(CF)	-1.1
	Year	94	325	31	69	13	4	1	21	23-0	4	75	.212	.272	.286	57	-19	10-6	.984	4	108	92	O-90(0-66-25)	-1.7
1989	Bal A	94	266	44	55	12	2	4	16	43-6	3	45	.207	.324	.312	82	-5	16-4	.985	-2	98	75	O-79(3-75-1)/D-8	-0.5
1990	Bal A	89	234	24	54	5	2	3	24	31-2	5	46	.231	.327	.308	83	-5	15-2	.987	4	114	86	O-63(44-21-1),D-11	0.0
1991	Bal A	113	256	40	59	12	3	2	27	38-0	5	44	.230	.338	.324	89	-2	12-5	.981	-3	93	74	*O-101(75-26-9)/D-2	-0.6
1992	Bal A★	159	623	100	169	28	10	21	80	98-14	9	98	.271	.373	.449	128	26	53-16	.980	5	106	89	*O-158(148-7-3)	3.2
1993	Bal A	142	560	87	147	36	8	13	66	82-4	10	99	.262	.363	.425	108	8	24-12	.993	-3	98	81	*O-140(126-18-3)/D-2	0.2
1994	Bal A	111	453	78	119	25	5	12	48	57-3	10	75	.263	.356	.419	95	-3	31-1	.996	-2	101	55	*O-109(76-38-5)	-0.1
1995	Bal A	143	554	108	145	33	10	16	64	87-4	10	111	.262	.371	.444	109	10	26-7	.989	-12	91	11	*O-142(121-40-0)	-0.2
1996	†Bal A★	149	579	117	172	37	5	50	110	76-1	**22**	106	.297	.396	.637	157	51	21-8	.992	-8	92	113	*O-143(CF)/D-2	4.2
1997	†Bal A★	151	590	97	170	39	7	18	73	84-6	**19**	105	.288	.393	.469	128	28	18-12	.989	-12	89	32	*O-124(CF),D-25	1.5
1998	Bal A	133	479	84	113	28	3	18	51	75-1	15	78	.236	.356	.420	103	4	21-7	.985	-14	87	13	*O-130(CF)	-0.6
1999	Bal A	150	564	109	159	28	5	24	81	96-7	**24**	105	.282	.404	.477	130	30	36-7	.997	-11	91	35	*O-136(9-129-0),D-10	2.3
2000	Bal A	141	506	89	130	26	0	19	50	92-5	8	103	.257	.375	.421	108	10	16-9	.997	-4	102	15	*O-127(16-88-24),D-11	0.4
2001	Bal A	131	430	50	87	12	3	8	45	60-4	8	77	.202	.311	.300	66	-21	12-4	.988	4	105	111	*O-120(56-6-66)/D-4	-2.0
2002	Cle A	34	80	4	13	4	0	1	5	18-2	2	23	.162	.327	.250	59	-4	4-0	.981	-2	96	0	O-29(14-16-2)/D	-0.5
Total	15	1834	6499	1062	1661	338	67	210	761	960-59	154	1190	.256	.362	.425	109	108	315-100	.989	-54	97	60	*O-1691(688-927-139)/D-76	5.6
ANDERSON, DAVE David Carter B 8.1.1960 Louisville, KY BR/TR 6-2/185# d5.8																								
1983	LA N	61	115	12	19	4	2	1	2	12-1	0	15	.165	.244	.261	40	-10	6-3	.969	-5	88	93	S-53/3	-1.1
1984	LA N	121	374	51	94	16	2	3	34	45-4	2	55	.251	.331	.329	88	-5	15-5	.965	19	106	109	*S-111,3-11	2.7
1985	†LA N	77	221	24	44	6	0	4	18	35-3	1	42	.199	.310	.281	69	-8	5-4	.957	9	116	151	3-51,S-25/2-2	0.2
1986	LA N	92	216	31	53	9	0	1	15	22-1	0	39	.245	.314	.301	76	-7	5-1	.976	0	101	116	3-51,S-34/2-5	-0.3
1987	LA N	108	265	32	62	12	3	1	13	24-1	1	43	.234	.299	.313	64	-14	9-5	.977	3	99	87	S-65,3-35/2-5	-0.4
1988	†LA N	116	285	31	71	10	2	2	20	32-4	1	45	.249	.325	.319	89	-3	4-2	.986	9	105	127	S-82,3-12,2-11	1.2
1989	LA N	87	140	15	32	2	0	1	14	17-1	0	26	.229	.310	.264	67	-6	2-0	.990	-8	73	114	S-33,3-18/2-7	-1.2
1990	SF N	60	100	14	35	5	1	1	6	3-0	0	20	.350	.369	.450	129	3	1-2	1.000	-4	97	65	S-29,2-13/1-3,3-2	0.0
1991	SF N	100	226	24	56	5	2	2	13	12-2	0	35	.248	.286	.314	71	-10	2-4	.956	-0	97	133	S-63,1-16,3-11/2-6	-0.9
1992	LA N	51	84	10	24	4	0	3	8	4-0	0	11	.286	.311	.440	115	1	0-4	.974	-1	82	106	3-26/S-7	0.0
Total	10	873	2026	244	490	73	12	19	143	206-17	5	331	.242	.312	.318	79	-59	49-30	.970	23	100	105	S-502,3-218/2-49,1-19	0.2
ANDERSON, DWAIN Dwain Cleaven B 11.23.1947 Oakland, CA BR/TR 5-11/165# d9.3																								
1971	Oak A	16	37	3	10	2	1	0	3	5-1	1	9	.270	.372	.378	115	1	0-1	.968	-2	92	112	S-10/2-5,3	-0.1
1972	Oak A	3	7	2	0	0	0	0	0	1-0	0	4	.000	.125	.000	-64	-1	0-0	1.000	-1	60	0	/S3	-0.2
	StL N	57	135	12	36	4	1	1	8	8-1	1	23	.267	.313	.333	85	-3	0-1	.952	1	96	86	S-43,3-13/2	0.1
1973	StL N	18	17	5	2	0	0	0	0	4-0	0	4	.118	.286	.118	16	-2	0-0	.500	-2	0	0	/S-3,O-2(CF)	-0.4
	SD N	53	107	11	13	0	0	0	3	14-0	0	29	.121	.223	.121	-2	-15	2-0	.932	-2	97	89	S-39/3-6	-1.4
	Year	71	124	16	15	0	0	0	3	18-0	0	33	.121	.232	.121	1	-17	2-0	.919	-4	94	86	S-42/3-6,O-2(CF)	-1.8
1974	Cle A	2	3	0	1	0	0	0	0	0-0	0	1	.333	.333	.333	93	0	0-0	1.000	-1	0	0	/2	-0.1
Total	4	149	306	33	62	6	2	1	14	32-2	2	70	.203	.282	.245	52	-20	2-2	.940	-6	94	87	/S-96,3-21,2-7,O-2(CF)	-2.1
ANDERSON, GOAT Edward John B 1.13.1880 Cleveland, OH D 3.15.1923 South Bend, IN BL/TR d4.11																								
1907	Pit N	127	413	73	85	3	1	1	12	80	6		.206	.343	.225	77	-5	27	.953	-0	94	107	*O-117(2-24-91)/2-5	-1.2
ANDERSON, FERRELL Ferrell Jack "Andy" B 1.9.1918 Maple City, KS D 3.12.1978 Joplin, MO BR/TR 6-1/200# d4.16																								
1946	Bro N	79	199	19	51	10	0	2	14	18	4	21	.256	.330	.337	89	-3	1	.964	0	*147*	*116*	C-70	0.1
1953	StL N	18	35	1	10	2	0	0	1	0	0	4	.286	.286	.343	63	-2	0-0	1.000	-1	*69*	*80*	C-12	-0.2
Total	2	97	234	20	61	12	0	2	15	18	4	25	.261	.324	.338	85	-5	1-0	.968	-0	*138*	*112*	/C-82	-0.1
ANDERSON, GARRET Garret Joseph B 6.30.1972 Los Angeles, CA BL/TL 6-3/190# d7.27																								
1994	Cal A	5	13	0	5	0	0	0	1	0-0	0	2	.385	.385	.385	98	0	0-0	1.000	1	160	0	/O-4(LF)	0.0
1995	Cal A	106	374	50	120	19	1	16	69	19-4	1	65	.321	.352	.505	122	11	6-2	.978	5	115	109	*O-100(99-1-1)/D	1.1

Year	Tm Lg	G	AB	R	H	2B	3B	HR	RBI	BB-IB	HP	SO	AVG	OBP	SLG	AOPS	ABR	SB-CS	FA	FR	Rng	Thr	G at Pos	BFW
1996	Cal A	150	607	79	173	33	2	12	72	27-5	0	84	.285	.314	.405	80	-20	7-9	.979	-2	105	48	*O-146(140-3-6)/D	-2.7
1997	Ana A	154	624	76	189	36	3	8	92	30-6	2	70	.303	.334	.409	94	-7	10-4	.992	10	111	149	*O-148(130-27-4)/D-4	-0.1
1998	Ana A	156	622	62	183	41	7	15	79	29-8	1	80	.294	.325	.455	100	-2	8-3	.983	5	108	104	*O-155(39-0-122)	-0.3
1999	Ana A	157	620	88	188	36	2	21	80	34-8	0	81	.303	.336	.469	104	2	3-4	.993	2	107	70	*O-153(32-116-6)/D-4	0.2
2000	Ana A	159	647	92	185	40	3	35	117	24-5	0	87	.286	.307	.519	103	-1	7-6	.990	-8	95	61	*O-148(0-137-15),D-10	-0.9
2001	Ana A	161	672	83	194	39	2	28	123	27-4	0	100	.289	.314	.478	103	0	13-6	.994	1	100	94	*O-149(144-12-0),D-12	-0.4
2002	†Ana A★	158	638	93	195	**56**	3	29	123	30-11	0	80	.306	.332	.539	128	24	6-4	.994	-2	97	80	*O-147(137-14-0),D-10	1.6
2003	Ana A★	159	638	80	201	**49**	4	29	116	31-10	0	83	.315	.345	.541	134	30	6-3	.997	13	112	151	*O-144(LF),D-15	3.5
Total	10	1365	5455	703	1633	349	27	193	872	251-61	4	732	.299	.328	.479	107	37	66-41	.989	25	105	95	*O-1294(869-310-154)/D-57	2.0

ANDERSON, GEORGE George Jendrus "Andy" (Born George Andrew Jendrus) B 9.26.1889 Cleveland, OH D 5.28.1962 Cleveland, OH BL/TR 5-8/160# d5.26

1914	Bro F	98	364	58	115	13	3	3	24	31	4	50	.316	.376	.393	110	0	16	.946	2	104	109	O-92(70-21-1)	-0.2
1915	Bro F	136	511	70	135	23	9	2	39	52	8	54	.264	.342	.356	97	-9	20	.956	-4	91	97	*O-134(40-12-82)	-2.1
1918	StL N	35	132	20	39	4	5	0	6	15	3	7	.295	.380	.402	143	7	0	.956	-3	94	49	O-35(RF)	0.2
Total	3	269	1007	148	289	40	17	5	69	98	15	111	.287	.359	.375	108	-2	36	.952	-5	96	94	O-261(110-33-118)	-2.1

ANDERSON, SPARKY George Lee B 2.22.1934 Bridgewater, SD BR/TR 5-9/170# d4.10 M26 C1 HF2000

1959	Phi N	152	477	42	104	9	3	0	34	42-1	1	53	.218	.282	.249	43	-39	6-9	.984	1	98	79	*2-152	-3.0

ANDERSON, HAL Harold B 2.10.1904 St.Louis, MO D 5.1.1974 St.Louis, MO BR/TR 5-11/160# d4.12

1932	Chi A	9	32	4	8	0	0	0	2	0	0	1	.250	.250	.250	32	-3	0-1	1.000	1	103	162	/O-9(CF)	-0.3

ANDERSON, HARRY Harry Walter B 9.10.1931 North East, MD D 6.11.1998 Greenville, DE BL/TR 6-3/210# d4.18

1957	Phi N	118	400	53	107	15	4	17	61	36-7	6	61	.268	.333	.452	113	7	2-3	.986	5	113	76	*O-109(107-0-2)	0.5
1958	Phi N	140	515	80	155	34	6	23	97	59-10	3	95	.301	.373	.524	137	28	0-2	.975	-7	93	63	O-87(LF),1-49	1.3
1959	Phi N	142	508	50	122	28	6	14	63	43-14	5	95	.240	.304	.402	85	-11	1-1	.980	10	105	158	*O-137(LF)	-1.0
1960	Phi N	38	93	10	23	2	0	5	12	10-1	2	19	.247	.333	.430	107	1	0-0	1.000	-1	101	94	O-16(LF),1-12	-0.1
	Cin N	42	66	6	11	3	0	1	9	11-0	0	20	.167	.282	.258	49	-4	0-0	.990	-1	88	67	1-15/O-4(2-0-2)	-0.6
	Year	80	159	16	34	5	0	6	21	21-1	2	39	.214	.311	.358	82	-4	0-0	.989	-1	85	54	1-27,O-20(18-0-2)	-0.7
1961	Cin N	4	4	0	1	0	0	0	0	0-0	0	1	.250	.250	.250	33	0	0-0	—	0			H	0.0
Total	5	484	1586	199	419	82	16	60	242	159-32	16	291	.264	.334	.450	109	21	3-6	.982	7	104	106	O-353(349-0-4)/1-76	0.1

ANDERSON, JIM James Lea B 2.23.1957 Los Angeles, CA BR/TR 6/170# d7.2 OF Total (2-LF 1-RF)

1978	Cal A	48	108	6	21	7	0	0	7	11-1	0	16	.194	.267	.259	51	-7	0-0	.955	-3	87	92	S-47/2	-0.6
1979	†Cal A	96	234	33	58	13	1	3	23	17-0	1	31	.248	.298	.350	78	-7	3-2	.949	-2	95	94	S-82,3-10/2-6,C-3	-0.3
1980	Sea A	116	317	46	72	7	0	8	30	27-1	3	39	.227	.292	.325	69	-14	2-4	.958	7	113	105	S-65,3-33/2-2,CD	-0.3
1981	Sea A	70	162	12	33	7	0	2	19	17-0	1	29	.204	.283	.284	61	-8	3-5	.947	1	104	115	S-68/3-2	-0.3
1983	Tex A	50	102	8	22	1	1	0	6	5-0	0	8	.216	.252	.245	38	-9	1-2	.962	3	137	84	S-27,2-17/3-3,O-3(2-0-1),CD	-0.4
1984	Tex A	39	47	2	5	0	0	0	1	4-0	0	7	.106	.176	.106	-19	-8	0-0	.989	4	106	127	S-31/3-6,2	-0.2
Total	6	419	970	107	211	35	2	13	86	81-2	5	130	.218	.280	.298	60	-53	9-13	.955	10	103	103	S-320/3-54,2-27,D-7,C-5,O-3L	-2.1

ANDERSON, JOHN John Joseph "Honest John" B 12.14.1873 Sarpsborg, Norway D 7.23.1949 Worcester, MA BB/TR 6-2/180# d9.8

1894	Bro N	17	63	14	19	1	3	1	19	3	0	3	.302	.333	.460	96	-1	7	.778	-3	0	0	O-16(15-1-0)/3	-0.4
1895	Bro N	103	423	77	122	11	14	10	89	12	5	29	.288	.316	.452	105	-1	24	.882	-8	68	117	*O-102(90-0-12)	-1.5
1896	Bro N	108	430	70	135	23	17	1	55	18	2	23	.314	.344	.453	116	7	37	.942	-2	97	172	O-68(33-9-26),1-42	0.0
1897	Bro N	117	492	93	160	28	12	4	85	17	7		.325	.357	.455	120	12	29	.936	-2	65	60	*O-115(LF)/1-3	-0.1
1898	Bro N	6	21	1	3	2	0	0	2	1	1		.143	.217	.238	31	-2	0	1.000	-0	0	0	/O-5(2-1-2)	-0.2
	Was N	110	430	70	131	28	18	9	71	23	12		.305	.357	.516	150	24	18	.948	7	155	88	O-93(13-78-2),1-17	2.3
	Bro N	19	69	11	19	3	4	0	8	5	1		.275	.333	.435	120	1	2	.966	0	0	0	O-17(LF)/1-2	0.0
	Year	135	520	82	153	33	**22**	9	81	29	14		.294	.348	**.494**	141	24	20	.952	7	**145**	98	*O-115(32-79-4),1-19	2.1
1899	Bro N	117	439	65	118	18	7	4	92	27	4		.269	.317	.369	86	-10	25	.933	-3	55	70	O-76(7-61-8),1-41	-1.6
1901	Mil A	138	576	90	190	46	7	8	99	24	3		.330	.360	.476	137	28	35	**.982**	4	99	106	*1-125,O-13(12-0-1)	2.5
1902	StL A	126	524	60	149	29	6	4	85	21	3		.284	.316	.385	95	-5	15	.985	-9	67	110	*1-126/O-3(2-0-1)	-1.5
1903	StL A	138	550	65	156	34	8	2	78	23	0		.284	.312	.385	111	7	16	.986	5	111	**113**	*1-133/O-7(2-3-2)	1.0
1904	NY A	143	558	62	155	27	12	3	82	23	6		.278	.313	.385	115	8	20	.956	0	76	35	*O-112(46-52-13),1-33	0.2
1905	NY A	32	99	12	23	3	1	0	14	8	1		.232	.296	.283	75	-3	9	.900	-1	139	0	O-22(1-19-2)/1-3	-0.5
	Was A	101	400	50	116	21	6	1	38	22	2		.290	.330	.380	130	13	22	.960	-1	64	38	O-97(16-3-78)/1-4	0.7
	Year	133	499	62	139	24	7	1	52	30	3		.279	.323	.361	117	9	31	.949	-2	76	32	*O-119(17-22-80)/1-7	0.2
1906	Was A	**151**	583	62	158	25	4	3	70	19	2		.271	.296	.343	105	1	**39**	.953	7	100	44	*O-151(LF)	-0.1
1907	Was A	87	333	33	96	12	4	0	44	34	3		.288	.359	.348	136	15	19	.983	-1	85	45	1-61,O-26(LF)	1.3
1908	Chi A	123	355	36	93	17	1	0	47	30	1		.262	.321	.315	109	4	21	.963	-4	97	317	O-87(13-2-72)/1-9	-0.3
Total	14	1636	6345	871	1843	328	124	50	978	310	53	55	.290	.329	.405	114	98	338	.939	-12	86	87	*O-1010(561-229-219),1-599/3	1.8

ANDERSON, KENT Kent McKay B 8.12.1963 Florence, SC BR/TR 6-1/180# d4.15 b-Mike

1989	Cal A	86	223	27	51	6	1	0	17	17-0	1	42	.229	.285	.265	57	-13	1-2	.972	8	109	134	S-70/2-7,3-5,O-2(RF),D	-0.1
1990	Cal A	49	143	16	44	6	1	1	5	13-1	1	19	.308	.369	.385	113	3	0-2	.964	7	97	116	S-28,3-16/2-5	1.1
Total	2	135	366	43	95	12	2	1	22	30-1	2	61	.260	.318	.311	79	-10	1-4	.969	14	105	129	/S-98,3-21,2-12,O-2(RF),D	1.0

ANDERSON, MARLON Marlon Ordell B 1.6.1974 Montgomery, AL BL/TR 5-11/190# d9.8

1998	Phi N	17	43	4	14	3	0	1	4	1-0	0	6	.326	.333	.465	108	0	2-0	.978	1	112	103	/2-9	0.2
1999	Phi N	129	452	48	114	26	4	5	54	24-1	2	61	.252	.292	.361	62	-27	13-2	.979	-7	95	86	*2-121	-2.6
2000	Phi N	41	162	10	37	8	1	1	15	12-0	0	22	.228	.282	.309	49	-13	2-2	.989	-2	90	121	2-41	-1.3
2001	Phi N	147	522	69	153	30	2	11	61	35-5	2	74	.293	.337	.421	98	-2	8-5	.982	4	106	104	*2-140	0.8
2002	Phi N	145	539	64	139	30	6	8	48	42-14	5	71	.258	.315	.380	90	-12	5-1	.970	-6	100	101	*2-143	-1.0
2003	TB A	145	482	59	130	27	3	6	67	41-5	3	60	.270	.328	.376	87	-8	19-3	.973	-17	96	108	*2-134/O-3(LF),D-4	-1.5
Total	6	624	2200	254	587	124	16	32	249	155-25	12	294	.267	.316	.381	82	-62	49-13	.977	-27	99	102	2-588/D-4,O-3(LF)	-5.4

ANDERSON, MIKE Michael Allen B 6.22.1951 Florence, SC BR/TR 6-2/200# d9.2 b-Kent

1971	Phi N	26	89	11	22	5	1	2	5	13-0	0	28	.247	.343	.393	108	1	0-0	.986	0	107	69	O-26(CF)	0.1
1972	Phi N	36	103	8	20	5	1	2	5	19-1	0	36	.194	.317	.320	80	-2	1-0	.987	4	111	257	O-35(0-3-34)	0.1
1973	Phi N	87	193	32	49	9	1	9	28	19-4	1	53	.254	.321	.451	110	2	0-3	.981	0	103	96	O-67(0-12-57)	-0.1
1974	Phi N	145	395	35	99	22	2	5	34	37-13	0	75	.251	.313	.354	83	-9	2-1	.980	10	**117**	160	*O-133(1-2-131)/1	-0.5
1975	Phi N	115	247	24	64	10	3	4	28	17-3	2	66	.259	.307	.372	86	-5	1-2	.977	4	109	131	*O-105(0-24-88)/1-3	-0.5
1976	StL N	86	199	17	58	8	1	1	12	26-4	1	30	.291	.371	.357	108	3	1-1	.982	3	108	131	O-58(24-2-33)/1-5	0.3
1977	StL N	94	154	18	34	4	1	4	17	14-0	0	31	.221	.286	.338	68	-8	2-3	.980	2	113	118	O-77(2-1-74)	-0.8
1978	Bal A	53	32	2	3	0	1	0	3	3-0	0	10	.094	.171	.156	-8	-5	0-0	.962	-1	92	0	O-47(41-2-6)	-0.7
1979	Phi N	79	78	12	18	4	0	1	2	13-0	0	14	.231	.341	.321	79	-2	1-2	.973	3	118	130	O-70(47-6-20)/P	-0.1
Total	9	721	1490	159	367	67	11	28	134	161-25	4	343	.246	.319	.362	88	-25	8-12	.980	26	111	135	O-618(115-78-443)/1-9,P	-2.2

ANDRES, ERNIE Ernest Henry "Junie" B 1.11.1918 Jeffersonville, IN BR/TR 6-1/200# d4.16

1946	Bos A	15	41	0	4	2	0	0	1	3	0	5	.098	.159	.146	-14	-6	0-0	1.000	1	114	45	3-15	-0.6

ANDREW, KIM Kim Darrell B 11.14.1953 Glendale, CA BR/TR 5-10/160# d4.16

1975	Bos A	2	2	0	1	0	0	0	0	0-0	0	0	.500	.500	.500	169	0	0-0	1.000	-0	76	0	/2-2	0.0

ANDREWS, SHANE Darrell Shane B 8.28.1971 Dallas, TX BR/TR 6-1/215# d4.26

1995	Mon N	84	220	27	47	10	1	8	31	17-2	1	68	.214	.271	.377	67	-11	1-1	.973	-1	104	32	3-51,1-29	-1.3
1996	Mon N	127	375	43	85	15	2	19	64	35-8	2	119	.227	.295	.429	86	-9	3-1	.955	16	115	81	*3-123	0.8
1997	Mon N	18	64	10	13	3	0	4	9	3-0	0	20	.203	.232	.438	73	-3	0-0	.895	3	121	204	3-18	0.0
1998	Mon N	150	492	48	117	30	1	25	69	58-3	0	137	.238	.314	.455	102	0	1-6	.954	18	**118**	109	*3-147	1.8
1999	Mon N	98	281	28	51	8	0	11	37	43-2	0	88	.181	.287	.327	57	-19	1-0	.932	-1	109	79	3-82,1-18/D	-1.9
	Chi N	19	67	13	17	4	0	5	14	7-1	1	21	.254	.329	.537	117	1	0-1	.955	-1	98	194	3-19/1	0.0
	Year	117	348	41	68	12	0	16	51	50-3	1	109	.195	.295	.368	69	-18	1-1	.936	-1	107	104	*3-101,1-19/D	-1.9
2000	Chi N	66	192	25	44	5	0	14	39	27-1	2	59	.229	.329	.474	102	0	1-1	.907	4	112	120	3-58/1-6	0.3
2002	Bos A	7	13	2	1	1	0	0	0	1-0	1	3	.077	.200	.154	-4	-2	0-0	1.000	1	147	287	/3-4,1-2,O(LF)D	-0.1
Total	7	569	1704	196	375	76	4	86	263	191-17	7	515	.220	.298	.421	85	-43	7-10	.946	40	113	100	3-502/1-56,D-2,O(LF)	-0.4

Year	Tm Lg	G	AB	R	H	2B	3B	HR	RBI	BB-IB	HP	SO	AVG	OBP	SLG	AOPS	ABR	SB-CS	FA	FR	Rng	Thr	G at Pos	BFW
ANDREWS, FRED Fred B 5.4.1952 Lafayette, LA BR/TR 5-8/163# d9.26																								
1976	Phi N	4	6	1	4	0	0	0	0	2-0	1	0	.667	.778	.667	304	2	1-1	1.000	-2	39	62	/2-4	0.1
1977	Phi N	12	23	3	4	0	1	0	2	1-0	0	5	.174	.200	.261	24	-3	1-0	1.000	3	127	197	/2-7	0.1
Total	2	16	29	4	8	0	1	0	2	3-0	1	5	.276	.353	.345	90	-1	2-1	1.000	1	97	151	/2-11	0.2
ANDREWS, ED George Edward B 4.5.1859 Painesville, OH D 8.12.1934 W.Palm Beach, FL BR/TR 5-8/160# d5.1 U3																								
1884	Phi N	109	420	74	93	21	2	0	23	9		42	.221	.238	.281	66	-16		.891	-20	95	78	*2-109	-2.8
1885	Phi N	103	421	77	112	15	3	0	23	32		25	.266	.318	.316	108	5		.921	1	61	44	*O-99(LF)/2-5	0.4
1886	Phi N	107	437	93	109	15	4	2	28	31		35	.249	.299	.316	86	-7	**56**	.903	3	118	73	*O-104(1-103-0)/2-3	-0.6
1887	Phi N	104	464	110	151	19	7	4	67	21	3	21	.325	.359	.422	110	5	57	.902	-7	102	33	*O-99(CF)/2-7,1	-0.4
1888	Phi N	124	528	75	126	14	4	3	44	21	3	41	.239	.272	.297	77	-14	35	.903	-6	111	129	*O-124(CF)	-2.4
1889	Phi N	10	39	10	11	1	0	0	7	2	0	4	.282	.317	.308	69	-2	7	.808	-1	51	0	/O-9(8-0-1),2	-0.3
	Ind N	40	173	32	53	11	0	0	22	5	1	10	.306	.330	.370	94	-2	7	.885	-2	140	75	O-40(CF)/2	-0.5
	Year	50	212	42	64	12	0	0	29	7	1	14	.302	.327	.358	89	-4	14	.867	-4	121	59	O-49(8-40-1)/2-2	-0.8
1890	Bro P	94	395	84	100	14	2	3	38	40	1	32	.253	.323	.322	68	-19	21	.912	-3	96	81	*O-94(1-89-4)	-2.0
1891	Cin AA	83	356	47	75	7	4	0	26	33	1	35	.211	.279	.253	48	-26	22	.961	15	165	118	O-83(LF)	-1.1
Total	8	774	3233	602	830	117	26	12	278	194	9	245	.257	.301	.320	82	-76	205	.912	-18	109	79	O-652(192-455-5),2-126/1	-9.7
ANDREWS, JIM James Pratt B 6.5.1865 Shelburne Falls, MA D 12.27.1907 Chicago, IL d4.19																								
1890	Chi N	53	202	32	38	4	2	3	17	23	2	41	.188	.278	.272	58	-11	11	.900	1	109	58	O-53(RF)	-1.0
ANDREWS, MIKE Michael Jay B 7.9.1943 Los Angeles, CA BR/TR 6-3/195# d9.18 b-Rob																								
1966	Bos A	5	18	1	3	0	0	0	0	0-0	0	2	.167	.167	.167	-4	-2	0-0	1.000	1	122	57	/2-5	-0.1
1967	†Bos A	142	494	79	130	20	0	8	40	62-4	2	72	.263	.346	.352	99	2	7-7	.976	-3	99	87	*2-139/S-6	1.0
1968	Bos A	147	536	77	145	22	1	7	45	81-1	3	57	.271	.368	.354	113	13	3-8	.976	6	101	113	*2-139/S-4,3	3.2
1969	Bos A★	121	464	79	136	26	2	15	59	71-0	5	53	.293	.390	.455	129	21	1-1	.972	-0	98	97	*2-120	3.0
1970	Bos A	151	589	91	149	28	1	17	65	81-0	3	63	.253	.344	.390	96	-1	2-1	.973	-30	83	73	*2-148	-2.2
1971	Chi A	109	330	45	93	16	0	12	47	67-1	1	36	.282	.400	.439	135	19	3-5	.956	-1	100	107	2-76,1-25	2.1
1972	Chi A	148	505	58	111	18	0	7	50	70-3	2	78	.220	.313	.297	82	-9	2-2	.973	-8	90	79	*2-145/1-5	-1.0
1973	Chi A	52	159	10	32	9	0	0	10	23-3	0	28	.201	.302	.258	57	-8	0-1	1.000	-1	89	20	D-30/1-9,2-6,3-5	-1.1
	†Oak A	18	21	1	4	1	0	0	0	3-0	0	1	.190	.292	.238	53	-1	0-0	.944	-0	76	106	/2-9,D-2	-0.1
	Year	70	180	11	36	10	0	0	10	26-3	0	29	.200	.301	.256	57	-9	0-1	.974	-1	79	96	D-32,2-15/1-9,3-5	-1.2
Total	8	893	3116	441	803	140	4	66	316	458-12	16	390	.258	.353	.369	104	34	18-25	.973	-36	95	91	2-787/1-39,D-32,S-10,3-6	4.8
ANDREWS, ROB Robert Patrick B 12.11.1952 Santa Monica, CA BR/TR 6/185# d4.7 b-Mike																								
1975	Hou N	103	277	29	66	5	4	0	19	31-4	0	34	.238	.310	.285	73	-11	12-5	.982	1	99	117	2-94/S-6	-0.3
1976	Hou N	109	410	42	105	8	5	0	23	33-1	0	27	.256	.312	.300	81	-11	7-3	.977	9	109	92	*2-107/S-3	0.6
1977	SF N	127	436	60	115	11	3	0	25	56-0	0	33	.264	.345	.303	76	-13	5-6	.964	-11	97	94	*2-115	-1.9
1978	SF N	79	177	21	39	3	3	1	11	20-1	0	18	.220	.299	.288	67	-8	5-1	.977	-0	99	83	2-62/S	-0.5
1979	SF N	75	154	22	40	3	0	2	13	8-0	0	9	.260	.289	.318	73	-6	4-1	.956	4	105	88	2-53/3-3	0.0
Total	5	493	1454	174	365	30	15	3	91	148-6	0	121	.251	.318	.298	76	-49	33-16	.972	2	102	96	2-431/S-10,3-3	-2.1
ANDREWS, STAN Stanley Joseph "Polo" (born Stanley Joseph Andruskewicz) B 4.17.1917 Lynn, MA D 6.10.1995 Bradenton, FL BR/TR 5-11/178# d6.11																								
1939	Bos N	13	26	1	6	0	0	0	1	1	0	2	.231	.259	.231	35	-2	0	.857	-2	*190*	*62*	C-10	-0.4
1940	Bos N	19	33	1	6	0	0	0	2	0	0	3	.182	.182	.182	1	-5	1	.944	-1	*99*	*83*	C-14	-0.5
1944	Bro N	4	8	1	1	0	0	0	1	1	0	2	.125	.222	.125	-1	-1	0	1.000	-0	*65*	*0*	/C-4	-0.1
1945	Bro N	21	49	5	8	0	1	0	2	5	1	4	.163	.255	.204	29	-5	0	.948	1	*99*	*178*	C-21	-0.3
	Phi N	13	33	3	11	2	0	1	6	1	0	5	.333	.353	.485	135	1	1	.950	-1	*75*	*81*	C-12	0.1
	Year	34	82	8	19	2	1	1	8	6	1	9	.232	.292	.317	70	-4	1	.949	-0	*90*	*142*	C-33	-0.2
Total	4	70	149	11	32	2	1	1	12	8	1	16	.215	.259	.262	46	-12	2	.938	-3	*106*	*110*	/C-61	-1.2
ANDREWS, WALLY William Walter B 9.18.1859 Philadelphia, PA D 1.20.1940 Indianapolis, IN BR/TR 6-3/170# d5.22																								
1884	Lou AA	14	49	10	10	5	1	0	8	4	0		.204	.264	.347	102	1		.950	-1	138	61	/1-9,3-3,O(LF)S	-0.1
1888	Lou AA	26	93	12	18	6	3	0	6	13	0		.194	.292	.323	99	0	5	.997	1	103	128	1-26	-0.1
Total	2	40	142	22	28	11	4	0	14	17	0		.197	.283	.331	100	1	5	.985	0	111	112	/1-35,3-3,SO(LF)	-0.2
ANDRUS, FRED Frederick Hotham B 8.23.1850 Washington, MI D 11.10.1937 Detroit, MI BR/TR 6-2/185# d7.25 ▲																								
1876	Chi N	8	36	6	11	3	0	0	2	0		5	.306	.306	.389	116	0		.714	-2	0	0	/O-8(1-3-5)	-0.1
1884	Chi N	1	5	3	1	0	0	0	0	1		0	.200	.333	.200	67	0		1.000	0	163	0	/P	0.0
Total	2	9	41	9	12	3	0	0	2	1		5	.293	.310	.366	110	0		.714	-2	0	0	/O-8(1-3-5),P	-0.1
ANDRUS, BILL William Morgan "Andy" B 7.25.1907 Beaumont, TX D 3.12.1982 Washington, DC BR/TR 6/185# d9.19																								
1931	Was A	3	7	0	0	0	0	0	1	0	0	1	.000	.000	.000	-99	-2	0-0	.750	-0	69	422	/3-2	-0.2
1937	Phi N	3	2	0	0	0	0	0	0	0	0	2	.000	.000	.000	-93	-1	0	—	-0	0	0	/3	-0.1
Total	2	6	9	0	0	0	0	0	1	0	0	3	.000	.000	.000	-98	-3	0-0	.750	-1	64	392	/3-3	-0.3
ANDRUS, WIMAN William Wiman B 10.14.1858 Orono, ON, CAN D 6.17.1935 Miles City, MT 5-6.5/155# d9.15																								
1885	Pro N	1	4	0	0	0	0	0	0	0		1	.000	.000	.000	-99	-1		1.000	1	132	0	/3	0.0
ANGLEY, TOM Thomas Samuel B 10.2.1904 Baltimore, MD D 10.26.1952 Wichita, KS BL/TR 5-8/190# d4.23																								
1929	Chi N	5	16	1	4	1	0	0	6	2	0	2	.250	.333	.313	61	-1	0	.968	1	*157*	*175*	/C-5	0.0
ANKENMAN, PAT Frederick Norman B 12.23.1912 Houston, TX D 1.13.1989 Houston, TX BR/TR 5-4/125# d4.16 Mil 1943																								
1936	StL N	1	3	0	0	0	0	0	0	0	0	3	.000	.000	.000	-99	-1	0	.600	-1	31	0	/S	-0.2
1943	Bro N	1	2	1	1	0	0	0	0	0	0	0	.500	.500	.500	189	0	0	1.000	0	91	230	/S	0.1
1944	Bro N	13	24	1	6	1	0	0	3	0	0	2	.250	.250	.292	53	-2	0	.971	0	119	48	2-11/S-2	-0.1
Total	3	15	29	2	7	1	0	0	3	0	0	5	.241	.241	.276	46	-3	0	.971	-1	119	48	/2-11,S-4	-0.2
ANNIS, BILL William Perley B 3.8.1857 Stoneham, MA D 6.10.1923 Kennebunkport, ME BR 5-7/150# d5.1																								
1884	Bos N	27	96	17	17	2	0	0	3	0		8	.177	.177	.198	18	-9		.900	-1	117	179	O-27(4-15-8)	-1.0
ANSON, CAP Adrian Constantine B 4.17.1852 Marshalltown, IA D 4.14.1922 Chicago, IL BR/TR 6/227# d5.6 M21 HF1939 OF NA (1-LF 5-CF 31-RF) OF Total (45-LF 3-CF 1-RF)																								
1871	Rok NA	**25**	120	29	39	**11**	3	0	16	2		1	.325	.336	.467	134	6	6-2	.763	1	114	76	*3-20/C-5,2-2,1O(LF)	0.4
1872	Ath NA	46	217	60	90	10	7	0	48	16		3	.415	**.455**	.525	200	26	6-6	.752	-10	74	99	*3-46	1.0
1873	Ath NA	**52**	254	53	101	9	2	0	36	5		2	.398	.409	.449	144	12	1-2	.920	-4	107	120	*1-36,3-11/C-3,2-3,O-3(CF)	0.5
1874	Ath NA	**55**	260	51	87	8	3	0	37	4		1	.335	.345	.388	124	5	6-0	.936	-5	120	138	1-24,3-20/O-8(RF),S-6,C	0.1
1875	Ath NA	69	326	84	106	15	3	0	58	4		2	.325	.333	.390	135	9	11-6	.922	11	249	121	1-32,O-25(0-2-23),C-13/3-5,M	1.9
1876	Chi N	**66**	309	63	110	9	7	2	59	12		8	.356	.380	.450	157	16		.849	14	113	168	*3-66/C-2	2.8
1877	Chi N	59	255	52	86	**19**	1	0	32	9		3	.337	.360	.420	129	8		**.883**	7	105	**213**	*3-40,C-31	1.5
1878	Chi N	60	261	55	89	12	2	0	40	13		1	.341	.372	.402	145	12		.825	-7	48	0	*O-48(45-3-0)/2-9,3-3,C-3	0.3
1879	Chi N	51	227	40	72	20	1	0	34	2		2	**.317**	.323	.414	133	8		.975	0	62	121	1-51/,M	0.6
1880	Chi N	**86**	356	54	120	24	1	1	**74**	14		12	.337	.362	.419	154	20		**.978**	0	72	89	*1-81/3-9,S2M	1.6
1881	Chi N	**84**	343	67	**137**	21	7	1	**82**	26		4	**.399**	**.442**	.510	**189**	**35**		**.975**	7	**144**	112	*1-84/C-2,SM	**3.6**
1882	Chi N	82	348	69	126	29	8	1	**83**	20		7	.362	.397	.500	177	30		.949	-0	**119**	112	*1-82/CM	2.0
1883	Chi N	**98**	413	70	127	36	5	0	68	18		9	.308	.336	.419	118	9		.964	3	**129**	117	*1-98/P-2,O(RF)CM	0.3
1884	Chi N	**112**	475	108	159	30	3	21	**102**	29		13	.335	.373	.543	170	37		.956	-0	123	**166**	*1-112/C-3,SPM	2.3
1885	†Chi N	112	464	100	144	**35**	7	7	**108**	34		13	.310	.357	.461	143	21		.958	-4	100	117	*1-112/CM	0.6
1886	†Chi N	125	504	117	187	35	11	10	**147**	55		19	.371	.433	.544	170	42	29	.963	9	144	**133**	*1-125,C-12,M	3.6
1887	Chi N	122	472	107	164	33	13	7	102	60	1	18	**.347**	.422	.517	141	26	27	.973	10	**156**	**114**	*1-122/CM	2.1
1888	Chi N	134	515	101	177	20	12	12	**84**	47	1	24	**.344**	**.400**	.499	172	42	28	**.986**	9	133	**127**	*1-134,M	3.8
1889	Chi N	134	518	100	177	32	7	7	117	86	5	19	.342	.440	.471	147	36	27	**.982**	8	**127**	98	*1-134,M	2.8
1890	Chi N	**139**	504	95	157	14	5	7	107	**113**	6	23	.312	**.443**	.401	141	34	29	.978	1	**105**	95	*1-135/C-3,2-2,M	2.0
1891	Chi N	136	540	81	157	24	8	8	**120**	75	1	29	.291	.378	.409	129	22	17	.981	8	129	**123**	*1-136/C-2,M	1.6
1892	Chi N	**146**	559	62	152	25	9	1	74	67	4	30	.272	.354	.354	113	10	13	.973	-6	86	78	*1-146/,M	0.4
1893	Chi N	103	398	70	125	24	2	0	91	68	1	12	.314	.415	.384	115	13	13	.981	-4	79	88	*1-101/,M	0.8
1894	Chi N	84	343	85	133	29	4	5	100	41	3	15	.388	.457	.539	132	20	17	.990	3	104	94	1-83/2M	1.7
1895	Chi N	122	474	87	159	23	6	2	91	55	3	23	.335	.408	.422	107	6	12	.985	-1	91	110	*1-122/,M	0.4

Year	Tm Lg	G	AB	R	H	2B	3B	HR	RBI	BB-IB	HP	SO	AVG	OBP	SLG	AOPS	ABR	SB-CS	FA	FR	Rng	Thr	G at Pos	BFW
1896	Chi N	108	402	72	133	18	2	2	90	49	3	10	.331	.407	.400	109	8	24	.983	-1	103	110	*1-98,C-10/,M	0.6
1897	Chi N	114	424	67	121	17	3	3	75	60	4		.285	.379	.361	92	-2	11	.975	1	112	117	*1-103,C-11/,M	0.0
Total	5 NA	247	1177	277	423	53	18	0	195	31	0	9	.359	.376	.435	146	58	30-16	.000	-7	83	97	3-102/1-93,O-37R,C-22,S-6,2-5	3.9
Total	22	2277	9104	1722	3012	529	124	97	1880	953	32	294	.331	.396	.448	139	453	247-0	.974	57	114	111	*1-2059,3-118/C-83,O-49L,2-13,PS	35.4

ANTHONY, ERIC Eric Todd B 11.8.1967 San Diego, CA BL/TL 6-2/195# d7.29

Year	Tm Lg	G	AB	R	H	2B	3B	HR	RBI	BB-IB	HP	SO	AVG	OBP	SLG	AOPS	ABR	SB-CS	FA	FR	Rng	Thr	G at Pos	BFW
1989	Hou N	25	61	7	11	2	0	4	7	9-2	0	16	.180	.286	.410	100	0	0-0	1.000	0	102	108	O-21(3-0-18)	0.0
1990	Hou N	84	239	26	46	8	0	10	29	29-3	2	78	.192	.279	.351	76	-8	5-0	.970	-3	91	105	O-71(13-0-59)	-1.2
1991	Hou N	39	118	11	18	6	0	1	7	12-1	0	41	.153	.227	.229	31	-11	1-0	.986	3	105	210	O-37(RF)	-0.9
1992	Hou N	137	440	45	105	15	1	19	80	38-5	1	98	.239	.298	.407	103	0	5-4	.973	-7	85	85	*O-115(1-2-113)	-1.2
1993	Hou N	145	486	70	121	19	4	15	66	49-2	2	88	.249	.319	.397	94	-5	3-5	.988	-7	93	67	*O-131(0-23-121)	-1.8
1994	Sea A	79	262	31	62	14	1	10	30	23-4	0	66	.237	.297	.412	79	-9	6-2	.985	-0	103	92	O-71(62-5-10)/D-4	-1.0
1995	†Cin N	47	134	19	36	6	0	5	23	13-2	0	30	.269	.327	.425	99	0	2-1	1.000	1	102	145	O-24(4-1-20),1-17	-0.1
1996	Cin N	47	123	22	30	6	0	8	13	22-2	0	36	.244	.359	.488	120	4	0-1	.949	-5	59	99	O-37(13-0-24)	-0.3
	Col N	32	62	10	15	2	0	4	9	10-0	0	20	.242	.342	.468	91	-1	0-1	1.000	-1	64	233	O-19(1-9-10)	-0.3
	Year	79	185	32	45	8	0	12	22	32-2	0	56	.243	.353	.481	107	2	0-2	.967	-6	61	141	O-56(14-9-34)	-0.6
1997	LA N	47	74	8	18	3	2	2	5	12-1	0	18	.243	.349	.419	108	1	2-0	.966	1	98	215	O-21(17-0-4)	0.2
Total	9	682	1999	249	462	81	8	78	269	217-22	5	491	.231	.305	.397	91	-29	24-14	.981	-17	91	105	O-547(114-40-416)/1-17,D-4	-6.6

ANTOLICK, JOE Joseph B 4.11.1916 Hokendauqua, PA D 6.25.2002 Catasauqua, PA BR/TR 6/185# d9.20

Year	Tm Lg	G	AB	R	H	2B	3B	HR	RBI	BB-IB	HP	SO	AVG	OBP	SLG	AOPS	ABR	SB-CS	FA	FR	Rng	Thr	G at Pos	BFW
1944	Phi N	4	6	1	2	0	0	0	0	1	0	0	.333	.429	.333	120	0	0	1.000	1	*57*	*0*	/C-3	0.1

ANTONELLI, JOHN John Lawrence B 7.15.1915 Memphis, TN D 4.18.1990 Memphis, TN BR/TR 5-10.5/165# d9.16

Year	Tm Lg	G	AB	R	H	2B	3B	HR	RBI	BB-IB	HP	SO	AVG	OBP	SLG	AOPS	ABR	SB-CS	FA	FR	Rng	Thr	G at Pos	BFW
1944	StL N	8	21	0	4	1	0	0	1	0	0	4	.190	.190	.238	20	-2	0	1.000	1	177	113	/1-3,3-3,2-2	-0.2
1945	StL N	2	3	0	0	0	0	0	0	0	0	1	.000	.000	.000	-98	-1	0	.667	-1	0	0	/3	-0.1
	Phi N	125	504	50	129	27	2	1	28	24	2	24	.256	.292	.323	73	-20	1	.959	-4	95	109	*3-108,2-23/1S	-2.1
	Year	127	507	50	129	27	2	1	28	24	2	25	.254	.291	.321	72	-20	1	.957	-4	94	108	*3-109,2-23/1S	-2.2
Total	2	135	528	50	133	28	2	1	29	24	2	29	.252	.287	.318	70	-23	1	.958	-3	95	106	3-112/2-25,1-4,S	-2.4

ANTONELLO, BILL William James B 5.19.1927 Brooklyn, NY D 3.4.1993 Fridley, MN BR/TR 5-11/185# d4.30

Year	Tm Lg	G	AB	R	H	2B	3B	HR	RBI	BB-IB	HP	SO	AVG	OBP	SLG	AOPS	ABR	SB-CS	FA	FR	Rng	Thr	G at Pos	BFW
1953	Bro N	40	43	9	7	1	1	1	4	2	0	11	.163	.200	.302	28	-5	0-0	.964	1	133	0	O-25(20-2-4)	-0.5

APARICIO, LUIS Luis Ernesto (Montiel) B 4.29.1934 Maracaibo, Venezuela BR/TR 5-9/160# d4.17 HF1984

Year	Tm Lg	G	AB	R	H	2B	3B	HR	RBI	BB-IB	HP	SO	AVG	OBP	SLG	AOPS	ABR	SB-CS	FA	FR	Rng	Thr	G at Pos	BFW
1956	Chi A	152	533	69	142	19	6	3	56	34-2	1	63	.266	.311	.341	71	-24	**21**-4	.954	-4	102	97	*S-152	-1.1
1957	Chi A	143	575	82	148	22	6	3	41	52-1	0	55	.257	.317	.332	78	-18	**28**-8	.972	-10	98	94	*S-142	-1.3
1958	Chi A★	145	557	76	148	20	9	2	40	35-2	1	38	.266	.309	.345	82	-15	**29**-6	.973	12	105	97	*S-145	1.3
1959	†Chi A★	152	612	98	157	18	5	6	51	53-1	3	40	.257	.316	.332	80	-17	**56**-13	**.970**	-6	98	96	*S-152	-0.2
1960	Chi A★	153	600	86	166	20	7	2	61	43-3	1	39	.277	.323	.343	82	-16	**51**-8	**.979**	**29**	**112**	116	*S-153	3.4
1961	Chi A★	156	625	90	170	24	4	6	45	38-0	1	33	.272	.313	.352	79	-20	**53**-13	**.962**	7	**106**	92	*S-156	0.7
1962	Chi A★	153	581	72	140	23	5	7	40	32-1	1	36	.241	.280	.334	65	-30	**31**-12	**.973**	12	105	115	*S-152	-0.3
1963	Bal A★	146	601	73	150	18	8	5	45	36-2	2	35	.250	.291	.331	78	-20	**40**-6	**.983**	-3	95	93	*S-145	-0.3
1964	Bal A✳	146	578	93	154	20	3	10	37	49-0	3	51	.266	.324	.363	92	-6	**57**-17	**.979**	4	101	121	*S-145	1.8
1965	Bal A	144	564	67	127	20	10	8	40	46-0	3	56	.225	.286	.339	76	-19	26-7	**.971**	-1	104	112	*S-141	-0.4
1966	†Bal A	151	659	97	182	25	8	6	41	33-2	1	42	.276	.311	.366	95	-6	25-11	**.978**	7	96	117	*S-151	1.8
1967	Bal A	134	546	55	127	22	5	4	31	29-2	1	44	.233	.270	.313	73	-19	18-5	.957	-15	89	96	*S-131	-2.3
1968	Chi A	155	622	55	164	24	4	4	36	33-3	2	43	.264	.302	.334	92	-7	17-11	.977	20	115	110	*S-154	3.0
1969	Chi A	156	599	77	168	24	5	5	51	66-1	2	29	.280	.352	.362	96	-2	24-4	.976	33	**119**	102	*S-154	5.4
1970	Chi A★	146	552	86	173	29	3	5	43	53-1	1	34	.313	.372	.404	110	10	8-3	.976	25	116	108	*S-146	5.3
1971	Bos A★	125	491	56	114	23	0	4	45	35-0	2	43	.232	.284	.303	63	-24	6-4	.971	-18	91	75	*S-121	-3.0
1972	Bos A✳	110	436	47	112	26	3	3	39	26-0	2	28	.257	.299	.351	89	-6	3-3	.968	-10	91	79	*S-109	-0.4
1973	Bos A	132	499	56	135	17	1	0	49	43-1	0	33	.271	.324	.309	76	-15	13-1	.966	-12	95	87	*S-132	-1.0
Total	18	2599	10230	1335	2677	394	92	83	791	736-22	27	742	.262	.311	.343	82	-254	506-136	.972	70	103	101	*S-2581	12.4

APPLING, LUKE Lucius Benjamin B 4.2.1907 High Point, NC D 1.3.1991 Cumming, GA BR/TR 5-10/183# d9.10 Mil 1944-45 M1 C9 HF1964

Year	Tm Lg	G	AB	R	H	2B	3B	HR	RBI	BB-IB	HP	SO	AVG	OBP	SLG	AOPS	ABR	SB-CS	FA	FR	Rng	Thr	G at Pos	BFW
1930	Chi A	6	26	2	8	2	0	0	2	0	0	0	.308	.308	.385	77	-1	2-0	.879	-2	92	26	/S-6	-0.2
1931	Chi A	96	297	36	69	13	4	1	28	29	1	27	.232	.303	.313	66	-15	9-2	.900	-9	102	79	S-76/2	-1.6
1932	Chi A	139	489	66	134	20	10	3	63	40	0	36	.274	.329	.374	87	-11	9-8	.929	15	112	114	S-85,2-30,3-14	1.1
1933	Chi A	**151**	612	90	197	36	10	6	85	56	0	29	.322	.379	.443	122	19	6-11	.939	9	**108**	119	*S-151	3.4
1934	Chi A	118	452	75	137	28	6	2	61	59	0	27	.303	.384	.405	100	2	3-1	.945	-7	98	74	*S-110/2-8	0.3
1935	Chi A	**153**	525	94	161	28	6	1	71	122	0	40	.307	.437	.389	112	18	12-6	.958	**25**	**113**	99	*S-153	5.1
1936	Chi A★	138	526	111	204	31	7	6	128	85	1	25	**.388**	.474	.508	137	37	10-6	.951	15	**108**	**129**	*S-137	5.4
1937	Chi A	**154**	574	98	182	42	8	4	77	86	1	28	.317	.407	.439	113	16	18-10	.944	17	**111**	**122**	*S-154	4.0
1938	Chi A	81	294	41	89	14	0	0	44	42	1	17	.303	.392	.350	85	-4	1-3	.953	2	112	72	S-78	0.2
1939	Chi A☆	148	516	82	162	16	6	0	56	105	0	37	.314	.430	.368	103	9	16-9	.951	-1	**102**	95	*S-148	1.8
1940	Chi A★	150	566	96	197	27	13	0	79	69	1	35	.348	.420	.442	122	21	3-5	.953	-3	99	101	*S-150	2.6
1941	Chi A☆	154	592	93	186	26	8	1	57	82	1	32	.314	.399	.390	111	13	12-8	.948	-4	103	101	*S-154	1.9
1942	Chi A	142	543	78	142	26	4	3	53	63	3	23	.262	.342	.341	94	-3	17-5	.948	-3	103	93	*S-141	0.7
1943	Chi A☆	**155**	585	63	192	33	2	3	80	90	1	29	**.328**	**.419**	.407	142	37	27-8	.957	8	106	112	*S-155	6.3
1945	Chi A	18	57	12	21	2	2	1	10	12	0	7	.368	.478	.526	197	8	1-0	.930	-1	100	64	S-17	0.9
1946	Chi A★	149	582	59	180	27	5	1	55	71	0	41	.309	.384	.378	118	17	6-4	.951	5	**113**	107	*S-149	3.2
1947	Chi A★	139	503	67	154	29	0	8	49	64	1	28	.306	.386	.412	126	20	8-6	.949	-9	104	91	*S-129/3-2	1.9
1948	Chi A	139	497	63	156	16	2	0	47	94	0	35	.314	.423	.354	112	15	10-4	.943	13	124	94	3-72,S-64	3.2
1949	Chi A	142	492	82	148	21	5	5	58	121	0	24	.301	.439	.394	125	27	7-12	.964	-3	**105**	90	*S-141	2.8
1950	Chi A	50	128	11	30	3	4	0	13	12	0	8	.234	.300	.320	61	-8	2-0	.967	1	92	96	S-20,1-13/2	-0.6
Total	20	2422	8856	1319	2749	440	102	45	1116	1302	11	528	.310	.399	.398	113	217	179-108	.948	68	106	101	*S-2218/3-88,2-40,1-13	42.4

ARAGON, ANGEL Angel (Valdes) "Pete" B 8.2.1890 Havana, Cuba D 1.24.1952 New York, NY BR/TR 5-5/150# d8.20 s-Jack

Year	Tm Lg	G	AB	R	H	2B	3B	HR	RBI	BB-IB	HP	SO	AVG	OBP	SLG	AOPS	ABR	SB-CS	FA	FR	Rng	Thr	G at Pos	BFW
1914	NY A	6	7	1	1	0	0	0	0	1	1	2	.143	.333	.143	44	0	0	—	-0	0	0	/O(CF)	0.0
1916	NY A	12	24	1	5	0	0	0	3	2	0	2	.208	.269	.208	43	-2	2	.864	1	143	0	/3-8,O-2(1-0-1)	-0.1
1917	NY A	14	45	2	3	1	0	0	2	2	0	2	.067	.106	.089	-40	-8	0	.933	0	92	0	/O-6(4-2-0),3-4,S-2	-0.9
Total	3	32	76	4	9	1	0	0	5	5	1	6	.118	.183	.132	-4	-10	2	.921	1	131	74	/3-12,O-9(5-3-1),S-2	-1.0

ARAGON, JACK Angel Valdes (Reyes) B 11.20.1915 Havana, Cuba D 4.4.1988 Clearwater, FL BR/TR 5-10/176# d8.13 Mil 1942-44 f-Angel

Year	Tm Lg	G	AB	R	H	2B	3B	HR	RBI	BB-IB	HP	SO	AVG	OBP	SLG	AOPS	ABR	SB-CS	FA	FR	Rng	Thr	G at Pos	BFW
1941	NY N	1	0	0	0	0	0	0	0	0	0	0	—	—	—	—	0	0	—	0			R	0.0

ARCHDEACON, MAURICE Maurice John "Flash" B 12.14.1897 St.Louis, MO D 9.5.1954 St.Louis, MO BL/TL 5-8/153# d9.17

Year	Tm Lg	G	AB	R	H	2B	3B	HR	RBI	BB-IB	HP	SO	AVG	OBP	SLG	AOPS	ABR	SB-CS	FA	FR	Rng	Thr	G at Pos	BFW
1923	Chi A	22	87	23	35	5	1	0	4	6	0	8	.402	.441	.483	145	6	2-3	.918	-2	93	45	O-20(0-18-2)	0.2
1924	Chi A	95	288	59	92	9	3	0	25	40	4	30	.319	.410	.372	106	5	11-7	.958	-1	96	126	O-77(CF)	0.1
1925	Chi A	10	9	2	1	0	0	0	0	2	0	1	.111	.273	.111	0	-1	0-0	1.000	0	113	0	/O(LF)	-0.1
Total	3	127	384	84	128	14	4	0	29	48	4	39	.333	.413	.391	112	10	13-10	.950	-3	95	107	/O-98(1-95-2)	0.2

ARCHER, JIMMY James Patrick B 5.13.1883 Dublin, Ireland D 3.29.1958 Milwaukee, WI BR/TR 5-10/168# d9.6

Year	Tm Lg	G	AB	R	H	2B	3B	HR	RBI	BB-IB	HP	SO	AVG	OBP	SLG	AOPS	ABR	SB-CS	FA	FR	Rng	Thr	G at Pos	BFW
1904	Pit N	7	20	1	3	0	0	0	1	0	0		.150	.150	.150	-7	-3	0	.919	0	*127*	*108*	/C-7,O(LF)	-0.2
1907	†Det A	18	42	6	5	0	0	0	0	4	0		.119	.196	.119	1	-5	0	.975	1	*113*	*103*	C-17/2	-0.2
1909	Chi N	80	261	31	60	9	2	1	30	12	1		.230	.266	.291	71	-10	5	.960	0	*129*	*89*	C-80	-0.2
1910	†Chi N	98	313	36	81	17	6	2	41	14	1	49	.259	.293	.371	94	-4	6	.970	5	*143*	*104*	C-49,1-40	0.5
1911	Chi N	116	387	41	98	18	5	4	41	18	1	43	.253	.288	.357	80	-13	5	.977	13	***160***	*84*	*C-102,1-10/2	0.9
1912	Chi N	120	385	35	109	20	2	5	58	22	5	36	.283	.330	.384	95	-3	7	.966	2	*131*	*92*	*C-118	0.9
1913	Chi N	111	368	38	98	14	7	2	44	19	5	27	.266	.311	.359	91	-5	4-5	.969	-0	112	109	*C-103/1-8	0.2
1914	Chi N	79	248	17	64	9	2	0	19	9	0	9	.258	.284	.310	77	-8	1	.973	-0	*93*	*101*	C-76	-0.2
1915	Chi N	97	309	21	75	11	5	1	27	11	2	38	.243	.273	.320	79	-9	5-6	.977	-3	*97*	*104*	C-88/1-4	-0.6
1916	Chi N	77	205	11	45	6	2	1	30	12	2	24	.220	.269	.283	63	-9	3	.979	-2	94	91	C-61/3	-0.6
1917	Chi N	2	2	0	0	0	0	0	0	0	0	1	.000	.000	.000	-93	0	0	—	0			H	-0.1
1918	Pit N	24	58	4	9	1	2	0	3	1	2	6	.155	.197	.241	32	-5	0	.989	5	*155*	*133*	C-21/1	0.2
	Bro N	9	22	3	6	0	1	0	0	1	0	5	.273	.304	.364	104	0	0	.968	0	*93*	*184*	/C-7	0.1
	Cin N	9	26	2	7	1	0	0	2	1	0	3	.269	.296	.308	86	0	0	1.000	1	*121*	*127*	/C-7,1	0.1

Year	Tm Lg	G	AB	R	H	2B	3B	HR	RBI	BB-IB	HP	SO	AVG	OBP	SLG	AOPS	ABR	SB-CS	FA	FR	Rng	Thr	G at Pos	BFW
	Year	42	106	9	22	2	3	0	5	3	2	14	.208	.243	.283	59	-6	0	.987	7	*136*	*142*	C-35/1-2	0.4
Total	12	847	2646	246	660	106	34	16	296	124	19	241	.249	.288	.333	80	-74	36-11	.971	25	*122*	*98*	C-736/1-64,2-2,30(LF)	0.8
ARCHIE, GEORGE George Albert B 4.27.1914 Nashville, TN D 9.20.2001 Nashville, TN BR/TR 6/170# d9.14 Mil 1942-45																								
1938	Det A	3	2	1	0	0	0	0	0	0	0	1	.000	.000	.000	-95	-1	0-0	—	0			H	-0.1
1941	Was A	105	379	45	102	20	4	3	48	30	1	42	.269	.324	.367	87	-8	8-4	.936	-4	100	83	3-73,1-23	-1.1
	StL A	9	29	3	11	3	0	0	5	7	0	3	.379	.500	.483	156	3	2-0	.975	0	120	60	/1-8	0.3
	Year	114	408	48	113	23	4	3	53	37	1	45	.277	.339	.375	92	-5	10-4	.936	-3	100	83	3-73,1-31	-0.8
1946	StL A	4	11	1	2	1	0	0	0	0	0	1	.182	.182	.273	25	-1	0-0	1.000	2	270	195	/1-3	0.0
Total	3	121	421	50	115	24	4	3	53	37	1	47	.273	.333	.371	90	-7	10-4	.936	-2	100	83	/3-73,1-34	-0.9
ARCIA, JOSE Jose Raimundo (Orta) B 8.22.1943 Havana, Cuba BR/TR 6-3/170# d4.10																								
1968	Chi N	59	84	15	16	4	0	1	8	3-0	0	24	.190	.218	.274	44	-6	0-0	1.000	0	114	0	O-17(5-13-0),2-10/S-7,3	-0.5
1969	SD N	120	302	35	65	11	3	0	10	14-0	2	47	.215	.255	.272	49	-21	14-7	.977	2	106	80	2-68,S-37/3-8,O-4(LF),1	-1.3
1970	SD N	114	229	28	51	9	3	0	17	12-1	7	36	.223	.282	.288	55	-15	3-6	.955	1	97	105	S-67,2-20/3-9,O-7(LF)	-0.9
Total	3	293	615	78	132	24	6	1	35	29-1	9	107	.215	.260	.278	51	-42	17-13	.950	4	99	93	S-111/2-98,O-28(16-13-0),3-18,1	-2.7
ARDELL, DAN Daniel Miers B 5.27.1941 Seattle, WA BL/TL 6-2/190# d9.14																								
1961	LA A	7	4	1	1	0	0	0	0	1-0	0	2	.250	.400	.250	70	0	0-0	1.000	-0	0	137	/1	0.0
ARDNER, JOE Joseph A. "Old Hoss" B 2.27.1858 Mt.Vernon, OH D 9.15.1935 Cleveland, OH BR/TR ?/160# d5.1																								
1884	Cle N	26	92	6	16	1	1	0	4	1		24	.174	.183	.207	21	-8		.866	-6	95	61	2-25/3	-1.2
1890	Cle N	84	323	28	72	13	1	0	35	17	2	40	.223	.266	.269	57	-18	9	.920	-6	98	118	2-84	-1.9
Total	2	110	415	34	88	14	2	0	39	18	2	64	.212	.248	.255	50	-26	9	.908	-12	97	106	2-109/3	-3.1
ARDOIN, DANNY Daniel Wayne B 7.8.1974 Mamou, LA BR/TR 6/205# d8.2																								
2000	Min A	15	32	4	4	1	0	1	5	8-0	0	10	.125	.300	.250	40	-3	0-0	.989	4	161	180	C-15	0.1
ARFT, HANK Henry Irven "Bow Wow" B 1.28.1922 Manchester, MO D 12.14.2002 St.Louis, MO BL/TL 5-10.5/190# d7.27																								
1948	StL A	69	248	25	59	10	3	5	38	45	0	43	.238	.355	.363	89	-3	1-2	.995	-0	96	111	1-69	-0.6
1949	StL A	6	5	1	1	1	0	0	2	0	0	1	.200	.200	.400	55	0	0-0	—	0			H	0.0
1950	StL A	98	280	45	75	16	4	1	32	46	2	48	.268	.375	.364	87	-4	3-2	.995	-1	96	67	1-84	-0.7
1951	StL A	112	345	44	90	16	5	7	42	41	0	34	.261	.339	.397	96	-3	4-6	.989	7	124	91	1-97	0.0
1952	StL A	15	28	1	4	3	1	0	4	5	0	7	.143	.273	.321	63	-1	0-0	.985	-0	81	164	1-10	-0.2
Total	5	300	906	116	229	46	13	13	118	137	2	133	.253	.352	.375	90	-11	8-10	.992	5	106	91	1-260	-1.5
ARIAS, ALEX Alejandro B 11.20.1967 New York, NY BR/TR 6-3/185# d5.12																								
1992	Chi N	32	99	14	29	6	0	0	7	11-0	2	13	.293	.375	.354	105	1	0-0	.967	-5	94	53	S-30	-0.1
1993	Fla N	96	249	27	67	5	1	2	20	27-0	3	18	.269	.344	.321	76	-8	1-1	.987	-7	101	82	2-30,3-22,S-18	-1.2
1994	Fla N	59	113	4	27	5	0	0	15	9-0	1	19	.239	.298	.283	52	-8	0-1	.985	-4	72	78	S-20,3-15	-1.1
1995	Fla N	94	216	22	58	9	2	3	26	22-1	2	20	.269	.337	.370	87	-4	1-0	.947	-0	98	83	S-36,3-21/2-6	-0.1
1996	Fla N	100	224	27	62	11	2	3	26	17-1	3	28	.277	.335	.384	92	-3	2-0	.956	2	99	144	3-59,S-20/12	0.2
1997	†Fla N	74	93	13	23	2	0	1	11	12-0	3	12	.247	.352	.301	76	-3	0-1	.971	-2	70	116	3-37,S-11	-0.4
1998	Phi N	56	133	17	39	8	0	1	16	13-3	1	18	.293	.358	.376	93	-1	2-0	.985	-3	96	54	S-38/3-5,2	-0.1
1999	Phi N	118	347	43	105	20	1	4	48	36-6	4	31	.303	.373	.401	94	-2	2-2	.988	-18	86	81	S-95/3-2,2	-1.3
2000	Phi N	70	155	17	29	9	0	2	15	16-2	3	28	.187	.271	.284	41	-14	1-0	.963	-6	90	90	S-39,3-10/2	-1.7
2001	SD N	70	137	19	31	9	0	2	12	17-1	1	22	.226	.312	.336	75	-5	1-0	.957	-4	137	83	3-18,1-17,2-13,S-13	-0.8
2002	NY A	6	7	0	0	0	0	0	0	1-0	0	2	.000	.125	.000	-63	-2	0-0	.750	-0	124	508	/3-4,S	-0.2
Total	11	775	1773	203	470	84	6	18	196	181-14	23	211	.265	.338	.350	81	-49	10-5	.973	-47	89	81	S-321,3-193/2-53,1-18	-6.8
ARIAS, GEORGE George Alberto B 3.12.1972 Tucson, AZ BR/TR 5-11/190# d4.2																								
1996	Cal A	84	252	19	60	8	1	6	28	16-2	0	50	.238	.284	.349	59	-17	2-0	.960	22	136	137	3-83/D	0.5
1997	Ana A	3	6	1	2	0	0	0	1	0-0	0	0	.333	.333	.333	75	0	0-0	1.000	0	168	0	/3D	0.0
	SD N	11	22	2	5	1	0	0	2	0-0	0	1	.227	.227	.273	33	-2	0-0	.941	0	116	0	/3-8	-0.2
1998	†SD N	20	36	4	7	1	1	1	4	3-0	2	16	.194	.293	.361	77	-1	0-0	.933	1	122	121	3-14/1	0.0
1999	SD N	55	164	20	40	8	0	7	20	6-0	0	54	.244	.271	.421	77	-7	0-0	.941	6	116	58	3-50	-0.1
Total	4	173	480	46	114	18	2	14	55	25-2	2	121	.237	.278	.371	65	-27	2-0	.952	29	128	104	3-156/D-2,1	0.2
ARLETT, BUZZ Russell Loris B 1.3.1899 Elmhurst, CA D 5.16.1964 Minneapolis, MN BB/TR 6-2/210# d4.14																								
1931	Phi N	121	418	65	131	26	7	18	72	45	5	39	.313	.387	.538	135	21	3	.955	1	97	122	O-94(RF),1-13	1.5
ARMAS, TONY Antonio Rafael (Machado) B 7.2.1953 Anzoategui, Venezuela BR/TR 6-1/200# d9.6 b-Marcos s-Tony																								
1976	Pit N	4	6	0	2	0	0	0	1	0-0	0	2	.333	.333	.333	89	0	0-0	1.000	0	101	0	/O-2(1-1-0)	0.0
1977	Oak A	118	363	26	87	8	2	13	53	20-2	0	99	.240	.274	.380	79	-12	1-2	.981	9	114	121	*O-112(3-84-30)/S	-0.6
1978	Oak A	91	239	17	51	6	1	2	13	10-2	2	62	.213	.250	.272	50	-17	1-2	.991	8	129	63	O-85(2-40-47)/D-3	-1.2
1979	Oak A	80	278	29	69	9	3	11	34	16-2	1	67	.248	.290	.421	95	-4	1-0	.976	6	115	124	O-80(12-17-53)	-0.1
1980	Oak A	158	628	87	175	18	8	35	109	29-4	2	128	.279	.310	.500	128	18	5-3	.975	11	114	137	*O-158(0-10-152)	2.0
1981	†Oak A★	**109**	440	51	115	24	3	**22**	76	19-6	2	115	.261	.294	.480	126	11	5-1	.993	5	110	95	*O-109(0-2-108)	1.1
1982	Oak A	138	536	58	125	19	2	28	89	33-5	1	128	.233	.275	.433	96	-6	2-2	.983	5	114	87	*O-135(0-5-133)/D	-0.8
1983	Bos A	145	574	77	125	23	2	36	107	29-0	2	131	.218	.254	.453	85	-15	0-1	.985	-1	103	70	*O-116(CF),D-27	-1.8
1984	Bos A☆	157	639	107	171	29	5	**43**	**123**	32-9	1	156	.268	.300	.531	120	14	1-3	.974	-9	94	48	*O-126(0-126-1),D-31	0.1
1985	Bos A	103	385	50	102	17	5	23	64	18-4	2	90	.265	.298	.514	114	5	0-0	.983	-6	88	63	O-79(16-69-2),D-19	-0.3
1986	†Bos A	121	425	40	112	21	4	11	58	24-1	2	77	.264	.305	.409	92	-6	0-3	.969	-6	93	70	*O-117(9-108-19)/D	-1.4
1987	Cal A	28	81	8	16	3	1	3	9	1-0	0	11	.198	.205	.370	51	-6	1-0	1.000	-2	87	0	O-27(2-0-26)	-0.9
1988	Cal A	120	368	42	100	20	2	13	49	22-0	0	87	.272	.311	.443	112	5	1-3	.986	-3	92	91	*O-113(74-36-10)/D-5	-0.2
1989	Cal A	60	202	22	52	7	1	11	30	7-2	0	48	.257	.280	.465	109	1	0-0	.990	1	99	115	O-47(5-1-42)/1-2,D-6	0.0
Total	14	1432	5164	614	1302	204	39	251	815	260-37	15	1201	.252	.287	.453	103	-12	18-20	.981	17	105	89	*O-1306(124-615-623)/D-93,1-2,S-	4.1
ARMAS, MARCOS Marcos Rafael (Ruiz) B 8.5.1969 Puerto Piritu, Venezuela BR/TR 6-5/195# d5.25 b-Tony																								
1993	Oak A	15	31	7	6	2	0	1	1	1-0	1	12	.194	.242	.355	62	-2	1-0	1.000	-1	65	53	1-12/O(RF)D	-0.3
ARMBRISTER, ED Edison Rosanda B 7.4.1948 Nassau, Bahamas BR/TR 5-11/160# d8.31																								
1973	†Cin N	18	37	5	8	3	1	1	5	2-0	0	8	.216	.250	.432	92	-1	0-0	.917	0	107	143	O-14(3-4-7)	-0.1
1974	Cin N	9	7	0	2	0	0	0	0	1-0	0	1	.286	.375	.286	88	0	0-0	1.000	-0	65	0	/O-4(2-0-2)	0.0
1975	†Cin N	59	65	9	12	1	0	0	2	5-0	1	19	.185	.254	.200	27	-6	3-1	.867	-3	57	0	O-19(10-4-7)	-1.0
1976	†Cin N	73	78	20	23	3	2	2	7	6-0	0	22	.295	.341	.462	124	2	7-3	.972	3	100	337	O-32(20-0-13)	0.5
1977	Cin N	65	78	12	20	4	3	1	5	10-0	0	21	.256	.337	.423	102	0	5-6	.903	0	81	272	O-27(20-0-7)	-0.1
Total	5	224	265	46	65	11	6	4	19	24-0	1	71	.245	.307	.377	88	-5	15-10	.925	-0	86	209	/O-96(55-8-36)	-0.7
ARMBRUSTER, CHARLIE Charles A. B 8.30.1880 Cincinnati, OH D 10.7.1964 Grants Pass, OR BR/TR 5-9/180# d7.17																								
1905	Bos A	35	91	13	18	4	0	0	6	18	1		.198	.336	.242	83	0	3	.944	-3	*123*	*75*	C-35	-0.1
1906	Bos A	72	201	9	29	6	1	0	6	25	1		.144	.242	.184	34	-14	2	.955	-4	*82*	*112*	C-66/1	-1.3
1907	Bos A	23	60	2	6	1	0	0	0	8	0		.100	.206	.117	3	-6	1	.935	1	*119*	*116*	C-21	-0.3
	Chi A	1	3	0	0	0	0	0	0	1	0		.000	.250	.000	-20	0	0	1.000	0	*153*	*82*	/C	0.0
	Year	24	63	2	6	1	0	0	0	9	0		.095	.208	.111	2	-7	1	.940	2	*121*	*114*	C-22	-0.3
Total	3	131	355	24	53	11	1	0	12	52	2		.149	.262	.186	42	-20	6	.949	-5	*101*	*102*	C-123/1	-1.7
ARMBRUSTER, HARRY Henry "Army" B 3.20.1882 Cincinnati, OH D 12.10.1953 Cincinnati, OH BL/TL 5-10/190# d4.30																								
1906	Phi A	91	265	40	63	6	3	2	24	43	4		.238	.353	.306	103	3	13	.971	0	98	51	O-74(0-40-34)	0.0
ARMSTRONG, GEORGE Noble George "Dodo" B 6.3.1924 Orange, NJ D 7.24.1993 Orange, NJ BR/TR 5-10/190# d4.26																								
1946	Phi A	8	6	0	1	1	0	0	0	1	0	1	.167	.286	.333	73	0	0-0	1.000	0	*0*	*392*	/C-4	0.0
ARMSTRONG, BOB Robert B 1850 Baltimore, MD 6-2/160# d6.26																								
1871	Kek NA	12	49	9	11	2	1	0	5	0		1	.224	.224	.306	50	-3	0-1	.816	1	132	0	O-12(0-11-1)	-0.2
ARNDT, HARRY Harry J. B 2.12.1879 South Bend, IN D 3.25.1921 South Bend, IN BR/TR d7.2																								
1902	Det A	10	34	4	5	0	1	0	7	6	0		.147	.275	.206	34	-3	0	.958	0	0	0	O-10(7-0-3)/1	-0.3
	Bal A	68	248	41	63	7	4	2	28	35	4		.254	.355	.339	89	-3	9	.872	1	121	52	O-62(1-0-61)/2-4,3-2,S	-0.4

Year	Tm Lg	G	AB	R	H	2B	3B	HR	RBI	BB-IB	HP	SO	AVG	OBP	SLG	AOPS	ABR	SB-CS	FA	FR	Rng	Thr	G at Pos	BFW
	Year	78	282	45	68	7	5	2	35	41	4		.241	.346	.323	83	-5	9	.885	1	104	45	O-72(8-0-64)/2-4,3-2,1S	-0.7
1905	StL N	113	415	40	101	11	6	2	36	24	3		.243	.290	.313	82	-10	13	.951	-10	96	87	2-90/O-9(RF),3-7,S-5	-2.0
1906	StL N	69	256	30	69	7	9	2	26	19	0		.270	.320	.391	127	6	5	.965	10	106	191	3-65/1O(RF)	2.0
1907	StL N	11	32	3	6	1	0	0	2	1	0		.188	.212	.219	36	-2	0	1.000	1	129	99	/1-4,3-3	-0.2
Total	4	271	985	118	244	26	20	6	99	85	7		.248	.312	.333	91	-12	27	.952	2	97	85	/2-94,O-82(8-0-74),3-77,S-6,1-6	-0.9
ARNDT, LARRY Larry Wayne B 2.25.1963 Fremont, OH BR/TR 6-1/195# d6.6																								
1989	Oak A	2	6	1	1	0	0	0	0	0-0	0	1	.167	.167	.167	-6	-1	0-0	1.000	0	132	241	/13	-0.1
ARNOLD, CHRIS Christopher Paul B 11.6.1947 Long Beach, CA BR/TR 5-10/160# d9.7																								
1971	SF N	6	13	2	3	0	0	1	3	1-0	0	2	.231	.286	.462	110	0	0-0	.917	-0	114	0	/2-3	0.0
1972	SF N	51	84	8	19	3	1	1	4	8-1	0	12	.226	.293	.321	74	-3	0-1	.970	-1	119	211	3-17/2-7,S-4	-0.3
1973	SF N	49	54	7	16	2	0	1	13	8-2	0	11	.296	.381	.389	111	1	0-0	.944	-3	48	0	/C-9,23	-0.1
1974	SF N	78	174	22	42	7	3	1	26	15-1	1	27	.241	.302	.333	75	-6	1-1	.974	-5	99	83	2-31/3-7,S	-0.9
1975	SF N	29	41	4	8	0	0	0	0	4-0	0	8	.195	.267	.195	28	-4	0-0	.923	1	93	230	/2-4,O-4(3-0-1)	-0.4
1976	SF N	60	69	4	15	0	1	0	5	6-1	0	16	.217	.276	.246	49	-5	0-0	1.000	4	188	67	/2-8,3-4,1S	-0.1
Total	6	273	435	47	103	12	5	4	51	42-5	1	76	.237	.303	.315	72	-17	1-2	.971	-4	107	76	/2-54,3-29,C-9,S-6,O-4(3-0-1),1	-1.8
ARNOLD, BILLY Willis S. B 3.2.1851 Middletown, CT D 1.17.1899 Albany, NY d4.26																								
1872	Man NA	2	7	2	1	0	0	0	0			0	.143	.143	.143	-13	-1	1-0	1.000	0	0	0	/O-2(RF)	0.0
ARNOVICH, MORRIE Morris "Snooker" B 11.16.1910 Superior, WI D 7.20.1959 Superior, WI BR/TR 5-10/168# d9.14 Mil 1942-45																								
1936	Phi N	13	48	4	15	3	0	1	7	1	2	3	.313	.353	.438	102	0	0	1.000	1	120	92	O-13(LF)	0.1
1937	Phi N	117	410	60	119	27	4	10	60	34	3	32	.290	.349	.449	107	4	5	.972	7	110	130	*O-107(97-9-1)	0.5
1938	Phi N	139	502	47	138	29	0	4	72	42	2	37	.275	.333	.357	92	-4	2	.983	17	**118**	174	*O-133(130-1-3)	0.6
1939	Phi N☆	134	491	68	159	25	2	5	67	58	2	28	.324	.397	.413	122	18	7	.983	14	**122**	124	*O-132(131-2-0)	2.4
1940	Phi N	39	141	13	28	2	1	0	12	14	1	15	.199	.276	.227	42	-11	0	.959	1	105	102	O-37(36-0-1)	-1.3
	†Cin N	62	211	17	60	10	2	0	21	13	0	10	.284	.326	.351	86	-4	1	1.000	3	105	120	O-60(57-0-3)	-0.4
	Year	101	352	30	88	12	3	0	33	27	1	25	.250	.305	.301	68	-15	1	.983	4	105	112	O-97(93-0-4)	-1.7
1941	NY N	85	207	25	58	8	3	2	22	23	0	14	.280	.352	.377	103	1	2	.982	1	98	148	O-61(LF)	0.0
1946	NY N	1	3	0	0	0	0	0	0	0	0	0	.000	.000	.000	-99	-1	0	1.000	-0	85	0	/O(LF)	-0.1
Total	7	590	2013	234	577	104	12	22	261	185	10	139	.287	.350	.383	100	3	17	.981	45	113	137	O-544(526-12-8)	1.8
ARUNDEL, TUG John Thomas B 6.30.1862 Romulus, NY D 9.5.1912 Auburn, NY d5.23																								
1882	Phi AA	1	5	0	0	0	0	0		0			.000	.000	.000	-94	-1		.800	-0			/C	-0.1
1884	Tol AA	15	47	6	4	0	0	0		3	0		.085	.140	.085	-24	-6		.946	5			C-15	0.0
1887	Ind N	43	157	13	31	4	0	0	13	8	1	12	.197	.241	.223	31	-14	8	.865	-8			C-42/O-2(RF),1	-1.7
1888	Was N	17	51	2	10	0	1	0	3	5	0	10	.196	.268	.235	66	-2	1	.840	-6			C-17	-0.6
Total	4	76	260	21	45	4	1	0	16	16	1	22	.173	.224	.196	25	-23	9	.882	-9			/C-75,O-2(RF),1	-2.4
ASADOOR, RANDY Randall Carl B 10.20.1962 Fresno, CA BR/TR 6-1/185# d9.14																								
1986	SD N	15	55	9	20	5	0	0	7	3-1	0	13	.364	.397	.455	137	3	1-2	.889	-0	103	41	3-15/2-2	0.2
ASBELL, JIM James Marion "Big Train" B 6.22.1914 Dallas, TX D 7.6.1967 San Mateo, CA BR/TR 6/195# d5.8																								
1938	Chi N	17	33	6	6	2	0	0	3	3	0	9	.182	.250	.242	35	-3	0	1.000	1	94	171	O-10(7-0-3)	-0.3
ASBJORNSON, CASPER Robert Anthony (Name Changed To Asby) B 6.19.1909 Concord, MA D 1.21.1970 Williamsport, PA BR/TR 6-1/196# d9.17																								
1928	Bos A	6	16	0	3	1	0	0	1	1	0	1	.188	.235	.250	28	-2	0-0	.917	-2	*69*	*134*	/C-6	-0.3
1929	Bos A	17	29	1	3	0	0	0	0	1	0	6	.103	.133	.103	-39	-6	0-0	.897	-2	*90*	*108*	C-15	-0.7
1931	Cin N	45	118	13	36	7	1	0	22	7	1	23	.305	.349	.381	102	0	0	.981	-1	*83*	*132*	C-31	0.1
1932	Cin N	29	58	5	10	2	0	1	4	0	1	15	.172	.186	.259	19	-7	0	.961	-1	*94*	*53*	C-16	-0.7
Total	4	97	221	19	52	10	1	1	27	9	2	45	.235	.272	.303	56	-15	0-0	.960	-5	*86*	*110*	/C-68	-1.6
ASHBURN, RICHIE Don Richard "Whitey" B 3.19.1927 Tilden, NE D 9.9.1997 New York, NY BL/TR 5-10/170# d4.20 HF1995																								
1948	Phi N★	117	463	78	154	17	4	2	40	60	1	22	.333	.410	.400	122	17	**32**	.981	9	109	156	*O-116(15-102-0)	2.2
1949	Phi N	**154**	662	84	188	18	11	1	37	58	1	38	.284	.343	.349	88	-12	9	.980	10	**112**	108	*O-154(CF)	-0.5
1950	†Phi N	151	594	84	180	25	**14**	2	41	63	2	32	.303	.372	.402	105	5	14	.988	-1	102	64	*O-147(CF)	0.0
1951	Phi N★	**154**	643	92	**221**	31	5	4	63	50	2	37	.344	.393	.426	122	21	29-6	.988	**21**	**125**	107	*O-154(CF)	4.2
1952	Phi N	**154**	613	93	173	31	6	1	42	75	2	30	.282	.362	.357	101	4	16-11	.980	8	103	147	*O-154(CF)	0.7
1953	Phi N★	**156**	622	110	**205**	25	9	2	57	61	5	35	.330	.394	.408	110	12	14-6	.990	18	**115**	126	*O-156(CF)	2.2
1954	Phi N	**153**	559	111	175	16	8	1	41	**125**	4	46	.313	**.441**	.376	116	23	11-8	.984	13	**116**	102	*O-153(CF)	2.8
1955	Phi N	140	533	91	180	32	9	3	42	105-5	3	36	**.338**	**.449**	.448	142	41	12-10	.983	5	108	94	*O-140(CF)	3.7
1956	Phi N	**154**	628	94	190	26	8	3	50	79-3	5	45	.303	.384	.384	110	12	10-1	.983	19	124	97	*O-154(CF)	2.6
1957	Phi N	**156**	626	93	186	26	8	0	33	**94**-1	4	44	.297	.390	.364	108	13	13-10	.987	**25**	**124**	162	*O-156(0-156-1)	3.0
1958	Phi N☆	152	615	98	**215**	24	**13**	2	33	**97**-7	4	48	**.350**	**.440**	.441	136	39	30-12	.984	12	120	63	*O-152(CF)	4.5
1959	Phi N	153	564	86	150	16	2	1	20	79-4	6	42	.266	.360	.307	79	-13	9-11	.971	-5	102	48	*O-149(CF)	-2.8
1960	Chi N	151	547	99	159	16	5	0	40	**116**-1	1	50	.291	**.415**	.338	110	16	16-4	.976	-4	95	99	*O-146(45-106-0)	0.7
1961	Chi N	109	307	49	79	7	4	0	19	55-2	3	27	.257	.373	.306	83	-5	7-6	.978	-7	82	77	O-76(14-62-0)	-1.5
1962	NY N★	135	389	60	119	7	3	7	28	81-2	0	39	.306	.424	.393	119	16	12-7	.975	-3	92	124	O-97(10-56-42)/2-2	0.8
Total	15	2189	8365	1322	2574	317	109	29	586	1198-25	43	571	.308	.396	.382	111	189	234-92	.983	119	110	105	*O-2104(84-1995-43)/2-2	22.6
ASHBY, ALAN Alan Dean B 7.8.1951 Long Beach, CA BB/TR (BL 1976) 6-2/190# d7.3 C1																								
1973	Cle A	11	29	4	5	1	0	1	3	2-0	0	11	.172	.226	.310	49	-2	0-0	.978	-3	150	37	C-11	-0.4
1974	Cle A	10	7	1	1	0	0	0	0	1-0	0	2	.143	.250	.143	15	-1	0-0	1.000	0	0	0	/C-9	-0.1
1975	Cle A	90	254	32	57	10	1	5	32	30-1	1	42	.224	.309	.331	81	-6	3-2	.990	-3	87	110	C-87/1-2,3D	-0.6
1976	Cle A	89	247	26	59	5	1	4	32	27-4	0	49	.239	.310	.316	86	-4	0-2	.987	3	82	117	C-86/1-2,3	0.2
1977	Tor A	124	396	25	83	16	3	2	29	50-3	2	51	.210	.301	.280	59	-22	0-2	.984	-0	125	117	*C-124	-1.7
1978	Tor A	81	264	27	69	15	0	9	29	28-4	1	32	.261	.333	.420	109	3	1-1	.986	-6	107	103	C-81	0.1
1979	Hou N	108	336	25	68	15	2	2	35	26-10	2	70	.202	.262	.277	51	-24	0-0	.987	1	102	83	*C-105	-1.9
1980	†Hou N	116	352	30	90	19	2	3	48	35-12	0	40	.256	.319	.347	94	-2	0-0	.991	-1	103	62	*C-114	0.1
1981	†Hou N	83	255	20	69	13	0	4	33	35-6	0	33	.271	.356	.369	112	5	0-2	.982	10	105	130	C-81	1.9
1982	Hou N	100	339	40	87	14	2	12	49	27-4	1	53	.257	.311	.416	111	3	2-0	.977	-7	75	69	C-95	0.1
1983	Hou N	87	275	31	63	18	1	8	34	31-4	0	38	.229	.303	.389	98	-1	0-0	.974	-8	83	86	C-85	-0.6
1984	Hou N	66	191	16	50	7	0	4	27	20-2	1	22	.262	.330	.361	103	1	0-0	.986	-4	76	122	C-63	0.0
1985	Hou N	65	189	20	53	8	0	8	25	24-2	1	27	.280	.363	.450	130	8	0-0	.978	-2	78	108	C-60	0.8
1986	†Hou N	120	315	24	81	15	0	7	38	39-9	0	56	.257	.333	.371	98	0	1-0	.985	-2	86	76	*C-103	0.2
1987	Hou N	125	386	53	111	16	0	14	63	50-2	1	52	.288	.367	.438	118	11	0-1	**.993**	-2	79	74	*C-110	1.3
1988	Hou N	73	227	19	54	10	0	7	33	29-3	0	36	.238	.319	.374	104	2	0-0	.991	-10	66	67	C-66	-0.5
1989	Hou N	22	61	4	10	1	1	0	3	7-0	1	8	.164	.257	.213	38	-5	0-0	1.000	-4	87	65	C-19	-0.8
Total	17	1370	4123	397	1010	183	13	90	513	461-66	11	622	.245	.320	.361	93	-34	7-10	.986	-36	92	92	*C-1299/1-4,3-2,D	-1.9
ASHFORD, TUCKER Thomas Steven B 12.4.1954 Memphis, TN BR/TR 6-1/195# d9.21																								
1976	SD N	4	5	0	3	1	0	0	0	1-0	0	0	.600	.667	.800	343	2	2-0	1.000	-0	90	0	/3	0.2
1977	SD N	81	249	25	54	18	0	3	24	21-4	1	35	.217	.278	.325	69	-11	2-3	.937	-8	102	122	3-74,S-10/2-4	-2.1
1978	SD N	75	155	11	38	11	0	3	26	14-1	0	31	.245	.301	.374	97	-1	1-0	.917	-11	47	68	3-32,2-18,1-14	-1.2
1980	Tex A	15	32	2	4	0	0	0	3	3-0	0	3	.125	.200	.125	-9	-5	0-0	.943	2	117	46	3-12/S-2	-0.3
1981	NY A	3	0	0	0	0	0	0	0	0-0	0	0	—	—	—	—	0	0-0	—	-1	0	0	/2-2	-0.1
1983	NY N	35	56	3	10	0	1	0	2	7-1	0	4	.179	.270	.214	36	-5	0-0	.957	-0	90	117	3-15,2-13/C	-0.6
1984	KC A	9	13	1	2	1	0	0	0	1-0	0	2	.154	.214	.231	23	-1	0-0	.909	-1	86	125	/3-9	-0.2
Total	7	222	510	42	111	31	1	6	55	47-6	1	75	.218	.282	.318	70	-21	5-3	.936	-19	93	105	3-143/2-37,1-14,S-12,C	-4.3
ASHLEY, BILLY Billy Manual B 7.11.1970 Trenton, MI BR/TR 6-7/227# d9.1																								
1992	LA N	29	95	6	21	5	0	2	6	5-0	0	34	.221	.260	.337	69	-4	0-0	.857	-3	72	123	O-27(1-0-26)	-0.9
1993	LA N	14	37	0	9	0	0	0	0	2-0	0	11	.243	.282	.243	45	-3	0-0	1.000	1	58	432	O-11(LF)	-0.3
1994	LA N	2	6	0	2	1	0	0	0	0-0	0	2	.333	.333	.500	121	0	0-0	1.000	-0	79	0	/O-2(LF)	0.0
1995	†LA N	81	215	17	51	5	0	8	27	25-4	2	88	.237	.320	.372	91	-3	0-0	.972	0	103	60	O-69(LF)	-0.6
1996	†LA N	71	110	18	22	2	1	9	25	21-1	1	44	.200	.331	.482	121	3	0-0	.952	-1	85	141	O-38(LF)	0.2

Year	Tm Lg	G	AB	R	H	2B	3B	HR	RBI	BB-IB	HP	SO	AVG	OBP	SLG	AOPS	ABR	SB-CS	FA	FR	Rng	Thr	G at Pos	BFW
1997	LA N	71	131	12	32	7	0	6	19	8-0	1	46	.244	.293	.435	95	-2	0-0	.911	-2	82	121	O-35(LF)	-0.4
1998	Bos A	13	24	3	7	3	0	3	7	2-0	0	11	.292	.346	.792	180	3	0-0	.857	0	0	377	/1-2,O-2(LF),D-5	0.3
Total	7	281	618	56	144	23	1	28	84	63-5	4	236	.233	.307	.409	95	-6	0-0	.941	-5	87	130	O-184(158-0-26)/D-5,1-2	-1.7
ASMUSSEN, TOM Thomas William B 9.26.1876 Chicago, IL D 8.21.1963 Arlington Heights, IL TR d8.10																								
1907	Bos N	2	5	0	0	0	0	0	0	0		0	.000	.000	.000	-99	-1	0	1.000	-1	49	82	/C-2	-0.2
ASPROMONTE, KEN Kenneth Joseph B 9.22.1931 Brooklyn, NY BR/TR 6/180# d9.2 M3 b-Bob																								
1957	Bos A	24	78	9	21	5	0	0	4	17-0	0	10	.269	.396	.333	97	1	0-1	.965	-3	102	81	2-24	0.0
1958	Bos A	6	16	0	2	0	0	0	0	3-0	0	1	.125	.263	.125	10	-2	0-0	.952	-2	57	81	/2-6	-0.4
	Was A	92	253	15	57	9	1	5	27	25-1	1	28	.225	.296	.328	73	-9	1-1	.964	1	105	93	2-72,3-11/S	-0.4
	Year	98	269	15	59	9	1	5	27	28-1	1	29	.219	.294	.316	69	-11	1-1	.963	-1	102	92	2-78,3-11/S	-0.8
1959	Was A	70	225	31	55	12	0	2	14	26-0	0	39	.244	.321	.324	79	-6	2-1	.960	-6	102	76	2-52,S-12/1O(LF)	-0.7
1960	Was A	4	3	0	0	0	0	0	0	0-0	0	1	.000	.000	.000	-99	-1	0-0	—	0			H	-0.1
	Cle A	117	459	65	133	20	1	10	48	53-0	2	32	.290	.364	.403	111	8	4-1	.976	-18	91	100	2-80,3-36	-0.3
	Year	121	462	65	133	20	1	10	48	53-0	2	33	.288	.362	.400	110	7	4-1	.976	-18	91	100	2-80,3-36	-0.4
1961	LA A	66	238	29	53	10	0	2	14	33-1	2	21	.223	.322	.290	58	-13	0-0	.970	14	112	116	2-62	0.6
	Cle A	22	70	5	16	6	1	0	5	6-0	0	3	.229	.286	.343	70	-3	0-0	.963	-3	106	67	2-21	-0.4
	Year	88	308	34	69	16	1	2	19	39-1	2	24	.224	.314	.302	61	-16	0-0	.969	11	111	106	2-83	0.2
1962	Cle A	20	28	4	4	2	0	0	1	6-1	0	5	.143	.286	.214	41	-2	0-0	1.000	-1	68	99	/2-6,3-3	-0.3
	Mil N	34	79	11	23	2	0	0	7	6-0	1	5	.291	.341	.316	82	-2	0-1	1.000	-0	103	95	2-12/3-6	-0.1
1963	Chi N	20	34	2	5	3	0	0	4	4-1	0	4	.147	.237	.235	35	-3	0-0	.951	2	132	104	/2-7,1-2	0.0
Total	7	475	1483	171	369	69	3	19	124	179-4	6	149	.249	.330	.338	82	-32	7-5	.969	-16	102	95	2-342/3-56,S-13,1-3,O(LF)	-2.1
ASPROMONTE, BOB Robert Thomas B 6.19.1938 Brooklyn, NY BR/TR 6-2/185# d9.19 b-Ken OF Total (60-LF 2-RF)																								
1956	Bro N	1	1	0	0	0	0	0	0	0-0	0	1	.000	.000	.000	-93	0	0-0	—	0			H	0.0
1960	LA N	21	55	1	10	1	0	1	6	0-0	1	6	.182	.196	.255	21	-6	1-0	.933	-1	85	107	S-15/3-4	-0.6
1961	LA N	47	58	7	14	3	0	0	2	4-0	0	12	.241	.290	.293	51	-4	0-0	.917	-0	108	0	/3-9,S-4,2-2	-0.4
1962	Hou N	149	534	59	142	18	4	11	59	46-4	8	54	.266	.332	.376	97	-2	4-5	.967	3	95	87	*3-142,S-11/2	0.0
1963	Hou N	136	468	42	100	9	5	8	49	40-4	1	57	.214	.276	.306	72	-18	3-1	.938	-10	90	22	*3-131/1	-3.2
1964	Hou N	157	553	51	155	20	3	12	69	35-7	8	54	.280	.329	.392	109	6	6-7	**.973**	-6	96	43	*3-155	-0.1
1965	Hou N	152	578	53	152	15	2	5	52	38-5	3	54	.263	.310	.322	85	-13	2-2	.962	6	107	106	*3-146/1-6,S-4	-0.9
1966	Hou N	152	560	55	141	16	3	8	52	35-7	2	63	.252	.297	.334	81	-16	0-4	**.962**	-2	94	65	*3-149/1-2,S-2	-2.1
1967	Hou N	137	486	51	143	24	5	6	58	45-11	2	44	.294	.354	.401	121	14	2-2	.963	-6	86	73	*3-133	0.7
1968	Hou N	124	409	25	92	9	2	1	46	35-9	2	57	.225	.285	.264	68	-16	1-0	.973	2	98	55	3-75,O-36(35-0-2)/1S	-1.8
1969	†Atl N	82	198	16	50	8	1	3	24	13-1	2	19	.253	.304	.348	82	-5	0-1	.975	-5	106	88	O-24(LF),3-23,S-18/2-2	-1.1
1970	Atl N	62	127	5	27	3	0	0	7	13-0	0	13	.213	.282	.236	39	-11	0-0	.938	-0	102	112	3-30/S-4,1O(LF)	-1.1
1971	NY N	104	342	21	77	9	1	5	33	29-4	0	25	.225	.285	.301	67	-15	0-2	.965	-6	81	71	3-97	-2.5
Total	13	1324	4369	386	1103	135	26	60	457	333-52	29	459	.252	.308	.336	86	-86	19-24	.960	-26	94	66	*3-1094/O-61L,S-59,1-11,2-5	-13.1
ASSELSTINE, BRIAN Brian Hanly B 9.23.1953 Santa Barbara, CA BL/TR 6-1/175# d9.14																								
1976	Atl N	11	33	2	7	0	0	1	3	1-0	0	2	.212	.229	.303	49	-2	0-0	1.000	-1	91	0	/O-9(0-7-2)	-0.4
1977	Atl N	83	124	12	26	6	0	4	17	9-1	0	10	.210	.263	.355	57	-8	1-0	.983	1	114	64	O-35(9-13-13)	-0.7
1978	Atl N	39	103	11	28	3	3	2	13	11-1	2	16	.272	.339	.417	103	0	2-1	.968	-1	100	47	O-35(0-11-31)	-0.2
1979	Atl N	8	10	1	1	0	0	0	0	1-1	0	2	.100	.182	.100	-20	-2	0-0	1.000	-0	55	0	/O(LF)	-0.2
1980	Atl N	87	218	18	62	13	1	3	25	11-3	1	37	.284	.318	.394	96	-1	1-3	.962	-9	79	0	O-61(29-32-2)	-1.3
1981	Atl N	56	86	8	22	5	0	2	10	5-0	0	7	.256	.297	.384	90	-1	1-0	.958	-0	96	100	O-16(4-0-12)	-0.2
Total	6	284	574	52	146	27	4	12	68	38-6	3	74	.254	.300	.378	83	-14	5-4	.971	-10	92	31	O-157(43-63-60)	-3.0
ASTROTH, JOE Joseph Henry B 9.1.1922 East Alton, IL BR/TR 5-9/187# d8.13																								
1945	Phi A	10	17	1	1	0	0	0	1	0	1	1	.059	.111	.059	-50	-3	0-0	.857	-1	96	137	/C-8	-0.4
1946	Phi A	4	7	0	1	0	0	0	0	0	0	2	.143	.143	.143	-20	-1	0-0	.889	-0	0	209	/C-4	-0.1
1949	Phi A	55	148	18	36	4	1	0	12	21	0	13	.243	.337	.284	67	-7	1-0	.979	0	105	115	C-44	-0.4
1950	Phi A	39	110	11	36	3	1	1	18	18	0	3	.327	.422	.400	113	3	0-0	.985	-5	87	50	C-38	0.0
1951	Phi A	64	187	30	46	10	2	2	19	18	0	13	.246	.312	.353	78	-6	0-1	.992	4	162	67	C-57	0.0
1952	Phi A	104	337	24	84	7	2	1	36	25	2	27	.249	.305	.291	62	-17	2-2	.992	-1	121	84	*C-102	-1.4
1953	Phi A	82	260	28	77	15	2	3	24	27	2	12	.296	.367	.404	104	2	1-0	.987	6	***151***	***130***	C-79	1.2
1954	Phi A	77	226	22	50	8	1	1	23	21	3	19	.221	.296	.279	58	-13	0-0	.988	-3	95	96	C-71	-1.3
1955	KC A	101	274	29	69	4	1	5	23	47-6	6	33	.252	.372	.328	89	-2	2-3	.989	-5	120	82	*C-100	-0.3
1956	KC A	8	13	0	1	0	0	0	0	0-0	0	1	.077	.077	.077	-59	-3	0-0	1.000	1	108	256	/C-8	-0.2
Total	10	544	1579	163	401	51	10	13	156	177-6	14	124	.254	.334	.324	77	-47	6-6	.987	-4	122	94	C-511	-2.9
ATHERTON, CHARLIE Charles Morgan Herbert "Prexy" B 11.19.1874 New Brunswick, NJ D 12.19.1935 Vienna, Austria BR/TR 5-10/160# d5.30																								
1899	Was N	65	242	28	60	5	6	0	23	21	2		.248	.313	.318	74	-9	2	.890	-5	86	69	3-63/O(RF)	-1.2
ATKINS, GARRETT Garrett Bernard B 12.12.1979 Orange, CA BR/TR 6-2/190# d8.3																								
2003	Col N	25	69	6	11	2	0	0	4	3-0	1	14	.159	.205	.188	3	-10	0-0	.850	-5	82	0	3-19	-1.4
ATKINSON, ED Edward B 1851 Baltimore, MD d10.22																								
1873	Was NA	2	8	2	0	0	0	0	0	0		0	.000	.000	.000	-99	-2	0-0	1.000	-0	0	0	/O-2(RF)	-0.1
ATKINSON, LEFTY Hubert Berley B 6.2.1906 Chicago, IL D 2.12.1961 Chicago, IL BL/TL 5-6.5/149# d8.5																								
1927	Was A	1	1	1	0	0	0	0	0	0	0	0	.000	.000	.000	-99	0	0-0	—	0			H	0.0
ATTREAU, DICK Richard Gilbert B 4.8.1897 Chicago, IL D 7.5.1964 Chicago, IL BL/TL 6/160# d9.14																								
1926	Phi N	17	61	9	14	1	1	0	5	6	0	5	.230	.299	.279	53	-4	0	.989	-2	62	77	1-17	-0.7
1927	Phi N	44	83	17	17	1	1	1	11	14	0	18	.205	.320	.277	60	-4	1	.989	-1	70	78	1-26	-0.7
Total	2	61	144	26	31	2	2	1	16	20	0	23	.215	.311	.278	57	-8	1	.989	-3	66	78	/1-43	-1.4
ATWELL, TOBY Maurice Dailey B 3.8.1924 Leesburg, VA D 1.25.2003 Purcellville, VA BL/TR 5-9.5/185# d4.15																								
1952	Chi N☆	107	362	36	105	16	3	2	31	40	1	22	.290	.362	.367	102	2	2-1	.977	-9	58	81	*C-101	-0.1
1953	Chi N	24	74	10	17	2	0	1	8	13	0	7	.230	.345	.297	68	-3	0-0	.940	-1	90	165	C-24	-0.3
	Pit N	53	139	11	34	6	0	0	17	20	3	12	.245	.352	.288	70	-5	0-0	.967	-4	69	108	C-45	-0.7
	Year	77	213	21	51	8	0	1	25	33	3	19	.239	.349	.291	69	-8	0-0	.957	-5	77	129	C-69	-1.0
1954	Pit N	96	287	36	83	8	4	3	26	43	3	21	.289	.384	.376	101	2	2-3	.990	-5	56	109	C-88	0.1
1955	Pit N	71	207	21	44	8	0	1	18	40-9	1	16	.213	.337	.266	65	-8	0-1	.992	1	79	91	C-67	-0.4
1956	Pit N	12	18	0	2	0	0	0	3	1-0	0	5	.111	.158	.111	-27	-3	0-0	1.000	1	154	109	/C-9	-0.2
	Mil N	15	30	2	5	1	0	2	7	4-1	0	1	.167	.265	.400	80	-1	0-0	1.000	-0	115	135	C-10	-0.1
	Year	27	48	2	7	1	0	2	10	5-1	0	6	.146	.226	.292	40	-4	0-0	1.000	1	131	125	C-19	-0.3
Total	5	378	1117	116	290	41	7	9	110	161-10	8	84	.260	.355	.333	86	-16	4-5	.980	-16	68	102	C-344	-1.7
ATWOOD, BILL William Franklin B 9.25.1911 Rome, GA D 9.14.1993 Snyder, TX BR/TR 5-11.5/190# d4.15																								
1936	Phi N	71	192	21	58	9	2	2	29	11	2	15	.302	.346	.401	92	-2	0	.972	-1	99	77	C-53	0.0
1937	Phi N	87	279	27	68	15	1	2	32	30	0	27	.244	.317	.326	69	-11	3	.968	-9	137	93	C-80	-1.6
1938	Phi N	102	281	27	55	8	1	3	28	25	0	26	.196	.261	.263	46	-21	0	.969	-7	58	***125***	C-94	-2.3
1939	Phi N	4	6	0	0	0	0	0	0	1	0	3	.000	.250	.000	-29	-1	1	1.000	-0	50	0	/C-2	-0.1
1940	Phi N	78	203	7	39	9	0	0	22	25	1	18	.192	.284	.236	47	-14	0	.989	0	91	105	C-69	-1.0
Total	5	342	961	82	220	41	4	7	112	93	3	89	.229	.299	.302	63	-49	4	.974	-17	95	102	C-298	-5.0
ATZ, JAKE John Jacob (born Jacob Henry Atz) B 7.1.1879 Washington, DC D 5.22.1945 New Orleans, LA BR/TR 5-9/150# d9.24																								
1902	Was A	3	10	1	1	0	0	0	0	0	0		.100	.100	.100	-44	-2	0	1.000	1	147	93	/2-3	-0.1
1907	Chi A	4	8	0	1	0	0	0	0	0	0		.125	.125	.125	-21	-1	0	1.000	1	177	469	/3-2,O(CF)	0.0
1908	Chi A	83	206	24	40	3	0	0	27	31	4		.194	.311	.209	71	-4	9	.936	-1	104	103	2-46,S-18/3	-0.6
1909	Chi A	119	381	39	90	18	3	0	22	38	2		.236	.309	.299	96	-1	14	.954	-5	99	115	*2-114/O-3(RF),S	-0.5
Total	4	209	605	64	132	21	3	0	49	69	6		.218	.304	.263	83	-8	23	.949	-5	101	111	2-163/S-19,O-4(0-1-3),3-3	-1.2
AUBREY, HARRY Harry Herbert "Chub" B 7.5.1880 St.Joseph, MO D 9.18.1953 Baltimore, MD BR/TR d4.22																								
1903	Bos N	96	325	26	69	8	2	0	27	18	5		.212	.264	.249	49	-22	7	.868	-12	99	56	S-94/2O(LF)	-3.1

Year	Tm Lg	G	AB	R	H	2B	3B	HR	RBI	BB-IB	HP	SO	AVG	OBP	SLG	AOPS	ABR	SB-CS	FA	FR	Rng	Thr	G at Pos	BFW
AUDE, RICH Richard Thomas B 7.13.1971 Van Nuys, CA BR/TR 6-5/180# d9.9																								
1993	Pit N	13	26	1	3	1	0	0	4	1-0	0	7	.115	.148	.154	-19	-4	0-0	1.000	-1	78	132	/1-7,O(LF)	-0.6
1995	Pit N	42	109	10	27	8	0	2	19	6-0	0	20	.248	.287	.376	72	-5	1-2	.996	-3	60	127	1-32	-1.0
1996	Pit N	7	16	0	4	0	0	0	1	0-0	0	8	.250	.250	.250	32	-2	0-0	.969	0	139	114	/1-4	-0.2
Total	3	62	151	11	34	9	0	2	24	7-0	0	35	.225	.259	.325	52	-11	1-2	.994	-3	70	127	/1-43,O(LF)	-1.8
AUERBACH, RICK Frederick Steven B 2.15.1950 Woodland Hills, CA BR/TR 6/165# d4.13																								
1971	Mil A	79	236	22	48	10	0	1	9	20-1	2	40	.203	.271	.258	51	-15	3-2	.963	-11	91	72	S-78	-1.9
1972	Mil A	153	554	50	121	16	3	2	30	43-5	2	62	.218	.277	.269	64	-25	24-8	.959	-17	96	97	*S-153	-2.5
1973	Mil A	6	10	2	1	1	0	0	0	0-0	0	1	.100	.100	.200	-18	-2	0-1	.833	-1	87	0	/S-2	-0.3
1974	†LA N	45	73	12	25	0	0	1	4	8-0	0	9	.342	.407	.384	127	3	4-2	.950	-2	86	84	S-19,2-16/3-3	0.3
1975	LA N	85	170	18	38	9	0	0	12	18-3	0	22	.224	.298	.276	63	-8	3-2	.960	-20	77	62	S-81/23	-2.3
1976	LA N	36	47	7	6	0	0	0	1	6-0	0	6	.128	.226	.128	2	-6	0-1	.943	1	89	154	S-12/3-8,2-7	-0.4
1977	Cin N	33	45	5	7	2	0	0	3	4-0	0	7	.156	.216	.200	15	-5	0-0	.976	0	98	84	2-19,S-12	-0.4
1978	Cin N	63	55	17	18	6	0	2	5	7-0	1	12	.327	.413	.545	166	5	1-0	.971	-0	102	103	S-26,2-10/3-3	0.7
1979	†Cin N	62	100	17	21	8	1	1	12	14-1	0	19	.210	.304	.340	76	-3	0-1	.933	-3	112	95	3-18,S-16/2-3	-0.5
1980	Cin N	24	33	5	11	1	1	1	4	3-0	0	5	.333	.389	.515	150	2	0-3	1.000	0	167	85	/S-3,3-3,2	0.2
1981	Sea A	38	84	12	13	3	0	1	6	4-0	1	15	.155	.200	.226	22	-9	1-1	.979	2	106	128	S-38	-0.4
Total	11	624	1407	167	309	56	5	9	86	127-10	6	198	.220	.286	.286	65	-63	36-21	.960	-51	93	89	S-440/2-57,3-36	-7.5
AUGUSTINE, DAVE David Ralph B 11.28.1949 Follansbee, WV BR/TR 6-2/174# d9.3																								
1973	Pit N	11	7	1	2	1	0	0	0	0-0	0	1	.286	.286	.429	98	0	0-0	1.000	0	72	578	/O-9(4-4-1)	0.0
1974	Pit N	18	22	3	4	0	0	0	0	0-0	0	5	.182	.182	.182	2	-3	0-1	1.000	3	132	483	O-11(1-6-4)	-0.1
Total	2	29	29	4	6	1	0	0	0	0-0	0	6	.207	.207	.241	26	-3	0-1	1.000	3	115	511	/O-20(5-10-5)	-0.1
AULDS, LESLIE Leycester Doyle "Tex" B 12.28.1920 Farmerville, LA D 10.13.1999 Hondo, TX BR/TR 6-2/185# d5.25																								
1947	Bos A	3	4	0	1	0	0	0	0	0	0	1	.250	.250	.250	37	0	0-0	1.000	0	*0*	*0*	/C-3	0.0
AULT, DOUG Douglas Reagan B 3.9.1950 Beaumont, TX BR/TL 6-3/200# d9.9																								
1976	Tex A	9	20	0	6	1	0	0	0	1-0	0	3	.300	.333	.350	98	0	0-0	1.000	-1	0	57	/1-4,D-3	-0.1
1977	Tor A	129	445	44	109	22	3	11	64	39-5	4	68	.245	.310	.382	87	-8	4-4	.987	6	**120**	82	*1-122/D-4	-1.0
1978	Tor A	54	104	10	25	1	1	3	7	17-1	1	14	.240	.352	.356	98	0	0-0	.979	-2	81	78	1-25/O-7(6-0-1),D-5	-0.3
1980	Tor A	64	144	12	28	5	1	3	15	14-0	2	23	.194	.273	.306	56	-9	0-1	1.000	2	135	100	1-32,D-21/O(LF)	-0.9
Total	4	256	713	66	168	29	5	17	86	71-6	7	108	.236	.309	.362	82	-17	4-5	.988	6	116	84	1-183/D-33,O-8(7-0-1)	-2.3
AURILIA, RICH Richard Santo B 9.2.1971 Brooklyn, NY BR/TR 6/170# d9.6																								
1995	SF N	9	19	4	9	3	0	2	4	1-0	0	2	.474	.476	.947	280	5	1-0	1.000	2	135	165	/S-6	0.7
1996	SF N	105	318	27	76	7	1	3	26	25-2	1	52	.239	.295	.296	59	-19	4-1	.973	-7	97	87	S-93,2-11	-1.9
1997	SF N	46	102	16	28	8	0	5	19	8-0	0	15	.275	.321	.500	116	2	1-1	.979	8	119	122	S-36	1.1
1998	SF N	122	413	54	110	27	2	9	49	31-3	2	62	.266	.319	.407	95	-4	3-3	.979	2	102	114	*S-120	0.6
1999	SF N	152	558	68	157	23	1	22	80	43-3	5	71	.281	.336	.444	103	1	2-3	.957	-3	99	108	*S-150	0.8
2000	†SF N	141	509	67	138	24	2	20	79	54-2	0	90	.271	.339	.444	104	2	1-2	.967	10	103	**130**	*S-140	2.1
2001	SF N★	156	636	114	**206**	37	5	37	97	47-2	0	83	.324	.369	.572	150	44	1-3	.975	-4	97	116	*S-149	4.9
2002	†SF N	133	538	76	138	35	2	15	61	37-0	4	90	.257	.305	.413	95	-8	1-2	**.980**	-10	90	**123**	*S-131	-0.9
2003	†SF N	129	505	65	140	26	1	13	58	36-0	1	82	.277	.325	.410	93	-6	2-2	.974	-19	89	109	*S-123/D	-1.5
Total	9	993	3598	491	1002	190	14	126	473	282-12	13	547	.278	.331	.444	105	17	16-17	.972	-21	98	115	S-948/2-11,D	5.9
AUSMUS, BRAD Bradley David B 4.14.1969 New Haven, CT BR/TR 5-11/195# d7.28																								
1993	SD N	49	160	18	41	8	1	5	12	6-0	0	28	.256	.283	.412	82	-5	2-0	.975	2	112	119	C-49	0.1
1994	SD N	101	327	45	82	12	1	7	24	30-12	1	63	.251	.314	.358	77	-11	5-1	.991	-3	92	104	C-99/1	-0.7
1995	SD N	103	328	44	96	16	4	5	34	31-3	2	56	.293	.353	.412	106	3	16-5	.992	5	134	127	*C-100/1	1.5
1996	SD N	50	149	16	27	4	0	1	13	13-0	3	27	.181	.261	.228	32	-15	1-4	.982	-3	104	116	C-46	-1.6
	Det A	75	226	30	56	12	0	4	22	26-1	2	45	.248	.328	.354	73	-9	3-4	.992	-2	92	130	C-73	-0.7
1997	†Hou N	130	425	45	113	25	1	4	44	38-4	3	78	.266	.326	.358	83	-10	14-6	.992	13	**187**	112	*C-129	1.2
1998	†Hou N	128	412	62	111	10	4	6	45	53-11	3	60	.269	.356	.357	91	-5	10-3	.992	5	128	91	*C-124	0.9
1999	Det A★	127	458	62	126	25	6	9	54	51-0	14	71	.275	.365	.415	98	0	12-9	**.998**	-3	133	94	*C-127	0.4
2000	Det A	150	523	75	139	25	3	7	51	69-0	6	79	.266	.357	.365	86	-9	11-5	.992	20	196	106	*C-150/123	1.9
2001	†Hou N	128	422	45	98	23	4	5	34	30-6	1	64	.232	.284	.341	58	-27	4-1	**.997**	15	151	124	*C-127	-0.4
2002	Hou N	130	447	57	115	19	3	6	50	38-3	6	71	.257	.322	.353	78	-16	2-3	.997	8	110	92	*C-129	-0.1
2003	Hou N	143	450	43	103	12	2	4	47	46-1	4	66	.229	.303	.291	54	-30	5-3	.997	25	97	124	*C-143	0.4
Total	11	1314	4327	542	1107	191	29	63	430	431-41	45	708	.256	.328	.357	79	-134	85-44	.993	82	133	110	*C-1296/1-3,32	2.9
AUSTIN, HENRY Henry C. B 1844 Brooklyn, NY D 9.3.1895 Amityville, NY d4.28																								
1873	Res NA	**23**	101	10	25	3	3	0	11	0		5	.248	.248	.337	78	-2	1-1	.722	-1	114	251	O-23(0-14-9)	-0.2
AUSTIN, JIMMY James Philip "Pepper" B 12.8.1879 Swansea, Wales D 3.6.1965 Laguna Beach, CA BB/TR 5-7.5/155# d4.19 M3 C18																								
1909	NY A	136	437	37	101	11	5	1	39	32	1		.231	.285	.286	80	-11	30	.928	13	105	**134**	*3-111,S-23/2	0.7
1910	NY A	133	432	46	94	11	4	2	36	47	7		.218	.305	.275	77	-10	22	.942	3	98	54	*3-133	-0.4
1911	StL A	148	541	84	141	25	11	2	45	69	6		.261	.351	.359	102	3	26	.931	19	**116**	123	*3-148	2.5
1912	StL A	149	536	57	135	14	8	2	44	38	4		.252	.306	.319	82	-14	28	.911	2	98	104	*3-149	-0.9
1913	StL A	142	489	56	130	18	6	2	42	45	8	51	.266	.338	.339	101	1	37	**.944**	6	104	101	*3-142,M	1.2
1914	StL A	130	466	55	111	16	4	0	30	40	1	59	.238	.300	.290	80	-12	20-23	.935	-1	99	98	*3-127	-1.4
1915	StL A	141	477	61	127	6	6	1	30	64	2	60	.266	.355	.310	103	4	18-15	.917	10	104	**143**	*3-141	1.7
1916	StL A	129	411	55	85	15	6	1	28	74	4	59	.207	.333	.280	89	-2	19	.939	-8	102	91	*3-124	-0.8
1917	StL A	127	455	61	109	18	8	0	19	50	3	46	.240	.319	.314	97	-1	13	.947	7	102	118	*3-121/S-6	1.0
1918	StL A	110	367	42	97	14	4	0	20	53	1	32	.264	.359	.324	109	6	18	.939	-15	88	59	S-57,3-48,M	-0.4
1919	StL A	106	396	54	94	9	9	1	21	42	2	31	.237	.314	.313	74	-14	8	.939	6	101	95	3-98	-0.5
1920	StL A	83	280	38	76	11	3	1	32	31	4	15	.271	.352	.343	82	-6	2-4	.943	0	96	106	3-75	-0.5
1921	StL A	27	66	8	18	2	1	0	2	4	1	7	.273	.324	.333	64	-4	2-1	.938	-2	87	0	S-14/2-6,3-2	-0.4
1922	StL A	15	31	6	9	3	1	0	1	3	0	2	.290	.353	.452	105	0	0-0	.957	-2	62	0	/3-9,2-2	-0.1
1923	StL A	1	0	0	0	0	0	0	0	0	0	0	—	—	—	—	0	0-0	—	0			/RM	0.0
1925	StL A	1	1	0	0	0	0	0	0	0	0	0	.000	.000	.000	-95	0	0-0	1.000	-0	0	0	/3	0.0
1926	StL A	1	2	1	1	1	0	0	1	0	0	0	.500	.500	1.000	272	1	1-0	1.000	0	80	955	/3	0.1
1929	StL A	1	1	0	0	0	0	0	0	0	0	1	.000	.000	.000	-96	0	0-0	1.000	0	236	0	/3	0.0
Total	18	1580	5388	661	1328	174	76	13	390	592	44	363	.246	.326	.314	90	-59	244-43	.933	38	102	105	*3-1431,S-100/2-9	1.8
AUTRY, CHICK Martin Gordon B 3.5.1903 Martindale, TX D 1.26.1950 Savannah, GA BR/TR 6/180# d4.20																								
1924	NY A	2	0	1	0	0	0	0	0	0	1	0	—	1.000	—	172	0	0-0	1.000	-0	*0*	*0*	/C-2	0.0
1926	Cle A	3	7	1	1	0	0	0	0	1	0	0	.143	.250	.143	4	-1	0-0	1.000	-0	*97*	*130*	/C-3	-0.1
1927	Cle A	16	43	5	11	4	1	0	7	0	0	6	.256	.256	.395	66	-2	0-0	.933	1	*133*	*167*	C-14	0.0
1928	Cle A	22	60	6	18	6	1	1	9	1	0	7	.300	.311	.483	105	0	0-0	.972	0	*100*	*64*	C-18	0.1
1929	Chi A	43	96	7	20	6	0	1	12	1	1	8	.208	.224	.302	35	-10	0-0	.940	-3	*98*	*78*	C-30	-1.1
1930	Chi A	34	71	1	18	1	1	0	5	4	0	8	.254	.293	.296	52	-5	0-0	.992	4	*108*	*139*	C-29	0.0
Total	6	120	277	21	68	17	3	2	33	7	2	29	.245	.269	.350	59	-18	0-0	.965	2	*107*	*109*	/C-96	-1.1
AUTRY, CHICK William Askew B 1.2.1885 Humboldt, TN D 1.16.1976 Santa Rosa, CA BL/TL 5-11/168# d9.18																								
1907	Cin N	7	25	3	5	0	0	0	0	1	0		.200	.231	.200	34	-2	0	.929	-1	0	0	/O-7(4-3-0)	-0.4
1909	Cin N	9	33	3	6	2	0	0	4	2	0		.182	.229	.242	46	-2	1	.956	0	152	71	/1-9	-0.2
	Bos N	65	199	16	39	4	0	0	13	21	2		.196	.279	.216	51	-11	5	.994	4	125	88	1-61/O-4(4-1-0)	-0.9
	Year	74	232	19	45	6	0	0	17	23	2		.194	.272	.220	51	-13	6	.989	5	129	86	1-70/O-4(4-1-0)	-1.1
Total	2	81	257	22	50	6	0	0	17	24	2		.195	.269	.218	49	-15	6	.989	4	129	86	/1-70,O-11(8-4-0)	-1.5
AVEN, BRUCE David Bruce B 3.4.1972 Orange, TX BR/TR 5-9/180# d8.27																								
1997	Cle A	13	19	4	4	1	0	0	2	1-0	0	5	.211	.250	.263	33	-2	0-1	1.000	1	125	268	O-13(10-1-2)	-0.1
1999	Fla N	137	381	57	110	19	2	12	70	44-1	9	82	.289	.370	.444	113	8	3-0	.984	1	103	73	*O-102(78-9-24)/D-6	0.7
2000	Pit N	72	148	18	37	11	0	5	25	5-0	0	31	.250	.275	.426	74	-7	2-3	.980	-3	87	0	O-41(17-8-20)	-1.0
	LA N	9	20	2	5	0	0	2	4	3-0	0	8	.250	.348	.550	130	1	0-0	1.000	-0	93	0	/O-9(LF)	0.0

Year	Tm Lg	G	AB	R	H	2B	3B	HR	RBI	BB-IB	HP	SO	AVG	OBP	SLG	AOPS	ABR	SB-CS	FA	FR	Rng	Thr	G at Pos	BFW
	Year	81	168	20	42	11	0	7	29	8-0	0	39	.250	.284	.440	80	-6	2-3	.984	-3	88	0	O-50(26-8-20)	-1.0
2001	LA N	21	24	3	8	2	0	1	2	0-0	2	5	.333	.385	.542	147	2	0-0	1.000	-0	78	0	/O-9(5-0-4)	0.1
2002	Cle A	7	17	1	2	0	0	0	0	4-0	0	4	.118	.286	.118	13	-2	1-0	1.000	-0	106	0	/O-7(5-1-1)	-0.2
Total	5	259	609	85	166	33	2	20	103	57-1	11	135	.273	.343	.432	100	0	6-4	.986	-1	100	58	O-181(124-19-51)/D-6	-0.5
AVERILL, EARL Earl Douglas B 9.9.1931 Cleveland, OH BR/TR 5-10/190# d4.19 f-Earl																								
1956	Cle A	42	93	12	22	6	0	3	14	14-1	1	25	.237	.343	.398	93	-1	0-1	.994	2	83	131	C-34	0.3
1958	Cle A	17	55	2	10	1	0	2	7	4-0	1	7	.182	.250	.309	54	-4	1-0	.863	-1	109	94	3-17	-0.5
1959	Chi N	74	186	22	44	10	0	10	34	15-1	2	39	.237	.298	.452	98	-1	0-1	.963	-3	58	70	C-32,3-13/O-5(LF),2-2	-0.3
1960	Chi N	52	102	14	24	4	0	1	13	11-1	1	16	.235	.310	.304	71	-4	1-1	.979	-7	63	64	C-34/3O(LF)	-1.0
	Chi A	10	14	2	3	0	0	0	2	4-0	0	2	.214	.389	.214	68	0	0-0	1.000	1	108	149	/C-5	0.1
1961	LA A	115	323	56	86	9	0	21	59	62-1	2	70	.266	.384	.489	119	10	1-0	.991	-4	75	91	C-88/O-9(LF),2	1.0
1962	LA A	92	187	21	41	9	0	4	22	43-3	1	47	.219	.366	.332	93	0	0-0	1.000	-1	88	86	O-49(LF)/C-6	-0.2
1963	Phi N	47	71	8	19	2	0	3	8	9-1	0	14	.268	.341	.423	123	2	0-0	.966	-0	94	147	C-20/O-8(LF),13	0.3
Total	7	449	1031	137	249	41	0	44	159	162-8	8	220	.242	.346	.409	101	2	3-3	.984	-13	74	98	C-219/O-72(LF),3-32,2-3,1	-0.3
AVERILL, EARL Howard Earl "Rock" B 5.21.1902 Snohomish, WA D 8.16.1983 Everett, WA BL/TR 5-9.5/172# d4.16 HF1975 s-Earl																								
1929	Cle A	**152**	597	110	198	43	13	18	96	63	3	53	.332	.398	.538	134	30	13-14	.966	-11	89	85	*O-152(CF)	1.0
1930	Cle A	139	534	102	181	33	8	19	119	56	2	48	.339	.404	.537	131	26	10-7	.949	-4	94	111	*O-134(0-132-2)	1.4
1931	Cle A	**155**	627	140	209	36	10	32	143	68	6	38	.333	.404	.576	147	41	9-9	.976	-4	98	76	*O-155(CF)	3.0
1932	Cle A	**153**	631	116	198	37	14	32	124	75	**6**	40	.314	.392	.569	137	33	5-8	.964	-7	94	90	*O-153(CF)	1.8
1933	Cle A★	**151**	599	83	180	39	16	11	92	54	5	29	.301	.363	.474	115	12	3-1	.971	-4	100	74	*O-149(CF)	0.4
1934	Cle A★	**154**	598	128	187	48	6	31	113	99	4	44	.313	.414	.569	149	46	5-3	.970	3	104	98	*O-154(CF)	4.1
1935	Cle A✳	140	563	109	162	34	13	19	79	70	1	58	.288	.368	.496	119	15	8-4	.982	-7	96	55	*O-139(CF)	0.5
1936	Cle A★	152	614	136	**232**	39	**15**	28	126	65	1	35	.378	.438	.627	159	55	3-3	.969	-7	93	86	*O-150(CF)	3.8
1937	Cle A★	**156**	609	121	182	33	11	21	92	88	0	65	.299	.387	.493	119	18	5-4	.976	-12	88	77	*O-156(CF)	0.2
1938	Cle A★	134	482	101	159	27	15	14	93	81	3	48	.330	.429	.535	143	34	5-2	.975	1	98	115	*O-131(0-118-13)	2.8
1939	Cle A	24	55	8	15	8	0	1	7	6	0	12	.273	.344	.473	111	1	0-1	1.000	-1	72	0	O-11(RF)	-0.1
	Det A	87	309	58	81	20	6	10	58	43	1	30	.262	.354	.463	100	-1	4-2	.976	-3	94	59	O-80(75-5-0)	-0.7
	Year	111	364	66	96	28	6	11	65	49	1	42	.264	.353	.464	102	1	4-3	.977	-5	92	53	O-91(75-5-11)	-0.8
1940	†Det A	64	118	10	33	4	1	2	20	5	0	14	.280	.309	.381	71	-5	0-0	.962	-1	69	190	O-22(7-11-5)	-0.7
1941	Bos N	8	17	2	2	0	0	0	2	1	1	4	.118	.211	.118	-6	-2	0	1.000	1	70	879	/O-4(1-3-0)	-0.2
Total	13	1669	6353	1224	2019	401	128	238	1164	774	33	518	.318	.395	.534	132	303	70-58	.970	-57	95	87	*O-1590(83-1477-31)	17.3
AVILA, BOBBY Roberto Francisco (Gonzales) B 4.2.1924 Veracruz, Mexico BR/TR 5-10/175# d4.30																								
1949	Cle A	31	14	3	3	0	0	0	3	1	0	3	.214	.267	.214	29	-1	0-0	1.000	2	187	110	/2-5	0.0
1950	Cle A	80	201	39	60	10	2	1	21	29	1	17	.299	.390	.383	102	2	5-0	.983	-9	80	108	2-62/S-2	-0.3
1951	Cle A	141	542	76	165	21	3	10	58	60	0	31	.304	.374	.410	118	14	14-8	.982	-3	97	88	*2-136	1.9
1952	Cle A★	150	597	102	179	26	**11**	7	45	67	1	36	.300	.371	.415	127	21	12-10	.966	-23	94	76	*2-149	0.6
1953	Cle A	141	559	85	160	22	3	8	55	58	2	27	.286	.355	.379	101	1	10-8	**.986**	13	**107**	108	*2-140	2.3
1954	†Cle A★	143	555	112	189	27	2	15	67	59	1	31	**.341**	.402	.477	139	30	9-7	.976	7	**106**	**114**	*2-141/S-7	4.8
1955	Cle A★	141	537	83	146	22	4	13	61	82-1	2	47	.272	.368	.400	103	5	1-4	.982	-2	91	107	*2-141	1.2
1956	Cle A	138	513	74	115	14	2	10	54	70-0	5	68	.224	.323	.318	68	-23	17-4	.977	-2	97	91	*2-135	-1.3
1957	Cle A	129	463	60	124	19	3	5	48	46-2	1	47	.268	.334	.354	89	-6	2-4	.983	-10	90	85	*2-107,3-16	-1.0
1958	Cle A	113	375	54	95	21	3	5	30	55-0	1	45	.253	.349	.365	100	2	5-7	.986	-10	90	103	2-82,3-33	-0.5
1959	Bal A	20	47	1	8	0	0	0	0	4-0	0	5	.170	.235	.170	14	-6	0-0	1.000	-2	85	0	O-10(1-0-9)/2-8,3	-0.8
	Bos A	22	45	7	11	0	0	3	6	6-0	0	11	.244	.333	.444	107	0	0-0	.975	-1	89	135	2-11	0.0
	Year	42	92	8	19	0	0	3	6	10-0	0	16	.207	.284	.304	61	-5	0-0	.967	-2	90	116	2-19,O-10(1-0-9)/3	-0.8
	Mil N	51	172	29	41	3	2	3	19	24-0	0	31	.238	.330	.331	84	-4	3-0	.967	-9	96	70	2-51	-0.8
Total	11	1300	4620	725	1296	185	35	80	467	561-3	14	399	.281	.359	.388	104	35	78-52	.979	-48	96	96	*2-1168/3-50,O-10(1-0-9),S-9	6.1
AVILES, RAMON Ramon Antonio (Miranda) B 1.22.1952 Manati, P.R. BR/TR 5-9/155# d7.10																								
1977	Bos A	1	0	0	0	0	0	0	0	0-0	0	0	—	—	—	—	0	0-0	1.000	0	137	0	/2	0.0
1979	Phi N	27	61	7	17	2	0	0	12	8-1	1	8	.279	.371	.311	86	-1	0-0	.977	-6	80	66	2-27	-0.6
1980	†Phi N	51	101	12	28	6	0	2	9	10-2	0	9	.277	.336	.396	100	0	0-0	.944	-6	87	112	S-29,2-15	-0.4
1981	†Phi N	38	28	2	6	1	0	0	3	3-0	0	5	.214	.290	.250	52	-2	0-0	1.000	1	118	90	2-20,3-13/S-5	-0.1
Total	4	117	190	21	51	9	0	2	24	21-3	1	22	.268	.341	.347	88	-3	0-0	.971	-12	83	89	/2-63,S-34,3-13	-1.1
AYALA, BENNY Benigno (Felix) B 2.7.1951 Yauco, P.R. BR/TR 6-1/185# d8.27																								
1974	NY N	23	68	9	16	1	0	2	8	7-0	1	17	.235	.308	.338	84	-2	0-0	.927	-0	105	76	O-20(18-0-2)	-0.3
1976	NY N	22	26	2	3	0	0	1	2	2-0	0	6	.115	.179	.231	16	-3	0-1	.889	1	111	410	/O-7(4-0-3)	-0.3
1977	StL N	1	3	0	1	0	0	0	0	0-0	0	1	.333	.333	.333	81	0	0-0	1.000	2	329	1378	/O(RF)	0.2
1979	†Bal A	42	86	15	22	5	0	6	13	6-1	0	9	.256	.298	.523	123	2	0-0	.974	-0	116	0	O-24(23-1-1),D-10	0.1
1980	Bal A	76	170	28	45	8	1	10	33	19-3	0	21	.265	.335	.500	128	6	0-0	1.000	0	79	221	D-41,O-19(16-1-2)	0.4
1981	Bal A	44	86	12	24	2	0	3	13	11-0	1	9	.279	.364	.407	123	3	0-1	1.000	2	109	2196	D-27/O-4(LF)	0.3
1982	Bal A	64	128	17	39	6	0	6	24	5-2	0	14	.305	.331	.492	123	3	1-1	.972	-1	103	0	O-25(LF),D-17/1-3	0.1
1983	†Bal A	47	104	12	23	7	0	4	13	9-0	0	18	.221	.278	.404	88	-2	0-0	.953	-1	101	0	O-24(19-0-5),D-11	-0.4
1984	Bal A	60	118	9	25	6	0	4	24	8-0	0	24	.212	.258	.364	73	-5	1-1	1.000	-1	74	0	D-34,O-13(11-0-2)	-0.7
1985	Cle A	46	76	10	19	7	0	2	15	4-1	0	17	.250	.284	.421	92	-1	0-0	.917	-1	86	132	O-20(LF)/D-3	-0.2
Total	10	425	865	114	217	42	1	38	145	71-7	2	136	.251	.305	.434	104	1	2-4	.958	-1	101	106	O-157(140-2-16),D-143/1-3	-0.8
AYLWARD, DICK Richard John "Dandy" B 6.4.1925 Baltimore, MD D 6.11.1983 Spring Valley, CA BR/TR 6/190# d5.1																								
1953	Cle A	4	3	0	0	0	0	0	0	0	0	1	.000	.000	.000	-99	-1	0-0	1.000	0	0	0	/C-4	-0.1
AYRAULT, JOE Joseph Allen B 10.8.1971 Rochester, MI BR/TR 6-3/190# d9.1																								
1996	Atl N	7	5	0	1	0	0	0	0	0-0	1	1	.200	.333	.200	43	0	0-0	1.000	-0	0	0	/C-7	-0.1
AZCUE, JOE Jose Joaquin (Lopez) B 8.18.1939 Cienfuegos, Cuba BR/TR 6/200# d8.3																								
1960	Cin N	14	31	1	3	0	0	0	3	2-0	0	6	.097	.152	.097	-30	-6	0-1	1.000	3	132	118	C-14	-0.3
1962	KC A	72	223	18	51	9	1	2	25	17-7	3	27	.229	.287	.305	58	-13	1-0	.985	2	84	119	C-70	-0.8
1963	KC A	2	4	0	0	0	0	0	0	0-0	0	1	.000	.000	.000	-95	-1	0-0	1.000	0	0	0	/C	-0.1
	Cle A	94	320	26	91	16	0	14	46	15-1	0	46	.284	.314	.466	117	6	1-1	.992	6	112	137	C-91	1.7
	Year	96	324	26	91	16	0	14	46	15-1	0	47	.281	.310	.460	114	5	1-1	**.992**	6	111	**136**	C-92	1.6
1964	Cle A	83	271	20	74	9	1	4	34	16-2	2	38	.273	.314	.358	88	-5	0-2	.993	-2	87	128	C-76	-0.4
1965	Cle A	111	335	16	77	7	0	2	35	27-8	3	54	.230	.290	.269	60	-17	2-1	.994	3	126	103	*C-108	-0.9
1966	Cle A	98	302	22	83	10	1	9	37	20-5	2	22	.275	.319	.404	108	3	0-2	.989	-3	**149**	106	C-97	0.4
1967	Cle A	86	295	33	74	12	5	11	34	22-0	3	35	.251	.307	.437	117	5	0-3	**.999**	8	**184**	93	C-86	1.8
1968	Cle A★	115	357	23	100	10	0	4	42	28-5	0	33	.280	.331	.342	106	3	1-1	**.996**	14	**177**	92	C-97	2.4
1969	Cle A	7	24	1	7	0	0	1	1	4-0	0	3	.292	.393	.417	122	1	0-0	.980	1	118	100	/C-6	0.2
	Bos A	19	51	7	11	2	0	0	3	4-1	0	5	.216	.273	.255	46	-4	0-0	.981	3	205	114	C-19	0.0
	Cal A	80	248	15	54	6	0	1	19	27-11	2	28	.218	.295	.254	59	-13	0-1	.992	9	128	111	C-80	-0.1
	Year	106	323	23	72	8	0	2	23	35-12	2	36	.223	.299	.266	62	-16	0-1	.989	13	139	111	*C-105	0.1
1970	Cal A	114	351	19	85	13	1	2	25	24-4	2	40	.242	.292	.302	67	-16	0-0	.991	-4	105	81	*C-112	-1.6
1972	Cal A	3	2	0	0	0	0	0	0	0-0	0	1	.000	.000	.000	-99	-1	0-0	1.000	1	0	0	/C-2	0.0
	Mil A	11	14	0	2	0	0	0	0	1-1	0	5	.143	.200	.143	3	-2	0-0	1.000	1	98	250	/C-9	-0.1
	Year	14	16	0	2	0	0	0	0	1-1	0	6	.125	.176	.125	-10	-2	0-0	1.000	1	93	238	C-11	-0.1
Total	11	909	2828	201	712	94	9	50	304	207-45	17	344	.252	.304	.344	85	-60	5-12	.992	42	131	107	C-868	2.2
AZOCAR, OSCAR Oscar Gregorio (Azocar) B 2.21.1965 Soro, Venezuela BL/TL 6-1/170# d7.17																								
1990	NY A	65	214	18	53	8	0	5	19	2-0	1	15	.248	.257	.355	70	-10	7-0	.991	1	99	117	O-57(47-0-12)/D	-0.9
1991	SD N	38	57	5	14	2	0	0	9	1-1	1	9	.246	.267	.281	54	-4	2-0	.875	-1	84	0	O-13(12-0-1)/1	-0.5
1992	SD N	99	168	15	32	6	0	0	8	9-1	0	12	.190	.230	.226	30	-16	1-0	.942	0	111	68	O-37(31-0-6)	-1.8
Total	3	202	439	38	99	16	0	5	36	12-2	2	36	.226	.248	.296	52	-30	10-0	.964	-0	102	90	O-107(90-0-19)/1D	-3.2
BABB, CHARLIE Charles Amos B 2.20.1873 Milwaukie, OR D 3.20.1954 Portland, OR BB/TR 5-10/165# d4.17																								
1903	NY N	121	424	68	105	15	8	0	46	45	**22**		.248	.350	.321	88	-4	22	.912	-7	93	93	*S-113/3-8	-0.7

Year	Tm Lg	G	AB	R	H	2B	3B	HR	RBI	BB-IB	HP	SO	AVG	OBP	SLG	AOPS	ABR	SB-CS	FA	FR	Rng	Thr	G at Pos	BFW
1904	Bro N	151	521	49	138	18	3	0	53	53	11		.265	.345	.311	106	7	34	.927	-2	97	81	*S-151	1.0
1905	Bro N	75	235	27	44	8	2	0	17	27	12		.187	.303	.238	67	-7	10	.923	-3	104	51	S-36,1-31/3-5,2-2	-1.0
Total	3	347	1180	144	287	41	13	0	116	125	45		.243	.339	.300	92	-4	66	.921	-12	96	82	S-300/1-31,3-13,2-2	-0.7

BABE, LOREN Loren Rolland "Bee Bee" B 1.11.1928 Pisgah, IA D 2.14.1984 Omaha, NE BL/TR 5-10/180# d8.19 C4

Year	Tm Lg	G	AB	R	H	2B	3B	HR	RBI	BB-IB	HP	SO	AVG	OBP	SLG	AOPS	ABR	SB-CS	FA	FR	Rng	Thr	G at Pos	BFW
1952	NY A	12	21	1	2	1	0	0	0	4	0	4	.095	.240	.143	9	-3	1-0	.909	1	132	233	/3-9	-0.1
1953	NY A	5	18	2	6	1	0	2	6	0	0	2	.333	.333	.722	185	2	0-0	.920	2	124	242	/3-5	0.3
	Phi A	103	343	34	77	16	2	0	20	35	2	20	.224	.300	.283	56	-21	0-1	.950	0	100	108	3-93/S	-2.1
	Year	108	361	36	83	17	2	2	26	35	2	22	.230	.302	.305	62	-19	0-1	.948	2	101	116	3-98/S	-1.8
Total	2	120	382	37	85	18	2	2	26	39	2	26	.223	.298	.296	59	-22	1-1	.946	3	103	123	3-107/S	-1.9

BABINGTON, CHARLIE Charles Percy B 5.4.1895 Cranston, RI D 3.22.1957 Providence, RI BR/TR 6/170# d7.20

Year	Tm Lg	G	AB	R	H	2B	3B	HR	RBI	BB-IB	HP	SO	AVG	OBP	SLG	AOPS	ABR	SB-CS	FA	FR	Rng	Thr	G at Pos	BFW
1915	NY N	28	33	5	8	3	1	0	2	0	1	4	.242	.265	.394	104	0	1	.909	-1	94	0	O-12(2-11-1)/1	-0.1

BABITT, SHOOTY Mack Neal B 3.9.1959 Oakland, CA BR/TR 5-8/174# d4.9

Year	Tm Lg	G	AB	R	H	2B	3B	HR	RBI	BB-IB	HP	SO	AVG	OBP	SLG	AOPS	ABR	SB-CS	FA	FR	Rng	Thr	G at Pos	BFW
1981	Oak A	54	156	10	40	1	3	0	14	13-1	0	13	.256	.314	.301	82	-4	5-4	.972	-21	81	38	2-52	-2.4

BACKMAN, WALLY Walter Wayne B 9.22.1959 Hillsboro, OR BB/TR 5-9/160# d9.2

Year	Tm Lg	G	AB	R	H	2B	3B	HR	RBI	BB-IB	HP	SO	AVG	OBP	SLG	AOPS	ABR	SB-CS	FA	FR	Rng	Thr	G at Pos	BFW
1980	NY N	27	93	12	30	1	1	0	9	11-1	1	14	.323	.396	.355	115	2	2-3	1.000	-9	73	58	2-20/S-8	-0.6
1981	NY N	26	36	5	10	2	0	0	0	4-0	0	7	.278	.350	.333	96	0	1-0	.946	-1	102	49	2-11/3	0.0
1982	NY N	96	261	37	71	13	2	3	22	49-1	0	47	.272	.387	.372	114	8	8-7	.964	-4	98	68	2-88/3-6,S	0.7
1983	NY N	26	42	6	7	0	1	0	3	2-0	0	8	.167	.205	.214	16	-5	0-0	1.000	-2	75	58	2-14/3-2	-0.8
1984	NY N	128	436	68	122	19	2	1	26	56-2	0	63	.280	.360	.339	99	2	32-9	.981	-6	89	106	*2-115/S-8	0.7
1985	NY N	145	520	77	142	24	5	1	38	36-1	1	72	.273	.320	.344	88	-9	30-12	**.989**	-11	93	96	*2-140/S	-1.0
1986	†NY N	124	387	67	124	18	2	1	27	36-1	0	32	.320	.376	.385	114	8	13-7	.966	-2	101	103	*2-113	1.3
1987	NY N	94	300	43	75	6	1	1	23	25-0	0	43	.250	.307	.287	62	-17	11-3	.983	-9	94	95	2-87	-2.0
1988	†NY N	99	294	44	89	12	0	0	17	41-1	1	49	.303	.388	.344	118	9	9-5	.989	-9	92	83	2-92	0.3
1989	Min A	87	299	33	69	9	2	1	26	32-0	1	45	.231	.306	.284	63	-14	1-1	.982	-17	87	73	2-84/D	-3.0
1990	†Pit N	104	315	62	92	21	3	2	28	42-1	1	53	.292	.374	.397	118	9	6-3	.920	-11	89	63	3-71,2-15	-0.1
1991	Phi N	94	185	20	45	12	0	0	15	30-0	0	30	.243	.344	.308	87	-1	3-2	.981	-11	71	84	2-36,3-20	-1.3
1992	Phi N	42	48	6	13	1	0	0	6	6-1	0	9	.271	.352	.292	84	-1	1-0	.968	4	167	157	2-10/3-2	0.3
1993	Sea A	10	29	2	4	0	0	0	0	1-0	0	8	.138	.167	.138	-17	-5	0-0	.857	-1	100	0	/3-9,2	-0.6
Total	14	1102	3245	482	893	138	19	10	240	371-9	5	480	.275	.349	.339	94	-14	117-52	.980	-88	92	90	2-826,3-111/S-18,D	-6.1

BACON, EDDIE Edgar Suter B 4.8.1895 Franklin Co., KY D 10.2.1963 Louisville, KY d8.13

Year	Tm Lg	G	AB	R	H	2B	3B	HR	RBI	BB-IB	HP	SO	AVG	OBP	SLG	AOPS	ABR	SB-CS	FA	FR	Rng	Thr	G at Pos	BFW
1917	Phi A	4	6	1	3	1	0	0	2	0	0	0	.500	.500	.667	259	1	0	1.000	1	404	0	/P	0.0

BADER, ART Arthur Herman B 9.21.1886 St.Louis, MO D 4.5.1957 St.Louis, MO BR/TR 5-9/160# d8.2

Year	Tm Lg	G	AB	R	H	2B	3B	HR	RBI	BB-IB	HP	SO	AVG	OBP	SLG	AOPS	ABR	SB-CS	FA	FR	Rng	Thr	G at Pos	BFW
1904	StL A	2	3	0	0	0	0	0	0	1	0		.000	.250	.000	-19	0	0	1.000	1	1002	0	/O(LF)	0.0

BADGRO, RED Morris Hiram B 12.1.1902 Orillia, WA D 7.13.1998 Kent, WA BL/TR 6/190# d6.20

Year	Tm Lg	G	AB	R	H	2B	3B	HR	RBI	BB-IB	HP	SO	AVG	OBP	SLG	AOPS	ABR	SB-CS	FA	FR	Rng	Thr	G at Pos	BFW
1929	StL A	54	148	27	42	12	0	1	18	11	2	15	.284	.342	.385	84	-3	1-0	.983	-2	96	30	O-37(RF)	-0.7
1930	StL A	89	234	30	56	18	3	1	27	13	2	27	.239	.285	.355	59	-15	3-5	.952	-0	89	154	O-61(4-14-43)	-1.9
Total	2	143	382	57	98	30	3	2	45	24	4	42	.257	.307	.366	69	-18	4-5	.962	-3	91	111	/O-98(4-14-80)	-2.6

BAERGA, CARLOS Carlos Obed (Ortiz) B 11.4.1968 Santurce, P.R. BB/TR 5-11/200# d4.14

Year	Tm Lg	G	AB	R	H	2B	3B	HR	RBI	BB-IB	HP	SO	AVG	OBP	SLG	AOPS	ABR	SB-CS	FA	FR	Rng	Thr	G at Pos	BFW
1990	Cle A	108	312	46	81	17	2	7	47	16-2	4	57	.260	.300	.394	94	-3	0-2	.944	-5	112	108	3-50,S-48/2-8	-0.7
1991	Cle A	158	593	80	171	28	2	11	69	48-5	6	74	.288	.346	.398	105	4	3-2	.944	17	114	88	3-89,2-75/S-2	2.3
1992	Cle A★	161	657	92	205	32	1	20	105	35-10	13	76	.312	.354	.455	129	24	10-2	.979	8	99	**121**	*2-160/D	3.8
1993	Cle A★	154	624	105	200	28	6	21	114	34-7	6	68	.321	.355	.486	126	20	15-4	.979	8	102	103	*2-150/D-4	3.6
1994	Cle A	103	442	81	139	32	2	19	80	10-1	6	45	.314	.333	.525	118	10	8-2	.973	4	104	101	*2-102/D	1.8
1995	†Cle A★	135	557	87	175	28	2	15	90	35-6	3	31	.314	.355	.452	108	5	11-2	.973	10	107	121	*2-134/D	2.2
1996	Cle A	100	424	54	113	25	0	10	55	16-0	7	25	.267	.302	.396	76	-17	1-1	.971	-1	101	96	*2-100	-1.2
	NY N	26	83	5	16	3	0	2	11	5-0	2	2	.193	.253	.301	48	-7	0-0	.990	-4	49	72	1-16/3-6,2	-1.1
1997	NY N	133	467	53	131	25	1	9	52	20-1	3	54	.281	.311	.396	88	-10	2-6	.978	1	105	**122**	*2-131	-0.5
1998	NY N	147	511	46	136	27	1	7	53	24-6	6	55	.266	.303	.364	77	-18	0-1	.986	-9	90	118	*2-144	-2.1
1999	SD N	33	80	6	20	1	0	2	5	6-0	2	14	.250	.318	.338	72	-4	1-0	1.000	-3	85	136	2-13,3-13/1-2,D	-0.6
	Cle A	22	57	4	13	0	0	1	5	4-1	0	10	.228	.274	.281	41	-5	1-1	.964	-1	88	50	3-15/2-6,D	-0.6
2002	Bos A	73	182	17	52	11	0	2	19	7-1	2	20	.286	.316	.379	83	-4	6-0	.983	2	109	68	D-32,2-17/3	-0.2
2003	Ari N	105	207	31	71	13	0	4	39	18-1	2	20	.343	.396	.464	113	5	1-1	.985	1	88	110	1-19,2-15/3-5,D-6	0.5
Total	12	1458	5196	707	1523	270	17	130	744	278-41	62	551	.293	.333	.427	102	0	59-24	.976	28	101	113	*2-1056,3-179/S-50,D-47,1-37	7.2

BAEZ, JOSE Jose Antonio (born Jose Antonio Mota (Baez)) B 12.31.1953 San Cristobal, D.R. BR/TR 5-8/160# d4.6

Year	Tm Lg	G	AB	R	H	2B	3B	HR	RBI	BB-IB	HP	SO	AVG	OBP	SLG	AOPS	ABR	SB-CS	FA	FR	Rng	Thr	G at Pos	BFW
1977	Sea A	91	305	39	79	14	1	1	17	19-1	1	20	.259	.305	.321	71	-12	6-1	.973	12	112	109	2-77/3D	0.5
1978	Sea A	23	50	8	8	0	1	0	2	6-1	0	7	.160	.250	.200	28	-5	1-0	.978	9	144	209	2-14/3-3,D	0.5
Total	2	114	355	47	87	14	2	1	19	25-2	1	27	.245	.297	.304	65	-17	7-1	.974	21	116	123	/2-91,D-4,3-4	1.0

BAEZ, KEVIN Kevin Richard B 1.10.1967 Brooklyn, NY BR/TR 6/160# d9.3

Year	Tm Lg	G	AB	R	H	2B	3B	HR	RBI	BB-IB	HP	SO	AVG	OBP	SLG	AOPS	ABR	SB-CS	FA	FR	Rng	Thr	G at Pos	BFW
1990	NY N	5	12	0	2	1	0	0	0	0-0	0	0	.167	.167	.250	13	-1	0-0	1.000	-0	79	66	/S-4	-0.2
1992	NY N	6	13	0	2	0	0	0	0	0-0	0	0	.154	.154	.154	-13	-2	0-0	.889	-0	98	95	/S-5	-0.2
1993	NY N	52	126	10	23	9	0	0	7	13-1	0	17	.183	.259	.254	38	-11	0-0	.967	-3	98	103	S-52	-1.1
Total	3	63	151	10	27	10	0	0	7	13-1	0	17	.179	.244	.245	33	-14	0-0	.962	-3	97	100	/S-61	-1.5

BAGWELL, JEFF Jeffery Robert B 5.27.1968 Boston, MA BR/TR 6/195# d4.8

Year	Tm Lg	G	AB	R	H	2B	3B	HR	RBI	BB-IB	HP	SO	AVG	OBP	SLG	AOPS	ABR	SB-CS	FA	FR	Rng	Thr	G at Pos	BFW
1991	Hou N	156	554	79	163	26	4	15	82	75-5	**13**	116	.294	.387	.437	141	33	7-4	.991	-4	89	89	*1-155	1.9
1992	Hou N	**162**	586	87	160	34	6	18	96	84-13	12	97	.273	.368	.444	137	32	10-6	.995	4	107	95	*1-159	2.6
1993	Hou N	142	535	76	171	37	4	20	88	62-6	3	73	.320	.388	.516	146	37	13-4	.993	4	106	103	*1-140	2.9
1994	Hou N★	110	400	**104**	147	32	2	39	**116**	65-14	4	65	.368	.451	**.750**	**220**	**73**	15-4	.991	16	**148**	108	*1-109/O(RF)	**7.7**
1995	Hou N	114	448	88	130	29	0	21	87	79-12	6	102	.290	.399	.496	145	34	12-5	.994	**18**	**151**	84	*1-114	3.9
1996	Hou N★	**162**	568	111	179	**48**	2	31	120	135-20	10	114	.315	.451	.570	182	80	21-7	.989	8	116	84	*1-162	7.1
1997	†Hou N★	**162**	566	109	162	40	2	43	135	127-27	16	122	.286	.425	.592	171	66	31-10	.993	8	118	118	*1-159/D	6.0
1998	†Hou N	147	540	124	164	33	1	34	111	109-8	7	90	.304	.424	.557	161	53	19-7	.995	11	125	102	*1-147	5.0
1999	†Hou N★	**162**	562	**143**	171	35	0	42	126	**149**-16	11	127	.304	.454	.591	165	**67**	30-11	.994	3	102	**116**	*1-161/D-2	**5.3**
2000	Hou N	159	590	**152**	183	37	1	47	132	107-11	15	116	.310	.424	.615	151	50	9-6	.994	2	103	97	*1-158/D	3.5
2001	†Hou N	161	600	126	173	43	4	39	130	106-5	6	135	.288	.397	.568	139	38	11-3	.992	15	**133**	101	*1-160	3.8
2002	Hou N	158	571	94	166	33	2	31	98	101-8	10	130	.291	.401	.518	139	33	7-3	.995	6	110	93	*1-153/D-4	2.5
2003	Hou N	160	605	109	168	28	2	39	100	88-3	6	119	.278	.373	.524	125	23	11-4	.994	5	110	98	*1-158	1.4
Total	13	1955	7125	1402	2137	455	30	419	1421	1287-148	119	1406	.300	.411	.549	154	619	196-74	.993	96	115	99	*1-1935/D-8,O(RF)	53.6

BAGWELL, BILL William Mallory "Big Bill" B 2.24.1896 Choudrant, LA D 10.5.1976 Choudrant, LA BL/TL 6-1/175# d4.17

Year	Tm Lg	G	AB	R	H	2B	3B	HR	RBI	BB-IB	HP	SO	AVG	OBP	SLG	AOPS	ABR	SB-CS	FA	FR	Rng	Thr	G at Pos	BFW
1923	Bos N	56	93	8	27	4	2	2	10	6	0	12	.290	.333	.441	107	0	0-0	1.000	0	105	71	O-22(LF)	0.0
1925	Phi A	36	50	4	15	2	1	0	10	2	0	2	.300	.327	.380	74	-2	0-0	.667	-1	34	0	/O-4(LF)	-0.3
Total	2	92	143	12	42	6	3	2	20	8	0	14	.294	.331	.420	95	-2	0-0	.973	-1	94	60	/O-26(LF)	-0.3

BAHRET, FRANK Frank F. B 1858 Poughkeepsie, NY D 3.30.1888 Poughkeepsie, NY 6-1/184# d4.17

Year	Tm Lg	G	AB	R	H	2B	3B	HR	RBI	BB-IB	HP	SO	AVG	OBP	SLG	AOPS	ABR	SB-CS	FA	FR	Rng	Thr	G at Pos	BFW
1884	Bal U	2	8	0	0	0	0	0		0			.000	.000	.000	-91	-2		1.000	-0	0	0	/O-2(0-1-1)	-0.2

BAILEY, GENE Arthur Eugene B 11.25.1893 Pearsall, TX D 11.14.1973 Houston, TX BR/TR 5-8/160# d9.10 Mil 1918

Year	Tm Lg	G	AB	R	H	2B	3B	HR	RBI	BB-IB	HP	SO	AVG	OBP	SLG	AOPS	ABR	SB-CS	FA	FR	Rng	Thr	G at Pos	BFW
1917	Phi A	5	12	1	1	0	0	0	0	1	0	1	.083	.154	.083	-28	-2	0	.833	-1	88	0	/O-4(LF)	-0.3
1919	Bos N	4	6	0	2	0	0	0	1	0	0	2	.333	.333	.333	105	0	1	1.000	0	119	0	/O-3(0-1-1)	0.0
1920	Bos N	13	24	2	2	0	0	0	0	3	0	3	.083	.185	.083	-22	-4	0-1	.929	0	96	141	/O-8(5-4-1)	-0.5
	Bos A	46	135	14	31	2	0	0	5	9	1	15	.230	.283	.244	42	-11	2-7	.986	-1	97	70	O-40(9-16-15)	-1.6
1923	Bro N	127	411	71	109	11	7	1	42	43	6	34	.265	.343	.333	81	-10	9-7	.959	-1	102	84	*O-100(25-60-17)/1-5	-1.7
1924	Bro N	18	46	7	11	3	0	1	4	7	0	6	.239	.340	.370	93	0	1-0	1.000	1	109	117	O-17(0-10-8)	0.0
Total	5	213	634	95	156	16	7	2	52	63	7	61	.246	.321	.303	69	-27	13-15	.965	-1	101	84	O-172(43-91-42)/1-5	-4.1

BAILEY, FRED Frederick Middleton "Penny" B 8.16.1895 Mt.Hope, WV D 8.16.1972 Huntington, WV BL/TL 5-11/150# d8.19 Mil 1918

Year	Tm Lg	G	AB	R	H	2B	3B	HR	RBI	BB-IB	HP	SO	AVG	OBP	SLG	AOPS	ABR	SB-CS	FA	FR	Rng	Thr	G at Pos	BFW
1916	Bos N	6	10	0	1	0	0	0	1	0	0	3	.100	.100	.100	-40	-2	0	1.000	-0	47	0	/O-2(LF)	-0.2

Year	Tm Lg	G	AB	R	H	2B	3B	HR	RBI	BB-IB	HP	SO	AVG	OBP	SLG	AOPS	ABR	SB-CS	FA	FR	Rng	Thr	G at Pos	BFW
1917	Bos N	50	110	9	21	2	1	1	5	9	3	25	.191	.270	.255	65	-4	3	.962	1	94	170	O-27(9-15-4)	-0.6
1918	Bos N	4	4	1	1	0	0	0	0	0	0	1	.250	.250	.250	55	0	0	—	0			H	0.0
Total	3	60	124	10	23	2	1	1	6	9	3	29	.185	.257	.242	57	-6	3	.963	1	92	162	/O-29(10-15-4)	-0.8
BAILEY, BILL Harry Lewis B 11.19.1881 Shawnee, OH D 10.27.1967 Seattle, WA BL/TR 5-10.5/170# d4.21																								
1911	NY A	5	9	1	1	0	0	0	0	0	0		.111	.111	.111	-36	-2	0	—	0	0	0	/O-2,3	-0.1
BAILEY, MARK John Mark B 11.4.1961 Springfield, MO BB/TR 6-5/195# d4.27 C2																								
1984	Hou N	108	344	38	73	16	1	9	34	53-4	2	71	.212	.318	.343	93	-2	0-1	.983	-4	83	97	*C-108	-0.2
1985	Hou N	114	332	47	88	14	0	10	45	67-13	1	70	.265	.389	.398	124	14	0-2	.979	-6	116	91	*C-110/1-2	1.3
1986	Hou N	57	153	9	27	5	0	4	15	28-6	0	45	.176	.302	.288	66	-7	1-1	.989	-0	80	131	C-53/1	-0.5
1987	Hou N	35	64	5	13	1	0	0	3	10-0	0	21	.203	.311	.219	45	-5	1-0	.985	-1	84	119	C-27	-0.5
1988	Hou N	8	23	1	3	0	0	0	0	5-0	0	6	.130	.286	.130	24	-2	0-1	.981	-0	87	80	/C-8	-0.3
1990	SF N	5	7	1	1	0	0	1	3	0-0	0	2	.143	.143	.571	90	0	0-0	1.000	0	0	0	/C	0.0
1992	SF N	13	26	0	4	1	0	0	1	3-0	0	7	.154	.241	.192	26	-3	0-0	1.000	-0	0	46	/C-7	-0.3
Total	7	340	949	101	209	37	1	24	101	166-23	3	222	.220	.337	.337	93	-5	2-5	.983	-11	93	100	C-314/1-3	-0.5
BAILEY, ED Lonas Edgar B 4.15.1931 Strawberry Plains, TN BL/TR 6-2/205# d9.26 b-Jim																								
1953	Cin N	2	8	1	3	1	0	0	1	1	0	3	.375	.444	.500	145	1	0-0	1.000	-1	*53*	*0*	/C-2	0.0
1954	Cin N	73	183	21	36	2	3	9	20	35	0	34	.197	.324	.388	83	-5	1-0	.973	-6	*167*	*84*	C-61	-0.8
1955	Cin N	21	39	3	8	1	1	1	4	4-0	3	10	.205	.326	.359	77	-1	0-0	.962	2	*142*	*136*	C-11	0.1
1956	Cin N★	118	383	59	115	8	2	28	75	52-11	3	50	.300	.385	.551	140	22	2-0	.984	1	*94*	*110*	*C-106	2.9
1957	Cin N★	122	391	54	102	15	2	20	48	73-9	2	69	.261	.377	.463	117	12	5-3	.991	-11	*111*	*88*	*C-115	0.7
1958	Cin N	112	360	39	90	23	1	11	59	47-10	1	61	.250	.337	.411	92	-3	2-2	.988	1	*125*	*107*	C-99	0.3
1959	Cin N	121	379	43	100	13	0	12	40	62-6	2	53	.264	.370	.393	101	3	2-0	.990	5	*133*	*124*	*C-117	1.4
1960	Cin N★	133	441	52	115	19	3	13	67	59-9	2	70	.261	.346	.406	105	4	1-0	.990	-8	*106*	***100***	*C-129	0.2
1961	Cin N	12	43	4	13	4	0	0	2	3-1	0	5	.302	.348	.395	95	0	0-0	.967	-3	*80*	*115*	C-12	-0.2
	SF N☆	107	340	39	81	9	1	13	51	42-6	4	41	.238	.324	.385	92	-4	1-5	.985	-1	*88*	*86*	*C-103/O(LF)	-0.1
	Year	119	383	43	94	13	1	13	53	45-7	4	46	.245	.326	.386	93	-4	1-5	.984	-3	*87*	*89*	*C-115/O(LF)	-0.3
1962	†SF N	96	254	32	59	9	1	17	45	42-5	6	42	.232	.351	.476	123	9	1-1	.987	-3	*122*	*52*	C-75	0.9
1963	SF N★	105	308	41	81	8	0	21	68	50-11	1	64	.263	.366	.494	147	20	0-6	.987	-3	*103*	*80*	C-88	2.1
1964	Mil N	95	271	30	71	10	1	5	34	34-2	1	39	.262	.343	.362	99	1	2-0	.982	-8	*130*	*67*	C-80	-0.3
1965	SF N	24	28	1	3	0	0	0	3	6-1	0	7	.107	.250	.107	9	-3	0-0	1.000	2	*151*	*116*	C-12/1-2	-0.1
	Chi N	66	150	13	38	6	0	5	23	34-6	0	28	.253	.385	.393	119	6	0-1	.981	-3	*91*	*90*	C-54/1-3	0.4
	Year	90	178	14	41	6	0	5	26	40-7	0	35	.230	.363	.348	102	2	0-1	.984	-1	*99*	*93*	C-66/1-5	0.3
1966	Cal A	5	3	0	0	0	0	0	0	1-0	0	1	.000	.250	.000	-22	0	0-0	—	0			H	0.0
Total	14	1212	3581	432	915	128	15	155	540	545-77	25	577	.256	.355	.429	110	62	17-18	.986	-34	*114*	*93*	*C-1064/1-5,O(LF)	7.5
BAILEY, BOB Robert Sherwood B 10.13.1942 Long Beach, CA BR/TR 6/188# d9.14 OF Total (399-LF 2-CF 3-RF)																								
1962	Pit N	14	42	6	7	2	1	0	6	6-0	0	10	.167	.271	.262	44	-3	1-1	.921	-0	103	87	3-12	-0.4
1963	Pit N	154	570	60	130	15	3	12	45	58-2	5	98	.228	.303	.328	82	-13	10-9	.933	9	112	**160**	*3-153/S-3	-0.6
1964	Pit N	143	530	73	149	26	3	11	51	44-1	1	78	.281	.336	.404	108	6	10-8	.943	5	108	111	*3-105,O-35(34-2-2)/S-2	0.9
1965	Pit N	159	626	87	160	28	3	11	49	70-1	0	93	.256	.330	.363	95	-3	10-14	.939	-13	94	117	*3-142,O-28(LF)	-2.1
1966	Pit N	126	380	51	106	19	3	13	46	47-4	2	65	.279	.360	.447	123	13	5-3	.956	1	107	114	3-96,O-20(LF)	1.3
1967	LA N	116	322	21	73	8	2	4	28	40-4	1	50	.227	.310	.301	84	-6	5-5	.941	-1	108	98	3-65,O-27(LF)/1-4,S	-1.0
1968	LA N	105	322	24	73	9	3	8	39	38-4	1	69	.227	.308	.348	105	2	1-2	.953	-1	95	91	3-90/SO(LF)	0.1
1969	Mon N	111	358	46	95	16	6	9	53	40-3	1	76	.265	.337	.419	111	5	3-3	.992	5	131	106	1-85,O-12(LF)/3	0.3
1970	Mon N	131	352	77	101	19	3	28	84	72-8	1	70	.287	.407	.597	166	35	5-3	.953	-2	95	62	3-48,O-44(LF),1-18	2.9
1971	Mon N	157	545	65	137	21	4	14	83	97-8	0	105	.251	.359	.382	111	12	13-7	**.960**	-1	102	71	*3-120,O-51(51-0-1)/1-9	0.8
1972	Mon N	143	489	55	114	10	4	16	57	59-7	1	112	.233	.315	.368	92	-5	6-7	.938	-1	103	97	*3-134/O-5(LF),1-3	-0.8
1973	Mon N	151	513	77	140	25	4	26	86	88-10	1	99	.273	.379	.489	134	26	5-8	.956	-1	102	88	*3-146/O-2(LF)	2.4
1974	Mon N	152	507	69	142	20	2	20	73	100-9	1	107	.280	.396	.446	129	24	4-7	.974	-8	72	158	O-78(LF),3-68	1.0
1975	Mon N	106	227	23	62	5	0	5	30	46-3	1	38	.273	.392	.361	107	5	4-4	.979	-1	89	103	O-61(LF)/3-3	0.1
1976	Cin N	69	124	17	37	6	1	6	23	16-1	0	26	.298	.376	.508	146	8	0-0	.974	-2	79	130	O-31(LF),3-10	0.5
1977	Cin N	49	79	9	20	2	1	2	11	12-2	0	10	.253	.348	.380	94	0	1-1	.975	0	123	108	1-19/O-3(LF)	-0.2
	Bos A	2	2	0	0	0	0	0	0	0-0	0	1	.000	.000	.000	-90	-1	0-0	—	0			H	-0.1
1978	Bos A	43	94	12	18	3	0	4	9	19-0	1	19	.191	.328	.351	84	-2	2-1	1.000	0	109	0	D-34/3O(LF)	-0.2
Total	17	1931	6082	772	1564	234	43	189	773	852-67	17	1126	.257	.347	.403	111	103	85-83	.946	-10	103	103	*3-1194,O-399L,1-138/D-34,S-7	4.9
BAILOR, BOB Robert Michael B 7.10.1951 Connellsville, PA BR/TR 5-11/170# d9.6 C4 OF Total (79-LF 105-CF 254-RF)																								
1975	Bal A	5	7	0	1	0	0	0	0	1-0	0	0	.143	.250	.143	14	-1	0-0	1.000	1	120	0	/S-2,2	0.0
1976	Bal A	9	6	2	2	0	1	0	0	0-0	0	0	.333	.333	.667	200	1	0-1	—	-0	0	0	/SD	0.0
1977	Tor A	122	496	62	154	21	5	5	32	17-1	2	26	.310	.335	.403	99	-2	15-6	.988	5	102	226	O-63(15-47-2),S-53/D-7	0.9
1978	Tor A	154	621	74	164	29	7	1	52	38-1	5	21	.264	.310	.338	81	-16	5-6	.964	11	109	165	*O-125(3-25-102),3-28/S-4	-1.2
1979	Tor A	130	414	50	95	11	5	1	38	36-2	6	27	.229	.297	.287	59	-24	14-8	.987	5	96	**203**	*O-118(4-4-113)/3-9,D	-2.3
1980	Tor A	117	347	44	82	14	2	1	16	36-3	2	33	.236	.311	.297	65	-16	12-8	.991	15	108	264	0-98(41-28-33),S-12,3-11/P-3,2D	-0.3
1981	NY N	51	81	11	23	3	1	0	8	8-0	1	11	.284	.352	.346	101	0	2-0	.955	-2	99	66	S-22,2-13,O-13(10-0-3)/3	0.1
1982	NY N	110	376	44	104	14	1	0	31	20-0	2	17	.277	.313	.319	79	-11	20-3	.984	1	107	85	S-60,2-56,3-21/O-4(3-1-0)	-0.1
1983	NY N	118	340	33	85	8	0	1	30	20-2	1	23	.250	.290	.282	61	-18	18-3	.969	6	107	113	S-75,2-50,3-11/O-3(2-0-1)	-0.2
1984	LA N	65	131	11	36	4	0	0	8	8-1	0	1	.275	.317	.305	76	-4	3-1	.944	3	85	68	2-23,3-17,S-16	0.2
1985	†LA N	74	118	8	29	3	1	0	7	3-0	1	5	.246	.270	.288	58	-7	1-0	.962	7	117	155	3-45,2-16/S-5,O(LF)	0.1
Total	11	955	2937	339	775	107	23	9	222	187-10	20	164	.264	.310	.325	76	-98	90-36	.980	54	105	207	0-425R,S-250,2-160,3-143/D-10,P	-2.8
BAINES, HAROLD Harold Douglass B 3.15.1959 Easton, MD BL/TL 6-2/195# d4.10																								
1980	Chi A	141	491	55	125	23	6	13	49	19-7	1	65	.255	.281	.405	87	-11	2-4	.963	-9	88	62	*O-137(RF)/D	-2.8
1981	Chi A	82	280	42	80	11	7	10	41	12-4	2	41	.286	.318	.482	131	9	6-2	.985	-0	82	197	O-80(RF)/D	0.6
1982	Chi A	161	608	89	165	29	8	25	105	49-10	0	95	.271	.321	.469	115	11	10-3	.980	-4	97	86	*O-161(1-3-160)	0.0
1983	†Chi A	156	596	76	167	33	2	20	99	49-13	1	85	.280	.333	.443	108	6	7-5	.973	-4	97	88	*O-155(1-20-142)	-0.5
1984	Chi A	147	569	72	173	28	10	29	94	54-9	0	75	.304	.361	**.541**	141	30	1-2	.981	-2	100	87	*O-147(0-7-147)	2.0
1985	Chi A★	160	640	86	198	29	3	22	113	42-8	1	89	.309	.348	.467	118	15	1-1	.994	1	101	78	*O-159(RF)/D	0.7
1986	Chi A★	145	570	72	169	29	2	21	88	38-9	2	89	.296	.338	.465	114	10	2-1	.984	8	105	153	*O-141(RF)/D-3	1.0
1987	Chi A★	132	505	59	148	26	4	20	93	46-2	1	82	.293	.352	.479	115	11	0-0	1.000	-1	83	0	*D-117/O-8(RF)	0.6
1988	Chi A	158	599	55	166	39	1	13	81	67-14	1	109	.277	.347	.411	113	12	0-0	.882	-1	67	167	*D-147/O-9(RF)	0.6
1989	Chi A★	96	333	55	107	20	1	13	56	60-13	1	52	.321	.423	.505	165	32	0-1	.981	-0	112	0	D-70,O-25(RF)	2.9
	Tex A	50	172	18	49	9	0	3	16	13-0	0	27	.285	.333	.390	102	0	0-2	.667	-0	111	0	D-46/O(RF)	-0.2
	Year	146	505	73	156	29	1	16	72	73-13	1	79	.309	.395	.465	144	32	0-3	.964	-0	112	0	*D-116,O-26(RF)	2.7
1990	Tex A	103	321	41	93	10	1	13	44	47-9	0	63	.290	.377	.449	131	14	0-1	.833	0	181	0	D-95/O-2(RF)	1.1
	†Oak A	32	94	11	25	5	0	3	21	20-1	0	17	.266	.381	.415	132	5	0-2	—	0	0	0	D-30	0.4
	Year	135	415	52	118	15	1	16	65	67-10	0	80	.284	.378	.441	131	19	0-3	.831	0	181	0	*D-125/O-2(RF)	1.5
1991	Oak A★	141	488	76	144	25	1	20	90	72-22	1	67	.295	.383	.473	145	32	0-1	.923	-0	77	198	*D-125,O-12(1-0-10)	2.7
1992	†Oak A	140	478	58	121	18	0	16	76	59-6	0	61	.253	.331	.391	109	6	1-3	.964	-2	84	0	*D-116,O-23(6-0-17)	-0.1
1993	Bal A	118	416	64	130	22	0	20	78	57-9	0	52	.313	.390	.510	136	22	0-0	—	0	0	0	*D-116	1.4
1994	Bal A	94	326	44	96	12	1	16	54	30-6	1	49	.294	.356	.485	109	3	0-0	—	0	0	0	D-91	-0.3
1995	Bal A	127	385	60	115	19	1	24	63	70-13	0	45	.299	.403	.540	142	25	0-2	—	0	0	0	*D-122	1.5
1996	Chi A	143	495	80	154	29	0	22	95	73-7	1	62	.311	.399	.503	133	28	3-1	—	0	0	0	*D-141	1.7
1997	Chi A	93	318	40	97	18	0	12	52	41-10	0	47	.305	.382	.475	128	14	0-1	—	0	0	0	D-86	0.8
	†Bal A	44	134	15	39	5	0	4	15	14-1	0	15	.291	.356	.418	105	1	0-0	—	-0	0	0	D-35/O(RF)	-0.1
	Year	137	452	55	136	23	0	16	67	55-11	0	62	.301	.375	.458	121	15	0-1	.913	-0	0	0	*D-121/O(RF)	0.7
1998	Bal A	104	293	40	88	17	0	9	57	32-4	1	40	.300	.369	.451	114	7	0-0	—	0	0	0	D-80	0.1
1999	Bal A★	107	345	57	111	16	1	24	81	43-3	0	38	.322	.395	.583	151	27	1-2	—	0	0	0	D-96	1.8
	†Cle A	28	85	5	23	2	0	1	22	11-0	0	10	.271	.354	.329	73	-3	0-0	—	0	0	0	D-25	-0.5
	Year	135	430	62	134	18	1	25	103	54-3	0	48	.312	.387	.533	134	22	1-2	—	0	0	0	*D-121	1.3
2000	Bal A	72	222	24	59	8	0	10	30	29-6	0	39	.266	.349	.437	103	1	0-0	—	0	0	0	D-62	-0.3
	†Chi A	24	61	2	13	5	0	1	9	7-1	0	11	.213	.294	.344	60	-4	0-0	—	0	0	0	D-16	-0.4
	Year	96	283	26	72	13	0	11	39	36-7	0	50	.254	.338	.417	93	-3	0-0	—	0	0	0	D-78	-0.7

Year	Tm Lg	G	AB	R	H	2B	3B	HR	RBI	BB-IB	HP	SO	AVG	OBP	SLG	AOPS	ABR	SB-CS	FA	FR	Rng	Thr	G at Pos	BFW
2001	Chi A	32	84	3	11	1	0	0	6	8-0	0	16	.131	.202	.143	-5	-13	0-0	—	0	0	0	D-22	-1.4
Total	22	2830	9908	1299	2866	488	49	384	1628	1062-187	14	1441	.289	.356	.465	121	290	34-34	.978	-16	97	97	*D-1644,O-1061(9-30-1039)	13.3
BAIRD, AL Albert Wells B 6.2.1895 Cleburne, TX D 11.27.1976 Shreveport, LA BR/TR 5-9/160# d9.10 Mil 1918																								
1917	NY N	10	24	1	7	0	0	0	4	2	0	2	.292	.346	.292	100	0	2	1.000	0	92	42	/2-7,S-3	0.1
1919	NY N	38	83	8	20	1	0	0	5	5	0	9	.241	.284	.253	63	-4	3	.898	5	120	127	2-24/S-9,3-5	0.2
Total	2	48	107	9	27	1	0	0	9	7	0	11	.252	.298	.262	71	-4	5	.921	6	113	106	/2-31,S-12,3-5	0.3
BAIRD, DOUG Howard Douglas B 9.27.1891 St.Charles, MO D 6.13.1967 Thomasville, GA BR/TR 5-9.5/148# d4.18 Mil 1918																								
1915	Pit N	145	512	49	112	26	12	1	53	37	4	88	.219	.277	.322	82	-12	29-12	.939	-2	95	83	*3-120,O-20(CF)/2-3	-1.1
1916	Pit N	128	430	41	93	10	7	1	28	24	3	49	.216	.263	.279	66	-18	20-16	.933	-9	96	108	3-80,2-29,O-16(10-5-1)	-3.1
1917	Pit N	43	135	17	35	6	1	0	18	20	0	19	.259	.355	.319	104	2	8	.935	-4	88	44	3-41/2-2	-0.1
	StL N	104	364	38	92	19	12	0	24	23	2	52	.253	.301	.371	108	2	18	.941	14	119	138	*3-103/O-2(CF)	2.2
	Year	147	499	55	127	25	13	0	42	43	2	71	.255	.316	.357	107	4	26	**.940**	10	110	**112**	*3-144/2-2,O-2(CF)	2.1
1918	StL N	82	316	41	78	12	8	2	25	25	1	42	.247	.304	.354	104	1	25	.967	11	118	81	3-81/SO(RF)	1.6
1919	Phi N	66	242	33	61	13	3	2	30	22	1	28	.252	.317	.355	95	-1	13	.950	9	108	157	3-66	1.1
	StL N	16	33	4	7	0	1	0	4	2	0	3	.212	.257	.273	63	-2	2	.773	-3	80	0	/3-8,2O(RF)	-0.5
	Bro N	20	60	6	11	0	1	0	8	1	0	10	.183	.197	.217	24	-6	3	1.000	1	106	84	3-17	-0.5
	Year	102	335	43	79	13	5	2	42	25	1	41	.236	.291	.322	81	-8	18	.946	7	106	132	3-91/2O(RF)	0.1
1920	Bro N	6	6	1	2	0	0	0	1	2	1	1	.333	.556	.333	154	1	0-0	.800	-0	98	0	/3-2	0.1
	NY N	7	8	0	1	0	0	0	0	1	0	3	.125	.222	.125	1	-1	0-0	1.000	1	120	303	/3-4	0.0
	Year	13	14	1	3	0	0	0	1	3	1	4	.214	.389	.214	76	0	0-0	.929	0	111	174	/3-6	0.1
Total	6	617	2106	230	492	86	45	6	191	157	12	295	.234	.291	.326	88	-34	118-28	.944	18	105	104	3-522/O-40(10-27-3),2-35,S	-0.3
BAKER, CHARLIE Charles Arthur B 1.15.1856 W.Boylston, MA D 1.15.1937 Manchester, NH BR/TR 5-4/140# d8.1																								
1884	CP U	15	57	5	8	2	0	1		0			.140	.140	.228	10	-8		.722	-1	127	0	O-11(RF)/S-3,2	-0.8
BAKER, CHUCK Charles Joseph B 12.6.1952 Seattle, WA BR/TR 5-11/180# d4.7																								
1978	SD N	44	58	8	12	1	0	0	3	2-0	0	15	.207	.233	.224	31	-6	0-0	.952	7	121	146	2-24,S-12	0.3
1980	SD N	9	22	0	3	1	0	0	0	0-0	0	4	.136	.136	.182	-13	-3	0-0	.963	-0	116	83	/S-8	-0.3
1981	Min A	40	66	6	12	0	3	0	6	1-0	0	8	.182	.194	.273	31	-6	0-0	.969	4	110	80	S-31/2-3,3D	-0.1
Total	3	93	146	14	27	2	3	0	9	3-0	0	27	.185	.201	.240	25	-15	0-0	.962	10	119	95	/S-51,2-27,D3	-0.1
BAKER, DAVE David Glenn B 11.25.1957 Lacona, IA BL/TR 6/185# d9.12 b-Doug																								
1982	Tor A	9	20	3	5	1	0	0	2	3-0	2	3	.250	.400	.300	88	0	0-0	.808	1	127	154	/3-8	0.0
BAKER, DEL Delmer David B 5.3.1892 Sherwood, OR D 9.11.1973 San Antonio, TX BR/TR 5-11.5/176# d4.16 M9 C20																								
1914	Det A	44	70	4	15	2	1	0	1	6	0	9	.214	.276	.271	63	-3	0-2	.920	-5	*88*	*86*	C-38	-0.8
1915	Det A	68	134	16	33	3	3	0	15	15	1	15	.246	.327	.313	87	-2	3-1	.940	-5	*99*	*93*	C-61	-0.3
1916	Det A	61	98	7	15	4	0	0	6	11	1	8	.153	.245	.194	31	-8	2	.975	-4	91	59	C-59	-1.0
Total	3	173	302	27	63	9	4	0	22	32	2	32	.209	.289	.265	63	-13	5-3	.948	-15	*94*	*80*	C-158	-2.1
BAKER, DOUG Douglas Lee B 4.3.1961 Fullerton, CA BB/TR 5-9/165# d7.2 b-Dave																								
1984	†Det A	43	108	15	20	4	1	0	12	7-0	1	22	.185	.241	.241	34	-10	3-0	.969	-5	93	108	S-39/2-5,D	-1.1
1985	Det A	15	27	4	5	1	0	0	1	0-0	0	9	.185	.185	.222	11	-3	0-0	.960	-3	62	50	S-12/2	-0.6
1986	Det A	13	24	1	3	1	0	0	0	2-0	0	7	.125	.192	.167	-1	-3	0-0	.970	-2	87	106	S-10/2-2,D	-0.4
1987	Det A	8	1	0	0	0	0	0	0	0-0	0	1	.000	.000	.000	-99	0	0-0	1.000	2	274	167	/S-6,23	0.1
1988	Min A	11	7	1	0	0	0	0	0	0-0	0	5	.000	.000	.000	-97	-2	0-0	1.000	-1	63	150	/S-9,23	-0.3
1989	Min A	43	78	17	23	5	1	0	9	9-0	2	18	.295	.378	.385	109	1	0-0	.982	-5	96	51	2-25,S-19/D	-0.3
1990	Min A	3	1	0	0	0	0	0	0	0-0	0	0	.000	.000	.000	-94	0	0-0	1.000	0	120	0	/2-3	0.0
Total	7	136	246	38	51	11	2	0	22	18-0	3	62	.207	.269	.268	49	-17	3-0	.973	-14	88	95	/S-95,2-38,D-3,3-2	-2.6
BAKER, GENE Eugene Walter B 6.15.1925 Davenport, IA D 12.1.1999 Davenport, IA BR/TR 6-1/170# d9.20 C1																								
1953	Chi N	7	22	1	5	1	0	0	0	1	0	4	.227	.261	.273	39	-2	1-0	.917	-2	73	77	/2-6	-0.4
1954	Chi N	135	541	68	149	32	5	13	61	47	2	55	.275	.333	.425	96	-4	4-5	.967	1	101	99	*2-134	0.6
1955	Chi N★	**154**	609	82	163	29	7	11	52	49-1	2	57	.268	.323	.392	89	-10	9-7	.967	6	100	102	*2-154	0.7
1956	Chi N	140	546	65	141	23	3	12	57	39-2	3	54	.258	.309	.377	85	-12	4-3	.969	13	**104**	101	*2-140	1.2
1957	Chi N	12	44	4	11	3	1	1	10	6-0	1	3	.250	.353	.432	111	1	0-0	.867	-3	72	45	3-12	-0.2
	Pit N	111	365	36	97	19	4	2	36	29-5	1	29	.266	.318	.356	84	-8	3-2	.955	-2	102	115	3-60,S-28,2-13	-0.8
	Year	123	409	40	108	22	5	3	46	35-5	2	32	.264	.322	.364	87	-7	3-2	.942	-5	97	103	3-72,S-28,2-13	-1.0
1958	Pit N	29	56	3	14	2	1	0	7	8-0	0	6	.250	.338	.321	80	-1	0-0	1.000	-1	88	0	3-11/2-3	-0.2
1960	†Pit N	33	37	5	9	0	0	0	4	2-0	0	9	.243	.275	.243	45	-3	0-0	1.000	1	112	301	/3-7,2	-0.2
1961	Pit N	9	10	1	1	0	0	0	0	3-1	0	2	.100	.308	.100	15	-1	0-0	1.000	1	165	0	/3-3	-0.1
Total	8	630	2230	265	590	109	21	39	227	184-9	9	219	.265	.321	.385	88	-40	21-17	.968	14	101	100	2-451/3-93,S-28	0.6
BAKER, FLOYD Floyd Wilson B 10.10.1916 Luray, VA BL/TR 5-9/160# d5.4 C4																								
1943	StL A	22	46	5	8	2	0	0	4	6	0	4	.174	.269	.217	42	-3	0-1	.961	-1	86	105	S-10/3	-0.4
1944	†StL A	44	97	10	17	3	0	0	5	11	0	5	.175	.259	.206	32	-8	2-0	.979	-2	88	50	2-17,S-16	-0.9
1945	Chi A	82	208	22	52	8	0	0	19	23	0	12	.250	.325	.288	81	-5	3-2	.971	1	104	68	3-58,2-11	-0.3
1946	Chi A	9	24	2	6	1	0	0	3	2	0	3	.250	.308	.292	71	-1	0-0	.962	0	102	68	/3-6	-0.1
1947	Chi A	105	371	61	98	12	3	0	22	66	0	28	.264	.375	.313	96	1	9-7	.980	14	121	148	*3-101/2S	1.5
1948	Chi A	104	335	47	72	8	3	0	18	73	2	26	.215	.359	.257	68	-12	4-10	.961	16	129	122	3-71,2-18/S	0.2
1949	Chi A	125	388	38	101	15	4	1	40	84	0	32	.260	.392	.327	94	1	3-1	**.977**	11	**115**	118	*3-122/S-3,2	1.2
1950	Chi A	83	186	26	59	7	0	0	11	32	0	10	.317	.417	.355	102	3	1-1	.987	3	105	71	3-53/2-3,O-2(LF)	0.5
1951	Chi A	82	133	24	35	6	1	0	14	25	0	12	.263	.380	.323	93	0	0-1	.924	-2	99	87	3-44/2-5,S-3	-0.2
1952	Was A	79	263	27	69	8	0	0	33	30	2	17	.262	.342	.293	81	-6	1-0	.994	-15	91	75	2-68/S-7,3	-1.7
1953	Was A	9	7	0	0	0	0	0	0	1	1	0	.000	.222	.000	-37	-1	0-0	.000	-1	0	0	/3	-0.2
	Bos A	81	172	22	47	4	2	0	24	24	1	10	.273	.365	.320	82	-4	0-2	.963	-1	100	97	3-37,2-16	-0.4
	Year	90	179	22	47	4	2	0	24	25	2	10	.263	.359	.307	78	-5	0-2	.952	-1	99	96	3-38,2-16	-0.6
1954	Bos A	21	20	1	4	2	0	0	3	0	0	1	.200	.200	.300	32	-2	0-0	.889	0	94	247	/3-7,2	-0.2
	Phi N	23	22	0	5	0	0	0	0	5	0	4	.227	.370	.227	60	-1	0-0	1.000	2	140	0	/3-7,2-2	0.1
1955	Phi N	5	8	0	0	0	0	0	0	0-0	0	1	.000	.000	.000	-99	-2	0-0	1.000	1	90	0	/3	-0.2
Total	13	874	2280	285	573	76	13	1	196	382-0	6	165	.251	.360	.297	82	-40	23-25	.971	26	114	111	3-510,2-143/S-41,O-2(LF)	-1.1
BAKER, FRANK Frank B 1.11.1944 Bartow, FL BL/TR 5-10/180# d7.27																								
1969	Cle A	52	172	21	44	5	3	3	15	14-0	1	34	.256	.312	.372	89	-3	2-1	.950	-0	91	152	O-46(LF)	-0.6
1971	Cle A	73	181	18	38	12	1	1	23	12-3	1	34	.210	.262	.304	55	-11	1-3	.985	-4	77	72	O-51(17-6-30)	-2.0
Total	2	125	353	39	82	17	4	4	38	26-3	2	68	.232	.286	.337	71	-14	3-4	.966	-4	84	112	/O-97(63-6-30)	-2.6
BAKER, FRANK Frank Watts B 10.29.1946 Meridian, MS BL/TR 6-2/178# d8.9																								
1970	NY A	35	117	6	27	4	1	0	11	14-0	2	26	.231	.323	.282	72	-4	1-2	.973	5	116	117	S-35	0.5
1971	NY A	43	79	9	11	2	0	0	2	16-3	0	22	.139	.281	.165	32	-7	3-0	.949	3	108	171	S-38	0.1
1973	†Bal A	44	63	10	12	1	2	1	11	7-0	0	7	.190	.268	.317	66	-3	0-0	.964	-2	89	164	S-32/2-7,13	-0.3
1974	†Bal A	24	29	3	5	1	0	0	0	3-0	0	5	.172	.250	.207	34	-2	0-0	.842	-3	101	93	S-17/2-3,3	-0.4
Total	4	146	288	28	55	8	3	1	24	40-3	2	60	.191	.292	.250	56	-16	4-2	.953	3	107	142	S-122/2-10,3-2,1	-0.1
BAKER, GEORGE George F. B 1859 St.Louis, MO d5.24																								
1883	Bal AA	7	22	0	5	0	0	0		0			.227	.227	.227	45	-1		.667	-2	67	192	/S-4,C-3,O(RF)	-0.3
1884	StL U	80	317	39	52	6	0	0		5			.164	.177	.183	9	-45		**.897**	15			C-68/2-4,O-4(2-1-2),3-3,S-2	-2.2
1885	StL N	38	131	5	16	0	0	0	5	9		28	.122	.179	.122	-1	-14		.865	-10			C-32/3-3,O-2(1-1-0),2	-2.1
1886	KC N	1	4	1	1	0	0	0	0	0		1	.250	.250	.250	49	0	0	.889	-0			/C	-0.1
Total	4	126	474	45	74	6	0	0	5	14		29	.156	.180	.169	8	-60	0	.887	2			C-104/O-7(3-2-3),3-6,S-6,2-5	-4.7
BAKER, HOWARD Howard Francis B 3.1.1888 Bridgeport, CT D 1.16.1964 Bridgeport, CT BR/TR 5-11/175# d8.11																								
1912	Cle A	11	30	1	5	0	0	0	2	5	0		.167	.286	.167	29	-3	0	.964	-1	72	0	3-10	-0.3
1914	Chi A	15	47	4	13	1	1	0	5	3	0	8	.277	.320	.340	100	0	2-1	.879	-2	96	67	3-15	-0.2
1915	Chi A	2	2	0	0	0	0	0	0	0	0	2	.000	.000	.000	-97	0	0	—	0			H	-0.1
	NY N	1	3	0	0	0	0	0	0	0	0	0	.000	.000	.000	-99	-1	0	1.000	0	128	0	/3	-0.1

Year	Tm Lg	G	AB	R	H	2B	3B	HR	RBI	BB-IB	HP	SO	AVG	OBP	SLG	AOPS	ABR	SB-CS	FA	FR	Rng	Thr	G at Pos	BFW
Total	3	29	82	5	18	1	1	0	7	8	0	10	.220	.289	.256	61	-4	2-1	.922	-3	88	38	/3-26	-0.7
BAKER, JACK Jack Edward B 5.4.1950 Birmingham, AL BR/TR 6-5/225# d9.11																								
1976	Bos A	12	23	1	3	0	0	1	2	1-0	0	5	.130	.160	.261	21	-2	0-0	.981	-1	74	134	/1-8,D	-0.4
1977	Bos A	2	3	0	0	0	0	0	0	0-0	0	1	.000	.000	.000	-90	-1	0-0	.857	0	193	0	/1	-0.1
Total	2	14	26	1	3	0	0	1	2	1-0	0	6	.115	.143	.231	8	-3	0-0	.966	-1	87	119	/1-9,D	-0.5
BAKER, JESSE Jesse (born Michael Myron Silverman) B 3.4.1895 Cleveland, OH D 7.29.1976 W.Los Angeles, CA BR/TR 5-4/140# d9.14																								
1919	Was A	1	0	0	0	0	0	0	1	0	0	0	—	—	—	—	0	0	1.000	0	146	0	/S	0.0
BAKER, FRANK John Franklin "Home Run" B 3.13.1886 Trappe, MD D 6.28.1963 Trappe, MD BL/TR 5-11/173# d9.21 HF1955																								
1908	Phi A	9	31	5	9	3	0	0	2	0	0		.290	.290	.387	112	0	0	1.000	1	108	0	/3-9	0.2
1909	Phi A	148	541	73	165	27	**19**	4	85	26	5		.305	.343	.447	146	25	20	.920	-10	89	95	*3-146	2.2
1910	†Phi A	146	561	83	159	25	15	2	74	34	4		.283	.329	.392	127	15	21	.920	2	96	**179**	*3-146	2.3
1911	†Phi A	148	592	96	198	42	14	**11**	115	40	2		.334	.379	.508	149	36	38	**.942**	-4	90	**125**	*3-148	3.5
1912	Phi A	149	577	116	200	40	21	**10**	**130**	50	6		.347	.404	.541	176	54	40	.941	8	103	119	*3-149	6.5
1913	†Phi A	149	564	116	190	34	9	**12**	**117**	63	10	31	.337	.413	.493	169	50	34	.921	9	100	95	*3-149	6.6
1914	†Phi A	150	570	84	182	23	10	**9**	89	53	3	37	.319	.380	.442	153	35	19-20	.955	9	99	99	*3-149	5.0
1916	NY A	100	360	46	97	23	2	10	52	36	5	30	.269	.344	.428	129	12	15	.940	1	100	90	3-96	1.7
1917	NY A	146	553	57	156	24	2	6	71	48	5	27	.282	.345	.365	116	10	18	.949	9	103	101	*3-146	2.6
1918	NY A	**126**	504	65	154	24	5	6	62	38	2	13	.306	.357	.409	128	16	8	**.972**	7	103	117	*3-126	2.9
1919	NY A	**141**	567	70	166	22	1	10	83	44	2	18	.293	.346	.388	105	3	13	.955	-5	95	**134**	*3-141	0.3
1921	†NY A	94	330	46	97	16	2	9	71	26	4	12	.294	.353	.436	98	-2	8-5	.959	5	107	118	3-83	0.8
1922	†NY A	69	234	30	65	12	3	7	36	15	2	14	.278	.327	.444	97	-2	1-3	.962	-10	84	68	3-60	-0.9
Total	13	1575	5984	887	1838	315	103	96	987	473	50	182	.307	.363	.442	136	252	235-28	.943	25	98	114	*3-1548	33.7
BAKER, DUSTY Johnnie B B 6.15.1949 Riverside, CA BR/TR 6-2/187# d9.7 M11 C5																								
1968	Atl N	6	5	0	2	0	0	0	0	0-0	0	1	.400	.400	.400	140	0	0-0	—	-0	0	0	/O-3(CF)	0.0
1969	Atl N	3	7	0	0	0	0	0	0	0-0	0	3	.000	.000	.000	-99	-2	0-0	1.000	-1	42	0	/O-3(CF)	-0.3
1970	Atl N	13	24	3	7	0	0	0	4	2-0	0	4	.292	.333	.292	69	-1	0-0	.800	-1	87	221	O-11(5-4-2)	-0.2
1971	Atl N	29	62	2	14	2	0	0	4	1-1	0	14	.226	.238	.258	38	-5	0-1	1.000	0	89	90	O-18(1-4-16)	-0.6
1972	Atl N	127	446	62	143	27	2	17	76	45-2	4	68	.321	.383	.504	139	24	4-7	.989	12	111	104	*O-123(30-121-3)	3.3
1973	Atl N	159	604	101	174	29	4	21	99	67-8	5	72	.288	.359	.454	116	15	24-3	.983	-4	92	90	*O-156(CF)	1.1
1974	Atl N	149	574	80	147	35	0	20	69	71-9	1	87	.256	.335	.422	107	6	18-7	.981	0	102	97	*O-148(0-102-112)	0.2
1975	Atl N	142	494	63	129	18	2	19	72	67-7	0	57	.261	.346	.421	109	6	12-7	.990	4	107	108	*O-136(0-12-129)	0.4
1976	LA N	112	384	36	93	13	0	4	39	31-3	1	54	.242	.298	.307	74	-13	2-4	.996	-6	97	43	*O-106(0-83-24)	-2.5
1977	†LA N	153	533	86	155	26	1	30	86	58-6	6	89	.291	.364	.512	134	25	2-6	.987	-8	82	84	*O-152(150-1-2)	0.9
1978	†LA N	149	522	62	137	24	1	11	66	47-2	3	66	.262	.325	.375	96	-3	12-3	.985	0	95	113	*O-145(LF)	-0.7
1979	LA N	151	554	86	152	29	1	23	88	56-0	1	70	.274	.340	.455	117	13	11-4	.990	6	99	123	*O-150(LF)	1.4
1980	LA N	153	579	80	170	26	4	29	97	43-4	3	66	.294	.339	.503	137	26	12-10	.991	-1	102	44	*O-151(151-1-1)	1.8
1981	†LA N★	103	400	48	128	17	3	9	49	29-1	1	43	.320	.363	.445	134	17	10-7	.990	-3	95	91	*O-101(LF)	1.0
1982	LA N★	147	570	80	171	19	1	23	88	56-5	3	62	.300	.361	.458	132	24	17-10	.975	-14	81	59	*O-144(144-0-1)	0.4
1983	†LA N	149	531	71	138	25	1	15	73	72-2	2	59	.260	.346	.395	107	7	7-1	.981	-6	97	39	*O-143(LF)	-0.4
1984	SF N	100	243	31	71	7	2	3	32	40-1	0	27	.292	.387	.374	120	8	4-1	.974	-2	101	24	O-62(29-0-33)	0.4
1985	Oak A	111	343	48	92	15	1	14	52	50-0	0	47	.268	.359	.440	128	14	2-1	.993	-2	72	78	1-58,O-35(32-0-5),D-13	0.8
1986	Oak A	83	242	25	58	8	0	4	19	27-1	0	37	.240	.314	.322	80	-6	0-1	1.000	-1	86	133	O-55(36-0-20),D-15/1-3	-1.1
Total	19	2039	7117	964	1981	320	23	242	1013	762-52	30	926	.278	.347	.432	116	155	137-73	.985	-24	96	84	*O-1842(1117-490-348)/1-61,D-28	5.9
BAKER, PHIL Philip B 9.19.1856 Philadelphia, PA D 6.4.1940 Washington, DC BL/TL 5-8/152# d5.1																								
1883	Bal AA	28	121	22	33	2	1	1		8			.273	.318	.331	106	1		.883	-5			C-19,O-14(1-1-12)/S	-0.3
1884	Was U	86	371	75	107	12	5	1		11			.288	.309	.356	104	-9		.955	-3	111	98	1-39,O-32(CF),C-27	-1.3
1886	Was N	81	325	37	72	6	5	1	34	20		32	.222	.267	.280	72	-11	16	.967	-5	63	97	1-56,O-21(1-7-14)/C-4	-1.9
Total	3	195	817	134	212	20	11	3	34	39		32	.259	.293	.322	92	-19	16	.963	-13			/1-95,O-67(2-40-26),C-50,S	-3.5
BAKER, TRACY Tracy Lee B 11.7.1891 Pendleton, OR D 3.14.1975 Placerville, CA BR/TR 6-1/180# d6.19																								
1911	Bos A	1	0	0	0	0	0	0	0	0	0		—	—	—	—	0	0	1.000	-0	0	0	/1	0.0
BAKER, BILL William Presley B 2.22.1911 Paw Creek, NC BR/TR 6/200# d5.4 Mil 1944-45 C1																								
1940	†Cin N	27	69	5	15	1	1	0	7	4	0	8	.217	.260	.261	44	-6	2	1.000	2	*114*	*54*	C-24	-0.2
1941	Cin N	2	1	0	0	0	0	0	0	1	0	1	.000	.500	.000	49	0	0	1.000	0	*0*	*0*	/C	0.0
	Pit N	35	67	5	15	3	0	0	6	11	0	0	.224	.333	.269	71	-2	0	.967	0	*113*	*102*	C-33	-0.1
	Year	37	68	5	15	3	0	0	6	12	0	1	.221	.338	.265	71	-2	0	.967	0	*111*	*100*	C-34	-0.1
1942	Pit N	18	17	1	2	0	0	0	2	1	0	0	.118	.167	.118	-16	-3	0	1.000	1	*126*	*0*	C-11	-0.2
1943	Pit N	63	172	12	47	6	3	1	26	22	3	6	.273	.365	.360	106	2	3	.979	3	*138*	*101*	C-56	0.8
1946	Pit N	53	113	7	27	4	0	1	8	12	0	6	.239	.312	.301	72	-4	0	.965	-4	*71*	*98*	C-41/1	-0.7
1948	StL N	45	119	13	35	10	1	0	15	15	0	7	.294	.373	.395	102	1	1	.994	2	*311*	*72*	C-36	0.5
1949	StL N	20	30	2	4	1	0	0	4	2	0	2	.133	.188	.167	-4	-4	0	1.000	-1	*146*	*0*	C-10	-0.5
Total	7	263	588	45	145	25	5	2	68	68	3	30	.247	.328	.316	79	-16	6	.983	2	*155*	*83*	C-212/1	-0.4
BAKO, PAUL Gabor Paul B 6.20.1972 Lafayette, LA BL/TR 6-2/205# d4.30																								
1998	Det A	96	305	23	83	12	1	3	30	23-4	0	82	.272	.319	.348	74	-12	1-1	.989	-7	88	130	C-94	-1.2
1999	Hou N	73	215	16	55	14	1	2	17	26-3	0	57	.256	.332	.358	77	-7	1-1	.988	7	130	103	C-71	0.4
2000	Hou N	1	2	0	0	0	0	0	0	0-0	0	1	.000	.000	.000	-95	-1	0-0	1.000	0	0	0	/C	0.0
	Fla N	56	161	10	39	6	1	0	14	22-7	1	48	.242	.335	.292	64	-9	0-0	.991	-3	87	127	C-56	-0.8
	†Atl N	24	58	8	11	4	0	2	6	5-3	0	15	.190	.254	.362	53	-4	0-0	.992	0	116	80	C-23/1	-0.3
	Year	81	221	18	50	10	1	2	20	27-10	1	64	.226	.312	.308	59	-14	0-0	.992	-3	94	114	C-80/1	-1.1
2001	†Atl N	61	137	19	29	10	1	2	15	20-2	0	34	.212	.312	.343	68	-6	1-0	.991	3	70	153	C-60	0.0
2002	Mil N	87	234	24	55	8	1	4	20	20-3	0	46	.235	.295	.329	68	-12	0-2	.991	-10	85	91	C-76	-1.9
2003	†Chi N	70	188	19	43	13	3	0	17	22-3	1	47	.229	.311	.330	69	-8	0-1	.987	-8	107	100	C-69	-1.3
Total	6	468	1300	119	315	67	8	13	119	138-25	2	330	.242	.314	.336	70	-59	3-5	.990	-18	96	114	C-450/1	-5.1
BALAZ, JOHN John Lawrence B 11.24.1950 Toronto, ON, CAN BR/TR 6-3/180# d9.10																								
1974	Cal A	14	42	4	10	0	0	1	5	2-0	1	10	.238	.289	.310	76	-1	0-0	1.000	-1	77	0	O-12(LF)	-0.4
1975	Cal A	45	120	10	29	8	1	1	10	5-0	0	25	.242	.270	.350	80	-4	0-0	1.000	1	93	188	O-27(19-0-8),D-11	-0.4
Total	2	59	162	14	39	8	1	2	15	7-0	1	35	.241	.275	.340	79	-5	0-0	1.000	-0	87	123	/O-39(31-0-8),D-11	-0.8
BALBONI, STEVE Stephen Charles B 1.16.1957 Brockton, MA BR/TR 6-3/225# d4.22																								
1981	NY A	4	7	2	2	1	1	0	2	1-0	0	4	.286	.375	.714	211	1	0-0	1.000	0	86	132	/1-3,D	0.1
1982	NY A	33	107	8	20	2	1	2	4	6-0	0	34	.187	.228	.280	40	-9	0-0	.990	-0	96	115	1-26/D-5	-1.1
1983	NY A	32	86	8	20	2	0	5	17	8-0	0	23	.233	.295	.430	101	0	0-0	.984	-1	82	121	1-23/D-4	-0.2
1984	†KC A	126	438	58	107	23	2	28	77	45-5	4	139	.244	.320	.498	122	12	0-0	.987	-2	98	107	*1-125/D	0.2
1985	†KC A	160	600	74	146	28	2	36	88	52-4	5	166	.243	.307	.477	111	7	1-1	.993	-5	90	101	*1-160	-0.8
1986	KC A	138	512	54	117	25	1	29	88	43-2	1	146	.229	.286	.451	96	-5	0-0	.987	-4	94	103	*1-137	-1.7
1987	KC A	121	386	44	80	11	1	24	60	34-1	2	97	.207	.273	.427	80	-13	0-0	.989	1	112	88	1-55,D-52	-1.6
1988	KC A	21	63	2	9	2	0	2	5	1-0	0	20	.143	.156	.270	17	-7	0-0	.980	-1	67	123	1-13/D-6	-1.0
	Sea A	97	350	44	88	15	1	21	61	23-2	1	67	.251	.298	.480	110	3	0-1	.994	-1	87	101	D-56,1-40	-0.3
	Year	118	413	46	97	17	1	23	66	24-2	1	87	.235	.277	.448	96	-4	0-1	.991	-2	83	106	D-62,1-53	-1.3
1989	NY A	110	300	33	71	12	2	17	59	25-5	3	67	.237	.296	.460	113	4	0-0	.994	-0	97	148	D-82,1-20	0.0
1990	NY A	116	266	24	51	6	0	17	34	35-2	3	91	.192	.291	.406	93	-3	0-0	.984	-3	49	121	D-72,1-28	-1.1
1993	Tex A	2	5	0	3	0	0	0	0	0-0	0	2	.600	.600	.600	233	1	0-0	—	0			/D-2	0.1
Total	11	960	3120	351	714	127	11	181	495	273-21	19	856	.229	.293	.451	100	-9	1-2	.989	-16	93	105	1-630,D-281	-7.4
BALCENA, BOBBY Robert Rudolph B 8.1.1925 San Pedro, CA D 1.5.1990 San Pedro, CA BR/TL 5-7/160# d9.16																								
1956	Cin N	7	2	2	0	0	0	0	0	0-0	0	1	.000	.000	.000	-94	-1	0-0	1.000	0	146	0	/O-2(LF)	-0.1
BALDELLI, ROCCO Rocco Daniel B 9.25.1981 Woonsocket, RI BR/TR 6-4/190# d3.31																								
2003	TB A	156	637	89	184	32	8	11	78	30-4	8	128	.289	.326	.416	96	-5	27-10	.989	10	107	**197**	*O-154(CF)/D-2	0.9

Year	Tm Lg	G	AB	R	H	2B	3B	HR	RBI	BB-IB	HP	SO	AVG	OBP	SLG	AOPS	ABR	SB-CS	FA	FR	Rng	Thr	G at Pos	BFW
BALDWIN, KID Clarence Geoghan B 11.1.1864 Newport, KY D 7.10.1897 Cincinnati, OH BR/TR 5-6/147# d7.27 OF Total (11-LF 13-CF 8-RF)																								
1884	KC U	50	191	19	37	6	3	0		4			.194	.210	.257	47	-18		.885	0			C-44,O-10(8-2-0)/23	-1.3
	CP U	1	1	0	1	0	0	0		0			1.000	1.000	1.000	511	0		1.000	-0			/C	0.0
	Year	51	192	19	38	6	3	0		4			.198	.214	.260	49	-18		.885	-0			C-45,O-10(8-2-0)/23	-1.3
1885	Cin AA	34	126	9	17	1	0	1	8	3	0		.135	.155	.167	2	-14		.863	-4			C-25/O-6(0-5-1),2-2,P-2,3	-1.4
1886	Cin AA	87	315	41	72	8	7	3	32	8	2		.229	.252	.327	78	-10	12	.891	-7			C-71,3-13/O-6(0-5-1)	-1.0
1887	Cin AA	96	388	46	98	15	10	1	57	6	4		.253	.271	.351	71	-18	13	.874	-2			*C-96/O-2(LF)	-0.9
1888	Cin AA	67	271	27	59	11	3	1	25	3	3		.218	.235	.292	65	-12	4	.918	-4			C-65/O-2(RF),1	-0.9
1889	Cin AA	60	223	34	55	14	2	1	34	5	3	32	.247	.273	.341	72	-9	7	.912	-1			C-55/O-4(1-1-2),31	-0.5
1890	Cin N	22	72	5	11	0	0	0	10	3	0	6	.153	.187	.153	-1	-9	2	.902	3	*125*	*119*	C-20/O-2(RF)	-0.4
	Phi AA	24	90	5	21	1	2	0	12	4	1		.233	.274	.289	66	-4	2	.887	-4	*83*	*100*	C-19/3-5	-0.6
Total	7	441	1677	186	371	56	27	7	178	36	13	38	.221	.243	.299	61	-94	40	.893	-17	*10*	*11*	C-396/O-32C,3-21,2-3,1-2,P-2	-7.0
BALDWIN, FRANK Frank De Witt B 12.25.1928 High Bridge, NJ BR/TR 5-11/195# d4.22																								
1953	Cin N	16	20	0	2	0	0	0	0	1	0	9	.100	.143	.100	-35	-4	0-0	1.000	-1	*69*	*0*	/C-6	-0.5
BALDWIN, HENRY Henry Clay "Ted" B 6.13.1894 Chadds Ford, PA D 2.24.1964 West Chester, PA BR/TR 5-11/180# d5.22																								
1927	Phi N	6	16	1	5	0	0	0	1	1	0	2	.313	.353	.313	78	0	0	.857	-1	98	94	/S-3,3-2	-0.1
BALDWIN, JEFF Jeffrey Allen B 9.5.1965 Milford, DE BL/TL 6-1/180# d5.22																								
1990	Hou N	7	8	1	0	0	0	0	0	1-0	0	2	.000	.111	.000	-69	-2	0-0	1.000	-0	67	0	/O-3(2-0-1)	-0.2
BALDWIN, REGGIE Reginald Conrad B 8.19.1954 River Rouge, MI BR/TR 6-1/195# d5.25																								
1978	Hou N	38	67	5	17	5	0	1	11	3-0	0	3	.254	.286	.373	89	-1	0-0	.955	-3	52	83	C-17	-0.4
1979	Hou N	14	20	0	4	1	0	0	1	0-0	0	1	.200	.200	.250	23	-2	0-0	1.000	-0	0	0	/C-3,1	-0.3
Total	2	52	87	5	21	6	0	1	12	3-0	0	4	.241	.267	.345	74	-3	0-0	.956	-4	49	78	/C-20,1	-0.7
BALDWIN, BILLY Robert Harvey B 6.9.1951 Tazewell, VA BL/TL 6/175# d7.29																								
1975	Det A	30	95	8	21	3	0	4	8	5-0	0	14	.221	.260	.379	75	-4	2-1	.983	2	100	220	O-25(0-13-13)/D	-0.3
1976	NY N	9	22	4	6	1	1	1	5	1-0	0	2	.273	.292	.545	146	1	0-0	.929	1	136	296	O-5(3-0-2)	0.2
Total	2	39	117	12	27	4	1	5	13	6-0	0	16	.231	.266	.410	87	-3	2-1	.972	3	106	233	/O-30(3-13-15),D	-0.1
BALENTI, MIKE Michael Richard B 7.3.1886 Calumet, OK D 8.4.1955 Altus, OK BR/TR 5-11/175# d7.19																								
1911	Cin N	8	8	2	2	0	0	0	0	0	0	1	.250	.250	.250	42	-1	3	.857	0	127	248	/S-2,O(CF)	0.0
1913	StL A	70	211	17	38	2	4	0	11	6	1	32	.180	.206	.227	28	-21	3	.923	-2	103	116	S-56/O-8(LF)	-2.1
Total	2	78	219	19	40	2	4	0	11	6	1	33	.183	.208	.228	28	-22	6	.922	-2	103	119	/S-58,O-9(8-1-0)	-2.1
BALES, LEE Wesley Owen B 12.4.1944 Los Angeles, CA BB/TR 5-10.5/165# d8.7																								
1966	Atl N	12	16	4	1	0	0	0	0	0-0	0	5	.063	.063	.063	-64	-4	0-0	1.000	1	125	69	/2-7,3-3	-0.2
1967	Hou N	19	27	4	3	0	0	0	2	8-0	0	7	.111	.306	.111	28	-2	1-1	.944	-1	88	0	/2-6,S	-0.3
Total	2	31	43	8	4	0	0	0	2	8-0	0	12	.093	.231	.093	-3	-6	1-1	.978	0	107	36	/2-13,3-3,S	-0.5
BALL, ART Arthur Clark B 4.1876 , KY D 12.26.1915 Chicago, IL TR ?/168# d8.1																								
1894	StL N	1	3	0	1	0	0	0	0	0	0	1	.333	.333	.333	61	0	0	.667	-1	0	0	/2	-0.1
1898	Bal N	32	81	7	15	2	0	0	8	7	1		.185	.258	.210	34	-7	2	.906	6	108	182	3-15,S-14/2-2,O(CF)	0.0
Total	2	33	84	7	16	2	0	0	8	7	1	1	.190	.261	.214	35	-7	2	.906	5	108	182	/3-15,S-14,2-3,O(CF)	-0.1
BALL, NEAL Cornelius B 4.22.1881 Grand Haven, MI D 10.15.1957 Bridgeport, CT BR/TR 5-7/145# d9.12																								
1907	NY A	15	44	5	9	1	1	0	4	1	0		.205	.222	.273	53	-3	1	.817	-3	95	68	S-11/2-5	-0.6
1908	NY A	132	446	35	110	16	2	0	38	21	2		.247	.284	.291	86	-7	32	.898	-6	100	62	*S-130/2	-1.1
1909	NY A	8	29	5	6	1	1	0	3	3	0		.207	.281	.310	86	-1	2	.917	-3	77	33	/2-8	-0.4
	Cle A	96	324	29	83	13	2	1	25	17	1		.256	.295	.318	90	-4	17	.914	-10	91	129	S-95	-1.2
	Year	104	353	34	89	14	3	1	28	20	1		.252	.294	.317	90	-5	19	.914	-13	91	129	S-95/2-8	-1.6
1910	Cle A	54	123	13	25	3	1	0	12	9	0		.203	.258	.244	56	-6	4	.927	-3	88	101	S-27/2-7,O-6(0-5-1),3-3	-1.0
1911	Cle A	116	412	45	122	14	9	3	45	27	0		.296	.339	.396	104	0	21	.945	3	105	111	2-94,3-17/S	0.5
1912	Cle A	40	132	12	30	4	1	0	14	9	0		.227	.277	.273	55	-8	7	.938	0	93	98	2-37	-0.7
	†Bos A	18	45	10	9	2	0	0	6	3	0		.200	.250	.244	40	-4	5	.927	-2	96	35	2-17	-0.6
	Year	58	177	22	39	6	1	0	20	12	0		.220	.270	.266	51	-11	12	.936	-2	94	84	2-54	-1.3
1913	Bos A	23	58	9	10	2	0	0	4	9	1	13	.172	.294	.207	46	-4	3	.902	-3	88	124	2-10/S-7,3	-0.6
Total	7	502	1613	163	404	56	17	4	151	99	4	13	.250	.295	.314	83	-37	92	.902	-28	96	89	S-271,2-179/3-21,O-6(0-5-1)	-5.7
BALL, JIM James Chandler B 2.22.1884 Harford Co., MD D 4.7.1963 Glendale, CA BR/TR 5-11/175# d9.21																								
1907	Bos N	10	36	3	6	2	0	0	3	2	0		.167	.211	.222	36	-3	0	.963	-2	*73*	*114*	C-10	-0.5
1908	Bos N	6	15	1	1	0	0	0	0	1	0		.067	.125	.067	-39	-2	0	.917	-1	*83*	*142*	/C-6	-0.3
Total	2	16	51	4	7	2	0	0	3	3	0		.137	.185	.176	14	-5	0	.949	-3	*76*	*123*	/C-16	-0.8
BALL, JEFF Jeffery D. B 4.17.1969 Merced, CA BR/TR 5-10/185# d6.10																								
1998	SF N	2	4	0	1	0	0	0	0	0-0	0	0	.250	.250	.250	34	0	0-0	1.000	-0	0	158	/1	-0.1
BALLENGER, PELHAM Pelham Ashby B 2.6.1894 Gilreath Mill, SC D 12.8.1948 Greenville, SC BR/TR 5-11/160# d5.7																								
1928	Was A	3	9	0	1	0	0	0	0	0	0	1	.111	.111	.111	-42	-2	0-0	1.000	1	161	236	/3-3	-0.1
BAMBERGER, HAL Harold Earl "Dutch" B 10.29.1924 Lebanon, PA BL/TR 6/173# d9.15																								
1948	NY N	7	12	0	1	0	0	0	0	1	0	2	.083	.154	.083	-34	-2	0	1.000	-0	102	0	/O-3(0-1-2)	-0.3
BANCKER, STUD John B Philadelphia, PA d4.19																								
1875	NH NA	19	72	3	11	0	0	0	2	0		3	.153	.153	.153	7	-6	1-0	.796	-4			C-14/2-4,3-3,S1	-0.8
BANCROFT, DAVE David James "Beauty" B 4.20.1891 Sioux City, IA D 10.9.1972 Superior, WI BB/TR 5-9.5/160# d4.14 M4 C3 HF1971																								
1915	†Phi N	**153**	563	85	143	18	2	7	30	77	2	62	.254	.346	.330	104	6	15-27	.928	5	101	105	*S-153	1.7
1916	Phi N	142	477	53	101	10	0	3	33	74	4	57	.212	.323	.252	75	-10	15	.933	25	110	113	*S-142	2.8
1917	Phi N	127	478	56	116	22	5	4	43	44	0	42	.243	.307	.335	93	-3	14	.936	**28**	112	111	*S-120/2-3,O-2(LF)	3.6
1918	Phi N	**125**	499	69	132	19	4	0	26	54	1	36	.265	.338	.319	94	-1	11	.928	16	104	102	*S-125	2.6
1919	Phi N	92	335	45	91	13	7	0	25	31	0	30	.272	.333	.352	99	0	8	.951	6	99	96	S-88	1.4
1920	Phi N	42	171	23	51	7	2	0	5	9	1	12	.298	.337	.363	96	-1	1-7	.981	9	106	131	S-42	1.0
	NY N	108	442	79	132	29	7	0	31	33	1	32	.299	.349	.396	115	9	7-5	.946	28	118	143	*S-108	4.6
	Year	150	613	102	183	36	9	0	36	42	2	44	.299	.346	.387	109	8	8-12	**.955**	**37**	**115**	**140**	*S-150	5.6
1921	†NY N	**153**	606	121	193	26	15	6	67	66	4	23	.318	.389	.441	119	18	17-10	.960	19	104	**141**	*S-153	5.3
1922	†NY N	**156**	651	117	209	41	5	4	60	79	3	27	.321	.397	.418	109	14	16-11	.941	22	108	114	*S-156	4.9
1923	†NY N	107	444	80	135	33	3	1	31	62	1	23	.304	.391	.399	110	10	8-7	.936	12	107	94	S-96,2-11	3.2
1924	Bos N	79	319	49	89	11	1	2	21	37	1	24	.279	.356	.339	91	-3	4-4	.961	-3	96	107	S-79,M	0.3
1925	Bos N	128	479	75	153	29	8	2	49	64	0	22	.319	.400	.426	122	19	7-4	**.945**	10	**108**	101	*S-125,M	3.9
1926	Bos N	127	453	70	141	18	6	1	44	64	2	29	.311	.399	.384	122	18	3	.956	-5	96	92	*S-123/3-2,M	2.6
1927	Bos N	111	375	44	91	13	4	1	31	43	1	36	.243	.322	.307	75	-13	5	.939	5	100	100	*S-104/3M	0.3
1928	Bro N	149	515	47	127	19	5	0	51	59	2	20	.247	.326	.303	66	-24	7	.948	2	98	72	*S-149	-0.6
1929	Bro N	104	358	35	99	11	3	1	44	29	0	11	.277	.331	.332	66	-19	7	.955	-3	94	69	*S-102	-1.1
1930	NY N	10	17	0	1	1	0	0	0	2	0	1	.059	.158	.118	-33	-4	0	.966	-0	96	0	/S-8	-0.3
Total	16	1913	7182	1048	2004	320	77	32	591	827	23	487	.279	.355	.358	98	16	145-75	.944	178	104	105	*S-1873/2-14,3-3,O-2(LF)	36.2
BANDO, CHRIS Christopher Michael B 2.4.1956 Cleveland, OH BB/TR 6/195# d8.13 C3 b-Sal																								
1981	Cle A	21	47	3	10	3	0	0	6	2-0	0	2	.213	.240	.277	51	-3	0-0	.967	-2	115	106	C-15/D-2	-0.5
1982	Cle A	66	184	13	39	6	1	3	16	24-1	0	30	.212	.299	.304	68	-8	0-0	.990	-6	107	108	C-63/3-2	-1.2
1983	Cle A	48	121	15	31	3	0	4	15	15-0	0	19	.256	.336	.380	94	-1	0-1	.995	0	135	128	C-43	0.1
1984	Cle A	75	220	38	64	11	0	12	41	33-5	0	35	.291	.377	.505	141	13	1-2	.982	-1	118	76	C-63/13D	1.4
1985	Cle A	73	173	11	24	4	1	0	13	22-0	0	21	.139	.234	.173	14	-21	0-1	.986	-8	65	114	C-67	-2.7
1986	Cle A	92	254	28	68	9	0	2	26	22-0	1	49	.268	.325	.327	81	-7	0-1	.990	-7	95	77	C-86	-1.0
1987	Cle A	89	211	20	46	9	0	5	16	12-0	0	28	.218	.260	.332	55	-14	0-0	.990	-2	100	111	C-86	-1.3
1988	Cle A	32	72	6	9	1	0	1	8	8-0	1	12	.125	.217	.181	14	-8	0-0	.979	2	111	128	C-32	-0.5

Year	Tm Lg	G	AB	R	H	2B	3B	HR	RBI	BB-IB	HP	SO	AVG	OBP	SLG	AOPS	ABR	SB-CS	FA	FR	Rng	Thr	G at Pos	BFW
	Det A	1	0	0	0	0	0	0	0	0-0	0	0	—	—	—	—	0	0-0	—	-0	0	0	/C	0.0
	Year	33	72	6	9	1	0	1	8	8-0	1	12	.125	.217	.181	14	-8	0-0	.979	2	110	127	C-33	-0.5
1989	Oak A	1	2	0	1	0	0	0	1	0-0	0	1	.500	.500	.500	189	0	0-0	1.000	1	0	0	/C	0.1
Total	9	498	1284	134	292	46	2	27	142	138-6	2	197	.227	.300	.329	73	-49	1-5	.987	-23	102	101	C-457/3-3,D-3,1	-5.6
BANDO, SAL Salvatore Leonard B 2.13.1944 Cleveland, OH BR/TR 6/205# d9.3 C2 b-Chris																								
1966	KC A	11	24	1	7	1	1	0	1	1-0	0	3	.292	.320	.417	113	0	0-0	.933	2	154	67	/3-7	0.3
1967	KC A	47	130	11	25	3	2	0	6	16-0	3	24	.192	.295	.246	64	-6	1-0	.959	9	122	106	3-44	0.4
1968	Oak A	162	605	67	152	25	5	9	67	51-6	7	78	.251	.314	.354	108	5	13-4	.964	-4	89	97	*3-162/O(LF)	0.2
1969	Oak A★	**162**	609	106	171	25	3	31	113	111-5	11	82	.281	.400	.484	153	48	1-4	.954	-8	95	106	*3-162	3.9
1970	Oak A	155	502	93	132	20	2	20	75	118-5	6	88	.263	.407	.430	137	32	6-10	.954	-13	88	76	*3-152	1.7
1971	†Oak A	153	538	75	146	23	1	24	94	86-11	8	55	.271	.377	.452	137	29	3-7	.971	-20	82	77	*3-153	0.8
1972	†Oak A★	152	535	64	126	20	3	15	77	78-17	9	55	.236	.341	.368	118	14	3-1	.960	0	102	108	*3-151/2	1.5
1973	†Oak A★	**162**	592	97	170	**32**	3	29	98	82-5	4	84	.287	.375	.498	153	43	4-2	.949	-29	80	90	*3-159/D-3	1.4
1974	†Oak A✳	146	498	84	121	21	2	22	103	86-4	5	79	.243	.352	.426	134	25	2-3	.946	-14	89	102	*3-141/D-3	1.0
1975	†Oak A	160	562	64	129	24	1	15	78	87-2	5	80	.230	.337	.356	98	1	7-1	.967	-20	85	126	*3-160	-1.8
1976	Oak A	158	550	75	132	18	2	27	84	76-1	4	74	.240	.335	.427	128	20	20-6	.962	-2	99	108	*3-155/S-5,D-2	2.0
1977	Mil A	159	580	65	145	27	3	17	82	75-3	3	89	.250	.336	.395	99	1	4-2	.966	-1	100	120	*3-135,D-24/2S	-0.2
1978	Mil A	152	540	85	154	20	6	17	78	72-4	6	52	.285	.371	.439	128	22	3-2	.968	8	113	103	*3-134,D-12/1-5	2.7
1979	Mil A	130	476	57	117	14	3	9	43	57-3	3	42	.246	.330	.345	82	-11	2-0	.963	-11	94	81	*3-109,D-19/1-4,P2	-2.3
1980	Mil A	78	254	28	50	12	1	5	31	29-2	1	35	.197	.278	.311	64	-12	5-3	.934	-2	99	114	3-57,D-15/1-7	-1.6
1981	†Mil A	32	65	10	13	4	0	2	9	6-1	0	3	.200	.268	.354	82	-2	1-1	.967	-1	94	145	3-15/1-9,D-2	-0.4
Total	16	2019	7060	982	1790	289	38	242	1039	1031-69	75	923	.254	.352	.408	120	209	75-46	.959	-104	94	100	*3-1896/D-80,1-25,S-6,2-3,PO(LF)	9.6
BANISTER, JEFF Jeffery Todd B 1.15.1965 Weatherford, OK BR/TR 6-2/200# d7.23																								
1991	Pit N	1	1	0	1	0	0	0	0	0-0	0	0	1.000	1.000	1.000	471	0	0-0	—	0			/H	0.0
BANKS, BRIAN Brian Glen B 9.28.1970 Mesa, AZ BB/TR 6-3/200# d9.9																								
1996	Mil A	4	7	2	4	2	0	1	2	1-0	0	2	.571	.625	1.286	353	3	0-0	1.000	0	67	0	/O-3(LF),1	0.2
1997	Mil A	28	68	9	14	1	0	1	8	6-0	0	17	.206	.267	.265	40	-6	0-1	.950	-1	71	0	O-15(15-0-1)/1-5,3D	-0.8
1998	Mil N	24	24	3	7	2	0	1	5	4-0	0	7	.292	.393	.500	133	1	0-0	1.000	-1	39	0	/C-5,1-2,3O(LF)	0.0
1999	Mil N	105	219	34	53	7	1	5	22	25-5	0	59	.242	.317	.352	70	-10	6-1	.992	-5	120	79	1-44,C-40/O-5(4-0-1)	-1.4
2002	Fla N	20	28	3	9	1	0	1	4	1-0	0	6	.321	.345	.464	119	0	0-0	1.000	-0	95	0	/O-8(3-0-5),13	0.0
2003	†Fla N	92	149	14	35	6	2	4	23	25-1	2	38	.235	.348	.383	96	0	2-1	.975	-2	89	69	O-33(23-0-10),1-12/D	-0.4
Total	6	273	495	65	122	19	3	13	64	62-6	2	129	.246	.330	.376	84	-12	8-3	.989	-9	111	92	/1-65,O-65(49-0-17),C-45,3-3,D-2	-2.4
BANKS, ERNIE Ernest "Mr. Cub" B 1.31.1931 Dallas, TX BR/TR 6-1/180# d9.17 C7 HF1977																								
1953	Chi N	10	35	3	11	1	1	2	6	4	0	5	.314	.385	.571	142	2	0-0	.981	2	112	133	S-10	0.5
1954	Chi N	**154**	593	70	163	19	7	19	79	40	7	50	.275	.326	.427	94	-7	6-10	.959	-2	99	99	*S-154	0.2
1955	Chi N★	**154**	596	98	176	29	9	44	117	45-6	2	72	.295	.345	.596	145	35	9-3	**.972**	3	102	100	*S-154	5.1
1956	Chi N☆	139	538	82	160	25	8	28	85	52-18	0	62	.297	.358	.530	137	27	6-9	.962	-13	88	100	*S-139	2.4
1957	Chi N★	**156**	594	113	169	34	6	43	102	70-11	3	85	.285	.360	.579	150	41	8-4	.975	-11	91	87	*S-100,3-58	3.9
1958	Chi N★	**154**	617	119	193	23	11	**47**	**129**	52-12	4	87	.313	.366	**.614**	157	47	4-4	.960	0	99	89	*S-154	5.9
1959	Chi N★	**155**	589	97	179	25	6	45	**143**	64-**20**	7	72	.304	.374	.596	156	46	2-4	**.985**	5	**107**	102	*S-154	6.2
1960	Chi N★	**156**	597	94	162	32	7	**41**	117	71-**28**	4	69	.271	.350	.554	145	36	1-3	**.977**	11	107	99	*S-156	**6.0**
1961	Chi N★	138	511	75	142	22	4	29	80	54-21	2	75	.278	.346	.507	122	15	1-2	.965	15	**115**	98	*S-104,O-23(LF)/1-7	3.6
1962	Chi N★	154	610	87	164	20	6	37	104	30-3	7	71	.269	.306	.503	110	5	5-1	.993	-2	97	97	*1-149/3-3	-0.5
1963	Chi N	130	432	41	98	20	1	18	64	39-16	4	73	.227	.292	.403	94	-3	0-3	.993	-2	95	110	*1-125	-1.5
1964	Chi N	157	591	67	156	29	6	23	95	36-11	3	84	.264	.307	.450	107	4	1-2	.994	10	**127**	101	*1-157	0.4
1965	Chi N★	163	612	79	162	25	3	28	106	55-19	6	64	.265	.328	.453	116	12	3-5	.992	-9	83	108	*1-162	-0.8
1966	Chi N	141	511	52	139	23	7	15	75	29-10	5	59	.272	.315	.432	105	2	0-1	.992	3	111	84	*1-130/3-8	-0.3
1967	Chi N★	151	573	68	158	26	4	23	95	27-8	3	93	.276	.310	.455	112	7	2-2	.993	0	101	101	*1-147	-0.2
1968	Chi N	150	552	71	136	27	0	32	83	27-4	5	67	.246	.287	.469	116	9	2-0	.996	-1	96	113	*1-147	0.0
1969	Chi N★	155	565	60	143	19	2	23	106	42-7	7	101	.253	.309	.416	91	-8	0-0	**.997**	-0	94	103	*1-153	-2.1
1970	Chi N	72	222	25	56	6	2	12	44	20-3	1	33	.252	.313	.459	94	-3	0-0	.993	-2	86	119	1-62	-0.9
1971	Chi N	39	83	4	16	2	0	3	6	6-1	0	14	.193	.247	.325	53	-5	0-0	1.000	0	94	99	1-20	-0.7
Total	19	2528	9421	1305	2583	407	90	512	1636	763-198	70	1236	.274	.330	.500	122	262	50-53	.994	10	100	103	*1-1259,*S-1125/3-69,O-23(LF)	27.2
BANKS, GEORGE George Edward B 9.24.1938 Pacolet Mills, SC D 3.1.1985 Spartanburg, SC BR/TR 5-11/185# d4.15																								
1962	Min A	63	103	22	26	0	2	4	15	21-0	1	27	.252	.372	.408	109	2	0-0	.962	-1	93	0	O-17(7-0-11)/3-6	0.0
1963	Min A	25	71	5	11	4	0	3	8	9-1	1	21	.155	.259	.338	65	-3	0-0	.910	0	98	119	3-21	-0.3
1964	Min A	1	1	0	0	0	0	0	0	0-0	0	1	.000	.000	.000	-99	0	0-0	—	0			H	0.0
	Cle A	9	17	6	5	1	0	2	3	6-0	0	6	.294	.478	.706	226	3	0-0	1.000	-0	95	0	/O-3(3-0-1),23	0.3
	Year	10	18	6	5	1	0	2	3	6-0	0	7	.278	.458	.667	210	3	0-0	1.000	-0	95	0	/O-3(3-0-1),23	0.3
1965	Cle A	4	5	0	1	1	0	0	0	1-0	0	3	.200	.333	.400	107	0	0-1	1.000	0	121	673	/3	0.0
1966	Cle A	4	4	0	1	0	0	0	1	0-0	0	1	.250	.250	.250	44	0	0-0	—	0			H	0.0
Total	5	106	201	33	44	6	2	9	27	37-1	2	59	.219	.340	.403	102	2	0-1	.919	-1	99	131	/3-29,O-20(10-0-12),2	0.0
BANKSTON, EVERETT Wilborn Everett B 5.25.1893 Barnesville, GA D 2.26.1970 Griffin, GA BL/TR 5-11/180# d8.15																								
1915	Phi A	11	36	6	5	1	1	1	2	2	1	5	.139	.205	.306	55	-2	1	.882	-1	85	95	/O-8(4-4-0)	-0.4
BANNING, JIM James M. B 6.11.1865 New York, NY D 10.14.1952 St.Paul, MN BL/TR 5-6/150# d9.27																								
1888	Was N	1	0	0	0	0	0	0	0	0	0	0	—	—	—	—	0	0	1.000	-0			/C	0.0
1889	Was N	2	1	0	0	0	0	0	0	0	0	0	.000	.000	.000	-99	0	0	1.000	1			/C-2	0.0
Total	2	3	1	0	0	0	0	0	0	0	0	0	.000	.000	.000	-99	0	0	1.000	1			/C-3	0.0
BANNISTER, ALAN Alan B 9.3.1951 Montebello, CA BR/TR 5-11/175# d7.13 OF Total (254-LF 72-CF 100-RF)																								
1974	Phi N	26	25	4	3	0	0	0	1	3-0	1	7	.120	.241	.120	3	-3	0-0	1.000	-1	89	0	/O-8(CF),S-2	-0.4
1975	Phi N	24	61	10	16	3	1	0	0	1-0	0	9	.262	.274	.344	68	-3	2-2	1.000	1	134	0	O-18(4-14-1)/2S	-0.2
1976	Chi A	73	145	19	36	6	2	0	8	14-1	1	21	.248	.317	.317	86	-2	12-4	.988	1	120	46	O-43(29-13-4),S-14/2-4,3D	0.0
1977	Chi A	139	560	87	154	20	3	3	57	54-1	2	49	.275	.335	.338	86	-10	4-3	.936	-30	82	62	*S-133/2-3,O-3(2-2-0)	-2.6
1978	Chi A	49	107	16	24	3	2	0	8	11-1	1	12	.224	.303	.290	67	-5	3-3	1.000	-1	102	0	D-19,O-15(8-7-0)/S-8,2-2	-0.6
1979	Chi A	136	506	71	144	28	8	2	55	43-1	3	40	.285	.342	.383	96	-2	22-6	.963	-15	92	68	2-65,O-47(47-0-2),3-12/1D	-1.3
1980	Chi A	45	130	16	25	6	0	0	9	12-5	0	16	.192	.259	.238	38	-11	5-2	1.000	-0	98	0	O-23(22-0-1),3-17	-1.2
	Cle A	81	262	41	86	17	4	1	32	28-1	0	25	.328	.388	.435	126	10	9-2	.968	-4	96	73	2-41,O-40(9-9-26)/3-3,S-2	0.8
	Year	126	392	57	111	23	4	1	41	40-6	0	41	.283	.346	.370	97	0	14-4	.981	-4	99	56	O-63(31-9-27),2-41,3-20/S-2	-0.4
1981	Cle A	68	232	36	61	11	1	1	17	16-2	0	19	.263	.309	.332	86	-4	16-2	.986	-3	108	93	O-35(18-6-17),2-30/1-2,S	-0.4
1982	Cle A	101	348	40	93	16	1	4	41	42-1	1	41	.267	.347	.353	94	-2	18-5	.991	-3	113	35	O-55(46-4-9),2-48/S-2,3D	-0.2
1983	Cle A	117	377	51	100	25	4	5	45	31-0	3	43	.265	.323	.393	93	-3	6-6	.969	-1	91	123	O-91(58-8-34),2-27/1-3,D-3	-0.7
1984	Hou N	9	20	2	4	2	0	0	0	2-0	0	2	.200	.273	.300	65	-1	0-0	.947	-1	75	51	/S-4,O(LF)	-0.1
	Tex A	47	112	20	33	2	1	2	9	21-0	1	17	.295	.407	.384	118	4	3-0	.959	-10	61	38	2-25/O-3(1-1-1),13D	-0.4
1985	Tex A	57	122	17	32	4	1	1	6	14-0	0	17	.262	.338	.336	84	-2	8-2	1.000	-1	92	0	D-21,O-14(9-0-5),2-10/3-5,1-4	-0.3
Total	12	972	3007	430	811	143	28	19	288	292-13	13	318	.270	.334	.355	90	-34	108-37	.983	-65	103	72	O-396L,2-256,S-167/D-66,3-40,1	-7.6
BANNON, JIMMY James Henry "Foxy Grandpa" B 5.5.1871 Amesbury, MA D 3.24.1948 Glen Rock, NJ BR/TR 5-5/160# d6.15 b-Tom ▲																								
1893	StL N	26	107	9	36	3	4	0	15	4	1	5	.336	.366	.439	113	1	8	.795	-5	59	0	O-24(1-0-23)/S-2,P	-0.4
1894	Bos N	128	494	130	166	29	10	13	114	62	4	42	.336	.414	.514	114	10	47	.873	17	**200**	**242**	*O-128(RF)/P	1.6
1895	Bos N	124	493	101	171	35	5	6	74	54	5	31	.347	.417	.475	120	16	28	.879	7	161	75	*O-123(1-0-122)/P	1.3
1896	Bos N	89	344	53	87	9	5	0	50	32	1	23	.253	.318	.308	62	-20	16	.901	-2	116	75	O-76(2-1-73)/2-6,S-5,3-3	-2.1
Total	4	367	1438	293	460	76	24	19	253	152	11	101	.320	.389	.446	104	7	99	.877	17	159	131	O-351(4-1-346)/S-7,2-6,3-3,P-3	0.4
BANNON, TOM Thomas Edward "Ward Six" B 5.8.1869 Amesbury, MA D 1.26.1950 Lynn, MA BR/TR 5-8/175# d5.10 b-Jimmy																								
1895	NY N	37	159	33	43	6	2	0	8	7	0	8	.270	.301	.333	65	-9	20	.894	1	261	130	O-21(13-0-8),1-16	-0.8
1896	NY N	2	7	1	1	1	0	0	0	1	0	1	.143	.250	.286	42	-1	0	.500	-1	0	0	/O-2(1-1-0)	-0.1
Total	2	39	166	34	44	7	2	0	8	8	0	9	.265	.299	.331	64	-10	20	.878	0	246	123	/O-23(14-1-8),1-16	-0.9

Year	Tm Lg	G	AB	R	H	2B	3B	HR	RBI	BB-IB	HP	SO	AVG	OBP	SLG	AOPS	ABR	SB-CS	FA	FR	Rng	Thr	G at Pos	BFW
BARAJAS, ROD Rodrigo Richard B 9.5.1975 Ontario, CA BR/TR 6-2/220# d9.25																								
1999	Ari N	5	16	3	4	1	0	1	3	1-0	0	1	.250	.294	.500	95	0	0-0	1.000	-2	189	0	/C-5	-0.2
2000	Ari N	5	13	1	3	0	0	1	3	0-0	0	4	.231	.231	.462	67	-1	0-0	1.000	-0	0	0	/C-5	-0.1
2001	†Ari N	51	106	9	17	3	0	3	9	4-0	0	26	.160	.191	.274	17	-14	0-0	.995	-17	66	91	C-50	-2.8
2002	†Ari N	70	154	12	36	10	0	3	23	10-4	3	25	.234	.288	.357	67	-8	1-0	.997	-15	147	81	C-69/1	-2.0
2003	Ari N	80	220	19	48	15	0	3	28	14-7	1	43	.218	.265	.327	49	-16	0-0	1.000	12	130	113	C-79	0.0
Total	5	211	509	44	108	29	0	11	66	29-11	4	99	.212	.257	.334	50	-39	1-0	.998	-22	121	93	C-208/1	-5.1
BARBARE, WALTER Walter Lawrence "Dinty" B 8.11.1891 Greenville, SC D 10.28.1965 Greenville, SC BR/TR 6/162# d9.17																								
1914	Cle A	15	52	6	16	2	2	0	5	2	1	5	.308	.345	.423	126	1	1-4	.933	1	120	148	3-14/S	0.2
1915	Cle A	77	246	15	47	3	1	0	11	10	4	27	.191	.235	.211	33	-21	6-5	.960	6	104	104	3-68/1	-1.4
1916	Cle A	13	48	3	11	1	0	0	3	4	0	9	.229	.288	.250	58	-2	0	.977	2	122	88	3-12	0.0
1918	Bos A	13	29	2	5	3	0	0	2	0	0	1	.172	.172	.276	36	-2	1	.826	-3	79	73	3-11/S	-0.5
1919	Pit N	85	293	34	80	11	5	1	34	18	1	18	.273	.317	.355	98	-1	11	.961	-8	82	110	3-80/2	-0.7
1920	Pit N	57	186	9	51	5	2	0	12	9	0	11	.274	.308	.323	79	-5	5-3	.923	-4	92	102	S-34,2-12/3-5	-0.7
1921	Bos N	134	550	66	166	22	7	0	49	24	0	28	.302	.331	.367	89	-9	11-4	.957	-15	94	89	*S-121/2-8,3-2	-1.0
1922	Bos N	106	373	38	86	5	4	0	40	21	0	22	.231	.272	.265	41	-34	2-0	.966	3	103	109	2-45,3-38,1-14	-2.7
Total	8	500	1777	173	462	52	21	1	156	88	6	121	.260	.297	.315	71	-73	37-16	.959	-18	96	105	3-230,S-157/2-66,1-15	-6.8
BARBARY, RED Donald Odell B 6.20.1920 Simpsonville, SC D 9.27.2003 Simpsonville, SC BR/TR 6-2/195# d5.22																								
1943	Was A	1	1	0	0	0	0	0	0	0	0	0	.000	.000	.000	-99	0	0-0	—	0			H	0.0
BARBEAU, JAP William Joseph B 6.10.1882 New York, NY D 9.10.1969 Milwaukee, WI BR/TR 5-5/140# d9.27																								
1905	Cle A	11	37	1	10	1	1	0	2	1	0		.270	.289	.351	102	0	1	.905	0	106	213	2-11	0.0
1906	Cle A	42	129	8	25	5	3	0	12	9	2		.194	.257	.279	69	-5	5	.830	-8	87	204	3-32/S-6	-1.3
1909	Pit N	91	350	60	77	16	3	0	25	37	4		.220	.302	.283	75	-9	19	.891	-18	83	89	3-85	-2.8
	StL N	48	175	23	44	3	0	0	5	28	5		.251	.370	.269	105	3	14	.901	-5	89	126	3-47	0.0
	Year	139	525	83	121	19	3	0	30	65	9		.230	.326	.278	85	-6	33	.895	-22	85	101	*3-132	-2.8
1910	StL N	7	21	4	4	0	1	0	2	3	0	3	.190	.292	.286	71	-1	0	.917	2	155	0	/3-6,2	0.1
Total	4	199	712	96	160	25	8	0	46	78	11	3	.225	.311	.282	82	-12	39	.884	-29	88	115	3-170/2-12,S-6	-4.0
BARBEE, DAVE David Monroe B 5.7.1905 Greensboro, NC D 7.1.1968 Albemarle, NC BR/TR 5-11.5/178# d7.29																								
1926	Phi A	19	47	7	8	1	1	1	5	2	1	4	.170	.220	.298	32	-5	0-0	1.000	0	101	95	O-10(RF)	-0.6
1932	Pit N	97	327	37	84	22	6	5	55	18	2	38	.257	.300	.407	89	-6	1	.975	4	111	103	O-78(77-1-0)	-0.6
Total	2	116	374	44	92	23	7	6	60	20	3	42	.246	.290	.393	82	-11	1-0	.977	4	110	102	/O-88(77-1-10)	-1.2
BARBER, CHARLIE Charles D. B 1854 Philadelphia, PA D 11.23.1910 Philadelphia, PA BR/TR d4.17																								
1884	Cin U	55	204	38	41	1	4	0		11			.201	.242	.245	44	-21		.837	3	111	82	3-55	-1.4
BARBER, TURNER Tyrus Turner B 7.9.1893 Lavinia, TN D 10.20.1968 Milan, TN BL/TR 5-11/170# d8.19																								
1915	Was A	20	53	9	16	1	1	0	6	6	1	7	.302	.383	.358	120	1	0-3	.952	0	78	177	O-19(3-0-16)	0.0
1916	Was A	15	33	3	7	0	1	1	5	2	0	3	.212	.257	.364	87	-1	0	.833	-1	90	0	O-10(6-0-4)	-0.3
1917	Chi N	7	28	2	6	1	0	0	2	2	0	8	.214	.267	.250	54	-1	1	1.000	1	90	242	/O-7(1-6-0)	-0.1
1918	†Chi N	55	123	11	29	3	2	0	10	9	1	16	.236	.293	.293	77	-3	3	.940	-2	92	62	O-27(4-17-15)/1-4	-0.8
1919	Chi N	76	230	26	72	9	4	0	21	14	1	17	.313	.355	.387	122	6	7	.949	-3	95	87	O-68(53-13-2)	0.0
1920	Chi N	94	340	27	90	10	5	0	50	9	3	26	.265	.290	.324	74	-12	5-6	.988	-6	73	85	1-69,O-17(6-8-3)/2-2	-2.3
1921	Chi N	127	452	73	142	14	4	1	54	41	6	24	.314	.379	.369	99	1	5-9	.970	2	90	152	*O-123(90-20-14)	-0.7
1922	Chi N	84	226	35	70	7	4	0	29	30	0	9	.310	.391	.376	97	0	7-4	.953	-3	93	78	O-47(31-0-16),1-16	-0.7
1923	Bro N	13	46	3	10	2	0	0	8	2	0	2	.217	.250	.261	36	-4	0-1	1.000	-1	84	86	O-12(CF)	-0.5
Total	9	491	1531	189	442	47	21	2	185	115	12	112	.289	.343	.351	93	-13	28-23	.959	-13	91	114	O-330(194-76-70)/1-89,2-2	-5.4
BARBERIE, BRET Bret Edward B 8.16.1967 Long Beach, CA BB/TR 5-11/180# d6.16																								
1991	Mon N	57	136	16	48	12	2	2	18	20-2	2	22	.353	.435	.515	171	14	0-0	.931	-1	109	93	S-19,2-10,3-10/1	1.5
1992	Mon N	111	285	26	66	11	0	1	24	47-3	8	62	.232	.354	.281	83	-3	9-5	.932	5	116	108	3-63,2-26/S	0.3
1993	Fla N	99	375	45	104	16	2	5	33	33-2	7	58	.277	.344	.371	87	-6	2-4	.982	7	105	102	2-97	0.5
1994	Fla N	107	372	40	112	20	2	5	31	23-3	9	65	.301	.356	.406	95	-2	2-0	.975	7	105	97	*2-106	1.0
1995	Bal A	90	237	32	57	14	0	2	25	36-0	6	50	.241	.351	.325	77	-6	3-3	.977	4	101	119	2-74/3-3,D-5	0.0
1996	Chi N	15	29	4	1	0	0	1	2	5-0	0	11	.034	.176	.138	-15	-5	0-1	1.000	-1	125	35	/2-6,3-2,S	-0.6
Total	6	479	1434	163	388	73	6	16	133	164-10	32	268	.271	.356	.363	92	-8	16-13	.980	21	104	101	2-319/3-78,S-21,D-5,1	2.7
BARBIERI, JIM James Patrick B 9.15.1941 Schenectady, NY BL/TR 5-7/155# d7.5																								
1966	†LA N	39	82	9	23	5	0	0	3	9-1	0	7	.280	.352	.341	102	1	2-0	.939	0	94	162	O-20(9-0-11)	0.0
BARCLAY, GEORGE George Oliver "Deerfoot" B 5.16.1876 Millville, PA D 4.3.1909 Philadelphia, PA BR/TR 5-10/162# d4.17																								
1902	StL N	137	543	79	163	14	2	3	53	31	6		.300	.345	.350	119	12	30	.904	-6	87	97	*O-137(LF)	-0.2
1903	StL N	108	419	37	104	10	8	0	42	15	2		.248	.278	.310	70	-19	12	.901	-7	87	0	*O-107(LF)	-3.2
1904	StL N	103	375	41	75	7	4	1	28	12	6		.200	.237	.248	52	-22	14	.947	-6	54	55	*O-103(LF)	-3.7
	Bos N	24	93	5	21	3	1	0	10	2	2		.226	.258	.280	68	-4	3	.935	-2	74	110	O-24(6-1-17)	-0.7
	Year	127	468	46	96	10	5	1	38	14	8		.205	.241	.254	55	-26	17	.945	-8	57	64	*O-127(109-1-17)	-4.4
1905	Bos N	29	108	5	19	1	0	0	7	2	2		.176	.205	.185	17	-11	2	.854	-4	54	109	O-28(LF)	-1.8
Total	4	401	1538	167	382	35	15	4	140	62	18		.248	.286	.298	79	-44	61	.911	-25	75	61	O-399(381-1-17)	-9.6
BARD, JOSH Joshua David B 3.30.1978 Ithaca, NY BB/TR 6-3/205# d8.23																								
2002	Cle A	24	90	9	20	5	0	3	12	4-0	0	13	.222	.255	.378	66	-5	0-0	.988	0	147	115	C-24	-0.3
2003	Cle A	91	303	25	74	13	1	8	36	22-1	0	53	.244	.293	.373	77	-11	0-2	.991	11	110	125	C-87/D	0.5
Total	2	115	393	34	94	18	1	11	48	26-1	0	66	.239	.284	.374	75	-16	0-2	.990	11	118	123	C-111/D	0.2
BARFIELD, JESSE Jesse Lee B 10.29.1959 Joliet, IL BR/TR 6-1/205# d9.3 C3																								
1981	Tor A	25	95	7	22	3	2	2	9	4-0	1	19	.232	.270	.368	77	-3	4-3	1.000	4	134	105	O-25(RF)	-0.1
1982	Tor A	139	394	54	97	13	2	18	58	42-3	3	79	.246	.323	.426	95	-3	1-4	.963	1	95	183	*O-137(1-3-136)/D	-0.9
1983	Tor A	128	388	58	98	13	3	27	68	22-0	4	110	.253	.296	.510	111	4	2-5	.966	8	107	**209**	*O-120(0-1-120)/D-5	0.4
1984	Tor A	110	320	51	91	14	1	14	49	35-5	2	81	.284	.357	.466	122	10	8-2	.952	6	113	178	O-88(0-9-79)/D-9	1.3
1985	†Tor A	155	539	94	156	34	9	27	84	66-5	4	143	.289	.369	.536	141	31	22-8	.989	15	107	**206**	*O-154(0-8-147)	3.9
1986	Tor A★	158	589	107	170	35	2	**40**	108	69-5	8	146	.289	.368	.559	145	37	8-8	.992	16	112	182	*O-157(0-18-147)	4.3
1987	Tor A	159	590	89	155	25	3	28	84	58-7	3	141	.263	.331	.458	104	3	3-5	.992	13	112	163	*O-158(0-13-152)	0.7
1988	Tor A	137	468	62	114	21	5	18	56	41-6	1	108	.244	.302	.425	102	0	7-3	.988	13	**114**	153	*O-136(0-13-132)/D	0.9
1989	Tor A	21	80	8	16	4	0	5	11	5-0	1	28	.200	.256	.438	94	-1	0-2	.979	2	94	246	O-21(1-0-20)	-0.1
	NY A	129	441	71	106	19	1	18	56	82-6	2	122	.240	.360	.410	119	14	5-3	.972	8	106	166	*O-129(0-18-120)	1.9
	Year	150	521	79	122	23	1	23	67	87-6	3	150	.234	.345	.415	115	13	5-5	.973	10	104	177	*O-150(1-18-140)	1.8
1990	NY A	153	476	69	117	21	2	25	78	82-4	5	150	.246	.359	.456	127	19	4-3	.973	7	104	158	*O-151(0-4-151)	2.1
1991	NY A	84	284	37	64	12	0	17	48	36-6	0	80	.225	.312	.447	107	2	1-0	1.000	9	112	177	O-81(1-0-81)	0.9
1992	NY A	30	95	8	13	2	0	2	7	9-2	0	27	.137	.210	.221	21	-10	1-1	.966	0	95	160	O-30(RF)	-1.2
Total	12	1428	4759	715	1219	216	30	241	716	551-49	34	1234	.256	.335	.466	116	103	66-47	.980	101	108	176	*O-1387(3-87-1340)/D-16	14.1
BARKER, AL Alfred L B 1.18.1839 Rockford, IL D 9.15.1912 Rockford, IL d6.1																								
1871	Rok NA	1	4	0	1	0	0	0	2	1		0	.250	.400	.250	97	0	0-0	1.000	-0	0	0	/O(LF)	0.0
BARKER, GLEN Glen F. B 5.10.1971 Albany, NY BB/TR 5-10/180# d4.7																								
1999	†Hou N	81	73	23	21	2	0	1	11	11-0	1	19	.288	.384	.356	91	0	17-6	.981	-0	94	158	O-57(3-47-8)/D	0.1
2000	Hou N	84	67	18	15	2	1	2	6	7-0	1	23	.224	.307	.373	67	-4	9-6	.985	1	117	72	O-69(2-63-4)	-0.2
2001	Hou N	70	24	12	2	0	0	0	1	3-0	2	6	.083	.233	.083	-10	-4	4-6	1.000	-0	112	0	O-60(CF)	-0.5
Total	3	235	164	53	38	4	1	3	18	21-0	4	48	.232	.330	.323	66	-8	30-18	.987	1	107	89	O-186(5-170-12)/D	-0.6
BARKER, KEVIN Kevin Stewart B 7.26.1975 Bristol, VA BL/TL 6-3/205# d8.19																								
1999	Mil N	38	117	13	33	3	0	3	23	9-1	0	19	.282	.331	.385	82	-4	1-0	.996	0	103	80	1-31	-0.6
2000	Mil N	40	100	14	22	5	0	2	9	20-0	1	21	.220	.352	.330	76	-3	1-0	.993	-3	73	96	1-32	-0.8
2002	SD N	7	19	0	3	0	0	0	0	1-0	0	6	.158	.200	.158	-3	-3	1-0	1.000	-1	30	108	/1-6	-0.4
Total	3	85	236	27	58	8	0	5	32	30-1	1	46	.246	.331	.343	74	-10	3-0	.995	-3	83	90	/1-69	-1.8

Year	Tm Lg	G	AB	R	H	2B	3B	HR	RBI	BB-IB	HP	SO	AVG	OBP	SLG	AOPS	ABR	SB-CS	FA	FR	Rng	Thr	G at Pos	BFW
BARKER, RAY Raymond Herrell "Buddy" B 3.12.1936 Martinsburg, WV BL/TR 6/192# d9.13																								
1960	Bal A	5	6	0	0	0	0	0	0	0-0	0	3	.000	.000	.000	-99	-2	0-0	—	-0	0	0	/O(LF)	-0.2
1965	Cle A	11	6	0	0	0	0	0	0	2-1	0	2	.000	.250	.000	-22	-1	0-0	1.000	-0	0	0	/1-3	-0.1
	NY A	98	205	21	52	11	0	7	31	20-5	3	46	.254	.326	.410	109	3	1-0	.991	7	153	113	1-61/3-3	0.7
	Year	109	211	21	52	11	0	7	31	22-6	3	48	.246	.324	.398	105	2	1-0	.991	6	152	112	1-64/3-3	0.6
1966	NY A	61	75	11	14	5	0	3	13	4-0	0	20	.187	.225	.373	72	-3	0-0	.987	5	199	72	1-47	0.1
1967	NY A	17	26	2	2	0	0	0	0	3-0	0	5	.077	.172	.077	-25	-4	0-0	.961	1	163	90	1-13	-0.4
Total	4	192	318	34	68	16	0	10	44	29-6	3	76	.214	.283	.358	84	-7	1-0	.987	12	166	99	1-124/3-3,O(LF)	0.1
BARKETT, ANDY Andrew Jon B 9.5.1974 Miami, FL BL/TL 6-1/205# d5.28																								
2001	Pit N	17	46	5	14	2	0	1	3	4-1	1	7	.304	.373	.413	101	0	1-0	1.000	1	92	180	O-10(9-0-2)/1-4,D	0.0
BARKLEY, RED John Duncan B 9.19.1913 Childress, TX D 12.12.2000 Waco, TX BR/TR 5-11/160# d9.2 gs-Brian																								
1937	StL A	31	101	9	27	6	0	0	14	14	0	17	.267	.357	.327	73	-4	1-0	.969	-4	90	88	2-31	-0.5
1939	Bos N	12	11	1	0	0	0	0	0	1	0	2	.000	.083	.000	-82	-3	0	.842	2	158	0	/S-7,3-4	-0.1
1943	Bro N	20	51	6	16	3	0	0	7	4	0	7	.314	.364	.373	113	1	1	.894	-3	89	109	S-18	-0.1
Total	3	63	163	16	43	9	0	0	21	19	0	26	.264	.341	.319	75	-6	2-0	.969	-5	90	88	/2-31,S-25,3-4	-0.7
BARKLEY, SAM Samuel E B 5.24.1858 Wheeling, WV D 4.20.1912 Wheeling, WV BR/TR 5-11.5/180# d5.1 M1																								
1884	Tol AA	104	435	71	133	**39**	9	1		22	2		.306	.342	.444	149	24		.930	26	111	106	*2-103/C-2	**4.8**
1885	†StL AA	106	418	67	112	18	10	3	53	25	2		.268	.312	.380	113	5		.921	12	111	106	*2-96,1-11	1.7
1886	Pit AA	122	478	77	127	31	8	1	69	58	0		.266	.345	.370	125	16	22	.936	1	94	118	*2-112/O-8(LF),1-2	1.8
1887	Pit N	89	340	44	76	10	4	1	35	30	4	24	.224	.294	.285	66	-14	6	.979	-8	76	82	1-53,2-36	-2.2
1888	KC AA	116	482	67	104	21	6	4	51	26	4		.216	.262	.309	78	-14	15	.938	-8	92	89	*2-116/,M	-1.6
1889	KC AA	45	176	36	50	6	2	0	23	15	0	20	.284	.340	.341	89	-3	8	.923	-10	89	96	2-41/1-4	-1.0
Total	6	582	2329	362	602	125	39	10	231	176	12	44	.258	.314	.359	105	14	51	.929	13	100	103	2-504/1-70,O-8(LF),C-2	3.5
BARLOW, TOM Thomas H. B 1852 , NY d5.2																								
1872	Atl NA	**37**	171	34	54	1	0	0	8	3		2	.316	.328	.322	86	-5	7-5	.758	-10			*C-36/S-4,3	-1.1
1873	Atl NA	**55**	269	48	74	0	2	1	12	5		1	.275	.288	.301	84	-3	3-4	.762	-16			*C-55/2S	-1.4
1874	Har NA	32	155	37	46	5	1	0	12	2		2	.297	.306	.342	102	0	**17**-4	.820	8	111	57	S-32	0.7
1875	NH NA	1	5	1	1	0	0	0	0	0		0	.200	.200	.200	45	0	0-0	.800	0	109	0	/S	0.0
	Atl NA	1	4	0	0	0	0	0	0	0		0	.000	.000	.000	-99	-1	0-0	.500	-1	0	0	/2	-0.2
	Year	2	9	1	1	0	0	0	0	0		0	.111	.111	.111	-26	-1	0-0	.800	-1	109	0	/S2	-0.2
Total	4 NA	126	604	120	175	6	3	1	32	10		5	.290	.301	.315	88	-9	27-13	.000	-18			/C-91,S-38,2-2,3	-2.0
BARMES, BRUCE Bruce Raymond "Squeaky" B 10.23.1929 Vincennes, IN BL/TR 5-8/165# d9.13																								
1953	Was A	5	5	1	1	0	0	0	0	0	0	0	.200	.200	.200	8	-1	0-0	1.000	0	149	0	/O(RF)	-0.1
BARMES, CLINT Clint Harold B 3.6.1979 Vincennes, IN BR/TR 6/170# d9.5																								
2003	Col N	12	25	2	8	2	0	0	2	0-0	2	10	.320	.357	.400	89	0	0-0	.958	1	108	99	S-12	0.2
BARNA, BABE Herbert Paul B 3.2.1915 Clarksburg, WV D 5.18.1972 Charleston, WV BL/TR 6-2/210# d9.16																								
1937	Phi A	14	36	10	14	2	0	2	9	2	0	6	.389	.421	.611	159	3	1-0	.800	-1	74	0	/O-9(LF),1	0.2
1938	Phi A	9	30	4	4	0	0	0	2	3	0	5	.133	.212	.133	-12	-5	0-0	.917	-0	81	205	/O-7(4-0-3)	-0.6
1941	NY N	10	42	5	9	3	0	1	5	2	0	6	.214	.250	.357	68	-2	0	1.000	0	75	222	O-10(2-0-8)	-0.3
1942	NY N	104	331	39	85	8	7	6	58	38	0	48	.257	.333	.378	107	2	3	.983	-4	91	67	O-89(88-0-1)	-0.8
1943	NY N	40	113	11	23	5	1	1	12	16	0	9	.204	.302	.292	72	-4	3	.984	-1	97	72	O-31(LF)	-0.7
	Bos A	30	112	19	19	4	1	2	10	15	0	24	.170	.268	.277	58	-6	2-1	.940	-3	73	140	O-29(LF)	-1.1
Total	5	207	664	88	154	22	9	12	96	76	0	98	.232	.311	.346	88	-12	9-1	.969	-9	87	93	O-175(163-0-12)/1	-3.3
BARNES, RED Emile B 12.25.1904 Suggsville, AL D 7.3.1959 Mobile, AL BL/TR 5-10.5/158# d9.29																								
1927	Was A	3	11	5	4	1	0	0	0	1	0	3	.364	.417	.455	127	1	0-0	1.000	0	57	383	/O-3(0-1-2)	0.1
1928	Was A	114	417	82	127	22	15	6	51	55	4	38	.305	.391	.472	127	17	7-3	.978	-4	88	131	*O-104(8-96-1)	0.8
1929	Was A	72	130	16	26	5	2	1	15	13	0	12	.200	.273	.292	45	-11	1-0	.877	-3	90	85	O-30(8-14-9)	-1.4
1930	Was A	12	12	1	2	1	0	0	0	0	0	3	.167	.167	.250	4	-2	0-0	—	0			H	-0.2
	Chi A	85	266	48	66	12	7	1	31	26	1	20	.248	.317	.357	73	-11	4-2	.939	-1	95	119	O-72(1-71-0)	-1.4
	Year	97	278	49	68	13	7	1	31	26	1	23	.245	.311	.353	70	-13	4-2	.939	-1	95	119	O-72(1-71-0)	-1.6
Total	4	286	836	152	225	41	24	8	97	95	5	76	.269	.347	.404	95	-6	12-5	.953	-8	90	125	O-209(17-182-12)	-2.1
BARNES, EPPIE Everett Duane B 12.1.1900 Ossining, NY D 11.17.1980 Mineola, NY BL/TL 5-9/175# d9.25																								
1923	Pit N	2	2	0	1	0	0	0	0	0	0	1	.500	.500	.500	161	0	0-0	1.000	0	568	382	/1	0.0
1924	Pit N	2	5	0	0	0	0	0	0	0	0	1	.000	.000	.000	-98	-1	0-0	1.000	0	205	0	/1	-0.1
Total	2	4	7	0	1	0	0	0	0	0	0	2	.143	.143	.143	-23	-1	0-0	1.000	1	304	104	/1-2	-0.1
BARNES, JOHN John Delbert B 4.24.1976 San Diego, CA BR/TR 6-2/176# d9.16																								
2000	Min A	11	37	5	13	4	0	0	2	2-0	2	6	.351	.415	.459	116	1	0-1	1.000	2	117	274	O-11(2-2-8)	0.3
2001	Min A	9	21	1	1	0	0	0	0	1-0	1	3	.048	.130	.048	-49	-5	0-0	.895	1	119	230	/O-9(3-0-6)	-0.4
Total	2	20	58	6	14	4	0	0	2	3-0	3	9	.241	.313	.310	59	-4	0-1	.959	3	118	258	/O-20(5-2-14)	-0.1
BARNES, HONEY John Francis B 1.31.1900 Fulton, NY D 6.18.1981 Lockport, NY BL/TR 5-10/175# d4.20																								
1926	NY A	1	0	0	0	0	0	0	0	1	0	0	—	1.000	—	179	0	0-0	—	0	*0*	*0*	/C	0.0
BARNES, LARRY Larry Richard B 7.23.1974 Bakersfield, CA BL/TL 6-1/195# d4.11																								
2001	Ana A	16	40	2	4	0	0	1	2	1-0	0	9	.100	.122	.175	-22	-7	0-0	1.000	-0	93	53	1-16/O(LF)	-0.9
2003	LA N	30	38	2	8	2	0	0	2	1-0	0	9	.211	.231	.263	30	-4	0-0	1.000	-0	57	95	/1-8,O-2(LF),D	-0.5
Total	2	46	78	4	12	2	0	1	4	2-0	0	18	.154	.175	.218	2	-11	0-0	1.000	-0	81	67	/1-24,O-3(LF),D	-1.4
BARNES, LUTE Luther Owens B 4.28.1947 Forest City, IA BR/TR 5-10/160# d8.6																								
1972	NY N	24	72	5	17	2	2	0	6	6-1	0	4	.236	.291	.319	76	-2	0-1	.959	1	95	140	2-14/S-6	-0.1
1973	NY N	3	2	2	1	0	0	0	1	0-0	0	1	.500	.500	.500	181	0	0-0	—	0			H	0.0
Total	2	27	74	7	18	2	2	0	7	6-1	0	5	.243	.296	.324	79	-2	0-1	.959	1	95	140	/2-14,S-6	-0.1
BARNES, ROSS Roscoe Charles B 5.8.1850 Mount Morris, NY D 2.5.1915 Chicago, IL BR/TR 5-8.5/145# d5.5 U1																								
1871	Bos NA	**31**	157	**66**	63	10	9	0	34	13		1	.401	.447	.580	186	17	11-6	.873	12	134	189	2-16,S-15	**1.8**
1872	Bos NA	45	230	81	**99**	**28**	2	1	44	9		4	**.430**	.452	**.583**	**205**	**28**	12-2	**.904**	26	**130**	**261**	*2-45	**3.5**
1873	Bos NA	**60**	320	**125**	**138**	**31**	**11**	2	60	**20**		2	**.431**	**.465**	**.616**	**201**	**38**	**43**-6	**.857**	19	**122**	127	*2-47,3-13	**4.2**
1874	Bos NA	51	259	72	88	12	4	0	39	8		2	.340	.360	.417	140	11	8-7	**.856**	18	**117**	**201**	*2-51/O(LF)	**1.9**
1875	Bos NA	78	393	**115**	**143**	20	4	1	58	7		3	.364	**.375**	.443	177	29	29-6	.877	**22**	110	163	*2-76/O-3(LF),S-2	**4.2**
1876	Chi N	**66**	322	**126**	**138**	**21**	**14**	1	59	**20**		8	**.429**	**.462**	**.590**	**222**	**40**		**.910**	7	106	118	*2-66/P	**4.2**
1877	Chi N	22	92	16	25	1	0	0	5	7		4	.272	.323	.283	83	-2		.838	-7	93	60	2-22	-0.7
1879	Cin N	77	323	55	86	9	2	1	30	16		25	.266	.301	.316	109	4		.855	0	104	99	*S-61,2-16	0.7
1881	Bos N	69	295	42	80	14	1	0	17	16		16	.271	.309	.325	104	3		.854	-3	100	82	*S-63/2-7	0.3
Total	5 NA	265	1359	459	531	101	30	4	235	57		12	.391	.415	.518	182	123	103-27	.000	97	119	184	2-235/S-17,3-13,O-4(LF)	15.6
Total	4	234	1032	239	329	45	17	2	111	59		53	.319	.356	.401	143	45		.855	-3	102	90	S-124,2-111/P	4.5
BARNES, SAM Samuel Thomas B 12.18.1899 Suggsville, AL D 2.19.1981 Montgomery, AL BL/TR 5-8/150# d9.14																								
1921	Det A	7	11	2	2	1	0	0	0	2	1	1	.182	.357	.273	63	0	0-0	.944	1	135	0	/2-2	0.0
BARNES, BILL William H. B Indianapolis, IN d9.27																								
1884	StP U	8	30	2	6	1	0	0		0			.200	.200	.233	57	-2		.727	-2	0	289	/O-8(CF)	-0.4
BARNES, SKEETER William Henry B 3.3.1957 Cincinnati, OH BR/TR 5-10/180# d9.6 OF Total (37-LF 11-CF 30-RF)																								
1983	Cin N	15	34	5	7	0	0	1	4	7-0	2	3	.206	.372	.294	84	0	2-2	1.000	-0	129	103	/1-7,3-7	-0.1
1984	Cin N	32	42	5	5	0	0	1	3	4-1	0	6	.119	.196	.190	8	-5	0-0	1.000	1	108	0	3-11/O-3(LF)	-0.5
1985	Mon N	19	26	0	4	1	0	0	0	0-0	0	2	.154	.154	.192	-4	-4	0-1	1.000	1	118	238	/3-4,O-3(1-0-2),1	-0.3
1987	StL N	4	4	1	1	0	0	1	3	0-0	0	0	.250	.250	1.000	208	1	0-0	—	-0	0	0	/3	0.0
1989	Cin N	5	3	1	0	0	0	0	0	0-0	0	0	.000	.000	.000	-97	-1	0-1	—	0			H	-0.1
1991	Det A	75	159	28	46	13	2	5	17	9-1	0	24	.289	.325	.491	121	4	10-7	1.000	-0	104	331	O-33(13-5-17),3-17/1-9,2-7,D-3	0.3

Year	Tm Lg	G	AB	R	H	2B	3B	HR	RBI	BB-IB	HP	SO	AVG	OBP	SLG	AOPS	ABR	SB-CS	FA	FR	Rng	Thr	G at Pos	BFW
1992	Det A	95	165	27	45	8	1	3	25	10-1	2	18	.273	.318	.388	97	-1	3-1	.919	3	113	126	3-39,1-17,O-15(4-6-5)/2-7,D-7	0.2
1993	Det A	84	160	24	45	8	1	2	27	11-0	0	19	.281	.318	.381	90	-2	5-5	.984	0	107	56	1-27,O-18(12-0-6),3-13,D-13,2-10/S-2	-0.5
1994	Det A	24	21	4	6	0	0	1	4	0-0	0	2	.286	.286	.429	81	-1	0-1	1.000	-0	56	86	1-15/O-4(LF),D	-0.2
Total	9	353	614	95	159	30	4	14	83	41-3	4	74	.259	.306	.389	90	-9	20-18	.938	3	108	107	/3-92,O-76L,1-76,D-24,2-24,S-2	-1.2
BARNEY, ED Edmund J. B 1.23.1890 Amery, WI D 10.4.1967 Rice Lake, WI BL/TR 5-10.5/178# d7.22																								
1915	NY A	11	36	1	7	0	0	0	8	3	0	6	.194	.256	.194	35	-3	2-1	1.000	0	96	76	O-10(3-7-0)	-0.4
	Pit N	32	99	16	27	1	2	0	5	11	3	12	.273	.363	.323	110	2	7-3	.972	0	109	61	O-26(3-22-1)	0.1
1916	Pit N	45	137	16	27	4	0	0	9	23	0	15	.197	.313	.226	66	-4	8	.964	3	117	107	O-40(20-20-0)	-0.4
Total	2	88	272	33	61	5	2	0	22	37	3	33	.224	.324	.257	78	-5	17-4	.971	4	112	87	/O-76(26-49-1)	-0.7
BARNHART, CLYDE Clyde Lee "Pooch" B 12.29.1895 Buck Valley, PA D 1.21.1980 Hagerstown, MD BR/TR 5-10/155# d9.22 s-Vic																								
1920	Pit N	12	46	5	15	4	2	0	5	1	0	2	.326	.340	.500	135	2	1-0	.971	0	107	176	3-12	0.3
1921	Pit N	124	449	66	116	15	13	3	62	32	3	36	.258	.312	.370	78	-15	3-3	.956	-19	84	94	*3-118	-2.8
1922	Pit N	75	209	30	69	7	5	1	38	25	0	7	.330	.402	.426	112	5	3-2	.918	-7	64	96	3-30,O-26(5-0-21)	-0.3
1923	Pit N	114	327	60	106	25	13	9	72	47	0	21	.324	.409	.563	151	24	5-7	.985	6	105	144	O-92(RF)	2.1
1924	Pit N	102	344	49	95	6	11	3	51	30	2	17	.276	.338	.384	91	-5	8-4	.970	1	108	76	O-88(RF)	-1.1
1925	†Pit N	142	539	85	175	32	11	4	114	59	0	25	.325	.391	.447	106	7	9-5	.962	-1	101	87	*O-138(LF)	-0.4
1926	Pit N	76	203	26	39	3	0	0	10	23	1	13	.192	.278	.207	30	-20	1	.991	1	100	100	O-61(54-0-8)	-2.3
1927	†Pit N	108	360	65	115	23	4	3	54	37	1	19	.319	.384	.431	110	7	2	.978	3	116	58	O-94(LF)	0.3
1928	Pit N	61	196	18	58	6	2	4	30	11	0	9	.296	.333	.408	89	-4	3	.971	-0	103	85	O-48(45-0-4)/3	-0.7
Total	9	814	2673	404	788	121	61	27	436	265	7	149	.295	.360	.416	100	1	35-21	.973	-17	105	90	O-547(336-0-213),3-161	-4.9
BARNHART, VIC Victor Dee B 9.1.1922 Hagerstown, MD BR/TR 6/188# d10.1 f-Clyde																								
1944	Pit N	1	2	0	1	0	0	0	0	1	0	1	.500	.667	.500	222	0	0	.889	0	146	0	/S	0.1
1945	Pit N	71	201	21	54	7	0	0	19	9	0	11	.269	.300	.303	65	-10	2	.928	1	100	111	S-60/3-4	-0.5
1946	Pit N	2	1	0	0	0	0	0	0	0	0	0	.000	.000	.000	-98	0	0	—	0			H	0.0
Total	3	74	204	21	55	7	0	0	19	10	0	12	.270	.304	.304	67	-10	2	.927	1	101	108	/S-61,3-4	-0.4
BARNIE, BILLY William Harrison "Bald Billy" B 1.26.1853 New York, NY D 7.15.1900 Hartford, CT TR 5-7/157# d5.7 M14 U1																								
1874	Har NA	45	190	21	35	4	2	0	20	1		13	.184	.188	.226	31	-15	2-2	.733	-8			C-30,O-29(0-4-25)/S	-1.7
1875	Wes NA	10	36	3	4	1	0	0	2	0		3	.111	.111	.139	-13	-4	0-0	.889	0	0	0	/O-7(0-3-4),C-3	-0.3
	Mut NA	9	34	1	5	0	0	0	1	1		0	.147	.171	.147	11	-3	0-0	.750	-3			/C-6,O-3(0-1-2)	-0.5
	Year	19	70	4	9	1	0	0	3	1		3	.129	.141	.143	-1	-7	0-0	.857	-2	0	0	O-10(0-4-6)/C-9	-0.8
1883	Bal AA	17	55	7	11	0	0	0		2			.200	.228	.200	38	-4		.846	-2			C-13/O-6(RF),SM	-0.4
1886	Bal AA	2	6	0	0	0	0	0	0	1	0		.000	.143	.000	-55	-1	0	—	-1	0	0	/O(CF)C	-0.2
Total	2 NA	64	260	25	44	5	2	0	23	2	0	16	.169	.176	.204	23	-22	2-2	.000	-10			/O-39(0-8-31),C-39,S	-2.5
Total	2	19	61	7	11	0	0	0	0	3	0	0	.180	.219	.180	29	-5	0-0	.848	-3			/C-14,O-7(0-1-6),S	-0.6
BARONE, DICK Richard Anthony B 10.13.1932 San Jose, CA BR/TR 5-9/165# d9.22																								
1960	Pit N	3	6	0	0	0	0	0	0	0-0	0	1	.000	.000	.000	-99	-2	0-0	.875	-1	69	0	/S-2	-0.2
BARR, SCOTTY Hyder Edward B 10.6.1886 Bristol, TN D 12.2.1934 Ft.Worth, TX BR/TR 6/175# d8.22																								
1908	Phi A	19	56	4	8	2	0	0	1	3	1		.143	.200	.179	22	-5	0	.923	-4	80	0	2-11/3-4,1-2,O-2(1-1-0)	-1.0
1909	Phi A	22	51	5	4	1	0	0	1	11	1		.078	.254	.098	12	-5	2	.947	-1	0	0	O-15(1-14-0)/1-7	-0.7
Total	2	41	107	9	12	3	0	0	2	14	2		.112	.228	.140	17	-10	2	.947	-5	0	0	/O-17(2-15-0),2-11,1-9,3-4	-1.7
BARRAGAN, CUNO Facundo Anthony B 6.20.1932 Sacramento, CA BR/TR 5-11/180# d9.1																								
1961	Chi N	10	28	3	6	0	0	1	2	2-0	0	7	.214	.267	.321	54	-2	0-0	1.000	-1	*97*	*112*	C-10	-0.2
1962	Chi N	58	134	11	27	6	1	0	12	21-1	0	28	.201	.306	.261	53	-8	0-2	.971	-6	*74*	*137*	C-55	-1.3
1963	Chi N	1	1	0	0	0	0	0	0	0-0	0	1	.000	.000	.000	-95	0	0-0	1.000	0	*0*	*0*	/C	0.0
Total	3	69	163	14	33	6	1	1	14	23-1	0	36	.202	.298	.270	53	-10	0-2	.975	-6	*77*	*133*	/C-66	-1.5
BARRANCA, GERMAN German (Costales) B 10.19.1956 Veracruz, Mexico BL/TR 6/160# d9.2																								
1979	KC A	5	5	3	3	1	0	0	0	0-0	0	0	.600	.600	.800	269	1	3-1	1.000	2	231	412	/23D	0.4
1980	KC A	7	0	3	0	0	0	0	0	0-0	0	0	—	—	—	—	0	0-0	—	0			/R	0.0
1981	Cin N	9	6	2	2	0	0	0	1	0-0	0	0	.333	.333	.333	88	0	0-0	—	0			/H	0.0
1982	Cin N	46	51	11	13	1	3	0	2	2-0	0	9	.255	.283	.392	85	-1	2-0	.824	-2	80	44	/2-6	-0.3
Total	4	67	62	19	18	2	3	0	3	2-0	0	9	.290	.313	.419	101	0	5-1	.893	0	113	125	/2-7,D3	0.1
BARRETT, JIMMY James Erigena B 3.28.1875 Athol, MA D 10.24.1921 Detroit, MI BL/TR 5-9/170# d9.13																								
1899	Cin N	26	92	30	34	2	4	0	10	18	1		.370	.477	.478	159	9	4	.936	-2	53	0	O-26(3-0-23)	0.5
1900	Cin N	137	545	114	172	11	7	5	42	72	5		.316	.400	.389	121	19	44	.929	2	133	122	*O-137(0-115-22)	1.2
1901	Det A	**135**	542	110	159	16	9	4	65	76	5		.293	.385	.378	107	8	26	.940	11	**178**	175	*O-135(CF)	1.2
1902	Det A	136	509	93	154	19	6	4	44	74	6		.303	.397	.387	116	15	24	.961	6	126	164	*O-136(CF)	1.3
1903	Det A	136	517	95	163	13	10	2	31	**74**	6		.315	**.407**	.391	144	33	27	.955	7	128	182	*O-136(CF)	3.4
1904	Det A	**162**	624	83	167	10	5	0	31	**79**	3		.268	.353	.300	111	12	15	.971	9	**163**	121	*O-162(CF)	1.5
1905	Det A	20	67	2	17	1	0	0	3	6	1		.254	.324	.269	88	-1	0	1.000	-1	0	0	O-18(CF)	-0.3
1906	Cin N	5	12	1	0	0	0	0	0	2	0		.000	.143	.000	-53	-2	0	1.000	1	294	1194	/O-4(RF)	-0.2
1907	Bos A	106	390	52	95	11	6	1	28	38	2		.244	.314	.310	100	1	3	.966	0	100	169	O-99(96-3-0)	-0.6
1908	Bos A	3	8	0	1	0	0	0	1	1	0		.125	.222	.125	13	-1	0	1.000	-0	0	0	/O-2(CF)	-0.1
Total	10	866	3306	580	962	83	47	16	255	440	29		.291	.379	.359	117	93	143	.954	32	135	150	O-855(99-707-49)	7.9
BARRETT, JOHN John B Brooklyn, NY d9.18																								
1872	Atl NA	8	34	6	7	1	0	0	2	0		1	.206	.206	.235	30	-3	1-0	.808	-1	0	0	/O-8(LF)	-0.2
BARRETT, JOHNNY John Joseph "Jack" B 12.18.1915 Lowell, MA D 8.17.1974 Seabrook Beach, NH BL/TL 5-10.5/170# d4.14																								
1942	Pit N	111	332	56	82	11	6	0	26	48	3	42	.247	.347	.316	92	-2	10	.973	6	109	137	O-94(15-5-74)	-0.1
1943	Pit N	130	290	41	67	12	3	1	32	32	4	23	.231	.316	.303	77	-8	5	.988	1	107	76	O-99(4-3-92)	-1.3
1944	Pit N	149	568	99	153	24	**19**	7	83	86	1	56	.269	.366	.415	115	12	**28**	.972	-2	102	76	*O-147(1-67-92)	0.3
1945	Pit N	142	507	97	130	29	4	15	67	79	0	68	.256	.357	.418	111	9	25	.976	-6	98	68	*O-132(0-75-57)	-0.3
1946	Pit N	32	71	7	12	3	0	0	6	8	0	11	.169	.253	.211	32	-6	1	.919	-1	93	69	O-21(0-12-9)	-0.9
	Bos N	24	43	3	10	3	0	0	6	12	0	1	.233	.400	.302	100	1	0	.962	-1	92	99	O-17(2-11-4)	0.0
	Year	56	114	10	22	6	0	0	12	20	0	12	.193	.313	.246	59	-5	1	.937	-2	93	82	O-38(2-23-13)	-0.9
Total	5	588	1811	303	454	82	32	23	220	265	8	201	.251	.349	.369	100	6	69	.974	-3	102	86	O-510(22-173-328)	-2.3
BARRETT, MARTY Martin F. B 11.1860 Port Henry, NY D 1.29.1910 Holyoke, MA BR/TR 5-9/170# d6.24																								
1884	Bos N	3	6	0	0	0	0	0	0	0		4	.000	.000	.000	-99	-1		.900	-1			/C-3	-0.2
	Ind AA	5	13	1	1	1	0	0		1	0		.077	.143	.154	-3	-1		.808	-2			/C-4,O(RF)	-0.3
Total	1	8	19	1	1	1	0	0	0	1	0	4	.053	.100	.105	-34	-2		.833	-3			/C-7,O(RF)	-0.5
BARRETT, MARTY Martin Glenn B 6.23.1958 Arcadia, CA BR/TR 5-10/176# d9.6 b-Tom																								
1982	Bos A	8	18	0	1	0	0	0	0	0-0	0	1	.056	.056	.056	-66	-4	0-0	1.000	4	157	124	/2-7	0.0
1983	Bos A	33	44	7	10	1	1	0	2	3-0	0	1	.227	.271	.295	54	-3	0-0	.984	-4	75	83	2-23/D-5	-0.6
1984	Bos A	139	475	56	144	23	3	3	45	42-2	1	25	.303	.358	.383	101	2	5-3	**.987**	0	103	72	*2-136	1.0
1985	Bos A	156	534	59	142	26	0	5	56	56-3	2	50	.266	.336	.343	84	-10	7-5	.987	16	103	101	*2-155	1.4
1986	†Bos A	158	625	94	179	39	4	4	60	65-0	1	31	.286	.353	.381	100	2	15-7	.982	-3	95	102	*2-158	0.9
1987	Bos A	137	559	72	164	23	0	3	43	51-0	1	38	.293	.351	.351	85	-10	15-2	**.988**	**33**	108	116	*2-137	3.1
1988	†Bos A	150	612	83	173	28	1	1	65	40-1	7	35	.283	.330	.337	85	-12	7-3	.990	5	90	100	*2-150	-0.2
1989	Bos A	86	336	31	86	18	0	1	27	32-0	2	12	.256	.320	.318	77	-9	4-1	.975	-0	97	99	2-80/D-4	-0.7
1990	†Bos A	62	159	15	36	4	0	0	13	15-1	1	13	.226	.294	.252	53	-10	4-0	.992	-2	97	79	2-60/3D	-0.9
1991	SD N	12	16	1	3	1	0	1	3	0-0	1	3	.188	.235	.438	83	0	0-0	1.000	1	101	291	/2-2,3-2	0.1
Total	10	941	3378	418	938	163	9	18	314	304-7	16	209	.278	.337	.347	86	-54	57-21	.986	51	99	98	2-908/D-10,3-3	4.1
BARRETT, MICHAEL Michael Patrick B 10.22.1976 Atlanta, GA BR/TR 6-3/185# d9.19																								
1998	Mon N	8	23	3	7	2	0	1	2	3-0	1	6	.304	.407	.522	144	2	0-0	.963	1	41	268	/C-3,3-3	0.3
1999	Mon N	126	433	53	127	32	3	8	52	32-4	3	39	.293	.345	.436	99	-1	0-2	.943	-5	102	40	3-66,C-59/S-2	-0.3
2000	Mon N	89	271	28	58	15	1	1	22	23-5	1	35	.214	.277	.288	42	-24	0-1	.891	-5	95	107	3-55,C-28	-2.6

Year	Tm Lg	G	AB	R	H	2B	3B	HR	RBI	BB-IB	HP	SO	AVG	OBP	SLG	AOPS	ABR	SB-CS	FA	FR	Rng	Thr	G at Pos	BFW
2001	Mon N	132	472	42	118	33	2	6	38	25-2	2	54	.250	.289	.367	67	-23	2-1	.993	-16	74	66	*C-131	-3.0
2002	Mon N	117	376	41	99	20	1	12	49	40-7	1	65	.263	.332	.418	92	-5	6-3	.989	11	101	88	*C-110/1-6	1.3
2003	Mon N	70	226	33	47	9	2	10	30	21-7	2	37	.208	.280	.398	68	-11	0-0	.998	0	195	70	C-68	-0.7
Total	6	542	1801	200	456	111	9	38	193	144-25	10	236	.253	.310	.388	77	-62	8-7	.991	-13	103	79	C-399,3-124/1-6,S-2	-5.0
BARRETT, BOB Robert Schley "Jumbo" B 1.27.1899 Atlanta, GA D 1.18.1982 Atlanta, GA BR/TR 5-11/175# d4.30																								
1923	Chi N	3	3	0	1	0	0	0	0	0	0	0	.333	.333	.333	76	0	0-0	—	0			H	0.0
1924	Chi N	54	133	12	32	2	3	5	21	7	0	29	.241	.279	.414	82	-4	1-0	.943	-2	98	93	2-25,1-10/3-8	-0.6
1925	Chi N	14	32	1	10	1	0	0	7	1	0	4	.313	.333	.344	72	-1	1-2	1.000	-1	35	356	/3-6,2-4	-0.3
	Bro N	1	1	0	0	0	0	0	1	0	0	0	.000	.000	.000	-99	0	0-0	—	0			H	0.0
	Year	15	33	1	10	1	0	0	8	1	0	4	.303	.324	.333	67	-2	1-2	1.000	-1	35	356	/3-6,2-4	-0.3
1927	Bro N	99	355	29	92	10	2	5	38	14	1	22	.259	.289	.341	68	-17	1	.920	-7	94	87	3-96	-1.8
1929	Bos A	68	126	15	34	10	0	0	19	10	0	6	.270	.324	.349	75	-4	3-1	.938	5	133	62	3-34/1-4,2-2,O(LF)	0.2
Total	5	239	650	57	169	23	5	10	86	32	1	61	.260	.296	.357	72	-26	6-3	.924	-5	100	85	3-144/2-31,1-14,O(LF)	-2.5
BARRETT, TOM Thomas Loren B 4.2.1960 San Fernando, CA BB/TR 5-9/157# d7.2 b-Marty																								
1988	Phi N	36	54	5	11	1	0	0	3	7-0	1	8	.204	.306	.222	53	-3	0-0	.959	2	123	104	2-10	-0.1
1989	Phi N	14	27	3	6	0	0	0	1	1-0	0	7	.222	.250	.222	36	-2	0-0	.978	2	86	197	/2-9	0.0
1992	Bos A	4	3	1	0	0	0	0	0	2-0	0	0	.000	.400	.000	19	0	0-0	1.000	-1	76	0	/2-2	-0.1
Total	3	54	84	9	17	1	0	0	4	10-0	1	15	.202	.295	.214	47	-5	0-0	.970	3	103	132	/2-21	-0.2
BARRETT, BILL William B Washington, DC d7.8																								
1871	Kek NA	1	5	1	1	1	0	0	1	0		0	.200	.200	.400	66	0	0-0	1.000	1			/C3	0.0
1872	Oly NA	1	4	0	0	0	0	0	0	0		0	.000	.000	.000	-99	-1	0-0	.400	-2			/C	-0.2
1873	Bal NA	1	4	0	1	0	0	0	0	0		0	.250	.250	.250	49	0	0-1	.667	-1	31	0	/SO(RF)	-0.1
Total	3 NA	3	13	1	2	1	0	0	1	0		0	.154	.154	.231	12	-1	0-1	.000	-2			/C-2,O(RF)S3	-0.3
BARRETT, BILL William Joseph "Whispering Bill" B 5.28.1900 Cambridge, MA D 1.26.1951 Cambridge, MA BR/TR 6/175# d5.13 OF Total (74-LF 28-CF 400-RF)																								
1921	Phi A	14	30	3	7	2	1	0	3	0	0	5	.233	.233	.367	51	-2	0-0	.925	1	116	29	/S-8,P-4,3-2,1	-0.1
1923	Chi A	44	162	17	44	7	2	2	23	9	0	24	.272	.310	.377	81	-5	12-3	.940	-1	100	100	O-40(40-1-0)/3	-0.7
1924	Chi A	119	406	52	110	18	5	2	56	30	3	38	.271	.326	.355	78	-15	15-10	.904	-14	87	91	S-77,O-28(25-3-0)/3-8	-2.1
1925	Chi A	81	245	44	89	23	3	3	40	24	0	27	.363	.420	.518	145	17	5-6	.943	-5	100	110	2-41,O-27(3-1-23)/S-4,3-4	1.1
1926	Chi A	111	368	46	113	31	4	6	61	25	1	26	.307	.353	.462	115	7	9-7	.969	-2	103	78	*O-102(1-0-102)/1-2	-0.2
1927	Chi A	147	556	62	159	35	9	4	83	52	0	46	.286	.347	.403	96	-3	20-13	.963	7	103	140	*O-147(0-12-136)	-0.7
1928	Chi A	76	235	34	65	11	2	3	26	14	1	30	.277	.320	.379	84	-6	8-4	.988	-1	104	187	O-37(4-1-32),2-25	-0.9
1929	Chi A	3	1	0	0	0	0	0	0	2	0	0	.000	.667	.000	87	0	0-0	—	0			H	0.0
	Bos A	111	370	57	100	23	4	3	35	51	3	38	.270	.363	.378	93	-2	11-8	.974	7	104	164	*O-109(1-10-101)/3	-0.3
	Year	114	371	57	100	23	4	3	35	53	3	38	.270	.365	.377	94	-2	11-8	.974	7	104	164	*O-109(1-10-101)/3	-0.3
1930	Bos A	6	18	3	3	1	0	0	1	1	0	3	.167	.211	.222	10	-2	0-0	1.000	-1	71	0	/O-5(RF)	-0.3
	Was A	6	4	0	0	0	0	0	0	1	0	2	.000	.200	.000	-44	-1	0-0	1.000	0	157	0	/O(RF)	-0.1
	Year	12	22	3	3	1	0	0	1	2	0	5	.136	.208	.182	-0	-3	0-0	1.000	-1	78	0	/O-6(RF)	-0.4
Total	9	718	2395	318	690	151	30	23	328	209	8	239	.288	.347	.405	97	-12	80-51	.964	-8	102	133	O-496R/S-89,2-66,3-16,P-4,1-3	-4.3
BARRIOS, JOSE Jose Manuel B 6.26.1957 New York, NY BR/TR 6-4/195# d4.23																								
1982	SF N	10	19	2	3	0	0	0	0	1-0	0	4	.158	.200	.158	1	-3	0-0	1.000	-1	0	111	/1-7	-0.4
BARRON, TONY Anthony Dirk B 8.17.1966 Portland, OR BR/TR 6/185# d6.2																								
1996	Mon N	1	1	0	0	0	0	0	0	0-0	0	1	.000	.000	.000	-98	0	0-0	—	0			/H	0.0
1997	Phi N	57	189	22	54	12	1	4	24	12-0	2	38	.286	.330	.423	97	-1	0-1	.983	3	121	82	O-53(RF)	-0.1
Total	2	58	190	22	54	12	1	4	24	12-0	2	39	.284	.329	.421	96	-1	0-1	.983	3	121	82	/O-53(RF)	-0.1
BARRON, RED David Irenus B 6.21.1900 Clarksville, GA D 10.4.1982 Atlanta, GA BR/TR 5-11.5/185# d6.10																								
1929	Bos N	10	21	3	4	1	0	0	1	1	0	4	.190	.227	.238	16	-3	2	.929	1	114	291	/O-6(LF)	-0.2
BARROWS, FRANK Franklin L. B 10.22.1846 Hudson, OH D 2.6.1922 Fitchburg, MA d5.20																								
1871	Bos NA	18	86	13	13	2	1	0	11	0		0	.151	.151	.198	-1	-11	1-0	.829	-2	52	0	O-17(13-0-4)/2	-0.8
BARROWS, CUKE Roland B 10.20.1883 Gray, ME D 2.10.1955 Gorham, ME BL/TR 5-8/158# d9.18																								
1909	Chi A	5	20	1	3	0	0	0	2	0	1		.150	.190	.150	8	-2	0	.923	1	228	562	/O-5(LF)	-0.2
1910	Chi A	6	20	0	4	0	0	0	1	3	0		.200	.304	.200	61	-1	0	.875	-1	77	0	/O-6(LF)	-0.2
1911	Chi A	13	46	5	9	2	0	0	4	7	1		.196	.315	.239	57	-2	2	1.000	-1	113	0	O-13(RF)	-0.4
1912	Chi A	8	13	0	3	0	0	0	2	2	0		.231	.333	.231	64	0	1	1.000	0	31	320	/O-3(RF)	-0.1
Total	4	32	99	6	19	2	0	0	9	12	2		.192	.292	.212	50	-5	3	.950	-1	129	176	/O-27(11-0-16)	-0.9
BARRY, JEFF Jeffrey Finas B 9.22.1969 Medford, OR BB/TR 6-1/190# d6.9																								
1995	NY N	15	15	2	2	1	0	0	0	1-0	0	8	.133	.188	.200	2	-2	0-0	1.000	0	134	0	/O-2(1-0-1)	-0.2
1998	Col N	15	34	4	6	1	0	0	2	2-0	0	11	.176	.216	.206	11	-4	0-0	1.000	1	115	207	O-10(1-8-5)	-0.3
1999	Col N	74	168	19	45	16	0	5	26	19-1	2	29	.268	.344	.452	79	-5	0-4	1.000	1	95	167	O-56(14-32-15)	-0.6
Total	3	104	217	25	53	18	0	5	28	22-1	2	48	.244	.314	.396	65	-11	0-4	1.000	2	99	170	/O-68(16-40-21)	-1.1
BARRY, SHAD John C. B 10.27.1878 Newburgh, NY D 11.27.1936 Los Angeles, CA BR/TR d5.30 OF Total (214-LF 39-CF 371-RF)																								
1899	Was N	78	247	31	71	7	5	1	33	12	3		.287	.328	.368	92	-4	11	.946	-9	80	0	O-23(20-0-3),1-22,S-13,3-13/2-7	-1.1
1900	Bos N	81	254	40	66	10	7	1	37	13	2		.260	.301	.366	74	-10	9	.956	-12	134	268	O-24(22-1-1),S-18,2-16,1-10/3	-2.1
1901	Bos N	11	40	3	7	2	0	0	6	2	1		.175	.233	.225	30	-4	1	.926	-0	68	0	O-11(LF)	-0.5
	Phi N	67	252	35	62	10	0	1	22	15	2		.246	.294	.298	70	-9	13	.903	-13	92	65	2-35,3-16,O-13(3-9-1)/S	-2.2
	Year	78	292	38	69	12	0	1	28	17	3		.236	.285	.288	64	-13	14	.903	-13	92	65	2-35,O-24(14-9-1),3-16/S	-2.7
1902	Phi N	**138**	543	65	156	20	6	3	58	44	2		.287	.343	.363	118	11	14	.939	-6	82	60	*O-137(7-0-130)/1	-0.1
1903	Phi N	138	550	75	152	24	5	1	60	30	6		.276	.321	.344	92	-6	26	.970	-2	94	52	*O-107(105-2-0),1-30/3	-1.4
1904	Phi N	35	122	15	25	2	0	0	3	11	2		.205	.281	.221	58	-6	2	.979	11	300	322	O-32(11-6-15)/3	0.4
	Chi N	73	263	29	69	7	2	1	26	17	1		.262	.310	.316	93	-2	12	.917	-4	74	0	O-30(0-13-17),1-18,3-16/S-8,2-2	-0.8
	Year	108	385	44	94	9	2	1	29	28	3		.244	.300	.286	82	-8	14	.955	7	195	172	O-62(11-19-32),1-18,3-17/S-8,2-2	-0.4
1905	Chi N	27	104	10	22	2	0	0	10	5	1		.212	.255	.231	43	-7	5	.982	0	106	87	1-26	-0.8
	Cin N	125	494	90	160	11	12	1	56	33	5		.324	.372	.401	118	10	16	.982	-7	79	117	*1-124/O-2(1-1-0)	0.1
	Year	152	598	100	182	13	12	1	66	38	6		.304	.352	.371	105	3	21	**.982**	-6	84	**112**	*1-150/O-2(1-1-0)	-0.7
1906	Cin N	73	279	38	80	10	5	1	33	26	3		.287	.354	.369	120	7	11	.993	-0	90	113	1-43,O-30(14-7-9)	0.4
	StL N	62	237	26	59	9	1	0	12	15	2		.249	.299	.295	89	-3	6	.930	-3	82	109	O-35(RF),1-21/3-6	-0.9
	Year	135	516	64	139	19	6	1	45	41	5		.269	.329	.335	107	4	17	.922	-3	130	52	O-65(14-7-44),1-64/3-6	-0.5
1907	StL N	81	294	30	73	5	2	0	19	28	3		.248	.320	.279	91	-2	4	.963	-5	103	0	O-81(RF)	-1.2
1908	StL N	74	268	24	61	8	1	0	11	19	3		.228	.286	.265	80	-6	9	.967	1	119	0	O-69(RF)/S-2	-0.9
	NY N	37	67	5	10	1	1	0	5	9	1		.149	.260	.194	43	-4	1	.971	-2	0	0	O-31(20-0-10)	-0.8
	Year	111	335	29	71	9	2	0	16	28	4		.212	.281	.251	71	-10	10	.968	-1	92	0	*O-100(20-0-79)/S-2	-1.7
Total	10	1100	4014	516	1073	128	47	10	391	279	37		.267	.321	.330	94	-35	140	.955	-50	106	58	O-625R,1-295/2-60,3-54,S-42	-11.9
BARRY, JACK John Joseph B 4.26.1887 Meriden, CT D 4.23.1961 Shrewsbury, MA BR/TR 5-9/158# d7.13 Mil 1918 M1																								
1908	Phi A	40	135	13	30	4	3	0	8	10	3		.222	.291	.296	85	-2	5	.966	-7	102	53	2-20,S-14/3-3	-0.9
1909	Phi A	124	409	56	88	11	2	1	23	44	10		.215	.307	.259	77	-8	17	.927	-26	88	**106**	*S-124	-3.5
1910	†Phi A	145	487	64	126	19	5	3	60	52	5		.259	.336	.337	112	8	14	.916	-27	87	**114**	*S-145	-1.6
1911	†Phi A	127	442	73	117	18	7	1	63	38	7		.265	.333	.344	90	-6	30	**.944**	-11	92	**108**	*S-127	-0.7
1912	Phi A	140	483	75	126	19	9	0	55	47	7		.261	.335	.337	96	-2	22	.925	-6	103	**125**	*S-139	0.1
1913	†Phi A	134	455	62	125	20	6	3	85	44	8	32	.275	.349	.365	111	7	15	.953	-5	96	116	*S-134	1.1
1914	†Phi A	140	467	57	113	12	0	0	42	53	4	34	.242	.324	.268	81	-9	22-13	.947	7	107	120	*S-140	0.9
1915	Phi A	54	194	16	43	6	2	0	15	15	2	9	.222	.284	.273	69	-8	6-5	.952	-2	95	87	S-54	-0.7
	†Bos A	78	248	30	65	13	2	0	26	24	6	11	.262	.342	.331	104	2	0	.962	-4	100	76	2-78	-0.1
	Year	132	442	46	108	19	4	0	41	39	8	20	.244	.317	.305	89	-6	6-5	.962	-6	100	76	2-78,S-54	-0.8
1916	Bos A	94	330	28	67	6	1	0	20	17	**17**	24	.203	.277	.227	52	-19	8	.974	1	102	81	2-94	-1.9
1917	Bos A	116	388	45	83	9	0	2	30	47	4	27	.214	.305	.253	71	-12	12	**.974**	-5	104	93	*2-116,M	-1.7
1919	Bos A	31	108	13	26	5	1	0	2	5	3	5	.241	.293	.306	72	-4	2	.922	-5	99	106	2-31	-0.9

Year	Tm Lg	G	AB	R	H	2B	3B	HR	RBI	BB-IB	HP	SO	AVG	OBP	SLG	AOPS	ABR	SB-CS	FA	FR	Rng	Thr	G at Pos	BFW
Total	11	1223	4146	532	1009	142	38	10	429	396	76	142	.243	.321	.303	88	-53	153-18	.935	-90	95	112	S-877,2-339/3-3	-9.9
BARRY, RICH Richard Donovan B 9.12.1940 Berkeley, CA BR/TR 6-4/205# d7.4																								
1969	Phi N	20	32	4	6	1	0	0	0	5-0	1	6	.188	.316	.219	54	-2	0-0	.938	0	134	0	/O-9(LF)	-0.2
BARTEE, KIMERA Kimera Anotchi B 7.21.1972 Omaha, NE BR/TR (BB 1998) 6/175# d4.3																								
1996	Det A	110	217	32	55	6	1	1	14	17-0	0	77	.253	.308	.304	56	-15	20-10	.991	3	119	23	O-99(4-95-2)/D-2	-1.0
1997	Det A	12	5	4	1	0	0	0	0	2-0	1	2	.200	.500	.200	93	0	3-1	1.000	-0	83	0	/O-6(3-3-0),D-3	0.0
1998	Det A	57	98	20	19	5	1	3	15	6-0	0	35	.194	.238	.357	52	-7	9-5	.964	2	105	239	O-29(11-18-1),D-10	-0.6
1999	Det A	41	77	11	15	1	3	0	3	9-0	0	20	.195	.279	.286	44	-7	3-3	.985	0	113	0	O-38(CF)/D	-0.7
2000	Cin N	11	4	2	0	0	0	0	0	0-0	1	2	.000	.200	.000	-43	-1	1-0	1.000	-0	68	0	/O-3(2-1-0)	-0.1
2001	Col N	12	15	0	0	0	0	0	1	2-1	1	5	.000	.158	.000	-42	-3	0-0	.889	-1	92	0	/O-10(9-2-0)	-0.4
Total	6	243	416	69	90	12	5	4	33	36-1	3	141	.216	.282	.298	48	-33	36-19	.983	4	114	52	O-185(29-157-3)/D-16	-2.8
BARTELL, DICK Richard William "Rowdy Richard" B 11.22.1907 Chicago, IL D 8.4.1995 Alameda, CA BR/TR 5-9/160# d10.2 Mil 1944-45 C7																								
1927	Pit N	1	2	0	0	0	0	0	0	2	0	0	.000	.500	.000	41	0	0	1.000	0	69	198	/S	0.0
1928	Pit N	72	233	27	71	8	4	1	36	21	6	18	.305	.377	.386	96	-1	4	.974	-2	96	110	2-39,S-27/3	0.1
1929	Pit N	143	610	101	184	40	13	2	57	40	2	29	.302	.347	.420	87	-13	11	.953	-6	94	89	S-74,2-70	-0.9
1930	Pit N	129	475	69	152	32	13	4	75	39	5	34	.320	.378	.467	102	2	8	.941	5	103	**115**	*S-126	1.8
1931	Phi N	135	554	88	160	43	7	0	34	27	3	38	.289	.325	.392	85	-11	6	.948	4	98	96	*S-133/2-3	0.3
1932	Phi N	**154**	614	118	189	48	7	1	53	64	6	47	.308	.379	.414	101	4	8	.963	9	102	82	*S-154	2.4
1933	Phi N★	**152**	587	78	159	25	5	1	37	56	5	46	.271	.340	.336	83	-11	6	.951	9	101	96	*S-152	0.9
1934	Phi N	146	604	102	187	30	4	0	37	64	**9**	59	.310	.384	.373	91	-4	13	.954	18	106	108	*S-146	2.4
1935	NY N	137	539	60	141	28	4	14	53	37	6	52	.262	.316	.406	94	-5	5	.954	7	101	102	*S-137	1.1
1936	†NY N	145	510	71	152	31	3	8	42	40	5	36	.298	.355	.418	109	7	6	.956	**43**	**122**	**125**	*S-144	**5.7**
1937	†NY N★	128	516	91	158	38	2	14	62	40	**10**	38	.306	.367	.469	124	18	5	.958	**36**	**114**	**134**	*S-128	**6.1**
1938	NY N	127	481	67	126	26	1	9	49	55	8	60	.262	.347	.376	98	1	4	.952	**26**	**111**	115	*S-127	3.6
1939	Chi N	105	336	37	80	24	2	3	34	42	**7**	25	.238	.335	.348	82	-7	6	.943	-4	94	93	*S-101/3	-0.3
1940	†Det A	139	528	76	123	24	3	7	53	76	5	53	.233	.335	.330	67	-25	12-2	.953	13	100	89	*S-139	0.1
1941	Det A	5	12	0	2	1	0	0	1	2	1	2	.167	.333	.250	51	-1	0-1	.920	-0	84	67	/S-5	-0.1
	NY N	104	373	44	113	20	0	5	35	52	4	29	.303	.394	.397	121	13	6	.959	-5	96	102	3-84,S-21	1.3
1942	NY N	90	316	53	77	10	3	5	24	44	**8**	34	.244	.351	.342	102	3	4	.965	3	109	140	3-52,S-31	1.0
1943	NY N	99	337	48	91	14	0	5	28	47	**7**	27	.270	.371	.356	110	7	5	.980	15	115	84	3-54,S-33	2.7
1946	NY N	5	2	0	0	0	0	0	0	0	0	0	.000	.000	.000	-99	-1	0	1.000	0	226	0	/3-4,2-2	0.0
Total	18	2016	7629	1130	2165	442	71	79	710	748	97	627	.284	.355	.391	96	-24	109-3	.953	171	104	102	*S-1679,3-196,2-114	28.2
BARTIROME, TONY Anthony Joseph B 5.9.1932 Pittsburgh, PA BL/TL 5-10/155# d4.19 Mil 1953 C3																								
1952	Pit N	124	355	32	78	10	3	0	16	26	0	37	.220	.273	.265	48	-25	3-3	.989	1	108	98	*1-118	-2.9
BARTLEY, BOYD Boyd Owen B 2.11.1920 Chicago, IL BR/TR 5-8.5/165# d5.30 Mil 1943-46																								
1943	Bro N	9	21	0	1	0	0	0	1	1	0	3	.048	.091	.048	-59	-4	0	.897	-0	99	72	/S-9	-0.4
BARTLING, IRV Henry Irving B 6.27.1914 Bay City, MI D 6.12.1973 Westland, MI BR/TR 6/175# d9.8																								
1938	Phi A	14	46	5	8	1	1	0	5	3	0	7	.174	.224	.239	17	-6	0-0	.914	-3	86	83	S-13/3	-0.8
BARTON, HARRY Harry Lamb B 1.20.1875 Chester, PA D 1.25.1955 Upland, PA BB/TR 5-6.5/155# d4.15																								
1905	Phi A	29	60	5	10	2	1	0	3	3	0		.167	.206	.233	39	-4	2	.954	-4	*101*	*124*	C-13/1-2,3-2,O(RF)	-0.8
BARTON, BOB Robert Wilbur B 7.30.1941 Norwood, OH BR/TR 6/175# d9.17																								
1965	SF N	4	7	1	4	0	0	0	1	0-0	0	0	.571	.571	.571	217	1	0-0	1.000	0	*74*	*0*	/C-2	0.1
1966	SF N	43	91	1	16	2	1	0	3	5-2	0	5	.176	.216	.220	22	-10	0-0	.994	4	*100*	*127*	C-39	-0.5
1967	SF N	7	19	0	4	0	0	0	1	0-0	1	2	.211	.250	.211	34	-2	0-0	1.000	0	*115*	*132*	/C-7	-0.1
1968	SF N	46	92	4	24	2	0	0	5	7-1	0	18	.261	.310	.283	80	-2	0-0	.995	7	*90*	*147*	C-45	0.7
1969	SF N	49	106	5	18	2	0	0	1	9-1	1	19	.170	.241	.189	22	-11	0-0	.985	-8	76	60	C-49	-1.9
1970	SD N	61	188	15	41	6	0	4	16	15-2	1	37	.218	.278	.314	61	-11	1-1	.995	4	71	148	C-59	-0.5
1971	SD N	121	376	23	94	17	2	5	23	35-11	2	49	.250	.317	.346	94	-3	0-5	.981	10	89	**147**	*C-119	1.1
1972	SD N	29	88	1	17	1	0	0	9	2-0	0	19	.193	.209	.205	20	-10	2-0	.989	-4	125	110	C-29	-1.3
1973	Cin N	3	1	0	0	0	0	0	0	1-0	0	0	.000	.500	.000	52	0	0-0	1.000	0	0	0	/C-2	0.0
1974	SD N	30	81	4	19	1	0	0	7	13-1	0	19	.235	.333	.247	69	-3	0-0	.981	6	87	245	C-29	0.4
Total	10	393	1049	54	237	31	3	9	66	87-18	5	168	.226	.287	.287	65	-51	3-6	.987	19	*89*	*140*	C-380	-2.0
BARTON, VINCE Vincent David B 2.1.1908 Edmonton, AL, CAN D 9.13.1973 Toronto, ON, CAN BL/TR 6/180# d7.17																								
1931	Chi N	66	239	45	57	10	1	13	50	21	**9**	40	.238	.323	.452	104	1	1	.964	-4	101	27	O-61(RF)	-0.7
1932	Chi N	36	134	19	30	2	3	3	15	8	1	22	.224	.273	.351	67	-7	0	1.000	-1	90	89	O-34(RF)	-1.0
Total	2	102	373	64	87	12	4	16	65	29	10	62	.233	.306	.416	91	-6	1	.976	-5	97	49	/O-95(RF)	-1.7
BARTOSCH, DAVE David Robert B 3.24.1917 St.Louis, MO BR/TR 6-1/190# d4.28																								
1945	StL N	24	47	9	12	1	0	0	1	6	0	3	.255	.340	.277	71	-2	0	.964	1	120	112	O-11(4-0-7)	-0.1
BASGALL, MONTY Romanus B 2.8.1922 Pfeifer, KS BR/TR 5-10.5/175# d4.19 C14																								
1948	Pit N	38	51	12	11	1	0	2	6	3	0	5	.216	.259	.353	63	-3	0	1.000	3	110	60	2-22	0.0
1949	Pit N	107	308	25	67	9	1	2	26	31	1	32	.218	.291	.273	51	-21	1	.972	-3	96	98	2-98/3-3	-2.0
1951	Pit N	55	153	15	32	5	2	0	9	12	1	14	.209	.271	.268	44	-12	0-0	.969	6	106	100	2-55	-0.4
Total	3	200	512	52	110	15	3	4	41	46	2	51	.215	.282	.279	50	-36	1-0	.973	5	100	96	2-175/3-3	-2.4
BASHANG, AL Albert C. B 8.22.1888 Cincinnati, OH D 6.23.1967 Cincinnati, OH BB/TR 5-8/150# d7.30																								
1912	Det A	6	12	3	1	0	0	0	0	3	0		.083	.267	.083	2	-1	0	1.000	-0	92	0	/O-6(5-1-0)	-0.2
1918	Bro N	2	5	0	1	0	0	0	0	0	0	0	.200	.200	.200	22	0	0	1.000	1	0	0	/O	0.0
Total	2	8	17	3	2	0	0	0	0	3	0	0	.118	.250	.118	8	-1	0	1.000	0	89	0	/O-7(5-1-0)	-0.2
BASHORE, WALT Walter Franklin (born Walter Franklin Beshore) B 10.6.1909 Harrisburg, PA D 9.26.1984 Sebring, FL BR/TR 6/170# d7.14																								
1936	Phi N	10	10	1	2	0	0	0	0	1	0	3	.200	.273	.200	26	-1	0	1.000	-1	58	0	/O-6(CF),3	-0.2
BASINSKI, EDDIE Edwin Frank "Bazooka" or "Fiddler" B 11.4.1922 Buffalo, NY BR/TR 6-1/172# d5.20																								
1944	Bro N	39	105	13	27	4	1	0	9	6	2	10	.257	.310	.314	77	-3	1	.960	-3	89	73	2-37/S-3	-0.5
1945	Bro N	108	336	30	88	9	4	0	33	11	4	33	.262	.293	.313	69	-15	0	.926	-10	92	119	*S-101/2-6	-1.9
1947	Pit N	56	161	15	32	6	2	4	17	18	0	27	.199	.279	.335	61	-10	0	.972	-5	95	102	2-56	-1.2
Total	3	203	602	58	147	19	7	4	59	35	6	70	.244	.292	.319	68	-28	1	.925	-19	92	117	S-104/2-99	-3.6
BASS, JOHN John E. B 1850 Baltimore, MD 5-6/150# d5.4																								
1871	Cle NA	22	89	18	27	1	**10**	3	18	3		4	.303	.326	.640	179	8	0-1	.779	-7	74	59	*S-22/C	0.1
1872	Atl NA	2	7	0	1	1	0	0	1	0		0	.143	.143	.286	24	-1	0-0	.500	-1	0	0	/O-2(RF)	-0.1
1877	Har N	1	4	1	1	0	0	0	0	0		0	.250	.250	.250	65	0		—	-0	0	0	/O(LF)	0.0
Total	2 NA	24	96	18	28	2	10	3	19	3		4	.292	.313	.615	166	7	0-1	.779	-7	74	59	/S-22,O-2(RF),C	0.0
BASS, KEVIN Kevin Charles B 5.12.1959 Redwood City, CA BB/TR 6/183# d4.9																								
1982	Mil A	18	9	4	0	0	0	0	0	1-0	0	1	.000	.100	.000	-74	-2	0-0	1.000	-1	72	0	O-14(0-6-8)/D-2	-0.3
	Hou N	12	24	2	1	0	0	0	1	0-0	0	8	.042	.042	.042	-83	-6	0-0	.917	-1	72	0	/O-7(4-4-0)	-0.8
1983	Hou N	88	195	25	46	7	3	2	18	6-1	0	27	.236	.257	.333	67	-10	2-2	.945	-3	93	37	O-52(0-5-47)	-1.6
1984	Hou N	121	331	33	86	17	5	2	29	6-1	3	57	.260	.279	.360	84	-9	5-5	.975	-0	101	93	O-81(0-31-52)	-1.3
1985	Hou N	150	539	72	145	27	5	16	68	31-1	6	63	.269	.315	.427	109	4	19-8	**.997**	4	105	117	*O-141(10-105-39)	0.7
1986	†Hou N★	157	591	83	184	33	5	20	79	38-11	6	72	.311	.357	.486	134	26	22-13	.984	3	104	107	*O-155(2-41-133)	2.3
1987	Hou N	157	592	83	168	31	5	19	85	53-13	4	77	.284	.344	.449	113	10	21-8	.987	4	104	109	*O-155(RF)	0.7
1988	Hou N	157	541	57	138	27	2	14	72	42-10	6	65	.255	.314	.390	106	3	31-6	.979	1	100	103	*O-147(RF)	0.4
1989	Hou N	87	313	42	94	19	4	5	44	29-3	1	44	.300	.357	.435	131	13	11-4	.985	4	109	127	O-84(31-0-53)	1.6
1990	SF N	61	214	25	54	9	1	7	32	14-3	2	26	.252	.303	.402	96	-2	2-2	.968	-7	79	51	O-55(RF)	-1.1
1991	SF N	124	361	43	84	10	4	10	40	36-8	4	56	.233	.307	.366	92	-5	7-4	.977	-0	90	142	*O-101(23-0-79)	-0.8
1992	SF N	89	265	25	71	11	3	7	30	16-1	1	53	.268	.310	.411	109	2	7-7	.983	-4	92	30	O-72(56-0-21)	-0.5
	NY N	46	137	15	37	12	2	2	9	7-2	0	17	.270	.303	.431	108	1	7-2	.987	2	115	58	O-39(28-0-13)	0.2

Year	Tm Lg	G	AB	R	H	2B	3B	HR	RBI	BB-IB	HP	SO	AVG	OBP	SLG	AOPS	ABR	SB-CS	FA	FR	Rng	Thr	G at Pos	BFW
	Year	135	402	40	108	23	5	9	39	23-3	1	70	.269	.308	.418	109	3	14-9	.985	-2	100	40	*O-111(84-0-34)	-0.3
1993	Hou N	111	229	31	65	18	0	3	37	26-3	1	31	.284	.359	.402	107	4	7-1	.989	-2	89	85	O-64(12-2-51)	0.0
1994	Hou N	82	203	37	63	15	1	6	35	28-6	1	24	.310	.393	.483	135	12	2-3	.977	-1	94	93	O-57(11-0-47)	0.7
1995	Bal A	111	295	32	72	12	0	5	32	24-0	2	47	.244	.303	.336	66	-15	8-8	.984	-0	101	72	O-77(32-0-53),D-19	-2.0
Total	14	1571	4839	609	1308	248	40	118	611	357-63	37	668	.270	.323	.411	106	26	151-73	.982	-2	100	97	*O-1301(209-194-953)/D-21	-1.8

BASS, RANDY Randy William B 3.13.1954 Lawton, OK BL/TR 6-1/210# d9.3

Year	Tm Lg	G	AB	R	H	2B	3B	HR	RBI	BB-IB	HP	SO	AVG	OBP	SLG	AOPS	ABR	SB-CS	FA	FR	Rng	Thr	G at Pos	BFW
1977	Min A	9	19	0	2	0	0	0	0	0-0	0	5	.105	.105	.105	-43	-4	0-0	—	0			/D-6	-0.4
1978	KC A	2	2	0	0	0	0	0	0	0-0	0	0	.000	.000	.000	-97	-1	0-0	—	0			H	-0.1
1979	Mon N	2	1	0	0	0	0	0	0	0-0	0	0	.000	.000	.000	-99	0	0-0	1.000	0	0	0	/1	0.0
1980	SD N	19	49	5	14	0	1	3	8	7-1	1	7	.286	.386	.510	157	4	0-0	.985	-1	83	104	1-15	0.2
1981	SD N	69	176	13	37	4	1	4	20	20-1	1	28	.210	.293	.313	78	-5	0-1	.993	3	124	101	1-50	-0.7
1982	SD N	13	30	1	6	0	0	1	8	2-0	1	4	.200	.265	.300	63	-2	0-0	1.000	-0	84	159	/1-9	-0.2
	Tex A	16	48	5	10	2	0	1	6	1-0	1	7	.208	.231	.313	53	-3	0-0	1.000	-0	83	156	/1-6,D-7	-0.4
Total	6	130	325	24	69	6	2	9	42	30-2	4	51	.212	.284	.326	76	-11	0-1	.993	1	109	112	/1-81,D-13	-1.6

BASS, DOC William Capers (Also Played One Game In 1918 Under Name Of Johnson) B 12.4.1899 Macon, GA D 1.12.1970 Macon, GA BL/TL 5-10/165# d7.29

Year	Tm Lg	G	AB	R	H	2B	3B	HR	RBI	BB-IB	HP	SO	AVG	OBP	SLG	AOPS	ABR	SB-CS	FA	FR	Rng	Thr	G at Pos	BFW
1918	Bos N	2	1	1	1	0	0	0	0	0	0	0	1.000	1.000	1.000	533	0	1	—	0			/H	0.1

BASSETT, CHARLEY Charles Edwin B 2.9.1863 Central Falls, RI D 5.28.1942 Pawtucket, RI BR/TR 5-10/150# d7.22

Year	Tm Lg	G	AB	R	H	2B	3B	HR	RBI	BB-IB	HP	SO	AVG	OBP	SLG	AOPS	ABR	SB-CS	FA	FR	Rng	Thr	G at Pos	BFW
1884	Pro N	27	79	10	11	2	1	0	6	4		15	.139	.181	.190	17	-7		.815	-2	100	75	3-13/S-7,O-2(1-1-0),2	-0.8
1885	Pro N	82	285	21	41	8	2	0	16	19		60	.144	.197	.186	25	-23		.900	3	103	114	2-39,S-23,3-20/C	-1.6
1886	KC N	90	342	41	89	19	8	2	32	36		43	.260	.331	.380	109	4	6	.886	9	111	95	S-82/3-8	1.3
1887	Ind N	119	452	41	104	14	6	1	47	25	5	31	.230	.278	.294	61	-23	25	**.931**	18	**115**	111	*2-119	-0.1
1888	Ind N	128	481	58	116	20	3	2	60	32	6	41	.241	.297	.308	91	-4	24	.922	-14	103	84	*2-128	-1.2
1889	Ind N	127	477	64	117	12	5	4	68	37	3	38	.245	.304	.317	72	-20	15	.937	13	**109**	**114**	*2-127	-0.2
1890	NY N	100	410	52	98	13	8	0	54	29	7	25	.239	.300	.310	78	-13	14	**.952**	19	**109**	107	*2-100	0.9
1891	NY N	130	524	60	136	19	8	4	68	36	4	29	.260	.312	.349	96	-4	16	**.908**	6	96	101	*3-121/2-9	0.4
1892	NY N	35	130	9	27	2	3	0	16	6	2	11	.208	.254	.269	59	-7	0	.938	8	115	79	2-30/3-5	0.2
	Lou N	79	313	36	67	5	5	2	35	15	0	19	.214	.250	.281	66	-14	16	.861	-1	109	118	3-73/2-6	-1.3
	Year	114	443	45	94	7	8	2	51	21	2	30	.212	.251	.278	64	-22	16	.858	7	109	119	3-78,2-36	-1.1
Total	9	917	3493	392	806	114	49	15	402	239	27	312	.231	.285	.304	76	-111	116	.932	59	109	102	2-559,3-240,S-112/O-2(1-1-0),C	-2.4

BASSLER, JOHNNY John Landis B 6.3.1895 Mechanics Grove, PA D 6.29.1979 Santa Monica, CA BL/TR 5-9/170# d7.11 C4

Year	Tm Lg	G	AB	R	H	2B	3B	HR	RBI	BB-IB	HP	SO	AVG	OBP	SLG	AOPS	ABR	SB-CS	FA	FR	Rng	Thr	G at Pos	BFW
1913	Cle A	1	2	0	0	0	0	0	0	0	0	0	.000	.000	.000	-97	-1	0	.500	-1	*62*	*0*	/C	-0.2
1914	Cle A	43	77	5	14	1	1	0	6	15	1	8	.182	.323	.221	61	-3	3-2	.946	-2	*88*	*129*	C-25/3O(RF)	-0.3
1921	Det A	119	388	37	119	18	5	0	56	58	3	16	.307	.401	.379	101	4	2-1	.975	-4	*88*	*115*	*C-114	0.8
1922	Det A	121	372	41	120	14	0	0	41	62	2	12	.323	.422	.360	109	10	2-1	.980	-9	*80*	*106*	*C-118	0.9
1923	Det A	135	383	45	114	12	3	0	49	76	0	13	.298	.414	.345	103	7	2-2	.988	9	*113*	***140***	*C-128	2.2
1924	Det A	124	379	43	131	20	3	1	68	62	3	11	.346	.441	.422	125	19	2-1	.979	-6	*94*	*104*	*C-122	2.0
1925	Det A	121	344	40	96	19	3	0	52	74	1	6	.279	.408	.352	96	3	1-1	.983	-10	*87*	*87*	*C-118	0.0
1926	Det A	66	174	20	53	8	1	0	22	45	0	6	.305	.447	.362	111	7	0-0	1.000	1	*85*	*124*	C-63	1.1
1927	Det A	81	200	19	57	7	0	0	24	45	0	9	.285	.416	.320	92	1	1-0	.974	-1	*91*	*101*	C-67	0.4
Total	9	811	2319	250	704	99	16	1	318	437	10	81	.304	.416	.361	104	47	13-8	.980	-21	*92*	*112*	C-756/O(RF)3	6.9

BASTIAN, CHARLIE Charles J. B 7.4.1860 Philadelphia, PA D 1.18.1932 Pennsauken, NJ BR/TR 5-6.5/145# d8.18

Year	Tm Lg	G	AB	R	H	2B	3B	HR	RBI	BB-IB	HP	SO	AVG	OBP	SLG	AOPS	ABR	SB-CS	FA	FR	Rng	Thr	G at Pos	BFW
1884	Wil U	**17**	60	6	12	1	3	2		3			.200	.238	.417	92	-3		.907	11	153	60	2-16/PS	0.8
	KC U	11	46	6	9	3	0	1		4			.196	.260	.326	88	-2		.950	1	108	83	2-11	-0.1
	Year	28	106	12	21	4	3	3		7			.198	.248	.377	90	-5		.923	12	135	69	2-27/PS	0.7
1885	Phi N	103	389	63	65	11	5	4	29	35		82	.167	.236	.252	59	-17		.890	8	102	117	*S-103	-0.6
1886	Phi N	105	373	46	81	9	11	2	38	33		73	.217	.281	.316	81	-9	29	**.945**	-5	**108**	59	*2-87,S-10/3-8	-1.0
1887	Phi N	60	221	33	47	11	1	1	21	19	3	29	.213	.284	.285	55	-13	11	.921	-11	92	95	2-39,S-18/3-4	-1.9
1888	Phi N	80	275	30	53	4	1	1	17	27	7	41	.193	.282	.225	60	-11	12	.945	10	116	59	2-65,3-14/S	0.1
1889	Chi N	46	155	19	21	0	0	0	10	25	0	46	.135	.256	.135	10	-19	1	.919	-3	103	58	S-45/2	-1.8
1890	Chi P	80	283	38	54	10	5	0	29	33	5	37	.191	.287	.261	45	-23	4	.880	-10	94	98	S-64,2-12/3-4	-2.5
1891	Cin AA	1	4	0	0	0	0	0	0	0	0	0	.000	.000	.000	-92	-1	0	1.000	1	118	199	/2	0.0
	Phi N	1	0	0	0	0	0	0	0	0	0	0	—	—	—	—	0	0	1.000	0	133	0	/S	0.0
Total	8	504	1806	241	342	49	26	11	144	179	15	308	.189	.268	.264	57	-98	57	.892	1	99	106	S-243,2-232/3-30,P	-7.0

BATCH, EMIL Emil "Heinie" or "Ace" B 1.21.1880 Brooklyn, NY D 8.23.1926 Brooklyn, NY BR/TR 5-7/170# d9.13

Year	Tm Lg	G	AB	R	H	2B	3B	HR	RBI	BB-IB	HP	SO	AVG	OBP	SLG	AOPS	ABR	SB-CS	FA	FR	Rng	Thr	G at Pos	BFW
1904	Bro N	28	94	9	24	1	2	2	7	1	1		.255	.271	.372	100	-1	6	.880	-1	104	100	3-28	-0.2
1905	Bro N	145	568	64	143	20	11	5	49	26	0		.252	.285	.352	96	-6	21	.887	-5	91	116	*3-145	-0.8
1906	Bro N	59	203	23	52	7	6	0	11	15	1		.256	.311	.350	115	2	3	.964	0	78	0	O-50(47-0-3)/3-2	0.0
1907	Bro N	116	388	38	96	10	3	0	31	23	1		.247	.291	.289	89	-6	7	.937	-4	95	109	*O-102(81-1-20)/3-2,2S	-1.9
Total	4	348	1253	134	315	38	22	7	98	65	3		.251	.290	.334	98	-11	37	.886	-11	93	112	3-177,O-152(128-1-23)/S2	-2.9

BATEMAN, JOHN John Alvin B 7.21.1940 Killeen, TX D 12.3.1996 Sand Springs, OK BR/TR 6-3/220# d4.19

Year	Tm Lg	G	AB	R	H	2B	3B	HR	RBI	BB-IB	HP	SO	AVG	OBP	SLG	AOPS	ABR	SB-CS	FA	FR	Rng	Thr	G at Pos	BFW
1963	Hou N	128	404	23	85	8	6	10	59	13-1	9	103	.210	.249	.334	71	-17	0-0	.971	-2	*89*	*104*	*C-115	-1.5
1964	Hou N	74	221	18	42	8	0	5	19	17-5	1	48	.190	.249	.294	56	-13	0-1	.987	3	*69*	*101*	C-72	-0.7
1965	Hou N	45	142	15	28	3	1	7	14	12-3	0	37	.197	.256	.380	83	-4	0-1	.985	1	*107*	*119*	C-39	-0.3
1966	Hou N	131	433	39	121	24	3	17	70	20-9	5	74	.279	.315	.467	123	12	0-0	.981	3	*102*	*90*	*C-121	2.2
1967	Hou N	76	252	16	48	9	0	2	17	17-11	2	53	.190	.245	.250	44	-18	0-0	.989	-2	*82*	*109*	C-71	-1.8
1968	Hou N	111	350	28	87	19	0	4	33	23-16	3	46	.249	.297	.337	93	-3	1-1	.985	-6	*67*	*62*	*C-108	-0.4
1969	Mon N	74	235	16	49	4	0	8	19	12-6	1	44	.209	.250	.328	60	-14	0-2	.985	-2	72	77	C-66	-1.4
1970	Mon N	139	520	51	123	21	5	15	68	28-9	1	75	.237	.275	.383	75	-21	8-4	.983	6	143	115	*C-137	-0.9
1971	Mon N	139	492	34	119	17	3	10	56	19-3	4	87	.242	.273	.350	76	-18	1-0	.985	-7	83	110	*C-137	-1.9
1972	Mon N	18	29	0	7	1	0	0	3	3-0	0	4	.241	.313	.276	67	-1	0-0	1.000	-1	281	0	/C-7	-0.2
	Phi N	82	252	10	56	9	0	3	17	8-6	1	39	.222	.246	.294	52	-16	0-1	.972	-1	86	110	C-80	-1.6
	Year	100	281	10	63	10	0	3	20	11-6	1	43	.224	.253	.292	54	-17	0-1	.973	-2	100	102	C-87	-1.8
Total	10	1017	3330	250	765	123	18	81	375	172-69	27	610	.230	.271	.350	77	-113	10-10	.982	-9	*94*	*99*	C-953	-8.5

BATES, CHARLIE Charles William B 9.17.1907 Philadelphia, PA D 1.29.1980 Topeka, KS BR/TR 5-10/165# d9.22

Year	Tm Lg	G	AB	R	H	2B	3B	HR	RBI	BB-IB	HP	SO	AVG	OBP	SLG	AOPS	ABR	SB-CS	FA	FR	Rng	Thr	G at Pos	BFW
1927	Phi A	9	38	5	9	2	2	0	2	3	0	5	.237	.293	.395	73	-2	3-1	.857	-1	91	98	/O-9(0-1-8)	-0.3

BATES, DEL Delbert Oakley B 6.12.1940 Seattle, WA BL/TR 6-2/195# d5.6

Year	Tm Lg	G	AB	R	H	2B	3B	HR	RBI	BB-IB	HP	SO	AVG	OBP	SLG	AOPS	ABR	SB-CS	FA	FR	Rng	Thr	G at Pos	BFW
1970	Phi N	22	60	1	8	2	0	0	1	6-1	4	15	.133	.257	.167	16	-7	0-1	.992	-0	62	125	C-20	-0.7

BATES, BUD Hubert Edgar B 3.16.1912 Los Angeles, CA D 4.29.1987 Long Beach, CA BR/TR 6/165# d9.16

Year	Tm Lg	G	AB	R	H	2B	3B	HR	RBI	BB-IB	HP	SO	AVG	OBP	SLG	AOPS	ABR	SB-CS	FA	FR	Rng	Thr	G at Pos	BFW
1939	Phi N	15	58	8	15	2	0	1	2	2	0	8	.259	.283	.345	70	-3	1	.978	1	116	82	O-14(1-13-0)	-0.2

BATES, JASON Jason Charles B 1.5.1971 Downey, CA BB/TR 5-11/170# d4.26

Year	Tm Lg	G	AB	R	H	2B	3B	HR	RBI	BB-IB	HP	SO	AVG	OBP	SLG	AOPS	ABR	SB-CS	FA	FR	Rng	Thr	G at Pos	BFW
1995	†Col N	116	322	42	86	17	4	8	46	42-3	2	70	.267	.355	.419	80	-8	3-6	.991	3	98	114	2-82,S-20,3-15	-0.3
1996	Col N	88	160	19	33	8	1	1	9	23-1	2	34	.206	.312	.287	48	-11	2-1	.978	-3	111	93	2-37,S-18,3-12	-1.2
1997	Col N	62	121	17	29	10	0	3	11	15-1	3	27	.240	.338	.397	74	-4	0-1	1.000	-4	71	148	2-22,S-16/3-6	-0.7
1998	Col N	53	74	10	14	3	0	0	3	8-1	0	21	.189	.268	.230	27	-8	0-0	.974	-5	89	62	2-17/3-3,S-3	-1.2
Total	4	319	677	88	162	38	5	12	69	88-6	7	152	.239	.332	.363	66	-31	5-8	.987	-9	97	108	2-158/S-57,3-36	-3.4

BATES, JOHNNY John William B 1.10.1884 Steubenville, OH D 2.10.1949 Steubenville, OH BL/TR 5-7/168# d4.12

Year	Tm Lg	G	AB	R	H	2B	3B	HR	RBI	BB-IB	HP	SO	AVG	OBP	SLG	AOPS	ABR	SB-CS	FA	FR	Rng	Thr	G at Pos	BFW
1906	Bos N	140	504	52	127	21	5	6	54	36	10		.252	.315	.349	110	5	9	.958	-11	70	91	*O-140(7-133-0)	-1.4
1907	Bos N	126	447	52	116	18	12	2	49	39	7		.260	.329	.367	118	9	11	.979	-3	107	111	*O-120(1-1-118)	0.0
1908	Bos N	127	445	48	115	14	6	1	29	35	2		.258	.315	.324	106	3	25	.948	-4	100	54	*O-117(101-8-8)	-0.9
1909	Bos N	63	236	27	68	15	3	1	23	20	4		.288	.354	.390	125	7	15	.945	5	178	0	O-60(LF)	0.9
	Phi N	77	266	43	78	11	1	1	15	28	2		.293	.365	.353	122	8	22	.959	-1	123	141	O-73(11-62-0)	0.4
	Year	140	502	70	146	26	4	2	38	48	6		.291	.360	.371	123	15	37	.952	4	**149**	75	*O-133(71-62-0)	1.3
1910	Phi N	135	498	91	152	26	11	3	61	61	4	49	.305	.385	.420	130	20	31	.954	5	101	131	*O-131(25-103-3)	2.0
1911	Cin N	148	518	89	151	24	13	1	61	103	6	59	.292	.415	.394	131	29	33	.966	1	103	96	*O-147(0-145-2)	2.0
1912	Cin N	81	239	45	69	12	7	1	29	47	0	16	.289	.406	.410	127	11	10	.950	5	103	151	O-65(1-64-0)	1.1

Year	Tm Lg	G	AB	R	H	2B	3B	HR	RBI	BB-IB	HP	SO	AVG	OBP	SLG	AOPS	ABR	SB-CS	FA	FR	Rng	Thr	G at Pos	BFW
1913	Cin N	131	407	63	113	13	7	6	51	67	6	30	.278	.387	.388	122	15	21-9	.946	2	96	131	*O-111(0-24-88)	1.3
1914	Cin N	58	155	29	39	7	5	2	15	28	4	17	.252	.380	.400	128	7	4	.913	-6	85	71	O-54(CF)	-0.3
	Chi N	9	8	2	1	0	0	0	1	1	1	1	.125	.300	.125	28	-1	0	1.000	0	196	0	/O-3(0-2-1)	0.0
	Year	67	163	31	40	7	5	2	16	29	5	18	.245	.376	.387	124	6	4	.917	-5	88	69	O-57(0-56-1)	-0.3
	Bal F	59	190	24	58	6	3	1	29	38	3	18	.305	.429	.384	119	5	6	.950	-1	99	92	O-59(12-48-0)	0.0
Total	9	1154	3913	565	1087	167	73	25	417	503	49	190	.278	.367	.377	121	118	187-9	.955	-7	103	100	*O-1080(218-644-220)	5.1
BATES, RAY Raymond B 2.8.1890 Paterson, NJ D 8.15.1970 Tucson, AZ BR/TR 6/165# d5.31 Mil 1918																								
1913	Cle A	27	30	4	5	0	2	0	4	3	1	9	.167	.265	.300	63	-2	3	.905	0	114	244	3-12/O-2(CF)	-0.1
1917	Phi A	127	485	47	115	20	7	2	66	21	6	39	.237	.277	.320	83	-12	12	.933	9	104	86	*3-124	0.0
Total	2	154	515	51	120	20	9	2	70	24	7	48	.233	.277	.318	82	-14	15	.932	9	104	93	3-136/O-2(CF)	-0.1
BATES, BILLY William Derrick B 12.7.1963 Houston, TX BL/TR 5-7/155# d8.17																								
1989	Mil A	7	14	3	3	0	0	0	0	0-0	0	1	.214	.214	.214	21	-2	2-0	.938	3	125	251	/2-7	0.2
1990	Mil A	14	29	6	3	1	0	0	2	4-0	0	7	.103	.206	.138	-0	-4	4-0	.962	-0	113	84	2-14	-0.3
	†Cin N	8	5	2	0	0	0	0	0	0-0	0	2	.000	.000	.000	-96	-1	2-1	1.000	-1	35	0	/2	-0.3
Total	2	29	48	11	6	1	0	0	2	4-0	0	10	.125	.189	.146	-4	-7	8-1	.953	1	111	125	/2-22	-0.4
BATHE, BILL William David B 10.14.1960 Downey, CA BR/TR 6-2/200# d4.12																								
1986	Oak A	39	103	9	19	3	0	5	11	2-0	1	20	.184	.208	.359	55	-7	0-0	.991	-3	64	92	C-39	-0.9
1989	†SF N	30	32	3	9	1	0	0	6	0-0	0	7	.281	.273	.313	72	-1	0-0	1.000	1	54	203	/C-7	-0.1
1990	SF N	52	48	3	11	0	1	3	12	7-2	0	12	.229	.321	.458	118	1	0-0	1.000	-0	111	113	/C-8	0.1
Total	3	121	183	15	39	4	1	8	29	9-2	1	39	.213	.251	.377	75	-7	0-0	.992	-3	67	97	/C-54	-0.9
BATISTA, TONY Leocadio Francisco B 12.9.1973 Puerto Plata, D.R. BR/TR 6/180# d6.3																								
1996	Oak A	74	238	38	71	10	2	6	25	19-0	1	49	.298	.350	.433	99	-1	7-3	.988	9	120	106	2-52,3-18/S-4,D-4	1.0
1997	Oak A	68	188	22	38	10	1	4	18	14-0	2	31	.202	.265	.330	55	-13	2-2	.970	7	112	96	S-61/3-4,2D	-0.2
1998	Ari N	106	293	46	80	16	1	18	41	18-0	3	52	.273	.318	.519	117	6	1-1	.994	-1	93	116	2-41,S-34,3-15	0.9
1999	Ari N	44	144	16	37	5	0	5	21	16-3	2	17	.257	.335	.396	85	-3	2-0	.979	9	114	123	S-43	0.9
	Tor A	98	375	61	107	25	1	26	79	22-1	4	79	.285	.328	.565	121	10	2-0	.975	8	106	104	S-98	2.4
2000	Tor A★	154	620	96	163	32	2	41	114	35-1	6	121	.263	.307	.519	101	-3	5-4	.963	12	107	**120**	*3-154	1.0
2001	Tor A	72	271	29	56	11	1	13	45	13-1	4	66	.207	.251	.399	66	-15	0-1	.953	7	111	173	3-72	-0.7
	Bal A	84	308	41	82	16	5	12	42	19-0	0	47	.266	.305	.468	106	1	5-1	.934	2	103	102	D-33,3-29,S-20	0.3
	Year	156	579	70	138	27	6	25	87	32-1	4	113	.238	.280	.435	87	-14	5-2	.948	9	109	153	*3-101,D-33,S-20	-0.4
2002	Bal A★	161	615	90	150	36	1	31	87	50-9	11	107	.244	.309	.457	106	4	5-4	.962	6	107	134	*3-154/D-7	1.1
2003	Bal A	161	631	76	148	20	1	26	99	28-4	5	102	.235	.270	.393	76	-26	4-3	.950	0	104	119	*3-154/D-7	-2.3
Total	8	1022	3683	515	932	181	15	182	571	234-19	38	671	.253	.302	.459	96	-40	33-19	.957	59	107	128	3-600,S-260/2-94,D-52	4.4
BATISTA, RAFAEL Rafael (Sanchez) B 10.20.1947 San Pedro De Macoris, D.R. BL/TL 6-1/195# d6.17																								
1973	Hou N	12	15	2	4	0	0	0	2	1-1	0	6	.267	.313	.267	62	-1	0-0	1.000	-0	56	40	/1-8	-0.1
1975	Hou N	10	10	0	3	1	0	0	0	0-0	0	4	.300	.300	.400	100	0	0-0	—	0			H	0.0
Total	2	22	25	2	7	1	0	0	2	1-1	0	10	.280	.308	.320	76	-1	0-0	1.000	-0	56	40	/1-8	-0.1
BATISTE, KEVIN Kevin Wade B 10.21.1966 Galveston, TX BR/TR 6-2/175# d6.13																								
1989	Tor A	6	8	1	2	0	0	0	0	0-0	0	5	.250	.250	.250	42	-1	0-0	1.000	0	135	0	/O-5(2-0-3)	0.0
BATISTE, KIM Kimothy Emil B 3.15.1968 New Orleans, LA BR/TR 6/193# d9.8																								
1991	Phi N	10	27	2	6	0	0	0	1	1-1	0	8	.222	.250	.222	34	-2	0-1	.970	1	111	113	/S-7	-0.2
1992	Phi N	44	136	9	28	4	0	1	10	4-1	0	18	.206	.224	.257	37	-12	0-0	.922	-11	76	79	S-41	-2.2
1993	†Phi N	79	156	14	44	7	1	5	29	3-2	1	29	.282	.298	.436	95	-2	0-1	.956	5	86	51	3-58,S-24	0.4
1994	Phi N	64	209	17	49	6	0	1	13	1-0	1	32	.234	.239	.278	34	-21	1-1	.919	-3	94	64	3-42,S-17	-2.2
1996	SF N	54	130	17	27	6	0	3	11	5-1	0	33	.208	.235	.323	48	-10	3-3	.847	-5	85	188	3-25/S-7	-1.6
Total	5	251	658	59	154	23	1	10	64	14-5	2	120	.234	.250	.318	52	-47	4-6	.908	-15	89	92	3-125/S-96	-5.8
BATSCH, BILL William McKinley B 5.18.1892 Mingo Junction, OH D 12.31.1963 Canton, OH BR/TR 5-10.5/168# d9.9																								
1916	Pit N	1	0	0	0	0	0	0	0	1	0	0	—	1.000	—	218	0	0	—	0			H	0.0
BATTAM, LARRY Lawrence J. B 5.1.1878 Brooklyn, NY D 1.27.1938 Brooklyn, NY 5-11/166# d9.28																								
1895	NY N	2	4	0	1	0	0	0	0	2	0	1	.250	.500	.250	99	0	0	.667	-1	83	0	/3-2	0.0
BATTEN, GEORGE George Burnett B 10.7.1891 Haddonfield, NJ D 8.4.1972 New Port Richey, FL BR/TR 5-11/165# d9.28																								
1912	NY A	1	3	0	0	0	0	0	0	0	0		.000	.000	.000	-94	-1	0	1.000	-0	55	0	/2	-0.1
BATTEY, EARL Earl Jesse B 1.5.1935 Los Angeles, CA D 11.15.2003 Gainesville, FL BR/TR 6-1/205# d9.10																								
1955	Chi A	5	7	1	2	0	0	0	0	1-0	1	1	.286	.444	.286	97	0	0-0	1.000	1	*0*	*181*	/C-5	0.1
1956	Chi A	4	4	1	1	0	0	0	0	1-0	0	1	.250	.400	.250	74	0	0-0	.800	-1	*0*	*0*	/C-3	-0.1
1957	Chi A	48	115	12	20	2	3	3	6	11-1	0	38	.174	.246	.322	54	-8	0-2	.989	3	*110*	*107*	C-43	-0.4
1958	Chi A	68	168	24	38	8	0	8	26	24-1	2	34	.226	.325	.417	106	2	1-0	.988	2	*98*	*105*	C-49	0.6
1959	Chi A	26	64	9	14	1	2	2	7	8-0	0	13	.219	.306	.391	91	-1	0-0	.990	2	*90*	*147*	C-20	0.2
1960	Was A	137	466	49	126	24	2	15	60	48-5	8	68	.270	.346	.427	110	7	4-5	.982	5	***134***	***140***	*C-136	1.7
1961	Min A	133	460	70	139	24	1	17	55	53-3	3	66	.302	.377	.470	118	13	3-3	.993	4	*106*	*80*	*C-131	2.3
1962	Min A★	148	522	58	146	20	3	11	57	57-3	0	48	.280	.348	.393	96	-2	0-0	.991	10	*145*	*107*	*C-147	1.5
1963	Min A★	147	508	64	145	17	1	26	84	61-8	8	75	.285	.369	.476	133	24	0-0	.994	8	133	79	*C-146	4.0
1964	Min A	131	405	33	110	17	1	12	52	51-6	1	49	.272	.348	.407	111	7	1-1	.990	-5	*108*	*100*	*C-125	0.9
1965	†Min A★	131	394	36	117	22	2	6	60	50-7	2	23	.297	.375	.409	119	12	0-0	.986	-0	*125*	*94*	*C-128	1.8
1966	Min A★	115	364	30	93	12	1	4	34	43-7	3	30	.255	.337	.327	87	-5	4-1	.995	8	*99*	*106*	*C-113	1.0
1967	Min A	48	109	6	18	3	1	0	8	13-1	0	24	.165	.254	.211	36	-8	0-0	.987	-1	68	89	C-41	-0.9
Total	13	1141	3586	393	969	150	17	104	449	421-42	28	470	.270	.349	.409	106	41	13-12	.990	36	*119*	*102*	*C-1087	12.7
BATTIN, JOE Joseph V. B 11.11.1851 Philadelphia, PA D 12.10.1937 Akron, OH BR/TR d8.11 M2 U2																								
1871	Cle NA	1	3	0	0	0	0	0	0	1		0	.000	.250	.000	-21	0	0-0	1.000	0	0	0	/O(RF)	0.0
1873	Ath NA	1	5	4	3	0	0	0	2	1		0	.600	.667	.600	260	1	0-0	.667	0	491	0	/O(CF)	0.1
1874	Ath NA	51	226	40	52	11	1	0	27	1		7	.230	.233	.288	61	-11	3-2	.813	3	108	174	*2-41/O-7(0-2-5),S-5	-0.8
1875	StL NA	67	284	31	71	6	3	0	33	0		6	.250	.250	.292	97	0	15-3	.861	14	**115**	130	*2-62/3-6,C-2,O(CF)	1.0
1876	StL N	**64**	283	34	85	11	4	0	46	6		6	.300	.315	.367	134	11		**.867**	15	**115**	**203**	*3-63/2	2.3
1877	StL N	57	226	28	45	3	7	1	22	6		17	.199	.220	.288	62	-10		.823	-3	114	161	3-32,2-21/O-5(CF),P	-0.9
1882	Pit AA	34	133	13	28	5	1	1		3			.211	.228	.286	76	-3		.876	17	137	135	3-34	1.3
1883	Pit AA	**98**	388	42	83	9	6	1		11			.214	.236	.276	67	-14		**.891**	29	**127**	97	*3-98/P-2,M	1.5
1884	Pit AA	43	158	10	28	1	2	0		3	1		.177	.198	.209	33	-12		.919	8	122	73	3-43,M	-0.3
	CP U	18	69	8	13	2	0	0		0			.188	.188	.217	23	-9		.908	8	125	151	3-18,M	0.0
	Bal U	17	59	3	6	1	0	0		0			.102	.102	.119	-30	-11		.813	2	122	60	3-17	-0.8
	Year	35	128	11	19	3	0	0		0			.148	.148	.172	-3	-20		.868	10	124	112	3-35	-0.8
1890	Syr AA	29	119	15	25	2	1	0	13	8	0		.210	.260	.244	54	-7	8	.794	-6	89	39	3-29	-1.1
Total	4 NA	120	518	75	126	17	4	0	62	3	0	13	.243	.248	.292	80	-10	18-5	.000	17	112	148	2-103/O-10(0-4-6),3-6,S-5,C-2	0.3
Total	6	360	1435	153	313	34	21	3	81	37	1	23	.218	.238	.277	67	-55	8-0	.870	69	120	121	3-334/2-22,O-5(CF),P-3	2.0
BATTLE, ALLEN Allen Zelmo B 11.29.1968 Grantham, NC BR/TR 6/170# d4.26																								
1995	StL N	61	118	13	32	5	0	0	2	15-0	1	26	.271	.358	.314	79	-3	3-3	.984	1	121	0	O-32(15-7-14)	-0.3
1996	Oak A	47	130	20	25	3	0	1	5	17-1	2	26	.192	.293	.238	38	-12	10-2	.988	-1	96	84	O-47(24-27-0)	-1.1
Total	2	108	248	33	57	8	0	1	7	32-1	3	52	.230	.324	.274	57	-15	13-5	.986	-0	107	48	/O-79(39-34-14)	-1.4
BATTLE, HOWARD Howard Dion B 3.25.1972 Biloxi, MS BR/TR 6/210# d9.5																								
1995	Tor A	9	15	3	3	0	0	0	0	4-0	0	8	.200	.368	.200	53	-1	1-0	1.000	-1	75	0	/3-6,D	-0.2
1996	Phi N	5	5	0	0	0	0	0	0	0-0	0	2	.000	.000	.000	-99	-1	0-0	—	-0	0	0	/3	-0.2
1999	†Atl N	15	17	2	6	0	0	1	5	2-0	0	3	.353	.421	.529	138	1	0-0	1.000	-0	76	0	/3-6	0.1
Total	3	29	37	5	9	0	0	1	5	6-0	0	13	.243	.349	.324	75	-1	1-0	1.000	-2	73	0	/3-13,D	-0.3

Year	Tm Lg	G	AB	R	H	2B	3B	HR	RBI	BB-IB	HP	SO	AVG	OBP	SLG	AOPS	ABR	SB-CS	FA	FR	Rng	Thr	G at Pos	BFW
BATTLE, JIM James Milton B 3.26.1901 Bailey, TX D 9.30.1965 Chico, CA BR/TR 6-1/170# d9.9																								
1927	Chi A	6	8	1	3	0	1	0	0	0	0	1	.375	.375	.625	160	0	0-0	1.000	-1	68	0	/3-4,S-2	0.0
BATTS, MATT Matthew Daniel B 10.16.1921 San Antonio, TX BR/TR 5-11/200# d9.10																								
1947	Bos A	7	16	3	8	1	0	1	5	1	0	1	.500	.529	.750	236	3	0-0	1.000	-0	121	98	/C-6	0.3
1948	Bos A	46	118	13	37	12	0	1	24	15	0	9	.314	.391	.441	115	3	0-0	.986	-1	120	88	C-41	0.4
1949	Bos A	60	157	23	38	9	1	3	31	25	1	22	.242	.350	.369	84	-3	1-0	.977	1	145	82	C-50	0.0
1950	Bos A	75	238	27	65	15	3	4	34	18	1	19	.273	.327	.412	80	-8	0-0	.994	1	121	64	C-73	-0.3
1951	Bos A	11	29	1	4	1	0	0	2	1	0	2	.138	.167	.172	-8	-4	0-0	.975	-0	138	148	C-11	-0.4
	StL A	79	248	26	75	17	1	5	31	21	0	21	.302	.357	.440	111	4	2-0	.960	-8	91	113	C-64	-0.1
	Year	90	277	27	79	18	1	5	33	22	0	23	.285	.338	.412	98	-1	2-0	.962	-8	96	117	C-75	-0.5
1952	Det A	56	173	11	41	4	1	3	13	14	1	22	.237	.298	.324	72	-7	1-0	.983	2	104	134	C-55	-0.2
1953	Det A	116	374	38	104	24	3	6	42	24	0	36	.278	.322	.406	97	-3	2-3	.986	-15	77	114	*C-103	-1.4
1954	Det A	12	21	1	6	1	0	0	5	2	0	4	.286	.333	.333	89	0	0-0	.967	1	153	167	/C-8	0.1
	Chi A	55	158	16	36	7	1	3	19	17	0	15	.228	.299	.342	74	-6	0-1	.992	5	124	104	C-42	0.1
	Year	67	179	17	42	8	1	3	24	19	0	19	.235	.303	.341	76	-6	0-1	.989	6	127	111	C-50	0.2
1955	Cin N	26	71	4	18	4	1	0	13	4-0	0	11	.254	.286	.338	63	-4	0-0	.986	0	119	81	C-21	-0.3
1956	Cin N	3	2	0	0	0	0	0	0	1-0	0	1	.000	.333	.000	0	0	0-0	—	0			H	0.0
Total	10	546	1605	163	432	95	11	26	219	143-0	3	163	.269	.329	.391	89	-25	6-4	.983	-15	108	102	C-474	-1.8
BAUER, HANK Henry Albert B 7.31.1922 E.St.Louis, IL BR/TR 6/192# d9.6 M8 C1																								
1948	NY A	19	50	6	9	1	1	1	9	6	0	13	.180	.268	.300	51	-4	1-0	.964	0	103	115	O-14(8-0-7)	-0.4
1949	†NY A	103	301	56	82	6	6	10	45	37	1	42	.272	.354	.432	107	1	2-2	.977	1	92	169	O-95(21-25-60)	-0.1
1950	†NY A	113	415	72	133	16	2	13	70	35	5	41	.320	.380	.463	118	10	2-3	.987	2	105	93	*O-110(36-0-82)	0.7
1951	†NY A	118	348	53	103	19	3	10	54	42	1	39	.296	.373	.454	128	13	5-2	.990	2	103	108	*O-107(51-1-62)	1.1
1952	†NY A★	141	553	86	162	31	6	17	74	50	3	61	.293	.355	.463	134	23	6-7	.984	-3	89	141	*O-139(18-0-122)	1.5
1953	†NY A★	133	437	77	133	20	6	10	57	59	6	45	.304	.394	.446	131	21	2-3	.992	3	102	123	*O-126(3-1-124)	1.8
1954	NY A★	114	377	73	111	16	5	12	54	40	0	42	.294	.360	.459	128	13	4-4	.989	-2	97	85	*O-108(8-0-104)	0.7
1955	†NY A	139	492	97	137	20	5	20	53	56-1	8	65	.278	.360	.461	122	14	8-4	.981	5	106	136	*O-133(5-0-131)/C	1.5
1956	†NY A	147	539	96	130	18	7	26	84	59-3	2	72	.241	.316	.445	103	-1	4-2	.969	-6	90	98	*O-146(7-0-143)	-1.1
1957	†NY A	137	479	70	124	22	**9**	18	65	42-4	4	64	.259	.321	.455	112	6	7-2	.986	-5	93	79	*O-135(3-0-134)	-0.3
1958	†NY A	128	452	62	121	22	6	12	50	32-1	1	56	.268	.316	.423	106	2	3-2	.980	-5	93	79	*O-123(2-0-121)	-0.7
1959	NY A	114	341	44	81	20	0	9	39	33-1	2	54	.238	.307	.375	90	-5	4-2	.972	-8	88	41	*O-111(4-0-108)	-1.6
1960	KC A	95	255	30	70	15	0	3	31	21-1	1	36	.275	.326	.369	89	-4	1-0	.978	-4	82	110	O-67(RF)	-1.0
1961	KC A	43	106	11	28	3	1	3	18	9-0	0	8	.264	.319	.396	89	-2	1-0	.958	-1	87	106	O-35(11-2-27),M	-0.5
Total	14	1544	5145	833	1424	229	57	164	703	521-11	34	638	.277	.346	.439	114	87	50-33	.982	-20	95	106	*O-1449(177-29-1292)/C	1.6
BAUGHMAN, JUSTIN Justin Reis B 8.1.1974 Mountain View, CA BR/TR 5-11/175# d5.17																								
1998	Ana A	63	196	24	50	9	1	1	20	6-0	1	36	.255	.277	.327	57	-13	10-4	.977	-1	101	64	2-59/S-3,D	-1.0
2000	Ana A	16	22	4	5	2	0	0	0	1-0	0	2	.227	.261	.318	44	-2	3-0	.958	-0	132	147	/2-5,S-5,D-4	-0.1
Total	2	79	218	28	55	11	1	1	20	7-0	1	38	.252	.275	.326	56	-15	13-4	.976	-2	103	70	/2-64,S-8,D-5	-1.1
BAUMANN, PADDY Charles John B 12.20.1885 Indianapolis, IN D 11.20.1969 Indianapolis, IN BR/TR 5-9/160# d8.10																								
1911	Det A	26	94	8	24	2	4	0	11	6	1		.255	.307	.362	82	-3	1	.956	4	116	77	2-23/O-3(RF)	0.1
1912	Det A	16	42	3	11	1	0	0	7	6	0		.262	.354	.286	86	0	4	.786	-2	95	0	/3-6,2-5,O-2(1-1-0)	-0.3
1913	Det A	50	191	31	57	7	4	1	22	16	0	18	.298	.353	.393	120	4	4	.943	-6	98	83	2-49	-0.1
1914	Det A	3	11	1	0	0	0	0	0	2	0	1	.000	.154	.000	-52	-2	0	1.000	-1	93	101	/2-3	-0.3
1915	NY A	76	219	30	64	13	1	2	28	28	3	32	.292	.380	.388	130	9	9-10	.978	1	96	113	2-43,3-19/O(CF)	1.0
1916	NY A	79	237	35	68	5	3	1	25	19	5	16	.287	.352	.346	108	2	10	.958	-6	94	30	O-28(12-1-15),3-26/2-9	-0.4
1917	NY A	49	110	10	24	2	1	0	8	4	0	9	.218	.246	.255	52	-7	2	.941	-6	70	126	2-18/O-7(4-1-2),3	-1.5
Total	7	299	904	118	248	30	13	4	101	81	9	76	.274	.340	.350	103	3	30-10	.953	-16	97	95	2-150/3-52,O-41(17-4-20)	-1.5
BAUMER, JIM James Sloan B 1.29,1931 Tulsa, OK D 7.8.1996 Paoli, PA BR/TR 6-2/185# d9.14																								
1949	Chi A	8	10	2	4	1	1	0	2	2	2	1	.400	.571	.700	243	2	0-0	.938	1	126	170	/S-7	0.3
1961	Cin N	10	24	0	3	0	0	0	0	0-0	0	9	.125	.125	.125	-33	-5	0-0	1.000	-1	80	49	/2-9	-0.5
Total	2	18	34	2	7	1	1	0	2	2-0	2	10	.206	.289	.294	55	-3	0-0	1.000	-0	80	49	/2-9,S-7	-0.2
BAUMGARTNER, JOHN John Edward B 5.29.1931 Birmingham, AL BR/TR 6-1/190# d4.14																								
1953	Det A	7	27	3	5	0	0	0	2	0	0	5	.185	.185	.185	0	-4	0-0	.913	-1	79	119	/3-7	-0.5
BAUMHOLTZ, FRANK Frank Conrad B 10.7.1918 Midvale, OH D 12.14.1997 Winter Springs, FL BL/TL (BR 1952 (1 game)) 5-10.5/175# d4.15																								
1947	Cin N	151	643	96	182	32	9	5	45	56	1	53	.283	.341	.384	93	-7	6	.977	-7	84	136	*O-150(0-29-136)	-1.9
1948	Cin N	128	415	57	123	19	5	4	30	27	3	32	.296	.344	.395	103	1	8	.987	3	100	145	*O-110(20-23-67)	0.0
1949	Cin N	27	81	12	19	5	3	1	8	6	1	8	.235	.295	.407	86	-2	0	.964	1	115	53	O-20(13-0-7)	-0.3
	Chi N	58	164	15	37	4	2	1	15	9	1	21	.226	.270	.293	52	-12	2	.986	-2	86	90	O-43(0-7-38)	-1.5
	Year	85	245	27	56	9	5	2	23	15	2	29	.229	.279	.331	64	-14	2	.976	-1	97	77	O-63(13-7-45)	-1.8
1951	Chi N	146	560	62	159	28	10	2	50	49	4	36	.284	.346	.380	94	-5	5-4	.975	-10	94	47	*O-140(17-64-60)	-2.1
1952	Chi N	103	409	59	133	17	4	4	35	27	3	27	.325	.371	.416	116	9	5-7	.974	3	107	99	*O-101(0-47-65)	0.7
1953	Chi N	133	520	75	159	36	7	3	25	42	1	36	.306	.359	.419	100	1	3-3	.980	-6	96	56	*O-130(0-69-64)	-1.0
1954	Chi N	90	303	38	90	12	6	4	28	20	1	15	.297	.340	.416	95	-3	1-3	.988	-4	95	37	O-71(10-61-13)	-1.1
1955	Chi N	105	280	23	81	12	5	1	27	16-2	1	24	.289	.325	.379	88	-5	0-1	.993	0	105	61	O-63(40-0-23)	-0.9
1956	Phi N	76	100	13	27	0	0	0	9	6-0	1	6	.270	.309	.270	61	-5	0-2	.962	1	98	185	O-15(0-1-14)	-0.6
1957	Phi N	2	2	0	0	0	0	0	0	0-0	0	0	.000	.000	.000	-99	-1	0-0	—	0			H	-0.1
Total	10	1019	3477	450	1010	165	51	25	272	258-2	17	258	.290	.342	.389	95	-29	30-20	.980	-22	96	88	O-843(100-301-487)	-8.8
BAUTISTA, DANNY Daniel (Alcantara) B 5.24.1972 Santo Domingo, D.R. BR/TR 5-11/170# d9.15																								
1993	Det A	17	61	6	19	3	0	1	9	1-0	0	10	.311	.317	.410	96	-1	3-1	1.000	1	103	207	O-16(0-9-8)/D	0.1
1994	Det A	31	99	12	23	4	1	4	15	3-0	0	18	.232	.255	.414	68	-5	1-2	1.000	0	109	0	O-30(0-14-16)/D	-0.6
1995	Det A	89	271	28	55	9	0	7	27	12-0	0	68	.203	.237	.314	42	-25	4-1	.988	-0	105	56	O-86(2-0-84)/D	-2.7
1996	Det A	25	64	12	16	2	0	2	8	9-0	0	15	.250	.342	.375	81	-2	1-2	.974	-1	102	0	O-22(12-0-12)/D	-0.4
	Atl N	17	20	1	3	0	0	0	1	2-0	1	5	.150	.261	.150	11	-3	0-0	1.000	-0	96	0	O-14(2-2-10)	-0.3
1997	†Atl N	64	103	14	25	3	2	3	9	5-1	1	24	.243	.282	.398	75	-4	2-0	.984	1	110	51	O-57(48-1-10)	-0.4
1998	†Atl N	82	144	17	36	11	0	3	17	7-0	0	21	.250	.281	.389	75	-5	1-0	.959	-4	79	0	O-58(53-1-4)/D	-1.1
1999	Fla N	70	205	32	59	10	1	5	24	4-0	1	30	.288	.303	.420	86	-6	3-0	.979	7	137	98	O-60(22-18-31)	0.1
2000	Fla N	44	89	9	17	4	0	4	12	5-0	0	20	.191	.234	.371	52	-7	1-0	.980	1	103	143	O-38(25-5-17)	-0.6
	Ari N	87	262	45	83	16	7	7	47	20-4	3	30	.317	.366	.511	117	6	5-2	.987	3	103	148	O-82(2-21-67)	0.6
	Year	131	351	54	100	20	7	11	59	25-4	3	50	.285	.333	.476	102	0	6-2	.985	4	103	147	*O-120(27-26-84)	0.0
2001	†Ari N	100	222	26	67	11	2	5	26	14-1	1	31	.302	.346	.437	95	-2	3-2	1.000	2	101	146	O-61(3-28-33)	-0.1
2002	Ari N	40	154	22	50	5	2	6	23	11-2	0	21	.325	.367	.500	119	3	4-2	.985	-3	92	0	O-39(0-5-37)	-0.1
2003	Ari N	88	284	29	78	16	3	4	36	21-2	4	50	.275	.330	.394	81	-8	3-2	.961	-7	88	23	O-79(3-18-59)	-1.7
Total	11	754	1978	253	531	94	18	51	254	114-10	11	343	.268	.310	.412	83	-59	31-14	.983	-0	102	71	O-642(172-122-388)/D-5	-7.2
BAXES, JIM Dimitrios Speros B 7.5.1928 San Francisco, CA D 11.14.1996 Garden Grove, CA BR/TR 6-1/190# d4.11 b-Mike																								
1959	LA N	11	33	4	10	1	0	2	5	4-0	1	7	.303	.395	.515	130	2	1-0	.952	3	129	113	3-10	0.5
	Cle A	77	247	35	59	11	0	15	34	21-0	0	47	.239	.299	.466	111	2	0-1	.956	-13	84	93	2-48,3-22	-0.8
Total	1	88	280	39	69	12	0	17	39	25-0	1	54	.246	.310	.471	113	4	1-1	.956	-10	84	93	/2-48,3-32	-0.3
BAXES, MIKE Michael B 12.18.1930 San Francisco, CA BR/TR 5-10/175# d4.17 b-Jim																								
1956	KC A	73	106	9	24	3	1	1	5	18-1	0	15	.226	.339	.302	70	-4	0-1	.944	2	114	75	S-62/2	0.0
1958	KC A	73	231	31	49	10	1	0	8	21-0	3	24	.212	.286	.264	52	-15	1-6	.969	-2	102	96	2-61/S-4	-1.5
Total	2	146	337	40	73	13	2	1	13	39-1	3	39	.217	.303	.276	58	-19	1-7	.946	-0	114	71	/S-66,2-62	-1.5
BAXTER, MOOSE John Morris B 7.27.1876 Chippewa Falls, WI D 8.7.1926 Portland, OR BL/TR 6-2/200# d4.19																								
1907	StL N	6	21	1	4	0	0	0	0	0	0		.190	.190	.190	20	-2	0	.921	-1	118	34	/1-6	-0.3
BAY, HARRY Harry Elbert "Deerfoot" B 1.17.1878 Pontiac, IL D 3.20.1952 Peoria, IL BL/TL 5-8/138# d7.23																								
1901	Cin N	41	157	25	33	1	2	1	3	13	1		.210	.275	.261	60	-8	4	.953	-1	60	217	O-40(0-25-15)	-1.1

Year	Tm Lg	G	AB	R	H	2B	3B	HR	RBI	BB-IB	HP	SO	AVG	OBP	SLG	AOPS	ABR	SB-CS	FA	FR	Rng	Thr	G at Pos	BFW
1902	Cin N	6	16	3	6	0	0	0	1	2	1		.375	.474	.375	148	1	0	.778	0	211	0	/O-3(LF)	0.1
	Cle A	108	455	71	132	10	5	0	23	36	1		.290	.343	.334	92	-4	22	**.973**	1	92	105	*O-107(24-79-4)	-0.8
1903	Cle A	**140**	579	94	169	15	12	1	35	29	3		.292	.329	.364	110	6	**45**	.950	-5	83	79	*O-140(26-114-0)	-0.7
1904	Cle A	132	506	69	122	12	9	3	36	43	5		.241	.307	.318	99	0	**38**	**.987**	6	105	166	*O-132(5-127-0)	0.0
1905	Cle A	144	552	90	166	18	10	0	22	36	5		.301	.349	.370	126	16	36	.970	-2	89	115	*O-144(CF)	0.8
1906	Cle A	68	280	47	77	8	3	0	14	26	0		.275	.337	.325	109	3	17	.979	-5	91	117	O-68(CF)	-0.6
1907	Cle A	34	95	14	17	1	1	0	7	10	2		.179	.271	.211	53	-5	7	.968	2	143	127	O-31(7-23-1)	-0.5
1908	Cle A	2	0	0	0	0	0	0	0	0	0		—	—	—	—	0	0	—	0			R	0.0
Total	8	675	2640	413	722	65	42	5	141	195	18		.273	.328	.336	103	9	169	.968	-4	93	122	O-665(65-580-20)	-2.8
BAY, JASON Jason Raymond B 9.20.1978 Trail, BC, CAN BR/TR 6-2/200# d5.23																								
2003	SD N	3	8	2	2	1	0	1	2	1-0	1	1	.250	.400	.750	210	1	0-0	1.000	1	159	0	/O-3(CF)	0.2
	Pit N	27	79	13	23	6	1	3	12	18-0	0	28	.291	.423	.506	138	5	3-1	.976	-2	85	67	O-26(24-2-1)	0.3
	Year	30	87	15	25	7	1	4	14	19-0	1	29	.287	.421	.529	144	7	3-1	.980	-1	91	61	O-29(24-5-1)	0.5
BAYLESS, DICK Harry Owen B 9.6.1883 Joplin, MO D 12.16.1920 Santa Rita, NM BL/TR 5-9/178# d9.9																								
1908	Cin N	19	71	7	16	1	0	1	3	6	2		.225	.304	.282	90	-1	0	.946	3	251	345	O-19(0-2-17)	0.1
BAYLOR, DON Don Edward B 6.28.1949 Austin, TX BR/TR 6-1/195# d9.18 M9 C5																								
1970	Bal A	8	17	4	4	0	0	0	4	2-0	0	3	.235	.300	.235	54	-1	1-1	1.000	0	125	0	/O-6(3-4-0)	-0.1
1971	Bal A	1	2	0	0	0	0	0	1	2-0	1	1	.000	.600	.000	83	0	0-0	1.000	0	195	0	/O(RF)	0.1
1972	Bal A	102	320	33	81	13	3	11	38	29-0	9	50	.253	.330	.416	118	7	24-2	.975	-4	100	35	O-84(35-13-48)/1-9	0.3
1973	†Bal A	118	405	64	116	20	4	11	51	35-3	**13**	48	.286	.357	.437	125	14	32-9	.981	-1	100	67	*O-110(LF)/1-6,D	1.1
1974	†Bal A	137	489	66	133	22	1	10	59	43-6	10	56	.272	.341	.382	112	8	29-12	.978	-16	85	11	*O-129(112-2-26)/1-8,D	-1.4
1975	Bal A	145	524	79	148	21	6	25	76	53-8	**13**	64	.282	.360	.489	148	32	32-17	.982	-6	91	77	*O-135(127-5-6)/1-2,D-7	2.0
1976	Oak A	157	595	85	147	25	1	15	68	58-4	**20**	72	.247	.329	.368	110	9	52-12	.981	-6	97	18	O-76(27-2-50),1-69,D-23	0.1
1977	Cal A	154	561	87	141	27	0	25	75	62-7	12	76	.251	.334	.433	113	11	26-12	.966	-2	97	59	O-77(48-11-19),D-61,1-18	0.5
1978	Cal A	158	591	103	151	26	0	34	99	56-9	**18**	71	.255	.332	.472	131	23	22-9	.974	-3	100	0	*D-102,O-39(LF),1-17	1.7
1979	†Cal A★	**162**	628	**120**	186	33	3	36	**139**	71-6	11	51	.296	.371	.530	147	42	22-12	.976	-3	101	43	O-97(78-0-19),D-65/1	3.2
1980	Cal A	90	340	39	85	12	2	5	51	24-4	11	32	.250	.316	.341	83	-8	6-6	.969	1	106	99	O-54(37-0-18),D-36	-1.1
1981	Cal A	103	377	52	90	18	1	17	66	42-1	7	51	.239	.322	.427	116	8	3-3	1.000	1	116	60	D-97/1-4,O(LF)	0.5
1982	†Cal A	157	608	80	160	24	1	24	93	57-7	7	69	.263	.329	.424	106	5	10-4	—	0	0	0	*D-155	0.1
1983	NY A	144	534	82	162	33	3	21	85	40-11	13	53	.303	.361	.494	139	29	17-7	1.000	0	101	0	*D-136/O-5(2-0-4),1	2.6
1984	NY A	134	493	84	129	29	1	27	89	38-6	**23**	68	.262	.341	.489	132	22	1-1	.889	-0	98	0	*D-127/O-5(1-0-4)	1.7
1985	NY A	142	477	70	110	24	1	23	91	52-6	**24**	90	.231	.330	.430	111	8	0-4	—	0	0	0	*D-140	0.3
1986	†Bos A	160	585	93	139	23	1	31	94	62-8	**35**	111	.238	.344	.439	112	11	3-5	.986	-2	43	74	*D-143,1-13/O-3(LF)	0.3
1987	Bos A	108	339	64	81	8	0	16	57	40-3	24	47	.239	.355	.404	100	1	5-2	—	0	0	0	D-97	-0.1
	†Min A	20	49	3	14	1	0	0	6	5-0	4	12	.286	.397	.306	87	0	0-1	—	0	0	0	D-14	-0.1
	Year	128	388	67	95	9	0	16	63	45-3	**28**	59	.245	.360	.392	98	1	5-3	—	0	0	0	*D-111	-0.2
1988	†Oak A	92	264	28	58	7	0	7	34	34-2	12	44	.220	.332	.326	89	-2	0-1	—	0	0	0	D-80	-0.5
Total	19	2292	8198	1236	2135	366	28	338	1276	805-91	267	1069	.260	.342	.436	119	219	285-120	.977	-41	97	46	*D-1285,O-822(623-37-195),1-148	11.2
BEACH, JACK Stonewall Jackson B 1862 Alexandria, VA D 7.23.1896 Alexandria, VA d5.1																								
1884	Was AA	8	31	3	3	2	0	0		0	0		.097	.097	.161	-20	-4		.667	-1	128	335	/O-8(1-0-7)	-0.4
BEADLE, DAVE David A. B 1.1864 New York, NY D 9.22.1925 New York, NY BL 6-2/200# d6.17																								
1884	Det N	1	3	0	0	0	0	0	0	0		2	.000	.000	.000	-99	-1		.500	-1	0	0	/O(1-0-1)C	-0.1
BEALL, JOHNNY John Woolf B 3.12.1882 Beltsville, MD D 6.13.1926 Beltsville, MD BL/TR 6/180# d4.17																								
1913	Cle A	6	6	0	1	0	0	0	1	0	0	2	.167	.167	.167	-2	-1	0	—	0			H	-0.1
	Chi A	17	60	10	16	0	1	2	3	0	1	0	.267	.279	.400	99	-1	1	.953	0	100	110	O-17(CF)	-0.2
	Year	23	66	10	17	0	1	2	4	0	1	2	.258	.269	.379	89	-2	1	.953	0	100	110	O-17(CF)	-0.3
1915	Cin N	10	34	3	8	1	0	0	3	5	1	10	.235	.350	.265	86	0	0-1	.960	1	99	153	O-10(9-1-0)	0.0
1916	Cin N	6	21	3	7	2	0	1	4	3	0	7	.333	.417	.571	207	3	1	1.000	1	82	334	/O-6(LF)	0.4
1918	StL N	19	49	2	11	1	0	0	6	3	0	6	.224	.269	.245	59	-2	0	1.000	-0	97	81	O-18(RF)	-0.4
Total	4	58	170	18	43	4	1	3	17	11	2	25	.253	.306	.341	95	-1	2-1	.972	1	97	136	/O-51(14-18-18)	-0.3
BEALL, BOB Robert Brooks B 4.24.1948 Portland, OR BB/TL 5-11/180# d5.12																								
1975	Atl N	20	31	2	7	2	0	0	1	6-0	0	9	.226	.351	.290	77	-1	0-0	.984	-0	91	104	/1-8	-0.2
1978	Atl N	108	185	29	45	8	0	1	16	36-0	1	27	.243	.368	.303	81	-3	4-5	.987	1	119	87	1-40/O-8(6-2-0)	-0.5
1979	Atl N	17	15	1	2	2	0	0	1	3-0	0	4	.133	.263	.267	46	-1	0-0	1.000	0	111	0	/1-3	-0.1
1980	Pit N	3	3	0	0	0	0	0	0	0-0	0	1	.000	.000	.000	-99	-1	0-0	—	0			/H	-0.1
Total	4	148	234	32	54	12	0	1	18	45-0	1	41	.231	.355	.295	76	-6	4-5	.987	0	114	87	/1-51,O-8(6-2-0)	-0.9
BEALS, TOMMY Thomas L. (a/k/a W.Thomas In 1871-1873) B 8.1850 , NY D 10.2.1915 San Francisco, CA BR 5-5/144# d7.27																								
1871	Oly NA	10	36	6	7	0	0	0	1	2		0	.194	.237	.194	27	-3	2-0	.778	2	92	0	/O-8(4-0-4),2-2	0.0
1872	Oly NA	**9**	36	6	11	1	1	0	5	1		1	.306	.324	.389	125	1	0-0	.853	1	146	95	/2-5,S-2,O-2(CF)	0.1
1873	Was NA	37	169	35	46	9	5	0	22	1		1	.272	.276	.385	97	0	3-0	.870	9	112	109	2-26,C-13/O(LF)	0.5
1874	Bos NA	19	97	20	19	3	4	0	17	0		2	.196	.196	.309	56	-5	0-1	.849	1	108	61	2-12/O-9(1-2-6)	-0.4
1875	Bos NA	35	155	38	41	2	6	0	16	3		1	.265	.278	.355	114	1	1-0	.867	-0	43	126	O-30(3-19-8)/2-8	0.1
1880	Chi N	13	46	4	7	0	0	0	3	1		6	.152	.170	.152	10	-4		.889	-4	55	0	O-10(RF)/2-3	-0.9
Total	5 NA	110	493	105	124	15	16	0	61	7		5	.252	.262	.347	90	-6	6-1	.000	13	112	115	/2-53,O-50(9-23-18),C-13,S-2	0.3
BEAMON, CHARLIE Charles Alfonzo Jr. B 12.4.1953 Oakland, CA BL/TL 6-1/183# d9.11 f-Charlie																								
1978	Sea A	10	11	2	2	0	0	0	0	1-0	0	1	.182	.250	.182	23	-1	0-0	1.000	1	279	109	/1-2,D-6	0.0
1979	Sea A	27	25	5	5	1	0	0	0	0-0	0	5	.200	.200	.240	18	-3	1-0	1.000	-0	125	0	/1-7,O-2(LF),D-5	-0.3
1981	Tor A	8	15	1	3	1	0	0	0	2-0	0	2	.200	.294	.267	59	-1	0-0	1.000	-0	0	0	/D-4,1	-0.1
Total	3	45	51	8	10	2	0	0	0	3-0	0	8	.196	.241	.235	32	-5	1-0	1.000	1	175	46	/D-15,1-10,O-2(LF)	-0.4
BEAMON, TREY Clifford B 2.11.1974 Dallas, TX BL/TR 6-3/195# d8.4																								
1996	Pit N	24	51	7	11	2	0	0	6	4-0	0	6	.216	.273	.255	39	-4	1-1	.960	-0	107	0	O-14(5-0-10)	-0.6
1997	SD N	43	65	5	18	3	0	0	7	2-0	1	17	.277	.309	.323	71	-3	1-2	.909	0	76	368	O-20(15-0-5)	-0.3
1998	Det A	28	42	4	11	4	0	0	2	5-0	0	13	.262	.340	.357	81	-1	1-0	1.000	1	200	0	D-11/O-4(2-0-2)	-0.1
Total	3	95	158	16	40	9	0	0	15	11-0	1	36	.253	.306	.310	63	-8	3-3	.944	1	99	172	/O-38(22-0-17),D-11	-1.0
BEAN, JOE Joseph William B 3.18.1874 Boston, MA D 2.15.1961 Atlanta, GA BR/TR 5-8/138# d4.28																								
1902	NY N	50	182	13	40	2	1	0	5	5	2		.220	.249	.242	52	-11	9	.880	-8	96	109	S-50	-1.8
BEAN, BILLY William Daro B 5.11.1964 Santa Ana, CA BL/TL 6-1/185# d4.25																								
1987	Det A	26	66	6	17	2	0	0	4	5-0	0	11	.258	.310	.288	63	-4	1-1	1.000	3	129	111	O-24(5-17-3)	-0.1
1988	Det A	10	11	2	2	0	1	0	0	0-0	0	2	.182	.182	.364	51	-1	0-0	1.000	0	83	0	/O-4(0-2-3),1-2,D	-0.1
1989	Det A	9	11	0	0	0	0	0	0	2-0	1	3	.000	.214	.000	-36	-2	0-0	.833	-1	88	0	/O-6(4-1-2),1-2	-0.3
	LA N	51	71	7	14	4	0	0	3	4-0	1	10	.197	.250	.254	45	-5	0-2	1.000	-0	103	0	O-44(28-11-7)	-0.7
1993	SD N	88	177	19	46	9	0	5	32	6-1	2	29	.260	.284	.395	81	-5	2-4	.987	1	94	250	O-54(11-17-32),1-12	-0.7
1994	SD N	84	135	7	29	5	1	0	14	7-1	0	25	.215	.248	.267	37	-13	0-1	1.000	0	110	0	O-39(17-7-15),1-16	-1.5
1995	SD N	4	7	1	0	0	0	0	0	1-0	0	4	.000	.125	.000	-66	-2	0-0	.750	-1	72	0	/O-4(LF)	-0.2
Total	6	272	478	42	108	20	2	5	53	25-2	4	84	.226	.266	.308	55	-32	3-8	.988	2	104	105	O-175(69-55-62)/1-32,D	-3.6
BEANE, BILLY William Lamar B 3.29.1962 Orlando, FL BR/TR 6-4/195# d9.13																								
1984	NY N	5	10	0	1	0	0	0	0	0-0	0	2	.100	.100	.100	-44	-2	0-1	1.000	-0	55	0	/O-5(2-1-2)	-0.3
1985	NY N	8	8	0	2	1	0	0	1	0-0	0	3	.250	.250	.375	74	0	0-0	1.000	-0	39	0	/O-2(1-0-1)	-0.1
1986	Min A	80	183	20	39	6	0	3	15	11-0	0	54	.213	.258	.295	49	-13	2-3	1.000	2	120	0	O-67(64-5-1)/D-5	-1.4
1987	Min A	12	15	1	4	2	0	0	1	0-0	0	6	.267	.267	.400	71	-1	0-0	1.000	0	152	0	/O-7(RF)	0.0
1988	Det A	6	6	1	1	0	0	0	1	0-0	0	2	.167	.167	.167	-7	-1	0-0	1.000	-0	93	0	/O-6(4-1-1)	-0.1
1989	Oak A	37	79	8	19	5	0	0	11	0-0	0	13	.241	.237	.304	54	-5	3-1	1.000	1	114	0	O-25(4-0-21)/1-4,C3D	-0.5
Total	6	148	301	30	66	14	0	3	29	11-0	0	80	.219	.246	.296	48	-22	5-5	1.000	2	116	0	O-112(75-7-33)/D-9,1-4,3C	-2.4

Year	Tm Lg	G	AB	R	H	2B	3B	HR	RBI	BB-IB	HP	SO	AVG	OBP	SLG	AOPS	ABR	SB-CS	FA	FR	Rng	Thr	G at Pos	BFW
BEARD, TED Cramer Theodore B 1.7.1921 Woodsboro, MD BL/TL 5-8/165# d9.5																								
1948	Pit N	25	81	15	16	1	3	0	7	12	2	18	.198	.316	.284	62	-4	5	1.000	-1	105	0	O-22(CF)	-0.6
1949	Pit N	14	24	1	2	0	0	0	1	2	0	2	.083	.154	.083	-34	-5	0	.900	-1	91	0	O-10(RF)	-0.6
1950	Pit N	61	177	32	41	6	2	4	12	27	0	45	.232	.333	.356	79	-5	3	.983	2	109	108	O-49(1-21-27)	-0.5
1951	Pit N	22	48	7	9	1	0	1	3	6	1	14	.188	.291	.271	51	-3	0-0	1.000	0	87	195	O-15(12-4-0)	-0.4
1952	Pit N	15	44	5	8	2	1	0	3	7	0	9	.182	.294	.273	57	-3	2-0	1.000	0	103	83	O-13(0-3-10)	-0.3
1957	Chi A	38	78	15	16	1	0	0	7	18-2	0	14	.205	.354	.218	59	-3	3-2	.974	2	89	342	O-28(0-3-25)	-0.3
1958	Chi A	19	22	5	2	0	0	1	2	6-0	0	5	.091	.286	.227	44	-2	3-0	1.000	-0	105	0	O-15(10-6-1)	-0.2
Total	7	194	474	80	94	11	6	6	35	78-2	3	107	.198	.315	.285	61	-25	16-2	.987	2	102	120	O-152(23-59-73)	-2.9
BEARD, OLLIE Oliver Perry B 5.2.1862 Lexington, KY D 5.28.1929 Cincinnati, OH BR/TR 5-11/180# d4.17																								
1889	Cin AA	**141**	558	96	159	13	14	1	77	35	1	39	.285	.328	.364	94	-8	36	.896	18	109	**126**	*S-141	1.2
1890	Cin N	122	492	64	132	17	15	3	72	44	2	13	.268	.331	.382	108	3	30	.897	-1	**108**	117	*S-113/3-9	0.5
1891	Lou AA	68	257	35	62	4	5	0	24	33	1	9	.241	.330	.296	80	-6	7	.879	3	105	150	3-61/S-7	-0.2
Total	3	331	1307	195	353	34	34	4	173	112	4	61	.270	.330	.357	97	-11	73	.896	20	109	121	S-261/3-70	1.5
BEASLEY, LEW Lewis Paige B 8.27.1948 Sparta, VA BL/TR 5-10/172# d5.21																								
1977	Tex A	25	32	5	7	1	0	0	3	2-0	0	2	.219	.257	.250	41	-3	1-1	.833	-3	53	0	O-18(14-0-4)/SD	-0.6
BEATTY, DESMOND Aloysius Desmond "Desperate" B 4.7.1893 Baltimore, MD D 10.6.1969 Norway, ME BR/TR 5-8.5/158# d9.28																								
1914	NY N	2	3	0	0	0	0	0	1	0	0	0	.000	.000	.000	-99	-1	0	.400	-1	47	0	/S3	-0.2
BEAUCHAMP, JIM James Edward B 8.21.1939 Vinita, OK BR/TR 6-2/205# d9.22 C8																								
1963	StL N	4	3	0	0	0	0	0	0	0-0	0	2	.000	.000	.000	-91	-1	0-0	—	0			H	-0.1
1964	Hou N	23	55	6	9	2	0	2	4	5-0	1	16	.164	.246	.309	58	-3	0-0	.913	-1	90	0	O-15(11-4-0)/1-2	-0.5
1965	Hou N	24	53	5	10	1	0	0	4	5-0	0	11	.189	.259	.208	36	-5	0-2	1.000	2	90	257	/O-9(LF),1-3	-0.5
	Mil N	4	3	0	0	0	0	0	0	1-0	0	1	.000	.250	.000	-23	0	0-1	1.000	-0	0	138	/1-2	-0.1
	Year	28	56	5	10	1	0	0	4	6-0	0	12	.179	.258	.196	32	-5	0-3	1.000	1	90	257	/O-9(LF),1-5	-0.6
1967	Atl N	4	3	0	0	0	0	0	1	0-0	0	0	.000	.000	.000	-99	-1	0-0	—	0			H	-0.1
1968	Cin N	31	57	10	15	2	0	2	14	4-1	0	19	.263	.306	.404	107	0	0-0	1.000	-0	104	0	O-13(1-11-1)/1	0.0
1969	Cin N	43	60	8	15	1	0	1	8	5-2	0	13	.250	.308	.317	71	-2	0-0	1.000	0	113	0	/O-9(5-4-0),1-3	-0.3
1970	Hou N	31	26	3	5	0	0	1	4	3-0	0	7	.192	.276	.308	59	-2	0-1	1.000	-1	83	0	O-16(13-3-0)	-0.3
	StL N	44	58	8	15	2	0	1	6	8-0	0	11	.259	.338	.345	85	-1	2-0	1.000	1	113	245	O-10(2-6-2)/1-5	0.0
	Year	75	84	11	20	2	0	2	10	11-0	0	18	.238	.320	.333	78	-3	2-1	1.000	1	101	145	O-26(15-9-2)/1-5	-0.3
1971	StL N	77	162	24	38	8	3	2	16	9-1	1	26	.235	.274	.358	76	-5	3-1	.982	-2	85	87	1-44/O(LF)	-1.1
1972	NY N	58	120	10	29	1	0	5	19	7-1	1	33	.242	.282	.375	90	-2	0-0	.979	-2	67	88	1-35/O-5(LF)	-0.7
1973	†NY N	50	61	5	17	1	1	0	14	7-1	0	11	.279	.343	.328	91	-1	1-0	.969	-1	73	123	1-11	-0.2
Total	10	393	661	79	153	18	4	14	90	54-6	3	150	.231	.288	.334	76	-23	6-5	.980	-4	90	89	1-106/O-78(47-28-3)	-3.9
BEAUMONT, GINGER Clarence Howeth B 7.23.1876 Rochester, WI D 4.10.1956 Burlington, WI BL/TR 5-8/190# d4.21																								
1899	Pit N	111	437	90	154	15	8	3	38	41	7		.352	.416	.444	136	23	31	.924	-0	123	140	*O-100(3-96-1)/1-2	1.5
1900	†Pit N	138	567	105	158	14	9	5	50	40	4		.279	.331	.362	90	-9	27	.944	-15	52	67	*O-138(CF)	-3.0
1901	Pit N	133	558	120	185	14	5	8	72	44	2		.332	.382	.418	128	20	36	.943	-7	47	52	*O-133(CF)	0.6
1902	Pit N	130	541	100	**193**	21	6	0	67	39	4		**.357**	.404	.418	148	31	33	.975	-2	85	204	*O-130(CF)	2.4
1903	†Pit N	**141**	613	**137**	**209**	30	6	7	68	44	5		.341	.390	.444	133	26	23	.948	-11	76	45	*O-141(CF)	0.8
1904	Pit N	153	615	97	**185**	12	12	3	54	34	1		.301	.338	.374	117	10	28	.968	-7	74	110	*O-153(CF)	-0.4
1905	Pit N	103	384	60	126	12	8	3	40	22	0		.328	.365	.424	131	13	21	.972	0	99	178	O-97(CF)	0.9
1906	Pit N	80	310	48	82	9	3	2	32	19	2		.265	.311	.332	96	-2	1	.945	-5	63	96	O-78(CF)	-1.2
1907	Bos N	150	580	67	**187**	19	14	4	62	37	3		.322	.366	.424	148	29	25	.962	4	150	**224**	*O-149(CF)	3.0
1908	Bos N	125	476	66	127	20	6	2	52	42	1		.267	.328	.347	117	9	13	.965	-3	112	80	*O-121(CF)	0.0
1909	Bos N	123	407	35	107	11	4	0	60	35	0		.263	.321	.310	92	-4	12	.969	1	101	80	*O-111(CF)	-0.9
1910	†Chi N	76	172	30	46	5	1	2	22	28	1	14	.267	.373	.343	110	3	4	.957	-2	98	73	O-56(15-34-7)	-0.1
Total	12	1463	5660	955	1759	182	82	39	617	425	30	14	.311	.362	.393	122	149	254	.956	-48	89	114	*O-1407(18-1380-8)/1-2	3.6
BEAVENS, ED Edward P. (a/k/a Edward P. Bevens) B 1848 Troy, NY TR 5-8/138# d5.9																								
1871	Tro NA	3	15	7	6	0	0	0	5	0		0	.400	.400	.400	129	0	2-0	.818	1	120	166	/2-3	0.1
1872	Atl NA	10	43	6	9	2	0	0	2	1		0	.209	.227	.256	41	-3	0-0	.683	-6	92	50	2-10/SO(LF)	-0.7
Total	2 NA	13	58	13	15	2	0	0	7	1		0	.259	.271	.293	62	-3	2-0	.000	-5	99	78	/2-13,O(LF)S	-0.6
BECHTEL, GEORGE George A. B 1848 Philadelphia, PA 5-11/165# d5.20 ▲																								
1871	Ath NA	20	94	24	33	9	1	1	21	2		2	.351	.365	.500	147	6	4-0	.821	1	124	354	O-15(1-3-11)/P-3,3-3	0.4
1872	Mut NA	51	247	61	74	11	3	0	42	7		3	.300	.319	.368	118	7	9-1	.823	-0	79	111	*O-50(13-0-37)/1	0.8
1873	Phi NA	**53**	258	53	63	12	1	1	39	9		1	.244	.270	.310	69	-10	2-1	.853	6	121	152	*O-52(0-2-50)/P-3	0.0
1874	Phi NA	32	151	29	42	4	5	1	34	2		1	.278	.288	.391	111	1	0-0	.731	-4	0	0	O-28(1-0-28)/P-6	-0.1
1875	Cen NA	**14**	61	12	17	5	0	0	7	1		1	.279	.290	.361	136	4	0-0	.791	-1	91	138	P-14	0.0
	Ath NA	35	164	33	46	6	2	0	20	1		3	.280	.285	.341	105	0	2-0	.810	0	73	101	O-31(0-3-29)/P-4	0.2
	Year	49	225	45	63	11	2	0	27	2		4	.280	.286	.347	113	2	2-0	.810	-1	73	101	O-31(0-3-29),P-18	0.2
1876	Lou N	14	55	2	10	1	0	0	2	0		1	.182	.182	.200	23	-5		.882	-1	49	0	O-14(RF)	-0.5
	NY N	2	10	2	3	0	0	0	0	0		0	.300	.300	.300	115	0		.429	-2	0	0	/O-2(CF)	-0.1
	Year	16	65	4	13	1	0	0	2	0		1	.200	.200	.215	34	-5		.750	-3	41	0	O-16(0-2-14)	-0.6
Total	5 NA	205	975	212	275	47	12	3	163	22		11	.282	.298	.364	105	8	17-2	.000	1	81	122	O-176(15-8-155)/P-30,3-3,1	1.3
BECK, CLYDE Clyde Eugene "Jersey" B 1.6.1900 Bassett, CA D 7.15.1988 Temple City, CA BR/TR 5-10/176# d5.19																								
1926	Chi N	30	81	10	16	0	0	1	4	7	0	15	.198	.261	.235	34	-8	0	.993	8	107	150	2-30	0.1
1927	Chi N	117	391	44	101	20	5	2	44	43	0	37	.258	.332	.350	83	-9	0	.969	11	106	107	2-99,3-17/S	0.6
1928	Chi N	131	483	72	124	18	4	3	52	58	4	58	.257	.341	.329	77	-15	3	.958	3	92	161	3-87,S-47/2	-0.2
1929	Chi N	54	190	28	40	7	0	0	9	19	0	24	.211	.282	.247	32	-20	3	.978	7	124	116	3-33,S-14	-0.9
1930	Chi N	83	244	32	52	7	0	6	34	36	0	32	.213	.314	.316	53	-19	2	.953	-3	96	99	S-57,2-24/3-2	-1.4
1931	Cin N	53	136	17	21	4	2	0	19	21	1	14	.154	.272	.213	34	-12	1	.960	0	103	204	3-38/S-6	-1.1
Total	6	468	1525	203	354	56	11	12	162	184	5	180	.232	.317	.307	63	-83	9	.959	27	103	163	3-177,2-154,S-125	-2.9
BECK, ERVE Ervin Thomas "Dutch" B 7.19.1878 Toledo, OH D 12.23.1916 Toledo, OH BR/TR 5-10/168# d9.19																								
1899	Bro N	8	24	2	4	2	0	0	2	0	0		.167	.167	.250	13	-3	0	.931	-1	126	52	/2-6,S-2	-0.3
1901	Cle A	135	539	78	156	26	8	6	79	23	1		.289	.320	.401	103	1	7	.927	-8	99	71	*2-132	-0.6
1902	Cin N	48	187	19	57	10	3	1	20	3	1		.305	.319	.406	113	2	2	.936	-2	99	93	2-32/1-6,O-6(3-0-3)	0.0
	Det A	41	162	23	48	4	0	2	22	4	0		.296	.313	.358	84	-4	3	.971	2	134	113	1-36/O-5(RF)	-0.3
Total	3	232	912	122	265	42	11	9	123	30	2		.291	.315	.390	99	-4	12	.929	-9	100	75	2-170/1-42,O-11(3-0-8),S-2	-1.2
BECK, FRED Frederick Thomas B 11.17.1886 Havana, IL D 3.12.1962 Havana, IL BL/TL 6-1/180# d4.14																								
1909	Bos N	96	334	20	66	5	6	2	27	17	4		.198	.245	.266	56	-19	5	.966	2	99	244	O-57(12-42-2),1-33	-2.2
1910	Bos N	154	571	52	157	32	9	**10**	64	19	7	55	.275	.307	.415	105	0	8	.963	0	100	108	*O-134(2-125-7),1-19	-0.7
1911	Cin N	41	87	7	16	1	2	2	20	1	0	13	.184	.193	.310	41	-8	2	1.000	-0	99	109	O-16(4-5-7)/1-6	-0.9
	Phi N	66	210	26	59	8	3	3	25	17	4	21	.281	.346	.390	105	1	3	.957	-3	87	94	O-61(11-1-50)	-0.5
	Year	107	297	33	75	9	5	5	45	18	4	34	.253	.304	.367	88	-7	5	.966	-3	89	97	O-77(15-6-57)/1-6	-1.4
1914	Chi F	**157**	555	51	155	23	4	11	77	44	8	66	.279	.341	.395	106	-5	9	.982	-13	66	119	*1-157	-2.4
1915	Chi F	121	373	35	83	9	3	5	38	24	4	38	.223	.277	.303	67	-24	4	.992	-6	70	105	*1-117	-3.6
Total	5	635	2130	191	536	78	27	33	251	122	27	193	.252	.301	.360	89	-55	31	.984	-20	72	110	1-332,O-268(29-173-66)	-10.3
BECK, ZINN Zinn Bertram B 9.30.1885 Steubenville, OH D 3.19.1981 W.Palm Beach, FL BR/TR 5-10.5/160# d9.14																								
1913	StL N	10	30	4	5	1	0	0	2	4	0	10	.167	.265	.200	34	-2	1	.833	0	107	94	/S-5,3-5	-0.2
1914	StL N	137	457	42	106	15	11	3	45	28	4	32	.232	.282	.333	84	-12	14	.935	3	108	**150**	*3-122,S-16	-0.4
1915	StL N	70	223	21	52	9	4	0	15	12	3	31	.233	.282	.309	79	-6	3-10	.935	1	110	126	3-62/S-4,2-2	-0.7
1916	StL N	62	184	8	41	7	1	0	10	14	1	21	.223	.281	.272	71	-6	3	.910	-2	98	100	3-52/12	-0.8
1918	NY A	11	8	0	0	0	0	0	1	0	0	1	.000	.000	.000	-98	-2	0	1.000	0	197	205	/1-5,3	-0.2
Total	5	290	902	75	204	32	16	3	73	58	8	95	.226	.279	.307	76	-28	21-10	.932	2	107	132	3-242/S-25,1-6,2-3	-2.3

Year	Tm Lg	G	AB	R	H	2B	3B	HR	RBI	BB-IB	HP	SO	AVG	OBP	SLG	AOPS	ABR	SB-CS	FA	FR	Rng	Thr	G at Pos	BFW
BECKENDORF, HEINIE Henry Ward B 6.15.1884 New York, NY D 9.15.1949 Jackson Heights, NY BR/TR 5-9/174# d4.16																								
1909	Det A	15	27	1	7	1	0	0	1	2	0		.259	.310	.296	88	0	0	.957	-0	*96*	*88*	C-15	0.0
1910	Det A	3	7	0	3	0	0	0	2	1	0		.429	.500	.429	179	1	0	.909	-0	*115*	*54*	/C-2	0.1
	Was A	37	103	8	15	1	0	0	10	5	3		.146	.207	.155	14	-10	0	.991	2	*103*	*64*	C-36	-0.6
	Year	40	110	8	18	1	0	0	12	6	3		.164	.227	.173	26	-9	0	.988	1	*104*	*63*	C-38	-0.5
Total	2	55	137	9	25	2	0	0	13	8	3		.182	.243	.197	39	-9	0	.983	1	*102*	*68*	/C-53	-0.5
BECKER, BEALS David Beals B 7.5.1886 ElDorado, KS D 8.16.1943 Huntington Park, CA BL/TL 5-9/170# d4.19																								
1908	Pit N	20	65	4	10	0	1	0	0	2	1		.154	.191	.185	20	-6	2	1.000	1	226	0	O-17(RF)	-0.7
	Bos N	43	171	13	47	3	1	0	7	7	0		.275	.303	.304	96	-1	7	.941	-1	182	93	O-43(0-1-42)	-0.4
	Year	63	236	17	57	3	2	0	7	9	1		.242	.272	.271	74	-8	9	.958	-0	195	66	O-60(0-1-59)	-1.1
1909	Bos N	152	562	60	138	15	6	6	24	47	1		.246	.305	.326	91	-7	21	.932	-2	123	150	*O-152(RF)	-1.7
1910	NY N	80	126	18	36	2	4	3	24	14	0	25	.286	.357	.437	131	4	11	.972	3	107	178	O-45(6-23-14)/1	0.6
1911	†NY N	88	172	28	45	11	1	1	20	26	0	22	.262	.359	.355	97	0	19	.975	1	101	129	O-55(17-6-33)	-0.1
1912	†NY N	125	402	66	106	18	8	6	58	54	2	35	.264	.354	.393	101	1	30	.958	3	99	125	*O-117(1-93-26)	-0.3
1913	Cin N	30	108	11	32	5	3	0	14	6	0	12	.296	.333	.398	109	1	0-4	.971	1	110	77	O-28(9-8-11)	-0.1
	Phi N	88	306	53	99	19	10	9	44	22	0	30	.324	.369	.539	151	19	11-12	.983	-1	103	58	O-77(42-36-2)/1	1.2
	Year	118	414	64	131	24	13	9	58	28	0	42	.316	.360	.502	140	20	11-16	.980	-0	105	63	*O-105(51-44-13)/1	1.1
1914	Phi N	138	514	76	167	25	5	9	66	37	0	59	.325	.370	.446	133	20	16	.947	4	108	108	*O-126(87-32-8)	1.9
1915	†Phi N	112	338	38	83	16	4	11	35	26	1	48	.246	.301	.414	114	5	12-15	.943	-6	99	46	O-98(90-0-8)	-0.9
Total	8	876	2764	367	763	114	43	45	292	241	5	231	.276	.335	.397	112	36	129-31	.955	4	114	106	O-758(252-199-313)/1-2	-0.5
BECKER, HEINZ Heinz Reinhard "Dutch" B 8.26.1915 Berlin, Germany D 11.11.1991 Dallas, TX BB/TR (BL 1946) 6-2/200# d4.21																								
1943	Chi N	24	69	5	10	0	0	0	2	9	0	6	.145	.244	.145	14	-8	0	.983	1	132	66	1-18	-0.8
1945	†Chi N	67	133	25	38	8	2	2	27	17	2	16	.286	.375	.421	124	5	0	1.000	-1	72	132	1-28	0.2
1946	Chi N	9	7	0	2	0	0	0	1	1	0	1	.286	.375	.286	91	0	0	—	0			H	0.0
	Cle A	50	147	15	44	10	1	0	17	23	2	18	.299	.401	.381	127	7	1-0	.995	-0	91	95	1-44	0.6
1947	Cle A	2	2	0	0	0	0	0	0	0	0	1	.000	.000	.000	-99	-1	0-0	—	0			H	-0.1
Total	4	152	358	45	94	18	3	2	47	50	4	42	.263	.359	.346	102	3	1-0	.994	-0	94	100	/1-90	-0.1
BECKER, JOE Joseph Edward B 6.25.1908 St.Louis, MO D 1.11.1998 Sunset Hills, MO BR/TR 6-1/180# d5.10 C16																								
1936	Cle A	22	50	5	9	3	1	1	11	5	0	4	.180	.255	.340	45	-5	0-0	.977	-2	*89*	*42*	C-15	-0.6
1937	Cle A	18	33	3	11	2	1	0	2	3	1	4	.333	.405	.455	116	1	0-0	.949	-1	*82*	*205*	C-12	0.1
Total	2	40	83	8	20	5	2	1	13	8	1	8	.241	.315	.386	73	-4	0-0	.964	-3	*86*	*112*	/C-27	-0.5
BECKER, MARTY Martin Henry B 12.25.1893 Tiffin, OH D 9.25.1957 Cincinnati, OH BB/TL 5-8.5/155# d9.8																								
1915	NY N	17	52	5	13	2	0	0	3	2	0	9	.250	.278	.288	76	-2	3	.917	1	86	230	O-16(0-16-1)	-0.1
BECKER, RICH Richard Godhard B 2.1.1972 Aurora, IL BL/TL (BB 1993-94, 95 (part)) 5-10/199# d9.10																								
1993	Min A	3	7	3	2	2	0	0	0	5-0	0	4	.286	.583	.571	211	2	1-1	.875	-0	109	0	/O-3(CF)	0.2
1994	Min A	28	98	12	26	3	0	1	8	13-0	0	25	.265	.351	.327	76	-3	6-1	.989	4	124	135	O-26(1-23-2)/D	0.2
1995	Min A	106	392	45	93	15	1	2	33	34-0	4	95	.237	.303	.296	57	-25	8-9	.986	7	104	**227**	*O-105(2-99-5)	-1.7
1996	Min A	148	525	92	153	31	4	12	71	68-1	2	118	.291	.372	.434	102	3	19-5	.993	17	**114**	**209**	*O-146(15-121-10)	2.1
1997	Min A	132	443	61	117	22	3	10	45	62-1	1	130	.264	.354	.395	94	-2	17-5	.985	1	105	78	*O-128(9-114-14)	0.1
1998	NY N	49	100	15	19	4	2	3	10	21-2	0	42	.190	.331	.360	83	-2	3-1	.984	3	106	238	O-41(17-14-13)	0.0
	Bal A	79	113	22	23	1	0	3	11	22-0	2	34	.204	.343	.292	69	-5	2-0	.984	-3	87	46	O-60(5-13-43)/D	-0.8
1999	Mil N	89	139	15	35	5	2	5	16	33-0	0	38	.252	.395	.424	109	3	5-0	.970	0	93	160	O-50(16-19-17)/D-2	0.3
	Oak A	40	125	21	33	3	0	1	10	25-0	2	43	.264	.395	.312	87	-1	3-2	.986	0	85	197	O-39(17-32-8)	-0.1
2000	Oak A	23	47	11	11	2	0	1	5	11-0	1	17	.234	.390	.340	89	0	1-0	.949	2	111	306	O-19(8-14-1)/D-2	0.2
	Det A	92	238	48	58	12	0	7	34	56-0	0	70	.244	.383	.382	99	2	1-2	.956	-3	94	78	O-80(14-24-47)/D-3	-0.3
	Year	115	285	59	69	14	0	8	39	67-0	1	87	.242	.384	.375	97	2	2-2	.954	-1	97	116	O-99(22-38-48)/D-5	-0.1
Total	8	789	2227	345	570	100	12	45	243	350-4	12	616	.256	.358	.372	89	-28	66-26	.983	29	104	158	O-697(104-476-160)/D-9	0.2
BECKERT, GLENN Glenn Alfred B 10.12.1940 Pittsburgh, PA BR/TR 6-1/190# d4.12 Mil 1966																								
1965	Chi N	154	614	73	147	21	3	3	30	28-0	3	52	.239	.275	.298	60	-33	6-8	.973	8	109	103	*2-153	-1.5
1966	Chi N	153	656	73	188	23	7	1	59	26-0	4	36	.287	.317	.348	84	-15	10-4	.970	-15	96	86	*2-152/S	-1.6
1967	Chi N	146	597	91	167	32	3	5	40	30-1	0	25	.280	.314	.369	91	-7	10-3	.968	3	105	103	*2-144	1.0
1968	Chi N	155	643	**98**	189	28	4	4	37	31-0	2	20	.294	.326	.369	102	2	8-4	.977	9	103	117	*2-155	2.8
1969	Chi N★	131	543	69	158	22	1	1	37	24-0	6	24	.291	.325	.341	78	-15	6-0	.965	11	**112**	91	*2-129	0.6
1970	Chi N★	143	591	99	170	15	6	3	36	32-0	0	22	.288	.323	.349	72	-24	4-1	.970	13	107	105	*2-138/O(CF)	-0.1
1971	Chi N★	131	530	80	181	18	5	2	42	24-0	0	24	.342	.367	.406	104	3	3-2	.986	-1	100	89	*2-129	1.2
1972	Chi N★	120	474	51	128	22	2	3	43	23-1	2	17	.270	.304	.344	76	-14	2-1	.976	15	**112**	101	*2-118	0.9
1973	Chi N	114	372	38	95	13	0	0	29	30-1	2	15	.255	.313	.290	64	-17	0-2	.984	-7	98	88	2-88	-2.1
1974	SD N	64	172	11	44	1	0	0	7	11-0	0	8	.256	.301	.262	61	-9	0-0	.938	-10	84	67	2-36/3	-1.8
1975	SD N	9	16	2	6	1	0	0	0	1-0	0	0	.375	.412	.438	145	1	0-0	1.000	-0	106	0	/3-4	0.1
Total	11	1320	5208	685	1473	196	31	22	360	260-3	19	243	.283	.318	.345	81	-128	49-25	.973	25	104	98	*2-1242/3-5,O(CF)S	-0.5
BECKLEY, JAKE Jacob Peter "Eagle Eye" B 8.4.1867 Hannibal, MO D 6.25.1918 Kansas City, MO BL/TL 5-10/200# d6.20 HF1971																								
1888	Pit N	71	283	35	97	15	3	0	27	7	2	22	.343	.363	.417	162	20	20	.979	-3	73	110	1-71	1.0
1889	Pit N	123	522	91	157	24	10	9	97	29	6	29	.301	.345	.437	130	19	11	.982	2	98	111	*1-122/O(RF)	0.8
1890	Pit P	121	516	109	167	38	**22**	9	120	42	6	32	.324	.381	.535	156	40	18	.976	-0	97	91	*1-121	2.3
1891	Pit N	133	554	94	162	20	19	4	73	44	8	46	.292	.353	.419	128	18	13	.982	13	**147**	90	*1-133	1.6
1892	Pit N	151	614	102	145	21	19	10	96	31	14	44	.236	.288	.381	102	-3	30	.978	20	**163**	101	*1-151	1.5
1893	Pit N	**131**	542	108	164	32	19	5	106	54	20	26	.303	.386	.459	127	21	15	.986	11	**130**	106	*1-131	2.5
1894	Pit N	132	537	123	185	36	19	7	122	43	19	16	.345	.412	.521	125	22	21	.978	5	115	94	*1-132	2.0
1895	Pit N	130	534	104	175	31	19	5	111	24	21	20	.328	.380	.485	129	22	20	.978	-7	75	98	*1-130	1.2
1896	Pit N	59	217	44	55	7	5	3	32	22	10	28	.253	.349	.373	94	-1	8	.982	-0	99	120	1-56/O-3(CF),2	-0.2
	NY N	46	182	37	55	8	4	6	38	9	5	7	.302	.352	.489	124	5	11	.982	-1	96	69	1-45/O-2(LF)	0.4
	Year	105	399	81	110	15	9	9	70	31	15	35	.276	.351	.426	108	4	19	.982	-1	98	98	*1-101/O-5(2-3-0),2	0.2
1897	NY N	17	68	8	17	2	3	1	11	2	3		.250	.301	.412	90	-2	2	.973	2	152	130	1-17	0.0
	Cin N	97	365	76	126	17	9	7	76	18	12		.345	.395	.499	127	12	23	.979	-3	85	114	*1-97	0.8
	Year	114	433	84	143	19	12	8	87	20	15		.330	.380	.485	121	11	25	.978	-1	96	117	*1-114	0.8
1898	Cin N	118	459	86	135	20	12	4	72	28	10		.294	.348	.416	111	5	6	.983	-1	92	107	*1-118	0.3
1899	Cin N	135	517	87	172	27	16	3	99	40	10		.333	.392	.464	132	22	20	.986	5	107	97	*1-135	2.4
1900	Cin N	141	558	98	190	26	10	2	94	40	4		.341	.389	.434	130	23	23	.980	5	115	**115**	*1-140	2.5
1901	Cin N	140	580	78	178	36	13	3	79	28	7		.307	.346	.429	133	23	4	.977	-4	89	104	*1-140	1.6
1902	Cin N	129	531	82	175	23	7	5	69	34	6		.330	.377	.427	135	21	15	.983	-2	87	**119**	*1-129/P	1.7
1903	Cin N	120	459	85	150	29	10	2	81	42	1		.327	.384	.447	123	13	23	.976	4	114	96	*1-119	1.4
1904	StL N	142	551	72	179	22	9	1	67	35	9		.325	.375	.403	147	30	17	.988	-12	67	113	*1-142	1.7
1905	StL N	134	514	48	147	20	10	1	57	30	6		.286	.333	.370	113	7	12	.982	-8	80	79	*1-134	-0.3
1906	StL N	87	320	29	79	16	6	0	44	13	3		.247	.283	.334	96	-3	3	.987	-4	78	90	1-85	-1.0
1907	StL N	32	115	6	24	3	0	0	7	1	1		.209	.222	.235	45	-8	0	.988	-2	71	107	1-32	-1.2
Total	20	2389	9538	1602	2934	473	244	87	1578	616	183	270	.308	.361	.436	126	306	315	.981	19	102	102	*1-2380/O-6(2-3-1),P2	23.0
BECQUER, JULIO Julio (Villegas) B 12.20.1931 Havana, Cuba BL/TL 5-11.5/178# d9.13																								
1955	Was A	10	14	1	3	0	0	0	1	0-0	0	1	.214	.214	.214	16	-2	0-0	1.000	0	205	124	/1-2	-0.1
1957	Was A	105	186	14	42	6	2	2	22	10-2	1	29	.226	.269	.312	59	-11	3-3	1.000	-0	90	86	1-43	-1.4
1958	Was A	86	164	10	39	3	0	0	12	8-3	0	21	.238	.270	.256	47	-12	1-2	.994	5	149	74	1-42/O(LF)	-1.0
1959	Was A	108	220	20	59	12	5	1	26	8-2	1	17	.268	.296	.382	85	-5	3-2	.990	1	113	102	1-53	-0.7
1960	Was A	110	298	41	75	15	7	4	35	12-3	1	35	.252	.282	.389	81	-10	1-3	.989	-3	86	92	1-77/P	-1.8
1961	LA A	11	8	0	0	0	0	0	0	1-0	0	5	.000	.111	.000	-61	-2	0-0	1.000	0	133	0	/1-5	-0.2
	Min A	57	84	13	20	1	2	5	18	2-1	0	12	.238	.253	.476	86	-3	0-1	1.000	0	62	130	1-18/O-5(LF),P	-0.3
	Year	68	92	13	20	1	2	5	18	3-1	0	17	.217	.240	.435	72	-5	0-1	1.000	0	71	114	1-23/O-5(LF),P	-0.5
1963	Min A	1	0	1	0	0	0	0	0	0-0	0	0	—	—	—	—	0	0-0	—	0			H	0.0
Total	7	488	974	100	238	37	16	12	114	41-11	3	120	.244	.276	.352	70	-45	8-11	.993	3	105	91	1-240/O-6(LF),P-2	-5.5

Year	Tm Lg	G	AB	R	H	2B	3B	HR	RBI	BB-IB	HP	SO	AVG	OBP	SLG	AOPS	ABR	SB-CS	FA	FR	Rng	Thr	G at Pos	BFW
BEDELL, HOWIE Howard William B 9.29.1935 Clearfield, PA BL/TR 6-1/185# d4.10 C2																								
1962	Mil N	58	138	15	27	1	2	0	2	11-0	0	22	.196	.255	.232	33	-14	1-0	.955	-1	111	0	O-45(44-2-0)	-1.6
1968	Phi N	9	7	0	1	0	0	0	1	1-0	0	0	.143	.222	.143	20	-1	0-0	—	0			H	-0.1
Total	2	67	145	15	28	1	2	0	3	12-0	0	22	.193	.253	.228	32	-15	1-0	.955	-1	111	0	/O-45(44-2-0)	-1.7
BEDFORD, GENE William Eugene B 12.2.1896 Dallas, TX D 10.6.1977 San Antonio, TX BB/TR 5-8/170# d6.25																								
1925	Cle A	2	3	1	0	0	0	0	0	0	0	1	.000	.000	.000	-99	-1	0-0	1.000	-1	57	0	/2-2	-0.2
BEECHER, ED Edward Harry B 7.2.1860 Guilford, CT D 9.12.1935 Hartford, CT BL/TL 5-10/185# d6.28																								
1887	Pit N	41	169	15	41	8	0	2	22	7	2	8	.243	.281	.325	73	-6	8	.915	5	167	79	O-41(18-22-1)	-0.2
1889	Was N	42	179	20	53	9	0	0	30	5	1	4	.296	.319	.346	91	-2	3	.861	-2	93	64	O-39(1-0-38)/1-3	-0.4
1890	Buf P	126	536	69	159	22	10	3	90	29	7	23	.297	.341	.392	104	3	14	.810	-5	102	72	*O-126(119-0-7)/P	-0.4
1891	Was AA	58	235	35	57	11	3	2	28	27	5	9	.243	.333	.340	97	0	17	.824	0	116	142	O-58(52-6-0)	-0.1
	Phi AA	16	71	9	15	2	4	0	7	3	0	4	.211	.243	.352	70	-4	7	1.000	-0	81	0	O-16(RF)	-0.4
	Year	74	306	44	72	13	7	2	35	30	5	13	.235	.314	.343	91	-4	24	.845	-0	110	116	O-74(52-6-16)	-0.5
Total	4	283	1190	148	325	52	17	7	177	71	15	48	.273	.322	.363	94	-9	49	.843	-2	112	84	O-280(190-28-62)/1-3,P	-1.5
BEELER, JODIE Joseph Sam B 11.26.1921 Dallas, TX D 10.8.2002 Mesquite, TX BR/TR 6/170# d9.21																								
1944	Cin N	3	3	0	0	0	0	0	0	0	0	2	.000	.000	.000	-99	-1	0	.000	-1	0	0	/23	-0.2
BEGLEY, GENE Eugene T. B 6.7.1861 Brooklyn, NY d9.11																								
1886	NY N	5	16	1	2	0	0	0	1	1		3	.125	.176	.125	-7	-2	1	.864	-0			/C-3,O-2(RF)	-0.2
BEGLEY, JIM James Lawrence "Imp" B 9.19.1902 San Francisco, CA D 2.22.1957 San Francisco, CA BR/TR 5-6/145# d5.28																								
1924	Cin N	2	5	1	1	0	0	0	0	2	0	0	.200	.429	.200	75	0	0-0	.933	0	118	0	/2-2	0.0
BEHEL, STEVE Stephen Arnold Douglas B 11.6.1860 Earlville, IL D 2.15.1945 Los Angeles, CA d9.27																								
1884	Mil U	9	33	5	8	1	0	0		3			.242	.306	.273	141	1		1.000	-0	64	0	/O-9(LF)	0.1
1886	NY AA	59	224	32	46	5	2	0	17	22	1		.205	.279	.246	71	-6	16	.858	-4	76	0	O-59(26-33-0)	-1.0
Total	2	68	257	37	54	6	2	0	17	25	1		.210	.283	.249	76	-5	16	.865	-4	75	0	/O-68(35-33-0)	-0.9
BEJMA, OLLIE Alojzy Frank B 9.12.1907 South Bend, IN D 1.3.1995 South Bend, IN BR/TR 5-10/165# d4.24																								
1934	StL A	95	262	39	71	16	3	2	29	40	4	36	.271	.376	.378	87	-4	3-2	.952	-6	93	107	S-32,2-14,3-13/O-9(RF)	-0.6
1935	StL A	64	198	18	38	8	2	2	26	27	0	21	.192	.289	.283	46	-16	1-0	.952	-4	101	95	2-47/S-8,3-2	-1.6
1936	StL A	67	139	19	36	2	3	2	18	27	0	21	.259	.380	.360	81	-4	0-0	.963	-9	88	43	2-32/3-7,S	-0.9
1939	Chi A	90	307	52	77	9	3	8	44	36	1	27	.251	.331	.378	79	-11	1-3	.981	-8	95	84	2-81/S3	-1.3
Total	4	316	906	128	222	35	11	14	117	130	5	105	.245	.343	.354	75	-35	5-5	.967	-26	94	78	2-174/S-42,3-23,O-9(RF)	-4.4
BELANGER, MARK Mark Henry B 6.8.1944 Pittsfield, MA D 10.6.1998 New York, NY BR/TR 6-1/170# d8.7																								
1965	Bal A	11	3	1	1	0	0	0	0	0-0	0	0	.333	.333	.333	88	0	0-1	1.000	0	102	1105	/S-4	0.0
1966	Bal A	8	19	2	3	1	0	0	0	0-0	0	3	.158	.158	.211	5	-2	0-0	1.000	2	133	103	/S-6	0.0
1967	Bal A	69	184	19	32	5	0	1	10	12-1	0	46	.174	.224	.217	31	-16	6-1	.952	2	92	90	S-38,2-26/3-2	-1.0
1968	Bal A	145	472	40	98	13	0	2	21	40-2	4	114	.208	.272	.248	59	-23	10-1	.969	19	106	105	*S-145	1.2
1969	†Bal A	150	530	76	152	17	4	2	50	53-5	2	54	.287	.351	.345	95	-2	14-6	.968	-8	97	108	*S-148	0.8
1970	†Bal A	145	459	53	100	6	5	1	36	52-3	5	65	.218	.303	.259	56	-27	13-2	.970	-2	101	110	*S-143	-1.2
1971	†Bal A	150	500	67	133	19	4	0	35	73-6	7	48	.266	.365	.320	97	2	10-8	.978	-1	97	100	*S-149	1.9
1972	Bal A	113	285	36	53	9	1	2	16	18-1	2	53	.186	.236	.246	43	-20	6-3	.975	9	101	114	*S-105	-0.1
1973	†Bal A	154	470	60	106	15	1	0	27	49-1	5	54	.226	.302	.262	61	-23	13-6	.971	5	106	118	*S-154	0.1
1974	†Bal A	155	493	54	111	14	4	5	36	51-0	2	69	.225	.298	.300	75	-15	17-7	**.984**	3	**106**	110	*S-155	0.8
1975	Bal A	152	442	44	100	11	1	3	27	36-0	1	53	.226	.286	.276	63	-22	16-4	.978	**30**	**116**	**139**	*S-152	2.7
1976	Bal A★	153	522	66	141	22	2	1	40	51-0	2	64	.270	.336	.326	101	2	27-17	.982	16	**112**	111	*S-153	3.8
1977	Bal A	144	402	39	83	13	4	2	30	43-1	3	68	.206	.287	.274	58	-23	15-8	**.985**	19	108	117	*S-142	0.9
1978	Bal A	135	348	39	74	13	0	0	16	40-1	6	55	.213	.299	.250	61	-16	6-6	**.985**	**30**	**118**	119	*S-134	2.5
1979	†Bal A	101	198	28	33	6	2	0	9	29-0	1	33	.167	.273	.217	36	-17	5-1	.990	-4	93	99	S-98	-1.3
1980	Bal A	113	268	37	61	7	3	0	22	12-0	0	25	.228	.261	.276	48	-20	6-3	.975	-3	97	92	*S-109	-1.4
1981	Bal A	64	139	9	23	3	2	1	10	12-0	2	25	.165	.242	.237	39	-11	2-1	.973	-0	102	64	S-63	-0.6
1982	LA N	54	50	6	12	1	0	0	4	5-1	0	10	.240	.309	.260	62	-2	1-0	.953	-4	99	40	S-44/2	-0.4
Total	18	2016	5784	676	1316	175	33	20	389	576-22	42	839	.228	.300	.280	68	-235	167-75	.977	114	105	109	*S-1942/2-27,3-2	8.7
BELARDI, WAYNE Carroll Wayne B 9.5.1930 St.Helena, CA D 10.21.1993 Santa Cruz, CA BL/TL 6-1/185# d4.18																								
1950	Bro N	10	10	0	0	0	0	0	0	0	0	4	.000	.000	.000	-98	-3	0	1.000	-0	0	0	/1	-0.3
1951	Bro N	3	3	1	1	0	1	0	0	0	0	2	.333	.333	1.000	240	0	0-0	—	0			H	0.0
1953	†Bro N	69	163	19	39	3	2	11	34	16	1	40	.239	.311	.485	101	-1	0-0	.984	-1	95	124	1-38	-0.3
1954	Bro N	11	9	0	2	0	0	0	1	2	0	3	.222	.364	.222	55	-1	0-0	—	0			H	0.0
	Det A	88	250	27	58	7	1	11	24	33	5	34	.232	.330	.400	102	0	1-0	.988	2	111	89	1-79	-0.2
1955	Det A	3	3	0	0	0	0	0	0	0-0	0	1	.000	.000	.000	-99	-1	0-0	—	0			H	-0.1
1956	Det A	79	154	24	43	3	1	6	15	15-1	8	13	.279	.371	.429	111	3	0-0	.988	-1	94	78	1-31/O-2(2-0-1)	0.0
Total	6	263	592	71	143	13	5	28	74	66-1	14	97	.242	.330	.422	100	-3	1-0	.987	-0	103	95	1-149/O-2(2-0-1)	-0.9
BELCHER, KEVIN Kevin Donnell B 8.8.1967 Waco, TX BR/TR 6/170# d9.3																								
1990	Tex A	16	15	4	2	1	0	0	0	2-0	0	6	.133	.235	.200	23	-2	0-0	1.000	0	115	0	/O-9(2-5-2)	-0.1
BELDEN, IRA Ira Allison B 4.16.1874 Cleveland, OH D 7.15.1916 Lakewood, OH BL/TR 5-11/175# d9.17																								
1897	Cle N	8	30	5	8	0	2	0	4	2	1		.267	.333	.400	88	-1	0	1.000	1	159	0	/O-8(RF)	0.0
BELK, TIM Timothy William B 4.6.1970 Cincinnati, OH BR/TR 6-3/200# d6.25																								
1996	Cin N	7	15	2	3	0	0	0	0	1-0	0	2	.200	.250	.200	20	-2	0-0	1.000	-1	0	57	/1-6	-0.3
BELL, BUDDY David Gus B 8.27.1951 Pittsburgh, PA BR/TR 6-2/185# d4.15 M6 C3 f-Gus s-David s-Mike OF Total (11-LF 64-CF 66-RF)																								
1972	Cle A	132	466	49	119	21	1	9	36	34-8	3	29	.255	.310	.363	96	-2	5-6	.990	5	104	121	*O-123(0-63-65)/3-6	-0.3
1973	Cle A★	156	631	86	169	23	7	14	59	49-2	6	47	.268	.325	.393	100	-1	7-15	.958	27	117	**141**	*3-154/O-2(0-1-1)	2.2
1974	Cle A	116	423	51	111	15	1	7	46	35-1	3	29	.262	.322	.352	95	-3	1-3	.963	15	**115**	127	*3-115/D	1.1
1975	Cle A	153	553	66	150	20	4	10	59	51-6	1	72	.271	.332	.376	100	0	6-5	.950	-0	98	95	*3-153	-0.2
1976	Cle A	**159**	604	75	170	26	2	7	60	44-3	2	49	.281	.329	.366	105	4	3-8	.956	8	104	86	*3-158/1-2	0.9
1977	Cle A	129	479	64	140	23	4	11	64	45-5	1	63	.292	.351	.426	115	10	1-8	.960	13	110	106	*3-118,O-11(LF)	1.8
1978	Cle A	142	556	71	157	27	8	6	62	39-1	0	43	.282	.328	.392	103	1	1-3	.970	27	**116**	108	*3-139/D	2.5
1979	Tex A	**162**	670	89	200	42	3	18	101	30-4	3	45	.299	.327	.451	110	8	5-4	.969	28	**123**	84	*3-147,S-33	3.5
1980	Tex A★	129	490	76	161	24	4	17	83	40-11	0	39	.329	.379	.498	143	28	3-1	**.981**	27	115	100	*3-120/S-3	5.2
1981	Tex A★	97	360	44	106	16	1	10	64	42-10	3	30	.294	.364	.428	137	18	3-3	.961	**34**	**144**	110	3-96/S	5.2
1982	Tex A★	148	537	62	159	27	2	13	67	70-8	2	50	.296	.376	.426	127	23	5-4	**.976**	**38**	**127**	113	*3-145/S-4	5.7
1983	Tex A	156	618	75	171	35	3	14	66	50-5	4	48	.277	.332	.411	106	5	3-5	.967	18	**113**	88	*3-154	1.9
1984	Tex A★	148	553	88	174	36	5	11	83	63-8	3	54	.315	.382	.458	129	24	2-1	.958	24	**117**	104	*3-147	4.5
1985	Tex A	84	313	33	74	13	3	4	32	33-1	1	21	.236	.308	.335	76	-10	3-2	.942	17	122	139	3-83	0.6
	Cin N	67	247	28	54	15	2	6	36	34-2	0	27	.219	.311	.368	86	-4	0-1	.946	-11	77	117	3-67	-1.7
1986	Cin N	155	568	89	158	29	3	20	75	73-4	5	49	.278	.362	.445	117	15	2-8	.975	-5	97	111	*3-151/2	0.6
1987	Cin N	143	522	74	148	19	2	17	70	71-3	1	39	.284	.369	.425	105	6	4-1	**.979**	-24	82	73	*3-142	-2.0
1988	Cin N	21	54	3	10	0	0	0	3	7-1	0	8	.185	.270	.185	34	-4	0-0	.968	-1	89	105	3-13/1-2	-0.6
	Hou N	74	269	24	68	10	1	7	37	19-1	0	29	.253	.301	.375	97	-2	1-1	.924	-10	88	79	3-66/1-7	-1.4
	Year	95	323	27	78	10	1	7	40	26-2	0	32	.241	.295	.344	86	-7	1-1	.931	-11	88	83	3-79/1-9	-2.0
1989	Tex A	34	82	4	15	4	0	0	3	7-0	0	10	.183	.247	.232	35	-7	0-0	1.000	0	96	0	D-22/3-9,1	-0.8
Total	18	2405	8995	1151	2514	425	56	201	1106	836-84	38	776	.279	.341	.406	108	109	55-79	.964	229	110	104	*3-2183,O-136R/S-41,D-24,1-12,2	28.7
BELL, DAVID David Michael B 9.14.1972 Cincinnati, OH BR/TR 5-10/170# d5.3 f-Buddy gf-Gus b-Mike																								
1995	Cle A	2	2	0	0	0	0	0	0	0-0	0	0	.000	.000	.000	-99	-1	0-0	1.000	0	252	0	/3-2	0.0
	StL N	39	144	13	36	7	2	2	19	4-0	2	25	.250	.278	.368	69	-7	1-2	.967	-2	100	116	2-37/3-3	-0.8
1996	StL N	62	145	12	31	6	0	1	9	10-2	1	22	.214	.268	.276	45	-12	1-1	.953	4	110	24	3-45,2-20/S	-0.7
1997	StL N	66	142	9	30	7	2	1	12	10-2	0	28	.211	.261	.310	50	-11	1-0	.913	-4	99	34	3-35,2-23,S-13	-1.3
1998	StL N	4	9	0	2	1	0	0	0	0-0	0	3	.222	.222	.333	44	-1	0-0	1.000	-1	53	0	/3-4,2	-0.2

Year	Tm Lg	G	AB	R	H	2B	3B	HR	RBI	BB-IB	HP	SO	AVG	OBP	SLG	AOPS	ABR	SB-CS	FA	FR	Rng	Thr	G at Pos	BFW
	Cle A	107	340	37	89	21	2	10	41	22-4	2	54	.262	.306	.424	86	-8	0-4	.982	13	107	99	*2-101/3-6,1S	0.7
	Sea A	21	80	11	26	8	0	0	8	5-0	0	8	.325	.365	.425	105	1	0-0	.984	3	111	132	2-14/1-5,3-5,O(LF)	0.4
	Year	128	420	48	115	29	2	10	49	27-4	2	62	.274	.317	.424	89	-7	0-4	.982	16	108	103	*2-115,3-11/1-6,SO(LF)	1.1
1999	Sea A	157	597	92	160	31	2	21	78	58-0	2	90	.268	.331	.432	96	-4	7-4	.978	2	101	105	*2-154/1-4,S	0.4
2000	†Sea A	133	454	57	112	24	2	11	47	42-0	6	66	.247	.316	.381	79	-15	2-3	.944	-10	93	94	3-93,2-48/1-2,S	-2.1
2001	†Sea A	135	470	62	122	28	0	15	64	28-1	3	59	.260	.303	.415	93	-6	2-1	.961	2	102	112	*3-134/1-2	-0.3
2002	†SF N	154	552	82	144	29	2	20	73	54-2	9	80	.261	.333	.429	108	3	1-2	.973	-7	98	86	*3-139,2-12/S-3,1-2	-0.2
2003	Phi N	85	297	32	58	14	0	4	37	41-1	4	40	.195	.296	.283	57	-18	0-0	.966	6	106	117	3-85/2-3	-1.1
Total	9	965	3232	407	810	176	12	85	388	274-12	29	475	.251	.312	.391	85	-79	15-17	.960	5	101	93	3-551,2-413/S-20,1-16,O(LF)	-5.2

BELL, GUS David Russell B 11.15.1928 Louisville, KY D 5.7.1995 Montgomery, OH BL/TR 6-2/196# d5.30 s-Buddy gs-David gs-Mike

1950	Pit N	111	422	62	119	22	11	8	53	28	4	46	.282	.333	.443	99	-2	4	.977	5	**109**	131	*O-104(RF)	-0.1
1951	Pit N	149	600	80	167	27	**12**	16	89	42	4	41	.278	.330	.443	103	0	1-4	.986	1	95	136	*O-145(RF)	-0.4
1952	Pit N	131	468	53	117	21	5	16	59	36	2	72	.250	.306	.419	97	-4	1-4	.972	-7	90	73	*O-123(RF)	-1.7
1953	Cin N★	151	610	102	183	37	5	30	105	48	3	72	.300	.354	.525	124	21	0-2	.977	5	103	111	*O-151(0-145-6)	1.7
1954	Cin N★	153	619	104	185	38	7	17	101	48	4	58	.299	.349	.465	108	7	5-3	.986	-2	97	102	*O-153(CF)	-0.2
1955	Cin N	**154**	610	88	188	30	6	27	104	54-2	0	57	.308	.361	.510	122	19	4-4	.987	-13	91	34	*O-154(CF)	-0.2
1956	Cin N★	150	603	82	176	31	4	29	84	50-4	3	66	.292	.347	.501	117	15	6-2	.986	-11	84	110	*O-149(CF)	-0.3
1957	Cin N★	121	510	65	149	20	3	13	61	30-5	3	54	.292	.332	.420	95	-4	0-1	.988	-5	96	79	*O-121(CF)	-1.5
1958	Cin N	112	385	42	97	16	2	10	46	36-7	1	40	.252	.314	.382	80	-11	2-3	**.996**	-4	93	86	*O-107(20-87-0)	-2.1
1959	Cin N	148	580	59	170	27	2	19	115	29-1	2	44	.293	.325	.445	101	-1	2-3	**.996**	4	99	132	*O-145(6-0-141)	-0.3
1960	Cin N	143	515	65	135	19	5	12	62	29-3	1	40	.262	.300	.388	86	-11	4-3	.988	0	98	110	*O-131(41-0-97)	-1.7
1961	†Cin N	103	235	27	60	10	1	3	33	18-3	0	21	.255	.298	.345	72	-9	1-1	.991	-1	108	21	O-75(43-1-33)	-1.4
1962	NY N	30	101	8	15	2	0	1	6	10-0	0	7	.149	.221	.198	14	-12	0-1	.979	3	84	307	O-26(RF)	-1.2
	Mil N	79	214	28	61	11	3	5	24	12-2	0	17	.285	.322	.435	104	0	0-0	.987	-0	97	94	O-58(52-1-8)	-0.2
	Year	109	315	36	76	13	3	6	30	22-2	0	24	.241	.288	.359	74	-12	0-1	.984	3	92	174	O-84(52-1-34)	-1.4
1963	Mil N	3	3	0	1	0	0	0	0	0-0	0	0	.333	.333	.333	94	0	0-0	—	0			H	0.0
1964	Mil N	3	3	0	0	0	0	0	0	0-0	0	1	.000	.000	.000	-99	-1	0-0	—	0			H	-0.1
Total	15	1741	6478	865	1823	311	66	206	942	470-27	27	636	.281	.330	.445	102	7	30-31	.985	-27	96	101	*O-1642(162-811-683)	-9.7

BELL, DEREK Derek Nathaniel B 12.11.1968 Tampa, FL BR/TR 6-2/215# d6.28

1991	Tor A	18	28	5	4	0	0	0	1	6-0	1	5	.143	.314	.143	30	-2	3-2	.889	-2	75	0	O-13(7-6-0)	-0.5
1992	†Tor A	61	161	23	39	6	3	2	15	15-1	5	34	.242	.324	.354	86	-3	7-2	1.000	2	104	139	O-56(24-18-15)/D	-0.1
1993	SD N	150	542	73	142	19	1	21	72	23-5	12	122	.262	.303	.417	90	-10	26-5	.976	1	104	125	*O-125(1-119-6),3-19	-0.4
1994	SD N	108	434	54	135	20	0	14	54	29-5	1	88	.311	.354	.454	112	7	24-8	.962	-5	99	55	*O-108(CF)	0.6
1995	Hou N	112	452	63	151	21	2	8	86	33-2	8	71	.334	.385	.442	128	19	27-9	.963	-4	87	132	*O-110(0-30-82)	1.3
1996	Hou N	158	627	84	165	40	3	17	113	40-8	8	123	.263	.311	.418	99	-3	29-3	.977	2	95	153	*O-157(0-2-157)	-0.3
1997	†Hou N	129	493	67	136	29	3	15	71	40-3	12	94	.276	.344	.438	107	5	15-7	.967	-8	92	61	*O-125(0-36-89)/D	-0.6
1998	†Hou N	156	630	111	198	41	2	22	108	51-0	4	126	.314	.364	.490	127	25	13-3	.973	-3	95	78	*O-154(RF)	1.5
1999	†Hou N	128	509	61	120	22	0	12	66	50-1	4	129	.236	.306	.350	67	-26	18-6	.985	-14	79	49	*O-126(RF)	-4.3
2000	†NY N	144	546	87	145	31	1	18	69	65-0	6	125	.266	.348	.425	99	-1	8-4	.988	-7	90	58	*O-143(0-5-142)/P	-1.3
2001	Pit N	46	156	14	27	3	0	5	13	25-5	0	38	.173	.287	.288	49	-12	0-2	.988	-1	88	103	O-46(5-1-43)	-1.6
Total	11	1210	4578	642	1262	232	15	134	668	377-30	61	955	.276	.336	.421	100	-1	170-51	.975	-39	93	92	*O-1163(37-325-814)/3-19,D-2,P	-5.7

BELL, FERN Fernando Jerome Lee (born Fern Oran Bell) "Danny" B 1.21.1913 Ada, OK D 8.29.2000 Rancho Mirage, CA BR/TR 6/180# d4.17

1939	Pit N	83	262	44	75	5	8	2	34	42	0	18	.286	.385	.389	110	5	2	.975	-1	100	120	O-67(15-46-7)/3	0.2
1940	Pit N	6	3	0	0	0	0	0	1	1	0	1	.000	.250	.000	-26	0	0	—	0			H	0.0
Total	2	89	265	44	75	5	8	2	35	43	0	19	.283	.383	.385	109	5	2	.975	-1	100	120	/O-67(15-46-7),3	0.2

BELL, FRANK Frank Gustav B 1863 Cincinnati, OH D 4.14.1891 Cincinnati, OH 6/?# d7.7 b-Charlie

1885	Bro AA	10	29	5	5	0	1	0	2	0	1		.172	.200	.241	39	-2		.739	-4			/C-5,O-4(0-3-1),3-2	-0.5

BELL, GEORGE George Antonio (Mathey) B 10.21.1959 San Pedro De Macoris, D.R. BR/TR 6-1/190# d4.9 b-Juan

1981	Tor A	60	163	19	38	2	1	5	12	5-1	0	27	.233	.256	.350	69	-7	3-2	.969	2	110	108	O-44(26-0-18)/D-8	-0.7
1983	Tor A	39	112	5	30	5	4	2	17	4-1	2	17	.268	.305	.438	96	-1	1-1	.954	-1	98	45	O-34(28-0-6)/D-2	-0.4
1984	Tor A	159	606	85	177	39	4	26	87	24-2	8	86	.292	.326	.498	121	15	11-2	.971	-3	93	114	*O-147(66-0-90)/3-3,D-7	0.7
1985	†Tor A	157	607	87	167	28	6	28	95	43-6	8	90	.275	.327	.479	116	12	21-6	.968	-2	93	124	*O-157(LF)/3-2	0.5
1986	Tor A	159	641	101	198	38	6	31	108	41-3	2	62	.309	.349	.532	133	28	7-8	.966	-3	85	173	*O-147(LF),D-11/3-2	1.6
1987	Tor A★	156	610	111	188	32	4	47	**134**	39-9	7	75	.308	.352	.605	146	37	5-1	.960	-4	89	146	*O-148(LF)/23D	2.6
1988	Tor A	156	614	78	165	27	5	24	97	34-5	1	66	.269	.304	.446	108	4	4-2	.946	-12	85	94	*O-149(LF)/D-7	-1.3
1989	†Tor A	153	613	88	182	41	2	18	104	33-3	4	60	.297	.330	.458	124	18	4-3	.963	-10	92	48	*O-134(LF),D-19	0.3
1990	Tor A★	142	562	67	149	25	0	21	86	32-7	3	80	.265	.303	.422	100	-2	3-2	.979	-1	102	58	*O-106(LF),D-36	-0.8
1991	Chi N★	149	558	63	159	27	0	25	86	32-6	4	62	.285	.323	.468	116	10	2-6	.962	-10	84	74	*O-146(LF)	-0.6
1992	Chi A	155	627	74	160	27	0	25	112	31-8	6	97	.255	.294	.418	99	-4	5-2	.964	-2	87	0	*D-140,O-15(LF)	-1.0
1993	Chi A	102	410	36	89	17	2	13	64	13-2	4	49	.217	.243	.363	64	-24	1-1	—	0	0	0	*D-102	-3.0
Total	12	1587	6123	814	1702	308	34	265	1002	331-53	49	771	.278	.316	.469	113	86	67-36	.964	-45	91	104	*O-1227(1123-0-114),D-339/3-8,2	-2.1

BELL, JAY Jay Stuart B 12.11.1965 Eglin A.F.B., FL BR/TR 6-1/185# d9.29

1986	Cle A	5	14	3	5	2	0	1	4	2-0	0	3	.357	.438	.714	211	2	0-0	.778	-0	148	101	/2-2,D-2	0.2
1987	Cle A	38	125	14	27	9	1	2	13	8-0	1	31	.216	.269	.352	62	-7	2-0	.947	-1	95	100	S-38	-0.4
1988	Cle A	73	211	23	46	5	1	2	21	21-0	1	53	.218	.289	.280	59	-11	4-2	.965	-17	84	83	S-72/D	-2.4
1989	Pit N	78	271	33	70	13	3	2	27	19-0	1	47	.258	.307	.351	91	-4	5-3	.968	-9	95	111	S-78	-0.7
1990	†Pit N	159	583	93	148	28	7	7	52	65-0	3	109	.254	.329	.362	94	-4	10-6	.970	1	102	112	*S-159	0.9
1991	†Pit N	157	608	96	164	32	8	16	67	52-1	4	99	.270	.330	.428	114	10	10-6	.968	8	106	108	*S-156	3.1
1992	†Pit N	159	632	87	167	36	6	9	55	55-0	4	103	.264	.326	.383	102	1	7-5	.973	15	**112**	112	*S-159	3.0
1993	Pit N★	154	604	102	187	32	9	9	51	77-6	6	122	.310	.392	.437	122	22	16-10	**.986**	22	112	106	*S-154	5.4
1994	Pit N	110	424	68	117	35	4	9	45	49-1	3	82	.276	.353	.441	105	4	2-0	.973	18	**115**	99	*S-110	3.0
1995	Pit N	138	530	79	139	28	4	13	55	55-1	4	110	.262	.336	.404	92	-6	2-5	.978	11	105	105	*S-136/3-3	1.4
1996	Pit N	151	527	65	132	29	3	13	71	54-5	5	108	.250	.323	.391	86	-11	6-4	**.986**	6	**106**	82	*S-151	0.6
1997	KC A	153	573	89	167	28	3	21	92	71-2	4	101	.291	.368	.461	113	12	10-6	.985	8	106	111	*S-149/3-4	3.0
1998	Ari N	155	549	79	138	29	5	20	67	81-3	7	129	.251	.353	.432	106	6	3-5	.971	-11	101	99	*S-138,2-15	0.5
1999	†Ari N★	151	589	132	170	32	6	38	112	82-2	4	132	.289	.374	.557	132	28	7-4	.968	-19	87	99	*2-148/SD	1.6
2000	Ari N	149	565	87	151	30	6	18	68	70-0	3	88	.267	.348	.437	95	-5	7-3	.988	-3	94	101	*2-145/D	0.0
2001	†Ari N	129	428	59	106	24	1	13	46	65-3	4	79	.248	.349	.400	88	-6	0-1	.994	-11	84	105	2-80,3-40/D-3	-1.3
2002	Ari N	32	49	3	8	1	0	2	11	5-0	1	9	.163	.250	.306	45	-4	0-0	1.000	0	81	234	/3-6,1-5,2-2,S-2	-0.4
2003	NY N	72	116	11	21	1	0	0	3	22-1	2	38	.181	.319	.190	39	-10	0-0	.952	-4	93	101	2-14,3-14,1-13,S-12/D	-1.3
Total	18	2063	7398	1123	1963	394	67	195	860	853-25	57	1443	.265	.343	.416	101	17	91-60	.975	14	105	104	*S-1515,2-406/3-67,1-18,D-10	16.2

BELL, RUDY John (born Rudolph Fred Baerwald) B 1.1.1881 Wausau, WI D 7.28.1955 Albuquerque, NM BR/TR 5-8.5/158# d9.16

1907	NY A	17	52	4	11	2	1	0	3	3	1		.212	.268	.288	72	-2	4	.897	-1	0	0	O-17(12-0-5)	-0.4

BELL, JUAN Juan (Mathey) B 3.29.1968 San Pedro De Macoris, D.R. BR/TR (BB 1995) 5-11/176# d9.6 b-George

1989	Bal A	8	4	2	0	0	0	0	0	0-0	0	1	.000	.000	.000	-99	-1	1-0	1.000	1	172	263	/2-2,S-2,D-4	0.0
1990	Bal A	5	2	1	0	0	0	0	0	0-0	0	1	.000	.000	.000	-99	-1	0-0	1.000	0	101	0	/SD	-0.1
1991	Bal A	100	209	26	36	9	2	1	15	8-0	0	51	.172	.201	.249	25	-22	0-0	.973	-2	106	97	2-77,S-15/O(LF)D	-2.3
1992	Phi N	46	147	12	30	3	1	1	8	18-5	1	29	.204	.292	.259	58	-8	5-0	.972	2	100	88	S-46	-0.2
1993	Phi N	24	65	5	13	6	1	0	7	5-0	1	12	.200	.268	.323	58	-4	0-1	.909	-1	95	93	S-22	-0.4
	Mil A	91	286	42	67	6	2	5	29	36-0	1	64	.234	.321	.322	75	-10	6-6	.983	-4	87	111	2-47,S-40/O-3(0-1-2),D-2	-1.0
1994	Mon N	38	97	12	27	4	0	2	10	15-0	0	21	.278	.372	.381	97	0	4-0	.991	4	116	128	2-25/3-3,S	0.6
1995	Bos A	17	26	7	4	2	0	1	2	2-0	0	10	.154	.207	.346	41	-2	0-0	.857	-1	79	30	/S-6,2-5,3	-0.3
Total	7	329	836	107	177	30	6	10	71	84-5	3	189	.212	.284	.298	60	-48	16-7	.981	-2	102	110	2-156,S-133/D-11,3-4,O-4(1-1-2)	-3.7

BELL, KEVIN Kevin Robert B 7.13.1955 Los Angeles, CA BR/TR 6/195# d6.16

1976	Chi A	68	230	24	57	7	6	5	20	18-0	1	56	.248	.302	.396	104	0	2-1	.970	-1	91	84	3-67/D	-0.1
1977	Chi A	9	28	4	5	1	0	1	6	3-0	0	8	.179	.250	.321	57	-2	0-0	.909	1	87	159	/S-5,3-4,O(LF)	-0.1
1978	Chi A	54	68	9	13	0	0	2	5	5-0	1	19	.191	.257	.279	50	-5	1-0	.946	6	121	124	3-52/D	0.1

Year	Tm Lg	G	AB	R	H	2B	3B	HR	RBI	BB-IB	HP	SO	AVG	OBP	SLG	AOPS	ABR	SB-CS	FA	FR	Rng	Thr	G at Pos	BFW
1979	Chi A	70	200	20	49	8	1	4	22	15-0	0	43	.245	.296	.355	75	-7	2-4	.923	2	106	90	3-68/S-2	-0.7
1980	Chi A	92	191	16	34	5	2	1	11	29-1	0	37	.178	.284	.241	46	-14	0-0	.925	2	109	91	3-83/S-3,D-3	-1.3
1982	Oak A	4	9	1	3	1	0	0	0	0-0	0	2	.333	.333	.444	117	0	0-0	.857	-0	71	216	/3-3,D	0.0
Total	6	297	726	74	161	22	9	13	64	70-1	2	165	.222	.289	.331	73	-28	5-5	.940	9	104	97	3-277/S-10,D-6,O(LF)	-2.1

BELL, LES Lester Rowland B 12.14.1901 Harrisburg, PA D 12.26.1985 Hershey, PA BR/TR 5-11/165# d9.18

Year	Tm Lg	G	AB	R	H	2B	3B	HR	RBI	BB-IB	HP	SO	AVG	OBP	SLG	AOPS	ABR	SB-CS	FA	FR	Rng	Thr	G at Pos	BFW
1923	StL N	15	51	5	19	2	1	0	9	9	0	7	.373	.467	.451	146	4	1-0	.917	-2	97	94	S-15	0.4
1924	StL N	17	57	5	14	3	2	1	5	3	1	7	.246	.295	.421	91	-1	0-0	.905	-4	78	75	S-17	-0.3
1925	StL N	**153**	586	80	167	29	9	11	88	43	0	47	.285	.334	.422	89	-10	4-5	.924	1	99	143	*3-153/S	-0.1
1926	†StL N	155	581	85	189	33	14	17	100	54	0	62	.325	.383	.518	135	28	9	.950	-24	83	100	*3-155	1.3
1927	StL N	115	390	48	101	26	6	9	65	34	1	63	.259	.320	.426	95	-3	5	.904	-16	83	98	*3-100,S-10	-1.2
1928	Bos N	**153**	591	58	164	36	7	10	91	40	0	45	.277	.323	.413	96	-5	1	.948	7	102	122	*3-153	1.1
1929	Bos N	139	483	58	144	23	5	9	72	50	0	42	.298	.364	.422	98	-1	4	.953	-21	83	79	*3-127/2S	-1.3
1930	Chi N	74	248	35	69	15	4	5	47	24	0	27	.278	.342	.431	85	-6	1	.948	-2	90	126	3-70/1-2	-0.4
1931	Chi N	75	252	30	71	17	1	4	32	19	0	22	.282	.332	.405	95	-2	0	.944	4	103	162	3-70	0.5
Total	9	896	3239	404	938	184	49	66	509	276	2	322	.290	.346	.438	102	4	25-5	.939	-57	92	116	3-828/S-44,1-2,2	0.0

BELL, MIKE Michael Allen B 4.22.1968 Lewiston, NY BL/TL 6-1/175# d5.2

Year	Tm Lg	G	AB	R	H	2B	3B	HR	RBI	BB-IB	HP	SO	AVG	OBP	SLG	AOPS	ABR	SB-CS	FA	FR	Rng	Thr	G at Pos	BFW
1990	Atl N	36	45	8	11	5	1	1	5	2-0	1	9	.244	.292	.467	99	0	0-1	.981	1	130	79	1-24	-0.1
1991	Atl N	17	30	4	4	0	0	1	1	2-0	0	7	.133	.188	.233	17	-3	1-0	.975	-0	97	142	1-14	-0.4
Total	2	53	75	12	15	5	1	2	6	4-0	1	16	.200	.250	.373	67	-3	1-1	.979	0	116	107	/1-38	-0.5

BELL, MIKE Michael John B 12.7.1974 Cincinnati, OH BR/TR 6-2/195# d7.20 f-Buddy gf-Gus b-David

Year	Tm Lg	G	AB	R	H	2B	3B	HR	RBI	BB-IB	HP	SO	AVG	OBP	SLG	AOPS	ABR	SB-CS	FA	FR	Rng	Thr	G at Pos	BFW
2000	Cin N	19	27	5	6	0	0	2	4	4-0	0	7	.222	.323	.444	89	-1	0-0	.900	2	150	193	3-13	0.1

BELL, BEAU Roy Chester B 8.20.1907 Bellville, TX D 9.14.1977 College Station, TX BR/TR 6-2/185# d4.16

Year	Tm Lg	G	AB	R	H	2B	3B	HR	RBI	BB-IB	HP	SO	AVG	OBP	SLG	AOPS	ABR	SB-CS	FA	FR	Rng	Thr	G at Pos	BFW
1935	StL A	76	220	20	55	8	2	3	17	16	1	16	.250	.304	.345	65	-12	1-1	.918	-4	92	68	O-37(10-0-27),1-15/3-3	-1.9
1936	StL A	**155**	616	100	212	40	12	11	123	60	1	55	.344	.403	.502	119	18	4-1	.974	0	103	85	*O-142(12-0-133),1-17	0.8
1937	StL A☆	**156**	642	82	**218**	**51**	8	14	117	53	1	54	.340	.391	.509	124	24	2-2	.984	3	87	**178**	*O-131(RF),1-26/3-2	1.5
1938	StL A	147	526	91	138	35	3	13	84	71	0	46	.262	.350	.414	91	-7	1-3	.979	3	106	104	*O-132(RF)/1-4	-1.2
1939	StL A	11	32	4	7	1	0	1	5	4	1	3	.219	.324	.344	69	-1	0-0	1.000	-0	105	0	/O-9(LF)	-0.2
	Det A	54	134	14	32	4	2	0	24	24	1	16	.239	.358	.299	65	-7	0-1	1.000	2	99	179	O-37(LF)	-0.6
	Year	65	166	18	39	5	2	1	29	28	2	19	.235	.352	.307	66	-8	0-1	1.000	2	100	143	O-46(LF)	-0.8
1940	Cle A	120	444	55	124	22	2	4	58	34	1	41	.279	.332	.365	83	-11	2-2	.971	0	107	69	O-97(RF),1-14	-1.7
1941	Cle A	48	104	12	20	4	3	0	9	10	1	8	.192	.270	.288	50	-8	1-2	1.000	-2	94	0	O-14(RF),1-10	-1.2
Total	7	767	2718	378	806	165	32	46	437	272	7	239	.297	.362	.432	99	-4	11-12	.976	2	100	109	O-599(68-0-534)/1-86,3-5	-4.5

BELL, TERRY Terence William B 10.27.1962 Dayton, OH BR/TR 6/195# d9.3

Year	Tm Lg	G	AB	R	H	2B	3B	HR	RBI	BB-IB	HP	SO	AVG	OBP	SLG	AOPS	ABR	SB-CS	FA	FR	Rng	Thr	G at Pos	BFW
1986	KC A	8	3	0	0	0	0	0	0	2-0	0	1	.000	.400	.000	20	0	0-0	1.000	-1	117	0	/C-8	-0.1
1987	Atl N	1	1	0	0	0	0	0	0	0-0	0	1	.000	.000	.000	-95	0	0-0	—	0			/H	0.0
Total	2	9	4	0	0	0	0	0	0	2-0	0	2	.000	.333	.000	-0	0	0-0	1.000	-1	117	0	/C-8	-0.1

BELLA, ZEKE John B 8.23.1930 Greenwich, CT BR/TL 5-11/185# d9.11

Year	Tm Lg	G	AB	R	H	2B	3B	HR	RBI	BB-IB	HP	SO	AVG	OBP	SLG	AOPS	ABR	SB-CS	FA	FR	Rng	Thr	G at Pos	BFW
1957	NY A	5	10	0	1	0	0	0	0	1-0	0	2	.100	.182	.100	-21	-2	0-0	1.000	1	106	402	/O-4(1-0-3)	-0.1
1959	KC A	47	82	10	17	2	1	1	9	9-0	1	14	.207	.293	.293	60	-4	0-0	1.000	0	83	240	O-25(11-0-14)/1	-0.5
Total	2	52	92	10	18	2	1	1	9	10-0	1	16	.196	.282	.272	52	-6	0-0	1.000	1	88	273	/O-29(12-0-17),1	-0.6

BELLAN, STEVE Esteban Enrique B 1850 , Cuba D 8.8.1932 Havana, Cuba 5-6/154# d5.9

Year	Tm Lg	G	AB	R	H	2B	3B	HR	RBI	BB-IB	HP	SO	AVG	OBP	SLG	AOPS	ABR	SB-CS	FA	FR	Rng	Thr	G at Pos	BFW
1871	Tro NA	**29**	128	26	32	3	3	0	23	9	2		.250	.299	.320	77	-4	4-4	.713	-2	83	100	*3-28/S	-0.4
1872	Tro NA	23	115	22	30	4	0	0	17	0	0		.261	.261	.296	70	-4	1-0	.673	-7	69	0	/S-9,3-8,O-6(CF)	-0.8
1873	Mut NA	8	32	4	7	2	0	0	3	2	0		.219	.265	.281	63	-1	0-0	.488	-6	46	327	/3-7,2-3	-0.5
Total	3 NA	60	275	52	69	9	3	0	43	11	2		.251	.280	.305	73	-9	5-4	.000	-14	76	141	/3-43,S-10,O-6(CF),2-3	-1.7

BELLE, ALBERT Albert Jojuan "Joey" B 8.25.1966 Shreveport, LA BR/TR 6-2/210# d7.15

Year	Tm Lg	G	AB	R	H	2B	3B	HR	RBI	BB-IB	HP	SO	AVG	OBP	SLG	AOPS	ABR	SB-CS	FA	FR	Rng	Thr	G at Pos	BFW
1989	Cle A	62	218	22	49	8	4	7	37	12-0	2	55	.225	.269	.394	84	-6	2-2	.979	1	102	97	O-44(15-0-31),D-17	-0.8
1990	Cle A	9	23	1	4	0	0	1	3	1-0	0	6	.174	.208	.304	42	-2	0-0	—	-0	0	0	/O(LF)D	-0.2
1991	Cle A	123	461	60	130	31	2	28	95	25-2	5	99	.282	.323	.540	134	19	3-1	.952	1	98	168	O-89(88-0-2),D-32	1.7
1992	Cle A	153	585	81	152	23	1	34	112	52-5	4	128	.260	.320	.477	124	16	8-2	.969	-4	92	30	*D-100,O-52(LF)	0.9
1993	Cle A★	159	594	93	172	36	3	38	**129**	76-13	8	96	.290	.370	.552	147	40	23-12	.986	11	106	170	*O-150(LF)/D-9	4.3
1994	Cle A★	106	412	90	147	35	2	36	101	58-9	5	71	.357	.438	.714	191	58	9-6	.973	-3	89	103	*O-104(LF)/D-2	4.5
1995	†Cle A★	143	546	**121**	173	**52**	1	**50**	**126**	73-5	6	80	.317	.401	**.690**	175	61	5-2	.981	-1	99	70	*O-142(LF)/D	5.1
1996	†Cle A★	158	602	124	187	38	3	48	**148**	99-15	7	87	.311	.410	.623	158	56	11-0	.970	-2	94	101	*O-152(LF)/D-6	4.5
1997	Chi A☆	**161**	634	90	174	45	1	30	116	53-6	6	105	.274	.332	.491	117	15	4-4	.972	2	116	10	*O-154(LF)/D-7	0.9
1998	Chi A	**163**	609	113	200	48	2	49	152	81-10	1	84	.328	.399	**.655**	**175**	**69**	6-4	.976	2	102	115	*O-159(LF)/D-4	**5.9**
1999	Bal A	161	610	108	181	36	1	37	117	101-15	7	82	.297	.400	.541	143	43	17-3	.985	-5	83	159	*O-154(RF)/D-7	3.1
2000	Bal A	141	559	71	157	37	1	23	103	52-11	4	68	.281	.342	.474	110	8	0-5	.986	-0	98	107	*O-110(RF),D-31	-0.1
Total	12	1539	5853	974	1726	389	21	381	1239	683-91	55	961	.295	.369	.564	144	377	88-41	.976	1	99	106	*O-1311(1017-0-297),D-222	29.8

BELLHORN, MARK Mark Christian B 8.23.1974 Boston, MA BB/TR 6-1/195# d6.10 OF Total (1-LF 3-CF 3-RF)

Year	Tm Lg	G	AB	R	H	2B	3B	HR	RBI	BB-IB	HP	SO	AVG	OBP	SLG	AOPS	ABR	SB-CS	FA	FR	Rng	Thr	G at Pos	BFW
1997	Oak A	68	224	33	51	9	1	6	19	32-0	0	70	.228	.324	.357	79	-7	7-1	.951	7	103	114	3-40,2-17/SD	0.3
1998	Oak A	11	12	1	1	1	0	0	1	3-0	1	4	.083	.313	.167	30	-1	2-0	1.000	-0	144	0	/3-5,S-2,2D	-0.1
2000	Oak A	9	13	2	2	0	0	0	0	2-0	0	6	.154	.267	.154	11	-2	0-0	1.000	-1	37	0	/2-2,3-2,S	-0.2
2001	Oak A	38	74	11	10	1	2	1	4	7-0	0	37	.135	.210	.243	19	-9	0-0	.953	-2	99	74	2-12/3-9,S-5,O(RF)D	-1.0
2002	Chi N	146	445	86	115	24	4	27	56	76-3	6	144	.258	.374	.512	137	23	7-5	.980	-8	93	98	2-77,3-36,1-22,S-12/O(LF)	1.8
2003	Chi N	51	139	15	29	7	1	2	22	29-1	1	46	.209	.341	.317	77	-4	3-3	.938	-1	96	58	3-42	-0.4
	Col N	48	110	12	26	3	0	0	4	21-0	2	32	.236	.368	.264	60	-5	2-3	.973	-1	105	59	2-20,3-15/S-6,O-5(0-3-2),1	-0.6
	Year	99	249	27	55	10	1	2	26	50-1	3	78	.221	.353	.293	68	-10	5-6	.944	-1	98	56	3-57,2-20/S-6,O-5(0-3-2),1	-1.0
Total	6	371	1017	160	234	45	8	36	106	170-4	10	339	.230	.345	.396	95	-5	21-12	.946	-5	94	67	3-149,2-129/S-27,1-23,D-9,O-7C	-0.2

BELLIARD, RAFAEL Rafael Leonidas (Matias) B 10.24.1961 Pueblo Nuevo, D.R. BR/TR (BB 1982) 5-6/150# d9.6

Year	Tm Lg	G	AB	R	H	2B	3B	HR	RBI	BB-IB	HP	SO	AVG	OBP	SLG	AOPS	ABR	SB-CS	FA	FR	Rng	Thr	G at Pos	BFW
1982	Pit N	9	2	3	1	0	0	0	0	0-0	0	0	.500	.500	.500	175	0	1-0	1.000	0	91	0	/S-4	0.1
1983	Pit N	4	1	1	0	0	0	0	0	0-0	0	1	.000	.000	.000	-98	0	0-0	1.000	1	170	300	/S-3	0.0
1984	Pit N	20	22	3	5	0	0	0	0	0-0	0	1	.227	.227	.227	28	-2	4-1	.889	-3	64	113	S-12/2	-0.5
1985	Pit N	17	20	1	4	0	0	0	1	0-0	0	5	.200	.200	.200	12	-2	0-0	.947	1	112	72	S-12	0.0
1986	Pit N	117	309	33	72	5	2	0	31	26-6	3	54	.233	.298	.262	55	-19	12-2	.970	10	114	90	S-96,2-23	0.2
1987	Pit N	81	203	26	42	4	3	1	15	20-6	3	25	.207	.286	.271	49	-15	5-1	.979	2	99	85	S-71/2-7	-0.6
1988	Pit N	122	286	28	61	0	4	0	11	26-3	4	47	.213	.288	.241	54	-17	7-1	**.977**	-11	96	101	*S-117/2-3	-2.2
1989	Pit N	67	154	10	33	4	0	0	8	8-2	0	22	.214	.253	.240	43	-12	5-2	.978	-4	101	82	S-40,2-20/3-6	-1.4
1990	Pit N	47	54	10	11	3	0	0	6	5-0	1	13	.204	.283	.259	52	-3	1-2	1.000	-1	76	135	2-21,S-10/3-5	-0.5
1991	†Atl N	149	353	36	88	9	2	0	27	22-2	2	63	.249	.296	.286	61	-18	3-1	.967	7	106	100	*S-145	-0.3
1992	†Atl N	144	285	20	60	6	1	0	14	14-4	3	43	.211	.255	.239	38	-23	0-1	.969	-1	100	93	*S-139/2	-1.9
1993	†Atl N	91	79	6	18	5	0	0	6	4-0	3	13	.228	.291	.291	56	-5	0-0	1.000	6	113	144	S-58,2-24	0.3
1994	Atl N	46	120	9	29	7	1	0	9	2-1	2	29	.242	.264	.317	50	-9	0-2	.984	-7	72	78	S-26,2-18	-1.4
1995	†Atl N	75	180	12	40	2	1	0	7	6-2	2	28	.222	.255	.244	32	-18	2-2	.992	2	92	64	S-40,2-32	-1.2
1996	†Atl N	87	142	9	24	7	0	0	3	2-0	0	22	.169	.179	.218	4	-20	3-1	.983	7	105	115	S-63,2-15	-0.9
1997	Atl N	72	71	9	15	3	0	1	3	1-0	0	17	.211	.219	.296	33	-7	0-1	.990	-4	85	106	S-53/2-7	-0.9
1998	Atl N	7	20	1	5	0	0	0	1	0-0	0	1	.250	.250	.250	32	-2	0-0	.952	-1	75	128	/S-7	-0.3
Total	17	1155	2301	217	508	55	14	2	142	136-26	23	384	.221	.270	.259	46	-172	43-17	.974	2	100	95	S-896,2-172/3-11	-11.5

BELLIARD, RON Ronald B 4.7.1975 Bronx, NY. BR/TR 5-8/180# d9.12

Year	Tm Lg	G	AB	R	H	2B	3B	HR	RBI	BB-IB	HP	SO	AVG	OBP	SLG	AOPS	ABR	SB-CS	FA	FR	Rng	Thr	G at Pos	BFW
1998	Mil N	8	5	1	1	0	0	0	0	0-0	0	0	.200	.200	.200	6	-1	0-0	—	-0	0	0	/2	-0.1
1999	Mil N	124	457	60	135	29	4	8	58	64-0	0	59	.295	.379	.429	106	6	4-5	.978	-1	105	95	*2-119/3S	0.9
2000	Mil N	152	571	83	150	30	9	8	54	82-4	3	84	.263	.354	.389	90	-7	7-5	.976	1	102	**125**	*2-151	0.1
2001	Mil N	101	364	69	96	30	3	11	36	35-2	5	65	.264	.335	.453	104	2	5-2	.990	13	107	107	2-96	2.0
2002	Mil N	104	289	30	61	13	0	3	26	18-0	1	46	.211	.257	.287	47	-24	2-3	.975	-9	89	88	2-49,3-42	-3.2
2003	Col N	116	447	73	124	31	2	8	50	49-0	2	71	.277	.351	.409	86	-8	7-2	.973	-2	103	100	*2-113	-0.4
Total	6	605	2133	316	567	133	18	38	224	248-6	11	325	.266	.343	.398	89	-32	25-17	.978	2	103	107	2-529/3-43,S	-0.7

Year	Tm Lg	G	AB	R	H	2B	3B	HR	RBI	BB-IB	HP	SO	AVG	OBP	SLG	AOPS	ABR	SB-CS	FA	FR	Rng	Thr	G at Pos	BFW
BELLINGER, CLAY Clayton Daniel B 11.18.1968 Oneonta, NY BR/TR 6-3/195# d4.9 OF Total (32-LF 36-CF 7-RF)																								
1999	†NY A	32	45	12	9	2	0	1	2	1-0	0	10	.200	.217	.311	33	-5	1-0	1.000	1	89	65	3-16/1-8,O-2(LF),2SD	-0.4
2000	†NY A	98	184	33	38	8	2	6	21	17-1	5	48	.207	.288	.370	66	-10	5-0	.968	0	91	71	O-46(17-26-5),2-21,3-18,1-10/S-6	-0.8
2001	†NY A	51	81	12	13	1	1	5	12	4-0	1	23	.160	.207	.383	51	-7	1-2	1.000	3	81	0	O-25(13-10-2),3-17/1-6,S-2	-0.4
2002	Ana A	2	1	0	0	0	0	0	0	0-0	0	1	.000	.000	.000	-99	0	0-0	1.000	-0	0	0	/1-2	0.0
Total	4	183	311	57	60	11	3	12	35	22-1	6	82	.193	.257	.363	57	-22	7-2	.977	4	88	48	/O-73C,3-51,1-26,2-22,S-9,D-4	-1.6
BELLMAN, JACK John Hutchins "Happy Jack" B 3.4.1864 Taylorsville, KY D 12.8.1931 Louisville, KY d4.23																								
1889	StL AA	1	2	1	1	0	0	0	0	1	0	0	.500	.667	.500	207	0	0	1.000	-0			/C	0.0
BELLOIR, ROB Robert Edward B 7.13.1948 Heidelberg, Germany BR/TR 5-10/155# d8.2																								
1975	Atl N	43	105	11	23	2	1	0	9	7-0	0	8	.219	.268	.257	45	-8	0-0	.922	-6	100	81	S-38/2	-1.1
1976	Atl N	30	60	5	12	2	0	0	4	5-1	0	7	.200	.262	.233	39	-5	0-0	.929	-5	80	114	S-12,3-10/2-5	-0.9
1977	Atl N	6	1	2	0	0	0	0	0	0-0	0	0	.000	.000	.000	-89	0	0-0	1.000	0	141	0	/S-3	0.0
1978	Atl N	2	1	0	1	1	0	0	0	0-0	0	0	1.000	1.000	2.000	647	1	0-0	1.000	-0	141	0	/S3	0.1
Total	4	81	167	18	36	5	1	0	13	12-1	0	15	.216	.268	.257	45	-12	0-0	.924	-11	97	85	/S-54,3-11,2-6	-1.9
BELTRAN, CARLOS Carlos Ivan B 4.24.1977 Manati, P.R. BB/TR 6/175# d9.14																								
1998	KC A	14	58	12	16	5	3	0	7	3-0	1	12	.276	.317	.466	99	0	3-0	.978	1	127	0	O-14(CF)	0.1
1999	KC A	156	663	112	194	27	7	22	108	46-2	4	123	.293	.337	.454	99	-3	27-8	.972	-1	96	158	*O-154(CF)/D-2	0.0
2000	KC A	98	372	49	92	15	4	7	44	35-2	0	69	.247	.309	.366	68	-19	13-0	.975	-1	101	108	O-88(2-83-3)/D-7	-1.5
2001	KC A	155	617	106	189	32	12	24	101	52-2	5	120	.306	.362	.514	118	15	31-1	.988	5	102	158	*O-152(CF)/D-3	2.6
2002	KC A	**162**	637	114	174	44	7	29	105	71-1	4	135	.273	.346	.501	110	9	35-7	.983	1	99	148	*O-149(CF),D-12	1.5
2003	KC A	141	521	102	160	14	10	26	100	72-4	2	81	.307	.389	.522	122	17	41-4	.987	7	106	165	*O-130(CF)/D-8	3.1
Total	6	726	2868	495	825	137	43	108	465	279-11	16	540	.288	.350	.478	106	19	150-20	.981	11	101	148	O-687(2-682-3)/D-32	5.8
BELTRE, ADRIAN Adrian (Perez) B 4.7.1979 Santo Domingo, D.R. BR/TR 5-11/200# d6.24																								
1998	LA N	77	195	18	42	9	0	7	22	14-0	3	37	.215	.278	.369	73	-9	3-1	.925	6	114	127	3-74/S-2	-0.2
1999	LA N	152	538	84	148	27	5	15	67	61-12	6	105	.275	.352	.428	103	2	18-7	.932	-1	99	98	*3-152	0.4
2000	LA N	138	510	71	148	30	2	20	85	56-2	2	80	.290	.360	.475	116	12	12-5	.944	17	**110**	124	*3-138/S	3.0
2001	LA N	126	475	59	126	22	4	13	60	28-1	5	82	.265	.310	.411	92	-8	13-4	.952	6	100	88	*3-124/S-2	0.0
2002	LA N	159	587	70	151	26	5	21	75	37-4	4	96	.257	.303	.426	100	-7	7-5	.954	-10	92	63	*3-157	-1.5
2003	LA N	158	559	50	134	30	2	23	80	37-4	5	103	.240	.290	.424	89	-12	2-2	.957	9	98	**130**	*3-157/S	-0.2
Total	6	810	2864	352	749	144	18	99	389	233-23	25	503	.262	.320	.428	98	-22	55-24	.946	26	101	102	3-802/S-6	1.5
BELTRE, ESTEBAN Esteban (Valera) B 12.26.1967 Ingenio Quisquella, D.R. BR/TR 5-10/172# d9.3																								
1991	Chi A	8	6	0	1	0	0	0	0	1-0	0	1	.167	.286	.167	29	-1	1-0	1.000	-2	61	63	/S-8	-0.2
1992	Chi A	49	110	21	21	2	0	1	10	3-0	0	18	.191	.211	.236	26	-11	1-0	.924	-11	87	54	S-43/D-4	-2.0
1994	Tex A	48	131	12	37	5	0	0	12	16-0	0	25	.282	.358	.321	78	-4	2-5	.961	6	116	91	S-41/3-5,2	0.3
1995	Tex A	54	92	7	20	8	0	0	7	4-0	0	15	.217	.250	.304	42	-8	0-0	.969	-4	85	93	S-36,2-15/3	-0.9
1996	Bos A	27	62	6	16	2	0	0	6	4-0	0	14	.258	.299	.290	50	-5	1-0	1.000	-4	66	45	3-13/2-8,S-6,D	-0.7
Total	5	186	401	46	95	17	0	1	35	28-0	0	73	.237	.285	.287	51	-29	5-5	.951	-15	95	75	S-134/2-24,3-19,D-5	-3.5
BEMIS, HARRY Harry Parker B 2.1.1874 Farmington, NH D 5.23.1947 Cleveland, OH BR/TR 5-7.5/175# d4.23																								
1902	Cle A	93	317	42	99	12	7	1	29	19	8		.312	.366	.404	118	8	3	.964	1	*93*	***111***	C-87/O-2(RF),2	1.6
1903	Cle A	92	314	31	82	20	3	1	41	8	7		.261	.295	.354	96	-2	5	**.988**	-2	*102*	*97*	C-74,1-10/2	0.3
1904	Cle A	97	336	35	76	11	6	0	25	8	7		.226	.259	.295	76	-10	6	.958	1	*119*	*97*	C-79,1-13/2	-0.2
1905	Cle A	70	226	27	66	13	3	0	28	13	5		.292	.344	.376	127	7	3	.972	-4	*102*	*81*	C-58/2-4,3-2,1	1.0
1906	Cle A	93	297	28	82	13	5	2	30	12	3		.276	.311	.374	116	4	8	.963	-3	*116*	*75*	C-81	1.0
1907	Cle A	65	172	12	43	7	0	0	19	7	1		.250	.283	.291	82	-4	5	.957	-5	*99*	*79*	C-51/1-2	-0.5
1908	Cle A	91	277	23	62	9	1	0	33	7	4		.224	.253	.264	68	-10	14	.964	-1	*143*	*78*	C-76/1-2	-0.4
1909	Cle A	42	123	4	23	2	3	0	13	0	1		.187	.194	.252	39	-9	2	.971	1	*109*	*77*	C-36	-0.6
1910	Cle A	61	167	12	36	5	1	1	16	5	0		.216	.238	.275	60	-8	3	.961	-7	*84*	*101*	C-46	-1.2
Total	9	704	2229	214	569	92	29	5	234	79	36		.255	.292	.329	92	-24	49	.966	-18	*109*	*90*	C-588/1-28,2-7,3-2,O-2(RF)	1.0
BENARD, MARVIN Marvin Larry B 1.20.1971 Bluefields, Nicaragua BL/TL 5-10/180# d9.5																								
1995	SF N	13	34	5	13	2	0	1	4	1-0	0	7	.382	.400	.529	147	2	1-0	1.000	0	124	0	/O-7(CF)	0.3
1996	SF N	135	488	89	121	17	4	5	27	59-2	4	84	.248	.333	.330	79	-14	25-11	.984	6	110	104	*O-132(5-102-38)	-0.7
1997	†SF N	84	114	13	26	4	0	1	13	13-0	2	29	.228	.315	.289	62	-6	3-1	.967	-1	72	162	O-36(14-6-18)/D	-0.8
1998	SF N	121	286	41	92	21	1	3	36	34-1	2	39	.322	.396	.434	126	13	11-4	.982	-5	89	24	O-79(12-9-64)/D-2	0.6
1999	SF N	149	562	100	163	36	5	16	64	55-2	6	97	.290	.359	.457	113	11	27-14	.988	-3	100	67	*O-142(4-123-20)	0.8
2000	†SF N	149	560	102	147	27	6	12	55	63-0	6	97	.262	.342	.396	93	-6	22-7	.997	6	104	137	*O-141(21-128-38)	0.1
2001	SF N	129	392	70	104	19	2	15	44	29-2	4	66	.265	.320	.439	102	-1	10-5	.965	-0	101	94	*O-109(15-75-37)	-0.2
2002	SF N	65	123	16	34	9	2	1	13	7-0	1	26	.276	.321	.407	97	-1	5-1	1.000	3	113	213	O-38(14-6-20)	0.1
2003	SF N	46	71	5	14	3	1	0	4	4-0	0	9	.197	.237	.268	33	-7	1-0	1.000	3	139	224	O-21(17-0-4)	-0.4
Total	9	891	2630	441	714	138	21	54	260	265-7	25	454	.271	.343	.402	97	-9	105-43	.986	8	103	101	O-705(102-456-239)/D-3	-0.2
BENAVIDES, FREDDIE Alfredo B 4.7.1966 Laredo, TX BR/TR 6-2/180# d5.14 C1																								
1991	Cin N	24	63	11	18	1	0	0	3	1-1	1	15	.286	.303	.302	69	-3	1-0	.974	0	102	61	S-20/2-3	-0.1
1992	Cin N	74	173	14	40	10	1	1	17	10-4	1	34	.231	.277	.318	66	-8	0-1	1.000	-1	93	61	2-37,S-34/3	-0.8
1993	Col N	74	213	20	61	10	3	3	26	6-1	0	27	.286	.305	.404	76	-8	3-2	.937	-5	92	67	S-48,2-19/3-5,1	-0.9
1994	Mon N	47	85	8	16	5	1	0	6	3-1	1	15	.188	.222	.271	28	-9	0-0	.976	-6	71	88	2-36/3-5,1-3,S-3	-1.5
Total	4	219	534	53	135	26	5	4	52	20-7	3	91	.253	.282	.343	65	-28	4-3	.948	-12	95	92	S-105/2-95,3-11,1-4	-3.3
BENCH, JOHNNY Johnny Lee B 12.7.1947 Oklahoma City, OK BR/TR 6-1/208# d8.28 HF1989 OF Total (55-LF 2-CF 54-RF)																								
1967	Cin N	26	86	7	14	3	1	1	6	5-0	0	19	.163	.207	.256	29	-8	0-1	.995	3	*83*	*118*	C-26	-0.4
1968	Cin N★	154	564	67	155	40	2	15	82	31-8	2	96	.275	.311	.433	115	10	1-5	.991	5	*116*	*109*	*C-154	2.5
1969	Cin N★	148	532	83	156	23	1	26	90	49-7	4	86	.293	.353	.487	128	19	6-6	.992	6	**193**	104	*C-147	3.2
1970	†Cin N★	158	605	97	177	35	4	**45**	**148**	54-9	0	102	.293	.345	.587	146	36	5-2	.986	20	**211**	89	*C-139,O-24(15-2-6),1-12/3	6.0
1971	Cin N★	149	562	80	134	19	2	27	61	49-7	0	83	.238	.299	.423	105	1	2-1	.988	11	162	83	*C-141,1-12,O-12(10-0-3)/3-3	1.8
1972	†Cin N★	147	538	87	145	22	2	**40**	**125**	100-**23**	2	84	.270	.379	.541	**171**	**52**	6-6	.992	7	**250**	86	*C-129,O-17(RF)/1-7,3-4	**6.6**
1973	†Cin N★	152	557	83	141	17	3	25	104	83-14	0	83	.253	.345	.429	121	16	4-1	.995	10	**204**	79	*C-134,O-23(RF)/1-4,3	3.2
1974	Cin N★	160	621	108	174	38	2	33	**129**	80-15	3	90	.280	.363	.507	144	36	5-4	.993	14	**212**	86	*C-137,3-36/1-5	5.7
1975	†Cin N★	142	530	83	150	39	1	28	110	65-12	2	108	.283	.359	.519	140	29	11-0	.989	18	**198**	82	*C-121,O-19(16-0-3)/1-9	5.4
1976	†Cin N★	135	465	62	109	24	1	16	74	81-6	2	95	.234	.348	.394	108	8	13-2	**.997**	7	136	101	*C-128/O-5(LF),1	2.4
1977	Cin N★	142	494	67	136	34	2	31	109	58-8	1	95	.275	.348	.540	133	23	2-4	.987	3	143	81	*C-135/O-8(7-0-1),1-4,3	3.0
1978	Cin N✳	120	393	52	102	17	1	23	73	50-10	1	83	.260	.340	.483	129	15	4-2	.989	8	**150**	100	*C-107,1-11/O-2(1-0-1)	2.7
1979	†Cin N★	130	464	73	128	19	0	22	80	67-8	0	73	.276	.364	.459	123	16	4-2	.986	5	134	92	*C-126/1-2	2.8
1980	Cin N★	114	360	52	90	12	0	24	68	41-2	0	64	.250	.327	.483	124	11	4-2	.991	-11	107	81	*C-105	0.4
1981	Cin N	52	178	14	55	8	0	8	25	17-3	0	21	.309	.369	.489	139	9	0-2	.983	-2	84	123	1-38/C-7	0.5
1982	Cin N	119	399	44	103	16	0	13	38	37-2	0	58	.258	.320	.396	98	-2	1-2	.917	-17	80	62	*3-107/1-8,C	-2.2
1983	Cin N★	110	310	32	79	15	2	12	54	24-1	0	38	.255	.308	.432	100	-1	0-1	.933	-7	87	85	3-42,1-32/C-5,O(LF)	-1.1
Total	17	2158	7658	1091	2048	381	24	389	1376	891-135	19	1278	.267	.342	.476	127	270	68-43	.990	80	*170*	*91*	*C-1742,3-195,1-145,O-111L	42.5
BENEDICT, ART Arthur Melville B 3.31.1862 Cornwall, IL D 1.20.1948 Denver, CO BR/TR d5.14																								
1883	Phi N	3	15	3	4	1	0	0	4	0		4	.267	.267	.333	89	0		.571	-3	62	0	/2-3	-0.3
BENEDICT, BRUCE Bruce Edwin B 8.18.1955 Birmingham, AL BR/TR 6-1/190# d8.18 C3																								
1978	Atl N	22	52	3	13	2	0	0	1	6-2	0	6	.250	.328	.288	66	-2	0-0	.990	-0	80	188	C-22	-0.2
1979	Atl N	76	204	14	46	11	0	0	15	33-3	0	18	.225	.331	.279	64	-9	1-3	.984	-7	78	84	C-76	-1.4
1980	Atl N	120	359	18	91	14	1	2	34	28-8	1	36	.253	.308	.315	72	-13	3-3	.988	6	**140**	93	*C-120	-0.2
1981	Atl N★	90	295	26	78	12	1	5	35	33-4	3	21	.264	.341	.363	98	0	1-1	.986	5	88	**131**	C-90	0.9
1982	†Atl N	118	386	34	95	11	1	3	44	37-9	3	40	.246	.315	.303	71	-14	4-4	**.993**	4	110	93	*C-118	-0.6
1983	Atl N★	134	423	43	126	13	1	2	43	61-16	1	24	.298	.385	.348	98	2	1-3	.992	9	92	102	*C-134	1.6
1984	Atl N	95	300	26	67	8	1	4	25	34-3	1	25	.223	.301	.297	65	-14	1-2	.991	-7	96	71	C-95	-1.8
1985	Atl N	70	208	12	42	6	0	0	20	22-1	1	12	.202	.279	.231	42	-16	0-1	.989	-7	85	102	C-70	-2.2
1986	Atl N	64	160	11	36	10	1	0	13	15-1	2	10	.225	.298	.300	62	-8	1-0	.993	-4	173	86	C-57	-1.0

Year	Tm Lg	G	AB	R	H	2B	3B	HR	RBI	BB-IB	HP	SO	AVG	OBP	SLG	AOPS	ABR	SB-CS	FA	FR	Rng	Thr	G at Pos	BFW
1987	Atl N	37	95	4	14	1	0	1	5	17-0	0	15	.147	.277	.189	25	-10	0-1	.989	0	77	90	C-35	-0.9
1988	Atl N	90	236	11	57	7	0	0	19	19-1	0	26	.242	.296	.271	61	-11	0-2	.989	3	109	120	C-89	-0.5
1989	Atl N	66	160	12	31	3	0	1	6	23-4	1	18	.194	.299	.231	52	-9	0-0	.995	8	107	139	C-65	0.2
Total	12	982	2878	214	696	98	6	18	260	328-52	13	251	.242	.320	.299	71	-104	12-20	.990	10	105	102	C-971	-6.1
BENES, JOE Joseph Anthony "Bananas" B 1.8.1901 Long Island City, NY D 3.7.1975 Elmhurst, NY BR/TR 5-8.5/158# d5.9																								
1931	StL N	10	12	1	2	0	0	0	0	2	1	1	.167	.333	.167	37	-1	0	1.000	-0	109	78	/S-6,2-2,3	-0.1
BENGOUGH, BENNY Bernard Oliver B 7.27.1898 Niagara Falls, NY D 12.22.1968 Philadelphia, PA BR/TR 5-7.5/168# d5.18 C19																								
1923	NY A	19	53	1	7	2	0	0	3	4	0	2	.132	.193	.170	-4	-8	0-0	.973	1	*130*	*111*	C-19	-0.7
1924	NY A	11	16	4	5	1	1	0	3	2	0	0	.313	.389	.500	128	1	0-0	1.000	2	*125*	*69*	C-11	0.3
1925	NY A	95	283	17	73	14	2	0	23	19	0	9	.258	.305	.322	60	-18	0-2	**.993**	6	*96*	*114*	C-94	-0.7
1926	NY A	36	84	9	32	6	0	0	14	7	1	4	.381	.435	.452	134	5	1-0	.973	5	*100*	*171*	C-35	1.1
1927	†NY A	31	85	6	21	3	3	0	10	4	0	4	.247	.281	.353	66	-5	0-3	.986	7	*126*	*90*	C-30	0.3
1928	†NY A	58	161	12	43	3	1	0	9	7	1	8	.267	.302	.298	60	-10	0-0	.992	3	*95*	*116*	C-58	-0.3
1929	NY A	23	62	5	12	2	1	0	7	0	0	2	.194	.194	.258	16	-8	0-0	.982	-3	*90*	*71*	C-23	-1.0
1930	NY A	44	102	10	24	4	2	0	12	3	0	8	.235	.257	.314	46	-9	1-0	.990	4	*103*	*97*	C-44	-0.2
1931	StL A	40	140	6	35	4	1	0	12	4	0	4	.250	.271	.293	46	-11	0-3	.986	1	*104*	*98*	C-37	-0.8
1932	StL A	54	139	13	35	7	1	0	15	12	0	4	.252	.311	.317	60	-8	0-1	.989	5	*118*	*135*	C-47	-0.1
Total	10	411	1125	83	287	46	12	0	108	62	2	45	.255	.295	.317	59	-71	2-9	.988	31	*105*	*113*	C-398	-2.1
BENIQUEZ, JUAN Juan Jose (Torres) B 5.13.1950 San Sebastian, P.R. BR/TR 5-11/165# d9.4 OF Total (295-LF 735-CF 184-RF)																								
1971	Bos A	16	57	8	17	2	0	0	4	3-0	0	4	.298	.333	.333	83	-1	3-1	.895	-8	61	56	S-15	-0.8
1972	Bos A	33	99	10	24	4	1	1	8	7-0	0	11	.242	.287	.333	81	-2	2-0	.900	1	108	114	S-27	0.3
1974	Bos A	106	389	60	104	14	3	5	33	25-2	1	61	.267	.313	.357	86	-7	19-11	.978	-2	104	58	O-97(7-91-0)/D-4	-1.2
1975	†Bos A	78	254	43	74	14	4	2	17	25-1	2	26	.291	.358	.402	106	2	7-10	.991	1	119	104	O-44(31-13-2),D-20,3-14	-0.1
1976	Tex A	145	478	49	122	14	4	0	33	39-1	3	56	.255	.315	.301	79	-12	17-6	.986	13	109	**178**	*O-141(CF)/2	-0.1
1977	Tex A	123	424	56	114	19	6	10	50	43-0	1	43	.269	.336	.413	102	1	26-18	.988	-2	96	115	*O-123(CF)	-0.3
1978	Tex A	127	473	61	123	17	3	11	50	20-1	3	59	.260	.292	.378	88	-10	10-12	.972	-10	89	98	*O-126(CF)	-2.3
1979	NY A	62	142	19	36	6	1	4	17	9-0	2	17	.254	.299	.394	90	-2	3-3	.981	1	95	137	O-60(18-38-4)/3-3	-0.2
1980	Sea A	70	237	26	54	10	0	6	21	17-0	0	25	.228	.278	.346	70	-10	2-3	.957	-1	104	70	O-65(2-63-0)/D	-1.3
1981	Cal A	58	166	18	30	5	0	3	13	15-0	1	16	.181	.251	.265	49	-11	2-1	.959	-4	95	0	O-55(15-36-7)/D	-1.8
1982	†Cal A	112	196	25	52	11	2	3	24	15-1	1	21	.265	.321	.388	93	-2	3-0	.983	-6	77	92	*O-107(37-25-51)	-1.0
1983	Cal A	92	315	44	96	15	0	3	34	15-0	4	29	.305	.343	.381	100	0	4-2	.968	-0	94	141	O-84(38-30-31)/D-6	-0.3
1984	Cal A	110	354	60	119	17	0	8	39	18-0	3	43	.336	.370	.452	128	13	0-3	.971	0	104	85	O-98(64-8-50)	0.9
1985	Cal A	132	411	54	125	13	5	8	42	34-3	5	46	.304	.364	.418	114	8	4-3	1.000	-9	84	26	O-71(18-36-22),1-46,D-14/3S	-0.5
1986	Bal A	113	343	48	103	15	0	6	36	40-1	3	49	.300	.372	.397	113	8	2-3	.963	-1	108	34	O-54(44-3-9),3-25,D-16,1-14	0.3
1987	KC A	57	174	14	41	7	0	3	26	11-1	1	26	.236	.282	.328	60	-10	0-0	1.000	-7	81	0	O-22(17-2-4),D-15/1-6,3-6	-1.9
	Tor A	39	81	6	23	5	1	5	21	5-0	1	13	.284	.330	.556	127	3	0-0	.875	-2	62	0	D-15/O-7(3-0-4),1-2	0.1
	Year	96	255	20	64	12	1	8	47	16-1	2	39	.251	.297	.400	82	-7	0-0	.976	-9	77	0	D-30,O-29(20-2-8)/1-8,3-6	-1.8
1988	Tor A	27	58	9	17	2	0	1	8	8-0	0	6	.293	.373	.379	112	1	0-0	—	-0	0	0	D-19/O(LF)	0.1
Total	17	1500	4651	610	1274	190	30	79	476	349-11	31	551	.274	.327	.379	95	-31	104-76	.977	-35	98	95	*O-1155C,D-111/1-68,3-49,S-43,2	-10.1
BENITEZ, YAMIL Yamil Antonio B 10.5.1972 San Juan, P.R. BR/TR 6-2/180# d9.16																								
1995	Mon N	14	39	8	15	2	1	2	7	1-0	0	7	.385	.400	.641	163	3	0-2	.950	0	101	160	O-14(3-4-8)	0.2
1996	Mon N	11	12	0	2	0	0	0	2	0-0	0	4	.167	.167	.167	-11	-2	0-0	.500	-0	52	0	/O-4(3-0-1)	-0.2
1997	KC A	53	191	22	51	7	1	8	21	10-0	1	49	.267	.307	.440	90	-4	2-2	.965	-1	108	0	O-52(31-0-22)	-0.7
1998	Ari N	91	206	17	41	7	1	9	30	14-1	4	46	.199	.262	.374	65	-12	2-2	.972	4	115	129	O-62(49-0-13)/D-2	-1.0
Total	4	169	448	47	109	16	3	19	60	25-1	5	106	.243	.290	.420	82	-15	4-6	.963	2	110	69	O-132(86-4-44)/D-2	-1.7
BENJAMIN, STAN Alfred Stanley B 5.20.1914 Framingham, MA BR/TR 6-2/194# d9.16																								
1939	Phi N	12	50	4	7	2	1	0	2	1	0	6	.140	.157	.220	0	-7	1	.867	0	98	240	/O-7(4-2-2),3-5	-0.7
1940	Phi N	8	9	1	2	0	0	0	1	1	0	1	.222	.300	.222	48	-1	0	1.000	1	108	871	/O-2(RF)	0.0
1941	Phi N	129	480	47	113	20	7	3	27	20	0	81	.235	.266	.325	68	-23	17	.980	-1	92	132	*O-110(2-26-86)/1-8,2-2,3	-3.1
1942	Phi N	78	210	24	47	8	3	2	8	10	1	27	.224	.262	.319	73	-8	5	.976	1	92	207	O-45(0-25-21),1-15	-1.1
1945	Cle A	14	21	1	7	2	0	0	3	0	0	0	.333	.333	.429	126	1	0-1	1.000	2	108	547	/O-4(3-0-1)	0.2
Total	5	241	770	77	176	32	11	5	41	32	1	115	.229	.260	.318	66	-38	23-1	.975	2	93	173	O-168(9-53-112)/1-23,3-6,2-2	-4.7
BENJAMIN, MIKE Michael Paul B 11.22.1965 Euclid, OH BR/TR 6/169# d7.7 OF Total (RF)																								
1989	SF N	14	6	6	1	0	0	0	0	0-0	0	1	.167	.167	.167	-5	-1	0-0	1.000	-1	74	0	/S-8	-0.1
1990	SF N	22	56	7	12	3	1	2	3	3-1	0	10	.214	.254	.411	83	-2	1-0	.988	4	122	117	S-21	0.4
1991	SF N	54	106	12	13	3	0	2	8	7-2	2	26	.123	.188	.208	13	-13	3-0	.984	11	120	131	S-51/3	0.1
1992	SF N	40	75	4	13	2	1	1	3	4-1	0	15	.173	.215	.267	38	-7	1-0	.991	-1	101	102	S-33/3-2	-0.5
1993	SF N	63	146	22	29	7	0	4	16	9-2	4	23	.199	.264	.329	59	-9	0-0	.991	12	103	230	2-23,S-23,3-16	0.5
1994	SF N	38	62	9	16	5	1	1	9	5-1	3	16	.258	.343	.419	102	0	5-0	.968	7	156	172	S-18,2-10/3-5	0.9
1995	SF N	68	186	19	41	6	0	3	12	8-3	1	51	.220	.256	.301	48	-15	11-1	.964	1	114	53	3-43,S-16/2-8	-1.0
1996	Phi N	35	103	13	23	5	1	4	13	12-5	2	21	.223	.316	.408	88	-2	3-1	.954	-2	99	78	S-31/2	-0.1
1997	Bos A	49	116	12	27	9	1	0	7	4-0	1	27	.233	.262	.328	52	-8	2-3	.929	3	137	140	3-19,S-16/2-5,1-4,PD	-0.4
1998	†Bos A	124	349	46	95	23	0	4	39	15-1	6	73	.272	.312	.372	76	-12	3-0	.994	4	89	95	2-87,S-20,3-11,1-10/D-2	-0.3
1999	Pit N	110	368	42	91	26	7	1	37	20-3	2	90	.247	.288	.364	64	-21	10-1	.982	**35**	128	148	S-93,2-12/3-6	2.1
2000	Pit N	93	233	28	63	18	2	2	19	12-0	3	45	.270	.313	.391	77	-8	5-4	.974	25	150	116	3-34,S-30,2-27/1	1.8
2002	Pit N	108	120	7	18	2	1	0	3	7-0	1	31	.150	.202	.183	5	-17	0-4	.979	4	104	91	3-62,S-15,2-11/10(RF)	-1.4
Total	13	818	1926	227	442	109	15	24	169	106-19	25	429	.229	.277	.339	61	-115	44-14	.980	102	118	116	S-375,3-199,2-184/1-16,D-3,OP	2.0
BENNERS, IKE Isaac B. B 6.7.1856 Philadelphia, PA D 4.18.1932 Philadelphia, PA BL ?/175# d5.1																								
1884	Bro AA	49	189	25	38	11	5	1		7	2		.201	.237	.328	82	-4		.821	-4	11	0	O-49(LF)	-0.8
	Wil U	6	22	0	1	0	0	0		1			.045	.087	.045	-57	-5		.750	-0	62	357	/O-6(0-3-3)	-0.5
Total	1	55	211	25	39	11	5	1		8			.185	.222	.299	66	-9		.813	-5	17	43	/O-55(49-3-3)	-1.3
BENNETT, CHARLIE Charles Wesley B 11.21.1854 New Castle, PA D 2.24.1927 Detroit, MI BR/TR 5-11/180# d5.1 OF Total (25-LF 25-CF 20-RF)																								
1878	Mil N	49	184	16	45	9	0	1	12	10		26	.245	.284	.310	89	-2		.831	-12			C-35,O-20(0-16-4)	-1.3
1880	Wor N	51	193	20	44	9	3	0	18	10		30	.228	.266	.306	86	-3		.913	0			C-46/O-6(0-3-3)	-0.2
1881	Det N	76	299	44	90	18	7	7	64	18		37	.301	.341	.478	149	16		**.962**	17			*C-70/3-5,O-3(1-2-0)	3.2
1882	Det N	84	342	43	103	16	10	5	51	20		33	.301	.340	.450	151	19		.945	6			*C-65,3-11/2-7,S1	2.8
1883	Det N	92	371	56	113	34	7	5	55	26		59	.305	.350	.474	155	26		**.944**	2			*C-72,2-15,O-12(1-4-7)	3.0
1884	Det N	90	341	37	90	18	6	3	40	36		40	.264	.334	.378	132	15		.917	3			*C-80/O-5(1-0-4),S-4,321	2.2
1885	Det N	91	349	49	94	24	13	5	60	47		37	.269	.356	.456	161	25		.919	5			C-62,O-19(18-0-1),3-10	3.3
1886	Det N	72	235	37	57	13	5	4	34	48		29	.243	.371	.391	127	10	4	**.955**	13			C-69/O-4(3-0-1),S	2.5
1887	†Det N	46	160	26	39	6	5	3	20	30	0	22	.244	.363	.400	108	2	7	.951	7			C-45/O(LF)1	1.0
1888	Det N	74	258	32	68	12	4	5	29	31	2	40	.264	.347	.399	136	12	4	**.966**	8			C-73/1	2.5
1889	Bos N	82	247	42	57	8	2	4	28	21	2	43	.231	.296	.328	70	-11	7	**.955**	7			C-82	0.2
1890	Bos N	85	281	59	60	17	2	3	40	72	2	56	.214	.377	.320	96	2	6	**.959**	19	***128***	*86*	C-85	2.5
1891	Bos N	75	256	35	55	9	3	5	39	42	3	61	.215	.332	.332	84	-5	3	**.960**	18	*127*	*89*	C-75	1.7
1892	†Bos N	35	114	19	23	4	0	1	16	27	0	23	.202	.355	.263	80	-1	6	.948	5	*132*	*72*	C-35	0.6
1893	Bos N	60	191	34	40	6	0	4	27	40	2	36	.209	.352	.304	69	-8	5	.953	2	*131*	*58*	C-60	-0.1
Total	15	1062	3821	549	978	203	67	55	533	478	11	572	.256	.340	.387	118	97	42	.942	100	*35*	*21*	C-954/O-70L,3-27,2-23,S-6,1-4	23.9
BENNETT, GARY Gary David B 4.17.1972 Waukegan, IL BR/TR 6/190# d9.24																								
1995	Phi N	1	1	0	0	0	0	0	0	0-0	0	1	.000	.000	.000	-99	0	0-0	—	0			/H	0.0
1996	Phi N	6	16	0	4	0	0	0	1	2-1	0	6	.250	.333	.250	56	-1	0-0	1.000	3	177	212	/C-5	0.2
1998	Phi N	9	31	4	9	0	0	0	3	5-0	0	5	.290	.378	.290	81	-1	0-0	1.000	-4	559	0	/C-9	-0.4
1999	Phi N	36	88	7	24	4	0	1	21	4-0	0	11	.273	.298	.352	64	-5	0-0	.971	-6	78	46	C-32	-0.9
2000	Phi N	31	74	8	18	5	0	2	5	13-0	2	15	.243	.371	.392	92	0	0-0	.995	1	111	87	C-31	0.2
2001	NY N	1	1	0	1	0	0	0	0	0-0	0	0	1.000	1.000	1.000	443	1	0-0	—	0			/H	0.0
	Phi N	26	75	8	16	3	1	1	6	9-1	0	19	.213	.294	.320	61	-4	0-0	.987	-2	129	99	C-24	-0.4
	Col N	19	55	7	15	3	0	1	4	3-3	1	5	.273	.317	.382	66	-3	0-0	1.000	-3	63	48	C-19	-0.5

Year	Tm Lg	G	AB	R	H	2B	3B	HR	RBI	BB-IB	HP	SO	AVG	OBP	SLG	AOPS	ABR	SB-CS	FA	FR	Rng	Thr	G at Pos	BFW
	Year	46	131	15	32	6	1	2	10	12-4	1	24	.244	.308	.351	66	-7	0-0	.992	-5	102	78	C-43	-0.9
2002	Col N	90	291	26	77	10	2	4	26	15-2	6	45	.265	.314	.354	68	-14	1-3	.992	-13	115	55	C-90	-2.3
2003	SD N	96	307	26	73	15	0	2	42	24-3	2	48	.238	.296	.306	64	-17	3-0	.996	-24	88	64	C-91	-3.4
Total	8	315	939	86	237	40	3	11	108	75-10	11	155	.252	.313	.337	68	-44	4-3	.992	-48	117	64	C-301	-7.5
BENNETT, HERSCHEL Herschel Emmett B 9.21.1896 Elwood, MO D 9.9.1964 Springfield, MO BL/TR 5-9.5/160# d4.19																								
1923	StL A	5	4	0	0	0	0	0	0	1	0	1	.000	.200	.000	-42	-1	0-0	1.000	0	116	0	/O(CF)	-0.1
1924	StL A	41	94	16	31	4	3	1	11	3	2	6	.330	.364	.468	107	0	1-0	.966	-1	84	109	O-21(12-0-9)	-0.1
1925	StL A	93	298	46	83	11	6	2	37	18	2	16	.279	.324	.376	73	-13	4-10	.916	-1	91	155	O-73(41-12-21)	-2.1
1926	StL A	80	225	33	60	14	2	1	26	22	2	21	.267	.337	.360	78	-7	2-1	.950	3	98	174	O-50(36-6-9)	-0.8
1927	StL A	93	256	40	68	12	2	3	30	14	3	21	.266	.311	.363	72	-11	6-2	.946	1	110	86	O-55(12-2-42)	-1.3
Total	5	312	877	135	242	41	13	7	104	58	9	65	.276	.327	.376	77	-32	13-13	.937	2	98	136	O-200(101-21-81)	-4.4
BENNETT, FRED James Fred "Red" B 3.15.1902 Atkins, AR D 5.12.1957 Atkins, AR BR/TR 5-9/185# d4.13																								
1928	StL A	7	8	0	2	1	0	0	0	0	0	2	.250	.250	.375	60	0	0-0	1.000	0	158	0	/O(RF)	0.0
1931	Pit N	32	89	6	25	5	0	1	7	7	0	4	.281	.333	.371	90	-1	0	.951	-0	90	143	O-21(3-0-18)	-0.3
Total	2	39	97	6	27	6	0	1	7	7	0	6	.278	.327	.371	87	-1	0-0	.953	-0	93	138	/O-22(3-0-19)	-0.3
BENNETT, JOE Joseph Rosenblum B 7.2.1900 New York, NY D 7.11.1987 Morro Bay, CA BR/TR 5-9/168# d7.5																								
1923	Phi N	1	0	0	0	0	0	0	0	0	0	0	—	—	—	—	0	0-0	1.000	0	154	0	/3	0.0
BENNETT, PUG Justin Titus B 2.20.1874 Ponca, NE D 9.12.1935 Kirkland, WA BR/TR 5-11/165# d4.12																								
1906	StL N	153	595	66	156	16	7	1	34	56	8		.262	.334	.318	108	6	20	.948	-8	99	83	*2-153	-0.1
1907	StL N	87	324	20	72	8	2	0	21	21	1		.222	.272	.259	69	-12	7	.939	-10	89	88	2-83/3-3	-2.5
Total	2	240	919	86	228	24	9	1	55	77	9		.248	.312	.297	94	-6	27	.945	-18	96	85	2-236/3-3	-2.6
BENSON, VERN Vernon Adair B 9.19.1924 Granite Quarry, NC BL/TR 5-11/180# d7.31 Mil 1943-45 M1 C18																								
1943	Phi A	2	2	0	0	0	0	0	0	0	0	0	.000	.000	.000	-99	-1	0-0	—	0			H	-0.1
1946	Phi A	7	5	1	0	0	0	0	0	1	0	3	.000	.167	.000	-51	-1	0-0	1.000	0	203	0	/O-2(LF)	-0.1
1951	StL N	13	46	8	12	3	1	1	7	6	0	8	.261	.346	.435	108	1	0-0	.950	1	125	190	/3-9,O-4(LF)	0.1
1952	StL N	20	47	6	9	2	0	2	5	5	0	9	.191	.269	.362	73	-2	0-0	.889	-0	114	159	3-15	-0.2
1953	StL N	13	4	2	0	0	0	0	0	1	0	2	.000	.200	.000	-42	-1	0-0	—	0			H	-0.1
Total	5	55	104	17	21	5	1	3	12	13	0	22	.202	.291	.356	75	-4	0-0	.911	1	118	170	/3-24,O-6(LF)	-0.4
BENTLEY, JACK John Needles B 3.8.1895 Sandy Spring, MD D 10.24.1969 Olney, MD BL/TL 5-11.5/200# d9.6 ▲																								
1913	Was A	3	3	0	0	0	0	0	0	0	0	0	.000	.000	.000	-98	0	0	1.000	0	154	0	/P-3	0.0
1914	Was A	30	40	7	11	2	0	0	4	0	0	5	.275	.275	.325	77	2	0	.930	-1	86	85	P-30	0.0
1915	Was A	4	2	0	0	0	0	0	0	0	0	1	.000	.000	.000	-98	0	0	.750	-0	61	0	/P-4	0.0
1916	Was A	2	0	0	0	0	0	0	0	0	0	0	—	—	—	—	0	0	1.000	0	352	0	/P-2	0.0
1923	†NY N	52	89	9	38	6	2	1	14	3	0	4	.427	.446	.573	169	15	0-0	.977	-1	89	47	P-31	0.0
1924	†NY N	46	98	12	26	5	1	0	6	3	0	13	.265	.287	.337	68	4	0-0	.979	-1	94	139	P-28	0.0
1925	NY N	64	99	10	30	5	2	3	18	9	0	11	.303	.361	.485	119	3	0-0	.930	-1	89	91	P-28/O-3(RF),1	-0.1
1926	Phi N	75	240	19	62	12	3	2	27	5	0	4	.258	.273	.358	66	-12	0	.993	-1	90	81	1-56/P-7	-1.6
	NY N	3	4	0	1	0	0	0	0	0	0	0	.250	.250	.250	35	0	0	—	-0	0	0	/P	0.0
	Year	78	244	19	63	12	3	2	27	5	0	4	.258	.273	.357	65	-13	0	.993	-1	90	81	1-56/P-8	-1.6
1927	NY N	8	9	1	2	0	0	1	2	1	0	1	.222	.300	.556	125	0	0	.750	-0	91	0	/P-4,1-2	0.0
Total	9	287	584	58	170	30	8	7	71	21	0	39	.291	.316	.406	91	12	0-0	.949	-5	90	84	P-138/1-59,O-3(RF)	-1.7
BENTON, BUTCH Alfred Lee B 8.24.1957 Tampa, FL BR/TR 6-1/190# d9.14																								
1978	NY N	4	4	1	2	0	0	0	2	0-0	1	0	.500	.600	.500	218	1	0-0	1.000	-0	0	0	/C	0.1
1980	NY N	12	21	0	1	0	0	0	0	2-0	1	4	.048	.167	.048	-39	-4	0-0	.935	-2	96	47	/C-8	-0.6
1982	Chi N	4	7	0	1	0	0	0	1	0-0	0	1	.143	.143	.143	-19	-1	0-0	1.000	2	87	0	/C-4	0.1
1985	Cle A	31	67	5	12	4	0	0	7	3-2	0	9	.179	.208	.239	24	-7	0-0	.957	-5	118	95	C-26	-1.1
Total	4	51	99	6	16	4	0	0	10	5-2	2	14	.162	.213	.202	16	-11	0-0	.959	-5	109	77	/C-39	-1.5
BENTON, STAN Stanley W. "Rabbit" B 9.29.1901 Cannel City, KY D 6.7.1984 Mesquite, TX BR/TR 5-7/150# d9.13																								
1922	Phi N	6	19	1	4	1	0	0	3	2	0	1	.211	.286	.263	39	-2	0-0	.889	-1	103	0	/2-5	-0.2
BENZINGER, TODD Todd Eric B 2.11.1963 Dayton, KY BB/TR 6-1/190# d6.21																								
1987	Bos A	73	223	36	62	11	1	8	43	22-3	2	41	.278	.344	.444	105	2	5-4	.987	9	131	157	O-61(14-5-47)/1-2	0.7
1988	†Bos A	120	405	47	103	28	1	13	70	22-4	1	80	.254	.293	.425	95	-4	2-3	.991	-3	78	89	1-85,O-48(5-0-43)/D	-1.4
1989	Cin N	161	628	79	154	28	3	17	76	44-13	2	120	.245	.293	.381	89	-10	3-7	.995	-12	69	84	*1-158	-3.8
1990	†Cin N	118	376	35	95	14	2	5	46	19-4	4	69	.253	.291	.340	71	-15	3-4	.992	-1	86	102	1-95,O-10(LF)	-2.5
1991	Cin N	51	123	7	23	3	2	1	11	10-2	0	20	.187	.244	.268	43	-10	2-0	.986	1	113	62	1-21,O-15(LF)	-1.1
	KC A	78	293	29	86	15	3	2	40	17-2	3	46	.294	.338	.386	99	0	2-6	.996	-7	68	89	1-75/D	-1.4
1992	LA N	121	293	24	70	16	2	4	31	15-1	0	54	.239	.272	.348	77	-10	2-4	.989	-1	97	37	O-51(18-0-33),1-42	-1.5
1993	SF N	86	177	25	51	7	2	6	26	13-1	0	35	.288	.332	.452	112	2	0-0	1.000	-3	66	120	1-40/O-7(LF),3	-0.4
1994	SF N	107	328	32	87	13	2	9	31	17-4	2	84	.265	.304	.399	86	-8	2-1	.994	-5	83	102	1-99	-2.1
1995	SF N	9	10	2	2	0	0	1	2	2-1	0	3	.200	.308	.500	120	0	0-0	1.000	-1	0	200	/1-5	0.0
Total	9	924	2856	316	733	135	18	66	376	181-35	14	552	.257	.301	.386	88	-53	21-29	.994	-22	77	94	1-622,O-192(69-5-123)/D-2,3	-13.5
BERARDINO, JOHNNY John "Bernie" B 5.1.1917 Los Angeles, CA D 5.19.1996 Los Angeles, CA BR/TR 6/180# d4.22 Mil 1942-45 C1																								
1939	StL A	126	468	42	120	24	5	5	58	37	2	36	.256	.314	.361	71	-22	6-2	.958	-1	99	76	*2-114/3-8,S-2	-1.4
1940	StL A	142	523	71	135	31	4	16	85	32	0	46	.258	.301	.424	84	-15	6-8	.939	10	**105**	112	*S-112,2-13/3-9	0.3
1941	StL A	128	469	48	127	30	4	5	89	41	2	27	.271	.332	.384	86	-10	3-5	.954	-10	91	104	*S-123/3	-1.2
1942	StL A	29	74	11	21	6	0	1	10	4	1	2	.284	.329	.405	104	0	3-1	.950	-0	73	76	/S-6,3-6,1-5,2-4	0.1
1946	StL A	144	582	70	154	29	5	5	68	34	1	58	.265	.306	.357	81	-16	2-4	.972	-2	101	91	*2-143	-1.2
1947	StL A	90	306	29	80	22	1	1	20	44	2	26	.261	.358	.350	95	0	6-5	.977	-4	90	99	2-86	0.1
1948	Cle A	66	147	19	28	5	1	2	10	27	3	16	.190	.328	.279	64	-7	0-1	.988	2	99	110	2-20,1-18,S-12/3-3	-0.5
1949	Cle A	50	116	11	23	6	1	0	13	14	2	14	.198	.295	.267	50	-8	0-1	.935	-3	97	68	3-25/2-8,S-3	-1.1
1950	Cle A	4	5	1	2	0	0	0	3	1	0	0	.400	.500	.400	137	0	0-0	1.000	-0	66	86	/23	0.0
	Pit N	40	131	12	27	3	1	1	12	19	0	11	.206	.307	.267	51	-9	0	.964	2	112	102	2-36/3-3	-0.5
1951	StL A	39	119	13	27	7	1	0	13	17	0	18	.227	.324	.303	68	-5	1-1	.917	-5	77	84	3-31/2-2,1O(LF)	-1.0
1952	Cle A	35	32	5	3	0	0	0	2	10	0	8	.094	.310	.094	17	-3	0-1	.960	1	138	66	/2-8,S-8,3-4,1-2	-0.2
	Pit N	19	56	2	8	4	0	0	4	4	0	6	.143	.200	.214	14	-6	0-0	.960	4	125	109	2-18	-0.2
Total	11	912	3028	334	755	167	23	36	387	284	13	268	.249	.316	.355	77	-101	27-29	.968	-6	101	91	2-453,S-266/3-91,1-26,O(LF)	-6.8
BERBERET, LOU Louis Joseph B 11.20.1929 Long Beach, CA BL/TR 5-11/212# d9.17																								
1954	NY A	5	5	1	2	0	0	0	3	1	0	1	.400	.500	.400	154	0	0-0	1.000	1	*0*	*0*	/C-3	0.1
1955	NY A	2	5	1	2	0	0	0	2	1-0	0	0	.400	.500	.400	147	0	0-0	1.000	0	*0*	*0*	/C	0.1
1956	Was A	95	207	25	54	6	3	4	27	46-9	3	33	.261	.402	.377	107	4	0-0	.997	-2	*82*	*134*	C-59	0.5
1957	Was A	99	264	24	69	11	2	7	36	41-5	2	38	.261	.359	.398	110	5	0-1	**1.000**	-5	*75*	***144***	C-77	0.4
1958	Was A	5	6	0	1	0	0	0	0	4-0	0	1	.167	.500	.167	94	0	0-0	.917	0	*55*	*252*	/C-2	0.1
	Bos A	57	167	11	35	5	3	2	18	31-1	1	32	.210	.337	.311	74	-5	0-2	.984	-4	*131*	*88*	C-49	-0.7
	Year	62	173	11	36	5	3	2	18	35-1	1	33	.208	.344	.306	76	-5	0-2	.981	-3	*128*	*94*	C-51	-0.6
1959	Det A	100	338	38	73	8	2	13	44	35-1	0	59	.216	.284	.367	75	-13	0-0	.989	-6	*115*	*107*	C-95	-1.5
1960	Det A	85	232	18	45	4	0	5	23	41-4	1	31	.194	.313	.276	60	-12	2-0	.993	-0	*96*	*106*	C-81	-0.8
Total	7	448	1224	118	281	34	10	31	153	200-20	7	195	.230	.337	.350	86	-21	2-3	.992	-16	*98*	*116*	C-367	-1.8
BERBLINGER, JEFF Jeffrey James B 11.19.1970 Wichita, KS BR/TR 6/190# d9.7																								
1997	StL N	7	5	1	0	0	0	0	0	0-0	0	1	.000	.000	.000	-99	-1	0-0	1.000	1	108	258	/2-4	-0.1
BERG, DAVE David Scott B 9.3.1970 Roseville, CA BR/TR 5-11/185# d4.2 OF Total (7-LF 15-RF)																								
1998	Fla N	81	182	18	57	11	0	2	21	26-1	0	46	.313	.393	.407	119	6	3-0	1.000	0	84	86	2-27,3-25,S-17	0.9
1999	Fla N	109	304	42	87	18	1	3	25	27-0	2	59	.286	.348	.382	90	-5	2-2	.969	1	108	62	S-37,2-29,3-19/O-3(LF)	0.0
2000	Fla N	82	210	23	53	14	1	1	21	25-0	5	46	.252	.340	.343	78	-6	3-0	.957	-5	98	110	S-49,3-13,2-11	-0.6
2001	Fla N	82	215	26	52	12	1	4	16	14-0	2	39	.242	.292	.363	71	-10	0-1	.965	-7	101	111	2-34,S-19,3-16	-1.4
2002	Tor A	109	374	42	101	26	2	4	39	26-1	5	57	.270	.322	.382	84	-8	0-2	.966	-3	99	115	2-52,3-20,S-13,O-13(3-0-10),1-10/D-8	-1.0

Year	Tm Lg	G	AB	R	H	2B	3B	HR	RBI	BB-IB	HP	SO	AVG	OBP	SLG	AOPS	ABR	SB-CS	FA	FR	Rng	Thr	G at Pos	BFW
2003	Tor A	61	161	26	41	6	1	4	18	11-0	0	34	.255	.301	.379	77	-6	0-1	.978	-6	92	61	2-24,3-17/O-6(1-0-5),1-2,SD	-1.1
Total	6	524	1446	177	391	87	6	18	140	129-2	14	281	.270	.333	.376	86	-29	8-6	.980	-19	98	95	2-177,S-136,3-110/O-22R,D-15,1	-3.2
BERG, MOE Morris B 3.2.1902 New York, NY D 5.29.1972 Belleville, NJ BR/TR 6-1/185# d6.27 C2																								
1923	Bro N	49	129	9	24	3	2	0	6	2	0	5	.186	.198	.240	16	-16	1-0	.906	-5	93	83	S-47/2	-1.6
1926	Chi A	41	113	4	25	6	0	0	7	6	0	9	.221	.261	.274	41	-10	0-2	.948	4	106	147	S-31/2-2,3	-0.4
1927	Chi A	35	69	4	17	4	0	0	4	4	0	10	.246	.288	.304	55	-5	0-0	.952	-4	117	87	2-11,C-10/S-6,3-3	-0.7
1928	Chi A	76	224	25	55	16	0	0	29	14	4	25	.246	.302	.317	64	-12	3-1	.990	7	*139*	*96*	C-73	0.0
1929	Chi A	107	352	32	101	7	0	0	47	17	2	16	.287	.323	.307	64	-19	5-1	.982	-1	*99*	*101*	*C-106	-1.2
1930	Chi A	20	61	4	7	3	0	0	7	1	0	5	.115	.129	.164	-27	-12	0-0	.986	-0	*95*	*126*	C-20	-1.1
1931	Cle A	10	13	1	1	1	0	0	0	1	0	1	.077	.143	.154	-21	-2	0-0	.889	0	*174*	*247*	/C-8	-0.2
1932	Was A	75	195	16	46	8	1	1	26	8	0	13	.236	.266	.303	48	-16	1-1	1.000	6	*168*	*105*	C-75	-0.6
1933	Was A	40	65	8	12	3	0	2	9	4	0	5	.185	.232	.323	46	-5	0-0	1.000	2	*221*	*72*	C-35	-0.2
1934	Was A	33	86	5	21	4	0	0	6	6	1	4	.244	.301	.291	55	-6	2-0	.988	-3	*149*	*87*	C-31	-0.6
	Cle A	29	97	4	25	3	1	0	9	1	0	7	.258	.265	.309	47	-8	0-0	.980	2	*127*	*68*	C-28	-0.4
	Year	62	183	9	46	7	1	0	15	7	1	11	.251	.283	.301	51	-14	2-0	.983	-1	*137*	*76*	C-59	-1.0
1935	Bos A	38	98	13	28	5	0	2	12	5	0	3	.286	.320	.398	79	-3	0-0	.991	3	*111*	*145*	C-37	0.1
1936	Bos A	39	125	9	30	4	1	0	19	2	2	6	.240	.264	.288	34	-14	0-0	.986	9	*96*	*158*	C-39	-0.2
1937	Bos A	47	141	13	36	3	1	0	20	5	0	4	.255	.281	.291	43	-13	0-0	.979	2	*115*	*91*	C-47	-0.8
1938	Bos A	10	12	0	4	0	0	0	0	0	0	1	.333	.333	.333	64	-1	0-0	1.000	0	*113*	*155*	/C-7,1	0.0
1939	Bos A	14	33	3	9	1	0	1	5	2	0	3	.273	.314	.394	77	-1	0-0	.965	2	*101*	*178*	C-13	0.1
Total	15	663	1813	150	441	71	6	6	206	78	9	117	.243	.278	.299	49	-143	12-5	.986	24	*127*	*107*	C-529/S-84,2-14,3-4,1	-7.8
BERGAMO, AUGIE August Samuel B 2.14.1917 Detroit, MI D 8.19.1974 Grosse Pointe, MI BL/TL 5-9/165# d4.25																								
1944	†StL N	80	192	35	55	6	3	2	19	35	1	23	.286	.399	.380	118	6	0	.988	-4	94	0	O-50(31-1-19)/1-2	0.0
1945	StL N	94	304	51	96	17	2	3	44	43	0	21	.316	.401	.414	124	12	0	.969	2	101	140	O-77(7-0-70)/1-2	0.9
Total	2	174	496	86	151	23	5	5	63	78	1	44	.304	.400	.401	122	18	0	.975	-2	98	87	O-127(38-1-89)/1-4	0.9
BERGEN, MARTY Martin B 10.25.1871 N.Brookfield, MA D 1.19.1900 N.Brookfield, MA TR 5-10/170# d4.17 b-Bill																								
1896	Bos N	65	245	39	66	6	4	4	37	11	3	22	.269	.309	.376	75	-10	6	.920	8	*113*	*115*	C-63/1	0.3
1897	†Bos N	87	327	47	81	11	3	2	45	18	4		.248	.295	.318	58	-21	5	.963	14	*154*	*71*	C-85/O(CF)	0.1
1898	Bos N	120	446	62	125	16	5	3	60	13	1		.280	.302	.359	85	-11	9	.962	5	*117*	*92*	*C-117/1-2	0.4
1899	Bos N	72	260	32	67	11	3	1	34	10	2		.258	.290	.335	65	-13	4	.955	6	*119*	*96*	C-72	-0.1
Total	4	344	1278	180	339	44	15	10	176	52	10	22	.265	.299	.347	72	-55	24	.954	33	*126*	*92*	C-337/1-3,O(CF)	0.7
BERGEN, BILL William Aloysius B 6.13.1878 N.Brookfield, MA D 12.19.1943 Worcester, MA BR/TR 6/184# d5.6 b-Marty																								
1901	Cin N	87	308	15	55	6	4	1	17	8	0		.179	.199	.234	27	-30	2	.970	-3	*110*	*105*	C-87	-2.5
1902	Cin N	89	322	19	58	8	3	0	36	14	0		.180	.214	.224	32	-26	2	.959	19	***125***	*101*	C-89	0.2
1903	Cin N	58	207	21	47	4	2	0	19	7	0		.227	.252	.266	43	-16	2	.980	4	*123*	*102*	C-58	-0.6
1904	Bro N	96	329	17	60	4	2	0	12	9	0		.182	.204	.207	28	-29	3	.959	13	*100*	*111*	C-93/1	-0.7
1905	Bro N	79	247	12	47	3	2	0	22	7	0		.190	.213	.219	31	-22	4	.954	0	*82*	*128*	C-76	-1.5
1906	Bro N	103	353	9	56	3	3	0	19	7	0		.159	.175	.184	13	-38	2	.977	1	*97*	*104*	*C-103	-2.9
1907	Bro N	51	138	2	22	3	0	0	14	1	0		.159	.165	.181	9	-15	1	.968	-2	*87*	*123*	C-51	-1.5
1908	Bro N	99	302	8	53	8	2	0	15	5	0		.175	.189	.215	30	-25	1	**.989**	10	*87*	*105*	C-99	-0.6
1909	Bro N	112	346	16	48	1	1	1	15	10	0		.139	.163	.156	-1	-42	4	.976	11	*93*	***125***	*C-112	-2.3
1910	Bro N	89	249	11	40	2	1	0	14	6	0	39	.161	.180	.177	4	-31	0	.981	13	*99*	***114***	C-89	-1.1
1911	Bro N	84	227	8	30	3	1	0	10	14	0	42	.132	.183	.154	-6	-33	2	**.981**	5	*87*	***118***	C-84	-2.2
Total	11	947	3028	138	516	45	21	2	193	88	0	81	.170	.194	.201	20	-307	23	.972	73	*99*	*112*	C-941/1	-15.7
BERGER, BRANDON Brandon Charles B 2.21.1975 Covington, KY BR/TR 5-11/205# d9.9																								
2001	KC A	6	16	4	5	1	1	2	2	2-0	0	2	.313	.389	.875	202	2	0-0	1.000	-1	69	0	/O-5(LF),D	0.1
2002	KC A	51	134	16	27	5	1	6	17	8-2	2	32	.201	.255	.388	61	-8	1-0	1.000	2	101	221	O-36(14-4-21),D-10/1	-0.8
2003	KC A	13	32	3	7	0	0	0	3	5-0	0	4	.219	.324	.219	42	-3	0-0	1.000	0	96	211	O-11(RF)/D	-0.3
Total	3	70	182	23	39	6	2	8	22	15-2	2	38	.214	.280	.401	70	-9	1-0	1.000	1	96	194	/O-52(19-4-32),D-12,1	-1.0
BERGER, CLARENCE Clarence Edward B 11.1.1894 E.Cleveland, OH D 6.30.1959 Washington, DC BL/TR 6/185# d9.23																								
1914	Pit N	6	13	2	1	0	0	0	0	1	0	4	.077	.143	.077	-36	-2	0	1.000	-1	53	0	/O-5(RF)	-0.3
BERGER, JOHNNY John Henne B 8.27.1901 Philadelphia, PA D 5.7.1979 Lake Charles, LA BR/TR 5-9/165# d4.20																								
1922	Phi A	2	1	0	1	0	0	0	0	0	0	0	1.000	1.000	1.000	412	0	1-0	1.000	0	*0*	*0*	/C-2	0.1
1927	Was A	9	15	1	4	0	0	0	1	2	0	3	.267	.353	.267	63	-1	0-0	.926	-0	*144*	*0*	/C-9	-0.1
Total	2	11	16	1	5	0	0	0	1	2	0	3	.313	.389	.313	85	-1	1-0	.935	0	*129*	*0*	/C-11	0.0
BERGER, TUN John Henry B 12.6.1867 Pittsburgh, PA D 6.10.1907 Pittsburgh, PA TR ?/204# d5.9																								
1890	Pit N	104	391	64	104	18	4	0	40	35	7	23	.266	.337	.332	108	6	11	.912	-13	160	54	O-41(4-3-36),S-33,C-21/2-6,3	-0.3
1891	Pit N	43	134	15	32	2	1	1	14	12	3	10	.239	.315	.291	79	-3	4	.920	-10	*106*	*112*	C-18,2-17/S-6,O-2(0-1-1)	-1.0
1892	Was N	26	97	9	14	2	1	0	3	7	1	9	.144	.210	.186	20	-9	3	.872	-7	84	54	S-18/C-9	-1.4
Total	3	173	622	88	150	22	6	1	57	54	11	42	.241	.313	.301	87	-6	18	.837	-30	84	53	/S-57,C-48,O-43(4-4-37),2-23,3	-2.7
BERGER, JOE Joseph August "Fats" B 12.20.1886 St.Louis, MO D 3.5.1956 Rock Island, IL BR/TR 5-10.5/170# d4.11																								
1913	Chi A	79	223	27	48	6	2	2	20	36	2	28	.215	.330	.287	82	-4	5	.959	3	111	82	2-71/S-4,3	0.0
1914	Chi A	48	148	11	23	3	1	0	3	13	0	9	.155	.224	.189	25	-14	2-8	.922	0	104	86	S-28,2-12/3-7	-1.6
Total	2	127	371	38	71	9	3	2	23	49	2	37	.191	.289	.248	60	-18	7-8	.956	3	110	89	/2-83,S-32,3-8	-1.6
BERGER, BOZE Louis William B 5.13.1910 Baltimore, MD D 11.3.1992 Bethesda, MD BR/TR 6-2/180# d8.17																								
1932	Cle A	1	1	0	0	0	0	0	0	0	0	1	.000	.000	.000	-94	0	0-0	1.000	0	98	0	/S	0.0
1935	Cle A	124	461	62	119	27	5	5	43	34	1	97	.258	.310	.371	74	-19	7-5	.964	12	106	119	*2-120/S-3,1-2,3	0.1
1936	Cle A	28	52	1	9	2	0	0	3	1	0	14	.173	.189	.212	-1	-9	0-0	.959	1	93	56	/1-8,2-8,3-7,S-2	-0.6
1937	Chi A	52	130	19	31	5	0	5	13	15	1	24	.238	.322	.392	79	-5	1-1	.931	-1	101	118	3-40/2S	-0.4
1938	Chi A	118	470	60	102	15	3	3	36	43	1	80	.217	.284	.281	41	-44	4-1	.946	-8	108	119	S-67,2-42/3-9	-4.0
1939	Bos A	20	30	4	9	2	0	0	2	1	0	10	.300	.323	.367	73	-1	0-0	.947	1	97	48	S-10/3-5,2-2	0.0
Total	6	343	1144	146	270	51	8	13	97	94	3	226	.236	.296	.329	57	-78	12-7	.954	5	104	111	2-173/S-84,3-62,1-10	-4.9
BERGER, WALLY Walter Anton B 10.10.1905 Chicago, IL D 11.30.1988 Redondo Beach, CA BR/TR 6-2/198# d4.15																								
1930	Bos N	151	555	98	172	27	14	38	119	54	4	69	.310	.375	.614	139	31	3	.966	3	106	98	*O-145(LF)	2.0
1931	Bos N	**156**	617	94	199	44	8	19	84	55	2	70	.323	.380	.512	143	37	13	.977	4	102	118	*O-156(CF)/1	3.6
1932	Bos N	145	602	90	185	34	6	17	73	33	3	66	.307	.346	.468	121	17	5	**.993**	-2	100	79	*O-134(CF),1-11	1.0
1933	Bos N★	137	528	84	165	37	8	27	106	41	3	77	.313	.365	.566	**177**	50	2	.977	-2	103	61	*O-136(CF)	4.7
1934	Bos N★	150	615	92	183	35	8	34	121	49	3	65	.298	.352	.546	148	38	2	.978	-6	94	80	*O-150(CF)	2.7
1935	Bos N★	150	589	91	174	39	4	**34**	**130**	50	4	80	.295	.355	.548	151	40	3	.965	9	**119**	67	*O-149(CF)	4.4
1936	Bos N☆	138	534	88	154	23	3	25	91	53	8	84	.288	.361	.483	134	25	1	.966	-3	99	95	*O-133(CF)	1.8
1937	Bos N	30	113	14	31	9	1	5	22	11	1	33	.274	.344	.504	140	6	0	1.000	-1	94	52	O-28(LF)	0.3
	†NY N	59	199	40	58	11	2	12	43	18	3	30	.291	.359	.548	141	11	3	.965	-3	88	97	O-52(3-46-3)	0.6
	Year	89	312	54	89	20	3	17	65	29	4	63	.285	.354	.532	141	17	3	.976	-5	90	82	O-80(31-46-3)	0.9
1938	NY N	16	32	5	6	0	0	0	4	2	0	4	.188	.235	.188	17	-4	0	1.000	0	120	0	/O-9(0-8-1)	-0.4
	Cin N	99	407	74	125	23	4	16	56	29	2	44	.307	.356	.501	137	19	2	.966	-2	95	94	O-98(LF)	1.2
	Year	115	439	79	131	23	4	16	60	31	2	48	.298	.347	.478	128	15	2	.970	-2	97	85	*O-107(98-8-1)	0.8
1939	†Cin N	97	329	36	85	15	1	14	44	36	5	63	.258	.341	.438	107	3	1	.970	-8	80	99	O-95(66-29-0)	-0.9
1940	Cin N	2	2	0	0	0	0	0	0	0	0	1	.000	.000	.000	-99	-1	0	—	0			H	-0.1
	Phi N	20	41	3	13	2	0	1	5	4	0	7	.317	.378	.439	130	2	1	.947	-1	103	0	O-11(4-2-5)/1	0.1
	Year	22	43	3	13	2	0	1	5	4	0	8	.302	.362	.419	119	1	1	.947	-1	103	0	O-11(4-2-5)/1	0.0
Total	11	1350	5163	809	1550	299	59	242	898	435	38	693	.300	.359	.522	140	274	36	.974	-11	100	86	*O-1296(344-943-9)/1-13	21.0
BERGERON, PETER Peter Francis B 11.9.1977 Greenfield, MA BL/TR 6-2/185# d9.7																								
1999	Mon N	16	45	12	11	2	0	0	1	9-0	0	5	.244	.370	.289	72	-2	0-0	.967	2	118	287	O-13(13-3-0)	0.0
2000	Mon N	148	518	80	127	25	7	5	31	58-0	0	100	.245	.320	.349	67	-26	11-13	.985	5	99	**201**	*O-146(32-117-0)	-2.2
2001	Mon N	102	375	53	79	11	4	3	16	28-2	5	87	.211	.275	.285	44	-32	10-7	.996	-4	95	113	*O-101(CF)	-3.4

Year	Tm Lg	G	AB	R	H	2B	3B	HR	RBI	BB-IB	HP	SO	AVG	OBP	SLG	AOPS	ABR	SB-CS	FA	FR	Rng	Thr	G at Pos	BFW
2002	Mon N	31	123	24	23	3	2	0	7	22-0	0	44	.187	.310	.244	47	-10	10-3	.974	-2	100	0	O-31(CF)	-1.1
Total	4	297	1061	169	240	41	13	8	55	117-2	5	236	.226	.305	.312	57	-70	31-23	.986	1	98	149	O-291(45-252-0)	-6.7
BERGH, JOHN John Baptist B 10.8.1857 Boston, MA D 4.17.1883 Boston, MA d8.5																								
1876	Phi N	1	4	0	0	0	0	0	0	0		2	.000	.000	.000	-99	-1		1.000	-0	0	0	/O(CF)C	-0.1
1880	Bos N	11	40	2	8	3	0	0	0	2		5	.200	.238	.275	76	-1		.844	-3			C-11	-0.3
Total	2	12	44	2	8	3	0	0	0	2		7	.182	.217	.250	59	-2		.841	-3			/C-12,O(CF)	-0.4
BERGHAMMER, MARTY Martin Andrew "Pepper" B 6.18.1888 Elliott, PA D 12.21.1957 Pittsburgh, PA BL/TR 5-9/172# d9.8																								
1911	Chi A	2	5	0	0	0	0	0	0	0	1		.000	.167	.000	-54	-1	0	1.000	-0	51	0	/2-2	-0.1
1913	Cin N	74	188	25	41	4	1	1	13	10	3	29	.218	.269	.266	53	-12	16-10	.909	4	107	97	S-54,2-13	-0.5
1914	Cin N	77	112	15	25	2	0	0	6	10	0	18	.223	.287	.241	56	-6	4	.906	6	124	68	S-33,2-13	0.1
1915	Pit F	132	469	96	114	10	6	0	33	83	12	44	.243	.371	.290	88	-9	26	**.943**	-15	90	113	*S-132	-1.6
Total	4	285	774	136	180	16	7	1	52	103	16	91	.233	.335	.275	75	-28	46-10	.931	-5	97	106	S-219/2-28	-2.1
BERGMAN, AL Alfred Henry "Dutch" B 9.27.1890 Peru, IN D 6.20.1961 Fort Wayne, IN BR/TR 5-7/155# d8.29																								
1916	Cle A	8	14	2	3	0	1	0	0	2	0	4	.214	.313	.357	95	0	0	.889	-1	92	0	/2-3	-0.1
BERGMAN, DAVE David Bruce B 6.6.1953 Evanston, IL BL/TL 6-1.5/185# d8.26																								
1975	NY A	7	17	0	0	0	0	0	0	2-0	0	4	.000	.105	.000	-69	-4	0-0	.917	1	109	258	/O-6(RF)	-0.4
1977	NY A	5	4	1	1	0	0	0	1	0-0	0	0	.250	.200	.250	37	0	0-0	1.000	0	157	0	/O-3(1-1-1),1-2	0.0
1978	Hou N	104	186	15	43	5	1	0	12	39-9	0	32	.231	.361	.269	86	-1	2-0	.993	-3	80	109	1-66,O-29(LF)	-0.7
1979	Hou N	13	15	4	6	0	0	1	2	0-0	0	3	.400	.400	.600	179	1	0-0	1.000	-0	0	93	/1-4	0.1
1980	†Hou N	90	78	12	20	6	1	0	3	10-2	0	10	.256	.341	.359	104	1	1-0	.995	1	116	158	1-59/O-5(3-0-2)	0.1
1981	Hou N	6	6	1	1	0	0	1	1	0-0	0	0	.167	.167	.667	134	0	0-0	1.000	0	626	0	/1	0.0
	SF N	63	145	16	37	9	0	3	13	19-3	0	18	.255	.339	.379	106	2	2-0	.992	2	136	99	1-33,O-15(LF)	0.2
	Year	69	151	17	38	9	0	4	14	19-3	0	18	.252	.333	.391	108	2	2-0	.992	2	140	98	1-34,O-15(LF)	0.2
1982	SF N	100	121	22	33	3	1	4	14	18-3	0	11	.273	.364	.413	118	3	3-0	.991	-0	92	76	1-69/O-6(4-0-3)	0.1
1983	SF N	90	140	16	40	4	1	6	24	24-2	1	21	.286	.394	.457	140	8	2-1	.994	3	129	87	1-50/O-6(LF)	0.9
1984	†Det A	120	271	42	74	8	5	7	44	33-2	3	40	.273	.351	.417	115	6	3-4	.989	5	122	103	*1-114/O-2(1-0-1)	0.5
1985	Det A	69	140	8	25	2	0	3	7	14-0	0	15	.179	.250	.257	41	-12	0-0	.991	-1	93	88	1-44/O(LF)D	-1.5
1986	Det A	65	130	14	30	6	1	1	9	21-0	0	16	.231	.338	.315	79	-3	0-0	.986	1	118	119	1-41/O-2(1-0-1),D-8	-0.4
1987	†Det A	91	172	25	47	7	3	6	22	30-4	1	23	.273	.379	.453	127	8	0-1	.992	-2	91	98	1-65/O-7(3-0-4),D-7	0.2
1988	Det A	116	289	37	85	14	0	5	35	38-2	0	34	.294	.372	.394	121	10	0-2	.990	1	110	86	1-64,D-30,O-13(LF)	0.5
1989	Det A	137	385	38	103	13	1	7	37	44-3	2	44	.268	.345	.361	102	2	1-3	.993	5	**119**	88	*1-123/O(LF)D	-0.1
1990	Det A	100	205	21	57	10	1	2	26	33-3	0	17	.278	.375	.366	108	4	3-2	.995	-1	83	93	D-51,1-27/O-5(LF)	-0.1
1991	Det A	86	194	23	46	10	1	7	29	35-2	0	40	.237	.351	.407	108	3	1-1	.997	-0	100	106	1-49,D-13/O-4(LF)	-0.1
1992	Det A	87	181	17	42	3	0	1	10	20-1	0	19	.232	.305	.265	62	-9	1-0	.986	-3	80	84	1-55,D-12/O(LF)	-1.6
Total	17	1349	2679	312	690	100	16	54	289	380-36	7	347	.258	.348	.367	102	19	19-14	.992	8	107	97	1-866,D-133,O-106(88-1-18)	-2.3
BERKENSTOCK, NATE Nathan B 1831 , PA D 2.23.1900 Philadelphia, PA d10.30																								
1871	Ath NA	1	4	0	0	0	0	0	0	0		3	.000	.000	.000	-99	-1	0-0	1.000	0	0	0	/O(RF)	0.0
BERKLEBACH, FRANK Frank Pierce B 7.27.1853 Philadelphia, PA D 6.10.1932 Merchantville, NJ 6/182# d7.4																								
1884	Cin AA	6	25	3	6	0	1	0	3	0	2		.240	.296	.320	96	0		.667	-1	0	0	/O-6(LF)	-0.2
BERKMAN, LANCE William Lance B 2.10.1976 Waco, TX BB/TL 6-1/205# d7.16																								
1999	Hou N	34	93	10	22	2	0	4	15	12-0	0	21	.237	.321	.387	80	-3	5-1	.955	-2	94	0	O-27(22-0-8)/1	-0.5
2000	Hou N	114	353	76	105	28	1	21	67	56-1	1	73	.297	.388	.561	131	18	6-2	.968	0	99	107	O-96(40-0-63)/1-2	1.4
2001	†Hou N★	156	577	110	191	**55**	5	34	126	92-5	13	121	.331	.430	.620	160	57	7-9	.981	-2	100	61	*O-155(128-40-7)	4.7
2002	Hou N★	158	578	106	169	35	2	42	**128**	107-20	4	118	.292	.405	.578	152	44	8-4	.977	-10	88	70	*O-156(76-122-12)	3.3
2003	Hou N	153	538	110	155	35	6	25	93	107-13	9	108	.288	.412	.515	134	32	5-3	.989	-3	92	108	*O-153(153-1-0)	2.3
Total	5	615	2139	412	642	155	14	126	429	374-39	27	441	.300	.407	.562	143	148	31-19	.979	-16	94	81	O-587(419-163-90)/1-3	11.2
BERMAN, BOB Robert Leon B 1.24.1899 New York, NY D 8.2.1988 Bridgeport, CT BR/TR 5-7.5/158# d6.4																								
1918	Was A	2	0	0	0	0	0	0	0	0	0	0	—	—	—	—	0	0	1.000	0	*0*	*0*	/C	0.0
BERNARD, CURT Curtis Henry B 2.18.1878 Parkersburg, WV D 4.10.1955 Culver City, CA BL/TR 5-10/150# d9.17																								
1900	NY N	20	71	9	18	2	0	0	8	6	2		.254	.329	.282	73	-2	1	.929	-2	39	0	O-19(RF)/S	-0.4
1901	NY N	23	76	11	17	0	2	0	6	7	0		.224	.289	.276	67	-3	2	.800	-2	189	0	O-15(0-8-7)/2-4,S-2,3	-0.6
Total	2	43	147	20	35	2	2	0	14	13	2		.238	.309	.279	70	-5	3	.857	-4	110	0	/O-34(0-8-26),2-4,S-3,3	-1.0
BERNAZARD, TONY Antonio (Garcia) B 8.24.1956 Caguas, P.R. BB/TR 5-9/160# d7.13																								
1979	Mon N	22	40	11	12	2	0	1	8	15-0	1	12	.300	.500	.425	156	5	1-2	.982	-3	97	54	2-14	0.2
1980	Mon N	82	183	26	41	7	1	5	18	17-4	0	41	.224	.289	.355	79	-6	9-2	.976	-1	104	90	2-39,S-22	-0.3
1981	Chi A	**106**	384	53	106	14	4	6	34	54-6	2	66	.276	.367	.380	118	11	4-4	.987	6	103	91	*2-104/S	2.3
1982	Chi A	137	540	90	138	25	9	11	56	67-0	2	88	.256	.337	.396	101	2	11-0	.985	31	**112**	119	*2-137	4.2
1983	Chi A	59	233	30	61	16	2	2	26	17-0	0	45	.262	.306	.373	85	-5	2-1	.976	2	111	99	2-59	0.1
	Sea A	80	300	35	80	18	1	6	30	38-3	2	52	.267	.351	.393	101	2	21-8	.971	5	100	89	2-79	1.3
	Year	139	533	65	141	34	3	8	56	55-3	2	97	.265	.332	.385	94	-3	23-9	.973	7	105	93	*2-138	1.4
1984	Cle A	140	439	44	97	15	4	2	38	43-0	2	70	.221	.290	.287	60	-23	20-13	.971	2	103	101	*2-136/D	-1.5
1985	Cle A	153	500	73	137	26	3	11	59	69-2	1	72	.274	.361	.404	111	10	17-9	.978	-10	97	83	*2-147/S	0.8
1986	Cle A	146	562	88	169	28	4	17	73	53-5	6	77	.301	.362	.456	125	20	17-8	.979	3	104	91	*2-146	3.0
1987	Cle A	79	293	39	70	12	1	11	30	25-2	1	49	.239	.300	.399	83	-8	7-4	.983	-14	90	71	2-78	-1.7
	Oak A	61	214	34	57	14	1	3	19	30-0	0	30	.266	.354	.383	103	2	4-4	.953	-15	85	64	2-59/D-3	-1.0
	Year	140	507	73	127	26	2	14	49	55-2	1	79	.250	.323	.393	91	-6	11-8	.971	-30	88	68	*2-137/D-3	-2.7
1991	Det A	6	12	0	2	0	0	0	0	0-0	0	4	.167	.167	.167	-7	-2	0-0	.900	1	165	328	/2-2,D-2	-0.1
Total	10	1071	3700	523	970	177	30	75	391	428-22	17	606	.262	.339	.387	100	8	113-55	.978	7	102	92	2-1000/S-24,D-6	7.3
BERNHARDT, JUAN Juan Ramon (Coradin) B 8.31.1953 San Pedro De Macoris, D.R. BR/TR 5-11/160# d7.10																								
1976	NY A	10	21	1	4	1	0	0	1	0-0	0	4	.190	.190	.238	25	-2	0-0	.800	-1	77	0	/O-4(1-0-3),3D	-0.3
1977	Sea A	89	305	32	74	9	2	7	30	5-0	2	26	.243	.259	.354	66	-16	2-3	.982	1	102	28	D-54,3-21/1-8	-1.8
1978	Sea A	54	165	13	38	9	0	2	12	9-1	1	10	.230	.270	.321	67	-7	1-1	.989	0	151	87	1-25,3-22/D-2	-1.0
1979	Sea A	1	1	0	1	0	0	0	0	0-0	0	0	1.000	1.000	1.000	434	0	0-0	—	0			/H	0.0
Total	4	154	492	46	117	19	2	9	43	14-1	3	40	.238	.261	.339	66	-25	3-4	.965	0	94	26	/D-58,3-44,1-33,O-4(1-0-3)	-3.1
BERNIER, CARLOS Carlos (Rodriguez) B 1.28.1927 Juana Diaz, P.R. D 4.6.1989 Juana Diaz, P.R. BR/TR 5-9/180# d4.22																								
1953	Pit N	105	310	48	66	7	8	3	31	51	4	53	.213	.332	.316	70	-13	15-14	.970	3	107	111	O-86(11-57-18)	-1.5
BERO, JOHNNY John George B 12.22.1922 Gary, WV D 5.11.1985 Gardena, CA BL/TR 6/170# d9.26																								
1948	Det A	4	9	2	0	0	0	0	0	1	0	1	.000	.100	.000	-70	-2	0-0	1.000	-1	59	0	/2-2	-0.3
1951	StL A	61	160	24	34	5	0	5	17	26	0	30	.213	.323	.338	76	-5	1-1	.954	-7	97	73	S-55/2	-0.9
Total	2	65	169	26	34	5	0	5	17	27	0	31	.201	.311	.320	69	-7	1-1	.954	-8	97	73	/S-55,2-3	-1.2
BERRA, DALE Dale Anthony B 12.13.1956 Ridgewood, NJ BR/TR 6/190# d8.22 f-Yogi																								
1977	Pit N	17	40	0	7	1	0	0	3	1-0	0	8	.175	.195	.200	6	-5	0-0	.973	-0	88	62	3-14	-0.6
1978	Pit N	56	135	16	28	2	0	6	14	13-3	2	20	.207	.285	.356	75	-5	3-1	.908	-5	91	161	3-55/S-2	-1.1
1979	Pit N	44	123	11	26	5	0	3	15	11-2	0	17	.211	.272	.325	61	-7	0-0	.940	-7	86	101	S-22,3-22	-1.2
1980	Pit N	93	245	21	54	8	2	6	31	16-6	1	52	.220	.269	.343	69	-11	2-0	.968	-11	98	138	3-48,S-45/2-4	-1.9
1981	Pit N	81	232	21	56	12	0	2	27	17-4	3	34	.241	.302	.319	74	-8	11-1	.976	-6	100	114	3-42,S-30,2-18	-0.9
1982	Pit N	156	529	64	139	25	5	10	61	33-12	4	83	.263	.306	.386	91	-7	6-6	.961	5	103	90	*S-153/3-6	1.4
1983	Pit N	161	537	51	135	25	1	10	52	61-**19**	0	84	.251	.327	.358	88	-8	8-5	.963	14	100	108	*S-161	2.4
1984	Pit N	136	450	31	100	16	0	9	52	34-8	1	78	.222	.273	.318	67	-20	1-3	.955	-2	103	86	*S-135/3	-1.0
1985	NY A	48	109	8	25	5	1	1	8	7-0	0	20	.229	.276	.321	64	-6	1-1	.917	2	107	160	3-41/S-6	-0.4
1986	NY A	42	108	10	25	7	0	2	13	9-0	1	14	.231	.294	.352	77	-3	0-0	.972	-0	93	88	S-19,3-18/D-4	-0.2
1987	Hou N	19	45	3	8	3	0	0	2	8-3	0	12	.178	.296	.244	49	-3	0-0	.963	-2	96	53	S-18/2-3	-0.4
Total	11	853	2553	236	603	109	9	49	278	210-57	12	422	.236	.294	.344	76	-83	32-17	.959	-12	99	92	S-591,3-247/2-25,D-4	-3.9

BERRA, YOGI Lawrence Peter B 5.12.1925 St.Louis, MO BL/TR 5-8/194# d9.22 M7 C20 HF1972 s-Dale

Year	Tm Lg	G	AB	R	H	2B	3B	HR	RBI	BB-IB	HP	SO	AVG	OBP	SLG	AOPS	ABR	SB-CS	FA	FR	Rng	Thr	G at Pos	BFW
1946	NY A	7	22	3	8	1	0	2	4	1	0	1	.364	.391	.682	193	2	0-0	1.000	2	94	187	/C-6	0.4
1947	†NY A	83	293	41	82	15	3	11	54	13	0	12	.280	.310	.464	115	3	0-1	.972	-5	86	55	C-51,O-24(12-0-12)	0.0
1948	NY A☆	125	469	70	143	24	10	14	98	25	1	24	.305	.341	.488	120	9	3-3	.979	-2	92	115	C-71,O-50(RF)	0.8
1949	†NY A★	116	415	59	115	20	2	20	91	22	6	25	.277	.323	.480	111	2	2-1	.989	10	81	108	*C-109	1.7
1950	†NY A★	151	597	116	192	30	6	28	124	55	4	12	.322	.383	.533	136	29	4-2	.985	4	128	103	*C-148	3.8
1951	†NY A★	141	547	92	161	19	4	27	88	44	3	20	.294	.350	.492	131	19	5-4	.984	9	115	124	*C-141	3.5
1952	†NY A★	142	534	97	146	17	1	30	98	66	4	24	.273	.358	.478	139	26	2-3	.992	1	93	102	*C-140	3.5
1953	†NY A★	137	503	80	149	23	5	27	108	50	3	32	.296	.363	.523	142	27	0-3	.986	7	122	85	*C-133	3.8
1954	NY A★	151	584	88	179	28	6	22	125	56	4	29	.307	.367	.488	139	29	0-1	.990	7	**132**	97	*C-149/3	4.4
1955	†NY A★	147	541	84	147	20	3	27	108	60-6	7	20	.272	.349	.470	121	14	1-0	.984	4	**134**	76	*C-145	2.5
1956	†NY A★	140	521	93	155	29	2	30	105	65-7	5	29	.298	.378	.534	144	32	3-2	.986	6	125	95	*C-135/O(LF)	4.3
1957	†NY A★	134	482	74	121	14	2	24	82	57-10	1	24	.251	.329	.438	110	6	1-2	.995	12	116	140	*C-121/O-6(5-0-1)	2.4
1958	†NY A★	122	433	60	115	17	3	22	90	35-5	2	35	.266	.319	.471	120	10	3-0	**1.000**	4	100	**128**	C-88,O-21(RF)/1-2	1.8
1959	NY A★	131	472	64	134	25	1	19	69	43-5	4	38	.284	.347	.462	125	16	1-2	**.997**	6	127	101	*C-116/O-7(1-0-6)	2.7
1960	†NY A★	120	359	46	99	14	1	15	62	38-6	3	23	.276	.347	.446	120	10	2-1	.989	-3	116	98	C-63,O-36(20-0-17)	0.8
1961	†NY A★	119	395	62	107	11	0	22	61	35-4	2	28	.271	.330	.466	117	8	2-0	.988	2	98	108	O-87(81-0-8),C-15	0.6
1962	†NY A★	86	232	25	52	8	0	10	35	24-4	2	18	.224	.297	.388	87	-5	0-1	.990	4	175	131	C-31,O-28(LF)	-0.1
1963	†NY A	64	147	20	43	6	0	8	28	15-2	1	17	.293	.360	.497	139	8	1-0	.988	8	82	55	C-35	1.8
1965	NY N	4	9	1	2	0	0	0	0	0-0	0	3	.222	.222	.222	27	-1	0-0	.941	0	114	0	/C-2	-0.1
Total	19	2120	7555	1175	2150	321	49	358	1430	704-49	52	414	.285	.348	.482	126	244	30-26	.989	74	115	103	*C-1699,O-260(148-0-115)/1-2,3	38.6

BERRAN, DENNIS Dennis Martin B 10.8.1887 Merrimac, MA D 4.28.1943 Boston, MA BL/TL d8.11

Year	Tm Lg	G	AB	R	H	2B	3B	HR	RBI	BB-IB	HP	SO	AVG	OBP	SLG	AOPS	ABR	SB-CS	FA	FR	Rng	Thr	G at Pos	BFW
1912	Chi A	2	4	1	1	0	0	0	0	0	0	0	.250	.250	.250	44	0	0	1.000	-0	66	0	/O-2(LF)	-0.1

BERRES, RAY Raymond Frederick B 8.31.1907 Kenosha, WI BR/TR 5-9/170# d4.24 C20

Year	Tm Lg	G	AB	R	H	2B	3B	HR	RBI	BB-IB	HP	SO	AVG	OBP	SLG	AOPS	ABR	SB-CS	FA	FR	Rng	Thr	G at Pos	BFW
1934	Bro N	39	79	7	17	4	0	0	3	1	0	16	.215	.225	.266	32	-8	0	.969	-2	93	148	C-37	-0.8
1936	Bro N	105	267	16	64	10	1	1	13	14	1	35	.240	.280	.296	55	-17	1	.988	10	65	125	*C-105	-0.3
1937	Pit N	2	6	0	1	0	0	0	0	0	0	0	.167	.167	.167	-9	-1	0	1.000	0	67	173	/C-2	0.0
1938	Pit N	40	100	7	23	2	0	0	6	8	0	10	.230	.287	.250	48	-7	0	.993	3	98	139	C-40	-0.2
1939	Pit N	81	231	22	53	6	1	0	16	11	1	25	.229	.267	.264	44	-19	1	.993	0	112	88	C-80	-1.5
1940	Pit N	21	32	2	6	0	0	0	2	1	0	1	.188	.212	.188	11	-4	0	.980	1	69	178	C-21	-0.3
	Bos N	85	229	12	44	4	1	0	14	18	0	19	.192	.251	.218	32	-22	0	.981	1	102	121	C-85	-1.7
	Year	106	261	14	50	4	1	0	16	19	0	20	.192	.246	.215	29	-26	0	.981	2	98	128	*C-106	-2.0
1941	Bos N	120	279	21	56	10	0	1	19	17	0	20	.201	.247	.247	41	-22	2	**.995**	4	93	117	*C-120	-1.3
1942	NY N	12	32	0	6	0	0	0	1	2	0	3	.188	.235	.188	24	-3	0	.973	-1	147	40	C-12	-0.4
1943	NY N	20	28	1	4	1	0	0	0	1	0	2	.143	.172	.179	1	-4	0	.981	2	90	187	C-17	-0.2
1944	NY N	16	17	4	8	0	0	1	2	1	1	0	.471	.526	.647	230	3	0	1.000	0	112	241	C-12	0.4
1945	NY N	20	30	4	5	0	0	0	2	2	0	3	.167	.219	.167	8	-4	0	1.000	1	187	41	C-20	-0.2
Total	11	561	1330	96	287	37	3	3	78	76	3	134	.216	.260	.255	43	-108	4	.989	19	95	118	C-551	-6.5

BERROA, ANGEL Angel Maria (Selmo) B 1.27.1980 Santo Domingo, D.R. BR/TR 6/175# d9.18

Year	Tm Lg	G	AB	R	H	2B	3B	HR	RBI	BB-IB	HP	SO	AVG	OBP	SLG	AOPS	ABR	SB-CS	FA	FR	Rng	Thr	G at Pos	BFW
2001	KC A	15	53	8	16	2	0	0	4	3-0	0	10	.302	.339	.340	74	-2	2-0	.953	1	114	108	S-14	0.1
2002	KC A	20	75	8	17	7	1	0	5	7-1	1	10	.227	.301	.347	64	-4	3-0	.964	4	116	92	S-20	0.2
2003	KC A	158	567	92	163	28	7	17	73	29-3	18	100	.287	.338	.451	94	-5	21-5	.968	3	105	98	*S-158	1.2
Total	3	193	695	108	196	37	8	17	82	39-4	19	120	.282	.334	.432	90	-11	26-5	.967	8	107	98	S-192	1.5

BERROA, GERONIMO Geronimo Emiliano Letta (born Emiliano Letta (Berroa)) B 3.18.1965 Santo Domingo, D.R. BR/TR 6/195# d4.5

Year	Tm Lg	G	AB	R	H	2B	3B	HR	RBI	BB-IB	HP	SO	AVG	OBP	SLG	AOPS	ABR	SB-CS	FA	FR	Rng	Thr	G at Pos	BFW
1989	Atl N	81	136	7	36	4	0	2	9	7-1	0	32	.265	.301	.338	80	-4	0-1	.971	3	135	72	O-34(1-0-33)	-0.2
1990	Atl N	7	4	0	0	0	0	0	0	1-1	0	1	.000	.200	.000	-38	-1	0-0	1.000	-0	86	0	/O-3(LF)	-0.1
1992	Cin N	13	15	2	4	1	0	0	0	2-0	1	1	.267	.389	.333	103	0	0-1	1.000	0	50	1067	/O-3(LF)	0.0
1993	Fla N	14	34	3	4	1	0	0	0	2-0	0	7	.118	.167	.147	-14	-6	0-0	.833	-1	63	181	/O-9(1-0-8)	-0.7
1994	Oak A	96	340	55	104	18	2	13	65	41-0	3	62	.306	.379	.485	134	18	7-2	1.000	3	116	169	D-44,O-42(36-0-7)/1-9	1.6
1995	Oak A	141	546	87	152	22	3	22	88	63-2	1	98	.278	.351	.451	114	11	7-4	.971	2	105	118	D-72,O-71(17-0-54)	0.4
1996	Oak A	153	586	101	170	32	1	36	106	47-0	4	122	.290	.344	.532	120	16	0-3	.980	-3	80	151	D-91,O-61(17-0-54)	0.3
1997	Oak A	73	261	40	81	12	0	16	42	36-2	1	58	.310	.395	.540	144	17	3-2	.986	-3	87	38	O-43(RF),D-32	0.9
	†Bal A	83	300	48	78	13	0	10	48	40-2	3	62	.260	.347	.403	100	1	1-2	.959	-2	95	43	D-42,O-40(RF)	-0.6
	Year	156	561	88	159	25	0	26	90	76-4	4	120	.283	.369	.467	120	18	4-4	.955	-5	91	40	O-83(RF),D-74	0.3
1998	Cle A	20	65	6	13	3	1	0	3	7-0	0	17	.200	.278	.277	44	-5	1-0	1.000	1	104	130	O-14(LF)/D-5	-0.5
	Det A	52	126	17	30	4	1	1	10	17-1	2	27	.238	.338	.310	70	-5	0-1	1.000	-0	101	0	D-37/O-4(2-0-2)	-0.8
	Year	72	191	23	43	7	2	1	13	24-1	2	44	.225	.318	.298	61	-11	1-1	1.000	1	104	113	D-42,O-18(16-0-2)	-1.3
1999	Tor A	22	62	11	12	3	0	1	6	9-0	2	15	.194	.315	.290	55	-4	0-0	1.000	0	111	0	D-17/O-2(LF)	-0.5
2000	LA N	24	31	2	8	0	1	0	5	4-1	0	8	.258	.343	.323	74	-1	0-0	1.000	1	135	0	/O-6(4-0-2),1-2	-0.1
Total	11	779	2506	379	692	113	9	101	382	276-10	17	510	.276	.349	.449	109	37	19-16	.977	0	99	112	D-340,O-332(100-0-243)/1-11	-0.3

BERRY, KEN Allen Kent B 5.10.1941 Kansas City, MO BR/TR 5-11/180# d9.9

Year	Tm Lg	G	AB	R	H	2B	3B	HR	RBI	BB-IB	HP	SO	AVG	OBP	SLG	AOPS	ABR	SB-CS	FA	FR	Rng	Thr	G at Pos	BFW
1962	Chi A	3	6	2	2	0	0	0	0	0-0	0	0	.333	.333	.333	80	0	0-0	1.000	1	93	882	/O-2(1-1-1)	0.1
1963	Chi A	4	5	2	1	0	0	0	0	1-0	0	1	.200	.333	.200	55	0	0-0	.857	0	199	0	/O-2(LF),2	0.0
1964	Chi A	12	32	4	12	1	0	1	4	5-0	0	3	.375	.459	.500	171	3	0-1	1.000	-1	77	0	O-12(CF)	0.2
1965	Chi A	157	472	51	103	17	4	12	42	28-5	5	96	.218	.268	.347	79	-15	4-2	.980	3	110	104	*O-156(CF)	-1.7
1966	Chi A	147	443	50	120	20	2	8	34	28-4	2	63	.271	.316	.379	106	3	7-10	.991	-1	91	132	*O-141(101-13-41)	-0.7
1967	Chi A★	147	485	49	117	14	4	7	41	46-4	3	68	.241	.310	.330	93	-5	9-8	.992	-6	88	97	*O-143(50-38-86)	-2.2
1968	Chi A	153	504	49	127	21	2	7	32	25-1	1	64	.252	.288	.343	90	-7	6-6	.981	-2	98	108	*O-151(0-149-2)	-1.6
1969	Chi A	130	297	25	69	12	2	4	18	24-5	3	50	.232	.296	.327	71	-12	1-2	**1.000**	1	101	121	*O-120(2-116-2)	-1.5
1970	Chi A	141	463	45	128	12	2	7	50	43-10	6	61	.276	.344	.356	90	-5	6-4	.988	-1	102	103	*O-138(CF)	-1.0
1971	Cal A	111	298	29	66	17	0	3	22	18-0	3	33	.221	.269	.309	69	-13	3-2	.988	4	111	91	*O-101(8-94-0)	-1.3
1972	Cal A	119	409	41	118	15	3	5	39	35-2	2	47	.289	.347	.377	122	11	5-3	**1.000**	8	106	**191**	*O-116(CF)	1.8
1973	Cal A	136	415	48	118	11	2	3	36	26-0	1	50	.284	.327	.342	96	-3	1-6	**.997**	4	113	63	*O-129(15-111-4)	-0.4
1974	Mil A	98	267	21	64	9	2	1	24	18-0	3	26	.240	.295	.300	72	-10	3-1	.995	5	107	169	O-82(5-74-5),D-13	-0.7
1975	Cle A	25	40	6	8	1	0	0	1	1-0	1	7	.200	.238	.225	31	-4	0-1	.926	1	111	130	O-18(LF)/D-5	-0.4
Total	14	1383	4136	422	1053	150	23	58	343	298-31	30	569	.255	.308	.344	90	-57	45-46	.989	16	102	115	*O-1311(202-1018-141)/D-18,2	-9.4

BERRY, CHARLIE Charles Francis B 10.18.1902 Phillipsburg, NJ D 9.6.1972 Evanston, IL BR/TR 6/185# d6.15 C5 U21 f-Charlie

Year	Tm Lg	G	AB	R	H	2B	3B	HR	RBI	BB-IB	HP	SO	AVG	OBP	SLG	AOPS	ABR	SB-CS	FA	FR	Rng	Thr	G at Pos	BFW
1925	Phi A	10	14	1	3	1	0	0	3	0	0	2	.214	.214	.286	24	-2	0-0	.900	-1	122	0	/C-4	-0.2
1928	Bos A	80	177	18	46	7	3	1	19	21	1	19	.260	.342	.350	84	-4	1-1	.959	-8	73	132	C-63	-0.9
1929	Bos A	77	207	19	50	11	4	1	21	15	3	29	.242	.302	.348	69	-10	2-6	.983	3	106	130	C-72	-0.5
1930	Bos A	88	256	31	74	9	6	6	35	16	0	22	.289	.331	.441	98	-2	2-0	.988	8	**165**	104	C-85	1.0
1931	Bos A	111	357	41	101	16	2	6	49	29	0	38	.283	.337	.389	96	-3	4-0	.985	-0	116	98	*C-102	0.4
1932	Bos A	10	32	0	6	3	0	0	6	3	0	4	.188	.257	.281	40	-3	0-0	.944	-1	66	105	C-10	-0.3
	Chi A	72	226	33	69	15	6	4	31	21	0	23	.305	.364	.478	124	8	3-0	.981	-2	81	156	C-70	1.0
	Year	82	258	33	75	18	6	4	37	24	0	25	.291	.351	.453	114	5	3-0	**.977**	-3	79	**150**	C-80	0.7
1933	Chi A	86	271	25	69	8	3	2	28	17	1	16	.255	.301	.328	70	-13	0-0	.987	-10	84	76	C-83	-1.7
1934	Phi A	99	269	14	72	10	2	0	34	22	0	23	.268	.323	.320	69	-13	1-0	.987	-2	86	110	C-99	-0.9
1935	Phi A	62	190	14	48	7	3	3	29	10	0	20	.253	.290	.368	70	-10	0-0	.987	-1	72	145	C-56	-0.8
1936	Phi A	13	17	0	1	1	0	0	1	6	0	2	.059	.304	.118	8	-2	0-0	.971	-0	77	117	C-12	-0.2
1938	Phi A	1	2	0	0	0	0	0	0	0	0	0	.000	.000	.000	-99	-1	0-0	1.000	0	0	857	/C	0.0
Total	11	709	2018	196	539	88	29	23	256	160	5	196	.267	.322	.374	83	-55	13-7	.982	-14	101	115	C-657	-3.1

BERRY, CHARLIE Charles Joseph B 9.6.1860 Elizabeth, NJ D 1.22.1940 Phillipsburg, NJ BR/TR 5-11/175# d4.30 s-Charlie

Year	Tm Lg	G	AB	R	H	2B	3B	HR	RBI	BB-IB	HP	SO	AVG	OBP	SLG	AOPS	ABR	SB-CS	FA	FR	Rng	Thr	G at Pos	BFW
1884	Alt U	7	25	2	6	0	0	0		0			.240	.240	.240	45	-2		.862	-5	54	0	/2-7	-0.6
	KC U	29	118	15	29	6	1	1		1			.246	.252	.339	89	-5		.887	1	102	83	2-22/O-8(1-7-0),3	-0.3
	CP U	7	27	4	3	2	0	0		0			.111	.111	.185	-12	-4		.833	-0	95	46	/2-7	-0.4
	Year	43	170	21	38	8	1	1		1			.224	.228	.300	64	-13		.871	-4	92	59	2-36/O-8(1-7-0),3	-1.3

BERRY, CLAUDE Claude Elzy "Admiral" B 2.14.1880 Losantville, IN D 2.1.1974 Richmond, IN BR/TR 5-7/165# d4.22

Year	Tm Lg	G	AB	R	H	2B	3B	HR	RBI	BB-IB	HP	SO	AVG	OBP	SLG	AOPS	ABR	SB-CS	FA	FR	Rng	Thr	G at Pos	BFW
1904	Chi A	3	1	1	0	0	0	0	0	1	0		.000	.500	.000	68	0	0	1.000	0	0	175	/C-3	0.1

Year	Tm Lg	G	AB	R	H	2B	3B	HR	RBI	BB-IB	HP	SO	AVG	OBP	SLG	AOPS	ABR	SB-CS	FA	FR	Rng	Thr	G at Pos	BFW
1906	Phi A	10	30	2	7	0	0	0	2	2	0		.233	.281	.233	60	-1	1	.938	3	*107*	*180*	C-10	0.3
1907	Phi A	8	19	2	4	2	0	0	1	2	0		.211	.286	.316	90	0	0	.944	-2	*84*	*64*	/C-8	-0.1
1914	Pit F	124	411	35	98	18	9	2	36	26	0	50	.238	.284	.341	70	-26	6	.970	1	*103*	*101*	*C-122	-1.5
1915	Pit F	100	292	32	56	11	1	1	26	29	2	42	.192	.269	.247	46	-25	7	.980	6	*116*	*101*	C-99	-1.2
Total	5	245	753	72	165	31	10	3	65	60	2	92	.219	.279	.299	61	-52	14	.971	8	*108*	*104*	C-242	-2.4
BERRY, NEIL Cornelius John B 1.11.1922 Kalamazoo, MI BR/TR 5-10/170# d4.20																								
1948	Det A	87	256	46	68	8	1	0	16	37	0	23	.266	.358	.305	75	-8	1-3	.930	-1	98	113	S-41,2-26	-0.6
1949	Det A	109	329	38	78	9	1	0	18	27	2	24	.237	.299	.271	51	-24	4-2	.970	-8	93	86	2-95/S-4	-2.6
1950	Det A	39	40	9	10	1	0	0	7	6	0	11	.250	.348	.275	59	-2	0-0	.944	2	100	181	S-12/2-2,3	0.0
1951	Det A	67	157	17	36	5	2	0	9	10	0	15	.229	.275	.287	52	-11	4-2	.944	3	112	81	S-38,2-10/3-7	-0.6
1952	Det A	73	189	22	43	4	3	0	13	22	1	19	.228	.311	.280	65	-9	1-3	.965	3	105	78	S-66/3-2	-0.4
1953	StL A	57	99	14	28	1	2	0	11	9	0	10	.283	.343	.333	82	-3	1-2	.825	-3	77	35	3-18,2-15/S-6	-0.5
	Chi A	5	8	1	1	0	0	0	0	1	0	1	.125	.222	.125	-4	-1	0-0	1.000	1	162	63	/2-3	0.0
	Year	62	107	15	29	1	2	0	11	10	0	11	.271	.333	.318	75	-4	1-2	.825	-2	77	35	3-18,2-18/S-6	-0.5
1954	Bal A	5	9	1	1	0	0	0	0	1	0	2	.111	.200	.111	-14	-1	0-0	1.000	0	90	113	/S-5	-0.1
Total	7	442	1087	148	265	28	9	0	74	113	3	105	.244	.317	.286	62	-59	11-12	.949	-4	105	95	S-172,2-151/3-28	-4.8
BERRY, JOE Joseph Howard Jr. "Nig" B 12.31.1894 Philadelphia, PA D 4.29.1976 Philadelphia, PA BB/TR 5-10.5/159# d7.18 f-Joe																								
1921	NY N	9	6	0	2	0	1	0	2	1	0	1	.333	.429	.667	185	1	0-0	.875	0	155	0	/2-7	0.1
1922	NY N	6	0	0	0	0	0	0	0	0	0	0	—	—	—	—	0	0-0	—	0			R	0.0
Total	2	15	6	0	2	0	1	0	2	1	0	1	.333	.429	.667	185	1	0-0	.875	0	155	0	/2-7	0.1
BERRY, JOE Joseph Howard Sr. "Hodge" B 9.10.1872 Wheeling, WV D 3.13.1961 Allenwood, NJ BB/TR 5-9/172# d9.4 s-Joe																								
1902	Phi N	1	4	0	1	0	0	0	1	1	0		.250	.400	.250	101	0	1	1.000	-1	*57*	*0*	/C	-0.1
BERRY, SEAN Sean Robert B 3.22.1966 Santa Monica, CA BR/TR 5-11/210# d9.17																								
1990	KC A	8	23	2	5	1	1	0	4	2-0	0	5	.217	.280	.348	76	-1	0-0	.944	-0	78	148	/3-8	-0.1
1991	KC A	31	60	5	8	3	0	0	1	5-0	1	23	.133	.212	.183	10	-7	0-0	.970	5	134	73	3-30	-0.2
1992	Mon N	24	57	5	19	1	0	1	4	1-0	0	11	.333	.345	.404	112	1	2-1	.879	-3	73	45	3-20	-0.3
1993	Mon N	122	299	50	78	15	2	14	49	41-6	2	70	.261	.348	.465	112	6	12-2	.936	1	101	105	3-96	1.0
1994	Mon N	103	320	43	89	19	2	11	41	32-7	3	50	.278	.347	.453	106	3	14-0	.938	-10	84	78	*3-100	-0.3
1995	Mon N	103	314	38	100	22	1	14	55	25-1	2	53	.318	.367	.529	130	13	3-8	.947	2	97	153	3-83/1-3	1.3
1996	Hou N	132	431	55	121	38	1	17	95	23-1	9	58	.281	.328	.492	123	13	12-6	.922	-1	99	76	*3-110	1.4
1997	†Hou N	96	301	37	77	24	1	8	43	25-1	5	53	.256	.318	.422	97	-1	1-5	.921	-1	102	94	3-85/D-3	-0.3
1998	†Hou N	102	299	48	94	17	1	13	52	31-3	7	50	.314	.387	.508	138	17	3-1	.953	-0	97	105	3-87/D	1.8
1999	Mil N	106	259	26	59	11	1	2	23	17-0	3	50	.228	.281	.301	49	-21	0-0	.989	-3	80	109	1-64	-2.8
2000	Mil N	32	46	1	7	2	0	1	2	4-0	0	13	.152	.220	.261	21	-6	0-1	1.000	-3	36	82	/3-9	-0.9
	Bos A	1	4	0	0	0	0	0	0	0-0	0	2	.000	.000	.000	-97	-1	0-0	—	-1	0	0	/3	-0.2
Total	11	860	2413	310	657	153	10	81	369	206-19	32	438	.272	.334	.445	105	16	47-24	.937	-15	96	98	3-629/1-67,D-4	0.4
BERRY, TOM Thomas Haney B 12.31.1842 Chester, PA D 6.6.1915 Chester, PA 5-6/140# d9.2																								
1871	Ath NA	1	4	0	1	0	0	0	0	0		0	.250	.250	.250	45	0	0-0	.000	-0	0	0	/O(RF)	0.0
BERRYHILL, DAMON Damon Scott B 12.3.1963 South Laguna, CA BB/TR 6/205# d9.5																								
1987	Chi N	12	28	2	5	1	0	0	1	3-0	0	5	.179	.258	.214	26	-3	0-1	.909	-5	80	34	C-11	-0.8
1988	Chi N	95	309	19	80	19	1	7	38	17-5	0	56	.259	.295	.395	93	-3	1-0	.982	-0	113	**149**	C-90	0.2
1989	Chi N	91	334	37	86	13	0	5	41	16-4	2	54	.257	.291	.341	76	-11	1-0	.992	-0	179	90	C-89	-0.6
1990	Chi N	17	53	6	10	4	0	1	9	5-1	0	14	.189	.254	.321	54	-3	0-0	.978	-2	109	37	C-15	-0.5
1991	Chi N	62	159	13	30	7	0	5	14	11-1	1	41	.189	.244	.327	57	-9	1-2	.967	-7	101	61	C-48	-1.6
	Atl N	1	1	0	0	0	0	0	0	0-0	0	1	.000	.000	.000	-94	0	0-0	1.000	0	0	0	/C	0.0
	Year	63	160	13	30	7	0	5	14	11-1	1	42	.188	.243	.325	56	-10	1-2	.967	-7	100	60	C-49	-1.6
1992	†Atl N	101	307	21	70	16	1	10	43	17-4	1	67	.228	.268	.384	79	-9	0-2	.998	-9	83	71	C-84	-1.5
1993	†Atl N	115	335	24	82	18	2	8	43	21-1	2	64	.245	.291	.382	78	-11	0-0	.990	7	105	92	*C-105	0.2
1994	Bos A	82	255	30	67	17	2	6	34	19-0	0	59	.263	.312	.416	82	-7	0-1	.995	-1	70	111	C-67/D-6	-0.4
1995	Cin N	34	82	6	15	3	0	2	11	10-2	0	19	.183	.260	.293	49	-6	0-0	.988	1	109	80	C-29/1	-0.4
1997	†SF N	73	167	17	43	8	0	3	23	20-5	0	29	.257	.335	.359	85	-3	0-0	.990	1	101	112	C-51/1	0.0
Total	10	683	2030	175	488	106	6	47	257	139-23	6	409	.240	.288	.368	77	-65	3-6	.988	-15	111	96	C-590/D-6,1-2	-5.4
BERTE, HARRY Harry Thomas B 5.10.1872 Covington, KY D 5.6.1952 Los Angeles, CA TR 5-10/160# d9.17																								
1903	StL N	4	15	1	5	0	0	0	1	1	0		.333	.375	.333	106	0	0	.778	-3	67	137	/2-3,S	-0.3
BERTELL, DICK Richard George B 11.21.1935 Oak Park, IL D 12.20.1999 Mission Viejo, CA BR/TR 6-0.5/200# d9.22																								
1960	Chi N	5	15	0	2	0	0	0	2	3-0	0	1	.133	.263	.133	17	-2	0-0	1.000	-1	*62*	*263*	/C-5	-0.2
1961	Chi N	92	267	20	73	7	1	2	33	15-3	0	33	.273	.308	.330	70	-12	0-0	.982	2	*106*	*110*	C-90	-0.7
1962	Chi N	77	215	19	65	6	2	2	18	13-5	1	30	.302	.343	.377	90	-3	0-1	.986	-10	*74*	*126*	C-76	-1.0
1963	Chi N	100	322	15	75	7	2	2	14	24-6	0	41	.233	.284	.286	62	-16	0-2	.988	15	***146***	***160***	C-99	0.3
1964	Chi N	112	353	29	84	11	3	4	35	33-8	2	67	.238	.305	.320	74	-12	2-1	.981	-6	*122*	*110*	*C-110	-1.3
1965	Chi N	34	84	6	18	2	0	0	7	11-2	0	10	.214	.302	.238	54	-5	0-0	.981	2	*90*	*201*	C-34	-0.1
	SF N	22	48	1	9	1	0	0	3	7-3	0	5	.188	.291	.208	42	-3	0-0	.992	2	*120*	*49*	C-22	-0.1
	Year	56	132	7	27	3	0	0	10	18-5	0	15	.205	.298	.227	50	-8	0-0	.986	4	*101*	*144*	C-56	-0.2
1967	Chi N	2	6	1	1	0	1	0	0	0-0	0	1	.167	.167	.500	80	0	0-0	1.000	-0	*86*	*173*	/C-2	0.0
Total	7	444	1310	91	327	34	9	10	112	106-27	3	188	.250	.305	.312	70	-53	2-4	.985	3	*114*	*131*	C-438	-3.1
BERTHRONG, HARRY Henry W. B 1.1.1844 Mumford, NY D 4.28.1928 Chelsea, MA TR 5-6.5/140# d5.5																								
1871	Oly NA	17	73	17	17	1	1	0	8	4		2	.233	.273	.274	61	-3	3-1	.806	-4	0	0	O-12(11-1-0)/2-5,C	-0.4
BERTOIA, RENO Reno Peter B 1.8.1935 St.Vito Udine, Italy BR/TR 5-11.5/185# d9.22																								
1953	Det A	1	1	0	0	0	0	0	0	0	0	1	.000	.000	.000	-99	0	0-0	.500	-1	0	0	/2	-0.1
1954	Det A	54	37	13	6	2	0	1	2	5	0	9	.162	.262	.297	54	-2	1-0	.969	8	175	109	2-15/3-8,S-3	0.6
1955	Det A	38	68	13	14	2	1	1	10	5-1	0	11	.206	.253	.309	54	-5	0-0	.923	3	113	196	3-14/2-6,S-5	-0.1
1956	Det A	22	66	7	12	2	0	1	5	6-0	1	12	.182	.260	.258	37	-6	0-0	.982	5	111	122	2-18/3-2	0.0
1957	Det A	97	295	28	81	16	2	4	28	19-2	4	43	.275	.326	.383	91	-4	2-3	.953	-14	82	60	3-83/S-7,2-2	-1.9
1958	Det A	86	240	28	56	6	0	6	27	20-2	2	35	.233	.290	.333	68	-10	5-2	.950	4	104	100	3-68/S-5,O(LF)	-0.7
1959	Was A	90	308	33	73	10	0	8	29	29-3	1	48	.237	.302	.347	79	-9	2-5	.971	-5	102	84	2-71/3-5,S	-1.1
1960	Was A	121	460	44	122	17	7	4	45	26-2	8	58	.265	.313	.359	83	-12	3-5	.961	-4	101	81	*3-112,2-21	-1.8
1961	Min A	35	104	17	22	2	0	1	8	20-1	0	12	.212	.333	.260	59	-5	0-0	.900	-5	88	48	3-32	-1.1
	KC A	39	120	12	29	2	0	0	13	9-0	0	15	.242	.286	.258	48	-9	1-0	.942	5	119	94	3-29/2-6	-0.3
	Det A	24	46	6	10	1	0	1	4	3-0	0	8	.217	.265	.304	50	-3	2-0	.931	-1	84	109	3-13/2-7,S	-0.4
	Year	98	270	35	61	5	0	2	25	32-1	0	35	.226	.302	.267	53	-18	3-0	.923	-2	100	76	3-74,2-13/S	-1.8
1962	Det A	5	0	3	0	0	0	0	0	0-0	0	0	—	—	—	—	0	0-0	1.000	-0	163	0	/2S3	0.0
Total	10	612	1745	204	425	60	10	27	171	142-11	16	252	.244	.303	.336	73	-65	16-15	.949	-7	98	84	3-367,2-148/S-23,O(LF)	-6.9
BESCHER, BOB Robert Henry B 2.25.1884 London, OH D 11.29.1942 London, OH BB/TL 6-1/200# d9.5																								
1908	Cin N	32	114	16	31	5	5	0	17	9	2		.272	.336	.404	140	5	10	1.000	3	46	190	O-32(LF)	0.6
1909	Cin N	124	446	73	107	17	6	1	34	56	8		.240	.335	.312	102	3	**54**	.953	0	85	105	*O-117(115-0-2)	-0.4
1910	Cin N	150	589	95	147	20	10	4	48	81	4	75	.250	.344	.338	104	4	**70**	.947	2	108	81	*O-150(LF)	-0.3
1911	Cin N	153	599	106	165	32	10	1	45	102	5	78	.275	.385	.367	115	18	**81**	.954	-8	87	95	*O-153(LF)	0.3
1912	Cin N	145	548	**120**	154	29	11	4	38	83	6	61	.281	.381	.396	116	16	**67**	.963	2	**110**	68	*O-143(LF)	1.1
1913	Cin N	141	511	86	132	22	11	1	37	**94**	3	68	.258	.377	.350	109	11	38-23	.968	4	100	119	*O-138(LF)	1.0
1914	NY N	135	512	82	138	23	4	6	35	45	6	48	.270	.336	.365	112	8	36	.960	1	103	90	*O-126(15-111-0)	0.0
1915	StL N	130	486	71	128	15	7	4	34	52	6	53	.263	.342	.348	109	6	27-19	.971	-2	100	78	*O-129(128-0-1)	-0.2
1916	StL N	151	561	78	132	24	8	6	43	60	6	50	.235	.316	.339	102	2	39-12	.953	-0	98	114	*O-151(151-2-1)	0.0
1917	StL N	42	110	10	17	1	1	1	8	20	1	13	.155	.290	.209	56	-5	3	.984	-5	88	0	O-32(27-4-0)	-1.3
1918	Cle A	25	60	12	20	2	1	0	6	17	1	5	.333	.487	.400	153	6	3	.969	0	92	135	O-17(0-3-14)	0.5
Total	11	1228	4536	749	1171	190	74	28	345	619	48	451	.258	.353	.351	109	74	428-54	.960	-3	97	94	*O-1188(1052-120-18)	1.3

Year	Tm Lg	G	AB	R	H	2B	3B	HR	RBI	BB-IB	HP	SO	AVG	OBP	SLG	AOPS	ABR	SB-CS	FA	FR	Rng	Thr	G at Pos	BFW
BESTICK, WILLIAM William B New York, NY d6.10																								
1872	Eck NA	4	14	0	4	0	0	0	0	0		0	.286	.286	.286	90	0	0-0	.760	-2			/C-4,S	-0.1
BESWICK, JIM James William B 2.12.1958 Wilkinsburg, PA BB/TR 6-1/180# d8.9																								
1978	SD N	17	20	2	1	0	0	0	0	1-0	0	7	.050	.095	.050	-63	-4	0-0	1.000	-0	99	0	/O-6(0-2-4)	-0.5
BETCHER, FRANK Franklin Lyle (born Franklin Lyle Bettger) B 2.15.1888 Philadelphia, PA D 11.27.1981 Wynnewood, PA BB/TR 5-11/173# d5.21																								
1910	StL N	35	89	7	18	2	0	0	6	7	2	14	.202	.276	.225	48	-6	1	.928	0	105	72	S-12/3-7,2-6,O-2(1-1-0)	-0.6
BETEMIT, WILSON Wilson B 11.2.1981 Santo Domingo, D.R. BB/TR 6-2/155# d9.18																								
2001	Atl N	8	3	1	0	0	0	0	0	2-0	0	3	.000	.400	.000	17	0	1-0	—	-0	0	0	/S	0.0
BETHEA, BILL William Lamar "Spot" B 1.1.1942 Houston, TX BR/TR 6/175# d9.13																								
1964	Min A	10	30	4	5	1	0	0	2	4-0	0	4	.167	.265	.200	31	-3	0-0	1.000	-1	89	138	/2-7,S-3	-0.3
BETTENCOURT, LARRY Lawrence Joseph B 9.22.1905 Newark, CA D 9.15.1978 New Orleans, LA BR/TR 5-11/195# d6.2																								
1928	StL A	67	159	30	45	9	4	4	24	22	2	19	.283	.377	.465	117	4	2-1	.946	-6	88	59	3-41/O-2(RF),C	0.0
1931	StL A	74	206	27	53	9	2	3	26	31	1	35	.257	.357	.364	87	-3	4-3	.963	-1	94	118	O-58(2-0-56)	-0.7
1932	StL A	27	30	4	4	1	0	1	3	7	0	6	.133	.297	.267	45	-2	1-0	1.000	0	122	0	/O-4(2-0-3),3-2	-0.2
Total	3	168	395	61	102	19	6	8	53	60	3	60	.258	.360	.397	95	-1	7-4	.966	-6	95	111	/O-64(4-0-61),3-43,C	-0.9
BETZEL, BRUNO Christian Frederick Albert John Henry David B 12.6.1894 Chattanooga, OH D 2.7.1965 W.Hollywood, FL BR/TR 5-9/158# d9.3																								
1914	StL N	7	9	2	0	0	0	0	0	1	0	1	.000	.100	.000	-70	-2	0	1.000	1	157	0	/2-4,3	-0.1
1915	StL N	117	367	42	92	12	4	0	27	18	3	48	.251	.291	.305	80	-9	10-13	.937	4	112	74	*3-105/2-3,S-2	-0.6
1916	StL N	142	510	49	119	15	11	1	37	39	0	77	.233	.288	.312	85	-10	22-16	.960	**29**	**112**	132	*2-113,3-33/O-7(1-2-4)	2.3
1917	StL N	106	328	24	71	4	3	1	17	20	2	47	.216	.266	.256	62	-15	9	.962	12	113	138	2-75,O-23(12-1-9)/3-4	-0.4
1918	StL N	76	230	18	51	6	7	0	13	12	0	16	.222	.260	.309	76	-8	8	.914	-2	103	60	3-34,O-21(1-7-15),2-10	-1.2
Total	5	448	1444	135	333	37	25	2	94	90	5	189	.231	.278	.295	76	-44	49-29	.956	44	113	132	2-205,3-177/O-51(14-10-28),S-2	-0.0
BEVACQUA, KURT Kurt Anthony B 1.23.1947 Miami Beach, FL BR/TR 6-1/185# d6.22 OF Total (47-LF 25-RF)																								
1971	Cle A	55	137	9	28	3	1	3	13	4-1	0	28	.204	.222	.307	46	-10	0-0	.971	-3	91	53	2-36/O-5(2-0-3),3-3,S-2	-1.3
1972	Cle A	19	35	2	4	0	0	1	1	3-1	0	10	.114	.184	.200	14	-4	0-0	.900	0	65	0	O-11(8-0-3)/3	-0.5
1973	KC A	99	276	39	71	8	3	2	40	25-1	1	42	.257	.317	.330	78	-8	2-3	.935	-10	81	92	3-40,2-16,D-16,O-10(5-0-5)/1-9	-2.1
1974	Pit N	18	35	1	4	1	0	0	0	2-1	0	10	.114	.162	.143	-15	-6	0-0	.955	-2	71	0	/3-8,O(LF)	-0.8
	KC A	39	90	10	19	0	0	0	3	9-0	1	20	.211	.290	.211	43	-6	1-1	.987	-3	54	154	1-14,3-13/2-7,S-2,D-3	-1.1
1975	Mil A	104	258	30	59	14	0	2	24	26-1	1	45	.229	.300	.306	72	-9	3-4	.948	-6	90	108	3-60,2-32/S-5,1-3,D	-1.4
1976	Mil A	12	7	3	1	0	0	0	0	0-0	0	0	.143	.143	.143	-17	-1	0-0	1.000	1	257	0	/2-2,D-3	0.0
1977	Tex A	39	96	13	32	7	2	5	28	6-1	0	13	.333	.365	.604	159	7	0-1	1.000	-1	61	0	O-14(6-0-8),3-11/1-5,2-5,D-3	0.6
1978	Tex A	90	248	21	55	12	0	6	30	18-0	0	31	.222	.271	.343	72	-10	1-2	.877	-5	95	88	3-49,D-16,2-13/1	-1.6
1979	SD N	114	297	23	75	12	4	1	34	38-2	0	25	.253	.331	.330	88	-4	2-5	.954	2	105	135	3-64,2-16/1-8,O-8(LF)	-0.5
1980	SD N	62	71	4	19	6	1	0	12	6-0	0	1	.268	.321	.380	102	0	1-1	.929	-0	109	127	3-13/O-4(LF),2-2,1	0.0
	Pit N	22	43	1	7	1	0	0	4	6-0	1	7	.163	.280	.186	32	-4	0-0	.958	1	117	90	/3-9,1-2	-0.4
	Year	84	114	5	26	7	1	0	16	12-0	1	8	.228	.305	.307	75	-4	1-1	.947	0	114	105	3-22/O-4(LF),1-3,2-2	-0.4
1981	Pit N	29	27	2	7	1	0	1	4	4-0	0	6	.259	.333	.407	112	1	0-0	.941	1	128	214	/2-4,3-2	0.2
1982	SD N	64	123	15	31	9	0	0	24	17-4	0	22	.252	.333	.325	93	0	2-0	.989	-1	94	72	1-30/O-3(2-0-1),3	-0.3
1983	SD N	74	156	17	38	7	0	2	24	18-1	0	33	.244	.320	.327	83	-3	0-3	.995	1	89	93	1-27,3-12,O-12(9-0-3)	-0.5
1984	†SD N	59	80	7	16	3	0	1	9	14-1	1	19	.200	.326	.275	71	-3	0-0	1.000	-2	87	114	1-20,3-10/O-3(1-0-2)	-0.6
1985	SD N	71	138	17	33	6	0	3	25	25-5	0	17	.239	.349	.348	99	1	0-0	.946	0	93	145	3-33/1-9,O(LF)	0.0
Total	15	970	2117	214	499	90	11	27	275	221-19	5	329	.236	.305	.327	78	-59	12-20	.938	-28	94	121	3-329,2-133,1-129/O-72L,D-42,S-9	-10.3
BEVAN, HAL Harold Joseph B 11.15.1930 New Orleans, LA D 10.5.1968 New Orleans, LA BR/TR 6-2/198# d4.24																								
1952	Bos A	1	1	0	0	0	0	0	0	0	0	0	.000	.000	.000	-93	0	0-0	—	-0	0	0	/3	0.0
	Phi A	8	17	1	6	0	0	0	4	0	0	1	.353	.353	.353	91	0	2-0	1.000	0	105	0	/3-6	0.0
	Year	9	18	1	6	0	0	0	4	0	0	1	.333	.333	.333	81	-1	2-0	1.000	0	102	0	/3-7	0.0
1955	KC A	3	3	0	0	0	0	0	0	0-0	0	0	.000	.000	.000	-99	-1	0-0	1.000	-0	0	0	/3	-0.1
1961	Cin N	3	3	1	1	0	0	1	1	0-0	0	2	.333	.333	1.333	311	1	0-0	—	0			H	0.1
Total	3	15	24	2	7	0	0	1	5	0-0	0	3	.292	.292	.417	89	0	2-0	1.000	0	97	0	/3-8	0.0
BEVILLE, MONTE Henry Monte B 2.24.1875 Dublin, IN D 1.24.1955 Grand Rapids, MI BL/TR 5-11/180# d4.24																								
1903	NY A	82	258	23	50	14	1	0	29	16	4		.194	.252	.256	49	-15	4	.960	-7	*105*	*81*	C-75/1-3	-1.6
1904	NY A	9	22	2	6	2	0	0	2	2	0		.273	.333	.364	115	1	0	.906	-2	56	0	/1-4,C-3	-0.1
	Det A	54	174	14	36	5	1	0	13	8	2		.207	.250	.247	59	-8	2	.957	-4	*86*	*82*	C-30,1-24	-1.1
	Year	63	196	16	42	7	1	0	15	10	2		.214	.260	.260	66	-7	2	.950	-5	*86*	*83*	C-33,1-28	-1.2
Total	2	145	454	39	92	21	2	0	44	26	6		.203	.255	.258	56	-22	6	.957	-12	*99*	*82*	C-108/1-31	-2.8
BIANCALANA, BUDDY Roland Americo B 2.2.1960 Larkspur, CA BB/TR 5-11/160# d9.12																								
1982	KC A	3	2	0	1	0	1	0	0	1-0	0	0	.500	.667	1.500	474	1	0-0	1.000	2	199	137	/S-3	0.3
1983	KC A	6	15	2	3	0	0	0	0	0-0	0	7	.200	.200	.200	10	-2	1-0	.914	2	138	97	/S-6	0.1
1984	†KC A	66	134	18	26	6	1	2	9	6-0	0	44	.194	.229	.299	44	-11	1-2	.946	-2	116	85	S-33,2-29/D	-0.9
1985	†KC A	81	138	21	26	5	1	1	6	17-0	0	34	.188	.277	.261	48	-10	1-4	.961	4	110	98	S-74/2-4,D-2	-0.1
1986	KC A	100	190	24	46	4	4	2	8	15-0	0	50	.242	.298	.337	71	-8	5-1	.946	-5	97	102	S-89,2-12	-0.6
1987	KC A	37	47	4	10	1	0	1	7	1-0	0	10	.213	.229	.298	37	-4	0-0	.886	-3	102	73	S-22,2-12/D	-0.6
	Hou N	18	24	1	1	0	0	0	0	1-0	0	12	.042	.080	.042	-69	-6	0-0	.889	-2	78	53	S-16/2-3	-0.8
Total	6	311	550	70	113	16	7	6	30	41-0	0	157	.205	.261	.293	50	-40	8-7	.945	-4	106	95	S-243/2-60,D-4	-2.6
BIANCO, TOMMY Thomas Anthony B 12.16.1952 Rockville Centre, NY BB/TR 5-11/190# d5.28																								
1975	Mil A	18	34	6	6	1	0	0	0	3-0	1	7	.176	.263	.206	34	-3	0-0	.941	-0	108	0	/3-7,1-5,D-2	-0.4
BIASATTI, HANK Henry Arcado B 1.14.1922 Beano, Italy D 4.20.1996 Dearborn, MI BL/TL 5-11/175# d4.23																								
1949	Phi A	21	24	6	2	2	0	0	2	8	0	5	.083	.313	.167	30	-2	0-0	.979	-1	59	78	/1-8	-0.3
BICHETTE, DANTE Alphonse Dante B 11.18.1963 W.Palm Beach, FL BR/TR 6-3/225# d9.5																								
1988	Cal A	21	46	1	12	2	0	0	8	0-0	0	7	.261	.240	.304	59	-3	0-0	.979	2	107	261	O-21(3-17-5)	-0.1
1989	Cal A	48	138	13	29	7	0	3	15	6-0	0	24	.210	.240	.326	60	-8	3-0	.990	6	116	232	O-40(12-6-23)/D	-0.2
1990	Cal A	109	349	40	89	15	1	15	53	16-1	3	79	.255	.292	.433	103	-1	5-2	.965	2	93	195	*O-105(51-16-53)	-0.1
1991	Mil A	134	445	53	106	18	3	15	59	22-4	1	107	.238	.272	.393	85	-12	14-8	.976	9	109	160	*O-127(1-7-120)/3	-0.6
1992	Mil A	112	387	37	111	27	2	5	41	16-3	3	74	.287	.318	.406	104	1	18-7	.990	-5	90	87	*O-101(0-1-101)/D-4	-0.5
1993	Col N	141	538	93	167	43	5	21	89	28-2	7	99	.310	.348	.526	113	10	14-8	.973	9	112	137	*O-137(0-9-134)	1.3
1994	Col N★	116	484	74	147	33	2	27	95	19-3	4	70	.304	.334	.548	107	5	21-8	.991	-1	94	116	*O-116(RF)	0.0
1995	†Col N★	139	579	102	**197**	38	2	**40**	**128**	22-5	4	96	.340	.364	**.620**	120	17	13-9	.986	-8	82	103	*O-136(120-0-35)	0.3
1996	Col N★	159	633	114	198	39	3	31	141	45-4	6	105	.313	.359	.531	107	7	31-12	.967	-12	87	49	*O-156(19-0-138)	-1.0
1997	Col N	151	561	81	173	31	2	26	118	30-1	3	90	.308	.343	.510	98	-1	6-5	.987	-6	89	46	*O-139(128-0-16)/D-5	-1.3
1998	Col N★	161	662	97	**219**	48	2	22	122	28-2	1	76	.331	.357	.509	103	4	14-4	.965	6	99	138	*O-156(134-0-29)/D	0.5
1999	Col N	151	593	104	177	38	2	34	133	54-3	2	84	.298	.354	.541	97	-2	6-6	.951	0	87	193	*O-144(LF)/D-2	-0.8
2000	Cin N	125	461	67	136	27	2	16	76	41-3	4	69	.295	.353	.466	104	2	5-2	.969	3	101	148	*O-121(RF)	0.0
	Bos A	30	114	13	33	5	0	7	14	8-0	0	22	.289	.336	.518	109	1	0-0	—	0	0	0	D-30	-0.1
2001	Bos A	107	391	45	112	30	1	12	49	20-1	3	76	.286	.325	.460	103	1	2-2	.955	-2	85	137	O-53(37-0-16),D-46	-0.6
Total	14	1704	6381	934	1906	401	27	274	1141	355-32	41	1078	.299	.336	.499	104	21	152-73	.974	2	95	128	*O-1552(649-56-907)/D-89,3	-3.2
BIECHER, ED Edward "Scrap Iron" B 5.1876 , IN D 7.15.1939 St.Louis, MO d9.26																								
1897	StL N	3	12	1	4	0	0	0	1	0	0		.333	.333	.333	78	0	1	1.000	-0	0	0	/O-3(LF)	-0.1
1898	Cle N	8	25	1	5	2	0	0	0	0	0		.200	.200	.280	38	-2	0	.846	-1	121	0	/O-8(CF)	-0.3
Total	2	11	37	2	9	2	0	0	1	0	0		.243	.243	.297	51	-2	1	.895	-1	83	0	/O-11(3-8-0)	-0.4
BIELASKI, OSCAR Oscar B 3.21.1847 Washington, DC D 11.8.1911 Washington, DC BR/TR 5-10.5/170# d4.24																								
1872	Nat NA	10	46	13	8	0	0	0	3	0		0	.174	.174	.174	6	-6	0-0	.737	-1	0	0	O-10(RF)	-0.4
1873	Was NA	38	173	35	49	3	2	0	20	4		6	.283	.299	.324	88	-2	1-3	.755	2	128	0	*O-38(2-0-36)	0.1
1874	Bal NA	43	187	24	45	0	0	0	8	2		4	.241	.249	.241	58	-9	3-1	.806	5	156	72	*O-43(0-1-43)/1	-0.1

Year	Tm Lg	G	AB	R	H	2B	3B	HR	RBI	BB-IB	HP	SO	AVG	OBP	SLG	AOPS	ABR	SB-CS	FA	FR	Rng	Thr	G at Pos	BFW
1875	Chi NA	51	201	21	48	1	0	0	11	2		5	.239	.246	.244	70	-6	5-5	.748	-1	140	130	*O-51(4-0-48)	-0.4
1876	Chi N	32	139	24	29	3	0	0	10	2		3	.209	.220	.230	45	-9		.763	-3	76	106	O-32(RF)	-1.0
Total	4 NA	142	607	93	150	4	2	0	42	8		15	.247	.257	.260	66	-23	9-9	.000	5	132	68	O-142(6-1-137)/1	-0.8
BIERBAUER, LOU Louis W. B 9.28.1865 Erie, PA D 1.31.1926 Erie, PA BL/TR 5-8/140# d4.17 ▲																								
1886	Phi AA	137	522	56	118	17	5	2	47	21	0		.226	.256	.289	70	-20	19	.910	-5	**104**	85	*2-133/C-4,S-2,P-2	-1.7
1887	Phi AA	126	530	74	144	19	7	1	82	13	0		.272	.289	.340	75	-20	40	.921	-7	99	87	*2-126/P	-1.8
1888	Phi AA	134	535	83	143	20	9	0	80	25	1		.267	.301	.338	105	2	34	.916	22	**110**	95	*2-121,3-13/P	2.6
1889	Phi AA	130	549	80	167	27	7	7	105	29	4	30	.304	.344	.417	118	11	17	.941	36	107	127	*2-130/C	4.3
1890	Bro P	**133**	589	128	180	31	11	7	99	40	0	15	.306	.350	.431	102	-2	16	.931	21	**112**	113	*2-133	1.9
1891	Pit N	121	500	60	103	13	6	1	47	28	3	19	.206	.252	.262	51	-33	12	.929	-0	98	82	*2-121	-2.6
1892	Pit N	**152**	649	81	153	20	9	8	65	25	0	29	.236	.264	.331	79	-20	11	.950	29	**117**	102	*2-152	1.4
1893	Pit N	128	528	84	150	19	11	4	94	36	4	12	.284	.335	.384	93	-8	11	**.959**	14	105	123	*2-128	1.0
1894	Pit N	131	528	87	160	20	13	3	109	26	2	10	.303	.338	.407	80	-20	19	.939	6	109	93	*2-131	-0.6
1895	Pit N	118	470	54	122	13	11	1	71	19	2	8	.260	.291	.340	66	-26	18	.947	9	**108**	102	*2-118	-0.9
1896	Pit N	59	258	33	74	10	6	0	39	5	0	7	.287	.300	.372	80	-9	7	.966	8	108	127	2-59	0.1
1897	StL N	12	46	1	10	0	0	0	1	0	0		.217	.217	.217	15	-6	2	.921	-1	97	91	2-12	-0.6
1898	StL N	4	9	0	0	0	0	0	0	1	0		.000	.100	.000	-69	-2	0	.429	-1	83	0	/2-2,S3	-0.3
Total	13	1385	5713	821	1524	209	95	34	839	268	16	130	.267	.301	.354	84	-153	206	.935	130	107	102	*2-1366/3-14,C-5,P-4,S-3	2.8
BIERMAN, CHARLIE Charles S. B 1845 Hoboken, NJ D 8.4.1879 Hoboken, NJ 6/180# d6.21																								
1871	Kek NA	1	2	0	0	0	0	0	0	1		0	.000	.333	.000	6	0	0-0	.818	-0	0	0	/1	0.0
BIESER, STEVE Steven Ray B 8.4.1967 Perryville, MO BL/TR 5-10/170# d4.1																								
1997	NY N	47	69	16	17	3	0	0	4	7-1	4	20	.246	.346	.290	72	-2	2-3	1.000	2	112	287	O-21(9-13-1)/C-2	-0.1
1998	Pit N	13	11	2	3	1	0	0	1	2-0	0	2	.273	.385	.364	97	0	0-0	—	-0	0	0	/O(LF)	0.0
Total	2	60	80	18	20	4	0	0	5	9-1	4	22	.250	.351	.300	76	-2	2-3	1.000	2	109	279	/O-22(10-13-1),C-2	-0.1
BIGBEE, CARSON Carson Lee "Skeeter" B 3.31.1895 Waterloo, OR D 10.17.1964 Portland, OR BL/TR 5-9/157# d8.25 b-Lyle																								
1916	Pit N	43	164	17	41	3	6	0	3	7	1	14	.250	.285	.341	91	-3	8	.946	-5	85	85	2-23,O-19(LF)/3	-0.9
1917	Pit N	133	469	46	112	11	6	0	21	37	5	16	.239	.301	.288	79	-11	19	.961	-4	107	64	*O-107(85-5-17),2-16/S-2	-2.3
1918	Pit N	92	310	47	79	11	3	1	19	42	0	10	.255	.344	.319	99	2	19	.958	0	93	129	O-92(87-0-5)	-0.3
1919	Pit N	125	478	61	132	11	4	2	27	37	3	26	.276	.332	.328	95	-2	31	.971	15	**119**	128	*O-124(50-75-0)	0.6
1920	Pit N	137	550	78	154	19	15	4	32	45	6	28	.280	.341	.391	106	4	31-15	.971	3	103	104	*O-133(128-6-0)	0.3
1921	Pit N	147	632	100	204	23	17	3	42	41	0	19	.323	.364	.427	106	5	21-20	.977	12	105	142	*O-146(133-13-0)	0.3
1922	Pit N	150	614	113	215	29	15	5	99	56	1	13	.350	.405	.471	124	23	24-15	.956	14	**111**	**146**	*O-150(146-4-0)	2.3
1923	Pit N	123	499	79	149	18	7	0	54	43	1	15	.299	.355	.363	88	-8	10-9	.990	8	111	105	*O-122(LF)	-1.1
1924	Pit N	89	282	42	74	4	1	0	15	26	3	12	.262	.331	.284	65	-13	15-7	.943	1	101	118	O-75(LF)	-1.7
1925	†Pit N	66	126	31	30	7	0	0	8	7	0	8	.238	.278	.294	43	-11	2-2	.942	1	106	105	O-42(30-2-10)	-1.2
1926	Pit N	42	68	15	15	3	1	2	4	3	1	0	.221	.264	.382	69	-3	2	.966	1	101	175	O-21(17-4-0)	-0.4
Total	11	1147	4192	629	1205	139	75	17	324	344	21	161	.287	.345	.369	96	-17	182-68	.966	44	107	119	*O-1031(892-109-32)/2-39,S-2,3	-4.4
BIGBEE, LYLE Lyle Randolph "Al" B 8.22.1893 Sweet Home, OR D 8.5.1942 Portland, OR BL/TR 6/180# d4.15 b-Carson ▲																								
1920	Phi A	38	75	5	14	2	0	1	8	9	1	12	.187	.282	.253	42	-6	1-0	.857	-3	85	0	O-13(11-0-1),P-12	-0.8
1921	Pit N	5	2	0	0	0	0	0	0	0	0	1	.000	.000	.000	-97	0	0-0	1.000	-0	96	0	/P-5	0.0
Total	2	43	77	5	14	2	0	1	8	9	1	13	.182	.276	.247	39	-6	1-0	1.000	-3	103	0	/P-17,O-13(11-0-1)	-0.8
BIGBIE, LARRY Larry Robert B 11.4.1977 Hobart, IN BL/TL 6-4/190# d6.23																								
2001	Bal A	47	131	15	30	6	0	2	11	17-1	0	42	.229	.318	.321	73	-5	4-1	1.000	-2	91	91	O-40(5-18-17)	-0.6
2002	Bal A	16	34	1	6	1	0	0	3	1-0	0	11	.176	.194	.206	9	-5	1-0	1.000	0	117	0	O-12(6-1-6)	-0.4
2003	Bal A	83	287	43	87	15	1	9	31	29-3	0	60	.303	.365	.456	120	9	7-1	.994	2	102	105	O-80(76-2-5)	0.8
Total	3	146	452	59	123	22	1	11	45	47-4	0	113	.272	.339	.398	98	-1	12-2	.996	1	100	94	O-132(87-21-28)	-0.2
BIGELOW, ELLIOT Elliot Allardice "Babe" or "Gilly" B 10.13.1897 Tarpon Springs, FL D 8.10.1933 Tampa, FL BL/TL 5-11/185# d4.18																								
1929	Bos A	100	211	23	60	16	0	1	26	23	1	18	.284	.357	.374	91	-2	1-4	.944	-2	85	125	O-59(2-2-55)	-0.8
BIGGIO, CRAIG Craig Alan B 12.14.1965 Smithtown, NY BR/TR 5-11/180# d6.26 OF Total (26-LF 189-CF 2-RF)																								
1988	Hou N	50	123	14	26	6	1	3	5	7-2	0	29	.211	.254	.350	74	-5	6-1	.991	6	67	121	C-50	0.5
1989	Hou N	134	443	64	114	21	2	13	60	49-8	6	64	.257	.336	.402	115	9	21-3	.990	-20	66	67	*C-125/O-5(1-4-0)	0.0
1990	Hou N	150	555	53	153	24	2	4	42	53-1	3	79	.276	.342	.348	93	-4	25-11	.985	-5	78	104	*C-113,O-50(17-34-2)	-0.2
1991	Hou N★	149	546	79	161	23	4	4	46	53-3	2	71	.295	.358	.374	113	10	19-6	.990	-10	89	84	*C-139/2-3,O-2(1-1-0)	1.1
1992	Hou N★	**162**	613	96	170	32	3	6	39	94-9	7	95	.277	.378	.369	118	20	38-15	.984	-27	84	84	*2-161	0.0
1993	Hou N	155	610	98	175	41	5	21	64	77-7	10	93	.287	.373	.474	130	29	15-17	.982	-0	95	101	*2-155	3.3
1994	Hou N★	114	437	88	139	**44**	5	6	56	62-1	8	58	.318	.411	.483	139	30	**39**-4	.988	-4	98	89	*2-113	3.7
1995	Hou N★	141	553	**123**	167	30	2	22	77	80-1	**22**	85	.302	.406	.483	145	41	33-8	.986	-6	100	82	*2-141	4.5
1996	Hou N★	**162**	605	113	174	24	4	15	75	75-0	**27**	72	.288	.386	.415	122	24	25-7	.988	-2	96	70	*2-162	3.2
1997	†Hou N★	**162**	619	**146**	191	37	8	22	81	84-6	**34**	107	.309	.415	.501	145	46	47-10	.979	25	**111**	116	*2-160/D	**8.3**
1998	†Hou N★	160	646	123	210	**51**	2	20	88	64-6	23	113	.325	.403	.503	141	42	50-8	.980	-0	102	98	*2-159/D	5.6
1999	†Hou N	160	639	123	188	**56**	0	16	73	88-9	11	107	.294	.386	.457	115	19	28-14	.985	19	100	**124**	*2-155/O-6(LF),D-2	4.3
2000	Hou N	101	377	67	101	13	5	8	35	61-3	16	73	.268	.388	.393	94	-1	12-2	.987	-5	99	87	*2-100	0.1
2001	†Hou N	155	617	118	180	35	3	20	70	66-4	**28**	100	.292	.382	.455	110	13	7-4	.984	-16	90	96	*2-154/D	0.4
2002	Hou N	145	577	96	146	36	3	15	58	50-2	17	111	.253	.330	.404	91	-9	16-2	.988	-4	88	96	*2-142/O(LF)	-0.4
2003	Hou N	153	628	102	166	44	2	15	62	57-3	**27**	116	.264	.350	.412	94	-3	8-4	.997	-5	94	111	*O-150(CF)	-0.6
Total	16	2253	8588	1503	2461	517	51	210	931	1020-65	241	1373	.287	.375	.432	117	261	389-116	.984	-54	97	95	*2-1605,C-427,O-214C/D-5	33.8
BIGLER, PETE Ivan Edward B 12.13.1892 Bradford, OH D 4.1.1975 Coldwater, MI BR/TR 5-9/150# d5.6																								
1917	StL A	1	0	0	0	0	0	0	0	0	0	0	—	—	—	—	0	0	—	0			/R	0.0
BIGNELL, GEORGE George William B 7.18.1858 Taunton, MA D 1.16.1925 Providence, RI 5-9/160# d9.27																								
1884	Mil U	4	9	4	2	0	0	0		1			.222	.300	.222	112	0		.951	1			/C-4	0.1
BIITTNER, LARRY Lawrence David B 7.27.1945 Pocahontas, IA BL/TL 6-2/205# d7.17																								
1970	Was A	2	2	0	0	0	0	0	0	0-0	0	0	.000	.000	.000	-99	-1	0-0	—	0			H	-0.1
1971	Was A	66	171	12	44	4	1	0	16	16-3	1	20	.257	.323	.292	80	-4	1-0	.940	1	95	227	O-41(7-0-38)/1-3	-0.6
1972	Tex A	137	382	34	99	18	1	3	31	29-5	2	37	.259	.313	.335	98	-1	1-3	.991	1	126	82	1-65,O-65(28-8-32)	-0.9
1973	Tex A	83	258	19	65	8	2	1	12	20-0	1	21	.252	.307	.310	78	-8	1-0	.980	3	93	177	O-57(19-2-38),1-20/D-3	-0.9
1974	Mon N	18	26	2	7	1	0	0	3	0-0	0	2	.269	.269	.308	58	-2	0-0	1.000	1	107	444	/O-4(LF)	-0.1
1975	Mon N	121	346	34	109	13	5	3	28	34-8	0	33	.315	.376	.408	113	6	2-1	.972	-0	95	127	O-93(35-4-55)	0.2
1976	Mon N	11	32	2	6	1	0	0	1	0-0	0	3	.188	.188	.219	14	-4	0-0	.947	1	125	189	/O-7(3-0-4)	-0.3
	Chi N	78	192	21	47	13	1	0	17	10-3	1	6	.245	.286	.323	66	-8	0-2	.985	5	174	92	1-33,O-24(22-0-3)	-0.8
	Year	89	224	23	53	14	1	0	18	10-3	1	9	.237	.272	.308	59	-12	0-2	.985	6	174	92	1-33,O-31(25-0-7)	-1.1
1977	Chi N	138	493	74	147	28	1	12	62	35-2	1	36	.298	.345	.432	97	-2	2-1	.987	4	139	93	1-80,O-52(LF)/P	-0.4
1978	Chi N	120	343	32	88	15	1	4	50	23-4	1	37	.257	.300	.341	72	-13	0-1	.987	5	149	120	1-62,O-29(LF)	-1.4
1979	Chi N	111	272	35	79	13	3	3	50	21-1	0	23	.290	.339	.393	91	-3	1-1	.925	-3	70	113	O-44(23-1-21),1-32	-0.9
1980	Chi N	127	273	21	68	12	2	1	34	18-2	2	33	.249	.294	.319	68	-12	1-3	.996	2	105	62	1-41,O-38(20-0-17)	-1.5
1981	Cin N	42	61	1	13	4	0	0	8	4-1	0	4	.213	.258	.279	52	-4	0-0	1.000	1	75	48	/1-8,O-3(RF)	-0.3
1982	Cin N	97	184	18	57	9	2	2	24	17-2	2	16	.310	.369	.413	118	5	1-0	.978	1	96	113	O-31(26-0-6),1-15	0.4
1983	Tex A	66	116	5	32	5	1	0	18	9-5	0	16	.276	.323	.336	85	-2	0-0	.987	1	139	99	1-22/O-2(RF),D-9	-0.2
Total	14	1217	3151	310	861	144	20	29	354	236-36	11	287	.273	.324	.359	87	-53	10-12	.970	23	91	133	O-490(268-15-219),1-381/D-12,P	-7.8
BILARDELLO, DANN Dann James B 5.26.1959 Santa Cruz, CA BR/TR 6/190# d4.11																								
1983	Cin N	109	298	27	71	18	0	9	38	15-3	1	49	.238	.274	.389	80	-9	2-1	.991	-2	104	121	*C-105	-0.7
1984	Cin N	68	182	16	38	7	0	2	10	19-3	1	34	.209	.287	.280	57	-10	0-1	.992	3	121	129	C-68	-0.5
1985	Cin N	42	102	6	17	0	0	1	9	4-1	1	15	.167	.206	.196	12	-12	0-0	.986	7	122	179	C-42	-0.4
1986	Mon N	79	191	12	37	5	0	4	17	14-3	0	32	.194	.249	.283	47	-15	1-0	.982	-1	104	80	C-77	-1.3
1989	Pit N	33	80	11	18	6	0	2	8	2-0	0	18	.225	.244	.375	77	-3	1-2	.970	1	76	134	C-33	0.0
1990	Pit N	19	37	1	2	0	0	0	3	4-1	0	10	.054	.146	.054	-44	-7	0-0	1.000	3	192	128	C-19	-0.4

Year	Tm Lg	G	AB	R	H	2B	3B	HR	RBI	BB-IB	HP	SO	AVG	OBP	SLG	AOPS	ABR	SB-CS	FA	FR	Rng	Thr	G at Pos	BFW
1991	SD N	15	26	4	7	2	1	0	5	3-0	0	4	.269	.345	.423	111	0	0-0	1.000	4	109	128	C-13	0.5
1992	SD N	17	33	2	4	1	0	0	1	4-1	0	8	.121	.216	.152	6	-4	0-0	1.000	1	51	173	C-14	-0.2
Total	8	382	949	79	194	39	1	18	91	65-12	3	170	.204	.257	.305	55	-60	4-4	.988	17	109	124	C-371	-3.0
BILKO, STEVE Stephen Thomas B 11.13.1928 Nanticoke, PA D 3.7.1978 Wilkes-Barre, PA BR/TR 6-1/230# d9.22																								
1949	StL N	6	17	3	5	2	0	0	2	5	0	6	.294	.455	.412	128	1	0	1.000	0	109	26	/1-5	0.1
1950	StL N	10	33	1	6	1	0	0	2	4	0	10	.182	.270	.212	27	-3	0	.989	1	123	98	/1-9	-0.3
1951	StL N	21	72	5	16	4	0	2	12	9	0	10	.222	.309	.361	79	-2	0-0	.984	0	106	104	1-19	-0.3
1952	StL N	20	72	7	19	6	1	1	6	4	0	15	.264	.303	.417	97	0	0-0	.995	5	184	83	1-20	0.4
1953	StL N	154	570	72	143	23	3	21	84	70	1	125	.251	.334	.412	93	-6	0-1	.991	9	**121**	106	*1-154	-0.5
1954	StL N	8	14	1	2	0	0	0	1	3	0	1	.143	.294	.143	18	-2	0-0	1.000	2	299	102	/1-6	0.0
	Chi N	47	92	11	22	8	1	4	12	11	0	24	.239	.320	.478	104	0	0-0	1.000	6	200	94	1-22	0.5
	Year	55	106	12	24	8	1	4	13	14	0	25	.226	.317	.434	92	-1	0-0	1.000	8	214	95	1-28	0.5
1958	Cin N	31	87	12	23	4	2	4	17	10-0	0	20	.264	.330	.494	111	1	0-0	.995	-1	81	106	1-21	-0.1
	LA N	47	101	13	21	1	2	7	18	8-0	0	37	.208	.264	.465	86	-3	0-0	.995	2	127	100	1-25	-0.2
	Year	78	188	25	44	5	4	11	35	18-0	0	57	.234	.295	.479	98	-2	0-0	.995	1	104	103	1-46	-0.3
1960	Det A	78	222	20	46	11	2	9	25	27-0	0	31	.207	.292	.396	82	-6	0-1	.991	-1	96	94	1-62	-1.1
1961	LA A	114	294	49	82	16	1	20	59	58-2	0	81	.279	.395	.544	134	16	1-1	.989	4	114	84	1-86/O-3(RF)	1.5
1962	LA A	64	164	26	47	9	1	8	38	25-0	2	35	.287	.374	.500	141	10	1-1	.995	-1	91	97	1-50	0.7
Total	10	600	1738	220	432	85	13	76	276	234-2	3	395	.249	.336	.444	103	6	2-4	.992	25	119	97	1-479/O-3(RF)	0.7
BILLINGS, JOSH John Augustus B 11.30.1892 Grantville, KS D 12.30.1981 Santa Monica, CA BR/TR 5-11/165# d9.9 Mil 1918																								
1913	Cle A	1	3	0	0	0	0	0	0	0	0	3	.000	.000	.000	-97	-1	0	.857	0	*125*	*99*	/C	-0.1
1914	Cle A	11	8	3	2	1	0	0	0	1	0	1	.250	.333	.375	109	0	1	.813	1	*0*	*147*	/C-3	0.1
1915	Cle A	8	21	2	4	1	0	0	0	0	0	6	.190	.190	.238	28	-2	1	1.000	-0	*94*	*63*	/C-7,O(CF)	-0.2
1916	Cle A	22	31	2	5	0	0	0	1	2	0	11	.161	.212	.161	12	-3	0	.981	2	126	76	C-12	-0.1
1917	Cle A	66	129	8	23	3	2	0	9	8	3	21	.178	.243	.233	42	-9	2	.974	2	*108*	*118*	C-48	-0.4
1918	Cle A	2	3	0	1	0	0	0	0	0	0	0	.333	.333	.333	92	0	0	1.000	0	*0*	*0*	/C	0.0
1919	StL A	38	76	9	15	1	1	0	3	1	1	12	.197	.218	.237	27	-8	0	.982	3	*102*	*128*	C-26/1	-0.3
1920	StL A	66	155	19	43	5	2	0	11	11	7	10	.277	.353	.335	80	-4	1-0	.967	-4	*92*	*104*	C-40	-0.5
1921	StL A	20	46	2	10	0	0	0	4	0	0	7	.217	.217	.217	11	-6	0-0	.982	1	*110*	*88*	C-12	-0.5
1922	StL A	5	7	0	3	1	0	0	1	0	0	0	.429	.429	.571	153	1	0-0	1.000	-0	*64*	*191*	/C-3	0.0
1923	StL A	4	9	0	0	0	0	0	0	0	0	2	.000	.000	.000	-95	-3	0-0	.917	0	*141*	*173*	/C-4	-0.2
Total	11	243	488	45	106	12	5	0	29	23	11	73	.217	.268	.262	47	-35	5-0	.970	4	*102*	*109*	C-157/1O(CF)	-2.2
BILLINGS, DICK Richard Arlin B 12.4.1942 Detroit, MI BR/TR 6-1/195# d9.11 OF Total (78-LF 1-CF 15-RF)																								
1968	Was A	12	33	3	6	1	0	1	3	5-0	0	13	.182	.282	.303	82	-1	0-0	.929	1	93	219	/O-8(LF),3-4	-0.1
1969	Was A	27	37	3	5	0	0	0	0	6-0	0	8	.135	.256	.135	13	-4	0-1	1.000	0	78	0	/O-6(5-1-0),3	-0.5
1970	Was A	11	24	3	6	2	0	1	1	2-0	0	3	.250	.308	.458	114	0	0-0	1.000	-2	86	178	/C-8	-0.1
1971	Was A	116	349	32	86	14	0	6	48	21-1	5	54	.246	.296	.338	85	-8	2-5	.992	-4	62	121	C-62,O-32(22-0-12)/3-2	-1.2
1972	Tex A	133	469	41	119	15	1	5	58	29-5	2	77	.254	.296	.322	89	-8	1-5	.981	-1	77	136	C-92,O-41(39-0-2)/3-5,1	-1.0
1973	Tex A	81	280	17	50	11	0	3	32	20-2	2	43	.179	.237	.250	39	-23	1-1	.975	-16	66	110	C-72/O-4(3-0-1),1-3,D-2	-3.8
1974	Tex A	16	31	2	7	1	0	0	0	4-0	0	6	.226	.314	.258	68	-1	2-0	1.000	0	136	91	C-13/O(LF)D	0.0
	StL N	1	5	0	1	0	0	0	0	0-0	0	1	.200	.200	.200	12	-1	0-0	1.000	0	0	0	/C	-0.1
1975	StL N	3	3	0	0	0	0	0	0	0-0	0	2	.000	.000	.000	-97	-1	0-0	—	0			H	-0.1
Total	8	400	1231	101	280	44	1	16	142	87-8	9	207	.227	.281	.304	73	-47	6-12	.984	-22	72	122	C-248/O-92L,3-12,1-4,D-3	-6.9
BINKS, GEORGE George Alvin "Bingo" (born George Alvin Binkowski) B 7.11.1916 Chicago, IL BL/TL 6/175# d9.23																								
1944	Was A	5	12	0	3	0	0	0	0	0	0	1	.250	.250	.250	45	-1	0-0	1.000	-0	97	0	/O-3(RF)	-0.1
1945	Was A	145	550	62	153	32	6	6	81	34	3	52	.278	.324	.391	117	9	11-7	.977	5	106	117	*O-128(27-79-26),1-20	0.8
1946	Was A	65	134	13	26	3	0	0	12	6	0	16	.194	.229	.216	26	-14	1-0	1.000	1	112	53	O-28(15-9-5)	-1.5
1947	Phi A	104	333	33	86	19	4	2	34	23	1	36	.258	.308	.357	83	-8	8-2	.965	2	101	149	O-75(25-0-51),1-13	-1.0
1948	Phi A	17	41	2	4	1	0	0	2	2	0	2	.098	.140	.122	-30	-8	1-0	1.000	0	92	146	O-14(2-0-12)	-0.8
	StL A	15	23	2	5	0	0	0	1	2	0	1	.217	.280	.217	32	-2	0-0	1.000	-1	96	0	/O-5(2-0-3),1-4	-0.3
	Year	32	64	4	9	1	0	0	3	4	0	3	.141	.191	.156	-7	-10	1-0	1.000	-1	93	106	O-19(4-0-15)/1-4	-1.1
Total	5	351	1093	112	277	55	10	8	130	67	4	108	.253	.299	.344	86	-24	21-9	.977	7	104	118	O-253(71-88-100)/1-37	-2.9
BIRAS, STEVE Stephen Alexander B 2.26.1922 E.St.Louis, IL D 4.21.1965 St.Louis, MO BR/TR 5-11/185# d9.15																								
1944	Cle A	2	2	0	2	0	0	0	2	0	0	0	1.000	1.000	1.000	491	1	0-0	.667	-0	77	0	/2	0.1
BIRCHALL, JUD Adoniram Judson B 9.12.1855 Philadelphia, PA D 12.22.1887 Philadelphia, PA d5.2																								
1882	Phi AA	**75**	338	65	89	12	1	0	27	8			.263	.280	.305	91	-4		.860	0	80	0	*O-74(LF)/2	-0.5
1883	Phi AA	96	448	95	108	10	1	1	24	20			.241	.274	.275	70	-16		.809	5	116	0	*O-96(LF)	-1.2
1884	Phi AA	54	221	36	57	2	2	0		4	5		.258	.287	.285	82	-5		.838	2	65	62	O-52(51-0-1)/3-2	-0.4
Total	3	225	1007	196	254	24	4	1	51	32	5		.252	.279	.287	80	-25		.832	7	92	15	O-222(221-0-1)/3-2,2	-2.1
BIRD, FRANK Frank Zepherin "Dodo" B 3.10.1869 Spencer, MA D 5.20.1958 Worcester, MA BR/TR 5-10/195# d4.16																								
1892	StL N	17	50	9	10	3	1	1	1	6	0	11	.200	.286	.360	100	0	2	.920	-3	*96*	*96*	C-17	-0.2
BIRD, GEORGE George Raymond B 6.23.1850 Stillman Valley, IL D 11.9.1940 Rockford, IL BR/TR 5-9/150# d5.6																								
1871	Rok NA	**25**	106	19	28	2	5	0	13	3		2	.264	.284	.377	92	-1	1-0	.756	-5	66	0	*O-25(1-25-0)	-0.4
BIRDSALL, DAVE David Solomon B 7.16.1838 New York, NY D 12.30.1896 Boston, MA BR/TR 5-9/126# d5.5																								
1871	Bos NA	29	152	51	46	3	3	0	24	4		4	.303	.321	.362	93	-2	6-0	.769	0	110	208	*O-27(RF)/C-7	0.0
1872	Bos NA	16	76	11	16	3	0	0	15	1		0	.211	.221	.250	42	-5	0-2	.826	2			C-12/O-7(4-0-3)	-0.3
1873	Bos NA	3	11	4	1	0	0	0	0	2		0	.091	.231	.091	-1	-1	1-0	.200	-2	0	0	/O-3(1-0-3)	-0.2
Total	3 NA	48	239	66	63	6	3	0	39	7		4	.264	.285	.314	73	-8	7-2	.000	0			/O-37(5-0-33),C-19	-0.5
BIRMINGHAM, JOE Joseph Leo "Dode" B 8.6.1884 Elmira, NY D 4.24.1946 Tampico, Mexico BR/TR 5-10/185# d9.12 M4																								
1906	Cle A	10	40	5	11	2	1	0	6	1	0		.275	.293	.375	110	0	2	1.000	1	155	0	/O-9(LF),3	0.0
1907	Cle A	137	476	55	112	10	9	1	33	16	3		.235	.265	.300	79	-13	23	.949	12	**168**	213	*O-133(17-101-16)/S-3	-0.8
1908	Cle A	122	413	32	88	10	1	2	38	19	3		.213	.253	.257	65	-16	15	.957	4	**148**	**179**	*O-121(1-119-1)/S	-2.0
1909	Cle A	100	343	29	99	10	5	1	38	19	4		.289	.333	.356	113	4	12	.948	2	124	75	O-98(CF)	0.2
1910	Cle A	104	367	41	84	11	2	0	35	23	5		.229	.284	.270	72	-12	18	.961	11	107	**159**	*O-103(1-102-0)/3	-0.6
1911	Cle A	125	447	55	136	18	5	2	51	15	5		.304	.334	.380	98	-3	16	.973	3	101	110	*O-102(3-96-3),3-16	-0.6
1912	Cle A	107	369	49	94	19	3	1	45	26	4		.255	.311	.331	81	-9	15	.952	2	93	129	O-96(3-93-0)/1-9,M	-1.4
1913	Cle A	47	131	16	37	9	1	0	15	8	0	22	.282	.324	.366	99	0	7	.974	-2	102	39	O-36(4-32-0),M	-0.5
1914	Cle A	19	47	2	6	0	0	0	4	2	0	5	.128	.163	.128	-12	-7	0-1	1.000	-0	92	90	O-14(0-6-8),M	-0.9
Total	9	771	2633	284	667	89	27	7	265	129	24	27	.253	.294	.316	84	-56	108-1	.958	33	125	141	O-712(38-647-28)/3-18,1-9,S-4	-6.6
BISCHOFF, JOHN John George "Smiley" B 10.28.1894 Granite City, IL D 12.28.1981 Granite City, IL BR/TR 5-7/165# d4.18																								
1925	Chi A	7	11	1	1	0	0	0	0	1	0	5	.091	.167	.091	-35	-2	0-0	1.000	-0	*110*	*212*	/C-4	-0.2
	Bos A	41	133	13	37	9	1	1	16	6	0	11	.278	.309	.383	75	-6	1-2	.952	-4	*70*	*100*	C-40	-0.7
	Year	48	144	14	38	9	1	1	16	7	0	16	.264	.298	.361	67	-8	1-2	.955	-4	*72*	*106*	C-44	-0.9
1926	Bos A	59	127	6	33	11	2	0	19	15	1	16	.260	.343	.378	91	-2	1-3	.974	-4	*66*	*87*	C-46	-0.4
Total	2	107	271	20	71	20	3	1	35	22	1	32	.262	.320	.369	78	-10	2-5	.964	-8	*69*	*97*	/C-90	-1.3
BISHOP, FRANK Frank H. B 9.21.1860 Belvidere, IL D 6.18.1929 Chicago, IL d5.27																								
1884	CP U	4	16	1	3	1	0	0		0			.188	.188	.250	32	-2		.667	-2	49	0	/3-3,S	-0.3
BISHOP, MAX Max Frederick "Tilly" or "Camera Eye" B 9.5.1899 Waynesboro, PA D 2.24.1962 Waynesboro, PA BL/TR 5-8.5/165# d4.15																								
1924	Phi A	91	294	52	75	13	2	2	21	54	5	30	.255	.380	.333	84	-4	4-3	.969	10	114	108	2-80	0.7
1925	Phi A	105	368	66	103	18	4	4	27	87	2	37	.280	.420	.383	98	4	5-9	.957	5	**109**	90	*2-104	0.9
1926	Phi A	122	400	77	106	20	2	0	33	116	1	41	.265	.431	.325	94	5	4-5	**.987**	6	102	95	*2-119	1.3
1927	Phi A	117	372	80	103	15	1	0	22	105	5	28	.277	.442	.323	95	6	8-6	.967	2	103	85	*2-106	1.0
1928	Phi A	126	472	104	149	27	5	6	50	100	3	36	.316	.438	.432	126	25	6-10	**.978**	-6	92	92	*2-125	1.9
1929	†Phi A	129	475	102	110	19	6	3	36	**128**	3	44	.232	.398	.316	83	-5	1-4	.970	-20	88	77	*2-129	-2.1
1930	†Phi A	130	441	117	111	27	6	10	38	128	6	60	.252	.426	.408	108	13	3-2	.976	-1	101	81	*2-127	1.4

Year	Tm Lg	G	AB	R	H	2B	3B	HR	RBI	BB-IB	HP	SO	AVG	OBP	SLG	AOPS	ABR	SB-CS	FA	FR	Rng	Thr	G at Pos	BFW
1931	†Phi A	130	497	115	146	30	4	5	37	112	2	51	.294	.426	.400	111	15	3-1	.984	2	98	116	*2-130	2.4
1932	Phi A	114	409	89	104	24	2	5	37	110	0	43	.254	.412	.359	98	6	2-2	**.988**	-1	100	106	*2-106	1.1
1933	Phi A	117	391	80	115	27	1	4	42	106	1	46	.294	.446	.399	124	23	1-5	.975	-7	101	70	*2-113	2.0
1934	Bos A	97	253	65	66	13	1	1	22	82	2	22	.261	.445	.332	96	5	3-2	.990	3	98	105	2-57,1-15	0.9
1935	Bos A	60	122	19	28	3	1	1	14	28	1	14	.230	.377	.295	71	-4	0-2	.978	-3	93	55	2-34,1-11/S-2	-0.6
Total	12	1338	4494	966	1216	236	35	41	379	1156	31	452	.271	.423	.366	102	89	40-51	.976	-10	100	91	*2-1230/1-26,S-2	10.9
BISHOP, MIKE Michael David B 11.5.1958 Santa Maria, CA BR/TR 6-2/188# d4.16																								
1983	NY N	3	8	2	1	1	0	0	0	3-0	0	4	.125	.364	.250	74	0	0-0	.944	-0	86	79	/C-3	0.0
BISLAND, RIVINGTON Rivington Martin B 2.17.1890 New York, NY D 1.11.1973 Salzburg, Austria BR/TR 5-9/155# d9.13																								
1912	Pit N	1	1	0	0	0	0	0	0	0	0	0	.000	.000	.000	-99	0	0	—	0			H	0.0
1913	StL A	12	44	3	6	0	0	0	3	2	1	5	.136	.191	.136	-4	-6	0	.963	-3	89	66	S-12	-0.9
1914	Cle A	18	57	9	6	1	0	0	2	6	0	2	.105	.190	.123	-5	-7	2-5	.962	0	100	92	S-15/3	-0.8
Total	3	31	102	12	12	1	0	0	5	8	1	7	.118	.189	.127	-6	-13	2-5	.962	-2	95	81	/S-27,3	-1.7
BISSONETTE, DEL Delphia Louis B 9.6.1899 Winthrop, ME D 6.9.1972 Augusta, ME BL/TL 5-11/180# d4.11 M1 C2																								
1928	Bro N	**155**	587	90	188	30	13	25	106	70	4	75	.320	.396	.543	145	38	5	.987	-3	90	74	*1-155	2.4
1929	Bro N	116	431	68	121	28	10	12	75	46	1	58	.281	.351	.476	105	2	2	.987	-9	67	74	*1-113	-1.3
1930	Bro N	146	572	102	192	33	13	16	113	56	1	66	.336	.396	.523	121	19	4	.987	-9	78	**118**	*1-146	0.1
1931	Bro N	152	587	90	170	19	14	12	87	59	0	53	.290	.354	.431	111	8	4	.990	-6	79	104	*1-152	-1.3
1933	Bro N	35	114	9	28	7	0	1	10	2	0	17	.246	.259	.333	71	-5	2	.988	-0	97	100	1-32	-0.8
Total	5	604	2291	359	699	117	50	66	391	233	6	269	.305	.371	.486	119	62	17	.988	-28	80	94	1-598	-0.9
BITTMAN, RED Henry Peter B 7.22.1862 Cincinnati, OH D 11.8.1929 Cincinnati, OH d10.10																								
1889	KC AA	4	14	2	4	0	0	0	2	1	0	1	.286	.333	.286	73	-1	1	1.000	1	112	104	/2-4	0.0
BJORKMAN, GEORGE George Anton B 8.26.1956 Ontario, CA BR/TR 6-2/190# d7.10																								
1983	Hou N	29	75	8	17	4	0	2	14	16-4	1	29	.227	.370	.360	110	2	0-0	.993	-3	95	73	C-29	0.0
BLACK, JOHN John Falcnor "Jack" (born John Falcnor Haddow) B 2.23.1890 Covington, KY D 3.20.1962 Rutherford, NJ BR/TR 6-1/185# d6.20																								
1911	StL A	54	186	13	28	4	0	0	7	10	2		.151	.202	.172	5	-24	4	.972	0	111	121	1-54	-2.6
BLACK, BILL John William "Jigger" B 8.12.1899 Philadelphia, PA D 1.14.1968 Philadelphia, PA BL/TR 5-11/168# d5.4																								
1924	Chi A	6	5	0	1	0	0	0	0	0	0	0	.200	.200	.200	3	-1	0-0	—	-0	0	0	/2	-0.1
BLACK, BOB Robert Benjamin B 12.10.1862 Cincinnati, OH D 3.21.1933 Sioux City, IA 5-5.5/155# d8.19 ▲																								
1884	KC U	38	146	25	36	14	2	1		10			.247	.295	.390	122	0		.784	-0	94	0	O-19(5-7-7),P-16/2-6,S	-0.1
BLACKABY, ETHAN Ethan Allen B 7.24.1940 Cincinnati, OH BL/TL 5-11/190# d9.6																								
1962	Mil N	6	13	0	2	1	0	0	0	1-0	0	8	.154	.214	.231	20	-1	0-0	1.000	-0	75	0	/O-3(2-1-0)	-0.2
1964	Mil N	9	12	0	1	0	0	0	1	1-0	0	2	.083	.154	.083	-31	-2	0-0	.500	-1	40	0	/O-5(2-0-3)	-0.3
Total	2	15	25	0	3	1	0	0	1	2-0	0	10	.120	.185	.160	-4	-3	0-0	.800	-1	60	0	/O-8(4-1-3)	-0.5
BLACKBURN, EARL Earl Stuart B 11.1.1892 Leesville, OH D 8.3.1966 Mansfield, OH BR/TR 5-11/180# d9.17																								
1912	Pit N	1	0	0	0	0	0	0	0	0	0	0	—	—	—	—	0	0	1.000	0	*0*	*0*	/C	0.0
	Cin N	1	0	0	0	0	0	0	0	1	0	0	—	1.000	—	191	0	0	1.000	0	*0*	*0*	/C	0.1
	Year	2	0	0	0	0	0	0	0	1	0	0	—	1.000	—	190	0	0	1.000	0	*0*	*0*	/C-2	0.1
1913	Cin N	17	27	1	7	0	0	0	3	2	0	5	.259	.310	.259	64	-1	2-1	.848	-2	108	86	C-12	-0.2
1915	Bos N	3	6	0	1	0	0	0	0	2	0	1	.167	.375	.167	70	0	0	1.000	-0	*94*	*126*	/C-3	0.0
1916	Bos N	47	110	12	30	4	4	0	7	9	0	21	.273	.328	.382	123	3	2	.972	3	173	67	C-44	1.0
1917	Chi N	2	2	0	0	0	0	0	0	0	0	0	.000	.000	.000	-93	0	0	—	0			H	-0.1
Total	5	71	145	13	38	4	4	0	10	14	0	27	.262	.327	.345	107	2	4-1	.954	2	*156*	*71*	/C-61	0.8
BLACKBURNE, LENA Russell Aubrey "Slats" B 10.23.1886 Clifton Heights, PA D 2.29.1968 Riverside, NJ BR/TR 5-11/160# d4.14 M2 C13																								
1910	Chi A	75	242	16	42	3	1	0	10	19	4		.174	.245	.194	39	-17	4	.911	11	107	117	S-74	-0.4
1912	Chi A	5	1	0	0	0	0	0	0	1	0		.000	.500	.000	48	0	1	.800	0	57	570	/S-4,3	0.0
1914	Chi A	144	474	52	105	10	5	1	35	66	6	58	.222	.324	.270	80	-9	25-15	.963	4	**109**	67	*2-143	-0.3
1915	Chi A	96	283	33	61	5	1	0	25	35	1	34	.216	.304	.240	61	-13	13-11	.949	-9	88	108	3-83/S-9	-2.2
1918	Cin N	125	435	34	99	8	10	1	45	25	1	30	.228	.271	.299	75	-15	6	.938	11	99	**126**	*S-125	0.5
1919	Bos N	31	80	5	21	3	1	0	4	6	1	7	.262	.322	.325	99	0	3	.948	1	96	103	3-24/12S	0.2
	Phi N	72	291	32	58	10	5	2	19	10	1	22	.199	.228	.289	51	-18	2	.933	7	114	94	3-72/1	-1.0
	Year	103	371	37	79	13	6	2	23	16	2	29	.213	.249	.296	61	-18	5	**.937**	8	**110**	96	3-96/1-2,2S	-0.8
1927	Chi A	1	1	1	1	0	0	0	1	0	0	0	1.000	1.000	1.000	431	0	0-0	—	0			H	0.0
1929	Chi A	1	0	0	0	0	0	0	0	0	0	0	—	—	—	—	0	0-0	—	0	0	0	/PM	0.0
Total	8	550	1807	173	387	39	23	4	139	162	14	151	.214	.284	.268	67	-72	54-26	.927	25	102	124	S-213,3-180,2-144/1-2,P	-3.2
BLACKERBY, GEORGE George Franklin B 11.10.1903 Luther, OK D 5.30.1987 Wichita Falls, TX BR/TR 6-1/176# d8.10																								
1928	Chi A	30	83	8	21	0	0	0	12	4	0	10	.253	.287	.253	44	-7	2-1	.953	-1	95	54	O-20(LF)	-0.9
BLACKWELL, FRED Fredrick William "Blacky" B 9.7.1891 Bowling Green, KY D 12.8.1975 Morgantown, KY BL/TR 5-11.5/160# d9.25 Mil 1918																								
1917	Pit N	3	10	1	2	0	0	0	2	0	0	3	.200	.200	.200	22	-1	0	1.000	0	*84*	*102*	/C-3	-0.1
1918	Pit N	8	13	1	2	0	0	0	4	3	0	4	.154	.313	.154	42	-1	0	.926	0	*148*	*87*	/C-8	0.0
1919	Pit N	24	65	3	14	3	0	0	4	3	1	9	.215	.261	.262	55	-3	0	.964	0	*135*	*75*	C-22	-0.1
Total	3	35	88	5	18	3	0	0	10	6	1	16	.205	.263	.239	50	-5	0	.961	1	*132*	*80*	/C-33	-0.2
BLACKWELL, TIM Timothy P B 8.19.1952 San Diego, CA BB/TR 5-11/180# d7.3																								
1974	Bos A	44	122	9	30	1	1	0	8	10-1	1	21	.246	.308	.270	63	-6	1-1	.971	-4	82	105	C-44	-0.8
1975	Bos A	59	132	15	26	3	2	0	6	19-0	1	13	.197	.303	.250	53	-8	0-0	.984	1	82	104	C-57/D-2	-0.5
1976	Phi N	4	8	0	2	0	0	0	0	0-0	0	1	.250	.250	.250	41	-1	0-0	1.000	1	0	0	/C-4	0.1
1977	Phi N	1	0	1	0	0	0	0	0	0-0	0	0	—	—	—	—	0	0-0	1.000	0	0	0	/C	0.0
	Mon N	16	22	3	2	1	0	0	0	2-1	0	7	.091	.167	.136	-18	-4	0-0	.925	-3	48	0	C-14	-0.7
	Year	17	22	4	2	1	0	0	0	2-1	0	7	.091	.167	.136	-18	-4	0-0	.929	-3	46	0	C-15	-0.7
1978	Chi N	49	103	8	23	3	0	0	7	23-1	1	17	.223	.367	.252	68	-3	0-0	.987	4	101	44	C-49	0.3
1979	Chi N	63	122	8	20	3	1	0	12	32-1	1	25	.164	.338	.205	48	-7	0-0	.975	-4	85	105	C-63	-1.0
1980	Chi N	103	320	24	87	16	4	5	30	41-6	0	62	.272	.352	.394	101	2	0-1	.982	13	99	**158**	*C-103	2.0
1981	Chi N	58	158	21	37	10	2	1	11	23-4	0	23	.234	.331	.342	87	-2	2-1	.993	-6	61	115	C-56	-0.6
1982	Mon N	23	42	2	8	2	1	0	3	3-0	0	11	.190	.244	.286	47	-3	0-0	.985	-2	71	86	C-18	-0.4
1983	Mon N	6	15	0	3	1	0	0	2	1-0	0	3	.200	.250	.267	43	-1	0-0	.935	-2	39	0	/C-5	-0.3
Total	10	426	1044	91	238	40	11	6	80	154-14	4	183	.228	.328	.305	73	-33	3-3	.981	0	84	110	C-414/D-2	-1.9
BLADES, RAY Francis Raymond B 8.6.1896 Mt.Vernon, IL D 5.18.1979 Lincoln, IL BR/TR 5-7.5/163# d8.19 M3 C11																								
1922	StL N	37	130	27	39	2	4	3	21	25	4	21	.300	.428	.446	132	8	3-3	.931	-1	103	169	O-29(28-0-1)/S-4,3	0.4
1923	StL N	98	317	48	78	21	5	5	44	37	9	46	.246	.342	.391	95	-1	4-2	.967	6	110	138	O-83(81-1-3)/3-4	-0.1
1924	StL N	131	456	86	142	21	13	11	68	35	10	38	.311	.373	.487	131	19	7-9	.956	-1	**114**	55	*O-109(106-3-1)/2-7,3-7	0.9
1925	StL N	122	462	112	158	37	8	12	57	59	6	47	.342	.423	.535	140	30	6-8	.979	9	**114**	127	*O-114(LF)/3	2.7
1926	StL N	107	416	81	127	17	12	8	43	62	**11**	57	.305	.409	.462	129	19	6	.980	0	101	94	*O-105(LF)	1.1
1927	StL N	61	180	33	57	8	5	2	29	28	2	22	.317	.414	.450	127	8	3	.914	-9	74	0	O-50(29-0-21)	-0.4
1928	†StL N	51	85	9	20	7	1	1	19	20	2	26	.235	.393	.376	100	1	0	.972	-1	87	56	O-19(4-0-15)	-0.1
1930	†StL N	45	101	26	40	6	2	4	25	21	1	15	.396	.504	.614	163	12	1	.957	-1	107	33	O-32(13-0-21)	0.7
1931	†StL N	35	67	10	19	4	0	1	5	10	2	7	.284	.392	.388	106	1	1	.871	-2	83	70	O-20(7-0-13)	-0.2
1932	StL N	80	201	35	46	10	1	3	29	34	0	31	.229	.340	.333	80	-5	2	.975	-1	106	42	O-62(13-0-49)/3	-0.9
Total	10	767	2415	467	726	133	51	50	340	331	47	310	.301	.395	.460	123	92	33-22	.963	-1	105	87	O-623(500-4-124)/3-14,2-7,S-4	4.1
BLADT, RICK Richard Alan B 12.9.1946 Santa Cruz, CA BR/TR 6-1/160# d6.15																								
1969	Chi N	10	13	1	2	0	0	0	1	0-0	0	5	.154	.154	.154	-12	-2	0-0	1.000	1	141	401	/O-7(2-5-1)	-0.1
1975	NY A	52	117	13	26	3	1	1	11	11-0	1	8	.222	.292	.291	67	-5	6-2	.973	2	106	154	O-51(CF)	-0.4
Total	2	62	130	14	28	3	1	1	12	11-0	1	13	.215	.280	.277	58	-7	6-2	.976	3	109	178	/O-58(2-56-1)	-0.5

Year	Tm Lg	G	AB	R	H	2B	3B	HR	RBI	BB-IB	HP	SO	AVG	OBP	SLG	AOPS	ABR	SB-CS	FA	FR	Rng	Thr	G at Pos	BFW
BLAEMIRE, RAE Rae Bertrum B 2.8.1911 Gary, IN D 12.23.1975 Champaign, IL BR/TR 6/178# d9.13																								
1941	NY N	2	5	0	2	0	0	0	0	0	0	0	.400	.400	.400	123	0	0	1.000	-0	*0*	*0*	/C-2	0.0
BLAIR, FOOTSIE Clarence Vick B 7.13.1900 Enterprise, OK D 7.1.1982 Texarkana, TX BL/TR 6-1/180# d4.28																								
1929	†Chi N	26	72	10	23	5	0	1	8	3	0	4	.319	.347	.431	91	-1	1	.897	-0	88	0	/3-8,1-7,2-2	-0.1
1930	Chi N	134	578	97	158	24	12	6	59	20	7	58	.273	.306	.388	66	-35	9	.958	4	105	101	*2-115,3-13	-2.4
1931	Chi N	86	240	31	62	19	4	3	29	14	1	26	.258	.302	.408	88	-5	1	.956	-7	89	67	2-44,1-23/3	-1.1
Total	3	246	890	138	243	48	16	10	96	37	8	88	.273	.308	.397	73	-41	11	.958	-4	101	94	2-161/1-30,3-22	-3.6
BLAIR, BUDDY Louis Nathan B 9.10.1910 Columbia, MS D 6.7.1996 Monroe, LA BL/TR 6/186# d4.14 Mil 1943-45																								
1942	Phi A	137	484	48	135	26	8	5	66	30	3	30	.279	.325	.397	103	0	1-6	.931	-5	95	84	*3-126	-0.3
BLAIR, PAUL Paul L D B 2.1.1944 Cushing, OK BR/TR (BB 1971 (part)) 6/171# d9.9 OF Total (31-LF 1801-CF 58-RF)																								
1964	Bal A	8	1	0	0	0	0	0	0	0-0	0	1	.000	.000	.000	-99	0	0-1	1.000	0	187	0	/O-6(CF)	-0.1
1965	Bal A	119	364	49	85	19	2	5	25	32-3	4	52	.234	.302	.338	80	-9	8-5	.992	0	103	112	*O-116(CF)	-1.3
1966	†Bal A	133	303	35	84	20	2	6	33	15-0	0	36	.277	.309	.416	109	3	5-6	.990	-1	103	77	*O-127(2-125-0)	-0.1
1967	Bal A	151	552	72	162	27	**12**	11	64	50-3	5	68	.293	.353	.446	137	25	8-6	.985	9	113	151	*O-146(CF)	3.2
1968	Bal A	141	421	48	89	22	1	7	38	37-4	2	60	.211	.277	.318	80	-10	4-2	.993	4	104	135	*O-132(CF)/3	-1.0
1969	†Bal A★	150	625	102	178	32	5	26	76	40-0	2	72	.285	.327	.477	122	15	20-6	.988	12	114	144	*O-150(CF)	2.6
1970	†Bal A	133	480	79	128	24	2	18	65	56-1	3	93	.267	.344	.438	114	9	24-11	.990	11	121	122	*O-128(CF)/3	1.9
1971	†Bal A	141	516	75	135	24	8	10	44	32-2	1	94	.262	.306	.397	99	-3	14-11	.991	-4	101	48	*O-138(CF)	-1.2
1972	Bal A	142	477	47	111	20	8	8	49	25-0	0	78	.233	.267	.358	84	-12	7-8	.991	5	109	122	*O-139(CF)	-1.2
1973	†Bal A★	146	500	73	140	25	3	10	64	43-4	0	72	.280	.334	.402	108	5	18-8	.990	6	105	139	*O-144(CF)/D	0.9
1974	†Bal A	151	552	77	144	27	4	17	62	43-0	2	59	.261	.313	.417	113	8	27-9	.985	-1	106	62	*O-151(CF)	0.6
1975	Bal A	140	440	51	96	13	4	5	31	25-0	0	82	.218	.257	.300	62	-24	17-11	.991	-1	101	93	*O-138(CF)/1D	-2.9
1976	Bal A	145	375	29	74	16	0	3	16	22-2	2	49	.197	.245	.264	52	-23	15-6	.979	-1	104	71	*O-139(CF)/D	-2.7
1977	†NY A	83	164	20	43	4	3	4	25	9-1	2	16	.262	.303	.396	91	-3	3-2	.969	-1	101	28	O-79(6-42-33)/D	-0.5
1978	†NY A	75	125	10	22	5	0	2	13	9-0	0	17	.176	.231	.264	40	-10	1-1	.989	-2	98	84	O-64(1-49-16)/2-5,S-4,3-3	-1.4
1979	NY A	2	5	0	1	0	0	0	0	0-0	0	1	.200	.200	.200	8	-1	0-0	1.000	0	173	0	/O-2(0-1-1)	0.0
	Cin N	75	140	7	21	4	1	2	15	11-3	0	27	.150	.209	.236	22	-16	0-0	.992	2	109	96	O-67(16-56-2)	-1.5
1980	NY A	12	2	2	0	0	0	0	0	0-0	0	0	.000	.000	.000	-99	-1	0-0	1.000	0	155	0	O-12(6-1-6)	0.0
Total	17	1947	6042	776	1513	282	55	134	620	449-23	23	877	.250	.302	.382	96	-47	171-93	.988	40	107	104	*O-1878C/2-5,3-5,S-4,D-4,1	-4.7
BLAIR, WALTER Walter Allen "Heavy" B 10.13.1883 Landrus, PA D 8.20.1948 Lewisburg, PA BR/TR 6/185# d9.17 M1																								
1907	NY A	7	22	1	4	0	0	0	1	2	0		.182	.250	.182	35	-2	0	.922	1	*99*	*112*	/C-7	0.0
1908	NY A	76	211	9	40	5	1	1	13	11	2		.190	.237	.237	53	-11	4	.956	-12	*74*	*99*	C-60/O-9(2-0-7),1-3	-2.1
1909	NY A	42	110	5	23	2	2	0	11	7	2		.209	.269	.264	68	-4	2	.964	-5	*86*	*87*	C-42	-0.7
1910	NY A	6	22	2	5	0	1	0	2	0	0		.227	.227	.318	67	-1	0	.970	-1	*87*	*125*	/C-6	-0.2
1911	NY A	85	222	18	43	9	2	0	26	16	3		.194	.257	.252	40	-18	2	.970	2	*96*	*105*	C-84/1	-1.0
1914	Buf F	128	378	22	92	11	2	0	33	32	1	64	.243	.304	.283	59	-27	6	.984	11	*114*	*100*	*C-128	-0.6
1915	Buf F	98	290	23	65	15	3	2	20	18	2	32	.224	.274	.317	65	-19	4	**.981**	-2	*75*	***119***	C-97,M	-1.4
Total	7	442	1255	80	272	42	11	3	106	86	10	96	.217	.272	.275	56	-82	18	.974	-6	*93*	*105*	C-424/O-9(2-0-7),1-4	-6.0
BLAKE, HARRY Harry Cooper B 6.16.1874 Portsmouth, OH D 10.14.1919 Chicago, IL BR/TR 5-7/165# d7.7																								
1894	Cle N	73	296	51	78	15	4	1	51	30	2	22	.264	.335	.351	63	-18	1	.932	2	133	148	O-73(0-4-69)	-1.5
1895	†Cle N	85	318	50	88	10	1	3	45	31	1	33	.277	.343	.343	73	-13	11	.898	-5	99	113	O-84(RF)	-1.8
1896	†Cle N	104	383	66	92	12	5	1	43	46	0	30	.240	.322	.305	62	-21	10	.944	-2	110	143	*O-103(0-12-92)/S	-2.5
1897	Cle N	32	117	17	30	3	1	1	15	12	1		.256	.331	.325	70	-5	5	.989	3	63	238	O-32(2-25-5)	-0.4
1898	Cle N	136	474	65	116	18	7	0	58	69	1		.245	.342	.312	89	-4	12	.952	6	133	74	*O-136(1-22-114)/1-2	-0.4
1899	StL N	97	292	50	70	9	4	2	41	43	2		.240	.341	.318	80	-7	16	.979	1	85	100	O-87(9-69-9)/2-4,S1C	-1.0
Total	6	527	1880	299	474	67	22	8	253	231	7	85	.252	.336	.324	73	-68	55	.948	6	111	120	O-515(12-132-373)/2-4,1-3,S-2,C	-7.6
BLAKE, CASEY William Casey B 8.23.1973 Des Moines, IA BR/TR 6-2/195# d8.14																								
1999	Tor A	14	39	6	10	2	0	1	1	2-0	0	7	.256	.293	.385	70	-2	0-0	1.000	3	119	230	3-14	0.1
2000	Min A	7	16	1	3	2	0	0	1	3-0	1	7	.188	.333	.313	67	-1	0-0	1.000	-1	70	0	/3-5,1D	-0.2
2001	Min A	13	22	1	7	1	0	0	2	3-1	0	8	.318	.400	.364	101	0	1-0	.800	-0	83	0	/3-5,1-3,D-4	0.0
	Bal A	6	15	2	2	0	0	1	2	1-0	0	4	.133	.188	.333	35	-2	2-0	.967	-1	0	80	/1-5,D	-0.3
	Year	19	37	3	9	1	0	1	4	4-1	0	12	.243	.317	.351	76	-1	3-0	.979	-2	49	77	/1-8,3-5,D-5	-0.3
2002	Min A	9	20	2	4	1	0	0	1	2-0	0	7	.200	.273	.250	40	-2	0-0	.846	-2	64	128	/3-5,1-3	-0.3
2003	Cle A	152	557	80	143	35	0	17	67	38-1	10	109	.257	.312	.411	93	-6	7-9	.952	6	108	128	*3-140,1-31	-0.2
Total	5	201	669	92	169	41	0	19	74	49-2	11	142	.253	.310	.399	88	-13	10-9	.952	5	106	130	3-169/1-43,D-6	-0.9
BLAKELY, LINC Lincoln Howard B 2.12.1912 Oakland, CA D 9.28.1976 Oakland, CA BR/TR 6/180# d4.29																								
1934	Cin N	34	102	11	23	1	1	0	10	5	1	14	.225	.269	.255	42	-9	1	.987	3	109	211	O-28(6-22-0)	-0.6
BLAKISTON, BOB Robert J. (born Robert J. Blackstone) B 10.2.1855 San Francisco, CA D 12.25.1918 San Francisco, CA 5-8.5/180# d5.2																								
1882	Phi AA	72	281	40	64	4	1	0	20	9			.228	.252	.249	65	-11		.855	-1	154	0	O-38(0-4-34),3-34/2	-1.1
1883	Phi AA	44	167	26	41	3	3	0	26	9			.246	.284	.299	81	-4		.857	-1	93	0	O-37(2-35-0)/1-6,3-5	-0.5
1884	Phi AA	32	128	21	33	6	0	0		11	4		.258	.336	.305	104	1		.911	-3	53	119	O-28(0-27-1)/3-2,12S	-0.2
	Ind AA	6	18	0	4	1	0	0		1	0		.222	.263	.278	79	0		.884	-1	155	0	/1-5,O(RF)	-0.1
	Year	38	146	21	37	7	0	0		12	4		.253	.327	.301	101	1		.914	-3	51	115	O-29(0-27-3)/1-6,3-2,2S	-0.3
Total	3	154	594	87	142	14	4	0	46	30	4		.239	.280	.276	79	-14		.874	-5	103	37	O-104(2-66-37)/3-41,1-12,2-2,S	-1.9
BLALOCK, HANK Hank Joe B 11.21.1980 San Diego, CA BL/TR 6-1/192# d4.1																								
2002	Tex A	49	147	16	31	8	0	3	17	20-1	1	43	.211	.306	.327	66	-7	0-0	.943	-5	88	86	3-46	-1.1
2003	Tex A★	143	567	89	170	33	3	29	90	44-1	1	97	.300	.350	.522	116	12	2-3	.959	6	99	128	*3-141/2-4	1.8
Total	2	192	714	105	201	41	3	32	107	64-2	2	140	.282	.340	.482	106	5	2-3	.955	1	96	118	3-187/2-4	0.7
BLANCHARD, JOHNNY John Edwin B 2.26.1933 Minneapolis, MN BL/TR 6-1/198# d9.25																								
1955	NY A	1	3	0	0	0	0	0	0	1-0	0	0	.000	.250	.000	-29	-1	0-0	1.000	0	*0*	*0*	/C	0.0
1959	NY A	49	59	6	10	1	0	2	4	7-0	0	12	.169	.258	.288	51	-4	0-0	.963	-1	*137*	*0*	C-12/O-8(1-0-7),1	-0.6
1960	†NY A	53	99	8	24	3	1	4	14	6-1	1	17	.242	.292	.414	94	-2	0-0	.988	5	*166*	*66*	C-28	0.4
1961	†NY A	93	243	38	74	10	1	21	54	27-9	4	28	.305	.382	.613	170	23	1-0	.990	1	*143*	*87*	C-48,O-15(8-0-7)	2.5
1962	†NY A	93	246	33	57	7	0	13	39	28-0	1	32	.232	.309	.419	98	-1	0-0	.987	-4	96	83	O-47(15-0-32),C-15/1-2	-0.8
1963	†NY A	76	218	22	49	4	0	16	45	26-3	0	30	.225	.305	.463	114	3	0-0	.987	-6	74	54	O-64(22-0-42)	-0.7
1964	†NY A	77	161	18	41	8	0	7	28	24-4	0	24	.255	.344	.435	115	4	1-0	.984	-1	*160*	*54*	C-25,O-14(6-0-8)/1-3	0.3
1965	NY A	12	34	1	5	1	0	1	3	7-2	0	3	.147	.286	.265	60	-2	0-0	.961	-1	*99*	*120*	C-12	-0.2
	KC A	52	120	10	24	2	0	2	11	8-1	1	16	.200	.250	.267	49	-8	0-0	1.000	-5	91	0	O-20(1-0-19),C-14	-1.4
	Year	64	154	11	29	3	0	3	14	15-3	1	19	.188	.259	.266	52	-10	0-0	.971	-6	*77*	*104*	C-26,O-20(1-0-19)	-1.6
	Mil N	10	10	1	1	0	0	1	2	2-0	0	1	.100	.250	.400	79	0	0-0	—	0	0	0	/O(LF)	0.0
Total	8	516	1193	137	285	36	2	67	200	136-20	7	163	.239	.317	.441	109	12	2-0	.987	-13	86	57	O-169(54-0-115),C-155/1-6	-0.5
BLANCO, DAMASO Damaso (Caripe) B 11.12.1941 Curiepe, Venezuela BR/TR 5-10/165# d5.26																								
1972	SF N	39	20	5	7	1	0	0	2	4-0	0	3	.350	.440	.400	144	2	2-1	.889	-1	91	182	3-19/S-8,2-3	0.1
1973	SF N	28	12	4	0	0	0	0	0	1-0	0	2	.000	.077	.000	-74	-3	0-0	1.000	-1	50	0	/3-7,S-5,2-3	-0.4
1974	SF N	5	1	0	0	0	0	0	0	0-0	0	1	.000	.000	.000	-96	0	1-0	—	0			H	0.0
Total	3	72	33	9	7	1	0	0	2	5-0	0	6	.212	.308	.242	58	-1	3-1	.929	-2	81	139	/3-26,S-13,2-6	-0.3
BLANCO, HENRY Henry Ramon B 8.29.1971 Caracas, Venezuela BR/TR 5-11/170# d7.25																								
1997	LA N	3	5	1	2	0	0	1	1	0-0	0	1	.400	.400	1.000	273	1	0-0	1.000	-0	0	0	/13	0.1
1999	Col N	88	263	30	61	12	3	6	28	34-1	1	38	.232	.320	.369	58	-17	1-1	.992	19	102	**161**	C-86/O(LF)	0.7
2000	Mil N	93	284	29	67	24	0	7	31	36-6	0	60	.236	.318	.394	81	-8	0-3	.991	14	184	**165**	C-88	1.0
2001	Mil N	104	314	33	66	18	3	6	31	34-6	2	72	.210	.290	.344	65	-17	3-1	.992	10	131	113	*C-102	0.0
2002	†Atl N	81	221	17	45	9	1	6	22	20-5	1	51	.204	.267	.335	61	-14	0-2	.993	-0	106	115	C-79	-1.0
2003	Atl N	55	151	11	30	8	0	1	13	10-2	1	21	.199	.252	.272	37	-14	0-0	.996	-4	67	109	C-52	-1.5
Total	6	424	1238	121	271	71	7	27	126	134-20	5	243	.219	.295	.353	64	-69	4-7	.992	38	125	135	C-407/O(LF)31	-0.7

Year	Tm Lg	G	AB	R	H	2B	3B	HR	RBI	BB-IB	HP	SO	AVG	OBP	SLG	AOPS	ABR	SB-CS	FA	FR	Rng	Thr	G at Pos	BFW
BLANCO, OSSIE Oswaldo Carlos (Diaz) B 9.8.1945 Caracas, Venezuela BR/TR 6/185# d5.26																								
1970	Chi A	34	66	4	13	0	0	0	8	3-0	0	14	.197	.225	.197	19	-7	0-1	.993	-0	103	83	1-22/O(LF)	-0.9
1974	Cle A	18	36	1	7	0	0	0	2	7-0	0	4	.194	.326	.194	53	-2	0-3	.992	-2	50	104	1-16/D	-0.6
Total	2	52	102	5	20	0	0	0	10	10-0	0	18	.196	.263	.196	31	-9	0-4	.993	-2	76	94	/1-38,DO(LF)	-1.5
BLANK, COONIE Frank Ignatz B 10.18.1892 St.Louis, MO D 12.8.1961 St.Louis, MO BR/TR 5-11/165# d8.15																								
1909	StL N	1	2	0	0	0	0	0	0	0	0		.000	.000	.000	-99	0	0	1.000	-0	_55_	_0_	/C	-0.1
BLANKENSHIP, CLIFF Clifford Douglas B 4.10.1880 Columbus, GA D 4.26.1956 Oakland, CA BR/TR 5-10.5/165# d4.17																								
1905	Cin N	19	56	8	11	1	1	0	7	4	0		.196	.250	.250	44	-4	1	.960	-3	47	97	1-15	-0.7
1907	Was A	37	102	4	23	2	0	0	6	3	0		.225	.248	.245	62	-5	3	.991	-1	_85_	_123_	C-22/1-9	-0.4
1909	Was A	39	60	4	15	1	0	0	9	0	0		.250	.250	.267	66	-3	2	.907	-6	_69_	_83_	C-17/O-4(1-1-2)	-0.8
Total	3	95	218	16	49	4	1	0	22	7	0		.225	.249	.252	58	-12	6	.964	-9	_80_	_110_	/C-39,1-24,O-4(1-1-2)	-1.9
BLANKENSHIP, LANCE Lance Robert B 12.6.1963 Portland, OR BR/TR 6/185# d9.4 OF Total (71-LF 66-CF 71-RF)																								
1988	Oak A	10	3	1	0	0	0	0	0	0-0	0	1	.000	.000	.000	-99	-1	0-1	1.000	-1	42	0	/2-4,D-4	-0.2
1989	†Oak A	58	125	22	29	5	1	1	4	8-0	0	31	.232	.276	.312	68	-6	5-1	1.000	1	120	80	O-25(4-0-21),2-24,D-10	-0.5
1990	†Oak A	86	136	18	26	3	0	0	10	20-0	0	23	.191	.295	.213	46	-9	3-1	.947	-2	99	62	3-28,O-28(10-1-17),2-20/1D	-1.1
1991	Oak A	90	185	33	46	8	0	3	21	23-0	3	42	.249	.336	.341	95	-1	12-3	.983	10	107	107	2-45,O-28(18-0-11),3-14/D-6	1.2
1992	†Oak A	123	349	59	84	24	1	3	34	82-2	6	57	.241	.393	.341	113	13	21-7	.992	7	104	117	2-78,O-51(22-16-20)/1-7,D-3	2.3
1993	Oak A	94	252	43	48	8	1	2	23	67-0	2	64	.190	.363	.254	74	-5	13-5	.994	-0	109	29	O-66(17-49-2),2-19/1-6,S-2,D-5	-0.4
Total	6	461	1050	176	233	48	3	9	92	200-2	11	218	.222	.350	.299	86	-9	54-18	.987	15	112	33	O-198L,2-190/3-42,D-34,1-14,S-2	1.3
BLANKS, LARVELL Larvell B 1.28.1950 Del Rio, TX BR/TR 5-8/167# d7.19																								
1972	Atl N	33	85	10	28	5	0	1	7	7-0	0	12	.329	.376	.424	117	2	0-0	1.000	5	116	113	2-18/S-4,3-2	0.9
1973	Atl N	17	18	1	4	0	0	0	0	1-0	0	3	.222	.263	.222	33	-2	0-0	—	-1	0	0	/3-3,2-2,S-2	-0.3
1974	Atl N	3	8	0	2	0	0	0	1	0-0	0	0	.250	.250	.250	38	-1	0-0	.889	-1	111	0	/S-2	-0.1
1975	Atl N	141	471	49	110	13	3	3	38	38-1	2	43	.234	.292	.293	61	-25	4-3	.960	-8	106	85	*S-129,2-12	-1.9
1976	Cle A	104	328	45	92	8	7	5	41	30-0	0	31	.280	.337	.393	116	6	1-2	.977	-7	86	116	S-56,2-46/3-2,D-3	0.6
1977	Cle A	105	322	43	92	10	4	6	38	19-1	1	37	.286	.324	.398	100	-1	3-0	.960	-11	83	75	S-66,3-18,2-12/D-6	-0.6
1978	Cle A	70	193	19	49	10	0	2	20	10-0	0	16	.254	.285	.337	77	-6	0-0	.926	-4	98	100	S-43,2-17/3-3,D	-0.6
1979	Tex A	68	120	13	24	5	0	1	15	11-0	0	9	.200	.259	.267	45	-9	0-0	.972	-7	90	108	S-49,2-16/D	-1.3
1980	Atl N	88	221	23	45	6	0	2	12	16-1	0	27	.204	.255	.258	43	-17	1-2	.947	13	117	138	S-56,3-43/2	-0.3
Total	9	629	1766	203	446	57	14	20	172	132-3	3	178	.253	.302	.335	78	-53	9-7	.957	-21	99	94	S-407,2-124/3-71,D-11	-3.6
BLASINGAME, DON Don Lee B 3.16.1932 Corinth, MS BL/TR 5-10/165# d9.20																								
1955	StL N	5	16	4	6	1	0	0	0	6-1	0	0	.375	.545	.438	165	2	1-1	.955	0	124	37	/2-3,S-2	0.3
1956	StL N	150	587	94	153	22	7	0	27	72-0	3	52	.261	.344	.322	81	-14	8-8	.986	17	106	132	2-98,S-49/3-2	1.3
1957	StL N	**154**	650	108	176	25	7	8	58	71-4	1	49	.271	.343	.368	89	-8	21-9	.984	20	**110**	**125**	*2-154	2.5
1958	StL N★	143	547	71	150	19	10	2	36	57-2	1	47	.274	.343	.356	83	-13	20-5	.964	-2	100	95	*2-137	-0.3
1959	StL N	150	615	90	178	26	7	1	24	67-2	2	42	.289	.361	.359	87	-9	15-15	.979	**20**	**107**	103	*2-150	2.0
1960	SF N	136	523	72	123	12	8	2	31	49-1	2	53	.235	.302	.300	70	-22	14-2	.979	-10	92	82	*2-133	-2.1
1961	SF N	3	1	1	0	0	0	0	0	2-0	0	1	.000	.667	.000	100	0	0-0	—	0			H	0.0
	†Cin N	123	450	59	100	18	4	1	21	39-0	2	38	.222	.286	.287	52	-31	4-3	.972	-18	90	67	*2-116	-3.9
	Year	126	451	60	100	18	4	1	21	41-0	2	39	.222	.288	.286	53	-30	4-3	.972	-18	90	67	*2-116	-3.9
1962	Cin N	141	494	77	139	9	7	2	35	63-2	2	44	.281	.364	.340	88	-7	4-3	.976	-11	93	76	*2-137	-0.6
1963	Cin N	18	31	4	5	2	0	0	0	7-0	0	5	.161	.316	.226	57	-1	0-1	.974	-0	76	138	2-11/3-2	-0.1
	Was A	69	254	29	65	10	2	2	12	24-1	0	18	.256	.320	.335	84	-5	3-2	.991	10	109	130	2-64	1.1
1964	Was A	143	506	56	135	17	2	1	34	40-1	0	44	.267	.320	.314	78	-15	8-5	.977	-19	98	85	*2-135	-2.4
1965	Was A	129	403	47	90	8	8	1	18	35-1	2	45	.223	.287	.290	66	-19	5-4	.984	-1	98	103	*2-110	-1.3
1966	Was A	68	200	18	43	9	0	1	11	18-0	0	21	.215	.280	.275	61	-10	2-1	.984	0	101	105	2-58/S	-0.6
	KC A	12	19	1	3	0	0	0	1	2-0	0	3	.158	.238	.158	17	-2	0-1	1.000	-0	104	96	/2-4	-0.3
	Year	80	219	19	46	9	0	1	12	20-0	0	24	.210	.276	.265	57	-12	2-2	.985	-0	101	104	2-62/S	-0.9
Total	12	1444	5296	731	1366	178	62	21	308	552-15	15	462	.258	.329	.327	78	-154	105-60	.979	6	100	99	*2-1310/S-52,3-4	-4.4
BLATNIK, JOHNNY John Louis B 3.10.1921 Bridgeport, OH BR/TR 6/195# d4.21																								
1948	Phi N	121	415	56	108	27	8	6	45	31	2	77	.260	.315	.407	96	-4	3	.946	-0	100	110	*O-105(LF)	-1.2
1949	Phi N	6	8	3	1	0	0	0	0	4	0	1	.125	.417	.125	53	0	0	1.000	-0	84	0	/O-2(RF)	0.0
1950	Phi N	4	4	0	1	0	0	0	0	2	0	3	.250	.500	.250	106	0	0	1.000	0	114	0	/O(LF)	0.0
	StL N	7	20	0	3	0	0	0	1	3	0	2	.150	.261	.150	11	-3	0	.875	-0	66	279	/O-7(2-0-7)	-0.3
	Year	11	24	0	4	0	0	0	1	5	0	5	.167	.310	.167	29	-2	0	.900	-0	73	239	/O-8(3-0-7)	-0.3
Total	3	138	447	59	113	27	8	6	46	40	2	83	.253	.317	.389	91	-7	3	.945	-1	98	115	O-115(108-0-9)	-1.5
BLATTNER, BUDDY Robert Garnett B 2.8.1920 St.Louis, MO BR/TR 6-0.5/180# d4.18 Mil 1943-45																								
1942	StL N	19	23	3	1	0	0	0	1	3	1	6	.043	.185	.043	-29	-4	0	.900	-1	92	68	S-13/2-3	-0.4
1946	NY N	126	420	63	107	18	6	11	49	56	**6**	52	.255	.351	.405	113	8	12	.976	4	101	93	*2-114/1	1.9
1947	NY N	55	153	28	40	9	2	0	13	21	0	19	.261	.351	.346	85	-3	4	.947	-1	110	64	2-34,3-11	-0.2
1948	NY N	8	20	3	4	1	0	0	0	3	0	2	.200	.304	.250	51	-1	2	1.000	2	152	129	/2-7	0.1
1949	Phi N	64	97	15	24	6	0	5	21	19	0	17	.247	.371	.464	126	4	0	.981	-6	87	69	2-15,3-12/S	-0.1
Total	5	272	713	112	176	34	8	16	84	102	7	96	.247	.347	.384	102	4	18	.971	-1	103	87	2-173/3-23,S-14,1	1.3
BLAUSER, JEFF Jeffrey Michael B 11.8.1965 Los Gatos, CA BR/TR 6/170# d7.5 OF Total (1-LF 3-CF)																								
1987	Atl N	51	165	11	40	6	3	2	15	18-1	3	34	.242	.328	.352	76	-6	7-3	.962	4	116	93	S-50	0.4
1988	Atl N	18	67	7	16	3	1	2	7	2-0	1	11	.239	.268	.403	87	-1	0-1	.967	1	143	69	/2-9,S-8	0.0
1989	Atl N	142	456	63	123	24	2	12	46	38-2	1	101	.270	.325	.410	107	4	5-2	.929	-16	97	85	3-78,2-39,S-30/O-2(CF)	-1.0
1990	Atl N	115	386	46	104	24	3	8	39	35-1	5	70	.269	.338	.409	99	0	3-5	.961	-3	100	90	S-93,2-14/3-9,O(CF)	0.4
1991	†Atl N	129	352	49	91	14	3	11	54	54-4	2	59	.259	.358	.409	109	6	5-6	.948	-14	83	91	S-85,2-32,3-18	-0.5
1992	†Atl N	123	343	61	90	19	3	14	46	46-2	4	82	.262	.354	.458	122	11	5-5	.968	-14	91	75	*S-106,2-21/3	0.1
1993	†Atl N★	161	597	110	182	29	2	15	73	85-0	**16**	109	.305	.401	.436	124	25	16-6	.970	-16	93	106	*S-161	2.3
1994	Atl N	96	380	56	98	21	4	6	45	38-0	5	64	.258	.329	.382	84	-9	1-3	.970	4	100	85	S-96	0.2
1995	†Atl N	115	431	60	91	16	2	12	31	57-2	12	107	.211	.319	.341	72	-17	8-5	.970	3	97	102	*S-115	-0.5
1996	†Atl N	83	265	48	65	14	1	10	35	40-3	6	54	.245	.356	.419	98	0	6-0	.926	-14	89	95	S-79	-0.6
1997	†Atl N★	151	519	90	160	31	4	17	70	70-6	20	101	.308	.405	.482	130	27	5-1	.973	-18	88	107	*S-149/D	2.0
1998	†Chi N	119	361	49	79	11	3	4	26	60-1	8	93	.219	.340	.299	68	-15	2-2	.965	-22	88	58	*S-106	-2.9
1999	Chi N	104	200	41	48	5	2	9	26	26-0	8	52	.240	.347	.420	95	-2	2-2	.961	-5	78	92	2-25,S-22,3-18/O(LF)	-0.5
Total	13	1407	4522	691	1187	217	33	122	513	569-22	91	937	.262	.354	.406	101	23	65-41	.964	-110	93	91	*S-1100,2-140,3-124/O-4C,D	-0.6
BLAYLOCK, MARV Marvin Edward B 9.30.1929 Ft.Smith, AR D 10.23.1993 Conway, AR BL/TL 6-1.5/175# d9.26																								
1950	NY N	1	1	0	0	0	0	0	0	0	0	0	.000	.000	.000	-99	0	0	—	0			H	0.0
1955	Phi N	113	259	30	54	7	7	3	24	31-2	1	43	.208	.293	.324	66	-13	6-1	.991	2	98	69	1-77/O-6(4-0-2)	-1.4
1956	Phi N	136	460	61	117	14	8	10	50	50-2	2	86	.254	.327	.385	93	-5	5-1	.992	-4	85	91	*1-124/O(RF)	-1.5
1957	Phi N	37	26	5	4	0	0	2	4	3-0	3	8	.154	.313	.385	89	0	0-0	1.000	0	76	0	1-12/O(RF)	-0.1
Total	4	287	746	96	175	21	15	15	78	84-4	6	137	.235	.314	.363	83	-18	11-2	.992	-2	89	82	1-213/O-8(4-0-5)	-3.0
BLEFARY, CURT Curtis Le Roy B 7.5.1943 Brooklyn, NY D 1.28.2001 Pompano Beach, FL BL/TR 6-2/195# d4.14 OF Total (323-LF 232-RF)																								
1965	Bal A	144	462	72	120	23	4	22	70	88-4	3	73	.260	.381	.470	138	26	4-2	.979	1	96	122	*O-136(63-0-73)	2.1
1966	†Bal A	131	419	73	107	14	3	23	64	73-3	6	56	.255	.371	.468	142	26	1-4	.976	-3	90	81	*O-109(LF),1-20	1.6
1967	Bal A	155	554	69	134	19	5	22	81	73-11	8	94	.242	.337	.413	122	16	4-4	.968	11	94	188	*O-103(86-0-19),1-52	1.9
1968	Bal A	137	451	50	90	8	1	15	39	65-11	4	66	.200	.301	.322	90	-4	6-3	.962	-6	102	183	O-92(55-0-46),C-40,1-12	-1.6
1969	Hou N	155	542	66	137	26	7	12	67	77-10	4	79	.253	.347	.393	110	9	8-7	.987	6	**109**	96	*1-152/O(LF)	0.2
1970	NY A	99	269	34	57	6	0	9	37	43-3	3	37	.212	.324	.335	87	-4	1-3	.972	-9	80	21	O-79(RF)/1-6	-1.8
1971	NY A	21	36	4	7	1	0	1	2	3-0	0	5	.194	.256	.306	62	-2	0-0	.875	-0	70	335	/O-6(RF),1-4	-0.3
	†Oak A	50	101	15	22	2	0	5	12	15-2	1	15	.218	.325	.386	103	0	0-1	.975	-2	63	112	C-14,O-14(8-0-6)/3-5,2-2	-0.2
	Year	71	137	19	29	3	0	6	14	18-2	1	20	.212	.308	.365	93	-1	0-1	.958	-2	85	233	O-20(8-0-12),C-14/3-5,1-4,2-2	-0.5
1972	Oak A	8	11	1	5	2	0	0	1	0-0	0	1	.455	.417	.636	234	2	0-0	—	-0	0	0	/12O(LF)	0.2
	SD N	74	102	10	20	3	0	3	9	19-3	0	18	.196	.320	.314	88	-1	0-0	.982	-3	50	125	C-12/1-6,3-3,O-3(RF)	-0.5

Year	Tm Lg	G	AB	R	H	2B	3B	HR	RBI	BB-IB	HP	SO	AVG	OBP	SLG	AOPS	ABR	SB-CS	FA	FR	Rng	Thr	G at Pos	BFW
Total	8	974	2947	394	699	104	20	112	382	456-47	29	444	.237	.342	.400	115	68	24-24	.972	-5	93	126	O-544L,1-253/C-66,3-8,2-3	1.6
BLESSITT, IKE Isaiah B 9.30.1949 Detroit, MI BR/TR 5-11/185# d9.7																								
1972	Det A	4	5	0	0	0	0	0	0	0-0	0	2	.000	.000	.000	-97	-1	0-0	1.000	0	168	0	/O(1-0-1)	-0.1
BLIGH, NED Edwin Forrest B 6.30.1864 Brooklyn, NY D 4.18.1892 Brooklyn, NY BR/TR 5-11/172# d6.26																								
1886	Bal AA	3	9	0	0	0	0	0	0	1	0		.000	.100	.000	-69	-2	0	.833	-1			/C-3	-0.3
1888	Cin AA	3	5	0	0	0	0	0	0	0	0		.000	.000	.000	-95	-1	0	1.000	-0			/C-2,O(RF)	-0.1
1889	Col AA	28	93	6	13	1	1	0	5	4	3	14	.140	.200	.172	7	-12	2	.927	-3			C-28	-1.1
1890	Col AA	8	29	2	6	2	0	0	5	2	0		.207	.258	.276	62	-1	0	.933	1	*105*	*141*	/C-8	0.0
	†Lou AA	24	73	9	15	0	0	1	9	9	0		.205	.293	.247	60	-4	1	.921	2	*135*	*82*	C-24	0.0
	Year	32	102	11	21	2	0	1	14	11	0		.206	.283	.255	61	-5	1	.925	3	*127*	*98*	C-32	0.0
Total	4	66	209	17	34	3	1	1	19	16	3	14	.163	.232	.201	28	-20	3	.923	-2	*65*	*50*	/C-65,O(RF)	-1.5
BLISS, FRANK Frank Eugene B 12.10.1852 Chicago, IL D 1.8.1929 Nashville, TN d6.20																								
1878	Mil N	2	8	1	1	0	0	0	0	0		0	.125	.125	.125	-17	-1		1.000	-1	93	0	/3C	-0.1
BLISS, JACK John Joseph Albert B 1.9.1882 Vancouver, WA D 10.23.1968 Temple City, CA BR/TR 5-9/185# d5.10																								
1908	StL N	44	136	9	29	4	0	1	5	8	2		.213	.267	.265	73	-4	3	.992	-2	*67*	*117*	C-43	-0.2
1909	StL N	35	113	12	25	2	1	1	8	12	2		.221	.307	.283	89	-1	2	.951	-2	*79*	*96*	C-32	-0.1
1910	StL N	16	33	2	2	0	0	0	3	4	0	8	.061	.162	.061	-36	-6	0	.980	-2	*73*	*80*	C-13	-0.7
1911	StL N	97	258	36	59	6	4	1	27	42	2	25	.229	.341	.295	81	-5	5	.952	-15	*75*	*105*	C-84/S	-1.4
1912	StL N	49	114	11	28	3	1	0	18	19	4	14	.246	.372	.289	84	-1	3	.973	-6	*69*	*96*	C-41	-0.4
Total	5	241	654	70	143	15	6	3	61	85	10	47	.219	.318	.274	76	-17	13	.966	-27	*73*	*103*	C-213/S	-2.8
BLOCK, BRUNO James John (born James John Blochowicz) B 3.13.1885 Wisconsin Rapids, WI D 8.6.1937 S.Milwaukee, WI BR/TR 5-9/185# d8.5																								
1907	Was A	24	57	3	8	2	1	0	2	2	0		.140	.169	.211	23	-5	0	.949	-4	*78*	*102*	C-21	-0.9
1910	Chi A	55	152	12	32	1	1	0	9	13	0		.211	.273	.230	60	-7	3	.964	2	*120*	*102*	C-47	0.0
1911	Chi A	39	115	11	35	6	1	1	18	6	0		.304	.339	.400	109	1	0	.972	0	*145*	*74*	C-38	0.4
1912	Chi A	46	136	8	35	5	6	0	26	7	0		.257	.294	.382	96	-2	1	.980	2	*99*	*93*	C-46	0.3
1914	Chi F	45	106	8	21	4	1	0	14	11	0	17	.198	.274	.255	47	-10	1	.966	3	*140*	*88*	C-34	-0.5
Total	5	209	566	42	131	18	10	1	69	39	0	17	.231	.281	.304	74	-23	5	.969	3	*120*	*91*	C-186	-0.7
BLOCK, CY Seymour B 5.4.1919 Brooklyn, NY BR/TR 6/180# d9.7 Mil 1943-45																								
1942	Chi N	9	33	6	12	1	1	0	4	3	0	3	.364	.417	.455	161	2	2	.917	-2	70	59	/3-8,2	0.1
1945	†Chi N	2	7	1	1	0	0	0	1	0	0	0	.143	.143	.143	-21	-1	0	1.000	1	147	0	/23	-0.1
1946	Chi N	6	13	2	3	0	0	0	0	4	0	0	.231	.412	.231	86	0	0	1.000	1	105	582	/3-4	0.1
Total	3	17	53	9	16	1	1	0	5	7	0	3	.302	.383	.358	118	1	2	.947	-1	82	195	/3-13,2-2	0.1
BLOCKER, TERRY Terry Fennell B 8.18.1959 Columbia, SC BL/TL 6-2/195# d4.11																								
1985	NY N	18	15	1	1	0	0	0	0	1-0	0	2	.067	.125	.067	-46	-3	0-0	1.000	-0	75	0	/O-5(3-1-1)	-0.4
1988	Atl N	66	198	13	42	4	2	2	10	10-3	0	20	.212	.250	.283	50	-13	1-1	.994	1	108	37	O-61(CF)	-1.4
1989	Atl N	26	31	1	7	1	0	0	1	1-0	0	5	.226	.250	.258	44	-2	1-0	1.000	-0	93	0	/O-8(2-2-4),P	-0.2
Total	3	110	244	15	50	5	2	2	11	12-3	0	27	.205	.242	.266	44	-18	2-1	.994	0	106	33	/O-74(5-64-5),P	-2.0
BLOGG, WES Wesley Collins B 1855 Norfolk, VA D 3.10.1897 Baltimore, MD 5-8/155# d6.20																								
1883	Pit AA	9	34	0	5	0	0	0		0			.147	.147	.147	-5	-4		.881	-2			/C-6,O-3(RF)	-0.5
BLOMBERG, RON Ronald Mark "Boomer" B 8.23.1948 Atlanta, GA BL/TR 6-1/205# d9.10																								
1969	NY A	4	6	0	3	0	0	0	0	1-0	0	0	.500	.571	.500	210	1	0-0	1.000	-0	70	0	/O-2(LF)	0.1
1971	NY A	64	199	30	64	6	2	7	31	14-3	0	23	.322	.363	.477	146	11	2-4	.970	-4	91	27	O-57(RF)	0.4
1972	NY A	107	299	36	80	22	1	14	49	38-4	3	26	.268	.355	.488	155	21	0-2	.985	-7	72	127	1-95	0.7
1973	NY A	100	301	45	99	13	1	12	57	34-4	0	25	.329	.395	.498	156	23	2-0	.980	1	122	128	D-55,1-41	2.0
1974	NY A	90	264	39	82	11	2	10	48	29-2	2	33	.311	.375	.481	150	17	2-1	1.000	1	108	175	D-58,O-19(2-0-17)	1.7
1975	NY A	34	106	18	27	8	2	4	17	13-1	0	10	.255	.336	.481	131	4	0-0	1.000	0	112	0	D-27/O(RF)	0.3
1976	NY A	1	2	0	0	0	0	0	0	0-0	0	0	.000	.000	.000	-99	-1	0-0	—	0			/D	-0.1
1978	Chi A	61	156	16	36	7	0	5	22	11-2	0	17	.231	.280	.372	81	-4	0-0	.986	-1	69	35	D-36/1-7	-0.7
Total	8	461	1333	184	391	67	8	52	224	140-16	5	134	.293	.360	.473	142	72	6-7	.983	-10	86	122	D-177,1-143/O-79(4-0-75)	4.4
BLONG, JOE Joseph Myles B 9.17.1853 St.Louis, MO D 9.17.1892 St.Louis, MO BR/TR d5.4 ▲																								
1875	RS NA	16	68	3	10	2	0	0	5	0		7	.147	.147	.176	13	-5	1-0	.927	3	134	82	P-15/O-4(2-2-0)	0.1
1876	StL N	62	264	30	62	7	4	0	30	2		9	.235	.241	.292	81	-5		.895	-1	124	123	*O-62(RF)/P	-0.5
1877	StL N	58	218	17	47	8	3	0	13	4		22	.216	.230	.280	63	-8		.835	-2	86	0	*O-40(13-4-23),P-25	-0.7
Total	2	120	482	47	109	15	7	0	43	6		31	.226	.236	.286	72	-13		.867	-3	110	77	O-102(13-4-85)/P-26	-1.2
BLOODWORTH, JIMMY James Henry B 7.26.1917 Tallahassee, FL D 8.17.2002 Apalachicola, FL BR/TR 5-11/180# d9.14 Mil 1944-46																								
1937	Was A	15	50	3	11	2	1	0	8	5	0	8	.220	.291	.300	51	-4	0-1	.946	-1	102	98	2-14	-0.4
1939	Was A	83	318	34	92	24	1	4	40	10	1	26	.289	.313	.409	90	-6	3-1	.972	12	101	135	2-73/O-5(RF)	0.9
1940	Was A	119	469	47	115	17	8	11	70	16	1	71	.245	.272	.386	73	-23	3-1	.978	14	97	106	2-96,1-17/3-6	-0.4
1941	Was A	142	506	59	124	24	3	7	66	41	1	58	.245	.303	.346	75	-20	1-1	.971	**27**	**109**	114	*2-132/3-6,S	1.5
1942	Det A	137	533	62	129	23	1	13	57	35	5	63	.242	.295	.362	78	-17	2-8	.972	10	**104**	75	*2-134/S-2	-0.1
1943	Det A	129	474	41	114	23	4	6	52	29	3	59	.241	.289	.344	79	-14	4-7	.972	15	104	86	*2-129	0.8
1946	Det A	76	249	25	61	8	1	5	36	12	2	26	.245	.285	.345	71	-10	3-3	.974	-1	94	107	2-71	-0.8
1947	Pit N	88	316	27	79	9	0	7	48	16	2	39	.250	.290	.345	66	-16	1	.979	-16	84	95	2-87	-2.8
1949	Cin N	134	452	40	118	27	1	9	59	27	1	36	.261	.304	.385	83	-12	1	.981	-4	100	93	2-92,1-23/3-8	-1.2
1950	Cin N	4	14	1	3	1	0	0	1	2	0	0	.214	.313	.286	58	-1	0	1.000	-2	58	0	/2-4	-0.2
	†Phi N	54	96	6	22	2	0	0	13	6	0	12	.229	.275	.250	40	-9	0	1.000	-1	96	100	2-27/1-7,3-2	-0.8
	Year	58	110	7	25	3	0	0	14	8	0	12	.227	.280	.255	42	-9	0	1.000	-3	91	86	2-31/1-7,3-2	-1.0
1951	Phi N	21	42	2	6	0	0	0	1	3	0	9	.143	.200	.143	-6	-6	1-0	1.000	-1	99	64	/2-8,1-6	-0.7
Total	11	1002	3519	347	874	160	20	62	451	202	16	407	.248	.292	.358	74	-138	19-22	.975	52	100	98	2-867/1-53,3-22,O-5(RF),S-3	-4.2
BLOOMFIELD, BUD Clyde Stalcup B 1.5.1936 Oklahoma City, OK BR/TR 5-11.5/175# d9.25																								
1963	StL N	1	0	0	0	0	0	0	0	0-0	0	0	—	—	—	—	0	0-0	—	-0	0	0	/3	0.0
1964	Min A	7	7	1	1	0	0	0	0	0-0	0	0	.143	.143	.143	-20	-1	0-0	1.000	1	128	212	/2-3,S-2	0.0
Total	2	8	7	1	1	0	0	0	0	0-0	0	0	.143	.143	.143	-20	-1	0-0	1.000	1	128	212	/2-3,S-2,3	0.0
BLOOMQUIST, WILLIE William Paul B 11.27.1977 Bremerton, WA BR/TR 5-11/185# d9.1 OF Total (17-LF 1-RF)																								
2002	Sea A	12	33	11	15	4	0	0	7	5-0	0	2	.455	.526	.576	200	5	3-1	1.000	1	121	0	/O-7(LF),2-4	0.6
2003	Sea A	89	196	30	49	7	2	1	14	19-1	1	39	.250	.317	.321	72	-8	4-1	.970	-6	80	65	3-37,S-18,D-12,O-11(10-0-1)/2-7,1-3	-1.3
Total	2	101	229	41	64	11	2	1	21	24-1	1	41	.279	.348	.358	91	-3	7-2	.970	-6	80	65	/3-37,S-18,O-18L,D-12,2-11,1-3	-0.7
BLOSSER, GREG Gregory Brent B 6.26.1971 Manatee, FL BL/TL 6-3/200# d9.5																								
1993	Bos A	17	28	1	2	1	0	0	1	2-0	0	7	.071	.133	.107	-33	-5	1-0	1.000	1	105	328	/O-9(LF),D	-0.5
1994	Bos A	5	11	2	1	0	0	0	1	4-0	0	4	.091	.333	.091	16	-1	0-0	.727	0	184	0	/O-3(1-0-2),D	-0.1
Total	2	22	39	3	3	1	0	0	2	6-0	0	11	.077	.200	.103	-16	-6	1-0	.870	1	129	229	/O-12(10-0-2),D-2	-0.6
BLOTT, JACK John Leonard B 8.24.1902 Girard, OH D 6.11.1964 Ann Arbor, MI BR/TR 6/210# d7.30																								
1924	Cin N	2	1	0	0	0	0	0	0	0	0	0	.000	.000	.000	-99	0	0-0	1.000	-0	*0*	*0*	/C	0.0
BLOWERS, MIKE Michael Roy B 4.24.1965 Wurzburg, W.Germany BR/TR 6-2/210# d9.1 OF Total (16-LF 6-RF)																								
1989	NY A	13	38	2	10	0	0	0	3	3-0	0	13	.263	.317	.263	66	-2	0-0	.852	-4	62	148	3-13	-0.5
1990	NY A	48	144	16	27	4	0	5	21	12-1	1	50	.188	.255	.319	59	-8	1-0	.899	-11	74	51	3-45/D-2	-2.0
1991	NY A	15	35	3	7	0	0	1	1	4-0	0	3	.200	.282	.286	57	-2	0-0	.870	-3	77	49	3-14	-0.5
1992	Sea A	31	73	7	14	3	0	1	2	6-0	0	20	.192	.253	.274	47	-5	0-0	.984	1	90	193	3-29/1-3	-0.5
1993	Sea A	127	379	55	106	23	3	15	57	44-3	2	98	.280	.357	.475	120	11	1-5	.951	7	107	75	*3-117/O-2(1-0-1),C1D	1.6
1994	Sea A	85	270	37	78	13	0	9	49	25-2	1	60	.289	.348	.437	100	0	2-2	.939	5	108	64	3-48,1-20/O-9(8-0-1),D-9	0.3
1995	†Sea A	134	439	59	113	24	1	23	96	53-0	0	128	.257	.335	.474	107	4	2-1	.947	-14	79	43	*3-126/1-7,O-5(2-0-3)	-0.8
1996	LA N	92	317	31	84	19	2	6	38	37-2	1	77	.265	.341	.394	102	1	0-0	.951	-18	72	66	3-90/1-6,S	-1.6
1997	†Sea A	68	150	22	44	5	0	5	20	21-1	0	33	.293	.376	.427	111	3	0-0	.990	1	125	93	1-49,3-10/O-6(5-0-1),D	0.1

Year	Tm Lg	G	AB	R	H	2B	3B	HR	RBI	BB-IB	HP	SO	AVG	OBP	SLG	AOPS	ABR	SB-CS	FA	FR	Rng	Thr	G at Pos	BFW
1998	Oak A	129	409	56	97	24	2	11	71	39-1	1	116	.237	.302	.386	80	-13	1-0	.927	-9	96	95	*3-120/1-8,D-2	-1.9
1999	Sea A	19	46	2	11	1	0	2	7	4-0	0	12	.239	.300	.391	76	-2	0-0	1.000	1	125	163	1-14/3-4,D	-0.2
Total	11	761	2300	290	591	116	8	78	365	248-10	6	610	.257	.329	.416	97	-13	7-8	.938	-44	89	74	3-616,1-108/O-22L,D-18,SC	-6.0
BLUE, BERT Bird Wayne B 12.9.1877 Bettsville, OH D 9.2.1929 Detroit, MI BR/TR 6-3/200# d6.15																								
1908	StL A	11	24	2	9	1	2	0	1	3	0		.375	.444	.583	232	3	0	.942	1	*141*	*57*	/C-8	0.5
	Phi A	6	18	2	3	0	0	0	1	0	0		.167	.167	.167	8	-2	0	1.000	0	*73*	*123*	/C-6	-0.1
	Year	17	42	4	12	1	2	0	2	3	0		.286	.333	.405	136	1	0	.967	1	*113*	*84*	C-14	0.4
BLUE, LU Luzerne Atwell B 3.5.1897 Washington, DC D 7.28.1958 Alexandria, VA BB/TL 5-10/165# d4.14																								
1921	Det A	153	585	103	180	33	11	5	75	103	5	47	.308	.416	.427	116	20	13-17	.990	-6	85	68	*1-152	0.1
1922	Det A	145	584	131	175	31	9	6	45	82	7	48	.300	.392	.414	114	15	8-5	.991	0	101	101	*1-144	0.6
1923	Det A	129	504	100	143	27	7	1	46	96	4	40	.284	.402	.371	106	11	10-11	.992	5	113	79	*1-129	0.5
1924	Det A	108	395	81	123	26	7	2	53	64	4	26	.311	.413	.428	119	14	9-4	.986	3	114	93	*1-108	1.0
1925	Det A	150	532	91	163	18	9	3	94	83	3	29	.306	.403	.391	104	6	19-5	.988	1	102	94	*1-148	0.0
1926	Det A	128	429	92	123	24	14	1	52	90	2	18	.287	.413	.415	115	13	13-7	.985	-6	82	108	*1-109/O(CF)	0.0
1927	Det A	112	365	71	95	17	9	1	42	71	2	28	.260	.384	.364	94	-1	13-7	.984	-2	98	**120**	*1-104	-0.8
1928	StL A	**154**	549	116	154	32	11	14	80	105	4	43	.281	.400	.455	120	20	12-7	.989	2	106	103	*1-154	1.2
1929	StL A	151	573	111	168	40	10	6	61	126	2	32	.293	.422	.429	115	21	12-6	.994	-3	92	107	*1-151	0.7
1930	StL A	117	425	85	100	27	5	4	42	81	4	44	.235	.363	.351	79	-11	12-7	.987	-0	104	100	*1-111	-1.6
1931	Chi A	155	589	119	179	23	15	1	62	127	3	60	.304	.430	.399	126	32	13-3	.990	-3	95	81	*1-155	1.5
1932	Chi A	112	373	51	93	21	2	0	43	64	3	21	.249	.364	.316	83	-6	17-6	.986	8	**138**	**116**	*1-105	-0.5
1933	Bro N	1	1	0	0	0	0	0	0	0	0	0	.000	.000	.000	-99	0	0	1.000	-0	0	0	/1	0.0
Total	13	1615	5904	1151	1696	319	109	44	695	1092	43	436	.287	.402	.401	109	134	151-85	.989	-2	101	96	*1-1571/O(CF)	2.7
BLUEGE, OSSIE Oswald Louis B 10.24.1900 Chicago, IL D 10.14.1985 Edina, MN BR/TR 5-11/162# d4.24 M5 C3 b-Otto OF Total (LF)																								
1922	Was A	19	61	5	12	1	0	0	2	7	2	7	.197	.300	.213	37	-5	1-0	.925	-2	95	101	3-17/S-2	-0.6
1923	Was A	109	379	48	93	15	7	2	42	48	8	53	.245	.343	.338	84	-8	5-3	.936	4	103	**144**	*3-106/2-4	0.3
1924	†Was A	117	402	59	113	15	4	2	49	39	9	36	.281	.358	.353	86	-8	7-5	.943	-13	92	65	*3-102,2-10/S-4	-1.4
1925	†Was A	145	522	77	150	27	4	4	79	59	2	56	.287	.362	.377	89	-7	16-15	.953	1	100	108	*3-144/S-4	0.1
1926	Was A	139	487	69	132	19	8	3	65	70	5	46	.271	.368	.361	93	-3	12-9	.952	-16	91	64	*3-134/S-8	-1.0
1927	Was A	146	503	71	138	21	10	1	66	57	5	47	.274	.354	.362	87	-9	15-5	.961	15	**112**	71	*3-146	1.5
1928	Was A	146	518	78	154	33	7	2	75	46	**8**	27	.297	.364	.400	101	2	18-6	.960	10	**110**	**133**	*3-144/2	2.2
1929	Was A	64	220	35	65	6	0	5	31	19	1	15	.295	.354	.391	91	-3	6-4	.967	4	117	132	3-35,2-14,S-10	0.4
1930	Was A	134	476	64	138	27	7	3	69	51	8	40	.290	.368	.395	93	-3	15-8	.964	-1	101	91	*3-134	0.4
1931	Was A	152	570	82	155	25	7	8	98	50	5	39	.272	.336	.382	88	-11	16-10	**.960**	-7	94	97	*3-152/S	-1.1
1932	Was A	149	507	64	131	22	4	5	64	83	4	41	.258	.367	.347	87	-6	9-7	.970	5	105	**119**	*3-149	0.3
1933	†Was A	140	501	63	131	14	0	6	71	55	3	34	.261	.338	.325	77	-15	6-7	.965	-10	97	116	*3-138	-2.1
1934	Was A	99	285	39	70	9	2	0	11	23	2	15	.246	.306	.291	57	-19	2-1	.950	7	120	136	3-41,S-30/2-5,O-5(LF)	-0.7
1935	Was A★	100	320	44	84	14	3	0	34	37	1	21	.262	.341	.325	75	-11	2-2	.967	2	99	85	S-58,3-25/2-4	-0.4
1936	Was A	90	319	43	92	12	1	1	55	38	6	16	.288	.375	.342	83	-7	5-3	.993	4	97	108	2-52,S-23,3-15	0.2
1937	Was A	42	127	12	36	4	2	1	13	13	1	9	.283	.355	.370	87	-3	1-1	.952	-2	96	100	S-28/1-2,3-2	-0.2
1938	Was A	58	184	25	48	12	1	0	21	21	1	11	.261	.340	.337	75	-7	3-1	.990	0	104	101	2-38,S-10/13	-0.3
1939	Was A	18	59	5	9	0	0	0	3	7	0	2	.153	.242	.153	3	-9	1-0	.989	0	127	114	1-11/2-2,S-2,3-2	-0.8
Total	18	1867	6440	883	1751	276	67	43	848	723	71	515	.272	.352	.356	85	-132	140-87	.957	3	102	104	*3-1487,S-180,2-130/1-14,0-5L	-3.2
BLUEGE, OTTO Otto Adam "Squeaky" B 7.20.1909 Chicago, IL D 6.28.1977 Chicago, IL BR/TR 5-10/154# d4.12 b-Ossie																								
1932	Cin N	1	0	1	0	0	0	0	0	0	0	0	—	—	—	—	0	0	—	0			R	0.0
1933	Cin N	108	291	17	62	6	2	0	18	26	0	29	.213	.278	.247	52	-18	0	.937	-8	99	98	S-95,2-10/3	-2.1
Total	2	109	291	18	62	6	2	0	18	26	0	29	.213	.278	.247	52	-18	0	.937	-8	99	98	/S-95,2-10,3	-2.1
BLUHM, RED Harvey Fred B 6.27.1894 Cleveland, OH D 5.7.1952 Flint, MI BR/TR 5-11/165# d7.3																								
1918	Bos A	1	1	0	0	0	0	0	0	0	0	0	.000	.000	.000	-99	0	0	—	0			H	0.0
BLUM, GEOFF Geoffrey Edward B 4.26.1973 Redwood City, CA BB/TR (BL 2000 (part)) 6-3/193# d8.9 OF Total (45-LF 4-RF)																								
1999	Mon N	45	133	21	32	7	2	8	18	17-3	0	25	.241	.327	.504	109	1	1-0	.928	-13	82	48	S-42/2-2	-0.8
2000	Mon N	124	343	40	97	20	2	11	45	26-2	3	60	.283	.335	.449	94	-4	1-4	.952	12	117	70	3-55,S-44,2-13,1-11	0.9
2001	Mon N	148	453	57	107	25	0	9	50	43-8	10	94	.236	.313	.351	71	-19	9-5	.966	2	103	105	3-72,O-35(LF),2-25,1-14/S-4	-1.7
2002	Hou N	130	368	45	104	20	4	10	52	49-5	1	70	.283	.367	.440	110	5	2-0	.971	15	113	147	*3-104,O-10(9-0-3)/S-2,12	2.0
2003	Hou N	123	420	51	110	19	0	10	52	20-1	2	50	.262	.295	.379	72	-18	0-0	.971	-7	96	144	3-83,2-25,S-11/1-6,O-2(1-0-1)	-2.3
Total	5	570	1717	214	450	91	8	48	217	155-19	16	299	.262	.326	.408	87	-35	13-9	.967	8	107	124	3-314,S-103/2-66,O-47L,1-32	-1.9
BOAK, CHET Chester Robert B 6.19.1935 New Castle, PA D 11.28.1983 Emporium, PA BR/TR 6/180# d9.18																								
1960	KC A	5	13	1	2	0	0	0	1	0-0	1	2	.154	.200	.154	1	-2	0-0	.957	0	100	133	/2-5	-0.1
1961	Was A	5	7	0	0	0	0	0	0	1-0	0	1	.000	.125	.000	-64	-2	1-0	1.000	-0	91	0	/2	-0.2
Total	2	10	20	1	2	0	0	0	1	1-0	1	3	.100	.174	.100	-22	-4	1-0	.962	-0	98	110	/2-6	-0.3
BOARDMAN, FREDERICK Frederick d8.29																								
1874	Bal NA	1	4	0	1	0	0	0	0	0		0	.250	.250	.250	61	0	0-0	—	0	0	0	/O(RF)	0.0
BOBB, RANDY Mark Randall B 1.1.1948 Los Angeles, CA D 6.13.1982 Carnelian Bay, CA BR/TR 6-1/185# d8.15																								
1968	Chi N	7	8	0	1	0	0	0	0	1-0	0	2	.125	.222	.125	6	-1	0-0	1.000	0	*110*	*140*	/C-7	-0.1
1969	Chi N	3	2	0	0	0	0	0	0	0-0	0	1	.000	.000	.000	-89	0	0-0	1.000	-1	35	0	/C-2	-0.1
Total	2	10	10	0	1	0	0	0	0	1-0	0	3	.100	.182	.100	-14	-1	0-0	1.000	-0	*92*	*106*	/C-9	-0.2
BOCACHICA, HIRAM Hiram (Colon) B 3.4.1976 Ponce, P.R. BR/TR 5-11/165# d9.13																								
2000	LA N	8	10	2	3	0	0	0	0	0-0	0	2	.300	.300	.300	56	-1	0-0	1.000	3	252	255	/2-2	0.2
2001	LA N	75	133	15	31	11	1	2	9	9-0	1	33	.233	.287	.376	75	-5	4-1	.941	-4	100	95	2-19,O-13(10-0-3)/3-8	-0.8
2002	LA N	49	65	12	14	3	0	4	9	5-0	0	19	.215	.271	.446	94	-1	1-1	.960	-1	99	0	O-22(19-3-2)	-0.3
	Det A	34	103	14	23	4	0	4	8	5-0	0	22	.223	.259	.379	71	-5	2-2	.966	0	91	235	O-32(1-27-4)/2-2,D	-0.5
2003	Det A	6	22	1	1	1	0	0	0	0-0	0	7	.045	.045	.091	-71	-5	0-0	1.000	0	80	377	/O-6(1-5-0)	-0.5
Total	4	172	333	44	72	19	1	10	26	19-0	1	83	.216	.261	.369	67	-17	7-4	.962	-2	93	160	/O-73(31-35-9),2-23,3-8,D	-1.9
BOCCABELLA, JOHN John Dominic B 6.29.1941 San Francisco, CA BR/TR 6-1/200# d9.2																								
1963	Chi N	24	74	7	14	4	1	1	5	6-0	0	21	.189	.247	.311	57	-4	0-1	.996	-1	80	180	1-24	-0.8
1964	Chi N	9	23	4	9	2	1	0	6	0-0	0	3	.391	.391	.565	159	2	0-0	1.000	-0	97	84	/1-5,O-2(LF)	0.1
1965	Chi N	6	12	2	4	0	0	2	4	1-0	0	2	.333	.385	.833	227	2	0-0	1.000	-0	117	0	/1-2,O(LF)	0.1
1966	Chi N	75	206	22	47	9	0	6	25	14-1	0	39	.228	.274	.359	74	-7	0-1	.981	2	94	143	O-33(LF),1-30/C-5	-0.9
1967	Chi N	25	35	0	6	1	1	0	8	3-1	1	7	.171	.250	.257	45	-3	0-0	1.000	-0	112	0	/O-9(4-0-5),1-3,C	-0.3
1968	Chi N	7	14	0	1	0	0	0	1	2-0	0	2	.071	.176	.071	-19	-2	0-0	1.000	-0	*180*	*0*	/C-4,O(LF)	-0.2
1969	Mon N	40	86	4	9	2	0	1	6	6-1	1	30	.105	.170	.163	-6	-12	1-0	1.000	-1	79	181	C-32	-1.3
1970	Mon N	61	145	18	39	3	1	5	17	11-2	0	24	.269	.321	.407	94	-2	0-1	.993	6	178	111	1-33,C-24/3	0.3
1971	Mon N	74	177	15	39	11	0	3	15	14-2	1	26	.220	.278	.333	73	-6	0-1	.979	-3	118	97	C-37,1-37/3-2	-1.1
1972	Mon N	83	207	14	47	8	1	1	10	9-3	1	29	.227	.259	.290	56	-12	1-2	.983	6	99	164	C-73/1-7,3	-0.6
1973	Mon N	118	403	25	94	13	0	7	46	26-8	1	57	.233	.279	.318	63	-21	1-1	.980	5	100	119	*C-117/1	-1.1
1974	SF N	29	80	6	11	3	0	0	5	4-2	0	6	.138	.176	.175	-1	-11	0-0	.991	-1	110	46	C-26	-1.1
Total	12	551	1462	117	320	56	5	26	148	96-20	5	246	.219	.267	.317	62	-76	3-7	.984	13	*101*	*124*	C-319,1-142/O-46(41-0-5),3-4	-6.9
BOCEK, MILT Milton Francis B 7.16.1912 Chicago, IL BR/TR 6-1/185# d9.3																								
1933	Chi A	11	22	3	8	1	0	1	3	4	0	6	.364	.462	.545	173	3	0-0	1.000	-1	76	0	/O-6(3-1-2)	0.2
1934	Chi A	19	38	3	8	1	0	0	3	5	0	5	.211	.302	.237	39	-3	0-0	1.000	2	117	238	O-10(9-1-0)	-0.2
Total	2	30	60	6	16	2	0	1	6	9	0	11	.267	.362	.350	86	0	0-0	1.000	1	106	175	/O-16(12-2-2)	0.0
BOCHTE, BRUCE Bruce Anton B 11.12.1950 Pasadena, CA BL/TL 6-3/200# d7.19																								
1974	Cal A	57	196	24	53	4	1	5	26	18-0	1	23	.270	.332	.378	111	2	6-3	.985	-3	96	87	O-39(32-5-3),1-24	-0.4
1975	Cal A	107	375	41	107	19	3	3	48	45-5	2	43	.285	.362	.376	118	10	3-4	.987	-6	75	103	*1-105/D	-0.5
1976	Cal A	146	466	53	120	17	1	2	49	64-11	2	53	.258	.346	.311	101	4	4-5	.988	1	104	55	O-86(71-0-18),1-59/D	-0.6
1977	Cal A	25	100	12	29	4	0	2	8	7-0	0	4	.290	.336	.390	101	0	3-2	1.000	0	79	304	O-24(CF)/D	0.0

Year	Tm Lg	G	AB	R	H	2B	3B	HR	RBI	BB-IB	HP	SO	AVG	OBP	SLG	AOPS	ABR	SB-CS	FA	FR	Rng	Thr	G at Pos	BFW
	Cle A	112	392	52	119	19	1	5	43	40-3	0	38	.304	.364	.395	112	8	3-2	.966	3	109	130	O-76(74-3-1),1-36/D	0.5
	Year	137	492	64	148	23	1	7	51	47-3	0	42	.301	.358	.394	110	8	6-4	.974	3	102	173	*O-100(74-27-1),1-36/D-2	0.5
1978	Sea A	140	486	58	128	25	3	11	51	60-3	1	47	.263	.342	.395	108	7	3-4	.984	-5	84	114	O-91(82-19-0),D-43/1	-0.4
1979	Sea A★	150	554	81	175	38	6	16	100	67-8	2	64	.316	.385	.493	134	29	2-2	.991	5	114	103	*1-147	2.4
1980	Sea A	148	520	62	156	34	4	13	78	72-13	0	81	.300	.381	.456	128	23	2-3	.996	7	119	116	*1-133,D-11	2.1
1981	Sea A	99	335	39	87	16	0	6	30	47-5	2	53	.260	.354	.361	102	3	1-3	.995	-4	94	97	1-82,O-14(LF)/D	-0.7
1982	Sea A	144	509	58	151	21	0	12	70	67-5	3	71	.297	.380	.409	114	13	8-5	.988	-5	83	91	O-99(99-1-0),1-34,D-12	0.1
1984	Oak A	148	469	58	124	23	0	5	52	52-3	0	59	.264	.333	.345	96	-1	2-5	.993	-13	68	98	*1-144/D-2	-2.3
1985	Oak A	137	424	48	125	17	1	14	60	49-6	0	58	.295	.367	.439	129	18	3-1	.990	-10	73	86	*1-128	0.2
1986	Oak A	125	407	57	104	13	1	6	43	65-3	0	68	.256	.357	.337	98	1	3-2	.991	0	100	86	*1-115/D	-0.5
Total	12	1538	5233	643	1478	250	21	100	658	653-65	13	662	.282	.360	.396	114	117	43-41	.992	-29	93	98	*1-1008,O-429(372-52-22)/D-74	-0.1

BOCHY, BRUCE Bruce Douglas B 4.16.1955 Landes De Bussac, France BR/TR 6-4/210# d7.19 M9 C2

Year	Tm Lg	G	AB	R	H	2B	3B	HR	RBI	BB-IB	HP	SO	AVG	OBP	SLG	AOPS	ABR	SB-CS	FA	FR	Rng	Thr	G at Pos	BFW
1978	Hou N	54	154	8	41	8	0	3	15	11-4	0	35	.266	.311	.377	100	0	0-0	.974	-1	71	128	C-53	0.1
1979	Hou N	56	129	11	28	4	0	1	6	13-4	1	25	.217	.294	.271	59	-7	0-0	.970	-3	80	121	C-55	-0.9
1980	†Hou N	22	22	0	4	1	0	0	0	5-1	1	7	.182	.357	.227	72	0	0-0	1.000	-1	74	0	C-10/1	-0.1
1982	NY N	17	49	4	15	4	0	2	8	4-0	0	6	.306	.358	.510	141	3	0-0	.961	0	82	139	C-16/1	0.4
1983	SD N	23	42	2	9	1	1	0	3	0-0	0	9	.214	.205	.286	39	-4	0-0	1.000	1	151	186	C-11	-0.3
1984	†SD N	37	92	10	21	5	1	4	15	3-0	0	21	.228	.250	.435	90	-2	0-1	.988	1	98	69	C-36	0.0
1985	SD N	48	112	16	30	2	0	6	13	6-1	0	30	.268	.305	.446	109	1	0-0	.988	-4	76	88	C-46	-0.2
1986	SD N	63	127	16	32	9	0	8	22	14-3	0	23	.252	.326	.512	130	5	1-0	.991	1	91	107	C-48	0.8
1987	SD N	38	75	8	12	3	0	2	11	11-1	0	21	.160	.264	.280	47	-6	0-1	.962	-5	86	15	C-23	-1.1
Total	9	358	802	75	192	37	2	26	93	67-14	2	177	.239	.298	.388	92	-10	1-2	.979	-10	85	103	C-298/1-2	-1.3

BOCKMAN, EDDIE Joseph Edward B 7.26.1920 Santa Ana, CA BR/TR 5-9/175# d9.11

Year	Tm Lg	G	AB	R	H	2B	3B	HR	RBI	BB-IB	HP	SO	AVG	OBP	SLG	AOPS	ABR	SB-CS	FA	FR	Rng	Thr	G at Pos	BFW
1946	NY A	4	12	2	1	1	0	0	0	1	0	4	.083	.154	.167	-10	-2	0-0	.933	1	77	375	/3-4	-0.1
1947	Cle A	46	66	8	17	2	2	1	14	5	0	17	.258	.310	.394	97	-1	0-0	.946	5	135	241	3-12/2-4,SO(LF)	0.4
1948	Pit N	70	176	23	42	7	1	4	23	17	1	35	.239	.309	.358	79	-6	2	.962	7	119	129	3-51/2	0.2
1949	Pit N	79	220	21	49	6	1	6	19	23	0	31	.223	.296	.341	69	-10	3	.959	5	108	120	3-68/2-5	-0.5
Total	4	199	474	54	109	16	4	11	56	46	1	87	.230	.299	.350	74	-19	5-0	.958	18	114	143	3-135/2-10,O(LF)S	0.0

BODIE, PING Frank Stephan (born Francesco Stephano Pezzolo) B 10.8.1887 San Francisco, CA D 12.17.1961 San Francisco, CA BR/TR 5-8/195# d4.22

Year	Tm Lg	G	AB	R	H	2B	3B	HR	RBI	BB-IB	HP	SO	AVG	OBP	SLG	AOPS	ABR	SB-CS	FA	FR	Rng	Thr	G at Pos	BFW
1911	Chi A	145	551	75	159	27	13	4	97	49	1		.289	.348	.407	114	9	14	.969	-2	94	111	*O-128(0-107-21),2-16	-0.2
1912	Chi A	138	472	58	139	24	7	5	72	43	4		.294	.358	.407	123	14	12	.969	-10	88	63	*O-130(8-72-50)	-0.4
1913	Chi A	127	406	39	107	14	8	8	48	35	2	57	.264	.325	.397	112	4	5	.968	-5	94	81	*O-119(43-76-0)	-0.8
1914	Chi A	107	327	21	75	9	5	3	29	21	1	35	.229	.278	.315	79	-10	12-11	.959	-3	89	120	O-95(2-92-1)	-2.3
1917	Phi A	148	557	51	162	28	11	7	74	53	3	40	.291	.356	.418	138	24	13	.963	7	93	**168**	*O-145(LF)/1	2.8
1918	NY A	91	324	36	83	12	6	3	46	27	3	24	.256	.319	.358	102	0	6	.971	4	97	139	O-90(LF)	-0.1
1919	NY A	134	475	45	132	27	8	6	59	36	4	46	.278	.334	.406	107	3	15	.959	-11	89	68	*O-134(0-129-5)	-1.8
1920	NY A	129	471	63	139	26	12	7	79	40	0	30	.295	.350	.446	106	3	6-14	.968	-12	88	77	*O-129(CF)	-2.1
1921	NY A	31	87	5	15	2	2	0	12	8	0	8	.172	.242	.241	23	-11	0-1	.944	-3	75	90	O-25(5-20-0)	-1.4
Total	9	1050	3670	393	1011	169	72	43	516	312	18	240	.275	.335	.396	110	36	83-26	.965	-35	91	102	O-995(293-625-77)/2-16,1	-6.3

BOECKEL, TONY Norman Doxie B 8.25.1892 Los Angeles, CA D 2.16.1924 LaJolla, CA BR/TR 5-10.5/175# d7.23 Mil 1918

Year	Tm Lg	G	AB	R	H	2B	3B	HR	RBI	BB-IB	HP	SO	AVG	OBP	SLG	AOPS	ABR	SB-CS	FA	FR	Rng	Thr	G at Pos	BFW
1917	Pit N	64	219	16	58	11	1	0	23	8	2	31	.265	.297	.324	88	-3	6	.935	-3	95	89	3-62	-0.5
1919	Pit N	45	152	18	38	9	2	0	16	18	1	20	.250	.333	.336	98	0	11	.930	-7	88	38	3-45	-0.5
	Bos N	95	365	42	91	11	5	1	26	35	1	13	.249	.317	.315	94	-2	10	.960	1	104	85	3-93	0.1
	Year	140	517	60	129	20	7	1	42	53	2	33	.250	.322	.321	95	-2	21	.951	-6	99	70	*3-138	-0.4
1920	Bos N	**153**	582	70	156	28	5	3	62	38	1	50	.268	.314	.349	94	-5	18-15	.936	-6	91	110	*3-149/S-3,2	-0.8
1921	Bos N	**153**	592	93	185	20	13	10	84	52	2	41	.313	.370	.441	120	17	20-15	.933	-13	91	67	*3-153	1.3
1922	Bos N	119	402	61	116	19	6	6	47	35	2	32	.289	.349	.410	99	-1	14-8	.952	-9	86	75	*3-106	-0.2
1923	Bos N	148	568	72	169	32	4	7	79	51	2	31	.298	.357	.405	105	5	11-8	.939	-9	94	100	*3-147/S	0.4
Total	6	777	2880	372	813	130	36	27	337	237	11	218	.282	.339	.381	102	11	90-46	.941	-45	93	86	3-755/S-4,2	-0.2

BOEHMER, LEN Leonard Joseph Stephen B 6.28.1941 Flinthill, MO BR/TR 6-1/192# d6.18

Year	Tm Lg	G	AB	R	H	2B	3B	HR	RBI	BB-IB	HP	SO	AVG	OBP	SLG	AOPS	ABR	SB-CS	FA	FR	Rng	Thr	G at Pos	BFW
1967	Cin N	2	3	0	0	0	0	0	0	0-0	0	0	.000	.000	.000	-90	-1	0-0	1.000	-0	100	0	/2	-0.1
1969	NY A	45	108	5	19	4	0	0	7	8-2	0	10	.176	.233	.213	26	-11	0-1	.995	1	98	103	1-21/3-8,2S	-1.2
1971	NY A	3	5	0	0	0	0	0	0	0-0	0	0	.000	.000	.000	-99	-1	0-0	1.000	-0	51	0	/3	-0.2
Total	3	50	116	5	19	4	0	0	7	8-2	0	10	.164	.218	.198	18	-13	0-1	.995	0	98	103	/1-21,3-9,2-2,S	-1.5

BOGAR, TIM Timothy Paul B 10.28.1966 Indianapolis, IN BR/TR 6-2/198# d4.21 OF Total (LF)

Year	Tm Lg	G	AB	R	H	2B	3B	HR	RBI	BB-IB	HP	SO	AVG	OBP	SLG	AOPS	ABR	SB-CS	FA	FR	Rng	Thr	G at Pos	BFW
1993	NY N	78	205	19	50	13	0	3	25	14-2	3	29	.244	.300	.351	75	-7	0-1	.972	9	109	99	S-66/3-7,2-6	0.6
1994	NY N	50	52	5	8	0	0	2	5	4-1	0	11	.154	.211	.269	25	-6	1-0	.909	5	81	0	3-22,1-14/S-7,2O(LF)	-0.1
1995	NY N	78	145	17	42	7	0	1	21	9-0	0	25	.290	.329	.359	85	-3	1-0	.971	3	97	55	S-27,3-25,1-10/2-7,O(LF)	0.1
1996	NY N	91	89	17	19	4	0	0	6	8-0	2	20	.213	.287	.258	49	-6	1-3	1.000	1	70	113	1-32,3-25,S-19/2-8	-0.6
1997	Hou N	97	241	30	60	14	4	4	30	24-1	3	42	.249	.320	.390	89	-4	4-1	.985	11	109	140	S-80,3-14/1	1.2
1998	Hou N	79	156	12	24	4	1	1	8	9-2	2	36	.154	.208	.212	11	-21	2-1	.989	5	116	77	S-55,2-11,3-11/D	-1.3
1999	†Hou N	106	309	44	74	16	2	4	31	38-5	4	52	.239	.328	.343	72	-13	3-5	.977	26	117	144	S-90,3-12/2	1.7
2000	Hou N	110	304	32	63	9	2	7	33	35-7	3	56	.207	.292	.319	52	-23	1-1	.971	3	106	102	S-95/2-2,P-2,3	-1.3
2001	LA N	12	15	4	5	2	0	2	2	2-0	0	1	.333	.412	.867	235	3	0-0	1.000	-2	0	128	/1-3,S-2,3	0.1
Total	9	701	1516	180	345	69	9	24	161	143-18	17	272	.228	.298	.332	65	-80	13-12	.978	61	111	116	S-441,3-118/1-60,2-36,P-2,O-2L,D	0.4

BOGENER, TERRY Terry Wayne B 9.28.1955 Hannibal, MO BL/TL 6/193# d6.14

Year	Tm Lg	G	AB	R	H	2B	3B	HR	RBI	BB-IB	HP	SO	AVG	OBP	SLG	AOPS	ABR	SB-CS	FA	FR	Rng	Thr	G at Pos	BFW
1982	Tex A	24	60	6	13	2	1	1	4	4-0	2	8	.217	.288	.333	74	-2	2-0	1.000	-1	84	0	O-16(4-10-2)/D-4	-0.4

BOGGS, WADE Wade Anthony B 6.15.1958 Omaha, NE BL/TR 6-2/197# d4.10 C1

Year	Tm Lg	G	AB	R	H	2B	3B	HR	RBI	BB-IB	HP	SO	AVG	OBP	SLG	AOPS	ABR	SB-CS	FA	FR	Rng	Thr	G at Pos	BFW
1982	Bos A	104	338	51	118	14	1	5	44	35-4	0	21	.349	.406	.441	126	14	1-0	.994	20	156	95	1-49,3-44/O(LF)D	3.0
1983	Bos A	153	582	100	210	44	7	5	74	92-2	1	36	**.361**	**.444**	.486	147	44	3-3	.947	4	103	112	*3-153	4.4
1984	Bos A	158	625	109	203	31	4	6	55	89-6	0	44	.325	.407	.416	123	25	3-2	.959	22	111	100	*3-156/D-2	4.4
1985	Bos A★	161	653	107	**240**	42	3	8	78	96-5	4	61	**.368**	**.450**	.478	149	51	2-1	.965	9	104	94	*3-161	5.6
1986	†Bos A★	149	580	107	207	47	2	8	71	**105**-14	0	44	**.357**	**.453**	.486	156	54	0-4	.953	6	99	118	*3-149	**5.4**
1987	Bos A★	147	551	108	200	40	6	24	89	105-**19**	2	48	**.363**	**.461**	.588	**173**	**65**	1-3	.965	8	102	129	*3-145/1D	**6.5**
1988	†Bos A★	155	584	**128**	214	**45**	6	5	58	**125-18**	3	34	**.366**	**.476**	.490	165	**63**	2-3	.971	3	92	69	*3-151/D-3	**6.4**
1989	Bos A★	156	621	**113**	205	**51**	7	3	54	107-**19**	7	51	.330	**.430**	.449	141	42	2-6	.958	3	95	111	*3-152/D-3	4.3
1990	†Bos A★	155	619	89	187	44	5	6	63	87-**19**	1	68	.302	.386	.418	120	21	0-0	.946	-15	86	63	*3-152/D-3	0.6
1991	Bos A★	144	546	93	181	42	2	8	51	89-**25**	0	32	.332	.421	.460	138	34	1-2	.968	5	99	133	*3-140	3.8
1992	Bos A★	143	514	62	133	22	4	7	50	74-**19**	4	31	.259	.353	.358	94	-2	1-3	.952	-0	98	**118**	*3-117,D-21	-0.3
1993	NY A★	143	560	83	169	26	1	2	59	74-4	0	49	.302	.378	.363	105	8	0-1	**.970**	21	**121**	**131**	*3-134/D-8	2.9
1994	NY A★	97	366	61	125	19	1	11	55	61-3	1	29	.342	.433	.489	144	28	2-1	.962	9	**116**	137	3-93/1-4	3.4
1995	†NY A★	126	460	76	149	22	4	5	63	74-5	0	50	.324	.412	.422	120	18	1-1	**.981**	-2	96	62	*3-117/1-9	1.5
1996	†NY A★	132	501	80	156	29	2	2	41	67-7	0	32	.311	.389	.389	99	2	1-2	.974	-4	91	116	*3-123/D-4	-0.1
1997	†NY A	104	353	55	103	23	1	4	28	48-3	0	38	.292	.373	.397	103	4	0-1	.978	2	100	131	3-76,D-19/P	0.4
1998	TB A	123	435	51	122	23	4	7	52	46-6	0	54	.280	.348	.400	93	-4	3-2	.973	1	101	108	3-78,D-33	-0.4
1999	TB A	90	292	40	88	14	1	2	29	38-2	0	23	.301	.377	.377	94	-1	1-0	.942	-7	83	116	3-74/1-4,PD	-0.7
Total	18	2440	9180	1513	3010	578	61	118	1014	1412-180	23	745	.328	.415	.443	130	466	24-35	.962	84	101	107	*3-2215,D-107/1-67,P-2,O(LF)	51.1

BOHNE, SAM Samuel Arthur (born Samuel Arthur Cohen) B 10.22.1896 San Francisco, CA D 5.23.1977 Palo Alto, CA BR/TR 5-8.5/175# d9.9 OF Total (1-LF 4-RF)

Year	Tm Lg	G	AB	R	H	2B	3B	HR	RBI	BB-IB	HP	SO	AVG	OBP	SLG	AOPS	ABR	SB-CS	FA	FR	Rng	Thr	G at Pos	BFW
1916	StL N	14	38	3	9	0	0	0	0	4	0	6	.237	.310	.237	69	-1	3	.870	-3	98	63	S-14	-0.4
1921	Cin N	**153**	613	98	175	28	16	3	44	54	4	38	.285	.347	.398	101	1	26-22	.973	10	97	120	*2-102,3-53	1.6
1922	Cin N	112	383	53	105	14	5	3	51	39	2	18	.274	.344	.360	83	-9	13-8	.958	13	114	128	2-85,S-20	0.8
1923	Cin N	139	539	77	136	18	10	3	47	48	2	37	.252	.316	.340	74	-21	16-19	.975	9	104	86	2-96,3-35/S-9,1	-0.8
1924	Cin N	100	349	42	89	15	9	4	46	18	1	24	.255	.293	.384	81	-11	9-6	.941	-5	95	74	2-48,S-40,3-12	-1.0
1925	Cin N	73	214	24	55	9	1	2	24	14	0	14	.257	.303	.336	65	-12	6-4	.933	-5	98	102	S-49,2-10/O-4(1-0-4),1-2,3-2	-1.1
1926	Cin N	25	54	8	11	0	2	0	5	4	0	8	.204	.259	.278	46	-5	1	.931	-2	100	91	S-20	-0.5
	Bro N	47	125	4	25	3	2	1	11	12	0	9	.200	.270	.280	49	-9	1	.965	5	109	60	2-31,3-15	-0.3
	Year	72	179	12	36	3	4	1	16	16	0	17	.201	.267	.279	48	-14	2	.965	3	109	60	2-31,S-20,3-15	-0.8

Year	Tm Lg	G	AB	R	H	2B	3B	HR	RBI	BB-IB	HP	SO	AVG	OBP	SLG	AOPS	ABR	SB-CS	FA	FR	Rng	Thr	G at Pos	BFW
Total	7	663	2315	309	605	87	45	16	228	193	9	154	.261	.321	.359	81	-67	75-59	.966	23	103	102	2-372,S-152,3-117/O-4R,1-3	-1.7
BOISCLAIR, BRUCE Bruce Armand B 12.9.1952 Putnam, CT BL/TL 6-2/190# d9.11																								
1974	NY N	7	12	0	3	1	0	0	1	1-0	0	4	.250	.308	.333	81	0	0-0	.923	2	112	837	/O-5(2-3-0)	0.1
1976	NY N	110	286	42	82	13	3	2	13	28-5	0	55	.287	.350	.374	112	5	9-5	.981	0	104	66	O-87(35-39-20)	0.2
1977	NY N	127	307	41	90	21	1	4	44	31-0	1	57	.293	.359	.407	110	5	6-4	.959	-4	101	20	O-91(30-9-55)/1-9	-0.2
1978	NY N	107	214	24	48	7	1	4	15	23-3	0	43	.224	.293	.322	77	-7	3-3	.983	2	115	71	O-69(12-2-58)/1	-0.9
1979	NY N	59	98	7	18	5	1	0	4	3-0	1	24	.184	.210	.255	29	-10	0-2	1.000	0	97	137	O-24(8-0-17)/1	-1.2
Total	5	410	917	114	241	47	6	10	77	86-8	2	183	.263	.324	.360	94	-7	18-14	.975	0	105	71	O-276(87-53-150)/1-11	-2.0
BOKEN, BOB Robert Anthony B 2.23.1908 Maryville, IL D 10.6.1988 Las Vegas, NV BR/TR 6-2/165# d4.25																								
1933	Was A	55	133	19	37	5	2	3	26	9	0	16	.278	.324	.414	95	-2	0-0	.969	-3	103	94	2-31,3-19,S-10	-0.2
1934	Was A	11	27	5	6	1	1	0	6	3	0	1	.222	.300	.333	66	-2	2-0	.864	1	112	268	/3-6,2	0.0
	Chi A	81	297	30	70	9	1	3	40	15	1	32	.236	.275	.303	47	-24	2-1	.929	-15	92	69	2-57,S-22	-3.2
	Year	92	324	35	76	10	2	3	46	18	1	33	.235	.277	.306	49	-26	4-1	.929	-14	92	73	2-58,S-22/3-6	-3.2
Total	2	147	457	54	113	15	4	6	72	27	1	49	.247	.291	.337	62	-28	4-1	.941	-17	95	79	/2-89,S-32,3-25	-3.4
BOLAND d9.4																								
1875	Atl NA	1	4	0	0	0	0	0	0	0		0	.000	.000	.000	-99	-1	0-0	.750	-0	55	0	/3	-0.1
BOLAND, ED Edward John B 4.18.1908 Long Island City, NY D 2.5.1993 Clearwater, FL BL/TL 5-10/165# d9.18																								
1934	Phi N	8	30	2	9	1	1	0	5	0	0	2	.300	.300	.400	76	-1	1	.778	-1	55	207	/O-7(RF)	-0.2
1935	Phi N	30	47	5	10	0	0	0	4	4	0	6	.213	.275	.213	30	-5	1	.833	-2	88	0	O-10(2-2-6)	-0.6
1944	Was A	19	59	4	16	4	0	0	14	0	0	6	.271	.271	.339	77	-2	0-0	.889	0	92	245	O-14(RF)	-0.3
Total	3	57	136	11	35	5	1	0	23	4	0	14	.257	.279	.309	59	-8	2-0	.852	-2	83	161	/O-31(2-2-27)	-1.1
BOLD, CHARLIE Charles Dickens "Dutch" B 10.27.1894 Karlskrona, Sweden D 7.29.1978 Chelsea, MA BR/TR 6-2/185# d8.24																								
1914	StL A	2	1	0	0	0	0	0	0	0	0	1	.000	.000	.000	-99	0	0	.500	-0	0	0	/1	-0.1
BOLES, CARL Carl Theodore B 10.31.1934 Center Point, AR BR/TR 5-11/185# d8.2																								
1962	SF N	19	24	4	9	0	0	0	1	0-0	0	6	.375	.375	.375	104	0	0-0	.833	-0	94	0	/O-7(LF)	-0.1
BOLEY, JOE John Peter (born John Peter Bolinsky) B 7.19.1896 Mahanoy City, PA D 12.30.1962 Mahanoy City, PA BR/TR 5-11/170# d4.12																								
1927	Phi A	118	370	49	115	18	8	1	52	26	3	14	.311	.361	.411	95	-4	8-5	.951	-7	97	88	*S-114	0.1
1928	Phi A	132	425	49	112	20	3	0	49	32	1	11	.264	.317	.325	67	-20	5-1	.949	-17	87	78	*S-132	-2.3
1929	†Phi A	91	303	36	76	17	6	2	47	24	2	16	.251	.310	.366	71	-14	1-0	.963	-11	87	104	S-88/3	-1.4
1930	†Phi A	121	420	41	116	22	2	4	55	32	5	26	.276	.335	.367	74	-16	0-0	**.970**	-6	88	99	*S-120	-0.9
1931	†Phi A	67	224	26	51	9	3	0	20	15	2	13	.228	.282	.295	49	-17	1-1	.954	-8	87	111	S-62/2	-2.0
1932	Phi A	10	34	2	7	2	0	0	4	1	0	4	.206	.229	.265	26	-4	0-1	.897	-4	76	44	S-10	-0.7
	Cle A	1	4	0	1	0	0	0	0	0	0	0	.250	.250	.250	28	0	0-0	—	-0	0	0	/S	-0.1
	Year	11	38	2	8	2	0	0	4	1	0	4	.211	.231	.263	27	-4	0-1	.897	-4	75	43	S-11	-0.8
Total	6	540	1780	203	478	88	22	7	227	130	13	84	.269	.323	.354	72	-75	15-8	.957	-53	89	93	S-527/23	-7.3
BOLGER, JIM James Cyril "Dutch" B 2.23.1932 Cincinnati, OH BR/TR 6-2/180# d6.24																								
1950	Cin N	2	1	0	0	0	0	0	0	0	0	0	.000	.000	.000	-99	0	0	—	-0	0	0	/O-2(LF)	0.0
1951	Cin N	2	0	1	0	0	0	0	0	0	0	0	—	—	—	—	0	1-0	—	0			R	0.0
1954	Cin N	5	3	1	1	0	0	0	0	0	0	1	.333	.333	.333	72	0	0-0	—	-0	0	0	/O-2(CF)	0.0
1955	Chi N	64	160	19	33	5	4	0	7	9-1	2	17	.206	.257	.287	45	-13	2-2	.955	-2	105	28	O-51(3-49-0)	-1.8
1957	Chi N	112	273	28	75	4	1	5	29	10-1	3	36	.275	.303	.352	78	-9	0-1	.987	2	111	91	O-63(24-28-17)/3-3	-1.1
1958	Chi N	84	120	15	27	4	1	1	11	9-0	1	20	.225	.285	.300	56	-8	0-1	.940	-0	106	61	O-37(28-6-5)	-1.0
1959	Cle A	8	7	0	0	0	0	0	0	1-0	0	1	.000	.125	.000	-65	-2	0-0	—	0			H	-0.2
	Phi N	35	48	1	4	1	0	0	1	3-1	0	8	.083	.135	.104	-34	-9	0-0	.938	-0	110	0	/O-9(7-1-1)	-1.0
Total	7	312	612	65	140	14	6	6	48	32-3	6	83	.229	.272	.301	54	-41	3-4	.966	-1	108	61	O-164(64-86-23)/3-3	-5.1
BOLICK, FRANK Frank Charles B 6.28.1966 Ashland, PA BB/TR 5-10/180# d4.5																								
1993	Mon N	95	213	25	45	13	0	4	24	23-2	4	37	.211	.298	.329	65	-10	1-0	.992	4	135	106	1-51,3-24	-0.9
1998	Ana A	21	45	3	7	2	0	1	2	11-0	0	8	.156	.321	.267	55	-3	0-0	1.000	-1	72	0	/3-7,1O(RF)D	-0.3
Total	2	116	258	28	52	15	0	5	26	34-2	4	45	.202	.302	.318	64	-13	1-0	.992	3	134	109	/1-52,3-31,D-9,O(RF)	-1.2
BOLLING, FRANK Frank Elmore B 11.16.1931 Mobile, AL BR/TR 6-1/175# d4.13 Mil 1955 b-Milt																								
1954	Det A	117	368	46	87	15	2	6	38	36	0	51	.236	.302	.337	77	-12	3-5	.974	-20	88	77	*2-113	-2.8
1956	Det A	102	366	53	103	21	7	7	45	42-1	2	51	.281	.354	.434	108	4	6-2	.978	-9	95	92	*2-102	0.3
1957	Det A	146	576	72	149	27	6	15	40	57-3	2	64	.259	.327	.405	96	-3	4-9	.980	-5	98	106	*2-146	0.1
1958	Det A	**154**	610	91	164	25	4	14	75	54-1	4	54	.269	.328	.392	92	-6	6-4	**.985**	11	106	96	*2-154	1.6
1959	Det A	127	459	56	122	18	3	13	55	45-2	7	37	.266	.339	.403	98	-1	2-2	.987	4	99	101	*2-126	1.2
1960	Det A	139	536	64	136	20	4	9	59	40-2	2	48	.254	.308	.356	77	-18	7-4	.978	-7	95	91	*2-138	-1.4
1961	Mil N★	148	585	86	153	16	4	15	56	57-1	3	62	.262	.329	.379	93	-6	7-3	**.988**	-1	110	107	*2-148	0.6
1962	Mil N★	122	406	45	110	17	4	9	43	35-3	4	45	.271	.333	.399	99	-1	2-2	**.989**	-3	101	106	*2-119	0.6
1963	Mil N	142	542	73	132	18	2	5	43	41-3	3	47	.244	.299	.312	77	-16	2-1	.981	1	101	133	*2-141	-0.3
1964	Mil N	120	352	35	70	11	1	5	34	21-3	2	44	.199	.245	.278	48	-25	0-1	**.985**	-4	95	**119**	*2-117	-2.2
1965	Mil N	148	535	55	141	26	3	7	50	24-6	0	41	.264	.295	.363	84	-12	0-4	.976	-10	94	98	*2-147	-1.2
1966	Atl N	75	227	16	48	7	0	1	18	10-3	1	14	.211	.244	.256	40	-18	1-1	.983	-11	88	91	2-67	-2.7
Total	12	1540	5562	692	1415	221	40	106	556	462-28	30	558	.254	.313	.366	85	-114	40-38	.982	-53	98	102	*2-1518	-6.2
BOLLING, JACK John Edward B 2.20.1917 Mobile, AL D 4.13.1998 Panama City, FL BL/TL 5-11/168# d6.10 Mil 1944-46																								
1939	Phi N	69	211	27	61	11	0	3	13	11	0	10	.289	.324	.384	92	-3	6	.982	2	123	77	1-48	-0.5
1944	Bro N	56	131	21	46	14	1	1	25	14	1	4	.351	.418	.496	159	11	0	.991	1	114	30	1-27	1.1
Total	2	125	342	48	107	25	1	4	38	25	1	14	.313	.361	.427	118	8	6	.985	3	120	60	/1-75	0.6
BOLLING, MILT Milton Joseph B 8.9.1930 Mississippi City, MS BR/TR 6-1/180# d9.10 b-Frank																								
1952	Bos A	11	36	4	8	1	0	1	3	3	0	5	.222	.282	.333	66	-2	0-1	.984	3	124	80	S-11	0.2
1953	Bos A	109	323	30	85	12	1	5	28	23	3	41	.263	.318	.353	77	-11	1-4	.956	5	104	110	*S-109	0.1
1954	Bos A	113	370	42	92	20	3	6	36	47	4	55	.249	.337	.368	84	-7	2-4	.946	9	**111**	97	*S-107/3-5	1.1
1955	Bos A	6	5	0	1	0	0	0	0	0-0	0	1	.200	.200	.200	7	-1	0-0	.800	-0	109	0	/S-2	-0.1
1956	Bos A	45	118	19	25	3	2	3	8	18-1	1	20	.212	.319	.347	68	-6	0-1	.947	-4	94	78	S-26,3-11/2	-0.9
1957	Bos A	1	1	0	0	0	0	0	0	0-0	0	0	.000	.000	.000	-95	0	0-0	—	0			H	0.0
	Was A	91	277	29	63	12	1	4	19	18-0	2	59	.227	.277	.321	64	-14	2-2	.982	7	110	94	2-53,S-37/3	-0.2
	Year	92	278	29	63	12	1	4	19	18-0	2	59	.227	.276	.320	64	-14	2-2	.982	7	110	94	2-53,S-37/3	-0.2
1958	Det A	24	31	3	6	2	0	0	0	5-0	0	7	.194	.306	.258	53	-2	0-0	.946	1	96	151	S-13/23	-0.1
Total	7	400	1161	127	280	50	7	19	94	114-1	10	188	.241	.313	.345	74	-43	5-12	.952	20	107	100	S-305/2-55,3-18	0.1
BOLLWEG, DON Donald Raymond B 2.12.1921 Wheaton, IL D 5.26.1996 Wheaton, IL BL/TL 6-1/190# d9.28																								
1950	StL N	4	11	1	2	0	0	0	1	1	0	1	.182	.250	.182	15	-1	0	1.000	-1	0	115	/1-4	-0.2
1951	StL N	6	9	1	1	1	0	0	2	0	0	1	.111	.111	.222	-13	-1	0-0	.941	-1	0	155	/1-2	-0.2
1953	†NY A	70	155	24	46	6	4	6	24	21	1	31	.297	.384	.503	143	9	1-0	.983	-4	66	116	1-43	0.4
1954	Phi A	103	268	35	60	15	3	5	24	35	3	33	.224	.319	.358	85	-5	1-0	.978	2	119	83	1-71	-0.7
1955	KC A	12	9	1	1	0	0	0	2	3-2	0	2	.111	.333	.111	23	-1	0-0	1.000	-0	0	377	/1-3	-0.1
Total	5	195	452	62	110	22	7	11	53	60-2	4	68	.243	.337	.396	100	1	2-0	.980	-3	95	98	1-123	-0.8
BOLTON, CECIL Cecil Glenford "Glenn" B 2.13.1904 Booneville, MS D 8.25.1993 Jackson, MS BL/TR 6-4/195# d9.21																								
1928	Cle A	4	13	1	2	0	2	0	0	2	0	2	.154	.267	.462	87	-1	0-0	.955	-1	42	93	/1-4	-0.2
BOLTON, CLIFF William Clifton B 4.10.1907 High Point, NC D 4.21.1979 Lexington, NC BL/TR 5-9/160# d4.20																								
1931	Was A	23	43	3	11	1	1	0	6	1	0	5	.256	.273	.326	56	-3	0-0	.947	-3	*103*	*92*	C-13	-0.5
1933	†Was A	33	39	4	16	1	1	0	6	6	1	3	.410	.500	.487	164	4	0-0	.889	-1	*160*	*75*	/C-9,O(RF)	0.3
1934	Was A	42	148	12	40	9	1	1	17	11	0	9	.270	.321	.365	80	-5	2-0	.981	-3	*152*	*120*	C-39	-0.4
1935	Was A	110	375	47	114	18	11	2	55	58	1	13	.304	.399	.427	117	11	0-1	.971	-23	*75*	*87*	*C-106	-0.5
1936	Was A	86	289	41	84	18	4	2	51	25	1	12	.291	.349	.401	90	-5	1-2	.979	-2	*86*	***114***	C-83	-0.2

Year	Tm Lg	G	AB	R	H	2B	3B	HR	RBI	BB-IB	HP	SO	AVG	OBP	SLG	AOPS	ABR	SB-CS	FA	FR	Rng	Thr	G at Pos	BFW
1937	Det A	27	57	6	15	2	0	1	7	8	0	6	.263	.354	.351	76	-2	0-0	.982	0	*89*	*121*	C-13	-0.1
1941	Was A	14	11	0	0	0	0	0	1	1	0	2	.000	.083	.000	-80	-3	0-0	1.000	0	*0*	*0*	/C-3	-0.3
Total	7	335	962	113	280	49	18	6	143	110	3	50	.291	.366	.398	98	-3	3-3	.974	-32	*94*	*102*	C-266/O(RF)	-1.7

BOND, WALT Walter Franklin B 10.19.1937 Denmark, TN D 9.14.1967 Houston, TX BL/TR 6-7/228# d4.19

1960	Cle A	40	131	19	29	2	1	5	18	13-2	3	14	.221	.302	.366	84	-3	4-1	1.000	1	108	92	O-36(5-11-20)	-0.3
1961	Cle A	38	52	7	9	1	1	2	7	6-0	1	10	.173	.267	.346	65	-3	1-0	1.000	1	102	161	O-12(0-1-11)	-0.3
1962	Cle A	12	50	10	19	3	0	6	17	4-1	0	9	.380	.426	.800	228	9	1-0	1.000	-0	108	0	O-12(3-0-10)	0.8
1964	Hou N	148	543	63	138	16	7	20	85	38-8	8	90	.254	.310	.420	110	5	2-2	.989	-10	75	83	1-76,O-71(28-1-42)	-1.4
1965	Hou N	117	407	46	107	17	2	7	47	42-8	5	51	.263	.337	.366	106	4	2-1	.983	-4	95	91	1-74,O-38(18-0-21)	-0.7
1967	Min A	10	16	4	5	1	0	1	5	3-0	0	1	.313	.400	.563	174	2	0-0	.875	0	160	0	/O-3(LF)	0.2
Total	6	365	1199	149	307	40	11	41	179	106-19	17	175	.256	.323	.410	110	14	10-4	.974	-12	100	38	O-172(57-13-104),1-150	-1.7

BONDS, BARRY Barry Lamar B 7.24.1964 Riverside, CA BL/TL 6-1/190# d5.30 f-Bobby

1986	Pit N	113	413	72	92	26	3	16	48	65-2	2	102	.223	.330	.416	102	2	36-7	.983	4	108	140	*O-110(CF)	1.1
1987	Pit N	150	551	99	144	34	9	25	59	54-3	3	88	.261	.329	.492	114	9	32-10	.986	16	117	172	*O-145(101-46-1)	2.4
1988	Pit N	144	538	97	152	30	5	24	58	72-14	2	82	.283	.368	.491	147	34	17-11	.980	2	107	60	*O-136(135-3-0)	3.3
1989	Pit N	159	580	96	144	34	6	19	58	93-22	1	93	.248	.351	.426	126	22	32-10	.984	12	111	154	*O-156(LF)	3.5
1990	†Pit N★	151	519	104	156	32	3	33	114	93-15	3	83	.301	.406	**.565**	**172**	**54**	52-13	.983	8	107	126	*O-150(149-2-0)	**6.5**
1991	†Pit N	153	510	95	149	28	5	25	116	107-25	4	73	.292	**.410**	.514	**163**	**49**	43-13	.991	6	106	147	*O-150(150-4-0)	5.7
1992	†Pit N★	140	473	**109**	147	36	5	34	103	**127-32**	5	69	.311	**.456**	**.624**	**207**	**76**	39-8	.991	-0	104	57	*O-139(LF)	**8.0**
1993	SF N★	159	539	129	181	38	4	**46**	**123**	126-**43**	2	79	.336	**.458**	**.677**	**207**	**90**	29-12	.984	-3	100	59	*O-157(LF)	**8.0**
1994	SF N★	112	391	89	122	18	1	37	81	**74-18**	6	43	.312	.426	.647	184	51	29-9	.986	1	92	144	*O-112(LF)	4.9
1995	SF N★	**144**	506	109	149	30	7	33	104	**120-22**	5	83	.294	**.431**	.577	169	**57**	31-10	.980	5	104	130	*O-143(LF)	**5.7**
1996	SF N★	158	517	122	159	27	3	42	129	**151-30**	1	76	.308	.461	.615	189	78	40-7	.980	4	104	114	*O-152(149-6-0)	**7.8**
1997	†SF N★	159	532	123	155	26	5	40	101	**145-34**	8	87	.291	.446	.585	173	66	37-8	.984	-0	100	95	*O-159(LF)	6.3
1998	SF N★	156	552	120	167	44	7	37	122	130-**29**	8	92	.303	.438	.609	184	75	28-12	.984	-1	105	20	*O-155(LF)	6.8
1999	SF N	102	355	91	93	20	2	34	83	73-9	3	62	.262	.389	.617	162	34	15-2	.984	-0	100	69	O-96(LF)/D-4	3.1
2000	†SF N✳	143	480	129	147	28	4	49	106	**117**-22	3	77	.306	.440	.688	**195**	**75**	11-3	.989	5	104	99	*O-141(LF)	**7.0**
2001	SF N★	153	476	129	156	32	2	**73**	137	**177**-35	9	93	.328	**.515**	**.863**	**267**	**136**	13-3	.977	-4	94	82	*O-143(LF)/D-6	**12.0**
2002	†SF N★	143	403	117	149	31	2	46	110	**198-68**	9	47	**.370**	**.582**	**.799**	**278**	**129**	9-2	.968	-2	100	49	*O-135(LF)/D-5	**11.7**
2003	†SF N★	130	390	111	133	22	1	45	90	**148-61**	10	58	.341	**.529**	**.749**	**235**	**94**	7-0	.992	2	106	67	*O-123(LF)/D-6	**8.8**
Total	18	2569	8725	1941	2595	536	74	658	1742	2070-484	84	1387	.297	.433	.602	181	1131	500-140	.984	53	104	99	*O-2502(2343-171-1)/D-21	112.6

BONDS, BOBBY Bobby Lee B 3.15.1946 Riverside, CA D 8.23.2003 San Carlos, CA BR/TR 6-1/190# d6.25 C8 s-Barry

1968	SF N	81	307	55	78	10	5	9	35	38-0	1	84	.254	.336	.407	123	9	16-7	.978	-1	98	92	O-80(0-35-62)	0.5
1969	SF N	158	622	**120**	161	25	6	32	90	81-3	10	187	.259	.351	.473	132	27	45-4	.978	-1	104	77	*O-155(0-77-99)	2.8
1970	SF N	157	663	134	200	36	10	26	78	77-7	2	189	.302	.375	.504	135	33	48-10	.969	6	105	131	*O-157(1-32-141)	3.7
1971	†SF N★	155	619	110	178	32	4	33	102	62-6	5	137	.288	.355	.512	146	36	26-8	**.994**	2	104	92	*O-154(0-33-133)	3.5
1972	SF N	153	626	118	162	29	5	26	80	60-4	5	137	.259	.326	.446	116	12	44-6	.978	5	115	70	*O-153(0-12-143)	1.8
1973	SF N★	160	643	**131**	182	34	4	39	96	87-9	4	148	.283	.370	.530	141	37	43-17	.970	6	115	84	*O-158(0-2-158)	3.9
1974	SF N	150	567	97	145	22	8	21	71	95-8	4	134	.256	.364	.434	118	15	41-11	.966	2	107	106	*O-148(0-8-141)	1.5
1975	NY A★	145	529	93	143	26	3	32	85	89-8	3	137	.270	.375	.512	152	38	30-17	.987	5	107	122	*O-129(1-44-90),D-12	3.9
1976	Cal A	99	378	48	100	10	3	10	54	41-6	3	90	.265	.337	.386	120	10	30-15	.977	3	101	130	O-98(RF)/D	0.9
1977	Cal A	158	592	103	156	23	9	37	115	74-5	2	141	.264	.342	.520	138	30	41-18	.986	-0	104	53	*O-140(RF),D-18	2.4
1978	Chi A	26	90	8	25	4	0	2	8	10-1	0	10	.278	.347	.389	107	1	6-2	.956	0	89	188	O-22(RF)/D-3	0.1
	Tex A	130	475	85	126	15	4	29	82	69-6	2	110	.265	.356	.497	139	24	37-20	.970	-1	90	154	*O-111(RF),D-18	1.9
	Year	156	565	93	151	19	4	31	90	79-7	2	120	.267	.355	.480	133	25	43-22	.968	-1	90	159	*O-133(RF),D-21	2.0
1979	Cle A	146	538	93	148	24	1	25	85	74-4	8	135	.275	.367	.463	123	19	34-23	.979	7	116	107	*O-116(RF),D-29	1.8
1980	StL N	86	231	37	47	5	3	5	24	33-3	2	74	.203	.305	.316	72	-8	15-5	.967	-0	97	107	O-70(63-0-15)	-1.0
1981	Chi N	45	163	26	35	7	1	6	19	24-5	2	44	.215	.323	.380	95	-1	5-6	.982	-3	94	65	O-45(0-42-3)	-0.5
Total	14	1849	7043	1258	1886	302	66	332	1024	914-75	53	1757	.268	.353	.471	129	282	461-169	.977	29	105	100	*O-1736(65-285-1472)/D-81	27.2

BONE, GEORGE George Drummond B 8.28.1876 New Haven, CT D 5.26.1918 West Haven, CT BB/TR 5-7/152# d9.18

1901	Mil A	12	43	6	13	2	0	0	6	4	0		.302	.362	.349	103	0	0	.869	-1	87	148	S-12	0.0

BONGIOVANNI, NINO Anthony Thomas B 12.21.1911 New Orleans, LA BL/TL 5-10/175# d4.23

1938	Cin N	2	7	0	2	1	0	0	0	0	0	0	.286	.286	.429	97	0	0	1.000	0	123	0	/O-2(LF)	0.0
1939	†Cin N	66	159	17	41	6	0	0	16	9	0	8	.258	.298	.296	60	-9	0	.989	1	119	31	O-39(6-1-32)	-1.0
Total	2	68	166	17	43	7	0	0	16	9	0	8	.259	.297	.301	61	-9	0	.990	1	119	29	/O-41(8-1-32)	-1.0

BONILLA, JUAN Juan Guillermo B 2.12.1955 Santurce, P.R. BR/TR 5-9/170# d4.9

1981	SD N	99	369	30	107	13	2	1	25	25-5	2	23	.290	.337	.344	101	0	4-9	.976	-8	98	108	2-97	-0.5
1982	SD N	45	182	21	51	6	2	0	8	11-0	1	15	.280	.325	.335	90	-3	0-1	.975	-4	100	100	2-45	-0.5
1983	SD N	152	556	55	132	17	4	4	45	50-11	3	40	.237	.301	.304	71	-22	3-0	.986	-9	97	104	*2-149	-2.3
1985	NY A	8	16	0	2	1	0	0	2	0-0	0	3	.125	.125	.188	-16	-3	0-0	.955	0	109	105	/2-7	-0.2
1986	Bal A	102	284	33	69	10	1	1	18	25-0	3	21	.243	.311	.296	67	-13	0-0	.981	-4	90	107	2-70,3-33/D-2	-1.3
1987	NY A	23	55	6	14	3	0	1	3	5-0	0	6	.255	.317	.364	81	-1	0-0	.965	-2	91	89	2-22/3D	-0.3
Total	6	429	1462	145	375	50	9	7	101	116-16	9	108	.256	.314	.317	79	-42	7-10	.980	-27	96	104	2-390/3-34,D-3	-5.1

BONILLA, BOBBY Roberto Martin Antonio B 2.23.1963 Bronx, NY BB/TR 6-3/240# d4.9 OF Total (206-LF 10-CF 698-RF)

1986	Chi A	75	234	27	63	10	2	2	26	33-2	1	49	.269	.361	.355	93	-1	4-1	.989	1	110	79	O-43(39-4-4),1-30	-0.3
	Pit N	63	192	28	46	6	2	1	17	29-1	1	39	.240	.342	.307	79	-5	4-4	.974	-0	85	94	O-51(37-6-24)/1-4,3-4	-0.8
1987	Pit N	141	466	58	140	33	3	15	77	39-4	2	64	.300	.351	.481	119	13	3-5	.932	-10	92	93	3-89,O-46(17-0-34)/1-6	-0.2
1988	Pit N★	159	584	87	160	32	7	24	100	85-19	4	82	.274	.366	.476	143	35	3-5	.935	3	108	66	*3-159	3.8
1989	Pit N★	163	616	96	173	37	10	24	86	76-20	1	93	.281	.358	.490	146	37	8-8	.929	5	108	121	*3-156/1-8,O(RF)	4.2
1990	†Pit N★	160	625	112	175	39	7	32	120	45-9	1	103	.280	.322	.518	135	26	4-3	.961	-5	91	73	*O-149(RF),3-14/1-3	1.6
1991	†Pit N★	157	577	102	174	**44**	6	18	100	90-8	2	67	.302	.391	.492	151	43	2-4	.989	3	93	113	*O-104(RF),3-67/1-4	4.4
1992	NY N	128	438	62	109	23	0	19	70	66-10	1	73	.249	.348	.432	121	14	4-3	.992	4	108	93	*O-121(RF)/1-6	1.4
1993	NY N★	139	502	81	133	21	3	34	87	72-11	0	96	.265	.352	.522	133	23	3-3	.969	-2	88	125	O-85(RF),3-52/1-6	1.7
1994	NY N	108	403	60	117	24	1	20	67	55-9	0	101	.290	.374	.504	128	17	1-3	.942	6	111	153	*3-107	2.3
1995	NY N★	80	317	49	103	25	4	18	53	31-10	1	48	.325	.385	.599	160	27	0-3	.882	-5	88	122	3-46,O-31(LF),1-10	1.9
	Bal A	61	237	47	79	12	4	10	46	23-0	1	31	.333	.392	.544	139	13	0-2	.971	1	94	83	O-39(1-0-38),3-24	1.1
1996	†Bal A	159	595	107	171	27	5	28	116	75-7	5	85	.287	.363	.491	116	15	1-3	.975	-8	86	107	*O-108(RF),D-44/1-9,3-4	-0.2
1997	†Fla N	153	562	77	167	39	3	17	96	73-8	5	94	.297	.378	.468	127	24	6-6	.938	-17	81	115	*3-149/1-2,D-3	0.8
1998	Fla N	28	97	11	27	5	0	4	15	12-1	0	22	.278	.355	.454	118	3	0-1	.922	-4	84	117	3-26	-0.1
	LA N	72	236	28	56	6	1	7	30	29-3	0	37	.237	.315	.360	84	-6	1-1	.912	-9	80	85	3-59,O-12(LF)	-1.5
	Year	100	333	39	83	11	1	11	45	41-4	0	59	.249	.326	.387	94	-3	1-2	.915	-13	81	95	3-85,O-12(LF)	-1.6
1999	†NY N	60	119	12	19	5	0	4	18	19-1	1	16	.160	.277	.303	49	-10	0-1	.974	1	100	168	O-25(2-0-23)/1-4,D-3	-1.0
2000	†Atl N	114	239	23	61	13	3	5	28	37-2	1	51	.255	.356	.397	90	-3	0-0	.927	-10	57	34	O-64(63-0-1)/3D	-1.4
2001	StL N	93	174	17	37	7	0	5	21	23-3	1	53	.213	.308	.339	68	-8	1-1	.992	-2	61	139	1-33,O-10(4-0-6)/PD	-1.3
Total	16	2113	7213	1084	2010	408	61	287	1173	912-128	28	1204	.279	.358	.472	125	257	45-57	.931	-49	100	108	3-957,O-889R,1-125/D-53,P	16.4

BONIN, LUTHER Ernest Luther "Bonnie" B 1.13.1888 Greenhill, IN D 1.3.1966 Sycamore, OH BL/TR 5-9.5/178# d4.13

1913	StL A	1	1	0	0	0	0	0	0	0	0	0	.000	.000	.000	-99	0	0	—	0			H	0.0
1914	Buf F	20	76	6	14	4	1	0	4	7	0	11	.184	.253	.263	40	-8	3	.970	0	94	122	O-20(RF)	-0.9
Total	2	21	77	6	14	4	1	0	4	7	0	11	.182	.250	.260	38	-8	3	.970	0	94	122	/O-20(RF)	-0.9

BONNELL, BARRY Robert Barry B 10.27.1953 Clermont County, OH BR/TR 6-3/200# d5.4 OF Total (395-LF 344-CF 214-RF)

1977	Atl N	100	360	41	108	11	0	1	45	37-8	2	32	.300	.368	.339	81	-8	7-5	.989	6	124	76	O-75(2-63-10),3-32	-0.4
1978	Atl N	117	304	36	73	11	3	1	16	20-1	0	30	.240	.287	.306	59	-17	12-6	.984	7	105	159	*O-105(53-55-11),3-15	-1.2
1979	Atl N	127	375	47	97	20	3	12	45	26-2	3	55	.259	.311	.424	92	-5	8-7	.983	-1	92	106	*O-124(77-74-0)/3	-0.9
1980	Tor A	130	463	55	124	22	4	13	56	37-2	2	59	.268	.322	.417	97	-2	3-4	.973	-1	92	164	*O-122(5-57-61)/D-3	-0.8
1981	Tor A	66	227	21	50	7	4	4	28	12-0	1	25	.220	.262	.339	68	-10	4-3	.975	1	103	112	O-66(9-18-41)	-1.3
1982	Tor A	140	437	59	128	26	3	6	49	32-4	3	51	.293	.342	.407	97	-1	14-2	.979	-6	93	45	*O-125(99-39-7)/3-9,D-6	-0.8
1983	Tor A	121	377	49	120	21	3	10	54	33-5	0	52	.318	.369	.469	123	12	10-7	.986	-1	94	95	*O-117(62-22-51)/3-4,D	0.6

Year	Tm Lg	G	AB	R	H	2B	3B	HR	RBI	BB-IB	HP	SO	AVG	OBP	SLG	AOPS	ABR	SB-CS	FA	FR	Rng	Thr	G at Pos	BFW
1984	Sea A	110	363	42	96	15	4	8	48	25-3	2	51	.264	.315	.394	96	-3	5-2	.994	-3	89	153	O-94(70-16-20),3-10/1-5,D-8	-0.9
1985	Sea A	48	111	9	27	8	0	1	10	6-1	0	19	.243	.282	.342	70	-5	1-2	.976	-0	101	164	O-22(9-0-13)/1-5,D-2	-0.6
1986	Sea A	17	51	4	10	2	0	0	4	1-0	0	13	.196	.208	.235	21	-6	0-1	.941	1	99	0	/O-9(LF),1-8,D-2	-0.6
Total	10	976	3068	363	833	143	24	56	355	229-26	13	387	.272	.323	.389	89	-45	64-39	.982	2	97	114	O-859L/3-71,D-22,1-18	-6.9
BONNER, FRANK Frank J B 8.20.1869 Lowell, MA D 12.31.1905 Kansas City, MO BR/TR 5-7.5/169# d4.26																								
1894	†Bal N	33	118	27	38	10	2	0	24	17	1	5	.322	.412	.441	101	1	12	.904	-9	82	74	2-27/O-4(2-1-1),3-2,S	-0.5
1895	Bal N	11	42	9	14	1	1	0	7	5	0	1	.333	.404	.405	106	0	4	.742	-4	76	159	3-11	-0.2
	StL N	15	59	3	8	0	1	1	8	1	1	8	.136	.164	.220	-1	-10	2	.656	-5	72	0	3-10/O-5(RF),C	-1.2
	Year	26	101	12	22	1	2	1	15	6	1	9	.218	.269	.297	46	-9	6	.698	-8	74	83	3-21/O-5(RF),C	-1.4
1896	Bro N	9	34	8	6	2	0	0	5	2	2	8	.176	.263	.235	34	-3	1	.915	0	129	84	/2-9	-0.2
1899	Was N	85	347	41	95	20	4	2	44	18	2		.274	.313	.372	88	-6	6	.940	3	102	94	2-85	0.1
1902	Cle A	34	132	14	37	6	0	0	14	5	1		.280	.312	.326	80	-4	1	.907	-6	95	39	2-34	-0.9
	Phi A	11	44	2	8	0	0	0	3	0	1		.182	.200	.182	6	-6	0	.937	-1	95	80	2-11	-0.7
	Year	45	176	16	45	6	0	0	17	5	2		.256	.284	.290	61	-10	1	.915	-7	95	50	2-45	-1.6
1903	Bos N	48	173	11	38	5	0	1	10	7	3		.220	.262	.266	53	-11	2	.957	-1	99	145	2-24,S-22	-1.0
Total	6	246	949	115	244	44	8	4	115	55	11	22	.257	.305	.333	73	-39	28	.931	-21	99	87	2-190/S-23,3-23,O-9(2-1-6),C	-4.6
BONNER, BOBBY Robert Averill B 8.12.1956 Uvalde, TX BR/TR 6/185# d9.12																								
1980	Bal A	4	4	1	0	0	0	0	1	0-0	0	0	.000	.000	.000	-99	-1	0-0	.889	-0	110	91	/S-3	-0.1
1981	Bal A	10	27	6	8	2	0	0	2	1-0	0	4	.296	.310	.370	99	0	1-0	.976	2	109	163	/S-9	0.3
1982	Bal A	41	77	8	13	3	1	0	5	3-0	0	12	.169	.198	.234	19	-9	0-0	.959	-12	76	62	S-38/2-3	-1.8
1983	Bal A	6	0	0	0	0	0	0	0	0-0	0	0	—	—	—	—	0	0-0	1.000	-1	0	0	/2-5,D	-0.1
Total	4	61	108	15	21	5	1	0	8	4-0	0	16	.194	.219	.259	34	-10	1-0	.960	-10	85	85	/S-50,2-8,D	-1.7
BONURA, ZEKE Henry John B 9.20.1908 New Orleans, LA D 3.9.1987 New Orleans, LA BR/TR 6/210# d4.17 Mil 1941-45																								
1934	Chi A	127	510	86	154	35	4	27	110	64	0	31	.302	.380	.545	132	23	0-2	**.996**	4	109	81	*1-127	1.3
1935	Chi A	138	550	107	162	34	4	21	92	57	3	28	.295	.364	.485	115	11	4-0	.994	2	105	93	*1-138	0.1
1936	Chi A	148	587	120	194	39	7	12	138	94	4	29	.330	.426	.482	119	22	4-2	**.996**	11	**134**	**118**	*1-146	1.7
1937	Chi A	116	447	79	154	41	2	19	100	49	2	24	.345	.412	.573	146	32	5-1	.989	-2	97	**132**	*1-115	1.9
1938	Was A	137	540	72	156	27	3	22	114	44	3	29	.289	.346	.472	111	6	2-2	**.993**	3	109	107	*1-129	-0.4
1939	NY N	123	455	75	146	26	6	11	85	46	4	22	.321	.388	.477	130	20	1	.992	6	118	104	*1-122	1.5
1940	Was A	79	311	41	85	16	3	3	45	40	1	13	.273	.358	.373	96	-1	2-0	.982	-4	85	97	1-79	-1.1
	Chi N	49	182	20	48	14	0	4	20	10	0	4	.264	.302	.407	96	-1	1	.991	6	151	99	1-44	0.0
Total	7	917	3582	600	1099	232	29	119	704	404	17	180	.307	.380	.487	121	112	19-7	.992	26	112	104	1-900	5.0
BOOE, EVERETT Everett Little B 9.28.1891 Mocksville, NC D 5.21.1969 Kenedy, TX BL/TR 5-8.5/165# d4.13																								
1913	Pit N	29	80	9	16	0	2	0	2	6	0	9	.200	.256	.250	47	-6	2-4	1.000	1	89	162	O-22(1-21-0)	-0.8
1914	Ind F	20	31	5	7	1	0	0	6	7	0	6	.226	.368	.258	65	-2	4	.778	-1	96	0	/O-5(4-1-0),S-3	-0.3
	Buf F	76	241	29	54	9	2	0	14	21	1	50	.224	.289	.278	54	-19	8	.959	-3	97	90	O-58(23-0-35)/S-8,3-2,2	-2.6
	Year	96	272	34	61	10	2	0	20	28	1	56	.224	.299	.276	55	-21	12	.944	-5	97	84	O-63(27-1-35),S-11/3-2,2	-2.9
Total	2	125	352	43	77	10	4	0	22	34	1	65	.219	.289	.270	54	-27	14-4	.959	-4	95	102	/O-85(28-22-35),S-11,3-2,2	-3.7
BOOKER, BUDDY Richard Lee B 5.28.1942 Lynchburg, VA BL/TR 5-10/170# d6.4																								
1966	Cle A	18	28	6	6	1	0	2	5	2-0	0	6	.214	.267	.464	105	0	0-0	.964	-3	*115*	*74*	C-12	-0.2
1968	Chi A	5	5	0	0	0	0	0	0	1-0	0	2	.000	.167	.000	-46	-1	0-0	1.000	-1	28	0	/C-3	-0.2
Total	2	23	33	6	6	1	0	2	5	3-0	0	8	.182	.250	.394	83	-1	0-0	.967	-3	*106*	*67*	/C-15	-0.4
BOOKER, ROD Roderick Stewart B 9.4.1958 Los Angeles, CA BL/TR 6/175# d4.29																								
1987	StL N	44	47	9	13	1	1	0	8	7-1	0	7	.277	.370	.340	88	-1	2-0	.960	1	105	57	2-18/3-4,S	0.2
1988	StL N	18	35	6	12	3	0	0	3	4-0	0	3	.343	.410	.429	140	2	2-2	.889	-2	85	0	3-13/2	0.0
1989	StL N	10	8	1	2	0	0	0	0	0-0	0	1	.250	.250	.250	42	-1	0-0	.867	1	149	177	/2-5,3	0.0
1990	Phi N	73	131	19	29	5	2	0	10	15-7	0	26	.221	.301	.290	64	-6	3-1	.976	-11	76	93	S-27,2-23,3-10	-1.6
1991	Phi N	28	53	3	12	1	0	0	7	1-1	0	7	.226	.236	.245	37	-5	0-0	1.000	-5	75	29	S-20/3-3	-0.9
Total	5	173	274	38	68	10	3	0	28	27-9	0	44	.248	.315	.307	72	-11	7-3	.985	-16	76	68	/S-48,2-47,3-31	-2.3
BOOL, AL Albert J. B 8.24.1897 Lincoln, NE D 9.27.1981 Lincoln, NE BR/TR 5-11/180# d9.29																								
1928	Was A	2	7	0	1	0	0	0	1	0	0	0	.143	.143	.143	-25	-1	0-0	1.000	0	*111*	*121*	/C-2	-0.1
1930	Pit N	78	216	30	56	12	4	7	46	25	0	29	.259	.336	.449	87	-5	0	.967	1	*95*	*135*	C-65	0.0
1931	Bos N	49	85	5	16	1	0	0	6	9	0	13	.188	.266	.200	28	-9	0	.989	-0	*103*	*101*	C-37	-0.8
Total	3	129	308	35	73	13	4	7	53	34	0	42	.237	.313	.373	71	-15	0-0	.973	1	*98*	*125*	C-104	-0.9
BOONE, AARON Aaron John B 3.9.1973 LaMesa, CA BR/TR 6-2/190# d6.20 b-Bret f-Bob gf-Ray																								
1997	Cin N	16	49	5	12	1	0	0	5	2-0	0	5	.245	.275	.265	42	-4	1-0	.917	-0	100	0	3-13/2	-0.4
1998	Cin N	58	181	24	51	13	2	2	28	15-1	5	36	.282	.350	.409	99	0	6-1	.950	0	103	82	3-52/2S	0.2
1999	Cin N	139	472	56	132	26	5	14	72	30-2	8	79	.280	.330	.445	92	-7	17-6	.958	2	103	89	*3-136/S-6	-0.2
2000	Cin N	84	291	44	83	18	0	12	43	24-1	10	52	.285	.356	.471	105	3	6-1	.964	3	103	144	3-84/S-2	0.7
2001	Cin N	103	381	54	112	26	2	14	62	29-1	8	71	.294	.351	.483	109	6	6-3	.936	5	114	94	*3-103	1.1
2002	Cin N	**162**	606	83	146	38	2	26	87	56-4	10	111	.241	.314	.439	97	-7	32-8	.954	16	**122**	**142**	*3-154,S-16	1.6
2003	Cin N★	106	403	61	110	19	3	18	65	35-2	5	74	.273	.339	.469	110	5	15-3	.945	10	114	124	3-83,2-19/S-5	1.9
	†NY A	54	189	31	48	13	0	6	31	11-0	3	30	.254	.302	.418	90	-3	8-0	.961	5	109	83	3-54	0.4
Total	7	722	2572	358	694	154	14	92	393	202-11	49	458	.270	.332	.448	99	-7	91-22	.951	41	111	110	3-679/S-30,2-21	5.3
BOONE, BRET Bret Robert B 4.6.1969 ElCajon, CA BR/TR 5-10/180# d8.19 b-Aaron f-Bob gf-Ray																								
1992	Sea A	33	129	15	25	4	0	4	15	4-0	1	34	.194	.224	.318	50	-9	1-1	.965	1	104	94	2-32/3-6	-0.8
1993	Sea A	76	271	31	68	12	2	12	38	17-1	4	52	.251	.301	.443	97	-3	2-3	.991	-5	89	116	2-74/D	-0.4
1994	Cin N	108	381	59	122	25	2	12	68	24-1	8	74	.320	.368	.491	124	14	3-4	.974	-18	88	95	*2-106/3-2	0.0
1995	†Cin N	138	513	63	137	34	2	15	68	41-0	6	84	.267	.326	.429	98	-2	5-1	**.994**	-8	94	**127**	*2-138	-0.2
1996	Cin N	142	520	56	121	21	3	12	69	31-0	3	100	.233	.275	.354	65	-28	3-2	**.991**	3	98	95	*2-141	-1.8
1997	Cin N	139	443	40	99	25	1	7	46	45-4	4	101	.223	.298	.332	65	-23	5-5	**.997**	-4	94	95	*2-136	-2.1
1998	Cin N☆	157	583	76	155	38	1	24	95	48-3	4	104	.266	.324	.458	102	1	6-4	.988	-7	94	101	*2-156	0.2
1999	†Atl N	152	608	102	153	38	1	20	63	47-0	5	112	.252	.310	.416	82	-19	14-9	.982	2	**107**	90	*2-151	-0.9
2000	SD N	127	463	61	116	18	2	19	74	50-7	5	97	.251	.326	.421	95	-5	8-4	.977	-5	94	102	*2-126	-0.4
2001	†Sea A★	158	623	118	206	37	3	37	**141**	40-5	9	110	.331	.372	.578	156	49	5-5	.986	-16	93	106	*2-156/D-2	3.8
2002	Sea A	155	608	88	169	34	3	24	107	53-4	6	102	.278	.339	.462	115	13	12-5	**.989**	-18	91	94	*2-153/D	0.3
2003	Sea A★	159	622	111	183	35	5	35	117	68-3	7	125	.294	.366	.535	139	35	16-3	.990	-15	91	**117**	*2-158	2.9
Total	12	1544	5764	820	1554	321	25	221	901	468-28	62	1095	.270	.328	.449	104	23	80-46	.987	-91	94	103	*2-1527/3-8,D-4	0.6
BOONE, IKE Isaac Morgan B 2.17.1897 Samantha, AL D 8.1.1958 Northport, AL BL/TR 6/195# d4.22 b-Danny																								
1922	NY N	2	2	0	1	0	0	0	0	0	0	1	.500	.500	.500	157	0	0-0	—	0			H	0.0
1923	Bos A	5	15	1	4	0	1	0	2	1	0	0	.267	.313	.400	86	0	0-1	.929	-0	114	0	/O-4(CF)	-0.1
1924	Bos A	128	487	72	164	31	4	13	98	54	1	32	.337	.404	.497	131	23	2-2	.976	-9	82	96	*O-124(RF)	0.3
1925	Bos A	133	476	79	157	34	5	9	68	60	1	19	.330	.406	.479	124	19	1-4	.941	-9	90	73	*O-118(RF)	0.0
1927	Chi A	29	53	10	12	4	0	1	11	3	0	4	.226	.268	.358	63	-3	0-0	1.000	-1	100	0	O-11(1-0-10)	-0.4
1930	Bro N	40	101	13	30	9	1	3	13	14	0	8	.297	.383	.495	111	2	0	.960	-0	105	63	O-27(LF)	0.0
1931	Bro N	6	5	0	1	0	0	0	0	1	0	1	.200	.333	.200	47	0	0	—	0			H	0.0
1932	Bro N	13	21	2	3	1	0	0	2	5	0	2	.143	.308	.190	38	-2	0	1.000	0	83	245	/O-8(2-0-6)	-0.1
Total	8	356	1160	177	372	79	11	26	194	138	2	67	.321	.394	.475	121	39	3-7	.960	-19	88	82	O-292(30-4-258)	-0.3
BOONE, LUTE Lute Joseph "Danny" B 5.6.1890 Pittsburgh, PA D 7.29.1982 Pittsburgh, PA BR/TR 5-9/160# d9.9																								
1913	NY A	6	12	3	4	0	0	0	1	3	0	1	.333	.467	.333	134	1	0	.857	-1	87	0	/S-4	0.0
1914	NY A	106	370	34	82	8	2	0	21	31	2	41	.222	.285	.254	63	-17	10-18	.960	18	111	115	2-90/3-9,O(RF)	-0.2
1915	NY A	130	431	44	88	12	2	5	43	41	8	53	.204	.285	.276	68	-17	14-17	.965	**21**	**117**	**140**	*2-115,S-11/3-4	0.3
1916	NY A	46	124	14	23	4	0	1	8	8	3	10	.185	.252	.242	47	-8	7	.973	3	119	148	3-25,S-12/2-8	-0.4
1918	Pit N	27	91	7	18	3	0	0	3	8	0	6	.198	.263	.231	49	-5	1	.921	-3	95	60	S-26/2	-0.8
Total	5	315	1028	102	215	27	4	6	76	91	13	111	.209	.282	.261	63	-46	32-35	.964	37	114	128	2-214/S-53,3-38,O(RF)	-1.1

Year	Tm Lg	G	AB	R	H	2B	3B	HR	RBI	BB-IB	HP	SO	AVG	OBP	SLG	AOPS	ABR	SB-CS	FA	FR	Rng	Thr	G at Pos	BFW
BOONE, RAY Raymond Otis "Ike" B 7.27.1923 San Diego, CA BR/TR 6-1/188# d9.3 s-Bob gs-Bret gs-Aaron																								
1948	†Cle A	6	5	0	2	1	0	0	1	0	0	1	.400	.400	.600	168	0	0-0	.889	0	129	0	/S-4	0.1
1949	Cle A	86	258	39	65	4	4	4	26	38	2	17	.252	.352	.345	87	-5	0-2	.947	0	97	117	S-76	-0.1
1950	Cle A	109	365	53	110	14	6	7	58	56	2	27	.301	.397	.430	116	10	4-3	.945	-7	93	96	*S-102	0.8
1951	Cle A	151	544	65	127	14	1	12	51	48	5	36	.233	.302	.329	75	-21	5-3	.957	-1	98	106	*S-151	-1.3
1952	Cle A	103	316	57	83	8	2	7	45	53	2	33	.263	.372	.367	113	7	0-1	.941	-4	98	102	S-96/3-2,2	0.9
1953	Cle A	34	112	21	27	1	2	4	21	24	0	21	.241	.375	.393	110	2	1-2	.952	1	100	122	S-31	0.6
	Det A	101	385	73	120	16	6	22	93	48	5	47	.312	.395	.556	156	30	2-1	.958	1	99	125	3-97/S-3	3.0
	Year	135	497	94	147	17	8	26	114	72	5	68	.296	.390	.519	146	32	3-3	.958	3	99	125	3-97,S-34	3.6
1954	Det A★	148	543	76	160	19	7	20	85	71	2	53	.295	.376	.466	133	24	4-2	.964	2	103	80	*3-148/S	2.6
1955	Det A	135	500	61	142	22	7	20	**116**	50-2	1	49	.284	.346	.476	123	14	1-1	.953	-2	98	133	*3-126	1.2
1956	Det A★	131	481	77	148	14	6	25	81	77-8	3	46	.308	.403	.518	142	30	0-0	.959	-4	91	83	*3-130	2.5
1957	Det A	129	462	48	126	25	3	12	65	57-6	3	47	.273	.353	.418	108	6	1-1	.990	-12	61	101	*1-117/3-4	-1.3
1958	Det A	39	114	16	27	4	1	6	20	14-1	1	13	.237	.323	.447	103	0	0-2	.988	-1	82	101	1-32	-0.3
	Chi A	77	246	25	60	12	1	7	41	18-1	1	33	.244	.295	.386	89	-4	1-1	.986	-2	91	85	1-63	-1.1
	Year	116	360	41	87	16	2	13	61	32-2	2	46	.242	.304	.406	93	-4	1-3	.986	-3	88	90	1-95	-1.4
1959	Chi A	9	21	3	5	0	0	1	5	7-0	0	5	.238	.400	.381	126	1	1-0	.955	0	141	45	/1-6	0.1
	KC A	61	132	19	36	6	0	2	12	27-2	0	17	.273	.396	.364	108	3	1-0	.983	1	117	70	1-38/3-3	0.3
	Year	70	153	22	41	6	0	3	17	34-2	0	22	.268	.397	.366	111	4	2-0	.980	2	121	66	1-44/3-3	0.4
	Mil N	13	15	3	3	0	0	1	2	4-0	0	2	.200	.368	.400	114	0	0-0	1.000	-0	63	224	/1-3	0.0
1960	Mil N	7	12	3	3	1	0	0	4	5-0	0	1	.250	.471	.333	135	1	0-0	1.000	0	117	104	/1-4	0.1
	Bos A	34	78	6	16	1	0	1	11	11-0	0	15	.205	.300	.256	51	-5	0-0	.994	-0	86	103	1-22	-0.7
Total	13	1373	4589	645	1260	162	46	151	737	608-20	27	463	.275	.361	.429	115	93	21-19	.958	-28	98	103	3-510,S-464,1-285/2	7.4
BOONE, BOB Robert Raymond B 11.19.1947 San Diego, CA BR/TR 6-2/202# d9.10 M6 C1 f-Ray s-Bret s-Aaron																								
1972	Phi N	16	51	4	14	1	0	1	4	5-2	0	7	.275	.333	.353	95	0	1-0	.936	-4	140	101	C-14	-0.4
1973	Phi N	145	521	42	136	20	2	10	61	41-8	0	36	.261	.311	.365	86	-11	3-4	.990	14	120	**138**	*C-145	0.9
1974	Phi N	146	488	41	118	24	3	3	52	35-9	4	29	.242	.295	.322	70	-20	3-1	.976	-3	89	112	*C-146	-1.6
1975	Phi N	97	289	28	71	14	2	2	20	32-6	1	14	.246	.322	.329	78	-8	1-3	.990	2	138	117	C-92/3-3	-0.3
1976	†Phi N★	121	361	40	98	18	2	4	54	45-14	1	44	.271	.348	.366	101	2	2-5	.993	-8	125	62	*C-108/1-4	-0.3
1977	†Phi N	132	440	55	125	26	4	11	66	42-5	2	54	.284	.343	.436	105	3	5-5	.989	7	119	85	*C-131/3-2	1.5
1978	†Phi N★	132	435	48	123	18	4	12	62	46-10	1	37	.283	.347	.425	115	9	2-5	**.991**	-1	133	84	*C-129/1-3,O(LF)	1.2
1979	Phi N★	119	398	38	114	21	3	9	58	49-9	2	33	.286	.367	.422	111	8	1-4	.988	-3	**152**	101	*C-117/3-2	0.9
1980	†Phi N	141	480	34	110	23	1	9	55	48-12	1	41	.229	.299	.338	74	-16	3-4	.979	3	102	108	*C-138	-0.9
1981	†Phi N	76	227	19	48	7	0	4	24	22-2	0	16	.211	.279	.295	61	-12	2-2	.985	-12	72	78	C-75	-2.3
1982	†Cal A	143	472	42	121	17	0	7	58	39-2	0	34	.256	.310	.337	79	-14	0-2	.989	15	**193**	**130**	*C-143	0.7
1983	Cal A★	142	468	46	120	18	0	9	52	24-1	0	42	.256	.289	.353	77	-16	4-3	.980	10	148	111	*C-142	0.0
1984	Cal A	139	450	33	91	16	1	3	32	25-1	0	45	.202	.242	.262	40	-37	3-3	.984	8	148	93	*C-137	-2.3
1985	Cal A	150	460	37	114	17	0	5	55	37-2	3	35	.248	.306	.317	72	-17	1-2	.987	10	**154**	104	*C-147	-0.2
1986	†Cal A	144	442	48	98	12	2	7	49	43-1	0	30	.222	.287	.305	63	-23	1-0	.988	19	**210**	94	*C-144	0.2
1987	Cal A	128	389	42	94	18	0	3	33	35-0	1	36	.242	.304	.311	66	-18	0-2	.983	5	**207**	92	*C-127/D	-0.9
1988	Cal A	122	352	38	104	17	0	5	39	29-2	2	26	.295	.352	.386	110	5	2-2	.986	-3	118	127	*C-121	0.8
1989	KC A	131	405	33	111	13	2	1	43	49-4	2	37	.274	.351	.323	93	-2	3-2	.991	11	138	110	*C-129	1.7
1990	KC A	40	117	11	28	3	0	0	9	17-0	0	12	.239	.336	.265	71	-4	1-1	.985	-3	78	78	C-40	-0.4
Total	19	2264	7245	679	1838	303	26	105	826	663-90	20	608	.254	.315	.346	82	-171	38-50	.986	66	140	104	*C-2225/1-7,3-7,DO(LF)	-1.7
BOOTH d5.1																								
1875	NH NA	1	2	0	0	0	0	0	0	0		1	.000	.000	.000	-99	0	0-0	.500	-0	66	0	/S	-0.1
BOOTH, AMOS Amos Smith "Darling" B 9.14.1853 Cincinnati, OH D 7.1.1921 Miamisburg, OH BR/TR 5-9/159# d4.25 ▲ OF Total (1-LF 3-RF)																								
1876	Cin N	63	272	31	71	3	0	0	14	9		11	.261	.285	.272	101	3		.760	-16	77	0	3-24,C-24,S-22/O-3(RF),P-3	-1.0
1877	Cin N	44	157	16	27	2	1	0	13	12		10	.172	.231	.197	41	-9		.853	-5	107	28	S-13,C-12,P-12,2-10/3-3,O(LF)	-0.9
1880	Cin N	1	2	0	0	0	0	0	0	0		0	.000	.000	.000	-99	0		—	-0	0	0	/3	-0.1
1882	Bal AA	1	3	0	0	0	0	0		0			.000	.000	.000	-99	-1		1.000	0	66	0	/3	-0.1
	Lou AA	1	4	0	0	0	0	0		0			.000	.000	.000	-99	-1		1.000	-0	103	0	/2	-0.1
	Year	2	7	0	0	0	0	0		0			.000	.000	.000	-99	-1		1.000	0	66	0	/32	-0.2
Total	4	110	438	47	98	5	1	0	27	21		21	.224	.259	.240	73	-8		.746	-21			/C-36,S-35,3-29,P-15,2-11,O-4R	-2.2
BOOTH, EDDIE Edward H. B Brooklyn, NY d4.26																								
1872	Man NA	**24**	116	25	37	5	2	0	15	0		1	.319	.319	.397	126	4	0-2	.775	4	120	92	2-20/O-4(0-3-1)	0.4
	Atl NA	15	62	10	19	4	0	0	7	0		0	.306	.306	.371	92	-1	0-2	.808	2	358	0	O-14(6-0-8)/2	0.0
	Year	39	178	35	56	9	2	0	22	0		1	.315	.315	.388	111	2	0-4	.780	6	121	97	2-21,O-18(6-3-9)	0.4
1873	Res NA	18	74	11	21	5	2	0	6	0		1	.284	.284	.405	111	1	0-0	.875	-3	41	0	O-17(15-0-2)/2	-0.1
	Atl NA	16	70	8	14	3	1	0	7	2		0	.200	.222	.271	51	-3	0-1	.788	0	130	0	O-16(0-4-12)	-0.2
	Year	34	144	19	35	8	3	0	13	2		1	.243	.253	.340	82	-2	0-1	.831	-3	84	0	O-33(15-4-14)/2	-0.3
1874	Atl NA	44	185	24	47	4	3	1	16	3		3	.254	.266	.324	100	2	0-0	.809	-8	48	0	*O-44(LF)/2	-0.4
1875	Mut NA	68	281	33	56	3	4	0	18	0		2	.199	.199	.238	49	-15	4-3	.827	1	**158**	103	*O-63(3-1-60)/2-8	-0.9
1876	NY N	**57**	228	17	49	2	1	0	7	2		4	.215	.222	.232	59	-8		.764	-5	132	0	*O-53(0-2-51)/2-5,P	-1.2
Total	4 NA	185	788	111	194	24	12	1	69	5		7	.246	.251	.311	81	-12	4-8	.000	-3	130	41	O-158(68-8-83)/2-31	-1.2
BOOTY, JOSH Joshua Gibson B 4.29.1975 Starkville, MS BR/TR 6-3/210# d9.24																								
1996	Fla N	2	2	1	1	0	0	0	0	0-0	0	0	.500	.500	.500	170	0	0-0	—	-0	0	0	/3	0.0
1997	Fla N	4	5	2	3	0	0	0	1	1-0	0	1	.600	.667	.600	246	1	0-0	.857	1	174	387	/3-4	0.2
1998	Fla N	7	19	0	3	1	0	0	3	3-0	0	8	.158	.273	.211	31	-2	0-0	.833	-1	95	83	/3-7	-0.3
Total	3	13	26	3	7	1	0	0	4	4-0	0	9	.269	.367	.308	84	-1	0-0	.840	-0	109	143	/3-12	-0.1
BORCHARD, JOE Joseph Edward B 11.25.1978 Panorama City, CA BB/TR 6-5/220# d9.2																								
2002	Chi A	16	36	5	8	0	0	2	5	1-0	0	14	.222	.243	.389	63	-2	0-0	1.000	-1	90	0	O-15(10-5-3)	-0.3
2003	Chi A	16	49	5	9	1	0	1	5	5-0	0	18	.184	.246	.265	39	-4	0-1	1.000	-2	83	0	O-16(CF)	-0.6
Total	2	32	85	10	17	1	0	3	10	6-0	0	32	.200	.245	.318	49	-6	0-1	1.000	-3	86	0	/O-31(10-21-3)	-0.9
BORDAGARAY, FRENCHY Stanley George B 1.3.1910 Coalinga, CA D 4.13.2000 Ventura, CA BR/TR 5-7.5/175# d4.17																								
1934	Chi A	29	87	12	28	3	1	0	2	3	0	8	.322	.344	.379	84	-2	1-2	.938	-1	86	156	O-17(2-1-14)	-0.4
1935	Bro N	120	422	69	119	19	6	1	39	17	6	29	.282	.319	.363	85	-10	18	.980	2	95	164	*O-105(17-61-27)	-1.1
1936	Bro N	125	372	63	117	21	3	4	31	17	1	42	.315	.346	.419	104	2	12	.991	2	111	117	O-92(14-46-33),2-11/3-6	0.1
1937	StL N	96	300	43	88	11	4	1	37	15	2	25	.293	.331	.367	88	-6	11	.942	-6	82	32	3-50,O-28(3-7-15)	-1.1
1938	StL N	81	156	19	44	5	1	0	21	8	2	9	.282	.325	.327	76	-5	2	.959	0	112	133	O-29(6-14-9)/3-4	-0.6
1939	†Cin N	63	122	19	24	5	1	0	12	9	0	10	.197	.252	.254	36	-11	3	1.000	-0	104	47	O-43(21-3-19)/2-2	-1.3
1941	†NY A	36	73	10	19	1	0	0	4	6	1	8	.260	.325	.274	61	-4	1-0	.967	-1	94	75	O-19(6-0-13)	-0.5
1942	Bro N	48	58	11	14	2	0	0	5	3	0	3	.241	.279	.276	62	-3	2	1.000	0	117	0	O-17(0-10-7)	-0.3
1943	Bro N	89	268	47	81	18	2	0	19	30	3	15	.302	.379	.384	120	9	6	.989	-7	99	147	O-53(28-6-20),3-25	0.0
1944	Bro N	130	501	85	141	26	4	6	51	36	1	22	.281	.331	.385	103	1	3	.945	-15	79	78	3-98,O-25(5-15-8)	-1.4
1945	Bro N	113	273	32	70	9	6	2	49	29	0	15	.256	.328	.355	91	-4	7	.886	-9	86	72	3-57,O-22(9-7-6)	-1.3
Total	11	930	2632	410	745	120	28	14	270	173	16	186	.283	.331	.366	91	-33	66-2	.982	-32	103	113	O-450(111-170-171),3-240/2-13	-7.9
BORDERS, PAT Patrick Lance B 5.14.1963 Columbus, OH BR/TR 6-2/200# d4.6																								
1988	Tor A	56	154	15	42	6	3	5	21	3-0	0	24	.273	.285	.448	102	-1	0-0	.973	2	120	160	C-43/23D	0.4
1989	†Tor A	94	241	22	62	11	1	3	29	11-2	1	45	.257	.290	.349	81	-7	2-1	.980	1	88	136	C-68,D-18	-0.4
1990	Tor A	125	346	36	99	24	2	15	49	18-2	0	57	.286	.319	.497	123	9	0-1	.993	4	110	128	*C-115/D	1.9
1991	†Tor A	105	291	22	71	17	0	5	36	11-1	1	45	.244	.271	.354	70	-13	0-0	.993	13	98	107	*C-102	0.5
1992	†Tor A	138	480	47	116	26	2	13	53	33-3	2	75	.242	.290	.385	85	-11	1-1	.991	4	83	103	*C-137	0.1
1993	†Tor A	138	488	38	124	30	0	9	55	20-2	2	66	.254	.285	.371	75	-19	2-2	.986	1	80	102	*C-138	-0.8
1994	Tor A	85	295	24	73	13	1	3	26	15-0	0	50	.247	.284	.329	57	-20	1-1	.988	6	84	128	C-85	-0.8
1995	KC A	52	143	14	33	8	1	4	13	7-1	0	22	.231	.267	.385	66	-8	0-0	1.000	1	196	97	C-45/D-3	-0.4
	Hou N	11	35	1	4	0	0	0	0	2-1	0	7	.114	.162	.114	-27	-7	0-0	.987	1	118	198	C-11	-0.5
1996	StL N	26	69	3	22	3	0	0	4	1-0	0	14	.319	.329	.362	83	-2	0-1	.984	5	198	127	C-17/1	0.3

Year	Tm Lg	G	AB	R	H	2B	3B	HR	RBI	BB-IB	HP	SO	AVG	OBP	SLG	AOPS	ABR	SB-CS	FA	FR	Rng	Thr	G at Pos	BFW
	Cal A	19	57	6	13	3	0	2	8	3-0	0	11	.228	.267	.386	62	-4	0-1	.984	2	69	113	C-19	0.0
	Chi A	31	94	6	26	1	0	3	6	5-0	0	18	.277	.313	.383	79	-4	0-0	.982	-3	75	129	C-30/D	-0.4
	Year	50	151	12	39	4	0	5	14	8-0	0	29	.258	.296	.384	72	-7	0-1	.983	-0	73	123	C-49/D	-0.4
1997	Cle A	55	159	17	47	7	1	4	15	9-0	2	27	.296	.341	.428	96	-1	0-2	1.000	0	84	96	C-53	0.1
1998	Cle A	54	160	12	38	6	0	0	6	10-0	2	40	.237	.289	.275	47	-13	0-2	.974	-4	97	88	C-53/3	-1.4
1999	Cle A	6	20	2	6	0	1	0	3	0-0	0	3	.300	.300	.400	73	-1	0-1	.943	-2	36	0	/C-5	-0.3
	Tor A	6	14	1	3	0	0	1	3	1-0	0	2	.214	.267	.429	72	-1	0-0	1.000	-0	0	200	/C-3,3D	-0.1
	Year	12	34	3	9	0	1	1	6	1-0	0	5	.265	.286	.412	73	-2	0-1	.955	-3	27	51	/C-8,D-3,3	-0.4
2001	Sea A	5	6	1	3	0	0	0	0	0-0	0	1	.500	.500	.500	175	1	0-0	.923	-0	150	153	/C-5	0.0
2002	Sea A	4	4	0	2	1	0	0	1	0-0	0	1	.500	.500	.750	234	1	0-0	1.000	-0	0	0	/C-2,D-2	0.1
2003	Sea A	12	14	1	2	1	0	0	1	1-0	0	5	.143	.200	.214	10	-2	0-0	1.000	1	111	308	/C-7,3-2	-0.1
Total	15	1022	3070	268	786	157	12	67	329	150-12	10	513	.256	.291	.380	79	-103	6-13	.988	30	97	115	C-938/D-35,3-5,12	-1.8
BORDICK, MIKE Michael Todd B 7.21.1965 Marquette, MI BR/TR 5-11/175# d4.11																								
1990	†Oak A	25	14	0	1	0	0	0	0	1-0	0	4	.071	.133	.071	-43	-3	0-0	1.000	-3	79	0	3-10/S-9,2-7	-0.6
1991	Oak A	90	235	21	56	5	1	0	21	14-0	3	37	.238	.289	.268	59	-14	3-4	.972	-6	96	89	S-84/2-5,3	-1.5
1992	†Oak A	154	504	62	151	19	4	3	48	40-2	9	59	.300	.358	.371	111	8	12-6	.987	5	101	98	2-95,S-70	2.1
1993	Oak A	159	546	60	136	21	2	3	48	60-2	11	58	.249	.332	.311	80	-14	10-10	.982	-15	92	99	*S-159/2	-1.7
1994	Oak A	**114**	391	38	99	18	4	2	37	38-1	3	44	.253	.320	.335	77	-13	7-2	.974	6	98	95	*S-112/2-4	0.2
1995	Oak A	126	428	46	113	13	0	8	44	35-2	5	48	.264	.325	.350	81	-13	11-3	.983	8	95	113	*S-126/D	0.6
1996	Oak A	155	525	46	126	18	4	5	54	52-0	1	59	.240	.307	.318	60	-33	5-6	.979	10	108	113	*S-155	-1.1
1997	†Bal A	153	509	55	120	19	1	7	46	33-1	2	66	.236	.283	.318	59	-32	0-2	.980	-3	97	105	*S-153	-2.2
1998	Bal A	151	465	59	121	29	1	13	51	39-0	10	65	.260	.328	.411	93	-5	6-7	.990	21	107	102	*S-150	2.4
1999	Bal A	160	631	93	175	35	7	10	77	54-1	5	102	.277	.334	.403	92	-8	14-4	**.989**	**35**	114	**125**	*S-159	3.7
2000	Bal A★	100	391	70	116	22	1	16	59	34-0	1	71	.297	.350	.481	114	8	6-5	.979	-13	89	81	*S-100	0.2
	†NY N	56	192	18	50	8	0	4	21	15-0	2	28	.260	.321	.365	76	-8	3-1	.968	-7	90	77	S-56	-1.0
2001	Bal A	58	229	32	57	13	0	7	30	17-1	6	36	.249	.314	.397	92	-3	9-3	.977	-5	92	76	S-58	-0.3
2002	Bal A	117	367	37	85	19	3	8	36	35-0	3	63	.232	.302	.365	81	-10	7-4	**.998**	**26**	**117**	**125**	*S-117	2.4
2003	Tor A	102	343	39	94	18	2	5	54	33-0	2	60	.274	.340	.382	89	-5	3-1	.987	12	100	124	S-69,3-22,2-13/D	1.2
Total	14	1720	5770	676	1500	257	30	91	626	500-10	63	800	.260	.323	.362	83	-145	96-58	.982	71	101	105	*S-1577,2-125/3-33,D-2	4.4
BORGMANN, GLENN Glenn Dennis B 5.25.1950 Paterson, NJ BR/TR 6-4/210# d7.1																								
1972	Min A	56	175	11	41	4	0	3	14	25-8	0	25	.234	.325	.309	86	-2	0-0	.965	2	124	91	C-56	0.2
1973	Min A	12	34	7	9	2	0	0	9	6-0	0	10	.265	.375	.324	95	0	0-0	1.000	-4	90	76	C-12	-0.3
1974	Min A	128	345	33	87	8	1	3	45	39-0	1	44	.252	.323	.307	82	-7	2-1	**.997**	-2	89	108	*C-128	-0.4
1975	Min A	125	352	34	73	15	2	2	33	47-1	2	59	.207	.303	.278	65	-15	0-1	.989	2	102	**120**	*C-125	-0.9
1976	Min A	24	65	10	16	3	0	1	6	19-0	0	7	.246	.417	.338	120	3	1-1	.976	-2	68	117	C-24	0.2
1977	Min A	17	43	12	11	1	0	2	7	11-0	0	9	.256	.407	.419	128	2	0-0	1.000	-3	53	98	C-17	0.0
1978	Min A	49	123	16	26	4	1	3	15	18-0	0	17	.211	.306	.333	80	-3	0-0	.990	1	129	120	C-46/D	0.0
1979	Min A	31	70	4	14	3	0	0	8	12-0	0	11	.200	.317	.243	52	-4	1-0	.993	3	78	81	C-31	0.0
1980	Chi A	32	87	10	19	2	0	2	14	14-0	0	9	.218	.320	.310	76	-3	0-0	1.000	5	106	169	C-32	0.3
Total	9	474	1294	137	296	42	4	16	151	191-9	3	191	.229	.325	.304	79	-29	4-3	.989	1	99	112	C-471/D	-0.9
BORKOWSKI, BOB Robert Vilarian B 1.27.1926 Dayton, OH BR/TR 6/182# d4.22																								
1950	Chi N	85	256	27	70	7	4	4	29	16	1	30	.273	.319	.379	84	-7	1	.975	-2	99	56	O-65(7-29-30)/1	-1.2
1951	Chi N	58	89	9	14	1	0	0	10	3	0	16	.157	.185	.169	-4	-13	0-0	.933	-0	109	68	O-25(7-9-9)	-1.4
1952	Cin N	126	377	42	95	11	4	4	24	26	0	53	.252	.300	.334	76	-13	1-3	.991	-2	103	58	*O-103(15-64-26)/1-5	-2.0
1953	Cin N	94	249	32	67	11	1	7	29	21	1	41	.269	.328	.406	89	-4	0-1	.982	-3	94	71	O-67(3-3-61)/1-2	-0.9
1954	Cin N	73	162	13	43	12	1	1	19	8	1	18	.265	.299	.370	73	-6	0-2	1.000	1	107	114	O-36(13-0-23)/1-3	-0.8
1955	Cin N	25	18	1	3	1	0	0	1	1-0	0	2	.167	.211	.222	14	-2	0-0	1.000	0	151	0	O-11(LF)/1	-0.2
	Bro N	9	19	2	2	0	0	0	0	1-0	0	6	.105	.150	.105	-30	-4	0-0	1.000	-1	84	0	/O-9(3-2-4)	-0.4
	Year	34	37	3	5	1	0	0	1	2-0	0	8	.135	.179	.162	-8	-6	0-0	1.000	-0	103	0	O-20(14-2-4)/1	-0.6
Total	6	470	1170	126	294	43	10	16	112	76-0	3	166	.251	.298	.346	71	-49	2-6	.982	-6	101	66	O-316(59-107-153)/1-12	-6.9
BOROM, RED Edward Jones B 10.30.1916 Spartanburg, SC BL/TR 5-10/175# d4.23																								
1944	Det A	7	14	1	1	0	0	0	1	2	0	2	.071	.188	.071	-23	-2	0-0	.950	0	154	44	/2-4,S	-0.2
1945	†Det A	55	130	19	35	4	0	0	9	7	0	8	.269	.307	.300	72	-5	4-2	.966	4	119	96	2-28/3-4,S-2	0.1
Total	2	62	144	20	36	4	0	0	10	9	0	10	.250	.294	.278	62	-7	4-2	.964	5	123	90	/2-32,3-4,S-3	-0.1
BOROS, STEVE Stephen B 9.3.1936 Flint, MI BR/TR 6/185# d6.19 M3 C10																								
1957	Det A	24	41	4	6	1	0	0	2	1-0	0	8	.146	.167	.171	-7	-6	0-0	.906	1	122	63	/3-9,S-5	-0.6
1958	Det A	6	2	0	0	0	0	0	0	0-0	0	0	.000	.000	.000	-93	-1	0-0	1.000	0	0	0	/2	-0.1
1961	Det A	116	396	51	107	18	2	5	62	68-2	8	42	.270	.382	.364	99	3	4-2	.953	-20	80	70	*3-116	-1.7
1962	Det A	116	356	46	81	14	1	16	47	53-3	3	62	.228	.331	.407	95	-2	3-1	.931	-15	80	90	*3-105/2-6	-1.7
1963	Chi N	41	90	9	19	5	1	3	7	12-0	0	19	.211	.304	.389	93	-1	0-2	.975	-2	83	77	1-14,O-11(RF)	-0.5
1964	Cin N	117	370	31	95	12	3	2	31	47-14	2	43	.257	.342	.322	86	-5	4-1	.961	-2	92	109	*3-114	-0.7
1965	Cin N	2	0	0	0	0	0	0	0	0-0	0	0	—	—	—	—	0	0-0	1.000	0	114	0	/3-2	0.0
Total	7	422	1255	141	308	50	7	26	149	181-19	13	174	.245	.344	.359	90	-12	11-6	.948	-37	85	89	3-346/1-14,O-11(RF),2-7,S-5	-5.3
BORTON, BABE William Baker B 8.14.1888 Marion, IL D 7.29.1954 Berkeley, CA BL/TL 6/178# d9.2																								
1912	Chi A	31	105	15	39	3	1	0	17	8	0		.371	.416	.419	143	6	1	.997	0	92	103	1-30	0.5
1913	Chi A	28	80	9	22	5	0	0	13	23	1	5	.275	.442	.338	130	6	1	.991	-2	71	136	1-26	0.3
	NY A	33	108	8	14	2	0	0	11	18	1	19	.130	.260	.148	20	-10	1	.978	4	157	87	1-33	-0.8
	Year	61	188	17	36	7	0	0	24	41	2	24	.191	.342	.229	68	-5	2	.984	2	118	109	1-59	-0.5
1915	StL F	**159**	549	**97**	157	20	14	3	83	**92**	7	64	.286	.395	.390	115	8	17	.993	-10	65	**113**	*1-159	-0.6
1916	StL A	66	98	10	22	1	2	1	12	19	0	13	.224	.350	.306	102	1	1	.991	-1	73	69	1-22	-0.1
Total	4	317	940	139	254	31	17	4	136	160	9	101	.270	.381	.352	108	11	21	.991	-8	80	108	1-270	-0.7
BOSCH, DON Donald John B 7.15.1942 San Francisco, CA BB/TR 5-10/160# d9.19																								
1966	Pit N	3	2	0	0	0	0	0	0	0-0	0	0	.000	.000	.000	-99	-1	0-0	—	-0	0	0	/O(CF)	-0.1
1967	NY N	44	93	7	13	0	1	0	2	5-0	0	24	.140	.184	.161	-0	-12	3-1	1.000	0	97	142	O-39(CF)	-1.4
1968	NY N	50	111	14	19	1	0	3	7	9-1	0	33	.171	.231	.261	48	-7	0-2	.974	3	115	166	O-33(4-30-0)	-0.7
1969	Mon N	49	112	13	20	5	0	1	4	8-0	0	20	.179	.233	.250	35	-10	1-0	.964	-1	98	67	O-32(2-29-1)	-1.2
Total	4	146	318	34	52	6	1	4	13	22-1	0	77	.164	.217	.226	28	-30	4-3	.979	2	104	127	O-105(6-99-1)	-3.4
BOSETTI, RICK Richard Alan B 8.5.1953 Redding, CA BR/TR 5-11/185# d9.9																								
1976	Phi N	13	18	6	5	1	0	0	0	1-0	0	3	.278	.316	.333	82	0	3-0	1.000	0	86	377	/O-6(1-4-1)	0.0
1977	StL N	41	69	12	16	0	0	0	3	6-0	1	11	.232	.303	.232	47	-5	4-4	1.000	2	100	227	O-35(27-7-3)	-0.5
1978	Tor A	136	568	61	147	25	5	5	42	30-0	3	65	.259	.299	.347	80	-16	6-10	.986	14	112	194	*O-135(CF)	-0.5
1979	Tor A	**162**	619	59	161	35	2	8	65	22-0	3	70	.260	.286	.362	73	-24	13-12	.974	9	105	167	*O-162(CF)	-1.7
1980	Tor A	53	188	24	40	7	1	4	18	15-1	2	29	.213	.277	.324	62	-10	4-6	.985	-4	88	112	O-51(CF)	-1.6
1981	Tor A	25	47	5	11	2	0	0	4	2-0	0	6	.234	.265	.277	53	-3	0-2	1.000	0	107	0	O-19(5-13-2)/D	-0.4
	†Oak A	9	19	4	2	0	0	0	1	3-0	0	3	.105	.227	.105	-2	-2	0-0	1.000	0	129	0	/O-5(0-4-1),D-2	-0.2
	Year	34	66	9	13	2	0	0	5	5-0	0	9	.197	.254	.227	38	-5	0-2	1.000	0	111	0	O-24(5-17-3)/D-3	-0.6
1982	Oak A	6	15	1	3	0	0	0	0	0-0	0	1	.200	.200	.200	11	-2	0-0	1.000	2	116	643	/O-6(CF)	0.0
Total	7	445	1543	172	385	70	8	17	133	79-1	9	188	.250	.288	.338	71	-62	30-34	.982	25	105	173	O-419(33-382-7)/D-3	-4.9
BOSLEY, THAD Thaddis B 9.17.1956 Oceanside, CA BL/TL 6-3/175# d6.29 C5																								
1977	Cal A	58	212	19	63	10	2	0	19	16-0	1	32	.297	.346	.363	98	0	5-4	.963	-1	110	28	O-55(20-35-1)	-0.2
1978	Chi A	66	219	25	59	5	1	2	13	13-1	0	32	.269	.308	.329	79	-6	12-11	.975	3	114	82	O-64(15-39-14)	-0.6
1979	Chi A	36	77	13	24	1	1	1	8	9-0	0	14	.312	.384	.390	109	1	4-1	.967	4	149	143	O-28(22-1-5)/D	0.5
1980	Chi A	70	147	12	33	2	0	2	14	10-3	0	27	.224	.272	.279	52	-10	3-2	.958	-0	108	38	O-52(32-18-4)	-1.2
1981	†Mil A	42	105	11	24	2	0	0	3	6-0	0	13	.229	.270	.248	53	-7	2-1	.966	-2	93	54	O-37(7-8-22)/D	-1.0
1982	Sea A	22	46	3	8	1	0	0	2	4-0	0	8	.174	.240	.196	21	-5	3-1	1.000	-3	44	128	O-19(15-3-2)	-0.8
1983	Chi N	43	72	12	21	4	1	2	12	10-1	0	12	.292	.373	.458	125	3	1-1	1.000	1	102	102	O-20(16-1-3)	0.3
1984	†Chi N	55	98	17	29	2	2	2	14	13-2	0	22	.296	.375	.418	113	2	5-1	.976	0	99	139	O-33(11-2-21)	0.2

Year	Tm Lg	G	AB	R	H	2B	3B	HR	RBI	BB-IB	HP	SO	AVG	OBP	SLG	AOPS	ABR	SB-CS	FA	FR	Rng	Thr	G at Pos	BFW
1985	Chi N	108	180	25	59	6	3	7	27	20-1	0	29	.328	.391	.511	137	9	5-1	.988	2	133	0	O-55(46-7-8)	1.1
1986	Chi N	87	120	15	33	4	1	1	9	18-3	0	24	.275	.370	.350	92	-1	3-0	.969	-2	86	0	O-41(32-2-8)	-0.3
1987	KC A	80	140	13	39	6	1	1	16	9-2	0	26	.279	.318	.357	78	-4	0-0	.966	-1	96	0	O-28(13-1-14),D-13	-0.6
1988	KC A	15	21	1	4	0	0	0	2	2-1	0	6	.190	.250	.190	28	-2	0-0	1.000	-0	83	0	/O-6(1-4-1),D-4	-0.2
	Cal A	35	75	9	21	5	0	0	7	6-0	0	12	.280	.321	.347	93	0	1-1	.965	1	120	0	O-26(24-0-2)/D-2	0.0
	Year	50	96	10	25	5	0	0	9	8-1	0	18	.260	.306	.313	78	-3	1-1	.967	1	117	0	O-32(25-4-3)/D-6	-0.2
1989	Tex A	37	40	5	9	2	0	1	9	3-0	0	11	.225	.273	.350	75	-1	2-0	1.000	2	216	603	/O-8(6-0-2),D-5	0.1
1990	Tex A	30	29	3	4	0	0	1	3	4-1	0	7	.138	.242	.241	36	-3	1-0	1.000	-1	51	0	/O-9(7-1-1),D-4	-0.4
Total	14	784	1581	183	430	50	12	20	158	143-15	1	275	.272	.330	.357	89	-24	47-24	.972	4	109	57	O-481(267-122-108)/D-30	-3.1
BOSS, HARLEY Elmer Harley "Lefty" B 11.19.1908 Hodge, LA D 5.15.1964 Nashville, TN BL/TL 5-11.5/185# d7.19																								
1928	Was A	12	12	1	3	0	0	0	2	3	0	1	.250	.400	.250	75	0	0-0	.970	-1	0	106	/1-5	-0.1
1929	Was A	28	66	9	18	2	1	0	6	2	0	6	.273	.294	.333	61	-4	0-0	.977	0	117	126	1-18	-0.5
1930	Was A	3	3	0	0	0	0	0	0	0	0	0	.000	.000	.000	-99	-1	0-0	1.000	-0	0	0	/1	-0.1
1933	Cle A	112	438	54	118	17	7	1	53	25	1	27	.269	.310	.347	71	-20	2-5	.994	5	119	112	*1-110	-2.5
Total	4	155	519	64	139	19	8	1	61	30	1	34	.268	.309	.341	69	-25	2-5	.992	5	116	113	1-134	-3.2
BOSTICK, HENRY Henry Landers (born Henry Lipschitz) B 1.12.1895 Boston, MA D 9.16.1968 Denver, CO BR/TR d5.18																								
1915	Phi A	2	7	0	0	0	0	0	2	1	0	1	.000	.125	.000	-65	-1	0	1.000	-1	78	0	/3-2	-0.2
BOSTOCK, LYMAN Lyman Wesley B 11.22.1950 Birmingham, AL D 9.23.1978 Gary, IN BL/TR 6-1/180# d4.8																								
1975	Min A	98	369	52	104	21	5	0	29	28-2	0	42	.282	.331	.366	96	-2	2-3	.985	-5	97	43	O-92(12-28-55)/D	-1.2
1976	Min A	128	474	75	153	21	9	4	60	33-5	1	37	.323	.364	.430	131	17	12-6	.988	1	99	115	*O-124(0-121-3)	1.6
1977	Min A	153	593	104	199	36	12	14	90	51-5	6	59	.336	.389	.508	146	38	16-7	.989	-2	99	93	*O-149(60-90-3)	3.4
1978	Cal A	147	568	74	168	24	4	5	71	59-8	2	36	.296	.362	.379	113	12	15-12	.989	4	109	69	*O-146(0-58-90)/D	0.9
Total	4	526	2004	305	624	102	30	23	250	171-20	9	174	.311	.365	.427	124	65	45-28	.988	-2	102	82	O-511(72-297-151)/D-2	4.7
BOSTON, DARYL Daryl Lamont B 1.4.1963 Cincinnati, OH BL/TL 6-3/203# d5.13																								
1984	Chi A	35	83	8	14	3	1	0	3	4-0	0	20	.169	.207	.229	20	-9	6-0	.910	-2	95	130	O-34(0-30-5)/D	-1.0
1985	Chi A	95	232	20	53	13	1	3	15	14-1	0	44	.228	.271	.332	62	-12	8-6	.989	3	101	168	O-93(0-90-4)/D-2	-1.1
1986	Chi A	56	199	29	53	11	3	5	22	21-3	0	33	.266	.335	.427	103	1	9-5	.969	1	107	105	O-53(CF)/D	0.2
1987	Chi A	103	337	51	87	21	2	10	29	25-2	0	68	.258	.307	.421	89	-6	12-6	.991	-1	100	58	O-92(51-45-0)/D-5	-0.8
1988	Chi A	105	281	37	61	12	2	15	31	21-5	0	44	.217	.271	.434	95	-4	9-3	.951	-1	101	97	O-85(44-43-1)/D-5	-0.5
1989	Chi A	101	218	34	55	3	4	5	23	24-3	0	31	.252	.325	.372	99	-1	7-2	.971	1	110	54	O-75(57-2-21)/D-9	-0.1
1990	Chi A	5	1	0	0	0	0	0	0	0-0	0	0	.000	.000	.000	-99	0	1-0	—	-0	0	0	/O(RF)D	0.0
	NY N	115	366	65	100	21	2	12	45	28-2	2	50	.273	.328	.440	110	4	18-7	.986	-5	95	65	*O-109(1-108-0)	0.0
1991	NY N	137	255	40	70	16	4	4	21	30-0	0	42	.275	.350	.416	116	6	15-8	.981	-0	104	52	*O-115(9-74-37)	0.5
1992	NY N	130	289	37	72	14	2	11	35	38-6	3	60	.249	.338	.426	118	7	12-6	.993	-2	90	141	O-95(66-16-14)	0.5
1993	Col N	124	291	46	76	15	1	14	40	26-1	2	57	.261	.325	.464	93	-3	1-6	.985	-4	85	111	O-79(41-31-9)	-1.0
1994	NY A	52	77	11	14	2	0	4	14	6-0	1	20	.182	.250	.364	58	-5	0-1	1.000	-0	74	221	O-16(7-7-2)/D-9	-0.6
Total	11	1058	2629	378	655	131	22	83	278	237-23	8	469	.249	.312	.410	95	-22	98-50	.977	-10	98	96	O-847(276-499-94)/D-35	-3.9
BOSWELL, KEN Kenneth George B 2.23.1946 Austin, TX BL/TR 6/172# d9.18																								
1967	NY N	11	40	2	9	3	0	1	4	1-0	0	5	.225	.233	.375	76	-1	0-0	.971	2	127	70	/2-6,3-4	0.1
1968	NY N	75	284	37	74	7	2	4	11	16-0	1	27	.261	.300	.342	93	-3	7-2	.965	-4	98	91	2-69	0.0
1969	†NY N	102	362	48	101	14	7	3	32	36-3	2	47	.279	.347	.381	102	1	7-3	.959	-14	92	100	2-96	-0.7
1970	NY N	105	351	32	89	13	2	5	44	41-8	2	32	.254	.331	.345	82	-8	5-4	.996	-10	91	86	*2-101	-1.2
1971	NY N	116	392	46	107	20	1	5	40	36-4	2	31	.273	.334	.367	101	1	5-2	.973	-26	78	86	*2-109	-1.9
1972	NY N	100	355	35	75	9	1	9	33	32-1	0	35	.211	.274	.318	70	-15	2-2	.990	-23	72	97	2-94	-3.5
1973	†NY N	76	110	12	25	2	1	2	14	12-2	0	11	.227	.303	.318	74	-4	0-0	.973	0	90	116	3-17/2-3	-0.4
1974	NY N	96	222	19	48	6	1	2	15	18-1	1	19	.216	.277	.279	57	-13	0-1	1.000	5	92	69	2-28,3-20/O-7(2-0-5)	-0.7
1975	Hou N	86	178	16	43	8	2	0	21	30-7	1	12	.242	.349	.309	92	-1	0-3	.991	-5	102	74	2-31,3-23	-0.6
1976	Hou N	91	126	12	33	8	1	0	18	8-2	0	8	.262	.301	.341	92	-2	1-0	.933	-4	81	152	3-16/2-3,O(LF)	-0.5
1977	Hou N	72	97	7	21	1	1	0	12	10-1	0	12	.216	.287	.247	50	-7	0-0	1.000	-1	81	118	2-26/3-2	-0.8
Total	11	930	2517	266	625	91	19	31	244	240-29	9	239	.248	.313	.337	85	-52	27-17	.979	-79	87	90	2-566/3-82,O-8(3-0-5)	-10.2
BOTTARINI, JOHN John Charles B 9.14.1908 Crockett, CA D 10.8.1976 Jemez Springs, NM BR/TR 6/190# d4.22																								
1937	Chi N	26	40	3	11	3	0	1	7	5	1	10	.275	.370	.425	111	1	0	1.000	0	*115*	*134*	C-18/O(LF)	0.2
BOTTOMLEY, JIM James Leroy "Sunny Jim" B 4.23.1900 Oglesby, IL D 12.11.1959 St.Louis, MO BL/TL 6/180# d8.18 M1 C1 HF1974																								
1922	StL N	37	151	29	49	8	5	5	35	6	2	13	.325	.358	.543	136	7	3-1	.986	-3	65	81	1-34	0.2
1923	StL N	134	523	79	194	34	14	8	94	45	4	44	.371	.425	.535	155	42	4-6	.986	-12	61	88	*1-130	1.9
1924	StL N	137	528	87	167	31	12	14	111	35	3	35	.316	.362	.500	131	22	5-4	.982	-11	67	94	*1-133/2	0.1
1925	StL N	**153**	619	92	**227**	**44**	12	21	128	47	2	36	.367	.413	.578	147	43	3-4	.987	-3	91	107	*1-153	2.7
1926	†StL N	154	603	98	180	**40**	14	19	**120**	58	4	52	.299	.364	.506	127	22	4	.989	-15	61	101	*1-154	-0.3
1927	StL N	152	574	95	174	31	15	19	124	74	5	49	.303	.387	.509	134	28	8	.989	-12	73	**130**	*1-152	0.6
1928	†StL N	149	576	123	187	42	**20**	**31**	**136**	71	3	54	.325	.402	.628	163	51	10	.987	-14	61	94	*1-148	2.5
1929	StL N	146	560	108	176	31	12	29	137	70	1	54	.314	.391	.568	133	28	3	.991	-5	83	102	*1-145	1.2
1930	†StL N	131	487	92	148	33	7	15	97	44	5	36	.304	.368	.493	102	1	5	.990	-14	53	111	*1-124	-1.8
1931	†StL N	108	382	73	133	34	5	9	75	34	1	24	.348	.403	.534	144	25	3	.987	-4	81	118	1-93	1.2
1932	StL N	91	311	45	92	16	3	11	48	25	1	32	.296	.350	.473	115	7	2	.986	-3	81	108	1-74	-0.4
1933	Cin N	145	549	57	137	23	9	13	83	42	7	28	.250	.311	.395	102	0	3	.991	-9	78	102	*1-145	-2.4
1934	Cin N	142	556	72	158	31	11	11	78	33	0	40	.284	.324	.439	105	2	1	.989	-4	93	92	*1-139	-1.5
1935	Cin N	107	399	44	103	21	1	1	49	18	2	24	.258	.294	.323	68	-18	3	.992	-2	88	101	1-97	-2.9
1936	StL A	140	544	72	162	39	11	12	95	44	3	55	.298	.354	.476	100	-2	0-0	.992	-9	67	80	*1-140	-2.1
1937	StL A	65	109	11	26	7	0	1	12	18	0	15	.239	.346	.330	71	-4	1-0	.995	1	113	86	1-24,M	-0.5
Total	16	1991	7471	1177	2313	465	151	219	1422	664	43	591	.310	.369	.500	124	254	58-15	.988	-120	74	101	*1-1885/2	-1.5
BOUCHEE, ED Edward Francis B 3.7.1933 Livingston, MT BL/TL 6-1/205# d9.19																								
1956	Phi N	9	22	0	6	2	0	0	1	5-0	0	6	.273	.407	.364	112	1	0-0	1.000	-0	69	123	/1-6	0.0
1957	Phi N	154	574	78	168	35	8	17	76	84-6	**14**	91	.293	.394	.470	136	33	1-0	.988	6	**110**	77	*1-154	3.1
1958	Phi N	89	334	55	86	19	5	9	39	51-4	0	74	.257	.355	.425	107	5	1-0	.993	-1	95	74	1-89	-0.1
1959	Phi N	136	499	75	142	29	4	15	74	70-4	5	74	.285	.375	.449	117	15	0-4	.986	-2	95	89	*1-134	0.4
1960	Phi N	22	65	1	17	4	0	0	8	9-2	1	11	.262	.355	.323	89	0	0-0	.994	0	107	81	1-22	-0.1
	Chi N	98	299	33	71	11	1	5	44	45-4	2	51	.237	.335	.331	86	-4	2-0	.991	-1	98	86	1-80	-1.0
	Year	120	364	34	88	15	1	5	52	54-6	3	62	.242	.339	.330	86	-5	2-0	.992	-0	100	85	*1-102	-1.1
1961	Chi N	112	319	49	79	12	3	12	38	58-7	5	77	.248	.371	.417	108	6	1-4	.983	1	112	115	*1-107	0.0
1962	NY N	50	87	7	14	2	0	3	10	18-2	0	17	.161	.302	.287	59	-5	0-0	.976	4	195	100	1-19	-0.2
Total	7	670	2199	298	583	114	21	61	290	340-29	27	401	.265	.368	.419	112	51	5-8	.988	7	105	88	1-611	2.1
BOUCHER, AL Alexander Francis "Bo" B 11.13.1881 Franklin, MA D 6.23.1974 Torrance, CA BR/TR 5-8.5/156# d4.16																								
1914	StL F	147	516	62	119	26	4	2	49	52	2	88	.231	.304	.308	64	-33	13	.916	-4	95	79	*3-147	-3.6
BOUCHER, MEDRIC Medric Charles Francis B 3.12.1886 St.Louis, MO D 3.12.1974 Martinez, CA BR/TR 5-10/165# d5.20																								
1914	Bal F	16	16	2	5	1	1	0	2	1	0	1	.313	.353	.500	127	0	0	.950	0	*151*	*41*	/C-7,1O(RF)	0.1
	Pit F	1	1	0	0	0	0	0	0	0	0	0	.000	.000	.000	-99	0	0	—	0			H	0.0
	Year	17	17	2	5	1	1	0	2	1	0	1	.294	.333	.471	114	0	0	.950	0	*151*	*41*	/C-7,1O(RF)	0.1
BOUDREAU, LOU Louis B 7.17.1917 Harvey, IL D 8.20.2001 Olympia Fields, IL BR/TR 5-11/185# d9.9 M16 HF1970																								
1938	Cle A	1	1	0	0	0	0	0	0	1	0	0	.000	.500	.000	36	0	0-0	—	-0	0	0	/3	0.0
1939	Cle A	53	225	42	58	15	4	0	19	28	0	24	.258	.340	.360	82	-6	2-1	.953	6	109	95	S-53	0.4
1940	Cle A★	**155**	627	97	185	46	10	9	101	73	2	39	.295	.370	.443	113	14	6-3	**.968**	12	100	**134**	*S-155	3.5
1941	Cle A★	148	579	95	149	**45**	8	10	56	85	3	57	.257	.355	.415	108	9	9-4	**.966**	13	103	101	*S-147	3.2
1942	Cle A★	147	506	57	143	18	10	2	58	75	4	39	.283	.379	.370	118	15	7-16	**.965**	-2	101	124	*S-146,M	2.0
1943	Cle A☆	152	539	69	154	32	7	3	67	90	0	31	.286	.388	.388	135	29	4-7	**.970**	**25**	108	**126**	*S-152/CM	**6.8**
1944	Cle A☆	150	584	91	191	**45**	5	3	67	73	5	39	**.327**	.406	.437	146	39	11-3	**.978**	20	103	123	*S-149/CM	**7.5**
1945	Cle A✱	97	345	50	106	24	1	3	48	35	2	20	.307	.374	.409	133	15	0-4	.983	4	94	120	S-97,M	2.7

Year	Tm Lg	G	AB	R	H	2B	3B	HR	RBI	BB-IB	HP	SO	AVG	OBP	SLG	AOPS	ABR	SB-CS	FA	FR	Rng	Thr	G at Pos	BFW
1946	Cle A	140	515	51	151	30	6	6	62	40	1	14	.293	.345	.410	118	11	6-7	**.970**	17	99	105	*S-139,M	3.7
1947	Cle A★	150	538	79	165	**45**	3	4	67	67	4	10	.307	.388	.424	129	24	1-0	**.982**	19	106	**123**	*S-148,M	5.3
1948	†Cle A★	152	560	116	199	34	6	18	106	98	2	9	.355	.453	.534	166	58	3-2	**.975**	8	103	**121**	*S-151/CM	**7.1**
1949	Cle A	134	475	53	135	20	3	4	60	70	4	10	.284	.381	.364	100	2	0-1	.982	8	105	131	S-88,3-38/1-6,2M	1.5
1950	Cle A	81	260	23	70	13	2	1	29	31	1	5	.269	.349	.346	81	-7	1-2	.986	2	95	106	S-61/1-8,2-2,3-2,M	-0.2
1951	Bos A	82	273	37	73	18	1	5	47	30	6	12	.267	.353	.396	93	-2	1-0	.951	1	104	126	S-52,3-15/1-2	0.2
1952	Bos A	4	2	1	0	0	0	0	2	0	0	0	.000	.000	.000	-93	-1	0-0	1.000	-0	151	0	/S3M	-0.1
Total	15	1646	6029	861	1779	385	66	68	789	796	34	309	.295	.380	.415	121	200	51-50	.973	134	102	119	*S-1539/3-57,1-16,2-3,C-3	43.6

BOURJOS, CHRIS Christopher B 10.16.1955 Chicago, IL BR/TR 6/185# d8.31

Year	Tm Lg	G	AB	R	H	2B	3B	HR	RBI	BB-IB	HP	SO	AVG	OBP	SLG	AOPS	ABR	SB-CS	FA	FR	Rng	Thr	G at Pos	BFW
1980	SF N	13	22	4	5	1	0	1	2	2-0	0	7	.227	.292	.409	96	0	0-0	1.000	-1	67	0	/O-6(2-0-4)	-0.1

BOURNIGAL, RAFAEL Rafael Antonio (Pelletier) B 5.12.1966 Azua, D.R. BR/TR 5-11/165# d9.1

Year	Tm Lg	G	AB	R	H	2B	3B	HR	RBI	BB-IB	HP	SO	AVG	OBP	SLG	AOPS	ABR	SB-CS	FA	FR	Rng	Thr	G at Pos	BFW
1992	LA N	10	20	1	3	1	0	0	0	1-0	1	2	.150	.227	.200	22	-2	0-0	.967	0	91	157	/S-9	-0.1
1993	LA N	8	18	0	9	1	0	0	3	0-0	0	2	.500	.500	.556	193	2	0-0	1.000	0	47	0	/2-4,S-4	0.3
1994	LA N	40	116	2	26	3	1	0	11	9-1	2	5	.224	.291	.267	50	-9	0-0	.981	-4	87	109	S-40	-1.0
1996	Oak A	88	252	33	61	14	2	0	18	16-0	1	19	.242	.290	.313	54	-18	4-3	.993	3	109	99	2-64,S-23	-1.1
1997	Oak A	79	222	29	62	9	0	1	20	16-1	4	19	.279	.339	.333	78	-7	2-1	.980	5	114	91	S-74/2-7	0.3
1998	Oak A	85	209	23	47	11	0	1	19	10-1	2	11	.225	.265	.292	46	-17	6-1	1.000	-3	93	102	2-48,S-38/D	-1.5
1999	Sea A	55	95	16	26	5	0	2	14	7-0	0	6	.274	.317	.389	83	-3	0-0	.987	2	105	116	S-28,2-17/3-8,O(LF)D	0.1
Total	7	365	932	104	234	44	3	4	85	59-3	10	64	.251	.301	.318	62	-54	12-5	.986	3	103	101	S-216,2-140/3-8,D-2,O(LF)	-3.0

BOURQUE, PAT Patrick Daniel B 3.23.1947 Worcester, MA BL/TL 6/210# d9.6

Year	Tm Lg	G	AB	R	H	2B	3B	HR	RBI	BB-IB	HP	SO	AVG	OBP	SLG	AOPS	ABR	SB-CS	FA	FR	Rng	Thr	G at Pos	BFW
1971	Chi N	14	37	3	7	0	1	1	3	3-0	0	9	.189	.250	.324	54	-2	0-0	.957	2	187	73	1-11	-0.2
1972	Chi N	11	27	3	7	1	0	0	5	2-0	0	2	.259	.310	.296	66	-1	0-0	1.000	1	148	162	/1-7	-0.1
1973	Chi N	57	139	11	29	6	0	7	20	16-1	2	21	.209	.297	.403	86	-3	1-1	.986	4	145	109	1-38	-0.2
	†Oak A	23	42	8	8	4	1	2	9	15-2	0	10	.190	.390	.476	155	4	0-0	1.000	-1	0	111	D-15/1-5	0.3
1974	Oak A	73	96	6	22	4	0	1	16	15-1	0	20	.229	.327	.302	90	-1	0-2	.988	-1	83	127	1-39/D-8	-0.4
	Min A	23	64	5	14	2	0	1	8	7-0	0	11	.219	.296	.297	69	-2	0-0	.987	3	168	99	1-21	-0.1
	Year	96	160	11	36	6	0	2	24	22-1	0	31	.225	.315	.300	82	-3	0-2	.988	2	125	113	1-60/D-8	-0.5
Total	4	201	405	36	87	17	2	12	61	58-4	2	73	.215	.313	.356	87	-5	1-3	.985	9	138	110	1-121/D-23	-0.7

BOWA, LARRY Lawrence Robert B 12.6.1945 Sacramento, CA BB/TR 5-10/155# d4.7 M5 C13

Year	Tm Lg	G	AB	R	H	2B	3B	HR	RBI	BB-IB	HP	SO	AVG	OBP	SLG	AOPS	ABR	SB-CS	FA	FR	Rng	Thr	G at Pos	BFW
1970	Phi N	145	547	50	137	17	6	0	34	21-1	0	48	.250	.277	.303	57	-35	24-13	.979	-23	91	79	*S-143/2	-4.1
1971	Phi N	159	650	74	162	18	5	0	25	36-2	5	61	.249	.293	.292	66	-29	28-11	**.987**	5	105	95	*S-157	-0.3
1972	Phi N	152	579	67	145	11	**13**	1	31	32-1	2	51	.250	.291	.320	72	-23	17-9	**.987**	2	101	97	*S-150	-0.4
1973	Phi N	122	446	42	94	11	3	0	23	24-8	1	31	.211	.252	.249	38	-38	10-6	.979	2	96	113	*S-122	-2.3
1974	Phi N★	**162**	669	97	184	19	10	1	36	23-0	1	52	.275	.298	.338	75	-25	39-11	**.984**	-13	90	103	*S-162	-1.4
1975	Phi N★	136	583	79	178	18	9	2	38	24-0	2	32	.305	.334	.377	94	-7	24-6	.962	-11	90	104	*S-135	0.1
1976	†Phi N★	156	624	71	155	15	9	0	49	32-3	0	31	.248	.283	.301	65	-31	30-8	.975	-14	95	105	*S-156	-2.4
1977	†Phi N	154	624	93	175	19	3	4	41	32-2	0	32	.280	.313	.340	73	-25	32-3	.983	3	103	111	*S-154	0.1
1978	†Phi N★	156	654	78	192	31	5	3	43	24-1	1	40	.294	.319	.370	91	-9	27-5	**.986**	6	102	112	*S-156	1.8
1979	Phi N★	147	539	74	130	17	11	0	31	61-5	1	32	.241	.316	.314	71	-21	20-9	**.991**	-6	96	96	*S-146	-1.1
1980	†Phi N	147	540	57	144	16	4	2	39	24-7	3	28	.267	.300	.322	70	-22	21-6	.975	-20	92	80	*S-147	-2.5
1981	†Phi N	103	360	34	102	14	3	0	31	26-2	0	17	.283	.331	.339	87	-6	16-7	.975	-7	99	83	*S-102	-0.2
1982	Chi N	142	499	50	123	15	7	0	29	39-5	1	38	.246	.302	.305	68	-21	8-3	.973	-22	89	81	*S-140	-3.0
1983	Chi N	147	499	73	133	20	5	2	43	35-1	0	30	.267	.312	.339	77	-16	7-3	**.984**	26	**112**	122	*S-145	2.6
1984	†Chi N	133	391	33	87	14	2	0	17	28-5	0	24	.223	.274	.269	49	-26	10-4	.974	12	106	93	*S-132	-0.1
1985	Chi N	72	195	13	48	6	4	0	13	11-2	0	20	.246	.285	.318	62	-10	5-1	.970	4	107	93	S-66	0.0
	NY N	14	19	2	2	1	0	0	2	2-0	0	2	.105	.190	.158	-2	-3	0-0	.882	-2	50	140	/S-9,2-4	-0.4
	Year	86	214	15	50	7	4	0	15	13-2	0	22	.234	.276	.304	57	-13	5-1	.965	2	103	96	S-75/2-4	-0.4
Total	16	2247	8418	987	2191	262	99	15	525	474-45	17	569	.260	.300	.320	71	-347	318-105	.980	-58	98	99	*S-2222/2-5	-13.6

BOWCOCK, BENNY Benjamin James B 10.28.1879 Fall River, MA D 6.16.1961 Taunton, MA BR/TR 5-7/150# d9.18

Year	Tm Lg	G	AB	R	H	2B	3B	HR	RBI	BB-IB	HP	SO	AVG	OBP	SLG	AOPS	ABR	SB-CS	FA	FR	Rng	Thr	G at Pos	BFW
1903	StL A	14	50	7	16	3	1	1	10	3	0		.320	.358	.480	154	3	1	.885	-6	79	85	2-14	-0.2

BOWDEN, TIM David Timon B 8.15.1891 McDonough, GA D 10.25.1949 Emory, GA BL/TR 5-10/175# d9.17

Year	Tm Lg	G	AB	R	H	2B	3B	HR	RBI	BB-IB	HP	SO	AVG	OBP	SLG	AOPS	ABR	SB-CS	FA	FR	Rng	Thr	G at Pos	BFW
1914	StL A	7	9	0	2	0	0	0	0	1	0	6	.222	.300	.222	60	0	0	1.000	0	123	0	/O-4(0-1-3)	-0.1

BOWEN, CHICK Emmons Joseph B 7.26.1897 New Haven, CT D 8.9.1948 New Haven, CT BR/TR 5-7/165# d9.15

Year	Tm Lg	G	AB	R	H	2B	3B	HR	RBI	BB-IB	HP	SO	AVG	OBP	SLG	AOPS	ABR	SB-CS	FA	FR	Rng	Thr	G at Pos	BFW
1919	NY N	3	5	0	1	0	0	0	1	1	0	2	.200	.333	.200	63	0	0	1.000	-0	108	0	/O-2(0-1-1)	0.0

BOWEN, ROB Robert McClure B 2.24.1981 Bedford, TX BB/TR 6-2/210# d9.1

Year	Tm Lg	G	AB	R	H	2B	3B	HR	RBI	BB-IB	HP	SO	AVG	OBP	SLG	AOPS	ABR	SB-CS	FA	FR	Rng	Thr	G at Pos	BFW
2003	Min A	7	10	0	1	0	0	0	1	0-0	0	4	.100	.091	.100	-47	-2	0-0	.944	-2	18	0	/C-7	-0.4

BOWEN, SAM Samuel Thomas B 9.18.1952 Brunswick, GA BR/TR 5-9/170# d8.25

Year	Tm Lg	G	AB	R	H	2B	3B	HR	RBI	BB-IB	HP	SO	AVG	OBP	SLG	AOPS	ABR	SB-CS	FA	FR	Rng	Thr	G at Pos	BFW
1977	Bos A	3	2	0	0	0	0	0	0	0-0	0	2	.000	.000	.000	-90	-1	0-0	1.000	0	229	0	/O-3(2-1-0)	0.0
1978	Bos A	6	7	3	1	0	0	1	1	1-0	0	2	.143	.250	.571	112	0	0-0	1.000	-1	28	0	/O-4(1-3-0)	-0.1
1980	Bos A	7	13	0	2	0	0	0	0	2-0	0	3	.154	.267	.154	17	-1	1-0	1.000	2	142	290	/O-6(1-4-1)	0.0
Total	3	16	22	3	3	0	0	1	1	3-0	0	7	.136	.240	.273	38	-2	1-0	1.000	1	110	172	/O-13(4-8-1)	-0.1

BOWENS, SAM Samuel Edward B 3.23.1939 Wilmington, NC D 3.28.2003 Wilmington, NC BR/TR 6-1.5/195# d9.7

Year	Tm Lg	G	AB	R	H	2B	3B	HR	RBI	BB-IB	HP	SO	AVG	OBP	SLG	AOPS	ABR	SB-CS	FA	FR	Rng	Thr	G at Pos	BFW
1963	Bal A	15	48	8	16	3	1	1	9	4-1	0	5	.333	.385	.500	151	3	1-1	.952	-2	86	0	O-13(RF)	0.1
1964	Bal A	139	501	58	132	25	2	22	71	42-1	4	99	.263	.323	.453	114	9	4-3	.981	3	107	103	*O-135(32-0-120)	0.4
1965	Bal A	84	203	16	33	4	1	7	20	10-0	0	41	.163	.199	.296	39	-17	7-1	.982	2	111	86	O-68(11-0-58)	-1.9
1966	Bal A	89	243	26	51	9	1	6	20	17-2	5	52	.210	.275	.329	74	-8	9-3	.960	3	99	187	O-68(32-4-41)	-1.0
1967	Bal A	62	120	13	22	2	1	5	12	11-0	1	43	.183	.258	.342	76	-4	3-4	.977	-1	87	111	O-32(16-0-16)	-0.8
1968	Was A	57	115	14	22	4	0	4	7	11-0	0	39	.191	.262	.330	81	-3	0-0	.957	0	100	142	O-27(11-3-14)	-0.5
1969	Was A	33	57	6	11	1	0	0	4	5-0	0	14	.193	.258	.211	34	-5	1-1	.971	-0	102	77	O-30(6-3-22)	-0.7
Total	7	479	1287	141	287	48	6	45	143	100-4	10	293	.223	.283	.375	87	-25	25-13	.974	5	103	115	O-373(108-10-284)	-4.4

BOWERMAN, FRANK Frank Eugene "Mike" B 12.5.1868 Romeo, MI D 11.30.1948 Romeo, MI BR/TR 6-2/190# d8.24 M1

Year	Tm Lg	G	AB	R	H	2B	3B	HR	RBI	BB-IB	HP	SO	AVG	OBP	SLG	AOPS	ABR	SB-CS	FA	FR	Rng	Thr	G at Pos	BFW
1895	Bal N	1	1	0	0	0	0	0	0	0	0	0	.000	.000	.000	-97	0	0	1.000	0	0	0	/C	0.0
1896	Bal N	4	16	0	2	0	0	0	4	1	0	0	.125	.176	.125	-20	-3	0	.900	-0	118	167	/C-3,1	-0.2
1897	†Bal N	38	130	16	41	5	0	1	21	1	2		.315	.331	.377	87	-3	3	.948	-0	103	76	C-36	0.0
1898	Bal N	5	16	5	7	1	0	0	1	2	1		.438	.526	.500	191	2	1	.950	-0	115	163	/C-4	0.2
	Pit N	69	241	17	66	6	3	0	29	7	1		.274	.297	.324	79	-8	4	.946	2	104	106	C-59/1-9	0.0
	Year	74	257	22	73	7	3	0	30	9	2		.284	.313	.335	87	-5	5	.946	2	105	110	C-63/1-9	0.2
1899	Pit N	110	427	51	111	16	10	3	53	12	5		.260	.288	.365	79	-15	10	.947	13	121	109	C-80,1-28	0.5
1900	NY N	80	270	25	65	5	3	1	42	6	4		.241	.268	.293	57	-17	10	.929	11	110	**125**	C-75/S-2	0.1
1901	NY N	59	191	20	38	5	3	0	14	7	2		.199	.235	.257	44	-14	3	.950	4	96	113	C-46/2-3,S-3,3-3,1	-0.6
1902	NY N	109	373	38	93	14	6	0	27	13	1		.249	.276	.319	85	-8	12	.954	2	96	**111**	C-100/1-3	0.3
1903	NY N	64	210	22	58	6	2	1	31	6	3		.276	.306	.338	81	-6	5	.977	3	118	85	C-55/1-4,O(CF)	0.2
1904	NY N	93	289	38	67	11	4	2	27	16	7		.232	.288	.318	84	-6	7	.977	8	**143**	98	C-79/1-9,2-2,P	1.0
1905	NY N	98	297	37	80	8	1	3	41	12	11		.269	.322	.333	93	-2	6	.982	5	150	80	C-72,1-17/2	0.9
1906	NY N	103	285	23	65	7	3	1	42	15	3		.228	.274	.284	72	-10	5	.984	7	113	109	C-67,1-20	0.3
1907	NY N	96	311	31	81	8	2	0	32	17	5		.260	.309	.299	88	-5	11	.990	-2	127	91	C-62,1-29	-0.1
1908	Bos N	86	254	16	58	8	1	1	25	13	3		.228	.274	.280	78	-7	4	.971	-3	88	94	C-63,1-11	-0.5
1909	Bos N	33	99	6	21	2	0	0	4	2	0		.212	.228	.232	41	-7	0	.928	-1	91	90	C-27,M	-0.6
Total	15	1048	3410	345	853	102	38	13	393	130	48	0	.250	.287	.314	77	-109	81	.963	48	114	102	C-829,1-132/2-6,S-5,3-3,P0(CF)	1.5

BOWERS, BRENT Brent Raymond B 5.2.1971 Bridgeview, IL BL/TR 6-3/200# d8.16

Year	Tm Lg	G	AB	R	H	2B	3B	HR	RBI	BB-IB	HP	SO	AVG	OBP	SLG	AOPS	ABR	SB-CS	FA	FR	Rng	Thr	G at Pos	BFW
1996	Bal A	21	39	6	12	2	0	0	3	0-0	0	7	.308	.308	.359	68	-2	0-0	1.000	1	95	250	O-21(LF)	-0.1

BOWERS, BILLY Grover Bill B 3.25.1922 Parkin, AR D 9.17.1996 Wynne, AR BL/TR 5-9.5/176# d4.24

Year	Tm Lg	G	AB	R	H	2B	3B	HR	RBI	BB-IB	HP	SO	AVG	OBP	SLG	AOPS	ABR	SB-CS	FA	FR	Rng	Thr	G at Pos	BFW
1949	Chi A	26	78	5	15	2	1	0	6	4	0	5	.192	.232	.244	27	-9	1-1	.980	0	102	132	O-20(3-10-8)	-0.9

Year	Tm Lg	G	AB	R	H	2B	3B	HR	RBI	BB-IB	HP	SO	AVG	OBP	SLG	AOPS	ABR	SB-CS	FA	FR	Rng	Thr	G at Pos	BFW
BOWES, FRANK Frank M. B 1865 Bath, NY D 1.21.1895 New York, NY TR 5-9/160# d4.17																								
1890	Bro AA	61	232	28	51	5	2	0	24	7	1		.220	.246	.259	50	-16	11	.813	-11	*82*	*96*	C-25,O-19(4-2-13),3-13/1-3,S-2	-2.2
BOWIE, JIM James R. B 2.17.1965 Tokyo, Japan BL/TL 6/205# d8.3																								
1994	Oak A	6	14	0	3	0	0	0	0	0-0	0	2	.214	.214	.214	12	-2	0-0	1.000	-0	66	138	/1-6	-0.2
BOWLIN, WELDON Lois Weldon "Hoss" B 12.10.1940 Paragould, AR BR/TR 5-9/155# d9.16																								
1967	KC A	2	5	0	1	0	0	0	0	0-0	0	0	.200	.200	.200	19	-1	0-0	1.000	0	133	0	/3-2	0.0
BOWLING, STEVE Stephen Shaddon B 6.26.1952 Tulsa, OK BR/TR 6/185# d9.7																								
1976	Mil A	14	42	4	7	2	0	0	2	2-0	0	5	.167	.205	.214	23	-4	0-0	.975	1	118	116	O-13(CF)/D	-0.3
1977	Tor A	89	194	19	40	8	1	1	13	37-1	0	42	.206	.330	.273	67	-8	2-3	.987	8	98	304	O-87(20-24-47)	-0.3
Total	2	103	236	23	47	10	1	1	15	39-1	0	47	.199	.310	.263	60	-12	2-3	.985	9	101	276	O-100(20-37-47)/D	-0.6
BOWMAN, ELMER Elmari Wilhelm "Big Bow" B 3.19.1897 Proctor, VT D 12.17.1985 Los Angeles, CA BR/TR 6-0.5/193# d8.3																								
1920	Was A	2	1	0	0	0	0	0	0	1	0	0	.000	.500	.000	42	0	0-0	—	0			H	0.0
BOWMAN, ERNIE Ernest Ferrell B 7.28.1935 Johnson City, TN BR/TR 5-10/160# d4.12																								
1961	SF N	38	38	10	8	0	2	0	2	1-0	0	8	.211	.231	.316	45	-3	2-0	.885	-1	92	65	2-13,S-12/3-7	-0.3
1962	†SF N	46	42	9	8	1	0	1	4	1-0	1	10	.190	.227	.286	37	-4	0-1	1.000	1	115	29	2-17,3-11,S-10	-0.2
1963	SF N	81	125	10	23	3	0	0	4	0-0	0	15	.184	.181	.208	13	-14	1-2	.952	-2	93	89	S-40,2-26,3-12	-1.5
Total	3	165	205	29	39	4	2	1	10	2-0	1	33	.190	.200	.244	24	-21	3-3	.950	-1	98	80	/S-62,2-56,3-30	-2.0
BOWMAN, BOB Robert Leroy B 5.10.1931 Laytonville, CA BR/TR 6-1/195# d4.16																								
1955	Phi N	3	3	0	0	0	0	0	0	0-0	0	0	.000	.000	.000	-99	-1	0-0	1.000	0	134	0	/O-2(1-0-1)	-0.1
1956	Phi N	6	16	2	3	0	1	1	2	0-0	0	6	.188	.188	.500	78	-1	0-0	.833	-1	75	0	/O-5(0-1-4)	-0.2
1957	Phi N	99	237	31	63	8	2	6	23	27-1	6	50	.266	.352	.392	104	2	0-0	.929	1	98	162	O-81(3-0-79)	0.0
1958	Phi N	91	184	31	53	11	2	8	24	16-2	0	30	.288	.343	.500	122	5	0-1	.988	-1	105	30	O-57(20-1-37)	0.2
1959	Phi N	57	79	7	10	0	0	2	5	5-0	0	23	.127	.176	.203	1	-12	0-0	1.000	1	114	101	O-20(11-2-7)/P-5	-1.1
Total	5	256	519	71	129	19	5	17	54	48-3	6	109	.249	.317	.403	93	-7	0-1	.955	0	102	108	O-165(35-4-128)/P-5	-1.2
BOWMAN, BILL William George B 1869 Chicago, IL 5-11/180# d6.18																								
1891	Chi N	15	45	2	4	1	0	0	5	5	1	9	.089	.196	.111	-10	-6	0	.915	-2	*130*	*99*	C-15	-0.7
BOWSER, RED James Harvey B 9.20.1881 Freeport, PA D 5.22.1943 Moundsville, WV d9.13																								
1910	Chi A	1	2	0	0	0	0	0	0	0	0		.000	.000	.000	-99	0	0	—	0	0	0	/O	-0.1
BOYD, FRANK Frank Jay B 4.2.1868 West Middletown, PA D 12.16.1937 Oil City, PA BR/TR ?/168# d5.18																								
1893	Cle N	2	5	3	1	1	0	0	3	1	0	0	.200	.333	.400	89	0	0	1.000	0	*98*	*174*	/C-2	0.0
BOYD, JAKE Jacob Henry B 1.19.1874 Martinsburg, WV D 8.12.1932 Gettysburg, PA TL ?/160# d9.20 ▲																								
1894	Was N	6	21	1	3	0	0	0	1	1	0	4	.143	.182	.143	-22	-4	2	.833	1	410	0	/O-3(1-0-2),P-3	-0.1
1895	Was N	52	159	29	43	5	1	1	16	20	7	28	.270	.376	.333	85	-2	2	.786	-7	82	160	O-21(3-0-18),P-15,2-10/S-8,3	-0.8
1896	Was N	4	13	1	1	0	0	0	1	1	1	1	.077	.200	.077	-25	-1	0	.909	0	113	0	/P-4	0.0
Total	3	62	193	31	47	5	1	1	18	22	8	33	.244	.345	.295	66	-7	4	.794	-6	132	136	/O-24(4-0-20),P-22,2-10,S-8,3	-0.9
BOYD, BOB Robert Richard "The Rope" B 10.1.1925 Potts Camp, MS BL/TL 5-10/170# d9.8																								
1951	Chi A	12	18	3	3	0	1	0	4	3	0	3	.167	.286	.278	54	-1	0-0	1.000	-1	38	244	/1-6	-0.2
1953	Chi A	55	165	20	49	6	2	3	23	13	1	11	.297	.352	.412	103	0	1-4	1.000	-1	84	97	1-29,O-16(15-0-1)	-0.4
1954	Chi A	29	56	10	10	3	0	0	5	4	0	3	.179	.233	.232	27	-6	2-0	.955	-0	108	175	O-13(LF),1-12	-0.6
1956	Bal A	70	225	28	70	8	3	2	11	30-2	1	14	.311	.395	.400	119	7	0-5	.990	-4	68	92	1-60/O-8(3-0-5)	-0.2
1957	Bal A	141	485	73	154	16	8	4	34	55-3	2	31	.318	.388	.408	126	18	2-4	.991	-3	91	100	*1-132/O(LF)	0.7
1958	Bal A	125	401	58	124	21	5	7	36	25-1	2	24	.309	.350	.439	123	12	1-1	.994	0	98	106	1-99	0.6
1959	Bal A	128	415	42	110	20	2	3	41	29-1	1	14	.265	.312	.345	83	-10	3-1	.985	-9	71	**108**	*1-109	-2.5
1960	Bal A	71	82	9	26	5	2	0	9	6-1	0	5	.317	.364	.427	114	2	0-0	1.000	-0	77	136	1-17	0.1
1961	KC A	26	48	7	11	2	0	0	9	1-0	0	2	.229	.240	.271	37	-4	0-2	1.000	-1	46	68	/1-8	-0.6
	Mil N	36	41	3	10	0	0	0	3	1-0	0	7	.244	.256	.244	38	-4	0-0	1.000	1	280	149	/1-3	-0.3
Total	9	693	1936	253	567	81	23	19	175	167-8	7	114	.293	.349	.388	105	14	9-17	.991	-17	84	103	1-475/O-38(32-0-6)	-3.4
BOYD, BILL William J. B 12.22.1852 New York, NY D 9.30.1912 Jamaica, NY d4.22 M1 U1																								
1872	Mut NA	36	170	27	44	6	1	1	32	6		7	.259	.284	.324	92	0	4-2	.730	-12	75	54	*3-34/2O(RF)	-0.9
1873	Atl NA	48	228	31	63	5	4	1	30	2		4	.276	.283	.346	96	1	1-1	.716	3	172	84	*O-43(RF)/3-8	0.4
1874	Har NA	26	117	22	41	8	4	0	19	1		2	.350	.356	.487	160	7	1-0	.664	-9	75	159	3-25/O(RF)	-0.2
1875	Atl NA	36	151	14	44	11	0	1	10	1		0	.291	.296	.384	154	10	0-0	.774	-7	95	59	2-15,O-12(RF)/3-9,1-2,PSM	0.2
Total	4 NA	146	666	94	192	30	9	3	91	10		13	.288	.299	.374	119	18	6-3	.000	-24	79	88	/3-76,O-57(RF),2-16,1-2,SP	-0.5
BOYER, CLETE Cletis Leroy B 2.9.1937 Cassville, MO BR/TR 6/182# d6.5 C10 b-Cloyd b-Ken																								
1955	KC A	47	79	3	19	1	0	0	6	3-0	0	17	.241	.268	.253	40	-7	0-0	.963	2	89	120	S-12,3-11,2-10	-0.4
1956	KC A	67	129	15	28	3	1	1	4	11-1	1	24	.217	.284	.279	49	-10	1-1	.971	11	120	117	2-51/3-7	0.3
1957	KC A	10	0	0	0	0	0	0	0	0-0	0	0	—	—	—	—	0	0-0	—	-0	0	0	/23	0.0
1959	NY A	47	114	4	20	2	0	0	3	6-2	0	23	.175	.215	.193	14	-14	1-0	.990	4	100	110	S-26,3-16	-0.8
1960	†NY A	124	393	54	95	20	1	14	46	23-1	3	85	.242	.285	.405	90	-7	2-3	.967	21	121	133	3-99,S-33	1.5
1961	†NY A	148	504	61	113	19	5	11	55	63-4	2	83	.224	.308	.347	80	-14	1-3	.967	**28**	**117**	**139**	*3-141,S-12/O(RF)	1.2
1962	†NY A	158	566	85	154	24	1	18	68	51-8	3	106	.272	.331	.413	104	2	3-2	.964	**33**	**121**	**150**	*3-157	3.4
1963	†NY A	152	557	59	140	20	3	12	54	33-11	2	91	.251	.295	.363	84	-13	4-2	.954	22	108	134	*3-141/S-9,2	1.0
1964	†NY A	147	510	43	111	10	5	8	52	36-11	1	93	.218	.269	.304	59	-30	6-1	.968	12	**111**	140	*3-123,S-21	-1.6
1965	NY A	148	514	69	129	23	6	18	58	39-10	2	79	.251	.304	.424	106	2	4-1	.968	**25**	**116**	**164**	*3-147/S-2	2.8
1966	NY A	144	500	59	120	22	4	14	57	46-4	2	48	.240	.303	.384	101	0	6-0	.966	17	124	78	3-85,S-59	2.4
1967	Atl N	154	572	63	140	18	3	26	96	39-3	2	81	.245	.292	.423	105	1	6-3	**.970**	6	98	124	*3-150/S-6	0.7
1968	Atl N	71	273	19	62	7	2	4	17	16-3	2	32	.227	.275	.311	75	-9	2-0	.981	3	100	140	3-69	-0.6
1969	†Atl N	144	496	57	124	16	1	14	57	55-6	4	87	.250	.328	.371	96	-3	3-7	**.965**	7	104	83	*3-141	0.2
1970	Atl N	134	475	44	117	14	1	16	62	41-8	1	71	.246	.305	.381	79	-15	2-5	.954	11	112	94	*3-126/S-5	-0.6
1971	Atl N	30	98	10	24	1	0	6	19	8-2	0	11	.245	.299	.439	101	0	0-0	.961	2	113	133	3-25/S	0.1
Total	16	1725	5780	645	1396	200	33	162	654	470-74	25	931	.242	.299	.372	87	-117	41-28	.965	200	112	126	*3-1439,S-186/2-63,O(RF)	9.6
BOYER, KEN Kenton Lloyd B 5.20.1931 Liberty, MO D 9.7.1982 St.Louis, MO BR/TR 6-2/200# d4.12 M3 C2 b-Clete b-Cloyd																								
1955	StL N	147	530	78	140	27	2	18	62	37-5	1	67	.264	.311	.425	94	-6	22-17	.952	2	103	**104**	*3-139,S-18	-0.4
1956	StL N★	150	595	91	182	30	2	26	98	38-7	1	65	.306	.347	.494	123	18	8-3	.961	9	**109**	**149**	*3-149	2.8
1957	StL N	142	544	79	144	18	3	19	62	44-8	1	77	.265	.318	.414	94	-6	12-8	**.996**	-3	102	27	*O-105(CF),3-41	-1.4
1958	StL N	150	570	101	175	21	9	23	90	49-8	3	53	.307	.360	.496	121	16	11-6	.962	**24**	**115**	**135**	*3-144/O-6(CF),S	4.0
1959	StL N★	149	563	86	174	18	5	28	94	67-7	2	77	.309	.384	.508	127	22	12-6	.956	13	**109**	**133**	*3-143,S-12	3.5
1960	StL N★	151	552	95	168	26	10	32	97	56-10	4	77	.304	.370	.562	139	30	8-7	.959	16	107	**149**	*3-146	4.5
1961	StL N★	153	589	109	194	26	11	24	95	68-9	1	91	.329	.397	.533	132	28	6-3	.951	14	**116**	75	*3-153	4.0
1962	StL N★	160	611	92	178	27	5	24	98	75-7	1	104	.291	.369	.470	113	12	12-7	.956	4	102	120	*3-160	1.6
1963	StL N★	159	617	86	176	28	2	24	111	70-10	2	90	.285	.358	.454	121	19	1-0	.925	-17	91	98	*3-159	0.2
1964	†StL N★	**162**	628	100	185	30	10	24	**119**	70-12	2	85	.295	.365	.489	128	24	3-5	.951	-0	102	**118**	*3-162	2.3
1965	StL N	144	535	71	139	18	2	13	75	57-3	1	73	.260	.328	.374	90	-6	2-7	**.968**	-10	93	80	*3-143	-2.0
1966	NY N	136	496	62	132	28	2	14	61	30-5	0	64	.266	.304	.415	101	0	4-3	.951	15	**116**	127	*3-130/1-2	1.5
1967	NY N	56	166	17	39	7	2	3	13	26-3	0	22	.235	.335	.355	100	1	2-1	.949	2	112	104	3-44/1-8	0.3
	Chi A	57	180	17	47	5	1	4	21	7-0	0	25	.261	.287	.367	96	-2	0-2	.957	-1	101	87	3-33,1-18	-0.5
1968	Chi A	10	24	0	3	0	0	0	0	1-0	0	6	.125	.160	.125	-13	-3	0-0	.900	-1	84	140	/3-5,1	-0.5
	LA N	83	221	20	60	7	2	6	41	16-3	1	34	.271	.317	.403	127	6	2-2	.922	-4	90	77	3-34,1-32	0.1
1969	LA N	25	34	0	7	2	0	0	4	2-0	0	7	.206	.250	.265	48	-2	0-0	.971	-0	91	236	/1-4	-0.3
Total	15	2034	7455	1104	2143	318	68	282	1141	713-97	20	1017	.287	.349	.462	115	151	105-77	.952	63	105	115	*3-1785,O-111(CF)/1-65,S-31	19.7
BOYLAND, DOE Dorian Scott B 1.6.1955 Chicago, IL BL/TL 6-4/200# d9.4																								
1978	Pit N	6	8	1	2	0	0	0	1	0-0	0	1	.250	.250	.250	38	-1	0-0	1.000	-0	0	0	/1	-0.1
1979	Pit N	4	3	0	0	0	0	0	0	0-0	0	2	.000	.000	.000	-96	-1	0-0	—	0			/H	-0.1

Year	Tm Lg	G	AB	R	H	2B	3B	HR	RBI	BB-IB	HP	SO	AVG	OBP	SLG	AOPS	ABR	SB-CS	FA	FR	Rng	Thr	G at Pos	BFW
1981	Pit N	11	8	0	0	0	0	0	0	1-0	0	3	.000	.111	.000	-64	-2	0-0	—	0			/H	-0.2
Total	3	21	19	1	2	0	0	0	1	1-0	0	6	.105	.150	.105	-26	-4	0-0	1.000	-0	0	0	/1	-0.4
BOYLE, EDDIE Edward J. B 5.8.1874 Cincinnati, OH D 2.9.1941 Cincinnati, OH BR/TR 6-3/200# d4.17 b-Jack																								
1896	Lou N	3	9	0	0	0	0	0	0	2	0	2	.000	.182	.000	-52	-2	0	.938	-0	*78*	*93*	/C-3	-0.2
	Pit N	2	5	0	0	0	0	0	0	0	0	1	.000	.000	.000	-99	-1	0	.833	-1	*75*	*75*	/C-2	-0.2
	Year	5	14	0	0	0	0	0	0	2	0	3	.000	.125	.000	-68	-3	0	.909	-1	*77*	*88*	/C-5	-0.4
BOYLE, HENRY Henry J. "Handsome Henry" B 9.20.1860 Philadelphia, PA D 5.25.1932 Philadelphia, PA BR/TR d7.9 ▲ OF Total (54-LF 18-CF 13-RF)																								
1884	StL U	65	262	41	68	10	3	4		9			.260	.284	.366	93	-11		.885	4	137	140	O-43(40-2-2),P-19/3-4,S21	-0.4
1885	StL N	72	258	24	52	9	1	1	21	13		38	.202	.240	.256	64	-9		.907	-4	86	172	P-42,O-31(12-10-9)/2-2	-0.8
1886	StL N	30	108	8	27	2	2	1	13	5		19	.250	.283	.333	93	-1	0	.852	0	112	90	P-25/O-6(0-5-1)	0.0
1887	Ind N	41	141	17	27	9	1	2	13	9	2	18	.191	.250	.312	57	-8	2	.912	-6	67	134	P-38/O-4(2-1-1)	-0.4
1888	Ind N	37	125	13	18	2	0	1	6	6	1	31	.144	.189	.184	19	-11	1	.933	2	120	59	P-37/1	0.1
1889	Ind N	46	155	17	38	10	0	1	17	9	1	23	.245	.291	.329	72	-6	4	.958	-5	69	0	P-46/3	-0.2
Total	6	291	1049	120	230	42	7	10	70	51	4	129	.219	.258	.301	69	-46	7	.912	-8	87	103	P-207/O-84L,3-5,2-3,1-2,S	-1.7
BOYLE, JIM James John B 1.19.1904 Cincinnati, OH D 12.24.1958 Cincinnati, OH BR/TR 6/180# d6.20 b-Buzz																								
1926	NY N	1	0	0	0	0	0	0	0	0	0	0	—	—	—	—	0	0	—	0	*0*	*0*	/C	0.0
BOYLE, JACK John Anthony "Honest Jack" B 3.22.1866 Cincinnati, OH D 1.7.1913 Cincinnati, OH BR/TR 6-4/190# d10.8 b-Eddie OF Total (6-LF 2-CF 7-RF)																								
1886	Cin AA	1	5	0	1	0	0	0	0	0	0		.200	.200	.200	25	0	0	.769	-1			/C	-0.1
1887	†StL AA	88	350	48	66	3	1	2	41	20	2		.189	.237	.220	25	-38	7	**.897**	-9			C-86/O-2(RF),1-2,3	-3.3
1888	†StL AA	71	257	33	62	8	1	1	23	13	3		.241	.286	.292	77	-8	11	**.932**	13			C-70/O(CF)	1.1
1889	StL AA	99	347	54	85	11	5	3	42	21	7	42	.245	.301	.331	71	-16	5	.947	9			C-80,3-12/O-5(3-0-2),1-4,2	-0.1
1890	Chi P	100	369	56	96	9	5	1	49	44	5	29	.260	.347	.320	76	-13	11	.940	-2	*116*	*98*	C-50,3-30,S-16/1-7,O-2(RF)	-0.8
1891	StL AA	121	434	76	122	18	8	5	79	44	12	35	.281	.363	.394	102	-1	18	.936	-3	*116*	*78*	C-91,S-25/3-7,O-3(1-1-1),2-3,1-3	0.3
1892	NY N	120	436	52	80	8	8	0	32	36	4	41	.183	.252	.239	49	-28	10	.922	-3	*70*	***152***	C-79,1-40/O-2(LF),S-2	-2.3
1893	Phi N	116	504	105	144	29	9	4	81	41	10	30	.286	.351	.403	100	-1	22	.988	6	119	101	*1-112/C-6,2-2	0.4
1894	Phi N	117	510	103	152	23	10	4	89	46	3	27	.298	.360	.406	86	-12	23	.982	0	98	106	*1-117/32	-0.9
1895	Phi N	**133**	565	90	143	17	4	0	67	35	5	23	.253	.302	.297	55	-39	13	.973	-6	84	82	*1-133	-3.7
1896	Phi N	40	145	17	43	4	1	1	28	6	5	7	.297	.346	.359	87	-3	3	.920	-7	*102*	*81*	C-28,1-12	-0.6
1897	Phi N	75	288	37	73	9	1	2	36	19	3		.253	.306	.313	65	-15	3	.962	-6	*103*	*89*	C-50,1-24	-1.4
1898	Phi N	6	22	0	2	0	1	0	3	1	0		.091	.130	.182	-11	-3	0	.919	-1	120	94	/1-4,C-3	-0.4
Total	13	1087	4232	671	1069	139	54	23	570	326	59	234	.253	.315	.327	72	-177	126	.929	-9	*55*	*56*	C-544,1-458/3-51,S-43,O-15R,2-7	-11.8
BOYLE, JACK John Bellew B 7.9.1889 Morris, IL D 4.3.1971 Ft.Lauderdale, FL BL/TR 5-11.5/165# d6.28																								
1912	Phi N	15	25	4	7	1	0	0	2	1	0	5	.280	.308	.320	67	-1	0	.905	3	164	292	/3-6,S-2	0.2
BOYLE, BUZZ Ralph Francis B 2.9.1908 Cincinnati, OH D 11.12.1978 Cincinnati, OH BL/TL 5-11.5/170# d9.11 b-Jim																								
1929	Bos N	17	57	8	15	2	1	1	2	6	0	11	.263	.333	.386	81	-2	2	1.000	1	106	101	O-17(LF)	-0.2
1930	Bos N	1	1	0	0	0	0	0	0	0	0	1	.000	.000	.000	-99	0	0	—	-0	0	0	/O(CF)	0.0
1933	Bro N	93	338	38	101	13	4	0	31	16	0	24	.299	.331	.361	102	0	7	.975	-3	103	32	O-90(45-34-10)	-0.7
1934	Bro N	128	472	88	144	26	10	7	48	51	3	44	.305	.376	.447	126	18	8	.970	9	103	**189**	*O-121(18-19-86)	1.9
1935	Bro N	127	475	51	129	17	9	4	44	43	0	45	.272	.332	.371	90	-7	7	.963	4	99	152	*O-124(0-17-107)	-0.9
Total	5	366	1343	185	389	58	24	12	125	116	3	125	.290	.347	.395	105	9	24	.970	11	102	135	O-353(80-71-203)	0.1
BRACK, GIBBY Gilbert Herman B 3.29.1908 Chicago, IL D 1.20.1960 Greenville, TX BR/TR 5-9/170# d4.23																								
1937	Bro N	112	372	60	102	27	9	5	38	44	0	93	.274	.351	.435	111	6	9	.969	2	102	130	*O-101(37-44-21)	0.4
1938	Bro N	40	56	10	12	2	1	1	6	4	0	14	.214	.267	.339	64	-3	1	1.000	3	124	350	O-13(7-0-6)	-0.1
	Phi N	72	282	40	81	20	4	4	28	18	1	30	.287	.332	.429	111	4	2	.964	-0	103	88	O-68(12-38-24)	0.1
	Year	112	338	50	93	22	5	5	34	22	1	44	.275	.321	.414	102	0	3	.969	3	106	123	O-81(19-38-30)	0.0
1939	Phi N	91	270	40	78	21	4	6	41	26	0	49	.289	.351	.463	121	8	1	.959	-3	98	102	O-48(2-6-40),1-19	0.0
Total	3	315	980	150	273	70	18	16	113	92	1	186	.279	.341	.436	111	15	13	.967	2	103	122	O-230(58-88-91)/1-19	0.4
BRADFORD, BUDDY Charles William B 7.25.1944 Mobile, AL BR/TR 5-11/191# d9.9																								
1966	Chi A	14	28	3	4	0	0	0	0	2-0	0	6	.143	.200	.143	0	-4	0-0	.833	-1	57	0	/O-9(5-0-4)	-0.6
1967	Chi A	24	20	6	2	1	0	0	1	1-1	0	7	.100	.143	.150	-14	-3	1-0	.900	-1	75	0	O-14(6-1-8)	-0.5
1968	Chi A	103	281	32	61	11	0	5	24	23-2	2	67	.217	.277	.310	78	-7	8-4	.965	-1	103	78	O-99(35-25-58)	-1.5
1969	Chi A	93	273	36	70	8	2	11	27	34-4	4	75	.256	.347	.421	109	3	5-2	.961	-5	89	91	O-88(0-48-59)	-0.5
1970	Chi A	32	91	8	17	3	0	2	8	10-0	0	30	.187	.265	.286	51	-6	1-2	.979	-2	86	65	O-27(2-20-9)	-1.0
	Cle A	75	163	25	32	6	1	7	23	21-1	1	43	.196	.290	.374	79	-5	0-1	.984	1	115	36	O-64(1-58-5)/3	-0.6
	Year	107	254	33	49	9	1	9	31	31-1	1	73	.193	.281	.343	69	-11	1-3	.982	-1	105	46	O-91(3-78-14)/3	-1.6
1971	Cle A	20	38	4	6	2	1	0	3	6-1	0	10	.158	.273	.263	48	-3	0-0	.930	1	122	123	O-18(CF)	-0.2
	Cin N	79	100	17	20	3	0	2	12	14-4	3	23	.200	.316	.290	74	-3	4-2	.986	-0	89	98	O-66(36-26-5)	-0.5
1972	Chi A	35	48	13	13	2	0	2	8	4-0	1	13	.271	.340	.438	127	2	3-2	1.000	0	100	109	O-28(3-22-3)	0.1
1973	Chi A	53	168	24	40	3	1	8	15	17-1	2	43	.238	.316	.411	100	-1	4-5	.992	3	94	257	O-51(1-48-2)	0.0
1974	Chi A	39	96	16	32	2	0	5	10	13-0	1	11	.333	.414	.510	162	8	1-2	.980	1	103	118	O-32(10-0-24)/D	0.7
1975	Chi A	25	58	8	9	3	1	2	15	8-0	3	22	.155	.274	.345	78	-2	3-2	.966	-0	98	90	O-18(3-0-15)/D-4	-0.3
	StL N	50	81	12	22	1	0	4	15	12-0	0	24	.272	.366	.432	117	2	0-2	.935	1	123	85	O-25(3-1-21)	0.1
1976	Chi A	55	160	20	35	5	2	4	14	19-2	2	37	.219	.309	.350	92	-2	6-0	.978	-2	104	0	O-48(2-0-46)/D-3	-0.4
Total	11	697	1605	224	363	50	8	52	175	184-16	19	411	.226	.311	.364	91	-21	36-24	.971	-6	99	92	O-587(107-267-259)/D-8,3	-5.2
BRADFORD, VIC Henry Victor B 3.5.1915 Brownsville, TN D 6.10.1994 Paris, KY BR/TR 6-2/190# d5.1 Mil 1944-46																								
1943	NY N	6	5	1	1	0	0	0	1	1	0	1	.200	.333	.200	55	0	0	1.000	0	185	0	/O(LF)	0.0
BRADLEY, AL Albert Joseph B 5.23.1856 Bradys Bend, PA D 2.5.1937 Altoona, PA 5-10/185# d5.21																								
1884	Was U	1	3	0	0	0	0	0		2			.000	.400	.000	32	0		1.000	0	0	0	/O(CF)	0.0
BRADLEY, GEORGE George Washington "Grin" B 7.13.1852 Reading, PA D 10.2.1931 Philadelphia, PA BR/TR 5-10.5/175# d5.4 ▲ OF Total (11-LF 19-CF 16-RF)																								
1875	StL NA	60	254	28	62	7	3	0	24	1		19	.244	.247	.295	96	0	3-3	.896	0	108	193	*P-60/S-2,2O(LF)	-0.1
1876	StL N	**64**	265	29	66	7	6	0	28	3		12	.249	.257	.321	97	3		.919	2	96	188	*P-64	0.0
1877	Chi N	55	214	31	52	7	3	0	12	6		19	.243	.264	.304	70	-8		**.950**	-2	101	100	*P-50,3-16/1-3,O(RF)	-0.3
1879	Tro N	63	251	36	62	9	5	0	23	1		20	.247	.250	.323	93	-2		.867	6	130	0	P-54/3-5,1-3,O(RF)S	0.3
1880	Pro N	82	309	32	70	7	6	0	23	5		38	.227	.239	.288	80	-7		.858	17	**147**	**166**	*3-57,P-28/O-7(1-0-6),1-2	1.2
1881	Det N	1	4	0	0	0	0	0	0	0		0	.000	.000	.000	-96	-1		.667	-1	38	396	/S	-0.1
	Cle N	60	241	21	60	10	1	2	18	4		25	.249	.261	.324	88	-3		.865	-12	76	83	3-48/P-6,S-6,O(LF)	-1.2
	Year	61	245	21	60	10	1	2	18	4		25	.245	.257	.318	84	-4		.865	-12	76	83	3-48/S-7,P-6,O(LF)	-1.3
1882	Cle N	30	115	16	21	5	0	0	6	4		16	.183	.210	.226	41	-7		.897	3	**151**	**607**	P-18/O-9(5-4-0),1-6	-0.2
1883	Cle N	4	16	0	5	0	1	0	1	0		1	.313	.313	.438	126	0		.792	-1	79	178	/S-4	0.0
	Phi AA	76	312	47	73	8	5	1	36	8			.234	.253	.301	71	-11		.779	1	118	129	3-44,P-26,O-11(CF)/1-2	-0.5
1884	Cin U	58	226	31	43	4	7	0		7			.190	.215	.270	43	-24		.912	-1	105	152	P-41,O-16(4-4-8)/S-5,1-2	-1.0
1886	Phi AA	13	48	1	4	0	1	0	1	1	0		.083	.102	.125	-29	-7	2	.849	1	115	49	S-13	-0.6
1888	Bal AA	1	3	0	0	0	0	0	0	0	0		.000	.000	.000	-99	-1	0	.600	-1	34	0	/S	-0.2
Total	10	507	2004	244	456	57	35	3	148	39	0	131	.228	.242	.295	72	-68	2-0	.896	12	110	136	P-287,3-170/O-46C,S-31,1-18	-2.6
BRADLEY, GEORGE George Washington B 4.1.1914 Greenwood, AR D 10.19.1982 Lawrenceburg, TN BR/TR 6-1.5/185# d4.28																								
1946	StL A	4	12	2	2	1	0	0	3	0	0	1	.167	.167	.250	15	-1	0-0	1.000	-0	86	0	/O-3(CF)	-0.2
BRADLEY, HUGH Hugh Frederick "Corns" B 5.23.1885 Grafton, MA D 1.26.1949 Worcester, MA BR/TR 5-10/175# d4.25																								
1910	Bos A	32	83	8	14	6	2	0	7	5	0		.169	.216	.289	57	-4	2	.995	-1	69	115	1-21/C-3,O(RF)	-0.7
1911	Bos A	12	41	9	13	2	0	1	4	2	1		.317	.364	.439	125	1	1	.993	1	101	126	1-12	0.1
1912	Bos A	40	137	16	26	11	1	1	19	15	1		.190	.275	.307	63	-7	3	.989	0	94	80	1-40	-0.7
1914	Pit F	118	427	41	131	20	6	0	61	27	8	27	.307	.359	.382	103	-5	7	.990	-0	98	83	*1-118	-0.8
1915	Pit F	26	66	3	18	4	1	0	6	4	0	5	.273	.314	.364	91	-2	2	.952	-1	99	0	O-15(RF)	-0.4
	Bro F	37	126	7	31	3	2	0	18	4	0	9	.246	.269	.302	61	-9	6	.996	3	156	47	1-26/O-7(RF),C	-0.8
	New F	12	33	0	5	0	0	0	2	2	2	3	.152	.243	.152	13	-4	2	.986	-1	23	94	/1-8	-0.7
	Year	75	225	10	54	7	3	0	26	10	2	17	.240	.278	.298	63	-15	10	.994	0	125	58	1-34,O-22(RF)/C	-1.9

Year	Tm Lg	G	AB	R	H	2B	3B	HR	RBI	BB-IB	HP	SO	AVG	OBP	SLG	AOPS	ABR	SB-CS	FA	FR	Rng	Thr	G at Pos	BFW
Total	5	277	913	84	238	46	12	2	117	59	12	44	.261	.314	.344	84	-30	23	.991	-1	99	84	1-225/O-23(RF),C-4	-4.0
BRADLEY, JACK John Thomas B 9.20.1893 Denver, CO D 3.18.1969 Tulsa, OK BR/TR 5-11/175# d6.18																								
1916	Cle A	2	3	0	0	0	0	0	0	0	0	1	.000	.000	.000	-94	-1	0	1.000	-0	51	0	/C	-0.1
BRADLEY, MARK Mark Allen B 12.3.1956 Elizabethtown, KY BR/TR 6-1/180# d9.3																								
1981	LA N	9	6	2	1	1	0	0	0	0-0	0	1	.167	.167	.333	41	0	0-0	1.000	1	91	704	/O-6(1-0-5)	0.0
1982	LA N	8	3	1	1	0	0	0	0	0-0	0	0	.333	.333	.333	89	0	0-0	1.000	-0	76	0	/O-3(1-0-2)	0.0
1983	NY N	73	104	10	21	4	0	3	5	11-1	0	35	.202	.278	.327	68	-5	4-2	1.000	-0	91	133	O-35(14-7-16)	-0.6
Total	3	90	113	13	23	5	0	3	5	11-1	0	36	.204	.274	.327	67	-5	4-2	1.000	0	91	171	/O-44(16-7-23)	-0.6
BRADLEY, MILTON Milton Obelle B 4.15.1978 Harbor City, CA BB/TR 6/180# d7.19																								
2000	Mon N	42	154	20	34	8	1	2	15	14-0	1	32	.221	.288	.325	53	-11	2-1	.979	1	96	262	O-40(CF)	-0.9
2001	Mon N	67	220	19	49	16	3	1	19	19-0	1	62	.223	.287	.336	59	-13	7-4	.988	4	111	145	O-65(13-52-2)	-0.9
	Cle A	10	18	3	4	1	0	0	0	2-0	0	3	.222	.300	.278	53	-1	1-1	.929	0	98	361	/O-9(0-8-1),D	-0.1
2002	Cle A	98	325	48	81	18	3	9	38	32-2	0	58	.249	.317	.406	92	-4	6-3	.982	3	99	205	O-94(CF)/D	0.0
2003	Cle A	101	377	61	121	34	2	10	56	64-8	5	73	.321	.421	.501	148	31	17-7	.992	-2	94	133	O-93(CF)/D-8	3.0
Total	4	318	1094	151	289	77	9	22	128	131-10	7	228	.264	.345	.411	98	2	33-16	.985	6	99	178	O-301(13-287-3)/D-10	1.1
BRADLEY, PHIL Philip Poole B 3.11.1959 Bloomington, IN BR/TR 6/185# d9.2																								
1983	Sea A	23	67	8	18	2	0	0	5	8-0	0	5	.269	.342	.299	77	-2	3-1	.974	-3	76	94	O-21(CF)/D	-0.4
1984	Sea A	124	322	49	97	12	4	0	24	34-2	3	61	.301	.373	.363	106	4	21-8	.992	1	105	51	*O-117(48-68-14)/D-3	0.4
1985	Sea A★	159	641	100	192	33	8	26	88	55-4	12	129	.300	.365	.498	133	29	22-9	.986	-1	97	99	*O-159(126-28-10)	2.3
1986	Sea A	143	526	88	163	27	4	12	50	77-1	8	134	.310	.405	.445	130	26	21-12	.996	-6	85	120	*O-140(138-5-0)	1.4
1987	Sea A	158	603	101	179	38	10	14	67	84-2	8	119	.297	.387	.463	119	19	40-10	.983	-5	87	122	*O-158(LF)	1.2
1988	Phi N	154	569	77	150	30	5	11	56	54-0	**16**	106	.264	.341	.392	109	8	11-9	.990	5	102	151	*O-153(153-3-1)	0.8
1989	Bal A	144	545	83	151	23	10	11	55	70-4	7	103	.277	.364	.417	124	19	20-6	.990	-6	93	46	*O-140(LF)/D-2	1.1
1990	Bal A	72	289	39	78	9	1	4	26	30-2	7	35	.270	.352	.349	100	1	10-4	.987	-1	98	65	O-70(LF)/D-2	-0.1
	Chi A	45	133	20	30	5	1	0	5	20-3	4	26	.226	.344	.278	78	-3	7-3	.973	-1	100	54	O-38(23-14-6)/D-7	-0.4
	Year	117	422	59	108	14	2	4	31	50-5	**11**	61	.256	.349	.327	93	-2	17-7	.982	-1	99	62	*O-108(93-14-6)/D-9	-0.5
Total	8	1022	3695	565	1058	179	43	78	376	432-18	65	718	.286	.369	.421	118	101	155-62	.988	-17	94	98	O-996(856-139-31)/D-15	6.3
BRADLEY, SCOTT Scott William B 3.22.1960 Glen Ridge, NJ BL/TR 5-11/185# d9.9																								
1984	NY A	9	21	3	6	1	0	0	2	1-0	0	1	.286	.318	.333	84	0	0-0	1.000	-0	103	0	/O-5(LF),C-3	-0.1
1985	NY A	19	49	4	8	2	1	0	1	1-0	1	5	.163	.196	.245	20	-6	0-0	.923	-2	56	118	/C-3,D-9	-0.7
1986	Chi A	9	21	3	6	0	0	0	0	1-0	2	0	.286	.375	.286	81	0	0-2	—	-0	0	0	/O(LF)D	-0.1
	Sea A	68	199	17	60	8	3	5	28	12-4	2	7	.302	.344	.447	113	3	1-0	.990	-6	103	75	C-59/D-3	0.0
	Year	77	220	20	66	8	3	5	28	13-4	4	7	.300	.347	.432	110	3	1-2	.990	-6	103	75	C-59/D-9,O(LF)	-0.1
1987	Sea A	102	342	34	95	15	1	5	43	15-1	3	18	.278	.310	.371	77	-12	0-1	.983	-3	84	86	C-82/3-8,O-2(RF),D-6	-1.2
1988	Sea A	103	335	45	86	17	1	4	33	17-1	2	16	.257	.295	.349	77	-11	1-1	.991	5	84	102	C-85/O-4(RF),3-3,1-2,D-4	-0.1
1989	Sea A	103	270	21	74	16	0	3	37	21-4	1	23	.274	.322	.367	93	-2	1-1	.993	-0	74	75	C-70/1-2,O(LF)D	0.1
1990	Sea A	101	233	11	52	9	0	1	28	15-2	0	20	.223	.264	.275	52	-15	0-1	.995	1	78	97	C-63/3-5,1D	-1.1
1991	Sea A	83	172	10	35	7	0	0	11	19-2	0	19	.203	.280	.244	47	-12	0-0	.993	-5	80	46	C-65/3-4,1D	-1.5
1992	Sea A	2	1	0	0	0	0	0	0	1-0	0	1	.000	.500	.000	51	0	0-0	1.000	1	0	0	/C	0.1
	Cin N	5	5	1	2	0	0	0	1	1-0	0	0	.400	.500	.400	154	0	0-0	1.000	-1	36	0	/C-2	0.0
Total	9	604	1648	149	424	75	6	18	184	104-14	11	110	.257	.302	.343	76	-55	3-6	.990	-10	83	83	C-433/D-42,3-20,O-13(7-0-6),1-6	-4.6
BRADLEY, BILL William Joseph B 2.13.1878 Cleveland, OH D 3.11.1954 Cleveland, OH BR/TR 6/185# d8.26 M2																								
1899	Chi N	35	129	26	40	6	1	2	18	12	2		.310	.378	.419	121	4	4	.884	-4	97	157	3-30/S-5	0.1
1900	Chi N	122	444	63	125	21	8	5	49	27	5		.282	.330	.399	104	1	14	.882	14	**111**	75	*3-106,1-15	1.6
1901	Cle A	133	516	95	151	28	13	1	55	26	8		.293	.336	.403	109	5	15	**.930**	12	102	125	*3-133/P	1.9
1902	Cle A	**137**	550	104	187	39	12	11	77	27	4		.340	.375	.515	151	36	11	.923	12	107	107	*3-137	4.8
1903	Cle A	136	536	101	168	36	22	6	68	25	3		.313	.348	.496	154	33	21	.924	11	**114**	130	*3-136	4.8
1904	Cle A	**154**	609	94	183	32	8	6	83	26	5		.300	.334	.409	136	23	23	**.955**	9	104	132	*3-154	4.0
1905	Cle A	146	541	63	145	34	6	0	51	27	15		.268	.321	.353	112	8	22	**.945**	13	108	141	*3-146,M	2.7
1906	Cle A	82	302	32	83	16	2	2	25	18	4		.275	.324	.361	116	6	13	.966	1	103	80	3-82	1.0
1907	Cle A	139	498	48	111	20	1	0	34	35	9		.223	.286	.267	76	-12	20	**.938**	6	**101**	**130**	*3-139	-0.3
1908	Cle A	148	548	70	133	24	7	1	46	29	13		.243	.297	.318	99	-1	18	.939	-25	88	110	*3-118,S-30	-2.5
1909	Cle A	95	334	30	62	6	3	0	22	19	3		.186	.236	.222	43	-22	8	.957	-5	94	164	3-87/1-3,2-3	-2.9
1910	Cle A	61	214	12	42	3	0	0	12	10	1		.196	.236	.210	39	-15	6	.956	-2	95	86	3-61	-1.8
1914	Bro F	7	6	1	3	1	0	0	3	0	0	0	.500	.500	.667	218	1	0	—	0			HM	0.1
1915	KC F	66	203	15	38	9	1	0	9	9	1	18	.187	.225	.241	33	-22	6	.949	-3	98	60	3-61	-2.6
Total	14	1461	5430	754	1471	275	84	34	552	290	73	18	.271	.317	.371	108	45	181	.933	40	103	118	*3-1390/S-35,1-18,2-3,P	10.9
BRADSHAW, DALLAS Dallas Carl "Windy" B 11.23.1895 Wolf Creek, IL D 12.11.1939 Herrin, IL BL/TR 5-7/145# d6.5																								
1917	Phi A	2	4	0	0	0	0	0	0	0	0	1	.000	.000	.000	-99	-1	0	1.000	0	61	196	/2	-0.1
BRADSHAW, GEORGE George Thomas B 9.12.1924 Salisbury, NC D 11.4.1994 Hendersonville, NC BR/TR 6-2/185# d8.10																								
1952	Was A	10	23	3	5	2	0	0	6	1	1	2	.217	.280	.304	65	-1	0-0	.917	-2	*83*	*0*	/C-9	-0.3
BRADSHAW, TERRY Terry Leon B 2.3.1969 Franklin, VA BL/TR 6/180# d5.4																								
1995	StL N	19	44	6	10	1	1	0	2	2-0	0	10	.227	.261	.295	46	-4	1-2	.952	1	121	202	O-10(6-3-1)	-0.3
1996	StL N	15	21	4	7	1	0	0	3	3-0	0	2	.333	.417	.381	113	1	0-1	1.000	-1	50	0	/O-7(4-3-1)	-0.1
Total	2	34	65	10	17	2	1	0	5	5-0	0	12	.262	.314	.323	69	-3	1-3	.960	-0	97	135	/O-17(10-6-2)	-0.4
BRADY d9.25																								
1875	Chi NA	1	4	1	1	0	1	0	0	0		0	.250	.250	.750	231	0	0-0	.625	-0	247	0	/O(CF)	0.0
BRADY, BRIAN Brian Phelan B 7.11.1962 Elmhurst, NY BL/TL 5-11/185# d4.16																								
1989	Cal A	2	2	0	1	1	0	0	1	0-0	0	1	.500	.500	1.000	319	1	0-0	—	-0	0	0	/O(RF)	0.1
BRADY, CLIFF Clifford Francis B 3.6.1897 St.Louis, MO D 9.25.1974 Belleville, IL BR/TR 5-5.5/140# d8.8																								
1920	Bos A	53	180	16	41	5	1	0	12	13	1	12	.228	.284	.267	48	-14	0-1	.974	11	124	95	2-53	-0.2
BRADY, BOB Robert Jay B 11.8.1922 Lewistown, PA D 4.22.1996 Manchester, CT BL/TR 6-1/175# d8.24																								
1946	Bos N	3	5	0	1	0	0	0	0	1	0	1	.200	.333	.200	52	0	0	.857	-0	*47*	*275*	/C	0.0
1947	Bos N	1	1	0	0	0	0	0	0	0	0	0	.000	.000	.000	-99	0	0	—	0			H	0.0
Total	2	4	6	0	1	0	0	0	0	1	0	1	.167	.286	.167	29	0	0	.857	-0	*47*	*275*	/C	0.0
BRADY, STEVE Stephen A. B 7.14.1851 Worcester, MA D 11.1.1917 Hartford, CT 5-9.5/165# d7.23																								
1874	Har NA	27	118	19	37	5	1	0	14	2		10	.314	.325	.373	117	2	1-2	.662	-9	58	0	3-16,O-11(0-5-6)/S	-0.6
1875	Was NA	21	91	7	13	0	0	0	3	0		4	.143	.143	.143	-0	-9	5-0	.815	-5	107	26	2-18/O-2(1-0-1),C1	-1.2
	Har NA	1	4	0	0	0	0	0	0	0		1	.000	.000	.000	-95	-1	0-0	1.000	1	454	0	/O(CF)	0.0
	Year	22	95	7	13	0	0	0	3	0		5	.137	.137	.137	-5	-10	5-0	.815	-4	107	26	2-18/O-3(1-1-1),C1	-1.2
1883	NY AA	**97**	432	69	117	12	6	0		11			.271	.289	.326	94	-4		.961	3	121	101	*1-81,O-16(RF)	-0.8
1884	†NY AA	**112**	485	102	122	11	3	1		21	0		.252	.283	.293	90	-5		.918	2	124	38	*O-110(RF)/1-5,2	-0.4
1885	NY AA	**108**	434	60	128	14	5	3	58	25	6		.295	.342	.371	131	16		.879	-5	58	88	*O-105(RF)/1-4,2-2,3	0.9
1886	NY AA	124	466	56	112	8	5	0	39	35	3		.240	.298	.279	88	-4	16	.836	-4	123	27	*O-123(RF)/1	-0.8
Total	2 NA	49	213	26	50	5	1	0	17	2	0	15	.235	.242	.268	68	-8	6-2	.815	-13	107	26	/2-18,3-16,O-14(1-6-7),1CS	-1.8
Total	4	441	1817	287	479	45	19	4	97	92	9	0	.264	.302	.316	100	3	16-0	.877	-4	102	63	O-354(RF)/1-91,2-3,3	-1.1
BRADY, DOUG Stephen Douglas B 11.23.1969 Jacksonville, IL BB/TR 5-11/165# d9.5																								
1995	Chi A	12	21	4	4	1	0	0	3	2-0	0	4	.190	.261	.238	32	-2	0-1	1.000	3	141	108	/2-6,D-3	0.1
BRAGAN, BOBBY Robert Randall "Nig" B 10.30.1917 Birmingham, AL BR/TR 5-10.5/175# d4.16 Mil 1945-46 M7 C2																								
1940	Phi N	132	474	36	105	14	1	7	44	28	0	34	.222	.265	.300	58	-29	2	.936	4	105	100	*S-132/3-2	-1.5
1941	Phi N	154	557	37	140	19	3	4	69	26	0	29	.251	.285	.318	72	-23	7	.944	-7	95	88	*S-154/2-2,3	-2.0
1942	Phi N	109	335	17	73	12	2	2	15	20	1	21	.218	.264	.284	63	-17	0	.939	8	108	106	S-78,C-22/2-4,3-3	-0.2
1943	Bro N	74	220	17	58	7	2	2	24	15	0	16	.264	.311	.341	88	-4	0	.973	0	*97*	*114*	C-57,3-12	-0.1

Year	Tm Lg	G	AB	R	H	2B	3B	HR	RBI	BB-IB	HP	SO	AVG	OBP	SLG	AOPS	ABR	SB-CS	FA	FR	Rng	Thr	G at Pos	BFW
1944	Bro N	94	266	26	71	8	4	0	17	13	1	14	.267	.304	.327	79	-8	2	.954	-3	91	64	S-51,C-35/3-6,2	-0.7
1947	†Bro N	25	36	3	7	2	0	0	3	7	0	3	.194	.326	.250	53	-2	1	1.000	2	*88*	*94*	C-21	0.1
1948	Bro N	9	12	0	2	0	0	0	0	1	0	0	.167	.231	.167	9	-2	0	1.000	-0	*70*	*214*	/C-5	-0.2
Total	7	597	1900	136	456	62	12	15	172	110	2	117	.240	.282	.309	69	-85	12	.941	4	100	93	S-415,C-140/3-24,2-7	-4.6

BRAGG, DARREN Darren William B 9.7.1969 Waterbury, CT BL/TR 5-9/180# d4.12

Year	Tm Lg	G	AB	R	H	2B	3B	HR	RBI	BB-IB	HP	SO	AVG	OBP	SLG	AOPS	ABR	SB-CS	FA	FR	Rng	Thr	G at Pos	BFW
1994	Sea A	8	19	4	3	1	0	0	2	2-1	0	5	.158	.238	.211	17	-2	0-0	1.000	-0	47	0	/O-3(LF),D-3	-0.3
1995	Sea A	52	145	20	34	5	1	3	12	18-1	4	37	.234	.331	.345	77	-5	9-0	.989	6	112	280	O-47(32-0-17)/D-2	0.1
1996	Sea A	69	195	36	53	12	1	7	25	33-4	2	35	.272	.376	.451	110	4	8-5	.992	4	106	186	O-63(48-5-16)	0.6
	Bos A	58	222	38	56	14	1	3	22	36-2	2	39	.252	.357	.365	83	-5	6-4	.986	2	100	140	O-58(7-47-29)	-0.3
	Year	127	417	74	109	26	2	10	47	69-6	4	74	.261	.366	.405	95	-1	14-9	.989	6	103	162	*O-121(55-52-45)	0.3
1997	Bos A	153	513	65	132	35	2	9	57	61-5	3	102	.257	.337	.386	87	-8	10-6	.987	6	105	142	*O-150(1-118-41)/3	-0.3
1998	†Bos A	129	409	51	114	29	3	8	57	42-0	6	99	.279	.351	.423	99	0	5-3	**.996**	-3	97	75	*O-124(7-12-112)/D-4	-0.7
1999	StL N	93	273	38	71	12	1	6	26	44-1	3	67	.260	.369	.377	89	-3	3-0	.982	0	95	157	O-88(22-43-33)	-0.4
2000	Col N	71	149	16	33	7	1	3	21	17-1	0	41	.221	.296	.342	50	-12	4-1	1.000	-3	84	0	O-43(34-0-9)	-1.5
2001	NY N	18	57	4	15	6	0	0	5	4-0	1	23	.263	.323	.368	82	-1	3-2	1.000	-1	78	114	O-16(8-2-10)	-0.3
	NY A	5	4	1	1	1	0	0	0	0-0	0	1	.250	.250	.500	89	0	0-0	1.000	0	118	0	/O-3(RF)	0.0
2002	†Atl N	109	212	34	57	15	2	3	15	24-0	2	52	.269	.347	.401	99	-1	5-2	.971	-1	100	67	O-63(12-18-36)/D-3	-0.3
2003	†Atl N	104	162	21	39	5	1	0	9	13-1	2	38	.241	.305	.284	55	-11	2-1	.988	-4	86	36	O-78(29-21-35)	-1.6
Total	10	869	2360	328	608	142	13	42	251	294-16	25	539	.258	.343	.382	86	-44	55-24	.988	6	99	122	O-736(203-266-341)/D-12,3	-5.0

BRAGGS, GLENN Glenn Erick B 10.17.1962 San Bernardino, CA BR/TR 6-3/210# d7.18

Year	Tm Lg	G	AB	R	H	2B	3B	HR	RBI	BB-IB	HP	SO	AVG	OBP	SLG	AOPS	ABR	SB-CS	FA	FR	Rng	Thr	G at Pos	BFW
1986	Mil A	58	215	19	51	8	2	4	18	11-0	1	47	.237	.274	.349	67	-10	1-1	.910	-0	103	141	O-56(51-3-5)/D-2	-1.3
1987	Mil A	132	505	67	136	28	7	13	77	47-7	4	96	.269	.332	.430	98	-1	12-5	.972	10	**128**	71	*O-123(RF)/D-8	0.3
1988	Mil A	72	272	30	71	14	0	10	42	14-0	5	60	.261	.307	.423	102	0	6-4	.978	1	114	29	O-54(RF),D-18	-0.1
1989	Mil A	144	514	77	127	12	3	15	66	42-4	4	111	.247	.305	.370	91	-7	17-5	.972	-1	100	77	*O-132(127-0-9),D-13	-1.1
1990	Mil A	37	113	17	28	5	0	3	13	12-2	3	21	.248	.328	.372	98	0	5-3	.965	3	131	48	O-32(13-0-20)/D-2	0.2
	†Cin N	72	201	22	60	9	1	6	28	26-1	3	43	.299	.385	.443	122	7	3-4	.968	6	102	266	O-60(26-0-35)	1.1
1991	Cin N	85	250	36	65	10	0	11	39	23-3	2	46	.260	.323	.432	108	2	11-3	.966	1	112	52	O-74(55-0-27)	0.3
1992	Cin N	92	266	40	63	16	3	8	38	36-5	2	48	.237	.330	.410	106	3	3-1	.946	-7	78	85	O-79(56-0-29)	-0.6
Total	7	692	2336	308	601	102	16	70	321	211-22	24	472	.257	.322	.405	98	-6	58-26	.963	13	108	92	O-610(328-3-302)/D-43	-1.2

BRAIN, DAVE David Leonard B 1.24.1879 Hereford, England D 5.25.1959 Los Angeles, CA BR/TR 5-10/170# d4.24 OF Total (26-LF 15-CF 5-RF)

Year	Tm Lg	G	AB	R	H	2B	3B	HR	RBI	BB-IB	HP	SO	AVG	OBP	SLG	AOPS	ABR	SB-CS	FA	FR	Rng	Thr	G at Pos	BFW
1901	Chi A	5	20	2	7	1	0	0	5	1	0		.350	.381	.400	120	1	0	.909	0	96	189	/2-5	0.1
1903	StL N	119	464	44	107	8	15	1	60	25	0		.231	.270	.319	70	-22	21	.908	7	104	121	S-72,3-46	-1.1
1904	StL N	127	488	57	130	24	12	7	72	17	0		.266	.291	.408	120	8	18	.927	-3	100	108	S-59,3-30,O-19(7-11-1),2-13/1-4	0.8
1905	StL N	44	158	11	36	4	5	1	17	8	1		.228	.269	.335	82	-4	4	.910	-7	83	36	S-29/3-6,O-6(0-4-2)	-1.1
	Pit N	85	307	31	79	17	6	3	46	15	2		.257	.296	.381	99	-2	8	.923	6	116	152	3-78/S-4	0.7
	Year	129	465	42	115	21	11	4	63	23	3		.247	.287	.366	93	-6	12	.929	-1	117	141	3-84,S-33/O-6(0-4-2)	-0.4
1906	Bos N	139	525	43	131	19	5	5	45	29	3		.250	.293	.333	98	-4	11	.917	25	116	**152**	*3-139	2.8
1907	Bos N	133	509	60	142	24	9	**10**	56	29	5		.279	.324	.420	134	17	10	.916	24	**121**	**148**	*3-130/O-3(LF)	4.8
1908	Cin N	16	55	4	6	0	0	0	1	8	0		.109	.222	.109	7	-6	0	.947	-1	0	0	O-16(LF)	-0.8
	NY N	11	17	2	3	0	0	0	1	2	0		.176	.263	.176	39	-1	1	.867	-2	92	0	/2-3,O-3(RF),3-2,S	-0.4
	Year	27	72	6	9	0	0	0	2	10	0		.125	.232	.125	14	-7	1	.947	-3	0	0	O-19(16-0-2)/2-3,3-2,S	-1.2
Total	7	679	2543	254	641	97	52	27	303	134	11		.252	.292	.363	101	-13	73	.913	50	116	142	3-431,S-165/O-47L,2-21,1-4	5.8

BRAINERD, FRED Frederick F. B 2.17.1892 Champaign, IL D 4.17.1959 Galveston, TX BR/TR 6/176# d10.6

Year	Tm Lg	G	AB	R	H	2B	3B	HR	RBI	BB-IB	HP	SO	AVG	OBP	SLG	AOPS	ABR	SB-CS	FA	FR	Rng	Thr	G at Pos	BFW
1914	NY N	2	5	1	1	0	0	0	0	1	0	0	.200	.333	.200	62	0	0	.923	0	94	130	/2-2	0.0
1915	NY N	91	249	31	50	7	2	1	21	21	1	44	.201	.266	.257	62	-12	6-7	.988	4	149	141	1-43,3-15/S-9,2O(CF)	-1.0
1916	NY N	2	7	0	0	0	0	0	0	0	0	0	.000	.000	.000	-99	-2	0	.625	-1	46	0	/3-2	-0.4
Total	3	95	261	32	51	7	2	1	21	22	1	44	.195	.261	.249	58	-14	6-7	.988	3	149	141	/1-43,3-17,S-9,2-3,O(CF)	-1.4

BRAMHALL, ART Arthur Washington B 2.22.1909 Oak Park, IL D 9.4.1985 Madison, WI BR/TR 5-11/170# d4.18

Year	Tm Lg	G	AB	R	H	2B	3B	HR	RBI	BB-IB	HP	SO	AVG	OBP	SLG	AOPS	ABR	SB-CS	FA	FR	Rng	Thr	G at Pos	BFW
1935	Phi N	2	1	0	0	0	0	0	0	0	0	0	.000	.000	.000	-91	0	0	1.000	0	146	0	/S3	0.0

BRANCATO, AL Albert "Bronk" B 5.29.1919 Philadelphia, PA BR/TR 5-9.5/188# d9.7 Mil 1942-45

Year	Tm Lg	G	AB	R	H	2B	3B	HR	RBI	BB-IB	HP	SO	AVG	OBP	SLG	AOPS	ABR	SB-CS	FA	FR	Rng	Thr	G at Pos	BFW
1939	Phi A	21	68	12	14	5	0	1	8	8	1	4	.206	.299	.324	60	-4	1-0	.939	-1	106	48	3-20/S	-0.4
1940	Phi A	107	298	42	57	11	2	1	23	28	2	36	.191	.265	.252	36	-29	3-1	.949	-3	96	85	S-80,3-25	-2.5
1941	Phi A	144	530	60	124	20	9	2	49	59	0	49	.234	.311	.317	68	-25	1-5	.915	-17	101	88	*S-139/3-7	-3.3
1945	Phi A	10	34	3	4	1	0	0	0	1	0	3	.118	.143	.147	-16	-5	0-0	.959	-1	88	86	S-10	-0.6
Total	4	282	930	117	199	37	11	4	80	96	3	92	.214	.290	.290	54	-63	5-6	.927	-21	99	87	S-230/3-52	-6.8

BRAND, RON Ronald George B 1.13.1940 Los Angeles, CA BR/TR 5-8/170# d5.26 OF Total (14-LF 5-CF 2-RF)

Year	Tm Lg	G	AB	R	H	2B	3B	HR	RBI	BB-IB	HP	SO	AVG	OBP	SLG	AOPS	ABR	SB-CS	FA	FR	Rng	Thr	G at Pos	BFW
1963	Pit N	46	66	8	19	2	0	1	7	10-0	1	11	.288	.390	.364	118	2	0-0	.968	4	*107*	*97*	C-33/2-2,3-2	0.7
1965	Hou N	117	391	27	92	6	3	2	37	19-2	6	34	.235	.281	.281	63	-20	10-5	.988	-5	*104*	*99*	*C-102/3-6,O-5(LF)	-2.2
1966	Hou N	56	123	12	30	2	0	0	10	9-3	2	13	.244	.301	.260	64	-6	0-2	.986	-3	*98*	*50*	C-25/2-9,O-3(LF),3	-0.8
1967	Hou N	84	215	22	52	8	1	0	18	23-7	2	17	.242	.321	.288	78	-5	4-0	.998	-3	*80*	*102*	C-67/2O(LF)	-0.4
1968	Hou N	43	81	7	13	2	0	0	4	9-0	2	11	.160	.261	.185	36	-6	1-1	1.000	1	*68*	*84*	C-29/3O(RF)	-0.4
1969	Mon N	103	287	19	74	12	0	0	20	30-4	1	19	.258	.327	.300	77	-8	2-3	.985	-7	75	118	C-84/O-2(1-1-0)	-1.3
1970	Mon N	72	126	10	30	2	3	0	9	9-0	0	16	.238	.287	.302	59	-8	2-1	.952	1	117	120	S-19,3-12/C-9,O-5(1-3-1),2-3	-0.5
1971	Mon N	47	56	3	12	0	0	0	1	3-0	0	5	.214	.254	.214	34	-5	1-1	.957	5	126	135	S-22/3-4,O-4(3-1-0),C2	0.1
Total	8	568	1345	108	322	34	7	3	106	112-16	14	126	.239	.303	.282	68	-56	20-13	.988	-7	*88*	*100*	C-350/S-41,3-26,O-21L,2-16	-4.8

BRANDT, JACKIE John George B 4.28.1934 Omaha, NE BR/TR 5-11/170# d4.21 Mil 1957-58

Year	Tm Lg	G	AB	R	H	2B	3B	HR	RBI	BB-IB	HP	SO	AVG	OBP	SLG	AOPS	ABR	SB-CS	FA	FR	Rng	Thr	G at Pos	BFW
1956	StL N	27	42	9	12	3	0	1	3	4-0	1	5	.286	.362	.429	111	1	0-1	1.000	1	115	81	O-26(3-3-20)	0.1
	NY N	98	351	45	105	16	8	11	47	17-2	0	31	.299	.330	.484	116	6	3-4	.989	-1	98	130	O-96(86-3-26)	0.0
	Year	125	393	54	117	19	8	12	50	21-2	1	36	.298	.333	.478	116	7	3-5	.990	0	100	123	*O-122(89-6-46)	0.1
1958	SF N	18	52	7	13	1	0	0	3	6-0	0	5	.250	.328	.269	62	-3	1-0	1.000	-1	103	0	O-14(11-1-3)	-0.4
1959	SF N	137	429	63	116	16	5	12	57	35-2	0	69	.270	.324	.415	98	-3	11-4	.984	-0	99	137	*O-116(111-4-6),3-18/1-3,2	-0.8
1960	Bal A	145	511	73	130	24	6	15	65	47-3	3	69	.254	.317	.413	98	-3	5-3	.983	-2	96	121	*O-142(17-102-51)/3-2,1	-1.1
1961	Bal A★	139	516	93	153	18	5	16	72	62-0	1	51	.297	.371	.444	122	16	10-2	.974	-7	94	73	*O-136(21-120-34)/3	0.5
1962	Bal A	143	505	76	129	29	5	19	75	55-2	4	64	.255	.330	.446	115	10	9-3	.976	-3	97	127	*O-138(0-109-30)/3-2	0.2
1963	Bal A	142	451	49	112	15	5	15	61	34-3	0	85	.248	.298	.404	99	-2	4-5	.986	2	105	114	*O-134(30-92-39)/3	-0.7
1964	Bal A	137	523	66	127	25	1	13	47	45-5	3	104	.243	.305	.369	87	-9	1-4	.981	7	106	142	*O-134(10-131-0)	-0.9
1965	Bal A	96	243	35	59	17	0	8	24	21-0	0	40	.243	.303	.412	99	0	1-2	.961	3	105	159	O-84(39-37-22)	-0.2
1966	Phi N	82	164	16	41	6	1	1	15	17-2	0	36	.250	.317	.317	78	-4	0-2	.988	-1	91	107	O-71(17-49-6)	-0.8
1967	Phi N	16	19	1	2	1	0	0	1	0-0	0	6	.105	.105	.158	-25	-3	0-0	1.000	-0	59	0	/O-3(LF)	-0.4
	Hou N	41	89	7	21	4	1	1	15	8-1	0	9	.236	.296	.337	85	-2	0-0	.991	-1	77	46	1-14/O-6(LF),3	-0.4
	Year	57	108	8	23	5	1	1	16	8-1	0	15	.213	.265	.306	65	-5	0-0	.991	-1	77	46	1-14/O-9(LF),3	-0.8
Total	11	1221	3895	540	1020	175	37	112	485	351-20	12	574	.262	.323	.412	102	4	45-30	.980	-4	100	119	*O-1100(354-651-237)/3-25,1-18,2	-4.9

BRANNAN, OTIS Otis Owen B 3.13.1899 Greenbrier, AR D 6.6.1967 Little Rock, AR BL/TR 5-9/160# d4.11

Year	Tm Lg	G	AB	R	H	2B	3B	HR	RBI	BB-IB	HP	SO	AVG	OBP	SLG	AOPS	ABR	SB-CS	FA	FR	Rng	Thr	G at Pos	BFW
1928	StL A	135	483	68	118	18	3	10	66	60	4	19	.244	.333	.356	79	-15	3-9	.964	-6	101	98	*2-135	-1.9
1929	StL A	23	51	4	15	1	0	1	8	4	0	4	.294	.345	.373	82	-1	0-0	.975	0	105	76	2-19	-0.1
Total	2	158	534	72	133	19	3	11	74	64	4	23	.249	.334	.358	79	-16	3-9	.966	-6	101	96	2-154	-2.0

BRANNOCK, MIKE Michael J. B 1853 Guelph, ON, CAN 5-8/162# d10.21

Year	Tm Lg	G	AB	R	H	2B	3B	HR	RBI	BB-IB	HP	SO	AVG	OBP	SLG	AOPS	ABR	SB-CS	FA	FR	Rng	Thr	G at Pos	BFW
1871	Chi NA	3	14	2	1	0	0	0	0	0		0	.071	.071	.071	-53	-3	0-0	.500	-2	40	0	/3-3	-0.3
1875	Chi NA	2	9	2	1	0	0	0	0	0		0	.111	.111	.111	-22	-1	2-0	.500	-1	83	0	/3-2	-0.2
Total	2 NA	5	23	4	2	0	0	0	0	0		0	.087	.087	.087	-43	-4	2-0	.000	-3	59	0	/3-5	-0.5

BRANOM, DUD Edgar Dudley B 11.30.1897 Sulphur Springs, TX D 2.4.1980 Sun City, AZ BL/TL 6-1/190# d4.12

Year	Tm Lg	G	AB	R	H	2B	3B	HR	RBI	BB-IB	HP	SO	AVG	OBP	SLG	AOPS	ABR	SB-CS	FA	FR	Rng	Thr	G at Pos	BFW
1927	Phi A	30	94	8	22	1	0	0	13	2	0	5	.234	.250	.245	27	-10	2-1	.973	-0	108	105	1-26	-1.2

BRANSFIELD, KITTY William Edward B 1.7.1875 Worcester, MA D 5.1.1947 Worcester, MA BR/TR 5-11/207# d8.22 U1

Year	Tm Lg	G	AB	R	H	2B	3B	HR	RBI	BB-IB	HP	SO	AVG	OBP	SLG	AOPS	ABR	SB-CS	FA	FR	Rng	Thr	G at Pos	BFW
1898	Bos N	5	9	2	2	0	1	0	1	0	0		.222	.222	.444	85	0	0	.889	-1	*97*	*0*	/C-4,1	-0.1
1901	Pit N	139	566	92	167	26	16	0	91	29	5		.295	.335	.398	109	5	23	.981	-10	66	117	*1-139	-0.8

Year	Tm Lg	G	AB	R	H	2B	3B	HR	RBI	BB-IB	HP	SO	AVG	OBP	SLG	AOPS	ABR	SB-CS	FA	FR	Rng	Thr	G at Pos	BFW
1902	Pit N	102	413	49	126	21	8	0	69	17	2		.305	.336	.395	121	9	23	.984	-7	69	82	*1-101	0.0
1903	†Pit N	127	505	69	134	23	7	2	57	33	3		.265	.314	.350	87	-10	13	.981	5	117	**136**	*1-127	-0.7
1904	Pit N	139	520	47	116	17	9	0	60	22	3		.223	.259	.290	68	-21	11	.981	-2	97	**121**	*1-139	-2.8
1905	Phi N	151	580	55	150	23	9	3	76	27	2		.259	.294	.345	93	-7	27	.985	-2	94	99	*1-151	-1.2
1906	Phi N	140	524	47	144	28	5	1	60	16	3		.275	.300	.353	104	0	12	.980	-1	100	86	*1-139	-0.5
1907	Phi N	94	348	25	81	15	2	0	38	14	0		.233	.262	.287	73	-12	8	.978	-3	93	101	1-92	-1.8
1908	Phi N	144	527	53	160	25	7	3	71	23	2		.304	.335	.395	128	15	30	.986	-1	98	111	*1-143	1.3
1909	Phi N	140	527	47	154	27	6	1	59	18	3		.292	.319	.372	114	6	17	**.989**	7	**117**	108	*1-138	1.1
1910	Phi N	123	427	39	102	17	4	3	52	20	1	34	.239	.275	.319	71	-18	10	.982	-4	83	**130**	*1-110	-2.6
1911	Phi N	23	43	4	11	1	1	0	3	0	0	5	.256	.256	.326	61	-3	1	.987	0	95	47	/1-8	-0.3
	Chi N	3	10	0	4	2	0	0	0	2	0	2	.400	.500	.600	207	2	0	1.000	-0	62	398	/1-3	0.1
	Year	26	53	4	15	3	1	0	3	2	0	7	.283	.309	.377	91	-1	1	.991	-0	86	143	1-11	-0.2
Total	12	1330	4999	529	1351	225	75	13	637	221	24	41	.270	.304	.353	97	-34	175	.983	-18	94	110	*1-1291/C-4	-8.3
BRANSON, JEFF Jeffery Glenn B 1.26.1967 Waynesboro, MS BL/TR 6/180# d4.12																								
1992	Cin N	72	115	12	34	7	1	0	15	5-2	0	16	.296	.322	.374	95	-1	0-1	.946	2	103	161	2-33/3-8,S	0.1
1993	Cin N	125	381	40	92	15	1	3	22	19-2	0	73	.241	.275	.310	57	-24	4-1	.978	0	96	94	S-59,2-45,3-14/1	-1.8
1994	Cin N	58	109	18	31	4	1	6	16	5-2	0	16	.284	.316	.505	110	1	0-0	.980	-5	69	57	2-19,3-18/S-8,1-2	-0.3
1995	†Cin N	122	331	43	86	18	2	12	45	44-14	2	69	.260	.345	.435	106	3	2-1	.971	13	107	**191**	3-98,S-32/2-6,1	1.8
1996	Cin N	129	311	34	76	16	4	9	37	31-4	1	67	.244	.312	.408	89	-6	2-0	.932	-4	102	157	3-64,S-38,2-31	-0.6
1997	Cin N	65	98	9	15	3	1	1	5	7-1	0	23	.153	.210	.235	16	-13	1-0	.971	-0	95	202	3-27,2-14,S-11	-1.2
	†Cle A	29	72	5	19	4	0	2	7	7-0	1	17	.264	.329	.403	89	-1	0-2	.986	-1	104	91	2-19/3-6,S-2,D	-0.1
1998	†Cle A	63	100	6	20	4	1	1	9	3-0	1	21	.200	.221	.290	31	-11	0-0	.960	0	88	155	2-31,3-20/1-3,S-2	-0.9
2000	LA N	18	17	3	4	1	0	0	0	1-0	0	6	.235	.278	.294	47	-1	0-0	1.000	-1	68	0	/S-7,2-3,3-3	-0.2
2001	LA N	13	21	3	6	0	0	0	0	0-0	0	4	.286	.286	.286	52	-2	0-0	1.000	-1	96	93	/2-6,S-2,3	-0.2
Total	9	694	1555	173	383	72	11	34	156	122-25	4	312	.246	.300	.372	77	-55	9-5	.957	2	103	161	3-259,2-207,S-162/1-7,D	-3.4
BRANT, MARSHALL Marshall Lee B 9.17.1955 Garberville, CA BR/TR 6-5/185# d10.1																								
1980	NY A	3	6	0	0	0	0	0	0	0-0	0	3	.000	.000	.000	-99	-2	0-0	1.000	0	135	181	/1-2,D	-0.2
1983	Oak A	5	14	2	2	0	0	0	2	0-0	0	3	.143	.143	.143	-22	-2	0-0	.905	-1	0	161	/1-3,D	-0.4
Total	2	8	20	2	2	0	0	0	2	0-0	0	6	.100	.100	.100	-47	-4	0-0	.935	-1	44	167	/1-5,D-2	-0.6
BRANTLEY, MICKEY Michael Charles B 6.17.1961 Catskill, NY BR/TR 5-10/180# d8.9 C1																								
1986	Sea A	27	102	12	20	3	2	3	7	10-0	0	21	.196	.268	.353	67	-5	1-1	.983	-1	81	222	O-25(1-25-0)	-0.7
1987	Sea A	92	351	52	106	23	2	14	54	24-0	0	44	.302	.344	.499	115	7	13-4	.982	-5	89	68	O-82(6-51-35)/D-8	0.1
1988	Sea A	149	577	76	152	25	4	15	56	26-0	2	64	.263	.296	.399	89	-10	18-7	.982	-0	103	65	*O-147(118-49-4)/D-2	-1.3
1989	Sea A	34	108	14	17	5	0	0	8	7-0	0	7	.157	.207	.204	16	-12	2-2	1.000	1	109	68	O-23(12-0-11)/D-7	-1.3
Total	4	302	1138	154	295	56	8	32	125	67-0	2	136	.259	.300	.407	89	-20	34-14	.984	-6	97	81	O-277(137-125-50)/D-17	-3.2
BRANYAN, RUSSELL Russell Oles B 12.19.1975 Warner Robins, GA BL/TR 6-3/195# d9.26																								
1998	Cle A	1	4	0	0	0	0	0	0	0-0	0	2	.000	.000	.000	-97	-1	0-0	1.000	-0	75	0	/3	-0.1
1999	Cle A	11	38	4	8	2	0	1	6	3-0	1	19	.211	.286	.342	57	-3	0-0	.960	3	159	0	/3-8,D-3	0.0
2000	Cle A	67	193	32	46	7	2	16	38	22-1	4	76	.238	.327	.544	113	3	0-0	.968	1	114	123	O-33(18-0-15),D-23/3	0.1
2001	†Cle A	113	315	48	73	16	2	20	54	38-1	3	132	.232	.316	.486	107	2	1-1	.930	-2	95	77	3-72,O-33(31-0-2)/D-7	0.0
2002	Cle A	50	161	16	33	4	0	8	17	17-0	0	65	.205	.278	.379	74	-7	1-2	.986	-2	87	180	O-42(LF)/3-8,D	-1.0
	Cin N	84	217	34	53	9	1	16	39	34-3	2	86	.244	.349	.516	125	7	3-1	.951	-0	93	235	O-25(LF),1-18,3-16/D-4	0.4
2003	Cin N	74	176	22	38	12	0	9	26	27-0	1	69	.216	.322	.438	98	-1	0-0	.968	6	153	153	3-20,O-17(LF),1-14/D	0.4
Total	6	400	1104	156	251	50	5	70	180	141-5	11	449	.227	.318	.472	103	0	5-4	.968	7	96	162	O-150(133-0-17),3-126/D-39,1-32	-0.2
BRASHEAR, ROY Roy Parks B 1.3.1874 Ashtabula, OH D 4.20.1951 Los Angeles, CA BR/TR 5-11/205# d4.25 b-Kitty																								
1902	StL N	110	388	36	107	8	2	1	40	32	1		.276	.333	.314	104	2	9	.980	-5	92	120	1-67,2-21,O-16(1-7-8)/S-3	-0.4
1903	Phi N	20	75	9	17	3	0	0	4	6	0		.227	.284	.267	59	-4	2	.918	-3	84	124	2-18/1-2	-0.7
Total	2	130	463	45	124	11	2	1	44	38	1		.268	.325	.307	96	-2	11	.978	-8	92	119	/1-69,2-39,O-16(1-7-8),S-3	-1.1
BRATCHER, JOE Joseph Warlick "Goobers" B 7.22.1898 Grand Saline, TX D 10.13.1977 Fort Worth, TX BL/TR 5-8.5/140# d8.26																								
1924	StL N	4	1	1	0	0	0	0	0	0	0	0	.000	.000	.000	-99	0	0-0	—	-0	0	0	/O(CF)	0.0
BRATSCHI, FRED Frederick Oscar "Fritz" B 1.16.1892 Alliance, OH D 1.10.1962 Massillon, OH BR/TR 5-10/170# d7.24																								
1921	Chi A	16	28	0	8	1	0	0	3	0	0	2	.286	.286	.321	55	-2	0-0	1.000	1	88	350	/O-5(1-0-4)	-0.1
1926	Bos A	72	167	12	46	10	1	0	19	14	1	15	.275	.335	.347	81	-5	0-1	.949	-5	80	30	O-37(29-0-8)	-1.2
1927	Bos A	1	1	0	0	0	0	0	0	0	0	0	.000	.000	.000	-99	0	0-0	—	0			H	0.0
Total	3	89	196	12	54	11	1	0	22	14	1	17	.276	.327	.342	76	-7	0-1	.956	-4	81	66	/O-42(30-0-12)	-1.3
BRAUN, STEVE Stephen Russell B 5.8.1948 Trenton, NJ BL/TR 5-10/180# d4.6 C1 OF Total (465-LF 35-RF)																								
1971	Min A	128	343	51	87	12	2	5	35	48-4	5	50	.254	.350	.344	95	0	8-3	.933	-10	81	54	3-73,2-28,S-10/O-2(LF)	-0.8
1972	Min A	121	402	40	116	21	0	2	50	45-1	2	38	.289	.360	.356	109	7	4-5	.970	-10	100	103	3-74,2-20,S-11/O-9(8-0-1)	-0.3
1973	Min A	115	361	46	102	28	5	6	42	74-8	3	48	.283	.408	.438	133	21	4-3	.941	-7	91	114	*3-102/O-6(LF)	1.2
1974	Min A	129	453	53	127	12	1	8	40	56-4	2	51	.280	.361	.364	106	5	4-4	.964	2	89	143	*O-108(LF),3-17	0.1
1975	Min A	136	453	70	137	18	3	11	45	66-5	1	55	.302	.389	.428	130	20	0-2	.971	-2	96	84	*O-106(LF)/1-9,3-2,2D	1.2
1976	Min A	122	417	73	120	12	3	3	61	67-2	1	43	.288	.384	.353	115	12	12-4	.971	2	111	203	D-71,O-32(30-0-3),3-16	1.2
1977	Sea A	139	451	51	106	19	1	5	31	80-2	2	59	.235	.351	.315	84	-6	8-3	.975	4	98	159	*O-100(LF),D-32/3	-0.7
1978	Sea A	32	74	11	17	4	0	3	15	9-1	0	5	.230	.310	.405	101	0	1-0	1.000	-0	81	0	D-14/O-4(2-0-2)	-0.1
	†KC A	64	137	16	36	10	1	0	14	28-1	0	16	.263	.386	.350	106	3	3-2	.964	-2	108	63	O-33(LF),3-11	0.0
	Year	96	211	27	53	14	1	3	29	37-2	0	21	.251	.360	.370	105	3	4-2	.967	-2	105	56	O-37(35-0-2),D-14,3-11	-0.1
1979	KC A	58	116	15	31	2	0	4	10	22-2	0	11	.267	.384	.388	107	2	0-0	1.000	1	85	353	O-18(LF),D-11/3-2	0.2
1980	KC A	14	23	0	1	0	0	0	1	2-0	0	2	.043	.120	.043	-53	-5	0-0	1.000	-1	27	0	/O-5(3-0-2),D	-0.6
	Tor A	37	55	4	15	2	0	1	9	8-1	0	5	.273	.365	.364	96	0	0-0	1.000	0	437	0	D-13/3	0.0
	Year	51	78	4	16	2	0	1	10	10-1	0	7	.205	.295	.269	54	-5	0-0	1.000	-1	27	0	D-14/O-5(3-0-2),3	-0.6
1981	StL N	44	46	9	9	2	1	0	2	15-0	0	7	.196	.393	.283	92	1	1-0	1.000	1	114	346	O-12(6-0-6)/3	0.2
1982	†StL N	58	62	6	17	4	0	0	4	11-0	0	10	.274	.384	.339	103	1	0-0	1.000	-2	62	0	/O-8(6-0-2),3-5	-0.1
1983	StL N	78	92	8	25	2	1	3	7	21-0	0	7	.272	.404	.413	128	5	0-1	1.000	0	84	0	O-22(18-0-5)/3-4	0.4
1984	StL N	86	98	6	27	3	1	0	16	17-0	0	17	.276	.383	.327	104	1	0-0	1.000	-2	48	123	O-19(12-0-7)/3	-0.1
1985	†StL N	64	67	7	16	4	0	1	6	10-1	1	9	.239	.342	.343	94	0	0-0	1.000	1	107	205	O-14(7-0-7)	0.0
Total	15	1425	3650	466	989	155	19	52	388	579-32	17	433	.271	.371	.367	108	67	45-27	.973	-23	94	136	O-498L,3-310,D-151/2-49,S-21,1-9	1.8
BRAVO, ANGEL Angel Alfonso (Urdaneta) B 8.4.1942 Maracaibo, Venezuela BL/TL 5-8/150# d6.6																								
1969	Chi A	27	90	10	26	4	2	1	3	3-0	1	5	.289	.319	.411	98	-1	2-0	.978	-2	90	0	O-25(2-24-3)	-0.3
1970	†Cin N	65	65	10	18	1	1	0	3	9-0	0	13	.277	.365	.323	86	-1	0-1	.947	0	100	204	O-22(5-12-5)	-0.1
1971	Cin N	5	5	0	1	0	0	0	0	0-0	0	1	.200	.200	.200	14	-1	0-0	—	0			H	-0.1
	SD N	52	58	6	9	2	0	0	6	8-1	1	12	.155	.265	.190	34	-5	0-1	.833	-2	41	0	/O-9(5-3-1)	-0.8
	Year	57	63	6	10	2	0	0	6	8-1	1	13	.159	.260	.190	33	-5	0-1	.833	-2	41	0	/O-9(5-3-1)	-0.9
Total	3	149	218	26	54	7	3	1	12	20-1	2	31	.248	.315	.321	77	-8	2-2	.957	-4	84	46	/O-56(12-39-9)	-1.3
BRAY, BUSTER Clarence Wilbur B 4.1.1913 Birmingham, AL D 9.4.1982 Evansville, IN BL/TL 6/170# d4.18																								
1941	Bos N	4	11	2	1	1	0	0	1	1	0	2	.091	.167	.182	-2	-2	0	1.000	-0	98	0	/O-3(CF)	-0.2
BRAZILL, FRANK Frank Leo B 8.11.1899 Spangler, PA D 11.3.1976 Oakland, CA BL/TR 5-11.5/175# d4.13																								
1921	Phi A	66	177	17	48	3	1	0	19	23	2	21	.271	.361	.299	70	-7	2-4	.984	-2	98	114	1-36/3-9	-1.1
1922	Phi A	6	13	0	1	0	0	0	1	0	0	1	.077	.077	.077	-58	-3	0-0	.750	-1	50	0	/3-2	-0.4
Total	2	72	190	17	49	3	1	0	20	23	2	22	.258	.344	.284	62	-10	2-4	.984	-4	98	114	/1-36,3-11	-1.5
BREAM, SID Sidney Eugene B 8.3.1960 Carlisle, PA BL/TL 6-4/220# d9.1																								
1983	LA N	15	11	0	2	0	0	0	2	2-0	0	2	.182	.308	.182	39	-1	0-0	1.000	-0	0	116	/1-4	-0.1
1984	LA N	27	49	2	9	3	0	0	6	6-2	0	9	.184	.263	.245	47	-3	1-0	1.000	2	153	102	1-14	-0.2
1985	LA N	24	53	4	7	0	0	3	6	7-3	0	10	.132	.230	.302	50	-4	0-0	.994	2	151	72	1-16	-0.3
	Pit N	26	95	14	27	7	0	3	15	11-2	0	14	.284	.355	.453	127	4	0-2	.992	2	124	102	1-25	0.3
	Year	50	148	18	34	7	0	6	21	18-5	0	24	.230	.310	.399	100	0	0-2	.993	4	134	91	1-41	0.0

Year	Tm Lg	G	AB	R	H	2B	3B	HR	RBI	BB-IB	HP	SO	AVG	OBP	SLG	AOPS	ABR	SB-CS	FA	FR	Rng	Thr	G at Pos	BFW
1986	Pit N	154	522	73	140	37	5	16	77	60-5	1	73	.268	.341	.450	115	11	13-7	.989	21	**152**	95	*1-153/O-2(LF)	2.4
1987	Pit N	149	516	64	142	25	3	13	65	49-11	0	69	.275	.336	.411	97	-3	9-8	.988	8	122	106	*1-144	-0.4
1988	Pit N	148	462	50	122	37	0	10	65	47-6	1	64	.264	.328	.409	114	9	9-9	.995	19	**152**	98	*1-138	1.9
1989	Pit N	19	36	3	8	3	0	0	4	12-0	0	10	.222	.417	.306	113	2	0-4	.992	-0	94	66	1-13	-0.1
1990	†Pit N	147	389	39	105	23	2	15	67	48-5	2	65	.270	.349	.455	125	14	8-4	.993	10	133	**113**	*1-142	1.6
1991	†Atl N	91	265	32	67	12	0	11	45	25-5	0	31	.253	.313	.423	100	0	0-3	.996	1	103	114	1-85	-0.6
1992	†Atl N	125	372	30	97	25	1	10	61	46-2	1	51	.261	.340	.414	107	5	6-0	.989	0	103	97	*1-120	-0.1
1993	†Atl N	117	277	33	72	14	1	9	35	31-3	0	43	.260	.332	.415	98	-1	4-2	.996	6	123	122	1-90	-0.2
1994	Hou N	46	61	7	21	5	0	0	7	9-1	0	9	.344	.429	.426	131	3	0-1	.986	2	207	141	1-10	0.5
Total	12	1088	3108	351	819	191	12	90	455	353-45	5	450	.264	.336	.420	107	36	50-40	.992	72	130	104	1-954/O-2(LF)	4.7
BREAZEALE, JIM James Leo B 10.3.1949 Houston, TX BL/TR 6-2/210# d9.13																								
1969	Atl N	2	1	1	0	0	0	0	0	2-0	0	0	.000	.667	.000	101	0	0-0	.833	-0	0	0	/1	0.0
1971	Atl N	10	21	1	4	0	0	1	3	0-0	0	3	.190	.182	.333	43	-2	0-0	1.000	-0	68	82	/1-4	-0.3
1972	Atl N	52	85	10	21	2	0	5	17	6-1	0	12	.247	.297	.447	100	0	0-1	1.000	-2	36	95	1-16/3	-0.4
1978	Chi A	25	72	8	15	3	0	3	13	8-0	0	10	.208	.284	.375	84	-2	0-0	.992	-3	29	75	1-19/D-4	-0.6
Total	4	89	179	20	40	5	0	9	33	16-1	0	25	.223	.284	.402	88	-4	0-1	.993	-6	36	82	/1-40,D-4,3	-1.3
BREDE, BRENT Brent David B 9.13.1971 Belleville, IL BL/TL 6-4/190# d9.8																								
1996	Min A	10	20	2	6	0	1	0	2	1-0	0	5	.300	.333	.400	83	-1	0-0	1.000	1	127	304	/O-7(RF)	0.0
1997	Min A	61	190	25	52	11	1	3	21	21-0	1	38	.274	.347	.389	91	-2	7-2	.957	-3	90	0	O-42(3-0-40),1-15/D	-0.7
1998	Ari N	98	212	23	48	9	3	2	17	24-2	2	43	.226	.311	.325	68	-10	1-0	.964	-2	92	67	O-58(26-0-39),1-12/D	-1.4
Total	3	169	422	50	106	20	5	5	40	46-2	3	86	.251	.328	.358	79	-13	8-2	.964	-4	93	52	O-107(29-0-86)/1-27,D-2	-2.1
BREEDEN, DANNY Danny Richard B 6.27.1942 Albany, GA BR/TR 5-11.5/185# d7.24 b-Hal																								
1969	Cin N	3	8	0	1	0	0	0	1	0-0	0	3	.125	.125	.125	-28	-1	0-0	.941	-1	65	0	/C-3	-0.2
1971	Chi N	25	65	3	10	1	0	0	4	9-0	1	18	.154	.263	.169	23	-6	0-0	.975	3	101	56	C-25	-0.2
Total	2	28	73	3	11	1	0	0	5	9-0	1	21	.151	.250	.164	18	-7	0-0	.972	3	96	49	/C-28	-0.4
BREEDEN, HAL Harold Noel B 6.28.1944 Albany, GA BR/TL 6-2/200# d4.7 b-Danny																								
1971	Chi N	23	36	1	5	1	0	1	2	2-0	0	7	.139	.184	.250	19	-4	0-0	.982	1	164	39	/1-8	-0.4
1972	Mon N	42	87	6	20	2	0	3	10	7-1	0	15	.230	.281	.356	80	-2	0-0	.994	-0	91	84	1-26/O(LF)	-0.5
1973	Mon N	105	258	36	71	10	6	15	43	29-3	2	45	.275	.353	.535	138	12	0-1	.991	3	118	99	1-66	1.0
1974	Mon N	79	190	14	47	13	0	2	20	24-0	0	35	.247	.330	.347	85	-3	0-1	.987	0	104	127	1-56	-0.7
1975	Mon N	24	37	4	5	2	0	0	1	7-3	0	5	.135	.273	.189	29	-3	0-0	.989	-1	77	72	1-12	-0.5
Total	5	273	608	61	148	28	6	21	76	69-7	2	107	.243	.321	.413	99	0	0-2	.990	3	110	102	1-168/O(LF)	-1.1
BREEDING, MARV Marvin Eugene B 3.8.1934 Decatur, AL BR/TR 6/175# d4.19																								
1960	Bal A	152	551	69	147	25	2	3	43	35-2	3	80	.267	.313	.336	77	-18	10-4	.977	7	101	111	*2-152	0.1
1961	Bal A	90	244	32	51	8	0	1	16	14-1	0	33	.209	.250	.254	37	-22	5-2	.970	3	98	122	2-80	-1.3
1962	Bal A	95	240	27	59	10	1	2	18	8-0	1	41	.246	.273	.321	63	-13	2-2	.977	10	113	120	2-73/S3	0.2
1963	Was A	58	197	20	54	7	2	1	14	7-0	0	21	.274	.299	.345	80	-6	1-1	.914	-1	99	20	3-29,2-22/S-2	-0.5
	LA N	20	36	6	6	0	0	0	1	2-0	0	5	.167	.211	.167	11	-4	1-0	.972	-2	93	0	2-17/S3	-0.6
Total	4	415	1268	154	317	50	5	7	92	66-3	4	180	.250	.288	.314	65	-63	19-9	.975	18	103	112	2-344/3-31,S-4	-2.1
BREMER, HERB Herbert Frederick B 10.26.1913 Chicago, IL D 11.28.1979 Columbus, GA BR/TR 6/195# d9.16																								
1937	StL N	11	33	2	7	1	0	0	3	2	0	4	.212	.257	.242	36	-3	0	.979	-0	*81*	*107*	C-10	-0.3
1938	StL N	50	151	14	33	5	1	2	14	9	0	36	.219	.262	.305	53	-10	1	.977	2	*91*	*123*	C-50	-0.6
1939	StL N	9	9	0	1	0	0	0	1	0	0	2	.111	.111	.111	-38	-2	0	1.000	0	*67*	*0*	/C-8	-0.2
Total	3	70	193	16	41	6	1	2	18	11	0	42	.212	.255	.285	45	-15	1	.979	2	*88*	*115*	/C-68	-1.1
BRENEGAN, SAM Olaf Selmar B 9.1.1890 Galesville, WI D 4.20.1956 Galesville, WI BL/TR 6-2/185# d4.24																								
1914	Pit N	1	0	0	0	0	0	0	0	0	0	0	—	—	—	—	0	0	—	-0	*0*	*0*	/C	0.0
BRENLY, BOB Robert Earl B 2.25.1954 Coshocton, OH BR/TR 6-2/210# d8.14 M3 C5																								
1981	SF N	19	45	5	15	2	1	1	4	6-0	1	4	.333	.423	.489	161	4	0-1	.964	-4	104	50	C-14/3-3,O(LF)	0.0
1982	SF N	65	180	26	51	4	1	4	15	18-4	1	26	.283	.348	.383	106	1	6-2	.961	-3	85	143	C-61/3	0.1
1983	SF N	104	281	36	63	12	2	7	34	37-6	2	48	.224	.317	.356	89	-4	10-7	.983	6	110	**132**	C-90,1-10/O-2(1-0-1)	0.5
1984	SF N★	145	506	74	147	28	0	20	80	48-3	3	52	.291	.352	.464	133	22	6-9	.986	-13	100	125	*C-127,1-22/O-3(1-0-2)	1.2
1985	SF N	133	440	41	97	16	1	19	56	57-5	2	62	.220	.311	.391	100	0	1-4	.984	-4	99	103	*C-110,3-17,1-10	-0.2
1986	SF N	149	472	60	116	26	0	16	62	74-10	3	97	.246	.350	.403	113	10	10-6	**.995**	2	126	121	*C-101,3-45,1-19	1.5
1987	†SF N	123	375	55	100	19	1	18	51	47-3	3	85	.267	.348	.467	121	11	10-7	.988	13	115	140	*C-108/1-6,3-2	2.7
1988	SF N	73	206	13	39	7	0	5	22	20-3	2	40	.189	.265	.296	64	-10	1-2	.984	-1	118	73	C-69	-0.8
1989	Tor A	48	88	9	15	3	1	1	6	10-0	0	17	.170	.255	.261	47	-6	1-0	.975	-3	53	81	D-28,C-13/1-5	-1.0
	SF N	12	22	2	4	2	0	0	3	1-1	0	7	.182	.208	.273	40	-2	0-0	1.000	0	278	39	C-12	-0.1
Total	9	871	2615	321	647	119	7	91	333	318-35	17	438	.247	.330	.403	107	26	45-38	.984	-7	109	118	C-705/1-72,3-68,D-28,O-6(3-0-3)	3.9
BRENNAN, JIM Jack (born John Gottlieb Dorn) B 1862 St.Louis, MO ?/155# d4.20																								
1884	StL U	56	231	38	50	6	1	0		12			.216	.255	.251	52	-20		.891	2			C-33,O-16(7-4-6)/3-7,S	-1.4
1885	StL N	3	10	0	1	0	0	0	1	1		1	.100	.182	.100	-7	-1		.750	-1	0	0	/O-2(LF),3	-0.2
1888	KC AA	34	118	5	20	2	0	0	6	3	2		.169	.203	.186	24	-10	3	.884	-2			C-25/O-5(2-1-2),3-5	-0.9
1889	Phi AA	31	113	12	25	4	0	0	15	10	0	15	.221	.285	.257	55	-6	1	.818	-2			C-13/O-7(0-4-3),2-7,3-4	-0.6
1890	Cle P	59	233	32	59	3	7	0	26	13	4	29	.253	.304	.326	74	-9	8	.845	-12	*70*	*104*	C-42,3-14/O-6(2-0-4)	-1.5
Total	5	183	705	87	155	15	8	0	48	39	6	45	.220	.267	.264	55	-46	12	.869	-15	*27*	*39*	C-113/O-36(13-9-15),3-31,2-7,S	-4.6
BRENZEL, BILL William Richard B 3.3.1910 Oakland, CA D 6.12.1979 Oakland, CA BR/TR 5-10/173# d4.13																								
1932	Pit N	9	24	0	1	1	0	0	2	0	0	4	.042	.042	.083	-69	-6	0	1.000	1	*89*	*46*	/C-9	-0.5
1934	Cle A	15	51	4	11	3	0	0	3	2	0	1	.216	.245	.275	33	-5	0-0	1.000	2	*112*	*103*	C-15	-0.3
1935	Cle A	52	142	12	31	5	1	0	14	6	0	10	.218	.250	.268	33	-15	2-2	.975	-4	*105*	*113*	C-51	-1.6
Total	3	76	217	16	43	9	1	0	19	8	0	15	.198	.227	.249	23	-26	2-2	.985	-2	*105*	*102*	/C-75	-2.4
BRESNAHAN, ROGER Roger Philip "The Duke Of Tralee" B 6.11.1879 Toledo, OH D 12.4.1944 Toledo, OH BR/TR 5-9/200# d8.27 M5 C6 HF1945 y OF Total (19-LF 221-CF 41-RF)																								
1897	Was N	6	16	1	6	0	0	0	3	1	0		.375	.412	.375	109	0	0	1.000	-1	75	0	/P-6,O(CF)	0.0
1900	Chi N	2	2	0	0	0	0	0	0	0	0		.000	.000	.000	-99	-1	0	—	-0	*0*	*0*	/C	-0.1
1901	Bal A	86	295	40	79	9	9	1	32	23	1		.268	.323	.369	88	-6	10	.919	-12	*98*	*85*	C-69/O-8(7-0-1),3-4,P-2,2-2	-1.1
1902	Bal A	65	235	30	64	8	6	4	34	21	2		.272	.337	.409	102	0	12	.880	-7	92	89	3-30,C-22,O-15(CF)	-0.5
	NY N	51	178	16	51	9	3	1	22	16	2		.287	.352	.388	130	6	6	.946	0	191	126	0-27(RF),C-16/1-4,S-4,3	0.8
1903	NY N	113	406	87	142	30	8	4	55	61	7		.350	.443	.493	161	36	34	.965	-0	122	235	0-84(4-79-1),1-13,C-11/3-4	3.1
1904	NY N	109	402	81	114	22	7	5	33	58	5		.284	.381	.410	138	21	13	.954	-1	123	314	0-93(7-81-5),1-10/S-4,23	1.6
1905	†NY N	104	331	58	100	18	3	0	46	50	11		.302	.411	.375	132	18	11	.970	8	***152***	*100*	C-87/O-8(0-2-4)	3.4
1906	NY N	124	405	69	114	22	4	0	43	81	**15**		.281	**.419**	.356	139	26	25	.974	6	*118*	***120***	C-82,O-40(0-39-3)	4.2
1907	NY N	110	328	57	83	9	7	4	38	61	6		.253	.380	.360	128	14	15	.986	-2	*125*	*81*	C-95/1-6,O-2(CF),3	2.3
1908	NY N	140	449	70	127	25	3	1	54	**83**	6		.283	.401	.359	136	25	14	.985	-5	*125*	*85*	*C-139	3.8
1909	StL N	72	234	27	57	4	1	0	23	46	1		.244	.370	.269	105	5	11	.960	-9	*74*	*118*	C-59/2-9,3M	0.1
1910	StL N	88	234	35	65	15	3	0	27	55	2	17	.278	.419	.368	135	15	13	.961	-15	*74*	*99*	C-77/O-2(1-1-0),PM	0.8
1911	StL N	81	227	22	63	17	8	3	41	45	3	19	.278	.404	.463	146	16	4	.968	-10	*76*	*110*	C-77/2-2,M	1.2
1912	StL N	48	108	8	36	7	2	1	15	14	2	9	.333	.419	.463	145	7	4	.974	2	*79*	*125*	C-28,M	1.1
1913	Chi N	69	162	20	37	5	2	1	21	21	2	11	.228	.324	.302	79	-4	7-1	.963	-2	109	98	C-58	0.0
1914	Chi N	101	248	42	69	10	4	0	24	49	2	20	.278	.401	.351	125	11	14	.978	-4	*88*	*101*	C-85,2-14/O(CF)	1.5
1915	Chi N	77	221	19	45	8	1	1	19	29	0	23	.204	.296	.262	70	-7	19-3	.982	1	*99*	*101*	C-68,M	0.3
Total	17	1446	4481	682	1252	218	71	26	530	714	67	99	.279	.386	.377	126	182	212-4	.971	-52	*106*	*99*	C-974,O-281C/3-42,1-33,2-28,P-9,S	22.5
BRESSLER, RUBE Raymond Bloom B 10.23.1894 Coder, PA D 11.7.1966 Cincinnati, OH BR/TL 6/187# d4.24 Mil 1918 ▲																								
1914	Phi A	29	51	6	11	1	1	0	4	6	1	7	.216	.310	.275	79	4	0	.941	-3	61	138	P-29	0.0
1915	Phi A	33	55	9	8	0	1	1	4	9	1	13	.145	.277	.236	56	1	0	.900	0	106	0	P-32	0.0
1916	Phi A	4	5	1	1	0	1	0	1	0	0	0	.200	.200	.600	147	1	0	1.000	-0	47	0	/P-4	0.0
1917	Cin N	3	5	0	1	0	0	0	0	0	0	2	.200	.200	.200	24	0	0	1.000	-0	39	0	/P-2	0.0

Year	Tm Lg	G	AB	R	H	2B	3B	HR	RBI	BB-IB	HP	SO	AVG	OBP	SLG	AOPS	ABR	SB-CS	FA	FR	Rng	Thr	G at Pos	BFW
1918	Cin N	23	62	10	17	5	0	0	6	5	0	4	.274	.328	.355	110	1	0	.982	3	137	152	P-17/O-3(3-0-1)	0.1
1919	Cin N	61	165	22	34	3	4	2	17	23	2	15	.206	.311	.309	89	-2	2	.965	1	111	63	O-48(41-0-7),P-13	-0.4
1920	Cin N	21	30	4	8	1	0	0	3	1	0	4	.267	.290	.300	71	-1	1-0	1.000	-1	109	502	P-10/O-3(0-1-2),1-2	-0.2
1921	Cin N	109	323	41	99	18	6	1	54	39	2	20	.307	.385	.409	115	9	5-5	.953	-5	100	56	O-85(9-0-76)/1-6	-0.3
1922	Cin N	52	53	7	14	0	2	0	8	4	0	4	.264	.316	.340	70	-3	1-0	1.000	-1	0	0	/1-3,O-2(1-0-1)	-0.3
1923	Cin N	54	119	25	33	3	1	0	18	20	4	4	.277	.399	.319	93	0	3-1	.983	-2	79	73	1-22/O-6(3-0-3)	-0.2
1924	Cin N	115	383	41	133	14	13	4	49	22	4	20	.347	.389	.483	134	17	9-10	.990	2	122	104	1-50,O-49(45-0-4)	1.0
1925	Cin N	97	319	43	111	17	6	4	61	40	2	16	.348	.424	.476	133	18	9-5	.982	-5	79	126	1-52,O-38(36-0-2)	0.7
1926	Cin N	86	297	58	106	15	9	1	51	37	3	20	.357	.433	.478	149	22	3	.970	-5	95	52	O-80(LF)/1-4	1.1
1927	Cin N	124	467	43	136	14	8	3	77	32	1	22	.291	.338	.375	94	-5	4	.972	5	104	132	*O-120(LF)	-0.9
1928	Bro N	145	501	78	148	29	13	4	70	80	5	33	.295	.398	.429	118	16	2	**.985**	-6	93	68	*O-137(LF)	-0.1
1929	Bro N	136	456	72	145	22	8	9	77	67	1	27	.318	.406	.461	117	14	4	.954	1	107	87	*O-122(LF)	0.5
1930	Bro N	109	335	53	100	12	8	3	52	51	2	19	.299	.394	.409	96	-1	4	.995	7	118	83	O-90(LF)/1-7	-0.1
1931	Bro N	67	153	22	43	4	5	0	26	11	0	10	.281	.329	.373	89	-3	0	.982	-2	91	58	O-35(23-7-3)/1	-0.6
1932	Phi N	27	83	9	19	6	1	0	6	2	0	5	.229	.247	.325	47	-6	0	1.000	3	110	360	O-18(LF)	-0.4
	StL N	10	19	0	3	0	0	0	2	0	0	1	.158	.158	.158	-14	-3	0	1.000	-0	104	0	/O-4(LF)	-0.3
	Year	37	102	9	22	6	1	0	8	2	0	6	.216	.231	.294	37	-9	0	1.000	3	109	298	O-22(LF)	-0.7
Total	19	1305	3881	544	1170	164	87	32	586	449	28	246	.301	.378	.413	110	79	47-21	.971	-8	102	85	O-840(732-8-99),1-147,P-107	-0.4
BRESSOUD, EDDIE Edward Francis B 5.2.1932 Los Angeles, CA BR/TR 6-1/175# d6.14																								
1956	NY N	49	163	15	37	4	2	0	9	12-1	1	20	.227	.284	.276	52	-11	1-0	.950	-8	92	90	S-48	-1.6
1957	NY N	49	127	11	34	2	2	5	10	4-1	2	19	.268	.299	.433	94	-2	0-1	.940	-1	105	88	S-33,3-12	-0.1
1958	SF N	66	137	19	36	5	3	0	8	14-1	0	22	.263	.331	.343	81	-4	0-1	.966	-4	93	87	2-57/3-6,S-4	-0.5
1959	SF N	104	315	36	79	17	2	9	26	28-6	0	55	.251	.311	.403	91	-5	0-0	.974	-7	96	72	S-92/123	-0.5
1960	SF N	116	386	37	87	19	6	9	43	35-12	2	72	.225	.290	.376	87	-8	1-2	.960	0	101	82	*S-115	0.1
1961	SF N	59	114	14	24	6	0	3	11	11-4	0	23	.211	.276	.342	66	-6	1-1	.964	-7	78	76	S-34/3-3,2	-1.1
1962	Bos A	153	599	79	166	40	9	14	68	46-4	2	118	.277	.329	.444	103	2	2-3	.965	25	**110**	107	*S-153	3.9
1963	Bos A	140	497	61	129	23	6	20	60	52-2	2	93	.260	.329	.451	113	9	1-1	.962	-13	88	93	*S-137	0.8
1964	Bos A☆	158	566	86	166	41	3	15	55	72-4	1	99	.293	.372	.456	123	21	1-1	.972	-7	93	78	*S-158	2.8
1965	Bos A	107	296	29	67	11	1	8	25	29-4	1	77	.226	.297	.351	79	-8	0-1	.963	-0	93	100	S-86/3-2,O(LF)	-0.2
1966	NY N	133	405	48	91	15	5	10	49	47-4	1	107	.225	.304	.360	87	-7	2-2	.960	10	107	106	S-94,3-32/1-9,2-7	1.0
1967	†StL N	52	67	8	9	1	1	1	1	9-1	0	18	.134	.237	.224	33	-6	0-0	.929	-4	89	106	S-48/3	-0.9
Total	12	1186	3672	443	925	184	40	94	365	359-44	12	723	.252	.319	.401	96	-25	9-13	.963	-17	97	91	*S-1002/2-66,3-57,1-10,O(LF)	3.7
BRETON, JIM John Frederick B 7.15.1891 Chicago, IL D 5.30.1973 Beloit, WI BR/TR 5-10.5/178# d8.25																								
1913	Chi A	12	30	1	5	1	1	0	2	1	0	5	.167	.194	.267	35	-3	0	.938	2	152	112	/S-7,3-3	0.0
1914	Chi A	81	231	21	49	7	2	0	24	24	2	42	.212	.292	.260	67	-9	9-6	.910	0	107	63	3-79	-0.7
1915	Chi A	16	36	3	5	1	0	0	1	5	1	9	.139	.262	.167	27	-3	2-1	.882	-2	74	126	3-14/2S	-0.5
Total	3	109	297	25	59	9	3	0	27	30	3	56	.199	.279	.249	59	-15	11-7	.906	1	103	69	/3-96,S-8,2	-1.2
BRETT, GEORGE George Howard B 5.15.1953 Glen Dale, WV BL/TR 6/200# d8.2 HF1999 b-Ken OF Total (22-LF 14-RF)																								
1973	KC A	13	40	2	5	2	0	0	0	0-0	0	5	.125	.125	.175	-15	-6	0-0	.974	2	126	88	3-13	-0.4
1974	KC A	133	457	49	129	21	5	2	47	21-3	0	38	.282	.313	.363	89	-7	8-5	.948	-7	102	56	*3-132/S	-1.6
1975	KC A	159	634	84	**195**	35	**13**	11	89	46-6	2	49	.308	.353	.456	125	19	13-10	.949	2	104	86	*3-159/S	2.0
1976	†KC A★	159	645	94	**215**	34	**14**	7	67	49-4	1	36	**.333**	.377	.462	145	35	21-11	.948	3	103	86	*3-157/S-4	4.1
1977	†KC A★	139	564	105	176	32	13	22	88	55-9	2	24	.312	.373	.532	143	33	14-12	.957	18	114	**137**	*3-135/SD	4.6
1978	†KC A★	128	510	79	150	**45**	8	9	62	39-6	1	35	.294	.342	.467	123	16	23-7	.961	4	104	108	*3-128/S	2.0
1979	KC A★	154	645	119	**212**	42	**20**	23	107	51-14	0	36	.329	.376	.563	147	40	17-10	.944	14	114	99	*3-149/1-8,D	4.9
1980	†KC A✶	117	449	87	175	33	9	24	118	58-16	1	22	**.390**	**.454**	**.664**	**203**	**65**	15-6	.955	4	106	123	*3-112/1	**6.6**
1981	†KC A★	89	347	42	109	27	7	6	43	27-7	1	23	.314	.361	.484	144	19	14-6	.946	-10	91	46	3-88	1.0
1982	KC A★	144	552	101	166	32	9	21	82	71-14	1	51	.301	.378	.505	141	32	6-1	.959	-7	96	83	*3-134,O-12(LF)	2.3
1983	KC A★	123	464	90	144	38	2	25	93	57-13	1	39	.310	.385	**.563**	157	38	0-1	.919	-16	87	117	*3-102,1-14,O-13(6-0-7)/D	1.8
1984	†KC A★	104	377	42	107	21	3	13	69	38-6	0	37	.284	.344	.459	121	11	0-2	.949	4	110	114	*3-101	1.2
1985	†KC A★	155	550	108	184	38	5	30	112	103-**31**	3	49	.335	.436	**.585**	**178**	**65**	9-1	.967	5	105	116	*3-152/D	6.7
1986	KC A✶	124	441	70	128	28	4	16	73	80-**18**	4	45	.290	.401	.481	137	27	1-2	.952	-1	99	88	*3-115/S-2,D-7	2.3
1987	KC A	115	427	71	124	18	2	22	78	72-14	1	47	.290	.388	.496	131	21	6-3	.993	-3	88	101	1-83,D-21,3-11	1.2
1988	KC A★	157	589	90	180	42	3	24	103	82-15	3	51	.306	.389	.509	149	42	14-3	.992	-7	81	102	*1-124,D-33/S	2.7
1989	KC A	124	457	67	129	26	3	12	80	59-14	3	47	.282	.362	.431	125	17	14-4	.998	4	106	82	*1-104,D-17/O-2(LF)	1.4
1990	KC A	142	544	82	179	**45**	7	14	87	56-14	0	63	**.329**	.387	.515	154	40	9-2	.993	-3	86	98	*1-102,D-32/O-9(2-0-7),3	3.0
1991	KC A	131	505	77	129	40	2	10	61	58-10	0	75	.255	.327	.402	102	2	2-0	.989	-1	69	72	*D-118,1-10	-0.3
1992	KC A	152	592	55	169	35	5	7	61	35-6	6	69	.285	.330	.397	101	0	8-6	.987	-0	109	70	*D-132,1-15/3-3	-0.6
1993	KC A	145	560	69	149	31	3	19	75	39-9	3	67	.266	.312	.434	94	-6	7-5	—	0	0	0	*D-140	-1.5
Total	21	2707	10349	1583	3154	665	137	317	1595	1096-229	33	908	.305	.369	.487	135	503	201-97	.951	4	103	98	*3-1692,D-506,1-461/O-36L,S-11	43.4
BREWER, TONY Anthony Bruce B 11.25.1957 Coushatta, LA BR/TR 5-11/190# d8.1 b-Mike																								
1984	LA N	24	37	3	4	1	0	1	4	4-1	0	9	.108	.195	.216	16	-4	1-0	1.000	-1	72	0	O-10(8-0-2)	-0.6
BREWER, MIKE Michael Quinn B 10.24.1959 Shreveport, LA BR/TR 6-5/190# d6.11 b-Tony																								
1986	KC A	12	18	0	3	1	0	0	0	2-0	0	6	.167	.250	.222	29	-2	0-1	1.000	-1	85	0	/O-9(RF),D	-0.3
BREWER, ROD Rodney Lee B 2.24.1966 Eustis, FL BL/TL 6-3/210# d9.5																								
1990	StL N	14	25	4	6	1	0	0	2	0-0	0	4	.240	.240	.280	42	-2	0-0	.981	1	167	143	/1-9	-0.2
1991	StL N	19	13	0	1	0	0	0	1	0-0	0	5	.077	.077	.077	-56	-3	0-0	1.000	0	107	86	1-15/O-3(RF)	-0.3
1992	StL N	29	103	11	31	6	0	0	10	8-0	1	12	.301	.354	.359	107	1	0-1	1.000	1	102	102	1-27/O-4(LF)	0.0
1993	StL N	110	147	15	42	8	0	2	20	17-5	1	26	.286	.359	.381	102	1	1-0	.960	-2	103	57	O-33(15-0-19),1-32/P	-0.3
Total	4	172	288	30	80	15	0	2	33	25-5	2	47	.278	.336	.351	92	-3	1-1	.995	-0	100	117	/1-83,O-40(19-0-22),P	-0.8
BREWSTER, CHARLIE Charles Lawrence B 12.27.1916 Marthaville, LA D 10.1.2000 Alma, GA BR/TR 5-8.5/175# d5.2																								
1943	Cin N	7	8	0	1	0	0	0	0	0	0	1	.125	.125	.125	-28	-1	0	1.000	-0	72	177	/2-2	-0.1
	Phi N	49	159	13	35	2	0	0	12	10	2	19	.220	.275	.233	49	-11	1	.901	-18	79	70	S-46	-2.7
	Year	56	167	13	36	2	0	0	12	10	2	20	.216	.268	.228	45	-12	1	.901	-18	79	70	S-46/2-2	-2.8
1944	Chi N	10	44	4	11	2	0	0	2	5	0	7	.250	.327	.295	76	-1	0	.903	-1	86	148	S-10	-0.1
1946	Cle A	3	2	0	0	0	0	0	0	1	0	1	.000	.333	.000	-1	0	0-0	1.000	0	151	0	/S	0.0
Total	3	69	213	17	47	4	0	0	14	16	2	28	.221	.281	.239	52	-13	1-0	.902	-18	81	85	/S-57,2-2	-2.9
BRICKELL, FRITZ Fritz Darrell B 3.19.1935 Wichita, KS D 10.15.1965 Wichita, KS BR/TR 5-5.5/157# d4.30 f-Fred																								
1958	NY A	2	0	0	0	0	0	0	0	0-0	0	0	—	—	—	—	0	0-0	1.000	0	165	0	/2-2	0.0
1959	NY A	18	39	4	10	1	0	1	4	1-0	0	10	.256	.275	.359	75	-2	0-0	.925	-1	108	46	S-15/2-3	-0.1
1961	LA A	21	49	3	6	0	0	0	3	6-0	0	9	.122	.218	.122	-6	-7	0-0	.901	-1	84	120	S-17	-0.7
Total	3	41	88	7	16	1	0	1	7	7-0	0	19	.182	.242	.227	26	-9	0-0	.911	-2	94	88	/S-32,2-5	-0.8
BRICKELL, FRED George Frederick B 11.9.1906 Saffordville, KS D 4.8.1961 Wichita, KS BL/TR 5-7/160# d8.19 s-Fritz																								
1926	Pit N	24	55	11	19	3	1	0	4	3	2	6	.345	.400	.436	119	2	0	.920	1	88	279	O-14(LF)	0.2
1927	†Pit N	32	21	6	6	1	0	1	4	1	0	0	.286	.318	.476	103	0	0	1.000	0	208	0	/O-3(0-1-2)	0.0
1928	Pit N	81	202	34	65	4	4	3	41	20	0	18	.322	.383	.426	107	2	5	.958	3	108	157	O-50(44-0-8)	0.1
1929	Pit N	60	118	13	37	4	2	0	17	7	0	12	.314	.352	.381	80	-4	3	1.000	2	110	151	O-27(14-0-13)	-0.3
1930	Pit N	68	219	36	65	9	3	1	14	15	0	20	.297	.342	.379	74	-9	3	.951	-1	102	73	O-61(11-50-0)	-1.1
	Phi N	53	240	33	59	12	6	0	17	13	2	21	.246	.290	.346	49	-20	1	.963	2	104	135	O-53(CF)	-1.9
	Year	121	459	69	124	21	9	1	31	28	2	41	.270	.315	.362	61	-30	4	.958	1	103	105	*O-114(11-103-0)	-3.0
1931	Phi N	130	514	77	130	14	5	1	31	42	5	39	.253	.316	.305	63	-26	5	.978	0	103	79	*O-122(CF)	-3.0
1932	Phi N	45	66	9	22	6	1	0	2	4	2	5	.333	.389	.455	112	2	2	.935	1	99	230	O-12(1-11-0)	0.2
1933	Phi N	8	13	2	4	1	1	0	1	1	0	0	.308	.357	.538	136	1	0	1.000	1	130	354	/O-4(LF)	0.1
Total	8	501	1448	221	407	54	23	6	131	106	11	121	.281	.335	.363	75	-52	19	.967	9	104	119	O-346(88-237-23)	-5.7
BRICKLEY, GEORGE George Vincent B 7.19.1894 Everett, MA D 2.23.1947 Everett, MA BR/TR 5-9/180# d9.26																								
1913	Phi A	5	12	0	2	0	1	0	0	0	1	4	.167	.231	.333	66	-1	0	1.000	-0	66	0	/O-4(RF)	-0.1

Year	Tm Lg	G	AB	R	H	2B	3B	HR	RBI	BB-IB	HP	SO	AVG	OBP	SLG	AOPS	ABR	SB-CS	FA	FR	Rng	Thr	G at Pos	BFW
BRIDEWESER, JIM James Ehrenfeld B 2.13.1927 Lancaster, OH D 8.25.1989 ElToro, CA BR/TR 6/165# d9.29																								
1951	NY A	2	8	1	3	0	0	0	0	0	0	1	.375	.375	.375	107	0	0-0	.818	-0	87	225	/S-2	0.0
1952	NY A	42	38	12	10	0	0	0	2	3	0	5	.263	.317	.263	67	-2	0-0	.935	1	132	94	S-22/2-4,3	-0.1
1953	NY A	7	3	3	3	0	1	0	3	1	0	0	1.000	1.000	1.667	631	2	0-0	.833	-0	0	0	/S-3	0.2
1954	Bal A	73	204	18	54	7	2	0	12	15	1	27	.265	.317	.319	81	-6	1-1	.944	-8	95	89	S-48,2-19	-1.0
1955	Chi A	34	58	6	12	3	2	0	4	3-0	0	7	.207	.246	.328	52	-4	0-0	.949	3	108	142	S-26/3-3,2-2	0.0
1956	Chi A	10	11	0	2	1	0	0	1	0-0	1	3	.182	.250	.273	37	-1	0-0	.938	-0	110	50	S-10	-0.1
	Det A	70	156	23	34	4	0	0	10	20-2	0	19	.218	.307	.244	47	-12	3-1	.987	6	113	117	S-32,2-31/3-4	-0.2
	Year	80	167	23	36	5	0	0	11	20-2	1	22	.216	.303	.246	46	-13	3-1	.979	5	112	105	S-42,2-31/3-4	-0.3
1957	Bal A	91	142	16	38	7	1	1	18	21-2	0	16	.268	.362	.352	102	1	2-0	.943	-0	98	112	S-74/3-3,2	0.5
Total	7	329	620	79	156	22	6	1	50	63-4	2	78	.252	.322	.311	75	-22	6-2	.946	-0	101	108	S-217/2-57,3-11	-0.7
BRIDGES, ROCKY Everett Lamar B 8.7.1927 Refugio, TX BR/TR 5-8/175# d4.17 C7																								
1951	Bro N	63	134	13	34	7	0	1	15	10	0	10	.254	.306	.328	69	-6	0-0	.871	-1	98	148	3-40,2-10/S-9	-0.6
1952	Bro N	51	56	9	11	3	0	0	2	7	0	9	.196	.286	.250	49	-4	0-1	.986	6	112	162	2-24,S-13/3-6	0.3
1953	Cin N	122	432	52	98	13	2	1	21	37	0	42	.227	.288	.273	47	-34	6-3	.976	14	106	**122**	*2-115/S-6,3-3	-1.1
1954	Cin N	53	52	4	12	1	0	0	2	7	0	7	.231	.322	.250	50	-4	0-1	1.000	6	122	73	S-20,2-19,3-13	0.3
1955	Cin N	95	168	20	48	4	0	1	18	15-2	0	19	.286	.341	.327	75	-6	1-1	.965	4	106	95	3-59,S-26/2-9	-0.1
1956	Cin N	71	19	9	4	0	0	0	1	4-0	0	3	.211	.348	.211	52	-1	1-2	.966	3	97	85	3-51/2-8,S-7,O(LF)	0.2
1957	Cin N	5	1	1	0	0	0	0	0	1-0	0	1	.000	.500	.000	46	0	0-0	1.000	-1	0	0	/2-2,S3	-0.1
	Was A	120	391	40	89	17	2	3	47	40-4	2	32	.228	.298	.304	67	-17	0-2	.971	23	111	93	*S-108,2-14/3	1.5
1958	Was A☆	116	377	38	99	14	3	5	28	27-1	3	32	.263	.315	.355	86	-8	0-3	.976	9	105	97	*S-112/2-3,3-3	1.0
1959	Det A	116	381	38	102	16	3	3	35	30-2	1	35	.268	.320	.349	80	-10	1-2	.952	-1	93	**110**	*S-110/2-5	-0.3
1960	Det A	10	5	0	1	0	0	0	0	0-0	0	0	.200	.200	.200	8	-1	0-0	1.000	2	143	0	/3-7,S-3	0.1
	Cle A	10	27	1	9	0	0	0	3	1-1	0	2	.333	.357	.333	91	0	0-0	1.000	1	122	78	/S-7,3-3	0.1
	Year	20	32	1	10	0	0	0	3	1-1	0	2	.313	.333	.313	76	-1	0-0	1.000	2	114	108	3-10,S-10	0.2
	StL N	3	0	0	0	0	0	0	0	0-0	0	0	—	—	—	—	0	0-0	1.000	1	64	288	/2-3	0.1
1961	LA A	84	229	20	55	5	1	2	15	26-0	1	37	.240	.320	.297	59	-13	1-0	.988	9	110	67	2-58,S-25/3-4	0.2
Total	11	919	2272	245	562	80	11	16	187	205-10	7	229	.247	.310	.313	67	-104	10-15	.968	74	104	99	S-447,2-270,3-191/O(LF)	1.6
BRIDWELL, AL Albert Henry B 1.4.1884 Friendship, OH D 1.23.1969 Portsmouth, OH BL/TR 5-9/170# d4.16 OF Total (3-LF 2-CF 14-RF)																								
1905	Cin N	82	254	17	64	3	1	0	17	19	2		.252	.309	.272	66	-10	8	.944	4	105	122	3-43,O-18(3-2-13)/2-7,S-5,1	-0.6
1906	Bos N	120	459	41	104	9	1	0	22	44	2		.227	.297	.251	73	-14	6	.930	18	104	101	*S-119/O(RF)	0.9
1907	Bos N	140	509	49	111	8	2	0	26	61	6		.218	.309	.242	73	-13	17	**.942**	5	102	111	*S-140	-0.5
1908	NY N	147	467	53	133	14	1	0	46	52	6		.285	.364	.319	113	10	20	.933	9	103	98	*S-147	2.7
1909	NY N	145	476	59	140	11	5	0	55	67	4		.294	.386	.338	123	16	32	.940	2	99	115	*S-145	2.5
1910	NY N	142	492	74	136	15	7	0	48	73	4	23	.276	.374	.335	107	8	14	.946	4	95	96	*S-141	1.7
1911	NY N	76	263	28	71	10	1	0	31	33	3	10	.270	.358	.316	86	-3	8	.917	5	104	96	S-76	0.6
	Bos N	51	182	29	53	5	0	0	10	33	1	8	.291	.403	.319	95	1	2	.950	-4	100	83	S-51	0.0
	Year	127	445	57	124	15	1	0	41	66	4	18	.279	.377	.317	90	-2	10	.929	0	102	91	*S-127	0.6
1912	Bos N	31	106	6	25	5	1	0	14	5	0	5	.236	.270	.302	55	-7	2	.936	-5	89	112	S-31	-1.0
1913	Chi N	136	405	35	97	6	6	1	37	74	1	28	.240	.358	.291	87	-4	12-16	.948	3	100	96	*S-136	0.5
1914	StL F	117	381	46	90	6	5	1	33	71	2	18	.236	.359	.286	73	-17	9	.944	-4	96	96	*S-103,2-11	-1.4
1915	StL F	65	175	20	40	3	2	0	9	25	1	6	.229	.328	.269	65	-10	6	.952	1	104	76	2-42,3-15/1	-0.9
Total	11	1252	4169	457	1064	95	32	2	348	557	32	98	.255	.347	.295	89	-43	136-16	.939	36	100	102	*S-1094/2-60,3-58,O-19R,1-2	4.5
BRIEF, BUNNY Anthony Vincent (born Anthony John Grzeszkowski) B 7.3.1892 Remus, MI D 2.10.1963 Milwaukee, WI BR/TR 6/185# d9.22																								
1912	StL A	15	42	9	13	3	0	0	5	6	1		.310	.408	.381	131	2	2	.826	-1	109	0	/O-9(LF),1-4	0.1
1913	StL A	85	258	24	56	11	6	1	26	21	3	46	.217	.284	.318	78	-8	3	.986	-1	93	122	1-62/O-8(LF)	-1.2
1915	Chi A	48	154	13	33	6	2	2	17	16	4	28	.214	.305	.318	84	-3	8-6	.986	-2	86	104	1-46	-0.7
1917	Pit N	36	115	15	25	5	1	2	11	15	2	21	.217	.318	.330	96	0	4	.988	2	121	107	1-34	0.1
Total	4	184	569	61	127	25	9	5	59	58	10	95	.223	.306	.325	87	-9	17-6	.987	-3	98	114	1-146/O-17(LF)	-1.7
BRIGGS, CHARLIE Charles R. B 9.1860 Batavia, IL D 3.10.1920 Seattle, WA 5-7/170# d5.2																								
1884	CP U	49	182	29	31	8	2	1		11			.170	.218	.253	42	-18		.814	-6	69	79	O-37(3-28-6),2-12/S-2	-2.2
BRIGGS, DAN Dan Lee B 11.18.1952 Scotia, CA BL/TL 6/180# d9.10																								
1975	Cal A	13	31	3	7	1	0	1	3	2-0	0	6	.226	.273	.355	82	-1	0-2	.953	-1	36	111	/1-6,O-5(LF),D-2	-0.3
1976	Cal A	77	248	19	53	13	2	1	14	13-3	1	47	.214	.254	.294	65	-12	0-3	.993	1	101	122	1-44,O-40(2-32-9)/D	-1.7
1977	Cal A	59	74	6	12	2	0	1	4	8-1	0	14	.162	.241	.230	31	-7	0-0	.993	0	110	75	1-45,O-13(0-12-1)	-0.8
1978	Cle A	15	49	4	8	0	1	1	1	4-0	0	9	.163	.226	.265	38	-4	0-0	1.000	2	120	90	O-15(RF)	-0.4
1979	SD N	104	227	34	47	4	3	8	30	18-5	5	45	.207	.277	.357	77	-9	2-1	.986	5	137	72	1-50,O-44(25-16-3)	-0.7
1981	Mon N	9	11	0	1	0	0	0	0	0-0	0	3	.091	.091	.091	-48	-2	0-1	1.000	0	161	81	/1-3,O-3(1-2-1)	-0.3
1982	Chi N	48	48	1	6	0	0	0	1	0-0	1	9	.125	.143	.125	-24	-8	0-0	.875	1	77	800	O-10(8-1-1)/1-4	-0.8
Total	7	325	688	67	134	20	6	12	53	45-9	7	133	.195	.249	.294	56	-43	2-7	.989	8	114	94	1-152,O-130(41-63-30)/D-3	-5.0
BRIGGS, GRANT Grant B 3.16.1865 Pittsburgh, PA D 5.31.1928 Pittsburgh, PA 5-11/170# d4.17																								
1890	Syr AA	86	316	44	57	6	5	0	21	16	1		.180	.222	.231	37	-26	7	.928	-10	*78*	*101*	C-46,O-33(4-25-4)/3-5,S-4	-2.9
1891	Lou AA	1	4	0	1	0	0	0	0	0	0	0	.250	.250	.250	44	0	0	1.000	-0	*79*	*103*	/C	0.0
1892	StL N	22	55	2	4	1	0	0	1	5	1	14	.073	.164	.091	-24	-8	2	.902	-8	*96*	*81*	C-15/O-8(2-1-5)	-1.5
1895	Lou N	1	3	0	0	0	0	0	0	0	0	1	.000	.000	.000	-99	-1	0	1.000	-0	*108*	*0*	/C	-0.1
Total	4	110	378	46	62	7	5	0	22	21	2	15	.164	.212	.209	27	-35	9	.925	-19	*82*	*96*	/C-63,O-41(6-26-9),3-5,S-4	-4.5
BRIGGS, JOHNNY John Edward B 3.10.1944 Paterson, NJ BL/TL 6-1/195# d4.17																								
1964	Phi N	61	66	16	17	2	0	1	6	9-0	0	12	.258	.347	.333	94	0	1-1	.957	1	113	163	O-19(9-9-1)/1	0.0
1965	Phi N	93	229	47	54	9	4	4	23	42-1	0	44	.236	.349	.362	104	3	3-2	.982	-4	90	63	O-66(4-62-0)	-0.3
1966	Phi N	81	255	43	72	13	5	10	23	41-3	0	55	.282	.380	.490	140	15	3-2	.977	-6	86	67	O-69(2-68-0)	0.8
1967	Phi N	106	332	47	77	12	4	9	30	41-1	0	72	.232	.315	.373	96	-2	3-5	.979	-2	103	40	O-94(31-65-1)	-0.8
1968	Phi N	110	338	36	86	13	1	7	31	58-4	1	72	.254	.364	.361	119	11	8-5	.968	-3	98	24	O-65(10-34-21),1-36	0.3
1969	Phi N	124	361	51	86	20	3	12	46	64-3	0	78	.238	.351	.410	116	10	9-6	.971	4	112	107	*O-108(76-32-12)/1-2	0.9
1970	Phi N	110	341	43	92	15	7	9	47	39-5	0	65	.270	.342	.434	110	4	5-4	.980	7	120	113	O-95(79-11-15)	0.6
1971	Phi N	10	22	3	4	1	0	0	3	6-1	0	2	.182	.357	.227	69	-1	0-0	.846	-0	89	246	/O-8(LF)	-0.1
	Mil A	125	375	51	99	11	1	21	59	71-7	1	79	.264	.378	.467	141	22	1-2	.958	5	113	127	O-65(55-0-11),1-60	2.0
1972	Mil A	135	418	58	111	14	1	21	65	54-4	1	67	.266	.347	.455	141	21	1-2	.980	0	104	82	*O-106(98-12-0),1-28	1.5
1973	Mil A	142	488	78	120	20	7	18	57	87-6	2	83	.246	.361	.426	124	18	15-9	.968	3	101	90	*O-137(LF)/D	1.3
1974	Mil A	154	554	72	140	30	8	17	73	71-2	0	102	.253	.337	.428	120	14	9-7	.973	0	98	91	*O-149(148-1-0)/D-2	0.6
1975	Mil A	28	74	12	22	1	0	3	5	20-0	0	13	.297	.447	.432	149	6	0-2	.962	2	110	204	O-21(LF)/D	0.7
	Min A	87	264	44	61	9	2	7	39	60-10	0	41	.231	.371	.360	106	5	6-2	.983	9	165	97	1-49,O-35(20-0-17)/D-2	0.9
	Year	115	338	56	83	10	2	10	44	80-10	0	54	.246	.388	.376	116	11	6-4	.983	11	108	134	O-56(41-0-17),1-49/D-3	1.6
Total	12	1366	4117	601	1041	170	43	139	507	663-47	5	785	.253	.355	.416	121	126	64-49	.973	16	103	87	*O-1037(698-294-78),1-176/D-6	8.4
BRIGHT, HARRY Harry James B 9.22.1929 Kansas City, MO D 3.13.2000 Sacramento, CA BR/TR 6/190# d8.7																								
1958	Pit N	15	24	4	6	1	0	1	3	1-0	0	6	.250	.269	.417	84	-1	0-0	1.000	0	112	0	/3-7	-0.1
1959	Pit N	40	48	4	12	1	0	3	8	5-0	0	10	.250	.321	.458	105	0	0-0	1.000	-1	81	0	/O-4(3-0-1),3-3,2	-0.1
1960	Pit N	4	4	0	0	0	0	0	0	0-0	0	2	.000	.000	.000	-99	-1	0-0	—	0			H	-0.1
1961	Was A	72	183	20	44	6	0	4	21	19-1	0	23	.240	.310	.339	75	-7	0-2	.928	5	116	164	3-40/C-8,2	-0.2
1962	Was A	113	392	55	107	15	4	17	67	26-0	2	51	.273	.319	.462	109	3	2-1	.989	1	109	107	1-99/C-3,3	-0.2
1963	Cin N	1	1	0	0	0	0	0	0	0-0	0	1	.000	.000	.000	-97	0	0-0	1.000	-0	0	0	/1	0.0
	†NY A	60	157	15	37	7	0	7	23	13-1	1	31	.236	.297	.414	98	-1	0-0	.985	-4	42	159	1-35,3-12	-0.7
1964	NY A	4	5	0	1	0	0	0	0	1-0	0	1	.200	.333	.200	52	0	0-0	1.000	-0	0	0	/1-2	-0.1
1965	Chi N	27	25	1	7	1	0	0	4	0-0	0	8	.280	.269	.320	67	-1	0-0	—	0			H	-0.1
Total	8	336	839	99	214	31	4	32	126	65-2	3	133	.255	.309	.416	96	-8	2-3	.988	1	93	118	1-137/3-63,C-11,O-4(3-0-1),2-2	-1.6
BRILEY, GREG Gregory "Peewee" B 5.24.1965 Greenville, NC BL/TR 5-8/165# d6.27																								
1988	Sea A	13	36	6	9	2	0	1	4	5-1	0	6	.250	.333	.389	100	0	0-1	.929	-2	64	0	O-11(LF)	-0.3
1989	Sea A	115	394	52	105	22	4	13	52	39-1	5	82	.266	.336	.442	115	8	11-5	.958	1	96	92	*O-105(96-0-10),2-10/D-2	0.7

Year	Tm Lg	G	AB	R	H	2B	3B	HR	RBI	BB-IB	HP	SO	AVG	OBP	SLG	AOPS	ABR	SB-CS	FA	FR	Rng	Thr	G at Pos	BFW
1990	Sea A	125	337	40	83	18	2	5	29	37-0	1	48	.246	.319	.356	89	-5	16-4	.989	-1	100	67	*O-107(43-0-67)/D-4	-0.6
1991	Sea A	139	381	39	99	17	3	2	26	27-0	0	51	.260	.307	.336	78	-12	23-11	.980	-4	93	82	*O-125(94-4-46)/23D	-1.8
1992	Sea A	86	200	18	55	10	0	5	12	4-0	1	31	.275	.290	.400	92	-3	9-2	.967	-5	89	56	O-42(27-13-4),D-12/2-4,3-4	-0.8
1993	Fla N	120	170	17	33	6	0	3	12	12-0	1	42	.194	.250	.282	40	-15	6-2	.986	1	107	80	O-67(32-1-36)	-1.5
Total	6	598	1518	172	384	75	9	29	135	124-2	8	260	.253	.310	.372	88	-27	65-25	.975	-10	96	76	O-457(303-18-163)/D-20,2-15,3-5	-4.3
BRINKER, BILL William Hutchinson "Dode" B 8.30.1883 Warrensburg, MO D 2.5.1965 Arcadia, CA BB/TR 6-1/190# d4.24																								
1912	Phi N	9	18	1	4	1	0	0	2	2	0	3	.222	.300	.278	55	-1	0	.778	-1	84	0	/3-2,O-2(1-1-0)	-0.2
BRINKMAN, CHUCK Charles Ernest B 9.16.1944 Cincinnati, OH BR/TR 6-1/185# d7.10 b-Ed																								
1969	Chi A	14	15	2	1	0	0	0	0	1-0	0	5	.067	.125	.067	-43	-3	0-0	1.000	-1	103	57	C-14	-0.4
1970	Chi A	9	20	4	5	1	0	0	0	3-0	0	3	.250	.348	.300	77	0	0-0	.974	0	303	101	/C-9	0.0
1971	Chi A	15	20	0	4	0	0	0	1	3-1	0	5	.200	.304	.200	44	-1	0-0	1.000	-2	33	196	C-14	-0.3
1972	Chi A	35	52	1	7	0	0	0	0	4-0	0	7	.135	.196	.135	-0	-6	0-0	.985	3	80	150	C-33	-0.3
1973	Chi A	63	139	13	26	6	0	1	10	11-0	1	37	.187	.252	.252	41	-11	0-0	.987	4	105	114	C-63	-0.5
1974	Chi A	8	14	1	2	0	0	0	0	1-0	0	3	.143	.200	.143	-0	-2	0-0	1.000	-2	73	57	/C-8	-0.4
	Pit N	4	7	1	1	0	0	0	1	0-0	0	0	.143	.125	.143	-21	-1	0-0	1.000	-1	157	0	/C-4	-0.2
Total	6	148	267	22	46	7	0	1	12	23-1	1	60	.172	.240	.210	28	-24	0-0	.988	1	109	117	/C-145	-2.1
BRINKMAN, ED Edwin Albert B 12.8.1941 Cincinnati, OH BR/TR 6/170# d9.6 C8 b-Chuck																								
1961	Was A	4	11	0	1	0	0	0	0	1-0	0	1	.091	.167	.091	-30	-2	0-0	.889	0	113	181	/3-3	-0.2
1962	Was A	54	133	8	22	7	1	0	4	11-0	0	28	.165	.228	.233	25	-14	1-0	.942	-2	89	104	S-38,3-10	-1.4
1963	Was A	145	514	44	117	20	3	7	45	31-4	4	86	.228	.276	.319	67	-24	5-3	.950	4	110	109	*S-143	-0.7
1964	Was A	132	447	54	100	20	3	8	34	26-1	4	99	.224	.271	.336	68	-20	2-2	.969	-0	103	102	*S-125	-1.0
1965	Was A	154	444	35	82	13	2	5	35	38-7	2	82	.185	.251	.257	46	-32	1-2	.964	-2	94	92	*S-150	-2.5
1966	Was A	158	582	42	133	18	9	7	48	29-4	0	105	.229	.263	.326	70	-25	7-9	.965	10	108	95	*S-158	-0.3
1967	Was A	109	320	21	60	9	2	1	18	24-1	4	58	.188	.252	.237	47	-21	1-3	**.979**	2	**108**	99	*S-109	-1.2
1968	Was A	77	193	12	36	3	0	0	6	19-5	0	31	.187	.259	.202	43	-13	0-0	.967	-4	105	74	S-74/2-2,O(LF)	-1.4
1969	Was A	151	576	71	153	18	5	2	43	50-3	5	42	.266	.328	.325	88	-9	2-2	.976	20	113	104	*S-150	2.9
1970	Was A	158	625	63	164	17	2	1	40	60-0	5	41	.262	.330	.301	79	-17	8-9	.974	**31**	**117**	105	*S-157	3.3
1971	Det A	159	527	40	120	18	2	1	37	44-7	7	54	.228	.293	.275	60	-27	1-4	.980	4	102	94	*S-159	-0.5
1972	†Det A	**156**	516	42	105	19	1	6	49	38-9	3	51	.203	.259	.279	59	-26	0-0	**.990**	2	98	89	*S-156	-0.6
1973	Det A★	**162**	515	55	122	16	4	7	40	34-1	1	79	.237	.284	.324	67	-24	0-1	.968	-17	90	89	*S-162	-2.2
1974	Det A	153	502	55	111	15	3	14	54	29-0	3	71	.221	.266	.347	73	-19	2-0	.972	6	101	92	*S-151/3-2	0.6
1975	StL N	28	75	6	18	4	0	1	6	7-2	1	10	.240	.306	.333	77	-2	0-0	.948	0	97	108	S-24	0.0
	Tex A	1	2	0	0	0	0	0	0	0-0	0	1	.000	.000	.000	-99	-1	0-0	1.000	-0	82	0	/3	-0.1
	NY A	44	63	2	11	4	1	0	2	3-0	1	6	.175	.224	.270	40	-5	0-0	.933	-6	84	112	S-39/2-3,3-3	-0.9
	Year	45	65	2	11	4	1	0	2	3-0	1	7	.169	.217	.262	35	-6	0-0	.933	-6	84	112	S-39/3-4,2-3	-1.0
Total	15	1845	6045	550	1355	201	38	60	461	444-44	40	845	.224	.280	.300	65	-281	30-35	.970	50	103	97	*S-1795/3-19,2-5,O(LF)	-6.2
BRINKOPF, LEON Leon Clarence B 10.20.1926 Cape Girardeau, MO D 7.2.1998 Cape Girardeau, MO BR/TR 5-11.5/185# d4.18																								
1952	Chi N	9	22	1	4	0	0	0	2	4	0	5	.182	.308	.182	38	-2	0-0	.955	-1	110	30	/S-6	-0.3
BRIODY, FATTY Charles F. "Alderman" B 8.13.1858 Lansingburg, NY D 6.22.1903 Chicago, IL TR 5-8.5/190# d6.16																								
1880	Tro N	1	4	0	0	0	0	0	0	0		0	.000	.000	.000	-95	-1		.700	-1			/C	-0.2
1882	Cle N	53	194	30	50	13	0	0	13	9		13	.258	.291	.325	101	1		.902	1			C-53	0.6
1883	Cle N	40	145	23	34	5	1	0	10	3		13	.234	.250	.283	62	-7		.900	5			C-33/2-4,1-2,3	0.1
1884	Cle N	43	148	17	25	6	0	1	12	6		19	.169	.201	.230	34	-11		.922	10			C-42/O(RF)	0.3
	Cin U	22	89	11	30	2	2	0		1			.337	.344	.404	117	-1		.943	12			C-22	1.1
1885	StL N	62	215	14	42	9	0	1	17	12		23	.195	.238	.251	62	-8		.893	-7			C-60/O(CF)32	-1.0
1886	KC N	56	215	14	51	10	3	0	29	3		35	.237	.248	.312	65	-10	0	.919	-1			C-54/O-2(0-1-1),1	-0.6
1887	Det N	33	128	24	29	6	1	1	26	9	1	10	.227	.283	.313	63	-7	6	.907	6			C-33	0.2
1888	KC AA	13	48	1	10	1	0	0	8	1	0		.208	.224	.229	43	-3	0	.896	-3			C-13	-0.5
Total	8	323	1186	134	271	52	7	3	<u>115</u>	44	1	<u>113</u>	.228	.257	.292	68	-47	6	.910	22			C-311/2-5,O-4(0-2-2),1-3,3-2	0.0
BRISTOW, GEORGE George T. B 5.1870 Paw Paw, IL TR d4.15																								
1899	Cle N	3	8	0	1	1	0	0	0	0	1		.125	.222	.250	32	-1	0	1.000	1	279	0	/O-3(1-0-2)	0.0
BRITO, BERNARDO Bernardo B 12.4.1963 San Cristobal, D.R. BR/TR 6-1/190# d9.15																								
1992	Min A	8	14	1	2	1	0	0	2	0-0	0	4	.143	.133	.214	-1	-2	0-1	.750	-0	86	0	/O-3(LF),D	-0.3
1993	Min A	27	54	8	13	2	0	4	9	1-0	0	20	.241	.255	.500	97	-1	0-0	1.000	1	97	272	O-10(LF)/D-7	-0.1
1995	Min A	5	5	1	1	0	0	1	1	0-0	1	3	.200	.333	.800	183	1	0-0	—	0			/D-3	0.0
Total	3	40	73	10	16	3	0	5	12	1-0	1	27	.219	.237	.466	85	-2	0-1	.941	0	95	211	/O-13(LF),D-11	-0.4
BRITO, JORGE Jorge Manuel (Uceta) B 6.22.1966 Moncion, D.R. BR/TR 6-1/190# d4.30																								
1995	Col N	18	51	5	11	3	0	0	7	2-0	1	17	.216	.259	.275	32	-5	1-0	.991	4	160	108	C-18	0.0
1996	Col N	8	14	1	1	0	0	0	0	1-0	2	8	.071	.235	.071	-12	-2	0-0	1.000	3	97	64	/C-8	0.1
Total	2	26	65	6	12	3	0	0	7	3-0	3	25	.185	.254	.231	23	-7	1-0	.994	6	143	96	/C-26	0.1
BRITO, JUAN Juan Ramon B 11.7.1979 Santiago, D.R. BR/TR 5-11/205# d5.3																								
2002	KC A	9	23	1	7	2	0	0	1	0-0	0	3	.304	.304	.391	74	-1	0-0	.978	-1	53	230	/C-9	-0.1
BRITO, TILSON Tilson Manuel (Jiminez) B 5.28.1972 Santo Domingo, D.R. BR/TR 6/175# d4.1																								
1996	Tor A	26	80	10	19	7	0	1	7	10-0	3	18	.237	.344	.363	79	-2	1-1	.956	-1	99	124	2-18/S-5,D-2	-0.1
1997	Tor A	49	126	9	28	3	0	0	8	9-0	2	28	.222	.281	.246	40	-11	1-0	.989	-2	96	103	2-25,3-17/S-8	-1.1
	Oak A	17	46	8	13	2	1	2	6	1-0	0	10	.283	.298	.500	105	0	0-0	.920	2	124	151	3-10/S-6,2-2	0.2
	Year	66	172	17	41	5	1	2	14	10-0	2	38	.238	.285	.314	57	-11	1-0	.961	-1	100	124	2-27,3-27,S-14	-0.9
Total	2	92	252	27	60	12	1	3	21	20-0	5	56	.238	.305	.329	64	-13	2-1	.974	-1	100	124	/2-45,3-27,S-19,D-2	-1.0
BRITTAIN, GUS August Schuster B 11.29.1909 Wilmington, NC D 2.16.1974 Wilmington, NC BR/TR 5-10/192# d7.22																								
1937	Cin N	3	6	0	1	0	0	0	0	0	0	3	.167	.167	.167	-10	-1	0	1.000	0	*0*	*0*	/C	-0.1
BRITTON, GIL Stephen Gilbert B 9.21.1891 Parsons, KS D 6.20.1983 Parsons, KS BR/TR 5-10/160# d9.20																								
1913	Pit N	3	12	0	0	0	0	0	0	0	0	2	.000	.000	.000	-99	-3	0	.824	-1	95	183	/S-3	-0.4
BROCK, GREG Gregory Allen B 6.14.1957 McMinnville, OR BL/TR 6-3/205# d9.1																								
1982	LA N	18	17	1	2	1	0	0	1	1-1	0	5	.118	.167	.176	-4	-2	0-0	1.000	-0	0	0	/1-3	-0.3
1983	†LA N	146	455	64	102	14	2	20	66	83-12	1	81	.224	.343	.396	105	5	5-1	.991	6	114	94	*1-140	0.3
1984	LA N	88	271	33	61	6	0	14	34	39-3	0	37	.225	.319	.402	104	1	8-0	.995	7	129	99	1-83	0.5
1985	†LA N	129	438	64	110	19	0	21	66	54-4	0	72	.251	.332	.438	118	10	4-2	.994	5	113	97	*1-122	0.8
1986	LA N	115	325	33	76	13	0	16	52	37-5	0	60	.234	.309	.422	108	2	2-5	.996	13	148	70	1-99	0.9
1987	Mil A	141	532	81	159	29	3	13	85	57-4	6	63	.299	.371	.438	111	10	5-4	.993	5	112	95	*1-141	0.6
1988	Mil A	115	364	53	77	16	1	6	50	63-16	3	48	.212	.329	.310	81	-7	6-2	.993	10	**135**	110	*1-114/D	-0.4
1989	Mil A	107	373	40	99	16	0	12	52	43-8	3	49	.265	.345	.405	112	7	6-1	.995	-4	87	106	*1-100/D-7	-0.3
1990	Mil A	123	367	42	91	23	0	7	50	43-9	2	45	.248	.324	.368	96	-1	4-2	.995	-4	89	96	*1-115	-1.2
1991	Mil A	31	60	9	17	4	0	1	6	14-1	0	9	.283	.419	.400	131	4	1-1	1.000	-1	76	116	1-25	0.1
Total	10	1013	3202	420	794	141	6	110	462	434-63	15	469	.248	.338	.399	105	29	41-18	.994	37	114	96	1-942/D-8	1.0
BROCK, JOHN John Roy B 10.16.1896 Hamilton, IL D 10.27.1951 Clayton, MO BR/TR 5-6.5/165# d8.10																								
1917	StL N	7	15	4	6	1	0	0	2	0	0	2	.400	.400	.467	170	1	2	.944	-0	*140*	*92*	/C-4	0.1
1918	StL N	27	52	9	11	2	0	0	4	3	0	10	.212	.255	.250	56	-3	5	.951	-2	*81*	*137*	C-18/O(RF)	-0.4
Total	2	34	67	13	17	3	0	0	6	3	0	12	.254	.286	.299	81	-2	7	.949	-2	*93*	*128*	/C-22,O(RF)	-0.3
BROCK, LOU Louis Clark B 6.18.1939 ElDorado, AR BL/TL (BR 1976 (1 game)) 5-11.5/170# d9.10 HF1985																								
1961	Chi N	4	11	1	1	0	0	0	0	1-0	0	3	.091	.167	.091	-29	-2	0-0	.750	-1	85	0	/O-3(CF)	-0.3
1962	Chi N	123	434	73	114	24	7	9	35	35-4	3	96	.263	.319	.412	92	-5	16-7	.965	-3	97	99	*O-106(CF)	-1.0
1963	Chi N	148	547	79	141	19	11	9	37	31-2	4	122	.258	.300	.382	91	-8	24-12	.973	10	109	155	*O-140(RF)	-0.7
1964	Chi N	52	215	30	54	9	2	2	14	13-0	2	40	.251	.300	.340	77	-7	10-3	.959	0	88	195	O-52(0-2-51)	-0.9

Year	Tm Lg	G	AB	R	H	2B	3B	HR	RBI	BB-IB	HP	SO	AVG	OBP	SLG	AOPS	ABR	SB-CS	FA	FR	Rng	Thr	G at Pos	BFW
	†StL N	103	419	81	146	21	9	12	44	27-0	2	87	.348	.387	.527	143	24	33-15	.949	2	103	105	*O-102(99-2-4)	2.3
	Year	155	634	111	200	30	11	14	58	40-0	4	127	.315	.358	.464	121	18	43-18	.953	2	98	135	*O-154(99-4-55)	1.4
1965	StL N	155	631	107	182	35	8	16	69	45-6	10	116	.288	.345	.445	110	9	63-27	.959	3	102	126	*O-153(150-2-7)	0.8
1966	StL N	156	643	94	183	24	12	15	46	31-6	3	134	.285	.320	.429	106	3	**74**-18	.936	-6	95	79	*O-154(122-0-34)	-0.3
1967	†StL N★	159	689	**113**	206	32	12	21	76	24-6	6	109	.299	.327	.472	128	21	**52**-18	.956	1	102	120	*O-157(LF)	2.0
1968	†StL N	159	660	92	184	**46**	**14**	6	51	46-7	3	124	.279	.328	.418	125	19	**62**-12	.952	-1	103	86	*O-156(LF)	2.1
1969	StL N	157	655	97	195	33	10	12	47	50-15	2	115	.298	.349	.434	118	14	**53**-14	.949	-3	94	81	*O-157(LF)	0.9
1970	StL N	155	664	114	202	29	5	13	57	60-12	1	99	.304	.361	.422	107	7	51-15	.962	-7	91	78	*O-152(149-0-3)	-0.3
1971	StL N★	157	640	**126**	200	37	7	7	61	76-5	1	107	.313	.385	.425	125	24	**64**-19	.951	-7	92	68	*O-157(156-0-1)	1.6
1972	StL N☆	153	621	81	193	26	8	3	42	47-12	1	93	.311	.359	.393	115	12	**63**-18	.952	-7	88	60	*O-149(LF)	0.5
1973	StL N	160	650	110	193	29	8	7	63	71-15	0	112	.297	.364	.398	112	12	**70**-20	.963	-6	93	27	*O-159(LF)	0.5
1974	StL N★	153	635	105	194	25	7	3	48	61-16	2	88	.306	.368	.381	111	10	**118**-33	.967	-4	93	73	*O-152(LF)	1.2
1975	StL N★	136	528	78	163	27	6	3	47	38-6	3	64	.309	.359	.400	106	5	56-16	.966	-2	101	53	*O-128(LF)	0.2
1976	StL N	133	498	73	150	24	5	4	67	35-7	1	75	.301	.344	.394	109	6	56-19	.983	-3	94	72	*O-123(LF)	0.1
1977	StL N	141	489	69	133	22	6	2	46	30-2	2	74	.272	.317	.354	81	-14	35-24	.954	-6	91	29	*O-130(LF)	-2.6
1978	StL N	92	298	31	66	9	0	0	12	17-2	0	29	.221	.263	.252	45	-22	17-5	.975	-5	86	36	O-79(LF)	-3.1
1979	StL N★	120	405	56	123	15	4	5	38	23-1	3	43	.304	.342	.398	101	0	21-12	.958	-4	84	100	O-98(LF)	-0.7
Total	19	2616	10332	1610	3023	486	141	149	900	761-124	49	1730	.293	.343	.410	109	108	938-307	.959	-49	96	84	*O-2507(2164-115-240)	2.3

BROCK, TARRIK Tarrik Jumaan B 12.25.1973 Goleta, CA BL/TL 6-3/170# d3.29

Year	Tm Lg	G	AB	R	H	2B	3B	HR	RBI	BB-IB	HP	SO	AVG	OBP	SLG	AOPS	ABR	SB-CS	FA	FR	Rng	Thr	G at Pos	BFW
2000	Chi N	13	12	1	2	0	0	0	0	4-0	0	4	.167	.375	.167	45	-1	1-1	.889	-0	97	0	O-10(9-2-0)	-0.1

BRODERICK, MATT Matthew Thomas B 12.1.1877 Lattimer, PA D 2.26.1940 Freeland, PA BR/TR 5-6.5/135# d5.1

Year	Tm Lg	G	AB	R	H	2B	3B	HR	RBI	BB-IB	HP	SO	AVG	OBP	SLG	AOPS	ABR	SB-CS	FA	FR	Rng	Thr	G at Pos	BFW
1903	Bro N	2	2	0	0	0	0	0	0	0	0		.000	.000	.000	-99	-1	0	1.000	0	0	1331	/2	0.0

BRODIE, STEVE Walter Scott B 9.11.1868 Warrenton, VA D 10.30.1935 Baltimore, MD BL/TR 5-11/180# d4.21

Year	Tm Lg	G	AB	R	H	2B	3B	HR	RBI	BB-IB	HP	SO	AVG	OBP	SLG	AOPS	ABR	SB-CS	FA	FR	Rng	Thr	G at Pos	BFW
1890	Bos N	132	514	77	152	19	9	0	67	66	11	20	.296	.387	.368	111	9	29	**.953**	2	82	140	*O-132(2-19-114)	0.8
1891	Bos N	133	523	84	136	13	6	2	78	63	10	39	.260	.351	.319	85	-10	25	.951	8	122	**294**	*O-133(1-102-31)	-0.5
1892	StL N	154	602	85	153	10	9	4	60	52	4	31	.254	.318	.321	98	-2	28	.943	1	91	76	*O-137(1-121-17),2-16/3-2	-0.9
1893	StL N	107	469	71	149	16	8	2	79	33	11	16	.318	.376	.399	106	3	41	.951	5	112	181	*O-107(0-102-5)	0.1
	Bal N	25	97	18	35	7	2	0	19	12	3	2	.361	.446	.474	142	7	8	.963	-1	55	0	O-25(2-24-0)	0.3
	Year	132	566	89	184	23	10	2	98	45	14	18	.325	.389	.412	112	10	49	.953	4	103	152	*O-132(2-126-5)	0.4
1894	†Bal N	**129**	573	134	210	25	11	3	113	18	13	8	.366	.399	.464	103	1	42	.950	-7	65	81	*O-129(CF)	-1.1
1895	†Bal N	**131**	528	85	184	27	10	2	134	26	14	15	.348	.394	.449	114	10	35	.965	3	119	51	*O-131(CF)	0.4
1896	†Bal N	**132**	516	98	153	19	11	2	87	36	18	17	.297	.363	.388	96	-3	25	.972	7	115	137	*O-132(CF)	-0.4
1897	Pit N	100	370	47	108	7	12	2	53	25	7		.292	.348	.392	99	-2	11	**.983**	2	83	39	*O-100(CF)	-0.5
1898	Pit N	42	156	15	41	5	0	0	21	6	3		.263	.303	.295	73	-6	3	.958	2	67	76	O-42(CF)	-0.6
	Bal N	23	98	12	30	3	2	0	19	5	1		.306	.346	.378	105	0	3	.923	1	144	0	O-23(CF)	0.0
	Year	65	254	27	71	8	2	0	40	11	4		.280	.320	.327	86	-5	6	.946	3	95	48	O-65(CF)	-0.6
1899	Bal N	137	531	82	164	26	1	3	87	31	23		.309	.373	.379	101	2	19	**.979**	-1	73	95	*O-137(0-136-1)	-0.7
1901	Bal A	83	306	41	95	6	6	2	41	25	8		.310	.378	.389	108	4	9	.963	-2	40	0	O-83(11-72-0)	-0.2
1902	NY N	110	420	37	118	8	2	3	42	22	6		.281	.326	.331	104	1	11	.953	7	157	**215**	*O-110(CF)	0.4
Total	12	1438	5703	886	1728	191	89	25	900	420	132	148	.303	.365	.381	102	14	289	.959	26	97	119	*O-1421(17-1243-168)/2-16,3-2	-2.9

BROGNA, RICO Rico Joseph B 4.18.1970 Turners Falls, MA BL/TL 6-2/200# d8.8

Year	Tm Lg	G	AB	R	H	2B	3B	HR	RBI	BB-IB	HP	SO	AVG	OBP	SLG	AOPS	ABR	SB-CS	FA	FR	Rng	Thr	G at Pos	BFW
1992	Det A	9	26	3	5	1	0	1	3	3-0	0	5	.192	.276	.346	73	-1	0-0	.982	0	126	151	/1-8,D-2	-0.1
1994	NY N	39	131	16	46	11	2	7	20	6-0	0	29	.351	.380	.626	158	10	1-0	.997	1	110	112	1-35	0.8
1995	NY N	134	495	72	143	27	2	22	76	39-7	2	111	.289	.342	.485	119	12	0-0	**.998**	0	100	101	*1-131	0.1
1996	NY N	55	188	18	48	10	1	7	30	19-1	0	50	.255	.318	.431	101	0	0-0	.996	-2	84	114	1-52	-0.7
1997	Phi N	148	543	68	137	36	1	20	81	33-4	0	116	.252	.293	.433	88	-12	12-3	.994	9	114	89	*1-145	-1.4
1998	Phi N	153	565	77	150	36	3	20	104	49-8	0	125	.265	.319	.446	99	-2	7-7	.996	13	126	89	*1-151	-0.4
1999	Phi N	157	619	90	172	29	4	24	102	54-7	2	132	.278	.336	.454	95	-6	8-5	.995	8	120	96	*1-157	-1.2
2000	Phi N	38	129	12	32	14	0	1	13	7-1	2	28	.248	.295	.380	69	-6	1-0	.996	-1	83	86	1-34	-0.9
	Bos A	43	56	8	11	3	0	1	8	3-0	0	13	.196	.237	.304	35	-6	0-0	.983	-2	74	87	1-37/D-2	-0.8
2001	Atl N	72	206	15	51	9	0	3	21	14-1	1	46	.248	.297	.335	62	-12	3-1	.994	3	122	73	1-67	-1.3
Total	9	848	2958	379	795	176	13	106	458	227-29	7	655	.269	.320	.445	96	-23	32-16	.995	30	112	94	1-817/D-4	-5.9

BROHAMER, JACK John Anthony B 2.26.1950 Maywood, CA BL/TR (BB 1972 (part)) 5-10/165# d4.18

Year	Tm Lg	G	AB	R	H	2B	3B	HR	RBI	BB-IB	HP	SO	AVG	OBP	SLG	AOPS	ABR	SB-CS	FA	FR	Rng	Thr	G at Pos	BFW
1972	Cle A	136	527	49	123	13	2	5	35	27-0	1	46	.233	.271	.294	66	-23	3-2	.977	4	106	103	*2-132/3	-1.2
1973	Cle A	102	300	29	66	12	1	4	29	32-3	0	23	.220	.291	.307	69	-12	0-2	.971	10	108	103	2-97	0.3
1974	Cle A	101	315	33	85	11	1	2	30	26-0	3	22	.270	.329	.330	92	-3	2-1	.987	4	107	107	2-99	0.7
1975	Cle A	69	217	15	53	5	0	6	16	14-0	0	14	.244	.289	.350	80	-6	2-2	.976	-1	91	123	2-66	-0.4
1976	Chi A	119	354	33	89	12	2	7	40	44-9	3	28	.251	.333	.356	103	2	1-3	.984	14	106	98	*2-117/3	2.3
1977	Chi A	59	152	26	39	10	3	2	20	21-4	1	8	.257	.347	.401	105	2	0-0	.923	-3	112	146	3-38,2-18/D	-0.1
1978	Bos A	81	244	34	57	14	1	1	25	25-1	0	13	.234	.300	.311	67	-10	1-3	.974	-6	91	97	3-30,D-25,2-23	-1.8
1979	Bos A	64	192	25	51	7	1	1	11	15-1	0	15	.266	.316	.328	71	-8	0-3	.982	-1	95	92	2-36,3-22	-0.8
1980	Bos A	21	57	5	18	2	0	1	6	4-0	0	3	.316	.361	.404	104	0	0-0	.900	-1	92	150	3-13/2-4,D-3	-0.1
	Cle A	53	142	13	32	5	1	1	15	14-4	0	6	.225	.291	.296	62	-7	0-1	.979	-4	93	90	2-47/D	-1.0
	Year	74	199	18	50	7	1	2	21	18-4	0	9	.251	.311	.327	74	-7	0-1	.981	-5	95	83	2-51,3-13/D-4	-1.1
Total	9	805	2500	262	613	91	12	30	227	222-22	8	178	.245	.306	.327	79	-65	9-17	.979	14	102	102	2-639,3-105/D-30	-2.1

BRONKIE, HERMAN Herman Charles "Dutch" B 3.31.1885 S.Manchester, CT D 5.27.1968 Somers, CT BR/TR 5-9/165# d9.20

Year	Tm Lg	G	AB	R	H	2B	3B	HR	RBI	BB-IB	HP	SO	AVG	OBP	SLG	AOPS	ABR	SB-CS	FA	FR	Rng	Thr	G at Pos	BFW
1910	Cle A	5	10	1	2	0	0	0	0	1	0		.200	.273	.200	48	-1	1	.625	-2	46	0	/3-3,S	-0.3
1911	Cle A	2	6	0	1	0	0	0	0	0	0		.167	.167	.167	-7	-1	0	1.000	-0	37	0	/3-2	-0.1
1912	Cle A	6	16	1	0	0	0	0	0	1	0		.000	.059	.000	-80	-4	0	.917	1	128	120	/3-6	-0.2
1914	Chi N	1	1	1	1	1	0	0	1	0	0	0	1.000	1.000	2.000	786	1	0	.000	-1	0	0	/3	0.0
1918	StL N	18	68	7	15	3	0	1	7	2	0	4	.221	.243	.309	70	-3	0	.984	0	107	63	3-18	-0.2
1919	StL A	67	196	23	50	6	4	0	14	23	1	23	.255	.336	.327	84	-4	2	.939	4	115	133	3-34,2-16/1-2	0.1
1922	StL A	23	64	7	18	4	1	0	2	6	0	7	.281	.343	.375	84	-1	0-2	.917	-0	88	245	3-18	-0.1
Total	7	122	361	40	87	14	5	1	24	33	1	34	.241	.306	.316	74	-13	3-2	.931	2	105	132	/3-82,2-16,1-2,S	-0.8

BROOKENS, TOM Thomas Dale B 8.10.1953 Chambersburg, PA BR/TR 5-10/170# d7.10 OF Total (2-CF 6-RF)

Year	Tm Lg	G	AB	R	H	2B	3B	HR	RBI	BB-IB	HP	SO	AVG	OBP	SLG	AOPS	ABR	SB-CS	FA	FR	Rng	Thr	G at Pos	BFW
1979	Det A	60	190	23	50	5	2	4	21	11-0	2	40	.263	.309	.374	81	-6	10-3	.945	8	123	148	3-42,2-19/D	0.4
1980	Det A	151	509	64	140	25	9	10	66	32-3	1	71	.275	.315	.418	98	-3	13-11	.931	6	105	100	*3-138/2-9,SD	0.1
1981	Det A	71	239	19	58	10	1	4	25	14-0	2	43	.243	.284	.343	79	-7	5-3	.952	3	104	114	3-71	-0.5
1982	Det A	140	398	40	92	15	3	9	58	27-0	0	63	.231	.277	.352	72	-16	5-9	.939	5	113	112	*3-113,2-26/S-9,O(CF)	-1.4
1983	Det A	138	332	50	71	13	3	6	32	29-2	2	46	.214	.276	.325	68	-15	10-4	.928	6	101	129	*3-103,S-30,2-10/D	-0.8
1984	†Det A	113	224	32	55	11	4	5	26	19-0	1	33	.246	.306	.397	94	-2	6-6	.969	6	104	172	3-68,S-28,2-26/D	0.6
1985	Det A	156	485	54	115	34	6	7	47	27-0	0	78	.237	.277	.375	77	-16	14-5	.943	3	99	106	*3-151/S-8,2-3,CD	-1.4
1986	Det A	98	281	42	76	11	2	3	25	20-0	1	42	.270	.319	.356	84	-6	11-8	.955	-8	99	76	3-35,2-31,S-14,D-14/O-3(0-1-3)	-1.3
1987	†Det A	143	444	59	107	15	3	13	59	33-3	2	63	.241	.295	.376	80	-14	7-4	.954	-4	101	73	*3-122,S-16,2-11	-1.7
1988	Det A	136	441	62	107	23	5	5	38	44-2	3	74	.243	.313	.351	90	-6	4-4	.952	-4	96	78	*3-136/S-3,2	-1.0
1989	NY A	66	168	14	38	6	0	4	14	11-1	0	27	.226	.272	.333	71	-7	1-3	.926	-5	95	60	3-51/S-7,2-5,O-3(RF),D-3	-1.3
1990	Cle A	64	154	18	41	7	2	1	20	14-1	0	25	.266	.322	.357	92	-2	0-0	.923	3	122	103	3-35,2-21/S-3,1-2,D	0.2
Total	12	1336	3865	477	950	175	40	71	431	281-12	14	605	.246	.296	.367	83	-100	86-60	.943	19	103	102	*3-1065,2-162,S-119/D-23,O-7R,1C	-8.1

BROOKS, HUBIE Hubert B 9.24.1956 Los Angeles, CA BR/TR 6/200# d9.4 OF Total (7-LF 576-RF)

Year	Tm Lg	G	AB	R	H	2B	3B	HR	RBI	BB-IB	HP	SO	AVG	OBP	SLG	AOPS	ABR	SB-CS	FA	FR	Rng	Thr	G at Pos	BFW
1980	NY N	24	81	8	25	2	1	1	10	5-0	2	9	.309	.364	.395	115	2	1-1	.966	-1	91	58	3-23	0.0
1981	NY N	98	358	34	110	21	2	4	38	23-2	1	65	.307	.345	.411	117	8	9-5	.924	1	104	93	3-93/O-3(1-0-2),S	0.8
1982	NY N	126	457	40	114	21	2	2	40	28-5	5	76	.249	.297	.317	73	-16	6-3	.931	-9	95	78	*3-126	-2.9
1983	NY N	150	586	53	147	18	4	5	58	24-2	4	96	.251	.284	.321	68	-27	6-4	.950	6	**112**	106	*3-145/2-7	-2.5
1984	NY N	153	561	61	159	23	2	16	73	48-15	2	79	.283	.341	.417	114	10	6-5	.929	-12	87	102	*3-129,S-26	-0.2
1985	Mon N	156	605	67	163	34	7	13	100	34-6	5	79	.269	.310	.413	108	4	6-9	.958	-35	90	89	*S-155	-1.7
1986	Mon N★	80	306	50	104	18	5	14	58	25-3	2	60	.340	.388	.569	164	25	4-2	.958	-7	96	82	S-80	2.7
1987	Mon N★	112	430	57	113	22	3	14	72	24-2	1	72	.263	.301	.426	88	-9	4-3	.953	-23	87	91	*S-109	-2.1
1988	Mon N	151	588	61	164	35	2	20	90	35-3	1	108	.279	.318	.447	113	9	7-3	.968	-5	93	111	*O-149(RF)	0.0

Year	Tm Lg	G	AB	R	H	2B	3B	HR	RBI	BB-IB	HP	SO	AVG	OBP	SLG	AOPS	ABR	SB-CS	FA	FR	Rng	Thr	G at Pos	BFW
1989	Mon N	148	542	56	145	30	1	14	70	39-2	4	108	.268	.317	.404	105	3	6-11	.964	-6	92	84	*O-140(RF)	-1.1
1990	LA N	153	568	74	151	28	1	20	91	33-10	6	108	.266	.307	.424	104	1	2-5	.964	-7	90	90	*O-150(RF)	-1.3
1991	NY N	103	357	48	85	11	1	16	50	44-8	3	62	.238	.324	.409	106	3	3-1	.972	-2	96	90	*O-100(RF)	-0.1
1992	Cal A	82	306	28	66	13	0	8	36	12-3	1	46	.216	.247	.337	62	-17	3-3	.986	-0	97	71	D-70/1-6	-2.1
1993	KC A	75	168	14	48	12	0	1	24	11-1	1	27	.286	.331	.375	85	-3	0-1	.966	1	98	157	O-40(6-0-34)/1-3,D-9	-0.4
1994	KC A	34	61	5	14	2	0	1	14	2-0	0	10	.230	.239	.311	43	-5	1-0	1.000	-0	45	117	D-19/1-4	-0.7
Total	15	1645	5974	656	1608	290	31	149	824	387-62	38	1005	.269	.315	.403	100	-12	64-56	.966	-99	93	97	O-582R,3-516,S-371/D-98,1-13,2-7	-11.6
BROOKS, JERRY Jerome Edward B 3.23.1967 Syracuse, NY BR/TR 6/195# d9.6																								
1993	LA N	9	9	2	2	1	0	1	1	0-0	0	2	.222	.222	.667	135	0	0-0	—	-0	0	0	/O-2(RF)	0.0
1996	Fla N	8	5	2	2	0	1	0	3	1-0	1	1	.400	.571	.800	266	1	0-0	1.000	-0	129	0	/O-2(RF),1	0.1
Total	2	17	14	4	4	1	1	1	4	1-0	1	3	.286	.375	.714	191	1	0-0	1.000	-1	75	0	/O-4(RF),1	0.1
BROOKS, MANDY Jonathan Joseph (born Jonathan Joseph Brozek) B 8.18.1897 Milwaukee, WI D 6.17.1962 Kirkwood, MO BR/TR 5-9/165# d5.30																								
1925	Chi N	90	349	55	98	25	7	14	72	19	2	28	.281	.322	.513	108	2	10-3	.977	3	105	111	O-89(CF)	0.3
1926	Chi N	26	48	7	9	1	0	1	6	5	1	5	.188	.278	.271	48	-4	0	1.000	1	97	161	O-18(4-5-9)	-0.3
Total	2	116	397	62	107	26	7	15	78	24	3	33	.270	.316	.484	101	-2	10-3	.979	4	104	117	O-107(4-94-9)	0.0
BROOKS, BOBBY Robert B 11.1.1945 Los Angeles, CA D 10.11.1994 Harbor City, CA BR/TR 5-8.5/165# d9.1																								
1969	Oak A	29	79	13	19	5	0	3	10	20-1	1	24	.241	.396	.418	135	5	0-2	1.000	-1	84	116	O-21(16-0-5)	0.3
1970	Oak A	7	18	2	6	1	0	2	5	1-0	0	7	.333	.368	.722	201	2	0-1	1.000	-1	53	0	/O-5(4-0-2)	0.1
1972	Oak A	15	39	4	7	0	0	0	5	8-1	0	8	.179	.319	.179	54	-2	0-1	.930	1	137	0	O-11(CF)	-0.2
1973	Cal A	4	7	0	1	0	0	0	0	0-0	0	3	.143	.143	.143	-21	-1	0-0	—	-0	0	0	/O(LF)	-0.2
Total	4	55	143	19	33	6	0	5	20	29-2	1	42	.231	.362	.378	116	4	0-4	.964	-1	95	65	/O-38(21-11-7)	0.0
BROSIUS, SCOTT Scott David B 8.15.1966 Hillsboro, OR BR/TR 6-1/185# d8.7 OF Total (37-LF 68-CF 74-RF)																								
1991	Oak A	36	68	9	16	5	0	2	4	3-0	0	11	.235	.268	.397	86	-2	3-1	1.000	-1	67	59	2-18,O-13(5-0-10)/3-7,D	-0.2
1992	Oak A	38	87	13	19	2	0	4	13	3-1	2	13	.218	.258	.379	82	-3	3-0	1.000	-3	75	112	O-20(4-0-19),3-12/1-3,SD	-0.6
1993	Oak A	70	213	26	53	10	1	6	25	14-0	1	37	.249	.296	.390	89	-4	6-0	.991	-2	97	81	O-46(8-34-6),1-11,3-10/S-6,D-2	-0.5
1994	Oak A	96	324	31	77	14	1	14	49	24-0	2	57	.238	.289	.417	88	-7	2-6	.946	5	102	125	3-93/O-7(2-2-4),1	-0.3
1995	Oak A	123	389	69	102	19	2	17	46	41-0	8	67	.262	.342	.452	111	6	4-2	.918	-2	107	89	3-60,O-49(8-22-22),1-18/2-3,S-3,D-2	0.2
1996	Oak A	114	428	73	130	25	0	22	71	59-4	7	85	.304	.393	.516	131	22	7-2	.969	15	121	124	*3-109,1-10/O-4(3-2-0)	3.5
1997	Oak A	129	479	59	97	20	1	11	41	34-1	4	102	.203	.259	.317	51	-36	9-4	.977	17	122	124	*3-107,S-30,O-22(6-6-11)	-1.7
1998	†NY A★	152	530	86	159	34	0	19	98	52-1	10	97	.300	.371	.472	123	19	11-8	.948	9	106	145	*3-150/1-3,O(RF)	2.7
1999	†NY A	133	473	64	117	26	1	17	71	39-2	6	74	.247	.307	.414	84	-12	9-3	**.962**	4	100	97	*3-132/D	-0.6
2000	†NY A	135	470	57	108	20	0	16	64	45-1	2	73	.230	.299	.374	70	-23	0-3	.968	-3	92	99	*3-134/1-2,O-2(1-0-1),D	-2.4
2001	†NY A	120	428	57	123	25	2	13	49	34-2	5	83	.287	.343	.446	106	4	3-1	.935	2	97	107	*3-120/O-2(CF)	0.7
Total	11	1146	3889	544	1001	200	8	141	531	348-12	47	699	.257	.323	.422	95	-36	57-30	.956	41	105	114	3-934,O-166R/1-48,S-40,2-21,D-8	0.8
BROSKIE, SIG Sigmund Theodore "Chops" B 3.23.1911 Iselin, PA D 5.17.1975 Canton, OH BR/TR 5-11.5/200# d9.11																								
1940	Bos N	11	22	1	6	1	0	0	4	1	0	2	.273	.304	.318	76	-1	0	.935	0	*125*	*148*	C-11	0.0
BROTTEM, TONY Anton Christian B 4.30.1892 Halstad, MN D 8.5.1929 Chicago, IL BR/TR 6-0.5/176# d4.17 Mil 1918																								
1916	StL N	26	33	3	6	1	0	0	4	3	0	10	.182	.250	.212	43	-2	1	.950	-1	75	172	C-15/O-2(0-1-1)	-0.3
1918	StL N	2	4	0	0	0	0	0	0	1	0	0	.000	.200	.000	-39	-1	0	1.000	1	384	0	/1-2	0.0
1921	Was A	4	7	1	1	0	0	0	0	2	0	1	.143	.333	.143	26	-1	0-0	1.000	1	*143*	*81*	/C-4	0.0
	Pit N	30	91	6	22	2	0	0	9	3	0	11	.242	.266	.264	40	-8	0-1	.983	-0	*135*	*86*	C-29	-0.7
Total	3	62	135	10	29	3	0	0	13	9	0	22	.215	.264	.237	38	-12	1-1	.977	1	*124*	*103*	/C-48,1-2,O-2(0-1-1)	-1.0
BROUGHTON, CAL Cecil Calvert B 12.28.1860 Magnolia, WI D 3.15.1939 Evansville, WI BR/TR 5-10/180# d5.2																								
1883	Cle N	4	10	2	2	0	0	0	1	2		2	.200	.333	.200	68	0		.950	0			/C-4	0.0
	Bal AA	9	32	1	6	0	0	0		1			.188	.212	.188	29	-3		.825	-2			/C-8,O(RF)	-0.4
1884	Mil U	11	39	5	12	5	0	0		0			.308	.308	.436	227	5		.937	-1			/C-7,O-5(1-4-0)	0.4
1885	StL AA	4	17	1	1	0	0	0	1	0	0		.059	.059	.059	-60	-3		.889	-1			/C-4	-0.3
	NY AA	11	41	1	6	1	0	0	1	1	0		.146	.167	.171	7	-4		.860	-1			C-11	-0.4
	Year	15	58	2	7	1	0	0	2	1	0		.121	.136	.138	-14	-7		.867	-2			C-15	-0.7
1888	Det N	1	4	0	0	0	0	0	0	0	0	0	.000	.000	.000	-99	-1	0	1.000	1			/C	0.0
Total	4	40	143	10	27	6	0	0	3	4	0	2	.189	.211	.231	43	-6	0	.887	-4			/C-35,O-6(1-4-1)	-0.7
BROUHARD, MARK Mark Steven B 5.22.1956 Burbank, CA BR/TR 6-1/210# d4.12																								
1980	Mil A	45	125	17	29	6	0	5	16	7-0	1	24	.232	.278	.400	86	-3	1-0	.964	0	121	0	D-21,O-12(4-0-8),1-10	-0.4
1981	Mil A	60	186	19	51	6	3	2	20	7-1	2	41	.274	.305	.371	100	-1	1-1	.990	3	95	206	O-51(7-0-46)/D-7	-0.1
1982	†Mil A	40	108	16	29	4	1	4	10	9-0	2	17	.269	.336	.435	117	2	0-3	.986	2	119	103	O-30(7-0-23)/D-7	0.2
1983	Mil A	56	185	25	51	10	1	7	23	9-0	2	39	.276	.315	.454	118	4	0-4	.991	3	122	30	O-42(38-0-8),D-11	0.3
1984	Mil A	66	197	20	47	7	0	6	22	16-3	2	36	.239	.298	.365	87	-4	0-3	.983	5	107	186	O-52(48-0-4)/D-8	-0.2
1985	Mil A	37	108	11	28	7	2	1	13	5-1	1	26	.259	.298	.389	87	-2	0-0	.964	-2	98	0	O-29(10-0-21)/D	-0.5
Total	6	304	909	108	235	40	7	25	104	53-5	10	183	.259	.305	.400	99	-4	2-11	.983	11	109	112	O-216(114-0-110)/D-55,1-10	-0.7
BROUSSARD, BEN Benjamin Isaac B 9.24.1976 Beaumont, TX BL/TL 6-2/220# d6.22																								
2002	Cle A	39	112	10	27	4	0	4	9	7-1	1	25	.241	.292	.384	79	-4	0-0	.960	-2	91	66	O-32(LF)/1-4,D-3	-0.7
2003	Cle A	116	386	53	96	21	3	16	55	32-2	5	75	.249	.312	.443	100	-1	5-2	.991	-2	96	98	*1-114	-1.2
Total	2	155	498	63	123	25	3	20	64	39-3	6	100	.247	.308	.430	95	-5	5-2	.991	-4	95	97	1-118/O-32(LF),D-3	-1.9
BROUTHERS, ART Arthur H. B 11.25.1882 Montgomery, AL D 9.28.1959 Charleston, SC TR 6-1/?# d4.14																								
1906	Phi A	37	144	18	30	5	1	0	14	5	1		.208	.240	.257	54	-8	4	.900	-3	86	0	3-35/2	-1.1
BROUTHERS, DAN Dennis Joseph "Big Dan" B 5.8.1858 Sylvan Lake, NY D 8.2.1932 E.Orange, NJ BL/TL (BR 1882 (1 game)) 6-2/207# d6.23 HF1945 ▲																								
1879	Tro N	39	168	17	46	12	1	4	17	1		18	.274	.278	.429	138	7		.926	-5	63	59	1-37/P-3	0.1
1880	Tro N	3	12	0	2	0	0	0	1	1		0	.167	.231	.167	35	-1		.893	-1	0	70	/1-3	-0.2
1881	Buf N	65	270	60	86	18	9	**8**	45	18		22	.319	.361	**.541**	182	25		.797	-6	72	62	O-35(33-0-2),1-30	1.5
1882	Buf N	**84**	351	71	**129**	23	11	6	63	21		7	**.368**	**.403**	**.547**	**198**	**38**		**.974**	1	84	84	*1-84	2.8
1883	Buf N	**98**	425	85	**159**	41	**17**	3	**97**	16		17	**.374**	**.397**	**.572**	**186**	**43**		.961	1	108	82	*1-97/3P	3.0
1884	Buf N	94	398	82	130	22	15	14	79	33		20	.327	.378	**.563**	**186**	38		.964	0	112	93	*1-93/3	2.7
1885	Buf N	98	407	87	146	32	11	7	59	34		10	.359	.408	**.543**	199	44		.975	-2	76	92	*1-98	3.1
1886	Det N	121	489	139	181	**40**	15	**11**	72	66		16	.370	.445	**.581**	**203**	**63**	21	.968	-8	58	123	*1-121	3.9
1887	†Det N	123	500	**153**	169	**36**	20	12	101	71	6	9	.338	**.426**	.562	**166**	**46**	34	.969	-4	80	103	*1-123	2.6
1888	Det N	129	522	**118**	160	**33**	11	9	66	68	12	13	.307	.399	.464	172	**47**	34	.971	-2	101	94	*1-129	3.3
1889	Bos N	126	485	105	181	26	9	7	118	66	**14**	6	**.373**	.462	.507	161	42	22	.974	1	104	**119**	*1-126	2.8
1890	Bos P	123	460	117	152	36	9	1	97	99	18	17	.330	**.466**	.454	137	32	28	.963	2	119	109	*1-123	1.8
1891	Bos AA	130	486	117	170	26	19	5	109	87	24	20	**.350**	**.471**	**.512**	**184**	**60**	31	.978	-7	63	121	*1-130	3.5
1892	Bro N	152	588	121	**197**	30	20	5	**124**	84	16	30	**.335**	.432	.480	**182**	**64**	31	.982	12	129	82	*1-152	**6.8**
1893	Bro N	77	282	57	95	21	11	2	59	52	6	10	.337	.450	.511	163	29	9	.986	4	113	110	1-77	2.6
1894	†Bal N	123	525	137	182	39	23	9	128	67	5	9	.347	.425	.560	130	25	38	.976	-2	95	110	*1-123	1.7
1895	Bal N	5	23	2	6	2	0	0	5	1	0	1	.261	.292	.348	63	-1	0	1.000	0	119	322	/1-5	-0.1
	Lou N	24	97	13	30	10	1	2	15	11	0	2	.309	.380	.495	133	5	1	.953	-2	79	87	1-24	0.2
	Year	29	120	15	36	12	1	2	20	12	0	3	.300	.364	.467	119	4	1	.960	-2	86	126	1-29	0.1
1896	Phi N	57	218	42	75	13	3	1	41	44	4	11	.344	.462	.445	141	17	7	.983	-3	74	116	1-57	1.2
1904	NY N	2	5	0	0	0	0	0	0	0	0		.000	.000	.000	-96	-1	0	1.000	-0	0	0	/1	-0.1
Total	19	1673	6711	1523	2296	460	205	106	1296	840	105	238	.342	.423	.519	169	622	256	.971	-20	94	102	*1-1633/O-35(33-0-2),P-4,3-2	43.2
BROVIA, JOE Joseph John "Ox" B 2.18.1922 Davenport, CA D 8.15.1994 Santa Cruz, CA BL/TR 6-3/195# d7.3																								
1955	Cin N	21	18	0	2	0	0	0	4	1-0	0	6	.111	.150	.111	-25	-3	0-0	—	0			H	-0.3
BROWER, FRANK Frank Willard "Turkeyfoot" B 3.26.1893 Gainesville, VA D 11.20.1960 Baltimore, MD BL/TR 6-2/180# d8.14 ▲																								
1920	Was A	36	119	21	37	7	2	1	13	9	3	11	.311	.374	.429	115	3	1-1	.900	-1	85	141	O-20(1-0-19)/1-9,3	0.1
1921	Was A	83	203	31	53	12	3	1	35	18	3	7	.261	.330	.365	81	-6	1-1	.917	4	112	148	O-46(RF)/1-4	-0.6
1922	Was A	139	471	61	138	20	6	9	71	52	10	25	.293	.375	.418	112	9	8-6	.978	-3	100	70	*O-121(RF)/1-7	-0.3

Year	Tm Lg	G	AB	R	H	2B	3B	HR	RBI	BB-IB	HP	SO	AVG	OBP	SLG	AOPS	ABR	SB-CS	FA	FR	Rng	Thr	G at Pos	BFW
1923	Cle A	126	397	77	113	25	8	16	66	62	8	32	.285	.392	.509	136	21	6-5	.988	-1	100	110	*1-112/O-4(1-0-3)	1.3
1924	Cle A	66	107	16	30	10	1	3	20	27	2	9	.280	.434	.477	133	7	1-1	.990	1	117	67	1-26/P-4,O-3(2-0-1)	0.5
Total	5	450	1297	206	371	74	20	30	205	168	26	84	.286	.379	.443	117	34	17-14	.952	-0	101	96	O-194(4-0-190),1-158/P-4,3	1.0
BROWER, LOUIS Louis Lester B 7.1.1900 Cleveland, OH D 3.4.1994 Tyler, TX BR/TR 5-10/155# d6.13																								
1931	Det A	21	62	3	10	1	0	0	6	8	2	5	.161	.278	.177	21	-7	1-0	.886	-6	71	95	S-20/2-2	-1.1
BROWER, BOB Robert Richard B 1.10.1960 Jamaica, NY BR/TR 5-11/185# d9.3																								
1986	Tex A	21	9	3	1	1	0	0	0	0-0	0	3	.111	.111	.222	-12	-1	1-2	1.000	-1	79	0	O-17(16-1-1)/D	-0.3
1987	Tex A	127	303	63	79	10	3	14	46	36-0	0	66	.261	.338	.452	107	3	15-9	.964	-4	95	47	*O-106(45-67-6)/D-7	-0.3
1988	Tex A	82	201	29	45	7	0	1	11	27-0	0	38	.224	.316	.274	65	-9	10-5	.972	-3	89	81	O-59(26-33-4),D-13	-1.3
1989	NY A	26	69	9	16	3	0	2	3	6-0	0	11	.232	.293	.362	85	-2	3-1	.970	3	131	142	O-25(1-9-15)/D	0.2
Total	4	256	582	104	141	21	3	17	60	69-0	0	118	.242	.322	.376	89	-9	29-17	.968	-4	97	68	O-207(88-110-26)/D-22	-1.7
BROWN, ADRIAN Adrian Demond B 2.7.1974 McComb, MS BB/TR 6/175# d5.16																								
1997	Pit N	48	147	17	28	6	0	1	10	13-0	4	18	.190	.273	.252	38	-13	8-4	.987	-1	90	169	O-38(0-35-3)	-1.4
1998	Pit N	41	152	20	43	4	1	0	5	9-0	0	18	.283	.323	.322	70	-7	4-0	.977	1	103	137	O-38(3-34-1)	-0.5
1999	Pit N	116	226	34	61	5	2	4	17	33-2	1	39	.270	.364	.363	85	-5	5-3	.966	-4	90	82	O-96(4-29-66)	-0.9
2000	Pit N	104	308	64	97	18	3	4	28	29-1	0	34	.315	.373	.432	104	2	13-1	.976	-1	93	164	O-92(7-71-15)	0.3
2001	Pit N	8	31	3	6	0	0	1	2	3-0	0	3	.194	.265	.290	43	-3	2-1	1.000	-0	104	0	O-7(CF)	-0.3
2002	Pit N	91	208	20	45	10	2	1	21	19-0	1	34	.216	.284	.298	56	-14	10-6	.974	-4	92	34	O-71(0-64-9)	-1.9
2003	†Bos A	9	15	2	3	0	0	0	1	1-0	0	4	.200	.250	.200	20	-2	2-0	1.000	-0	85	0	/O-9(3-6-0)	-0.2
Total	7	417	1087	160	283	43	8	11	84	107-3	6	150	.260	.329	.345	75	-42	44-15	.976	-10	93	110	O-351(17-246-94)	-4.9
BROWN, BRANT Brant Michael B 6.22.1971 Porterville, CA BL/TL 6-3/220# d6.15																								
1996	Chi N	29	69	11	21	1	0	5	9	2-1	1	17	.304	.329	.536	122	2	3-3	1.000	2	151	35	1-18	0.2
1997	Chi N	46	137	15	32	7	1	5	15	7-0	3	28	.234	.286	.409	77	-5	2-1	1.000	0	102	204	O-27(LF),1-12	-0.7
1998	†Chi N	124	347	56	101	17	7	14	48	30-2	1	95	.291	.348	.501	116	7	4-5	.963	-3	101	20	*O-102(48-69-0)/1-7	0.2
1999	Pit N	130	341	49	79	20	3	16	58	22-3	4	114	.232	.283	.449	82	-11	3-4	.981	1	108	96	O-82(0-23-59)/1-7,D-6	-1.3
2000	Fla N	41	73	4	14	6	0	2	6	3-0	0	33	.192	.224	.356	45	-7	1-0	.923	-1	85	0	O-13(8-0-5)/1-5	-0.7
	Chi N	54	89	7	14	1	0	3	10	10-0	1	29	.157	.248	.270	32	-10	2-1	1.000	1	110	0	O-28(18-9-3)/1-7	-1.0
	Year	95	162	11	28	7	0	5	16	13-0	1	62	.173	.237	.309	38	-16	3-1	.980	-0	102	0	O-41(26-9-8),1-12	-1.7
Total	5	424	1056	142	261	52	11	45	146	74-6	10	316	.247	.301	.445	89	-24	15-14	.975	1	104	65	O-252(101-101-67)/1-56,D-6	-3.3
BROWN, CURTIS Curtis B 9.14.1945 Sacramento, CA BR/TR 5-11/180# d5.27 b-Leon																								
1973	Mon N	1	4	0	0	0	0	0	0	0-0	0	0	.000	.000	.000	-97	-1	0-0	1.000	0	159	0	/O(LF)	-0.1
BROWN, DARRELL Darrell Wayne B 10.29.1955 Oklahoma City, OK BB/TR 6/184# d4.11																								
1981	Det A	16	4	4	1	0	0	0	0	0-0	0	1	.250	.250	.250	43	0	1-0	1.000	-0	70	0	/O-6(1-2-3),D-4	0.0
1982	Oak A	8	18	2	6	0	1	0	3	1-0	0	2	.333	.368	.444	128	1	1-0	1.000	-1	90	0	/O-7(1-0-6),D	0.0
1983	Min A	91	309	40	84	6	2	0	22	10-0	1	28	.272	.297	.304	64	-16	3-3	.995	-4	95	44	O-81(5-76-0)/D-3	-2.1
1984	Min A	95	260	36	71	9	3	1	19	14-1	0	16	.273	.309	.342	77	-9	4-1	.993	3	109	115	O-55(19-35-0),D-13	-0.7
Total	4	210	591	82	162	15	6	1	44	25-1	1	47	.274	.304	.325	71	-24	9-4	.994	-2	100	70	O-149(26-113-9)/D-21	-2.8
BROWN, DELOS Delos Hight B 10.4.1892 Anna, IL D 12.21.1964 Carbondale, IL BR/TR 5-9/160# d6.12																								
1914	Chi A	1	1	0	0	0	0	0	0	0	0	1	.000	.000	.000	-99	0	0	—	0			H	0.0
BROWN, DEE Dermal Bram B 3.27.1978 Bronx, NY BL/TR 5-11/210# d9.14																								
1998	KC A	5	3	2	0	0	0	0	0	0-0	0	1	.000	.000	.000	-97	-1	0-0	1.000	0	144	0	/O-2(RF),D-3	-0.1
1999	KC A	12	25	1	2	0	0	0	0	2-0	0	7	.080	.148	.080	-39	-5	0-0	.929	2	195	501	/O-3(LF),D-2	-0.4
2000	KC A	15	25	4	4	1	0	0	4	3-0	0	9	.160	.250	.200	15	-3	0-0	1.000	1	145	0	/O-5(LF)	-0.3
2001	KC A	106	380	39	93	19	0	7	40	22-4	1	81	.245	.286	.350	62	-21	5-3	.988	-3	91	58	O-83(77-4-3),D-20	-2.8
2002	KC A	16	51	5	12	3	1	1	7	4-0	0	20	.235	.291	.392	71	-2	0-0	.923	-1	71	0	/O-8(LF),D-5	-0.4
2003	KC A	50	132	16	30	7	0	2	14	8-1	2	37	.227	.280	.326	53	-9	1-1	.985	3	120	132	O-33(17-0-17),D-11	-0.8
Total	6	204	616	67	141	30	1	10	65	39-5	3	155	.229	.277	.330	54	-41	6-4	.981	0	100	79	O-134(110-4-22)/D-41	-4.8
BROWN, DRUMMOND Drummond Nicol B 1.31.1885 Los Angeles, CA D 1.27.1927 Parkville, MO BR/TR 6/180# d4.25																								
1913	Bos N	15	34	3	11	1	0	1	2	2	0	9	.324	.361	.441	126	1	0	.960	-3	92	58	C-12	-0.1
1914	KC F	31	58	4	11	3	0	0	5	7	0	6	.190	.277	.241	44	-5	1	.954	2	*106*	*116*	C-23/1-2	-0.2
1915	KC F	77	227	13	55	10	1	1	26	12	3	23	.242	.289	.308	71	-13	3	.961	-2	*94*	*103*	C-65/1	-1.0
Total	3	123	319	20	77	14	1	2	33	21	3	38	.241	.294	.310	72	-17	4	.960	-3	*96*	*101*	C-100/1-3	-1.3
BROWN, ED Edward P. B Chicago, IL TR ?/178# d8.19 ▲																								
1882	StL AA	17	60	4	11	0	0	0		4			.183	.234	.183	41	-4		.808	-2	92	0	O-15(2-0-13)/2-2,P	-0.5
1884	Tol AA	42	153	13	27	3	0	0		2	0		.176	.187	.196	24	-13		.815	-8	77	24	3-40/O-2(LF),CP	-1.8
Total	2	59	213	17	38	3	0	0		6	0		.178	.201	.192	29	-17		.815	-10	77	24	/3-40,O-17(4-0-13),P-2,2-2,C	-2.3
BROWN, EDDIE Edward William "Glass Arm Eddie" B 7.17.1891 Milligan, NE D 9.10.1956 Vallejo, CA BR/TR 6-3/190# d9.26																								
1920	NY N	3	8	1	1	1	0	0	0	0	0	3	.125	.125	.250	6	-1	0-0	1.000	-0	97	0	/O-2(CF)	-0.2
1921	NY N	70	128	16	36	6	2	0	12	4	4	11	.281	.324	.359	80	-4	1-0	.956	-1	101	56	O-30(2-26-2)	-0.6
1924	Bro N	114	455	56	140	30	4	5	78	26	0	15	.308	.345	.424	108	5	3-5	.975	-4	106	26	*O-114(CF)	-0.4
1925	Bro N	**153**	618	88	189	39	11	5	99	22	2	18	.306	.332	.429	95	-6	3-4	.972	1	108	49	*O-153(CF)	-1.2
1926	Bos N	**153**	612	71	**201**	31	8	2	84	23	2	20	.328	.355	.415	117	12	5	.965	3	110	69	*O-153(73-80-0)	0.6
1927	Bos N	**155**	558	64	171	35	6	2	75	28	0	20	.306	.340	.401	106	4	11	.980	3	**111**	74	*O-150(LF)/1	-0.4
1928	Bos N	142	523	45	140	28	2	2	59	24	4	22	.268	.305	.340	72	-22	6	.960	-3	103	58	*O-129(80-50-1)/1	-3.3
Total	7	790	2902	341	878	170	33	16	407	127	12	109	.303	.334	.400	99	-12	29-9	.970	-1	108	56	O-731(305-425-3)/1-2	-5.5
BROWN, RANDY Edwin Randolph B 8.29.1944 Leesburg, FL BL/TR 5-7/170# d9.11																								
1969	Cal A	13	25	3	4	1	0	0	0	6-0	0	1	.160	.323	.200	52	-1	0-0	1.000	0	77	143	C-10/O(CF)	-0.1
1970	Cal A	5	4	0	0	0	0	0	0	0-0	0	0	.000	.000	.000	-99	-1	0-0	1.000	-2	42	0	/C-5	-0.3
Total	2	18	29	3	4	1	0	0	0	6-0	0	1	.138	.286	.172	32	-2	0-0	1.000	-2	70	113	/C-15,O(CF)	-0.4
BROWN, EMIL Emil Quincy B 12.29.1974 Chicago, IL BR/TR 6-2/195# d4.3																								
1997	Pit N	66	95	16	17	2	1	2	6	10-1	7	32	.179	.304	.284	54	-6	5-1	.948	2	117	134	O-42(30-8-4)	-0.5
1998	Pit N	13	39	2	10	1	0	0	3	1-0	1	11	.256	.293	.282	51	-3	0-0	1.000	2	119	333	O-10(9-1-1)	-0.1
1999	Pit N	6	14	0	2	1	0	0	0	0-0	0	3	.143	.143	.214	-11	-2	0-0	1.000	0	113	0	/O-6(LF)	-0.2
2000	Pit N	50	119	13	26	5	0	3	16	11-0	3	34	.218	.299	.336	61	-7	3-1	1.000	0	90	165	O-38(14-12-18)	-0.7
2001	Pit N	61	123	18	25	4	1	3	13	15-1	2	42	.203	.300	.325	60	-7	10-4	.988	1	99	216	O-54(2-51-2)	-0.5
	SD N	13	14	3	1	0	0	0	0	1-0	0	7	.071	.133	.071	-49	-3	2-0	1.000	-1	83	0	O-11(4-6-2)	-0.3
	Year	74	137	21	26	4	1	3	13	16-1	2	49	.190	.284	.299	51	-10	12-4	.989	1	97	188	O-65(6-57-4)	-0.8
Total	5	209	404	52	81	13	2	8	38	38-2	13	129	.200	.289	.302	53	-28	20-6	.983	5	102	176	O-161(65-78-27)	-2.3
BROWN, FRED Fred Herbert B 4.12.1879 Ossipee, NH D 2.3.1955 Somersworth, NH BR/TR 5-10.5/190# d5.4																								
1901	Bos N	7	14	1	2	0	0	0	2	0	0		.143	.143	.143	-16	-2	0	1.000	1	205	0	/O-5(3-0-2)	-0.2
1902	Bos N	2	6	1	2	1	0	0	0	0	0		.333	.333	.500	155	0	0	1.000	0	726	0	/O-2(RF)	0.1
Total	2	9	20	2	4	1	0	0	2	0	0		.200	.200	.250	30	-2	0	1.000	1	314	0	/O-7(3-0-4)	-0.1
BROWN, IKE Isaac B 4.13.1942 Memphis, TN D 5.17.2001 Memphis, TN BR/TR 6-1/205# d6.17 OF Total (44-LF 7-RF)																								
1969	Det A	70	170	24	39	4	3	5	12	26-4	2	43	.229	.338	.376	96	-1	2-3	.962	-8	96	77	2-45,3-12/O-3(1-0-2),S	-0.7
1970	Det A	56	94	17	27	5	0	4	15	13-0	1	26	.287	.376	.468	132	4	0-0	.935	-7	65	65	2-23/O-4(3-0-1),3	-0.2
1971	Det A	59	110	20	28	1	0	8	19	19-1	0	25	.255	.359	.482	133	5	0-1	1.000	-0	92	45	1-17/O-9(8-0-1),2-8,3-4,S	0.4
1972	†Det A	51	84	12	21	3	0	2	10	17-1	0	23	.250	.376	.357	115	3	1-2	1.000	5	188	103	0-22(20-0-3),1-13/2-3,S3	0.6
1973	Det A	42	76	12	22	2	1	1	9	15-1	0	13	.289	.407	.382	115	2	0-1	.983	-0	123	87	1-21,O-12(LF)/3-2,D-2	0.0
1974	Det A	2	2	0	0	0	0	0	0	0-0	0	0	.000	.000	.000	-97	-1	0-0	1.000	0	64	0	/3-2	0.0
Total	6	280	536	85	137	15	4	20	65	90-7	3	130	.256	.364	.410	115	12	3-7	.956	-11	89	75	/2-79,1-51,O-50L,3-22,S-3,D-2	0.1
BROWN, JIM James Donaldson "Don" or "Moose" B 3.31.1897 Laurel, MD BR/TR 6/178# d9.13																								
1915	StL N	1	2	0	1	0	0	0	0	2	0	1	.500	.750	.500	281	1	0	1.000	-0	61	0	/O(CF)	0.1
1916	Phi A	14	42	6	10	2	1	1	5	4	0	9	.238	.304	.405	119	1	0	.895	-1	79	155	O-12(0-6-6)	-0.1

Year	Tm Lg	G	AB	R	H	2B	3B	HR	RBI	BB-IB	HP	SO	AVG	OBP	SLG	AOPS	ABR	SB-CS	FA	FR	Rng	Thr	G at Pos	BFW
Total	2	15	44	6	11	2	1	1	5	6	0	10	.250	.340	.409	131	2	0	.900	-1	78	145	/O-13(0-7-6)	0.0

BROWN, JIMMY James Roberson B 4.25.1910 Jamesville, NC D 12.29.1977 Bath, NC BB/TR 5-8.5/165# d4.23 Mil 1944-45 C3

Year	Tm Lg	G	AB	R	H	2B	3B	HR	RBI	BB-IB	HP	SO	AVG	OBP	SLG	AOPS	ABR	SB-CS	FA	FR	Rng	Thr	G at Pos	BFW
1937	StL N	138	525	86	145	20	9	2	53	27	1	29	.276	.313	.360	81	-15	10	.964	-14	101	85	*2-112,S-25/3	-2.1
1938	StL N	108	382	50	115	12	6	0	38	27	2	9	.301	.350	.364	91	-4	7	.968	-0	100	120	2-49,S-30,3-24	0.1
1939	StL N	147	645	88	192	31	8	3	51	32	4	18	.298	.335	.384	87	-12	4	.957	-4	101	98	*S-104,2-50	-0.6
1940	StL N	107	454	56	127	17	4	0	30	24	1	15	.280	.317	.335	76	-15	9	.977	-17	93	107	2-48,3-41,S-28	-2.7
1941	StL N	132	549	81	168	28	9	3	56	45	4	22	.306	.363	.406	109	7	2	.965	2	101	102	*3-123,2-11	1.4
1942	†StL N★	145	606	75	155	28	4	1	71	52	0	11	.256	.315	.320	80	-15	4	.970	-7	89	125	2-82,3-66,S-12	-1.5
1943	StL N	34	110	6	20	4	2	0	8	6	0	1	.182	.224	.255	37	-9	0	.978	2	98	102	2-19/3-9,S-6	-0.7
1946	Pit N	79	241	23	58	6	0	0	12	18	0	5	.241	.293	.266	58	-13	3	.960	-2	99	82	S-30,2-21/3-9	-1.3
Total	8	890	3512	465	980	146	42	9	319	231	12	110	.279	.326	.352	84	-76	39	.968	-42	97	103	2-392,3-273,S-235	-7.4

BROWN, JIM James W. H. B 12.12.1860 Clinton Co., PA D 4.6.1908 Williamsport, PA d4.17 ▲

Year	Tm Lg	G	AB	R	H	2B	3B	HR	RBI	BB-IB	HP	SO	AVG	OBP	SLG	AOPS	ABR	SB-CS	FA	FR	Rng	Thr	G at Pos	BFW
1884	Alt U	21	88	12	22	2	2	1		1			.250	.258	.352	82	-5		.615	-3	60	0	O-14(2-4-8),P-11	-0.6
	NY N	1	3	0	0	0	0	0	0	0		1	.000	.000	.000	-98	-1		.333	-0	54	0	/P	0.0
	StP U	6	16	5	5	4	0	0		1			.313	.353	.563	320	4		.706	0	148	0	/P-6,1O(RF)	0.1
1886	Phi AA	1	3	0	0	0	0	0	0	0	0		.000	.000	.000	-99	-1	0	1.000	-0	73	0	/P	0.0
Total	2	29	110	17	27	6	2	1	0	2	0	1	.245	.259	.364	92	-3	0	.741	-4	117	0	/P-19,O-15(2-4-9),1	-0.5

BROWN, JARVIS Jarvis Ardel B 3.26.1967 Waukegan, IL BR/TR 5-7/170# d7.2

Year	Tm Lg	G	AB	R	H	2B	3B	HR	RBI	BB-IB	HP	SO	AVG	OBP	SLG	AOPS	ABR	SB-CS	FA	FR	Rng	Thr	G at Pos	BFW
1991	†Min A	38	37	10	8	0	0	0	0	2-0	0	8	.216	.256	.216	31	-4	7-1	.955	-2	74	0	O-32(3-11-19)/D-4	-0.5
1992	Min A	35	15	8	1	0	0	0	0	2-0	1	4	.067	.222	.067	-15	-2	2-2	.952	-0	108	0	O-31(4-9-18)/D-2	-0.3
1993	SD N	47	133	21	31	9	2	0	8	15-0	6	26	.233	.335	.331	78	-3	3-3	.982	4	121	104	O-43(5-40-0)	0.0
1994	Atl N	17	15	3	2	1	0	1	1	0-0	0	2	.133	.133	.400	31	-2	0-0	1.000	0	108	0	/O-9(3-4-2)	-0.2
1995	Bal A	18	27	2	4	1	0	0	1	7-0	0	9	.148	.324	.185	36	-2	1-1	1.000	-2	73	0	O-17(0-13-5)	-0.4
Total	5	155	227	44	46	11	2	1	10	26-0	7	49	.203	.303	.282	57	-13	13-7	.978	-0	104	53	O-132(15-77-44)/D-6	-1.4

BROWN, JAKE Jerald Ray B 3.22.1948 Sumrall, MS D 12.18.1981 Houston, TX BR/TR 6-2/200# d5.17

Year	Tm Lg	G	AB	R	H	2B	3B	HR	RBI	BB-IB	HP	SO	AVG	OBP	SLG	AOPS	ABR	SB-CS	FA	FR	Rng	Thr	G at Pos	BFW
1975	SF N	41	43	6	9	3	0	0	4	5-0	0	13	.209	.292	.279	57	-2	0-0	.857	-0	87	211	O-14(9-1-4)	-0.3

BROWN, CHRIS John Christopher B 8.15.1961 Jackson, MS BR/TR 6-2/210# d9.3

Year	Tm Lg	G	AB	R	H	2B	3B	HR	RBI	BB-IB	HP	SO	AVG	OBP	SLG	AOPS	ABR	SB-CS	FA	FR	Rng	Thr	G at Pos	BFW
1984	SF N	23	84	6	24	7	0	1	11	9-0	1	19	.286	.358	.405	119	3	2-1	.900	-2	88	72	3-23	0.0
1985	SF N	131	432	50	117	20	3	16	61	38-4	**11**	78	.271	.345	.442	125	14	2-3	**.971**	4	97	74	*3-120	1.6
1986	SF N★	116	416	57	132	16	3	7	49	33-4	9	43	.317	.376	.421	127	15	13-9	.933	-10	88	100	*3-111/S-2	0.3
1987	SF N	38	132	17	32	6	0	6	17	9-1	3	16	.242	.306	.424	95	-1	1-3	.905	-3	88	87	3-37/S	-0.6
	SD N	44	155	17	36	3	0	6	23	11-0	3	30	.232	.294	.368	77	-6	3-1	.942	-4	88	170	3-43	-1.0
	Year	82	287	34	68	9	0	12	40	20-1	6	46	.237	.299	.394	86	-7	4-4	.923	-7	88	132	3-80/S	-1.6
1988	SD N	80	247	14	58	6	0	2	19	19-3	3	49	.235	.295	.283	69	-10	0-0	.949	2	101	143	3-72	-0.8
1989	Det A	17	57	3	11	3	0	0	4	1-0	0	17	.193	.203	.246	28	-6	0-0	.909	-1	84	138	3-17	-0.7
Total	6	449	1523	164	410	61	6	38	184	120-12	30	252	.269	.333	.392	105	9	21-17	.943	-15	93	105	3-423/S-3	-1.2

BROWN, LINDSAY John Lindsay "Red" B 7.22.1911 Mason, TX D 1.1.1967 San Antonio, TX BR/TR 5-10/160# d7.13

Year	Tm Lg	G	AB	R	H	2B	3B	HR	RBI	BB-IB	HP	SO	AVG	OBP	SLG	AOPS	ABR	SB-CS	FA	FR	Rng	Thr	G at Pos	BFW
1937	Bro N	48	115	16	31	3	1	0	6	3	0	17	.270	.288	.313	62	-6	1	.937	2	100	123	S-45	-0.2

BROWN, JOE Joseph E. B 4.4.1859 Warren, PA D 6.28.1888 Warren, PA 5-10/162# d8.16 ▲

Year	Tm Lg	G	AB	R	H	2B	3B	HR	RBI	BB-IB	HP	SO	AVG	OBP	SLG	AOPS	ABR	SB-CS	FA	FR	Rng	Thr	G at Pos	BFW
1884	Chi N	15	61	6	13	1	0	0	3	0		15	.213	.213	.230	36	-5		.750	-1	98	0	/O-9(0-1-9),P-7,1C	-0.3
1885	Bal AA	5	19	2	3	0	0	0	0	0	0		.158	.158	.158	-0	-2		1.000	0	80	0	/P-4,2	0.0
Total	2	20	80	8	16	1	0	0	3	0	0	15	.200	.200	.213	28	-7		.895	-1	96	0	/P-11,O-9(0-1-9),2C1	-0.3

BROWN, KEVIN Kevin Lee B 4.21.1973 Valparaiso, IN BR/TR 6-2/200# d9.12

Year	Tm Lg	G	AB	R	H	2B	3B	HR	RBI	BB-IB	HP	SO	AVG	OBP	SLG	AOPS	ABR	SB-CS	FA	FR	Rng	Thr	G at Pos	BFW
1996	Tex A	3	4	1	0	0	0	0	1	2-0	1	2	.000	.375	.000	20	0	0-0	1.000	1	0	221	/C-2,D	0.1
1997	Tex A	4	5	1	2	0	0	1	1	0-0	0	0	.400	.400	1.000	237	1	0-0	.900	-0	101	0	/C-4	0.1
1998	Tor A	52	110	17	29	7	1	2	15	9-0	2	31	.264	.320	.400	89	-2	0-0	.993	3	84	107	C-52	0.3
1999	Tor A	2	9	1	4	2	0	0	1	0-0	0	3	.444	.444	.667	176	1	0-0	1.000	-1	130	155	/C-2	0.1
2000	Mil N	5	17	3	4	3	0	0	1	1-0	0	5	.235	.278	.412	72	-1	0-0	.957	-2	70	0	/C-5	-0.3
2001	Mil N	17	43	7	9	0	1	4	12	2-0	1	18	.209	.261	.535	100	-1	0-0	1.000	-2	77	131	C-16	-0.1
2002	Bos A	2	1	0	0	0	0	0	0	0-0	0	0	.000	.000	.000	-98	0	0-0	1.000	-0	0	0	/C-2	0.0
Total	7	85	189	30	48	12	2	7	31	14-0	4	59	.254	.311	.450	96	-2	0-0	.990	-2	81	105	/C-83,D	0.2

BROWN, LARRY Larry Leslie B 3.1.1940 Shinnston, WV BR/TR 5-11/165# d7.6 b-Dick

Year	Tm Lg	G	AB	R	H	2B	3B	HR	RBI	BB-IB	HP	SO	AVG	OBP	SLG	AOPS	ABR	SB-CS	FA	FR	Rng	Thr	G at Pos	BFW
1963	Cle A	74	247	28	63	6	0	5	18	22-0	1	27	.255	.316	.340	85	-5	4-3	.938	-9	97	68	S-46,2-27	-0.9
1964	Cle A	115	335	33	77	12	1	12	40	24-3	2	55	.230	.283	.379	84	-8	1-2	.981	9	109	92	*2-103/S-4	0.8
1965	Cle A	124	438	52	111	22	2	8	40	38-0	2	62	.253	.315	.368	93	-4	5-7	.977	3	95	108	S-95,2-26	0.8
1966	Cle A	105	340	29	78	12	0	3	17	36-3	3	58	.229	.309	.291	73	-11	0-1	.961	-6	94	94	S-90,2-10	-1.0
1967	Cle A	152	485	38	110	16	2	7	37	53-6	6	62	.227	.308	.311	84	-9	4-4	.967	-3	93	109	*S-150	0.1
1968	Cle A	154	495	43	116	18	3	6	35	43-10	5	46	.234	.300	.319	90	-6	1-1	.966	-16	84	95	*S-154	-1.1
1969	Cle A	132	469	48	112	10	2	4	24	44-2	1	43	.239	.304	.294	66	-21	5-3	.959	-8	92	99	*S-101,3-29/2-5	-1.8
1970	Cle A	72	155	17	40	5	2	0	15	20-1	0	14	.258	.339	.316	79	-4	1-0	.950	0	91	108	S-27,3-17,2-16	0.0
1971	Cle A	13	50	4	11	1	0	0	5	3-0	1	3	.220	.278	.240	44	-4	0-0	.980	-6	61	45	S-13	-0.9
	Oak A	70	189	14	37	2	1	1	9	7-0	1	19	.196	.228	.233	31	-18	1-2	.959	-1	93	134	S-31,2-23,3-10	-1.6
	Year	83	239	18	48	3	1	1	14	10-0	2	22	.201	.239	.234	35	-21	1-2	.965	-7	82	104	S-44,2-23,3-10	-2.5
1972	Oak A	47	142	11	26	2	0	0	4	13-1	0	8	.183	.250	.197	37	-11	0-0	.974	-2	96	117	2-46/3	-1.2
1973	†Bal A	17	28	4	7	0	0	1	5	5-0	0	4	.250	.353	.357	104	0	0-0	.880	-2	77	155	3-15/2	-0.2
1974	Tex A	54	76	10	15	2	0	0	5	9-0	0	13	.197	.279	.224	48	-5	0-0	.931	3	119	171	3-47/2-8,S	-0.2
Total	12	1129	3449	331	803	108	13	47	254	317-26	22	414	.233	.300	.313	76	-106	22-23	.964	-37	91	99	S-712,2-265,3-119	-7.2

BROWN, LEON Leon B 11.16.1949 Sacramento, CA BR/TR 6/185# d5.19 b-Curtis

Year	Tm Lg	G	AB	R	H	2B	3B	HR	RBI	BB-IB	HP	SO	AVG	OBP	SLG	AOPS	ABR	SB-CS	FA	FR	Rng	Thr	G at Pos	BFW
1976	NY N	64	70	11	15	3	0	0	2	4-0	0	4	.214	.257	.257	49	-5	2-4	1.000	3	102	254	O-43(39-28-6)	-0.4

BROWN, LEW Lewis J. "Blower" B 2.1.1858 Leominster, MA D 1.15.1889 Boston, MA BR/TR 5-10.5/185# d6.17

Year	Tm Lg	G	AB	R	H	2B	3B	HR	RBI	BB-IB	HP	SO	AVG	OBP	SLG	AOPS	ABR	SB-CS	FA	FR	Rng	Thr	G at Pos	BFW
1876	Bos N	45	195	23	41	6	6	2	21	3		22	.210	.222	.333	82	-4		.856	1			C-45/O(0-1-1)	-0.2
1877	Bos N	58	221	27	56	12	8	1	31	6		33	.253	.273	.394	104	0		.897	15			*C-55/1-4	1.5
1878	Pro N	58	243	44	74	21	6	1	43	7		37	.305	.324	.453	153	14		.880	3			*C-45,1-15/O(RF)P	1.6
1879	Pro N	53	229	23	59	13	4	2	38	4		24	.258	.270	.376	112	3		.847	-6			C-48/O-6(RF)	-0.1
	Chi N	6	21	2	6	1	0	0	3	1		4	.286	.318	.333	109	0		.974	0	138	206	/1-6	0.0
	Year	59	250	25	65	14	4	2	41	5		28	.260	.275	.372	112	3		.847	-5			C-48/O-6(RF),1-6	-0.1
1881	Det N	27	108	16	26	3	1	3	14	3		16	.241	.261	.370	93	-1		.959	-1	84	134	1-27	-0.3
	Pro N	18	75	9	18	3	1	0	10	4		13	.240	.278	.307	85	-1		.833	-2	42	0	O-13(RF)/1-5	-0.3
	Year	45	183	25	44	6	2	3	24	7		29	.240	.268	.344	90	-2		.960	-3	80	136	1-32,O-13(RF)	-0.6
1883	Bos N	14	54	5	13	4	1	0	9	3		6	.241	.281	.352	89	-1		.943	-2	43	111	1-14	-0.3
	Lou AA	14	60	6	11	2	1	0		1			.183	.197	.250	46	-3		.891	-2	121	91	1-14/C	-0.6
1884	Bos U	85	325	50	75	18	3	1		13			.231	.260	.314	74	-20		.914	10			C-54,1-33/O-2(RF),P	-0.7
Total	7	378	1531	205	379	83	31	10	169	45		155	.248	.269	.362	99	-13		.884	17			C-248,1-118/O-23(0-1-23),P-2	0.6

BROWN, MARTY Marty Leo B 1.23.1963 Lawton, OK BR/TR 6-1/190# d9.4

Year	Tm Lg	G	AB	R	H	2B	3B	HR	RBI	BB-IB	HP	SO	AVG	OBP	SLG	AOPS	ABR	SB-CS	FA	FR	Rng	Thr	G at Pos	BFW
1988	Cin N	10	16	0	3	1	0	0	2	1-0	0	2	.188	.235	.250	38	-1	0-1	1.000	-0	100	0	/3-8	-0.2
1989	Cin N	16	30	2	5	1	0	0	4	4-0	0	9	.167	.257	.200	34	-3	0-0	.913	0	116	147	3-11	-0.2
1990	Bal A	9	15	1	3	0	0	0	0	1-0	0	7	.200	.250	.200	28	-1	0-0	1.000	-1	47	0	/2-3,3-2,D-4	-0.3
Total	3	35	61	3	11	2	0	0	6	6-0	0	18	.180	.250	.213	34	-5	0-1	.943	-1	108	88	/3-21,D-4,2-3	-0.7

BROWN, MIKE Michael Charles B 12.29.1959 San Francisco, CA BR/TR 6-2/195# d7.21

Year	Tm Lg	G	AB	R	H	2B	3B	HR	RBI	BB-IB	HP	SO	AVG	OBP	SLG	AOPS	ABR	SB-CS	FA	FR	Rng	Thr	G at Pos	BFW
1983	Cal A	31	104	12	24	5	1	3	9	7-0	0	20	.231	.279	.385	81	-3	1-0	.949	-2	76	167	O-31(18-3-11)	-0.6
1984	Cal A	62	148	19	42	8	3	7	22	13-1	0	23	.284	.342	.520	136	7	0-2	.968	-2	78	181	O-44(2-0-43)/D-3	0.2
1985	Cal A	60	153	23	41	9	1	4	20	7-0	1	21	.268	.304	.418	96	-1	0-1	1.000	1	100	115	O-48(1-1-46)/D-7	-0.3
	Pit N	57	205	29	68	18	2	5	33	22-4	0	27	.332	.391	.512	154	15	2-2	.938	-4	85	81	O-56(RF)	0.8
1986	Pit N	87	243	18	53	7	0	4	26	27-3	0	32	.218	.293	.296	62	-12	2-3	.973	-3	92	59	O-71(RF)	-2.1
1988	Cal A	18	50	4	11	2	0	0	3	1-0	0	12	.220	.235	.260	40	-4	0-0	.946	1	103	226	O-18(18-0-2)	-0.4

Year	Tm Lg	G	AB	R	H	2B	3B	HR	RBI	BB-IB	HP	SO	AVG	OBP	SLG	AOPS	ABR	SB-CS	FA	FR	Rng	Thr	G at Pos	BFW
Total	5	315	903	105	239	49	7	23	113	77-8	1	135	.265	.321	.411	102	2	5-8	.964	-10	88	115	O-268(39-4-229)/D-10	-2.4
BROWN, OLIVER Oliver S. B 1849 Brooklyn, NY D 9.23.1932 Brooklyn, NY d8.1																								
1872	Atl NA	4	15	0	2	0	0	0	0	0		1	.133	.133	.133	-15	-2	0-0	.889	0	0	0	/O-4(RF)	-0.1
1875	Atl NA	3	10	0	0	0	0	0	0	0		0	.000	.000	.000	-99	-2	0-0	.833	-1	0	0	/1-2,O-2(0-1-1)	-0.2
Total	2 NA	7	25	0	2	0	0	0	0	0		1	.080	.080	.080	-46	-4	0-0	.000	-0	0	0	/O-6(0-1-5),1-2	-0.3
BROWN, OLLIE Ollie Lee "Downtown" B 2.11.1944 Tuscaloosa, AL BR/TR 6-3/200# d9.10 b-Oscar																								
1965	SF N	6	10	0	2	1	0	0	0	0-0	0	2	.200	.200	.300	38	-1	0-0	1.000	0	113	0	/O-4(RF)	-0.1
1966	SF N	115	348	32	81	7	1	7	33	33-7	2	66	.233	.303	.319	71	-13	2-5	.978	-3	84	159	*O-114(1-16-107)	-2.6
1967	SF N	120	412	44	110	12	1	13	53	25-7	4	65	.267	.312	.396	104	1	0-2	.985	-6	90	62	*O-115(0-10-111)	-1.4
1968	SF N	40	95	7	22	4	0	0	11	3-0	2	23	.232	.270	.274	64	-4	1-0	1.000	-2	83	60	O-35(3-3-30)	-0.8
1969	SD N	151	568	76	150	18	3	20	61	44-3	3	97	.264	.319	.412	108	4	10-6	.976	2	100	122	*O-148(RF)	-0.2
1970	SD N	139	534	79	156	34	1	23	89	34-8	0	78	.292	.331	.489	123	15	5-3	.964	1	99	126	*O-137(RF)	0.9
1971	SD N	145	484	36	132	16	0	9	55	52-5	3	74	.273	.346	.362	108	6	3-3	.982	2	96	88	*O-134(0-1-134)	0.1
1972	SD N	23	70	3	12	2	0	0	3	5-2	0	9	.171	.224	.200	24	-7	0-0	1.000	0	108	80	O-17(RF)	-0.9
	Oak A	20	54	5	13	1	0	1	4	6-1	0	14	.241	.317	.315	93	0	1-1	1.000	-1	97	0	O-16(0-9-9)	-0.2
	Mil A	66	179	21	50	8	0	3	25	17-3	1	24	.279	.342	.374	116	4	0-2	.992	9	124	227	O-56(RF)/3	1.0
	Year	86	233	26	63	9	0	4	29	23-4	1	38	.270	.336	.361	111	3	1-3	.994	8	118	176	O-72(0-9-65)/3	0.8
1973	Mil A	97	296	28	83	10	1	7	32	33-1	2	53	.280	.355	.392	113	6	4-1	1.000	-1	21	0	D-82/O-4(RF)	0.3
1974	Hou N	27	69	8	15	1	0	3	6	4-0	0	15	.217	.260	.362	76	-3	0-0	1.000	1	132	0	O-20(RF)	-0.3
	Phi N	43	99	11	24	5	2	4	13	6-1	0	20	.242	.286	.455	101	-1	0-1	.921	-2	83	67	O-33(24-0-9)	-0.5
	Year	70	168	19	39	6	2	7	19	10-1	0	35	.232	.275	.417	91	-3	0-1	.961	-1	103	39	O-53(24-0-29)	-0.8
1975	Phi N	84	145	19	44	12	0	6	26	15-1	0	29	.303	.369	.510	137	7	1-1	1.000	-1	103	0	O-63(23-0-48)	0.4
1976	†Phi N	92	209	30	53	10	1	5	30	33-5	0	33	.254	.350	.383	106	3	2-1	.949	2	100	162	O-75(9-0-69)	0.2
1977	†Phi N	53	70	5	17	3	1	1	13	4-1	0	14	.243	.280	.357	68	-3	1-1	1.000	-1	79	135	O-21(15-0-7)	-0.5
Total	13	1221	3642	404	964	144	11	102	454	314-45	17	616	.265	.324	.394	103	14	30-27	.977	1	97	110	O-992(75-39-910)/D-82,3	-4.6
BROWN, OSCAR Oscar Lee B 2.8.1946 Long Beach, CA BR/TR 6/175# d9.3 b-Ollie																								
1969	Atl N	7	4	2	1	0	0	0	0	0-0	0	1	.250	.250	.250	40	0	0-0	1.000	-0	90	0	/O-3(0-2-1)	0.0
1970	Atl N	28	47	6	18	2	1	1	7	7-0	1	7	.383	.464	.532	159	4	0-2	.960	-1	93	0	O-25(8-12-5)	0.2
1971	Atl N	27	43	4	9	4	0	0	5	3-0	0	8	.209	.261	.302	56	-2	0-0	1.000	0	66	118	O-15(6-7-3)	-0.3
1972	Atl N	76	164	19	37	5	1	3	16	4-0	0	29	.226	.244	.323	55	-10	0-2	.899	4	111	254	O-59(28-3-28)	-1.0
1973	Atl N	22	58	3	12	3	0	0	0	3-0	0	10	.207	.246	.259	37	-5	0-0	1.000	1	119	102	O-13(5-3-5)	-0.5
Total	5	160	316	34	77	14	2	4	28	17-0	1	55	.244	.284	.339	68	-13	0-4	.939	4	104	164	O-115(47-27-42)	-1.6
BROWN, DICK Richard Ernest B 1.17.1935 Shinnston, WV D 4.17.1970 Baltimore, MD BR/TR 6-3/190# d6.20 b-Larry																								
1957	Cle A	34	114	10	30	4	0	4	22	4-1	0	23	.263	.281	.404	88	-3	1-1	.986	-0	*79*	*108*	C-33	-0.2
1958	Cle A	68	173	20	41	5	0	7	20	14-1	3	27	.237	.304	.387	91	-2	1-0	.987	1	*90*	*127*	C-62	0.1
1959	Cle A	48	141	15	31	7	0	5	16	11-1	3	39	.220	.288	.376	85	-3	0-0	.996	1	*92*	*104*	C-48	0.0
1960	Chi A	16	43	4	7	0	0	3	5	3-0	0	11	.163	.217	.372	57	-3	0-0	.986	2	*110*	*146*	C-14	-0.1
1961	Det A	93	308	32	82	12	2	16	45	22-2	0	57	.266	.312	.474	105	0	0-2	.990	2	*116*	***131***	C-91	0.6
1962	Det A	134	431	40	104	12	0	12	40	21-7	2	66	.241	.279	.353	67	-22	0-1	.994	5	*113*	*76*	*C-132	-1.1
1963	Bal A	59	171	13	42	7	0	2	13	15-6	1	35	.246	.310	.322	80	-4	1-0	.986	2	123	85	C-58	0.1
1964	Bal A	88	230	24	59	6	0	8	32	12-4	1	45	.257	.294	.387	89	-4	2-0	.988	2	*83*	*92*	C-84	0.2
1965	Bal A	96	255	17	59	9	1	5	30	17-8	1	53	.231	.278	.333	73	-10	2-2	.983	4	*105*	***132***	C-92	-0.2
Total	9	636	1866	175	455	62	3	62	223	119-30	11	356	.244	.291	.380	83	-51	7-6	.989	19	*104*	*106*	C-614	-0.6
BROWN, ROBERT Robert d7.29																								
1874	Bal NA	2	9	0	0	0	0	0	0	0		0	.000	.000	.000	-99	-2	0-0	.727	-1	78	0	/S-2	-0.2
BROWN, BOBBY Robert William "Doc" B 10.25.1924 Seattle, WA BL/TR 6-1/180# d9.22 Mil 1952																								
1946	NY A	7	24	1	8	1	0	0	1	4	0	0	.333	.429	.375	124	1	0-0	1.000	-2	73	39	/S-5,3-2	0.0
1947	†NY A	69	150	21	45	6	1	1	18	21	1	9	.300	.390	.373	114	4	0-2	.932	-7	73	73	3-27,S-11/O-3(0-2-1)	-0.4
1948	NY A	113	363	62	109	19	5	3	48	48	1	16	.300	.383	.405	111	7	0-1	.946	-13	84	104	3-41,S-26,2-17/O-4(3-0-1)	-0.4
1949	†NY A	104	343	61	97	14	4	6	61	38	3	18	.283	.359	.399	101	0	4-3	.949	-3	94	88	3-86/O-3(1-0-2)	-0.4
1950	†NY A	95	277	33	74	4	2	4	37	39	1	18	.267	.360	.339	82	-7	3-1	.958	-4	94	89	3-82	-1.0
1951	†NY A	103	313	44	84	15	2	6	51	47	3	18	.268	.369	.387	108	5	1-1	.955	-6	91	86	3-90	-0.1
1952	NY A	29	89	6	22	2	0	1	14	9	1	6	.247	.323	.303	80	-2	1-1	.894	2	118	73	3-24	-0.1
1954	NY A	28	60	5	13	1	0	1	7	8	0	3	.217	.304	.283	65	-3	0-1	1.000	1	102	78	3-17	-0.3
Total	8	548	1619	233	452	62	14	22	237	214	10	88	.279	.367	.376	100	5	9-10	.948	-32	93	87	3-369/S-42,2-17,O-10(4-2-4)	-2.7
BROWN, BOBBY Rogers Lee B 5.24.1954 Norfolk, VA BB/TR (BL 1979) 6-1/205# d4.5																								
1979	Tor A	4	10	1	0	0	0	0	0	2-0	0	1	.000	.167	.000	-50	-2	0-0	1.000	0	110	0	/O-4(2-0-2)	-0.2
	NY A	30	68	7	17	3	1	0	3	2-0	0	17	.250	.271	.324	61	-4	2-1	.949	-0	113	0	O-27(7-20-0)/D	-0.4
	Year	34	78	8	17	3	1	0	3	4-0	0	18	.218	.256	.282	46	-6	2-1	.955	-0	113	0	O-31(9-20-2)/D	-0.6
1980	†NY A	137	412	65	107	12	5	14	47	29-4	0	82	.260	.306	.415	98	-3	27-8	.972	3	105	88	*O-131(28-81-25)/D	0.0
1981	†NY A	31	62	5	14	1	0	0	6	5-0	0	15	.226	.279	.242	53	-4	4-2	.949	3	126	166	O-29(6-11-14)/D-2	-0.2
1982	Sea A	79	245	29	59	7	1	4	17	17-2	0	32	.241	.288	.327	67	-11	28-6	.968	2	105	128	O-68(51-14-4)/D-3	-0.7
1983	SD N	57	225	40	60	5	3	5	22	23-0	0	38	.267	.333	.382	102	0	27-9	.963	-4	97	24	O-54(52-4-0)	-0.3
1984	†SD N	85	171	28	43	7	2	3	29	11-0	0	33	.251	.292	.368	86	-4	16-4	.971	2	115	69	O-53(27-13-16)	-0.1
1985	SD N	79	84	8	13	3	0	0	6	5-0	0	20	.155	.200	.190	11	-10	6-4	1.000	0	79	246	O-28(9-9-12)	-1.1
Total	7	502	1277	183	313	38	12	26	130	94-6	0	238	.245	.295	.355	80	-38	110-34	.968	6	106	87	O-394(182-152-73)/D-7	-3.0
BROWN, ROOSEVELT Roosevelt Lawayne B 8.3.1975 Vicksburg, MS BL/TR 5-11/195# d5.18																								
1999	Chi N	33	64	6	14	6	1	1	10	2-0	0	14	.219	.239	.391	58	-4	1-0	.955	-2	70	122	O-18(13-5-1)	-0.6
2000	Chi N	45	91	11	32	8	0	3	14	4-0	1	22	.352	.378	.538	133	5	0-1	1.000	2	110	104	O-28(24-1-5)	0.5
2001	Chi N	39	83	13	22	6	1	4	22	7-0	1	12	.265	.326	.506	118	2	0-0	.952	-2	77	0	O-22(21-1-3)/D-3	-0.1
2002	Chi N	111	204	14	43	12	0	3	23	23-0	3	50	.211	.299	.314	66	-11	2-2	.975	-1	99	42	O-64(48-13-4)/D	-1.3
Total	4	228	442	44	111	32	2	11	69	36-0	5	98	.251	.311	.407	89	-8	3-3	.975	-2	93	58	O-132(106-20-13)/D-4	-1.5
BROWN, SAM Samuel Wakefield B 5.21.1878 Webster, PA D 11.8.1931 Mount Pleasant, PA BR/TR d4.21																								
1906	Bos N	71	231	12	48	6	1	0	20	13	4		.208	.262	.242	59	-11	4	.970	-2	*85*	*124*	C-35,O-13(6-4-1),3-12/1-3,2-2	-1.1
1907	Bos N	70	208	17	40	6	0	0	14	12	4		.192	.250	.221	48	-12	0	.970	-4	*80*	*111*	C-63/1-2	-1.1
Total	2	141	439	29	88	12	1	0	34	25	8		.200	.256	.232	54	-23	4	.970	-6	*82*	*116*	/C-98,O-13(6-4-1),3-12,1-5,2-2	-2.2
BROWN, TOMMY Thomas Michael "Buckshot" B 12.6.1927 Brooklyn, NY BR/TR 6-1/170# d8.3 Mil 1946-47 OF Total (87-LF 6-RF)																								
1944	Bro N	46	146	17	24	4	0	0	8	8	0	17	.164	.208	.192	13	-17	0	.925	-10	82	87	S-46	-2.5
1945	Bro N	57	196	13	48	3	4	2	19	6	0	16	.245	.267	.332	66	-11	3	.918	-6	97	92	S-55/O(RF)	-1.2
1947	Bro N	15	34	3	8	1	0	0	2	1	0	6	.235	.257	.265	37	-3	0	1.000	1	102	0	/3-6,O-3(LF),S	-0.2
1948	Bro N	54	145	18	35	4	0	2	20	7	1	17	.241	.281	.310	58	-9	1	.936	-3	84	120	3-43/1	-1.2
1949	†Bro N	41	89	14	27	2	0	3	18	6	0	8	.303	.347	.427	102	0	0	.931	-0	110	55	O-27(LF)	-0.2
1950	Bro N	48	86	15	25	2	1	8	20	11	1	9	.291	.378	.616	153	6	0	.917	1	101	191	O-16(LF)	0.5
1951	Bro N	11	25	2	4	2	0	0	1	2	0	4	.160	.222	.240	24	-3	0-0	.909	-0	83	224	/O-5(LF)	-0.3
	Phi N	78	196	24	43	2	1	10	32	15	1	21	.219	.278	.393	80	-7	1-2	.966	-6	106	0	O-32(LF),2-14,1-12/3	-1.6
	Year	89	221	26	47	4	1	10	33	17	1	25	.213	.272	.376	73	-10	1-2	.957	-7	102	39	O-37(LF),2-14,1-12/3	-1.9
1952	Phi N	18	25	2	4	1	0	1	2	4	0	3	.160	.276	.320	65	-1	0-0	1.000	0	142	0	/1-3,O-3(LF)	-0.1
	Chi N	61	200	24	64	11	0	3	24	12	0	24	.320	.358	.420	114	4	1-2	.911	-16	82	75	S-39,2-10/1-5	-1.1
	Year	79	225	26	68	12	0	4	26	16	0	27	.302	.349	.409	109	3	1-2	.911	-16	82	75	S-39,2-10/1-8,O-3(LF)	-1.2
1953	Chi N	65	138	19	27	7	1	2	13	13	3	17	.196	.279	.304	51	-10	1-0	.903	-5	92	77	S-25/O-6(1-0-5)	-1.2
Total	9	494	1280	151	309	39	7	31	159	85	6	142	.241	.292	.355	74	-51	7-4	.916	-45	89	86	S-166/O-93L,3-50,2-24,1-21	-9.1
BROWN, TOM Thomas Tarlton B 9.21.1860 Liverpool, England D 10.25.1927 Washington, DC BL/TR 5-10/168# d7.6 M2 U4 ▲																								
1882	Bal AA	45	181	30	55	5	2	1	23	6			.304	.326	.370	146	9		.728	-1	155	82	O-45(RF)/P-2	0.7
1883	Col AA	**97**	420	69	115	12	7	5	32	20			.274	.307	.371	127	14		.808	-1	121	123	*O-96(RF)/P-3	1.1
1884	Col AA	107	451	93	123	9	11	5	32	24	4		.273	.315	.375	135	18		.847	-6	88	180	*O-107(RF)/P-4	1.0
1885	Pit AA	108	437	81	134	16	12	4	68	34	7		.307	.366	.426	152	27		.828	-5	111	61	*O-108(RF)/P-2	1.8

Year	Tm Lg	G	AB	R	H	2B	3B	HR	RBI	BB-IB	HP	SO	AVG	OBP	SLG	AOPS	ABR	SB-CS	FA	FR	Rng	Thr	G at Pos	BFW
1886	Pit AA	115	460	106	131	11	11	1	51	56	2		.285	.365	.363	129	17	30	.837	6	**156**	**381**	*O-115(1-1-115)/P	1.9
1887	Pit N	47	192	30	47	3	4	0	6	11	1	40	.245	.289	.302	69	-8	12	.870	2	112	0	O-47(CF)	-0.7
	Ind N	36	140	20	25	3	0	2	9	8	1	25	.179	.228	.243	32	-13	13	.813	-3	110	156	O-36(0-17-19)	-1.4
	Year	83	332	50	72	6	4	2	15	19	2	65	.217	.263	.277	53	-21	25	.851	-1	111	65	O-83(0-64-19)	-2.1
1888	Bos N	107	420	62	104	10	7	9	49	30	1	68	.248	.299	.369	109	4	46	.896	-6	94	80	*O-107(6-2-99)	-0.4
1889	Bos N	90	362	93	84	10	5	2	24	59	1	56	.232	.341	.304	76	-11	63	.901	2	73	33	O-90(88-0-2)	-1.0
1890	Bos P	128	543	146	149	23	14	4	61	86	3	84	.274	.377	.390	98	-1	79	.911	2	136	172	*O-128(CF)	-0.3
1891	Bos AA	137	589	**177**	**189**	30	**21**	5	72	70	4	96	.321	.397	.469	150	37	**106**	.878	-12	95	150	*O-137(CF)	1.8
1892	Lou N	153	660	105	150	16	8	2	45	47	5	94	.227	.284	.285	78	-18	78	.919	12	149	154	*O-153(CF)	-1.4
1893	Lou N	122	529	104	127	15	7	5	54	56	5	63	.240	.319	.323	77	-17	**66**	.929	26	**192**	**273**	*O-122(CF)	0.1
1894	Lou N	**130**	541	123	137	22	14	9	57	60	3	74	.253	.331	.396	80	-19	66	.912	2	97	147	*O-130(CF)	-2.0
1895	StL N	84	355	73	78	11	4	1	31	48	2	44	.220	.316	.282	56	-23	34	.951	7	120	166	O-84(1-83-0)	-1.7
	Was N	34	134	25	32	8	3	2	16	18	0	16	.239	.329	.388	85	-3	8	.909	-5	23	0	O-34(CF)	-0.8
	Year	118	489	98	110	19	7	3	47	66	2	60	.225	.320	.311	64	-26	42	.942	2	95	123	*O-118(1-117-0)	-2.5
1896	Was N	116	435	87	128	17	6	2	59	58	6	49	.294	.385	.375	101	3	28	.928	-4	45	46	*O-116(0-114-2)	-0.6
1897	Was N	116	469	91	137	17	2	5	45	52	1		.292	.364	.369	94	-3	25	.928	-2	102	149	*O-115(CF)/,M	-1.0
1898	Was N	16	55	8	9	1	0	0	2	5	0		.164	.233	.182	19	-6	3	.925	0	49	0	O-15(CF)/,M	-0.6
Total	17	1788	7373	1523	1954	239	138	64	736	748	46	709	.265	.336	.361	101	7	657	.890	14	113	144	*O-1785(96-1098-593)/P-12	-3.5
BROWN, TOM Thomas William B 12.12.1940 Laureldale, PA BB/TL 6-1/190# d4.8																								
1963	Was A	61	116	8	17	4	0	1	4	11-0	1	45	.147	.227	.207	23	-12	2-1	1.000	-2	82	0	O-16(10-5-1),1-14	-1.6
BROWN, WILLARD Willard Jessie B 6.26.1915 Shreveport, LA D 8.8.1996 Houston, TX BR/TR 5-11.5/200# d7.19																								
1947	StL A	21	67	4	12	3	0	1	6	0	0	7	.179	.179	.269	23	-7	2-2	1.000	1	124	0	O-18(0-1-17)	-0.8
BROWN, GATES William James B 5.2.1939 Crestline, OH BL/TR 5-11/220# d6.19 C7																								
1963	Det A	55	82	16	22	3	1	2	14	8-0	1	13	.268	.333	.402	104	0	2-1	1.000	4	138	320	O-16(LF)	0.4
1964	Det A	123	426	65	116	22	6	15	54	31-0	4	53	.272	.326	.458	114	7	11-4	.981	4	113	76	*O-106(LF)	0.7
1965	Det A	96	227	33	58	14	2	10	43	17-1	0	33	.256	.305	.467	115	4	6-0	.973	1	113	31	O-56(49-0-7)	0.3
1966	Det A	88	169	27	45	5	1	7	27	18-2	2	19	.266	.337	.432	119	4	3-0	.980	-0	78	194	O-43(LF)	0.3
1967	Det A	51	91	17	17	1	1	2	9	13-0	0	15	.187	.286	.286	68	-4	0-0	1.000	-0	85	102	O-20(LF)	-0.5
1968	†Det A	67	92	15	34	7	2	6	15	12-1	0	4	.370	.442	.685	231	15	0-0	1.000	-1	78	120	O-17(LF)/1	1.5
1969	Det A	60	93	13	19	1	2	1	6	5-0	1	17	.204	.250	.290	49	-7	0-0	.906	1	127	108	O-14(LF)	-0.7
1970	Det A	81	124	18	28	3	0	3	24	20-0	1	14	.226	.331	.323	82	-2	0-0	.950	-0	102	76	O-26(LF)	-0.4
1971	Det A	82	195	37	66	2	3	11	29	21-2	2	17	.338	.408	.549	163	16	4-2	.986	-2	90	78	O-56(LF)	1.2
1972	†Det A	103	252	33	58	5	0	10	31	26-3	2	28	.230	.304	.369	97	-1	3-0	.977	5	123	118	O-72(LF)	0.2
1973	Det A	125	377	48	89	11	1	12	50	52-6	1	41	.236	.328	.366	90	-4	1-1	1.000	-0	43	0	*D-119/O-2(LF)	-0.8
1974	Det A	73	99	7	24	2	0	4	17	10-2	0	15	.242	.312	.384	96	-1	0-0	—	0	0	0	D-13	-0.1
1975	Det A	47	35	1	6	2	0	1	3	9-1	1	6	.171	.356	.314	87	0	0-0	—	0			H	-0.1
Total	13	1051	2262	330	582	78	19	84	322	242-18	15	275	.257	.330	.420	109	27	30-8	.977	12	107	99	O-428(421-0-7),D-132/1	2.0
BROWN, WILLARD William M. "Big Bill" or "California" B 1866 San Francisco, CA D 12.20.1897 San Francisco, CA BR/TR 6-2/190# d5.10 OF Total (2-LF 5-CF 13-RF)																								
1887	NY N	49	170	17	37	3	2	0	25	10	3	15	.218	.273	.259	51	-11	10	.914	-2			C-46/3-3,O-2(RF)	-0.8
1888	†NY N	20	59	4	16	1	0	0	6	1	0	8	.271	.283	.288	84	-1	1	.893	-1			C-20	-0.1
1889	†NY N	40	139	16	36	10	0	1	29	9	3	9	.259	.318	.353	87	-2	6	.846	-5			C-37/O-3(CF)	-0.5
1890	NY P	60	230	47	64	8	4	4	43	13	1	13	.278	.320	.400	84	-7	5	.900	-4	*100*	*107*	C-34,O-13(2-0-11)/1-9,3-3,2-2	-0.8
1891	Phi N	115	441	62	107	20	4	0	50	34	4	35	.243	.303	.306	75	-14	7	**.989**	4	111	113	*1-97,C-19/O-2(CF)	-1.6
1893	Bal N	7	32	5	4	3	0	0	5	1	0	3	.125	.152	.219	-2	-5	0	.985	-0	80	67	/1-7	-0.4
	Lou N	111	461	80	140	23	7	1	85	50	1	32	.304	.373	.390	112	10	9	.989	-1	86	103	*1-111/C	0.7
	Year	118	493	85	144	26	7	1	90	51	1	35	.292	.360	.379	104	5	9	**.988**	-1	86	101	*1-118/C	0.3
1894	Lou N	13	48	5	10	2	0	0	9	5	0	7	.208	.283	.250	31	-5	1	.977	4	231	67	1-13	-0.1
	StL N	3	9	0	1	0	0	0	0	0	0	2	.111	.111	.111	-46	-2	0	1.000	0	120	107	/1-3	-0.2
	Year	16	57	5	11	2	0	0	9	5	0	9	.193	.258	.228	19	-8	1	.982	4	211	74	1-16	-0.3
Total	7	418	1589	236	415	70	17	6	252	123	12	124	.261	.319	.338	82	-37	39	.987	-5	105	103	1-240,C-157/O-20R,3-6,2-2	-3.8
BROWN, BILL William Verna "Verna" B 7.8.1893 Coleman, TX D 5.13.1965 Lubbock, TX BL/TL 5-8/185# d8.15																								
1912	StL A	9	20	0	4	0	0	0	1	0	0		.200	.200	.200	15	-2	0	.909	-0	111	0	/O-7(6-1-0)	-0.3
BROWNE, BYRON Byron Ellis B 12.27.1942 St.Joseph, MO BR/TR 6-2/200# d9.9																								
1965	Chi N	4	6	0	0	0	0	0	0	0-0	0	2	.000	.000	.000	-98	-2	0-0	.667	-0	78	0	/O-4(LF)	-0.2
1966	Chi N	120	419	46	102	15	7	16	51	40-1	5	143	.243	.316	.427	103	1	3-3	.967	-5	98	40	*O-114(67-42-10)	-0.9
1967	Chi N	10	19	3	3	2	0	0	2	4-1	0	5	.158	.304	.263	61	-1	1-1	1.000	-0	107	0	/O-8(0-2-6)	-0.1
1968	Hou N	10	13	0	3	0	0	0	1	4-0	0	6	.231	.412	.231	99	0	0-0	1.000	1	119	375	/O-2(RF)	0.1
1969	StL N	22	53	9	12	0	1	1	7	11-1	0	14	.226	.359	.321	92	0	0-0	1.000	4	130	320	O-16(5-5-8)	0.3
1970	Phi N	104	270	29	67	17	2	10	36	33-5	0	72	.248	.327	.437	107	2	1-2	.975	1	105	86	O-88(6-23-61)	0.0
1971	Phi N	58	68	5	14	3	0	3	5	8-0	0	23	.206	.289	.382	89	-1	0-0	1.000	-2	79	0	O-30(17-4-10)	-0.4
1972	Phi N	21	21	2	4	0	0	0	0	1-0	0	8	.190	.227	.190	19	-2	0-0	1.000	-1	37	0	/O-9(0-3-6)	-0.3
Total	8	349	869	94	205	37	10	30	102	101-8	5	273	.236	.318	.405	98	-3	5-6	.973	-2	101	74	O-271(99-79-103)	-1.5
BROWNE, EARL Earl James "Snitz" B 3.5.1911 Louisville, KY D 1.12.1993 Whittier, CA BL/TL 6/175# d9.12																								
1935	Pit N	9	32	6	8	2	0	0	6	2	0	8	.250	.294	.313	61	-2	0	1.000	0	93	70	/1-9	-0.2
1936	Pit N	8	23	7	7	1	2	0	3	1	0	4	.304	.333	.522	124	0	0	1.000	1	95	385	/O-4(LF),1	0.1
1937	Phi N	105	332	42	97	19	3	6	52	21	4	41	.292	.342	.422	98	-1	4	.980	3	94	146	O-54(8-5-43),1-23	-0.3
1938	Phi N	21	74	4	19	4	0	0	8	5	0	11	.257	.304	.311	71	-3	0	.978	-0	101	78	1-16/O-2(LF)	-0.5
Total	4	143	461	59	131	26	5	6	69	29	4	64	.284	.332	.401	93	-6	4	.983	4	96	156	/O-60(14-5-43),1-49	-0.9
BROWNE, GEORGE George Edward B 1.12.1876 Richmond, VA D 12.9.1920 Hyde Park, NY BL/TR 5-10.5/160# d9.27																								
1901	Phi N	8	26	2	5	1	0	0	4	1	1		.192	.250	.231	39	-2	2	1.000	-0	0	0	/O-8(6-1-1)	-0.3
1902	Phi N	70	281	41	73	7	1	0	26	16	2		.260	.304	.292	84	-5	11	.910	6	137	36	O-70(LF)	-0.4
	NY N	53	216	30	69	9	5	0	14	9	3		.319	.355	.407	137	8	13	.895	-1	92	52	O-53(51-0-2)	0.4
	Year	123	497	71	142	16	6	0	40	25	5		.286	.326	.342	107	3	24	.904	4	118	43	*O-123(121-0-2)	0.0
1903	NY N	141	591	105	185	20	3	3	45	43	4		.313	.364	.372	106	5	27	.918	-6	66	91	*O-141(1-0-140)	-0.7
1904	NY N	150	596	**99**	169	16	5	4	39	39	4		.284	.332	.347	105	3	24	.925	-6	106	148	*O-149(RF)	-1.0
1905	†NY N	127	536	95	157	16	14	4	43	20	2		.293	.321	.397	111	4	26	.915	-9	54	29	*O-127(RF)	-1.1
1906	NY N	122	477	61	126	10	4	0	38	27	0		.264	.304	.302	87	-9	32	.934	-5	113	87	*O-121(RF)	-2.1
1907	NY N	127	458	54	119	11	10	5	37	31	1		.260	.308	.360	106	1	15	.941	-7	88	137	*O-121(RF)	-1.2
1908	Bos N	138	536	61	122	10	6	1	34	36	0		.228	.276	.274	77	-15	17	.950	2	111	181	*O-138(12-17-109)	-2.3
1909	Chi N	12	39	7	8	0	1	0	1	5	0		.205	.295	.256	70	-1	3	.944	-1	73	0	O-12(0-11-1)	-0.3
	Was A	103	393	40	107	15	5	1	16	17	3		.272	.308	.344	111	3	13	.935	-3	92	96	*O-101(63-4-34)	-0.5
1910	Was A	7	22	1	4	0	0	0	0	1	0		.182	.217	.182	26	-2	0	.667	-1	64	0	/O-5(LF)	-0.4
	Chi A	30	112	17	27	4	1	0	4	12	0		.241	.315	.295	95	0	5	.952	-3	79	53	O-29(0-20-9)	-0.6
	Year	37	134	18	31	4	1	0	4	13	0		.231	.299	.276	84	-2	5	.917	-5	77	46	O-34(5-20-9)	-1.0
1911	Bro N	8	12	1	4	0	0	0	2	1	0	1	.333	.385	.333	106	0	2	1.000	-0	121	0	/O-2(RF)	0.0
1912	Phi N	6	5	0	1	0	0	0	0	1	0	0	.200	.333	.200	45	0	0	—	0			H	0.0
Total	12	1102	4300	614	1176	119	55	18	303	259	20	1	.273	.318	.339	100	-10	190	.927	-36	93	100	*O-1077(208-53-816)	-10.5
BROWNE, JERRY Jerome Austin B 2.13.1966 Christiansted, V.I. BB/TR 5-10/170# d9.6 OF Total (98-LF 67-CF 25-RF)																								
1986	Tex A	12	24	6	10	2	0	0	3	1-0	0	4	.417	.440	.500	151	2	0-2	.923	-2	86	97	/2-8	0.0
1987	Tex A	132	454	63	123	16	6	1	38	61-0	2	50	.271	.358	.339	87	-7	27-17	.980	-4	92	77	*2-130/D	-0.4
1988	Tex A	73	214	26	49	9	2	1	17	25-0	0	32	.229	.308	.304	71	-8	7-5	.958	-25	75	62	2-70/D	-3.3
1989	Cle A	153	598	83	179	31	4	5	45	68-10	1	64	.299	.370	.390	113	13	14-6	.979	-38	87	70	*2-151/D-2	-2.1
1990	Cle A	140	513	92	137	26	5	6	50	72-1	2	46	.267	.353	.372	105	6	12-7	.985	-11	96	73	*2-139	-0.1
1991	Cle A	107	290	28	66	5	2	1	29	27-0	1	29	.228	.292	.269	57	-17	2-4	.964	-3	98	65	2-47,O-17(LF),3-15/D-7	-2.1
1992	†Oak A	111	324	43	93	12	2	3	40	40-0	4	40	.287	.366	.364	113	7	3-3	.965	-7	89	108	3-58,O-43(17-23-6),2-19/SD	0.0
1993	Oak A	76	260	27	65	13	0	2	19	22-0	0	17	.250	.306	.323	74	-9	4-0	.985	-0	109	33	O-56(30-26-4),3-13/2-3,1-2	-1.0
1994	Fla N	101	329	42	97	17	4	3	30	52-3	2	23	.295	.392	.398	104	5	3-0	.931	-1	90	118	3-62,O-30(23-7-4),2-15	0.5

Year	Tm Lg	G	AB	R	H	2B	3B	HR	RBI	BB-IB	HP	SO	AVG	OBP	SLG	AOPS	ABR	SB-CS	FA	FR	Rng	Thr	G at Pos	BFW
1995	Fla N	77	184	21	47	4	0	1	17	25-0	1	20	.255	.346	.293	71	-7	1-1	.959	6	109	158	O-29(11-11-11),2-27/3-7	0.0
Total	10	982	3190	431	866	135	25	23	288	393-14	13	325	.271	.351	.351	94	-15	73-45	.977	-85	90	71	2-609,O-175L,3-155/D-12,1-2,S	-8.5

BROWNE, PIDGE Prentice Almont B 3.21.1929 Peekskill, NY D 6.3.1997 Houston, TX BL/TL 6-1/190# d4.13

Year	Tm Lg	G	AB	R	H	2B	3B	HR	RBI	BB-IB	HP	SO	AVG	OBP	SLG	AOPS	ABR	SB-CS	FA	FR	Rng	Thr	G at Pos	BFW
1962	Hou N	65	100	8	21	4	2	1	10	13-0	0	9	.210	.298	.320	72	-4	0-0	.983	1	118	74	1-26	-0.4

BROWNING, PETE Louis Rogers "The Gladiator" B 6.17.1861 Louisville, KY D 9.10.1905 Louisville, KY BR/TR 6/180# d5.2 OF Total (477-LF 490-CF 35-RF)

Year	Tm Lg	G	AB	R	H	2B	3B	HR	RBI	BB-IB	HP	SO	AVG	OBP	SLG	AOPS	ABR	SB-CS	FA	FR	Rng	Thr	G at Pos	BFW
1882	Lou AA	69	288	67	109	17	3	5		26			**.378**	**.430**	**.510**	**229**	**41**		.890	9	104	117	2-42,S-18,3-13	**4.6**
1883	Lou AA	84	358	95	121	15	9	4		23			.338	.378	.464	183	34		.861	-9	48	81	O-48(34-11-3),S-26,3-10/2-3,1	2.2
1884	Lou AA	103	447	101	150	33	8	4	47	13	2		.336	.357	.472	176	37		.806	-12	67	81	3-52,O-24(1-23-0),1-23/2-4,P	2.1
1885	Lou AA	**112**	481	98	**174**	34	10	9	73	25	0		**.362**	**.393**	.530	**190**	**48**		.900	3	104	115	*O-112(CF)	**4.2**
1886	Lou AA	112	467	86	159	29	6	2	68	30	7		.340	.389	.441	151	27	26	.791	-13	74	29	*O-112(31-82-0)	0.9
1887	Lou AA	134	547	137	220	35	16	4	118	55	8		.402	.464	.547	178	59	103	.868	-6	93	152	*O-134(CF)	3.8
1888	Lou AA	99	383	58	120	22	8	3	72	37	4		.313	.380	.436	164	29	36	.888	-1	104	226	*O-99(20-79-0)	2.3
1889	Lou AA	83	324	39	83	19	5	2	32	34	0	30	.256	.327	.364	98	0	21	.882	-4	74	96	O-83(LF)	-0.6
1890	Cle P	118	493	112	184	**40**	8	5	93	75	3	36	**.373**	.459	.517	**175**	**60**	35	.893	5	82	82	*O-118(LF)	**4.9**
1891	Pit N	50	203	35	59	14	1	4	28	27	1	31	.291	.377	.429	138	11	4	.904	3	92	0	O-50(48-0-2)	1.1
	Cin N	55	216	29	74	10	3	0	33	24	2	23	.343	.413	.417	141	12	12	.924	-2	65	128	O-55(54-1-0)	0.8
	Year	105	419	64	133	24	4	4	61	51	3	54	.317	.395	.422	139	23	16	.913	1	78	66	*O-105(102-1-2)	1.9
1892	Lou N	21	77	10	19	4	0	0	4	12	0	7	.247	.348	.299	104	1	5	.911	-1	28	269	O-21(LF)	-0.2
	Cin N	83	307	47	93	12	5	3	52	40	0	26	.303	.383	.404	140	16	8	.917	-3	98	0	O-82(23-46-16)/1-2	0.7
	Year	104	384	57	112	16	5	3	56	52	0	33	.292	.376	.383	133	18	13	.916	-4	83	57	*O-103(44-46-16)/1-2	0.5
1893	Lou N	57	220	38	78	11	3	1	37	44	2	15	.355	.466	.445	155	22	8	.881	-4	51	44	O-57(44-0-13)	1.2
1894	StL N	2	7	1	1	0	0	0	0	0	0	0	.143	.143	.143	-31	-2	0	1.000	-0	0	0	/O-2(CF)	-0.2
	Bro N	1	2	1	2	0	0	0	2	1	0	0	1.000	1.000	1.000	412	1	0	1.000	-0	0	0	/O(RF)	0.1
	Year	3	9	2	3	0	0	0	2	1	0	0	.333	.400	.333	80	0	0	1.000	-1	0	0	/O-3(0-2-1)	-0.1
Total	13	1183	4820	954	1646	295	85	46	659	466	29	168	.341	.403	.467	164	396	258	.883	-36	82	103	O-998C/3-75,2-49,S-44,1-26,P	27.9

BRUBAKER, BILL Wilbur Lee B 11.7.1910 Cleveland, OH D 4.2.1978 Laguna Hills, CA BR/TR 6-2/185# d9.8 gs-Dennis

Year	Tm Lg	G	AB	R	H	2B	3B	HR	RBI	BB-IB	HP	SO	AVG	OBP	SLG	AOPS	ABR	SB-CS	FA	FR	Rng	Thr	G at Pos	BFW
1932	Pit N	7	24	3	10	3	0	0	4	3	0	4	.417	.481	.542	178	3	1	.909	0	103	176	/3-7	0.3
1933	Pit N	2	2	0	0	0	0	0	0	0	0	0	.000	.000	.000	-99	-1	0	1.000	0	148	0	/3	0.0
1934	Pit N	3	6	0	2	1	0	0	1	1	0	0	.333	.429	.500	144	0	0	1.000	1	139	395	/3-3	0.1
1935	Pit N	6	11	1	0	0	0	0	0	2	0	5	.000	.154	.000	-53	-2	0	.889	-0	96	0	/3-5	-0.3
1936	Pit N	145	554	77	160	27	4	6	102	50	4	96	.289	.352	.384	96	-2	5	.940	-12	90	49	*3-145	-0.9
1937	Pit N	120	413	57	105	20	4	6	48	47	3	51	.254	.335	.366	90	-5	2	.952	5	**108**	116	*3-115/S-3,1	0.4
1938	Pit N	45	112	18	33	5	0	3	19	9	0	14	.295	.347	.420	109	1	2	.875	-3	85	137	3-18/1-9,S-3,O(LF)	-0.1
1939	Pit N	100	345	41	80	23	1	7	43	29	3	51	.232	.297	.365	78	-11	3	.950	5	102	100	2-65,3-32/S	-0.1
1940	Pit N	38	78	8	15	3	1	0	7	8	0	16	.192	.267	.256	45	-6	0	.955	4	117	133	3-19/S-8,1-4	-0.2
1943	Bos N	13	19	3	8	3	0	0	1	2	0	2	.421	.476	.579	207	3	0	.778	-1	95	0	/3-5,1-3	0.2
Total	10	479	1564	208	413	85	10	22	225	151	10	239	.264	.333	.373	90	-20	13	.938	-2	102	85	3-350/2-65,1-17,S-15,O(LF)	-0.6

BRUCE, LOU Louis R. B 1.16.1877 St.Regis, NY D 2.9.1968 Ilion, NY BL/TR 5-5/145# d6.22 ▲

Year	Tm Lg	G	AB	R	H	2B	3B	HR	RBI	BB-IB	HP	SO	AVG	OBP	SLG	AOPS	ABR	SB-CS	FA	FR	Rng	Thr	G at Pos	BFW
1904	Phi A	30	101	9	27	3	0	0	8	5	0		.267	.302	.297	85	-2	2	.969	-0	131	350	O-25(11-10-5)/P-2,23	-0.3

BRUCKER, EARLE Earle Francis Jr. B 8.29.1925 Los Angeles, CA BL/TR 6-2/210# d10.2 f-Earle

Year	Tm Lg	G	AB	R	H	2B	3B	HR	RBI	BB-IB	HP	SO	AVG	OBP	SLG	AOPS	ABR	SB-CS	FA	FR	Rng	Thr	G at Pos	BFW
1948	Phi A	2	6	0	1	1	0	0	0	1	0	1	.167	.286	.333	64	0	0-0	1.000	0	*0*	*0*	/C-2	0.0

BRUCKER, EARLE Earle Francis Sr. B 5.6.1901 Albany, NY D 5.8.1981 San Diego, CA BR/TR 5-11/175# d4.19 M1 C11 s-Earle

Year	Tm Lg	G	AB	R	H	2B	3B	HR	RBI	BB-IB	HP	SO	AVG	OBP	SLG	AOPS	ABR	SB-CS	FA	FR	Rng	Thr	G at Pos	BFW
1937	Phi A	102	317	40	82	16	5	6	37	48	0	30	.259	.356	.397	91	-4	1-2	.971	-5	*87*	*106*	C-92	-0.4
1938	Phi A	53	171	26	64	21	1	3	35	19	0	16	.374	.437	.561	152	15	1-1	.986	-4	*79*	*87*	C-44/1	1.2
1939	Phi A	62	172	18	50	15	1	3	31	24	1	16	.291	.381	.442	112	4	0-1	1.000	-6	*72*	*84*	C-47	0.1
1940	Phi A	23	46	3	9	1	1	0	2	6	0	3	.196	.288	.261	44	-4	0-0	.966	0	*71*	*134*	C-13	-0.3
1943	Phi A	1	1	0	0	0	0	0	0	0	0	0	.000	.000	.000	-99	0	0-0	—	0			H	0.0
Total	5	241	707	87	205	53	8	12	105	97	1	65	.290	.376	.438	108	11	2-4	.980	-15	*81*	*98*	C-196/1	0.6

BRUETT, J. T. Joseph Timothy B 10.8.1967 Milwaukee, WI BL/TL 5-11/175# d6.3

Year	Tm Lg	G	AB	R	H	2B	3B	HR	RBI	BB-IB	HP	SO	AVG	OBP	SLG	AOPS	ABR	SB-CS	FA	FR	Rng	Thr	G at Pos	BFW
1992	Min A	56	76	7	19	4	0	0	2	6-1	1	12	.250	.313	.303	71	-3	6-3	.979	-1	94	81	O-45(5-20-22)/D-3	-0.4
1993	Min A	17	20	2	5	2	0	0	1	1-0	1	4	.250	.318	.350	79	-1	0-0	.857	-1	105	0	O-13(2-4-8)	-0.1
Total	2	73	96	9	24	6	0	0	3	7-1	2	16	.250	.314	.313	73	-4	6-3	.952	-1	96	64	/O-58(7-24-30),D-3	-0.5

BRUGGY, FRANK Frank Leo B 5.4.1891 Elizabeth, NJ D 4.5.1959 Elizabeth, NJ BR/TR 5-11/195# d4.13

Year	Tm Lg	G	AB	R	H	2B	3B	HR	RBI	BB-IB	HP	SO	AVG	OBP	SLG	AOPS	ABR	SB-CS	FA	FR	Rng	Thr	G at Pos	BFW
1921	Phi N	96	277	28	86	11	2	5	28	23	3	37	.310	.370	.419	100	1	6-2	.953	-11	*69*	*104*	C-86/1-2	-0.4
1922	Phi A	53	111	10	31	7	0	0	9	6	1	11	.279	.322	.342	71	-5	1-2	.925	-2	*113*	*121*	C-31	-0.5
1923	Phi A	54	105	4	22	3	0	1	6	4	1	9	.210	.245	.267	34	-10	1-1	.950	-1	*110*	*131*	C-34/1-5	-1.0
1924	Phi A	50	113	9	30	6	0	0	8	8	0	15	.265	.314	.319	63	-6	4-0	.928	-6	*98*	*83*	C-44	-0.9
1925	Cin N	6	14	2	3	0	0	0	1	2	0	0	.214	.313	.214	38	-1	0-0	.870	-1	*85*	*107*	/C-6	-0.2
Total	5	259	620	53	172	27	2	6	52	43	5	72	.277	.329	.356	76	-21	12-5	.941	-19	*88*	*106*	C-201/1-7	-3.0

BRUMBAUGH, CLIFF Clifford Michael B 4.21.1974 Wilmington, DE BR/TR 6-2/205# d5.30

Year	Tm Lg	G	AB	R	H	2B	3B	HR	RBI	BB-IB	HP	SO	AVG	OBP	SLG	AOPS	ABR	SB-CS	FA	FR	Rng	Thr	G at Pos	BFW
2001	Tex A	7	10	1	0	0	0	0	0	1-0	0	5	.000	.091	.000	-70	-3	0-0	1.000	-0	84	0	/O-6(2-0-4)	-0.3
	Col N	14	36	5	10	2	0	1	4	2-0	0	9	.278	.316	.417	71	-1	0-1	1.000	-1	94	0	O-11(4-0-8)	-0.3
Total	1	21	46	6	10	2	0	1	4	3-0	0	14	.217	.265	.326	44	-4	0-1	1.000	-1	91	0	/O-17(6-0-12)	-0.6

BRUMFIELD, JACOB Jacob Donnell B 5.27.1965 Bogalusa, LA BR/TR 6/185# d4.6

Year	Tm Lg	G	AB	R	H	2B	3B	HR	RBI	BB-IB	HP	SO	AVG	OBP	SLG	AOPS	ABR	SB-CS	FA	FR	Rng	Thr	G at Pos	BFW
1992	Cin N	24	30	6	4	0	0	0	2	2-1	1	4	.133	.212	.133	-0	-4	6-0	1.000	2	132	279	O-16(7-8-1)	-0.1
1993	Cin N	103	272	40	73	17	3	6	23	21-4	1	47	.268	.321	.419	97	-2	20-8	.978	3	101	156	O-96(24-68-5)/2-4	0.3
1994	Cin N	68	122	36	38	10	2	4	11	15-0	0	18	.311	.381	.525	136	7	6-3	.987	2	117	65	O-43(14-24-6)	0.9
1995	Pit N	116	402	64	109	23	2	4	26	37-0	5	71	.271	.339	.368	85	-8	22-12	.969	5	109	159	*O-104(CF)	-0.1
1996	Pit N	29	80	11	20	9	0	2	8	5-1	0	17	.250	.291	.438	87	-1	3-1	.946	-2	82	110	O-22(CF)	-0.3
	Tor A	90	308	52	79	19	2	12	52	24-1	4	58	.256	.316	.448	91	-5	12-3	.982	1	96	165	O-83(18-39-37)/D-5	-0.4
1997	Tor A	58	174	22	36	5	1	2	20	14-0	1	31	.207	.268	.282	44	-15	4-4	1.000	3	98	266	O-47(14-24-10)/D-4	-1.3
1999	LA N	18	17	4	5	0	1	0	1	0-0	0	5	.294	.294	.412	81	-1	0-0	1.000	0	122	0	O-11(7-4-0)	-0.1
	Tor A	62	170	25	40	8	3	2	19	19-0	0	39	.235	.307	.353	68	-8	1-2	.978	3	110	161	O-53(10-36-8)/D-6	-0.6
Total	7	568	1575	260	404	91	14	32	162	137-7	12	290	.257	.318	.393	84	-37	74-33	.979	17	104	163	O-475(94-329-67)/D-15,2-4	-1.7

BRUMLEY, MIKE Anthony Michael B 4.9.1963 Oklahoma City, OK BB/TR 5-10/165# d6.16 s-Mike OF Total (9-LF 6-CF 3-RF)

Year	Tm Lg	G	AB	R	H	2B	3B	HR	RBI	BB-IB	HP	SO	AVG	OBP	SLG	AOPS	ABR	SB-CS	FA	FR	Rng	Thr	G at Pos	BFW
1987	Chi N	39	104	8	21	2	2	1	9	10-1	1	30	.202	.276	.288	49	-8	7-1	.965	1	101	123	S-34/2	-0.2
1989	Det A	92	212	33	42	5	2	1	11	14-0	1	45	.198	.251	.255	44	-16	8-4	.980	-14	86	49	S-42,2-24,3-11/O-4(1-1-2),D-8	-2.8
1990	Sea A	62	147	19	33	5	4	0	7	10-0	0	22	.224	.272	.313	63	-8	2-0	.983	-2	92	88	S-47/2-6,3-3,O-2(1-1-0),D	-0.6
1991	Bos A	63	118	16	25	5	0	0	5	10-0	0	22	.212	.273	.254	45	-9	2-0	.950	7	119	69	S-31,3-17/2-7,O-4(CF),D-2	0.1
1992	Bos A	2	1	0	0	0	0	0	0	0-0	0	0	.000	.000	.000	-94	0	0-0	—	0			/H	0.0
1993	Hou N	8	10	1	3	0	0	0	2	1-0	0	3	.300	.364	.300	83	0	0-1	—	-0	0	0	/3SO(1-0-1)	-0.1
1994	Oak A	11	25	0	6	0	0	0	2	1-0	0	8	.240	.269	.240	36	-3	0-0	.929	-2	86	102	/2-4,3-4,O-3(LF),S	-0.4
1995	Hou N	18	18	1	1	0	0	1	2	0-0	0	6	.056	.056	.222	-33	-4	1-0	1.000	-1	42	0	/S-3,O-3(LF),13	-0.4
Total	8	295	635	78	131	17	8	3	38	46-1	2	136	.206	.261	.272	47	-48	20-6	.972	-10	97	82	S-159/2-42,3-37,O-17L,D-11,1	-4.4

BRUMLEY, MIKE Tony Mike B 7.10.1938 Granite, OK BL/TR 5-10/195# d4.18 f-Mike

Year	Tm Lg	G	AB	R	H	2B	3B	HR	RBI	BB-IB	HP	SO	AVG	OBP	SLG	AOPS	ABR	SB-CS	FA	FR	Rng	Thr	G at Pos	BFW
1964	Was A	136	426	36	104	19	2	2	35	40-6	1	54	.244	.309	.312	74	-14	1-1	.991	-8	*97*	*108*	*C-132	-1.7
1965	Was A	79	216	15	45	4	0	3	15	20-6	2	33	.208	.280	.269	58	-12	1-1	.990	0	*102*	*101*	C-66	-0.9
1966	Was A	9	18	1	2	1	0	0	0	0-0	0	2	.111	.111	.167	-22	-3	0-0	1.000	-0	*178*	*190*	/C-7	-0.3
Total	3	224	660	52	151	24	2	5	50	60-12	3	89	.229	.295	.294	67	-29	2-2	.991	-7	*100*	*107*	C-205	-2.9

BRUMMER, GLENN Glenn Edward B 11.23.1954 Olney, IL BR/TR 6/200# d5.25

Year	Tm Lg	G	AB	R	H	2B	3B	HR	RBI	BB-IB	HP	SO	AVG	OBP	SLG	AOPS	ABR	SB-CS	FA	FR	Rng	Thr	G at Pos	BFW
1981	StL N	21	30	2	6	1	0	0	2	1-0	0	2	.200	.219	.233	30	-3	0-0	1.000	-1	84	98	C-19	-0.4
1982	†StL N	35	64	4	15	4	0	0	8	0-0	0	12	.234	.234	.297	47	-5	2-0	.970	-1	161	49	C-32	-0.5
1983	StL N	45	87	7	24	7	0	0	9	10-1	0	11	.276	.351	.356	96	0	1-3	.978	-5	99	68	C-41	-0.4
1984	StL N	28	58	3	12	0	0	1	3	3-0	0	7	.207	.246	.259	43	-5	0-0	.973	2	164	117	C-26	-0.2
1985	Tex A	49	108	7	30	4	0	0	5	11-1	2	22	.278	.355	.315	84	-2	1-5	.989	-8	84	40	C-47/O(RF)D	-1.0

Year	Tm Lg	G	AB	R	H	2B	3B	HR	RBI	BB-IB	HP	SO	AVG	OBP	SLG	AOPS	ABR	SB-CS	FA	FR	Rng	Thr	G at Pos	BFW
Total	5	178	347	23	87	16	0	1	27	25-2	2	54	.251	.304	.305	70	-15	4-8	.981	-12	115	66	C-165/DO(RF)	-2.5
BRUNANSKY, TOM Thomas Andrew B 8.20.1960 Covina, CA BR/TR 6-4/211# d4.9																								
1981	Cal A	11	33	7	5	0	0	3	6	8-0	0	10	.152	.317	.424	112	1	1-0	.938	2	107	363	O-11(LF)	0.2
1982	Min A	127	463	77	126	30	1	20	46	71-0	8	101	.272	.377	.471	128	21	1-2	.986	11	123	91	*O-127(3-38-97)	2.6
1983	Min A	151	542	70	123	24	5	28	82	61-4	4	95	.227	.308	.445	101	0	2-5	.985	13	114	146	*O-146(0-38-119)/D-4	0.6
1984	Min A	155	567	75	144	21	0	32	85	57-2	0	94	.254	.320	.460	109	6	4-5	.984	0	95	135	*O-153(RF)/D	-0.3
1985	Min A★	157	567	71	137	28	4	27	90	71-7	0	86	.242	.320	.448	103	2	5-3	.984	1	96	135	*O-155(0-1-155)	-0.5
1986	Min A	157	593	69	152	28	1	23	75	53-4	1	98	.256	.315	.423	97	-3	12-4	.982	3	105	97	*O-152(0-1-152)/D-2	-0.7
1987	†Min A	155	532	83	138	22	2	32	85	74-5	4	104	.259	.352	.489	116	13	11-11	.990	3	104	108	*O-138(58-0-107),D-17	0.7
1988	Min A	14	49	5	9	1	0	1	6	7-0	0	11	.184	.286	.265	54	-3	1-2	.864	-3	70	0	O-13(1-0-12)/D	-0.7
	StL N	143	523	69	128	22	4	22	79	79-6	4	82	.245	.345	.428	121	15	16-6	**.996**	-1	92	136	*O-143(1-0-143)	1.2
1989	StL N	158	556	67	133	29	3	20	85	59-3	2	107	.239	.312	.410	102	1	5-9	.977	-2	96	107	*O-155(0-1-155)/1	-0.8
1990	StL N	19	57	5	9	3	0	1	2	12-0	1	10	.158	.310	.263	60	-3	0-0	.950	0	106	83	O-17(RF)	-0.3
	†Bos A	129	461	61	123	24	5	15	71	54-7	3	105	.267	.342	.438	113	8	5-10	.982	4	113	83	*O-121(0-1-121)/D-7	0.6
1991	Bos A	142	459	54	105	24	1	16	70	49-2	3	72	.229	.303	.390	87	-8	1-2	.989	0	105	56	*O-137(0-1-136)/D	-1.2
1992	Bos A	138	458	47	122	31	3	15	74	66-2	0	96	.266	.354	.445	116	11	2-5	.980	0	101	99	O-92(RF),1-28,D-17	0.6
1993	Mil A	80	224	20	41	7	3	6	29	25-0	0	59	.183	.265	.321	58	-14	3-4	.987	3	113	86	O-71(RF)/D-6	-1.5
1994	Mil A	16	28	2	6	2	0	0	0	1-0	0	9	.214	.241	.286	34	-3	0-0	1.000	-1	46	0	/O-6(RF),1-2,D-2	-0.4
	Bos A	48	177	22	42	10	1	10	34	23-1	0	48	.237	.319	.475	98	-1	0-2	.989	-2	101	33	O-42(14-0-33)/1-5,D-3	-0.6
	Year	64	205	24	48	12	1	10	34	24-1	0	57	.234	.309	.449	90	-4	0-2	.989	-3	98	31	O-48(14-0-39)/1-7,D-5	-1.0
Total	14	1800	6289	804	1543	306	33	271	919	770-43	30	1187	.245	.327	.434	105	43	69-70	.984	33	104	108	*O-1679(88-81-1569)/D-61,1-36	-0.5
BRUNSBERG, ARLO Arlo Adolph B 8.15.1940 Fertile, MN BL/TR 6/195# d9.23																								
1966	Det A	2	3	1	1	1	0	0	0	0-0	1	0	.333	.500	.667	227	1	0-0	1.000	-0	*0*	*0*	/C-2	0.0
BRUNTLETT, ERIC Eric Kevin B 3.29.1978 Lafayette, IN BR/TR 6/200# d6.27																								
2003	Hou N	31	54	3	14	3	0	1	4	0-0	0	10	.259	.255	.370	59	-3	0-0	.963	-2	66	68	S-10/2-9,O-2(1-0-1),3	-0.4
BRUSH, BOB Robert B 3.8.1875 Osage, IA D 4.2.1944 San Bernardino, CA d4.20																								
1907	Bos N	2	2	0	0	0	0	0	0	0	0		.000	.000	.000	-99	0	0	1.000	-0	0	0	/1	-0.1
BRUTON, BILL William Haron B 11.9.1925 Panola, AL D 12.5.1995 Marshallton, DE BL/TR 6-0.5/169# d4.13																								
1953	Mil N	151	613	82	153	18	14	1	41	44	6	100	.250	.306	.330	70	-29	**26**-11	.979	0	98	111	*O-150(CF)	-3.3
1954	Mil N	142	567	89	161	20	7	4	30	40	4	78	.284	.336	.365	88	-11	**34**-13	.981	-1	94	**134**	*O-141(CF)	-1.6
1955	Mil N	149	636	106	175	30	12	9	47	43-6	4	72	.275	.325	.403	97	-5	**25**-11	.968	9	106	148	*O-149(CF)	-0.2
1956	Mil N	147	525	73	143	23	**15**	8	56	26-11	1	63	.272	.304	.419	99	-4	8-6	.969	-3	100	92	*O-145(CF)	-1.4
1957	Mil N	79	306	41	85	16	9	5	30	19-4	1	35	.278	.317	.438	110	3	11-4	.981	-4	94	83	O-79(CF)	-0.4
1958	†Mil N	100	325	47	91	11	3	3	28	27-4	2	37	.280	.336	.360	93	-4	4-1	.977	-7	90	86	O-96(CF)	-1.4
1959	Mil N	133	478	72	138	22	6	6	41	35-2	1	54	.289	.338	.397	104	2	13-5	.991	-2	101	83	*O-133(CF)	-0.5
1960	Mil N	151	629	**112**	180	27	**13**	12	54	41-1	2	97	.286	.330	.428	115	10	22-13	.986	-7	92	88	*O-149(CF)	-0.4
1961	Det A	160	596	99	153	15	5	17	63	61-0	3	66	.257	.327	.384	87	-12	22-6	.988	7	116	52	*O-155(CF)	-0.7
1962	Det A	147	561	90	156	27	5	16	74	55-0	5	67	.278	.346	.430	104	4	14-7	.983	7	117	73	*O-145(CF)	0.7
1963	Det A	145	524	84	134	21	8	8	48	59-3	0	70	.256	.330	.372	93	-4	14-7	.991	1	110	72	*O-138(CF)	-0.7
1964	Det A	106	296	42	82	11	5	5	33	32-1	0	54	.277	.347	.399	105	2	14-5	.987	-1	91	147	O-81(10-70-1)	0.1
Total	12	1610	6056	937	1651	241	102	94	545	482-32	29	793	.273	.328	.393	96	-48	207-89	.981	-0	102	97	*O-1561(10-1550-1)	-9.8
BRUYETTE, ED Edward T. B 8.31.1874 Manawa, WI D 8.5.1940 Peshastin, WA BL/TR 5-10/170# d8.6																								
1901	Mil A	26	82	7	15	3	0	0	4	12	1		.183	.295	.220	46	-5	1	.778	-4	45	0	O-21(CF)/2-3,S3	-1.0
BRYAN, BILLY William Ronald B 12.4.1938 Morgan, GA BL/TR 6-4/200# d9.12																								
1961	KC A	9	19	2	3	0	0	1	2	2-0	0	7	.158	.238	.316	46	-2	0-0	1.000	-1	*128*	*0*	/C-4	-0.2
1962	KC A	25	74	5	11	2	1	2	7	5-0	0	32	.149	.203	.284	28	-8	0-0	.976	-3	*80*	*28*	C-22	-1.0
1963	KC A	24	65	11	11	1	1	3	7	9-5	0	22	.169	.270	.354	69	-3	0-0	.981	2	101	29	C-24	0.1
1964	KC A	93	220	19	53	9	2	13	36	16-1	0	69	.241	.290	.477	107	1	0-0	.991	-9	*56*	*83*	C-65	-0.6
1965	KC A	108	325	36	82	11	5	14	51	29-5	2	87	.252	.315	.446	116	6	0-0	.984	-8	*68*	*83*	C-95	0.2
1966	KC A	32	76	0	10	4	0	0	7	6-0	0	17	.132	.193	.184	10	-9	0-0	.965	-2	*78*	*132*	C-21/1-3	-1.1
	NY A	27	69	5	15	2	0	4	5	5-0	0	19	.217	.270	.420	99	0	0-0	.988	1	*125*	*133*	C-14/1-3	0.1
	Year	59	145	5	25	6	0	4	12	11-0	0	36	.172	.229	.297	52	-9	0-0	.975	-1	*99*	*132*	C-35/1-6	-1.0
1967	NY A	16	12	1	2	0	0	1	2	5-0	0	3	.167	.412	.417	151	1	0-0	1.000	0	0	0	/C	0.1
1968	Was A	40	108	7	22	3	0	3	8	14-2	1	27	.204	.301	.315	90	-1	0-1	.983	-3	85	107	C-28	-0.3
Total	8	374	968	86	209	32	9	41	125	91-13	3	283	.216	.284	.395	91	-15	0-1	.984	-21	*76*	*81*	C-274/1-6	-2.7
BRYANT, DEREK Derek Roszell B 10.9.1951 Lexington, KY BR/TR 5-11/185# d4.24																								
1979	Oak A	39	106	8	19	2	1	0	13	10-1	0	10	.179	.246	.217	29	-11	0-0	1.000	-1	93	94	O-33(25-0-10)/D-2	-1.3
BRYANT, DON Donald Ray B 7.13.1941 Jasper, FL BR/TR 6-5/200# d7.17 C7																								
1966	Chi N	13	26	2	8	2	0	0	4	1-0	1	4	.308	.357	.385	105	0	1-0	.978	-0	*99*	*100*	C-10	0.1
1969	Hou N	31	59	2	11	1	0	1	6	4-1	1	13	.186	.250	.254	42	-5	0-0	.993	-1	59	21	C-28	-0.5
1970	Hou N	15	24	2	5	0	0	0	3	1-0	0	8	.208	.231	.208	22	-3	0-0	.957	-2	26	125	C-13	-0.5
Total	3	59	109	6	24	3	0	1	13	6-1	2	25	.220	.271	.275	53	-8	1-0	.983	-4	*61*	*59*	/C-51	-0.9
BRYANT, GEORGE George F. B 2.10.1857 Bridgeport, CT D 6.12.1907 Boston, MA d8.6																								
1885	Det N	1	4	0	0	0	0	0	1	0		2	.000	.000	.000	-99	-1		1.000	-0	46	339	/2	-0.1
BRYANT, RALPH Ralph Wendell B 5.20.1961 Fort Gaines, GA BL/TR 6-2/200# d9.8																								
1985	LA N	6	6	0	2	0	0	0	1	0-0	0	2	.333	.333	.333	90	0	0-0	—	-0	0	0	/O-3(2-0-1)	0.0
1986	LA N	27	75	15	19	4	2	6	13	5-0	1	25	.253	.305	.600	156	5	0-1	.953	1	110	131	O-26(RF)	0.4
1987	LA N	46	69	7	17	2	1	2	10	10-2	1	24	.246	.346	.391	99	0	2-1	.917	-1	97	0	O-19(8-0-12)	-0.2
Total	3	79	150	22	38	6	3	8	24	15-2	2	51	.253	.325	.493	125	5	2-2	.940	-0	103	79	/O-48(10-0-39)	0.2
BRYE, STEVE Stephen Robert B 2.4.1949 Alameda, CA BR/TR 6/190# d9.3																								
1970	Min A	9	11	1	2	1	0	0	2	2-0	0	4	.182	.308	.273	60	-1	0-0	1.000	-1	66	0	/O-6(6-0-1)	-0.1
1971	Min A	28	107	10	24	1	0	3	11	7-0	0	15	.224	.270	.318	65	-5	3-1	.966	1	93	231	O-28(25-7-0)	-0.6
1972	Min A	100	253	18	61	9	3	0	12	17-1	1	38	.241	.292	.300	73	-9	3-1	.994	9	114	165	O-93(74-20-2)	-0.4
1973	Min A	92	278	39	73	9	5	6	33	35-1	0	43	.263	.343	.396	104	2	3-5	.986	2	108	71	O-87(12-72-4)/D	0.0
1974	Min A	135	488	52	138	32	1	2	41	22-1	5	59	.283	.319	.365	94	-4	1-3	**.997**	-2	97	120	*O-129(0-128-1)	-1.0
1975	Min A	86	246	41	62	13	1	9	34	21-2	2	37	.252	.315	.423	106	1	2-1	.983	-0	93	146	O-72(19-5-48)/D-6	-0.2
1976	Min A	87	258	33	68	11	0	2	23	13-0	0	31	.264	.295	.329	82	-6	1-2	.987	-6	88	21	O-78(11-57-17)/D-3	-1.6
1977	Mil A	94	241	27	60	14	3	7	28	16-0	1	39	.249	.297	.419	93	-3	1-0	1.000	7	111	173	O-83(29-43-17)/D-6	0.2
1978	Pit N	66	115	16	27	7	0	1	9	11-1	1	10	.235	.305	.322	73	-4	2-1	.983	-1	96	85	O-47(28-7-12)	-0.6
Total	9	697	1997	237	515	97	13	30	193	144-6	10	276	.258	.309	.365	90	-29	16-14	.991	9	101	119	O-623(204-339-102)/D-16	-4.3
BUBSER, HAL Harold Fred B 9.28.1895 Chicago, IL D 6.22.1959 Melrose Park, IL BR/TR 5-11/170# d4.15																								
1922	Chi A	3	3	0	0	0	0	0	0	0	0	2	.000	.000	.000	-99	-1	0-0	—	0			H	-0.1
BUCHA, JOHNNY John George B 1.22.1925 Allentown, PA D 4.28.1996 Bethlehem, PA BR/TR 5-11/190# d5.2																								
1948	StL N	2	1	0	0	0	0	0	0	1	0	0	.000	.500	.000	43	0	0	1.000	-0	*0*	*0*	/C	0.0
1950	StL N	22	36	1	5	1	0	0	1	4	0	7	.139	.225	.167	5	-5	0	.959	-0	*146*	*86*	C-17	-0.5
1953	Det A	60	158	17	35	9	0	1	14	20	0	14	.222	.309	.297	65	-7	1-1	.984	-6	*81*	*118*	C-56	-1.1
Total	3	84	195	18	40	10	0	1	15	25	0	21	.205	.295	.272	53	-12	1-1	.980	-6	*92*	*112*	/C-74	-1.6
BUCHANAN, BRIAN Brian James B 7.21.1973 Miami, FL BR/TR 6-4/230# d5.19																								
2000	Min A	30	82	10	19	3	0	1	8	8-0	1	22	.232	.301	.305	54	-6	0-2	1.000	-2	77	67	O-25(2-0-24)/D-2	-0.9
2001	Min A	69	197	28	54	12	0	10	32	19-0	2	58	.274	.342	.487	113	4	1-1	.973	-0	105	45	O-46(7-0-39),D-19	0.0
2002	Min A	44	135	19	34	5	1	5	15	6-0	2	33	.252	.294	.415	85	-4	2-1	1.000	1	127	0	O-24(RF),D-17	-0.4
	SD N	48	92	12	27	5	0	6	13	9-0	1	26	.293	.363	.543	152	6	0-1	1.000	-0	108	79	1-15,O-14(RF)	0.4
2003	SD N	115	198	29	52	10	2	8	29	24-1	3	51	.263	.346	.455	119	5	6-2	1.000	1	114	144	O-43(15-0-29),1-24/D-5	0.4

Year	Tm Lg	G	AB	R	H	2B	3B	HR	RBI	BB-IB	HP	SO	AVG	OBP	SLG	AOPS	ABR	SB-CS	FA	FR	Rng	Thr	G at Pos	BFW
Total	4	306	704	98	186	35	3	30	97	66-1	9	190	.264	.332	.450	106	5	9-7	.987	-1	103	72	0-152(24-0-130)/D-43,1-39	-0.5
BUCHEK, JERRY Gerald Peter B 5.9.1942 St.Louis, MO BR/TR 5-11/185# d6.30																								
1961	StL N	31	90	6	12	2	0	0	9	0-0	2	28	.133	.151	.156	-16	-15	0-0	.912	-4	87	127	S-31	-1.7
1963	StL N	3	4	0	1	0	0	0	0	0-0	0	2	.250	.250	.250	41	0	0-0	1.000	0	74	387	/S	0.0
1964	†StL N	35	30	7	6	0	2	0	1	3-0	0	11	.200	.273	.333	64	-2	0-0	.929	3	134	81	S-20/2-9,3	0.2
1965	StL N	55	166	17	41	8	3	3	21	13-2	0	46	.247	.300	.386	84	-4	1-0	.994	7	107	122	2-33,S-18/3	0.8
1966	StL N	100	284	23	67	10	4	4	25	23-4	0	71	.236	.288	.342	75	-10	0-5	.974	-7	106	134	2-49,S-48/3-4	-1.2
1967	NY N	124	411	35	97	11	2	14	41	26-5	2	101	.236	.283	.375	89	-8	3-5	.977	4	100	93	2-95,3-17/S-9	0.3
1968	NY N	73	192	8	35	4	0	1	11	10-5	3	53	.182	.234	.219	36	-15	1-1	.935	-1	95	111	3-37,2-12/O-9(LF)	-1.8
Total	7	421	1177	96	259	35	11	22	108	75-16	7	312	.220	.269	.325	67	-54	5-11	.978	2	103	107	2-198,S-127/3-60,O-9(LF)	-3.4
BUCHER, JIM James Quinter B 3.11.1911 Manassas, VA BL/TR 5-11/170# d4.18																								
1934	Bro N	47	84	12	19	5	2	0	8	4	0	7	.226	.261	.333	61	-5	1	.920	-2	93	117	2-20/3-6	-0.6
1935	Bro N	123	473	72	143	22	1	7	58	10	0	33	.302	.317	.397	93	-6	4	.950	-2	100	113	2-41,3-39,O-37(21-0-16)	-0.7
1936	Bro N	110	370	49	93	12	8	2	41	29	0	27	.251	.306	.343	74	-15	5	.910	-6	108	86	3-39,2-32,O-30(7-0-23)	-2.0
1937	Bro N	125	380	44	96	11	2	4	37	20	3	18	.253	.295	.324	67	-18	5	.951	-10	79	97	2-49,3-43/O-6(4-1-1)	-2.4
1938	StL N	17	57	7	13	3	1	0	7	2	0	2	.228	.254	.316	53	-4	0	.955	-3	81	115	2-14/3	-0.6
1944	Bos A	80	277	39	76	9	2	4	31	19	2	13	.274	.326	.365	98	-1	3-3	.958	-4	96	119	3-44,2-21	-0.4
1945	Bos A	52	151	19	34	4	3	0	11	7	1	13	.225	.264	.291	60	-8	1-3	.940	1	111	125	3-32/2-2	-0.9
Total	7	554	1792	242	474	66	19	17	193	91	6	113	.265	.302	.351	78	-57	19-6	.939	-25	102	102	3-204,2-179/O-73(32-1-40)	-7.6
BUCKLEY, KEVIN Kevin John B 1.16.1959 Quincy, MA BR/TR 6-1/200# d9.4																								
1984	Tex A	5	7	1	2	1	0	0	0	2-0	0	4	.286	.444	.429	138	1	0-0	—	0			/D-3	0.0
BUCKLEY, DICK Richard D. B 9.21.1858 Troy, NY D 12.12.1929 Pittsburgh, PA BR/TR 5-10/195# d4.20																								
1888	Ind N	71	260	28	71	9	3	5	22	6	0	24	.273	.289	.388	112	3	4	.898	-14			C-51,3-22/O(RF)1	-0.7
1889	Ind N	68	260	35	67	11	0	8	41	15	1	32	.258	.301	.392	91	-5	5	.877	-13			C-55,3-12/O(LF)1	-1.2
1890	NY N	70	266	39	68	11	0	2	26	23	4	35	.256	.324	.320	88	-4	3	.931	7	*98*	*127*	C-62/3-8	0.7
1891	NY N	75	253	23	55	9	1	4	31	11	3	30	.217	.258	.308	67	-11	3	.958	4	*82*	*106*	C-74/3	-0.1
1892	StL N	121	410	43	93	17	4	5	52	22	5	34	.227	.275	.324	85	-9	7	.937	-9	*95*	*85*	*C-119/1-2	-0.7
1893	StL N	9	23	2	4	1	0	0	1	0	0	0	.174	.174	.217	4	-3	0	.914	0	*86*	*100*	/C-9	-0.2
1894	StL N	29	89	5	16	1	2	1	3	6	1	3	.180	.240	.270	23	-12	1	.936	2	*106*	*118*	C-27/1	-0.6
	Phi N	43	160	18	47	7	3	1	26	6	2	13	.294	.327	.394	75	-7	0	.966	-1	*92*	*90*	C-42/1	-0.4
	Year	72	249	23	63	8	5	2	29	12	3	16	.253	.295	.349	56	-20	1	.954	1	*97*	*100*	C-69/1-2	-1.0
1895	Phi N	38	112	20	28	6	1	0	14	9	5	17	.250	.333	.321	69	-5	2	.919	-1	*93*	*84*	C-38	-0.2
Total	8	524	1833	213	449	72	14	26	216	98	21	188	.245	.291	.342	81	-53	25	.931	-25	*73*	*78*	C-477/3-43,1-6,O-2(1-0-1)	-3.4
BUCKNER, BILL William Joseph B 12.14.1949 Vallejo, CA BL/TL 6/185# d9.21 C2																								
1969	LA N	1	1	0	0	0	0	0	0	0-0	0	0	.000	.000	.000	-99	0	0-0	—	0			H	0.0
1970	LA N	28	68	6	13	3	1	0	4	3-1	0	7	.191	.225	.265	32	-7	0-1	1.000	1	121	81	O-20(19-0-1)/1	-0.7
1971	LA N	108	358	37	99	15	1	5	41	11-4	5	18	.277	.306	.366	96	-3	4-1	.994	4	110	91	O-86(6-0-81),1-11	-0.4
1972	LA N	105	383	47	122	14	3	5	37	17-2	1	13	.319	.348	.410	118	7	10-3	.992	2	112	24	O-61(19-0-52),1-35	0.5
1973	LA N	140	575	68	158	20	0	8	46	17-5	3	34	.275	.297	.351	83	-15	12-2	.998	-2	94	137	1-93,O-48(35-0-13)	-2.6
1974	†LA N	145	580	83	182	30	3	7	58	30-10	4	24	.314	.351	.412	118	12	31-13	.976	-6	94	44	*O-137(134-0-4)/1-6	0.0
1975	LA N	92	288	30	70	11	2	6	31	17-7	2	15	.243	.286	.358	82	-8	8-3	.986	2	108	80	O-72(LF)	-1.0
1976	LA N	154	642	76	193	28	4	7	60	26-6	1	26	.301	.326	.389	105	2	28-9	.985	-2	99	62	*O-153(149-0-5)/1	-0.7
1977	Chi N	122	426	40	121	27	0	11	60	21-2	1	23	.284	.314	.425	88	-7	7-5	.990	-2	92	102	1-99	-1.6
1978	Chi N	117	446	47	144	26	1	5	74	18-5	0	17	.323	.345	.419	102	1	7-5	.995	7	128	103	*1-105	0.2
1979	Chi N	149	591	72	168	34	7	14	66	30-6	2	28	.284	.319	.437	96	-4	9-4	.995	15	136	103	*1-140	0.3
1980	Chi N	145	578	69	187	41	3	10	68	30-11	0	18	**.324**	.353	.457	117	13	1-2	.993	5	123	91	1-94,O-50(42-0-12)	1.1
1981	Chi N★	**106**	421	45	131	**35**	3	10	75	26-9	1	16	.311	.349	.480	129	15	5-2	.984	0	105	99	*1-105	1.0
1982	Chi N	161	657	93	201	34	5	15	105	36-7	5	26	.306	.342	.441	116	13	15-5	.993	12	125	72	*1-161	1.7
1983	Chi N	153	626	79	175	**38**	6	16	66	25-5	5	30	.280	.310	.436	101	-1	12-4	.992	22	**153**	116	*1-144,O-15(LF)	1.3
1984	Chi N	21	43	3	9	0	0	0	2	1-1	1	1	.209	.239	.209	26	-4	0-0	1.000	1	126	114	/1-7,O-2(LF)	-0.3
	Bos A	114	439	51	122	21	2	11	67	24-5	5	38	.278	.321	.410	97	-2	2-2	.986	6	117	75	*1-113	-0.4
1985	Bos A	162	673	89	201	46	3	16	110	30-5	2	36	.299	.325	.447	106	5	18-4	.992	**25**	**150**	96	*1-162	2.2
1986	†Bos A	153	629	73	168	39	2	18	102	40-9	4	25	.267	.311	.421	98	-3	6-4	.989	20	**142**	93	*1-138,D-15	0.8
1987	Bos A	75	286	23	78	6	1	2	42	13-1	0	19	.273	.299	.322	65	-15	1-3	.991	2	109	88	1-74	-1.7
	Cal A	57	183	16	56	12	1	3	32	9-1	0	7	.306	.337	.432	106	1	1-0	1.000	-0	62	30	D-39/1-5	0.0
	Year	132	469	39	134	18	2	5	74	22-2	0	26	.286	.314	.365	80	-14	2-3	.992	2	106	85	1-79,D-39	-1.7
1988	Cal A	19	43	1	9	0	0	0	9	4-0	0	0	.209	.271	.209	39	-4	2-0	1.000	0	1146	972	D-11/1	-0.3
	KC A	89	242	18	62	14	0	3	34	13-5	0	19	.256	.290	.351	79	-7	3-1	.994	-0	91	70	D-42,1-21	-1.0
	Year	108	285	19	71	14	0	3	43	17-5	0	19	.249	.287	.330	73	-10	5-1	.973	0	97	75	D-53,1-22	-1.3
1989	KC A	79	176	7	38	4	1	1	16	6-2	0	11	.216	.240	.267	43	-14	1-0	.985	-1	89	113	1-24,D-19	-1.7
1990	Bos A	22	43	4	8	0	0	1	3	3-2	0	2	.186	.234	.256	37	-4	0-0	1.000	-0	86	73	1-15	-0.5
Total	22	2517	9397	1077	2715	498	49	174	1208	450-111	42	453	.289	.321	.408	99	-29	183-73	.992	112	125	97	*1-1555,O-644(493-0-168),D-126	-3.8
BUDASKA, MARK Mark David B 12.27.1952 Sharon, PA BB/TL 6/180# d6.6																								
1978	Oak A	4	4	0	1	1	0	0	0	1-0	0	2	.250	.400	.500	160	0	0-0	.500	-1	42	0	/O-2(1-0-1)	0.0
1981	Oak A	9	32	3	5	1	0	0	2	4-0	0	10	.156	.250	.188	29	-3	0-1	—	0			/D-9	-0.4
Total	2	13	36	3	6	2	0	0	2	5-0	0	12	.167	.268	.222	44	-3	0-1	.500	-1	42	0	/D-9,O-2(1-0-1)	-0.4
BUDD B Cleveland, OH d9.10																								
1890	Cle P	1	4	0	0	0	0	0	0	0	0	3	.000	.000	.000	-99	-1	0	1.000	0	0	0	/O(LF)	-0.1
BUDDIN, DON Donald Thomas B 5.5.1934 Turbeville, SC BR/TR 5-11/178# d4.17																								
1956	Bos A	114	377	49	90	24	0	5	37	65-1	4	62	.239	.352	.342	76	-11	2-0	.953	7	105	**123**	*S-113	0.6
1958	Bos A	136	497	74	118	25	2	12	43	82-1	4	106	.237	.349	.368	92	-3	0-4	.958	14	108	107	*S-136	2.2
1959	Bos A	151	485	75	117	24	1	10	53	92-0	5	99	.241	.366	.357	95	1	6-1	.949	-10	96	95	*S-150	0.4
1960	Bos A	124	428	62	105	21	5	6	36	62-5	1	59	.245	.338	.360	87	-6	4-2	.951	-4	96	90	*S-124	0.0
1961	Bos A	115	339	58	89	22	3	6	42	72-7	2	45	.263	.394	.398	110	9	2-1	.956	-0	98	101	*S-109	1.8
1962	Hou N	40	80	10	13	4	1	2	10	17-2	1	17	.162	.316	.313	75	-2	0-0	.952	2	103	106	S-27/3-9	0.1
	Det A	31	83	14	19	3	0	0	4	20-0	1	16	.229	.385	.265	76	-2	1-0	.978	-3	85	107	S-19/2-5,3-2	-0.3
Total	6	711	2289	342	551	123	12	41	225	410-16	18	404	.241	.358	.359	90	-14	15-8	.954	6	100	103	S-678/3-11,2-5	4.8
BUDZINSKI, MARK Mark Joseph B 8.26.1973 Baltimore, MD BL/TL 6-2/180# d8.3																								
2003	Cin N	4	7	0	0	0	0	0	0	0-0	0	4	.000	.000	.000	-99	-2	0-0	1.000	0	133	0	/O(CF)	-0.2
BUECHELE, STEVE Steven Bernard B 9.26.1961 Lancaster, CA BR/TR 6-2/190# d7.19																								
1985	Tex A	69	219	22	48	6	3	6	21	14-2	2	38	.219	.271	.356	70	-10	3-2	.969	7	107	132	3-69/2	-0.5
1986	Tex A	153	461	54	112	19	2	18	54	35-1	5	98	.243	.302	.410	90	-8	5-8	.968	15	108	81	*3-137,2-33/O-2(LF)	0.5
1987	Tex A	136	363	45	86	20	0	13	50	28-3	1	66	.237	.290	.399	81	-10	2-2	.964	-5	97	65	*3-123,2-18/O-2(LF)	-1.6
1988	Tex A	155	503	68	126	21	4	16	58	65-6	5	79	.250	.342	.404	105	5	2-4	.962	7	106	97	*3-153/2-2	1.1
1989	Tex A	155	486	60	114	22	2	16	59	36-0	5	107	.235	.294	.387	89	-8	1-3	.969	19	106	98	*3-145,2-18/SD	1.0
1990	Tex A	91	251	30	54	10	0	7	30	27-1	2	63	.215	.294	.339	77	-8	1-0	.966	5	104	48	3-88/2-4	-0.2
1991	Tex A	121	416	58	111	17	2	18	66	39-4	5	69	.267	.335	.447	117	9	0-4	**.991**	15	115	92	*3-111,2-13/S-4	2.3
	†Pit N	31	114	16	28	5	1	4	19	10-0	2	28	.246	.315	.412	105	1	0-1	.956	-0	100	106	3-31	0.0
1992	Pit N	80	285	27	71	14	1	8	43	34-4	2	61	.249	.331	.389	105	2	0-2	.957	1	109	80	3-80	0.3
	Chi N	65	239	25	66	9	3	1	21	18-2	5	44	.276	.338	.351	94	-2	1-1	.960	1	105	59	3-63/2-2	0.0
	Year	145	524	52	137	23	4	9	64	52-6	7	105	.261	.334	.372	100	1	1-3	**.958**	3	**107**	71	*3-143/2-2	0.3
1993	Chi N	133	460	53	125	27	2	15	65	48-5	5	87	.272	.345	.437	110	7	1-1	**.975**	-2	99	121	*3-129/1-6	0.6
1994	Chi N	104	339	33	82	11	1	14	52	39-2	4	80	.242	.325	.404	91	-5	1-0	.974	-11	84	90	3-99/1-6,2	-1.5
1995	Chi N	32	106	10	20	2	0	1	9	11-0	0	19	.189	.265	.236	34	-10	0-0	.942	-2	93	59	3-32	-1.2
	Tex A	9	24	0	3	0	0	0	0	4-1	0	3	.125	.250	.125	1	-4	0-0	1.000	-0	84	161	/3-9	-0.3
Total	11	1334	4266	501	1046	183	21	137	547	408-31	43	842	.245	.316	.394	94	-41	17-28	.968	50	103	90	*3-1269/2-92,1-12,S-5,O-4(LF),D	0.5

Year	Tm Lg	G	AB	R	H	2B	3B	HR	RBI	BB-IB	HP	SO	AVG	OBP	SLG	AOPS	ABR	SB-CS	FA	FR	Rng	Thr	G at Pos	BFW
BUELOW, CHARLIE Charles John B 1.12.1877 Dubuque, IA D 5.4.1951 Dubuque, IA BR/TR d6.1																								
1901	NY N	22	72	3	8	4	0	0	4	2	1		.111	.147	.167	-10	-10	0	.853	3	131	109	3-17/2-2	-0.7
BUELOW, FRITZ Frederick William Alexander B 2.13.1876 Berlin, Germany D 12.27.1933 Detroit, MI BR/TR 5-10.5/170# d9.28																								
1899	StL N	7	15	4	7	0	2	0	2	2	1		.467	.556	.733	246	3	0	1.000	-0	*141*	*30*	/C-4,O-2(LF)	0.3
1900	StL N	6	17	2	4	0	0	0	3	0	0		.235	.235	.235	30	-2	0	.864	-1	*100*	*104*	/C-4,O(LF)	-0.2
1901	Det A	70	231	28	52	5	5	2	29	11	3		.225	.269	.316	59	-14	2	.967	6	*118*	*108*	C-69	-0.1
1902	Det A	66	224	23	50	5	2	2	29	9	1		.223	.256	.290	50	-16	3	.927	-5	*84*	*119*	C-63/1-2	-1.4
1903	Det A	63	192	24	41	3	6	1	13	6	3		.214	.249	.307	68	-8	4	.961	-3	*79*	*112*	C-60/1-2	-0.7
1904	Det A	42	136	6	15	1	1	0	5	8	0		.110	.160	.132	-7	-17	2	.975	-1	*87*	*110*	C-42	-1.6
	Cle A	42	119	11	21	4	1	0	5	11	1		.176	.252	.227	52	-6	2	.979	2	*118*	*85*	C-42	0.0
	Year	84	255	17	36	5	2	0	10	19	1		.141	.204	.176	21	-23	4	.977	1	*102*	*98*	C-84	-1.6
1905	Cle A	75	239	11	41	4	1	1	18	6	2		.172	.198	.209	29	-20	7	.960	-4	*102*	*105*	C-60/O-8(RF),1-3,3-2	-2.0
1906	Cle A	34	86	7	14	2	0	0	7	9	1		.163	.250	.186	38	-6	0	.938	1	*128*	*115*	C-33/1	-0.2
1907	StL A	26	75	9	11	1	0	0	1	7	0		.147	.220	.160	21	-6	0	.983	-0	*89*	*126*	C-25	-0.5
Total	9	431	1334	125	256	25	18	6	112	69	12		.192	.238	.251	46	-92	20	.960	-5	*100*	*109*	C-402/O-11(3-0-8),1-8,3-2	-6.4
BUES, ART Arthur Frederick B 3.3.1888 Milwaukee, WI D 11.7.1954 Whitefish Bay, WI BR/TR 5-11/184# d4.17																								
1913	Bos N	2	1	0	0	0	0	0	0	0	0	1	.000	.000	.000	-98	0	0	—	-0	0	0	/23	-0.1
1914	Chi N	14	45	3	10	1	1	0	4	5	0	6	.222	.300	.289	76	-1	1	.968	-2	76	0	3-12	-0.3
Total	2	16	46	3	10	1	1	0	4	5	0	7	.217	.294	.283	72	-1	1	.968	-2	75	0	/3-13,2	-0.4
BUFFINTON, CHARLIE Charles G. B 6.14.1861 Fall River, MA D 9.23.1907 Fall River, MA BR/TR 6-1/180# d5.17 M1 ▲																								
1882	Bos N	15	50	5	13	1	0	0	4	2		3	.260	.288	.280	83	-1		.615	-2	108	0	/O-7(RF),P-5,1-4	-0.3
1883	Bos N	86	341	28	81	8	3	1	26	6		24	.238	.251	.287	62	-16		.756	-6	93	197	O-51(0-13-40),P-43/1-2	-1.4
1884	Bos N	87	352	48	94	18	3	1	39	16		12	.267	.299	.344	102	1		.946	-3	98	64	P-67,O-13(0-13-1),1-11	-0.4
1885	Bos N	82	338	26	81	12	3	1	33	3		26	.240	.246	.302	79	-8		.912	1	121	178	P-51,O-18(1-11-6),1-15	-0.6
1886	Bos N	44	176	27	51	4	1	1	30	6		12	.290	.313	.341	102	0	3	.968	-5	54	73	1-19,P-18/O-9(0-1-8)	-0.6
1887	Phi N	66	269	34	72	12	1	1	46	11	1	3	.268	.299	.331	70	-11	8	.931	3	144	236	P-40,O-22(7-7-8),1-10	-0.5
1888	Phi N	46	160	14	29	4	1	0	12	7	0	5	.181	.216	.219	37	-11	1	.939	9	**141**	168	P-46/O(LF)	0.4
1889	Phi N	47	154	16	32	2	0	0	21	9	1	5	.208	.256	.221	31	-15	0	.916	1	107	131	P-47/O(LF)	0.0
1890	Phi P	42	150	24	41	3	2	1	24	9	1	3	.273	.319	.340	74	-6	1	.864	1	105	210	P-36/O-5(1-2-2),1-3,M	0.0
1891	Bos AA	58	181	16	34	2	1	1	16	19	1	15	.188	.269	.227	43	-14	0	.934	5	134	119	P-48,O-10(5-0-6)/1-4	0.0
1892	Bal N	13	43	7	15	1	1	0	4	3	0	6	.349	.391	.419	141	4	1	.892	1	138	115	P-13	0.0
Total	11	586	2214	245	543	67	16	7	255	91	4	114	.245	.276	.299	71	-77	14	.916	6	116	147	P-414,O-137(16-47-78)/1-68	-3.4
BUFORD, DAMON Damon Jackson B 6.12.1970 Baltimore, MD BR/TR 5-10/170# d5.4 f-Don																								
1993	Bal A	53	79	18	18	5	0	2	9	9-0	1	19	.228	.315	.367	79	-2	2-2	.984	1	98	146	O-30(5-24-1),D-17	-0.3
1994	Bal A	4	2	2	1	0	0	0	0	0-0	0	1	.500	.500	.500	151	0	0-0	—	-0	0	0	/O(LF)D	0.0
1995	Bal A	24	32	6	2	0	0	0	2	6-0	0	7	.063	.205	.063	-24	-6	3-1	1.000	1	126	0	O-24(0-15-9)	-0.4
	NY N	44	136	24	32	5	0	4	12	19-0	5	28	.235	.346	.360	91	-1	7-7	.972	-2	92	93	O-39(25-16-0)	-0.4
1996	†Tex A	90	145	30	41	9	0	6	20	15-0	0	34	.283	.348	.469	99	0	8-5	1.000	-1	95	101	O-80(14-25-44)	-0.2
1997	Tex A	122	366	49	82	18	0	8	39	30-0	3	83	.224	.287	.339	60	-22	18-7	.990	3	105	129	*O-117(CF)/D-3	-1.5
1998	†Bos A	86	216	37	61	14	4	10	42	22-1	1	43	.282	.349	.523	121	6	5-5	1.000	-1	94	116	O-67(CF),D-15/23	0.4
1999	†Bos A	91	297	39	72	15	2	6	38	21-0	2	74	.242	.294	.367	66	-16	9-2	.985	1	100	127	O-84(5-82-0)/D-5	-1.3
2000	Chi N	150	495	64	124	18	3	15	48	47-3	8	118	.251	.324	.390	82	-15	4-6	.986	-4	103	49	*O-148(2-140-7)	-1.9
2001	Chi N	35	85	11	15	2	0	3	8	4-0	0	23	.176	.213	.306	34	-9	0-0	1.000	-1	101	0	O-34(0-33-1)	-1.0
Total	9	699	1853	280	448	86	9	54	218	173-4	20	430	.242	.311	.385	77	-65	56-35	.989	-3	101	93	O-624(52-519-62)/D-41,32	-6.6
BUFORD, DON Donald Alvin B 2.2.1937 Linden, TX BB/TR 5-8/165# d9.14 C5 s-Damon																								
1963	Chi A	12	42	9	12	1	2	0	5	5-0	0	7	.286	.354	.405	116	1	1-0	.955	-4	62	65	/3-9,2-2	-0.3
1964	Chi A	135	442	62	116	14	6	4	30	46-2	5	62	.262	.337	.348	94	-3	12-7	.968	-7	91	132	2-92,3-37	-0.3
1965	Chi A	155	586	93	166	22	5	10	47	67-4	4	76	.283	.358	.389	120	17	17-7	.981	10	103	**124**	*2-139,3-41	**4.1**
1966	Chi A	**163**	607	85	148	26	7	8	52	69-3	3	71	.244	.323	.349	100	1	51-22	.939	2	**116**	**118**	*3-133,2-37,O-11(8-0-3)	1.0
1967	Chi A	156	535	61	129	10	9	4	32	65-3	1	51	.241	.322	.316	93	-4	34-21	.948	6	108	100	*3-121,2-51/O(LF)	0.6
1968	Bal A	130	426	65	120	13	4	15	46	57-5	4	46	.282	.367	.437	144	24	27-12	1.000	2	107	106	O-65(27-41-2),2-58/3-2	3.3
1969	†Bal A	144	554	99	161	31	3	11	64	96-7	5	62	.291	.397	.417	128	26	19-18	.983	-4	93	67	*O-128(LF),2-10/3-6	1.3
1970	†Bal A	144	504	99	137	15	2	17	66	109-8	8	55	.272	.406	.411	125	24	16-8	.987	2	98	160	*O-130(LF)/2-3,3-3	1.9
1971	†Bal A★	122	449	**99**	130	19	4	19	54	89-15	7	62	.290	.413	.477	153	36	15-7	.987	0	103	84	*O-115(114-0-1)	3.3
1972	Bal A	125	408	46	84	6	2	5	22	69-10	4	83	.206	.326	.267	76	-9	8-3	.989	-4	91	74	*O-105(104-0-1)	-2.2
Total	10	1286	4553	718	1203	157	44	93	418	672-57	41	575	.264	.362	.379	115	113	200-105	.988	3	97	100	O-555(512-41-7),2-392,3-352	12.7
BUHNER, JAY Jay Campbell B 8.13.1964 Louisville, KY BR/TR 6-3/205# d9.11																								
1987	NY A	7	22	0	5	2	0	0	1	1-0	0	6	.227	.261	.318	53	-1	0-0	1.000	0	78	259	/O-7(2-3-2)	-0.2
1988	NY A	25	69	8	13	0	0	3	13	3-0	3	25	.188	.250	.319	60	-4	0-0	.964	1	107	218	O-22(3-16-3)	-0.3
	Sea A	60	192	28	43	13	1	10	25	25-1	3	68	.224	.320	.458	111	3	1-1	.993	7	112	206	O-59(1-2-55)	0.8
	Year	85	261	36	56	13	1	13	38	28-1	6	93	.215	.302	.421	98	-1	1-1	.985	8	111	209	O-81(4-18-58)	0.5
1989	Sea A	58	204	27	56	15	1	9	33	19-0	2	55	.275	.341	.490	128	7	1-4	.966	-1	90	140	O-57(0-2-56)	0.3
1990	Sea A	51	163	16	45	12	0	7	33	17-1	4	50	.276	.357	.479	131	7	2-2	.966	-5	77	41	O-40(0-1-39),D-10	0.1
1991	Sea A	137	406	64	99	14	4	27	77	53-5	6	117	.244	.337	.498	128	15	0-1	.981	7	102	177	*O-131(1-3-131)	1.8
1992	Sea A	152	543	69	132	16	3	25	79	71-2	6	146	.243	.333	.422	111	7	0-6	.994	4	97	135	*O-150(0-2-150)	0.4
1993	Sea A	158	563	91	153	28	3	27	98	100-11	2	144	.272	.379	.476	128	25	2-5	.978	-9	88	75	*O-148(RF),D-10	0.6
1994	Sea A	101	358	74	100	23	4	21	68	66-3	5	63	.279	.394	.542	137	22	0-1	.990	3	96	166	O-96(0-1-95)/D-4	1.8
1995	†Sea A	126	470	86	123	23	0	40	121	60-7	1	120	.262	.343	.566	131	20	0-1	.989	-9	82	67	*O-120(RF)/D-4	0.4
1996	Sea A★	150	564	107	153	29	0	44	138	84-5	9	159	.271	.369	.557	131	27	0-1	.989	-6	87	90	*O-142(RF)/D-8	1.2
1997	†Sea A	157	540	104	131	18	2	40	109	119-3	5	175	.243	.383	.506	131	27	0-0	**.997**	-2	97	53	*O-154(RF)/D-2	1.7
1998	Sea A	72	244	33	59	7	1	15	45	38-0	1	71	.242	.344	.463	108	3	0-0	.985	1	100	110	O-70(RF)/D	0.0
1999	Sea A	87	266	37	59	11	0	14	38	69-0	5	100	.222	.388	.421	110	7	0-0	.993	-4	79	126	O-85(RF)/1	-0.1
2000	†Sea A	112	364	50	92	20	0	26	82	59-3	4	98	.253	.361	.522	124	14	0-2	1.000	-3	94	63	*O-104(RF)/D	0.5
2001	†Sea A	19	45	4	10	2	0	2	5	8-0	0	9	.222	.340	.400	100	0	0-0	1.000	-1	88	0	O-12(10-0-2)/D-4	-0.1
Total	15	1472	5013	798	1273	233	19	310	965	792-41	56	1406	.254	.359	.494	124	179	6-24	.988	-17	93	109	*O-1397(17-30-1356)/D-44,1	8.9
BUKER, HARRY Henry L. "Happy" B 1859 Chicago, IL D 8.10.1899 Chicago, IL ?/140# d6.11																								
1884	Det N	30	111	5	15	1	0	0	3	4		15	.135	.165	.144	-2	-13		.867	1	109	106	S-19,O-11(RF)	-1.0
BULLARD, GEORGE George Donald "Curly" B 10.24.1928 Lynn, MA D 12.23.2002 Lynn, MA BR/TR 5-9.5/165# d9.17																								
1954	Det A	4	1	0	0	0	0	0	0	0	0	0	.000	.000	.000	-99	0	0-0	.800	0	116	0	/S	0.0
BULLAS, SIM Simeon Edward B 4.10.1861 Cleveland, OH D 1.14.1908 Cleveland, OH 5-7.5/150# d5.2																								
1884	Tol AA	13	45	4	4	0	1	0		1	0		.089	.109	.133	-21	-6		.909	-3			C-12/O-2(LF)	-0.8
BULLETT, SCOTT Scott Douglas B 12.25.1968 Martinsburg, WV BL/TL (BB 1993) 6-2/200# d9.3																								
1991	Pit N	11	4	2	0	0	0	0	0	0-0	1	3	.000	.200	.000	-40	-1	1-1	1.000	-0	82	0	/O-3(1-1-1)	-0.1
1993	Pit N	23	55	2	11	0	2	0	4	3-0	0	15	.200	.237	.273	37	-5	3-2	1.000	-1	92	124	O-19(0-18-1)	-0.6
1995	Chi N	104	150	19	41	5	7	3	22	12-2	1	30	.273	.331	.460	108	1	8-3	.968	-2	94	51	O-64(54-12-0)	-0.1
1996	Chi N	109	165	26	35	5	0	3	16	10-0	0	54	.212	.256	.297	44	-14	7-3	.986	3	119	111	O-58(28-11-22)	-1.1
Total	4	247	374	49	87	10	9	6	42	25-2	2	102	.233	.283	.356	68	-19	19-9	.983	1	103	87	O-144(83-42-24)	-1.9
BULLING, BUD Terry Charles "Terry" B 12.15.1952 Lynwood, CA BR/TR 6-1/200# d7.3																								
1977	Min A	15	32	2	5	1	0	0	5	5-1	0	5	.156	.270	.188	28	-3	0-0	.952	-1	57	34	C-10/D-3	-0.4
1981	Sea A	62	154	15	38	3	0	2	15	21-0	1	20	.247	.341	.305	84	-2	0-0	.977	-6	80	103	C-62	-0.7
1982	Sea A	56	154	17	34	7	0	1	8	19-2	0	16	.221	.306	.286	62	-8	2-1	.991	2	103	123	C-56	-0.3
1983	Sea A	5	5	0	0	0	0	0	0	0-0	0	0	.000	.000	.000	-96	-1	0-0	1.000	0	155	0	/C-5	-0.1
Total	4	138	345	34	77	11	0	3	28	45-3	1	41	.223	.315	.281	66	-14	2-1	.983	-5	90	105	C-133/D-3	-1.5
BULLOCK, ERIC Eric Gerald B 2.16.1960 Los Angeles, CA BL/TL 5-11/185# d8.26																								
1985	Hou N	18	25	3	7	2	0	0	2	1-0	0	3	.280	.308	.360	89	0	0-1	.750	-1	83	0	/O-7(4-0-3)	-0.2

Year	Tm Lg	G	AB	R	H	2B	3B	HR	RBI	BB-IB	HP	SO	AVG	OBP	SLG	AOPS	ABR	SB-CS	FA	FR	Rng	Thr	G at Pos	BFW
1986	Hou N	6	21	0	1	0	0	0	1	0-0	0	3	.048	.048	.048	-76	-5	2-0	.875	-1	71	0	/O-6(LF)	-0.6
1988	Min A	16	17	3	5	0	0	0	3	3-0	0	1	.294	.400	.294	95	0	1-0	.875	0	175	0	/O-4(3-0-2),D-2	0.1
1989	Phi N	6	4	1	0	0	0	0	0	0-0	0	2	.000	.000	.000	-99	-1	0-0	1.000	0	194	0	/O-3(0-1-2)	-0.1
1990	Mon N	4	2	0	1	0	0	0	0	0-0	0	0	.500	.500	.500	183	0	0-0	—	0			/H	0.0
1991	Mon N	73	72	6	16	4	0	1	6	9-0	0	13	.222	.305	.319	78	-2	6-1	1.000	0	100	0	/O-9(6-0-3),1-3	-0.1
1992	Mon N	8	5	0	0	0	0	0	0	0-0	0	1	.000	.000	.000	-99	-1	0-0	—	0			/H	-0.2
Total	7	131	146	13	30	6	0	1	12	13-0	0	23	.205	.269	.267	52	-9	9-2	.892	-1	98	0	/O-29(19-1-10),1-3,D-2	-1.1
BUMBRY, AL Alonza Benjamin (born Alonza Benjamin Bumbrey) B 4.21.1947 Fredericksburg, VA BL/TR 5-8/175# d9.5 C9																								
1972	Bal A	9	11	5	4	0	1	0	0	0-0	0	0	.364	.364	.545	164	1	1-1	1.000	0	119	0	/O-2(LF)	0.1
1973	†Bal A	110	356	73	120	15	**11**	7	34	34-0	3	49	.337	.398	.500	153	25	23-10	.978	-7	86	36	O-86(62-1-29)/D-7	1.5
1974	†Bal A	94	270	35	63	10	3	1	19	21-2	1	46	.233	.288	.304	74	-10	12-4	.953	0	96	159	O-67(LF)/D-7	-1.2
1975	Bal A	114	349	47	94	19	4	2	32	32-3	4	81	.269	.336	.364	105	3	16-3	1.000	-2	87	70	D-48,O-39(35-3-1)/3	-0.1
1976	Bal A	133	450	71	113	15	7	9	36	43-2	1	76	.251	.316	.376	109	4	42-10	.989	0	99	113	*O-116(82-57-0),D-10	0.5
1977	Bal A	133	518	74	164	31	3	4	41	45-4	2	88	.317	.371	.411	121	17	19-8	.991	1	102	76	*O-130(52-112-0)	1.6
1978	Bal A	33	114	21	27	5	2	2	6	17-0	2	15	.237	.346	.368	108	2	5-3	.985	-1	93	111	O-28(16-17-0)	0.0
1979	†Bal A	148	569	80	162	29	1	7	49	43-3	3	74	.285	.336	.376	96	-3	37-12	.982	-4	97	76	*O-146(5-146-0)	-0.4
1980	Bal A★	160	645	118	205	29	9	9	53	78-8	3	75	.318	.392	.433	128	27	44-11	.990	5	110	62	*O-160(1-160-0)	3.6
1981	Bal A	101	392	61	107	18	2	1	27	51-2	2	51	.273	.358	.337	102	3	22-15	.992	-2	96	100	*O-100(CF)	0.0
1982	Bal A	150	562	77	147	20	4	5	40	44-4	0	77	.262	.314	.338	80	-16	10-5	.986	6	108	98	*O-147(3-146-0)/D	-1.1
1983	†Bal A	124	378	63	104	14	4	3	31	31-2	0	33	.275	.328	.357	91	-5	12-5	.988	-2	99	54	*O-104(17-99-0),D-11	-0.7
1984	Bal A	119	344	47	93	12	1	3	24	25-0	0	35	.270	.317	.337	84	-8	9-5	.988	3	101	125	O-99(28-82-0)/D-9	-0.6
1985	SD N	68	95	6	19	3	0	1	10	7-0	0	9	.200	.255	.263	46	-7	2-0	.939	0	126	0	O-17(12-5-1)	-0.7
Total	14	1496	5053	778	1422	220	52	54	402	471-30	21	709	.281	.343	.378	104	33	254-92	.986	-4	100	85	*O-1241(382-928-31)/D-93,3	2.5
BUNCE, JOSH Joshua B 5.10.1847 Brooklyn, NY D 4.28.1912 Brooklyn, NY d8.27																								
1877	Har N	1	4	0	0	0	0	0	0	0		0	.000	.000	.000	-99	-1		1.000	-0	0	0	/O(LF)	-0.1
BURBRINK, NELSON Nelson Edward B 12.28.1921 Cincinnati, OH D 4.12.2001 Largo, FL BR/TR 5-10/195# d6.5																								
1955	StL N	58	170	11	47	8	1	0	15	14-1	1	13	.276	.333	.335	79	-5	1-1	.979	-2	*106*	*118*	C-55	-0.5
BURCH, AL Albert William B 10.7.1883 Albany, NY D 10.5.1926 Brooklyn, NY BL/TR 5-8.5/160# d6.19																								
1906	StL N	91	335	40	89	5	1	0	11	37	0		.266	.339	.287	99	1	15	.934	-1	131	210	O-91(0-58-33)	-0.5
1907	StL N	48	154	18	35	3	1	0	5	17	0		.227	.304	.260	79	-3	7	.922	-1	152	235	O-48(CF)	-0.7
	Bro N	40	120	12	35	2	2	0	12	11	0		.292	.351	.342	127	4	5	.890	2	180	0	O-36(27-5-5)/2	0.4
	Year	88	274	30	70	5	3	0	17	28	0		.255	.325	.296	100	0	12	.908	1	164	134	O-84(27-53-5)/2	-0.3
1908	Bro N	123	456	45	111	8	4	2	18	33	0		.243	.294	.292	91	-6	15	.971	9	**151**	156	*O-116(47-44-28)	-0.4
1909	Bro N	152	601	80	163	20	6	1	30	51	1		.271	.329	.329	108	5	38	.955	2	106	77	*O-151(41-102-9)/1	0.0
1910	Bro N	103	352	41	83	8	3	1	20	22	0	30	.236	.281	.284	67	-16	13	.957	-2	91	110	O-70(0-26-45),1-13	-2.3
1911	Bro N	54	167	18	38	2	3	0	7	15	0	22	.228	.291	.275	61	-9	3	.972	1	102	97	O-43(0-41-3)/2-3	-1.1
Total	6	611	2185	254	554	48	20	4	103	186	1	52	.254	.312	.299	91	-24	96	.950	11	126	130	O-555(115-324-123)/1-14,2-4	-4.6
BURCH, ERNIE Ernest A. B 9.9.1856 DeKalb Co., IL D 10.12.1892 Guthrie, OK BL 5-10/190# d8.15																								
1884	Cle N	32	124	9	26	4	0	0	7	5		24	.210	.240	.242	50	-7		.899	5	162	94	O-32(23-0-9)	-0.3
1886	Bro AA	113	456	78	119	22	6	2	72	39	1		.261	.321	.349	109	5	16	.884	-10	56	89	*O-113(LF)	-0.7
1887	Bro AA	49	188	47	55	4	4	2	26	29	3		.293	.395	.388	118	6	15	.899	1	101	56	O-49(LF)	0.4
Total	3	194	768	134	200	30	10	4	105	73	4	24	.260	.328	.341	102	4	31	.891	-4	85	81	O-194(185-0-9)	-0.6
BURDA, BOB Edward Robert B 7.16.1938 St.Louis, MO BL/TL 5-11/180# d8.25																								
1962	StL N	7	14	0	1	0	0	0	0	3-0	0	1	.071	.235	.071	-12	-2	1-0	.917	-0	113	0	/O-6(1-0-5)	-0.3
1965	SF N	31	27	0	3	0	0	0	5	5-0	0	6	.111	.235	.111	6	-3	0-0	.969	-1	0	49	1-11/O(LF)	-0.5
1966	SF N	37	43	3	7	3	0	0	2	2-0	0	5	.163	.196	.233	19	-5	0-0	1.000	-0	106	0	/1-7,O-4(3-0-1)	-0.5
1969	SF N	97	161	20	37	8	0	6	27	21-3	0	12	.230	.317	.391	100	0	0-1	.995	-0	92	93	1-45,O-19(5-0-15)	-0.3
1970	SF N	28	23	1	6	0	0	0	3	5-2	1	2	.261	.414	.261	86	0	0-0	.933	-1	0	63	/1-8,O(LF)	-0.1
	Mil A	78	222	19	55	9	0	4	20	16-1	3	17	.248	.303	.342	78	-7	1-0	.987	-5	76	87	O-64(RF)/1-7	-1.6
1971	StL N	65	71	6	21	0	0	1	12	10-2	1	11	.296	.386	.338	104	1	0-0	1.000	1	127	61	1-13/O(RF)	0.1
1972	Bos A	45	73	4	12	1	0	2	9	8-3	0	11	.164	.241	.260	48	-5	0-0	.992	-0	81	103	1-15/O(LF)	-0.7
Total	7	388	634	53	142	21	0	13	78	70-11	5	65	.224	.302	.319	74	-21	2-1	.992	-8	84	82	1-106/O-97(12-0-86)	-3.9
BURDOCK, JACK John Joseph "Black Jack" B 4.1852 Brooklyn, NY D 11.27.1931 Brooklyn, NY BR/TR 5-9.5/158# d5.2 M1 U3																								
1872	Atl NA	**37**	174	27	47	3	0	0	14	1		1	.270	.274	.287	62	-10	0-1	.743	-7	94	22	*S-36/C-4,2-2	-1.3
1873	Atl NA	**55**	245	56	62	7	1	2	36	7		4	.253	.274	.314	83	-2	3-2	.818	-0	105	94	*2-55/C-2	-0.5
1874	Mut NA	61	273	45	75	11	4	1	26	1		5	.275	.277	.355	98	-1	4-1	**.820**	10	93	97	*3-60/O-3(2-1-0)	0.6
1875	Har NA	74	350	72	103	12	5	0	35	3		13	.294	.300	.357	121	6	20-11	**.895**	-3	84	134	*2-73/3-2,C	-0.1
1876	Har N	**69**	309	66	80	9	1	0	23	13		16	.259	.289	.294	87	-5		.895	2	89	98	*2-69/3	0.0
1877	Har N	58	277	35	72	6	0	0	9	2		16	.260	.265	.282	81	-5		**.903**	7	99	128	*2-55/3-3	0.4
1878	Bos N	**60**	246	37	64	12	6	0	25	3		17	.260	.269	.358	97	-2		**.918**	**21**	**103**	**151**	*2-60	2.0
1879	Bos N	**84**	359	64	86	10	3	0	36	9		28	.240	.258	.284	77	-9		.911	12	100	147	*2-84	0.6
1880	Bos N	**86**	356	58	90	17	4	2	35	8		26	.253	.269	.340	108	3		**.923**	15	100	101	*2-86	2.1
1881	Bos N	73	282	36	67	12	4	1	24	7		18	.238	.256	.319	84	-5		.911	-8	91	98	*2-72/S	-1.0
1882	Bos N	83	319	36	76	6	7	0	27	9		24	.238	.259	.301	79	-8		**.932**	6	99	82	*2-83	0.0
1883	Bos N	96	400	80	132	27	8	5	88	14		35	.330	.353	.475	145	21		.921	1	93	103	*2-96/,M	2.2
1884	Bos N	87	361	65	97	14	4	6	49	15		52	.269	.298	.380	112	5		**.922**	2	100	82	*2-87/3	0.9
1885	Bos N	45	169	18	24	5	0	0	7	8		18	.142	.181	.172	15	-15		.917	-3	96	83	2-45	-1.6
1886	Bos N	59	221	26	48	6	1	0	25	11		27	.217	.254	.253	56	-11	3	.904	-10	92	87	2-59	-1.8
1887	Bos N	65	237	36	61	6	0	0	29	18	4	22	.257	.320	.283	68	-9	19	.882	-16	94	124	2-65	-2.0
1888	Bos N	22	79	5	16	0	0	0	4	2	1	5	.203	.232	.203	38	-6	1	.903	-1	100	116	2-22	-0.6
	Bro AA	70	246	15	30	1	2	1	8	8	5		.122	.166	.154	3	-27	9	.904	-3	104	101	2-70	-2.5
1891	Bro N	3	12	1	1	0	0	0	1	1	0	1	.083	.154	.083	-31	-2	0	1.000	-0	106	88	/2-3	-0.2
Total	4 NA	227	1042	200	287	33	10	3	111	12	0	23	.275	.284	.335	95	-7	27-15	.000	-1	93	116	2-130/3-62,S-36,C-7,O-3(2-1-0)	-1.3
Total	14	960	3873	578	944	131	40	15	390	128	10	305	.244	.270	.310	83	-75	32-0	.912	26	97	106	2-956/3-5,S	-1.5
BURG, JOE Joseph Peter B 6.4.1882 Chicago, IL D 4.28.1969 Joliet, IL BR/TR 5-10/150# d9.26																								
1910	Bos N	13	46	7	15	0	1	0	10	7	0	12	.326	.415	.370	124	2	5	.867	1	123	58	3-12/S	0.3
BURGESS, SMOKY Forrest Harrill B 2.6.1927 Caroleen, NC D 9.15.1991 Asheville, NC BL/TR 5-8/187# d4.19																								
1949	Chi N	46	56	4	15	0	0	1	12	4	0	4	.268	.317	.321	73	-2	0	1.000	1	*78*	*250*	/C-8	-0.1
1951	Chi N	94	219	21	55	4	2	2	20	21	0	12	.251	.317	.315	69	-10	2-0	.980	-4	*58*	*129*	C-64	-1.1
1952	Phi N	110	371	49	110	27	2	6	56	49	1	21	.296	.380	.429	125	15	3-1	.978	-4	*94*	*97*	*C-104	1.8
1953	Phi N	102	312	31	91	17	5	4	36	37	2	17	.292	.370	.417	105	4	3-2	**.993**	-4	*102*	*46*	C-95	0.4
1954	Phi N★	108	345	41	127	27	5	4	46	42	0	11	.368	.432	.510	146	26	1-5	.975	-3	*111*	*69*	C-91	2.5
1955	Phi N	7	21	4	4	2	0	1	1	3-1	0	1	.190	.292	.429	90	0	0-0	1.000	1	*90*	*0*	/C-6	0.1
	Cin N★	116	421	67	129	15	3	20	77	47-4	1	35	.306	.373	.499	123	14	1-1	.986	-3	*120*	*62*	*C-107	1.6
	Year	123	442	71	133	17	3	21	78	50-5	1	36	.301	.369	.495	122	14	1-1	.987	-3	*118*	*59*	*C-113	1.7
1956	Cin N	90	229	28	63	10	0	12	39	26-4	0	18	.275	.346	.476	112	4	0-1	1.000	-2	*91*	*77*	C-55	0.5
1957	Cin N	90	205	29	58	14	1	14	39	24-5	0	16	.283	.353	.566	134	10	0-0	.988	-5	*117*	*80*	C-45	0.7
1958	Cin N	99	251	28	71	12	1	6	31	22-3	1	20	.283	.343	.410	93	-2	0-0	.988	3	*131*	*86*	C-58	0.4
1959	Pit N★	114	377	41	112	28	5	11	59	31-9	2	16	.297	.349	.485	122	12	0-0	.984	-12	*99*	*91*	*C-101	0.5
1960	†Pit N★	110	337	33	99	15	2	7	39	35-12	0	13	.294	.356	.412	110	5	0-1	**.994**	3	*152*	*75*	C-89	1.2
1961	Pit N★	100	323	37	98	17	3	12	52	30-8	2	16	.303	.365	.486	123	11	1-0	**.991**	-7	*135*	*55*	C-92	0.8
1962	Pit N	103	360	38	118	19	2	13	61	31-9	0	19	.328	.375	.500	134	17	0-1	.988	-7	*91*	*66*	*C-101	1.5
1963	Pit N	91	264	20	74	10	1	6	37	24-8	1	14	.280	.338	.394	111	4	0-1	.990	-7	*80*	*94*	C-72	0.0
1964	Pit N☆	68	171	9	42	3	1	2	17	13-3	1	14	.246	.303	.310	73	-6	2-1	.992	-5	*96*	*76*	C-44	-0.9
	Chi A	7	5	1	1	0	0	1	1	2-2	0	0	.200	.429	.800	239	1	0-0	—	0			H	0.1
1965	Chi A	80	77	2	22	4	0	2	24	11-4	0	7	.286	.371	.416	132	4	0-0	1.000	0	*70*	*144*	/C-5	0.4
1966	Chi A	79	67	0	21	5	0	0	15	11-2	1	8	.313	.412	.388	143	5	0-0	1.000	-0	*0*	*0*	/C-2	0.5

Year	Tm Lg	G	AB	R	H	2B	3B	HR	RBI	BB-IB	HP	SO	AVG	OBP	SLG	AOPS	ABR	SB-CS	FA	FR	Rng	Thr	G at Pos	BFW
1967	Chi A	77	60	2	8	1	0	2	11	14-6	1	8	.133	.303	.250	69	-2	0-0	—	0			H	-0.2
Total	18	1691	4471	485	1318	230	33	126	673	477-80	13	270	.295	.362	.446	116	110	13-14	.988	-54	*107*	*77*	*C-1139	10.7
BURGESS, TOM Thomas Roland "Tim" B 9.1.1927 London, ON, CAN BL/TL 6/180# d4.17 C2																								
1954	StL N	17	21	2	1	1	0	0	1	3	0	9	.048	.167	.095	-29	-4	0-0	.750	-1	65	0	/O-4(RF)	-0.5
1962	LA A	87	143	17	28	7	1	2	13	36-8	0	20	.196	.354	.301	82	-2	2-0	.997	-3	68	101	1-35/O-2(LF)	-0.6
Total	2	104	164	19	29	8	1	2	14	39-8	0	29	.177	.332	.274	67	-6	2-0	.997	-3	68	101	/1-35,O-6(2-0-4)	-1.1
BURGO, BILL William Ross B 11.5.1919 Johnstown, PA D 10.19.1988 Morgan City, LA BR/TR 5-8/185# d9.22																								
1943	Phi A	17	70	12	26	4	2	1	9	4	2	1	.371	.421	.529	178	7	0-2	.979	1	108	137	O-17(LF)	0.7
1944	Phi A	27	88	6	21	2	0	1	3	7	3	3	.239	.316	.295	76	-3	1-3	.955	1	119	52	O-22(14-0-8)	-0.4
Total	2	44	158	18	47	6	2	2	12	11	5	4	.297	.362	.399	121	4	1-5	.965	2	114	88	/O-39(31-0-8)	0.3
BURICH, BILL William Max B 5.29.1918 Calumet, MI BR/TR 6/180# d4.15 Mil 1943-46																								
1942	Phi N	25	80	3	23	1	0	0	7	6	0	13	.287	.337	.300	92	-1	2	.917	-4	83	54	S-19/3-3	-0.3
1946	Phi N	2	1	1	0	0	0	0	0	0	0	0	.000	.000	.000	-99	0	0	—	-0	0	0	/3	0.0
Total	2	27	81	4	23	1	0	0	7	6	0	13	.284	.333	.296	89	-1	2	.917	-4	83	54	/S-19,3-4	-0.3
BURK, MACK Mack Edwin B 4.21.1935 Nacogdoches, TX BR/TR 6-4/180# d5.25 Mil 1957-58																								
1956	Phi N	15	1	3	1	0	0	0	0	0-0	0	0	1.000	1.000	1.000	449	0	0-0	1.000	0	*0*	*0*	/C	0.0
1958	Phi N	1	1	0	0	0	0	0	0	0-0	0	1	.000	.000	.000	-99	0	0-0	—	0			H	0.0
Total	2	16	2	3	1	0	0	0	0	0-0	0	1	.500	.500	.500	171	0	0-0	1.000	0	*0*	*0*	/C	0.0
BURKAM, CHRIS Chauncey De Pew B 10.13.1892 Benton Harbor, MI D 5.9.1964 Kalamazoo, MI BL/TR 5-11/175# d6.24																								
1915	StL A	1	1	0	0	0	0	0	0	0	0	1	.000	.000	.000	-99	0	0	—	0			H	0.0
BURKE, DAN Daniel L. B 10.25.1868 Abington, MA D 3.20.1933 Taunton, MA BR/TR 5-10/190# d4.18																								
1890	Roc AA	32	102	14	22	1	0	0	9	17	1		.216	.333	.225	70	-2	2	.944	-1	189	122	O-29(0-19-10)/C-4,1-2	-0.3
	Syr AA	9	20	1	0	0	0	0	0	5	1		.000	.231	.000	-35	-3	0	.900	-1	*79*	*65*	/C-9	-0.3
	Year	41	122	15	22	1	0	0	9	22	2		.180	.315	.189	53	-5	2	.944	-2	189	122	O-29(0-19-10),C-13/1-2	-0.6
1892	Bos N	1	4	0	0	0	0	0	0	0	0	2	.000	.000	.000	-92	-1	0	.900	0	*107*	*80*	/C	0.0
Total	2	42	126	15	22	1	0	0	9	22	2	2	.175	.307	.183	48	-6	2	.944	-2	189	122	/O-29(0-19-10),C-14,1-2	-0.6
BURKE, EDDIE Edward D. B 10.6.1866 Northumberland, PA D 11.26.1907 Utica, NY BL/TR 5-6/161# d4.19																								
1890	Phi N	100	430	85	113	16	11	4	50	49	8	40	.263	.349	.379	109	5	38	.904	1	138	113	*O-96(CF)/2-4	0.2
	Pit N	31	124	17	26	5	2	1	7	14	1	9	.210	.295	.306	85	-2	6	.911	0	38	71	O-31(CF)	-0.2
	Year	131	554	102	139	21	13	5	57	63	9	49	.251	.337	.363	105	3	44	.906	1	114	103	*O-127(CF)/2-4	0.0
1891	Mil AA	35	144	31	34	9	0	2	21	12	10	19	.236	.337	.340	78	-5	7	.918	2	131	254	O-35(CF)	-0.3
1892	Cin N	15	41	6	6	1	0	0	4	9	0	4	.146	.300	.171	44	-2	2	1.000	-1	136	330	O-14(3-5-6)/3	-0.3
	NY N	89	363	81	94	10	5	6	41	46	5	37	.259	.350	.364	118	9	42	.857	-5	98	74	2-59,O-30(LF)	0.4
	Year	104	404	87	100	11	5	6	45	55	5	41	.248	.345	.344	110	7	44	.857	-6	98	74	2-59,O-44(33-5-6)/3	0.1
1893	NY N	135	537	122	150	23	10	9	80	51	**25**	32	.279	.369	.410	106	5	54	.911	0	82	41	*O-135(LF)	-0.6
1894	†NY N	138	574	124	176	23	11	4	77	39	10	35	.307	.361	.406	85	-15	36	.934	-6	71	58	*O-138(LF)	-2.6
1895	NY N	39	167	38	43	6	2	1	12	7	3	9	.257	.299	.335	65	-9	14	.914	1	128	144	O-39(LF)	-1.0
	Cin N	56	228	52	61	8	6	1	28	22	4	14	.268	.343	.368	80	-7	19	.899	1	89	99	O-56(56-0-1)	-0.9
	Year	95	395	90	104	14	8	2	40	29	7	23	.263	.325	.354	74	-16	33	.905	2	105	117	O-95(95-0-1)	-1.9
1896	Cin N	122	521	120	177	24	9	1	52	41	4	29	.340	.392	.426	108	6	53	.935	-1	73	73	*O-122(116-5-1)	-0.5
1897	Cin N	95	387	71	103	17	1	1	41	29	6		.266	.327	.323	67	-18	22	.940	5	78	152	*O-95(94-0-1)	-1.9
Total	8	855	3516	747	983	142	57	30	413	319	76	228	.280	.352	.378	94	-33	293	.921	-2	90	93	O-791(611-172-9)/2-63,3	-7.7
BURKE, FRANK Frank Aloysius B 2.16.1880 Carbon Co., PA D 9.17.1946 Los Angeles, CA TR d9.14																								
1906	NY N	8	9	2	3	1	1	0	1	1	0		.333	.400	.667	227	1	1	.667	-1	0	0	/O-4(0-3-1)	0.1
1907	Bos N	43	129	6	23	0	1	0	8	11	0		.178	.243	.194	37	-9	3	.955	-3	60	0	O-36(32-4-1)	-1.7
Total	2	51	138	8	26	1	2	0	9	12	0		.188	.253	.225	50	-8	4	.942	-4	57	0	/O-40(32-7-2)	-1.6
BURKE, GLENN Glenn Lawrence B 11.16.1952 Oakland, CA D 5.30.1995 San Leandro, CA BR/TR 6/195# d4.9																								
1976	LA N	25	46	9	11	2	0	0	5	3-0	1	8	.239	.300	.283	67	-2	3-2	.971	-2	89	0	O-20(5-15-0)	-0.5
1977	†LA N	83	169	16	43	8	0	1	13	5-1	1	22	.254	.280	.320	61	-10	13-5	.971	-7	81	31	O-74(5-64-6)	-1.7
1978	LA N	16	19	2	4	0	0	0	2	0-0	0	4	.211	.211	.211	18	-2	1-0	1.000	-1	69	0	O-15(4-11-0)	-0.3
	Oak A	78	200	19	47	6	1	1	14	10-1	0	26	.235	.270	.290	61	-11	15-8	.987	0	109	27	O-67(13-45-14)/1D	-1.2
1979	Oak A	23	89	4	19	2	1	0	4	4-1	0	10	.213	.247	.258	39	-8	3-1	1.000	0	93	115	O-23(22-0-2)	-0.9
Total	4	225	523	50	124	18	2	2	38	22-3	2	70	.237	.270	.291	56	-33	35-16	.983	-10	94	38	O-199(49-135-22)/D-2,1	-4.6
BURKE, JAMIE James Eugene B 9.24.1971 Roseburg, OR BR/TR 6/195# d5.9																								
2001	Ana A	9	5	1	1	0	0	0	0	0-0	0	2	.200	.200	.200	6	-1	0-0	1.000	1	82	0	/C-8,1D	0.0
2003	Chi A	6	8	0	3	0	0	0	2	0-0	0	0	.375	.375	.375	98	0	0-0	1.000	-1	57	0	/C-4,1D	-0.1
Total	2	15	13	1	4	0	0	0	2	0-0	0	2	.308	.308	.308	62	-1	0-0	1.000	-1	66	0	/C-12,D-2,1-2	-0.1
BURKE, JIMMY James Timothy "Sunset Jimmy" B 10.12.1874 St.Louis, MO D 3.26.1942 St.Louis, MO BR/TR 5-7/160# d10.6 M4 C15																								
1898	Cle N	13	38	1	4	1	0	0	1	2	0		.105	.150	.132	-19	-6	1	.853	-2	93	0	3-13	-0.8
1899	StL N	2	6	1	2	0	0	0	0	1	0		.333	.429	.333	108	0	0	.923	1	131	277	/2-2	0.1
1901	Mil A	64	233	24	48	8	0	0	26	17	2		.206	.266	.240	43	-17	6	.860	-8	92	53	3-64	-2.1
	Chi A	42	148	20	39	5	0	0	21	12	2		.264	.327	.297	76	-4	11	.867	-4	98	97	S-31,3-11	-0.6
	Year	106	381	44	87	13	0	0	47	29	4		.228	.290	.262	56	-21	17	.859	-12	95	44	3-75,S-31	-2.7
	Pit N	14	51	4	10	0	0	0	4	4	1		.196	.268	.196	35	-4	0	.877	2	124	224	3-14	-0.1
1902	Pit N	60	203	24	60	12	2	0	26	17	3		.296	.359	.374	122	6	9	.895	-3	102	88	2-27,O-18(7-0-11)/3-9,S-4	0.3
1903	StL N	115	431	55	123	13	3	0	42	23	3		.285	.326	.329	90	-6	28	.911	9	107	**138**	3-93,2-15/O-5(4-0-1)	0.5
1904	StL N	118	406	37	92	10	3	0	37	15	10		.227	.271	.266	69	-15	17	.897	-7	94	84	*3-118	-2.0
1905	StL N	122	431	34	97	9	5	1	30	21	9		.225	.275	.276	67	-18	15	.924	4	104	90	*3-122,M	-1.2
Total	7	550	1947	200	475	58	13	1	187	112	30		.244	.295	.289	73	-64	87	.899	-8	101	91	3-444/2-44,S-35,O-23(11-0-12)	-5.9
BURKE, JOE Joseph Aloysius B 12.7.1867 Nashville, TN D 11.3.1940 Cincinnati, OH 5-7/160# d9.26																								
1890	StL AA	2	6	3	4	0	0	0	2	1	1		.667	.750	.667	278	2	0	.750	-0	131	0	/3-2	0.1
1891	Cin AA	1	4	0	1	0	0	0	1	0	0	2	.250	.250	.250	40	0	0	1.000	1	134	0	/2	0.0
Total	2	3	10	3	5	0	0	0	3	1	1	2	.500	.583	.500	193	2	0	.750	1	131	0	/3-2,2	0.1
BURKE, LEO Leo Patrick B 5.6.1934 Hagerstown, MD BR/TR 5-10/190# d9.7 OF Total (7-LF 1-CF 37-RF)																								
1958	Bal A	7	11	4	5	1	0	1	4	1-0	0	2	.455	.500	.818	271	3	0-0	1.000	-1	63	0	/O-3(1-1-1),3	0.2
1959	Bal A	5	10	0	2	0	0	0	1	0-0	1	5	.200	.273	.200	33	-1	0-0	1.000	-1	64	0	/2-2,3-2	-0.2
1961	LA A	6	5	0	0	0	0	0	0	0-0	0	1	.000	.000	.000	-90	-1	0-0	—	0			H	-0.1
1962	LA A	19	64	8	17	1	0	4	14	5-1	1	11	.266	.329	.469	115	1	0-0	.958	-2	98	0	O-12(4-0-8)/3-4,S	-0.2
1963	StL N	30	49	6	10	2	1	1	5	4-0	0	12	.204	.264	.347	68	-2	0-0	1.000	-1	123	0	O-11(2-0-9)/3-5	-0.4
	Chi N	27	49	4	9	0	0	2	7	4-1	0	13	.184	.241	.306	55	-3	0-1	.925	1	116	127	2-10/1-4	-0.2
	Year	57	98	10	19	2	1	3	12	8-1	0	25	.194	.252	.327	61	-5	0-1	1.000	0	123	0	O-11(2-0-9),2-10/3-5,1-4	-0.6
1964	Chi N	59	103	11	27	3	1	1	14	7-1	1	31	.262	.315	.340	81	-3	0-0	1.000	-1	98	93	O-18(RF)/2-5,3-4,1-2,C	-0.4
1965	Chi N	12	10	0	2	0	0	0	0	0-0	0	4	.200	.200	.200	13	-1	0-0	1.000	-0	*0*	*0*	/C-2,O(RF)	-0.1
Total	7	165	301	33	72	7	2	9	45	21-3	3	79	.239	.294	.365	81	-7	0-1	.985	-5	100	38	/O-45R,2-17,3-16,1-6,C-3,S	-1.4
BURKE, LES Leslie Kingston "Buck" B 12.18.1902 Lynn, MA D 5.6.1975 Danvers, MA BL/TR 5-9/168# d5.2																								
1923	Det A	7	10	2	1	0	0	0	2	0	0	1	.100	.100	.100	-48	-2	0-0	.500	-1	44	0	/3-2,2	-0.3
1924	Det A	72	241	30	61	10	4	0	17	22	2	20	.253	.321	.328	69	-12	2-4	.957	-2	102	102	2-58/S-6	-1.3
1925	Det A	77	180	32	52	6	3	0	24	17	2	8	.289	.357	.356	82	-5	4-1	.962	4	105	115	2-52	0.0
1926	Det A	38	75	9	17	1	0	0	4	7	1	3	.227	.301	.240	42	-6	1-2	.942	1	106	123	2-15/3-7,S	-0.5
Total	4	194	506	73	131	17	7	0	47	46	5	32	.259	.327	.320	67	-25	7-7	.958	1	104	109	2-126/3-9,S-7	-2.1
BURKE, MIKE Michael E. B Cincinnati, OH D 6.9.1889 Albany, NY BR/TR 6/190# d5.1																								
1879	Cin N	28	117	13	26	3	0	0	8	2		5	.222	.235	.248	63	-4		.786	-6	87	70	S-19/O-5(0-1-4),3-5	-0.9

Year	Tm Lg	G	AB	R	H	2B	3B	HR	RBI	BB-IB	HP	SO	AVG	OBP	SLG	AOPS	ABR	SB-CS	FA	FR	Rng	Thr	G at Pos	BFW
BURKE, PAT Patrick Edward B 5.13.1901 St.Louis, MO D 7.7.1965 St.Louis, MO BR/TR 5-10.5/170# d9.23																								
1924	StL A	1	3	0	0	0	0	0	1		0	0	.000	.000	.000	-94	-1	0-0	—	-0	0	0	/3	-0.1
BURKETT, JESSE Jesse Cail "Crab" B 12.4.1868 Wheeling, WV D 5.27.1953 Worcester, MA BL/TL 5-8/155# d4.22 C1 HF1946 ▲																								
1890	NY N	101	401	67	124	23	13	4	60	33	3	52	.309	.366	.461	140	19	14	.824	1	142	115	O-90(11-2-77),P-21	1.3
1891	Cle N	40	167	29	45	7	4	0	13	23	0	19	.269	.358	.359	105	1	1	.892	-2	82	90	O-40(6-2-35)	-0.1
1892	†Cle N	145	608	119	167	15	14	6	66	67	1	59	.275	.348	.375	114	9	36	.904	2	84	159	*O-145(LF)	-0.2
1893	Cle N	125	511	145	178	25	15	6	82	98	7	23	.348	.459	.491	144	36	39	.849	-7	89	115	*O-125(LF)	1.4
1894	Cle N	125	523	138	187	27	14	8	94	84	1	27	.358	.447	.509	125	24	28	.915	-4	81	106	*O-125(LF)/P	0.7
1895	†Cle N	**132**	555	153	**225**	22	13	5	83	74	8	32	**.405**	.482	.519	149	44	41	.884	-4	84	98	*O-132(131-0-1)	2.3
1896	†Cle N	133	586	**160**	**240**	27	16	6	72	49	7	19	**.410**	.461	.541	155	46	34	.926	29	**184**	181	*O-133(LF)	5.7
1897	Cle N	127	517	129	198	28	7	2	60	76	7		.383	.468	.476	142	37	28	.949	-1	100	94	*O-127(127-1-0)	2.1
1898	Cle N	150	624	114	213	18	9	0	42	69	9		.341	.415	.399	135	32	19	.938	-7	81	67	*O-150(148-1-1)	1.2
1899	StL N	141	558	116	221	21	8	7	71	67	2		.396	.463	.500	160	49	25	.938	-3	92	54	*O-140(139-0-1)/2	3.1
1900	StL N	**141**	559	88	203	11	15	7	68	62	3		.363	.429	.474	150	39	32	.934	6	89	123	*O-141(140-1-0)	3.0
1901	StL N	**142**	601	**142**	**226**	20	15	10	75	59	10		**.376**	**.440**	.509	**184**	**66**	27	.923	-1	93	88	*O-142(LF)	**5.5**
1902	StL A	138	553	97	169	29	9	5	52	71	5		.306	.390	.418	126	22	23	.924	5	94	144	*O-137(LF)/PS3	1.9
1903	StL A	132	515	73	151	20	7	3	40	52	3		.293	.361	.377	125	18	17	.941	-3	69	112	*O-132(LF)	0.7
1904	StL A	147	575	72	156	15	10	2	27	78	5		.271	.363	.343	132	25	12	.942	5	145	92	*O-147(LF)	2.4
1905	Bos A	148	573	78	147	12	13	4	47	67	4		.257	.339	.344	115	11	13	.929	-2	67	0	*O-148(LF)	0.1
Total	16	2067	8426	1720	2850	320	182	75	952	1029	75	231	.338	.415	.446	140	478	389	.917	13	96	99	*O-2054(1936-7-115)/P-23,3S2	31.1
BURKHART, MORGAN Morgan B 1.29.1972 St.Louis, MO BB/TL 5-11/225# d6.27																								
2000	Bos A	25	73	16	21	3	0	4	18	17-1	4	25	.288	.442	.493	134	5	0-0	.964	-1	52	42	D-19/1-5,O(LF)	0.3
2001	Bos A	11	33	3	6	1	0	1	4	1-0	0	11	.182	.206	.303	31	-3	0-0	1.000	-0	68	117	/1-5,D-6	-0.4
2003	KC A	6	15	1	3	0	0	0	1	1-0	0	2	.200	.250	.200	18	-2	0-0	1.000	-0	0	140	/1-2,D-2	-0.2
Total	3	42	121	20	30	4	0	5	23	19-1	4	38	.248	.366	.405	95	0	0-0	.986	-1	50	96	/D-27,1-12,O(LF)	-0.3
BURKS, ELLIS Ellis Rena B 9.11.1964 Vicksburg, MS BR/TR 6-2/205# d4.30																								
1987	Bos A	133	558	94	152	30	2	20	59	41-0	2	98	.272	.324	.441	98	-3	27-6	.988	7	99	**269**	*O-132(CF)/D	0.7
1988	†Bos A	144	540	93	159	37	5	18	92	62-1	3	89	.294	.367	.481	131	24	25-9	.977	3	103	147	*O-142(CF)/D-2	2.8
1989	Bos A	97	399	73	121	19	6	12	61	36-2	5	52	.303	.365	.471	127	14	21-5	.977	-0	98	137	O-95(CF)/D	1.6
1990	†Bos A✱	152	588	89	174	33	8	21	89	48-4	1	82	.296	.349	.486	126	19	9-11	.994	-10	88	97	*O-143(CF)/D-6	0.6
1991	Bos A	130	474	56	119	33	3	14	56	39-2	6	81	.251	.314	.422	97	-2	6-11	.993	-10	91	33	*O-126(CF)/D-2	-1.5
1992	Bos A	66	235	35	60	8	3	8	30	25-2	1	48	.255	.327	.417	101	0	5-2	.984	-10	72	88	O-63(CF)/D	-1.0
1993	†Chi A	146	499	75	137	24	4	17	74	60-2	4	97	.275	.352	.441	116	11	6-9	.982	-0	106	60	*O-146(0-21-132)	0.3
1994	Col N	42	149	33	48	8	3	13	24	16-3	0	39	.322	.388	.678	147	10	3-1	.964	-4	85	98	O-39(CF)	0.7
1995	†Col N	103	278	41	74	10	6	14	49	39-0	2	72	.266	.359	.496	96	-2	7-3	.970	1	109	83	O-80(23-65-1)	0.0
1996	Col N★	156	613	**142**	211	45	8	40	128	61-2	6	114	.344	.408	**.639**	138	35	32-6	.983	-2	97	71	*O-152(129-32-0)	3.2
1997	Col N	119	424	91	123	19	2	32	82	47-0	3	75	.290	.363	.571	114	8	7-2	.982	-5	87	104	*O-112(66-89-0)	0.3
1998	Col N	100	357	54	102	22	5	16	54	39-0	2	80	.286	.355	.510	103	2	3-7	.975	-5	89	84	O-98(45-78-0)	-0.6
	SF N	42	147	22	45	6	1	5	22	19-1	3	31	.306	.387	.463	133	8	8-1	.989	-3	96	39	O-41(0-36-10)	0.6
	Year	142	504	76	147	28	6	21	76	58-1	5	111	.292	.365	.496	110	8	11-8	.979	-8	91	70	*O-139(45-114-10)	0.0
1999	SF N	120	390	73	110	19	0	31	96	69-2	6	86	.282	.394	.569	152	32	7-5	.991	-0	105	45	*O-107(RF)/D-3	2.5
2000	†SF N	122	393	74	135	21	5	24	96	56-5	1	49	.344	.419	.606	169	43	5-1	.982	2	109	64	*O-108(RF)/D-2	3.8
2001	†Cle A	124	439	83	123	29	1	28	74	62-2	5	85	.280	.369	.542	136	24	5-1	1.000	-0	79	202	*D-102,O-20(18-0-2)	1.6
2002	Cle A	138	518	92	156	28	0	32	91	44-3	6	108	.301	.362	.541	138	28	2-3	1.000	-1	66	0	*D-127/O-6(LF)	1.7
2003	Cle A	55	198	27	52	11	1	6	28	27-2	3	46	.263	.360	.419	108	3	1-1	1.000	0	154	0	D-51/O-2(LF)	0.0
Total	17	1989	7199	1247	2101	402	63	351	1205	790-33	59	1332	.292	.364	.511	124	254	179-84	.983	-35	96	100	*O-1612(289-1062-360),D-298	17.3
BURLESON, RICK Richard Paul "Rooster" B 4.29.1951 Lynwood, CA BR/TR 5-10/165# d5.4 C5																								
1974	Bos A	114	384	36	109	22	0	4	44	21-0	2	34	.284	.320	.372	93	-3	3-3	.957	-3	99	86	S-88,2-31/3-2	0.6
1975	†Bos A	158	580	66	146	25	1	6	62	45-1	3	44	.252	.305	.329	74	-20	8-5	.963	2	103	110	*S-158	0.1
1976	Bos A	152	540	75	157	27	1	7	42	60-2	5	37	.291	.365	.383	107	7	14-9	.957	3	103	101	*S-152	2.9
1977	Bos A★	154	663	80	194	36	7	3	52	47-1	2	69	.293	.338	.382	87	-11	13-12	.970	20	107	**125**	*S-154	2.3
1978	Bos A✱	145	626	75	155	32	5	5	49	40-2	4	71	.248	.295	.339	71	-24	8-8	.981	20	109	113	*S-144	1.0
1979	Bos A★	153	627	93	174	32	5	5	60	35-0	3	54	.278	.315	.368	80	-18	9-5	**.980**	30	113	108	*S-153	2.8
1980	Bos A	155	644	89	179	29	2	8	51	62-0	2	51	.278	.341	.366	90	-7	12-13	.974	**31**	110	**136**	*S-155	3.8
1981	Cal A★	109	430	53	126	17	1	5	33	42-2	3	38	.293	.357	.372	111	7	4-6	.979	27	115	123	*S-109	4.6
1982	Cal A	11	45	4	7	1	0	0	2	6-2	0	3	.156	.255	.178	21	-5	0-0	.986	4	126	157	S-11	0.1
1983	Cal A	33	119	22	34	7	0	0	11	12-0	0	12	.286	.348	.345	93	-1	0-2	.969	2	110	82	S-31	0.4
1984	Cal A	7	4	2	0	0	0	0	0	0-0	0	2	.000	.000	.000	-99	-1	0-0	—	0			/H	-0.1
1986	†Cal A	93	271	35	77	14	0	5	29	33-1	1	32	.284	.363	.391	107	4	1-3	.984	-5	96	72	D-38,S-37/2-6,3-4	0.0
1987	Bal A	62	206	26	43	14	1	2	14	17-0	3	30	.209	.279	.316	59	-12	0-2	.977	-6	93	109	2-55/D-7	-1.5
Total	13	1346	5139	656	1401	256	23	50	449	420-11	28	477	.273	.328	.361	87	-84	72-68	.971	126	108	113	*S-1192/2-92,D-45,3-6	17.0
BURNETT, HERCULES Hercules H. B 8.13.1865 Louisville, KY D 10.4.1936 Louisville, KY BR 5-11/177# d6.26																								
1888	Lou AA	1	4	1	0	0	0	0	0	1	0		.000	.200	.000	-34	-1	1	.667	-0	0	0	/O(RF)	-0.1
1895	Lou N	5	17	6	7	0	1	2	3	2	0	2	.412	.474	.882	262	4	2	.769	-1	147	0	/O-4(CF),1	0.2
Total	2	6	21	7	7	0	1	2	3	3	0	2	.333	.417	.714	212	3	3	.750	-1	110	0	/O-5(0-4-1),1	0.1
BURNETT, JOHNNY John Henderson B 11.1.1904 Bartow, FL D 8.12.1959 Tampa, FL BL/TR 5-11/175# d5.7																								
1927	Cle A	17	8	5	0	0	0	0	0	0	0	3	.000	.000	.000	-99	-2	1-0	.833	1	163	284	/2-2	-0.2
1928	Cle A	3	10	3	5	0	0	0	1	0	0	1	.500	.500	.500	162	1	0-0	.867	0	95	189	/S-2	0.1
1929	Cle A	19	33	2	5	1	0	0	2	1	1	2	.152	.200	.182	-1	-5	0-0	.923	2	135	64	S-10/2-8	-0.2
1930	Cle A	54	170	28	53	13	0	0	20	17	1	8	.312	.378	.388	91	-1	2-2	.973	-1	107	42	3-27,S-19	0.1
1931	Cle A	111	427	85	128	25	5	1	52	39	1	25	.300	.360	.389	92	-5	5-2	.938	-1	99	108	S-63,2-35,3-21/O(RF)	0.1
1932	Cle A	129	512	81	152	23	5	4	53	46	4	27	.297	.359	.385	87	-9	2-5	.946	-19	97	83	*S-103,2-26	-1.9
1933	Cle A	83	261	39	71	11	2	1	29	23	1	14	.272	.333	.341	76	-9	3-2	.938	-2	101	98	S-41,2-17,3-12	-0.7
1934	Cle A	72	208	28	61	11	2	3	30	18	1	11	.293	.352	.409	94	-2	1-1	.981	-6	85	88	3-42/S-9,2-3,O-2(1-0-1)	-0.6
1935	StL A	70	206	17	46	10	1	0	26	19	0	16	.223	.289	.282	46	-17	1-0	.939	-3	104	123	3-31,S-18,2-12	-1.6
Total	9	558	1835	288	521	94	15	9	213	163	9	107	.284	.345	.366	81	-49	15-12	.935	-29	100	95	S-265,3-133,2-103/O-3(1-0-2)	-4.9
BURNETT, JACK John P. B 12.2.1889 , MO D 9.8.1929 Taft, CA d7.2																								
1907	StL N	59	206	18	49	8	4	0	12	15	2		.238	.296	.316	95	-2	5	.955	-5	102	49	O-59(CF)	-1.0
BURNITZ, JEROMY Jeromy Neal B 4.15.1969 Westminster, CA BL/TR 6/190# d6.21																								
1993	NY N	86	263	49	64	10	6	13	38	38-4	1	66	.243	.339	.475	117	6	3-6	.977	1	101	113	O-79(0-20-61)	0.3
1994	NY N	45	143	26	34	4	0	3	15	23-0	1	45	.238	.347	.329	78	-4	1-1	.970	-6	77	32	O-42(RF)	-1.2
1995	Cle A	9	7	4	4	1	0	0	0	0-0	0	0	.571	.571	.714	229	1	0-0	1.000	1	191	0	/O-6(5-1-0),D-2	0.2
1996	Cle A	71	128	30	36	10	0	7	26	25-1	2	31	.281	.406	.523	133	8	2-1	1.000	-1	105	0	O-30(10-6-14),D-15	0.5
	Mil A	23	72	8	17	4	0	2	14	8-1	2	16	.236	.321	.375	75	-3	2-0	.975	-2	81	71	O-22(0-8-14)	-0.5
	Year	94	200	38	53	14	0	9	40	33-2	4	47	.265	.377	.470	113	5	4-1	.988	-3	93	36	O-52(10-14-28),D-15	0.0
1997	Mil A	153	494	85	139	37	8	27	85	75-8	5	111	.281	.382	.553	139	29	20-13	.975	-3	89	153	*O-149(5-26-124)	2.0
1998	Mil N	161	609	92	160	28	1	38	125	70-7	4	158	.263	.339	.499	118	14	7-4	.972	-2	98	92	*O-161(0-1-161)	0.5
1999	Mil N★	130	467	87	126	33	2	33	103	91-7	16	124	.270	.402	.561	143	34	7-3	.982	0	100	92	*O-127(RF)/D-3	2.6
2000	Mil N	161	564	91	131	29	2	31	98	99-10	14	121	.232	.356	.456	106	7	6-4	.979	-2	96	113	*O-158(RF)/D	-0.3
2001	Mil N	154	562	104	141	32	4	34	100	80-9	5	150	.251	.347	.504	120	16	0-4	.981	1	97	127	*O-153(RF)	0.8
2002	NY N	154	479	65	103	15	0	19	54	58-5	10	135	.215	.311	.365	84	-14	10-7	.966	-4	96	80	*O-140(RF)/D	-2.5
2003	NY N	65	234	38	64	18	0	18	45	21-6	4	55	.274	.344	.581	140	13	1-4	.986	-1	104	50	O-65(10-21-48)	0.9
	LA N	61	230	25	47	4	0	13	32	14-3	1	57	.204	.252	.391	69	-13	4-0	.946	-5	79	90	O-60(54-12-2)	-1.9
	Year	126	464	63	111	22	0	31	77	35-9	5	112	.239	.299	.487	105	1	5-4	.970	-6	92	69	*O-125(64-33-50)	-1.0
Total	11	1273	4252	704	1066	225	23	238	735	602-61	65	1069	.251	.350	.482	116	94	63-47	.976	-22	95	100	*O-1192(84-95-1044)/D-22	1.4
BURNS, C.B. Charles Birmingham B 5.15.1879 Bay View, MD D 6.6.1968 Havre De Grace, MD BR/TR 6/175# d8.19																								
1902	Bal A	1	1	0	1	0	0	0	0	0	0		1.000	1.000	1.000	436	0	0	—	0			H	0.0

Year	Tm Lg	G	AB	R	H	2B	3B	HR	RBI	BB-IB	HP	SO	AVG	OBP	SLG	AOPS	ABR	SB-CS	FA	FR	Rng	Thr	G at Pos	BFW
BURNS, ED Edward James B 10.31.1888 San Francisco, CA D 5.30.1942 Monterey, CA BR/TR 5-6/165# d6.25																								
1912	StL N	1	1	0	0	0	0	0	1	0	0	0	.000	.000	.000	-99	0	0	—	0	*0*	*0*	/C	0.0
1913	Phi N	17	30	3	6	3	0	0	3	6	1	3	.200	.351	.300	83	0	2	.980	-2	94	90	C-15	-0.1
1914	Phi N	70	139	8	36	3	4	0	16	20	0	12	.259	.352	.338	99	0	5	.947	-5	*73*	*122*	C-55	-0.2
1915	†Phi N	67	174	11	42	5	0	0	16	20	2	12	.241	.327	.270	81	-3	1	.981	-1	*106*	*93*	C-62	0.1
1916	Phi N	78	219	14	51	8	1	0	14	16	3	18	.233	.294	.279	74	-6	3	.981	-6	105	90	C-75/SO(CF)	-0.7
1917	Phi N	20	49	2	10	1	0	0	6	1	0	5	.204	.220	.224	35	-4	2	.971	-0	*108*	*131*	C-15	-0.4
1918	Phi N	68	184	10	38	1	1	0	9	20	1	9	.207	.288	.223	53	-10	1	.981	-4	*96*	*111*	C-68	-1.0
Total	7	321	796	48	183	21	6	0	65	83	7	59	.230	.308	.271	73	-23	14	.974	-19	*97*	*103*	C-291/O(CF)S	-2.3
BURNS, GEORGE George Henry "Tioga George" B 1.31.1893 Niles, OH D 1.7.1978 Kirkland, WA BR/TR 6-1.5/180# d4.14																								
1914	Det A	137	478	55	139	22	5	5	57	32	**12**	56	.291	.351	.389	119	10	23-13	.982	-6	91	106	*1-137	0.2
1915	Det A	105	392	49	99	18	3	5	50	22	5	51	.253	.301	.352	91	-6	9-3	.986	-4	90	123	*1-104	-1.2
1916	Det A	135	479	60	137	22	6	4	73	22	7	30	.286	.327	.382	109	3	12	.985	-10	72	97	*1-124	-1.1
1917	Det A	119	407	42	92	14	10	1	40	15	6	33	.226	.264	.317	77	-14	3	.990	-4	84	72	*1-104	-2.3
1918	Phi A	**130**	505	61	**178**	22	9	6	70	23	**8**	25	.352	.390	.467	157	32	8	.983	6	**124**	**132**	*1-128/O-2(1-0-1)	3.8
1919	Phi A	126	470	63	139	29	9	8	57	19	**12**	18	.296	.339	.447	118	9	15	.980	2	120	83	1-86,O-34(RF)	0.7
1920	Phi A	22	60	1	14	3	0	1	7	6	1	7	.233	.313	.333	71	-2	4-0	.958	0	84	164	O-13(RF)	-0.2
	†Cle A	44	56	7	15	4	1	0	13	4	2	3	.268	.339	.375	86	-1	1-0	.979	1	159	21	1-12/O(RF)	0.0
	Year	66	116	8	29	7	1	1	20	10	3	10	.250	.326	.353	78	-4	5-0	.958	1	83	161	O-14(RF),1-12	-0.2
1921	Cle A	84	244	52	88	21	4	0	49	13	2	19	.361	.398	.480	121	8	3-1	.990	2	111	108	1-73	0.6
1922	Bos A	147	558	71	171	32	5	12	73	20	9	28	.306	.341	.446	104	1	8-2	.987	-1	103	101	*1-140	-0.7
1923	Bos A	146	551	91	181	47	5	7	82	45	7	33	.328	.386	.470	124	20	9-7	.990	-1	97	90	*1-146	0.8
1924	Cle A	129	462	64	143	37	5	4	68	29	15	27	.310	.370	.437	106	4	14-5	.987	9	**130**	90	*1-127	0.6
1925	Cle A	127	488	69	164	41	4	6	79	24	3	24	.336	.371	.473	112	8	16-11	.989	1	102	92	*1-126	0.0
1926	Cle A	151	603	97	**216**	**64**	3	4	114	28	8	33	.358	.394	.494	130	27	13-7	.988	1	107	115	*1-151	1.8
1927	Cle A	140	549	84	175	51	2	3	78	42	7	27	.319	.375	.435	109	9	13-11	.990	4	112	99	*1-139	0.3
1928	Cle A	82	209	29	52	12	1	5	30	17	6	11	.249	.323	.388	85	-5	2-3	.984	2	126	108	1-53	-0.6
	NY A	4	4	1	2	0	0	0	0	0	0	1	.500	.500	.500	169	0	0-0	1.000	-0	0	0	/1-2	0.0
	Year	86	213	30	54	12	1	5	30	17	6	12	.254	.326	.390	87	-4	2-3	.985	2	125	107	1-55	-0.6
1929	NY A	9	9	0	0	0	0	0	0	0	0	4	.000	.000	.000	-99	-3	0-0	—	0			H	-0.3
	†Phi A	29	49	5	13	5	0	1	11	2	0	3	.265	.294	.429	81	-1	1-0	1.000	-0	77	110	1-19	-0.2
	Year	38	58	5	13	5	0	1	11	2	0	7	.224	.250	.362	55	-4	1-0	1.000	-0	77	110	1-19	-0.5
Total	16	1866	6573	901	2018	444	72	72	951	363	110	433	.307	.354	.429	112	99	154-63	.987	2	104	101	*1-1671/O-50(1-0-49)	2.2
BURNS, GEORGE George Joseph B 11.24.1889 Utica, NY D 8.15.1966 Gloversville, NY BR/TR 5-7/160# d10.3 C1																								
1911	NY N	6	17	2	1	0	0	0	0	1	0	0	.059	.111	.059	-50	-3	0	1.000	-1	89	0	/O-6(1-4-1)	-0.4
1912	NY N	29	51	11	15	4	0	0	3	8	1	8	.294	.400	.373	109	1	7	1.000	1	94	163	O-23(13-5-5)	0.2
1913	†NY N	150	605	81	173	37	4	2	54	58	4	74	.286	.352	.370	106	7	40-35	.963	1	101	102	*O-150(119-0-32)	-0.3
1914	NY N	154	561	**100**	170	35	10	3	60	89	5	53	.303	.403	.417	149	**39**	**62**	.950	0	106	82	*O-154(102-0-54)	3.4
1915	NY N	**155**	622	83	169	27	14	3	51	56	1	57	.272	.333	.375	121	15	27-20	.960	-7	93	72	*O-155(140-0-15)	-0.1
1916	NY N	**155**	623	**105**	174	24	8	5	41	63	1	47	.279	.346	.368	126	20	37-26	.962	-0	97	117	*O-155(LF)	1.4
1917	†NY N	152	597	**103**	180	25	13	5	45	**75**	1	55	.302	.380	.412	148	36	40	.974	2	105	83	*O-152(LF)	3.5
1918	NY N	119	465	80	135	22	6	4	51	43	3	37	.290	.354	.389	129	17	40	.965	9	**125**	80	*O-119(LF)	2.3
1919	NY N	139	534	**86**	162	30	9	2	46	**82**	0	37	.303	**.396**	.404	142	33	**40**	**.990**	2	105	85	*O-139(LF)	3.1
1920	NY N	154	631	**115**	181	35	9	6	46	**76**	2	48	.287	.365	.399	121	20	22-22	.983	11	**123**	74	*O-154(154-1-0)	2.3
1921	†NY N	149	605	111	181	28	9	4	61	**80**	6	24	.299	.386	.395	107	10	19-20	.972	-7	96	75	*O-149(90-59-0)/3	-0.9
1922	Cin N	**156**	631	104	180	20	10	1	53	78	2	38	.285	.366	.353	88	-9	30-23	.976	-4	95	97	*O-156(0-109-47)	-2.2
1923	Cin N	**154**	614	99	168	27	13	3	45	**101**	0	46	.274	.376	.375	101	5	12-14	.960	-6	101	60	*O-154(0-3-151)	-1.5
1924	Cin N	93	336	43	86	19	2	2	33	29	0	21	.256	.315	.342	77	-10	3-6	.963	2	99	129	O-90(12-1-79)	-1.7
1925	Phi N	88	349	65	102	29	1	1	22	33	0	20	.292	.353	.390	82	-8	4-8	.990	2	102	99	O-88(66-4-22)	-1.4
Total	15	1853	7241	1188	2077	362	108	41	611	872	26	565	.287	.366	.384	115	173	383-174	.970	6	103	88	*O-1844(1262-186-406)/3	7.7
BURNS, JIM James M. B St.Louis, MO D 2.17.1909 Chicago, IL 5-7/168# d9.25																								
1888	KC AA	15	66	13	20	0	0	0	4	1	3		.303	.343	.303	101	0	6	.853	1	155	300	O-15(LF)	0.1
1889	KC AA	134	579	103	176	23	11	5	97	20	7	68	.304	.335	.408	105	-1	56	.913	-8	44	65	*O-134(CF)/3	-1.1
1891	Was AA	20	82	15	26	6	0	0	10	6	2	10	.317	.378	.390	126	3	2	.771	-4	31	0	O-20(0-5-16)/S	-0.1
Total	3	169	727	131	222	29	11	5	111	27	12	78	.305	.341	.396	107	2	64	.897	-10	53	81	O-169(15-139-16)/S3	-1.1
BURNS, JACK John Irving "Slug" B 8.31.1907 Cambridge, MA D 4.18.1975 Brighton, MA BL/TL 5-10.5/175# d9.17 C5																								
1930	StL A	8	30	5	9	3	0	0	2	5	0	5	.300	.400	.400	100	0	0-0	1.000	1	138	165	/1-8	0.1
1931	StL A	144	570	75	148	27	7	4	70	42	1	58	.260	.312	.353	72	-25	19-12	.993	19	**159**	114	*1-143	-1.8
1932	StL A	150	617	111	188	33	8	11	70	61	1	43	.305	.368	.438	102	2	17-11	.992	5	111	99	*1-150	-0.7
1933	StL A	144	556	89	160	43	4	7	71	56	0	51	.288	.353	.417	97	-1	11-11	.992	3	108	114	*1-143	-1.3
1934	StL A	**154**	612	86	157	28	8	13	73	62	2	47	.257	.327	.392	78	-22	9-3	.992	-0	97	98	*1-154	-3.3
1935	StL A	143	549	77	157	28	1	5	67	68	1	49	.286	.366	.368	86	-9	3-2	.992	-9	74	92	*1-141	-2.9
1936	StL A	9	14	2	3	1	0	0	1	3	0	1	.214	.353	.286	58	-1	0-0	1.000	-0	73	120	/1-2	-0.1
	Det A	138	558	96	158	36	3	4	63	79	3	45	.283	.375	.380	87	-9	4-8	.994	1	99	109	*1-138	-2.1
	Year	147	572	98	161	37	3	4	64	82	3	46	.281	.374	.378	86	-10	4-8	.994	1	99	109	*1-140	-2.2
Total	7	890	3506	541	980	199	31	44	417	376	8	299	.280	.351	.392	87	-65	63-47	.992	19	108	105	1-879	-12.1
BURNS, JACK John Joseph B 5.13.1880 Avoca, PA D 6.24.1957 Waterford, CT BR/TR 5-10/160# d9.11																								
1903	Det A	11	37	2	10	0	0	0	3	1	2		.270	.325	.270	82	-1	0	.981	2	109	135	2-11	0.1
1904	Det A	4	16	3	2	0	0	0	1	1	0		.125	.176	.125	-4	-2	1	.952	-1	72	77	/2-4	-0.4
Total	2	15	53	5	12	0	0	0	4	2	2		.226	.281	.226	57	-3	1	.973	0	98	118	/2-15	-0.3
BURNS, JOE Joseph Francis B 3.26.1889 Ipswich, MA D 7.12.1987 Beverly, MA BL/TL 5-11/170# d6.19																								
1910	Cin N	1	1	0	1	0	0	0	0	0	0	0	1.000	1.000	1.000	506	0	1	—	0			H	0.1
1913	Det A	4	13	0	5	0	0	0	1	2	1	4	.385	.500	.385	162	1	0	1.000	-0	99	0	/O-4(LF)	0.1
Total	2	5	14	0	6	0	0	0	1	2	1	4	.429	.529	.429	184	1	1	1.000	-0	99	0	/O-4(LF)	0.2
BURNS, JOE Joseph Francis B 2.25.1900 Trenton, NJ D 1.7.1986 Trenton, NJ BR/TR 6/175# d4.18																								
1924	Chi A	8	19	1	2	0	0	0	0	0	0	2	.105	.105	.105	-47	-4	0-0	.933	-1	*72*	*56*	/C-6	-0.5
BURNS, JOE Joseph James B 6.17.1916 Bryn Mawr, PA D 6.24.1974 Bryn Mawr, PA BR/TR 5-10.5/175# d4.24																								
1943	Bos N	52	135	12	28	3	0	1	5	8	2	25	.207	.262	.252	49	-9	2	.933	2	116	125	3-34/O-4(1-1-2)	-0.7
1944	Phi A	28	75	5	18	2	0	1	8	4	0	8	.240	.278	.307	68	-3	0-1	.919	-5	79	98	3-17/2-9	-0.9
1945	Phi A	31	90	7	23	1	1	0	3	4	0	17	.256	.287	.289	68	-4	0-1	1.000	-2	83	63	O-19(RF)/3-5,1	-0.8
Total	3	111	300	24	69	6	1	2	16	16	2	50	.230	.274	.277	60	-16	2-2	.920	-5	104	110	/3-56,O-23(1-1-21),2-9,1	-2.4
BURNS, PAT Patrick d8.11																								
1884	Bal AA	6	25	3	5	2	1	0		3	0		.200	.286	.360	105	0		.953	-1	46	70	/1-6	-0.1
	Bal U	1	4	0	2	0	0	0		0			.500	.500	.500	185	0		.917	-0	0	238	/1	0.0
Total	1	7	29	3	7	2	1	0		3			.241	.313	.379	117	0		.947	-1	39	96	/1-7	-0.1
BURNS, DICK Richard Simon B 12.26.1863 Holyoke, MA D 11.16.1937 Holyoke, MA BL/TL 5-7/140# d5.3 ▲																								
1883	Det N	37	140	11	26	7	1	0	5	2		22	.186	.197	.250	36	-10		.758	-4	89	132	O-24(1-1-23),P-17	-0.9
1884	Cin U	79	350	84	107	17	**12**	4		5			.306	.315	.457	122	-3		.827	-2	95	78	O-44(6-33-7),P-40/S-2	-0.4
1885	StL N	14	54	2	12	2	1	0	4	3		8	.222	.263	.296	86	-1		.682	-2	93	334	O-14(CF)/P	-0.3
Total	3	130	544	97	145	26	14	4	9	10		30	.267	.280	.388	98	-14		.785	-8	93	135	/O-82(7-48-30),P-58,S-2	-1.6
BURNS, TOM Thomas Everett B 3.30.1857 Honesdale, PA D 3.19.1902 Jersey City, NJ BR/TR 5-7/152# d5.1 M3 U1 OF Total (10-LF 2-CF 2-RF)																								
1880	Chi N	85	333	47	103	17	3	0	43	12		23	.309	.333	.378	133	11		.864	-25	76	54	*S-79/3-9,C-2,P	-1.1
1881	Chi N	**84**	342	41	95	20	3	4	42	14		22	.278	.306	.389	112	4		.870	-4	96	88	*S-80/3-3,2-3	0.4
1882	Chi N	**84**	355	55	88	23	6	0	48	15		28	.248	.278	.346	95	-2		.911	-2	93	119	2-43,S-41	-0.1
1883	Chi N	97	405	69	119	37	7	2	67	13		31	.294	.316	.435	116	7		.872	3	106	113	*S-79,2-19/O(LF)	1.1
1884	Chi N	83	343	54	84	14	2	7	44	13		50	.245	.272	.359	89	-5		.838	-4	**103**	113	*S-80/3-3	-0.6

Year	Tm Lg	G	AB	R	H	2B	3B	HR	RBI	BB-IB	HP	SO	AVG	OBP	SLG	AOPS	ABR	SB-CS	FA	FR	Rng	Thr	G at Pos	BFW
1885	†Chi N	111	445	82	121	23	9	7	71	16		48	.272	.297	.411	112	3		.844	-4	101	114	*S-111/2	0.2
1886	†Chi N	112	445	64	123	18	10	3	65	14		40	.276	.298	.382	92	-7	15	.890	11	106	101	*3-112	0.5
1887	Chi N	115	424	57	112	20	10	3	60	34	1	32	.264	.320	.380	83	-12	32	.872	17	110	**134**	*3-107/O-8(6-2-0)	0.6
1888	Chi N	134	483	60	115	12	6	3	70	26	3	49	.238	.281	.306	81	-11	34	.905	17	105	89	*3-134	0.8
1889	Chi N	**136**	525	64	135	27	6	4	66	32	2	57	.257	.302	.354	79	-18	18	.880	-3	100	**124**	*3-136	-1.6
1890	Chi N	**139**	538	86	149	17	6	5	86	57	2	45	.277	.348	.359	102	1	44	.898	2	101	**122**	*3-139	0.4
1891	Chi N	59	243	36	55	8	1	1	17	21	0	21	.226	.288	.280	66	-11	18	.892	-1	90	150	3-53/S-4,O-2(LF)	-1.0
1892	Pit N	12	39	7	8	0	0	0	4	3	0	8	.205	.262	.205	41	-3	1	.690	-4	58	0	/3-8,O-3(1-0-2),M	-0.7
Total	13	1251	4920	722	1307	236	69	39	683	270	8	454	.266	.305	.365	96	-43	162	.886	2	102	115	3-704,S-474/2-66,O-14L,C-2,P	-1.1
BURNS, TOMMY Thomas P. "Oyster" B 9.6.1864 Philadelphia, PA D 11.11.1928 Brooklyn, NY BL/TR 5-8/183# d8.18 ▲ OF Total (100-LF 15-CF 781-RF)																								
1884	Wil U	2	7	0	1	0	1	0		1			.143	.250	.429	99	0		.778	-0	101	0	/S-2	0.0
	Bal AA	35	131	34	39	2	6	6	23	7	3		.298	.348	.542	179	10		.826	-4	64	210	O-24(RF),2-10/P-2,3	0.6
1885	Bal AA	78	321	47	74	11	6	5	37	16	6		.231	.280	.349	99	0		.908	1	193	254	O-45(1-0-44),P-15,S-10/3-6,2-6,1	0.1
1887	Bal AA	140	551	122	188	33	19	9	99	63	5		.341	.414	.519	169	53	58	.841	-17	84	85	*S-98,3-42/P-3,2	3.2
1888	Bal AA	79	325	54	97	18	9	4	42	24	1		.298	.349	.446	158	21	23	.855	-7	29	42	O-56(46-0-10),S-23/P-5,3-2,2	1.1
	Bro AA	52	204	40	58	9	6	2	25	14	3		.284	.339	.417	142	9	21	.851	-9	90	84	S-36,O-14(CF)/2-3	0.1
	Year	131	529	94	155	27	15	6	67	38	4		.293	.345	.435	152	30	44	.847	-16	24	35	O-70(46-14-10),S-59/P-5,2-4,3-2	1.2
1889	†Bro AA	131	504	105	153	19	13	5	100	68	4	26	.304	.391	.423	131	22	32	.920	-7	97	113	*O-113(RF),S-19	1.2
1890	†Bro N	119	472	102	134	22	12	**13**	**128**	51	4	42	.284	.359	.464	139	21	21	.941	-2	120	108	*O-116(RF)/3-3	1.6
1891	Bro N	123	470	75	134	24	13	4	83	53	0	30	.285	.358	.417	126	15	21	.922	-1	91	164	*O-113(RF)/S-6,3-5	1.2
1892	Bro N	141	542	88	171	27	18	4	96	65	6	42	.315	.395	.454	162	42	33	.937	-12	78	95	*O-129(2-0-127)/3-7,S-5	2.2
1893	Bro N	109	415	68	112	22	8	7	60	36	4	16	.270	.334	.412	103	0	14	.932	-0	109	136	*O-108(0-1-108)/S	-0.4
1894	Bro N	126	513	107	182	32	14	5	109	44	3	18	.355	.409	.501	127	24	30	.949	-5	72	78	*O-126(RF)	1.0
1895	Bro N	20	76	7	14	0	1	0	7	8	1	2	.184	.271	.211	27	-8	0	.918	1	132	156	O-19(LF)	-0.8
	NY N	33	114	21	35	5	3	1	25	14	1	6	.307	.388	.430	113	3	10	.870	-2	123	0	O-32(LF)/1	-0.1
	Year	53	190	28	49	5	4	1	32	22	2	8	.258	.341	.342	80	-5	10	.893	-1	127	67	O-51(LF)/1	-0.9
Total	11	1188	4645	870	1392	224	129	65	834	464	41	182	.300	.368	.445	135	212	263	.920	-64	94	114	O-895R,S-200/3-66,P-25,2-21,1-2	11.0
BURR, ALEX Alexander Thomson B 11.1.1893 Chicago, IL D 10.12.1918 Cazaux, France BR/TR 6-3.5/190# d4.21																								
1914	NY A	1	0	0	0	0	0	0	0	0	0	0	—	—	—	—	0	0	—	-0	0	0	/O(CF)	0.0
BURRELL, BUSTER Frank Andrew B 12.22.1866 Weymouth, MA D 5.8.1962 Weymouth, MA BR/TR 5-10/165# d8.1																								
1891	NY N	15	53	1	5	0	0	0	1	3	1	12	.094	.158	.094	-27	-9	2	.856	-6	*82*	*104*	C-15/O(CF)	-1.3
1895	Bro N	12	28	7	4	0	0	1	5	4	0	3	.143	.250	.250	32	-3	0	.838	-1	*129*	*77*	C-12	-0.3
1896	Bro N	62	206	19	62	11	3	0	23	15	0	13	.301	.348	.383	98	0	1	.928	-6	*104*	*74*	C-60	-0.1
1897	Bro N	33	103	15	25	2	0	2	18	10	0		.243	.310	.320	70	-4	1	.884	-5	*89*	*93*	C-27/1-4	-0.6
Total	4	122	390	42	96	13	3	3	47	32	1	28	.246	.305	.318	70	-16	4	.896	-18	*100*	*83*	C-114/1-4,O(CF)	-2.3
BURRELL, PAT Patrick Brian B 10.10.1976 Eureka Springs, AR BR/TR 6-4/230# d5.24																								
2000	Phi N	111	408	57	106	27	1	18	79	63-2	1	139	.260	.359	.463	105	4	0-0	.988	-6	60	80	1-58,O-48(LF)/D-4	-0.8
2001	Phi N	155	539	70	139	29	2	27	89	70-7	5	162	.258	.346	.469	112	10	2-1	.972	0	87	186	*O-146(LF)/D-5	0.4
2002	Phi N	157	586	96	165	39	2	37	116	89-9	3	153	.282	.376	.544	150	41	1-0	.979	-5	92	80	*O-157(LF)	3.0
2003	Phi N	146	522	57	109	31	4	21	64	72-2	4	142	.209	.309	.404	90	-9	0-0	.976	-4	94	84	*O-140(LF)/D-2	-1.8
Total	4	569	2055	280	519	126	9	103	348	294-20	13	596	.253	.348	.473	116	46	3-1	.976	-14	91	125	O-491(LF)/1-58,D-11	0.8
BURRIGHT, LARRY Larry Allen "Possum" B 7.10.1937 Roseville, IL BR/TR 5-11/170# d4.12																								
1962	LA N	115	249	35	51	6	5	4	30	21-5	0	67	.205	.264	.317	60	-15	4-3	.962	5	104	75	*2-109/S	-0.4
1963	NY N	41	100	9	22	2	1	0	3	8-1	2	25	.220	.291	.260	59	-5	1-0	.946	7	115	80	S-19,2-15/3	0.5
1964	NY N	3	7	0	0	0	0	0	0	0-0	0	0	.000	.000	.000	-99	-2	0-0	1.000	2	145	164	/2-3	0.1
Total	3	159	356	44	73	8	6	4	33	29-6	2	92	.205	.267	.295	56	-22	5-3	.964	14	109	87	2-127/S-20,3	0.2
BURRIS, PAUL Paul Robert B 7.21.1923 Hickory, NC D 10.3.1999 Charlotte, NC BR/TR 6/190# d10.2																								
1948	Bos N	2	4	0	2	0	0	0	0	0	0	0	.500	.500	.500	174	0	0	1.000	1	*0*	*0*	/C-2	0.1
1950	Bos N	10	23	1	4	1	0	0	3	1	0	2	.174	.208	.217	13	-3	0	1.000	1	*87*	*0*	/C-8	-0.2
1952	Bos N	55	168	14	37	4	0	2	21	7	1	19	.220	.256	.280	50	-12	0-0	1.000	-3	*91*	*68*	C-50	-1.3
1953	Mil N	2	1	0	0	0	0	0	0	0	0	0	.000	.000	.000	-99	0	0-0	1.000	0	*0*	*0*	/C-2	0.0
Total	4	69	196	15	43	5	0	2	24	8	1	21	.219	.254	.276	47	-15	0-0	1.000	-2	*88*	*57*	/C-62	-1.4
BURROUGHS, HENRY Henry S. B 1845 , NJ D 3.31.1878 Newark, NJ 5-8/147# d5.5																								
1871	Oly NA	12	63	11	15	2	3	1	14	1		1	.238	.250	.413	91	-1	0-0	.706	-2	107	0	/O-8(4-0-4),3-5,2	-0.1
1872	Oly NA	2	7	1	1	0	0	0	0	1		0	.143	.250	.143	25	-1	0-0	.625	-0	305	0	/O-2(CF)	-0.1
Total	2 NA	14	70	12	16	2	3	1	14	2		1	.229	.250	.386	85	-2	0-0	.000	-2	162	0	/O-10(4-2-4),3-5,2	-0.2
BURROUGHS, JEFF Jeffrey Alan B 3.7.1951 Long Beach, CA BR/TR 6-1/200# d7.20 s-Sean																								
1970	Was A	6	12	1	2	0	0	0	1	2-0	0	5	.167	.286	.167	29	-1	0-0	1.000	-0	89	0	/O-3(RF)	-0.2
1971	Was A	59	181	20	42	9	0	5	25	22-0	1	55	.232	.319	.365	99	0	1-0	.966	-2	90	98	O-50(34-0-23)	-0.5
1972	Tex A	22	65	4	12	1	0	1	3	5-0	0	22	.185	.243	.246	48	-4	0-2	.935	-1	85	154	O-19(17-0-2)/1	-0.8
1973	Tex A	151	526	71	147	17	1	30	85	67-3	1	88	.279	.355	.487	143	30	0-0	.975	10	112	139	*O-148(43-0-106)/1-3,D	3.2
1974	Tex A★	152	554	84	167	33	2	25	**118**	91-12	5	104	.301	.397	.504	164	**50**	2-3	.972	-13	81	89	*O-150(RF)/1-2,D	3.0
1975	Tex A	152	585	81	132	20	0	29	94	79-11	1	155	.226	.315	.409	105	3	4-4	.966	-15	83	77	*O-148(RF)/D-3	-2.0
1976	Tex A	158	604	71	143	22	2	18	86	69-4	2	93	.237	.315	.369	98	-1	0-0	.987	-6	89	104	*O-155(RF)/D-3	-1.6
1977	Atl N	154	579	91	157	19	1	41	114	86-2	0	126	.271	.362	.520	120	17	4-1	.974	-12	86	77	*O-154(RF)	-0.2
1978	Atl N☆	153	488	72	147	30	6	23	77	**117**-12	0	92	.301	**.432**	.529	151	40	1-2	.975	-4	85	115	*O-146(LF)	3.1
1979	Atl N	116	397	49	89	14	1	11	47	73-7	3	75	.224	.347	.348	84	-6	2-2	.963	-3	86	102	*O-110(LF)	-1.5
1980	Atl N	99	278	35	73	14	0	13	51	35-6	2	57	.263	.347	.453	118	7	1-1	.977	-7	89	0	O-73(LF)	-0.3
1981	Sea A	89	319	32	81	13	1	10	41	41-3	0	64	.254	.339	.395	107	3	0-1	.985	-11	72	65	O-87(1-0-86)/D	-1.3
1982	Oak A	113	285	42	79	13	2	16	48	45-0	0	61	.277	.372	.505	146	19	1-3	.981	-2	97	0	D-48,O-34(17-0-18)	1.3
1983	Oak A	121	401	43	108	15	1	10	56	47-4	0	79	.269	.341	.387	108	5	0-2	—	0	0	0	*D-114	0.1
1984	Oak A	58	71	5	15	1	0	2	8	18-0	0	23	.211	.367	.310	97	1	0-0	1.000	-0	55	0	D-23/O-4(LF)	0.0
1985	†Tor A	86	191	19	49	9	3	6	28	34-1	0	36	.257	.366	.429	115	5	0-1	—	0	0	0	D-75	0.2
Total	16	1689	5536	720	1443	230	20	240	882	831-65	15	1135	.261	.355	.439	120	168	16-22	.974	-65	88	90	*O-1281(445-0-845),D-269/1-6	2.5
BURROUGHS, SEAN Sean Patrick B 9.12.1980 Atlanta, GA BL/TR 6-2/200# d4.2 f-Jeff																								
2002	SD N	63	192	18	52	5	1	1	11	12-1	1	30	.271	.317	.323	79	-7	2-0	.935	0	93	61	3-48,2-13	-0.6
2003	SD N	146	517	62	148	27	6	7	58	44-4	11	75	.286	.352	.402	107	5	7-2	.966	1	95	105	*3-137	0.8
Total	2	209	709	80	200	32	7	8	69	56-5	12	105	.282	.343	.381	99	-2	9-2	.959	1	95	95	3-185/2-13	0.2
BURRUS, DICK Maurice Lennon B 1.29.1898 Hatteras, NC D 2.2.1972 Elizabeth City, NC BL/TL 5-11/175# d6.23																								
1919	Phi A	70	194	17	50	3	4	0	8	9	1	25	.258	.294	.314	70	-9	2	.986	-3	91	72	1-38,O-10(0-2-8)	-1.4
1920	Phi A	71	135	11	25	8	0	0	10	5	2	7	.185	.225	.244	24	-15	0-3	.989	-1	97	142	1-31/O-2(RF)	-1.7
1925	Bos N	152	588	82	200	41	4	5	87	51	3	29	.340	.396	.449	126	26	8-9	**.990**	1	102	87	*1-151	1.4
1926	Bos N	131	486	59	131	21	1	3	61	37	2	16	.270	.324	.335	85	-10	4	.991	12	**140**	88	*1-128	-0.6
1927	Bos N	72	220	22	70	8	3	0	32	17	1	10	.318	.370	.382	110	3	3	.972	1	120	103	1-61	0.0
1928	Bos N	64	137	15	37	6	0	3	13	19	2	8	.270	.367	.380	101	1	1	.977	-2	87	101	1-32	-0.3
Total	6	560	1760	206	513	87	12	11	211	138	11	95	.291	.347	.373	97	-4	18-12	.986	8	114	92	1-441/O-12(0-2-10)	-2.6
BURT, FRANK Frank J. B Camden, NJ d5.2																								
1882	Bal AA	10	36	2	4	2	1	0		1			.111	.135	.222	20	-3		.815	-1	40	335	O-10(LF)	-0.4
BURTON, ELLIS Ellis Narrington B 8.12.1936 Los Angeles, CA BB/TR 5-11/165# d9.18																								
1958	StL N	8	30	5	7	0	1	2	4	3-0	1	8	.233	.324	.500	110	0	0-1	1.000	-1	88	0	/O-7(5-0-2)	-0.1
1960	StL N	29	28	5	6	1	0	0	2	4-0	0	14	.214	.313	.250	52	-2	0-2	1.000	-1	84	0	O-23(14-5-4)	-0.3
1963	Cle A	26	31	6	6	3	0	1	1	4-0	0	4	.194	.286	.387	87	0	0-0	1.000	-1	53	182	O-16(9-0-7)	-0.2
	Chi N	93	322	45	74	16	1	12	41	36-1	4	59	.230	.311	.398	98	0	6-3	.975	-7	82	104	O-90(1-76-21)	-1.1
1964	Chi N	42	105	12	20	3	2	2	7	17-0	0	22	.190	.303	.314	71	-4	4-0	.981	-3	94	0	O-29(1-21-11)	-0.7
1965	Chi N	17	40	6	7	1	0	0	4	1-0	0	10	.175	.186	.200	11	-5	1-0	1.000	0	96	190	O-12(2-10-0)	-0.5

Year	Tm Lg	G	AB	R	H	2B	3B	HR	RBI	BB-IB	HP	SO	AVG	OBP	SLG	AOPS	ABR	SB-CS	FA	FR	Rng	Thr	G at Pos	BFW
Total	5	215	556	79	120	24	4	17	59	65-1	5	117	.216	.300	.365	85	-11	11-6	.981	-11	84	86	O-177(32-112-45)	-2.9
BUSBY, JIM James Franklin B 1.8.1927 Kenedy, TX D 7.8.1996 Augusta, GA BR/TR 6-1/175# d4.23 C18																								
1950	Chi A	18	48	5	10	0	0	0	4	1	0	5	.208	.224	.208	12	-7	0-2	.964	1	92	233	O-12(0-12-1)	-0.7
1951	Chi A★	143	477	59	135	15	2	5	68	40	4	46	.283	.344	.354	91	-7	26-11	.982	7	106	127	*O-139(CF)	-0.1
1952	Chi A	16	39	5	5	0	0	0	0	2	0	7	.128	.171	.128	-16	-6	0-2	1.000	1	118	0	O-16(CF)	-0.7
	Was A	129	512	58	125	24	4	2	47	22	4	48	.244	.281	.318	69	-24	5-6	.993	6	114	38	*O-128(CF)	-2.3
	Year	145	551	63	130	24	4	2	47	24	4	55	.236	.273	.305	62	-30	5-8	.994	7	**114**	35	*O-144(CF)	-3.0
1953	Was A	150	586	68	183	28	7	6	82	38	4	45	.312	.358	.415	111	8	13-6	.988	13	113	112	*O-150(CF)	1.4
1954	Was A	**155**	628	83	187	22	7	7	80	43	3	56	.298	.342	.389	107	3	17-2	.988	5	**114**	40	*O-155(CF)	0.4
1955	Was A	47	191	23	44	6	2	6	14	13-1	0	22	.230	.279	.377	79	-7	5-0	.993	-1	104	35	O-47(CF)	-0.9
	Chi A	99	337	38	82	13	4	1	27	25-0	0	37	.243	.294	.315	62	-19	7-3	.984	1	100	111	O-99(CF)	-2.2
	Year	146	528	61	126	19	6	7	41	38-1	0	59	.239	.289	.337	68	-26	12-3	.987	0	101	85	*O-146(CF)	-3.1
1956	Cle A	135	494	72	116	17	3	12	50	43-2	4	47	.235	.301	.354	71	-22	8-3	.989	0	109	37	*O-133(CF)	-2.7
1957	Cle A	30	74	9	14	2	1	2	4	1-0	0	8	.189	.200	.324	41	-7	0-1	.978	0	103	85	O-26(2-25-0)	-0.8
	Bal A	86	288	31	72	10	1	3	19	23-0	0	36	.250	.304	.323	77	-10	6-3	.984	2	103	128	O-85(CF)	-1.3
	Year	116	362	40	86	12	2	5	23	24-0	0	44	.238	.284	.323	69	-17	6-4	.983	2	103	121	*O-111(2-110-0)	-2.1
1958	Bal A	113	215	32	51	7	2	3	19	24-0	3	37	.237	.320	.330	84	-4	6-4	**.995**	2	114	25	*O-103(CF)/3	-0.6
1959	Bos A	61	102	16	23	8	0	1	5	5-0	1	18	.225	.266	.333	61	-5	0-1	.980	0	104	75	O-34(8-25-1)	-0.7
1960	Bos A	1	0	0	0	0	0	0	0	0-0	0	0	—	—	—	—	0	0-0	—	-0	0	0	/O(LF)	0.0
	Bal A	79	159	25	41	7	1	0	12	20-1	0	14	.258	.341	.314	79	-4	2-3	.985	2	116	70	O-71(CF)	-0.5
	Year	80	159	25	41	7	1	0	12	20-1	0	14	.258	.341	.314	79	-4	2-3	.985	2	116	70	O-72(1-71-0)	-0.5
1961	Bal A	75	89	15	23	3	1	0	6	8-0	0	10	.258	.316	.315	73	-3	2-0	.987	2	112	135	O-71(CF)	-0.2
1962	Hou N	15	11	2	2	0	0	0	1	2-0	0	3	.182	.308	.182	38	-1	0-1	1.000	-0	91	0	O-10(1-8-1)/C	-0.2
Total	13	1352	4250	541	1113	162	35	48	438	310-4	23	439	.262	.314	.350	82	-115	97-48	.988	39	109	76	*O-1280(12-1267-3)/C3	-12.1
BUSBY, PAUL Paul Miller "Red" B 8.25.1918 Waynesboro, MS BL/TR 6-1/175# d9.14																								
1941	Phi N	10	16	3	5	0	0	0	2	0	0	1	.313	.313	.313	79	-1	0	1.000	-0	78	0	/O-3(0-2-1)	-0.1
1943	Phi N	26	40	13	10	1	0	0	5	2	0	1	.250	.286	.275	65	-2	2	1.000	0	121	0	O-10(2-0-8)	-0.3
Total	2	36	56	16	15	1	0	0	7	2	0	2	.268	.293	.286	69	-3	2	1.000	-0	115	0	/O-13(2-2-9)	-0.4
BUSCH, ED Edgar John B 11.16.1917 Lebanon, IL D 1.17.1987 St.Clair Co., IL BR/TR 5-10/175# d9.30																								
1943	Phi A	4	17	2	5	0	0	0	0	1	1	2	.294	.368	.294	95	0	0-1	.941	-2	55	39	/S-4	-0.2
1944	Phi A	140	484	41	131	11	3	0	40	29	1	17	.271	.313	.306	78	-15	5-3	.940	-21	93	74	*S-111,2-27/3-4	-2.7
1945	Phi A	126	416	37	104	10	3	0	35	32	1	9	.250	.305	.288	73	-15	2-3	.952	1	105	93	*S-116/2-2,3-2,1	-0.6
Total	3	270	917	80	240	21	6	0	75	62	3	28	.262	.311	.298	76	-30	7-7	.946	-22	98	83	S-231/2-29,3-6,1	-3.5
BUSCH, MIKE Michael Anthony B 7.7.1968 Davenport, IA BR/TR 6-5/249# d8.30																								
1995	LA N	13	17	3	4	0	0	3	6	0-0	0	7	.235	.235	.765	165	1	0-0	.875	-1	76	0	3-10/1-2	0.0
1996	LA N	38	83	8	18	4	0	4	17	5-0	0	33	.217	.261	.410	80	-3	0-0	.932	-3	73	36	3-23/1	-0.6
Total	2	51	100	11	22	4	0	7	23	5-0	0	40	.220	.257	.470	94	-2	0-0	.923	-4	73	30	/3-33,1-3	-0.6
BUSH, HOMER Homer Giles B 11.12.1972 East St.Louis, IL BR/TR 5-11/180# d8.16																								
1997	NY A	10	11	2	4	0	0	0	3	0-0	0	0	.364	.364	.364	91	0	0-0	.913	1	137	92	/2-8,D	0.1
1998	†NY A	45	71	17	27	3	0	1	5	5-0	0	19	.380	.421	.465	135	4	6-3	.971	-3	73	50	2-24,D-12/3-3,S-2	0.1
1999	Tor A	128	485	69	155	26	4	5	55	21-0	6	82	.320	.353	.421	96	-4	32-8	.984	10	109	107	*2-109,S-18	1.6
2000	Tor A	76	297	38	64	8	0	1	18	18-0	5	60	.215	.271	.253	33	-31	9-4	.986	18	113	128	2-75	-0.8
2001	Tor A	78	271	32	83	11	1	3	27	8-1	6	50	.306	.336	.387	89	-4	13-4	.990	19	115	141	2-78	1.9
2002	Tor A	23	78	9	18	2	0	1	2	2-0	2	12	.231	.268	.295	48	-6	2-0	.990	-2	95	84	2-22/D	-0.6
	Fla N	40	54	7	12	0	0	0	5	3-0	0	13	.222	.263	.222	33	-6	2-1	.962	-7	64	37	2-12/S-4	-1.3
Total	6	400	1267	174	363	50	5	11	115	57-1	19	236	.287	.325	.360	76	-47	64-20	.985	36	108	114	2-328/S-24,D-14,3-3	1.0
BUSH, DONIE Owen Joseph B 10.8.1887 Indianapolis, IN D 3.28.1972 Indianapolis, IN BB/TR 5-6/140# d9.18 M7																								
1908	Det A	20	68	13	20	1	1	0	4	7	0		.294	.360	.338	122	2	2	.938	-2	93	140	S-20	0.1
1909	†Det A	157	532	114	145	18	2	0	33	**88**	4		.273	.380	.314	114	15	53	.925	0	**110**	73	*S-157	2.3
1910	Det A	142	496	90	130	13	4	3	34	**78**	2		.262	.365	.323	108	8	49	**.940**	10	**110**	61	*S-141/3	2.6
1911	Det A	150	561	126	130	18	5	1	36	**98**	3		.232	.349	.287	74	-15	40	.925	13	**112**	72	*S-150	0.8
1912	Det A	144	511	107	118	14	8	2	38	**117**	3		.231	.377	.301	98	6	37	.929	27	**121**	88	*S-144	4.2
1913	Det A	**153**	597	98	150	19	10	1	40	80	4	32	.251	.344	.322	96	-1	44	.938	2	106	94	*S-153	1.2
1914	Det A	**157**	596	97	150	18	4	0	32	**112**	3	54	.252	.373	.295	98	6	35-26	.944	**32**	**114**	106	*S-157	5.1
1915	Det A	155	561	99	128	12	8	1	44	118	2	44	.228	.364	.283	89	-1	35-27	.937	6	105	109	*S-155	1.4
1916	Det A	145	550	73	124	5	9	0	34	75	1	42	.225	.319	.267	74	-16	19	.954	-16	96	73	*S-144	-2.5
1917	Det A	147	581	**112**	163	18	3	0	24	80	2	40	.281	.370	.322	111	12	34	.932	-17	95	64	*S-147	0.6
1918	Det A	**128**	500	74	117	10	3	0	22	79	1	31	.234	.340	.266	86	-5	9	.931	-20	91	54	*S-128	-1.7
1919	Det A	129	509	82	124	11	6	0	26	75	2	36	.244	.343	.289	80	-11	22	.943	-10	95	80	*S-129	-1.2
1920	Det A	141	506	85	133	18	5	1	33	73	1	32	.263	.357	.324	83	-9	15-7	.938	-15	95	69	*S-140	-1.4
1921	Det A	104	402	72	113	6	5	0	27	45	1	23	.281	.355	.321	74	-15	8-11	.949	-6	101	87	S-81,2-23	-1.2
	Was A	23	84	15	18	1	0	0	2	12	0	4	.214	.313	.226	41	-7	2-2	.932	-2	99	119	S-21	-0.7
	Year	127	486	87	131	7	5	0	29	57	1	27	.270	.347	.305	69	-22	10-13	.946	-8	101	93	*S-102,2-23	-1.9
1922	Was A	41	134	17	32	4	1	0	7	21	0	7	.239	.342	.284	68	-6	1-1	.957	2	106	183	3-37/2	-0.2
1923	Was A	10	22	6	9	0	0	0	0	0	0	1	.409	.409	.409	122	1	1-1	.813	-1	90	0	/3-5,2-2,M	0.0
Total	16	1946	7210	1280	1804	186	74	9	436	1158	29	346	.250	.356	.300	91	-36	406-75	.936	3	104	81	*S-1867/3-43,2-26	9.4
BUSH, RANDY Robert Randall B 10.5.1958 Dover, DE BL/TL 6-1/186# d5.1																								
1982	Min A	55	119	13	29	6	1	4	13	8-0	3	28	.244	.305	.412	93	-1	0-0	1.000	-0	88	0	D-26/O-6(LF)	-0.3
1983	Min A	124	373	43	93	24	3	11	56	34-8	7	51	.249	.323	.418	99	0	0-1	1.000	1	165	38	*D-103/1-3	-0.3
1984	Min A	113	311	46	69	17	1	11	43	31-6	4	60	.222	.292	.389	85	-6	1-2	1.000	-0	0	154	D-89/1-2	-1.0
1985	Min A	97	234	26	56	13	3	10	35	24-1	5	30	.239	.321	.449	103	1	3-0	.969	-3	92	0	O-41(39-0-4),D-28/1	-0.4
1986	Min A	130	357	50	96	19	7	7	45	39-2	4	63	.269	.347	.420	105	3	5-3	.977	-3	100	37	*O-102(90-0-13)/1-3,D-6	-0.4
1987	†Min A	122	293	46	74	10	2	11	46	43-5	3	49	.253	.349	.413	99	0	10-3	.982	-4	99	25	O-75(2-0-72)/1-9,D-9	-0.5
1988	Min A	136	394	51	103	20	3	14	51	58-14	9	49	.261	.365	.434	120	13	8-6	.979	-1	101	56	*O-109(1-0-108)/1-6,D-7	0.9
1989	Min A	141	391	60	103	17	4	14	54	48-6	3	73	.263	.347	.435	112	7	5-8	.986	3	109	111	*O-109(34-1-88),1-25/D-5	0.4
1990	Min A	73	181	17	44	8	0	6	18	21-2	6	27	.243	.338	.387	97	0	0-3	1.000	0	103	57	O-32(2-0-32),D-29/1-6	-0.3
1991	†Min A	93	165	21	50	10	1	6	23	24-3	3	25	.303	.401	.485	137	9	0-2	1.000	-1	95	54	O-38(7-0-32),1-12,D-10	0.6
1992	Min A	100	182	14	39	8	1	2	22	11-3	2	37	.214	.263	.302	57	-11	1-1	1.000	-0	110	0	O-24(3-0-21),D-24/1-8	-1.3
1993	Min A	35	45	1	7	2	0	0	3	7-1	0	13	.156	.269	.200	28	-4	0-0	1.000	-1	0	132	/1-4,O(RF)D	-0.5
Total	12	1219	3045	388	763	154	26	96	409	348-51	49	505	.251	.334	.413	101	11	33-29	.983	-9	101	53	O-537(184-1-371),D-341/1-79	-3.1
BUSHONG, DOC Albert John B 9.15.1856 Philadelphia, PA D 8.19.1908 Brooklyn, NY BR/TR 5-11/165# d7.19																								
1875	Atl NA	1	5	0	3	0	1	0	0	0		0	.600	.600	1.000	511	2	0-0	.800	-0			/C	0.1
1876	Phi N	5	21	4	1	0	0	0	1	0		0	.048	.048	.048	-69	-4		.769	-2			/C-5	-0.5
1880	Wor N	41	146	13	25	3	0	0	19	1		16	.171	.177	.192	23	-12		.918	13			C-40/O(RF)3	0.2
1881	Wor N	76	275	35	64	7	4	0	21	21		23	.233	.287	.287	77	-7		.918	9			*C-76	0.4
1882	Wor N	69	253	20	40	4	1	1	15	5		17	.158	.174	.194	18	-23		.897	-3			*C-69	-1.8
1883	Cle N	63	215	15	37	5	0	0	9	7		19	.172	.198	.195	21	-20		.909	13			C-63	-0.1
1884	Cle N	62	203	24	48	6	1	0	10	17		11	.236	.295	.276	78	-5		.886	0			C-62/O(CF)	0.1
1885	†StL AA	85	300	42	80	13	5	0	21	11	2		.267	.297	.343	97	-2		.932	12			*C-85/3	1.6
1886	†StL AA	107	386	56	86	8	0	1	31	31	0		.223	.281	.251	64	-16	12	**.942**	15			*C-106/1	0.7
1887	†StL AA	53	201	35	51	4	0	0	26	11	2		.254	.299	.274	55	-13	14	.927	4			C-52/O-2(RF),3-2	-0.4
1888	Bro AA	69	253	23	53	5	1	0	16	5	2		.209	.231	.237	50	-15	9	.915	-4			C-69	-1.2
1889	†Bro AA	25	84	15	13	1	0	0	8	9	0	7	.155	.237	.167	16	-9	2	.894	-0			C-25	-0.7
1890	†Bro N	16	55	5	13	2	0	0	7	6	0	4	.236	.311	.273	70	-2	2	.913	-2	*86*	62	C-15/O-2(CF)	-0.2
Total	12	671	2392	287	511	58	12	2	184	124	6	97	.214	.254	.250	55	-128	39-0	.916	57	*2*	*2*	C-667/O-6(0-3-3),3-4,1	-1.9
BUSKEY, JOE Joseph Henry "Jazzbow" B 12.18.1902 Cumberland, MD D 4.11.1949 Cumberland, MD BR/TR 5-10/175# d4.19																								
1926	Phi N	5	8	1	0	0	0	0	0	1	0	1	.000	.111	.000	-65	-2	0	.810	-1	93	48	/S-5	-0.3

Year	Tm Lg	G	AB	R	H	2B	3B	HR	RBI	BB-IB	HP	SO	AVG	OBP	SLG	AOPS	ABR	SB-CS	FA	FR	Rng	Thr	G at Pos	BFW
BUSKEY, MIKE Michael Thomas B 1.13.1949 San Francisco, CA BR/TR 5-11/160# d9.2																								
1977	Phi N	6	7	1	2	0	1	0	1	0-0	1	1	.286	.375	.571	143	0	0-0	.882	1	102	227	/S-6	0.1
BUSSE, RAY Raymond Edward B 9.25.1948 Daytona Beach, FL BR/TR 6-4/175# d7.24																								
1971	Hou N	10	34	2	5	3	0	0	4	2-0	0	9	.147	.194	.235	22	-3	0-0	.929	-6	56	0	/S-5,3-3	-1.0
1973	StL N	24	70	6	10	4	2	2	5	5-2	0	21	.143	.200	.343	48	-5	0-1	.898	1	107	136	S-23	-0.3
	Hou N	15	17	1	1	0	0	0	0	1-0	0	12	.059	.111	.059	-52	-4	0-0	1.000	1	120	89	/S-5,3-3	-0.3
	Year	39	87	7	11	4	2	2	5	6-2	0	33	.126	.183	.287	28	-9	0-1	.906	1	108	132	S-28/3-3	-0.6
1974	Hou N	19	34	3	7	1	0	0	0	3-0	0	12	.206	.270	.235	44	-3	0-0	.864	-0	120	77	/3-8	-0.3
Total	3	68	155	12	23	8	2	2	9	11-2	0	54	.148	.205	.265	31	-15	0-1	.908	-5	98	107	/S-33,3-14	-1.9
BUTCHER, HANK Henry Joseph B 7.12.1886 Chicago, IL D 12.28.1979 Hazel Crest, IL BR/TR 5-10/180# d7.8																								
1911	Cle A	38	133	22	32	7	3	1	11	11	1		.241	.303	.361	84	-3	9	.984	1	104	102	O-34(24-4-6)	-0.3
1912	Cle A	26	82	9	16	4	1	1	10	6	0		.195	.250	.305	57	-5	1	.920	1	106	113	O-21(LF)	-0.5
Total	2	64	215	31	48	11	4	2	21	17	1		.223	.283	.340	74	-8	10	.956	2	105	106	/O-55(45-4-6)	-0.8
BUTERA, SAL Salvatore Philip B 9.25.1952 Richmond Hill, NY BR/TR 6/190# d4.10 C3																								
1980	Min A	34	85	4	23	1	0	0	2	3-0	1	6	.271	.300	.282	57	-5	0-0	.950	-6	115	111	C-32/D-2	-1.0
1981	Min A	62	167	13	40	7	1	0	18	22-0	0	14	.240	.325	.293	75	-5	0-0	.970	5	131	147	C-59/1D	0.3
1982	Min A	54	126	9	32	2	0	0	8	17-0	1	12	.254	.347	.270	70	-4	0-0	.988	3	91	101	C-53	0.0
1983	Det A	4	5	1	1	0	0	0	0	0-0	0	0	.200	.200	.200	11	-1	0-0	.929	1	107	0	/C-4	0.0
1984	Mon N	3	3	0	0	0	0	0	0	1-0	0	0	.000	.250	.000	-26	0	0-0	1.000	1	90	0	/C-2	0.0
1985	Mon N	67	120	11	24	1	0	3	12	13-1	1	12	.200	.281	.283	63	-6	0-0	.984	-6	64	76	C-66/P	-1.1
1986	Cin N	56	113	14	27	6	1	2	16	21-3	0	10	.239	.356	.363	95	0	0-0	.979	-2	105	86	C-53/P	-0.1
1987	Cin N	5	11	1	2	0	0	1	2	1-0	0	6	.182	.250	.455	78	0	0-0	.920	0	49	240	/C-5	0.0
	†Min A	51	111	7	19	5	0	1	12	7-0	0	16	.171	.217	.243	22	-13	0-0	.983	-5	65	123	C-51	-1.6
1988	Tor A	23	60	3	14	2	1	1	6	1-0	0	9	.233	.246	.350	65	-3	0-0	.991	-1	110	71	C-23	-0.3
Total	9	359	801	63	182	24	3	8	76	86-4	3	85	.227	.302	.295	65	-37	0-0	.978	-12	97	107	C-348/D-3,P-2,1	-3.8
BUTKA, ED Edward Luke "Babe" B 1.7.1916 Canonsburg, PA BR/TR 6-3/193# d9.26																								
1943	Was A	3	9	0	3	1	0	0	1	0	0	3	.333	.333	.444	132	0	0-0	1.000	1	217	57	/1-3	0.1
1944	Was A	15	41	1	8	1	0	0	1	2	0	11	.195	.233	.220	31	-4	0-0	.972	-0	109	84	1-14	-0.5
Total	2	18	50	1	11	2	0	0	2	2	0	14	.220	.250	.260	48	-4	0-0	.977	1	127	80	/1-17	-0.4
BUTLER, ART Arthur Edward (born Arthur Edward Bouthillier) B 12.19.1887 Fall River, MA D 10.7.1984 Fall River, MA BR/TR 5-9/160# d4.14																								
1911	Bos N	27	68	11	12	2	0	0	2	6	2	6	.176	.263	.206	30	-6	0	.930	-2	107	45	3-14/2-4,S	-0.9
1912	Pit N	43	154	19	42	4	2	1	17	15	0	13	.273	.337	.344	88	-3	2	.960	-15	80	75	2-43	-1.7
1913	Pit N	82	214	40	60	9	3	0	20	32	2	14	.280	.379	.350	114	6	9-5	.919	-15	82	75	2-28,S-26/3-2,O-2(RF)	-0.7
1914	StL N	86	274	29	55	12	3	1	24	39	5	23	.201	.311	.277	76	-6	14	.927	-16	93	90	S-83/O(CF)	-1.8
1915	StL N	130	469	73	119	12	5	1	31	47	1	34	.254	.323	.307	91	-4	26-14	.916	-32	88	84	*S-125/2-2	-3.1
1916	StL N	86	110	9	23	5	0	0	7	7	0	12	.209	.256	.255	57	-5	3	.882	-3	77	0	O-15(2-9-4)/2-8,S3	-1.0
Total	6	454	1289	181	311	44	13	3	101	146	10	102	.241	.323	.303	85	-18	54-19	.919	-83	89	82	S-236/2-85,O-18(2-10-6),3-17	-9.2
BUTLER, BRETT Brett Morgan B 6.15.1957 Los Angeles, CA BL/TL 5-10/160# d8.20																								
1981	Atl N	40	126	17	32	2	3	0	4	19-0	0	17	.254	.352	.317	89	-1	9-1	.987	-0	103	70	O-37(25-11-5)	-0.1
1982	†Atl N	89	240	35	52	2	0	0	7	25-0	0	35	.217	.291	.225	44	-17	21-8	1.000	-6	87	56	O-77(CF)	-2.3
1983	Atl N	151	549	84	154	21	**13**	5	37	54-3	2	56	.281	.344	.393	98	-2	39-23	.987	6	101	140	*O-143(109-38-4)	0.0
1984	Cle A	159	602	108	162	25	9	3	49	86-1	4	62	.269	.361	.355	98	2	52-22	.991	2	101	123	*O-156(0-155-1)	0.6
1985	Cle A	152	591	106	184	28	14	5	50	63-2	1	42	.311	.377	.431	122	19	47-20	**.998**	14	108	199	*O-150(CF)/D	3.4
1986	Cle A	161	587	92	163	17	**14**	4	51	70-1	4	65	.278	.356	.375	102	2	32-15	.993	1	101	104	*O-159(CF)	0.4
1987	Cle A	137	522	91	154	25	8	9	41	91-0	1	55	.295	.399	.425	119	18	33-16	.990	7	112	66	*O-136(CF)	2.4
1988	SF N	157	568	**109**	163	27	9	6	43	97-4	4	64	.287	.393	.398	134	30	43-20	.988	-3	101	43	*O-155(CF)	3.0
1989	†SF N	154	594	100	168	22	4	4	36	59-2	3	69	.283	.349	.354	105	5	31-16	.986	4	104	137	*O-152(CF)	0.9
1990	SF N	160	622	108	**192**	20	9	3	44	90-1	6	62	.309	.397	.384	122	23	51-19	.986	-8	99	44	*O-159(CF)	1.8
1991	LA N★	161	615	**112**	182	13	5	2	38	**108**-4	1	79	.296	.401	.343	114	18	38-28	**1.000**	-5	97	91	*O-161(CF)	1.0
1992	LA N	157	553	86	171	14	11	3	39	95-2	3	67	.309	.413	.391	131	27	41-21	.995	-7	92	108	*O-155(CF)	2.2
1993	LA N	156	607	80	181	21	10	1	42	86-1	5	69	.298	.387	.371	111	14	39-19	**1.000**	-11	90	72	*O-155(CF)	0.7
1994	LA N	111	417	79	131	13	**9**	8	33	68-0	2	52	.314	.411	.446	133	23	27-8	.993	1	99	138	*O-111(CF)	2.7
1995	NY N	90	367	54	114	13	7	1	25	43-2	0	42	.311	.381	.392	108	5	21-7	.995	-0	98	124	O-90(CF)	0.8
	†LA N	39	146	24	40	5	2	0	13	24-0	0	9	.274	.368	.336	98	1	11-1	.987	-4	87	0	O-38(CF)	-0.1
	Year	129	513	78	154	18	**9**	1	38	67-2	0	51	.300	.377	.376	106	6	32-8	.993	-5	95	87	*O-128(CF)	0.7
1996	LA N	34	131	22	35	1	1	0	8	9-0	1	22	.267	.313	.290	67	-6	8-3	.987	-1	101	62	O-34(CF)	-0.6
1997	LA N	105	343	52	97	8	3	0	18	42-0	1	40	.283	.363	.324	88	-5	15-10	1.000	-1	95	88	O-91(47-49-0)/D	-0.7
Total	17	2213	8180	1359	2375	277	131	54	578	1129-23	38	907	.290	.377	.376	110	156	558-257	.992	-13	99	100	*O-2159(181-1986-10)/D-2	16.1
BUTLER, FRANK Frank Dean "Stuffy" or "Goldbrick" B 7.18.1860 Savannah, GA D 7.10.1945 Jacksonville, FL BL/TL 5-7/155# d7.30																								
1895	NY N	5	22	5	6	1	0	0	2	1	0	1	.273	.304	.318	62	-1	0	1.000	-0	0	0	/O-5(4-0-1)	-0.2
BUTLER, KID Frank Edward B 5.1861 Boston, MA D 4.9.1921 S.Boston, MA 5-6/140# d5.20																								
1884	Bos U	71	255	36	43	15	0	0		12			.169	.206	.227	32	-29		.810	-4	67	58	O-53(37-7-9),2-12/S-6,3-2	-3.0
BUTLER, JOHN John Albert (a/k/a Frederick King In 1901) B 7.26.1879 Boston, MA D 2.2.1950 Boston, MA BR/TR 5-7/170# d9.28																								
1901	Mil A	1	3	0	0	0	0	0	0	1	0		.000	.250	.000	-28	0	0	1.000	-1	*46*	*0*	/C	-0.1
1904	StL N	12	37	0	6	1	0	0	1	4	1		.162	.262	.189	42	-2	0	.968	-2	*82*	*67*	C-12	-0.4
1906	Bro N	1	0	0	0	0	0	0	0	0	0		—	—	—	—	0	0	1.000	0	*0*	*297*	/C	0.0
1907	Bro N	30	79	6	10	1	0	0	2	9	0		.127	.216	.139	12	-8	0	.946	-5	*85*	*99*	C-28/O(LF)	-1.2
Total	4	44	119	6	16	2	0	0	3	14	1		.134	.231	.151	21	-10	0	.953	-8	*83*	*90*	/C-42,O(LF)	-1.7
BUTLER, JOHNNY John Stephen "Trolley Line" B 3.20.1893 Fall River, KS D 4.29.1967 Seal Beach, CA BR/TR 6/175# d4.18 C1																								
1926	Bro N	147	501	54	135	27	5	1	68	54	5	44	.269	.346	.349	89	-6	6	.949	-2	95	68	*S-102,3-42/2-8	0.5
1927	Bro N	149	521	39	124	13	6	2	57	34	6	33	.238	.292	.298	58	-32	9	.959	-5	87	98	S-90,3-60	-2.3
1928	Chi N	62	174	17	47	7	0	0	16	19	3	7	.270	.352	.310	75	-5	2	.950	5	109	93	3-59/S-2	0.3
1929	StL N	17	55	5	9	1	1	0	5	4	0	5	.164	.220	.218	9	-8	0	.964	-1	78	0	/3-9,S-8	-0.7
Total	4	375	1251	115	315	48	12	3	146	111	14	89	.252	.320	.317	70	-51	17	.954	-3	91	82	S-202,3-170/2-8	-2.2
BUTLER, BRENT Justin Brent B 2.11.1978 Laurinburg, NC BR/TR 6/180# d7.4																								
2001	Col N	53	119	17	29	7	1	1	14	7-0	1	7	.244	.287	.345	52	-8	1-1	.959	-2	103	118	2-23,S-10/3-9	-0.9
2002	Col N	113	344	55	89	18	4	9	42	10-3	5	40	.259	.287	.413	74	-15	2-6	.974	-9	101	101	2-72,3-33,S-13	-2.1
2003	Col N	37	90	13	19	3	1	1	4	7-2	1	13	.211	.276	.300	44	-8	1-0	.988	-4	99	74	2-20/3-8,S-4	-1.0
Total	3	203	553	85	137	28	6	11	60	24-5	7	60	.248	.285	.380	64	-31	4-7	.973	-14	101	99	2-115/3-50,S-27	-4.0
BUTLER, RICH Richard Dwight B 5.1.1973 Toronto, ON, CAN BL/TR 6-1/180# d9.6 b-Rob																								
1997	Tor A	7	14	3	4	1	0	0	2	2-0	0	3	.286	.375	.357	92	0	0-1	1.000	-0	83	0	/O-3(LF),D	-0.1
1998	TB A	72	217	25	49	3	3	7	20	15-0	2	37	.226	.278	.364	65	-12	4-2	1.000	1	100	109	O-61(39-0-22)	-1.3
1999	TB A	7	20	2	3	1	0	0	0	2-0	0	4	.150	.227	.200	10	-3	0-0	1.000	-1	80	0	/O-6(2-0-4)	-0.3
Total	3	86	251	30	56	5	3	7	22	19-0	2	44	.223	.280	.351	62	-15	4-3	1.000	-0	98	95	/O-70(44-0-26),D	-1.7
BUTLER, DICK Richard H. B Brooklyn, NY d6.16																								
1897	Lou N	10	38	3	7	0	0	0	2	0	0		.184	.184	.184	-3	-6	1	.818	-3	*93*	*119*	C-10	-0.7
1899	Was N	12	36	4	10	0	1	0	1	2	0		.278	.316	.333	79	-1	1	.892	-4	*77*	*133*	C-11	-0.4
Total	2	22	74	7	17	0	1	0	3	2	0		.230	.250	.257	37	-7	2	.852	-6	*85*	*126*	/C-21	-1.1
BUTLER, ROB Robert Frank John B 4.10.1970 E.York, ON, CAN BL/TL 5-11/185# d6.12 b-Rich																								
1993	†Tor A	17	48	8	13	4	0	0	2	7-0	1	12	.271	.375	.354	97	0	2-2	.970	0	118	0	O-16(15-1-0)	0.0
1994	Tor A	41	74	13	13	0	1	0	5	7-0	1	8	.176	.250	.203	20	-9	0-1	.977	-1	96	0	O-31(17-13-2)/D	-1.0
1997	Phi N	43	89	10	26	9	1	0	13	5-0	0	8	.292	.326	.416	94	-1	1-0	1.000	2	92	334	O-25(4-14-8)	0.1
1999	Tor A	8	7	1	1	0	0	0	1	0-0	1	0	.143	.250	.143	4	-1	0-0	1.000	-0	49	0	/O-2(LF),D-3	-0.1
Total	4	109	218	32	53	13	2	0	21	19-0	3	28	.243	.309	.321	66	-11	3-3	.982	1	99	113	/O-74(38-28-10),D-4	-1.0

Year	Tm Lg	G	AB	R	H	2B	3B	HR	RBI	BB-IB	HP	SO	AVG	OBP	SLG	AOPS	ABR	SB-CS	FA	FR	Rng	Thr	G at Pos	BFW
BUTLER, BILL William J. B 1861 New Orleans, LA d6.29																								
1884	Ind AA	9	31	7	7	3	2	0		1	0		.226	.250	.452	128	1		.700	-1	157	0	/O-9(1-1-7)	0.0
BUTLER, KID Willis Everett B 8.9.1887 Franklin, PA D 2.22.1964 Richmond, CA BR/TR 5-11/155# d4.30																								
1907	StL A	20	59	4	13	2	0	0	6	2	0		.220	.246	.254	60	-3	1	.940	0	118	70	2-11/3-5,S	-0.2
BUTTERY, FRANK Frank B 5.13.1851 Silvermine, CT D 12.16.1902 Silvermine, CT d4.26 ▲																								
1872	Man NA	18	93	16	20	0	0	0	7	0		2	.215	.215	.215	35	-7	0-0	.842	-0	131	0	/P-8,O-8(RF),3-5	-0.3
BUZAS, JOE Joseph John B 10.2.1919 Alpha, NJ D 3.19.2003 Salt Lake City, UT BR/TR 6-1/180# d4.17																								
1945	NY A	30	65	8	17	2	1	0	6	2	0	5	.262	.284	.323	73	-3	2-0	.898	-2	100	89	S-12	-0.4
BYERS, BURLEY Burley (born Christopher A. Bayer) B 12.19.1875 Louisville, KY D 5.30.1933 Louisville, KY ?/175# d6.17																								
1899	Lou N	1	3	0	0	0	0	0	0	0	0		.000	.000	.000	-99	-1	0	.600	-1	36	0	/S	-0.2
BYERS, BILL James William B 10.3.1877 Bridgeton, IN D 9.8.1948 Baltimore, MD BL/TR 5-7/210# d4.15																								
1904	StL N	19	60	3	13	0	0	0	4	1	0		.217	.230	.217	40	-4	0	.971	-2	*89*	*55*	C-16/1	-0.5
BYERS, RANDY Randell Parker B 10.2.1964 Bridgeton, NJ BL/TR 6-2/180# d9.7																								
1987	SD N	10	16	1	5	1	0	0	1	1-0	0	5	.313	.353	.375	96	0	1-0	1.000	0	83	391	/O-5(LF)	0.0
1988	SD N	11	10	0	2	1	0	0	0	0-0	0	5	.200	.200	.300	42	-1	0-0	—	-0	0	0	/O-2(1-0-1)	-0.1
Total	2	21	26	1	7	2	0	0	1	1-0	0	10	.269	.296	.346	77	-1	1-0	1.000	0	80	379	/O-7(6-0-1)	-0.1
BYRD, JIM James Edward B 10.3.1968 Wewahitchka, FL BR/TR 6-1/185# d5.31																								
1993	Bos A	2	0	0	0	0	0	0	0	0-0	0	0	—	—	—	—	0	0-0	—	0			/R	0.0
BYRD, MARLON Marlon Jerrard B 8.30.1977 Boynton Beach, FL BR/TR 6/225# d9.8																								
2002	Phi N	10	35	2	8	2	0	1	1	1-0	0	8	.229	.250	.371	66	-2	0-2	1.000	-1	82	0	O-10(0-8-2)	-0.4
2003	Phi N	135	495	86	150	28	4	7	45	44-3	7	94	.303	.366	.418	111	9	11-1	.984	-4	99	72	*O-131(CF)	0.9
Total	2	145	530	88	158	30	4	8	46	45-3	7	102	.298	.359	.415	109	7	11-3	.984	-5	98	67	O-141(0-139-2)	0.5
BYRD, SAMMY Samuel Dewey "Babe Ruth's Legs" B 10.15.1907 Bremen, GA D 5.11.1981 Mesa, AZ BR/TR 5-10.5/175# d5.11																								
1929	NY A	62	170	32	53	12	0	5	28	28	0	18	.312	.409	.471	135	10	1-4	.950	3	110	128	O-54(6-16-32)	0.8
1930	NY A	92	218	46	62	12	2	6	31	30	0	18	.284	.371	.440	110	4	5-1	.992	1	110	48	O-85(47-12-26)	0.1
1931	NY A	115	248	51	67	18	2	3	32	29	1	26	.270	.349	.395	101	1	5-0	.974	0	106	58	O-88(26-34-34)	-0.1
1932	†NY A	105	209	49	62	12	1	8	30	30	0	20	.297	.385	.478	129	10	1-2	.964	-1	98	96	O-91(11-70-11)	0.6
1933	NY A	85	107	26	30	6	1	2	11	15	0	12	.280	.369	.411	113	2	0-1	.987	3	131	42	O-71(23-15-35)	0.3
1934	NY A	106	191	32	47	8	0	3	23	18	2	22	.246	.318	.335	73	-8	1-2	**.988**	6	**132**	44	*O-104(34-13-59)	-0.5
1935	Cin N	121	416	51	109	25	4	9	52	37	0	51	.262	.322	.406	97	-2	4	.970	-1	98	109	*O-115(39-76-0)	-0.7
1936	Cin N	59	141	17	35	8	0	2	13	11	0	11	.248	.303	.348	80	-4	0	.989	1	112	43	O-37(15-22-0)	-0.4
Total	8	745	1700	304	465	101	10	38	220	198	3	178	.274	.350	.412	104	13	17-10	.975	11	109	78	O-645(201-258-197)	0.1
BYRNE, BOBBY Robert Matthew B 12.31.1884 St.Louis, MO D 12.31.1964 Wayne, PA BR/TR 5-7.5/145# d4.11																								
1907	StL N	149	559	55	143	11	5	0	29	35	6		.256	.307	.293	91	-7	21	.920	21	112	117	*3-148/S	2.0
1908	StL N	127	439	27	84	7	1	0	14	23	4		.191	.238	.212	46	-27	16	.925	10	105	91	*3-122/S-4	-1.6
1909	StL N	105	421	61	90	13	6	1	33	46	7		.214	.302	.280	86	-6	21	.922	13	116	74	*3-105	1.1
	†Pit N	46	168	31	43	6	2	0	7	32	4		.256	.387	.315	109	4	8	.987	3	115	60	3-46	1.0
	Year	151	589	92	133	19	8	1	40	78	11		.226	.327	.290	93	-1	29	**.939**	16	**116**	70	*3-151	2.1
1910	Pit N	148	602	101	**178**	**43**	12	2	52	66	1	27	.296	.366	.417	121	17	36	.929	-7	101	56	*3-148	1.4
1911	Pit N	153	598	96	155	24	17	2	52	67	8	41	.259	.342	.366	94	-5	23	.930	-2	100	112	*3-152	-0.3
1912	Pit N	130	528	99	152	31	11	3	35	54	4	40	.288	.358	.405	110	8	20	**.948**	-24	76	90	*3-130	-1.2
1913	Pit N	113	448	54	121	22	0	1	47	29	5	28	.270	.322	.326	89	-6	10-16	.940	-10	83	96	*3-110	-1.7
	Phi N	19	58	9	13	1	0	1	4	5	2	3	.224	.308	.293	69	-2	2-3	.963	0	104	0	3-15	-0.2
	Year	132	506	63	134	23	0	2	51	34	7	31	.265	.320	.322	86	-8	12-19	.943	-10	86	84	*3-125	-1.9
1914	Phi N	126	467	61	127	12	1	0	26	45	2	44	.272	.339	.302	85	-7	9	.934	-1	109	47	*2-101,3-22	-0.6
1915	†Phi N	105	387	50	81	6	4	0	21	39	5	28	.209	.290	.245	62	-17	4-12	**.969**	-5	94	75	*3-105	-2.5
1916	Phi N	48	141	22	33	10	1	0	9	14	1	7	.234	.308	.319	89	-1	6	.933	1	99	149	3-40	0.1
1917	Phi N	13	14	1	5	0	0	0	0	1	0	2	.357	.400	.357	128	0	0	1.000	-1	33	0	/3-4	0.0
	Chi A	1	1	0	0	0	0	0	0	0	0	0	.000	.000	.000	-98	0	0	1.000	0	154	0	/2	0.0
Total	11	1283	4831	667	1225	186	60	10	329	456	49	220	.254	.324	.323	91	-49	176-31	.934	-1	99	90	*3-1147,2-102/S-5	-2.5
BYRNES, ERIC Eric James B 2.16.1976 Redwood City, CA BR/TR 6-2/200# d8.22																								
2000	Oak A	10	10	5	3	0	0	0	0	0-0	1	1	.300	.364	.300	72	0	2-1	1.000	0	131	0	/O-4(1-0-3),D-2	0.0
2001	†Oak A	19	38	9	9	1	0	3	5	4-0	1	6	.237	.326	.500	113	1	1-0	.933	-2	74	0	O-12(8-2-5)/D-5	-0.1
2002	†Oak A	90	94	24	23	4	2	3	11	4-0	3	17	.245	.291	.426	89	-2	3-0	.982	-3	84	56	O-79(52-10-22)/D-6	-0.5
2003	†Oak A	121	414	64	109	27	9	12	51	42-4	2	71	.263	.333	.459	105	3	10-2	.991	-11	80	92	*O-117(44-82-2)/D-2	-0.7
Total	4	240	556	102	144	32	11	18	67	50-4	7	95	.259	.326	.453	102	2	16-3	.986	-15	81	78	O-212(105-94-32)/D-15	-1.3
BYRNES, JIM James Joseph B 1.5.1880 San Francisco, CA D 7.31.1941 San Francisco, CA BR/TR 5-9/150# d4.19																								
1906	Phi A	10	23	2	4	0	1	0	0	0	0		.174	.174	.261	34	-2	0	.889	-0	*103*	*122*	/C-9	-0.2
BYRNES, MILT Milton John "Skippy" B 11.15.1916 St.Louis, MO D 2.1.1979 St.Louis, MO BL/TL 5-10.5/170# d4.21																								
1943	StL A	129	429	58	120	28	7	4	50	53	2	49	.280	.362	.406	122	13	1-4	**.997**	7	104	150	*O-114(23-66-26)	1.4
1944	†StL A	128	407	63	120	20	4	4	45	68	0	50	.295	.396	.393	119	13	1-7	.976	0	105	73	*O-122(41-52-36)	0.6
1945	StL A	133	442	53	110	29	4	8	59	78	1	84	.249	.363	.387	112	10	1-3	.988	7	111	105	*O-125(31-56-47)/1-2	1.0
Total	3	390	1278	174	350	77	15	16	154	199	3	183	.274	.373	.395	117	36	3-14	.987	14	107	109	O-361(95-174-109)/1-2	3.0
CABALLERO, PUTSY Ralph Joseph B 11.5.1927 New Orleans, LA BR/TR 5-11/175# d9.14																								
1944	Phi N	4	4	0	0	0	0	0	0	0	0	1	.000	.000	.000	-99	-1	0	.889	1	119	0	/3-2	-0.1
1945	Phi N	9	1	1	0	0	0	0	1	0	0	0	.000	.000	.000	-99	0	0	.857	0	87	417	/3-5	0.0
1947	Phi N	2	7	2	1	0	0	0	0	1	0	0	.143	.250	.143	7	-1	0	1.000	0	117	102	/2-2,3	-0.1
1948	Phi N	113	351	33	86	12	1	0	19	24	0	18	.245	.293	.285	58	-21	7	.962	5	103	114	3-79,2-23	-1.5
1949	Phi N	29	68	8	19	3	0	0	3	0	0	3	.279	.279	.324	63	-4	0	.981	0	92	106	2-21/S	-0.2
1950	†Phi N	46	24	12	4	0	0	0	0	2	0	2	.167	.231	.167	7	-3	1	.950	2	127	146	/2-5,3-4,S-2	-0.1
1951	Phi N	84	161	15	30	3	2	1	11	12	0	7	.186	.243	.248	33	-16	1-2	.985	-1	95	109	2-54/3-3,S	-1.5
1952	Phi N	35	42	10	10	3	0	0	6	2	0	3	.238	.273	.310	62	-2	1-0	.857	-0	110	148	/S-8,2-7,3-7	-0.2
Total	8	322	658	81	150	21	3	1	40	41	0	34	.228	.273	.274	49	-48	10-2	.968	7	96	104	2-112,3-101/S-12	-3.7
CABELL, ENOS Enos Milton B 10.8.1949 Fort Riley, KS BR/TR 6-5/185# d9.17 OF Total (42-LF 1-CF 72-RF)																								
1972	Bal A	3	5	0	0	0	0	0	1	0-0	0	0	.000	.000	.000	-97	-1	0-0	1.000	-0	0	134	/1	-0.2
1973	Bal A	32	47	12	10	2	0	1	3	3-0	0	7	.213	.250	.319	63	-2	1-3	.991	-2	54	149	1-23/3	-0.6
1974	†Bal A	80	174	24	42	4	2	3	17	7-1	0	20	.241	.269	.339	77	-6	5-3	.995	-0	109	118	1-28,O-22(1-0-22),3-19/2D	-0.9
1975	Hou N	117	348	43	92	17	6	2	43	18-1	3	53	.264	.303	.365	92	-6	12-3	.973	3	85	231	O-67(37-0-32),1-25,3-22	-0.5
1976	Hou N	144	586	85	160	13	7	2	43	29-1	2	79	.273	.309	.329	89	-11	35-8	.958	-2	97	88	*3-143/1-3	-1.0
1977	Hou N	150	625	101	176	36	7	16	68	27-2	3	55	.282	.313	.438	109	4	42-22	.948	-1	97	76	*3-144/1-8,S	0.3
1978	Hou N	**162**	660	92	195	31	8	7	71	22-1	5	80	.295	.321	.398	109	4	33-15	.958	-7	91	58	*3-153,1-14/S	-0.4
1979	Hou N	155	603	60	164	30	5	6	67	21-7	3	68	.272	.299	.368	86	-14	37-18	.957	-20	76	54	*3-132,1-51	-3.8
1980	†Hou N	152	604	69	167	23	8	2	55	26-6	1	84	.276	.305	.351	90	-11	21-13	.927	-12	89	71	*3-150/1	-2.7
1981	SF N	96	396	41	101	20	1	2	36	10-0	1	47	.255	.274	.326	71	-16	6-7	.987	-2	**134**	99	1-69,3-22	-2.6
1982	Det A	125	464	45	121	17	3	2	37	15-2	1	48	.261	.284	.323	67	-22	15-6	.992	-1	123	127	1-83,3-59/O-3(1-0-2)	-2.7
1983	Det A	121	392	62	122	23	5	5	46	16-2	1	41	.311	.335	.434	114	6	4-8	.997	5	121	108	*1-106/3-4,SD	0.4
1984	Hou N	127	436	52	135	17	3	8	44	21-5	1	47	.310	.341	.417	121	10	8-11	.993	-1	95	**123**	*1-112	0.1
1985	Hou N	60	143	20	35	8	1	2	14	16-0	0	15	.245	.321	.357	92	-1	3-1	.994	-1	92	106	1-49	-0.4
	†LA N	57	192	20	56	11	0	0	22	14-1	0	21	.292	.340	.349	96	-1	6-2	.920	3	117	137	3-32,1-21/O-4(1-0-3)	0.1
	Year	117	335	40	91	19	1	2	36	30-1	0	36	.272	.332	.352	94	-2	9-3	.993	2	79	90	1-70,3-32/O-4(1-0-3)	-0.3
1986	LA N	107	277	27	71	11	0	2	29	14-2	2	26	.256	.294	.318	75	-10	10-4	.987	3	105	85	1-61,O-16(2-1-13)/3-7	-1.1
Total	15	1688	5952	753	1647	263	56	60	596	259-31	23	691	.277	.308	.370	93	-77	238-124	.944	-33	92	74	3-888,1-655,O-112R/D-9,S-3,2	-16.0

Year	Tm Lg	G	AB	R	H	2B	3B	HR	RBI	BB-IB	HP	SO	AVG	OBP	SLG	AOPS	ABR	SB-CS	FA	FR	Rng	Thr	G at Pos	BFW
CABRERA, ALEX Alexander Alberto B 12.24.1971 Caripito, Venezuela BR/TR 6-2/220# d6.26																								
2000	Ari N	31	80	10	21	2	1	5	14	4-0	1	21	.262	.299	.500	96	-1	0-0	1.000	1	84	104	1-15,O-12(1-0-11)	-0.1
CABRERA, AL Alfredo A. B 5.11.1881 Canary Islands, Spain D 1964 Batabano, Cuba TR d5.16																								
1913	StL N	1	2	0	0	0	0	0	0	0	0	0	.000	.000	.000	-99	-1	0	—	-0	0	0	/S	-0.1
CABRERA, FRANCISCO Francisco (Paulino) B 10.10.1966 Santo Domingo, D.R. BR/TR 6-4/193# d7.24																								
1989	Tor A	3	12	1	2	1	0	0	0	1-0	0	3	.167	.231	.250	36	-1	0-0	—	0			/D-3	-0.1
	Atl N	4	14	0	3	2	0	0	0	0-0	0	3	.214	.214	.357	59	-1	0-0	1.000	-1	69	68	/1-2,C	-0.2
1990	Atl N	63	137	14	38	5	1	7	25	5-0	0	21	.277	.301	.482	106	0	1-0	.990	-1	90	64	1-48/C-3	-0.3
1991	†Atl N	44	95	7	23	6	0	4	23	6-0	0	20	.242	.284	.432	94	-1	1-1	.987	-1	104	78	C-17,1-14	-0.2
1992	†Atl N	12	10	2	3	0	0	2	3	1-0	0	1	.300	.364	.900	233	2	0-0	—	-0	0	0	/C	0.1
1993	†Atl N	70	83	8	20	3	0	4	11	8-1	0	21	.241	.308	.422	92	-1	0-0	1.000	2	174	69	1-12/C-2	0.0
Total	5	196	351	32	89	17	1	17	62	21-1	0	69	.254	.294	.453	99	-2	2-1	.989	-1	113	66	/1-76,C-24,D-3	-0.7
CABRERA, JOLBERT Jolbert Alexis B 12.8.1972 Cartagena, Colombia BR/TR 6/177# d4.12 b-Orlando OF Total (103-LF 127-CF 65-RF)																								
1998	Cle A	1	2	0	0	0	0	0	0	0-0	0	1	.000	.000	.000	-97	-1	0-0	1.000	0	122	0	/S	0.0
1999	Cle A	30	37	6	7	1	0	0	0	1-0	1	8	.189	.231	.216	14	-5	3-0	.957	1	109	0	O-16(4-12-0)/2-6	-0.3
2000	Cle A	100	175	27	44	3	1	2	15	8-0	2	15	.251	.290	.314	53	-13	6-4	.989	4	105	145	O-74(24-26-29),2-19/S-8,D-2	-0.9
2001	†Cle A	141	287	50	75	16	3	1	38	16-0	6	41	.261	.312	.348	73	-11	10-4	.978	-0	93	40	O-83(36-35-18),2-28,3-27,S-14/D	-1.0
2002	Cle A	38	72	5	8	1	0	0	7	5-0	1	13	.111	.177	.125	-17	-12	1-1	1.000	-1	89	0	O-34(5-16-13)/2-3,D	-1.3
	LA N	10	12	3	4	1	0	0	1	2-0	0	2	.333	.429	.417	137	1	0-0	1.000	1	158	0	/O-4(3-0-1),3-3,2	0.1
2003	LA N	128	347	43	98	32	2	6	37	17-3	10	62	.282	.332	.438	105	3	6-4	.967	-4	67	143	O-63(31-38-4),2-59/S-9,1-8,3-5	0.0
Total	6	448	932	134	236	54	6	9	98	49-3	20	142	.253	.303	.353	72	-38	26-13	.981	-0	90	85	O-274C,2-116/3-35,S-32,1-8,D-4	-3.4
CABRERA, MIGUEL Jose Miguel (Torres) B 4.18.1983 Maracay, Venezuela BR/TR 6-2/180# d6.20																								
2003	†Fla N	87	314	39	84	21	3	12	62	25-3	2	84	.268	.325	.468	108	3	0-2	.972	-4	102	151	O-55(LF),3-34	-0.3
CABRERA, ORLANDO Orlando Luis B 11.2.1974 Cartagena, Colombia BR/TR 5-11/165# d9.3 b-Jolbert																								
1997	Mon N	16	18	4	4	0	0	0	2	1-0	0	3	.222	.263	.222	29	-2	1-2	.875	1	150	126	/S-6,2-4	-0.1
1998	Mon N	79	261	44	73	16	5	3	22	18-1	0	27	.280	.325	.414	94	-3	6-2	.984	-5	91	69	S-52,2-28	-0.2
1999	Mon N	104	382	48	97	23	5	8	39	18-4	3	38	.254	.293	.403	76	-16	2-2	.979	15	107	98	*S-102	0.6
2000	Mon N	125	422	47	100	25	1	13	55	25-3	1	28	.237	.279	.393	66	-23	4-4	.981	8	108	104	*S-124/2	-0.6
2001	Mon N	**162**	626	64	173	41	6	14	96	43-5	4	54	.276	.324	.428	91	-9	19-7	**.986**	**29**	**113**	105	*S-162	3.3
2002	Mon N	153	563	64	148	43	1	7	56	48-4	2	53	.263	.321	.380	81	-17	25-7	.962	21	113	103	*S-153	1.9
2003	Mon N	**162**	626	95	186	47	2	17	80	52-3	1	64	.297	.347	.460	100	1	24-2	.975	6	101	104	*S-162	2.3
Total	7	801	2898	366	781	195	20	62	350	205-20	11	267	.269	.318	.415	85	-69	81-26	.976	76	107	101	S-761/2-33	7.2
CACEK, CRAIG Craig Thomas B 9.10.1954 Hollywood, CA BR/TR 6-1/200# d6.18																								
1977	Hou N	7	20	0	1	0	0	0	1	1-0	0	3	.050	.095	.050	-66	-5	0-0	.981	-1	31	161	/1-6	-0.7
CACERES, EDGAR Edgar F. B 6.6.1964 Barquisimeto, Venezuela BB/TR 6-1/170# d6.8																								
1995	KC A	55	117	13	28	6	2	1	17	8-0	1	15	.239	.291	.350	66	-6	2-2	.992	0	102	66	2-36/S-8,1-6,3-3,D-3	-0.5
CADY, CHARLIE Charles B. B 12.1865 Chicago, IL D 6.7.1909 Kankakee, IL 5-11/180# d9.5 ▲																								
1883	Cle N	3	11	0	0	0	0	0	0	1		5	.000	.083	.000	-73	-2		1.000	-0	0	0	/O-2(RF),P	-0.1
1884	CP U	6	20	4	2	1	1	0		1			.100	.143	.250	17	-3		.909	-0	76	0	/P-4,O-2(CF)	-0.1
	KC U	2	3	0	0	0	0	0		0			.000	.000	.000	-99	-1		.600	-2			/C2	-0.3
	Year	8	23	4	2	1	1	0		1			.087	.125	.217	2	-4		.909	-2	76	0	/P-4,O-2(CF),C2	-0.4
Total	2	11	34	4	2	1	1	0	0	2		5	.059	.111	.147	-23	-6		.917	-3			/P-5,O-4(0-2-2),2C	-0.5
CADY, HICK Forrest Leroy (born Forrest Leroy Bergland) B 1.26.1886 Bishop Hill, IL D 3.3.1946 Cedar Rapids, IA BR/TR 6-2/179# d4.26																								
1912	†Bos A	47	135	19	35	13	2	0	9	10	3		.259	.324	.385	98	0	0	.990	9	*126*	*93*	C-43/1-4	1.2
1913	Bos A	40	96	10	24	5	2	0	6	5	1	14	.250	.294	.344	84	-2	1	.992	4	*98*	*91*	C-39	0.4
1914	Bos A	61	159	14	41	6	1	0	8	12	0	22	.258	.310	.308	86	-3	2-1	.971	2	*121*	*109*	C-58	0.4
1915	†Bos A	78	205	25	57	10	2	0	17	19	1	25	.278	.342	.346	109	2	0-2	.980	4	*117*	*87*	C-77	1.2
1916	†Bos A	78	162	5	31	6	3	0	13	15	1	16	.191	.264	.265	59	-9	0	.967	-5	126	72	C-63/1-3	-1.1
1917	Bos A	17	46	4	7	1	1	0	2	1	0	6	.152	.170	.217	18	-5	0	.959	1	*125*	*99*	C-14	-0.4
1919	Phi N	34	98	6	21	6	0	1	19	4	1	8	.214	.252	.306	63	-4	1	.984	-6	*74*	*111*	C-29	-0.9
Total	7	355	901	83	216	47	11	1	74	66	7	91	.240	.297	.320	82	-21	4-3	.979	8	*115*	*93*	C-323/1-7	0.8
CAFEGO, TOM Thomas B 8.21.1911 Whipple, WV D 10.29.1961 Detroit, MI BL/TR 5-10/160# d9.3																								
1937	StL A	4	4	1	0	0	0	0	0	0	0	1	.000	.000	.000	-99	-1	0-0	.500	-0	83	0	/O(LF)	-0.1
CAFFIE, JOE Joseph Clifford "Rabbit" B 2.14.1931 Ramer, AL BL/TR 5-10.5/180# d9.13																								
1956	Cle A	12	38	7	13	0	0	0	1	4-0	2	8	.342	.432	.342	104	1	3-2	1.000	1	106	134	O-10(LF)	0.1
1957	Cle A	32	89	14	24	2	1	3	10	4-2	0	11	.270	.301	.416	95	-1	0-1	.976	0	118	0	O-19(3-0-18)	-0.3
Total	2	44	127	21	37	2	1	3	11	8-2	2	19	.291	.343	.394	99	0	3-3	.984	1	114	46	/O-29(13-0-18)	-0.2
CAFFYN, BEN Benjamin Thomas B 2.10.1880 Peoria, IL D 11.22.1942 Peoria, IL BL/TL 5-10/175# d8.21																								
1906	Cle A	30	103	16	20	4	0	0	3	12	2		.194	.291	.233	65	-3	2	.909	-3	60	308	O-29(28-1-0)	-0.9
CAGE, WAYNE Wayne Levell B 11.23.1951 Monroe, LA BL/TL 6-4/205# d4.22																								
1978	Cle A	36	98	11	24	6	1	4	13	9-0	0	28	.245	.308	.449	112	1	1-2	.988	1	140	131	D-20,1-11	0.1
1979	Cle A	29	56	6	13	2	0	1	6	5-0	0	16	.232	.295	.321	66	-3	0-2	1.000	0	126	72	/1-7,D-9	-0.3
Total	2	65	154	17	37	8	1	5	19	14-0	0	44	.240	.304	.403	94	-2	1-4	.992	1	135	111	/D-29,1-18	-0.2
CAHILL, JOHN John Patrick Parnell "Patsy" B 4.30.1865 San Francisco, CA D 10.31.1901 Pleasanton, CA BR/TR 5-7.5/168# d5.31 ▲																								
1884	Col AA	59	210	28	46	3	3	0		6	2		.219	.248	.262	72	-6		.843	-0	79	0	O-56(LF)/S-5,P-2	-0.7
1886	StL N	125	463	43	92	17	6	1	32	9		79	.199	.214	.268	49	-28	16	.866	2	141	131	*O-124(0-1-123)/P-2,S3	-2.5
1887	Ind N	68	263	22	54	4	3	0	26	9	1	5	.205	.234	.243	34	-24	34	.826	-5	108	49	O-56(0-3-53)/3-9,P-6,S	-2.4
Total	3	252	936	93	192	24	12	1	58	24	3	84	.205	.227	.260	49	-58	50	.851	-4	119	81	O-236(56-4-176)/3-10,P-10,S-7	-5.6
CAHILL, TOM Thomas H. B 10.1868 Fall River, MA D 12.25.1894 Scranton, PA 5-7/150# d4.9																								
1891	Lou AA	119	430	68	109	17	7	3	44	41	6	51	.253	.327	.347	94	-4	38	.930	-8	*83*	*122*	C-55,S-49,O-12(9-2-1)/2-6,3-2	-0.5
CAIRO, MIGUEL Miguel Jesus B 5.4.1974 Anaco, Venezuela BR/TR 6/160# d4.17 OF Total (47-LF 11-RF)																								
1996	Tor A	9	27	5	6	2	0	0	1	2-0	1	9	.222	.300	.296	52	-2	0-0	1.000	-1	77	95	/2-9	-0.2
1997	Chi N	16	29	7	7	1	0	0	1	2-0	1	3	.241	.313	.276	54	-2	0-0	1.000	0	83	129	/2-9,S-2	-0.1
1998	TB A	150	515	49	138	26	5	5	46	24-0	6	44	.268	.307	.367	73	-21	19-8	.978	17	107	122	*2-148/D-2	0.4
1999	TB A	120	465	61	137	15	5	3	36	24-0	7	46	.295	.335	.368	79	-15	22-7	.986	27	**111**	**117**	*2-117/D-2	1.9
2000	TB A	119	375	49	98	18	2	1	34	29-0	2	34	.261	.314	.328	65	-20	28-7	.983	5	99	111	*2-108/D-2	-0.6
2001	Chi N	66	123	20	35	3	1	2	9	16-1	0	21	.285	.364	.374	97	0	2-1	.900	-4	73	145	3-40,2-11/S	-0.4
	†StL N	27	33	5	11	5	0	1	7	2-0	0	2	.333	.371	.576	141	2	0-0	1.000	-0	174	0	/O-6(LF),2-5,3-3,1S	0.2
	Year	93	156	25	46	8	1	3	16	18-1	0	23	.295	.366	.417	106	2	2-1	.882	-5	71	142	3-43,2-16/O-6(LF),S-2,1	-0.2
2002	†StL N	108	184	28	46	9	2	2	23	13-2	3	36	.250	.307	.353	79	-7	1-1	.905	-2	94	0	O-24(19-0-5),2-18/3-7,S-6,1-4,D-3	-0.8
2003	StL N	92	261	41	64	15	2	5	32	13-1	6	30	.245	.289	.375	77	-10	4-1	.986	-14	87	75	2-40,O-27(22-0-6),3-12/S-7,1-3	-2.2
Total	8	707	2012	265	542	94	17	19	189	125-4	26	225	.269	.317	.361	76	-75	76-25	.982	29	104	113	2-465/3-62,O-57L,S-17,D-9,1-8	-1.8
CAITHAMER, GEORGE George Theodore "Sidee" B 7.22.1910 Chicago, IL D 6.1.1954 Chicago, IL BR/TR 5-10/168# d9.17																								
1934	Chi A	5	19	1	6	1	0	0	3	1	0	5	.316	.350	.368	83	0	0-0	.958	-1	*59*	*75*	/C-5	-0.1
CALDERON, IVAN Ivan (Perez) B 3.19.1962 Fajardo, PR D 12.27.2003 Loiza, PR BR/TR 6-1/220# d8.10																								
1984	Sea A	11	24	2	5	1	0	1	1	2-0	0	5	.208	.269	.375	77	-1	1-0	1.000	0	110	0	O-11(4-6-1)	-0.1
1985	Sea A	67	210	37	60	16	4	8	28	19-1	2	45	.286	.349	.514	132	9	4-2	.981	1	95	151	O-53(33-1-22)/1-2,D-3	0.7
1986	Sea A	37	131	13	31	5	0	2	13	6-0	1	33	.237	.275	.321	61	-7	3-1	.937	-1	86	187	O-32(2-2-31)	-0.9
	Chi A	13	33	3	10	2	1	0	2	3-1	0	6	.303	.361	.424	109	0	0-0	.900	0	135	0	/O-5(LF),D-6	0.0
	Year	50	164	16	41	7	1	2	15	9-1	1	39	.250	.293	.341	71	-7	3-1	.932	-1	90	170	O-37(7-2-31)/D-6	-0.9
1987	Chi A	144	542	93	159	38	2	28	83	60-6	1	109	.293	.362	.526	129	23	10-5	.984	-1	101	76	*O-139(6-0-135)/D-3	1.4

Year	Tm Lg	G	AB	R	H	2B	3B	HR	RBI	BB-IB	HP	SO	AVG	OBP	SLG	AOPS	ABR	SB-CS	FA	FR	Rng	Thr	G at Pos	BFW
1988	Chi A	73	264	40	56	14	0	14	35	34-2	0	66	.212	.299	.424	101	0	4-4	.954	-1	96	119	O-67(4-0-63)/D-3	-0.3
1989	Chi A	157	622	83	178	34	9	14	87	43-7	3	94	.286	.332	.437	119	14	7-1	.978	-2	99	104	*O-103(17-0-89),D-36,1-26	0.8
1990	Chi A	158	607	85	166	44	2	14	74	51-7	1	79	.273	.327	.422	111	9	32-16	.975	-1	100	84	*O-130(130-0-3),D-27/1-2	0.5
1991	Mon N★	134	470	69	141	22	3	19	75	53-4	3	64	.300	.368	.481	141	26	31-16	.974	-1	104	43	*O-122(LF)/1-4	2.3
1992	Mon N	48	170	19	45	14	2	3	24	14-1	1	22	.265	.323	.424	111	2	1-2	.988	-1	92	100	O-46(LF)	0.0
1993	Bos A	73	213	25	47	8	2	1	19	21-1	1	28	.221	.291	.291	54	-14	4-2	1.000	1	111	69	O-47(9-2-39),D-19	-1.5
	Chi A	9	26	1	3	2	0	0	3	0-0	0	5	.115	.115	.192	-19	-4	0-0	—	0			/D-6	-0.5
	Year	82	239	26	50	10	2	1	22	21-1	1	33	.209	.274	.280	47	-18	4-2	1.000	1	111	69	O-47(9-2-39),D-25	-2.0
Total	10	924	3312	470	901	200	25	104	444	306-30	13	556	.272	.333	.442	113	57	97-49	.976	-5	100	90	O-755(378-11-383),D-103/1-34	2.4
CALDERONE, SAM Samuel Francis B 2.6.1926 Beverly, NJ BR/TR 5-10.5/185# d4.19 Mil 1951																								
1950	NY N	34	67	9	20	1	0	1	12	2	0	5	.299	.319	.358	77	-2	0	.972	-2	*156*	*81*	C-33	-0.3
1953	NY N	35	45	4	10	2	0	0	8	1	0	4	.222	.239	.267	31	-5	0-0	.966	0	*157*	*101*	C-31	-0.4
1954	Mil N	22	29	3	11	2	0	0	5	4	0	4	.379	.441	.448	146	2	0-0	1.000	2	*102*	*67*	C-16	0.4
Total	3	91	141	16	41	5	0	1	25	7	0	13	.291	.322	.348	76	-5	0-0	.978	-0	*144*	*84*	/C-80	-0.3
CALDWELL, BRUCE Bruce B 2.8.1906 Ashton, RI D 2.15.1959 West Haven, CT BR/TR 6/195# d6.30																								
1928	Cle A	18	27	2	6	1	1	0	3	2	1	2	.222	.300	.333	66	-1	1-0	1.000	0	97	159	O-10(RF)/1	-0.2
1932	Bro N	7	11	2	1	0	0	0	2	2	0	2	.091	.231	.091	-10	-2	0	.875	-1	0	53	/1-6	-0.3
Total	2	25	38	4	7	1	1	0	5	4	1	4	.184	.279	.263	44	-3	1-0	1.000	-1	97	159	/O-10(RF),1-7	-0.5
CALDWELL, RAY Raymond Benjamin "Rube" or "Sum" B 4.26.1888 Corydon, PA D 8.17.1967 Salamanca, NY BL/TR 6-2/190# d9.9 ▲																								
1910	NY A	6	6	0	0	0	0	0	0	0	0		.000	.000	.000	-95	-1	0	1.000	-0	66	0	/P-6	0.0
1911	NY A	59	147	14	40	4	1	0	17	11	0		.272	.323	.313	73	-5	5	.953	-2	76	103	P-41,O-11(5-0-5)	-0.3
1912	NY A	44	76	18	18	1	2	0	6	5	0		.237	.284	.303	64	-4	4	.938	1	111	125	P-30/O(LF)	0.0
1913	NY A	59	97	10	28	3	2	0	11	3	0	15	.289	.310	.361	96	-1	3	**1.000**	-1	87	63	P-27/O-3(0-1-2)	-0.1
1914	NY A	59	113	9	22	4	0	0	10	7	1	24	.195	.248	.230	44	-8	2-1	.967	-4	74	101	P-31/1-6	-0.5
1915	NY A	72	144	27	35	4	1	4	20	9	0	32	.243	.288	.368	96	8	4-3	**.988**	-3	80	161	P-36	0.0
1916	NY A	45	93	6	19	2	0	0	4	2	0	17	.204	.221	.226	34	-8	1	.960	-0	93	111	P-21/O-2	0.0
1917	NY A	63	124	12	32	6	1	2	12	16	0	16	.258	.343	.371	117	3	2	.973	-2	88	43	P-32/O-8(0-5-3)	-0.1
1918	NY A	65	151	14	44	10	0	1	18	13	1	23	.291	.352	.377	117	3	2	.977	-3	73	49	P-24,O-19(2-12-5)	-0.1
1919	Bos A	33	48	5	13	1	1	0	4	0	0	9	.271	.271	.333	73	-2	0	.950	-2	78	0	P-18/O-2(LF)	-0.1
	Cle A	6	23	4	8	4	0	0	2	0	0	4	.348	.348	.522	134	3	0	.900	-1	56	0	/P-6	0.0
	Year	39	71	9	21	5	1	0	6	0	0	13	.296	.296	.394	97	-1	0	.933	-3	70	0	P-24/O-2(LF)	-0.1
1920	†Cle A	41	89	17	19	3	0	0	7	10	1	13	.213	.300	.247	45	1	0-2	.917	-3	80	0	P-34	0.0
1921	Cle A	38	53	2	11	4	0	1	3	2	0	5	.208	.236	.340	45	0	0-0	.930	-0	93	83	P-37	0.0
Total	12	590	1164	138	289	46	8	8	114	78	3	158	.248	.297	.322	78	-11	23-6	.960	-21	83	80	P-343/O-46(11-18-15),1-6	-1.2
CALHOUN, JACK John Charles "Red" B 12.14.1879 Pittsburgh, PA D 2.27.1947 Cincinnati, OH BR/TR 6/185# d6.27																								
1902	StL N	20	64	3	10	2	1	0	8	8	1		.156	.260	.219	50	-4	1	.972	-1	89	66	3-12/1-5,O(RF)	-0.5
CALHOUN, BILL William Davitte "Mary" B 6.23.1890 Rockmart, GA D 1.28.1955 Sandersville, GA BL/TL 6/180# d4.24																								
1913	Bos N	6	13	0	1	0	0	0	0	0	0	3	.077	.077	.077	-55	-3	0	.970	-0	67	70	/1-3	-0.3
CALLAGHAN, MARTY Martin Francis B 6.9.1900 Norwood, MA D 6.23.1975 Norfolk, MA BL/TL 5-10/157# d4.13																								
1922	Chi N	74	175	31	45	7	4	0	20	17	1	17	.257	.326	.343	71	-7	2-3	.946	-4	96	38	O-53(12-10-31)	-1.4
1923	Chi N	61	129	18	29	1	3	0	14	8	1	18	.225	.275	.279	47	-10	2-5	.969	-0	100	98	O-38(19-0-19)	-1.4
1928	Cin N	81	238	29	69	11	4	0	24	27	0	10	.290	.362	.370	93	-2	5	.980	-1	97	97	O-69(48-22-1)	-0.6
1930	Cin N	79	225	28	62	9	2	0	16	19	1	25	.276	.335	.333	66	-12	1	.986	1	106	71	O-54(16-38-0)	-1.3
Total	4	295	767	106	205	28	13	0	74	71	3	70	.267	.332	.338	72	-31	10-8	.973	-4	100	77	O-214(95-70-51)	-4.7
CALLAGHAN, PAT Patrick J. B New York, NY d5.1																								
1884	Ind AA	61	258	38	67	8	5	2		8	0		.260	.282	.353	109	2		.812	-9	83	67	3-61	-0.5
CALLAHAN, DAVE David Joseph B 7.20.1888 Ottawa, IL D 10.28.1969 Ottawa, IL BL/TR 5-10/165# d9.14																								
1910	Cle A	13	44	6	8	1	0	0	2	4	1		.182	.265	.205	47	-3	5	1.000	-0	123	0	O-12(LF)	-0.4
1911	Cle A	6	16	1	4	0	1	0	0	1	0		.250	.294	.375	85	-1	0	.875	1	64	342	/O-4(CF)	0.0
Total	2	19	60	7	12	1	1	0	2	5	1		.200	.273	.250	58	-4	5	.972	1	111	71	/O-16(12-4-0)	-0.4
CALLAHAN, ED Edward Joseph B 12.11.1857 Boston, MA D 2.5.1947 New York, NY d7.19																								
1884	StL U	1	3	0	0	0	0	0		0			.000	.000	.000	-97	-1		1.000	1	707	0	/O(LF)	0.0
	KC U	3	11	0	4	0	0	0		0			.364	.364	.364	139	0		.800	1	139	192	/S-3	0.1
	Bos U	4	13	2	5	0	0	0		1			.385	.429	.385	151	1		.750	-1	0	0	/O-4(1-0-3)	0.0
	Year	8	27	2	9	0	0	0		1			.333	.357	.333	117	0		.778	1	86	0	/O-5(2-0-3),S-3	0.1
CALLAHAN, NIXEY James Joseph B 3.18.1874 Fitchburg, MA D 10.4.1934 Boston, MA BR/TR 5-10.5/180# d5.12 M7 ▲ OF Total (401-LF 30-CF 59-RF)																								
1894	Phi N	9	21	4	5	0	0	0	0	0	0	7	.238	.238	.238	15	-1	0	.923	1	125	0	/P-9	0.0
1897	Chi N	94	360	60	105	18	6	3	47	10	5		.292	.320	.400	86	-9	12	.918	3	102	95	2-30,P-23,O-21(12-9-0),S-18/3-2	-0.3
1898	Chi N	43	164	27	43	7	5	0	22	4	0		.262	.280	.366	85	-5	3	.947	-2	93	145	P-31/O-9(1-0-8),S21	-0.3
1899	Chi N	47	150	21	39	4	3	0	18	8	2		.260	.306	.327	76	-5	9	.904	4	128	95	P-35/O-9(0-7-2),S-2,2	0.0
1900	Chi N	32	115	16	27	3	2	0	9	6	0		.235	.273	.296	59	2	5	.975	6	131	104	P-32	0.0
1901	Chi A	45	118	15	39	7	3	1	19	10	0		.331	.383	.466	138	6	10	.944	4	**135**	159	P-27/3-6,2-2	0.2
1902	Chi A	70	218	27	51	7	2	0	13	6	2		.234	.261	.284	53	-14	4	.941	4	129	**250**	P-35,O-23(6-3-15)/S	-0.4
1903	Chi A	118	439	47	128	26	5	2	56	20	1		.292	.324	.387	118	9	24	.895	-5	106	47	*3-102/O-8(6-0-2),P-3,M	0.6
1904	Chi A	132	482	66	126	23	2	0	54	39	1		.261	.318	.317	105	5	29	.977	-13	81	0	*O-104(LF),2-28,M	-1.6
1905	Chi A	96	345	50	94	18	6	1	43	29	4		.272	.336	.368	128	11	26	.956	-5	104	0	O-93(71-1-21)	0.2
1911	Chi A	120	466	64	131	13	5	3	60	15	2		.281	.306	.350	86	-12	45	.963	-11	85	56	*O-114(93-10-11)	-2.8
1912	Chi A	111	408	45	111	9	7	1	52	12	3		.272	.298	.336	84	-11	19	.939	-16	81	22	*O-107(LF),M	-3.2
1913	Chi A	6	9	0	2	0	0	0	1	0	0	2	.222	.222	.222	30	-1	0	1.000	-0	108	0	/O(LF)M	-0.1
Total	13	923	3295	442	901	135	46	11	394	159	20	9	.273	.311	.352	94	-25	186	.953	-30	94	26	O-489L,P-195,3-110/2-62,S-22,1	-7.7
CALLAHAN, JIM James Timothy "Red" (born James Timothy Callaghan) B 1.12.1879 Allegheny Co., PA D 3.9.1968 Carnegie, PA BR/TR 5-9/145# d5.25																								
1902	NY N	1	4	0	0	0	0	0	0	1	0		.000	.200	.000	-38	-1	0	—	0	0	0	/O(RF)	-0.1
CALLAHAN, LEO Leo David B 8.9.1890 Jamaica Plain, MA D 5.2.1982 Erie, PA BL/TL 5-8/142# d4.9																								
1913	Bro N	33	41	6	7	3	1	0	3	4	0	5	.171	.244	.293	52	-3	0	.857	-1	105	0	/O-8(2-4-2)	-0.4
1919	Phi N	81	235	26	54	14	4	1	9	29	1	19	.230	.317	.336	90	-2	5	.950	2	91	162	O-58(12-9-38)	-0.4
Total	2	114	276	32	61	17	5	1	12	33	1	24	.221	.306	.330	84	-5	5	.941	1	92	148	/O-66(14-13-40)	-0.8
CALLAHAN, WESLEY Wesley Leroy B 7.3.1888 Lyons, IN D 9.13.1953 Dayton, OH BR/TR 5-7.5/155# d9.7																								
1913	StL N	7	14	0	4	0	0	0	1	2	0	2	.286	.375	.286	91	0	1	.920	0	112	119	/S-6	0.1
CALLAWAY, FRANK Frank Burnett B 2.26.1898 Knoxville, TN D 8.21.1987 Knoxville, TN BR/TR 6/170# d9.17																								
1921	Phi A	14	50	7	12	1	1	0	4	2	1	11	.240	.283	.300	49	-4	1-0	.878	-5	96	28	S-14	-0.7
1922	Phi A	29	48	5	13	0	2	0	4	0	0	13	.271	.271	.354	60	-3	0-0	.880	0	126	112	2-11/3-5,S-4	-0.2
Total	2	43	98	12	25	1	3	0	8	2	1	24	.255	.277	.327	54	-7	1-0	.889	-5	96	26	/S-18,2-11,3-5	-0.9
CALLISON, JOHNNY John Wesley B 3.12.1939 Qualls, OK BL/TR 5-10/175# d9.9																								
1958	Chi A	18	64	10	19	4	2	1	12	6-0	0	14	.297	.352	.469	128	2	1-0	.976	1	98	164	O-18(LF)	0.2
1959	Chi A	49	104	12	18	3	0	3	12	13-0	1	20	.173	.271	.288	54	-7	0-1	.983	1	92	161	O-41(LF)	-0.8
1960	Phi N	99	288	36	75	11	5	9	30	45-2	0	70	.260	.360	.427	114	7	0-4	.989	5	114	103	O-86(32-16-47)	0.7
1961	Phi N	138	455	74	121	20	11	9	47	69-5	3	76	.266	.363	.418	109	7	10-4	.967	1	101	98	*O-124(90-1-35)	0.2
1962	Phi N★	157	603	107	181	26	**10**	23	83	54-1	6	96	.300	.363	.491	131	25	10-3	.980	19	**117**	183	*O-152(3-5-151)	3.4
1963	Phi N	157	626	96	178	36	11	26	78	50-4	2	111	.284	.339	.502	140	31	8-3	.994	18	**111**	**220**	*O-157(2-1-156)	4.1
1964	Phi N★	**162**	654	101	179	30	10	31	104	36-3	6	95	.274	.316	.492	126	19	6-3	.988	14	113	160	*O-162(2-0-162)	2.3
1965	Phi N☆	160	619	93	162	25	**16**	32	101	57-2	6	117	.262	.328	.509	135	26	6-5	.982	15	110	**196**	*O-159(RF)	3.1
1966	Phi N	155	612	93	169	**40**	7	11	55	56-4	3	83	.276	.338	.418	109	9	8-8	.990	1	101	110	*O-154(RF)	-0.2
1967	Phi N	149	556	62	145	30	5	14	64	55-17	3	63	.261	.329	.408	109	7	6-12	.977	5	106	112	*O-147(RF)	-0.1

Year	Tm Lg	G	AB	R	H	2B	3B	HR	RBI	BB-IB	HP	SO	AVG	OBP	SLG	AOPS	ABR	SB-CS	FA	FR	Rng	Thr	G at Pos	BFW
1968	Phi N	121	398	46	97	18	4	14	40	42-4	3	70	.244	.319	.415	119	9	4-3	**1.000**	0	96	113	*O-109(RF)	0.2
1969	Phi N	134	495	66	131	29	5	16	64	49-11	3	73	.265	.332	.440	119	12	2-1	.990	12	**119**	124	*O-129(RF)	1.8
1970	Chi N	147	477	65	126	23	2	19	68	60-11	3	63	.264	.348	.440	98	0	7-2	.973	-0	100	90	*O-144(0-3-143)	-0.7
1971	Chi N	103	290	27	61	12	1	8	38	36-8	2	55	.210	.298	.341	71	-10	2-1	.982	-2	102	51	O-89(1-0-88)	-1.8
1972	NY A	92	275	28	71	10	0	9	34	18-1	0	34	.258	.299	.393	110	2	3-0	.992	-2	92	79	O-74(RF)	-0.3
1973	NY A	45	136	10	24	4	0	1	10	4-0	0	24	.176	.197	.228	21	-15	1-1	.960	-2	82	103	O-32(RF),D-10	-2.0
Total	16	1886	6652	926	1757	321	89	226	840	650-73	41	1064	.264	.331	.441	114	124	74-51	.984	84	107	136	*O-1777(189-26-1586)/D-10	10.1
CALLOWAY, RON Ronald Isiah B 9.4.1976 San Jose, CA BL/TL 6-1/210# d3.31																								
2003	Mon N	126	340	36	81	17	1	9	52	20-1	2	80	.238	.282	.374	64	-19	9-2	.983	1	105	76	O-97(50-2-47)	-2.0
CALVO, JACK Jacinto (Gonzalez) (Born Jacinto Del Calvo) B 6.11.1894 Havana, Cuba D 6.15.1965 Miami, FL BL/TL 5-10/156# d5.9																								
1913	Was A	17	33	5	8	0	0	1	2	1	0	4	.242	.265	.333	73	-1	0	.900	-0	64	212	O-13(6-0-7)	-0.2
1920	Was A	17	23	5	1	0	1	0	2	2	0	2	.043	.120	.130	-35	-5	0-0	1.000	-1	79	0	O-10(6-1-3)	-0.6
Total	2	34	56	10	9	0	1	1	4	3	0	6	.161	.203	.250	27	-6	0-0	.938	-1	69	137	/O-23(12-1-10)	-0.8
CAMELLI, HANK Henry Richard B 12.12.1914 Gloucester, MA D 7.14.1996 Wellesley, MA BR/TR 5-11/190# d10.3																								
1943	Pit N	1	3	1	0	0	0	0	0	1	0	0	.000	.250	.000	-24	0	0	1.000	0	*0*	*0*	/C	0.0
1944	Pit N	63	125	14	37	5	1	1	10	18	0	12	.296	.385	.376	110	2	0	.959	2	*100*	*85*	C-61	0.7
1945	Pit N	1	2	0	0	0	0	0	0	1	0	0	.000	.333	.000	-3	0	0	1.000	0	*0*	*0*	/C	0.0
1946	Pit N	42	96	8	20	2	2	0	5	8	0	9	.208	.269	.271	52	-6	0	.971	1	*69*	*117*	C-39	-0.4
1947	Bos N	52	150	10	29	8	1	1	11	18	0	18	.193	.280	.280	50	-11	0	.977	2	*83*	*90*	C-51	-0.6
Total	5	159	376	33	86	15	4	2	26	46	0	39	.229	.313	.306	70	-15	0	.970	5	*84*	*93*	C-153	-0.3
CAMERON, JACK James Stanley "Happy Jack" B 9.22.1884 Cape Breton, NS, CAN D 7.12.1963 Charlotte, NC TR 5-10/170# d9.13																								
1906	Bos N	18	61	3	11	0	0	0	4	2	0		.180	.206	.180	21	-6	0	.852	-1	150	193	O-16(15-0-1)/P-2	-0.8
CAMERON, MIKE Michael Terrance B 1.8.1973 LaGrange, GA BR/TR 6-1/170# d8.27																								
1995	Chi A	28	38	4	7	2	0	1	2	3-0	0	15	.184	.244	.316	46	-3	0-0	1.000	1	111	108	O-28(0-3-26)	-0.3
1996	Chi A	11	11	1	1	0	0	0	0	1-0	0	3	.091	.167	.091	-34	-2	0-1	1.000	-0	79	0	/O-8(2-4-5),D-2	-0.3
1997	Chi A	116	379	63	98	18	3	14	55	55-1	5	105	.259	.356	.433	110	7	23-2	.985	13	**124**	88	*O-112(0-102-37)/D-4	2.2
1998	Chi A	141	396	53	83	16	5	8	43	37-0	6	101	.210	.285	.336	63	-23	27-11	.988	2	106	83	*O-138(0-136-2)	-1.7
1999	Cin N	146	542	93	139	34	9	21	66	80-2	6	145	.256	.357	.469	104	4	38-12	.979	-1	104	88	*O-146(CF)	0.8
2000	†Sea A	155	543	96	145	28	4	19	78	78-0	9	133	.267	.365	.438	106	7	24-7	.985	1	106	68	*O-155(0-155-1)	1.1
2001	†Sea A★	150	540	99	144	30	5	25	110	69-3	10	155	.267	.353	.480	126	21	34-5	.986	5	110	96	*O-149(CF)/D	3.2
2002	Sea A	158	545	84	130	26	5	25	80	79-3	7	176	.239	.340	.442	110	9	31-8	.988	3	107	76	*O-155(CF)	1.7
2003	Sea A	147	534	74	135	31	5	18	76	70-1	5	137	.253	.344	.431	106	6	17-7	.992	16	**126**	45	*O-147(CF)	2.4
Total	9	1052	3528	567	882	185	36	131	510	472-10	48	970	.250	.343	.434	104	26	194-53	.987	39	111	77	*O-1038(2-997-71)/D-7	9.1
CAMILLI, DOLPH Adolph Louis B 4.23.1907 San Francisco, CA D 10.21.1997 San Mateo, CA BL/TL 5-10/185# d9.9 Def 1943 Mil 1944-45 s-Doug																								
1933	Chi N	16	58	8	13	2	1	2	7	4	0	11	.224	.274	.397	90	-1	3	.994	2	130	166	1-16	-0.1
1934	Chi N	32	120	17	33	8	0	4	19	5	2	25	.275	.315	.442	102	0	1	.988	2	123	108	1-32	-0.1
	Phi N	102	378	52	100	20	3	12	68	48	2	69	.265	.350	.429	95	-2	3	.985	-3	92	97	*1-102	-1.4
	Year	134	498	69	133	28	3	16	87	53	4	94	.267	.342	.432	96	-2	4	.986	-1	99	100	*1-134	-1.5
1935	Phi N	**156**	602	88	157	23	5	25	83	65	3	113	.261	.336	.440	97	-3	9	.987	-2	98	92	*1-156	-1.9
1936	Phi N	151	530	106	167	29	13	28	102	116	3	84	.315	.441	.577	156	47	5	.988	-11	77	93	*1-150	2.2
1937	Phi N	131	475	101	161	23	7	27	80	90	2	82	.339	**.446**	.587	165	47	6	**.994**	4	108	92	*1-131	3.8
1938	Bro N	146	509	106	128	25	11	24	100	**119**	0	101	.251	.393	.485	137	30	6	.995	-1	95	104	*1-145	1.5
1939	Bro N★	**157**	565	105	164	30	12	26	104	**110**	4	107	.290	.409	.524	144	38	1	.990	9	122	106	*1-157	3.2
1940	Bro N	142	512	92	147	29	13	23	96	89	4	83	.287	.397	.529	145	33	9	.992	-5	84	79	*1-140	1.4
1941	†Bro N✶	149	529	92	151	29	6	**34**	**120**	104	4	115	.285	.407	.556	162	**46**	3	.989	1	101	99	*1-148	3.3
1942	Bro N	150	524	89	132	23	7	26	109	97	3	85	.252	.372	.471	144	31	10	.992	-1	94	121	*1-150	1.7
1943	Bro N	95	353	56	87	15	6	6	43	65	1	48	.246	.365	.374	113	8	2	.992	-1	94	91	1-95	0.3
1945	Bos A	63	198	24	42	5	2	2	19	35	0	38	.212	.330	.288	78	-4	2-0	.991	2	110	132	1-54	-0.5
Total	12	1490	5353	936	1482	261	86	239	950	947	28	961	.277	.388	.492	134	270	60-0	.990	-5	98	100	*1-1476	13.4
CAMILLI, DOUG Douglas Joseph B 9.22.1936 Philadelphia, PA BR/TR 5-11/195# d9.25 C6 f-Dolph																								
1960	LA N	6	24	4	8	2	0	1	3	1-0	1	4	.333	.385	.542	141	1	0-0	.980	0	*115*	*68*	/C-6	0.2
1961	LA N	13	30	3	4	0	0	3	4	1-0	0	9	.133	.161	.433	47	-3	0-0	.986	1	*93*	*111*	C-12	-0.1
1962	LA N	45	88	16	25	5	2	4	22	12-1	0	21	.284	.366	.523	145	6	0-0	.983	-3	*105*	*51*	C-39	0.4
1963	LA N	49	117	9	19	1	1	3	10	11-6	0	22	.162	.234	.265	47	-9	0-0	.977	4	*137*	*58*	C-47	-0.3
1964	LA N	50	123	1	22	3	0	0	10	8-1	0	19	.179	.226	.203	25	-12	0-0	.990	5	*152*	*113*	C-46	-0.6
1965	Was A	75	193	13	37	6	1	3	18	16-2	1	34	.192	.257	.280	53	-12	0-0	.980	-0	*103*	*110*	C-59	-1.1
1966	Was A	44	107	5	22	4	0	2	8	3-0	1	19	.206	.234	.299	53	-7	0-0	.990	3	*137*	*148*	C-39	-0.3
1967	Was A	30	82	5	15	1	0	2	5	4-0	0	16	.183	.221	.268	46	-6	0-0	.993	-5	76	117	C-24	-1.0
1969	Was A	1	3	0	1	0	0	0	0	0-0	0	2	.333	.333	.333	92	0	0-0	1.000	0	0	0	/C	0.0
Total	9	313	767	56	153	22	4	18	80	56-10	3	146	.199	.256	.309	61	-42	0-0	.984	5	*119*	*100*	C-273	-2.8
CAMILLI, LOU Louis Steven B 9.24.1946 ElPaso, TX BB/TR 5-10/170# d8.9																								
1969	Cle A	13	14	0	0	0	0	0	0	0-0	0	3	.000	.000	.000	-97	-4	0-0	1.000	2	91	83	3-13	-0.2
1970	Cle A	16	15	0	0	0	0	0	0	2-0	0	2	.000	.118	.000	-62	-3	0-0	1.000	1	143	0	/S-3,2-2,3	-0.3
1971	Cle A	39	81	5	16	2	0	0	0	8-1	0	10	.198	.270	.222	37	-7	0-0	.938	-3	95	50	S-23,2-16	-0.8
1972	Cle A	39	41	2	6	2	0	0	3	3-0	0	8	.146	.205	.195	19	-4	0-0	1.000	-1	79	91	/S-8,2-2	-0.5
Total	4	107	151	7	22	4	0	0	3	13-1	0	23	.146	.213	.172	11	-18	0-0	.951	-2	94	56	/S-34,2-20,3-14	-1.8
CAMINITI, KEN Kenneth Gene B 4.21.1963 Hanford, CA BB/TR 6/200# d7.16																								
1987	Hou N	63	203	10	50	7	1	3	23	12-1	0	44	.246	.287	.335	67	-10	0-0	.949	2	92	127	3-61	-0.9
1988	Hou N	30	83	5	15	2	0	1	7	5-0	0	18	.181	.225	.241	36	-7	0-0	.948	-1	96	57	3-28	-0.9
1989	Hou N	161	585	71	149	31	3	10	72	51-9	3	93	.255	.316	.369	99	-1	4-1	.954	11	108	103	*3-160	1.2
1990	Hou N	153	541	52	131	20	2	4	51	48-7	0	97	.242	.302	.309	71	-22	9-4	.945	-9	93	108	*3-149	-3.1
1991	Hou N	152	574	65	145	30	3	13	80	46-7	5	85	.253	.312	.383	101	0	4-5	.948	14	107	114	*3-152	1.4
1992	Hou N	135	506	68	149	31	2	13	62	44-13	1	68	.294	.350	.441	129	19	10-4	.966	-7	88	88	*3-129	1.4
1993	Hou N	143	543	75	142	31	0	13	75	49-10	0	88	.262	.321	.390	93	-5	8-5	.942	11	103	106	*3-143	0.7
1994	Hou N★	111	406	63	115	28	2	18	75	43-13	2	71	.283	.352	.495	125	15	4-3	.969	5	103	102	*3-108	2.0
1995	SD N	143	526	74	159	33	0	26	94	69-8	1	94	.302	.380	.513	139	31	12-5	.936	14	106	122	*3-143	4.6
1996	†SD N★	146	546	109	178	37	2	40	130	78-16	4	99	.326	.408	.621	179	64	11-5	.954	15	112	128	*3-145	7.7
1997	SD N★	137	486	92	141	28	0	26	90	80-9	3	118	.290	.389	.508	145	34	11-2	.941	16	**121**	84	*3-133	5.2
1998	†SD N	131	452	87	114	29	0	29	82	71-4	4	108	.252	.353	.509	135	24	6-2	.931	-9	90	80	*3-126	1.6
1999	†Hou N	78	273	45	78	11	1	13	56	46-4	3	58	.286	.386	.476	121	10	6-2	.932	4	103	150	3-75	1.4
2000	Hou N	59	208	42	63	13	0	15	45	42-8	1	37	.303	.419	.582	142	15	3-0	.915	-7	85	77	3-58	0.8
2001	Tex A	54	185	24	43	8	1	9	25	22-2	2	41	.232	.318	.432	93	-2	0-0	.940	-1	97	105	3-53	-0.3
	†Atl N	64	171	12	38	9	0	6	16	21-1	0	44	.222	.306	.380	75	-7	0-1	.977	-3	80	91	1-33,3-13/D	-1.2
Total	15	1760	6288	894	1710	348	17	239	983	727-112	29	1163	.272	.347	.447	117	158	88-39	.946	53	102	106	*3-1676/1-33,D	21.6
CAMP, HOWIE Howard Lee "Red" B 7.1.1893 Munford, AL D 5.8.1960 Eastaboga, AL BL/TR 5-9/169# d9.19 Mil 1918																								
1917	NY A	5	21	3	6	1	0	0	0	1	0	2	.286	.318	.333	98	0	0	.857	0	82	263	/O-5(0-4-1)	0.0
CAMP, LEW Robert Plantagenet Llewellyn B 2.23.1868 Columbus, OH D 10.1.1948 Omaha, NE BL/TR 6/175# d8.26 b-Kid																								
1892	StL N	42	145	19	30	3	1	2	13	17	1	27	.207	.294	.283	79	-3	12	.780	-13	78	68	3-39/O-3(0-2-1)	-1.5
1893	Chi N	38	156	37	41	7	7	2	17	19	1	19	.263	.347	.436	109	1	30	.847	-5	79	71	3-16,O-11(CF)/2-9,S-3	-0.3
1894	Chi N	8	33	1	6	2	0	0	1	1	0	6	.182	.206	.242	7	-5	0	.830	-4	68	92	/2-8	-0.7
Total	3	88	334	57	77	12	8	4	31	37	2	52	.231	.311	.350	85	-7	42	.801	-22	78	69	/3-55,2-17,O-14(0-13-1),S-3	-2.5
CAMPANELLA, ROY Roy B 11.19.1921 Philadelphia, PA D 6.26.1993 Woodland Hills, CA BR/TR 5-8/200# d4.20 HF1969																								
1948	Bro N	83	279	32	72	11	3	9	45	36	1	45	.258	.345	.416	102	1	3	.981	8	*130*	*146*	C-78	1.2
1949	†Bro N★	130	436	65	125	22	2	22	82	67	3	36	.287	.385	.498	130	20	3	.985	5	***140***	*110*	*C-127	3.1
1950	Bro N★	126	437	70	123	19	3	31	89	55	2	51	.281	.364	.551	134	21	1	.985	-3	*126*	*92*	*C-123	2.4

Year	Tm Lg	G	AB	R	H	2B	3B	HR	RBI	BB-IB	HP	SO	AVG	OBP	SLG	AOPS	ABR	SB-CS	FA	FR	Rng	Thr	G at Pos	BFW
1951	Bro N★	143	505	90	164	33	1	33	108	53	4	51	.325	.393	.590	158	41	1-2	.986	12	**254**	107	*C-140	5.9
1952	†Bro N★	128	468	73	126	18	1	22	97	57	3	59	.269	.352	.453	120	13	8-4	**.994**	-3	147	101	*C-122	1.8
1953	†Bro N★	144	519	103	162	26	3	41	**142**	67	4	58	.312	.395	.611	154	41	4-2	.989	5	**166**	98	*C-140	5.0
1954	Bro N★	111	397	43	82	14	3	19	51	42	2	49	.207	.285	.401	74	-17	1-4	.989	-1	148	109	*C-111	-1.3
1955	†Bro N✶	123	446	81	142	20	1	32	107	56-9	6	41	.318	.395	.583	153	35	2-3	.992	4	118	73	*C-121	4.3
1956	†Bro N★	124	388	39	85	6	1	20	73	66-15	1	61	.219	.333	.394	88	-6	1-0	.985	4	134	88	*C-121	0.5
1957	Bro N	103	330	31	80	9	0	13	62	34-6	4	50	.242	.316	.388	81	-8	1-0	**.993**	15	**136**	108	*C-100	1.2
Total	10	1215	4205	627	1161	178	18	242	856	533-30	30	501	.276	.360	.500	123	141	25-15	.988	46	153	102	*C-1183	24.1
CAMPANERIS, BERT Dagoberto (Blanco) "Campy" (born Dagoberto Campaneria (Blanco)) B 3.9.1942 Pueblo Nuevo, Cuba BR/TR 5-10/160# d7.23 OF Total (68-LF 2-CF 1-RF)																								
1964	KC A	67	269	27	69	14	3	4	22	15-0	4	41	.257	.306	.375	86	-5	10-2	.981	-3	98	64	S-38,O-27(LF)/3-6	-0.6
1965	KC A	144	578	67	156	23	**12**	6	42	41-0	**9**	71	.270	.326	.382	103	1	**51**-19	.938	-11	93	81	*S-109,O-39(38-2-1)/PC123	0.1
1966	KC A	142	573	82	153	29	10	5	42	25-1	5	72	.267	.302	.379	98	-3	**52**-10	.971	-15	89	92	*S-138	0.2
1967	KC A	147	601	85	149	29	6	3	32	36-2	7	82	.248	.297	.331	89	-9	**55**-16	.954	-13	88	92	*S-145	-0.3
1968	Oak A★	159	642	87	**177**	25	9	4	38	50-2	4	69	.276	.330	.361	116	11	**62**-22	.956	8	102	106	*S-155/O-3(LF)	4.3
1969	Oak A	135	547	71	142	15	2	2	25	30-2	4	62	.260	.302	.305	74	-21	62-8	.967	-3	103	100	*S-125	0.3
1970	Oak A	147	603	97	168	28	4	22	64	36-1	4	73	.279	.321	.448	115	9	**42**-10	.973	2	99	115	*S-143	3.5
1971	†Oak A	134	569	80	143	18	4	5	47	29-1	2	64	.251	.287	.323	75	-21	34-7	.960	3	98	120	*S-133	0.4
1972	†Oak A☆	149	625	85	150	25	2	8	32	32-0	2	88	.240	.278	.325	84	-15	**52**-14	.977	5	101	113	*S-148	1.7
1973	†Oak A★	151	601	89	150	17	6	4	46	50-1	4	79	.250	.308	.318	82	-15	34-10	.969	-3	101	103	*S-149	0.4
1974	†Oak A★	134	527	77	153	18	8	2	41	47-2	0	81	.290	.347	.366	113	9	34-15	.966	-2	98	104	*S-133/D	2.5
1975	†Oak A★	137	509	69	135	15	3	4	46	50-2	7	71	.265	.337	.330	92	-4	24-12	.962	-16	93	82	*S-137	-0.4
1976	Oak A	149	536	67	137	14	1	1	52	63-0	3	80	.256	.331	.291	89	-5	54-12	.969	-1	106	79	*S-149	2.0
1977	Tex A★	150	552	77	140	19	7	5	46	47-1	4	86	.254	.314	.341	78	-17	27-20	.968	26	**113**	113	*S-149	2.3
1978	Tex A	98	269	30	50	5	3	1	17	20-0	2	36	.186	.245	.238	37	-23	22-4	.954	4	104	93	S-89/D-4	-0.7
1979	Tex A	8	9	2	1	0	0	0	0	1-0	0	3	.111	.200	.111	-14	-1	1-0	.962	3	117	219	/S-8	0.2
	†Cal A	85	239	27	56	4	4	0	15	19-0	2	32	.234	.294	.285	59	-14	12-4	.957	11	102	142	S-82/D	0.6
	Year	93	248	29	57	4	4	0	15	20-0	2	35	.230	.290	.278	57	-16	13-4	.957	14	103	146	S-90/D	0.8
1980	Cal A	77	210	32	53	8	1	2	18	14-0	1	33	.252	.300	.329	75	-8	10-5	.957	-9	86	99	S-64/2D	-1.0
1981	Cal A	55	82	11	21	2	1	1	10	5-0	0	10	.256	.295	.341	84	-2	5-2	.900	-8	83	106	3-45/S-3,2-2	-1.1
1983	NY A	60	143	19	46	5	0	0	11	8-0	0	9	.322	.355	.357	101	0	6-7	.964	-1	119	127	2-32,3-24	-0.1
Total	19	2328	8684	1181	2249	313	86	79	646	618-15	64	1142	.259	.311	.342	89	-133	649-199	.964	-23	99	101	*S-2097/3-76,O-69L,2-36,D-8,1CP	14.3
CAMPANIS, AL Alexander Sebastian (born Alessandro Campani) B 11.2.1916 Kos, Dodecanese Islands D 6.21.1998 Fullerton, CA BB/TR 6/185# d9.23 Mil 1944-45 s-Jim																								
1943	Bro N	7	20	3	2	0	0	0	0	4	0	5	.100	.250	.100	3	-2	0	1.000	1	90	106	/2-7	-0.1
CAMPANIS, JIM James Alexander B 2.9.1944 New York, NY BR/TR 6/195# d9.20 f-Al																								
1966	LA N	1	1	0	0	0	0	0	0	0-0	0	0	.000	.000	.000	-99	0	0-0	1.000	0	0	0	/C	0.0
1967	LA N	41	62	3	10	1	0	2	2	9-1	0	14	.161	.268	.274	60	-3	0-0	.990	-0	119	75	C-23	-0.3
1968	LA N	4	11	0	1	0	0	0	0	1-0	0	2	.091	.167	.091	-23	-2	0-0	.960	1	141	329	/C-4	-0.1
1969	KC A	30	83	4	13	5	0	0	5	5-1	0	19	.157	.202	.217	18	-9	0-0	.982	1	67	78	C-26	-0.8
1970	KC A	31	54	6	7	0	0	2	2	4-1	1	14	.130	.203	.241	22	-6	0-0	.986	-3	36	162	C-13/O(RF)	-0.9
1973	Pit N	6	6	0	1	0	0	0	0	0-0	0	0	.167	.167	.167	-8	-1	0-0	—	0			H	-0.1
Total	6	113	217	13	32	6	0	4	9	19-3	1	49	.147	.218	.230	27	-21	0-0	.983	-1	79	111	/C-67,O(RF)	-2.2
CAMPAU, COUNT Charles Columbus B 10.17.1863 Detroit, MI D 4.3.1938 New Orleans, LA BL/TR 5-11/160# d7.7 M1																								
1888	Det N	70	251	28	51	5	3	1	18	19	0	36	.203	.259	.259	65	-10	27	.933	-4	85	138	O-70(RF)	-1.4
1890	StL AA	75	314	68	101	9	12	**9**	75	26	0		.322	.374	.513	141	12	36	.934	2	106	36	O-74(39-2-33)/31M	1.1
1894	Was N	2	7	1	1	0	0	0	0	1	0	4	.143	.250	.143	-3	-1	0	1.000	-0	0	0	/O-2(LF)	-0.1
Total	3	147	572	97	153	14	15	10	93	46	0	40	.267	.322	.397	109	1	63	.934	-2	95	84	O-146(41-2-103)/13	-0.4
CAMPBELL, VIN Arthur Vincent B 1.30.1888 St.Louis, MO D 11.16.1969 Towson, MD BL/TR 6/185# d6.6																								
1908	Chi N	1	1	0	0	0	0	0	0	0			.000	.000	.000	-96	0	0	—	0			H	0.0
1910	Pit N	97	282	42	92	9	5	4	21	26	4	23	.326	.391	.436	133	12	17	.895	-4	100	83	O-74(38-17-18)	0.5
1911	Pit N	42	93	12	29	3	1	0	10	8	0	7	.312	.366	.366	101	0	6	.923	-2	101	38	O-21(9-1-11)	-0.2
1912	Bos N	145	624	102	185	32	9	3	48	32	3	44	.296	.334	.391	96	-5	19	.938	-5	99	89	*O-144(CF)	-2.0
1914	Ind F	134	544	92	173	23	11	7	44	37	6	47	.318	.368	.439	108	-2	26	.925	-8	88	95	*O-132(1-94-37)	-1.8
1915	New F	127	525	78	163	18	10	1	44	29	5	35	.310	.352	.389	115	1	24	.947	-9	87	84	*O-126(0-12-115)	-1.7
Total	6	546	2069	326	642	85	36	15	167	132	18	156	.310	.357	.408	109	6	92	.929	-27	93	86	O-497(48-268-181)	-5.2
CAMPBELL, BRUCE Bruce Douglas B 10.20.1909 Chicago, IL D 6.17.1995 Ft.Myers Beach, FL BL/TR 6-1/185# d9.12 Mil 1942-45																								
1930	Chi A	5	10	4	5	1	1	0	5	1	0	2	.500	.545	.800	245	2	0-0	1.000	0	128	0	/O-4(LF)	0.2
1931	Chi A	4	17	4	7	2	0	2	5	0	1	4	.412	.444	.882	256	4	0-0	.900	-0	101	0	/O-4(LF)	0.3
1932	Chi A	7	18	3	4	1	0	0	2	0	0	2	.222	.222	.278	31	-2	0-1	1.000	-0	81	0	/O-4(3-0-1)	-0.3
	StL A	139	593	83	169	35	11	14	85	40	6	102	.285	.336	.452	97	-5	7-5	.935	4	107	119	*O-139(RF)	-0.9
	Year	146	611	86	173	36	11	14	87	40	**6**	104	.283	.333	.447	95	-6	7-6	.935	3	106	117	*O-143(3-0-140)	-1.2
1933	StL A	148	567	87	157	38	8	16	106	69	2	77	.277	.357	.457	108	6	10-4	.950	-5	87	134	*O-144(RF)	-0.6
1934	StL A	138	481	62	134	25	6	9	74	51	2	64	.279	.350	.412	88	-9	5-4	.935	1	97	147	*O-123(RF)	-1.5
1935	Cle A	80	308	56	100	26	3	7	54	31	2	33	.325	.390	.497	126	12	2-1	.992	-7	88	32	O-75(RF)	0.1
1936	Cle A	76	172	35	64	15	2	6	30	19	2	17	.372	.440	.587	150	14	2-1	.960	0	95	121	O-47(RF)	1.1
1937	Cle A	134	448	82	135	42	11	4	61	67	0	49	.301	.392	.471	116	13	4-5	.978	-0	91	129	*O-123(RF)	0.4
1938	Cle A	133	511	90	148	27	12	12	72	53	3	57	.290	.360	.460	106	3	11-7	.967	1	97	124	*O-122(RF)	-0.4
1939	Cle A	130	450	84	129	23	13	8	72	67	3	48	.287	.383	.449	116	12	7-6	.942	-4	87	134	*O-115(RF)	0.0
1940	†Det A	103	297	56	84	15	5	8	44	45	2	28	.283	.381	.448	104	3	2-7	.959	-1	97	108	O-74(RF)	-0.4
1941	Det A	141	512	72	141	28	10	15	93	68	3	67	.275	.364	.457	105	4	3-3	.976	-8	95	41	*O-133(RF)	-1.2
1942	Was A	122	378	41	105	17	5	5	63	37	1	34	.278	.344	.389	107	3	0-6	.955	0	109	63	O-87(20-0-68)	-0.4
Total	13	1360	4762	759	1382	295	87	106	766	548	27	584	.290	.367	.455	108	60	53-50	.956	-20	95	107	*O-1194(31-0-1164)	-3.6
CAMPBELL, SOUP Clarence B 3.7.1915 Sparta, VA D 2.16.2000 Sparta, VA BL/TR 6-1/188# d4.21 Mil 1942-46																								
1940	Cle A	35	62	8	14	1	0	0	2	7	0	12	.226	.304	.242	45	-5	0-0	1.000	1	121	0	O-16(8-5-4)	-0.5
1941	Cle A	104	328	36	82	10	4	3	35	31	1	21	.250	.317	.332	75	-12	1-9	.981	0	101	92	O-78(20-59-0)	-1.7
Total	2	139	390	44	96	11	4	3	37	38	1	33	.246	.315	.318	70	-17	1-9	.984	1	104	80	/O-94(28-64-4)	-2.2
CAMPBELL, DAVE David Wilson B 1.14.1942 Manistee, MI BR/TR 6/185# d9.17																								
1967	Det A	2	2	0	0	0	0	0	0	0-0	0	1	.000	.000	.000	-97	0	0-0	.500	-0	0	0	/1	-0.1
1968	Det A	9	8	1	1	0	0	1	2	1-0	0	3	.125	.222	.500	111	0	0-0	1.000	-1	64	113	/2-5	0.0
1969	Det A	32	39	4	4	1	0	0	2	4-0	1	15	.103	.205	.128	-5	-5	0-1	.967	-2	41	137	1-13/2-5,3	-0.9
1970	SD N	154	581	71	127	28	2	12	40	40-2	1	115	.219	.268	.336	64	-32	18-6	.974	18	111	96	*2-153	-0.2
1971	SD N	108	365	38	83	14	2	7	29	37-0	0	75	.227	.299	.334	85	-8	9-6	.968	2	111	95	2-69,3-40/S-4,1-2,O-2(LF)	-0.2
1972	SD N	33	100	6	24	5	0	0	3	11-2	0	12	.240	.315	.290	79	-3	0-4	.988	1	101	53	3-31/2	-0.4
1973	SD N	33	98	2	22	3	0	0	8	7-1	0	15	.224	.271	.255	52	-6	1-1	.979	4	103	107	2-27/1-3,3-2	-0.2
	StL N	13	21	1	0	0	0	0	1	1-0	0	6	.000	.043	.000	-87	-5	0-0	.933	-3	68	41	/2-6	-0.8
	Hou N	9	15	1	4	2	0	0	2	0-0	0	4	.267	.267	.400	83	0	0-0	1.000	2	161	146	/3-5,1-2,O(LF)	0.1
	Year	55	134	4	26	5	0	0	11	8-1	0	25	.194	.234	.231	33	-12	1-1	.975	3	98	98	2-33/3-7,1-5,O(LF)	-0.9
1974	Hou N	35	23	4	2	1	0	0	2	1-0	0	8	.087	.125	.130	-30	-4	1-0	.895	2	102	198	/2-9,1-6,3-2,O(LF)	-0.2
Total	8	428	1252	128	267	54	4	20	89	102-5	2	254	.213	.272	.311	64	-63	29-18	.971	22	109	96	2-275/3-81,1-27,O-4(LF),S-4	-2.9
CAMPBELL, JIM James Robert B 6.24.1937 Palo Alto, CA BR/TR 6/190# d7.17																								
1962	Hou N	27	86	6	19	4	0	3	6	6-0	0	23	.221	.272	.372	77	-3	0-0	.970	2	77	111	C-25	0.0
1963	Hou N	55	158	9	35	3	0	4	19	10-3	0	40	.222	.268	.316	72	-6	0-0	.979	-1	88	95	C-42	-0.6
Total	2	82	244	15	54	7	0	7	25	16-3	0	63	.221	.269	.336	74	-9	0-0	.975	0	84	101	/C-67	-0.6
CAMPBELL, JIM James Robert B 1.10.1943 Hartsville, SC BL/TR 6/205# d4.11																								
1970	StL N	13	13	0	3	0	0	0	1	0-0	0	3	.231	.231	.231	24	-1	0-0	—	0			H	-0.1
CAMPBELL, JOE Joseph Earl B 3.10.1944 Louisville, KY BR/TR 6-1/175# d5.3																								
1967	Chi N	1	3	0	0	0	0	0	0	0-0	0	3	.000	.000	.000	-96	-1	0-0	—	-0	0	0	/O(RF)	-0.1

Year	Tm Lg	G	AB	R	H	2B	3B	HR	RBI	BB-IB	HP	SO	AVG	OBP	SLG	AOPS	ABR	SB-CS	FA	FR	Rng	Thr	G at Pos	BFW
CAMPBELL, HUTCH Marc Thaddeus B 11.29.1884 Punxsutawney, PA D 2.13.1946 New Bethlehem, PA BB/TR 5-9/155# d9.30																								
1907	Pit N	2	4	0	1	0	0	0	1	1	0		.250	.400	.250	102	0	0	.889	0	132	0	/S-2	0.0
CAMPBELL, MAT Mathew B 8.1.1850 , Ireland D 1.12.1926 Scotch Plains, NJ d4.28 b-Hugh																								
1873	Res NA	21	84	9	12	2	0	0	2	2		6	.143	.163	.167	-2	-10	1-0	.938	-2	75	89	1-18/S-3,O(RF)	-0.8
CAMPBELL, PAUL Paul McLaughlin B 9.1.1917 Paw Creek, NC BL/TL 5-10/185# d4.15 Mil 1943-45																								
1941	Bos A	1	0	0	0	0	0	0	0	0	0	0	—	—	—	—	0	0-0	—	0			R	0.0
1942	Bos A	26	15	4	1	0	0	0	0	1	0	5	.067	.125	.067	-44	-3	1-0	1.000	0	162	0	/O-4(CF)	-0.3
1946	†Bos A	28	26	3	3	1	0	0	0	2	0	7	.115	.179	.154	-6	-4	0-0	1.000	-0	50	81	/1-5	-0.4
1948	Det A	59	83	15	22	1	1	1	11	1	0	10	.265	.274	.337	60	-5	0-0	.969	2	164	71	1-27	-0.4
1949	Det A	87	255	38	71	15	4	3	30	24	1	32	.278	.343	.404	97	-2	3-3	.988	-3	83	108	1-74	-0.7
1950	Det A	3	1	1	0	0	0	0	0	0	0	0	.000	.000	.000	-97	0	0-0	—	0			H	0.0
Total	6	204	380	61	97	17	5	4	41	28	1	54	.255	.308	.358	76	-14	4-3	.984	-1	98	99	1-106/O-4(CF)	-1.8
CAMPBELL, RON Ronald Thomas B 4.5.1940 Chattanooga, TN BR/TR 6-1/180# d9.1																								
1964	Chi N	26	92	7	25	6	1	1	10	1-0	0	21	.272	.277	.391	83	-2	0-1	.941	7	131	98	2-26	0.7
1965	Chi N	2	2	0	0	0	0	0	0	0-0	0	0	.000	.000	.000	-98	-1	0-0	—	0			H	-0.1
1966	Chi N	24	60	4	13	1	0	0	4	6-2	0	5	.217	.284	.233	46	-4	1-1	.980	3	124	97	S-11/3-7	-0.1
Total	3	52	154	11	38	7	1	1	14	7-2	0	26	.247	.276	.325	67	-7	1-2	.941	10	131	98	/2-26,S-11,3-7	0.5
CAMPBELL, SAM Samuel B Philadelphia, PA d10.11																								
1890	Phi AA	2	5	0	0	0	0	0	0	1	0		.000	.167	.000	-51	-1	0	.833	-1	25	0	/2-2	-0.2
CAMPBELL, GILLY William Gilthorpe B 2.13.1908 Kansas City, KS D 2.21.1973 Los Angeles, CA BL/TR 5-7.5/182# d4.25																								
1933	Chi N	46	89	11	25	3	1	1	10	7	2	4	.281	.347	.371	105	1	0	.949	-1	*142*	*83*	C-20	0.1
1935	Cin N	88	218	26	56	7	0	3	30	42	1	7	.257	.379	.330	95	1	3	.986	-1	*90*	*117*	C-66/1-5,O(LF)	0.3
1936	Cin N	89	235	28	63	13	1	1	40	43	1	14	.268	.384	.345	104	4	2	.984	3	*97*	*119*	C-71/1	1.1
1937	Cin N	18	40	3	11	2	0	0	2	5	0	1	.275	.356	.325	90	0	0	.967	-1	*80*	*86*	C-17	0.0
1938	Bro N	54	126	10	31	5	0	0	11	19	2	9	.246	.354	.286	76	-3	0	.958	-1	*82*	*121*	C-44	-0.1
Total	5	295	708	78	186	30	2	5	93	116	6	35	.263	.371	.332	96	3	5	.975	0	*95*	*113*	C-218/1-6,O(LF)	1.4
CAMPOS, FRANK Francisco Jose (Lopez) B 5.11.1924 Havana, Cuba BL/TL 5-11/180# d9.11																								
1951	Was A	8	26	4	11	3	1	0	3	0	0	1	.423	.423	.615	182	3	0-0	1.000	-1	74	0	/O-7(RF)	0.2
1952	Was A	53	112	9	29	6	1	0	8	1	2	13	.259	.278	.330	71	-5	0-0	.978	-1	104	0	O-23(13-1-10)	-0.7
1953	Was A	10	9	0	1	0	0	0	2	1	0	0	.111	.200	.111	-14	-1	0-0	—	0			H	-0.1
Total	3	71	147	13	41	9	2	0	13	2	2	14	.279	.298	.367	86	-3	0-0	.981	-2	99	0	/O-30(13-1-17)	-0.6
CAMPUSANO, SIL Silvestre (Diaz) B 12.31.1965 Santo Domingo, D.R. BR/TR 6/175# d4.4																								
1988	Tor A	73	142	14	31	10	2	2	12	9-0	4	33	.218	.282	.359	78	-4	0-0	.934	-2	96	82	O-69(15-35-19)/D-2	-0.7
1990	Phi N	66	85	10	18	1	1	2	9	6-0	1	16	.212	.269	.318	62	-5	1-0	.976	-3	78	78	O-47(16-25-7)	-0.8
1991	Phi N	15	35	2	4	0	0	1	2	1-0	0	10	.114	.139	.200	-6	-5	0-0	1.000	1	111	177	O-15(1-15-0)	-0.5
Total	3	154	262	26	53	11	3	5	23	16-0	5	59	.202	.260	.324	62	-14	1-0	.953	-4	93	94	O-131(32-75-26)/D-2	-2.0
CANALE, GEORGE George Anthony B 8.11.1965 Memphis, TN BL/TR 6-1/190# d9.3																								
1989	Mil A	13	26	5	5	1	0	1	3	2-0	0	3	.192	.250	.346	67	-1	0-1	.989	-1	70	58	1-11	-0.3
1990	Mil A	10	13	4	1	1	0	0	0	2-0	0	6	.077	.200	.154	0	-2	0-1	1.000	0	124	24	/1-6,D-3	-0.2
1991	Mil A	21	34	6	6	2	0	3	10	8-0	0	6	.176	.318	.500	130	2	0-0	.983	2	166	85	1-19	0.3
Total	3	44	73	15	12	4	0	4	13	12-0	0	15	.164	.276	.384	85	-1	0-2	.988	2	127	65	/1-36,D-3	-0.2
CANATE, WILLIE Emisael William (Librada) B 12.11.1971 Maracaibo, Venezuela BR/TR 6/170# d4.16																								
1993	†Tor A	38	47	12	10	0	0	1	3	6-0	1	15	.213	.309	.277	60	-3	1-1	1.000	2	111	205	O-31(17-6-9)/D	-0.1
CANAVAN, JIM James Edward B 11.26.1866 New Bedford, MA D 5.27.1949 New Bedford, MA BR/TR 5-8/160# d4.8 OF Total (105-LF 10-CF 106-RF)																								
1891	Cin AA	101	426	74	97	13	14	7	66	27	5	44	.228	.282	.373	80	-16	21	.860	-14	95	85	*S-101	-2.3
	Mil AA	35	142	33	38	2	4	3	21	16	0	10	.268	.342	.401	94	-3	7	.864	-2	107	44	2-24,S-11	-0.3
	Year	136	568	107	135	15	18	10	87	43	5	54	.238	.297	.380	84	-18	28	.860	-15	96	80	*S-112,2-24	-2.6
1892	Chi N	118	439	48	73	10	11	0	32	48	0	48	.166	.248	.239	47	-29	33	.923	-11	96	86	*2-112/O-4(1-3-0),S-2	-3.3
1893	Cin N	121	461	65	104	13	7	5	64	51	2	20	.226	.305	.317	64	-26	31	.931	-0	76	0	*O-117(96-6-16)/2-5,3	-2.9
1894	Cin N	103	364	81	100	16	10	13	74	64	0	25	.275	.383	.481	104	1	13	.897	-1	64	153	*O-97(8-1-90)/S-3,3-2,21	-0.4
1897	Bro N	63	240	25	52	9	3	2	34	26	2		.217	.299	.304	63	-13	9	.909	-17	84	84	2-63	-2.4
Total	5	541	2072	326	464	63	49	30	291	232	9	147	.224	.305	.345	74	-86	114	.917	-45	73	66	O-218R,2-205,S-117/3-3,1	-11.6
CANCEL, ROBINSON Robinson Castro B 5.4.1976 Lajas, P.R. BR/TR 6/195# d9.3																								
1999	Mil N	15	44	5	8	2	0	0	5	2-0	1	12	.182	.234	.227	18	-6	0-0	.980	3	83	107	C-15	-0.2
CANDAELE, CASEY Casey Todd B 1.12.1961 Lompoc, CA BB/TR 5-9/165# d6.5 OF Total (86-LF 78-CF 38-RF)																								
1986	Mon N	30	104	9	24	4	1	0	6	5-0	0	15	.231	.264	.288	53	-7	3-5	.983	1	103	96	2-24/3-4	-0.6
1987	Mon N	138	449	62	122	23	4	1	23	38-3	2	28	.272	.330	.347	78	-14	7-10	.985	3	106	77	2-68,O-67(8-45-16),S-25/1	-1.0
1988	Mon N	36	116	9	20	5	1	0	4	10-1	0	11	.172	.238	.233	34	-10	1-0	.988	-1	100	94	2-35	-1.1
	Hou N	21	31	2	5	3	0	0	1	1-0	0	6	.161	.188	.258	28	-3	0-1	1.000	2	121	105	2-10/O-5(0-3-2),3	-0.1
	Year	57	147	11	25	8	1	0	5	11-1	0	17	.170	.228	.238	33	-13	1-1	.990	1	104	96	2-45/O-5(0-3-2),3	-1.2
1990	Hou N	130	262	30	75	8	6	3	22	31-5	1	42	.286	.364	.397	112	5	7-5	1.000	1	111	55	O-58(36-12-13),2-49,S-13/3	0.6
1991	Hou N	151	461	44	121	20	7	4	50	40-7	0	49	.262	.319	.362	97	-2	9-3	.982	5	100	94	*2-109,O-26(18-5-4),3-11	0.6
1992	Hou N	135	320	19	68	12	1	1	18	24-3	3	36	.213	.269	.266	56	-19	7-1	.968	8	107	124	S-65,3-29,O-21(20-1-1)/2-9	-0.7
1993	Hou N	75	121	18	29	8	0	1	7	10-0	0	14	.240	.298	.331	70	-5	2-3	1.000	-2	69	57	2-19,O-17(4-12-2),S-14/3-4	-0.7
1996	†Cle A	24	44	8	11	2	0	1	4	1-0	0	9	.250	.267	.364	58	-3	0-0	1.000	6	130	219	2-11/3-3,S	0.3
1997	Cle A	14	26	5	8	1	0	0	4	1-0	0	1	.308	.333	.346	75	-1	1-0	1.000	4	174	124	/2-9,3D	0.4
Total	9	754	1934	206	483	86	20	11	139	161-19	6	211	.250	.308	.332	78	-59	37-28	.987	26	102	94	2-343,O-194L,S-118/3-54,D1	-2.3
CANGELOSI, JOHN John Anthony B 3.10.1963 Brooklyn, NY BB/TL 5-8/160# d6.3																								
1985	Chi A	5	2	2	0	0	0	0	0	0-0	1	1	.000	.333	.000	1	0	0-0	1.000	-1	31	0	/O-3(CF),D-2	-0.1
1986	Chi A	137	438	65	103	16	3	2	32	71-0	7	61	.235	.349	.299	77	-11	50-17	.969	-7	90	102	*O-129(29-98-5)/D-3	-1.5
1987	Pit N	104	182	44	50	8	3	4	18	46-1	3	33	.275	.427	.418	125	10	21-6	.962	0	99	129	O-47(27-16-8)	1.1
1988	Pit N	75	118	18	30	4	1	0	8	17-0	1	16	.254	.353	.305	92	0	9-4	.963	0	117	0	O-24(11-12-3)/P	0.0
1989	Pit N	112	160	18	35	4	2	0	9	35-2	3	20	.219	.365	.269	88	0	11-8	.973	1	114	67	O-46(12-24-10)	0.0
1990	Pit N	58	76	13	15	2	0	0	1	11-0	1	12	.197	.307	.224	50	-5	7-2	1.000	-1	86	0	O-12(3-9-0)	-0.6
1992	Tex A	73	85	12	16	2	0	1	6	18-0	0	16	.188	.330	.247	66	-3	6-5	.964	3	106	212	O-65(36-24-10)/D-6	-0.2
1994	NY N	62	111	14	28	4	0	0	4	19-1	2	20	.252	.371	.288	76	-3	5-1	1.000	4	104	264	O-50(24-13-19)	0.0
1995	Hou N	90	201	46	64	5	2	2	18	48-2	4	42	.318	.457	.393	137	15	21-5	.950	-1	95	116	O-59(26-32-1)/P	1.6
1996	Hou N	108	262	49	69	11	4	1	16	44-0	5	41	.263	.378	.347	101	3	17-9	.975	1	97	156	O-78(53-29-0)	0.3
1997	†Fla N	103	192	28	47	8	0	1	12	19-1	3	33	.245	.321	.302	68	-9	5-1	1.000	1	112	46	O-58(34-23-6)/P	-0.8
1998	Fla N	104	171	19	43	8	0	1	10	30-0	1	23	.251	.365	.316	86	-2	2-3	.969	-1	96	56	O-45(9-33-8)/D	-0.4
1999	Col N	7	6	0	1	1	0	0	0	0-0	0	4	.167	.167	.333	18	-1	0-0	1.000	0	226	0	/O(LF)	-0.1
Total	13	1038	2004	328	501	73	15	12	134	358-7	31	322	.250	.370	.319	90	-6	154-61	.972	-1	99	114	O-617(265-317-70)/D-12,P-3	-0.7
CANIZARO, JAY Jason Kyle B 7.4.1973 Beaumont, TX BR/TR 5-9/170# d4.28																								
1996	SF N	43	120	11	24	4	1	2	8	9-0	1	38	.200	.260	.300	50	-9	0-2	.972	-1	103	89	2-35/S-7	-0.9
1999	SF N	12	18	5	8	2	0	1	9	1-0	0	2	.444	.474	.722	212	3	1-0	1.000	-1	89	74	/2-4	0.2
2000	Min A	102	346	43	93	21	1	7	40	24-0	1	57	.269	.318	.396	76	-13	4-2	.982	-24	86	71	2-90/D-2	-3.0
2002	Min A	38	112	14	24	8	1	0	11	10-0	1	22	.214	.280	.304	56	-7	0-1	.990	-4	91	90	2-30/3-8	-1.0
Total	4	195	596	73	149	35	3	10	68	44-0	3	119	.250	.303	.369	71	-26	5-5	.981	-29	90	78	2-159/3-8,S-7,D-2	-4.7
CANNELL, RIP Virgin Wirt B 1.23.1880 S.Bridgton, ME D 8.26.1948 Bridgton, ME BL/TR 5-10.5/180# d4.14																								
1904	Bos N	100	346	32	81	5	1	0	18	23	2		.234	.286	.254	70	-12	10	.897	-10	44	26	O-93(15-10-69)	-2.9
1905	Bos N	154	567	52	140	14	4	0	36	51	2		.247	.311	.286	80	-13	17	.935	-11	69	117	*O-154(3-149-3)	-3.3
Total	2	254	913	84	221	19	5	0	54	74	4		.242	.302	.274	76	-25	27	.923	-21	60	83	O-247(18-159-72)	-6.2

Year	Tm Lg	G	AB	R	H	2B	3B	HR	RBI	BB-IB	HP	SO	AVG	OBP	SLG	AOPS	ABR	SB-CS	FA	FR	Rng	Thr	G at Pos	BFW
CANNIZZARO, CHRIS Christopher John B 5.3.1938 Oakland, CA BR/TR 6/190# d4.17 C3																								
1960	StL N	7	9	0	2	0	0	0	1	1-0	0	3	.222	.273	.222	42	-1	0-0	1.000	1	*121*	*136*	/C-6	0.1
1961	StL N	6	2	0	1	0	0	0	0	0-0	0	0	.500	.500	.500	151	0	0-0	1.000	0	*0*	*0*	/C-5	0.0
1962	NY N	59	133	9	32	2	1	0	9	19-1	1	26	.241	.335	.271	65	-6	1-1	.973	-1	*88*	*168*	C-56/O(RF)	-0.5
1963	NY N	16	33	4	8	1	0	0	4	1-0	0	8	.242	.257	.273	54	-2	0-0	1.000	0	*127*	*114*	C-15	-0.2
1964	NY N	60	164	11	51	10	0	0	10	14-2	1	28	.311	.367	.372	112	3	0-5	.988	1	*84*	*132*	C-53	0.5
1965	NY N	114	251	17	46	8	2	0	7	28-4	2	60	.183	.270	.231	44	-18	0-2	.977	7	*91*	***148***	*C-112	-0.8
1968	Pit N	25	58	5	14	2	2	1	7	9-4	0	13	.241	.343	.397	123	2	0-0	.976	-1	*106*	*97*	C-25	0.3
1969	SD N☆	134	418	23	92	14	3	4	33	42-8	0	81	.220	.290	.297	68	-18	0-1	.988	-10	92	118	*C-132	-2.4
1970	SD N	111	341	27	95	13	3	5	42	48-8	1	49	.279	.366	.378	105	4	2-7	.980	-9	116	89	*C-110	-0.2
1971	SD N	21	63	2	12	1	0	1	8	11-0	1	10	.190	.320	.254	69	-2	0-0	.992	-0	118	68	C-19	-0.1
	Chi N	71	197	18	42	8	1	5	23	28-2	1	24	.213	.311	.340	74	-6	0-0	.983	-12	81	99	C-70	-1.6
	Year	92	260	20	54	9	1	6	31	39-2	2	34	.208	.314	.319	73	-8	0-0	.985	-12	90	92	C-89	-1.7
1972	LA N	73	200	14	48	6	0	2	18	31-5	0	38	.240	.341	.300	86	-3	0-1	.983	-6	99	56	C-72	-0.6
1973	LA N	17	21	0	4	0	0	0	3	3-1	0	3	.190	.280	.190	38	-2	0-0	1.000	-2	100	0	C-13	-0.4
1974	SD N	26	60	2	11	1	0	0	4	6-0	0	11	.183	.258	.200	31	-6	0-0	.979	-2	93	87	C-26	-0.7
Total	13	740	1950	132	458	66	12	18	169	241-35	7	354	.235	.319	.309	77	-55	3-17	.983	-31	*97*	*109*	C-714/O(RF)	-6.6
CANNON, JOE Joseph Jerome B 7.13.1953 Camp Lejeune, NC BL/TR 6-3/193# d9.22																								
1977	Hou N	9	17	3	2	2	0	0	1	0-0	0	5	.118	.118	.235	-9	-3	1-1	1.000	0	125	0	/O-3(LF)	-0.3
1978	Hou N	8	18	1	4	0	0	0	1	0-0	0	1	.222	.222	.222	26	-2	0-1	.778	-1	87	0	/O-5(3-2-0)	-0.3
1979	Tor A	61	142	14	30	1	1	1	5	1-0	0	34	.211	.217	.254	26	-15	12-2	1.000	3	104	176	O-50(17-0-40)	-1.2
1980	Tor A	70	50	16	4	0	0	0	4	0-0	1	14	.080	.098	.080	-48	-10	2-2	.968	-1	80	96	O-33(18-16-0)/D	-1.2
Total	4	148	227	34	40	3	1	1	11	1-0	1	54	.176	.183	.211	7	-30	15-6	.977	1	98	136	/O-91(41-18-40),D	-3.0
CANSECO, JOSE Jose (Capas) B 7.2.1964 Havana, Cuba BR/TR 6-4/240# d9.2 twb-Ozzie																								
1985	Oak A	29	96	16	29	3	0	5	13	4-0	0	31	.302	.330	.490	130	3	1-1	.951	1	104	117	O-26(13-1-16)	0.3
1986	Oak A☆	157	600	85	144	29	1	33	117	65-1	8	175	.240	.318	.457	118	14	15-7	.958	-7	98	39	*O-155(124-0-46)/D	0.1
1987	Oak A	159	630	81	162	35	3	31	113	50-2	2	157	.257	.310	.470	111	8	15-3	.975	6	104	141	*O-130(LF),D-30	1.0
1988	†Oak A★	158	610	120	187	34	0	**42**	**124**	78-10	10	128	.307	.391	**.569**	**172**	60	40-16	.978	2	99	123	*O-144(RF),D-13	6.0
1989	†Oak A✱	65	227	40	61	9	1	17	57	23-4	2	69	.269	.333	.542	151	14	6-3	.976	2	105	120	O-56(RF)/D-5	1.4
1990	†Oak A★	131	481	83	132	14	2	37	101	72-8	5	158	.274	.371	.543	160	39	19-10	.995	1	102	109	O-88(RF),D-43	3.6
1991	Oak A	154	572	115	152	32	1	**44**	122	78-7	9	152	.266	.359	.556	159	46	26-6	.965	-7	96	54	*O-131(RF),D-24	3.8
1992	Oak A✱	97	366	66	90	11	0	22	72	48-1	3	104	.246	.335	.456	127	13	5-7	.988	1	103	95	O-77(RF),D-20	0.9
	Tex A	22	73	8	17	4	0	4	15	15-1	3	24	.233	.385	.452	139	5	1-0	.970	1	126	0	O-13(RF)/D-8	0.5
	Year	119	439	74	107	15	0	26	87	63-2	6	128	.244	.344	.456	129	17	6-7	.985	2	106	81	O-90(RF),D-28	1.4
1993	Tex A	60	231	30	59	14	1	10	46	16-2	3	62	.255	.308	.455	107	1	6-6	.970	-1	92	110	O-49(RF)/P	-0.3
1994	Tex A	111	429	88	121	19	2	31	90	69-8	5	114	.282	.386	.552	139	26	15-8	—	0	0	0	*D-111	1.7
1995	†Bos A	102	396	64	121	25	1	24	81	42-4	7	93	.306	.378	.556	136	21	4-0	1.000	-0	64	0	*D-101/O(RF)	1.4
1996	Bos A	96	360	68	104	22	1	28	82	63-3	6	82	.289	.400	.589	144	25	3-1	1.000	-1	80	140	D-84,O-11(10-0-2)	1.7
1997	Oak A	108	388	56	91	19	0	23	74	51-1	3	122	.235	.325	.461	105	2	8-2	.938	-4	86	73	D-56,O-44(19-0-27)	-0.6
1998	Tor A	151	583	98	138	26	0	46	107	65-5	6	159	.237	.318	.518	112	8	29-17	.960	-1	95	101	D-78,O-73(50-0-26)	-0.1
1999	TB A✱	113	430	75	120	18	1	34	95	58-3	7	135	.279	.369	.563	133	21	3-0	1.000	0	77	338	*D-106/O-6(LF)	1.3
2000	TB A	61	218	31	56	15	0	9	30	41-1	4	65	.257	.383	.450	111	5	2-0	—	0	0	0	D-60	0.2
	†NY A	37	111	16	27	3	0	6	19	23-1	0	37	.243	.365	.432	104	1	0-0	.818	-0	118	0	D-26/O-5(4-0-1)	-0.1
	Year	98	329	47	83	18	0	15	49	64-2	4	102	.252	.377	.444	109	7	2-0	.730	-0	118	0	D-86/O-5(4-0-1)	0.1
2001	Chi A	76	256	46	66	8	0	16	49	45-1	1	75	.258	.366	.477	117	7	2-1	1.000	-1	34	0	D-68/O-2(RF)	0.2
Total	17	1887	7057	1186	1877	340	14	462	1407	906-63	84	1942	.266	.353	.515	132	319	200-88	.971	-8	99	94	*O-1011(356-1-679),D-834/P	23.0
CANSECO, OZZIE Osvaldo (Capas) B 7.2.1964 Havana, Cuba BR/TR 6-2/220# d7.18 twb-Jose																								
1990	Oak A	9	19	1	2	1	0	0	1	1-0	0	10	.105	.150	.158	-14	-3	0-0	1.000	-0	86	0	/O-2(1-0-1),D-4	-0.3
1992	StL N	9	29	7	8	5	0	0	3	7-0	0	4	.276	.417	.448	150	3	0-0	.889	-2	48	0	/O-8(7-0-1)	0.0
1993	StL N	6	17	0	3	0	0	0	0	1-0	0	3	.176	.222	.176	8	-2	0-0	.500	-2	13	0	/O-5(LF)	-0.4
Total	3	24	65	8	13	6	0	0	4	9-0	0	17	.200	.297	.292	67	-2	0-0	.857	-4	42	0	/O-15(13-0-2),D-4	-0.7
CANTZ, BART Bartholomew L. B 1.29.1860 Philadelphia, PA D 2.12.1943 Philadelphia, PA d7.25																								
1888	Bal AA	37	126	7	21	2	1	0	9	2	0		.167	.180	.198	22	-11	0	.904	-7			C-33/O-4(1-0-3)	-1.5
1889	Bal AA	20	69	6	12	2	0	0	8	4	0	14	.174	.219	.203	20	-7	2	.860	-5			C-18/O-2(RF)	-0.9
1890	Phi AA	5	22	1	1	0	0	0	1	0	0		.045	.045	.045	-74	-5	0	.893	-2	*84*	*127*	/C-5	-0.6
Total	3	62	217	14	34	4	1	0	18	6	0	14	.157	.179	.184	11	-23	2	.890	-14	*8*	*12*	/C-56,O-6(1-0-5)	-3.0
CAPRA, NICK Nick Lee B 3.8.1958 Denver, CO BR/TR 5-8/165# d9.6																								
1982	Tex A	13	15	2	4	0	0	1	1	3-0	1	4	.267	.421	.467	151	1	2-1	1.000	2	131	586	/O-9(4-1-4)	0.3
1983	Tex A	8	2	2	0	0	0	0	0	0-0	0	0	.000	.000	.000	-99	-1	0-0	—	-0	0	0	/O-4(1-1-2)	-0.1
1985	Tex A	8	8	1	1	0	0	0	0	0-0	0	0	.125	.125	.125	-31	-1	0-0	1.000	1	158	0	/O-8(1-3-4)	-0.1
1988	KC A	14	29	3	4	1	0	0	0	2-0	0	3	.138	.194	.172	3	-4	1-0	1.000	-1	77	0	O-11(2-7-2)/D	-0.5
1991	Tex A	2	0	1	0	0	0	0	0	1-0	0	0	—	1.000	—	205	0	0-0	1.000	0	242	0	/O-2(1-1-0)	0.1
Total	5	45	54	9	9	1	0	1	1	6-0	1	7	.167	.262	.241	41	-5	3-1	1.000	2	111	175	/O-34(9-13-12),D	-0.3
CAPRI, PAT Patrick Nicholas B 11.27.1918 New York, NY D 6.14.1989 New York, NY BR/TR 6-0.5/170# d7.16																								
1944	Bos N	7	1	1	0	0	0	0	0	0	0	1	.000	.000	.000	-96	0	0	1.000	1	287	732	/2	0.0
CAPRON, RALPH Ralph Earl B 6.16.1889 Minneapolis, MN D 9.19.1980 Los Angeles, CA BL/TR 5-11.5/165# d4.25																								
1912	Pit N	1	0	0	0	0	0	0	0	0	0	0	—	—	—	—	0	0	—	0			R	0.0
1913	Phi N	2	1	1	0	0	0	0	0	0	0	0	.000	.000	.000	-96	0	0	—	-0	0	0	/O(LF)	0.0
Total	2	3	1	1	0	0	0	0	0	0	0	0	.000	.000	.000	-96	0	0	.000	-0	0	0	/O(LF)	0.0
CARABALLO, RAMON Ramon (Sanchez) B 5.23.1969 Rio San Juan, D.R. BB/TR 5-7/150# d9.9																								
1993	Atl N	6	0	0	0	0	0	0	0	0-0	0	0	—	—	—	—	0	0-0	1.000	1	116	0	/2-5	0.1
1995	StL N	34	99	10	20	4	1	2	3	6-0	3	33	.202	.269	.323	55	-7	3-2	.956	4	115	139	2-24	-0.1
Total	2	40	99	10	20	4	1	2	3	6-0	3	33	.202	.269	.323	55	-7	3-2	.958	5	115	134	/2-29	0.0
CARBINE, JOHN John C. B 10.12.1855 Syracuse, NY D 9.11.1915 Chicago, IL 6/187# d5.8																								
1875	Wes NA	10	36	0	3	0	0	0	2	0		1	.083	.083	.083	-40	-5	0-0	.950	1	154	111	1-10	-0.4
1876	Lou N	7	25	3	4	0	0	0	1	0		0	.160	.160	.160	6	-3		.878	-0	88	219	/1-6,O(RF)	-0.3
CARBO, BERNIE Bernardo B 8.5.1947 Detroit, MI BL/TR 6/175# d9.2																								
1969	Cin N	4	3	0	0	0	0	0	0	0-0	0	2	.000	.000	.000	-95	-1	0-0	—	0			H	-0.1
1970	†Cin N	125	365	54	113	19	3	21	63	94-9	4	77	.310	.454	.551	168	42	10-4	.979	-1	93	101	*O-119(118-0-1)	3.4
1971	Cin N	106	310	33	68	20	1	5	20	54-4	2	56	.219	.338	.339	94	0	2-1	.982	1	94	118	O-90(LF)	-0.4
1972	Cin N	19	21	2	3	0	0	0	0	6-1	1	3	.143	.357	.143	50	-1	0-0	1.000	0	146	0	/O-4(RF)	-0.1
	StL N	99	302	42	78	13	1	7	34	57-9	5	56	.258	.381	.377	119	11	0-1	.967	7	103	236	O-92(RF)/3	1.3
	Year	118	323	44	81	13	1	7	34	63-10	6	59	.251	.380	.362	115	10	0-1	.969	7	104	228	O-96(RF)/3	1.2
1973	StL N	111	308	42	88	18	0	8	40	58-7	1	52	.286	.397	.422	128	15	2-0	.978	3	104	139	O-94(2-0-93)	1.5
1974	Bos A	117	338	40	84	20	0	12	61	58-7	4	90	.249	.364	.414	116	9	4-3	.994	0	100	82	O-87(33-0-56),D-15	0.5
1975	†Bos A	107	319	64	82	21	3	15	50	83-5	1	69	.257	.409	.483	140	21	2-4	.976	1	100	114	O-85(38-0-47),D-13	1.7
1976	Bos A	17	55	5	13	4	0	2	6	8-1	0	17	.236	.333	.418	106	1	1-0	1.000	0	100	0	D-15/O(LF)	0.0
	Mil A	69	183	20	43	7	0	3	15	33-3	0	55	.235	.352	.322	100	2	1-2	1.000	5	122	243	O-33(4-0-29),D-24	0.5
	Year	86	238	25	56	11	0	5	21	41-4	0	72	.235	.348	.345	102	2	2-2	1.000	5	122	239	D-39,O-34(5-0-29)	0.5
1977	Bos A	86	228	36	66	6	1	15	34	47-3	0	72	.289	.409	.522	136	13	1-2	.951	2	111	115	O-67(8-0-59)/D-7	1.2
1978	Bos A	17	46	7	12	3	0	1	6	8-0	0	8	.261	.370	.391	103	1	1-1	1.000	1	155	0	/O-9(1-0-8),D-8	0.1
	Cle A	60	174	21	50	8	0	4	16	20-1	1	31	.287	.362	.402	117	4	1-0	1.000	-1	23	0	D-49/O-4(RF)	0.2
	Year	77	220	28	62	11	0	5	22	28-1	1	39	.282	.364	.400	113	5	2-1	.976	1	127	0	D-57,O-13(1-0-12)	0.3
1979	StL N	52	64	6	18	1	0	3	12	10-0	0	22	.281	.368	.438	121	2	1-0	1.000	-2	57	0	O-17(4-0-13)	0.0
1980	StL N	14	11	0	2	0	0	0	0	1-0	0	0	.182	.250	.182	22	-1	0-0	—	0			H	-0.2
	Pit N	7	6	0	2	0	0	0	1	1-0	0	1	.333	.429	.333	114	0	0-0	—	0			/H	0.0

Year	Tm Lg	G	AB	R	H	2B	3B	HR	RBI	BB-IB	HP	SO	AVG	OBP	SLG	AOPS	ABR	SB-CS	FA	FR	Rng	Thr	G at Pos	BFW
	Year	21	17	0	4	0	0	0	1	2-0	0	1	.235	.316	.235	55	-1	0-0	—	0				-0.2
Total	12	1010	2733	372	722	140	9	96	358	538-50	19	611	.264	.387	.427	125	118	26-18	.978	17	101	131	O-702(299-0-406),D-131/3	9.6

CARDENAL, JOSE Jose Rosario Domec (born Jose Rosario Domec (Cardenal)) B 10.7.1943 Matanzas, Cuba BR/TR 5-10/150# d4.14 C10 OF Total (427-LF 847-CF 549-RF)

Year	Tm Lg	G	AB	R	H	2B	3B	HR	RBI	BB-IB	HP	SO	AVG	OBP	SLG	AOPS	ABR	SB-CS	FA	FR	Rng	Thr	G at Pos	BFW
1963	SF N	9	5	1	1	0	0	0	2	1-0	0	1	.200	.333	.200	58	0	0-1	—	-0	0	0	/O-2(0-1-1)	-0.1
1964	SF N	20	15	3	0	0	0	0	0	2-0	0	3	.000	.118	.000	-62	-3	2-0	.909	1	97	642	O-16(8-2-6)	-0.2
1965	Cal A	134	512	58	128	23	2	11	57	27-1	2	72	.250	.287	.367	87	-10	37-15	.964	0	99	**217**	*O-129(CF)/3-2,2	-1.1
1966	Cal A	154	561	67	155	15	3	16	48	34-5	4	69	.276	.320	.399	109	5	24-11	.992	2	103	111	*O-146(7-140-0)	0.4
1967	Cal A	108	381	40	90	13	5	6	27	15-0	2	63	.236	.268	.344	83	-10	10-5	.986	3	102	173	*O-101(27-70-17)	-1.1
1968	Cle A	157	583	78	150	21	7	7	44	39-3	2	74	.257	.305	.353	101	-1	40-18	.974	7	108	124	*O-153(CF)	0.4
1969	Cle A	146	557	75	143	26	3	11	45	49-3	0	58	.257	.314	.373	89	-8	36-6	.982	2	108	109	*O-142(1-141-0)/3-5	-0.4
1970	StL N	148	552	73	162	32	6	10	74	45-0	1	70	.293	.348	.428	104	3	26-9	.969	-9	91	78	*O-134(0-133-1)	-0.7
1971	StL N	89	301	37	73	12	4	7	48	29-1	0	35	.243	.303	.379	90	-4	12-3	.969	7	118	162	O-83(0-8-78)	0.1
	Mil A	53	198	20	51	10	0	3	32	13-0	1	20	.258	.297	.354	88	-3	9-5	.979	3	107	183	O-52(0-45-7)	-0.2
1972	Chi N	143	533	96	155	24	6	17	70	55-3	1	58	.291	.356	.454	117	12	25-14	.971	-9	85	112	*O-137(8-16-125)	-0.3
1973	Chi N	145	522	80	158	33	2	11	68	58-9	5	62	.303	.375	.437	116	14	19-7	.980	-5	92	106	*O-142(1-2-142)	0.4
1974	Chi N	143	542	75	159	35	3	13	72	56-3	1	67	.293	.359	.441	118	14	23-9	.965	4	101	157	*O-137(32-1-108)	1.3
1975	Chi N	154	574	85	182	30	2	9	68	77-5	4	50	.317	.397	.423	124	22	34-12	.976	9	107	126	*O-151(137-0-18)	2.7
1976	Chi N	136	521	64	156	25	2	8	47	32-0	1	39	.299	.339	.401	101	1	23-14	.981	3	97	116	*O-128(127-0-2)	-0.3
1977	Chi N	100	226	33	54	12	1	3	18	28-2	1	30	.239	.324	.341	71	-8	5-4	.989	-4	84	30	O-62(54-6-2)/2S	-1.6
1978	†Phi N	87	201	27	50	12	0	4	33	23-2	0	16	.249	.323	.368	93	-2	2-3	.990	-5	71	136	1-50,O-13(10-0-4)	-1.0
1979	Phi N	29	48	4	10	3	0	0	9	8-1	0	8	.208	.321	.271	61	-2	1-0	1.000	-1	85	0	O-12(9-0-6)/1	-0.4
	NY N	11	37	8	11	4	0	2	4	6-0	1	3	.297	.409	.568	170	4	1-0	1.000	-1	102	0	/O-9(RF),1-2	0.3
	Year	40	85	12	21	7	0	2	13	14-1	1	11	.247	.360	.400	106	1	2-0	1.000	-2	93	0	O-21(9-0-15)/1-3	-0.1
1980	NY N	26	42	4	7	1	0	0	4	6-0	0	4	.167	.265	.190	32	-4	0-1	1.000	1	141	268	/O-6(2-0-4),1-5	-0.4
	†KC A	25	53	8	18	2	0	0	5	5-0	0	5	.340	.377	.377	112	1	0-0	.970	-1	84	150	O-23(4-0-19)	0.0
Total	18	2017	6964	936	1913	333	46	138	775	608-38	26	807	.275	.333	.395	102	21	329-137	.976	9	100	129	*O-1778C/1-58,3-7,2-2,S	-2.2

CARDENAS, LEO Leonardo Lazaro (Alfonso) "Chico" B 12.17.1938 Matanzas, Cuba BR/TR 5-10/163# d7.25

Year	Tm Lg	G	AB	R	H	2B	3B	HR	RBI	BB-IB	HP	SO	AVG	OBP	SLG	AOPS	ABR	SB-CS	FA	FR	Rng	Thr	G at Pos	BFW
1960	Cin N	48	142	13	33	2	4	1	12	6-0	0	32	.232	.264	.324	59	-9	0-0	.958	2	104	132	S-47	-0.4
1961	†Cin N	74	198	23	61	18	1	5	24	15-1	0	39	.308	.353	.485	119	6	1-0	.973	-4	94	72	S-63	0.6
1962	Cin N	153	589	77	173	31	4	10	60	39-4	5	99	.294	.341	.411	98	-1	2-5	.972	-10	95	89	*S-149	0.1
1963	Cin N	158	565	42	133	22	4	7	48	23-6	4	101	.235	.270	.326	69	-23	3-5	**.972**	-2	93	99	*S-157	-1.4
1964	Cin N★	**163**	597	61	150	32	2	9	69	41-10	2	110	.251	.299	.357	82	-14	4-4	.960	-11	85	97	*S-163	-1.2
1965	Cin N★	156	557	65	160	25	11	11	57	60-**25**	1	100	.287	.355	.431	113	11	1-4	.975	-2	90	93	*S-155	2.2
1966	Cin N★	**160**	568	59	145	25	4	20	81	45-**18**	1	87	.255	.309	.419	93	-6	9-4	**.980**	-15	87	88	*S-160	-0.6
1967	Cin N	108	379	30	97	14	3	2	21	34-16	2	77	.256	.320	.325	76	-10	4-5	.971	-10	90	87	*S-108	-1.2
1968	Cin N★	137	452	45	106	13	2	7	41	36-18	2	83	.235	.292	.319	79	-11	2-1	.955	-25	90	81	*S-136	-2.9
1969	†Min A	160	578	67	162	24	4	10	70	66-12	4	96	.280	.353	.388	106	6	5-6	.965	23	112	**134**	*S-160	5.0
1970	†Min A	160	588	67	145	34	4	11	65	42-2	4	101	.247	.300	.374	84	-14	2-5	.978	5	100	100	*S-160	0.9
1971	Min A☆	153	554	59	146	25	4	18	75	51-5	1	69	.264	.321	.421	107	4	3-3	**.985**	0	95	96	*S-153	2.4
1972	Cal A	150	551	25	123	11	2	6	42	35-4	2	73	.223	.272	.283	69	-23	1-2	.970	8	98	90	*S-150	0.2
1973	Cle A	72	195	9	42	4	0	0	12	13-0	0	42	.215	.264	.236	41	-15	1-4	.964	-12	84	86	S-67/3-5	-2.2
1974	Tex A	34	92	5	25	3	0	0	7	2-1	0	14	.272	.287	.304	72	-4	1-0	1.000	2	106	29	3-21,S-10/D-4	-0.1
1975	Tex A	55	102	15	24	2	0	1	5	14-0	0	12	.235	.328	.284	75	-3	0-0	.956	8	122	153	3-43/S-5,2-3	0.5
Total	16	1941	6707	662	1725	285	49	118	689	522-122	28	1135	.257	.311	.367	88	-106	39-48	.971	-43	94	96	*S-1843/3-69,D-4,2-3	1.9

CARDONA, JAVIER Javier Peterson B 9.15.1975 Santurce, P.R. BR/TR 6-1/185# d5.31

Year	Tm Lg	G	AB	R	H	2B	3B	HR	RBI	BB-IB	HP	SO	AVG	OBP	SLG	AOPS	ABR	SB-CS	FA	FR	Rng	Thr	G at Pos	BFW
2000	Det A	26	40	1	7	1	0	1	2	0-0	1	9	.175	.190	.275	18	-5	0-0	.973	-4	99	58	C-26	-0.7
2001	Det A	46	96	10	25	8	0	1	10	2-0	1	12	.260	.280	.375	75	-4	0-1	.980	-8	199	111	C-44/D	-0.9
2002	SD N	15	39	2	4	1	0	0	2	2-0	0	10	.103	.143	.128	-28	-8	0-0	.976	-2	134	131	C-14	-0.9
Total	3	87	175	13	36	10	0	2	14	4-0	2	31	.206	.228	.297	39	-17	0-1	.977	-13	161	102	/C-84,D	-2.5

CAREW, ROD Rodney Cline B 10.1.1945 Gatun, Canal Zone BL/TR 6/182# d4.11 C10 HF1991 OF Total (LF)

Year	Tm Lg	G	AB	R	H	2B	3B	HR	RBI	BB-IB	HP	SO	AVG	OBP	SLG	AOPS	ABR	SB-CS	FA	FR	Rng	Thr	G at Pos	BFW
1967	Min A★	137	514	66	150	22	7	8	51	37-4	2	91	.292	.341	.409	112	7	5-9	.976	-2	97	86	*2-134	1.6
1968	Min A★	127	461	46	126	27	2	1	42	26-1	1	71	.273	.312	.347	95	-2	12-4	.968	-5	96	77	*2-117/S-4	0.5
1969	†Min A★	123	458	79	152	30	4	8	56	37-0	3	72	**.332**	.386	.467	135	22	19-8	.970	-6	102	116	*2-118	2.5
1970	†Min A✳	51	191	27	70	12	3	4	28	11-0	2	28	.366	.407	.524	153	13	4-6	.961	-5	101	99	2-45/1	1.0
1971	Min A★	147	577	88	177	16	10	2	48	45-1	1	81	.307	.356	.380	106	4	6-7	.976	-21	87	80	*2-142/3-2	-1.0
1972	Min A★	142	535	61	170	21	6	0	51	43-9	2	60	**.318**	.369	.379	118	13	12-6	.978	2	100	103	*2-139	2.6
1973	Min A★	149	580	98	**203**	30	**11**	6	62	62-9	2	55	**.350**	.411	.471	143	35	41-16	.984	10	98	96	*2-147	**5.8**
1974	Min A★	153	599	86	**218**	30	5	3	55	74-9	1	49	**.364**	**.433**	.446	149	42	38-16	.960	13	100	104	*2-148	**6.9**
1975	Min A★	143	535	89	192	24	4	14	80	64-**18**	1	40	**.359**	**.421**	.497	159	43	35-9	.973	12	106	95	*2-123,1-14/D-2	6.7
1976	Min A★	156	605	97	200	29	12	9	90	67-14	1	52	.331	.395	.463	149	38	49-22	.989	-3	97	**113**	*1-152/2-7	2.7
1977	Min A★	155	616	**128**	**239**	38	**16**	14	100	69-**15**	3	55	**.388**	**.449**	.570	**179**	**70**	23-13	.994	7	114	**124**	*1-151/2-4,D	**6.6**
1978	Min A★	152	564	85	188	26	10	5	70	78-**19**	1	62	**.333**	**.411**	.441	138	32	27-7	.989	-0	105	111	*1-148/2-4,O(LF)	2.7
1979	†Cal A✳	110	409	78	130	15	3	3	44	73-7	0	46	.318	.419	.391	125	19	18-8	.988	-8	72	108	*1-103/D-6	0.6
1980	Cal A★	144	540	74	179	34	7	3	59	59-7	1	38	.331	.396	.437	132	26	23-15	.994	-4	82	81	*1-103,D-32	1.4
1981	Cal A★	93	364	57	111	17	1	2	21	45-7	0	45	.305	.380	.374	118	11	16-9	.995	-1	98	114	1-90/D-2	0.5
1982	†Cal A✳	138	523	88	167	25	5	3	44	67-5	2	49	.319	.396	.403	121	18	10-17	.992	1	106	105	*1-134	0.7
1983	Cal A★	129	472	66	160	24	2	2	44	57-9	1	48	.339	.409	.411	128	22	6-7	.994	-9	72	112	1-89,D-24/2-2	0.6
1984	Cal A★	93	329	42	97	8	1	3	31	40-1	0	39	.295	.367	.353	102	2	4-3	.981	-3	99	108	1-83/D	-0.5
1985	Cal A	127	443	69	124	17	3	2	39	64-9	1	47	.280	.371	.345	99	2	5-5	.994	-10	73	**128**	*1-116	-1.6
Total	19	2469	9315	1424	3053	445	112	92	1015	1018-144	25	1028	.328	.393	.429	131	417	353-187	.991	-32	94	111	*1-1184,*2-1130/D-68,S-4,3-2,O	40.3

CAREY, ANDY Andrew Arthur (born Andrew Arthur Hexem) B 10.18.1931 Oakland, CA BR/TR 6-1/195# d5.2

Year	Tm Lg	G	AB	R	H	2B	3B	HR	RBI	BB-IB	HP	SO	AVG	OBP	SLG	AOPS	ABR	SB-CS	FA	FR	Rng	Thr	G at Pos	BFW
1952	NY A	16	40	6	6	0	0	0	1	3	0	10	.150	.209	.150	1	-5	0-0	.889	-1	102	185	3-14/S	-0.7
1953	NY A	51	81	14	26	5	0	4	8	9	0	12	.321	.389	.531	152	6	2-1	.988	5	121	172	3-40/S-2,2	1.1
1954	NY A	122	411	60	124	14	6	8	65	43	7	38	.302	.373	.423	123	13	5-5	.967	13	105	**141**	*3-120	2.5
1955	†NY A	135	510	73	131	19	**11**	7	47	44-6	1	51	.257	.313	.378	88	-11	3-3	.954	10	102	**138**	*3-135	-0.2
1956	†NY A	132	422	54	100	18	2	7	50	45-4	2	53	.237	.310	.339	75	-16	9-6	.947	-3	101	**102**	*3-131	-1.9
1957	†NY A	85	247	30	63	6	5	6	33	15-3	5	42	.255	.309	.393	92	-4	2-2	.977	1	101	72	3-81	-0.3
1958	†NY A	102	315	39	90	19	4	12	45	34-4	6	43	.286	.363	.486	137	16	1-2	.961	10	107	125	3-99	2.6
1959	NY A	41	101	11	26	1	0	3	9	7-0	0	17	.257	.306	.356	84	-3	1-1	.916	-1	85	203	3-34	-0.4
1960	NY A	4	3	1	1	0	0	0	1	0-0	0	1	.333	.333	.333	86	0	0-0	1.000	-0	143	0	/3-2,O(LF)	0.0
	KC A	102	343	30	80	14	4	12	53	26-0	1	52	.233	.287	.402	84	-9	0-0	.975	3	101	136	3-91	-0.6
	Year	106	346	31	81	14	4	12	54	26-0	1	53	.234	.287	.402	85	-9	0-0	.975	3	101	135	3-93/O(LF)	-0.6
1961	KC A	39	123	20	30	6	2	3	11	15-0	2	23	.244	.336	.398	94	-1	0-0	.944	2	105	165	3-39	0.0
	Chi A	56	143	21	38	12	3	0	14	11-0	2	24	.266	.323	.392	93	-1	0-1	.961	-4	95	57	3-54	-0.6
	Year	95	266	41	68	18	5	3	25	26-0	4	47	.256	.329	.395	93	-2	0-1	.953	-2	100	108	3-93	-0.6
1962	LA N	53	111	12	26	5	1	2	13	16-1	1	23	.234	.333	.351	90	-1	0-0	.932	-1	94	76	3-42	-0.2
Total	11	938	2850	371	741	119	38	64	350	268-18	27	389	.260	.327	.396	97	-16	23-21	.958	35	102	124	3-882/S-3,O(LF)2	1.3

CAREY, SCOOPS George C. B 12.4.1870 Pittsburgh, PA D 12.17.1916 E.Liverpool, OH BR/TR 5-11/175# d4.26

Year	Tm Lg	G	AB	R	H	2B	3B	HR	RBI	BB-IB	HP	SO	AVG	OBP	SLG	AOPS	ABR	SB-CS	FA	FR	Rng	Thr	G at Pos	BFW
1895	†Bal N	123	490	59	128	21	6	1	75	27	4	32	.261	.305	.335	63	-29	2	**.987**	-7	65	**112**	*1-123/O(CF)S3	-2.9
1898	Lou N	8	32	1	6	1	1	0	1	1	0		.188	.212	.281	42	-3	0	.961	-0	118	92	/1-8	-0.3
1902	Was A	120	452	46	142	35	11	0	60	20	5		.314	.350	.440	117	10	3	**.989**	4	107	76	*1-120	1.1
1903	Was A	48	183	8	37	3	2	0	23	4	1		.202	.223	.240	38	-14	0	.977	-3	81	75	1-47	-1.9
Total	4	299	1157	114	313	60	20	1	159	52	10	32	.271	.308	.360	80	-36	5	.986	-5	86	91	1-298/3SO(CF)	-4.0

CAREY, MAX Max George "Scoops" (born Maximilian Carnarius) B 1.11.1890 Terre Haute, IN D 5.30.1976 Miami, FL BB/TR 5-11.5/170# d10.3 M2 C1 HF1961

Year	Tm Lg	G	AB	R	H	2B	3B	HR	RBI	BB-IB	HP	SO	AVG	OBP	SLG	AOPS	ABR	SB-CS	FA	FR	Rng	Thr	G at Pos	BFW
1910	Pit N	2	6	2	3	0	1	0	2	2	0	1	.500	.625	.833	307	2	0	1.000	1	149	239	/O-2(LF)	0.3
1911	Pit N	129	427	77	110	15	10	5	43	44	7	75	.258	.337	.375	95	-4	27	.975	7	**121**	66	*O-122(46-76-0)	-0.3
1912	Pit N	150	587	114	177	23	8	5	66	61	5	79	.302	.372	.394	111	10	45	.968	3	106	77	*O-150(145-6-0)	0.6
1913	Pit N	154	620	**99**	172	23	10	5	49	55	3	67	.277	.339	.371	107	6	**61**-17	.961	11	107	127	*O-154(144-11-0)	1.7

Year	Tm Lg	G	AB	R	H	2B	3B	HR	RBI	BB-IB	HP	SO	AVG	OBP	SLG	AOPS	ABR	SB-CS	FA	FR	Rng	Thr	G at Pos	BFW
1914	Pit N	156	593	76	144	25	**17**	1	31	59	2	56	.243	.313	.347	101	-1	38	.966	7	105	117	*O-154(LF)	-0.1
1915	Pit N	140	564	76	143	26	5	3	27	57	4	58	.254	.326	.333	101	2	**36**-17	.982	11	109	126	*O-139(LF)	1.0
1916	Pit N	154	599	90	158	23	11	7	42	59	7	58	.264	.337	.374	117	13	**63**-19	.983	22	113	**166**	*O-154(21-134-0)	3.6
1917	Pit N	155	588	82	174	21	12	1	51	58	10	38	.296	.369	.378	125	20	**46**	.979	21	**121**	136	*O-153(CF)	3.4
1918	Pit N	**126**	468	70	128	14	6	3	48	**62**	4	25	.274	.363	.348	113	10	**58**	.958	13	110	**146**	*O-126(CF)	1.6
1919	Pit N	66	244	41	75	10	2	0	9	25	2	24	.307	.376	.365	119	7	18	.947	1	114	63	O-63(CF)	0.4
1920	Pit N	130	485	74	140	18	4	1	35	59	3	31	.289	.369	.348	104	5	**52**-10	.967	-5	103	52	*O-129(CF)	-0.1
1921	Pit N	140	521	85	161	34	4	7	56	70	4	30	.309	.395	.430	115	16	37-12	.957	5	**115**	71	*O-139(CF)	1.8
1922	Pit N	**155**	629	140	207	28	12	10	70	**80**	4	26	.329	.408	.459	122	23	**51**-2	.969	10	109	116	*O-155(3-152-0)	3.5
1923	Pit N	153	610	120	188	32	**19**	6	63	73	7	28	.308	.388	.452	119	18	**51**-8	.962	12	108	137	*O-153(CF)	3.0
1924	Pit N	149	599	113	178	30	9	8	55	58	7	17	.297	.366	.417	108	8	**49**-13	.965	2	103	97	*O-149(CF)	1.0
1925	†Pit N	133	542	109	186	39	13	5	44	66	4	19	.343	.418	.491	123	22	**46**-11	.950	4	99	**160**	*O-130(CF)	2.4
1926	Pit N	86	324	46	72	14	5	0	28	30	0	14	.222	.288	.296	55	-21	10	.943	1	104	104	O-82(CF)	-2.3
	Bro N	27	100	18	26	3	1	0	7	8	0	5	.260	.315	.310	70	-4	0	.933	-3	100	0	O-27(CF)	-0.8
	Year	113	424	64	98	17	6	0	35	38	0	19	.231	.294	.300	58	-25	10	.941	-2	103	78	*O-109(CF)	-3.1
1927	Bro N	144	538	70	143	30	10	1	54	64	1	18	.266	.345	.364	90	-6	32	.970	3	101	112	*O-141(1-38-108)	-1.4
1928	Bro N	108	296	41	73	11	0	2	19	47	2	24	.247	.354	.304	74	-9	18	.986	1	102	109	O-95(1-75-35)	-1.2
1929	Bro N	19	23	2	7	0	0	0	1	3	1	2	.304	.407	.304	81	0	0	1.000	-0	101	0	/O-4(0-2-2)	-0.1
Total	20	2476	9363	1545	2665	419	159	70	800	1040	77	695	.285	.361	.386	107	117	738-109	.966	127	108	111	*O-2421(656-1645-145)	18.0
CAREY, PAUL Paul Stephan B 1.8.1968 Boston, MA BL/TR 6-4/215# d5.25																								
1993	Bal A	18	47	1	10	1	0	0	3	5-0	0	14	.213	.288	.234	41	-4	0-0	.970	-2	21	122	/1-9,D-5	-0.6
CAREY, ROGER Roger J. d7.9																								
1887	NY N	1	4	0	0	0	0	0	2	0	0	1	.000	.000	.000	-99	-1	0	.800	0	143	193	/2	-0.1
CAREY, TOM Thomas Francis Aloysius "Scoops" B 10.11.1906 Hoboken, NJ D 2.21.1970 Rochester, NY BR/TR 5-8.5/170# d7.19 Mil 1943-45 C2																								
1935	StL A	76	296	29	86	18	4	0	42	13	0	11	.291	.320	.378	77	-11	0-2	.961	-3	100	93	2-76	-1.0
1936	StL A	134	488	58	133	27	6	1	57	27	3	25	.273	.315	.359	64	-29	2-1	.967	-1	**105**	86	*2-128/S	-2.0
1937	StL A	130	487	54	134	24	1	1	40	21	1	26	.275	.306	.335	61	-30	1-2	.983	-2	99	89	2-87,S-44/3	-2.2
1939	Bos A	54	161	17	39	6	2	0	20	3	2	9	.242	.265	.304	44	-14	0-0	1.000	6	111	106	2-35,S-10	-0.6
1940	Bos A	43	62	4	20	4	0	0	7	2	0	1	.323	.344	.387	86	-1	0-0	.953	3	121	162	S-20/2-4,3-4	0.3
1941	Bos A	25	21	7	4	0	0	0	2	0	0	2	.190	.190	.190	1	-3	0-0	1.000	2	105	169	/2-9,S-8,3	-0.1
1942	Bos A	1	1	0	1	0	0	0	1	0	0	0	1.000	1.000	1.000	448	0	0-0	1.000	-0	0	0	/2	0.0
1946	Bos A	3	5	0	1	0	0	0	0	0	0	1	.200	.200	.200	11	-1	0-0	.900	1	139	202	/2-3	0.0
Total	8	466	1521	169	418	79	13	2	169	66	6	75	.275	.308	.348	63	-89	3-5	.973	5	103	91	2-343/S-83,3-6	-5.6
CAREY, TOM Thomas John B 1849 Brooklyn, NY BR/TR 5-8/145# d5.4 M2 U2																								
1871	Kek NA	**19**	87	16	20	2	0	0	10	2		1	.230	.247	.253	43	-6	5-0	.857	0	96	74	2-19	-0.4
1872	Bal NA	42	196	42	57	7	0	2	27	2		2	.291	.298	.357	96	-2	4-1	.815	-13	63	39	2-29/S-9,3-3,O-3(RF),1	-1.1
1873	Bal NA	56	291	76	98	18	3	1	55	1		4	.337	.339	.430	127	10	2-3	.847	-3	94	106	*2-54/3-4,S-3,M	0.2
1874	Mut NA	64	287	56	82	10	3	1	38	2		4	.286	.291	.352	102	0	3-0	.776	-19	80	61	*S-51,2-13,M	-1.6
1875	Har NA	**86**	382	63	101	6	2	0	38	1		3	.264	.266	.291	89	-6	13-3	.844	-13	83	136	*S-86/2	-1.7
1876	Har N	68	289	51	78	7	0	0	26	3		4	.270	.277	.294	84	-6		.882	0	99	84	*S-68	-0.2
1877	Har N	**60**	274	38	70	3	2	1	20	0		9	.255	.255	.292	81	-5		.826	-7	107	84	*S-60	-0.8
1878	Pro N	61	253	33	60	10	3	0	24	0		14	.237	.237	.300	76	-7		.874	2	107	55	*S-61	-0.2
1879	Cle N	80	335	30	80	14	1	0	32	5		20	.239	.250	.287	77	-8		.864	-3	99	67	*S-80	-0.7
Total	5 NA	267	1243	253	358	43	8	4	168	8		14	.288	.293	.345	99	-4	27-7	.000	-47	82	105	S-149,2-116/3-7,O-3(RF),1	-4.6
Total	4	269	1151	152	288	34	6	1	102	8		47	.250	.255	.293	79	-26		.862	-8	103	72	S-269	-1.9
CARGO, BOBBY Robert J. B 10.1868 Pittsburgh, PA D 4.27.1904 Atlanta, GA BR/TR d10.6																								
1892	Pit N	2	4	0	1	0	0	0	0	0	0	0	.250	.250	.250	51	0	0	.636	-0	109	404	/S-2	-0.1
CARISCH, FRED Frederick Behlmer B 11.14.1881 Fountain City, WI D 4.19.1977 San Gabriel, CA BR/TR 5-10.5/174# d8.31 C2																								
1903	Pit N	5	18	4	6	4	0	1	5	0	0		.333	.333	.722	192	2	0	.969	1	*143*	*102*	/C-4	0.3
1904	Pit N	37	125	9	31	3	1	0	8	9	0		.248	.299	.288	79	-3	3	.984	2	*108*	*109*	C-22,1-14	0.1
1905	Pit N	32	107	7	22	0	3	0	8	2	1		.206	.227	.262	44	-8	1	.973	3	*126*	*97*	C-30	-0.3
1906	Pit N	4	12	0	1	0	0	0	0	1	0		.083	.154	.083	-25	-2	1	.909	-1	*114*	*107*	/C-4	-0.2
1912	Cle A	24	69	4	19	3	1	0	5	1	0		.275	.286	.348	78	-2	3	.952	4	*103*	*125*	C-23	0.4
1913	Cle A	82	222	11	48	4	2	0	26	21	1	19	.216	.287	.252	56	-12	6	.971	14	*126*	*94*	C-79	0.8
1914	Cle A	40	102	8	22	3	2	0	5	12	0	18	.216	.298	.284	72	-3	2-2	.962	-1	*89*	*90*	C-38	-0.2
1923	Det A	2	0	0	0	0	0	0	0	0	0	0	—	—	—	—	0	0-0	1.000	-0	*0*	*0*	/C-2	0.0
Total	8	226	655	43	149	17	9	1	57	46	2	37	.227	.280	.285	66	-28	16-2	.968	22	*115*	*99*	C-202/1-14	0.9
CARL, FRED Frederick E. B 9.8.1858 Baltimore, MD D 5.4.1919 Washington, DC BL/TL 5-6/158# d7.25																								
1889	Lou AA	25	99	13	20	2	2	0	13	16	0	22	.202	.313	.263	66	-4	0	.735	0	128	125	O-18(2-4-12)/2-6,3	-0.3
CARL, LEW Lewis Adolph B 1836 Baltimore, MD D 5.19.1885 Newark, NJ d9.9																								
1874	Bal NA	1	3	0	0	0	0	0	0	0		0	.000	.000	.000	-99	-1	0-0	.250	-1			/C	-0.1
CARLETON, JIM James Leslie B 8.20.1848 , NY D 4.25.1910 Detroit, MI 5-8/155# d5.4																								
1871	Cle NA	**29**	127	31	32	8	1	0	18	8		3	.252	.296	.331	85	-1	2-1	.898	-3	87	78	*1-29	-0.2
1872	Cle NA	7	38	8	12	1	0	0	4	1		0	.316	.333	.342	114	1	1-0	.956	2	483	135	/1-7	0.2
Total	2 NA	36	165	39	44	9	1	0	22	9		3	.267	.305	.333	91	0	3-1	.000	-1	165	89	/1-36	0.0
CARLIN, JIM James Arthur B 2.23.1918 Wylam, AL BR/TR 5-11/165# d7.26 Mil 1942-45																								
1941	Phi N	16	21	2	3	1	0	1	2	3	0	4	.143	.250	.333	66	-1	0	1.000	-1	55	0	/O-9(0-4-5),3-2	-0.2
CARLISLE, WALTER Walter G. "Rosy" B 7.6.1883 Yorkshire, England D 5.27.1945 Los Angeles, CA BB/TR 5-9/154# d5.8																								
1908	Bos A	3	10	0	1	0	0	0	0	1	0		.100	.182	.100	-8	-1	1	1.000	1	298	0	/O-3(LF)	-0.1
CARLSTROM, SWEDE Albin Oscar B 10.26.1886 Elizabeth, NJ D 4.28.1935 Elizabeth, NJ BR/TR 6/167# d9.12																								
1911	Bos A	2	6	0	1	0	0	0	0	0	0		.167	.167	.167	-7	-1	0	1.000	0	108	165	/S-2	0.0
CARLYLE, CLEO Hiram Cleo B 9.7.1902 Fairburn, GA D 11.12.1967 Los Angeles, CA BL/TR 6/170# d5.16 b-Roy																								
1927	Bos A	95	278	31	65	12	8	1	28	36	1	40	.234	.324	.345	75	-11	4-4	.965	-2	88	132	O-83(30-3-50)	-1.8
CARLYLE, ROY Roy Edward "Dizzy" B 12.10.1900 Buford, GA D 11.22.1956 Norcross, GA BL/TR 6-2.5/195# d4.16 b-Cleo																								
1925	Was A	1	1	0	0	0	0	0	0	0	0	1	.000	.000	.000	-99	0	0-0	—	0			H	0.0
	Bos A	93	276	36	90	20	3	7	49	16	1	28	.326	.365	.496	117	6	1-1	.909	-5	93	70	O-67(43-0-24)	-0.4
	Year	94	277	36	90	20	3	7	49	16	1	29	.325	.364	.495	116	6	1-1	.909	-5	93	70	O-67(43-0-24)	-0.4
1926	Bos A	45	165	22	47	6	2	2	16	4	2	18	.285	.310	.382	82	-5	0-0	.904	-5	81	88	O-38(RF)	-1.3
	NY A	35	62	3	20	5	1	0	11	4	1	9	.323	.373	.435	112	1	0-0	.941	-1	85	96	O-15(RF)	0.0
	Year	80	227	25	67	11	3	2	27	8	3	27	.295	.328	.396	91	-4	0-0	.911	-5	82	90	O-53(RF)	-1.3
Total	2	174	504	61	157	31	6	9	76	24	4	56	.312	.348	.450	105	2	1-1	.910	-11	88	78	O-120(43-0-77)	-1.7
CARMAN, GEORGE George Wartman B 3.29.1866 Philadelphia, PA D 6.16.1929 Lancaster, PA d9.4																								
1890	Phi AA	28	97	9	17	2	0	0	7	8	1		.175	.245	.196	30	-9	5	.767	-9	86	74	S-15,O-10(RF)/2-2,3	-1.5
CARMEL, DUKE Leon James B 4.23.1937 New York, NY BL/TL 6-3/202# d9.10																								
1959	StL N	10	23	2	3	1	0	0	3	1-0	0	6	.130	.167	.174	-9	-4	0-1	1.000	-0	97	0	O-10(2-8-3)	-0.5
1960	StL N	4	3	0	0	0	0	0	0	1-0	0	1	.000	.250	.000	-23	0	1-1	1.000	0	275	125	/1-2,O(RF)	0.0
1963	StL N	57	44	9	10	1	0	1	2	9-0	0	11	.227	.358	.318	88	0	0-0	.974	2	154	0	O-38(26-6-8)/1	0.1
	NY N	47	149	11	35	5	3	3	18	16-2	0	37	.235	.307	.369	93	-1	2-2	.980	-3	93	70	O-21(CF),1-18	-0.7
	Year	104	193	20	45	6	3	4	20	25-2	0	48	.233	.320	.358	90	-2	2-2	.977	-1	117	43	O-59(26-27-8),1-19	-0.6
1965	NY A	6	8	0	0	0	0	0	0	0-0	0	5	.000	.000	.000	-99	-2	0-0	1.000	0	175	0	/1-2	-0.2
Total	4	124	227	22	48	7	3	4	23	27-2	0	60	.211	.294	.322	73	-7	3-4	.981	-1	113	36	/O-70(28-35-12),1-23	-1.3

Year	Tm Lg	G	AB	R	H	2B	3B	HR	RBI	BB-IB	HP	SO	AVG	OBP	SLG	AOPS	ABR	SB-CS	FA	FR	Rng	Thr	G at Pos	BFW
CARNETT, EDDIE Edwin Elliott "Lefty" B 10.21.1916 Springfield, MO BL/TL 6/185# d4.19 Mil 1945-46																								
1941	Bos N	2	0	0	0	0	0	0	0	0	0	0	—	—	—	—	0	0	—	0	0	0	/P-2	0.0
1944	Chi A	126	457	51	126	18	8	1	60	26	5	35	.276	.322	.357	95	-4	5-2	.949	-5	97	92	O-88(62-25-6),1-25/P-2	-1.5
1945	Cle A	30	73	5	16	7	0	0	7	2	1	9	.219	.250	.315	66	-3	0-1	.971	-0	100	68	O-16(8-1-7)/P-2	-0.5
Total	3	158	530	56	142	25	8	1	67	28	6	44	.268	.312	.351	91	-7	5-3	.952	-5	97	88	O-104(70-26-13)/1-25,P-6	-2.0
CARNEY, JOHN John Joseph "Handsome Jack" B 11.10.1866 Salem, MA D 10.19.1925 Litchfield, NH BR/TR 5-10.5/175# d4.24																								
1889	Was N	69	273	25	63	7	0	1	29	14	1	14	.231	.271	.267	54	-17	12	.957	-6	67	85	1-53,O-16(1-0-15)	-2.5
1890	Buf P	28	107	11	29	3	0	0	13	7	3	14	.271	.333	.299	76	-3	2	.972	-1	79	107	1-24/O-4(1-0-3)	-0.5
	Cle P	25	89	15	31	5	3	0	21	14	1	5	.348	.442	.472	157	8	6	.857	-2	97	0	O-19(RF)/1-6	0.4
	Year	53	196	26	60	8	3	0	34	21	4	19	.306	.385	.378	113	5	8	.969	-4	72	115	1-30,O-23(1-0-22)	-0.1
1891	Cin AA	99	367	47	102	10	8	3	43	35	3	18	.278	.346	.373	98	-3	15	.974	1	111	71	1-99	-1.0
	Mil AA	31	110	22	33	5	2	3	23	13	3	8	.300	.389	.464	120	2	5	.986	4	160	101	1-31	0.3
	Year	130	477	69	135	15	10	6	66	48	6	26	.283	.356	.394	103	-1	20	.977	4	123	78	*1-130	-0.7
Total	3	252	946	120	258	30	13	7	129	83	11	59	.273	.338	.354	92	-13	40	.971	-5	102	85	1-213/O-39(2-0-37)	-3.3
CARNEY, PAT Patrick Joseph "Doc" B 8.7.1876 Holyoke, MA D 1.9.1953 Worcester, MA BL/TL 6/200# d9.20 ▲																								
1901	Bos N	13	55	6	16	2	1	0	6	3	1		.291	.339	.364	95	0	0	.933	-2	0	0	O-13(RF)	-0.3
1902	Bos N	137	522	75	141	17	4	2	65	42	12		.270	.339	.330	105	5	27	.930	-8	106	158	*O-137(3-0-135)/P-2	-1.0
1903	Bos N	110	392	37	94	12	4	1	49	28	4		.240	.297	.298	73	-14	10	.953	-3	86	135	O-92(3-0-90),P-10/1	-1.9
1904	Bos N	78	279	24	57	5	2	0	11	12	1		.204	.240	.237	49	-17	6	.953	-1	145	181	O-71(2-9-60)/P-4,1	-2.1
Total	4	338	1248	142	308	36	11	3	131	85	18		.247	.304	.300	82	-26	43	.942	-14	105	151	O-313(8-9-298)/P-16,1-2	-5.3
CARNEY, BILL William John B 3.25.1874 St.Paul, MN D 7.31.1938 Hopkins, MN BB/TR 5-10/?# d8.22																								
1904	Chi N	2	7	0	0	0	0	0	0	1	0		.000	.125	.000	-60	-1	0	1.000	0	580	0	/O-2(RF)	-0.1
CARPENTER, BUBBA Charles Sydney B 7.23.1968 Dallas, TX BL/TL 6-1/195# d5.13																								
2000	Col N	15	27	4	6	0	0	3	5	4-0	0	13	.222	.323	.556	93	0	0-0	1.000	-1	39	0	/O-6(5-0-1),D-2	-0.2
CARPENTER, HICK Warren William B 8.16.1855 Grafton, MA D 4.18.1937 San Diego, CA BR/TL 5-11/186# d5.1																								
1879	Syr N	65	261	30	53	6	0	0	20	2		15	.203	.209	.226	49	-13		.948	-5	117	72	1-34,3-18,O-11(RF)/2-3	-1.7
1880	Cin N	77	300	32	72	6	4	0	23	2		15	.240	.245	.287	80	-7		.853	-0	89	109	*3-67/1-9,S	-0.5
1881	Wor N	**83**	347	40	75	12	2	2	31	3		19	.216	.223	.280	54	-19		.848	3	104	100	*3-83	-1.3
1882	Cin AA	**80**	351	78	**120**	15	5	1	67	10			.342	.360	.422	154	18		**.835**	-3	92	93	*3-80	1.5
1883	Cin AA	95	435	99	130	18	4	3	40	19			.299	.328	.379	120	9		.870	-5	92	68	*3-95	0.5
1884	Cin AA	108	474	80	121	16	2	4	60	6	4		.255	.271	.323	89	-7		.881	-9	86	135	*3-108/O(RF)	-1.3
1885	Cin AA	**112**	473	89	131	12	8	2	61	9	3		.277	.295	.349	101	-1		.860	-7	90	104	*3-112	-0.6
1886	Cin AA	111	458	67	101	8	5	2	61	18	8		.221	.262	.273	66	-20	8	.841	-7	99	136	*3-111	-2.2
1887	Cin AA	127	498	70	124	12	6	1	50	19	4		.249	.282	.303	62	-28	44	.846	-14	95	95	*3-127	-3.2
1888	Cin AA	136	551	68	147	14	5	3	67	5	5		.267	.280	.327	89	-10	59	.866	-14	97	81	*3-136	-2.0
1889	Cin AA	123	486	67	127	23	6	0	63	18	4	41	.261	.293	.333	76	-17	47	.835	-25	82	87	*3-121/1-2	-3.5
1892	StL N	1	3	0	1	0	0	0	0	1	0	1	.333	.500	.333	161	0	0	.714	-0	90	0	/3	0.0
Total	12	1118	4637	720	1202	142	47	18	543	112	28	91	.259	.281	.322	86	-95	158	.853	-86	92	98	*3-1059/1-45,O-12(RF),2-3,S	-14.3
CARR, CHARLIE Charles Carbitt B 12.27.1876 Coatesville, PA D 11.25.1932 Memphis, TN BR/TR 6-2/195# d9.15																								
1898	Was N	20	73	6	14	2	0	0	4	2	0		.192	.213	.219	24	-7	2	.950	-2	84	114	1-20	-0.9
1901	Phi A	2	8	0	1	0	0	0	0	0	0		.125	.125	.125	-29	-1	0	.926	0	174	0	/1-2	-0.1
1903	Det A	135	548	59	154	23	11	2	79	10	2		.281	.296	.374	103	0	10	.982	13	**134**	90	*1-135	1.0
1904	Det A	92	360	29	77	13	3	0	40	14	1		.214	.245	.267	64	-15	6	.983	16	169	109	1-92	-0.1
	Cle A	32	120	9	27	5	1	0	7	4	0		.225	.250	.283	69	-4	0	.973	-0	105	94	1-32	-0.6
	Year	124	480	38	104	18	4	0	47	18	1		.217	.246	.271	65	-20	6	**.980**	16	**152**	105	*1-124	-0.7
1905	Cle A	89	306	29	72	12	4	1	31	13	0		.235	.266	.310	82	-7	12	.991	-1	89	96	1-87	-1.1
1906	Cin N	22	94	9	18	2	3	0	10	2	1		.191	.216	.277	51	-6	0	.983	1	112	147	1-22	-0.7
1914	Ind F	115	441	44	129	11	10	3	69	26	1	47	.293	.333	.383	86	-16	19	**.991**	1	98	110	*1-115	-1.9
Total	7	507	1950	185	492	68	32	6	240	71	5	47	.252	.280	.329	81	-56	49	.984	27	120	102	1-505	-4.4
CARR, CHUCK Charles Lee Glenn B 8.10.1967 San Bernardino, CA BB/TR (BR 1995 (part)) 5-10/165# d4.28																								
1990	NY N	4	2	0	0	0	0	0	0	0-0	0	2	.000	.000	.000	-99	-1	1-0	—	-0	0	0	/O(LF)	0.0
1991	NY N	12	11	1	2	0	0	0	1	0-0	0	2	.182	.182	.182	3	-1	1-0	1.000	1	153	0	/O-9(CF)	-0.1
1992	StL N	22	64	8	14	3	0	0	3	9-0	0	6	.219	.315	.266	68	-2	10-2	1.000	-0	100	98	O-19(5-9-6)	-0.1
1993	Fla N	142	551	75	147	19	2	4	41	49-0	2	74	.267	.327	.330	73	-20	**58**-22	.985	7	112	99	*O-139(CF)	-0.7
1994	Fla N	106	433	61	114	19	2	2	30	22-1	5	71	.263	.305	.330	64	-23	32-8	.980	6	118	72	*O-104(CF)	-1.1
1995	Fla N	105	308	54	70	20	0	2	20	46-1	2	49	.227	.330	.312	71	-11	25-11	.987	6	111	**179**	*O-103(CF)	-0.2
1996	Mil A	27	106	18	29	6	1	1	11	6-0	0	21	.274	.310	.377	71	-5	5-4	1.000	5	123	271	O-27(CF)	0.0
1997	Mil A	26	46	3	6	3	0	0	0	2-0	1	11	.130	.184	.196	-1	-7	1-0	1.000	-1	77	152	O-23(CF)/D	-0.8
	†Hou N	63	192	34	53	11	2	4	17	15-2	2	37	.276	.333	.417	99	-1	11-5	.966	-1	98	126	O-59(1-58-0)	-0.1
Total	8	507	1713	254	435	81	7	13	123	149-4	12	273	.254	.316	.332	70	-71	144-52	.984	22	111	122	O-484(7-472-6)/D	-3.1
CARR, LEW Lewis Smith B 8.15.1872 Union Springs, NY D 6.15.1954 Moravia, NY BR/TR 6-2/200# d7.4																								
1901	Pit N	9	28	2	7	1	1	0	4	2	2		.250	.344	.357	100	0	0	.886	-3	82	130	/S-9,3	-0.3
CARRASQUEL, CHICO Alfonso (Colon) B 1.23.1928 Caracas, Venezuela BR/TR 6/170# d4.18																								
1950	Chi A	141	524	72	148	21	5	4	46	66	5	46	.282	.368	.365	91	-6	0-2	.961	11	**107**	106	*S-141	1.2
1951	Chi A★	147	538	41	142	22	4	2	58	46	3	39	.264	.325	.331	79	-16	14-4	**.975**	12	**110**	108	*S-147	0.6
1952	Chi A	100	359	36	89	7	4	1	42	33	2	27	.248	.315	.298	71	-15	2-2	.964	-11	89	88	S-99	-2.1
1953	Chi A★	149	552	72	154	30	4	2	47	38	4	47	.279	.330	.359	83	-13	5-3	**.976**	5	100	94	*S-149	0.5
1954	Chi A★	**155**	620	106	158	28	3	12	62	85	5	67	.255	.348	.368	93	-4	7-6	**.975**	13	103	110	*S-155	2.3
1955	Chi A★	145	523	83	134	11	2	11	52	61-0	4	59	.256	.335	.348	83	-13	1-1	.973	4	101	102	*S-144	0.3
1956	Cle A	141	474	60	115	15	1	7	48	52-0	6	61	.243	.323	.323	70	-20	0-4	.967	-20	84	85	*S-141/3	-3.0
1957	Cle A	125	392	37	108	14	1	8	57	41-2	8	53	.276	.351	.378	102	2	0-2	.960	-8	93	84	*S-122	0.3
1958	Cle A	49	156	14	40	6	0	2	21	14-1	0	12	.256	.318	.333	81	-4	0-0	.931	-13	76	80	S-32,3-14	-1.5
	KC A	59	160	19	34	5	1	2	13	21-0	0	15	.213	.304	.294	64	-8	0-1	.976	-4	92	175	3-32,S-22	-1.1
	Year	108	316	33	74	11	1	4	34	35-1	0	27	.234	.311	.313	72	-12	0-1	.947	-17	83	72	S-54,3-46	-2.6
1959	Bal A	114	346	28	77	13	0	4	28	34-1	1	41	.223	.292	.295	64	-17	2-3	.970	-7	96	133	S-89,2-22/3-2,1	-1.7
Total	10	1325	4644	568	1199	172	25	55	474	491-4	38	467	.258	.333	.342	82	-114	31-28	.969	-19	98	99	*S-1241/3-49,2-22,1	-4.2
CARREON, CAM Camilo B 8.6.1937 Colton, CA D 9.2.1987 Tucson, AZ BR/TR 6/198# d9.27 s-Mark																								
1959	Chi A	1	1	0	0	0	0	0	0	0-0	0	0	.000	.000	.000	-99	0	0-0	1.000	0	*0*	*0*	/C	0.0
1960	Chi A	8	17	2	4	0	0	0	2	1-0	0	3	.235	.278	.235	41	-1	0-0	1.000	0	*117*	*137*	/C-7	-0.1
1961	Chi A	78	229	32	62	5	1	4	27	21-2	0	24	.271	.331	.354	85	-5	0-1	.995	5	*121*	*89*	C-71	0.2
1962	Chi A	106	313	31	80	19	1	4	37	33-2	1	37	.256	.328	.361	86	-6	1-1	.995	2	*79*	*79*	C-93	0.1
1963	Chi A	101	270	28	74	10	1	2	35	23-2	1	32	.274	.332	.341	91	-3	1-1	.987	-1	91	99	C-92	0.0
1964	Chi A	37	95	12	26	5	0	0	4	7-3	1	13	.274	.330	.326	86	-2	0-0	.987	-1	*152*	*94*	C-34	-0.1
1965	Cle A	19	52	6	12	2	1	1	7	9-3	0	6	.231	.344	.365	101	0	1-1	1.000	1	*132*	*116*	C-19	0.2
1966	Bal A	4	9	2	2	2	0	0	2	3-0	0	2	.222	.417	.444	150	1	0-0	1.000	-0	*142*	*0*	/C-3	0.1
Total	8	354	986	113	260	43	4	11	114	97-12	3	117	.264	.331	.349	87	-16	3-4	.993	6	*103*	*90*	C-320	0.4
CARREON, MARK Mark Steven B 7.19.1963 Chicago, IL BR/TL 6/195# d9.8 f-Cam																								
1987	NY N	9	12	0	3	0	0	0	1	1-0	0	1	.250	.308	.250	53	-1	0-1	.800	-0	87	0	/O-5(LF)	-0.2
1988	NY N	7	9	5	5	2	0	1	1	2-0	0	1	.556	.636	1.111	413	4	0-0	1.000	-1	26	0	/O-4(LF)	0.3
1989	NY N	68	133	20	41	6	0	6	16	12-0	1	17	.308	.370	.489	151	9	2-3	.983	-1	103	0	O-39(18-0-21)	0.7
1990	NY N	82	188	30	47	12	0	10	26	15-0	2	29	.250	.312	.473	113	3	1-0	1.000	-3	92	40	O-60(16-36-13)	0.0
1991	NY N	106	254	18	66	6	0	4	21	12-2	2	26	.260	.297	.331	77	-8	2-1	.971	-4	82	122	O-77(43-22-22)	-1.4
1992	Det A	101	336	34	78	11	1	10	41	22-2	1	57	.232	.278	.360	78	-11	3-1	.979	1	105	91	O-83(64-1-19),D-13	-1.3
1993	SF N	78	150	22	49	9	1	7	33	13-2	1	16	.327	.373	.540	149	10	1-0	.943	-3	76	90	O-41(9-5-30)/1-3	0.6
1994	SF N	51	100	8	27	4	0	3	20	7-0	2	20	.270	.324	.400	94	-1	0-0	.978	-2	98	0	O-33(10-0-24)	-0.4
1995	SF N	117	396	53	119	24	0	17	65	23-1	4	37	.301	.343	.490	121	11	0-1	.993	-7	79	103	1-81,O-22(3-0-19)	-0.4

Year	Tm Lg	G	AB	R	H	2B	3B	HR	RBI	BB-IB	HP	SO	AVG	OBP	SLG	AOPS	ABR	SB-CS	FA	FR	Rng	Thr	G at Pos	BFW
1996	SF N	81	292	40	76	22	3	9	51	22-2	3	33	.260	.317	.449	104	1	2-3	.986	-5	77	114	1-73/O-5(3-0-2)	-1.1
	Cle A	38	142	16	46	12	0	2	14	11-0	3	9	.324	.385	.451	111	3	1-1	.994	-2	85	88	1-34/O-5(0-4-1),D-2	-0.2
Total	10	738	2012	246	557	108	5	69	289	140-9	19	246	.277	.327	.438	108	20	12-11	.974	-25	92	74	0-374(175-68-151),1-191/D-15	-3.4
CARRIGAN, BILL William Francis "Rough" B 10.22.1883 Lewiston, ME D 7.8.1969 Lewiston, ME BR/TR 5-9/175# d7.7 M7																								
1906	Bos A	37	109	5	23	0	0	0	10	5	1		.211	.252	.211	45	-7	3	.940	-4	*84*	*104*	C-35	-0.8
1908	Bos A	57	149	13	35	5	2	0	14	3	1		.235	.255	.295	77	-4	1	.955	5	*102*	*118*	C-47/1-3	0.5
1909	Bos A	94	280	25	83	13	2	1	36	17	2		.296	.341	.368	121	7	2	.972	2	*112*	*105*	C-77/1-8	1.9
1910	Bos A	114	342	36	85	11	1	3	53	23	6		.249	.307	.313	92	-3	10	.962	-16	*100*	*84*	*C-110	-1.0
1911	Bos A	72	232	29	67	6	1	1	30	26	5		.289	.373	.336	99	1	5	.972	-0	*96*	*106*	C-62/1-6	0.6
1912	†Bos A	87	266	34	70	7	1	0	24	38	2		.263	.359	.297	84	-4	7	**.970**	-4	*110*	*86*	C-87	-0.1
1913	Bos A	87	256	17	62	15	5	0	28	27	2	26	.242	.319	.340	91	-3	6	.979	-7	*87*	*109*	C-82,M	-0.3
1914	Bos A	82	178	18	45	5	1	1	22	40	2	18	.253	.395	.309	112	6	1-2	**.984**	8	*126*	*83*	C-78,M	2.1
1915	†Bos A	46	95	10	19	3	0	0	7	16	1	12	.200	.321	.232	68	-3	0	.975	7	*128*	*106*	C-44,M	0.8
1916	†Bos A	33	63	7	17	2	1	0	11	11	0	3	.270	.378	.333	113	2	2	1.000	5	151	58	C-27,M	0.9
Total	10	709	1970	194	506	67	14	6	235	206	22	59	.257	.334	.314	94	-8	37-2	.971	-3	*107*	*96*	C-649/1-17	4.6
CARRILLO, MATIAS Matias (Garcia) B 2.24.1963 Los Mochis, Mexico BL/TL 5-11/190# d5.23																								
1991	Mil A	3	0	0	0	0	0	0	0	0-0	0	0	—	—	—	—	0	0-0	—	-0	0	0	/O-3(LF)	0.0
1993	Fla N	24	55	4	14	6	0	0	3	1-0	1	7	.255	.281	.364	67	-2	0-0	1.000	-1	85	0	O-16(4-5-9)	-0.4
1994	Fla N	80	136	13	34	7	0	0	9	9-0	0	31	.250	.295	.301	55	-9	3-3	.982	0	81	246	O-49(20-8-25)	-1.0
Total	3	107	191	17	48	13	0	0	12	10-0	1	38	.251	.291	.319	58	-11	3-3	.987	-1	81	174	/O-68(27-13-34)	-1.4
CARROLL, DIXIE Dorsey Lee B 5.9.1891 Paducah, KY D 10.13.1984 Jacksonville, FL BL/TR 5-11/165# d9.12																								
1919	Bos N	15	49	10	13	3	1	0	7	7	2	1	.265	.379	.367	130	2	5	.921	1	89	255	O-13(6-8-1)	0.3
CARROLL, CHICK Edward B 1868 , AR D 7.13.1908 Chicago, IL d4.17																								
1884	Was U	4	16	1	4	0	0	0		0			.250	.250	.250	54	-1		.500	-1	98	0	/O-4(LF)	-0.2
CARROLL, FRED Frederick Herbert B 7.2.1864 Sacramento, CA D 11.7.1904 San Rafael, CA BR/TR 5-11/185# d5.1 OF Total (144-LF 67-CF 108-RF)																								
1884	Col AA	69	252	46	70	13	5	6		13	5		.278	.326	.440	161	18		.944	7			C-54,O-15(12-2-1)	2.6
1885	Pit AA	71	280	45	75	13	8	0	30	7	5		.268	.298	.371	112	3		.926	1			C-60,O-12(10-2-0)	0.8
1886	Pit AA	122	486	92	140	28	11	5	64	52	4		.288	.362	.422	146	27	20	.921	0			C-70,O-27(15-10-2),1-25/S	2.7
1887	Pit N	102	421	71	138	24	15	6	54	36	2	21	.328	.383	.499	154	32	23	.833	-16	114	0	O-46(8-33-5),C-40,1-17/S	1.4
1888	Pit N	97	366	62	91	14	5	2	48	32	10	31	.249	.326	.331	120	11	18	.897	-11			C-54,O-38(31-2-5)/1-5,3	0.4
1889	Pit N	91	318	80	105	21	11	2	51	85	11	26	.330	**.486**	.484	**190**	**50**	19	.930	-8			C-43,O-41(24-12-5)/1-7,3	3.7
1890	Pit P	111	416	95	124	20	7	2	71	75	11	22	.298	.418	.394	128	25	35	.856	-13	*103*	*69*	C-56,O-49(42-6-1)/1-7	1.2
1891	Pit N	91	353	55	77	13	4	4	48	48	2	36	.218	.315	.312	85	-6	22	.915	4	81	80	O-91(2-0-89)	-0.2
Total	8	754	2892	546	820	146	66	27	366	348	50	136	.284	.370	.408	137	160	137	.913	-35	*15*	*10*	C-377,O-319L/1-61,3-2,S-2	12.6
CARROLL, JAMEY Jamey Blake B 2.18.1974 Evansville, IN BR/TR 5-10/175# d9.11																								
2002	Mon N	16	71	16	22	5	3	1	6	4-0	0	12	.310	.347	.507	115	1	1-0	.917	-1	98	71	3-13/S-3,2	0.0
2003	Mon N	105	227	31	59	10	1	1	10	19-0	3	39	.260	.323	.326	64	-11	5-2	.969	10	128	93	3-67,S-14,2-11/D	0.0
Total	2	121	298	47	81	15	4	2	16	23-0	3	51	.272	.328	.369	76	-10	6-2	.960	9	121	88	/3-80,S-17,2-12,D	0.0
CARROLL, SCRAPPY John E. B 8.27.1860 Buffalo, NY D 11.14.1942 Buffalo, NY BR 5-7.5/?# d9.27																								
1884	StP U	**9**	31	3	3	1	0	0		2			.097	.152	.129	-26	-6		.824	3	305	334	/O-8(RF),3-2	-0.2
1885	Buf N	13	40	1	3	0	0	0	1	2		8	.075	.119	.075	-35	-6		.917	2	202	0	O-13(7-6-0)	-0.4
1887	Cle AA	57	216	30	43	5	1	0	19	15	4		.199	.264	.231	40	-17	19	.843	-3	86	47	O-54(14-0-40)/3-3,2	-1.7
Total	3	79	287	34	49	6	1	0	20	19	4	8	.171	.232	.199	26	-29	19	.853	1	126	68	/O-75(21-6-48),3-5,2	-2.3
CARROLL, PAT Patrick B 3.1853 Philadelphia, PA D 2.14.1916 Philadelphia, PA d5.10																								
1884	Alt U	11	49	4	13	1	0	0		1			.265	.280	.286	71	-3		.920	-2			/C-8,O-3(RF)	-0.4
	Phi U	5	19	1	3	1	0	0		0			.158	.158	.211	12	-3		.804	-2			/C-5	-0.4
	Year	16	68	5	16	2	0	0		1			.235	.246	.265	56	-6		.865	-4			C-13/O-3(RF)	-0.8
CARROLL, DOC Ralph Arthur "Red" B 12.28.1891 Worcester, MA D 6.27.1983 Worcester, MA BR/TR 6/170# d6.27																								
1916	Phi A	10	22	1	2	0	0	0	0	1	1	8	.091	.167	.091	-24	-3	0	.942	-2	63	214	C-10	-0.5
CARROLL, CLIFF Samuel Clifford B 10.18.1859 Clay Grove, IA D 6.12.1923 Portland, OR BB/TR 5-8/163# d8.3																								
1882	Pro N	10	41	4	5	0	0	0	2	0		4	.122	.122	.122	-21	-5		1.000	1	94	508	O-10(2-0-8)	-0.4
1883	Pro N	58	238	37	63	12	3	1	20	4		28	.265	.277	.353	87	-4		.902	3	80	209	O-58(56-1-1)	-0.2
1884	†Pro N	113	452	90	118	16	4	3	54	29		39	.261	.306	.334	103	2		.904	0	46	34	*O-113(LF)	0.0
1885	Pro N	104	426	62	99	12	3	1	40	29		29	.232	.281	.282	85	-6		.886	4	51	75	*O-104(LF)	-0.5
1886	Was N	111	433	73	99	11	6	2	22	44		26	.229	.300	.296	88	-4	31	.862	-0	101	106	*O-111(109-1-1)	-0.6
1887	Was N	103	420	79	104	17	4	4	37	17	9	30	.248	.291	.336	79	-11	40	.902	1	105	183	*O-103(102-1-0)	-1.1
1888	Pit N	5	20	1	0	0	0	0	0	0	0	8	.000	.000	.000	-99	-5	2	.667	-1	128	0	/O-5(1-0-4)	-0.6
1890	Chi N	136	582	134	166	16	6	7	65	53	7	34	.285	.352	.369	106	3	34	.936	11	114	151	*O-136(112-0-24)	1.0
1891	Chi N	130	515	87	132	20	8	7	80	50	15	42	.256	.340	.367	106	4	31	.915	-5	75	153	*O-130(0-1-130)	-0.1
1892	StL N	101	407	82	111	14	8	4	49	47	11	22	.273	.363	.376	130	17	30	.901	5	119	27	*O-101(99-0-3)	1.2
1893	Bos N	120	438	80	98	7	5	2	54	88	5	28	.224	.360	.276	65	-20	29	.917	2	89	127	*O-120(33-0-89)	-2.1
Total	11	991	3972	729	995	125	47	31	423	361	47	290	.251	.320	.329	93	-29	197	.905	21	87	119	O-991(731-4-260)	-3.4
CARROLL, TOM Thomas Edward B 9.17.1936 Jamaica, NY BR/TR 6-3/186# d5.7 Mil 1958																								
1955	†NY A	14	6	3	2	0	0	0	0	0-0	0	2	.333	.333	.333	81	0	0-0	.875	1	177	0	/S-4	0.1
1956	NY A	36	17	11	6	0	0	0	0	1-0	0	3	.353	.389	.353	100	0	1-0	.857	3	262	452	3-11/S	0.3
1959	KC A	14	7	1	1	0	0	0	1	0-0	0	1	.143	.143	.143	-21	-1	0-0	1.000	2	144	66	/S-9,3-3	0.1
Total	3	64	30	15	9	0	0	0	1	1-0	0	6	.300	.323	.300	69	-1	1-0	.813	5	234	373	/3-14,S-14	0.5
CARSON, KIT Walter Lloyd B 11.15.1912 Colton, CA D 6.21.1983 Long Beach, CA BL/TL 6/180# d7.21																								
1934	Cle A	5	18	4	5	2	1	0	1	2	0	3	.278	.350	.500	115	0	0-0	1.000	-1	41	0	/O-4(RF)	0.0
1935	Cle A	16	22	1	5	2	0	0	1	2	0	6	.227	.292	.318	57	-1	0-1	1.000	-0	105	0	/O-4(RF)	-0.2
Total	2	21	40	5	10	4	1	0	2	4	0	9	.250	.318	.400	83	-1	0-1	1.000	-1	78	0	/O-8(RF)	-0.2
CARSWELL, FRANK Frank Willis "Tex" or "Wheels" B 11.6.1919 Palestine, TX D 10.16.1998 Houston, TX BR/TR 6/195# d4.17																								
1953	Det A	16	15	2	4	0	0	0	2	3	0	1	.267	.389	.267	81	0	0-0	1.000	-0	60	0	/O-3(LF)	0.0
CARTER, GARY Gary Edmund B 4.8.1954 Culver City, CA BR/TR 6-2/215# d9.16 HF2002																								
1974	Mon N	9	27	5	11	0	1	1	6	1-0	0	2	.407	.414	.593	174	2	2-0	1.000	0	338	58	/C-6,O-2(RF)	0.3
1975	Mon N★	144	503	58	136	20	1	17	68	72-8	1	83	.270	.360	.416	111	9	5-2	.974	-9	92	17	O-92(RF),C-66/3	-0.1
1976	Mon N	91	311	31	68	8	1	6	38	30-2	1	43	.219	.287	.309	67	-14	0-2	.994	11	146	138	C-60,O-36(2-0-34)	-0.3
1977	Mon N	154	522	86	148	29	2	31	84	58-5	5	103	.284	.356	.525	138	28	5-5	.990	4	103	87	*C-146/O(LF)	3.7
1978	Mon N	157	533	76	136	27	1	20	72	62-11	5	70	.255	.336	.422	113	9	10-6	.989	22	149	104	*C-152/1	4.0
1979	Mon N★	141	505	74	143	26	5	22	75	40-3	5	62	.283	.338	.485	124	15	3-2	.989	22	138	122	*C-138	4.4
1980	Mon N★	154	549	76	145	25	5	29	101	58-11	1	78	.264	.331	.486	127	18	3-2	**.993**	25	138	103	*C-149	5.2
1981	†Mon N★	100	374	48	94	20	2	16	68	35-4	1	35	.251	.313	.444	113	5	1-5	.993	13	157	108	*C-100/1	2.2
1982	Mon N★	154	557	91	163	32	1	29	97	78-11	6	64	.293	.381	.510	146	36	2-5	.991	25	133	109	*C-153	**6.9**
1983	Mon N★	145	541	63	146	37	3	17	79	51-7	7	57	.270	.336	.444	116	12	1-1	**.995**	25	151	115	*C-144/1	4.4
1984	Mon N★	159	596	75	175	32	1	27	**106**	64-9	6	57	.294	.366	.487	145	36	2-2	.993	4	112	91	*C-143,1-25	4.5
1985	NY N✳	149	555	83	156	17	1	32	100	69-16	6	46	.281	.365	.488	141	30	1-1	.992	9	120	98	*C-143/1-6,O(RF)	4.6
1986	†NY N★	132	490	81	125	14	2	24	105	62-9	6	63	.255	.337	.439	118	12	1-0	.991	8	102	82	*C-122/1-9,O-4(2-0-2),3	2.5
1987	NY N★	139	523	55	123	18	2	20	83	42-1	1	73	.235	.290	.392	84	-15	0-0	.991	1	99	91	*C-135/1-4,O(RF)	-0.8
1988	†NY N★	130	455	39	110	16	2	11	46	34-1	7	52	.242	.301	.358	94	-4	0-2	.990	-10	75	74	*C-119,1-10/3	-0.9
1989	NY N	50	153	14	28	8	0	2	15	12-0	0	15	.183	.241	.275	50	-10	0-0	.980	-5	68	132	C-47/1	-1.4
1990	SF N	92	244	24	62	10	0	9	27	25-3	1	31	.254	.324	.406	104	1	1-1	.992	-5	85	93	C-80/1-3	0.0
1991	LA N	101	248	22	61	14	0	6	26	22-1	7	26	.246	.323	.375	98	0	2-2	.988	4	81	121	C-68,1-10	0.6
1992	Mon N	95	285	24	62	18	1	5	29	33-4	2	37	.218	.299	.340	83	-6	0-4	.989	-3	58	135	C-85/1-5	-0.6
Total	19	2296	7971	1025	2092	371	31	324	1225	848-106	68	997	.262	.335	.439	116	164	39-42	.991	140	120	104	*C-2056,O-137(5-0-132)/1-76,3-3	39.2

Year	Tm Lg	G	AB	R	H	2B	3B	HR	RBI	BB-IB	HP	SO	AVG	OBP	SLG	AOPS	ABR	SB-CS	FA	FR	Rng	Thr	G at Pos	BFW
CARTER, HOWIE John Howard B 10.13.1904 New York, NY D 7.24.1991 New York, NY BR/TR 5-10/154# d6.21																								
1926	Cin N	5	1	0	0	0	0	0	0	0	0	0	.000	.000	.000	-99	0	0	1.000	0	172	0	/2-3,S	0.0
CARTER, JOE Joseph Chris B 3.7.1960 Oklahoma City, OK BR/TR 6-3/215# d7.30 OF Total (775-LF 432-CF 624-RF)																								
1983	Chi N	23	51	6	9	1	1	0	1	0-0	0	21	.176	.176	.235	13	-6	1-0	1.000	-0	100	0	O-16(14-2-1)	-0.7
1984	Cle A	66	244	32	67	6	1	13	41	11-0	1	48	.275	.307	.467	109	2	2-4	.956	4	103	253	O-59(48-14-0)/1-7	0.2
1985	Cle A	143	489	64	128	27	0	15	59	25-2	2	74	.262	.298	.409	93	-6	24-6	.983	7	108	137	*O-135(122-4-30),1-11/23D	-0.1
1986	Cle A	162	663	108	200	36	9	29	**121**	32-3	5	95	.302	.335	.514	130	25	29-7	.976	4	113	114	*O-104(45-9-78),1-70	2.3
1987	Cle A	149	588	83	155	27	2	32	106	27-6	9	105	.264	.304	.480	103	0	31-6	.983	-7	77	86	1-84,O-62(42-13-14)/D-5	-0.9
1988	Cle A	157	621	85	168	36	6	27	98	35-6	7	82	.271	.314	.478	116	11	27-5	.985	0	101	106	*O-156(CF)	1.4
1989	Cle A	**162**	651	84	158	32	4	35	105	39-8	8	112	.243	.292	.465	109	4	13-5	.978	-2	96	72	*O-146(56-103-1),1-11/D-8	0.0
1990	SD N	**162**	634	79	147	27	1	24	115	48-18	7	93	.232	.290	.391	86	-14	22-6	.988	2	104	143	*O-150(51-112-0),1-14	-1.3
1991	†Tor A★	**162**	638	89	174	42	3	33	108	49-12	**10**	112	.273	.330	.503	124	19	20-9	.974	-3	91	127	*O-151(57-0-100),D-11	1.2
1992	†Tor A★	158	622	97	164	30	7	34	119	36-4	11	109	.264	.309	.498	119	12	12-5	.971	1	100	119	*O-129(6-0-123),D-24/1-4	0.9
1993	†Tor A★	155	603	92	153	33	5	33	121	47-5	9	113	.254	.312	.489	113	8	8-3	.974	-5	97	70	*O-151(55-0-96)/D-3	-0.3
1994	Tor A★	111	435	70	118	25	2	27	103	33-6	2	64	.271	.317	.524	114	7	11-0	.991	-3	100	53	*O-110(RF)/D	0.1
1995	Tor A	139	558	70	141	23	0	25	76	37-5	3	87	.253	.300	.428	88	-12	12-1	.975	0	99	108	*O-128(116-20-0)/1-7,D-5	-1.4
1996	Tor A★	157	625	84	158	35	7	30	107	44-2	7	106	.253	.306	.475	95	-8	7-6	.961	-13	74	94	*O-115(LF),1-41,D-15	-2.8
1997	Tor A	157	612	76	143	30	4	21	102	40-5	7	105	.234	.284	.399	76	-24	8-2	.972	-2	108	33	D-65,O-51(41-0-10),1-42	-3.4
1998	Bal A	85	283	36	70	15	1	11	34	18-4	2	48	.247	.297	.424	86	-7	3-1	.962	3	115	132	O-50(3-0-47),D-32/1	-0.7
	SF N	41	105	15	31	7	0	7	29	6-0	0	13	.295	.322	.562	138	5	1-0	1.000	-3	62	0	O-17(4-0-14),1-16	0.1
Total	16	2189	8422	1170	2184	432	53	396	1445	527-86	90	1387	.259	.306	.464	104	16	231-66	.977	-18	99	103	*O-1730L,1-308,D-176/32	-5.4
CARTER, BLACKIE Otis Leonard B 9.30.1902 Langley, SC D 9.10.1976 Greenville, SC BR/TR 5-10/175# d10.3																								
1925	NY N	1	4	0	0	0	0	0	0	0	0	1	.000	.000	.000	-99	-1	0-0	1.000	1	46	1047	/O(LF)	-0.1
1926	NY N	5	17	4	4	1	0	1	1	1	0	0	.235	.278	.471	100	0	0	.917	-0	112	0	/O-4(3-0-1)	-0.1
Total	2	6	21	4	4	1	0	1	1	1	0	1	.190	.227	.381	61	-1	0-0	.929	0	100	185	/O-5(4-0-1)	-0.2
CARTER, STEVE Steven Jerome B 12.3.1964 Charlottesville, VA BL/TR 6-4/201# d4.16																								
1989	Pit N	9	16	2	2	1	0	1	3	2-1	0	5	.125	.222	.375	70	-1	0-0	1.000	-1	51	0	/O-5(RF)	-0.2
1990	Pit N	5	5	0	1	0	0	0	0	0-0	0	1	.200	.200	.200	11	-1	0-0	1.000	0	155	0	/O-3(1-2-1)	0.0
Total	2	14	21	2	3	1	0	1	3	2-1	0	6	.143	.217	.333	56	-2	0-0	1.000	-1	73	0	/O-8(1-2-6)	-0.2
CARTWRIGHT, ED Edward Charles "Jumbo" B 10.6.1859 Johnstown, PA D 9.3.1933 St.Petersburg, FL BR/TR 5-10/220# d7.10																								
1890	StL AA	75	300	70	90	12	4	8	60	29	3		.300	.367	.447	123	6	26	.976	-1	85	101	1-75	-0.1
1894	Was N	**132**	507	88	149	35	13	12	106	57	8	43	.294	.374	.485	109	7	31	.973	-1	100	71	*1-132	0.4
1895	Was N	122	472	95	156	34	17	3	90	54	1	41	.331	.400	.494	131	22	50	.984	15	**149**	86	*1-122	2.9
1896	Was N	**133**	499	76	138	15	10	1	62	54	2	44	.277	.350	.353	85	-10	28	.978	0	100	86	*1-133	-0.9
1897	Was N	33	124	19	29	4	0	0	15	8	1		.234	.286	.266	46	-10	9	.963	2	143	92	1-33	-0.7
Total	5	495	1902	348	562	100	44	24	333	202	15	128	.295	.368	.432	106	15	144	.977	16	113	85	1-495	1.6
CARTY, RICO Ricardo Adolfo Jacobo (born Ricardo Adolfo Jacobo (Carty)) B 9.1.1939 San Pedro De Macoris, D.R. BR/TR 6-3/200# d9.15 OF Total (789-LF 1-CF 18-RF)																								
1963	Mil N	2	2	0	0	0	0	0	0	0-0	0	2	.000	.000	.000	-99	-1	0-0	—	0			H	-0.1
1964	Mil N	133	455	72	150	28	4	22	88	43-4	3	78	.330	.388	.554	162	38	1-2	.978	2	105	78	*O-121(118-1-2)	3.5
1965	Mil N	83	271	37	84	18	1	10	35	17-0	3	44	.310	.355	.494	136	13	1-4	.958	0	103	84	O-73(LF)	0.9
1966	Atl N	151	521	73	170	25	2	15	76	60-7	0	74	.326	.391	.468	137	28	4-6	.971	3	106	96	*O-126(126-0-1),C-17/1-2,3	2.5
1967	Atl N	134	444	41	113	16	2	15	64	49-10	1	70	.255	.329	.401	110	6	4-3	.959	-2	100	92	*O-112(97-0-15)/1-9	-0.4
1969	†Atl N	104	304	47	104	15	0	16	58	32-3	0	28	.342	.401	.549	164	26	0-2	.952	-3	96	0	O-79(LF)	1.9
1970	Atl N★	136	478	84	175	23	3	25	101	77-6	2	46	**.366**	**.454**	.584	167	49	1-2	.974	-0	105	57	*O-133(LF)	4.0
1972	Atl N	86	271	31	75	12	2	6	29	44-4	0	33	.277	.378	.402	111	6	0-0	.979	2	104	63	O-78(LF)	0.5
1973	Tex A	86	306	24	71	12	0	3	33	36-2	1	39	.232	.311	.301	77	-8	2-0	1.000	-1	96	62	O-53(LF),D-31	-1.3
	Chi N	22	70	4	15	0	0	1	8	6-0	0	10	.214	.276	.257	45	-5	0-0	.947	-0	104	0	O-19(LF)	-0.7
	Oak A	7	8	1	2	1	0	1	1	2-0	0	1	.250	.400	.750	230	1	0-0	—	0			/D-2	0.1
1974	Cle A	33	91	6	33	5	0	1	16	5-0	0	9	.363	.396	.451	144	5	0-0	.985	-2	22	147	D-14/1-8	0.3
1975	Cle A	118	383	57	118	19	1	18	64	45-3	2	31	.308	.378	.504	149	25	2-2	.990	-1	100	113	D-72,1-26,O-12(LF)	2.0
1976	Cle A	152	552	67	171	34	0	13	83	67-9	0	45	.310	.379	.442	143	32	1-1	1.000	-1	41	97	*D-137,1-12/O(LF)	2.8
1977	Cle A	127	461	50	129	23	1	15	80	56-6	0	51	.280	.355	.432	118	13	1-2	1.000	1	226	263	*D-123/1-2	0.9
1978	Tor A	104	387	51	110	16	0	20	68	36-5	0	41	.284	.340	.481	127	13	1-1	—	0	0	0	*D-101	1.0
	Oak A	41	141	19	39	5	1	11	31	21-2	0	16	.277	.368	.560	167	12	0-0	—	0	0	0	D-41	1.1
	Year	145	528	70	149	21	1	31	99	57-7	0	57	.282	.348	.502	138	25	1-1	.789	0	0	0	*D-142	2.1
1979	Tor A	132	461	48	118	26	0	12	55	46-4	1	45	.256	.322	.390	91	-5	3-1	—	0	0	0	*D-129	-0.9
Total	15	1651	5606	712	1677	278	17	204	890	642-65	13	663	.299	.369	.464	132	248	21-26	.970	-2	103	68	O-807L,D-650/1-59,C-17,3	18.1
CARUSO, MIKE Michael John B 5.27.1977 Queens, NY BL/TR 6-1/172# d3.31																								
1998	Chi A	133	523	81	160	17	6	5	55	14-0	7	38	.306	.331	.390	90	-10	22-6	.944	-8	98	107	*S-131	-0.5
1999	Chi A	136	529	60	132	11	4	2	35	20-0	3	36	.250	.280	.297	47	-44	12-14	.957	-23	92	94	*S-132/D-2	-5.6
2002	KC A	12	20	3	2	0	0	0	0	1-0	0	2	.100	.143	.100	-30	-4	0-0	1.000	-1	135	0	/S-5,2-4,3-2	-0.4
Total	3	281	1072	144	294	28	10	7	90	35-0	10	76	.274	.302	.339	66	-58	34-20	.951	-32	95	99	S-268/2-4,3-2,D-2	-6.5
CARUTHERS, BOB Robert Lee "Parisian Bob" B 1.5.1864 Memphis, TN D 8.5.1911 Peoria, IL BL/TR 5-7/138# d9.7 M1 U2 ▲																								
1884	StL AA	23	82	15	22	2	0	2		4	0		.268	.302	.366	113	1		.750	-4	47	0	O-16(RF),P-13	-0.3
1885	†StL AA	60	222	37	50	10	2	1	12	20	0		.225	.289	.302	83	-4		.902	-1	97	**233**	P-53/O-7(6-0-1)	-0.1
1886	†StL AA	87	317	91	106	21	14	4	61	64	1		.334	.448	.527	196	38	26	.897	-4	80	112	P-44,O-43(1-0-42)/2-2	1.3
1887	†StL AA	98	364	102	130	23	11	8	73	66	6		.357	.463	.547	164	33	49	.903	8	121	56	O-54(3-2-50),P-39/1-7	1.8
1888	Bro AA	94	335	58	77	10	5	5	53	45	4		.230	.328	.334	113	7	23	.899	-1	58	183	O-51(4-16-31),P-44	0.1
1889	†Bro AA	59	172	45	43	8	3	2	31	44	2	17	.250	.408	.366	121	8	9	.968	1	103	166	P-56/O-3(0-1-2),1-2	0.0
1890	†Bro N	71	238	46	63	7	4	1	29	47	5	18	.265	.397	.340	115	8	13	.860	-1	74	0	O-39(37-1-1),P-37	0.0
1891	Bro N	56	171	24	48	5	3	2	23	25	0	13	.281	.372	.380	120	5	4	.940	-1	108	91	P-38,O-17(1-2-14)/2	0.0
1892	StL N	143	513	76	142	16	8	3	69	86	5	29	.277	.386	.357	131	25	24	.892	-9	74	46	*O-122(6-7-110),P-16/2-6,1-4,M	0.7
1893	Chi N	1	3	0	0	0	0	0	0	1	0	0	.000	.250	.000	-32	-1	0	1.000	-0	0	0	/O(CF)	-0.1
	Cin N	13	48	14	14	2	0	1	8	15	1	2	.292	.469	.396	128	3	4	.857	-1	45	0	O-13(RF)	0.1
	Year	14	51	14	14	2	0	1	8	16	1	2	.275	.456	.373	119	3	4	.862	-1	43	0	O-14(0-1-13)	0.0
Total	10	705	2465	508	695	104	50	29	359	417	24	79	.282	.391	.400	135	123	152	.875	-14	90	87	O-366(58-30-280),P-340/1-13,2-9	3.5
CASANOVA, PAUL Paulino (Ortiz) B 12.21.1941 Colon, Cuba BR/TR 6-4/200# d9.18																								
1965	Was A	5	13	2	4	1	0	0	1	1-0	0	3	.308	.357	.385	112	0	0-0	.938	-2	*67*	*0*	/C-4	-0.1
1966	Was A	122	429	45	109	16	5	13	44	14-2	1	78	.254	.278	.406	95	-5	1-2	.981	-5	*126*	*99*	*C-119	-0.5
1967	Was A☆	141	528	47	131	19	1	9	53	17-5	2	65	.248	.273	.339	84	-13	1-1	.984	1	153	92	*C-137	-0.6
1968	Was A	96	322	19	63	6	0	4	25	7-1	0	52	.196	.210	.252	42	-24	0-1	.989	-8	119	87	C-92	-3.3
1969	Was A	124	379	26	82	9	2	4	37	18-7	3	52	.216	.254	.282	54	-25	0-0	.992	-3	110	85	*C-122	-2.4
1970	Was A	104	328	25	75	17	3	6	30	10-2	1	47	.229	.251	.354	69	-16	0-0	.988	0	166	96	*C-100	-1.2
1971	Was A	94	311	19	63	9	1	5	26	14-1	1	52	.203	.238	.286	51	-22	0-3	.985	-3	112	75	C-83	-2.4
1972	Atl N	49	136	8	28	3	0	2	10	4-2	0	28	.206	.229	.272	38	-11	0-1	.975	-8	176	78	C-43	-1.9
1973	Atl N	82	236	18	51	7	0	7	18	11-3	1	36	.216	.254	.335	58	-14	0-2	.977	-7	54	153	C-78	-2.0
1974	Atl N	42	104	5	21	0	0	0	8	5-2	0	17	.202	.232	.202	23	-11	0-0	.986	-2	101	134	C-33	-1.2
Total	10	859	2786	214	627	87	12	50	252	101-25	9	430	.225	.252	.319	64	-141	2-10	.985	-35	*126*	*96*	C-811	-15.6
CASANOVA, RAUL Raul B 8.23.1972 Humacao, P.R. BB/TR 6/192# d5.24																								
1996	Det A	25	85	6	16	1	0	4	9	6-0	0	18	.188	.242	.341	45	-8	0-0	.978	-4	45	150	C-22/D-3	-1.0
1997	Det A	101	304	27	74	10	1	5	24	26-1	3	48	.243	.308	.332	68	-15	1-1	.985	1	74	108	C-92/D	-0.8
1998	Det A	16	42	4	6	2	0	1	3	5-0	1	10	.143	.250	.262	33	-4	0-0	.967	1	78	182	C-14	-0.2
2000	Mil N	86	231	20	57	13	3	6	36	26-1	4	48	.247	.331	.407	87	-5	1-2	.990	-3	95	65	C-72/D-3	-0.4
2001	Mil N	71	192	21	50	10	0	11	33	12-2	1	29	.260	.303	.484	103	0	0-0	.991	-6	71	90	C-56/D-2	-0.3
2002	Mil N	31	87	3	16	1	0	1	8	10-4	1	18	.184	.273	.230	38	-8	0-0	.994	-2	68	137	C-28	-0.9
	Bal A	2	1	0	0	0	0	0	0	0-0	0	1	.000	.000	.000	-99	0	0-0	1.000	0	0	0	/C-2	0.0
Total	6	332	942	81	219	37	4	28	113	85-8	10	172	.232	.301	.369	73	-40	2-3	.987	-13	76	104	C-286/D-9	-3.6

Year	Tm Lg	G	AB	R	H	2B	3B	HR	RBI	BB-IB	HP	SO	AVG	OBP	SLG	AOPS	ABR	SB-CS	FA	FR	Rng	Thr	G at Pos	BFW
CASE, GEORGE George Washington B 11.11.1915 Trenton, NJ D 1.23.1989 Trenton, NJ BR/TR 6/183# d9.8 C4																								
1937	Was A	22	90	14	26	6	2	0	11	3	0	5	.289	.312	.400	82	-3	2-1	.945	-0	112	50	O-22(8-1-14)	-0.4
1938	Was A	107	433	69	132	27	3	2	40	39	0	28	.305	.362	.395	96	-2	11-6	.964	-6	93	73	*O-101(0-19-82)	-1.2
1939	Was A✫	128	530	103	160	20	7	2	35	56	0	36	.302	.369	.377	98	-1	**51**-17	.955	-2	103	66	*O-123(7-79-38)	-0.2
1940	Was A	**154**	656	109	192	29	5	5	56	52	5	39	.293	.349	.375	94	-6	**35**-10	.970	-3	99	86	*O-154(0-118-36)	-0.9
1941	Was A	153	649	95	176	32	8	2	53	51	1	37	.271	.325	.354	84	-17	**33**-9	.975	12	108	153	*O-151(115-0-36)	-0.9
1942	Was A	125	513	101	164	26	2	5	43	44	3	30	.320	.377	.407	122	15	**44**-6	.951	-3	105	43	*O-120(86-0-34)	1.3
1943	Was A★	141	613	**102**	180	36	5	1	52	41	3	27	.294	.341	.374	113	9	**61**-14	.985	2	106	76	*O-140(18-0-122)	1.1
1944	Was A✱	119	464	63	116	14	2	2	32	49	3	22	.250	.326	.302	83	-9	49-18	.970	2	108	70	*O-114(83-7-28)	-1.1
1945	Was A✱	123	504	72	148	19	5	1	31	49	3	27	.294	.360	.357	118	12	30-16	.979	9	108	137	*O-123(87-15-27)	1.5
1946	Cle A	118	484	46	109	23	4	1	22	34	3	38	.225	.280	.295	65	-24	**28**-11	.983	-6	90	65	*O-118(LF)	-3.9
1947	Was A	36	80	11	12	1	0	0	2	8	0	8	.150	.227	.162	10	-10	5-1	.963	1	113	73	O-21(12-4-5)	-1.0
Total	11	1226	5016	785	1415	233	43	21	377	426	21	297	.282	.341	.358	95	-36	349-109	.970	5	103	87	*O-1187(534-243-422)	-5.7
CASEY, DENNIS Dennis Patrick B 3.30.1858 Binghamton, NY D 1.19.1909 Binghamton, NY BL/TR 5-9/164# d8.18 b-Dan																								
1884	Wil U	2	8	1	2	1	0	0		0			.250	.250	.375	85	0		1.000	0	0	0	/O-2(CF)	0.0
	Bal AA	37	149	20	37	7	4	3		5	0		.248	.273	.409	115	2		.898	0	79	208	O-37(CF)	0.1
1885	Bal AA	63	264	50	76	10	5	3	29	21	3		.288	.347	.398	137	12		.821	-5	96	0	O-63(CF)	0.4
Total	2	102	421	71	115	18	9	6	29	26	3		.273	.320	.401	128	14		.847	-5	89	71	O-102(CF)	0.5
CASEY, DOC James Patrick B 3.15.1870 Lawrence, MA D 12.31.1936 Detroit, MI BB/TR 5-6/157# d9.14																								
1898	Was N	28	112	13	31	2	0	0	15	3	1		.277	.302	.295	71	-4	15	.893	-2	101	120	3-22/S-4,C-3	-0.5
1899	Was N	9	34	3	4	2	0	0	2	2	0		.118	.167	.176	-6	-5	1	.853	-1	87	209	/3-9	-0.5
	Bro N	134	525	75	141	14	8	1	43	25	9		.269	.313	.331	75	-19	27	.892	-16	88	107	*3-134	-3.0
	Year	143	559	78	145	16	8	1	45	27	9		.259	.304	.322	70	-24	28	.889	-16	88	113	*3-143	-3.5
1900	Bro N	1	3	0	1	0	0	0	1	0	1		.333	.500	.333	125	0	0	1.000	0	103	0	/3	0.0
1901	Det A	128	540	105	153	16	9	2	46	32	10		.283	.335	.357	88	-9	34	.887	3	**112**	137	*3-127	-0.3
1902	Det A	132	520	69	142	18	7	3	55	44	7		.273	.338	.352	90	-7	22	.904	3	106	87	*3-132	0.0
1903	Chi N	112	435	56	126	8	3	1	40	19	3		.290	.324	.329	88	-8	11	.915	-19	84	47	*3-112	-2.3
1904	Chi N	136	548	71	147	20	4	1	43	18	7		.268	.300	.325	93	-6	21	.911	-10	91	84	*3-134/C-2	-1.3
1905	Chi N	144	526	66	122	21	10	1	56	41	6		.232	.295	.316	79	-14	22	**.949**	-10	94	50	*3-142/S	-2.2
1906	Bro N	149	571	71	133	17	8	0	34	52	8		.233	.306	.291	93	-4	22	.919	-16	93	64	*3-149	-1.8
1907	Bro N	141	527	55	122	19	3	0	19	34	3		.231	.282	.279	82	-11	16	.955	-7	95	87	*3-138	-1.7
Total	10	1114	4341	584	1122	137	52	9	354	270	55		.258	.310	.320	85	-87	191	.915	-74	96	84	*3-1100/C-5,S-5	-13.6
CASEY, JOE Joseph Felix B 8.15.1887 Boston, MA D 6.2.1966 Melrose, MA BR/TR 5-9/180# d10.1																								
1909	Det A	3	5	1	0	0	0	0	0	1	0		.000	.167	.000	-45	-1	0	1.000	1	*125*	*193*	/C-3	0.0
1910	Det A	23	62	3	12	3	0	0	2	2	1		.194	.231	.242	45	-4	1	.964	3	*114*	*104*	C-22	0.2
1911	Det A	15	33	2	5	0	0	0	3	3	0		.152	.222	.152	5	-4	0	.956	-2	*103*	*84*	C-12/O-3(CF)	-0.5
1918	Was A	9	17	3	4	0	0	0	2	2	0	2	.235	.316	.235	67	-1	0	1.000	1	*105*	*72*	/C-8	0.1
Total	4	50	117	9	21	3	0	0	7	8	1	2	.179	.238	.205	32	-10	1	.970	4	*111*	*100*	/C-45,O-3(CF)	-0.2
CASEY, BOB Orrin Robinson B 1.26.1859 Adolphustown, ON, CAN D 11.28.1936 Syracuse, NY 5-11/190# d7.17																								
1882	Det N	9	39	5	9	2	1	1	7	0		15	.231	.231	.410	101	0		.667	-5	58	0	/3-8,2	-0.5
CASEY, SEAN Sean Thomas B 7.2.1974 Willingboro, NJ BL/TR 6-4/215# d9.12																								
1997	Cle A	6	10	1	2	0	0	0	1	1-0	1	2	.200	.333	.200	42	-1	0-0	1.000	-0	0	0	/1D	-0.1
1998	Cin N	96	302	44	82	21	1	7	52	43-3	3	45	.272	.365	.417	105	4	1-1	.994	-8	62	104	1-86	-1.2
1999	Cin N★	151	594	103	197	42	3	25	99	61-13	9	88	.332	.399	.539	131	30	0-2	.995	-15	59	101	*1-148/D	0.0
2000	Cin N	133	480	69	151	33	2	20	85	52-4	7	80	.315	.385	.517	124	19	1-0	.995	-10	72	107	*1-129	-0.2
2001	Cin N★	145	533	69	165	40	0	13	89	43-8	9	63	.310	.369	.458	108	8	3-1	.994	-10	74	84	*1-136/D-3	-1.4
2002	Cin N	120	425	56	111	25	0	6	42	43-6	5	47	.261	.334	.362	85	-10	2-1	.993	-2	96	101	*1-108/D	-2.3
2003	Cin N	147	573	71	167	19	3	14	80	51-4	2	58	.291	.350	.408	99	-1	4-0	.996	-10	78	87	*1-144	-2.3
Total	7	798	2917	413	875	180	9	85	448	294-38	36	383	.300	.369	.455	110	49	11-5	.995	-55	73	97	1-752/D-8	-7.5
CASH, DAVE David B 6.11.1948 Utica, NY BR/TR 5-11/175# d9.13 C1																								
1969	Pit N	18	61	8	17	3	1	0	4	9-0	0	9	.279	.371	.361	108	1	2-0	.990	6	129	82	2-17	0.9
1970	†Pit N	64	210	30	66	7	6	1	28	17-3	1	25	.314	.365	.419	113	3	5-2	.974	8	103	127	2-55	1.5
1971	†Pit N	123	478	79	138	17	4	2	34	46-0	0	33	.289	.349	.354	101	1	13-5	.987	-1	102	120	*2-105,3-24/S-3	0.8
1972	†Pit N	99	425	58	120	22	4	3	30	22-1	0	31	.282	.316	.374	98	-2	9-9	.992	25	114	136	2-97	3.0
1973	Pit N	116	436	59	118	21	2	2	31	38-0	0	36	.271	.328	.342	88	-6	2-5	.979	5	103	75	2-92,3-17	0.3
1974	Phi N★	**162**	687	89	206	26	11	2	58	46-4	9	33	.300	.351	.378	100	0	20-8	.977	31	109	127	*2-162	4.4
1975	Phi N★	**162**	699	111	**213**	40	3	4	57	56-5	4	34	.305	.356	.388	103	4	13-6	.981	18	104	**123**	*2-162	3.4
1976	†Phi N★	160	666	92	189	14	**12**	1	56	54-3	2	13	.284	.337	.345	92	-8	10-12	**.988**	10	96	**126**	*2-158	1.1
1977	Mon N	153	650	91	188	42	7	0	43	52-5	2	33	.289	.343	.375	96	-3	21-12	.986	-15	96	79	*2-153	-0.9
1978	Mon N	159	658	66	166	26	3	3	43	37-2	0	29	.252	.291	.315	70	-27	12-6	**.986**	-7	98	103	*2-159	-2.8
1979	Mon N	76	187	24	60	11	1	2	19	12-0	0	12	.321	.358	.422	114	4	7-4	.971	-5	99	75	2-47	0.2
1980	SD N	130	397	25	90	14	2	1	23	35-5	0	21	.227	.287	.280	63	-20	6-5	.987	6	104	102	*2-123	-0.9
Total	12	1422	5554	732	1571	243	56	21	426	424-28	18	309	.283	.334	.358	93	-53	120-74	.984	81	103	110	*2-1330/3-41,S-3	11.0
CASH, KEVIN Kevin Forrest B 12.6.1977 Tampa, FL BR/TR 6/185# d9.6																								
2002	Tor A	7	14	1	2	0	0	0	0	1-0	0	4	.143	.200	.143	-6	-2	0-0	.968	0	79	88	/C-7	-0.2
2003	Tor A	34	106	10	15	3	0	1	8	4-0	1	22	.142	.179	.198	-0	-16	0-0	.995	-4	130	78	C-34	-1.7
Total	2	41	120	11	17	3	0	1	8	5-0	1	26	.142	.181	.192	-1	-18	0-0	.991	-3	124	79	/C-41	-1.9
CASH, NORM Norman Dalton B 11.10.1934 Justiceburg, TX D 10.12.1986 Beaver Island, MI BL/TL 6/190# d6.18																								
1958	Chi A	13	8	2	2	0	0	0	0	0-0	0	1	.250	.250	.250	39	-1	0-0	1.000	-0	126	0	/O-4(1-0-3)	-0.1
1959	†Chi A	58	104	16	25	0	1	4	16	18-3	5	9	.240	.372	.375	109	2	1-1	.984	-1	86	93	1-31	-0.1
1960	Det A	121	353	64	101	16	3	18	63	65-1	6	58	.286	.402	.501	140	22	4-2	.991	-0	99	86	1-99/O-4(3-0-1)	1.7
1961	Det A★	159	535	119	**193**	22	8	41	132	124-**19**	9	85	**.361**	**.487**	.662	198	83	11-5	.992	5	108	96	*1-157	**7.6**
1962	Det A	148	507	94	123	16	2	39	89	104-12	**13**	82	.243	.382	.513	134	28	6-3	.992	7	114	80	*1-146/O-3(RF)	2.5
1963	Det A	147	493	67	133	19	1	26	79	89-8	6	76	.270	.386	.471	135	27	2-3	.994	3	105	87	*1-142	2.2
1964	Det A	144	479	63	123	15	5	23	83	70-4	3	66	.257	.351	.453	121	15	2-1	**.997**	4	108	93	*1-137	1.1
1965	Det A	142	467	79	124	23	1	30	82	77-5	4	62	.266	.371	.512	147	31	6-6	.992	6	113	95	*1-139	2.9
1966	Det A★	160	603	98	168	18	3	32	93	66-4	4	91	.279	.351	.478	133	26	2-1	.988	4	108	96	*1-158	2.1
1967	Det A	152	488	64	118	16	5	22	72	81-9	4	100	.242	.352	.430	127	19	3-2	**.995**	10	121	99	*1-146	2.2
1968	†Det A	127	411	50	108	15	1	25	63	39-7	3	70	.263	.329	.487	141	19	1-1	.992	9	**127**	91	*1-117	2.4
1969	Det A	142	483	81	135	15	4	22	74	63-5	6	80	.280	.368	.464	126	18	2-1	.994	7	**114**	98	*1-134	1.4
1970	Det A	130	370	58	96	18	2	15	53	72-6	5	58	.259	.383	.441	127	17	0-1	.989	3	110	83	*1-114	1.2
1971	Det A★	135	452	72	128	10	3	32	91	59-7	7	86	.283	.372	.531	148	28	1-0	.992	1	101	96	*1-131	2.1
1972	†Det A★	137	440	51	114	16	0	22	61	50-13	4	64	.259	.338	.445	128	15	0-2	.993	2	102	103	*1-134	0.8
1973	Det A	121	363	51	95	19	0	19	40	47-7	8	73	.262	.357	.471	124	12	1-0	.991	2	107	85	*1-114/D-3	0.7
1974	Det A	53	149	17	34	3	2	7	12	19-2	3	30	.228	.327	.416	109	2	1-1	.985	-0	101	83	1-44	-0.2
Total	17	2089	6705	1046	1820	241	41	377	1103	1043-112	90	1091	.271	.374	.488	138	363	43-30	.992	60	109	92	*1-1943/O-11(4-0-7),D-3	30.5
CASH, RON Ronald Forrest B 11.20.1949 Atlanta, GA BR/TR 6/180# d9.4																								
1973	Det A	14	39	8	16	1	1	0	6	5-0	0	5	.410	.467	.487	161	3	0-0	.900	0	104	357	/O-7(LF),3-6	0.4
1974	Det A	20	62	6	14	2	0	0	5	0-0	0	11	.226	.222	.258	38	-5	0-1	.979	-1	87	93	1-15/3-4	-0.9
Total	2	34	101	14	30	3	1	0	11	5-0	0	16	.297	.324	.347	89	-2	0-1	.979	-1	87	93	/1-15,3-10,O-7(LF)	-0.5
CASIMIRO, CARLOS Carlos Rafael B 11.8.1976 San Pedro De Macoris, D.R. BR/TR 5-11/179# d7.31																								
2000	Bal A	2	8	0	1	1	0	0	3	0-0	0	2	.125	.125	.250	-9	-1	0-0	—	0			/D-2	-0.1
CASKIN, ED Edward James B 12.30.1851 Danvers, MA D 10.9.1924 Danvers, MA BR/TR 5-9.5/165# d5.1																								
1879	Tro N	70	304	32	78	13	2	0	21	2		14	.257	.261	.313	95	-1		.902	6	121	94	S-42,C-22/2-6	0.7
1880	Tro N	82	333	36	75	5	4	0	28	7		24	.225	.241	.264	68	-12		.885	6	112	73	*S-82/C-2	-0.2
1881	Tro N	63	234	33	53	7	1	0	21	13		29	.226	.267	.265	65	-9		.906	3	102	94	*S-63	-0.4

Year	Tm Lg	G	AB	R	H	2B	3B	HR	RBI	BB-IB	HP	SO	AVG	OBP	SLG	AOPS	ABR	SB-CS	FA	FR	Rng	Thr	G at Pos	BFW
1883	NY N	95	383	47	91	11	2	1	40	14		25	.238	.264	.285	68	-15		.855	-5	98	62	*S-81,2-13/C	-1.5
1884	NY N	100	351	49	81	11	1	1	40	34		55	.231	.299	.276	80	-7		.883	5	98	**125**	*S-96/C-6	0.1
1885	StL N	71	262	31	47	3	0	0	12	12		22	.179	.215	.191	34	-18		.884	-3	101	56	3-69/C-2,S	-1.9
1886	NY N	1	4	1	2	0	0	0	1	0		1	.500	.500	.500	203	0	0	1.000	-1	0	0	/S	0.0
Total	7	482	1871	229	427	50	10	2	163	82		170	.228	.261	.269	70	-62	0	.883	11	104	90	S-366/3-69,C-33,2-19	-3.2
CASSADY, HARRY Harry Delbert (born Harry Delbert Cassaday) B 7.20.1880 Bellflower, IL D 4.19.1969 Fresno, CA BL/TL 5-8/145# d8.8																								
1904	Pit N	12	44	8	9	0	0	0	3	2	0		.205	.239	.205	36	-3	2	.867	-0	243	0	O-12(RF)	-0.4
1905	Was A	10	30	1	4	0	0	0	1	0	0		.133	.133	.133	-16	-4	0	1.000	1	113	0	/O-9(RF)	-0.4
Total	2	22	74	9	13	0	0	0	4	2	0		.176	.197	.176	17	-7	2	.933	1	184	0	/O-21(RF)	-0.8
CASSIDY, JOHN John P. B 1857 Brooklyn, NY D 7.2.1891 Brooklyn, NY BR/TL 5-8/168# d4.24 ▲ OF Total (1-LF 147-CF 411-RF)																								
1875	Atl NA	41	166	14	29	3	2	1	6	0		4	.175	.175	.235	47	-7	0-0	.782	-4	110	43	P-30,O-12(1-0-11),1-10/2-2	-0.5
	NH NA	6	22	3	3	1	0	0	1	0		1	.136	.136	.182	11	-2	0-1	.988	1	84	149	/1-6	-0.1
	Year	47	188	17	32	4	2	1	7	0		5	.170	.170	.229	43	-9	0-1	.782	-3	110	43	P-30,1-16,O-12(1-0-11)/2-2	-0.6
1876	Har N	12	47	6	13	2	0	0	8	1		0	.277	.292	.319	95	0		1.000	1	189	0	/O-8(RF),1-4	0.1
1877	Har N	**60**	251	43	95	10	5	0	27	3		3	.378	.386	.458	184	24		.722	-5	147	117	*O-58(0-1-57)/P-2	1.6
1878	Chi N	60	256	33	68	7	1	0	29	9		11	.266	.291	.301	89	-3		.810	7	190	**265**	*O-60(RF)/C	0.3
1879	Tro N	9	37	4	7	1	0	0	1	2		4	.189	.231	.216	52	-2		.889	-1	76	0	/O-8(0-3-5),1-2	-0.3
1880	Tro N	**83**	352	40	89	14	8	0	29	12		34	.253	.277	.338	102	0		.880	-4	95	28	*O-82(0-47-35)/2	-0.5
1881	Tro N	**85**	370	57	82	13	3	1	11	18		21	.222	.258	.281	66	-15		.872	-12	87	0	*O-84(CF)/S	-2.8
1882	Tro N	29	121	14	21	3	1	0	9	3		16	.174	.194	.215	32	-9		.778	-8	66	140	O-16(0-12-4),3-13	-1.6
1883	Pro N	89	366	46	87	16	5	0	42	9		38	.238	.256	.309	69	-14		.864	-0	133	73	*O-88(1-0-87)/21	-1.3
1884	Bro AA	106	433	57	109	11	6	2		19	2		.252	.286	.319	96	-2		.847	-8	132	162	*O-101(RF)/3-4,S	-1.0
1885	Bro AA	54	221	36	47	6	2	1	28	8	3		.213	.250	.271	64	-9		.852	-6	83	197	O-54(RF)	-1.4
Total	10	587	2454	336	618	83	31	4	184	84	5	127	.252	.278	.316	89	-30		.845	-35	122	108	O-559R/3-17,1-7,S-2,2-2,P-2,C	-6.9
CASSIDY, JOE Joseph Phillip B 2.8.1883 Chester, PA D 3.25.1906 Chester, PA BR/TR d4.18																								
1904	Was A	152	581	63	140	12	**19**	1	33	15	4		.241	.265	.332	90	-10	17	.937	7	96	111	S-99,O-32(1-20-11),3-23	-0.1
1905	Was A	151	576	67	124	16	4	1	43	25	2		.215	.250	.262	65	-24	23	.934	**35**	**115**	104	*S-151	1.7
Total	2	303	1157	130	264	28	23	2	76	40	6		.228	.258	.297	78	-34	40	.935	42	108	107	S-250/O-32(1-20-11),3-23	1.6
CASSIDY, PETE Peter Francis B 4.8.1873 Wilmington, DE D 7.9.1929 Wilmington, DE BR/TR 5-10/165# d4.18																								
1896	Lou N	49	184	16	39	1	1	0	12	7	4	7	.212	.256	.228	29	-19	5	.973	-7	89	56	1-38,S-11	-2.2
1899	Bro N	6	20	2	3	1	0	0	4	1	2		.150	.261	.200	27	-2	1	1.000	-2	77	0	/3-3,S-2	-0.4
	Was N	46	178	21	56	13	0	3	32	9	5		.315	.365	.438	121	5	5	.970	-2	92	111	1-37/3-6,S-3	0.3
	Year	52	198	23	59	14	0	3	36	10	7		.298	.353	.414	111	3	6	.970	-5	92	111	1-37/3-9,S-5	-0.1
Total	2	101	382	39	98	15	1	3	48	17	11	*7*	.257	.307	.325	72	-16	11	.972	-11	91	84	/1-75,S-16,3-9	-2.3
CASSINI, JACK Jack Dempsey "Gabby" or "Scat" B 10.26.1919 Dearborn, MI BR/TR 5-10/175# d4.19																								
1949	Pit N	8	0	3	0	0	0	0	0	0	0	0	—	—	—	—	0	0	—	0			R	0.0
CASTELLANO, PEDRO Pedro Orlando (Arrieta) B 3.11.1970 Lara, Venezuela BR/TR 6-1/175# d5.30																								
1993	Col N	34	71	12	13	2	0	3	7	8-0	0	16	.183	.266	.338	52	-5	1-1	.909	-2	97	61	3-13,1-10/S-5,2-4	-0.7
1995	Col N	4	5	0	0	0	0	0	0	2-0	0	3	.000	.286	.000	-13	-1	0-0	1.000	-1	0	0	/3-3	-0.1
1996	Col N	13	17	1	2	0	0	0	2	3-1	1	6	.118	.286	.118	9	-2	0-0	1.000	1	167	136	/2-3,3O(LF)	-0.1
Total	3	51	93	13	15	2	0	3	9	13-1	1	25	.161	.271	.280	40	-8	1-1	.917	-2	89	53	/3-17,1-10,2-7,S-5,O(LF)	-0.9
CASTIGLIA, JIM James Vincent B 9.30.1918 Passaic, NJ BL/TR 5-11/200# d4.14 Mil 1942-45																								
1942	Phi A	16	18	2	7	0	0	0	2	1	0	3	.389	.421	.389	129	1	0-0	.875	-1	*72*	*198*	/C-3	0.0
CASTIGLIONE, PETE Peter Paul B 2.13.1921 Greenwich, CT BR/TR 5-11/175# d9.10																								
1947	Pit N	13	50	6	14	0	0	0	1	2	0	5	.280	.308	.280	55	-3	0	.970	-0	100	74	S-13	-0.3
1948	Pit N	4	2	0	0	0	0	0	0	0	0	0	.000	.000	.000	-98	-1	1	1.000	0	145	0	/S	-0.1
1949	Pit N	118	448	57	120	20	2	6	43	20	0	43	.268	.299	.362	74	-17	2	.957	4	103	128	3-98,S-17/O-2(RF)	-1.3
1950	Pit N	94	263	29	67	10	3	3	22	23	1	23	.255	.317	.350	73	-11	1	.970	-11	86	115	3-35,S-29/2-9,1-3	-2.0
1951	Pit N	132	482	62	126	19	4	7	42	34	1	28	.261	.311	.361	78	-16	2-2	.957	8	115	103	3-99,S-28	-0.7
1952	Pit N	67	214	27	57	9	1	4	18	17	1	8	.266	.323	.374	90	-3	3-3	.951	4	111	64	3-57/1O(LF)	0.0
1953	Pit N	45	159	14	33	2	1	4	21	5	1	14	.208	.236	.308	41	-15	1-1	.978	4	113	64	3-43	-1.1
	StL N	67	52	9	9	2	0	0	3	2	0	5	.173	.204	.212	9	-7	0-0	.967	4	121	211	3-51/2-9,S-3	-0.3
	Year	112	211	23	42	4	1	4	24	7	1	19	.199	.228	.284	33	-22	1-1	.976	8	114	90	3-94/2-9,S-3	-1.4
1954	StL N	5	0	1	0	0	0	0	0	0	0	0	—	—	—	—	0	0-0	1.000	0	142	0	/3-5	0.0
Total	8	545	1670	205	426	62	11	24	150	103	4	126	.255	.300	.349	71	-73	10-6	.960	12	108	102	3-388/S-91,2-18,1-4,O-3(1-0-2)	-5.8
CASTILLA, VINNY Vinicio (Soria) B 7.4.1967 Oaxaca, Mexico BR/TR 6-1/185# d9.1																								
1991	Atl N	12	5	1	1	0	0	0	0	0-0	0	2	.200	.200	.200	12	-1	0-0	1.000	-1	65	0	S-12	-0.2
1992	Atl N	9	16	1	4	1	0	0	1	1-1	1	4	.250	.333	.313	79	0	0-0	.875	-0	72	0	/3-4,S-4	0.0
1993	Col N	105	337	36	86	9	7	9	30	13-4	2	45	.255	.283	.404	71	-15	2-5	.975	4	103	105	*S-104	-0.5
1994	Col N	52	130	16	43	11	1	3	18	7-1	0	23	.331	.357	.500	105	1	2-1	.984	-0	98	119	S-18,2-14/3-9,1-2	0.3
1995	†Col N★	139	527	82	163	34	2	32	90	30-2	4	87	.309	.347	.564	106	4	2-8	.958	-7	99	87	*3-137/S-5	-0.3
1996	Col N	160	629	97	191	34	0	40	113	35-7	5	88	.304	.343	.548	106	5	7-2	.960	**34**	**130**	**150**	*3-160	4.0
1997	Col N	159	612	94	186	25	2	40	113	44-9	8	108	.304	.356	.547	108	7	2-4	.954	12	116	135	*3-157	1.9
1998	Col N★	**162**	645	108	206	28	4	46	144	40-7	6	89	.319	.362	.589	120	17	5-9	.970	0	102	125	*3-162/S	1.7
1999	Col N	158	615	83	169	24	1	33	102	53-7	1	75	.275	.331	.478	80	-19	2-3	.954	-1	101	107	*3-157	-1.8
2000	TB A	85	331	22	73	9	1	6	42	14-3	3	41	.221	.254	.308	43	-30	1-2	.967	14	126	135	3-83	-1.4
2001	TB A	24	93	7	20	6	0	2	9	3-0	1	22	.215	.247	.344	54	-6	0-0	.934	2	101	119	3-24	-0.4
	†Hou N	122	445	62	120	28	1	23	82	32-3	3	86	.270	.320	.492	101	0	1-4	.963	9	107	91	*3-121/S-3	0.9
2002	†Atl N	143	543	56	126	23	2	12	61	22-4	7	69	.232	.268	.348	64	-33	4-1	**.982**	-18	91	90	*3-139	-4.9
2003	†Atl N	147	542	65	150	28	3	22	76	26-3	3	86	.277	.310	.461	99	-4	1-2	.955	0	104	106	*3-147	-0.2
Total	13	1477	5470	730	1538	260	24	268	881	320-51	44	825	.281	.323	.484	94	-74	29-41	.961	49	108	113	*3-1300,S-147/2-14,1-2	-0.9
CASTILLO, ALBERTO Alberto Terrero B 2.10.1970 San Juan De La Maguana, D.R. BR/TR 6/185# d5.28																								
1995	NY N	13	29	2	3	0	0	0	0	3-0	1	9	.103	.212	.103	-14	-5	1-0	.974	3	198	154	C-12	-0.1
1996	NY N	6	11	1	4	0	0	0	0	0-0	0	4	.364	.364	.364	97	0	0-0	1.000	-1	76	0	/C-6	-0.1
1997	NY N	35	59	3	12	1	0	0	7	9-0	0	16	.203	.304	.220	43	-5	0-1	.987	2	159	42	C-34	-0.1
1998	NY N	38	83	13	17	4	0	2	7	9-0	1	17	.205	.290	.325	63	-5	0-2	.990	2	137	188	C-35/D	-0.1
1999	StL N	93	255	21	67	8	0	4	31	24-1	2	48	.263	.326	.341	70	-12	0-0	.991	11	159	157	C-91	0.4
2000	Tor A	66	185	14	39	7	0	1	16	21-0	0	36	.211	.287	.265	41	-17	0-0	.993	9	133	116	C-66	-0.4
2001	Tor A	66	131	9	26	4	0	1	4	7-0	3	30	.198	.255	.252	34	-13	1-1	.989	7	98	103	C-66	-0.3
2002	NY A	15	37	3	5	1	1	0	4	1-0	0	12	.135	.158	.216	-2	-6	0-0	.990	3	79	166	C-14	-0.2
2003	SF N	11	15	2	3	1	0	1	4	0-0	0	5	.200	.200	.467	69	-1	0-0	.975	2	219	0	C-10	0.1
Total	9	343	805	68	176	26	1	9	73	74-1	7	177	.219	.287	.287	49	-64	2-4	.990	38	137	128	C-334/D	-0.8
CASTILLO, TONY Anthony B 6.14.1957 San Jose, CA BR/TR 6-4/190# d9.22																								
1978	SD N	5	8	0	1	0	0	0	1	0-0	0	2	.125	.125	.125	-33	-1	0-0	.950	1	226	187	/C-5	0.0
CASTILLO, BRAULIO Braulio Robinson Medrano (born Medrano (Castillo)) B 5.13.1968 Elias Pina, D.R. BR/TR 6/160# d8.18																								
1991	Phi N	28	52	3	9	3	0	0	2	1-0	0	15	.173	.189	.231	18	-6	1-1	.977	0	98	208	O-26(0-24-2)	-0.6
1992	Phi N	28	76	12	15	3	1	2	7	4-0	0	15	.197	.237	.342	62	-4	1-0	.956	-1	102	0	O-24(2-6-16)	-0.6
Total	2	56	128	15	24	6	1	2	9	5-0	0	30	.188	.218	.297	44	-10	2-1	.966	-1	100	98	/O-50(2-30-18)	-1.2
CASTILLO, MANNY Esteban Manuel Antonio (Cabrera) B 4.1.1957 Santo Domingo, D.R. BB/TR 5-9/160# d9.1																								
1980	KC A	7	10	1	2	0	0	0	0	0-0	0	0	.200	.200	.200	10	-1	0-0	1.000	0	103	0	/3-3,2D	-0.1
1982	Sea A	138	506	49	130	29	1	3	49	22-2	2	35	.257	.286	.336	70	-21	2-8	.938	-16	81	74	*3-130/2-9	-4.2
1983	Sea A	91	203	13	42	6	3	0	24	7-2	1	20	.207	.233	.266	37	-18	1-1	.971	8	112	94	3-55,1-11/2-5,PD	-1.1
Total	3	236	719	63	174	35	4	3	73	29-4	3	55	.242	.270	.314	59	-40	3-9	.949	-8	89	78	3-188/2-15,1-11,D-8,P	-5.4

Year	Tm Lg	G	AB	R	H	2B	3B	HR	RBI	BB-IB	HP	SO	AVG	OBP	SLG	AOPS	ABR	SB-CS	FA	FR	Rng	Thr	G at Pos	BFW
CASTILLO, JUAN Juan (Bryas) B 1.25.1962 San Pedro De Macoris, D.R. BB/TR (BR 1988-89) 5-11/162# d4.12																								
1986	Mil A	26	54	6	9	0	1	0	5	5-0	1	12	.167	.250	.204	24	-6	1-1	1.000	-2	83	77	2-17/S-4,3-2,O(RF)D	-0.7
1987	Mil A	116	321	44	72	11	4	3	28	33-0	3	76	.224	.302	.312	62	-18	15-7	.973	-11	90	93	2-97,S-13/3-7	-2.2
1988	Mil A	54	90	10	20	0	0	0	2	3-0	0	14	.222	.247	.222	32	-8	2-0	.932	0	129	105	2-18,3-17,S-13/O(LF)D	-0.7
1989	Mil A	3	4	0	0	0	0	0	3	0-0	0	2	.000	.000	.000	-99	-1	0-0	1.000	0	90	83	/2-3	-0.1
Total	4	199	469	60	101	11	5	3	38	41-0	4	104	.215	.282	.279	51	-33	18-8	.972	-13	93	92	2-135/S-30,3-26,D-5,O-2(1-0-1)	-3.7
CASTILLO, LUIS Luis Antonio (Donato) B 9.12.1975 San Pedro De Macoris, D.R. BB/TR 5-11/145# d8.8																								
1996	Fla N	41	164	26	43	2	1	1	8	14-0	0	46	.262	.320	.305	68	-8	17-4	.986	7	104	143	2-41	0.3
1997	Fla N	75	263	27	63	8	0	0	8	27-0	0	53	.240	.310	.270	56	-17	16-10	.971	-3	94	106	2-70	-1.6
1998	Fla N	44	153	21	31	3	2	1	10	22-0	1	33	.203	.307	.268	56	-10	3-0	.970	-1	93	105	2-44	-0.8
1999	Fla N	128	487	76	147	23	4	0	28	67-0	0	85	.302	.384	.366	97	1	50-17	.976	-12	97	88	*2-126	0.0
2000	Fla N	136	539	101	180	17	3	2	17	78-0	0	86	.334	.418	.388	110	13	**62**-22	.983	-4	98	92	*2-136	2.0
2001	Fla N	134	537	76	141	16	10	2	45	67-0	1	90	.263	.344	.341	81	-15	33-16	.980	10	104	**118**	*2-133	0.3
2002	Fla N★	146	606	86	185	18	5	2	39	55-4	2	76	.305	.364	.361	100	-3	**48**-15	.981	-12	97	94	*2-144	-0.2
2003	†Fla N★	152	595	99	187	19	6	6	39	63-0	2	60	.314	.381	.397	108	8	21-19	.986	4	103	99	*2-152	1.7
Total	8	856	3344	512	977	106	31	14	194	393-4	6	529	.292	.367	.355	93	-31	250-103	.980	-11	99	101	2-846	1.7
CASTILLO, MARTY Martin Horace B 1.16.1957 Long Beach, CA BR/TR 6-1/190# d8.19																								
1981	Det A	6	8	1	1	0	0	0	0	0-0	0	2	.125	.125	.125	-27	-1	0-0	1.000	2	147	642	/3-4,CO(LF)	0.1
1982	Det A	1	0	0	0	0	0	0	0	0-0	0	0	—	—	—	—	0	0-0	1.000	-0	7	0	/C	0.0
1983	Det A	67	119	10	23	4	0	2	10	7-0	0	22	.193	.238	.277	42	-10	2-0	.990	0	94	82	3-58,C-10	-1.0
1984	†Det A	70	141	16	33	5	2	4	17	10-0	0	33	.234	.285	.383	83	-4	1-0	.970	-6	101	111	C-36,3-33/D	-0.8
1985	Det A	57	84	4	10	2	0	2	5	2-0	0	19	.119	.138	.214	-5	-12	0-2	.977	0	109	157	C-32,3-25	-1.2
Total	5	201	352	31	67	11	2	8	32	19-0	0	76	.190	.231	.301	46	-27	3-2	.978	-4	97	91	3-120/C-80,DO(LF)	-2.9
CASTILLO, CARMEN Monte Carmelo B 6.8.1958 San Pedro De Macoris, D.R. BR/TR 6-1/190# d7.17																								
1982	Cle A	47	120	11	25	4	0	2	11	6-2	2	17	.208	.258	.292	51	-8	0-0	.978	1	123	0	O-43(19-8-20)/D-2	-0.9
1983	Cle A	23	36	9	10	2	1	1	3	4-0	1	6	.278	.366	.472	124	1	1-1	.929	1	99	343	O-19(RF)/D	0.2
1984	Cle A	87	211	36	55	9	2	10	36	21-0	2	32	.261	.329	.464	116	4	1-3	.933	-2	106	57	O-70(RF)/D-2	-0.1
1985	Cle A	67	184	27	45	5	1	11	25	11-0	3	40	.245	.298	.462	105	0	3-0	.953	-0	116	0	O-51(RF)/D-9	-0.1
1986	Cle A	85	205	34	57	9	0	8	32	9-0	1	48	.278	.310	.439	103	0	2-1	.939	2	106	209	O-37(RF),D-35	0.0
1987	Cle A	89	220	27	55	17	0	11	31	16-0	0	52	.250	.296	.477	101	0	1-1	1.000	1	92	264	D-43,O-23(1-0-22)	-0.1
1988	Cle A	66	176	12	48	8	0	4	14	5-1	1	31	.273	.297	.386	87	-3	6-2	.933	-2	96	49	O-45(30-0-16)/D-9	-0.6
1989	Min A	94	218	23	56	13	3	8	33	15-1	1	40	.257	.305	.454	105	1	1-2	.976	2	113	81	O-67(7-0-61),D-16	0.1
1990	Min A	64	137	11	30	4	0	0	12	3-1	1	23	.219	.239	.248	35	-12	0-1	.923	-1	104	0	D-35,O-21(2-0-21)	-1.5
1991	Min A	9	12	0	2	0	1	0	0	0-0	1	2	.167	.231	.333	52	-1	0-0	1.000	0	126	0	/O-4(1-0-3),D-2	-0.1
Total	10	631	1519	190	383	71	8	55	197	90-5	13	291	.252	.298	.418	93	-18	15-11	.953	3	109	80	O-380(60-8-320),D-154	-3.1
CASTINO, JOHN John Anthony B 10.23.1954 Evanston, IL BR/TR 5-11/175# d4.6																								
1979	Min A	148	393	49	112	13	8	5	52	27-0	1	72	.285	.331	.397	92	-5	5-2	.963	9	109	**136**	*3-143/S-5	0.2
1980	Min A	150	546	67	165	17	7	13	64	29-1	0	67	.302	.336	.430	101	-1	7-5	.961	21	114	122	*3-138,S-18	2.0
1981	Min A	101	381	41	102	13	**9**	6	36	18-3	1	52	.268	.301	.396	94	-5	4-5	**.975**	17	113	125	3-98/2-4	1.1
1982	Min A	117	410	48	99	12	6	6	37	36-1	2	51	.241	.304	.344	76	-14	2-5	.995	-0	90	100	2-96,3-21/O-6(5-1-0),D	-1.1
1983	Min A	142	563	83	156	30	4	11	57	62-1	1	54	.277	.348	.403	103	3	4-2	.990	10	104	92	*2-132/3-8,D	2.0
1984	Min A	8	27	5	12	1	0	0	3	5-2	0	2	.444	.531	.481	174	3	0-0	1.000	-1	81	74	/3-8	0.2
Total	6	666	2320	293	646	86	34	41	249	177-8	5	298	.278	.329	.398	95	-19	22-19	.967	56	112	126	3-416,2-232/S-23,O-6(5-1-0),D-2	4.4
CASTINO, VINCE Vincent Charles B 10.11.1917 Willisville, IL D 3.6.1967 Sacramento, CA BR/TR 5-9/175# d6.24																								
1943	Chi A	33	101	14	23	1	0	2	16	12	0	11	.228	.310	.297	78	-3	0-0	.971	-5	*88*	*47*	C-30	-0.6
1944	Chi A	29	78	8	18	5	0	0	3	10	1	13	.231	.326	.295	79	-2	0-1	.990	1	*120*	*137*	C-26	0.1
1945	Chi A	26	36	2	8	1	0	0	4	3	0	7	.222	.282	.250	56	-2	0-0	.951	-1	*160*	*111*	C-25	-0.3
Total	3	88	215	24	49	7	0	2	23	25	1	31	.228	.311	.288	75	-7	0-1	.976	-5	*112*	*92*	/C-81	-0.8
CASTLE, DON Donald Hardy B 2.1.1950 Kokomo, IN BL/TL 6-1/205# d9.11																								
1973	Tex A	4	13	0	4	1	0	0	2	1-0	0	3	.308	.357	.385	114	0	0-0	—	0			/D-3	0.0
CASTLE, JOHN John Francis B 6.1.1883 Honey Brook, PA D 4.13.1929 Philadelphia, PA 5-10.5/?# d4.25																								
1910	Phi N	3	4	1	1	0	0	0	0	0	0	0	.250	.250	.250	44	0	1	—	-0	0	0	/O-2(1-1-0)	0.0
CASTLEMAN, FOSTER Foster Ephraim B 1.1.1931 Nashville, TN BR/TR 6/175# d8.4																								
1954	NY N	13	12	0	3	0	0	0	1	0	1	3	.250	.308	.250	47	-1	0-0	—	-0	0	0	/3-2	-0.1
1955	NY N	15	28	3	6	1	0	2	4	2-0	0	4	.214	.267	.464	89	-1	0-0	1.000	-2	73	57	/2-6,3	-0.2
1956	NY N	124	385	33	87	16	3	14	45	15-2	2	50	.226	.256	.392	72	-17	2-1	.947	3	108	61	*3-107/S-2,2	-1.4
1957	NY N	18	37	7	6	2	0	1	1	2-0	0	8	.162	.205	.297	33	-4	0-0	.867	-1	101	106	/3-7,2S	-0.5
1958	Bal A	98	200	15	34	5	0	3	14	16-2	3	34	.170	.242	.240	35	-18	2-0	.964	-15	85	95	S-91/2-4,3-4,O(LF)	-2.8
Total	5	268	662	58	136	24	3	20	65	35-4	6	99	.205	.250	.341	60	-41	4-1	.944	-14	107	63	3-121/S-94,2-12,O(LF)	-5.0
CASTRO, JUAN Juan Gabriel B 6.20.1972 Los Mochis, Mexico BR/TR 5-10/165# d9.2																								
1995	LA N	11	4	0	1	0	0	0	0	1-0	0	1	.250	.400	.250	84	0	0-0	1.000	1	153	0	/3-7,S-4	0.1
1996	†LA N	70	132	16	26	5	3	0	5	10-0	0	27	.197	.254	.280	44	-11	1-0	.982	-5	90	137	S-30,3-23/2-9,O(LF)	-1.4
1997	LA N	40	75	3	11	3	1	0	4	7-1	0	20	.147	.220	.213	15	-10	0-0	1.000	-2	82	77	S-22,2-14/3-3	-1.1
1998	LA N	89	220	25	43	7	0	2	14	15-0	0	37	.195	.245	.255	34	-22	0-0	.954	3	102	143	S-47,2-38,3-12	-1.5
1999	LA N	2	1	0	0	0	0	0	0	0-0	0	1	.000	.000	.000	-99	0	0-0	1.000	1	408	463	/2S	0.1
2000	Cin N	82	224	20	54	12	2	4	23	14-1	0	33	.241	.283	.366	62	-14	0-2	.994	-7	95	101	S-57,2-21/3-7	-1.6
2001	Cin N	96	242	27	54	10	0	3	13	13-2	0	50	.223	.261	.302	43	-21	0-0	.944	-14	89	68	S-46,2-37,3-19/1	-3.1
2002	Cin N	54	82	5	18	3	0	2	11	7-0	0	18	.220	.278	.329	61	-5	0-0	.964	-0	96	125	S-25,2-17/13	-0.4
2003	Cin N	113	320	28	81	14	1	9	33	18-1	0	58	.253	.290	.387	77	-12	2-3	.984	-1	108	94	2-56,3-30,S-24/1	-1.0
Total	9	557	1300	124	288	54	7	20	103	85-5	0	245	.222	.267	.320	53	-95	3-5	.975	-24	93	111	S-256,2-193,3-102/1-3,O(LF)	-9.9
CASTRO, LOUIS Louis Manuel "Jud" B 1877 , Colombia D 9.24.1941 New York, NY BR/TR 5-7/?# d4.23																								
1902	Phi A	42	143	18	35	8	1	1	15	4	0		.245	.265	.336	63	-8	2	.918	-11	82	70	2-36/O-3(0-2-1),S	-1.8
CASTRO, RAMON Ramon Abraham B 3.1.1976 Vega Baja, P.R. BR/TR 6-3/225# d8.27																								
1999	Fla N	24	67	4	12	4	0	2	4	10-3	0	14	.179	.282	.328	58	-4	0-0	.992	-1	141	143	C-24	-0.4
2000	Fla N	50	138	10	33	4	0	2	14	16-7	1	36	.239	.318	.312	64	-8	0-0	.980	-1	93	128	C-50	-0.6
2001	Fla N	7	11	0	2	0	0	0	1	1-0	0	1	.182	.250	.182	15	-1	0-0	1.000	-1	94	0	/C-3	-0.2
2002	Fla N	54	101	11	24	4	0	6	18	14-3	0	24	.238	.322	.455	112	1	0-0	1.000	-4	78	119	C-37/D	-0.1
2003	Fla N	40	53	6	15	2	0	5	8	4-0	0	11	.283	.333	.604	144	3	0-0	.982	-1	176	0	C-18/D	0.3
Total	5	175	370	31	86	14	0	15	45	45-13	1	86	.232	.313	.392	85	-9	0-0	.988	-7	106	117	C-132/D-2	-1.0
CATALANOTTO, FRANK Frank John B 4.27.1974 Smithtown, NY BL/TR 6/170# d9.3 OF Total (165-LF 59-RF)																								
1997	Det A	13	26	2	8	2	0	0	3	3-0	0	7	.308	.379	.385	101	0	0-0	1.000	-2	81	0	/2-6,D-3	-0.1
1998	Det A	89	213	23	60	13	2	6	25	12-1	4	39	.282	.325	.446	99	-1	3-2	.974	-0	86	108	2-31,D-23,1-18/3-3	-0.3
1999	Det A	100	286	41	79	19	0	11	35	15-1	9	49	.276	.327	.458	98	-1	3-4	1.000	-10	72	130	1-32,2-32,3-21/D-9	-1.2
2000	Tex A	103	282	55	82	13	2	10	42	33-0	6	36	.291	.375	.457	108	4	6-2	.966	-5	101	73	2-49,D-20,1-17/O(RF)	0.0
2001	Tex A	133	463	77	153	31	5	11	54	39-3	8	55	.330	.391	.490	126	19	15-5	.995	-1	106	36	O-92(78-0-15),2-13,3-11/1-5,D-5	1.6
2002	Tex A	68	212	42	57	16	6	3	23	25-0	8	27	.269	.364	.443	109	3	9-5	.971	-3	84	0	O-26(LF),2-23,1-15/D-8	-0.1
2003	Tor A	133	489	83	146	34	6	13	59	35-1	6	62	.299	.351	.472	113	9	2-2	.993	-8	79	74	*O-100(61-0-43),D-21/1-5	-0.4
Total	7	639	1971	323	585	128	21	54	241	162-6	41	275	.297	.359	.465	111	33	38-20	.992	-28	91	50	O-219L,2-154/1-92,D-89,3-35	-0.5
CATER, DANNY Danny Anderson B 2.25.1940 Austin, TX BR/TR 5-11.5/180# d4.14 OF Total (293-LF 2-CF 16-RF)																								
1964	Phi N	60	152	13	45	9	1	1	13	7-1	0	15	.296	.325	.388	102	0	1-0	.981	1	95	212	O-39(36-1-2)/1-7,3	-0.1
1965	Chi A	142	514	74	139	18	4	14	55	33-0	3	65	.270	.316	.403	110	5	3-3	.978	-13	72	74	*O-127(127-1-0),3-11/1-3	-1.7
1966	Chi A	21	60	3	11	1	1	0	4	0-0	1	10	.183	.194	.233	25	-6	3-1	.909	-2	78	0	O-18(16-0-3)	-1.0
	KC A	116	425	47	124	16	3	7	52	28-2	1	37	.292	.334	.393	113	6	1-4	.994	-4	96	107	1-53,3-42,O-22(21-0-1)	-0.4
	Year	137	485	50	135	17	4	7	56	28-2	2	47	.278	.317	.373	102	0	4-5	.994	-6	96	107	1-53,3-42,O-40(37-0-4)	-1.4

Year	Tm Lg	G	AB	R	H	2B	3B	HR	RBI	BB-IB	HP	SO	AVG	OBP	SLG	AOPS	ABR	SB-CS	FA	FR	Rng	Thr	G at Pos	BFW
1967	KC A	142	529	55	143	17	4	4	46	34-9	4	56	.270	.317	.340	98	-2	4-5	.916	-10	76	36	3-56,O-55(LF),1-44	-2.0
1968	Oak A	147	504	53	146	28	3	6	62	35-3	2	43	.290	.336	.393	127	16	8-7	**.995**	-3	87	108	*1-121,O-20(19-0-2)/2	0.5
1969	Oak A	152	584	64	153	24	2	10	76	28-3	2	40	.262	.296	.361	87	-12	1-4	.992	2	112	114	*1-132,O-20(19-0-1)/2-4	-2.4
1970	NY A	155	582	64	175	26	5	6	76	34-6	2	44	.301	.340	.393	108	4	4-2	.992	-4	98	96	*1-131,3-42/O-7(RF)	-0.9
1971	NY A	121	428	39	118	16	5	4	50	19-4	2	25	.276	.308	.364	96	-4	0-3	.995	10	159	110	1-78,3-52	-0.1
1972	Bos A	92	317	32	75	17	1	8	39	15-2	2	33	.237	.270	.372	87	-6	0-1	.993	5	121	88	1-90	-0.9
1973	Bos A	63	195	30	61	12	0	1	24	10-1	1	22	.313	.348	.390	102	1	0-0	.997	2	88	134	1-37,3-21/D-3	-0.1
1974	Bos A	56	126	14	31	5	0	5	20	10-1	2	13	.246	.309	.405	98	0	1-0	1.000	0	100	63	1-23,D-14	-0.2
1975	StL N	22	35	3	8	2	0	0	2	1-1	0	3	.229	.250	.286	47	-3	0-0	.981	-0	99	80	1-12	-0.3
Total	12	1289	4451	491	1229	191	29	66	519	254-33	22	406	.276	.316	.377	102	-1	26-30	.994	-16	107	105	1-731,0-308L,3-225/D-17,2-5	-9.6

CATES, ELI Eli Eldo B 1.26.1877 Greens Fork, IN D 5.29.1964 Anderson, IN BR/TR 5-9.5/175# d4.20 ▲

Year	Tm Lg	G	AB	R	H	2B	3B	HR	RBI	BB-IB	HP	SO	AVG	OBP	SLG	AOPS	ABR	SB-CS	FA	FR	Rng	Thr	G at Pos	BFW
1908	Was A	40	59	5	11	1	1	0	3	6	1		.186	.273	.237	72	-2	0	.907	-0	118	107	P-19/2-3	-0.1

CATHER, TED Theodore Physick B 5.20.1889 Chester, PA D 4.9.1945 Elkton, MD BR/TR 5-10.5/178# d9.23

Year	Tm Lg	G	AB	R	H	2B	3B	HR	RBI	BB-IB	HP	SO	AVG	OBP	SLG	AOPS	ABR	SB-CS	FA	FR	Rng	Thr	G at Pos	BFW
1912	StL N	5	19	4	8	1	1	0	2	0	0	4	.421	.421	.579	176	2	1	.944	1	110	213	/O-5(0-4-1)	0.2
1913	StL N	67	183	16	39	8	4	0	12	9	0	24	.213	.250	.301	58	-11	7-6	.915	-2	86	139	O-57(14-1-42)/P1	-1.6
1914	StL N	39	99	11	27	7	0	0	13	3	0	15	.273	.294	.343	90	-1	4	.981	1	99	129	O-28(23-5-0)	-0.2
	†Bos N	50	145	19	43	11	2	0	27	7	2	28	.297	.338	.400	120	3	7	.953	-3	85	81	O-48(23-7-20)	-0.1
	Year	89	244	30	70	18	2	0	40	10	2	43	.287	.320	.377	108	2	11	.966	-2	91	101	O-76(46-12-20)	-0.3
1915	Bos N	40	102	10	21	3	1	2	18	15	2	19	.206	.319	.314	96	0	2-4	.902	-3	75	72	O-32(31-0-2)	-0.6
Total	4	201	548	60	138	30	8	2	72	34	4	90	.252	.300	.347	91	-7	21-10	.938	-6	87	113	O-170(91-17-65)/1P	-2.3

CATON, HOWDY James Howard "Buster" B 7.16.1896 Zanesville, OH D 1.8.1948 Zanesville, OH BR/TR 5-6/165# d9.17 Mil 1918

Year	Tm Lg	G	AB	R	H	2B	3B	HR	RBI	BB-IB	HP	SO	AVG	OBP	SLG	AOPS	ABR	SB-CS	FA	FR	Rng	Thr	G at Pos	BFW
1917	Pit N	14	57	6	12	1	2	0	4	6	0	7	.211	.286	.298	77	-2	0	.895	-3	99	75	S-14	-0.4
1918	Pit N	80	303	37	71	5	7	0	17	32	2	16	.234	.312	.297	83	-6	12	.928	-7	101	112	S-79	-0.9
1919	Pit N	39	102	13	18	1	2	0	5	12	0	10	.176	.263	.225	46	-7	2	.927	-9	65	65	S-17,3-14/O(CF)	-1.6
1920	Pit N	98	352	29	83	11	5	0	27	33	2	19	.236	.305	.295	71	-13	4-9	.929	-22	89	97	S-96	-3.3
Total	4	231	814	85	184	18	16	0	53	83	4	52	.226	.301	.287	72	-28	18-9	.926	-41	93	99	S-206/3-14,O(CF)	-6.2

CATTERSON, TOM Thomas Henry B 8.25.1884 Warwick, RI D 2.5.1920 Portland, ME BL/TL 5-10/170# d9.19

Year	Tm Lg	G	AB	R	H	2B	3B	HR	RBI	BB-IB	HP	SO	AVG	OBP	SLG	AOPS	ABR	SB-CS	FA	FR	Rng	Thr	G at Pos	BFW
1908	Bro N	19	68	5	13	1	1	1	2	5	1		.191	.257	.279	74	-2	0	.976	0	42	0	O-18(LF)	-0.4
1909	Bro N	9	18	0	4	0	0	0	1	3	0		.222	.333	.222	75	0	0	.833	-1	0	0	/O-6(CF)	-0.2
Total	2	28	86	5	17	1	1	1	3	8	1		.198	.274	.267	75	-2	0	.957	-1	35	0	/O-24(18-6-0)	-0.6

CAULFIELD, JAKE John Joseph B 11.23.1917 Los Angeles, CA D 12.16.1986 San Francisco, CA BR/TR 5-11/170# d4.24

Year	Tm Lg	G	AB	R	H	2B	3B	HR	RBI	BB-IB	HP	SO	AVG	OBP	SLG	AOPS	ABR	SB-CS	FA	FR	Rng	Thr	G at Pos	BFW
1946	Phi A	44	94	13	26	8	0	0	10	4	0	11	.277	.306	.362	87	-2	0-0	.929	-4	85	87	S-31/3	-0.4

CAUSEY, WAYNE James Wayne B 12.26.1936 Ruston, LA BL/TR 5-10.5/175# d6.5

Year	Tm Lg	G	AB	R	H	2B	3B	HR	RBI	BB-IB	HP	SO	AVG	OBP	SLG	AOPS	ABR	SB-CS	FA	FR	Rng	Thr	G at Pos	BFW
1955	Bal A	68	175	14	34	2	1	1	9	17-1	1	25	.194	.269	.234	39	-16	0-1	.912	-6	101	122	3-55/2-7,S	-2.2
1956	Bal A	53	88	7	15	0	1	1	4	8-0	0	23	.170	.237	.227	26	-10	0-0	.980	1	117	130	3-30/2-7	-0.9
1957	Bal A	14	10	2	2	0	0	0	1	5-2	1	2	.200	.471	.200	105	1	0-0	.960	1	125	80	/2-6,3-5	0.2
1961	KC A	104	312	37	86	14	1	8	49	37-0	0	28	.276	.348	.404	100	0	0-0	.955	15	115	110	3-88,S-11/2-9	1.6
1962	KC A	117	305	40	77	14	1	4	38	41-5	2	30	.252	.340	.344	82	-6	2-0	.953	1	96	66	S-51,3-26/2-9	0.0
1963	KC A	139	554	72	155	32	4	8	44	56-3	0	54	.280	.345	.395	101	3	4-2	.978	15	107	102	*S-135/3-2	3.0
1964	KC A	157	604	82	170	31	4	8	49	88-3	7	65	.281	.377	.386	110	13	0-1	.967	-7	92	86	*S-131,2-17/3-9	2.0
1965	KC A	144	513	48	134	17	8	3	34	61-4	2	48	.261	.341	.343	97	-1	1-3	.972	-11	95	94	S-62,2-45,3-35	-0.6
1966	KC A	28	79	1	18	0	0	0	5	7-1	0	6	.228	.284	.228	53	-5	1-0	.871	-5	56	141	3-15,S-10	-0.9
	Chi A	78	164	23	40	8	2	0	13	24-0	0	13	.244	.333	.317	97	0	2-0	.980	-8	97	62	2-60/S3	-0.3
	Year	106	243	24	58	8	2	0	18	31-1	0	19	.239	.318	.288	83	-5	3-0	.980	-12	97	62	2-60,3-15,S-11	-1.2
1967	Chi A	124	292	21	66	10	3	1	28	32-4	1	35	.226	.302	.291	80	-7	2-5	.978	-4	109	94	2-96/S-2	-0.7
1968	Chi A	59	100	8	18	2	0	0	7	14-2	1	7	.180	.284	.200	49	-6	0-0	.971	-5	93	87	2-41	-1.0
	Cal A	4	11	0	0	0	0	0	0	0-0	0	1	.000	.000	.000	-99	-3	0-0	1.000	1	132	184	/2-4	-0.2
	Year	63	111	8	18	2	0	0	7	14-2	1	8	.162	.260	.180	36	-8	0-0	.975	-4	97	98	2-45	-1.2
	Atl N	16	37	2	4	0	1	1	4	0-0	0	4	.108	.103	.243	3	-5	0-0	1.000	-3	72	68	/2-6,S-2,3-2	-0.8
Total	11	1105	3244	357	819	130	26	35	285	390-25	15	341	.252	.333	.341	89	-42	12-12	.969	-13	99	89	S-406,2-307,3-268	-0.8

CAVANAUGH, JOHN John J. B 6.5.1900 Scranton, PA D 1.14.1961 New Brunswick, NJ BR/TR 5-9/158# d7.7

Year	Tm Lg	G	AB	R	H	2B	3B	HR	RBI	BB-IB	HP	SO	AVG	OBP	SLG	AOPS	ABR	SB-CS	FA	FR	Rng	Thr	G at Pos	BFW
1919	Phi N	1	1	0	0	0	0	0	0	0	0	1	.000	.000	.000	-93	0	0	—	-0	0	0	/3	0.0

CAVARRETTA, PHIL Philip Joseph B 7.19.1916 Chicago, IL BL/TL 5-11.5/175# d9.16 M3 C4

Year	Tm Lg	G	AB	R	H	2B	3B	HR	RBI	BB-IB	HP	SO	AVG	OBP	SLG	AOPS	ABR	SB-CS	FA	FR	Rng	Thr	G at Pos	BFW
1934	Chi N	7	21	5	8	0	1	1	6	2	0	3	.381	.435	.619	182	2	1	1.000	1	148	151	/1-5	0.2
1935	†Chi N	146	589	85	162	28	12	8	82	39	2	61	.275	.322	.404	93	-7	4	.986	2	108	**128**	*1-145	-1.8
1936	Chi N	124	458	55	125	18	1	9	56	17	5	36	.273	.306	.376	81	-14	8	.987	-2	95	113	*1-115	-2.5
1937	Chi N	106	329	43	94	18	7	5	56	32	0	35	.286	.349	.429	106	3	7	.972	2	90	191	O-55(7-47-1),1-43	0.0
1938	†Chi N	92	268	29	64	11	4	1	28	14	4	27	.239	.287	.321	65	-13	4	.962	-2	84	138	O-52(7-8-37),1-28	-2.0
1939	Chi N	22	55	4	15	3	1	0	0	4	0	3	.273	.322	.364	82	-1	2	.991	-1	76	94	1-13/O(RF)	-0.3
1940	Chi N	65	193	34	54	11	4	2	22	31	3	18	.280	.388	.409	122	7	3	.991	-1	94	138	1-52	0.2
1941	Chi N	107	346	46	99	18	4	6	40	53	2	28	.286	.384	.413	129	15	2	.992	-5	97	69	O-66(8-53-6),1-33	0.6
1942	Chi N	136	482	59	130	28	4	3	54	71	1	42	.270	.365	.363	118	14	7	.989	0	97	72	O-70(4-67-0),1-61	0.7
1943	Chi N	143	530	93	154	27	9	8	73	75	3	42	.291	.382	.421	134	25	3	.987	-11	74	95	*1-134/O-7(CF)	0.7
1944	Chi N★	152	614	106	**197**	35	15	5	82	67	3	42	.321	.390	.451	137	31	4	.992	-7	80	107	*1-139,O-13(CF)	1.7
1945	†Chi N✳	132	498	94	177	34	10	6	97	81	4	34	**.355**	**.449**	.500	167	50	5	.993	-1	92	104	*1-120,O-11(LF)	4.1
1946	Chi N★	139	510	89	150	28	10	8	78	88	3	54	.294	.401	.435	140	30	2	.967	3	108	80	O-86(7-13-78),1-51	3.0
1947	Chi N★	127	459	56	144	22	5	2	63	58	0	35	.314	.391	.397	114	11	2	.977	-2	90	149	*O-100(69-26-8),1-24	0.3
1948	Chi N	111	334	41	93	16	5	3	40	35	1	29	.278	.349	.383	102	1	4	.998	1	110	147	1-41,O-40(30-0-10)	-0.2
1949	Chi N	105	360	46	106	22	4	8	49	45	1	31	.294	.374	.444	122	12	2	.993	9	142	89	1-70,O-25(3-0-21)	1.7
1950	Chi N	82	256	49	70	11	1	10	31	40	2	31	.273	.376	.441	115	7	1	.986	0	107	88	1-67/O-3(RF)	0.5
1951	Chi N	89	206	24	64	7	1	6	28	27	1	28	.311	.393	.442	122	7	0-0	.994	3	122	110	1-53,M	0.9
1952	Chi N	41	63	7	15	1	1	1	8	9	0	3	.238	.333	.333	84	-1	0-0	.991	1	129	136	1-13,M	-0.1
1953	Chi N	27	21	3	6	3	0	0	3	6	0	3	.286	.444	.429	126	1	0-0	—	0			HM	0.1
1954	Chi A	71	158	21	50	6	0	3	24	26	2	12	.316	.417	.411	124	7	4-0	.993	-2	83	114	1-44/O-9(2-0-7)	0.4
1955	Chi A	6	4	1	0	0	0	0	0	0-0	0	1	.000	.000	.000	-97	-1	0-0	1.000	-0	0	0	/1-3	-0.1
Total	22	2030	6754	990	1977	347	99	95	920	820-0	37	598	.293	.372	.416	118	186	65-0	.990	-10	99	105	*1-1254,O-538(148-234-172)	8.1

CAVENEY, IKE James Christopher B 12.10.1894 San Francisco, CA D 7.6.1949 San Francisco, CA BR/TR 5-9/168# d4.12

Year	Tm Lg	G	AB	R	H	2B	3B	HR	RBI	BB-IB	HP	SO	AVG	OBP	SLG	AOPS	ABR	SB-CS	FA	FR	Rng	Thr	G at Pos	BFW
1922	Cin N	118	394	41	94	12	9	3	54	29	6	33	.239	.301	.338	66	-21	6-6	.934	-5	100	**121**	*S-118	-1.3
1923	Cin N	138	488	58	135	21	9	4	63	26	1	41	.277	.315	.381	84	-13	5-4	.942	-1	98	109	*S-138	0.1
1924	Cin N	95	337	36	92	19	1	4	32	14	4	21	.273	.310	.371	83	-8	2-3	.924	-3	99	112	S-90/2-5	-0.2
1925	Cin N	115	358	38	89	9	5	2	47	28	0	31	.249	.303	.318	60	-22	2-0	.941	5	105	**129**	*S-111	-0.6
Total	4	466	1577	173	410	61	24	13	196	97	11	126	.260	.307	.354	74	-64	15-13	.936	-4	100	117	S-457/2-5	-2.0

CEDENO, ANDUJAR Andujar (Donastorg) B 8.21.1969 LaRomana, D.R. D 10.28.2000 Santo Domingo, D.R. BR/TR 6-1/168# d9.2 b-Domingo

Year	Tm Lg	G	AB	R	H	2B	3B	HR	RBI	BB-IB	HP	SO	AVG	OBP	SLG	AOPS	ABR	SB-CS	FA	FR	Rng	Thr	G at Pos	BFW
1990	Hou N	7	8	0	0	0	0	0	0	0-0	0	5	.000	.000	.000	-99	-2	0-0	.833	-2	39	0	/S-3	-0.4
1991	Hou N	67	251	27	61	13	2	9	36	9-1	1	74	.243	.270	.418	97	-3	4-3	.930	-18	80	104	S-66	-1.7
1992	Hou N	71	220	15	38	13	2	2	13	14-2	3	71	.173	.232	.277	46	-16	2-0	.959	-8	96	77	S-70	-2.1
1993	Hou N	149	505	69	143	24	4	11	56	48-9	3	97	.283	.346	.412	107	5	9-7	.955	-21	91	99	*S-149/3	-0.6
1994	Hou N	98	342	38	90	26	0	9	49	29-15	8	79	.263	.334	.418	100	0	1-1	.947	1	101	**122**	S-95	0.9
1995	SD N	120	390	42	82	16	2	6	31	28-7	5	92	.210	.271	.308	54	-27	5-3	.965	-3	96	93	*S-116/3	-2.1
1996	SD N	49	154	10	36	2	1	3	18	9-2	1	32	.234	.279	.318	61	-10	3-2	.946	-1	106	115	S-47/3-2	-0.8
	Det A	52	179	19	35	4	2	7	20	4-0	0	37	.196	.213	.358	41	-18	2-1	.948	-2	106	70	S-51/3	-1.5
	Hou N	3	2	1	0	0	0	0	0	2-0	0	1	.000	.500	.000	50	0	0-0	1.000	2	194	440	/S-2,3	0.2
Total	7	616	2051	221	485	98	13	47	223	143-36	21	488	.236	.292	.366	78	-71	26-17	.952	-52	95	99	S-599/3-6	-8.1

CEDENO, CESAR Cesar (Encarnacion) B 2.25.1951 Santo Domingo, D.R. BR/TR 6-2/195# d6.20

Year	Tm Lg	G	AB	R	H	2B	3B	HR	RBI	BB-IB	HP	SO	AVG	OBP	SLG	AOPS	ABR	SB-CS	FA	FR	Rng	Thr	G at Pos	BFW
1970	Hou N	90	355	46	110	21	4	7	42	15-2	2	57	.310	.340	.451	115	6	17-4	.968	-2	108	19	O-90(0-75-17)	0.4
1971	Hou N	161	611	85	161	**40**	6	10	81	25-5	3	102	.264	.293	.398	97	-4	20-9	.989	-6	85	59	*O-157(11-125-30)/1-2	-1.5

Year	Tm Lg	G	AB	R	H	2B	3B	HR	RBI	BB-IB	HP	SO	AVG	OBP	SLG	AOPS	ABR	SB-CS	FA	FR	Rng	Thr	G at Pos	BFW
1972	Hou N★	139	559	103	179	**39**	8	22	82	56-5	5	62	.320	.385	.537	163	46	55-21	.981	2	103	108	*O-137(CF)	5.2
1973	Hou N★	139	525	86	168	35	2	25	70	41-7	7	79	.320	.376	.537	151	36	56-15	.981	6	109	117	*O-136(CF)	4.6
1974	Hou N★	160	610	95	164	29	5	26	102	64-6	4	103	.269	.338	.461	129	21	57-17	.993	6	109	110	*O-157(CF)	3.1
1975	Hou N	131	500	93	144	31	3	13	63	62-9	7	52	.288	.371	.440	135	25	50-17	.982	-4	96	96	*O-131(CF)	2.3
1976	Hou N★	150	575	89	171	26	5	18	83	55-9	1	51	.297	.357	.454	143	30	58-15	.980	-2	99	119	*O-146(CF)	3.4
1977	Hou N	141	530	92	148	36	8	14	71	47-7	11	50	.279	.346	.457	126	19	61-14	**.997**	1	98	156	*O-137(CF)	2.8
1978	Hou N	50	192	31	54	8	2	7	23	15-1	0	24	.281	.333	.453	127	6	23-2	.987	4	118	73	O-50(CF)	1.4
1979	Hou N	132	470	57	123	27	4	6	54	64-8	3	52	.262	.348	.374	105	5	30-13	.981	-10	55	122	1-91,O-40(CF)	-0.9
1980	†Hou N	137	499	71	154	32	8	10	73	66-11	1	72	.309	.389	.465	150	35	48-15	.977	-5	95	98	*O-136(CF)	3.6
1981	†Hou N	82	306	42	83	19	0	5	34	24-2	1	31	.271	.321	.382	106	2	12-7	.991	-3	88	88	1-46,O-34(CF)	-0.4
1982	Cin N	138	492	52	142	35	1	8	57	41-2	4	41	.289	.346	.413	110	8	16-11	.990	-6	97	53	*O-131(CF)/1	0.0
1983	Cin N	98	332	40	77	16	0	9	39	33-2	3	53	.232	.302	.361	82	-8	13-9	.993	0	110	106	O-73(0-1-73),1-17	-1.4
1984	Cin N	110	380	59	105	24	2	10	47	25-4	1	54	.276	.321	.429	105	2	19-3	.980	2	108	143	O-77(52-14-19),1-44	0.2
1985	Cin N	83	220	24	53	12	0	3	30	19-1	3	35	.241	.307	.336	77	-6	9-5	.990	1	116	32	O-53(46-4-4),1-34	-0.8
	†StL N	28	76	14	33	4	1	6	19	5-2	0	7	.434	.463	.750	238	13	5-1	.993	-3	46	132	1-23/O-2(1-0-1)	1.0
	Year	111	296	38	86	16	1	9	49	24-3	3	42	.291	.347	.443	116	6	14-6	.993	-2	69	126	1-57,O-55(47-4-5)	0.2
1986	LA N	37	78	5	18	2	1	0	6	7-0	0	13	.231	.294	.282	64	-4	1-1	.944	-2	85	76	O-31(28-3-0)	-0.7
Total	17	2006	7310	1084	2087	436	60	199	976	664-83	56	938	.285	.347	.443	124	232	550-179	.985	-21	101	94	*O-1718(138-1457-144),1-258	22.3

CEDENO, DOMINGO Domingo Antonio (Donastorg) B 11.4.1968 LaRomana, D.R. BB/TR 6-1/170# d5.19 b-Andujar

Year	Tm Lg	G	AB	R	H	2B	3B	HR	RBI	BB-IB	HP	SO	AVG	OBP	SLG	AOPS	ABR	SB-CS	FA	FR	Rng	Thr	G at Pos	BFW
1993	Tor A	15	46	5	8	0	0	0	7	1-0	0	10	.174	.188	.174	-1	-7	1-0	.973	-2	107	69	S-10/2-5	-0.7
1994	Tor A	47	97	14	19	2	3	0	10	10-0	0	31	.196	.261	.278	42	-9	1-2	.935	-7	87	78	2-28/S-8,3-6,O(LF)	-1.4
1995	Tor A	51	161	18	38	6	1	4	14	10-0	2	35	.236	.289	.360	68	-8	0-1	.980	3	106	88	S-30,2-20/3	-0.3
1996	Tor A	77	282	44	79	10	2	2	17	15-0	2	60	.280	.320	.351	70	-13	5-3	.969	3	95	118	2-62/3-6,S-5	-0.6
	Chi A	12	19	2	3	2	0	0	3	0-0	0	4	.158	.143	.263	4	-3	1-0	—	-2	0	0	/2-2,S-2,D	-0.4
	Year	89	301	46	82	12	2	2	20	15-0	2	64	.272	.308	.346	66	-16	6-3	.969	1	93	116	2-64/S-7,3-6,D	-1.0
1997	Tex A	113	365	49	103	19	6	4	36	27-0	2	77	.282	.334	.400	86	-8	3-3	.960	-6	102	76	2-65,S-43/3-3,D-2	-0.8
1998	Tex A	61	141	19	37	9	1	2	21	10-0	0	32	.262	.309	.383	76	-5	2-1	.963	-7	87	79	S-35,D-14/2-7	-1.0
1999	Sea A	21	42	4	9	2	0	2	8	5-0	1	9	.214	.313	.405	83	-1	1-1	.941	2	120	112	S-20/23	0.1
	Phi N	32	66	5	10	4	0	1	5	5-0	0	22	.152	.211	.258	17	-9	0-1	.982	-2	88	68	S-19/2	-1.0
Total	7	429	1219	160	306	54	13	15	121	83-0	7	280	.251	.300	.354	67	-63	14-12	.964	-19	97	90	2-191,S-172/D-17,3-17,O(LF)	-6.1

CEDENO, ROGER Roger Leandro B 8.16.1974 Valencia, Venezuela BB/TR 6-1/165# d6.20

Year	Tm Lg	G	AB	R	H	2B	3B	HR	RBI	BB-IB	HP	SO	AVG	OBP	SLG	AOPS	ABR	SB-CS	FA	FR	Rng	Thr	G at Pos	BFW
1995	LA N	40	42	4	10	2	0	0	3	3-0	0	10	.238	.283	.286	57	-3	1-0	.977	2	135	0	O-36(19-13-5)	-0.1
1996	LA N	86	211	26	52	11	1	2	18	24-0	1	47	.246	.326	.336	82	-5	5-1	.983	1	105	73	O-71(20-50-4)	-0.4
1997	LA N	80	194	31	53	10	2	3	17	25-2	3	44	.273	.362	.392	106	2	9-1	.987	5	131	38	O-71(13-55-4)	0.9
1998	LA N	105	240	33	58	11	1	2	17	27-2	0	57	.242	.317	.321	73	-9	8-2	.978	-4	77	117	O-77(45-29-10)	-1.3
1999	†NY N	155	453	90	142	23	4	4	36	60-3	3	100	.313	.396	.408	108	8	66-17	.989	4	105	118	*O-149(13-21-127)/2	1.5
2000	Hou N	74	259	54	73	2	5	6	26	43-0	0	47	.282	.383	.398	93	-2	25-11	.978	-3	100	26	O-67(23-29-17)	-0.4
2001	Det A	131	523	79	153	14	11	6	48	36-1	2	83	.293	.337	.396	98	-4	55-15	.953	-12	87	68	*O-120(0-67-55)/D-7	-1.1
2002	NY N	149	511	65	133	19	2	7	41	42-1	2	92	.260	.318	.346	81	-17	25-4	.966	-5	100	26	*O-132(LF)	-2.3
2003	NY N	148	484	70	129	25	4	7	37	38-3	1	86	.267	.320	.378	84	-12	14-9	.987	1	104	71	*O-128(0-17-111)	-1.6
Total	9	968	2917	452	803	117	30	37	243	298-12	12	566	.275	.343	.374	91	-42	208-60	.977	-11	101	66	O-851(265-281-333)/D-7,2	-4.8

CEPEDA, ORLANDO Orlando Manuel (Penne) "Baby Bull" or "Cha Cha" B 9.17.1937 Ponce, P.R. BR/TR 6-2/210# d4.15 C1 HF1999 OF Total (214-LF 18-RF)

Year	Tm Lg	G	AB	R	H	2B	3B	HR	RBI	BB-IB	HP	SO	AVG	OBP	SLG	AOPS	ABR	SB-CS	FA	FR	Rng	Thr	G at Pos	BFW
1958	SF N	148	603	88	188	**38**	4	25	96	29-7	3	84	.312	.342	.512	126	21	15-11	.989	-2	96	95	*1-147	0.9
1959	SF N★	151	605	92	192	35	4	27	105	33-10	5	100	.317	.355	.522	134	27	23-9	.984	-5	97	89	*1-122,O-44(LF)/3-4	1.6
1960	SF N★	151	569	81	169	36	3	24	96	34-9	8	91	.297	.343	.497	135	26	15-6	.983	-2	103	141	O-91(LF),1-63	1.7
1961	SF N★	152	585	105	182	28	4	**46**	**142**	39-11	9	91	.311	.362	.609	158	45	12-8	.997	-2	84	79	1-81,O-80(64-0-17)	3.4
1962	†SF N★	162	625	105	191	26	1	35	114	37-8	6	97	.306	.347	.518	132	26	10-4	.991	-7	84	100	*1-160/O-2(1-0-1)	1.0
1963	SF N☆	156	579	100	183	33	4	34	97	37-11	10	70	.316	.366	.563	166	48	8-3	.985	-9	82	80	*1-150/O-3(LF)	3.2
1964	SF N★	142	529	75	161	27	2	31	97	43-7	8	83	.304	.361	.539	148	33	9-4	.986	-7	85	86	*1-139/O(LF)	2.0
1965	SF N	33	34	1	6	1	0	1	5	3-1	0	9	.176	.225	.294	49	-2	0-0	1.000	0	104	51	/1-4,O-2(LF)	-0.3
1966	SF N	19	49	5	14	2	0	3	15	4-2	1	11	.286	.352	.510	132	2	0-1	.778	-2	76	0	/O-8(LF),1-6	-0.1
	StL N	123	452	65	137	24	0	17	58	34-10	13	68	.303	.362	.469	130	20	9-8	.989	-5	85	118	*1-120	0.7
	Year	142	501	70	151	26	0	20	73	38-12	**14**	79	.301	.361	.473	130	22	9-9	.990	-7	82	118	*1-126/O-8(LF)	0.6
1967	†StL N★	151	563	91	183	37	0	25	**111**	62-23	**12**	75	.325	.399	.524	166	51	11-2	.993	1	101	92	*1-151	4.6
1968	†StL N	157	600	71	149	26	2	16	73	43-13	9	96	.248	.306	.378	107	4	8-6	.988	-5	92	100	*1-154	-1.2
1969	†Atl N	154	573	74	147	28	2	22	88	55-10	5	76	.257	.325	.428	109	7	12-5	.994	1	103	84	*1-153	-0.4
1970	Atl N	148	567	87	173	33	0	34	111	47-11	9	75	.305	.365	.543	133	26	6-5	.992	4	107	87	*1-148	1.7
1971	Atl N	71	250	31	69	10	1	14	44	22-7	0	29	.276	.330	.492	124	7	3-6	.992	1	108	107	1-63	0.2
1972	Atl N	28	84	6	25	3	0	4	9	7-1	0	17	.298	.352	.476	122	2	0-0	1.000	1	106	88	1-22	0.1
	Oak A	3	3	0	0	0	0	0	0	0-0	0	0	.000	.000	.000	-99	-1	0-0	—	0			H	-0.1
1973	Bos A	142	550	51	159	25	0	20	86	50-13	3	81	.289	.350	.444	116	12	0-2	—	0	0	0	*D-142	0.7
1974	KC A	33	107	3	23	5	0	1	18	9-0	1	16	.215	.282	.290	61	-5	1-0	—	0	0	0	D-26	-0.6
Total	17	2124	7927	1131	2351	417	27	379	1365	588-154	102	1169	.297	.350	.499	133	349	142-80	.990	-38	92	92	*1-1683,O-231L,D-168/3-4	19.1

CEPICKY, MATT Matthew William B 11.10.1977 St.Louis, MO BL/TR 6-2/215# d7.31

Year	Tm Lg	G	AB	R	H	2B	3B	HR	RBI	BB-IB	HP	SO	AVG	OBP	SLG	AOPS	ABR	SB-CS	FA	FR	Rng	Thr	G at Pos	BFW
2002	Mon N	32	74	7	16	3	0	3	15	4-1	0	21	.216	.256	.378	62	-5	0-0	1.000	-2	76	0	O-17(16-0-1)	-0.7
2003	Mon N	5	8	0	2	1	0	0	0	0-0	0	2	.250	.250	.375	55	-1	0-0	1.000	-1	27	0	/O-4(3-0-1)	-0.1
Total	2	37	82	7	18	4	0	3	15	4-1	0	23	.220	.256	.378	61	-6	0-0	1.000	-2	70	0	/O-21(19-0-2)	-0.8

CERMAK, ED Edward Hugo B 3.10.1882 Cleveland, OH D 11.22.1911 Cleveland, OH BR/TR 5-11/170# d9.9

Year	Tm Lg	G	AB	R	H	2B	3B	HR	RBI	BB-IB	HP	SO	AVG	OBP	SLG	AOPS	ABR	SB-CS	FA	FR	Rng	Thr	G at Pos	BFW
1901	Cle A	1	4	0	0	0	0	0	0	0	0		.000	.000	.000	-99	-1	0	1.000	1	450	1792	/O(RF)	0.0

CERONE, RICK Richard Aldo B 5.19.1954 Newark, NJ BR/TR 5-11/192# d8.17

Year	Tm Lg	G	AB	R	H	2B	3B	HR	RBI	BB-IB	HP	SO	AVG	OBP	SLG	AOPS	ABR	SB-CS	FA	FR	Rng	Thr	G at Pos	BFW
1975	Cle A	7	12	1	3	1	0	0	0	1-0	0	0	.250	.308	.333	81	0	0-0	1.000	-1	125	68	/C-7	-0.1
1976	Cle A	7	16	1	2	0	0	0	1	0-0	0	2	.125	.125	.125	-27	-3	0-0	.963	-1	86	59	/C-6,D	-0.3
1977	Tor A	31	100	7	20	4	0	1	10	6-0	0	12	.200	.245	.270	40	-8	0-0	.994	2	183	86	C-31	-0.6
1978	Tor A	88	282	25	63	8	2	3	20	23-0	1	32	.223	.284	.298	63	-14	0-3	.992	1	112	103	C-84/D-2	-1.1
1979	Tor A	136	469	47	112	27	4	7	61	37-1	1	40	.239	.294	.358	75	-17	1-4	.980	3	129	97	*C-136	-1.0
1980	†NY A	147	519	70	144	30	4	14	85	32-2	6	56	.277	.321	.432	108	5	1-3	.990	18	**172**	116	*C-147	2.7
1981	†NY A	71	234	23	57	13	2	2	21	12-0	0	24	.244	.276	.342	80	-7	0-2	.992	-3	116	80	C-69	-0.8
1982	NY A	89	300	29	68	10	0	5	28	19-1	1	27	.227	.271	.310	61	-16	0-2	.989	-11	100	69	C-89	-2.5
1983	NY A	80	246	18	54	7	0	2	22	15-1	1	29	.220	.267	.272	51	-17	0-0	.991	-6	103	60	C-78/3	-2.0
1984	NY A	38	120	8	25	3	0	2	13	9-0	1	15	.208	.269	.283	55	-7	1-0	.996	-1	120	104	C-38	-0.7
1985	Atl N	96	282	15	61	9	0	3	25	29-1	1	25	.216	.288	.280	57	-16	0-3	.986	-5	99	100	C-91	-2.0
1986	Mil A	68	216	22	56	14	0	4	18	15-0	1	28	.259	.304	.380	84	-5	1-1	.991	4	109	168	C-68	0.2
1987	NY A	113	284	28	69	12	1	4	23	30-0	4	46	.243	.320	.335	76	-9	0-1	**.998**	8	123	109	*C-111/P-2,1-2	0.2
1988	Bos A	84	264	31	71	13	1	3	27	20-0	3	32	.269	.326	.360	89	-4	0-0	**1.000**	-2	91	71	C-83/D	-0.2
1989	Bos A	102	296	28	72	16	1	4	48	34-1	2	40	.243	.320	.345	84	-6	0-0	.984	-3	73	116	C-97/O(RF)D	-0.3
1990	NY A	49	139	12	42	6	0	2	11	5-0	0	13	.302	.324	.388	99	-1	0-0	.995	2	146	158	C-35/2D	0.3
1991	NY N	90	227	18	62	13	0	2	16	30-2	1	24	.273	.360	.357	103	2	1-1	.987	2	**138**	121	C-81	0.8
1992	Mon N	33	63	10	17	4	0	1	7	3-0	1	5	.270	.313	.381	97	0	1-2	1.000	-1	82	66	C-28	-0.1
Total	18	1329	4069	393	998	190	15	59	436	320-9	24	450	.245	.301	.343	78	-123	6-22	.990	5	120	102	*C-1279/D-11,1-2,P-2,2O(RF)3	-7.5

CERV, BOB Robert Henry B 5.5.1926 Weston, NE BR/TR 6/202# d8.1

Year	Tm Lg	G	AB	R	H	2B	3B	HR	RBI	BB-IB	HP	SO	AVG	OBP	SLG	AOPS	ABR	SB-CS	FA	FR	Rng	Thr	G at Pos	BFW
1951	NY A	12	28	4	6	1	0	0	2	4	0	6	.214	.313	.250	55	-2	0-0	.875	-1	101	0	/O-9(RF)	-0.3
1952	NY A	36	87	11	21	3	2	1	8	9	0	22	.241	.313	.356	91	-1	0-1	1.000	0	102	68	O-27(15-12-0)	-0.3
1953	NY A	8	6	0	0	0	0	0	0	1	0	1	.000	.143	.000	-61	-1	0-0	—	0			H	-0.1
1954	NY A	56	100	14	26	6	0	5	13	11	0	17	.260	.330	.470	122	3	0-2	.897	-2	73	94	O-24(LF)	-0.1
1955	†NY A	55	85	17	29	4	2	3	22	7-0	3	16	.341	.411	.541	157	7	4-0	1.000	-1	88	105	O-20(13-7-1)	0.6
1956	†NY A	54	115	16	35	5	6	3	25	18-0	0	13	.304	.396	.530	148	8	0-1	.984	1	93	190	O-44(29-15-1)	0.7
1957	KC A	124	345	35	94	14	2	11	44	20-1	1	57	.272	.312	.420	97	-3	1-1	.964	-2	92	118	O-89(40-35-22)	-0.9
1958	KC A★	141	515	93	157	20	7	38	104	50-10	5	82	.305	.371	.592	158	39	3-3	.985	15	118	161	*O-136(LF)	4.6

Year	Tm Lg	G	AB	R	H	2B	3B	HR	RBI	BB-IB	HP	SO	AVG	OBP	SLG	AOPS	ABR	SB-CS	FA	FR	Rng	Thr	G at Pos	BFW
1959	KC A	125	463	61	132	22	4	20	87	35-5	3	87	.285	.332	.479	120	11	3-2	.980	2	100	107	*O-119(LF)	0.7
1960	KC A	23	78	14	20	1	1	6	12	10-1	0	17	.256	.337	.526	130	3	0-0	.977	2	95	290	O-21(LF)	0.4
	†NY A	87	216	32	54	11	1	8	28	30-2	3	36	.250	.349	.421	114	5	0-0	.982	3	98	173	O-51(50-1-1)/1-3	0.4
	Year	110	294	46	74	12	2	14	40	40-3	3	53	.252	.346	.449	119	8	0-0	.980	5	97	206	O-72(71-1-1)/1-3	0.8
1961	LA A	18	57	3	9	3	0	2	6	1-0	0	8	.158	.169	.316	25	-6	0-0	.944	-1	83	0	O-15(LF)	-0.8
	NY A	57	118	17	32	5	1	6	20	12-0	1	17	.271	.344	.483	125	4	1-0	.983	2	112	107	O-30(28-2-0)/1-3	0.4
	Year	75	175	20	41	8	1	8	26	13-0	1	25	.234	.289	.429	91	-3	1-0	.974	1	103	75	O-45(43-2-0)/1-3	-0.4
1962	NY A	14	17	1	2	1	0	0	0	2-0	1	3	.118	.250	.176	18	-2	0-0	1.000	-0	100	0	/O-3(1-0-2)	-0.2
	Hou N	19	31	2	7	0	0	2	3	2-0	0	10	.226	.273	.419	89	-1	0-0	.833	-0	59	373	/O-6(LF)	-0.1
Total	12	829	2261	320	624	96	26	105	374	212-19	17	392	.276	.340	.481	122	64	12-10	.976	18	101	135	O-594(497-72-36)/1-6	5.0
CEY, RON Ronald Charles B 2.15.1948 Tacoma, WA BR/TR 5-10/185# d9.3																								
1971	LA N	2	2	0	0	0	0	0	0	0-0	0	2	.000	.000	.000	-99	-1	0-0	—	0			H	-0.1
1972	LA N	11	37	3	10	1	0	1	3	7-0	1	10	.270	.400	.378	125	2	0-0	.900	-2	84	60	3-11	-0.1
1973	LA N	152	507	60	124	18	4	15	80	74-7	2	77	.245	.338	.385	106	5	1-1	.961	5	101	159	*3-146	1.0
1974	†LA N★	159	577	88	151	20	2	18	97	76-13	7	68	.262	.349	.397	115	12	1-1	.959	14	103	91	*3-158	2.6
1975	LA N★	158	566	72	160	29	2	25	101	78-15	7	74	.283	.372	.473	141	32	5-2	.960	-3	94	100	*3-158	3.0
1976	LA N★	145	502	69	139	18	3	23	80	89-13	3	74	.277	.386	.462	144	32	0-4	.965	9	111	91	*3-144	4.0
1977	†LA N★	153	564	77	136	22	3	30	110	93-6	2	106	.241	.347	.450	114	12	3-4	.964	12	105	129	*3-153	2.1
1978	†LA N★	159	555	84	150	32	0	23	84	96-9	7	96	.270	.380	.452	134	29	2-5	.966	3	102	107	*3-158	3.0
1979	LA N★	150	487	77	137	20	1	28	81	86-8	2	85	.281	.389	.499	143	32	3-3	**.977**	6	101	102	*3-150	3.6
1980	LA N	157	551	81	140	25	0	28	77	69-5	5	92	.254	.342	.452	122	17	2-2	.972	6	101	109	*3-157	2.1
1981	†LA N	85	312	42	90	15	2	13	50	40-3	3	55	.288	.372	.474	145	19	0-2	.941	4	100	119	3-84	2.1
1982	LA N	150	556	62	141	23	1	24	79	57-6	4	99	.254	.323	.428	113	8	3-2	.963	-1	100	103	*3-149	0.5
1983	Chi N	159	581	73	160	33	1	24	90	62-11	5	85	.275	.346	.460	117	14	0-0	.955	-13	95	47	*3-157	-0.2
1984	†Chi N	146	505	71	121	27	0	25	97	61-10	6	108	.240	.324	.442	105	4	3-2	**.967**	-12	88	96	*3-144	-1.1
1985	Chi N	145	500	64	116	18	2	22	63	58-9	4	106	.232	.316	.408	91	-6	1-1	.943	-8	99	87	*3-140	-1.7
1986	Chi N	97	256	42	70	21	0	13	36	44-1	3	66	.273	.384	.508	134	14	0-0	.952	-6	92	59	3-77	0.6
1987	Oak A	45	104	12	23	6	0	4	11	22-1	1	32	.221	.359	.394	108	2	0-0	.982	-2	25	71	D-30/1-7,3-3	-0.1
Total	17	2073	7162	977	1868	328	21	316	1139	1012-117	62	1235	.261	.354	.445	121	227	24-29	.961	11	100	101	*3-1989/D-30,1-7	21.3
CHACON, ELIO Elio (Rodriguez) B 10.26.1936 Caracas, Venezuela D 4.24.1992 Caracas, Venezuela BR/TR 5-9/160# d4.20																								
1960	Cin N	49	116	14	21	1	0	0	7	14-1	1	23	.181	.271	.190	29	-11	7-1	.980	1	99	115	2-43/O-2(RF)	-0.7
1961	†Cin N	61	132	26	35	4	2	2	5	21-0	2	22	.265	.374	.371	97	0	1-4	.989	1	101	91	2-42/O-7(3-0-5)	0.3
1962	NY N	118	368	49	87	10	3	2	27	76-3	1	64	.236	.368	.296	80	-7	12-7	.961	-6	100	86	*S-110/2-2,3	-0.4
Total	3	228	616	89	143	15	5	4	39	111-4	4	109	.232	.351	.292	74	-18	20-12	.961	-4	100	86	S-110/2-87,O-9(3-0-7),3	-0.8
CHADBOURNE, CHET Chester James "Pop" B 10.28.1884 Parkman, ME D 6.21.1943 Los Angeles, CA BL/TR 5-9/170# d9.17																								
1906	Bos A	11	43	7	13	1	0	0	3	3	0		.302	.348	.326	111	1	1	.926	2	131	78	2-11/S	0.3
1907	Bos A	10	38	0	11	0	0	0	1	7	0		.289	.400	.289	121	1	1	1.000	-0	78	0	O-10(LF)	0.1
1914	KC F	147	581	92	161	22	8	1	37	69	5	49	.277	.359	.348	97	-10	42	.965	9	95	**157**	*O-146(LF)	-0.7
1915	KC F	152	587	75	133	16	9	1	35	62	6	29	.227	.307	.290	71	-32	29	**.979**	-4	91	109	*O-152(5-147-0)	-5.1
1918	Bos N	27	104	9	27	2	1	0	6	5	1	5	.260	.300	.298	86	-2	5	.925	-3	90	57	O-27(CF)	-0.8
Total	5	347	1353	183	345	41	18	2	82	146	12	83	.255	.333	.316	86	-42	78	.969	4	92	123	O-335(161-174-0)/2-11,S	-6.2
CHALK, DAVE David Lee B 8.30.1950 Del Rio, TX BR/TR 5-10/175# d9.4																								
1973	Cal A	24	69	14	16	2	0	0	6	9-0	1	13	.232	.329	.261	74	-2	0-0	.962	2	96	148	S-22	0.3
1974	Cal A★	133	465	44	117	9	3	5	31	30-1	7	57	.252	.304	.316	84	-10	10-10	.938	6	91	93	S-99,3-38	0.5
1975	Cal A☆	149	513	59	140	24	2	3	56	66-4	2	49	.273	.353	.345	107	8	6-9	.976	5	99	100	*3-149	1.0
1976	Cal A	142	438	39	95	14	1	0	33	49-3	10	62	.217	.308	.253	71	-14	0-0	.971	3	98	83	*S-102,3-49	0.0
1977	Cal A	149	519	58	144	27	2	3	45	52-2	5	69	.277	.345	.355	96	-1	12-8	.948	-2	93	81	*3-141/2-7,S-4	-0.4
1978	Cal A	135	470	42	119	12	0	1	34	38-0	7	34	.253	.318	.285	74	-16	5-8	.955	-11	88	86	S-97,2-29,3-22/D	-1.9
1979	Tex A	9	8	0	2	0	0	0	0	0-0	0	0	.250	.250	.250	36	-1	0-0	1.000	0	210	0	/S-3,2D	0.0
	Oak A	66	212	15	47	6	0	2	13	29-0	1	14	.222	.317	.278	66	-9	2-1	.988	-10	89	78	2-37,S-16,3-16	-1.6
	Year	75	220	15	49	6	0	2	13	29-0	1	14	.223	.315	.277	65	-10	2-1	.988	-10	88	77	2-38,S-19,3-16/D-2	-1.6
1980	†KC A	69	167	19	42	10	1	1	20	18-0	2	27	.251	.326	.341	84	-3	1-1	.964	-7	95	54	3-33,2-17/SD	-0.9
1981	KC A	27	49	2	11	3	0	0	5	4-0	0	2	.224	.283	.286	65	-2	0-1	.955	-4	66	203	3-14,2-10/S	-0.7
Total	9	903	2910	292	733	107	9	15	243	295-10	35	327	.252	.325	.310	85	-50	36-38	.962	-19	95	101	3-462,S-345,2-101/D-9	-3.7
CHAMBERLAIN, JOE Joseph Jeremiah B 5.10.1910 San Francisco, CA D 1.28.1983 San Francisco, CA BR/TR 6-1/175# d4.17																								
1934	Chi A	43	141	13	34	5	1	2	17	6	0	38	.241	.272	.333	54	-10	1-1	.896	-5	112	66	S-26,3-14/2	-1.3
CHAMBERLAIN, WES Wesley Polk B 4.13.1966 Chicago, IL BR/TR 6-2/210# d8.31																								
1990	Phi N	18	46	9	13	3	0	2	4	1-0	0	9	.283	.298	.478	110	0	4-0	.958	-0	111	0	O-10(10-0-2)	0.1
1991	Phi N	101	383	51	92	16	3	13	50	31-0	2	73	.240	.300	.399	96	-3	9-4	.985	-1	99	70	O-98(95-0-3)	-0.7
1992	Phi N	76	275	26	71	18	0	9	41	10-2	1	55	.258	.285	.422	99	-2	4-0	.971	-2	97	72	O-73(28-0-48)	-0.5
1993	†Phi N	96	284	34	80	20	2	12	45	17-3	1	51	.282	.320	.493	117	6	2-1	.993	6	103	207	O-76(RF)	0.8
1994	Phi N	24	69	7	19	5	0	2	6	3-0	0	12	.275	.306	.435	88	-1	0-0	1.000	1	93	272	O-18(RF)	-0.1
	Bos A	51	164	13	42	9	1	4	20	12-2	0	38	.256	.307	.396	76	-6	0-2	1.000	3	105	207	O-34(RF),D-12	-0.6
1995	Bos A	19	42	4	5	1	0	1	1	3-0	0	11	.119	.178	.214	1	-6	1-0	.955	1	109	158	O-12(RF)/D-5	-0.6
Total	6	385	1263	144	322	72	6	43	167	77-7	4	249	.255	.299	.424	95	-12	20-7	.984	8	100	126	O-321(133-0-193)/D-17	-1.6
CHAMBERS, AL Albert Eugene B 3.24.1961 Harrisburg, PA BL/TL 6-4/217# d7.23																								
1983	Sea A	31	67	11	14	3	0	1	7	18-1	0	20	.209	.376	.299	85	0	0-1	1.000	-1	52	0	D-22/O-3(LF)	-0.2
1984	Sea A	22	49	4	11	1	0	1	4	3-0	0	12	.224	.269	.306	60	-3	2-1	.947	-1	89	0	O-13(LF)/D	-0.4
1985	Sea A	4	4	0	0	0	0	0	0	0-0	0	2	.000	.000	.000	-99	-1	0-0	—	0			/H	-0.1
Total	3	57	120	15	25	4	0	2	11	21-1	0	34	.208	.326	.292	71	-4	2-2	.955	-2	81	0	/D-23,O-16(LF)	-0.7
CHAMBLEE, JIM James Nathaniel B 5.6.1975 Denton, TX BR/TR 6-4/170# d8.24																								
2003	Cin N	2	2	0	0	0	0	0	0	0-0	0	2	.000	.000	.000	-99	-1	0-0	—	-0	0	0	/3	-0.1
CHAMBLISS, CHRIS Carroll Christopher B 12.26.1948 Dayton, OH BL/TR 6-1/215# d5.28 C8																								
1971	Cle A	111	415	49	114	20	4	9	48	40-1	2	83	.275	.341	.407	102	2	2-0	.992	-6	77	83	*1-108	-1.3
1972	Cle A	121	466	51	136	27	2	6	44	26-2	0	63	.292	.327	.397	112	6	3-4	.993	-8	74	109	*1-119	-1.4
1973	Cle A	155	572	70	156	30	2	11	53	58-8	3	76	.273	.342	.390	104	4	4-8	.991	4	110	107	*1-154	-0.7
1974	Cle A	17	67	8	22	4	0	0	7	5-1	0	5	.328	.375	.388	121	2	0-1	.982	-3	53	93	1-17	-0.3
	NY A	110	400	38	97	16	3	6	43	23-1	0	43	.243	.282	.343	81	-11	0-0	.992	6	120	101	*1-106	-1.5
	Year	127	467	46	119	20	3	6	50	28-2	0	48	.255	.296	.349	87	-9	0-1	.990	3	110	100	*1-123	-1.8
1975	NY A	150	562	66	171	38	4	9	72	29-9	1	50	.304	.336	.434	119	13	0-1	.991	4	106	97	*1-147	0.4
1976	†NY A★	156	641	79	188	32	6	17	96	27-1	3	80	.293	.323	.441	124	16	1-0	.994	-2	98	106	*1-155/D	0.1
1977	†NY A	157	600	90	172	32	6	17	90	45-5	2	73	.287	.336	.445	113	10	4-0	.989	-3	94	106	*1-157	-0.2
1978	†NY A	162	625	81	171	26	3	12	90	41-3	5	60	.274	.321	.382	100	-1	2-1	**.997**	4	105	102	*1-155/D-7	-0.7
1979	NY A	149	554	61	155	27	3	18	63	34-4	5	53	.280	.324	.437	106	3	3-2	.995	3	107	118	*1-134,D-16	-0.3
1980	Atl N	158	602	83	170	37	2	18	72	49-6	4	73	.282	.338	.440	113	10	7-3	.993	-2	97	**120**	*1-158	-0.1
1981	Atl N	**107**	404	44	110	25	2	8	51	44-10	1	41	.272	.343	.403	109	6	4-1	.997	6	117	97	*1-107	0.5
1982	†Atl N	157	534	57	144	25	2	20	86	57-13	0	57	.270	.337	.436	111	8	7-3	.993	11	**126**	**132**	*1-151	1.1
1983	Atl N	131	447	59	125	24	3	20	78	63-15	0	68	.280	.366	.481	124	16	2-7	.996	0	98	123	*1-126	0.7
1984	Atl N	135	389	47	100	14	0	9	44	58-12	1	54	.257	.350	.362	95	0	1-2	.993	-1	97	106	*1-109	-0.9
1985	Atl N	101	170	16	40	7	0	3	21	18-4	0	22	.235	.307	.329	74	-6	0-0	.997	1	110	109	1-39	-0.7
1986	Atl N	97	122	13	38	8	0	2	14	15-4	0	24	.311	.384	.426	117	4	0-2	.993	-2	53	124	1-20	0.0
1988	NY A	1	1	0	0	0	0	0	0	0-0	0	1	.000	.000	.000	-99	0	0-0	—	0			/H	0.0
Total	17	2175	7571	912	2109	392	42	185	972	632-99	27	926	.279	.334	.415	108	82	40-35	.993	12	101	108	*1-1962/D-24	-5.3
CHAMPION, MIKE Robert Michael B 2.10.1955 Montgomery, AL BR/TR 6/185# d9.14																								
1976	SD N	11	38	4	9	2	0	1	2	1-0	0	3	.237	.256	.368	82	-1	0-0	.940	-3	87	31	2-11	-0.4
1977	SD N	150	507	35	116	14	6	1	43	27-3	2	85	.229	.271	.286	55	-35	3-3	.974	-29	90	86	*2-149	-5.8

Year	Tm Lg	G	AB	R	H	2B	3B	HR	RBI	BB-IB	HP	SO	AVG	OBP	SLG	AOPS	ABR	SB-CS	FA	FR	Rng	Thr	G at Pos	BFW
1978	SD N	32	53	3	12	0	2	0	4	5-0	0	13	.226	.293	.302	72	-2	0-0	.932	1	120	151	2-20/3-4	-0.1
Total	3	193	598	42	137	16	8	2	49	33-3	2	101	.229	.272	.293	58	-38	3-3	.968	-31	92	88	2-180/3-4	-6.3

CHANCE, FRANK Frank Leroy "Husk" or "The Peerless Leader" B 9.9.1877 Fresno, CA D 9.15.1924 Los Angeles, CA BR/TR 6/190# d4.29 M11 HF1946

Year	Tm Lg	G	AB	R	H	2B	3B	HR	RBI	BB-IB	HP	SO	AVG	OBP	SLG	AOPS	ABR	SB-CS	FA	FR	Rng	Thr	G at Pos	BFW
1898	Chi N	53	147	32	41	4	3	1	14	7	6		.279	.338	.367	102	0	7	.950	-1	*155*	*74*	C-33,O-17(1-1-15)/1-3	-0.1
1899	Chi N	64	192	37	55	6	2	1	22	15	4		.286	.351	.354	96	-1	10	.950	0	*108*	*105*	C-57/O(LF)1	0.4
1900	Chi N	56	149	26	44	9	3	0	13	15	15		.295	.413	.396	129	8	8	.932	-3	*94*	*109*	C-51/1	0.8
1901	Chi N	69	241	38	67	12	4	0	36	29	9		.278	.376	.361	119	8	27	.932	-2	125	0	O-51(4-1-46),C-13/1-6	0.5
1902	Chi N	76	242	40	70	9	4	1	31	37	8		.289	.401	.372	143	15	29	.969	-2	89	105	1-38,C-30/O-4(RF)	1.6
1903	Chi N	125	441	83	144	24	10	2	81	78	10		.327	.439	.440	155	38	**67**	.972	-3	97	89	*1-121/C-2	3.1
1904	Chi N	124	451	89	140	16	10	6	49	36	16		.310	.382	.430	150	27	42	.990	11	**128**	101	*1-123/C	3.8
1905	Chi N	118	392	92	124	16	12	2	70	78	17		.316	**.450**	.434	157	35	38	.990	2	99	105	*1-115,M	3.5
1906	†Chi N	136	474	**103**	151	24	10	3	71	70	12		.319	.419	.430	156	35	**57**	.989	-1	92	125	*1-136,M	3.4
1907	†Chi N	111	382	58	112	19	2	1	49	51	13		.293	.395	.361	129	17	35	**.992**	7	119	**135**	*1-109,M	2.5
1908	†Chi N	129	452	65	123	27	4	2	55	37	8		.272	.338	.363	119	11	27	.989	5	110	111	*1-126,M	1.5
1909	Chi N	93	324	53	88	16	4	0	46	30	4		.272	.341	.346	110	4	29	.994	-2	82	115	1-92,M	0.1
1910	†Chi N	88	295	54	88	12	8	0	36	37	10	15	.298	.395	.393	131	13	16	.996	-1	83	111	1-87,M	1.1
1911	Chi N	31	88	23	21	6	3	1	17	25	5	13	.239	.432	.409	136	6	9	.990	-2	66	77	1-29,M	0.4
1912	Chi N	2	5	2	1	0	0	0	0	3	0	0	.200	.500	.200	96	0	1	1.000	-0	0	88	/1-2,M	0.0
1913	NY A	12	24	3	5	0	0	0	6	8	0	1	.208	.406	.208	81	0	1	1.000	0	106	47	/1-7,M	0.0
1914	NY A	1	0	0	0	0	0	0	0	0	0	0	—	—	—	—	0	0	1.000	-0	0	0	/1M	0.0
Total	17	1288	4299	798	1274	200	79	20	596	556	137	<u>29</u>	.296	.394	.394	135	216	403	.987	8	101	109	1-997,C-187/O-73(6-2-65)	22.6

CHANCE, BOB Robert B 9.10.1940 Statesboro, GA BL/TR 6-2/219# d9.4

Year	Tm Lg	G	AB	R	H	2B	3B	HR	RBI	BB-IB	HP	SO	AVG	OBP	SLG	AOPS	ABR	SB-CS	FA	FR	Rng	Thr	G at Pos	BFW
1963	Cle A	16	52	5	15	4	0	2	7	1-0	0	10	.288	.302	.481	116	1	0-1	.909	-1	95	0	O-14(RF)	-0.2
1964	Cle A	120	390	45	109	16	1	14	75	40-8	3	101	.279	.346	.433	118	10	3-3	.988	-11	52	81	1-81,O-31(1-0-30)	-0.8
1965	Was A	72	199	20	51	9	0	4	14	18-2	0	44	.256	.317	.362	94	-1	0-1	.988	-2	88	103	1-48/O-3(RF)	-0.7
1966	Was A	37	57	1	10	3	0	1	8	2-0	0	23	.175	.200	.281	38	-5	0-0	.974	-1	55	93	1-13	-0.7
1967	Was A	27	42	5	9	2	0	3	7	7-0	1	13	.214	.340	.476	144	3	0-0	1.000	-0	87	97	1-10	0.2
1969	Cal A	5	7	0	1	0	0	0	1	0-0	0	4	.143	.143	.143	-21	-1	0-0	.909	-0	0	0	/1	-0.2
Total	6	277	747	76	195	34	1	24	112	68-10	4	195	.261	.323	.406	106	7	3-5	.987	-16	66	90	1-153/O-48(1-0-47)	-2.4

CHANEY, DARREL Darrel Lee B 3.9.1948 Hammond, IN BB/TR (BL 1973 (part), 74-75) 6-1/190# d4.11

Year	Tm Lg	G	AB	R	H	2B	3B	HR	RBI	BB-IB	HP	SO	AVG	OBP	SLG	AOPS	ABR	SB-CS	FA	FR	Rng	Thr	G at Pos	BFW
1969	Cin N	93	209	21	40	5	2	0	15	24-4	1	75	.191	.278	.234	43	-16	1-0	.947	-14	91	102	S-91	-2.3
1970	†Cin N	57	95	7	22	3	0	1	4	3-1	1	26	.232	.263	.295	49	-7	1-1	.941	1	92	46	S-30,2-18/3-3	-0.4
1971	Cin N	10	24	2	3	0	0	0	1	1-0	0	3	.125	.160	.125	-19	-4	0-1	1.000	-1	86	26	/S-7,23	-0.5
1972	†Cin N	83	196	29	49	7	2	2	19	29-7	0	28	.250	.345	.337	101	1	1-3	.963	-12	90	84	S-64,2-12,3-10	-0.5
1973	†Cin N	105	227	27	41	7	1	0	14	26-5	1	50	.181	.267	.220	39	-19	4-3	.964	2	105	119	S-75,2-14,3-12	-0.9
1974	Cin N	117	135	27	27	6	1	2	16	26-6	0	33	.200	.327	.304	79	-3	1-2	.952	-1	86	49	3-81,2-38,S-12	-0.2
1975	†Cin N	71	160	18	35	6	0	2	26	14-2	0	38	.219	.280	.294	59	-9	3-0	.961	9	122	116	S-34,2-23,3-13	0.5
1976	Atl N	153	496	42	125	20	8	1	50	54-7	1	92	.252	.324	.331	82	-11	5-7	.950	5	102	93	*S-151/23	1.0
1977	Atl N	74	209	22	42	7	2	3	15	17-2	0	44	.201	.260	.297	44	-17	0-0	.979	9	104	72	S-41,2-24	-0.3
1978	Atl N	89	245	27	55	9	1	3	20	25-7	0	48	.224	.295	.306	62	-12	1-0	.976	-2	98	81	S-77/3-8,2	-0.8
1979	Atl N	63	117	15	19	5	0	0	10	19-2	0	34	.162	.277	.205	32	-10	2-1	.945	-5	92	86	S-39/2-5,3-4,C	-1.3
Total	11	915	2113	237	458	75	17	14	190	238-43	4	471	.217	.296	.288	61	-107	19-18	.959	-10	100	93	S-621,2-137,3-133/C	-5.7

CHANNELL, LES Lester Clark "Goat" or "Gint" B 3.3.1886 Crestline, OH D 5.8.1954 Denver, CO BL/TL 6/180# d5.11

Year	Tm Lg	G	AB	R	H	2B	3B	HR	RBI	BB-IB	HP	SO	AVG	OBP	SLG	AOPS	ABR	SB-CS	FA	FR	Rng	Thr	G at Pos	BFW
1910	NY A	6	19	3	6	0	0	0	3	2	0		.316	.381	.316	112	0	2	1.000	-0	111	0	/O-6(LF)	0.0
1914	NY A	1	1	0	1	1	0	0	0	0	0	0	1.000	1.000	2.000	803	1	0	—	0			H	0.1
Total	2	7	20	3	7	1	0	0	3	2	0	<u>0</u>	.350	.409	.400	145	1	2	1.000	-0	111	0	/O-6(LF)	0.1

CHANT, CHARLIE Charles Joseph B 8.7.1951 Bell, CA BR/TR 6/190# d9.12

Year	Tm Lg	G	AB	R	H	2B	3B	HR	RBI	BB-IB	HP	SO	AVG	OBP	SLG	AOPS	ABR	SB-CS	FA	FR	Rng	Thr	G at Pos	BFW
1975	Oak A	5	5	1	0	0	0	0	0	0-0	0	0	.000	.000	.000	-99	-1	0-0	1.000	-0	36	0	/O-5(3-0-2),D	-0.2
1976	StL N	15	14	0	2	0	0	0	0	0-0	0	4	.143	.143	.143	-19	-2	0-0	1.000	2	149	270	O-14(7-2-5)	-0.1
Total	2	20	19	1	2	0	0	0	0	0-0	0	4	.105	.105	.105	-40	-3	0-0	1.000	1	124	210	/O-19(10-2-7),D	-0.3

CHAPLIN, ED Bert Edgar (born Bert Edgar Chapman) B 9.25.1893 Pelzer, SC D 8.15.1978 Sanford, FL BL/TR 5-7/158# d9.4

Year	Tm Lg	G	AB	R	H	2B	3B	HR	RBI	BB-IB	HP	SO	AVG	OBP	SLG	AOPS	ABR	SB-CS	FA	FR	Rng	Thr	G at Pos	BFW
1920	Bos A	4	5	2	1	1	0	0	1	4	0	1	.200	.556	.400	163	1	0-0	.900	-0	*108*	*0*	/C-2	0.1
1921	Bos A	3	2	0	0	0	0	0	0	0	0	1	.000	.000	.000	-99	-1	0-0	1.000	0	*0*	*968*	/C	-0.1
1922	Bos A	28	69	8	13	1	1	0	6	9	0	9	.188	.282	.232	35	-7	2-1	.960	-2	*80*	*78*	C-21	-0.7
Total	3	35	76	10	14	2	1	0	7	13	0	11	.184	.303	.237	43	-7	2-1	.953	-2	*82*	*81*	/C-24	-0.7

CHAPMAN, CALVIN Calvin Louis B 12.20.1910 Courtland, MS D 4.1.1983 Batesville, MS BL/TR 5-9/160# d9.10

Year	Tm Lg	G	AB	R	H	2B	3B	HR	RBI	BB-IB	HP	SO	AVG	OBP	SLG	AOPS	ABR	SB-CS	FA	FR	Rng	Thr	G at Pos	BFW
1935	Cin N	15	53	6	18	1	0	0	3	4	0	5	.340	.386	.358	105	0	2	.949	-1	96	141	S-12/2-4	0.0
1936	Cin N	96	219	35	54	7	3	1	22	16	1	19	.247	.301	.320	72	-9	5	.961	-5	81	129	O-31(21-1-9),2-23/3	-1.5
Total	2	111	272	41	72	8	3	1	25	20	1	24	.265	.317	.327	78	-9	7	.961	-7	81	129	/O-31(21-1-9),2-27,S-12,3	-1.5

CHAPMAN, GLENN Glenn Justice "Pete" B 1.21.1906 Cambridge City, IN D 11.5.1988 Richmond, IN BR/TR 5-11.5/170# d4.18

Year	Tm Lg	G	AB	R	H	2B	3B	HR	RBI	BB-IB	HP	SO	AVG	OBP	SLG	AOPS	ABR	SB-CS	FA	FR	Rng	Thr	G at Pos	BFW
1934	Bro N	67	93	19	26	5	1	1	10	7	0	19	.280	.330	.387	96	-1	1	1.000	2	123	0	O-40(27-0-14),2-14	0.1

CHAPMAN, HARRY Harry E. B 10.26.1887 Severance, KS D 10.21.1918 Nevada, MO BR/TR 5-11/160# d10.6

Year	Tm Lg	G	AB	R	H	2B	3B	HR	RBI	BB-IB	HP	SO	AVG	OBP	SLG	AOPS	ABR	SB-CS	FA	FR	Rng	Thr	G at Pos	BFW
1912	Chi N	1	4	1	1	0	1	0	1	0	0	0	.250	.250	.750	169	0	1	1.000	1	*177*	*142*	/C	0.1
1913	Cin N	2	2	0	1	0	0	0	0	0	0	1	.500	.500	.500	187	0	0	—	0			H	0.0
1914	StL F	64	181	16	38	2	1	0	14	13	2	27	.210	.270	.232	36	-19	2	.973	-5	*83*	*98*	C-51/12O(CF)	-2.1
1915	StL F	62	186	19	37	6	3	1	29	22	0	24	.199	.284	.280	56	-14	4	.989	6	*107*	*98*	C-53	-0.4
1916	StL A	18	31	2	3	0	0	0	0	2	0	5	.097	.152	.097	-27	-5	0	.981	1	96	155	C-14	-0.4
Total	5	147	404	38	80	8	5	1	44	37	2	57	.198	.269	.250	43	-38	7	.982	2	*97*	*103*	C-119/O(CF)21	-2.8

CHAPMAN, JACK John Curtis "Death To Flying Things" B 5.8.1843 Brooklyn, NY D 6.10.1916 Brooklyn, NY TR 5-11/170# d5.5 M11

Year	Tm Lg	G	AB	R	H	2B	3B	HR	RBI	BB-IB	HP	SO	AVG	OBP	SLG	AOPS	ABR	SB-CS	FA	FR	Rng	Thr	G at Pos	BFW
1874	Atl NA	53	242	32	64	10	2	0	24	4		11	.264	.276	.322	103	4	2-1	.741	1	**167**	0	*O-53(0-1-52)/1	0.6
1875	StL NA	43	195	28	44	5	3	0	30	1		7	.226	.230	.282	84	-2	4-1	.733	-5	81	159	O-43(RF)/1	-0.3
1876	Lou N	17	67	4	16	1	0	0	5	1		3	.239	.250	.254	58	-3		.750	-3	78	0	O-17(5-1-11)/3M	-0.6
Total	2 NA	96	437	60	108	15	5	0	54	5		18	.247	.256	.304	95	2	6-2	.000	-4	126	75	/O-96(0-1-95),1-2	0.3

CHAPMAN, JOHN John Joseph B 10.15.1899 Centralia, PA D 11.3.1953 Philadelphia, PA BR/TR 5-10.5/175# d6.28

Year	Tm Lg	G	AB	R	H	2B	3B	HR	RBI	BB-IB	HP	SO	AVG	OBP	SLG	AOPS	ABR	SB-CS	FA	FR	Rng	Thr	G at Pos	BFW
1924	Phi A	19	71	7	20	4	1	0	7	4	1	8	.282	.329	.366	78	-2	0-0	.958	-5	73	116	S-19	-0.6

CHAPMAN, KELVIN Kelvin Keith B 6.2.1956 Willits, CA BR/TR 5-11/173# d4.5

Year	Tm Lg	G	AB	R	H	2B	3B	HR	RBI	BB-IB	HP	SO	AVG	OBP	SLG	AOPS	ABR	SB-CS	FA	FR	Rng	Thr	G at Pos	BFW
1979	NY N	35	80	7	12	1	2	0	4	5-0	0	15	.150	.198	.213	13	-10	0-0	.980	-2	86	121	2-22/3	-1.1
1984	NY N	75	197	27	57	13	0	3	23	19-0	2	30	.289	.356	.401	115	4	8-7	.979	-4	87	103	2-57/3-3	0.3
1985	NY N	62	144	16	25	3	0	0	7	9-0	2	15	.174	.231	.194	21	-15	5-4	.970	-10	82	79	2-48/3	-2.6
Total	3	172	421	50	94	17	2	3	34	33-0	4	60	.223	.284	.295	64	-21	13-11	.976	-16	85	98	2-127/3-5	-3.4

CHAPMAN, RAY Raymond Johnson B 1.15.1891 Beaver Dam, KY D 8.17.1920 New York, NY BR/TR 5-10/170# d8.30

Year	Tm Lg	G	AB	R	H	2B	3B	HR	RBI	BB-IB	HP	SO	AVG	OBP	SLG	AOPS	ABR	SB-CS	FA	FR	Rng	Thr	G at Pos	BFW
1912	Cle A	31	109	29	34	6	3	0	19	10	1		.312	.375	.422	124	3	10	.904	-7	77	98	S-31	-0.2
1913	Cle A	141	508	78	131	19	7	3	39	46	2	51	.258	.322	.341	91	-6	29	.936	-9	92	106	*S-138/O(RF)	-0.6
1914	Cle A	106	375	59	103	16	10	2	42	48	1	48	.275	.358	.387	119	9	24-9	.913	-13	86	77	S-72,2-33	0.5
1915	Cle A	**154**	570	101	154	14	17	3	67	70	3	82	.270	.353	.370	114	9	36-15	.944	10	100	66	*S-154	3.4
1916	Cle A	109	346	50	80	10	5	0	27	50	1	46	.231	.330	.289	81	-7	21-14	.935	7	102	92	S-52,3-36,2-16	0.6
1917	Cle A	**156**	563	98	170	28	13	2	36	61	0	65	.302	.370	.409	128	19	52	.938	**24**	**111**	107	*S-156	5.8
1918	Cle A	128	446	**84**	119	19	8	1	32	**84**	6	46	.267	.390	.352	113	12	35	.936	7	101	85	*S-128/O(CF)	3.0
1919	Cle A	115	433	75	130	23	10	3	53	31	3	38	.300	.351	.420	109	4	18	.944	2	100	107	*S-115	1.4
1920	Cle A	111	435	97	132	27	8	3	49	52	2	38	.303	.380	.423	109	7	13-9	.959	14	**106**	106	*S-111	2.7
Total	9	1051	3785	671	1053	162	81	17	364	452	19	<u>414</u>	.278	.358	.377	110	50	238-<u>47</u>	.939	34	100	94	S-957/2-49,3-36,O-2(0-1-1)	16.6

CHAPMAN, SAM Samuel Blake B 4.11.1916 Tiburon, CA BR/TR 6-1/190# d5.16 Mil 1942-45

Year	Tm Lg	G	AB	R	H	2B	3B	HR	RBI	BB-IB	HP	SO	AVG	OBP	SLG	AOPS	ABR	SB-CS	FA	FR	Rng	Thr	G at Pos	BFW
1938	Phi A	114	406	60	105	17	7	17	63	55	4	94	.259	.353	.461	105	1	3-4	.952	0	102	103	*O-110(103-8-0)	-0.4
1939	Phi A	140	498	74	134	24	6	15	64	51	1	62	.269	.338	.432	98	-4	11-4	.955	1	106	107	*O-117(CF),1-19	-0.6

Year	Tm Lg	G	AB	R	H	2B	3B	HR	RBI	BB-IB	HP	SO	AVG	OBP	SLG	AOPS	ABR	SB-CS	FA	FR	Rng	Thr	G at Pos	BFW
1940	Phi A	134	508	88	140	26	3	23	75	46	1	96	.276	.337	.474	110	6	2-6	.963	5	104	142	*O-129(CF)	0.5
1941	Phi A	143	552	97	178	29	9	25	106	47	2	49	.322	.378	.543	145	32	6-9	.967	12	106	**174**	*O-141(0-140-1)	3.7
1945	Phi A	9	30	3	6	2	0	0	1	2	0	4	.200	.250	.267	50	-2	0-0	1.000	-1	90	0	/O-8(CF)	-0.3
1946	Phi A★	146	545	77	142	22	5	20	67	54	0	66	.261	.327	.429	111	6	1-3	.970	8	108	134	*O-145(89-59-0)	0.5
1947	Phi A	149	551	84	139	18	5	14	83	65	0	70	.252	.331	.379	95	-4	3-4	.987	8	103	161	*O-146(12-134-0)	-0.1
1948	Phi A	123	445	58	115	18	6	13	70	55	1	50	.258	.341	.413	100	-2	6-1	.982	1	104	79	*O-118(CF)	-0.3
1949	Phi A	**154**	589	89	164	24	4	24	108	80	2	68	.278	.367	.455	121	16	3-4	.979	3	104	101	*O-154(CF)	1.4
1950	Phi A	144	553	93	139	20	6	23	95	68	4	79	.251	.338	.434	98	-4	3-3	.978	5	108	90	*O-140(CF)	-0.3
1951	Phi A	18	65	7	11	1	0	0	5	12	0	12	.169	.299	.185	32	-6	0-0	.957	-2	91	57	O-17(CF)	-0.8
	Cle A	94	246	24	56	9	1	6	36	27	0	32	.228	.304	.346	80	-8	3-0	.985	-4	93	40	O-84(38-44-7)/1	-1.4
	Year	112	311	31	67	10	1	6	41	39	0	44	.215	.303	.312	69	-14	3-0	.978	-6	93	44	*O-101(38-61-7)/1	-2.2
Total	11	1368	4988	754	1329	210	52	180	773	562	15	682	.266	.342	.438	107	31	41-38	.972	36	104	117	*O-1309(242-1068-8)/1-20	1.9

CHAPMAN, TRAVIS Travis Adrian B 6.5.1978 Jacksonville, FL BR/TR 6-2/180# d9.9

2003	Phi N	1	1	0	0	0	0	0	0	0-0	0	0	.000	.000	.000	-99	0	0-0	—	-0	0	0	/3	-0.1

CHAPMAN, BEN William Benjamin B 12.25.1908 Nashville, TN D 7.7.1993 Hoover, AL BR/TR 6/190# d4.15 M4 C1 ▲ OF Total (404-LF 583-CF 541-RF)

1930	NY A	138	513	74	162	31	10	10	81	43	2	58	.316	.371	.474	118	13	14-6	.912	-9	92	71	3-91,2-45	1.1
1931	NY A	149	600	120	189	28	11	17	122	75	5	77	.315	.396	.483	138	34	**61**-23	.963	6	106	125	*O-137(90-0-50),2-11	3.4
1932	†NY A	151	581	101	174	41	15	10	107	71	5	55	.299	.381	.473	126	24	**38**-18	.949	4	106	122	*O-150(81-0-86)	1.9
1933	NY A★	147	565	112	176	36	4	9	98	72	4	45	.312	.393	.437	127	25	**27**-18	.975	14	107	**190**	*O-147(76-0-77)	2.9
1934	NY A★	149	588	82	181	21	**13**	5	86	67	3	68	.308	.381	.413	113	11	26-16	.967	4	106	100	*O-149(41-87-23)	0.9
1935	NY A★	140	553	118	160	38	8	8	74	61	1	39	.289	.361	.430	110	8	17-10	.964	13	103	**243**	*O-138(CF)	1.7
1936	NY A	36	139	19	37	14	3	1	21	15	0	20	.266	.338	.432	92	-2	1-2	.965	1	106	93	O-36(CF)	-0.2
	Was A★	97	401	91	133	36	7	4	60	69	1	18	.332	.431	.486	133	25	19-7	.959	-1	97	112	O-97(CF)	2.1
	Year	133	540	110	170	50	10	5	81	84	1	38	.315	.408	.472	123	23	20-9	.961	-0	99	107	*O-133(CF)	1.9
1937	Was A	35	130	23	34	7	1	0	12	26	0	7	.262	.385	.331	86	-1	8-0	.957	-1	104	34	O-32(CF)	-0.2
	Bos A	113	423	76	130	23	11	7	57	57	1	35	.307	.391	.463	110	7	27-12	.985	5	114	85	*O-112(2-10-100)/S	0.6
	Year	148	553	99	164	30	12	7	69	83	1	42	.297	.389	.432	105	6	**35**-12	.978	4	**112**	74	*O-144(2-42-100)/S	0.4
1938	Bos A	127	480	92	163	40	8	6	80	65	0	33	.340	.418	.494	122	19	13-6	.966	5	106	130	*O-126(1-0-125)/3	1.6
1939	Cle A	149	545	101	158	31	9	6	82	87	2	30	.290	.390	.413	109	11	18-6	.971	-6	93	100	*O-146(2-137-9)	0.3
1940	Cle A	143	548	82	157	40	6	4	50	78	2	45	.286	.377	.403	105	8	13-7	.964	1	103	94	*O-140(62-18-62)	0.2
1941	Was A	28	110	9	28	6	0	1	10	10	0	6	.255	.317	.336	76	-4	2-2	.983	1	100	142	O-26(LF)	-0.4
	Chi A	57	190	26	43	9	1	2	19	19	0	14	.226	.297	.316	63	-10	2-2	.992	0	100	91	O-49(21-22-7)	-1.2
	Year	85	300	35	71	15	1	3	29	29	0	20	.237	.304	.323	68	-14	4-4	.989	1	100	108	O-75(47-22-7)	-1.6
1944	Bro N	20	38	11	14	4	0	0	11	5	0	4	.368	.442	.474	161	7	1	.900	-2	40	0	P-11	0.0
1945	Bro N	13	22	2	3	0	0	0	3	2	0	1	.136	.208	.136	-3	-1	0	.938	1	123	172	P-10	0.0
	Phi N	24	51	4	16	2	0	0	4	2	0	1	.314	.340	.353	95	0	0	.933	-1	80	183	O-10(2-6-2)/3-4,P-3,M	-0.2
	Year	37	73	6	19	2	0	0	7	4	0	2	.260	.299	.288	65	-4	0	.941	-1	117	152	P-13,O-10(2-6-2)/3-4	-0.2
1946	Phi N	1	1	1	0	0	0	0	0	0	0	0	.000	.000	.000	-99	0	0	—	0	0	0	/PM	0.0
Total	15	1717	6478	1144	1958	407	107	90	977	824	26	556	.302	.383	.440	115	174	287-135	.967	36	104	127	*O-1495C/3-96,2-56,P-25,S	14.5

CHAPMAN, FRED William Fred "Chappie" B 7.17.1916 Liberty, SC D 3.27.1997 Kannapolis, NC BR/TR 6-1/185# d9.15 Mil 1943-45

1939	Phi A	15	49	5	14	1	1	0	1	1	0	3	.286	.300	.347	66	-3	1-0	.899	-3	98	59	S-15	-0.4
1940	Phi A	26	69	6	11	1	0	0	4	6	0	10	.159	.227	.174	6	-10	1-1	.862	-6	88	88	S-25	-1.4
1941	Phi A	35	69	1	11	1	0	0	4	4	0	15	.159	.205	.174	1	-10	1-2	.917	-1	121	66	S-28/3-2,2	-1.1
Total	3	76	187	12	36	3	1	0	9	11	0	28	.193	.237	.219	20	-23	3-3	.889	-10	101	74	/S-68,3-2,2	-2.9

CHAPPAS, HARRY Harry Perry B 10.26.1957 Mt.Rainier, MD BB/TR 5-3/150# d9.7

1978	Chi A	20	75	11	20	1	0	0	6	6-0	1	11	.267	.318	.280	72	-3	1-2	1.000	1	107	66	S-20	0.0
1979	Chi A	26	59	9	17	1	0	1	4	5-0	1	5	.288	.354	.356	92	-1	1-1	.929	1	107	104	S-23	0.2
1980	Chi A	26	50	6	8	2	0	0	2	4-0	1	10	.160	.236	.200	21	-5	0-2	.981	3	113	139	S-19/2D	-0.2
Total	3	72	184	26	45	4	0	1	12	15-0	3	26	.245	.307	.283	65	-9	2-5	.967	5	108	95	/S-62,D-2,2	0.0

CHAPPELL, LARRY La Verne Ashford B 2.19.1890 McClusky, IL D 11.8.1918 San Francisco, CA BL/TR 6/186# d7.18

1913	Chi A	60	208	20	48	8	1	0	15	18	1	22	.231	.295	.279	69	-8	7	.952	-3	98	59	O-59(52-7-0)	-1.6
1914	Chi A	21	39	3	9	0	0	0	1	4	0	11	.231	.302	.231	61	-2	0	.929	-1	93	0	/O-9(7-0-2)	-0.4
1915	Chi A	1	1	0	0	0	0	0	0	0	0	0	.000	.000	.000	-97	0	0	—	0			H	0.0
1916	Cle A	3	2	0	0	0	0	0	0	1	0	0	.000	.333	.000	1	0	1	—	0			H	0.0
	Bos N	20	53	4	12	1	1	0	9	2	1	8	.226	.268	.283	72	-2	1	.957	-2	93	0	O-14(12-0-2)	-0.5
1917	Bos N	4	2	0	0	0	0	0	1	0	0	1	.000	.000	.000	-99	0	0	—	-0	0	0	/O(CF)	-0.1
Total	5	109	305	27	69	9	2	0	26	25	2	42	.226	.289	.269	66	-12	9	.951	-6	97	44	/O-83(71-8-4)	-2.6

CHARBONEAU, JOE Joseph B 6.17.1955 Belvidere, IL BR/TR 6-2/205# d4.11

1980	Cle A	131	453	76	131	17	2	23	87	49-0	3	70	.289	.358	.488	130	19	2-4	.963	-1	95	128	O-67(67-0-1),D-57	1.2
1981	Cle A	48	138	14	29	7	1	4	18	7-0	0	22	.210	.247	.362	75	-5	1-0	.963	-1	97	58	O-27(24-0-5),D-14	-0.8
1982	Cle A	22	56	7	12	2	1	2	9	5-0	1	7	.214	.286	.393	86	-1	0-0	.955	-3	72	0	O-18(9-0-8)/D	-0.5
Total	3	201	647	97	172	26	4	29	114	61-0	4	99	.266	.329	.453	115	13	3-4	.962	-4	92	94	O-112(100-0-14)/D-72	-0.1

CHARLES, ED Edwin Douglas B 4.29.1933 Daytona Beach, FL BR/TR 5-10/170# d4.11

1962	KC A	147	535	81	154	24	7	17	74	54-0	4	70	.288	.356	.454	111	9	20-4	.964	12	109	101	*3-140/2-2	2.3
1963	KC A	158	603	82	161	28	2	15	79	58-7	5	79	.267	.332	.395	99	0	15-8	.949	1	105	63	*3-158	0.1
1964	KC A	150	557	69	134	25	2	16	63	64-2	4	92	.241	.321	.379	92	-5	12-7	.954	-12	91	87	*3-147	-1.8
1965	KC A	134	480	55	129	19	7	8	56	44-0	4	72	.269	.332	.387	106	4	13-4	.971	3	98	104	*3-128/2S	0.9
1966	KC A	118	385	52	110	18	8	9	42	30-2	0	53	.286	.337	.444	127	12	12-5	.963	-1	103	108	*3-104/1O(LF)	1.2
1967	KC A	19	61	5	15	1	0	0	5	12-1	1	13	.246	.378	.262	95	1	1-0	.966	2	116	35	3-18	0.3
	NY N	101	323	32	77	13	2	3	31	24-1	7	58	.238	.300	.319	80	-8	4-1	.944	10	113	101	3-89	0.3
1968	NY N	117	369	41	102	11	1	15	53	28-4	2	57	.276	.328	.434	127	11	5-4	.954	-0	102	112	*3-106/1-2	1.2
1969	†NY N	61	169	21	35	8	1	3	18	18-3	1	31	.207	.286	.320	68	-7	4-2	.946	-1	96	131	3-52	-0.9
Total	8	1005	3482	438	917	147	30	86	421	332-20	28	525	.263	.330	.397	103	17	86-35	.957	15	102	95	3-942/1-3,2-3,O(LF)S	3.6

CHARLES, FRANK Franklin Scott B 2.23.1969 Fontana, CA BR/TR 6-4/210# d9.5

2000	Hou N	4	7	1	3	1	0	0	2	0-0	0	2	.429	.429	.571	142	0	0-0	1.000	1	61	0	/C	0.1

CHARLES, CHAPPY Raymond (born Charles Shuh Achenbach) B 3.25.1881 Phillipsburg, NJ D 8.4.1959 Bethlehem, PA BR/TR 5-11/175# d4.15

1908	StL N	121	454	39	93	14	3	1	17	19	1		.205	.238	.256	61	-22	15	.921	-6	98	26	2-65,S-31,3-23	-3.0
1909	StL N	99	339	33	80	7	3	0	29	31	5		.236	.309	.274	87	-5	7	.918	-8	96	108	2-71,S-26/3-2	-1.2
	Cin N	13	43	3	11	2	0	0	5	4	0		.256	.319	.302	94	0	2	.932	-1	107	34	2-10/S-3	-0.1
	Year	112	382	36	91	9	3	0	34	35	5		.238	.310	.277	87	-5	9	.920	-9	97	100	2-81,S-29/3-2	-1.3
1910	Cin N	4	15	1	2	0	1	0	0	0	0	1	.133	.133	.267	17	-2	0	.818	-1	82	119	/S-4	-0.3
Total	3	237	851	76	186	23	7	1	51	54	6	1	.219	.270	.266	72	-29	24	.920	-15	98	68	2-146/S-64,3-25	-4.6

CHARTAK, MIKE Michael George "Shotgun" B 4.28.1916 Brooklyn, NY D 7.25.1967 Cedar Rapids, IA BL/TL 6-2/180# d9.13

1940	NY A	11	15	2	2	1	0	0	3	5	0	5	.133	.350	.200	49	-1	0-0	1.000	-0	87	0	/O-3(RF)	-0.1
1942	NY A	5	5	0	0	0	0	0	0	0	0	0	.000	.000	.000	-99	-1	0-0	—	0			H	-0.1
	Was A	24	92	11	20	4	2	1	8	14	0	16	.217	.321	.337	86	-2	0-1	.926	0	103	116	O-24(RF)	-0.4
	StL A	73	237	37	59	11	2	9	43	40	2	27	.249	.362	.426	119	7	3-3	.974	5	104	199	O-64(RF)	0.8
	Year	102	334	48	79	15	4	10	51	54	2	43	.237	.346	.395	107	4	3-4	.962	5	104	177	O-88(RF)	0.3
1943	StL A	108	344	38	88	16	2	10	37	39	1	55	.256	.333	.401	112	5	1-3	.970	-0	109	78	O-77(RF),1-18	-0.2
1944	†StL A	35	72	8	17	2	1	1	7	6	1	9	.236	.304	.333	77	-2	0-0	1.000	0	88	63	1-12/O-7(4-0-3)	-0.3
Total	4	256	765	96	186	34	7	21	98	104	4	112	.243	.337	.388	105	6	4-7	.967	5	106	127	O-175(4-0-171)/1-30	-0.3

CHASE, HAL Harold Homer "Prince Hal" B 2.13.1883 Los Gatos, CA D 5.18.1947 Colusa, CA BR/TL (BL 1909 (1 game)) 6/175# d4.14 M2 OF Total (23-LF 26-CF 1-RF)

1905	NY A	128	465	60	116	16	6	3	49	15	3		.249	.277	.329	83	-11	22	.976	-9	78	125	*1-124/S-2,2	-2.4
1906	NY A	151	597	84	193	23	10	0	76	13	3		.323	.341	.395	118	10	28	.980	-2	95	89	*1-150/2	0.6
1907	NY A	125	498	72	143	23	3	2	68	19	1		.287	.315	.357	106	2	32	.973	0	103	84	*1-121/O-4(LF)	0.0
1908	NY A	106	405	50	104	11	3	1	36	15	1		.257	.285	.306	91	-5	27	.980	-3	91	73	1-98/2-3,O-3(LF),3P	-1.2

Year	Tm Lg	G	AB	R	H	2B	3B	HR	RBI	BB-IB	HP	SO	AVG	OBP	SLG	AOPS	ABR	SB-CS	FA	FR	Rng	Thr	G at Pos	BFW
1909	NY A	118	474	60	134	17	3	4	63	20	4		.283	.317	.357	112	5	25	.978	-2	100	89	*1-118/S	0.1
1910	NY A	130	524	67	152	20	5	3	73	16	1		.290	.312	.365	106	1	40	.981	-4	88	120	*1-130,M	-0.6
1911	NY A	133	527	82	166	32	7	3	62	21	1		.315	.342	.419	105	2	36	.974	-2	101	108	*1-124/O-7(CF),2-2,M	-0.3
1912	NY A	131	522	61	143	21	9	4	58	17	2		.274	.299	.372	86	-12	33	.979	-1	**111**	80	*1-122/2-7	-1.7
1913	NY A	39	146	15	31	2	4	0	9	11	0	13	.212	.268	.281	60	-8	5	.982	-4	88	97	1-29/2-5,O-5(CF)	-1.4
	Chi A	102	384	49	110	11	10	2	39	16	3	41	.286	.320	.383	107	0	9	.976	1	114	104	*1-102	-0.1
	Year	141	530	64	141	13	14	2	48	27	3	54	.266	.305	.355	94	-8	14	.977	-3	108	102	*1-131/2-5,O-5(CF)	-1.5
1914	Chi A	58	206	27	55	10	5	0	20	23	1	19	.267	.343	.364	114	4	9-4	.981	2	116	103	1-58	0.5
	Buf F	75	291	43	101	19	9	3	48	6	2	31	.347	.365	.505	133	7	10	.980	-1	99	89	1-73	0.5
1915	Buf F	145	567	85	165	31	10	**17**	89	20	1	50	.291	.316	.471	118	1	23	.983	0	103	101	*1-143/O(RF)	-0.3
1916	Cin N	142	542	66	**184**	29	12	4	82	19	1	48	**.339**	.363	.459	**155**	32	22-11	.986	-5	79	116	1-98,O-25(14-14-0),2-16	2.8
1917	Cin N	152	602	71	167	28	15	4	86	15	1	49	.277	.296	.394	115	7	21	.983	-3	98	103	*1-151	0.0
1918	Cin N	74	259	30	78	12	6	2	38	13	2	15	.301	.339	.417	133	9	5	.980	-2	93	146	1-67/O-2(LF)	0.6
1919	NY N	110	408	58	116	17	7	5	45	17	3	40	.284	.318	.397	115	6	16	.984	-1	101	**111**	*1-107	0.2
Total	15	1919	7417	980	2158	322	124	57	941	276	30	306	.291	.319	.391	110	50	363-15	.980	-35	98	102	*1-1815/O-47C,2-35,S-3,P3	-2.7
CHATHAM, BUSTER Charles L B 12.25.1901 West, TX D 12.15.1975 Waco, TX BR/TR 5-5/150# d6.1																								
1930	Bos N	112	404	48	108	20	11	5	56	37	2	41	.267	.332	.408	80	-14	8	.920	-11	88	158	3-92,S-17	-1.6
1931	Bos N	17	44	4	10	1	0	1	3	6	0	6	.227	.320	.318	75	-2	0	.762	-4	51	99	/S-6,3-6	-0.5
Total	2	129	448	52	118	21	11	6	59	43	2	47	.263	.331	.400	80	-16	8	.924	-15	90	155	/3-98,S-23	-2.1
CHATTERTON, JIM James M. B 10.14.1864 Brooklyn, NY D 12.15.1944 Tewksbury, MA d6.7																								
1884	KC U	4	15	4	2	1	0	0		2			.133	.235	.200	38	-1		1.000	1	589	0	/O-2(RF),1-2,P	-0.1
CHAVARRIA, OSSIE Osvaldo (Quijano) B 8.5.1940 Colon, Panama BR/TR 5-11/155# d4.14																								
1966	KC A	86	191	26	46	10	0	2	10	18-1	0	43	.241	.306	.325	84	-4	3-2	.939	-1	98	97	O-26(19-0-7),S-23,2-14/1-8,3-5	-0.3
1967	KC A	38	59	2	6	2	0	0	4	7-0	1	16	.102	.209	.136	4	-7	1-0	1.000	1	105	144	2-17/3-7,O-3(2-0-1),S-2	-0.5
Total	2	124	250	28	52	12	0	2	14	25-1	1	59	.208	.283	.280	65	-11	4-2	.990	0	104	112	/2-31,O-29(21-0-8),S-25,3-12,1-8	-0.8
CHAVEZ, ENDY Endy De Jesus B 2.7.1978 Valencia, Venezuela BL/TL 6/165# d5.29																								
2001	KC A	29	77	4	16	2	0	0	5	3-0	0	8	.208	.237	.234	23	-9	0-2	1.000	0	91	162	O-28(22-5-2)	-0.9
2002	Mon N	36	125	20	37	8	5	1	9	5-0	0	16	.296	.321	.464	99	-1	3-5	.989	5	109	402	O-35(CF)	0.3
2003	Mon N	141	483	66	121	25	5	5	47	31-3	0	59	.251	.294	.354	63	-27	18-7	.990	1	100	138	*O-135(CF)	-2.3
Total	3	206	685	90	174	35	10	6	61	39-3	0	83	.254	.293	.361	65	-37	21-14	.991	7	101	190	O-198(22-175-2)	-2.9
CHAVEZ, ERIC Eric Cesar B 12.7.1977 Los Angeles, CA BL/TR 6-1/195# d9.8																								
1998	Oak A	16	45	6	14	4	1	0	6	3-1	0	5	.311	.354	.444	109	1	1-1	1.000	2	109	119	3-13	0.2
1999	Oak A	115	356	47	88	21	2	13	50	46-4	0	56	.247	.333	.427	96	-2	1-1	.961	-8	90	81	*3-105/S-2,D-3	-0.8
2000	†Oak A	153	501	89	139	23	4	26	86	62-8	1	94	.277	.355	.495	116	11	2-2	.951	-6	99	66	*3-146/S-2	0.6
2001	†Oak A	151	552	91	159	43	0	32	114	41-9	4	99	.288	.338	.540	127	21	8-2	**.972**	12	**108**	119	*3-149/1SD	3.4
2002	†Oak A	153	585	87	161	31	3	34	109	65-13	1	119	.275	.348	.513	125	20	8-3	.961	12	**108**	105	*3-143/O(LF)D	3.3
2003	†Oak A	156	588	94	166	39	5	29	101	62-10	1	89	.282	.350	.514	123	19	8-3	.971	23	**112**	**137**	*3-154	4.2
Total	6	744	2627	414	727	161	15	134	466	279-45	7	462	.277	.346	.502	119	70	28-12	.965	36	105	104	3-710/D-13,S-5,O(LF)1	10.9
CHAVEZ, RAUL Raul Alexander B 3.18.1973 Valencia, Venezuela BR/TR 5-11/175# d8.30																								
1996	Mon N	4	5	1	1	0	0	0	0	1-0	0	1	.200	.333	.200	44	0	1-0	1.000	1	0	0	/C-3	0.0
1997	Mon N	13	26	0	7	0	0	0	2	0-0	0	5	.269	.259	.269	42	-2	1-0	1.000	1	121	108	C-13	-0.1
1998	Sea A	1	1	0	0	0	0	0	0	0-0	0	0	.000	.000	.000	-99	0	0-0	1.000	-0	0	0	/C	0.0
2000	Hou N	14	43	3	11	2	0	1	5	3-2	0	6	.256	.298	.372	66	-2	0-0	.986	-4	83	57	C-14	-0.6
2002	Hou N	2	4	1	1	1	0	0	0	1-0	1	0	.250	.500	.500	162	1	0-0	1.000	-1	0	0	/C-2	0.0
2003	Hou N	19	37	5	10	1	1	1	4	1-0	0	6	.270	.289	.432	81	-1	0-0	1.000	-1	223	150	C-16	-0.1
Total	6	53	116	10	30	4	1	2	11	6-2	1	18	.259	.296	.362	68	-4	2-0	.995	-5	121	88	/C-49	-0.8
CHEEK, HARRY Harry G. B 1879 Sedalia, MO D 6.25.1956 Paramus, NJ TR d4.30																								
1910	Phi N	2	4	1	2	1	0	0	0	0	0	0	.500	.500	.750	255	1	0	1.000	-1	*87*	*0*	/C-2	0.0
CHEN, CHIN-FENG Chin-Feng B 10.28.1977 Tainan City, Taiwan BR/TR 6-1/189# d9.14																								
2002	LA N	3	5	1	0	0	0	0	0	1-0	0	3	.000	.167	.000	-53	-1	0-0	1.000	0	163	0	/O(LF)	-0.1
2003	LA N	1	1	0	0	0	0	0	0	0-0	0	0	.000	.000	.000	-99	0	0-0	—	0			/H	0.0
Total	2	4	6	1	0	0	0	0	0	1-0	0	3	.000	.143	.000	-61	-1	0-0	1.000	0	163	0	/O(LF)	-0.1
CHERVINKO, PAUL Paul B 7.28.1910 Trauger, PA D 6.3.1976 Danville, IL BR/TR 5-8/185# d5.30																								
1937	Bro N	30	48	1	7	0	1	0	2	3	0	16	.146	.196	.188	5	-7	0	1.000	0	*81*	*85*	C-26	-0.5
1938	Bro N	12	27	0	4	0	0	0	3	2	0	0	.148	.207	.148	-1	-4	0	.974	0	*102*	*120*	C-12	-0.3
Total	2	42	75	1	11	0	1	0	5	5	0	16	.147	.200	.173	3	-11	0	.990	0	*90*	*99*	/C-38	-0.8
CHILDS, CUPID Clarence Algernon B 8.14.1867 Calvert Co., MD D 11.8.1912 Baltimore, MD BL/TR 5-8/185# d4.23																								
1888	Phi N	2	4	0	0	0	0	0	0	0	0	0	.000	.000	.000	-95	-1	0	.857	0	108	248	/2-2	-0.1
1890	Syr AA	126	493	109	170	**33**	14	2	89	72	6		.345	.434	.481	189	**61**	56	.928	14	105	103	*2-125/S	**6.8**
1891	Cle N	**141**	551	120	155	21	12	2	83	97	7	32	.281	.395	.374	119	18	39	.910	-12	99	84	*2-141	1.0
1892	†Cle N	145	558	**136**	177	14	11	3	53	117	9	20	.317	**.443**	.398	149	41	26	.938	-5	99	97	*2-145	3.9
1893	Cle N	124	485	145	158	19	10	3	65	120	4	12	.326	.463	.425	129	28	23	.926	9	107	101	*2-123	3.4
1894	Cle N	118	479	143	169	21	12	2	52	107	5	11	.353	.475	.459	121	24	17	.916	-1	101	99	*2-118	2.2
1895	†Cle N	120	466	96	134	15	4	4	90	74	6	24	.288	.392	.363	90	-5	20	.921	10	106	91	*2-120	0.9
1896	†Cle N	132	498	106	177	24	9	1	106	100	4	18	.355	.467	.446	133	31	25	.942	**39**	**117**	**147**	*2-132	6.3
1897	Cle N	114	444	105	150	15	9	1	61	74	2		.338	.435	.419	119	16	25	.944	18	106	116	*2-114	3.3
1898	Cle N	110	413	90	119	9	4	1	31	69	4		.288	.395	.337	112	11	9	.931	12	**110**	95	*2-110	2.5
1899	StL N	125	464	73	123	11	11	1	48	74	2		.265	.369	.343	93	-2	11	.934	-14	91	97	*2-125	-0.9
1900	Chi N	137	531	67	128	14	5	0	44	57	7		.241	.323	.286	71	-19	15	.935	15	110	105	*2-137	0.2
1901	Chi N	63	236	24	61	9	0	0	21	30	7		.258	.359	.297	95	1	3	.939	9	106	154	2-63	1.0
Total	13	1457	5622	1214	1721	205	101	20	743	991	63	117	.306	.416	.389	119	204	269	.930	94	105	106	*2-1455/S	30.5
CHILDS, PETE Peter Pierre B 11.15.1871 Philadelphia, PA D 2.15.1922 Philadelphia, PA TR d4.24																								
1901	StL N	29	79	12	21	1	0	0	8	14	2		.266	.389	.278	100	1	0	.907	-5	94	66	2-19/O-2(1-1-0),S	-0.3
	Chi N	60	210	23	48	5	1	0	14	26	2		.229	.319	.262	72	-6	4	.958	12	116	92	2-60	0.6
	Year	89	289	35	69	6	1	0	22	40	4		.239	.339	.266	80	-5	4	.947	7	111	86	2-79/O-2(1-1-0),S	0.3
1902	Phi N	123	403	25	78	5	0	0	25	34	0		.194	.256	.206	43	-26	6	.945	-8	97	53	*2-123	-3.6
Total	2	212	692	60	147	11	1	0	47	74	4		.212	.292	.231	59	-31	10	.946	-1	102	66	2-202/O-2(1-1-0),S	-3.3
CHILDS, SAM Samuel Beresford B 11.6.1861 East Hartford, CT D 5.21.1938 Denver, CO d5.31																								
1883	Col AA	1	4	0	0	0	0	0		0			.000	.000	.000	-99	-1		1.000	0	0	0	/1	-0.1
CHILES, PEARCE Pearce Nuget "What's The Use" B 5.28.1867 Deepwater, MO BR/TR 5-11/185# d4.18																								
1899	Phi N	97	338	57	108	28	7	2	76	16	1		.320	.352	.462	127	11	6	.944	-10	96	247	O-46(13-2-31),1-25,2-16	0.0
1900	Phi N	33	111	13	24	6	2	1	23	6	0		.216	.256	.333	63	-6	4	.987	-1	102	132	1-16,2-12/O-3(RF)	-0.6
Total	2	130	449	70	132	34	9	3	99	22	1		.294	.328	.430	111	5	10	.947	-11	90	232	/O-49(13-2-34),1-41,2-28	-0.6
CHILES, RICH Richard Francis B 11.22.1949 Sacramento, CA BL/TL 5-11/170# d4.20																								
1971	Hou N	67	119	12	27	5	1	2	15	6-0	1	20	.227	.268	.336	73	-5	0-1	1.000	-1	67	0	O-27(25-0-2)	-0.8
1972	Hou N	9	11	0	3	1	0	0	2	1-0	0	1	.273	.333	.364	100	0	0-0	1.000	0	149	0	/O-2(LF)	0.0
1973	NY N	8	25	2	3	2	0	0	1	0-0	0	2	.120	.120	.200	-13	-4	0-0	1.000	2	143	249	/O-8(CF)	-0.2
1976	Hou N	5	4	1	2	1	0	0	0	0-0	0	0	.500	.500	.750	276	1	0-0	1.000	0	427	0	/O(LF)	0.1
1977	Min A	108	261	31	69	16	1	3	36	23-2	2	17	.264	.323	.368	91	-3	0-1	.946	-2	97	0	D-61,O-22(1-0-21)	-0.7
1978	Min A	87	198	22	53	12	0	1	22	20-2	2	25	.268	.333	.343	91	-1	1-2	.965	0	101	88	O-61(58-0-3)/D-8	-0.4
Total	6	284	618	68	157	37	2	6	76	50-4	5	65	.254	.310	.350	85	-12	1-4	.972	-1	97	62	O-121(87-8-26)/D-69	-2.0
CHIOZZA, DINO Dino Joseph "Dynamo" B 6.30.1912 Memphis, TN D 4.23.1972 Memphis, TN BL/TR 6/170# d7.14 b-Lou																								
1935	Phi N	2	0	1	0	0	0	0	0	0	0	0	—	—	—	—	0	0	1.000	-0	0	0	/S-2	0.0

Year	Tm Lg	G	AB	R	H	2B	3B	HR	RBI	BB-IB	HP	SO	AVG	OBP	SLG	AOPS	ABR	SB-CS	FA	FR	Rng	Thr	G at Pos	BFW
CHIOZZA, LOU Louis Peo B 5.17.1910 Tallulah, LA D 2.28.1971 Memphis, TN BL/TR 6/172# d4.17 b-Dino																								
1934	Phi N	134	484	66	147	28	5	0	44	34	6	35	.304	.357	.382	86	-8	9	.938	-18	93	73	2-85,3-26,O-17(13-0-4)	-2.1
1935	Phi N	124	472	71	134	26	6	3	47	33	2	44	.284	.333	.383	84	-10	5	.947	4	**106**	74	*2-120/3-2	0.1
1936	Phi N	144	572	83	170	32	6	1	48	37	6	39	.297	.346	.379	87	-10	17	.972	-6	100	108	O-90(4-85-1),2-33,3-26	-1.5
1937	†NY N	117	439	49	102	11	2	4	29	20	0	30	.232	.266	.294	51	-31	6	.939	-4	96	81	3-93,O-12(CF)/2-2	-3.2
1938	NY N	57	179	15	42	7	2	3	17	12	0	7	.235	.283	.346	72	-8	5	.944	-3	109	49	2-34,O-16(5-10-0)/3	-0.9
1939	NY N	40	142	19	38	3	1	3	12	9	0	10	.268	.311	.366	81	-4	3	.915	-2	97	137	3-30/S-8	-0.5
Total	6	616	2288	303	633	107	22	14	197	145	14	165	.277	.324	.361	78	-71	45	.943	-28	102	70	2-274,3-178,O-135(22-107-5)/S-8	-8.1
CHIPPLE, WALT Walter John (born Walter John Chlipala) B 9.26.1918 Utica, NY D 6.8.1988 Tonawanda, NY BR/TR 6-0.5/168# d4.17																								
1945	Was A	18	44	4	6	0	0	0	5	5	0	6	.136	.224	.136	6	-5	0-1	.978	2	121	172	O-13(1-11-1)	-0.4
CHISM, TOM Thomas Raymond B 5.9.1955 Chester, PA BL/TL 6-1/195# d9.13																								
1979	Bal A	6	3	0	0	0	0	0	0	0-0	0	0	.000	.000	.000	-99	-1	0-0	1.000	-0	0	0	/1-4	-0.1
CHITI, HARRY Harry B 11.16.1932 Kincaid, IL D 1.31.2002 Haines City, FL BR/TR 6-3/225# d9.27 Mil 1953																								
1950	Chi N	3	6	0	2	0	0	0	0	0	0	0	.333	.333	.333	77	0	0	1.000	-0	*0*	*534*	/C	-0.1
1951	Chi N	9	31	1	11	2	0	0	5	2	0	2	.355	.394	.419	117	1	0-0	.913	-1	*63*	*188*	/C-8	0.0
1952	Chi N	32	113	14	31	5	0	5	13	5	0	8	.274	.305	.451	106	0	0-1	.984	2	*66*	*65*	C-32	0.4
1955	Chi N	113	338	24	78	6	1	11	41	25-8	1	68	.231	.282	.352	68	-17	0-0	.984	-4	*66*	***131***	*C-113	-1.5
1956	Chi N	72	203	17	43	6	4	4	18	19-3	1	35	.212	.281	.340	68	-10	0-0	.981	0	*78*	*136*	C-67	-0.7
1958	KC A	103	295	32	79	11	3	9	44	18-4	3	48	.268	.311	.417	98	-2	3-2	.987	1	*130*	*94*	C-83	0.3
1959	KC A	55	162	20	44	11	1	5	25	17-1	1	26	.272	.344	.444	113	3	0-1	.988	2	*115*	*72*	C-47	0.7
1960	KC A	58	190	16	42	7	0	5	28	17-0	1	33	.221	.288	.337	68	-9	1-0	.983	-3	*70*	*65*	C-52	-1.0
	Det A	37	104	9	17	0	0	2	5	10-1	0	12	.163	.235	.221	24	-11	0-3	.984	0	*100*	*123*	C-36	-1.1
	Year	95	294	25	59	7	0	7	33	27-1	1	45	.201	.269	.296	52	-20	1-3	.984	-3	*81*	*86*	C-88	-2.1
1961	Det A	5	12	0	1	0	0	0	0	1-0	0	2	.083	.154	.083	-34	-2	0-0	1.000	1	*115*	*303*	/C-5	-0.2
1962	NY N	15	41	2	8	1	0	0	0	1-0	1	8	.195	.233	.220	22	-5	0-0	.971	-1	*90*	*74*	C-14	-0.5
Total	10	502	1495	135	356	49	9	41	179	115-17	8	242	.238	.294	.365	77	-52	4-7	.983	-4	*89*	*107*	C-458	-3.7
CHOI, HEE SEOP Hee Seop B 3.16.1979 Chun-Nam, South Korea BL/TL 6-5/235# d9.3																								
2002	Chi N	24	50	6	9	1	0	2	4	7-0	0	15	.180	.281	.320	62	-3	0-0	.983	-1	81	133	1-22	-0.5
2003	Chi N	80	202	31	44	17	0	8	28	37-1	4	71	.218	.350	.421	102	2	1-1	.991	2	102	97	1-69	-0.2
Total	2	104	252	37	53	18	0	10	32	44-1	4	86	.210	.337	.401	94	-1	1-1	.990	1	98	104	/1-91	-0.7
CHOUINARD, FELIX Felix George B 10.5.1887 Chicago, IL D 4.28.1955 Hines, IL BR/TR 5-7/150# d9.11																								
1910	Chi A	24	82	6	16	3	2	0	9	8	1		.195	.275	.280	77	-2	4	.962	2	90	197	O-23(CF)/2	-0.1
1911	Chi A	14	17	3	3	0	0	0	0	0	0		.176	.176	.176	-2	-2	0	.857	1	103	313	/2-4,O-4(0-3-1)	-0.2
1914	Pit F	9	30	2	9	1	0	1	3	0	0	4	.300	.300	.433	99	-1	1	.917	-0	101	189	/2-4,O-3(2-1-0),S	-0.1
	Bro F	32	79	7	20	1	2	0	8	4	0	13	.253	.289	.316	65	-6	3	.929	1	106	119	O-20(5-14-2)	-0.6
	Bal F	5	9	3	4	0	0	0	1	0	0	1	.444	.444	.444	138	0	0	1.000	-0	96	0	/O-2(1-1-0)	0.0
	Year	46	118	12	33	2	2	1	12	4	0	18	.280	.303	.356	79	-6	4	.941	0	102	123	O-25(8-16-2)/2-4,S	-0.7
1915	Bro F	4	4	1	2	0	0	0	2	0	0	0	.500	.500	.500	183	0	0	1.000	-0	61	0	/O-2(1-1-0)	0.0
Total	4	88	221	22	54	5	4	1	23	12	1	18	.244	.286	.317	75	-11	8	.948	3	96	161	/O-54(9-43-3),2-9,S	-1.0
CHOZEN, HARRY Harry B 9.27.1915 Winnebago, MN D 9.16.1994 Houston, TX BR/TR 5-9.5/190# d9.21																								
1937	Cin N	1	4	0	1	0	0	0	0	0	0	0	.250	.250	.250	38	0	0	.833	-0	*42*	*0*	/C	-0.1
CHRISLEY, NEIL Barbra O'Neil B 12.16.1931 Calhoun Falls, SC BL/TR 6-3/187# d4.15																								
1957	Was A	26	51	6	8	2	1	0	3	7-0	0	7	.157	.259	.235	36	-5	0-0	.810	-1	80	139	O-11(4-0-7)	-0.7
1958	Was A	105	233	19	50	7	4	5	26	16-2	0	18	.215	.265	.343	67	-12	1-3	.992	2	99	147	O-69(38-7-25)/3	-1.4
1959	Det A	65	106	7	14	3	0	6	11	12-0	1	10	.132	.225	.330	48	-8	0-0	1.000	-1	98	0	O-21(3-1-17)	-1.0
1960	Det A	96	220	27	56	10	3	5	24	19-0	1	26	.255	.311	.395	89	-4	2-0	.981	-1	102	61	O-47(31-4-12)/1-2	-0.7
1961	Mil N	10	9	1	2	0	0	0	0	1-0	0	1	.222	.300	.222	44	-1	0-0	—	0			H	-0.1
Total	5	302	619	60	130	22	8	16	64	55-2	2	62	.210	.275	.349	69	-30	3-3	.975	-1	98	97	O-148(76-12-61)/1-2,3	-3.9
CHRISTENBURY, LLOYD Lloyd Reid "Low" B 10.19.1893 Mecklenburg Co., NC D 12.13.1944 Birmingham, AL BL/TR 5-7/165# d9.20																								
1919	Bos N	7	31	5	9	1	0	0	4	2	0	2	.290	.333	.323	102	0	0	.941	1	93	208	/O-7(LF)	0.1
1920	Bos N	65	106	17	22	2	2	0	14	13	1	12	.208	.300	.264	66	-4	0-1	.895	-3	84	86	O-14(0-7-7)/S-7,2-6,3-2	-0.8
1921	Bos N	62	125	34	44	6	2	3	16	21	1	7	.352	.449	.504	161	12	3-4	.914	-10	81	69	2-32/S-2,3-2	0.3
1922	Bos N	71	152	22	38	5	2	1	13	18	2	11	.250	.337	.329	76	-5	2-4	.946	2	109	139	O-32(30-0-2)/2-5,3-2	-0.6
Total	4	205	414	78	113	14	6	4	47	54	4	32	.273	.362	.365	101	3	5-9	.936	-10	102	141	/O-53(37-7-9),2-43,S-9,3-6	-1.0
CHRISTENSEN, BRUCE Bruce Ray B 2.22.1948 Madison, WI BL/TR 5-11/160# d7.17																								
1971	Cal A	29	63	4	17	1	0	0	3	6-1	0	5	.270	.333	.286	83	-1	0-1	.988	-2	97	123	S-24	-0.1
CHRISTENSEN, JOHN John Lawrence B 9.5.1960 Downey, CA BR/TR 6-3/205# d9.13																								
1984	NY N	5	11	2	3	2	0	0	3	1-0	0	2	.273	.308	.455	121	0	0-1	.500	-1	20	0	/O-5(3-0-2)	-0.1
1985	NY N	51	113	10	21	4	1	3	13	19-1	0	23	.186	.303	.319	76	-3	1-2	.956	-4	69	93	O-38(6-2-31)	-1.0
1987	Sea A	53	132	19	32	6	1	2	12	12-0	0	28	.242	.306	.348	69	-6	2-0	1.000	1	98	136	O-43(2-0-41)/D-8	-0.6
1988	Min A	23	38	5	10	4	0	0	5	3-1	2	5	.263	.349	.368	98	0	0-0	1.000	-0	99	0	O-17(RF)/D	0.0
Total	4	132	294	36	66	16	2	5	33	35-2	2	58	.224	.310	.344	77	-9	3-3	.977	-5	83	95	O-103(11-2-91)/D-9	-1.7
CHRISTENSEN, MC KAY McKay Andrew B 8.14.1975 Upland, CA BL/TL 5-11/180# d4.6																								
1999	Chi A	28	53	10	12	1	0	1	6	4-0	0	7	.226	.271	.302	49	-4	2-1	.943	-0	116	0	O-27(CF)	-0.4
2000	†Chi A	32	19	4	2	0	0	0	1	2-0	1	6	.105	.227	.105	-12	-3	1-1	1.000	0	91	235	O-29(CF)	-0.3
2001	Chi A	7	4	0	1	0	0	0	0	0-0	1	2	.250	.400	.250	74	0	0-0	1.000	-1	37	0	/O-6(CF)	-0.1
	LA N	28	49	7	16	2	0	1	7	3-0	3	10	.327	.400	.429	124	2	3-2	.917	-1	88	0	O-14(3-11-0)	0.0
2002	NY N	4	3	1	1	0	0	0	0	1-0	0	1	.333	.500	.333	135	0	0-0	1.000	0	190	0	/O-3(2-1-0)	0.0
Total	4	99	128	22	32	3	0	2	14	10-0	5	26	.250	.324	.320	69	-5	6-4	.951	-2	100	51	/O-79(5-74-0)	-0.8
CHRISTENSEN, CUCKOO Walter Niels "Seacap" B 10.24.1899 San Francisco, CA D 12.20.1984 Menlo Park, CA BL/TL 5-6.5/156# d4.13																								
1926	Cin N	114	329	41	115	15	7	0	41	40	4	18	.350	.426	.438	136	19	8	.978	-5	92	71	O-93(72-19-9)	0.9
1927	Cin N	57	185	25	47	6	0	0	16	20	1	16	.254	.330	.286	68	-8	4	.957	-2	87	119	O-50(11-35-4)	-1.2
Total	2	171	514	66	162	21	7	0	57	60	5	34	.315	.392	.383	112	11	12	.970	-7	90	88	O-143(83-54-13)	-0.3
CHRISTENSON, RYAN Ryan Alan B 3.28.1974 Redlands, CA BR/TR 5-11/175# d4.20																								
1998	Oak A	117	370	56	95	22	2	5	40	36-0	1	106	.257	.321	.368	81	-10	5-6	.983	2	104	105	*O-116(1-113-4)	-0.7
1999	Oak A	106	268	41	56	12	1	4	24	38-0	1	58	.209	.305	.306	60	-16	7-5	.969	-1	105	60	*O-104(CF)/D	-1.5
2000	†Oak A	121	129	31	32	2	2	4	18	19-0	1	33	.248	.349	.388	88	-2	1-2	.951	-2	92	78	*O-114(76-27-14)	-0.5
2001	Ari N	19	4	3	1	1	0	0	1	1-0	0	1	.250	.400	.500	123	0	1-0	1.000	-0	69	0	/O-5(4-1-0)	0.0
	Oak A	7	4	1	0	0	0	0	0	0-0	0	1	.000	.000	.000	-99	-1	0-0	1.000	-0	61	0	/O-4(1-1-3),D	-0.1
2002	Mil N	22	58	5	9	4	0	1	3	5-0	0	13	.155	.222	.276	33	-6	0-0	1.000	-1	103	0	O-21(6-16-0)	-0.7
2003	Tex A	60	165	22	29	7	0	2	16	15-0	3	44	.176	.255	.255	33	-16	2-2	1.000	-0	107	0	O-59(CF)	-1.6
Total	6	452	998	159	222	48	5	16	102	114-0	6	256	.222	.303	.329	65	-51	16-15	.979	-2	103	65	O-423(88-321-21)/D-2	-5.1
CHRISTIAN, BOB Robert Charles B 10.17.1945 Chicago, IL D 2.20.1974 San Diego, CA BR/TR 5-10/180# d9.2																								
1968	Det A	3	3	0	1	1	0	0	0	0-0	0	0	.333	.333	.667	191	0	0-0	1.000	-0	0	0	/1O(RF)	0.0
1969	Chi A	39	129	11	28	4	0	3	16	10-1	1	19	.217	.273	.318	63	-7	3-0	.958	-0	99	105	O-38(37-0-1)	-0.9
1970	Chi A	12	15	3	4	0	0	1	3	1-0	0	4	.267	.313	.467	108	0	0-0	1.000	-1	51	0	/O-4(LF)	-0.1
Total	3	54	147	14	33	5	0	4	19	11-1	1	23	.224	.278	.340	70	-7	3-0	.959	-1	96	98	/O-43(41-0-2),1	-1.0
CHRISTMAN, MARK Marquette Joseph B 10.21.1913 Maplewood, MO D 10.9.1976 St.Louis, MO BR/TR 5-11/180# d4.20																								
1938	Det A	95	318	35	79	6	4	1	44	27	0	21	.248	.307	.302	50	-25	5-2	.983	10	109	118	3-69,S-21	-1.1
1939	Det A	6	16	0	4	2	0	0	0	0	0	2	.250	.250	.375	54	-1	0-0	.900	-1	72	155	/3-5	-0.1
	StL A	79	222	27	48	6	3	0	20	20	0	10	.216	.281	.270	41	-20	2-1	.960	14	112	103	S-64/2	-0.2
	Year	85	238	27	52	8	3	0	20	20	0	12	.218	.279	.277	42	-22	2-1	.960	13	112	103	S-64/3-5,2	-0.3
1943	StL A	98	336	31	91	11	5	2	35	19	4	19	.271	.318	.351	94	-4	0-3	.991	2	111	78	3-37,S-24,1-20,2-14	-0.2

Year	Tm Lg	G	AB	R	H	2B	3B	HR	RBI	BB-IB	HP	SO	AVG	OBP	SLG	AOPS	ABR	SB-CS	FA	FR	Rng	Thr	G at Pos	BFW
1944	†StL A	148	547	56	148	25	1	6	83	47	3	37	.271	.332	.353	90	-6	5-2	**.972**	4	98	**125**	*3-145/1-3	-0.1
1945	StL A	78	289	32	80	7	4	4	34	19	3	19	.277	.328	.370	98	-2	1-0	.973	-1	94	94	3-77	-0.2
1946	StL A	128	458	40	118	22	2	1	41	22	2	29	.258	.295	.321	68	-20	0-2	.975	9	116	125	3-77,S-47	-0.9
1947	Was A	110	374	27	83	15	2	1	33	32	2	16	.222	.287	.281	60	-21	4-4	.978	-6	94	100	*S-106/2	-2.2
1948	Was A	120	409	38	106	17	2	1	40	25	1	19	.259	.303	.318	67	-21	0-3	.969	-25	85	75	*S-102/3-9,2-3	-4.0
1949	Was A	49	112	8	24	2	0	3	18	8	1	7	.214	.273	.313	56	-8	0-0	.967	3	122	157	3-23/1-6,S-4,2	-0.5
Total	9	911	3081	294	781	113	23	19	348	219	16	179	.253	.306	.324	71	-128	17-17	.975	8	104	115	3-442,S-368/1-29,2-20	-9.5
CHRISTMAS, STEVE Stephen Randall B 12.9.1957 Orlando, FL BL/TR 6/190# d9.1																								
1983	Cin N	9	17	0	1	0	0	0	1	1-0	0	3	.059	.105	.059	-50	-4	0-0	1.000	1	122	168	/C-7	-0.2
1984	Chi A	12	11	1	4	1	0	1	4	0-0	0	2	.364	.364	.727	185	1	0-0	1.000	0	6	0	/C	0.1
1986	Chi N	3	9	0	1	1	0	0	2	0-0	0	1	.111	.111	.222	-10	-1	0-0	1.000	0	32	224	/C1	-0.1
Total	3	24	37	1	6	2	0	1	7	1-0	0	6	.162	.179	.297	30	-4	0-0	1.000	1	102	175	/C-9,1	-0.2
CHRISTOPHER, JOE Joseph O'Neal B 12.13.1935 Frederiksted, V.I. BR/TR 5-10/176# d5.26																								
1959	Pit N	15	12	6	0	0	0	0	0	1-0	0	4	.000	.077	.000	-78	-3	0-0	1.000	0	119	0	/O-9(RF)	-0.3
1960	†Pit N	50	56	21	13	2	0	1	3	5-0	0	8	.232	.295	.321	68	-2	1-0	1.000	1	131	0	O-17(11-5-1)	-0.2
1961	Pit N	76	186	25	49	7	3	0	14	18-0	0	24	.263	.327	.333	76	-6	6-4	.978	-1	102	55	O-55(45-5-5)	-0.9
1962	NY N	119	271	36	66	10	2	6	32	35-0	4	42	.244	.338	.362	87	-4	11-3	.972	-1	97	96	O-94(19-34-42)	-0.7
1963	NY N	64	149	19	33	5	1	1	8	13-0	3	21	.221	.295	.289	68	-6	1-3	.983	-2	97	39	O-45(6-0-40)	-1.1
1964	NY N	154	543	78	163	26	8	16	76	48-5	6	92	.300	.360	.466	135	25	6-5	.974	-3	96	94	*O-145(7-10-129)	1.3
1965	NY N	148	437	38	109	18	3	5	40	35-3	6	82	.249	.311	.339	87	-7	4-4	.989	-2	99	47	*O-112(62-0-51)	-1.7
1966	Bos A	12	13	1	1	0	0	0	0	2-0	0	4	.077	.200	.077	-15	-2	0-0	1.000	-0	67	0	/O-2(LF)	-0.2
Total	8	638	1667	224	434	68	17	29	173	157-8	19	277	.260	.329	.374	96	-5	29-19	.979	-7	99	71	O-479(152-54-277)	-3.8
CHRISTOPHER, LOYD Loyd Eugene B 12.31.1919 Richmond, CA D 9.5.1991 Richmond, CA BR/TR 6-2/190# d4.20 b-Russ																								
1945	Bos A	8	14	4	4	0	0	0	4	3	0	2	.286	.412	.286	101	0	0-0	1.000	-0	78	0	/O-3(CF)	0.0
	Chi N	1	0	0	0	0	0	0	0	0	0	0	—	—	—	—	0	0	—	-0	0	0	/O(LF)	0.0
1947	Chi A	7	23	1	5	0	1	0	0	2	0	4	.217	.280	.304	65	-1	0-1	1.000	1	114	192	/O-7(LF)	-0.1
Total	2	16	37	5	9	0	1	0	4	5	0	6	.243	.333	.297	80	-1	0-1	1.000	1	104	143	/O-11(8-3-0)	-0.1
CHURCH, HI Hiram Lincoln B 11.23.1863 Central Square, NY D 2.23.1926 Jacksonville, FL d8.23																								
1890	Bro AA	3	9	1	1	0	0	0	0	0	0		.111	.111	.111	-36	-2	0	1.000	-1	0	0	/O-3(LF)	-0.2
CHURRY, JOHN John B 11.26.1900 Johnstown, PA D 2.8.1970 Zanesville, OH BR/TR 5-9/172# d5.24																								
1924	Chi N	6	7	0	1	1	0	0	0	2	0	0	.143	.333	.286	67	0	0-0	1.000	0	*90*	*135*	/C-3	0.0
1925	Chi N	3	6	1	3	0	0	0	1	0	0	0	.500	.500	.500	154	0	0-0	1.000	0	*61*	*422*	/C-3	0.0
1926	Chi N	2	4	0	0	0	0	0	0	1	0	2	.000	.200	.000	-42	-1	0	1.000	0	*0*	*0*	/C	-0.1
1927	Chi N	1	1	0	1	0	0	0	0	0	0	0	1.000	1.000	1.000	436	0	0	1.000	0	*0*	*0*	/C	0.1
Total	4	12	18	1	5	1	0	0	1	3	0	2	.278	.381	.333	89	-1	0-0	1.000	0	*52*	*170*	/C-8	0.0
CIAFFONE, LARRY Lawrence Thomas "Symphony Larry" B 8.17.1924 Brooklyn, NY D 12.14.1991 Brooklyn, NY BR/TR 5-9.5/185# d4.17																								
1951	StL N	5	5	0	0	0	0	0	0	1	0	2	.000	.167	.000	-51	-1	0-0	1.000	0	103	0	/O(LF)	-0.1
CIANFROCCO, ARCHI Angelo Dominic B 10.6.1966 Rome, NY BR/TR 6-5/215# d4.8 OF Total (8-LF 17-RF)																								
1992	Mon N	86	232	25	56	5	2	6	30	11-0	1	66	.241	.276	.358	80	-7	3-0	.993	1	117	81	1-56,3-19/O-5(LF)	-1.0
1993	Mon N	12	17	3	4	1	0	1	1	0-0	0	5	.235	.235	.471	80	-1	0-0	1.000	-0	62	173	1-11	-0.1
	SD N	84	279	27	68	10	2	11	47	17-1	3	64	.244	.289	.412	85	-7	2-0	.932	-7	76	85	3-64,1-31	-1.5
	Year	96	296	30	72	11	2	12	48	17-1	3	69	.243	.287	.416	85	-8	2-0	.932	-7	76	85	3-64,1-42	-1.6
1994	SD N	59	146	9	32	8	0	4	13	3-0	4	39	.219	.252	.356	59	-9	2-0	.920	3	106	42	3-37,1-16/S	-0.6
1995	SD N	51	118	22	31	7	0	5	31	11-1	2	28	.263	.333	.449	109	1	0-2	1.000	0	88	84	1-30,S-15/O-7(2-0-5),2-3,3-3	0.1
1996	†SD N	79	192	21	54	13	3	2	32	8-0	2	56	.281	.315	.411	96	-2	1-0	1.000	-5	96	83	1-33,3-11,S-10/O-8(1-0-7),2-6,C	-0.8
1997	SD N	89	220	25	54	12	0	4	26	25-1	3	80	.245	.328	.355	86	-4	7-1	.983	7	110	80	1-39,3-38,2-12/S-5,O-2(RF)	0.3
1998	SD N	40	72	4	9	3	0	1	5	5-0	1	22	.125	.192	.208	6	-10	1-0	1.000	1	138	136	1-19,3-13/2-3,O-3(RF)	-1.0
Total	7	500	1276	136	308	59	7	34	185	80-3	16	360	.241	.292	.379	81	-39	16-3	.994	0	113	91	1-235,3-185/S-31,O-25R,2-24,C	-4.6
CIAS, DARRYL Darryl Richard B 4.23.1957 New York, NY BR/TR 5-11/190# d4.27																								
1983	Oak A	19	18	1	6	1	0	0	1	2-0	0	4	.333	.400	.389	126	1	1-0	.967	-3	55	45	C-19	-0.2
CICERO, JOE Joseph Francis "Dode" B 11.18.1910 Atlantic City, NJ D 3.30.1983 Clearwater, FL BR/TR 5-8/167# d9.20																								
1929	Bos A	10	32	6	10	2	2	0	4	0	0	2	.313	.313	.500	108	0	0-0	1.000	-0	101	0	/O-7(1-6-0)	-0.1
1930	Bos A	18	30	5	5	1	2	0	4	1	0	5	.167	.194	.333	32	-4	0-0	—	-0	0	0	/O-5(1-0-4),3-2	-0.3
1945	Phi A	12	19	3	3	0	0	0	0	1	1	6	.158	.238	.158	16	-2	0-0	1.000	-0	91	0	/O-7(1-0-6)	-0.3
Total	3	40	81	14	18	3	4	0	8	2	1	13	.222	.250	.358	60	-6	0-0	1.000	-1	94	0	/O-19(3-6-10),3-2	-0.7
CIESLAK, TED Thaddeus Walter B 11.22.1912 Milwaukee, WI D 5.9.1993 Milwaukee, WI BR/TR 5-10/175# d4.18																								
1944	Phi N	85	220	18	54	10	0	2	11	21	1	17	.245	.314	.318	81	-5	1	.877	-12	81	14	3-48/O-5(LF)	-1.8
CIHOCKI, AL Albert Joseph B 5.7.1924 Nanticoke, PA BR/TR 5-11/185# d4.17																								
1945	Cle A	92	283	21	60	9	3	0	24	11	0	48	.212	.241	.265	49	-20	2-1	.946	-2	100	117	S-41,3-29,2-23	-1.9
CIHOCKI, ED Edward Joseph "Cy" B 5.9.1907 Wilmington, DE D 11.9.1987 Newark, DE BR/TR 5-8/163# d5.29																								
1932	Phi A	1	1	0	0	0	0	0	0	0	0	0	.000	.000	.000	-97	0	0-0	—	0			H	0.0
1933	Phi A	33	97	6	14	2	3	0	9	7	0	16	.144	.202	.227	13	-13	0-0	.904	-2	95	120	S-28/23	-1.3
Total	2	34	98	6	14	2	3	0	9	7	0	16	.143	.200	.224	12	-13	0-0	.904	-2	95	120	/S-28,32	-1.3
CIMOLI, GINO Gino Nicholas (born Gino Anichletto Cimoli) B 12.18.1929 San Francisco, CA BR/TR 6-2/200# d4.19																								
1956	†Bro N	73	36	3	4	1	0	0	4	1-1	0	8	.111	.135	.139	-24	-6	1-0	.946	1	132	0	O-62(52-8-3)	-0.7
1957	Bro N★	142	532	88	156	22	5	10	57	39-1	4	86	.293	.343	.410	93	-4	3-1	.979	-2	94	112	*O-138(81-24-51)	-1.4
1958	LA N	109	325	35	80	6	3	9	27	18-0	3	49	.246	.292	.366	71	-15	3-3	.974	-0	93	152	*O-104(34-68-12)	-2.0
1959	StL N	143	519	61	145	40	7	8	72	37-2	2	83	.279	.327	.430	94	-4	7-0	.979	-1	94	121	*O-141(43-45-55)	-1.0
1960	†Pit N	101	307	36	82	14	4	0	28	32-3	1	43	.267	.336	.339	85	-5	1-0	.964	-1	104	79	O-91(27-58-17)	-1.0
1961	Pit N	21	67	4	20	3	1	0	6	2-0	0	13	.299	.319	.373	83	-2	0-0	.971	-0	103	78	O-19(14-5-0)	-0.3
	Mil N	37	117	12	23	5	0	3	4	11-0	0	15	.197	.266	.316	57	-7	1-0	.985	-4	86	0	O-31(0-30-1)	-1.3
	Year	58	184	16	43	8	1	3	10	13-0	0	28	.234	.284	.337	67	-9	1-0	.980	-4	92	28	O-50(14-35-1)	-1.6
1962	KC A	152	550	67	151	20	**15**	10	71	40-2	2	89	.275	.323	.420	95	-6	2-1	.968	-6	90	102	*O-147(5-10-138)	-2.1
1963	KC A	145	529	56	139	19	11	4	48	39-3	2	72	.263	.313	.363	85	-11	3-1	.985	5	101	159	*O-136(2-13-130)	-1.6
1964	KC A	4	9	1	0	0	0	0	0	0-0	0	1	.000	.000	.000	-97	-2	0-0	1.000	0	117	0	/O-4(1-0-3)	-0.3
	Bal A	38	58	6	8	3	2	0	3	2-1	0	13	.138	.164	.259	16	-7	0-0	.893	-1	102	0	O-35(11-2-23)	-0.9
	Year	42	67	7	8	3	2	0	3	2-1	0	14	.119	.143	.224	1	-9	0-0	.912	-1	105	0	O-39(12-2-26)	-1.2
1965	Cal A	4	5	1	0	0	0	0	1	0-0	0	2	.000	.000	.000	-99	-1	0-0	1.000	0	121	0	/O(RF)	-0.1
Total	10	969	3054	370	808	133	48	44	321	221-13	14	474	.265	.315	.383	84	-70	21-6	.974	-10	96	112	O-909(270-263-434)	-12.7
CINTRON, ALEX Alexander B 12.17.1978 Humacao, P.R. BB/TR 6-1/170# d7.24																								
2001	Ari N	8	7	0	2	0	1	0	0	0-0	0	0	.286	.286	.571	107	0	0-0	1.000	0	112	0	/S-7	0.0
2002	†Ari N	38	75	11	16	6	0	0	4	12-2	0	13	.213	.322	.293	61	-4	0-0	1.000	-0	76	103	2-18/3-9,S-8	-0.3
2003	Ari N	117	448	70	142	26	6	13	51	29-0	2	33	.317	.359	.489	108	5	2-3	.979	-2	89	101	S-93,3-16/2-9	1.0
Total	3	163	530	81	160	32	7	13	55	41-2	2	46	.302	.352	.462	102	1	2-3	.978	-2	91	103	S-108/2-27,3-25	0.7
CIPRIANI, FRANK Frank Dominick B 4.14.1941 Buffalo, NY BR/TR 6/180# d9.8																								
1961	KC A	13	36	2	9	0	0	0	2	2-0	0	4	.250	.289	.250	45	-3	0-0	1.000	-0	105	0	O-11(RF)	-0.4
CIRILLO, JEFF Jeffrey Howard B 9.23.1969 Pasadena, CA BR/TR 6-2/190# d5.11																								
1994	Mil A	39	126	17	30	9	0	3	12	11-0	2	16	.238	.309	.381	73	-5	0-1	.965	-3	92	144	3-37/2	-0.8
1995	Mil A	125	328	57	91	19	4	9	39	47-0	4	42	.277	.371	.442	106	4	7-2	.938	10	117	**168**	*3-108,2-25/1-3,S-2	1.5
1996	Mil A	158	566	101	184	46	5	15	83	58-0	7	69	.325	.391	.504	120	20	4-9	.950	-14	92	69	*3-154/1-2,2D	0.4
1997	Mil A★	154	580	74	167	46	2	10	82	60-0	14	74	.288	.367	.426	106	8	4-3	.963	**24**	**117**	119	*3-150/D-2	3.1
1998	Mil N	156	604	97	194	31	1	14	68	79-3	4	88	.321	.402	.445	123	24	10-4	.976	22	113	**164**	*3-149/1-6	4.6
1999	Mil N	157	607	98	198	35	1	15	88	75-4	5	83	.326	.401	.461	120	22	7-4	.967	7	105	130	*3-155	2.9

Year	Tm Lg	G	AB	R	H	2B	3B	HR	RBI	BB-IB	HP	SO	AVG	OBP	SLG	AOPS	ABR	SB-CS	FA	FR	Rng	Thr	G at Pos	BFW
2000	Col N★	157	598	111	195	53	2	11	115	67-4	6	72	.326	.392	.477	96	0	3-4	.964	7	106	**144**	*3-155	0.7
2001	Col N	138	528	72	165	26	4	17	83	43-6	5	63	.313	.364	.473	95	-3	12-2	**.982**	18	**117**	105	*3-137	1.8
2002	Sea A	146	485	51	121	20	0	6	54	31-0	9	67	.249	.301	.328	71	-20	8-4	**.973**	1	92	118	*3-141,1-11	-1.7
2003	Sea A	87	258	24	53	11	0	2	23	24-1	5	32	.205	.284	.271	50	-19	1-1	.977	-10	78	60	3-85/1	-2.7
Total	10	1317	4680	702	1398	296	19	102	647	495-18	61	606	.299	.369	.435	102	31	56-34	.966	62	105	121	*3-1271/2-27,1-23,D-5,S-2	9.8
CISAR, GEORGE George Joseph B 8.25.1912 Chicago, IL BR/TR 6/175# d9.9																								
1937	Bro N	20	29	8	6	0	0	0	4	2	0	6	.207	.258	.207	27	-3	3	1.000	0	119	0	O-13(9-0-4)	-0.3
CISSELL, BILL Chalmer William B 1.3.1904 Perryville, MO D 3.15.1949 Chicago, IL BR/TR 5-11/170# d4.11																								
1928	Chi A	125	443	66	115	22	3	1	60	29	1	41	.260	.307	.330	68	-21	18-6	.938	1	102	107	*S-123	-0.5
1929	Chi A	**152**	618	83	173	27	12	5	62	28	1	53	.280	.312	.387	80	-22	25-17	.937	-3	100	97	*S-152	-0.8
1930	Chi A	141	562	82	152	28	9	2	48	28	2	32	.270	.307	.363	72	-26	16-9	.948	-9	97	88	*2-107,3-24,S-10	-2.7
1931	Chi A	109	409	42	90	13	5	1	46	16	4	26	.220	.256	.284	44	-35	18-6	.944	-7	97	96	S-83,2-23/3	-3.2
1932	Chi A	12	43	7	11	1	1	1	5	1	0	0	.256	.273	.395	76	-2	0-0	.928	-1	72	120	S-12	-0.2
	Cle A	131	541	78	173	35	6	6	93	28	1	25	.320	.354	.440	98	-2	18-15	.964	5	**106**	99	*2-129/S-6	0.9
	Year	143	584	85	184	36	7	7	98	29	1	25	.315	.349	.437	97	-4	18-15	.964	4	**106**	99	*2-129,S-18	0.7
1933	Cle A	112	409	53	94	21	3	6	33	31	0	29	.230	.284	.340	62	-24	6-6	.947	-3	98	68	2-62,S-46/3	-1.9
1934	Bos A	102	416	71	111	13	4	4	44	28	1	23	.267	.315	.346	66	-22	11-4	.959	-3	96	94	2-96/S-7,3-2	-1.7
1937	Phi A	34	117	15	31	7	0	1	14	17	0	10	.265	.358	.350	81	-3	0-0	.962	1	107	69	2-33	0.0
1938	NY N	38	149	19	40	6	0	2	18	6	0	11	.268	.297	.349	76	-5	1	.977	8	115	99	2-33/3-6	0.5
Total	9	956	3707	516	990	173	43	29	423	212	10	250	.267	.308	.360	73	-162	113-63	.958	-12	101	88	2-483,S-439/3-34	-9.6
CLABAUGH, MOOSE John William B 11.13.1901 Albany, MO D 7.11.1984 Tucson, AZ BL/TR 6/185# d8.30																								
1926	Bro N	11	14	2	1	1	0	0	1	0	1	1	.071	.133	.143	-26	-3	0	.600	-1	84	0	/O-2(LF)	-0.3
CLACK, BOBBY Robert S. "Gentlemanly Bob" (born Robert S. Clark) B 6.1850 , England D 10.22.1933 Danvers, MA BR/TR 5-9/153# d5.13																								
1874	Atl NA	33	135	22	23	1	0	0	13	4		2	.170	.194	.178	23	-10	0-0	.779	-3	110	0	O-31(1-30-0)/1-2	-1.0
1875	Atl NA	17	59	1	6	0	0	0	1	0		3	.102	.102	.102	-33	-7	0-0	.867	2	154	325	O-17(0-16-1)/1	-0.4
1876	Cin N	32	118	10	19	0	1	0	5	5		12	.161	.195	.178	29	-8		.736	-2	90	0	O-17(0-3-14)/2-8,1-5,3-3,P	-0.8
Total	2 NA	50	194	23	29	1	0	0	14	4		5	.149	.167	.155	7	-17	0-0	.000	-0	125	108	/O-48(1-46-1),1-3	-1.4
CLAIRE, DAVEY David Matthew B 11.17.1897 Ludington, MI D 1.7.1956 Las Vegas, NV BR/TR 5-8/164# d9.17																								
1920	Det A	3	7	1	1	0	0	0	0	0	0	0	.143	.143	.143	-25	-1	0-0	.800	-1	105	0	/S-3	-0.2
CLANCY, AL Albert Harrison B 8.14.1888 Santa Fe, NM D 10.17.1951 Las Cruces, NM BR/TR 5-10.5/175# d6.20																								
1911	StL A	3	5	0	0	0	0	0	0	0	1		.000	.167	.000	-54	-1	0	.800	0	120	532	/3-2	-0.1
CLANCY, BUD John William B 9.15.1900 Odell, IL D 9.26.1968 Ottumwa, IA BL/TL 6/170# d8.29																								
1924	Chi A	13	35	5	9	1	0	0	6	3	0	2	.257	.316	.286	58	-2	3-2	.947	-2	54	67	/1-8	-0.4
1925	Chi A	4	3	0	0	0	0	0	0	1	0	0	.000	.250	.000	-34	-1	0-0	—	0			H	-0.1
1926	Chi A	12	38	3	13	2	2	0	7	1	1	1	.342	.375	.500	132	1	0-0	.991	-0	94	153	1-10	0.1
1927	Chi A	130	464	46	139	21	2	3	53	24	2	24	.300	.337	.373	86	-10	4-3	.991	-1	97	85	*1-123	-1.9
1928	Chi A	130	487	64	132	19	11	2	37	42	2	25	.271	.331	.368	85	-12	6-9	.991	4	**112**	104	*1-128	-1.8
1929	Chi A	92	290	36	82	14	6	3	45	16	0	19	.283	.320	.403	86	-7	3-1	.991	2	113	83	1-74	-0.9
1930	Chi A	68	234	28	57	8	3	3	27	12	2	18	.244	.286	.342	61	-15	3-1	.995	-3	72	79	1-60	-2.0
1932	Bro N	53	196	14	60	4	2	0	16	6	0	13	.306	.327	.347	83	-5	0	.996	3	116	126	1-53	-0.7
1934	Phi N	20	49	8	12	0	0	1	7	6	1	4	.245	.339	.306	65	-2	0	1.000	-1	65	134	1-10	-0.4
Total	9	522	1796	204	504	69	26	12	198	111	8	106	.281	.325	.368	82	-53	19-16	.992	2	101	96	1-466	-8.1
CLANCY, BILL William Edward B 4.12.1879 Redfield, NY D 2.10.1948 Oriskany, NY BR/TR 6-2/180# d4.14																								
1905	Pit N	56	227	23	52	11	3	2	34	4	1		.229	.246	.330	69	-10	3	.983	-3	81	118	1-52/O-4(RF)	-1.4
CLANTON, UKE Eucal "Cat" B 2.19.1898 Powell, MO D 2.24.1960 Antlers, OK BL/TL 5-8/165# d9.21																								
1922	Cle A	1	1	0	0	0	0	0	0	0	0	1	.000	.000	.000	-99	0	0-0	.500	-0	0	0	/1	-0.1
CLAPINSKI, CHRIS Christopher Alan B 8.20.1971 Buffalo, NY BB/TR 6/175# d7.17																								
1999	Fla N	36	56	6	13	1	2	0	2	9-0	1	12	.232	.348	.321	75	-2	1-0	.882	-1	65	72	/3-9,S-6,O-3(LF),2-2,D	-0.2
2000	Fla N	34	49	12	15	4	1	1	7	5-0	0	7	.306	.370	.490	120	2	0-0	.933	-1	97	65	2-14/3-3,O-3(LF),S	0.1
Total	2	70	105	18	28	5	3	1	9	14-0	1	19	.267	.358	.400	96	0	1-0	.935	-2	101	64	/2-16,3-12,S-7,O-6(LF),D	-0.1
CLAPP, AARON Aaron Bronson B 7.1856 Ithaca, NY D 1.13.1914 Sayre, PA TR 5-8/175# d5.1 b-John																								
1879	Tro N	36	146	24	39	9	3	0	18	6		10	.267	.296	.370	126	5		.935	-3	63	80	1-25,O-11(7-1-3)	0.0
CLAPP, JOHN John Edgar B 7.17.1851 Ithaca, NY D 12.18.1904 Ithaca, NY BR/TR 5-7/194# d4.26 M6 b-Aaron OF Total (62-LF 19-CF 21-RF)																								
1872	Man NA	19	97	30	27	7	1	1	16	1		0	.278	.286	.402	116	2	2-1	.845	-1			C-19/S-2,1O(CF)M	0.1
1873	Ath NA	45	204	36	62	10	2	1	27	2		2	.304	.311	.387	99	-2	4-5	.893	2			*C-43/S-6,2O(CF)	-0.1
1874	Ath NA	39	165	46	48	7	4	3	19	1		1	.291	.295	.436	121	3	2-0	.861	7			C-27,O-15(0-1-14)/S	0.8
1875	Ath NA	60	292	65	77	8	7	0	39	7		1	.264	.281	.339	103	-1	9-5	.874	18			*C-60	1.5
1876	StL N	**64**	298	60	91	4	2	0	29	8		2	.305	.324	.332	125	9		.874	10			*C-61/O-4(0-1-3),2	1.8
1877	StL N	**60**	255	47	81	6	6	0	34	8		6	.318	.338	.388	135	10		.887	-5			*C-53,O-10(2-0-9)/1	0.6
1878	Ind N	**63**	263	42	80	10	2	0	29	13		8	.304	.337	.357	148	16		.890	-3	48	0	*O-44(LF),1-12/C-9,S-3,2M	0.9
1879	Buf N	70	292	47	77	12	5	1	36	11		11	.264	.290	.349	107	2		.906	-8			*C-63/O-7(RF),M	-0.4
1880	Cin N	80	323	33	91	16	4	1	20	21		10	.282	.326	.365	135	13		.897	19			*C-73,O-10(1-9-0),M	**3.2**
1881	Cle N	68	261	47	66	12	2	0	25	**35**		6	.253	.341	.314	113	7		.890	-3			C-48,O-21(15-6-0),M	0.4
1883	NY N	20	73	6	13	0	0	0	5	5		4	.178	.231	.178	27	-6		.895	3			C-16/O-5(0-3-2),M	-0.2
Total	4 NA	163	758	177	214	32	14	5	101	11		4	.282	.293	.381	107	2	17-11	.000	26			C-149/O-17(0-3-14),S-9,21	2.3
Total	7	425	1765	282	499	60	21	2	178	101		47	.283	.322	.344	122	51		.892	14			C-323,O-101L/1-13,S-3,2-2	6.3
CLAPP, STUBBY Richard Keith B 2.24.1973 Windsor, ON, CAN BL/TR 5-8/175# d6.18																								
2001	StL N	23	25	0	5	2	0	0	1	1-0	0	7	.200	.231	.280	31	-3	0-0	1.000	0	174	0	/2-4,O-4(LF)	-0.2
CLARE, DENNY Dennis J. B 1.1853 Brooklyn, NY D 11.26.1928 Brooklyn, NY d9.14																								
1872	Atl NA	2	7	1	1	0	0	0	0	0		0	.143	.143	.143	-10	-1	0-0	.857	-1	195	0	/2-2,S	-0.2
CLAREY, DOUG Douglas William B 4.20.1954 Los Angeles, CA BR/TR 6/180# d4.20																								
1976	StL N	9	4	2	1	0	0	1	2	0-0	0	1	.250	.250	1.000	240	1	0-0	1.000	-1	27	0	/2-7	-0.1
CLARK, ALLIE Alfred Aloysius B 6.16.1923 S.Amboy, NJ BR/TR 5-11/185# d8.5																								
1947	†NY A	24	67	9	25	5	0	1	14	5	0	2	.373	.417	.493	154	5	0-0	1.000	0	115	0	O-16(6-0-10)	0.4
1948	†Cle A	81	271	43	84	5	2	9	38	23	0	13	.310	.364	.443	117	5	0-2	.982	-3	89	95	O-65(21-0-44)/3-5,1	-0.2
1949	Cle A	35	74	8	13	4	0	1	9	4	0	7	.176	.218	.270	29	-8	0-0	1.000	-2	65	98	O-17(1-0-16)/1	-1.0
1950	Cle A	59	163	19	35	6	1	6	21	11	0	10	.215	.264	.374	64	-10	0-1	.987	-1	97	70	O-41(25-0-17)	-1.3
1951	Cle A	3	10	3	3	2	0	1	3	1	0	2	.300	.364	.800	221	2	0-0	1.000	-0	73	0	/O-3(RF)	0.1
	Phi A	56	161	20	40	10	1	4	22	15	2	7	.248	.320	.398	91	-2	2-0	.984	0	102	95	O-32(1-1-30),3-10	-0.2
	Year	59	171	23	43	12	1	5	25	16	2	9	.251	.323	.421	98	-1	2-0	.985	0	100	88	O-35(1-1-33),3-10	-0.1
1952	Phi A	71	186	23	51	12	0	7	29	10	1	19	.274	.315	.452	105	0	0-2	.988	-1	100	61	O-48(7-2-39)/1-2	-0.3
1953	Phi A	20	74	6	15	4	0	3	13	3	0	5	.203	.234	.378	61	-5	0-0	1.000	-0	92	117	O-19(RF)	-0.6
	Chi A	9	15	0	1	0	0	0	0	0	0	5	.067	.067	.067	-62	-3	0-0	1.000	-0	0	279	/1O(LF)	-0.4
	Year	29	89	6	16	4	0	3	13	3	0	10	.180	.207	.326	40	-8	0-0	1.000	-1	91	113	O-20(1-0-19)/1	-1.0
Total	7	358	1021	131	267	48	4	32	149	72	3	70	.262	.312	.410	92	-16	2-5	.988	-8	95	78	O-242(62-3-178)/3-15,1-5	-3.5
CLARK, DAD Alfred Robert "Fred" B 7.16.1873 San Francisco, CA D 7.26.1956 Ogden, UT BL/TL 5-11/170# d7.3																								
1902	Chi N	12	43	1	8	1	0	0	2	4	0		.186	.255	.209	45	-3	1	.938	-2	88	147	1-12	-0.5
CLARK, TONY Anthony Christopher B 6.15.1972 Newton, KS BB/TR 6-7/240# d9.3																								
1995	Det A	27	101	10	24	5	1	3	11	8-0	0	30	.238	.294	.396	78	-4	0-0	.985	-1	94	99	1-27	-0.7
1996	Det A	100	376	56	94	14	0	27	72	29-1	0	127	.250	.299	.503	99	-3	0-1	.993	-2	90	92	1-86,D-12	-1.4
1997	Det A	159	580	105	160	28	3	32	117	93-13	3	144	.276	.376	.500	128	25	1-3	.993	-3	94	101	*1-158/D	0.6

Year	Tm Lg	G	AB	R	H	2B	3B	HR	RBI	BB-IB	HP	SO	AVG	OBP	SLG	AOPS	ABR	SB-CS	FA	FR	Rng	Thr	G at Pos	BFW
1998	Det A	157	602	84	175	37	0	34	103	63-5	3	128	.291	.358	.522	125	22	3-3	.991	-0	104	111	*1-142,D-15	0.7
1999	Det A	143	536	74	150	29	0	31	99	64-7	6	133	.280	.361	.507	118	15	2-1	.992	2	106	95	*1-132,D-11	0.3
2000	Det A	60	208	32	57	14	0	13	37	24-2	0	51	.274	.349	.529	121	6	0-0	.993	3	121	104	1-58/D	0.4
2001	Det A★	126	428	67	123	29	3	16	75	62-10	1	108	.287	.374	.481	130	21	0-1	.996	-1	99	108	1-78,D-42	1.0
2002	Bos A	90	275	25	57	12	1	3	29	21-0	1	57	.207	.265	.291	47	-21	0-0	.992	4	118	99	1-85/D-2	-2.3
2003	NY N	125	254	29	59	13	0	16	43	24-2	1	73	.232	.300	.472	101	-1	0-0	.992	-4	71	83	1-80/O(LF)	-1.1
Total	9	987	3360	482	899	181	8	175	586	388-40	15	851	.268	.344	.482	113	60	6-9	.992	-3	100	100	1-846/D-84,O(LF)	-2.5
CLARK, EARL Bailey Earl B 11.6.1907 Washington, DC D 1.16.1938 Washington, DC BR/TR 5-10/160# d8.17																								
1927	Bos N	13	44	6	12	1	0	0	3	2	0	4	.273	.304	.295	66	-2	0	1.000	-0	114	0	O-13(10-3-0)	-0.3
1928	Bos N	28	112	18	34	9	1	0	10	4	2	8	.304	.339	.402	98	0	0	.987	-2	103	0	O-27(CF)	-0.3
1929	Bos N	84	279	43	88	13	3	1	30	12	1	30	.315	.346	.394	86	-6	6	.978	4	109	100	O-74(4-70-1)	-0.6
1930	Bos N	82	233	29	69	11	3	3	28	7	1	22	.296	.320	.408	77	-10	3	.977	3	118	55	O-63(1-40-22)	-0.8
1931	Bos N	16	50	8	11	2	0	0	4	7	0	4	.220	.316	.260	58	-3	1	.970	1	98	257	O-14(LF)	-0.3
1932	Bos N	50	44	11	11	2	0	0	4	2	0	7	.250	.283	.295	58	-3	1	1.000	3	136	394	O-16(6-3-6)	0.0
1933	Bos N	7	23	3	8	1	0	0	1	2	0	1	.348	.400	.391	138	1	0	1.000	-1	81	0	/O-6(3-3-0)	0.0
1934	StL A	13	41	4	7	2	0	0	1	1	0	3	.171	.190	.220	5	-6	0-0	1.000	0	115	0	/O-9(2-0-7)	-0.6
Total	8	293	826	122	240	41	7	4	81	37	4	79	.291	.324	.372	78	-29	11-0	.981	8	111	81	O-222(40-146-36)	-2.9
CLARK, BRADY Brady William B 4.18.1973 Portland, OR BR/TR 6-2/195# d9.3																								
2000	Cin N	11	11	1	3	1	0	0	2	0-0	0	2	.273	.273	.364	58	-1	0-0	1.000	1	237	0	/O-5(2-0-3)	0.0
2001	Cin N	89	129	22	34	3	0	6	18	22-1	1	16	.264	.373	.426	102	1	4-1	.981	-1	103	0	O-43(26-7-14)/D	0.0
2002	Cin N	51	66	6	10	3	0	0	9	6-2	1	9	.152	.233	.197	16	-8	1-2	.938	-1	78	0	O-22(15-3-6)	-1.1
	NY N	10	12	3	5	1	0	0	1	1-0	0	2	.417	.462	.500	164	1	0-0	1.000	-0	93	0	/O-6(1-2-3)	0.1
	Year	61	78	9	15	4	0	0	10	7-2	1	11	.192	.267	.244	38	-7	1-2	.950	-2	81	0	O-28(16-5-9)	-1.0
2003	Mil N	128	315	33	86	21	1	6	40	21-0	9	40	.273	.330	.403	94	-3	13-2	.973	5	114	100	*O-105(25-6-82)	0.0
Total	4	289	533	65	138	29	1	12	70	50-3	11	69	.259	.331	.385	87	-10	18-5	.973	3	110	68	O-181(69-18-108)/D	-1.0
CLARK, DANNY Daniel Curran B 1.18.1894 Meridian, MS D 5.23.1937 Meridian, MS BL/TR 5-9/167# d4.12																								
1922	Det A	83	185	31	54	11	3	3	26	15	0	11	.292	.345	.432	105	1	1-0	.945	-3	101	88	2-38/O-5(RF),3	-0.1
1924	Bos A	104	325	36	90	23	3	2	54	51	2	19	.277	.378	.385	97	1	4-7	.943	-0	105	56	3-94	0.4
1927	StL N	58	72	8	17	2	2	0	13	8	0	7	.236	.313	.319	67	-3	0	.929	1	118	81	O-9(RF)	-0.4
Total	3	245	582	75	161	36	8	5	93	74	2	37	.277	.360	.392	96	-1	5-7	.943	-2	105	56	/3-95,2-38,O-14(RF)	-0.1
CLARK, DAVE David Earl B 9.3.1962 Tupelo, MS BL/TR 6-2/210# d9.3 C2																								
1986	Cle A	18	58	10	16	1	0	3	9	7-0	0	11	.276	.348	.448	119	1	1-0	1.000	1	127	0	O-10(RF)/D-7	0.2
1987	Cle A	29	87	11	18	5	0	3	12	2-0	0	24	.207	.225	.368	53	-6	1-0	1.000	1	118	136	O-13(1-0-12),D-12	-0.6
1988	Cle A	63	156	11	41	4	1	3	18	17-2	0	28	.263	.333	.359	92	-2	0-2	.947	-2	89	0	D-27,O-23(10-1-15)	-0.6
1989	Cle A	102	253	21	60	12	0	8	29	30-5	0	63	.237	.317	.379	94	-2	0-2	.964	-3	70	0	D-55,O-21(12-0-11)	-0.8
1990	Chi N	84	171	22	47	4	2	5	20	8-1	0	40	.275	.304	.409	89	-3	7-1	1.000	-1	87	85	O-39(LF)	-0.5
1991	KC A	11	10	1	2	0	0	0	1	1-0	0	1	.200	.273	.200	33	-1	0-0	—	-0	0	0	/O(RF)D	-0.1
1992	Pit N	23	33	3	7	0	0	2	7	6-0	0	8	.212	.325	.394	106	0	0-0	1.000	-1	71	0	/O-8(1-0-7)	-0.1
1993	Pit N	110	277	43	75	11	2	11	46	38-5	1	58	.271	.358	.444	114	6	1-0	.957	-6	90	53	O-91(40-0-53)	-0.3
1994	Pit N	86	223	37	66	11	1	10	46	22-0	0	48	.296	.355	.489	117	5	2-2	.974	2	102	130	O-57(10-0-48)	0.4
1995	Pit N	77	196	30	55	6	0	4	24	24-1	1	38	.281	.359	.372	92	-2	3-3	.961	0	113	32	O-61(34-0-29)	-0.4
1996	Pit N	92	211	28	58	12	2	8	35	31-3	0	51	.275	.366	.464	115	5	2-1	.988	-1	93	102	O-61(34-0-28)	0.2
	†LA N	15	15	0	3	0	0	0	1	3-0	0	2	.200	.333	.200	49	-1	0-0	—	-0	0	0	/O(LF)	-0.1
	Year	107	226	28	61	12	2	8	36	34-3	0	53	.270	.364	.447	112	4	2-1	.988	-1	91	100	O-62(35-0-28)	0.1
1997	Chi N	102	143	19	43	8	0	5	32	19-3	2	34	.301	.386	.462	119	5	1-0	.953	2	113	165	O-25(24-0-1)/D-4	0.6
1998	†Hou N	93	131	12	27	7	0	0	4	14-1	1	45	.206	.288	.260	47	-10	1-1	.885	-2	79	102	O-22(9-0-13)/D-4	-1.2
Total	13	905	1964	248	518	81	8	62	284	222-21	5	451	.264	.338	.408	99	-5	19-12	.969	-11	96	73	O-433(215-1-228),D-110	-3.3
CLARK, GLEN Glen Ester B 3.7.1941 Austin, TX BB/TR 6-1/190# d6.3																								
1967	Atl N	4	4	0	0	0	0	0	0	0-0	0	1	.000	.000	.000	-99	-1	0-0	—	0			H	-0.1
CLARK, PEP Harry B 3.20.1883 Union City, OH D 6.8.1965 Milwaukee, WI BR/TR 5-7.5/175# d9.11																								
1903	Chi A	15	65	7	20	4	2	0	9	2	1		.308	.338	.431	135	3	5	.877	-1	118	58	3-15	0.3
CLARK, HOWIE Howard Roddy B 2.13.1974 San Diego, CA BL/TR 5-10/195# d7.16																								
2002	Bal A	14	53	3	16	5	0	0	4	3-0	2	6	.302	.362	.396	107	1	0-0	1.000	0	119	0	/O-4(LF),1D	0.1
2003	Tor A	38	70	9	25	3	1	0	7	3-0	2	6	.357	.400	.429	117	2	0-1	.957	1	114	239	3-13/O-5(4-0-1),2-3,1-2,SD	0.3
Total	2	52	123	12	41	8	1	0	11	6-0	4	12	.333	.383	.415	113	3	0-1	.957	1	114	239	/D-15,3-13,O-9(8-0-1),2-3,1-3,S	0.4
CLARK, JACK Jack Anthony B 11.10.1955 New Brighton, PA BR/TR 6-2/205# d9.12 C3 OF Total (11-LF 23-CF 1014-RF)																								
1975	SF N	8	17	3	4	0	0	0	2	1-0	0	2	.235	.263	.235	42	-1	1-0	1.000	0	110	0	/O-3(1-2-1),3-2	-0.1
1976	SF N	26	102	14	23	6	2	2	10	8-0	0	18	.225	.277	.382	85	-2	6-2	.987	3	113	168	O-26(5-20-8)	0.0
1977	SF N	136	413	64	104	17	4	13	51	49-2	2	73	.252	.332	.407	98	-1	12-4	.975	6	110	135	*O-114(0-1-113)	0.0
1978	SF N★	156	592	90	181	46	8	25	98	50-8	3	72	.306	.358	.537	155	41	15-11	.982	8	107	127	*O-152(RF)	4.2
1979	SF N★	143	527	84	144	25	2	26	86	63-6	1	95	.273	.348	.476	133	23	11-8	.982	2	97	118	*O-140(RF)/3-2	1.7
1980	SF N	127	437	77	124	20	8	22	82	74-13	2	52	.284	.382	.517	155	34	2-5	.967	-4	98	66	*O-120(RF)	2.3
1981	SF N	99	385	60	103	19	2	17	53	45-6	1	45	.268	.341	.460	129	14	1-1	.981	5	99	**168**	O-98(RF)	1.5
1982	SF N	157	563	90	154	30	3	27	103	90-7	1	91	.274	.372	.481	138	31	6-9	.980	-4	96	89	*O-155(RF)	1.8
1983	SF N	135	492	82	132	25	0	20	66	74-6	1	79	.268	.361	.441	126	19	5-3	.967	6	101	**183**	*O-133(RF)/1-2	1.9
1984	SF N	57	203	33	65	9	1	11	44	43-7	0	29	.320	.434	.537	179	24	1-1	.990	-1	90	82	O-54(RF)/1-4	2.0
1985	†StL N★	126	442	71	124	26	3	22	87	83-14	2	88	.281	.393	.502	151	34	1-4	.988	-9	81	**112**	*1-121,O-12(RF)	1.7
1986	StL N	65	232	34	55	12	2	9	23	45-4	1	61	.237	.362	.422	117	7	1-1	.995	-6	75	137	1-64	-0.3
1987	†StL N★	131	419	93	120	23	1	35	106	**136**-13	0	139	.286	**.459**	**.597**	**174**	54	1-2	.989	-5	92	116	*1-126/O(RF)	4.0
1988	NY A	150	496	81	120	14	0	27	93	113-6	2	141	.242	.381	.433	130	25	3-2	.951	-1	99	91	*D-112,O-19(5-0-14),1-10	1.9
1989	SD N	142	455	76	110	19	1	26	94	**132**-18	1	145	.242	.410	.459	149	37	6-2	.988	2	107	**119**	*1-131,O-12(RF)	3.2
1990	SD N	115	334	59	89	12	1	25	62	**104**-11	2	91	.266	.441	.533	166	37	4-3	.994	-1	95	104	*1-109	2.9
1991	Bos A	140	481	75	120	18	1	28	87	96-3	3	133	.249	.374	.466	126	20	0-2	—	0	0	0	*D-135	1.5
1992	Bos A	81	257	32	54	11	0	5	33	56-3	2	87	.210	.350	.311	83	-3	1-1	.992	0	106	74	D-64,1-13	-0.6
Total	18	1994	6847	1118	1826	332	39	340	1180	1262-127	24	1441	.267	.379	.476	138	393	77-61	.978	1	101	122	*O-1039R,1-580,D-311/3-4	29.6
CLARK, JIM James (born James Petrosky) B 9.21.1927 Baggaley, PA D 10.24.1990 Santa Monica, CA BR/TR 5-9/150# d8.17																								
1948	Was A	9	12	1	3	0	0	0	0	0	0	2	.250	.250	.250	34	-1	0-0	1.000	-0	95	0	/S3	-0.1
CLARK, JIM James Edward B 4.30.1947 Kansas City, KS BR/TR 6-1/190# d7.16																								
1971	Cle A	13	18	2	3	0	1	0	0	2-0	0	7	.167	.250	.278	45	-1	0-0	1.000	0	150	0	/O-3(2-0-1),1	-0.1
CLARK, JIM James Francis B 12.26.1887 Brooklyn, NY D 3.20.1969 Beaumont, TX BR/TR 5-11/175# d9.2																								
1911	StL N	14	18	2	3	0	1	0	3	3	0	4	.167	.286	.278	60	-1	2	1.000	-1	83	0	/O-8(1-6-1)	-0.2
1912	StL N	2	1	0	0	0	0	0	0	0	0	1	.000	.000	.000	-99	0	0	—	0			H	0.0
Total	2	16	19	2	3	0	1	0	3	3	0	5	.158	.273	.263	51	-1	2	1.000	-1	83	0	/O-8(1-6-1)	-0.2
CLARK, JERALD Jerald Dwayne B 8.10.1963 Crockett, TX BR/TR 6-4/202# d9.19 b-Phil																								
1988	SD N	6	15	0	3	1	0	0	3	0-0	0	4	.200	.200	.267	33	-1	0-0	1.000	1	152	496	/O-4(LF)	0.0
1989	SD N	17	41	5	8	2	0	1	7	3-0	0	9	.195	.250	.317	61	-2	0-1	.947	0	80	356	O-14(10-0-4)	-0.3
1990	SD N	53	101	12	27	4	1	5	11	5-0	0	24	.267	.299	.475	109	1	0-0	1.000	0	93	49	1-15,O-13(5-0-9)	0.0
1991	SD N	118	369	26	84	16	0	10	47	31-2	6	90	.228	.295	.352	80	-10	2-1	.994	-5	86	91	O-96(85-0-13),1-16	-2.0
1992	SD N	146	496	45	120	22	6	12	58	22-3	4	97	.242	.278	.383	85	-12	3-0	.990	7	110	153	*O-134(115-1-22),1-11	-1.0
1993	Col N	140	478	65	135	26	6	13	67	20-2	10	60	.282	.324	.444	89	-8	9-6	.966	-1	105	100	O-96(80-0-17),1-37	-1.6
1995	Min A	36	109	17	37	8	3	3	15	2-0	1	11	.339	.354	.550	132	4	3-0	1.000	-1	99	77	O-23(12-10-5),1-11/D-3	0.3
Total	7	516	1609	170	414	79	16	44	208	83-7	21	295	.257	.301	.408	89	-28	17-8	.983	2	102	124	0-380(311-11-70)/1-90,D-3	-4.6
CLARK, JERMAINE Jermaine Marcel B 9.29.1976 Berkeley, CA BL/TR 5-10/175# d4.3																								
2001	Det A	3	0	1	0	0	0	0	0	0-0	0	0	—	—	—	—	0	0-0	—	0			/R-2	0.0
2003	Tex A	10	9	0	0	0	0	0	0	3-0	0	0	.000	.250	.000	-24	-2	0-0	1.000	-8	16	0	/O-6(5-1-0),2-2,D	-1.0

Year	Tm Lg	G	AB	R	H	2B	3B	HR	RBI	BB-IB	HP	SO	AVG	OBP	SLG	AOPS	ABR	SB-CS	FA	FR	Rng	Thr	G at Pos	BFW
	SD N	1	2	0	0	0	0	0	1	0-0	0	1	.000	.000	.000	-99	-1	0-1	1.000	0	107	0	/O(LF)	-0.1
	Tex A	14	37	2	8	2	0	0	6	3-0	0	4	.216	.268	.270	41	-3	2-1	1.000	-1	16	0	O-11(LF)/2-5,D	-0.4
Total	2	28	48	3	8	2	0	0	7	6-0	0	5	.167	.250	.208	24	-6	2-2	1.000	-9	61	133	/O-18(17-1-0),2-7,D-2	-1.5
CLARK, CAP John Carrol B 9.19.1906 Snow Camp, NC D 2.16.1957 Fayetteville, NC BL/TR 5-11/180# d4.23																								
1938	Phi N	52	74	11	19	1	1	0	4	9	0	10	.257	.337	.297	78	-2	0	.936	-4	*57*	*107*	C-29	-0.5
CLARK, MEL Melvin Earl B 7.7.1926 Letart, WV BR/TR 6/180# d9.11																								
1951	Phi N	10	31	2	10	1	0	1	3	0	0	3	.323	.323	.452	108	0	0-1	1.000	-0	102	0	/O-7(1-0-6)	-0.1
1952	Phi N	47	155	20	52	6	4	1	15	6	1	13	.335	.364	.445	125	4	2-1	1.000	3	108	146	O-38(12-0-27)/3	0.6
1953	Phi N	60	198	31	59	10	4	0	19	11	1	17	.298	.338	.389	89	-3	1-0	.991	1	109	53	O-51(1-0-51)	-0.4
1954	Phi N	83	233	26	56	9	7	1	24	17	0	21	.240	.291	.352	67	-12	0-1	.961	4	101	192	O-63(21-0-42)	-1.2
1955	Phi N	10	32	3	5	3	0	0	1	3-0	0	4	.156	.229	.250	27	-3	0-0	1.000	3	114	401	/O-8(RF)	-0.1
1957	Det A	5	7	0	0	0	0	0	1	0-0	0	3	.000	.000	.000	-97	-2	0-0	1.000	0	143	0	/O-2(LF)	-0.2
Total	6	215	656	82	182	29	15	3	63	37-0	2	61	.277	.318	.381	85	-16	3-3	.983	9	106	140	O-169(37-0-134)/3	-1.4
CLARK, SPIDER Owen F. B 9.16.1867 Brooklyn, NY D 2.8.1892 Brooklyn, NY TR 5-10/150# d5.2 OF Total (5-LF 4-CF 34-RF)																								
1889	Was N	38	145	19	37	7	2	3	22	6	0	18	.255	.285	.393	94	-2	8	.887	4			C-14,S-13/O-9(RF),3-2,2-2	0.3
1890	Buf P	69	260	45	69	11	1	2	25	20	3	16	.265	.325	.338	84	-5	8	.938	-3	106	149	O-34(5-4-25),C-14,2-13/1-6,3-3,SP	-0.5
Total	2	107	405	64	106	18	3	5	47	26	3	34	.262	.311	.358	88	-7	16	.952	2			/O-43R,C-28,2-15,S-14,1-6,3-5,P	-0.2
CLARK, PHIL Phillip Benjamin B 5.6.1968 Crockett, TX BR/TR 6/200# d5.27 b-Jerald OF Total (52-LF 50-RF)																								
1992	Det A	23	54	3	22	4	0	1	5	6-1	0	9	.407	.467	.537	179	6	1-0	.931	1	138	0	O-13(4-0-9)/D-7	0.7
1993	SD N	102	240	33	75	17	0	9	33	8-2	5	31	.313	.345	.496	121	7	2-0	.963	10	142	254	O-36(22-0-15),1-24,C-11/3-5	1.5
1994	SD N	61	149	14	32	6	0	5	20	5-1	3	17	.215	.250	.356	59	-10	1-2	.992	-2	100	104	1-24,O-17(12-0-5)/C-5,3	-1.4
1995	SD N	75	97	12	21	3	0	2	7	8-1	1	18	.216	.278	.309	58	-6	0-2	1.000	-2	86	0	O-34(14-0-21)/1-2	-0.9
1996	Bos A	3	3	0	0	0	0	0	0	0-0	0	1	.000	.000	.000	-98	-1	0-0	1.000	0	0	0	/13D	-0.1
Total	5	264	543	62	150	30	0	17	65	27-5	9	76	.276	.317	.425	97	-4	4-4	.951	7	121	103	O-100L/1-51,C-16,D-8,3-7	-0.2
CLARK, BOBBY Robert Cale B 6.13.1955 Sacramento, CA BR/TR 6/190# d8.21																								
1979	†Cal A	19	54	8	16	2	2	1	5	5-0	0	11	.296	.356	.463	123	2	1-1	.978	4	132	372	O-19(16-3-2)	0.5
1980	Cal A	78	261	26	60	10	1	5	23	11-0	2	42	.230	.266	.333	65	-14	0-1	.982	8	122	119	O-77(33-46-0)	-0.7
1981	Cal A	34	88	12	22	2	1	4	19	7-0	0	18	.250	.305	.432	110	1	0-0	1.000	4	112	290	O-34(27-8-1)	0.4
1982	†Cal A	102	90	11	19	1	0	2	8	0-0	0	29	.211	.209	.289	36	-8	1-0	1.000	1	101	80	*O-102(24-24-57)	-0.9
1983	Cal A	76	212	17	49	9	1	5	21	9-0	0	45	.231	.261	.354	68	-10	0-0	1.000	-5	93	0	O-72(43-4-28)/3D	-1.8
1984	Mil A	58	169	17	44	7	2	2	16	16-0	1	35	.260	.326	.361	94	-1	1-5	.981	-8	80	0	O-56(3-42-16)	-1.2
1985	Mil A	29	93	6	21	3	0	0	8	7-0	0	19	.226	.277	.258	49	-7	1-1	1.000	2	116	61	O-27(1-17-12)	-0.6
Total	7	396	967	97	231	34	7	19	100	55-0	3	199	.239	.281	.347	74	-37	4-8	.990	6	105	91	O-387(147-144-116)/D-2,3	-4.3
CLARK, BOB Robert H. B 3.18.1863 Covington, KY D 8.21.1919 Covington, KY BR/TR 5-10/175# d4.17																								
1886	Bro AA	71	269	37	58	8	2	0	26	17	0		.216	.262	.260	63	-12	14	.864	-7			C-44,O-17(6-1-11),S-12	-1.3
1887	Bro AA	48	177	24	47	3	1	0	18	7	1		.266	.297	.294	64	-9	15	.871	-2			C-45/O-3(RF)	-0.6
1888	Bro AA	45	150	23	36	5	3	1	20	9	2		.240	.292	.333	100	0	11	.884	-2			C-36/O-8(1-1-6),1	0.1
1889	†Bro AA	53	182	32	50	5	2	0	22	26	1	7	.275	.368	.324	98	1	18	.870	-0			C-53	0.4
1890	†Bro N	43	151	24	33	3	3	0	15	15	4	8	.219	.306	.278	70	-6	10	.836	-15	*86*	*76*	C-42/O(RF)	-1.5
1891	Cin N	16	54	2	6	0	0	0	3	6	1	9	.111	.213	.111	-5	-7	3	.868	-4	*91*	*91*	C-16	-0.9
1893	Lou N	12	28	3	3	1	0	0	3	5	0	5	.107	.242	.143	4	-4	0	.947	-1	*102*	*149*	C-10/O(RF)S	-0.3
Total	7	288	1011	145	233	25	11	1	107	85	9	29	.230	.296	.280	71	-37	71	.867	-31	*23*	*22*	C-246/O-30(7-2-22),S-13,1	-4.1
CLARK, RON Ronald Bruce B 1.14.1943 Ft.Worth, TX BR/TR 5-10/175# d9.11 C6																								
1966	Min A	5	1	1	1	0	0	0	1	0-0	0	0	1.000	.500	1.000	448	0	0-0	—	-0	0	0	/3	0.0
1967	Min A	20	60	7	10	3	1	2	11	4-0	0	9	.167	.215	.350	61	-3	0-0	.891	-2	101	0	3-16	-0.5
1968	Min A	104	227	14	42	5	1	1	13	16-2	2	44	.185	.245	.229	42	-16	3-2	.932	-4	113	109	3-52,S-43,2-10	-1.9
1969	Min A	5	8	0	1	0	0	0	0	0-0	0	0	.125	.125	.125	-29	-1	0-0	1.000	-1	31	0	/3-2	-0.3
	Sea A	57	163	9	32	5	0	0	12	13-2	1	29	.196	.258	.227	38	-14	1-0	.966	-9	83	69	S-38,3-15/2-5,1	-2.0
	Year	62	171	9	33	5	0	0	12	13-2	1	29	.193	.253	.222	35	-15	1-0	.966	-10	83	69	S-38,3-17/2-5,1	-2.3
1971	Oak A	2	1	0	0	0	0	0	0	1-0	0	0	.000	.500	.000	53	0	0-0	—	0			H	0.0
1972	Oak A	14	15	1	4	2	0	0	1	2-0	0	4	.267	.353	.400	130	1	0-0	1.000	1	93	211	2-11/3-3	0.2
	Mil A	22	54	8	10	1	1	2	5	5-0	0	11	.185	.250	.352	81	-2	0-0	.963	4	142	108	2-11,3-10	0.3
	Year	36	69	9	14	3	1	2	6	7-0	0	15	.203	.273	.362	92	-1	0-0	.974	5	126	142	2-22,3-13	0.5
1975	Phi N	1	1	0	0	0	0	0	0	0-0	0	1	.000	.000	.000	-96	0	0-0	—	0			H	0.0
Total	7	230	530	40	100	16	3	5	43	41-4	3	98	.189	.249	.258	49	-35	4-2	.904	-12	106	89	/3-99,S-81,2-37,1	-4.2
CLARK, ROY Roy Elliott "Pepper" B 5.11.1874 New Haven, CT D 11.1.1925 Bridgeport, CT BL/TR 5-8/170# d4.19																								
1902	NY N	22	80	4	12	1	0	0	3	1	0		.150	.160	.162	-0	-10	5	.964	-1	88	174	O-21(3-9-9)	-1.2
CLARK, WILL William Nuschler B 3.13.1964 New Orleans, LA BL/TL 6-1/190# d4.8																								
1986	SF N	111	408	66	117	27	2	11	41	34-10	3	76	.287	.343	.444	122	12	4-7	.989	-3	93	102	*1-102	0.2
1987	†SF N	150	529	89	163	29	5	35	91	49-11	5	98	.308	.371	.580	155	40	5-17	.991	1	104	**125**	*1-139	2.7
1988	SF N★	**162**	575	102	162	31	6	29	**109**	**100-27**	4	129	.282	.386	.508	163	**51**	9-1	.993	-3	94	**120**	*1-158	4.0
1989	†SF N★	159	588	**104**	196	38	9	23	111	74-14	5	103	.333	.407	.546	177	60	8-3	.994	-1	100	115	*1-158	5.1
1990	SF N★	154	600	91	177	25	5	19	95	62-9	3	97	.295	.357	.448	127	22	8-2	.992	-1	101	108	*1-153	1.1
1991	SF N★	148	565	84	170	32	7	29	116	51-12	2	91	.301	.359	**.536**	154	38	4-2	**.997**	5	109	**119**	*1-144	3.4
1992	SF N★	144	513	69	154	40	1	16	73	73-23	4	82	.300	.384	.476	153	39	12-7	.993	1	103	**132**	*1-141	3.2
1993	SF N	132	491	82	139	27	2	14	73	63-6	6	68	.283	.367	.432	118	14	2-2	.988	-2	98	**127**	*1-129	0.1
1994	Tex A★	110	389	73	128	24	2	13	80	71-11	3	59	.329	.431	.501	141	28	5-1	.990	2	108	95	*1-107/D	1.9
1995	Tex A	123	454	85	137	27	3	16	92	68-6	4	50	.302	.389	.480	124	18	0-1	.994	1	102	**117**	*1-122/D	0.7
1996	†Tex A	117	436	69	124	25	1	13	72	64-5	5	67	.284	.377	.436	101	3	2-1	.996	-2	93	90	*1-117	-0.9
1997	Tex A	110	393	56	128	29	1	12	51	49-11	3	62	.326	.400	.496	127	17	0-0	.996	-1	95	101	*1-100/D-7	0.7
1998	†Tex A	149	554	98	169	41	1	23	102	72-5	3	97	.305	.384	.507	125	23	1-0	.989	-9	79	98	*1-134,D-15	0.1
1999	Bal A	77	251	40	76	15	0	10	29	38-2	2	42	.303	.395	.482	128	12	2-2	.995	2	111	101	1-63/D-3	0.7
2000	Bal A	79	256	49	77	15	1	9	28	47-3	4	45	.301	.413	.473	131	15	4-2	.991	-1	93	90	1-72/D-6	0.6
	†StL N	51	171	29	59	15	1	12	42	22-0	3	24	.345	.426	.655	168	18	1-0	.992	-2	84	94	1-50	1.2
Total	15	1976	7173	1186	2176	440	47	284	1205	937-155	59	1190	.303	.384	.497	138	410	67-48	.992	-14	98	111	*1-1889/D-33	24.8
CLARK, WILLIE William Otis "Wee Willie" B 8.16.1872 Pittsburgh, PA D 11.13.1932 Pittsburgh, PA BL 6/195# d6.20																								
1895	NY N	23	88	9	23	3	2	0	16	5	0	6	.261	.301	.341	67	-5	1	.974	1	119	124	1-23	-0.3
1896	NY N	72	247	38	72	12	4	0	33	15	8	12	.291	.352	.372	94	-2	8	.975	-4	75	105	1-65	-0.5
1897	NY N	116	431	63	122	17	12	1	75	37	9		.283	.352	.385	97	-2	18	.984	3	106	122	*1-107/O-7(LF),3	0.0
1898	Pit N	57	209	29	64	9	7	1	31	22	2		.306	.378	.431	134	9	0	.984	1	98	90	1-57	0.9
1899	Pit N	81	300	49	85	13	10	0	44	35	10		.283	.377	.393	112	6	11	.989	0	89	78	1-79	0.5
Total	5	349	1275	188	366	54	35	2	199	114	29	18	.287	.359	.389	104	6	38	.983	0	95	102	1-331/O-7(LF),3	0.6
CLARK, WIN William Winfield B 4.11.1875 Circleville, OH D 4.15.1959 Los Angeles, CA BR/TR 5-10/175# d7.12																								
1897	Lou N	4	16	2	3	0	0	0	2	1	0		.188	.235	.188	13	-2	1	.810	-2	75	80	/2-3,3	-0.3
CLARKE, ARTIE Arthur Franklin B 5.6.1865 Providence, RI D 11.14.1949 Brookline, MA BR/TR 5-8/155# d4.19																								
1890	NY N	101	395	55	89	12	8	0	49	32	4	38	.225	.290	.296	71	-16	44	.908	-2	*98*	*146*	C-36,O-33(3-1-30),3-16,2-15/S	-1.3
1891	NY N	48	174	17	33	2	2	0	21	15	0	16	.190	.254	.224	41	-13	5	.916	-11	*82*	*120*	C-42/3-5,O-2(0-1-1)	-1.9
Total	2	149	569	72	122	14	10	0	70	47	4	54	.214	.279	.274	62	-29	49	.912	-13	*90*	*132*	/C-78,O-35(3-2-31),3-21,2-15,S	-3.2
CLARKE, FRED Fred Clifford "Cap" B 10.3.1872 Winterset, IA D 8.14.1960 Winfield, KS BL/TR 5-10.5/165# d6.30 M19 C1 HF1945 b-Josh																								
1894	Lou N	76	314	55	86	11	7	7	48	26	4	27	.274	.337	.420	88	-8	26	.886	4	118	62	O-76(LF)	-0.8
1895	Lou N	**132**	550	96	191	21	5	4	82	34	10	24	.347	.396	.425	119	18	40	.881	13	103	80	*O-132(LF)	1.6
1896	Lou N	131	517	96	168	15	18	9	79	43	14	34	.325	.392	.476	133	24	34	.908	-1	99	38	*O-131(LF)	1.0
1897	Lou N	130	526	122	205	30	13	6	67	45	25		.390	.461	.530	**167**	**55**	59	.927	5	96	0	*O-129(128-3-0),M	4.1
1898	Lou N	149	599	116	184	23	12	3	47	48	15		.307	.373	.401	123	19	40	.940	7	90	58	*O-149(148-0-2),M	1.1
1899	Lou N	149	606	122	206	23	9	5	70	49	16		.340	.404	.432	130	26	49	.964	-1	89	34	*O-145(LF)/S-3,M	1.2

Year	Tm Lg	G	AB	R	H	2B	3B	HR	RBI	BB-IB	HP	SO	AVG	OBP	SLG	AOPS	ABR	SB-CS	FA	FR	Rng	Thr	G at Pos	BFW
1900	Pit N	106	399	84	110	15	12	3	32	51	7		.276	.368	.396	110	6	21	.944	2	55	58	*O-104(LF),M	-0.1
1901	Pit N	129	527	118	171	24	15	6	60	51	10		.324	.395	.461	143	30	23	.970	2	80	0	*O-127(LF)/S3M	2.4
1902	Pit N	113	459	103	145	27	14	2	53	51	**14**		.316	.401	.449	157	33	29	.958	-1	83	57	*O-113(110-0-4),M	2.6
1903	†Pit N	104	427	88	150	**32**	15	5	70	41	5		.351	.414	**.532**	**164**	35	21	.962	-8	71	95	*O-101(LF)/S-2,M	2.0
1904	Pit N	72	278	51	85	7	11	0	25	22	5		.306	.367	.410	136	11	11	.979	-1	44	76	O-70(LF),M	0.7
1905	Pit N	141	525	95	157	18	15	2	51	55	2		.299	.368	.402	126	17	24	.976	5	9	9	*O-137(LF),M	1.5
1906	Pit N	118	417	69	129	14	**13**	1	39	40	1		.309	.371	.412	138	18	18	.974	5	107	98	*O-110(LF),M	1.8
1907	Pit N	148	501	97	145	18	13	2	59	68	8		.289	.383	.389	140	26	37	**.987**	8	77	44	*O-144(LF),M	2.9
1908	Pit N	151	551	83	146	18	15	2	53	65	6		.265	.349	.363	127	18	24	.973	10	79	47	*O-151(150-1-0),M	2.3
1909	†Pit N	152	550	97	158	16	11	3	68	**80**	6		.287	.384	.373	124	19	31	**.987**	7	79	47	*O-152(LF),M	1.9
1910	Pit N	123	429	57	113	23	9	2	63	53	4	23	.263	.350	.373	105	3	12	.967	3	**113**	64	*O-118(LF),M	0.0
1911	Pit N	110	392	73	127	25	13	5	49	53	2	27	.324	.407	.492	146	24	10	.970	-1	108	56	*O-101(LF),M	1.9
1913	Pit N	9	13	0	1	1	0	0	0	0	0	0	.077	.077	.154	-37	-2	0	1.000	-0	77	0	/O-2(LF),M	-0.3
1914	Pit N	2	2	0	0	0	0	0	0	0	0	0	.000	.000	.000	-99	-1	0	—	0			HM	-0.1
1915	Pit N	1	2	0	1	0	0	0	0	0	0	0	.500	.500	.500	206	0	0	—	-0	0	0	/O(LF)M	0.0
Total	21	2246	8584	1622	2678	361	220	67	1015	875	154	135	.312	.386	.429	132	371	509	.952	59	83	49	*O-2193(2187-4-6)/S-6,3	27.7
CLARKE, HARRY Harry Corson B 1861 D 3.3.1923 Long Beach, CA d8.28																								
1889	Was N	1	3	0	0	0	0	0	0	0	0	1	.000	.000	.000	-99	-1	0	1.000	1	915	0	/O(RF)	0.0
CLARKE, HORACE Horace Meredith B 6.2.1940 Frederiksted, V.I. BB/TR 5-9/178# d5.13																								
1965	NY A	51	108	13	28	1	0	1	9	6-0	0	6	.259	.296	.296	70	-4	2-1	.923	2	117	113	3-17/2-7,S	-0.2
1966	NY A	96	312	37	83	10	4	6	28	27-4	1	24	.266	.324	.381	107	2	5-3	.970	-10	88	108	S-63,2-16/3-4	-0.1
1967	NY A	143	588	74	160	17	0	3	29	42-2	0	64	.272	.321	.316	92	-6	21-4	**.990**	16	**116**	97	*2-140	2.8
1968	NY A	148	579	52	133	6	1	2	26	23-0	0	46	.230	.258	.254	58	-32	20-7	.984	**29**	**119**	103	*2-139	1.3
1969	NY A	156	641	82	183	26	7	4	48	53-1	0	41	.285	.339	.367	101	0	33-13	.982	2	101	**119**	*2-156	1.7
1970	NY A	158	686	81	172	24	2	4	46	35-5	2	35	.251	.286	.309	68	-32	23-7	.979	-8	104	96	*2-157	-2.7
1971	NY A	159	625	76	156	23	7	2	41	64-2	2	43	.250	.321	.318	87	-11	17-7	.981	-3	106	98	*2-156	-0.2
1972	NY A	147	547	65	132	20	2	3	37	56-4	4	44	.241	.315	.302	87	-8	18-6	.985	15	**115**	116	*2-143	2.1
1973	NY A	148	590	60	155	21	0	2	35	47-0	2	48	.263	.317	.308	80	-15	11-10	.979	16	107	111	*2-147	1.0
1974	NY A	24	47	3	11	1	0	0	1	4-0	0	5	.234	.294	.255	60	-2	1-0	1.000	-1	88	62	2-20/D	-0.3
	SD N	42	90	5	17	1	0	0	4	8-0	0	6	.189	.255	.200	30	-9	0-0	.978	-0	100	51	2-21	-0.8
Total	10	1272	4813	548	1230	150	23	27	304	365-18	11	362	.256	.308	.313	82	-117	151-58	.983	59	109	104	*2-1102/S-64,3-21,D	4.6
CLARKE, NIG Jay Justin B 12.15.1882 Amherstburg, ON, CAN D 6.15.1949 River Rouge, MI BL/TR (BB 1907) 5-8/165# d4.26																								
1905	Cle A	5	9	2	1	1	0	0	1	1	0		.111	.200	.222	33	-1	0	1.000	-1	*76*	*55*	/C-5	-0.2
	Det A	3	7	1	3	0	0	1	1	0	1		.429	.500	.857	326	2	0	1.000	0	*71*	*116*	/C-2	0.2
	Cle A	37	114	9	23	5	1	0	8	10	0		.202	.266	.263	67	-4	0	.961	-2	*76*	*55*	C-37	-0.3
	Year	45	130	12	27	6	1	1	10	11	1		.208	.275	.292	79	-3	0	.965	-3	*103*	*92*	C-44	-0.3
1906	Cle A	57	179	22	64	12	4	1	21	13	1		.358	.404	.486	181	17	3	.982	2	*117*	*93*	C-54	2.5
1907	Cle A	120	390	44	105	19	6	3	33	35	2		.269	.333	.372	123	11	3	.961	-8	*100*	*87*	*C-115	1.5
1908	Cle A	97	290	34	70	8	6	1	27	30	1		.241	.315	.321	106	2	6	.969	-1	***137***	*101*	C-90	1.1
1909	Cle A	55	164	15	45	4	2	0	14	9	1		.274	.316	.323	98	-1	1	.952	-1	*106*	*111*	C-44	0.3
1910	Cle A	21	58	4	9	2	0	0	2	8	0		.155	.258	.190	40	-4	0	.974	-0	*90*	*121*	C-17	-0.2
1911	StL A	82	256	22	55	10	1	0	18	26	0		.215	.287	.262	56	-15	2	.926	-12	*76*	*104*	C-73/1-4	-2.1
1919	Phi N	26	62	4	15	3	0	0	2	4	1	5	.242	.299	.290	72	-2	1	.969	-2	*83*	*138*	C-22	-0.2
1920	Pit N	3	7	0	0	0	0	0	0	2	0	4	.000	.222	.000	-32	-1	0-0	1.000	1	*101*	*105*	/C-3	0.0
Total	9	506	1536	157	390	64	20	6	127	138	7	9	.254	.318	.333	102	4	16-0	.960	-23	*105*	*99*	C-462/1-4	2.6
CLARKE, JOSH Joshua Baldwin "Pepper" B 3.8.1879 Winfield, KS D 7.2.1962 Ventura, CA BL/TR 5-10/180# d6.15 b-Fred																								
1898	Lou N	6	18	0	3	0	0	0	0	1	0		.167	.211	.167	9	-2	0	.917	-0	0	0	/O-5(2-0-4)	-0.3
1905	StL N	50	167	31	43	3	2	3	18	27	0		.257	.361	.353	117	4	8	.942	-8	29	0	O-26(2-5-19),2-16/S-4	-0.4
1908	Cle A	131	492	70	119	8	4	1	21	76	4		.242	.348	.280	104	7	37	.963	-3	84	26	*O-131(130-1-0)	-0.5
1909	Cle A	4	12	1	0	0	0	0	0	2	0		.000	.143	.000	-52	-2	0	.600	-1	0	0	/O-4(LF)	-0.4
1911	Bos N	32	120	16	28	7	3	1	4	29	1	22	.233	.387	.367	103	2	6	.938	3	107	153	O-30(LF)	0.3
Total	5	223	809	118	193	18	9	5	43	135	5	22	.239	.351	.302	102	9	51	.949	-10	77	42	O-196(168-6-23)/2-16,S-4	-1.3
CLARKE, GREY Richard Grey "Noisy" B 9.26.1912 Fulton, AL D 11.25.1993 Kannapolis, NC BR/TR 5-9/183# d4.19																								
1944	Chi A	63	169	14	44	10	1	0	27	22	2	6	.260	.352	.331	97	0	0-4	.941	1	110	77	3-45	0.0
CLARKE, SUMPTER Sumpter Mills B 10.18.1897 Savannah, GA D 3.16.1962 Knoxville, TN BR/TR 5-11/170# d9.27 b-Rufe																								
1920	Chi N	1	3	0	1	0	0	0	0	0	0	1	.333	.333	.333	90	0	0-0	1.000	-0	91	0	/3	0.0
1923	Cle A	1	3	0	0	0	0	0	0	0	0	0	.000	.000	.000	-99	-1	0-0	1.000	0	0	0	/O	-0.1
1924	Cle A	35	104	17	24	6	1	0	11	6	0	12	.231	.273	.308	49	-8	0-0	1.000	-1	97	67	O-33(2-9-22)	-1.0
Total	3	37	110	17	25	6	1	0	11	6	0	13	.227	.267	.300	46	-9	0-0	1.000	-1	97	67	/O-34(2-9-22),3	-1.1
CLARKE, TOMMY Thomas Aloysius B 5.9.1888 New York, NY D 8.14.1945 Corona, NY BR/TR 5-11/175# d8.26 C5																								
1909	Cin N	18	52	8	13	3	2	0	10	6	0		.250	.328	.385	122	1	3	.965	2	*102*	*119*	C-17	0.5
1910	Cin N	64	151	19	42	6	5	1	20	19	3	17	.278	.370	.404	131	6	1	.971	2	*123*	*85*	C-56	1.3
1911	Cin N	86	203	20	49	6	7	1	25	25	1	22	.241	.328	.355	94	-2	4	.970	8	*133*	*86*	C-81/1	1.1
1912	Cin N	72	146	19	41	7	2	0	22	28	1	14	.281	.400	.356	111	4	9	.983	3	*98*	*99*	C-63	1.1
1913	Cin N	114	330	29	87	11	8	1	38	39	2	40	.264	.345	.355	100	1	2-1	.979	-5	99	89	*C-100	0.4
1914	Cin N	113	313	30	82	13	7	2	25	31	2	30	.262	.332	.367	105	2	6	.973	2	*92*	*98*	*C-106	1.2
1915	Cin N	96	226	23	65	7	2	0	21	33	1	22	.288	.381	.336	116	6	7-3	.981	-3	*93*	*91*	C-72	1.0
1916	Cin N	78	177	10	42	10	1	0	17	24	0	20	.237	.328	.305	97	1	8	.965	-9	75	96	C-51	-0.6
1917	Cin N	58	110	11	32	3	3	1	13	11	1	12	.291	.361	.400	139	5	2	.991	-3	*81*	*82*	C-29	0.4
1918	Chi N	1	0	0	0	0	0	0	0	0	0	0	—	—	—	—	0	0	—	0	*0*	*0*	/C	0.0
Total	10	700	1708	169	453	66	37	6	191	216	11	177	.265	.351	.358	109	24	42-4	.975	-4	*100*	*93*	C-576/1	6.4
CLARKE, BOILERYARD William Jones B 10.18.1868 New York, NY D 7.29.1959 Princeton, NJ BR/TR 5-11.5/170# d5.1																								
1893	Bal N	49	183	23	32	1	3	1	24	19	6	14	.175	.274	.230	34	-18	2	.909	-5	*90*	*100*	C-38,1-11	-1.6
1894	Bal N	28	100	18	24	8	0	1	19	16	3	14	.240	.361	.350	69	-5	2	.903	-1	*121*	*89*	C-23/1-5	-0.2
1895	†Bal N	67	241	38	70	15	3	0	35	13	9	18	.290	.350	.378	85	-5	8	.938	15	*149*	*115*	C-60/1-6	1.2
1896	Bal N	80	300	48	89	14	7	2	71	14	8	12	.297	.345	.410	97	-2	7	.948	-3	*111*	*86*	C-67,1-14	0.0
1897	†Bal N	64	241	32	65	7	1	1	38	9	9		.270	.320	.320	69	-11	5	.939	-9	*102*	*64*	C-59/1-4	-1.2
1898	Bal N	82	285	26	69	5	2	0	27	4	15		.242	.289	.274	60	-15	2	.962	3	*113*	*96*	C-70,1-10	-0.5
1899	Bos N	60	223	25	50	3	2	2	32	10	4		.224	.270	.283	47	-17	2	.940	3	*119*	*88*	C-60	-0.8
1900	Bos N	81	270	35	85	5	2	1	30	9	3		.315	.344	.359	84	-7	0	.928	4	*101*	*107*	C-67/1-8	0.3
1901	Was A	110	422	58	118	15	5	3	54	23	12		.280	.335	.360	94	-3	7	.952	-5	*108*	*96*	*C-107/1-3	0.2
1902	Was A	87	291	31	78	15	0	6	40	23	4		.268	.330	.381	96	-1	1	**.972**	-4	*99*	*102*	C-87	0.3
1903	Was A	126	465	35	111	14	6	2	38	15	7		.239	.273	.308	72	-16	12	.981	-14	80	94	1-88,C-37	-2.9
1904	Was A	85	275	23	58	8	1	0	17	17	5		.211	.269	.247	65	-10	5	.977	-4	*73*	*125*	C-52,1-29	-1.1
1905	NY N	31	50	2	9	0	0	1	4	4	0		.180	.241	.240	42	-4	1	.973	-1	66	96	1-15,C-12	-0.4
Total	13	950	3346	394	858	110	32	20	429	176	85	58	.256	.310	.326	75	-114	54	.947	-18	*106*	*98*	C-739,1-193	-6.7
CLARKE, STU William Stuart B 1.24.1906 San Francisco, CA D 8.26.1985 Hayward, CA BR/TR 5-8.5/160# d7.17																								
1929	Pit N	57	178	20	47	5	7	2	21	19	1	21	.264	.338	.404	81	-6	3	.919	-9	97	78	S-41,3-15/2	-0.9
1930	Pit N	4	9	2	4	0	1	0	2	1	0	0	.444	.500	.667	178	1	0	1.000	-1	64	0	/2-2	0.0
Total	2	61	187	22	51	5	8	2	23	20	1	21	.273	.346	.417	86	-5	3	.919	-9	97	78	/S-41,3-15,2-3	-0.9
CLARKSON, BUZZ James Buster B 3.13.1915 Hopkins, SC D 1.18.1989 Jeannette, PA BR/TR 5-11/210# d4.30																								
1952	Bos N	14	25	3	5	0	0	0	1	3	0	3	.200	.286	.200	38	-2	0-0	.938	-2	60	0	/S-6,3-2	-0.4
CLARY, ELLIS Ellis "Cat" B 9.11.1916 Valdosta, GA D 6.2.2000 Valdosta, GA BR/TR 5-8/160# d6.7 C7																								
1942	Was A	76	240	34	66	9	0	0	16	45	2	25	.275	.394	.313	101	4	2-0	.969	-15	86	75	2-69/3-2	-0.7
1943	Was A	73	254	36	65	19	1	0	19	44	2	31	.256	.370	.339	112	7	8-4	.945	-6	90	49	3-68/S	0.3
	StL A	23	69	15	19	2	0	0	5	11	0	6	.275	.375	.304	98	0	1-2	.972	0	107	135	3-14/2-3	0.1

Year	Tm Lg	G	AB	R	H	2B	3B	HR	RBI	BB-IB	HP	SO	AVG	OBP	SLG	AOPS	ABR	SB-CS	FA	FR	Rng	Thr	G at Pos	BFW
	Year	96	323	51	84	21	1	0	24	55	2	37	.260	.371	.331	109	7	9-6	.949	-5	93	62	3-82/2-3,S	0.4
1944	†StL A	25	49	6	13	1	1	0	4	12	0	9	.265	.410	.327	106	1	1-0	1.000	-0	94	118	3-11/2-6	0.1
1945	StL A	26	38	6	8	1	0	1	2	2	0	3	.211	.250	.316	61	-2	0-2	.947	0	106	171	3-16/2-3	-0.3
Total	4	223	650	97	171	32	2	1	46	114	4	74	.263	.376	.323	103	10	12-8	.953	-20	94	78	3-111/2-81,S	-0.5
CLAY, DAIN Dain Elmer "Sniffy" or "Ding-A-Ling" B 7.10.1919 Hicksville, OH D 8.28.1994 Chula Vista, CA BR/TR 5-10.5/160# d6.12																								
1943	Cin N	49	93	19	25	2	4	0	9	8	1	14	.269	.333	.376	106	0	1	.936	-2	81	103	O-33(1-29-3)	-0.3
1944	Cin N	110	356	51	89	15	0	0	17	17	3	18	.250	.290	.292	67	-16	8	.993	-2	103	45	O-98(5-93-0)	-2.2
1945	Cin N	153	656	81	184	29	2	1	50	37	2	58	.280	.321	.335	84	-15	19	.989	1	104	77	*O-152(CF)	-1.9
1946	Cin N	121	435	52	99	17	0	2	22	53	5	40	.228	.318	.280	73	-14	11	**.988**	-5	94	85	*O-120(11-107-2)	-2.5
Total	4	433	1540	203	397	63	6	3	98	115	11	130	.258	.314	.312	79	-45	39	.987	-9	99	73	O-403(17-381-5)	-6.9
CLAY, BILL Frederick C. B 11.23.1874 Baltimore, MD D 10.12.1917 York, PA TL ?/175# d8.8																								
1902	Phi N	3	8	1	2	0	0	0	1	0	0		.250	.250	.250	54	0	0	.750	-1	0	0	/O-3(LF)	-0.1
CLAYTON, ROYCE Royce Spencer B 1.2.1970 Burbank, CA BR/TR 6/183# d9.20																								
1991	SF N	9	26	0	3	1	0	0	2	1-0	0	6	.115	.148	.154	-15	-4	0-0	.880	-6	30	29	/S-8	-1.0
1992	SF N	98	321	31	72	7	4	4	24	26-3	0	63	.224	.281	.308	71	-14	8-4	.973	-2	99	107	S-94/3	-0.9
1993	SF N	153	549	54	155	21	5	6	70	38-2	5	91	.282	.331	.372	91	-7	11-10	.963	4	98	126	*S-153	0.7
1994	SF N	108	385	38	91	14	6	3	30	30-2	3	74	.236	.295	.327	66	-21	23-3	.973	8	106	105	*S-108	0.0
1995	SF N	138	509	56	124	29	3	5	58	38-1	3	109	.244	.298	.342	71	-22	24-9	.969	3	104	115	*S-136	-0.6
1996	†StL N	129	491	64	136	20	4	6	35	33-4	1	89	.277	.321	.371	83	-13	33-15	.972	0	101	101	*S-113	-0.2
1997	StL N★	154	576	75	153	39	5	9	61	33-4	3	109	.266	.306	.398	84	-15	30-10	.973	11	106	107	*S-153	1.1
1998	StL N	90	355	59	83	19	1	4	29	40-1	2	51	.234	.313	.327	70	-15	19-6	.970	5	111	96	S-89	-0.1
	†Tex A	52	186	30	53	12	1	5	24	13-0	1	32	.285	.330	.441	96	-1	5-5	.972	0	102	76	S-52	0.2
1999	†Tex A	133	465	69	134	21	5	14	52	39-1	4	100	.288	.346	.445	96	-3	8-6	.961	5	107	100	*S-133	1.0
2000	Tex A	148	513	70	124	21	5	14	54	42-1	3	92	.242	.301	.384	71	-24	11-7	.977	-6	95	87	*S-148	-1.8
2001	Chi A	135	433	62	114	21	4	9	60	33-2	3	72	.263	.315	.393	84	-11	10-7	.988	-1	103	94	*S-133	-0.2
2002	Chi A	112	342	51	86	14	2	7	35	20-0	3	67	.251	.295	.365	74	-13	5-1	.989	6	101	113	*S-109	0.1
2003	Mil N	146	483	49	110	16	1	11	39	49-10	3	92	.228	.301	.333	67	-24	5-2	.977	-15	96	82	*S-141	-2.7
Total	13	1605	5634	708	1438	255	46	97	573	435-31	34	1047	.255	.310	.368	79	-187	192-85	.973	14	102	102	*S-1570/3	-4.4
CLEMENS, CHET Chester Spurgeon B 5.10.1917 San Fernando, CA D 2.10.2002 San Clemente, CA BR/TR 6/175# d9.13 Mil 1944-46																								
1939	Bos N	9	23	2	5	0	0	0	1	1	0	3	.217	.250	.217	29	-2	1	.867	-1	102	0	/O-7(LF)	-0.3
1944	Bos N	19	17	7	3	1	1	0	2	2	0	2	.176	.263	.353	69	-1	0	1.000	0	123	0	/O-7(LF)	-0.1
Total	2	28	40	9	8	1	1	0	3	3	0	5	.200	.256	.275	46	-3	1	.905	-1	108	0	/O-14(LF)	-0.4
CLEMENS, CLEM Clement Lambert "Count" (born Clement Lambert Ulatowski) B 11.21.1886 Chicago, IL D 11.2.1967 St.Petersburg, FL BR/TR 5-11/176# d5.15																								
1914	Chi F	13	27	4	4	0	0	0	2	3	0	0	.148	.233	.148	6	-4	0	.950	-0	*144*	*69*	/C-8	-0.4
1915	Chi F	11	22	3	3	1	0	0	3	1	0	0	.136	.174	.182	0	-3	0	1.000	-0	*122*	*61*	/C-9,2-2	-0.3
1916	Chi N	10	15	0	0	0	0	0	0	1	0	6	.000	.063	.000	-72	-3	0	.941	0	128	101	/C-9	-0.3
Total	3	34	64	7	7	1	0	0	5	5	0	6	.109	.174	.125	-15	-10	0	.962	0	*132*	*76*	/C-26,2-2	-1.0
CLEMENS, DOUG Douglas Horace B 6.9.1939 Leesport, PA BL/TR 6/180# d10.2																								
1960	StL N	1	0	0	0	0	0	0	0	0-0	0	0	—	—	—	—	0	0-0	1.000	0	165	0	/O(RF)	0.0
1961	StL N	6	12	1	2	1	0	0	0	3-0	0	1	.167	.333	.250	53	-1	0-0	.667	-1	46	0	/O-3(2-0-2)	-0.2
1962	StL N	48	93	12	22	1	1	1	12	17-1	0	19	.237	.355	.301	71	-3	0-0	.974	-2	91	0	O-34(7-1-27)	-0.7
1963	StL N	5	6	1	1	0	0	1	2	1-0	0	2	.167	.286	.667	151	0	0-0	1.000	1	103	863	/O-3(2-0-1)	0.1
1964	StL N	33	78	8	16	4	3	1	9	6-0	1	16	.205	.271	.372	73	-3	0-0	.970	1	97	166	O-22(17-0-5)	-0.4
	Chi N	54	140	23	39	10	2	2	12	18-2	1	22	.279	.363	.421	116	4	0-0	.923	0	95	172	O-40(1-2-38)	0.2
	Year	87	218	31	55	14	5	3	21	24-2	2	38	.252	.331	.404	100	1	0-0	.937	1	96	170	O-62(18-2-43)	-0.2
1965	Chi N	128	340	36	75	11	0	4	26	38-4	2	53	.221	.300	.288	66	-14	5-8	.981	-1	93	132	*O-105(44-13-49)	-2.3
1966	Phi N	79	121	10	31	1	0	1	15	16-0	2	25	.256	.353	.289	81	-2	1-0	1.000	1	108	68	O-28(24-2-3)/1	-0.2
1967	Phi N	69	73	2	13	5	0	0	4	8-0	1	15	.178	.262	.247	48	-5	0-0	1.000	-1	64	0	O-10(9-0-1)	-0.6
1968	Phi N	29	57	6	12	1	1	2	8	7-1	0	13	.211	.292	.368	99	0	0-0	1.000	0	103	93	O-17(3-0-15)	-0.1
Total	9	452	920	99	211	34	7	12	88	114-8	7	166	.229	.317	.321	78	-24	6-8	.969	-2	95	119	O-263(109-18-142)/1	-4.2
CLEMENS, BOB Robert Baxter B 8.9.1886 Odessa, MO D 4.5.1964 Marshall, MO BR/TR 5-9/163# d9.17																								
1914	StL A	7	13	1	3	0	1	0	3	2	1	1	.231	.375	.385	134	1	0-2	.750	-0	76	201	/O-5(2-1-2)	-0.1
CLEMENT, WALLY Wallace Oakes B 7.21.1881 Auburn, ME D 11.1.1953 Coral Gables, FL BL/TR 5-11/175# d8.17																								
1908	Phi N	16	36	0	8	3	0	0	1	0	0		.222	.222	.306	66	-1	2	1.000	2	71	312	/O-8(LF)	0.0
1909	Phi N	3	3	0	0	0	0	0	0	0	0		.000	.000	.000	-99	-1	0	—	0			H	-0.1
	Bro N	92	340	35	88	8	4	0	17	18	0		.259	.296	.306	90	-5	11	.965	2	108	129	O-88(84-0-4)	-0.9
	Year	95	343	35	88	8	4	0	17	18	0		.257	.294	.303	88	-6	11	.965	2	108	129	O-88(84-0-4)	-1.0
Total	2	111	379	35	96	11	4	0	18	18	0		.253	.287	.303	86	-7	13	.970	4	104	149	/O-96(92-0-4)	-1.0
CLEMENTE, EDGARD Edgard Alexis (Velazquez) (born Edgard Alexis Velazquez) B 12.15.1975 Santurce, P.R. BR/TR 5-11/188# d9.10																								
1998	Col N	11	17	2	6	0	1	0	2	2-0	0	8	.353	.421	.471	110	0	0-0	.857	-1	56	0	/O-7(0-1-6)	-0.1
1999	Col N	57	162	24	41	10	2	8	25	7-0	0	46	.253	.282	.488	71	-8	0-0	.972	0	104	91	O-49(2-45-4)	-0.7
2000	Ana A	46	78	4	17	2	0	0	5	0-0	1	27	.218	.228	.244	19	-10	0-1	1.000	0	95	180	O-32(15-5-12),D-11	-1.0
Total	3	114	257	30	64	12	3	8	32	9-0	1	81	.249	.276	.412	60	-18	0-1	.974	-1	97	108	/O-88(17-51-22),D-11	-1.8
CLEMENTE, ROBERTO Roberto (Walker) "Bob" B 8.18.1934 Carolina, P.R. D 12.31.1972 San Juan, P.R. BR/TR 5-11/175# d4.17 HF1973																								
1955	Pit N	124	474	48	121	23	11	5	47	18-3	2	60	.255	.284	.382	76	-18	2-5	.978	11	**109**	181	*O-118(1-10-111)	-1.3
1956	Pit N	147	543	66	169	30	7	7	60	13-2	4	58	.311	.330	.431	105	3	6-6	.957	3	102	152	*O-139(26-22-101)/2-2,3	-0.1
1957	Pit N	111	451	42	114	17	7	4	30	23-1	0	45	.253	.288	.348	72	-19	0-4	.979	7	117	101	*O-109(0-14-97)	-1.8
1958	Pit N	140	519	69	150	24	10	6	50	31-1	0	41	.289	.327	.408	96	-4	8-2	.982	19	**122**	190	*O-135(RF)	1.1
1959	Pit N	105	432	60	128	17	7	4	50	15-2	3	51	.296	.322	.396	91	-7	2-3	.948	3	108	112	*O-104(RF)	-0.9
1960	†Pit N★	144	570	89	179	22	6	16	94	39-4	2	72	.314	.357	.458	121	16	4-5	.971	-2	90	139	*O-142(RF)	0.8
1961	Pit N★	146	572	100	201	30	10	23	89	35-10	3	59	**.351**	.390	.559	148	38	4-1	.969	10	98	**206**	*O-144(0-1-144)	3.8
1962	Pit N★	144	538	95	168	28	9	10	74	35-9	1	73	.312	.352	.454	115	11	6-4	.973	7	105	154	*O-142(RF)	0.7
1963	Pit N★	152	600	77	192	23	8	17	76	31-6	4	64	.320	.356	.470	135	26	12-2	.958	-7	90	96	*O-151(0-8-143)	1.1
1964	Pit N★	155	622	95	**211**	40	7	12	87	51-16	2	87	**.339**	.388	.484	145	38	5-2	.968	4	106	114	*O-154(RF)	3.3
1965	Pit N★	152	589	91	194	21	14	10	65	43-14	5	78	**.329**	.378	.463	136	27	8-0	.968	5	102	152	*O-145(0-5-143)	2.5
1966	Pit N★	154	638	105	202	31	11	29	119	46-13	0	109	.317	.360	.536	146	38	7-5	.965	10	113	153	*O-154(0-1-154)	3.8
1967	Pit N★	147	585	103	**209**	26	10	23	110	41-17	3	103	**.357**	.400	.554	170	51	9-1	.970	4	97	154	*O-145(0-2-144)	5.0
1968	Pit N	132	502	74	146	18	12	18	57	51-**27**	1	77	.291	.355	.482	152	31	2-3	.984	7	**116**	77	*O-131(RF)	3.1
1969	Pit N★	138	507	87	175	20	**12**	19	91	56-16	3	73	.345	.411	.544	170	47	4-1	.980	6	104	152	*O-135(RF)	4.8
1970	†Pit N★	108	412	65	145	22	10	14	60	38-14	2	66	.352	.407	.556	159	34	3-0	.966	3	98	171	*O-104(RF)	3.2
1971	†Pit N★	132	522	82	178	29	8	13	86	26-5	0	65	.341	.370	.502	146	29	1-2	.993	7	**112**	122	*O-124(RF)	3.1
1972	†Pit N✳	102	378	68	118	19	7	10	60	29-7	0	49	.312	.356	.479	140	18	0-0	1.000	3	115	72	O-94(RF)	1.8
Total	18	2433	9454	1416	3000	440	166	240	1305	621-167	35	1230	.317	.359	.475	130	359	83-46	.973	100	105	140	*O-2370(27-63-2302)/2-2,3	34.0
CLEMENTS, ED Edward B Philadelphia, PA d6.24																								
1890	Pit N	1	1	0	0	0	0	0	0	0	0	0	.000	.000	.000	-99	0	0	.400	-1	52	0	/S	-0.1
CLEMENTS, JACK John J. B 7.24.1864 Philadelphia, PA D 5.23.1941 Norristown, PA BL/TL 5-8.5/204# d4.22 M1 OF Total (8-LF 7-CF 26-RF)																								
1884	Phi U	41	177	37	50	13	2	3		9			.282	.317	.429	134	2		.764	-2	210	155	O-22(5-0-17),C-20/S	0.1
	Phi N	9	30	3	7	0	0	0	0	4		8	.233	.324	.233	82	0		.827	-2			/C-9	-0.1
1885	Phi N	52	188	14	36	11	3	1	14	2		30	.191	.200	.298	61	-8		.891	-4			C-41,O-11(2-7-2)	-0.9
1886	Phi N	54	185	15	38	5	1	0	11	7		34	.205	.234	.243	45	-12	4	.930	7			C-47/O-7(1-0-6)	-0.2
1887	Phi N	66	246	48	69	13	7	1	47	9	4	24	.280	.317	.402	93	-3	7	.940	8			C-59/3-4,S-3	0.8
1888	Phi N	86	326	26	80	8	4	1	32	10	4	36	.245	.276	.304	80	-8	3	.927	0			C-85/O(RF)	0.0
1889	Phi N	78	310	51	88	17	1	4	35	29	1	21	.284	.347	.384	96	-3	3	.916	-6			C-78	-0.2
1890	Phi N	97	381	64	120	23	8	7	74	45	3	30	.315	.392	.472	148	23	10	.944	4	*105*	*80*	C-91/1-5,M	3.0
1891	Phi N	107	423	58	131	29	4	4	75	43	5	19	.310	.380	.426	131	18	3	.927	-6	*93*	*86*	*C-107/1-2	1.8

Year	Tm Lg	G	AB	R	H	2B	3B	HR	RBI	BB-IB	HP	SO	AVG	OBP	SLG	AOPS	ABR	SB-CS	FA	FR	Rng	Thr	G at Pos	BFW
1892	Phi N	109	402	50	106	25	6	8	76	43	3	40	.264	.339	.415	128	14	7	.950	13	135	66	*C-109	3.3
1893	Phi N	94	376	64	107	20	3	17	80	39	5	29	.285	.360	.489	125	12	3	.942	-3	128	69	*C-92/1	1.4
1894	Phi N	48	171	26	60	6	5	3	36	26	9	9	.351	.461	.497	134	12	6	.940	-5	91	70	C-48	0.8
1895	Phi N	88	322	64	127	27	2	13	75	22	8	7	.394	.446	.612	170	34	3	.969	-8	94	89	*C-88	2.6
1896	Phi N	57	184	35	66	5	7	5	45	17	5	14	.359	.427	.543	157	15	2	.966	-3	104	103	C-53	1.4
1897	Phi N	55	185	18	44	4	2	6	36	12	6		.238	.305	.378	82	-6	3	.962	-2	103	80	C-49	-0.3
1898	StL N	99	335	39	86	19	5	3	41	21	7		.257	.314	.370	94	-4	1	.971	-12	74	90	C-86	-0.7
1899	Cle N	4	12	1	3	0	0	0	0	0	1		.250	.308	.250	58	-1	0	.938	-1	61	155	/C-4	-0.1
1900	Bos N	16	42	6	13	1	0	1	10	3	1		.310	.370	.405	101	0	0	.948	1	99	63	C-10	0.2
Total	17	1160	4295	619	1231	226	60	77	687	341	62	301	.287	.348	.421	116	85	55	.937	-21	71	55	*C-1076/O-41R,1-8,3-4,S-4	12.9
CLEMONS, VERNE Verne James "Stinger" or "Tubby" B 9.8.1891 Clemons, IA D 5.5.1959 Bay Pines, FL BR/TR 5-9.5/190# d4.22																								
1916	StL A	4	7	0	1	1	0	0	0	0	0	1	.143	.143	.286	30	-1	0	.889	-0	85	160	/C-2	-0.1
1919	StL N	88	239	14	63	13	2	2	22	26	0	13	.264	.336	.360	116	6	4	.982	3	104	97	C-75	1.6
1920	StL N	112	338	17	95	10	6	1	36	30	0	12	.281	.340	.355	103	2	1-1	.977	-7	85	90	*C-103	0.3
1921	StL N	117	341	29	109	16	2	2	48	33	0	17	.320	.380	.396	108	5	0-0	.985	-1	95	95	*C-107	1.0
1922	StL N	71	160	9	41	4	0	0	15	18	0	5	.256	.331	.281	62	-8	1-0	.996	2	106	121	C-63	-0.3
1923	StL N	57	130	6	37	9	1	0	13	10	2	11	.285	.345	.369	90	-1	0-0	.981	1	105	102	C-41	0.2
1924	StL N	25	56	3	18	3	0	0	6	2	0	3	.321	.345	.375	94	0	0-0	.983	-1	98	90	C-17	-0.1
Total	7	474	1271	78	364	56	11	5	140	119	2	62	.286	.348	.360	99	3	6-1	.983	-4	96	98	C-408	2.6
CLENDENON, DONN Donn Alvin B 7.15.1935 Neosho, MO BR/TR 6-3.5/210# d9.22																								
1961	Pit N	9	35	7	11	1	1	0	2	5-0	0	10	.314	.400	.400	113	1	0-0	1.000	0	96	129	/O-8(1-0-7)	0.0
1962	Pit N	80	222	39	67	8	5	7	28	26-3	1	58	.302	.376	.477	128	9	16-4	.990	-3	81	127	1-52,O-19(16-1-2)	0.4
1963	Pit N	154	563	65	155	28	7	15	57	39-3	5	136	.275	.326	.430	116	11	22-13	.991	5	114	131	*1-151	0.8
1964	Pit N	133	457	53	129	23	8	12	64	26-2	2	96	.282	.321	.446	115	8	12-8	.989	-1	98	123	*1-119	-0.1
1965	Pit N	162	612	89	184	32	14	14	96	48-7	5	128	.301	.351	.467	129	23	9-9	.984	2	112	132	*1-158/3	1.4
1966	Pit N	155	571	80	171	22	10	28	98	52-7	2	142	.299	.358	.520	141	30	8-7	.985	-1	103	146	*1-152	2.0
1967	Pit N	131	478	46	119	15	2	13	56	34-4	1	107	.249	.298	.370	90	-7	4-4	.988	5	122	118	*1-123	-1.1
1968	Pit N	158	584	63	150	20	6	17	87	47-4	1	163	.257	.309	.399	114	9	10-3	.990	8	124	112	*1-155	0.9
1969	Mon N	38	129	14	31	6	1	4	14	6-1	0	32	.240	.272	.395	85	-3	0-2	.987	3	144	112	1-24,O-11(9-1-1)	-0.3
	†NY N	72	202	31	51	5	0	12	37	19-4	2	62	.252	.321	.455	113	3	3-2	.984	-3	81	131	1-58/O(LF)	-0.4
	Year	110	331	45	82	11	1	16	51	25-5	2	94	.248	.303	.432	103	0	3-4	.985	0	100	125	1-82,O-12(10-1-1)	-0.7
1970	NY N	121	396	65	114	18	3	22	97	39-4	1	91	.288	.348	.515	129	15	4-1	.991	-0	96	102	*1-100	0.8
1971	NY N	88	263	29	65	10	0	11	37	21-3	1	78	.247	.302	.411	103	0	1-2	.985	-2	88	101	1-72	-0.8
1972	StL N	61	136	13	26	4	0	4	9	17-4	0	37	.191	.279	.309	68	-6	1-2	.986	2	127	132	1-36	-0.7
Total	12	1362	4648	594	1273	192	57	159	682	379-46	21	1140	.274	.328	.442	117	93	90-57	.988	15	108	124	*1-1200/O-39(27-2-10),3	2.9
CLEVELAND, ELMER Elmer Ellsworth B 9.15.1862 Washington, DC D 10.8.1913 Zimmerman, PA BR/TR 5-11/190# d8.29																								
1884	Cin U	29	115	24	37	9	2	0		4			.322	.345	.435	125	0		.843	1	99	0	3-29	0.2
1888	NY N	9	34	6	8	0	2	2	7	3	0	1	.235	.297	.529	161	2	1	.667	-4	42	0	/3-9	-0.2
	Pit N	30	108	10	24	2	1	2	9	5	2	23	.222	.270	.315	94	-1	3	.831	-5	90	86	3-30	-0.6
	Year	39	142	16	32	2	3	4	16	8	2	24	.225	.276	.366	111	2	4	.806	-10	80	67	3-39	-0.8
1891	Col AA	12	41	12	7	0	0	0	4	12	1	9	.171	.370	.171	59	-1	4	.843	1	111	43	3-12	0.0
Total	3	80	298	52	76	11	5	4	20	24	3	33	.255	.317	.366	111	0	8	.830	-8	93	37	/3-80	-0.6
CLIBURN, STAN Stanley Gene B 12.19.1956 Jackson, MS BR/TR 6/195# d5.6 twb-Stew																								
1980	Cal A	54	56	7	10	2	0	2	6	3-0	0	9	.179	.217	.321	48	-4	0-0	.971	-1	60	93	C-54	-0.5
CLIFT, HARLOND Harlond Benton "Darkie" B 8.12.1912 ElReno, OK D 4.27.1992 Yakima, WA BR/TR 5-11/180# d4.17																								
1934	StL A	147	572	104	149	30	10	14	56	84	2	100	.260	.357	.421	92	-7	7-2	.929	-14	89	98	*3-141	-1.4
1935	StL A	137	475	101	140	26	4	11	69	83	6	39	.295	.406	.436	113	12	0-3	.934	-6	102	63	*3-127/2-6	0.9
1936	StL A	152	576	145	174	40	11	20	73	115	7	68	.302	.424	.514	127	28	12-4	.951	5	105	99	*3-152	3.4
1937	StL A☆	155	571	103	175	36	7	29	118	98	6	80	.306	.413	.546	139	36	8-5	.947	41	129	141	*3-155	7.4
1938	StL A	149	534	119	155	25	7	34	118	118	5	67	.290	.423	.554	143	39	10-5	.962	15	102	105	*3-149	5.3
1939	StL A	151	526	90	142	25	2	15	84	111	5	55	.270	.402	.411	106	10	4-3	.953	13	107	99	*3-149	2.6
1940	StL A	150	523	92	143	29	5	20	87	104	2	62	.273	.396	.463	119	19	9-8	.959	9	110	104	*3-147	3.0
1941	StL A	154	584	108	149	33	9	17	84	113	0	93	.255	.376	.430	109	10	6-4	.959	5	104	94	*3-154	2.0
1942	StL A	143	541	108	148	39	4	7	55	106	2	48	.274	.394	.399	122	22	6-4	.941	-1	101	106	*3-141/S	2.6
1943	StL A	105	379	43	88	11	3	3	25	54	1	37	.232	.329	.301	83	-7	5-4	.950	16	118	98	*3-104	1.1
	Was A	8	30	4	9	0	0	0	4	5	1	3	.300	.417	.300	115	1	0-0	.968	-1	69	0	/3-8	0.0
	Year	113	409	47	97	11	3	3	29	59	2	40	.237	.336	.301	85	-6	5-4	.951	15	114	91	*3-112	1.1
1944	Was A	12	44	4	7	3	0	0	3	3	0	3	.159	.213	.227	27	-4	0-0	.842	-2	90	95	3-12	-0.7
1945	Was A	119	375	49	79	12	0	8	53	76	4	58	.211	.349	.307	99	4	2-1	.934	-4	98	95	*3-111	0.1
Total	12	1582	5730	1070	1558	309	62	178	829	1070	41	713	.272	.390	.441	115	163	69-43	.948	75	106	100	*3-1550/2-6,S	26.3
CLIFTON, FLEA Herman Earl B 12.12.1909 Cincinnati, OH D 12.22.1997 Cincinnati, OH BR/TR 5-10/160# d4.29																								
1934	Det A	16	16	3	1	0	0	0	1	1	0	2	.063	.118	.063	-52	-4	0-0	1.000	1	141	0	/3-4,2	-0.3
1935	†Det A	43	110	15	28	5	0	0	9	5	1	13	.255	.293	.300	56	-7	2-1	.934	-1	89	74	3-21/2-5,S-4	-0.7
1936	Det A	13	26	5	5	1	0	0	1	4	0	3	.192	.300	.231	33	-3	0-1	.926	-1	84	95	/S-6,3-2,2	-0.3
1937	Det A	15	43	4	5	1	0	0	2	7	0	10	.116	.240	.140	-2	-7	3-0	.958	-2	94	66	/3-7,S-4,2-3	-0.7
Total	4	87	195	27	39	7	0	0	13	17	1	28	.200	.268	.236	30	-21	5-2	.937	-3	94	85	/3-34,S-14,2-10	-2.0
CLINE, MONK John P. B 3.3.1858 Louisville, KY D 9.23.1916 Louisville, KY BL/TL 5-4/150# d7.4																								
1882	Bal AA	44	172	18	38	6	2	0		3			.221	.234	.279	79	-3		.825	4	165	87	O-39(1-38-0)/S-8,2-2,3	-0.1
1884	Lou AA	94	396	91	115	16	7	2	39	27	4		.290	.342	.381	142	20		.875	4	142	44	*O-90(8-81-3)/S-6	1.9
1885	Lou AA	2	9	0	2	1	0	0	2	0	0		.222	.222	.333	74	0		1.000	-0	0	0	/O(LF)3	0.0
1888	KC AA	73	293	45	69	13	2	0	19	20	2		.235	.289	.294	82	-6	29	.883	5	192	135	O-70(32-0-38)/2-3,3	-0.2
1891	Lou AA	19	70	11	21	3	1	0	11	16	0	2	.300	.430	.371	131	4	2	.929	-1	72	0	O-19(LF)	0.2
Total	5	232	940	165	245	39	12	2	71	66	6	2	.261	.313	.334	110	15	31	.868	12	157	78	O-219(61-119-41)/S-14,2-5,3-3	1.8
CLINE, TY Tyrone Alexander B 6.15.1939 Hampton, SC BL/TL 6-0.5/170# d9.14																								
1960	Cle A	7	26	2	8	1	1	0	2	0-0	0	4	.308	.308	.423	99	0	0-0	1.000	1	132	0	/O-6(CF)	0.0
1961	Cle A	12	43	9	9	2	1	0	1	6-0	2	1	.209	.333	.302	73	-1	1-0	1.000	-1	84	0	O-12(CF)	-0.3
1962	Cle A	118	375	53	93	15	5	2	28	28-0	5	50	.248	.308	.331	74	-14	5-4	.992	-3	101	62	*O-107(CF)	-2.0
1963	Mil N	72	174	17	41	2	1	0	10	10-0	2	31	.236	.283	.259	58	-9	2-1	.992	3	106	162	O-62(CF)	-0.8
1964	Mil N	101	116	22	35	4	2	1	13	8-0	3	22	.302	.359	.397	113	2	0-1	.982	2	110	296	O-54(3-49-2)/1-6	0.3
1965	Mil N	123	220	27	42	5	3	0	10	16-2	0	50	.191	.246	.241	37	-19	2-2	.969	4	110	162	O-86(17-58-12)/1-5	-1.9
1966	Chi N	7	17	3	6	0	0	0	2	0-0	0	2	.353	.353	.353	96	0	1-0	1.000	-0	94	0	/O-5(CF)	0.0
	Atl N	42	71	12	18	0	0	0	6	3-0	2	11	.254	.303	.254	56	-4	2-1	1.000	-0	125	160	O-19(7-5-10)/1-6	-0.5
	Year	49	88	15	24	0	0	0	8	3-0	2	13	.273	.312	.273	63	-4	3-1	1.000	-0	117	117	O-24(7-10-10)/1-6	-0.5
1967	Atl N	10	8	0	0	0	0	0	0	0-0	1	3	.000	.111	.000	-66	-2	0-0	1.000	0	129	0	/O(LF)	-0.2
	SF N	64	122	18	33	5	5	0	4	9-0	1	13	.270	.326	.393	106	1	2-1	1.000	-1	101	0	O-37(17-21-3)	-0.2
	Year	74	130	18	33	5	5	0	4	9-0	2	16	.254	.312	.369	96	-1	2-1	1.000	-1	101	0	O-38(18-21-3)	-0.4
1968	SF N	116	291	37	65	6	3	1	28	11-1	1	26	.223	.253	.275	59	-15	0-2	.971	1	100	171	O-70(48-13-10),1-24	-2.2
1969	Mon N	101	209	26	50	5	3	2	12	32-1	2	22	.239	.346	.321	87	-3	4-3	.988	1	110	103	O-41(7-35-0),1-17	-0.4
1970	Mon N	2	2	0	1	0	0	0	0	0-0	0	0	.500	.500	.500	169	0	0-0	—	0			H	0.0
	†Cin N	48	63	13	17	7	1	0	8	12-1	0	11	.270	.387	.413	114	2	1-2	.966	1	124	138	O-20(6-8-6)/1-2	0.2
	Year	50	65	13	18	7	1	0	8	12-1	0	11	.277	.390	.415	115	2	1-2	.966	1	124	138	O-20(6-8-6)/1-2	0.2
1971	Cin N	69	97	12	19	1	0	0	1	18-0	2	16	.196	.333	.206	57	-5	2-2	1.000	-1	95	0	O-28(6-21-1)/1-2	-0.7
Total	12	892	1834	251	437	53	25	6	125	153-5	21	262	.238	.304	.304	72	-67	22-19	.986	6	105	113	O-548(112-402-44)/1-62	-8.7
CLINES, GENE Eugene Anthony B 10.6.1946 San Pablo, CA BR/TR 5-9/170# d6.28 C17																								
1970	Pit N	31	37	4	15	2	0	0	3	2-0	0	5	.405	.436	.459	143	2	2-1	1.000	-1	45	0	/O-7(2-2-3)	0.1
1971	†Pit N	97	273	52	84	12	4	1	24	22-0	3	36	.308	.366	.392	115	6	15-6	.981	4	100	202	O-74(20-43-13)	0.9
1972	†Pit N	107	311	52	104	15	6	0	17	16-1	2	47	.334	.369	.421	127	10	12-6	.958	-2	91	138	O-83(38-17-39)	0.6

Year	Tm Lg	G	AB	R	H	2B	3B	HR	RBI	BB-IB	HP	SO	AVG	OBP	SLG	AOPS	ABR	SB-CS	FA	FR	Rng	Thr	G at Pos	BFW
1973	Pit N	110	304	42	80	11	3	1	23	26-0	3	36	.263	.327	.329	84	-6	8-7	.968	-2	96	121	O-77(7-45-25)	-1.2
1974	†Pit N	107	276	29	62	5	1	0	14	30-2	4	40	.225	.307	.250	60	-14	14-2	.989	5	111	137	O-78(19-51-11)	-1.0
1975	NY N	82	203	25	46	6	3	0	10	11-1	1	21	.227	.269	.286	57	-13	4-4	.982	5	95	297	O-60(35-34-2)	-1.1
1976	Tex A	116	446	52	123	12	3	0	38	16-0	4	52	.276	.304	.316	81	-12	11-9	.987	3	103	126	*O-103(96-5-4),D-10	-1.6
1977	Chi N	101	239	27	70	12	2	3	41	25-2	1	25	.293	.358	.397	93	-1	1-2	.986	-6	68	88	O-63(50-3-11)	-1.0
1978	Chi N	109	229	31	59	10	2	0	17	21-1	1	28	.258	.321	.319	71	-8	4-3	.978	-1	85	155	O-66(35-10-24)	-1.2
1979	Chi N	10	10	0	2	0	0	0	0	0-0	0	1	.200	.200	.200	9	-1	0-0	—	0			/H	-0.2
Total	10	870	2328	314	645	85	24	5	187	169-7	19	291	.277	.329	.341	88	-37	71-40	.979	6	95	151	O-611(302-210-132)/D-10	-5.7
CLINGMAN, BILLY William Frederick B 11.21.1869 Cincinnati, OH D 5.14.1958 Cincinnati, OH BB/TR 5-11/150# d9.9																								
1890	Cin N	7	27	2	7	1	0	0	5	1	0	0	.259	.286	.296	70	-1	0	.892	-1	107	181	/S-6,2	-0.1
1891	Cin AA	1	5	0	1	1	0	0	0	0	0	0	.200	.200	.400	66	0	0	.667	-1	84	0	/2	-0.1
1895	Pit N	107	386	69	99	16	4	0	45	41	2	43	.256	.331	.319	72	-15	19	.888	12	114	102	*3-107	0.0
1896	Lou N	121	423	57	99	10	2	2	37	57	3	51	.234	.329	.281	64	-20	19	.925	24	**114**	104	*3-121	0.5
1897	Lou N	115	403	61	92	14	7	2	47	37	5		.228	.301	.313	64	-21	14	**.947**	30	**124**	106	*3-115	0.9
1898	Lou N	**154**	538	65	138	12	6	0	50	51	5		.257	.327	.301	81	-12	15	.914	7	112	101	3-79,S-74/O(CF)2	0.0
1899	Lou N	110	369	68	97	15	5	2	45	46	3		.263	.349	.347	91	-3	13	.913	-3	106	112	*S-110	-0.1
1900	Chi N	47	159	15	33	6	0	0	11	17	2		.208	.292	.245	51	-10	6	.872	-11	91	107	S-47	-1.8
1901	Was A	137	480	66	116	10	7	2	55	42	4		.242	.308	.304	71	-18	10	**.932**	**22**	**107**	112	*S-137	0.7
1903	Cle A	21	64	10	18	1	1	0	7	11	0		.281	.387	.328	118	2	2	.932	1	114	64	2-11/S-7,3-3	0.4
Total	10	820	2854	413	700	86	32	8	302	303	24	94	.245	.323	.306	74	-98	98	.919	81	116	103	3-425,S-381/2-14,O(CF)	0.4
CLINTON, JIM James Lawrence "Big Jim" B 8.10.1850 New York, NY D 9.3.1921 Brooklyn, NY BR/TR 5-8.5/174# d5.18 U1 ▲ OF NA (8-CF 9-RF)																								
1872	Eck NA	25	98	11	24	4	1	0	6	0		3	.245	.245	.306	81	-1	0-1	.712	-4	105	0	3-11/O-9(0-7-2),2-3,C-2,S-2,P	-0.4
1873	Res NA	9	39	5	9	2	0	0	4	0		2	.231	.231	.282	56	-2	0-0	.687	-2	84	58	/3-9	-0.3
1874	Atl NA	2	11	3	2	1	0	0	2	0		2	.182	.182	.273	49	0	0-0	.444	-1	72	0	/2O(CF)	-0.1
1875	Atl NA	22	81	3	10	0	0	0	0	0		0	.123	.123	.123	-16	-8	0-0	.830	3	125	75	P-17/O-7(RF),1-5,2	0.0
1876	Lou N	16	65	8	22	2	0	0	0	0		0	.338	.338	.369	115	0		.783	0	168	231	O-14(RF)/1P	0.0
1882	Wor N	26	98	9	16	2	0	0	3	7		13	.163	.219	.184	30	-7		.734	-4	67	63	O-26(21-1-4)	-1.1
1883	Bal AA	94	399	69	125	16	8	0		27			.313	.357	.393	137	17		.842	4	102	85	*O-92(LF)/2-2	1.6
1884	Bal AA	104	437	82	118	12	6	4		29	13		.270	.334	.352	119	10		.807	-4	83	161	*O-104(37-67-0)/2	0.3
1885	Cin AA	105	408	48	97	5	5	0	34	15	7		.238	.277	.275	73	-13		.877	-2	78	114	*O-105(CF)	-1.7
1886	Bal AA	23	83	8	15	1	0	0	6	4	1		.181	.227	.193	33	-6	3	.894	-1	26	142	O-23(CF)	-0.7
Total	4 NA	58	229	22	45	7	1	0	12	0	0	7	.197	.197	.236	43	-11	0-1	.000	-4	94	29	/3-20,P-18,O-17R,1-5,2-5,S-2,C-2	-0.8
Total	6	368	1490	224	393	38	19	4	43	82	21	13	.264	.311	.323	101	1	3-0	.838	-6	85	123	O-364(150-196-18)/2-3,P1	-1.6
CLINTON, LOU Luciean Louis B 10.13.1937 Ponca City, OK D 12.6.1997 Wichita, KS BR/TR 6-1/185# d4.22																								
1960	Bos A	96	298	37	68	17	5	6	37	20-1	3	66	.228	.278	.379	75	-11	4-3	.966	1	112	77	O-89(RF)	-1.4
1961	Bos A	17	51	4	13	2	1	0	3	2-0	0	10	.255	.283	.333	63	-3	0-0	1.000	2	106	270	O-13(RF)	-0.2
1962	Bos A	114	398	63	117	24	10	18	75	34-3	1	79	.294	.349	.540	132	16	2-1	.979	0	100	104	*O-103(RF)	0.9
1963	Bos A	148	560	71	130	23	7	22	77	49-6	1	118	.232	.294	.416	94	-6	0-0	.982	7	**118**	73	*O-146(RF)	-1.0
1964	Bos A	37	120	15	31	4	3	3	6	9-1	0	33	.258	.310	.417	95	-1	1-0	1.000	4	106	308	O-35(RF)	0.1
	LA A	91	306	30	76	18	0	9	38	31-0	1	40	.248	.317	.395	108	3	3-0	.985	2	86	241	O-86(RF)	0.0
	Year	128	426	45	107	22	3	12	44	40-1	1	73	.251	.315	.401	104	2	4-0	.990	6	92	**261**	*O-121(RF)	0.1
1965	Cal A	89	222	29	54	12	3	1	8	23-1	1	37	.243	.316	.338	88	-3	2-3	.983	2	99	156	O-73(1-0-72)	-0.7
	KC A	1	1	0	0	0	0	0	0	0-0	0	0	.000	.000	.000	-99	0	0-0	—	-0	0	0	/O(RF)	0.0
	Cle A	12	34	2	6	1	0	1	2	3-0	0	7	.176	.243	.294	51	-2	0-0	.941	0	91	189	/O-9(9-1-1)	-0.3
	Year	102	257	31	60	13	3	2	10	26-1	1	44	.233	.305	.331	83	-6	2-3	.977	2	98	160	O-83(10-1-74)	-1.0
1966	NY A	80	159	18	35	10	2	5	21	16-1	0	27	.220	.288	.403	101	0	0-0	.976	-1	97	77	O-63(5-1-57)	-0.4
1967	NY A	6	4	1	2	1	0	0	2	1-1	0	1	.500	.600	.750	308	1	0-0	—	-0	0	0	/O(LF)	0.1
Total	8	691	2153	270	532	112	31	65	269	188-14	7	418	.247	.308	.418	99	-6	12-7	.980	17	104	132	O-619(16-2-603)	-2.9
CLOUGH, ED Edgar George "Big Ed" or "Spec" B 10.28.1906 Wiconisco, PA D 1.30.1944 Harrisburg, PA BL/TL 6/188# d8.28 ▲																								
1924	StL N	7	14	0	1	0	0	0	1	0	0	3	.071	.071	.071	-63	-3	0-0	1.000	1	139	227	/O-6(5-0-1)	-0.2
1925	StL N	3	4	0	1	0	0	0	0	0	0	0	.250	.250	.250	28	0	0-0	1.000	-0	42	0	/P-3	0.0
1926	StL N	1	1	0	0	0	0	0	0	0	0	0	.000	.000	.000	-96	0	0	—	-0	0	0	/P	0.0
Total	3	11	19	0	2	0	0	0	1	0	0	3	.105	.105	.105	-44	-3	0-0	1.000	1	139	227	/O-6(5-0-1),P-4	-0.2
CLYBURN, DANNY Danny B 4.6.1974 Lancaster, SC BR/TR 6-3/220# d9.15																								
1997	Bal A	2	3	0	0	0	0	0	0	0-0	0	2	.000	.000	.000	-99	-1	0-0	—	-0	0	0	/O(LF)	-0.1
1998	Bal A	11	25	6	7	0	0	1	3	1-0	0	10	.280	.308	.400	83	-1	0-0	1.000	-0	108	0	/O-8(5-0-5),D	-0.1
1999	TB A	28	81	8	16	4	0	3	5	7-0	1	21	.198	.270	.358	58	-6	0-0	1.000	2	106	244	O-24(14-0-10)/D-4	-0.4
Total	3	41	109	14	23	4	0	4	8	8-0	1	33	.211	.271	.358	59	-8	0-0	1.000	2	105	188	/O-33(20-0-15),D-5	-0.6
CLYMER, OTIS Otis Edgar B 1.27.1876 Pine Grove, PA D 2.27.1926 St.Paul, MN BB/TR 5-11/180# d4.14																								
1905	Pit N	96	365	74	108	11	5	0	23	19	1		.296	.332	.353	102	0	23	.986	-2	61	188	O-89(4-0-85)/1	-0.6
1906	Pit N	11	45	7	11	0	1	0	1	3	0		.244	.292	.289	78	-1	1	.900	-1	69	0	O-11(RF)	-0.3
1907	Pit N	22	66	8	15	2	0	0	4	5	3		.227	.311	.258	77	-1	4	.923	-2	0	0	O-15(RF)/1	-0.5
	Was A	57	206	30	65	5	5	1	16	18	4		.316	.382	.403	163	15	18	.912	-2	64	0	O-51(27-1-24)/1	1.1
1908	Was A	110	368	32	93	11	4	1	35	20	0		.253	.291	.313	105	1	19	.933	-1	185	299	O-82(1-0-81),2-13/3-2	-0.4
1909	Was A	45	138	11	27	5	2	0	6	17	0		.196	.284	.261	76	-3	7	.922	-2	65	91	O-41(0-1-40)	-0.9
1913	Chi N	30	105	16	24	5	1	0	7	14	0	18	.229	.319	.295	76	-3	9-5	.933	-3	92	57	O-26(0-24-2)	-0.7
	Bos N	14	37	4	12	3	1	0	6	3	0	3	.324	.375	.459	135	2	2-1	.880	-1	104	0	O-11(1-7-4)	0.0
	Year	44	142	20	36	8	2	0	13	17	0	21	.254	.333	.338	91	-1	11-6	.918	-4	95	41	O-37(1-31-6)	-0.7
Total	6	385	1330	182	355	42	19	2	98	99	8	21	.267	.322	.332	106	10	83-6	.939	-15	94	142	0-326(33-33-262)/2-13,1-3,3-2	-2.3
CLYMER, BILL William Johnston "Derby Day Bill" B 12.18.1873 Philadelphia, PA D 12.26.1936 Philadelphia, PA d6.25 C1																								
1891	Phi AA	3	11	0	0	0	0	0	0	1	1	2	.000	.154	.000	-55	-2	1	.867	-1	55	0	/S-3	-0.3
COACHMAN, PETE Bobby Dean B 11.11.1961 Cottonwood, AL BR/TR 5-9/175# d8.18																								
1990	Cal A	16	45	3	14	3	0	0	5	1-0	2	7	.311	.354	.378	107	0	0-1	.958	0	100	183	/3-9,2-2,D-2	0.0
COAN, GIL Gilbert Fitzgerald B 5.18.1922 Monroe, NC BL/TR 6/180# d4.27																								
1946	Was A	59	134	17	28	3	2	3	9	7	4	37	.209	.269	.328	70	-6	2-2	.969	-1	102	0	O-29(27-0-2)	-1.0
1947	Was A	11	42	5	21	3	2	0	3	5	0	6	.500	.553	.667	245	8	2-1	1.000	1	103	128	O-11(RF)	0.9
1948	Was A	138	513	56	119	13	9	7	60	41	7	78	.232	.298	.333	70	-26	23-9	.970	12	**119**	116	*O-131(LF)	-2.1
1949	Was A	111	358	36	78	7	8	3	25	29	1	58	.218	.278	.307	56	-26	9-6	.975	0	98	115	O-97(68-29-0)	-3.1
1950	Was A	104	366	58	111	17	4	7	50	28	4	46	.303	.359	.429	106	2	10-5	.970	-0	105	55	O-98(95-3-1)	-0.4
1951	Was A	135	538	85	163	25	7	9	62	39	6	62	.303	.357	.426	113	8	8-5	.965	**18**	**121**	**162**	*O-132(LF)	1.6
1952	Was A	107	332	50	68	11	6	5	20	32	1	35	.205	.277	.319	68	-16	9-4	.984	0	101	77	O-86(LF)	-2.2
1953	Was A	68	168	28	33	1	4	2	17	22	3	23	.196	.301	.286	60	-10	7-0	1.000	3	114	62	O-46(45-1-0)	-0.8
1954	Bal A	94	265	29	74	11	1	2	20	16	1	17	.279	.320	.351	91	-4	9-4	.968	-3	100	21	O-67(36-32-0)	-1.1
1955	Bal A	61	130	18	31	7	1	1	11	13-0	1	15	.238	.313	.331	79	-4	4-2	.983	0	85	201	O-43(42-0-1)	-0.5
	Chi A	17	17	0	3	0	0	0	1	0-0	0	5	.176	.176	.176	-5	-3	0-0	1.000	0	127	0	/O-3(1-0-2)	-0.3
	Year	78	147	18	34	7	1	1	12	13-0	1	20	.231	.298	.313	68	-7	4-2	.984	0	86	195	O-46(43-0-3)	-0.8
	NY N	9	13	0	2	0	0	0	0	0-0	0	1	.154	.154	.154	-18	-2	0-0	1.000	-0	88	0	/O-6(1-2-4)	-0.3
1956	NY N	4	1	2	0	0	0	0	0	0-0	0	1	.000	.000	.000	-99	0	0-0	—	0			H	0.0
Total	11	918	2877	384	731	98	44	39	278	232-0	28	384	.254	.316	.359	84	-79	83-38	.973	29	108	99	O-749(664-67-21)	-9.3
COBB, JOE Joseph Stanley (born Joseph Stanley Serafin) B 1.24.1895 Hudson, PA D 12.24.1947 Allentown, PA BR/TR 5-9/170# d4.25 Mil 1918																								
1918	Det A	1	0	0	0	0	0	0	0	1	0	0	—	1.000	—	210	0	0	—	0			H	0.0
COBB, TY Tyrus Raymond "The Georgia Peach" B 12.18.1886 Narrows, GA D 7.17.1961 Atlanta, GA BL/TR 6-1/175# d8.30 M6 HF1936 OF Total (35-LF 2194-CF 706-RF)																								
1905	Det A	41	150	19	36	6	0	1	15	10	0		.240	.287	.300	86	-2	2	.958	2	141	96	O-41(2-39-0)	-0.2
1906	Det A	98	358	45	113	15	5	1	34	19	3		.316	.355	.394	131	12	23	.961	4	112	134	O-96(18-55-24)	1.2
1907	†Det A	150	605	97	**212**	28	14	5	**119**	24	5		**.350**	.380	**.468**	**164**	**40**	**53**	.961	12	156	**267**	*O-150(RF)	4.9
1908	†Det A	150	581	88	**188**	**36**	**20**	4	**108**	34	6		**.324**	.367	**.475**	**166**	**40**	39	.944	3	132	101	*O-150(RF)	4.1

Year	Tm Lg	G	AB	R	H	2B	3B	HR	RBI	BB-IB	HP	SO	AVG	OBP	SLG	AOPS	ABR	SB-CS	FA	FR	Rng	Thr	G at Pos	BFW
1909	†Det A	156	573	**116**	**216**	33	10	**9**	**107**	48	6		**.377**	**.431**	**.517**	**190**	**59**	**76**	.946	2	120	162	*O-156(RF)	**6.0**
1910	Det A	140	506	**106**	194	35	13	8	91	64	4		**.383**	**.456**	**.551**	**202**	61	65	.958	3	112	87	*O-137(0-111-26)	6.3
1911	Det A	146	591	**147**	**248**	**47**	**24**	8	**127**	44	8		**.420**	.467	**.621**	**193**	**72**	**83**	.957	7	111	95	*O-146(CF)	**6.6**
1912	Det A	140	553	120	**226**	30	23	7	83	43	5		**.409**	.456	**.584**	**203**	**72**	61	.940	-4	98	96	*O-140(CF)	5.6
1913	Det A	122	428	70	167	18	16	4	67	58	4	31	**.390**	**.467**	.535	**196**	54	51	.947	-1	97	112	*O-118(0-116-2)/2	4.6
1914	Det A	98	345	69	127	22	11	2	57	57	6	22	**.368**	.466	**.513**	188	41	35-17	.949	-14	79	61	O-96(CF)	2.3
1915	Det A	**156**	563	**144**	**208**	31	13	3	99	118	10	43	**.369**	**.486**	.487	**182**	**67**	**96**-38	.951	-9	88	95	*O-156(CF)	5.7
1916	Det A	145	542	**113**	201	31	10	5	68	78	2	39	.371	.452	.493	177	55	**68**-24	.953	-8	93	85	*O-143(CF)/1	4.6
1917	Det A	152	588	107	**225**	**44**	**24**	6	102	61	4	34	**.383**	**.444**	**.570**	**210**	**76**	**55**	.973	4	100	116	*O-152(0-123-29)	**7.4**
1918	Det A	111	421	83	161	19	**14**	3	64	41	2	21	**.382**	**.440**	.515	**196**	**48**	34	.975	-1	99	88	0-95(0-92-3),1-13/P-2,23	**4.3**
1919	Det A	124	497	92	**191**	36	13	1	70	38	1	22	**.384**	.429	.515	168	45	28	.973	-6	88	107	*O-123(CF)	3.1
1920	Det A	112	428	86	143	28	8	2	63	58	2	28	.334	.416	.451	133	23	15-10	.966	-11	90	57	*O-112(CF)	0.4
1921	Det A	128	507	124	197	37	16	12	101	56	3	19	.389	.452	.596	167	52	22-15	.970	6	96	**169**	*O-121(CF),M	4.8
1922	Det A	137	526	99	211	42	16	4	99	55	4	24	.401	.462	.565	172	58	9-13	.980	-5	93	96	*O-134(0-133-1),M	4.2
1923	Det A	145	556	103	189	40	7	6	88	66	3	14	.340	.413	.469	135	30	9-10	.969	3	107	92	*O-141(CF),M	2.5
1924	Det A	155	625	115	211	38	10	4	79	85	1	18	.338	.418	.450	126	27	23-14	**.986**	0	101	82	*O-155(CF),M	2.0
1925	Det A	121	415	97	157	31	12	12	102	65	5	12	.378	.468	.598	**171**	48	13-9	.948	-5	96	82	*O-105(0-101-4)/PM	3.5
1926	Det A	79	233	48	79	18	5	4	62	26	1	2	.339	.408	.511	137	13	9-4	.950	-5	89	80	O-55(15-39-1),M	0.5
1927	Phi A	134	490	104	175	32	7	5	93	67	5	12	.357	.440	.482	131	26	22-16	.969	-5	96	73	*O-127(0-52-75)	1.2
1928	Phi A	95	353	54	114	27	4	1	40	34	4	16	.323	.389	.431	112	8	6-8	.964	-1	104	85	O-85(RF)	-0.1
Total	24	3035	11434	2246	4189	724	295	117	1938	1249	94	357	.366	.433	.512	167	1025	897-178	.961	-29	104	108	*O-2934C/1-14,P-3,2-2,3	85.5
COBLE, DAVE David Lamar B 12.24.1912 Monroe, NC D 10.15.1971 Orlando, FL BR/TR 6-1/183# d5.1																								
1939	Phi N	15	25	2	7	1	0	0	0	0	0	3	.280	.280	.320	63	-1	0	.938	-2	*49*	*121*	C-13	-0.3
COCHRAN, GEORGE George Leslie B 2.12.1889 Rusk, TX D 5.21.1960 Harbor City, CA TR d7.29																								
1918	Bos A	24	60	7	7	0	0	0	3	10	2	6	.117	.264	.117	15	-6	3	.960	-1	102	133	3-22/S	-0.7
COCHRANE, DAVE David Carter B 1.31.1963 Riverside, CA BB/TR 6-2/180# d9.2 OF Total (42-LF 12-RF)																								
1986	Chi A	19	62	4	12	2	0	1	2	5-1	0	22	.194	.254	.274	42	-5	0-0	.872	-4	95	33	3-18/S	-0.9
1989	Sea A	54	102	13	24	4	1	3	7	14-0	1	27	.235	.333	.382	98	0	0-2	.905	-5	89	151	S-30/1-9,3-9,2-4,0-3(LF),C-2	-0.6
1990	Sea A	15	20	0	3	0	0	0	0	0-0	0	8	.150	.150	.150	-16	-3	0-0	1.000	1	58	0	/S-5,1-3,3-3,C	-0.2
1991	Sea A	65	178	16	44	13	0	2	22	9-0	1	38	.247	.286	.354	76	-6	0-1	.969	-6	84	0	O-26(23-0-3),C-19,3-13/1-4,D	-1.2
1992	Sea A	65	152	10	38	5	0	2	12	12-0	1	34	.250	.309	.322	77	-5	1-0	.879	-1	83	293	O-25(16-0-9),C-21,3-10/1-3,S-3,D-2,2	-0.6
Total	5	218	514	43	121	24	1	8	43	40-1	3	129	.235	.294	.333	73	-19	1-3	.925	-15	82	125	/O-54L,3-53,C-43,S-39,1-19,2-5,D	-3.5
COCHRANE, MICKEY Gordon Stanley B 4.6.1903 Bridgewater, MA D 6.28.1962 Lake Forest, IL BL/TR 5-10.5/180# d4.14 M5 C1 HF1947																								
1925	Phi A	134	420	69	139	21	5	6	55	44	2	19	.331	.397	.448	107	5	7-4	.984	-5	*96*	*80*	*C-133	0.7
1926	Phi A	120	370	50	101	8	9	8	47	56	0	15	.273	.369	.408	97	-2	5-2	.975	12	*109*	*96*	*C-115	1.7
1927	Phi A	126	432	80	146	20	6	12	80	50	2	7	.338	.409	.495	127	17	9-6	.986	5	***117***	*72*	*C-123	2.8
1928	Phi A	131	468	92	137	26	12	10	57	76	3	25	.293	.395	.464	122	17	7-5	.966	5	*109*	*63*	*C-130	2.8
1929	†Phi A	135	514	113	170	37	8	7	95	69	2	8	.331	.412	.475	123	21	7-7	.983	6	*93*	*62*	*C-135	3.3
1930	†Phi A	130	487	110	174	42	5	10	85	55	1	18	.357	.424	.526	133	27	5-0	**.993**	6	*99*	*77*	*C-130	3.8
1931	†Phi A	122	459	87	160	31	6	17	89	56	3	21	.349	.423	.553	146	31	2-3	.986	11	***128***	*89*	*C-117	4.5
1932	Phi A	139	518	118	152	35	4	23	112	100	4	22	.293	.412	.510	132	29	0-1	**.993**	9	*107*	*92*	*C-137/O(LF)	4.2
1933	Phi A	130	429	104	138	30	4	15	60	106	3	22	.322	**.459**	.515	156	43	8-6	.989	-6	*88*	*82*	*C-128	4.1
1934	†Det A★	129	437	74	140	32	1	2	76	78	4	26	.320	.428	.412	117	17	8-4	.988	1	***135***	*119*	*C-124,M	2.4
1935	†Det A☆	115	411	93	131	33	3	5	47	96	4	15	.319	.452	.450	139	32	5-5	.989	-0	***129***	*83*	*C-110,M	3.6
1936	Det A	44	126	24	34	8	0	2	17	46	0	15	.270	.465	.381	111	6	1-1	.983	-6	*118*	*61*	C-42,M	0.2
1937	Det A	27	98	27	30	10	1	2	12	25	1	4	.306	.452	.490	134	7	0-1	1.000	-2	*89*	*69*	C-27,M	0.6
Total	13	1482	5169	1041	1652	333	64	119	832	857	29	217	.320	.419	.478	127	250	64-45	.985	37	*109*	*82*	*C-1451/O(LF)	34.7
COCKMAN, JIM James B 4.26.1873 Guelph, ON, CAN D 9.28.1947 Guelph, ON, CAN BR/TR 5-6/145# d9.28																								
1905	NY A	13	38	5	4	0	0	0	2	4	0		.105	.190	.105	-5	-4	2	.875	-2	90	0	3-13	-0.6
COCKRELL, ALAN Atlee Alan B 12.5.1962 Kansas City, KS BR/TR 6-2/210# d9.7 C1																								
1996	Col N	9	8	0	2	1	0	0	2	0-0	0	4	.250	.222	.375	50	-1	0-0	—	-0	0	0	/O(RF)	-0.1
COFFEY, JACK John Francis B 1.28.1887 New York, NY D 2.14.1966 Bronx, NY BR/TR 5-11/178# d6.23																								
1909	Bos N	73	257	21	48	4	4	0	20	11	3		.187	.229	.233	41	-19	2	.896	-7	102	67	S-73	-2.6
1918	Det A	22	67	7	14	0	2	0	4	8	1	6	.209	.303	.269	75	-2	2	.957	-2	89	64	2-22	-0.4
	Bos A	15	44	5	7	1	0	1	2	3	0	2	.159	.213	.250	40	-3	2	.955	1	115	0	3-14/2	-0.2
	Year	37	111	12	21	1	2	1	6	11	1	8	.189	.268	.261	62	-6	4	.959	-0	93	61	2-23,3-14	-0.6
Total	2	110	368	33	69	5	6	1	26	22	4	8	.188	.241	.242	48	-24	6	.896	-7	102	67	/S-73,2-23,3-14	-3.2
COFFIE, IVANON Ivanon Angelino B 5.16.1977 Willemstad, Curacao, Netherlands Antilles BL/TR 6-1/190# d7.15																								
2000	Bal A	23	60	6	13	4	1	0	6	5-0	1	11	.217	.284	.317	56	-4	1-0	.971	0	113	40	3-15/S-4,D	-0.3
COGGINS, FRANK Franklin B 5.22.1944 Griffin, GA BB/TR 6-2/187# d9.10																								
1967	Was A	19	75	9	23	3	0	1	8	2-0	0	17	.307	.321	.387	114	1	1-0	.964	3	121	101	2-19	0.6
1968	Was A	62	171	15	30	6	1	0	7	9-2	0	33	.175	.215	.222	34	-14	1-1	.953	-5	92	109	2-52	-1.7
1972	Chi N	6	1	1	0	0	0	0	0	1-0	0	0	.000	.500	.000	48	0	0-0	—	0			H	0.0
Total	3	87	247	25	53	9	1	1	15	12-2	0	50	.215	.249	.271	59	-13	2-1	.957	-2	100	107	/2-71	-1.1
COGGINS, RICH Richard Allen B 12.7.1950 Indianapolis, IN BL/TL 5-8/170# d8.29																								
1972	Bal A	16	39	5	13	4	0	0	1	1-0	0	6	.333	.350	.436	129	1	0-2	1.000	4	172	148	O-13(0-9-6)	0.5
1973	†Bal A	110	389	54	124	19	9	7	41	28-2	0	24	.319	.363	.468	134	16	17-9	.987	1	102	88	*O-101(0-39-76)/D	1.4
1974	†Bal A	113	411	53	100	13	3	4	32	29-3	5	31	.243	.299	.319	81	-11	26-6	.984	-3	102	37	*O-105(2-30-87)	-1.6
1975	Mon N	13	37	1	10	3	1	0	4	1-0	0	7	.270	.289	.405	87	-1	0-0	1.000	-1	89	0	O-10(9-0-2)	-0.2
	NY A	51	107	7	24	1	0	1	6	7-0	0	16	.224	.272	.262	52	-7	3-3	.970	1	105	118	O-36(3-25-8)/D-9	-0.7
1976	NY A	7	4	1	1	0	0	0	1	0-0	0	1	.250	.250	.250	47	0	1-0	1.000	0	201	0	/O-2(0-1-1),D	0.0
	Chi A	32	96	4	15	2	0	0	5	6-0	0	15	.156	.206	.177	13	-11	3-1	1.000	-3	81	52	O-26(6-2-23)	-1.6
	Year	39	100	5	16	2	0	0	6	6-0	0	16	.160	.208	.180	14	-11	4-1	1.000	-2	84	51	O-28(6-3-24)/D	-1.6
Total	5	342	1083	125	287	42	13	12	90	72-5	5	100	.265	.312	.361	93	-13	50-21	.986	-1	103	67	O-293(20-106-203)/D-11	-2.2
COGSWELL, ED Edward B 2.25.1854 , England D 7.27.1888 Fitchburg, MA BR/TR 5-8/150# d7.11																								
1879	Bos N	49	236	51	76	8	1	1	18	8		5	.322	.344	.377	135	9		.967	1	78	120	1-49	0.6
1880	Tro N	47	209	41	63	7	3	0	13	11		10	.301	.336	.364	130	6		.961	1	117	76	1-47	0.5
1882	Wor N	13	51	10	7	1	0	0	1	6		6	.137	.228	.157	26	-4		.937	-1	82	128	1-13	-0.6
Total	3	109	496	102	146	16	4	1	32	25		21	.294	.328	.349	121	11		.960	1	95	102	1-109	0.5
COHEN, ALTA Alta Albert "Schoolboy" B 12.25.1908 New York, NY D 3.11.2003 Maplewood, NJ BL/TL 5-10.5/170# d4.15																								
1931	Bro N	1	3	1	2	0	0	0	0	0	0	0	.667	.667	.667	261	1	0	1.000	1	46	1623	/O(RF)	0.2
1932	Bro N	9	32	1	5	1	0	0	1	3	0	7	.156	.229	.188	14	-4	0	.850	1	73	517	/O-8(5-3-0)	-0.4
1933	Phi N	19	32	6	6	1	0	0	1	6	0	4	.188	.316	.219	49	-2	0	1.000	0	116	0	/O-7(LF)	-0.2
Total	3	29	67	8	13	2	0	0	2	9	0	11	.194	.289	.224	42	-5	0	.925	2	90	369	/O-16(12-3-1)	-0.4
COHEN, ANDY Andrew Howard B 10.25.1904 Baltimore, MD D 10.29.1988 ElPaso, TX BR/TR 5-8/155# d6.6 M1 C1 b-Syd																								
1926	NY N	32	35	4	9	0	1	0	8	1	0	2	.257	.278	.314	60	-2	0	.792	0	123	0	2-10,S-10/3-2	-0.2
1928	NY N	129	504	64	138	24	7	9	59	31	2	17	.274	.318	.403	87	-11	3	.969	2	103	115	*2-126/S-3,3	-0.6
1929	NY N	101	347	40	102	12	2	5	47	11	2	15	.294	.319	.383	73	-16	3	.964	10	108	106	2-94/S3	-0.3
Total	3	262	886	108	249	36	10	14	114	43	4	34	.281	.317	.392	81	-29	6	.964	11	105	110	2-230/S-14,3-4	-1.1
COKER, JIMMIE Jimmie Goodwin B 3.28.1936 Holly Hill, SC D 10.29.1991 Throckmorton, TX BR/TR 5-11/195# d9.11																								
1958	Phi N	2	6	0	1	0	0	0	0	0-0	0	0	.167	.167	.167	-12	-1	0-0	1.000	-0	*52*	*0*	/C-2	-0.1
1960	Phi N	81	252	18	54	5	3	6	34	23-2	4	45	.214	.289	.329	69	-11	0-3	.982	-2	*63*	*137*	C-76	-1.1
1961	Phi N	11	25	3	10	1	0	1	4	7-1	0	4	.400	.531	.560	193	4	1-0	.984	-1	*86*	*46*	C-11	0.4
1962	Phi N	5	3	0	0	0	0	0	1	1-0	0	2	.000	.200	.000	-27	-1	0-0	—	0			H	-0.1

Year	Tm Lg	G	AB	R	H	2B	3B	HR	RBI	BB-IB	HP	SO	AVG	OBP	SLG	AOPS	ABR	SB-CS	FA	FR	Rng	Thr	G at Pos	BFW
1963	SF N	4	5	0	1	0	0	0	0	1-0	0	2	.200	.333	.200	58	0	0-0	1.000	-1	*0*	*0*	/C-2	-0.1
1964	Cin N	11	32	3	10	2	0	1	4	3-1	0	5	.313	.371	.469	130	1	0-0	1.000	2	*83*	*172*	C-11	0.4
1965	Cin N	24	61	3	15	2	0	2	9	8-1	0	16	.246	.329	.377	93	0	0-0	.993	3	*86*	*89*	C-19	0.3
1966	Cin N	50	111	9	28	3	0	4	14	8-1	0	5	.252	.300	.387	83	-3	0-1	.979	2	*73*	*171*	C-39/O-2(LF)	0.0
1967	Cin N	45	97	8	18	2	1	2	4	4-1	0	20	.186	.218	.289	39	-8	0-1	.976	0	*82*	*113*	C-34	-0.7
Total	9	233	592	44	137	15	4	16	70	55-7	4	99	.231	.299	.351	77	-19	1-5	.983	4	*72*	*129*	C-194/O-2(LF)	-1.0
COLANGELO, MIKE Michael Gus B 10.22.1976 Teaneck, NJ BR/TR 6-1/185# d6.13																								
1999	Ana A	1	2	0	1	0	0	0	0	1-0	0	0	.500	.667	.500	205	0	0-0	1.000	1	72	2192	/O(LF)	0.1
2001	SD N	50	91	10	22	3	3	2	8	8-0	1	30	.242	.310	.407	91	-2	0-0	.979	-0	95	74	O-40(25-14-4)	-0.3
2002	Oak A	20	23	2	4	1	0	0	0	1-0	1	2	.174	.240	.217	23	-3	0-0	1.000	-1	95	0	O-19(14-1-5)	-0.3
Total	3	71	116	12	27	4	3	2	8	10-0	2	32	.233	.305	.371	80	-5	0-0	.985	-0	94	100	/O-60(40-15-9)	-0.5
COLAVITO, ROCKY Rocco Domenico B 8.10.1933 New York, NY BR/TR 6-3/190# d9.10 C6																								
1955	Cle A	5	9	3	4	2	0	0	0	0-0	0	2	.444	.444	.667	189	1	0-0	1.000	1	133	463	/O-2(RF)	0.2
1956	Cle A	101	322	55	89	11	4	21	65	49-0	2	46	.276	.372	.531	134	15	0-1	.968	-1	99	89	O-98(RF)	1.0
1957	Cle A	134	461	66	116	26	0	25	84	71-0	1	80	.252	.348	.471	124	16	1-6	.962	8	**118**	127	*O-130(RF)	1.8
1958	Cle A	143	489	80	148	26	3	41	113	84-6	2	89	.303	.405	**.620**	183	57	0-2	.981	-0	99	127	*O-129(1-0-129),1-11/P	5.1
1959	Cle A★	**154**	588	90	151	24	0	**42**	111	71-8	2	86	.257	.337	.512	135	27	3-3	.985	5	**114**	81	*O-154(RF)	2.5
1960	Det A	145	555	67	138	18	1	35	87	53-4	4	80	.249	.317	.474	108	4	3-6	.976	1	101	119	*O-144(RF)	-0.2
1961	Det A★	**163**	583	129	169	30	2	45	140	113-2	2	75	.290	.402	.580	156	49	1-2	.975	8	105	132	*O-161(150-0-20)	4.7
1962	Det A★	**161**	601	90	164	30	2	37	112	96-7	2	68	.273	.371	.514	132	29	2-0	.992	12	111	105	*O-161(LF)	3.1
1963	Det A	160	597	91	162	29	2	22	91	84-9	1	78	.271	.358	.437	119	18	0-0	.988	5	105	89	*O-159(142-0-23)	1.4
1964	KC A★	160	588	89	161	31	2	34	102	83-4	5	56	.274	.366	.507	136	31	3-1	.973	-1	100	105	*O-159(3-0-157)	2.0
1965	Cle A★	**162**	592	92	170	25	2	26	**108**	**93**-11	3	63	.287	.383	.468	140	35	1-1	**1.000**	0	100	94	*O-162(1-0-162)	2.5
1966	Cle A★	151	533	68	127	13	0	30	72	76-4	3	81	.238	.336	.432	119	14	2-1	.982	4	104	127	*O-146(RF)	0.8
1967	Cle A	63	191	10	46	9	0	5	21	24-0	1	31	.241	.329	.366	104	2	2-2	.962	-2	93	65	O-50(28-0-31)	-0.4
	Chi A	60	190	20	42	4	1	3	29	25-2	0	10	.221	.306	.300	85	-3	1-1	.977	-4	87	56	O-58(11-0-54)	-1.2
	Year	123	381	30	88	13	1	8	50	49-2	1	41	.231	.317	.333	95	-2	3-3	.970	-5	90	60	*O-108(39-0-85)	-1.6
1968	LA N	40	113	8	23	3	0	3	11	15-1	0	18	.204	.295	.310	89	-1	0-1	1.000	0	98	104	O-33(21-0-13)	-0.4
	NY A	39	91	13	20	2	2	5	13	14-0	1	17	.220	.330	.451	139	4	0-0	.933	-4	63	69	O-28(6-0-22)/P	-0.2
Total	14	1841	6503	971	1730	283	21	374	1159	951-58	29	880	.266	.359	.489	132	298	19-27	.980	32	104	106	*O-1774(524-0-1285)/1-11,P-2	22.7
COLBERN, MIKE Michael Malloy B 4.19.1955 Santa Monica, CA BR/TR 6-3/205# d7.18																								
1978	Chi A	48	141	11	38	5	1	2	20	1-0	2	36	.270	.281	.362	80	-4	0-1	.969	-1	96	104	C-47/D	-0.4
1979	Chi A	32	83	5	20	5	1	0	8	4-0	0	25	.241	.276	.325	61	-5	0-0	.971	-0	77	161	C-32	-0.4
Total	2	80	224	16	58	10	2	2	28	5-0	2	61	.259	.279	.348	73	-9	0-1	.970	-2	89	126	/C-79,D	-0.8
COLBERT, CRAIG Craig Charles B 2.13.1965 Iowa City, IA BR/TR 6/190# d4.6																								
1992	SF N	49	126	10	29	5	2	1	16	9-0	0	22	.230	.277	.325	76	-5	1-0	.994	-3	122	98	C-35/3-9,2-2	-0.6
1993	SF N	23	37	2	6	2	0	1	5	3-1	0	13	.162	.225	.297	40	-3	0-0	.982	2	271	81	C-10/2-2,3	-0.1
Total	2	72	163	12	35	7	2	2	21	12-1	0	35	.215	.266	.319	67	-8	1-0	.990	-1	156	94	/C-45,3-10,2-4	-0.7
COLBERT, NATE Nathan B 4.9.1946 St.Louis, MO BR/TR 6-2/209# d4.14																								
1966	Hou N	19	7	3	0	0	0	0	0	0-0	0	4	.000	.000	.000	-99	-2	0-0	—	0			H	-0.2
1968	Hou N	20	53	5	8	1	0	0	4	1-0	0	23	.151	.164	.170	1	-6	1-1	.952	-1	104	157	O-11(3-5-3)/1-5	-1.0
1969	SD N	139	483	64	123	20	9	24	66	45-7	3	123	.255	.322	.482	128	15	6-4	.990	0	107	85	*1-134	0.5
1970	SD N	156	572	84	148	17	6	38	86	56-8	4	150	.259	.328	.509	126	17	3-5	.991	-8	84	95	*1-153/3	-0.4
1971	SD N★	156	565	81	149	25	3	27	84	63-6	4	119	.264	.339	.462	135	25	5-2	.993	3	104	92	*1-153	1.6
1972	SD N★	151	563	87	141	27	2	38	111	70-14	2	127	.250	.333	.508	147	33	15-6	.996	6	112	88	*1-150	2.9
1973	SD N★	145	529	73	143	25	2	22	80	54-9	8	146	.270	.343	.450	130	21	9-8	.992	5	111	100	*1-144	1.3
1974	SD N	119	368	53	76	16	0	14	54	62-6	1	108	.207	.319	.364	96	-1	10-2	.988	9	133	80	1-79,O-48(LF)	0.2
1975	Det A	45	156	16	23	4	2	4	18	17-0	0	52	.147	.231	.276	41	-13	0-2	.982	-4	72	80	1-44/D	-2.2
	Mon N	38	81	10	14	4	1	4	11	5-3	1	31	.173	.230	.395	68	-4	0-0	.988	-1	83	123	1-22	-0.7
1976	Mon N	14	40	5	8	2	0	2	6	9-1	0	16	.200	.347	.400	107	1	3-1	1.000	1	90	644	/O-7(LF),1-6	0.2
	Oak A	2	5	0	0	0	0	0	0	1-1	0	3	.000	.167	.000	-50	-1	0-0	—	0			/D-2	-0.1
Total	10	1004	3422	481	833	141	25	173	520	383-55	23	902	.243	.322	.451	120	85	52-31	.991	10	103	91	1-890/O-66(58-5-3),D-3,3	2.1
COLBRUNN, GREG Gregory Joseph B 7.26.1969 Fontana, CA BR/TR 6/200# d7.9																								
1992	Mon N	52	168	12	45	8	0	2	18	6-1	2	34	.268	.294	.351	85	-4	3-2	.992	-1	90	81	1-47	-0.9
1993	Mon N	70	153	15	39	9	0	4	23	6-1	1	33	.255	.282	.392	76	-5	4-2	.995	-1	94	101	1-61	-1.0
1994	Fla N	47	155	17	47	10	0	6	31	9-0	2	27	.303	.345	.484	111	2	1-1	.988	-2	91	92	1-41	-0.3
1995	Fla N	138	528	70	146	22	1	23	89	22-4	6	69	.277	.311	.453	99	-4	11-3	.996	-3	90	97	*1-134	-1.7
1996	Fla N	141	511	60	146	26	2	16	69	25-1	14	76	.286	.333	.438	106	3	4-5	.995	4	111	**124**	*1-134	-0.6
1997	Min A	70	217	24	61	14	0	5	26	8-1	1	38	.281	.307	.415	86	-5	1-2	.988	-0	103	135	1-64/D-2	-1.0
	†Atl N	28	54	3	15	3	0	2	9	2-0	1	11	.278	.316	.444	94	-1	0-0	.984	0	120	60	1-14/D-3	-0.1
1998	Col N	62	122	12	38	8	2	2	13	8-0	1	23	.311	.359	.459	93	-1	3-3	.992	1	125	93	1-27/O-5(RF),C	-0.2
	†Atl N	28	44	6	13	3	0	1	10	2-0	3	11	.295	.367	.432	109	1	1-0	1.000	0	84	41	/1-9,O(RF)D	0.0
	Year	90	166	18	51	11	2	3	23	10-0	4	34	.307	.361	.452	98	0	4-3	.993	1	115	81	1-36/O-6(RF),D-3,C	-0.2
1999	†Ari N	67	135	20	44	5	3	5	24	12-0	4	23	.326	.392	.519	129	6	1-1	.996	1	116	105	1-39/3-2,D-2	0.4
2000	Ari N	116	329	48	103	22	1	15	57	43-2	10	45	.313	.405	.523	129	17	0-1	.989	1	102	96	1-99/3D	0.8
2001	†Ari N	59	97	12	28	8	0	4	18	9-0	4	14	.289	.373	.495	115	3	0-0	.987	-1	160	107	1-14,3-10	0.1
2002	†Ari N	72	171	30	57	16	2	10	27	13-1	0	19	.333	.378	.626	150	11	0-0	.993	-4	64	71	1-40/3-5,D-3	0.5
2003	Sea A	22	58	7	16	1	1	3	7	4-0	0	16	.276	.323	.483	112	1	0-1	.989	-1	68	64	1-14/D-4	-0.2
Total	12	972	2742	336	798	155	12	98	421	169-11	49	439	.291	.340	.464	107	24	29-21	.993	-4	99	102	1-737/D-19,3-18,O-6(RF),C	-4.2
COLE, ALEX Alexander B 8.17.1965 Fayetteville, NC BL/TL 6/170# d7.27																								
1990	Cle A	63	227	43	68	5	4	0	13	28-0	1	38	.300	.379	.357	107	3	40-9	.961	-1	99	104	O-59(CF)/D	0.7
1991	Cle A	122	387	58	114	17	3	0	21	58-2	1	47	.295	.386	.354	106	6	27-17	.970	0	102	118	*O-107(8-101-0)/D-6	0.5
1992	Cle A	41	97	11	20	1	0	0	5	10-0	1	21	.206	.284	.216	44	-7	9-2	.971	-2	80	81	O-24(18-5-2)/D-4	-0.9
	†Pit N	64	205	33	57	3	7	0	10	18-1	0	46	.278	.335	.361	99	-1	7-4	.989	-1	87	151	O-53(0-1-52)	-0.3
1993	Col N	126	348	50	89	9	4	0	24	43-3	2	58	.256	.339	.305	64	-17	30-13	.982	-1	98	111	O-93(CF)	-1.5
1994	Min A	105	345	68	102	15	5	4	23	44-2	1	60	.296	.375	.403	101	2	29-8	.969	1	107	79	*O-100(16-84-0)/D	0.6
1995	Min A	28	79	10	27	3	2	1	14	8-0	1	15	.342	.409	.468	127	3	1-3	.938	-1	93	109	O-23(CF)/D-2	0.1
1996	Bos A	24	72	13	16	5	1	0	7	8-0	0	11	.222	.296	.319	56	-5	5-3	.974	-2	79	90	O-24(CF)	-0.6
Total	7	573	1760	286	493	58	26	5	117	217-8	7	296	.280	.360	.351	91	-16	148-59	.971	-8	98	107	O-483(42-390-54)/D-14	-1.4
COLE, DICK Richard Roy B 5.6.1926 Long Beach, CA BR/TR 6-2/175# d4.27 C1																								
1951	StL N	15	36	4	7	1	0	0	3	6	0	5	.194	.310	.222	45	-3	0-0	.969	3	142	125	2-14	0.1
	Pit N	42	106	9	25	4	0	1	11	15	0	9	.236	.331	.302	69	-4	0-1	.981	-1	92	77	2-34/S-8	-0.4
	Year	57	142	13	32	5	0	1	14	21	0	14	.225	.325	.282	63	-7	0-1	.978	2	105	90	2-48/S-8	-0.3
1953	Pit N	97	235	29	64	13	1	0	23	38	0	26	.272	.374	.336	87	-2	2-2	.965	-5	95	85	S-77/2-7,1	-0.2
1954	Pit N	138	486	40	131	22	5	1	40	41	0	48	.270	.323	.342	75	-17	0-0	.949	-8	100	68	S-66,3-55,2-17	-1.9
1955	Pit N	77	239	16	54	8	3	0	21	18-1	2	22	.226	.285	.285	53	-16	0-0	.935	1	103	112	3-33,2-24,S-12	-1.3
1956	Pit N	72	99	7	21	2	1	0	9	11-0	0	9	.212	.291	.253	49	-7	0-0	.947	-3	106	163	3-18,2-12/S-6	-1.0
1957	Mil N	15	14	1	1	0	0	0	0	3-1	0	5	.071	.235	.071	-13	-2	0-0	.952	0	89	212	2-10/13	-0.2
Total	6	456	1215	106	303	50	10	2	107	132-2	2	124	.249	.322	.312	69	-51	2-3	.961	-13	98	78	S-169,2-118,3-107/1-2	-4.9
COLE, STU Stewart Bryan B 2.7.1966 Charlotte, NC BR/TR 6-1/175# d9.5																								
1991	KC A	9	7	1	1	0	0	0	0	2-0	0	2	.143	.333	.143	37	-1	0-0	1.000	-1	111	0	/2-5,SD	-0.2
COLE, WILLIS Willis Russell B 1.6.1882 Milton Junction, WI D 10.11.1965 Madison, WI BR/TR 5-8/170# d8.22																								
1909	Chi A	46	165	17	39	7	3	0	16	16	1		.236	.308	.315	101	0	3	.889	-5	85	84	O-46(CF)	-0.8
1910	Chi A	22	80	6	14	2	1	0	2	4	1		.175	.224	.225	42	-6	0	.974	1	77	205	O-22(CF)	-0.7
Total	2	68	245	23	53	9	4	0	18	20	2		.216	.281	.286	82	-6	3	.912	-5	82	122	/O-68(CF)	-1.5

Year	Tm Lg	G	AB	R	H	2B	3B	HR	RBI	BB-IB	HP	SO	AVG	OBP	SLG	AOPS	ABR	SB-CS	FA	FR	Rng	Thr	G at Pos	BFW
COLEMAN, CHOO CHOO Clarence B 8.25.1937 Orlando, FL BL/TR 5-9/165# d4.16																								
1961	Phi N	34	47	3	6	1	0	0	4	2-0	1	8	.128	.180	.149	-12	-8	0-0	.977	-1	*92*	*114*	C-14	-0.8
1962	NY N	55	152	24	38	7	2	6	17	11-2	1	24	.250	.303	.441	96	-1	2-4	.995	-6	*80*	*120*	C-44	-0.6
1963	NY N	106	247	22	44	0	0	3	9	24-3	5	49	.178	.264	.215	39	-19	5-5	.969	2	*117*	*142*	C-91/O(LF)	-1.6
1966	NY N	6	16	2	3	0	0	0	0	0-0	0	4	.188	.188	.188	5	-2	0-0	.963	-0	*96*	*79*	/C-5	-0.2
Total	4	201	462	51	91	8	2	9	30	37-5	7	85	.197	.266	.281	52	-30	7-9	.977	-4	*103*	*131*	C-154/O(LF)	-3.2
COLEMAN, CURT Curtis Hancock B 2.18.1887 Salem, OR D 7.1.1980 Newport, OR BL/TR 5-11/180# d4.13																								
1912	NY A	12	37	8	9	4	0	0	4	7	0		.243	.364	.351	99	0	0	.865	-0	113	67	3-10	0.1
COLEMAN, DAVE David Lee B 10.26.1950 Dayton, OH BR/TR 6-3/195# d4.13																								
1977	Bos A	11	12	1	0	0	0	0	0	1-0	0	3	.000	.077	.000	-69	-3	0-0	1.000	-1	59	0	/O-9(3-5-1)	-0.4
COLEMAN, JERRY Gerald Francis B 9.14.1924 San Jose, CA BR/TR 6/170# d4.20 Mil 1952 M1																								
1949	†NY A	128	447	54	123	21	5	2	42	63	2	44	.275	.367	.358	92	-4	8-6	**.981**	5	95	111	*2-122/S-4	0.7
1950	†NY A★	153	522	69	150	19	6	6	69	67	3	38	.287	.372	.381	96	-2	3-2	.977	-12	89	111	*2-152/S-6	-0.6
1951	†NY A	121	362	48	90	11	2	3	43	31	4	36	.249	.315	.315	73	-14	6-1	.968	6	96	123	*2-102,S-18	-0.2
1952	NY A	11	42	6	17	2	1	0	4	5	0	4	.405	.468	.500	180	5	0-1	.971	2	98	200	2-11	0.7
1953	NY A	8	10	1	2	0	0	0	0	0	0	2	.200	.200	.200	9	-1	0-0	1.000	1	102	191	/2-7,S	0.0
1954	NY A	107	300	39	65	7	1	3	21	26	0	29	.217	.278	.277	54	-20	3-0	.977	**15**	114	132	2-79,S-30/3	0.2
1955	†NY A	43	96	12	22	5	0	0	8	11-0	2	11	.229	.321	.281	64	-4	0-2	.966	-1	84	142	S-29,2-13/3	-0.4
1956	†NY A	80	183	15	47	5	1	0	18	12-2	1	33	.257	.305	.295	61	-11	1-2	.979	8	111	136	2-41,S-24,3-18	0.1
1957	†NY A	72	157	23	42	7	2	2	12	20-0	1	21	.268	.354	.376	101	1	1-1	.969	3	105	152	2-45,3-21/S-4	0.6
Total	9	723	2119	267	558	77	18	16	217	235-2	13	218	.263	.340	.339	83	-50	22-15	.976	26	98	122	2-572,S-116/3-41	1.1
COLEMAN, GORDY Gordon Calvin B 7.5.1934 Rockville, MD D 3.12.1994 Cincinnati, OH BL/TR 6-2/218# d9.19																								
1959	Cle A	6	15	5	8	0	1	0	2	1-0	0	2	.533	.563	.667	245	3	0-0	.955	0	184	46	/1-3	0.3
1960	Cin N	66	251	26	68	10	1	6	32	12-1	2	32	.271	.308	.390	89	-4	1-1	.998	7	136	132	1-66	-0.1
1961	†Cin N	150	520	63	149	27	4	26	87	45-11	2	67	.287	.341	.504	120	14	1-3	.991	6	**113**	78	*1-150	1.1
1962	Cin N	136	476	73	132	13	1	28	86	36-4	3	68	.277	.331	.485	113	7	2-3	.989	-1	96	96	*1-128	-0.3
1963	Cin N	123	365	38	90	20	2	14	59	29-1	2	51	.247	.303	.427	105	2	1-0	.987	2	104	94	*1-107	-0.2
1964	Cin N	89	198	18	48	6	2	5	27	13-1	1	30	.242	.291	.369	82	-5	2-0	.990	3	125	92	1-49	-0.4
1965	Cin N	108	325	39	98	19	0	14	57	24-4	1	38	.302	.348	.489	125	11	0-0	.991	-1	90	79	1-89	0.6
1966	Cin N	91	227	20	57	7	0	5	37	16-2	0	45	.251	.299	.348	73	-8	2-1	.986	-1	90	78	1-65	-1.3
1967	Cin N	4	7	0	0	0	0	0	0	1-1	0	0	.000	.125	.000	-55	-1	0-0	1.000	0	112	0	/1-2	-0.2
Total	9	773	2384	282	650	102	11	98	387	177-25	11	333	.273	.324	.448	106	19	9-8	.990	16	107	91	1-659	-0.5
COLEMAN, JOHN John Francis B 3.6.1863 Saratoga Springs, NY D 5.31.1922 Detroit, MI BL/TR (BB 1887) 5-9.5/170# d5.1 ▲																								
1883	Phi N	90	354	33	83	12	8	0	32	15		39	.234	.266	.314	83	-7		.886	6	111	53	P-65,O-31(19-12-0)/2	0.2
1884	Phi N	43	171	16	42	7	2	0	22	8		20	.246	.279	.310	89	-2		.844	3	120	224	O-27(3-19-5),P-21/1-2	0.0
	Phi AA	28	107	16	22	2	3	2		5	0		.206	.241	.336	81	-3		.743	-1	147	165	O-24(11-13-0)/P-3,1-2	-0.4
1885	Phi AA	96	398	71	119	15	11	3	70	25	3		.299	.345	.415	131	13		.844	1	153	170	*O-93(1-17-76)/P-8	1.0
1886	Phi AA	121	492	67	121	18	16	0	65	33	2		.246	.296	.348	100	-2	28	.862	2	122	160	*O-115(0-5-110)/1-6,P-3,2	-0.1
	Pit AA	11	43	3	15	2	1	0	9	2	0		.349	.378	.442	157	3	1	.786	-1	69	0	O-11(LF)	0.1
	Year	132	535	70	136	20	17	0	74	35	2		.254	.302	.355	105	1	29	.858	0	118	148	*O-126(11-5-110)/1-6,P-3,2	0.0
1887	Pit N	115	475	75	139	21	11	2	54	31	1	40	.293	.337	.396	111	8	25	.899	-1	83	83	*O-115(0-2-113)/1-2	0.5
1888	Pit N	116	438	49	101	11	4	0	26	29	4	52	.231	.285	.274	86	-5	15	.928	2	130	66	O-91(0-3-88),1-25	-0.6
1889	Phi AA	6	19	1	1	0	0	0	1	1	0	3	.053	.100	.053	-57	-4	1	.929	0	148	0	/P-5,O(LF)	0.0
1890	Pit N	3	11	1	2	0	0	0	0	3	0	0	.182	.357	.182	66	0	1	1.000	-1	0	0	/O-2(1-0-1),P-2	0.0
Total	8	629	2508	332	645	88	56	7	279	152	10	154	.257	.302	.345	101	1	71	.873	10	123	132	0-510(47-71-393),P-107/1-37,2-2	0.7
COLEMAN, MICHAEL Michael Donnell B 8.16.1975 Nashville, TN BR/TR 5-11/180# d9.1																								
1997	Bos A	8	24	2	4	1	0	0	2	0-0	0	11	.167	.167	.208	-3	-4	1-0	.941	-1	90	0	/O-7(CF)	-0.4
1999	Bos A	2	5	1	1	0	0	0	0	1-0	0	0	.200	.333	.200	39	0	0-0	—	-1	0	0	/O-2(1-1-0)	-0.1
2001	NY A	12	38	5	8	0	0	1	7	0-0	0	15	.211	.205	.289	30	-4	0-1	1.000	-2	51	0	/O-9(1-7-3),D-3	-0.6
Total	3	22	67	8	13	1	0	1	9	1-0	0	26	.194	.203	.254	19	-8	1-1	.960	-4	63	0	/O-18(2-15-3),D-3	-1.1
COLEMAN, ED Parke Edward B 12.1.1901 Canby, OR D 8.5.1964 Oregon City, OR BL/TR 6-2/200# d4.15																								
1932	Phi A	26	73	13	25	7	1	1	13	1	0	6	.342	.351	.507	115	1	1-0	1.000	2	92	299	O-16(RF)	0.2
1933	Phi A	102	388	48	109	26	3	6	68	19	2	51	.281	.318	.410	91	-6	0-0	.948	-2	105	63	O-89(1-0-88)	-1.3
1934	Phi A	101	329	53	92	14	6	14	60	29	2	34	.280	.342	.486	116	5	0-1	.980	1	94	134	O-86(RF)	0.1
1935	Phi A	10	13	0	1	0	0	0	0	0	0	3	.077	.077	.077	-61	-3	0-0	—	-0	0	0	/O(RF)	-0.3
	StL A	108	397	66	114	15	9	17	71	53	1	41	.287	.373	.499	118	9	0-2	.974	-2	90	131	*O-102(RF)	0.1
	Year	118	410	66	115	15	9	17	71	53	1	44	.280	.364	.485	113	7	0-2	.974	-2	90	131	*O-103(RF)	-0.2
1936	StL A	92	137	13	40	5	4	2	34	15	1	17	.292	.366	.431	93	-2	0-0	.939	-2	93	0	O-18(RF)	-0.4
Total	5	439	1337	193	381	67	23	40	246	117	6	152	.285	.345	.459	105	4	1-3	.966	-4	96	112	O-312(1-0-311)	-1.6
COLEMAN, RAY Raymond Leroy B 6.4.1922 Dunsmuir, CA BL/TR 5-11/170# d4.22																								
1947	StL A	110	343	34	89	9	7	2	30	26	1	32	.259	.314	.344	81	-10	2-5	.984	1	100	115	O-93(21-0-73)	-1.4
1948	StL A	17	29	2	5	0	1	0	2	2	0	5	.172	.226	.241	24	-3	1-0	.889	-1	88	0	/O-5(RF)	-0.4
	Phi A	68	210	32	51	6	6	0	21	31	0	17	.243	.340	.329	78	-7	4-3	.978	1	92	166	O-53(0-32-21)	-0.8
	Year	85	239	34	56	6	7	0	23	33	0	22	.234	.327	.318	72	-10	5-3	.972	0	92	153	O-58(0-32-26)	-1.2
1950	StL A	117	384	54	104	25	6	8	55	32	2	37	.271	.330	.430	90	-7	7-5	.985	3	107	86	O-98(27-43-28)	-0.8
1951	StL A	91	341	41	96	16	5	5	55	24	0	32	.282	.329	.402	94	-4	3-4	.975	2	100	138	O-87(47-5-42)	-0.7
	Chi A	51	181	21	50	8	7	3	21	15	0	14	.276	.332	.448	112	1	2-3	.980	3	117	69	O-51(23-29-12)	0.2
	Year	142	522	62	146	24	12	8	76	39	0	46	.280	.330	.418	100	-3	5-7	.977	5	106	113	*O-138(70-34-54)	-0.5
1952	Chi A	85	195	19	42	7	1	2	14	13	0	17	.215	.264	.292	54	-13	0-0	.978	2	104	129	O-73(28-33-15)	-1.4
	StL A	20	46	5	9	3	0	0	1	5	1	4	.196	.288	.261	52	-3	0-0	1.000	-0	107	0	O-16(5-5-6)	-0.4
	Year	105	241	24	51	10	1	2	15	18	1	21	.212	.269	.286	54	-15	0-0	.982	2	105	107	O-89(33-38-21)	-1.8
Total	5	559	1729	208	446	74	33	20	199	148	4	158	.258	.318	.374	84	-46	19-20	.980	11	103	112	O-476(151-147-202)	-5.7
COLEMAN, BOB Robert Hunter B 9.26.1890 Huntingburg, IN D 7.16.1959 Boston, MA BR/TR 6-2/190# d6.13 M3 C3																								
1913	Pit N	24	50	5	9	2	0	0	9	7	0	8	.180	.281	.220	46	-3	0	.978	-3	83	89	C-24	-0.5
1914	Pit N	73	150	11	40	4	1	1	14	15	0	32	.267	.333	.327	101	0	3	.977	2	*113*	*89*	C-72	0.7
1916	Cle A	19	28	3	6	2	0	0	4	7	0	6	.214	.371	.286	92	0	0	.972	-1	99	136	C-12	0.0
Total	3	116	228	19	55	8	1	1	27	29	0	46	.241	.327	.298	87	-3	3	.976	-2	*105*	*94*	C-108	0.2
COLEMAN, VINCE Vincent Maurice B 9.22.1961 Jacksonville, FL BB/TR 6/185# d4.18																								
1985	†StL N	151	636	107	170	20	10	1	40	50-1	0	115	.267	.320	.335	84	-14	**110**-25	.979	5	101	143	*O-150(138-17-10)	0.0
1986	StL N	154	600	94	139	13	8	0	29	60-0	2	98	.232	.301	.280	63	-31	**107**-14	.972	-1	96	111	*O-149(131-20-0)	-2.1
1987	†StL N	151	623	121	180	14	10	3	43	70-0	3	126	.289	.363	.358	90	-8	**109**-22	.970	-0	93	146	*O-150(LF)	0.2
1988	StL N★	153	616	77	160	20	10	3	38	49-4	1	111	.260	.313	.339	87	-11	**81**-27	.971	-3	92	152	*O-150(127-24-0)	-1.0
1989	StL N★	145	563	94	143	21	9	2	28	50-0	2	90	.254	.316	.334	84	-12	**65**-10	.962	-10	86	63	*O-142(LF)	-1.7
1990	StL N	124	497	73	145	18	9	6	39	35-1	2	88	.292	.340	.400	103	1	**77**-17	.981	2	96	135	*O-120(118-0-2)	1.0
1991	NY N	72	278	45	71	7	5	1	17	39-0	0	47	.255	.347	.327	91	-2	37-14	.979	-7	82	135	O-70(CF)	-0.7
1992	NY N	71	229	37	63	11	1	2	21	27-3	2	41	.275	.355	.358	104	2	24-9	.991	-2	93	73	O-61(41-21-0)	0.1
1993	NY N	92	373	64	104	14	8	2	25	21-1	0	58	.279	.316	.375	86	-9	38-13	.982	-3	96	76	O-90(LF)	-1.1
1994	KC A	104	438	61	105	14	12	2	33	29-0	1	72	.240	.285	.340	59	-29	50-8	.962	-4	79	155	O-99(LF)/D-5	-2.7
1995	KC A	75	293	39	84	13	4	4	20	27-1	1	48	.287	.348	.399	93	-3	26-9	.975	-5	74	143	O-69(57-2-13)/D-4	-0.8
	†Sea A	40	162	27	47	10	2	1	9	10-1	1	32	.290	.335	.395	88	-3	16-7	.988	2	116	84	O-38(LF)	-0.1
	Year	115	455	66	131	23	6	5	29	37-2	2	80	.288	.343	.398	91	-6	42-16	.980	-3	89	122	*O-107(95-2-13)/D-4	-0.9
1996	Cin N	33	84	10	13	1	1	1	4	9-0	0	31	.155	.237	.226	23	-10	12-2	.968	0	92	203	O-20(LF)	-0.8
1997	Det A	6	14	0	1	0	0	0	0	1-0	0	3	.071	.133	.071	-45	-3	0-0	1.000	-0	84	0	/O-3(2-1-0),D	-0.3
Total	13	1371	5406	849	1425	176	89	28	346	477-12	15	960	.264	.324	.345	83	-132	752-177	.974	-26	92	123	*O-1311(1153-155-25)/D-10	-10.0
COLES, CAD Cadwallader B 1.17.1886 Rock Hill, SC D 6.30.1942 Miami, FL BL/TR 6-0.5/174# d4.16																								
1914	KC F	78	194	17	49	7	3	1	25	5	0	30	.253	.271	.335	67	-13	6	.889	-5	77	82	O-39(3-31-6)/1-3	-2.2

Year	Tm Lg	G	AB	R	H	2B	3B	HR	RBI	BB-IB	HP	SO	AVG	OBP	SLG	AOPS	ABR	SB-CS	FA	FR	Rng	Thr	G at Pos	BFW
COLES, CHUCK Charles Edward B 6.27.1931 Fredericktown, PA D 1.25.1996 Myrtle Beach, SC BL/TL 5-9/180# d9.19																								
1958	Cin N	5	11	0	2	1	0	0	2	2-0	0	6	.182	.308	.273	52	-1	0-0	1.000	0	132	0	/O-4(3-1-0)	-0.1
COLES, DARNELL Darnell B 6.2.1962 San Bernardino, CA BR/TR 6-1/185# d9.4 OF Total (123-LF 228-RF)																								
1983	Sea A	27	92	9	26	7	0	1	6	7-0	0	12	.283	.333	.391	95	0	0-3	.941	-2	84	136	3-26	-0.4
1984	Sea A	48	143	15	23	3	1	0	6	17-0	2	26	.161	.259	.196	28	-14	2-1	.918	-4	82	130	3-42/O-3(LF),D-3	-1.9
1985	Sea A	27	59	8	14	4	0	1	5	9-0	1	17	.237	.338	.356	93	0	0-1	.918	1	113	130	S-15/3-7,O-2(LF),D-2	0.2
1986	Det A	142	521	67	142	30	2	20	86	45-3	6	84	.273	.333	.453	113	9	6-2	.938	-4	97	105	*3-133/S-2,O-2(RF),D-7	0.3
1987	Det A	53	149	14	27	5	1	4	15	15-1	2	23	.181	.263	.309	54	-10	0-1	.847	-1	109	87	3-36/1-9,O-8(2-0-6),SD	-1.2
	Pit N	40	119	20	27	8	0	6	24	19-2	1	20	.227	.333	.445	105	1	1-3	1.000	-4	63	60	O-26(1-0-26),3-10/1	-0.5
1988	Pit N	68	211	20	49	13	1	5	36	20-1	3	41	.232	.299	.374	96	-1	1-1	.990	-5	92	0	O-55(RF)/13	-0.8
	Sea A	55	195	32	57	10	1	10	34	17-0	4	26	.292	.356	.508	134	9	3-2	.986	-4	75	122	O-47(43-0-4)/1D	0.4
1989	Sea A	146	535	54	135	21	3	10	59	27-1	6	61	.252	.294	.359	81	-15	5-4	.975	7	101	136	O-89(7-0-83),3-26,1-18,D-12	-1.2
1990	Sea A	37	107	9	23	5	1	2	16	4-1	1	17	.215	.248	.336	62	-6	0-0	.970	1	91	0	O-20(RF)/3-6,1-4,D	-0.6
	Det A	52	108	13	22	2	0	1	4	12-1	0	21	.204	.281	.250	50	-7	0-4	1.000	2	96	0	D-30,O-11(4-0-9)/3-8	-0.8
	Year	89	215	22	45	7	1	3	20	16-2	1	38	.209	.265	.293	56	-13	0-4	.977	3	92	0	O-31(4-0-29),D-31,3-14/1-4	-1.4
1991	SF N	11	14	1	3	0	0	0	0	0-0	0	2	.214	.214	.214	22	-2	0-0	—	-1	0	0	/O-3(RF),1	-0.2
1992	Cin N	55	141	16	44	11	2	3	18	3-0	0	15	.312	.322	.482	123	4	1-0	1.000	0	103	38	3-23,1-20/O-5(3-0-2)	0.3
1993	Tor A	64	194	26	49	9	1	4	26	16-1	4	29	.253	.319	.371	85	-4	1-1	.957	-6	91	45	O-44(31-0-13),3-16/1D	-1.1
1994	Tor A	48	143	15	30	6	1	4	15	10-0	1	25	.210	.263	.350	57	-10	0-0	.980	-2	108	63	O-29(24-0-5),1-10/3-7,D	-1.3
1995	StL N	63	138	13	31	7	0	3	16	16-1	3	20	.225	.316	.341	74	-5	0-0	.951	-8	64	32	3-22,1-18/O(LF)	-1.3
1997	Col N	21	22	1	7	1	0	1	2	0-0	1	6	.318	.348	.500	97	0	0-0	1.000	-0	123	0	/3-3,O-2(LF)	0.0
Total	14	957	2891	333	709	142	14	75	368	237-12	35	445	.245	.307	.382	88	-51	20-23	.923	-30	97	93	3-366,0-347R/1-84,D-67,S-18	-10.1
COLETTA, CHRIS Christopher Michael B 8.2.1944 Brooklyn, NY BL/TL 5-11/190# d8.15																								
1972	Cal A	14	30	5	9	1	0	1	7	1-0	0	4	.300	.323	.433	131	1	0-0	1.000	-1	35	0	/O-7(5-0-2)	-0.1
COLGAN, ED William H. B E.St.Louis, IL D 8.8.1895 Great Falls, MT ?/180# d5.3																								
1884	Pit AA	48	161	10	25	4	1	0		3	0		.155	.171	.193	18	-14		.906	1			C-44/O-4(2-0-2)	-0.9
COLLIER, LOU Louis Keith B 8.21.1973 Chicago, IL BR/TR 5-10/170# d6.28																								
1997	Pit N	18	37	3	5	0	0	0	3	1-0	0	11	.135	.158	.135	-22	-7	1-0	1.000	1	116	106	S-18	-0.5
1998	Pit N	110	334	30	82	13	6	2	34	31-6	6	70	.246	.316	.338	73	-13	2-2	.960	1	100	96	*S-107	-0.5
1999	Mil N	74	135	18	35	9	0	2	21	14-0	0	32	.259	.325	.370	77	-5	3-2	.948	-8	88	52	S-31,O-10(9-0-1)/3-7,2-4	-1.1
2000	Mil N	14	32	9	7	1	0	1	2	6-0	0	4	.219	.333	.344	75	-1	0-0	1.000	1	86	401	O-10(5-7-0)/3	-0.1
2001	Mil N	50	127	19	32	8	1	2	14	17-0	1	30	.252	.340	.378	89	-2	5-1	.976	1	108	99	O-23(12-11-0),3-16/D	0.0
2002	Mon N	13	11	3	1	1	0	0	0	1-1	1	3	.091	.231	.182	12	-1	0-0	1.000	-1	90	0	/O-7(3-3-1),2-2,3	-0.2
2003	Bos A	4	1	0	0	0	0	0	0	0-0	0	0	.000	.000	.000	-98	0	0-1	1.000	0	167	0	/3-2,O-2(1-1-0)	-0.1
Total	7	283	677	82	162	32	7	7	74	70-7	8	150	.239	.314	.338	71	-29	11-6	.962	-6	99	90	S-156/0-52(30-22-2),3-27,2-6,D	-2.5
COLLINS d9.12																								
1892	StL N	1	2	0	0	0	0	0	0	0	0	2	.000	.000	.000	-99	0	0	1.000	0	0	0	/O(RF)	-0.1
COLLINS, CHUB Charles Augustine B 10.12.1857 Dundas, ON, CAN D 5.20.1914 Dundas, ON, CAN BB 5-11.5/165# d5.1																								
1884	Buf N	45	169	24	30	6	0	0	20	14		36	.178	.240	.213	42	-11		.914	2	105	94	2-42/S-3	-0.6
	Ind AA	38	138	18	31	3	1	0		9	0		.225	.272	.261	77	-3		.886	-6	90	58	2-38	-0.7
1885	Det N	14	55	8	10	0	2	0	6	0		11	.182	.182	.255	40	-4		.792	-5	83	73	S-14	-0.9
Total	2	97	362	50	71	9	3	0	26	23		47	.196	.244	.238	55	-18		.901	-9	98	77	/2-80,S-17	-2.2
COLLINS, WILSON Cyril Wilson B 5.7.1889 Pulaski, TN D 2.28.1941 Knoxville, TN BR/TR 5-9.5/165# d5.12																								
1913	Bos N	16	3	3	1	0	0	0	0	0	0	1	.333	.333	.333	89	0	0	1.000	0	180	0	/O-9(5-3-1)	0.0
1914	Bos N	27	35	5	9	0	0	0	1	2	0	8	.257	.297	.257	66	-2	0	.917	-0	120	0	O-19(9-3-7)	-0.3
Total	2	43	38	8	10	0	0	0	1	2	0	9	.263	.300	.263	68	-2	0	.926	-0	125	0	/O-28(14-6-8)	-0.3
COLLINS, DAN Daniel Thomas B 7.12.1854 St.Louis, MO D 9.21.1883 New Orleans, LA d6.8 ▲																								
1874	Chi NA	3	12	1	1	1	0	0	0	0		2	.083	.083	.167	-22	-2	1-0	1.000	0	243	0	/P-2,O-2(RF),S	-0.1
1876	Lou N	7	28	3	4	1	0	0	9	0		2	.143	.143	.179	5	-3		.909	1	179	492	/O-7(0-2-5)	-0.2
COLLINS, DAVE David S B 10.20.1952 Rapid City, SD BB/TL 5-11/175# d6.7 C6																								
1975	Cal A	93	319	41	85	13	4	3	29	36-1	1	55	.266	.340	.361	106	3	24-10	.988	3	112	59	O-75(74-1-0),D-12	0.3
1976	Cal A	99	365	45	96	12	1	4	28	40-2	0	55	.263	.335	.334	103	2	32-19	.994	2	110	64	O-71(52-19-0),D-22	0.0
1977	Sea A	120	402	46	96	9	3	5	28	33-0	3	66	.239	.299	.313	69	-18	25-10	.985	1	95	127	O-73(67-3-3),D-40	-1.9
1978	Cin N	102	102	13	22	1	0	0	7	15-0	0	18	.216	.311	.225	54	-6	7-7	.969	1	103	140	O-24(3-17-4)	-0.6
1979	†Cin N	122	396	59	126	16	4	3	35	27-2	2	48	.318	.364	.402	108	4	16-9	.976	-4	101	31	O-91(45-3-50),1-10	-0.3
1980	Cin N	144	551	94	167	20	4	3	35	53-2	3	68	.303	.366	.370	106	6	79-21	.986	4	112	60	*O-141(18-119-6)	1.9
1981	Cin N	95	360	63	98	18	6	3	23	41-1	6	41	.272	.355	.381	107	5	26-10	.977	0	108	60	O-94(1-0-93)	0.3
1982	NY A	111	348	41	88	12	3	3	25	28-3	5	49	.253	.315	.330	80	-10	13-8	.992	-1	98	145	O-60(20-20-25),1-52/D	-1.5
1983	Tor A	118	402	55	109	12	4	1	34	43-1	2	67	.271	.343	.328	81	-9	31-7	.989	10	**115**	105	*O-112(112-2-1)/1-5,D	0.0
1984	Tor A	128	441	59	136	24	**15**	2	44	33-0	9	41	.308	.366	.444	119	12	60-14	.991	-2	87	110	*O-108(106-2-0)/1-6,D-4	1.3
1985	Oak A	112	379	52	95	16	4	4	29	29-2	1	37	.251	.303	.346	84	-9	29-8	.978	2	113	17	O-91(LF)	-0.8
1986	Det A	124	419	44	113	18	2	1	27	44-0	2	49	.270	.340	.329	84	-8	27-12	.995	1	109	34	O-94(76-10-11),D-24	-0.9
1987	Cin N	57	85	19	25	5	0	0	5	11-0	2	12	.294	.388	.353	94	0	9-0	1.000	1	135	0	O-21(18-2-1)	0.3
1988	Cin N	99	174	12	41	6	2	0	14	11-0	2	27	.236	.286	.293	65	-8	7-2	.965	-1	96	139	O-35(13-5-18)/1-3	-1.0
1989	Cin N	78	106	12	25	4	0	0	7	10-0	0	17	.236	.302	.274	63	-5	3-1	1.000	3	165	0	O-16(LF)	-0.2
1990	StL N	99	58	12	13	1	0	0	3	13-2	0	10	.224	.366	.241	70	-2	7-1	1.000	-4	0	72	1-49,O-12(4-1-8)	-0.5
Total	16	1701	4907	667	1335	187	52	32	373	467-16	38	660	.272	.338	.351	93	-43	395-139	.986	15	107	71	*O-1118(716-204-220),1-125,D-104	-3.6
COLLINS, EDDIE Edward Trowbridge Jr. B 11.23.1916 Lansdowne, PA D 11.2.2000 Jennersville, PA BL/TR 5-10/175# d7.4 Mil 1942-45 f-Eddie																								
1939	Phi A	32	21	6	5	1	0	0	0	0	0	3	.238	.238	.286	34	-2	1-0	1.000	0	202	0	/O-6(RF),2	-0.2
1941	Phi A	80	219	29	53	6	3	0	12	20	0	24	.242	.305	.297	61	-13	2-1	.968	1	113	65	O-50(4-9-38)	-1.4
1942	Phi A	20	34	6	8	2	0	0	4	4	0	2	.235	.316	.294	72	-1	1-0	.800	-1	70	0	/O-9(1-3-6)	-0.3
Total	3	132	274	41	66	9	3	0	16	24	0	29	.241	.302	.296	61	-16	4-1	.959	0	113	56	/O-65(5-12-50),2	-1.9
COLLINS, EDDIE Edward Trowbridge Sr. "Cocky" (a/k/a Edward T. Sullivan In 1906) B 5.2.1887 Millerton, NY D 3.25.1951 Boston, MA BL/TR 5-9/175# d9.17 Mil 1918 M3 C2 HF1939 s-Eddie																								
1906	Phi A	6	15	2	3	0	0	0	0	0	0		.200	.200	.200	25	-1	1	.900	-1	91	0	/S-3,23	-0.2
1907	Phi A	14	23	0	8	0	1	0	2	0	0		.348	.348	.435	146	1	0	.833	-1	78	99	/S-6	0.0
1908	Phi A	102	330	39	90	18	7	1	40	16	3		.273	.312	.379	116	5	8	.944	-10	89	34	2-47,S-28,O-10(2-3-5)	-0.5
1909	Phi A	**153**	571	104	198	30	10	3	56	62	6		.347	.416	.450	170	48	63	**.967**	4	93	114	*2-152/S	5.9
1910	†Phi A	153	581	81	188	16	15	3	81	49	6		.324	.382	.418	152	34	**81**	**.972**	30	**104**	**136**	*2-153	7.0
1911	†Phi A	132	493	92	180	22	13	3	73	62	15		.365	.451	.481	163	46	38	.967	-0	90	107	*2-132	4.6
1912	Phi A	**153**	543	**137**	189	25	11	0	64	101	0		.348	.450	.435	159	50	63	.955	14	103	**125**	*2-153	6.4
1913	†Phi A	148	534	**125**	184	23	13	3	73	85	7	37	.345	.441	.453	165	49	55	.965	16	**106**	107	*2-148	**7.0**
1914	†Phi A	152	526	**122**	181	23	14	2	85	97	6	31	.344	**.452**	.452	**179**	**58**	58-30	**.970**	2	91	116	*2-152	6.9
1915	Chi A	**155**	521	118	173	22	10	4	77	**119**	5	27	.332	.460	.436	163	50	46-30	**.974**	11	104	103	*2-155	**6.6**
1916	Chi A	**155**	545	87	168	14	17	0	52	86	3	36	.308	.405	.396	139	29	40-21	**.976**	-7	91	**131**	*2-155	2.9
1917	†Chi A	**156**	564	91	163	18	12	0	67	89	3	16	.289	.389	.363	127	22	53	.969	-26	85	110	*2-156	-0.1
1918	Chi A	97	330	51	91	8	2	2	30	73	0	13	.276	.407	.330	121	14	22	.974	-1	95	131	2-96	1.6
1919	†Chi A	**140**	518	87	165	19	7	4	80	68	2	27	.319	.400	.405	126	20	**33**	.974	3	97	**125**	*2-140	2.7
1920	Chi A	153	602	117	224	38	13	3	76	69	2	19	.372	.438	.493	146	43	20-8	**.976**	10	99	115	*2-153	5.4
1921	Chi A	139	526	79	177	20	10	2	58	66	2	11	.337	.412	.424	115	15	12-10	**.968**	31	**112**	115	*2-136	4.4
1922	Chi A	154	598	92	194	20	12	1	69	73	3	16	.324	.401	.403	110	12	20-12	**.976**	-13	93	87	*2-154	0.4
1923	Chi A	145	505	89	182	22	5	5	67	84	4	8	.360	.455	.453	141	37	**48**-29	.975	-6	99	93	*2-142	3.4
1924	Chi A	152	556	108	194	27	7	6	86	89	3	16	.349	.441	.455	136	35	**42**-17	**.977**	-10	95	94	*2-150,M	3.0
1925	Chi A	118	425	80	147	26	3	3	80	87	4	8	.346	.461	.442	137	32	19-6	.970	-13	93	110	*2-116,M	2.3
1926	Chi A	106	375	66	129	32	4	1	62	62	3	8	.344	.441	.459	140	27	13-8	.973	-8	93	99	*2-101,M	2.1
1927	Phi A	95	226	50	76	12	1	1	15	56	0	9	.336	.468	.412	123	12	6-2	.965	-5	88	107	2-56/S	0.9
1928	Phi A	36	33	3	10	3	0	0	7	4	0	4	.303	.378	.394	100	0	0-0	—	-1	0	0	/2-2,S	-0.1

Year	Tm Lg	G	AB	R	H	2B	3B	HR	RBI	BB-IB	HP	SO	AVG	OBP	SLG	AOPS	ABR	SB-CS	FA	FR	Rng	Thr	G at Pos	BFW
1929	Phi A	9	7	0	0	0	0	0	0	2	0	0	.000	.222	.000	-37	-1	0-0	—	0			H	-0.1
1930	Phi A	3	2	1	1	0	0	0	0	0	0	0	.500	.500	.500	148	0	0-0	—	0			H	0.0
Total	25	2826	9949	1821	3315	438	187	47	1300	1499	77	286	.333	.424	.429	142	637	741-173	.970	21	97	111	*2-2650/S-40,O-10(2-3-5),3	72.5
COLLINS, HUB Hubert B. B 4.15.1864 Louisville, KY D 5.21.1892 Brooklyn, NY BR/TR 5-8/160# d9.4 OF Total (241-LF 31-CF)																								
1886	Lou AA	27	101	12	29	3	2	0	10	5	0		.287	.321	.356	106	0	7	.885	-2	46	0	O-24(22-2-0)/3-2,S21	-0.2
1887	Lou AA	130	559	122	162	22	8	1	66	39	2		.290	.338	.363	94	-6	71	.887	-7	103	27	*O-109(LF),2-10/1-8,S-4,3	-1.2
1888	Lou AA	116	485	117	149	26	11	2	50	41	4		.307	.366	.419	154	30	62	.890	3	124	162	O-82(57-26-0),2-19,S-15	2.9
	Bro AA	12	42	16	13	5	1	0	3	9	1		.310	.442	.476	195	5	9	.897	-2	88	106	2-12	0.3
	Year	128	527	133	162	**31**	12	2	53	50	5		.307	.373	.423	158	36	71	.890	0	124	162	O-82(57-26-0),2-31,S-15	3.2
1889	†Bro AA	**138**	560	139	149	18	3	2	73	80	7	41	.266	.365	.320	95	0	65	.929	-3	101	91	*2-138	0.2
1890	†Bro N	**129**	510	**148**	142	32	7	3	69	85	3	47	.278	.385	.386	124	20	85	.945	3	104	118	*2-129	2.4
1891	Bro N	107	435	82	120	16	5	3	31	59	2	63	.276	.365	.356	111	8	32	.910	-21	91	58	2-72,O-35(32-3-0)	-1.0
1892	Bro N	21	87	17	26	5	1	0	17	14	0	13	.299	.396	.379	140	5	4	.925	-2	0	0	O-21(LF)	0.1
Total	7	680	2779	653	790	127	38	11	319	332	19	164	.284	.365	.369	115	62	335	.928	-32	99	92	2-381,O-271L/S-20,1-9,3-3	3.5
COLLINS, RIPPER James Anthony B 3.30.1904 Altoona, PA D 4.15.1970 New Haven, CT BB/TL 5-9/165# d4.18 C3																								
1931	†StL N	89	279	34	84	20	10	4	59	18	3	24	.301	.350	.487	118	6	1	.995	4	123	104	1-68/O-3(1-0-2)	0.4
1932	StL N	149	549	82	153	28	8	21	91	38	3	67	.279	.329	.474	110	6	4	.999	-1	83	107	1-81,O-60(15-0-45)	-0.6
1933	StL N	132	493	66	153	26	7	10	68	38	3	49	.310	.363	.452	125	16	7	.994	3	102	83	*1-123	0.8
1934	†StL N	**154**	600	116	200	40	12	**35**	128	57	2	50	.333	.393	**.615**	155	46	2	.991	8	**118**	99	*1-154	3.7
1935	StL N★	150	578	109	181	36	10	23	122	65	3	45	.313	.385	.529	138	31	0	.987	1	102	102	*1-150	1.7
1936	StL N★	103	277	48	81	15	3	13	48	48	1	30	.292	.399	.509	143	18	1	.990	-1	93	104	1-61/O-9(1-0-8)	1.1
1937	Chi N★	115	456	77	125	16	5	16	71	32	5	46	.274	.329	.436	102	0	2	.991	1	101	106	*1-111	-1.0
1938	†Chi N	143	490	78	131	22	8	13	61	54	3	48	.267	.344	.424	107	5	1	**.996**	8	118	108	*1-135	0.0
1941	Pit N	49	62	5	13	2	2	0	11	6	0	14	.210	.279	.306	65	-3	0	.947	1	180	85	1-11/O-3(RF)	-0.3
Total	9	1084	3784	615	1121	205	65	135	659	356	23	373	.296	.360	.492	125	125	18	.992	23	107	101	1-894/O-75(17-0-58)	5.8
COLLINS, JIMMY James Joseph B 1.16.1870 Buffalo, NY D 3.6.1943 Buffalo, NY BR/TR 5-9/178# d4.19 M6 HF1945																								
1895	Bos N	11	38	10	8	3	0	1	8	4	1	4	.211	.302	.368	67	-2	0	.714	-2	81	0	O-10(RF)	-0.3
	Lou N	96	373	65	104	17	5	6	49	33	9	16	.279	.352	.399	100	1	12	.926	20	116	95	3-77,O-18(0-7-11)/2-2,S	1.7
	Year	107	411	75	112	20	5	7	57	37	10	20	.273	.347	.397	96	-2	12	.926	19	116	95	3-77,O-28(0-7-21)/2-2,S	1.4
1896	Bos N	84	304	48	90	10	9	1	46	30	8	12	.296	.374	.398	98	-1	10	.909	16	118	137	3-80/S-4	1.4
1897	†Bos N	134	529	103	183	28	13	6	132	41	7		.346	.400	.482	125	18	14	.917	19	113	129	*3-134	3.3
1898	Bos N	**152**	597	107	196	35	5	**15**	111	40	7		.328	.377	.479	138	27	12	.932	12	101	104	*3-152	3.9
1899	Bos N	151	599	98	166	28	11	5	92	40	12		.277	.335	.386	89	-11	12	.943	18	109	115	*3-151	0.8
1900	Bos N	**142**	586	104	178	25	5	6	95	34	10		.304	.352	.394	94	-6	23	.935	10	96	113	*3-141/S	0.6
1901	Bos A	**138**	564	108	187	42	16	6	94	34	5		.332	.375	.495	142	31	19	.914	13	106	**142**	*3-138,M	4.2
1902	Bos A	108	429	71	138	21	10	6	61	24	2		.322	.360	.459	123	12	18	**.954**	8	105	96	*3-107,M	2.1
1903	†Bos A	130	540	88	160	33	17	5	72	24	2		.296	.329	.448	125	14	23	**.952**	10	103	**149**	*3-130,M	2.9
1904	Bos A	156	631	85	171	33	13	3	67	27	5		.271	.306	.379	110	6	19	.945	5	104	121	*3-156,M	1.7
1905	Bos A	131	508	66	140	26	5	4	65	37	4		.276	.330	.370	120	12	18	.923	5	103	115	*3-131,M	2.2
1906	Bos A	37	142	17	39	8	4	1	16	4	0		.275	.295	.408	120	2	1	.911	2	107	64	3-32,M	0.5
1907	Bos A	41	158	13	46	8	0	0	10	10	0		.291	.333	.342	116	3	4	.874	-6	89	53	3-41	-0.2
	Phi A	99	364	38	99	21	0	0	35	24	8		.272	.331	.330	108	5	4	.904	-2	94	116	3-98	0.5
	Year	140	522	51	145	29	0	0	45	34	8		.278	.332	.333	110	8	8	.895	-9	93	98	*3-139	0.3
1908	Phi A	115	433	34	94	14	3	0	30	20	4		.217	.258	.263	65	-17	5	.928	-7	92	109	*3-115	-2.3
Total	14	1725	6795	1055	1999	352	116	65	983	426	84	32	.294	.343	.409	112	94	194	.929	122	104	117	*3-1683/O-28(0-7-21),S-6,2-2	23.0
COLLINS, ZIP John Edgar B 5.2.1892 Brooklyn, NY D 12.19.1983 Manassas, VA BL/TL 5-11/152# d7.31																								
1914	Pit N	49	182	14	44	2	0	0	15	8	1	10	.242	.277	.253	61	-9	3	.962	1	103	107	O-49(0-11-40)	-1.2
1915	Pit N	101	354	51	104	8	5	1	23	24	1	38	.294	.340	.353	112	4	6-7	.942	1	104	103	O-89(CF)	-0.2
	Bos N	5	14	3	4	1	1	0	0	2	0	1	.286	.375	.500	171	1	1	1.000	0	88	245	/O-4(LF)	0.2
	Year	106	368	54	108	9	6	1	23	26	1	39	.293	.342	.359	114	5	7-7	.944	2	103	108	O-93(4-89-0)	0.0
1916	Bos N	93	268	39	56	1	6	1	18	18	1	42	.209	.261	.269	66	-12	4	.947	-1	89	131	O-78(26-27-27)	-2.0
1917	Bos N	9	27	3	4	0	1	0	2	0	0	4	.148	.148	.222	14	-3	0	1.000	-0	118	0	/O-5(1-0-4)	-0.4
1921	Phi A	24	71	14	20	5	1	0	5	6	2	5	.282	.354	.380	87	-1	1-2	.915	-0	100	116	O-20(CF)	-0.3
Total	5	281	916	124	232	17	14	2	63	58	5	100	.253	.301	.309	85	-20	15-9	.946	1	99	112	O-245(31-147-71)	-3.9
COLLINS, SHANO John Francis B 12.4.1885 Charlestown, MA D 9.10.1955 Newton, MA BR/TR 6/185# d4.21 M2 gs-Bob Gallagher																								
1910	Chi A	97	315	29	62	10	8	1	24	25	1		.197	.258	.289	74	-11	10	.949	2	96	118	O-66(19-7-40),1-28	-1.4
1911	Chi A	106	370	48	97	16	12	4	48	20	5		.262	.309	.403	101	-2	14	.978	4	118	117	1-98/2-3,O-3(LF)	-0.1
1912	Chi A	153	579	75	168	34	10	2	81	29	5		.290	.330	.394	110	5	27	.969	0	100	70	*O-105(1-17-85),1-46	-0.2
1913	Chi A	148	535	53	128	26	9	1	47	32	3	60	.239	.286	.327	80	-16	22	.949	2	111	87	*O-147(2-0-145)	-2.3
1914	Chi A	154	598	61	164	34	9	3	65	27	6	49	.274	.312	.376	108	3	30-24	.970	1	100	103	*O-154(7-45-103)	-0.7
1915	Chi A	153	576	73	148	24	17	2	85	28	6	50	.257	.298	.368	96	-7	38-19	.963	-0	106	96	*O-104(20-21-64),1-47	-1.3
1916	Chi A	143	527	74	128	28	12	0	42	59	3	51	.243	.323	.342	98	-1	16	.959	5	104	119	*O-137(23-2-112)/1-4	-0.4
1917	†Chi A	82	252	38	59	13	3	1	14	10	2	27	.234	.269	.321	78	-8	14	.992	3	119	72	O-73(9-0-64)	-0.9
1918	Chi A	103	365	30	100	18	11	1	56	17	2	19	.274	.310	.392	111	2	7	.973	12	117	151	O-93(16-34-42)/1-5	0.9
1919	†Chi A	63	179	21	50	6	3	1	16	7	3	11	.279	.317	.363	90	-3	3	.957	4	115	135	O-46(2-7-37)/1-8	-0.1
1920	Chi A	133	495	70	150	21	10	1	63	23	4	24	.303	.339	.392	93	-7	12-9	.988	-7	82	106	*1-116,O-13(2-1-10)	-1.7
1921	Bos A	141	542	63	155	29	12	4	69	18	4	38	.286	.314	.406	85	-16	15-8	.966	4	99	124	*O-139(1-44-94)/1-3	-1.9
1922	Bos A	135	472	33	128	24	7	1	52	7	5	30	.271	.289	.358	68	-24	7-9	.951	-4	104	49	*O-117(11-45-63)/1	-3.7
1923	Bos A	97	342	41	79	10	5	0	18	11	5	29	.231	.265	.289	46	-29	7-8	.953	-0	86	172	O-89(0-57-32)	-3.4
1924	Bos A	89	240	37	70	17	5	0	28	18	3	17	.292	.349	.404	94	-3	4-6	.957	-8	79	66	O-56(18-11-27),1-12	-1.5
1925	Bos A	2	3	1	1	0	0	0	1	0	0	0	.333	.333	.333	70	0	0-0	—	-0	0	0	/O(CF)	0.0
Total	16	1799	6390	747	1687	310	133	22	709	331	57	405	.264	.306	.364	90	-117	226-83	.962	17	103	103	*O-1343(133-292-918),1-368/2-3	-18.7
COLLINS, JOE Joseph Edward (born Joseph Edward Kollonige) B 12.3.1922 Scranton, PA D 8.30.1989 Union, NJ BL/TL 6/185# d9.25																								
1948	NY A	5	5	0	1	1	0	0	2	0	0	1	.200	.200	.400	58	0	0-0	—	0			H	0.0
1949	NY A	7	10	2	1	0	0	0	4	6	0	2	.100	.438	.100	46	0	0-0	.920	-1	0	60	/1-5	-0.1
1950	†NY A	108	205	47	48	8	3	8	28	31	0	34	.234	.335	.420	95	-2	5-0	.987	0	101	111	1-99/O-2(RF)	-0.3
1951	†NY A	125	262	52	75	8	5	9	48	34	0	23	.286	.368	.458	127	9	9-7	.987	5	126	110	*1-114,O-15(RF)	1.1
1952	†NY A	122	428	69	120	16	8	18	59	55	1	47	.280	.364	.481	142	23	4-2	.990	-3	90	**124**	*1-119	1.7
1953	†NY A	127	387	72	104	11	2	17	44	59	0	36	.269	.365	.439	121	11	2-6	.989	1	106	116	*1-113/O-4(RF)	0.5
1954	NY A	130	343	67	93	20	2	12	46	51	0	37	.271	.365	.446	126	13	2-2	.992	2	108	**142**	*1-117	1.0
1955	†NY A	105	278	40	65	9	1	13	45	44-2	2	32	.234	.339	.414	104	2	0-2	.998	7	135	146	1-73,O-27(RF)	0.4
1956	†NY A	100	262	38	59	5	3	7	43	34-2	1	33	.225	.313	.347	78	-9	3-1	.990	5	103	60	O-51(25-7-24),1-43	-0.7
1957	†NY A	79	149	17	30	1	0	2	10	24-2	0	18	.201	.310	.248	56	-9	2-1	.987	-1	93	107	1-32,O-15(2-2-11)	-1.1
Total	10	908	2329	404	596	79	24	86	329	338-6	4	263	.256	.350	.421	112	38	27-21	.990	16	110	124	1-715,O-114(27-9-83)	2.5
COLLINS, KEVIN Kevin Michael "Casey" B 8.4.1946 Springfield, MA BL/TR 6-2/190# d9.1																								
1965	NY N	11	23	3	4	1	0	0	0	1-0	0	9	.174	.208	.217	21	-2	0-1	1.000	-0	112	142	/3-7,S-3	-0.3
1967	NY N	4	10	1	1	0	0	0	0	0-0	0	3	.100	.100	.100	-43	-2	1-0	1.000	0	132	0	/2-2	-0.2
1968	NY N	58	154	12	31	5	2	1	13	7-2	0	37	.201	.233	.279	54	-9	0-1	.955	-5	86	122	3-40/2-6,S	-1.6
1969	NY N	16	40	1	6	3	0	1	2	3-1	0	10	.150	.209	.300	40	-3	0-0	.925	1	113	114	3-14	-0.2
	Mon N	52	96	5	23	5	1	2	12	8-0	0	16	.240	.292	.375	87	-2	0-0	1.000	-5	76	40	2-20,3-16	-0.7
	Year	68	136	6	29	8	1	3	14	11-1	0	26	.213	.268	.353	73	-5	0-0	.917	-4	93	95	3-30,2-20	-0.9
1970	Det A	25	24	2	5	1	0	1	3	1-0	0	10	.208	.240	.375	67	-1	0-0	1.000	0	158	0	/1	-0.1
1971	Det A	35	41	6	11	2	1	1	4	0-0	0	12	.268	.268	.439	94	-1	0-0	1.000	1	114	0	/3-4,O-2(1-0-1),2	0.0
Total	6	201	388	30	81	17	4	6	34	20-3	0	97	.209	.245	.320	62	-20	1-2	.944	-8	91	109	/3-81,2-29,S-4,O-2(1-0-1),1	-3.1
COLLINS, ORTH Orth Stein "Buck" B 4.27.1880 Lafayette, IN D 12.13.1949 Ft.Lauderdale, FL BL/TR 6/150# d6.1																								
1904	NY A	5	17	3	6	1	1	0	1	1	0		.353	.389	.529	180	1	0	1.000	3	1145	0	/O-5(0-5-1)	0.4
1909	Was A	8	7	0	0	0	0	0	0	0	0		.000	.000	.000	-99	-2	0	1.000	-0	0	0	/O-2(0-1-1),P	-0.2
Total	2	13	24	3	6	1	1	0	1	1	0		.250	.280	.375	104	-1	0	1.000	3	954	0	/O-7(0-6-2),P	0.2

Year	Tm Lg	G	AB	R	H	2B	3B	HR	RBI	BB-IB	HP	SO	AVG	OBP	SLG	AOPS	ABR	SB-CS	FA	FR	Rng	Thr	G at Pos	BFW
COLLINS, RIP Robert Joseph B 9.18.1909 Pittsburgh, PA D 4.19.1969 Pittsburgh, PA BR/TR 5-11/176# d4.28																								
1940	Chi N	47	120	11	25	3	0	1	14	14	1	18	.208	.296	.258	55	-7	4	.951	-3	104	109	C-42	-0.8
1944	NY A	3	3	0	1	0	0	0	0	1	0	0	.333	.500	.333	136	0	0-0	1.000	0	0	0	/C-3	0.1
Total	2	50	123	11	26	3	0	1	14	15	1	18	.211	.302	.260	58	-7	4-0	.953	-3	101	105	/C-45	-0.7
COLLINS, PAT Tharon Leslie B 9.13.1896 Sweet Sprgs., MO D 5.20.1960 Kansas City, KS BR/TR 5-9/178# d9.5																								
1919	StL A	11	21	2	3	1	0	0	1	4	0	2	.143	.280	.190	32	-2	0	.929	-0	107	87	/C-5	-0.2
1920	StL A	23	28	5	6	1	0	0	6	3	0	5	.214	.290	.250	43	-2	0-0	1.000	-1	82	61	/C-7	-0.3
1921	StL A	58	111	9	27	3	0	1	10	16	0	17	.243	.339	.297	60	-6	1-0	.961	-1	113	80	C-31	-0.5
1922	StL A	63	127	14	39	6	0	8	23	21	0	21	.307	.405	.543	140	8	0-1	.980	4	133	92	C-28/1-5	1.2
1923	StL A	85	181	9	32	8	0	3	30	15	0	45	.177	.240	.271	32	-18	0-0	.980	-0	96	102	C-47	-1.6
1924	StL A	32	54	9	17	2	0	1	11	11	0	14	.315	.431	.407	110	1	0-1	.969	-1	95	107	C-20	0.1
1926	†NY A	102	290	41	83	11	3	7	35	73	2	57	.286	.433	.417	124	15	3-2	.971	1	89	95	*C-100	2.2
1927	†NY A	92	251	38	69	9	3	7	36	54	2	24	.275	.407	.418	118	9	0-1	.976	-3	103	59	C-89	1.1
1928	†NY A	70	136	18	30	5	0	6	14	35	0	16	.221	.380	.390	106	3	0-0	.977	-4	88	100	C-70	0.2
1929	Bos N	7	5	1	0	0	0	0	2	3	0	1	.000	.375	.000	2	-1	0	1.000	0	91	75	/C-6	0.0
Total	10	543	1204	146	306	46	6	33	168	235	4	202	.254	.378	.385	98	7	4-5	.974	-5	99	87	C-403/1-5	2.2
COLLINS, BILLY William J. B 1863 Dublin, Ireland D 6.8.1893 Brooklyn, NY BR ?/150# d8.1																								
1887	NY AA	1	4	0	1	0	0	0	0	0	0		.250	.250	.250	42	0	0	.250	-2			/C	-0.2
1889	Phi AA	1	4	0	1	0	0	0	1	1	0	0	.250	.400	.250	88	0	1	.800	-1			/C	0.0
1890	Phi AA	1	1	0	0	0	0	0	0	0	0		.000	.000	.000	-99	0	0	.500	-1	67	0	/S	-0.1
1891	Cle N	2	3	0	0	0	0	0	0	0	0	0	.000	.000	.000	-96	-1	0	—	1	0	0	/O(RF)C	0.0
Total	4	5	12	0	2	0	0	0	1	1	0	0	.167	.231	.167	14	-1	1	.737	-2			/C-3,O(RF)S	-0.3
COLLINS, BILL William Shirley B 3.27.1882 Chesterton, IN D 6.26.1961 San Bernardino, CA BB/TR 6/170# d4.14																								
1910	Bos N	151	584	67	141	6	7	3	40	43	13	48	.241	.308	.291	72	-22	36	**.977**	8	108	109	*O-151(129-10-13)	-2.4
1911	Bos N	17	44	8	6	1	1	0	8	1	0	8	.136	.156	.205	0	-6	4	1.000	1	127	61	O-13(3-8-2)/3	-0.6
	Chi N	7	3	2	1	1	0	0	0	1	0	0	.333	.500	.667	225	1	0	1.000	0	101	0	/O-4(2-2-0)	0.1
	Year	24	47	10	7	2	1	0	8	2	0	8	.149	.184	.234	16	-6	4	1.000	1	126	59	O-17(5-10-2)/3	-0.5
1913	Bro N	32	95	8	18	1	0	0	4	8	2	11	.189	.267	.200	33	-8	2-4	.921	-2	102	29	O-27(13-15-0)	-1.4
1914	Buf F	21	47	6	7	2	2	0	2	1	0	8	.149	.167	.277	19	-7	0	.864	1	75	260	O-15(2-1-13)	-0.6
Total	4	228	773	91	173	11	10	3	54	54	15	75	.224	.287	.276	60	-42	42-4	.966	8	106	105	O-210(149-36-28)/3	-4.9
COLLVER, BILL William J. B 3.21.1867 Clyde, OH D 3.24.1888 Detroit, MI d7.4																								
1885	Bos N	1	4	0	0	0	0	0	0	0		1	.000	.000	.000	-99	-1		—	-0	0	0	/O(RF)	-0.1
COLMAN, FRANK Frank Lloyd B 3.2.1918 London, ON, CAN D 2.19.1983 London, ON, CAN BL/TL 5-11/188# d9.12																								
1942	Pit N	10	37	2	5	0	0	1	2	2	0	2	.135	.179	.216	15	-4	0	1.000	1	93	285	/O-8(RF)	-0.4
1943	Pit N	32	59	9	16	2	2	0	4	8	0	7	.271	.358	.373	108	1	0	1.000	-0	111	0	O-11(RF)	-0.1
1944	Pit N	99	226	30	61	9	5	6	53	25	1	27	.270	.345	.434	113	4	0	.964	-1	103	77	O-53(3-0-50)/1-6	0.0
1945	Pit N	77	153	18	32	11	1	4	30	9	0	16	.209	.253	.373	70	-7	0	.993	1	131	83	1-22,O-12(6-0-5)	-0.8
1946	Pit N	26	53	3	9	3	0	1	6	2	1	7	.170	.214	.283	39	-4	0	1.000	0	100	142	/O-8(4-0-4),1-2	-0.5
	NY A	5	15	2	4	0	0	1	5	1	0	1	.267	.313	.467	114	0	0-0	1.000	-0	110	0	/O-5(RF)	0.0
1947	NY A	22	28	2	3	0	0	2	6	2	0	6	.107	.167	.321	34	-3	0-0	1.000	1	96	450	/O-6(LF)	-0.3
Total	6	271	571	66	130	25	8	15	106	49	2	66	.228	.291	.378	85	-13	0-0	.980	1	102	93	O-103(19-0-83)/1-30	-2.1
COLON, CRIS Cristobal B 1.3.1969 LaGuaira, Venezuela BB/TR 6-2/180# d9.18																								
1992	Tex A	14	36	5	6	0	0	0	1	1-0	0	8	.167	.189	.167	0	-5	0-0	.946	0	104	63	S-14	-0.4
COLUCCIO, BOB Robert Pasquali B 10.2.1951 Centralia, WA BR/TR 5-11/183# d4.15																								
1973	Mil A	124	438	65	98	21	8	15	58	54-2	3	92	.224	.311	.411	105	2	13-6	.992	8	110	165	*O-108(18-14-79),D-11	0.6
1974	Mil A	138	394	42	88	13	4	6	31	43-2	3	61	.223	.305	.322	81	-10	15-9	.989	6	108	109	*O-131(4-103-34)/D-2	-0.8
1975	Mil A	22	62	8	12	0	1	1	5	11-0	1	11	.194	.320	.274	70	-2	1-4	1.000	-0	102	67	O-22(CF)	-0.4
	Chi A	61	161	22	33	4	2	4	13	13-1	1	34	.205	.269	.329	67	-8	4-0	.980	1	104	113	O-59(14-3-44)/D	-0.8
	Year	83	223	30	45	4	3	5	18	24-1	2	45	.202	.284	.314	68	-10	5-4	.987	1	103	98	O-81(14-25-44)/D	-1.2
1977	Chi A	20	37	4	10	0	0	0	7	6-0	0	2	.270	.356	.270	79	-1	0-2	1.000	1	101	113	O-19(9-8-3)	-0.1
1978	StL N	5	3	0	0	0	0	0	0	1-0	0	2	.000	.250	.000	-25	0	0-0	1.000	-0	91	0	/O-2(1-0-1)	-0.1
Total	5	370	1095	141	241	38	15	26	114	128-5	8	202	.220	.305	.353	87	-19	33-21	.990	15	107	126	O-341(46-150-161)/D-14	-1.6
COMBS, EARLE Earle Bryan "The Kentucky Colonel" B 5.14.1899 Pebworth, KY D 7.21.1976 Richmond, KY BL/TR 6/185# d4.16 C16 HF1970																								
1924	NY A	24	35	10	14	5	0	0	2	4	0	2	.400	.462	.543	159	3	0-1	1.000	-1	98	0	O-11(5-3-3)	0.2
1925	NY A	150	593	117	203	36	13	3	61	65	4	43	.342	.411	.462	123	23	12-13	.979	-5	98	73	*O-150(12-138-0)	0.8
1926	†NY A	145	606	113	181	31	12	8	55	47	3	23	.299	.352	.429	105	2	8-6	.970	-8	103	57	*O-145(CF)	-1.2
1927	†NY A	152	648	137	**231**	36	**23**	6	64	62	2	31	.356	.414	.511	143	40	15-6	.968	-6	104	39	*O-152(CF)	2.8
1928	†NY A	149	626	118	194	33	**21**	7	56	77	2	33	.310	.387	.463	127	24	11-8	.980	0	106	66	*O-149(CF)	1.7
1929	NY A	142	586	119	202	33	15	3	65	69	0	32	.345	.414	.468	135	33	12-7	.966	-7	94	69	*O-141(CF)	1.9
1930	NY A	137	532	129	183	30	**22**	7	82	74	0	26	.344	.424	.523	145	38	16-10	.969	-4	99	51	*O-135(60-45-30)	2.3
1931	NY A	138	563	120	179	31	13	5	58	68	3	34	.318	.394	.446	128	24	11-3	.974	-8	95	49	*O-129(CF)	1.3
1932	†NY A	144	591	143	190	32	10	9	65	81	2	16	.321	.405	.455	129	28	3-9	.967	-9	94	52	*O-139(42-115-1)	1.1
1933	NY A	122	417	86	125	22	16	5	64	47	1	19	.300	.372	.465	128	16	6-4	.975	-5	98	41	*O-104(23-80-2)	0.7
1934	NY A	63	251	47	80	13	5	2	25	40	0	9	.319	.412	.434	127	12	3-1	.993	-3	99	21	O-62(12-51-0)	0.7
1935	NY A	89	298	47	84	7	4	3	35	36	0	10	.282	.359	.362	92	-3	1-3	.993	-1	102	39	*O-70(57-13-1)	-0.8
Total	12	1455	5746	1186	1866	309	154	58	632	670	17	278	.325	.397	.462	127	240	98-71	.974	-56	99	53	*O-1387(211-1161-37)	11.5
COMBS, MERL Merrill Russell B 12.11.1919 Los Angeles, CA D 7.7.1981 Riverside, CA BL/TR 6/172# d9.12 C2																								
1947	Bos A	17	68	8	15	1	0	1	6	9	2	9	.221	.329	.279	65	-3	0-0	1.000	3	117	181	3-17	0.0
1949	Bos A	14	24	5	5	1	0	0	1	9	0	0	.208	.424	.250	75	0	0-0	.923	-1	81	120	/3-9,S	-0.1
1950	Bos A	1	0	0	0	0	0	0	0	1	0	0	—	1.000	—	158	0	0-0	—	0			H	0.0
	Was A	37	102	19	25	1	0	0	6	22	0	16	.245	.379	.255	68	-4	0-0	.966	0	107	89	S-30	-0.2
	Year	38	102	19	25	1	0	0	6	23	0	16	.245	.384	.255	69	-3	0-0	.966	0	107	89	S-30	-0.2
1951	Cle A	19	28	2	5	2	0	0	2	2	0	3	.179	.233	.250	32	-3	0-0	.960	3	131	87	S-16	0.0
1952	Cle A	52	139	11	23	1	1	1	10	14	0	15	.165	.242	.209	28	-14	0-1	.972	8	115	113	S-49/2-3	-0.4
Total	5	140	361	45	73	6	1	2	25	57	2	43	.202	.314	.241	52	-24	0-1	.968	13	113	101	/S-96,3-26,2-3	-0.7
COMER, WAYNE Harry Wayne B 2.3.1944 Shenandoah, VA BR/TR 5-10/175# d9.17																								
1967	Det A	4	3	0	1	0	0	0	0	0-0	0	0	.333	.333	.333	95	0	0-0	—	-0	0	0	/O(CF)	0.0
1968	†Det A	48	48	8	6	0	1	1	3	2-0	0	7	.125	.160	.229	16	-5	0-0	1.000	0	113	0	O-27(26-0-1)/C	-0.6
1969	Sea A	147	481	88	118	18	1	15	54	82-2	1	79	.245	.354	.380	108	8	18-7	.980	7	105	**161**	*O-139(20-92-46)/C3	1.1
1970	Mil A	13	17	1	1	0	0	0	1	0-0	0	3	.059	.059	.059	-67	-4	0-0	1.000	0	109	0	/O-5(1-2-2)	-0.4
	Was A	77	129	21	30	4	0	0	8	22-0	1	16	.233	.346	.264	75	-3	4-1	.960	-2	91	84	O-58(18-21-20)/3	-0.7
	Year	90	146	22	31	4	0	0	9	22-0	1	19	.212	.318	.240	59	-7	4-1	.962	-2	92	79	O-63(19-23-22)/3	-1.1
1972	Det A	27	9	1	1	0	0	0	1	0-0	0	1	.111	.100	.111	-33	-1	0-1	1.000	-1	69	0	O-17(15-1-1)	-0.3
Total	5	316	687	119	157	22	2	16	67	106-2	2	106	.229	.331	.336	90	-5	22-9	.978	4	102	131	O-247(80-117-70)/3-2,C-2	-0.9
COMISKEY, CHARLIE Charles Albert "Commy" or "The Old Roman" B 8.15.1859 Chicago, IL D 10.26.1931 Eagle River, WI BR/TR 6/180# d5.2 M12 HF1939 ▲																								
1882	StL AA	78	329	58	80	9	5	1	45	4			.243	.252	.310	85	-6		.967	-1	73	73	*1-77/P-2	-1.3
1883	StL AA	96	401	87	118	17	9	2	64	11			.294	.313	.397	120	7		.963	-1	70	**135**	*1-96/O(LF)M	-0.2
1884	StL AA	108	460	76	109	17	6	2	84	5	5		.237	.253	.313	81	-11		.969	2	101	116	*1-108/2PM	-1.7
1885	†StL AA	83	340	68	87	15	7	2	44	14	4		.256	.293	.359	101	-1		.969	1	110	92	*1-83,M	-0.6
1886	†StL AA	131	578	95	147	15	9	3	76	10	0		.254	.267	.327	82	-16	41	.975	5	125	125	*1-122/2-9,O-2(RF),M	-2.0
1887	†StL AA	125	538	139	180	22	5	4	103	27	7		.335	.374	.416	109	3	117	.976	4	**135**	115	*1-116/2-9,O-3(RF),M	-0.2
1888	†StL AA	**137**	576	102	157	22	5	6	83	12	4		.273	.292	.359	98	-5	72	.970	-4	95	109	*1-133/O-5(0-2-3),2-3,M	-2.0
1889	StL AA	137	587	105	168	28	10	3	102	19	3	19	.286	.312	.383	86	-16	65	.970	-1	95	106	*1-134/O-3(0-1-2),2-3,PM	-2.4
1890	Chi P	88	377	53	92	11	3	0	59	14	3	17	.244	.277	.289	49	-29	34	.965	-3	92	106	1-88,M	-3.2
1891	StL AA	**139**	572	84	148	16	2	2	88	33	7	25	.259	.307	.304	65	-29	38	.979	4	110	106	*1-139/O-2(LF),M	-3.3
1892	Cin N	141	551	61	125	14	6	3	71	32	4	16	.227	.274	.290	72	-20	30	.984	1	96	**132**	*1-141,M	-1.9

Year	Tm Lg	G	AB	R	H	2B	3B	HR	RBI	BB-IB	HP	SO	AVG	OBP	SLG	AOPS	ABR	SB-CS	FA	FR	Rng	Thr	G at Pos	BFW
1893	Cin N	64	259	38	57	12	1	0	26	11	2	2	.220	.257	.274	40	-23	9	.979	-6	59	143	1-64,M	-2.5
1894	Cin N	63	228	26	61	9	0	0	38	5	4	5	.268	.295	.307	44	-22	10	.973	-3	82	101	1-62/O(RF)M	-1.9
Total	13	1390	5796	992	1529	207	68	28	883	197	43	84	.264	.293	.337	81	-168	416	.973	-3	99	113	*1-1363/2-25,O-17(3-3-11),P-4	-23.2
COMMAND, JIM James Dalton "Igor" B 10.15.1928 Grand Rapids, MI BL/TR 6-2/200# d6.20																								
1954	Phi N	9	18	1	4	1	0	1	6	2	0	4	.222	.300	.444	91	0	0-0	.929	-0	96	0	/3-6	-0.1
1955	Phi N	5	5	0	0	0	0	0	0	0-0	0	0	.000	.000	.000	-99	-1	0-0	—	0			H	-0.1
Total	2	14	23	1	4	1	0	1	6	2-0	0	4	.174	.240	.348	52	-1	0-0	.929	-0	96	0	/3-6	-0.2
COMOROSKY, ADAM Adam Anthony B 12.9.1905 Swoyersville, PA D 3.2.1951 Swoyersville, PA BR/TR 5-10/167# d9.13																								
1926	Pit N	8	15	2	4	1	1	0	0	1	0	2	.267	.313	.467	102	0	1	1.000	-0	108	0	/O-6(LF)	0.0
1927	Pit N	18	61	5	14	1	0	0	4	3	0	1	.230	.266	.246	35	-6	0	.978	1	123	65	O-16(15-1-0)	-0.6
1928	Pit N	51	176	22	52	6	3	2	34	15	1	6	.295	.354	.398	92	-2	1	.968	1	113	52	O-49(38-9-5)	-0.4
1929	Pit N	127	473	86	152	26	11	6	97	40	2	22	.321	.377	.461	104	2	19	.963	-1	102	73	*O-121(LF)	-0.7
1930	Pit N	152	597	112	187	47	**23**	12	119	51	4	33	.313	.371	.529	114	12	14	.969	2	102	107	*O-152(130-30-0)	0.3
1931	Pit N	99	350	37	85	12	1	1	48	34	0	28	.243	.310	.291	63	-18	11	.978	3	110	81	O-90(89-0-1)	-2.0
1932	Pit N	108	370	54	106	18	4	4	46	25	3	20	.286	.337	.389	96	-2	7	.981	5	116	62	O-92(74-18-0)	-0.1
1933	Pit N	64	162	18	46	8	1	1	15	4	0	9	.284	.301	.364	89	-3	2	1.000	-1	101	42	O-30(LF)	-0.5
1934	Cin N	127	446	46	115	12	6	0	40	34	3	23	.258	.315	.312	70	-19	1	.970	-1	107	48	*O-122(47-9-66)	-2.7
1935	Cin N	59	137	22	34	3	1	2	14	7	1	14	.248	.290	.328	68	-7	1	.953	1	105	116	O-40(25-10-5)	-0.7
Total	10	813	2787	404	795	134	51	28	417	214	14	158	.285	.339	.400	91	-43	57	.972	10	107	74	O-718(575-77-77)	-7.4
COMPTON, PETE Anna Sebastian "Bash" B 9.28.1889 San Marcos, TX D 2.3.1978 Kansas City, MO BL/TL 5-11/170# d9.6																								
1911	StL A	28	107	9	29	4	0	0	5	8	0		.271	.322	.308	79	-3	2	.917	1	94	149	O-28(RF)	-0.3
1912	StL A	103	268	26	75	6	4	2	30	22	2		.280	.339	.354	102	0	11	.925	2	112	99	O-72(50-0-22)	-0.1
1913	StL A	63	100	14	18	5	2	2	17	13	0	13	.180	.274	.330	79	-3	2	.862	-2	79	85	O-21(8-5-8)	-0.6
1915	StL F	2	8	0	2	0	0	0	3	0	0	0	.250	.250	.250	39	-1	0	1.000	-0	62	0	/O-2(CF)	-0.1
	Bos N	35	116	10	28	7	1	1	12	8	0	11	.241	.290	.345	96	-1	4-1	.971	0	108	58	O-31(0-20-11)	-0.2
1916	Bos N	34	98	13	20	2	0	0	8	7	1	7	.204	.264	.224	53	-5	5	.939	-1	101	64	O-30(3-26-1)	-0.9
	Pit N	5	16	1	1	0	0	0	0	2	1	5	.063	.211	.063	-14	-2	0	.917	-0	120	0	/O-5(RF)	-0.3
	Year	39	114	14	21	2	0	0	8	9	2	12	.184	.256	.202	43	-7	5	.936	-1	104	53	O-35(3-26-6)	-1.2
1918	NY N	21	60	5	13	0	1	0	5	5	0	4	.217	.277	.250	62	-3	2	.971	1	106	169	O-19(12-2-5)	-0.2
Total	6	291	773	78	186	24	8	5	80	65	4	40	.241	.303	.312	83	-18	26-1	.933	1	104	95	O-208(73-55-80)	-2.7
COMPTON, MIKE Michael Lynn B 8.15.1944 Stamford, TX BR/TR 5-10/180# d4.17																								
1970	Phi N	47	110	8	18	0	1	1	7	9-3	2	22	.164	.240	.209	22	-13	0-0	.986	-1	87	119	C-40	-1.2
CONATSER, CLINT Clinton Astor "Connie" (born Astor Clinton Conatser) B 7.24.1921 Los Angeles, CA BR/TR 5-11/182# d4.21																								
1948	†Bos N	90	224	30	62	9	3	3	23	32	1	27	.277	.370	.384	106	3	0	.974	-2	99	68	O-76(24-52-0)	-0.1
1949	Bos N	53	152	10	40	6	0	3	16	14	0	19	.263	.325	.362	89	-3	0	.951	1	103	151	O-44(15-13-16)	-0.3
Total	2	143	376	40	102	15	3	6	39	46	1	46	.271	.352	.375	99	0	0	.965	-1	101	102	O-120(39-65-16)	-0.4
CONCEPCION, DAVE David Ismael (Benitez) B 6.17.1948 Aragua, Venezuela BR/TR 6-1/180# d4.6 OF Total (CF)																								
1970	†Cin N	101	265	38	69	6	3	1	19	23-5	3	45	.260	.324	.317	73	-10	10-2	.945	-3	101	110	S-93/2-3	-0.2
1971	Cin N	130	327	24	67	4	4	1	20	18-2	0	51	.205	.246	.251	42	-26	9-3	.974	-2	99	**115**	*S-112,2-10/3-7,O-5(CF)	-1.8
1972	†Cin N	119	378	40	79	13	2	2	29	32-8	2	65	.209	.272	.270	58	-21	13-6	.969	1	103	122	*S-114/3-9,2	-0.7
1973	Cin N✶	89	328	39	94	18	3	8	46	21-3	1	55	.287	.327	.433	116	6	22-5	.974	6	104	110	S-88/O-2(CF)	2.6
1974	Cin N	160	594	70	167	25	1	14	82	44-10	6	79	.281	.335	.397	106	4	41-6	.963	11	105	113	*S-160/O(CF)	4.1
1975	†Cin N★	140	507	62	139	23	1	5	49	39-4	2	51	.274	.326	.353	88	-9	33-6	.977	17	109	**141**	*S-130/3-6	3.0
1976	†Cin N★	152	576	74	162	28	7	9	69	49-11	1	68	.281	.335	.401	107	5	21-10	.968	17	105	105	*S-150	4.2
1977	Cin N★	156	572	59	155	26	3	8	64	46-6	0	77	.271	.322	.369	84	-13	29-7	**.986**	16	100	115	*S-156	2.3
1978	Cin N★	153	565	75	170	33	4	6	67	51-4	1	83	.301	.357	.405	113	11	23-10	.969	4	100	83	*S-152	3.3
1979	†Cin N✶	149	590	91	166	25	3	16	84	64-5	0	73	.281	.348	.415	108	7	19-7	.967	20	107	120	*S-148	4.5
1980	Cin N★	156	622	72	162	31	8	5	77	37-2	1	107	.260	.300	.360	84	-14	12-2	.978	-9	91	112	*S-155/2	-0.5
1981	Cin N★	106	421	57	129	28	0	5	67	37-1	1	61	.306	.358	.409	117	10	4-5	.960	8	98	113	*S-106	3.1
1982	Cin N★	147	572	48	164	25	4	5	53	45-4	0	61	.287	.337	.371	96	-3	13-6	.977	19	101	112	*S-145/13	3.3
1983	Cin N	143	528	54	123	22	0	1	47	56-9	0	81	.233	.303	.280	61	-26	14-9	.979	-6	93	83	*S-139/3-6,1	-1.9
1984	Cin N	154	531	46	130	26	1	4	58	52-5	0	72	.245	.307	.320	75	-17	22-6	.978	-27	83	71	*S-104,3-54/1-6	-3.4
1985	Cin N	155	560	59	141	19	2	7	48	50-3	3	67	.252	.314	.330	77	-17	16-12	.962	-31	87	75	*S-151/3-5	-3.5
1986	Cin N	90	311	42	81	13	2	3	30	26-1	0	43	.260	.314	.344	79	-9	13-2	.965	-1	101	97	S-60,1-12,2-10,3-10	-0.2
1987	Cin N	104	279	32	89	15	0	1	33	28-5	0	24	.319	.377	.384	99	1	4-3	.992	5	102	126	2-59,1-26,3-13/S-2	0.7
1988	Cin N	84	197	11	39	9	0	0	8	18-5	0	23	.198	.265	.244	45	-14	3-2	.994	3	99	127	2-46,1-16,S-13/3-9,P	-1.0
Total	19	2488	8723	993	2326	389	48	101	950	736-93	21	1186	.267	.322	.357	88	-135	321-109	.971	47	99	106	*S-2178,2-130,3-120/1-62,O-8C,P	17.9
CONCEPCION, ONIX Onix Cardona (Cardona) B 10.5.1957 Dorado, P.R. BR/TR 5-6/180# d8.30																								
1980	†KC A	12	15	1	2	0	0	0	2	0-0	0	1	.133	.133	.133	-26	-3	0-0	.833	-2	81	39	/S-6	-0.5
1981	KC A	2	0	0	0	0	0	0	0	0-0	0	0	—	—	—	—	0	0-0	—	-0	0	0	/S	0.0
1982	KC A	74	205	17	48	9	1	0	15	5-0	1	18	.234	.256	.288	49	-15	2-1	.948	-8	100	100	S-46,2-24/D	-1.8
1983	KC A	80	219	22	53	11	3	0	20	12-0	1	12	.242	.282	.320	66	-11	10-3	.913	-7	89	132	3-31,2-28,S-21/D	-1.4
1984	†KC A	90	287	36	81	9	2	1	23	14-0	3	33	.282	.319	.338	82	-7	9-6	.972	9	114	114	S-85/2-6,3	1.1
1985	†KC A	131	314	32	64	5	1	2	20	16-0	6	29	.204	.255	.245	38	-27	4-4	.959	6	**114**	94	*S-128/2-2	-1.1
1987	Pit N	1	1	0	1	0	0	0	0	0-0	0	0	1.000	1.000	1.000	429	0	0-0	—	0			/H	0.0
Total	7	390	1041	108	249	34	7	3	80	47-0	11	93	.239	.278	.294	58	-63	25-14	.960	-3	109	100	S-287/2-60,3-32,D-2	-3.7
CONDE, RAMON Ramon Luis (Roman) "Wito" B 12.29.1934 Juana Diaz, P.R. BR/TR 5-8/172# d7.17																								
1962	Chi A	14	16	0	0	0	0	0	1	3-0	0	3	.000	.158	.000	-54	-4	0-0	.889	-1	65	0	/3-7	-0.5
CONE, FRED Joseph Frederick B 5.1848 Rockford, IL D 4.13.1909 Chicago, IL 5-9.5/171# d5.5																								
1871	Bos NA	19	77	17	20	3	1	0	16	8	2		.260	.329	.325	86	-1	12-1	.854	-1	90	0	O-18(18-0-1)	0.1
CONGALTON, BUNK William Millar B 1.24.1875 Guelph, ON, CAN D 8.19.1937 Cleveland, OH BL/TL 5-11/190# d4.18																								
1902	Chi N	47	188	16	45	3	0	1	27	7	0		.239	.267	.271	68	-8	4	.988	0	96	67	O-47(0-5-43)	-1.0
1905	Cle A	12	47	4	17	0	0	0	5	2	0		.362	.388	.362	136	2	3	.923	-1	152	0	O-12(RF)	0.0
1906	Cle A	117	419	51	134	13	5	3	50	24	3		.320	.361	.396	139	18	12	.957	-9	41	0	*O-114(21-1-93)	0.4
1907	Cle A	9	22	2	4	0	0	0	2	4	0		.182	.308	.182	56	-1	0	1.000	0	125	0	/O-6(RF)	-0.1
	Bos A	124	496	44	142	11	8	2	47	20	3		.286	.318	.353	115	6	13	.969	-3	113	119	*O-123(RF)	-0.3
	Year	133	518	46	146	11	8	2	49	24	3		.282	.317	.346	112	5	13	.971	-2	114	113	*O-129(RF)	-0.4
Total	4	309	1172	117	342	27	13	6	131	57	6		.292	.328	.352	116	17	32	.967	-12	85	59	O-302(21-6-277)	-1.0
CONIGLIARO, TONY Anthony Richard B 1.7.1945 Revere, MA D 2.24.1990 Salem, MA BR/TR 6-3/185# d4.16 b-Billy																								
1964	Bos A	111	404	69	117	21	2	24	52	35-1	5	78	.290	.354	.530	135	19	2-4	.973	2	101	139	*O-106(81-25-2)	1.5
1965	Bos A	138	521	82	140	21	5	**32**	82	51-6	5	116	.269	.338	.512	131	20	4-2	.976	9	**116**	128	*O-137(0-2-135)	2.1
1966	Bos A	150	558	77	148	26	7	28	93	52-8	5	112	.265	.330	.487	120	14	0-2	.973	-4	94	96	*O-146(RF)	-0.1
1967	Bos A★	95	349	59	100	11	5	20	67	27-2	5	58	.287	.341	.519	141	17	4-6	.983	3	114	86	O-95(RF)	1.3
1969	Bos A	141	506	57	129	21	3	20	82	48-6	4	111	.255	.321	.427	103	1	2-4	.981	-11	88	39	*O-137(RF)	-1.9
1970	Bos A	146	560	89	149	20	1	36	116	43-4	8	93	.266	.324	.498	116	10	4-2	.977	-3	98	75	*O-146(RF)	0.0
1971	Cal A	74	266	23	59	18	0	4	15	23-1	1	52	.222	.285	.335	81	-7	3-3	.994	4	109	122	O-72(RF)	-0.7
1975	Bos A	21	57	8	7	1	0	2	9	8-0	0	9	.123	.221	.246	32	-5	1-0	—	0	0	0	D-15	-0.6
Total	8	876	3221	464	849	139	23	166	516	287-28	33	629	.264	.327	.476	118	69	20-23	.979	-0	102	95	O-839(81-27-733)/D-15	1.6
CONIGLIARO, BILLY William Michael B 8.15.1947 Revere, MA BR/TR 6/190# d4.11 b-Tony																								
1969	Bos A	32	80	14	23	6	2	4	7	9-0	1	23	.287	.367	.563	149	5	1-1	.926	-5	57	0	O-24(3-18-6)	-0.1
1970	Bos A	114	398	59	108	16	3	18	58	35-0	7	73	.271	.339	.462	112	6	3-7	.968	2	102	122	*O-108(77-25-20)	0.0
1971	Bos A	101	351	42	92	26	1	11	33	25-4	0	68	.262	.310	.436	102	1	3-2	.983	-1	101	81	*O-100(1-79-20)	-0.3
1972	Mil A	52	191	22	44	6	2	7	16	8-0	0	54	.230	.261	.393	95	-3	1-0	.992	5	121	138	O-50(2-6-45)	0.0
1973	†Oak A	48	110	5	22	2	2	0	14	9-1	0	26	.200	.252	.255	48	-8	1-0	1.000	3	104	227	O-40(21-18-3)/2	-0.7
Total	5	347	1130	142	289	56	10	40	128	86-5	8	244	.256	.311	.429	103	1	9-10	.980	3	102	114	O-322(104-146-94)/2	-1.1

Year	Tm Lg	G	AB	R	H	2B	3B	HR	RBI	BB-IB	HP	SO	AVG	OBP	SLG	AOPS	ABR	SB-CS	FA	FR	Rng	Thr	G at Pos	BFW
CONINE, JEFF Jeffrey Guy B 6.27.1966 Tacoma, WA BR/TR 6-1/220# d9.16																								
1990	KC A	9	20	3	5	2	0	0	2	2-0	0	5	.250	.318	.350	88	0	0-0	.977	-0	99	146	/1-9	-0.1
1992	KC A	28	91	10	23	5	2	0	9	8-1	0	23	.253	.313	.352	84	-2	0-0	1.000	-1	88	71	O-23(22-0-1)/1-4	-0.5
1993	Fla N	**162**	595	75	174	24	3	12	79	52-2	5	135	.292	.351	.403	97	-2	2-2	.992	-2	90	104	*O-147(LF),1-43	-1.1
1994	Fla N☆	**115**	451	60	144	27	6	18	82	40-4	1	92	.319	.373	.525	128	18	1-2	.974	1	103	71	O-97(LF),1-46	1.3
1995	Fla N★	133	483	72	146	26	2	25	105	66-5	1	94	.302	.379	.520	136	26	2-0	.976	0	96	101	*O-118(LF),1-14	2.1
1996	Fla N	157	597	84	175	32	2	26	95	62-1	4	121	.293	.360	.484	125	22	1-4	.975	2	86	114	*O-128(LF),1-48	1.4
1997	†Fla N	151	405	46	98	13	1	17	61	57-3	2	89	.242	.337	.405	98	-1	2-0	.992	9	**127**	112	*1-145/O(LF)	-0.2
1998	KC A	93	309	30	79	26	0	8	43	26-1	2	68	.256	.312	.417	87	-6	3-0	.993	-4	92	84	O-80(50-0-31),1-12/D-3	-1.3
1999	Bal A	139	444	54	129	31	1	13	75	30-0	3	40	.291	.335	.453	104	2	0-3	.993	-3	88	130	1-99,D-20,O-13(7-0-6)/3-4	-1.1
2000	Bal A	119	409	53	116	20	2	13	46	36-1	2	53	.284	.341	.438	101	0	4-3	.932	4	107	136	3-44,1-39,D-20,O-19(7-0-12)	-0.1
2001	Bal A	139	524	75	163	23	2	14	97	64-6	5	75	.311	.386	.443	126	22	12-8	.994	-2	83	94	1-80,O-36(22-0-16),3-17,D-12	1.0
2002	Bal A	116	451	44	123	26	4	15	63	25-6	2	66	.273	.307	.448	105	1	8-0	.990	-8	79	115	*1-103/O-6(LF),D-7	-1.5
2003	Bal A	124	493	75	143	33	3	15	80	37-5	5	60	.290	.338	.460	115	10	5-0	.992	-2	97	102	*1-118/O-8(6-0-2),3	-0.2
	†Fla N	25	84	13	20	3	0	5	15	13-0	0	10	.238	.337	.452	109	1	0-0	1.000	2	105	210	O-25(LF)	0.2
Total	13	1510	5356	694	1538	291	28	181	852	518-35	32	931	.287	.349	.453	112	91	40-22	.992	-3	102	108	1-760,O-701(636-0-68)/3-66,D-62	-0.1
CONLAN, JOCKO John Bertrand B 12.6.1899 Chicago, IL D 4.16.1989 Scottsdale, AZ BL/TL 5-7.5/165# d7.6 U24 HF1974																								
1934	Chi A	63	225	35	56	11	3	0	16	19	1	7	.249	.310	.324	62	-13	2-2	.955	-3	89	116	O-54(0-54-4)	-1.7
1935	Chi A	65	140	20	40	7	1	0	15	14	1	6	.286	.355	.350	81	-4	3-3	.961	-0	96	120	O-37(0-21-16)	-0.5
Total	2	128	365	55	96	18	4	0	31	33	2	13	.263	.327	.334	69	-17	5-5	.957	-3	92	117	/O-91(0-75-20)	-2.2
CONLON, JOCKO Arthur Joseph B 12.10.1897 Woburn, MA D 8.5.1987 Falmouth, MA BR/TR 5-7/145# d4.17																								
1923	Bos N	59	147	23	32	3	0	0	17	11	6	11	.218	.299	.238	45	-11	0-3	.955	-2	102	77	2-36/S-6,3-4	-1.2
CONN, BERT Albert Thomas B 9.22.1879 Philadelphia, PA D 11.2.1944 Philadelphia, PA TR 6/178# d9.16 ▲																								
1898	Phi N	1	3	1	1	0	1	0	1	0	0		.333	.333	1.000	291	1	0	1.000	-0	58	0	/P	0.0
1900	Phi N	6	9	4	3	1	0	0	1	0	0		.333	.333	.444	115	1	0	.667	-1	23	0	/P-4	0.0
1901	Phi N	5	18	2	4	1	0	0	0	0	1		.222	.263	.278	56	-1	0	.880	-2	93	0	/2-5	-0.2
Total	3	12	30	7	8	2	1	0	2	0	1		.267	.290	.400	95	1	0	.880	-2	93	0	/2-5,P-5	-0.2
CONNALLY, FRITZIE Fritzie Lee B 5.19.1958 Bryan, TX BR/TR 6-3/210# d9.9																								
1983	Chi N	8	10	0	1	0	0	0	0	0-0	0	5	.100	.100	.100	-42	-2	0-0	1.000	0	109	0	/3-3	-0.2
1985	Bal A	50	112	16	26	4	0	3	15	19-0	1	21	.232	.346	.348	94	0	0-0	.976	-2	96	50	3-46/1-2,D	-0.2
Total	2	58	122	16	27	4	0	3	15	19-0	1	26	.221	.329	.328	83	-2	0-0	.977	-2	97	48	/3-49,1-2,D	-0.4
CONNATSER, BRUCE Broadus Milburn B 9.19.1902 Sevierville, TN D 1.27.1971 Terre Haute, IN BR/TR 5-11.5/170# d9.15																								
1931	Cle A	12	49	5	14	3	0	0	4	2	1	3	.286	.327	.347	73	-2	0-0	1.000	1	138	41	1-12	-0.2
1932	Cle A	23	60	8	14	3	1	0	4	4	0	8	.233	.281	.317	51	-4	1-0	1.000	0	108	75	1-14	-0.5
Total	2	35	109	13	28	6	1	0	8	6	1	11	.257	.302	.330	61	-6	1-0	1.000	2	123	58	/1-26	-0.7
CONNAUGHTON, FRANK Frank Henry B 1.1.1869 Clinton, MA D 12.1.1942 Boston, MA BR/TR 5-9/165# d5.28																								
1894	Bos N	46	171	42	59	9	2	2	33	16	2	8	.345	.407	.456	100	0	3	.892	0	106	87	S-33/C-7;O-4(2-2-0)	0.2
1896	NY N	88	315	53	82	3	2	2	43	25	2	7	.260	.319	.302	66	-16	22	.892	5	116	88	S-54,O-30(LF)	-0.9
1906	Bos N	12	44	3	9	0	0	0	1	3	1		.205	.271	.205	50	-3	1	.918	-1	88	54	S-11/2	-0.4
Total	3	146	530	98	150	12	4	4	77	44	5	<u>15</u>	.283	.344	.343	78	-19	26	.894	4	110	84	/S-98,O-34(32-2-0),C-7,2	-1.1
CONNELL, GENE Eugene Joseph B 5.10.1906 Hazleton, PA D 8.31.1937 Waverly, NY BR/TR 6-0.5/180# d7.4 b-Joe																								
1931	Phi N	6	12	1	3	0	0	0	0	0	0	3	.250	.250	.250	32	-1	0	1.000	-1	*57*	*104*	/C-6	-0.2
CONNELL, JOE Joseph Bernard B 1.16.1902 Bethlehem, PA D 9.21.1977 Trexlertown, PA BL/TL 5-8/165# d6.15 b-Gene																								
1926	NY N	2	1	1	0	0	0	0	0	0	0	0	.000	.000	.000	-99	0	0	—	0			H	0.0
CONNELL, PETE Peter J. (born Patrick J. O'Connell) B 1862 Brooklyn, NY D 5.5.1892 Brooklyn, NY 6-1/180# d9.3																								
1886	NY AA	1	5	0	0	0	0	0	0	0	0		.000	.000	.000	-99	-1	0	.667	-1	55	0	/3	-0.2
1890	Bro AA	11	40	7	9	2	1	0	3	7	0		.225	.340	.325	100	0	3	.830	-1	100	106	3-10/1	-0.1
Total	2	12	45	7	9	2	1	0	3	7	0		.200	.308	.289	80	-1	3	.820	-2	96	97	/3-11,1	-0.3
CONNELL, TERRY Terence G. B 6.17.1855 Philadelphia, PA D 3.25.1924 Narbeth, PA d6.20																								
1874	Chi NA	1	4	0	0	0	0	0	0	0		0	.000	.000	.000	-99	-1	0-0	.429	-1			/C	-0.1
CONNELLY, TOM Thomas Martin B 10.20.1897 Chicago, IL D 2.18.1941 Hines, IL BL/TR 5-11.5/165# d9.24																								
1920	NY A	1	1	0	0	0	0	0	0	0	0	0	.000	.000	.000	-97	0	0-0	—	0			H	0.0
1921	NY A	4	5	0	1	0	0	0	0	1	0	0	.200	.333	.200	38	0	0-0	1.000	0	146	0	/O-3(0-1-2)	0.0
Total	2	5	6	0	1	0	0	0	0	1	0	0	.167	.286	.167	18	0	0-0	1.000	0	146	0	/O-3(0-1-2)	0.0
CONNOLLY, ED Edward Joseph Sr. B 7.17.1908 Brooklyn, NY D 11.12.1963 Pittsfield, MA BR/TR 5-8.5/180# d9.20 s-Ed																								
1929	Bos A	5	8	0	0	0	0	0	0	0	0	2	.000	.000	.000	-99	-2	0-0	.889	-0	*104*	*124*	/C-5	-0.3
1930	Bos A	27	48	1	9	2	0	0	7	4	0	3	.188	.250	.229	23	-6	0-0	1.000	0	*141*	*122*	C-26	-0.4
1931	Bos A	42	93	3	7	1	0	0	3	5	1	18	.075	.131	.086	-44	-20	0-0	.981	-1	*116*	*82*	C-41	-1.8
1932	Bos A	75	222	9	50	8	4	0	21	20	0	27	.225	.289	.297	54	-16	0-1	.957	-2	*69*	*130*	C-75	-1.3
Total	4	149	371	13	66	11	4	0	31	29	1	50	.178	.239	.229	23	-44	0-1	.966	-3	*90*	*117*	C-147	-3.8
CONNOLLY, RED John M. B 1863 New York, NY D 3.2.1896 New York, NY BB d7.1																								
1886	StL N	2	7	0	0	0	0	0	0	0		3	.000	.000	.000	-99	-2	0	—	-0	0	0	/O-2(CF)	-0.2
CONNOLLY, JOEY Joseph Francis B 2.1.1884 N.Smithfield, RI D 9.1.1943 N.Smithfield, RI BL/TR 5-7.5/165# d4.10																								
1913	Bos N	126	427	79	120	18	11	5	57	66	1	47	.281	.379	.410	123	15	18-21	.954	-5	88	100	*O-124(LF)	0.0
1914	†Bos N	120	399	64	122	28	10	9	65	49	8	36	.306	.393	.494	164	33	12	.974	-1	84	144	*O-118(115-0-5)	2.9
1915	Bos N	104	305	48	91	14	8	0	23	39	5	35	.298	.387	.397	144	18	13-12	.971	1	98	103	O-93(81-3-9)	1.4
1916	Bos N	62	110	11	25	5	2	0	12	14	1	13	.227	.320	.309	98	0	5	.980	1	98	138	O-31(14-4-12)	0.0
Total	4	412	1241	202	358	65	31	14	157	168	15	131	.288	.380	.425	139	66	48-<u>33</u>	.967	-5	90	117	O-366(334-7-26)	4.3
CONNOLLY, JOE Joseph H. "Coaster Joe" B 6.4.1896 San Francisco, CA D 3.30.1960 San Francisco, CA BR/TR 6/170# d10.1																								
1921	NY N	2	4	0	0	0	0	0	0	1	0	1	.000	.200	.000	-42	-1	0-0	1.000	-0	101	0	/O(LF)	-0.1
1922	Cle A	12	45	6	11	2	1	0	6	5	0	8	.244	.320	.333	70	-2	1-0	.972	1	103	153	O-12(CF)	-0.2
1923	Cle A	52	109	25	33	10	1	3	25	13	0	7	.303	.377	.495	129	5	1-2	.957	-3	82	60	O-39(2-3-34)	-0.1
1924	Bos A	14	10	1	1	0	0	0	1	2	0	2	.100	.250	.100	-7	-2	0-0	1.000	0	130	0	/O-3(RF)	-0.2
Total	4	80	168	32	45	12	2	3	32	21	0	18	.268	.349	.417	100	0	2-2	.966	-2	91	86	/O-55(3-15-37)	-0.6
CONNOLLY, BUD Mervin Thomas "Mike" B 5.25.1901 San Francisco, CA D 6.12.1964 Berkeley, CA BR/TR 5-8/154# d5.3																								
1925	Bos A	43	107	12	28	7	1	0	21	23	0	9	.262	.392	.346	88	-1	0-3	.950	-4	88	75	S-34/3-2	-0.2
CONNOLLY, TOM Thomas Francis "Blackie" or "Ham" B 12.30.1892 Boston, MA D 5.14.1966 Boston, MA BL/TR 5-11/175# d5.12																								
1915	Was A	50	141	14	26	3	2	0	7	14	2	19	.184	.268	.234	49	-9	5-4	.970	-2	88	102	3-24,O-19(11-0-8)/S-4	-1.2
CONNOR, NED Edward B 1850 , NY 5-9/156# d5.18																								
1871	Tro NA	7	33	6	7	0	0	0	2	0		0	.212	.212	.212	22	-3	0-0	.878	-1	167	50	/1-4,O-3(RF)	-0.2
CONNOR, JIM James Matthew (born James Matthew O'Connor) B 5.11.1863 Port Jervis, NY D 9.3.1950 Providence, RI BR/TR 5-10.5/179# d7.11																								
1892	Chi N	9	34	0	2	0	0	0	0	1	1	7	.059	.111	.059	-48	-6	0	.917	-4	76	0	/2-9	-1.0
1897	Chi N	77	285	40	83	10	5	3	38	24	4		.291	.355	.393	94	-3	10	.936	19	118	138	2-76	1.6
1898	Chi N	138	505	51	114	9	9	0	67	42	3		.226	.289	.279	63	-25	11	.946	-7	100	143	*2-138	-2.4
1899	Chi N	69	234	26	48	7	1	0	24	18	1		.205	.265	.244	41	-19	6	.942	2	111	126	2-44,3-25	-1.3
Total	4	293	1058	117	247	26	15	3	129	85	9	<u>7</u>	.233	.296	.295	64	-53	27	.942	10	106	135	2-267/3-25	-3.1
CONNOR, JOE Joseph Francis B 12.8.1874 Waterbury, CT D 11.8.1957 Waterbury, CT BR/TR 6-2/185# d9.9 b-Roger																								
1895	StL N	2	7	0	0	0	0	0	1	0	0	2	.000	.000	.000	-99	-2	0	1.000	1	138	0	/3-2	-0.1
1900	Bos N	7	19	2	4	0	0	0	4	2	0		.211	.286	.211	34	-2	1	.971	2	*98*	*127*	/C-7	0.0
1901	Mil A	38	102	10	28	3	1	1	9	6	1		.275	.321	.353	91	-1	4	.949	-3	*74*	*120*	C-30/23O(CF)	-0.2

Year	Tm Lg	G	AB	R	H	2B	3B	HR	RBI	BB-IB	HP	SO	AVG	OBP	SLG	AOPS	ABR	SB-CS	FA	FR	Rng	Thr	G at Pos	BFW
	Cle A	37	121	13	17	3	1	0	6	7	2		.140	.200	.182	7	-15	2	.942	-1	*94*	*93*	C-32/O-4(RF),S	-1.3
	Year	75	223	23	45	6	2	1	15	13	3		.202	.255	.260	45	-17	6	.946	-4	*85*	*105*	C-62/O-5(0-1-4),23S	-1.5
1905	NY A	8	22	4	5	1	0	0	2	3	0		.227	.320	.273	79	0	1	.978	1	*117*	*142*	/C-6,1-2	0.2
Total	4	92	271	29	54	7	2	1	22	18	3	2	.199	.257	.251	43	-20	8	.952	-1	*89*	*111*	/C-75,O-5(0-1-4),3-3,1-2,S2	-1.4
CONNOR, ROGER Roger B 7.1.1857 Waterbury, CT D 1.4.1931 Waterbury, CT BL/TL 6-3/220# d5.1 M1 HF1976 b-Joe																								
1880	Tro N	**83**	340	53	113	18	8	3	47	13		21	.332	.357	.459	166	22		.821	-11	93	108	*3-83	1.3
1881	Tro N	**85**	367	55	107	17	6	2	31	15		20	.292	.319	.387	115	6		.950	2	128	105	*1-85	0.3
1882	Tro N	81	349	65	115	22	**18**	4	42	13		20	.330	.354	.530	188	33		.951	0	183	123	1-43,O-24(5-19-0),3-14	2.6
1883	NY N	**98**	409	80	146	28	15	1	50	25		16	.357	.394	.506	173	36		.958	3	125	75	*1-98	2.6
1884	NY N	**116**	477	98	151	28	4	4	82	38		32	.317	.367	.417	143	24		.860	-1	94	103	2-67,O-37(CF),3-12	2.2
1885	NY N	110	455	102	**169**	23	15	1	65	51		8	**.371**	**.435**	.495	**203**	**54**		.975	3	**109**	**138**	*1-110	**4.3**
1886	NY N	118	485	105	172	29	**20**	7	71	41		15	.355	.405	.540	183	48	17	.973	10	**147**	104	*1-118	4.2
1887	NY N	127	471	113	134	26	22	17	104	75	8	50	.285	.392	.541	164	44	43	**.993**	5	96	100	*1-127	3.1
1888	†NY N	134	481	98	140	15	17	14	71	**73**	4	44	.291	.389	.480	**178**	45	27	.982	1	88	100	*1-133/2	3.3
1889	†NY N	**131**	496	117	157	32	17	13	**130**	93	2	46	.317	.426	**.528**	166	46	21	.977	-8	56	96	*1-131/3	2.3
1890	NY P	123	484	133	169	24	15	**14**	103	88	1	32	.349	.450	**.548**	152	37	22	**.985**	10	**129**	**111**	*1-123	2.8
1891	NY N	129	479	112	139	29	13	7	94	83	4	39	.290	.399	.449	153	37	27	.983	1	96	112	*1-129	2.3
1892	Phi N	**155**	564	123	166	**37**	11	12	73	116	6	39	.294	.420	.463	167	53	22	**.985**	-6	71	118	*1-155	4.2
1893	NY N	135	511	111	156	25	8	11	105	91	3	26	.305	.413	.450	129	24	24	.974	2	110	83	*1-135/3	2.1
1894	NY N	22	82	10	24	7	0	1	14	8	0	0	.293	.356	.415	86	-2	2	.976	2	131	108	1-21/O(RF)	0.0
	StL N	99	380	83	122	28	25	7	79	51	6	17	.321	.410	.582	137	21	17	.974	5	122	114	*1-99	1.9
	Year	121	462	93	146	35	25	8	93	59	6	17	.316	.400	.552	128	19	19	**.974**	6	**123**	**113**	*1-120/O(RF)	1.9
1895	StL N	104	401	78	131	29	9	8	78	63	3	10	.327	.422	.504	140	27	9	.986	5	111	90	*1-104	2.5
1896	StL N	126	483	71	137	21	9	11	72	52	2	14	.284	.356	.433	112	8	10	**.988**	13	**139**	57	*1-126,M	1.7
1897	StL N	22	83	13	19	3	1	1	12	13	0		.229	.333	.325	76	-3	3	.984	-0	95	41	1-22	-0.3
Total	18	1998	7797	1620	2467	441	233	138	1323	1002	39	449	.316	.397	.486	154	560	244	.978	33	109	100	*1-1759,3-111/2-68,O-62(5-56-1)	43.4
CONNORS, JERRY Jeremiah B Cleveland, OH d7.11																								
1892	Phi N	1	3	0	0	0	0	0	0	0	0	1	.000	.000	.000	-99	-1	0	—	-0	0	0	/O(RF)	-0.1
CONNORS, CHUCK Kevin Joseph Aloysius B 4.10.1921 Brooklyn, NY D 11.10.1992 Los Angeles, CA BL/TL 6-5/190# d5.1																								
1949	Bro N	1	1	0	0	0	0	0	0	0	0	0	.000	.000	.000	-96	0	0	—	0			H	0.0
1951	Chi N	66	201	16	48	5	1	2	18	12	0	25	.239	.282	.303	56	-13	4-0	.984	-2	95	84	1-57	-1.5
Total	2	67	202	16	48	5	1	2	18	12	0	25	.238	.280	.302	56	-13	4-0	.984	-2	95	84	/1-57	-1.5
CONNORS, MERV Mervyn James B 1.23.1914 Berkeley, CA BR/TR 6-2/192# d9.4																								
1937	Chi A	28	103	12	24	4	1	2	12	14	0	19	.233	.325	.350	70	-5	2-1	.926	-2	98	158	3-28	-0.5
1938	Chi A	24	62	14	22	4	0	6	13	9	0	17	.355	.437	.710	178	7	0-0	.979	0	117	131	1-16	0.6
Total	2	52	165	26	46	8	1	8	25	23	0	36	.279	.367	.485	111	2	2-1	.926	-1	98	158	/3-28,1-16	0.1
CONROY, BEN Bernard Patrick B 3.14.1871 Philadelphia, PA D 11.25.1937 Philadelphia, PA ?/160# d4.21																								
1890	Phi AA	117	404	45	69	13	1	0	21	45	5		.171	.262	.208	39	-30	17	.893	-1	107	98	S-74,2-42/O(CF)	-2.5
CONROY, WID William Edward B 4.5.1877 Camden, NJ D 12.6.1959 Mt.Holly, NJ BR/TR 5-9/158# d4.25 C1 OF Total (224-LF 76-CF 10-RF)																								
1901	Mil A	131	503	74	129	20	6	5	64	36	8		.256	.316	.350	89	-7	21	.922	17	106	97	*S-118,3-12	1.3
1902	Pit N	99	365	55	89	10	6	1	47	24	5		.244	.299	.312	86	-7	10	.925	8	104	**132**	S-95/O-3(2-0-1)	0.4
1903	NY A	126	503	74	137	23	12	1	45	32	5		.272	.322	.372	101	1	33	.919	3	104	88	*3-123/S-4	0.7
1904	NY A	140	489	58	119	18	12	1	52	43	7		.243	.314	.335	100	1	30	.944	7	108	86	*3-110,S-27/O-3(CF)	1.2
1905	NY A	101	385	55	105	19	11	2	25	32	0		.273	.329	.395	116	6	25	.928	0	87	23	3-48,O-25(20-3-2),S-17,1-10/2-3	0.7
1906	NY A	148	567	67	139	17	10	4	54	47	0		.245	.303	.332	89	-7	32	.968	-2	95	38	O-97(37-66-0),S-49/3-2	-1.4
1907	NY A	140	530	58	124	12	11	3	51	30	3		.234	.279	.315	83	-12	41	.955	8	76	60	*O-100(LF),S-38	-1.0
1908	NY A	141	531	44	126	22	3	1	39	14	1		.237	.258	.296	79	-14	23	.939	14	107	83	*3-119,2-12,O-10(5-1-4)	0.3
1909	Was A	139	488	44	119	13	4	1	20	37	1		.244	.298	.293	91	-5	24	.938	3	103	95	*3-120,2-13/O-5(2-3-0),S	0.1
1910	Was A	103	351	36	89	11	3	1	27	30	1		.254	.314	.311	100	0	11	.961	1	94	102	3-46,O-46(44-0-2)/2-5	0.0
1911	Was A	106	349	40	81	11	4	2	28	20	4		.232	.282	.304	64	-18	12	.930	8	116	102	3-85,O-15(14-0-1)/2	-0.9
Total	11	1374	5061	605	1257	176	82	22	452	345	35		.248	.301	.329	91	-62	262	.934	67	104	86	3-665,S-349,O-304L/2-34,1-10	1.4
CONROY, BILL William Frederick "Pep" B 1.9.1899 Chicago, IL D 1.23.1970 Chicago, IL BR/TR 5-8.5/160# d4.18																								
1923	Was A	18	60	6	8	2	2	0	2	4	0	9	.133	.188	.233	11	-8	0-0	.926	-1	67	0	3-10/1-6,O(CF)	-0.9
CONROY, BILL William Gordon B 2.26.1915 Bloomington, IL D 11.13.1997 Citrus Heights, CA BR/TR 6/185# d9.21 Mil 1945																								
1935	Phi A	1	4	0	1	1	0	0	0	1	0	0	.250	.400	.500	133	0	0-0	1.000	0	*73*	*0*	/C	0.0
1936	Phi A	1	2	0	1	0	0	0	0	0	0	1	.500	.500	.500	151	0	0-0	1.000	-0	*0*	*0*	/C	0.0
1937	Phi A	26	60	4	12	1	1	0	3	7	0	9	.200	.284	.250	36	-6	1-0	1.000	-1	*87*	*79*	C-18/1	-0.5
1942	Bos A	83	250	22	50	4	2	4	20	40	2	47	.200	.315	.280	66	-11	2-0	.971	-0	*113*	*93*	C-83	-0.6
1943	Bos A	39	89	13	16	5	0	1	6	18	3	19	.180	.336	.270	77	-1	0-0	.969	0	*108*	*92*	C-38	0.1
1944	Bos A	19	47	6	10	2	0	0	4	11	0	9	.213	.362	.255	79	-1	0-0	.972	-0	*103*	*105*	C-19	0.0
Total	6	169	452	45	90	13	3	5	33	77	5	85	.199	.322	.274	66	-19	3-0	.974	-2	*107*	*91*	C-160/1	-1.0
CONSOLO, BILLY William Angelo B 8.18.1934 Cleveland, OH BR/TR 5-11/180# d4.20 C15																								
1953	Bos A	47	65	9	14	2	1	1	6	2	0	23	.215	.239	.323	48	-5	1-2	.808	5	121	185	3-16,2-11	0.0
1954	Bos A	91	242	23	55	7	1	1	11	33	2	69	.227	.324	.277	59	-12	2-1	.953	-2	97	84	S-50,3-18,2-12	-1.0
1955	Bos A	8	18	4	4	0	0	0	0	5-0	0	4	.222	.391	.222	63	-1	0-0	.889	-3	49	35	/2-4	-0.3
1956	Bos A	48	11	13	2	0	0	0	1	3-0	0	5	.182	.357	.182	41	-1	0-0	.920	4	207	215	2-25	0.3
1957	Bos A	68	196	26	53	6	1	4	19	23-0	0	48	.270	.345	.372	91	-2	1-3	.933	9	124	110	S-42,2-16/3-2	1.1
1958	Bos A	46	72	13	9	2	1	0	5	6-0	0	14	.125	.192	.181	3	-10	0-0	.925	4	91	124	2-13,S-11/3	-0.5
1959	Bos A	10	14	3	3	1	0	0	0	2-0	0	5	.214	.313	.286	63	-1	0-0	.818	-1	46	70	/S-2	-0.2
	Was A	79	202	25	43	5	3	0	10	36-0	0	54	.213	.332	.267	67	-8	1-0	.952	10	114	105	S-75/2-4	0.8
	Year	89	216	28	46	6	3	0	10	38-0	0	59	.213	.331	.269	66	-9	1-0	.948	9	112	104	S-77/2-4	0.6
1960	Was A	100	174	23	36	4	2	3	15	25-1	1	29	.207	.310	.305	68	-8	1-1	.938	-3	100	107	S-82,2-12/3-2	-0.6
1961	Min A	11	5	1	0	0	0	0	0	0-0	0	1	.000	.000	.000	-95	-1	0-0	1.000	-1	49	0	/2-3,S-3,3	-0.2
1962	Phi N	13	5	3	2	0	0	0	0	0-0	0	1	.400	.400	.400	119	0	0-0	—	-0	0	0	/3	0.0
	LA A	28	20	4	2	0	0	0	0	3-0	0	11	.100	.217	.100	-12	-3	2-0	.917	1	105	314	3-20/S-4,2	-0.1
	KC A	54	154	11	37	4	2	0	16	23-2	0	33	.240	.337	.292	68	-6	1-3	.950	0	104	93	S-48	-0.3
	Year	82	174	15	39	4	2	0	16	26-2	0	44	.224	.323	.270	61	-9	3-3	.944	2	107	88	S-52,3-20/2	-0.4
Total	10	603	1178	158	260	31	11	9	83	161-3	3	297	.221	.315	.289	63	-58	9-10	.945	24	109	101	S-317,2-101/3-61	-1.0
CONTI, JASON Stanley Jason B 1.27.1975 Pittsburgh, PA BL/TR 5-11/180# d6.29																								
2000	Ari N	47	91	11	21	4	3	1	15	7-2	1	30	.231	.293	.374	65	-5	3-0	.983	4	117	290	O-35(2-4-33)	-0.2
2001	Ari N	5	4	1	1	0	0	0	0	1-0	0	2	.250	.400	.250	70	0	0-0	—	-0	0	0	/O(RF)	0.0
2002	TB A	78	222	26	57	15	2	3	21	18-1	1	55	.257	.315	.383	86	-4	4-2	.966	7	114	214	O-74(21-28-28)	0.1
2003	Mil N	30	48	3	11	2	0	2	7	2-0	0	18	.229	.255	.396	69	-2	0-1	.909	1	133	139	O-20(1-1-19)	-0.2
Total	4	160	365	41	90	21	5	6	43	28-3	2	105	.247	.303	.381	78	-11	7-3	.963	12	117	223	O-130(24-33-81)	-0.3
CONWAY, CHARLIE Charles Connell B 4.28.1886 Youngstown, OH D 9.12.1968 Youngstown, OH BR/TR d4.15																								
1911	Was A	2	3	0	1	0	1	0	0	0	0		.333	.333	1.000	272	0	0	.000	-0	0	0	/O-2	0.0
CONWAY, JACK Jack Clements B 7.30.1919 Bryan, TX D 6.11.1993 Waco, TX BR/TR 5-11.5/175# d9.9 Mil 1942-45																								
1941	Cle A	2	2	0	1	0	0	0	1	0	0	0	.500	.500	.500	174	0	0-0	1.000	1	151	0	/S-2	0.1
1946	Cle A	68	258	24	58	6	2	0	18	20	0	36	.225	.281	.264	56	-16	2-2	.955	-9	85	74	2-50,S-14/3-3	-2.4
1947	Cle A	34	50	3	9	2	0	0	5	3	0	8	.180	.226	.220	25	-5	0-0	.877	-1	106	131	S-24/2-5,3	-0.5
1948	NY N	24	49	8	12	2	1	1	3	5	0	10	.245	.315	.388	89	-1	0	.985	4	120	143	2-13/S-6,3-3	0.3
Total	4	128	359	35	80	10	3	1	27	28	0	54	.223	.279	.276	57	-22	2-2	.962	-6	91	84	/2-68,S-46,3-7	-2.5
CONWAY, OWEN Owen Sylvester B 10.23.1890 New York, NY D 3.12.1942 Philadelphia, PA TR d6.21																								
1915	Phi A	4	15	2	1	0	0	0	0	0	0	3	.067	.067	.067	-62	-3	0	.750	0	115	197	/3-4	-0.3

Year	Tm Lg	G	AB	R	H	2B	3B	HR	RBI	BB-IB	HP	SO	AVG	OBP	SLG	AOPS	ABR	SB-CS	FA	FR	Rng	Thr	G at Pos	BFW
CONWAY, PETE Peter J. B 10.30.1866 Burmont, PA D 1.13.1903 Clifton Heights, PA BR/TR 5-10.5/162# d8.10 b-Jim ▲																								
1885	Buf N	29	90	7	10	5	0	1	7	5		28	.111	.158	.200	15	-8		.889	-1	112	0	P-27/O-2(RF),S1	-0.1
1886	KC N	51	194	22	47	8	2	1	18	5		34	.242	.261	.320	71	-7	3	.857	-3	122	172	O-31(3-20-8),P-23	-0.6
	Det N	12	43	10	8	1	0	2	3	1		8	.186	.205	.349	63	-2	0	.846	-1	101	0	P-11/O(LF)	0.0
	Year	63	237	32	55	9	2	3	21	6		42	.232	.251	.325	70	-9	3	.826	-3	89	49	P-34,O-32(4-20-8)	-0.6
1887	†Det N	24	95	16	22	5	1	1	7	2	0	9	.232	.247	.337	58	-6	0	**.979**	1	131	0	P-17/O-8(LF)	-0.2
1888	Det N	45	167	28	46	4	2	3	23	8	3	25	.275	.320	.377	120	4	1	.938	2	114	230	P-45/O(LF)	0.1
1889	Pit N	3	10	2	1	0	0	1	2	1	0	3	.100	.182	.400	67	-1	1	.875	0	139	0	/P-3,O(LF)	0.0
Total	5	164	599	85	134	23	5	9	60	22	3	107	.224	.255	.324	73	-20	5	.907	-0	110	99	P-126/O-44(14-20-10),1S	-0.8
CONWAY, RIP Richard Daniel B 4.18.1896 White Bear Lake, MN D 12.3.1971 St.Paul, MN BL/TR 5-6/160# d4.16 Mil 1918																								
1918	Bos N	14	24	4	4	0	0	0	2	2	0	4	.167	.231	.167	23	-2	1	.810	-3	61	0	/2-5,3	-0.6
CONWAY, BILL William F. B 11.28.1861 Lowell, MA D 12.28.1943 Somerville, MA BR/TR 5-8/170# d7.28 b-Dick																								
1884	Phi N	1	4	0	0	0	0	0	0	0		1	.000	.000	.000	-99	-1		1.000	0			/C	-0.1
1886	Bal AA	7	14	4	2	0	0	0	3	7	0		.143	.429	.143	84	1	0	.925	-3			/C-7	-0.2
Total	2	8	18	4	2	0	0	0	3	7	0	1	.111	.360	.111	52	0	0	.936	-3			/C-8	-0.3
CONWELL, ED Edward James "Irish" B 1.29.1890 Chicago, IL D 5.1.1926 Chicago, IL BR/TR 5-11/155# d9.22																								
1911	StL N	1	1	0	0	0	0	0	0	0	0	1	.000	.000	.000	-99	0	0	.000	-1	0	0	/3	-0.1
CONYERS, HERB Herbert Leroy B 1.8.1921 Cowgill, MO D 9.16.1964 Cleveland, OH BL/TR 6-4/205# d4.18																								
1950	Cle A	7	9	2	3	0	0	1	1	1	0	2	.333	.400	.667	175	1	1-0	1.000	-0	0	0	/1	0.1
COOGAN, DALE Dale Roger B 8.14.1930 Los Angeles, CA D 3.8.1989 Mission Viejo, CA BL/TL 6-1/190# d4.22																								
1950	Pit N	53	129	19	31	6	1	1	13	17	2	24	.240	.338	.326	73	-5	0	.980	2	135	96	1-32	-0.3
COOGAN, DAN Daniel George B 2.16.1875 Philadelphia, PA D 10.28.1942 Philadelphia, PA 5-8/128# d4.25																								
1895	Was N	26	77	9	17	2	1	0	7	13	0	6	.221	.333	.273	58	-4	1	.746	-9	81	71	S-18/C-5,O-2(RF),3	-1.0
COOK, JIM James Fitchie B 11.10.1879 Dundee, IL D 6.17.1949 St.Louis, MO BR/TR 5-9/163# d7.2																								
1903	Chi N	8	26	3	4	1	0	0	2	2	1		.154	.241	.192	25	-2	1	1.000	-1	0	0	/O-5(CF),2-2,1	-0.4
COOK, DOC Luther Almus B 6.24.1886 Whitt, TX D 6.30.1973 Lawrenceburg, TN BL/TR 6/170# d8.7																								
1913	NY A	20	72	9	19	2	1	0	1	10	2	4	.264	.369	.319	101	1	1	.939	-0	101	88	O-20(0-13-7)	-0.1
1914	NY A	132	470	59	133	11	3	1	40	44	9	60	.283	.356	.326	105	4	26-32	.949	-3	94	97	*O-127(1-10-116)	-1.2
1915	NY A	132	476	70	129	16	5	2	33	62	8	43	.271	.364	.338	111	8	29-18	.959	-1	93	123	*O-131(RF)	0.1
1916	NY A	4	10	0	1	0	0	0	1	0	0	2	.100	.100	.100	-39	-2	0	1.000	-0	98	0	/O-3(RF)	-0.2
Total	4	288	1028	138	282	29	9	3	75	116	19	109	.274	.359	.329	106	11	56-50	.953	-5	94	108	O-281(1-23-257)	-1.4
COOK, PAUL Paul B 5.5.1863 Caledonia, NY D 5.25.1905 Rochester, NY BR/TR 5-10/185# d9.13																								
1884	Phi N	3	12	0	1	0	0	0	0	0		2	.083	.083	.083	-50	-2		.818	-2			/C-3	-0.3
1886	Lou AA	66	262	28	54	5	2	0	14	10	0		.206	.235	.240	46	-17	6	.945	-7	98	104	1-43,C-21/O-2(1-0-1)	-2.3
1887	Lou AA	61	223	34	55	4	2	0	17	11	4		.247	.294	.283	60	-12	15	.916	-4			C-55/1-6	-1.0
1888	Lou AA	57	185	20	34	2	0	0	13	5	4		.184	.222	.195	35	-13	9	.901	-8			C-53/O-4(1-0-3),S	-1.6
1889	Lou AA	81	286	34	65	10	1	0	15	15	9	48	.227	.287	.269	60	-15	11	.925	3			C-74/O-7(0-2-5),S1	-0.5
1890	Bro P	58	218	32	55	3	3	0	31	14	2	18	.252	.303	.294	56	-15	7	.890	3	*129*	*120*	C-36,1-21/O(RF)	-0.8
1891	Lou AA	45	153	21	35	3	1	0	23	11	1	17	.229	.285	.261	57	-9	4	.909	-10	*83*	*105*	C-35,1-10	-1.5
	StL AA	7	25	3	5	0	0	0	1	1	1	2	.200	.259	.200	28	-2	0	.921	1	*116*	*88*	/C-7	0.0
	Year	52	178	24	40	3	1	0	24	12	2	19	.225	.281	.253	52	-11	4	.912	-8	*90*	*101*	/C-42,1-10	-1.5
Total	7	378	1364	172	304	27	9	0	114	67	21	87	.223	.270	.256	52	-85	52	.906	-22	*30*	*30*	C-284/1-81,O-14(2-2-10),S-2	-8.0
COOK, CLIFF Raymond Clifford B 8.20.1936 Dallas, TX BR/TR 6/188# d9.9																								
1959	Cin N	9	21	3	8	2	1	0	5	2-1	0	8	.381	.435	.571	161	2	1-0	.909	0	104	190	/3-9	0.2
1960	Cin N	54	149	9	31	7	0	3	13	8-1	0	51	.208	.247	.315	52	-10	0-0	.954	3	104	123	3-47/O-4(3-1-0)	-0.8
1961	Cin N	4	5	0	0	0	0	0	0	0-0	0	4	.000	.000	.000	-99	-1	0-0	1.000	0	155	0	/3	-0.1
1962	Cin N	6	5	0	0	0	0	0	0	0-0	0	2	.000	.000	.000	-97	-1	0-0	1.000	-0	0	0	/3-4	-0.2
	NY N	40	112	12	26	6	1	2	9	4-0	3	34	.232	.275	.357	68	-5	1-0	.875	-5	76	69	3-16,O-10(RF)	-1.1
	Year	46	117	12	26	6	1	2	9	4-0	3	36	.222	.264	.342	61	-7	1-0	.878	-5	73	66	3-20,O-10(RF)	-1.3
1963	NY N	50	106	9	15	2	1	2	8	12-4	0	37	.142	.229	.236	34	-9	0-1	1.000	2	96	182	O-21(8-1-12)/3-9,1-5	-0.9
Total	5	163	398	33	80	17	3	7	35	26-6	3	136	.201	.254	.312	54	-24	2-1	.937	0	102	101	/3-86,O-35(11-2-22),1-5	-2.9
COOKE, DUSTY Allen Lindsey B 6.23.1907 Swepsonville, NC D 11.21.1987 Raleigh, NC BL/TR 6-1/205# d4.15 M1 C5																								
1930	NY A	92	216	43	55	12	3	6	29	32	1	61	.255	.353	.421	100	0	4-6	.978	1	111	47	O-73(21-28-24)	-0.3
1931	NY A	27	39	10	13	1	0	1	6	8	0	11	.333	.447	.436	141	3	4-1	1.000	1	136	0	O-11(7-0-6)	0.3
1932	NY A	3	0	1	0	0	0	0	0	1	0	0	—	1.000	—	191	0	0-0	—	0			H	0.0
1933	Bos A	119	454	86	133	35	10	5	54	67	2	71	.293	.386	.447	121	16	7-5	.956	-5	98	62	*O-118(47-70-30)	0.6
1934	Bos A	74	168	34	41	8	5	1	26	36	0	25	.244	.377	.369	87	-2	7-2	.976	-2	95	33	O-44(9-14-21)	-0.5
1935	Bos A	100	294	51	90	18	6	3	34	46	0	24	.306	.400	.439	109	5	6-8	.972	-2	100	66	O-82(7-35-44)	-0.1
1936	Bos A	111	341	58	93	20	3	6	47	72	1	48	.273	.401	.402	93	-1	4-3	.972	-1	108	35	O-91(24-1-67)	-0.7
1938	Cin N	82	233	41	64	15	1	2	33	28	1	36	.275	.355	.373	103	2	0	.963	1	106	89	O-51(46-0-7)	0.0
Total	8	608	1745	324	489	109	28	24	229	290	5	276	.280	.384	.416	106	23	32-25	.969	-7	104	55	O-470(161-148-199)	-0.7
COOKE, FRED Frederick B. B Paulding, OH ?/ 16# d47.30																								
1897	Cle N	5	17	2	5	2	0	0	3	3	0		.294	.400	.412	109	0	0	.857	1	490	0	/O-5(RF)	0.1
COOKSON, BRENT Brent Adam B 9.7.1969 Van Nuys, CA BR/TR 5-11/200# d8.12																								
1995	KC A	22	35	2	5	1	0	0	5	2-0	0	7	.143	.189	.171	-5	-6	1-0	1.000	-0	98	0	O-12(10-0-2)/D-2	-0.6
1999	LA N	3	5	0	1	0	0	0	0	0-0	0	1	.200	.200	.200	2	-1	0-0	1.000	0	146	0	/O-3(2-0-1)	-0.1
Total	2	25	40	2	6	1	0	0	5	2-0	0	8	.150	.190	.175	-4	-7	1-0	1.000	-0	106	0	/O-15(12-0-3),D-2	-0.7
COOLBAUGH, MIKE Michael Robert B 6.5.1972 Binghamton, NY BR/TR 6-1/185# d7.16 b-Scott																								
2001	Mil N	39	70	10	14	6	0	2	7	5-0	2	16	.200	.273	.371	66	-4	0-0	.971	-1	92	189	3-27/S-3	-0.4
2002	StL N	5	12	0	1	0	0	0	0	1-0	0	3	.083	.154	.083	-35	-2	0-0	1.000	1	143	530	/3-4	-0.1
Total	2	44	82	10	15	6	0	2	7	6-0	2	19	.183	.256	.329	52	-6	0-0	.977	0	101	247	/3-31,S-3	-0.5
COOLBAUGH, SCOTT Scott Robert B 6.13.1966 Binghamton, NY BR/TR 5-11/185# d9.2 b-Mike																								
1989	Tex A	25	51	7	14	1	0	2	7	4-0	0	12	.275	.321	.412	105	0	0-0	.958	4	133	113	3-23/D-2	0.4
1990	Tex A	67	180	21	36	6	0	2	13	15-0	1	47	.200	.264	.267	49	-12	1-0	.941	6	111	118	3-66	-0.6
1991	SD N	60	180	12	39	8	1	2	15	19-2	1	45	.217	.294	.306	67	-8	0-3	.952	0	105	101	3-54	-0.9
1994	StL N	15	21	4	4	0	0	2	6	1-0	0	4	.190	.217	.476	79	-1	0-0	1.000	-1	0	146	/1-4,3-4	-0.2
Total	4	167	432	44	93	15	1	8	41	39-2	2	108	.215	.281	.310	65	-21	1-3	.949	11	112	108	3-147/1-4,D-2	-1.3
COOLEY, DUFF Duff Gordon "Dick" B 3.29.1873 Leavenworth, KS D 8.9.1937 Dallas, TX BL/TR 5-11/158# d7.27 OF Total (549-LF 479-CF 69-RF)																								
1893	StL N	29	107	20	37	2	3	0	21	8	0	9	.346	.391	.421	115	2	8	.947	-5	50	0	O-15(RF),C-10/S-5	-0.2
1894	StL N	54	206	35	61	3	1	1	21	12	0	16	.296	.335	.335	62	-13	7	.833	-11	15	63	O-39(8-4-28),3-13/S1	-2.0
1895	StL N	133	567	108	194	9	20	7	75	37	3	29	.342	.386	.466	121	14	27	.934	8	86	21	*O-125(116-8-1)/3-5,S-3,C	0.9
1896	StL N	40	166	29	51	5	3	0	13	7	0	3	.307	.335	.373	90	-3	12	.959	-3	33	0	O-40(LF)	-0.8
	Phi N	64	287	63	88	6	4	2	22	18	0	16	.307	.348	.376	92	-4	18	.901	-4	70	85	O-64(22-40-2)	-1.1
	Year	104	453	92	139	11	7	2	35	25	0	19	.307	.343	.375	91	-7	30	.923	-7	55	50	*O-104(62-40-2)	-1.9
1897	Phi N	**133**	566	124	186	14	13	4	40	51	2		.329	.386	.420	116	13	31	.960	3	84	162	*O-131(0-108-23)/1-2	0.7
1898	Phi N	149	629	123	196	24	12	4	55	48	4		.312	.364	.407	126	21	17	.943	1	73	40	*O-149(CF)	1.1
1899	Phi N	94	406	75	112	15	8	1	31	29	4		.276	.330	.360	92	-5	15	.971	-6	88	126	1-79,O-14(CF)/2	-1.0
1900	Pit N	66	249	30	50	8	1	0	22	14	0		.201	.243	.241	34	-23	9	.989	-5	53	118	1-66	-2.7
1901	Bos N	63	240	27	62	13	3	0	27	14	1		.258	.302	.338	78	-7	5	.943	-1	68	59	O-53(29-24-0),1-10	-1.1
1902	Bos N	135	548	73	162	26	8	0	58	34	2		.296	.339	.372	118	11	27	.952	-7	40	46	*O-127(94-33-0)/1-7	-0.3
1903	Bos N	138	553	76	160	26	10	1	70	44	0		.289	.342	.378	109	6	27	.952	-5	62	88	*O-126(124-3-0),1-13	-0.6
1904	Bos N	122	467	41	127	18	7	5	70	24	3		.272	.312	.373	115	7	14	.976	-7	20	82	*O-116(LF)/1-6	-0.7

Year	Tm Lg	G	AB	R	H	2B	3B	HR	RBI	BB-IB	HP	SO	AVG	OBP	SLG	AOPS	ABR	SB-CS	FA	FR	Rng	Thr	G at Pos	BFW
1905	Det A	97	377	25	93	11	9	1	32	26	1		.247	.297	.332	99	-2	7	.959	5	113	192	O-96(CF)	-0.1
Total	13	1317	5368	849	1579	180	102	26	557	366	20	73	.294	.342	.380	104	17	224	.945	-36	63	78	*O-1095L,1-184/3-18,C-11,S-9,2	-7.9

COOMBS, CECIL Cecil Lysander B 3.18.1888 Moweaqua, IL D 11.25.1975 Fort Worth, TX BR/TR 5-9/160# d8.7

Year	Tm Lg	G	AB	R	H	2B	3B	HR	RBI	BB-IB	HP	SO	AVG	OBP	SLG	AOPS	ABR	SB-CS	FA	FR	Rng	Thr	G at Pos	BFW
1914	Chi A	7	23	1	4	1	0	0	1	1	0	7	.174	.208	.217	28	-2	0-1	1.000	1	93	245	/O-7(CF)	-0.2

COOMBS, JACK John Wesley "Colby Jack" B 11.18.1882 LeGrand, IA D 4.15.1957 Palestine, TX BB/TR 6/185# d7.5 M1 C1 ▲

Year	Tm Lg	G	AB	R	H	2B	3B	HR	RBI	BB-IB	HP	SO	AVG	OBP	SLG	AOPS	ABR	SB-CS	FA	FR	Rng	Thr	G at Pos	BFW
1906	Phi A	24	67	9	16	2	0	0	3	1	1		.239	.261	.269	64	1	2	.967	-1	80	**288**	P-23	0.0
1907	Phi A	24	48	4	8	0	0	1	4	0	0		.167	.167	.229	25	-1	1	.979	-0	89	185	P-23	0.0
1908	Phi A	78	220	24	56	9	5	1	23	9	1		.255	.287	.355	101	-1	6	.990	5	106	194	O-47(1-11-35),P-26/1	0.3
1909	Phi A	37	83	4	14	4	0	0	10	4	1		.169	.216	.217	36	1	1	.973	-0	95	127	P-30	0.0
1910	†Phi A	46	132	20	29	3	0	0	9	7	2		.220	.270	.242	61	3	3	**.990**	-5	68	74	P-45	0.0
1911	†Phi A	52	141	31	45	6	1	2	23	8	0		.319	.356	.418	118	13	5	.913	-3	77	118	P-47	0.0
1912	Phi A	56	110	10	28	2	0	0	13	14	1		.255	.344	.273	80	6	1	**1.000**	-1	87	188	P-40	0.0
1913	Phi A	2	3	1	1	1	0	0	0	0	0	2	.333	.333	.667	195	1	0	.500	-0	0	0	/P-2	0.0
1914	Phi A	5	11	0	3	1	0	0	2	1	0	1	.273	.333	.364	114	0	0-1	1.000	-0	44	0	/P-2,O-2(CF)	0.0
1915	Bro N	29	75	8	21	1	1	0	5	2	0	17	.280	.299	.320	86	4	0-1	.980	-4	58	110	P-29	0.0
1916	†Bro N	27	61	2	11	2	0	0	3	2	0	10	.180	.206	.213	28	0	0	**1.000**	-6	36	82	P-27	0.0
1917	Bro N	32	44	4	10	0	1	0	2	4	0	9	.227	.292	.273	72	2	1	.971	-3	65	76	P-31	0.0
1918	Bro N	46	113	6	19	3	2	0	3	7	1	5	.168	.223	.230	38	-9	1	.962	-4	75	0	P-27,O-13(0-3-11)	-0.5
1920	Det A	2	2	0	0	0	0	0	0	0	0	0	.000	.000	.000	-99	0	0-0	1.000	-0	65	0	/P-2	0.0
Total	14	460	1110	123	261	34	10	4	100	59	7	44	.235	.278	.295	74	20	21-2	.966	-23	75	118	P-354/O-62(1-16-46),1	-0.2

COOMER, RON Ronald Bryan B 11.18.1966 Crest Hill, IL BR/TR 5-11/195# d8.1

Year	Tm Lg	G	AB	R	H	2B	3B	HR	RBI	BB-IB	HP	SO	AVG	OBP	SLG	AOPS	ABR	SB-CS	FA	FR	Rng	Thr	G at Pos	BFW
1995	Min A	37	101	15	26	3	1	5	19	9-0	1	11	.257	.324	.455	100	-1	0-1	.993	1	111	92	1-22,3-13/O(RF)D	-0.1
1996	Min A	95	233	34	69	12	1	12	41	17-1	0	24	.296	.340	.511	110	3	3-0	.993	2	161	83	1-57,O-23(RF)/3-9,D-3	0.1
1997	Min A	140	523	63	156	30	2	13	85	22-5	0	91	.298	.324	.438	96	-5	4-3	.966	-3	99	102	*3-119/1-9,O-7(RF),D-7	-0.7
1998	Min A	137	529	54	146	22	1	15	72	18-1	0	72	.276	.295	.406	80	-17	2-2	.972	-4	90	83	3-75,1-54,D-13/O-3(RF)	-2.5
1999	Min A★	127	467	53	123	25	1	16	65	30-1	1	69	.263	.307	.424	82	-14	2-1	.996	9	130	108	1-71,3-57/O(RF)D	-1.0
2000	Min A	140	544	64	147	29	1	16	82	36-2	4	50	.270	.317	.415	81	-17	2-0	.995	2	92	94	*1-124/3-5,D-9	-2.4
2001	Chi N	111	349	25	91	19	1	8	53	29-1	2	70	.261	.316	.390	87	-7	0-0	.954	1	91	105	3-76,1-36/D	-0.7
2002	†NY A	55	148	14	39	7	0	3	17	6-1	0	23	.264	.290	.372	75	-6	0-0	.882	-4	78	58	3-26,D-15,1-11	-1.1
2003	LA N	69	125	11	30	4	0	4	15	10-2	1	19	.240	.299	.368	78	-5	0-0	1.000	-0	115	96	1-24,3-11/D-4	-0.6
Total	9	911	3019	333	827	151	8	92	449	177-14	9	429	.274	.313	.421	87	-69	13-7	.996	3	115	97	1-408,3-391/D-63,O-35(RF)	-9.0

COON, WILLIAM William K. B 3.21.1855 , PA D 8.30.1915 Burlington, NJ d9.4

Year	Tm Lg	G	AB	R	H	2B	3B	HR	RBI	BB-IB	HP	SO	AVG	OBP	SLG	AOPS	ABR	SB-CS	FA	FR	Rng	Thr	G at Pos	BFW
1875	Ath NA	4	12	1	2	0	0	0	1	0		0	.167	.167	.167	15	-1	1-0	.810	-0			/C-4,O(RF)	-0.1
1876	Phi N	54	220	30	50	5	1	0	22	2		4	.227	.234	.259	65	-8		.761	-13	160	76	0-29(0-2-29),C-18/3-4,2-4,P-2	-1.8

COONEY, JIMMY James Edward "Scoops" B 8.24.1894 Cranston, RI D 8.7.1991 Warwick, RI BR/TR 5-11/160# d9.22 Mil 1918 f-Jimmy b-Johnny

Year	Tm Lg	G	AB	R	H	2B	3B	HR	RBI	BB-IB	HP	SO	AVG	OBP	SLG	AOPS	ABR	SB-CS	FA	FR	Rng	Thr	G at Pos	BFW
1917	Bos A	11	36	4	8	1	0	0	3	6	0	2	.222	.333	.250	79	-1	0	1.000	3	107	167	2-10/S	0.3
1919	NY N	5	14	3	3	0	0	0	1	0	0	0	.214	.214	.214	29	-1	0	1.000	0	100	170	/S-4,2	-0.1
1924	StL N	110	383	44	113	20	8	1	57	20	0	20	.295	.330	.397	96	-3	12-10	.969	4	97	102	S-99/3-7,2	1.1
1925	StL N	54	187	27	51	11	2	0	18	4	1	5	.273	.292	.353	62	-11	1-3	.976	-4	87	110	S-37,2-15/O(LF)	-1.2
1926	Chi N	141	513	52	129	18	5	1	47	23	3	10	.251	.288	.312	61	-29	11	**.972**	18	102	**120**	*S-141	0.4
1927	Chi N	33	132	16	32	2	0	0	6	8	0	7	.242	.286	.258	46	-10	1	.973	-1	97	66	S-33	-0.8
	Phi N	76	259	33	70	12	1	0	15	13	0	9	.270	.305	.324	68	-12	4	.980	15	110	114	S-74	1.0
	Year	109	391	49	102	14	1	0	21	21	0	16	.261	.299	.302	61	-22	5	**.978**	13	106	98	*S-107	0.2
1928	Bos N	18	51	2	7	0	0	0	3	2	0	5	.137	.170	.137	-20	-9	1	.982	1	99	150	S-11/2-4	-0.7
Total	7	448	1575	181	413	64	16	2	150	76	4	58	.262	.298	.327	67	-76	30-13	.974	34	100	110	S-400/2-31,3-7,O(LF)	0.0

COONEY, JIMMY James Joseph B 7.9.1865 Cranston, RI D 7.1.1903 Cranston, RI BB/TR 5-9/155# d4.19 s-Jimmy s-Johnny

Year	Tm Lg	G	AB	R	H	2B	3B	HR	RBI	BB-IB	HP	SO	AVG	OBP	SLG	AOPS	ABR	SB-CS	FA	FR	Rng	Thr	G at Pos	BFW
1890	Chi N	135	574	114	156	19	10	4	52	73	6	23	.272	.360	.361	106	5	45	**.936**	-1	98	114	*S-135/C	0.8
1891	Chi N	118	465	84	114	15	3	0	42	48	2	17	.245	.318	.290	78	-12	21	**.917**	9	**113**	102	*S-118	0.0
1892	Chi N	65	238	18	41	1	0	0	20	23	1	5	.172	.248	.176	29	-20	10	.912	-3	101	72	S-65	-1.9
	Was N	6	25	5	4	0	1	0	4	4	0	3	.160	.276	.240	58	-1	1	.862	-2	72	49	/S-6	-0.3
	Year	71	263	23	45	1	1	0	24	27	1	8	.171	.251	.183	31	-22	11	.908	-5	99	70	S-71	-2.2
Total	3	324	1302	221	315	35	14	4	118	148	9	48	.242	.324	.300	82	-28	77	.923	3	104	100	S-324/C	-1.4

COONEY, JOHNNY John Walter B 3.18.1901 Cranston, RI D 7.8.1986 Sarasota, FL BR/TL 5-10/165# d4.19 M1 C21 f-Jimmy b-Jimmy ▲

Year	Tm Lg	G	AB	R	H	2B	3B	HR	RBI	BB-IB	HP	SO	AVG	OBP	SLG	AOPS	ABR	SB-CS	FA	FR	Rng	Thr	G at Pos	BFW
1921	Bos N	8	5	0	1	0	0	0	0	0	0	1	.200	.200	.200	7	0	0-0	1.000	0	91	0	/P-8	0.0
1922	Bos N	4	8	0	0	0	0	0	0	0	0	1	.000	.000	.000	-99	-1	0-0	1.000	0	103	392	/P-4	0.0
1923	Bos N	42	66	7	25	1	0	0	3	4	0	2	.379	.414	.394	119	2	0-1	1.000	0	61	79	P-23,O-11(2-8-1)/1	0.1
1924	Bos N	55	130	10	33	2	1	0	4	9	0	5	.254	.302	.285	61	-7	0-4	.962	-1	72	132	P-34,O-16(0-15-1)/1	-0.5
1925	Bos N	54	103	17	33	7	0	0	13	3	1	6	.320	.346	.388	96	-1	1-0	.949	1	104	167	P-31/1-3,O(LF)	0.0
1926	Bos N	64	126	17	38	3	2	0	18	13	0	7	.302	.367	.357	105	1	6	.996	4	160	121	1-31,P-19/O(RF)	0.3
1927	Bos N	10	1	3	0	0	0	0	0	0	0	0	.000	.000	.000	-99	0	0	—	0			H	0.0
1928	Bos N	33	41	2	7	0	0	0	2	4	0	3	.171	.244	.171	11	-5	0	1.000	3	153	231	P-24/1-3,O-2(0-1-1)	0.0
1929	Bos N	41	72	10	23	4	1	0	6	3	1	3	.319	.355	.403	91	-1	1	1.000	2	121	0	O-16(4-10-2),P-14	0.0
1930	Bos N	4	3	0	0	0	0	0	0	0	0	0	.000	.000	.000	-99	-1	0	1.000	1	283	0	/P-2	0.0
1935	Bro N	10	29	3	9	0	1	0	1	3	0	2	.310	.375	.379	106	0	0	1.000	-0	109	0	O-10(CF)	0.0
1936	Bro N	130	507	71	143	17	5	0	30	24	0	15	.282	.315	.335	74	-19	3	**.994**	9	108	131	*O-130(CF)	-1.3
1937	Bro N	120	430	61	126	18	5	0	37	22	0	10	.293	.327	.358	85	-10	5	.976	5	108	105	*O-111(5-104-3)/1-2	-0.7
1938	Bos N	120	432	45	117	25	5	0	17	22	1	12	.271	.308	.352	90	-7	2	.982	-2	101	68	*O-110(17-15-84),1-13	-1.6
1939	Bos N	118	368	39	101	8	1	2	27	21	2	8	.274	.317	.318	77	-13	2	.992	2	99	128	*O-116(0-112-5)/1-2	-1.4
1940	Bos N	108	365	40	116	14	3	0	21	25	1	9	.318	.363	.373	109	5	4	.992	1	106	67	O-99(0-98-1)/1-7	0.2
1941	Bos N	123	442	52	141	25	2	0	29	27	0	15	.319	.358	.385	114	8	3	**.996**	3	104	106	*O-111(CF)/1-4	0.8
1942	Bos N	74	198	23	41	6	0	0	7	23	0	5	.207	.290	.237	56	-10	2	.984	-2	96	77	O-54(5-16-34),1-23	-1.7
1943	Bro N	37	34	7	7	0	0	0	2	4	0	3	.206	.289	.206	44	-2	1	1.000	0	0	89	/1-3,O-2(CF)	-0.3
1944	Bro N	7	4	0	3	0	0	0	1	0	0	0	.750	.750	.750	329	1	0	1.000	0	120	0	/O-2(1-1-0)	0.1
	NY A	10	8	1	1	0	0	0	1	1	0	0	.125	.222	.125	1	-1	0-0	1.000	0	173	0	/O-2(LF)	-0.1
Total	20	1172	3372	408	965	130	26	2	219	208	6	107	.286	.329	.342	87	-61	30-5	.988	25	105	98	O-794(37-633-133),P-159/1-93	-6.1

COONEY, PHIL Philip Clarence (born Philip Clarence Cohen) B 9.14.1882 New York, NY D 10.6.1957 New York, NY BL/TR 5-8/155# d9.27

Year	Tm Lg	G	AB	R	H	2B	3B	HR	RBI	BB-IB	HP	SO	AVG	OBP	SLG	AOPS	ABR	SB-CS	FA	FR	Rng	Thr	G at Pos	BFW
1905	NY A	1	3	0	0	0	0	0	0	0	0		.000	.000	.000	-90	-1	0	1.000	-0	74	0	/3	-0.1

COONEY, BILL William A. "Cush" B 4.7.1883 Boston, MA D 11.6.1928 Roxbury, MA TR d9.22

Year	Tm Lg	G	AB	R	H	2B	3B	HR	RBI	BB-IB	HP	SO	AVG	OBP	SLG	AOPS	ABR	SB-CS	FA	FR	Rng	Thr	G at Pos	BFW
1909	Bos N	5	10	0	3	0	0	0	0	0	0		.300	.300	.300	82	0	0	.500	-0	60	0	/P-3,2S	0.0
1910	Bos N	8	12	2	3	0	0	0	1	2	0	0	.250	.357	.250	74	0	0	—	-0	0	0	/O-2(RF)	0.0
Total	2	13	22	2	6	0	0	0	1	2	0	0	.273	.333	.273	78	0	0	.500	-0	60	0	/P-3,O-2(RF),S2	0.0

COOPER, CECIL Cecil Celester B 12.20.1949 Brenham, TX BL/TL 6-2/190# d9.8 C1

Year	Tm Lg	G	AB	R	H	2B	3B	HR	RBI	BB-IB	HP	SO	AVG	OBP	SLG	AOPS	ABR	SB-CS	FA	FR	Rng	Thr	G at Pos	BFW
1971	Bos A	14	42	9	13	4	1	0	3	5-1	1	4	.310	.388	.452	130	2	1-0	.988	-2	43	62	1-11	0.0
1972	Bos A	12	17	0	4	1	0	0	2	2-1	0	5	.235	.316	.294	78	0	0-0	1.000	-1	0	94	/1-3	-0.1
1973	Bos A	30	101	12	24	2	0	3	11	7-1	0	12	.238	.284	.347	73	-4	1-2	.984	-0	99	103	1-29	-0.7
1974	Bos A	121	414	55	114	24	1	8	43	32-3	1	74	.275	.327	.396	101	1	2-5	.983	-2	96	112	1-74,D-41	-1.0
1975	†Bos A	106	305	49	95	17	6	14	44	19-6	3	33	.311	.355	.544	140	15	1-4	.995	2	126	105	D-54,1-35	1.2
1976	Bos A	123	451	66	127	22	6	15	78	16-6	1	62	.282	.304	.457	109	3	7-1	.994	-2	91	96	1-66,D-53	-0.5
1977	Mil A	160	643	86	193	31	7	20	78	28-4	0	110	.300	.326	.463	113	9	13-8	.992	7	116	104	*1-148,D-10	0.6
1978	Mil A	107	407	60	127	23	2	13	54	32-3	0	72	.312	.359	.474	133	17	3-4	.988	4	125	108	1-84,D-19	1.5
1979	Mil A★	150	590	83	182	**44**	1	24	106	56-10	0	77	.308	.364	.508	134	28	15-3	.993	-8	84	103	*1-135,D-15	1.4
1980	Mil A★	153	622	96	219	33	4	25	**122**	39-15	2	42	.352	.387	.539	157	47	17-6	**.997**	5	115	**125**	*1-142,D-11	4.4
1981	†Mil A	106	416	70	133	**35**	1	12	60	28-2	3	30	.320	.363	.495	154	29	5-4	.992	1	109	**123**	*1-101/D-5	2.4
1982	†Mil A★	155	654	104	205	38	3	32	121	32-7	0	53	.313	.342	.528	145	37	2-3	.997	1	100	117	*1-154/D	2.7
1983	Mil A★	160	661	106	203	37	3	30	**126**	37-7	1	63	.307	.341	.508	142	35	2-1	.993	-10	79	100	*1-158/D-2	1.5
1984	Mil A	148	603	63	166	28	3	11	67	27-6	2	59	.275	.307	.386	95	-6	8-2	.991	3	108	100	*1-122,D-26	-1.1

Year	Tm Lg	G	AB	R	H	2B	3B	HR	RBI	BB-IB	HP	SO	AVG	OBP	SLG	AOPS	ABR	SB-CS	FA	FR	Rng	Thr	G at Pos	BFW
1985	Mil A★	154	631	82	185	39	8	16	99	30-3	2	77	.293	.322	.456	112	9	10-3	.986	-2	100	93	*1-123,D-30	-0.1
1986	Mil A	134	542	46	140	24	1	12	75	41-2	1	87	.258	.310	.373	83	-13	1-2	.988	-3	90	102	1-90,D-44	-2.3
1987	Mil A	63	250	25	62	13	0	6	36	17-2	0	51	.248	.293	.372	74	-10	1-1	—	0	0	0	D-62	-1.1
Total	17	1896	7349	1012	2192	415	47	241	1125	448-79	17	911	.298	.337	.466	121	199	89-49	.992	-8	101	107	*1-1475,D-373	8.8

COOPER, CLAUDE Claude William B 4.1.1892 Troup, TX D 1.21.1974 Plainview, TX BL/TL 5-9/158# d4.14 Mil 1918

Year	Tm Lg	G	AB	R	H	2B	3B	HR	RBI	BB-IB	HP	SO	AVG	OBP	SLG	AOPS	ABR	SB-CS	FA	FR	Rng	Thr	G at Pos	BFW
1913	†NY N	27	30	11	9	4	0	0	4	4	0	6	.300	.382	.433	132	2	3-3	.895	-0	106	108	O-15(6-10-0)	0.1
1914	Bro F	113	399	56	96	14	11	2	25	26	4	60	.241	.294	.346	74	-23	25	.926	-2	106	76	*O-101(45-21-38)	-3.2
1915	Bro F	**153**	527	75	155	26	12	2	63	77	4	78	.294	.388	.400	123	12	31	.958	13	111	150	*O-121(112-7-2),1-32	2.0
1916	Phi N	56	104	9	20	2	0	0	11	7	1	15	.192	.250	.212	41	-7	1	.945	-1	107	39	O-29(15-13-1)/1	-1.0
1917	Phi N	24	29	5	3	1	0	0	1	5	0	4	.103	.235	.138	15	-3	0	.923	-1	98	0	O-12(9-3-2)	-0.4
Total	5	373	1089	156	283	47	23	4	104	119	9	163	.260	.338	.356	95	-19	60-3	.943	10	108	108	O-278(187-54-43)/1-33	-2.5

COOPER, GARY Gary Clifton B 8.13.1964 Lynwood, CA BR/TR 6-1/200# d9.15

Year	Tm Lg	G	AB	R	H	2B	3B	HR	RBI	BB-IB	HP	SO	AVG	OBP	SLG	AOPS	ABR	SB-CS	FA	FR	Rng	Thr	G at Pos	BFW
1991	Hou N	9	16	1	4	1	0	0	2	3-0	0	6	.250	.368	.313	99	0	0-0	.833	-2	32	0	/3-4	-0.2

COOPER, GARY Gary Nathaniel B 12.22.1956 Savannah, GA BB/TR 6-3/175# d8.25

Year	Tm Lg	G	AB	R	H	2B	3B	HR	RBI	BB-IB	HP	SO	AVG	OBP	SLG	AOPS	ABR	SB-CS	FA	FR	Rng	Thr	G at Pos	BFW
1980	Atl N	21	2	3	0	0	0	0	0	0-0	0	1	.000	.000	.000	-97	-1	2-1	1.000	1	89	511	O-13(11-2-0)	0.0

COOPER, PAT Orge Patterson B 11.26.1917 Albemarle, NC D 3.15.1993 Charlotte, NC BR/TR 6-3/180# d5.11

Year	Tm Lg	G	AB	R	H	2B	3B	HR	RBI	BB-IB	HP	SO	AVG	OBP	SLG	AOPS	ABR	SB-CS	FA	FR	Rng	Thr	G at Pos	BFW
1946	Phi A	1	0	0	0	0	0	0	0	0	0	0	—	—	—	—	0	0-0	—	-0	0	0	/P	0.0
1947	Phi A	13	16	0	4	2	0	0	3	0	0	5	.250	.250	.375	71	-1	0-0	1.000	-0	0	125	/1	-0.1
Total	2	14	16	0	4	2	0	0	3	0	0	5	.250	.250	.375	71	-1	0-0	1.000	-0	0	125	/1P	-0.1

COOPER, SCOTT Scott Kendrick B 10.13.1967 St.Louis, MO BL/TR 6-3/205# d9.5

Year	Tm Lg	G	AB	R	H	2B	3B	HR	RBI	BB-IB	HP	SO	AVG	OBP	SLG	AOPS	ABR	SB-CS	FA	FR	Rng	Thr	G at Pos	BFW
1990	Bos A	2	1	0	0	0	0	0	0	0-0	0	1	.000	.000	.000	-96	0	0-0	—	0			/H	0.0
1991	Bos A	14	35	6	16	4	2	0	7	2-0	0	2	.457	.486	.686	210	5	0-0	.933	1	112	56	3-13	0.6
1992	Bos A	123	337	34	93	21	0	5	33	37-0	0	33	.276	.346	.383	98	0	1-1	.990	6	101	107	1-62,3-47/2SD	0.2
1993	Bos A★	156	526	67	147	29	3	9	63	58-15	5	81	.279	.355	.397	96	-1	5-2	.937	-11	89	87	*3-154/1-2,S	-1.1
1994	Bos A★	104	369	49	104	16	4	13	53	30-2	1	65	.282	.333	.453	97	-3	0-3	.944	10	**116**	125	*3-104	0.7
1995	StL N	118	374	29	86	18	2	3	40	49-3	3	85	.230	.321	.313	69	-16	0-3	.945	9	**111**	141	*3-110	-0.7
1997	KC A	75	159	12	32	6	1	3	15	17-0	2	32	.201	.283	.308	54	-11	1-1	1.000	-2	94	80	3-39/1-8,D-5	-1.3
Total	7	592	1801	197	478	94	12	33	211	193-20	11	299	.265	.337	.386	89	-26	7-10	.948	12	104	106	3-467/1-72,D-7,S-2,2	-1.6

COOPER, WALKER William Walker "Walk" B 1.8.1915 Atherton, MO D 4.11.1991 Scottsdale, AZ BR/TR 6-3/210# d9.25 Mil 1945 C2 b-Mort

Year	Tm Lg	G	AB	R	H	2B	3B	HR	RBI	BB-IB	HP	SO	AVG	OBP	SLG	AOPS	ABR	SB-CS	FA	FR	Rng	Thr	G at Pos	BFW
1940	StL N	6	19	3	6	1	0	0	2	2	0	2	.316	.381	.368	102	0	1	1.000	-0	*86*	*144*	/C-6	0.0
1941	StL N	68	200	19	49	9	1	1	20	13	0	14	.245	.291	.315	66	-9	1	.966	3	*123*	*122*	C-63	-0.3
1942	†StL N★	125	438	58	123	32	7	7	65	29	1	29	.281	.327	.434	113	6	4	.972	7	***158***	*103*	*C-115	2.1
1943	†StL N★	122	449	52	143	30	4	9	81	19	2	19	.318	.349	.463	128	14	1	.975	1	***169***	*75*	*C-112	2.3
1944	†StL N★	112	397	56	126	25	5	13	72	20	1	19	.317	.352	.504	136	17	4	.980	5	*146*	*74*	C-97	2.8
1945	StL N	4	18	3	7	0	0	0	1	0	0	1	.389	.389	.389	114	0	0	.966	0	*115*	*66*	/C-4	0.1
1946	NY N★	87	280	29	75	10	1	8	46	17	0	12	.268	.310	.396	99	-2	0	.972	-7	*87*	*103*	C-73	-0.6
1947	NY N★	140	515	79	157	24	8	35	122	24	3	43	.305	.339	.586	141	24	2	.979	-6	***163***	*67*	*C-132	2.5
1948	NY N★	91	290	40	77	12	0	16	54	28	1	29	.266	.332	.472	115	5	1	.979	-7	*118*	*44*	C-79	0.2
1949	NY N	42	147	14	31	4	2	4	21	7	3	8	.211	.261	.347	62	-9	0	.982	-1	*91*	*83*	C-40	-0.7
	Cin N☆	82	307	34	86	9	2	16	62	21	2	24	.280	.330	.479	113	4	0	.978	-3	*118*	*105*	C-77	0.6
	Year	124	454	48	117	13	4	20	83	28	5	32	.258	.308	.436	97	-5	0	.979	-3	*109*	*98*	*C-117	-0.1
1950	Cin N	15	47	3	9	3	0	0	4	0	0	5	.191	.191	.255	16	-6	0	.972	-0	*73*	*104*	C-13	-0.6
	Bos N☆	102	337	52	111	19	3	14	60	30	3	26	.329	.389	.528	148	23	1	.973	-3	*82*	*114*	C-88	2.4
	Year	117	384	55	120	22	3	14	64	30	3	31	.313	.367	.495	132	17	1	.973	-4	*81*	*113*	*C-101	1.8
1951	Bos N	109	342	42	107	14	1	18	59	28	1	18	.313	.367	.518	145	20	1-1	.981	-2	*78*	***138***	C-90	2.3
1952	Bos N	102	349	33	82	12	1	10	55	22	1	32	.235	.282	.361	80	-11	1-0	.983	-5	*93*	*114*	C-89	-1.1
1953	Mil N	53	137	12	30	6	0	3	16	12	1	15	.219	.287	.328	64	-7	1-0	.983	-3	*86*	*54*	C-35	-0.8
1954	Pit N	14	15	0	3	2	0	0	1	2	0	1	.200	.294	.333	64	-1	0-0	1.000	-0	*36*	*0*	/C-2	-0.1
	Chi N	57	158	21	49	10	2	7	32	21	2	23	.310	.398	.532	138	9	0-0	.978	-3	*59*	*132*	C-48	0.8
	Year	71	173	21	52	12	2	7	33	23	2	24	.301	.389	.514	132	9	0-0	.978	-3	*58*	*128*	C-50	0.7
1955	Chi N	54	111	11	31	8	1	7	15	6-1	1	19	.279	.322	.559	128	4	0-0	.961	-7	*58*	*96*	C-31	-0.2
1956	StL N	40	68	5	18	5	1	2	14	3-1	0	8	.265	.296	.456	98	0	0-0	.984	-2	*87*	*46*	C-16	-0.2
1957	StL N	48	78	7	21	5	1	3	10	5-1	0	10	.269	.310	.474	106	0	0-0	.957	-2	*93*	*87*	C-13	-0.1
Total	18	1473	4702	573	1341	240	40	173	812	309-3	22	357	.285	.332	.464	116	81	18-1	.977	-32	*118*	*93*	*C-1223	11.4

COQUILLETTE, TRACE Trace Robert B 6.4.1974 Carmichael, CA BR/TR 6/185# d9.7

Year	Tm Lg	G	AB	R	H	2B	3B	HR	RBI	BB-IB	HP	SO	AVG	OBP	SLG	AOPS	ABR	SB-CS	FA	FR	Rng	Thr	G at Pos	BFW
1999	Mon N	17	49	2	13	3	0	0	4	4-0	1	7	.265	.333	.327	70	-2	1-0	.944	-1	81	59	3-11/2-6	-0.2
2000	Mon N	34	59	6	12	4	0	1	8	7-0	0	19	.203	.284	.322	52	-4	0-0	.958	-1	105	93	3-19/2-8,O-2(2-0-1)	-0.5
Total	2	51	108	8	25	7	0	1	12	11-0	1	26	.231	.306	.324	60	-6	1-0	.952	-2	94	77	/3-30,2-14,O-2(2-0-1)	-0.7

CORA, ALEX Jose Alexander B 10.18.1975 Caguas, P.R. BL/TR 6/180# d6.7 b-Joey

Year	Tm Lg	G	AB	R	H	2B	3B	HR	RBI	BB-IB	HP	SO	AVG	OBP	SLG	AOPS	ABR	SB-CS	FA	FR	Rng	Thr	G at Pos	BFW
1998	LA N	29	33	1	4	0	1	0	0	2-0	1	8	.121	.194	.182	-0	-5	0-0	.956	3	83	117	S-21/2-4	-0.2
1999	LA N	11	30	2	5	1	0	0	3	0-0	1	4	.167	.194	.200	-0	-5	0-0	1.000	0	94	80	/S-8,2-3	-0.4
2000	LA N	109	353	39	84	18	6	4	32	26-4	7	53	.238	.302	.357	70	-18	4-1	.972	3	99	123	*S-101/2-8	-0.6
2001	LA N	134	405	38	88	18	3	4	29	31-6	8	58	.217	.285	.306	58	-27	0-2	.962	-5	97	88	*S-132/2	-2.2
2002	LA N	115	258	37	75	14	4	5	28	26-4	7	38	.291	.371	.434	123	7	7-2	.977	-3	94	105	S-61,2-40	1.0
2003	LA N	148	477	39	119	24	3	4	34	16-3	10	59	.249	.287	.338	66	-25	4-2	.978	31	106	**146**	*2-141,S-15	1.2
Total	6	546	1556	156	375	75	17	17	126	101-17	34	220	.241	.301	.344	71	-73	15-7	.969	28	97	104	S-338,2-197	-1.2

CORA, JOEY Jose Manuel (Amaro) B 5.14.1965 Caguas, P.R. BB/TR 5-8/152# d4.6 b-Alex

Year	Tm Lg	G	AB	R	H	2B	3B	HR	RBI	BB-IB	HP	SO	AVG	OBP	SLG	AOPS	ABR	SB-CS	FA	FR	Rng	Thr	G at Pos	BFW
1987	SD N	77	241	23	57	7	2	0	13	28-1	1	26	.237	.317	.282	63	-13	15-11	.975	1	109	82	2-66/S-6	-0.9
1989	SD N	12	19	5	6	1	0	0	1	1-0	0	0	.316	.350	.368	105	0	1-0	.960	1	110	93	/S-7,3-2,2	0.2
1990	SD N	51	100	12	27	3	0	0	2	6-1	0	9	.270	.311	.300	68	-4	8-3	.833	-7	50	49	S-21,2-15/C	-1.0
1991	Chi A	100	228	37	55	2	3	0	18	20-0	5	21	.241	.313	.276	67	-10	11-6	.970	-13	95	82	2-80/S-5,D-2	-2.2
1992	Chi A	68	122	27	30	7	1	0	9	22-1	4	13	.246	.371	.320	99	1	10-3	.984	-2	99	118	2-28,D-18/S-6,3-5	0.1
1993	†Chi A	153	579	95	155	15	13	2	51	67-0	9	63	.268	.351	.349	91	-6	20-8	.974	-17	93	89	*2-151/3-3	-1.4
1994	Chi A	90	312	55	86	13	4	2	30	38-0	2	32	.276	.353	.362	88	-5	8-4	.978	-9	84	106	2-84/D	-0.9
1995	†Sea A	120	427	64	127	19	2	3	39	37-0	6	31	.297	.359	.372	91	-5	18-7	.955	-16	84	72	*2-112/SD	-1.3
1996	Sea A	144	530	90	154	37	6	6	45	35-1	7	32	.291	.340	.417	91	-8	5-5	.979	-2	90	102	*2-140/3	-0.4
1997	†Sea A★	149	574	105	172	40	4	11	54	53-2	5	49	.300	.359	.441	110	9	6-7	.973	-7	86	91	*2-142	0.8
1998	Sea A	131	519	95	147	23	6	6	26	62-0	4	50	.283	.362	.385	95	-2	13-5	.962	-24	82	87	*2-130	-1.8
	†Cle A	24	83	16	19	4	0	0	6	11-0	1	9	.229	.326	.277	57	-5	2-1	.986	-11	65	60	2-21	-1.5
	Year	155	602	111	166	27	6	6	32	73-0	5	59	.276	.357	.370	90	-7	15-6	.965	-35	80	83	*2-151	-3.3
Total	11	1119	3734	624	1035	171	41	30	294	380-6	44	335	.277	.348	.369	90	-48	117-60	.971	-105	89	91	2-970/S-46,D-22,3-11,C	-10.3

CORBETT, GENE Eugene Louis B 10.25.1913 Winona, MN BL/TR 6-1.5/190# d9.19

Year	Tm Lg	G	AB	R	H	2B	3B	HR	RBI	BB-IB	HP	SO	AVG	OBP	SLG	AOPS	ABR	SB-CS	FA	FR	Rng	Thr	G at Pos	BFW
1936	Phi N	6	21	1	3	0	0	0	2	2	0	3	.143	.217	.143	-1	-3	0	1.000	-1	54	149	/1-6	-0.4
1937	Phi N	7	12	4	4	2	0	0	1	0	0	0	.333	.333	.500	114	0	0	.800	-1	92	0	/3-3,2	0.0
1938	Phi N	24	75	7	6	1	0	2	7	6	0	11	.080	.148	.173	-12	-12	0	.995	-1	86	88	1-22	-1.5
Total	3	37	108	12	13	3	0	2	10	8	0	14	.120	.181	.204	5	-15	0	.996	-2	79	101	/1-28,3-3,2	-1.9

CORBITT, CLAUDE Claude Elliott B 7.21.1915 Sunbury, NC D 5.1.1978 Cincinnati, OH BR/TR 5-10/170# d9.23

Year	Tm Lg	G	AB	R	H	2B	3B	HR	RBI	BB-IB	HP	SO	AVG	OBP	SLG	AOPS	ABR	SB-CS	FA	FR	Rng	Thr	G at Pos	BFW
1945	Bro N	2	4	1	2	0	0	0	0	1	0	0	.500	.600	.500	209	1	0	1.000	0	118	433	/3-2	0.1
1946	Cin N	82	274	25	68	10	1	1	16	23	1	13	.248	.309	.303	77	-9	3	.947	-6	101	109	S-77	-1.1
1948	Cin N	87	258	24	66	11	0	0	18	14	1	16	.256	.297	.298	64	-13	4	.973	-4	96	68	2-52,3-16,S-11	-1.4
1949	Cin N	44	94	10	17	1	0	0	3	9	0	1	.181	.252	.191	20	-11	1	.984	-5	77	127	S-18,2-17/3	-1.5
Total	4	215	630	60	153	22	1	1	37	47	2	30	.243	.297	.286	63	-32	8	.956	-15	96	106	S-106/2-69,3-19	-3.9

CORCORAN, ART Arthur Andrew "Bunny" B 11.23.1894 Roxbury, MA D 7.27.1958 Chelsea, MA TR 5-11/185# d9.9

Year	Tm Lg	G	AB	R	H	2B	3B	HR	RBI	BB-IB	HP	SO	AVG	OBP	SLG	AOPS	ABR	SB-CS	FA	FR	Rng	Thr	G at Pos	BFW
1915	Phi A	1	4	0	0	0	0	0	0	0	0	2	.000	.000	.000	-99	-1	0	1.000	-0	59	0	/3	-0.1

Year	Tm Lg	G	AB	R	H	2B	3B	HR	RBI	BB-IB	HP	SO	AVG	OBP	SLG	AOPS	ABR	SB-CS	FA	FR	Rng	Thr	G at Pos	BFW
CORCORAN, JOHN John A. B 1873 Cincinnati, OH D 11.2.1901 Cincinnati, OH TL d9.17																								
1895	Pit N	6	20	0	3	0	0	0	1	0	0	2	.150	.150	.150	-24	-4	0	.895	-1	100	0	/S-4,3-2	-0.4
CORCORAN, JACK John H. B 1860 Lowell, MA d5.1																								
1884	Bro AA	52	185	17	39	4	3	0		8	2		.211	.251	.265	68	-6		.873	-7			C-38/O-9(4-2-3),2-4,S-2,P	-1.0
CORCORAN, LARRY Lawrence J. B 8.10.1859 Brooklyn, NY D 10.14.1891 Newark, NJ BL/TR (TB 1884 (part)) ?/120# d5.1 b-Mike ▲																								
1880	Chi N	72	286	41	66	11	1	0	25	10		33	.231	.257	.276	76	-7		.957	5	114	117	*P-63/O-8(0-5-3),S-8	0.1
1881	Chi N	47	189	25	42	8	0	0	9	5		22	.222	.242	.265	57	-9		.893	-1	83	0	P-45/S-2,O(LF)	-0.1
1882	Chi N	40	169	23	35	10	2	1	24	6		18	.207	.234	.308	69	-6		.915	-0	95	55	P-39/3	0.0
1883	Chi N	68	263	40	55	12	7	0	25	6		62	.209	.227	.308	56	-15		.906	-2	94	113	P-56,O-13(8-4-1)/S-3,2	-0.4
1884	Chi N	64	251	43	61	3	4	1	19	10		33	.243	.272	.299	73	-9		.882	7	125	145	P-60/O-4(RF),S-2	0.3
1885	Chi N	7	22	6	6	1	0	0	4	6		1	.273	.429	.318	127	1		.905	-0	98	0	/P-7,S	0.0
	NY N	3	14	3	5	0	0	0	2	0		1	.357	.357	.357	133	1		1.000	1	177	1558	/P-3	0.0
	Year	10	36	9	11	1	0	0	6	6		2	.306	.405	.333	129	1		.935	1	122	464	P-10/S	0.0
1886	NY N	1	4	0	0	0	0	0	0	0		0	.000	.000	.000	-99	-1	0	.000	-1	0	0	/O(RF)	-0.1
	Was N	21	81	9	15	2	1	0	3	7		14	.185	.250	.235	52	-4	3	.619	-3	178	256	O-11(RF)/S-9,P-2	-0.6
	Year	22	85	9	15	2	1	0	3	7		16	.176	.239	.224	44	-5	3	.591	-4	166	239	O-12(RF)/S-9,P-2	-0.7
1887	Ind N	3	10	2	2	0	0	0	0	2	0	1	.200	.333	.200	53	-1	2	1.000	0	0	0	/O-2(0-1-1),P-2	0.0
Total	8	326	1289	192	287	47	15	2	111	52	0	187	.223	.253	.287	67	-50	5	.910	6	105	104	P-277/O-40(9-10-21),S-25,23	-0.8
CORCORAN, MICKEY Michael Joseph B 8.26.1882 Buffalo, NY D 12.9.1950 Buffalo, NY BR/TR 5-8/165# d9.15																								
1910	Cin N	14	46	3	10	3	0	0	7	5	1	9	.217	.308	.283	76	-1	0	.911	-2	108	86	2-14	-0.3
CORCORAN, TOMMY Thomas William "Corky" B 1.4.1869 New Haven, CT D 6.25.1960 Plainfield, CT BR/TR 5-9/164# d4.19 U1																								
1890	Pit P	123	503	80	117	14	13	1	61	38	2	45	.233	.289	.318	68	-24	43	.884	6	**106**	76	*S-123	-1.2
1891	Phi AA	133	511	84	130	11	15	7	71	29	10	56	.254	.307	.376	95	-8	30	**.911**	12	104	11	*S-133	0.7
1892	Bro N	151	613	77	145	11	6	1	74	34	4	51	.237	.281	.279	72	-22	39	**.925**	-6	96	93	*S-151	-1.9
1893	Bro N	115	459	61	126	11	10	2	58	27	2	12	.275	.318	.355	82	-14	14	.907	13	**111**	93	*S-115	0.5
1894	Bro N	129	576	123	173	21	20	5	92	25	0	17	.300	.329	.432	88	-15	33	.904	-4	99	79	*S-129	-1.0
1895	Bro N	128	540	83	145	17	10	2	69	23	3	11	.269	.302	.348	73	-23	17	.925	17	111	100	*S-128	0.0
1896	Bro N	132	532	63	154	15	7	3	73	15	1	13	.289	.310	.361	81	-17	16	.926	26	108	126	*S-132	1.3
1897	Cin N	109	445	76	128	30	5	3	57	13	2		.288	.311	.398	81	-14	15	.913	4	97	142	S-63,2-47	-0.5
1898	Cin N	153	619	80	155	28	15	2	87	26	2		.250	.283	.354	77	-23	19	.932	10	**108**	119	*S-153	-0.5
1899	Cin N	138	540	93	150	11	8	0	81	29	2		.278	.317	.328	76	-20	32	.930	0	98	115	*S-124,2-14	-1.1
1900	Cin N	127	523	64	128	21	9	1	54	22	2		.245	.278	.325	68	-25	27	.921	-7	97	114	*S-124/2-5	-2.3
1901	Cin N	31	115	14	24	3	3	0	15	11	0		.209	.278	.287	68	-5	6	.919	1	102	150	S-30	-0.2
1902	Cin N	138	538	54	136	18	4	0	54	11	0		.253	.268	.301	69	-21	20	.926	-11	92	101	*S-137/2	-3.0
1903	Cin N	115	459	61	113	18	7	2	73	12	1		.246	.267	.329	63	-25	12	.943	9	100	105	*S-115	-1.2
1904	Cin N	150	578	55	133	17	9	2	74	19	2		.230	.257	.301	66	-25	19	**.936**	0	100	109	*S-150	-2.1
1905	Cin N	151	605	70	150	21	11	2	85	23	1		.248	.277	.329	72	-23	28	**.952**	20	107	105	*S-151	0.2
1906	Cin N	117	430	29	89	13	1	1	33	19	1		.207	.242	.249	51	-25	8	.941	2	99	124	*S-117	-2.2
1907	NY N	62	226	21	60	9	2	0	24	7	0		.265	.288	.323	88	-4	9	.939	-8	98	71	2-62	-1.3
Total	18	2202	8812	1188	2256	289	155	34	1135	383	35	205	.256	.290	.336	74	-333	387	.924	84	102	100	*S-2075,2-129	-15.8
CORCORAN, TIM Timothy Michael B 3.19.1953 Glendale, CA BL/TL 5-11/175# d5.18																								
1977	Det A	55	103	13	29	3	0	3	15	6-1	0	9	.282	.315	.398	90	-2	0-1	1.000	-1	101	0	O-18(4-6-8)/D-3	-0.3
1978	Det A	116	324	37	86	13	1	1	27	24-2	5	27	.265	.322	.321	80	-8	3-2	.985	-4	93	84	*O-109(0-2-107)/D	-1.7
1979	Det A	18	22	4	5	1	0	0	6	4-1	0	2	.227	.333	.273	67	-1	1-1	1.000	1	142	391	/O-9(3-0-6),1-5,D-2	0.0
1980	Det A	84	153	20	44	7	1	3	18	22-2	1	10	.288	.379	.405	113	4	0-2	.985	-1	90	116	1-48,O-18(7-0-11)/D-5	-0.1
1981	Min A	22	51	4	9	3	0	0	4	6-0	0	7	.176	.259	.235	42	-4	0-0	1.000	0	103	84	1-16/D-3	-0.4
1983	Phi N	3	0	0	0	0	0	0	0	0-0	0	0	—	—	—	—	0	0-0	1.000	-0	0	0	/1-3	0.0
1984	Phi N	102	208	30	71	13	1	5	36	37-5	1	27	.341	.440	.486	158	19	0-1	.997	-2	91	70	1-51,O-17(4-0-13)	1.4
1985	Phi N	103	182	11	39	6	1	0	22	29-4	0	20	.214	.312	.258	63	-8	0-0	.993	-1	88	73	1-59/O-3(2-0-2)	-1.3
1986	NY N	6	7	1	0	0	0	0	0	2-1	0	0	.000	.222	.000	-34	-1	0-0	1.000	0	134	136	/1	-0.1
Total	9	509	1050	120	283	46	4	12	128	130-16	7	102	.270	.349	.355	96	-1	4-7	.993	-7	90	84	1-183,O-174(20-8-147)/D-14	-2.5
CORDERO, WIL Wilfredo (Nieva) B 10.3.1971 Mayaguez, P.R. BR/TR 6-2/190# d7.24 OF Total (397-LF 17-RF)																								
1992	Mon N	45	126	17	38	4	1	2	8	9-0	1	31	.302	.353	.397	113	2	0-0	.949	-8	85	72	S-35/2-9	-0.4
1993	Mon N	138	475	56	118	32	2	10	58	34-8	7	60	.248	.308	.387	81	-12	12-3	.941	-20	96	83	*S-134/3-2	-2.1
1994	Mon N★	110	415	65	122	30	3	15	63	41-3	6	62	.294	.363	.489	119	12	16-3	.952	-13	95	93	*S-109	1.1
1995	Mon N	131	514	64	147	35	2	10	49	36-4	9	88	.286	.341	.420	97	-2	9-5	.960	-25	87	78	*S-105,O-26(LF)	-1.9
1996	Bos A	59	198	29	57	14	0	3	37	11-4	2	31	.288	.330	.404	83	-5	2-1	.949	-2	97	66	2-37,D-13/1	-0.6
1997	Bos A	140	570	82	160	26	3	18	72	31-7	4	122	.281	.320	.432	93	-8	1-3	.992	-5	89	90	*O-137(LF)/2D	-1.8
1998	Chi A	96	341	58	91	18	2	13	49	22-0	3	66	.267	.314	.446	98	-2	2-1	.992	4	131	115	1-83,O-11(4-0-8)	-0.5
1999	†Cle A	54	194	35	58	15	0	8	32	15-0	6	37	.299	.364	.500	113	4	2-0	.981	-2	90	0	O-29(LF),D-23	0.0
2000	Pit N	89	348	46	98	24	3	16	51	25-1	4	58	.282	.336	.506	110	4	1-2	.983	-10	69	57	O-85(LF)/D	-1.0
	Cle A	38	148	18	39	11	2	0	17	7-0	3	18	.264	.310	.365	69	-7	0-0	1.000	2	110	96	O-38(LF)	-0.6
2001	Cle A	89	268	30	67	11	1	4	21	22-2	4	50	.250	.313	.343	73	-10	0-0	.985	-5	81	41	O-51(49-0-4),1-22,D-12	-1.9
2002	Cle A	6	18	1	4	0	0	0	1	0-0	0	3	.222	.222	.222	19	-2	0-0	1.000	2	107	916	/O-4(LF),1	-0.1
	Mon N	66	143	21	39	9	0	6	29	17-0	2	26	.273	.349	.462	108	1	2-0	.958	1	109	73	O-28(24-0-5),1-10/D-2	0.1
2003	Mon N	130	436	57	121	27	0	16	71	49-5	4	90	.278	.354	.450	99	0	1-1	.996	-6	82	96	*1-123/O(LF)D	-1.6
Total	12	1191	4194	579	1159	256	19	121	558	319-34	55	742	.276	.333	.433	96	-25	48-19	.980	-87	88	75	O-410L,S-383,1-240/D-55,2-47,3-2	-11.3
CORDOVA, MARTY Martin Keevin B 7.10.1969 Las Vegas, NV BR/TR 6/200# d4.26																								
1995	Min A	137	512	81	142	27	4	24	84	52-1	10	111	.277	.352	.486	116	11	20-7	.986	14	117	127	*O-137(132-11-0)	2.1
1996	Min A	145	569	97	176	46	1	16	111	53-4	8	96	.309	.371	.478	112	12	11-5	.991	5	107	87	*O-145(LF)	1.1
1997	Min A	103	378	44	93	18	4	15	51	30-2	3	92	.246	.305	.434	89	-8	5-3	.991	9	109	186	*O-101(LF)/D-2	-0.3
1998	Min A	119	438	52	111	20	2	10	69	50-3	5	103	.253	.333	.377	84	-10	3-6	.978	4	114	73	*O-115(LF)/D-4	-1.1
1999	Min A	124	425	62	121	28	3	14	70	48-2	9	96	.285	.365	.464	107	5	13-4	.927	-4	80	0	D-85,O-29(6-0-25)	-0.3
2000	Tor A	62	200	23	49	7	0	4	18	18-0	3	35	.245	.317	.340	64	-11	3-2	.982	-6	67	39	O-41(23-0-18),D-15	-1.9
2001	†Cle A	122	409	61	123	20	2	20	69	23-0	8	81	.301	.348	.506	120	11	0-3	.990	6	109	138	*O-106(83-2-30)/D-7	1.1
2002	Bal A	131	458	55	116	25	2	18	64	47-3	3	111	.253	.325	.434	105	3	1-6	.971	-5	86	46	O-72(LF),D-56	-1.0
2003	Bal A	9	30	5	7	1	0	1	4	8-1	1	5	.233	.410	.367	112	1	1-0	1.000	1	85	815	/O-4(LF),D-5	0.2
Total	9	952	3419	480	938	192	18	122	540	329-16	50	730	.274	.344	.448	103	14	57-36	.984	24	105	107	O-750(681-13-73),D-174	-0.1
COREY, FRED Frederick Harrison B 1857 S.Kingston, RI D 11.27.1912 Providence, RI BR/TR 5-7/160# d5.1 ▲ OF Total (8-LF 29-CF 46-RF)																								
1878	Pro N	7	21	3	3	0	0	0	1	0		2	.143	.143	.143	-6	-2		1.000	0	42	0	/P-5,2-2,1	-0.1
1880	Wor N	41	138	11	24	8	1	0	6	4		27	.174	.197	.246	45	-8		.759	-7	68	135	O-29(2-6-21),P-25/S-3,31	-1.0
1881	Wor N	51	203	22	45	8	4	0	10	5		10	.222	.240	.300	65	-9		.827	1	96	96	O-25(1-0-24),P-23/S-7	-0.4
1882	Wor N	64	255	33	63	7	12	0	29	5		31	.247	.262	.369	97	-2		.847	-5	100	58	S-26,P-21,O-15(5-10-0)/3-6,1-5	-0.6
1883	Phi AA	71	298	45	77	16	2	1	40	12			.258	.287	.336	91	-3		.799	-1	116	109	3-34,P-18,O-14(0-13-1)/2-9,SC	-0.3
1884	Phi AA	104	439	64	121	17	16	5		17	2		.276	.306	.421	127	10		**.887**	12	110	91	*3-104	2.2
1885	Phi AA	94	384	61	94	14	8	1	38	17	3		.245	.282	.331	88	-7		.872	7	106	103	*3-92/SP	0.2
Total	7	432	1738	239	427	70	43	7	124	60	5	70	.246	.273	.348	93	-21		.863	7	108	96	3-237/P-93,O-83R,S-38,2-11,1-7,C	0.0
COREY, MARK Mark Mundell B 11.3.1955 Tucumcari, NM BR/TR 6-2/200# d9.1																								
1979	Bal A	13	13	1	2	0	0	0	1	0-0	0	4	.154	.154	.154	-17	-2	1-0	1.000	0	116	0	O-11(RF)/D	-0.2
1980	Bal A	36	36	7	10	2	0	1	2	5-0	0	7	.278	.366	.417	115	1	0-1	1.000	-2	72	0	O-34(15-0-19)	-0.2
1981	Bal A	10	8	2	0	0	0	0	0	2-0	0	2	.000	.200	.000	-38	-1	0-0	1.000	0	78	388	/O-9(7-0-2)	-0.1
Total	3	59	57	10	12	2	0	1	3	7-0	0	13	.211	.297	.298	65	-2	1-1	1.000	-2	82	65	/O-54(22-0-32),D	-0.5
CORGAN, CHUCK Charles Howard B 12.4.1902 Wagoner, OK D 6.13.1928 Wagoner, OK BB/TR 5-11/180# d9.19																								
1925	Bro N	14	47	4	8	1	1	0	0	3	0	9	.170	.220	.234	16	-6	0-0	.908	1	115	56	S-14	-0.3
1927	Bro N	19	57	3	15	1	0	0	1	4	0	4	.263	.311	.281	59	-3	0	.969	0	116	65	2-13/S-3	-0.3
Total	2	33	104	7	23	2	1	0	1	7	0	13	.221	.270	.260	40	-9	0-0	.900	1	108	58	/S-17,2-13	-0.6

Year	Tm Lg	G	AB	R	H	2B	3B	HR	RBI	BB-IB	HP	SO	AVG	OBP	SLG	AOPS	ABR	SB-CS	FA	FR	Rng	Thr	G at Pos	BFW
CORHAN, ROY Roy George "Irish" B 10.21.1887 Indianapolis, IN D 11.24.1958 San Francisco, CA BR/TR 5-9.5/165# d4.20																								
1911	Chi A	43	131	14	28	6	2	0	8	15	2		.214	.304	.290	68	-5	2	.924	10	112	137	S-43	0.7
1916	StL N	92	295	30	62	6	3	0	18	20	2	31	.210	.265	.251	59	-14	15	.917	1	106	92	S-84	-0.9
Total	2	135	426	44	90	12	5	0	26	35	4	31	.211	.277	.263	62	-19	17	.920	10	108	107	S-127	-0.2
CORIDAN, PHIL Philip F. B 8.19.1858 Walpole, IN D 7.1.1915 Indianapolis, IN BL d7.16																								
1884	CP U	2	7	1	1	0	0	0		0			.143	.143	.143	-13	-1		.800	-1	81	0	/2-2,O(LF)	-0.2
CORKHILL, POP John Stewart B 4.11.1858 Parkesburg, PA D 4.3.1921 Pennsauken, NJ BL/TR 5-10/180# d5.1 ▲ OF Total (6-LF 615-CF 420-RF)																								
1883	Cin AA	88	375	53	81	10	8	2	46	3			.216	.222	.301	63	-17		**.930**	0	60	0	*O-85(0-15-70)/S-2,2-2,1-2	-1.5
1884	Cin AA	110	452	85	124	13	11	4	70	6	4		.274	.290	.378	111	3		**.934**	8	162	181	*O-92(RF),S-11/1-6,3-3,P	0.9
1885	Cin AA	**112**	440	64	111	10	8	1	53	7	7		.252	.275	.318	85	-9		.938	17	**189**	139	*O-110(RF)/P-8,1-3	0.6
1886	Cin AA	129	540	81	143	9	7	5	97	23	6		.265	.302	.335	96	-5	24	.918	-0	136	166	*O-112(RF),3-12/1-7,S-3,P	-0.5
1887	Cin AA	128	541	79	168	19	11	5	97	14	4		.311	.333	.414	105	0	30	**.952**	12	136	164	*O-128(0-121-7)/P-5	0.6
1888	Cin AA	118	490	68	133	11	9	1	74	15	4		.271	.299	.337	98	-4	27	.958	1	86	123	*O-116(4-112-0)/P-2,12	-0.7
	Bro AA	19	71	17	27	4	3	1	19	4	2		.380	.429	.563	217	9	3	.980	0	60	0	O-19(CF)	0.8
	Year	137	561	85	160	15	12	2	93	19	6		.285	.316	.365	113	5	30	.961	1	82	105	*O-135(4-131-0)/P-2,12	0.1
1889	†Bro AA	**138**	537	91	134	21	9	8	78	42	3	24	.250	.308	.367	91	-8	22	**.949**	9	131	146	*O-138(CF)/S1	-0.4
1890	Bro N	51	204	23	46	4	2	1	21	15	0	11	.225	.279	.279	62	-10	6	.977	2	71	62	O-48(CF)/1-6	-0.9
1891	Phi AA	83	349	50	73	7	7	0	31	26	2	15	.209	.268	.269	54	-23	12	.956	4	94	97	O-83(0-73-10)	-1.8
	Cin N	1	4	0	0	0	0	0	0	0	0	1	.000	.000	.000	-99	-1	0	1.000	0	0	0	/O(CF)	-0.1
	Pit N	41	145	16	33	1	1	3	20	7	1	10	.228	.268	.310	70	-6	7	.935	3	160	316	O-41(1-40-0)	-0.4
	Year	42	149	16	33	1	1	3	20	7	1	11	.221	.261	.302	65	-7	7	.939	3	150	296	O-42(1-41-0)	-0.5
1892	Pit N	68	256	23	47	1	4	0	25	12	3	19	.184	.229	.219	35	-21	6	.953	4	112	160	O-68(1-48-19)	-2.1
Total	10	1086	4404	650	1120	110	80	31	631	174	36	80	.254	.288	.337	87	-92	137	.947	58	122	134	*O-1041C/1-26,P-17,S-17,3-15,2-3	-5.5
CORRALES, PAT Patrick B 3.20.1941 Los Angeles, CA BR/TR 6/195# d8.2 M9 C19																								
1964	Phi N	2	1	1	0	0	0	0	0	1-0	0	0	.000	.500	.000	55	0	0-0	—	0			H	0.0
1965	Phi N	63	174	16	39	8	1	2	15	25-5	1	42	.224	.323	.316	83	-3	0-0	.982	-2	*105*	*88*	C-62	-0.3
1966	StL N	28	72	5	13	2	0	0	3	2-0	2	17	.181	.221	.208	21	-8	1-0	.975	6	*146*	*203*	C-27	-0.1
1968	Cin N	20	56	3	15	4	0	0	6	6-0	1	16	.268	.349	.339	101	1	0-0	.991	-0	*112*	*71*	C-20	0.1
1969	Cin N	29	72	10	19	5	0	1	5	8-0	1	17	.264	.346	.375	97	0	0-1	.986	1	87	52	C-29	0.2
1970	†Cin N	43	106	9	25	5	1	1	10	8-1	0	22	.236	.289	.330	65	-5	0-0	.983	1	196	103	C-42	-0.3
1971	Cin N	40	94	6	17	2	0	0	6	6-1	0	17	.181	.230	.202	24	-10	0-0	.980	-3	107	14	C-39	-1.2
1972	Cin N	2	1	0	0	0	0	0	0	2-1	0	0	.000	.667	.000	110	0	0-0	1.000	1	0	341	/C-2	0.1
	SD N	44	119	6	23	0	0	0	6	11-1	1	26	.193	.267	.193	35	-10	0-0	.993	-1	93	81	C-43	-1.0
	Year	46	120	6	23	0	0	0	6	13-2	1	26	.192	.276	.192	38	-10	0-0	.993	-0	91	88	C-45	-0.9
1973	SD N	29	72	7	15	2	1	0	3	6-1	1	10	.208	.275	.264	55	-5	0-0	.986	-5	71	76	C-28	-0.9
Total	9	300	767	63	166	28	3	4	54	75-10	7	167	.216	.291	.276	61	-40	1-1	.984	-3	*114*	*86*	C-292	-3.4
CORREIA, ROD Ronald Douglas B 9.13.1967 Providence, RI BR/TR 5-11/180# d6.20																								
1993	Cal A	64	128	12	34	5	0	0	9	6-0	4	20	.266	.319	.305	66	-6	2-4	.981	1	105	79	S-40,2-11/3-3,D-6	-0.3
1994	Cal A	6	17	4	4	1	0	0	0	0-0	2	0	.235	.316	.294	58	-1	0-0	1.000	-2	52	69	/2-5,S	-0.3
1995	Cal A	14	21	3	5	1	1	0	3	0-0	0	5	.238	.238	.381	58	-1	0-0	.850	-0	81	143	/S-7,2-3,3-2,D	-0.1
Total	3	84	166	19	43	7	1	0	12	6-0	6	25	.259	.309	.313	65	-8	2-4	.968	-1	102	89	/S-48,2-19,D-7,3-5	-0.7
CORRELL, VIC Victor Crosby B 2.5.1946 Washington, DC BR/TR 5-10/185# d10.4																								
1972	Bos A	1	4	1	2	0	0	0	1	0-0	0	1	.500	.500	.500	188	0	0-0	1.000	1	0	0	/C	0.1
1974	Atl N	73	202	20	48	15	1	4	29	21-3	4	38	.238	.317	.381	92	-2	0-0	.988	5	94	61	C-59	0.6
1975	Atl N	103	325	37	70	12	1	11	39	42-5	1	66	.215	.305	.360	82	-8	0-2	.973	-5	84	99	C-97	-1.0
1976	Atl N	69	200	26	45	6	2	5	16	21-5	1	37	.225	.302	.350	80	-6	0-1	.981	-3	76	110	C-65	-0.7
1977	Atl N	54	144	16	30	7	0	7	16	22-1	1	33	.208	.314	.403	82	-3	2-3	.973	-6	60	120	C-49	-0.8
1978	Cin N	52	105	9	25	7	0	1	6	8-3	0	17	.238	.292	.333	74	-4	0-2	.980	-3	118	110	C-52	-0.6
1979	Cin N	48	133	14	31	12	0	1	15	14-2	1	26	.233	.309	.346	78	-3	0-0	.992	-1	77	62	C-47	-0.2
1980	Cin N	10	19	1	8	1	0	0	3	0-0	0	2	.421	.421	.474	149	1	0-0	.919	-3	48	41	C-10	-0.1
Total	8	410	1132	124	259	60	4	29	125	128-19	8	220	.229	.310	.366	83	-25	2-8	.979	-15	83	92	C-380	-2.7
CORRIDEN, JOHN John Michael Jr. B 1.6.1918 Logansport, IN D 6.4.2001 Indianapolis, IN BB/TR 5-6/160# d4.20 f-Red																								
1946	Bro N	1	0	1	0	0	0	0	0	0	0	0	—	—	—	—	0	0	—	0			R	0.0
CORRIDEN, RED John Michael Sr. B 9.4.1887 Logansport, IN D 9.28.1959 Indianapolis, IN BR/TR 5-9/165# d9.8 M1 C18 s-John																								
1910	StL A	26	84	19	13	3	0	1	4	13	4		.155	.297	.226	68	-2	5	.902	2	115	49	S-14,3-12	0.1
1912	Det A	38	138	22	28	6	0	0	5	15	1		.203	.286	.246	54	-8	4	.929	-2	102	138	3-25/2-7,S-3	-0.9
1913	Chi N	46	97	13	17	3	0	2	9	10	0	14	.175	.252	.268	49	-7	4-3	.907	-2	102	127	S-37/2-2,3	-0.7
1914	Chi N	107	318	42	73	9	5	3	29	35	9	33	.230	.323	.318	91	-3	13	.894	-27	78	95	S-91/3-8,2-3	-2.6
1915	Chi N	6	3	1	0	0	0	0	0	2	2	1	.000	.571	.000	79	1	0	.667	-1	56	0	/3O(CF)	0.0
Total	5	223	640	97	131	21	5	6	47	75	16	48	.205	.304	.281	74	-19	26-3	.896	-29	88	94	S-145/3-47,2-12,O(CF)	-4.1
CORTAZZO, JESS John Francis B 9.26.1904 Wilmerding, PA D 3.4.1963 Pittsburgh, PA BR/TR 5-3.5/142# d9.1																								
1923	Chi A	1	1	0	0	0	0	0	0	0	0	0	.000	.000	.000	-99	0	0-0	—	0			H	0.0
COSCARART, JOE Joseph Marvin B 11.18.1909 Escondido, CA D 4.5.1993 Sequim, WA BR/TR 6/185# d4.26 b-Pete																								
1935	Bos N	86	284	30	67	11	2	1	29	16	0	28	.236	.277	.299	59	-17	2	.962	-3	120	87	3-41,S-27,2-15	-1.6
1936	Bos N	104	367	28	90	11	2	2	44	19	5	37	.245	.292	.302	64	-19	0	.935	1	109	136	3-97/S-6,2	-1.5
Total	2	190	651	58	157	22	4	3	73	35	5	65	.241	.285	.301	62	-36	2	.943	-2	112	123	3-138/S-33,2-16	-3.1
COSCARART, PETE Peter Joseph B 6.16.1913 Escondido, CA D 7.24.2002 Escondido, CA BR/TR 5-11.5/175# d4.26 b-Joe																								
1938	Bro N	32	79	10	12	3	0	0	6	9	2	18	.152	.256	.190	24	-8	0	.955	1	97	115	2-27	-0.6
1939	Bro N	115	419	59	116	22	2	4	43	46	4	56	.277	.354	.368	91	-4	10	.960	-10	98	102	*2-107/3-4,S-2	-0.7
1940	Bro N★	143	506	55	120	24	4	9	58	53	1	59	.237	.311	.354	78	-15	5	.958	-34	85	73	*2-140	-4.1
1941	†Bro N	43	62	13	8	1	0	0	5	7	0	12	.129	.217	.145	3	-8	1	.948	1	111	74	2-19/S	-0.7
1942	Pit N	133	487	57	111	12	4	3	29	38	3	56	.228	.288	.287	67	-21	2	.952	-19	97	80	*S-108,2-25	-3.3
1943	Pit N	133	491	57	119	19	6	0	48	46	0	48	.242	.307	.305	75	-16	4	.961	-3	103	105	2-85,S-47/3	-1.2
1944	Pit N	139	554	89	146	30	4	4	42	41	1	57	.264	.315	.354	85	-11	10	.967	-3	99	91	*2-136/S-4,O(RF)	-0.7
1945	Pit N	123	392	59	95	17	2	8	38	55	4	55	.242	.341	.357	91	-4	2	.978	21	**116**	**124**	*2-122/S	2.3
1946	Pit N	3	2	0	1	1	0	0	0	0	0	0	.500	.500	1.000	312	1	0	—	-0	0	0	/S	0.0
Total	9	864	2992	399	728	129	22	28	269	295	15	361	.243	.314	.329	78	-86	34	.963	-47	99	97	2-661,S-164/3-5,O(RF)	-9.0
COSEY, RAY Donald Ray B 2.15.1956 San Rafael, CA BL/TL 5-10/185# d4.14																								
1980	Oak A	9	9	0	1	0	0	0	0	0-0	0	0	.111	.111	.111	-42	-2	0-0	—	0			/H	-0.2
COSTELLO, DAN Daniel Francis "Dashing Dan" B 9.9.1891 Jessup, PA D 3.26.1936 Pittsburgh, PA BL/TR 6-0.5/185# d7.2																								
1913	NY A	2	2	1	1	0	0	0	0	0	0	0	.500	.500	.500	192	0	0	—	0			H	0.0
1914	Pit N	21	64	7	19	1	0	0	5	8	0	16	.297	.375	.313	110	1	2	.970	0	100	107	O-20(RF)	0.1
1915	Pit N	71	125	16	27	4	1	0	11	7	0	23	.216	.258	.264	59	-6	7-1	.893	-3	70	52	O-22(5-12-5)/1	-1.1
1916	Pit N	60	159	11	38	1	3	0	8	6	0	23	.239	.267	.283	68	-7	3	.976	-1	114	0	O-41(33-1-7)	-1.1
Total	4	154	350	35	85	6	4	0	24	21	0	62	.243	.286	.283	73	-12	12-1	.959	-4	101	37	/O-83(38-13-32),1	-2.1
COSTO, TIM Timothy Roger B 2.16.1969 Melrose Park, IL BR/TR 6-5/220# d9.18																								
1992	Cin N	12	36	3	8	2	0	0	2	5-0	0	6	.222	.310	.278	68	-1	0-0	1.000	0	104	203	1-12	-0.2
1993	Cin N	31	98	13	22	5	0	3	12	4-0	0	17	.224	.250	.367	64	-5	0-0	.980	0	104	56	O-26(11-0-16)/1-2,3-2	-0.7
Total	2	43	134	16	30	7	0	3	14	9-0	0	23	.224	.267	.343	66	-6	0-0	.980	1	104	56	/O-26(11-0-16),1-14,3-2	-0.9
COTA, HUMBERTO Humberto Figueroa B 2.7.1979 San Luis Rio Colorado, Mexico BR/TR 6/180# d9.9																								
2001	Pit N	7	9	0	2	0	0	0	1	0-0	0	5	.222	.222	.222	15	-1	0-0	1.000	1	0	0	/C-3	0.0
2002	Pit N	7	17	2	5	1	0	0	0	1-1	0	4	.294	.333	.353	84	0	0-0	1.000	1	262	83	/C-7	0.1
2003	Pit N	10	16	1	4	1	0	0	1	1-0	0	5	.250	.294	.313	57	-1	0-0	1.000	0	129	171	/C-4	-0.1
Total	3	24	42	3	11	2	0	0	2	2-1	0	14	.262	.295	.310	59	-2	0-0	1.000	2	184	99	/C-14	0.0

Year	Tm Lg	G	AB	R	H	2B	3B	HR	RBI	BB-IB	HP	SO	AVG	OBP	SLG	AOPS	ABR	SB-CS	FA	FR	Rng	Thr	G at Pos	BFW
COTE, HENRY Henry Joseph B 2.19.1864 Troy, NY D 4.28.1940 Troy, NY 5-9.5/165# d9.16																								
1894	Lou N	10	31	7	9	2	2	0	3	5	0	6	.290	.389	.484	117	1	2	.918	3	100	145	C-10	0.4
1895	Lou N	10	33	10	10	0	0	0	5	3	0	3	.303	.361	.303	77	-1	2	.872	-3	90	53	C-10	-0.3
Total	2	20	64	17	19	2	2	0	8	8	0	9	.297	.375	.391	98	0	4	.900	-0	95	102	/C-20	0.1
COTE, PETE Warren Peter B 8.30.1902 Cambridge, MA D 10.17.1987 Middleton, MA BR/TR 5-6/148# d6.18																								
1926	NY N	2	1	0	0	0	0	0	0	0	0	0	.000	.000	.000	-99	0	0	—	0			H	0.0
COTTER, ED Edward Christopher B 7.4.1904 Hartford, CT D 6.14.1959 Hartford, CT BR/TR 6/185# d6.12																								
1926	Phi N	17	26	3	8	0	1	0	1	1	0	4	.308	.333	.385	88	-1	1	.833	-1	111	0	/3-8,S-5	-0.1
COTTER, HOOKS Harvey Louis B 5.22.1900 Holden, MO D 8.6.1955 Los Angeles, CA BL/TL 5-10/160# d4.15																								
1922	Chi N	1	1	0	1	1	0	0	0	0	0	0	1.000	1.000	2.000	644	1	0-0	—	0			H	0.1
1924	Chi N	98	310	39	81	16	4	4	33	36	0	31	.261	.338	.377	91	-3	3-5	.989	4	119	99	1-90	-0.7
Total	2	99	311	39	82	17	4	4	33	36	0	31	.264	.340	.383	92	-2	3-5	.989	4	119	99	/1-90	-0.6
COTTER, DICK Richard Raphael B 10.12.1889 Manchester, NH D 4.4.1945 Brooklyn, NY BR/TR 5-11/172# d8.17																								
1911	Phi N	20	46	2	13	0	0	0	5	5	0	7	.283	.353	.283	78	-1	1	.975	-2	81	133	C-17	-0.2
1912	Chi N	26	54	6	15	0	2	0	10	6	1	13	.278	.361	.352	96	0	1	.954	-1	128	85	C-24	0.0
Total	2	46	100	8	28	0	2	0	15	11	1	20	.280	.357	.320	87	-1	2	.964	-3	107	107	/C-41	-0.2
COTTER, TOM Thomas B. B 9.30.1866 Waltham, MA D 11.22.1906 Brookline, MA BR/TR 5-10.5/149# d9.3																								
1891	Bos AA	6	12	1	3	0	0	0	4	1	0	2	.250	.308	.250	61	-1	0	.938	-0	154	106	/C-5,O(RF)	0.0
COTTIER, CHUCK Charles Keith B 1.8.1936 Delta, CO BR/TR 5-10.5/175# d4.17 M3 C18																								
1959	Mil N	10	24	1	3	1	0	0	1	3-0	0	7	.125	.222	.167	6	-3	0-0	.976	-0	106	43	2-10	-0.3
1960	Mil N	95	229	29	52	8	0	3	19	14-3	2	21	.227	.273	.301	63	-12	1-0	.968	5	109	90	2-92	-0.2
1961	Det A	10	7	2	2	0	0	0	1	1-0	0	1	.286	.375	.286	77	0	0-0	.889	0	22	110	/S-8,2-2	0.0
	Was A	101	337	37	79	14	4	2	34	30-1	1	51	.234	.296	.318	66	-17	9-1	.982	11	116	104	*2-100	0.4
	Year	111	344	39	81	14	4	2	35	31-1	1	52	.235	.297	.317	66	-17	9-1	.982	11	117	106	*2-102/S-8	0.4
1962	Was A	136	443	50	107	14	6	6	40	44-0	2	57	.242	.310	.341	76	-15	14-8	.981	20	106	**121**	*2-134	1.6
1963	Was A	113	337	30	69	16	4	5	21	24-6	0	63	.205	.257	.320	61	-18	2-1	.963	2	104	93	2-85,S-24/3	-0.8
1964	Was A	73	137	16	23	6	2	3	10	19-1	0	33	.168	.268	.307	60	-7	2-0	.982	5	105	123	2-53/3-3,S-2	0.1
1965	Was A	7	1	1	0	0	0	0	0	0-0	0	0	.000	.000	.000	-99	0	0-0	—	0			H	0.0
1968	Cal A	33	67	2	13	4	1	0	1	2-0	0	15	.194	.217	.284	53	-4	0-0	.963	-1	98	59	3-27/2-4	-0.6
1969	Cal A	2	2	0	0	0	0	0	0	0-0	0	0	.000	.000	.000	-99	-1	0-0	1.000	-0	79	0	/2-2	-0.1
Total	9	580	1584	168	348	63	17	19	127	137-11	5	248	.220	.282	.317	65	-77	28-10	.976	42	109	105	2-482/S-34,3-31	0.1
COTTO, HENRY Henry B 1.5.1961 New York, NY BR/TR 6-2/178# d4.5																								
1984	†Chi N	105	146	24	40	5	0	0	8	10-2	1	23	.274	.325	.308	72	-5	9-3	.984	7	131	123	O-88(47-34-10)	0.2
1985	NY A	34	56	4	17	1	0	1	6	3-0	0	12	.304	.339	.375	98	0	1-1	.977	1	100	185	O-30(14-20-1)	0.0
1986	NY A	35	80	11	17	3	0	1	6	2-0	0	17	.213	.229	.287	41	-7	3-0	1.000	1	108	77	O-29(11-19-0)/D	-0.6
1987	NY A	68	149	21	35	10	0	5	20	6-0	1	35	.235	.269	.403	76	-6	4-2	.989	-1	96	102	O-57(15-41-2)	-0.7
1988	Sea A	133	386	50	100	18	1	8	33	23-0	2	53	.259	.302	.373	85	-8	27-3	.992	-3	93	130	*O-120(CF)/D-2	-0.7
1989	Sea A	100	295	44	78	11	2	9	33	12-3	3	44	.264	.300	.407	94	-3	10-4	.988	3	95	212	O-90(57-30-14)/D-2	-0.1
1990	Sea A	127	355	40	92	14	3	4	33	22-2	4	52	.259	.307	.349	83	-9	21-3	.990	2	108	70	*O-118(41-18-67)/D-3	-0.6
1991	Sea A	66	177	35	54	6	2	6	23	10-0	2	27	.305	.347	.463	123	5	16-3	.981	3	116	88	O-56(38-19-8)/D-6	0.9
1992	Sea A	108	294	42	76	11	1	5	27	14-3	1	49	.259	.294	.354	80	-9	23-2	1.000	1	112	45	O-92(63-30-6)/D-3	-0.5
1993	Sea A	54	105	10	20	1	0	2	7	2-0	1	22	.190	.213	.257	25	-12	5-4	.983	1	117	0	O-34(23-9-4),D-15	-1.3
	Fla N	54	135	15	40	7	0	3	14	3-0	1	18	.296	.312	.415	89	-2	11-1	.977	2	120	46	O-46(13-15-21)	0.1
Total	10	884	2178	296	569	87	9	44	210	107-10	16	352	.261	.299	.370	83	-56	130-26	.989	16	106	104	O-760(322-355-133)/D-32	-3.3
COUGHLIN, DENNIS Dennis F. B 1844 , NY D 5.14.1913 Washington, DC d4.27																								
1872	Nat NA	8	37	5	11	1	0	0	7	0		0	.297	.297	.324	78	-1	0-0	.941	1	187	646	/O-5(CF),12S	-0.1
COUGHLIN, ED Edward E. B 8.5.1861 Hartford, CT D 12.25.1952 Hartford, CT d5.15																								
1884	Buf N	1	4	0	1	0	0	0	1	0		2	.250	.250	.250	56	0		.750	-0	0	0	/O(RF)P	0.0
COUGHLIN, BILL William Paul "Scranton Bill" B 7.12.1878 Scranton, PA D 5.7.1943 Scranton, PA BR/TR 5-9/140# d8.9																								
1899	Was N	6	24	2	3	0	1	0	3	1	0		.125	.160	.208	1	-4	1	.818	-1	85	0	/3-6	-0.4
1901	Was A	137	506	75	139	17	13	6	68	25	6		.275	.317	.395	98	-3	16	.922	3	92	85	*3-137	0.3
1902	Was A	123	469	84	141	27	4	6	71	26	8		.301	.348	.414	110	6	29	.926	7	106	60	3-66,S-31,2-26	1.5
1903	Was A	125	473	56	116	18	3	1	31	9	5		.245	.267	.302	69	-18	30	.952	3	98	96	*3-119/S-4,2-2	-1.2
1904	Was A	65	265	28	73	15	4	0	17	9	3		.275	.307	.362	113	3	10	.939	4	99	105	3-64	1.0
	Det A	56	206	22	47	6	0	0	17	5	3		.228	.257	.257	65	-8	1	.929	-5	99	38	3-56	-1.3
	Year	121	471	50	120	21	4	0	34	14	6		.255	.285	.316	92	-5	11	.935	-1	99	74	*3-120	-0.3
1905	Det A	137	489	48	123	20	6	0	44	34	7		.252	.309	.317	98	-1	16	.914	-7	96	98	*3-136	-0.5
1906	Det A	147	498	54	117	15	5	2	60	36	5		.235	.293	.297	83	-10	31	.940	-12	90	103	*3-147	-1.9
1907	†Det A	134	519	80	126	10	2	0	46	35	8		.243	.301	.270	79	-11	15	.930	-9	89	66	*3-133	-1.9
1908	†Det A	119	405	32	87	5	1	0	23	23	7		.215	.269	.232	61	-17	10	.941	-13	92	91	*3-119	-3.2
Total	9	1049	3854	481	972	133	39	15	380	203	52		.252	.299	.319	86	-63	159	.931	-30	94	86	3-983/S-35,2-28	-7.6
COUGHTRY, MARLAN James Marlan B 9.11.1934 Hollywood, CA BL/TR 6-1/170# d9.2																								
1960	Bos A	15	19	3	3	0	0	0	0	5-0	0	8	.158	.333	.158	36	-1	0-0	.909	-1	103	24	2-13/3	-0.2
1962	LA A	11	22	0	4	0	0	0	2	0-0	0	6	.182	.182	.182	-2	-3	0-0	.867	1	128	134	/3-5,2-2	-0.2
	KC A	6	11	1	2	0	0	0	1	4-0	0	3	.182	.400	.182	60	0	0-0	.917	1	155	151	/3-3	0.1
	Cle A	3	2	1	1	0	0	0	1	1-0	0	1	.500	.667	.500	226	1	0-0	—	0			H	0.1
	Year	20	35	2	7	0	0	0	4	5-0	0	10	.200	.300	.200	38	-3	0-0	.889	2	141	142	/3-8,2-2	0.0
Total	2	35	54	5	10	0	0	0	4	10-0	0	18	.185	.313	.185	37	-3	0-0	.915	1	106	80	/2-15,3-9	-0.2
COULSON, BOB Robert Jackson B 6.17.1887 Courtney, PA D 9.11.1953 Washington, PA BR/TR 5-10.5/175# d8.4																								
1908	Cin N	8	18	3	6	1	1	0	1	3	0		.333	.429	.500	202	2	0	1.000	1	126	0	/O-6(4-1-1)	0.3
1910	Bro N	25	89	14	22	3	4	1	13	6	1	14	.247	.302	.404	109	0	9	.922	0	101	111	O-25(RF)	-0.1
1911	Bro N	146	521	52	122	23	7	0	50	42	8	78	.234	.301	.305	73	-20	32	.968	0	101	102	*O-145(0-2-144)	-2.7
1914	Pit F	18	64	7	13	1	0	0	3	7	0	10	.203	.282	.219	38	-7	2	.931	-1	97	39	O-18(11-0-7)	-0.9
Total	4	197	692	76	163	28	12	1	67	58	9	102	.236	.303	.315	77	-25	43	.960	-0	101	95	O-194(15-3-177)	-3.4
COULTER, CHIP Thomas Lee B 6.5.1945 Steubenville, OH BB/TR 5-10/172# d9.18																								
1969	StL N	6	19	3	6	1	1	0	4	2-0	0	6	.316	.381	.474	138	1	0-1	.960	-1	100	146	/2-6	0.0
COUNSELL, CRAIG Craig John B 8.21.1970 South Bend, IN BL/TR 6/180# d9.17																								
1995	Col N	3	1	0	0	0	0	0	0	1-0	0	0	.000	.500	.000	36	0	0-0	1.000	-0	60	275	/S-3	0.0
1997	Col N	1	0	0	0	0	0	0	0	0-0	0	0	—	—	—	—	0	0-0	—	0			/R	0.0
	†Fla N	51	164	20	49	9	2	1	16	18-2	3	17	.299	.376	.396	108	3	1-1	.989	13	107	121	2-51	1.7
	Year	52	164	20	49	9	2	1	16	18-2	3	17	.299	.376	.396	107	2	1-1	.989	13	107	121	2-51	1.7
1998	Fla N	107	335	43	84	19	5	4	40	51-7	4	47	.251	.355	.373	97	0	3-0	.991	5	104	94	*2-104	1.0
1999	Fla N	37	66	4	10	1	0	0	2	5-0	0	10	.152	.211	.167	-3	-11	0-0	.980	-2	98	56	2-12	-1.1
	LA N	50	108	20	28	6	0	0	9	9-0	0	14	.259	.311	.315	64	-6	1-0	.993	3	114	79	2-38/S-2	-0.1
	Year	87	174	24	38	7	0	0	11	14-0	0	24	.218	.274	.259	39	-17	1-0	.989	2	110	73	2-50/S-2	-1.2
2000	Ari N	67	152	23	48	8	1	2	11	20-0	2	18	.316	.400	.421	105	2	3-3	.974	2	100	122	2-25,3-23/S-6	0.5
2001	†Ari N	141	458	76	126	22	3	4	38	61-3	2	76	.275	.359	.362	83	-9	6-8	.975	14	90	121	S-58,2-55,3-38/1-2	0.9
2002	Ari N	112	436	63	123	22	1	2	51	45-3	1	52	.282	.348	.351	82	-12	7-5	.974	16	109	84	3-94,S-22,2-13	0.6
2003	Ari N	89	303	40	71	6	3	3	21	41-0	2	32	.234	.328	.304	61	-17	11-4	.986	11	110	104	3-57,S-26,2-10/1-2	-0.3
Total	8	658	2023	289	539	93	15	16	188	251-15	14	266	.266	.349	.351	81	-50	32-21	.991	62	105	105	2-308,3-212,S-117/1-4	3.2
COURTNEY, CLINT Clinton Dawson "Scrap Iron" B 3.16.1927 Hall Summit, LA D 6.16.1975 Rochester, NY BL/TR 5-8/180# d9.29 C1																								
1951	NY A	1	2	0	0	0	0	0	0	0	1	1	.000	.333	.000	-5	0	0-0	.800	-0	0	511	/C	0.0
1952	StL A	119	413	38	118	24	3	5	50	39	1	26	.286	.349	.395	104	2	0-2	**.996**	1	97	**113**	*C-113	0.9

Year	Tm Lg	G	AB	R	H	2B	3B	HR	RBI	BB-IB	HP	SO	AVG	OBP	SLG	AOPS	ABR	SB-CS	FA	FR	Rng	Thr	G at Pos	BFW
1953	StL A	106	355	28	89	12	2	4	19	25	1	20	.251	.302	.330	69	-16	0-1	.980	-7	91	126	*C-103	-1.9
1954	Bal A	122	397	25	107	18	3	4	37	30	3	7	.270	.323	.360	95	-4	2-1	.990	-5	82	**125**	*C-111	-0.3
1955	Chi A	19	37	7	14	3	0	1	10	7-2	0	0	.378	.467	.541	168	4	0-0	1.000	0	113	54	C-17	0.5
	Was A	75	238	26	71	8	4	2	30	19-4	1	9	.298	.349	.391	105	1	0-0	.983	-9	78	128	C-67	-0.5
	Year	94	275	33	85	11	4	3	40	26-6	1	9	.309	.366	.411	114	5	0-0	.985	-9	83	117	C-84	0.0
1956	Was A	101	283	31	85	20	3	5	44	20-4	9	10	.300	.362	.445	113	5	0-5	.979	-11	75	134	C-76	-0.4
1957	Was A	91	232	23	62	14	1	6	27	16-5	12	11	.267	.346	.414	108	3	0-0	.994	-3	75	127	C-59	0.3
1958	Was A	134	450	46	113	18	0	8	62	48-3	9	23	.251	.332	.344	89	-5	1-5	.991	-8	60	115	*C-128	-0.9
1959	Was A	72	189	19	44	4	1	2	18	20-1	1	19	.233	.308	.296	68	-8	0-1	.987	-11	55	49	C-53	-1.7
1960	Bal A	83	154	14	35	3	0	1	12	30-3	8	14	.227	.374	.266	79	-2	0-1	.975	2	102	84	C-58	0.2
1961	KC A	1	1	0	0	0	0	0	0	0-0	0	0	.000	.000	.000	-98	0	0-0	—	0			H	0.0
	Bal A	22	45	3	12	2	0	0	4	10-0	0	3	.267	.400	.311	96	0	0-0	1.000	1	110	130	C-16	0.2
	Year	23	46	3	12	2	0	0	4	10-0	0	3	.261	.393	.304	92	0	0-0	1.000	1	110	130	C-16	0.2
Total	11	946	2796	260	750	126	17	38	313	264-22	46	143	.268	.339	.366	94	-20	3-16	.987	-50	81	115	C-802	-3.6
COURTNEY, ERNIE Edward Ernest B 1.20.1875 Des Moines, IA D 2.29.1920 Buffalo, NY BL/TR 5-8/168# d4.17 OF Total (40-LF 1-CF 6-RF)																								
1902	Bos N	48	165	23	36	3	0	0	17	13	4		.218	.291	.236	62	-7	3	.974	-0	92	0	O-39(36-1-3)/S-3	-1.0
	Bal A	1	4	3	2	0	1	0	1	1	0		.500	.600	1.000	324	1	0	1.000	0	66	0	/3	0.1
1903	NY A	25	79	7	21	3	3	1	8	7	2		.266	.341	.418	119	2	1	.916	1	116	122	S-19/2-4,1	0.3
	Det A	23	74	7	17	0	0	0	6	5	3		.230	.305	.230	64	-3	1	.938	-2	59	80	3-13/S-9	-0.5
	Year	48	153	14	38	3	3	1	14	12	5		.248	.324	.327	94	-1	2	.921	-1	116	94	S-28,3-13/2-4,1	-0.2
1905	Phi N	**155**	601	77	165	14	7	2	77	47	7		.275	.334	.331	102	2	17	.923	-20	83	73	*3-155	-1.4
1906	Phi N	116	398	53	94	12	2	0	42	45	1		.236	.315	.276	84	-6	6	.923	-9	90	86	3-96,1-13/O-3(RF),S	-1.5
1907	Phi N	130	440	42	107	17	4	2	43	55	6		.243	.335	.314	105	5	6	.907	-5	93	118	3-75,1-48/O-4(LF),2-2,S-2	0.1
1908	Phi N	60	160	14	29	3	0	0	6	15	2		.181	.260	.200	46	-9	1	.915	-3	96	46	3-22,1-13/2-5,S-2	-1.4
Total	6	558	1921	226	471	52	17	5	200	188	25		.245	.321	.298	91	-15	35	.920	-40	87	84	3-362/1-75,O-46L,S-36,2-11	-5.3
COUSINEAU, DEE Edward Thomas B 12.16.1898 Watertown, MA D 7.14.1951 Watertown, MA BR/TR 6/170# d10.6																								
1923	Bos N	1	2	1	2	0	0	0	2	0	0	0	1.000	1.000	1.000	447	1	0-0	—	0	0	0	/C	0.1
1924	Bos N	3	2	0	0	0	0	0	0	0	0	0	.000	.000	.000	-99	-1	0-0	.500	-0	0	0	/C-3	-0.1
1925	Bos N	1	0	0	0	0	0	0	0	0	0	0	—	—	—	—	0	0-0	—	0	0	0	/C	0.0
Total	3	5	4	1	2	0	0	0	2	0	0	0	.500	.500	.500	174	0	0-0	.500	-0	0	0	/C-5	0.0
COVENEY, JACK John Patrick B 6.10.1880 S.Natick, MA D 3.28.1961 Wayland, MA BR/TR 5-9/175# d9.19																								
1903	StL N	4	14	0	2	0	0	0	0	0	0		.143	.143	.143	-19	-2	0	.923	0	94	172	/C-4	-0.2
COVINGTON, SAM Clarence Calvert B 11.18.1894 Denison, TX D 1.4.1963 Denison, TX BL/TR 6-1/190# d8.25 Mil 1918 b-Tex																								
1913	StL A	20	60	3	9	0	1	0	4	4	0	6	.150	.203	.183	14	-7	3	.994	3	184	83	1-16	-0.4
1917	Bos N	17	66	8	13	2	0	1	10	5	1	5	.197	.264	.273	69	-2	1	.994	0	99	166	1-17	-0.3
1918	Bos N	3	3	0	1	0	0	0	0	0	0	0	.333	.333	.333	108	0	0	—	0			H	0.0
Total	3	40	129	11	23	2	1	1	14	9	1	11	.178	.237	.233	43	-9	4	.994	4	139	127	/1-33	-0.7
COVINGTON, WES John Wesley B 3.27.1932 Laurinburg, NC BL/TR 6-1/205# d4.19																								
1956	Mil N	75	138	17	39	4	0	2	16	16-3	1	20	.283	.361	.355	100	0	1-0	.979	-2	85	115	O-35(34-0-1)	-0.3
1957	†Mil N	96	328	51	93	4	8	21	65	29-7	2	44	.284	.339	.537	143	17	4-1	.981	0	90	155	O-89(LF)	1.3
1958	†Mil N	90	294	43	97	12	1	24	74	20-7	5	35	.330	.380	.622	175	30	0-0	.953	-4	90	60	O-82(LF)	2.2
1959	Mil N	103	373	38	104	17	3	7	45	26-8	3	41	.279	.329	.397	101	0	0-1	.962	-4	88	86	O-94(LF)	-1.0
1960	Mil N	95	281	25	70	16	1	10	35	15-1	1	37	.249	.288	.420	99	-2	1-2	.964	-4	91	39	O-72(LF)	-1.1
1961	Mil N	9	21	3	4	1	0	0	0	2-0	0	4	.190	.261	.238	36	-2	0-0	1.000	-1	52	0	/O-5(LF)	-0.3
	Chi A	22	59	5	17	1	0	4	15	4-1	0	5	.288	.333	.508	123	2	0-0	.900	-1	72	230	O-14(11-0-3)	0.0
	KC A	17	44	3	7	0	0	1	6	4-0	2	7	.159	.260	.227	31	-4	0-0	1.000	-1	82	0	O-12(11-0-1)	-0.6
	Year	39	103	8	24	1	0	5	21	8-1	2	12	.233	.301	.388	83	-3	0-0	.941	-2	76	131	O-26(22-0-4)	-0.6
	Phi N	57	165	23	50	9	0	7	26	15-1	0	17	.303	.355	.485	124	6	0-0	.950	-2	83	127	O-45(10-0-36)	0.2
1962	Phi N	116	304	36	86	12	1	9	44	19-1	2	44	.283	.324	.418	102	0	0-0	.944	-3	90	70	O-88(LF)	-0.6
1963	Phi N	119	353	46	107	24	1	17	64	26-7	2	56	.303	.354	.521	150	23	1-0	.937	-5	86	83	*O-101(LF)	1.5
1964	Phi N	129	339	37	95	18	0	13	58	38-6	3	50	.280	.355	.448	127	13	0-0	.972	-4	81	87	*O-99(97-1-2)	0.6
1965	Phi N	101	235	27	58	10	1	15	45	26-8	1	47	.247	.322	.489	128	8	0-0	.968	-0	101	71	O-64(LF)	0.5
1966	Chi N	9	11	0	1	0	0	0	0	1-1	0	2	.091	.167	.091	-26	-2	0-0	1.000	0	103	0	/O(LF)	-0.2
	†LA N	37	33	1	4	0	1	1	6	6-0	2	5	.121	.293	.273	63	-2	0-0	1.000	-0	60	0	/O-2(LF)	-0.2
	Year	46	44	1	5	0	1	1	6	7-1	2	7	.114	.264	.227	41	-4	0-0	1.000	-0	83	0	/O-3(LF)	-0.4
Total	11	1075	2978	355	832	128	17	131	499	247-51	24	414	.279	.337	.466	123	87	7-4	.961	-29	88	89	O-803(761-1-43)	2.0
COWAN, BILLY Billy Rolland B 8.28.1938 Calhoun City, MS BR/TR 6/170# d9.9																								
1963	Chi N	14	36	1	9	1	1	1	2	0-0	0	11	.250	.250	.417	84	-1	0-1	.917	-1	66	207	O-10(1-7-2)	-0.2
1964	Chi N	139	497	52	120	16	4	19	50	18-5	1	128	.241	.268	.404	83	-13	12-3	.968	-9	100	23	*O-134(CF)	-2.5
1965	NY N	82	156	16	28	8	2	3	9	4-1	1	45	.179	.205	.314	45	-12	3-2	1.000	-0	98	94	O-61(2-59-0)/2-2,S	-1.4
	Mil N	19	27	4	5	1	0	0	0	0-0	0	9	.185	.185	.222	14	-3	0-0	1.000	-0	106	0	O-10(7-3-0)	-0.4
	Year	101	183	20	33	9	2	3	9	4-1	1	54	.180	.202	.301	41	-15	3-2	1.000	-0	99	84	O-71(9-62-0)/2-2,S	-1.8
1967	Phi N	34	59	11	9	0	0	3	6	4-0	0	14	.153	.203	.305	44	-5	1-0	1.000	-1	97	0	O-20(16-0-4)/23	-0.7
1969	NY A	32	48	5	8	0	0	1	3	3-0	0	9	.167	.216	.229	25	-5	0-0	1.000	-0	82	140	O-14(8-4-2)	-0.6
	Cal A	28	56	10	17	1	0	4	10	3-1	1	9	.304	.350	.536	152	3	0-0	1.000	1	95	482	O-13(3-2-8)/1-6	0.4
	Year	60	104	15	25	1	0	5	13	6-1	1	18	.240	.288	.394	93	-2	0-0	1.000	1	88	301	O-27(11-6-10)/1-6	-0.2
1970	Cal A	68	134	20	37	9	1	5	25	11-2	1	29	.276	.336	.470	124	4	0-1	.929	-3	79	0	O-27(3-1-23),1-14/3-2	-0.1
1971	Cal A	74	174	12	48	8	0	4	20	7-1	0	41	.276	.304	.391	103	0	1-1	1.000	-0	108	47	O-40(38-0-2)/1-5	-0.3
1972	Cal A	3	3	0	0	0	0	0	0	0-0	0	2	.000	.000	.000	-99	-1	0-0	—	0			H	-0.1
Total	8	493	1190	131	281	44	8	40	125	50-10	4	297	.236	.269	.387	83	-33	17-8	.977	-13	98	58	O-329(78-210-41)/1-25,3-3,2-3,S	-5.9
COWENS, AL Alfred Edward B 10.25.1951 Los Angeles, CA D 3.11.2002 Downey, CA BR/TR 6-2/200# d4.6																								
1974	KC A	110	269	28	65	7	1	1	25	23-0	1	38	.242	.303	.286	67	-11	5-0	.988	2	89	219	*O-102(6-24-75)/3-2,D-4	-1.2
1975	KC A	120	328	44	91	13	8	4	42	28-1	4	36	.277	.340	.402	107	2	12-7	.978	-0	107	55	*O-113(22-35-65)/D-2	-0.2
1976	†KC A	152	581	71	154	23	6	3	59	26-0	3	50	.265	.298	.341	87	-11	23-16	.986	3	101	115	*O-148(0-12-142)/D	-1.8
1977	†KC A	**162**	606	98	189	32	14	23	112	41-4	8	64	.312	.361	.525	138	30	16-12	.982	0	96	127	*O-159(0-26-141)/D	2.2
1978	†KC A	132	485	63	133	24	8	5	63	31-3	6	54	.274	.319	.388	97	-2	14-6	.990	3	99	106	*O-127(0-16-119)/3-5,D-2	-0.5
1979	KC A	136	516	69	152	18	7	9	73	40-4	3	44	.295	.345	.409	102	1	10-8	.986	-7	99	29	*O-134(0-1-134)/D	-1.4
1980	Cal A	34	119	11	27	5	0	1	17	12-1	1	21	.227	.303	.294	66	-5	1-2	1.000	-0	95	133	O-30(3-10-19)/D	-0.7
	Det A	108	403	58	113	15	3	5	42	37-4	1	40	.280	.339	.370	93	-4	5-6	.986	-3	92	97	*O-107(RF)/D	-1.4
	Year	142	522	69	140	20	3	6	59	49-5	2	61	.268	.331	.352	87	-9	6-8	.989	-4	93	105	*O-137(3-10-126)/D-2	-2.1
1981	Det A	85	253	27	66	11	4	1	18	22-3	1	36	.261	.319	.348	90	-3	3-3	.994	-4	93	68	O-83(0-65-18)	-0.9
1982	Sea A	146	560	72	151	39	8	20	78	46-3	1	81	.270	.325	.475	114	10	11-7	.987	-2	94	133	*O-145(RF)/D	0.0
1983	Sea A	110	356	39	73	19	2	7	35	23-0	2	38	.205	.255	.329	58	-21	10-2	.985	2	101	157	O-70(2-4-65),D-34	-2.2
1984	Sea A	139	524	60	145	34	2	15	78	27-2	2	83	.277	.312	.435	106	4	9-5	.987	-4	92	108	*O-130(0-2-130)/D-7	-0.6
1985	Sea A	122	452	59	120	32	5	14	69	30-3	1	56	.265	.310	.451	105	3	0-0	.967	-1	92	140	*O-110(RF)/D-5	-0.4
1986	Sea A	28	82	5	15	4	0	0	6	3-0	0	18	.183	.209	.232	20	-9	1-0	.971	-0	87	161	O-19(1-0-18)/D	-1.0
Total	13	1584	5534	704	1494	276	68	108	717	389-28	34	659	.270	.319	.403	98	-16	120-74	.985	-12	96	111	*O-1477(34-195-1288)/D-61,3-7	-10.1
COX, STEVE Charles Steven B 10.31.1974 Delano, CA BL/TL 6-4/225# d9.19																								
1999	TB A	6	19	0	4	1	0	0	0	0-0	0	2	.211	.211	.263	20	-2	0-0	1.000	-1	52	157	/1-4,O-2(LF)	-0.3
2000	TB A	116	318	44	90	19	1	11	35	45-2	5	47	.283	.379	.453	111	7	1-2	.948	-1	107	94	O-56(26-0-30),1-24,D-17	0.0
2001	TB A	108	342	37	88	22	0	12	51	24-0	10	75	.257	.323	.427	97	-1	2-2	.998	0	96	101	1-78/O-8(6-0-2),D-4	-0.8
2002	TB A	148	560	65	142	30	1	16	72	60-5	7	116	.254	.330	.396	95	-4	5-0	.993	5	**119**	101	*1-110,D-35	-1.0
Total	4	378	1239	146	324	72	2	39	158	129-7	22	240	.262	.340	.417	99	0	8-4	.994	3	106	99	1-216/O-66(34-0-32),D-56	-2.1
COX, DICK Elmer Joseph B 9.30.1895 Pasadena, CA D 6.1.1966 Morro Bay, CA BR/TR 5-7.5/158# d4.16																								
1925	Bro N	122	434	68	143	23	10	7	64	37	0	29	.329	.382	.477	121	14	4-3	.968	-3	93	96	*O-111(3-0-108)	0.2
1926	Bro N	124	398	53	118	17	4	1	45	46	4	20	.296	.375	.367	102	3	6	.964	-3	95	86	*O-117(0-1-116)	-0.8
Total	2	246	832	121	261	40	14	8	109	83	4	49	.314	.379	.424	112	17	10-3	.966	-6	94	91	O-228(3-1-224)	-0.6

Year	Tm Lg	G	AB	R	H	2B	3B	HR	RBI	BB-IB	HP	SO	AVG	OBP	SLG	AOPS	ABR	SB-CS	FA	FR	Rng	Thr	G at Pos	BFW
COX, FRANK Francis Bernard "Runt" B 8.29.1857 Waltham, MA D 6.24.1928 Hartford, CT 5-6/?# d8.13																								
1884	Det N	27	102	6	13	3	1	0	4	2		36	.127	.144	.176	0	-11		.812	-3	99	106	S-27	-1.2
COX, JIM James Charles B 5.28.1950 Bloomington, IL BR/TR 5-11/175# d7.19																								
1973	Mon N	9	15	1	2	1	0	0	0	1-0	0	4	.133	.188	.200	7	-2	0-0	.950	-2	75	33	/2-7	-0.4
1974	Mon N	77	236	29	52	9	1	2	26	23-2	1	36	.220	.288	.292	61	-12	2-3	.968	5	104	106	2-72	-0.4
1975	Mon N	11	27	1	7	1	0	1	5	1-1	0	2	.259	.276	.407	87	-1	1-0	1.000	-1	103	145	/2-8	-0.1
1976	Mon N	13	29	2	5	0	1	0	2	2-0	0	2	.172	.226	.241	31	-3	0-0	.958	-1	86	96	2-11	-0.3
Total	4	110	307	33	66	11	2	3	33	27-3	1	44	.215	.276	.293	58	-18	3-3	.969	1	101	104	/2-98	-1.2
COX, DARRON James Darron B 11.21.1967 Oklahoma City, OK BR/TR 6-1/205# d4.6																								
1999	Mon N	15	25	2	6	1	0	1	2	0-0	2	5	.240	.296	.400	76	-1	0-0	.963	3	227	55	C-14	0.2
COX, JEFF Jeffrey Lindon B 11.9.1955 Los Angeles, CA BR/TR 5-11/170# d7.1 C4																								
1980	Oak A	59	169	20	36	3	0	0	9	14-0	0	23	.213	.273	.231	43	-13	8-5	.979	-18	86	72	2-58	-2.8
1981	Oak A	2	0	0	0	0	0	0	0	0-0	0	0	—	—	—	—	0	0-0	1.000	0	264	0	/2	0.0
Total	2	61	169	20	36	3	0	0	9	14-0	0	23	.213	.273	.231	43	-13	8-5	.979	-17	86	72	/2-59	-2.8
COX, LARRY Larry Eugene B 9.11.1947 Bluffton, OH D 2.17.1990 Bellefontaine, OH BR/TR 5-11/190# d4.18 C2																								
1973	Phi N	1	0	0	0	0	0	0	0	0-0	0	0	—	—	—	—	0	0-0	1.000	0	0	0	/C	0.0
1974	Phi N	30	53	5	9	2	0	0	4	4-0	1	9	.170	.241	.208	25	-5	0-0	.990	-3	76	19	C-29	-0.8
1975	Phi N	11	5	0	1	0	0	0	1	1-0	0	0	.200	.286	.200	49	0	1-0	1.000	-1	138	0	C-10	-0.1
1977	Sea A	35	93	6	23	6	0	2	6	10-0	0	12	.247	.320	.376	90	-1	1-1	.970	-4	72	158	C-35	-0.4
1978	Chi N	59	121	10	34	5	0	2	18	12-0	0	16	.281	.346	.372	90	-1	0-0	.967	-1	110	108	C-58	-0.1
1979	Sea A	100	293	32	63	11	3	4	36	22-0	0	39	.215	.266	.314	56	-19	2-1	.981	-7	68	119	C-99	-2.2
1980	Sea A	105	243	18	49	6	2	4	20	19-0	0	36	.202	.260	.292	50	-17	1-2	**.993**	7	102	108	*C-104	-0.7
1981	Tex A	5	13	0	3	1	0	0	0	0-0	0	4	.231	.231	.308	57	-1	0-0	1.000	1	43	0	/C-5	0.0
1982	Chi N	2	4	1	0	0	0	0	0	2-1	0	1	.000	.333	.000	1	0	0-0	1.000	1	48	306	/C-2	0.0
Total	9	348	825	72	182	31	5	12	85	70-1	1	117	.221	.280	.314	61	-44	5-4	.983	-8	86	110	C-343	-4.3
COX, BOBBY Robert Joseph B 5.21.1941 Tulsa, OK BR/TR 5-11/180# d4.14 M22 C1																								
1968	NY A	135	437	33	100	15	1	7	41	41-7	5	85	.229	.300	.316	90	-5	3-2	.957	-5	105	97	*3-132	-1.2
1969	NY A	85	191	17	41	7	1	2	17	34-7	1	41	.215	.332	.293	80	-4	0-1	.935	6	114	149	3-56/2-6	0.2
Total	2	220	628	50	141	22	2	9	58	75-14	6	126	.225	.310	.309	87	-9	3-3	.950	1	107	111	3-188/2-6	-1.0
COX, BILLY William Richard B 8.29.1919 Newport, PA D 3.30.1978 Harrisburg, PA BR/TR 5-10/150# d9.20 Mil 1942-45																								
1941	Pit N	10	37	4	10	3	1	0	2	3	0	2	.270	.325	.405	105	0	1	.943	1	118	142	S-10	0.2
1946	Pit N	121	411	32	119	22	6	2	36	26	1	15	.290	.333	.387	101	0	4	.935	-13	94	83	*S-114	-0.7
1947	Pit N	132	529	75	145	30	7	15	54	29	1	28	.274	.313	.442	96	-6	5	.968	-11	99	78	*S-129	-0.8
1948	Bro N	88	237	36	59	13	2	3	15	38	0	19	.249	.353	.359	90	-2	3	.958	-5	93	75	3-70/S-6,2	-0.7
1949	†Bro N	100	390	48	91	18	2	8	40	30	1	18	.233	.290	.351	68	-18	5	.964	7	100	145	*3-100	-1.2
1950	Bro N	119	451	62	116	17	2	8	44	35	0	24	.257	.311	.357	74	-18	6	**.957**	12	**108**	**165**	*3-107,2-13/S-9	-0.5
1951	Bro N	142	455	62	127	25	4	9	51	37	2	30	.279	.336	.411	98	-2	5-5	.967	-5	95	87	*3-139/S	-0.8
1952	†Bro N	116	455	56	118	12	3	6	34	25	2	32	.259	.301	.338	76	-16	10-12	.970	-7	88	175	*3-100,S-10/2-9	-2.5
1953	†Bro N	100	327	44	95	18	1	10	44	37	0	21	.291	.363	.443	106	4	2-2	.974	-2	90	123	3-89/S-6,2	0.1
1954	Bro N	77	226	26	53	9	2	2	17	21	0	13	.235	.297	.319	59	-14	0-0	.961	1	98	85	3-58,2-11/S-8	-1.2
1955	Bal A	53	194	25	41	7	2	3	14	17-0	0	16	.211	.275	.314	63	-11	1-2	.969	-5	100	71	3-37,2-18/S-6	-1.7
Total	11	1058	3712	470	974	174	32	66	351	298-0	7	218	.262	.318	.380	85	-83	42-21	.965	-27	96	124	3-700,S-299/2-53	-9.8
COX, TED William Ted B 1.24.1955 Oklahoma City, OK BR/TR 6-3/195# d9.18 OF Total (49-LF 5-RF)																								
1977	Bos A	13	58	11	21	3	1	1	6	3-0	0	6	.362	.393	.500	127	2	0-0	—	0	0	0	D-13	0.2
1978	Cle A	82	227	14	53	7	0	1	19	16-1	1	30	.233	.286	.278	60	-12	0-1	.980	-4	78	156	O-38(33-0-5),3-20,D-12/1-7,S	-2.0
1979	Cle A	78	189	17	40	6	0	4	22	14-1	2	27	.212	.272	.307	56	-12	3-4	.964	-1	95	142	3-52,O-16(LF)/2-4,D	-1.5
1980	Sea A	83	247	17	60	9	0	2	23	19-3	0	25	.243	.295	.304	64	-12	0-0	.945	-4	95	135	3-80	-1.7
1981	Tor A	16	50	6	15	4	0	2	9	5-0	0	10	.300	.364	.500	138	3	0-1	.897	-4	75	40	3-14/1D	-0.2
Total	5	272	771	65	189	29	1	10	79	57-5	3	98	.245	.298	.324	71	-31	3-6	.947	-14	91	120	3-166/O-54L,D-27,1-8,2-4,S	-5.2
COYNE, TOOTS Martin Albert B 10.20.1894 St.Louis, MO D 9.18.1939 St.Louis, MO TR d9.28																								
1914	Phi A	1	2	0	0	0	0	0	0	0	0	2	.000	.000	.000	-99	-1	0	1.000	-0	112	0	/3	-0.1
CRABTREE, ESTEL Estel Crayton "Crabby" B 8.19.1903 Crabtree, OH D 1.4.1967 Logan, OH BL/TR 6/168# d4.18 C2																								
1929	Cin N	1	1	0	0	0	0	0	0	0	0	0	.000	.000	.000	-99	0	0	—	0			H	0.0
1931	Cin N	117	443	70	119	12	12	4	37	23	3	33	.269	.309	.377	89	-10	3	.974	10	107	172	*O-101(9-16-76)/3-4,1-2	-0.5
1932	Cin N	108	402	38	110	14	9	2	35	23	2	26	.274	.316	.368	86	-9	2	.990	5	108	103	O-95(14-73-9)	-0.7
1933	StL N	23	34	6	9	3	0	0	3	2	0	3	.265	.306	.353	83	-1	1	.947	0	128	0	/O-7(0-4-3)	-0.1
1941	StL N	77	167	27	57	6	3	5	28	26	3	24	.341	.439	.503	154	13	1	1.000	-2	91	71	O-50(17-16-19)/3	1.0
1942	StL N	10	9	1	3	2	0	0	2	1	0	3	.333	.400	.556	166	1	0	—	0			H	0.1
1943	Cin N	95	254	25	70	12	0	2	26	25	2	17	.276	.345	.346	101	1	1	.939	-6	89	66	O-65(2-44-17)	-0.8
1944	Cin N	58	98	7	28	4	1	0	11	13	0	3	.286	.369	.347	106	1	0	1.000	-1	80	86	O-19(15-3-1)/1-2	-0.1
Total	8	489	1408	174	396	53	25	13	142	113	10	109	.281	.339	.382	100	-4	8	.976	6	101	111	O-337(57-156-125)/3-5,1-4	-1.1
CRADLE, RICKEY Rickey Nelson B 6.20.1973 Norfolk, VA BR/TR 6-2/180# d7.1																								
1998	Sea A	5	7	0	1	0	0	0	2	1-0	0	5	.143	.250	.143	6	-1	1-0	1.000	-0	57	0	/O-4(1-2-1)	-0.1
CRAFT, HARRY Harry Francis "Wildfire" B 4.19.1915 Ellisville, MS D 8.3.1995 Conroe, TX BR/TR 6-1/185# d9.19 M7 C5																								
1937	Cin N	10	42	7	13	2	1	0	4	1	0	3	.310	.326	.405	102	0	0	1.000	0	94	131	O-10(CF)	0.0
1938	Cin N	**151**	612	70	165	28	9	15	83	29	2	46	.270	.305	.418	100	-4	3	.983	7	110	112	*O-151(CF)	0.0
1939	†Cin N	134	502	58	129	20	7	13	67	27	3	54	.257	.299	.402	86	-12	5	.981	-3	91	122	*O-134(CF)	-1.9
1940	†Cin N	115	422	47	103	18	5	6	48	17	2	46	.244	.277	.353	72	-18	2	**.997**	0	103	76	*O-109(0-106-3)/1-2	-2.1
1941	Cin N	119	413	48	103	15	2	10	59	33	2	43	.249	.308	.368	90	-7	4	.983	-2	102	68	*O-115(CF)	-1.2
1942	Cin N	37	113	7	20	2	1	0	6	3	1	11	.177	.205	.212	22	-12	0	.987	2	101	147	O-33(CF)	-1.2
Total	6	566	2104	237	533	85	25	44	267	110	10	203	.253	.294	.380	85	-53	14	.986	4	102	100	O-552(0-549-3)/1-2	-6.4
CRAIG, ROD Rodney Paul B 1.12.1958 Los Angeles, CA BB/TR 6-1/195# d9.11																								
1979	Sea A	16	52	9	20	8	1	0	6	1-0	0	5	.385	.396	.577	156	4	1-1	.923	-2	87	0	O-15(RF)	0.1
1980	Sea A	70	240	30	57	15	1	3	20	17-3	2	35	.237	.293	.346	74	-9	3-6	.987	-5	90	45	O-63(3-58-2)	-1.6
1982	Cle A	49	65	7	15	2	0	0	1	4-0	0	6	.231	.275	.262	49	-5	3-1	.966	-1	105	0	O-22(11-4-7)/D-4	-0.5
1986	Chi A	10	10	3	2	0	0	0	0	2-0	0	2	.200	.333	.200	48	-1	0-0	—	-0	0	0	/O-2(1-0-1)	-0.1
Total	4	145	367	49	94	25	2	3	27	24-3	2	48	.256	.305	.360	80	-11	7-8	.977	-8	91	32	O-102(15-62-26)/D-4	-2.1
CRAMER, DOC Roger Maxwell "Flit" B 7.22.1905 Beach Haven, NJ D 9.9.1990 Manahawkin, NJ BL/TR 6-2/185# d9.18 C4																								
1929	Phi A	2	6	0	0	0	0	0	0	0	0	2	.000	.000	.000	-97	-2	0-0	1.000	0	167	0	/O(LF)	-0.2
1930	Phi A	30	82	12	19	1	1	0	6	2	0	8	.232	.250	.268	30	-9	0-0	.927	-1	97	85	O-21(6-13-2)/S	-1.0
1931	†Phi A	65	223	37	58	8	2	2	20	11	2	15	.260	.301	.341	64	-12	2-1	.979	0	97	118	O-55(2-47-6)	-1.3
1932	Phi A	92	384	73	129	27	6	3	46	17	2	27	.336	.367	.461	109	5	3-1	.976	4	110	98	O-86(0-45-42)	0.5
1933	Phi A	**152**	661	109	195	27	8	8	75	36	0	24	.295	.331	.396	91	-11	5-4	.971	-0	100	121	*O-152(CF)	-1.4
1934	Phi A	**153**	649	99	202	29	9	6	46	40	2	35	.311	.353	.411	100	-2	1-5	.985	2	101	102	*O-152(CF)	-0.5
1935	Phi A★	**149**	644	96	214	37	4	3	70	37	5	34	.332	.373	.416	105	4	6-7	.975	-1	104	51	*O-149(CF)	-0.2
1936	Bos A	154	643	99	188	31	7	0	41	49	5	20	.292	.347	.362	71	-29	4-6	.975	11	106	149	*O-154(CF)	-2.1
1937	Bos A☆	133	560	90	171	22	11	0	51	35	4	14	.305	.351	.384	82	-17	8-6	.969	2	103	98	*O-133(CF)	-1.7
1938	Bos A★	148	658	116	198	36	8	0	71	51	3	19	.301	.354	.380	80	-20	4-9	.986	6	104	106	*O-148(CF)/P	-1.9
1939	Bos A★	137	589	110	183	30	6	0	56	36	2	17	.311	.352	.382	85	-14	3-3	.984	-5	92	100	*O-135(CF)	-2.1
1940	Bos A☆	150	661	94	**200**	27	12	1	51	36	1	29	.303	.340	.384	84	-17	3-5	.969	-7	91	98	*O-149(16-96-37)	-2.9
1941	Was A	154	660	93	180	25	6	2	66	37	6	15	.273	.317	.338	77	-24	4-1	.984	-11	90	71	*O-152(CF)	-3.8
1942	Det A	151	630	71	166	26	4	0	43	43	3	18	.263	.314	.317	72	-24	4-4	.981	-4	90	139	*O-150(CF)	-3.3
1943	Det A	140	606	79	182	18	4	1	43	31	1	13	.300	.335	.348	93	-7	4-3	.989	-5	95	86	*O-138(CF)	-1.7
1944	Det A	143	578	69	169	20	9	2	42	37	2	21	.292	.337	.369	96	-4	6-5	.980	-12	86	95	*O-141(CF)	-2.1

Year	Tm Lg	G	AB	R	H	2B	3B	HR	RBI	BB-IB	HP	SO	AVG	OBP	SLG	AOPS	ABR	SB-CS	FA	FR	Rng	Thr	G at Pos	BFW
1945	†Det A	141	541	62	149	22	8	6	58	36	3	21	.275	.324	.379	97	-3	2-9	**.991**	-15	84	59	*O-140(CF)	-2.7
1946	Det A	68	204	26	60	8	2	1	26	15	0	8	.294	.342	.368	93	-2	3-0	1.000	-4	83	73	O-50(CF)	-0.7
1947	Det A	73	157	21	42	2	2	2	30	20	0	5	.268	.350	.344	91	-2	0-4	.965	-1	93	149	O-35(CF)	-0.5
1948	Det A	4	4	1	0	0	0	0	1	3	0	0	.000	.429	.000	19	0	0-0	1.000	-0	69	0	/O(CF)	0.0
Total	20	2239	9140	1357	2705	396	109	37	842	572	41	345	.296	.340	.375	87	-190	62-73	.979	-40	96	99	*O-2142(25-2031-87)/PS	-29.6
CRAMER, DICK William B. B Brooklyn, NY D 8.11.1885 Camden, NJ d5.12																								
1883	NY N	2	6	0	0	0	0	0	0	1		5	.000	.143	.000	-52	-1		—	-0	0	0	/O-2(0-1-1)	-0.1
CRANDALL, DEL Delmar Wesley B 3.5.1930 Ontario, CA BR/TR 6-1/195# d6.17 Mil 1951 M6 C1																								
1949	Bos N	67	228	21	60	10	1	4	34	9	0	18	.263	.291	.368	80	-8	2	.982	4	*99*	*117*	C-63	0.0
1950	Bos N	79	255	21	56	11	0	4	37	13	0	24	.220	.257	.310	52	-19	0	.967	0	*82*	*132*	C-75/1	-1.5
1953	Mil N✱	116	382	55	104	13	1	15	51	33	0	47	.272	.330	.429	102	0	2-1	.986	11	*90*	***140***	*C-108	1.6
1954	Mil N☆	138	463	60	112	18	2	21	64	40	3	56	.242	.305	.425	94	-6	0-3	.989	11	*97*	***117***	*C-136	1.0
1955	Mil N★	133	440	61	104	15	2	26	62	40-11	2	56	.236	.299	.457	103	0	2-1	.985	-2	***126***	*117*	*C-131	0.4
1956	Mil N✱	112	311	37	74	14	2	16	48	35-15	1	30	.238	.313	.450	110	4	1-2	**.996**	5	***147***	*100*	*C-109	1.3
1957	†Mil N	118	383	45	97	11	2	15	46	30-9	1	38	.253	.308	.410	98	-3	1-2	.987	-3	*87*	*116*	*C-102/O-9(1-0-9),1	-0.2
1958	†Mil N★	131	427	50	116	23	1	18	63	48-18	4	38	.272	.348	.457	122	14	4-1	**.990**	7	*126*	*105*	*C-124	2.7
1959	Mil N★	150	518	65	133	19	2	21	72	46-8	3	48	.257	.318	.423	105	2	5-1	**.994**	9	*163*	*89*	*C-146	1.9
1960	Mil N★	142	537	81	158	14	1	19	77	34-6	4	36	.294	.334	.430	118	12	4-6	.988	-7	***161***	*83*	*C-141	1.1
1961	Mil N	15	30	3	6	3	0	0	1	1-0	0	0	.200	.226	.300	40	-3	0-0	1.000	-1	*173*	*186*	/C-5	-0.3
1962	Mil N★	107	350	35	104	12	3	8	45	27-2	2	24	.297	.348	.417	108	4	3-4	**.994**	5	***160***	*101*	C-90/1-5	1.2
1963	Mil N	86	259	18	52	4	0	3	28	18-5	0	22	.201	.251	.251	46	-18	1-4	.991	2	*113*	*102*	C-75/1-7	-1.5
1964	SF N	69	195	12	45	8	1	3	11	22-9	0	21	.231	.309	.328	78	-5	0-3	.993	7	*95*	*95*	C-65	0.4
1965	Pit N	60	140	11	30	2	0	2	10	14-7	1	10	.214	.288	.271	59	-8	1-0	.996	4	*153*	*99*	C-60	-0.1
1966	Cle A	50	108	10	25	2	0	4	8	14-5	0	9	.231	.320	.361	95	-1	0-0	.991	8	*168*	*91*	C-49	1.0
Total	16	1573	5026	585	1276	179	18	179	657	424-95	21	477	.254	.312	.404	97	-35	26-28	.989	62	*126*	*107*	*C-1479/1-14,O-9(1-0-9)	9.0
CRANDALL, DOC James Otis B 10.8.1887 Wadena, IN D 8.17.1951 Bell, CA BR/TR 5-10.5/180# d4.24 C4 ▲																								
1908	NY N	34	72	8	16	4	0	2	6	4	1		.222	.273	.361	97	0	0	.985	-2	85	131	P-32/2	-0.1
1909	NY N	30	41	4	10	0	1	1	1	1	0		.244	.262	.366	93	2	0	.941	2	116	432	P-30	0.0
1910	NY N	45	73	10	25	2	4	1	13	5	0	7	.342	.385	.521	163	5	0	.984	-2	84	164	P-42/S	-0.1
1911	†NY N	61	113	12	27	1	4	2	21	8	1	16	.239	.295	.372	83	-4	2	.958	0	110	114	P-41/S-6,2-3	-0.1
1912	†NY N	50	80	9	25	6	2	0	19	6	0	7	.313	.360	.438	114	1	0	.957	-0	101	0	P-37/2-2,1	0.0
1913	†NY N	31	25	4	7	2	1	0	2	1	0	5	.280	.308	.440	111	0	0	1.000	1	120	0	P-24/2-2	0.1
	StL N	2	2	0	0	0	0	0	0	0	0	2	.000	.000	.000	-99	-1	0	—	0			H	-0.1
	†NY N	15	22	3	8	2	0	0	2	2	0	3	.364	.417	.455	148	3	0	1.000	1	120	0	P-11	0.0
	Year	48	49	7	15	4	1	0	4	3	0	10	.306	.346	.429	120	1	0	1.000	1	124	0	P-35/2-2	0.0
1914	StL F	118	278	40	86	16	5	2	41	58	0	32	.309	.429	.424	126	10	3	.926	-13	96	48	2-63,P-27/SO(CF)	-0.4
1915	StL F	84	141	18	40	2	2	1	19	27	2	15	.284	.406	.348	107	13	4	.958	1	103	105	P-51	0.0
1916	StL A	16	12	0	1	0	0	0	0	2	0	4	.083	.214	.083	-11	0	0	.000	-0	0	0	/P-2	0.0
1918	Bos N	14	28	1	8	0	0	0	2	4	0	3	.286	.375	.286	107	0	0	1.000	-0	101	302	/P-5,O-3(RF)	0.0
Total	10	500	887	109	253	35	19	9	126	118	4	94	.285	.372	.398	114	29	9	.962	-13	99	129	P-302/2-71,S-8,O-4(0-1-2),1	-0.7
CRANE, ED Edward Nicholas "Cannon-Ball" B 5.27.1862 Boston, MA D 9.20.1896 Rochester, NY BR/TR 5-10.5/204# d4.17 ▲																								
1884	Bos U	101	428	83	122	23	6	12		14			.285	.308	.451	129	2		.826	-6	126	125	O-57(18-0-39),C-42/1-5,P-4	-0.3
1885	Pro N	1	2	0	0	0	0	0	0	1		1	.000	.333	.000	15	0		.500	0	663	0	/O(LF)	0.0
	Buf N	13	51	5	14	0	1	2	9	3		8	.275	.315	.431	135	2		.769	-3	0	0	O-13(10-3-0)	-0.1
	Year	14	53	5	14	0	1	2	9	4		9	.264	.316	.415	131	2		.750	-2	38	0	O-14(11-3-0)	-0.1
1886	Was N	80	292	20	50	11	3	0	20	13		54	.171	.207	.229	35	-22	8	.866	1	113	162	O-68(8-9-51),P-10/C-4	-1.8
1888	†NY N	12	37	3	6	2	0	1	2	3	0	11	.162	.225	.297	66	1	1	.867	1	115	0	P-12	0.0
1889	†NY N	29	103	16	21	1	0	2	11	13	0	21	.204	.293	.272	58	-6	6	.762	-4	51	57	P-29/1	-0.2
1890	NY P	43	146	27	46	5	4	0	16	10	1	26	.315	.363	.404	96	7	5	.846	-4	83	0	P-43	0.0
1891	Cin AA	34	110	13	17	0	0	1	7	8	0	28	.155	.212	.182	12	-13	4	.822	-3	92	0	P-32/O-3(0-1-2)	-0.3
	Cin N	15	46	3	5	0	0	0	2	3	0	12	.109	.163	.109	-20	-3	3	.906	0	108	239	P-15	0.0
1892	NY N	48	163	20	40	1	1	0	14	11	1	30	.245	.297	.264	71	-6	2	.814	-2	85	140	P-47/O(RF)	-0.2
1893	NY N	12	26	8	12	1	0	0	3	7	0	0	.462	.576	.500	186	4	0	.889	-1	93	0	P-10/1O(RF)	0.0
	Bro N	3	5	1	2	1	0	0	0	0	0	0	.400	.400	.600	172	1	0	.500	-1	0	0	/P-2,O(RF)	0.0
	Year	15	31	9	14	2	0	0	3	7	0	0	.452	.553	.516	186	5	0	.850	-1	81	0	P-12/O-2(RF),1	0.0
Total	9	391	1409	199	335	45	15	18	84	86	2	191	.238	.283	.329	81	-33	29	.840	-21	86	59	P-204,O-145(37-13-95)/C-46,1-7	-2.9
CRANE, FRED Frederic William Hotchkiss B 11.4.1840 Old Saybrook, CT D 4.27.1925 Brooklyn, NY 5-9/135# d5.26																								
1873	Res NA	1	4	0	1	0	0	0	1	0		0	.250	.250	.250	53	0	0-0	.667	-1	79	0	/2	-0.1
1875	Atl NA	21	81	7	17	1	0	0	4	0		4	.210	.210	.222	58	-3	0-0	.953	2	255	136	1-20/SO(RF)	0.0
Total	2 NA	22	85	7	18	1	0	0	5	0		4	.212	.212	.224	57	-3	0-0	.953	1	255	136	/1-20,O(RF)S2	-0.1
CRANE, SAM Samuel Byren "Lucky" or "Red" B 9.13.1894 Harrisburg, PA D 11.12.1955 Philadelphia, PA BR/TR 5-11.5/154# d10.2																								
1914	Phi A	2	6	0	0	0	0	0	0	2	0	3	.000	.250	.000	-25	-1	0	.929	0	111	0	/S-2	-0.1
1915	Phi A	8	23	3	2	2	0	0	1	0	0	4	.087	.087	.174	-23	-4	0	.900	0	106	66	/S-6,2	-0.3
1916	Phi A	2	4	1	1	0	0	0	0	2	0	1	.250	.500	.250	132	0	0	1.000	0	120	0	/S-2	0.1
1917	Was A	32	95	6	17	2	0	0	4	4	0	14	.179	.212	.200	26	-9	0	.889	-4	90	108	S-32	-1.2
1920	Cin N	54	144	20	31	4	0	0	9	7	2	9	.215	.261	.243	46	-10	5-4	.945	-7	81	112	S-25,3-10/2-4,O-3(RF)	-1.7
1921	Cin N	73	215	20	50	10	2	0	16	14	4	14	.233	.292	.298	59	-12	2-5	.953	-14	85	106	S-63/3-2,O(RF)	-2.1
1922	Bro N	3	8	1	2	1	0	0	0	0	1	1	.250	.333	.375	83	0	0-0	.875	1	115	103	/S-3	0.1
Total	7	174	495	51	103	19	2	0	30	29	7	46	.208	.262	.255	46	-36	7-9	.931	-23	88	102	S-133/3-12,2-5,O-4(RF)	-5.2
CRANE, SAM Samuel Newhall B 1.2.1854 Springfield, MA D 6.26.1925 New York, NY BR/TR 6/190# d5.1 M2																								
1880	Buf N	10	31	4	4	0	0	0	2	1		8	.129	.156	.129	-2	-3		.866	-1	90	114	2-10/O(CF)M	-0.4
1883	NY AA	96	349	57	82	8	5	0		13			.235	.262	.287	73	-11		.859	-12	86	84	*2-96/O(CF)	-1.7
1884	Cin U	80	309	56	72	9	3	1		11			.233	.259	.291	62	-24		.858	-12	97	124	*2-80,M	-3.0
1885	Det N	68	245	23	47	4	6	1	20	13		45	.192	.233	.269	62	-11		.908	-4	93	72	2-68	-1.2
1886	Det N	47	185	24	26	2	2	1	12	8		34	.141	.176	.189	11	-20	8	.903	-1	96	134	2-38/S-8,O-4(1-0-3)	-1.8
	StL N	39	116	10	20	3	1	0	7	13		27	.172	.256	.216	48	-7	6	.897	-4	93	91	2-39	-0.8
	Year	86	301	34	46	5	3	1	19	21		61	.153	.208	.199	25	-27	14	.900	-5	95	113	2-77/S-8,O-4(1-0-3)	-2.6
1887	Was N	7	30	6	9	1	1	0	1	1	0	6	.300	.323	.400	106	0	5	.865	-0	98	139	/S-7	0.0
1890	NY N	2	6	0	0	0	0	0	0	0	0	0	.000	.000	.000	-99	-2	1	.778	-1	0	0	/1O(RF)	-0.2
	Pit N	22	82	3	16	3	0	0	3	0	1	7	.195	.205	.232	31	-7	5	.880	2	117	53	2-15/S-7,O(RF)	-0.4
	NY N	2	6	0	0	0	0	0	0	0	0	0	.000	.000	.000	-99	-2	0	1.000	0	114	433	/2-2	-0.1
	Year	26	94	3	16	3	0	0	3	0	1	7	.170	.179	.202	12	-11	6	.883	1	117	67	2-17/S-7,O-2(RF),1	-0.7
Total	7	373	1359	183	276	30	18	3	45	60	1	127	.203	.237	.258	53	-87	25	.878	-33	93	97	2-348/S-22,O-8(1-2-5),1	-9.6
CRAVATH, GAVY Clifford Carlton "Cactus" B 3.23.1881 Poway, CA D 5.23.1963 Laguna Beach, CA BR/TR 5-10.5/186# d4.18 M2 C1																								
1908	Bos A	94	277	43	71	10	11	1	34	38	4		.256	.354	.383	136	12	6	.925	-1	80	127	O-77(62-0-15)/1-5	0.8
1909	Chi A	19	50	7	9	0	0	1	8	19	0		.180	.406	.240	109	2	3	.944	-2	0	0	O-18(CF)	-0.1
	Was A	4	6	0	0	0	0	0	1	1	0		.000	.143	.000	-57	-1	0	1.000	1	685	0	/O(RF)	-0.1
	Year	23	56	7	9	0	0	1	9	20	0		.161	.382	.214	93	1	3	.947	-2	43	0	O-19(0-18-1)	-0.2
1912	Phi N	130	436	63	124	30	9	11	70	47	3	77	.284	.358	.470	118	10	15	.966	6	94	**154**	*O-113(30-14-73)	0.9
1913	Phi N	147	525	78	**179**	34	14	**19**	**128**	55	3	63	.341	.407	**.568**	**169**	**47**	10-11	.958	-8	84	106	*O-141(3-7-133)	3.0
1914	Phi N	149	499	76	149	27	8	**19**	100	83	3	72	.299	.402	.499	**157**	38	14	.930	1	85	148	*O-143(1-0-142)	3.3
1915	†Phi N	150	522	**89**	149	31	7	**24**	**115**	**86**	6	77	.285	**.393**	**.510**	**170**	**47**	11-9	.946	9	101	**173**	*O-149(RF)	**5.2**
1916	Phi N	137	448	70	127	21	8	11	70	64	5	89	.283	**.379**	.440	146	27	9	.966	-5	86	106	*O-130(RF)	1.7
1917	Phi N	140	503	70	141	29	16	**12**	83	70	1	57	.280	.369	.473	151	32	6	.946	-7	89	94	*O-139(RF)	2.0
1918	Phi N	121	426	43	99	27	5	**8**	54	54	1	46	.232	.320	.376	105	4	7	.931	-8	85	98	*O-118(7-0-110)	-1.2
1919	Phi N	83	214	34	73	18	5	**12**	45	35	2	21	.341	.438	.640	207	29	8	.914	-2	94	94	O-56(2-1-53),M	2.7
1920	Phi N	46	45	2	13	5	0	1	11	9	0	12	.289	.407	.467	144	3	0-0	.667	-1	43	0	/O-5(3-0-2),M	0.2
Total	11	1220	3951	575	1134	232	83	119	719	561	28	514	.287	.380	.478	149	250	89-20	.944	-18	88	122	*O-1090(108-40-947)/1-5	18.4

Year	Tm Lg	G	AB	R	H	2B	3B	HR	RBI	BB-IB	HP	SO	AVG	OBP	SLG	AOPS	ABR	SB-CS	FA	FR	Rng	Thr	G at Pos	BFW
CRAVER, BILL William H. B 6.1844 Troy, NY D 6.17.1901 Troy, NY BR/TR 5-9/160# d5.9 M4 OF NA (7-CF 5-RF)																								
1871	Tro NA	27	118	26	38	8	1	0	26	3		0	.322	.339	.407	112	2	6-3	.870	7	110	167	2-18/S-4,C-3,1-2,0(RF)M	0.5
1872	Bal NA	35	178	55	50	3	3	0	24	5		2	.281	.301	.331	90	-3	9-1	.876	7			C-27/2-5,0-4(RF),3-2,M	0.3
1873	Bal NA	41	197	45	57	9	3	0	26	2		3	.289	.296	.365	96	-1	5-4	.933	6			C-22,S-15/O-7(CF),1-3	0.3
1874	Phi NA	55	265	68	91	19	11	0	56	4		2	.343	.353	.498	164	18	11-3	.807	4	95	156	*2-54/C-5,1	1.5
1875	Cen NA	**14**	65	8	18	4	2	0	5	2		4	.277	.299	.400	153	4	1-0	.773	2	135	95	/S-9,3-4,1M	0.5
	Ath NA	54	260	71	83	11	11	2	40	4		5	.319	.330	.469	157	12	8-4	.856	-4	93	**174**	*2-54/C-2,3	0.4
	Year	68	325	79	101	15	**13**	2	45	6		9	.311	.323	.455	156	16	9-4	.856	-2	93	**174**	2-54/S-9,3-5,C-2,1	0.9
1876	NY N	56	246	24	55	4	0	0	22	2		7	.224	.230	.240	65	-7		.814	-24	69	41	2-42,C-11/S-6,M	-2.6
1877	Lou N	57	238	33	63	5	2	0	29	5		11	.265	.280	.303	71	-9		.904	-1	98	124	*S-57	-0.7
Total	5 NA	226	1083	273	337	54	31	2	177	20		16	.311	.324	.424	130	32	40-15	.000	22			2-131/C-59,S-28,0-12C,3-7,1-7	3.5
Total	2	113	484	57	118	9	2	0	51	7		18	.244	.255	.271	69	-16		.897	-26			/S-63,2-42,C-11	-3.3
CRAWFORD, CARL Carl Demonte B 8.5.1981 Houston, TX BL/TL 6-2/203# d7.20																								
2002	TB A	63	259	23	67	11	6	2	30	9-0	3	41	.259	.290	.371	76	-10	9-5	.994	6	118	127	O-63(LF)	-0.6
2003	TB A	151	630	80	177	18	9	5	54	26-4	1	102	.281	.309	.362	78	-22	**55**-10	.992	11	112	112	*O-146(137-13-0)/D	-0.8
Total	2	214	889	103	244	29	15	7	84	35-4	4	143	.274	.304	.364	77	-32	64-15	.992	17	114	117	O-209(200-13-0)/D	-1.4
CRAWFORD, PAT Clifford Rankin B 1.28.1902 Society Hill, SC D 1.25.1994 Morehead City, NC BL/TR 5-11/170# d4.18																								
1929	NY N	65	57	13	17	3	0	3	24	11	0	5	.298	.412	.509	127	3	1	1.000	-0	79	33	/1-7,3	0.2
1930	NY N	25	76	11	21	3	2	3	17	7	1	2	.276	.345	.487	100	0	0	.966	-1	93	108	2-18/1	-0.1
	Cin N	76	224	24	65	7	1	3	26	23	1	10	.290	.359	.371	81	-7	2	.969	-4	99	73	2-54,1-13	-0.9
	Year	101	300	35	86	10	3	6	43	30	2	12	.287	.355	.400	86	-7	2	.968	-6	97	82	2-72,1-14	-1.0
1933	StL N	91	224	24	60	8	2	0	21	14	2	9	.268	.317	.321	78	-6	1	.986	1	117	87	1-29,2-15/3-7	-0.7
1934	†StL N	61	70	3	19	2	0	0	16	5	0	3	.271	.320	.300	63	-4	0	.900	1	100	0	/3-9,2-4	-0.3
Total	4	318	651	75	182	23	5	9	104	60	4	29	.280	.344	.372	85	-14	4	.969	-4	99	87	/2-91,1-50,3-17	-1.8
CRAWFORD, FORREST Forrest A. B 5.10.1881 Rockdale, TX D 3.29.1908 Austin, TX BL/TR d7.30																								
1906	StL N	45	145	8	30	3	1	0	11	7	1		.207	.248	.241	55	-8	1	.927	-6	97	57	S-39/3-6	-1.5
1907	StL N	7	22	0	5	0	0	0	3	2	0		.227	.292	.227	65	-1	0	.912	-1	94	90	/S-7	-0.1
Total	2	52	167	8	35	3	1	0	14	9	1		.210	.254	.240	56	-9	1	.924	-7	97	62	/S-46,3-6	-1.6
CRAWFORD, GEORGE George d10.8																								
1890	Phi AA	5	17	1	2	0	0	0	3	0	0		.118	.118	.118	-31	-3	1	1.000	1	0	0	/O-4(RF),S	-0.2
CRAWFORD, GLENN Glenn Martin "Shorty" B 12.2.1913 North Branch, MI D 1.2.1972 Saginaw, MI BL/TR 5-9/165# d4.22																								
1945	StL N	4	3	0	0	0	0	0	0	1	0	0	.000	.250	.000	-26	0	0	—	-0	0	0	/O(LF)	-0.1
	Phi N	82	302	41	89	13	2	2	24	36	1	15	.295	.372	.371	110	5	5	.976	3	98	87	O-38(6-0-32),S-34,2-14	0.8
	Year	86	305	41	89	13	2	2	24	37	1	15	.292	.370	.367	108	5	5	.976	3	98	87	O-39(7-0-32),S-34,2-14	0.7
1946	Phi N	1	1	0	0	0	0	0	0	0	0	0	.000	.000	.000	-99	0	0	—	0			H	0.0
Total	2	87	306	41	89	13	2	2	24	37	1	15	.291	.369	.366	108	5	5	.976	3	98	87	/O-39(7-0-32),S-34,2-14	0.7
CRAWFORD, KEN Kenneth Daniel B 10.31.1894 South Bend, IN D 11.11.1976 Pittsburgh, PA BL/TR 5-9/145# d9.6																								
1915	Bal F	23	82	4	20	2	1	0	7	1	0	18	.244	.253	.293	52	-7	0	.978	-2	81	37	1-14/O-4(1-0-3)	-1.0
CRAWFORD, JAKE Rufus B 3.20.1928 Campbell, MO BR/TR 6-1.5/185# d9.7																								
1952	StL A	7	11	1	2	1	0	0	0	1	0	5	.182	.250	.273	44	-1	1-0	1.000	0	116	0	/O-3(0-2-1)	-0.1
CRAWFORD, SAM Samuel Earl "Wahoo Sam" B 4.18.1880 Wahoo, NE D 6.15.1968 Hollywood, CA BL/TL 6/190# d9.10 HF1957																								
1899	Cin N	31	127	25	39	3	7	1	20	2	0		.307	.318	.465	111	0	6	.970	3	212	183	O-31(9-22-0)	0.2
1900	Cin N	101	389	68	101	15	15	7	59	28	3		.260	.314	.429	107	1	14	.948	4	119	51	*O-95(70-12-12)	-0.4
1901	Cin N	131	515	91	170	20	16	**16**	104	37	3		.330	.378	.524	172	44	13	.923	2	124	134	*O-127(1-0-126)	3.9
1902	Cin N	140	555	92	185	18	**22**	3	78	47	1		.333	.386	.461	147	29	16	.932	3	130	105	*O-140(7-0-133)	2.7
1903	Det A	**137**	550	88	184	23	**25**	4	89	25	2		.335	.366	.489	159	36	18	.960	5	109	79	*O-137(45-0-92)	3.6
1904	Det A	150	562	49	143	22	16	2	73	44	0		.254	.309	.361	115	9	20	.973	5	110	177	*O-150(1-0-149)	0.7
1905	Det A	**154**	575	73	171	38	10	6	75	50	3		.297	.357	.430	148	31	22	**.988**	13	166	113	*O-103(RF),1-51	4.2
1906	Det A	145	563	65	166	25	16	2	72	38	1		.295	.341	.407	130	18	24	.984	5	136	60	*O-116(0-2-116),1-32	1.9
1907	†Det A	144	582	**102**	188	34	17	4	81	37	2		.323	.366	.460	157	35	18	.965	7	122	48	*O-144(CF)/1-2	3.9
1908	†Det A	152	591	102	184	33	16	**7**	80	37	3		.311	.355	.457	157	35	15	.970	-10	61	47	*O-134(CF),1-17	2.1
1909	†Det A	156	589	83	185	**35**	14	6	97	47	1		.314	.366	.452	151	33	30	.965	-15	38	50	*O-139(CF),1-18	1.2
1910	Det A	154	588	83	170	26	**19**	5	**120**	37	1		.289	.332	.423	128	16	20	.963	-8	102	49	*O-153(0-26-127)/1	0.1
1911	Det A	146	574	109	217	36	14	7	115	61	0		.378	.438	.526	160	47	37	.975	-13	86	63	*O-146(RF)	2.6
1912	Det A	149	581	81	189	30	21	4	109	42	2		.325	.373	.470	145	31	42	.984	-16	72	72	*O-149(RF)	0.6
1913	Det A	**153**	609	78	193	32	**23**	9	83	52	0	28	.317	.371	.489	154	37	13	.964	-11	91	63	*O-140(RF),1-13	1.9
1914	Det A	**157**	582	74	183	22	**26**	8	**104**	69	1	31	.314	.388	.483	157	38	25-16	.977	-10	82	86	*O-157(RF)	2.1
1915	Det A	**156**	612	81	183	31	**19**	4	**112**	66	0	29	.299	.367	.431	132	23	24-14	.974	-17	87	40	*O-156(RF)	-0.3
1916	Det A	100	322	41	92	11	13	0	42	37	0	10	.286	.359	.401	124	9	10	.978	-8	75	69	O-79(1-0-78)/1-2	-0.4
1917	Det A	61	104	6	18	4	0	2	12	4	0	6	.173	.204	.269	44	-8	0	.988	-3	22	62	1-15/O-3(RF)	-1.3
Total	19	2517	9570	1391	2961	458	309	97	1525	760	23	104	.309	.362	.452	143	464	367-30	.965	-65	100	78	*O-2299(134-479-1687),1-151	29.3
CRAWFORD, WILLIE Willie Murphy B 9.7.1946 Los Angeles, CA BL/TL 6-1/205# d9.16																								
1964	LA N	10	16	3	5	1	0	0	0	1-0	0	7	.313	.353	.375	113	0	1-1	1.000	0	125	0	/O-4(1-0-3)	0.0
1965	†LA N	52	27	10	4	0	0	0	0	2-0	0	8	.148	.207	.148	2	-4	2-0	1.000	1	190	0	/O-8(2-1-5)	-0.3
1966	LA N	6	0	1	0	0	0	0	0	0-0	0	0	—	—	—	—	0	0-0	—	0			R	0.0
1967	LA N	4	4	0	1	0	0	0	0	1-0	0	3	.250	.400	.250	98	0	0-0	.000	-0	0	0	/O(RF)	0.0
1968	LA N	61	175	25	44	12	1	4	14	20-0	2	64	.251	.335	.400	130	7	1-3	.966	3	107	205	O-48(45-1-4)	0.8
1969	LA N	129	389	64	96	17	5	11	41	49-3	0	85	.247	.331	.401	112	6	4-5	.973	-2	96	79	*O-113(56-22-38)	-0.2
1970	LA N	109	299	48	70	8	6	8	40	33-4	2	88	.234	.313	.381	89	-6	4-4	.960	4	105	157	O-94(34-4-64)	-0.7
1971	LA N	114	342	64	96	16	6	9	40	28-2	1	49	.281	.334	.442	126	10	5-2	.981	-4	91	86	O-97(63-5-35)	0.3
1972	LA N	96	243	28	61	7	3	8	27	35-3	2	55	.251	.349	.403	116	6	4-2	.983	-4	91	43	O-74(51-0-28)	-0.2
1973	LA N	145	457	75	135	26	2	14	66	78-12	1	91	.295	.396	.453	142	30	12-5	.978	-1	94	109	*O-138(11-5-125)	2.3
1974	†LA N	139	468	73	138	23	4	11	61	64-9	0	88	.295	.376	.432	132	21	7-8	.966	-9	94	34	*O-133(0-2-132)	0.5
1975	LA N	124	373	46	98	15	2	9	46	49-11	0	43	.263	.345	.386	108	5	5-5	.990	-2	105	29	*O-113(25-0-93)	-0.3
1976	StL N	120	392	49	119	17	5	9	50	37-6	1	53	.304	.360	.441	127	14	2-1	.982	-1	103	70	*O-107(3-0-105)	0.8
1977	Hou N	42	114	14	29	3	0	2	18	16-1	0	10	.254	.341	.333	91	-1	0-0	.959	-2	91	0	O-30(LF)	-0.4
	Oak A	59	136	7	25	7	1	1	16	18-4	0	20	.184	.277	.272	52	-9	0-0	.978	2	108	219	O-22(2-0-20),D-18	-0.8
Total	14	1210	3435	507	921	152	35	86	419	431-55	9	664	.268	.349	.408	117	79	47-36	.975	-14	98	82	O-982(323-40-653)/D-18	1.8
CREAMER, GEORGE George W. (born George W. Triebel) B 1855 Philadelphia, PA D 6.27.1886 Philadelphia, PA BR/TR 6-2/?# d5.1 M1																								
1878	Mil N	50	193	30	41	7	3	0	15	5		15	.212	.232	.280	63	-8		.839	-2	120	47	2-28,O-17(0-16-4)/3-6	-0.9
1879	Syr N	15	60	3	13	2	0	0	3	1		2	.217	.230	.250	65	-2		.825	-8	87	23	2-10/S-3,O-2(0-1-1)	-0.9
1880	Wor N	**85**	306	40	61	6	3	0	27	4		21	.199	.210	.239	47	-17		.883	-8	97	101	*2-85	-2.1
1881	Wor N	80	309	42	64	9	2	0	25	11		27	.207	.234	.249	49	-18		.904	-9	96	87	*2-80	-2.2
1882	Wor N	81	286	27	65	16	6	1	29	14		24	.227	.263	.336	88	-4		.907	11	**112**	107	*2-81	0.9
1883	Pit AA	91	369	54	94	7	9	0		20			.255	.293	.322	102	1		.897	8	102	101	*2-91	1.1
1884	Pit AA	98	339	38	62	8	5	0		16	2		.183	.224	.236	51	-18		**.937**	16	110	97	*2-98,M	0.2
Total	7	500	1862	234	400	55	28	1	99	71	2	89	.215	.244	.276	67	-66		.901	8	104	94	2-473/O-19(0-17-5),3-6,S-3	-3.9
CREDE, JOE Joseph B 4.26.1978 Jefferson City, MO BR/TR 6-3/195# d9.12																								
2000	Chi A	7	14	2	5	1	0	0	3	0-0	0	3	.357	.333	.429	96	0	0-0	.933	1	129	156	/3-6,D	0.1
2001	Chi A	17	50	1	11	1	1	0	7	3-0	1	11	.220	.273	.280	46	-4	1-0	1.000	-1	71	136	3-15	-0.5
2002	Chi A	53	200	28	57	10	0	12	35	8-0	0	40	.285	.311	.515	113	3	0-2	.938	-5	89	138	3-53	-0.3
2003	Chi A	151	536	68	140	31	2	19	75	32-1	6	75	.261	.308	.433	92	-7	1-1	.964	-0	95	121	*3-151	-0.6
Total	4	228	800	99	213	43	3	31	120	43-1	7	129	.266	.307	.444	94	-8	2-3	.959	-5	93	127	3-225/D	-1.3
CREE, BIRDIE William Franklin B 10.23.1882 Khedive, PA D 11.8.1942 Sunbury, PA BR/TR 5-6/150# d9.17																								
1908	NY A	21	78	5	21	0	2	0	4	7	2		.269	.345	.321	115	1	1	1.000	1	186	302	O-21(CF)	0.2

Year	Tm Lg	G	AB	R	H	2B	3B	HR	RBI	BB-IB	HP	SO	AVG	OBP	SLG	AOPS	ABR	SB-CS	FA	FR	Rng	Thr	G at Pos	BFW
1909	NY A	104	343	48	90	6	3	2	27	30	9		.262	.338	.315	105	3	10	.949	-1	100	93	O-79(24-32-25)/S-6,2-4,3	-0.1
1910	NY A	134	467	58	134	19	16	4	73	40	8		.287	.353	.422	135	18	28	.955	-8	92	67	*O-134(49-85-0)	0.4
1911	NY A	137	520	90	181	30	22	4	88	56	3		.348	.415	.513	149	33	48	.964	-2	99	90	*O-132(122-7-3)/S-4,2-2	2.4
1912	NY A	50	190	25	63	11	6	0	22	20	5		.332	.409	.453	138	10	12	.948	4	124	77	O-50(LF)	1.1
1913	NY A	145	534	51	145	25	6	1	63	50	4	51	.272	.338	.346	100	1	22	**.988**	-4	91	89	*O-144(LF)	-1.0
1914	NY A	77	275	45	85	18	5	0	40	30	6	24	.309	.389	.411	141	15	4-9	.976	4	109	98	O-76(CF)	1.2
1915	NY A	74	196	23	42	8	2	0	15	36	6	22	.214	.353	.276	88	0	7-8	.945	-4	89	84	O-53(0-37-16)	-0.9
Total	8	742	2603	345	761	117	62	11	332	269	43	97	.292	.368	.398	124	81	132-17	.965	-10	101	91	O-689(389-258-44)/S-10,2-6,3	3.3
CREEDEN, CONNIE Cornelius Stephen B 7.21.1915 Danvers, MA D 11.30.1969 Santa Ana, CA BL/TL 6-1/200# d4.28																								
1943	Bos N	5	4	0	1	0	0	0	1	1	0	0	.250	.400	.250	91	0	0	—	0			H	0.0
CREEDEN, PAT Patrick Francis "Whoops" B 5.23.1906 Newburyport, MA D 4.20.1992 Brockton, MA BL/TR 5-8/175# d4.14																								
1931	Bos A	5	8	0	0	0	0	0	0	1	0	3	.000	.111	.000	-73	-2	0-0	.846	-1	83	87	/2-2	-0.2
CREEGAN, MARTY Martin (born Marcus Kragen) B 1864 San Francisco, CA D 9.29.1920 San Francisco, CA ?/161# d4.17																								
1884	Was U	9	33	4	5	0	0	0		1			.152	.176	.152	0	-5		.667	-2	77	948	/O-6(0-5-1),C-3,3-2,1	-0.6
CREELY, GUS August L. B 6.6.1870 Florissant, MO D 4.22.1934 St.Louis, MO 5-6/150# d10.9																								
1890	StL AA	4	15	0	0	0	0	0	0	0	0		.000	.000	.000	-88	-4	1	.769	-2	76	0	/S-4	-0.5
CREGAN, PETE Peter James "Peekskill Pete" B 4.13.1875 Kingston, NY D 5.18.1945 New York, NY BR/TR 5-7.5/150# d9.8																								
1899	NY N	1	2	0	0	0	0	0	0	0	0		.000	.000	.000	-99	-1	0	1.000	-0	0	0	/O(RF)	-0.1
1903	Cin N	6	19	0	2	0	0	0	0	1	1		.105	.190	.105	-13	-3	0	.769	-1	0	0	/O-6(5-0-1)	-0.4
Total	2	7	21	0	2	0	0	0	0	1	1		.095	.174	.095	-21	-4	0	.786	-1	0	0	/O-7(5-0-2)	-0.5
CREGER, BERNIE Bernard Odell B 3.21.1927 Wytheville, VA D 11.30.1997 Lynchburg, VA BR/TR 6/175# d4.29																								
1947	StL N	15	16	3	3	1	0	0	0	1	0	3	.188	.235	.250	28	-2	1	.828	-2	96	58	S-13	-0.4
CRESPI, CREEPY Frank Angelo Joseph B 2.16.1918 St.Louis, MO D 3.1.1990 Florissant, MO BR/TR 5-8.5/175# d9.14 Mil 1943-46																								
1938	StL N	7	19	2	5	2	0	0	1	2	0	7	.263	.333	.368	88	0	0	.813	-3	66	111	/S-7	-0.3
1939	StL N	15	29	3	5	1	0	0	6	3	0	6	.172	.250	.207	23	-3	0	.962	-0	114	34	/2-6,S-4	-0.3
1940	StL N	3	11	2	3	1	0	0	0	1	0	2	.273	.333	.364	87	0	1	1.000	-1	27	0	/3-2,S	-0.1
1941	StL N	146	560	85	156	24	2	4	46	57	9	58	.279	.355	.350	93	-3	3	.962	-2	98	115	*2-145	0.4
1942	†StL N	93	292	33	71	4	2	0	35	27	1	29	.243	.309	.271	65	-13	4	.967	-6	85	101	2-83/S-5	-1.5
Total	5	264	911	125	240	32	4	4	88	90	10	102	.263	.336	.321	82	-19	8	.963	-13	94	109	2-234/S-17,3-2	-1.8
CRESPO, CESAR Cesar Antonio (Claudio) B 5.23.1979 Rio Piedras, P.R. BB/TR 5-11/170# d5.29 b-Felipe																								
2001	SD N	55	153	27	32	6	0	4	12	25-0	0	50	.209	.320	.327	74	-6	6-2	.970	-5	85	71	2-34,O-18(6-11-2)/3-2,S	-0.9
2002	SD N	25	29	5	5	2	0	0	0	3-0	0	6	.172	.250	.241	36	-3	-3-2	1.000	-1	57	903	/O-7(6-1-1),2-4,3-4,S	-0.4
Total	2	80	182	32	37	8	0	4	12	28-0	0	56	.203	.310	.313	69	-9	9-4	.971	-6	84	68	/2-38,O-25(12-12-3),3-6,S-2	-1.3
CRESPO, FELIPE Felipe Javier (Clausio) B 3.5.1973 Rio Piedras, P.R. BB/TR 5-11/195# d4.28 b-Cesar OF Total (41-LF 1-CF 34-RF)																								
1996	Tor A	22	49	6	9	4	0	0	4	12-0	3	13	.184	.375	.265	66	-2	1-0	.982	3	95	117	2-10/3-6,1-2	0.2
1997	Tor A	12	28	3	8	0	1	1	5	2-0	0	4	.286	.333	.464	105	0	0-0	.933	-2	54	100	/3-7,2D	-0.1
1998	Tor A	66	130	11	34	8	1	1	15	15-1	2	27	.262	.342	.362	84	-3	4-3	1.000	-1	102	54	O-42(19-1-24)/2-8,3-2,1D	-0.4
2000	†SF N	89	131	17	38	6	1	4	29	10-2	4	23	.290	.351	.443	109	2	3-2	.962	-2	83	0	O-26(18-0-9),1-11/2-7,D	-0.2
2001	SF N	40	66	8	13	1	0	4	10	7-1	2	26	.197	.286	.394	81	-2	1-1	.972	-2	44	111	1-16/2-2,O(RF)D	-0.6
	Phi N	33	41	1	7	3	1	0	5	4-0	0	8	.171	.234	.293	39	-4	0-0	1.000	1	160	718	/O-4(LF),1-2,2	-0.3
	Year	73	107	9	20	4	1	4	15	11-1	2	34	.187	.266	.355	65	-6	1-1	.977	-1	38	124	1-18/O-5(4-0-1),2-3,D	-0.9
Total	5	262	445	46	109	22	4	10	68	50-4	11	101	.245	.330	.380	86	-9	9-6	.989	-3	99	65	/O-73L,1-32,2-29,3-15,D-6	-1.4
CRIGER, LOU Louis B 2.3.1872 Elkhart, IN D 5.14.1934 Tucson, AZ BR/TR 5-10/165# d9.21																								
1896	Cle N	2	5	0	0	0	0	0	0	1	0	0	.000	.167	.000	-51	-1	1	1.000	1	*138*	*123*	/C	0.0
1897	Cle N	39	138	15	31	4	1	0	22	23	1		.225	.340	.268	58	-8	5	.937	0	*113*	*86*	C-37/1-2	-0.3
1898	Cle N	84	287	43	80	13	4	1	32	40	5		.279	.377	.362	113	7	2	.957	16	*114*	*101*	C-82	2.9
1899	StL N	77	258	39	66	4	5	2	44	28	2		.256	.333	.333	81	-7	14	.949	7	*125*	*97*	C-75	0.6
1900	StL N	80	288	31	78	8	6	2	38	4	2		.271	.286	.361	78	-10	5	.953	4	*94*	*104*	C-75/3	0.0
1901	Bos A	76	268	26	62	6	3	0	24	11	3		.231	.270	.276	52	-18	7	.967	19	*113*	*109*	C-68/1-8	0.7
1902	Bos A	83	266	32	68	16	6	0	28	27	0		.256	.324	.361	87	-4	7	.965	14	***133***	*104*	C-80/O(LF)	1.7
1903	†Bos A	96	317	41	61	7	10	3	31	26	1		.192	.256	.306	65	-15	5	.979	23	***125***	***114***	C-96	1.8
1904	Bos A	98	299	34	63	10	5	2	34	27	3		.211	.283	.298	79	-7	1	.981	18	***142***	*91*	C-95	2.3
1905	Bos A	109	313	33	62	6	7	1	36	54	3		.198	.322	.272	88	-2	5	.972	7	***127***	*104*	*C-109	1.7
1906	Bos A	7	17	0	3	1	0	0	1	1	0		.176	.222	.235	43	-1	1	.981	2	*112*	*70*	/C-6	0.2
1907	Bos A	75	226	12	41	4	0	0	14	19	2		.181	.251	.199	44	-14	2	.978	4	*112*	*100*	C-75	-0.3
1908	Bos A	84	237	12	45	4	2	0	25	13	0		.190	.232	.224	47	-14	1	.980	13	*102*	*108*	C-84	0.7
1909	StL A	74	212	15	36	1	1	0	9	25	1		.170	.261	.184	44	-13	2	.986	6	*98*	*96*	C-73	0.0
1910	NY A	27	69	3	13	2	0	0	4	10	0		.188	.291	.217	56	-3	0	.993	-1	*101*	*87*	C-27	-0.1
1912	StL A	1	2	1	0	0	0	0	0	0	0		.000	.000	.000	-99	-1	0	1.000	0	*120*	*104*	/C	0.0
Total	16	1012	3202	337	709	86	50	11	342	309	23	0	.221	.295	.290	72	-111	58	.971	133	*118*	*101*	C-984/1-10,O(LF)3	11.9
CRIPE, DAVE David Gordon B 4.7.1951 Ramona, CA BR/TR 6/180# d9.10																								
1978	KC A	7	13	1	2	0	0	0	1	0-0	0	2	.154	.154	.154	-13	-2	0-0	1.000	-3	15	0	/3-5	-0.5
CRISCIONE, DAVE David Gerald B 9.2.1951 Dunkirk, NY BR/TR 5-8/185# d7.17																								
1977	Bal A	7	9	1	3	0	0	1	1	0-0	0	1	.333	.333	.667	176	1	0-0	1.000	-1	88	0	/C-7	0.0
CRISCOLA, TONY Anthony Paul B 7.9.1915 Walla Walla, WA D 7.10.2001 LaJolla, CA BL/TR 5-11.5/180# d4.15																								
1942	StL A	91	158	17	47	9	2	1	13	8	0	13	.297	.331	.399	103	0	2-2	.955	-3	93	0	O-52(37-13-2)	-0.5
1943	StL A	29	52	4	8	0	0	0	1	8	0	7	.154	.267	.154	24	-5	0-0	.960	-1	103	0	O-13(10-2-1)	-0.7
1944	Cin N	64	157	14	36	3	2	0	14	14	1	12	.229	.297	.274	64	-8	0	.977	1	106	101	O-35(3-0-32)	-1.0
Total	3	184	367	35	91	12	4	1	28	30	1	32	.248	.307	.311	75	-13	2-2	.966	-3	100	47	O-100(50-15-35)	-2.2
CRISHAM, PAT Patrick J. B 6.4.1877 Amesbury, MA D 6.12.1915 Syracuse, NY 6/168# d5.5																								
1899	Bal N	53	172	23	50	5	3	0	20	4	1		.291	.311	.355	78	-6	4	.979	-1	94	37	1-26,C-22	-0.5
CRISP, COCO Covelli Loyce B 11.1.1979 Los Angeles, CA BB/TR 6/185# d8.15																								
2002	Cle A	32	127	16	33	9	2	1	9	11-0	0	19	.260	.314	.386	88	-2	4-1	.988	0	103	61	O-32(2-31-0)	-0.1
2003	Cle A	99	414	55	110	15	6	3	27	23-1	0	51	.266	.302	.353	75	-16	15-9	.995	-2	95	100	O-90(39-53-0)/D-7	-1.9
Total	2	131	541	71	143	24	8	4	36	34-1	0	70	.264	.305	.360	78	-18	19-10	.993	-2	97	90	O-122(41-84-0)/D-7	-2.0
CRISP, JOE Joseph Shelby B 7.8.1889 Higginsville, MO D 2.5.1939 Kansas City, MO BR/TR 6-4/200# d9.2																								
1910	StL A	1	1	0	0	0	0	0	0	0	0		.000	.000	.000	-99	0	0	1.000	-0	*45*	*0*	/C	0.0
1911	StL A	1	1	0	1	0	0	0	0	0	0		1.000	1.000	1.000	477	0	0	—	0			/H	0.0
Total	2	2	2	0	1	0	0	0	0	0	0		.500	.500	.500	206	0	0	1.000	-0	*45*	*0*	/C	0.0
CRISS, DODE Dode B 3.12.1885 Sherman, MS D 9.8.1955 Sherman, MS BL/TR 6-2/200# d4.20 ▲																								
1908	StL A	64	82	15	28	6	0	0	14	9	0		.341	.407	.415	166	7	1	.933	-1	189	0	O-11(RF)/P-9,1	0.6
1909	StL A	35	48	2	14	6	1	0	7	0	1		.292	.306	.458	152	6	0	1.000	-1	59	0	P-11	0.0
1910	StL A	70	91	11	21	4	2	1	11	11	1		.231	.320	.352	118	2	2	.983	-1	66	90	1-11/P-6	0.1
1911	StL A	58	83	10	21	3	1	2	15	11	1		.253	.347	.386	109	1	0	.956	-2	70	76	1-14/P-4	-0.1
Total	4	227	304	38	84	19	4	3	47	31	3		.276	.349	.395	133	16	3	.964	-4	72	0	/P-30,1-26,O-11(RF)	0.6
CRIST, CHES Chester Arthur "Squak" B 2.10.1882 Cozaddale, OH D 1.7.1957 Cincinnati, OH BR/TR 5-11/165# d5.18																								
1906	Phi N	6	11	1	0	0	0	0	0	0	1		.000	.083	.000	-74	-2	0	.800	-2	*71*	*43*	/C-6	-0.5
CRITZ, HUGHIE Hugh Melville B 9.17.1900 Starkville, MS D 1.10.1980 Greenwood, MS BR/TR 5-8/147# d5.31																								
1924	Cin N	102	413	67	133	15	14	3	35	19	0	18	.322	.352	.448	115	6	19-11	.956	2	102	101	2-96/S	1.1
1925	Cin N	144	541	74	150	14	8	2	51	34	1	17	.277	.321	.344	72	-24	13-13	.970	20	**110**	**126**	*2-144	-0.2
1926	Cin N	155	607	96	164	24	14	3	79	39	2	25	.270	.316	.371	87	-14	7	**.981**	**23**	**110**	**128**	*2-155	1.4

Year	Tm Lg	G	AB	R	H	2B	3B	HR	RBI	BB-IB	HP	SO	AVG	OBP	SLG	AOPS	ABR	SB-CS	FA	FR	Rng	Thr	G at Pos	BFW
1927	Cin N	113	396	50	110	10	8	4	49	16	0	18	.278	.306	.374	84	-11	7	.969	-1	103	114	*2-113	-0.9
1928	Cin N	**153**	641	95	190	21	11	5	52	37	0	24	.296	.335	.387	90	-12	18	.971	-15	98	124	*2-153	-2.2
1929	Cin N	107	425	55	105	17	9	1	50	27	0	21	.247	.292	.336	58	-30	9	**.974**	7	**112**	**115**	*2-106/S	-1.8
1930	Cin N	28	104	15	24	3	2	0	11	6	0	6	.231	.273	.298	40	-11	1	.987	-1	105	91	2-28	-0.9
	NY N	124	558	93	148	17	11	4	50	24	0	26	.265	.296	.357	58	-41	7	.972	8	98	106	*2-124	-2.7
	Year	152	662	108	172	20	13	4	61	30	0	32	.260	.292	.347	55	-51	8	**.974**	7	99	103	*2-152	-3.6
1931	NY N	66	238	33	69	7	2	4	17	8	0	17	.290	.313	.387	89	-5	4	.984	2	98	83	2-54	0.1
1932	NY N	151	659	90	182	32	7	2	50	34	1	27	.276	.313	.355	81	-18	3	.974	6	100	103	*2-151	-0.3
1933	†NY N	133	558	68	137	18	5	2	33	23	3	24	.246	.279	.306	68	-24	4	**.982**	**45**	**126**	118	*2-133	3.1
1934	NY N	137	571	77	138	17	1	6	40	19	2	24	.242	.269	.306	55	-38	3	**.978**	**27**	**114**	**125**	*2-137	-0.2
1935	NY N	65	219	19	41	0	3	2	14	3	0	10	.187	.198	.242	18	-27	2	.966	0	100	112	2-59	-2.2
Total	12	1478	5930	832	1591	195	95	38	531	289	9	257	.268	.303	.352	74	-249	97-24	.974	124	107	115	*2-1453/S-2	-5.7
CROCKETT, DAVEY Daniel Solomon B 10.5.1875 Roanoke, VA D 2.23.1961 Charlottesville, VA BL/TR 6-1/175# d7.11																								
1901	Det A	28	102	10	29	2	2	0	14	6	2		.284	.336	.343	85	-2	1	.968	-1	100	121	1-27	-0.3
CROFT, ART Arthur F. B 1.23.1855 St.Louis, MO D 3.16.1884 St.Louis, MO d5.4																								
1875	RS NA	**19**	75	5	15	3	0	0	2	0		2	.200	.200	.240	58	-2	5-1	.800	-3	0	0	O-19(10-7-2)	-0.4
1877	StL N	54	220	23	51	5	2	0	27	1		15	.232	.235	.273	63	-9		.971	-3	79	81	1-28,O-25(25-1-1)/2	-1.3
1878	Ind N	60	222	22	35	6	0	0	16	5		23	.158	.176	.185	22	-17		.963	-2	55	79	*1-51/O-9(LF)	-2.1
Total	2	114	442	45	86	11	2	0	43	6		38	.195	.205	.229	43	-26		.965	-5	63	80	/1-79,O-34(34-1-1),2	-3.4
CROFT, HARRY Henry T. B 8.1.1875 Chicago, IL D 12.11.1933 Oak Park, IL d5.19																								
1899	Lou N	2	2	0	0	0	0	0	0	0	0		.000	.000	.000	-99	-1	0	—	0			/H	-0.1
	Phi N	2	7	0	1	0	0	0	0	1	0		.143	.250	.143	9	-1	0	1.000	-0	111	0	/2-2	-0.1
	Year	4	9	0	1	0	0	0	0	1	0		.111	.200	.111	-14	-1	0	1.000	-0	111	0	/2-2	-0.2
1901	Chi N	3	12	1	4	0	0	0	4	0	0		.333	.333	.333	97	0	0	1.000	2	652	0	/O-3(RF)	0.2
Total	2	7	21	1	5	0	0	0	4	1	0		.238	.273	.238	47	-2	0	1.000	2	652	0	/O-3(RF),2-2	0.0
CROLIUS, FRED Fred Joseph B 12.16.1876 Jersey City, NJ D 8.25.1960 Ormond Beach, FL d4.19																								
1901	Bos N	49	200	22	48	4	1	1	13	9	10		.240	.306	.285	66	-9	6	.850	-8	48	69	O-49(0-3-46)	-1.8
1902	Pit N	9	38	4	10	2	1	0	7	0	0		.263	.263	.368	91	-1	0	1.000	-0	97	0	/O-9(RF)	-0.1
Total	2	58	238	26	58	6	2	1	20	9	10		.244	.300	.298	69	-10	6	.868	-8	55	60	/O-58(0-3-55)	-1.9
CROMARTIE, WARREN Warren Livingston B 9.29.1953 Miami Beach, FL BL/TL 6/192# d9.6																								
1974	Mon N	8	17	2	3	0	0	0	0	3-0	0	3	.176	.300	.176	34	-1	1-0	1.000	-1	76	0	/O-6(LF)	-0.2
1976	Mon N	33	81	8	17	1	0	0	2	1-0	0	5	.210	.220	.222	25	-8	1-2	.943	-1	98	74	O-20(5-0-16)	-1.1
1977	Mon N	155	620	64	175	41	7	5	50	33-3	4	40	.282	.321	.395	94	-6	10-3	.976	5	102	95	*O-155(153-0-4)	-0.7
1978	Mon N	159	607	77	180	32	6	10	56	33-5	7	60	.297	.337	.418	112	8	8-8	.978	17	**114**	180	*O-158(157-0-1)/1-4	1.8
1979	Mon N	158	659	84	181	46	5	8	46	38-19	1	78	.275	.313	.396	94	-7	8-7	.976	10	109	126	*O-158(LF)	-0.5
1980	Mon N	**162**	597	74	172	33	5	14	70	51-**24**	2	64	.288	.345	.430	115	12	8-8	.991	-5	90	87	*1-158/O-2(LF)	-0.4
1981	†Mon N	99	358	41	109	19	2	6	42	39-12	0	27	.304	.370	.419	123	12	2-3	.992	-4	75	90	1-62,O-38(RF)	0.2
1982	Mon N	144	497	59	126	24	3	14	62	69-15	3	60	.254	.346	.398	106	6	3-0	.979	6	114	107	*O-136(2-0-135)/1-9	0.6
1983	Mon N	120	360	37	100	26	2	3	43	43-7	1	48	.278	.352	.386	106	5	8-3	.973	11	124	187	*O-101(RF)/1	1.2
1991	KC A	69	131	13	41	7	2	1	20	15-0	0	18	.313	.381	.420	122	4	1-3	.996	-4	46	90	1-29/O-6(4-1-1),D	-0.2
Total	10	1107	3927	459	1104	229	32	61	391	325-85	18	403	.281	.336	.402	105	25	50-37	.977	36	111	127	O-780(487-1-296),1-263/D	0.7
CROMER, D.T. David Thomas B 3.19.1971 Lake City, SC BL/TL 6-2/190# d4.5 b-Tripp																								
2000	Cin N	35	47	7	16	4	0	2	8	1-1	1	14	.340	.360	.553	126	2	0-0	.964	-1	65	145	1-13	0.0
2001	Cin N	50	57	7	16	3	0	5	12	3-0	0	19	.281	.302	.596	123	2	0-0	.973	0	128	76	/1-8,D	0.1
Total	2	85	104	14	32	7	0	7	20	4-1	1	33	.308	.327	.577	124	4	0-0	.967	-1	91	117	/1-21,D	0.1
CROMER, TRIPP Roy Bunyan B 11.21.1967 Lake City, SC BR/TR 6-2/165# d9.7 b-D.T.																								
1993	StL N	10	23	1	2	0	0	0	0	1-0	0	6	.087	.125	.087	-43	-5	0-0	.912	-0	101	88	/S-9	-0.5
1994	StL N	2	0	1	0	0	0	0	0	0-0	0	0	—	—	—	—	0	0-0	.000	-1	0	0	/S-2	-0.1
1995	StL N	105	345	36	78	19	0	5	18	14-2	4	66	.226	.261	.325	54	-23	0-0	.960	-1	106	113	S-95,2-11	-1.7
1997	LA N	28	86	8	25	3	0	4	20	6-3	0	16	.291	.333	.465	116	2	0-1	.968	-3	84	85	2-17,S-10/3	0.0
1998	LA N	6	6	1	1	0	0	1	1	0-0	0	2	.167	.167	.667	113	0	0-0	—	0			/H	0.0
1999	LA N	33	52	5	10	0	0	2	8	5-0	0	10	.192	.263	.308	46	-5	0-0	1.000	4	134	169	/2-9,S-9,3-2,O-2(1-0-1),1	0.0
2000	Hou N	9	8	2	1	0	0	0	0	1-0	0	1	.125	.222	.125	-9	-1	0-0	.500	-1	124	0	/3-2,2S	-0.2
2003	Hou N	3	4	0	1	0	1	0	1	0-0	0	0	.250	.250	.750	141	0	0-0	1.000	1	202	445	/2	0.1
Total	8	196	524	54	118	22	1	12	48	27-5	4	101	.225	.266	.340	59	-32	0-1	.959	-0	106	110	S-126/2-39,3-5,O-2(1-0-1),1	-2.4
CROMPTON, NED Edward B 2.12.1889 Liverpool, England D 9.28.1950 Aspinwall, PA BL/TL 5-10.5/175# d9.13																								
1909	StL A	17	63	7	10	2	1	0	2	7	1		.159	.254	.222	54	-3	1	.909	1	178	191	O-17(LF)	-0.4
1910	Cin N	1	2	0	0	0	0	0	0	0	0	2	.000	.000	.000	-99	-1	0	—	-0	0	0	/O(CF)	-0.1
Total	2	18	65	7	10	2	1	0	2	7	1	2	.154	.247	.215	49	-4	1	.909	1	177	190	/O-18(17-1-0)	-0.5
CROMPTON, HERB Herbert Bryan "Workhorse" B 11.7.1911 Taylor Ridge, IL D 8.5.1963 Moline, IL BR/TR 6/185# d4.26																								
1937	Was A	2	3	0	1	0	0	0	0	0	0	0	.333	.333	.333	72	0	0-0	1.000	0	*0*	*449*	/C-2	0.0
1945	NY A	36	99	6	19	3	0	0	12	2	0	7	.192	.208	.222	24	-10	0-0	.984	-1	*80*	136	C-33	-1.0
Total	2	38	102	6	20	3	0	0	12	2	0	7	.196	.212	.225	25	-10	0-0	.984	-1	*78*	145	/C-35	-1.0
CRON, CHRIS Christopher John B 3.31.1964 Albuquerque, NM BR/TR 6-2/200# d8.15																								
1991	Cal A	6	15	0	2	0	0	0	0	2-0	0	5	.133	.235	.133	5	-2	0-0	1.000	1	202	26	/1-5,D	-0.1
1992	Chi A	6	10	0	0	0	0	0	0	0-0	0	4	.000	.000	.000	-99	-3	0-0	.923	0	162	69	/1-5,O(LF)	-0.3
Total	2	12	25	0	2	0	0	0	0	2-0	0	9	.080	.148	.080	-35	-5	0-0	.980	1	191	37	/1-10,O(LF)D	-0.4
CRONIN, DAN Daniel T. B 4.1.1857 S.Boston, MA D 11.30.1885 Boston, MA 5-8/170# d7.9																								
1884	CP U	1	4	1	1	0	0	0		0			.250	.250	.250	52	0		.200	-2	0	345	/2	-0.2
	StL U	1	5	0	0	0	0	0		0			.000	.000	.000	-97	-1		.000	-1	0	0	/O(LF)	-0.2
	Year	2	9	1	1	0	0	0		0			.111	.111	.111	-32	-2		.000	-3	0	345	/2O(LF)	-0.4
CRONIN, JIM James John B 8.7.1905 Richmond, CA D 6.10.1983 Concord, CA BB/TR 5-10.5/150# d7.4																								
1929	Phi A	25	56	7	13	2	1	0	4	5	0	7	.232	.295	.304	52	-4	0-0	.966	2	126	130	2-10/S-9,3-4	-0.1
CRONIN, JOE Joseph Edward B 10.12.1906 San Francisco, CA D 9.7.1984 Barnstable, MA BR/TR 5-11.5/180# d4.29 M15 HF1956																								
1926	Pit N	38	83	9	22	2	2	0	11	6	0	15	.265	.315	.337	72	-3	0	.977	5	105	150	2-27/S-7	0.2
1927	Pit N	12	22	2	5	1	0	0	3	2	0	3	.227	.292	.273	48	-2	0	1.000	-3	56	0	/2-7,S-4,1	-0.4
1928	Was A	63	227	23	55	10	4	0	25	22	0	27	.242	.309	.322	66	-11	4-0	.953	8	107	125	S-63	0.4
1929	Was A	145	494	72	139	29	8	8	61	85	1	37	.281	.388	.421	107	9	5-9	.923	5	**104**	106	*S-143/2	2.6
1930	Was A	**154**	587	127	203	41	9	13	126	72	5	36	.346	.422	.513	135	34	17-10	.960	**27**	**110**	111	*S-154	6.9
1931	Was A	**156**	611	103	187	44	13	12	126	81	4	52	.306	.391	.480	127	26	10-9	.950	13	101	**114**	*S-155	4.5
1932	Was A	143	557	95	177	43	**18**	6	116	66	3	45	.318	.393	.492	129	25	7-5	**.959**	7	103	111	*S-141	3.8
1933	†Was A★	152	602	89	186	**45**	11	5	118	87	2	49	.309	.398	.445	124	25	5-4	**.960**	6	106	118	*S-152,M	3.9
1934	Was A★	127	504	68	143	30	9	7	101	53	1	28	.284	.353	.421	103	1	8-0	.951	13	**114**	102	*S-127,M	2.4
1935	Bos A★	144	556	70	164	37	14	9	95	63	3	40	.295	.370	.460	106	5	3-3	.949	-15	95	98	*S-139/1-2,M	-0.1
1936	Bos A	81	295	36	83	22	4	2	43	32	1	21	.281	.354	.403	82	-8	1-3	.930	-5	98	89	S-60,3-21,M	-0.8
1937	Bos A★	148	570	102	175	40	4	18	110	84	6	73	.307	.402	.486	118	18	5-3	.958	-16	87	95	*S-148,M	1.2
1938	Bos A★	143	530	98	172	**51**	5	17	94	91	5	60	.325	.428	.536	134	32	7-5	.954	7	103	115	*S-142,M	4.4
1939	Bos A★	143	520	97	160	33	3	19	107	87	0	48	.308	.407	.492	124	22	6-6	.959	4	99	105	*S-142,M	3.2
1940	Bos A	149	548	104	156	35	6	24	111	83	1	65	.285	.380	.502	122	19	7-5	.948	-0	**105**	94	*S-146/3-2,M	2.7
1941	Bos A★	143	518	98	161	38	8	16	95	82	1	55	.311	.406	.508	137	30	1-4	.958	-1	99	85	*S-119,3-22/O(LF)M	3.5
1942	Bos A	45	79	7	24	3	0	4	24	15	0	21	.304	.415	.494	150	6	0-1	.865	-1	103	200	3-11/1-5,SM	0.5
1943	Bos A	59	77	8	24	4	0	5	29	11	0	4	.312	.398	.558	176	7	0-0	.968	-0	98	55	3-10,M	0.8
1944	Bos A	76	191	24	46	7	0	5	28	34	1	19	.241	.358	.356	106	3	1-4	.981	-2	93	90	1-49,M	-0.3
1945	Bos A	3	8	1	3	0	0	0	1	3	0	2	.375	.545	.375	165	1	0-0	1.000	1	148	355	/3-3,M	0.2
Total	20	2124	7579	1233	2285	515	118	170	1424	1059	34	700	.301	.390	.468	119	239	87-71	.951	53	102	105	*S-1843/3-69,1-57,2-35,O(LF)	39.6

Year	Tm Lg	G	AB	R	H	2B	3B	HR	RBI	BB-IB	HP	SO	AVG	OBP	SLG	AOPS	ABR	SB-CS	FA	FR	Rng	Thr	G at Pos	BFW
CRONIN, BILL William Patrick "Crungy" B 12.26.1902 W.Newton, MA D 10.26.1966 Newton, MA BR/TR 5-9/167# d7.4																								
1928	Bos N	3	2	1	0	0	0	0	0	1	0	0	.000	.333	.000	-6	0	0	1.000	0	*0*	*0*	/C-3	0.0
1929	Bos N	6	9	0	1	0	0	0	0	0	0	0	.111	.111	.111	-47	-2	0	1.000	1	*157*	*88*	/C-6	-0.1
1930	Bos N	66	178	19	45	9	1	0	17	4	2	8	.253	.277	.315	44	-16	0	.983	4	*117*	*90*	C-64	-0.7
1931	Bos N	51	107	8	22	6	1	0	10	7	2	5	.206	.267	.280	49	-8	0	.941	0	*105*	*94*	C-50	-0.6
Total	4	126	296	28	68	15	2	0	27	12	4	13	.230	.269	.294	43	-26	0	.968	5	*113*	*91*	C-123	-1.4
CROOKE, TOM Thomas Aloysius B 7.26.1884 Washington, DC D 4.5.1929 Quantico, VA BR/TR 6/180# d9.29																								
1909	Was A	3	7	2	2	1	0	0	2	2	0		.286	.444	.429	184	1	1	.969	-1	0	207	/1-3	0.0
1910	Was A	8	21	1	4	1	0	0	1	1	0		.190	.227	.238	48	-1	0	1.000	-0	75	97	/1-5	-0.2
Total	2	11	28	3	6	2	0	0	3	3	0		.214	.290	.286	85	0	1	.988	-1	47	138	/1-8	-0.2
CROOKS, JACK John Charles B 11.9.1865 St.Paul, MN D 2.2.1918 St.Louis, MO BR/TR 5-10/170# d9.26 M1																								
1889	Col AA	12	43	13	14	2	3	0	7	10	1	4	.326	.463	.512	187	6	10	.987	4	123	64	2-12	0.8
1890	Col AA	135	485	86	107	5	4	1	62	96	7		.221	.357	.254	86	-1	57	.937	-1	93	121	*2-134/3O(LF)	0.3
1891	Col AA	**138**	519	110	127	19	13	0	46	103	9	47	.245	.379	.331	110	14	50	**.957**	18	98	129	*2-138	3.2
1892	StL N	128	445	82	95	7	4	7	38	**136**	2	52	.213	.400	.294	116	22	23	.928	-5	94	96	*2-100,3-26/O-2(RF),M	2.0
1893	StL N	128	448	93	106	10	9	1	48	**121**	9	37	.237	.408	.306	91	2	31	.908	2	99	87	*3-123/S-4,C	0.6
1895	Was N	118	412	81	117	19	8	6	58	70	8	39	.284	.398	.413	111	10	36	**.956**	18	104	79	*2-118	2.6
1896	Was N	25	84	20	24	3	0	3	20	16	1	8	.286	.406	.429	120	3	2	.916	-2	86	60	2-20/3-4	0.1
	Lou N	39	122	19	29	5	1	2	15	20	2	8	.238	.354	.344	88	-1	8	.925	1	92	130	2-39	0.1
	Year	64	206	39	53	8	1	5	35	36	3	16	.257	.376	.379	101	2	10	.922	-2	90	107	2-59/3-4	0.2
1898	StL N	72	225	33	52	4	2	1	20	40	5		.231	.359	.280	82	-3	3	.959	2	99	81	2-66/3-3,S-2,O(1-1-0)	0.2
Total	8	795	2783	537	671	74	44	21	314	612	44	195	.241	.386	.322	102	52	220	.946	37	97	104	2-627,3-157/S-6,O-4(2-1-2),C	9.9
CROSBY, ED Edward Carlton B 5.26.1949 Long Beach, CA BL/TR 6-2/180# d7.12																								
1970	StL N	38	95	9	24	4	1	0	6	7-0	1	5	.253	.308	.316	67	-4	0-0	.954	2	109	94	S-35/3-3,2-2	0.0
1972	StL N	101	276	27	60	9	1	0	19	18-1	2	27	.217	.269	.257	51	-18	1-1	.979	-4	94	112	S-43,2-38,3-14	-1.7
1973	StL N	22	39	4	5	2	1	0	1	4-1	0	4	.128	.209	.231	22	-4	0-0	.938	-3	86	99	/S-7,2-5,3-4	-0.7
	†Cin N	36	51	4	11	1	1	0	5	7-1	2	12	.216	.333	.275	74	-2	0-1	.953	1	116	86	S-29/2-5	0.1
	Year	58	90	8	16	3	2	0	6	11-2	2	16	.178	.282	.256	52	-6	0-1	.950	-2	111	88	S-36,2-10/3-4	-0.6
1974	Cle A	37	86	11	18	3	0	0	6	6-0	0	12	.209	.258	.244	46	-6	0-1	.926	-3	71	99	3-18,S-13/2-3	-0.9
1975	Cle A	61	128	12	30	3	0	0	7	13-0	0	14	.234	.305	.258	60	-6	0-4	.974	-1	100	84	S-30,2-19,3-13	-0.5
1976	Cle A	2	2	0	1	0	0	0	0	0-0	0	0	.500	.500	.500	195	0	0-0	1.000	1	293	0	/3D	0.1
Total	6	297	677	67	149	22	4	0	44	55-3	5	74	.220	.282	.264	55	-40	1-7	.964	-7	104	92	S-157/2-72,3-53,D	-3.6
CROSBY, BUBBA Richard Stephen B 8.11.1976 Houston, TX BL/TL 5-11/180# d5.29																								
2003	LA N	9	12	0	1	0	0	0	1	0-0	0	3	.083	.083	.083	-60	-3	0-0	.667	-0	114	0	/O(LF)	-0.3
CROSBY, BOBBY Robert Edward B 1.12.1980 Lakewood, CA BR/TR 6-3/200# d9.2																								
2003	Oak A	11	12	1	0	0	0	0	0	1-0	1	5	.000	.143	.000	-57	-3	0-0	.889	2	165	144	/S-9,D-2	-0.1
CROSETTI, FRANKIE Frank Peter Joseph "Crow" B 10.4.1910 San Francisco, CA D 2.11.2002 Stockton, CA BR/TR 5-10/165# d4.12 Def 1944 C25																								
1932	†NY A	116	398	47	96	20	9	5	57	51	5	51	.241	.335	.374	88	-7	3-2	.937	-5	89	104	S-84,3-33/2	-0.5
1933	NY A	136	451	71	114	20	5	9	60	55	2	40	.253	.337	.379	95	-3	4-1	.936	-8	91	75	*S-133	-0.1
1934	NY A	138	554	85	147	22	10	11	67	61	**5**	58	.265	.344	.401	98	-3	5-6	.945	-11	91	111	*S-119,3-23/2	-0.5
1935	NY A	87	305	49	78	17	6	8	50	41	4	27	.256	.351	.430	107	3	3-1	.963	-7	94	88	S-87	0.2
1936	†NY A★	151	632	137	182	35	7	15	78	90	**12**	83	.288	.387	.437	107	9	18-7	.948	-13	94	96	*S-151	0.8
1937	†NY A	149	611	127	143	29	5	11	49	86	**12**	105	.234	.340	.352	74	-23	13-7	.948	0	98	101	*S-147	-1.1
1938	†NY A	**157**	631	113	166	35	3	9	55	106	**15**	97	.263	.382	.371	90	-5	**27**-12	.948	18	**106**	**119**	*S-157	2.4
1939	†NY A☆	**152**	656	109	153	25	5	10	56	65	**13**	81	.233	.315	.332	67	-34	11-7	**.968**	10	97	**148**	*S-152	-1.2
1940	NY A	145	546	84	106	23	4	4	31	72	**10**	77	.194	.299	.273	52	-39	14-8	.954	-13	97	91	*S-145	-3.9
1941	NY A	50	148	13	33	2	2	1	22	18	3	14	.223	.320	.284	62	-8	0-2	.944	5	100	107	S-32,3-13	-0.1
1942	†NY A	74	285	50	69	5	5	4	23	31	**9**	31	.242	.335	.337	91	-3	1-1	.951	0	88	140	3-62/S-8,2-2	-0.1
1943	†NY A	95	348	36	81	8	1	2	20	36	7	47	.233	.317	.279	74	-11	4-4	.946	-0	96	107	S-90	-0.4
1944	NY A	55	197	20	47	4	2	5	30	11	6	21	.239	.299	.355	84	-5	3-0	.960	-5	88	96	S-55	-0.5
1945	NY A	130	441	57	105	12	0	4	48	59	**10**	65	.238	.341	.293	81	-8	7-1	.946	-5	96	115	*S-126	-0.3
1946	NY A	28	59	4	17	3	0	0	3	8	1	2	.288	.382	.339	101	1	0-3	.940	5	124	146	S-24	0.6
1947	NY A	3	1	0	0	0	0	0	0	0	0	0	.000	.000	.000	-99	0	0-0	—	-0	0	0	/2S	-0.1
1948	NY A	17	14	4	4	0	1	0	0	2	0	0	.286	.375	.429	115	0	0-0	1.000	0	117	251	/2-6,S-5	0.0
Total	17	1683	6277	1006	1541	260	65	98	649	792	114	799	.245	.341	.354	84	-136	113-62	.949	-30	96	107	*S-1516,3-131/2-11	-4.8
CROSS, AMOS Amos C. B 1861 , Czechoslovakia D 7.16.1888 Cleveland, OH d4.22 b-Frank b-Lave																								
1885	Lou AA	35	130	11	37	2	1	0	14	0	1		.285	.290	.315	91	-2		.936	-0			C-35	0.1
1886	Lou AA	74	283	51	78	14	6	1	42	44	1		.276	.375	.378	129	11	13	.910	-7			C-51,1-20/S-2,O(LF)	0.5
1887	Lou AA	8	28	0	3	0	0	0	0	1	0		.107	.138	.107	-31	-5	0	.808	-2			/C-5,1-2,O(RF)	-0.6
Total	3	117	441	62	118	16	7	1	56	45	2		.268	.338	.342	108	4	13	.916	-10			/C-91,1-22,O-2(1-0-1),S-2	0.0
CROSS, CLARENCE Clarence (born Clarence Crause) B 3.4.1856 St.Louis, MO D 6.23.1931 Seattle, WA d5.5																								
1884	Alt U	2	7	1	4	1	0	0		2			.571	.667	.714	314	2		.500	-2	22	0	/3-2	0.0
	Phi U	2	9	0	2	0	0	0		0			.222	.222	.222	38	-1		.545	-2	84	0	/S-2	-0.2
	KC U	25	93	13	20	1	0	0		6			.215	.263	.226	57	-7		.836	4	137	68	S-24/3	-0.2
	Year	29	109	14	26	2	0	0		8			.239	.291	.257	76	-6		.813	1	133	62	S-26/3-3	-0.4
1887	NY AA	16	55	9	11	2	1	0	5	2	3		.200	.267	.273	53	-3	0	.833	-2	105	34	S-13/3-4	-0.4
Total	2	45	164	23	37	4	1	0	5	10	3		.226	.282	.262	67	-9	0	.818	-1	125	54	/S-39,3-7	-0.8
CROSS, FRANK Frank Atwell "Mickey" B 1.20.1873 Cleveland, OH D 11.2.1932 Geauga Lake, OH TR 5-9/161# d5.20 b-Amos b-Lave																								
1901	Cle A	1	5	0	3	0	0	0	0	0	0		.600	.600	.600	243	1	0	—	-0	0	0	/O(RF)	0.1
CROSS, JEFF Joffre James B 8.28.1918 Tulsa, OK D 7.23.1997 Huntsville, TX BR/TR 5-11/160# d9.27 Mil 1943-45																								
1942	StL N	1	4	0	1	0	0	0	1	0	0	0	.250	.250	.250	43	0	0	1.000	-0	123	0	/S	0.0
1946	StL N	49	69	17	15	3	0	0	6	10	0	8	.217	.316	.261	62	-3	4	.970	3	113	154	S-17/2-8,3	0.0
1947	StL N	51	49	4	5	1	0	0	3	10	0	6	.102	.254	.122	3	-7	0	.947	2	129	118	3-15,S-14/2-2	-0.4
1948	StL N	2	0	0	0	0	0	0	0	0	0	0	—	—	—	—	0	0	—	0			R	0.0
	Chi N	16	20	1	2	0	0	0	0	0	0	4	.100	.100	.100	-48	-4	0	.786	-3	79	0	/S-9,2	-0.7
	Year	18	20	1	2	0	0	0	0	0	0	4	.100	.100	.100	-47	-4	0	.786	-3	79	0	/S-9,2	-0.7
Total	4	119	142	22	23	4	0	0	10	20	0	18	.162	.265	.190	26	-14	4	.932	2	107	135	/S-41,3-16,2-11	-1.1
CROSS, LAVE Lafayette Napoleon B 5.12.1866 Milwaukee, WI D 9.6.1927 Toledo, OH BR/TR 5-8.5/155# d4.23 M1 b-Amos b-Frank OF Total (13-LF 34-CF 72-RF)																								
1887	Lou AA	54	203	32	54	8	3	0	26	15	1		.266	.320	.335	81	-5	15	.916	-2			C-44,O-10(3-1-6)	-0.3
1888	Lou AA	47	181	20	41	3	0	0	15	2	1		.227	.239	.243	56	-9	10	.929	2			C-37,O-12(2-0-10)/S-2	-0.4
1889	Phi AA	55	199	22	44	8	2	0	23	14	0	9	.221	.272	.281	58	-11	11	.934	14			C-55	0.6
1890	Phi P	63	245	42	73	7	8	3	47	12	0	6	.298	.331	.429	100	-2	5	.885	3	*98*	*120*	C-49,O-15(0-5-10)	0.3
1891	Phi AA	110	402	66	121	20	14	5	52	38	3	23	.301	.366	.458	135	16	14	.971	1	145	279	O-43(RF),C-43,3-24/S2	1.8
1892	Phi N	140	541	84	149	15	10	4	69	39	3	16	.275	.328	.362	109	4	18	.921	5	107	55	3-65,C-39,O-25(8-17-0),2-14/S-5	1.2
1893	Phi N	96	415	81	124	17	6	4	78	26	1	7	.299	.342	.398	96	-4	18	.974	15	*128*	*97*	C-40,3-30,O-10(0-9-1),S-10/1-6	1.2
1894	Phi N	122	542	128	210	35	10	7	132	31	3	7	.387	.424	.528	131	27	23	.916	23	**120**	**148**	*3-103,C-16/S-7,2	4.0
1895	Phi N	125	535	95	145	26	9	2	101	35	3	8	.271	.319	.364	76	-21	21	**.940**	32	**121**	121	*3-125	1.1
1896	Phi N	106	406	63	104	23	5	1	73	32	1	14	.256	.312	.345	74	-16	8	.937	13	110	95	3-61,S-37/2-6,O-2(CF),C	0.0
1897	Phi N	88	344	37	89	17	5	3	51	10	1		.259	.282	.363	71	-16	10	.912	-1	98	81	3-47,2-38/O-2(RF),S	-1.2
1898	StL N	151	602	71	191	28	8	3	79	28	0		.317	.348	.405	113	8	14	**.945**	20	**112**	90	*3-149/S-2	2.8
1899	Cle N	38	154	15	44	5	0	1	20	8	1		.286	.325	.338	88	-2	2	.955	5	98	99	3-38,M	0.3
	StL N	103	403	61	122	14	5	4	64	17	1		.303	.333	.392	96	-4	11	.960	31	122	178	*3-103	2.5
	Year	141	557	76	166	19	5	5	84	25	2		.298	.330	.377	94	-6	13	**.959**	36	**116**	**157**	*3-141	2.8
1900	StL N	16	61	6	18	1	0	0	6	1	0		.295	.306	.311	71	-3	1	.962	2	120	56	3-16	-0.1
	†Bro N	117	461	73	135	14	6	4	67	25	2		.293	.332	.375	90	-8	20	.943	3	101	61	*3-117	-0.3
	Year	133	522	79	153	15	6	4	73	26	2		.293	.329	.368	88	-11	21	**.945**	5	103	60	*3-133	-0.4

Year	Tm Lg	G	AB	R	H	2B	3B	HR	RBI	BB-IB	HP	SO	AVG	OBP	SLG	AOPS	ABR	SB-CS	FA	FR	Rng	Thr	G at Pos	BFW
1901	Phi A	100	424	82	139	28	12	2	73	19	1		.328	.358	.465	121	11	23	.919	7	107	49	*3-100	1.8
1902	Phi A	**137**	559	90	191	39	8	0	108	27	2		.342	.374	.440	120	15	25	.942	6	99	89	*3-137	2.3
1903	Phi A	**137**	559	60	163	22	4	2	90	10	0		.292	.304	.356	93	-6	14	.950	-3	88	100	*3-136/1	-0.5
1904	Phi A	**155**	607	73	176	31	10	1	71	13	5		.290	.310	.379	112	6	10	.936	-9	83	111	*3-155	0.2
1905	†Phi A	147	587	69	156	29	5	0	77	26	2		.266	.299	.332	98	-2	8	.928	-12	85	49	*3-147	-1.1
1906	Was A	130	494	55	130	14	6	1	46	28	0		.263	.303	.322	100	-1	19	**.952**	-4	93	65	*3-130	-0.1
1907	Was A	41	161	13	32	8	0	0	10	10	0		.199	.246	.248	62	-7	3	.978	8	124	46	3-41	0.3
Total	21	2278	9085	1338	2651	412	136	47	1378	466	31	90	.292	.329	.383	100	-30	303	.938	159	103	92	*3-1724,C-324,O-119R/S-65,2-60,1	16.4
CROSS, MONTE Montford Montgomery B 8.31.1869 Philadelphia, PA D 6.21.1934 Philadelphia, PA BR/TR 5-8.5/148# d9.27 U1																								
1892	Bal N	15	50	5	8	0	0	0	2	4	0	10	.160	.222	.160	16	-5	2	.864	-2	100	41	S-15	-0.6
1894	Pit N	13	43	14	19	1	5	2	13	5	2	4	.442	.520	.837	225	8	6	.924	-0	89	127	S-13	0.7
1895	Pit N	109	397	67	101	14	13	3	54	38	3	38	.254	.324	.378	85	-10	39	.884	-17	87	95	*S-108/2	-1.7
1896	StL N	125	427	66	104	10	6	6	52	58	6	48	.244	.342	.337	83	-9	40	.892	-13	94	54	*S-125	-1.3
1897	StL N	132	465	60	133	17	11	4	55	62	7		.286	.378	.396	107	6	38	.918	30	**117**	81	*S-132	3.6
1898	Phi N	149	525	68	135	25	5	1	50	55	8		.257	.337	.330	95	-1	20	.907	16	103	103	*S-149	2.1
1899	Phi N	**154**	557	85	143	25	6	3	65	56	10		.257	.335	.339	88	-7	26	.909	2	101	98	*S-154	0.2
1900	Phi N	131	466	59	94	11	3	3	62	51	6		.202	.289	.258	52	-30	19	.928	-7	94	119	*S-131	-2.8
1901	Phi N	139	483	49	95	14	1	1	44	52	5		.197	.281	.236	50	-29	24	.924	-16	93	65	*S-139	-4.0
1902	Phi A	**137**	497	72	115	22	2	3	59	32	8		.231	.289	.302	61	-26	17	.927	9	99	62	*S-137	-1.2
1903	Phi A	**137**	470	44	116	21	2	3	45	49	6		.247	.326	.319	90	-3	31	.940	8	92	78	*S-137/2	0.9
1904	Phi A	153	503	33	95	23	4	1	38	46	7		.189	.266	.256	62	-20	19	.937	-15	86	58	*S-153	-3.3
1905	†Phi A	79	252	28	67	17	2	0	24	19	6		.266	.332	.349	114	5	8	.929	-10	84	97	S-77/2-2	-0.3
1906	Phi A	134	445	32	89	23	3	1	40	50	7		.200	.291	.272	74	-11	22	.938	3	91	111	*S-134	-0.4
1907	Phi A	77	248	37	51	9	5	0	18	39	1		.206	.316	.282	89	-1	17	.954	8	97	84	S-74	0.9
Total	15	1684	5828	719	1365	232	68	31	621	616	82	100	.234	.316	.313	80	-133	328	.920	-4	96	84	*S-1678/2-4	-7.2
CROSSIN, FRANK Frank Patrick B 6.15.1891 Avondale, PA D 12.6.1965 Kingston, PA BR/TR 5-10/160# d9.24																								
1912	StL A	8	22	2	5	0	0	0	2	1	0		.227	.261	.227	41	-2	1	.920	-3	*70*	*81*	/C-8	-0.5
1913	StL A	4	4	1	1	0	0	0	0	1	1	1	.250	.500	.250	124	0	0	.857	-1	*85*	*73*	/C-2	0.0
1914	StL A	43	90	5	11	1	1	0	5	10	2	10	.122	.225	.156	15	-9	3	.934	-2	*101*	*90*	C-41	-0.8
Total	3	55	116	8	17	1	1	0	7	12	3	11	.147	.244	.172	25	-11	4	.930	-5	*96*	*88*	/C-51	-1.3
CROTTY, JOE Joseph P. B 12.24.1860 Cincinnati, OH D 6.22.1926 Minneapolis, MN BR/TR d5.4																								
1882	Lou AA	5	20	1	2	0	0	0		0			.100	.100	.100	-34	-3		.882	0			/C-5	-0.2
	StL AA	8	28	2	4	1	0	0		3			.143	.226	.179	37	-2		.882	-1			/C-7,O(CF)	-0.2
	Year	13	48	3	6	1	0	0		3			.125	.176	.146	10	-4		.882	-0			C-12/O(CF)	-0.4
1884	Cin U	21	84	11	22	4	2	1		1			.262	.271	.393	92	-4		.896	-3			C-21	-0.5
1885	Lou AA	39	129	14	20	2	0	0	7	3	3		.155	.193	.171	15	-12		.931	0			C-38/1	-0.8
1886	NY AA	14	47	6	8	0	1	0	2	4	1		.170	.250	.213	50	-3	3	.933	-0			C-14	-0.2
Total	4	87	308	34	56	7	3	1	9	11	4		.182	.220	.234	43	-24	3	.915	-4			/C-85,1O(CF)	-1.9
CROUCH, JACK Jack Albert "Roxy" B 10.12.1903 Salisbury, NC D 8.25.1972 Leesburg, FL BR/TR 5-9/165# d9.18																								
1930	StL A	6	14	1	2	1	0	0	1	1	0	3	.143	.200	.214	5	-2	0-0	1.000	1	*197*	*146*	/C-5	-0.1
1931	StL A	8	12	0	0	0	0	0	1	0	0	4	.000	.000	.000	-97	-3	0-0	.895	0	*171*	*87*	/C-7	-0.3
1933	StL A	19	30	1	5	0	0	1	5	2	0	6	.167	.219	.267	26	-3	0-0	1.000	-0	*88*	*206*	/C-9	-0.3
	Cin N	10	16	5	2	0	0	0	1	0	2	0	.125	.222	.125	1	-2	1	1.000	1	*84*	*70*	/C-6	-0.1
Total	3	43	72	7	9	1	0	1	8	3	2	13	.125	.182	.181	-3	-10	1-0	.976	1	*129*	*130*	/C-27	-0.8
CROUCHER, FRANK Frank Donald "Dingle" B 7.23.1914 San Antonio, TX D 5.21.1980 Houston, TX BR/TR 5-11/165# d4.18 Mil 1943-45																								
1939	Det A	97	324	38	87	15	0	5	40	16	0	42	.269	.303	.361	64	-18	2-2	.934	-6	98	93	S-93/2-3	-1.7
1940	†Det A	37	57	3	6	0	0	0	2	4	0	5	.105	.164	.105	-26	-11	0-0	.936	-2	100	35	S-26/2-7,3	-1.1
1941	Det A	136	489	51	124	21	4	2	39	33	3	72	.254	.305	.325	61	-28	2-0	.935	-4	94	96	*S-136	-2.1
1942	Was A	26	65	2	18	1	1	0	5	3	0	9	.277	.309	.323	79	-2	0-0	.950	1	116	75	2-18	0.0
Total	4	296	935	94	235	37	5	7	86	56	3	128	.251	.296	.324	58	-59	4-2	.934	-10	96	92	S-255/2-28,3	-4.9
CROUSE, BUCK Clyde Elsworth B 1.6.1897 Anderson, IN D 10.23.1983 Muncie, IN BL/TR 5-8/158# d8.1																								
1923	Chi A	23	70	6	18	2	1	1	7	3	1	4	.257	.297	.357	73	-3	0-0	.955	-2	*73*	*107*	C-22	-0.4
1924	Chi A	94	305	30	79	10	1	1	44	23	4	12	.259	.319	.308	64	-17	3-2	.945	-2	*80*	***127***	C-90	-1.2
1925	Chi A	54	131	18	46	7	0	2	25	12	1	4	.351	.410	.450	125	5	1-2	.952	-0	*185*	*138*	C-48	0.6
1926	Chi A	49	135	10	32	4	1	0	17	14	0	7	.237	.309	.281	57	-9	0-0	.985	2	*137*	*106*	C-45	-0.4
1927	Chi A	85	222	22	53	11	0	0	20	21	1	10	.239	.307	.288	57	-14	4-1	.972	7	***117***	*142*	C-81	-0.2
1928	Chi A	78	218	17	55	5	2	2	20	19	1	14	.252	.315	.321	68	-10	3-4	.959	2	*131*	*128*	C-76	-0.5
1929	Chi A	45	107	11	29	7	0	2	12	5	2	7	.271	.316	.393	82	-3	2-0	.979	3	*115*	*104*	C-40	0.3
1930	Chi A	42	118	14	30	8	1	0	15	17	0	10	.254	.348	.339	78	-3	1-1	.979	4	*107*	*120*	C-38	0.2
Total	8	470	1306	128	342	54	6	8	160	114	10	68	.262	.326	.331	72	-54	14-10	.964	13	*116*	*125*	C-440	-1.6
CROW, DON Donald Le Roy B 8.18.1958 Yakima, WA BR/TR 6-4/200# d7.25																								
1982	LA N	4	4	0	0	0	0	0	0	0-0	0	3	.000	.000	.000	-99	-1	0-0	1.000	-1	43	123	/C-4	-0.2
CROWE, GEORGE George Daniel "Big George" B 3.22.1921 Whiteland, IN BL/TL 6-2/212# d4.16																								
1952	Bos N	73	217	25	56	13	1	4	20	18	5	25	.258	.329	.382	100	0	0-1	.985	1	112	82	1-55	-0.1
1953	Mil N	47	42	6	12	2	0	2	6	2	1	7	.286	.333	.476	115	1	0-0	1.000	0	161	65	/1-9	0.1
1955	Mil N	104	303	41	85	12	4	15	55	45-8	1	44	.281	.374	.495	135	16	1-0	.989	2	111	88	1-79	1.3
1956	Cin N	77	144	22	36	2	1	10	23	11-1	2	28	.250	.312	.486	104	0	0-0	.988	2	128	69	1-32	0.1
1957	Cin N	133	494	71	134	20	1	31	92	32-3	1	62	.271	.314	.504	108	5	1-1	.989	-1	99	88	*1-120	-0.4
1958	Cin N☆	111	345	31	95	12	5	7	61	41-3	0	51	.275	.348	.400	94	-3	1-0	.992	-2	93	87	1-93/2	-0.9
1959	StL N	77	103	14	31	6	0	8	29	5-2	0	12	.301	.330	.592	132	4	0-0	1.000	2	172	104	1-14	0.6
1960	StL N	73	72	5	17	3	0	4	13	5-1	0	16	.236	.278	.444	89	-1	0-0	1.000	0	113	51	/1-5	-0.1
1961	StL N	7	7	0	1	0	0	0	0	0-0	0	1	.143	.143	.143	-22	-1	0-0	—	0			H	-0.1
Total	9	702	1727	215	467	70	12	81	299	159-18	10	246	.270	.333	.466	109	21	3-2	.990	5	106	86	1-407/2	0.5
CROWLEY, ED Edgar Jewel B 8.20.1906 Watkinsville, GA D 4.14.1970 Birmingham, AL BR/TR 6-1/180# d6.21																								
1928	Was A	2	1	0	0	0	0	0	0	0	0	0	.000	.000	.000	-99	0	0-0	.000	-1	0	0	/3-2	-0.1
CROWLEY, JOHN John A. B 1.12.1862 Lawrence, MA D 9.23.1896 Lawrence, MA 5-10/164# d5.1																								
1884	Phi N	48	168	26	41	7	3	0	19	15		21	.244	.306	.321	102	1		.832	-20			C-48	-1.3
CROWLEY, TERRY Terrence Michael B 2.16.1947 Staten Island, NY BL/TL 6/180# d9.4 C17																								
1969	Bal A	7	18	2	6	0	0	0	3	1-0	0	4	.333	.350	.333	97	0	0-0	1.000	0	135	179	/1-3,O-2(LF)	0.0
1970	†Bal A	83	152	25	39	5	0	5	20	35-3	0	26	.257	.394	.388	116	5	2-0	.973	-4	85	0	O-27(6-0-22),1-23	-0.1
1971	Bal A	18	23	2	4	0	0	0	1	3-0	0	4	.174	.269	.174	28	-2	0-0	1.000	-1	73	0	/O-6(1-0-5),1-2	-0.3
1972	Bal A	97	247	30	57	10	0	11	29	32-5	1	26	.231	.319	.405	112	4	0-0	.990	-3	87	49	O-68(3-0-65),1-15	-0.3
1973	†Bal A	54	131	16	27	4	0	3	15	16-1	1	14	.206	.297	.305	71	-5	0-0	.867	0	76	184	D-23,O-10(2-0-8)/1-7	-0.6
1974	Cin N	84	125	11	30	12	0	1	20	10-0	1	16	.240	.293	.360	86	-2	1-0	1.000	0	94	88	O-22(1-0-21)/1-7	-0.3
1975	†Cin N	66	71	8	19	6	0	1	11	7-1	0	6	.268	.333	.394	100	0	0-0	1.000	2	161	180	/1-4,O-4(3-0-1)	0.2
1976	Atl N	7	6	0	0	0	0	0	1	0-0	0	0	.000	.000	.000	-94	-2	0-0	—	0			H	-0.2
	Bal A	33	61	5	15	1	0	0	5	7-1	1	11	.246	.333	.262	81	-1	0-0	1.000	0	178	74	D-17/1	-0.1
1977	Bal A	18	22	3	8	1	0	1	9	1-0	0	3	.364	.391	.545	162	2	0-0	1.000	0	0	0	/1D	0.2
1978	Bal A	62	95	9	24	2	0	0	12	8-0	1	12	.253	.314	.274	72	-3	0-0	1.000	1	143	4397	D-17/O-2(LF),1	-0.3
1979	†Bal A	61	63	8	20	5	1	1	8	14-2	1	13	.317	.449	.476	155	6	0-0	1.000	-0	0	188	D-15/1-2	0.5
1980	Bal A	92	233	33	67	8	0	12	50	29-2	0	21	.288	.364	.476	130	10	0-0	1.000	2	357	52	D-65/1-3	0.9
1981	Bal A	68	134	12	33	6	0	4	25	29-5	0	12	.246	.376	.381	120	5	0-0	1.000	0	105	79	D-42/1-4	0.4
1982	Bal A	65	93	8	22	2	0	3	17	21-1	0	9	.237	.377	.355	103	1	0-0	.988	0	107	167	D-14,1-10	0.0
1983	Mon N	50	44	2	8	0	0	0	3	9-0	1	4	.182	.327	.182	47	-3	0-0	1.000	-1	0	116	/1-4	-0.4
Total	15	865	1518	174	379	62	1	42	229	222-21	7	181	.250	.345	.375	104	15	3-0	.980	-4	88	76	D-195,O-141(20-0-122)/1-87	-0.4

Year	Tm Lg	G	AB	R	H	2B	3B	HR	RBI	BB-IB	HP	SO	AVG	OBP	SLG	AOPS	ABR	SB-CS	FA	FR	Rng	Thr	G at Pos	BFW
CROWLEY, BILL William Michael B 4.8.1857 Philadelphia, PA D 7.14.1891 Gloucester, NJ BR/TR 5-7.5/159# d4.26 OF Total (82-LF 150-CF 254-RF)																								
1875	Phi NA	9	37	4	3	0	0	0	3	1		0	.081	.105	.081	-33	-5	0-0	.800	-1	80	0	/3-4,O-4(CF),1	-0.5
1877	Lou N	**61**	238	30	67	9	3	1	23	4		13	.282	.293	.357	88	-5		.849	7	**185**	121	*O-58(0-57-2)/S-2,C-2,32	0.0
1879	Buf N	60	261	41	75	9	5	0	30	6		14	.287	.303	.360	115	4		.809	-1	143	403	O-43(3-1-39),C-10/1-7,2-3	0.2
1880	Buf N	**85**	354	57	95	16	4	0	20	19		23	.268	.306	.336	115	6		.824	-2	126	80	*O-74(8-21-48),C-22	0.3
1881	Bos N	72	279	33	71	12	0	0	31	14		15	.254	.290	.297	89	-2		.880	-3	88	170	*O-72(0-47-26)	-0.6
1883	Phi AA	23	96	16	24	4	3	0	16	3			.250	.273	.354	92	-1		.810	-2	78	0	O-22(0-21-1)/1	-0.4
	Cle N	11	41	3	12	5	0	0	5	1		7	.293	.310	.415	119	1		.923	-2	0	0	O-11(RF)	-0.1
1884	Bos N	108	407	50	110	14	6	6	61	33		74	.270	.325	.378	121	10		.870	-7	96	168	*O-108(0-2-107)	0.2
1885	Buf N	92	344	29	83	14	1	1	36	21		32	.241	.285	.297	85	-5		.874	-4	47	37	*O-92(71-1-20)	-1.1
Total	7	512	2020	259	537	83	22	8	222	101		178	.266	.301	.341	103	8		.853	-13	103	136	O-480R/C-34,1-8,2-4,S-2,3	-1.5
CRUISE, WALTON Walton Edwin B 5.6.1890 Childersburg, AL D 1.9.1975 Sylacauga, AL BL/TR 6/175# d4.14 Mil 1918																								
1914	StL N	95	256	20	58	9	3	4	28	25	3	42	.227	.303	.332	90	-3	3	.976	-1	102	66	O-81(43-38-0)	-1.0
1916	StL N	3	3	0	2	0	0	0	0	1	0	0	.667	.750	.667	339	1	0	1.000	0	118	0	/O-2(1-1-0)	0.1
1917	StL N	153	529	70	156	20	10	5	59	38	1	73	.295	.343	.399	131	18	16	.965	-11	88	77	*O-152(49-85-26)	-0.1
1918	StL N	70	240	34	65	5	4	6	39	30	3	26	.271	.359	.400	136	11	2	.964	-8	83	51	O-65(48-0-17)	0.0
1919	StL N	9	21	0	2	1	0	0	0	1	0	6	.095	.136	.143	-17	-3	0	.833	-1	70	0	/O-5(0-4-1),1-2	-0.4
	Bos N	73	241	23	52	7	0	1	21	17	0	29	.216	.267	.257	61	-11	8	.978	-2	96	87	O-66(31-23-14)	-1.9
	Year	82	262	23	54	8	0	1	21	18	0	35	.206	.257	.248	55	-14	8	.971	-3	95	83	O-71(31-27-15)/1-2	-2.3
1920	Bos N	91	288	40	80	7	5	1	21	31	2	26	.278	.352	.347	106	3	5-3	.950	-6	81	99	O-82(RF)	-0.8
1921	Bos N	108	344	47	119	16	7	8	55	48	2	24	.346	.429	.503	154	29	10-8	.963	-1	115	18	*O-102(100-2-0)/1-2	2.0
1922	Bos N	104	352	51	98	15	10	4	46	44	1	20	.278	.360	.412	103	2	4-4	.948	2	113	76	*O-100(37-0-64)/1-2	-0.4
1923	Bos N	21	38	4	8	2	0	0	0	3	0	2	.211	.268	.263	42	-3	1-0	.952	-0	119	0	O-9(8-0-1)	-0.3
1924	Bos N	9	9	4	4	1	0	1	3	0	0	2	.444	.444	.889	260	2	0-0	—	0			H	0.2
Total	10	736	2321	293	644	83	39	30	272	238	12	250	.277	.348	.386	114	46	49-15	.962	-27	97	66	O-664(317-153-205)/1-6	-2.6
CRUMLING, GENE Eugene Leon B 4.5.1922 Wrightsville, PA BR/TR 6/180# d9.11																								
1945	StL N	6	12	0	1	0	0	0	1	0	0	1	.083	.083	.083	-52	-3	0	1.000	1	*83*	*183*	/C-6	-0.1
CRUMP, BUDDY Arthur Elliott B 11.29.1901 Norfolk, VA D 9.7.1976 Raleigh, NC BL/TL 5-10/156# d9.28																								
1924	NY N	1	4	0	0	0	0	0	1	0	0	1	.000	.000	.000	-99	-1	0-0	.500	-1	47	0	/O(CF)	-0.2
CRUTHERS, PRESS Charles Preston B 9.8.1890 Marshallton, DE D 12.27.1976 Kenosha, WI BR/TR 5-9/152# d9.29																								
1913	Phi A	3	12	0	3	1	0	0	0	0	0	0	.250	.250	.333	72	0	0	.923	-2	55	93	/2-3	-0.2
1914	Phi A	4	15	1	3	0	1	0	0	0	0	4	.200	.200	.333	63	-1	0-1	1.000	1	91	74	/2-4	-0.1
Total	2	7	27	1	6	1	1	0	0	0	0	4	.222	.222	.333	67	-1	0-1	.973	-1	76	82	/2-7	-0.3
CRUZ, TOMMY Cirilo (Dilan) B 2.15.1951 Arroyo, P.R. BL/TL 5-9/165# d9.4 b-Hector b-Jose																								
1973	StL N	3	0	1	0	0	0	0	0	0-0	0	0	—	—	—	—	0	0-0	—	-0	0	0	/O(LF)	0.0
1977	Chi A	4	2	1	0	0	0	0	0	0-0	0	0	.000	.000	.000	-99	-1	0-0	1.000	0	112	0	/O-2(LF)	-0.1
Total	2	7	2	2	0	0	0	0	0	0-0	0	0	.000	.000	.000	-99	-1	0-0	1.000	-0	75	0	/O-3(LF)	-0.1
CRUZ, DEIVI Deivi (Garcia) B 11.16.1972 Bani, D.R. BR/TR 5-11/160# d4.1																								
1997	Det A	147	436	35	105	26	0	2	40	14-0	0	55	.241	.263	.314	51	-32	3-6	.979	9	109	**112**	*S-147	-1.3
1998	Det A	135	454	52	118	22	3	5	45	13-0	3	55	.260	.284	.355	65	-25	3-4	.983	16	**115**	115	*S-135	0.1
1999	Det A	155	518	64	147	35	0	13	58	12-0	4	57	.284	.302	.427	84	-14	1-4	.983	7	104	103	*S-155	0.3
2000	Det A	156	583	68	176	46	5	10	82	13-2	4	43	.302	.318	.449	95	-6	1-4	.982	7	106	112	*S-156	1.1
2001	Det A	110	414	39	106	28	1	7	52	17-0	4	46	.256	.291	.379	79	-14	4-1	.964	-10	101	96	*S-109/3-7	-1.4
2002	SD N	151	514	49	135	28	2	7	47	22-2	3	58	.263	.294	.366	84	-17	2-3	.973	-8	98	91	*S-147/1	-1.5
2003	Bal A	152	548	61	137	24	2	14	65	13-1	2	49	.250	.269	.378	71	-25	1-2	.975	1	102	98	*S-147/D-5	-1.3
Total	7	1006	3467	368	924	209	13	58	389	104-5	20	363	.267	.290	.384	76	-133	15-24	.978	24	105	104	S-996/3-7,D-5,1	-4.0
CRUZ, ENRIQUE Enrique Michael B 11.21.1981 Santo Domingo, D.R. BR/TR 6-1/180# d4.2																								
2003	Mil N	60	71	6	6	1	0	0	2	4-0	1	30	.085	.145	.099	-36	-15	0-0	1.000	-4	82	54	S-13/2-6,3-2	-1.8
CRUZ, FAUSTO Fausto (Santiago) B 5.1.1972 Monte Cristi, D.R. BR/TR 5-10/165# d4.10																								
1994	Oak A	17	28	2	3	0	0	0	0	4-0	0	6	.107	.219	.107	-14	-5	0-0	.960	3	109	105	S-10/3-4,2	-0.1
1995	Oak A	8	23	0	5	0	0	0	5	3-0	0	5	.217	.286	.217	42	-2	1-1	.971	-1	104	37	/S-8	-0.2
1996	Det A	14	38	5	9	2	0	0	0	1-0	0	11	.237	.256	.289	38	-4	0-0	.906	-2	104	56	/2-8,S-4,D	-0.5
Total	3	39	89	7	17	2	0	0	5	8-0	0	22	.191	.253	.213	24	-11	1-1	.934	1	107	66	/S-22,2-9,3-4,D	-0.8
CRUZ, HECTOR Hector Louis (Dilan) "Heity" B 4.2.1953 Arroyo, P.R. BR/TR 5-11/170# d8.11 b-Tommy b-Jose																								
1973	StL N	11	11	1	0	0	0	0	0	1-0	0	3	.000	.083	.000	-75	-3	0-0	1.000	0	111	0	/O-5(1-4-0)	-0.3
1975	StL N	23	48	7	7	2	2	0	6	2-0	0	4	.146	.176	.271	23	-5	0-0	.800	-2	42	0	3-12/O-6(4-0-2)	-0.9
1976	StL N	151	526	54	120	17	1	13	71	42-7	2	119	.228	.286	.338	77	-17	1-0	.934	-23	89	68	*3-148	-4.4
1977	StL N	118	339	50	80	19	2	6	42	46-1	1	56	.236	.326	.357	85	-6	4-3	.964	-3	87	130	*O-106(27-0-85)/3-2	-1.4
1978	Chi N	30	76	8	18	5	0	2	9	3-1	0	6	.237	.266	.382	70	-3	0-0	1.000	-2	93	0	O-14(1-14-0)/3-7	-0.5
	SF N	79	197	19	44	8	1	6	24	21-2	1	39	.223	.301	.365	89	-3	0-2	.978	-2	97	159	O-53(31-17-14),3-14	-0.8
	Year	109	273	27	62	13	1	8	33	24-3	1	45	.227	.292	.370	83	-7	0-2	.983	-4	96	123	O-67(32-31-14),3-21	-1.3
1979	SF N	16	25	2	3	0	0	0	1	3-0	0	7	.120	.214	.120	-7	-4	0-0	1.000	-1	94	0	/O-6(5-0-1),3-2	-0.5
	†Cin N	74	182	24	44	10	2	4	27	31-3	0	39	.242	.350	.385	100	1	0-1	.984	4	100	185	O-69(13-23-49)	0.2
	Year	90	207	26	47	10	2	4	28	34-3	0	46	.227	.335	.353	89	-2	0-1	.985	3	100	176	O-75(18-23-50)/3-2	-0.3
1980	Cin N	52	75	5	16	4	1	1	5	8-1	0	16	.213	.289	.333	73	-3	0-0	.955	0	122	0	O-29(15-1-15)	-0.4
1981	Chi N	53	109	15	25	5	0	7	15	17-0	0	24	.229	.331	.468	120	3	2-2	.925	-1	97	0	3-18,O-16(8-0-10)	0.1
1982	Chi N	17	19	1	4	1	0	0	0	2-0	0	4	.211	.286	.263	53	-1	0-0	1.000	-1	30	0	/O-4(4-0-1)	-0.2
Total	9	624	1607	186	361	71	9	39	200	176-15	4	317	.225	.301	.353	81	-41	7-8	.975	-31	96	122	O-308(109-59-177),3-203	-9.1
CRUZ, HENRY Henry (Acosta) B 2.27.1952 Christiansted, V.I. BL/TL 6/175# d4.18																								
1975	LA N	53	94	8	25	3	1	0	5	7-0	0	6	.266	.317	.319	80	-3	1-1	.960	-2	89	0	O-41(17-23-4)	-0.7
1976	LA N	49	88	8	16	2	1	4	14	9-3	0	11	.182	.258	.364	76	-3	0-2	.976	-0	96	68	O-23(5-5-17)	-0.6
1977	Chi A	16	21	3	6	0	0	2	5	1-1	0	3	.286	.318	.571	137	1	0-0	.833	-1	57	0	/O-9(1-2-6)	-0.1
1978	Chi A	53	77	13	17	2	1	2	10	8-0	1	11	.221	.292	.351	82	-2	0-1	1.000	3	96	270	O-40(10-24-6)/D	0.0
Total	4	171	280	32	64	7	3	8	34	25-4	1	31	.229	.291	.361	84	-7	1-4	.974	-2	91	107	O-113(33-54-33)/D	-1.4
CRUZ, JACOB Jacob B 1.28.1973 Oxnard, CA BL/TL 6/175# d7.18																								
1996	SF N	33	77	10	18	3	0	3	10	12-0	2	24	.234	.352	.390	99	0	0-1	.977	0	106	75	O-23(6-0-17)	-0.1
1997	SF N	16	25	3	4	1	0	0	3	3-0	0	4	.160	.241	.200	20	-3	0-0	.933	2	124	535	O-11(2-0-10)	-0.1
1998	SF N	3	3	0	0	0	0	0	0	0-0	0	2	.000	.000	.000	-99	-1	0-0	—	0			/H	-0.1
	Cle A	1	1	0	0	0	0	0	0	0-0	0	1	.000	.000	.000	-97	0	0-0	—	0			/H	0.0
1999	Cle A	32	88	14	29	5	1	3	17	5-0	1	13	.330	.368	.511	117	2	0-2	1.000	0	115	0	O-24(11-15-2)/D-2	0.1
2000	Cle A	11	29	3	7	3	0	0	5	5-0	1	4	.241	.361	.345	81	0	1-0	1.000	0	91	277	/O-9(1-8-0),D-2	0.0
2001	Cle A	28	68	12	15	4	0	3	11	5-0	3	23	.221	.303	.412	85	-2	0-2	.976	0	116	0	O-22(3-15-5)	-0.2
	Col N	44	76	7	16	1	0	1	7	10-0	1	27	.211	.303	.263	41	-7	0-2	.931	-2	80	85	O-24(18-1-6)	-1.0
2002	Det A	35	88	12	24	3	1	2	6	13-0	3	20	.273	.377	.398	115	3	3-1	.929	-2	63	0	D-14,O-12(3-0-9)/1-4	-0.1
Total	7	203	455	61	113	20	2	12	59	53-0	11	118	.248	.337	.380	85	-8	4-8	.971	-1	100	82	O-125(44-39-49)/D-18,1-4	-1.5
CRUZ, JOSE Jose (Dilan) B 8.8.1947 Arroyo, P.R. BL/TL 6/175# d9.19 C7 b-Tommy b-Hector s-Jose																								
1970	StL N	6	17	2	6	1	0	0	1	4-0	1	0	.353	.500	.412	144	2	0-0	1.000	1	195	0	/O-4(1-0-3)	0.3
1971	StL N	83	292	46	80	13	2	9	27	49-6	1	35	.274	.377	.425	123	11	6-3	.975	-4	97	43	O-83(1-82-0)	0.5
1972	StL N	117	332	33	78	14	4	2	23	36-3	1	54	.235	.309	.319	81	-8	9-3	.979	4	104	162	*O-102(10-87-7)	-0.6
1973	StL N	132	406	51	92	22	5	10	57	51-4	1	66	.227	.310	.379	92	-5	10-4	.979	-2	112	24	*O-118(1-85-37)	-1.0
1974	StL N	107	161	24	42	4	3	5	20	20-5	0	27	.261	.341	.416	112	2	4-2	.975	1	110	84	O-53(21-8-24)/1	0.2
1975	Hou N	120	315	44	81	15	2	9	49	52-6	1	44	.257	.358	.403	121	11	6-3	.980	5	116	102	O-94(27-2-65)	1.2
1976	Hou N	133	439	49	133	21	5	4	61	53-5	0	46	.303	.377	.401	133	20	28-11	.972	7	108	118	*O-125(85-13-27)	2.4
1977	Hou N	157	579	87	173	31	10	17	87	69-13	0	67	.299	.368	.475	138	31	44-23	.973	-2	102	91	*O-155(0-6-155)	2.3
1978	Hou N	153	565	79	178	34	9	10	83	57-9	0	57	.315	.376	.460	144	33	37-9	.975	-2	112	33	*O-152(RF)/1-2	2.9

Year	Tm Lg	G	AB	R	H	2B	3B	HR	RBI	BB-IB	HP	SO	AVG	OBP	SLG	AOPS	ABR	SB-CS	FA	FR	Rng	Thr	G at Pos	BFW
1979	Hou N	157	558	73	161	33	7	9	72	72-16	0	66	.289	.367	.421	122	19	36-14	.959	1	104	59	*O-156(LF)	1.7
1980	†Hou N☆	160	612	79	185	29	7	11	91	60-13	0	66	.302	.360	.426	130	25	36-11	.969	7	101	136	*O-158(LF)	2.9
1981	†Hou N	107	409	53	109	16	5	13	55	35-4	0	49	.267	.319	.425	117	7	5-7	.984	4	116	54	*O-105(LF)	0.6
1982	Hou N	155	570	62	157	27	2	9	68	60-12	1	67	.275	.342	.377	110	9	21-11	.964	6	111	72	*O-155(LF)	0.9
1983	Hou N	160	594	85	**189**	28	8	14	92	65-10	1	86	.318	.385	.463	143	35	30-16	.979	-1	100	71	*O-160(LF)	2.9
1984	Hou N	160	600	96	187	28	13	12	95	73-10	0	68	.312	.381	.462	148	39	22-8	.976	2	101	87	*O-160(LF)	3.7
1985	Hou N★	141	544	69	163	34	4	9	79	43-10	0	74	.300	.349	.426	120	14	16-5	.971	4	100	122	*O-137(136-1-0)	1.4
1986	†Hou N	141	479	48	133	22	4	10	72	55-12	0	86	.278	.351	.403	111	7	3-4	.984	1	104	62	*O-134(LF)	0.2
1987	Hou N	126	365	47	88	17	4	11	38	36-3	0	65	.241	.307	.400	90	-7	4-1	.984	4	108	85	O-97(LF)	-0.6
1988	NY A	38	80	9	16	2	0	1	7	8-1	0	8	.200	.273	.262	51	-5	0-1	.889	-1	74	0	D-12/O-8(4-0-4)	-0.7
Total	19	2353	7917	1036	2251	391	94	165	1077	898-142	7	1031	.284	.354	.420	122	240	317-136	.974	35	106	82	*O-2156(1411-284-474)/D-12,1-3	21.2
CRUZ, JOSE Jose L. B 4.19.1974 Arroyo, P.R. BB/TR 6/190# d5.31 f-Jose																								
1997	Sea A	49	183	28	49	12	1	12	34	13-0	0	45	.268	.315	.541	119	4	1-0	.966	-3	99	35	O-49(LF)	0.0
	Tor A	55	212	31	49	7	0	14	34	28-2	0	72	.231	.316	.462	101	-1	6-2	.981	-2	89	89	O-55(51-4-0)	-0.4
	Year	104	395	59	98	19	1	26	68	41-2	0	117	.248	.315	.499	109	4	7-2	.974	-5	94	64	*O-104(100-4-0)	-0.4
1998	Tor A	105	352	55	89	14	3	11	42	57-3	0	99	.253	.354	.403	97	-1	11-4	.984	-1	97	113	*O-105(6-103-0)	0.0
1999	Tor A	106	349	63	84	19	3	14	45	64-5	0	91	.241	.358	.433	99	0	14-4	.990	7	112	129	*O-106(9-97-0)	0.9
2000	Tor A	**162**	603	91	146	32	5	31	76	71-3	2	129	.242	.323	.466	94	-8	15-5	.993	-4	96	109	*O-162(CF)	-0.8
2001	Tor A	146	577	92	158	38	4	34	88	45-4	1	138	.274	.326	.530	118	13	32-5	.990	-19	79	60	*O-143(14-133-0)	0.0
2002	Tor A	124	466	64	114	26	5	18	70	51-1	0	106	.245	.317	.438	95	-4	7-1	.992	3	101	127	*O-119(56-21-47)/D-2	-0.4
2003	†SF N	158	539	90	135	26	1	20	68	102-6	0	121	.250	.366	.414	107	9	5-8	.994	15	111	176	*O-158(0-3-157)	1.4
Total	7	905	3281	514	824	174	22	154	457	431-24	3	801	.251	.336	.458	103	12	91-29	.989	-5	98	113	O-897(185-523-204)/D-2	0.7
CRUZ, JULIO Julio Luis B 12.2.1954 Brooklyn, NY BB/TR 5-9/165# d7.4																								
1977	Sea A	60	199	25	51	3	1	1	7	24-1	0	29	.256	.336	.296	75	-6	15-6	.983	1	103	79	2-54/D	-0.1
1978	Sea A	147	550	77	129	14	1	1	25	69-0	1	66	.235	.319	.269	68	-21	59-10	**.987**	13	111	104	*2-141/S-5,D	0.9
1979	Sea A	107	414	70	112	16	2	1	29	62-0	0	61	.271	.363	.326	87	-5	49-9	.979	20	112	107	*2-107	2.7
1980	Sea A	119	422	66	88	9	3	2	16	59-0	1	49	.209	.306	.258	56	-24	45-7	.983	10	**106**	102	*2-115/D-3	-0.1
1981	Sea A	94	352	57	90	12	3	2	24	39-0	3	40	.256	.332	.324	87	-5	43-8	.982	12	107	108	2-92/S	1.9
1982	Sea A	154	549	83	133	22	5	8	49	57-1	3	71	.242	.316	.344	79	-15	46-13	.987	3	98	97	*2-151/S-2,3D	0.2
1983	Sea A	61	181	24	46	10	1	2	12	20-1	2	22	.254	.332	.354	86	-3	33-6	.984	6	99	96	2-60/D	1.2
	†Chi A	99	334	47	84	9	4	1	40	29-0	2	44	.251	.311	.311	71	-13	24-6	.983	12	107	113	2-97	0.7
	Year	160	515	71	130	19	5	3	52	49-1	4	66	.252	.318	.326	76	-16	57-12	.983	19	104	107	*2-157/D	1.9
1984	Chi A	143	415	42	92	14	4	5	43	45-0	0	58	.222	.295	.311	66	-19	14-6	.976	24	114	113	*2-141	1.3
1985	Chi A	91	234	28	46	2	3	0	15	32-0	2	40	.197	.297	.231	46	-17	8-5	.982	9	101	116	2-87/D-2	-0.4
1986	Chi A	81	209	38	45	2	0	0	19	42-0	0	28	.215	.343	.225	58	-11	7-2	.985	-8	96	97	2-78/D-3	-1.3
Total	10	1156	3859	557	916	113	27	23	279	478-3	14	508	.237	.321	.299	71	-139	343-78	.983	103	106	104	*2-1123/D-13,S-8,3	7.0
CRUZ, IVAN Luis Ivan B 5.3.1968 Fajardo, P.R. BL/TL 6-3/210# d7.18																								
1997	NY A	11	20	0	5	1	0	0	3	2-0	0	4	.250	.318	.300	63	-1	0-0	1.000	-0	0	0	/1-3,O(LF)D	-0.1
1999	Pit N	5	10	3	4	0	0	1	2	0-0	0	2	.400	.400	.700	171	1	0-0	1.000	0	149	356	/1O(RF)	0.1
2000	Pit N	8	11	0	1	0	0	0	0	0-0	0	8	.091	.091	.091	-55	-3	0-0	1.000	-0	0	0	/1	-0.3
2002	StL N	17	14	2	5	0	0	1	3	1-0	0	3	.357	.400	.571	160	1	0-0	1.000	0	95	0	/1-7	0.1
Total	4	41	55	5	15	1	0	2	8	3-0	0	17	.273	.310	.400	84	-2	0-0	1.000	-0	67	80	/1-12,D-4,O-2(1-0-1)	-0.2
CRUZ, TODD Todd Ruben B 11.23.1955 Highland Park, MI BR/TR 6/175# d9.4																								
1978	Phi N	3	4	0	2	0	0	0	2	0-0	0	0	.500	.500	.500	178	0	0-1	1.000	1	183	0	/S-2	0.1
1979	KC A	55	118	9	24	7	0	2	15	3-0	1	19	.203	.224	.314	44	-10	0-1	.974	-6	95	58	S-48/3-9	-1.2
1980	Cal A	18	40	5	11	3	0	1	5	5-1	0	8	.275	.356	.425	116	1	0-0	.860	-5	90	109	S-12/3-4,2O(LF)	-0.3
	Chi A	90	293	23	68	11	1	2	18	9-0	2	54	.232	.259	.297	52	-20	2-1	.956	4	105	86	S-90	-0.7
	Year	108	333	28	79	14	1	3	23	14-1	2	62	.237	.271	.312	60	-19	2-1	.948	-1	104	88	*S-102/3-4,2O(LF)	-1.0
1982	Sea A	136	492	44	113	20	2	16	57	12-1	2	95	.230	.246	.376	67	-25	2-10	.963	16	103	122	*S-136	0.2
1983	Sea A	65	216	21	41	4	2	7	21	7-2	2	56	.190	.221	.324	46	-17	1-3	.964	21	119	108	S-63	0.9
	†Bal A	81	221	16	46	9	1	3	27	15-0	1	52	.208	.259	.299	55	-14	3-4	.942	3	108	134	3-79/2-2	-1.3
	Year	146	437	37	87	13	3	10	48	22-2	3	108	.199	.241	.311	51	-31	4-7	.942	**24**	108	134	3-79,S-63/2-2	-0.4
1984	Bal A	96	142	15	31	4	0	3	9	8-0	1	33	.218	.263	.310	60	-8	1-4	.955	3	117	123	3-89/PD	-0.7
Total	6	544	1526	133	336	58	6	34	154	59-4	7	317	.220	.251	.333	59	-93	9-24	.960	37	106	103	S-351,3-181/2-3,DPO(LF)	-3.0
CUBBAGE, MIKE Michael Lee B 7.21.1950 Charlottesville, VA BL/TR 6/180# d4.7 M1 C14																								
1974	Tex A	9	15	0	0	0	0	0	0	0-0	0	4	.000	.000	.000	-99	-4	0-0	1.000	2	129	0	/3-3,2-2	-0.2
1975	Tex A	58	143	12	32	6	0	4	21	18-2	0	14	.224	.305	.350	87	-2	0-0	.962	1	112	105	2-37/3-3,D-2	0.1
1976	Tex A	14	32	2	7	0	0	0	0	7-0	0	7	.219	.359	.219	70	-1	0-0	1.000	-1	75	118	/2-5,3D	-0.2
	Min A	104	342	40	89	19	5	3	49	42-3	3	37	.260	.344	.371	108	5	1-1	.940	7	112	129	3-99/2-2,D-2	1.2
	Year	118	374	42	96	19	5	3	49	49-3	3	44	.257	.346	.358	105	4	1-1	.940	6	112	129	*3-100/D-8,2-7	1.0
1977	Min A	129	417	60	110	16	5	9	55	37-6	0	49	.264	.321	.391	95	-3	1-4	.952	14	**118**	133	*3-126/D	0.7
1978	Min A	125	394	40	111	12	7	7	57	40-3	1	44	.282	.348	.401	108	4	3-1	.971	7	113	**122**	*3-115/2-5	1.0
1979	Min A	94	243	26	67	10	1	2	23	39-2	0	26	.276	.371	.350	94	0	1-8	.928	-7	89	95	3-63,D-21/12	-1.1
1980	Min A	103	285	29	70	9	0	8	42	23-4	1	37	.246	.301	.361	76	-10	0-1	.996	8	124	108	1-72,3-32/2D	-0.6
1981	NY N	67	80	9	17	2	2	1	4	9-1	0	15	.213	.289	.325	76	-3	0-0	.963	0	112	0	3-12	-0.3
Total	8	703	1951	218	503	74	20	34	251	215-21	5	233	.258	.330	.369	94	-14	6-15	.952	31	111	121	3-454/1-73,2-53,D-33	0.6
CUCCINELLO, AL Alfred Edward B 11.26.1914 Long Island City, NY BR/TR 5-10/165# d5.17 b-Tony																								
1935	NY N	54	165	27	41	7	1	4	20	1	2	20	.248	.262	.376	70	-8	0	.951	1	102	119	2-48/3-2	-0.4
CUCCINELLO, TONY Anthony Francis "Cooch" or "Chick" B 11.8.1907 Long Island City, NY D 9.21.1995 Tampa, FL BR/TR 5-7/160# d4.15 C21 b-Al																								
1930	Cin N	125	443	64	138	22	5	10	78	47	2	44	.312	.380	.451	105	5	5	.920	-12	96	82	*3-109,2-15/S-4	0.0
1931	Cin N	**154**	575	67	181	39	11	2	93	54	0	28	.315	.374	.431	123	19	1	.969	7	103	**126**	*2-154	3.5
1932	Bro N	**154**	597	76	168	32	6	12	77	46	4	47	.281	.337	.415	103	3	5	.973	21	**109**	**118**	*2-154	3.2
1933	Bro N★	134	485	58	122	31	4	9	65	44	2	40	.252	.316	.388	105	3	4	.977	-17	88	87	*2-120,3-14	-0.7
1934	Bro N	140	528	59	138	32	2	14	94	49	1	45	.261	.325	.409	100	0	0	.974	9	107	90	*2-101,3-43	1.6
1935	Bro N	102	360	49	105	20	3	8	53	40	2	35	.292	.366	.431	116	9	3	.977	8	100	147	2-64,3-36	2.1
1936	Bos N	150	565	68	174	26	3	7	86	58	2	49	.308	.374	.402	116	15	1	.971	18	110	**141**	*2-150	4.0
1937	Bos N	**152**	575	77	156	36	4	11	80	61	0	40	.271	.341	.405	112	10	2	.967	-13	104	110	*2-151	0.7
1938	Bos N☆	147	555	62	147	25	2	9	76	52	3	32	.265	.331	.366	102	1	4	.974	-30	94	92	*2-147	-1.9
1939	Bos N	81	310	42	95	17	1	2	40	26	0	26	.306	.360	.387	109	4	5	.970	-5	97	121	2-80	0.5
1940	Bos N	34	126	14	34	9	0	0	19	8	1	9	.270	.319	.341	87	-2	1	.978	2	110	164	3-33	0.1
	NY N	88	307	26	64	9	2	5	36	16	0	42	.208	.248	.300	50	-22	1	.987	7	105	69	2-47,3-37	-1.2
	Year	122	433	40	98	18	2	5	55	24	1	51	.226	.269	.312	60	-25	2	.971	9	108	144	3-70,2-47	-1.1
1942	Bos N	40	104	8	21	3	0	1	8	9	0	11	.202	.265	.260	55	-6	1	.907	-0	90	188	3-20,2-14	-0.6
1943	Bos N	13	19	0	0	0	0	0	2	3	0	1	.000	.136	.000	-60	-4	0	.929	0	118	346	/3-4,2-2,S	-0.4
	Chi A	34	103	5	28	5	0	2	11	13	0	13	.272	.353	.379	114	2	3-1	.965	-1	92	100	3-30	0.2
1944	Chi A	38	130	5	34	3	0	0	17	8	0	16	.262	.304	.285	70	-5	0-0	.959	-1	98	97	3-30/2-6	-0.7
1945	Chi A✶	118	402	50	124	25	3	2	49	45	1	19	.308	.379	.400	130	17	6-2	.936	-6	101	109	*3-112	1.3
Total	15	1704	6184	730	1729	334	46	94	884	579	18	497	.280	.343	.394	105	49	42-3	.973	-14	102	112	*2-1205,3-468/S-5	11.7
CUDDYER, MICHAEL Michael Brent B 3.27.1979 Norfolk, VA BR/TR 6-2/202# d9.23																								
2001	Min A	8	18	1	4	2	0	0	1	2-0	0	6	.222	.300	.333	65	-1	1-0	.975	-1	68	111	/1-5,3-2,D	-0.2
2002	†Min A	41	112	12	29	7	0	4	13	8-0	1	30	.259	.311	.429	94	-1	2-0	.980	2	125	85	O-25(RF),3-10/1-6,D-3	0.0
2003	†Min A	35	102	14	25	1	3	4	8	12-0	0	19	.245	.325	.431	96	-1	1-1	1.000	-5	73	107	O-18(1-0-17)/3-7,1-5,2D	-0.7
Total	3	84	232	27	58	10	3	8	22	22-0	1	55	.250	.316	.422	93	-3	4-1	.986	-3	101	95	/O-43(1-0-42),3-19,1-16,D-6,2	-0.9
CUDWORTH, JIM James Alaric "Cuddy" B 8.22.1858 Fairhaven, MA D 12.21.1943 Middleboro, MA BR/TR 6/165# d7.27 ▲																								
1884	KC U	32	116	7	17	3	1	0		2			.147	.161	.190	7	-17		.963	2	123	132	1-19,O-12(CF)/P-2	-1.4

Year	Tm Lg	G	AB	R	H	2B	3B	HR	RBI	BB-IB	HP	SO	AVG	OBP	SLG	AOPS	ABR	SB-CS	FA	FR	Rng	Thr	G at Pos	BFW
CUETO, MANUEL Manuel "Patato" B 2.8.1892 Guanajay, Cuba D 6.29.1942 Regla, Cuba BR/TR 5-5/157# d6.25 OF Total (51-LF 5-CF 25-RF)																								
1914	StL F	19	43	2	4	0	0	0	2	5	0	7	.093	.188	.093	-21	-8	0	.941	-2	89	0	3-10/S-5,2-2	-1.0
1917	Cin N	56	140	10	28	3	0	1	11	16	1	17	.200	.287	.243	66	-5	4	.963	1	109	70	O-38(32-4-3)/2-6,C-5	-0.6
1918	Cin N	47	108	14	32	5	1	0	14	19	1	5	.296	.406	.361	137	6	4	.929	-7	92	60	O-19(12-1-4),2-10/S-9,C-6	0.0
1919	Cin N	29	88	10	22	2	0	0	4	10	2	4	.250	.340	.273	88	-1	5	.982	3	101	192	O-25(7-0-18)/3	0.1
Total	4	151	379	36	86	10	1	1	31	50	4	33	.227	.323	.266	80	-8	13	.964	-4	103	111	/O-82L,2-18,S-14,C-11,3-11	-1.5
CUFF, JOHN John Patrick B 6.1864 Jersey City, NJ D 12.5.1916 Hoboken, NJ d9.11																								
1884	Bal U	3	11	1	1	1	0	0		1			.091	.167	.182	5	-2		.920	1			/C-3	-0.1
CULBERSON, LEON Delbert Leon "Lee" B 8.6.1919 Halls, GA D 9.17.1989 Rome, GA BR/TR 5-11/180# d5.16																								
1943	Bos A	81	312	36	85	16	6	3	34	31	0	35	.272	.338	.391	111	4	14-0	.978	2	98	150	O-79(28-51-0)	0.6
1944	Bos A	75	282	41	67	11	5	2	21	20	0	20	.238	.288	.333	78	-9	6-4	.979	-1	99	94	O-72(CF)	-1.2
1945	Bos A	97	331	26	91	21	6	6	45	20	0	37	.275	.316	.429	113	4	4-3	.967	3	96	190	O-91(1-89-1)	0.4
1946	†Bos A	59	179	34	56	10	1	3	18	16	0	19	.313	.369	.430	116	4	3-2	.967	-3	95	31	O-49(6-18-26)/3-4	-0.1
1947	Bos A	47	84	10	20	1	0	0	11	12	3	10	.238	.354	.250	65	-3	1-1	.974	-1	92	162	O-25(5-4-16)/3-4	-0.5
1948	Was A	12	29	1	5	0	0	0	2	8	0	5	.172	.351	.172	43	-2	0-0	1.000	-1	74	162	O-11(CF)	-0.3
Total	6	371	1217	148	324	59	18	14	131	107	3	126	.266	.327	.379	100	-2	28-10	.974	0	96	134	O-327(40-245-43)/3-8	-1.1
CULLEN, JOHN John Joseph B 7.9.1852 New Orleans, LA D 2.11.1921 Ukiah, CA d8.18																								
1884	Wil U	9	31	2	6	0	0	0		1			.194	.219	.194	25	-4		.750	-2	63	0	/O-6(4-0-2),S-3	-0.5
CULLEN, TIM Timothy Leo B 2.16.1942 San Francisco, CA BR/TR 6-1/185# d8.8																								
1966	Was A	18	34	8	8	1	0	0	0	2-0	0	8	.235	.278	.265	57	-2	0-0	.889	0	79	110	/3-8,2-5	-0.2
1967	Was A	124	402	35	95	7	0	2	31	40-2	1	47	.236	.306	.269	74	-12	4-5	.951	15	121	114	S-69,2-46,3-15/O(RF)	1.1
1968	Chi A	72	155	16	31	7	0	2	13	15-5	1	23	.200	.275	.284	69	-6	0-0	.966	-2	109	113	2-71	-0.4
	Was A	47	114	8	31	4	2	1	16	7-1	2	12	.272	.323	.368	113	2	0-0	.968	-4	93	83	S-33,2-16/3-3	0.0
	Year	119	269	24	62	11	2	3	29	22-6	3	35	.230	.295	.320	87	-4	0-0	.965	-7	109	107	2-87,S-33/3-3	-0.4
1969	Was A	119	249	22	52	7	0	1	15	14-1	2	27	.209	.253	.249	44	-19	1-1	.981	4	103	102	*2-105/S-9,3	-1.1
1970	Was A	123	262	22	56	10	2	1	18	31-6	3	38	.214	.301	.279	65	-12	3-2	**.994**	12	111	119	*2-112/S-6	0.6
1971	Was A	125	403	34	77	13	4	2	26	33-4	0	47	.191	.252	.258	47	-29	2-0	.997	15	113	99	2-78,S-62	-0.3
1972	†Oak A	72	142	10	37	8	1	0	15	5-0	0	17	.261	.286	.331	88	-3	0-1	.952	-4	100	93	2-65/3-4,S	-0.4
Total	7	700	1761	155	387	57	9	9	134	147-19	9	219	.220	.282	.278	65	-81	10-9	.979	36	108	107	2-498,S-180/3-31,O(RF)	-0.7
CULLENBINE, ROY Roy Joseph B 10.18.1913 Nashville, TN D 5.28.1991 Mt.Clemens, MI BB/TR 6-1/190# d4.19																								
1938	Det A	25	67	12	19	1	3	0	9	12	0	9	.284	.392	.388	91	-1	2-0	1.000	0	104	88	O-17(LF)	-0.1
1939	Det A	75	179	31	43	9	2	6	23	34	0	29	.240	.362	.413	91	-2	0-1	.902	-2	96	70	O-46(24-4-19)/1-2	-0.7
1940	Bro N	22	61	8	11	1	0	1	9	23	0	11	.180	.405	.246	78	0	2	1.000	1	93	206	O-19(RF)	-0.1
	StL A	86	257	41	59	11	2	7	31	50	2	34	.230	.359	.370	87	-3	0-1	.975	1	94	105	O-57(11-0-49)/1-6	-0.8
1941	StL A★	149	501	82	159	29	9	9	98	121	2	43	.317	.452	.465	138	36	6-4	.964	-1	94	113	*O-120(108-7-5),1-22	2.6
1942	StL A	38	109	15	21	7	1	2	14	30	0	20	.193	.367	.330	95	1	0-1	.930	1	81	228	O-27(LF)/1-5	-0.1
	Was A	64	241	30	69	19	0	2	35	44	0	18	.286	.396	.390	123	10	1-2	.966	6	108	222	O-35(LF),3-28	1.5
	†NY A	21	77	16	28	7	0	2	17	18	0	2	.364	.484	.532	190	11	0-1	.980	1	111	128	O-19(RF)/1	1.0
	Year	123	427	61	118	33	1	6	66	92	0	40	.276	.405	.400	127	22	1-4	.959	8	100	199	O-81(62-0-19),3-28/1-6	2.4
1943	Cle A	138	488	66	141	24	4	8	56	96	1	58	.289	.407	.404	146	34	3-4	.981	3	96	**157**	*O-121(RF),1-13	2.9
1944	Cle A☆	154	571	98	162	34	5	16	80	87	2	49	.284	.380	.445	141	33	4-4	.967	-3	89	142	*O-151(0-1-150)	2.0
1945	Cle A	8	13	3	1	1	0	0	0	11	0	0	.077	.500	.154	97	2	0-0	1.000	-1	105	0	/O-4(RF),3-3	0.0
	†Det A	146	523	80	145	27	5	18	93	102	3	36	.277	.398	.451	137	29	2-0	.980	9	105	152	*O-146(2-0-145)	3.1
	Year	154	536	83	146	28	5	18	93	**113**	3	36	.272	.402	.444	137	31	2-0	.980	8	105	**150**	*O-150(2-0-149)/3-3	3.1
1946	Det A	113	328	63	110	21	0	15	56	88	1	39	.335	.477	.537	172	39	3-0	.965	2	86	191	O-81(12-0-69),1-21	3.9
1947	Det A	142	464	82	104	18	1	24	78	137	0	51	.224	.401	.422	125	23	3-2	.989	18	**144**	90	*1-138	3.6
Total	10	1181	3879	627	1072	209	32	110	599	853	11	399	.276	.408	.432	132	212	26-20	.969	32	96	146	0-843(236-12-600),1-208/3-31	18.8
CULLER, DICK Richard Broadus B 1.15.1915 High Point, NC D 6.16.1964 Chapel Hill, NC BR/TR 5-9.5/155# d9.19																								
1936	Phi A	9	38	3	9	0	0	0	1	1	0	3	.237	.256	.237	23	-5	0-0	.946	-2	71	86	/2-7,S-2	-0.6
1943	Chi A	53	148	9	32	5	1	0	11	16	1	11	.216	.297	.264	65	-6	4-5	.950	7	98	188	3-26,2-19/S-3	0.1
1944	Bos N	8	28	2	2	0	0	0	0	4	0	2	.071	.188	.071	-24	-5	0	.904	1	120	117	/S-8	-0.3
1945	Bos N	136	527	87	138	12	1	2	30	50	2	35	.262	.328	.300	75	-17	7	.954	-9	99	103	*S-126/3-6	-1.7
1946	Bos N	134	482	70	123	15	3	0	33	62	2	18	.255	.342	.299	82	-10	7	.948	-4	95	92	*S-132	-0.6
1947	Bos N	77	214	20	53	5	1	0	19	19	0	15	.248	.309	.280	59	-13	1	.967	2	109	88	S-77	-0.7
1948	Chi N	48	89	4	15	2	0	0	5	13	0	3	.169	.275	.191	29	-9	0	.968	10	120	99	S-43/2-2	0.3
1949	NY N	7	1	0	0	0	0	0	0	1	0	0	.000	.500	.000	45	0	0	.889	1	141	307	/S-7	0.1
Total	8	472	1527	195	372	39	6	2	99	166	5	87	.244	.320	.281	68	-65	19-5	.954	4	102	96	S-398/3-32,2-28	-3.4
CULLOP, NICK Henry Nicholas "Tomato Face" (born Heinrich Nicholas Kolop) B 10.16.1900 St.Louis, MO D 12.8.1978 Westerville, OH BR/TR 6/200# d4.14																								
1926	NY A	2	2	0	1	0	0	0	0	0	0	1	.500	.500	.500	164	0	0-0	—	0			H	0.0
1927	Was A	15	23	2	5	2	0	0	1	1	0	6	.217	.250	.304	44	-2	0-0	1.000	-0	102	0	/O-5(2-0-3),1	-0.2
	Cle A	32	68	9	16	2	3	1	8	9	1	19	.235	.333	.397	88	-2	0-4	.982	2	110	199	O-20(0-13-7)/P	-0.1
	Year	47	91	11	21	4	3	1	9	10	1	25	.231	.314	.374	78	-3	0-4	.984	2	109	172	O-25(2-13-10)/1P	-0.3
1929	Bro N	13	41	7	8	2	2	1	5	8	0	7	.195	.327	.415	84	-1	0	1.000	1	92	222	O-11(5-6-2)/1	-0.1
1930	Cin N	7	22	2	4	0	0	1	5	1	0	9	.182	.217	.318	29	-3	0	1.000	1	70	651	/O-5(CF)	-0.2
1931	Cin N	104	334	29	88	23	7	8	48	21	1	86	.263	.309	.446	107	1	1	.968	1	101	115	O-83(LF)	-0.2
Total	5	173	490	49	122	29	12	11	67	40	2	128	.249	.308	.424	96	-7	1-4	.975	4	101	153	O-124(90-24-12)/1-2,P	-0.8
CULMER, WIL Wilfred Hillard B 11.11.1958 Nassau, Bahamas BR/TR 6-4/210# d4.12																								
1983	Cle A	7	19	0	2	0	0	0	1	0-0	0	4	.105	.100	.105	-40	-4	0-1	1.000	-1	32	0	/O-4(RF),D-2	-0.5
CULP, BENNY Benjamin Baldy B 1.19.1914 Philadelphia, PA D 10.23.2000 Philadelphia, PA BR/TR 5-9/175# d9.17 Mil 1944-45 C2																								
1942	Phi N	1	0	0	0	0	0	0	0	0	0	0	—	—	—	—	0	0	.500	-0	*0*	*0*	/C	0.0
1943	Phi N	10	24	4	5	1	0	0	2	3	0	3	.208	.296	.250	61	-1	0	.958	-1	*103*	*62*	C-10	-0.2
1944	Phi N	4	2	1	0	0	0	0	0	0	0	0	.000	.000	.000	-99	-1	0	1.000	-0	*0*	*0*	/C	-0.1
Total	3	15	26	5	5	1	0	0	2	3	0	3	.192	.276	.231	49	-2	0	.926	-2	*95*	*57*	/C-12	-0.3
CUMMINGS, JACK John William B 4.1.1904 Pittsburgh, PA D 10.5.1962 W.Mifflin, PA BR/TR 6/195# d9.11																								
1926	NY N	7	16	3	5	3	0	0	4	4	0	2	.313	.450	.500	157	2	0	.958	0	*87*	*149*	/C-6	0.2
1927	NY N	43	80	8	29	6	1	2	14	5	1	10	.363	.407	.538	151	6	0	.974	-3	*113*	*77*	C-34	0.4
1928	NY N	33	27	4	9	2	0	2	9	3	0	4	.333	.400	.630	165	2	0	.833	-0	*0*	*0*	/C-4	0.2
1929	NY N	3	3	0	1	0	0	0	0	0	0	0	.333	.333	.333	66	0	0	1.000	-0	*0*	*0*	/C	0.0
	Bos N	3	6	0	1	0	0	0	1	0	0	2	.167	.167	.167	-18	-1	0	.667	-1	*85*	*0*	/C-3	-0.2
	Year	6	9	0	2	0	0	0	1	0	0	2	.222	.222	.222	11	-1	0	.714	-1	*74*	*0*	/C-4	-0.2
Total	4	89	132	15	45	11	1	4	28	12	1	18	.341	.400	.530	145	9	0	.947	-4	*101*	*84*	/C-48	0.6
CUMMINGS, MIDRE Midre Almeric B 10.14.1971 St.Croix, V.I. BL/TR 6/196# d9.10																								
1993	Pit N	13	36	5	4	1	0	0	3	4-0	0	9	.111	.195	.139	-7	-6	0-0	1.000	-1	97	0	O-11(5-5-1)	-0.6
1994	Pit N	24	86	11	21	4	0	1	12	4-0	1	18	.244	.283	.326	58	-5	0-0	.962	-0	104	67	O-24(18-5-4)	-0.6
1995	Pit N	59	152	13	37	7	1	2	15	13-3	0	30	.243	.303	.342	68	-7	1-0	.988	2	110	98	O-41(8-20-14)	-0.6
1996	Pit N	24	85	11	19	3	1	3	7	0-0	0	16	.224	.221	.388	56	-6	0-0	.980	-0	98	0	O-21(0-11-10)	-0.6
1997	Pit N	52	106	11	20	6	2	3	8	8-0	1	26	.189	.252	.368	59	-7	0-0	1.000	-1	98	71	O-25(14-0-11)	-0.8
	Phi N	63	208	24	63	16	4	1	23	23-0	0	30	.303	.369	.433	110	4	2-3	.991	-0	106	44	O-54(0-53-2)	0.3
	Year	115	314	35	83	22	6	4	31	31-0	1	56	.264	.330	.411	93	-4	2-3	.993	-1	104	52	O-79(14-53-13)	-0.5
1998	†Bos A	67	120	20	34	8	0	5	15	17-0	2	19	.283	.381	.475	118	4	3-3	.941	-1	85	0	D-29,O-17(RF)	0.0
1999	Min A	16	38	1	10	0	0	1	9	3-0	0	7	.263	.310	.342	66	-2	2-0	1.000	-1	75	0	/O-5(1-0-5),D-5	-0.2
2000	Min A	77	181	28	50	10	0	4	22	11-1	3	25	.276	.328	.398	79	-6	0-0	1.000	4	110	226	O-40(7-0-33),D-15	-0.4
	Bos A	21	25	1	7	0	0	0	2	6-0	0	3	.280	.419	.280	80	0	0-0	1.000	-0	106	0	/O-4(0-1-3),D	-0.1
	Year	98	206	29	57	10	0	4	24	17-1	3	28	.277	.341	.383	80	-6	0-0	1.000	3	110	201	O-44(7-1-36),D-16	-0.5
2001	†Ari N	20	20	1	6	1	0	0	1	0-0	0	4	.300	.286	.350	63	-1	0-0	1.000	0	216	0	/O-4(3-0-1)	-0.1
Total	9	436	1057	126	271	56	8	20	117	89-4	7	187	.256	.316	.381	79	-32	8-6	.987	2	105	72	O-246(56-95-101)/D-50	-3.7

Year	Tm Lg	G	AB	R	H	2B	3B	HR	RBI	BB-IB	HP	SO	AVG	OBP	SLG	AOPS	ABR	SB-CS	FA	FR	Rng	Thr	G at Pos	BFW
CUNNINGHAM, JOE Joseph Robert B 8.27.1931 Paterson, NJ BL/TL 6-1/190# d6.30 C1																								
1954	StL N	85	310	40	88	11	3	11	50	43	2	40	.284	.375	.445	112	6	1-1	.989	1	107	119	1-85	0.2
1956	StL N	4	3	1	0	0	0	0	0	1-0	0	1	.000	.250	.000	-25	-1	0-0	1.000	-0	0	0	/1	-0.1
1957	StL N	122	261	50	83	15	0	9	52	56-6	5	29	.318	.439	.479	146	22	3-3	1.000	-5	78	73	1-57,O-46(RF)	1.3
1958	StL N	131	337	61	105	20	3	12	57	82-3	3	23	.312	.449	.496	144	28	4-4	.997	-4	87	52	1-67,O-66(24-0-42)	1.9
1959	StL N★	144	458	65	158	28	6	7	60	88-9	5	47	.345	**.453**	.478	140	33	2-6	.972	-1	108	64	*O-121(20-0-109),1-35	2.5
1960	StL N	139	492	68	138	28	3	6	39	59-4	6	59	.280	.363	.386	97	1	1-7	.950	-6	95	61	*O-116(1-0-116),1-15	-1.3
1961	StL N	113	322	60	92	11	2	7	40	53-3	**11**	32	.286	.403	.398	104	5	1-0	.964	-7	95	29	O-86(1-1-85),1-10	-0.8
1962	Chi A	149	526	91	155	32	7	8	70	101-3	7	59	.295	.410	.428	128	27	3-3	**.994**	-5	86	103	*1-143/O-5(RF)	1.2
1963	Chi A	67	210	32	60	12	1	1	31	33-2	4	23	.286	.388	.367	116	7	1-0	.989	-6	63	94	1-58	-0.2
1964	Chi A	40	108	13	27	7	0	0	10	14-1	3	15	.250	.352	.315	90	-1	0-1	.996	-1	91	129	1-33	-0.3
	Was A	49	126	15	27	4	0	0	7	23-0	2	13	.214	.344	.246	68	-4	0-1	.997	-4	57	100	1-41	-1.1
	Year	89	234	28	54	11	0	0	17	37-1	5	28	.231	.348	.278	78	-5	0-2	.997	-5	72	113	1-74	-1.4
1965	Was A	95	201	29	46	9	1	3	20	46-0	1	27	.229	.375	.328	103	4	0-1	.986	-3	79	108	1-59	-0.3
1966	Was A	3	8	0	1	0	0	0	0	0-0	0	1	.125	.125	.125	-28	-1	0-0	1.000	1	347	73	/1-3	0.0
Total	12	1141	3362	525	980	177	26	64	436	599-31	49	369	.291	.403	.417	119	126	16-27	.993	-40	84	101	1-607,O-440(46-1-403)	3.0
CUNNINGHAM, RAY Raymond Lee B 1.17.1905 Mesquite, TX BR/TR 5-7.5/150# d9.16																								
1931	StL N	3	4	0	0	0	0	0	1	0	0	0	.000	.000	.000	-96	-1	0	1.000	1	184	0	/3-3	0.0
1932	StL N	11	22	4	4	1	0	0	0	3	0	4	.182	.280	.227	37	-2	0	1.000	2	92	0	/3-8,2-2	0.0
Total	2	14	26	4	4	1	0	0	1	3	0	4	.154	.241	.192	18	-3	0	1.000	2	109	0	/3-11,2-2	0.0
CUNNINGHAM, BILL William Aloysius B 7.30.1895 San Francisco, CA D 9.26.1953 Colusa, CA BR/TR 5-8/155# d7.14 C1																								
1921	NY N	40	76	10	21	2	1	1	12	3	1	3	.276	.313	.368	79	-2	0-1	1.000	-1	97	49	O-20(1-18-1)	-0.4
1922	†NY N	85	229	37	75	15	2	2	33	7	1	9	.328	.350	.437	101	0	4-5	.988	-1	96	93	O-71(2-68-0)/3	-0.4
1923	†NY N	79	203	22	55	7	1	5	27	10	0	9	.271	.305	.389	83	-6	5-2	.992	-1	89	120	O-68(10-58-0)/2-4	-0.8
1924	Bos N	114	437	44	119	15	8	1	40	32	3	27	.272	.326	.350	85	-10	8-5	.970	5	102	141	*O-109(95-15-0)	-1.2
Total	4	318	945	113	270	39	12	9	112	52	5	48	.286	.326	.381	88	-18	17-13	.982	3	97	119	O-268(108-159-1)/2-4,3	-2.8
CUNNINGHAM, BILL William John B 6.9.1888 Schenectady, NY D 2.21.1946 Schenectady, NY BR/TR 5-9/170# d9.12																								
1910	Was A	21	74	3	22	5	1	0	14	12	1		.297	.402	.392	156	6	4	.957	-2	94	105	2-21	0.5
1911	Was A	94	331	34	63	10	5	3	37	19	2		.190	.239	.278	45	-26	10	.932	-9	98	59	2-93	-3.4
1912	Was A	8	27	5	5	1	0	1	8	3	0		.185	.267	.333	71	-1	2	.962	-2	95	47	/2-7,S	-0.3
Total	3	123	432	42	90	16	6	4	59	34	3		.208	.271	.301	64	-21	16	.938	-12	97	66	2-121/S	-3.2
CURLEY, DOC Walter James B 3.12.1874 Upton, MA D 9.23.1920 Worcester, MA BR/TR d9.12																								
1899	Chi N	10	37	7	4	0	1	0	2	3	3		.108	.233	.162	9	-5	0	.907	-3	95	58	2-10	-0.7
CURREN, PETE Peter B Baltimore, MD ?/175# d9.12																								
1876	Phi N	3	12	5	4	1	0	0	2	0		0	.333	.333	.417	150	1		.588	-2			/C-2,O(RF)	-0.1
CURRIN, PERRY Perry Gilmore B 9.27.1928 Washington, DC BL/TR 6/175# d6.29																								
1947	StL A	3	2	0	0	0	0	0	0	1	0	0	.000	.333	.000	-3	0	0-0	1.000	1	115	477	/S	0.0
CURRY, TONY George Anthony B 12.22.1938 Nassau, Bahamas BL/TL 5-11/185# d4.12																								
1960	Phi N	95	245	26	64	14	2	6	34	16-2	1	53	.261	.308	.408	94	-2	0-2	.925	-4	94	44	O-64(51-3-14)	-1.1
1961	Phi N	15	36	3	7	2	0	0	3	1-0	0	8	.194	.216	.250	24	-4	0-0	.833	0	67	387	/O-8(LF)	-0.4
1966	Cle A	19	16	4	2	0	0	0	3	3-0	0	8	.125	.263	.125	16	-2	0-0	—	0			H	-0.2
Total	3	129	297	33	73	16	2	6	40	20-2	1	69	.246	.295	.374	82	-8	0-2	.915	-4	91	82	/O-72(59-3-14)	-1.7
CURRY, JIM James L. B 3.10.1893 Camden, NJ D 8.2.1938 Grenloch, NJ BR/TR 5-11/160# d10.2																								
1909	Phi A	1	4	1	1	0	0	0	0	0	0		.250	.250	.250	57	0	0	1.000	-0	105	0	/2	-0.1
1911	NY A	4	11	3	2	0	0	0	0	1	0		.182	.250	.182	20	-1	0	.773	-2	56	78	/2-4	-0.3
1918	Det A	5	20	1	5	1	0	0	0	0	1	0	.250	.286	.300	80	-1	0	.952	-2	92	0	/2-5	-0.2
Total	3	10	35	5	8	1	0	0	0	1	1	0	.229	.270	.257	56	-2	0	.867	-4	78	32	/2-10	-0.6
CURTIS, CHAD Chad David B 11.6.1968 Marion, IN BR/TR 5-10/175# d4.8																								
1992	Cal A	139	441	59	114	16	2	10	46	51-2	6	71	.259	.341	.372	100	1	43-18	.978	1	90	**199**	*O-135(48-35-62)/D	0.1
1993	Cal A	152	583	94	166	25	3	6	59	70-2	4	89	.285	.361	.369	95	-2	48-24	.980	7	105	155	*O-151(CF)/2-3	0.8
1994	Cal A	114	453	67	116	23	4	11	50	37-0	5	69	.256	.317	.397	82	-13	25-11	.988	7	109	146	*O-114(CF)	-0.3
1995	Det A	**144**	586	96	157	29	3	21	67	70-3	7	93	.268	.349	.435	104	4	27-15	.992	-8	93	66	*O-144(CF)	-0.2
1996	Det A	104	400	65	105	20	1	10	37	53-0	1	73	.262	.346	.393	88	-7	16-10	.965	-2	98	92	*O-104(48-80-0)	-0.9
	†LA N	43	104	20	22	5	0	2	9	17-0	0	15	.212	.322	.317	75	-3	2-1	.985	1	102	150	O-40(CF)	-0.2
1997	Cle A	22	29	8	6	1	0	3	5	7-0	0	10	.207	.361	.552	129	1	0-0	1.000	-0	104	0	O-19(3-12-4)	0.1
	†NY A	93	320	51	93	21	1	12	50	36-1	5	49	.291	.362	.475	120	10	12-6	.978	-5	87	117	O-92(53-43-5)	0.4
	Year	115	349	59	99	22	1	15	55	43-1	5	59	.284	.362	.481	120	11	12-6	.980	-5	88	107	*O-111(56-55-9)	0.5
1998	†NY A	151	456	79	111	21	1	10	56	75-3	7	80	.243	.355	.360	91	-3	21-5	.984	4	108	99	*O-148(100-45-9)/D-2	0.1
1999	†NY A	96	195	37	51	6	0	5	24	43-0	3	35	.262	.398	.369	100	2	8-4	.990	-4	86	55	O-81(72-6-3),D-14	-0.4
2000	Tex A	108	335	48	91	25	1	8	48	37-0	1	71	.272	.343	.424	92	-3	3-3	.965	-2	96	91	O-80(51-0-30),D-16	-0.9
2001	Tex A	38	115	24	29	3	0	3	10	14-0	1	21	.252	.338	.357	81	-3	7-1	.988	3	120	112	O-33(10-16-9)/D-2	0.1
Total	10	1204	4017	648	1061	195	16	101	461	510-11	40	676	.264	.349	.396	96	-16	212-98	.982	1	99	118	*O-1141(385-686-122)/D-35,2-3	-1.3
CURTIS, ERVIN Ervin Duane B 12.27.1861 Coldwater, MI D 2.14.1945 N.Adams, MA BL/TL 5-8.5/157# d7.15																								
1891	Cin N	27	108	11	29	3	3	1	13	9	1	19	.269	.331	.380	106	0	3	.862	-2	136	134	O-27(0-24-3)	-0.2
	Was AA	29	103	17	26	3	2	0	12	13	2	16	.252	.347	.320	96	0	2	.797	-1	141	0	O-29(0-20-9)	-0.2
Total	1	56	211	28	55	6	5	1	25	22	3	35	.261	.339	.351	101	0	5	.829	-3	138	68	/O-56(0-44-12)	-0.4
CURTIS, GENE Eugene Holmes "Eude" B 5.5.1883 Bethany, WV D 1.1.1919 Steubenville, OH BR/TR 6-3/220# d9.21																								
1903	Pit N	5	19	2	8	1	0	0	3	1	0		.421	.450	.474	158	1	0	.833	-1	129	0	/O-5(LF)	0.1
CURTIS, FRED Frederick Marion B 10.30.1880 Beaver Lake, MI D 4.5.1939 Minneapolis, MN BR/TR 6-1/?# d7.24																								
1905	NY A	2	9	0	2	1	0	0	2	1	0		.222	.300	.333	90	0	1	1.000	-0	72	0	/1-2	0.0
CURTIS, HARRY Harry Albert B 2.19.1883 Portland, ME D 8.1.1951 Evanston, IL TR 5-10.5/170# d8.28																								
1907	NY N	6	9	2	2	0	0	0	1	2	0		.222	.364	.222	81	0	2	.909	-0	*112*	107	/C-6	0.0
CURTRIGHT, GUY Guy Paxton B 10.18.1912 Holliday, MO D 8.23.1997 Sun City Center, FL BR/TR 5-11/200# d4.21																								
1943	Chi A	138	488	67	142	20	7	3	48	69	3	60	.291	.382	.379	123	17	13-12	.972	-2	102	66	*O-128(LF)	0.6
1944	Chi A	72	198	22	50	8	2	2	23	23	0	21	.253	.330	.343	94	-1	4-3	.948	3	98	207	O-51(35-0-17)	-0.2
1945	Chi A	98	324	51	91	15	7	4	32	39	0	29	.281	.358	.407	125	10	3-4	.986	1	100	110	O-84(26-46-13)	0.7
1946	Chi A	23	55	7	11	2	0	0	5	11	0	14	.200	.333	.236	63	-2	0-1	1.000	1	99	164	O-15(2-2-11)	-0.2
Total	4	331	1065	147	294	45	16	9	108	142	3	124	.276	.363	.374	115	24	20-20	.973	2	101	109	O-278(191-48-41)	0.9
CUSICK, TONY Andrew Daniel "Andy" B 12.1857 Fall River, MA D 8.6.1929 Chicago, IL BR/TR 5-9.5/190# d8.21																								
1884	Wil U	11	34	0	5	0	0	0		1			.147	.171	.147	-3	-5		.871	0			/C-6,S-3,O-3(1-1-1),23	-0.4
	Phi N	9	29	2	4	0	0	0	1	0		3	.138	.138	.138	-14	-4		.930	2			/C-9	-0.1
1885	Phi N	39	141	12	25	1	0	0	5	1		24	.177	.183	.184	19	-13		.808	-5			C-38/O(CF)	-1.4
1886	Phi N	29	104	10	23	5	1	0	4	3		14	.221	.243	.288	61	-5	1	.891	-3			C-25/O-3(1-0-2),1	-0.6
1887	Phi N	7	24	3	7	1	0	0	5	3	1	1	.292	.393	.333	98	0	0	.643	-4			/C-4,1-3,2	-0.3
Total	4	95	332	27	64	7	1	0	15	8	1	42	.193	.214	.220	35	-27	1	.844	-10			/C-82,O-7(2-2-3),1-4,S-3,2-2,3	-2.8
CUSICK, JACK John Peter B 6.12.1928 Weehawken, NJ D 11.17.1989 Englewood, NJ BR/TR 6/170# d4.24																								
1951	Chi N	65	164	16	29	3	2	2	16	17	0	29	.177	.254	.256	37	-15	2-1	.953	-2	104	78	S-56	-1.4
1952	Bos N	49	78	5	13	1	0	0	6	6	0	9	.167	.226	.179	14	-9	0-1	.969	-3	89	31	S-28/3-3	-1.1
Total	2	114	242	21	42	4	2	2	22	23	0	38	.174	.245	.231	30	-24	2-2	.958	-4	100	65	/S-84,3-3	-2.5
CUST, JACK John Joseph B 1.16.1979 Flemington, NJ BL/TR 6-2/200# d9.26																								
2001	Ari N	3	2	0	1	0	0	0	0	1-0	0	0	.500	.667	.500	197	0	0-0	—	-0	0	0	/O(LF)	0.0
2002	Col N	35	65	8	11	2	0	1	8	12-0	0	32	.169	.295	.246	42	-6	0-1	.960	-1	92	0	O-18(LF)	-0.8

Year	Tm Lg	G	AB	R	H	2B	3B	HR	RBI	BB-IB	HP	SO	AVG	OBP	SLG	AOPS	ABR	SB-CS	FA	FR	Rng	Thr	G at Pos	BFW
2003	Bal A	27	73	7	19	7	0	4	11	10-0	1	25	.260	.357	.521	133	4	0-0	1.000	0	254	0	D-23/O(LF)	0.2
Total	3	65	140	15	31	9	0	5	19	23-0	1	57	.221	.333	.393	88	-2	0-1	.964	-1	97	0	/D-23,O-20(LF)	-0.6

CUTHBERT, NED Edgar Edward B 6.20.1845 Philadelphia, PA D 2.6.1905 St.Louis, MO BR/TR 5-6/140# d5.20 M1 U1

Year	Tm Lg	G	AB	R	H	2B	3B	HR	RBI	BB-IB	HP	SO	AVG	OBP	SLG	AOPS	ABR	SB-CS	FA	FR	Rng	Thr	G at Pos	BFW
1871	Ath NA	**28**	150	47	37	7	5	3	30	10		2	.247	.294	.420	103	1	16-2	.890	4	93	0	*O-27(LF)/C	0.5
1872	Ath NA	**47**	260	83	88	10	0	1	47	6		10	.338	.353	.388	127	8	14-4	.858	-3	39	0	*O-47(LF)	0.6
1873	Phi NA	51	279	78	77	5	3	2	34	2		4	.276	.281	.337	80	-8	14-2	.842	-6	27	76	*O-51(LF)	-0.7
1874	Chi NA	58	295	65	79	6	1	2	24	5		5	.268	.280	.315	90	-3	8-0	.806	-1	121	66	*O-55(55-2-0)/C-4	0.0
1875	StL NA	68	319	68	78	9	2	0	17	3		8	.245	.252	.285	95	0	18-1	.860	-12	18	0	*O-67(65-2-0)/C-3,2	-0.5
1876	StL N	63	283	46	70	10	1	0	25	7		4	.247	.266	.290	90	-2		.843	-7	68	125	*O-63(LF)	-1.1
1877	Cin N	12	56	6	10	5	0	0	2	1		2	.179	.193	.268	49	-3		.830	4	219	413	O-12(LF)	0.1
1882	StL AA	60	233	28	52	16	5	0		17			.223	.276	.335	101	1		.896	-3	90	0	*O-60(LF),M	-0.3
1883	StL AA	21	71	3	12	1	0	0	3	4			.169	.213	.183	27	-6		.794	-1	127	0	O-20(18-1-1)/1	-0.7
1884	Bal U	44	168	29	34	5	0	0		10			.202	.247	.232	42	-17		.750	-5	104	0	O-44(CF)	-2.0
Total	5 NA	252	1303	341	359	37	11	8	152	26		29	.276	.290	.339	98	-2	70-9	.000	-18	56	31	O-247(245-4-0)/C-8,2	-0.1
Total	5	200	811	112	178	37	6	0	30	39		6	.219	.255	.280	73	-27		.833	-11	98	68	O-199(153-45-1)/1	-4.0

CUTSHAW, GEORGE George William "Clancy" B 7.29.1886 Wilmington, IL D 8.22.1973 San Diego, CA BR/TR 5-9/160# d4.25

Year	Tm Lg	G	AB	R	H	2B	3B	HR	RBI	BB-IB	HP	SO	AVG	OBP	SLG	AOPS	ABR	SB-CS	FA	FR	Rng	Thr	G at Pos	BFW
1912	Bro N	102	357	41	100	14	4	0	28	31	2	16	.280	.341	.342	91	-4	16	.958	4	108	80	2-91/3-5,S	0.1
1913	Bro N	147	592	72	158	23	13	7	80	39	3	22	.267	.315	.385	97	-5	39-17	.957	17	101	134	*2-147	1.8
1914	Bro N	153	583	69	150	22	12	2	78	30	3	32	.257	.297	.346	89	-10	34	.959	28	99	127	*2-153	2.1
1915	Bro N	**154**	566	68	139	18	9	0	62	34	4	35	.246	.293	.309	81	-14	28-23	**.971**	14	106	82	*2-154	0.1
1916	†Bro N	154	581	58	151	21	4	2	63	25	1	32	.260	.292	.320	85	-11	27-20	.958	6	101	88	*2-154	-0.4
1917	Bro N	135	487	42	126	17	7	4	49	21	2	26	.259	.292	.347	93	-5	22	.963	-11	94	71	*2-134	-1.6
1918	Pit N	**126**	463	56	132	16	10	5	68	27	1	18	.285	.326	.395	116	7	25	.964	-3	93	119	*2-126	0.7
1919	Pit N	**139**	512	49	124	15	8	3	51	30	2	22	.242	.287	.320	79	-14	36	**.980**	-9	89	107	*2-139	-2.2
1920	Pit N	131	488	56	123	16	8	0	47	23	1	10	.252	.287	.318	71	-19	17-14	.968	1	97	105	*2-129	-1.8
1921	Pit N	98	350	46	119	18	4	0	53	11	1	11	.340	.362	.414	102	1	14-5	.951	-23	85	92	2-84	-1.8
1922	Det A	132	499	57	133	14	8	2	61	20	4	13	.267	.300	.339	68	-25	11-5	.972	5	101	97	*2-132	-1.6
1923	Det A	45	143	15	32	1	2	0	13	9	2	5	.224	.279	.259	43	-12	2-1	.988	8	116	86	2-43/3-2	-0.4
Total	12	1516	5621	629	1487	195	89	25	653	300	26	242	.265	.305	.344	86	-111	271-85	.965	37	98	101	*2-1486/3-7,S	-5.0

CUYLER, KIKI Hazen Shirley B 8.30.1898 Harrisville, MI D 2.11.1950 Ann Arbor, MI BR/TR 5-10.5/180# d9.29 C4 HF1968

Year	Tm Lg	G	AB	R	H	2B	3B	HR	RBI	BB-IB	HP	SO	AVG	OBP	SLG	AOPS	ABR	SB-CS	FA	FR	Rng	Thr	G at Pos	BFW
1921	Pit N	1	3	0	0	0	0	0	0	0	0	1	.000	.000	.000	-97	-1	0-0	1.000	-0	90	0	/O(RF)	-0.1
1922	Pit N	1	0	0	0	0	0	0	0	0	0	0	—	—	—	—	0	0-0	—	0			R	0.0
1923	Pit N	11	40	4	10	1	1	0	2	5	1	3	.250	.348	.325	77	-1	2-3	.931	-0	105	88	O-11(10-3-0)	-0.3
1924	Pit N	117	466	94	165	27	16	9	85	30	7	62	.354	.402	.539	147	30	32-11	.943	3	98	145	*O-114(78-4-35)	2.7
1925	†Pit N	**153**	617	**144**	220	43	**26**	18	102	58	**13**	56	.357	.423	.598	148	44	41-13	.967	2	104	97	*O-153(0-25-129)	3.6
1926	Pit N	**157**	614	**113**	197	31	15	8	92	50	9	66	.321	.380	.459	119	16	**35**	.968	7	106	117	*O-157(62-79-18)	1.3
1927	Pit N	85	285	60	88	13	7	3	31	37	3	36	.309	.394	.435	114	7	20	.980	0	105	76	O-73(12-49-13)	0.3
1928	Chi N	133	499	92	142	25	9	17	79	51	7	61	.285	.359	.473	117	12	**37**	.982	1	91	140	*O-127(13-7-108)	0.2
1929	†Chi N	139	509	111	183	29	7	15	102	66	5	56	.360	.438	.532	139	34	**43**	.974	1	98	110	*O-129(16-8-114)	2.2
1930	Chi N	**156**	642	155	228	50	17	13	134	72	**10**	49	.355	.428	.547	133	37	**37**	.980	6	104	108	*O-156(29-0-131)	2.6
1931	Chi N	154	613	110	202	37	12	9	88	72	5	54	.330	.404	.473	133	31	13	.970	-9	93	68	*O-153(0-66-84)	1.5
1932	†Chi N	110	446	58	130	19	9	10	77	29	4	43	.291	.340	.442	109	5	9	.969	-11	87	65	*O-109(0-49-60)	-1.1
1933	Chi N	70	262	37	83	13	3	5	35	21	4	29	.317	.376	.447	135	12	4	.978	-5	91	39	O-69(35-15-19)	0.4
1934	Chi N★	142	559	80	189	**42**	8	6	69	31	4	62	.338	.377	.474	129	23	15	.971	-3	90	151	*O-142(0-136-6)	1.5
1935	Chi N	45	157	22	42	5	1	4	18	10	5	16	.268	.331	.389	92	-2	3	.981	-1	91	147	O-42(0-41-2)	-0.3
	Cin N	62	223	36	56	8	3	2	22	27	2	18	.251	.337	.341	85	-4	5	.985	-4	85	109	O-57(5-49-3)	-0.9
	Year	107	380	58	98	13	4	6	40	37	7	34	.258	.335	.361	88	-6	8	.983	-4	88	125	O-99(5-90-5)	-1.2
1936	Cin N	144	567	96	185	29	11	7	74	47	2	67	.326	.380	.453	132	25	16	.974	-5	94	87	*O-140(22-105-14)	1.5
1937	Cin N	117	406	48	110	12	4	0	32	36	2	50	.271	.333	.320	82	-10	10	.973	-5	86	107	*O-106(41-47-16)	-1.9
1938	Bro N	82	253	45	69	10	8	2	23	34	2	23	.273	.363	.399	107	3	6	.993	3	98	171	O-68(8-17-43)	0.3
Total	18	1879	7161	1305	2299	394	157	128	1065	676	85	752	.321	.386	.474	125	261	328-27	.972	-20	96	108	*O-1807(331-700-796)	13.5

CUYLER, MILT Milton B 10.7.1968 Macon, GA BB/TR 5-10/185# d9.6

Year	Tm Lg	G	AB	R	H	2B	3B	HR	RBI	BB-IB	HP	SO	AVG	OBP	SLG	AOPS	ABR	SB-CS	FA	FR	Rng	Thr	G at Pos	BFW
1990	Det A	19	51	8	13	3	1	0	8	5-0	0	10	.255	.316	.353	88	-1	1-2	.976	0	91	245	O-17(0-17-1)	-0.1
1991	Det A	154	475	77	122	15	7	3	33	52-0	5	92	.257	.335	.337	86	-9	41-10	.986	3	107	91	*O-151(1-150-0)	-0.1
1992	Det A	89	291	39	70	11	1	3	28	10-0	4	62	.241	.275	.316	65	-15	8-5	.983	-4	95	80	O-89(0-88-1)	-2.0
1993	Det A	82	249	46	53	11	7	0	19	19-0	3	53	.213	.276	.313	59	-16	13-2	.968	1	110	50	O-80(CF)	-1.1
1994	Det A	48	116	20	28	3	1	1	11	13-0	1	21	.241	.318	.310	64	-6	5-3	.975	-3	85	47	O-45(13-29-8)	-0.9
1995	Det A	41	88	15	18	1	4	0	5	8-0	0	16	.205	.271	.307	50	-7	2-1	.929	-1	92	111	O-36(34-1-1)/D-2	-0.9
1996	Bos A	50	110	19	22	1	2	2	12	13-0	3	19	.200	.299	.300	52	-9	7-3	.972	2	128	0	O-45(0-30-22)/D-2	-0.6
1998	Tex A	7	6	3	3	2	0	1	3	1-0	0	0	.500	.571	1.333	360	2	0-0	1.000	0	106	0	/O-3(CF),D-3	0.2
Total	8	490	1386	227	329	47	23	10	119	121-0	16	273	.237	.305	.326	71	-61	77-26	.977	-1	103	77	O-466(48-398-33)/D-7	-5.5

CYPERT, AL Alfred Boyd "Cy" B 8.8.1889 Little Rock, AR D 1.9.1973 Washington, DC BR/TR 5-10.5/150# d6.27

Year	Tm Lg	G	AB	R	H	2B	3B	HR	RBI	BB-IB	HP	SO	AVG	OBP	SLG	AOPS	ABR	SB-CS	FA	FR	Rng	Thr	G at Pos	BFW
1914	Cle A	1	1	0	0	0	0	0	0	0	0	1	.000	.000	.000	-96	0	0	—	-0	0	0	/3	0.0

DADE, PAUL Lonnie Paul B 12.7.1951 Seattle, WA BR/TR 6/195# d9.12

Year	Tm Lg	G	AB	R	H	2B	3B	HR	RBI	BB-IB	HP	SO	AVG	OBP	SLG	AOPS	ABR	SB-CS	FA	FR	Rng	Thr	G at Pos	BFW
1975	Cal A	11	30	5	6	4	0	0	1	6-0	0	7	.200	.333	.333	96	0	0-0	1.000	1	145	0	/O-3(1-0-2),3D	0.1
1976	Cal A	13	9	2	1	0	0	0	1	3-0	0	3	.111	.333	.111	36	-1	0-0	.750	1	88	1254	/O-4(3-0-1),2-2,3D	0.1
1977	Cle A	134	461	65	134	15	3	3	45	32-4	2	58	.291	.333	.356	93	-5	16-8	.989	-2	87	156	O-99(32-28-46),3-26/2D	-1.0
1978	Cle A	93	307	37	78	12	1	3	20	34-1	2	45	.254	.331	.329	88	-4	12-9	.962	3	109	111	O-81(1-7-75)/D-9	-0.6
1979	Cle A	44	170	22	48	4	1	3	18	12-1	0	22	.282	.326	.371	88	-3	12-6	.962	1	100	151	O-37(20-0-17)/3-2,D-4	-0.4
	SD N	76	283	38	78	19	2	1	19	14-0	2	48	.276	.311	.367	91	-4	13-5	.949	5	115	101	3-70/O-4(1-3-0)	0.1
1980	SD N	68	53	17	10	0	0	0	3	12-0	0	10	.189	.338	.189	54	-3	4-5	.846	-1	97	80	3-21/O-8(4-3-1),2	-0.5
Total	6	439	1313	186	355	54	7	10	107	113-6	6	193	.270	.328	.345	89	-20	57-33	.970	6	97	150	O-236(62-41-142),3-121/D-28,2-4	-2.2

DAGRES, ANGELO Angelo George "Junior" B 8.22.1934 Newburyport, MA BL/TL 5-11/175# d9.11

Year	Tm Lg	G	AB	R	H	2B	3B	HR	RBI	BB-IB	HP	SO	AVG	OBP	SLG	AOPS	ABR	SB-CS	FA	FR	Rng	Thr	G at Pos	BFW
1955	Bal A	8	15	5	4	0	0	0	3	1-0	0	2	.267	.278	.267	61	-1	0-0	.818	-1	100	0	/O-5(1-0-4)	-0.2

DAHLEN, BILL William Frederick "Bad Bill" B 1.5.1870 Nelliston, NY D 12.5.1950 Brooklyn, NY BR/TR 5-9/180# d4.22 M4 OF Total (36-LF 11-CF 11-RF)

Year	Tm Lg	G	AB	R	H	2B	3B	HR	RBI	BB-IB	HP	SO	AVG	OBP	SLG	AOPS	ABR	SB-CS	FA	FR	Rng	Thr	G at Pos	BFW
1891	Chi N	135	549	114	143	18	13	9	76	67	7	60	.260	.348	.390	115	10	21	.887	4	108	108	3-84,O-37(30-0-7),S-15	1.4
1892	Chi N	143	581	114	170	23	19	5	58	45	5	56	.293	.349	.423	132	19	60	.909	15	91	113	S-72,3-68/O-2(CF),2	3.6
1893	Chi N	116	485	113	146	28	15	5	64	58	5	30	.301	.381	.452	123	16	31	.892	6	101	86	*S-88,O-17(5-8-4),2-10/3-3	2.1
1894	Chi N	122	507	150	182	32	14	15	108	76	3	33	.359	.445	.566	135	29	43	.900	26	107	129	S-67,3-55	4.5
1895	Chi N	129	516	106	131	19	10	7	62	61	10	51	.254	.344	.370	79	-17	38	.904	35	**119**	128	*S-129/O(CF)	1.9
1896	Chi N	125	474	137	167	30	19	9	74	64	8	36	.352	.438	.553	154	38	51	.915	22	107	120	*S-125	5.5
1897	Chi N	75	276	67	80	18	8	6	40	43	7		.290	.399	.478	126	11	15	.930	24	110	152	S-75	3.3
1898	Chi N	142	521	96	151	35	8	1	79	58	23		.290	.385	.393	123	20	27	.921	20	**108**	**138**	*S-142	4.3
1899	Bro N	121	428	87	121	22	7	4	76	67	15		.283	.398	.395	115	13	29	.941	14	100	116	*S-110,3-11	2.9
1900	†Bro N	133	483	87	125	16	11	1	69	73	7		.259	.364	.344	90	-4	31	.938	21	107	110	*S-133	2.1
1901	Bro N	131	511	69	136	17	9	4	82	30	5		.266	.313	.358	92	-6	23	.929	14	103	97	*S-129/2-2	1.1
1902	Bro N	138	527	67	139	25	8	2	74	43	8		.264	.329	.353	110	6	20	.916	-6	98	76	*S-138	0.6
1903	Bro N	138	474	71	124	17	9	1	64	82	2		.262	.373	.342	107	9	34	**.948**	19	**109**	99	*S-138	3.1
1904	NY N	145	523	70	140	26	2	2	**80**	44	1		.268	.326	.337	100	1	47	.930	25	**108**	**139**	*S-145	3.2
1905	†NY N	148	520	67	126	20	4	7	81	62	12		.242	.337	.337	99	2	37	.948	20	102	114	*S-147/O(LF)	2.7
1906	NY N	143	471	63	113	18	3	1	49	76	10		.240	.357	.297	102	6	16	.938	2	101	79	*S-143	1.4
1907	NY N	143	464	40	96	20	1	0	34	51	4		.207	.291	.254	69	-15	11	.941	6	100	88	*S-143	-0.4
1908	Bos N	144	524	50	125	23	2	3	48	35	8		.239	.296	.307	94	-3	10	.952	**38**	**120**	**131**	*S-144	4.5
1909	Bos N	69	197	22	46	6	1	2	16	29	0		.234	.332	.305	93	-1	4	.908	6	117	99	S-49/2-6,3-2	0.8
1910	Bro N	3	2	0	0	0	0	0	0	0	0	0	.000	.000	.000	-99	-1	0	—	0			HM	-0.1
1911	Bro N	1	3	0	0	0	0	0	0	0	0	3	.000	.000	.000	-99	-1	0	1.000	1	159	246	/SM	0.0
Total	21	2444	9036	1590	2461	413	163	84	1234	1064	140	269	.272	.358	.382	109	132	548	.927	310	106	111	*S-2133,3-223/O-58L,2-19	48.5

Year	Tm Lg	G	AB	R	H	2B	3B	HR	RBI	BB-IB	HP	SO	AVG	OBP	SLG	AOPS	ABR	SB-CS	FA	FR	Rng	Thr	G at Pos	BFW
DAHLGREN, BABE Ellsworth Tenney B 6.15.1912 San Francisco, CA D 9.4.1996 Arcadia, CA BR/TR 6/190# d4.16 C1																								
1935	Bos A	149	525	77	138	27	7	9	63	56	3	67	.263	.337	.392	83	-14	6-5	.988	-6	86	89	*1-149	-3.3
1936	Bos A	16	57	6	16	3	1	1	7	7	0	1	.281	.359	.421	87	-1	2-1	.980	-0	99	78	1-16	-0.3
1937	NY A	1	1	0	0	0	0	0	0	0	0	0	.000	.000	.000	-99	0	0-0	—	0			H	0.0
1938	NY A	27	43	8	8	1	0	0	1	1	0	7	.186	.205	.209	4	-7	0-0	.826	-2	58	0	/3-8,1-6	-0.8
1939	†NY A	144	531	71	125	18	6	15	89	57	2	54	.235	.312	.377	76	-21	2-3	.991	-7	78	**133**	*1-144	-4.0
1940	NY A	**155**	568	51	150	24	4	12	73	46	5	54	.264	.325	.384	86	-13	1-1	.990	-11	74	116	*1-155	-3.7
1941	Bos N	44	166	20	39	8	1	7	30	16	1	13	.235	.306	.422	108	1	0	.993	2	116	136	1-39/3-5	-0.1
	Chi N	99	359	50	101	20	1	16	59	43	1	39	.281	.360	.476	139	18	2	.991	-8	64	105	1-98	0.1
	Year	143	525	70	140	28	2	23	89	59	2	52	.267	.343	.459	129	19	2	**.992**	-6	79	**114**	*1-137/3-5	0.0
1942	Chi N	17	56	4	12	1	0	0	6	4	0	2	.214	.267	.232	48	-4	0	.986	0	116	63	1-14	-0.5
	StL A	2	2	0	0	0	0	0	0	0	0	0	.000	.000	.000	-99	-1	0-0	—	0			H	-0.1
	Bro N	17	19	2	1	0	0	0	0	4	0	5	.053	.217	.053	-19	-3	0	1.000	1	143	192	1-10	-0.3
1943	Phi N★	136	508	55	146	19	2	5	56	50	2	39	.287	.354	.362	111	8	2	.988	-17	97	104	1-73,3-35,S-25/C	-1.2
1944	Pit N	**158**	599	67	173	28	7	12	101	47	6	56	.289	.347	.419	110	7	2	.987	9	126	85	*1-158	0.8
1945	Pit N	144	531	57	133	24	8	5	75	51	2	51	.250	.318	.354	84	-12	1	**.996**	2	99	108	*1-144	-1.8
1946	StL A	28	80	2	14	1	0	0	9	8	0	13	.175	.250	.188	22	-8	0-1	.981	1	126	81	1-24	-0.9
Total	12	1137	4045	470	1056	174	37	82	569	390	22	401	.261	.329	.383	92	-50	18-11	.990	-37	93	106	*1-1030/3-48,S-25,C	-16.1
DAILEY, JOHN John G. B Brooklyn, NY d4.29																								
1875	Was NA	27	110	16	20	5	4	0	13	0		1	.182	.182	.300	67	-3	3-2	.810	-2	114	39	S-20/3-5,2-2	-0.5
	Atl NA	2	8	3	1	0	0	0	0	0		1	.125	.125	.125	-15	-1	0-0	1.000	-2	0	0	/O-2(RF),1S	-0.3
	Year	29	118	19	21	5	4	0	13	0		2	.178	.178	.288	62	-4	3-2	.797	-4	108	37	S-21/3-5,2-2,O-2(RF),1	-0.8
DAILEY, VINCE Vincent Perry B 12.25.1864 Osceola, PA D 11.14.1919 Hornell, NY 6/200# d4.21																								
1890	Cle N	64	246	41	71	5	7	0	32	33	0	23	.289	.373	.366	118	6	17	.859	0	116	80	O-64(RF)/P-2	0.5
DAILY, CON Cornelius F. B 9.11.1864 Blackstone, MA D 6.14.1928 Brooklyn, NY BL 6/192# d6.9 b-Ed OF Total (8-LF 9-CF 28-RF)																								
1884	Phi U	2	8	0	0	0	0	0		0			.000	.000	.000	-99	-2		.857	-1			/C-2	-0.3
1885	Pro N	60	223	20	58	6	1	0	19	12		20	.260	.298	.296	95	-1		.876	1			C-48/1-7,O-6(1-3-2)	0.3
1886	Bos N	50	180	25	43	4	2	0	21	19		29	.239	.312	.283	84	-3	2	.911	-9			C-49/O(LF)	-0.7
1887	Bos N	36	120	12	19	5	0	0	13	9	2	8	.158	.229	.200	20	-13	7	.889	-2			C-36	-1.1
1888	Ind N	57	202	14	44	6	1	0	14	10	0	28	.218	.255	.257	62	-8	15	.893	-4			C-42/O-5(RF),3-5,1-5,2	-0.9
1889	Ind N	62	219	35	55	6	2	0	26	28	4	21	.251	.347	.297	79	-5	14	.887	-11			C-51/O-6(1-3-2),1-6,3	-1.2
1890	Bro P	46	168	20	42	6	3	0	35	15	1	14	.250	.315	.321	66	-9	6	.879	-0	129	80	C-40/1-6,O(RF)	-0.5
1891	Bro N	60	206	25	66	10	1	0	30	15	4	13	.320	.378	.379	121	6	7	.925	1	97	107	C-55/O-3(RF),S-2,1	1.0
1892	Bro N	80	278	38	65	10	1	0	28	38	1	21	.234	.328	.277	87	-2	18	.943	1	104	108	C-68,O-13(2-3-8)	0.4
1893	Bro N	61	215	33	57	4	2	1	32	20	5	12	.265	.342	.316	79	-6	13	.935	-1	99	80	C-51/O-9(2-0-7)	-0.2
1894	Bro N	67	234	40	60	14	7	0	32	31	3	22	.256	.351	.376	81	-7	8	.930	-5	90	101	C-60/1-7	-0.5
1895	Bro N	40	142	17	30	3	2	1	11	10	1	18	.211	.268	.282	45	-12	3	.956	1	132	64	C-39/O(LF)	-0.6
1896	Chi N	9	27	1	2	0	0	0	1	1	0	2	.074	.107	.074	-50	-6	1	.969	-1	93	104	/C-9	-0.6
Total	13	630	2222	280	541	74	22	2	262	208	21	208	.243	.314	.299	75	-68	94	.912	-33	62	55	C-550/O-45R,1-32,3-6,S-2,2	-4.9
DAILY, ED Edward M. B 9.7.1862 Providence, RI D 10.21.1891 Washington, DC BR/TR 5-10.5/174# d5.4 b-Con ▲																								
1885	Phi N	50	184	22	38	8	2	1	13	0		25	.207	.207	.288	60	0		.891	-4	88	78	P-50	0.0
1886	Phi N	79	309	40	70	17	1	4	50	7		34	.227	.244	.327	72	-11	23	.827	3	148	129	O-56(13-11-32),P-27	-0.5
1887	Phi N	26	106	18	30	11	1	1	17	3	0	9	.283	.303	.434	96	-1	8	.659	-4	64	0	O-22(1-20-1)/P-6	-0.5
	Was N	78	311	39	78	6	10	2	36	14	1	27	.251	.285	.354	82	-9	26	.855	-5	61	42	O-77(RF)/P	-1.2
	Year	104	417	57	108	17	11	3	53	17	1	36	.259	.290	.374	86	-9	34	.812	-9	62	34	O-99(1-20-78)/P-7	-1.7
1888	Was N	110	453	56	102	8	4	7	39	7	1	42	.225	.239	.307	78	-12	44	.912	4	114	113	*O-100(RF)/P-9,1	-0.8
1889	Col AA	136	578	105	148	22	8	3	70	38	1	65	.256	.303	.337	87	-11	60	.854	-3	105	65	*O-136(LF)/P-2	-1.5
1890	Bro AA	91	394	68	94	15	7	1	39	24	1		.239	.284	.320	81	-11	49	.892	3	147	100	O-64(RF),P-27	-0.5
	NY N	4	15	1	2	1	0	0	1	0	0	4	.133	.133	.200	-3	-2	0	.500	1	432	0	/O-3(1-0-2),P-2	0.0
	†Lou AA	23	80	24	20	0	2	0	9	13	0		.250	.355	.300	95	0	13	.925	2	166	203	P-12,O-11(0-2-9)	0.0
1891	Lou AA	22	64	10	16	2	0	0	8	8	1	6	.250	.342	.281	80	-1	4	.884	-0	105	0	P-15/O-7(2-0-5)	-0.1
	Was AA	21	79	13	18	2	0	0	6	11	0	10	.228	.322	.253	68	-3	8	.719	-3	59	117	O-21(RF)	-0.5
	Year	43	143	23	34	4	0	0	14	19	1	16	.238	.331	.266	73	-4	12	.750	-4	63	182	O-28(2-0-26),P-15	-0.6
Total	7	640	2573	396	616	92	35	19	288	125	5	222	.239	.276	.325	80	-61	235	.857	-6	108	87	O-497(153-33-311),P-151/1	-5.6
DAISEY, GEORGE George R. B 1857 Glouchester, NJ D 4.27.1931 Cumberland, MD 5-11/190# d5.31																								
1884	Alt U	1	4	0	0	0	0	0		0			.000	.000	.000	-99	-1		.000	-1	0	0	/O(LF)	-0.2
DALENA, PETE Peter Martin B 6.26.1960 Fresno, CA BL/TR 5-11/200# d7.7																								
1989	Cle A	5	7	0	1	1	0	0	0	0-0	0	3	.143	.143	.286	18	-1	0-0	—	0			/D	-0.1
DALESANDRO, MARK Mark Anthony B 5.14.1968 Chicago, IL BR/TR 6/185# d6.6																								
1994	Cal A	19	25	5	5	1	0	1	2	2-0	0	4	.200	.259	.360	57	-2	0-0	1.000	-2	223	0	C-11/3-5,O-2(LF)	-0.3
1995	Cal A	11	10	1	1	1	0	0	0	0-0	0	2	.100	.100	.200	-25	-2	0-0	1.000	-1	48	161	/C-8,O(LF)D	-0.3
1998	Tor A	32	67	8	20	5	0	2	14	1-0	0	6	.299	.304	.463	97	-1	0-0	.986	-6	97	75	C-18/3-8,1-2,O(RF)	-0.5
1999	Tor A	16	27	3	5	0	0	0	1	0-0	1	2	.185	.207	.185	3	-4	1-0	1.000	0	49	207	/C-8,3-2,D-5	-0.3
2001	Chi A	1	0	0	0	0	0	0	0	0-0	0	0	—	—	—	—	0	0-0	—	-0	0	0	/C	0.0
Total	5	79	129	17	31	7	0	3	17	3-0	1	14	.240	.259	.364	60	-9	1-0	.992	-9	103	91	/C-46,3-15,D-6,O-4(3-0-1),1-2	-1.4
DALEY, JOHN John Francis B 5.25.1887 Pittsburgh, PA D 8.31.1988 Mansfield, OH BR/TR 5-7.5/155# d7.19																								
1912	StL A	18	52	7	9	0	0	1	3	9	2		.173	.317	.231	60	-2	4	.833	-4	96	129	S-17	-0.5
DALEY, JUD Judson Lawrence B 3.14.1884 S.Coventry, CT D 1.26.1967 Gadsden, AL BL/TR 5-8/172# d9.19																								
1911	Bro N	19	65	8	15	2	1	0	7	2	3	8	.231	.286	.292	65	-3	2	.952	1	108	122	O-16(LF)	-0.3
1912	Bro N	61	199	22	51	9	1	1	13	24	2	17	.256	.342	.327	87	-3	2	.947	1	97	119	O-55(24-24-7)	-0.5
Total	2	80	264	30	66	11	2	1	20	26	5	25	.250	.329	.318	82	-6	4	.949	2	100	120	/O-71(40-24-7)	-0.8
DALEY, PETE Peter Harvey B 1.14.1930 Grass Valley, CA BR/TR 6/195# d5.3																								
1955	Bos A	17	50	4	11	2	1	0	5	3-0	0	6	.220	.264	.300	47	-4	0-0	1.000	2	83	71	C-14	-0.2
1956	Bos A	59	187	22	50	11	3	5	29	18-5	2	30	.267	.338	.439	92	-2	1-0	.992	-6	108	49	C-57	-0.5
1957	Bos A	78	191	17	43	10	0	3	25	16-4	1	31	.225	.288	.325	64	-9	0-0	**1.000**	0	144	63	C-77	-0.7
1958	Bos A	27	56	10	18	2	1	2	8	7-1	0	11	.321	.397	.500	136	3	0-0	.990	1	130	146	C-27	0.5
1959	Bos A	65	169	9	38	7	0	1	11	13-1	0	31	.225	.279	.284	53	-11	1-1	.996	4	132	102	C-58	-0.5
1960	KC A	73	228	19	60	10	2	5	25	16-1	0	41	.263	.311	.390	88	-4	0-0	.990	-4	68	78	C-61/O(LF)	-0.6
1961	Was A	72	203	12	39	7	1	2	17	14-3	0	37	.192	.244	.266	37	-19	0-1	.988	1	70	139	C-72	-1.5
Total	7	391	1084	93	259	49	8	18	120	87-15	3	187	.239	.297	.349	71	-46	2-2	.993	-3	103	90	C-366/O(LF)	-3.5
DALEY, TOM Thomas Francis "Pete" B 11.13.1884 DuBois, PA D 12.2.1934 Los Angeles, CA BL/TR 5-5/168# d8.29																								
1908	Cin N	14	46	5	5	0	0	0	1	3	2		.109	.196	.109	-2	-5	1	1.000	1	143	295	O-13(RF)	-0.6
1913	Phi A	62	141	13	36	2	1	0	11	13	2	28	.255	.327	.284	81	-3	4	.963	0	99	95	O-39(CF)	-0.6
1914	Phi A	28	86	17	22	1	3	0	7	12	0	14	.256	.347	.337	110	1	4-7	1.000	2	106	130	O-24(15-10-0)	0.0
	NY A	69	191	36	48	6	4	0	9	38	1	13	.251	.378	.325	112	5	8-8	.958	4	103	150	O-58(28-29-0)	0.5
	Year	97	277	53	70	7	7	0	16	50	1	27	.253	.369	.329	111	6	12-15	.969	6	104	144	O-82(43-39-0)	0.5
1915	NY A	10	8	2	2	0	0	0	1	2	0	2	.250	.400	.250	95	0	1	1.000	0	147	0	/O-2(1-0-1)	0.1
Total	4	183	472	73	113	9	8	0	29	68	5	57	.239	.341	.292	92	-2	18-15	.970	7	106	143	O-136(44-77-14)	-0.6
DALLESSANDRO, DOM Nicholas Dominic "Dim Dom" B 10.3.1913 Reading, PA D 4.29.1988 Indianapolis, IN BL/TL 5-6/168# d4.24 Mil 1945																								
1937	Bos A	68	147	18	34	7	1	0	11	27	0	16	.231	.351	.293	61	-8	2-1	.965	-2	91	44	O-35(30-1-4)	-1.1
1940	Chi N	107	287	33	77	19	6	1	36	34	1	13	.268	.348	.387	104	2	4	.969	-0	108	20	O-74(LF)	-0.2
1941	Chi N	140	486	73	132	36	2	6	85	68	1	37	.272	.362	.391	116	13	3	.987	-5	98	42	*O-131(69-62-0)	0.3
1942	Chi N	96	264	30	69	12	4	4	43	36	0	18	.261	.350	.383	119	7	4	.986	-1	92	115	O-66(31-32-4)	0.3
1943	Chi N	87	176	13	39	8	3	1	31	40	1	14	.222	.369	.318	101	2	1	.967	-3	92	51	O-45(31-14-0)	-0.3
1944	Chi N	117	381	53	116	19	4	8	74	61	0	29	.304	.400	.438	137	21	1	.982	-3	91	112	*O-106(91-16-0)	1.3

Year	Tm Lg	G	AB	R	H	2B	3B	HR	RBI	BB-IB	HP	SO	AVG	OBP	SLG	AOPS	ABR	SB-CS	FA	FR	Rng	Thr	G at Pos	BFW
1946	Chi N	65	89	4	20	2	2	1	9	23	0	12	.225	.384	.326	104	2	1	.971	-1	103	0	O-20(16-0-4)	0.0
1947	Chi N	66	115	18	33	7	1	1	14	21	0	11	.287	.397	.391	115	4	0	1.000	-1	95	55	O-28(LF)	0.1
Total	8	746	1945	242	520	110	23	22	303	310	3	150	.267	.369	.381	112	43	16-1	.980	-16	96	64	O-505(370-125-12)	0.4
DALRYMPLE, ABNER Abner Frank B 9.9.1857 Warren, IL D 1.25.1939 Warren, IL BL/TR 5-10.5/175# d5.1																								
1878	Mil N	**61**	271	52	96	10	4	0	15	6		29	**.354**	.368	.421	149	13		.832	7	69	120	*O-61(LF)	1.5
1879	Chi N	71	333	47	97	25	1	0	23	4		29	.291	.300	.372	113	5		.728	-15	24	55	*O-71(66-1-4)	-1.4
1880	Chi N	**86**	382	**91**	**126**	25	12	0	36	3		18	.330	.335	.458	156	20		.859	4	92	125	*O-86(LF)	1.8
1881	Chi N	82	362	72	117	22	4	1	37	15		22	.323	.350	.414	133	13		.835	-7	64	33	*O-82(LF)	0.1
1882	Chi N	**84**	397	96	117	25	11	1	36	14		18	.295	.319	.421	129	12		.877	0	42	114	*O-84(LF)	0.9
1883	Chi N	80	363	78	108	24	4	2	37	11		29	.298	.318	.402	108	3		.826	-2	65	99	*O-80(LF)	-0.1
1884	Chi N	111	521	111	161	18	9	22	69	14		39	.309	.327	.505	146	23		.882	0	78	133	*O-111(LF)	1.8
1885	†Chi N	**113**	492	109	135	27	12	**11**	61	46		42	.274	.336	.445	133	16		.879	-1	74	75	*O-113(112-1-0)	1.1
1886	†Chi N	82	331	62	77	7	12	3	26	33		44	.233	.302	.353	86	-7	16	.953	3	91	44	O-82(LF)	-0.6
1887	Pit N	92	358	45	76	18	5	2	31	45	6	43	.212	.311	.307	78	-8	29	.900	2	83	34	*O-92(LF)	-0.6
1888	Pit N	57	227	19	50	9	2	0	14	6	2	28	.220	.247	.278	73	-7	7	.909	-2	98	0	O-57(56-0-1)	-0.9
1891	Mil AA	32	135	31	42	7	5	1	22	7	0	18	.311	.345	.459	108	0	6	.909	-1	107	92	O-32(LF)	-0.2
Total	12	951	4172	813	1202	217	81	43	407	204	8	359	.288	.323	.410	120	83	58	.863	-10	72	79	O-951(944-2-5)	3.4
DALRYMPLE, CLAY Clayton Errol B 12.3.1936 Chico, CA BL/TR 6/199# d4.24																								
1960	Phi N	82	158	11	43	6	2	4	21	15-4	3	21	.272	.343	.411	106	1	0-0	.966	-4	*59*	*163*	C-48	-0.1
1961	Phi N	129	378	23	83	11	1	5	42	30-9	4	30	.220	.281	.294	54	-25	0-2	.978	-1	*85*	**178**	*C-122	-2.1
1962	Phi N	123	370	40	102	13	3	11	54	70-7	4	32	.276	.393	.416	122	15	1-3	.987	-6	*113*	**112**	*C-119	1.4
1963	Phi N	142	452	40	114	15	3	10	40	45-15	5	55	.252	.327	.365	100	1	0-2	.981	-0	*88*	*120*	*C-142	0.7
1964	Phi N	127	382	36	91	16	3	6	46	39-6	0	40	.238	.303	.343	84	-7	0-1	.991	4	*117*	*111*	*C-124	0.2
1965	Phi N	103	301	14	64	5	5	4	23	34-7	0	37	.213	.292	.302	69	-13	0-1	.993	12	*108*	**148**	*C-102	0.4
1966	Phi N	114	331	30	81	13	3	4	39	60-10	3	57	.245	.365	.338	97	2	0-0	.993	-3	*108*	*94*	*C-110	0.4
1967	Phi N	101	268	12	46	7	1	3	21	36-6	1	49	.172	.271	.239	47	-18	1-2	.994	16	*115*	*113*	C-97	0.2
1968	Phi N	85	241	19	50	9	1	3	26	22-9	1	57	.207	.272	.290	70	-9	1-2	.990	-2	*127*	*95*	C-80	-0.9
1969	†Bal A	37	80	8	19	1	1	3	6	13-1	0	8	.237	.340	.387	103	0	0-0	1.000	-0	123	175	C-30	0.1
1970	Bal A	13	32	4	7	1	0	1	3	7-2	0	4	.219	.350	.344	94	0	0-0	1.000	4	87	241	C-11	0.5
1971	Bal A	23	49	6	10	1	0	1	6	16-1	1	13	.204	.409	.286	101	1	0-0	.971	3	173	135	C-18	0.5
Total	12	1079	3042	243	710	98	23	55	327	387-77	22	403	.233	.322	.335	85	-52	3-13	.987	22	*106*	*127*	*C-1003	1.3
DALRYMPLE, BILL William Dunn B 2.7.1891 Baltimore, MD D 7.14.1967 San Diego, CA TR d7.6																								
1915	StL A	3	2	0	0	0	0	0	0	0	0	0	.000	.000	.000	-99	-1	0	1.000	0	233	0	/3	0.0
DALTON, JACK Talbot Percy B 7.3.1885 Henderson, TN BR/TR 5-10.5/187# d6.20																								
1910	Bro N	77	273	33	62	9	4	1	21	26	4	30	.227	.304	.300	79	-8	5	.966	1	101	110	O-72(RF)	-1.0
1914	Bro N	128	442	65	141	13	8	1	45	53	3	39	.319	.396	.391	131	19	19	.965	-9	93	50	*O-116(5-109-2)	0.2
1915	Buf F	132	437	68	128	17	3	2	46	50	2	38	.293	.368	.359	103	-3	28	.966	-4	99	71	*O-119(10-60-52)	-1.5
1916	Det A	8	11	1	2	0	0	0	0	0	0	5	.182	.182	.182	9	-1	0	1.000	-0	103	0	/O-4(1-0-3)	-0.2
Total	4	345	1163	167	333	39	15	4	112	129	9	112	.286	.362	.356	107	7	52	.966	-12	97	72	O-311(16-169-129)	-2.5
DALY, BERT Albert Joseph B 4.8.1881 Bayonne, NJ D 9.3.1952 Bayonne, NJ BR/TR 5-9/170# d8.7																								
1903	Phi A	10	21	2	4	0	2	0	4	1	0		.190	.227	.381	76	-1	0	.700	-3	69	0	/2-4,3-3,S	-0.4
DALY, SUN James J. B 1.6.1865 Port Henry, NY D 4.30.1938 Albany, NY BL ?/184# d9.30																								
1892	Bal N	13	48	5	12	0	2	0	7	1	0	4	.250	.265	.333	79	-2	0	.923	1	105	209	O-13(10-3-0)	-0.2
DALY, JOE Joseph John B 9.21.1868 Conshohocken, PA D 3.21.1943 Philadelphia, PA TR 5-8/157# d9.19 b-Tom																								
1890	Phi AA	21	75	8	21	4	1	0	7	3	0		.280	.308	.360	97	-1	1	.900	-5	168	0	O-14(3-8-3)/C-9	-0.4
1891	Cle N	1	3	0	0	0	0	0	0	0	0	2	.000	.000	.000	-96	-1	0	1.000	0	0	0	/O(RF)	-0.1
1892	Bos N	1	0	0	0	0	0	0	0	0	0	0	—	—	—	—	0	0	1.000	0	*0*	*0*	/C	0.0
Total	3	23	78	8	21	4	1	0	7	3	0	2	.269	.296	.346	90	-2	1	.909	-4	153	0	/O-15(3-8-4),C-10	-0.5
DALY, TOM Thomas Daniel B 12.12.1891 St.John, NB, CAN D 11.7.1946 Medford, MA BR/TR 5-11.5/171# d9.23 C14																								
1913	Chi A	1	3	0	0	0	0	0	0	0	0	0	.000	.000	.000	-99	-1	0	1.000	0	*127*	*97*	/C	0.0
1914	Chi A	62	133	13	31	2	0	0	8	7	0	13	.233	.271	.248	57	-7	3-4	.909	-5	72	47	O-23(14-0-10)/3-5,C-4,1-2	-1.5
1915	Chi A	29	47	5	9	1	0	0	3	5	0	9	.191	.269	.213	43	-3	0	.958	-1	*178*	*55*	C-19/1	-0.3
1916	Cle A	31	73	3	16	1	1	0	8	1	0	2	.219	.230	.260	45	-5	0	.982	-1	108	107	C-25/O(RF)	-0.5
1918	Chi N	1	1	0	0	0	0	0	0	0	0	0	.000	.000	.000	-98	0	0	.667	-0	*0*	*0*	/C	-0.1
1919	Chi N	25	50	4	11	0	1	0	1	2	0	5	.220	.250	.260	53	-3	0	.956	-1	*95*	*61*	C-18	-0.4
1920	Chi N	44	90	12	28	6	0	0	13	2	1	6	.311	.333	.378	102	0	1-1	.981	-1	*100*	*85*	C-29	0.1
1921	Chi N	51	143	12	34	7	1	0	22	8	0	8	.238	.278	.301	53	-10	1-2	.973	2	*100*	*105*	C-47	-0.5
Total	8	244	540	49	129	17	3	0	55	25	1	43	.239	.274	.281	59	-29	5-7	.972	-6	*109*	*89*	C-144/O-24(14-0-11),3-5,1-3	-3.2
DALY, TOM Thomas Peter "Tido" B 2.7.1866 Philadelphia, PA D 10.29.1938 Brooklyn, NY BB/TR 5-7/170# d4.30 b-Joe OF Total (9-LF 17-CF 29-RF)																								
1887	Chi N	74	256	45	53	10	4	2	17	22	0	25	.207	.270	.301	52	-18	29	**.935**	29			C-64/O-8(2-3-3),S-2,2-2,1-2	1.4
1888	Chi N	65	219	34	42	2	6	0	29	10	1	26	.192	.230	.256	51	-13	10	.939	14			C-62/O-4(0-1-3)	0.6
1889	Was N	71	250	39	75	13	5	1	40	38	1	28	.300	.394	.404	131	12	18	.917	4			C-57/1-8,2-4,0-3(1-0-2),S	1.8
1890	†Bro N	82	292	55	71	9	4	5	43	32	4	43	.243	.326	.353	97	-1	20	.953	2	*87*	*82*	C-69,1-12/O(RF)	0.5
1891	Bro N	58	200	29	50	11	5	2	27	21	2	34	.250	.327	.385	108	2	7	.881	-6	*97*	*48*	C-26,1-15,S-11/O-7(RF)	-0.3
1892	Bro N	124	446	76	114	15	6	4	51	64	5	62	.256	.355	.343	116	11	34	.897	-10	84	96	3-57,O-30(5-13-12),C-27,2-10	0.3
1893	Bro N	126	470	94	136	21	14	8	70	76	0	65	.289	.388	.445	127	20	32	.915	-26	96	55	2-82,3-45	-0.2
1894	Bro N	124	496	135	168	22	10	8	82	77	5	42	.339	.433	.472	127	27	51	.909	-21	91	87	*2-124	0.9
1895	Bro N	121	460	90	129	17	8	2	68	52	3	52	.280	.357	.365	94	-2	28	.931	-22	92	85	*2-121	-1.5
1896	Bro N	67	224	43	63	13	6	3	29	33	5	25	.281	.385	.433	122	9	19	.909	-7	93	115	2-66/C	0.4
1898	Bro N	23	73	11	24	3	1	0	11	14	1		.329	.443	.397	142	5	6	.993	3	107	127	2-23	0.8
1899	Bro N	141	498	95	156	24	9	5	88	69	12		.313	.409	.428	127	22	43	.929	16	104	**131**	*2-141	3.9
1900	†Bro N	97	343	72	107	17	3	4	55	46	6		.312	.403	.414	118	11	27	.921	-7	91	105	2-93/1-3,O-2(1-0-1)	0.7
1901	Bro N	133	520	88	164	**38**	10	3	90	42	4		.315	.371	.444	132	22	31	.944	10	94	98	*2-133	3.2
1902	Chi A	137	489	57	110	22	3	1	54	55	0		.225	.303	.288	68	-20	19	.957	-15	90	129	*2-137	-3.2
1903	Chi A	43	150	20	31	11	0	0	19	20	1		.207	.304	.280	80	-2	6	.948	-13	81	77	2-43	-1.6
	Cin N	80	307	42	90	14	9	1	38	16	2		.293	.332	.407	99	-2	5	.937	-7	97	86	2-79	-0.8
Total	16	1566	5693	1025	1583	262	103	49	811	687	52	402	.278	.361	.386	107	83	385	.931	-56	94	100	*2-1058,C-306,3-102/O-55R,1-40,S	6.9
DAM, BILL Elbridge Rust B 4.4.1885 Cambridge, MA D 6.22.1930 Quincy, MA BL/TL d8.23																								
1909	Bos N	1	2	1	1	1	0	0	0	1	0		.500	.667	1.000	398	1	0	1.000	-0	0	0	/O(LF)	0.1
DAMASKA, JACK Jack Lloyd B 8.21.1937 Beaver Falls, PA BR/TR 5-11/168# d7.3																								
1963	StL N	5	5	1	1	0	0	0	1	0-0	0	4	.200	.200	.200	14	-1	0-0	—	-0	0	0	/2O(LF)	-0.1
DAMON, JOHNNY Johnny David B 11.5.1973 Fort Riley, KS BL/TL 6/175# d8.12																								
1995	KC A	47	188	32	53	11	5	3	23	12-0	1	22	.282	.324	.441	97	-2	7-0	.991	-4	92	0	O-47(0-44-4)	-0.4
1996	KC A	145	517	61	140	22	5	6	50	31-3	3	64	.271	.313	.368	72	-23	25-5	.983	-0	106	54	*O-144(0-89-63)/D	-2.0
1997	KC A	146	472	70	130	12	8	8	48	42-2	3	70	.275	.338	.386	86	-10	16-10	.988	5	112	67	*O-136(48-65-47)/D-5	-0.8
1998	KC A	**161**	642	104	178	30	10	18	66	58-4	4	84	.277	.339	.439	98	-3	26-12	.990	-2	96	101	*O-158(14-130-24)	-0.4
1999	KC A	145	583	101	179	39	9	14	77	67-5	3	50	.307	.379	.477	115	14	36-6	.987	0	102	85	*O-140(132-8-3)/D-4	1.3
2000	KC A	159	655	**136**	214	42	10	16	88	65-4	1	60	.327	.382	.495	117	18	**46**-9	.986	2	105	80	*O-133(67-69-0),D-25	2.2
2001	†Oak A	155	644	108	165	34	4	9	49	61-1	5	70	.256	.324	.363	81	-17	27-12	.991	-6	98	44	*O-154(67-86-5)	-2.2
2002	Bos A★	154	623	118	178	34	**11**	14	63	65-5	6	70	.286	.356	.443	109	9	31-6	.997	-5	93	92	*O-151(CF)/D	0.9
2003	†Bos A	145	608	103	166	32	6	12	67	68-4	2	74	.273	.345	.405	96	-3	30-6	**.997**	-2	98	109	*O-144(CF)/D	0.1
Total	9	1257	4932	833	1403	256	68	100	531	469-28	28	564	.284	.347	.425	98	-17	244-66	.990	-12	101	76	*O-1207(328-786-146)/D-37	-1.3
DAMRAU, HARRY Harry Robert (Also Known As Arthur Lee Whitehorn) B 9.11.1890 Newburgh, NY D 8.21.1957 Staten Island, NY BR/TR 5-10/178# d9.17																								
1915	Phi A	16	56	4	11	1	0	0	3	5	0	17	.196	.262	.214	44	-4	1-1	.870	-2	90	36	3-16	-0.6

Year	Tm Lg	G	AB	R	H	2B	3B	HR	RBI	BB-IB	HP	SO	AVG	OBP	SLG	AOPS	ABR	SB-CS	FA	FR	Rng	Thr	G at Pos	BFW
DANIEL, JAKE Handley Jacob B 4.22.1911 Roanoke, AL D 4.23.1996 LaGrange, GA BL/TL 5-11/175# d7.24																								
1937	Bro N	12	27	3	5	1	0	0	3	3	0	4	.185	.267	.222	34	-2	0	1.000	-0	77	66	/1-7	-0.3
DANIELS, BERT Bertram Elmer B 10.31.1882 Danville, IL D 6.6.1958 Cedar Grove, NJ BR/TR 5-10/170# d6.25																								
1910	NY A	95	356	68	90	13	8	1	17	41	**16**		.253	.356	.343	112	7	41	.957	-1	107	73	O-85(79-6-0)/3-6,1-4	0.1
1911	NY A	131	462	74	132	16	9	2	31	48	18		.286	.375	.372	102	3	40	.941	-5	101	73	*O-120(8-86-26)	-1.0
1912	NY A	135	496	72	136	25	11	2	41	51	**18**		.274	.363	.381	106	5	37	.945	3	115	74	*O-131(92-0-39)	0.2
1913	NY A	94	320	52	69	13	5	0	22	44	**18**	36	.216	.343	.287	85	-3	27	.966	1	97	114	O-87(RF)	-0.7
1914	Cin N	71	269	29	59	9	7	0	19	19	2	40	.219	.276	.305	70	-11	14	.974	-2	100	66	O-71(11-26-38)	-1.9
Total	5	526	1903	295	486	76	40	5	130	203	72	76	.255	.349	.345	98	1	159	.953	-4	105	79	O-494(190-118-190)/3-6,1-4	-3.3
DANIELS, TONY Frederick Clinton B 12.28.1924 Gastonia, NC BR/TR 5-9.5/185# d6.12																								
1945	Phi N	76	230	15	46	3	2	0	10	12	3	22	.200	.249	.230	35	-21	1	.955	4	107	94	2-75/3	-1.4
DANIELS, JACK Harold Jack "Sour Mash Jack" B 12.21.1927 Chester, PA BL/TL 5-10/165# d4.18																								
1952	Bos N	106	219	31	41	5	1	2	14	28	3	30	.187	.288	.247	51	-14	3-3	.977	-1	96	102	O-87(13-0-75)	-1.9
DANIELS, KAL Kalvoski B 8.20.1963 Vienna, GA BL/TR 5-11/195# d4.9																								
1986	Cin N	74	181	34	58	10	4	6	23	22-1	2	30	.320	.398	.519	145	12	15-2	.967	-0	113	0	O-47(LF)	1.3
1987	Cin N	108	368	73	123	24	1	26	64	60-11	1	62	.334	.429	.617	166	37	26-8	.968	-1	101	78	O-94(LF)	3.4
1988	Cin N	140	495	95	144	29	1	18	64	87-10	3	94	.291	**.397**	.463	141	31	27-6	.982	-1	100	119	*O-137(LF)	3.2
1989	Cin N	44	133	26	29	11	0	2	9	36-1	2	28	.218	.390	.346	109	4	6-4	1.000	0	88	188	O-38(LF)	0.3
	LA N	11	38	7	13	2	0	2	8	7-0	0	5	.342	.435	.553	187	5	3-0	1.000	-0	102	0	O-11(LF)	0.5
	Year	55	171	33	42	13	0	4	17	43-1	2	33	.246	.399	.392	125	9	9-4	1.000	0	91	149	O-49(LF)	0.8
1990	LA N	130	450	81	133	23	1	27	94	68-1	3	104	.296	.389	.531	156	36	4-3	.987	1	87	161	*O-127(LF)	3.3
1991	LA N	137	461	54	115	15	1	17	73	63-4	1	116	.249	.337	.397	109	6	6-1	.979	-2	88	132	*O-132(LF)	0.2
1992	LA N	35	104	9	24	5	0	2	8	10-0	1	30	.231	.302	.337	83	-2	0-0	.964	-2	69	116	O-21(LF)/1-8	-0.6
	Chi N	48	108	12	27	6	0	4	17	12-0	1	24	.250	.328	.417	108	1	0-2	1.000	-1	70	277	O-28(LF)	-0.1
	Year	83	212	21	51	11	0	6	25	22-0	2	54	.241	.315	.377	95	-1	0-2	.984	-3	70	204	O-49(LF)/1-8	-0.7
Total	7	727	2338	391	666	125	8	104	360	365-28	14	493	.285	.382	.479	137	130	87-26	.980	-6	93	124	O-635(LF)/1-8	11.5
DANIELS, LAW Lawrence Long B 7.14.1862 Newton, MA D 1.7.1929 Waltham, MA BR/TR 5-10/170# d4.25 OF Total (24-LF 14-CF 7-RF)																								
1887	Bal AA	48	165	23	41	5	1	0	32	8	1		.248	.287	.291	65	-7	7	.845	-8			C-26,O-15(10-5-0)/1-4,2-2,S3	-1.2
1888	KC AA	61	218	32	45	2	0	2	28	14	3		.206	.264	.243	59	-10	20	.855	-3	174	253	O-30(14-9-7),C-29/3-2,S	-1.1
Total	2	109	383	55	86	7	1	2	60	22	4		.225	.274	.264	62	-17	27	.859	-12			/C-55,O-45L,1-4,3-3,S-2,2-2	-2.3
DANNER, BUCK Henry Frederick B 6.8.1891 Dedham, MA D 9.19.1949 Dedham, MA BR/TR 5-11/140# d9.17																								
1915	Phi A	3	12	1	3	0	0	0	0	0	0	1	.250	.250	.250	51	-1	1	.750	-2	51	0	/S-3	-0.3
DANNING, HARRY Harry "Harry The Horse" B 9.6.1911 Los Angeles, CA BR/TR 6-1/190# d7.30 Mil 1943-45 b-Ike																								
1933	NY N	3	2	0	0	0	0	0	0	1	0	0	.000	.333	.000	2	0	0	1.000	0	*0*	*0*	/C	0.0
1934	NY N	53	97	8	32	7	0	1	7	1	0	9	.330	.337	.433	107	1	1	.989	0	*112*	*124*	C-37	0.2
1935	NY N	65	152	16	37	11	1	2	20	9	0	16	.243	.286	.368	76	-5	0	.978	2	*124*	*102*	C-44	-0.1
1936	†NY N	32	69	3	11	2	2	0	4	1	1	5	.159	.183	.246	15	-9	0	.988	2	*138*	*83*	C-24	-0.6
1937	†NY N	93	292	30	84	12	4	8	51	18	1	20	.288	.331	.438	106	1	0	.982	1	*161*	*101*	C-86	0.7
1938	NY N☆	120	448	59	137	26	3	9	60	23	4	40	.306	.345	.438	113	7	1	.984	-2	*121*	*60*	*C-114	1.2
1939	NY N☆	135	520	79	163	28	5	16	74	35	2	42	.313	.359	.479	122	15	4	.991	6	*82*	*105*	*C-132	2.9
1940	NY N★	140	524	65	157	34	4	13	91	35	5	31	.300	.349	.454	119	13	3	.980	9	***135***	*89*	*C-131	3.1
1941	NY N★	130	459	58	112	22	4	7	56	30	1	25	.244	.292	.355	80	-14	1	.993	7	*117*	*100*	*C-116/1	0.1
1942	NY N	119	408	45	114	20	3	1	34	34	0	29	.279	.335	.350	100	0	3	.979	-0	*126*	*73*	*C-116	0.7
Total	10	890	2971	363	847	162	26	57	397	187	14	217	.285	.330	.415	104	9	13	.985	25	*121*	*89*	C-801/1	8.2
DANNING, IKE Isaac B 1.20.1905 Los Angeles, CA D 3.30.1983 Santa Monica, CA BR/TR 5-10/160# d9.21 b-Harry																								
1928	StL A	2	6	0	3	0	0	0	1	1	0	2	.500	.571	.500	178	1	0-0	.917	0	*123*	*220*	/C-2	0.1
DANTONIO, FATS John James B 12.31.1918 New Orleans, LA D 5.28.1993 New Orleans, LA BR/TR 5-8/165# d9.18																								
1944	Bro N	3	7	0	1	0	0	0	0	0	0	1	.143	.143	.143	-20	-1	0	.846	-1	*65*	*0*	/C-3	-0.2
1945	Bro N	47	128	12	32	6	1	0	12	11	0	6	.250	.309	.313	74	-5	3	.929	-5	*108*	*76*	C-45	-0.7
Total	2	50	135	12	33	6	1	0	12	11	0	7	.244	.301	.304	69	-6	3	.923	-5	*105*	*72*	/C-48	-0.9
DANZIG, BABE Harold Paul B 4.30.1887 Binghamton, NY D 7.14.1931 San Francisco, CA BR/TR 6-2/205# d4.12																								
1909	Bos A	6	13	0	2	0	0	0	0	2	1		.154	.313	.154	47	-1	0	.960	-1	0	212	/1-3	-0.2
DAPPER, CLIFF Clifford Roland B 1.2.1920 Los Angeles, CA BR/TR 6-2/190# d4.19 Mil 1943-45																								
1942	Bro N	8	17	2	8	1	0	1	9	2	0	2	.471	.526	.706	255	3	0	1.000	0	*145*	*82*	/C-8	0.4
DARINGER, CLIFF Clifford Clarence "Shanty" B 4.10.1885 Hayden, IN D 12.26.1971 Sacramento, CA BL/TR 5-7.5/155# d4.20 b-Rolla																								
1914	KC F	64	160	12	42	2	1	0	16	11	3	7	.262	.322	.287	70	-9	9	.944	5	122	94	S-24,3-19,2-14	-0.2
DARINGER, ROLLA Rolla Harrison B 11.15.1888 N.Vernon, IN D 5.23.1974 Seymour, IN BL/TR 5-10/155# d9.19 b-Cliff																								
1914	StL N	2	4	1	2	1	0	0	0	1	0	2	.500	.600	.750	304	1	0	.667	-1	81	373	/S	0.1
1915	StL N	10	23	3	2	0	0	0	0	9	0	5	.087	.344	.087	33	-1	0-1	.947	-2	91	151	S-10	-0.3
Total	2	12	27	4	4	1	0	0	0	10	0	7	.148	.378	.185	72	0	0-1	.927	-2	90	171	/S-11	-0.2
DARK, ALVIN Alvin Ralph "Blackie" B 1.7.1922 Comanche, OK BR/TR 5-11/185# d7.14 M13 C2 OF Total (39-LF 4-RF)																								
1946	Bos N	15	13	0	3	3	0	0	1	0	0	3	.231	.231	.462	93	0	0	.905	1	143	110	S-12/O(LF)	0.1
1948	†Bos N	137	543	85	175	39	6	3	48	24	2	36	.322	.353	.433	114	9	4	.963	-14	95	95	*S-133	0.4
1949	Bos N	130	529	74	146	23	5	3	53	31	1	43	.276	.317	.355	85	-13	5	.961	-3	98	100	*S-125/3-4	-0.8
1950	NY N	**154**	587	79	164	36	5	16	67	39	6	60	.279	.331	.440	100	-1	9	.962	-11	97	**106**	*S-154	-0.3
1951	†NY N★	156	646	114	196	**41**	7	14	69	42	6	39	.303	.352	.454	114	12	12-7	.944	4	100	**123**	*S-156	2.6
1952	NY N☆	151	589	92	177	29	3	14	73	47	5	39	.301	.357	.431	117	13	6-6	.965	5	96	**120**	*S-150	2.7
1953	NY N	**155**	647	126	194	41	6	23	88	28	6	34	.300	.335	.488	109	7	7-2	.967	8	105	107	*S-110,2-26,O-17(13-0-4)/3-8,P	2.5
1954	†NY N★	**154**	644	98	189	26	6	20	70	27	5	40	.293	.325	.446	98	-4	5-3	.956	2	102	105	*S-154	1.1
1955	NY N	115	475	77	134	20	3	9	45	22-2	5	32	.282	.319	.394	88	-9	2-1	.962	-12	93	94	*S-115	-1.1
1956	NY N	48	206	19	52	12	0	2	17	8-0	1	13	.252	.279	.340	67	-10	0-0	.961	-7	89	86	S-48	-1.3
	StL N	100	413	54	118	14	7	4	37	21-0	2	33	.286	.320	.383	89	-7	3-1	.959	-1	100	104	S-99	0.0
	Year	148	619	73	170	26	7	6	54	29-0	3	46	.275	.307	.368	82	-17	3-1	.960	-8	96	98	*S-147	-1.3
1957	StL N	140	583	80	169	25	8	4	64	29-4	4	56	.290	.326	.381	88	-10	3-4	.965	8	102	117	*S-139/3	0.9
1958	StL N	18	64	7	19	0	0	1	5	2-0	0	6	.297	.318	.344	72	-3	0-0	.943	-2	95	105	/S-8,3-8	-0.4
	Chi N	114	464	54	137	16	4	3	43	29-1	5	23	.295	.339	.366	89	-7	1-1	.949	1	99	105	*3-111	-0.6
	Year	132	528	61	156	16	4	4	48	31-1	5	29	.295	.337	.364	87	-10	1-1	.948	-0	99	100	*3-119/S-8	-1.0
1959	Chi N	136	477	60	126	22	9	6	45	55-9	3	50	.264	.342	.386	95	-3	1-1	.948	1	106	103	*3-131/1-4,S	-0.2
1960	Phi N	55	198	29	48	5	1	3	14	19-2	2	14	.242	.315	.323	75	-7	1-1	.953	-5	89	78	3-53/1	-1.2
	Mil N	50	141	16	42	6	2	1	18	7-2	1	13	.298	.329	.390	106	1	0-0	.960	-2	96	94	O-25(LF),1-10/3-4,2-3	-0.3
	Year	105	339	45	90	11	3	4	32	26-4	3	27	.265	.321	.351	88	-6	1-1	.954	-6	88	76	3-57,O-25(LF),1-11/2-3	-1.5
Total	14	1828	7219	1064	2089	358	72	126	757	430-20	54	534	.289	.333	.411	98	-32	59-27	.960	-26	99	107	*S-1404,3-320/O-43L,2-29,1-15,P	4.1
DARLING, DELL Conrad B 12.21.1861 Erie, PA D 11.20.1904 Erie, PA BR/TR 5-8/170# d7.3																								
1883	Buf N	6	18	1	3	0	0	0	1	2		5	.167	.250	.167	29	-1		.875	-2			/C-6	-0.3
1887	Chi N	38	141	28	45	7	4	3	20	22	0	18	.319	.411	.489	132	6	19	.786	2	132	189	O-20(RF),C-20	0.8
1888	Chi N	20	75	12	16	3	1	2	7	3	1	12	.213	.253	.360	87	-1	0	.932	1			C-20	0.2
1889	Chi N	36	120	14	23	1	1	0	7	25	0	22	.192	.331	.217	52	-7	5	.960	2			C-36	-0.2
1890	Chi P	58	221	45	57	12	4	2	39	29	3	28	.258	.352	.376	91	-3	5	.957	-8	88	99	1-29,S-15/C-9,O-7(RF),2-3,3-2	-1.0
1891	StL AA	17	53	9	7	1	3	0	9	10	0	11	.132	.270	.264	46	-4	0	.894	-0	*117*	*117*	C-17/2-2,S	-0.3
Total	6	175	628	109	151	24	13	7	83	91	4	96	.240	.340	.354	87	-10	29	.923	-4	22	22	C-108/1-29,O-27(RF),S-16,2-5,3-2	-0.8
DARR, MIKE Michael Curtis B 3.21.1976 Corona, CA D 2.15.2002 Phoenix, AZ BL/TR 6-3/205# d5.23																								
1999	SD N	25	48	6	13	1	0	2	3	5-0	0	18	.271	.340	.417	98	0	2-1	1.000	-0	110	0	O-22(0-3-21)	-0.1

Year	Tm Lg	G	AB	R	H	2B	3B	HR	RBI	BB-IB	HP	SO	AVG	OBP	SLG	AOPS	ABR	SB-CS	FA	FR	Rng	Thr	G at Pos	BFW
2000	SD N	58	205	21	55	14	4	1	30	23-1	0	45	.268	.342	.390	91	-3	9-1	1.000	5	107	203	O-57(8-19-47)	0.2
2001	SD N	105	289	36	80	13	1	2	34	39-3	1	72	.277	.363	.349	94	-1	6-2	.990	5	112	123	O-93(5-29-69)	0.2
Total	3	188	542	63	148	28	5	5	67	67-4	1	135	.273	.353	.371	93	-4	17-4	.994	10	110	142	O-172(13-51-137)	0.3
DARRAGH, JIMMY James S. B 7.17.1866 Ebensburg, PA D 8.12.1939 Rochester, PA 6-2.5/180# d5.13																								
1891	Lou AA	1	2	0	1	0	0	0	0	0	0	0	.500	.500	.500	188	0	0	1.000	0	353	0	/1	0.0
DARWIN, BOBBY Arthur Bobby Lee B 2.16.1943 Los Angeles, CA BR/TR 6-2/200# d9.30																								
1962	LA A	1	1	0	0	0	0	0	0	0-0	0	1	.000	.000	.000	-99	0	0-0	.000	-0	0	0	/P	0.0
1969	LA N	6	0	1	0	0	0	0	0	0-0	0	0	—	—	—	—	0	0-0	—	-0	0	0	/P-3	0.0
1971	LA N	11	20	2	5	1	0	1	4	2-0	0	9	.250	.318	.450	123	1	0-0	1.000	0	131	0	/O-4(RF)	0.1
1972	Min A	145	513	48	137	20	2	22	80	38-4	8	145	.267	.326	.442	122	13	2-3	.980	-8	92	84	*O-142(9-86-47)	-0.1
1973	Min A	145	560	69	141	20	2	18	90	46-5	3	137	.252	.309	.391	93	-6	5-2	.980	-4	88	142	*O-140(RF)/D	-1.7
1974	Min A	152	575	67	152	13	7	25	94	37-2	14	127	.264	.322	.442	115	9	1-3	.970	-7	93	75	*O-142(RF)	-0.7
1975	Min A	48	169	26	37	6	0	5	18	18-1	4	44	.219	.307	.343	83	-4	2-0	.969	-4	56	140	O-27(RF),D-19	-0.9
	Mil A	55	186	19	46	6	2	8	23	11-0	3	54	.247	.300	.430	104	0	4-1	.978	3	103	165	O-43(25-0-20)/D-9	0.1
	Year	103	355	45	83	12	2	13	41	29-1	7	98	.234	.304	.389	94	-4	6-1	.975	-1	84	155	O-70(25-0-47),D-28	-0.8
1976	Mil A	25	73	6	18	3	1	1	5	6-1	2	16	.247	.321	.356	100	0	0-0	.977	1	117	79	O-21(0-1-21)/D	0.0
	Bos A	43	106	9	19	5	2	3	13	2-0	3	35	.179	.216	.349	57	-6	1-0	.964	0	103	111	O-17(3-0-14),D-16	-0.7
	Year	68	179	15	37	8	3	4	18	8-1	5	51	.207	.260	.352	73	-7	1-0	.972	1	111	92	O-38(3-1-35),D-17	-0.7
1977	Bos A	4	9	1	2	1	0	0	1	0-0	0	4	.222	.222	.333	44	-1	0-0	.500	-0	225	0	/O(RF)D	-0.1
	Chi N	11	12	2	2	1	0	0	0	0-0	0	5	.167	.167	.250	9	-2	0-0	—	-0	0	0	/O(RF)	-0.2
Total	9	646	2224	250	559	76	16	83	328	160-13	37	577	.251	.311	.412	103	4	15-9	.976	-19	91	106	O-538(37-87-417)/D-48,P-4	-4.2
DASCENZO, DOUG Douglas Craig B 6.30.1964 Cleveland, OH BB/TL 5-8/160# d9.2																								
1988	Chi N	26	75	9	16	3	0	0	4	9-1	0	4	.213	.298	.253	57	-4	6-1	1.000	2	118	121	O-20(CF)	-0.1
1989	Chi N	47	139	20	23	1	0	1	12	13-0	0	13	.165	.234	.194	23	-14	6-3	1.000	-1	103	0	O-45(8-37-1)	-1.6
1990	Chi N	113	241	27	61	9	5	1	26	21-2	1	18	.253	.312	.344	76	-8	15-6	1.000	2	108	44	*O-107(65-38-22)/P	-0.7
1991	Chi N	118	239	40	61	11	0	1	18	24-2	2	26	.255	.327	.314	78	-6	14-7	.985	-4	95	0	O-86(32-59-16)/P-3	-1.1
1992	Chi N	139	376	37	96	13	4	0	20	27-2	0	32	.255	.304	.311	73	-14	6-8	.978	-6	93	36	*O-122(25-80-28)	-2.4
1993	Tex A	76	146	20	29	5	1	2	10	8-0	0	22	.199	.239	.288	43	-12	2-0	.990	3	100	216	O-68(16-35-25)/D-2	-1.0
1996	SD N	21	9	3	1	0	0	0	0	1-0	0	2	.111	.200	.111	-16	-2	0-1	1.000	-1	58	0	O-10(0-1-9)	-0.2
Total	7	540	1225	156	287	42	10	5	90	103-7	3	117	.234	.293	.297	64	-60	49-26	.990	-4	100	53	O-458(146-270-101)/P-4,D-2	-7.1
DASHIELL, WALLY John Wallace B 5.9.1902 Jewett, TX D 5.20.1972 Pensacola, FL BR/TR 5-9.5/170# d4.20																								
1924	Chi A	1	2	0	0	0	0	0	0	0	0	0	.000	.000	.000	-99	-1	0-0	.667	-1	48	0	/S	-0.1
DATZ, JEFF Jeffrey William B 11.28.1959 Camden, NJ BR/TR 6-4/220# d9.5 C1																								
1989	Det A	7	10	0	2	0	0	0	0	1-0	1	1	.200	.333	.200	55	-1	0-0	1.000	1	0	146	/C-6,D	0.1
DAUBACH, BRIAN Brian Michael B 2.11.1972 Belleville, IL BL/TR 6-1/201# d9.10																								
1998	Fla N	10	15	0	3	1	0	0	3	1-0	1	5	.200	.294	.267	51	-1	0-0	1.000	-0	50	155	/1-4	-0.2
1999	†Bos A	110	381	61	112	33	3	21	73	36-0	3	92	.294	.360	.562	126	15	0-1	.983	-0	101	80	1-61,D-43/O-2(LF),3	0.6
2000	Bos A	142	495	55	123	32	2	21	76	44-2	6	130	.248	.315	.448	88	-10	1-1	.996	2	102	79	1-83,D-41/O-8(7-0-1),3	-1.7
2001	Bos A	122	407	54	107	28	3	22	71	53-7	5	108	.263	.350	.509	123	14	1-0	.988	0	101	83	*1-106,O-14(6-0-8)	0.4
2002	Bos A	137	444	62	118	24	2	20	78	51-4	7	126	.266	.348	.464	112	8	2-1	.990	-4	85	95	1-60,O-48(35-0-13),D-28	-0.4
2003	Chi A	95	183	26	42	11	0	6	21	34-1	1	54	.230	.352	.388	95	0	1-0	.996	-1	99	84	1-45,D-14,O-12(3-0-9)	-0.5
Total	6	616	1925	258	505	129	10	90	322	219-14	23	515	.262	.342	.480	109	26	5-3	.990	-3	98	84	1-359,D-126/O-84(53-0-31),3-2	-1.8
DAUBERT, HARRY Harry "Jake" B 6.19.1892 Columbus, OH D 1.8.1944 Detroit, MI BR/TR 6/160# d9.4																								
1915	Pit N	1	1	0	0	0	0	0	0	0	0	1	.000	.000	.000	-99	0	0	—	0			H	0.0
DAUBERT, JAKE Jacob Ellsworth B 4.7.1884 Shamokin, PA D 10.9.1924 Cincinnati, OH BL/TL 5-10.5/160# d4.14																								
1910	Bro N	144	552	67	146	15	15	8	50	47	5	53	.264	.328	.389	112	5	23	.989	-3	87	94	*1-144	-0.1
1911	Bro N	149	573	89	176	17	8	5	45	51	2	56	.307	.366	.391	117	12	32	.989	2	104	**107**	*1-149	1.0
1912	Bro N	145	559	81	172	19	16	3	66	48	6	45	.308	.369	.415	119	13	29	**.993**	1	97	87	*1-143	1.0
1913	Bro N	139	508	76	178	17	7	2	52	44	3	40	**.350**	.405	.423	133	23	25-21	.991	3	105	**128**	*1-139	2.1
1914	Bro N	126	474	89	156	17	7	6	45	30	5	34	**.329**	.375	.432	137	20	25	.993	-6	71	107	*1-126	1.2
1915	Bro N	150	544	62	164	21	8	2	47	57	1	48	.301	.369	.381	125	17	11-13	.993	8	126	84	*1-150	2.2
1916	†Bro N	127	478	75	151	16	7	3	33	38	4	39	.316	.371	.397	132	19	21-7	**.993**	3	106	85	*1-126	2.4
1917	Bro N	125	468	59	122	4	4	2	30	51	6	30	.261	.341	.299	94	-1	11	.991	6	**121**	76	*1-125	0.2
1918	Bro N	108	396	50	122	12	**15**	2	47	27	5	18	.308	.360	.429	141	18	10	.991	-0	94	71	*1-105	1.7
1919	†Cin N	**140**	537	79	148	10	12	2	44	35	2	23	.276	.322	.350	105	2	11	.989	-1	95	109	*1-140	-0.4
1920	Cin N	142	553	97	168	28	13	4	48	47	3	29	.304	.362	.423	127	19	11-13	.990	-8	75	101	*1-140	0.6
1921	Cin N	136	516	69	158	18	12	2	64	24	3	16	.306	.341	.399	100	-2	12-6	.993	3	106	109	*1-136	-0.7
1922	Cin N	**156**	610	114	205	15	**22**	12	66	56	3	21	.336	.395	.492	130	25	14-17	**.994**	-0	97	**124**	*1-156	1.1
1923	Cin N	125	500	63	146	27	10	2	54	40	4	20	.292	.349	.398	99	-1	11-12	.993	6	**122**	104	*1-121	-0.4
1924	Cin N	102	405	47	114	14	9	1	31	28	2	17	.281	.331	.368	88	-7	5-10	.990	7	130	104	*1-102	-1.0
Total	15	2014	7673	1117	2326	250	165	56	722	623	54	489	.303	.360	.401	117	162	251-99	.991	20	102	100	*1-2002	10.9
DAUER, RICH Richard Fremont B 7.27.1952 San Bernardino, CA BR/TR 6/180# d9.11 C9																								
1976	Bal A	11	39	0	4	0	0	0	3	1-0	1	3	.103	.143	.103	-28	-6	0-0	1.000	-2	82	118	2-10	-0.9
1977	Bal A	96	304	38	74	15	1	5	25	20-0	2	28	.243	.294	.349	79	-9	1-0	.982	11	109	126	2-83/3-9,D-2	0.6
1978	Bal A	133	459	57	121	23	0	6	46	26-0	0	22	.264	.301	.353	89	-7	0-4	.998	5	95	115	2-87,3-52/D	0.0
1979	†Bal A	142	479	63	123	20	0	9	61	36-2	1	36	.257	.305	.355	82	-13	0-1	.979	-11	91	115	*2-103,3-44	-1.9
1980	Bal A	152	557	71	158	32	0	2	63	46-1	3	19	.284	.338	.352	91	-5	3-2	.991	3	94	**124**	*2-137,3-35	0.4
1981	Bal A	96	369	41	97	27	0	4	38	27-0	3	18	.263	.317	.369	98	-1	0-0	**.989**	-10	90	110	2-94/3-4	-0.6
1982	Bal A	158	558	75	156	24	2	8	57	50-1	1	34	.280	.337	.373	96	-2	0-1	.987	-29	84	91	*2-123,3-61	-2.6
1983	†Bal A	140	459	49	108	19	0	5	41	47-2	2	29	.235	.306	.309	72	-17	1-1	.988	-22	89	94	*2-131,3-17	-3.2
1984	Bal A	127	397	29	101	26	0	2	24	24-1	0	23	.254	.296	.335	76	-13	1-3	.980	-9	98	106	*2-123/3-3	-1.6
1985	Bal A	85	208	25	42	7	0	2	14	20-0	1	7	.202	.275	.264	50	-14	0-1	.990	2	103	106	2-73,3-17/1	-0.9
Total	10	1140	3829	448	984	193	3	43	372	297-7	14	219	.257	.310	.343	83	-87	6-13	.987	-61	94	109	2-964,3-242/D-3,1	-10.7
DAUGHERTY, DOC Harold Ray B 10.12.1927 Paris, PA BR/TR 6/180# d4.22																								
1951	Det A	1	1	0	0	0	0	0	0	0	0	1	.000	.000	.000	-99	0	0-0	—	0			H	0.0
DAUGHERTY, JACK John Michael B 7.3.1960 Hialeah, FL BB/TL 6/195# d9.1																								
1987	Mon N	11	10	1	1	1	0	0	1	0-0	0	3	.100	.100	.200	-22	-2	0-0	1.000	0	383	0	/1	-0.1
1989	Tex A	52	106	15	32	4	2	1	10	11-0	1	21	.302	.364	.406	117	3	2-1	1.000	1	116	81	1-23/O-5(4-0-1),D-8	0.3
1990	Tex A	125	310	36	93	20	2	6	47	22-0	2	49	.300	.347	.435	118	7	0-0	.982	-0	71	183	O-42(39-0-4),1-30,D-21	0.4
1991	Tex A	58	144	8	28	3	2	1	11	16-1	0	23	.194	.270	.264	51	-10	1-0	.981	-2	91	64	O-37(34-0-3),1-11/D	-1.3
1992	Tex A	59	127	13	26	9	0	0	9	16-1	1	21	.205	.295	.276	64	-6	2-1	.939	0	94	98	O-26(16-1-11),D-13/1-8	-0.7
1993	Hou N	4	3	0	1	0	0	0	0	0-0	0	0	.333	.333	.333	82	0	0-0	—	0	0	0	/1O(RF)	0.0
	Cin N	46	59	7	13	2	0	2	9	11-0	0	15	.220	.338	.356	87	-1	0-0	.917	-2	67	0	O-16(11-0-5)/1-2	-0.3
	Year	50	62	7	14	2	0	2	9	11-0	0	15	.226	.338	.355	87	-1	0-0	.923	-1	72	0	O-17(11-0-6)/1-3	-0.3
Total	6	355	759	80	194	39	6	10	87	76-2	4	132	.256	.322	.362	92	-9	5-2	.969	-2	80	127	O-127(104-1-25)/1-76,D-43	-1.7
DAUGHTERS, BOB Robert Francis "Red" B 8.5.1914 Cincinnati, OH D 8.22.1988 Southbury, CT BR/TR 6-2/185# d4.24																								
1937	Bos A	1	0	1	0	0	0	0	0	0	0	0	—	—	—	—	0	0-0	—	0			R	0.0
DAULTON, DARREN Darren Arthur B 1.3.1962 Arkansas City, KS BL/TR 6-2/190# d9.25 C1																								
1983	Phi N	2	3	1	1	0	0	0	0	1-0	0	1	.333	.500	.333	137	0	0-0	1.000	-0	51	0	/C-2	0.0
1985	Phi N	36	103	14	21	3	1	4	11	16-0	0	37	.204	.311	.369	87	-2	3-0	.994	1	90	101	C-28	0.1
1986	Phi N	49	138	18	31	4	0	8	21	38-3	1	41	.225	.391	.428	123	6	2-3	.985	-4	78	104	C-48	0.3
1987	Phi N	53	129	10	25	6	0	3	13	16-1	0	37	.194	.281	.310	55	-8	0-0	.991	-1	99	68	C-40/1	-0.8
1988	Phi N	58	144	13	30	6	0	1	12	17-1	0	26	.208	.288	.271	61	-7	2-1	.977	-8	93	65	C-44/1	-1.4
1989	Phi N	131	368	29	74	12	2	8	44	52-8	2	58	.201	.303	.310	76	-11	2-1	.984	-3	109	98	*C-126	-0.8
1990	Phi N	143	459	62	123	30	1	12	57	72-9	2	72	.268	.367	.416	116	13	7-1	.989	6	**151**	87	*C-139	2.9

Year	Tm Lg	G	AB	R	H	2B	3B	HR	RBI	BB-IB	HP	SO	AVG	OBP	SLG	AOPS	ABR	SB-CS	FA	FR	Rng	Thr	G at Pos	BFW
1991	Phi N	89	285	36	56	12	0	12	42	41-4	2	66	.196	.297	.365	88	-4	5-0	.985	-14	84	51	C-88	-1.3
1992	Phi N★	145	485	80	131	32	5	27	**109**	88-11	6	103	.270	.385	.524	157	39	11-2	.987	-3	122	92	*C-141	4.9
1993	†Phi N★	147	510	90	131	35	4	24	105	117-12	2	111	.257	.392	.482	136	32	5-0	.991	-6	124	88	*C-146	3.6
1994	Phi N	69	257	43	77	17	1	15	56	33-2	1	43	.300	.380	.549	136	14	4-1	.994	7	78	99	C-68	2.5
1995	Phi N★	98	342	44	85	19	3	9	55	55-2	5	52	.249	.359	.401	100	2	3-0	.994	-3	100	86	C-95	0.5
1996	Phi N	5	12	3	2	0	0	0	0	7-0	1	5	.167	.500	.167	85	1	0-0	1.000	-1	80	0	/O-5(LF)	0.0
1997	Phi N	84	269	46	71	13	6	11	42	54-4	1	57	.264	.381	.480	126	12	4-0	.979	5	121	137	O-70(RF)/1-3,D-6	1.4
	†Fla N	52	126	22	33	8	2	3	21	22-1	1	17	.262	.371	.429	115	4	2-1	.984	-2	83	98	1-39/O-3(1-0-3),D	-0.1
	Year	136	395	68	104	21	8	14	63	76-5	2	74	.263	.378	.463	123	15	6-1	.979	3	118	134	O-73(1-0-73),1-42/D-7	1.3
Total	14	1161	3630	511	891	197	25	137	588	629-58	24	726	.245	.357	.427	114	91	50-10	.989	-27	111	86	C-965/O-78(6-0-73),1-44,D-7	11.8
DAVALILLO, YO-YO Pompeyo Antonio (Romero) B 6.30.1931 Caracas, Venezuela BR/TR 5-3/140# d8.1 b-Vic																								
1953	Was A	19	58	10	17	1	0	0	2	1	0	7	.293	.305	.310	68	-3	1-0	.935	-2	90	96	S-17	-0.3
DAVALILLO, VIC Victor Jose (Romero) B 7.31.1936 Cabimas, Venezuela BL/TL 5-7/155# d4.9 b-Yo-Yo OF Total (131-LF 752-CF 196-RF)																								
1963	Cle A	90	370	44	108	18	5	7	36	16-0	1	41	.292	.321	.424	108	3	3-3	.988	9	121	180	O-89(CF)	0.9
1964	Cle A	150	577	64	156	26	2	6	51	34-2	1	77	.270	.309	.354	85	-12	21-11	.986	2	102	107	*O-143(CF)	-1.4
1965	Cle A★	142	505	67	152	19	1	5	40	35-9	0	50	.301	.344	.372	103	2	26-7	.988	4	112	92	*O-134(CF)	0.6
1966	Cle A	121	344	42	86	6	4	3	19	24-6	0	37	.250	.297	.317	77	-11	8-6	.986	2	107	118	*O-108(CF)	-1.3
1967	Cle A	139	359	47	103	17	5	2	22	10-0	1	30	.287	.307	.379	101	-1	6-7	.986	-0	104	97	*O-125(1-125-0)	-0.6
1968	Cle A	51	180	15	43	2	3	2	13	3-0	1	19	.239	.254	.317	74	-7	8-6	.967	2	108	156	O-49(3-2-48)	-1.0
	Cal A	93	339	34	101	15	4	1	18	15-1	0	34	.298	.326	.375	117	5	17-10	.995	5	116	75	O-86(0-70-17)	0.8
	Year	144	519	49	144	17	7	3	31	18-1	1	53	.277	.301	.355	102	-2	25-16	.987	7	**113**	105	*O-135(3-72-65)	-0.2
1969	Cal A	33	71	10	11	1	1	0	1	6-1	1	5	.155	.231	.197	22	-8	3-0	1.000	-0	108	0	O-22(0-2-20)/1-3	-0.9
	StL N	63	98	15	26	3	0	2	10	7-0	0	8	.265	.314	.357	87	-2	1-1	1.000	0	113	0	O-23(2-10-11)/P-2	-0.3
1970	StL N	111	183	29	57	14	3	1	33	13-1	0	19	.311	.355	.437	109	2	4-1	.972	1	97	157	O-54(12-33-13)	0.3
1971	†Pit N	99	295	48	84	14	6	1	33	11-1	2	31	.285	.312	.383	97	-2	10-2	.983	1	105	143	O-61(11-20-31),1-16	-0.4
1972	†Pit N	117	368	59	117	19	2	4	28	26-6	3	44	.318	.367	.413	124	12	14-1	.979	1	105	65	O-97(64-7-26)/1-8	1.1
1973	Pit N	59	83	9	15	1	0	1	3	2-0	0	7	.181	.200	.229	19	-10	0-2	.977	2	165	108	1-10,O-10(7-0-3)	-1.0
	†Oak A	38	64	5	12	1	0	0	4	3-1	0	4	.188	.224	.203	22	-7	0-0	.967	0	100	103	O-19(8-1-10)/1-8,D-2	-0.8
1974	Oak A	17	23	0	4	0	0	0	1	2-1	0	2	.174	.231	.174	22	-2	0-0	1.000	-1	49	0	/O-6(2-2-2),D-4	-0.4
1977	†LA N	24	48	3	15	2	0	0	4	0-0	0	6	.313	.313	.354	79	-2	0-0	1.000	-1	75	0	O-12(2-4-8)	-0.3
1978	†LA N	75	77	15	24	1	1	1	11	3-0	0	7	.312	.333	.390	103	0	2-1	1.000	-1	91	0	O-25(16-2-7)/1	-0.1
1979	LA N	29	27	2	7	1	0	0	2	2-0	0	0	.259	.310	.296	67	-1	2-0	1.000	-0	80	0	/O-3(LF)	-0.1
1980	LA N	7	6	1	1	0	0	0	0	0-0	0	1	.167	.167	.167	-7	-1	0-0	1.000	0	0	1230	/1	-0.1
Total	16	1458	4017	509	1122	160	37	36	329	212-29	10	422	.279	.315	.364	94	-42	125-58	.986	26	108	105	*O-1066C/1-47,D-6,P-2	-5.0
DaVANON, JERRY Frank Gerald B 8.21.1945 Oceanside, CA BR/TR 5-11/175# d4.11 s-Jeff																								
1969	SD N	24	59	4	8	1	0	0	3	3-0	0	12	.136	.177	.153	-7	-9	0-3	.932	1	93	53	2-15/S-7	-0.9
	StL N	16	40	7	12	3	0	1	7	6-1	0	8	.300	.391	.450	135	2	0-0	.958	2	105	90	S-16	0.6
	Year	40	99	11	20	4	0	1	10	9-1	0	20	.202	.269	.273	53	-6	0-3	.959	3	118	97	S-23,2-15	-0.3
1970	StL N	11	18	2	2	1	0	0	0	2-0	0	5	.111	.200	.167	-1	-3	0-0	1.000	2	88	442	/3-5,2-3	0.0
1971	Bal A	38	81	14	19	5	0	0	4	12-0	1	20	.235	.340	.296	82	-1	0-0	.970	-5	86	74	2-20,S-11/3-3,1	-0.5
1973	Cal A	41	49	6	12	3	0	0	2	3-0	0	9	.245	.288	.306	73	-2	1-2	.927	-2	100	101	S-14,2-12/3-7	-0.3
1974	StL N	30	40	4	6	1	0	0	4	4-0	2	5	.150	.255	.175	24	-4	0-1	.840	-3	70	87	S-14/3-8,2-7,O(RF)	-0.7
1975	Hou N	32	97	15	27	4	2	1	10	16-1	1	7	.278	.386	.392	125	4	2-0	.944	3	102	102	S-21/2-9,3-3	1.0
1976	Hou N	61	107	19	31	3	3	1	20	21-1	1	12	.290	.408	.402	144	7	0-2	.980	2	134	63	2-17,S-17/3-9	1.1
1977	StL N	9	8	2	0	0	0	0	0	1-0	0	2	.000	.111	.000	-68	-2	0-0	.923	0	129	0	/2-5	-0.2
Total	8	262	499	73	117	21	5	3	50	68-3	5	80	.234	.331	.315	86	-8	3-8	.936	-1	99	107	S-100/2-88,3-35,O(RF)1	0.1
DaVANON, JEFF Jeffrey Graham B 12.8.1973 San Diego, CA BB/TR 6/180# d9.7 f-Jerry																								
1999	Ana A	7	20	4	4	0	1	1	4	2-0	0	7	.200	.273	.450	81	-1	0-1	1.000	-1	60	0	/O-5(3-0-2),D-2	-0.2
2001	Ana A	40	88	7	17	2	1	5	9	11-0	0	29	.193	.280	.409	77	-3	1-3	.980	-0	86	205	O-29(0-13-17)/D-6	-0.5
2002	Ana A	16	30	3	5	3	0	1	4	2-0	0	6	.167	.219	.367	52	-2	1-0	1.000	-0	101	0	O-10(2-4-4)/D-4	-0.2
2003	Ana A	123	330	56	93	16	1	12	43	42-0	1	59	.282	.360	.445	117	9	17-5	.983	4	118	41	*O-115(8-31-91)/D	1.1
Total	4	186	468	70	119	21	3	19	60	57-0	1	101	.254	.333	.434	103	3	19-9	.983	3	109	68	O-159(13-48-114)/D-13	0.2
DAVENPORT, JIM James Houston B 8.17.1933 Siluria, AL BR/TR 5-11/175# d4.15 M1 C15																								
1958	SF N	134	434	70	111	22	3	12	41	33-0	7	64	.256	.317	.403	92	-6	1-3	.960	-7	97	89	*3-130/S-5	-1.4
1959	SF N	123	469	65	121	16	3	6	38	28-0	2	65	.258	.301	.343	73	-19	0-1	**.978**	-1	98	88	*3-121/S	-2.1
1960	SF N	112	363	43	91	15	3	6	38	26-1	4	58	.251	.306	.358	87	-7	0-2	**.961**	-0	100	82	*3-103/S-7	-0.8
1961	SF N	137	436	64	121	28	4	12	65	45-1	2	65	.278	.342	.443	112	8	4-3	**.965**	4	98	111	*3-132	1.1
1962	†SF N★	144	485	83	144	25	5	14	58	45-3	2	76	.297	.357	.456	119	13	2-5	.952	-1	98	**122**	*3-141	1.1
1963	SF N	147	460	40	116	19	3	4	36	32-4	0	87	.252	.297	.333	83	-10	5-2	.962	-8	87	56	*3-127,2-22/S	-1.8
1964	SF N	116	297	24	70	10	6	2	26	29-2	0	46	.236	.299	.330	77	-9	2-0	.979	-4	90	61	S-64,3-41,2-30	-0.8
1965	SF N	106	271	29	68	14	3	4	31	21-2	1	47	.251	.304	.369	87	-5	0-0	.949	-14	95	72	3-39,S-37,2-26	-1.6
1966	SF N	111	305	42	76	6	2	9	30	22-2	1	40	.249	.300	.370	83	-7	1-1	.961	-10	99	78	S-58,3-36,2-21/1-2	-1.4
1967	SF N	124	295	42	81	10	3	5	30	39-6	4	50	.275	.366	.380	116	7	1-4	1.000	1	101	109	3-64,S-28,2-12	1.0
1968	SF N	113	272	27	61	1	1	1	17	26-0	0	32	.224	.292	.246	63	-12	0-3	.960	-5	92	111	3-82,S-17/2	-2.1
1969	SF N	112	303	20	73	10	1	2	42	29-1	0	37	.241	.304	.300	72	-11	0-1	.967	-2	96	111	*3-104/1SO(RF)	-1.5
1970	SF N	22	37	3	9	1	0	0	4	7-1	0	6	.243	.356	.270	73	-1	0-0	1.000	-4	46	0	3-10	-0.5
Total	13	1501	4427	552	1142	177	37	77	456	382-23	23	673	.258	.318	.367	90	-59	16-25	.964	-52	96	96	*3-1130,S-219,2-112/1-3,O(RF)	-10.8
DAVID, ANDRE Andre Anter B 5.18.1958 Hollywood, CA BL/TL 6/170# d6.29																								
1984	Min A	33	48	5	12	2	0	1	5	7-2	1	11	.250	.351	.354	93	0	0-0	1.000	-1	74	0	O-14(10-0-4)/D-2	-0.2
1986	Min A	5	5	0	1	0	0	0	0	0-0	1	2	.200	.333	.200	48	0	0-0	—	0			/D	0.0
Total	2	38	53	5	13	2	0	1	5	7-2	2	13	.245	.349	.340	89	0	0-0	1.000	-1	74	0	/O-14(10-0-4),D-3	-0.2
DAVIDSON, CLAUDE Claude Boucher "Davey" B 10.13.1896 Boston, MA D 4.18.1956 Weymouth, MA BL/TR 5-11/155# d4.25																								
1918	Phi A	31	81	4	15	1	0	0	4	5	0	9	.185	.233	.198	29	-7	0	.943	-1	91	99	2-15/O-8(1-0-7),3	-1.0
1919	Was A	2	7	1	3	0	0	0	0	1	0	1	.429	.500	.429	163	1	0	1.000	-0	90	0	/3-2	0.1
Total	2	33	88	5	18	1	0	0	4	6	0	10	.205	.255	.216	41	-6	0	.943	-1	91	99	/2-15,O-8(1-0-7),3-3	-0.9
DAVIDSON, CLEATUS Cleatus La Von B 11.1.1976 Bartow, FL BB/TR 5-10/170# d5.30																								
1999	Min A	12	22	3	3	0	0	0	3	0-0	0	4	.136	.136	.136	-29	-4	2-0	.973	4	162	221	/2-6,S-4	0.1
DAVIDSON, HOMER Homer Hurd "Divvy" B 10.14.1884 Cleveland, OH D 7.26.1948 Detroit, MI BR/TR 5-10.5/155# d4.25																								
1908	Cle A	9	4	2	0	0	0	0	0	0	0		.000	.000	.000	-99	-1	1	1.000	1	*0*	*124*	/C-5,O(RF)	0.0
DAVIDSON, MARK John Mark B 2.15.1961 Knoxville, TN BR/TR 6-2/190# d6.20																								
1986	Min A	36	68	5	8	3	0	0	2	6-0	0	22	.118	.189	.162	-3	-10	2-3	.980	-0	111	0	O-31(20-5-7)/D-3	-1.1
1987	†Min A	102	150	32	40	4	1	1	14	13-1	0	26	.267	.321	.327	71	-6	9-2	1.000	1	103	102	O-86(36-20-33)/D-9	-0.5
1988	Min A	100	106	22	23	7	0	1	10	10-0	1	20	.217	.288	.311	67	-4	3-3	.955	5	132	137	O-91(4-4-84)/3D	-0.1
1989	Hou N	33	65	7	13	2	1	1	5	7-0	0	14	.200	.278	.308	70	-3	1-0	1.000	-0	104	0	O-23(7-3-15)	-0.4
1990	Hou N	57	130	12	38	5	1	1	11	10-1	0	18	.292	.340	.369	99	0	0-3	.981	4	131	37	O-51(26-1-27)	0.1
1991	Hou N	85	142	10	27	6	0	2	15	12-0	2	28	.190	.263	.275	54	-9	0-0	1.000	1	108	47	O-63(32-4-32)	-1.0
Total	6	413	661	88	149	27	3	6	57	58-2	3	128	.225	.289	.303	64	-32	15-11	.983	10	116	67	O-345(125-37-198)/D-15,3	-3.0
DAVIDSON, BILL William Simpson B 5.10.1884 Lafayette, IN D 5.23.1954 Lincoln, NE BR/TR 5-10/170# d9.29																								
1909	Chi N	2	7	2	1	0	0	0	0	1	0		.143	.250	.143	22	-1	1	1.000	-0	0	0	/O-2(1-1-0)	-0.1
1910	Bro N	136	509	48	121	13	7	0	34	24	4	54	.238	.277	.291	68	-23	27	.961	-11	92	60	*O-131(0-127-4)	-4.3
1911	Bro N	87	292	33	68	3	4	1	26	16	1	21	.233	.275	.281	58	-18	18	.956	-6	99	37	O-74(CF)	-3.0
Total	3	225	808	83	190	16	11	1	60	41	5	75	.235	.276	.286	64	-42	46	.959	-17	94	51	O-207(1-202-4)	-7.4
DAVIES, CHICK Lloyd Garrison B 3.6.1892 Peabody, MA D 9.5.1973 Middletown, CT BL/TL 5-8/145# d7.11 ▲																								
1914	Phi A	19	46	6	11	3	1	0	5	5	0	13	.239	.314	.348	103	0	1	.926	-1	111	0	O-10(9-0-1)/P	-0.1
1915	Phi A	56	132	13	24	5	3	0	11	14	2	31	.182	.270	.265	62	-6	2-4	.973	4	99	193	O-32(7-21-4)/P-4	-0.6

Year	Tm Lg	G	AB	R	H	2B	3B	HR	RBI	BB-IB	HP	SO	AVG	OBP	SLG	AOPS	ABR	SB-CS	FA	FR	Rng	Thr	G at Pos	BFW
1925	NY N	4	6	1	0	0	0	0	0	0	0	1	.000	.000	.000	-99	-2	0-0	1.000	0	182	0	/P-2,O(RF)	-0.1
1926	NY N	38	18	4	4	0	0	0	1	3	0	5	.222	.333	.222	53	1	0	.938	1	118	174	P-38	0.0
Total	4	117	202	24	39	8	4	0	17	22	2	50	.193	.279	.272	65	-7	3-4	.938	4	124	214	/P-45,O-43(16-21-6)	-0.8
DAVIS, LEFTY Alphonzo De Ford B 2.4.1875 Nashville, TN D 2.4.1919 Collins, NY BL/TL 5-10/170# d4.18																								
1901	Bro N	25	91	11	19	2	0	0	7	10	0		.209	.287	.231	50	-6	4	.822	-5	0	0	O-24(12-2-10)/2	-1.1
	Pit N	87	335	87	105	8	11	2	33	56	2		.313	.415	.421	138	19	22	.975	5	158	273	O-86(RF)	2.0
	Year	112	426	98	124	10	11	2	40	66	2		.291	.389	.380	120	13	26	.942	1	126	**217**	*O-110(12-2-96)/2	0.9
1902	Pit N	59	232	52	65	7	3	0	20	35	1		.280	.377	.336	116	6	19	.945	-2	78	58	O-59(RF)	0.1
1903	NY A	104	372	54	88	10	0	0	25	43	2		.237	.319	.263	72	-11	11	.906	-8	60	35	*O-102(95-1-6)/S	-2.6
1907	Cin N	73	266	28	61	5	5	1	25	23	1		.229	.293	.297	82	-6	9	.972	3	113	124	O-70(0-69-1)	-0.7
Total	4	348	1296	232	338	32	19	3	110	167	6		.261	.348	.322	98	2	65	.939	-6	95	116	O-341(107-72-162)/S2	-2.3
DAVIS, ALVIN Alvin Glenn B 9.9.1960 Riverside, CA BL/TR 6-1/195# d4.11																								
1984	Sea A★	152	567	80	161	34	3	27	116	97-16	7	78	.284	.391	.497	147	41	5-4	.992	-2	90	80	*1-147/D-7	2.9
1985	Sea A	155	578	78	166	33	1	18	78	90-7	2	71	.287	.381	.441	125	24	1-2	.992	-3	91	93	*1-154	1.1
1986	Sea A	135	479	66	130	18	1	18	72	76-10	3	68	.271	.373	.426	116	13	0-3	.986	1	106	122	*1-101,D-32	0.6
1987	Sea A	157	580	86	171	37	2	29	100	72-6	2	84	.295	.370	.516	126	23	0-0	.994	-5	87	107	*1-157	0.8
1988	Sea A	140	478	67	141	24	1	18	69	95-13	4	53	.295	.412	.462	139	31	1-1	.994	-5	80	**116**	*1-115,D-25	1.7
1989	Sea A	142	498	84	152	30	1	21	95	101-15	6	49	.305	.424	.496	155	43	0-1	.992	-4	90	107	*1-125,D-14	3.0
1990	Sea A	140	494	63	140	21	0	17	68	85-10	4	68	.283	.387	.429	128	23	0-2	.994	-1	89	94	D-87,1-52	1.5
1991	Sea A	145	462	39	102	15	1	12	69	56-9	0	78	.221	.299	.335	77	-15	0-3	1.000	-0	85	134	*D-126,1-14	-2.1
1992	Cal A	40	104	5	26	8	0	0	16	13-2	0	9	.250	.331	.327	85	-1	0-0	.995	0	105	119	1-22/D-9	-0.3
Total	9	1206	4240	568	1189	220	10	160	683	685-88	28	558	.280	.380	.450	127	182	7-16	.992	-19	90	103	1-887,D-300	9.2
DAVIS, BILL Arthur Willard B 6.6.1942 Graceville, MN BL/TL 6-7/215# d9.16																								
1965	Cle A	10	10	0	3	1	0	0	0	0-0	0	1	.300	.300	.400	96	0	0-0	—	0			H	0.0
1966	Cle A	23	38	2	6	1	0	1	4	6-0	0	9	.158	.267	.263	55	-2	0-0	.981	0	107	116	/1-9	-0.3
1969	SD N	31	57	1	10	1	0	0	1	8-0	1	18	.175	.288	.193	39	-4	0-0	.992	-1	68	108	1-14	-0.7
Total	3	64	105	3	19	3	0	1	5	14-0	1	28	.181	.281	.238	50	-6	0-0	.988	-1	83	111	/1-23	-1.0
DAVIS, BROCK Bryshear Barnett B 10.19.1943 Oakland, CA BL/TL 5-10/168# d4.9																								
1963	Hou N	34	55	7	11	2	0	1	2	4-1	0	10	.200	.254	.291	60	-3	0-0	.864	-1	93	152	O-14(5-6-3)	-0.4
1964	Hou N	1	3	0	0	0	0	0	0	1-0	0	1	.000	.250	.000	-24	0	0-0	1.000	0	101	0	/O(LF)	-0.1
1966	Hou N	10	27	2	4	1	0	0	1	5-0	0	4	.148	.281	.185	35	-2	1-0	1.000	-0	109	0	/O-7(CF)	-0.2
1970	Chi N	6	3	0	0	0	0	0	0	0-0	0	1	.000	.000	.000	-89	-1	0-0	—	-0	0	0	/O(CF)	-0.1
1971	Chi N	106	301	22	77	7	5	0	28	35-0	2	34	.256	.335	.312	74	-9	0-6	.982	2	104	104	O-93(3-85-5)	-1.3
1972	Mil A	85	154	17	49	2	0	0	12	12-0	0	23	.318	.365	.331	111	2	6-4	.970	-1	95	88	O-43(19-19-5)	-0.1
Total	6	242	543	48	141	12	5	1	43	57-1	2	73	.260	.331	.306	79	-13	7-10	.973	-1	101	98	O-159(28-118-13)	-2.2
DAVIS, CHILI Charles Theodore B 1.17.1960 Kingston, Jamaica BB/TR 6-3/210# d4.10																								
1981	SF N	8	15	1	2	0	0	0	0	1-0	0	2	.133	.188	.133	-8	-2	2-0	1.000	-0	92	0	/O-6(1-2-3)	-0.2
1982	SF N	154	641	86	167	27	6	19	76	45-2	2	115	.261	.308	.410	100	-2	24-13	.972	5	104	163	*O-153(13-142-1)	0.2
1983	SF N	137	486	54	113	21	2	11	59	55-6	0	108	.233	.305	.352	86	-9	10-12	.976	4	108	105	*O-133(0-121-12)	-1.0
1984	SF N★	137	499	87	157	21	6	21	81	42-6	1	74	.315	.368	.507	149	30	12-8	.971	3	106	121	*O-123(1-67-57)	3.1
1985	SF N	136	481	53	130	25	2	13	56	62-12	0	74	.270	.349	.412	119	13	15-7	.980	7	110	123	*O-126(0-36-91)	1.6
1986	SF N★	153	526	71	146	28	3	13	70	84-23	1	96	.278	.375	.416	125	21	16-13	.972	-1	104	83	*O-148(0-53-117)	1.3
1987	†SF N	149	500	80	125	22	1	24	76	72-15	2	109	.250	.344	.442	113	9	16-9	.975	-7	91	78	*O-135(18-114-36)	0.0
1988	Cal A	158	600	81	161	29	3	21	93	56-14	0	118	.268	.326	.432	115	11	9-10	.942	-10	89	103	*O-153(0-3-154)/D-3	-0.5
1989	Cal A	154	560	81	152	24	1	22	90	61-12	0	109	.271	.340	.436	120	15	3-0	.979	-11	87	56	*O-147(LF)/D-6	0.0
1990	Cal A	113	412	58	109	17	1	12	58	61-4	0	89	.265	.357	.398	114	9	1-2	.965	-3	79	159	D-60,O-52(46-0-7)	0.3
1991	†Min A	153	534	84	148	34	1	29	93	95-13	1	117	.277	.385	.507	139	31	5-6	1.000	0	280	0	*D-150/O-2(LF)	2.6
1992	Min A	138	444	63	128	27	2	12	66	73-11	3	76	.288	.386	.439	128	20	4-5	1.000	0	130	0	*D-125/O-4(1-0-3),1	1.6
1993	Cal A	153	573	74	139	32	0	27	112	71-12	1	135	.243	.327	.440	101	0	4-1	—	-0	0	0	*D-150/P	-0.9
1994	Cal A★	108	392	72	122	18	1	26	84	69-11	1	84	.311	.410	.561	147	29	3-2	1.000	0	124	0	*D-106/O-2(LF)	2.0
1995	Cal A	119	424	81	135	23	0	20	86	89-12	0	79	.318	.429	.514	148	35	3-3	—	0	0	0	*D-119	2.5
1996	Cal A	145	530	73	155	24	0	28	95	86-11	0	99	.292	.387	.496	122	20	5-2	—	0	0	0	*D-143	1.0
1997	KC A	140	477	71	133	20	0	30	90	85-16	1	96	.279	.386	.509	129	22	6-3	—	0	0	0	*D-133	1.3
1998	†NY A	35	103	11	30	7	0	3	9	14-1	0	18	.291	.373	.447	117	3	0-1	—	0	0	0	D-34	0.0
1999	†NY A	146	476	59	128	25	1	19	78	73-7	2	100	.269	.366	.445	108	7	4-1	—	0	0	0	*D-132	-0.1
Total	19	2436	8673	1240	2380	424	30	350	1372	1194-188	15	1698	.274	.360	.451	120	262	142-98	.971	-13	99	106	*O-1184(231-538-481),D-1161/P1	14.8
DAVIS, DOUG Douglas Raymond B 9.24.1962 Bloomsburg, PA BR/TR 6/180# d7.8 C1																								
1988	Cal A	6	12	1	0	0	0	0	0	0-0	1	3	.000	.077	.000	-79	-3	0-0	1.000	-2	99	226	/C-3,3-3	-0.6
1992	Tex A	1	1	0	1	0	0	0	0	0-0	0	0	1.000	1.000	1.000	479	0	0-0	—	-0	0	0	/C	0.0
Total	2	7	13	1	1	0	0	0	0	0-0	1	3	.077	.143	.077	-38	-3	0-0	1.000	-3	92	210	/C-4,3-3	-0.6
DAVIS, ERIC Eric Keith B 5.29.1962 Los Angeles, CA BR/TR 6-3/185# d5.19																								
1984	Cin N	57	174	33	39	10	1	10	30	24-0	1	48	.224	.320	.466	114	3	10-2	.992	5	114	158	O-51(2-46-10)	0.9
1985	Cin N	56	122	26	30	3	3	8	18	7-0	0	39	.246	.287	.516	114	1	16-3	.987	3	112	158	O-47(24-28-5)	0.6
1986	Cin N	132	415	97	115	15	3	27	71	68-5	1	100	.277	.378	.523	140	24	80-11	.975	0	111	27	*O-121(72-71-16)	3.5
1987	Cin N★	129	474	120	139	23	4	37	100	84-8	1	134	.293	.399	.593	152	37	50-6	.990	16	**124**	136	*O-128(4-124-0)	**5.8**
1988	Cin N	135	472	81	129	18	3	26	93	65-10	3	124	.273	.363	.489	138	24	35-3	.981	-9	92	34	*O-130(0-125-5)	2.1
1989	Cin N★	131	462	74	130	14	2	34	101	68-12	1	116	.281	.367	.541	154	32	21-7	.984	-7	97	31	*O-125(4-118-3)	2.8
1990	†Cin N	127	453	84	118	26	2	24	86	60-6	2	100	.260	.347	.486	122	14	21-3	.993	-1	94	148	*O-122(56-66-0)	1.5
1991	Cin N	89	285	39	67	10	0	11	33	48-5	5	92	.235	.353	.386	104	3	14-2	.985	2	106	120	O-81(7-77-0)	0.7
1992	LA N	76	267	21	61	8	1	5	32	36-2	3	71	.228	.325	.322	86	-4	19-1	.961	-7	84	0	O-74(69-5-4)	-1.1
1993	LA N	108	376	57	88	17	0	14	53	41-6	1	88	.234	.308	.391	92	-5	33-5	.991	5	107	93	*O-103(101-3-0)	0.2
	Det A	23	75	14	19	1	1	6	15	14-1	0	18	.253	.371	.533	141	4	2-2	.981	0	111	0	O-18(CF)/D-5	0.4
1994	Det A	37	120	19	22	4	0	3	13	18-0	0	45	.183	.290	.292	50	-9	5-0	.989	-2	96	56	O-35(CF)	-0.8
1996	Cin N	129	415	81	119	20	0	26	83	70-3	6	121	.287	.394	.523	140	26	23-9	.989	-1	105	51	*O-126(14-115-0)/1	2.7
1997	†Bal A	42	158	29	48	11	0	8	25	14-0	1	47	.304	.358	.525	132	7	6-0	.975	-5	68	0	O-30(RF),D-12	0.2
1998	Bal A	131	452	81	148	29	1	28	89	44-0	5	108	.327	.388	.582	151	34	7-6	.992	-3	90	88	O-72(0-11-64),D-53	2.3
1999	StL N	58	191	27	49	9	2	5	30	30-1	1	49	.257	.359	.403	92	-2	5-4	1.000	0	96	126	O-51(0-3-50)/D-2	-0.4
2000	†StL N	92	254	38	77	14	0	6	40	36-0	1	60	.303	.389	.429	107	4	1-1	.968	-1	108	28	O-69(RF)/D-4	0.0
2001	SF N	74	156	17	32	7	3	4	22	13-0	1	38	.205	.269	.365	67	-9	1-1	.962	-0	106	44	O-48(RF)/D	-1.1
Total	17	1626	5321	938	1430	239	26	282	934	740-59	33	1398	.269	.359	.482	125	184	349-66	.984	-5	102	74	*O-1431(353-845-304)/D-77,1	20.3
DAVIS, GEORGE George Stacey B 8.23.1870 Cohoes, NY D 10.17.1940 Philadelphia, PA BB/TR 5-9/180# d4.19 M3 HF1998 OF Total (12-LF 243-CF 48-RF)																								
1890	Cle N	**136**	526	98	139	22	9	6	73	53	4	34	.264	.336	.375	109	6	22	.946	12	**158**	182	*O-133(0-129-4)/2-2,S	1.2
1891	Cle N	136	570	115	165	35	12	3	89	53	4	29	.289	.354	.409	117	11	42	.931	8	**154**	32	*O-116(4-111-1),3-22/P-3	1.5
1892	†Cle N	144	597	95	144	27	12	5	82	58	3	51	.241	.312	.352	97	-4	36	.914	-8	95	76	3-79,O-44(0-3-41),S-20/2-3	-1.1
1893	NY N	133	549	112	195	22	27	11	119	42	9	20	.355	.410	.554	154	38	37	.884	-1	99	**114**	*3-133/S	3.2
1894	†NY N	124	486	125	171	27	19	9	93	67	4	10	.352	.434	.541	135	28	42	.908	-1	99	104	*3-124	2.2
1895	NY N	110	430	108	146	36	9	5	101	55	2	12	.340	.417	.500	139	27	48	.881	11	103	150	3-80,1-14,2-10/O-7(5-0-2),M	3.2
1896	NY N	124	494	98	158	25	12	5	99	50	4	24	.320	.387	.449	124	17	48	.917	15	109	99	3-74,S-45/O-3(LF),1-3	3.0
1897	NY N	131	521	112	184	31	10	10	**135**	43	7		.353	.410	.509	146	34	65	.926	20	99	**139**	*S-130	5.1
1898	NY N	121	486	80	149	20	5	2	86	32	1		.307	.351	.381	113	8	26	.933	**30**	101	112	*S-121	4.0
1899	NY N	109	419	69	141	22	5	1	59	38	2		.337	.394	.420	128	17	35	**.946**	**46**	**112**	119	*S-109	**6.1**
1900	NY N	114	426	69	136	20	4	3	61	35	4		.319	.376	.406	121	14	29	**.944**	**29**	**111**	105	*S-114,M	4.3
1901	NY N	130	491	69	148	26	7	7	65	40	2		.301	.356	.426	131	20	27	.939	24	102	89	*S-113,3-17,M	4.6
1902	Chi A	132	485	76	145	27	7	3	93	65	4		.299	.386	.402	124	20	31	**.951**	-3	96	**134**	*S-129/1-3	2.0
1903	NY N	4	15	2	4	0	0	0	1	1	0		.267	.313	.267	63	-1	0	.870	-2	68	0	/S-4	-0.2
1904	Chi A	152	563	75	142	27	15	1	69	43	5		.252	.311	.359	116	10	32	.937	18	107	**149**	*S-152	3.7
1905	Chi A	151	550	74	153	29	1	1	55	60	4		.278	.353	.340	125	19	31	**.948**	16	110	**137**	*S-151	**4.4**
1906	†Chi A	133	484	63	134	26	6	0	80	41	4		.277	.338	.355	120	13	27	.946	13	110	121	*S-129/2	3.2

Year	Tm Lg	G	AB	R	H	2B	3B	HR	RBI	BB-IB	HP	SO	AVG	OBP	SLG	AOPS	ABR	SB-CS	FA	FR	Rng	Thr	G at Pos	BFW
1907	Chi A	132	466	59	111	16	2	1	52	47	4		.238	.313	.288	95	-1	15	.949	7	**108**	138	*S-132	1.2
1908	Chi A	128	419	41	91	14	1	0	26	41	7		.217	.298	.255	81	-6	22	.960	2	109	97	2-95,S-23/1-4	-0.4
1909	Chi A	28	68	5	9	1	0	0	2	10	1		.132	.253	.147	28	-5	4	.986	1	143	93	1-17/2-2	-0.5
Total	20	2372	9045	1545	2665	453	163	73	1440	874	75	180	.295	.362	.405	121	265	619	.940	236	104	122	*S-1374,3-529,O-303C,2-113/1P	50.7
DAVIS, KIDDO George Willis B 2.12.1902 Bridgeport, CT D 3.4.1983 Bridgeport, CT BR/TR 5-11/178# d6.15																								
1926	NY A	1	0	0	0	0	0	0	0	0	0	0	—	—	—	—	0	0-0	—	-0	0	0	/O(RF)	0.0
1932	Phi N	137	576	100	178	39	6	5	57	44	1	56	.309	.359	.424	98	0	16	.975	8	108	122	*O-133(1-132-0)	0.4
1933	†NY N	126	434	61	112	20	4	7	37	25	0	30	.258	.298	.371	92	-6	10	.988	-9	85	92	*O-120(CF)	-1.9
1934	StL N	16	33	6	10	3	0	1	4	3	0	1	.303	.361	.485	117	1	1	.960	1	110	174	/O-9(CF)	0.1
	Phi N	100	393	50	115	25	5	3	48	27	0	28	.293	.338	.405	86	-7	1	.991	13	115	178	*O-100(CF)	0.3
	Year	116	426	56	125	28	5	4	52	30	0	29	.293	.340	.411	89	-6	2	.988	14	**115**	178	*O-109(CF)	0.4
1935	NY N	47	91	16	24	7	1	2	6	10	1	4	.264	.343	.429	108	1	2	.977	-1	97	49	O-21(2-2-17)	-0.1
1936	†NY N	47	67	6	16	1	0	0	5	6	0	5	.239	.301	.254	51	-5	0	1.000	2	107	229	O-22(6-11-6)	-0.3
1937	NY N	56	76	20	20	10	0	0	9	10	1	7	.263	.356	.395	103	1	1	.932	-2	93	0	O-37(11-25-0)	-0.2
	Cin N	40	136	19	35	6	0	1	5	16	1	6	.257	.340	.324	85	-2	1	.959	-1	104	33	O-35(9-26-0)	-0.5
	Year	96	212	39	55	16	0	1	14	26	2	13	.259	.346	.349	90	-1	2	.951	-3	100	22	O-72(20-51-0)	-0.7
1938	Cin N	5	18	3	5	1	0	0	0	1	0	4	.278	.316	.333	81	0	0	1.000	0	92	265	/O-5(2-0-5)	0.0
Total	8	575	1824	281	515	112	16	19	171	142	4	141	.282	.336	.393	92	-17	32-0	.980	11	102	117	O-483(31-425-29)	-2.2
DAVIS, GERRY Gerald Edward B 12.25.1958 Trenton, NJ BR/TR 6/185# d9.20																								
1983	SD N	5	15	3	5	2	0	0	1	3-0	0	4	.333	.444	.467	158	1	1-0	1.000	0	91	306	/O-5(RF)	0.2
1985	SD N	44	58	10	17	3	1	0	2	5-0	0	7	.293	.349	.379	105	0	0-0	.952	0	87	263	O-23(7-1-14)	0.0
Total	2	49	73	13	22	5	1	0	3	8-0	0	11	.301	.370	.397	117	1	1-0	.967	1	88	276	/O-28(7-1-19)	0.2
DAVIS, GLENN Glenn Earle B 3.28.1961 Jacksonville, FL BR/TR 6-3/210# d9.2																								
1984	Hou N	18	61	6	13	5	0	2	8	4-0	0	12	.213	.258	.393	88	-1	0-0	.988	2	144	109	1-16	0.0
1985	Hou N	100	350	51	95	11	0	20	64	27-6	7	68	.271	.332	.474	128	12	0-0	.985	-2	97	109	1-89/O-9(RF)	0.5
1986	†Hou N★	158	574	91	152	32	3	31	101	64-6	9	72	.265	.344	.493	133	25	3-1	.992	2	98	85	*1-156	1.8
1987	Hou N	151	578	70	145	35	2	27	93	47-10	5	84	.251	.310	.458	105	2	4-1	.991	3	101	79	*1-151	-0.4
1988	Hou N	152	561	78	152	26	0	30	99	53-20	11	77	.271	.341	.478	140	28	4-3	**.996**	1	96	99	*1-151	1.9
1989	Hou N★	158	581	87	156	26	1	34	89	69-17	7	123	.269	.350	.492	144	33	4-2	.992	2	106	92	*1-156	2.5
1990	Hou N	93	327	44	82	15	4	22	64	46-17	**8**	54	.251	.357	.523	143	19	8-3	.995	-5	82	93	1-91	0.9
1991	Bal A	49	176	29	40	9	1	10	28	16-0	5	29	.227	.307	.460	115	3	4-0	.976	4	152	116	1-36,D-12	0.5
1992	Bal A	106	398	46	110	15	2	13	48	37-2	2	65	.276	.338	.422	110	5	1-0	1.000	-0	65	59	*D-103/1-2	0.1
1993	Bal A	30	113	8	20	3	0	1	9	7-0	1	29	.177	.230	.230	24	-12	0-1	.990	-1	86	112	1-22/D-7	-1.6
Total	10	1015	3719	510	965	177	13	190	603	370-78	55	613	.259	.332	.467	124	114	28-11	.991	6	101	93	1-870,D-122/O-9(RF)	6.2
DAVIS, HARRY Harry Albert "Stinky" B 5.7.1908 Shreveport, LA D 3.3.1997 Shreveport, LA BL/TL 5-10.5/160# d4.13																								
1932	Det A	141	590	92	159	32	13	4	74	60	2	53	.269	.339	.388	84	-14	12-7	.989	-4	87	105	*1-141	-3.0
1933	Det A	66	173	24	37	8	2	0	14	22	0	8	.214	.303	.283	55	-11	2-3	.978	-5	57	104	1-44	-2.0
1937	StL A	120	450	89	124	25	3	3	35	71	0	26	.276	.374	.364	86	-7	7-6	.991	-4	86	98	*1-112/O(RF)	-2.0
Total	3	327	1213	205	320	65	18	7	123	153	2	87	.264	.347	.364	81	-32	21-16	.988	-13	82	102	1-297/O(RF)	-7.0
DAVIS, HARRY Harry H (born Harry Davis) "Jasper" B 7.19.1873 Philadelphia, PA D 8.11.1947 Philadelphia, PA BR/TR 5-10/180# d9.21 M1 C6 OF Total (50-LF 19-CF 11-RF)																								
1895	NY N	7	24	1	7	0	1	0	6	2	0	0	.292	.346	.375	88	-1	1	.957	0	118	108	/1-7	-0.1
1896	NY N	64	233	43	64	11	10	2	50	31	5	20	.275	.372	.433	115	5	16	.883	-6	34	0	O-40(39-1-0),1-23	-0.3
	Pit N	44	168	24	32	5	6	0	23	13	2	21	.190	.257	.292	46	-14	9	.966	0	98	82	1-35,O-10(9-0-1)/S	-1.3
	Year	108	401	67	96	16	16	2	73	44	7	41	.239	.325	.374	87	-9	25	.973	-6	96	91	1-58,O-50(48-1-1)/S	-1.6
1897	Pit N	111	429	70	131	10	**28**	2	63	26	10		.305	.359	.473	123	11	21	.965	-12	84	78	1-64,3-32,O-14(0-7-9)/S	-0.1
1898	Pit N	58	222	31	65	9	13	1	24	12	1		.293	.332	.464	130	6	7	.980	-1	85	99	1-53/O-6(CF)	0.4
	Lou N	37	138	18	30	5	2	1	16	7	0		.217	.255	.304	61	-8	6	.967	-0	124	111	1-34/2-2,O(RF)	-0.8
	Was N	1	3	0	0	0	0	0	0	0	0		.000	.000	.000	-99	-1	0	.875	-0	0	0	/1	-0.1
	Year	96	363	49	95	14	15	2	40	19	1		.262	.300	.399	102	-2	13	.974	-2	99	103	1-88/O-7(0-6-1),2-2	-0.5
1899	Was N	18	64	3	12	2	3	0	8	8	1		.188	.288	.313	65	-3	2	.988	-1	48	53	1-18	-0.4
1901	Phi A	117	496	92	152	28	10	8	76	23	2		.306	.340	.452	113	7	21	.976	8	133	97	*1-117	1.1
1902	Phi A	133	561	89	172	**43**	8	6	92	30	1		.307	.343	.444	112	8	28	.984	8	122	76	*1-128/O-5(CF)	1.3
1903	Phi A	106	420	77	125	28	7	6	55	24	5		.298	.343	.440	128	14	24	.972	-1	98	77	*1-104/O-2(LF)	1.2
1904	Phi A	102	404	54	125	21	11	**10**	62	23	2		.309	.350	.490	156	24	12	.983	-1	88	79	*1-102	2.3
1905	†Phi A	150	607	**93**	173	**47**	6	**8**	**83**	43	2		.285	.334	.422	137	25	36	.985	0	92	71	*1-150	2.4
1906	Phi A	145	551	94	161	42	7	**12**	**96**	49	5		.292	.355	.459	150	32	23	.975	0	100	109	*1-145	3.2
1907	Phi A	149	582	84	155	**35**	8	**8**	87	42	2		.266	.318	.395	124	15	20	.977	4	109	79	*1-149	1.7
1908	Phi A	147	513	65	127	23	9	5	62	61	4		.248	.332	.357	116	11	20	.986	1	96	68	*1-147	1.0
1909	Phi A	149	530	73	142	22	11	4	75	51	5		.268	.338	.374	122	14	20	.988	-6	80	98	*1-149	0.6
1910	†Phi A	139	492	61	122	19	4	1	41	53	9		.248	.332	.309	102	3	17	.986	-5	79	**126**	*1-139	-0.5
1911	†Phi A	57	183	27	36	9	1	1	22	24	2		.197	.297	.273	60	-9	2	.977	2	113	94	1-53	-0.8
1912	Cle A	2	5	0	0	0	0	0	0	0	0		.000	.000	.000	-97	-1	0	.941	0	233	137	/1-2,M	-0.1
1913	Phi A	7	17	2	6	2	0	0	4	1	0	4	.353	.389	.471	155	1	0	1.000	1	173	101	/1-6	0.2
1914	Phi A	5	7	0	3	0	0	0	2	1	1	0	.429	.556	.429	204	1	0-2	1.000	-0	0	0	/1	0.0
1915	Phi A	5	3	0	1	0	0	0	4	0	0	0	.333	.333	.333	103	0	0	—	0	0	0	/1	0.0
1916	Phi A	1	0	0	0	0	0	0	0	1	0	0	—	1.000	—	213	0	0	—	0			H	0.0
1917	Phi A	1	1	0	0	0	0	0	0	0	0	0	.000	.000	.000	-99	0	0	—	0			H	0.0
Total	22	1755	6653	1001	1841	361	145	75	951	525	59	45	.277	.335	.408	119	140	285-2	.980	-9	99	89	*1-1628/O-78L,3-32,2-2,S-2	10.9
DAVIS, TOMMY Herman Thomas B 3.21.1939 Brooklyn, NY BR/TR 6-2/205# d9.22 C1 OF Total (1101-LF 122-CF 56-RF)																								
1959	LA N	1	1	0	0	0	0	0	0	0-0	0	1	.000	.000	.000	-93	0	0-0	—	0			H	0.0
1960	LA N	110	352	43	97	18	1	11	44	13-2	2	35	.276	.302	.426	92	-5	6-2	.975	-2	88	117	O-87(24-55-10)/3-5	-1.0
1961	LA N	132	460	60	128	13	2	15	58	32-4	2	53	.278	.325	.413	87	-9	10-4	.973	-1	109	57	O-86(44-39-30),3-59	-1.2
1962	LA N★	163	665	120	**230**	27	9	27	**153**	33-6	2	65	**.346**	.374	.535	151	44	18-6	.961	-2	104	99	*O-146(134-13-5),3-39	3.7
1963	†LA N★	146	556	69	181	19	3	16	88	29-5	4	59	**.326**	.359	.457	144	30	15-10	.969	-2	96	100	*O-129(120-14-3),3-40	2.2
1964	LA N	152	592	70	163	20	5	14	86	29-6	4	68	.275	.311	.397	106	2	11-8	.982	6	107	96	*O-148(LF)	0.0
1965	LA N	17	60	3	15	1	1	0	9	2-1	0	4	.250	.270	.300	66	-3	2-1	1.000	0	93	128	O-16(LF)	-0.4
1966	†LA N	100	313	27	98	11	1	3	27	16-4	0	36	.313	.345	.383	111	4	3-3	.972	-1	91	115	O-79(LF)/3-2	-0.1
1967	NY N	154	577	72	174	32	0	16	73	31-10	7	71	.302	.342	.440	125	18	9-3	.975	-2	102	61	*O-149(LF)/1	1.1
1968	Chi A	132	456	30	122	5	3	8	50	16-3	0	48	.268	.289	.344	91	-7	4-2	.962	-4	87	112	*O-116(115-0-4)/1-6	-2.0
1969	Sea A	123	454	52	123	29	1	6	80	30-5	4	46	.271	.318	.379	97	-2	19-4	.967	-9	85	36	*O-112(LF)/1	-1.5
	Hou N	24	79	2	19	3	0	1	9	8-0	1	9	.241	.318	.316	80	-2	1-1	1.000	-0	88	102	O-21(20-1-0)	-0.4
1970	Hou N	57	213	24	60	12	2	3	30	7-1	0	25	.282	.305	.399	91	-4	8-3	.949	-2	86	116	O-53(LF)	-0.8
	Oak A	66	200	17	58	9	1	1	27	8-1	1	18	.290	.318	.360	91	-3	2-4	.963	-5	74	43	O-45(43-0-2)/1-8	-1.2
	Chi N	11	42	4	11	2	0	2	8	1-0	0	1	.262	.279	.452	83	-1	0-0	.938	-1	98	0	O-10(LF)	-0.2
1971	†Oak A	79	219	26	71	8	1	3	42	15-1	0	19	.324	.363	.411	123	6	7-1	.989	4	150	102	1-35,O-16(LF)/2-3,3-2	0.9
1972	Chi N	15	26	3	7	1	0	0	6	2-0	0	3	.269	.321	.308	72	-1	0-1	1.000	-0	77	0	/1-3,O-2(1-0-1)	-0.2
	Bal A	26	82	9	21	3	0	0	6	6-0	0	18	.256	.307	.293	77	-2	2-0	1.000	1	104	0	O-18(17-0-1)/1-3	-0.3
1973	†Bal A	137	552	53	169	20	3	7	89	30-3	1	56	.306	.341	.391	107	4	11-3	.971	-0	107	127	*D-127/1-4	0.2
1974	†Bal A	158	626	67	181	20	1	11	84	34-9	3	49	.289	.325	.377	106	3	6-2	—	0	0	0	*D-155	0.0
1975	Bal A	116	460	43	130	14	1	6	57	23-2	0	52	.283	.315	.357	96	-4	2-0	—	0	0	0	*D-111	-0.7
1976	Cal A	72	219	16	58	5	0	3	26	15-3	1	18	.265	.312	.329	95	-2	0-1	1.000	-0	0	0	D-54/1	-0.4
	KC A	8	19	1	5	0	0	0	0	1-0	0	0	.263	.300	.263	65	-1	0-0	—	0			/D-3	-0.1
	Year	80	238	17	63	5	0	3	26	16-3	1	18	.265	.311	.324	92	-3	0-1	1.000	-0	0	0	D-57/1	-0.5
Total	18	1999	7223	811	2121	272	35	153	1052	381-66	32	754	.294	.329	.405	109	65	136-59	.970	-19	96	85	*O-1233L,D-450,3-147/1-62,2-3	-2.4
DAVIS, IKE Isaac Marion B 6.14.1895 Pueblo, CO D 4.2.1984 Tucson, AZ BR/TR 5-7/140# d4.23																								
1919	Was A	8	14	0	0	0	0	0	0	0	0	6	.000	.000	.000	-99	-4	0	.857	-2	24	101	/S-4	-0.6
1924	Chi A	10	33	5	8	1	1	0	4	2	0	5	.242	.286	.333	61	-2	0-0	.940	1	120	63	S-10	-0.1
1925	Chi A	146	562	105	135	31	9	0	61	71	7	58	.240	.333	.327	72	-23	19-14	.937	7	106	**113**	*S-144	-0.1

Year	Tm Lg	G	AB	R	H	2B	3B	HR	RBI	BB-IB	HP	SO	AVG	OBP	SLG	AOPS	ABR	SB-CS	FA	FR	Rng	Thr	G at Pos	BFW
Total	3	164	609	110	143	32	10	0	65	73	7	69	.235	.324	.320	68	-29	19-14	.936	6	105	110	S-158	-0.8
DAVIS, IRA J. Ira "Slats" B 7.8.1870 Philadelphia, PA D 12.21.1942 Brooklyn, NY ?/162# d4.22																								
1899	NY N	6	17	3	4	1	1	0	2	0	0		.235	.235	.412	79	-1	1	.750	-0	114	289	/S-3,1-2	-0.1
DAVIS, JACKE Jacke Sylvesta B 3.5.1936 Carthage, TX BR/TR 5-11/160# d4.19																								
1962	Phi N	48	75	9	16	0	1	1	6	4-0	0	20	.213	.253	.280	44	-6	1-0	.926	-1	104	0	O-26(16-5-7)	-0.8
DAVIS, JUMBO James J. B 9.5.1861 New York, NY D 2.14.1921 St.Louis, MO BL/TR 5-11/195# d7.27 U1																								
1884	KC U	7	29	3	6	0	0	0		0			.207	.207	.207	30	-3		.633	-1	119	0	/3-7	-0.4
1886	Bal AA	60	216	23	42	5	2	1	20	11	2		.194	.240	.250	55	-11	12	.848	4	96	71	3-60	-0.6
1887	Bal AA	130	485	81	150	23	19	8	109	28	5		.309	.353	.485	141	24	49	.826	1	116	56	3-87,S-43	2.3
1888	KC AA	121	491	70	131	22	8	3	61	20	6		.267	.304	.363	106	1	42	.843	29	**139**	**141**	*3-113/S-8	2.9
1889	KC AA	62	241	40	64	4	3	0	30	17	2	35	.266	.319	.307	74	-9	25	.803	-3	103	111	3-62	-1.0
	StL AA	2	4	1	0	0	0	0	0	1	0	1	.000	.200	.000	-36	-1	0	1.000	-0	0	0	/SO(LF)	-0.1
	Year	64	245	41	64	4	3	0	30	18	2	36	.261	.317	.302	72	-10	25	.803	-4	103	111	3-62/SO(LF)	-1.1
1890	StL AA	21	71	8	18	3	1	0	13	9	0		.254	.338	.324	83	-2	5	.731	-3	105	60	3-21	-0.4
	Bro AA	38	142	33	43	9	2	2	28	15	4		.303	.385	.437	147	9	10	.845	-4	105	132	3-38	0.5
	Year	59	213	41	61	12	3	2	41	24	4		.286	.369	.399	123	6	15	.800	-6	105	105	3-59	0.1
1891	Was AA	12	44	7	14	3	2	0	9	7	0	5	.318	.412	.477	162	4	8	.820	-1	91	94	3-12	0.3
Total	7	453	1723	266	468	69	37	14	270	108	19	41	.272	.322	.379	107	12	151	.824	22	115	99	3-400/S-52,O(LF)	3.5
DAVIS, J.J. Jerry C. B 10.25.1978 Glendora, CA BR/TR 6-4/250# d9.4																								
2002	Pit N	9	10	1	1	0	0	0	0	0-0	1	4	.100	.182	.100	-21	-2	0-0	1.000	-0	68	0	/O-4(RF)	-0.2
2003	Pit N	19	35	1	7	0	0	1	4	3-0	0	13	.200	.263	.286	42	-3	0-1	1.000	-0	85	191	O-10(RF)	-0.4
Total	2	28	45	2	8	0	0	1	4	3-0	1	17	.178	.245	.244	28	-5	0-1	1.000	-1	81	149	/O-14(RF)	-0.6
DAVIS, JODY Jody Richard B 11.12.1956 Gainesville, GA BR/TR 6-3/210# d4.21																								
1981	Chi N	56	180	14	46	5	1	4	21	21-3	1	28	.256	.333	.361	94	-1	0-1	.972	1	118	130	C-56	0.2
1982	Chi N	130	418	41	109	20	2	12	52	36-4	1	92	.261	.316	.404	99	-1	0-1	.984	5	115	114	*C-129	1.0
1983	Chi N	151	510	56	138	31	2	24	84	33-5	2	93	.271	.315	.480	113	7	0-2	.984	-12	101	78	*C-150	0.1
1984	†Chi N★	150	523	55	134	25	2	19	94	47-15	1	99	.256	.315	.421	97	-2	5-6	.984	8	101	105	*C-146	1.1
1985	Chi N	142	482	47	112	30	0	17	58	48-5	0	83	.232	.300	.400	85	-9	1-0	.990	3	86	**133**	*C-138	0.0
1986	Chi N★	148	528	61	132	27	2	21	74	41-4	0	110	.250	.300	.428	92	-7	0-1	.992	10	137	**142**	*C-145/1	1.0
1987	Chi N	125	428	57	106	12	2	19	51	52-2	2	91	.248	.331	.418	93	-4	1-2	.989	-1	95	113	*C-123	-0.1
1988	Chi N	88	249	19	57	9	0	6	33	29-3	1	51	.229	.309	.337	83	-5	0-3	.995	-2	109	92	C-74	-0.5
	Atl N	2	8	2	2	0	0	1	3	0-0	0	1	.250	.250	.625	137	0	0-0	1.000	1	95	135	/C-2	0.1
	Year	90	257	21	59	9	0	7	36	29-3	1	52	.230	.307	.346	84	-5	0-3	.995	-1	109	93	C-76	-0.4
1989	Atl N	78	231	12	39	5	0	4	19	23-3	1	61	.169	.246	.242	39	-18	0-0	.985	1	131	117	C-72/1-2	-1.5
1990	Atl N	12	28	0	2	0	0	0	1	3-0	0	3	.071	.161	.071	-32	-5	0-0	1.000	1	166	120	/1-6,C-4	-0.4
Total	10	1082	3585	364	877	164	11	127	490	333-44	9	712	.245	.307	.403	91	-45	7-16	.987	15	109	113	*C-1039/1-9	1.0
DAVIS, JOHN John Humphrey "Red" B 7.15.1915 Wilkes-Barre, PA D 4.26.2002 Laurel, MS BR/TR 5-11/172# d9.9 Mil 1942-45																								
1941	NY N	21	70	8	15	3	0	0	5	8	0	12	.214	.295	.257	55	-4	0	.970	1	108	108	3-21	-0.2
DAVIS, CRASH Lawrence Columbus B 7.14.1919 Canon, GA D 8.31.2001 Greensboro, NC BR/TR 6/173# d6.15 Mil 1943-45																								
1940	Phi A	23	67	4	18	1	1	0	9	3	1	10	.269	.310	.313	63	-4	1-0	.963	0	96	85	2-19/S	-0.2
1941	Phi A	39	105	8	23	3	0	0	8	11	0	16	.219	.293	.248	45	-8	0-0	.952	-2	108	94	2-20,1-12	-0.9
1942	Phi A	86	272	31	61	8	1	2	26	21	1	30	.224	.282	.283	60	-15	1-0	.965	-9	91	55	2-57,S-26/1-3	-1.9
Total	3	148	444	43	102	12	2	2	43	35	2	56	.230	.289	.279	57	-27	2-0	.961	-10	96	70	/2-96,S-27,1-15	-3.0
DAVIS, MARK Mark Anthony B 11.25.1964 San Diego, CA BR/TR 6/180# d7.2 b-Mike																								
1991	Cal A	3	2	0	0	0	0	0	0	0-0	0	0	.000	.000	.000	-99	-1	0-0	.500	-0	71	0	/O-3(RF)	-0.1
DAVIS, BEN Mark Christopher B 3.10.1977 Chester, PA BB/TR 6-4/195# d9.25																								
1998	SD N	1	1	0	0	0	0	0	0	0-0	0	0	.000	.000	.000	-99	0	0-0	1.000	0	0	0	/C	0.0
1999	SD N	76	266	29	65	14	1	5	30	25-3	0	70	.244	.307	.361	75	-11	2-1	.986	-6	115	94	C-74	-1.1
2000	SD N	43	130	12	29	6	0	3	14	14-1	0	35	.223	.297	.338	65	-7	1-1	.996	-0	103	72	C-38/D	-0.5
2001	SD N	138	448	56	107	20	0	11	57	66-5	4	112	.239	.337	.357	89	-6	4-4	.990	-6	94	115	*C-135/1-2	-0.5
2002	Sea A	80	228	24	59	10	1	7	43	18-1	2	58	.259	.313	.404	94	-3	1-1	.998	3	138	120	C-77/1-2	0.4
2003	Sea A	80	246	25	58	18	0	6	42	18-2	0	61	.236	.284	.382	77	-8	0-0	.991	3	114	107	C-73/D	-0.1
Total	6	418	1319	146	318	68	2	32	186	141-12	6	336	.241	.313	.368	82	-35	8-7	.991	-7	110	106	C-398/1-4,D-2	-1.8
DAVIS, MIKE Michael Dwayne B 6.11.1959 San Diego, CA BL/TL 6-3/185# d4.10 b-Mark																								
1980	Oak A	51	95	11	20	2	1	1	8	7-0	0	14	.211	.262	.284	54	-6	2-1	1.000	2	116	201	O-18(5-0-13)/1-7,D-6	-0.5
1981	†Oak A	17	20	0	1	1	0	0	0	2-0	0	4	.050	.136	.100	-33	-3	0-0	1.000	0	160	0	/O-2(LF),1D	-0.4
1982	Oak A	23	75	12	30	4	0	1	10	2-0	0	8	.400	.416	.493	155	5	3-2	.946	1	141	0	O-13(8-3-5)/1-7	0.5
1983	Oak A	128	443	61	122	24	4	8	62	27-1	5	74	.275	.322	.402	105	2	32-15	.974	11	111	186	*O-121(0-21-110)/D-3	0.9
1984	Oak A	134	382	47	88	18	3	9	46	31-2	1	66	.230	.285	.364	85	-8	14-9	.961	7	121	85	*O-127(1-16-121)/D-4	-0.7
1985	Oak A	154	547	92	157	34	1	24	82	50-8	2	99	.287	.348	.484	135	26	24-10	.979	5	116	59	*O-151(0-31-138)	2.6
1986	Oak A	142	489	77	131	28	3	19	55	34-2	1	91	.268	.314	.454	115	9	27-4	.973	6	**113**	106	*O-139(0-34-120)	1.4
1987	Oak A	139	494	69	131	32	1	22	72	42-5	1	94	.265	.320	.468	114	9	19-7	.942	-8	97	38	*O-124(RF),D-14	-0.3
1988	†LA N	108	281	29	55	11	2	2	17	25-0	0	59	.196	.260	.270	55	-17	7-3	.961	-4	89	94	O-76(1-23-63)	-2.4
1989	LA N	67	173	21	43	7	1	5	19	16-1	0	28	.249	.309	.387	101	0	6-5	.987	-2	90	43	O-48(16-0-34)	-0.5
Total	10	963	2999	419	778	161	16	91	371	236-19	10	537	.259	.313	.415	105	17	134-56	.968	18	109	91	O-819(33-128-728)/D-30,1-15	0.6
DAVIS, ODIE Odie Ernest B 8.13.1955 San Antonio, TX BR/TR 6-1/178# d9.3																								
1980	Tex A	17	8	0	1	0	0	0	0	0-0	0	2	.125	.125	.125	-32	-1	0-0	.880	1	124	109	S-13/3	0.0
DAVIS, OTIS Otis Allen "Scat" B 9.24.1920 Charleston, AR BL/TR 6/160# d4.22																								
1946	Bro N	1	0	1	0	0	0	0	0	0	0	0	—	—	—	—	0	0	—	0			R	0.0
DAVIS, DICK Richard Earl B 9.25.1953 Long Beach, CA BR/TR 6-3/195# d7.12																								
1977	Mil A	22	51	7	14	2	0	0	6	1-0	0	8	.275	.278	.314	64	-3	0-0	1.000	-2	67	0	O-12(LF)/D-6	-0.5
1978	Mil A	69	218	28	54	10	1	5	26	7-0	2	23	.248	.273	.372	81	-6	2-5	1.000	1	108	123	D-34,O-28(18-4-8)	-0.9
1979	Mil A	91	335	51	89	13	1	12	41	16-0	0	46	.266	.298	.418	91	-6	3-3	.973	-1	103	39	D-53,O-35(32-0-3)	-1.0
1980	Mil A	106	365	50	99	26	2	4	30	11-0	3	43	.271	.297	.386	89	-6	5-3	.971	-1	87	112	D-63,O-38(13-0-27)	-1.1
1981	†Phi N	45	96	12	32	6	1	2	19	8-0	1	13	.333	.387	.479	139	5	1-2	.974	-2	86	55	O-32(1-0-31)	0.2
1982	Phi N	28	68	5	19	3	1	2	7	2-0	0	9	.279	.296	.441	103	0	1-0	1.000	0	114	0	O-16(RF)	-0.1
	Tor A	3	7	0	2	0	0	0	2	0-0	0	1	.286	.250	.286	53	0	0-0	1.000	0	97	0	/O(LF)D	-0.1
	Pit N	39	77	7	14	2	1	2	10	5-0	0	9	.182	.224	.312	49	-6	1-0	.971	-2	93	0	O-28(1-0-27)	-0.9
Total	6	403	1217	160	323	62	7	27	141	50-0	6	152	.265	.294	.394	89	-22	13-13	.981	-6	95	58	O-190(78-4-112),D-157	-4.4
DAVIS, BRANDY Robert Brandon B 9.10.1928 Newark, DE BR/TR 6/170# d4.15 C1																								
1952	Pit N	55	95	14	17	1	1	0	1	11	0	28	.179	.264	.211	32	-9	9-2	.932	-0	105	95	O-29(9-9-12)	-0.9
1953	Pit N	12	39	5	8	2	0	0	2	0	0	3	.205	.205	.256	20	-5	0-2	.955	-0	114	0	/O-9(LF)	-0.6
Total	2	67	134	19	25	3	1	0	3	11	0	31	.187	.248	.224	29	-14	9-4	.938	-1	107	69	/O-38(18-9-12)	-1.5
DAVIS, BOB Robert John Eugene B 3.1.1952 Pryor, OK BR/TR 6/180# d4.6																								
1973	SD N	5	11	1	1	0	0	0	0	0-0	0	5	.091	.091	.091	-54	-2	0-0	.941	0	66	87	/C-5	-0.2
1975	SD N	43	128	6	30	3	2	0	7	11-3	3	31	.234	.310	.289	71	-5	0-0	.986	0	100	99	C-43	-0.3
1976	SD N	51	83	7	17	0	1	0	5	5-1	0	13	.205	.244	.229	40	-7	0-0	.965	0	105	117	C-47	-0.6
1977	SD N	48	94	9	17	2	0	1	10	5-2	2	24	.181	.235	.234	30	-10	0-0	.975	-6	194	124	C-46	-1.5
1978	SD N	19	40	3	8	1	0	0	2	1-1	0	5	.200	.220	.225	26	-4	0-1	.960	-4	78	123	C-16	-0.9
1979	Tor A	32	89	6	11	2	0	1	8	6-0	1	15	.124	.188	.180	-0	-13	0-0	.984	-2	118	87	C-32	-1.4
1980	Tor A	91	218	18	47	11	0	4	19	12-0	1	25	.216	.260	.321	56	-14	0-0	.983	-2	101	87	C-89	-1.3
1981	Cal A	1	2	0	0	0	0	0	0	0-0	0	0	.000	.000	.000	-99	-1	0-0	1.000	-1	21	0	/C	-0.1
Total	8	290	665	50	131	19	3	6	51	40-7	7	118	.197	.249	.262	42	-56	0-1	.978	-15	115	100	C-279	-6.3

Year	Tm Lg	G	AB	R	H	2B	3B	HR	RBI	BB-IB	HP	SO	AVG	OBP	SLG	AOPS	ABR	SB-CS	FA	FR	Rng	Thr	G at Pos	BFW
DAVIS, RON Ronald Everette B 10.21.1941 Roanoke Rapids, NC D 9.5.1992 Houston, TX BR/TR 6/180# d8.1																								
1962	Hou N	6	14	1	3	0	0	0	1	1-0	0	7	.214	.267	.214	33	-1	1-0	1.000	0	112	0	/O-5(CF)	-0.1
1966	Hou N	48	194	21	48	10	1	2	19	13-2	4	26	.247	.308	.340	86	-4	2-2	.982	4	97	292	O-48(CF)	-0.1
1967	Hou N	94	285	31	73	19	1	7	38	17-2	2	48	.256	.303	.404	104	1	5-3	.976	2	98	170	O-80(63-11-8)	-0.1
1968	Hou N	52	217	22	46	10	1	1	12	13-0	4	48	.212	.268	.281	67	-9	0-4	.971	3	110	123	O-52(CF)	-1.1
	†StL N	33	79	11	14	4	2	0	5	5-0	0	17	.177	.221	.278	51	-5	1-0	.979	2	109	200	O-25(2-10-14)	-0.4
	Year	85	296	33	60	14	3	1	17	18-0	4	65	.203	.255	.280	63	-14	1-4	.973	5	110	144	O-77(2-62-14)	-1.5
1969	Pit N	62	64	10	15	1	1	0	4	7-0	0	14	.234	.310	.281	68	-3	0-0	.933	-2	76	78	O-51(22-12-20)	-0.6
Total	5	295	853	96	199	44	6	10	79	56-4	10	160	.233	.287	.334	82	-21	9-9	.974	9	100	175	O-261(87-138-42)	-2.4
DAVIS, RUSS Russell Stuart B 9.13.1969 Birmingham, AL BR/TR 6/170# d7.6																								
1994	NY A	4	14	0	2	0	0	0	1	0-0	0	4	.143	.143	.143	-27	-3	0-0	1.000	-1	82	0	/3-4	-0.3
1995	†NY A	40	98	14	27	5	2	2	12	10-0	1	26	.276	.349	.429	102	0	0-0	.968	-2	92	23	3-34/1-2,D-4	-0.2
1996	Sea A	51	167	24	39	9	0	5	18	17-1	2	50	.234	.312	.377	73	-7	2-0	.933	-10	75	57	3-51	-1.5
1997	Sea A	119	420	57	114	29	1	20	63	27-2	2	100	.271	.317	.488	108	3	6-2	.939	-3	95	**122**	*3-117/D	0.2
1998	Sea A	141	502	68	130	30	1	20	82	34-1	3	134	.259	.305	.442	93	-7	4-3	.906	-3	101	131	*3-137/O-3(LF)	-0.8
1999	Sea A	124	432	55	106	17	1	21	59	32-1	5	111	.245	.304	.435	88	-10	3-3	.959	-15	87	78	*3-124/S-2	-2.2
2000	†SF N	80	180	27	47	5	0	9	24	9-0	2	29	.261	.302	.439	91	-4	0-3	.933	-11	68	52	3-43/1-6,D-3	-1.5
2001	SF N	53	167	16	43	13	1	7	17	17-2	1	49	.257	.326	.473	112	3	1-0	.890	-12	74	122	3-46/D	-0.8
Total	8	612	1980	261	508	108	6	84	276	146-7	16	503	.257	.310	.444	94	-25	16-11	.932	-56	89	98	3-556/D-9,1-8,O-3(LF),S-2	-7.1
DAVIS, STEVE Steven Michael B 12.30.1953 Oakland, CA BR/TR 6-1/200# d9.23																								
1979	Chi N	3	4	0	0	0	0	0	1	0-0	0	0	.000	.000	.000	-91	-1	0-0	1.000	-0	143	0	/2-2,3	-0.1
DAVIS, TOMMY Thomas James B 5.21.1973 Mobile, AL BR/TR 6-1/195# d5.14																								
1999	Bal A	5	6	0	1	0	0	0	0	0-0	0	2	.167	.167	.167	-15	-1	0-0	.909	-0	40	253	/C-4,1	-0.1
DAVIS, TOD Thomas Oscar B 7.24.1924 Los Angeles, CA D 12.31.1978 W.Covina, CA BR/TR 6-2/190# d4.27																								
1949	Phi A	31	75	7	20	0	1	1	6	9	0	16	.267	.345	.333	83	-2	0-0	.912	-1	84	114	S-14,3-12/2	-0.2
1951	Phi A	11	15	0	1	0	0	0	0	1	0	3	.067	.125	.067	-46	-3	0-0	1.000	-0	0	0	/2-2,3	-0.3
Total	2	42	90	7	21	0	1	1	6	10	0	19	.233	.310	.289	61	-5	0-0	.912	-1	84	114	/S-14,3-13,2-3	-0.5
DAVIS, TRENCH Trench Neal B 9.12.1960 Baltimore, MD BL/TL 6-3/171# d6.4																								
1985	Pit N	2	7	1	1	0	0	0	0	0-0	0	0	.143	.143	.143	-20	-1	1-0	.667	-1	52	0	/O-2(CF)	-0.2
1986	Pit N	15	23	2	3	0	0	0	1	0-0	0	4	.130	.125	.130	-27	-4	0-0	.917	0	87	350	/O-7(CF)	-0.4
1987	Atl N	6	3	0	0	0	0	0	0	0-0	0	1	.000	.000	.000	-95	-1	0-0	—	0			/H	-0.1
Total	3	23	33	3	4	0	0	0	1	0-0	0	5	.121	.118	.121	-32	-6	1-0	.867	-1	78	263	/O-9(CF)	-0.7
DAVIS, SPUD Virgil Lawrence B 12.20.1904 Birmingham, AL D 8.14.1984 Birmingham, AL BR/TR 6-1/197# d4.30 M1 C9																								
1928	StL N	2	5	1	1	0	0	0	1	1	0	0	.200	.333	.200	42	0	0	.750	-1	*86*	*0*	/C-2	-0.1
	Phi N	67	163	16	46	2	0	3	18	15	0	11	.282	.343	.350	79	-5	0	.980	-1	*75*	*152*	C-49	-0.3
	Year	69	168	17	47	2	0	3	19	16	0	11	.280	.342	.345	78	-5	0	.971	-2	*75*	*145*	C-51	-0.4
1929	Phi N	98	263	31	90	18	0	7	48	19	2	17	.342	.391	.490	110	4	1	.961	-10	*92*	*103*	C-89	-0.1
1930	Phi N	106	329	41	103	16	1	14	65	17	1	20	.313	.349	.495	94	-4	1	.986	-9	*73*	*110*	C-96	-0.6
1931	Phi N	120	393	30	128	32	1	4	51	36	0	28	.326	.382	.443	112	9	0	.994	-1	*75*	*118*	*C-114	1.4
1932	Phi N	125	402	44	135	23	5	14	70	40	2	39	.336	.399	.522	130	18	1	.987	-3	*88*	*82*	*C-120	2.2
1933	Phi N	141	495	51	173	28	3	9	65	32	5	24	.349	.395	.473	130	21	2	.983	-10	*74*	*106*	*C-132	1.9
1934	†StL N	107	347	45	104	22	4	9	65	34	2	27	.300	.366	.464	113	7	0	.988	2	*106*	*97*	C-94	1.4
1935	StL N	102	315	28	100	24	2	1	60	33	2	30	.317	.386	.416	111	7	0	**.992**	-2	*114*	*33*	C-81/1-5	0.9
1936	StL N	112	363	24	99	26	2	4	59	35	3	34	.273	.342	.388	97	-1	0	.985	-7	*116*	*99*	*C-103/3-2	-0.2
1937	Cin N	76	209	19	56	10	1	3	33	23	0	15	.268	.341	.368	97	0	0	.980	4	*74*	*102*	C-59	0.7
1938	Cin N	12	36	3	6	1	0	0	1	5	1	6	.167	.286	.194	35	-3	0	.962	0	*154*	*119*	C-11	-0.2
	Phi N	70	215	11	53	7	0	2	23	14	0	14	.247	.293	.307	67	-10	1	.980	-10	*60*	*94*	C-63	-1.7
	Year	82	251	14	59	8	0	2	24	19	1	20	.235	.292	.291	62	-13	1	.977	-10	*75*	*98*	C-74	-1.9
1939	Phi N	87	202	10	62	8	1	0	23	24	1	20	.307	.383	.356	103	2	0	**1.000**	-6	*54*	*124*	C-85	0.0
1940	Pit N	99	285	23	93	14	1	5	39	35	2	20	.326	.404	.435	132	14	0	.967	-5	*73*	***139***	C-87	1.4
1941	Pit N	57	107	3	27	4	1	0	6	11	0	11	.252	.322	.308	78	-3	0	1.000	-0	*101*	*90*	C-49	-0.1
1944	Pit N	54	93	6	28	7	0	2	14	10	0	8	.301	.369	.441	122	3	0	.966	0	*95*	*94*	C-35	0.5
1945	Pit N	23	33	2	8	2	0	0	6	2	1	2	.242	.306	.303	67	-1	0	.968	-0	*91*	*111*	C-13	-0.1
Total	16	1458	4255	388	1312	244	22	77	647	386	22	326	.308	.369	.430	108	58	6	.984	-59	*85*	*102*	*C-1282/1-5,3-2	7.0
DAVIS, BUTCH Wallace McArthur B 6.19.1958 Martin Co., NC BR/TR 6/190# d8.23																								
1983	KC A	33	122	13	42	2	6	2	18	4-0	0	19	.344	.359	.508	137	5	4-3	.977	0	112	36	O-33(LF)	0.4
1984	KC A	41	116	11	17	3	0	2	12	10-0	0	19	.147	.211	.224	21	-13	4-3	.959	-0	104	90	O-35(34-1-1)/D-2	-1.5
1987	Pit N	7	7	3	1	1	0	0	0	1-0	0	3	.143	.250	.286	41	-1	0-0	1.000	0	218	0	/O(LF)	0.0
1988	Bal A	13	25	2	6	1	0	0	0	0-0	0	8	.240	.240	.280	46	-2	1-0	1.000	1	119	256	O-10(2-0-8)/D	-0.1
1989	Bal A	5	6	1	1	1	0	0	0	0-0	0	3	.167	.167	.333	39	0	0-0	1.000	-0	91	0	/O-3(2-0-1),D	-0.1
1991	LA N	1	1	0	0	0	0	0	0	0-0	0	0	.000	.000	.000	-99	0	0-0	—	0			/H	0.0
1993	Tex A	62	159	24	39	10	4	3	20	5-1	1	28	.245	.273	.415	85	-4	3-1	.960	2	118	85	O-44(23-10-17),D-11	-0.4
1994	Tex A	4	17	2	4	3	0	0	0	0-0	0	3	.235	.235	.412	63	-1	1-0	1.000	0	75	343	/O-4(RF)	0.0
Total	8	166	453	56	110	21	10	7	50	20-1	1	83	.243	.274	.380	78	-16	13-7	.969	4	111	89	O-130(95-11-31)/D-15	-1.7
DAVIS, WILLIE William Henry B 4.15.1940 Mineral Springs, AR BL/TL 6-2.5/181# d9.8																								
1960	LA N	22	88	12	28	6	1	2	10	4-2	0	12	.318	.348	.477	116	2	3-5	.981	-1	93	60	O-22(CF)	-0.2
1961	LA N	128	339	56	86	19	6	12	45	27-4	5	46	.254	.316	.451	93	-4	12-5	.983	3	**115**	68	*O-114(CF)	-0.2
1962	LA N	157	600	103	171	18	**10**	21	85	42-10	6	72	.285	.334	.453	117	12	32-7	.963	5	107	131	*O-156(1-155-0)	1.7
1963	†LA N	156	515	60	126	19	8	9	60	25-6	3	61	.245	.281	.365	92	-8	25-11	.978	11	110	184	*O-153(CF)	0.0
1964	LA N	157	613	91	180	23	7	12	77	22-1	1	59	.294	.316	.413	112	7	42-13	.983	13	**116**	160	*O-155(CF)	2.0
1965	†LA N	142	558	52	133	24	3	10	57	14-3	7	81	.238	.263	.346	76	-20	25-9	.967	-1	104	76	*O-141(CF)	-2.5
1966	†LA N	153	624	74	177	31	6	11	61	15-2	4	68	.284	.302	.405	104	0	21-10	.970	2	106	91	*O-152(CF)	-0.2
1967	LA N	143	569	65	146	27	9	6	41	29-5	3	65	.257	.295	.367	97	-5	20-6	.971	-5	96	77	*O-138(CF)	-1.3
1968	LA N	160	643	86	161	24	10	7	31	31-4	1	88	.250	.284	.351	98	-5	36-10	.973	-2	99	95	*O-158(CF)	-0.8
1969	LA N	129	498	66	155	23	8	11	59	33-5	4	39	.311	.356	.456	136	22	24-10	.979	-2	99	106	*O-125(CF)	2.0
1970	LA N	146	593	92	181	23	**16**	8	93	29-2	1	54	.305	.335	.438	111	6	38-14	.992	6	105	144	*O-143(0-139-4)	1.1
1971	LA N★	158	641	84	198	33	10	10	74	23-3	0	47	.309	.330	.438	124	16	20-8	.981	1	106	80	*O-157(CF)	1.6
1972	LA N	149	615	81	178	22	7	19	79	27-4	1	61	.289	.317	.441	117	10	20-3	.987	0	101	110	*O-146(CF)	1.0
1973	LA N★	152	599	82	171	29	9	16	77	29-12	5	62	.285	.320	.444	116	9	17-5	.980	-9	97	64	*O-146(CF)	-0.1
1974	Mon N	153	611	86	180	27	9	12	89	27-9	3	69	.295	.322	.427	104	1	25-7	.969	-4	102	90	*O-151(CF)	-0.4
1975	Tex A	42	169	16	42	8	2	5	17	4-0	1	25	.249	.270	.408	90	-3	13-5	.990	-3	94	35	O-42(CF)	-0.7
	StL N	98	350	41	102	19	6	6	50	14-1	4	27	.291	.319	.431	105	1	10-1	.970	3	112	88	O-89(8-15-71)	0.2
1976	SD N	141	493	61	132	18	10	5	46	19-2	2	34	.268	.295	.375	98	-5	14-2	.992	3	110	77	*O-128(CF)	-0.4
1979	†Cal A	43	56	9	14	2	1	0	2	4-0	0	7	.250	.300	.321	70	-2	1-0	1.000	-0	100	0	/O-7(1-0-6),D-6	-0.3
Total	18	2429	9174	1217	2561	395	138	182	1053	418-75	51	977	.279	.311	.412	106	34	398-131	.978	20	105	102	*O-2323(10-2237-81)/D-6	2.5
DAWKINS, GOOKIE Travis Sentell B 5.12.1979 Newberry, SC BR/TR 6-1/180# d9.3																								
1999	Cin N	7	7	1	1	0	0	0	0	0-0	1	4	.143	.250	.143	3	-1	0-0	1.000	-1	69	88	/S-7	-0.2
2000	Cin N	14	41	5	9	2	0	0	3	2-1	0	7	.220	.256	.268	32	-4	0-0	.965	2	102	179	S-14	-0.2
2002	Cin N	31	48	2	6	2	0	0	0	6-0	0	21	.125	.222	.167	6	-7	2-1	.944	-7	82	64	S-21/2-3	-1.2
2003	KC A	3	2	0	0	0	0	0	0	1-0	0	2	.000	.333	.000	-1	0	0-0	1.000	0	113	0	/2-3	0.0
Total	4	55	98	8	16	4	0	0	3	9-1	1	34	.163	.241	.204	17	-12	2-1	.957	-6	89	114	/S-42,2-6	-1.6
DAWSON, ANDRE Andre Nolan B 7.10.1954 Miami, FL BR/TR 6-3/195# d9.11																								
1976	Mon N	24	85	9	20	4	1	0	7	5-1	0	13	.235	.278	.306	63	-4	1-2	.969	1	112	64	O-24(8-14-2)	-0.5
1977	Mon N	139	525	64	148	26	9	19	65	34-4	2	93	.282	.326	.474	116	9	21-7	.989	1	102	98	*O-136(13-129-3)	1.0
1978	Mon N	157	609	84	154	24	8	25	72	30-3	**12**	128	.253	.299	.442	106	1	28-11	.988	4	99	189	*O-153(CF)	0.7
1979	Mon N	155	639	90	176	24	12	25	92	27-5	6	115	.275	.309	.468	111	5	35-10	.988	-9	96	60	*O-153(CF)	-0.2

Year	Tm Lg	G	AB	R	H	2B	3B	HR	RBI	BB-IB	HP	SO	AVG	OBP	SLG	AOPS	ABR	SB-CS	FA	FR	Rng	Thr	G at Pos	BFW
1980	Mon N	151	577	96	178	41	7	17	87	44-7	**6**	69	.308	.358	.492	137	28	34-9	.986	7	106	140	*O-147(CF)	4.0
1981	†Mon N★	103	394	71	119	21	3	24	64	35-14	**7**	50	.302	.365	.553	157	28	26-4	.980	12	**121**	140	*O-103(CF)	4.6
1982	Mon N★	148	608	107	183	37	7	23	83	34-4	8	96	.301	.343	.498	131	23	39-10	.982	8	116	91	*O-147(CF)	3.7
1983	Mon N★	159	633	104	**189**	36	10	32	113	38-12	**9**	81	.299	.338	.539	143	33	25-11	.980	-0	104	76	*O-157(CF)	3.4
1984	Mon N	138	533	73	132	23	6	17	86	41-2	2	80	.248	.301	.409	103	0	13-5	.975	8	116	121	*O-134(RF)	0.2
1985	Mon N	139	529	65	135	27	2	23	91	29-8	4	92	.255	.295	.444	112	5	13-4	.973	-2	97	103	*O-131(0-24-123)	-0.2
1986	Mon N	130	496	65	141	32	2	20	78	37-11	6	79	.284	.338	.478	125	15	18-12	.986	-4	89	110	*O-127(RF)	0.5
1987	Chi N★	153	621	90	178	24	2	**49**	**137**	32-7	7	103	.287	.328	.568	127	20	11-3	.986	1	98	119	*O-152(RF)	1.4
1988	Chi N★	157	591	78	179	31	8	24	79	37-12	4	73	.303	.344	.504	136	25	12-4	.989	-2	95	98	*O-147(RF)	2.1
1989	†Chi N★	118	416	62	105	18	6	21	77	35-13	1	62	.252	.307	.476	114	6	8-5	.987	1	107	67	*O-112(RF)	0.4
1990	Chi N★	147	529	72	164	28	5	27	100	42-**21**	2	65	.310	.358	.535	134	23	16-2	.981	-4	90	103	*O-139(RF)	1.8
1991	Chi N★	149	563	69	153	21	4	31	104	22-3	5	80	.272	.302	.488	114	7	4-5	.988	-7	90	66	*O-137(RF)	-0.6
1992	Chi N	143	542	60	150	27	2	22	90	30-8	4	70	.277	.316	.456	114	8	6-2	.992	-8	81	115	*O-139(RF)	-0.3
1993	Bos A	121	461	44	126	29	1	13	67	17-4	13	49	.273	.313	.425	92	-6	2-1	1.000	-0	112	0	D-97,O-20(RF)	-1.3
1994	Bos A	75	292	34	70	18	0	16	48	9-3	4	53	.240	.271	.466	82	-10	2-2	—	0	0	0	D-74	-1.4
1995	Fla N	79	226	30	58	10	3	8	37	9-1	8	45	.257	.305	.434	93	-3	0-0	.908	-4	84	89	O-59(12-0-47)	-1.0
1996	Fla N	42	58	6	16	2	0	2	14	2-0	1	13	.276	.311	.414	92	-1	0-0	.833	-1	52	0	/O-6(LF)	-0.2
Total	21	2627	9927	1373	2774	503	98	438	1591	589-143	111	1509	.279	.323	.482	119	212	314-109	.983	1	100	104	*O-2323(39-1027-1284),D-171	18.1
DAY, BOOTS Charles Frederick B 8.31.1947 Ilion, NY BL/TL 5-9/160# d6.15																								
1969	StL N	11	6	1	0	0	0	0	0	1-0	0	1	.000	.143	.000	-57	-1	0-0	—	-0	0	0	/O(CF)	-0.1
1970	Chi N	11	8	2	2	0	0	0	0	0-0	0	3	.250	.250	.250	31	-1	0-0	.875	1	116	763	/O-7(CF)	0.0
	Mon N	41	108	14	29	4	0	0	5	6-2	0	18	.269	.307	.306	65	-5	3-2	.987	3	125	65	O-35(5-30-0)	-0.4
	Year	52	116	16	31	4	0	0	5	6-2	0	21	.267	.303	.302	61	-6	3-2	.976	3	124	121	O-42(5-37-0)	-0.4
1971	Mon N	127	371	53	105	10	2	4	33	33-5	1	39	.283	.342	.353	97	-1	9-4	.982	7	107	**176**	*O-120(3-118-0)	0.4
1972	Mon N	128	386	32	90	7	4	0	30	29-3	1	44	.233	.288	.272	59	-21	3-6	.979	-4	93	109	*O-117(0-103-15)	-3.2
1973	Mon N	101	207	36	57	7	0	4	28	21-1	0	28	.275	.342	.367	93	-2	0-3	1.000	-2	78	68	O-51(12-45-6)	-0.7
1974	Mon N	52	65	8	12	0	0	0	2	5-0	0	8	.185	.239	.185	20	-7	0-0	1.000	-1	91	0	O-16(14-0-2)	-0.9
Total	6	471	1151	146	295	28	6	8	98	95-11	2	141	.256	.314	.312	75	-38	15-15	.983	4	99	124	O-347(34-304-23)	-4.9
DAYETT, BRIAN Brian Kelly B 1.22.1957 New London, CT BR/TR 5-10/180# d9.11																								
1983	NY A	11	29	3	6	0	1	0	5	2-0	0	4	.207	.258	.276	49	-2	0-0	1.000	2	142	167	/O-9(LF)	-0.1
1984	NY A	64	127	14	31	8	0	4	23	9-0	1	14	.244	.295	.402	96	-1	0-0	.988	1	102	115	O-62(55-0-10)/D	-0.2
1985	Chi N	22	26	1	6	0	0	1	4	0-0	1	6	.231	.259	.346	61	-1	0-0	1.000	-0	106	0	O-10(LF)	-0.2
1986	Chi N	24	67	7	18	4	0	4	11	6-0	0	10	.269	.316	.507	118	1	0-1	1.000	-1	88	72	O-24(15-1-12)	-0.1
1987	Chi N	97	177	20	49	14	1	5	25	20-0	0	37	.277	.348	.452	106	2	0-0	1.000	-2	88	68	O-78(68-0-12)	-0.2
Total	5	218	426	45	110	26	2	14	68	37-0	2	71	.258	.316	.427	99	-1	0-1	.995	-1	97	89	O-183(158-1-34)/D	-0.8
DEAL, CHARLIE Charles Albert B 10.30.1891 Wilkinsburg, PA D 9.16.1979 Covina, CA BR/TR 6/160# d7.19																								
1912	Det A	42	142	13	32	4	2	0	11	9	0		.225	.272	.282	60	-8	4	.942	6	129	46	3-41	0.0
1913	Det A	16	50	3	11	0	2	0	3	1	0	7	.220	.235	.300	57	-3	2	.862	1	124	135	3-15	-0.2
	Bos N	10	36	6	11	1	0	0	3	2	1	1	.306	.359	.333	96	0	1-2	.935	-3	83	34	2-10	-0.3
1914	†Bos N	79	257	17	54	13	2	0	23	20	1	23	.210	.270	.276	63	-12	4	.948	-2	95	85	3-74/S	-1.3
1915	StL F	65	223	21	72	12	4	1	27	12	0	16	.323	.357	.426	114	1	10	.951	7	111	110	3-65	1.0
1916	StL A	23	74	7	10	1	0	0	10	6	0	8	.135	.200	.149	5	-9	4	.970	-2	91	136	3-22/2	-1.1
	Chi N	2	8	2	2	1	0	0	3	0	0	0	.250	.250	.375	82	0	0	1.000	1	167	296	/3-2	0.1
1917	Chi N	135	449	46	114	11	3	0	47	19	0	18	.254	.284	.292	71	-16	10	.957	8	99	102	*3-130	-0.5
1918	†Chi N	119	414	43	99	9	3	2	34	21	2	13	.239	.279	.290	72	-15	11	.942	-6	92	112	*3-118	-1.9
1919	Chi N	116	405	37	117	23	5	2	52	12	4	12	.289	.316	.385	110	4	11	**.973**	6	97	93	*3-116	1.4
1920	Chi N	129	450	48	108	10	5	3	39	20	8	14	.240	.285	.304	68	-19	5-8	**.973**	11	109	101	*3-128	-0.7
1921	Chi N	115	422	52	122	19	8	3	66	13	0	9	.289	.310	.393	85	-10	3-5	**.973**	13	109	89	*3-112	0.8
Total	10	851	2930	295	752	104	34	11	318	135	16	121	.257	.293	.327	79	-87	65-15	.958	40	103	99	3-823/2-11,S	-2.7
DEAL, LINDSAY Fred Lindsay B 9.3.1911 Lenoir, NC D 4.18.1979 Little Rock, AR BL/TR 6/175# d9.13																								
1939	Bro N	4	7	0	0	0	0	0	0	0	0	2	.000	.000	.000	-97	-2	0	1.000	-0	91	0	/O(CF)	-0.2
DEAL, SNAKE John Wesley B 1.21.1879 Lancaster, PA D 5.9.1944 Harrisburg, PA BR/TR 6/164# d7.9																								
1906	Cin N	65	231	13	48	4	3	0	21	6	0		.208	.228	.251	47	-15	15	.985	2	113	80	1-65	-1.6
DEALY, PAT Patrick E. B Burlington, VT D 12.16.1924 Buffalo, NY BR/TR 5-8/145# d9.30																								
1884	StP U	5	15	2	2	0	0	0		0			.133	.133	.133	-35	-3		.871	2			/C-4,O(RF)	-0.1
1885	Bos N	35	130	18	29	4	1	1	9	2		14	.223	.235	.292	72	-4		.903	0			C-29/3-3,O-2(1-1-0),S-2,1	-0.1
1886	Bos N	15	46	9	15	1	1	0	3	4		4	.326	.380	.391	139	2	5	.929	-2			C-14/O(LF)	0.1
1887	Was N	58	212	33	55	8	2	1	18	8	2	8	.259	.293	.330	78	-6	36	.931	-4			C-28,S-23/O-5(4-1-0),3-5	-0.7
1890	Syr AA	18	66	9	12	1	0	0	4	5	1		.182	.250	.197	36	-5	4	.900	-5	*77*	*94*	C-10/3-6,O-2(0-1-1)	-0.9
Total	5	131	469	71	113	14	4	2	34	19	3	26	.241	.275	.301	75	-16	45	.914	-10	*8*	*10*	/C-85,S-25,3-14,O-11(6-3-2),1	-1.7
DEAN, CHUBBY Alfred Lovell B 8.24.1915 Mt.Airy, NC D 12.21.1970 Riverside, NJ BL/TL 5-11/181# d4.14 Mil 1943-46 ▲																								
1936	Phi A	111	342	41	98	21	3	1	48	24	2	24	.287	.337	.374	77	-13	3-2	.989	-1	97	93	1-77	-1.8
1937	Phi A	104	309	36	81	14	4	2	31	42	0	10	.262	.350	.353	79	-9	2-1	.991	-2	89	81	1-78/P-2	-1.7
1938	Phi A	16	20	3	6	2	0	0	1	1	0	4	.300	.333	.400	85	2	0-0	1.000	1	184	0	/P-6	0.0
1939	Phi A	80	77	12	27	4	0	0	19	8	0	4	.351	.412	.403	111	9	0-0	.935	1	131	258	P-54	0.0
1940	Phi A	67	90	6	26	2	0	0	6	16	0	9	.289	.396	.311	88	-1	0-0	.976	1	125	54	P-30/1	0.0
1941	Phi A	27	37	0	9	2	0	0	9	4	0	3	.243	.317	.297	65	-2	0-0	1.000	0	93	96	P-18/1	0.0
	Cle A	17	25	2	4	1	0	0	2	3	0	2	.160	.250	.200	21	1	0-0	1.000	1	155	0	/P-8	0.0
	Year	44	62	2	13	3	0	0	11	7	0	5	.210	.290	.258	48	-5	0-0	1.000	1	118	57	P-26/1	0.0
1942	Cle A	70	101	4	27	1	0	0	7	11	0	7	.267	.339	.277	79	8	0-0	.939	-3	69	0	P-27	0.0
1943	Cle A	41	46	2	9	0	0	0	5	6	0	2	.196	.288	.196	45	1	0-0	.929	-1	71	106	P-17	0.0
Total	8	533	1047	106	287	47	7	3	128	115	2	65	.274	.347	.341	79	-4	5-3	.964	-4	107	79	P-162,1-157	-3.5
DEAN, TOMMY Tommy Douglas B 8.30.1945 Iuka, MS BR/TR 6/165# d9.17																								
1967	LA N	12	28	1	4	1	0	0	2	0-0	0	9	.143	.143	.179	-9	-4	0-0	.981	3	114	191	S-12	0.0
1969	SD N	101	273	14	48	9	2	2	9	27-4	1	54	.176	.251	.245	42	-22	0-3	.978	-6	100	77	S-97/2-2	-2.0
1970	SD N	61	158	18	35	5	1	2	13	11-3	0	29	.222	.271	.304	56	-10	2-0	.974	-4	93	97	S-55	-0.8
1971	SD N	41	70	2	8	0	0	0	1	4-0	0	13	.114	.162	.114	-22	-11	1-0	.969	-1	94	95	S-28,3-11/2	-1.1
Total	4	215	529	35	95	15	3	4	25	42-7	1	105	.180	.240	.242	36	-47	3-3	.976	-8	98	92	S-192/3-11,2-3	-3.9
DEANE, HARRY John Henry B 5.6.1846 Trenton, NJ D 5.31.1925 Indianapolis, IN 5-7/150# d7.20 M1																								
1871	Kek NA	6	22	3	4	0	1	0	2	2		0	.182	.250	.273	49	-2	0-0	1.000	2	0	0	/O-6(LF),M	0.0
1874	Bal NA	**47**	203	29	50	8	1	0	13	4		3	.246	.261	.296	79	-4	2-1	.818	-5	94	143	*O-46(CF)/2-2,S	-0.7
Total	2 NA	53	225	32	54	8	2	0	15	6		3	.240	.260	.293	75	-6	2-1	.000	-3	83	126	/O-52(6-46-0),2-2,S	-0.7
DEAR, BUDDY Paul Stanford B 12.1.1905 Norfolk, VA D 8.29.1989 Radford, VA BR/TR 5-8/143# d9.9																								
1927	Was A	2	1	1	0	0	0	0	0	0	0	0	.000	.000	.000	-99	0	0-0	—	-0	0	0	/2	0.0
DeARMOND, CHARLIE Charles Hommer "Hummer" B 2.13.1877 Okeana, OH D 12.17.1933 Morning Sun, OH BR/TR 5-10/165# d9.19																								
1903	Cin N	11	39	10	11	2	1	0	7	3	1		.282	.349	.385	98	0	1	.878	-1	74	92	3-11	-0.1
DEASLEY, JOHN John B 1.1861 Philadelphia, PA D 12.25.1910 Philadelphia, PA d6.17 b-Pat																								
1884	Was U	31	134	20	29	1	1	0		3			.216	.234	.239	45	-13		.836	1	99	141	S-31	-1.0
	KC U	13	40	3	7	2	0	0		2			.175	.214	.225	38	-4		.833	1	109	207	S-13	-0.2
	Year	44	174	23	36	3	1	0		5			.207	.229	.236	44	-17		.835	3	102	158	S-44	-1.2
DEASLEY, PAT Thomas H. B 11.17.1857 , Ireland D 4.1.1943 Philadelphia, PA BR/TR 5-8.5/154# d5.18 b-John OF Total (3-LF 12-CF 29-RF)																								
1881	Bos N	43	147	13	35	5	2	0	8	5		10	.238	.263	.299	80	-3		.914	-1			C-28/O-7(0-2-6),S-7,1-2	-0.3
1882	Bos N	67	264	36	70	8	0	0	29	7		22	.265	.284	.295	86	-4		**.958**	2			*C-56,O-14(1-0-13)/S	0.2
1883	StL AA	58	206	27	53	2	1	0	15	6			.257	.278	.277	75	-6		**.930**	8			C-56/O-2(CF)	0.6
1884	StL AA	75	254	27	52	5	4	0		7	3		.205	.235	.256	58	-12		.919	9			*C-75/O-2(1-0-1),1	0.3

Year	Tm Lg	G	AB	R	H	2B	3B	HR	RBI	BB-IB	HP	SO	AVG	OBP	SLG	AOPS	ABR	SB-CS	FA	FR	Rng	Thr	G at Pos	BFW
1885	NY N	54	207	22	53	5	1	0	24	9		20	.256	.287	.290	88	-3		.935	7			C-54/O-2(CF),S	0.8
1886	NY N	41	143	18	38	6	1	0	17	4		12	.266	.286	.322	84	-3	2	.925	4			C-30,O-15(1-6-8)	0.2
1887	NY N	30	118	12	37	5	0	0	23	9	1	7	.314	.367	.356	107	2	3	.867	-10			C-24/3-7,S	-0.5
1888	Was N	34	127	6	20	1	0	0	4	2	0	18	.157	.171	.165	8	-13	2	.922	6			C-31/O(RF)S2	-0.4
Total	8	402	1466	161	358	37	9	0	120	49	4	89	.244	.271	.282	75	-42	7	.927	25			C-354/O-43R,S-11,3-7,1-3,2	0.9
DeBERRY, HANK John Herman B 12.29.1894 Savannah, TN D 9.10.1951 Savannah, TN BR/TR 5-11/195# d9.12 Mil 1918																								
1916	Cle A	15	33	7	9	4	0	0	4	6	0	9	.273	.385	.394	126	1	0	1.000	-1	94	91	C-14	0.1
1917	Cle A	25	33	3	9	2	0	0	1	2	1	7	.273	.333	.333	96	0	0	.968	1	110	113	/C-9	0.1
1922	Bro N	85	259	29	78	10	1	3	35	20	1	9	.301	.354	.382	91	-3	4-1	.971	-5	75	94	C-81	-0.3
1923	Bro N	78	235	21	67	11	6	1	48	20	2	12	.285	.346	.396	98	-1	2-1	.971	4	84	106	C-60	0.7
1924	Bro N	77	218	20	53	10	3	3	26	20	0	21	.243	.307	.358	80	-6	0-1	.993	12	108	92	C-63	1.0
1925	Bro N	67	193	26	50	8	1	2	24	16	2	8	.259	.322	.342	72	-8	2-2	.981	8	86	118	C-55	0.3
1926	Bro N	48	115	6	33	11	0	0	13	8	0	5	.287	.333	.383	94	-1	0	.976	3	79	82	C-37	0.5
1927	Bro N	68	201	15	47	3	2	1	21	17	0	8	.234	.294	.284	55	-13	1	.988	15	79	133	C-67	0.6
1928	Bro N	82	258	19	65	8	2	0	23	18	0	15	.252	.301	.298	58	-16	3	.977	9	75	**114**	C-80	-0.2
1929	Bro N	68	210	13	55	11	1	1	25	17	0	15	.262	.317	.338	64	-12	1	.991	-3	59	94	C-68	-0.9
1930	Bro N	35	95	11	28	3	0	0	14	4	0	10	.295	.323	.326	58	-6	0	.978	7	101	74	C-35	0.2
Total	11	648	1850	170	494	81	16	11	234	148	6	119	.267	.323	.346	76	-65	13-5	.982	51	82	103	C-569	2.1
DEBUS, ADAM Adam Joseph B 10.7.1892 Chicago, IL D 5.13.1977 Chicago, IL BR/TR 5-10.5/150# d7.14 Mil 1918																								
1917	Pit N	38	131	9	30	5	4	0	7	7	2	14	.229	.279	.328	83	-3	2	.898	-7	91	60	S-21,3-18	-1.0
DeCINCES, DOUG Douglas Vernon B 8.29.1950 Burbank, CA BR/TR 6-2/194# d9.9 OF Total (LF)																								
1973	Bal A	10	18	2	2	0	0	0	3	1-0	0	5	.111	.158	.111	-23	-3	0-0	.895	1	121	224	/3-8,2-2,S	-0.2
1974	Bal A	1	1	0	0	0	0	0	0	1-0	0	0	.000	.500	.000	55	0	0-0	1.000	0	121	0	/3	0.0
1975	Bal A	61	167	20	42	6	3	4	23	13-2	1	32	.251	.306	.395	105	0	0-1	.947	6	122	153	3-34,S-13,2-11/1-2	0.7
1976	Bal A	129	440	36	103	17	2	11	42	29-1	2	68	.234	.284	.357	93	-6	8-4	.941	-5	93	53	*3-109,2-17,1-11/S-2,D	-1.1
1977	Bal A	150	522	63	135	28	3	19	69	64-6	2	86	.259	.339	.433	117	13	8-8	.958	-3	99	128	*3-148/12D	0.7
1978	Bal A	142	511	72	146	37	1	28	80	46-2	2	81	.286	.346	.526	152	34	7-7	.975	11	103	117	*3-130,2-12	4.3
1979	†Bal A	120	422	67	97	27	1	16	61	54-5	3	68	.230	.318	.412	100	1	5-3	.964	-3	95	105	*3-120	-0.4
1980	Bal A	145	489	64	122	23	2	16	64	49-5	3	83	.249	.319	.403	98	-1	11-6	.960	26	**117**	**154**	*3-142/1	2.3
1981	Bal A	100	346	49	91	23	2	13	55	41-2	1	32	.263	.341	.454	128	13	0-3	.942	-2	92	**173**	*3-100/1O(LF)	0.9
1982	†Cal A	153	575	94	173	42	5	30	97	66-7	1	80	.301	.369	.548	149	40	7-5	.961	23	122	132	*3-153/S-2	5.9
1983	Cal A★	95	370	49	104	19	3	18	65	32-2	0	56	.281	.332	.495	127	13	2-0	.955	8	113	129	3-84,D-10	1.9
1984	Cal A	146	547	77	147	23	3	20	82	53-4	0	79	.269	.327	.431	111	7	4-1	.964	0	103	87	*3-140/D-5	0.6
1985	Cal A	120	427	50	104	22	1	20	78	47-11	2	71	.244	.317	.440	107	4	1-4	.958	-2	98	**132**	*3-111/D-3	-0.1
1986	†Cal A	140	512	69	131	20	3	26	96	52-4	2	74	.256	.325	.459	112	8	2-2	.965	-3	93	93	*3-132/SD	0.3
1987	Cal A	133	453	65	106	23	0	16	63	70-6	2	87	.234	.337	.391	96	-1	3-4	.948	-6	99	109	*3-128/1-4,SD	-0.9
	StL N	4	9	1	2	2	0	0	1	0-0	0	2	.222	.222	.444	70	0	0-0	.833	1	158	0	/3-3	0.0
Total	15	1649	5809	778	1505	312	29	237	879	618-57	21	904	.259	.329	.445	116	122	58-48	.958	54	103	118	*3-1543/2-43,D-24,1-20,S-20,O	14.9
DECKER, HARRY Earle Harry B 9.3.1864 Lockport, IL BR/TR 5-11/180# d8.23 OF Total (12-LF 4-CF 8-RF)																								
1884	Ind AA	4	15	1	4	1	0	0		1	0		.267	.313	.333	114	0		.870	-2			/C-4	-0.2
	KC U	23	75	8	10	2	0	0		5			.133	.188	.160	7	-11		.813	2	181	162	O-16(6-4-6),C-11	-0.7
1886	Det N	14	54	2	12	1	0	0	6	2		9	.222	.250	.241	48	-3	0	.871	2			C-14/O(LF)	0.0
	Was N	7	23	0	5	1	1	0	1	1		5	.217	.250	.348	87	0	0	.946	0			/C-4,3-2,S	0.0
	Year	21	77	2	17	2	1	0	7	3		14	.221	.250	.273	59	-4	0	.886	2			C-18/3-2,O(LF)S	0.0
1889	Phi N	11	30	4	3	0	0	0	2	2	0	5	.100	.156	.100	-25	-5	1	.857	-1	98	119	/2-7,C-3,O(LF)	-0.5
1890	Phi N	5	19	5	7	1	0	0	2	4	0	1	.368	.478	.421	159	2	4	.938	-2	158	205	/1-2,O-2(LF),C	0.0
	Pit N	92	354	52	97	14	3	5	38	26	0	36	.274	.324	.373	116	7	8	.909	-37	65	93	C-70,1-16/O-4(2-0-2),2S	-2.3
	Year	97	373	57	104	15	3	5	40	30	0	37	.279	.333	.375	119	9	12	.909	-39	65	92	C-71,1-18/O-6(4-0-2),2S	-2.3
Total	4	156	570	72	138	20	4	5	49	41	0	56	.242	.293	.318	87	-10	13	.903	-38	42	60	C-107/O-24L,1-18,2-8,S-2,3-2	-3.7
DECKER, FRANK Frank B 2.26.1856 St.Louis, MO D 2.5.1940 St.Louis, MO BR/TR d6.25																								
1879	Syr N	3	10	0	1	0	0	0	0	0		3	.100	.100	.100	-38	-1		.714	-2			/C-2,O(RF)1	-0.3
1882	StL AA	2	8	0	2	0	0	0	1	0			.250	.250	.250	66	0		.813	-1	98	94	/2-2	-0.1
Total	2	5	18	0	3	0	0	0	1	0		3	.167	.167	.167	12	-1		.813	-2			/2-2,C-2,1O(RF)	-0.4
DECKER, GEORGE George A "Gentleman George" B 6.1.1869 York, PA D 6.7.1909 Patton, CA BL/TL 6-1/180# d7.11 OF Total (189-LF 34-CF 111-RF)																								
1892	Chi N	78	291	32	66	6	7	1	28	20	0	49	.227	.277	.306	75	-10	9	.876	-7	125	154	O-62(RF),2-16	-1.8
1893	Chi N	81	328	57	89	9	8	2	48	24	2	22	.271	.325	.366	85	-9	22	.878	-6	182	161	O-33(23-0-10),1-27,2-20/S-2	-1.4
1894	Chi N	93	393	76	122	17	7	8	93	24	5	20	.310	.358	.450	89	-10	23	.974	-7	56	86	1-49,O-29(0-23-6)/3-8,2-2,S	-1.4
1895	Chi N	73	297	51	82	9	7	2	41	17	4	22	.276	.324	.374	75	-13	11	.910	-7	36	0	O-57(25-8-24),1-11/3-3,S2	-1.9
1896	Chi N	107	421	68	118	23	11	5	61	23	0	14	.280	.318	.423	91	-9	20	.928	-3	104	0	O-71(67-3-1),1-36	-1.5
1897	Chi N	111	428	72	124	12	7	5	63	24	4		.290	.333	.386	86	-11	11	.925	-2	120	48	O-75(74-0-1),1-38/2	-1.6
1898	StL N	76	286	26	74	10	0	1	45	20	3		.259	.314	.304	76	-9	4	.980	-7	48	67	1-75	-1.5
	Lou N	42	148	27	44	4	3	0	19	9	1		.297	.342	.365	104	0	9	.993	-0	82	96	1-32/O-6(RF)	0.0
	Year	118	434	53	118	14	3	1	64	29	4		.272	.323	.325	85	-9	13	**.984**	-7	58	75	*1-107/O-6(RF)	-1.5
1899	Lou N	39	138	14	37	8	1	1	18	12	2		.268	.336	.362	92	-1	3	.968	-3	77	102	1-39	-0.4
	Was N	4	9	0	0	0	0	0	0	0	0		.000	.000	.000	-99	-3	0	.955	-0	97	72	/1-2,O(RF)	-0.3
	Year	43	147	14	37	8	1	1	18	12	2		.252	.317	.340	80	-4	3	.968	-3	78	100	1-41/O(RF)	-0.7
Total	8	704	2739	423	756	98	51	25	416	173	21	127	.276	.324	.376	84	-75	112	.900	-41	117	57	O-334L,1-309/2-40,3-11,S-4	-11.8
DECKER, STEVE Steven Michael B 10.25.1965 Rock Island, IL BR/TR 6-3/205# d9.18																								
1990	SF N	15	54	5	16	2	0	3	8	1-0	0	10	.296	.309	.500	123	1	0-0	.989	2	109	134	C-15	0.4
1991	SF N	79	233	11	48	7	1	5	24	16-1	3	44	.206	.262	.309	63	-12	0-1	.984	1	115	103	C-78	-0.8
1992	SF N	15	43	3	7	1	0	0	1	6-0	1	7	.163	.280	.186	36	-3	0-0	1.000	3	537	40	C-15	0.0
1993	Fla N	8	15	0	0	0	0	0	1	3-0	0	3	.000	.158	.000	-48	-3	0-0	.968	1	70	78	/C-5	-0.2
1995	Fla N	51	133	12	30	2	1	3	13	19-1	0	22	.226	.318	.323	71	-6	1-0	.985	5	117	94	C-46/1-2	0.2
1996	SF N	57	122	16	28	1	0	1	12	15-4	0	26	.230	.309	.262	56	-8	0-0	1.000	2	90	110	C-30/1-3,3-2	-0.4
	Col N	10	25	8	8	2	0	1	8	3-0	0	3	.320	.393	.520	112	1	1-0	1.000	2	188	88	C-10	0.3
	Year	67	147	24	36	3	0	2	20	18-4	0	29	.245	.323	.306	68	-7	1-0	1.000	4	112	105	C-40/1-3,3-2	-0.1
1999	Ana A	28	63	5	15	6	0	0	5	13-0	1	9	.238	.372	.333	84	-1	0-0	.987	-2	101	91	C-17/1-6,D-3	-0.2
Total	7	263	688	60	152	21	2	13	72	76-6	5	124	.221	.299	.314	68	-31	2-1	.988	13	143	98	C-216/1-11,D-3,3-2	-0.7
DEDE, ARTIE Arthur Richard B 7.12.1895 Brooklyn, NY D 9.6.1971 Keene, NH BR/TR 5-9/155# d10.4																								
1916	Bro N	1	1	0	0	0	0	0	0	0	0	0	.000	.000	.000	-97	0	0	1.000	-0	0	0	/C	-0.1
DEDEAUX, ROD Raoul Martial B 2.17.1915 New Orleans, LA BR/TR 5-11/160# d9.28																								
1935	Bro N	2	4	0	1	0	0	0	1	0	0	0	.250	.250	.250	36	0	0	.857	0	116	159	/S-2	0.0
DEE, JIM James D. B Buffalo, NY d7.30																								
1884	Pit AA	12	40	0	5	0	0	0		1	0		.125	.146	.125	-11	-5		.860	1	106	193	S-12	-0.3
DEE, SHORTY Maurice Leo B 10.4.1889 Halifax, NS, CAN D 8.12.1971 Jamaica Plain, MA BR/TR 5-6/155# d9.14																								
1915	StL A	1	3	1	0	0	0	0	0	1	0	0	.000	.250	.000	-26	0	0-1	.500	-1	36	0	/S	-0.2
DEER, ROB Robert George B 9.29.1960 Orange, CA BR/TR 6-3/210# d9.4																								
1984	SF N	13	24	5	4	0	0	3	3	7-0	1	10	.167	.375	.542	160	2	1-1	.905	-0	111	0	/O-9(LF)	0.1
1985	SF N	78	162	22	30	5	1	8	20	23-0	0	71	.185	.283	.377	88	-3	0-1	.982	-3	94	46	O-37(21-0-17),1-10	-0.9
1986	Mil A	134	466	75	108	17	3	33	86	72-3	3	179	.232	.336	.494	119	12	5-2	.974	4	110	90	*O-131(1-0-131)/1-4	0.9
1987	Mil A	134	474	71	113	15	2	28	80	86-6	5	186	.238	.360	.456	112	9	12-4	.974	6	110	124	*O-123(98-0-29),1-12/D-4	1.0
1988	Mil A	135	492	71	124	24	0	23	85	51-4	7	153	.252	.328	.441	113	9	9-5	.990	3	100	124	*O-133(54-2-79)/D	0.8
1989	Mil A	130	466	72	98	18	2	26	65	60-5	4	158	.210	.305	.425	105	2	4-8	.972	1	102	105	*O-125(2-1-123)/D-5	-0.3
1990	Mil A	134	440	57	92	15	1	27	69	64-6	4	147	.209	.313	.432	108	4	2-3	.970	8	107	176	*O-117(RF),1-21/D	0.7
1991	Det A	134	448	64	80	14	2	25	64	89-1	0	175	.179	.314	.386	91	-5	1-3	.978	4	108	78	*O-132(RF)/D-2	-0.6

Year	Tm Lg	G	AB	R	H	2B	3B	HR	RBI	BB-IB	HP	SO	AVG	OBP	SLG	AOPS	ABR	SB-CS	FA	FR	Rng	Thr	G at Pos	BFW
1992	Det A	110	393	66	97	20	1	32	64	51-1	3	131	.247	.337	.547	143	21	4-2	.983	0	100	106	*O-106(RF)/D-2	1.9
1993	Det A	90	323	48	70	11	0	14	39	38-1	3	120	.217	.302	.381	84	-8	3-2	.975	2	108	79	O-86(0-2-84)/D-4	-1.0
	Bos A	38	143	18	28	6	1	7	16	20-0	2	49	.196	.303	.399	82	-4	2-0	.970	3	127	75	O-36(RF)/D-2	-0.2
	Year	128	466	66	98	17	1	21	55	58-1	5	169	.210	.303	.386	83	-12	5-2	.973	5	114	78	*O-122(0-2-120)/D-6	-1.2
1996	SD N	25	50	9	9	3	0	4	9	14-0	0	30	.180	.359	.480	126	2	0-0	1.000	-0	106	0	O-18(1-0-17)	0.1
Total	11	1155	3881	578	853	148	13	230	600	575-27	32	1409	.220	.324	.442	108	41	43-31	.977	27	106	104	*O-1053(186-5-871)/1-47,D-21	2.5
DEES, CHARLIE Charles Henry B 6.24.1935 Birmingham, AL BL/TL 6-1/173# d5.26																								
1963	LA A	60	202	23	62	11	1	3	27	11-1	8	31	.307	.362	.416	126	7	3-3	.986	-3	83	95	1-56	0.1
1964	LA A	26	26	3	2	1	0	0	1	1-0	1	4	.077	.143	.115	-30	-5	1-2	.981	-0	100	203	1-12	-0.6
1965	Cal A	12	32	1	5	0	0	0	1	1-1	0	8	.156	.182	.156	-3	-4	1-2	.986	-1	45	90	/1-8	-0.7
Total	3	98	260	27	69	12	1	3	29	13-2	9	43	.265	.319	.354	95	-2	5-7	.986	-4	80	102	/1-76	-1.2
DeFATE, TONY Clyde Herbert B 2.22.1895 Kansas City, MO D 9.3.1963 New Orleans, LA BR/TR 5-8.5/158# d4.18																								
1917	StL N	14	14	0	2	0	0	0	1	4	0	5	.143	.333	.143	50	-1	0	1.000	0	101	0	/3-5,2	-0.1
	Det A	3	2	1	0	0	0	0	0	0	0	1	.000	.000	.000	-99	0	0	1.000	-0	102	0	/2	-0.1
Total	1	17	16	1	2	0	0	0	1	4	0	6	.125	.300	.125	33	-1	0	1.000	-0	101	0	/3-5,2-2	-0.2
DeFREITES, ARTURO Arturo Marcelino (Simon) B 4.26.1953 San Pedro De Macoris, D.R. BR/TR 6-2/195# d9.7																								
1978	Cin N	9	19	1	4	1	0	1	2	1-0	0	4	.211	.238	.421	84	-1	0-0	1.000	0	97	131	/1-6	-0.1
1979	Cin N	23	34	2	7	2	0	0	4	0-0	0	16	.206	.200	.265	27	-3	0-0	.974	-1	0	154	/1-6,O(RF)	-0.5
Total	2	32	53	3	11	3	0	1	6	1-0	0	20	.208	.214	.321	47	-4	0-0	.988	-1	52	142	/1-12,O(RF)	-0.6
DeGROFF, RUBE Edward Arthur B 9.2.1879 Hyde Park, NY D 12.17.1955 Poughkeepsie, NY BL/TL 5-11/?# d9.22																								
1905	StL N	15	56	3	14	2	1	0	5	5	0		.250	.311	.321	91	-1	1	.909	0	149	197	O-15(0-8-7)	-0.1
1906	StL N	1	4	1	0	0	0	0	0	0	0		.000	.000	.000	-99	-1	0	—	-0	0	0	/O(RF)	-0.1
Total	2	16	60	4	14	2	1	0	5	5	0		.233	.292	.300	80	-2	1	.909	-0	148	196	/O-16(0-8-8)	-0.2
DeHAAN, KORY Korwin Jay B 7.16.1976 Pella, IA BL/TR 6-2/187# d4.25																								
2000	SD N	90	103	19	21	7	0	2	13	5-0	0	39	.204	.239	.330	45	-9	4-2	1.000	1	99	188	O-60(10-4-49)/D	-0.8
2002	SD N	12	11	1	1	0	0	0	0	0-0	0	6	.091	.091	.091	-56	-3	0-0	1.000	-0	108	0	/O-9(6-2-1)	-0.3
Total	2	102	114	20	22	7	0	2	13	5-0	0	45	.193	.225	.307	36	-12	4-2	1.000	1	100	168	/O-69(16-6-50),D	-1.1
DEHLMAN, HERMAN Herman J. "Dutch" B 1852 Brooklyn, NY D 3.13.1885 Wilkes-Barre, PA d5.2 U1																								
1872	Atl NA	**37**	164	30	37	4	1	0	15	3		1	.226	.240	.262	46	-13	4-2	.928	-1	89	49	*1-37	-0.9
1873	Atl NA	54	219	50	52	5	1	0	18	11		9	.237	.274	.269	69	-5	5-0	.926	-3	72	87	*1-54/S	-0.4
1874	Atl NA	53	218	40	49	3	1	0	18	7		5	.225	.249	.248	68	-5	2-0	.944	-1	89	45	*1-53	-0.4
1875	StL NA	67	254	42	57	12	2	0	14	**11**		21	.224	.257	.287	98	2	23-9	**.955**	1	92	113	*1-67/O-2(RF)	0.6
1876	StL N	**64**	245	40	45	6	0	0	9	9		10	.184	.213	.208	43	-13		.958	0	71	138	*1-64	-1.4
1877	StL N	32	119	24	22	4	0	0	11	7		21	.185	.230	.218	44	-7		.931	-4	41	102	1-31/O(LF)	-1.0
Total	4 NA	211	855	162	195	24	5	0	65	32		36	.228	.256	.268	71	-21	34-11	.000	-4	86	78	1-211/O-2(RF),S	-1.1
Total	2	96	364	64	67	10	0	0	20	16		31	.184	.218	.212	43	-20		.950	-3	61	126	/1-95,O(LF)	-2.4
DEIDEL, JIM James Lawrence B 6.6.1949 Denver, CO BR/TR 6-2/195# d5.31																								
1974	NY A	2	2	0	0	0	0	0	0	0-0	0	0	.000	.000	.000	-99	-1	0-0	1.000	1	0	316	/C-2	0.0
DEININGER, PEP Otto Charles B 10.10.1877 Wasseralfingen, Germany D 9.25.1950 Boston, MA BL/TL 5-8.5/180# d4.26 ▲																								
1902	Bos A	2	6	0	2	1	1	0	0	0	0		.333	.333	.833	210	1	0	1.000	-1	29	882	/P-2	0.0
1908	Phi N	1	0	0	0	0	0	0	0	0	0		—	—	—	—	0	0	—	-0	0	0	/O(CF)	0.0
1909	Phi N	55	169	22	44	9	0	0	16	11	1		.260	.309	.314	93	-1	5	.989	-1	87	0	O-45(1-38-6)/2	-0.5
Total	3	58	175	22	46	10	1	0	16	11	1		.263	.310	.331	97	0	5	.989	-2	87	0	/O-46(1-39-6),P-2,2	-0.5
DEISEL, PAT Edward B 4.29.1876 Ripley, OH D 4.17.1948 Cincinnati, OH BR/TR 5-5 /145# d8.21																								
1902	Bro N	1	3	0	2	0	0	0	1	1	1		.667	.800	.667	351	1	0	1.000	0	*70*	*0*	/C	0.1
1903	Cin N	2	0	0	0	0	0	0	0	1	0		—	1.000	—	174	0	0	—	0	*0*	*0*	/C	0.0
Total	2	3	3	0	2	0	0	0	1	2	1		.667	.833	.667	352	1	0	1.000	0	*64*	*0*	/C-2	0.1
DEITRICK, BILL William Alexander B 4.20.1902 Hanover Co., VA D 5.6.1946 Bethesda, MD BR/TR 5-10/160# d9.19																								
1927	Phi N	5	6	1	1	0	0	0	0	0	0	0	.167	.167	.167	-10	-1	0	.750	-1	46	220	/S-5	-0.2
1928	Phi N	52	100	13	20	6	0	0	7	17	1	10	.200	.322	.260	52	-6	1	1.000	0	101	208	O-21(17-1-3)/S-8	-0.7
Total	2	57	106	14	21	6	0	0	7	17	1	10	.198	.315	.255	49	-7	1	1.000	-1	101	208	/O-21(17-1-3),S-13	-0.9
DEJAN, MIKE Michael Dan B 1.13.1915 Cleveland, OH D 2.2.1953 W.Los Angeles, CA BL/TL 6-1/185# d7.13																								
1940	Cin N	12	16	1	3	0	1	0	2	3	0	3	.188	.316	.313	73	-1	0	1.000	-0	90	0	/O-2(LF)	-0.1
DeJESUS, DAVID David Christopher B 12.20.1979 Brooklyn, NY BL/TL 6/170# d9.2																								
2003	KC A	12	7	0	2	0	1	0	0	1-0	1	2	.286	.444	.571	146	0	0-0	1.000	-1	30	0	/O-9(0-8-1)	-0.1
DeJESUS, IVAN Ivan (Alvarez) B 1.9.1953 Santurce, P.R. BR/TR 5-11/175# d9.13																								
1974	LA N	3	3	1	1	0	0	0	0	0-0	0	2	.333	.333	.333	91	0	0-0	1.000	-1	0	0	/S-2	-0.1
1975	LA N	63	87	10	16	2	1	0	2	11-0	0	15	.184	.276	.230	43	-7	1-2	.974	1	104	112	S-63	-0.2
1976	LA N	22	41	4	7	2	1	0	2	4-0	0	9	.171	.244	.268	46	-3	0-1	.950	3	119	124	S-13/3-7	0.1
1977	Chi N	155	624	91	166	31	7	3	40	56-4	4	90	.266	.328	.353	75	-21	24-12	.962	**46**	**125**	108	*S-154	4.2
1978	Chi N	160	619	**104**	172	24	7	3	35	74-5	2	78	.278	.356	.354	88	-7	41-12	.967	15	**113**	103	*S-160	3.1
1979	Chi N	160	636	92	180	26	10	5	52	59-1	2	82	.283	.345	.379	89	-9	24-20	.959	8	103	100	*S-160	1.4
1980	Chi N	157	618	78	160	26	3	3	33	60-2	4	81	.259	.327	.325	77	-17	44-16	.969	10	106	99	*S-156	1.4
1981	Chi N	**106**	403	49	78	8	4	0	13	46-2	0	61	.194	.276	.233	44	-29	21-9	.959	9	101	112	*S-106	-0.8
1982	Phi N	161	536	53	128	21	5	3	59	54-9	2	70	.239	.309	.313	73	-18	14-4	.973	-3	95	94	*S-154/3-7	-0.4
1983	†Phi N	158	497	60	126	15	7	4	45	53-18	0	77	.254	.323	.336	85	-10	11-4	.966	-17	91	71	*S-158	-1.1
1984	Phi N	144	435	40	112	15	3	0	35	43-7	2	76	.257	.325	.306	77	-12	12-5	.951	-18	98	78	*S-141	-1.6
1985	†StL N	59	72	11	16	5	0	0	7	4-0	0	16	.222	.260	.292	55	-4	2-2	1.000	-2	121	128	3-20,S-13	-0.6
1986	NY A	7	4	1	0	0	0	0	0	1-0	0	1	.000	.200	.000	-40	-1	0-0	.900	-2	53	0	/S-7	-0.2
1987	SF N	9	10	0	2	0	0	0	1	0-0	0	2	.200	.200	.200	7	-1	0-1	.840	1	132	100	/S-9	0.0
1988	Det A	7	17	1	3	0	0	0	0	1-0	0	4	.176	.222	.176	14	-2	0-0	.893	-2	88	100	/S-7	-0.4
Total	15	1371	4602	595	1167	175	48	21	324	466-48	16	664	.254	.323	.326	76	-141	194-88	.963	48	104	95	*S-1303/3-34	4.8
DeJOHN, MARK Mark Stephen B 9.18.1953 Middletown, CT BB/TR 5-11/170# d4.28 C6																								
1982	Det A	24	21	1	4	2	0	0	1	4-0	0	4	.190	.320	.286	68	-1	1-0	.978	3	98	140	S-20/3-4,2	0.3
DeKONING, BILL William Callahan B 12.19.1918 Brooklyn, NY D 7.26.1979 Palm Harbor, FL BR/TR 5-11/185# d5.27																								
1945	NY N	3	1	0	0	0	0	0	0	0	0	1	.000	.000	.000	-99	0	0	1.000	-0	*0*	*0*	/C-2	0.0
DeLA ROSA, TOMAS Tomas Agramonte B 1.28.1978 LaVictoria, D.R. BR/TR 5-10/165# d7.17																								
2000	Mon N	32	66	7	19	3	1	2	9	7-0	1	11	.288	.365	.455	103	0	2-1	.980	2	107	55	S-29	0.4
2001	Mon N	1	1	0	0	0	0	0	0	0-0	0	0	.000	.000	.000	-98	0	0-0	—	0			/H	0.0
Total	2	33	67	7	19	3	1	2	9	7-0	1	11	.284	.360	.448	100	0	2-1	.980	2	107	55	/S-29	0.4
DELAHANTY, ED Edward James "Big Ed" B10.30.1867 Cleveland, OH D7.2.1903 Niagara Falls, ON, CAN BR/TR 6-1/170# d5.22 HF1945 b-Frank b-Jim b-Joe b-Tom OF Total (1056-LF 250-CF 40-RF)																								
1888	Phi N	74	290	40	66	12	2	1	31	12	1	26	.228	.261	.293	72	-9	38	.872	-9	94	101	2-56,O-17(10-1-6)	-1.7
1889	Phi N	56	246	37	72	13	3	0	27	14	1	17	.293	.333	.370	89	-5	19	.956	-8	80	0	O-31(30-0-1),2-24/S	-1.1
1890	Cle P	115	517	107	153	26	13	3	64	24	8	30	.296	.337	.414	109	5	25	.830	-6	99	98	S-76,2-20,O-18(4-11-3)/3-3,1	0.1
1891	Phi N	128	543	92	132	19	9	5	86	33	8	50	.243	.296	.339	83	-14	25	.909	-4	139	108	*O-99(2-95-2),1-27/2-3	-2.2
1892	Phi N	123	477	79	146	30	**21**	6	91	31	9	32	.306	.360	**.495**	158	30	29	.944	4	125	148	*O-121(1-120-0)/3-4	2.4
1893	Phi N	132	595	145	219	35	18	**19**	**146**	47	10	20	.368	.423	**.583**	167	**53**	37	.948	24	149	181	*O-117(100-17-0),2-15/1-6	**5.4**
1894	Phi N	116	495	148	200	39	19	4	133	60	7	16	.404	.475	.584	158	50	21	.927	12	147	106	*O-90(84-0-6),1-12/3-9,S-8,2-6	4.2
1895	Phi N	116	480	149	194	**49**	10	11	106	86	6	31	.404	**.500**	.617	**186**	**69**	46	.944	-2	100	105	*O-103(98-5-0)/S-9,2-6,3	4.6
1896	Phi N	123	499	131	198	**44**	17	**13**	**126**	62	9	22	.397	.472	**.631**	**192**	**68**	37	.952	11	125	101	*O-99(LF),1-22/2	5.8
1897	Phi N	129	530	109	200	40	15	5	96	60	3		.377	.444	.538	163	50	26	.970	9	125	56	*O-129(128-0-1)/1	4.0
1898	Phi N	144	548	115	183	36	9	4	92	77	11		.334	.426	.454	159	**48**	**58**	.964	7	100	103	*O-144(LF)	3.9

Year	Tm Lg	G	AB	R	H	2B	3B	HR	RBI	BB-IB	HP	SO	AVG	OBP	SLG	AOPS	ABR	SB-CS	FA	FR	Rng	Thr	G at Pos	BFW
1899	Phi N	146	581	135	**238**	**55**	9	9	**137**	55	4		**.410**	.464	**.582**	**193**	**76**	30	.969	2	120	72	*O-143(LF)	5.9
1900	Phi N	131	539	82	174	32	10	2	109	41	7		.323	.378	.430	124	18	16	.981	-4	88	109	*1-130	1.3
1901	Phi N	139	542	106	192	**38**	16	8	108	65	4		.354	.427	.528	173	52	29	.949	-3	85	83	O-84(82-1-1),1-58	4.1
1902	Was A	123	473	103	178	**43**	14	10	93	62	4		**.376**	**.453**	**.590**	**186**	**58**	16	.961	2	76	0	*O-111(LF),1-13	5.0
1903	Was A	42	156	22	52	11	1	1	21	12	2		.333	.388	.436	144	9	3	.962	2	139	86	O-40(20-0-20)/1	0.9
Total	16	1837	7511	1600	2597	522	186	101	1466	741	94	244	.346	.411	.505	152	558	455	.951	36	118	95	*O-1346L,1-271,2-131/S-94,3-17	42.6

DELAHANTY, FRANK Frank George "Pudgie" B 1.29.1883 Cleveland, OH D 7.22.1966 Cleveland, OH BR/TR 5-9/160# d8.23 b-Ed b-Jim b-Joe b-Tom

Year	Tm Lg	G	AB	R	H	2B	3B	HR	RBI	BB-IB	HP	SO	AVG	OBP	SLG	AOPS	ABR	SB-CS	FA	FR	Rng	Thr	G at Pos	BFW
1905	NY A	9	27	0	6	1	0	0	2	1	0		.222	.250	.259	55	-1	0	.932	-1	68	0	/1-5,O-3(LF)	-0.3
1906	NY A	92	307	37	73	11	8	2	41	16	3		.238	.282	.345	87	-6	11	.954	3	62	42	O-86(LF)	-0.9
1907	Cle A	15	52	3	9	0	1	0	4	4	0		.173	.232	.212	41	-4	2	.917	0	166	0	O-15(9-0-6)	-0.5
1908	NY A	37	125	12	32	1	2	0	10	10	1		.256	.316	.296	98	0	9	.957	-0	49	0	O-36(LF)	-0.3
1914	Buf F	79	274	29	55	4	7	2	27	23	1	19	.201	.265	.288	50	-25	21	.976	-4	91	73	O-78(LF)	-3.4
	Pit F	41	159	25	38	4	4	1	7	11	2	11	.239	.297	.333	72	-9	7	.984	-2	102	90	O-36(13-1-23)/2-4	-1.3
	Year	120	433	54	93	8	11	3	34	34	3	30	.215	.277	.305	58	-35	28	.979	-5	94	78	*O-114(91-1-23)/2-4	-4.7
1915	Pit F	14	42	3	10	1	0	0	3	1	0	0	.238	.256	.262	46	-4	0	1.000	1	108	154	O-11(LF)	-0.3
Total	6	287	986	109	223	22	22	5	94	66	7	30	.226	.280	.308	70	-49	50	.964	-3	81	53	O-265(236-1-29)/1-5,2-4	-7.0

DELAHANTY, JIM James Christopher B 6.20.1879 Cleveland, OH D 10.17.1953 Cleveland, OH BR/TR 5-10.5/170# d4.19 b-Ed b-Frank b-Joe b-Tom OF Total (176-LF 1-CF 12-RF)

Year	Tm Lg	G	AB	R	H	2B	3B	HR	RBI	BB-IB	HP	SO	AVG	OBP	SLG	AOPS	ABR	SB-CS	FA	FR	Rng	Thr	G at Pos	BFW
1901	Chi N	17	63	4	12	2	0	0	4	3	1		.190	.239	.222	35	-5	5	.877	-2	88	108	3-17/2	-0.6
1902	NY N	7	26	3	6	1	0	0	3	1	0		.231	.259	.269	64	-1	0	.917	-1	0	0	/O-7(RF)	-0.2
1904	Bos N	142	499	56	142	27	8	3	60	27	9		.285	.333	.389	127	15	16	.888	2	102	88	*3-113,2-18/O-9(8-1-0),P	2.0
1905	Bos N	125	461	50	119	11	8	5	55	28	10		.258	.315	.349	100	-1	12	.962	-7	98	24	*O-124(123-0-1)/P	-1.6
1906	Cin N	115	379	63	106	21	4	1	39	45	10		.280	.371	.364	124	13	21	.903	-15	85	34	*3-105/S-5,O-2(LF)	0.1
1907	StL A	33	95	8	21	3	0	0	6	5	2		.221	.275	.253	68	-3	6	.889	-2	86	50	3-21/O-4(RF),2-2	-0.5
	Was A	108	404	44	118	18	7	2	54	36	12		.292	.367	.386	152	25	18	.941	-10	88	75	2-68,3-27/O-9(LF),1-4	1.8
	Year	141	499	52	139	21	7	2	60	41	14		.279	.350	.361	135	21	24	.942	-11	89	74	2-70,3-48,O-13(10-0-4)/1-4	1.3
1908	Was A	83	287	33	91	11	4	1	30	24	3		.317	.376	.394	164	20	16	.963	-0	96	103	2-80	2.4
1909	Was A	90	302	18	67	13	5	1	21	23	6		.222	.290	.308	93	-2	4	.956	-1	94	89	2-85	-0.3
	†Det A	46	150	29	38	10	1	0	20	17	9		.253	.364	.333	115	4	9	.943	-5	101	88	2-46	0.0
	Year	136	452	47	105	23	6	1	41	40	15		.232	.316	.316	101	2	13	.951	-6	97	89	*2-131	-0.3
1910	Det A	106	378	67	111	16	2	3	45	43	9		.294	.379	.370	126	14	15	.940	-15	91	95	*2-106	0.0
1911	Det A	144	542	83	184	30	14	3	94	56	10		.339	.411	.463	137	28	15	.978	-13	45	48	1-71,2-59,3-13	1.5
1912	Det A	79	266	34	76	14	1	0	41	42	7		.286	.397	.346	117	9	9	.930	-3	107	130	2-44,O-33(LF)	0.6
1914	Bro F	74	214	28	62	13	5	0	15	25	3	21	.290	.372	.397	110	1	4	.957	-12	83	76	2-55/1-5	-1.1
1915	Bro F	17	25	0	6	1	0	0	2	3	1	3	.240	.345	.280	77	-1	1	.857	-1	102	0	/2-4	-0.2
Total	13	1186	4091	520	1159	191	59	19	489	378	92	24	.283	.357	.373	122	116	151	.946	-83	95	89	2-568,3-296,O-188L/1-80,S-5,P-2	3.9

DELAHANTY, JOE Joseph Nicholas B 10.18.1875 Cleveland, OH D 1.29.1936 Cleveland, OH BR/TR 5-9/168# d9.30 b-Ed b-Frank b-Jim b-Tom

Year	Tm Lg	G	AB	R	H	2B	3B	HR	RBI	BB-IB	HP	SO	AVG	OBP	SLG	AOPS	ABR	SB-CS	FA	FR	Rng	Thr	G at Pos	BFW
1907	StL N	7	22	3	7	0	0	1	2	0	0		.318	.318	.455	147	1	3	.933	-0	0	0	/O-7(LF)	0.0
1908	StL N	140	499	37	127	14	11	1	44	32	7		.255	.309	.333	110	4	11	.977	-3	64	23	*O-138(LF)	-0.8
1909	StL N	123	411	28	88	16	4	2	54	42	3		.214	.292	.287	85	-7	10	.985	-11	90	90	O-63(14-45-7)/2-48	-2.4
Total	3	270	932	68	222	30	15	4	100	74	10		.238	.301	.315	100	-2	24	.978	-15	70	43	O-208(159-45-7)/2-48	-3.2

DELAHANTY, TOM Thomas James B 3.9.1872 Cleveland, OH D 1.10.1951 Sanford, FL BL/TR 5-8/175# d9.29 b-Ed b-Frank b-Jim b-Joe

Year	Tm Lg	G	AB	R	H	2B	3B	HR	RBI	BB-IB	HP	SO	AVG	OBP	SLG	AOPS	ABR	SB-CS	FA	FR	Rng	Thr	G at Pos	BFW
1894	Phi N	1	4	0	1	0	0	0	0	0	0	1	.250	.250	.250	21	-1	0	.875	-1	55	0	/2	-0.1
1896	Cle N	16	56	11	13	4	0	0	4	8	1	4	.232	.338	.304	66	-2	4	.823	-3	96	44	3-16	-0.4
	Pit N	1	3	1	1	0	0	0	0	0	0	0	.333	.333	.333	79	0	0	.750	-0	73	295	/S	0.0
	Year	17	59	12	14	4	0	0	4	8	1	4	.237	.338	.305	67	-3	4	.823	-3	96	44	3-16/S	-0.4
1897	Lou N	1	4	1	1	1	0	0	2	0	0		.250	.250	.500	99	0	0	.333	-1	0	0	/2	-0.1
Total	3	19	67	13	16	5	0	0	6	8	1	5	.239	.329	.313	66	-3	4	.823	-5	96	44	/3-16,2-2,S	-0.6

DeLA HOZ, MIKE Miguel Angel (Piloto) B 10.2.1938 Havana, Cuba BR/TR 5-11/175# d7.22

Year	Tm Lg	G	AB	R	H	2B	3B	HR	RBI	BB-IB	HP	SO	AVG	OBP	SLG	AOPS	ABR	SB-CS	FA	FR	Rng	Thr	G at Pos	BFW
1960	Cle A	49	160	20	41	6	2	6	23	9-0	1	12	.256	.290	.431	98	-1	0-0	.950	-9	89	57	S-38/3-8	-0.8
1961	Cle A	61	173	20	45	10	0	3	23	7-0	2	10	.260	.295	.370	79	-6	0-0	.969	-3	110	23	2-17,S-17,3-16	-0.5
1962	Cle A	12	12	0	1	0	0	0	0	0-0	0	3	.083	.083	.083	-57	-3	0-0	1.000	0	154	0	/2-2	-0.3
1963	Cle A	67	150	15	40	10	0	5	25	9-0	1	29	.267	.313	.433	107	1	0-0	.962	7	115	120	2-34/3-6,S-2,O-2(LF)	1.1
1964	Mil N	78	189	25	55	7	1	4	12	14-4	2	22	.291	.346	.402	109	2	1-1	.968	-3	96	68	2-25,3-25/S-8	0.1
1965	Mil N	81	176	15	45	3	2	2	11	8-1	2	21	.256	.293	.330	75	-6	0-1	.963	-5	84	103	S-41,3-22,2-10/1	-1.0
1966	Atl N	71	110	11	24	3	0	2	7	5-1	0	18	.218	.250	.300	52	-7	0-1	.950	-2	90	80	3-30/2-8,S	-1.0
1967	Atl N	74	143	10	29	3	0	3	14	4-3	0	14	.203	.224	.287	46	-11	1-0	1.000	-2	86	134	2-23,3-22/S	-1.3
1969	Cin N	1	1	0	0	0	0	0	0	0-0	0	1	.000	.000	.000	-95	0	0-0	—	0			H	0.0
Total	9	494	1114	116	280	42	5	25	115	56-9	8	130	.251	.290	.365	82	-31	2-3	.936	-17	94	95	3-129,2-119,S-108/O-2(LF),1	-3.7

DeLANCEY, BILL William Pinkney B 11.28.1911 Greensboro, NC D 11.28.1946 Phoenix, AZ BL/TR 5-11.5/185# d9.11

Year	Tm Lg	G	AB	R	H	2B	3B	HR	RBI	BB-IB	HP	SO	AVG	OBP	SLG	AOPS	ABR	SB-CS	FA	FR	Rng	Thr	G at Pos	BFW
1932	StL N	8	26	1	5	0	2	0	2	2	0	1	.192	.250	.346	57	-2	0	.930	0	*76*	*217*	/C-8	-0.1
1934	†StL N	93	253	41	80	18	3	13	40	41	1	37	.316	.414	.565	150	19	1	.980	3	*105*	*103*	C-77	2.5
1935	StL N	103	301	37	84	14	5	6	41	42	1	34	.279	.369	.419	107	4	0	.971	-2	*110*	*31*	C-83	0.7
1940	StL N	15	18	0	4	0	0	0	2	0	0	2	.222	.222	.222	22	-2	0	.929	0	*82*	*75*	C-12	-0.2
Total	4	219	598	79	173	32	10	19	85	85	2	74	.289	.380	.472	121	19	1	.972	1	*106*	*71*	C-180	2.9

DELANEY, BILL William L. B 3.4.1863 Cincinnati, OH D 3.1.1942 Canton, OH BR/TR 5-10/170# d8.21

Year	Tm Lg	G	AB	R	H	2B	3B	HR	RBI	BB-IB	HP	SO	AVG	OBP	SLG	AOPS	ABR	SB-CS	FA	FR	Rng	Thr	G at Pos	BFW
1890	Cle N	36	116	16	22	1	1	1	7	21	0	19	.190	.314	.241	64	-5	5	.926	-6	88	125	2-36	-0.8

DeLA ROSA, JESUS Jesus (born (De La Rosa)) B 8.5.1953 Santo Domingo, D.R. BR/TR 6-1/153# d8.2

Year	Tm Lg	G	AB	R	H	2B	3B	HR	RBI	BB-IB	HP	SO	AVG	OBP	SLG	AOPS	ABR	SB-CS	FA	FR	Rng	Thr	G at Pos	BFW
1975	Hou N	3	3	1	1	1	0	0	0	0-0	0	0	.333	.333	.667	186	0	0-0	—	0			H	0.0

DELGADO, ALEX Alexander B 1.11.1971 Palmerejo, Venezuela BR/TR 6/160# d4.4

Year	Tm Lg	G	AB	R	H	2B	3B	HR	RBI	BB-IB	HP	SO	AVG	OBP	SLG	AOPS	ABR	SB-CS	FA	FR	Rng	Thr	G at Pos	BFW
1996	Bos A	26	20	5	5	0	0	0	1	3-0	0	3	.250	.348	.250	54	-1	0-0	.889	-0	51	0	C-14/O-6(5-0-2),3-4,12	-0.2

DELGADO, CARLOS Carlos Juan (Hernandez) B 6.25.1972 Mayaguez, P.R. BL/TR 6-3/220# d10.1

Year	Tm Lg	G	AB	R	H	2B	3B	HR	RBI	BB-IB	HP	SO	AVG	OBP	SLG	AOPS	ABR	SB-CS	FA	FR	Rng	Thr	G at Pos	BFW
1993	Tor A	2	1	0	0	0	0	0	0	1-0	0	0	.000	.500	.000	47	0	0-0	1.000	0	0	0	/CD	0.0
1994	Tor A	43	130	17	28	2	0	9	24	25-4	3	46	.215	.352	.438	103	1	1-1	.966	-4	75	79	O-41(LF)/C	-0.5
1995	Tor A	37	91	7	15	3	0	3	11	6-0	0	26	.165	.212	.297	32	-10	0-0	1.000	1	113	101	O-17(LF)/1-4,D-7	-0.9
1996	Tor A	138	488	68	132	28	2	25	92	58-2	9	139	.270	.353	.490	112	9	0-0	.983	-3	71	95	*D-108,1-27	-0.3
1997	Tor A	153	519	79	136	42	3	30	91	64-9	8	133	.262	.350	.528	125	19	0-3	.988	-6	80	105	*1-119,D-32	-0.1
1998	Tor A	142	530	94	155	43	1	38	115	73-13	11	139	.292	.385	.592	150	41	3-0	.992	-6	83	95	*1-141/D	2.0
1999	Tor A	152	573	113	156	39	0	44	134	86-7	15	141	.272	.377	.571	136	33	1-1	.990	-2	96	100	*1-147/D-5	1.5
2000	Tor A★	**162**	569	115	196	**57**	1	41	137	123-18	**15**	104	.344	.470	.664	178	77	0-1	.991	-10	78	105	*1-162	4.6
2001	Tor A	**162**	574	102	160	31	1	39	102	111-22	16	136	.279	.408	.540	144	42	3-0	.994	-5	90	121	*1-161	2.1
2002	Tor A	143	505	103	140	34	2	33	108	102-18	13	126	.277	.406	.549	147	39	1-0	.991	-1	99	99	*1-140/D-3	2.4
2003	Tor A★	161	570	117	172	38	1	42	**145**	109-23	19	137	.302	.426	.593	**163**	**59**	0-0	.993	1	102	109	*1-147,D-14	4.2
Total	11	1295	4550	815	1290	317	11	304	959	758-116	109	1127	.284	.395	.558	142	310	9-6	.992	-34	89	105	*1-1048,D-171/O-58(LF),C-2	15.0

DELGADO, PUCHY Luis Felipe (Robles) B 2.2.1954 Hatillo, P.R. BB/TL 5-11/170# d9.6

Year	Tm Lg	G	AB	R	H	2B	3B	HR	RBI	BB-IB	HP	SO	AVG	OBP	SLG	AOPS	ABR	SB-CS	FA	FR	Rng	Thr	G at Pos	BFW
1977	Sea A	13	22	4	4	0	0	0	2	1-0	0	8	.182	.217	.182	10	-3	0-0	1.000	1	105	219	O-13(1-2-10)	-0.2

DELGADO, WILSON Wilson (Duran) B 7.15.1972 San Cristobal, D.R. BB/TR 5-11/165# d9.24

Year	Tm Lg	G	AB	R	H	2B	3B	HR	RBI	BB-IB	HP	SO	AVG	OBP	SLG	AOPS	ABR	SB-CS	FA	FR	Rng	Thr	G at Pos	BFW
1996	SF N	6	22	3	8	0	0	0	2	1-0	2	5	.364	.440	.364	120	1	1-0	.960	-2	68	79	/S-6	0.0
1997	SF N	8	7	1	1	1	0	0	0	0-0	0	2	.143	.143	.286	9	-1	0-0	1.000	-1	96	137	/2-3,S	-0.1
1998	SF N	10	12	1	2	1	0	0	1	1-0	0	3	.167	.231	.250	28	-1	0-0	1.000	0	105	174	/S-6	-0.1
1999	SF N	35	71	7	18	2	1	0	3	5-0	1	9	.254	.312	.310	62	-4	1-0	.932	-4	102	142	S-20,2-15	-0.7
2000	NY A	31	45	6	11	1	0	1	4	5-0	0	9	.244	.314	.333	66	-2	1-0	.950	-3	91	53	2-14,S-11/3-5	-0.4
	KC A	33	83	15	22	1	0	0	7	6-0	0	17	.265	.311	.277	50	-6	1-1	.976	12	151	138	2-19,S-12/3-3	0.6
	Year	64	128	21	33	2	0	1	11	11-0	0	26	.258	.312	.297	56	-9	2-1	.986	9	130	108	2-33,S-23/3-8	0.2
2001	KC A	14	25	1	3	0	0	0	1	3-0	0	10	.120	.214	.120	-8	-4	0-0	1.000	1	134	113	/S-6,3-3,2-2	-0.3
2002	StL N	12	20	2	4	2	0	2	5	0-0	0	6	.200	.200	.600	105	0	0-0	1.000	-3	63	32	/S-8	-0.2

Year	Tm Lg	G	AB	R	H	2B	3B	HR	RBI	BB-IB	HP	SO	AVG	OBP	SLG	AOPS	ABR	SB-CS	FA	FR	Rng	Thr	G at Pos	BFW
2003	StL N	43	77	8	13	3	0	0	3	3-0	1	10	.169	.207	.208	10	-10	0-0	1.000	-3	117	78	2-12,3-11,S-11	-1.3
	Ana A	19	50	4	16	0	0	0	4	8-0	0	8	.320	.414	.320	101	1	0-0	.867	0	98	212	/3-9,S-9,2	0.1
Total	8	211	412	48	98	11	1	3	30	32-0	4	79	.238	.297	.291	54	-26	4-1	.966	-2	94	105	/S-90,2-66,3-31	-2.4
DelGRECO, BOBBY Robert George B 4.7.1933 Pittsburgh, PA BR/TR 5-11/190# d4.16																								
1952	Pit N	99	341	34	74	14	2	1	20	38	3	70	.217	.301	.279	60	-18	6-5	.977	2	102	119	O-93(1-88-4)	-2.0
1956	Pit N	14	20	4	4	0	0	2	3	3-0	0	3	.200	.304	.500	114	0	0-0	1.000	0	112	0	/O-7(CF),3-3	0.0
	StL N	102	270	29	58	16	2	5	18	32-3	6	50	.215	.308	.344	76	-8	1-1	.987	-6	94	46	O-99(CF)	-1.9
	Year	116	290	33	62	16	2	7	21	35-3	6	53	.214	.307	.355	79	-8	1-1	.987	-6	95	44	*O-106(CF)/3-3	-1.9
1957	Chi N	20	40	2	8	2	0	0	3	10-0	0	17	.200	.360	.250	69	-1	1-0	.967	0	88	238	O-16(CF)	-0.2
	NY A	8	7	3	3	0	0	0	0	2-0	0	2	.429	.556	.429	175	1	1-0	1.000	0	110	0	/O-6(CF)	0.1
1958	NY A	12	5	1	1	0	0	0	0	1-0	0	1	.200	.333	.200	52	0	0-1	1.000	0	113	0	O-12(11-1-0)	-0.1
1960	Phi N	100	300	48	71	16	4	10	26	54-0	1	64	.237	.355	.417	110	6	1-5	.970	7	112	150	O-89(0-87-2)	0.7
1961	Phi N	41	112	14	29	5	0	2	11	12-1	3	17	.259	.344	.357	88	-1	0-0	1.000	-1	106	43	O-32(1-31-0)/23	-0.3
	KC A	74	239	34	55	14	1	5	21	30-2	1	31	.230	.317	.360	79	-7	1-0	.983	3	100	220	O-73(CF)	-0.6
1962	KC A	132	338	61	86	21	1	9	38	49-0	**13**	62	.254	.370	.402	103	4	4-1	.984	10	**118**	**193**	*O-124(33-95-4)	1.1
1963	KC A	121	306	40	65	7	1	8	29	40-1	5	52	.212	.311	.320	74	-10	1-2	.981	-0	105	88	*O-110(24-85-6)/3-2	-1.5
1965	Phi N	8	4	1	0	0	0	0	0	0-0	0	3	.000	.000	.000	-99	-1	0-0	—	0	0	0	/O-4(LF)	-0.1
Total	9	731	1982	271	454	95	11	42	169	271-7	32	372	.229	.330	.352	84	-35	16-15	.981	14	105	129	O-665(74-588-16)/3-6,2	-4.8
DELIS, JUAN Juan Francisco B 2.27.1928 Santiago De Cuba, Cuba BR/TR 5-11/170# d4.16																								
1955	Was A	54	132	12	25	3	1	0	11	3-0	2	15	.189	.219	.227	21	-15	1-2	.918	-1	112	144	3-24/O-8(2-0-6),2	-1.7
DELKER, EDDIE Edward Alberts B 4.17.1906 Palo Alto, PA D 5.14.1997 Pottsville, PA BR/TR 5-10.5/170# d4.28																								
1929	StL N	22	40	5	6	0	1	0	3	2	2	12	.150	.227	.200	7	-6	0	.750	-3	68	0	/S-9,2-7,3-3	-0.8
1931	StL N	1	2	0	1	1	0	0	2	0	0	0	.500	.500	1.000	283	1	0	1.000	-0	0	0	/3	0.0
1932	StL N	20	42	1	5	4	0	0	2	8	0	7	.119	.260	.214	28	-4	0	1.000	3	111	155	2-10/3-5,S-4	-0.1
	Phi N	30	62	7	10	1	1	1	7	6	0	14	.161	.235	.258	29	-6	0	.925	-4	89	52	2-27	-1.0
	Year	50	104	8	15	5	1	1	9	14	0	21	.144	.246	.240	29	-10	0	.946	-2	95	78	2-37/3-5,S-4	-1.1
1933	Phi N	25	41	6	7	3	1	0	1	0	0	12	.171	.171	.293	27	-4	0	.968	3	121	64	2-17/3-4	0.0
Total	4	98	187	19	29	9	3	1	15	16	2	45	.155	.229	.251	26	-19	0	.952	-2	100	76	/2-61,3-13,S-13	-1.9
DELLAERO, JASON Jason Christopher B 12.17.1976 Mount Kisco, NY BB/TR 6-2/195# d9.7																								
1999	Chi A	11	33	1	3	0	0	0	2	1-0	0	13	.091	.114	.091	-46	-7	0-0	.917	-2	96	71	S-11	-0.8
DELLUCCI, DAVID David Michael B 10.31.1973 Baton Rouge, LA BL/TL 5-10/180# d6.3																								
1997	Bal A	17	27	3	6	1	0	1	3	4-1	1	7	.222	.344	.370	89	0	0-0	1.000	2	168	281	/O-9(3-0-6),D-5	0.1
1998	Ari N	124	416	43	108	19	**12**	5	51	33-2	3	103	.260	.318	.399	87	-9	3-5	.987	2	109	42	*O-117(95-19-15)	-1.2
1999	Ari N	63	109	27	43	7	1	1	15	11-0	3	24	.394	.463	.505	144	8	2-0	1.000	-1	93	81	O-31(13-4-19)/D	0.7
2000	Ari N	34	50	2	15	3	0	0	2	4-0	0	9	.300	.352	.360	78	-2	0-2	1.000	0	107	0	O-12(1-0-11)	-0.2
2001	†Ari N	115	217	28	60	10	2	10	40	22-4	2	52	.276	.349	.479	105	1	2-1	.989	-2	100	0	O-58(8-18-35)	-0.2
2002	†Ari N	97	229	34	56	11	2	7	29	28-5	1	55	.245	.326	.402	87	-5	2-4	.967	-4	86	60	O-64(20-2-45)/D-3	-1.2
2003	Ari N	70	165	18	40	11	3	2	19	19-1	3	45	.242	.328	.382	78	-5	9-0	.976	-1	103	40	O-53(4-9-43)	-0.6
	†NY A	21	51	8	9	1	0	1	4	4-0	2	13	.176	.263	.255	38	-5	3-0	1.000	1	103	117	O-18(2-1-16)/D-2	-0.4
Total	7	541	1264	163	337	63	20	27	163	125-13	15	308	.267	.338	.412	92	-17	21-12	.985	-3	102	49	O-362(146-53-190)/D-11	-3.0
DELMAS, BERT Albert Charles B 5.20.1911 San Francisco, CA D 12.4.1979 Huntington Beach, CA BL/TR 5-11/165# d9.10																								
1933	Bro N	12	28	4	7	0	0	0	0	1	0	7	.250	.276	.250	53	-2	0	.912	-3	82	75	2-10	-0.4
DeLOS SANTOS, LUIS Luis Manuel (Martinez) B 12.29.1966 San Cristobal, D.R. BR/TR 6-5/205# d9.7																								
1988	KC A	11	22	1	2	1	1	0	1	4-0	0	4	.091	.231	.227	29	-2	0-0	1.000	-0	50	125	/1-5,D-3	-0.3
1989	KC A	28	87	6	22	3	1	0	6	5-0	0	14	.253	.293	.310	71	-4	0-0	.986	-0	97	121	1-27	-0.6
1991	Det A	16	30	1	5	2	0	0	0	2-0	0	4	.167	.219	.233	25	-3	0-0	1.000	-1	155	0	/O-3(LF),1-2,3-2,D-9	-0.4
Total	3	55	139	8	29	6	2	0	7	11-0	0	22	.209	.267	.281	53	-9	0-0	.988	-1	91	121	/1-34,D-12,O-3(LF),3-2	-1.3
DelSAVIO, GARTON Garton Orville B 11.26.1913 New York, NY BR/TR 5-9.5/165# d4.24																								
1943	Phi N	4	11	0	1	0	0	0	0	1	0	0	.091	.167	.091	-26	-2	0	.857	-1	98	44	/S-4	-0.3
DELSING, JIM James Henry B 11.13.1925 Rudolph, WI BL/TR 5-10/175# d4.21																								
1948	Chi A	20	63	5	12	0	0	0	5	5	1	12	.190	.261	.190	22	-7	0-0	1.000	-1	93	90	O-15(CF)	-0.8
1949	NY A	9	20	5	7	1	0	1	3	1	0	2	.350	.381	.550	145	1	0-0	1.000	-1	71	0	/O-5(CF)	0.0
1950	NY A	12	10	2	4	0	0	0	2	2	0	0	.400	.500	.400	137	1	0-0	—	0			H	0.1
	StL A	69	209	25	55	5	2	0	15	20	0	23	.263	.328	.306	61	-12	1-4	.994	2	106	91	O-53(CF)	-1.2
	Year	81	219	27	59	5	2	0	17	22	0	23	.269	.336	.311	65	-12	1-4	.994	2	106	91	O-53(CF)	-1.1
1951	StL A	131	449	59	112	20	2	8	45	56	4	39	.249	.338	.356	85	-9	2-9	.983	8	108	128	*O-124(4-118-4)	-0.7
1952	StL A	93	298	34	76	13	6	1	34	25	5	29	.255	.323	.349	85	-7	3-3	.986	3	109	71	O-85(34-44-10)	-0.8
	Det A	33	113	14	31	2	1	3	15	11	1	8	.274	.344	.389	103	0	1-0	.958	-0	104	52	O-32(LF)	-0.2
	Year	126	411	48	107	15	7	4	49	36	6	37	.260	.329	.360	90	-6	4-3	.979	2	108	65	*O-117(66-44-10)	-1.0
1953	Det A	138	479	77	138	26	6	11	62	66	5	39	.288	.380	.436	121	16	1-3	.992	-6	96	60	*O-133(CF)	0.3
1954	Det A	122	371	39	92	24	2	6	38	49	1	38	.248	.336	.372	96	-1	4-4	**.996**	3	107	75	*O-108(90-5-16)	-0.5
1955	Det A	114	356	49	85	15	2	10	60	48-2	1	40	.239	.328	.376	92	-4	2-0	.995	-6	91	39	*O-101(98-3-0)	-1.5
1956	Det A	10	12	0	0	0	0	0	0	3-0	1	3	.000	.250	.000	-29	-2	0-0	1.000	-0	88	0	/O-3(LF)	-0.2
	Chi A	55	41	11	5	3	0	0	2	10-0	0	13	.122	.294	.195	31	-4	1-0	.957	1	119	164	O-29(13-7-9)	-0.3
	Year	65	53	11	5	3	0	0	2	13-0	1	16	.094	.284	.151	17	-6	1-0	.962	1	114	135	O-32(16-7-9)	-0.5
1960	KC A	16	40	2	10	3	0	0	5	3-0	0	5	.250	.302	.325	69	-2	0-0	1.000	1	122	0	O-10(LF)	-0.2
Total	10	822	2461	322	627	112	21	40	286	299-2	19	251	.255	.339	.366	91	-30	15-23	.989	3	102	76	O-698(284-383-39)	-6.0
DeMAESTRI, JOE Joseph Paul "Oats" B 12.9.1928 San Francisco, CA BR/TR 6/174# d4.19																								
1951	Chi A	56	74	8	15	0	2	1	3	5	0	11	.203	.253	.297	49	-6	0-4	.959	2	121	141	S-27,2-11/3-8	-0.4
1952	StL A	81	186	13	42	9	1	1	18	8	0	25	.226	.258	.301	54	-12	0-1	.939	-5	98	81	S-77/23	-1.5
1953	Phi A	111	420	53	107	17	3	6	35	24	1	39	.255	.297	.352	72	-18	0-1	.964	-17	92	74	*S-108	-2.7
1954	Phi A	146	539	49	124	16	3	8	40	20	3	63	.230	.258	.315	57	-34	1-4	.965	-6	96	85	*S-142/23	-3.1
1955	KC A	123	457	42	114	14	1	6	37	20-1	3	47	.249	.284	.324	63	-26	3-5	.964	-12	97	93	*S-122	-2.9
1956	KC A	133	434	41	101	16	1	6	39	25-2	3	73	.233	.277	.316	57	-29	3-3	.964	9	**109**	110	*S-132/2-2	-1.0
1957	KC A☆	135	461	44	113	14	6	9	33	22-1	2	82	.245	.280	.360	73	-19	6-1	**.980**	-3	96	98	*S-134	-1.1
1958	KC A	139	442	32	97	11	1	6	38	16-1	1	84	.219	.247	.290	47	-33	1-0	**.980**	6	106	110	*S-137	-1.7
1959	KC A	118	352	31	86	16	5	6	34	28-8	4	65	.244	.305	.369	83	-9	1-0	.957	2	**104**	94	*S-115	0.2
1960	†NY A	49	35	8	8	1	0	0	2	0-0	0	9	.229	.229	.257	33	-3	0-0	.952	3	93	134	2-19,S-17	0.1
1961	NY A	30	41	1	6	0	0	0	2	0-0	0	13	.146	.146	.146	-23	-7	0-0	.981	5	131	162	S-18/2-5,3-4	-0.2
Total	11	1121	3441	322	813	114	23	49	281	168-13	17	511	.236	.274	.325	62	-196	15-19	.967	-15	101	96	*S-1029/2-39,3-14	-14.3
DEMAREE, FRANK Joseph Franklin (born Joseph Franklin Dimaria) B 6.10.1910 Winters, CA D 8.30.1958 Los Angeles, CA BR/TR 5-11.5/185# d7.22																								
1932	†Chi N	23	56	4	14	3	0	0	6	2	1	7	.250	.288	.304	60	-3	0	1.000	1	92	173	O-17(4-9-4)	-0.3
1933	Chi N	134	515	68	140	24	6	6	51	22	2	42	.272	.304	.377	94	-6	4	.965	-4	94	130	*O-133(10-123-0)	-1.4
1935	†Chi N	107	385	60	125	19	4	2	66	26	1	23	.325	.369	.410	108	5	6	.973	-2	88	157	O-98(0-69-29)	0.0
1936	Chi N★	**154**	605	93	212	34	3	16	96	49	1	30	.350	.400	.496	137	32	4	.968	-2	97	107	*O-154(36-0-118)	2.0
1937	Chi N★	**154**	615	104	199	36	6	17	115	57	1	31	.324	.382	.485	129	25	6	.980	-0	97	107	*O-154(RF)	1.5
1938	†Chi N	129	476	63	130	15	7	8	62	45	4	34	.273	.341	.384	96	-2	1	.972	-6	85	112	*O-125(9-0-119)	-1.6
1939	NY N	150	560	68	170	27	2	11	79	66	4	40	.304	.381	.418	116	13	2	.986	-8	90	86	*O-150(1-116-36)	0.0
1940	NY N	121	460	68	139	18	6	7	61	45	0	39	.302	.364	.413	113	8	5	.980	-8	89	65	*O-119(9-74-37)	-0.4
1941	NY N	16	35	3	6	0	0	0	1	4	0	1	.171	.256	.171	22	-4	0	1.000	0	98	156	O-10(1-8-1)	-0.4
	Bos N	48	113	20	26	5	2	2	15	12	0	5	.230	.304	.363	91	-2	2	1.000	-1	88	58	O-28(9-7-12)	-0.4
	Year	64	148	23	32	5	2	2	16	16	0	6	.216	.293	.318	74	-5	2	1.000	-1	91	85	O-38(10-15-13)	-0.8
1942	Bos N	64	187	18	42	5	0	3	24	17	0	10	.225	.289	.299	74	-6	2	1.000	3	109	101	O-49(27-0-22)	-0.8
1943	†StL N	39	86	5	25	2	0	0	9	8	0	4	.291	.351	.314	89	-1	1	1.000	-1	99	58	O-23(12-0-12)	-0.3
1944	StL A	16	51	4	13	2	0	0	6	6	0	3	.255	.333	.294	76	-1	0-0	.969	-0	101	88	O-16(15-0-1)	-0.2
Total	12	1155	4144	578	1241	190	36	72	591	359	14	269	.299	.357	.415	110	58	33-0	.978	-29	93	106	*O-1076(133-406-545)	-2.3

DeMARS, BILLY William Lester "Kid" B 8.26.1925 Brooklyn, NY BR/TR 5-10/160# d5.18 C19

Year	Tm Lg	G	AB	R	H	2B	3B	HR	RBI	BB-IB	HP	SO	AVG	OBP	SLG	AOPS	ABR	SB-CS	FA	FR	Rng	Thr	G at Pos	BFW
1948	Phi A	18	29	3	5	0	0	0	1	5	0	3	.172	.294	.172	26	-3	0-0	.927	2	110	144	/S-9,23	-0.1
1950	StL A	61	178	25	44	5	1	0	13	22	0	13	.247	.330	.287	57	-11	0-1	.933	-9	88	81	S-54/3-5	-1.7
1951	StL A	1	4	1	1	0	0	0	0	1	0	0	.250	.400	.250	76	0	0-0	1.000	-0	109	93	/S	0.0
Total	3	80	211	29	50	5	1	0	14	28	0	16	.237	.326	.270	53	-14	0-1	.933	-8	91	89	/S-64,3-6,2	-1.8

DeMERIT, JOHN John Stephen "Thumper" B 1.8.1936 West Bend, WI BR/TR 6-1.5/195# d6.18

Year	Tm Lg	G	AB	R	H	2B	3B	HR	RBI	BB-IB	HP	SO	AVG	OBP	SLG	AOPS	ABR	SB-CS	FA	FR	Rng	Thr	G at Pos	BFW
1957	†Mil N	33	34	8	5	0	0	0	1	0-0	0	8	.147	.147	.147	-22	-6	1-0	1.000	1	133	0	O-13(2-11-0)	-0.6
1958	Mil N	3	3	1	2	0	0	0	0	0-0	0	0	.667	.667	.667	278	1	0-0	1.000	0	132	0	/O-2(0-1-1)	0.1
1959	Mil N	11	5	4	1	0	0	0	0	1-0	0	2	.200	.333	.200	51	0	0-0	1.000	1	195	0	/O-4(3-1-0)	0.0
1961	Mil N	32	74	5	12	3	0	2	5	5-0	1	19	.162	.225	.284	36	-7	0-0	1.000	1	111	125	O-21(2-5-15)	-0.7
1962	NY N	14	16	3	3	0	0	1	1	2-0	0	4	.188	.278	.375	72	-1	0-0	1.000	-0	79	0	/O-9(3-2-4)	-0.1
Total	5	93	132	21	23	3	0	3	7	8-0	1	33	.174	.227	.265	32	-13	1-0	1.000	2	118	76	/O-49(10-20-20)	-1.3

DEMETER, DON Donald Lee B 6.25.1935 Oklahoma City, OK BR/TR 6-4/190# d9.18

Year	Tm Lg	G	AB	R	H	2B	3B	HR	RBI	BB-IB	HP	SO	AVG	OBP	SLG	AOPS	ABR	SB-CS	FA	FR	Rng	Thr	G at Pos	BFW
1956	Bro N	3	3	1	1	0	0	1	1	0-0	0	1	.333	.333	1.333	297	1	0-0	1.000	0	114	0	/O(CF)	0.1
1958	LA N	43	106	11	20	2	0	5	8	5-0	0	32	.189	.225	.349	48	-9	2-3	1.000	-1	108	0	O-39(11-25-4)	-1.1
1959	†LA N	139	371	55	95	11	1	18	70	16-1	6	87	.256	.294	.437	86	-9	5-6	.983	-3	97	92	*O-124(CF)	-1.8
1960	LA N	64	168	23	46	7	1	9	29	8-1	1	34	.274	.306	.488	108	1	0-1	.989	-3	90	65	O-62(0-61-1)	-0.4
1961	LA N	15	29	3	5	0	0	1	2	3-0	0	6	.172	.250	.276	36	-3	0-0	.950	1	113	138	O-14(0-3-12)	-0.3
	Phi N	106	382	54	98	18	4	20	68	19-2	5	74	.257	.300	.482	105	0	2-1	.995	4	101	142	O-79(23-44-17),1-22	0.0
	Year	121	411	57	103	18	4	21	70	22-2	5	80	.251	.297	.467	99	-3	2-1	.990	4	102	142	O-93(23-47-29),1-22	-0.3
1962	Phi N	153	550	85	169	24	3	29	107	41-6	10	93	.307	.359	.520	139	29	2-7	.937	-6	95	96	*3-105,O-63(23-42-4)/1	1.8
1963	Phi N	154	515	63	133	20	2	22	83	31-10	6	93	.258	.306	.433	112	7	1-4	**1.000**	2	95	112	*O-119(41-80-0),3-43,1-26	0.2
1964	Det A	134	441	57	113	22	1	22	80	17-6	5	85	.256	.290	.460	104	0	4-1	1.000	-2	100	60	O-88(24-52-13),1-23	-0.6
1965	Det A	122	389	50	108	16	4	16	58	23-3	6	65	.278	.325	.463	121	9	4-2	.988	-5	102	27	O-82(1-56-25),1-34	0.0
1966	Det A	32	99	12	21	5	0	5	12	3-0	0	19	.212	.235	.414	81	-3	1-0	.985	4	120	134	O-27(4-20-3)/1-4	0.0
	Bos A	73	226	31	66	13	1	9	29	5-1	1	42	.292	.305	.478	111	3	1-0	.982	-3	91	95	O-57(0-55-3)/1-2	-0.2
	Year	105	325	43	87	18	1	14	41	8-1	1	61	.268	.284	.458	102	0	2-0	.984	0	100	108	O-84(4-75-6)/1-6	-0.2
1967	Bos A	20	43	7	12	5	0	1	4	3-0	0	11	.279	.326	.465	122	1	0-0	1.000	1	97	175	O-12(3-1-9)/3	0.2
	Cle A	51	121	15	25	4	0	5	12	6-1	2	16	.207	.256	.364	80	-3	0-0	.985	2	109	116	O-35(13-28-1)/3	-0.3
	Year	71	164	22	37	9	0	6	16	9-1	2	27	.226	.274	.390	92	-2	0-0	.988	2	106	130	O-47(16-29-10)/3-2	-0.1
Total	11	1109	3443	467	912	147	17	163	563	180-31	42	658	.265	.307	.459	108	24	22-25	.990	-11	100	81	O-802(143-592-92),3-150,1-112	-2.4

DEMETER, STEVE Stephen B 1.27.1935 Homer City, PA BR/TR 5-9.5/185# d7.29 C1

Year	Tm Lg	G	AB	R	H	2B	3B	HR	RBI	BB-IB	HP	SO	AVG	OBP	SLG	AOPS	ABR	SB-CS	FA	FR	Rng	Thr	G at Pos	BFW
1959	Det A	11	18	1	2	1	0	0	1	0-0	0	1	.111	.111	.167	-24	-3	0-0	.909	0	95	196	/3-4	-0.3
1960	Cle A	4	5	0	0	0	0	0	0	0-0	0	1	.000	.000	.000	-99	-1	0-0	1.000	-0	40	373	/3-3	-0.2
Total	2	15	23	1	2	1	0	0	1	0-0	0	2	.087	.087	.130	-40	-4	0-0	.933	0	79	249	/3-7	-0.5

DEMMITT, RAY Charles Raymond B 2.2.1884 Illiopolis, IL D 2.19.1956 Glen Ellyn, IL BL/TR 5-8/170# d4.12

Year	Tm Lg	G	AB	R	H	2B	3B	HR	RBI	BB-IB	HP	SO	AVG	OBP	SLG	AOPS	ABR	SB-CS	FA	FR	Rng	Thr	G at Pos	BFW
1909	NY A	123	427	68	105	12	12	4	30	55	6		.246	.340	.358	120	11	16	.908	-2	145	193	*O-109(0-70-39)	0.3
1910	StL A	10	23	4	4	1	0	0	2	3	1		.174	.296	.217	65	-1	0	1.000	1	108	198	/O-8(RF)	0.0
1914	Det A	1	0	0	0	0	0	0	0	0	0	0	—	—	—	—	0	0	—	0			R	0.0
	Chi A	146	515	63	133	13	12	2	46	61	6	48	.258	.344	.342	108	5	12-20	.953	-6	81	119	*O-142(127-4-12)	-1.3
	Year	147	515	63	133	13	12	2	46	61	6	48	.258	.344	.342	108	5	12-20	.953	-6	81	119	*O-142(127-4-12)	-1.3
1915	Chi A	9	6	0	0	0	0	0	0	1	0	2	.000	.143	.000	-55	-1	0	1.000	0	107	0	/O-3(1-0-2)	-0.1
1917	StL A	14	53	6	15	1	2	0	7	0	1	8	.283	.296	.377	109	0	1	1.000	-2	86	0	O-14(RF)	-0.2
1918	StL A	116	405	45	114	23	5	1	61	38	2	35	.281	.346	.370	120	10	10	.951	9	104	**164**	*O-114(RF)	1.4
1919	StL A	79	202	19	48	11	2	1	19	14	1	27	.238	.290	.327	71	-8	3	.868	-4	80	103	O-49(RF)	-1.5
Total	7	498	1631	205	419	61	33	8	165	172	17	120	.257	.334	.349	108	16	42-20	.934	-4	105	147	O-439(128-74-238)	-1.4

DeMONTREVILLE, GENE Eugene Napoleon B 3.26.1874 St.Paul, MN D 2.18.1935 Memphis, TN BR/TR 5-8/165# d8.20 b-Lee

Year	Tm Lg	G	AB	R	H	2B	3B	HR	RBI	BB-IB	HP	SO	AVG	OBP	SLG	AOPS	ABR	SB-CS	FA	FR	Rng	Thr	G at Pos	BFW
1894	Pit N	2	8	0	2	0	0	0	0	1	0	4	.250	.333	.250	43	-1	0	.889	-0	116	0	/S-2	-0.1
1895	Was N	12	46	7	10	1	3	0	9	3	0	4	.217	.265	.370	63	-3	5	.929	4	105	138	S-12	0.1
1896	Was N	**133**	533	94	183	24	5	8	77	29	3	27	.343	.381	.452	119	13	28	.890	19	**110**	88	*S-133	3.3
1897	Was N	**133**	566	92	193	27	8	3	93	21	1		.341	.366	.433	111	7	30	.886	10	104	118	*S-99,2-33	1.9
1898	Bal N	151	567	93	186	19	2	0	86	52	10		.328	.394	.369	117	15	49	.944	3	101	81	*2-123,S-28	2.3
1899	Chi N	82	310	43	87	6	3	0	40	17	5		.281	.328	.319	80	-9	26	.902	7	108	123	S-82	0.2
	Bal N	60	240	40	67	13	4	1	36	10	2		.279	.313	.379	85	-6	21	.961	4	102	70	2-60	0.1
	Year	142	550	83	154	19	7	1	76	27	7		.280	.322	.345	82	-14	47	.902	11	108	123	S-82,2-60	0.3
1900	Bro N	69	234	34	57	8	1	0	28	10	3		.244	.283	.286	54	-15	21	.952	-1	97	83	2-48,S-12/3-7,O(CF)1	-1.3
1901	Bos N	**140**	577	83	173	14	4	5	72	17	1		.300	.321	.364	90	-9	25	**.954**	1	99	93	*2-120,3-20	-0.7
1902	Bos N	124	481	51	125	16	5	0	53	12	0		.260	.278	.314	82	-12	23	.940	-17	88	59	*2-112,S-10	-3.0
1903	Was A	12	44	0	12	2	0	0	3	0	0		.273	.273	.318	75	-1	0	.931	-3	79	24	2-11/S	-0.5
1904	StL A	4	9	0	1	0	0	0	0	2	0		.111	.273	.111	25	-1	0	1.000	-0	95	0	/2-3	-0.1
Total	11	922	3615	537	1096	130	35	17	497	174	25	35	.303	.340	.373	97	-22	228	.948	24	97	74	2-510,S-379/3-27,1O(CF)	2.2

DeMONTREVILLE, LEE Leon B 9.23.1875 Washington Co., MN D 3.22.1962 Pelham Manor, NY BR/TR 5-7/140# d7.10 b-Gene

Year	Tm Lg	G	AB	R	H	2B	3B	HR	RBI	BB-IB	HP	SO	AVG	OBP	SLG	AOPS	ABR	SB-CS	FA	FR	Rng	Thr	G at Pos	BFW
1903	StL N	26	70	8	17	3	1	0	7	8	2		.243	.338	.314	89	-1	3	.901	-2	104	152	S-15/2-4,O(RF)	-0.2

DEMPSEY, RICK John Rikard B 9.13.1949 Fayetteville, TN BR/TR (BB 1982 (part)) 6/190# d9.23 C4 OF Total (6-LF 17-RF)

Year	Tm Lg	G	AB	R	H	2B	3B	HR	RBI	BB-IB	HP	SO	AVG	OBP	SLG	AOPS	ABR	SB-CS	FA	FR	Rng	Thr	G at Pos	BFW
1969	Min A	5	6	1	3	1	0	0	0	1-0	0	0	.500	.571	.667	240	1	0-0	.833	-1	63	0	/C-3	0.0
1970	Min A	5	7	1	0	0	0	0	0	1-0	0	1	.000	.125	.000	-62	-2	0-0	.923	-1	40	0	/C-3	-0.2
1971	Min A	6	13	2	4	1	0	0	0	1-0	0	1	.308	.357	.385	107	0	0-0	.944	1	46	170	/C-6	0.1
1972	Min A	25	40	0	8	1	0	0	0	6-0	0	8	.200	.304	.225	56	-2	0-0	.986	-2	118	109	C-23	-0.4
1973	NY A	6	11	0	2	0	0	0	0	1-0	0	3	.182	.250	.182	24	-1	0-0	.818	-3	65	0	/C-5	-0.4
1974	NY A	43	109	12	26	3	0	2	12	8-0	0	7	.239	.288	.321	77	-3	1-0	.978	6	291	150	C-31/O-2(1-0-1),D	0.4
1975	NY A	71	145	18	38	8	0	1	11	21-1	0	15	.262	.353	.338	98	1	0-0	.977	2	83	72	C-19,D-18/O-8(1-0-7),3	0.2
1976	NY A	21	42	1	5	0	0	0	2	5-0	0	4	.119	.213	.119	-1	-5	0-0	1.000	3	160	119	/C-9,O-4(RF)	-0.3
	Bal A	59	174	11	37	2	0	0	10	13-0	2	17	.213	.275	.224	50	-11	1-1	.987	11	197	114	C-58/O-3(1-0-2)	0.2
	Year	80	216	12	42	2	0	0	12	18-0	2	21	.194	.263	.204	40	-16	1-1	.988	13	192	115	C-67/O-7(1-0-6)	-0.1
1977	Bal A	91	270	27	61	7	4	3	34	34-1	2	34	.226	.314	.315	78	-8	2-3	.977	7	181	117	C-91	0.2
1978	Bal A	136	441	41	114	25	0	6	32	48-2	0	54	.259	.327	.356	99	1	7-3	.985	4	138	108	*C-135	1.1
1979	†Bal A	124	368	48	88	23	0	6	41	38-1	0	37	.239	.307	.351	81	-9	0-1	.990	27	159	105	*C-124	2.1
1980	Bal A	119	362	51	95	26	3	9	40	36-1	3	45	.262	.333	.425	108	4	3-1	.987	11	118	**131**	*C-112/O-6(3-0-3),1-2,D	2.0
1981	Bal A	92	251	24	54	10	1	6	15	32-1	1	36	.215	.306	.335	85	-5	0-1	**.998**	5	**154**	87	C-90/D	0.4
1982	Bal A	125	344	35	88	15	1	5	36	46-1	0	37	.256	.339	.349	91	-3	0-3	.991	1	143	71	*C-124/D	0.2
1983	†Bal A	128	347	33	80	16	2	4	32	40-1	3	54	.231	.311	.323	78	-10	1-1	**.997**	19	129	93	*C-128	1.3
1984	Bal A	109	330	37	76	11	0	11	34	40-0	1	58	.230	.312	.364	89	-5	1-2	.992	-6	102	68	*C-108	-0.7
1985	Bal A	132	362	54	92	19	0	12	52	50-0	1	87	.254	.345	.406	108	5	0-1	.987	-11	95	83	*C-131	-0.1
1986	Bal A	122	327	42	68	15	1	13	29	45-0	3	78	.208	.309	.379	87	-5	1-0	.990	4	102	95	*C-121	0.3
1987	Cle A	60	141	16	25	10	0	1	9	23-0	1	29	.177	.295	.270	51	-9	0-0	.984	1	102	112	C-59	-0.6
1988	†LA N	77	167	25	42	13	0	7	30	25-0	0	44	.251	.338	.455	133	8	1-0	.989	2	99	99	C-74	1.4
1989	LA N	79	151	16	27	7	0	4	16	30-3	1	37	.179	.319	.305	80	-3	1-0	.984	4	131	160	C-62	0.4
1990	LA N	62	128	13	25	5	0	2	15	23-0	0	29	.195	.318	.281	68	-5	1-0	.992	-1	96	130	C-53	-0.4
1991	Mil A	61	147	15	34	5	0	4	21	23-1	0	20	.231	.329	.347	91	-1	0-2	.993	-2	101	81	C-56/P-2,1	-0.1
1992	Bal A	8	9	2	1	0	0	0	0	2-0	0	1	.111	.273	.111	11	-1	0-0	1.000	-2	64	0	/C-8	-0.3
Total	24	1766	4692	525	1093	223	12	96	471	592-13	18	736	.233	.319	.347	88	-68	20-19	.988	78	131	100	*C-1633/O-23R,D-22,1-3,P-2,3	6.8

DENNEHEY, TOD Thomas Francis B 5.12.1899 Philadelphia, PA D 8.8.1977 Philadelphia, PA BL/TL 5-10/180# d4.21

Year	Tm Lg	G	AB	R	H	2B	3B	HR	RBI	BB-IB	HP	SO	AVG	OBP	SLG	AOPS	ABR	SB-CS	FA	FR	Rng	Thr	G at Pos	BFW
1923	Phi N	9	24	4	7	2	0	0	2	1	0	3	.292	.320	.375	74	-1	0-1	1.000	0	121	0	/O-9(7-0-2)	-0.1

DENNING, OTTO Otto George "Dutch" B 12.28.1912 Hays, KS D 5.25.1992 Chicago, IL BR/TR 6/180# d4.15

Year	Tm Lg	G	AB	R	H	2B	3B	HR	RBI	BB-IB	HP	SO	AVG	OBP	SLG	AOPS	ABR	SB-CS	FA	FR	Rng	Thr	G at Pos	BFW
1942	Cle A	92	214	15	45	14	0	1	19	18	1	14	.210	.275	.290	62	-11	0-0	**.992**	1	*108*	*89*	C-78/O-2(LF)	-0.7
1943	Cle A	37	129	8	31	6	0	0	13	5	0	1	.240	.269	.287	67	-6	3-1	.966	-4	78	135	1-34	-1.2
Total	2	129	343	23	76	20	0	1	32	23	1	15	.222	.272	.289	64	-17	3-1	.992	-3	*108*	*89*	/C-78,1-34,O-2(LF)	-1.9

Year	Tm Lg	G	AB	R	H	2B	3B	HR	RBI	BB-IB	HP	SO	AVG	OBP	SLG	AOPS	ABR	SB-CS	FA	FR	Rng	Thr	G at Pos	BFW
DENNY, JERRY Jeremiah Dennis (born Jeremiah Dennis Eldridge) B 3.16.1859 New York, NY D 8.16.1927 Houston, TX BR/TR 5-11.5/180# d5.2 OF Total (1-LF 2-CF 7-RF)																								
1881	Pro N	**85**	320	38	77	16	2	1	24	5		44	.241	.252	.313	78	-8		.840	6	106	92	*3-85	0.0
1882	Pro N	**84**	329	54	81	10	9	2	42	4		46	.246	.255	.350	92	-4		.861	11	114	72	*3-84	0.8
1883	Pro N	**98**	393	73	108	26	8	8	55	9		48	.275	.291	.443	116	7		**.876**	10	96	115	*3-98	1.6
1884	†Pro N	110	439	57	109	22	9	6	59	14		58	.248	.272	.380	105	2		.874	-5	86	52	*3-99/1-9,2-3,C	-0.2
1885	Pro N	83	318	40	71	14	4	3	24	12		53	.223	.252	.321	87	-5		.869	1	96	96	*3-83	-0.3
1886	StL N	119	475	58	122	24	6	9	62	14		68	.257	.278	.389	108	4	16	.895	**25**	**116**	**161**	*3-117/S-3	2.8
1887	Ind N	122	510	86	165	34	12	11	97	13	3	22	.324	.344	.502	137	23	29	.889	21	113	102	*3-116/S-4,O(RF)2	3.9
1888	Ind N	126	524	92	137	27	7	12	63	9	2	79	.261	.277	.408	114	6	32	.894	16	109	95	*3-96,S-25/2-5,O(CF)P	2.4
1889	Ind N	133	578	96	163	24	0	18	112	27	0	63	.282	.314	.417	101	-3	22	**.913**	13	**107**	53	*3-123/2-7,S-5	1.0
1890	NY N	114	437	50	93	18	7	3	42	28	6	62	.213	.270	.307	68	-20	11	.889	7	95	89	*3-106/S-7,2	-1.0
1891	NY N	4	16	0	4	1	0	0	1	0	0	3	.250	.250	.313	66	-1	2	.700	-2	24	190	/3-4	-0.3
	Cle N	36	138	17	31	5	0	0	21	12	1	23	.225	.291	.261	59	-7	3	.884	-0	105	26	3-29/O-7(1-1-6)	-0.6
	Phi N	19	73	5	21	1	1	0	11	4	0	6	.288	.325	.329	88	-1	1	.977	-1	36	75	1-12/3-7	-0.3
	Year	59	227	22	56	7	1	0	33	16	1	32	.247	.299	.286	69	-9	6	.876	-4	98	59	3-40,1-12/O-7(1-1-6)	-1.2
1893	Lou N	44	175	22	43	5	4	1	22	9	0	15	.246	.283	.337	70	-9	4	.920	2	99	87	S-42/3-2	-0.4
1894	Lou N	60	221	26	61	11	7	0	32	13	3	12	.276	.325	.389	77	-9	10	.874	3	104	121	3-60	-0.4
Total	13	1237	4946	714	1286	238	76	74	667	173	15	602	.260	.287	.384	98	-25	130	.882	106	104	93	*3-1109/S-86,1-21,2-17,O-9R,PC	9.0
DENSON, DREW Andrew B 11.16.1965 Cincinnati, OH BB/TR 6-5/210# d9.13																								
1989	Atl N	12	36	1	9	1	0	0	5	3-0	0	9	.250	.308	.278	67	-2	1-0	.988	2	170	46	1-12	0.0
1993	Chi A	4	5	0	1	0	0	0	0	0-0	0	2	.200	.200	.200	8	-1	0-0	.800	-0	0	176	/1-3	-0.1
Total	2	16	41	1	10	1	0	0	5	3-0	0	11	.244	.295	.268	60	-3	1-0	.977	1	159	55	/1-15	-0.1
DENT, BUCKY Russell Earl (born B 11.25.1951 Savannah, GA BR/TR 5-11/181# d6.1 M2 C11																								
1973	Chi A	40	117	17	29	2	0	0	10	10-0	1	18	.248	.308	.265	62	-6	2-3	.963	7	118	96	S-36/2-3,3	0.4
1974	Chi A	154	496	55	136	15	3	5	45	28-0	3	48	.274	.316	.347	89	-8	3-4	.972	6	100	112	*S-154	1.6
1975	Chi A★	157	602	52	159	29	4	3	58	36-3	0	48	.264	.301	.341	81	-16	2-4	**.981**	18	106	101	*S-157	2.1
1976	Chi A	158	562	44	138	18	4	2	52	43-3	2	45	.246	.300	.302	77	-17	3-5	.976	-4	94	96	*S-158	-0.4
1977	†NY A	158	477	54	118	18	4	8	49	39-0	1	28	.247	.300	.352	80	-14	1-1	.974	-10	95	108	*S-158	-0.8
1978	†NY A	123	379	40	92	11	1	5	40	23-1	2	24	.243	.286	.317	72	-15	3-1	.981	-5	97	91	*S-123	-0.7
1979	NY A	141	431	47	99	14	2	2	32	37-1	1	30	.230	.287	.285	58	-26	0-0	.977	32	**116**	122	*S-141	2.0
1980	†NY A★	141	489	57	128	26	2	5	52	48-1	2	37	.262	.327	.354	89	-6	0-3	**.982**	12	105	84	*S-141	1.9
1981	NY A★	73	227	20	54	11	0	7	27	19-0	2	17	.238	.300	.379	97	-1	0-1	.970	-2	91	117	S-73	0.4
1982	NY A	59	160	11	27	1	1	0	9	8-0	0	11	.169	.207	.188	10	-20	0-0	.962	6	108	89	S-58	-0.9
	Tex A	46	146	16	32	9	0	1	14	13-0	0	10	.219	.280	.301	64	-7	0-0	.980	0	105	107	S-45	-0.2
	Year	105	306	27	59	10	1	1	23	21-0	0	21	.193	.242	.242	35	-28	0-0	.970	7	107	97	*S-103	-1.1
1983	Tex A	131	417	36	99	15	2	2	34	23-0	1	31	.237	.278	.297	60	-24	3-7	**.979**	-12	97	98	*S-129/D	-2.4
1984	KC A	11	9	2	3	0	0	0	1	1-0	0	2	.333	.400	.333	105	0	0-0	1.000	-3	53	0	/S-9,3-2	-0.3
Total	12	1392	4512	451	1114	169	23	40	423	328-9	15	349	.247	.297	.321	74	-160	17-29	.976	46	101	102	*S-1382/3-3,2-3,D	2.7
DENTE, SAM Samuel Joseph "Blackie" B 4.26.1922 Harrison, NJ D 4.21.2002 Montclair, NJ BR/TR 5-11/175# d7.10																								
1947	Bos A	46	168	14	39	4	2	0	11	19	0	15	.232	.310	.280	60	-9	0-1	.939	-3	96	138	3-46	-1.2
1948	StL A	98	267	26	72	11	2	0	22	22	1	8	.270	.328	.326	72	-11	1-3	.958	1	102	86	S-76/3-6	-0.7
1949	Was A	153	590	48	161	24	4	1	53	31	0	24	.273	.309	.332	71	-27	4-4	.957	-7	101	82	*S-153	-2.5
1950	Was A	**155**	603	56	144	20	5	2	59	39	1	19	.239	.286	.299	52	-46	1-1	.952	-1	104	87	*S-128,2-29	-3.6
1951	Was A	88	273	21	65	8	1	0	29	25	0	10	.238	.302	.275	58	-16	3-0	.962	-1	102	97	S-65,2-10/3-5	-1.2
1952	Chi A	62	145	12	32	0	1	0	11	5	2	8	.221	.257	.234	37	-13	0-0	.942	2	89	109	S-27,3-18/2-6,O-6(4-0-2),1-2	-1.0
1953	Chi A	2	0	0	0	0	0	0	0	0	0	0	—	—	—	—	0	0-0	—	-0	0	0	/S	0.0
1954	†Cle A	68	169	18	45	7	1	1	19	14	0	4	.266	.319	.337	79	-5	0-0	.971	-2	100	131	S-60/2-7	-0.3
1955	Cle A	73	105	10	27	4	0	0	10	12-1	0	8	.257	.331	.295	68	-4	0-0	.976	6	113	100	S-53,3-13/2-4	0.3
Total	9	745	2320	205	585	78	16	4	214	167-1	4	96	.252	.303	.305	62	-131	9-9	.958	-6	102	92	S-563/3-88,2-56,O-6(4-0-2),1-2	-10.2
DePANGHER, MIKE Michael Anthony B 9.11.1858 Marysville, CA D 7.7.1915 San Francisco, CA BL 5-8/190# d8.8																								
1884	Phi N	4	10	0	2	0	0	0	0	1		3	.200	.273	.200	54	0		.920	0			/C-4	0.0
DEPASTINO, JOE Joseph Bernard B 9.4.1973 Philadelphia, PA BR/TR 6-2/210# d8.5																								
2003	NY N	2	2	0	0	0	0	0	0	0-0	0	1	.000	.000	.000	-99	-1	0-0	1.000	0	0	0	/C	-0.1
DePHILLIPS, TONY Anthony Andrew B 9.20.1912 New York, NY D 5.5.1994 Port Jefferson, NY BR/TR 6-2/185# d4.25																								
1943	Cin N	35	20	0	2	1	0	0	2	1	0	5	.100	.143	.150	-16	-3	0	.981	3	*126*	*100*	C-35	0.1
DERBY, GENE Eugene A. B 2.3.1860 Fitchburg, MA D 9.13.1917 Waterbury, CT 5-7/160# d9.3																								
1885	Bal AA	10	31	4	4	0	0	0	2	1	1		.129	.182	.129	-1	-3		.952	1			/C-9,O(LF)	-0.2
DERNIER, BOB Robert Eugene B 1.5.1957 Kansas City, MO BR/TR 6/165# d9.7																								
1980	Phi N	10	7	5	4	0	0	0	1	1-0	0	0	.571	.625	.571	224	1	3-0	1.000	1	185	0	/O-3(CF)	0.3
1981	Phi N	10	4	0	3	0	0	0	0	0-0	0	0	.750	.750	.750	313	1	2-1	1.000	-0	62	0	/O-5(CF)	0.1
1982	Phi N	122	370	56	92	10	2	4	21	36-0	1	69	.249	.315	.319	77	-11	42-12	.981	8	**124**	83	*O-119(0-70-62)	-0.1
1983	†Phi N	122	221	41	51	10	0	1	15	18-0	0	21	.231	.287	.290	61	-11	35-7	.988	5	120	91	*O-107(12-68-31)	-0.2
1984	†Chi N	143	536	94	149	26	5	3	32	63-0	2	60	.278	.356	.362	94	-2	45-17	.986	-1	104	67	*O-140(1-139-0)	0.0
1985	Chi N	121	469	63	119	20	3	1	21	40-1	3	44	.254	.315	.316	70	-18	31-8	.972	1	112	58	*O-116(CF)	-1.4
1986	Chi N	108	324	32	73	14	1	4	18	22-1	0	41	.225	.275	.312	57	-19	27-2	.987	-1	107	58	*O-105(CF)	-1.6
1987	Chi N	93	199	38	63	4	4	8	21	19-0	1	19	.317	.379	.497	125	7	16-7	.989	-4	85	83	O-71(CF)	0.3
1988	Phi N	68	166	19	48	3	1	1	10	9-0	1	19	.289	.330	.337	90	-2	13-6	.980	0	101	116	O-54(0-53-1)	-0.2
1989	Phi N	107	187	26	32	5	0	1	13	14-0	0	28	.171	.225	.214	27	-18	4-3	.970	0	108	48	O-74(28-29-20)	-2.0
Total	10	904	2483	374	634	92	16	23	152	222-2	8	301	.255	.318	.333	77	-72	218-63	.982	10	110	72	O-794(41-660-114)	-4.8
DeROSA, MARK Mark Thomas B 2.26.1975 Passaic, NJ BR/TR 6-1/185# d9.2 OF Total (5-LF 5-RF)																								
1998	Atl N	5	3	2	1	0	0	0	0	0-0	0	1	.333	.333	.333	76	0	0-0	1.000	-1	37	0	/S-4	-0.1
1999	Atl N	7	8	0	0	0	0	0	0	0-0	0	2	.000	.000	.000	-99	-2	0-0	1.000	0	87	0	/S-2	-0.2
2000	Atl N	22	13	9	4	1	0	0	3	2-0	0	1	.308	.400	.385	99	0	0-0	1.000	-2	59	85	S-10	-0.1
2001	†Atl N	66	164	27	47	8	0	3	20	12-6	5	19	.287	.350	.390	90	-2	2-1	.960	-0	100	91	S-48/2-5,3O(LF)D	0.1
2002	†Atl N	72	212	24	63	9	2	5	23	12-3	3	24	.297	.339	.429	104	0	2-3	.974	6	116	131	2-32,S-19/O-7(2-0-5),3-4	0.8
2003	†Atl N	103	266	40	70	14	0	6	22	16-0	5	49	.263	.316	.383	82	-7	1-0	.984	4	105	119	2-29,3-25,S-20/O-2(LF),1D	-0.1
Total	6	275	666	102	185	32	2	14	68	42-9	13	96	.278	.330	.395	89	-11	5-4	.974	8	103	113	S-103/2-66,3-30,O-10L,D-5,1	0.4
DERRICK, CLAUD Claud Lester "Deek" B 6.11.1886 Burton, GA D 7.15.1974 Clayton, GA BR/TR 6/175# d9.8																								
1910	Phi A	2	1	0	0	0	0	0	0	0	0		.000	.000	.000	-99	0	0	.500	-1	0	0	/S	-0.1
1911	Phi A	36	100	14	23	1	2	0	5	7	2		.230	.294	.280	61	-5	7	.960	-0	99	113	2-21/S-6,1-3,3-2	-0.5
1912	Phi A	21	58	7	14	0	1	0	7	5	1		.241	.313	.276	71	-2	1	.884	-1	109	93	S-18	-0.2
1913	NY A	23	65	7	19	1	0	1	7	5	1	8	.292	.352	.354	106	0	2	.874	-2	102	108	S-17/3-4,2	0.0
1914	Cin N	3	6	2	2	1	0	0	1	0	0	0	.333	.333	.500	142	0	1	.889	0	94	203	/S-2	0.1
	Chi N	28	96	5	21	3	1	0	13	5	0	13	.219	.257	.271	57	-5	2	.895	-3	94	85	/S-28	-0.7
	Year	31	102	7	23	4	1	0	14	5	0	13	.225	.262	.284	62	-5	3	.894	-3	94	90	S-30	-0.6
Total	5	113	326	35	79	6	4	1	33	22	4	21	.242	.298	.294	72	-12	13	.892	-6	99	88	/S-72,2-22,3-6,1-3	-1.4
DERRICK, MIKE James Michael B 9.19.1943 Columbia, SC BL/TR 6/190# d4.9																								
1970	Bos A	24	33	3	7	1	0	0	5	0-0	0	11	.212	.206	.242	23	-3	0-1	1.000	0	140	0	/O-2(LF),1	-0.4
DERRY, RUSS Alva Russell B 10.7.1916 Princeton, MO BL/TR 6-1/180# d7.4																								
1944	NY A	38	114	14	29	3	0	4	14	20	0	19	.254	.366	.386	111	2	1-0	.949	-1	92	93	O-28(16-0-12)	-0.1
1945	NY A	78	253	37	57	6	2	13	45	31	1	49	.225	.312	.419	107	1	1-0	.978	-0	105	68	O-68(10-44-15)	-0.2
1946	Phi A	69	184	17	38	8	5	0	14	27	1	54	.207	.311	.304	73	-7	0-0	.985	4	116	87	O-50(45-2-5)	-0.6
1949	StL N	2	2	0	0	0	0	0	0	0	0	2	.000	.000	.000	-96	-1	0	—	0			H	-0.1
Total	4	187	553	68	124	17	7	17	73	78	2	124	.224	.322	.373	95	-5	2-0	.976	3	106	80	O-146(71-46-32)	-1.0

Year	Tm Lg	G	AB	R	H	2B	3B	HR	RBI	BB-IB	HP	SO	AVG	OBP	SLG	AOPS	ABR	SB-CS	FA	FR	Rng	Thr	G at Pos	BFW
DeSA, JOE Joseph B 7.27.1959 Honolulu, HI D 12.20.1986 San Juan, P.R. BL/TL 5-11/170# d9.6																								
1980	StL N	7	11	0	3	0	0	0	0	0-0	0	2	.273	.273	.273	51	-1	0-0	1.000	-0	0	0	/1O(RF)	-0.1
1985	Chi A	28	44	5	8	2	0	2	7	3-1	0	6	.182	.234	.364	58	-3	0-0	1.000	1	149	71	/1-9,O(LF)D	-0.2
Total	2	35	55	5	11	2	0	2	7	3-1	0	8	.200	.241	.345	57	-4	0-0	1.000	1	137	65	/1-10,D-4,O-2(1-0-1)	-0.3
DESAUTELS, GENE Eugene Abraham "Red" B 6.13.1907 Worcester, MA D 11.5.1994 Flint, MI BR/TR 5-11/170# d6.22 Mil 1944-45																								
1930	Det A	42	126	13	24	4	2	0	9	7	1	9	.190	.239	.254	25	-15	2-0	.996	3	74	115	C-42	-0.8
1931	Det A	3	11	1	1	0	0	0	1	0	0	1	.091	.091	.091	-50	-2	0-0	1.000	-0	58	233	/C-3	-0.3
1932	Det A	28	72	8	17	2	0	0	2	13	1	11	.236	.360	.264	62	-3	0-0	.984	2	103	93	C-24	0.0
1933	Det A	30	42	5	6	1	0	0	4	4	1	6	.143	.234	.167	8	-6	0-0	.976	0	73	69	C-30	-0.4
1937	Bos A	96	305	33	74	10	3	0	27	36	1	26	.243	.325	.295	55	-21	1-2	**.993**	4	111	70	C-94	-1.1
1938	Bos A	108	333	47	97	16	2	2	48	57	1	31	.291	.396	.369	89	-3	1-1	.985	4	110	106	*C-108	0.7
1939	Bos A	76	226	26	55	14	0	0	21	33	0	13	.243	.340	.305	64	-11	3-1	.994	7	95	118	C-73	0.0
1940	Bos A	71	222	19	50	7	1	0	17	32	2	13	.225	.328	.266	54	-14	0-1	.992	-6	97	79	C-70	-1.6
1941	Cle A	66	189	20	38	5	1	1	17	14	1	12	.201	.260	.254	38	-18	1-0	.997	5	122	94	C-66	-0.8
1942	Cle A	62	162	14	40	5	0	0	9	12	1	13	.247	.303	.278	68	-7	1-0	.975	-5	102	51	C-61	-0.9
1943	Cle A	68	185	14	38	6	1	0	19	11	0	16	.205	.250	.249	49	-13	2-0	.982	3	147	78	C-66	-0.7
1945	Cle A	10	9	1	1	0	0	0	0	1	0	1	.111	.200	.111	-9	-1	0-0	1.000	0	95	135	C-10	-0.1
1946	Phi A	52	130	10	28	3	1	0	13	12	0	16	.215	.282	.254	51	-9	1-1	.989	3	118	160	C-52	-0.4
Total	13	712	2012	211	469	73	11	3	187	232	9	168	.233	.315	.285	57	-123	12-6	.989	20	107	94	C-699	-6.4
DeSHIELDS, DELINO Delino Lamont B 1.15.1969 Seaford, DE BL/TR 6-1/170# d4.9 OF Total (118-LF 3-CF 1-RF)																								
1990	Mon N	129	499	69	144	28	6	4	45	66-3	4	96	.289	.375	.393	116	14	42-22	.981	-5	99	101	*2-128	1.4
1991	Mon N	151	563	83	134	15	4	10	51	95-2	2	151	.238	.347	.332	94	-1	56-23	.962	-21	95	91	*2-148	-1.5
1992	Mon N	135	530	82	155	19	8	7	56	54-4	3	108	.292	.359	.398	116	11	46-15	.976	-22	89	91	*2-134	-0.2
1993	Mon N	123	481	75	142	17	7	2	29	72-3	3	64	.295	.389	.372	101	4	43-10	.983	7	**108**	101	*2-123	2.2
1994	LA N	89	320	51	80	11	3	2	33	54-0	0	53	.250	.357	.322	85	-5	27-7	.986	5	105	99	2-88,S-10	0.7
1995	†LA N	127	425	66	109	18	3	8	37	63-4	1	83	.256	.353	.369	100	1	39-14	.980	-5	98	83	*2-113	0.5
1996	†LA N	154	581	75	130	12	8	5	41	53-7	1	124	.224	.287	.298	60	-36	48-11	.975	-20	91	87	*2-154	-4.1
1997	StL N	150	572	92	169	26	**14**	11	58	55-1	3	72	.295	.357	.448	111	8	55-14	.972	-8	96	108	*2-147	1.4
1998	StL N	117	420	74	122	21	8	7	44	56-2	0	61	.290	.371	.429	111	8	26-10	.983	-10	93	97	*2-111/1	0.5
1999	Bal A	96	330	46	87	11	2	6	34	37-0	1	52	.264	.339	.364	83	-9	11-8	.977	-5	94	93	2-93	-0.9
2000	Bal A	151	561	84	166	43	5	10	86	69-2	1	82	.296	.369	.444	111	12	37-10	.975	-16	90	69	2-96,O-41(39-2-0),D-10	0.3
2001	Bal A	58	188	29	37	8	2	3	21	31-1	1	42	.197	.312	.309	69	-8	11-1	.967	-3	88	68	O-47(46-1-0)/D-8	-1.0
	Chi N	68	163	26	45	9	3	2	16	28-0	0	35	.276	.380	.405	109	3	12-1	.976	-3	89	63	O-33(LF),2-16/3-5,1	0.2
2002	Chi N	67	146	20	28	6	1	3	10	21-2	0	38	.192	.292	.308	63	-9	10-1	.970	2	99	67	2-41/O(RF)	-0.3
Total	13	1615	5779	872	1548	244	74	80	561	754-31	20	1061	.268	.352	.377	98	-7	463-147	.977	-104	96	92	*2-1392,O-122L/D-18,S-10,3-5,1-2	-0.8
DESTRADE, ORESTES Orestes (Cucuas) B 5.8.1962 Santiago De Cuba, Cuba BB/TR 6-4/210# d9.11																								
1987	NY A	9	19	5	5	0	0	0	1	5-0	0	5	.263	.417	.263	87	0	0-0	1.000	-0	62	103	/1-3,D-2	0.0
1988	Pit N	36	47	2	7	1	0	1	3	5-0	0	17	.149	.226	.234	34	-4	0-0	1.000	-1	47	73	/1-8	-0.6
1993	Fla N	153	569	61	145	20	3	20	87	58-8	3	130	.255	.324	.406	90	-9	0-2	.987	-9	82	93	*1-152	-3.3
1994	Fla N	39	130	12	27	4	0	5	15	19-1	2	32	.208	.316	.354	73	-5	1-0	.983	-3	75	100	1-37	-1.1
Total	4	237	765	80	184	25	3	26	106	87-9	5	184	.241	.319	.383	84	-18	1-2	.987	-13	79	94	1-200/D-2	-5.0
DETHERAGE, BOB Robert Wayne B 9.20.1954 Springfield, MO BR/TR 6/180# d4.11																								
1980	KC A	20	26	2	8	2	0	1	7	1-0	0	4	.308	.333	.500	124	1	1-1	1.000	-2	75	0	O-20(12-0-11)	-0.2
DeTORE, GEORGE George Francis B 11.11.1906 Utica, NY D 2.7.1991 Utica, NY BR/TR 5-8/170# d9.14 C1																								
1930	Cle A	3	12	0	2	1	0	0	2	0	0	2	.167	.167	.250	4	-2	0-0	.750	-1	50	243	/3-3	-0.3
1931	Cle A	30	56	3	15	6	0	0	7	8	0	2	.268	.359	.375	88	-1	0-2	.958	2	156	0	3-13,S-10/2-3	0.2
Total	2	33	68	3	17	7	0	0	9	8	0	4	.250	.329	.353	74	-3	0-2	.929	1	131	58	/3-16,S-10,2-3	-0.1
DETWEILER, DUCKY Robert Sterling B 2.15.1919 Trumbauersville, PA BR/TR 5-11/178# d9.12 Mil 1943-45																								
1942	Bos N	12	44	3	14	2	1	0	5	2	0	7	.318	.348	.409	123	1	0	.929	-2	80	104	3-12	-0.1
1946	Bos N	1	1	0	0	0	0	0	0	0	0	0	.000	.000	.000	-99	0	0	—	0			H	0.0
Total	2	13	45	3	14	2	1	0	5	2	0	7	.311	.340	.400	118	1	0	.929	-2	80	104	/3-12	-0.1
DEVAREZ, CESAR Cesar Salvatore (Santana) B 9.22.1969 San Francisco De Macoris, D.R. BR/TR 5-10/175# d6.2																								
1995	Bal A	6	4	0	0	0	0	0	0	0-0	0	0	.000	.000	.000	-99	-1	0-0	1.000	0	32	0	/C-6	-0.1
1996	Bal A	10	18	3	2	0	1	0	0	1-0	0	3	.111	.158	.222	-5	-3	0-0	1.000	-0	67	69	C-10	-0.3
Total	2	16	22	3	2	0	1	0	0	1-0	0	3	.091	.130	.182	-22	-4	0-0	1.000	0	59	54	/C-16	-0.4
DEVEREAUX, MIKE Michael B 4.10.1963 Casper, WY BR/TR 6/195# d9.2																								
1987	LA N	19	54	7	12	3	0	0	4	3-0	0	10	.222	.263	.278	45	-4	3-1	1.000	-1	81	111	O-18(11-2-5)	-0.5
1988	LA N	30	43	4	5	1	0	0	2	2-0	0	10	.116	.156	.140	-15	-7	0-1	1.000	-0	102	0	O-26(0-17-8)	-0.8
1989	Bal A	122	391	55	104	14	3	8	46	36-0	2	60	.266	.329	.379	103	1	22-11	.983	0	109	16	*O-112(4-80-35)/D-5	0.1
1990	Bal A	108	367	48	88	18	1	12	49	28-0	0	48	.240	.291	.392	93	-5	13-12	.983	2	108	78	*O-104(CF)/D-3	-0.5
1991	Bal A	149	608	82	158	27	10	19	59	47-2	2	115	.260	.313	.431	109	4	16-9	.993	4	104	131	*O-149(1-148-0)	0.7
1992	Bal A	156	653	76	180	29	11	24	107	44-1	4	94	.276	.321	.464	116	10	10-8	.989	-8	96	54	*O-155(CF)	0.1
1993	Bal A	131	527	72	132	31	3	14	75	43-0	1	99	.250	.306	.400	85	-12	3-3	.988	-6	90	111	*O-130(CF)	-1.7
1994	Bal A	85	301	35	61	8	2	9	33	22-0	1	72	.203	.256	.332	49	-25	1-2	.995	-2	97	71	O-84(CF)/D	-2.5
1995	Chi A	92	333	48	102	21	1	10	55	25-3	0	51	.306	.352	.465	117	8	6-6	.985	4	114	75	O-90(0-9-87)	0.6
	†Atl N	29	55	7	14	3	0	1	8	2-0	0	11	.255	.281	.364	66	-3	2-0	1.000	2	138	0	O-27(14-9-4)	-0.1
1996	†Bal A	127	323	49	74	11	2	8	34	34-0	2	53	.229	.305	.350	66	-18	8-2	.983	2	99	131	*O-112(35-30-62),D-10	-1.7
1997	Tex A	29	72	8	15	3	0	0	7	7-0	0	10	.208	.275	.250	37	-7	1-0	1.000	-2	92	0	O-28(5-3-24)	-0.9
1998	LA N	9	13	0	4	1	0	0	1	3-0	0	2	.308	.438	.385	126	1	0-1	1.000	1	128	489	/O-5(1-3-1)	0.1
Total	12	1086	3740	491	949	170	33	105	480	296-6	12	635	.254	.308	.401	91	-57	85-56	.988	-5	102	82	*O-1040(71-774-226)/D-19	-7.1
DEVINE, MICKEY William Patrick B 5.9.1892 Albany, NY D 10.1.1937 Albany, NY BR/TR 5-10/165# d8.2																								
1918	Phi N	4	8	0	1	1	0	0	0	0	0	1	.125	.125	.250	13	-1	0	.909	-0	110	58	/C-3	-0.1
1920	Bos A	8	12	1	2	0	0	0	0	1	0	2	.167	.231	.167	7	-2	1-0	.955	0	102	53	/C-5	-0.1
1925	NY N	21	33	6	9	3	0	0	4	2	0	3	.273	.314	.364	76	-1	0-0	.933	0	113	116	C-11/3	0.0
Total	3	33	53	7	12	4	0	0	4	3	0	6	.226	.268	.302	51	-4	1-0	.936	0	110	91	/C-19,3	-0.2
DeVIVEIROS, BERNIE Bernard John B 4.19.1901 Oakland, CA D 7.5.1994 Oakland, CA BR/TR 5-7/160# d9.13																								
1924	Chi A	1	1	0	0	0	0	0	0	0	0	0	.000	.000	.000	-99	0	0-0	.333	-1	0	0	/S	-0.1
1927	Det A	24	22	4	5	1	0	0	2	2	0	8	.227	.292	.273	46	-2	1-0	.913	-0	107	160	S-14/3	-0.1
Total	2	25	23	4	5	1	0	0	2	2	0	8	.217	.280	.261	40	-2	1-0	.846	-1	97	144	/S-15,3	-0.2
DEVLIN, ART Arthur McArthur B 10.16.1879 Washington, DC D 9.18.1948 Jersey City, NJ BR/TR 6/175# d4.14 C2																								
1904	NY N	130	474	81	133	16	8	1	66	62	6		.281	.371	.354	119	13	33	.907	5	108	81	*3-130	2.3
1905	†NY N	153	525	74	129	14	7	2	61	66	13		.246	.344	.310	94	-1	**59**	.932	6	103	91	*3-153	0.9
1906	NY N	148	498	76	149	23	8	2	65	74	6		.299	.396	.390	142	28	54	.944	**29**	**122**	136	*3-148	6.6
1907	NY N	143	491	61	136	16	2	1	54	63	**15**		.277	.376	.324	116	14	38	.940	-2	96	69	*3-140/S-3	1.8
1908	NY N	**157**	534	59	135	18	4	2	45	62	14		.253	.346	.313	106	7	19	**.947**	12	105	110	*3-157	2.6
1909	NY N	143	491	61	130	19	8	0	56	65	10		.265	.362	.336	115	12	26	.934	17	110	**125**	*3-143	3.5
1910	NY N	147	493	71	128	17	5	2	67	62	9	32	.260	.353	.327	98	1	28	.933	6	101	102	*3-147	1.1
1911	NY N	95	260	42	71	16	2	0	25	42	6	19	.273	.386	.350	103	4	9	.944	4	111	34	3-79/1-6,2-6,S-6	1.0
1912	Bos N	124	436	59	126	18	8	0	54	51	3	37	.289	.367	.367	99	1	11	.992	-1	95	79	1-69,S-26,3-26/O(LF)	0.0
1913	Bos N	73	210	19	48	7	5	0	12	29	2	17	.229	.328	.310	81	-5	8-8	.973	5	106	45	3-69	0.2
Total	10	1313	4412	603	1185	164	57	10	505	576	84	105	.269	.364	.338	109	74	285-8	.938	81	107	97	*3-1192/1-75,S-35,2-6,O(LF)	20.0
DEVLIN, JIM James Alexander B 1849 Philadelphia, PA D 10.10.1883 Philadelphia, PA BR/TR 5-11/175# d4.21 ▲																								
1873	Phi NA	23	99	18	24	4	4	0	10	2		4	.242	.257	.364	79	-3	0-0	.938	-2	150	171	1-12/3-6,S-4,O-2(RF)	-0.4
1874	Chi NA	45	203	26	58	5	0	0	26	2		9	.286	.293	.310	93	-2	2-1	.930	-2	63	57	1-24,O-17(RF)/3-5	-0.2
1875	Chi NA	**69**	318	60	92	17	6	0	40	4		4	.289	.298	.381	133	10	6-1	.934	1	134	71	1-42,P-28/O-4(0-3-1)	0.7

Year	Tm Lg	G	AB	R	H	2B	3B	HR	RBI	BB-IB	HP	SO	AVG	OBP	SLG	AOPS	ABR	SB-CS	FA	FR	Rng	Thr	G at Pos	BFW
1876	Lou N	68	298	38	94	14	1	0	28	1		11	.315	.318	.369	109	1		.941	2	102	147	*P-68/1	0.1
1877	Lou N	**61**	268	38	72	6	3	1	27	7		27	.269	.287	.325	78	-1		.933	2	111	158	*P-61	0.0
Total	3 NA	137	620	104	174	26	10	0	76	8		17	.281	.290	.355	110	5	8-2	.000	-3	114	81	/1-78,P-28,O-23(0-3-20),3-11,S-4	0.1
Total	2	129	566	76	166	20	4	1	55	8		38	.293	.303	.348	94	0		.937	4	106	152	P-129/1	0.1
DEVLIN, JIM James Raymond B 8.25.1922 Plains, PA BL/TR 5-11.5/165# d4.27																								
1944	Cle A	1	1	0	0	0	0	0	0	0	0	0	.000	.000	.000	-99	0	0-0	1.000	0	*0*	*0*	/C	0.0
DeVOGT, REX Rex Eugene B 1.4.1888 Clare, MI D 11.9.1935 Alma, MI BR/TR 5-9/170# d4.17																								
1913	Bos N	3	6	0	0	0	0	0	0	0	0	3	.000	.000	.000	-98	-2	0	.941	1	137	142	/C-3	-0.1
DEVORE, JOSH Joshua D. B 11.13.1887 Murray City, OH D 10.6.1954 Chillicothe, OH BL/TL 5-6/160# d9.25																								
1908	NY N	5	6	1	1	0	0	0	2	1	0		.167	.286	.167	43	0	1	1.000	-0	0	0	/O-2(RF)	-0.1
1909	NY N	22	28	6	4	1	0	0	1	2	2		.143	.250	.179	33	-2	3	.824	-1	103	0	O-12(3-10-1)	-0.3
1910	NY N	133	490	92	149	11	10	2	27	46	6	67	.304	.371	.380	119	11	43	.929	-7	81	116	*O-130(106-2-22)	-0.3
1911	†NY N	149	565	96	158	19	10	3	50	81	6	69	.280	.376	.365	104	6	61	.934	0	89	143	*O-149(104-0-48)	-0.1
1912	†NY N	106	327	66	90	14	6	2	37	51	5	43	.275	.381	.373	104	4	27	.918	-5	86	106	O-96(76-1-19)	-0.5
1913	NY N	16	21	4	4	0	1	0	1	3	1	4	.190	.320	.286	73	-1	6-2	1.000	0	68	214	/O-8(1-5-2)	0.0
	Cin N	66	217	30	58	6	4	3	14	12	1	21	.267	.309	.373	95	-3	17-7	.920	-2	88	126	O-57(0-57-1)	-0.7
	Phi N	23	39	9	11	1	0	0	5	4	1	7	.282	.364	.308	89	0	0	.889	-0	81	185	O-14(8-6-0)	-0.1
	Year	105	277	43	73	7	5	3	20	19	3	32	.264	.318	.357	92	-4	23-9	.919	-2	86	138	O-79(9-68-3)	-0.8
1914	Phi N	30	53	5	16	2	0	0	7	4	0	5	.302	.351	.340	99	0	0	.947	3	86	399	/O-9(7-2-0)	0.2
	†Bos N	51	128	22	29	4	0	1	5	18	1	14	.227	.327	.281	82	-2	2	.915	-4	79	79	O-42(23-20-0)	-0.8
	Year	81	181	27	45	6	0	1	12	22	1	19	.249	.333	.298	87	-2	2	.923	-1	80	147	O-51(30-22-0)	-0.6
Total	7	601	1874	331	520	58	31	11	149	222	23	230	.277	.361	.359	103	13	160-9	.925	-16	85	126	O-519(328-103-95)	-2.7
DeVORMER, AL Albert E. B 8.19.1891 Grand Rapids, MI D 8.29.1966 Grand Rapids, MI BR/TR 6-0.5/175# d8.4																								
1918	Chi A	8	19	2	5	2	0	0	0	0	0	4	.263	.263	.368	90	0	1	1.000	-1	*106*	*79*	/C-6,O(RF)	-0.1
1921	†NY A	22	49	6	17	4	0	0	7	2	0	4	.347	.373	.429	102	0	2-0	.950	-1	*109*	*91*	C-17	0.1
1922	NY A	24	59	8	12	4	1	0	11	1	0	6	.203	.217	.305	34	-6	0-0	.968	-1	*128*	*104*	C-17/1	-0.6
1923	Bos A	74	209	20	54	7	3	0	18	6	1	21	.258	.282	.321	58	-14	3-0	.979	-1	*81*	*107*	C-55/1-2	-1.0
1927	NY N	68	141	14	35	3	1	2	21	11	2	11	.248	.312	.326	71	-6	1	.953	-3	*122*	*103*	C-54/1-3	-0.7
Total	5	196	477	50	123	20	5	2	57	20	3	46	.258	.292	.333	65	-26	7-0	.967	-6	*103*	*103*	C-149/1-6,O(RF)	-2.3
DeVOY, WALT Walter Joseph B 3.14.1886 St.Louis, MO D 12.17.1953 St.Louis, MO BR/TR 5-11/165# d9.13																								
1909	StL A	19	69	7	17	3	1	0	8	3	0		.246	.278	.319	95	-1	4	.944	-0	127	0	O-16(RF)/1-3	-0.2
DeWILLIS, JEFF Jeffrey Allen B 4.13.1965 Houston, TX BR/TR 6-2/170# d4.19																								
1987	Tor A	13	25	2	3	1	0	1	2	2-0	0	12	.120	.185	.280	21	-3	0-0	.964	-1	174	160	C-13	-0.3
DEXTER, CHARLIE Charles Dana B 6.15.1876 Evansville, IN D 6.9.1934 Cedar Rapids, IA BR/TR 5-7/155# d4.17 OF Total (8-LF 159-CF 236-RF)																								
1896	Lou N	107	402	65	112	18	7	3	37	17	6	34	.279	.318	.381	87	-9	21	.903	-9	*79*	*120*	C-55,O-47(0-46-1)	-1.4
1897	Lou N	76	257	43	72	12	5	2	46	21	3		.280	.342	.389	96	-2	12	.907	-1	252	404	O-32(3-14-16),C-23,3-14/S-2	-0.2
1898	Lou N	112	421	76	132	13	5	1	66	26	7		.314	.363	.375	113	7	44	.958	-3	99	62	O-95(RF)/2-8,C-7	0.1
1899	Lou N	81	298	47	76	7	1	1	34	21	5		.255	.315	.295	68	-13	21	.943	2	141	68	O-72(1-0-71)/S-6	-1.3
1900	Chi N	40	125	7	25	5	0	2	20	1	1		.200	.213	.288	39	-11	2	.943	4	*95*	*136*	C-22,O-13(RF)/2	-0.5
1901	Chi N	116	460	46	123	9	5	1	66	16	7		.267	.302	.315	82	-11	22	.982	2	131	106	1-54,3-25,O-21(1-9-11),2-13/C-3	-1.0
1902	Chi N	71	273	31	62	13	0	2	26	19	5		.227	.290	.297	83	-5	13	.846	-14	70	99	3-41,1-22,O-10(1-4-5)	-2.0
	Bos N	48	183	33	47	3	0	1	18	16	2		.257	.323	.290	88	-2	16	.901	-3	100	78	S-22,2-19/O-7(0-4-3),3	-0.5
	Year	119	456	64	109	16	0	3	44	35	7		.239	.303	.294	85	-7	29	.847	-17	70	98	3-42,1-22,S-22,2-19,O-17(1-8-8)	-2.5
1903	Bos N	123	457	82	102	15	1	3	34	61	6		.223	.323	.280	75	-12	32	.941	-9	91	165	*O-106(2-82-21)/S-9,C-6	-2.4
Total	8	774	2876	430	751	95	24	16	347	198	42	34	.261	.318	.328	85	-58	183	.942	-30	114	138	O-403R,C-116/3-81,1-76,2-41,S-39	-9.2
DIAZ, ALEX Alexis B 10.5.1968 Brooklyn, NY BB/TR 5-11/180# d7.25																								
1992	Mil A	22	9	5	1	0	0	0	1	0-0	0	0	.111	.111	.111	-38	-2	3-2	1.000	0	109	0	O-11(2-10-0)/D-2	-0.2
1993	Mil A	32	69	9	22	2	0	0	1	0-0	0	12	.319	.319	.348	80	-2	5-3	.979	-0	99	77	O-28(4-12-13)/D	-0.3
1994	Mil A	79	187	17	47	5	7	1	17	10-1	0	19	.251	.285	.369	65	-11	5-5	.993	1	96	150	O-73(0-58-20)/2-2,D	-1.0
1995	†Sea A	103	270	44	67	14	0	3	27	13-2	2	27	.248	.286	.333	60	-16	18-8	.987	-1	94	122	O-88(17-69-4)	-1.5
1996	Sea A	38	79	11	19	2	0	1	5	2-0	2	8	.241	.274	.304	47	-7	6-3	.982	3	139	77	O-28(19-5-5)/D	-0.4
1997	Tex A	28	90	8	20	4	0	2	12	5-0	1	13	.222	.268	.333	54	-6	1-1	.980	1	104	137	O-23(3-0-20)/2	-0.6
1998	SF N	34	62	5	8	2	0	0	5	0-0	0	15	.129	.129	.161	-26	-12	1-1	1.000	1	105	268	O-21(4-15-3)	-1.0
1999	Hou N	30	50	3	11	2	0	1	7	3-0	0	13	.220	.264	.320	48	-4	2-2	.900	-0	64	258	/O-8(7-0-1)	-0.5
Total	8	366	816	102	195	31	7	8	75	33-3	5	107	.239	.271	.324	53	-60	41-25	.986	5	100	133	O-280(56-169-66)/D-5,2-3,1	-5.5
DIAZ, BO Baudilio Jose (Seijas) B 3.23.1953 Cua, Venezuela D 11.23.1990 Caracas, Venezuela BR/TR 5-11/190# d9.6																								
1977	Bos A	2	1	0	0	0	0	0	0	0-0	0	1	.000	.000	.000	-90	0	0-0	1.000	1	0	0	/C-2	0.0
1978	Cle A	44	127	12	30	4	0	2	11	4-0	0	17	.236	.260	.315	61	-7	0-0	.971	-5	112	92	C-44	-1.0
1979	Cle A	15	32	0	5	2	0	0	1	2-0	0	6	.156	.206	.219	15	-4	0-0	.958	-0	72	76	C-15	-0.4
1980	Cle A	76	207	15	47	11	2	3	32	7-3	0	27	.227	.250	.343	61	-12	1-0	.989	2	78	83	C-75	-0.8
1981	Cle A★	63	182	25	57	19	0	7	38	13-2	1	23	.313	.359	.533	157	13	2-2	.975	-3	122	84	C-51/D-3	1.2
1982	Phi N	144	525	69	151	29	1	18	85	36-5	3	87	.288	.333	.450	116	10	3-6	.989	-4	103	101	*C-144	1.1
1983	†Phi N	136	471	49	111	17	0	15	64	38-4	2	57	.236	.295	.367	84	-12	1-4	.986	18	106	114	*C-134	1.1
1984	Phi N	27	75	5	16	4	0	1	9	5-0	0	13	.213	.256	.307	58	-4	0-0	.992	-1	89	89	C-23	-0.5
1985	Phi N	26	76	9	16	5	1	2	16	6-0	0	7	.211	.268	.382	78	-2	0-0	.972	2	86	125	C-24	0.0
	Cin N	51	161	12	42	8	0	3	15	15-0	1	18	.261	.324	.366	89	-2	0-0	.988	13	116	98	C-51	1.3
	Year	77	237	21	58	13	1	5	31	21-0	1	25	.245	.307	.371	86	-4	0-0	.983	15	107	106	C-75	1.3
1986	Cin N	134	474	50	129	21	0	10	56	40-0	0	52	.272	.327	.380	91	-6	1-1	.984	3	115	98	*C-134	0.2
1987	Cin N★	140	496	49	134	28	1	15	82	19-1	5	73	.270	.300	.421	86	-11	1-0	.992	3	116	117	*C-137	-0.3
1988	Cin N	92	315	26	69	9	0	10	35	7-4	1	41	.219	.236	.343	63	-17	0-2	.990	5	126	127	C-88	-0.8
1989	Cin N	43	132	6	27	5	0	1	8	6-3	0	7	.205	.239	.265	43	-10	0-2	.984	-1	96	55	C-43	-1.0
Total	13	993	3274	327	834	162	5	87	452	198-22	13	429	.255	.297	.387	87	-64	9-17	.986	30	108	103	C-965/D-3	0.1
DIAZ, CARLOS Carlos Francisco B 12.24.1964 Elizabeth, NJ BR/TR 6-3/195# d5.8																								
1990	Tor A	9	3	1	1	0	0	0	0	0-0	0	2	.333	.333	.333	85	0	0-0	1.000	2	97	197	/C-9	0.2
DIAZ, EDDY Eddy Javier B 9.29.1971 Barquisimeto, Venezuela BR/TR 5-10/160# d4.17																								
1997	Mil A	16	50	4	11	2	1	0	7	1-0	0	5	.220	.235	.300	38	-5	0-0	1.000	1	100	132	2-14/3S	-0.3
DIAZ, EDGAR Edgar (Serrano) B 2.8.1964 Santurce, P.R. BR/TR 6/155# d9.16																								
1986	Mil A	5	13	0	3	0	0	0	0	1-0	0	3	.231	.286	.231	41	-1	0-0	.875	-3	62	70	/S-5	-0.3
1990	Mil A	86	218	27	59	2	2	0	14	21-0	1	32	.271	.338	.298	80	-6	3-2	.950	-5	96	93	S-65,2-15/3-7,D	-0.6
Total	2	91	231	27	62	2	2	0	14	22-0	1	35	.268	.335	.294	78	-7	3-2	.946	-8	93	91	/S-70,2-15,3-7,D	-0.9
DIAZ, EDWIN Edwin (Rosario) B 1.15.1975 Bayamon, P.R. BR/TR 5-11/172# d3.31																								
1998	Ari N	3	7	0	0	0	0	0	0	0-0	0	2	.000	.000	.000	-99	-2	0-0	.938	1	125	141	/2-3	-0.1
1999	Ari N	4	5	2	2	2	0	0	1	3-1	0	1	.400	.625	.800	256	2	0-0	1.000	-0	250	0	/2-2,S-2	0.1
Total	2	7	12	2	2	2	0	0	1	3-1	0	3	.167	.333	.333	73	0	0-0	.947	1	146	118	/2-5,S-2	0.0
DIAZ, EINAR Einar Antonio B 12.28.1972 Chiriqui, Panama BR/TR 5-10/165# d9.9																								
1996	Cle A	4	1	0	0	0	0	0	0	0-0	0	0	.000	.000	.000	-99	0	0-0	1.000	0	0	0	/C-4	0.0
1997	Cle A	5	7	1	1	1	0	0	1	0-0	0	2	.143	.143	.286	8	-1	0-0	.955	0	26	262	/C-5	-0.1
1998	†Cle A	17	48	8	11	1	0	2	9	3-0	2	2	.229	.286	.375	72	-2	0-0	.973	2	105	124	C-17	0.0
1999	†Cle A	119	392	43	110	21	1	3	32	23-0	5	41	.281	.328	.362	73	-16	11-4	.988	3	96	112	*C-119	-0.4
2000	Cle A	75	250	29	68	14	2	4	25	11-0	8	29	.272	.323	.392	78	-9	4-2	.994	17	120	104	C-74/3	1.2
2001	†Cle A	134	437	54	121	34	1	4	56	17-0	16	44	.277	.328	.387	86	-8	1-2	.992	14	111	**133**	*C-134/2	1.4
2002	Cle A	102	320	34	66	19	0	2	16	17-1	6	27	.206	.258	.284	45	-25	0-1	.989	3	65	**149**	*C-100	-1.6
2003	Tex A	101	334	30	86	14	1	4	35	9-0	10	32	.257	.294	.341	63	-18	3-1	.989	5	110	99	*C-101	-0.6
Total	8	557	1789	199	463	104	5	19	174	80-1	47	177	.259	.306	.354	70	-79	19-10	.990	45	100	121	C-554/23	-0.1

DIAZ, JUAN Juan Carlos B 2.19.1974 San Jose De Las Lajas, Cuba BR/TR 6-2/228# d6.12

Year	Tm Lg	G	AB	R	H	2B	3B	HR	RBI	BB-IB	HP	SO	AVG	OBP	SLG	AOPS	ABR	SB-CS	FA	FR	Rng	Thr	G at Pos	BFW
2002	Bos A	4	7	2	2	1	0	1	2	1-0	0	2	.286	.375	.857	210	1	0-0	1.000	-0	0	0	/1D	0.1

DIAZ, MARIO Mario Rafael (Torres) B 1.10.1962 Humacao, P.R. BR/TR 5-10/160# d9.12

Year	Tm Lg	G	AB	R	H	2B	3B	HR	RBI	BB-IB	HP	SO	AVG	OBP	SLG	AOPS	ABR	SB-CS	FA	FR	Rng	Thr	G at Pos	BFW
1987	Sea A	11	23	4	7	0	1	0	3	0-0	0	4	.304	.304	.391	79	-1	0-0	.972	3	130	155	S-10	0.2
1988	Sea A	28	72	6	22	5	0	0	9	3-0	0	5	.306	.329	.375	94	-1	0-0	.985	-6	73	75	S-21/2-4,13	-0.5
1989	Sea A	52	74	9	10	0	0	1	7	7-0	0	7	.135	.210	.176	9	-9	0-0	.930	-15	64	36	S-37,2-14/3-3	-2.3
1990	NY N	16	22	0	3	1	0	0	1	0-0	0	3	.136	.130	.182	-13	-3	0-0	.958	1	131	42	S-10/2	-0.2
1991	Tex A	96	182	24	48	7	0	1	22	15-0	0	18	.264	.318	.319	79	-5	0-1	.962	-3	91	91	S-65,2-20/3-8,D	-0.5
1992	Tex A	19	31	2	7	1	0	0	1	1-1	0	2	.226	.250	.258	44	-2	0-1	.975	-2	83	30	S-16/2-3,3	-0.5
1993	Tex A	71	205	24	56	10	1	2	24	8-0	1	13	.273	.297	.361	81	-6	1-0	.986	-3	93	88	S-57,3-12/1	-0.5
1994	Fla N	32	77	10	25	4	2	0	11	6-0	1	6	.325	.376	.429	107	1	0-0	.964	1	105	211	3-11/2-7,S-7	0.2
1995	Fla N	49	87	5	20	3	0	1	6	1-0	0	12	.230	.239	.299	41	-8	0-0	.944	-1	97	179	/2-9,S-5,3-3	-0.8
Total	9	374	773	84	198	31	4	5	84	41-1	2	70	.256	.292	.326	69	-34	1-2	.972	-24	88	81	S-228/2-58,3-39,1-2,D	-4.9

DIAZ, MATT Matthew E. B 3.3.1978 Portland, OR BR/TR 6-1/200# d7.19

Year	Tm Lg	G	AB	R	H	2B	3B	HR	RBI	BB-IB	HP	SO	AVG	OBP	SLG	AOPS	ABR	SB-CS	FA	FR	Rng	Thr	G at Pos	BFW
2003	TB A	4	9	2	1	0	0	0	0	1-0	0	3	.111	.200	.111	-15	-2	0-0	.857	1	274	0	/O(LF)D	-0.1

DIAZ, MIKE Michael Anthony B 4.15.1960 San Francisco, CA BR/TR 6-2/195# d9.15

Year	Tm Lg	G	AB	R	H	2B	3B	HR	RBI	BB-IB	HP	SO	AVG	OBP	SLG	AOPS	ABR	SB-CS	FA	FR	Rng	Thr	G at Pos	BFW
1983	Chi N	6	7	2	2	1	0	0	1	0-0	0	0	.286	.286	.429	91	0	0-0	1.000	-1	37	0	/C-3	-0.1
1986	Pit N	97	209	22	56	9	0	12	36	19-0	2	43	.268	.330	.483	120	5	0-1	.966	-3	96	50	O-38(37-0-1),1-20/3-5,C	0.0
1987	Pit N	103	241	28	58	8	2	16	48	31-3	3	42	.241	.326	.490	114	4	1-0	.960	-1	86	105	O-37(27-0-10),1-32/C-8	0.1
1988	Pit N	47	74	6	17	3	0	0	5	16-1	0	13	.230	.367	.270	87	0	0-0	1.000	-2	66	0	O-19(9-0-9)/1-6,C	-0.3
	Chi A	40	152	12	36	6	0	3	12	5-0	1	30	.237	.266	.336	67	-7	0-1	.987	-1	95	92	1-39/D	-1.2
Total	4	293	683	70	169	27	2	31	102	71-4	6	128	.247	.319	.429	103	2	1-2	.988	-8	91	88	/1-97,O-94(73-0-20),C-13,3-5,D	-1.5

DICKEN, PAUL Paul Franklin B 10.2.1943 DeLand, FL BR/TR 6-5/195# d6.7

Year	Tm Lg	G	AB	R	H	2B	3B	HR	RBI	BB-IB	HP	SO	AVG	OBP	SLG	AOPS	ABR	SB-CS	FA	FR	Rng	Thr	G at Pos	BFW
1964	Cle A	11	11	0	0	0	0	0	0	0-0	0	5	.000	.000	.000	-99	-3	0-0	—	0			H	-0.3
1966	Cle A	2	2	0	0	0	0	0	0	0-0	0	1	.000	.000	.000	-99	-1	0-0	—	0			H	-0.1
Total	2	13	13	0	0	0	0	0	0	0-0	0	6	.000	.000	.000	-99	-4	0-0	.988	0				-0.4

DICKERSON, BUTTERCUP Lewis Pessano B 10.11.1858 Tyaskin, MD D 7.23.1920 Baltimore, MD BL/TR 5-6/140# d7.15

Year	Tm Lg	G	AB	R	H	2B	3B	HR	RBI	BB-IB	HP	SO	AVG	OBP	SLG	AOPS	ABR	SB-CS	FA	FR	Rng	Thr	G at Pos	BFW
1878	Cin N	29	123	17	38	5	1	0	9	0		7	.309	.309	.366	134	4		.877	-2	13	0	O-29(10-19-0)	0.1
1879	Cin N	**81**	350	73	102	18	**14**	2	57	3		27	.291	.297	.440	147	17		.801	-4	50	48	*O-81(LF)	0.7
1880	Tro N	30	119	15	23	2	2	0	10	2		3	.193	.207	.244	49	-6		.903	4	91	207	O-30(0-29-1)/S	-0.4
	Wor N	31	133	22	39	8	6	0	20	1		2	.293	.299	.444	136	4		.852	-4	53	155	O-31(CF)	-0.1
	Year	61	252	37	62	10	8	0	30	3		5	.246	.255	.349	96	-2		.883	0	72	181	O-61(0-60-1)/S	-0.5
1881	Wor N	80	367	48	116	18	6	1	31	8		8	.316	.331	.406	123	9		.892	9	131	169	*O-80(79-0-1)	1.2
1883	Pit AA	85	354	62	88	15	1	0		18			.249	.285	.297	91	-2		.798	-1	184	97	*O-78(1-30-47)/S-8,2-2	-0.3
1884	StL U	46	211	49	77	15	1	0		8			.365	.388	.445	147	7		.895	4	113	144	O-42(LF)/3-4	0.8
	Bal AA	13	56	9	12	2	1	0		4	2		.214	.290	.286	85	-1		.941	-2	47	0	O-12(RF)/3	-0.2
	Lou AA	8	28	6	4	0	2	1		3	0		.143	.226	.393	103	0		.813	0	149	0	/O-8(1-5-3)	0.0
	Year	21	84	15	16	2	3	1		7	2		.190	.269	.321	91	-1		.879	-2	86	0	O-20(1-5-15)/3	-0.2
1885	Buf N	5	21	1	1	1	0	0	0	1		4	.048	.091	.095	-38	-3		1.000	1	226	0	/O-5(2-3-0)	-0.3
Total	7	408	1762	302	500	84	34	4	127	48		51	.284	.304	.377	118	29		.854	6	104	108	O-396(216-117-64)/S-9,3-5,2-2	1.5

DICKEY, GEORGE George Willard "Skeets" B 7.10.1915 Kensett, AR D 6.16.1976 DeWitt, AR BB/TR 6-2/180# d9.21 Mil 1943-45 b-Bill

Year	Tm Lg	G	AB	R	H	2B	3B	HR	RBI	BB-IB	HP	SO	AVG	OBP	SLG	AOPS	ABR	SB-CS	FA	FR	Rng	Thr	G at Pos	BFW
1935	Bos A	5	11	1	0	0	0	0	1	1	0	3	.000	.083	.000	-72	-3	0-0	1.000	-1	*74*	*0*	/C-4	-0.3
1936	Bos A	10	23	0	1	1	0	0	0	2	0	3	.043	.120	.087	-46	-5	0-0	.912	0	*95*	*193*	C-10	-0.4
1941	Chi A	32	55	6	11	1	0	2	8	5	0	7	.200	.267	.327	57	-4	0-0	1.000	1	*102*	*68*	C-17	-0.2
1942	Chi A	59	116	6	27	3	0	1	17	9	0	11	.233	.288	.284	63	-6	0-0	.918	-3	*98*	*54*	C-29	-0.8
1946	Chi A	37	78	8	15	1	0	0	1	12	0	13	.192	.300	.205	45	-5	0-2	1.000	2	*84*	*106*	C-30	-0.3
1947	Chi A	83	211	15	47	6	0	1	27	34	0	25	.223	.331	.265	69	-8	4-2	.985	-1	*79*	*105*	C-80	-0.5
Total	6	226	494	36	101	12	0	4	54	63	0	62	.204	.294	.253	53	-31	4-4	.974	-2	*86*	*95*	C-170	-2.5

DICKEY, BILL William Malcolm B 6.6.1907 Bastrop, LA D 11.12.1993 Little Rock, AR BL/TR 6-1.5/185# d8.15 Mil 1944-45 M1 C10 HF1954 b-George

Year	Tm Lg	G	AB	R	H	2B	3B	HR	RBI	BB-IB	HP	SO	AVG	OBP	SLG	AOPS	ABR	SB-CS	FA	FR	Rng	Thr	G at Pos	BFW
1928	NY A	10	15	1	3	1	1	0	2	0	0	2	.200	.200	.400	56	-1	0-0	1.000	-1	*71*	*102*	/C-6	-0.2
1929	NY A	130	447	60	145	30	6	10	65	14	1	16	.324	.346	.485	120	10	4-6	.979	2	*108*	*86*	*C-127	1.8
1930	NY A	109	366	55	124	25	7	5	65	21	0	14	.339	.375	.486	122	11	7-1	.977	-10	*85*	*92*	*C-101	0.8
1931	NY A	130	477	65	156	17	10	6	78	39	0	20	.327	.378	.442	122	14	2-1	**.996**	-1	*101*	*110*	*C-125	2.0
1932	†NY A	108	423	66	131	20	4	15	84	34	0	13	.310	.361	.482	123	13	2-4	.987	-2	*105*	*74*	*C-108	1.6
1933	NY A☆	130	478	58	152	24	8	14	97	47	2	14	.318	.381	.490	138	25	3-4	.993	5	*152*	*97*	*C-127	3.5
1934	NY A★	104	395	56	127	24	4	12	72	38	2	18	.322	.384	.494	134	19	0-3	.986	-0	*99*	*85*	*C-104	2.3
1935	NY A	120	448	54	125	26	6	14	81	35	6	11	.279	.339	.458	111	5	1-1	**.995**	3	*128*	*90*	*C-118	1.4
1936	†NY A★	112	423	99	153	26	8	22	107	46	3	16	.362	.428	.617	161	39	0-2	.976	3	***149***	*101*	*C-107	4.2
1937	†NY A★	140	530	87	176	35	2	29	133	73	4	22	.332	.417	.570	145	38	3-2	.991	16	***139***	*86*	*C-137	5.6
1938	†NY A★	132	454	84	142	27	4	27	115	75	2	22	.313	.412	.568	144	32	3-0	.987	6	*128*	*85*	*C-126	4.1
1939	†NY A★	128	480	98	145	23	3	24	105	77	4	37	.302	.403	.512	135	27	5-0	**.989**	14	***145***	*75*	*C-126	4.5
1940	NY A★	106	372	45	92	11	1	9	54	48	2	32	.247	.336	.355	83	-9	0-3	.994	2	*139*	*104*	*C-102	-0.2
1941	†NY A★	109	348	35	99	15	5	7	71	45	3	17	.284	.371	.417	110	5	2-1	**.994**	3	***139***	*88*	*C-104	1.3
1942	†NY A✳	82	268	28	79	13	1	2	37	26	1	11	.295	.359	.373	108	3	2-2	.976	7	***184***	*105*	C-80	1.4
1943	†NY A☆	85	242	29	85	18	2	4	33	41	0	12	.351	.445	.492	173	25	2-1	.994	4	*170*	*83*	C-71	3.4
1946	NY A★	54	134	10	35	8	0	2	10	19	1	12	.261	.357	.366	101	1	0-1	.987	7	*125*	*131*	C-39,M	1.0
Total	17	1789	6300	930	1969	343	72	202	1209	678	31	289	.313	.382	.486	128	257	36-32	.988	57	*130*	*91*	*C-1708	38.5

DICKSHOT, JOHNNY John Oscar "Ugly" (born John Oscar Dicksus) B 1.24.1910 Waukegan, IL D 11.4.1997 Waukegan, IL BR/TR 6/195# d4.16

Year	Tm Lg	G	AB	R	H	2B	3B	HR	RBI	BB-IB	HP	SO	AVG	OBP	SLG	AOPS	ABR	SB-CS	FA	FR	Rng	Thr	G at Pos	BFW
1936	Pit N	9	9	2	2	0	0	0	1	1	0	2	.222	.300	.222	42	-1	0	—	-0	0	0	/O(CF)	-0.1
1937	Pit N	82	264	42	67	8	4	3	33	26	1	36	.254	.323	.348	82	-7	0	.950	-1	94	115	O-64(58-0-6)	-1.1
1938	Pit N	29	35	3	8	0	0	0	4	8	0	5	.229	.372	.229	68	-1	3	1.000	-0	103	0	O-10(5-0-5)	-0.2
1939	NY N	10	34	3	8	0	0	0	5	5	0	3	.235	.333	.235	55	-2	0	1.000	-0	78	130	O-10(RF)	-0.3
1944	Chi A	62	162	18	41	8	5	0	15	13	1	10	.253	.313	.364	94	-2	2-0	.974	-0	95	103	O-40(35-0-5)	-0.4
1945	Chi A	130	486	74	147	19	10	4	58	48	1	41	.302	.366	.407	128	16	18-3	.971	0	97	115	*O-124(LF)	1.3
Total	6	322	990	142	273	35	19	7	116	101	3	97	.276	.345	.371	104	3	23-3	.968	-2	95	110	O-249(222-1-26)	-0.8

DIDIER, BOB Robert Daniel B 2.16.1949 Hattiesburg, MS BB/TR 6/190# d4.7 C5

Year	Tm Lg	G	AB	R	H	2B	3B	HR	RBI	BB-IB	HP	SO	AVG	OBP	SLG	AOPS	ABR	SB-CS	FA	FR	Rng	Thr	G at Pos	BFW
1969	†Atl N	114	352	30	90	16	1	0	32	34-5	0	39	.256	.321	.307	76	-10	1-3	.994	-4	86	78	*C-114	-1.0
1970	Atl N	57	168	9	25	2	1	0	7	12-4	1	11	.149	.210	.173	3	-23	1-0	.988	-5	63	101	C-57	-2.6
1971	Atl N	51	155	9	34	4	1	0	5	6-5	0	17	.219	.248	.258	41	-12	0-0	1.000	-0	126	47	C-50	-1.1
1972	Atl N	13	40	5	12	2	1	0	5	2-0	1	4	.300	.341	.400	103	0	0-0	1.000	1	67	96	C-11	0.1
1973	Det A	7	22	3	10	1	0	0	1	3-0	0	0	.455	.520	.500	177	3	0-0	1.000	2	85	96	/C-7	0.4
1974	Bos A	5	14	0	1	0	0	0	1	2-2	0	1	.071	.176	.071	-22	-2	0-0	.968	-1	44	104	/C-5	-0.3
Total	6	247	751	56	172	25	4	0	51	59-16	2	72	.229	.286	.273	55	-44	2-3	.994	-7	87	79	C-244	-4.5

DIEHL, ERNIE Ernest Guy B 10.2.1877 Cincinnati, OH D 11.6.1958 Miami, FL BR/TR 6-1/190# d5.31

Year	Tm Lg	G	AB	R	H	2B	3B	HR	RBI	BB-IB	HP	SO	AVG	OBP	SLG	AOPS	ABR	SB-CS	FA	FR	Rng	Thr	G at Pos	BFW
1903	Pit N	1	3	0	1	0	0	0	0	0	0		.333	.333	.333	87	0	0	—	-0	0	0	/O(LF)	0.0
1904	Pit N	12	37	6	6	0	0	0	4	6	2		.162	.311	.162	46	-2	3	1.000	1	158	0	/O-7(2-0-5),S-4	-0.1
1906	Bos N	3	11	1	5	0	1	0	0	0	0		.455	.455	.636	247	2	0	1.000	-0	0	0	/O-2(LF),S	0.1
1909	Bos N	1	4	1	2	1	0	0	0	0	0		.500	.500	.750	275	1	0	.800	1	485	0	/O(LF)	0.1
Total	4	17	55	8	14	1	1	0	4	6	2		.255	.349	.309	101	1	3	.944	1	170	0	/O-11(6-0-5),S-5	0.1

DIERING, CHUCK Charles Edward Allen B 2.5.1923 St.Louis, MO BR/TR 5-10/165# d4.15

Year	Tm Lg	G	AB	R	H	2B	3B	HR	RBI	BB-IB	HP	SO	AVG	OBP	SLG	AOPS	ABR	SB-CS	FA	FR	Rng	Thr	G at Pos	BFW
1947	StL N	105	74	22	16	3	1	2	11	19	1	22	.216	.383	.365	95	0	3	1.000	3	118	190	O-75(13-31-31)	0.3
1948	StL N	7	7	2	0	0	0	0	0	2	0	2	.000	.222	.000	-33	-1	1	1.000	1	102	672	/O-5(LF)	-0.1
1949	StL N	131	369	60	97	21	8	3	38	35	1	49	.263	.328	.388	87	-7	1	.987	6	**112**	100	*O-124(0-123-1)	-0.3
1950	StL N	89	204	34	51	12	0	3	18	35	0	38	.250	.360	.353	84	-3	1	.989	7	111	157	O-81(0-78-3)	0.2
1951	StL N	64	85	9	22	5	1	0	8	6	0	15	.259	.308	.341	74	-3	0-1	1.000	3	116	149	O-44(6-33-5)	-0.2
1952	NY N	41	23	2	4	1	1	0	2	4	0	3	.174	.296	.304	66	-1	0-2	1.000	2	135	137	O-36(27-4-5)	-0.1

Year	Tm Lg	G	AB	R	H	2B	3B	HR	RBI	BB-IB	HP	SO	AVG	OBP	SLG	AOPS	ABR	SB-CS	FA	FR	Rng	Thr	G at Pos	BFW
1954	Bal A	128	418	35	108	14	1	2	29	56	4	57	.258	.349	.311	89	-4	3-7	.983	10	107	**159**	*O-119(CF)	-0.2
1955	Bal A	137	371	38	95	16	2	3	31	57-1	0	45	.256	.355	.334	93	-2	5-8	.976	6	**110**	121	*O-107(2-105-0),3-34,S-12	-0.1
1956	Bal A	50	97	15	18	4	0	1	4	23-0	0	19	.186	.342	.258	65	-4	2-5	1.000	2	107	210	O-40(7-34-2)/3-2	-0.5
Total	9	752	1648	217	411	76	14	14	141	237-1	6	250	.249	.345	.338	86	-25	16-23	.987	38	111	145	O-631(60-527-47)/3-36,S-12	-1.0
DIETZ, DICK Richard Allen B 9.18.1941 Crawfordsville, IN BR/TR 6-1/195# d6.18																								
1966	SF N	13	23	1	1	0	0	0	0	0-0	1	9	.043	.083	.043	-62	-5	0-0	1.000	-1	*97*	*157*	/C-6	-0.6
1967	SF N	56	120	10	27	3	0	4	19	25-0	1	44	.225	.358	.350	106	2	0-1	.983	-1	*99*	*102*	C-43	0.3
1968	SF N	98	301	21	82	14	2	6	38	34-3	1	68	.272	.347	.392	122	9	1-1	.976	-7	*76*	*82*	C-90	0.7
1969	SF N	79	244	28	56	8	1	11	35	53-3	3	53	.230	.372	.406	120	9	0-0	.973	-1	107	96	C-73	1.2
1970	SF N★	148	493	82	148	36	2	22	107	109-10	3	106	.300	.426	.515	154	45	0-1	.984	-21	80	56	*C-139	2.9
1971	†SF N	142	453	58	114	19	0	19	72	97-8	4	86	.252	.387	.419	131	24	1-3	.982	-9	102	45	*C-135	2.1
1972	LA N	27	56	4	9	1	0	1	6	14-2	0	11	.161	.329	.232	63	-2	2-0	1.000	4	142	136	C-22	0.3
1973	Atl N	83	139	22	41	8	1	3	24	49-4	0	25	.295	.474	.432	143	13	0-0	.989	-2	121	76	1-36,C-20	1.0
Total	8	646	1829	226	478	89	6	66	301	381-30	13	402	.261	.390	.425	130	95	4-6	.980	-37	*92*	*70*	C-528/1-36	7.9
DIETZEL, ROY Leroy Louis B 1.9.1931 Baltimore, MD BR/TR 6/190# d9.2																								
1954	Was A	9	21	1	5	0	0	0	1	5	0	4	.238	.385	.238	78	0	0-0	.960	-1	110	104	/2-7,3-2	0.0
DIFANI, JAY Clarence Joseph B 12.21.1923 Crystal City, MO BR/TR 6/170# d4.23																								
1948	Was A	2	2	0	0	0	0	0	0	0	0	2	.000	.000	.000	-99	-1	0-0	—	0			H	-0.1
1949	Was A	2	1	0	1	1	0	0	0	0	0	0	1.000	1.000	2.000	699	1	0-0	1.000	0	149	0	/2	0.1
Total	2	4	3	0	1	1	0	0	0	0	0	2	.333	.333	.667	166	0	0-0	1.000	0	149	0	/2	0.0
DIFELICE, MIKE Michael William B 5.28.1969 Philadelphia, PA BR/TR 6-2/205# d9.1																								
1996	StL N	4	7	0	2	1	0	0	2	0-0	0	1	.286	.286	.429	86	0	0-0	1.000	0	52	161	/C-4	0.0
1997	StL N	93	260	16	62	10	1	4	30	19-0	3	61	.238	.297	.331	65	-14	1-1	.991	15	95	122	C-91/1	0.7
1998	TB A	84	248	17	57	12	3	3	23	15-0	1	56	.230	.274	.339	58	-16	0-0	.993	11	111	**132**	C-84	0.0
1999	TB A	51	179	21	55	11	0	6	27	8-0	3	23	.307	.346	.469	105	1	0-0	.987	4	143	108	C-51	0.7
2000	TB A	60	204	23	49	13	1	6	19	12-0	0	40	.240	.280	.402	71	-10	0-0	.980	5	94	119	C-59	-0.1
2001	TB A	48	149	13	31	5	1	2	9	8-0	3	39	.208	.259	.295	47	-12	1-1	.982	4	113	123	C-48	-0.5
	Ari N	12	21	1	1	0	0	0	1	0-0	1	10	.048	.091	.048	-59	-5	0-0	.982	0	383	158	C-12	-0.4
2002	†StL N	70	174	17	40	11	0	4	19	17-3	1	42	.230	.297	.362	79	-6	0-0	.991	5	124	68	C-61	0.2
2003	KC A	62	189	29	48	16	1	3	25	9-0	4	30	.254	.299	.397	73	-7	1-0	.994	5	78	127	C-58/D-2	0.2
Total	8	484	1431	137	345	79	7	28	155	88-3	16	302	.241	.290	.365	69	-69	3-2	.989	49	111	117	C-468/D-2,1	0.8
DIGNAN, STEVE Stephen E. B 4.16.1859 Boston, MA D 7.11.1881 Boston, MA d6.1																								
1880	Bos N	8	34	4	11	1	0	0	4	0		3	.324	.324	.353	133	1		.684	-0	148	501	/O-8(1-0-7)	0.1
	Wor N	3	10	1	3	0	1	0	2	0		1	.300	.300	.500	153	0		.750	-1	0	0	/O-3(CF)	0.0
	Year	11	44	5	14	1	1	0	6	0		4	.318	.318	.386	137	1		.696	-1	116	393	O-11(1-3-7)	0.1
DILLARD, DON David Donald B 1.8.1937 Greenville, SC BL/TR 6-1/200# d4.24																								
1959	Cle A	10	10	0	4	0	0	0	1	0-0	0	2	.400	.400	.400	125	0	0-0	—	0			H	0.0
1960	Cle A	6	7	0	1	0	0	0	0	1-0	0	3	.143	.250	.143	9	-1	0-0	—	-0	0	0	/O(RF)	-0.1
1961	Cle A	74	147	27	40	5	0	7	17	15-1	0	28	.272	.340	.449	112	2	0-0	1.000	-0	107	0	O-39(14-24-1)	0.1
1962	Cle A	95	174	22	40	5	1	5	14	11-1	0	25	.230	.276	.356	71	-8	0-1	.965	-3	85	62	O-50(28-20-4)	-1.2
1963	Mil N	67	119	9	28	6	4	1	12	5-0	1	21	.235	.270	.378	86	-3	0-2	.951	2	88	356	O-30(24-5-1)	-0.3
1965	Mil N	20	19	1	3	0	0	1	3	0-0	0	6	.158	.158	.316	30	-2	0-0	—	0	0	0	/O(LF)	-0.2
Total	6	272	476	59	116	16	5	14	47	32-2	1	85	.244	.292	.387	86	-12	0-3	.976	-1	93	120	O-121(67-49-7)	-1.7
DILLARD, PAT Robert Lee B 6.12.1873 Chattanooga, TN D 7.22.1907 Denver, CO BL/TR 6/180# d4.21																								
1900	StL N	57	183	24	42	5	2	0	12	13	1		.230	.284	.279	56	-11	7	.942	-3	136	0	O-26(0-20-6),3-21/S-3	-1.4
DILLARD, STEVE Stephen Bradley B 2.8.1951 Memphis, TN BR/TR 6-1/180# d9.28																								
1975	Bos A	1	5	2	2	0	0	0	0	0-0	0	0	.400	.400	.400	117	0	1-0	1.000	1	136	147	/2	0.1
1976	Bos A	57	167	22	46	14	0	1	15	17-1	0	20	.275	.341	.377	99	0	6-4	.918	-7	102	168	3-18,2-17,S-12/D-7	-0.5
1977	Bos A	66	141	22	34	7	0	1	13	7-0	0	13	.241	.270	.312	54	-9	4-3	.967	-1	99	97	2-45/S-9,D-6	-0.7
1978	Det A	56	130	21	29	5	2	0	7	6-0	0	11	.223	.257	.292	53	-9	1-2	.958	-0	98	128	2-41/D-4	-0.8
1979	Chi N	89	166	31	47	6	1	5	24	17-4	1	24	.283	.351	.422	101	0	1-0	.988	5	98	104	2-60/3-9	0.8
1980	Chi N	100	244	31	55	8	1	4	27	20-2	1	54	.225	.285	.316	63	-12	2-2	.908	-2	111	95	3-51,2-38/S-2	-1.3
1981	Chi N	53	119	18	26	7	1	2	11	8-0	0	20	.218	.268	.345	70	-5	0-0	.974	4	118	122	2-32/3-7,S-2	0.0
1982	Chi A	16	41	1	7	3	1	0	5	1-0	0	5	.171	.190	.293	30	-4	0-1	.959	2	118	57	2-16	-0.2
Total	8	438	1013	148	246	50	6	13	102	76-7	2	147	.243	.295	.343	73	-39	15-12	.973	2	101	100	2-250/3-85,S-25,D-17	-2.6
DILLHOEFER, PICKLES William Martin B 10.13.1894 Cleveland, OH D 2.23.1922 St.Louis, MO BR/TR 5-7/154# d4.16 Mil 1918																								
1917	Chi N	42	95	3	12	1	1	0	8	2	0	9	.126	.144	.158	-7	-12	1	.985	6	*101*	*132*	C-37	-0.4
1918	Phi N	8	11	0	1	0	0	0	0	1	0	1	.091	.167	.091	-19	-2	2	.923	-1	*93*	*92*	/C-6	-0.2
1919	StL N	45	108	11	23	3	2	0	12	8	0	6	.213	.267	.278	68	-4	5	.967	-2	*99*	*92*	C-39	-0.5
1920	StL N	76	224	26	59	8	3	0	13	13	0	7	.263	.304	.326	84	-5	2-1	.953	-5	*90*	*86*	C-74	-0.4
1921	StL N	76	162	19	39	4	4	0	15	11	0	7	.241	.289	.315	61	-10	2-1	.953	-0	*100*	*105*	C-69	-0.6
Total	5	247	600	59	134	16	10	0	48	35	0	30	.223	.266	.283	58	-33	12-2	.961	-2	*96*	*100*	C-225	-2.1
DILLINGER, BOB Robert Bernard "Duke" B 9.17.1918 Glendale, CA BR/TR 5-11.5/170# d4.16																								
1946	StL A	83	225	33	63	6	3	0	11	19	2	32	.280	.341	.333	85	-4	8-1	.922	-3	94	93	3-54/S	-0.7
1947	StL A	137	571	70	168	23	6	3	37	56	4	38	.294	.361	.371	102	2	**34**-13	.958	5	102	83	*3-137	1.0
1948	StL A	153	644	110	**207**	34	10	2	44	65	1	34	.321	.385	.415	110	9	**28**-11	.955	-16	83	96	*3-153	-0.5
1949	StL A★	137	544	68	176	22	13	1	51	51	3	40	.324	.385	.417	108	5	**20**-14	.938	-18	83	65	*3-133	-1.3
1950	Phi A	84	356	55	110	21	9	3	41	31	1	20	.309	.366	.444	109	3	5-3	.957	-1	100	95	3-84	0.2
	Pit N	58	222	23	64	8	2	1	9	13	0	22	.288	.328	.356	77	-8	4	.957	1	101	110	3-51	-0.7
1951	Pit N	12	43	3	10	3	0	0	0	1	0	0	.233	.250	.302	47	-3	2-0	.963	-1	85	0	3-10	-0.4
	Chi A	89	299	39	90	6	4	0	20	15	1	17	.301	.337	.348	87	-7	5-5	.930	-6	94	82	3-70	-1.4
Total	6	753	2904	401	888	123	47	10	213	251	12	203	.306	.363	.391	100	-3	106-47	.948	-40	92	86	3-692/S	-3.8
DILLON, POP Frank Edward B 10.17.1873 Normal, IL D 9.12.1931 Pasadena, CA BL/TR 6-1/185# d9.8																								
1899	Pit N	30	121	21	31	5	0	0	20	5	0		.256	.286	.298	60	-7	5	.988	1	111	89	1-30	-0.5
1900	Pit N	5	18	3	2	1	0	0	1	0	0		.111	.111	.167	-24	-3	0	.981	1	189	86	/1-5	-0.2
1901	Det A	74	281	40	81	14	6	1	42	15	0		.288	.324	.391	94	-3	14	.979	3	114	135	1-74	-0.2
1902	Det A	66	243	21	50	6	3	0	22	16	0		.206	.255	.255	41	-20	2	.976	5	140	111	1-66	-1.6
	Bal A	2	7	1	2	0	1	0	0	2	0		.286	.444	.571	173	1	0	.960	0	159	0	/1-2	0.1
	Year	68	250	22	52	6	4	0	22	18	0		.208	.261	.264	45	-19	2	.975	5	141	107	1-68	-1.5
1904	Bro N	135	511	60	132	18	6	0	31	40	1		.258	.313	.317	97	-1	13	.982	4	112	96	*1-134	0.0
Total	5	312	1181	146	298	44	16	1	116	78	1		.252	.299	.319	79	-33	34	.980	14	120	107	1-311	-2.4
DILLON, JOHN John d5.8 b-Packy																								
1875	RS NA	1	1	0	0	0	0	0	0	0		0	.000	.000	.000	-99	0	0-0	—	-0	0	0	/S	0.0
DILLON, PACKY Packard Andrew B St.Louis, MO D 1.8.1890 Guelph, ON, CAN d5.4 b-John																								
1875	RS NA	3	13	1	3	1	0	0	1	0		0	.231	.231	.308	94	0	0-0	.923	-2			/C-3	-0.2
DILONE, MIGUEL Miguel Angel (Reyes) B 11.1.1954 Santiago, D.R. BB/TR 6/160# d9.2																								
1974	Pit N	12	2	3	0	0	0	0	0	1-0	0	0	.000	.333	.000	-1	0	2-0	1.000	0	188	0	/O-2(0-1-1)	0.0
1975	Pit N	18	6	8	0	0	0	0	0	0-0	0	1	.000	.000	.000	-99	-2	2-2	1.000	-0	103	0	/O-2(CF)	-0.2
1976	Pit N	16	17	7	4	0	0	0	0	0-0	0	0	.235	.235	.235	34	-2	5-1	1.000	1	146	0	/O-3(1-2-0)	0.0
1977	Pit N	29	44	5	6	0	0	0	0	2-0	0	3	.136	.174	.136	-15	-7	12-0	1.000	0	95	152	O-17(9-7-2)	-0.5
1978	Oak A	135	258	34	59	8	0	1	14	23-0	1	30	.229	.294	.271	63	-12	50-23	.985	4	117	59	O-99(47-25-36),D-11/3-3	-0.9
1979	Oak A	30	91	15	17	1	2	1	6	6-0	0	7	.187	.237	.275	40	-8	6-5	.959	-2	99	0	O-25(5-0-20)	-1.2
	Chi N	43	36	14	11	0	0	0	1	2-0	0	5	.306	.342	.306	71	-1	15-5	1.000	-0	102	0	O-22(4-18-0)	0.0
1980	Cle A	132	528	82	180	30	9	0	40	28-1	2	45	.341	.375	.432	120	14	61-18	.973	-1	102	85	*O-118(90-23-13),D-11	1.6

Year	Tm Lg	G	AB	R	H	2B	3B	HR	RBI	BB-IB	HP	SO	AVG	OBP	SLG	AOPS	ABR	SB-CS	FA	FR	Rng	Thr	G at Pos	BFW
1981	Cle A	72	269	33	78	5	5	0	19	18-1	0	28	.290	.334	.346	98	-2	29-10	.971	4	107	184	O-56(LF),D-11	0.3
1982	Cle A	104	379	50	89	12	3	3	25	25-0	2	36	.235	.286	.306	63	-20	33-5	.964	-3	95	55	O-97(96-1-0)/D	-2.2
1983	Cle A	32	68	15	13	3	1	0	7	10-0	0	5	.191	.295	.265	53	-4	5-1	1.000	1	116	0	O-19(LF)	-0.4
	Chi A	4	3	1	0	0	0	0	0	0-0	0	0	.000	.000	.000	-96	-1	1-0	1.000	0	108	0	/O-2(CF),D-2	-0.1
	Year	36	71	16	13	3	1	0	7	10-0	0	5	.183	.284	.254	47	-5	6-1	1.000	1	116	0	O-21(19-2-0)/D-2	-0.5
	Pit N	7	0	1	0	0	0	0	0	0-0	0	0	—	—	—	—	0	2-0	—	0			/R	0.0
1984	Mon N	88	169	28	47	8	2	1	10	17-0	1	18	.278	.346	.367	106	1	27-2	.987	1	113	37	O-41(LF)	0.7
1985	Mon N	51	84	10	16	0	2	0	6	6-0	0	11	.190	.242	.238	38	-8	7-3	.974	-0	101	96	O-22(8-13-2)	-0.8
	SD N	27	46	8	10	0	1	0	1	4-0	0	8	.217	.280	.261	53	-3	10-3	.917	-1	86	145	O-14(4-9-1)	-0.3
	Year	78	130	18	26	0	3	0	7	10-0	0	19	.200	.255	.246	43	-11	17-6	.952	-1	95	115	O-36(12-22-3)	-1.1
Total	12	800	2000	314	530	67	25	6	129	142-2	6	197	.265	.315	.333	81	-55	267-78	.975	4	105	76	O-539(380-103-75)/D-36,3-3	-4.0
DiMAGGIO, DOM Dominic Paul "The Little Professor" B 2.12.1917 San Francisco, CA BR/TR 5-9/168# d4.16 Mil 1943-45 b-Joe b-Vince																								
1940	Bos A	108	418	81	126	32	6	8	46	41	2	46	.301	.367	.464	109	6	7-6	.977	6	96	208	O-94(11-59-26)	0.7
1941	Bos A★	144	584	117	165	37	6	8	58	90	**7**	57	.283	.385	.408	107	10	13-6	.964	4	102	137	*O-144(CF)	1.0
1942	Bos A☆	151	622	110	178	36	8	14	48	70	6	52	.286	.364	.437	121	17	16-10	.987	13	107	**169**	*O-151(CF)	2.7
1946	†Bos A★	142	534	85	169	24	7	7	73	66	1	58	.316	.393	.427	122	18	10-6	.985	2	104	94	*O-142(CF)	1.7
1947	Bos A	136	513	75	145	21	5	8	71	74	3	62	.283	.376	.390	105	6	10-6	.977	15	109	**213**	*O-134(CF)	1.8
1948	Bos A	**155**	648	127	185	40	4	9	87	101	2	58	.285	.383	.401	104	7	10-2	.981	9	109	98	*O-155(CF)	1.2
1949	Bos A★	145	605	126	186	34	5	8	60	96	2	55	.307	.404	.420	110	12	9-7	.977	6	106	130	*O-144(CF)	1.3
1950	Bos A★	141	588	**131**	193	30	**11**	7	70	82	4	68	.328	.414	.452	111	12	**15**-4	.983	3	101	126	*O-140(CF)	1.3
1951	Bos A★	146	639	**113**	189	34	4	12	72	73	2	53	.296	.370	.418	103	3	4-7	.973	-8	92	99	*O-146(CF)	-1.0
1952	Bos A★	128	486	81	143	20	1	6	33	57	2	61	.294	.371	.377	100	2	6-8	.975	-4	91	130	*O-123(CF)	-0.6
1953	Bos A	3	3	0	1	0	0	0	0	0	0	1	.333	.333	.333	76	0	0-0	—	0			H	0.0
Total	11	1399	5640	1046	1680	308	57	87	618	750	31	571	.298	.383	.419	109	93	100-62	.978	46	102	138	*O-1373(11-1338-26)	10.1
DiMAGGIO, JOE Joseph Paul "Joltin' Joe" or "The Yankee Clipper" B 11.25.1914 Martinez, CA D 3.8.1999 Hollywood, FL BR/TR 6-2/193# d5.3 Mil 1943-45 C2 HF1955 b-Dom b-Vince																								
1936	†NY A★	138	637	132	206	44	**15**	29	125	24	4	39	.323	.352	.576	130	23	4-0	.978	8	100	**171**	*O-138(66-55-18)	2.2
1937	†NY A★	151	621	**151**	215	35	15	**46**	167	64	5	37	.346	.412	**.673**	168	60	3-0	.962	6	102	148	*O-150(CF)	5.7
1938	†NY A★	145	599	129	194	32	13	32	140	59	2	21	.324	.386	.581	140	33	6-1	.963	-2	92	143	*O-145(CF)	2.6
1939	†NY A★	120	462	108	176	32	6	30	126	52	4	20	**.381**	.448	.671	**185**	59	3-0	.986	5	102	129	*O-117(CF)	**5.5**
1940	NY A★	132	508	93	179	28	9	31	133	61	3	30	**.352**	.425	.626	**176**	56	1-2	.978	-4	101	51	*O-130(CF)	**4.5**
1941	†NY A★	139	541	122	193	43	11	30	**125**	76	4	13	.357	.440	.643	186	68	4-2	.978	6	102	138	*O-139(CF)	6.6
1942	†NY A★	**154**	610	123	186	29	13	21	114	68	2	36	.305	.376	.498	148	37	4-2	.981	-3	98	88	*O-154(CF)	3.1
1946	NY A☆	132	503	81	146	20	8	25	95	59	2	24	.290	.367	.511	142	26	1-0	.982	2	95	**179**	*O-131(CF)	2.6
1947	†NY A★	141	534	97	168	31	10	20	97	64	3	32	.315	.391	.522	154	38	3-0	**.997**	-14	87	23	*O-139(CF)	2.2
1948	NY A★	153	594	110	190	26	11	**39**	**155**	67	**8**	30	.320	.396	.598	164	50	1-1	.972	1	107	67	*O-152(CF)	4.5
1949	†NY A★	76	272	58	94	14	6	14	67	55	2	18	.346	.459	.596	178	32	0-1	.985	-4	99	20	O-76(CF)	2.5
1950	†NY A★	139	525	114	158	33	10	32	122	80	1	33	.301	.394	**.585**	152	39	0-0	.976	-4	99	79	*O-137(CF)/1	3.0
1951	†NY A☆	116	415	72	109	22	4	12	71	61	6	36	.263	.365	.422	117	11	0-0	.990	1	100	103	*O-113(CF)	0.8
Total	13	1736	6821	1390	2214	389	131	361	1537	790	46	369	.325	.398	.579	156	532	30-9	.978	-1	99	106	*O-1721(66-1638-18)/1	45.8
DiMAGGIO, VINCE Vincent Paul B 9.6.1912 Martinez, CA D 10.3.1986 N.Hollywood, CA BR/TR 5-11/183# d4.19 b-Dom b-Joe																								
1937	Bos N	132	493	56	126	18	4	13	69	39	1	111	.256	.311	.387	98	-4	8	.982	8	99	**180**	*O-130(0-129-1)	0.1
1938	Bos N	150	540	71	123	28	3	14	61	65	2	134	.228	.313	.369	96	-3	11	.973	10	109	148	*O-149(CF)/2	0.4
1939	Cin N	8	14	1	1	1	0	0	2	2	0	10	.071	.188	.143	-10	-2	0	1.000	1	100	275	/O-7(3-3-1)	-0.2
1940	Cin N	2	4	2	1	0	0	0	0	1	0	0	.250	.400	.250	82	0	0	1.000	-0	103	0	/O(RF)	0.0
	Pit N	110	356	59	103	26	0	19	54	37	5	83	.289	.364	.522	143	21	11	.979	1	94	166	*O-108(1-103-4)	1.9
	Year	112	360	61	104	26	0	19	54	38	5	83	.289	.365	.519	142	21	11	.979	1	94	**164**	*O-109(1-103-5)	1.9
1941	Pit N	151	528	73	141	27	5	21	100	68	3	100	.267	.354	.456	128	19	10	.976	2	104	91	*O-151(CF)	1.7
1942	Pit N	143	496	57	118	22	3	15	75	52	1	87	.238	.311	.385	101	-1	10	.978	12	111	151	*O-138(CF)	0.9
1943	Pit N★	**157**	580	64	144	41	2	15	88	70	0	126	.248	.329	.403	107	6	11	.985	12	**113**	110	*O-156(CF)/S	1.4
1944	Pit N★	109	342	41	82	20	4	9	50	33	0	83	.240	.307	.401	94	-3	6	.984	-1	97	100	*O-101(CF)/3	-0.7
1945	Phi N	127	452	64	116	25	3	19	84	43	0	91	.257	.321	.451	117	8	12	.994	9	105	165	*O-121(CF)	1.3
1946	Phi N	6	19	1	4	1	0	0	1	0	0	7	.211	.211	.263	35	-2	0	1.000	-0	96	0	/O-6(CF)	-0.2
	NY N	15	25	2	0	0	0	0	0	2	0	5	.000	.074	.000	-78	-6	0	.967	0	125	0	O-13(CF)	-0.6
	Year	21	44	3	4	1	0	0	1	2	0	12	.091	.130	.114	-31	-8	0	.975	-0	116	0	O-19(CF)	-0.8
Total	10	1110	3849	491	959	209	24	125	584	412	12	837	.249	.324	.413	108	33	79	.981	52	105	137	*O-1081(4-1070-7)/3S2	6.0
DIMMEL, MIKE Michael Wayne B 10.16.1954 Albert Lea, MN BR/TR 6/180# d9.2																								
1977	Bal A	25	5	8	0	0	0	0	0	0-0	0	1	.000	.000	.000	-99	-1	1-0	1.000	2	151	314	O-23(0-1-22)	0.0
1978	Bal A	8	0	2	0	0	0	0	0	0-0	0	0	—	—	—	—	0	0-1	.667	-0	89	0	/O-7(1-1-5)	-0.1
1979	StL N	6	3	1	1	0	0	0	0	0-0	0	0	.333	.333	.333	82	0	0-1	1.000	-0	105	0	/O-5(5-1-0)	-0.1
Total	3	39	8	11	1	0	0	0	0	0-0	0	1	.125	.125	.125	-33	-1	1-2	.952	1	132	202	/O-35(6-3-27)	-0.2
DINEEN, KERRY Kerry Michael B 7.1.1952 Englewood, NJ BL/TL 5-11/165# d6.14																								
1975	NY A	7	22	3	8	1	0	0	1	2-0	0	1	.364	.417	.409	136	1	0-0	1.000	1	128	0	/O-7(CF)	0.1
1976	NY A	4	7	0	2	0	0	0	1	1-0	0	2	.286	.375	.286	96	0	1-1	.900	0	128	0	/O-4(0-2-2)	0.0
1978	Phi N	5	8	0	2	1	0	0	0	1-0	0	0	.250	.333	.375	97	0	0-0	1.000	-0	58	0	/O(LF)	0.0
Total	3	16	37	3	12	2	0	0	2	4-0	0	3	.324	.390	.378	120	1	1-1	.967	1	121	0	/O-12(1-9-2)	0.1
DINGES, VANCE Vance George B 5.29.1915 Elizabeth, NJ D 10.4.1990 Harrisonburg, VA BL/TL 6-2/175# d4.17																								
1945	Phi N	109	397	46	114	15	4	1	36	35	1	17	.287	.346	.353	97	-1	5	.986	2	98	195	O-65(16-18-33),1-42	-0.5
1946	Phi N	50	104	7	32	5	1	1	10	9	0	12	.308	.363	.404	121	3	2	.985	1	115	89	1-26/O(LF)	0.3
Total	2	159	501	53	146	20	5	2	46	44	1	29	.291	.350	.363	102	2	7	.986	3	94	96	/1-68,O-66(17-18-33)	-0.2
DiPIETRO, BOB Robert Louis Paul B 9.1.1927 San Francisco, CA BR/TR 5-11/185# d9.23																								
1951	Bos A	4	11	0	1	0	0	0	0	1	0	1	.091	.167	.091	-26	-2	0-0	.833	0	71	501	/O-3(RF)	-0.2
DiSARCINA, GARY Gary Thomas B 11.19.1967 Malden, MA BR/TR 6-1/178# d9.23																								
1989	Cal A	2	0	0	0	0	0	0	0	0-0	0	0	—	—	—	—	0	0-0	—	-0	0	0	/S	0.0
1990	Cal A	18	57	8	8	1	1	0	0	3-0	0	10	.140	.183	.193	5	-8	1-0	.940	0	113	82	S-14/2-3	-0.6
1991	Cal A	18	57	5	12	2	0	0	3	3-0	2	4	.211	.274	.246	45	-4	0-0	.915	-4	89	33	S-10/2-7,3-2	-0.8
1992	Cal A	157	518	48	128	19	0	3	42	20-0	7	50	.247	.283	.301	64	-26	9-7	.967	3	99	108	*S-157	-1.1
1993	Cal A	126	416	44	99	20	1	3	45	15-0	6	38	.238	.273	.313	56	-27	5-7	.975	-8	96	98	*S-126	-2.6
1994	Cal A	112	389	53	101	14	2	3	33	18-0	2	28	.260	.294	.329	60	-24	3-7	.983	3	104	96	*S-110	-1.3
1995	Cal A★	99	362	61	111	28	6	5	41	20-0	2	25	.307	.344	.459	108	4	7-4	.986	-11	92	79	S-98	0.1
1996	Cal A	150	536	62	137	26	4	5	48	21-0	2	36	.256	.286	.347	59	-35	2-1	.971	7	106	91	*S-150	-1.5
1997	Ana A	154	549	52	135	28	2	4	47	17-0	4	29	.246	.271	.326	56	-37	7-8	.977	-13	95	87	*S-153	-3.7
1998	Ana A	157	551	73	158	39	3	3	56	21-0	8	51	.287	.321	.385	82	-14	11-7	.980	-6	94	101	*S-157	-0.7
1999	Ana A	81	271	32	62	7	1	1	29	15-0	2	32	.229	.273	.273	41	-25	2-2	.963	2	104	111	S-81	-1.6
2000	Ana A	12	38	6	15	2	0	1	11	1-0	1	3	.395	.425	.526	135	2	0-1	.934	6	139	154	S-12	0.7
Total	12	1086	3744	444	966	186	20	28	355	154-0	36	306	.258	.292	.341	66	-194	47-44	.973	-21	99	96	*S-1069/2-10,3-2	-13.1
DISTEFANO, BENNY Benito James B 1.23.1962 Brooklyn, NY BL/TL 6-1/195# d5.18																								
1984	Pit N	45	78	10	13	1	2	3	9	5-1	1	13	.167	.226	.346	59	-5	0-1	.946	4	135	224	O-20(7-0-15),1-17	-0.3
1986	Pit N	31	39	3	7	1	0	1	5	1-0	0	5	.179	.190	.282	31	-4	0-0	1.000	0	136	0	/O-9(RF),1	-0.4
1988	Pit N	16	29	6	10	3	1	1	6	3-1	0	4	.345	.394	.621	194	3	0-0	1.000	0	100	34	/1-5,O-2(RF)	0.3
1989	Pit N	96	154	12	38	8	0	2	15	17-3	3	30	.247	.333	.338	96	0	1-0	.981	-4	73	93	1-48/C-3,O(RF)	-0.7
1992	Hou N	52	60	4	14	0	2	0	7	5-1	1	14	.233	.303	.300	75	-2	0-0	1.000	2	141	318	O-12(7-0-5)/1-6	-0.1
Total	5	240	360	35	82	13	5	7	42	31-6	5	66	.228	.296	.350	85	-8	1-1	.985	1	91	95	/1-77,O-44(14-0-32),C-3	-1.2
DISTEL, DUTCH George Adam B 4.15.1896 Madison, IN D 2.12.1967 Madison, IN BR/TR 5-9/165# d6.21																								
1918	StL N	8	17	3	3	1	1	0	1	2	0	3	.176	.263	.353	90	0	0	.900	-1	118	63	/2-5,S-2,O(RF)	-0.2
DITTMER, JACK John Douglas B 1.10.1928 Elkader, IA BL/TR 6-1/175# d6.17																								
1952	Bos N	93	326	26	63	7	2	7	41	26	1	26	.193	.255	.291	53	-22	1-0	.982	-1	100	94	2-90	-1.8

Year	Tm Lg	G	AB	R	H	2B	3B	HR	RBI	BB-IB	HP	SO	AVG	OBP	SLG	AOPS	ABR	SB-CS	FA	FR	Rng	Thr	G at Pos	BFW
1953	Mil N	138	504	54	134	22	1	9	63	18	1	35	.266	.293	.367	75	-20	1-0	.965	-23	88	105	*2-138	-3.2
1954	Mil N	66	192	22	47	8	0	6	20	19	3	17	.245	.319	.380	88	-4	0-1	.977	-2	100	89	2-55	-0.3
1955	Mil N	38	72	4	9	1	1	1	4	4-1	0	15	.125	.171	.208	0	-11	0-0	.977	-1	96	80	2-28	-1.0
1956	Mil N	44	102	8	25	4	0	1	6	8-0	0	8	.245	.300	.314	69	-4	0-0	.979	0	106	91	2-42	-0.2
1957	Det A	16	22	3	5	1	0	0	2	2-1	0	1	.227	.292	.273	54	-1	0-0	1.000	-1	63	0	/3-3,2	-0.2
Total	6	395	1218	117	283	43	4	24	136	77-2	5	102	.232	.280	.333	66	-62	2-1	.974	-27	95	97	2-354/3-3	-6.7
DIVIS, MOXIE Edward George B 1.16.1894 Cleveland, OH D 12.19.1955 Lakewood, OH d8.4																								
1916	Phi A	3	6	0	1	0	0	0	1	0	0	2	.167	.167	.167	0	-1	0	1.000	1	46	720	/O(LF)	0.0
DIXON, LEO Leo Moses B 9.4.1894 Chicago, IL D 4.11.1984 Chicago, IL BR/TR 5-11/170# d4.14																								
1925	StL A	76	205	27	46	11	1	1	19	24	4	42	.224	.318	.302	55	-14	3-2	.981	4	*91*	*153*	C-75	-0.6
1926	StL A	33	89	7	17	3	1	0	8	11	2	14	.191	.294	.247	40	-8	1-4	.977	3	*135*	*137*	C-33	-0.4
1927	StL A	36	103	6	20	3	1	0	12	7	0	6	.194	.245	.243	26	-12	0-1	.937	1	*118*	*142*	C-35	-0.9
1929	Cin N	14	30	0	5	2	0	0	2	3	0	7	.167	.242	.233	19	-4	0	1.000	2	*113*	*121*	C-14	-0.1
Total	4	159	427	40	88	19	3	1	41	45	6	69	.206	.291	.272	43	-38	4-7	.971	9	*109*	*144*	C-157	-2.0
DOBBEK, DAN Daniel John B 12.6.1934 Ontonagon, MI BL/TR 6/195# d9.9																								
1959	Was A	16	60	8	15	1	2	1	5	5-1	0	13	.250	.308	.383	89	-1	0-0	1.000	-0	99	109	O-16(RF)	-0.2
1960	Was A	110	248	32	54	8	2	10	30	35-7	1	41	.218	.316	.387	90	-4	4-3	.973	-0	99	128	O-78(12-58-17)	-0.7
1961	Min A	72	125	12	21	3	1	4	14	13-1	2	18	.168	.255	.304	47	-10	1-2	.985	1	115	51	O-48(32-10-13)	-1.1
Total	3	198	433	52	90	12	5	15	49	53-9	3	72	.208	.297	.363	77	-15	5-5	.980	1	103	105	O-142(44-68-46)	-2.0
DOBBS, JOHN John Gordon B 6.3.1875 Chattanooga, TN D 9.9.1934 Charlotte, NC BL/TR 5-9.5/170# d4.20																								
1901	Cin N	109	435	71	119	17	4	2	27	36	6		.274	.338	.345	105	4	19	.948	-6	89	117	*O-100(CF)/3-8	-0.6
1902	Cin N	63	256	39	76	7	3	1	16	19	1		.297	.348	.359	108	2	7	.963	6	121	86	O-63(LF)	0.5
	Chi N	59	235	31	71	8	2	0	35	18	0		.302	.352	.353	121	6	3	.977	2	106	332	O-59(CF)	0.5
	Year	122	491	70	147	15	5	1	51	37	1		.299	.350	.356	114	8	10	.970	8	114	198	*O-122(63-59-0)	1.0
1903	Chi N	16	61	8	14	1	1	0	4	7	2		.230	.329	.279	76	-2	0	1.000	0	46	0	O-16(CF)	-0.2
	Bro N	111	414	61	98	15	7	2	59	48	5		.237	.323	.321	86	-6	23	.966	2	72	109	*O-110(CF)	-1.0
	Year	127	475	69	112	16	8	2	63	55	7		.236	.324	.316	85	-8	23	.970	2	69	95	*O-126(CF)	-1.2
1904	Bro N	101	363	36	90	16	2	0	30	28	1		.248	.304	.303	90	-4	11	.936	-2	54	0	O-92(2-86-3)/2-2,S-2	-1.0
1905	Bro N	123	460	59	117	21	4	2	36	31	2		.254	.304	.330	96	-2	15	.938	-5	72	24	*O-123(CF)	-1.3
Total	5	582	2224	305	585	85	23	7	207	187	17		.263	.325	.331	98	-2	78	.954	-3	81	92	O-563(65-494-3)/3-8,S-2,2-2	-3.1
DOBY, LARRY Lawrence Eugene B 12.13.1923 Camden, SC D 6.18.2003 Montclair, NJ BL/TR 6-1/182# d7.5 M1 C7 HF1998																								
1947	Cle A	29	32	3	5	1	0	0	2	1	0	11	.156	.182	.188	3	-4	0-0	1.000	-1	111	0	/2-4,1S	-0.5
1948	†Cle A	121	439	83	132	23	9	14	66	54	5	77	.301	.384	.490	135	21	9-9	.955	-3	94	128	*O-114(0-68-46)	1.3
1949	Cle A★	147	547	106	153	25	3	24	85	91	**7**	90	.280	.389	.468	129	23	10-9	.976	-11	92	61	*O-147(0-117-39)	0.7
1950	Cle A★	142	503	110	164	25	5	25	102	98	6	71	.326	**.442**	.545	**156**	**47**	8-6	.987	-9	99	17	*O-140(CF)	3.2
1951	Cle A★	134	447	84	132	27	5	20	69	101	3	81	.295	.428	.512	**163**	45	4-1	.977	-2	98	99	*O-132(CF)	3.8
1952	Cle A★	140	519	**104**	143	26	8	**32**	104	90	0	111	.276	.383	**.541**	**166**	46	5-2	.986	1	101	100	*O-136(CF)	4.4
1953	Cle A★	149	513	92	135	18	5	29	102	96	6	121	.263	.385	.487	138	29	3-2	.984	-10	90	81	*O-146(CF)	1.2
1954	†Cle A★	153	577	94	157	18	4	**32**	**126**	85	3	94	.272	.364	.484	130	23	3-1	.995	1	100	98	*O-153(CF)	1.8
1955	Cle A☆	131	491	91	143	17	5	26	75	61-8	2	100	.291	.369	.505	129	19	2-0	.994	-6	93	80	*O-129(CF)	0.8
1956	Chi A	140	504	89	135	22	3	24	102	102-6	4	105	.268	.392	.466	125	21	0-1	.987	-3	103	43	*O-137(CF)	1.1
1957	Chi A	119	416	57	120	27	2	14	79	56-3	2	79	.288	.373	.464	127	17	2-3	.985	-9	93	39	*O-110(CF)	0.3
1958	Cle A	89	247	41	70	10	1	13	45	26-2	0	49	.283	.348	.490	132	10	0-2	1.000	1	101	148	O-68(8-59-1)	0.8
1959	Det A	18	55	5	12	3	1	0	4	8-0	0	9	.218	.313	.309	69	-2	0-0	.960	-0	92	125	O-16(11-0-5)	-0.3
	Chi A	21	58	1	14	1	1	0	9	2-0	0	13	.241	.267	.293	54	-4	1-0	.955	-1	88	144	O-12(1-2-10)/1-2	-0.5
	Year	39	113	6	26	4	2	0	13	10-0	0	22	.230	.290	.301	62	-6	1-0	.957	-1	90	134	O-28(12-2-15)/1-2	-0.8
Total	13	1533	5348	960	1515	243	52	253	970	871-19	38	1011	.283	.386	.490	137	291	47-36	.983	-50	96	79	*O-1440(20-1329-101)/2-4,1-3,S	18.1
DODD, ONA Ona Melvin. B 10.14.1886 Springtown, TX D 12.17.1956 Carter, OK BR/TR 5-8/150# d7.26																								
1912	Pit N	5	9	0	0	0	0	0	1	1	0	3	.000	.100	.000	-73	-2	0	1.000	0	109	0	/3-4,2	-0.2
DODD, TOM Thomas Marion B 8.15.1958 Portland, OR BR/TR 6/190# d7.25																								
1986	Bal A	8	13	1	3	0	0	1	2	2-0	1	2	.231	.375	.462	128	1	0-0	—	-0	0	0	/3D	0.0
DODGE, JOHN John Lewis B 4.27.1889 Bolivar, TN D 6.19.1916 Mobile, AL BR/TR 5-11.5/165# d8.29																								
1912	Phi N	30	92	3	11	1	0	0	3	4	0	11	.120	.156	.130	-20	-15	2	1.000	4	119	177	3-23/2-5,S	-1.1
1913	Phi N	3	3	0	1	0	0	0	0	2	0	0	.333	.600	.333	164	1	0	1.000	-0	85	0	/S-3	0.0
	Cin N	94	323	35	78	8	8	4	45	10	2	34	.241	.269	.353	77	-12	11-7	.908	3	108	86	3-91	-0.7
	Year	97	326	35	79	8	8	4	45	12	2	34	.242	.274	.353	78	-11	11-7	.908	2	108	86	3-91/S-3	-0.7
Total	2	127	418	38	90	9	8	4	48	16	2	45	.215	.248	.304	55	-26	13-7	.926	6	110	104	3-114/2-5,S-4	-1.8
DODSON, PAT Patrick Neal B 10.11.1959 Santa Monica, CA BL/TL 6-4/210# d9.5																								
1986	Bos A	9	12	3	5	2	0	1	3	3-0	0	3	.417	.533	.833	264	3	0-0	1.000	-1	38	230	/1-7	0.2
1987	Bos A	26	42	4	7	3	0	2	6	8-1	0	13	.167	.288	.381	77	-1	0-0	1.000	-2	43	115	1-21/D	-0.4
1988	Bos A	17	45	5	8	3	1	1	1	6-0	0	17	.178	.275	.356	72	-2	0-0	1.000	1	119	64	1-17	-0.1
Total	3	52	99	12	20	8	1	4	10	17-1	0	33	.202	.314	.424	97	0	0-0	1.000	-1	77	104	/1-45,D	-0.3
DOERR, BOBBY Robert Pershing B 4.7.1918 Los Angeles, CA BR/TR 5-11/175# d4.20 Mil 1944-45 C8 HF1986																								
1937	Bos A	55	147	22	33	5	1	2	14	18	1	25	.224	.313	.313	56	-10	2-4	.973	2	103	104	2-47	-0.6
1938	Bos A	145	509	70	147	26	7	5	80	59	0	39	.289	.363	.397	86	-11	5-10	.968	9	103	**121**	*2-145	0.4
1939	Bos A	127	525	75	167	28	2	12	73	38	1	32	.318	.365	.448	103	2	1-10	.976	**27**	**115**	110	*2-126	3.0
1940	Bos A	151	595	87	173	37	10	22	105	57	0	53	.291	.353	.497	113	10	10-5	.977	13	103	103	*2-151	3.1
1941	Bos A★	132	500	74	141	28	4	16	93	43	0	43	.282	.339	.450	105	2	1-3	.971	-1	101	95	*2-132	0.8
1942	Bos A☆	144	545	71	158	35	5	15	102	67	1	55	.290	.369	.455	127	20	4-4	**.975**	12	103	117	*2-142	4.1
1943	Bos A★	**155**	604	78	163	32	3	16	75	62	1	59	.270	.339	.412	117	12	8-8	**.990**	9	104	115	*2-155	3.2
1944	Bos A★	125	468	95	152	30	10	15	81	58	0	31	.325	.399	**.528**	166	40	5-2	.976	2	98	101	*2-125	5.1
1946	†Bos A★	151	583	95	158	34	9	18	116	66	1	67	.271	.346	.453	115	11	5-6	**.986**	**27**	108	**126**	*2-151	4.8
1947	Bos A★	146	561	79	145	23	10	17	95	59	0	47	.258	.329	.426	101	-1	3-3	.981	**25**	**111**	**115**	*2-146	3.3
1948	Bos A★	140	527	94	150	23	6	27	111	83	4	49	.285	.386	.505	129	22	3-2	.993	9	102	**116**	*2-138	3.7
1949	Bos A	139	541	91	167	30	9	18	109	75	0	33	.309	.393	.497	126	19	2-2	.980	**27**	109	**119**	*2-139	5.1
1950	Bos A★	149	586	103	172	29	**11**	27	120	67	1	42	.294	.367	.519	114	9	3-4	**.988**	9	99	99	*2-149	2.4
1951	Bos A★	106	402	60	116	21	2	13	73	57	1	33	.289	.378	.448	112	8	2-1	.981	6	99	118	*2-106	1.9
Total	14	1865	7093	1094	2042	381	89	223	1247	809	11	608	.288	.362	.461	114	133	54-64	.980	178	104	112	*2-1852	40.3
DOHERTY, JOHN John Michael B 8.22.1951 Woburn, MA BL/TL 5-11/185# d6.1																								
1974	Cal A	74	223	20	57	14	1	3	15	8-1	0	13	.256	.280	.368	91	-4	2-1	.991	-2	83	100	1-70/D-2	-1.0
1975	Cal A	30	94	7	19	3	0	1	12	8-1	0	12	.202	.262	.266	54	-6	1-1	.983	-1	83	93	1-26/D	-1.0
Total	2	104	317	27	76	17	1	4	27	16-2	0	25	.240	.275	.338	80	-10	3-2	.989	-3	83	98	/1-96,D-3	-2.0
DOLAN, COZY Albert J. (born James Alberts) B 12.23.1889 Chicago, IL D 12.10.1958 Chicago, IL BR/TR 5-10/160# d8.15 C3 OF Total (126-LF 48-CF 33-RF)																								
1909	Cin N	3	6	2	1	0	0	0	0	2	0		.167	.375	.167	69	0	0	.750	-1	85	334	/3-3	-0.1
1911	NY A	19	69	19	21	1	2	0	6	8	1		.304	.385	.377	106	1	12	.947	-1	90	159	3-19	0.0
1912	NY A	18	60	15	12	1	3	0	11	5	1		.200	.273	.317	64	-3	5	.768	-4	88	43	3-17	-0.7
	Phi N	11	50	8	14	2	2	0	7	1	0	10	.280	.294	.400	83	-2	3	.872	-1	94	64	3-11	-0.2
1913	Phi N	55	126	15	33	4	0	0	8	1	1	21	.262	.273	.294	59	-7	9-4	.905	-6	87	0	O-12(8-0-4),S-10/2-9,3-4,1	-1.3
	Pit N	35	133	22	27	5	2	0	9	15	1	14	.203	.289	.271	63	-6	14-7	.937	-1	97	171	3-35	-0.6
	Year	90	259	37	60	9	2	0	17	16	2	35	.232	.282	.282	61	-13	23-11	.932	-7	97	161	3-39,O-12(8-0-4),S-10/2-9,1	-1.9
1914	StL N	126	421	76	101	16	3	4	32	55	5	74	.240	.335	.321	96	0	42	.955	-11	93	77	O-96(90-1-5),3-27	-1.6
1915	StL N	111	322	53	90	14	9	2	38	34	4	37	.280	.356	.398	127	11	17-11	.929	-8	98	38	O-98(28-47-24)	-0.2
1922	NY N	1	0	0	0	0	0	0	0	0	0	0	—	—	—	—	0	0-0	—	0			R	0.0
Total	7	379	1187	210	299	43	21	6	111	121	13	156	.252	.328	.339	95	-6	102-22	.940	-33	95	55	0-206L,3-116/S-10,2-9,1	-4.7

Year	Tm Lg	G	AB	R	H	2B	3B	HR	RBI	BB-IB	HP	SO	AVG	OBP	SLG	AOPS	ABR	SB-CS	FA	FR	Rng	Thr	G at Pos	BFW
DOLAN, JOE Joseph B 2.24.1873 Baltimore, MD D 3.24.1938 Omaha, NE TR 5-10/155# d8.11																								
1896	Lou N	44	165	14	35	2	1	3	18	9	0	12	.212	.253	.291	45	-14	6	.940	7	108	118	S-44	-0.4
1897	Lou N	36	133	10	28	2	2	0	7	8	3		.211	.271	.256	41	-12	6	.849	-5	83	72	S-18,2-18	-1.3
1899	Phi N	61	222	27	57	6	3	1	30	11	2		.257	.298	.324	73	-9	3	.915	-6	107	47	2-61	-1.2
1900	Phi N	74	257	39	51	7	3	1	27	16	5		.198	.259	.261	44	-20	10	.931	0	111	81	3-31,2-29,S-12	-1.7
1901	Phi N	10	37	0	3	0	0	0	2	2	0		.081	.128	.081	-38	-7	0	.973	-1	96	157	2-10	-0.8
	Phi A	98	338	50	73	21	2	1	38	26	5		.216	.282	.299	58	-19	3	.881	12	116	132	S-61,3-35/2O(RF)	-0.3
Total	5	323	1152	140	247	38	11	6	122	72	15	12	.214	.270	.282	51	-81	28	.902	8	107	118	S-135,2-119/3-66,O(RF)	-5.7
DOLAN, BIDDY Leon Mark B 7.9.1881 Onalaska, WI D 7.15.1950 Indianapolis, IN BR/TR 6/?# d4.16																								
1914	Ind F	32	103	13	23	4	2	1	15	12	2	13	.223	.316	.330	69	-6	5	.979	1	113	82	1-31	-0.7
DOLAN, COZY Patrick Henry B 12.3.1872 Cambridge, MA D 3.29.1907 Louisville, KY BL/TL 5-10/160# d4.26 ▲																								
1895	Bos N	26	83	12	20	4	1	0	7	6	1	7	.241	.300	.313	54	-6	3	.949	3	138	145	P-25/O(CF)	0.1
1896	Bos N	6	14	4	2	0	0	0	0	0	0	1	.143	.143	.143	-23	-2	0	.765	-0	79	0	/P-6	0.0
1900	Chi N	13	48	5	13	1	0	0	2	2	0		.271	.300	.292	66	-2	2	.826	-1	63	0	O-13(RF)	-0.4
1901	Chi N	43	171	29	45	1	2	0	16	7	1		.263	.296	.292	74	-6	3	.878	1	163	209	O-41(RF)	-0.7
	Bro N	66	253	33	66	11	1	0	29	17	2		.261	.313	.312	79	-6	7	.967	0	123	104	O-64(2-57-5)	-0.9
	Year	109	424	62	111	12	3	0	45	24	3		.262	.306	.304	77	-12	10	.931	1	140	149	*O-105(2-57-46)	-1.6
1902	Bro N	**141**	592	72	166	16	7	1	54	33	5		.280	.324	.336	103	1	24	.936	-11	53	45	*O-141(1-140-0)	-1.7
1903	Chi A	27	104	16	27	5	1	0	7	6	2		.260	.313	.327	96	0	5	.971	0	125	68	1-19/O-4(2-2-0)	-0.1
	Cin N	93	385	64	111	20	3	0	58	28	2		.288	.340	.356	88	-6	11	.937	-3	97	73	O-93(RF)	-1.2
1904	Cin N	129	465	88	132	8	10	6	51	39	2		.284	.342	.383	113	6	19	.939	-2	105	0	*O-102(0-7-95),1-24	-0.1
1905	Cin N	22	77	7	18	2	1	0	4	7	1		.234	.306	.286	69	-3	2	.965	-3	86	87	1-13/O-9(1-0-8)	-0.7
	Bos N	112	433	44	119	11	7	3	48	27	3		.275	.322	.353	103	1	21	.946	3	129	54	*O-111(RF)/P-2,1-2	-0.1
	Year	134	510	51	137	13	8	3	52	34	4		.269	.319	.343	97	-3	23	.931	-0	121	51	*O-120(1-0-119),1-15/P-2	-0.8
1906	Bos N	**152**	549	54	136	20	4	0	39	55	2		.248	.318	.299	95	-2	17	.928	-1	**146**	87	*O-144(2-0-143)/2-7,P-2,1	-1.0
Total	9	830	3174	428	855	99	37	10	315	227	21	8	.269	.322	.333	94	-25	114	.931	-15	108	65	O-723(8-207-509)/1-59,P-35,2-7	-6.8
DOLAN, TOM Thomas J. B 1.10.1859 New York, NY D 1.16.1913 St.Louis, MO BR/TR 5-11/185# d9.30																								
1879	Chi N	1	4	0	0	0	0	0	0	0		2	.000	.000	.000	-94	-1		1.000	1			/C	0.0
1882	Buf N	22	89	12	14	0	1	0	8	2		11	.157	.176	.180	14	-9		.941	-4			C-18/O-4(1-2-1),3-2	-1.0
1883	StL AA	81	295	32	63	9	2	1	18	9			.214	.237	.268	59	-14		.957	11			C-42,O-40(19-19-2)/P	-0.1
1884	StL AA	35	137	19	36	6	2	0		6	1		.263	.299	.336	103	0		.873	-6			C-34/O-2(1-1-0)	-0.3
	StL U	19	69	9	13	3	0	0		4			.188	.233	.232	40	-7		.897	7			C-14/3-3,O-2(0-1-1)	0.1
1885	StL N	3	9	1	2	0	0	0	0	2		1	.222	.364	.222	99	0		.810	-1			/C-3	-0.1
1886	StL N	15	44	8	11	3	0	0	1	7		9	.250	.353	.318	113	1	2	.928	5			C-15	0.7
	Bal AA	38	125	13	19	3	2	0	12	8	0		.152	.203	.208	30	-10	8	.918	-4			C-35/O-3(LF)	-1.0
1888	StL AA	11	36	1	7	1	0	0	1	1	0		.194	.216	.222	37	-3	1	.914	0			C-11	-0.2
Total	7	225	808	95	165	25	7	1	40	39	1	23	.204	.242	.256	57	-43	11	.916	9			C-173/O-51(24-23-4),3-5,P	-1.9
DOLE, LESTER Lester Carrington B 7.8.1855 Meriden, CT D 12.10.1918 Concord, NH 5-11/?# d5.27																								
1875	NH NA	1	4	1	2	0	0	0	0	0		0	.500	.500	.500	285	1	0-0	.750	-0	0	0	/O(CF)	0.0
DOLJACK, FRANK Frank Joseph "Dolie" B 10.5.1907 Cleveland, OH D 1.23.1948 Cleveland, OH BR/TR 5-11/175# d9.4																								
1930	Det A	20	74	10	19	5	1	3	17	2	1	11	.257	.286	.473	87	-2	0-1	.930	1	106	130	O-20(0-4-16)	-0.3
1931	Det A	63	187	20	52	13	3	4	20	15	1	17	.278	.335	.444	100	-1	3-2	.925	2	101	183	O-54(3-44-8)	-0.1
1932	Det A	8	26	5	10	1	0	1	7	2	0	2	.385	.429	.538	143	2	1-0	1.000	-1	67	0	/O-6(LF)	0.1
1933	Det A	42	147	18	42	5	2	0	22	14	0	13	.286	.348	.347	83	-4	2-6	.941	1	92	160	O-37(32-0-5)	-0.6
1934	†Det A	56	120	15	28	7	1	1	19	13	1	15	.233	.313	.333	67	-6	2-1	.943	0	98	174	O-30(6-12-12)/1-3	-0.6
1943	Cle A	3	7	0	0	0	0	0	0	1	0	2	.000	.125	.000	-66	-1	0-0	1.000	-0	75	0	/O-2(1-0-1)	-0.2
Total	6	192	561	68	151	31	7	9	85	47	3	60	.269	.329	.398	87	-12	8-10	.934	2	97	161	O-149(48-60-42)/1-3	-1.7
DONAHUE, SHE Charles Michael B 6.29.1877 Oswego, NY D 8.28.1947 New York, NY BR/TR 5-9/?# d4.29																								
1904	StL N	4	15	1	4	0	0	0	2	0	0		.267	.267	.267	68	-1	3	.846	-2	70	125	/2-3,S	-0.3
	Phi N	58	200	21	43	4	0	0	14	3	0		.215	.227	.235	44	-14	7	.857	-14	85	92	S-29,3-24/1-3,2-2	-2.9
	Year	62	215	22	47	4	0	0	16	3	0		.219	.229	.237	46	-14	10	.852	-16	84	91	S-30,3-24/2-5,1-3	-3.2
DONAHUE, JIM James Augustus B 1.8.1862 Lockport, IL D 4.19.1935 Lockport, IL BR/TR 6/175# d4.19 OF Total (38-LF 28-CF 6-RF)																								
1886	NY AA	49	186	14	37	0	0	0	9	10	3		.199	.251	.199	45	-11	1	.803	-2	56	0	O-32(12-21-1),C-19	-1.1
1887	NY AA	60	220	33	62	4	1	1	29	21	2		.282	.350	.323	92	-1	6	.890	-6			C-51/O-5(0-2-3),1-4,32	-0.3
1888	KC AA	88	337	29	79	11	3	1	28	21	1		.234	.281	.294	79	-9	12	.902	-8			C-67,O-18(12-5-1)/3-5,2	-1.0
1889	KC AA	67	252	30	59	5	4	0	32	21	0	20	.234	.293	.286	61	-14	12	.887	-6			C-46,O-14(LF),3-10	-1.4
1891	Col AA	77	280	27	61	4	3	0	35	31	1	18	.218	.298	.254	62	-13	2	.942	-9	*74*	*115*	C-75/O(RF)1	-1.5
Total	5	341	1275	133	298	24	11	2	133	104	7	38	.234	.295	.275	70	-48	33	.911	-31	*22*	*34*	C-258/O-70L,3-16,1-5,2-2	-5.3
DONAHUE, JIGGS John Augustus B 7.13.1879 Springfield, OH D 7.19.1913 Columbus, OH BL/TL 6-1/178# d9.10 b-Pat																								
1900	Pit N	3	10	1	2	0	1	0	3	0	0		.200	.200	.400	63	-1	1	.889	-1	*148*	*42*	/C-2,O(RF)	-0.1
1901	Pit N	2	0	0	0	0	0	0	0	0	0		—	—	—	—	0	0	—	-0	*0*	*0*	/CO(LF)	0.0
	Mil A	37	107	10	34	5	4	0	16	10	2		.318	.387	.439	135	5	4	.933	-4	*77*	*105*	C-19,1-13	0.3
1902	StL A	30	89	11	21	1	1	1	7	12	0		.236	.327	.303	76	-3	2	.956	-1	*116*	*104*	C-23/1-5	-0.2
1904	Chi A	102	367	46	91	9	7	1	48	25	1		.248	.298	.319	99	-1	18	.979	7	133	126	*1-101	0.5
1905	Chi A	149	533	71	153	22	4	1	76	44	4		.287	.346	.349	126	17	32	**.988**	7	116	**142**	*1-149	2.3
1906	†Chi A	**154**	556	70	143	17	7	1	57	48	3		.257	.320	.318	103	2	36	**.988**	9	119	107	*1-154	0.9
1907	Chi A	**157**	609	75	158	16	4	0	68	28	3		.259	.295	.299	93	-6	27	**.994**	21	**141**	118	*1-157	1.2
1908	Chi A	93	304	22	62	8	2	0	22	25	3		.204	.271	.243	69	-10	14	.994	4	114	95	1-83	-0.8
1909	Chi A	2	4	0	0	0	0	0	2	1	0		.000	.200	.000	-38	-1	0	1.000	-0	0	0	/1-2	-0.1
	Was A	84	283	13	67	12	1	0	28	22	1		.237	.294	.286	87	-4	9	.984	-4	79	73	1-81	-1.0
	Year	86	287	13	67	12	1	0	30	23	1		.233	.293	.282	86	-4	9	.984	-4	78	72	1-83	-1.1
Total	9	813	2862	319	731	90	31	4	327	215	17		.255	.311	.313	99	-2	143	.987	38	119	115	1-745/C-45,O-2(1-0-1)	3.0
DONAHUE, JOHN John Frederick "Jiggs" B 4.19.1894 Roxbury, MA D 10.3.1949 Boston, MA BB/TR 5-8/170# d9.25																								
1923	Bos A	10	36	5	10	4	0	0	1	4	0	5	.278	.350	.389	94	0	0-1	1.000	3	105	294	/O-9(RF)	0.1
DONAHUE, PAT Patrick William B 11.8.1884 Springfield, OH D 1.31.1966 Springfield, OH BR/TR 6/175# d5.29 b-Jiggs																								
1908	Bos A	35	86	8	17	2	0	1	6	9	2		.198	.289	.256	75	-2	0	.959	1	*99*	*91*	C-32/1-3	0.2
1909	Bos A	65	177	14	42	4	1	2	25	17	1		.237	.308	.305	92	-2	2	.982	-1	*113*	*97*	C-58	0.4
1910	Bos A	2	4	0	0	0	0	0	0	0	0		.000	.000	.000	-98	-1	0	1.000	0	*120*	*0*	/C	-0.1
	Phi A	14	34	2	5	0	0	0	4	3	1		.147	.237	.147	21	-3	1	1.000	3	*114*	*118*	C-13	0.1
	Cle A	2	6	0	1	0	0	0	0	0	0		.167	.167	.167	4	-1	0	1.000	-0	*83*	*75*	/C-2,1	-0.1
	Phi A	1	1	0	0	0	0	0	0	0	0		.000	.000	.000	-99	0	0	1.000	0	*114*	*118*	/C	0.0
	Year	19	45	2	6	0	0	0	4	3	1		.133	.204	.133	6	-5	1	1.000	3	*109*	*110*	C-17/1	-0.1
Total	3	119	308	24	65	6	1	3	35	29	4		.211	.287	.266	75	-9	3	.978	4	*108*	*97*	C-107/1-4	0.5
DONAHUE, TIM Timothy Cornelius "Bridget" B 6.8.1870 Raynham, MA D 6.12.1902 Taunton, MA BL/TR 5-11/180# d7.28																								
1891	Bos AA	4	7	0	0	0	0	0	0	0	0	5	.000	.000	.000	-99	-2	0	.833	-1	*111*	*74*	/C-4	-0.2
1895	Chi N	63	219	29	59	9	1	2	36	20	3	25	.269	.339	.347	72	-9	5	.915	-5	*94*	*70*	C-63	-0.7
1896	Chi N	57	188	27	41	10	1	0	20	11	4	15	.218	.276	.282	45	-15	11	.934	-1	*93*	*104*	C-57	-0.9
1897	Chi N	58	188	28	45	7	3	0	21	9	2		.239	.281	.309	54	-13	3	.949	1	*87*	*121*	C-55/S-2,1	-0.6
1898	Chi N	122	396	52	87	12	3	0	39	49	8		.220	.318	.265	68	-15	17	.962	16	*154*	*86*	*C-122	1.2
1899	Chi N	92	278	39	69	9	3	0	29	34	7		.248	.345	.302	80	-6	10	.951	4	*107*	*97*	C-91/1	0.6
1900	Chi N	67	216	21	51	10	1	0	17	19	5		.236	.313	.292	70	-8	8	.928	-7	*95*	*79*	C-66/2	-0.8
1902	Was A	3	8	0	2	0	0	0	1	0	0		.250	.250	.250	39	-1	0	1.000	-0	*89*	*142*	/C-3	-0.1
Total	8	466	1500	196	354	57	12	2	163	142	29	45	.236	.314	.294	66	-69	54	.943	9	*112*	*92*	C-461/1-2,S-2,2	-1.5
DONALDSON, JOHN John David B 5.5.1943 Charlotte, NC BL/TR 5-11/165# d8.26																								
1966	KC A	15	30	4	4	0	0	0	1	3-0	0	4	.133	.212	.133	2	-4	1-0	1.000	-2	62	42	/2-9	-0.6

Year	Tm Lg	G	AB	R	H	2B	3B	HR	RBI	BB-IB	HP	SO	AVG	OBP	SLG	AOPS	ABR	SB-CS	FA	FR	Rng	Thr	G at Pos	BFW
1967	KC A	105	377	27	104	16	5	0	28	37-3	2	39	.276	.343	.345	107	4	6-3	.982	-15	88	70	*2-101/S	-0.2
1968	Oak A	127	363	37	80	9	2	2	27	45-0	2	44	.220	.307	.273	82	-7	5-5	.971	-2	102	95	2-98/3-5,S	-0.2
1969	Oak A	12	13	1	1	0	0	0	0	2-1	0	4	.077	.200	.077	-21	-2	0-0	.857	0	136	155	/2	-0.2
	Sea A	95	338	22	79	8	3	1	19	36-5	0	36	.234	.307	.284	67	-15	6-1	.974	-6	94	87	2-90/3-2,S	-1.4
	Year	107	351	23	80	8	3	1	19	38-6	0	40	.228	.303	.276	64	-17	6-1	.972	-5	94	88	2-91/3-2,S	-1.6
1970	Oak A	41	89	4	22	2	1	1	11	9-3	0	6	.247	.316	.326	80	-3	1-0	.986	-5	95	68	2-21/S-6,3	-0.5
1974	Oak A	10	15	1	2	0	0	0	0	0-0	0	0	.133	.133	.133	-25	-2	0-0	.962	2	152	207	/2-7,3-3	-0.1
Total	6	405	1225	96	292	35	11	4	86	132-12	4	133	.238	.313	.295	81	-29	19-9	.976	-27	95	83	2-327/3-11,S-9	-3.2
DONDERO, LEN Leonard Peter "Mike" B 9.12.1903 Newark, CA D 1.1.1999 Fremont, CA BR/TR 5-11/178# d4.21																								
1929	StL A	19	31	2	6	0	0	1	8	0	0	4	.194	.194	.290	22	-4	0-0	.857	-2	59	0	3-10/2-5	-0.5
DONLIN, MIKE Michael Joseph "Turkey Mike" B 5.30.1878 Peoria, IL D 9.24.1933 Hollywood, CA BL/TL 5-9/170# d7.19 ▲																								
1899	StL N	66	266	49	86	9	6	6	27	17	1		.323	.366	.470	126	8	20	.873	-8	91	102	O-51(1-50-0),1-13/S-3,P-3	-0.4
1900	StL N	78	276	40	90	8	6	10	48	14	1		.326	.361	.507	139	12	14	.922	-4	110	311	O-47(2-35-10),1-21	0.5
1901	Bal A	121	476	107	162	23	13	5	67	53	2		.340	.409	.475	138	25	33	.918	8	118	83	O-74(73-1-0),1-47	2.5
1902	Cin N	34	143	30	41	5	4	0	9	9	1		.287	.333	.378	109	1	9	.877	-2	107	83	O-32(30-0-2)/PS	-0.3
1903	Cin N	126	496	110	174	25	18	7	67	56	3		.351	.420	.516	150	31	26	.900	-5	86	96	*O-118(70-0-48)/1-7	1.9
1904	Cin N	60	236	42	84	11	7	1	38	18	2		.356	.406	.475	158	16	21	.872	-1	126	58	O-53(52-0-1)/1-6	1.2
	NY N	42	132	17	37	7	3	2	14	10	2		.280	.340	.424	130	4	1	.918	-4	26	104	O-37(23-11-3)	-0.1
	Year	102	368	59	121	18	10	3	52	28	4		.329	.382	.457	148	20	22	.886	-5	88	75	O-90(75-11-4)/1-6	1.1
1905	†NY N	150	606	**124**	216	31	16	7	80	56	2		.356	.413	.495	166	49	33	.934	-13	87	97	*O-150(4-147-0)	3.0
1906	NY N	37	121	15	38	5	1	1	14	11	0		.314	.371	.397	136	5	9	.929	-5	0	0	O-29(CF)/1	-0.1
1908	NY N	155	593	71	198	26	13	6	106	23	5		.334	.364	.452	153	32	30	.977	-0	106	23	*O-155(29-0-127)	2.8
1911	NY N	12	12	3	4	0	0	1	1	0	0	1	.333	.333	.583	150	1	2	1.000	-0	74	0	/O-3(0-2-1)	0.0
	Bos N	56	222	33	70	16	1	2	34	22	0	17	.315	.377	.423	115	5	7	.912	-3	93	100	O-56(CF)	-0.2
	Year	68	234	36	74	16	1	3	35	22	0	18	.316	.375	.432	117	6	9	.913	-3	93	99	O-59(0-58-1)	-0.2
1912	Pit N	77	244	27	77	9	8	2	35	20	1	16	.316	.370	.443	124	7	8	.982	-0	100	94	O-62(2-10-51)	0.3
1914	NY N	35	31	1	5	1	1	1	3	3	0	5	.161	.235	.355	77	-1	0	—	0			H	-0.1
Total	12	1049	3854	669	1282	176	97	51	543	312	20	39	.333	.386	.468	142	195	213	.924	-37	94	88	O-867(286-341-243)/1-95,P-4,S-4	11.0
DONNELLY, JIM James B. B 7.19.1865 New Haven, CT D 3.5.1915 New Haven, CT BR/TR 5-10.5/155# d8.11																								
1884	Ind AA	40	134	22	34	2	2	0		5	4		.254	.301	.299	99	0		.850	-4	72	78	3-24/S-8,O-6(2-2-2),2-2	-0.3
1885	Det N	56	211	24	49	4	3	1	22	10		29	.232	.267	.294	81	-5		.850	-2	94	56	3-56	-0.6
1886	KC N	113	438	51	88	11	3	0	38	36		57	.201	.262	.240	50	-26	16	.845	1	107	87	*3-113	-2.2
1887	Was N	117	425	51	85	9	6	1	46	16	3	26	.200	.234	.256	39	-35	42	.867	16	**120**	115	*3-115/S-2	-1.5
1888	Was N	122	428	43	86	9	4	0	23	20	3	16	.201	.242	.241	58	-20	44	.875	-1	103	92	*3-117/S-5	-1.9
1889	Was N	4	13	3	2	0	0	0	0	2	0	0	.154	.267	.154	20	-1	1	.667	-1	89	153	/3-4	-0.2
1890	StL AA	11	42	11	14	0	0	0	3	8	1		.333	.451	.333	115	1	5	.795	-2	71	270	3-11	0.0
1891	Col AA	17	54	6	13	0	0	0	9	13	0	5	.241	.388	.241	85	0	7	.855	2	119	179	3-17	0.2
1896	Bal N	106	396	70	130	14	10	0	71	34	4	11	.328	.387	.414	110	5	38	.884	-4	99	106	*3-106	0.3
1897	Pit N	44	161	22	31	4	0	0	14	16	1		.193	.270	.217	31	-16	14	.920	2	106	19	3-44	-1.2
	NY N	23	85	19	16	3	0	0	11	9	0		.188	.266	.224	31	-8	6	.869	-3	89	82	3-23	-1.0
	Year	67	246	41	47	7	0	0	25	25	1		.191	.268	.220	31	-24	20	.905	-1	100	39	3-67	-2.2
1898	StL N	1	1	0	1	0	0	0	0	0	0		1.000	1.000	1.000	463	0	0	.500	-0	135	0	/3	0.0
Total	11	654	2388	322	549	56	28	2	237	169	16	144	.230	.285	.279	66	-105	173	.865	3	104	94	3-631/S-15,O-6(2-2-2),2-2	-8.4
DONNELLY, JIM James J. 5-10.5/155# d7.11																								
1884	KC U	6	23	2	3	1	0	0		1			.130	.167	.174	4	-3		.536	-4	73	0	/3-5,C	-0.6
DONNELLY, JOHN John B Elizabeth, NJ d4.14 b-Pete																								
1873	Was NA	30	137	15	35	2	0	0	19	1		0	.255	.261	.270	60	-6	0-0	.750	0	83	119	S-13,2-12/O-6(CF),3	-0.5
1874	Phi NA	6	22	2	5	0	0	0	2	0		0	.227	.227	.227	45	-1	0-0	.667	-2	0	0	/O-3(RF),S-2,2	-0.3
Total	2 NA	36	159	17	40	2	0	0	21	1		0	.252	.256	.264	58	-7	0-0	.000	-2	81	107	/S-15,2-13,O-9(0-6-3),3	-0.8
DONNELLY, PETE Peter J. B 10.8.1849 Philadelphia, PA D 10.1.1890 Jersey City, NJ d5.13 b-John																								
1871	Kek NA	9	34	7	7	1	1	0	3	1		2	.206	.229	.294	48	-2	0-0	.714	-4	0	0	/O-9(2-1-6),3-2	-0.4
DONNELS, CHRIS Chris Barton B 4.21.1966 Los Angeles, CA BL/TR 6/185# d5.7																								
1991	NY N	37	89	7	20	2	0	0	5	14-1	0	19	.225	.330	.247	65	-4	1-1	1.000	4	114	106	1-15,3-11	-0.1
1992	NY N	45	121	8	21	4	0	0	6	17-0	0	25	.174	.275	.207	39	-9	1-0	.941	2	109	78	3-29,2-12	-0.8
1993	Hou N	88	179	18	46	14	2	2	24	19-0	0	33	.257	.327	.391	95	-1	2-0	.898	-1	108	152	3-31,1-23/2	-0.3
1994	Hou N	54	86	12	23	5	0	3	5	13-0	0	18	.267	.364	.430	112	2	1-0	1.000	-0	89	0	3-14/1-4,2-4	0.2
1995	Hou N	19	30	4	9	0	0	0	2	3-2	0	6	.300	.364	.300	83	-1	0-0	.818	-3	57	232	/3-9,2	-0.3
	Bos A	40	91	13	23	2	2	2	11	9-0	0	18	.253	.317	.385	80	-3	0-0	.927	-0	92	58	3-27/1-8,2-3	-0.3
2000	LA N	27	34	8	10	3	0	4	9	6-1	0	7	.294	.390	.735	190	5	0-0	1.000	-1	143	0	/O-6(LF),1-4,3-2,2	0.3
2001	LA N	66	88	8	15	2	0	3	8	12-2	1	25	.170	.277	.295	52	-7	0-0	.897	0	110	115	3-14/1-7,P	-0.7
2002	†Ari N	74	80	5	19	4	1	3	16	10-1	0	14	.237	.312	.425	90	-2	0-0	1.000	-2	67	0	3-26/1	-0.4
Total	8	450	798	83	186	36	5	17	86	103-7	1	165	.233	.319	.355	82	-20	5-1	.932	-2	98	94	3-163/1-62,2-22,O-6(LF),P	-2.4
DONOHUE, ALEX Alexander B 1869 Altoona, PA d8.24																								
1891	Phi N	6	22	2	7	1	0	0	2	1	1	3	.318	.375	.364	113	0	0	1.000	-1	0	0	/O-4(CF),S-2	-0.1
DONOHUE, TOM Thomas James B 11.15.1952 Mineola, NY BR/TR 6/185# d4.6																								
1979	Cal A	38	107	13	24	3	1	3	14	3-0	2	29	.224	.259	.355	66	-6	2-0	.981	-8	86	122	C-38	-1.2
1980	Cal A	84	218	18	41	4	1	2	14	7-0	1	63	.188	.216	.243	26	-23	5-1	.986	-13	67	98	C-84	-3.3
Total	2	122	325	31	65	7	2	5	28	10-0	3	92	.200	.230	.280	40	-29	7-1	.985	-21	73	105	C-122	-4.5
DONOVAN, FRED Frederick Maurice B 7.4.1864 , NH D 3.7.1916 Bloomington, IL BR/TR d6.23																								
1895	Cle N	3	12	1	1	0	0	0	1	1	0	2	.083	.154	.083	-36	-3	0	.938	-0	*124*	*55*	/C-3	-0.2
DONOVAN, JERRY Jeremiah Francis B 9.3.1876 Lock Haven, PA D 6.27.1938 St.Petersburg, FL BR/TR d4.12 b-Tom																								
1906	Phi N	61	166	11	33	4	0	0	15	6	2		.199	.236	.223	43	-11	2	.955	-4	*90*	*80*	C-53/SO(LF)	-1.2
DONOVAN, MIKE Michael Berchman B 10.18.1881 Brooklyn, NY D 2.3.1938 New York, NY BR/TR 5-8/155# d5.29																								
1904	Cle A	2	2	0	0	0	0	0	0	0	0		.000	.000	.000	-99	0	0	—	-0	0	0	/S	-0.1
1908	NY A	5	19	2	5	1	0	0	2	0	0		.263	.263	.316	87	0	0	1.000	1	86	0	/3-5	0.1
Total	2	7	21	2	5	1	0	0	2	0	0		.238	.238	.286	69	0	0	1.000	1	86	0	/3-5,S	0.0
DONOVAN, PATSY Patrick Joseph B 3.16.1865 County Cork, Ireland D 12.25.1953 Lawrence, MA BL/TL 5-11.5/175# d4.19 M11																								
1890	Bos N	32	140	17	36	0	0	0	9	8	2	17	.257	.307	.257	60	-8	10	.891	-4	80	108	O-32(CF)	-1.1
	†Bro N	28	105	17	23	5	1	0	8	5	2	5	.219	.268	.286	61	-5	3	1.000	1	63	109	O-28(1-24-3)	-0.5
	Year	60	245	34	59	5	1	0	17	13	4	22	.241	.290	.269	61	-13	13	.952	-3	72	108	O-60(1-56-3)	-1.6
1891	Lou AA	105	439	73	141	10	3	2	53	30	8	18	.321	.375	.371	115	8	27	.912	3	79	0	*O-105(LF)	0.7
	Was AA	17	70	9	14	1	0	0	3	4	0	5	.200	.243	.214	33	-6	1	.857	-2	78	154	O-17(0-13-4)	-0.7
	Year	122	509	82	155	11	3	2	56	34	8	23	.305	.358	.350	104	2	28	.907	1	79	18	*O-122(105-13-4)	0.0
1892	Was N	40	163	29	39	3	3	0	12	11	2	13	.239	.295	.294	81	-4	16	.844	1	142	210	O-40(14-0-26)	-0.5
	Pit N	90	388	77	114	15	3	2	26	20	3	16	.294	.333	.363	110	4	40	.872	-2	129	133	O-90(1-1-90)	-0.2
	Year	130	551	106	153	18	6	2	38	31	5	29	.278	.322	.343	102	0	56	.862	-1	133	157	*O-130(15-1-116)	-0.7
1893	Pit N	113	499	114	158	5	8	2	56	42	3	8	.317	.373	.371	100	0	46	.937	-2	86	133	*O-112(RF)	-0.6
1894	Pit N	**133**	577	147	175	21	10	4	76	36	5	12	.303	.350	.395	80	-20	41	.933	6	101	91	*O-133(RF)	-1.6
1895	Pit N	126	522	115	162	18	6	1	59	48	8	19	.310	.377	.374	99	2	36	.961	-6	59	49	*O-126(0-1-125)	-0.8
1896	Pit N	**131**	573	113	183	20	5	3	59	35	11	18	.319	.370	.387	104	4	48	.954	6	128	169	*O-131(RF)	0.3
1897	Pit N	120	479	82	154	16	7	0	57	25	4		.322	.360	.384	100	0	34	.949	1	101	154	*O-120(RF),M	-0.5
1898	Pit N	147	610	112	184	16	9	0	37	34	7		.302	.346	.357	103	2	41	.928	-2	101	87	*O-147(RF)	-0.7
1899	Pit N	122	536	82	156	11	7	1	56	17	5		.291	.319	.343	82	-15	26	.942	-13	48	61	*O-122(0-1-121),M	-3.1
1900	StL N	126	503	78	159	11	1	0	61	38	3		.316	.368	.342	97	-1	**45**	.951	-4	78	95	*O-124(RF)	-1.0
1901	StL N	130	531	92	161	23	5	1	73	27	6		.303	.344	.371	113	9	28	.979	2	114	193	*O-129(RF),M	0.5

Year	Tm Lg	G	AB	R	H	2B	3B	HR	RBI	BB-IB	HP	SO	AVG	OBP	SLG	AOPS	ABR	SB-CS	FA	FR	Rng	Thr	G at Pos	BFW
1902	StL N	126	502	70	158	12	4	0	35	28	10		.315	.363	.355	127	16	34	.959	9	**177**	126	*O-126(RF),M	2.0
1903	StL N	105	410	63	134	15	3	0	39	25	3		.327	.370	.378	117	9	25	.952	0	115	138	*O-105(RF),M	0.5
1904	Was A	125	436	30	100	6	0	0	19	24	1		.229	.271	.243	64	-18	17	.963	9	111	99	*O-122(0-2-120),M	-1.6
1906	Bro N	7	21	1	5	0	0	0	0	0	0		.238	.238	.238	53	-1	0	1.000	-0	0	0	/O-6(RF),M	-0.2
1907	Bro N	1	1	0	0	0	0	0	0	0	0		.000	.000	.000	-99	0	0	1.000	0	0	0	/O(RF)M	0.0
Total	17	1824	7505	1321	2256	208	75	16	738	457	83	131	.301	.348	.355	98	-24	518	.941	5	101	112	*O-1816(121-74-1623)	-9.1
DONOVAN, TOM Thomas Joseph B 1.1.1873 West Troy, NY D 3.25.1933 Watervliet, NY BR/TR 6-2/168# d9.10 b-Jerry																								
1901	Cle A	18	71	9	18	3	1	0	5	0	0		.254	.254	.324	62	-4	1	.862	0	209	0	O-18(RF)/P	-0.4
DONOVAN, BILL William Edward "Wild Bill" B 10.13.1876 Lawrence, MA D 12.9.1923 Forsyth, NY BR/TR 5-11/190# d4.22 M4 C1 ▲ OF Total (15-LF 8-CF 14-RF)																								
1898	Was N	39	103	11	17	2	2	2	8	4	2		.165	.211	.282	41	-9	2	.933	1	156	444	O-20(6-6-8),P-17/S2	-0.5
1899	Bro N	5	13	2	3	1	0	0	0	0	0		.231	.231	.308	46	0	0	.857	-0	79	0	/P-5	0.0
1900	Bro N	5	13	0	0	0	0	0	2	0	0		.000	.000	.000	-94	-2	0	1.000	1	154	0	/P-5	0.0
1901	Bro N	46	135	16	23	3	0	2	13	8	0		.170	.217	.237	31	-1	1	.927	-1	84	176	P-45	0.0
1902	Bro N	48	161	16	28	3	2	1	16	9	2		.174	.227	.236	43	-11	7	.948	1	94	97	P-35/1-8,O-4(2-0-2),2	-0.3
1903	Det A	40	124	11	30	3	2	0	12	4	0		.242	.266	.298	71	-5	3	.938	-3	70	92	P-35/S-2,2O(CF)	-0.1
1904	Det A	46	140	12	38	2	1	1	6	3	0		.271	.287	.321	95	-1	2	.967	-2	93	67	P-34/1-8,O(RF)	-0.3
1905	Det A	44	130	16	25	4	0	0	5	12	1		.192	.266	.223	55	-6	8	.933	-1	78	118	P-34/O-8(7-0-1),2-2	-0.1
1906	Det A	28	91	5	11	0	1	0	0	1	0		.121	.130	.143	-14	-12	6	.961	-2	97	53	P-25/2-3,O(CF)	-0.3
1907	†Det A	37	109	20	29	7	2	0	19	6	0		.266	.304	.367	110	7	4	.945	-6	66	0	P-32	0.0
1908	†Det A	30	82	5	13	1	0	0	2	10	0		.159	.250	.171	36	0	2	.917	-6	53	0	P-29	0.0
1909	†Det A	22	45	6	9	0	0	0	1	2	1		.200	.250	.200	41	0	0	.974	-2	67	88	P-21	0.0
1910	Det A	26	69	6	10	1	0	0	2	5	0		.145	.203	.159	13	-2	0	.955	-6	50	112	P-26	0.0
1911	Det A	24	60	11	12	3	1	1	6	11	0		.200	.324	.333	79	3	1	.935	-5	54	0	P-20	0.0
1912	Det A	6	13	3	1	0	0	0	0	1	0		.077	.143	.077	-38	-2	0	1.000	-1	35	0	/P-3,1-2,O-2(RF)	-0.2
1915	NY A	10	12	1	1	0	0	0	0	1	0	6	.083	.154	.083	-29	-1	0	1.000	-1	70	0	/P-9,M	0.0
1916	NY A	1	0	0	0	0	0	0	0	0	0	0	—	—	—	—	0	0	—	-0	0	0	/PM	0.0
1918	Det A	2	2	1	1	0	0	0	1	0	0	0	.500	.500	.500	210	0	0	1.000	-0	62	0	/P-2	0.0
Total	18	459	1302	142	251	30	11	7	93	77	6	6	.193	.241	.249	49	-42	36	.944	-32	76	81	P-378/O-37L,1-18,2-8,S-3	-1.8
DOOIN, RED Charles Sebastian B 6.12.1879 Cincinnati, OH D 5.14.1952 Rochester, NY BR/TR 5-9.5/165# d4.18 M5																								
1902	Phi N	94	333	20	77	7	3	0	35	10	4		.231	.262	.270	64	-15	8	.950	-6	83	110	C-84/O-6(LF)	-1.4
1903	Phi N	62	188	18	41	5	1	0	14	8	1		.218	.254	.255	47	-14	9	.940	-7	85	114	C-51/1O(RF)	-1.5
1904	Phi N	108	355	41	86	11	4	6	36	8	1		.242	.261	.346	90	-6	15	.938	-3	85	113	C-96/1-4,O-3(1-2-0),3	0.0
1905	Phi N	113	380	45	95	13	5	0	36	10	0		.250	.269	.311	75	-13	12	.965	11	120	96	*C-107/3	0.9
1906	Phi N	113	351	25	86	19	1	0	32	13	1		.245	.274	.305	80	-9	15	.948	-9	90	80	*C-107	-0.9
1907	Phi N	101	313	18	66	8	4	0	14	15	2		.211	.252	.262	62	-15	10	.959	8	124	92	C-94/2O(LF)	0.3
1908	Phi N	133	435	28	108	17	4	0	41	17	4		.248	.283	.306	85	-8	20	.966	19	**130**	**110**	*C-132	2.8
1909	Phi N	141	468	42	105	14	1	2	38	21	4		.224	.264	.271	66	-20	14	.958	6	102	97	*C-140	0.0
1910	Phi N	103	331	30	80	13	4	0	30	22	0	17	.242	.289	.305	71	-13	10	.956	-6	96	97	C-91/O-3(1-1-1),M	-1.0
1911	Phi N	74	247	18	81	15	1	1	16	14	1	12	.328	.366	.409	115	5	6	.967	-2	91	91	C-74,M	1.0
1912	Phi N	69	184	20	43	9	0	0	22	5	2	12	.234	.262	.283	46	-14	8	.958	-1	90	98	C-58,M	-1.1
1913	Phi N	55	129	6	33	4	1	0	13	3	0	9	.256	.273	.302	62	-7	1-4	.962	1	112	93	C-50,M	-0.3
1914	Phi N	53	118	10	21	2	0	1	8	4	0	14	.178	.205	.220	25	-11	4	.967	-3	73	114	C-40/O-2(LF),M	-1.2
1915	Cin N	10	31	2	10	0	0	0	0	2	0	5	.323	.364	.323	106	0	1	.915	-3	87	62	C-10	-0.2
	NY N	46	124	9	27	2	2	0	9	3	0	15	.218	.236	.266	55	-8	0-2	.964	-3	90	112	C-46	-0.8
	Year	56	155	11	37	2	2	0	9	5	0	20	.239	.262	.277	66	-7	1-2	.956	-5	89	103	C-56	-1.0
1916	NY N	15	17	1	2	0	0	0	0	0	0	3	.118	.118	.118	-29	-3	0	.972	0	131	25	C-15	-0.2
Total	15	1290	4004	333	961	139	31	10	344	155	20	87	.240	.272	.298	72	-151	133-6	.957	5	102	99	*C-1195/O-16(11-3-2),1-5,3-2,2	-3.6
DOOLAN, MICKEY Michael Joseph "Doc" (born Michael Joseph Doolittle) B 5.7.1880 Ashland, PA D 11.1.1951 Orlando, FL BR/TR 5-10.5/170# d4.14 C7																								
1905	Phi N	136	492	53	125	27	11	1	48	24	2		.254	.292	.360	97	-4	17	.935	-16	96	86	*S-135	-1.5
1906	Phi N	**154**	535	41	123	19	7	1	55	27	2		.230	.270	.297	77	-17	16	.930	8	100	100	*S-154	-0.4
1907	Phi N	145	509	33	104	19	7	1	47	25	1		.204	.243	.275	63	-24	18	.929	15	105	125	*S-145	-0.5
1908	Phi N	129	445	29	104	25	4	2	49	17	3		.234	.267	.321	85	-9	5	.939	-2	100	86	*S-129	-0.7
1909	Phi N	147	493	39	108	12	10	1	35	37	2		.219	.276	.290	75	-16	10	.939	24	**105**	114	*S-147	1.4
1910	Phi N	148	536	58	141	31	6	2	57	35	6	56	.263	.315	.354	92	-6	16	**.948**	18	**108**	116	*S-148	1.7
1911	Phi N	146	512	51	122	23	6	1	49	44	2	65	.238	.301	.313	71	-21	14	.936	17	104	**116**	*S-145	0.6
1912	Phi N	146	532	47	137	26	6	1	62	34	2	59	.258	.305	.335	70	-23	6	.950	10	104	83	*S-146	-0.2
1913	Phi N	151	518	32	113	12	6	1	43	29	2	68	.218	.262	.270	50	-35	17-8	.941	9	103	113	*S-148/2-3	-1.5
1914	Bal F	145	486	58	119	23	6	1	53	40	7	47	.245	.311	.323	71	-27	30	**.949**	**34**	**112**	109	*S-145	1.7
1915	Bal F	119	404	41	75	13	7	2	21	24	4	39	.186	.238	.267	41	-40	10	.946	32	111	132	*S-119	0.1
	Chi F	24	86	9	23	1	1	0	9	2	1	7	.267	.292	.302	72	-5	5	.914	-1	107	56	S-24	-0.5
	Year	143	490	50	98	14	8	2	30	26	5	46	.200	.248	.273	46	-45	15	**.941**	**31**	**110**	**119**	*S-143	-0.4
1916	Chi N	28	70	4	15	2	1	0	5	8	0	7	.214	.295	.271	67	-2	0	.918	0	105	86	S-24	-0.1
	NY N	18	51	4	12	3	1	1	3	2	0	4	.235	.264	.392	106	0	1	.975	2	105	112	S-16/2-2	0.3
	Year	46	121	8	27	5	2	1	8	10	0	11	.223	.282	.322	82	-3	1	.939	2	105	96	S-40/2-2	0.2
1918	Bro N	92	308	14	55	8	2	0	18	22	0	24	.179	.233	.218	38	-23	8	**.968**	10	101	99	2-91	-1.3
Total	13	1728	5977	513	1376	244	81	15	554	370	34	376	.230	.279	.306	71	-252	173-8	.940	160	104	106	*S-1625/2-96	-0.9
DOOMS, HARRY Henry E. "Jack" B 1.30.1867 St.Louis, MO D 12.14.1899 St.Louis, MO d8.7																								
1892	Lou N	1	4	0	0	0	0	0	0	1	0	3	.000	.200	.000	-42	-1	0	.000	-1	0	0	/O(RF)	-0.1
DORAN, TOM Thomas J. "Long Tom" B 12.2.1880 Westchester Co., NY D 6.22.1910 New York, NY BL/TR 5-11/152# d4.19																								
1904	Bos A	12	32	1	4	0	1	0	0	4	1		.125	.243	.188	35	-2	1	.898	-3	131	41	C-11	-0.5
1905	Bos A	3	3	0	0	0	0	0	0	0	0		.000	.000	.000	-99	-1	0	1.000	0	0	330	/C	0.0
	Det A	34	94	8	15	3	0	0	4	8	3		.160	.248	.191	40	-6	2	.963	-6	69	103	C-32	-1.0
	Year	37	97	8	15	3	0	0	4	8	3		.155	.241	.186	35	-7	2	.964	-5	68	106	C-33	-1.0
1906	Bos A	2	3	1	0	0	0	0	0	0	0		.000	.000	.000	-99	-1	0	1.000	0	91	137	/C-2	-0.1
Total	3	51	132	10	19	3	1	0	4	12	4		.144	.236	.182	33	-10	3	.950	-8	84	91	/C-46	-1.6
DORAN, BILL William Donald B 5.28.1958 Cincinnati, OH BB/TR 5-11/175# d9.6 C1																								
1982	Hou N	26	97	11	27	3	0	0	6	4-0	0	11	.278	.304	.309	79	-3	5-0	.975	-4	94	111	2-26	-0.4
1983	Hou N	154	535	70	145	12	7	8	39	86-11	0	67	.271	.371	.364	112	11	12-12	.979	3	99	117	*2-153	2.2
1984	Hou N	147	548	92	143	18	11	4	41	66-7	2	69	.261	.341	.356	104	3	21-12	.986	8	106	104	*2-139,S-13	2.0
1985	Hou N	148	578	84	166	31	6	14	59	71-6	0	69	.287	.362	.434	126	21	23-15	.980	6	100	112	*2-147	3.7
1986	†Hou N	145	550	92	152	29	3	6	37	81-7	2	57	.276	.368	.373	109	10	42-19	.974	-34	78	81	*2-144	-1.4
1987	Hou N	**162**	625	82	177	23	3	16	79	82-3	3	64	.283	.365	.406	109	10	31-11	**.992**	-13	91	72	*2-162/S-3	0.9
1988	Hou N	132	480	66	119	18	1	7	53	65-3	1	60	.248	.338	.333	97	0	17-4	**.987**	2	99	101	*2-130	0.9
1989	Hou N	142	507	65	111	25	2	8	58	59-2	2	63	.219	.301	.323	82	-11	22-3	.980	-25	90	84	*2-138	-3.1
1990	Hou N	109	344	49	99	21	2	6	32	71-1	0	53	.288	.405	.413	131	19	18-9	.989	-12	96	87	2-99	1.0
	Cin N	17	59	10	22	8	0	1	5	8-1	0	5	.373	.448	.559	168	6	5-0	.985	1	111	97	2-12/3-4	0.9
	Year	126	403	59	121	29	2	7	37	79-2	0	58	.300	.411	.434	137	26	23-9	.988	-11	98	88	*2-111/3-4	1.9
1991	Cin N	111	361	51	101	12	2	6	35	46-1	0	39	.280	.359	.374	103	3	5-4	.981	-9	91	108	2-88/O-6(LF),1-4	-0.5
1992	Cin N	132	387	48	91	16	2	8	47	64-9	0	40	.235	.342	.349	94	-1	7-4	.988	-6	92	106	*2-104,1-25	-0.6
1993	Mil A	28	60	7	13	4	0	0	6	6-1	0	3	.217	.284	.283	55	-4	1-0	.964	-3	79	67	2-17/1-4	-0.6
Total	12	1453	5131	727	1366	220	39	84	497	709-52	10	600	.266	.354	.373	107	64	209-93	.983	-85	94	97	*2-1359/1-33,S-16,O-6(LF),3-4	5.0
DORAN, BILL William James B 6.14.1898 San Francisco, CA D 3.9.1978 Santa Monica, CA BL/TR 5-11.5/175# d6.23																								
1922	Cle A	3	2	0	1	0	0	0	0	1	0	0	.500	.667	.500	206	0	0-0	—	-0	0	0	/3-2	0.0
DORGAN, JERRY Jeremiah F. B 1856 Meriden, CT D 6.10.1891 New Haven, CT BL/TR ?/165# d7.8 b-Mike																								
1880	Wor N	10	35	2	7	1	0	0	1	0		1	.200	.200	.229	41	-2		.750	-2	0	0	/O-9(RF),C	-0.4
1882	Phi AA	44	181	25	51	9	1	0	24	4			.282	.297	.343	108	1		.880	-2			C-25,O-22(1-1-20)/3	0.0
1884	Ind AA	34	141	22	42	6	1	0		2	2		.298	.317	.355	122	3		.793	-3	156	102	O-29(RF)/C-5	0.1

Year	Tm Lg	G	AB	R	H	2B	3B	HR	RBI	BB-IB	HP	SO	AVG	OBP	SLG	AOPS	ABR	SB-CS	FA	FR	Rng	Thr	G at Pos	BFW
	Bro AA	4	13	2	4	0	0	0		0	0		.308	.308	.308	101	0		.921	1			/C-4	0.1
	Year	38	154	24	46	6	1	0		2	2		.299	.316	.351	120	3		.793	-1	156	102	O-29(RF)/C-9	0.2
1885	Det N	39	161	23	46	6	2	0	24	8		10	.286	.320	.348	115	3		.857	-3	71	200	O-39(0-1-38)	0.0
Total	4	131	531	74	150	22	4	0	49	14		11	.282	.303	.339	109	5		.817	-9			/O-99(1-2-96),C-35,3	-0.2
DORGAN, MIKE Michael Cornelius B 10.2.1853 Middletown, CT D 4.26.1909 Hartford, CT BR/TR 5-9/180# d5.8 M3 b-Jerry ▲ OF Total (29-LF 17-CF 556-RF)																								
1877	StL N	**60**	266	45	82	9	7	0	23	9		13	.308	.331	.395	135	11		.824	-7	54	198	*O-50(20-1-29),C-12/3-2,S2	0.2
1879	Syr N	59	270	38	72	11	5	1	17	4		13	.267	.277	.356	120	7		.954	-6	143	46	1-21,O-16(RF),3-11/S-6,C-4,P-2,2M	0.1
1880	Pro N	79	321	45	79	10	1	0	31	10		18	.246	.269	.283	90	-3		.858	-1	135	146	*O-77(RF)/3-2,PM	-0.3
1881	Wor N	51	220	36	61	5	0	0	18	8		4	.277	.303	.300	85	-4		.953	-0	82	72	1-26,O-23(RF)/S-2,M	-0.5
	Det N	8	34	5	8	1	0	0	5	1		0	.235	.257	.265	62	-1		1.000	-1	70	0	/O-5(0-4-1),3-2,1	-0.2
	Year	59	254	41	69	6	0	0	23	9		4	.272	.297	.295	82	-5		.897	-1	101	76	O-28(0-4-24),1-27/S-2,3-2	-0.7
1883	NY N	64	261	32	61	11	3	0	27	2		23	.234	.240	.299	63	-12		.847	-8	50	45	O-59(0-9-51)/C-6,P	-1.7
1884	NY N	83	341	61	94	11	6	1	48	13		27	.276	.302	.352	103	0		.851	-2	93	124	O-64(2-2-60),P-14/C-6,2-3	-0.2
1885	NY N	89	347	60	113	17	8	0	46	11		24	.326	.346	.421	149	18		.905	-4	66	212	*O-88(RF)/1	1.3
1886	NY N	118	442	61	129	19	4	2	79	29		37	.292	.335	.367	112	7	9	.888	-10	57	122	*O-116(6-1-110)/1-3	-0.4
1887	NY N	71	283	41	73	10	0	0	34	15	3	20	.258	.302	.293	69	-11	22	.870	-3	47	0	O-69(1-0-68)/1-2	-1.2
1890	Syr AA	33	139	19	30	8	0	0	18	16	1		.216	.301	.273	77	-3	8	.900	-2	92	77	O-33(RF)	-0.4
Total	10	715	2924	443	802	112	34	4	346	118	4	179	.274	.303	.340	102	9	39	.867	-43	77	126	0-600R/1-54,C-28,P-18,3-17,S-9,2-3.3	
DORMAN, RED Charles Dwight "Curlie" B 10.3.1900 Jacksonville, IL D 12.7.1974 Anaheim, CA BR/TR 5-10.5/180# d8.21																								
1928	Cle A	25	77	12	28	6	0	0	11	9	0	6	.364	.430	.442	128	4	1-0	.915	-2	97	43	O-24(5-19-0)	0.1
DORMAN, CHARLIE Charles William "Slats" B 4.23.1898 San Francisco, CA D 11.15.1928 San Francisco, CA BR/TR 6-2/185# d5.14																								
1923	Chi A	1	2	0	1	0	0	0	0	0	0	0	.500	.500	.500	166	0	0-0	1.000	-0	*0*	*391*	/C	0.0
DORSETT, BRIAN Brian Richard B 4.9.1961 Terre Haute, IN BR/TR 6-3/220# d9.8																								
1987	Cle A	5	11	2	3	0	0	1	3	0-0	1	3	.273	.333	.545	127	0	0-0	1.000	-1	45	0	/C-4	-0.1
1988	Cal A	7	11	0	1	0	0	0	2	1-0	0	5	.091	.167	.091	-26	-2	0-0	1.000	0	126	178	/C-7	-0.1
1989	NY A	8	22	3	8	1	0	0	4	1-0	0	3	.364	.391	.409	127	1	0-0	1.000	-0	209	104	/C-8	0.1
1990	NY A	14	35	2	5	2	0	0	0	2-0	0	4	.143	.189	.200	9	-4	0-0	1.000	-1	71	0	/C-9,D-5	-0.6
1991	SD N	11	12	0	1	0	0	0	1	0-0	0	3	.083	.083	.083	-51	-2	0-0	1.000	0	244	0	/1-2	-0.2
1993	Cin N	25	63	7	16	4	0	2	12	3-0	0	14	.254	.288	.413	85	-2	0-0	1.000	2	118	61	C-18/1-3	0.2
1994	Cin N	76	216	21	53	8	0	5	26	21-7	1	33	.245	.313	.352	74	-8	0-0	.991	3	133	104	C-73/1	-0.2
1996	Chi N	17	41	3	5	0	0	1	3	4-0	0	8	.122	.196	.195	5	-6	0-0	1.000	4	405	94	C-15	-0.1
Total	8	163	411	38	92	15	0	9	51	32-7	2	73	.224	.281	.326	62	-23	0-0	.995	6	157	92	C-134/1-6,D-5	-1.0
DORSEY, JERRY Jeremiah B 1885 Oakland, CA BL/TL 5-11/175# d9.23																								
1911	Pit N	2	6	0	0	0	0	0	0	0	0	1	.000	.000	.000	-96	-2	0	1.000	0	118	0	/O(CF)	-0.2
DOSCHER, HERM John Henry Sr. B 12.20.1852 New York, NY D 3.20.1934 Buffalo, NY BR/TR 5-10/182# d9.4 U4 s-Jack																								
1872	Atl NA	6	24	4	9	0	0	0	5	0		1	.375	.375	.375	112	0	0-1	.714	0	142	0	/O-6(RF)	0.0
1873	Atl NA	1	6	1	1	0	0	0	1	0		0	.167	.167	.167	-1	-1	0-0	.500	-1	0	0	/O(CF)	-0.1
1875	Was NA	22	81	5	15	4	0	0	5	0		6	.185	.185	.235	46	-4	1-0	.752	0	114	31	3-22	-0.4
1879	Tro N	47	191	16	42	8	0	0	18	2		10	.220	.228	.262	65	-6		.806	-3	100	111	3-47	-0.7
	Chi N	3	11	1	2	0	0	0	1	0		3	.182	.182	.182	19	-1		.700	-1	90	0	/3-3	-0.2
	Year	50	202	17	44	8	0	0	19	2		13	.218	.225	.257	62	-7		.800	-4	99	105	3-50	-0.9
1881	Cle N	5	19	2	4	0	0	0	0	0		2	.211	.211	.211	35	-1		.895	-0	91	126	/3-5	-0.2
1882	Cle N	25	104	7	25	2	0	0	10	0		11	.240	.240	.260	63	-4		.857	-1	96	73	3-22/O-2(LF),S	-0.4
Total	3 NA	29	111	10	25	4	0	0	11	0		7	.225	.225	.261	62	-5	1-1	.752	-1	114	31	/3-22,O-7(0-1-6)	-0.5
Total	3	80	325	26	73	10	0	0	29	2		26	.225	.229	.255	61	-12		.823	-5	98	97	/3-77,O-2(LF),S	-1.5
DOSTER, DAVID David Eric B 10.8.1970 Ft.Wayne, IN BR/TR 5-10/185# d6.16																								
1996	Phi N	39	105	14	28	8	0	1	8	7-0	0	21	.267	.313	.371	79	-3	0-0	.973	-2	90	85	2-24/3	-0.4
1999	Phi N	99	97	9	19	2	0	3	10	12-1	0	23	.196	.282	.309	49	-8	1-0	.993	7	104	132	2-77/3-6,S-5	0.1
Total	2	138	202	23	47	10	0	4	18	19-1	0	44	.233	.297	.342	64	-11	1-0	.984	6	97	110	2-101/3-7,S-5	-0.3
DOTTERER, DUTCH Henry John B 11.11.1931 Syracuse, NY D 10.9.1999 Syracuse, NY BR/TR 6/209# d9.25																								
1957	Cin N	4	12	0	1	0	0	0	2	1-0	0	2	.083	.154	.083	-32	-2	0-0	1.000	-0	*99*	*0*	/C-4	-0.3
1958	Cin N	11	28	1	7	1	0	1	2	2-0	0	4	.250	.300	.393	77	-1	0-0	.981	2	*120*	*136*	/C-8	0.2
1959	Cin N	52	161	21	43	7	0	2	17	16-1	0	23	.267	.328	.348	79	-4	0-0	.992	1	*126*	*91*	C-51	-0.1
1960	Cin N	33	79	4	18	5	0	2	11	13-0	0	10	.228	.337	.367	91	0	0-1	.979	0	*113*	*155*	C-31	0.0
1961	Was A	7	19	1	5	2	0	0	1	3-0	0	5	.263	.364	.368	98	0	0-0	1.000	1	*70*	*357*	/C-7	0.2
Total	5	107	299	27	74	15	0	5	33	35-1	0	44	.247	.323	.348	79	-7	0-1	.988	4	*117*	*129*	C-101	-0.0
DOUGHERTY, CHARLIE Charles William B 2.7.1862 Darlington, WI D 2.18.1925 Milwaukee, WI d4.17																								
1884	Alt U	23	85	6	22	5	0	0		2			.259	.276	.318	78	-5		.854	-3	90	30	2-16/O-8(2-2-4),S	-0.6
DOUGHERTY, PATSY Patrick Henry B 10.27.1876 Andover, NY D 4.30.1940 Bolivar, NY BL/TR 6-2/190# d4.19																								
1902	Bos A	108	438	77	150	12	6	0	34	42	6		.342	.407	.397	120	14	20	.899	-10	61	41	*O-102(LF)/3	-0.1
1903	†Bos A	139	590	**107**	**195**	19	12	4	59	33	6		.331	.372	.424	131	22	35	.952	4	103	84	*O-139(LF)	1.8
1904	Bos A	49	195	33	53	5	4	0	4	25	0		.272	.355	.338	113	4	10	.925	-0	72	240	O-49(LF)	0.1
	NY A	106	452	80	128	13	10	6	22	19	3		.283	.316	.396	119	8	11	.925	-8	120	36	*O-106(LF)	-0.6
	Year	155	647	**113**	181	18	14	6	26	44	3		.280	.329	.379	117	12	21	.925	-8	104	102	*O-155(LF)	-0.5
1905	NY A	116	418	56	110	9	6	3	29	28	6		.263	.319	.335	96	-2	17	.898	-3	97	75	*O-108(LF)/3	-1.2
1906	NY A	12	52	3	10	2	0	0	4	0	0		.192	.192	.231	29	-4	0	1.000	2	197	315	O-12(LF)	-0.3
	†Chi A	75	253	30	59	9	4	1	27	19	3		.233	.295	.312	92	-2	11	.985	-2	105	55	O-74(LF)	-0.9
	Year	87	305	33	69	11	4	1	31	19	3		.226	.278	.298	81	-7	11	.987	1	118	91	O-86(LF)	-1.2
1907	Chi A	148	533	69	144	17	2	1	59	36	5		.270	.322	.315	107	5	33	.946	-7	98	98	*O-148(LF)	-1.2
1908	Chi A	138	482	68	134	11	6	0	45	58	10		.278	.367	.326	128	18	**47**	.947	-15	47	28	*O-128(LF)	-0.5
1909	Chi A	139	491	71	140	23	13	1	55	51	6		.285	.359	.391	143	25	36	.942	-14	57	0	*O-138(LF)	0.4
1910	Chi A	127	443	45	110	8	6	1	43	41	4		.248	.318	.300	98	-1	22	.923	-12	81	59	*O-121(LF)	-2.3
1911	Chi A	76	211	39	61	10	9	0	32	26	5		.289	.380	.422	128	8	19	.933	-6	80	72	O-56(LF)	0.0
Total	10	1233	4558	678	1294	138	78	17	413	378	54		.284	.346	.360	117	95	261	.935	-70	85	65	*O-1181(LF)/3-2	-4.8
DOUGLAS, JOHN John Franklin B 9.14.1917 Thayer, WV D 2.11.1984 Miami, FL BL/TL 6-2.5/195# d4.21																								
1945	Bro N	5	9	0	0	0	0	0	0	2	0	4	.000	.182	.000	-47	-2	0	.971	-1	0	44	/1-4	-0.3
DOUGLASS, ASTYANAX Astyanax Saunders B 9.19.1899 Covington, TX D 1.26.1975 ElPaso, TX BL/TR 6-1/190# d7.30																								
1921	Cin N	4	7	1	1	0	0	0	0	0	0	1	.143	.143	.143	-25	-1	0-0	1.000	0	*114*	*185*	/C-4	-0.1
1925	Cin N	7	17	1	3	0	0	0	1	1	0	3	.176	.222	.176	3	-3	0-0	.889	-1	*79*	*172*	/C-7	-0.3
Total	2	11	24	2	4	0	0	0	1	1	0	4	.167	.200	.167	-4	-4	0-0	.926	-1	*89*	*176*	/C-11	-0.4
DOUGLASS, KLONDIKE William Bingham B 5.10.1872 Boston, PA D 12.13.1953 Bend, OR BL/TR 6/200# d4.23 OF Total (68-LF 9-CF 55-RF)																								
1896	StL N	81	296	42	78	6	4	1	28	35	5	15	.264	.351	.321	81	-7	18	.894	-4	134	111	O-74(29-5-41)/C-6,S-2	-1.2
1897	StL N	126	519	77	170	15	3	6	50	52	13		.328	.402	.403	115	14	12	.948	-22	*68*	*108*	C-61,O-44(28-2-14),1-17/3-7,S	-0.4
1898	Phi N	146	582	105	150	26	4	2	48	55	11		.258	.333	.326	93	-3	18	.976	2	105	83	*1-146	-0.1
1899	Phi N	77	275	26	70	6	6	0	27	10	6		.255	.296	.320	71	-12	7	.970	2	*109*	*95*	C-66/3-4,1-4,O(CF)	-0.4
1900	Phi N	50	160	23	48	9	4	0	25	13	2		.300	.360	.406	112	3	7	.934	-9	*78*	*101*	C-47/3-2	-0.2
1901	Phi N	51	173	14	56	6	1	0	23	11	2		.324	.371	.370	113	3	10	.979	2	*103*	*62*	C-41/1-6,O-2(1-1-0)	0.8
1902	Phi N	109	408	37	95	12	3	0	37	23	0		.233	.274	.277	70	-15	6	.986	-6	84	68	1-69,C-29,O-10(LF)	-2.2
1903	Phi N	105	377	43	96	5	4	1	36	28	1		.255	.308	.297	75	-13	6	.985	-1	91	80	1-97	-1.5
1904	Phi N	3	10	1	3	0	0	0	1	0	1		.300	.364	.300	109	0	0	.970	-1	52	72	/1-3	0.0
Total	9	748	2800	368	766	85	29	10	275	227	41	15	.274	.337	.335	91	-30	84	.981	-36	94	78	1-342,C-250,O-131L/3-13,S-3	-5.2
DOUTHIT, TAYLOR Taylor Lee B 4.22.1901 Little Rock, AR D 5.28.1986 Fremont, CA BR/TR 5-11.5/175# d9.14																								
1923	StL N	9	27	3	5	0	2	0	0	0	0	4	.185	.185	.333	35	-3	1-0	1.000	1	104	168	/O-7(3-0-4)	-0.3
1924	StL N	53	173	24	48	13	1	0	13	16	3	19	.277	.349	.364	93	-1	4-3	.976	3	113	99	O-50(9-22-19)	-0.1

Year	Tm Lg	G	AB	R	H	2B	3B	HR	RBI	BB-IB	HP	SO	AVG	OBP	SLG	AOPS	ABR	SB-CS	FA	FR	Rng	Thr	G at Pos	BFW
1925	StL N	30	73	13	20	3	1	1	8	2	2	6	.274	.312	.384	75	-3	0-0	.981	1	113	61	O-21(4-16-1)	-0.3
1926	†StL N	139	530	96	163	20	4	3	52	55	2	46	.308	.375	.377	99	1	23	.958	7	**111**	100	*O-138(1-137-0)	0.2
1927	StL N	130	488	81	128	29	6	5	50	52	2	45	.262	.336	.377	88	-8	6	.964	-1	107	55	*O-125(1-122-1)	-1.4
1928	†StL N	**154**	648	111	191	35	3	3	43	84	**10**	36	.295	.384	.372	97	2	11	.984	13	**120**	66	*O-154(CF)	0.8
1929	StL N	150	613	128	206	42	7	9	62	79	5	49	.336	.416	.471	118	21	8	.974	-1	107	55	*O-150(CF)	1.3
1930	†StL N	**154**	664	109	201	41	10	7	93	60	4	38	.303	.364	.426	87	-13	4	.964	0	106	65	*O-154(CF)	-1.7
1931	StL N	36	133	21	44	11	2	1	21	11	1	9	.331	.386	.466	123	5	1	.972	-1	106	0	O-36(0-35-1)	0.2
	Cin N	95	374	42	98	9	1	0	24	42	2	24	.262	.340	.291	76	-12	4	.983	1	104	72	O-95(CF)	-1.3
	Year	131	507	63	142	20	3	1	45	53	3	33	.280	.352	.337	89	-6	5	.980	-0	105	52	*O-131(0-130-1)	-1.1
1932	Cin N	96	333	28	81	12	1	0	25	31	2	29	.243	.311	.285	64	-16	3	.985	2	106	79	O-88(2-86-0)	-1.6
1933	Cin N	1	0	1	0	0	0	0	0	0	0	0	—	—	—	—	0	0	—	0			R	0.0
	Chi N	27	71	8	16	5	0	0	5	11	0	7	.225	.329	.296	80	-1	2	.930	-1	84	238	O-18(5-13-0)	-0.2
	Year	28	71	9	16	5	0	0	5	11	0	7	.225	.329	.296	80	-1	2	.930	-1	84	238	O-18(5-13-0)	-0.2
Total	11	1074	4127	665	1201	220	38	29	396	443	33	312	.291	.364	.384	93	-28	67-3	.972	24	109	72	*O-1036(25-984-26)	-4.4
DOW, CLARENCE Clarence G. B 10.2.1854 Charlestown, MA D 3.11.1893 West Somerville, MA d9.22																								
1884	Bos U	1	6	1	2	0	0	0		0			.333	.333	.333	104	0		1.000	1	544	0	/O(CF)	0.1
DOWD, JOHN John Leo (born John Leo O'Dowd) B 1.3.1891 Weymouth, MA D 1.31.1981 Ft.Lauderdale, FL BR/TR 5-8/170# d7.3																								
1912	NY A	10	31	1	6	1	0	0	0	6	1		.194	.342	.226	60	-1	0	.840	-3	96	31	S-10	-0.3
DOWD, SNOOKS Raymond Bernard B 12.20.1897 Springfield, MA D 4.4.1962 Northampton, MA BR/TR 5-8/163# d4.27																								
1919	Det A	1	0	0	0	0	0	0	0	0	0	0	—	—	—	—	0	0	—	0			R	0.0
	Phi A	13	18	4	3	0	0	0	6	0	0	5	.167	.167	.167	-6	-3	2	.800	0	138	129	/2-3,S-2,3O(CF)	-0.2
	Year	14	18	4	3	0	0	0	6	0	0	5	.167	.167	.167	-6	-3	2	.800	0	138	129	/2-3,S-2,3O(CF)	-0.2
1926	Bro N	2	8	0	0	0	0	0	0	0	0	0	.000	.000	.000	-99	-2	0	1.000	-1	39	0	/2-2	-0.4
Total	2	16	26	4	3	0	0	0	6	0	0	5	.115	.115	.115	-36	-5	2	.875	-1	92	69	/2-5,S-2,O(CF)3	-0.6
DOWD, TOMMY Thomas Jefferson "Buttermilk Tommy" B 4.20.1869 Holyoke, MA D 7.2.1933 Holyoke, MA BR/TR 5-8/173# d4.8 M2 OF Total (284-LF 331-CF 350-RF)																								
1891	Bos AA	4	11	1	1	0	0	0	0	0	0	1	.091	.091	.091	-49	-2	0	—	-0	0	0	/O-4(RF)	-0.2
	Was AA	112	464	66	120	9	10	1	44	19	2	44	.259	.291	.328	81	-15	39	.885	-13	94	75	*2-107/O-5(LF)	-2.1
	Year	116	475	67	121	9	10	1	44	19	2	45	.255	.286	.322	78	-17	39	.885	-13	94	75	*2-107/O-9(5-0-4)	-2.3
1892	Was N	144	584	94	142	9	10	1	50	34	1	49	.243	.286	.298	79	-17	49	.891	-19	95	83	2-98,O-23(7-0-16),3-18/S-6	-3.1
1893	StL N	132	581	114	164	18	7	1	54	49	2	23	.282	.340	.343	81	-16	59	.944	3	121	196	*O-132(64-5-63)/2	-1.9
1894	StL N	123	524	92	142	16	8	4	62	54	2	33	.271	.341	.355	68	-28	31	.930	-7	73	89	*O-117(48-0-69)/2-7,3	-3.2
1895	StL N	130	508	95	164	19	17	7	74	31	3	31	.323	.365	.469	116	9	32	.928	-4	67	76	*O-116(14-36-66),3-17/2-2	-0.1
1896	StL N	126	521	93	138	17	11	5	46	42	2	19	.265	.322	.369	85	-13	40	.920	-13	92	63	2-78,O-48(CF),M	-2.2
1897	StL N	35	145	25	38	9	1	0	9	6	0		.262	.291	.338	67	-7	11	.915	-7	0	0	O-30(CF)/2-5,M	-1.3
	Phi N	91	391	68	114	14	4	0	43	19	0		.292	.324	.348	80	-12	30	.919	-5	98	169	O-73(0-23-50),2-19	-1.7
	Year	126	536	93	152	23	5	0	52	25	0		.284	.316	.345	76	-19	41	.918	-12	68	117	*O-103(0-53-50),2-24	-3.0
1898	StL N	139	586	70	143	17	7	0	32	30	5		.244	.287	.297	66	-28	16	.920	-13	64	69	*O-129(9-42-82),2-11	-4.5
1899	Cle N	147	605	81	168	17	6	2	35	48	2		.278	.333	.336	90	-8	28	.954	-2	47	26	*O-147(CF)	-1.7
1901	Bos A	**138**	594	104	159	18	7	3	52	38	3		.268	.315	.337	82	-15	33	.937	1	61	85	*O-137(LF)/1-2,3	-1.9
Total	10	1321	5514	903	1493	163	88	24	501	370	22	200	.271	.319	.345	82	-152	368	.933	-78	71	97	O-961R,2-328/3-37,S-6,1-2	-23.9
DOWELL, KEN Kenneth Allen B 1.19.1961 Sacramento, CA BR/TR 5-9/160# d6.24																								
1987	Phi N	15	39	4	5	0	0	0	1	2-0	0	5	.128	.171	.128	-19	-7	0-0	1.000	-1	98	99	S-15	-0.6
DOWIE, JOE Joseph E. B 7.15.1865 New Orleans, LA D 3.4.1917 New Orleans, LA 5-8/150# d7.10																								
1889	Bal AA	20	75	12	17	5	0	0	8	2	2	10	.227	.266	.293	58	-4	5	.947	0	54	0	O-20(RF)	-0.4
DOWNEY, RED Alexander Cummings B 2.6.1889 Aurora, IN D 7.10.1949 Detroit, MI BL/TL 5-11/174# d9.14																								
1909	Bro N	19	78	7	20	1	0	0	8	2			.256	.275	.269	71	-3	4	1.000	-1	83	0	O-19(0-3-16)	-0.5
DOWNEY, TOM Thomas Edward B 1.1.1884 Lewiston, ME D 8.3.1961 Passaic, NJ BR/TR 5-10/178# d5.7																								
1909	Cin N	119	416	39	96	9	6	1	32	32	1		.231	.287	.288	79	-11	16	.909	-6	98	124	*S-119/C	-1.4
1910	Cin N	111	378	43	102	9	3	2	32	34	3	28	.270	.335	.325	97	-2	12	.879	-8	95	64	S-68,3-41	-0.6
1911	Cin N	111	360	50	94	16	7	0	36	44	2	38	.261	.345	.344	97	-1	10	.906	-11	94	72	S-93/2-6,3-5,1-2,O(RF)	-0.5
1912	Phi N	54	171	27	50	6	3	1	23	21	0	20	.292	.370	.380	99	0	3	.893	-5	87	49	3-46/S-3	-0.4
	Chi N	13	22	4	4	0	2	0	4	1	0	5	.182	.217	.364	58	-2	0	.792	-0	108	0	/S-5,3-3,2	-0.2
	Year	67	193	31	54	6	5	1	27	22	0	25	.280	.353	.378	95	-2	3	.892	-6	88	47	3-49/S-8,2	-0.6
1914	Buf F	151	541	69	118	20	3	2	42	40	1	55	.218	.273	.277	49	-47	35	**.962**	10	**109**	110	*2-129,S-16/3-5	-3.6
1915	Buf F	92	282	24	56	9	1	1	19	26	1	26	.199	.269	.248	45	-25	11	.930	-1	89	106	2-48,3-35/S-2,1	-2.7
Total	6	651	2170	256	520	69	25	7	188	198	8	172	.240	.306	.304	74	-88	87	.901	-20	96	91	S-306,2-184,3-135/1-3,O(RF)C	-9.4
DOWNING, BRIAN Brian Jay B 10.9.1950 Los Angeles, CA BR/TR 5-10/194# d5.31																								
1973	Chi A	34	73	5	13	1	0	2	4	10-1	0	17	.178	.277	.274	54	-4	0-0	1.000	5	95	144	O-13(8-0-6),C-11/3-8,D	0.0
1974	Chi A	108	293	41	66	12	1	10	39	51-3	2	72	.225	.344	.375	104	3	0-1	.994	-2	79	105	C-63,O-39(5-0-34)/D-9	0.2
1975	Chi A	138	420	58	101	12	1	7	41	76-5	3	75	.240	.356	.324	93	0	13-4	.990	2	106	114	*C-137/D	1.0
1976	Chi A	104	317	38	81	14	0	3	30	40-0	1	55	.256	.338	.328	96	0	7-3	.988	-7	91	101	C-93,D-11	-0.4
1977	Chi A	69	169	28	48	4	2	4	25	34-0	2	21	.284	.402	.402	123	7	1-2	.983	2	67	102	C-61/O-3(2-0-1),D-2	1.0
1978	Cal A	133	412	42	105	15	0	7	46	52-2	6	47	.255	.345	.342	98	1	3-2	.993	-7	71	138	*C-128/D-2	-0.1
1979	†Cal A★	148	509	87	166	27	3	12	75	77-4	5	57	.326	.418	.462	142	35	3-3	.985	-19	81	75	*C-129,D-18	2.0
1980	Cal A	30	93	5	27	6	0	2	25	12-1	0	12	.290	.364	.419	119	3	0-2	1.000	-3	43	22	C-16,D-13	0.0
1981	Cal A	93	317	47	79	14	0	9	41	46-1	4	35	.249	.351	.379	110	6	1-1	.990	-4	87	28	O-56(LF),C-37/D-5	0.1
1982	†Cal A	158	623	109	175	37	2	28	84	86-1	5	58	.281	.368	.482	132	30	2-1	**1.000**	-1	95	94	*O-158(LF)	2.2
1983	Cal A	113	403	68	99	15	1	19	53	62-4	5	59	.246	.352	.429	115	10	1-2	.994	-2	88	133	O-84(LF),D-26	0.3
1984	Cal A	156	539	65	148	28	2	23	91	70-3	7	66	.275	.360	.462	128	22	0-4	**1.000**	-4	95	54	*O-131(LF),D-21	1.1
1985	Cal A	150	520	80	137	23	1	20	85	78-3	13	61	.263	.371	.427	119	17	5-3	.992	-4	93	64	*O-121(LF),D-25	0.8
1986	†Cal A	152	513	90	137	27	4	20	95	90-2	17	84	.267	.389	.452	131	27	4-4	.989	-4	94	57	*O-138(LF),D-10	1.6
1987	Cal A	155	567	110	154	29	3	29	77	**106**-6	17	85	.272	.400	.487	139	38	5-5	1.000	-3	76	96	*D-118,O-34(LF)	2.8
1988	Cal A	135	484	80	117	18	2	25	64	81-5	14	63	.242	.362	.442	129	22	3-4	—	0	0	0	*D-132	1.7
1989	Cal A	142	544	59	154	25	2	14	59	56-3	6	87	.283	.354	.414	118	14	0-2	—	0	0	0	*D-141	0.9
1990	Cal A	96	330	47	90	18	2	14	51	50-2	6	45	.273	.374	.467	138	18	0-0	—	0	0	0	D-87	1.6
1991	Tex A	123	407	76	113	17	2	17	49	58-7	8	70	.278	.377	.455	132	19	1-1	—	0	0	0	*D-109	1.6
1992	Tex A	107	320	53	89	18	0	10	39	62-2	8	58	.278	.407	.428	139	21	1-0	—	0	0	0	D-93	1.9
Total	20	2344	7853	1188	2099	360	28	275	1073	1197-55	129	1127	.267	.370	.425	122	289	50-44	.995	-52	92	75	D-824,O-777(737-0-41),C-675/3-8	20.3
DOWNS, RED Jerome Willis B 8.22.1883 Neola, IA D 10.19.1939 Council Bluffs, IA BR/TR 5-11/155# d5.2																								
1907	Det A	105	374	28	82	13	5	1	42	13	2		.219	.249	.289	69	-14	3	.930	-21	91	40	2-80,O-20(12-8-0)/S3	-4.0
1908	†Det A	84	289	28	64	10	3	1	35	5	1		.221	.237	.287	67	-11	2	.925	-4	104	88	2-82/3	-1.7
1912	Bro N	9	32	2	8	3	0	0	3	1	0	5	.250	.273	.344	71	-1	3	.881	-2	100	61	/2-9	-0.3
	Chi N	43	95	9	25	4	3	1	14	9	0	17	.263	.327	.400	99	-1	5	.907	2	101	147	2-16/S-9,3-5	0.2
	Year	52	127	11	33	7	3	1	17	10	0	22	.260	.314	.386	92	-2	8	.896	0	101	110	2-25/S-9,3-5	-0.1
Total	3	241	790	67	179	30	11	3	94	28	3	22	.227	.256	.304	72	-27	13	.924	-25	98	70	2-187/O-20(12-8-0),S-10,3-7	-5.8
DOWSE, TOM Thomas Joseph B 8.12.1866 Mohill, Ireland D 12.14.1946 Riverside, CA BR/TR 5-11/175# d4.21																								
1890	Cle N	40	159	20	33	2	1	0	9	12	1	22	.208	.267	.233	47	-11	3	.870	0	177	226	O-26(6-3-19),1-10/C-3,P	-1.1
1891	Col AA	55	201	24	45	7	0	0	22	13	2	22	.224	.278	.259	57	-11	2	.919	-14	*74*	*81*	C-51/O-5(2-0-3)	-1.8
1892	Lou N	41	145	10	21	2	0	0	7	2	3	15	.145	.173	.159	1	-18	1	.918	-1	*90*	*120*	C-29,1-11/O-3(RF),2	-1.6
	Cin N	1	4	0	0	0	0	0	0	0	0	0	.000	.000	.000	-99	-1	0	1.000	-0	*139*	*0*	/C	-0.1
	Phi N	16	54	3	10	0	0	0	6	2	1	4	.185	.228	.185	25	-5	1	.973	2	*133*	*68*	C-15	-0.2
	Was N	7	27	5	7	1	0	0	2	0	0	3	.259	.259	.296	70	-1	0	.800	-1	0	0	/O-4(LF),C-3	-0.1
	Year	65	230	18	38	3	0	0	15	4	4	22	.165	.193	.178	13	-25	2	.931	-0	*102*	*104*	C-48,1-11/O-7(4-0-3),2	-2.0
Total	3	160	590	62	116	12	1	0	46	29	7	66	.197	.243	.220	38	-47	7	.921	-15	*88*	*91*	C-102/O-38(12-3-25),1-21,2P	-4.9

Year	Tm Lg	G	AB	R	H	2B	3B	HR	RBI	BB-IB	HP	SO	AVG	OBP	SLG	AOPS	ABR	SB-CS	FA	FR	Rng	Thr	G at Pos	BFW
DOYLE, BRIAN Brian Reed B 1.26.1955 Glasgow, KY BL/TR 5-10/160# d4.30 b-Denny																								
1978	†NY A	39	52	6	10	0	0	0	0	0-0	0	3	.192	.192	.192	9	-7	0-3	.989	4	109	131	2-29/S-7,3-5	-0.2
1979	NY A	20	32	2	4	2	0	0	5	3-0	0	1	.125	.200	.188	5	-4	0-0	.944	-2	116	107	2-13/3-6	-0.6
1980	NY A	34	75	8	13	1	0	1	5	6-0	0	7	.173	.235	.227	27	-8	1-1	.953	0	93	59	2-20,S-12/3-2	-0.6
1981	Oak A	17	40	2	5	0	0	0	3	1-0	0	2	.125	.146	.125	-22	-6	0-1	1.000	-3	86	65	2-17	-1.0
Total	4	110	199	18	32	3	0	1	13	10-0	0	13	.161	.201	.191	10	-25	1-5	.977	-1	99	91	/2-79,S-19,3-13	-2.4
DOYLE, CONNY Cornelius J. B 1862 , Ireland D 7.29.1921 ElPaso, TX 5-10/185# d6.23																								
1883	Phi N	16	68	3	15	3	2	0	3	0		15	.221	.221	.324	69	-3		.788	-1	85	0	O-16(LF)	-0.4
1884	Pit AA	15	58	8	17	3	2	0		2	0		.293	.317	.414	138	2		.818	-1	41	0	O-14(LF)/S	0.1
Total	2	31	126	11	32	6	4	0	3	2	0	15	.254	.266	.365	101	-1		.800	-2	65	0	/O-30(LF),S	-0.3
DOYLE, DANNY Howard James B 1.24.1917 McLoud, OK BB/TR 6-1/195# d9.14 Mil 1944-45																								
1943	Bos A	13	43	2	9	1	0	0	6	7	0	9	.209	.320	.233	62	-2	0-1	.964	-2	*87*	*91*	C-13	-0.4
DOYLE, JIM James Francis B 12.25.1881 Detroit, MI D 2.1.1912 Syracuse, NY BR/TR 5-10/168# d5.4																								
1910	Cin N	7	13	1	2	2	0	0	1	0	0	2	.154	.154	.308	36	-1	0	.875	-1	44	0	/3-3,O(CF)	-0.2
1911	Chi N	130	472	69	133	23	12	5	62	40	2	54	.282	.340	.413	110	5	19	.922	8	**116**	**145**	*3-127	1.6
Total	2	137	485	70	135	25	12	5	63	40	2	56	.278	.336	.410	109	4	19	.921	7	115	142	3-130/O(CF)	1.4
DOYLE, JEFF Jeffrey Donald B 10.2.1956 Havre, MT BB/TR 5-9/160# d9.13																								
1983	StL N	13	37	4	11	1	2	0	2	1-1	0	3	.297	.316	.432	105	0	0-0	.966	-0	91	164	2-12	0.0
DOYLE, JACK John Joseph "Dirty Jack" B 10.25.1869 Killorglin, Ireland D 12.31.1958 Holyoke, MA BR/TR 5-9/155# d8.27 M2 U1 OF Total (13-LF 45-CF 76-RF)																								
1889	Col AA	11	36	6	10	1	1	0	3	6	0	6	.278	.381	.361	118	1	9	.897	-2			/C-7,O-3(RF),2-2	0.0
1890	Col AA	77	298	47	80	17	7	2	44	13	0		.268	.299	.393	111	2	27	.887	-4	*105*	*97*	C-38,S-25/O-9(2-6-1),2-6,3-3	0.1
1891	Cle N	69	250	43	69	14	4	0	43	26	3	44	.276	.351	.364	104	2	24	.897	-5	*92*	*113*	C-29,O-21(4-8-10),3-20/S	-0.1
1892	Cle N	24	88	17	26	4	1	1	14	6	0	10	.295	.340	.398	118	2	5	.875	0	143	257	O-12(1-0-11)/C-9,1S	0.2
	NY N	90	366	61	109	22	1	5	55	18	3	30	.298	.336	.404	126	10	42	.864	-20	91	62	2-31,C-26,O-17(0-10-7),3-13/S-7	-0.6
	Year	114	454	78	135	26	2	6	69	24	3	40	.297	.337	.403	124	12	47	.890	-20	*86*	*150*	C-35,2-31,O-29(1-10-18),3-13/S-8,1	-0.4
1893	NY N	82	318	56	102	17	5	1	51	27	5	12	.321	.383	.415	111	5	40	.919	-1	*98*	*130*	C-48,O-29(0-21-8)/S-4,3-3,1	0.6
1894	†NY N	107	427	94	157	30	8	3	103	37	3	3	.368	.422	.496	121	16	44	.965	-1	106	90	*1-101/C-6	1.2
1895	NY N	82	319	52	100	21	3	1	66	24	2	12	.313	.365	.408	101	1	35	.968	-3	108	78	1-58,2-13/3-6,C-4,M	0.0
1896	†Bal N	118	487	116	165	29	4	1	101	42	8	15	.339	.400	.421	115	13	73	.974	-12	64	126	*1-118/2	0.0
1897	†Bal N	114	460	91	163	29	4	2	87	29	1		.354	.394	.448	122	15	62	.979	4	118	**126**	*1-114	1.6
1898	Was N	43	177	26	54	2	2	2	26	7	1		.305	.335	.373	103	0	9	.963	-1	96	93	1-38/2-5,M	-0.2
	NY N	82	297	42	84	15	3	1	43	12	3		.283	.317	.364	98	-2	14	.860	2	189	152	O-38(6-0-32),1-24,S-15/3-5,C-2	-0.1
	Year	125	474	68	138	17	5	3	69	19	4		.291	.324	.367	100	-2	23	.970	0	102	85	1-62,O-38(6-0-32),S-15/2-5,3-5,C-2	-0.3
1899	NY N	119	452	56	135	16	7	3	77	33	4		.299	.352	.385	106	3	35	.976	6	129	102	*1-114/C-5	0.9
1900	NY N	133	505	69	135	24	1	1	66	34	3		.267	.317	.325	81	-12	34	.971	7	130	112	*1-133	-0.5
1901	Chi N	75	285	21	66	9	2	0	39	7	5		.232	.263	.277	59	-15	8	.973	7	145	87	1-75	-1.0
1902	NY N	51	193	22	58	13	0	0	18	11	1		.301	.341	.368	120	5	12	.991	5	134	108	1-51	0.9
	Was A	78	312	52	77	15	2	1	20	29	0		.247	.311	.317	74	-11	6	.929	-7	100	60	2-68/1-7,O-4(RF),C-2	-1.7
1903	Bro N	**139**	524	84	164	27	6	0	91	54	5		.313	.383	.387	123	18	34	.981	2	103	107	*1-139	1.7
1904	Bro N	8	22	2	5	1	0	0	2	6	1		.227	.414	.273	116	1	1	1.000	1	138	30	/1-8	0.2
	Phi N	66	236	20	52	10	3	1	22	19	1		.220	.281	.301	83	-5	4	.977	4	124	89	1-65/2	-0.3
	Year	74	258	22	57	11	3	1	24	25	2		.221	.295	.298	86	-4	5	.980	5	126	83	1-73/2	-0.1
1905	NY A	1	3	0	0	0	0	0	0	0	0		.000	.000	.000	-90	-1	0	.833	-1	0	0	/1	-0.2
Total	17	1569	6055	977	1811	316	64	25	971	440	49	132	.299	.351	.385	106	48	518	.975	-18	113	104	*1-1048,C-176,O-133R,2-127/S3	2.7
DOYLE, JOE Joseph K. B Cincinnati, OH d4.20																								
1872	Nat NA	9	41	6	11	1	0	0	9	0		0	.268	.268	.293	62	-2	0-0	.667	-4	86	0	/S-8,2	-0.5
DOYLE, LARRY Lawrence Joseph "Laughing Larry" B 7.31.1886 Caseyville, IL D 3.1.1974 Saranac Lake, NY BL/TR 5-10/165# d7.22																								
1907	NY N	69	227	16	59	3	0	0	16	20	0		.260	.320	.273	83	-4	3	.917	-21	81	32	2-69	-2.9
1908	NY N	104	377	65	116	16	9	0	33	22	5		.308	.354	.398	134	13	17	.935	-8	96	108	*2-102	0.7
1909	NY N	147	570	86	**172**	27	11	6	49	45	7		.302	.360	.419	140	25	31	.940	-17	84	**116**	*2-144	1.0
1910	NY N	151	575	97	164	21	14	8	69	71	5	26	.285	.369	.412	128	20	39	.930	-18	91	100	*2-151	0.3
1911	†NY N	143	526	102	163	25	**25**	13	77	71	5	39	.310	.397	.527	153	35	38	.944	-21	85	88	*2-141	1.6
1912	†NY N	143	558	98	184	33	8	10	90	56	2	20	.330	.393	.471	132	25	36	.948	-3	93	**131**	*2-143	2.3
1913	†NY N	132	482	67	135	25	6	5	73	59	5	29	.280	.364	.388	114	11	38-14	.955	-14	87	118	*2-130	0.2
1914	NY N	145	539	87	140	19	8	5	63	58	10	25	.260	.343	.353	111	8	17	.959	-17	89	119	*2-145	-0.7
1915	NY N	150	591	86	**189**	**40**	10	4	70	32	3	28	**.320**	.358	.442	150	34	22-18	.947	-9	94	**112**	*2-147	2.8
1916	NY N	113	441	55	118	24	10	2	47	27	4	23	.268	.316	.381	120	9	17	.960	14	103	123	*2-113	2.8
	Chi N	9	38	6	15	5	1	1	7	1	0	1	.395	.410	.658	203	4	2	.982	4	122	265	/2-9	0.9
	Year	122	479	61	133	29	11	3	54	28	4	24	.278	.323	.403	127	14	19	**.962**	18	104	**134**	*2-122	3.7
1917	Chi N	135	476	48	121	19	5	6	61	48	0	28	.254	.323	.353	99	0	5	.952	2	94	96	*2-128	0.5
1918	NY N	75	257	38	67	7	4	3	36	37	0	10	.261	.354	.354	118	7	10	.969	-7	101	90	2-73	0.1
1919	NY N	113	381	61	110	14	10	7	52	31	5	17	.289	.350	.433	136	16	12	.956	7	**106**	**130**	*2-100	2.7
1920	NY N	137	471	48	134	21	2	4	50	47	2	28	.285	.352	.363	107	6	11-9	.967	-23	91	106	*2-133	-1.7
Total	14	1766	6509	960	1887	299	123	74	793	625	53	274	.290	.357	.408	126	209	298-41	.949	-133	92	109	*2-1728	10.6
DOYLE, DENNY Robert Dennis B 1.17.1944 Glasgow, KY BL/TR 5-9/175# d4.7 b-Brian																								
1970	Phi N	112	413	43	86	10	7	2	16	33-3	0	64	.208	.266	.281	48	-32	6-5	.978	-17	83	83	*2-103	-4.4
1971	Phi N	95	342	34	79	12	1	3	24	19-0	5	31	.231	.280	.298	64	-16	4-2	.967	8	106	106	2-91	-0.2
1972	Phi N	123	442	33	110	14	2	1	26	31-2	0	33	.249	.295	.296	68	-19	6-7	.982	-11	92	90	*2-119	-2.5
1973	Phi N	116	370	45	101	9	3	3	26	31-8	0	32	.273	.327	.338	83	-9	1-3	.974	3	103	100	*2-114	0.0
1974	Cal A	147	511	47	133	19	2	1	34	25-2	1	49	.260	.295	.311	79	-15	6-7	.983	18	105	91	*2-146/S-2	1.2
1975	Cal A	8	15	0	1	0	0	0	0	1-0	0	1	.067	.125	.067	-48	-3	0-0	.926	1	112	70	/2-6,3	-0.2
	†Bos A	89	310	50	96	21	2	4	36	14-0	1	11	.310	.339	.429	107	3	5-7	.974	-22	90	70	2-84/3-6,S-2	-1.6
	Year	97	325	50	97	21	2	4	36	15-0	1	12	.298	.329	.412	102	0	5-7	.970	-21	91	70	2-90/3-7,S-2	-1.8
1976	Bos A	117	432	51	108	15	5	0	26	22-0	0	39	.250	.285	.308	66	-19	8-5	.977	-13	97	100	*2-112	-2.7
1977	Bos A	137	455	54	109	13	6	2	49	29-3	4	50	.240	.289	.308	57	-28	2-4	.979	-7	100	110	*2-137	-2.9
Total	8	944	3290	357	823	113	28	16	237	205-18	11	310	.250	.295	.316	70	-138	38-40	.977	-40	97	95	2-912/3-7,S-4	-13.3
DOZIER, D. J. William Henry B 9.21.1965 Norfolk, VA BR/TR 6/202# d5.6																								
1992	NY N	25	47	4	9	2	0	0	2	4-0	1	19	.191	.264	.234	44	-3	4-0	.971	1	122	0	O-17(LF)	-0.3
DRAKE, DELOS Delos Daniel B 12.3.1886 Girard, OH D 10.3.1965 Findlay, OH BR/TL 5-11.5/170# d4.30																								
1911	Det A	95	315	37	88	9	9	1	36	17	4		.279	.324	.375	90	-6	20	.942	-6	102	33	O-83(74-5-5)/1-2	-1.5
1914	StL F	138	514	51	129	18	8	3	42	31	1	57	.251	.295	.335	68	-32	17	.957	-0	103	98	*O-116(69-36-11),1-18	-4.1
1915	StL F	102	343	32	91	23	4	1	41	23	1	27	.265	.313	.364	86	-11	6	.974	-1	103	83	O-97(7-62-33)/1	-1.9
Total	3	335	1172	120	308	50	21	5	119	71	6	84	.263	.308	.354	79	-49	43	.959	-7	103	76	O-296(150-103-49)/1-21	-7.5
DRAKE, LARRY Larry Francis B 5.4.1921 McKinney, TX D 7.14.1985 Houston, TX BL/TR 6-1.5/195# d7.20																								
1945	Phi A	1	2	0	0	0	0	0	0	0	0	2	.000	.000	.000	-99	-1	0-0	1.000	0	116	0	/O(LF)	-0.1
1948	Was A	4	7	0	2	0	0	0	1	1	0	3	.286	.375	.286	79	0	0-0	1.000	-0	95	0	/O-2(RF)	0.0
Total	2	5	9	0	2	0	0	0	1	1	0	5	.222	.300	.222	44	-1	0-0	1.000	-0	102	0	/O-3(1-0-2)	-0.1
DRAKE, LYMAN Lyman Daniel B 2.9.1852 Berea, OH D 2.6.1932 Muskegon, MI 6/?# d6.29																								
1884	Was AA	2	7	0	2	1	0	0	2	0	0		.286	.286	.429	147	0		.000	-1	0	0	/O-2(RF)	0.0
DRAKE, SAMMY Samuel Harrison B 10.7.1934 Little Rock, AR BB/TR 5-11/175# d4.17 b-Solly																								
1960	Chi N	15	15	5	1	0	0	0	0	1-0	0	4	.067	.125	.067	-46	-3	0-0	1.000	-1	77	0	/3-6,2-2	-0.4
1961	Chi N	13	5	1	0	0	0	0	0	1-0	0	1	.000	.167	.000	-50	-1	0-0	1.000	0	157	0	/O(RF)	-0.1
1962	NY N	25	52	2	10	0	0	0	7	6-1	0	12	.192	.276	.192	28	-5	0-0	.977	-1	94	105	2-10/3-6	-0.6
Total	3	53	72	8	11	0	0	0	7	8-1	0	17	.153	.237	.153	8	-9	0-0	.978	-2	91	97	/2-12,3-12,O(RF)	-1.1

Year	Tm Lg	G	AB	R	H	2B	3B	HR	RBI	BB-IB	HP	SO	AVG	OBP	SLG	AOPS	ABR	SB-CS	FA	FR	Rng	Thr	G at Pos	BFW
DRAKE, SOLLY Solomon Louis B 10.23.1930 Little Rock, AR BB/TR 6/170# d4.17 b-Sammy																								
1956	Chi N	65	215	29	55	9	1	2	15	23-0	1	35	.256	.331	.335	81	-5	9-5	.993	0	103	78	O-53(CF)	-0.7
1959	LA N	9	8	2	2	0	0	0	0	1-0	0	3	.250	.333	.250	54	0	1-0	.667	-0	82	0	/O-4(RF)	-0.1
	Phi N	67	62	10	9	1	0	0	3	8-0	0	15	.145	.243	.161	10	-8	5-5	1.000	1	133	0	O-37(22-11-9)	-0.8
	Year	76	70	12	11	1	0	0	3	9-0	0	18	.157	.253	.171	15	-8	6-5	.974	1	128	0	O-41(22-11-13)	-0.9
Total	2	141	285	41	66	10	1	2	18	32-0	1	53	.232	.311	.295	64	-13	15-10	.989	1	108	62	/O-94(22-64-13)	-1.6
DRANSFELDT, KELLY Kelly Daniel B 4.16.1975 Joliet, IL BR/TR 6-2/195# d5.1																								
1999	Tex A	16	53	3	10	1	0	1	5	3-0	0	12	.189	.232	.264	25	-6	0-0	.966	4	118	118	S-16	-0.1
2000	Tex A	16	26	2	3	2	0	0	2	1-0	0	14	.115	.148	.192	-14	-5	0-0	1.000	3	125	143	S-14/2-2	-0.1
2001	Tex A	4	3	0	0	0	0	0	0	0-0	0	0	.000	.000	.000	-97	-1	0-0	1.000	0	176	0	/S-3,3	-0.1
Total	3	36	82	5	13	3	0	1	7	4-0	0	26	.159	.198	.232	9	-12	0-0	.977	7	122	122	/S-33,2-2,3	-0.3
DRAUBY, JAKE Jacob C. B 1865 Harrisburg, PA 5-10/163# d10.3																								
1892	Was N	10	34	3	7	0	1	0	3	2	0	12	.206	.250	.265	57	-2	0	.763	-2	88	135	3-10	-0.3
DREESEN, BILL William Richard B 7.26.1904 New York, NY D 11.9.1971 Mt.Vernon, NY BL/TR 5-7.5/160# d5.1																								
1931	Bos N	48	180	38	40	10	4	1	10	23	0	23	.222	.310	.339	77	-6	1	.910	-4	102	14	3-47	-0.9
DRESCHER, BILL William Clayton "Dutch" B 5.23.1921 Congers, NY D 5.15.1968 Haverstraw, NY BL/TR 6-2/190# d4.19																								
1944	NY A	4	7	0	1	0	0	0	0	0	0	0	.143	.143	.143	-18	-1	0-0	.875	-0	*0*	*0*	/C	-0.1
1945	NY A	48	126	10	34	3	1	0	15	8	0	5	.270	.313	.310	77	-4	0-2	.991	-6	*68*	*93*	C-33	-0.9
1946	NY A	5	6	0	2	1	0	0	1	0	0	0	.333	.333	.500	129	0	0-0	1.000	1	*0*	*0*	/C-3	0.1
Total	3	57	139	10	37	4	1	0	16	8	0	5	.266	.306	.309	75	-5	0-2	.985	-5	*63*	*86*	/C-37	-0.9
DRESSEN, CHUCK Charles Walter B 9.20.1898 Decatur, IL D 8.10.1966 Detroit, MI BR/TR 5-5.5/146# d4.17 M16 C12																								
1925	Cin N	76	215	35	59	8	2	3	19	12	2	4	.274	.319	.372	78	-8	5-3	.951	4	118	115	3-47/2-5,O-4(3-0-1)	-0.1
1926	Cin N	127	474	76	126	27	11	4	48	49	3	31	.266	.338	.395	99	-1	0	.966	16	**122**	101	*3-123/SO(LF)	2.2
1927	Cin N	144	548	78	160	36	10	2	55	71	3	32	.292	.376	.405	113	13	7	**.967**	12	116	96	*3-142/S-2	3.3
1928	Cin N	135	498	72	145	26	3	1	59	43	6	22	.291	.355	.361	89	-7	10	.938	-2	103	110	*3-135	0.0
1929	Cin N	110	401	49	98	22	3	1	36	41	4	21	.244	.321	.322	63	-23	8	.932	-13	89	70	3-98/2-8	-2.7
1930	Cin N	33	19	0	4	0	0	0	1	1	0	3	.211	.250	.211	14	-3	0	1.000	1	197	0	3-10/2-3	-0.1
1931	Cin N	5	15	0	1	0	0	0	0	1	0	1	.067	.125	.067	-50	-3	0	.846	-0	99	144	/3-4	-0.4
1933	NY N	16	45	3	10	4	0	0	3	1	0	4	.222	.239	.311	57	-3	0	.972	-0	87	129	3-16	-0.3
Total	8	646	2215	313	603	123	29	11	221	219	18	118	.272	.343	.369	89	-35	30-3	.953	18	109	98	3-575/2-16,O-5(4-0-1),S-3	1.9
DRESSEN, LEE Lee August B 7.23.1889 Ellinwood, KS D 6.30.1931 Diller, NE BL/TL 6/165# d4.21																								
1914	StL N	46	103	16	24	2	1	0	7	11	0	20	.233	.307	.272	73	-3	2	.982	-1	89	116	1-38	-0.5
1918	Det A	31	107	10	19	1	2	0	3	21	2	10	.178	.323	.224	68	-3	2	.988	-4	55	62	1-30	-0.8
Total	2	77	210	26	43	3	3	0	10	32	2	30	.205	.316	.248	71	-6	4	.985	-5	71	87	/1-68	-1.3
DREW, CAMERON Cameron Steward B 2.12.1964 Boston, MA BL/TR 6-5/230# d9.9																								
1988	Hou N	7	16	1	3	0	1	0	1	0-0	0	1	.188	.188	.313	43	-1	0-0	1.000	0	123	0	/O-5(3-0-2)	-0.1
DREW, DAVE David d5.14																								
1884	Phi U	2	9	1	4	0	0	0		0			.444	.444	.444	184	1		—	0	0	0	/P2S	0.0
	Was U	13	53	8	16	1	2	0		1			.302	.315	.396	118	-1		.806	1	91	0	/S-8,1-5,O(CF)	0.0
	Year	15	62	9	20	1	2	0		1			.323	.333	.403	127	0		.813	1	88	0	/S-9,1-5,P2O(CF)	0.0
DREW, J.D. David Jonathan B 11.20.1975 Tallahassee, FL BL/TR 6-1/190# d9.8 b-Tim																								
1998	StL N	14	36	9	15	3	1	5	13	4-0	0	10	.417	.463	.972	271	9	0-0	1.000	1	111	168	O-11(6-2-5)	0.9
1999	StL N	104	368	72	89	16	6	13	39	50-0	6	77	.242	.340	.424	92	-5	19-3	.972	2	101	174	O-98(1-97-0)	0.1
2000	†StL N	135	407	73	120	17	2	18	57	67-4	6	99	.295	.401	.479	121	15	17-9	.966	2	108	85	*O-127(24-26-98)	1.3
2001	†StL N	109	375	80	121	18	5	27	73	57-4	4	75	.323	.414	.613	163	36	13-3	.973	-1	99	104	*O-107(1-20-97)	3.2
2002	†StL N	135	424	61	107	19	1	18	56	57-4	8	104	.252	.349	.429	111	5	8-2	.987	-2	103	54	*O-120(0-6-119)	-0.1
2003	StL N	100	287	60	83	13	3	15	42	36-0	3	48	.289	.374	.512	134	14	2-2	.994	4	106	161	O-75(1-26-53)	1.5
Total	6	597	1897	355	535	86	18	96	280	271-12	27	413	.282	.377	.498	126	74	59-19	.977	7	103	111	O-538(33-177-372)	6.9
DREWS, FRANK Frank John B 5.25.1916 Buffalo, NY D 4.22.1972 Buffalo, NY BR/TR 5-10/175# d8.13																								
1944	Bos N	46	141	14	29	9	1	0	10	25	1	14	.206	.329	.284	71	-4	0	.959	1	98	102	2-46	-0.1
1945	Bos N	49	147	13	30	4	1	0	19	16	0	18	.204	.282	.245	47	-10	0	.976	2	111	111	2-48	-0.6
Total	2	95	288	27	59	13	2	0	29	41	1	32	.205	.306	.264	59	-14	0	.967	3	104	106	/2-94	-0.7
DRIESSEN, DAN Daniel B 7.29.1951 Hilton Head Island, SC BL/TR 5-11/190# d6.9																								
1973	†Cin N	102	366	49	110	15	2	4	47	24-4	2	37	.301	.346	.385	108	3	8-3	.946	-4	93	139	3-87,1-35/O(RF)	-0.2
1974	Cin N	150	470	63	132	23	6	7	56	48-5	1	62	.281	.347	.400	111	7	10-5	.915	-15	86	101	*3-126,1-47/O-3(RF)	-1.0
1975	†Cin N	88	210	38	59	8	1	7	38	35-2	2	30	.281	.386	.429	124	8	10-3	.986	-3	101	144	1-41,O-29(10-0-19)	0.3
1976	†Cin N	98	219	32	54	11	1	7	44	43-2	0	32	.247	.362	.402	116	6	14-1	.997	-2	93	124	1-40,O-20(LF)	0.4
1977	Cin N	151	536	75	161	31	4	17	91	64-8	3	85	.300	.375	.468	123	19	31-13	.994	-3	86	106	*1-148	0.9
1978	Cin N	153	524	68	131	23	3	16	70	75-7	4	79	.250	.345	.397	108	7	28-9	**.996**	1	98	79	*1-151	0.2
1979	†Cin N	150	515	72	129	24	3	18	75	62-11	3	77	.250	.330	.414	102	2	11-5	.993	-5	87	105	*1-143	-1.1
1980	Cin N	154	524	81	139	36	1	14	74	**93**-17	**6**	68	.265	.377	.418	123	22	19-6	.995	-5	85	102	*1-151	1.0
1981	Cin N	82	233	35	55	14	0	7	33	40-3	2	31	.236	.349	.386	108	4	2-4	.995	-7	60	104	1-74	-0.8
1982	Cin N	149	516	64	139	25	1	17	57	82-8	2	62	.269	.368	.421	119	16	11-6	**.998**	-8	73	109	*1-144	-0.1
1983	Cin N	122	386	57	107	17	1	12	57	75-10	0	51	.277	.390	.420	121	15	6-4	**.996**	-4	84	82	*1-112	0.4
1984	Cin N	81	218	27	61	13	0	7	28	37-2	0	25	.280	.378	.436	124	9	2-1	.991	-4	72	64	1-70	0.1
	Mon N	51	169	20	43	11	0	9	32	17-6	0	15	.254	.321	.479	128	6	0-1	.995	-3	75	117	1-45	0.0
	Year	132	387	47	104	24	0	16	60	54-8	0	40	.269	.354	.455	126	14	2-2	.992	-7	73	86	*1-115	0.1
1985	Mon N	91	312	31	78	18	0	6	25	33-9	2	29	.250	.324	.365	99	0	2-2	.997	2	109	118	1-88	-0.4
	SF N	54	181	22	42	8	0	3	22	17-3	1	22	.232	.297	.326	79	-5	0-0	.998	-1	89	83	1-49	-0.9
	Year	145	493	53	120	26	0	9	47	50-12	3	51	.243	.314	.351	92	-5	2-2	.997	2	102	106	*1-137	-1.3
1986	SF N	15	16	2	3	2	0	0	0	4-1	0	4	.188	.350	.313	89	0	0-0	1.000	0	143	0	/1-4	0.0
	Hou N	17	24	5	7	1	0	1	3	5-1	0	2	.292	.414	.458	144	2	0-0	1.000	-1	60	106	1-12	0.1
	Year	32	40	7	10	3	0	1	3	9-2	0	6	.250	.388	.400	122	2	0-0	1.000	-0	84	76	1-16	0.1
1987	†StL N	24	60	5	14	2	0	1	11	7-1	0	8	.233	.309	.317	66	-3	0-0	.993	-0	95	104	1-21	-0.4
Total	15	1732	5479	746	1464	282	23	153	763	761-100	28	719	.267	.356	.411	113	118	154-63	.995	-59	87	101	*1-1375,3-213/O-53(30-0-23)	-1.5
DRILL, LEW Lewis L B 5.9.1877 Browerville, MN D 7.4.1969 St.Paul, MN BR/TR 5-6/186# d4.23																								
1902	Was A	38	123	21	34	7	2	1	16	16	2		.276	.369	.390	110	2	0	.919	-10	*94*	*78*	C-28/2-4,O-4(1-0-3),3	-0.5
	Bal A	2	8	2	2	0	0	0	0	0	0		.250	.250	.250	37	-1	0	1.000	0	*93*	*272*	/C1	0.0
	Was A	33	98	12	24	3	2	0	13	10	2		.245	.327	.316	78	-3	5	.926	-4	*94*	*78*	C-25/O-4(RF),2	-0.4
	Year	73	229	35	60	10	4	1	29	26	4		.262	.347	.354	94	-1	5	.924	-13	*97*	*86*	C-54/O-8(1-0-7),2-5,31	-0.9
1903	Was A	51	154	11	39	9	3	0	23	15	3		.253	.331	.351	103	1	4	.966	-7	*76*	*90*	C-47/1-3	-0.1
1904	Was A	46	142	17	38	7	2	1	11	21	6		.268	.385	.366	140	8	3	.934	-6	*73*	*102*	C-29,O-14(0-3-11)	0.6
	Det A	51	160	7	39	6	1	0	13	20	2		.244	.335	.294	103	2	2	.950	-6	*83*	*96*	C-49/1-2	0.0
	Year	97	302	24	77	13	3	1	24	41	8		.255	.359	.328	121	10	5	.944	-12	*79*	*98*	C-78,O-14(0-3-11)/1-2	0.6
1905	Det A	72	211	17	55	9	0	0	24	32	3		.261	.366	.303	112	5	7	.970	-6	*72*	*92*	C-71	0.7
Total	4	293	896	87	231	41	10	2	100	114	18		.258	.353	.333	108	14	21	.953	-39	*80*	*92*	C-250/O-22(1-3-18),1-6,2-5,3	0.3
DRISCOLL, DENNIS Dennis F. D 2.21.1901 Providence, RI d7.25																								
1885	Buf N	7	19	2	3	0	0	0	0	2		5	.158	.238	.158	29	-1		.719	-4	70	41	/2-7	-0.5
DRISCOLL, JIM James Bernard B 5.14.1944 Medford, MA BL/TR 5-11/175# d6.17																								
1970	Oak A	21	52	2	10	0	0	1	2	2-0	1	15	.192	.236	.250	35	-5	0-0	.967	-3	94	143	/2-7,S-7	-0.7
1972	Tex A	15	18	0	0	0	0	0	0	2-1	0	3	.000	.100	.000	-72	-4	0-0	.900	1	107	203	/2-4,3-2	-0.3
Total	2	36	70	2	10	0	0	1	2	4-1	1	18	.143	.200	.186	9	-9	0-0	.950	-2	97	155	/2-11,S-7,3-2	-1.0

Year	Tm Lg	G	AB	R	H	2B	3B	HR	RBI	BB-IB	HP	SO	AVG	OBP	SLG	AOPS	ABR	SB-CS	FA	FR	Rng	Thr	G at Pos	BFW
DRISCOLL, DENNY John F. B 11.19.1855 Lowell, MA D 7.11.1886 Lowell, MA BL/TL 5-10.5/160# d7.1 ▲																								
1880	Buf N	18	65	1	10	1	0	0	4	1		7	.154	.167	.169	14	-6		.895	0	96	466	O-14(CF)/P-6	-0.4
1882	Pit AA	23	80	12	11	2	0	1		3			.138	.169	.200	25	-2		.885	-4	75	111	P-23	0.0
1883	Pit AA	41	148	19	27	2	1	0		4			.182	.204	.209	35	-10		.890	5	**146**	97	P-41/O-4(0-2-2),3	0.2
1884	Lou AA	13	48	5	9	1	0	0	1	2	0		.188	.220	.208	42	-3		.816	2	181	561	P-13/O-2(1-1-0)	0.1
Total	4	95	341	37	57	6	1	1	5	10	0	7	.167	.191	.199	30	-21		.872	3	127	165	/P-83,O-20(1-17-2),3	-0.1
DRISCOLL, PADDY John Leo B 1.11.1895 Evanston, IL D 6.28.1968 Chicago, IL BR/TR 5-8.5/155# d6.12 Mil 1918																								
1917	Chi N	13	28	2	3	1	0	0	3	2	0	6	.107	.167	.143	-4	-3	2	.882	0	114	166	/2-8,3-2,S	-0.4
DRISSEL, MIKE Michael F. B 12.19.1864 St.Louis, MO D 2.26.1913 St.Louis, MO BR/TR 5-11/?# d9.5																								
1885	StL AA	6	20	0	1	0	0	0	0	0	0		.050	.050	.050	-65	-4		.971	0			/C-6	-0.3
DROPO, WALT Walter "Moose" B 1.30.1923 Moosup, CT BR/TR 6-5/220# d4.19																								
1949	Bos A	11	41	3	6	2	0	0	1	3	0	7	.146	.205	.195	6	-6	0-0	1.000	-1	54	118	1-11	-0.7
1950	Bos A★	136	559	101	180	28	8	34	**144**	45	5	75	.322	.378	.583	130	22	0-0	.988	-3	90	104	*1-134	1.3
1951	Bos A	99	360	37	86	14	0	11	57	38	0	52	.239	.312	.369	76	-13	0-0	.987	-0	100	98	1-93	-1.6
1952	Bos A	37	132	13	35	7	1	6	27	11	2	22	.265	.331	.470	112	2	0-0	.994	-1	85	95	1-35	0.0
	Det A	115	459	56	128	17	3	23	70	26	2	63	.279	.320	.479	120	8	2-2	.989	1	99	95	*1-115	0.5
	Year	152	591	69	163	24	4	29	97	37	4	85	.276	.323	.477	118	10	2-2	.990	-0	96	95	*1-150	0.5
1953	Det A	152	606	61	150	30	3	13	96	29	6	69	.248	.289	.371	78	-21	2-0	.990	13	**131**	77	*1-150	-1.7
1954	Det A	107	320	27	90	14	2	4	44	24	0	41	.281	.328	.375	95	-3	0-1	.996	2	104	88	1-95	-0.7
1955	Chi A	141	453	55	127	15	2	19	79	42-8	2	71	.280	.343	.448	109	4	0-1	.995	-5	79	**103**	*1-140	-0.9
1956	Chi A	125	361	42	96	13	1	8	52	37-2	3	51	.266	.334	.374	87	-7	1-0	**.993**	-4	83	111	*1-117	-1.6
1957	Chi A	93	223	24	57	2	0	13	49	16-2	0	40	.256	.300	.439	101	-1	0-1	.987	2	122	108	1-69	-0.3
1958	Chi A	28	52	3	10	1	0	2	8	5-0	1	11	.192	.271	.327	67	-3	0-0	1.000	1	114	81	1-16	-0.3
	Cin N	63	162	18	47	7	2	7	31	12-0	1	31	.290	.335	.488	111	2	0-0	1.000	2	112	97	1-43	0.2
1959	Cin N	26	39	4	4	1	0	1	2	4-0	1	7	.103	.205	.205	9	-5	0-0	1.000	2	141	120	1-23	-0.4
	Bal A	62	151	17	42	9	0	6	21	12-0	0	20	.278	.329	.457	117	3	0-0	.990	-3	73	134	1-54/3-2	-0.2
1960	Bal A	79	179	16	48	8	0	4	21	20-0	1	19	.268	.343	.380	97	0	0-1	.993	-1	88	127	1-67/3	-0.5
1961	Bal A	14	27	1	7	0	0	1	2	4-0	0	3	.259	.355	.370	97	0	0-0	1.000	1	121	203	1-12	0.0
Total	13	1288	4124	478	1113	168	22	152	704	328-12	24	582	.270	.326	.432	100	-18	5-6	.992	2	99	100	*1-1174/3-3	-6.9
DRUMRIGHT, KEITH Keith Alan B 10.21.1954 Springfield, MO BL/TR 5-10/170# d9.1																								
1978	Hou N	17	55	5	9	0	0	0	2	3-0	0	4	.164	.207	.164	5	-7	0-1	.944	-2	94	102	2-17	-0.9
1981	†Oak A	31	86	8	25	1	1	0	11	4-0	0	4	.291	.319	.326	91	-1	0-0	.989	-4	88	61	2-19/D-5	-0.4
Total	2	48	141	13	34	1	1	0	13	7-0	0	8	.241	.275	.262	58	-8	0-1	.969	-5	91	80	/2-36,D-5	-1.3
DUCEY, ROB Robert Thomas B 5.24.1965 Toronto, ON, CAN BL/TR 6-2/180# d5.1																								
1987	Tor A	34	48	12	9	1	0	1	6	8-0	0	10	.188	.298	.271	53	-3	2-0	1.000	-1	97	0	O-28(17-11-3)/D	-0.4
1988	Tor A	27	54	15	17	4	1	0	6	5-0	0	7	.315	.361	.426	123	2	1-0	1.000	-3	70	116	O-26(1-25-0)/D	-0.1
1989	Tor A	41	76	5	16	4	0	0	7	9-1	0	25	.211	.294	.263	59	-4	2-1	1.000	2	102	170	O-35(16-2-18)/D	-0.3
1990	Tor A	19	53	7	16	5	0	0	7	7-0	1	15	.302	.387	.396	119	2	1-1	1.000	-1	104	0	O-19(LF)	0.1
1991	†Tor A	39	68	8	16	2	2	1	4	6-0	0	26	.235	.297	.368	80	-2	2-0	.892	-2	89	95	O-24(18-1-6)/D-2	-0.4
1992	Tor A	23	21	3	1	1	0	0	0	0-0	0	10	.048	.048	.095	-58	-4	0-1	1.000	-1	85	0	O-13(3-2-8)/D-4	-0.6
	Cal A	31	59	4	14	3	0	0	2	5-0	0	12	.237	.292	.288	64	-3	2-3	.944	-0	94	176	O-20(17-1-2)/D	-0.4
	Year	54	80	7	15	4	0	0	2	5-0	0	22	.188	.233	.237	32	-7	2-4	.957	-1	92	129	O-33(20-3-10)/D-5	-1.0
1993	Tex A	27	85	15	24	6	3	2	9	10-2	0	17	.282	.351	.494	132	4	2-3	1.000	-1	91	65	O-26(1-14-13)	0.1
1994	Tex A	11	29	1	5	1	0	0	1	2-0	0	1	.172	.226	.207	13	-4	0-0	.882	-1	87	0	O-10(RF)	-0.5
1997	†Sea A	76	143	25	41	15	2	5	10	6-0	0	31	.287	.311	.524	115	3	3-3	.986	-2	88	130	O-69(43-12-19)	-0.1
1998	Sea A	97	217	30	52	18	2	5	23	23-2	9	61	.240	.336	.410	93	-2	4-3	.970	2	111	102	O-83(23-6-61)	-0.2
1999	Phi N	104	188	29	49	10	2	8	33	38-1	0	57	.261	.383	.463	110	4	2-1	1.000	1	110	41	O-58(39-9-11)/D-2	0.4
2000	Phi N	70	106	16	20	3	1	6	20	20-0	0	36	.189	.317	.406	80	-4	1-0	.919	-2	82	76	O-26(24-1-1)/D-5	-0.6
	Tor A	5	13	2	2	1	0	0	1	2-0	0	2	.154	.267	.231	27	-1	0-0	.889	0	135	0	/O-3(2-0-1)	-0.1
	Phi N	42	46	8	10	1	0	0	5	9-1	0	11	.217	.333	.239	51	-3	0-0	1.000	-7	82	76	/O-7(4-1-2)	-1.1
2001	Phi N	30	27	4	6	1	0	1	4	6-0	0	11	.222	.364	.370	93	0	0-0	1.000	0	134	0	/O-3(1-1-1)	0.0
	Mon N	27	46	6	11	2	0	2	8	10-0	1	14	.239	.379	.413	105	1	0-1	1.000	1	117	160	O-14(9-3-3)/D-3	0.1
	Year	57	73	10	17	3	0	3	12	16-0	1	25	.233	.374	.397	101	1	0-1	1.000	1	120	136	O-17(10-4-4)/D-3	0.1
Total	13	703	1279	190	309	78	13	31	146	166-7	11	346	.242	.331	.396	91	-14	22-17	.976	-13	93	83	O-464(237-89-159)/D-20	-4.1
DUDRA, JOHN John Joseph B 5.27.1916 Assumption, IL D 10.24.1965 Pana, IL BR/TR 5-11.5/175# d9.7 Mil 1942-45																								
1941	Bos N	14	25	3	9	3	1	0	3	3	0	4	.360	.429	.560	185	3	0	.933	0	116	182	/2-5,3-5,1S	0.3
DUFF, PAT Patrick Henry B 5.6.1875 Providence, RI D 9.11.1925 Providence, RI TR 5-10/?# d4.16																								
1906	Was A	1	1	0	0	0	0	0	0	0	0		.000	.000	.000	-99	0	0	—	0			H	0.0
DUFFEE, CHARLIE Charles Edward "Home Run" B 1.27.1866 Mobile, AL D 12.24.1894 Mobile, AL BR/TR d4.17 OF Total (152-LF 257-CF 48-RF)																								
1889	StL AA	137	509	93	124	15	11	16	86	60	3	81	.244	.327	.411	97	-7	21	.936	14	**167**	136	*O-132(1-132-0)/3-5,2-2	0.3
1890	StL AA	98	378	68	104	11	7	3	54	37	3		.275	.344	.365	96	-5	20	.951	8	144	324	O-66(1-65-0),3-33/S	0.1
1891	Col AA	137	552	86	166	28	4	10	90	42	3	36	.301	.353	.420	129	19	41	.927	6	138	142	*O-128(73-55-0)/3-7,S-2	1.8
1892	Was N	132	492	64	122	12	11	6	51	36	2	33	.248	.302	.354	101	-2	28	.913	18	**166**	**174**	*O-125(73-5-48)/3-6,1-4	0.6
1893	Cin N	4	12	3	2	1	0	0	0	5	0	0	.167	.412	.250	76	0	0	.400	-2	0	0	/O-4(LF)	-0.2
Total	5	508	1943	314	518	67	33	35	281	180	11	150	.267	.332	.389	106	5	110	.927	43	154	175	0-455C/3-51,1-4,S-3,2-2	2.6
DUFFY, ED Edward Charles B 1844 , Ireland D 6.21.1889 Brooklyn, NY TR 5-7.5/152# d5.8																								
1871	Chi NA	26	121	30	28	5	0	0	15	3		2	.231	.250	.273	45	-10	11-4	.750	-4	95	95	*S-26/3	-0.8
DUFFY, FRANK Frank Thomas B 10.14.1946 Oakland, CA BR/TR 6-1/180# d9.4																								
1970	Cin N	6	11	1	2	2	0	0	0	1-0	0	2	.182	.250	.364	62	-1	1-0	1.000	1	127	221	/S-5	0.1
1971	Cin N	13	16	0	3	1	0	0	1	1-0	0	2	.188	.235	.250	38	-1	0-0	.944	3	144	165	S-10	0.3
	†SF N	21	28	4	5	0	0	0	2	0-0	0	10	.179	.179	.179	1	-4	0-0	.968	2	104	164	/S-6,23	-0.1
	Year	34	44	4	8	1	0	0	3	1-0	0	12	.182	.200	.205	15	-5	0-0	.955	5	124	165	S-16/23	0.2
1972	Cle A	130	385	23	92	16	4	3	27	31-5	1	54	.239	.297	.325	82	-9	6-2	.977	-3	98	106	*S-126	0.3
1973	Cle A	116	361	34	95	16	4	8	50	25-0	2	41	.263	.312	.396	97	-2	6-6	**.986**	16	106	109	*S-115	2.6
1974	Cle A	158	549	62	128	18	0	8	48	30-0	0	64	.233	.272	.310	68	-24	7-8	.980	-8	102	90	*S-158	-1.6
1975	Cle A	146	482	44	117	22	2	1	47	27-0	2	60	.243	.283	.303	66	-22	10-10	.977	15	109	101	*S-145	0.9
1976	Cle A	133	392	38	83	11	2	2	30	29-2	2	50	.212	.268	.265	58	-21	10-0	**.983**	3	91	**114**	*S-132	-0.2
1977	Cle A	122	334	30	67	13	2	4	31	21-0	0	47	.201	.247	.287	47	-25	8-3	.967	-10	96	99	*S-121	-2.3
1978	Bos A	64	104	12	27	5	0	0	4	6-0	1	11	.260	.306	.308	66	-5	1-1	.960	-2	86	64	3-22,S-21,2-12/D-6	-0.5
1979	Bos A	6	3	0	0	0	0	0	0	0-0	0	1	.000	.000	.000	-95	-1	0-0	1.000	-1	55	0	/2-3,1	-0.1
Total	10	915	2665	248	619	104	14	26	240	171-7	8	342	.232	.279	.311	69	-115	49-30	.977	17	101	104	S-839/3-23,2-16,D-6,1	-0.6
DUFFY, HUGH Hugh B 11.26.1866 Cranston, RI D 10.19.1954 Boston, MA BR/TR 5-7/168# d6.23 M8 C1 HF1945 OF Total (574-LF 677-CF 437-RF)																								
1888	Chi N	71	298	60	84	10	4	7	41	9	1	32	.282	.305	.413	118	5	13	.910	3	162	210	O-67(3-0-64)/S-3,3	0.7
1889	Chi N	**136**	584	144	182	21	7	12	89	46	2	30	.312	.364	.433	116	10	52	.894	-16	76	46	*O-126(RF),S-10	-0.6
1890	Chi P	**138**	596	**161**	**191**	36	16	7	82	59	2	20	.320	.384	.470	122	17	78	.917	9	130	103	*O-137(0-17-120)	1.9
1891	Bos AA	127	536	134	180	20	8	9	**110**	61	4	29	.336	.408	.453	149	34	85	.917	-2	104	70	*O-124(7-2-118)/3-3,S	2.7
1892	†Bos N	147	612	125	184	28	12	5	81	60	1	37	.301	.364	.410	123	15	51	.942	-13	74	92	*O-146(CF)/3-2	-0.6
1893	Bos N	**131**	560	147	203	23	7	6	118	50	1	13	**.363**	.416	.461	123	17	44	.953	-5	67	138	*O-131(0-128-3)	0.3
1894	Bos N	125	539	160	**237**	**51**	16	**18**	145	66	1	15	**.440**	.502	.694	172	64	48	.927	3	131	105	*O-124(4-121-0)/S-2	4.5
1895	Bos N	131	533	112	188	30	6	9	100	65	5	17	.353	.428	.482	125	21	42	.946	3	106	194	*O-131(CF)	1.2
1896	Bos N	131	527	97	158	16	8	5	113	52	2	19	.300	.365	.389	93	-6	39	.957	-5	84	48	*O-120(114-6-0)/2-9,S-2	-1.8
1897	†Bos N	134	550	130	187	25	10	**11**	129	52	6		.340	.403	.482	125	19	41	.975	-2	64	62	*O-129(LF)/2-6,S-2	0.5
1898	Bos N	**152**	568	97	169	13	3	8	108	59	1		.298	.365	.373	106	4	29	.956	1	83	45	*O-152(115-39-0)/31C	-0.6
1899	Bos N	147	588	103	164	29	7	5	102	39	3		.279	.327	.378	85	-14	26	.970	-7	38	18	*O-147(138-8-1)	-3.1
1900	Bos N	55	181	27	55	5	4	2	31	16	0		.304	.360	.409	100	-1	11	.957	-1	74	118	O-49(44-5-0)/2	-0.5
1901	Mil A	79	285	40	86	15	9	2	45	16	1		.302	.341	.439	121	7	12	.967	-4	54	0	O-77(12-65-0),M	-0.1

Year	Tm Lg	G	AB	R	H	2B	3B	HR	RBI	BB-IB	HP	SO	AVG	OBP	SLG	AOPS	ABR	SB-CS	FA	FR	Rng	Thr	G at Pos	BFW
1904	Phi N	18	46	10	13	1	1	0	5	13		0	.283	.441	.348	150	4	3	.850	-2	73	0	O-14(8-6-0),M	0.2
1905	Phi N	15	40	7	12	2	1	0	3	1		0	.300	.317	.400	117	1	0	.909	-0	76	0	/O-8(0-3-5),M	0.0
1906	Phi N	1	1	0	0	0	0	0	0	0		0	.000	.000	.000	-99	0	0	—	0			HM	0.0
Total	17	1738	7044	1554	2293	325	119	106	1302	664	30	<u>212</u>	.326	.386	.451	121	197	574	.943	-37	87	84	*O-1682C/S-20,2-16,3-7,C1	4.7
DUGAN, JOE Joseph Anthony "Jumping Joe" B 5.12.1897 Mahanoy City, PA D 7.7.1982 Norwood, MA BR/TR 5-11/160# d7.5																								
1917	Phi A	43	134	9	26	8	0	0	16	3	3	16	.194	.229	.254	48	-9	0	.917	1	108	76	S-39/2-2	-0.6
1918	Phi A	121	411	26	80	11	3	3	34	16	3	55	.195	.230	.258	47	-29	4	.930	17	106	126	S-86,2-34	-0.6
1919	Phi A	104	387	25	105	17	2	1	30	11	5	30	.271	.300	.333	77	-13	9	.929	1	99	96	S-98/2-4,3-2	-0.5
1920	Phi A	123	491	65	158	40	5	3	60	19	3	51	.322	.351	.442	108	5	5-8	.948	3	94	129	3-60,S-32,2-31	1.0
1921	Phi A	119	461	54	136	22	6	10	58	28	5	45	.295	.342	.434	96	-4	5-1	.953	-22	84	85	*3-119	-1.7
1922	Bos A	84	341	45	98	22	3	3	38	9	1	28	.287	.308	.396	83	-10	2-3	.943	-7	102	101	3-64,S-21	-1.2
	†NY A	60	252	44	72	9	1	3	25	13	4	21	.286	.331	.365	79	-8	1-0	.967	-8	89	96	3-60	-1.2
	Year	144	593	89	170	31	4	6	63	22	5	49	.287	.318	.383	81	-18	3-3	**.954**	-16	96	**99**	*3-124,S-21	-2.4
1923	†NY A	146	644	111	182	30	7	7	67	25	2	41	.283	.311	.384	81	-21	4-2	**.974**	-13	91	113	*3-146	-2.4
1924	NY A	148	610	105	184	31	7	3	56	31	5	33	.302	.341	.390	88	-13	1-2	.962	-12	86	94	*3-148/2-2	-1.5
1925	NY A	102	404	50	118	19	4	0	31	19	4	20	.292	.330	.359	76	-16	2-4	.970	6	102	101	3-96	-0.5
1926	†NY A	123	434	39	125	19	5	1	64	25	1	16	.288	.328	.362	81	-13	2-4	.955	-13	89	53	*3-122	-2.0
1927	†NY A	112	387	44	104	24	3	2	43	27	3	37	.269	.321	.362	79	-12	1-4	.938	-18	91	78	*3-111	-2.4
1928	†NY A	94	312	33	86	15	0	6	34	16	3	15	.276	.317	.381	85	-7	1-0	.952	-16	79	91	3-91/2	-1.7
1929	Bos N	60	125	14	38	10	0	0	15	8	0	8	.304	.346	.384	84	-3	0	.918	-7	81	96	3-24/S-5,2-2,O-2(LF)	-0.7
1931	Det A	8	17	1	4	0	0	0	0	0	0	3	.235	.235	.235	23	-2	0-0	.900	-1	81	0	/3-5	-0.2
Total	14	1447	5410	665	1516	277	46	42	571	250	42	419	.280	.317	.372	82	-155	37-<u>28</u>	.957	-88	90	92	*3-1048,S-281/2-76,O-2(LF)	-16.2
DUGAN, BILL William H. B 1864 New York, NY D 7.24.1921 New York, NY d8.5 b-Ed																								
1884	Ric AA	9	28	4	3	1	0	0		0		1	.107	.138	.143	-8	-3		.889	-3			/C-9	-0.5
	KC U	3	6	0	0	0	0	0		0			.000	.000	.000	-99	-2		.400	-1	0	0	/O-3(1-2-0)	-0.2
Total	1	12	34	4	3	1	0	0		0			.088	.114	.118	-26	-5		.889	-3			/C-9,O-3(1-2-0)	-0.7
DUGAS, GUS Augustin Joseph B 3.24.1907 St.Jean De Matha, PQ, CAN D 4.14.1997 Colchester, CT BL/TL 5-9/165# d9.17																								
1930	Pit N	9	31	8	9	2	0	0	1	7	0	4	.290	.421	.355	90	0	0	.864	-1	93	90	/O-9(RF)	-0.1
1932	Pit N	55	97	13	23	3	3	3	12	7	0	11	.237	.288	.423	90	-2	0	.952	-1	110	0	O-20(6-1-13)	-0.4
1933	Phi N	37	71	4	12	3	0	0	9	1	0	9	.169	.181	.211	10	-8	0	.984	0	111	70	1-11/O(CF)	-1.0
1934	Was A	24	19	2	1	1	0	0	1	3	0	3	.053	.182	.105	-25	-4	0-0	1.000	0	124	0	/O-2(0-1-1)	-0.3
Total	4	125	218	27	45	9	3	3	23	18	0	27	.206	.267	.317	54	-14	0-<u>0</u>	.926	-1	105	29	/O-32(6-3-23),1-11	-1.8
DUGDALE, DAN Daniel Edward B 10.28.1864 Peoria, IL D 3.9.1934 Seattle, WA 5-8/180# d5.20																								
1886	KC N	12	40	4	7	0	0	0	2	2		13	.175	.214	.175	18	-4	1	.884	-2			/C-7,O-6(0-1-5)	-0.5
1894	Was N	38	134	19	32	4	2	0	16	13	0	14	.239	.306	.299	48	-12	7	.874	-8	*71*	*112*	C-33/3-3,O-2(LF)	-1.3
Total	2	50	174	23	39	4	2	0	18	15	0	27	.224	.286	.270	42	-16	8	.877	-10	<u>*59*</u>	<u>*92*</u>	<u>/C-40,O-8(2-1-5),3-3</u>	<u>-1.8</u>
DUGEY, OSCAR Oscar Joseph "Jake" B 10.25.1887 Palestine, TX D 1.1.1966 Dallas, TX BR/TR 5-8/160# d9.13 C5																								
1913	Bos N	5	8	1	2	0	0	0	0	1	0	1	.250	.333	.250	67	0	0	.500	-1	67	0	/3-2,2S	-0.1
1914	Bos N	58	109	17	21	2	0	1	10	10	1	15	.193	.267	.239	51	-7	10	.933	-2	96	77	O-16(RF),2-16/3	-1.0
1915	†Phi N	42	39	4	6	1	0	0	0	7	0	5	.154	.283	.179	41	-2	2-1	.941	2	134	49	2-14	-0.1
1916	Phi N	41	50	9	11	3	0	0	1	9	0	8	.220	.339	.280	88	0	3	.967	2	113	75	2-12	0.2
1917	Phi N	44	72	12	14	4	1	0	9	4	0	9	.194	.237	.278	55	-4	2	.871	-1	84	43	2-15/O-4(1-2-0)	-0.6
1920	Bos N	5	0	2	0	0	0	0	0	0	0	0	—	—	—	—	0	0-0	—	0			R	0.0
Total	6	195	278	45	54	10	1	1	20	31	1	38	.194	.277	.248	58	-13	17-<u>1</u>	.915	-2	100	64	/2-58,O-20(1-2-16),3-3,S	-1.6
DUGGAN, JIM James Elmer "Mer" B 6.1.1885 Whiteland, IN D 12.5.1951 Indianapolis, IN BL/TL 5-10/165# d6.29																								
1911	StL A	1	4	1	0	0	0	0	1	1		0	.000	.200	.000	-44	-1	0	1.000	0	125	324	/1	-0.1
DUNBAR, TOM Thomas Jerome B 11.24.1959 Graniteville, SC BL/TL 6-2/192# d9.7																								
1983	Tex A	12	24	3	6	0	0	0	3	5-0	0	7	.250	.379	.250	79	0	3-1	.875	-2	51	0	/O-9(2-0-7),D	-0.2
1984	Tex A	34	97	9	25	2	0	2	10	6-1	0	16	.258	.301	.340	75	-3	1-0	.939	-2	85	0	O-20(9-0-11)/D-6	-0.6
1985	Tex A	45	104	7	21	4	0	1	5	12-3	1	9	.202	.291	.269	54	-6	0-3	.933	-3	57	0	D-18,O-14(12-0-3)	-1.1
Total	3	91	225	19	52	6	0	3	18	23-4	1	32	.231	.305	.298	66	-9	4-4	.929	-7	70	0	/O-43(23-0-21),D-25	-1.9
DUNCAN, DAVE David Edwin B 9.26.1945 Dallas, TX BR/TR 6-2/200# d5.6 C26																								
1964	KC A	25	53	2	9	0	1	1	5	2-0	0	20	.170	.200	.264	27	-6	0-0	.981	1	*61*	*112*	C-22	-0.4
1967	KC A	34	101	9	19	4	0	5	11	4-0	0	50	.188	.219	.376	75	-4	0-1	.979	-4	55	53	C-32	-0.8
1968	Oak A	82	246	15	47	4	0	7	28	25-3	1	68	.191	.266	.293	73	-8	1-2	.987	-1	88	104	C-79	-0.7
1969	Oak A	58	127	11	16	3	0	3	22	19-4	0	41	.126	.236	.220	31	-12	0-0	.982	-12	81	100	C-56	-2.4
1970	Oak A	86	232	21	60	7	0	10	29	22-2	0	38	.259	.320	.418	107	1	0-0	.978	2	100	97	C-73	0.6
1971	†Oak A☆	103	363	39	92	13	1	15	40	28-2	1	77	.253	.307	.419	106	1	1-1	.984	-2	88	67	*C-102	0.5
1972	†Oak A	121	403	39	88	13	0	19	59	34-5	5	68	.218	.283	.392	106	1	0-2	.993	-4	97	90	*C-113	0.2
1973	Cle A	95	344	43	80	11	1	17	43	35-1	3	86	.233	.309	.419	101	0	3-3	.988	-6	70	84	C-86/D-9	-0.3
1974	Cle A	136	425	45	85	10	1	16	46	42-3	2	91	.200	.274	.341	77	-14	0-4	.976	-7	124	73	*C-134/1-3,D	-1.7
1975	Bal A	96	307	30	63	7	0	12	41	16-0	1	82	.205	.245	.345	70	-14	0-0	.982	-3	**152**	78	C-95	-1.3
1976	Bal A	93	284	20	58	7	0	4	17	25-0	1	56	.204	.271	.271	63	-14	0-0	.985	-11	103	77	C-93	-2.2
Total	11	929	2885	274	617	79	4	109	341	252-20	14	677	.214	.279	.357	85	-69	5-13	.984	-49	*100*	*83*	C-885/D-10,1-3	-8.5
DUNCAN, JIM James William B 7.1.1871 Saltsburg, PA D 10.16.1901 Foxburg, PA BR/TR 5-8/140# d7.18																								
1899	Was N	15	47	5	11	2	0	0	5	4		0	.234	.294	.277	57	-3	1	.940	-2	*77*	*117*	C-14	-0.4
	Cle N	31	105	9	24	2	3	2	9	4		0	.229	.257	.362	74	-5	0	.971	-6	76	104	1-17,C-14	-0.9
	Year	46	152	14	35	4	3	2	14	8		0	.230	.269	.336	69	-7	1	.904	-9	*70*	*117*	C-28,1-17	-1.3
DUNCAN, JEFF Jeffrey Matthew B 12.9.1978 Harvey, IL BL/TL 6-2/180# d5.20																								
2003	NY N	56	139	13	27	0	2	1	10	17-3	2	41	.194	.291	.245	43	-12	4-2	1.000	5	134	0	O-52(1-52-0)	-0.7
DUNCAN, PAT Louis Baird B 10.6.1893 Coalton, OH D 7.17.1960 Columbus, OH BR/TR 5-9/170# d7.16 Mil 1918-19																								
1915	Pit N	3	5	0	1	0	0	0	0	0	0	1	.200	.200	.200	22	0	0	1.000	-0	74	0	/O(CF)	-0.1
1919	†Cin N	31	90	9	22	3	3	2	17	8	0	7	.244	.306	.411	118	2	2	.982	0	103	94	O-27(LF)	0.1
1920	Cin N	**154**	576	75	170	16	11	2	83	42	7	42	.295	.350	.372	109	7	18-18	.964	2	106	87	*O-154(LF)	-0.1
1921	Cin N	145	532	57	164	27	10	2	60	44	5	33	.308	.367	.408	110	8	7-18	.971	5	106	101	*O-145(129-16-1)	-0.3
1922	Cin N	151	607	94	199	44	12	8	94	40	1	31	.328	.370	.479	120	17	12-28	.971	1	100	100	*O-151(LF)	-0.1
1923	Cin N	147	566	92	185	26	8	7	83	30	2	27	.327	.363	.438	113	9	15-13	**.993**	-5	93	78	*O-146(144-3-0)	-0.8
1924	Cin N	96	319	34	86	21	6	2	37	20	0	23	.270	.313	.392	89	-5	1-7	.927	-10	83	41	O-83(82-0-1)	-2.3
Total	7	727	2695	361	827	137	50	23	374	184	15	164	.307	.355	.420	110	38	55-<u>84</u>	.970	-6	100	86	O-707(687-20-2)	-3.6
DUNCAN, MARIANO Mariano (Nalasco) B 3.13.1963 San Pedro De Macoris, D.R. BR/TR (BB 1985-87) 6/185# d4.9 OF Total (88-LF 2-CF 6-RF)																								
1985	†LA N	142	562	74	137	24	6	6	39	38-4	3	113	.244	.293	.340	79	-17	38-8	.954	-7	99	86	*S-123,2-19	-0.5
1986	LA N	109	407	47	93	7	0	8	30	30-1	2	78	.229	.284	.305	67	-20	48-13	.951	-1	98	75	*S-106	-0.4
1987	LA N	76	261	31	56	8	1	6	18	17-1	2	62	.215	.267	.322	57	-17	11-1	.930	5	104	102	S-67/2-7,O-2(1-0-1)	-0.4
1989	LA N	49	84	9	21	5	1	0	8	0-0	2	15	.250	.267	.333	72	-3	3-3	.943	0	107	161	S-16/2-8,O-7(4-0-4)	-0.3
	Cin N	45	174	23	43	10	1	3	13	8-0	3	36	.247	.292	.368	85	-4	6-2	.955	-6	87	80	S-44/2-5	-0.6
	Year	94	258	32	64	15	2	3	21	8-0	5	51	.248	.284	.357	81	-7	9-5	.952	-5	91	96	S-60,2-13/O-7(4-0-4)	-0.9
1990	†Cin N	125	435	67	133	22	**11**	10	55	24-4	4	67	.306	.345	.476	119	10	13-7	.973	4	98	93	*2-115,S-12/O(LF)	1.8
1991	Cin N	100	333	46	86	7	4	12	40	12-0	3	57	.258	.288	.411	92	-6	5-4	.974	-4	90	95	2-62,S-32/O-7(6-2-0)	-0.7
1992	Phi N	142	574	71	153	40	3	8	50	17-0	5	108	.267	.292	.389	92	-8	23-3	.976	-10	103	36	O-65(LF),2-52,S-42/3-4	-1.3
1993	†Phi N	124	496	68	140	26	4	11	73	12-0	4	88	.282	.304	.417	92	-7	6-5	.969	-18	95	76	2-65,S-59	-1.9
1994	Phi N★	88	347	49	93	22	1	8	48	17-1	4	72	.268	.306	.406	83	-9	10-2	.972	-8	100	107	2-37,3-28,S-19/1-6	-1.2
1995	Phi N	52	196	20	56	12	1	3	23	0-0	1	43	.286	.285	.403	80	-6	1-2	.957	9	102	131	2-24,S-14,1-12/3	0.3
	†Cin N	29	69	16	20	2	1	3	13	5-0	0	19	.290	.329	.478	113	1	0-1	.963	-3	76	81	/2-7,1-6,S-6,O-3(LF)	-0.2
	Year	81	265	36	76	14	2	6	36	5-0	1	62	.287	.297	.423	88	-6	1-3	.958	6	96	119	2-31,S-20,1-18/O-3(LF),3	0.1
1996	†NY A	109	400	62	136	34	3	8	56	9-1	1	77	.340	.352	.500	113	7	4-3	.975	1	96	93	*2-104/3-3,O-3(2-0-1),D-2	1.1

Year	Tm Lg	G	AB	R	H	2B	3B	HR	RBI	BB-IB	HP	SO	AVG	OBP	SLG	AOPS	ABR	SB-CS	FA	FR	Rng	Thr	G at Pos	BFW
1997	NY A	50	172	16	42	8	0	1	13	6-0	0	39	.244	.270	.308	51	-13	2-1	.976	1	106	93	2-41/O-6(LF),D-2	-0.9
	Tor A	39	167	20	38	6	0	0	12	6-0	3	39	.228	.267	.263	39	-15	4-2	.984	3	98	106	2-39	-1.0
	Year	89	339	36	80	14	0	1	25	12-0	3	78	.236	.268	.286	45	-28	6-3	.980	4	102	100	2-80/O-6(LF),D-2	-1.9
Total	12	1279	4677	619	1247	233	37	87	491	201-12	37	913	.267	.300	.388	86	-107	174-57	.972	-34	96	94	2-585,S-540/O-94L,3-36,1-24,D-4	-6.2
DUNCAN, TAYLOR Taylor McDowell B 5.12.1953 Memphis, TN BR/TR 6/170# d9.15																								
1977	StL N	8	12	2	4	0	0	1	2	2-0	0	1	.333	.400	.583	172	1	0-0	1.000	-2	35	0	/3-5	-0.1
1978	Oak A	104	319	25	82	15	2	2	37	19-0	0	38	.257	.296	.335	82	-8	1-2	.953	-11	83	28	3-84,2-11/SD	-2.2
Total	2	112	331	27	86	15	2	3	39	21-0	0	39	.260	.301	.344	86	-7	1-2	.953	-13	81	27	/3-89,2-11,D-7,S	-2.3
DUNCAN, VERN Vernon Van Duke B 1.6.1890 Clayton, NC D 6.1.1954 Daytona Beach, FL BL/TR 5-9/155# d9.11																								
1913	Phi N	8	12	3	5	1	0	0	1	0	0	3	.417	.417	.500	155	1	0	1.000	0	61	418	/O-3(1-0-2)	0.1
1914	Bal F	157	557	99	160	20	8	2	53	67	**11**	55	.287	.375	.363	98	-7	13	.914	-6	93	99	*O-148(36-101-11)/3-8,2	-2.3
1915	Bal F	146	531	68	142	18	4	2	43	54	2	40	.267	.337	.328	85	-17	19	.965	-4	103	113	*O-124(60-64-0),3-21/2	-3.0
Total	3	311	1100	170	307	39	12	4	97	121	13	98	.279	.357	.347	93	-23	32	.939	-9	97	108	O-275(97-165-13)/3-29,2-2	-5.2
DUNDON, GUS Augustus Joseph B 7.10.1874 Columbus, OH D 9.1.1940 Pittsburgh, PA BR/TR 5-10/165# d4.14																								
1904	Chi A	108	373	40	85	9	3	0	36	30	4		.228	.292	.268	81	-7	19	**.973**	-13	95	95	*2-103/3-3,S-2	-2.2
1905	Chi A	106	364	30	70	7	3	0	22	23	4		.192	.248	.228	53	-19	14	.983	4	106	95	*2-100/S-6	-1.6
1906	Chi A	33	96	7	13	1	0	0	4	11	0		.135	.224	.146	17	-9	4	.921	1	96	90	2-18,S-14	-0.8
Total	3	247	833	77	168	17	6	0	62	64	8		.202	.265	.236	61	-35	37	.972	-8	100	95	2-221/S-22,3-3	-4.6
DUNDON, ED Edward Joseph "Dummy" B 7.10.1859 Columbus, OH D 8.18.1893 Columbus, OH TR 6/170# d6.2 ▲																								
1883	Col AA	26	93	8	15	1	0	0		3			.161	.188	.172	18	-8		.804	1	104	**299**	P-20/O-9(6-2-1),2	-0.1
1884	Col AA	26	86	6	12	2	2	0		5	1		.140	.196	.209	35	-6		.966	3	125	460	O-16(14-1-1),P-11/1-3	-0.2
Total	2	52	179	14	27	3	2	0		8	1		.151	.191	.190	26	-14		.857	4	106	309	/P-31,O-25(20-3-2),1-3,2	-0.3
DUNGAN, SAM Samuel Morrison B 7.29.1866 Ferndale, CA D 3.16.1939 Santa Ana, CA BR 5-11/180# d4.12																								
1892	Chi N	113	433	46	123	19	7	0	53	35	6	19	.284	.346	.360	112	6	15	.905	-9	42	52	*O-113(37-0-76)	-0.9
1893	Chi N	107	465	86	138	23	7	2	64	29	9	8	.297	.350	.389	98	-2	11	.920	3	112	74	*O-107(1-0-106)	-0.4
1894	Chi N	10	39	5	9	2	0	0	3	7	0	1	.231	.348	.282	50	-3	1	1.000	1	140	267	O-10(RF)	-0.2
	Lou N	8	32	6	11	1	0	0	3	4	0	1	.344	.417	.375	99	0	2	.941	-0	69	274	/O-8(RF)	0.0
	Year	18	71	11	20	3	0	0	6	11	0	2	.282	.378	.324	70	-3	3	.971	1	104	271	O-18(RF)	-0.2
1900	Chi N	6	15	1	4	0	0	0	1	1	0		.267	.313	.267	63	-1	0	.800	-1	0	0	/O-3(CF)	-0.2
1901	Was A	**138**	559	70	179	26	12	1	73	40	2		.320	.368	.415	118	14	9	.947	-4	117	136	*O-104(1-0-103),1-35	0.5
Total	5	382	1543	214	464	71	26	3	197	116	17	29	.301	.356	.386	107	14	38	.924	-9	88	94	O-345(39-3-303)/1-35	-1.2
DUNHAM, LEE Leland Huffield B 6.9.1902 Atlanta, IL D 5.11.1961 Atlanta, IL BL/TL 5-11/185# d4.17																								
1926	Phi N	5	4	0	1	0	0	0	1	0	0	1	.250	.250	.250	33	0	0	1.000	-0	0	0	/1-2	0.0
DUNLAP, FRED Frederick C. "Sure Shot" B 5.21.1859 Philadelphia, PA D 12.1.1902 Philadelphia, PA BR/TR 5-8/165# d5.1 M4																								
1880	Cle N	**85**	373	61	103	**27**	9	4	30	7		32	.276	.289	.429	143	17		.911	7	**103**	**134**	*2-85	2.6
1881	Cle N	80	351	60	114	25	4	3	24	18		24	.325	.358	.444	159	25		.909	7	101	111	*2-79/3	3.2
1882	Cle N	**84**	364	68	102	19	4	0	28	23		26	.280	.323	.354	121	10		.900	18	**112**	**165**	*2-84,M	2.8
1883	Cle N	93	396	81	129	34	2	4	37	22		21	.326	.361	.452	147	24		.911	7	95	126	*2-93/O(RF)	2.9
1884	StL U	101	449	**160**	**185**	39	8	**13**		29			**.412**	**.448**	**.621**	**213**	**50**		**.926**	**30**	**111**	**214**	*2-100/O(RF)PM	**7.1**
1885	StL N	106	423	70	114	11	5	2	25	41		24	.270	.334	.333	124	14		**.934**	**27**	**113**	119	*2-106,M	4.1
1886	StL N	71	285	53	76	15	2	3	32	28		30	.267	.332	.365	119	8	7	.931	14	105	133	2-71/O(CF)	2.2
	Det N	51	196	32	56	8	3	4	37	16		21	.286	.340	.418	125	6	13	.918	4	107	119	2-51	1.0
	Year	122	481	85	132	23	5	7	69	44		51	.274	.335	.387	122	14	20	.926	17	106	127	*2-122/O(CF)	3.2
1887	†Det N	65	272	60	72	13	10	5	45	25	0	12	.265	.327	.441	107	2	15	.948	23	107	168	2-65/P	2.2
1888	Pit N	82	321	41	84	12	4	1	36	16	3	30	.262	.303	.333	112	5	24	.940	11	104	143	2-82	1.8
1889	Pit N	121	451	59	106	19	0	2	65	46	2	33	.235	.309	.290	75	-13	21	**.950**	-4	98	95	*2-121,M	-1.2
1890	Pit N	17	64	9	11	1	1	0	3	7	1	6	.172	.264	.219	46	-4	2	.873	-2	105	48	2-17	-0.5
	NY P	1	4	1	2	0	0	0	0	0	0	0	.500	.500	.500	154	0	0	1.000	-1	47	0	/2	0.0
1891	Was AA	8	25	4	5	1	1	0	4	5	1	4	.200	.355	.320	98	0	3	.818	-2	98	93	/2-8	-0.1
Total	12	965	3974	759	1159	224	53	41	366	283	7	263	.292	.340	.406	132	144	85	.924	137	105	136	2-963/O-3(0-1-2),P-2,3	28.1
DUNLAP, GRANT Grant Lester "Snap" B 12.20.1923 Stockton, CA BR/TR 6-2/180# d4.21																								
1953	StL N	16	17	2	6	0	1	1	3	0	0	2	.353	.353	.647	154	1	0-0	—	-0	0	0	/O(RF)	0.1
DUNLAP, BILL William James B 5.1.1909 Palmer, MA D 11.29.1980 Reading, PA BR/TR 5-11/170# d9.2																								
1929	Bos N	10	29	6	12	0	1	1	4	4	0	4	.414	.485	.586	171	3	0	.889	-1	103	0	/O-9(8-0-1)	0.2
1930	Bos N	16	29	3	2	1	0	0	0	0	0	6	.069	.069	.103	-61	-8	0	1.000	0	129	0	/O-7(0-2-5)	-0.7
Total	2	26	58	9	14	1	1	1	4	4	0	10	.241	.290	.345	57	-5	0	.939	-0	113	0	/O-16(8-2-6)	-0.5
DUNLEAVY, JACK John Francis B 9.14.1879 Harrison, NJ D 4.11.1944 S.Norwalk, CT BL/TL 5-6/167# d5.30 ▲																								
1903	StL N	61	193	23	48	3	3	0	10	13	3		.249	.306	.295	74	-7	10	.972	5	200	349	O-38(6-0-32),P-14	-0.2
1904	StL N	51	172	23	40	7	3	1	14	16	2		.233	.305	.326	99	0	8	.987	2	120	145	O-44(5-3-36)/P-7	0.0
1905	StL N	119	435	52	105	8	8	1	25	55	1		.241	.328	.303	91	-3	15	.962	7	**165**	184	*O-118(13-0-115)/2	-0.1
Total	3	231	800	98	193	18	14	2	49	84	6		.241	.318	.306	89	-10	33	.969	15	163	210	O-200(24-3-183)/P-21,2	-0.3
DUNLOP, GEORGE George Henry B 7.19.1888 Meriden, CT D 12.12.1972 Meriden, CT BR/TR 5-10/170# d9.9																								
1913	Cle A	7	17	3	4	1	0	0	0	0	0	5	.235	.235	.294	53	-1	0	.923	1	83	0	/S-4,3-3	0.0
1914	Cle A	1	3	0	0	0	0	0	0	1	0	1	.000	.250	.000	-23	0	0	1.000	-1	49	0	/S	-0.1
Total	2	8	20	3	4	1	0	0	0	1	0	6	.200	.238	.250	42	-1	0	.929	-0	75	0	/S-5,3-3	-0.1
DUNN, ADAM Adam Troy B 11.9.1979 Houston, TX BL/TR 6-6/240# d7.20																								
2001	Cin N	66	244	54	64	18	1	19	43	38-2	4	74	.262	.371	.578	134	13	4-2	.986	2	108	69	O-63(30-0-38)	1.2
2002	Cin N★	158	535	84	133	28	2	26	71	128-13	9	170	.249	.400	.454	125	23	19-9	.959	-4	90	136	*O-118(112-0-17),1-44/D	1.1
2003	Cin N	116	381	70	82	12	1	27	57	74-8	10	126	.215	.354	.465	114	9	8-2	.955	3	110	80	*O-102(99-0-4),1-19/D-2	0.8
Total	3	340	1160	208	279	58	4	72	171	240-23	23	370	.241	.379	.484	124	45	31-13	.964	1	101	101	O-283(241-0-59)/1-63,D-3	3.1
DUNN, JACK John Joseph B 10.6.1872 Meadville, PA D 10.22.1928 Towson, MD BR/TR 5-9/?# d5.6 ▲ OF Total (8-LF 10-CF 41-RF)																								
1897	Bro N	36	131	20	29	4	0	0	17	4	0		.221	.244	.252	33	-13	2	.911	-2	111	119	P-25/2-4,O-3(LF),3-3,S	-0.4
1898	Bro N	51	167	21	41	0	1	0	19	7	1		.246	.280	.257	54	-10	3	.939	-1	88	75	P-41/O-4(1-2-1),S-4,3-2	-0.3
1899	Bro N	43	122	21	30	2	1	0	16	3	1		.246	.270	.279	49	-9	3	.963	2	110	47	P-41/S	0.1
1900	Bro N	10	26	2	6	0	0	0	1	1	0		.231	.259	.231	34	-1	0	.960	1	139	0	P-10	0.0
	Phi N	10	33	3	10	1	0	0	5	0	0		.303	.303	.333	76	1	1	.920	-1	90	0	P-10	0.0
	Year	20	59	5	16	1	0	0	6	1	0		.271	.283	.288	56	1	1	.940	0	112	0	P-20	0.0
1901	Phi N	2	1	1	1	0	0	0	0	1	0		1.000	1.000	1.000	471	1	0	1.000	-0	79	0	/P-2	0.0
	Bal A	96	362	41	90	9	4	0	36	21	6		.249	.301	.296	63	-18	10	.872	-12	88	61	3-67,S-19/P-9,2O(CF)	-2.5
1902	NY N	100	342	26	72	11	1	0	14	20	1		.211	.256	.249	56	-18	13	.962	-5	90	178	O-43(0-3-40),S-36,3-18/P-3,2-2	-2.3
1903	NY N	78	257	35	62	15	1	0	37	15	3		.241	.291	.307	68	-11	12	.907	-3	94	207	S-27,3-25,2-19/O(LF)	-1.2
1904	NY N	64	181	27	56	12	2	1	19	11	2		.309	.356	.414	132	7	11	.914	-4	97	296	3-28,S-10/2-9,O-7(3-4-0),P	0.4
Total	8	490	1622	197	397	54	10	1	164	83	14		.245	.287	.292	66	-71	55	.890	-25	91	114	3-143,P-142/S-98,O-59R,2-35	-6.2
DUNN, JOE Joseph Edward B 3.11.1885 Springfield, OH D 3.19.1944 Springfield, OH BR/TR 5-9/160# d9.12																								
1908	Bro N	20	64	3	11	3	0	0	5	0	0		.172	.172	.219	26	-6	0	.957	4	*92*	*149*	C-20	0.0
1909	Bro N	10	25	1	4	1	0	0	2	0	1		.160	.192	.200	23	-2	0	.952	-1	*89*	*75*	/C-7	-0.3
Total	2	30	89	4	15	4	0	0	7	0	1		.169	.178	.213	25	-8	0	.956	3	*91*	*131*	/C-27	-0.3
DUNN, RON Ronald Ray B 1.24.1950 Oklahoma City, OK BR/TR 5-11/180# d9.3																								
1974	Chi N	23	68	6	20	7	0	2	15	12-3	0	8	.294	.400	.485	141	4	0-0	.917	-6	86	57	2-21/3-6	-0.1
1975	Chi N	32	44	2	7	3	0	1	6	6-0	0	17	.159	.250	.295	52	-3	0-0	.957	-1	105	0	3-11/O-2(LF),2	-0.4
Total	2	55	112	8	27	10	0	3	21	18-3	0	25	.241	.341	.411	106	1	0-0	.918	-7	86	56	/2-22,3-17,O-2(LF)	-0.5
DUNN, STEVE Stephen B. B 12.21.1858 London, ON, CAN D 5.5.1933 London, ON, CAN BL 5-9.5/173# d9.27																								
1884	StP U	**9**	32	2	8	2	0	0		0			.250	.250	.313	128	0		.972	1	241	70	/1-9,3	0.1

Year	Tm Lg	G	AB	R	H	2B	3B	HR	RBI	BB-IB	HP	SO	AVG	OBP	SLG	AOPS	ABR	SB-CS	FA	FR	Rng	Thr	G at Pos	BFW
DUNN, STEVE Steven Robert B 4.18.1970 Champaign, IL BL/TL 6-4/225# d5.3																								
1994	Min A	14	35	2	8	5	0	0	4	1-0	0	12	.229	.250	.371	57	-2	0-0	.990	1	134	134	1-12	-0.2
1995	Min A	5	6	0	0	0	0	0	0	1-0	0	3	.000	.143	.000	-59	-1	0-0	1.000	-0	0	322	/1-3	-0.2
Total	2	19	41	2	8	5	0	0	4	2-0	0	15	.195	.233	.317	40	-3	0-0	.990	1	125	147	/1-15	-0.4
DUNN, TODD Todd Kent B 7.29.1970 Tulsa, OK BR/TR 6-5/220# d9.8																								
1996	Mil A	6	10	2	3	1	0	0	1	0-0	0	3	.300	.300	.400	72	0	0-0	1.000	-0	105	0	/O-6(1-1-4)	-0.1
1997	Mil A	44	118	17	27	5	0	3	9	2-0	0	39	.229	.242	.347	51	-9	3-0	.909	-0	108	87	O-27(19-2-7),D-14	-1.0
Total	2	50	128	19	30	6	0	3	10	2-0	0	42	.234	.246	.352	53	-9	3-0	.920	-1	108	76	/O-33(20-3-11),D-14	-1.1
DUNSTON, SHAWON Shawon Donnell B 3.21.1963 Brooklyn, NY BR/TR 6-1/175# d4.9 OF Total (107-LF 75-CF 70-RF)																								
1985	Chi N	74	250	40	65	12	4	4	18	19-3	0	42	.260	.310	.388	85	-5	11-3	.958	18	116	92	S-73	2.2
1986	Chi N	150	581	66	145	37	3	17	68	21-5	3	114	.250	.278	.411	82	-16	13-11	.961	21	**104**	104	*S-149	2.0
1987	Chi N	95	346	40	85	18	3	5	22	10-1	1	68	.246	.267	.358	62	-20	12-3	.969	4	99	93	S-94	-0.5
1988	Chi N☆	155	575	69	143	23	6	9	56	16-8	2	108	.249	.271	.357	76	-20	30-9	.973	14	106	90	*S-151	0.9
1989	†Chi N	138	471	52	131	20	6	9	60	30-15	1	86	.278	.320	.403	99	-1	19-11	.972	5	102	114	*S-138	1.5
1990	Chi N★	146	545	73	143	22	8	17	66	15-1	3	87	.262	.283	.426	87	-13	25-5	.970	-1	99	95	*S-144	0.1
1991	Chi N	142	492	59	128	22	7	12	50	23-5	4	64	.260	.292	.407	92	-7	21-6	.968	-0	98	100	*S-142	0.6
1992	Chi N	18	73	8	23	3	1	0	2	3-0	0	13	.315	.342	.384	103	0	2-3	.986	-2	90	101	S-18	-0.1
1993	Chi N	7	10	3	4	2	0	0	2	0-0	0	1	.400	.400	.600	166	1	0-0	1.000	-0	0	0	/S-2	0.1
1994	Chi N	88	331	38	92	19	0	11	35	16-3	2	48	.278	.313	.435	94	-4	3-8	.966	-7	94	98	S-84	-0.6
1995	Chi N	127	477	58	141	30	6	14	69	10-3	6	75	.296	.317	.472	107	2	10-5	.969	-8	97	73	*S-125	0.4
1996	SF N	82	287	27	86	12	2	5	25	13-0	1	40	.300	.331	.408	98	-2	8-0	.957	-1	99	108	S-78	0.4
1997	Chi N	114	419	57	119	18	4	9	41	8-0	3	64	.284	.300	.411	82	-13	29-7	.970	-16	82	81	*S-108/O-7(LF)	-1.8
	Pit N	18	71	14	28	4	1	5	16	0-0	0	11	.394	.389	.690	174	7	3-1	.965	2	109	74	S-18	1.0
	Year	132	490	71	147	22	5	14	57	8-0	3	75	.300	.312	.451	96	-6	32-8	.969	-15	86	80	*S-126/O-7(LF)	-0.8
1998	Cle A	62	156	26	37	11	3	3	12	6-0	1	18	.237	.265	.404	70	-8	9-2	.978	-3	100	76	2-24,S-14,O-12(11-1-0)/D-7	-0.7
	SF N	36	51	10	9	2	0	3	8	0-0	3	10	.176	.222	.392	61	-3	0-2	.938	-4	32	0	/S-9,O-6(CF),2	-0.7
1999	StL N	62	150	23	46	5	2	5	25	2-0	3	23	.307	.327	.467	98	-1	6-3	1.000	-0	103	100	O-23(9-11-4)/1-8,S-7,3-5,D-2	-0.2
	†NY N	42	93	12	32	6	1	0	16	0-0	2	16	.344	.354	.430	101	0	4-1	.978	1	102	97	O-27(9-16-5)/3	0.1
	Year	104	243	35	78	11	3	5	41	2-0	5	39	.321	.337	.453	99	-1	10-4	.988	0	102	98	O-50(18-27-9)/1-8,S-7,3-6,D-2	-0.1
2000	†StL N	98	216	28	54	11	2	12	43	6-0	3	47	.250	.278	.486	88	-6	3-1	.989	1	115	44	O-58(41-9-13)/S-8,1-6,3-5,D	-0.6
2001	SF N	88	186	26	52	10	3	9	25	2-0	2	32	.280	.293	.511	110	1	3-1	.966	2	102	178	O-60(12-23-26)/1D	0.2
2002	†SF N	72	147	7	34	5	0	1	9	3-0	1	33	.231	.250	.286	46	-13	1-0	1.000	-4	79	0	O-49(18-9-22)/1SD	-1.8
Total	18	1814	5927	736	1597	292	62	150	668	203-44	41	1000	.269	.296	.416	88	-121	212-82	.967	21	99	95	*S-1363,O-242L/2-25,1-16,D-14,3	2.5
DUNWOODY, TODD Todd Franklin B 4.11.1975 Lafayette, IN BL/TL 6-1/190# d5.10																								
1997	Fla N	19	50	7	13	2	2	2	7	7-0	1	21	.260	.362	.500	129	2	2-0	.929	-1	101	0	O-14(6-8-0)	0.1
1998	Fla N	116	434	53	109	27	7	5	28	21-0	4	113	.251	.292	.380	79	-15	5-1	.989	7	113	141	*O-111(CF)	-0.6
1999	Fla N	64	186	20	41	6	3	2	20	12-0	1	41	.220	.270	.317	51	-15	3-4	.981	-3	89	110	O-55(8-44-5)	-1.8
2000	KC A	61	178	12	37	9	0	1	23	8-0	1	42	.208	.238	.275	31	-19	3-0	.976	-2	101	0	O-40(14-19-9),D-11	-2.0
2001	Chi N	33	61	6	13	4	0	1	3	3-0	0	14	.213	.250	.328	50	-5	0-1	.973	1	120	112	O-26(15-6-7)	-0.4
2002	Cle A	2	6	0	0	0	0	0	0	0-0	0	3	.000	.000	.000	-99	-2	0-0	1.000	-1	32	0	/O-2(1-0-1)	-0.2
Total	6	295	915	98	213	48	12	11	81	51-0	7	234	.233	.277	.348	63	-54	13-6	.982	3	105	100	O-248(44-188-22)/D-11	-4.9
DURAN, DAN Daniel James B 3.16.1954 Palo Alto, CA BL/TL 5-11/190# d4.17																								
1981	Tex A	13	16	1	4	0	0	0	0	1-0	0	1	.250	.294	.250	61	-1	0-0	1.000	0	65	335	/O-7(LF),1	-0.1
DURANT, MIKE Michael Joseph B 9.14.1969 Columbus, OH BR/TR 6-2/200# d4.3																								
1996	Min A	40	81	15	17	3	0	0	5	10-0	0	15	.210	.293	.247	39	-8	3-0	.975	5	151	81	C-37	0.0
DURAZO, ERUBIEL Erubiel (Cardenas) B 1.23.1974 Hermosillo, Mexico BL/TL 6-3/225# d7.26																								
1999	†Ari N	52	155	31	51	4	2	11	30	26-1	1	43	.329	.422	.594	154	13	1-1	1.000	-1	83	84	1-44	0.8
2000	Ari N	67	196	35	52	11	0	8	33	34-2	1	43	.265	.373	.444	103	2	1-0	.989	-4	70	90	1-60	-0.6
2001	†Ari N	92	175	34	47	11	0	12	38	28-1	2	49	.269	.372	.537	124	7	0-0	.993	1	94	105	1-38/O-2(RF),D-7	0.5
2002	†Ari N	76	222	46	58	12	2	16	48	49-2	2	60	.261	.395	.550	138	13	0-1	.984	-3	79	73	1-56/O-2(RF),D-6	0.4
2003	†Oak A	154	537	92	139	29	0	21	77	100-12	2	105	.259	.374	.430	111	13	1-1	.981	-5	46	103	*D-121,1-33	-0.3
Total	5	441	1285	238	347	67	4	68	226	237-18	8	300	.270	.383	.487	122	48	3-3	.989	-12	75	89	1-231,D-134/O-4(RF)	0.8
DURBIN, KID Blaine Alphonsus B 9.10.1886 Lamar, MO D 9.11.1943 Kirkwood, MO BL/TL 5-8/155# d4.24 ▲																								
1907	Chi N	11	18	2	6	0	0	0	0	1	0		.333	.368	.333	113	0	0	1.000	1	106	0	/P-5,O-5(1-0-4)	0.1
1908	Chi N	14	28	3	7	1	0	0	0	2	1		.250	.323	.286	91	0	0	1.000	-1	0	0	O-11(CF)	-0.1
1909	Cin N	6	5	1	1	0	0	0	0	1	0		.200	.333	.200	66	0	0	—	0			H	0.0
	Pit N	1	0	0	0	0	0	0	0	0	0		—	—	—	—	0	0	—	0			R	0.0
	Year	7	5	1	1	0	0	0	0	1	0		.200	.333	.200	65	0	0	—	0				0.0
Total	3	32	51	6	14	1	0	0	0	4	1		.275	.339	.294	96	0	0	1.000	1	151	0	/O-16(1-11-4),P-5	0.0
DURHAM, JOE Joseph Vann "Pop" B 7.31.1931 Newport News, VA BR/TR 6-1/186# d9.10 Mil 1955																								
1954	Bal A	10	40	4	9	0	0	1	3	4	0	7	.225	.295	.300	68	-2	0-0	.917	-1	90	0	O-10(10-1-0)	-0.4
1957	Bal A	77	157	19	29	2	0	4	17	16-1	0	42	.185	.259	.274	49	-12	1-1	1.000	-1	101	45	O-59(36-5-25)	-1.5
1959	StL N	6	5	2	0	0	0	0	0	0-0	0	1	.000	.000	.000	-94	-1	0-0	1.000	0	190	0	/O(RF)	-0.1
Total	3	93	202	25	38	2	0	5	20	20-1	0	50	.188	.260	.272	49	-15	1-1	.979	-2	99	34	/O-70(46-6-26)	-2.0
DURHAM, LEON Leon B 7.31.1957 Cincinnati, OH BL/TL 6-2/210# d5.27																								
1980	StL N	96	303	42	82	15	4	8	42	18-1	1	55	.271	.309	.426	101	0	8-5	.987	10	103	255	O-78(35-2-43)/1-8	0.6
1981	Chi N	87	328	42	95	14	6	10	35	27-6	0	53	.290	.344	.460	121	8	25-11	.970	-3	100	58	O-83(RF)/1-3	0.2
1982	Chi N☆	148	539	84	168	33	7	22	90	66-14	2	77	.312	.388	.521	148	36	28-14	.963	-3	98	116	*O-143(0-74-89)/1	3.0
1983	Chi N★	100	337	58	87	18	8	12	55	66-12	3	83	.258	.381	.466	128	15	12-6	.966	-11	82	34	O-95(51-40-4)/1-6	0.2
1984	†Chi N	137	473	86	132	30	4	23	96	69-11	1	86	.279	.369	.505	132	22	16-8	.994	3	107	96	*1-130	1.8
1985	Chi N	153	542	58	153	32	2	21	75	64-**24**	0	99	.282	.357	.465	116	13	7-6	.995	3	106	98	*1-151	0.6
1986	Chi N	141	484	66	127	18	7	20	65	67-16	1	98	.262	.350	.452	112	8	8-7	.995	-7	80	90	*1-141	-0.9
1987	Chi N	131	439	70	120	22	1	27	63	51-9	0	92	.273	.348	.513	120	12	2-2	.990	-10	68	92	*1-123	-0.6
1988	Chi N	24	73	10	16	6	1	3	6	9-2	0	20	.219	.305	.452	110	1	0-1	.995	1	110	114	1-20	0.0
	Cin N	21	51	4	11	3	0	1	2	5-1	0	12	.216	.286	.333	74	-2	0-0	.993	-1	69	86	1-17	-0.4
	Year	45	124	14	27	9	1	4	8	14-3	0	32	.218	.297	.403	95	-1	0-1	.994	-0	93	102	1-37	-0.4
1989	StL N	29	18	2	1	1	0	0	1	2-0	1	4	.056	.182	.111	-11	-3	0-1	.961	0	145	209	1-18	-0.3
Total	10	1067	3587	522	992	192	40	147	530	444-96	9	679	.277	.356	.475	122	110	106-61	.994	-19	93	95	1-618,O-399(86-116-219)	4.2
DURHAM, RAY Ray B 11.30.1971 Charlotte, NC BB/TR 5-8/170# d4.26																								
1995	Chi A	125	471	68	121	27	6	7	51	31-2	6	83	.257	.309	.384	83	-13	18-5	.973	-22	86	78	*2-122/D	-2.5
1996	Chi A	156	557	79	153	33	5	10	65	58-4	10	95	.275	.350	.406	96	-2	30-4	.984	-21	96	84	*2-150/D-3	-1.0
1997	Chi A	155	634	106	172	27	5	11	53	61-0	6	96	.271	.337	.382	92	-7	33-16	.974	-29	91	77	*2-153/D	-2.6
1998	Chi A★	158	635	126	181	35	8	19	67	73-3	6	105	.285	.363	.455	115	14	36-9	.976	1	103	**128**	*2-158	2.6
1999	Chi A	153	612	109	181	30	8	13	60	73-1	4	105	.296	.373	.435	105	6	34-11	.974	-6	98	97	*2-148/D-4	1.0
2000	†Chi A★	151	614	121	172	35	9	17	75	75-0	7	105	.280	.361	.450	103	4	25-13	.980	4	99	**122**	*2-151	1.4
2001	Chi A	152	611	104	163	42	10	20	65	64-3	4	110	.267	.337	.466	106	5	23-10	.986	6	107	94	*2-150/D	1.9
2002	Chi A	96	345	71	103	20	2	9	48	49-0	5	59	.299	.390	.446	121	13	20-5	.968	6	103	107	2-92	2.4
	†Oak A	54	219	43	60	14	4	6	22	24-1	2	34	.274	.350	.457	112	4	6-2	.967	3	121	175	D-43,2-11	0.5
	Year	150	564	114	163	34	6	15	70	73-1	7	93	.289	.374	.450	118	17	26-7	.968	9	105	115	*2-103,D-43	2.9
2003	†SF N	110	410	61	117	30	5	8	33	50-2	3	82	.285	.366	.441	113	9	7-7	.990	3	108	103	*2-105	1.5
Total	9	1310	5108	888	1423	293	62	120	539	558-16	53	874	.279	.353	.431	104	33	232-82	.978	-56	99	100	*2-1240/D-53	5.2
DURNBAUGH, BOBBY Robert Eugene "Scroggy" B 1.15.1933 Dayton, OH BR/TR 5-8/170# d9.22																								
1957	Cin N	2	1	0	0	0	0	0	0	0-0	0	0	.000	.000	.000	-93	0	0-0	.500	-0	100	0	/S-2	-0.1
DURNING, GEORGE George Dewey B 5.9.1898 Philadelphia, PA D 4.18.1986 Tampa, FL BR/TR 5-11/175# d9.12																								
1925	Phi N	5	14	3	5	0	0	0	1	2	0	1	.357	.438	.357	97	0	0-0	1.000	2	121	315	/O-4(RF)	0.1

Year	Tm Lg	G	AB	R	H	2B	3B	HR	RBI	BB-IB	HP	SO	AVG	OBP	SLG	AOPS	ABR	SB-CS	FA	FR	Rng	Thr	G at Pos	BFW
DUROCHER, LEO Leo Ernest "Lippy" B 7.27.1905 W.Springfield, MA D 10.7.1991 Palm Springs, CA BR/TR (BB 1928-29) 5-10/160# d10.2 M24 C4 HF1994																								
1925	NY A	2	1	1	0	0	0	0	0	0	0	0	.000	.000	.000	-99	0	0-0	—	0			H	0.0
1928	†NY A	102	296	46	80	8	6	0	31	22	3	52	.270	.327	.338	77	-10	1-4	.948	5	108	106	2-66,S-29	-0.2
1929	NY A	106	341	53	84	4	5	0	32	34	3	33	.246	.320	.287.	62	-20	3-1	.958	20	111	114	S-93,2-12	1.0
1930	Cin N	119	354	31	86	15	3	3	32	20	2	45	.243	.287	.328	51	-29	0	.959	11	107	111	*S-103,2-13	-0.7
1931	Cin N	121	361	26	82	11	5	1	29	18	0	32	.227	.264	.294	53	-26	0	.965	0	102	**121**	*S-120	-1.8
1932	Cin N	143	457	43	99	22	5	1	33	36	1	40	.217	.275	.293	55	-29	3	.960	-12	97	99	*S-142	-3.1
1933	Cin N	16	51	6	11	1	0	1	3	4	0	5	.216	.273	.294	63	-3	0	.953	3	115	95	S-16	0.1
	StL N	123	395	45	102	18	4	2	41	26	1	32	.258	.306	.339	80	-10	3	.961	-5	93	86	*S-123	-0.7
	Year	139	446	51	113	19	4	3	44	30	1	37	.253	.302	.334	78	-13	3	**.960**	-3	96	87	*S-139	-0.6
1934	†StL N	146	500	62	130	26	5	3	70	33	2	40	.260	.308	.350	71	-20	2	.957	-4	90	111	*S-146	-1.3
1935	StL N	143	513	62	136	23	5	8	78	29	0	46	.265	.304	.376	79	-16	4	.963	6	99	113	*S-142	0.0
1936	StL N★	136	510	57	146	22	3	1	58	29	2	47	.286	.327	.347	82	-13	3	**.971**	-11	92	92	*S-136	-1.4
1937	StL N	135	477	46	97	11	3	1	47	38	0	36	.203	.262	.245	38	-42	6	.959	-14	92	90	*S-134	-4.6
1938	Bro N★	141	479	41	105	18	5	1	56	47	3	30	.219	.293	.284	58	-27	3	**.966**	-3	95	105	*S-141	-2.1
1939	Bro N	116	390	42	108	21	6	1	34	27	1	24	.277	.325	.369	83	-9	2	.957	-11	93	110	*S-113/3M	-1.3
1940	Bro N☆	62	160	10	37	9	1	1	14	12	0	13	.231	.285	.319	62	-8	1	.959	-3	92	91	S-53/2-4,M	-0.8
1941	Bro N	18	42	2	12	1	0	0	6	1	0	3	.286	.302	.310	70	-2	0	.917	-0	110	70	S-12/2M	-0.1
1943	Bro N	6	18	1	4	0	0	0	1	1	0	2	.222	.263	.222	41	-1	0	1.000	1	62	141	/S-6,M	-0.1
1945	Bro N	2	5	1	1	0	0	0	2	0	0	0	.200	.200	.200	11	-1	0	1.000	0	119	156	/2-2,M	0.0
Total	17	1637	5350	575	1320	210	56	24	567	377	18	480	.247	.299	.320	66	-266	31-5	.961	-15	97	103	*S-1509/2-98,3	-17.1
DURRETT, RED Elmer Cable B 2.3.1921 Sherman, TX D 1.17.1992 Waxahachie, TX BL/TL 5-10/170# d9.14																								
1944	Bro N	11	32	3	5	1	0	1	1	7	0	10	.156	.308	.281	68	-1	0	.933	1	124	111	/O-9(0-5-4)	-0.1
1945	Bro N	8	16	2	2	0	0	0	0	3	0	3	.125	.263	.125	10	-2	0	1.000	-0	93	0	/O-4(CF)	-0.2
Total	2	19	48	5	7	1	0	1	1	10	0	13	.146	.293	.229	48	-3	0	.947	1	116	82	/O-13(0-9-4)	-0.3
DURRINGTON, TRENT Trent John B 8.27.1975 Sydney, Australia BR/TR 5-10/172# d8.6																								
1999	Ana A	43	122	14	22	2	0	0	2	9-0	0	28	.180	.237	.197	12	-17	4-3	.966	-4	96	80	2-41	-1.8
2000	Ana A	4	3	0	0	0	0	0	0	0-0	0	0	.000	.000	.000	-97	-1	0-0	1.000	-1	67	0	/2	-0.2
2003	Ana A	12	14	5	2	0	0	0	1	3-0	0	0	.143	.294	.143	22	-2	1-1	1.000	-2	70	0	/2-5,3-4,O(LF)D	-0.3
Total	3	59	139	19	24	2	0	0	3	12-0	0	28	.173	.238	.187	11	-20	5-4	.968	-7	94	73	/2-47,3-4,D-2,O(LF)	-2.3
DURST, CEDRIC Cedric Montgomery B 8.23.1896 Austin, TX D 2.16.1971 San Diego, CA BL/TL 5-11/160# d5.30																								
1922	StL A	15	12	5	4	1	0	0	0	0	0	1	.333	.333	.417	91	0	0-0	.857	-0	133	0	/O-6(1-4-1)	0.0
1923	StL A	45	85	11	18	2	0	5	11	8	0	14	.212	.280	.412	76	-4	0-0	1.000	-2	98	0	O-10(4-5-1)/1-8	-0.7
1926	StL A	80	219	32	52	7	5	3	16	22	1	19	.237	.310	.356	70	-11	0-5	.980	1	108	90	O-57(5-42-10)/1-4	-1.4
1927	†NY A	65	129	18	32	4	3	0	25	6	0	7	.248	.281	.326	59	-9	0-3	.980	-1	95	41	O-36(13-6-17)/1-2	-1.2
1928	†NY A	74	135	18	34	2	1	2	10	7	0	9	.252	.289	.326	63	-8	1-0	.983	1	105	79	O-33(13-5-15)/1-3	-0.9
1929	NY A	92	202	32	52	3	3	4	31	15	0	25	.257	.309	.361	77	-8	3-2	.987	6	128	89	O-72(46-6-20)/1	-0.6
1930	NY A	8	19	0	3	1	0	0	5	0	0	1	.158	.158	.211	-8	-3	0-0	1.000	0	128	0	/O-6(LF)	-0.3
	Bos A	102	302	29	74	19	5	1	24	17	2	24	.245	.290	.351	64	-17	3-1	.968	-2	98	65	O-75(46-0-29)	-2.3
	Year	110	321	29	77	20	5	1	29	17	2	25	.240	.282	.343	60	-20	3-1	.970	-2	100	61	O-81(52-0-29)	-2.6
Total	7	481	1103	145	269	39	17	15	122	75	3	100	.244	.294	.351	67	-60	7-11	.979	2	108	71	O-295(134-68-93)/1-18	-7.4
DUSAK, ERV Ervin Frank "Four Sack" B 7.29.1920 Chicago, IL D 11.6.1994 Glendale Heights, IL BR/TR 6-2/185# d9.18 Mil 1943-45 ▲ OF Total (105-LF 106-CF 67-RF)																								
1941	StL N	6	14	1	2	0	0	0	3	2	0	6	.143	.250	.143	12	-2	1	1.000	1	152	0	/O-4(1-2-1)	-0.1
1942	StL N	12	27	4	5	3	0	0	3	3	0	7	.185	.267	.296	60	-1	0	1.000	1	124	0	/O-8(5-0-3),3	0.0
1946	†StL N	100	275	38	66	9	1	9	42	33	0	63	.240	.321	.378	94	-3	7	.993	7	100	203	O-77(72-5-0),3-11/2-2	-0.1
1947	StL N	111	328	56	93	7	3	6	28	50	0	34	.284	.378	.378	97	0	1	.970	4	95	195	O-89(22-28-47)/3-7	0.0
1948	StL N	114	311	60	65	9	2	6	19	49	0	55	.209	.317	.309	66	-14	3	.992	-2	94	76	O-68(2-55-12),2-29/3-9,PS	-1.6
1949	StL N	1	0	1	0	0	0	0	0	0	0	0	—	—	—	—	0	0	—	0			R	0.0
1950	StL N	23	12	0	1	1	0	0	0	0	0	3	.083	.083	.167	-34	-2	0	1.000	1	108	211	P-14/O-2(CF)	0.0
1951	StL N	5	2	1	1	0	0	1	1	0	0	1	.500	.500	2.000	537	1	0-0	1.000	0	169	0	/P-5	0.0
	Pit N	21	39	6	12	3	0	1	7	3	0	11	.308	.357	.462	115	1	0-0	1.000	-3	70	0	O-12(1-10-1)/P-3,2-2,3-2	-0.2
	Year	26	41	7	13	3	0	2	8	3	0	12	.317	.364	.537	136	2	0-0	1.000	-3	70	0	O-12(1-10-1)/P-8,2-2,3-2	-0.2
1952	Pit N	20	27	1	6	0	0	1	3	2	0	8	.222	.276	.333	66	-1	0-0	.818	0	65	453	O-11(2-4-3)	-0.1
Total	9	413	1035	168	251	32	6	24	106	142	0	188	.243	.334	.355	84	-21	12-0	.981	9	97	159	O-271C/2-33,3-30,P-23,S	-2.1
DWIGHT, AL Albert Ward B 1.4.1856 New York, NY D 2.20.1903 San Francisco, CA d6.19																								
1884	KC U	12	43	8	10	2	0	0	2				.233	.267	.279	75	-2		.953	0			C-10/O(CF)2	-0.2
DWYER, JIM James Edward "Pig Pen" B 1.3.1950 Evergreen Park, IL BL/TL 5-10/175# d6.10																								
1973	StL N	28	57	7	11	1	1	0	0	1-0	0	5	.193	.207	.246	25	-6	0-0	1.000	-1	97	0	O-20(9-10-1)	-0.8
1974	StL N	74	86	13	24	1	0	2	11	11-2	1	16	.279	.360	.360	105	1	0-0	1.000	1	102	103	O-25(8-1-16)/1-3	0.1
1975	StL N	21	31	4	6	1	0	0	1	4-0	0	6	.194	.286	.226	42	-2	0-0	1.000	1	126	0	/O-9(5-3-2)	-0.2
	Mon N	60	175	22	50	7	1	3	20	23-0	0	30	.286	.365	.389	106	2	4-1	.959	1	90	214	O-52(46-3-3)	0.1
	Year	81	206	26	56	8	1	3	21	27-0	0	36	.272	.353	.364	96	0	4-1	.966	2	94	188	O-61(51-6-5)	-0.1
1976	Mon N	50	92	7	17	3	1	0	5	11-1	0	10	.185	.269	.239	44	-7	0-0	.970	-1	92	0	O-19(15-0-5)	-1.0
	NY N	11	13	2	2	0	0	0	0	2-1	0	1	.154	.267	.154	23	-1	0-0	1.000	0	107	0	/O-2(RF)	-0.2
	Year	61	105	9	19	3	1	0	5	13-2	0	11	.181	.269	.229	42	-8	0-0	.972	-1	93	0	O-21(15-0-7)	-1.2
1977	StL N	13	31	3	7	1	0	0	2	4-0	2	5	.226	.351	.258	68	-1	0-0	1.000	-1	89	0	O-12(3-0-10)	-0.3
1978	StL N	34	65	8	14	3	0	1	4	9-1	1	3	.215	.320	.308	77	-2	1-0	.952	-3	59	73	O-22(18-0-5)	-0.5
	SF N	73	173	22	39	9	2	5	22	28-3	0	29	.225	.327	.387	105	2	6-0	.987	3	98	330	O-36(3-26-9),1-29	0.4
	Year	107	238	30	53	12	2	6	26	37-4	1	32	.223	.325	.366	97	0	7-0	.979	0	84	235	O-58(21-26-14),1-29	-0.1
1979	Bos A	76	113	19	30	7	0	2	14	17-1	1	9	.265	.361	.381	96	0	3-1	.981	1	128	111	1-25,O-19(6-1-12)/D-4	0.0
1980	Bos A	93	260	41	74	11	1	9	38	28-5	2	23	.285	.357	.438	111	4	3-2	.975	-0	83	170	O-65(11-29-27),D-12/1-9	0.2
1981	Bal A	68	134	16	30	0	1	3	10	20-0	0	19	.224	.318	.306	83	-3	0-2	.977	-0	105	75	O-59(43-2-19)/1-3,D	-0.6
1982	Bal A	71	148	28	45	4	3	6	15	27-4	0	24	.304	.407	.493	148	11	2-0	.976	-3	100	0	O-49(16-0-37)/1D	0.6
1983	†Bal A	100	196	37	56	17	1	8	38	31-3	0	29	.286	.382	.505	145	13	1-1	.966	-1	111	35	O-56(7-0-49),D-10/1-4	1.0
1984	Bal A	76	161	22	41	9	1	2	21	23-0	0	24	.255	.337	.360	98	1	0-2	.966	0	99	119	O-52(1-0-51)/D-3	-0.2
1985	Bal A	101	233	35	58	8	3	7	36	37-2	1	31	.249	.353	.399	109	4	0-3	.993	3	109	105	O-78(46-0-33)/D-3	0.3
1986	Bal A	94	160	18	39	13	1	8	31	23-1	2	31	.244	.339	.488	126	6	0-2	1.000	3	110	300	O-24(8-0-16),D-24/1	0.7
1987	Bal A	92	241	54	66	7	1	15	33	37-4	1	57	.274	.371	.498	132	11	4-1	1.000	-0	104	51	D-41,O-30(3-0-29)	0.9
1988	Bal A	35	53	3	12	0	0	0	3	12-3	0	11	.226	.364	.226	73	-1	0-0	1.000	0	240	0	D-17/O-2(1-0-1)	-0.1
	Min A	20	41	6	12	1	0	2	15	13-1	1	8	.293	.464	.463	159	4	0-0	—	0	0	0	D-13	0.4
	Year	55	94	9	24	1	0	2	18	25-4	1	19	.255	.410	.330	113	3	0-0	1.000	0	240	0	D-30/O-2(1-0-1)	0.3
1989	Min A	88	225	34	71	11	0	3	23	28-1	0	23	.316	.390	.404	117	6	2-0	—	-0	0	0	D-74/O(RF)	0.4
	Mon N	13	10	1	3	1	0	0	2	1-0	0	1	.300	.364	.400	116	0	0-0	—	0			H	0.0
1990	Min A	37	63	7	12	0	0	1	5	12-1	0	7	.190	.320	.238	55	-4	0-0	1.000	0	279	0	D-23/O-2(1-0-1)	-0.4
Total	18	1328	2761	409	719	115	17	77	349	402-34	12	402	.260	.353	.398	107	38	26-15	.979	3	99	113	O-634(250-75-329),D-226/1-75	0.8
DWYER, JOHN John E. d5.16																								
1882	Cle N	1	3	0	0	0	0	0	1	0		0	.000	.000	.000	-99	-1		—	-1	0	0	/O(LF)C	-0.1
DWYER, DOUBLE JOE Joseph Michael B 3.27.1903 Orange, NJ D 10.21.1992 Glen Ridge, NJ BL/TL 5-9/186# d4.20																								
1937	Cin N	12	11	2	3	0	0	0	1	1	0	0	.273	.333	.273	70	0	0	—	0			H	0.0
DYBZINSKI, JERRY Jerome Matthew B 7.7.1955 Cleveland, OH BR/TR 6-2/180# d4.11																								
1980	Cle A	114	248	32	57	11	1	1	23	13-0	2	35	.230	.273	.294	55	-15	4-1	.971	14	110	93	S-73,2-29/3-4,D-2	0.6
1981	Cle A	48	57	10	17	0	0	0	6	5-0	0	8	.298	.355	.298	91	-1	7-1	.970	2	104	73	S-34/2-3,3-3,D	0.5
1982	Cle A	80	212	19	49	6	2	0	22	21-0	3	25	.231	.305	.278	63	-10	3-5	.957	16	117	95	S-77/3-3	1.1
1983	†Chi A	127	256	30	59	10	1	1	32	18-0	2	29	.230	.283	.289	57	-15	11-4	.966	-2	93	96	*S-118/3-9	-0.7
1984	Chi A	94	132	17	31	5	1	1	10	13-0	2	12	.235	.311	.311	70	-5	7-2	.974	6	114	121	S-76,3-14/2D	0.7
1985	Pit N	5	4	0	0	0	0	0	0	0-0	0	0	.000	.000	.000	-99	-1	0-0	.900	0	118	0	/S-5	-0.1
Total	6	468	909	108	213	32	5	3	93	70-0	9	109	.234	.293	.290	61	-47	32-13	.966	36	107	97	S-383/3-33,2-33,D-4	2.1

Year	Tm Lg	G	AB	R	H	2B	3B	HR	RBI	BB-IB	HP	SO	AVG	OBP	SLG	AOPS	ABR	SB-CS	FA	FR	Rng	Thr	G at Pos	BFW
DYCK, JIM James Robert B 2.3.1922 Omaha, NE D 1.11.1999 Cheney, WA BR/TR 6-2/205# d9.27																								
1951	StL A	4	15	1	1	0	0	0	0	1	0	1	.067	.125	.067	-46	-3	0-0	1.000	0	80	107	/3-4	-0.3
1952	StL A	122	402	60	108	22	3	15	64	50	3	68	.269	.354	.450	119	10	0-4	.962	7	110	91	3-74,O-48(39-8-2)	1.3
1953	StL A	112	334	38	71	15	1	9	27	38	3	40	.213	.299	.344	72	-14	3-2	.981	-1	105	148	O-55(32-19-8),3-51	-1.7
1954	Cle A	2	1	0	1	0	0	0	1	1	0	0	1.000	1.000	1.000	441	1	0-0	—	0			H	0.1
1955	Bal A	61	197	32	55	13	1	2	22	28-1	1	21	.279	.372	.386	112	4	1-0	.989	-0	100	116	O-45(LF),3-17	0.2
1956	Bal A	11	23	3	5	2	0	0	0	10-0	0	5	.217	.455	.304	112	2	0-0	.923	1	77	410	/O-9(LF)	0.2
	Cin N	18	11	5	1	0	0	0	0	3-0	0	5	.091	.286	.091	7	-1	0-0	1.000	-0	0	0	/13	-0.1
Total	6	330	983	139	242	52	5	26	114	131-1	7	140	.246	.339	.389	98	-1	4-6	.982	6	104	121	O-157(125-27-10),3-147/1	-0.3
DYE, JERMAINE Jermaine Terrell B 1.28.1974 Oakland, CA BR/TR 6-4/210# d5.17																								
1996	†Atl N	98	292	32	82	16	0	12	37	8-0	3	67	.281	.304	.459	93	-4	1-4	.950	-0	110	43	O-92(25-4-71)	-0.8
1997	KC A	75	263	26	62	14	0	7	22	17-0	1	51	.236	.284	.369	67	-13	2-1	.966	6	111	152	O-75(1-0-75)	-1.0
1998	KC A	60	214	24	50	5	1	5	23	11-2	1	46	.234	.270	.336	56	-15	2-2	.987	7	128	93	O-59(RF)	-1.0
1999	KC A	158	608	96	179	44	8	27	119	58-4	1	119	.294	.354	.526	119	16	2-3	.984	14	113	151	*O-157(RF)/D	2.0
2000	KC A★	157	601	107	193	41	2	33	118	69-6	3	99	.321	.390	.561	133	31	0-1	.976	-3	95	108	*O-146(RF),D-10	1.8
2001	KC A	97	367	50	100	14	0	13	47	30-3	6	68	.272	.333	.417	90	-6	7-1	.984	-3	96	79	O-93(0-2-92)/D-4	-1.2
	†Oak A	61	232	41	69	17	1	13	59	27-3	1	44	.297	.366	.547	138	13	2-0	.972	-2	80	174	O-61(RF)	0.8
	Year	158	599	91	169	31	1	26	106	57-6	7	112	.282	.346	.467	107	7	9-1	.979	-6	90	117	*O-154(0-2-153)/D-4	-0.4
2002	†Oak A	131	488	74	123	27	1	24	86	52-2	10	108	.252	.333	.459	108	6	2-0	.972	-14	77	29	*O-111(RF),D-19	-1.4
2003	†Oak A	65	221	28	38	6	0	4	20	25-2	3	42	.172	.261	.253	37	-20	1-0	1.000	-4	88	30	O-61(1-3-60)/D-3	-2.6
Total	8	902	3286	478	896	184	13	138	531	297-22	29	644	.273	.335	.463	102	8	19-12	.977	1	100	98	O-855(27-9-832)/D-37	-3.4
DYER, BEN Benjamin Franklin B 2.13.1893 Chicago, IL D 8.7.1959 Kenosha, WI BR/TR 5-11/170# d5.23 Mil 1918 OF Total (1-LF 2-RF)																								
1914	NY N	7	4	1	1	0	0	0	0	0	0	1	.250	.250	.250	50	0	1	1.000	0	142	331	/S-6,2	0.0
1915	NY N	7	19	4	4	0	1	0	0	4	1	3	.211	.375	.316	117	1	0	.889	-1	93	0	/3-6,S	0.0
1916	Det A	4	14	4	4	1	0	0	1	1	0	1	.286	.333	.357	104	0	0	1.000	-1	80	0	/S-4	-0.1
1917	Det A	30	67	6	14	5	0	0	0	2	0	17	.209	.232	.284	57	-4	3	.846	-1	95	106	S-14/3-8	-0.4
1918	Det A	13	18	1	5	0	0	0	2	0	0	6	.278	.278	.278	71	-1	0	1.000	1	185	0	/P-2,1-2,O-2(1-0-1),2	0.0
1919	Det A	44	85	11	21	4	0	0	15	8	0	19	.247	.312	.294	72	-3	0	.953	1	110	0	3-23,S-11/O(RF)	-0.1
Total	6	105	207	27	49	10	1	0	18	15	1	47	.237	.291	.295	74	-7	4	.937	-0	110	0	/3-37,S-36,O-3R,1-2,P-2,2-2	-0.6
DYER, DUFFY Don Robert B 8.15.1945 Dayton, OH BR/TR 6/195# d9.21 C11																								
1968	NY N	1	3	0	1	0	0	0	0	1-0	0	1	.333	.500	.333	153	0	0-0	1.000	0	*0*	*0*	/C	0.0
1969	†NY N	29	74	5	19	3	1	3	12	4-0	0	22	.257	.295	.446	103	0	0-0	.991	-2	97	58	C-19	-0.2
1970	NY N	59	148	8	31	1	0	2	12	21-4	0	32	.209	.308	.257	53	-10	1-1	.991	0	96	140	C-57	-0.7
1971	NY N	59	169	13	39	7	1	2	18	14-4	1	45	.231	.292	.320	75	-6	1-0	.992	-2	80	105	C-53	-0.6
1972	NY N	94	325	33	75	17	3	8	36	28-9	5	71	.231	.299	.375	94	-3	0-1	.993	17	123	**144**	C-91/O(RF)	1.9
1973	NY N	70	189	9	35	6	1	1	9	13-1	2	40	.185	.245	.243	36	-17	0-1	.994	-2	109	117	C-60	-1.7
1974	NY N	63	142	14	30	1	1	0	10	18-2	1	15	.211	.302	.232	53	-9	0-0	.982	-7	87	96	C-45	-1.5
1975	†Pit N	48	132	8	30	5	2	3	16	6-0	1	22	.227	.266	.364	74	-6	0-0	.990	5	194	100	C-36	0.1
1976	Pit N	69	184	12	41	8	0	3	9	29-10	3	35	.223	.336	.315	85	-2	0-0	.994	6	120	125	C-58	0.7
1977	Pit N	94	270	27	65	11	1	3	19	54-11	3	49	.241	.370	.322	86	-2	6-0	**.996**	-0	100	98	C-93	0.3
1978	Pit N	58	175	7	37	8	1	0	13	18-3	3	32	.211	.294	.269	56	-10	2-1	.991	-1	72	96	C-55	-0.9
1979	Mon N	28	74	4	18	6	0	1	8	9-4	0	17	.243	.325	.365	89	-1	0-0	.993	4	79	115	C-27	0.4
1980	Det A	48	108	11	20	1	0	4	11	13-1	0	34	.185	.273	.306	57	-7	0-0	.986	-4	71	44	C-37,D-10	-1.0
1981	Det A	2	0	0	0	0	0	0	0	0-0	0	0	—	—	—	—	0	0-0	—	-0	0	0	/C-2	0.0
Total	14	722	1993	151	441	74	11	30	173	228-49	19	415	.221	.306	.315	73	-73	10-4	.992	14	*104*	*110*	C-634/D-10,O(RF)	-3.2
DYER, EDDIE Edwin Hawley B 10.11.1900 Morgan City, LA D 4.20.1964 Houston, TX BL/TL 5-11.5/168# d7.8 M5 ▲																								
1922	StL N	6	3	1	1	1	0	0	0	0	0	0	.333	.333	.667	159	1	0-0	1.000	0	0	0	/P-2	0.0
1923	StL N	35	45	17	12	3	0	2	5	3	0	5	.267	.313	.467	105	0	1-0	1.000	-0	114	0	/O-8(7-2-0),P-4	0.0
1924	StL N	50	76	8	18	2	3	0	8	3	0	8	.237	.266	.342	63	-5	1-0	.909	1	119	57	P-29/O(CF)	0.0
1925	StL N	31	31	4	3	1	0	0	0	3	0	1	.097	.176	.129	-20	-2	1-1	.917	0	114	85	P-27	0.0
1926	StL N	6	2	1	1	0	0	0	0	0	0	0	.500	.500	.500	164	0	0	1.000	0	134	0	/P-6	0.0
1927	StL N	1	0	0	0	0	0	0	0	1	0	0	—	1.000	—	181	0	0	—	-0	0	0	/P	0.0
Total	6	129	157	31	35	7	3	2	13	10	0	14	.223	.269	.344	61	-6	3-1	.921	1	112	58	/P-69,O-9(7-3-0)	0.0
DYKES, JIMMY James Joseph B 11.10.1896 Philadelphia, PA D 6.15.1976 Philadelphia, PA BR/TR 5-9/185# d5.6 Mil 1918 M21 C10 OF Total (2-LF 4-CF 1-RF)																								
1918	Phi A	59	186	13	35	3	3	0	13	19	1	32	.188	.267	.237	51	-11	3	.940	9	111	127	2-56/3	-0.2
1919	Phi A	17	49	4	9	1	0	0	1	7	0	11	.184	.286	.204	38	-4	0	.945	3	129	73	2-16	0.0
1920	Phi A	142	546	81	140	25	4	8	35	55	9	73	.256	.334	.361	83	-13	6-9	.957	16	**110**	71	*2-108,3-34	0.4
1921	Phi A	**155**	613	88	168	32	13	16	77	60	15	75	.274	.353	.447	102	1	6-5	.954	21	109	104	*2-155	2.4
1922	Phi A	145	501	66	138	23	7	12	68	55	10	98	.275	.359	.421	100	0	6-2	.945	-5	96	75	*3-141/2-5	0.4
1923	Phi A	124	416	50	105	28	1	4	43	35	5	40	.252	.318	.353	76	-15	6-4	.964	2	106	95	*2-102,S-20/3-2	-0.8
1924	Phi A	110	410	68	128	26	6	3	50	38	1	60	.312	.372	.427	105	3	1-3	.961	10	109	103	2-77,3-27/S-4	1.5
1925	Phi A	122	465	93	150	32	11	5	55	46	8	49	.323	.393	.471	111	8	3-2	.944	6	94	62	3-64,2-58/S-2	1.8
1926	Phi A	124	429	54	123	32	5	1	44	49	8	34	.287	.370	.392	94	-2	6-2	.950	16	107	128	3-82,2-44/S	2.0
1927	Phi A	121	417	61	135	33	6	3	60	44	4	23	.324	.394	.453	113	9	2-3	.989	-3	90	100	1-82,3-25/S-5,O-5(0-4-1),2-3,P-2	0.2
1928	Phi A	85	242	39	67	11	0	5	30	27	5	21	.277	.361	.384	93	-1	2-1	.982	-2	95	92	2-32,S-22,3-20/1-8,O(LF)	0.0
1929	†Phi A	119	401	76	131	34	6	13	79	51	**7**	25	.327	.412	.539	138	24	8-3	.928	-17	80	79	S-60,3-48,2-12	1.7
1930	†Phi A	125	435	69	131	28	4	6	73	74	**10**	53	.301	.414	.425	109	10	3-3	.960	-13	82	90	*3-123/O(LF)	0.4
1931	†Phi A	101	355	48	97	28	2	3	46	49	6	47	.273	.371	.389	94	-1	1-2	.974	-2	93	149	3-87,S-15	0.1
1932	Phi A	153	558	71	148	29	5	7	90	77	4	65	.265	.358	.373	87	-9	8-2	**.980**	-9	89	89	*3-141,S-10/2	-1.1
1933	Chi A★	**151**	554	49	144	22	6	1	68	69	**12**	37	.260	.354	.327	85	-9	3-7	.953	-1	**109**	83	*3-151	-0.6
1934	Chi A☆	127	456	52	122	17	4	7	82	64	4	28	.268	.363	.368	86	-8	1-1	.944	-5	113	59	3-74,1-27,2-27,M	-1.0
1935	Chi A	117	403	45	116	24	2	4	61	59	2	28	.288	.381	.387	97	0	4-3	.953	-6	96	96	3-98,1-16/2-3,M	-0.4
1936	Chi A	127	435	62	116	16	3	7	60	61	4	36	.267	.362	.366	77	-15	1-3	.951	-6	104	71	*3-125,M	-1.6
1937	Chi A	30	85	10	26	5	0	1	23	9	0	7	.306	.372	.400	95	0	0-0	.993	0	65	108	1-15,3-11,M	-0.1
1938	Chi A	26	89	9	27	4	2	2	13	10	0	8	.303	.374	.461	105	1	0-0	.941	-3	92	76	2-23/S3M	-0.1
1939	Chi A	2	1	0	0	0	0	0	0	0	0	0	.000	.000	.000	-97	0	0-0	.667	-0	0	0	/3-2,M	-0.1
Total	22	2282	8046	1108	2256	453	90	108	1071	958	115	850	.280	.365	.399	96	-32	70-55	.952	11	98	95	*3-1257,2-722,1-148,S-140/O-7C,P	4.9
DYKSTRA, LENNY Leonard Kyle "Nails" B 2.10.1963 Santa Ana, CA BL/TL 5-10/167# d5.3																								
1985	NY N	83	236	40	60	9	3	1	19	30-0	1	24	.254	.338	.331	91	-2	15-2	.994	6	114	167	O-74(CF)	0.6
1986	†NY N	147	431	77	127	27	7	8	45	58-1	0	55	.295	.377	.445	130	19	31-7	.990	4	110	125	*O-139(1-138-0)	2.7
1987	NY N	132	431	86	123	37	3	10	43	40-3	4	67	.285	.352	.455	118	12	27-7	.988	-1	103	73	*O-118(CF)	1.3
1988	†NY N	126	429	57	116	19	3	8	33	30-2	3	43	.270	.321	.385	107	3	30-8	.996	5	**114**	71	*O-112(CF)	1.2
1989	NY N	56	159	27	43	12	1	3	13	23-0	2	15	.270	.362	.415	130	7	13-1	.984	2	118	46	O-51(CF)	1.2
	Phi N	90	352	39	78	20	3	4	19	37-1	1	38	.222	.297	.330	79	-9	17-11	.991	2	98	207	O-88(CF)	-0.9
	Year	146	511	66	121	32	4	7	32	60-1	3	53	.237	.318	.356	95	-2	30-12	.988	4	105	152	*O-139(CF)	0.3
1990	Phi N★	149	590	106	**192**	35	3	9	60	89-14	7	48	.325	**.418**	.441	137	36	33-5	.987	7	**113**	84	*O-149(CF)	4.8
1991	Phi N	63	246	48	73	13	5	3	12	37-1	1	20	.297	.391	.427	131	12	24-4	.977	1	111	87	O-63(CF)	1.7
1992	Phi N	85	345	53	104	18	0	6	39	40-4	3	32	.301	.375	.406	123	12	30-5	.989	6	113	123	O-85(CF)	2.3
1993	†Phi N	161	637	**143**	**194**	44	6	19	66	**129**-9	2	64	.305	.420	.482	144	48	37-12	.979	4	113	24	*O-160(CF)	5.6
1994	Phi N✳	84	315	68	86	26	5	5	24	68-11	2	44	.273	.404	.435	116	12	15-4	.984	4	114	88	O-82(CF)	1.8
1995	Phi N★	62	254	37	67	15	1	2	18	33-2	3	28	.264	.353	.354	87	-3	10-5	.987	1	109	59	O-61(9-52-0)	-0.2
1996	Phi N	40	134	21	35	6	3	3	13	26-2	2	25	.261	.387	.418	112	3	3-1	1.000	6	127	170	O-39(CF)	0.9
Total	12	1278	4559	802	1298	281	43	81	404	640-50	31	503	.285	.375	.419	120	150	285-72	.987	46	111	94	*O-1221(10-1213-0)	23.0
DYLER, JOHN John F. B 6.1852 Louisville, KY d7.22 U1																								
1882	Lou AA	1	4	0	0	0	0	0		0			.000	.000	.000	-99	-1		—	-0	0	0	/O(LF)	-0.1
EADDY, DON Donald Johnson B 2.16.1934 Grand Rapids, MI BR/TR 5-11/165# d4.24																								
1959	Chi N	15	1	3	0	0	0	0	0	0-0	0	1	.000	.000	.000	-99	0	0-0	.500	-0	115	0	/3	-0.1

Year	Tm Lg	G	AB	R	H	2B	3B	HR	RBI	BB-IB	HP	SO	AVG	OBP	SLG	AOPS	ABR	SB-CS	FA	FR	Rng	Thr	G at Pos	BFW
EAGAN, TRUCK Charles Eugene B 8.10.1877 San Francisco, CA D 3.19.1949 San Francisco, CA BR/TR 5-11/190# d5.1																								
1901	Pit N	4	12	0	1	0	0	0	2	0	0		.083	.083	.083	-50	-2	1	.923	-1	105	0	/S-3	-0.3
	Cle A	5	18	2	3	0	1	0	2	1	0		.167	.211	.278	36	-2	0	1.000	1	139	0	/2-5,3	-0.1
Total	1	9	30	2	4	0	1	0	4	1	0		.133	.161	.200	2	-4	1	1.000	0	139	0	/2-5,S-3,3	-0.4
EAGAN, BILL William "Bad Bill" B 6.1.1869 Camden, NJ D 2.13.1905 Denver, CO d4.8																								
1891	StL AA	82	297	49	65	11	4	4	43	44	3	53	.219	.326	.323	75	-11	21	.929	18	116	93	2-82	0.8
1893	Chi N	6	19	3	5	0	0	0	2	5	0	5	.263	.417	.263	83	0	4	.912	0	106	144	/2-6	0.0
1898	Pit N	19	61	14	20	2	3	0	5	8	6		.328	.453	.459	165	6	1	.914	1	106	147	2-17	0.7
Total	3	107	377	66	90	13	7	4	50	57	9	58	.239	.352	.342	88	-5	26	.926	19	114	105	2-105	1.5
EAGLE, BILL William Lycurgus B 7.25.1877 Rockville, MD D 4.27.1951 Churchton, MD d8.20																								
1898	Was N	4	13	0	4	1	0	0	2	0	0		.308	.308	.385	98	0	0	.750	-0	281	0	/O-4(1-0-1)	0.0
EAKLE, CHARLIE Charles Emory B 9.27.1887 , MD D 6.15.1959 Baltimore, MD d8.20																								
1915	Bal F	2	7	0	2	1	0	0	0	0	0	0	.286	.286	.429	97	0	1	.600	-2	47	0	/2-2	-0.2
EARL, HOWARD Howard J. "Slim Jim" B 2.27.1869 , MA D 12.22.1916 North Bay, NY 6-2/180# d4.19																								
1890	Chi N	92	384	57	95	10	3	7	51	18	2	47	.247	.285	.344	80	-13	17	.861	-6	107	71	O-49(RF),2-39/S-4,1-3	-1.5
1891	Mil AA	31	129	21	32	5	2	1	17	5	1	13	.248	.281	.341	65	-7	3	.978	-2	38	98	O-30(RF)/1-2	-0.8
Total	2	123	513	78	127	15	5	8	68	23	3	60	.248	.284	.343	76	-20	20	.904	-7	79	82	/O-79(RF),2-39,1-5,S-4	-2.3
EARL, SCOTT William Scott B 9.18.1960 Seymour, IN BR/TR 5-11/165# d9.10																								
1984	Det A	14	35	3	4	0	1	0	1	0-0	0	9	.114	.114	.171	-22	-6	1-0	.959	0	85	166	2-14	-0.5
EARLE, BILLY William Moffat "The Little Globetrotter" B 11.10.1867 Philadelphia, PA D 5.30.1946 Omaha, NE BR/TR 5-10.5/170# d4.27																								
1889	Cin AA	53	169	37	45	4	7	4	31	30	3	24	.266	.386	.444	132	7	26	.776	-4	133	175	O-26(2-1-23),C-23/1-5	0.3
1890	StL AA	22	73	16	17	3	1	0	12	7	2		.233	.317	.301	72	-3	6	.955	3	100	105	C-18/0-3(RF),S32	0.1
1892	Pit N	5	13	5	7	2	0	0	3	4	0	1	.538	.647	.692	304	4	2	.909	-0	108	106	/C-5	0.4
1893	Pit N	27	95	21	24	4	4	2	15	7	0	6	.253	.304	.442	99	-1	1	.959	0	98	71	C-27	0.1
1894	Lou N	21	65	10	23	1	0	0	7	9	0	3	.354	.432	.369	102	1	2	.954	3	98	169	C-18/1230(LF)	0.4
	Bro N	14	50	13	17	6	0	0	6	6	1	2	.340	.421	.460	121	2	4	.930	-2	90	139	C-12/2	0.1
	Year	35	115	23	40	7	0	0	13	15	1	5	.348	.427	.409	110	4	6	.944	1	95	157	C-30/2-2,130(LF)	0.5
Total	5	142	465	102	133	20	12	6	74	63	6	36	.286	.378	.419	114	10	41	.929	-1	75	87	C-103/O-30(3-1-26),1-6,2-3,3-2,S	1.4
EARLY, JAKE Jacob Willard B 5.19.1915 Kings Mountain, NC D 5.31.1985 Melbourne, FL BL/TR 5-11/168# d5.4 Mil 1944-45																								
1939	Was A	32	84	8	22	7	2	0	14	5	0	14	.262	.303	.393	83	-3	0-0	.963	-1	165	50	C-24	-0.2
1940	Was A	80	206	26	53	8	4	5	14	23	1	22	.257	.335	.408	98	-1	0-1	.969	2	88	135	C-56	0.3
1941	Was A	104	355	42	102	20	7	10	54	24	3	38	.287	.338	.468	117	6	0-1	.965	-10	93	114	*C-100	0.2
1942	Was A	104	353	31	72	14	2	3	46	37	1	37	.204	.281	.280	59	-20	0-0	.981	-4	94	**133**	C-98	-1.8
1943	Was A★	126	423	37	109	23	3	5	60	53	4	43	.258	.346	.362	111	7	5-3	.980	-4	113	94	*C-122	1.1
1946	Was A	64	189	13	38	6	0	4	18	23	0	27	.201	.288	.296	67	-9	0-0	.960	-2	96	146	C-64	-0.7
1947	StL A	87	214	25	48	9	3	3	19	54	0	34	.224	.381	.336	98	2	0-1	.989	-5	73	125	C-85	0.1
1948	Was A	97	246	22	54	7	2	1	28	36	1	33	.220	.322	.276	62	-13	2-1	.991	1	115	**185**	C-92	-0.7
1949	Was A	53	138	12	34	4	0	1	11	26	1	11	.246	.370	.297	79	-3	0-1	.973	-5	82	101	C-53	-0.6
Total	9	747	2208	216	532	98	23	32	264	281	11	259	.241	.330	.350	89	-34	7-8	.976	-28	99	124	C-694	-2.3
EASLER, MIKE Michael Anthony B 11.29.1950 Cleveland, OH BL/TR 6-1/196# d9.5 C6																								
1973	Hou N	6	7	1	0	0	0	0	0	2-1	0	4	.000	.222	.000	-34	-1	0-0	.500	-1	27	0	/O-2(1-0-1)	-0.2
1974	Hou N	15	15	0	1	0	0	0	0	0-0	0	5	.067	.067	.067	-65	-3	0-0	—	0			H	-0.4
1975	Hou N	5	5	0	0	0	0	0	0	0-0	0	1	.000	.000	.000	-99	-1	0-0	—	0			H	-0.2
1976	Cal A	21	54	6	13	1	1	0	4	2-1	0	11	.241	.259	.296	69	-2	1-1	—	0	0	0	D-16	-0.3
1977	Pit N	10	18	3	8	2	0	1	5	0-0	0	1	.444	.421	.722	202	2	0-0	1.000	-0	103	0	/O-4(1-0-3)	0.2
1979	†Pit N	55	54	8	15	1	1	2	11	8-0	0	13	.278	.371	.444	116	1	0-1	—	-1	0	0	/O-4(2-0-2)	0.0
1980	Pit N	132	393	66	133	27	3	21	74	43-6	0	65	.338	.396	.583	170	37	5-9	.986	-1	100	74	*O-119(91-0-42)	3.0
1981	Pit N★	95	339	43	97	18	5	7	42	24-7	0	45	.286	.328	.431	112	4	4-7	.980	6	104	163	O-90(72-0-25)	0.5
1982	Pit N	142	475	52	131	27	2	15	58	40-12	6	85	.276	.337	.436	112	8	1-1	.973	-1	98	78	*O-138(137-0-3)	0.1
1983	Pit N	115	381	44	117	17	2	10	54	22-1	3	64	.307	.349	.441	115	7	4-2	.965	-5	88	84	*O-105(LF)	-0.2
1984	Bos A	156	601	87	188	31	5	27	91	58-4	4	134	.313	.376	.516	138	31	1-1	.976	3	138	82	*D-126,1-29	2.8
1985	Bos A	155	568	71	149	29	4	16	74	53-1	3	129	.262	.325	.412	97	-2	0-1	.914	-2	88	0	*D-130,O-20(18-0-2)	-0.9
1986	NY A	146	490	64	148	26	2	14	78	49-13	0	87	.302	.362	.449	122	15	3-2	.958	0	122	0	*D-129,O-11(8-0-3)	1.1
1987	Phi N	33	110	7	31	4	0	1	10	6-0	0	20	.282	.316	.345	74	-4	0-1	.981	2	101	222	O-30(LF)	-0.4
	NY A	65	167	13	47	6	0	4	21	14-0	1	32	.281	.337	.389	94	-1	1-0	1.000	-1	89	106	D-32,O-15(14-0-1)	-0.3
Total	14	1151	3677	465	1078	189	25	118	522	321-46	17	696	.293	.349	.454	118	91	20-26	.974	0	97	97	O-538(479-0-82),D-433/1-29	4.8
EASLEY, DAMION Jacinto Damion B 11.11.1969 New York, NY BR/TR 5-11/185# d8.13																								
1992	Cal A	47	151	14	39	5	0	1	12	8-0	3	26	.258	.307	.311	74	-5	9-5	.970	5	108	175	3-45/S-3	0.0
1993	Cal A	73	230	33	72	13	2	2	22	28-2	3	35	.313	.392	.413	114	6	6-6	.978	-11	88	74	2-54,3-14/D	-0.3
1994	Cal A	88	316	41	68	16	1	6	30	29-0	4	48	.215	.288	.329	58	-20	4-5	.953	-4	92	54	3-47,2-40	-2.2
1995	Cal A	114	357	35	77	14	2	4	35	32-1	6	47	.216	.288	.300	55	-24	5-2	.981	-8	93	79	2-88,S-25	-2.5
1996	Cal A	28	45	4	7	1	0	2	7	6-0	0	12	.156	.255	.311	42	-4	0-0	.943	-1	103	182	S-13/2-9,3-3,O-2(CF),D-2	-0.4
	Det A	21	67	10	23	1	0	2	10	4-0	1	13	.343	.384	.448	111	1	3-1	.974	1	111	67	/2-8,S-8,3-2,D	0.3
	Year	49	112	14	30	2	0	4	17	10-0	1	25	.268	.331	.393	83	-3	3-1	.951	-0	103	154	S-21,2-17/3-5,D-3,O-2(CF)	-0.1
1997	Det A	151	527	97	139	37	3	22	72	68-3	16	102	.264	.362	.471	117	15	28-13	.981	-9	102	100	*2-137,S-21/D-4	1.4
1998	Det A★	153	594	84	161	38	2	27	100	39-2	16	112	.271	.332	.478	107	5	15-5	**.985**	**26**	**113**	118	*2-140,S-30/D-2	3.7
1999	Det A	151	549	83	146	30	1	20	65	51-2	19	124	.266	.346	.434	98	-2	11-3	.989	7	99	115	*2-147,S-19	1.3
2000	Det A	126	464	76	120	27	2	14	58	55-1	11	79	.259	.350	.416	96	-2	13-4	**.990**	11	110	118	*2-125	1.5
2001	Det A	154	585	77	146	27	7	11	65	52-3	13	90	.250	.323	.376	88	-10	10-5	.982	13	**112**	106	*2-153	1.0
2002	Det A	85	304	29	68	14	1	8	30	27-3	11	43	.224	.307	.355	81	-8	1-3	.980	4	108	93	2-84	-0.1
2003	TB A	36	107	8	20	3	1	1	7	2-0	0	18	.187	.202	.262	21	-13	0-0	.922	-5	91	51	3-23/2-4,D-8	-1.6
Total	12	1227	4296	591	1086	226	22	120	513	401-17	103	749	.253	.329	.399	90	-61	105-52	.984	28	104	104	2-989,3-134,S-119/D-18,0-2(CF)	2.1
EAST, CARL Carlton William B 8.27.1894 Marietta, GA D 1.15.1953 Whitesburg, GA BL/TR 6-2/178# d8.24																								
1915	StL A	1	1	0	0	0	0	0	0	0	0	0	.000	.000	.000	-99	0	0	—	-0	0	0	/P	0.0
1924	Was A	2	6	1	2	1	0	0	2	2	0	1	.333	.500	.500	163	1	0-0	.800	-0	107	0	/O-2(RF)	0.0
Total	2	3	7	1	2	1	0	0	2	2	0	1	.286	.444	.429	134	1	0-0	.800	-1	107	0	/O-2(RF),P	0.0
EAST, HARRY Henry H. B 4.1863 St.Louis, MO D 6.2.1905 St.Louis, MO d6.17																								
1882	Bal AA	1	4	0	0	0	0	0		0			.000	.000	.000	-99	-1		.600	-1	88	0	/3	-0.1
EASTER, LUKE Luscious Luke B 8.4.1915 Jonestown, MS D 3.29.1979 Euclid, OH BL/TR 6-4.5/240# d8.11 C1																								
1949	Cle A	21	45	6	10	3	0	0	2	8	0	6	.222	.340	.289	68	-2	0-1	1.000	-2	61	0	O-12(RF)	-0.4
1950	Cle A	141	540	96	151	20	4	28	107	70	**10**	95	.280	.373	.487	123	17	0-3	.991	-3	91	94	*1-128,O-13(RF)	0.8
1951	Cle A	128	486	65	131	12	5	27	103	37	9	71	.270	.333	.481	125	13	0-1	.988	-9	75	98	*1-125	-0.1
1952	Cle A	127	437	63	115	10	3	31	97	44	5	84	.263	.337	.513	144	22	1-1	.983	1	107	91	*1-118	2.0
1953	Cle A	68	211	26	64	9	0	7	31	15	4	35	.303	.361	.445	120	5	0-2	.981	-2	88	123	1-56	0.0
1954	Cle A	6	6	0	1	0	0	0	0	0	0	2	.167	.167	.167	-8	-1	0-0	—	0			H	-0.1
Total	6	491	1725	256	472	54	12	93	340	174	28	293	.274	.350	.481	126	54	1-8	.986	-14	90	98	1-427/O-25(RF)	2.2
EASTERDAY, HENRY Henry P. B 9.16.1864 Philadelphia, PA D 3.30.1895 Philadelphia, PA BR/TR 5-6/145# d6.23																								
1884	Phi U	28	115	12	28	5	0	0		5			.243	.275	.287	76	-6		.875	7	123	111	S-28	0.1
1888	KC AA	115	401	42	76	7	6	3	37	31	5		.190	.256	.259	61	-18	23	**.888**	26	**125**	92	*S-115	1.0
1889	Col AA	95	324	43	56	5	8	4	34	41	2	57	.173	.270	.275	58	-18	10	.890	15	109	81	S-89/2-5,3	-0.1
1890	Col AA	58	197	25	31	5	1	1	17	23	1		.157	.249	.208	37	-15	5	.879	5	107	133	S-58	-0.7
	Phi AA	19	68	17	10	1	0	1	3	10	0		.147	.256	.206	37	-5	4	.876	-1	97	104	S-19	-0.5
	Lou AA	7	24	2	2	0	0	0	1	2	1		.083	.185	.083	-21	-4	1	.886	0	123	66	/S-6,3	-0.3
	Year	84	289	44	43	6	1	2	21	35	2		.149	.245	.197	32	-24	10	.879	5	106	122	S-83/3	-1.5

Year	Tm Lg	G	AB	R	H	2B	3B	HR	RBI	BB-IB	HP	SO	AVG	OBP	SLG	AOPS	ABR	SB-CS	FA	FR	Rng	Thr	G at Pos	BFW
Total	4	322	1129	141	203	23	15	9	92	112	9	57	.180	.259	.251	54	-66	43	.885	52	115	98	S-315/2-5,3-2	-0.5
EASTERLING, PAUL Paul B 9.28.1905 Reidsville, GA D 3.15.1993 Reidsville, GA BR/TR 5-11/180# d4.11																								
1928	Det A	43	114	17	37	7	1	3	12	8	1	24	.325	.374	.482	122	3	2-1	.921	-1	101	67	O-34(32-0-2)	0.0
1930	Det A	29	79	7	16	6	0	1	14	6	0	18	.203	.259	.316	44	-7	0-1	1.000	1	91	216	O-25(8-1-16)	-0.7
1938	Phi A	4	7	1	2	0	0	0	0	1	0	2	.286	.375	.286	70	0	0-0	.750	-0	81	0	/O(CF)	-0.1
Total	3	76	200	25	55	13	1	4	26	15	1	44	.275	.329	.410	88	-4	2-2	.938	-0	97	116	/O-60(40-2-18)	-0.8
EASTERLY, TED Theodore Harrison B 4.20.1885 Lincoln, NE D 7.6.1951 Clearlake Highlands, CA BL/TR 5-8/165# d4.17																								
1909	Cle A	98	287	32	75	14	10	1	27	13	0		.261	.293	.390	111	2	8	.965	3	*105*	*110*	C-76	1.3
1910	Cle A	110	363	34	111	16	6	0	55	21	0		.306	.344	.383	126	10	10	.964	-9	*82*	*103*	C-65,O-32(RF)	0.7
1911	Cle A	99	287	34	93	19	5	1	37	8	1		.324	.345	.436	116	5	6	.910	-6	100	94	O-54(0-2-52),C-22	-0.2
1912	Cle A	65	186	17	55	4	0	2	21	7	2		.296	.328	.349	91	-3	3	.958	-1	*91*	*92*	C-51	0.0
	Chi A	30	55	5	20	2	0	0	14	2	0		.364	.386	.400	129	2	2	.964	-2	*87*	*86*	C-10/O(LF)	0.1
	Year	95	241	22	75	6	0	2	35	9	2		.311	.341	.361	100	-1	5	.959	-3	*90*	*91*	C-61/O(LF)	0.1
1913	Chi A	60	97	3	23	1	0	0	8	4	0	9	.237	.267	.247	51	-6	2	.976	3	*140*	*84*	C-19	-0.2
1914	KC F	134	436	58	146	20	12	1	67	31	4	25	.335	.384	.443	130	11	10	.969	-16	*92*	*93*	*C-128	0.5
1915	KC F	110	309	32	84	12	5	3	32	21	1	15	.272	.320	.372	99	-7	2	.969	3	*98*	*96*	C-88	0.4
Total	7	706	2020	215	607	88	38	8	261	107	8	49	.300	.338	.394	112	14	43	.965	-27	*95*	*97*	C-459/O-87(1-2-84)	2.6
EASTERWOOD, ROY Roy Charles "Shag" B 1.12.1915 Waxahachie, TX D 8.24.1984 Graham, TX BR/TR 6-0.5/196# d4.21																								
1944	Chi N	17	33	1	7	2	0	1	2	1	0	11	.212	.235	.364	67	-2	0	1.000	-0	*108*	*125*	C-12	-0.1
EASTON, JOHN John David "Goose" B 3.4.1933 Trenton, NJ D 7.28.2001 Princeton, NJ BR/TR 6-2/185# d6.19																								
1955	Phi N	1	0	0	0	0	0	0	0	0-0	0	0	—	—	—	—	0	0-0	—	0			R	0.0
1959	Phi N	3	3	0	0	0	0	0	0	0-0	0	3	.000	.000	.000	-98	-1	0-0	—	0			H	-0.1
Total	2	4	3	0	0	0	0	0	0	0-0	0	3	.000	.000	.000	-98	-1	0-0	1.000	0				-0.1
EAYRS, EDDIE Edwin B 11.10.1890 Blackstone, MA D 11.30.1969 Warwick, RI BL/TL 5-7/160# d6.30 ▲																								
1913	Pit N	4	6	0	1	0	0	0	0	0	0	1	.167	.167	.167	-5	0	0	.667	-0	97	0	/P-2	0.0
1920	Bos N	87	244	31	80	5	2	1	24	30	4	18	.328	.410	.377	133	12	4-3	.950	-3	87	85	O-63(43-7-13)/P-7	0.5
1921	Bos N	15	15	0	1	0	0	0	1	0	0	4	.067	.067	.067	-68	-2	0-0	—	-0	0	0	/P-2	0.0
	Bro N	8	6	1	1	0	0	0	1	2	0	0	.167	.375	.167	47	0	0-0	—	-0	0	0	/O(RF)	0.0
	Year	23	21	1	2	0	0	0	2	2	0	4	.095	.174	.095	-27	-4	0-0	—	-0	0	0	/P-2,O(RF)	0.0
Total	3	114	271	32	83	5	2	1	26	32	4	23	.306	.388	.351	116	10	4-3	.950	-4	87	85	/O-64(43-7-14),P-11	0.5
EBRIGHT, HI Hiram C. "Buck" B 6.12.1859 Lancaster Co., PA D 10.24.1916 Milwaukee, WI BR/TR d4.24																								
1889	Was N	16	59	7	15	2	2	1	6	3	1	8	.254	.302	.407	103	0	1	.875	3			/C-9,O-4(RF),S-3	0.3
ECHEVARRIA, ANGEL Angel Santos B 5.25.1971 Bridgeport, CT BR/TR 6-4/215# d7.15																								
1996	Col N	26	21	2	6	0	0	0	6	2-0	1	5	.286	.346	.286	63	-1	0-0	1.000	-1	19	0	O-11(4-0-7)	-0.2
1997	Col N	15	20	4	5	2	0	0	0	2-0	0	5	.250	.318	.350	61	-1	0-0	1.000	0	58	481	/O-7(2-2-3)	-0.1
1998	Col N	19	29	7	11	3	0	1	9	2-0	2	3	.379	.455	.586	141	2	0-0	1.000	-1	89	116	/1-4,O-4(3-0-1)	0.1
1999	Col N	102	191	28	56	7	0	11	35	17-0	3	34	.293	.360	.503	91	-3	1-3	.985	2	107	151	O-49(20-0-31),1-10	-0.4
2000	Col N	10	9	0	1	0	0	0	2	0-0	0	2	.111	.111	.111	-35	-2	0-0	1.000	-0	0	262	/1-2,O(LF)	-0.2
	Mil N	31	42	3	9	2	0	1	4	7-0	0	9	.214	.327	.333	69	-2	0-0	1.000	0	109	119	/1-9,O-5(2-0-3)	-0.2
	Year	41	51	3	10	2	0	1	6	7-0	0	11	.196	.293	.294	47	-4	0-0	1.000	-0	98	134	1-11/O-6(3-0-3)	-0.4
2001	Mil N	75	133	12	34	11	0	5	13	8-0	3	29	.256	.310	.451	96	-1	0-1	.931	-3	75	0	O-23(19-0-5),1-10/D	-0.6
2002	Chi N	50	98	14	30	7	0	3	21	8-0	1	17	.306	.351	.469	124	3	0-0	.971	1	138	123	O-19(8-0-11),1-13	0.3
Total	7	328	543	70	152	32	0	21	90	46-0	10	104	.280	.343	.455	94	-5	1-4	.972	-2	94	125	O-119(59-2-61)/1-48,D	-1.3
ECHOLS, JOHNNY John Gresham B 1.9.1917 Atlanta, GA D 11.13.1972 Atlanta, GA BR/TR 5-10.5/175# d5.24																								
1939	StL N	2	0	0	0	0	0	0	0	0	0	0	—	—	—	—	0	0	—	0			R	0.0
ECKHARDT, OX Oscar George B 12.23.1901 Yorktown, TX D 4.22.1951 Yorktown, TX BL/TR 6-1/185# d4.16																								
1932	Bos N	8	8	1	2	0	0	0	1	0	0	1	.250	.250	.250	36	-1	0	—	0			H	-0.1
1936	Bro N	16	44	5	8	1	0	1	6	5	0	2	.182	.265	.273	45	-3	0	1.000	0	111	87	O-10(RF)	-0.4
Total	2	24	52	6	10	1	0	1	7	5	0	3	.192	.263	.269	43	-4	0	1.000	0	111	87	/O-10(RF)	-0.5
ECKSTEIN, DAVID David Mark B 1.20.1975 Sanford, FL BR/TR 5-6.5/170# d4.3																								
2001	Ana A	153	582	82	166	26	2	4	41	43-0	**21**	60	.285	.355	.357	87	-9	29-4	.971	-12	98	90	*S-126,2-14,D-14	-0.7
2002	†Ana A	152	608	107	178	22	6	8	63	45-0	**27**	44	.293	.363	.388	101	3	21-13	.977	-13	96	106	*S-147/D-3	0.1
2003	Ana A	120	452	59	114	22	1	3	31	36-0	15	45	.252	.325	.325	76	-14	16-5	.984	-3	94	94	*S-116/D-3	-0.7
Total	3	425	1642	248	458	70	9	15	135	124-0	63	149	.279	.350	.360	89	-20	66-22	.977	-28	96	97	S-389/D-20,2-14	-1.3
EDEN, CHARLIE Charles M. B 1.18.1855 Lexington, KY D 9.17.1920 Cincinnati, OH BL/TL ?/168# d8.17 ▲																								
1877	Chi N	15	55	9	12	0	1	0	5	3		6	.218	.259	.255	56	-3		.679	-2	78	229	O-15(RF)	-0.4
1879	Cle N	81	353	40	96	**31**	7	3	34	6		20	.272	.284	.425	131	13		.808	-4	118	138	*O-80(0-1-79)/1-3,C	0.8
1884	Pit AA	32	122	12	33	7	4	1		7	6		.270	.341	.418	148	7		.759	-4	72	0	O-31(CF)/P-2	0.2
1885	Pit AA	98	405	57	103	18	6	0	38	17	8		.254	.298	.328	99	0		.814	-16	43	71	*O-96(LF)/P-4,3-2	-1.6
Total	4	226	935	118	244	56	18	4	77	33	14	26	.261	.296	.372	115	17		.793	-26	77	97	O-222(96-32-94)/P-6,1-3,3-2,C	-1.0
EDEN, MIKE Edward Michael B 5.22.1949 Fort Clayton, Canal Zone BB/TR 5-10/170# d8.2																								
1976	Atl N	5	8	0	0	0	0	0	1	0-0	0	0	.000	.000	.000	-94	-2	0-0	1.000	0	128	114	/2-2	-0.2
1978	Chi A	10	17	1	2	0	0	0	0	4-0	0	0	.118	.286	.118	17	-2	0-0	.905	-0	91	136	/S-5,2-4	-0.2
Total	2	15	25	1	2	0	0	0	1	4-0	0	0	.080	.207	.080	-16	-4	0-0	1.000	0	85	141	/2-6,S-5	-0.4
EDINGTON, STUMP Jacob Frank B 7.4.1891 Koleen, IN D 11.11.1969 Bastrop, LA BL/TL 5-8/170# d6.20																								
1912	Pit N	15	53	4	16	0	2	0	12	3	0	1	.302	.339	.377	97	-1	0	1.000	1	101	155	O-14(RF)	0.0
EDLER, DAVE David Delmar B 8.5.1956 Sioux City, IA BR/TR 6/185# d9.4																								
1980	Sea A	28	89	11	20	1	0	3	9	8-1	0	16	.225	.289	.337	70	-4	2-3	.965	1	107	101	3-28	-0.4
1981	Sea A	29	78	7	11	3	0	0	5	11-0	1	13	.141	.250	.179	26	-7	3-3	.884	-4	89	90	3-26/S	-1.3
1982	Sea A	40	104	14	29	2	2	2	18	11-1	0	13	.279	.345	.394	100	0	4-2	.922	1	93	78	3-31/O-2(1-0-1),D-2	0.0
1983	Sea A	29	63	2	12	1	1	1	4	5-0	1	11	.190	.257	.286	49	-5	3-3	.875	-3	75	39	3-13/1-5,O(RF)D	-0.9
Total	4	126	334	34	72	7	3	6	36	35-2	2	53	.216	.291	.308	66	-16	12-11	.922	-6	94	84	/3-98,D-8,1-5,O-3(1-0-2),S	-2.6
EDMONDS, JIM James Patrick B 6.27.1970 Fullerton, CA BL/TL 6-1/190# d9.9																								
1993	Cal A	18	61	5	15	4	1	0	4	2-1	0	16	.246	.270	.344	62	-3	0-2	.981	5	140	354	O-17(1-1-15)	0.0
1994	Cal A	94	289	35	79	13	1	5	37	30-3	1	72	.273	.343	.377	85	-6	4-2	.981	9	**122**	215	O-77(59-5-19),1-22	-0.2
1995	Cal A★	141	558	120	162	30	4	33	107	51-4	5	130	.290	.352	.536	129	22	1-4	.998	12	116	119	*O-139(CF)	3.1
1996	Cal A	114	431	73	131	28	3	27	66	46-2	4	101	.304	.375	.571	135	22	4-0	.997	1	104	94	*O-111(CF)/D	2.2
1997	Ana A	133	502	82	146	27	0	26	80	60-5	4	80	.291	.368	.500	125	19	5-7	.985	8	111	159	*O-115(CF),1-11/D-8	2.4
1998	Ana A	154	599	115	184	42	1	25	91	57-7	1	114	.307	.368	.506	124	21	7-5	.988	2	103	109	*O-153(CF)	2.3
1999	Ana A	55	204	34	51	17	2	5	23	28-0	0	45	.250	.339	.426	95	-1	5-4	.992	2	105	144	O-42(CF)/1-2,D-9	0.0
2000	†StL N★	152	525	129	155	25	0	42	108	103-3	6	167	.295	.411	.583	148	42	10-3	.989	3	105	120	*O-146(CF)/1-6	4.3
2001	†StL N	150	500	95	152	38	1	30	110	93-12	4	136	.304	.410	.564	152	43	5-5	.982	-5	93	156	*O-147(CF)/1-2	3.8
2002	†StL N	144	476	96	148	31	2	28	83	86-14	8	134	.311	.420	.561	165	46	4-3	.986	6	107	147	*O-139(CF)	5.2
2003	StL N★	137	447	89	123	32	2	39	89	77-6	4	127	.275	.385	.617	163	42	1-3	.986	13	**116**	178	*O-129(1-128-0)/D-2	5.3
Total	11	1292	4592	873	1346	287	17	260	798	633-57	37	1122	.293	.380	.533	135	247	46-38	.988	55	108	142	*O-1215(61-1126-34)/1-43,D-20	28.4
EDMONDSON, BOB Robert E. B 4.30.1879 Paris, KY D 8.14.1931 Lawrence, KS BR/TR 5-11/185# d9.15 ▲																								
1906	Was A	3	3	1	1	0	0	0	0	0	0		.333	.333	.333	114	0	0	1.000	0	166	0	/P-2,O(RF)	0.0
1908	Was A	26	80	5	15	4	1	0	2	7	1		.188	.261	.262	77	-2	0	.878	-2	75	140	O-24(1-9-14)	-0.6
Total	2	29	83	6	16	4	1	0	2	7	1		.193	.264	.265	78	-2	0	.878	-2	74	139	/O-25(1-9-15),P-2	-0.6
EDMONSON, EDDIE Earl Edward B 11.20.1889 Hopewell, PA D 5.10.1971 Leesburg, FL BL/TR 6/175# d10.4																								
1913	Cle A	2	5	0	0	0	0	0	0	0	0	0	.000	.000	.000	-97	-1	0	1.000	-0	0	0	/1O	-0.2

Year	Tm Lg	G	AB	R	H	2B	3B	HR	RBI	BB-IB	HP	SO	AVG	OBP	SLG	AOPS	ABR	SB-CS	FA	FR	Rng	Thr	G at Pos	BFW
EDWARDS, BRUCE Charles Bruce "Bull" B 7.15.1923 Quincy, IL D 4.25.1975 Sacramento, CA BR/TR 5-7/194# d6.23																								
1946	Bro N	92	292	24	78	13	5	1	25	34	2	20	.267	.348	.356	99	0	1	.982	8	**152**	108	C-91	1.3
1947	†Bro N★	130	471	53	139	15	8	9	80	49	2	55	.295	.364	.418	103	2	2	.983	6	93	106	*C-128	1.4
1948	Bro N	96	286	36	79	17	2	8	54	26	2	28	.276	.341	.434	105	2	4	.984	-3	138	119	C-48,O-21(LF),3-14/1	0.0
1949	†Bro N	64	148	24	31	3	0	8	25	25	0	15	.209	.324	.392	87	-3	0	.990	-1	153	101	C-41/O-4(LF),3	-0.2
1950	Bro N	50	142	16	26	4	1	8	16	13	1	22	.183	.256	.394	67	-8	1	.980	-2	128	126	C-38/1-2	-0.8
1951	Bro N	17	36	6	9	2	0	1	8	1	0	3	.250	.270	.389	74	-1	0-0	1.000	1	232	70	/C-9	-0.1
	Chi N☆	51	141	19	33	9	2	3	17	16	1	14	.234	.316	.390	87	-2	1-2	.962	-4	57	92	C-28/1-9	-0.5
	Year	68	177	25	42	11	2	4	25	17	1	17	.237	.308	.390	85	-4	1-2	.971	-3	93	88	C-37/1-9	-0.6
1952	Chi N	50	94	7	23	2	2	1	12	8	0	12	.245	.304	.340	77	-3	0-0	.989	-2	56	69	C-22/2	-0.5
1954	Chi N	4	3	1	0	0	0	0	1	2	0	2	.000	.400	.000	15	0	0-0	—	0			H	0.0
1955	Was A	30	57	5	10	2	0	0	3	16-0	0	6	.175	.356	.211	58	-2	0-1	.980	3	112	179	C-22/3-5	0.1
1956	Cin N	7	5	0	1	0	0	0	0	0-0	0	2	.200	.200	.200	8	-1	0-0	.000	-1	0	0	/C-2,23	-0.1
Total	10	591	1675	191	429	67	20	39	241	190-0	8	179	.256	.335	.390	93	-16	9-3	.982	3	118	109	C-429/O-25(LF),3-21,1-12,2-2	0.6
EDWARDS, DAVE David Leonard B 2.24.1954 Los Angeles, CA BR/TR 6/177# d9.11 b-Marshall b-Mike																								
1978	Min A	15	44	7	11	3	0	1	3	7-0	2	13	.250	.377	.386	113	1	1-1	.950	3	114	352	O-15(10-8-0)	0.3
1979	Min A	96	229	42	57	8	0	8	35	24-1	1	45	.249	.323	.389	88	-4	6-3	.983	3	104	142	O-86(37-31-23)/D-3	-0.3
1980	Min A	81	200	26	50	9	1	2	20	12-1	1	51	.250	.294	.335	68	-9	2-1	.932	-1	96	164	O-72(27-47-2)/D-3	-1.1
1981	SD N	58	112	13	24	4	1	2	13	11-0	0	24	.214	.282	.321	77	-4	3-1	.970	3	99	236	O-49(11-2-40)	-0.2
1982	SD N	71	55	7	10	2	0	1	2	1-0	0	14	.182	.196	.273	32	-5	0-0	.944	-1	108	0	O-45(18-25-2)/1	-0.7
Total	5	321	640	95	152	26	2	14	73	55-2	4	147	.237	.301	.350	77	-21	12-6	.958	7	102	169	O-267(103-113-67)/D-6,1	-2.0
EDWARDS, HANK Henry Albert B 1.29.1919 Elmwood Place, OH D 6.22.1988 Santa Ana, CA BL/TL 6/190# d9.10 Mil 1944-45																								
1941	Cle A	16	68	10	15	1	1	1	6	2	0	4	.221	.243	.309	47	-6	0-0	.929	-1	72	203	O-16(2-0-14)	-0.8
1942	Cle A	13	48	6	12	2	1	0	7	5	0	8	.250	.321	.333	89	-1	2-1	.968	-1	99	0	O-12(CF)	-0.2
1943	Cle A	92	297	38	82	18	6	3	28	30	0	34	.276	.343	.407	127	9	4-8	.983	-3	95	76	O-74(CF)	0.2
1946	Cle A	124	458	62	138	33	**16**	10	54	43	0	48	.301	.361	.509	151	28	1-3	.968	2	102	128	*O-123(0-1-122)	2.7
1947	Cle A	108	393	54	102	12	3	15	59	31	1	55	.260	.315	.420	106	0	1-3	.990	-3	99	44	*O-100(39-0-67)	-0.9
1948	Cle A	55	160	27	43	9	2	3	18	18	1	18	.269	.346	.406	102	0	1-1	.987	-2	98	36	O-41(RF)	-0.3
1949	Cle A	5	15	3	4	0	0	1	1	1	0	2	.267	.313	.467	107	0	0-0	1.000	-0	91	0	/O-5(RF)	-0.1
	Chi N	58	176	25	51	8	4	7	21	19	0	22	.290	.359	.500	131	7	0	.988	-1	89	103	O-51(18-0-34)	0.4
1950	Chi N	41	110	13	40	11	1	2	21	10	0	13	.364	.417	.536	150	8	0	.976	-2	85	108	O-29(RF)	0.6
1951	Bro N	35	31	1	7	3	0	0	3	4	0	9	.226	.314	.323	70	-1	0-0	—	0			H	-0.1
	Cin N	41	127	14	40	9	1	3	20	13	0	17	.315	.379	.472	126	5	0-2	.985	-2	102	0	O-34(26-0-8)	0.1
	Year	76	158	15	47	12	1	3	23	17	0	26	.297	.366	.443	115	4	0-2	.985	-2	102	0	O-34(26-0-8)	0.0
1952	Cin N	74	184	24	52	7	6	6	28	19	0	22	.283	.350	.484	129	6	0-3	.988	0	105	63	O-51(33-0-18)	0.3
	Chi A	8	18	2	6	0	0	0	1	0	0	2	.333	.333	.333	85	0	0-0	1.000	0	115	0	/O-3(LF)	-0.1
1953	StL A	65	106	6	21	3	0	0	9	13	0	10	.198	.286	.226	39	-9	0-1	1.000	0	97	142	O-21(11-4-7)	-1.0
Total	11	735	2191	285	613	116	41	51	276	208	2	264	.280	.343	.440	119	46	9-22	.981	-12	97	81	O-560(132-91-345)	0.8
EDWARDS, DOC Howard Rodney B 12.10.1936 Red Jacket, WV BR/TR 6-2/215# d4.21 M3 C8																								
1962	Cle A	53	143	13	39	6	0	3	9	9-0	2	14	.273	.325	.378	91	-2	0-0	.992	5	119	101	C-39	0.5
1963	Cle A	10	31	6	8	2	0	0	0	2-2	0	6	.258	.303	.323	76	-1	0-0	.988	3	157	68	C-10	0.3
	KC A	71	240	16	60	12	0	6	35	11-6	2	23	.250	.287	.375	80	-7	0-1	.987	-4	63	101	C-63	-0.8
	Year	81	271	22	68	14	0	6	35	13-8	2	29	.251	.289	.369	79	-7	0-1	.987	-1	76	97	C-73	-0.5
1964	KC A	97	294	25	66	10	0	5	28	13-0	3	40	.224	.265	.310	57	-17	0-1	.986	-5	60	83	C-79/1-7	-2.1
1965	KC A	6	20	1	3	0	0	0	0	1-0	0	2	.150	.190	.150	-2	-3	0-0	1.000	-0	69	93	/C-6	-0.3
	NY A	45	100	3	19	3	0	1	9	13-6	1	14	.190	.289	.250	55	-6	1-2	.986	2	113	102	C-43	-0.3
	Year	51	120	4	22	3	0	1	9	14-6	1	16	.183	.274	.233	46	-8	1-2	.988	1	107	101	C-49	-0.6
1970	Phi N	35	78	5	21	0	0	0	6	4-3	1	10	.269	.313	.269	59	-5	0-0	.970	1	47	191	C-34	-0.3
Total	5	317	906	69	216	33	0	15	87	53-17	9	109	.238	.287	.325	68	-41	1-4	.986	0	79	104	C-274/1-7	-3.0
EDWARDS, JOHNNY John Alban B 6.10.1938 Columbus, OH BL/TR 6-4/220# d6.27																								
1961	†Cin N	52	145	14	27	5	0	2	14	18-4	1	28	.186	.279	.262	45	-11	1-0	.982	-3	80	87	C-52	-1.2
1962	Cin N	133	452	47	115	28	5	8	50	45-9	1	70	.254	.322	.392	88	-7	1-1	.987	12	107	97	*C-130	1.1
1963	Cin N★	148	495	46	128	19	4	11	67	45-5	4	93	.259	.322	.380	99	0	1-5	**.995**	14	95	100	*C-148	2.1
1964	Cin N★	126	423	47	119	23	1	7	55	34-9	1	65	.281	.331	.390	100	1	1-2	.992	16	90	104	*C-120	2.4
1965	Cin N☆	114	371	47	99	22	2	17	51	50-16	1	45	.267	.353	.474	123	13	0-0	.990	4	80	124	*C-110	2.2
1966	Cin N	98	282	24	54	8	0	6	39	31-8	0	42	.191	.269	.284	50	-19	1-3	.992	2	73	97	C-98	-1.3
1967	Cin N	80	209	10	43	6	0	2	20	16-8	0	28	.206	.261	.263	46	-14	1-4	.990	9	88	89	C-73	-0.3
1968	†StL N	85	230	14	55	9	1	3	29	16-0	1	20	.239	.287	.326	86	-4	1-1	.992	2	135	73	C-54	0.1
1969	Hou N	151	496	52	115	20	6	6	50	53-12	2	69	.232	.306	.333	81	-13	2-1	**.994**	8	105	129	*C-151	0.3
1970	Hou N	140	458	46	101	16	4	7	49	51-16	1	63	.221	.299	.319	69	-21	1-0	**.995**	11	117	**140**	*C-139	-0.3
1971	Hou N	106	317	18	74	13	4	1	23	26-9	0	38	.233	.291	.309	72	-12	1-1	**.995**	9	120	111	*C-104	0.1
1972	Hou N	108	332	33	89	16	2	5	40	50-12	1	39	.268	.358	.373	113	8	2-4	.988	-9	78	85	*C-105	0.2
1973	Hou N	79	250	24	61	10	2	5	27	19-7	2	23	.244	.301	.360	83	-6	1-0	.989	-3	70	84	C-76	-0.6
1974	Hou N	50	117	8	26	7	1	1	10	11-3	1	12	.222	.292	.325	76	-4	1-1	.989	3	64	71	C-32	0.1
Total	14	1470	4577	430	1106	202	32	81	524	465-118	16	635	.242	.311	.353	85	-89	15-23	.992	76	96	105	*C-1392	4.9
EDWARDS, MARSHALL Marshall Lynn B 8.27.1952 Fort Lewis, WA BL/TL 5-9/157# d4.11 b-David twb-Mike																								
1981	†Mil A	40	58	10	14	1	1	0	4	0-0	0	2	.241	.241	.293	56	-4	6-2	.979	-1	92	79	O-36(2-21-14)/D	-0.5
1982	†Mil A	69	178	24	44	4	1	2	14	4-0	0	8	.247	.261	.315	62	-10	10-4	.984	1	109	57	O-54(4-13-41)/D-6	-1.1
1983	Mil A	51	74	14	22	1	1	0	5	1-0	0	9	.297	.303	.338	84	-2	5-5	1.000	2	102	225	O-35(12-12-13)/D-4	-0.1
Total	3	160	310	48	80	6	3	2	23	5-0	0	19	.258	.267	.316	66	-16	21-11	.987	2	104	105	O-125(18-46-68)/D-11	-1.7
EDWARDS, MIKE Michael Donald B 11.24.1976 Goshen, NY BR/TR 6-1/180# d9.20																								
2003	Oak A	4	4	0	1	0	0	0	0	2-0	0	1	.250	.500	.250	106	0	0-0	—	-0	0	0	/O-2(LF),D-2	0.0
EDWARDS, MIKE Michael Lewis B 8.27.1952 Fort Lewis, WA BR/TR 5-10/154# d9.10 b-Dave twb-Marshall																								
1977	Pit N	7	6	1	0	0	0	0	0	0-0	1	3	.000	.143	.000	-56	-1	0-2	1.000	1	120	143	/2-4	-0.1
1978	Oak A	142	414	48	113	16	2	1	23	16-0	2	32	.273	.303	.329	82	-11	27-21	.964	-23	87	92	*2-133/S-9,D-4	-3.0
1979	Oak A	122	400	35	93	12	2	1	23	15-0	2	37	.233	.263	.280	49	-30	10-6	.962	-13	95	61	*2-113/S-3,D-2	-3.6
1980	Oak A	46	59	10	14	0	0	0	3	1-0	0	5	.237	.250	.237	37	-5	1-1	.971	-3	101	74	2-23/O(RF)D	-0.8
Total	4	317	879	94	220	28	4	2	49	32-0	5	77	.250	.280	.298	63	-47	38-30	.964	-38	92	77	2-273/S-12,D-11,O(RF)	-7.5
EDWARDS, RALPH Ralph Strunk B 12.14.1882 Brewster, NY D 1.5.1949 White Plains, NY BR/TR 5-9/165# d9.17																								
1915	Phi A	2	5	0	0	0	0	0	0	0	0	3	.000	.000	.000	-99	-1	0	1.000	-1	50	0	/2	-0.2
EENHOORN, ROBERT Robert Franciscus B 2.9.1968 Rotterdam, Netherlands BR/TR 6-3/170# d4.27																								
1994	NY A	3	4	1	2	1	0	0	0	0-0	0	0	.500	.500	.750	225	1	0-0	1.000	-1	41	206	/S-3	0.0
1995	NY A	5	14	1	2	1	0	0	2	1-0	0	3	.143	.200	.214	8	-2	0-0	1.000	-1	82	123	/2-3,S-2	-0.2
1996	NY A	12	14	2	1	0	0	0	2	2-0	0	3	.071	.167	.071	-31	-3	0-0	1.000	1	75	138	2-10/3-2	-0.2
	Cal A	6	15	1	4	0	0	0	0	0-0	0	2	.267	.267	.267	35	-2	0-0	.875	-1	74	52	/S-4,2-2	-0.2
	Year	18	29	3	5	0	0	0	2	2-0	0	5	.172	.212	.172	3	-4	0-0	.971	-1	85	137	2-12/S-4,3-2	-0.4
1997	Ana A	11	20	2	7	1	0	1	6	0-0	0	2	.350	.333	.550	130	1	0-0	.833	-3	59	0	/3-5,2-3,S-2	-0.2
Total	4	37	67	7	16	3	0	1	10	3-0	0	10	.239	.260	.328	53	-5	0-0	.963	-5	78	117	/2-18,S-11,3-7	-0.8
EGAN, BEN Arthur Augustus B 11.20.1883 Augusta, NY D 2.18.1968 Sherrill, NY BR/TR 6/195# d9.29 C2																								
1908	Phi A	2	6	1	1	1	0	0	0	1	0		.167	.286	.333	95	0	0	.933	-0	76	105	/C-2	0.0
1912	Phi A	49	138	9	24	3	4	0	13	6	0		.174	.208	.254	33	-13	3	.958	4	135	122	C-46	-0.6
1914	Cle A	29	88	7	20	2	1	0	11	3	3	20	.227	.277	.273	63	-4	0-1	.975	2	91	116	C-27	0.0
1915	Cle A	42	120	4	13	3	0	0	6	8	0	14	.108	.164	.133	-11	-17	0	.970	6	115	107	C-40	-0.8
Total	4	122	352	21	58	9	5	0	30	18	3	34	.165	.212	.219	27	-34	3-1	.966	11	116	115	C-115	-1.4
EGAN, JIM James K. "Troy Terrier" B 1858 Derby, CT D 9.26.1884 New Haven, CT TL d5.15 ▲																								
1882	Tro N	30	115	15	23	3	2	0	10	1		21	.200	.207	.261	51	-6		.625	-6	62	132	O-18(2-16-0),P-12/C-2	-0.8

Year	Tm Lg	G	AB	R	H	2B	3B	HR	RBI	BB-IB	HP	SO	AVG	OBP	SLG	AOPS	ABR	SB-CS	FA	FR	Rng	Thr	G at Pos	BFW
EGAN, DICK Richard Joseph B 6.23.1884 Portland, OR D 7.7.1947 Oakland, CA BR/TR 5-11/162# d9.15 OF Total (11-LF 2-CF 14-RF)																								
1908	Cin N	18	68	8	14	3	1	0	5	2	0		.206	.229	.279	64	-3	7	.891	-2	92	202	2-18	-0.6
1909	Cin N	127	480	59	132	14	3	2	53	37	2		.275	.329	.329	105	3	39	.950	**24**	**117**	112	*2-116,S-10	3.0
1910	Cin N	135	474	70	116	11	5	0	46	53	1	38	.245	.322	.289	82	-10	41	.961	-10	101	80	*2-131/S-3	-2.0
1911	Cin N	153	558	80	139	11	5	1	56	59	1	50	.249	.322	.292	75	-18	37	.949	10	109	103	*2-152	-0.6
1912	Cin N	149	507	69	125	14	5	0	52	56	2	26	.247	.324	.294	72	-19	24	**.973**	1	101	85	*2-149	-1.5
1913	Cin N	60	195	15	55	7	3	0	22	15	0	13	.282	.333	.349	95	-1	6-10	.972	-1	96	113	2-37,S-17/3-2	-0.2
1914	Bro N	106	337	30	76	10	3	1	21	22	0	25	.226	.273	.282	64	-16	8	.914	-10	94	74	S-83,3-10/O-3(0-2-1),2-2,1	-2.2
1915	Bro N	3	3	0	0	0	0	0	0	0	0	0	.000	.000	.000	-98	-1	0	—	0			H	-0.1
	Bos N	83	220	20	57	9	1	0	21	28	0	18	.259	.343	.309	102	2	3-4	.974	1	101	86	O-24(11-0-13),2-22,S-10/1-9,3-4	0.2
	Year	86	223	20	57	9	1	0	21	28	0	18	.256	.339	.305	100	1	3-4	.974	1	101	86	O-24(11-0-13),2-22,S-10/1-9,3-4	0.1
1916	Bos N	83	238	23	53	8	3	0	16	19	0	21	.223	.280	.282	76	-7	2	.949	-18	83	60	2-59,S-12/3-8	-2.7
Total	9	917	3080	374	767	87	29	4	292	291	6	191	.249	.315	.300	82	-70	167-14	.956	-5	104	98	2-686,S-135/O-27R,3-24,1-10	-6.7
EGAN, TOM Thomas Patrick B 6.9.1946 Los Angeles, CA BR/TR (BB 1974 (part), 75) 6-4/218# d5.27																								
1965	Cal A	18	38	3	10	0	1	0	1	3-0	0	12	.263	.317	.316	82	-1	0-0	1.000	-0	*135*	*49*	C-16	-0.1
1966	Cal A	7	11	0	0	0	0	0	0	1-0	0	5	.000	.083	.000	-76	-3	0-0	1.000	1	*157*	*108*	/C-6	-0.2
1967	Cal A	1	1	0	0	0	0	0	0	0-0	0	0	.000	.000	.000	-99	0	0-0	1.000	0	0	0	/C	0.0
1968	Cal A	16	43	2	5	1	0	1	4	2-0	0	15	.116	.156	.209	10	-5	0-0	1.000	0	53	91	C-14	-0.5
1969	Cal A	46	120	7	17	1	0	5	16	17-2	1	41	.142	.248	.275	50	-8	0-1	.985	4	96	147	C-46	-0.3
1970	Cal A	79	210	14	50	6	0	4	20	14-1	1	67	.238	.286	.324	71	-9	0-0	.988	-5	81	97	C-79	-1.1
1971	Chi A	85	251	29	60	11	1	10	34	26-1	4	94	.239	.320	.410	102	1	1-0	.986	2	59	82	C-77/1	0.7
1972	Chi A	50	141	8	27	3	0	2	9	4-0	2	48	.191	.224	.255	42	-11	0-0	.986	4	65	109	C-46	-0.6
1974	Cal A	43	94	4	11	0	0	0	4	8-0	1	40	.117	.194	.117	-9	-13	1-0	.996	5	59	125	C-41	-0.7
1975	Cal A	28	70	7	16	3	1	0	3	5-0	0	14	.229	.280	.300	69	-3	0-0	.965	-2	46	158	C-28	-0.4
Total	10	373	979	74	196	25	3	22	91	80-4	9	336	.200	.266	.299	62	-52	2-1	.987	9	*72*	*108*	C-354/1	-3.2
EGGERT, ELMER Elmer Albert "Mose" B 1.29.1902 Rochester, NY D 4.9.1971 Rochester, NY BR/TR 5-9/160# d4.27																								
1927	Bos A	5	3	0	0	0	0	0	0	1	0	1	.000	.250	.000	-31	-1	0-0	—	-0	0	0	/2	-0.1
EGGLER, DAVE David Daniel B 4.30.1851 Brooklyn, NY D 4.5.1902 Buffalo, NY BR/TR 5-9/165# d5.18																								
1871	Mut NA	**33**	147	37	47	7	3	0	18	4		3	.320	.338	.408	124	6	14-3	.910	5	78	158	*O-33(CF)	0.8
1872	Mut NA	**56**	290	**94**	97	20	0	0	19	8		9	.334	.352	.403	141	17	**18**-6	**.917**	14	**194**	181	*O-56(1-55-0)	2.2
1873	Mut NA	**53**	266	82	90	13	4	0	35	6		2	.338	.353	.417	129	9	3-2	.856	4	81	79	*O-53(CF)/3	0.9
1874	Phi NA	**58**	299	70	95	13	8	0	31	5		1	.318	.329	.415	132	9	5-6	**.906**	7	111	198	*O-57(7-50-0)/2-2	1.2
1875	Ath NA	66	295	66	89	13	7	0	33	1		10	.302	.304	.393	126	6	6-5	**.921**	4	68	**162**	*O-66(2-65-0)	0.7
1876	Phi N	39	174	28	52	4	0	0	19	2		4	.299	.307	.322	111	2		.913	3	87	55	O-39(1-37-1)	0.3
1877	Chi N	33	136	20	36	3	0	0	20	1		5	.265	.270	.287	67	-5		.861	2	132	290	O-33(CF)	-0.4
1879	Buf N	78	317	41	66	5	7	0	27	11		41	.208	.235	.268	64	-13		.919	-7	63	113	*O-78(CF)	-2.2
1883	Bal AA	53	202	15	38	2	0	0	7	1			.188	.192	.198	25	-17		.916	-0	61	76	O-53(CF)	-1.7
	Buf N	38	153	13	38	2	1	0	13	2		29	.248	.258	.275	61	-8		.845	-4	43	70	O-38(1-37-0)	-1.1
1884	Buf N	63	241	25	47	3	1	0	20	6		54	.195	.215	.216	35	-18		.887	0	111	51	O-63(2-61-0)	-1.9
1885	Buf N	6	24	0	2	0	0	0	0	2		4	.083	.154	.083	-21	-3		.938	0	79	0	/O-6(CF)	-0.3
Total	5 NA	266	1297	349	418	66	22	0	136	24		25	.322	.335	.407	131	47	46-22	.000	33	109	157	O-265(10-256-0)/2-2,3	5.8
Total	6	310	1247	142	279	19	9	0	106	25		137	.224	.239	.253	56	-62		.894	-5	80	98	O-310(4-305-1)	-7.3
EHRET, RED Philip Sydney B 8.31.1868 Louisville, KY D 7.28.1940 Cincinnati, OH BR/TR 6/175# d7.7 ▲																								
1888	KC AA	17	63	4	12	4	0	0	4	1	0		.190	.203	.254	43	-4	1	.750	-2	0	0	O-10(5-2-3)/P-7,21	-0.4
1889	Lou AA	67	258	27	65	6	6	1	31	4	0	23	.252	.263	.333	71	-12	4	.891	-2	123	121	P-45,O-22(6-1-15)/S32	-0.6
1890	†Lou AA	43	146	11	31	2	1	0	10	1	0		.212	.218	.240	36	-3	1	.859	-3	89	105	P-43	0.0
1891	Lou AA	26	91	9	22	2	1	0	9	5	0	15	.242	.281	.286	63	1	3	.871	-0	108	235	P-26	0.0
1892	Pit N	40	132	12	34	2	0	0	19	7	0	22	.258	.295	.273	72	3	1	.855	-4	81	41	P-39	0.0
1893	Pit N	40	136	16	24	3	0	1	17	10	0	18	.176	.233	.221	21	-6	1	.893	1	115	0	P-39	0.0
1894	Pit N	46	135	6	23	4	1	0	11	8	0	22	.170	.217	.215	4	-11	0	.859	-2	93	86	P-46	0.0
1895	StL N	37	96	13	21	2	1	1	9	6	0	12	.219	.265	.292	44	-2	0	.848	-0	106	0	P-37	0.0
1896	Cin N	34	102	10	20	2	0	1	20	10	0	12	.196	.268	.245	33	-10	2	.923	0	100	138	P-34/1	0.0
1897	Cin N	34	66	6	13	2	0	0	6	4	1		.197	.254	.227	26	-3	2	.957	-1	79	292	P-34	0.0
1898	Lou N	13	40	3	9	3	1	0	4	1	1		.225	.262	.350	76	1	0	.800	-2	77	0	P-12	0.0
Total	11	397	1265	117	274	32	11	4	140	57	2	124	.217	.252	.269	44	-46	15	.882	-15	100	97	P-362/O-32(11-3-18),1-2,2-2,3S	-1.0
EIBEL, HACK Henry Hack B 12.6.1893 Brooklyn, NY D 10.16.1945 Macon, GA BL/TL 5-11/220# d6.13 ▲																								
1912	Cle A	1	3	0	0	0	0	0	0	0	0		.000	.000	.000	-97	-1	0	—	-0	0	0	/O(RF)	-0.1
1920	Bos A	29	43	4	8	2	0	0	6	3	0	6	.186	.239	.233	26	-5	1-1	.800	1	54	0	/O-5(3-0-2),P-3,1	-0.5
Total	2	30	46	4	8	2	0	0	6	3	0	6	.174	.224	.217	19	-6	1-1	.800	-2	52	0	/O-6(3-0-3),P-3,1	-0.6
EICHRODT, IKE Frederick George B 1.6.1903 Chicago, IL D 7.14.1965 Indianapolis, IN BR/TR 5-11.5/167# d9.7																								
1925	Cle A	15	52	4	12	3	1	0	4	2	0	7	.231	.259	.327	48	-4	0-0	.938	-2	96	0	O-13(CF)	-0.6
1926	Cle A	37	80	14	25	7	1	0	7	2	0	11	.313	.329	.425	95	-1	1-0	.976	1	100	173	O-27(19-6-2)	-0.1
1927	Cle A	85	267	24	59	19	2	0	25	16	0	25	.221	.265	.307	48	-21	2-3	.979	5	98	183	O-81(13-64-5)	-1.9
1931	Chi A	34	117	9	25	5	1	0	15	1	0	8	.214	.220	.274	31	-12	0-0	1.000	-1	104	0	O-32(0-30-3)	-1.3
Total	4	171	516	51	121	34	5	0	51	21	0	51	.234	.264	.320	52	-38	3-3	.979	4	99	128	O-153(32-113-10)	-3.9
EISENREICH, JIM James Michael B 4.18.1959 St.Cloud, MN BL/TL 5-11/195# d4.6																								
1982	Min A	34	99	10	30	6	0	2	9	11-0	1	13	.303	.378	.424	117	3	0-0	.973	0	113	0	O-30(CF)	0.3
1983	Min A	2	7	1	2	1	0	0	0	1-0	0	1	.286	.375	.429	116	0	0-0	1.000	1	105	771	/O-2(CF)	0.1
1984	Min A	12	32	1	7	1	0	0	3	2-1	0	4	.219	.250	.250	41	-3	2-0	1.000	-1	61	0	/O-3(0-2-1),D-6	-0.3
1987	KC A	44	105	10	25	8	2	4	21	7-2	0	13	.238	.278	.467	93	-2	1-1	—	0	0	0	D-26	-0.2
1988	KC A	82	202	26	44	8	1	1	19	6-1	0	31	.218	.236	.282	45	-15	9-3	.965	1	117	0	O-64(30-15-21),D-13	-1.6
1989	KC A	134	475	64	139	33	7	9	59	37-9	0	44	.293	.341	.448	122	13	27-8	.989	-1	103	56	*O-123(26-67-58),D-10	1.3
1990	KC A	142	496	61	139	29	7	5	51	42-2	1	51	.280	.335	.397	106	4	12-14	**.996**	-1	98	73	*O-138(70-19-78)/D-2	-0.3
1991	KC A	135	375	47	113	22	3	2	47	20-1	1	35	.301	.333	.392	101	0	5-3	.973	-6	87	21	*O-105(59-13-42),1-15/D	-0.9
1992	KC A	113	353	31	95	13	3	2	28	24-4	0	36	.269	.313	.340	81	-9	11-6	.995	-2	105	18	O-88(24-1-66)/D-8	-1.4
1993	†Phi N	153	362	51	115	17	4	7	54	26-5	1	36	.318	.363	.445	117	8	5-0	.996	7	118	86	*O-137(1-3-133)/1	1.1
1994	Phi N	104	290	42	87	15	4	4	43	33-3	1	31	.300	.371	.421	104	3	6-2	.989	4	115	69	O-93(0-5-90)	0.3
1995	Phi N	129	377	46	119	22	2	10	55	38-4	1	44	.316	.375	.464	120	12	10-0	**1.000**	3	**115**	32	*O-111(39-6-68)	1.2
1996	Phi N	113	338	45	122	24	3	3	41	31-9	1	32	.361	.413	.476	133	18	11-1	.977	2	111	59	O-91(43-3-50)	1.7
1997	†Fla N	120	293	36	82	19	1	2	34	30-4	1	28	.280	.345	.372	93	-2	0-0	.987	-2	94	68	O-55(43-0-13),1-29/D-4	-0.8
1998	Fla N	30	64	9	16	1	0	1	7	4-1	0	14	.250	.294	.313	63	-4	2-0	.965	-2	38	102	1-10/O-8(5-0-3)	-0.6
	LA N	75	127	12	25	2	2	0	6	12-1	0	22	.197	.266	.244	38	-12	4-0	.971	0	104	90	O-24(22-0-2)/1-9,D-2	-1.2
	Year	105	191	21	41	3	2	1	13	16-2	0	36	.215	.275	.267	46	-16	6-0	.977	-2	103	71	O-32(27-0-5),1-19/D-2	-1.8
Total	15	1422	3995	492	1160	221	39	52	477	324-47	8	435	.290	.341	.404	103	14	105-38	.988	2	106	52	*O-1072(362-166-625)/D-72,1-64	-1.3
ELAND d4.14																								
1873	Mar NA	1	3	0	0	0	0	0	0	0		0	.000	.000	.000	-99	-1	0-0	.667	-0	0	0	/O(RF)	-0.1
ELBERFELD, KID Norman Arthur "The Tabasco Kid" B 4.13.1875 Pomeroy, OH D 1.13.1944 Chattanooga, TN BR/TR 5-7/158# d5.30 M1																								
1898	Phi N	14	38	1	9	4	0	0	7	5	7		.237	.420	.342	124	3	0	.795	-5	70	57	3-14	-0.2
1899	Cin N	41	138	23	36	4	2	0	22	15	11		.261	.378	.319	90	0	5	.878	-6	90	75	S-24,3-18	-0.4
1901	Det A	121	432	76	133	21	11	3	76	57	7		.308	.397	.428	123	16	23	.907	19	104	**134**	*S-121	3.5
1902	Det A	130	488	70	127	17	6	1	64	55	11		.260	.348	.326	86	-7	19	.921	12	**105**	111	*S-130	0.8
1903	Det A	35	132	29	45	5	3	0	19	11	5		.341	.412	.424	156	10	6	.932	5	107	89	S-34/3	1.6
	NY A	90	349	49	100	18	5	0	45	22	10		.287	.346	.367	107	4	16	.914	4	100	130	S-90	1.1
	Year	125	481	78	145	23	8	0	64	33	**15**		.301	.365	.383	120	13	22	**.919**	9	102	**119**	*S-124/3	2.7
1904	NY A	122	445	55	117	13	5	2	46	37	13		.263	.337	.328	106	5	18	.933	11	**108**	125	*S-122	2.2
1905	NY A	111	390	48	102	18	2	0	53	23	16		.262	.329	.318	95	-1	18	.908	-4	98	104	*S-108	-0.1
1906	NY A	99	346	59	106	11	5	2	31	30	10		.306	.378	.384	126	12	19	.925	-1	100	61	S-98	1.5

Year	Tm Lg	G	AB	R	H	2B	3B	HR	RBI	BB-IB	HP	SO	AVG	OBP	SLG	AOPS	ABR	SB-CS	FA	FR	Rng	Thr	G at Pos	BFW
1907	NY A	120	447	61	121	17	6	0	51	36	13		.271	.343	.336	108	5	22	.930	13	104	78	*S-118	2.4
1908	NY A	19	56	11	11	3	0	0	5	6	5		.196	.328	.250	87	0	1	.916	-2	92	35	S-17,M	-0.1
1909	NY A	106	379	47	90	9	5	0	26	28	14		.237	.314	.288	89	-4	23	.943	4	93	112	S-61,3-44	0.4
1910	Was A	127	455	53	114	9	2	2	42	35	13		.251	.322	.292	97	-1	19	**.943**	-5	94	100	*3-113,2-10/S-3	-0.3
1911	Was A	127	404	58	110	19	4	0	47	65	**25**		.272	.405	.339	110	13	24	.957	7	98	99	2-68,3-52	2.2
1914	Bro N	30	62	7	14	1	0	0	1	2	5	4	.226	.304	.242	62	-3	0	.901	-3	77	122	S-18/2	-0.6
Total	14	1292	4561	647	1235	169	56	10	535	427	165	4	.271	.355	.339	105	52	213	.920	51	102	105	S-944,3-242/2-79	14.0
ELDER, GEORGE George Rezin B 3.10.1921 Lebanon, KY BL/TR 5-11/180# d7.22																								
1949	StL A	41	44	9	11	3	0	0	2	4	0	11	.250	.313	.318	64	-2	0-0	1.000	1	129	0	O-10(LF)	-0.2
ELIA, LEE Lee Constantine B 7.16.1937 Philadelphia, PA BR/TR 5-11/175# d4.23 M4 C13																								
1966	Chi A	80	195	16	40	5	2	3	22	15-3	2	39	.205	.265	.297	67	-9	0-1	.954	3	107	124	S-75	-0.1
1968	Chi N	15	17	1	3	0	0	0	3	0-0	1	6	.176	.222	.176	20	-2	0-0	1.000	-1	68	0	/S-2,23	-0.3
Total	2	95	212	17	43	5	2	3	25	15-3	3	45	.203	.262	.288	63	-11	0-1	.954	3	107	123	/S-77,32	-0.4
ELKO, PETE Peter "Piccolo Pete" B 6.17.1918 Wilkes-Barre, PA D 9.17.1993 Wilkes-Barre, PA BR/TR 5-11/185# d9.17																								
1943	Chi N	9	30	1	4	0	0	0	0	4	0	5	.133	.235	.133	8	-4	0	.852	-2	87	69	/3-9	-0.6
1944	Chi N	7	22	2	5	1	0	0	0	0	0	1	.227	.227	.273	40	-2	0	1.000	0	94	140	/3-6	-0.2
Total	2	16	52	3	9	1	0	0	0	4	0	6	.173	.232	.192	22	-6	0	.902	-2	89	92	/3-15	-0.8
ELLAM, ROY Roy "Whitey" or "Slippery" B 2.8.1886 W.Conshohocken, PA D 10.28.1948 Conshohocken, PA BR/TR 5-10.5/203# d9.18																								
1909	Cin N	10	21	4	4	0	1	1	4	7	0		.190	.393	.429	156	2	1	.895	-1	93	158	/S-9	0.1
1918	Pit N	26	77	9	10	1	1	0	2	17	2	17	.130	.302	.169	43	-4	2	.924	-6	87	69	S-26	-1.0
Total	2	36	98	13	14	1	2	1	6	24	2	17	.143	.323	.224	67	-2	3	.917	-7	88	90	/S-35	-0.9
ELLERBE, FRANK Francis Rogers "Governor" B 12.25.1895 Marion Co., SC D 7.8.1988 Latta, SC BR/TR 5-10.5/165# d8.28																								
1919	Was A	28	105	13	29	4	1	0	16	2	0	15	.276	.290	.333	75	-4	5	.945	-3	89	50	S-28	-0.5
1920	Was A	101	336	38	98	14	2	0	36	19	1	23	.292	.331	.345	82	-9	5-4	.934	-6	100	65	3-75,S-19/O(RF)	-1.2
1921	Was A	10	10	1	2	0	1	0	1	0	0	2	.200	.200	.400	52	-1	0-0	—	0			H	-0.1
	StL A	105	430	65	124	20	12	2	49	22	3	42	.288	.327	.405	81	-14	1-6	.953	1	97	44	*3-105	-0.8
	Year	115	440	66	126	20	13	2	50	22	3	44	.286	.325	.405	81	-15	1-6	.953	1	97	44	*3-105	-0.9
1922	StL A	91	342	42	84	16	3	1	33	25	3	36	.246	.303	.319	60	-20	1-1	.955	12	107	117	3-91	-0.3
1923	StL A	18	49	6	9	0	0	0	1	1	0	5	.184	.200	.184	1	-7	0-1	.967	-2	81	111	3-14	-0.8
1924	StL A	21	61	7	12	3	0	0	2	2	0	3	.197	.222	.246	19	-8	0-1	.953	1	91	231	3-21	-0.6
	Cle A	46	120	7	31	1	3	1	14	1	1	10	.258	.270	.342	56	-9	0-0	.975	5	120	38	3-39/2-2	-0.2
	Year	67	181	14	43	4	3	1	16	3	1	13	.238	.254	.309	44	-17	0-1	.967	5	109	111	3-60/2-2	-0.8
Total	6	420	1453	179	389	58	22	4	152	72	8	136	.268	.306	.346	68	-72	12-13	.952	8	102	81	3-345/S-47,2-2,O(RF)	-4.5
ELLICK, JOE Joseph J. B 4.3.1854 Cincinnati, OH D 4.21.1923 Kansas City, KS 5-10/162# d5.13 M1 U1																								
1875	RS NA	7	27	1	6	1	0	0	1	0		1	.222	.222	.259	74	0	1-0	.471	-4	60	0	/3-5,O-2(CF)	-0.4
1878	Mil N	3	13	2	2	0	0	0	1	0		1	.154	.154	.154	1	-1		.769	-2			/C-2,3P	-0.3
1880	Wor N	5	18	1	1	0	0	0	0	1		2	.056	.105	.056	-40	-3		.882	0	116	0	/3-5	-0.2
1884	CP U	**92**	394	71	93	11	0	0		16			.236	.266	.264	61	-30		.903	-0	98	52	O-57(3-0-54),S-33/2-4,M	-2.6
	KC U	2	8	0	0	0	0	0		0			.000	.000	.000	-99	-2		.778	-1	88	0	/2O(RF)	-0.3
	Bal U	7	27	2	4	0	0	0		2			.148	.207	.148	8	-4		.714	-1	107	0	/S-6,O(RF)	-0.4
	Year	101	429	73	97	11	0	0		18			.226	.257	.252	55	-36		.894	-2	101	94	O-59(3-0-56),S-39/2-5	-3.3
Total	3	109	460	76	100	11	0	0	1	19		3	.217	.248	.241	50	-40		.894	-3			/O-59(3-0-56),S-39,3-6,2-5,C-2,P	-3.8
ELLIOT, LARRY Lawrence Lee B 3.5.1938 San Diego, CA BL/TL 6-2/200# d4.19																								
1962	Pit N	8	10	2	3	0	0	1	2	0-0	0	1	.300	.300	.600	135	0	0-0	1.000	-0	90	0	/O-3(RF)	0.0
1963	Pit N	4	4	0	0	0	0	0	0	0-0	0	3	.000	.000	.000	-99	-1	0-0	—	0			H	-0.1
1964	NY N	80	224	27	51	8	0	9	22	28-2	3	55	.228	.320	.384	100	1	1-2	.985	-1	103	53	O-63(4-57-4)	-0.3
1966	NY N	65	199	24	49	14	2	5	32	17-1	0	46	.246	.306	.412	100	0	0-1	.912	1	83	287	O-54(25-0-31)	-0.3
Total	4	157	437	53	103	22	2	15	56	45-3	3	105	.236	.311	.398	99	0	1-3	.956	-0	94	159	O-120(29-57-38)	-0.7
ELLIOTT, ALLEN Allen Clifford "Ace" B 12.25.1897 St.Louis, MO D 5.6.1979 St.Louis, MO BL/TR 6/170# d6.14																								
1923	Chi N	53	168	21	42	8	2	2	29	2	2	12	.250	.267	.357	63	-10	3-3	.992	-2	80	106	1-52	-1.4
1924	Chi N	10	14	0	2	0	0	0	0	0	0	1	.143	.143	.143	-23	-2	0-0	1.000	-0	43	88	1-10	-0.3
Total	2	63	182	21	44	8	2	2	29	2	2	13	.242	.258	.341	57	-12	3-3	.992	-2	77	104	/1-62	-1.7
ELLIOTT, CARTER Carter Ward B 11.29.1893 Atchison, KS D 5.21.1959 Palm Springs, CA BL/TR 5-11/165# d9.10																								
1921	Chi N	12	28	5	7	2	0	0	0	5	0	3	.250	.364	.321	83	0	0-0	.964	2	104	85	S-10	0.2
ELLIOTT, GENE Eugene Birminghouse B 2.8.1889 Fayette Co., PA D 1.5.1976 Huntingdon, PA BL/TR 5-7/150# d4.13																								
1911	NY A	5	13	1	1	1	0	0	1	2	0		.077	.200	.154	-1	-2	0	—	-1	0	0	/O-2(RF),3	-0.2
ELLIOTT, ROWDY Harold Bell B 7.8.1890 Kokomo, IN D 2.12.1934 San Francisco, CA BR/TR 5-9/160# d9.24 Mil 1918																								
1910	Bos N	3	2	0	0	0	0	0	0	0	0	0	.000	.000	.000	-96	0	0	1.000	-0	*0*	*0*	/C	-0.1
1916	Chi N	23	55	5	14	3	0	0	3	3	0	5	.255	.293	.309	77	-1	1	.969	-1	97	78	C-18	-0.1
1917	Chi N	85	223	18	56	8	5	0	28	11	2	11	.251	.292	.332	84	-4	4	.969	4	*97*	*115*	C-73	0.6
1918	Chi N	5	10	0	0	0	0	0	0	2	0	1	.000	.167	.000	-47	-2	0	.952	0	*113*	*114*	/C-5	-0.1
1920	Bro N	41	112	13	27	4	0	1	13	3	1	6	.241	.267	.304	62	-6	0-0	.964	1	*102*	*117*	C-39	-0.1
Total	5	157	402	36	97	15	5	1	44	19	3	23	.241	.281	.311	73	-13	5-0	.967	5	*99*	*110*	C-136	0.2
ELLIOTT, HARRY Harry Lewis B 12.30.1923 San Francisco, CA BR/TR 5-9/175# d8.1																								
1953	StL N	24	59	6	15	6	1	1	6	3	1	8	.254	.302	.441	91	-1	0-0	1.000	0	111	75	O-17(15-0-2)	-0.1
1955	StL N	68	117	9	30	4	0	1	12	11-3	1	9	.256	.321	.316	71	-5	0-2	.978	-1	103	56	O-28(8-0-20)	-0.7
Total	2	92	176	15	45	10	1	2	18	14-3	2	17	.256	.314	.358	78	-6	0-2	.988	-0	106	64	/O-45(23-0-22)	-0.8
ELLIOTT, RANDY Randy Lee B 6.5.1951 Oxnard, CA BR/TR 6-2/190# d9.10																								
1972	SD N	14	49	5	10	3	1	0	6	2-0	0	11	.204	.235	.306	57	-3	0-0	1.000	1	131	0	O-13(RF)	-0.3
1974	SD N	13	33	5	7	1	0	1	2	7-1	0	9	.212	.350	.333	96	0	0-1	1.000	-2	49	0	O-11(7-0-4)/1	-0.3
1977	SF N	73	167	17	40	5	1	7	26	8-1	1	24	.240	.275	.407	82	-5	0-2	.973	2	93	200	O-46(LF)	-0.6
1980	Oak A	14	39	4	5	3	0	0	1	1-0	0	13	.128	.150	.205	-4	-6	0-0	—	0	0	0	D-11	-0.6
Total	4	114	288	31	62	12	2	8	35	18-2	1	57	.215	.262	.354	69	-14	0-3	.982	0	94	127	/O-70(53-0-17),D-11,1	-1.8
ELLIOTT, BOB Robert Irving "Mr. Team" B 11.26.1916 San Francisco, CA D 5.4.1966 San Diego, CA BR/TR 6/185# d9.2 M1 C1																								
1939	Pit N	32	129	18	43	10	3	3	19	9	0	4	.333	.377	.527	143	7	0	.978	0	110	39	O-30(CF)	0.7
1940	Pit N	148	551	88	161	34	11	5	64	45	2	28	.292	.348	.421	112	9	13	.978	2	104	107	*O-147(4-31-113)	0.3
1941	Pit N★	141	527	74	144	24	10	3	76	64	1	52	.273	.353	.374	105	4	6	.970	-0	106	76	*O-139(4-2-134)	-0.4
1942	Pit N★	143	560	75	166	26	7	9	89	52	2	35	.296	.358	.416	123	16	2	.927	-1	102	82	*3-142/O(LF)	2.1
1943	Pit N	156	581	82	183	30	12	7	101	56	1	24	.315	.376	.444	132	23	4	.949	-4	101	**137**	*3-151/2-2,S	2.3
1944	Pit N★	143	538	85	160	28	16	10	108	75	0	42	.297	.383	.465	132	24	9	.944	-4	97	96	*3-140/S	2.2
1945	Pit N✶	144	541	80	157	36	6	8	108	64	1	38	.290	.366	.423	115	12	5	.928	7	108	126	3-81,O-61(RF)	1.6
1946	Pit N	140	486	50	128	25	3	5	68	64	2	44	.263	.351	.358	99	1	6	.995	6	108	89	O-92(RF),3-43	0.4
1947	Bos N✶	150	555	93	176	35	5	22	113	87	0	60	.317	.410	.517	148	41	3	**.956**	-2	105	103	*3-148	3.8
1948	†Bos N★	151	540	99	153	24	5	23	100	**131**	0	57	.283	.423	.474	145	41	6	.945	-12	97	78	*3-150	2.9
1949	Bos N	139	482	77	135	29	5	17	76	90	2	38	.280	.395	.467	138	29	0	.963	11	**108**	**99**	*3-130	4.0
1950	Bos N	142	531	94	162	28	5	24	107	68	2	67	.305	.386	.512	143	34	2	.952	-17	87	89	*3-137	1.6
1951	Bos N★	136	480	73	137	29	2	15	70	65	0	56	.285	.371	.448	128	20	2-0	.941	-8	93	103	*3-127	1.3
1952	NY N	98	272	33	62	6	2	10	35	36	2	20	.228	.323	.375	92	-3	1-0	.978	-1	85	151	O-65(52-0-15),3-13	-0.8
1953	StL A	48	160	19	40	7	1	5	29	30	0	18	.250	.368	.400	105	2	0-1	.954	-1	96	103	3-45	0.0
	Chi A	67	208	24	54	11	1	4	32	31	1	21	.260	.358	.380	96	0	1-1	.963	-5	91	74	3-58/O-2(LF)	-0.6
	Year	115	368	43	94	18	2	9	61	61	1	39	.255	.363	.389	100	2	1-2	.959	-7	93	87	*3-103/O-2(LF)	-0.6
Total	15	1978	7141	1064	2061	382	94	170	1195	967	16	604	.289	.375	.440	124	260	60-2	.947	-28	99	99	*3-1365,O-537(63-63-415)/S-2,2-2	21.4

Year	Tm Lg	G	AB	R	H	2B	3B	HR	RBI	BB-IB	HP	SO	AVG	OBP	SLG	AOPS	ABR	SB-CS	FA	FR	Rng	Thr	G at Pos	BFW
ELLIS, BEN Alfred Benjamin B 7.1870 New York, NY D 7.26.1931 Schenectady, NY 5-10/165# d7.16																								
1896	Phi N	4	16	0	1	0	0	0	0	3	0	6	.063	.211	.063	-26	-3	0	.800	-1	69	126	/S-2,3-2	-0.3
ELLIS, RUBE George William B 11.17.1885 Downey, CA D 3.13.1938 Rivera, CA BL/TL 6/170# d4.15																								
1909	StL N	149	575	76	154	10	9	3	46	54	3		.268	.334	.332	114	8	18	.955	13	135	175	*O-145(144-0-1)	1.4
1910	StL N	142	550	87	142	18	8	4	54	62	5	70	.258	.339	.342	102	2	25	.942	2	93	**139**	*O-141(LF)	-0.5
1911	StL N	155	555	69	139	20	11	2	66	66	2	64	.250	.332	.337	90	-7	9	.938	0	101	100	*O-148(LF)	-1.4
1912	StL N	109	305	47	82	18	2	4	33	34	0	36	.269	.342	.380	100	0	6	.929	-1	103	83	O-76(65-4-7)	-0.4
Total	4	555	1985	279	517	66	30	13	199	216	10	<u>170</u>	.260	.336	.344	101	3	58	.943	14	109	130	O-510(498-4-8)	-0.9
ELLIS, JOHN John Charles B 8.21.1948 New London, CT BR/TR 6-2.5/225# d5.17																								
1969	NY A	22	62	2	18	4	0	1	8	1-0	1	11	.290	.308	.403	103	0	0-2	.978	-3	33	96	C-15	-0.3
1970	NY A	78	226	24	56	12	1	7	29	18-0	2	47	.248	.305	.403	100	-1	0-1	.992	-2	123	100	1-53/3-5,C-2	-0.6
1971	NY A	83	238	16	58	12	1	3	34	23-5	6	42	.244	.322	.340	95	-1	0-0	.990	-3	89	134	1-65/C-2	-1.0
1972	NY A	52	136	13	40	5	1	5	25	8-0	0	22	.294	.333	.456	138	5	0-0	.965	2	109	72	C-25/1-8	0.8
1973	Cle A	127	437	59	118	12	2	14	68	46-2	3	57	.270	.339	.403	108	4	0-0	.980	-17	105	96	C-72,D-38,1-12	-1.2
1974	Cle A	128	477	58	136	23	6	10	64	32-3	1	53	.285	.330	.421	116	9	1-2	.992	-4	86	100	1-69,C-42,D-21	0.0
1975	Cle A	92	296	22	68	11	1	7	32	14-2	2	33	.230	.266	.345	72	-12	0-1	.976	-6	97	114	C-84/1-2,D-3	-1.5
1976	Tex A	11	31	4	13	2	0	1	8	0-0	0	4	.419	.419	.581	187	3	0-0	1.000	-0	195	100	/C-7,D-3	0.3
1977	Tex A	49	119	7	28	7	0	4	15	8-2	0	26	.235	.283	.395	82	-3	0-0	1.000	-2	59	32	C-16,D-15/1-8	-0.6
1978	Tex A	34	94	7	23	4	0	3	17	6-0	0	20	.245	.282	.383	88	-2	0-1	.958	-2	120	59	C-22/D-7	-0.3
1979	Tex A	111	316	33	90	12	0	12	61	15-1	2	55	.285	.318	.437	103	0	2-2	.978	-3	71	94	D-62,1-30/C-7	-0.6
1980	Tex A	73	182	12	43	9	1	1	23	14-1	1	23	.236	.290	.313	69	-8	3-0	.992	-2	65	83	1-39,D-20/C-3	-1.2
1981	Tex A	23	58	2	8	3	0	1	7	5-1	1	10	.138	.219	.241	34	-5	0-1	.993	-1	86	144	1-18/D	-0.7
Total	13	883	2672	259	699	116	13	69	391	190-17	19	403	.262	.312	.392	99	-11	6-10	.989	-42	86	103	1-304,C-297,D-170/3-5	-6.9
ELLIS, MARK Mark William B 6.6.1977 Rapid City, SD BR/TR 5-11/180# d4.9																								
2002	†Oak A	98	345	58	94	16	4	6	35	44-1	4	54	.272	.359	.394	101	1	4-2	.978	6	101	93	2-85/S-8,3-7,D	1.1
2003	†Oak A	154	553	78	137	31	5	9	52	48-4	7	94	.248	.313	.371	80	-16	6-2	.982	30	113	105	*2-153	2.1
Total	2	252	898	136	231	47	9	15	87	92-5	11	148	.257	.331	.380	88	-15	10-4	.981	36	109	101	2-238/S-8,3-7,D	3.2
ELLIS, ROB Robert Walter B 7.3.1950 Grand Rapids, MI BR/TR 5-11/180# d6.18																								
1971	Mil A	36	111	9	22	2	0	0	6	12-0	1	24	.198	.278	.216	43	-8	0-2	.923	-6	70	144	3-19,O-15(1-1-13)	-1.7
1974	Mil A	22	48	4	14	2	0	0	4	4-0	0	11	.292	.346	.333	97	0	0-0	1.000	1	78	493	O-11(4-0-8)/3D	0.1
1975	Mil A	6	7	3	2	0	0	0	0	0-0	0	0	.286	.286	.286	62	0	0-0	1.000	-1	17	0	/O-5(LF),D	-0.2
Total	3	64	166	16	38	4	0	0	10	16-0	1	35	.229	.297	.253	59	-8	0-2	.976	-5	80	160	/O-31(10-1-21),3-20,D-10	-1.8
ELLISON, BABE Herbert Spencer "Bert" B 11.15.1895 Rutland, AR D 8.11.1955 San Francisco, CA BR/TR 5-11/170# d9.18 Mil 1918																								
1916	Det A	2	7	0	1	0	0	0	1	0	0	1	.143	.143	.143	-14	-1	0	1.000	-1	26	0	/3-2	-0.2
1917	Det A	9	29	2	5	1	2	1	4	6	1	3	.172	.333	.448	139	1	0	.980	-2	17	96	/1-9	-0.1
1918	Det A	7	23	1	6	1	0	0	2	3	0	1	.261	.346	.304	100	0	1	1.000	1	104	0	/O-4(RF),2-3	0.1
1919	Det A	56	134	18	29	4	0	0	11	13	1	24	.216	.291	.246	53	-8	4	.966	-2	99	80	2-25,O-10(1-1-8)/S	-1.1
1920	Det A	61	155	11	34	7	2	0	21	8	0	26	.219	.258	.290	46	-13	4-1	.997	3	114	61	1-38/O-4(0-2-2),3	-1.0
Total	5	135	348	32	75	13	4	1	39	30	2	55	.216	.282	.284	58	-21	9-<u>1</u>	.994	-2	94	68	/1-47,2-28,O-18(1-3-14),3-3,S	-2.3
ELLISON, JASON Jason Brett B 4.4.1978 Quincy, CA BR/TR 5-10/180# d5.9																								
2003	SF N	7	10	1	1	0	0	0	0	0-0	0	1	.100	.100	.100	-49	-2	0-0	1.000	-0	77	0	/O-4(3-1-0)	-0.3
ELMORE, VERDO Verdo Wilson "Ellie" B 12.10.1899 Gordo, AL D 8.5.1969 Birmingham, AL BL/TR 5-11/185# d9.11																								
1924	StL A	7	17	2	3	3	0	0	0	1	0	3	.176	.222	.353	44	-1	0-0	.000	-1	0	0	/O-3(RF)	-0.2
ELSH, ROY Eugene Reybold B 3.1.1892 Penns Grove, NJ D 11.12.1978 Philadelphia, PA BR/TR 5-9/165# d4.19																								
1923	Chi A	81	209	28	52	7	2	0	24	16	1	23	.249	.305	.301	61	-12	16-8	.957	2	109	108	O-57(50-6-1)	-1.3
1924	Chi A	60	147	21	45	9	1	0	11	10	0	14	.306	.350	.381	91	-2	6-1	.953	-1	104	79	O-38(2-5-31)/1-2	-0.4
1925	Chi A	32	48	6	9	1	0	0	4	5	0	7	.188	.264	.208	22	-6	2-0	.964	2	117	183	O-16(2-3-11)/1-3	-0.4
Total	3	173	404	55	106	17	3	0	39	31	1	44	.262	.317	.319	67	-20	24-9	.957	2	108	107	O-111(54-14-43)/1-5	-2.1
ELSTER, KEVIN Kevin Daniel B 8.3.1964 San Pedro, CA BR/TR 6-2/200# d9.2																								
1986	†NY N	19	30	3	5	1	0	0	0	3-1	0	8	.167	.242	.200	24	-3	0-0	.962	2	112	108	S-19	0.0
1987	NY N	5	10	1	4	2	0	0	1	0-0	0	1	.400	.400	.600	169	1	0-0	.909	-0	98	0	/S-3	0.1
1988	†NY N	149	406	41	87	11	1	9	37	35-12	3	47	.214	.282	.313	74	-15	2-0	.977	2	93	98	*S-148	-0.3
1989	NY N	151	458	52	106	25	2	10	55	34-11	2	77	.231	.283	.360	88	-8	4-3	.976	7	95	96	*S-150	1.0
1990	NY N	92	314	36	65	20	1	9	45	30-2	1	54	.207	.274	.363	75	-11	2-0	.960	10	96	94	S-92	0.7
1991	NY N	115	348	33	84	16	2	6	36	40-6	1	53	.241	.318	.351	90	-4	2-3	.970	5	104	82	*S-107	0.8
1992	NY N	6	18	0	4	0	0	0	0	0-0	0	2	.222	.222	.222	27	-2	0-0	1.000	-1	76	121	/S-5	-0.2
1994	NY A	7	20	0	0	0	0	0	0	1-0	0	6	.000	.048	.000	-90	-6	0-0	1.000	2	130	171	/S-7	-0.3
1995	NY A	10	17	1	2	1	0	0	0	1-0	0	5	.118	.167	.176	-11	-3	0-0	1.000	-1	88	59	S-10/2	-0.3
	Phi N	26	53	10	11	4	1	1	9	7-1	1	14	.208	.302	.377	80	-2	0-0	.982	-1	90	139	S-19/1-4,3-2	-0.2
1996	†Tex A	157	515	79	130	32	2	24	99	52-1	2	138	.252	.317	.462	91	-9	4-1	.981	5	99	99	*S-157	0.8
1997	Pit N	39	138	14	31	6	2	7	25	21-0	1	39	.225	.327	.449	100	0	0-2	.994	4	109	91	S-39	0.6
1998	Tex A	84	297	33	69	10	1	8	37	33-0	2	66	.232	.311	.354	70	-13	0-2	.976	-2	105	87	S-84	-0.9
2000	LA N	80	220	29	50	8	0	14	32	38-5	0	52	.227	.341	.455	105	1	0-0	.946	-9	92	80	S-55/3-8,1	-0.3
Total	13	940	2844	332	648	136	12	88	376	295-39	13	562	.228	.300	.377	83	-74	14-11	.974	23	98	94	S-895/3-10,1-5,2	1.5
ELY, BONES William Frederick B 6.7.1863 N.Girard, PA D 1.10.1952 Berkeley, CA BR/TR 6-1/155# d6.19 I OF Total (74-LF 9-CF 1-RF)																								
1884	Buf N	1	4	0	0	0	0	0	0	0		2	.000	.000	.000	-97	-1		.000	-0	0	0	/O(RF)P	-0.1
1886	Lou AA	10	32	5	5	0	0	0	6	2	0		.156	.206	.156	13	-3	1	1.000	-0	106	0	/P-6,O-5(4-1-0)	-0.2
1890	Syr AA	119	496	72	130	16	6	0	64	31	2		.262	.308	.319	95	-4	44	.914	10	87	28	O-78(70-8-0),S-36/1-4,2-2,3P	0.4
1891	Bro N	31	111	9	17	0	1	0	11	7	0	9	.153	.203	.171	9	-13	4	.870	5	116	93	S-28/3-2,2	-0.7
1893	StL N	44	178	25	45	1	6	0	16	17	0	13	.253	.318	.326	71	-8	2	.905	-5	91	90	S-44	-0.9
1894	StL N	127	510	85	156	20	12	12	89	30	0	34	.306	.344	.463	93	-10	23	.901	1	101	95	*S-126/2P	-0.2
1895	StL N	118	471	68	122	16	2	1	47	19	0	18	.259	.288	.308	54	-33	29	.925	5	101	100	*S-118	-1.8
1896	Pit N	128	537	85	153	15	9	3	77	33	0	33	.285	.326	.363	85	-13	18	.918	-6	98	95	*S-128	-1.0
1897	Pit N	133	516	63	146	20	8	2	74	25	1		.283	.317	.364	83	-14	10	.927	5	100	81	*S-133	-0.3
1898	Pit N	148	519	49	110	14	5	2	44	24	0		.212	.247	.270	49	-36	6	**.943**	8	106	100	*S-148	-1.9
1899	Pit N	139	526	67	146	18	6	3	72	22	5		.278	.313	.352	82	-14	8	.928	-5	102	90	*S-133/2-6	-1.1
1900	†Pit N	130	475	60	116	6	6	0	51	17	1		.244	.272	.282	53	-33	6	.935	11	106	**133**	*S-130	-1.3
1901	Pit N	65	240	18	50	6	3	0	28	6	2		.208	.234	.258	41	-19	5	.916	-3	104	112	S-64/3	-1.9
	Phi A	45	171	11	37	6	2	0	16	3	0		.216	.230	.275	38	-15	6	.913	2	106	108	S-45	-1.1
1902	Was A	105	381	39	100	11	2	1	62	21	0		.262	.301	.310	69	-16	3	.923	-7	99	67	*S-105	-1.9
Total	14	1343	5167	656	1333	149	68	24	657	257	11	<u>109</u>	.258	.295	.327	70	-232	165	.923	21	102	97	*S-1238/O-84L,2-10,P-9,3-4,1-4	-14.0
EMERSON, CHESTER Chester Arthur "Chuck" B 10.27.1889 Stow, ME D 7.2.1971 Augusta, ME BL/TR 5-8/165# d9.27																								
1911	Phi A	7	18	2	4	0	0	0	0	6	0		.222	.417	.222	82	0	1	1.000	-0	132	0	/O-7(0-1-6)	-0.1
1912	Phi A	1	1	0	0	0	0	0	0	0	0		.000	.000	.000	-99	0	0	—	0			H	0.0
Total	2	8	19	2	4	0	0	0	0	6	0		.211	.400	.211	74	0	1	1.000	-0	132	0	/O-7(0-1-6)	-0.1
EMERY, CAL Calvin Wayne B 6.28.1937 Centre Hall, PA BL/TL 6-2/205# d7.15 C1																								
1963	Phi N	16	19	0	3	1	0	0	0	0-0	0	2	.158	.158	.211	5	-2	0-0	1.000	-0	0	0	/1-2	-0.3
EMERY, SPOKE Herrick Smith B 12.10.1898 Bay City, MI D 6.2.1975 Cape Canaveral, FL BR/TR 5-9/165# d7.18																								
1924	Phi N	5	3	3	2	0	0	0	0	0	0	0	.667	.667	.667	230	1	0-1	1.000	0	165	0	/O(LF)	0.0
EMMER, FRANK Frank William B 2.17.1896 Crestline, OH D 10.18.1963 Homestead, FL BR/TR 5-8/150# d4.25																								
1916	Cin N	42	89	8	13	3	1	0	2	7	0	27	.146	.208	.202	27	-8	1	.899	-0	109	63	S-29/O-2(LF),23	-0.7
1926	Cin N	80	224	22	44	7	6	0	18	13	1	30	.196	.244	.281	42	-19	1	.918	-9	101	99	S-79	-2.1
Total	2	122	313	30	57	10	7	0	20	20	1	57	.182	.234	.259	38	-27	2	.913	-9	103	90	S-108/O-2(LF),32	-2.8

Year	Tm Lg	G	AB	R	H	2B	3B	HR	RBI	BB-IB	HP	SO	AVG	OBP	SLG	AOPS	ABR	SB-CS	FA	FR	Rng	Thr	G at Pos	BFW
EMMERICH, BOB Robert George B 8.1.1897 New York, NY D 11.22.1948 Bridgeport, CT BR/TR 5-3/155# d9.22																								
1923	Bos N	13	24	3	2	0	0	0	0	2	0	3	.083	.154	.083	-37	-5	1-1	1.000	0	101	148	/O-8(CF)	-0.5
ENCARNACION, ANGELO Angelo Benjamin B 4.18.1969 Santo Domingo, D.R. BR/TR 5-8/180# d5.2																								
1995	Pit N	58	159	18	36	7	2	2	10	13-5	0	28	.226	.285	.333	61	-9	1-1	.979	6	95	143	C-55	-0.1
1996	Pit N	7	22	3	7	2	0	0	1	0-0	0	5	.318	.318	.409	88	0	0-0	.951	-2	79	53	/C-7	-0.2
1997	Ana A	11	17	2	7	1	0	1	4	0-0	0	1	.412	.412	.647	171	2	2-0	.940	1	49	61	C-11	0.3
Total	3	76	198	23	50	10	2	3	15	13-5	0	34	.253	.299	.369	73	-7	3-1	.971	5	89	126	/C-73	0.0
ENCARNACION, JUAN Juan De Dios B 3.8.1976 Las Matas De Farfan, D.R. BR/TR 6-2/160# d9.2																								
1997	Det A	11	33	3	7	1	1	1	5	3-0	2	12	.212	.316	.394	84	-1	3-1	1.000	-0	106	0	O-10(0-2-10)	-0.1
1998	Det A	40	164	30	54	9	4	7	21	7-0	1	31	.329	.354	.561	134	7	7-4	.985	-5	68	145	O-39(8-13-21)/D	0.1
1999	Det A	132	509	62	130	30	6	19	74	14-1	9	113	.255	.287	.450	84	-15	33-12	.968	1	100	123	*O-131(118-22-1)	-1.4
2000	Det A	141	547	75	158	25	6	14	72	29-1	7	90	.289	.330	.433	94	-7	16-4	.987	-5	100	43	*O-141(CF)	-0.7
2001	Det A	120	417	52	101	19	7	12	52	25-1	6	93	.242	.292	.408	86	-10	9-5	.977	-7	94	68	*O-116(0-56-63)/D	-1.9
2002	Cin N	83	321	43	89	11	2	16	51	26-0	1	63	.277	.330	.474	110	2	9-4	.977	4	112	102	O-82(0-59-31)	0.6
	Fla N	69	263	34	69	11	3	8	34	20-0	3	50	.262	.317	.418	100	-2	12-5	.993	-0	99	91	O-67(0-12-61)	-0.5
	Year	152	584	77	158	22	5	24	85	46-0	4	113	.271	.324	.449	106	0	21-9	.983	4	106	97	*O-149(0-71-92)	0.1
2003	†Fla N	156	601	80	162	37	6	19	94	37-0	4	82	.270	.313	.446	100	-2	19-8	**1.000**	6	110	70	*O-155(RF)	-0.3
Total	7	752	2855	379	770	143	35	96	403	161-3	33	534	.270	.313	.445	97	-28	108-43	.984	-6	101	82	O-741(126-305-342)/D-2	-4.2
ENCARNACION, MARIO Mario (Gonzalez) B 9.24.1975 Bani, D.R. BR/TR 6-2/210# d8.26																								
2001	Col N	20	62	3	14	1	0	0	3	5-0	0	14	.226	.284	.242	31	-6	2-1	1.000	1	109	87	O-20(14-0-6)	-0.6
2002	Chi N	3	7	0	0	0	0	0	0	2-0	0	3	.000	.222	.000	-34	-1	0-0	1.000	0	193	0	/O-2(LF)	-0.1
Total	2	23	69	3	14	1	0	0	3	7-0	0	17	.203	.276	.217	26	-7	2-1	1.000	1	116	80	/O-22(16-0-6)	-0.7
ENDICOTT, BILL William Franklin B 9.4.1918 Acorn, MO BL/TL 5-11.5/175# d4.21																								
1946	StL N	20	20	2	4	3	0	0	3	4	0	4	.200	.333	.350	90	0	0	1.000	0	120	0	/O-2(LF)	0.0
ENGLE, CLYDE Arthur Clyde "Hack" B 3.19.1884 Dayton, OH D 12.26.1939 Boston, MA BR/TR 5-10/190# d4.12 OF Total (142-LF 111-CF 26-RF)																								
1909	NY A	135	492	66	137	20	5	3	71	47	5		.278	.347	.358	122	13	18	.946	15	99	122	*O-134(119-16-0)	2.3
1910	NY A	5	13	0	3	0	0	0	0	2	0		.231	.333	.231	73	0	1	.857	-0	105	0	/O-3(LF)	-0.1
	Bos A	106	363	59	96	18	7	2	38	31	2		.264	.326	.369	115	6	12	.915	-2	108	100	3-51,2-27,O-15(0-13-2)/S-7	0.6
	Year	111	376	59	99	18	7	2	38	33	2		.263	.326	.364	113	5	13	.915	-2	108	100	3-51,2-27,O-18(3-13-2)/S-7	0.5
1911	Bos A	146	514	58	139	13	3	2	48	51	6		.270	.343	.319	86	-8	24	.975	-1	107	86	1-65,3-51,2-13,O-10(3-7-0)	-1.0
1912	†Bos A	58	171	32	40	5	3	0	18	28	2		.234	.348	.298	81	-3	12	.977	-7	60	114	1-25,2-15,3-11/S-2,O(RF)	-1.0
1913	Bos A	143	498	75	144	17	12	2	50	53	5	41	.289	.363	.384	116	10	28	.987	-7	69	75	*1-133/O-2(0-1-1)	-0.1
1914	Bos A	59	134	14	26	2	0	0	9	14	1	11	.194	.275	.209	46	-9	4-9	.976	-4	56	106	1-29/2-5,3-3,O(RF)	-1.8
	Buf F	32	110	12	28	4	1	0	12	11	1	18	.255	.328	.309	73	-6	5	.889	-5	63	65	3-23/O-9(3-0-7)	-1.1
1915	Buf F	141	501	56	131	22	8	3	71	34	3	43	.261	.312	.355	86	-18	24	.969	-7	100	56	*O-100(14-74-13),2-21,3-17/1	-3.3
1916	Cle A	11	26	1	4	0	0	0	1	0	0	6	.154	.154	.154	-7	-3	0	.810	-2	98	0	/3-7,1-2,O(RF)	-0.6
Total	8	836	2822	373	748	101	39	12	318	271	25	119	.265	.335	.341	97	-18	128-9	.959	-20	99	102	O-276L,1-255,3-163/2-81,S-9	-6.1
ENGLE, CHARLIE Charlie August "Cholly" B 8.27.1903 New York, NY D 10.12.1983 San Antonio, TX BR/TR 5-8/145# d9.14																								
1925	Phi A	1	0	0	0	0	0	0	0	0	0	0	—	—	—	—	0	0-0	—	-0	0	0	/S	0.0
1926	Phi A	19	19	7	2	0	0	0	0	10	1	6	.105	.433	.105	43	-1	0-0	.930	1	111	147	S-16	0.1
1930	Pit N	67	216	34	57	10	1	0	15	22	1	20	.264	.335	.319	59	-14	1	.975	-1	113	65	3-24,S-23,2-10	-1.0
Total	3	87	235	41	59	10	1	0	15	32	2	26	.251	.346	.302	59	-15	1-0	.937	-0	105	89	/S-40,3-24,2-10	-0.9
ENGLE, DAVE Ralph David B 11.30.1956 San Diego, CA BR/TR 6-3/216# d4.14 C3 OF Total (17-LF 1-CF 119-RF)																								
1981	Min A	82	248	29	64	14	4	5	32	13-1	1	37	.258	.295	.407	95	-2	0-1	.980	1	106	83	O-76(RF)/3D	-0.6
1982	Min A	58	186	20	42	7	2	4	16	10-0	1	22	.226	.269	.349	67	-9	0-0	.985	3	115	158	O-34(2-1-32),D-20	-0.9
1983	Min A	120	374	46	114	22	4	8	43	28-1	1	39	.305	.350	.449	115	8	2-1	.973	-12	96	76	C-73,D-29/O-4(RF)	-0.2
1984	Min A☆	109	391	56	104	20	1	4	38	26-3	0	22	.266	.308	.353	80	-10	0-1	.981	-0	92	94	C-86,D-22	-0.8
1985	Min A	70	172	28	44	8	2	7	25	21-1	0	28	.256	.333	.448	106	2	2-2	.984	2	184	28	D-38,C-17/O-3(LF)	0.2
1986	Det A	35	86	6	22	7	0	0	4	7-0	0	13	.256	.312	.337	77	-2	0-0	1.000	-1	83	123	1-23/O-4(2-0-2),C-3,D-5	-0.4
1987	Mon N	59	84	7	19	4	0	1	14	6-1	0	11	.226	.278	.310	54	-6	1-0	1.000	1	122	182	O-11(9-0-2)/C-6,1-2,3	-0.5
1988	Mon N	34	37	4	8	3	0	0	1	5-0	0	5	.216	.310	.297	72	-1	0-0	1.000	0	65	96	/C-9,O-4(1-0-3),3	-0.1
1989	Mil A	27	65	5	14	3	0	2	8	4-0	0	13	.215	.261	.354	72	-3	0-0	.973	0	125	94	1-18/C-3,D-3	-0.4
Total	9	594	1643	201	431	88	13	31	181	120-7	3	190	.262	.311	.388	90	-23	5-5	.979	-7	99	83	C-197,O-136R,D-118/1-43,3-3	-3.7
ENGLISH, CHARLIE Charles Dewie B 4.8.1910 Darlington, SC D 6.25.1999 Pasadena, CA BR/TR 5-9.5/160# d7.23																								
1932	Chi A	24	63	7	20	3	1	1	8	3	0	7	.317	.348	.444	111	1	0-0	.821	-3	100	89	3-13/S	-0.1
1933	Chi A	3	9	2	4	2	0	0	1	1	0	1	.444	.500	.667	216	2	0-0	.923	-1	82	148	/2-3	0.1
1936	NY N	6	1	0	0	0	0	0	0	0	0	0	.000	.000	.000	-99	0	0	—	-0	0	0	/2	0.0
1937	Cin N	17	63	1	15	3	1	0	4	0	0	2	.238	.238	.317	52	-5	0	.958	2	112	106	3-15/2-2	-0.2
Total	4	50	136	10	39	8	2	1	13	4	0	10	.287	.307	.397	90	-2	0-0	.897	-2	106	98	/3-28,2-6,S	-0.2
ENGLISH, WOODY Elwood George B 3.2.1906 Fredonia, OH D 9.26.1997 Newark, OH BR/TR 5-10/155# d4.26																								
1927	Chi N	87	334	46	97	14	4	1	28	16	1	26	.290	.325	.365	84	-8	1	.940	2	105	94	S-84/3	0.3
1928	Chi N	116	475	68	142	22	4	2	34	30	2	28	.299	.343	.375	89	-8	4	.946	7	101	119	*S-114/3-2	1.1
1929	†Chi N	144	608	131	168	29	3	1	52	68	3	50	.276	.352	.339	72	-25	13	.955	14	102	116	*S-144	0.5
1930	Chi N	**156**	638	152	214	36	17	14	59	100	6	72	.335	.430	.511	125	31	3	.973	-11	88	126	3-83,S-78	2.9
1931	Chi N	**156**	634	117	202	38	8	2	53	68	7	80	.319	.391	.413	114	16	12	.965	1	96	78	*S-138,3-18	2.7
1932	†Chi N	127	522	70	142	23	7	3	47	55	2	73	.272	.344	.360	90	-6	5	.957	1	98	79	3-93,S-38	0.1
1933	Chi N★	105	398	54	104	19	2	3	41	53	0	44	.261	.348	.342	98	1	5	**.973**	-8	92	68	*3-103/S	-0.3
1934	Chi N	109	421	65	117	26	5	3	31	48	1	65	.278	.353	.385	99	1	6	.971	-1	76	89	S-56,3-46/2-7	0.5
1935	Chi N	34	84	11	17	2	0	2	8	20	2	4	.202	.368	.298	81	-1	1	.868	-3	94	97	3-16,S-12	-0.2
1936	Chi N	64	182	33	45	9	0	0	20	40	4	28	.247	.394	.297	86	0	1	.976	4	105	121	S-42,3-17/2	0.7
1937	Bro N	129	378	45	90	16	2	1	42	65	0	55	.238	.350	.299	77	-9	4	.956	-14	90	76	*S-116,2-11	-1.5
1938	Bro N	34	72	9	18	2	0	0	7	8	1	11	.250	.333	.278	68	-3	2	.958	0	99	147	3-21/2-3,S-3	-0.2
Total	12	1261	4746	801	1356	236	52	32	422	571	29	536	.286	.366	.378	95	-11	57	.957	-8	97	98	S-826,3-400/2-22	6.6
ENGLISH, GIL Gilbert Raymond B 7.2.1909 Glenola, NC D 8.31.1996 Trinity, NC BR/TR 5-11/180# d9.20																								
1931	NY N	3	8	0	0	0	0	0	0	1	0	3	.000	.111	.000	-69	-2	0	1.000	-0	86	0	/3-3	-0.2
1932	NY N	59	204	22	46	7	5	2	19	5	0	20	.225	.244	.338	56	-14	0	.931	2	106	157	3-39,S-23	-0.9
1936	Det A	1	1	0	0	0	0	0	0	0	0	1	.000	.000	.000	-99	0	0-0	1.000	0	111	0	/3	0.0
1937	Det A	18	65	6	17	1	0	1	6	6	1	4	.262	.333	.323	65	-4	1-1	.962	-5	82	66	2-12/3-6	-0.7
	Bos N	79	269	25	78	5	2	2	37	23	1	27	.290	.348	.346	98	-1	3	.958	-5	101	114	3-71	-0.4
1938	Bos N	53	165	17	41	6	0	2	21	15	1	16	.248	.315	.321	84	-4	1	.956	-3	103	48	3-43/O-3(LF),2-2,S-2	-0.5
1944	Bro N	27	79	4	12	3	0	1	7	6	0	7	.152	.212	.228	24	-8	0	.918	-3	106	94	S-13,3-11/2-2	-1.1
Total	6	240	791	74	194	22	7	8	90	56	3	78	.245	.298	.321	72	-33	5-1	.950	-14	101	104	3-174/S-38,2-16,O-3(LF)	-3.8
ENNIS, DEL Delmer B 6.8.1925 Philadelphia, PA D 2.8.1996 Huntingdon Valley, PA BR/TR 6/195# d4.28																								
1946	Phi N★	141	540	70	169	30	6	17	73	39	4	65	.313	.364	.485	144	28	5	.975	10	111	126	*O-138(138-0-1)	2.9
1947	Phi N	139	541	71	149	25	6	12	81	37	3	51	.275	.325	.410	98	-4	9	.979	4	103	112	*O-135(135-0-2)	-1.0
1948	Phi N	152	589	86	171	40	4	30	95	47	2	58	.290	.345	.525	135	26	2	.957	3	101	134	*O-151(RF)	2.3
1949	Phi N	**154**	610	92	184	39	11	25	110	59	4	61	.302	.367	.525	140	33	2	.966	-1	97	114	*O-154(LF)	2.0
1950	†Phi N	153	595	92	185	34	8	31	**126**	56	2	59	.311	.372	.551	142	34	2	.970	-3	99	87	*O-149(14-1-140)	2.5
1951	Phi N★	144	532	76	142	20	5	15	73	68	2	42	.267	.352	.408	105	5	4-2	.969	-2	97	109	*O-135(26-0-116)	-0.2
1952	Phi N	151	592	90	171	30	10	20	107	47	0	65	.289	.341	.475	125	18	6-4	.970	-5	93	92	*O-149(120-0-31)	0.3
1953	Phi N	152	578	79	165	22	3	29	125	57	5	53	.285	.355	.484	117	13	1-3	.980	-3	94	108	*O-150(LF)	0.0
1954	Phi N	145	556	73	145	23	2	25	119	50	2	60	.261	.318	.444	98	-3	2-1	.957	-2	103	79	*O-142(72-0-71)/1	-1.3
1955	Phi N★	146	564	82	167	24	7	29	120	46-8	2	46	.296	.346	.518	129	22	4-2	.987	1	102	84	*O-145(143-0-3)	1.4
1956	Phi N	153	630	80	164	23	3	26	95	33-8	3	62	.260	.299	.430	95	-7	7-3	.962	23	**178**	**160**	*O-153(LF)	1.2
1957	StL N	136	490	61	140	24	3	24	105	37-3	1	50	.286	.332	.494	117	11	1-3	.943	-17	77	35	*O-127(74-0-53)	-1.3
1958	StL N	106	329	22	86	18	1	3	47	15-3	1	35	.261	.290	.350	67	-15	0-1	.993	1	83	196	O-84(LF)	-2.0

Year	Tm Lg	G	AB	R	H	2B	3B	HR	RBI	BB-IB	HP	SO	AVG	OBP	SLG	AOPS	ABR	SB-CS	FA	FR	Rng	Thr	G at Pos	BFW
1959	Cin N	5	12	1	4	0	0	0	1	2-1	0	2	.333	.429	.333	103	0	0-0	1.000	-0	99	0	/O-3(LF)	0.0
	Chi A	26	96	10	21	6	0	2	7	4-0	0	10	.219	.250	.344	62	-5	0-0	.909	-3	65	146	O-25(LF)	-0.9
Total	14	1903	7254	985	2063	358	69	288	1284	597-23	31	719	.284	.340	.472	117	156	45-19	.969	7	101	107	*O-1840(1291-1-568)/1	5.9
ENNIS, RUSS Russell Elwood "Hack" B 3.10.1897 Superior, WI D 1.21.1949 Superior, WI BR/TR 5-11.5/160# d9.19																								
1926	Was A	1	0	0	0	0	0	0	0	0	0	0	—	—	—	—	0	0-0	—	-0	0	0	/C	0.0
ENRIGHT, GEORGE George Albert B 5.9.1954 New Britain, CT BR/TR 5-11/175# d8.8																								
1976	Chi A	2	1	0	0	0	0	0	0	0-0	0	0	.000	.000	.000	-99	0	0-0	1.000	-1	17	282	/C-2	-0.1
ENS, MUTZ Anton B 11.8.1884 St.Louis, MO D 6.28.1950 St.Louis, MO BL/TL 6-1/180# d9.2 b-Jewel																								
1912	Chi A	3	6	0	0	0	0	0	0	0	0		.000	.000	.000	-99	-2	0	.857	-1	0	162	/1-3	-0.2
ENS, JEWEL Jewel Winklemeyer B 8.24.1889 St.Louis, MO D 1.17.1950 Syracuse, NY BR/TR 5-10.5/165# d4.29 M3 C13 b-Mutz																								
1922	Pit N	47	142	18	42	7	3	0	17	7	2	9	.296	.338	.387	85	-3	3-0	.951	-13	74	52	2-29/3-3,1-2,S	-1.4
1923	Pit N	12	29	3	8	1	1	0	5	0	0	3	.276	.276	.379	70	-1	2-0	.975	-0	0	135	/1-4,3-3	-0.1
1924	Pit N	5	10	2	3	0	0	0	0	0	0	3	.300	.300	.300	60	-1	0-0	1.000	-0	71	51	/1-5	-0.1
1925	Pit N	3	5	2	1	0	0	1	2	0	0	1	.200	.200	.800	133	0	0-0	1.000	-0	0	0	/1-3	0.0
Total	4	67	186	25	54	8	4	1	24	7	2	16	.290	.323	.392	83	-5	5-0	.951	-14	74	52	/2-29,1-14,3-6,S	-1.6
ENSBERG, MORGAN Morgan Paul B 8.26.1975 Redondo Beach, CA BR/TR 6-2/210# d9.20																								
2000	Hou N	4	7	0	2	0	0	0	0	0-0	0	1	.286	.286	.286	43	-1	0-0	.667	-1	55	0	/3	-0.1
2002	Hou N	49	132	14	32	7	2	3	19	18-0	3	25	.242	.346	.394	93	-2	2-0	.929	3	108	68	3-43	0.2
2003	Hou N	127	385	69	112	15	1	25	60	48-1	6	60	.291	.377	.530	128	16	7-2	.967	4	98	109	*3-111/D	2.1
Total	3	180	524	83	146	22	3	28	79	66-1	9	86	.279	.368	.492	118	13	9-2	.953	6	101	97	3-155/D	2.2
ENWRIGHT, CHARLIE Charles Massey B 10.6.1887 Sacramento, CA D 1.19.1917 Sacramento, CA BL/TR 5-10/?# d4.19																								
1909	StL N	3	7	1	1	0	0	0	1	2	0		.143	.333	.143	51	0	0	.444	-3	34	0	/S-2	-0.4
ENZENROTH, JACK Clarence Herman B 11.4.1885 Mineral Point, WI D 2.21.1944 Detroit, MI BR/TR 5-7/160# d5.1																								
1914	StL A	3	6	0	1	0	0	0	0	2	1	3	.167	.444	.167	88	0	0-1	.923	-1	*96*	*41*	/C-3	0.0
	KC F	26	67	7	12	4	1	0	5	5	0	19	.179	.236	.269	39	-7	0	.965	-2	*91*	*105*	C-24	-0.8
1915	KC F	14	19	3	3	0	0	0	3	6	0	0	.158	.360	.158	50	-1	0	.973	1	*112*	*130*	/C-8	0.1
Total	2	43	92	10	16	4	1	0	8	13	1	22	.174	.283	.239	47	-8	0-1	.963	-1	*96*	*105*	/C-35	-0.7
EPPARD, JIM James Gerhard B 4.27.1960 South Bend, IN BL/TL 6-2/180# d9.8																								
1987	Cal A	8	9	2	3	0	0	0	0	2-0	0	0	.333	.455	.333	118	0	0-0	1.000	-0	55	0	/O(RF)	0.0
1988	Cal A	56	113	7	32	3	1	0	14	11-0	0	15	.283	.347	.327	92	-1	0-0	.971	1	116	0	O-17(LF),D-10/1-6	-0.1
1989	Cal A	12	12	0	3	0	0	0	2	1-0	0	4	.250	.308	.250	60	-1	0-0	1.000	-0	0	154	/1-4	-0.1
1990	Tor A	6	5	0	1	0	0	0	0	0-0	1	2	.200	.333	.200	52	0	0-0	—	0			/H	0.0
Total	4	82	139	9	39	3	1	0	16	14-0	1	21	.281	.351	.317	90	-2	0-0	.972	0	112	0	/O-18(17-0-1),1-10,D-10	-0.2
EPPS, AUBREY Aubrey Lee "Yo-Yo" B 3.3.1912 Memphis, TN D 11.13.1984 Ackerman, MS BR/TR 5-10/170# d9.29																								
1935	Pit N	1	4	1	3	0	1	0	3	0	0	0	.750	.750	1.250	414	2	0	.750	-1	*43*	*0*	/C	0.1
EPPS, HAL Harold Franklin B 3.26.1914 Athens, GA BL/TL 6/175# d9.9 Mil 1945-46																								
1938	StL N	17	50	8	15	0	0	1	3	2	0	4	.300	.327	.360	84	-1	2	.963	-1	103	0	O-10(CF)	-0.2
1940	StL N	11	15	6	3	0	0	0	1	0	0	3	.200	.200	.200	10	-2	0	.800	-0	99	0	O-3(CF)	-0.2
1943	StL A	8	35	2	10	4	0	0	1	3	0	4	.286	.342	.400	114	1	1-1	1.000	-1	91	0	/O-8(CF)	0.0
1944	StL A	22	62	15	11	1	1	0	3	14	1	14	.177	.338	.226	59	-3	0-1	.962	1	96	176	O-18(CF)	-0.3
	Phi A	67	229	27	60	8	8	0	13	18	0	18	.262	.316	.367	96	-2	2-1	.973	-2	96	79	O-60(0-44-16)	-0.7
	Year	89	291	42	71	9	9	0	16	32	1	32	.244	.321	.337	88	-5	2-2	.970	-1	96	102	O-78(0-62-16)	-1.0
Total	4	125	391	58	99	13	9	1	21	37	1	43	.253	.319	.340	86	-7	5-3	.968	-3	96	81	/O-99(0-83-16)	-1.4
EPSTEIN, MIKE Michael Peter "Superjew" B 4.4.1943 Bronx, NY BL/TL 6-3.5/230# d9.16																								
1966	Bal A	6	11	1	2	0	1	0	3	1-0	0	3	.182	.250	.364	75	0	0-0	1.000	0	91	121	/1-4	-0.1
1967	Bal A	9	13	0	2	0	0	0	0	3-0	0	5	.154	.313	.154	42	-1	0-0	1.000	-0	55	108	/1-3	-0.1
	Was A	96	284	32	65	7	4	9	29	38-5	6	74	.229	.331	.377	114	5	1-4	.987	-1	104	127	1-80	-0.2
	Year	105	297	32	67	7	4	9	29	41-5	6	79	.226	.330	.367	110	4	1-4	.988	-1	102	126	1-83	-0.3
1968	Was A	123	385	40	90	8	2	13	33	48-5	13	91	.234	.338	.366	117	9	1-1	.987	-1	103	97	*1-110	0.2
1969	Was A	131	403	73	112	18	1	30	85	85-10	10	99	.278	.414	.551	178	46	2-5	.990	-4	91	105	*1-118	3.3
1970	Was A	140	430	55	110	15	3	20	56	73-6	9	117	.256	.371	.444	131	21	2-3	.992	-5	88	105	*1-122	0.6
1971	Was A	24	85	6	21	1	1	1	9	12-1	4	31	.247	.366	.318	101	1	1-0	.992	-2	77	142	1-24	-0.3
	†Oak A	104	329	43	77	13	0	18	51	62-5	8	71	.234	.368	.438	130	15	0-3	.995	-2	89	137	1-96	0.6
	Year	128	414	49	98	14	1	19	60	74-6	**12**	102	.237	.367	.413	124	16	1-3	**.994**	-3	86	**138**	*1-120	0.3
1972	†Oak A	138	455	63	123	18	2	26	70	68-9	11	68	.270	.376	.490	166	39	0-1	.990	-0	102	108	*1-137	3.1
1973	Tex A	27	85	9	16	3	0	1	6	14-0	3	19	.188	.317	.259	69	-3	0-0	.991	-1	77	79	1-25	-0.6
	Cal A	91	312	30	67	8	2	8	32	34-2	5	54	.215	.300	.330	84	-7	0-0	.993	1	97	82	1-86	-1.3
	Year	118	397	39	83	11	2	9	38	48-2	8	73	.209	.304	.315	81	-10	0-0	.993	-1	93	81	*1-111	-1.9
1974	Cal A	18	62	10	10	2	0	4	6	10-0	1	13	.161	.288	.387	98	0	0-0	.993	1	119	91	1-18	0.0
Total	9	907	2854	362	695	93	16	130	380	448-43	70	645	.244	.358	.424	130	125	7-17	.991	-13	95	108	1-823	5.2
ERAUTT, JOE Joseph Michael "Stubby" B 9.1.1921 Vibank, SK, CAN D 10.6.1976 Portland, OR BR/TR 5-9/175# d5.9 b-Eddie																								
1950	Chi A	16	18	0	4	0	0	0	1	1	0	3	.222	.263	.222	26	-2	0-0	1.000	1	*57*	*220*	/C-5	-0.1
1951	Chi A	16	25	3	4	1	0	0	0	3	1	2	.160	.276	.200	31	-2	0-0	.977	2,	*112*	*116*	C-12	0.0
Total	2	32	43	3	8	1	0	0	1	4	1	5	.186	.271	.209	29	-4	0-0	.983	2	*99*	*140*	/C-17	-0.1
ERICKSON, HANK Henry Nels "Popeye" B 11.11.1907 Chicago, IL D 12.13.1964 Louisville, KY BR/TR 6-1/185# d4.17																								
1935	Cin N	37	88	9	23	3	2	1	4	6	2	4	.261	.323	.375	90	-1	0	.972	2	*93*	*155*	C-25	0.2
ERMER, CAL Calvin Coolidge B 11.10.1923 Baltimore, MD BR/TR 6-0.5/175# d9.26 M2 C4																								
1947	Was A	1	3	0	0	0	0	0	0	0	0	0	.000	.000	.000	-99	-1	0-0	1.000	0	101	0	/2	-0.1
ERNAGA, FRANK Frank John B 8.22.1930 Susanville, CA BR/TR 6-1/195# d5.24																								
1957	Chi N	20	35	9	11	3	2	2	7	9-0	0	14	.314	.455	.686	204	6	0-0	.950	0	121	0	O-10(3-0-7)	0.5
1958	Chi N	9	8	0	1	0	0	0	0	0-0	0	2	.125	.125	.125	-34	-2	0-0	—	0			H	-0.2
Total	2	29	43	9	12	3	2	2	7	9-0	0	16	.279	.404	.581	163	4	0-0	.950	0	121	0	/O-10(3-0-7)	0.3
ERSTAD, DARIN Darin Charles B 6.4.1974 Jamestown, ND BL/TL 6-2/195# d6.14																								
1996	Cal A	57	208	34	59	5	1	4	20	17-1	0	29	.284	.333	.375	80	-7	3-3	.976	-1	106	67	O-48(11-36-1)	-0.7
1997	Ana A	139	539	99	161	34	4	16	77	51-4	4	86	.299	.360	.466	115	12	23-8	.990	-6	82	88	*1-126/O(CF)D	-0.3
1998	Ana A★	133	537	84	159	39	3	19	82	43-7	6	77	.296	.353	.486	115	12	20-6	.992	-2	87	99	O-72(70-3-0),1-70/D-2	0.4
1999	Ana A	142	585	84	148	22	5	13	53	47-3	1	101	.253	.308	.374	74	-25	13-7	.999	12	96	91	1-78,O-69(67-2-0)/D-2	-2.1
2000	Ana A★	157	676	121	**240**	39	6	25	100	64-9	1	82	.355	.409	.541	135	37	28-8	.992	9	**113**	107	*O-136(112-30-0),D-20/1-3	3.9
2001	Ana A	157	631	89	163	35	1	9	63	62-7	10	113	.258	.331	.360	81	-16	24-10	**.998**	6	106	119	*O-146(CF),1-12/D-4	-0.7
2002	†Ana A	150	625	99	177	28	4	10	73	27-4	2	67	.283	.313	.389	86	-14	23-3	.998	19	**122**	147	*O-143(CF)/1-5,D-4	1.0
2003	Ana A	67	258	35	65	7	1	4	17	18-1	4	40	.252	.309	.333	73	-11	9-1	1.000	4	114	69	O-66(CF)	-0.4
Total	8	1002	4059	645	1172	209	25	100	485	329-36	28	595	.289	.344	.426	99	-12	143-46	.995	40	112	116	O-681(260-427-1),1-294/D-41	1.1
ERWIN, TEX Ross Emil B 12.22.1885 Forney, TX D 4.5.1953 Rochester, NY BL/TR 6/185# d8.26																								
1907	Det A	4	5	0	1	0	0	0	1	1	0		.200	.333	.200	68	0	0	.909	-0	*94*	*134*	/C-4	0.0
1910	Bro N	81	202	15	38	3	1	1	10	24	1	12	.188	.278	.228	49	-13	3	.949	-1	*94*	*111*	C-68	-0.8
1911	Bro N	91	218	30	59	13	2	7	34	31	2	23	.271	.367	.445	132	10	5	.971	-7	*79*	*109*	C-74	0.8
1912	Bro N	59	133	14	28	3	0	2	14	18	0	16	.211	.305	.278	62	-7	1	.949	-2	*92*	*94*	C-41	-0.6
1913	Bro N	20	31	6	8	1	0	0	3	4	0	5	.258	.343	.290	80	-1	0-1	.950	-2	90	57	C-13	-0.2
1914	Bro N	9	11	0	5	0	0	0	1	2	0	1	.455	.538	.455	192	1	1	1.000	-1	*69*	*121*	/C-4	0.1
	Cin N	12	35	5	11	3	0	1	7	2	0	3	.314	.351	.486	144	2	0	.962	0	*107*	*74*	C-12	0.3
	Year	21	46	5	16	3	0	1	8	4	0	4	.348	.400	.478	157	3	1	.966	-0	*102*	*81*	C-16	0.4
Total	6	276	635	70	150	23	3	11	70	82	3	60	.236	.326	.334	90	-8	10-1	.957	-13	*89*	*103*	C-216	-0.4

Year	Tm Lg	G	AB	R	H	2B	3B	HR	RBI	BB-IB	HP	SO	AVG	OBP	SLG	AOPS	ABR	SB-CS	FA	FR	Rng	Thr	G at Pos	BFW
ESASKY, NICK Nicholas Andrew B 2.24.1960 Hialeah, FL BR/TR 6-3/205# d6.19																								
1983	Cin N	85	302	41	80	10	5	12	46	27-1	3	99	.265	.328	.450	111	3	6-2	.935	-9	87	81	3-84	-0.7
1984	Cin N	113	322	30	62	10	5	10	45	52-3	0	103	.193	.301	.348	79	-9	1-2	.910	-8	94	67	3-82,1-25	-2.1
1985	Cin N	125	413	61	108	21	0	21	66	41-3	4	102	.262	.332	.465	115	8	3-4	.946	-1	91	147	3-62,O-54(LF),1-12	0.3
1986	Cin N	102	330	35	76	17	2	12	41	47-0	1	97	.230	.325	.403	96	-1	0-2	.991	-2	74	96	1-70,O-42(LF)/3	-0.9
1987	Cin N	100	346	48	94	19	2	22	59	29-3	0	76	.272	.327	.529	117	7	0-0	.994	-9	63	102	1-93/3O(LF)	-0.8
1988	Cin N	122	391	40	95	17	2	15	62	48-4	4	104	.243	.327	.412	108	5	7-2	.994	-6	76	95	*1-116	-0.9
1989	Bos A	154	564	79	156	26	5	30	108	66-9	3	117	.277	.355	.500	130	22	1-2	.996	0	94	97	*1-153/O(LF)	1.1
1990	Atl N	9	35	2	6	0	0	0	0	4-0	0	14	.171	.256	.171	19	-4	0-0	.944	-1	81	102	/1-9	-0.6
Total	8	810	2703	336	677	120	21	122	427	314-23	15	712	.250	.329	.446	109	31	18-14	.993	-36	78	96	1-478,3-230/O-98(LF)	-4.6
ESCALERA, NINO Saturnino Cuadrado B 12.1.1929 Santurce, P.R. BL/TR 5-10/165# d4.17																								
1954	Cin N	73	69	15	11	1	1	0	3	7	0	11	.159	.234	.203	15	-9	1-0	.962	2	125	422	O-14(1-3-10)/1-8,S	-0.7
ESCALONA, FELIX Felix Eduardo B 3.12.1979 Puerto Cabello, Venezuela BR/TR 6/185# d4.4																								
2002	TB A	59	157	17	34	8	2	0	9	3-0	7	44	.217	.262	.293	49	-12	7-2	.945	-2	106	118	S-26,2-25/3-4,D	-1.0
2003	TB A	10	27	2	5	2	0	0	2	2-0	0	6	.185	.241	.259	33	-3	1-0	1.000	2	96	147	/S-8,23	0.0
Total	2	69	184	19	39	10	2	0	11	5-0	7	50	.212	.259	.288	46	-15	8-2	.961	-1	103	126	/S-34,2-26,3-5,D	-1.0
ESCHEN, JIM James Godrich B 8.21.1891 Brooklyn, NY D 9.27.1960 Sloatsburg, NY BR/TR 5-10.5/160# d7.10 s-Larry																								
1915	Cle A	15	42	11	10	1	0	0	2	5	0	9	.238	.319	.262	73	-1	0-1	.968	0	115	64	O-10(CF)	-0.2
ESCHEN, LARRY Lawrence Edward B 9.22.1920 Suffern, NY BR/TR 6/180# d6.16 f-Jim																								
1942	Phi A	12	11	0	0	0	0	0	0	4	0	6	.000	.267	.000	-22	-2	0-0	.824	-2	48	0	/S-7,2	-0.4
ESCOBAR, ALEX Alexander Jose B 9.6.1978 Valencia, Venezuela BR/TR 6-1/185# d5.8																								
2001	NY N	18	50	3	10	1	0	3	8	3-0	0	19	.200	.245	.400	66	-3	1-0	.935	1	88	375	O-15(0-9-7)	-0.2
2003	Cle A	28	99	16	27	2	0	5	14	7-1	1	33	.273	.324	.444	104	0	1-0	.969	3	111	201	O-25(RF)	0.2
Total	2	46	149	19	37	3	0	8	22	10-1	1	52	.248	.298	.430	92	-3	2-0	.958	4	103	262	/O-40(0-9-32)	0.0
ESCOBAR, ANGEL Angel Rubenque (Rivas) B 5.12.1965 LaSabana, Venezuela BB/TR 6/160# d5.17																								
1988	SF N	3	3	1	1	0	0	0	0	0-0	0	0	.333	.333	.333	96	0	0-0	1.000	0	0	0	/S3	0.0
ESCOBAR, JOSE Jose Elias (Sanchez) B 10.30.1960 Las Flores, Venezuela BR/TR 5-10/140# d4.13																								
1991	Cle A	10	15	0	3	0	0	0	1	1-0	0	4	.200	.250	.200	26	-2	0-0	1.000	-1	51	0	/S-5,2-4,3	-0.2
ESMOND, JIMMY James Joseph B 10.8.1889 Albany, NY D 6.26.1948 Troy, NY BR/TR 5-11/167# d4.20																								
1911	Cin N	73	198	27	54	4	6	1	11	17	0	30	.273	.330	.369	99	-1	7	.918	-3	85	121	S-44,3-14/2-2	-0.1
1912	Cin N	82	231	24	45	5	3	1	40	20	0	31	.195	.259	.255	42	-19	11	.930	-8	87	82	S-74	-2.2
1914	Ind F	151	542	74	160	23	**15**	2	49	40	0	48	.295	.344	.404	93	-13	25	.919	-8	98	96	*S-151	-1.2
1915	New F	**155**	569	79	147	20	11	4	62	59	1	54	.258	.329	.353	98	-12	18	.939	1	101	109	*S-155	0.1
Total	4	461	1540	204	406	52	35	8	162	136	1	163	.264	.324	.358	88	-45	61	.929	-18	96	101	S-424/3-14,2-2	-3.4
ESPINO, JUAN Juan (Reyes) B 3.16.1956 Bonao, D.R. BR/TR 6-1/190# d6.25																								
1982	NY A	3	2	0	0	0	0	0	0	0-0	0	1	.000	.000	.000	-99	-1	0-0	1.000	-0	0	0	/C-3	-0.1
1983	NY A	10	23	1	6	0	0	1	3	1-0	0	5	.261	.280	.391	89	0	0-0	1.000	-1	96	43	C-10	-0.2
1985	NY A	9	11	0	4	0	0	0	0	0-0	0	0	.364	.364	.364	102	0	0-0	1.000	0	108	0	/C-9	0.0
1986	NY A	27	37	1	6	2	0	0	5	2-0	0	9	.162	.200	.216	15	-4	0-0	.987	0	84	50	C-27	-0.4
Total	4	49	73	2	16	2	0	1	8	3-0	0	15	.219	.244	.288	48	-5	0-0	.993	-1	89	39	/C-49	-0.7
ESPINOZA, ALVARO Alvaro Alberto B 2.19.1962 Valencia, Venezuela BR/TR 6/181# d9.14																								
1984	Min A	1	0	0	0	0	0	0	0	0-0	0	0	—	—	—	—	0	0-0	—	0	0	0	/S	0.0
1985	Min A	32	57	5	15	2	0	0	9	1-0	1	9	.263	.288	.298	58	-3	0-1	.949	1	112	113	S-31	-0.1
1986	Min A	37	42	4	9	1	0	0	1	1-0	0	10	.214	.233	.238	28	-4	0-1	.941	-1	130	105	2-19,S-18	-0.4
1988	NY A	3	3	0	0	0	0	0	0	0-0	0	0	.000	.000	.000	-99	-1	0-0	1.000	-0	31	0	/2-2,S	-0.1
1989	NY A	146	503	51	142	23	1	0	41	14-1	1	60	.282	.301	.332	80	-14	3-3	.970	19	108	118	*S-146	1.4
1990	NY A	150	438	31	98	12	2	2	20	16-0	5	54	.224	.258	.274	49	-31	1-2	.977	**23**	**108**	107	*S-150	0.2
1991	NY A	148	480	51	123	23	2	5	33	16-0	2	57	.256	.282	.344	72	-19	4-1	.969	21	107	**129**	*S-147/3-2,P	1.2
1993	Cle A	129	263	34	73	15	0	4	27	8-0	1	36	.278	.298	.380	82	-7	2-2	.937	-6	96	81	3-99,S-35/2-2	-1.2
1994	Cle A	90	231	27	55	13	0	1	19	6-0	1	33	.238	.258	.307	46	-19	1-3	.915	16	101	68	3-37,S-36,2-20/1-3	-0.1
1995	†Cle A	66	143	15	36	4	0	2	17	2-0	1	16	.252	.264	.322	52	-11	0-2	.966	-4	108	97	2-22,3-22,S-19/1-2,D-3	-1.3
1996	Cle A	59	112	12	25	4	2	4	11	6-0	3	18	.223	.279	.402	70	-6	1-1	.947	1	79	73	3-20,1-18,S-16/2-5,D	-0.5
	NY N	48	134	19	41	7	2	4	16	4-0	0	19	.306	.324	.478	114	2	0-2	.900	-3	93	40	3-38/S-7,2-2,1	-0.1
1997	Sea A	33	72	3	13	1	0	0	7	2-0	1	12	.181	.213	.194	7	-10	1-1	.965	2	84	57	S-17,2-14/3	-0.6
Total	12	942	2478	252	630	105	9	22	201	76-1	16	324	.254	.279	.331	66	-123	13-19	.971	68	107	117	S-624,3-219/2-86,1-24,D-4,P	-1.6
ESPOSITO, SAMMY Samuel B 12.15.1931 Chicago, IL BR/TR 5-9/165# d9.28 Mil 1952																								
1952	Chi A	1	4	0	1	0	0	0	0	0	0	2	.250	.250	.250	39	0	0-1	.500	-1	38	0	/S	-0.2
1955	Chi A	3	4	3	0	0	0	0	0	1-0	0	0	.000	.200	.000	-41	-1	0-0	1.000	-1	0	0	/3-2	-0.1
1956	Chi A	81	184	30	42	8	2	3	25	41-0	2	19	.228	.371	.342	89	-1	1-2	.962	2	105	181	3-61,S-19/2-3	0.0
1957	Chi A	94	176	26	36	3	0	2	15	38-0	0	27	.205	.344	.256	66	-7	5-1	.960	10	109	143	3-53,S-22/2-4,O(CF)	0.5
1958	Chi A	98	81	16	20	3	0	0	3	12-1	2	6	.247	.358	.284	81	-1	1-1	.979	5	125	74	3-63,S-22/2-2,O(LF)	0.5
1959	†Chi A	69	66	12	11	1	0	1	5	11-1	0	16	.167	.282	.227	43	-5	0-1	.979	4	97	47	3-45,S-14/2-2	-0.1
1960	Chi A	57	77	14	14	5	0	1	11	10-1	0	20	.182	.273	.286	53	-5	0-0	.929	0	108	110	3-37,S-11/2-5	-0.5
1961	Chi A	63	94	12	16	5	0	1	8	12-0	0	21	.170	.259	.255	40	-8	0-0	.976	6	119	219	3-28,S-20,2-11	0.0
1962	Chi A	75	81	14	19	1	0	0	4	17-1	0	13	.235	.367	.247	69	-3	0-1	.846	1	92	65	3-41,S-20/2-7	-0.1
1963	Chi A	1	0	0	0	0	0	0	0	0-0	0	0	—	—	—	—	0	0-0	—	0			R	0.0
	KC A	18	25	3	5	1	0	0	2	3-0	0	3	.200	.276	.240	47	-2	0-0	1.000	-6	54	41	/2-7,S-4,3-3	-0.7
	Year	19	25	3	5	1	0	0	2	3-0	0	3	.200	.276	.240	47	-2	0-0	1.000	-6	54	41	/2-7,S-4,3-3	-0.7
Total	10	560	792	130	164	27	2	8	73	145-4	4	127	.207	.330	.277	66	-33	7-7	.957	20	107	136	3-333,S-133/2-41,O-2(1-1-0)	-0.7
ESPY, CECIL Cecil Edward B 1.20.1963 San Diego, CA BB/TR 6-3/195# d9.2 OF Total (95-LF 263-CF 89-RF)																								
1983	LA N	20	11	4	3	1	0	0	1	1-0	0	2	.273	.333	.364	94	0	0-0	1.000	0	123	0	O-15(CF)	0.0
1987	Tex A	14	8	1	0	0	0	0	0	1-0	0	3	.000	.111	.000	-67	-2	2-0	1.000	1	122	439	/O-8(5-0-3)	-0.1
1988	Tex A	123	347	46	86	17	6	2	39	20-1	1	83	.248	.288	.349	76	-12	33-10	.972	2	99	223	O-98(52-46-8),D-12/S-3,C-2,12	-0.8
1989	Tex A	142	475	65	122	12	7	3	31	38-2	2	99	.257	.313	.331	81	-13	45-20	.990	-1	100	87	*O-133(3-131-1)/D-3	-1.2
1990	Tex A	52	71	10	9	0	0	0	1	10-0	0	20	.127	.235	.127	4	-9	11-5	1.000	2	117	93	O-39(4-28-9)/2D	-0.7
1991	†Pit N	43	82	7	20	4	0	1	11	5-0	0	17	.244	.281	.329	74	-3	4-0	.966	2	106	219	O-35(2-25-11)	-0.1
1992	†Pit N	112	194	21	50	7	3	1	20	15-2	0	40	.258	.310	.340	85	-4	6-3	.955	-3	91	38	O-82(11-18-56)	-0.9
1993	Cin N	40	60	6	14	2	0	0	5	14-0	0	13	.233	.368	.267	76	-1	2-2	.931	1	101	214	O-18(18-0-1)	-0.1
Total	8	546	1248	160	304	43	16	7	108	104-5	3	277	.244	.301	.321	74	-44	103-40	.977	4	101	136	O-428C/D-19,S-3,2-2,C-2,1	-3.9
ESSEGIAN, CHUCK Charles Abraham B 8.9.1931 Boston, MA BR/TR 5-11/202# d4.15																								
1958	Phi N	39	114	15	28	5	2	5	16	12-0	0	34	.246	.317	.456	103	0	0-0	.952	-1	100	45	O-30(28-2-0)	-0.3
1959	StL N	17	39	2	7	2	1	0	5	1-0	0	13	.179	.200	.282	25	-4	0-0	1.000	0	74	225	/O-9(LF)	-0.5
	†LA N	24	46	6	14	6	0	1	5	4-1	0	11	.304	.360	.500	118	1	0-0	1.000	-1	81	0	O-10(4-0-6)	0.0
	Year	41	85	8	21	8	1	1	10	5-1	0	24	.247	.289	.400	76	-3	0-0	1.000	-1	78	96	O-19(13-0-6)	-0.5
1960	LA N	52	79	8	17	3	0	3	11	8-1	0	24	.215	.284	.367	73	-3	0-0	.968	0	110	82	O-18(13-0-5)	-0.4
1961	Bal A	1	1	0	0	0	0	0	0	0-0	0	0	.000	.000	.000	-99	0	0-0	—	0			H	0.0
	KC A	4	6	1	2	1	0	0	1	1-0	0	2	.333	.429	.500	145	0	0-0	1.000	0	149	0	/O(LF)	0.1
	Cle A	60	166	25	48	7	1	12	35	10-0	1	33	.289	.328	.560	138	8	0-0	.968	2	102	190	O-49(16-19-16)	0.8
	Year	65	173	26	50	8	1	12	36	11-0	1	35	.289	.330	.555	137	8	0-0	.969	2	104	183	O-50(17-19-16)	0.9
1962	Cle A	106	336	59	92	12	0	21	50	42-2	7	68	.274	.363	.497	134	16	0-0	.994	-3	94	22	O-90(88-1-1)	0.9
1963	KC A	101	231	23	52	9	0	5	27	19-0	1	48	.225	.285	.329	68	-10	0-0	.990	1	104	61	O-53(LF)	-1.2
Total	6	404	1018	139	260	45	4	47	150	97-4	9	233	.255	.323	.446	106	8	0-0	.981	-1	99	70	O-260(212-22-28)	-0.6
ESSIAN, JIM James Sarkis B 1.2.1951 Detroit, MI BR/TR 6-2/195# d9.15 M1 OF Total (3-LF 1-RF)																								
1973	Phi N	2	3	0	0	0	0	0	0	0-0	0	1	.000	.000	.000	-97	-1	0-0	—	-0	0	0	/C	-0.1

Year	Tm Lg	G	AB	R	H	2B	3B	HR	RBI	BB-IB	HP	SO	AVG	OBP	SLG	AOPS	ABR	SB-CS	FA	FR	Rng	Thr	G at Pos	BFW
1974	Phi N	17	20	1	2	0	0	0	0	2-0	0	1	.100	.182	.100	-19	-3	0-0	.976	-2	50	90	C-15/13	-0.5
1975	Phi N	2	1	1	1	0	0	0	1	1-0	0	0	1.000	1.000	1.000	439	1	0-0	1.000	0	0	798	/C-2	0.1
1976	Chi A	78	199	20	49	7	0	0	21	23-0	1	28	.246	.326	.281	79	-4	2-1	.974	0	124	128	C-77/1-2,3	-0.1
1977	Chi A	114	322	50	88	18	2	10	44	52-1	1	35	.273	.374	.435	120	11	1-4	.986	0	98	121	*C-111/3-2	1.5
1978	Oak A	126	278	21	62	9	1	3	26	44-1	0	22	.223	.326	.295	81	-5	2-1	.981	9	92	**158**	*C-119/1-3,2D	0.8
1979	Oak A	98	313	34	76	16	0	8	40	25-1	2	29	.243	.295	.371	85	-7	0-1	.981	7	70	163	C-70,3-10/1-4,O-4(3-0-1),D-3	0.2
1980	Oak A	87	285	19	66	11	0	5	29	30-0	0	18	.232	.302	.323	78	-9	1-3	.987	5	102	172	C-68,D-11/1	-0.1
1981	Chi A	27	52	6	16	3	0	0	5	4-0	0	5	.308	.357	.365	111	1	0-1	.990	1	96	100	C-25/3-2	0.2
1982	Sea A	48	153	14	42	8	0	3	20	11-0	1	7	.275	.327	.386	92	-1	2-0	.994	-0	50	62	C-48	0.1
1983	Cle A	48	93	11	19	4	0	2	11	16-0	0	8	.204	.315	.312	72	-3	0-1	.989	-1	96	125	C-47/3	-0.3
1984	Oak A	63	136	17	32	9	0	2	10	23-0	1	17	.235	.348	.346	100	1	1-1	.985	3	79	176	C-59/3D	0.7
Total	12	710	1855	194	453	85	3	33	207	231-3	6	171	.244	.327	.347	90	-19	9-13	.984	22	91	139	C-642/3-18,D-16,1-11,O-4L,2	2.5

ESTALELLA, BOBBY Robert M B 8.23.1974 Hialeah, FL BR/TR 6-1/200# d9.17 gf-Bobby

Year	Tm Lg	G	AB	R	H	2B	3B	HR	RBI	BB-IB	HP	SO	AVG	OBP	SLG	AOPS	ABR	SB-CS	FA	FR	Rng	Thr	G at Pos	BFW
1996	Phi N	7	17	5	6	0	0	2	4	1-0	0	6	.353	.389	.706	179	2	1-0	1.000	-0	309	81	/C-4	0.2
1997	Phi N	13	29	9	10	1	0	4	9	7-0	0	7	.345	.472	.793	224	6	0-0	1.000	-3	214	34	C-11	0.3
1998	Phi N	47	165	16	31	6	1	8	20	13-0	1	49	.188	.247	.382	63	-10	0-0	.988	-10	77	55	C-47	-1.7
1999	Phi N	9	18	2	3	0	0	0	1	4-0	0	7	.167	.318	.167	27	-2	0-1	.976	-1	56	61	/C-7	-0.2
2000	†SF N	106	299	45	70	22	3	14	53	57-9	2	92	.234	.357	.468	116	8	3-0	.993	13	106	101	*C-106	2.6
2001	SF N	29	93	11	19	5	1	3	10	11-2	1	28	.204	.295	.376	78	-3	0-0	1.000	2	107	82	C-28	0.0
	NY A	3	4	1	0	0	0	0	0	1-0	1	2	.000	.333	.000	-1	-1	0-0	1.000	1	111	0	/C-3	0.0
2002	Col N	38	112	17	23	8	0	8	25	14-0	0	33	.205	.285	.491	91	-2	0-1	.995	-3	99	58	C-38	-0.3
2003	Col N	46	140	17	28	7	0	7	21	19-0	1	55	.200	.294	.400	71	-6	2-0	.985	0	86	127	C-46	-0.3
Total	8	298	877	123	190	49	5	46	143	127-11	6	279	.217	.316	.441	93	-8	6-2	.992	-1	102	86	C-290	0.6

ESTALELLA, BOBBY Roberto (Ventoza) B 4.25.1911 Cardenas, Cuba D 1.6.1991 Hialeah, FL BR/TR 5-8/180# d9.7 gs-Bobby

Year	Tm Lg	G	AB	R	H	2B	3B	HR	RBI	BB-IB	HP	SO	AVG	OBP	SLG	AOPS	ABR	SB-CS	FA	FR	Rng	Thr	G at Pos	BFW
1935	Was A	15	51	7	16	2	0	2	10	17	0	7	.314	.485	.471	153	6	1-0	.895	1	126	44	3-15	0.7
1936	Was A	13	9	2	2	0	2	0	0	4	0	5	.222	.462	.667	186	1	0-0	—	0			H	0.1
1939	Was A	82	280	51	77	18	6	8	41	40	1	27	.275	.368	.468	121	9	2-3	.964	-3	97	59	O-74(70-0-4)	0.1
1941	StL A	46	83	7	20	6	1	0	14	18	0	13	.241	.376	.337	87	-1	0-0	1.000	-2	78	0	O-17(15-0-2)	-0.3
1942	Was A	133	429	68	119	24	5	8	65	85	3	42	.277	.400	.413	130	22	5-2	.941	-5	94	26	3-78,O-36(17-2-17)	1.9
1943	Phi A	117	367	43	95	14	4	11	63	52	1	44	.259	.352	.409	123	11	1-3	.975	1	106	67	O-97(95-1-1)	0.6
1944	Phi A	140	506	54	151	17	9	7	60	59	2	60	.298	.374	.409	125	17	3-3	.988	-1	96	104	*O-128(5-103-25)/1-6	1.2
1945	Phi A	126	451	45	135	25	6	8	52	74	1	46	.299	.399	.435	142	27	1-6	.988	-6	92	91	*O-124(9-118-0)	1.7
1949	Phi A	8	20	2	5	0	0	0	3	1	0	2	.250	.286	.250	44	-2	0-0	1.000	1	99	230	/O-6(RF)	-0.1
Total	9	680	2196	279	620	106	33	44	308	350	8	246	.282	.383	.421	127	90	13-17	.982	-12	97	83	O-482(211-224-55)/3-93,1-6	5.9

ESTERBROOK, DUDE Thomas John B 6.20.1857 Staten Is., NY D 4.30.1901 Middletown, NY BR/TR 5-11/167# d5.1 M1 OF Total (40-LF 24-CF 12-RF)

Year	Tm Lg	G	AB	R	H	2B	3B	HR	RBI	BB-IB	HP	SO	AVG	OBP	SLG	AOPS	ABR	SB-CS	FA	FR	Rng	Thr	G at Pos	BFW
1880	Buf N	64	253	20	61	12	1	0	35	0		15	.241	.241	.296	80	-5		.939	-2	147	86	1-47,O-15(1-14-0)/2-6,SC	-0.9
1882	Cle N	45	179	13	44	4	3	0	19	5		12	.246	.266	.302	85	-3		.893	7	133	263	O-45(38-7-0)/1	0.3
1883	NY AA	**97**	407	55	103	9	7	0		15			.253	.280	.310	86	-7		.871	-6	84	92	*3-97	-1.0
1884	†NY AA	**112**	477	110	150	29	11	1		12	10		.314	.345	.428	154	29		.886	9	102	109	*3-112	3.5
1885	NY N	88	359	48	92	14	5	2	44	4		28	.256	.264	.340	96	-3		.885	-1	92	**153**	*3-84/O-4(1-0-3)	-0.3
1886	NY N	123	473	62	125	20	6	3	43	8		43	.264	.277	.351	89	-8	13	**.895**	-6	89	69	*3-123	-1.1
1887	NY AA	26	101	11	17	1	0	0	7	6	1		.168	.222	.178	13	-12	8	.950	-6	121	93	/1-9,O-7(0-3-5),S-5,2-5	-1.5
1888	Ind N	64	246	21	54	8	0	0	17	2	2	20	.220	.232	.252	53	-13	11	.976	-3	89	97	1-61/3-3	-2.1
	Lou AA	23	93	9	21	6	0	0	7	3	2		.226	.265	.290	80	-2	5	.962	0	120	74	1-23	-0.4
1889	Lou AA	11	44	8	14	3	0	0	9	5	1	2	.318	.400	.386	127	2	6	.931	-0	140	58	/1-8,O-2(RF),SM	0.1
1890	NY N	45	197	29	57	14	1	0	29	10	3	8	.289	.333	.371	105	1	12	.984	0	86	101	1-45	-0.2
1891	Bro N	3	8	1	3	0	0	0	0	0	1	1	.375	.444	.375	140	0	0	1.000	-1	0	0	/O-2(RF),2	0.0
Total	11	701	2837	387	741	120	34	6	210	70	20	129	.261	.284	.334	94	-21	55	.884	-8	92	102	3-419,1-194/O-75L,2-12,S-7,C	-3.6

ESTRADA, FRANK Francisco (Soto) B 2.12.1948 Navojoa, Mexico BR/TR 5-8/182# d9.14

Year	Tm Lg	G	AB	R	H	2B	3B	HR	RBI	BB-IB	HP	SO	AVG	OBP	SLG	AOPS	ABR	SB-CS	FA	FR	Rng	Thr	G at Pos	BFW
1971	NY N	1	2	0	1	0	0	0	0	0-0	0	0	.500	.500	.500	187	0	0-0	1.000	-1	0	0	/C	0.0

ESTRADA, JOHNNY Johnny P. B 6.27.1976 Hayward, CA BB/TR 5-11/209# d5.15

Year	Tm Lg	G	AB	R	H	2B	3B	HR	RBI	BB-IB	HP	SO	AVG	OBP	SLG	AOPS	ABR	SB-CS	FA	FR	Rng	Thr	G at Pos	BFW
2001	Phi N	89	298	26	68	15	0	8	37	16-6	4	32	.228	.273	.359	64	-17	0-0	.993	-3	138	76	C-89	-1.4
2002	Phi N	10	17	0	2	1	0	0	2	2-1	0	2	.118	.211	.176	6	-2	0-0	1.000	-1	53	0	C-10	-0.3
2003	Atl N	16	36	2	11	0	0	0	2	0-0	3	3	.306	.359	.306	76	-1	0-0	1.000	-3	72	0	C-14	-0.4
Total	3	115	351	28	81	16	0	8	41	18-7	7	37	.231	.279	.345	63	-20	0-0	.994	-6	128	65	C-113	-2.1

ETCHEBARREN, ANDY Andrew Auguste B 6.20.1943 Whittier, CA BR/TR 6-1/197# d9.26 C10

Year	Tm Lg	G	AB	R	H	2B	3B	HR	RBI	BB-IB	HP	SO	AVG	OBP	SLG	AOPS	ABR	SB-CS	FA	FR	Rng	Thr	G at Pos	BFW
1962	Bal A	2	6	0	2	0	0	0	1	0-0	0	2	.333	.333	.333	85	0	0-0	.875	-1	*51*	*0*	/C-2	-0.1
1965	Bal A	5	6	1	1	0	0	1	4	0-0	0	2	.167	.167	.667	123	0	0-0	1.000	1	*112*	*174*	/C-5	0.2
1966	†Bal A☆	121	412	49	91	14	6	11	50	38-12	5	106	.221	.293	.364	89	-6	0-1	.989	-8	*90*	***121***	*C-121	-0.9
1967	Bal A☆	112	330	29	71	13	0	7	35	38-9	2	80	.215	.298	.318	83	-6	1-0	.989	-3	80	73	*C-110	-0.4
1968	Bal A	74	189	20	44	11	2	5	20	19-4	3	46	.233	.311	.392	112	3	0-0	.998	6	119	81	C-70	1.4
1969	†Bal A	73	217	29	54	9	2	3	26	28-8	7	42	.249	.350	.350	96	0	1-2	.990	8	300	87	C-72	1.1
1970	†Bal A	78	230	19	56	10	1	4	28	21-2	3	41	.243	.313	.348	82	-6	4-1	.984	-1	124	58	C-76	-0.3
1971	†Bal A	70	222	21	60	8	0	9	29	16-2	1	40	.270	.321	.428	112	3	1-4	.986	2	152	126	C-70	0.7
1972	Bal A	71	188	11	38	6	1	2	21	17-2	3	43	.202	.276	.277	64	-8	0-2	.992	8	196	98	C-70	0.2
1973	†Bal A	54	152	16	39	9	1	2	23	12-1	2	21	.257	.317	.368	94	-1	1-1	.991	0	139	90	C-51	0.1
1974	†Bal A	62	180	13	40	8	0	2	15	6-0	1	26	.222	.249	.300	60	-10	1-0	.976	4	167	79	C-60	-0.3
1975	Bal A	8	20	0	4	1	0	0	3	0-0	0	3	.200	.200	.250	28	-2	0-0	1.000	-1	79	125	/C-7	-0.2
	Cal A	31	100	10	28	0	1	3	17	14-1	0	19	.280	.365	.390	123	3	1-0	.981	-2	93	94	C-31	0.2
	Year	39	120	10	32	1	1	3	20	14-1	0	22	.267	.341	.367	108	1	1-0	.983	-3	91	99	C-38	0.0
1976	Cal A	103	247	15	56	9	1	0	21	24-0	4	37	.227	.305	.271	74	-7	0-2	.980	-3	82	**128**	*C-102	-0.7
1977	Cal A	80	114	11	29	2	2	0	14	12-0	0	19	.254	.320	.307	77	-4	3-1	.987	-4	74	86	C-80	-0.5
1978	Mil A	4	5	1	2	1	0	0	2	1-0	0	2	.400	.500	.600	207	1	0-0	1.000	2	0	112	/C-4	0.2
Total	15	948	2618	245	615	101	17	49	309	246-41	31	529	.235	.306	.343	88	-40	13-14	.987	10	*129*	*96*	C-931	0.7

ETCHISON, BUCK Clarence Hampton B 1.27.1915 Baltimore, MD D 1.24.1980 Cambridge, MD BL/TL 6-1/190# d9.22

Year	Tm Lg	G	AB	R	H	2B	3B	HR	RBI	BB-IB	HP	SO	AVG	OBP	SLG	AOPS	ABR	SB-CS	FA	FR	Rng	Thr	G at Pos	BFW
1943	Bos N	10	19	2	6	3	0	0	2	2	0	2	.316	.381	.474	148	1	0	.956	-1	72	211	/1-6	0.0
1944	Bos N	109	308	30	66	16	0	8	33	33	1	50	.214	.292	.344	76	-10	1	.993	-2	89	102	1-85	-1.7
Total	2	119	327	32	72	19	0	8	35	35	1	52	.220	.298	.352	79	-9	1	.991	-3	88	107	/1-91	-1.7

ETHERIDGE, BOBBY Bobby Lamar "Luke" B 11.25.1942 Greenville, MS BR/TR 5-9/170# d7.16

Year	Tm Lg	G	AB	R	H	2B	3B	HR	RBI	BB-IB	HP	SO	AVG	OBP	SLG	AOPS	ABR	SB-CS	FA	FR	Rng	Thr	G at Pos	BFW
1967	SF N	40	115	13	26	7	2	1	15	7-0	5	12	.226	.297	.348	86	-2	0-0	.925	-3	90	161	3-37	-0.5
1969	SF N	56	131	13	34	9	0	1	10	19-0	1	26	.260	.358	.351	101	1	0-0	.899	-3	99	91	3-39/S	-0.2
Total	2	96	246	26	60	16	2	2	25	26-0	6	38	.244	.330	.350	94	-1	0-0	.911	-6	95	123	/3-76,S	-0.7

ETTEN, NICK Nicholas Raymond Thomas B 9.19.1913 Spring Grove, IL D 10.18.1990 Hinsdale, IL BL/TL 6-2/198# d9.8

Year	Tm Lg	G	AB	R	H	2B	3B	HR	RBI	BB-IB	HP	SO	AVG	OBP	SLG	AOPS	ABR	SB-CS	FA	FR	Rng	Thr	G at Pos	BFW
1938	Phi A	22	81	6	21	6	2	0	11	9	0	7	.259	.333	.383	81	-3	1-0	.987	-2	69	96	1-22	-0.6
1939	Phi A	43	155	20	39	11	2	3	29	16	0	11	.252	.322	.406	87	-3	0-0	.990	-3	77	79	1-41	-0.9
1941	Phi N	151	540	78	168	27	4	14	79	82	3	33	.311	.405	.454	147	37	9	.984	-3	96	92	*1-150	2.1
1942	Phi N	139	459	37	121	21	3	8	41	67	0	26	.264	.357	.375	120	14	3	.985	0	105	93	*1-135	0.2
1943	†NY A	154	583	78	158	35	5	14	107	76	0	31	.271	.355	.420	126	20	3-7	.989	-12	72	**119**	*1-154	-0.3
1944	NY A	**154**	573	88	168	25	4	**22**	91	**97**	4	29	.293	.399	.466	142	35	4-2	.989	3	108	106	*1-154	3.1
1945	NY A✱	**152**	565	77	161	24	4	18	**111**	90	4	23	.285	.387	.437	133	26	2-3	.989	-11	79	**121**	*1-152	0.8
1946	NY A	108	323	37	75	14	1	9	49	38	1	35	.232	.315	.365	88	-5	0-1	.991	-0	98	116	1-84	-0.9
1947	Phi N	14	41	5	10	4	0	1	8	5	0	4	.244	.326	.415	99	0	0	.990	1	141	46	1-11	0.1
Total	9	937	3320	426	921	167	25	89	526	480	12	199	.277	.371	.423	125	121	22-13	.988	-25	91	105	1-903	3.6

EUNICK, FRED Fernandas Bowen B 4.22.1892 Baltimore, MD D 12.9.1959 Baltimore, MD BR/TR 5-6/148# d8.29

Year	Tm Lg	G	AB	R	H	2B	3B	HR	RBI	BB-IB	HP	SO	AVG	OBP	SLG	AOPS	ABR	SB-CS	FA	FR	Rng	Thr	G at Pos	BFW
1917	Cle A	1	2	0	0	0	0	0	0	0	0	0	.000	.000	.000	-93	0	0	1.000	-0	107	0	/3	-0.1

Year	Tm Lg	G	AB	R	H	2B	3B	HR	RBI	BB-IB	HP	SO	AVG	OBP	SLG	AOPS	ABR	SB-CS	FA	FR	Rng	Thr	G at Pos	BFW
EUSEBIO, TONY Raul Antonio Bare (born Raul Antontio Bare (Eusebio)) B 4.27.1967 San Jose De Los Llanos, D.R. BR/TR 6-2/180# d8.8																								
1991	Hou N	10	19	4	2	1	0	0	0	6-0	0	8	.105	.320	.158	41	-1	0-0	.981	1	139	74	/C-9	0.0
1994	Hou N	55	159	18	47	9	1	5	30	8-0	0	33	.296	.320	.459	108	1	0-1	.993	-3	90	152	C-52	0.1
1995	Hou N	113	368	46	110	21	1	6	58	31-1	3	59	.299	.354	.410	110	5	0-2	.993	-9	106	97	*C-103	0.2
1996	Hou N	58	152	15	41	7	2	1	19	18-2	0	20	.270	.343	.362	95	-1	0-1	.996	-4	95	79	C-47	-0.3
1997	†Hou N	60	164	12	45	2	0	1	18	19-1	4	27	.274	.364	.305	80	-4	0-1	.987	-2	86	62	C-43	-0.4
1998	†Hou N	66	182	13	46	6	1	1	36	18-2	1	31	.253	.320	.313	70	-8	1-0	.992	5	147	83	C-54	0.0
1999	†Hou N	103	323	31	88	15	0	4	33	40-4	0	67	.272	.353	.356	81	-8	0-0	.994	8	162	78	C-98	0.5
2000	Hou N	74	218	24	61	18	0	7	33	25-2	4	45	.280	.361	.459	101	1	0-0	.988	-9	99	58	C-68	-0.4
2001	†Hou N	59	154	16	39	8	0	5	14	17-3	3	34	.253	.339	.403	86	-3	0-0	.991	-2	117	70	C-48	-0.2
Total	9	598	1739	179	479	87	5	30	241	182-15	15	324	.275	.346	.383	92	-18	1-5	.992	-16	117	85	C-522	-0.5
EUSTACE, FRANK Frank John B 11.7.1873 New York, NY D 10.16.1932 Pottsville, PA 5-9/160# d4.16																								
1896	Lou N	25	100	18	17	2	2	1	11	6	0	14	.170	.217	.260	26	-11	4	.841	-6	89	54	S-22/2-3	-1.4
EVANS d6.1																								
1875	NH NA	1	4	1	2	0	0	0	1	0		0	.500	.500	.500	285	1	0-0	—	-0	0	0	/O(LF)	0.1
EVANS, AL Alfred Hubert B 9.28.1916 Kenly, NC D 4.6.1979 Wilson, NC BR/TR 5-11/190# d9.13 Mil 1943-44																								
1939	Was A	7	21	2	7	0	0	0	1	5	0	2	.333	.462	.333	115	1	0-0	.964	0	137	120	/C-6	0.1
1940	Was A	14	25	1	8	2	0	0	7	6	0	7	.320	.452	.400	131	2	1-0	1.000	-1	76	57	/C-9	0.2
1941	Was A	53	159	16	44	8	4	1	19	9	0	18	.277	.315	.396	91	-3	0-3	.969	-1	97	113	C-51	-0.2
1942	Was A	74	223	22	51	4	1	0	10	25	1	36	.229	.309	.256	60	-11	3-0	.961	-5	96	126	C-67	-1.3
1944	Was A	14	22	5	2	0	0	0	0	2	0	6	.091	.167	.091	-27	-4	0-0	.933	-1	73	101	/C-8	-0.5
1945	Was A	51	150	19	39	11	2	2	19	17	1	22	.260	.339	.400	125	5	2-1	.973	-4	105	54	C-41	0.3
1946	Was A	88	272	30	69	10	4	2	30	30	2	28	.254	.332	.342	94	-2	1-2	.966	-10	91	72	C-81	-0.9
1947	Was A	99	319	17	77	8	3	2	23	28	0	25	.241	.303	.304	71	-13	2-1	.989	-1	94	117	C-94	-1.0
1948	Was A	93	228	19	59	6	3	2	28	38	1	20	.259	.367	.338	91	-2	1-1	.983	-2	112	154	C-85	0.0
1949	Was A	109	321	32	87	12	3	2	42	50	0	19	.271	.369	.346	92	-3	4-1	**.992**	-14	79	105	*C-107	-1.1
1950	Was A	90	289	24	68	8	3	2	30	29	2	21	.235	.309	.304	61	-18	0-0	.987	-10	65	68	C-88	-2.2
1951	Bos A	12	24	1	3	1	0	0	2	4	0	2	.125	.250	.167	13	-3	0-0	1.000	0	130	0	C-10	-0.2
Total	12	704	2053	188	514	70	23	13	211	243	7	206	.250	.332	.326	82	-51	14-9	.979	-49	91	101	C-647	-6.8
EVANS, BARRY Barry Steven B 11.30.1956 Atlanta, GA BR/TR 6-1/180# d9.4																								
1978	SD N	24	90	7	24	1	1	0	4	4-1	0	10	.267	.295	.300	73	-4	0-0	.947	2	116	103	3-24	-0.3
1979	SD N	56	162	9	35	5	0	1	14	5-0	0	16	.216	.237	.265	40	-14	0-2	.952	4	114	151	3-53/S-2,2	-1.2
1980	SD N	73	125	11	29	3	2	1	14	17-1	0	21	.232	.317	.312	83	-3	1-1	.983	-5	79	54	3-43,2-19/S-4,1	-0.8
1981	SD N	54	93	11	30	5	0	0	7	9-2	0	9	.323	.371	.376	125	3	2-2	.969	-4	76	45	3-24,1-10/2-6,S-2	-0.1
1982	NY A	17	31	2	8	3	0	0	2	6-0	1	6	.258	.395	.355	109	1	0-0	1.000	-1	87	73	/2-8,3-6,S-4	0.0
Total	5	224	501	40	126	17	3	2	41	41-4	1	62	.251	.304	.309	77	-17	3-5	.960	-4	103	102	3-150/2-34,S-12,1-11	-2.4
EVANS, DARRELL Darrell Wayne B 5.26.1947 Pasadena, CA BL/TR 6-2/205# d4.20 C1 OF Total (LF)																								
1969	Atl N	12	26	3	6	0	0	0	1	1-0	0	8	.231	.250	.231	38	-2	0-0	.917	-2	70	0	/3-6	-0.4
1970	Atl N	12	44	4	14	1	1	0	9	7-0	1	5	.318	.423	.386	112	1	0-0	.941	1	120	0	3-12	0.2
1971	Atl N	89	260	42	63	11	1	12	38	39-4	1	54	.242	.338	.431	111	4	2-3	.937	7	111	115	3-72/O-3(LF)	1.1
1972	Atl N	125	418	67	106	12	0	19	71	90-4	4	58	.254	.384	.419	119	15	4-2	.941	14	114	92	*3-123	2.9
1973	Atl N★	161	595	114	167	25	8	41	104	**124**-8	3	104	.281	.403	.556	153	46	6-3	.953	17	**118**	111	*3-146,1-20	6.3
1974	Atl N	160	571	99	137	21	3	25	79	**126**-9	6	88	.240	.381	.419	119	20	4-2	.955	27	114	**154**	*3-160	4.7
1975	Atl N	156	567	82	138	22	2	22	73	105-5	2	106	.243	.361	.406	109	10	12-3	.938	**31**	**123**	**141**	*3-156/1-3	4.3
1976	Atl N	44	139	11	24	0	0	1	10	30-0	0	33	.173	.320	.194	45	-9	3-0	.994	1	96	84	1-36/3-7	-1.1
	SF N	92	257	42	57	9	1	10	36	42-4	0	38	.222	.329	.381	99	0	6-1	.991	8	138	88	1-83/3-5	0.4
	Year	136	396	53	81	9	1	11	46	72-4	0	71	.205	.326	.316	80	-9	9-1	.992	10	124	87	*1-119,3-12	-0.7
1977	SF N	144	461	64	117	18	3	17	72	69-3	3	50	.254	.351	.416	106	5	9-6	.937	1	104	63	O-81(LF),1-41,3-35	0.1
1978	SF N	159	547	82	133	24	2	20	78	105-12	0	64	.243	.360	.404	119	18	4-5	.952	5	101	99	*3-155	2.1
1979	SF N	160	562	68	142	23	2	17	70	91-14	2	80	.253	.356	.391	112	12	6-7	.943	14	107	94	*3-159	2.3
1980	SF N	154	556	69	147	23	0	20	78	83-6	2	65	.264	.359	.414	119	16	17-5	.946	12	107	118	*3-140,1-14	2.9
1981	SF N	102	357	51	92	13	4	12	48	54-8	2	33	.258	.356	.417	122	11	2-3	.953	8	105	70	3-87,1-12	1.7
1982	SF N	141	465	64	119	20	4	16	61	77-7	2	64	.256	.360	.419	119	14	5-4	.933	4	94	93	3-84,1-49,S-13	1.5
1983	SF N★	142	523	94	145	29	3	30	82	84-12	2	81	.277	.378	.516	151	37	6-6	.993	5	109	68	*1-113,3-32/S-9	3.6
1984	†Det A	131	401	60	93	11	1	16	63	77-10	0	70	.232	.353	.384	105	5	2-2	.997	3	135	102	D-62,1-47,3-19	0.4
1985	Det A	151	505	81	125	17	0	**40**	94	85-12	1	85	.248	.356	.519	137	27	0-4	.984	13	143	95	*1-113,D-33/3-7	3.0
1986	Det A	151	507	78	122	15	0	29	85	91-5	1	105	.241	.356	.442	116	13	3-2	.998	13	141	108	*1-105,D-42/3-2	1.8
1987	†Det A	150	499	90	128	20	0	34	99	100-8	2	84	.257	.379	.501	138	31	6-5	.997	13	136	110	*1-105,D-44/3-7	3.4
1988	Det A	144	437	48	91	9	0	22	64	84-4	1	89	.208	.337	.380	104	4	1-4	.993	5	125	86	D-72,1-65	0.1
1989	Atl N	107	276	31	57	6	1	11	39	41-6	0	46	.207	.303	.355	87	-5	0-1	.985	7	162	104	1-50,3-28	-0.1
Total	21	2687	8973	1344	2223	329	36	414	1354	1605-141	35	1410	.248	.361	.431	119	273	98-68	.946	207	110	110	*3-1442,1-856,D-253/O-84L,S-22	41.2
EVANS, DWIGHT Dwight Michael "Dewey" B 11.3.1951 Santa Monica, CA BR/TR 6-2/205# d9.16 C2																								
1972	Bos A	18	57	2	15	3	1	1	6	7-0	0	13	.263	.344	.404	115	1	0-0	1.000	1	82	240	O-17(16-0-1)	0.1
1973	Bos A	119	282	46	63	13	1	10	32	40-2	1	52	.223	.320	.383	92	-2	5-0	.995	-0	101	67	*O-113(17-2-95)/D-2	-0.7
1974	Bos A	133	463	60	130	19	8	10	70	38-2	2	77	.281	.335	.421	110	5	4-4	.990	12	**126**	89	*O-122(1-3-120)/D-7	1.1
1975	†Bos A	128	412	61	113	24	6	13	56	47-3	4	60	.274	.353	.456	118	10	3-4	.987	19	**130**	164	*O-115(RF)/D-7	2.2
1976	Bos A	146	501	61	121	34	5	17	62	57-4	6	92	.242	.324	.431	107	5	6-7	**.994**	7	105	138	*O-145(0-8-140)/D	0.4
1977	Bos A	73	230	39	66	9	2	14	36	28-0	0	58	.287	.363	.526	125	8	4-2	.992	-1	105	48	O-63(0-14-54)/D-6	0.4
1978	Bos A★	147	497	75	123	24	2	24	63	65-2	2	119	.247	.336	.449	108	5	8-5	.982	1	100	127	*O-142(0-3-140)/D-4	-0.1
1979	Bos A	152	489	69	134	24	1	21	58	69-7	1	76	.274	.364	.456	114	11	6-9	.988	5	103	136	*O-149(RF)	0.5
1980	Bos A	148	463	72	123	37	5	18	60	64-6	5	98	.266	.358	.484	123	16	3-1	.982	-2	96	102	*O-144(0-1-144)/D-2	0.7
1981	Bos A★	**108**	412	84	122	19	4	**22**	71	**85**-1	1	85	.296	.415	.522	160	**35**	3-2	.993	6	109	108	*O-108(1-0-107)	3.7
1982	Bos A	**162**	609	122	178	37	7	32	98	112-1	1	125	.292	**.402**	.534	146	43	3-2	.973	-1	104	77	O-161(RF)/D	3.3
1983	Bos A	126	470	74	112	19	4	22	58	70-5	2	97	.238	.338	.436	104	3	3-0	.987	1	105	77	O-99(RF),D-21	-0.1
1984	Bos A	**162**	630	**121**	186	37	8	32	104	96-2	4	115	.295	.388	.532	146	42	3-1	.994	-4	97	72	*O-161(RF)	3.0
1985	Bos A	159	617	110	162	29	1	29	78	**114**-4	5	105	.263	.378	.454	123	24	7-2	.990	-4	94	87	*O-152(RF)/D-7	1.2
1986	†Bos A	152	529	86	137	33	2	26	97	97-4	6	117	.259	.376	.476	131	27	3-3	.983	0	101	102	*O-149(RF)/D	1.8
1987	Bos A★	154	541	109	165	37	2	34	123	**106**-6	3	98	.305	.417	.569	155	48	4-6	.982	-8	71	111	1-79,O-77(RF)/D-4	2.8
1988	†Bos A	149	559	96	164	31	7	21	111	76-3	1	99	.293	.375	.487	135	27	5-1	.987	-6	101	91	O-85(0-1-84),1-64/D-6	1.6
1989	Bos A	146	520	82	148	27	3	20	100	99-1	3	84	.285	.397	.463	135	29	3-3	.981	-1	100	88	O-77(RF),D-69	2.3
1990	†Bos A	123	445	66	111	18	3	13	63	67-5	4	73	.249	.349	.391	103	3	3-4	—	0	0	0	*D-122	-0.1
1991	Bal A	101	270	35	73	9	1	6	38	54-2	2	54	.270	.393	.378	120	11	2-3	.984	-0	92	133	O-67(RF),D-21	0.7
Total	20	2606	8996	1470	2446	483	73	385	1384	1391-60	53	1697	.272	.370	.470	126	351	78-59	.987	24	103	103	*O-2146(35-32-2092),D-282,1-143	24.8
EVANS, JOE Joseph Patton "Doc" B 5.15.1895 Meridian, MS D 8.9.1953 Gulfport, MS BR/TR 5-9/160# d7.3 Mil 1918 OF Total (172-LF 85-CF 54-RF)																								
1915	Cle A	42	109	17	28	4	2	0	11	22	0	12	.257	.382	.330	111	3	6-1	.885	-0	118	21	3-30/2-2	0.4
1916	Cle A	33	82	4	12	1	0	0	1	7	0	12	.146	.213	.159	11	-9	4	.915	3	120	67	3-28	-0.7
1917	Cle A	132	385	36	73	4	5	2	33	42	1	44	.190	.271	.242	53	-22	12	.939	1	**107**	111	*3-127	-2.0
1918	Cle A	79	243	38	64	6	7	1	22	30	0	29	.263	.344	.358	102	1	7	.932	1	102	123	3-74	0.4
1919	Cle A	21	14	9	1	0	0	0	0	2	0	1	.071	.188	.071	-24	-2	1	.923	2	221	0	/S-6	0.0
1920	†Cle A	56	172	32	60	9	9	0	23	15	1	3	.349	.404	.506	136	8	6-2	.966	1	107	129	O-43(LF)/S-6	0.8
1921	Cle A	57	153	36	51	11	0	0	21	19	1	5	.333	.410	.405	107	3	4-1	.933	3	105	162	O-47(LF)	0.3
1922	Cle A	75	145	35	39	6	2	0	22	8	0	4	.269	.307	.338	67	-7	11-2	.969	0	117	24	O-49(30-17-3)	-0.8
1923	Was A	106	372	42	98	15	3	0	38	27	0	18	.263	.313	.320	70	-17	6-4	.982	-5	93	63	O-72(2-65-5),3-21/1-5	-2.3
1924	StL A	77	209	30	53	3	3	0	19	24	0	12	.254	.330	.297	59	-13	4-4	.969	1	113	53	O-49(38-1-10)	-1.6
1925	StL A	55	159	27	50	12	0	0	20	16	0	6	.314	.377	.390	90	-2	6-2	1.000	2	115	67	O-47(12-2-36)	-0.2
Total	11	733	2043	306	529	71	31	3	210	212	3	152	.259	.329	.328	79	-57	67-16	.971	8	107	80	O-307L,3-280/S-12,1-5,2-2	-5.7
EVANS, STEVE Louis Richard B 2.17.1885 Cleveland, OH D 12.28.1943 Cleveland, OH BL/TL 5-10/175# d4.16																								
1908	NY N	2	2	0	1	0	0	0	0	0	0		.500	.500	.500	209	0	0	—	-0	0	0	/O(CF)	0.0

Year	Tm Lg	G	AB	R	H	2B	3B	HR	RBI	BB-IB	HP	SO	AVG	OBP	SLG	AOPS	ABR	SB-CS	FA	FR	Rng	Thr	G at Pos	BFW
1909	StL N	143	498	67	129	17	6	2	56	66	14		.259	.362	.329	122	17	14	.947	-3	99	**209**	*O-141(RF)/1-2	0.9
1910	StL N	151	506	73	122	21	8	2	73	78	**31**	63	.241	.376	.326	109	12	10	.968	-3	101	84	*O-141(RF),1-10	0.3
1911	StL N	154	547	74	161	24	13	5	71	46	**19**	52	.294	.369	.413	122	16	13	.972	-3	101	81	*O-150(RF)	0.5
1912	StL N	135	491	59	139	23	9	6	72	36	**17**	51	.283	.353	.403	109	6	11	.942	1	98	121	*O-134(RF)	-0.1
1913	StL N	97	245	18	61	15	6	1	31	20	6	28	.249	.321	.371	99	0	5-5	.983	-1	109	63	O-74(2-1-71)/1	-0.6
1914	Bro F	145	514	93	179	41	**15**	12	96	50	10	49	.348	.416	**.556**	**165**	**39**	18	.941	-1	101	80	*O-112(36-1-76),1-27	3.3
1915	Bro F	63	216	44	64	14	4	3	30	35	7	22	.296	.411	.440	140	11	7	.960	-1	93	103	O-61(RF)/1	0.7
	Bal F	88	340	50	107	20	6	1	37	28	7	34	.315	.379	.418	120	5	8	.925	-3	85	115	O-88(RF)/1-4	-0.2
	Year	151	556	94	171	**34**	10	4	67	63	**14**	56	.308	.392	.426	128	16	15	.940	-5	88	110	*O-149(RF)/1-5	0.5
Total	8	978	3359	478	963	175	67	32	466	359	111	<u>299</u>	.287	.374	.407	125	106	86-<u>5</u>	.955	-16	99	112	O-902(38-3-862)/1-45	4.8

EVANS, TOM Thomas John B 7.9.1974 Kirkland, WA BR/TR 6-1/200# d9.2

Year	Tm Lg	G	AB	R	H	2B	3B	HR	RBI	BB-IB	HP	SO	AVG	OBP	SLG	AOPS	ABR	SB-CS	FA	FR	Rng	Thr	G at Pos	BFW
1997	Tor A	12	38	7	11	2	0	1	2	2-0	1	10	.289	.341	.421	97	0	0-1	.917	2	122	56	3-12	0.1
1998	Tor A	7	10	0	0	0	0	0	0	1-0	0	2	.000	.091	.000	-73	-3	0-0	.889	-1	48	0	/3-7	-0.3
2000	Tex A	23	54	10	15	4	0	0	5	10-0	1	13	.278	.394	.352	91	0	0-3	.909	1	108	140	3-21/1D	0.0
Total	3	42	102	17	26	6	0	1	7	13-0	2	25	.255	.347	.343	78	-3	0-4	.910	2	106	95	/3-40,D1	-0.2

EVANS, JAKE Uriah L. P. "Bloody Jake" B 9.1856 Baltimore, MD D 1.16.1907 Baltimore, MD TR 5-8/154# d5.1 I OF Total (25-LF 17-CF 411-RF)

Year	Tm Lg	G	AB	R	H	2B	3B	HR	RBI	BB-IB	HP	SO	AVG	OBP	SLG	AOPS	ABR	SB-CS	FA	FR	Rng	Thr	G at Pos	BFW
1879	Tro N	72	280	30	65	9	5	0	17	5		18	.232	.246	.300	84	-4		.884	18	187	**197**	*O-72(2-7-64)	1.2
1880	Tro N	47	180	31	46	8	1	0	22	7		15	.256	.283	.311	96	-1		.906	-0	87	205	O-47(0-6-41)/P	-0.1
1881	Tro N	83	315	35	76	11	5	0	28	14		30	.241	.274	.308	78	-8		.926	11	140	150	*O-83(RF)	0.3
1882	Wor N	80	334	33	71	10	4	0	25	7		22	.213	.229	.266	57	-16		.910	17	**195**	47	*O-68(0-4-64),S-11/32P	0.0
1883	Cle N	90	332	36	79	13	2	0	31	8		38	.238	.256	.289	66	-13		.902	3	144	34	*O-86(RF)/S-3,3-3,2P	-1.0
1884	Cle N	80	313	32	81	18	3	1	38	15		49	.259	.293	.345	97	-1		**.917**	8	125	115	*O-76(23-0-53)/2-4,S-2	0.5
1885	Bal AA	20	77	18	17	1	1	0	7	7	4		.221	.318	.260	85	-1		.894	1	140	277	O-20(RF)	0.0
Total	7	472	1831	215	435	70	21	1	168	63	4	<u>172</u>	.238	.264	.300	78	-44		.907	58	149	124	O-452R/S-16,2-6,3-4,P-3	0.9

EVERETT, CARL Carl Edward B 6.3.1971 Tampa, FL BB/TR 6/190# d7.1

Year	Tm Lg	G	AB	R	H	2B	3B	HR	RBI	BB-IB	HP	SO	AVG	OBP	SLG	AOPS	ABR	SB-CS	FA	FR	Rng	Thr	G at Pos	BFW
1993	Fla N	11	19	0	2	0	0	0	0	1-0	0	9	.105	.150	.105	-29	-4	1-0	.857	-1	58	0	/O-8(CF)	-0.5
1994	Fla N	16	51	7	11	1	0	2	6	3-0	0	15	.216	.259	.353	56	-4	4-0	1.000	1	102	234	O-16(1-8-8)	-0.2
1995	NY N	79	289	48	75	13	1	12	54	39-2	2	67	.260	.352	.436	110	4	2-5	.981	2	96	165	O-77(0-10-68)	0.2
1996	NY N	101	192	29	46	8	1	1	16	21-2	4	53	.240	.326	.307	72	-7	6-0	.935	4	126	162	O-55(8-15-37)	-0.3
1997	NY N	142	443	58	110	28	3	14	57	32-3	7	102	.248	.308	.420	92	-7	17-9	.971	-1	98	120	*O-128(9-71-65)	-0.9
1998	†Hou N	133	467	72	138	34	4	15	76	44-2	3	102	.296	.359	.482	122	15	14-12	.987	6	106	162	*O-123(0-121-5)	2.0
1999	†Hou N	123	464	86	151	33	3	25	108	50-5	11	94	.325	.398	.571	145	33	27-7	.978	-4	89	167	*O-121(2-118-16)/D-2	3.1
2000	Bos A★	137	496	82	149	32	4	34	108	52-5	8	113	.300	.373	.587	135	25	11-4	.980	-3	90	184	*O-126(CF)/D-5	2.2
2001	Bos A	102	409	61	105	24	4	14	58	27-3	13	104	.257	.323	.438	97	-2	9-2	.974	-9	85	79	O-93(0-84-9)/D-7	-0.9
2002	Tex A	105	374	47	100	16	0	16	62	33-4	6	77	.267	.333	.439	99	-1	2-3	.969	-8	91	0	O-83(18-33-39),D-18	-1.2
2003	Tex A★	74	270	53	74	13	3	18	51	31-2	5	48	.274	.356	.544	123	9	4-1	.986	1	97	157	O-72(40-15-33)/D	0.8
	Chi A	73	256	40	77	14	0	10	41	22-4	10	36	.301	.377	.473	122	9	4-3	.987	-1	98	112	O-68(8-66-1)/D-3	0.8
	Year	147	526	93	151	27	3	28	92	53-6	15	84	.287	.366	.510	122	18	8-4	.986	1	97	136	*O-140(48-81-34)/D-4	1.6
Total	11	1096	3730	583	1038	216	23	161	637	355-32	69	820	.278	.350	.478	113	70	101-46	.977	-13	96	135	O-970(86-675-281)/D-36	5.1

EVERETT, ADAM Jeffrey Adam B 2.2.1977 Austell, GA BR/TR 6/156# d8.30

Year	Tm Lg	G	AB	R	H	2B	3B	HR	RBI	BB-IB	HP	SO	AVG	OBP	SLG	AOPS	ABR	SB-CS	FA	FR	Rng	Thr	G at Pos	BFW
2001	Hou N	9	3	1	0	0	0	0	0	0-0	0	1	.000	.000	.000	-95	-1	1-0	.667	-0	89	214	/S-6	-0.1
2002	Hou N	40	88	11	17	3	0	0	4	12-1	1	19	.193	.297	.227	41	-8	3-0	.962	5	113	120	S-34	0.0
2003	Hou N	128	387	51	99	18	3	8	51	28-6	9	66	.256	.320	.380	78	-13	8-1	.970	14	103	102	*S-128	1.2
Total	3	177	478	63	116	21	3	8	55	40-7	10	86	.243	.314	.349	71	-22	12-1	.966	19	105	106	S-168	1.1

EVERITT, BILL William Lee "Wild Bill" B 12.13.1868 Ft.Wayne, IN D 1.19.1938 Denver, CO BL/TR 6-0.5/185# d4.18

Year	Tm Lg	G	AB	R	H	2B	3B	HR	RBI	BB-IB	HP	SO	AVG	OBP	SLG	AOPS	ABR	SB-CS	FA	FR	Rng	Thr	G at Pos	BFW
1895	Chi N	**133**	550	129	197	16	10	3	88	33	4	42	.358	.399	.440	109	6	47	.854	-8	97	61	*3-130/2-3	0.0
1896	Chi N	**132**	575	130	184	16	13	2	46	41	2	43	.320	.367	.403	99	-2	46	.882	-13	86	65	*3-97,O-35(27-6-2)	-1.4
1897	Chi N	92	379	63	119	14	7	5	39	36	0		.314	.373	.427	107	3	26	.864	-6	92	83	3-83/O-8(4-4-0)	-0.2
1898	Chi N	149	596	102	190	15	6	0	69	53	3		.319	.377	.364	113	11	28	.974	-3	96	**144**	*1-149	0.7
1899	Chi N	136	536	87	166	17	5	1	74	31	3		.310	.351	.366	99	-1	30	.971	8	**140**	130	*1-136	0.6
1900	Chi N	23	91	10	24	4	0	0	17	3	0		.264	.287	.308	67	-4	2	.979	-2	72	104	1-23	-0.6
1901	Was A	33	115	14	22	3	2	0	8	15	3		.191	.301	.252	55	-6	7	.967	-4	49	68	1-33	-1.0
Total	7	698	2842	535	902	85	43	11	341	212	15	<u>85</u>	.317	.368	.389	102	7	186	.973	-26	108	129	1-341,3-310/O-43(31-10-2),2-3	-1.9

EVERS, JOHNNY John Joseph "Crab" or "Trojan" B 7.21.1881 Troy, NY D 3.28.1947 Albany, NY BL/TR 5-9/125# d9.1 M3 C7 HF1946 b-Joe

Year	Tm Lg	G	AB	R	H	2B	3B	HR	RBI	BB-IB	HP	SO	AVG	OBP	SLG	AOPS	ABR	SB-CS	FA	FR	Rng	Thr	G at Pos	BFW
1902	Chi N	26	90	7	20	0	0	0	2	3	2		.222	.263	.222	51	-5	1	.990	1	112	81	2-18/S-8	-0.4
1903	Chi N	124	464	70	136	27	7	0	52	19	3		.293	.325	.381	104	1	25	.937	-14	95	116	*2-110,S-11/3-2	-1.2
1904	Chi N	152	532	49	141	14	7	0	47	28	4		.265	.307	.318	93	-6	26	.943	28	**109**	125	*2-152	2.5
1905	Chi N	99	340	44	94	11	2	1	37	27	2		.276	.333	.329	94	-2	19	.937	-1	94	137	2-99	-0.2
1906	†Chi N	**154**	533	65	136	17	6	1	51	36	2		.255	.305	.315	88	-8	49	.947	2	97	118	*2-153/3	-0.6
1907	†Chi N	151	508	66	127	18	4	2	51	38	5		.250	.309	.313	89	-6	46	.964	**27**	**113**	126	*2-151	2.5
1908	†Chi N	126	416	83	125	19	6	0	37	66	5		.300	.402	.375	143	25	36	.960	-1	99	122	*2-122/O(RF)	2.8
1909	Chi N	127	463	88	122	19	6	1	24	73	4		.263	.369	.337	116	13	28	.942	1	100	79	*2-126	1.7
1910	Chi N	125	433	87	114	11	7	0	28	108	2	18	.263	.413	.321	115	17	28	.950	-3	97	108	*2-125	1.6
1911	Chi N	46	155	29	35	4	3	0	7	34	2	10	.226	.372	.290	86	-1	6	.975	-2	99	132	2-33,3-11	-0.3
1912	Chi N	143	478	73	163	23	11	1	63	74	2	18	.341	**.431**	.441	139	30	16	.959	6	**104**	122	*2-143	3.7
1913	Chi N	136	446	81	127	20	5	3	49	50	3	14	.285	.361	.372	109	7	11-18	.960	**28**	**113**	**135**	*2-136,M	3.4
1914	†Bos N	139	491	81	137	20	3	1	40	87	2	26	.279	.390	.338	118	17	12	**.976**	6	99	**145**	*2-139	2.7
1915	Bos N	83	278	38	73	4	1	1	22	50	0	16	.263	.375	.295	109	6	7-8	.959	-2	95	112	2-82	0.5
1916	Bos N	71	241	33	52	4	1	0	15	40	1	19	.216	.330	.241	80	-3	5	.951	-15	88	120	2-71	-2.0
1917	Bos N	24	83	5	16	0	0	0	0	13	0	8	.193	.302	.193	56	-4	1	.950	-4	97	129	2-24	-0.8
	Phi N	56	183	20	41	5	1	1	12	30	0	13	.224	.333	.279	85	-2	8	.983	1	108	78	2-49/3-7	0.1
	Year	80	266	25	57	5	1	1	12	43	0	21	.214	.324	.252	77	-5	9	.973	-3	104	95	2-73/3-7	-0.7
1922	Chi A	1	3	0	0	0	0	0	1	2	0	0	.000	.400	.000	12	0	0-0	1.000	-0	85	0	/2	0.0
1929	Bos N	1	0	0	0	0	0	0	0	0	0	0	—	—	—	—	0	0	.000	-1	0	0	/2	-0.1
Total	18	1784	6137	919	1659	216	70	12	538	778	39	<u>142</u>	.270	.356	.334	106	79	324-<u>26</u>	.955	58	101	119	*2-1735/3-21,S-19,O(RF)	15.9

EVERS, JOE Joseph Francis B 9.10.1891 Troy, NY D 1.4.1949 Albany, NY BR/TR 5-9/135# d4.24 b-Johnny

Year	Tm Lg	G	AB	R	H	2B	3B	HR	RBI	BB-IB	HP	SO	AVG	OBP	SLG	AOPS	ABR	SB-CS	FA	FR	Rng	Thr	G at Pos	BFW
1913	NY N	1	0	0	0	0	0	0	0	0	0	0	—	—	—	—	0	0	—	0			R	0.0

EVERS, TOM Thomas Francis B 3.31.1852 Troy, NY D 3.23.1925 Washington, DC TL d5.25

Year	Tm Lg	G	AB	R	H	2B	3B	HR	RBI	BB-IB	HP	SO	AVG	OBP	SLG	AOPS	ABR	SB-CS	FA	FR	Rng	Thr	G at Pos	BFW
1882	Bal AA	1	4	0	0	0	0	0		0			.000	.000	.000	-99	-1		.500	-2	0	0	/2	-0.3
1884	Was U	109	427	54	99	6	1	0		7			.232	.244	.251	52	-38		.869	15	103	83	*2-109	-1.7
Total	2	110	431	54	99	6	1	0		7			.230	.242	.248	51	-39		.866	13	102	82	2-110	-2.0

EVERS, HOOT Walter Arthur B 2.8.1921 St.Louis, MO D 1.25.1991 Houston, TX BR/TR 6-2/185# d9.16 Mil 1943-45 C1

Year	Tm Lg	G	AB	R	H	2B	3B	HR	RBI	BB-IB	HP	SO	AVG	OBP	SLG	AOPS	ABR	SB-CS	FA	FR	Rng	Thr	G at Pos	BFW
1941	Det A	1	4	0	0	0	0	0	0	0	0	2	.000	.000	.000	-91	-1	0-0	—	-0	0	0	/O(RF)	-0.1
1946	Det A	81	304	42	81	8	4	4	33	34	2	43	.266	.344	.359	91	-3	7-1	.975	-5	96	38	O-76(1-76-0)	-1.0
1947	Det A	126	460	67	136	24	5	10	67	45	6	49	.296	.366	.435	119	11	8-7	.978	3	103	123	*O-123(CF)	1.1
1948	Det A★	139	538	81	169	33	6	10	103	51	4	31	.314	.378	.454	117	13	3-4	.973	-4	99	70	*O-138(CF)	0.4
1949	Det A	132	432	68	131	21	6	7	72	70	2	38	.303	.403	.428	120	14	6-7	.994	8	108	133	*O-123(81-42-2)	1.3
1950	Det A★	143	526	100	170	35	**11**	21	103	71	4	40	.323	.408	.551	139	31	5-9	**.997**	3	96	129	*O-139(139-3-0)	1.9
1951	Det A	116	393	47	88	15	2	11	46	40	1	47	.224	.297	.356	76	-15	5-3	.976	-4	93	99	*O-108(66-45-1)	-2.4
1952	Det A	1	1	0	1	0	0	0	0	0	0	0	1.000	1.000	1.000	454	0	0-0	—	0			H	0.0
	Bos A	106	401	53	105	17	4	14	59	29	4	55	.262	.318	.429	99	-2	5-2	.974	1	98	114	*O-105(90-12-20)	-0.8
	Year	107	402	53	106	17	4	14	59	29	4	55	.264	.320	.430	100	-2	5-2	.974	1	98	114	*O-105(90-12-20)	-0.8
1953	Bos A	99	300	39	72	10	1	11	31	23	3	41	.240	.301	.390	81	-9	2-1	.988	-3	97	52	O-93(78-16-0)	-1.6
1954	Bos A	6	8	1	0	0	0	0	0	0	0	2	.000	.000	.000	-90	-2	0-0	1.000	-0	83	0	/O(LF)	-0.2
	NY N	12	11	1	1	0	0	1	3	0	0	6	.091	.091	.364	12	-2	0-0	1.000	0	149	0	/O-4(2-2-0)	-0.1
	Det A	30	60	5	11	4	0	0	5	5	1	8	.183	.258	.250	40	-5	1-0	1.000	1	108	99	O-24(17-2-6)	-0.5
1955	Bal A	60	185	21	44	10	1	6	30	19-0	0	28	.238	.307	.400	96	-2	2-1	.991	-2	103	28	O-55(10-16-31)	-0.5

Year	Tm Lg	G	AB	R	H	2B	3B	HR	RBI	BB-IB	HP	SO	AVG	OBP	SLG	AOPS	ABR	SB-CS	FA	FR	Rng	Thr	G at Pos	BFW
	Cle A	39	66	10	19	7	1	2	9	3-0	0	12	.288	.314	.515	117	1	0-1	1.000	1	105	96	O-25(15-9-2)	0.1
	Year	99	251	31	63	17	2	8	39	22-0	0	40	.251	.309	.430	101	-1	2-2	.993	-1	103	44	O-80(25-25-33)	-0.4
1956	Cle A	3	0	1	0	0	0	0	0	1-0	0	0	—	1.000	—	180	0	0-0	—	0			H	0.0
	Bal A	48	112	20	27	3	0	1	4	24-0	0	18	.241	.375	.295	85	-1	1-0	.985	0	109	46	O-36(3-2-34)	-0.2
	Year	51	112	21	27	3	0	1	4	25-0	0	18	.241	.380	.295	86	-1	1-0	.985	0	109	46	O-36(3-2-34)	-0.2
Total	12	1142	3801	556	1055	187	41	98	565	415-0	27	420	.278	.353	.426	106	28	45-36	.983	-1	100	94	*O-1051(503-486-97)	-2.6

EWELL, GEORGE George W. B 2.1851 Philadelphia, PA D 10.20.1910 Philadelphia, PA d6.26

Year	Tm Lg	G	AB	R	H	2B	3B	HR	RBI	BB-IB	HP	SO	AVG	OBP	SLG	AOPS	ABR	SB-CS	FA	FR	Rng	Thr	G at Pos	BFW
1871	Cle NA	1	3	0	0	0	0	0	0	0		0	.000	.000	.000	-99	-1	0-0	1.000	0	0	0	/O(RF)	0.0

EWING, REUBEN Reuben (born Reuben Cohen) B 11.30.1899 Odessa, Russia D 10.5.1970 W.Hartford, CT BR/TR 5-4.5/150# d6.21

Year	Tm Lg	G	AB	R	H	2B	3B	HR	RBI	BB-IB	HP	SO	AVG	OBP	SLG	AOPS	ABR	SB-CS	FA	FR	Rng	Thr	G at Pos	BFW
1921	StL N	3	1	0	0	0	0	0	0	0	0	1	.000	.000	.000	-99	0	0-0	1.000	0	258	0	/S	0.0

EWING, SAM Samuel James B 4.9.1949 Lewisburg, TN BL/TL 6-3/200# d9.11

Year	Tm Lg	G	AB	R	H	2B	3B	HR	RBI	BB-IB	HP	SO	AVG	OBP	SLG	AOPS	ABR	SB-CS	FA	FR	Rng	Thr	G at Pos	BFW
1973	Chi A	11	20	1	3	1	0	0	2	2-0	0	6	.150	.227	.200	20	-2	0-0	1.000	1	163	190	/1-4	-0.2
1976	Chi A	19	41	3	9	2	1	0	2	2-0	0	8	.220	.256	.317	67	-2	0-0	1.000	-0	0	0	D-12/1	-0.2
1977	Tor A	97	244	24	70	8	2	4	34	19-4	0	42	.287	.338	.385	95	-2	1-1	.957	-4	85	36	O-46(15-0-31),D-27/1-2	-0.9
1978	Tor A	40	56	3	10	0	0	2	9	5-2	0	9	.179	.242	.286	48	-4	0-0	1.000	0	118	0	/O-3(RF),D-9	-0.4
Total	4	167	361	31	92	11	3	6	47	28-6	0	65	.255	.308	.352	81	-10	1-1	.959	-3	86	35	/O-49(15-0-34),D-48,1-7	-1.7

EWING, BUCK William B 10.17.1859 Hoagland, OH D 10.20.1906 Cincinnati, OH BR/TR 5-10/188# d9.9 M7 HF1939 b-John I OF Total (9-LF 34-CF 193-RF)

Year	Tm Lg	G	AB	R	H	2B	3B	HR	RBI	BB-IB	HP	SO	AVG	OBP	SLG	AOPS	ABR	SB-CS	FA	FR	Rng	Thr	G at Pos	BFW
1880	Tro N	13	45	1	8	1	0	0	5	1		3	.178	.196	.200	33	-3		.864	-3			C-10/O-4(RF)	-0.6
1881	Tro N	67	272	40	68	14	7	0	25	7		8	.250	.269	.353	89	-4		.915	19			C-44,S-22/O-2(LF),3	1.6
1882	Tro N	74	328	67	89	16	11	2	29	10		15	.271	.293	.405	127	10		.887	14	119	171	3-44,C-25/2-4,O(CF)1P	2.4
1883	NY N	88	376	90	114	11	13	**10**	41	20		14	.303	.338	.481	147	20		.922	7			C-63,O-14(0-10-4),2-11/S-4,3	2.8
1884	NY N	94	382	90	106	15	**20**	3	41	28		22	.277	.327	.445	137	15		.933	14			*C-80,O-12(3-1-8)/S-3,3P	3.1
1885	NY N	81	342	81	104	15	12	6	63	13		17	.304	.330	.471	159	20		.918	6			C-63,O-14(1-3-10)/3-8,S1P	2.9
1886	NY N	73	275	59	85	11	7	4	31	16		17	.309	.347	.444	138	11	18	.921	7			C-50,O-23(2-18-3)/1-2	1.9
1887	NY N	77	318	83	97	17	13	6	44	30	3	33	.305	.370	.497	146	20	26	.863	-1	95	75	3-51,2-19/C-8	1.7
1888	†NY N	103	415	83	127	18	15	6	58	24	3	28	.306	.348	.465	159	27	53	.947	6			C-78,3-21/S-4,P-2	3.8
1889	†NY N	99	407	91	133	23	13	4	87	37	0	32	.327	.383	.477	139	20	34	.937	16			*C-97/P-3,O(LF)	3.7
1890	NY P	83	352	98	119	19	15	8	72	39	1	12	.338	.406	.545	141	17	36	**.949**	8	*100*	*111*	C-81/2PM	2.5
1891	NY N	14	49	8	17	2	1	0	18	5	0	5	.347	.407	.429	150	3	5	.881	-1	121	107	/2-8,C-6	0.2
1892	NY N	105	393	58	122	10	15	8	76	38	0	26	.310	.371	.473	157	25	42	.974	3	132	86	1-73,C-30/2-2	2.8
1893	Cle N	116	500	117	172	28	15	6	122	41	0	18	.344	.394	.496	128	17	47	.927	-1	73	77	*O-112(0-1-112)/2-5,1C	0.8
1894	Cle N	53	211	32	53	12	4	2	39	24	0	9	.251	.328	.374	66	-13	18	.912	-2	83	105	O-52(RF)/2	-1.3
1895	Cin N	105	434	90	138	24	13	5	94	30	1	22	.318	.363	.468	109	3	34	.976	8	139	110	*1-105,M	0.9
1896	Cin N	69	263	41	73	14	4	1	38	29	0	13	.278	.349	.373	85	-6	41	.980	5	133	108	1-69,M	-0.1
1897	Cin N	1	1	0	0	0	0	0	0	0	1		.000	.500	.000	36	0	0	.800	-0	0	0	/1M	0.0
Total	18	1315	5363	1129	1625	250	178	71	883	392	9	294	.303	.351	.456	130	182	354	.931	104	*17*	*22*	C-636,1-253,O-235R,3-127/2-51,SP	29.1

EWOLDT, ART Arthur Lee "Sheriff" B 1.8.1894 Paullina, IA D 12.8.1977 Des Moines, IA BR/TR 5-10/165# d9.17

Year	Tm Lg	G	AB	R	H	2B	3B	HR	RBI	BB-IB	HP	SO	AVG	OBP	SLG	AOPS	ABR	SB-CS	FA	FR	Rng	Thr	G at Pos	BFW
1919	Phi A	9	32	2	7	1	0	0	2	1	0	5	.219	.242	.250	38	-3	0	1.000	0	99	0	/3-9	-0.2

EZZELL, HOMER Homer Estell B 2.28.1896 Victoria, TX D 8.3.1976 San Antonio, TX BR/TR 5-10/158# d4.22

Year	Tm Lg	G	AB	R	H	2B	3B	HR	RBI	BB-IB	HP	SO	AVG	OBP	SLG	AOPS	ABR	SB-CS	FA	FR	Rng	Thr	G at Pos	BFW
1923	StL A	88	279	31	68	6	0	0	14	15	2	20	.244	.287	.265	44	-23	4-3	.961	3	98	100	3-73/2-8	-1.5
1924	Bos A	90	277	35	75	8	4	0	32	14	2	21	.271	.311	.329	65	-16	12-5	.984	8	125	68	3-64,S-21/C	-0.1
1925	Bos A	58	186	40	53	6	4	0	15	19	0	18	.285	.351	.360	81	-6	9-7	.916	-6	99	62	3-47/2-9	-0.9
Total	3	236	742	106	196	20	8	0	61	48	4	59	.264	.312	.313	61	-45	25-15	.957	5	106	80	3-184/S-21,2-17,C	-2.5

FAATZ, JAY Jayson S. B 10.24.1860 Weedsport, NY D 4.10.1923 Syracuse, NY BR/TR 6-4/196# d8.22 M1

Year	Tm Lg	G	AB	R	H	2B	3B	HR	RBI	BB-IB	HP	SO	AVG	OBP	SLG	AOPS	ABR	SB-CS	FA	FR	Rng	Thr	G at Pos	BFW
1884	Pit AA	29	112	18	27	2	3	0		1	4		.241	.274	.313	92	-1		.963	-1	64	108	1-29	-0.4
1888	Cle AA	120	470	73	124	10	2	0	51	12	21		.264	.312	.294	97	-1	64	**.989**	2	90	86	*1-120	-0.8
1889	Cle N	117	442	50	102	12	5	2	38	17	10	28	.231	.275	.294	60	-26	27	.981	6	120	105	*1-117	-2.7
1890	Buf P	32	111	18	21	0	2	1	16	9	8	5	.189	.297	.252	52	-7	2	.982	-2	48	89	1-32,M	-1.0
Total	4	298	1135	159	274	24	12	3	105	39	43	33	.241	.293	.292	77	-35	93	.982	5	95	96	1-298	-4.9

FABREGAS, JORGE Jorge B 3.13.1970 Miami, FL BL/TR 6-3/205# d4.24

Year	Tm Lg	G	AB	R	H	2B	3B	HR	RBI	BB-IB	HP	SO	AVG	OBP	SLG	AOPS	ABR	SB-CS	FA	FR	Rng	Thr	G at Pos	BFW
1994	Cal A	43	127	12	36	3	0	0	16	7-1	0	18	.283	.321	.307	62	-7	2-1	.987	-2	85	88	C-41	-0.6
1995	Cal A	73	227	24	56	10	0	1	22	17-0	0	28	.247	.298	.304	58	-14	0-2	.986	3	122	120	C-73	-0.7
1996	Cal A	90	254	18	73	6	0	2	26	17-3	0	27	.287	.326	.335	69	-12	0-1	.989	0	81	105	C-89/D	-0.7
1997	Ana A	21	38	2	3	1	0	0	3	3-0	0	3	.079	.146	.105	-33	-8	0-0	.989	1	196	54	C-21	-0.5
	Chi A	100	322	31	90	10	1	7	48	11-0	1	43	.280	.302	.382	81	-10	1-1	.988	2	94	124	C-92/1	-0.3
	Year	121	360	33	93	11	1	7	51	14-0	1	46	.258	.285	.353	68	-18	1-1	.988	3	107	115	*C-113/1	-0.8
1998	Ari N	50	151	8	30	4	0	1	15	13-1	1	26	.199	.263	.245	36	-14	0-0	.996	7	114	201	C-41	-0.5
	NY N	20	32	3	6	0	0	1	5	1-0	0	6	.188	.212	.281	29	-4	0-0	.971	3	57	147	C-12	0.0
	Year	70	183	11	36	4	0	2	20	14-1	1	32	.197	.255	.251	35	-18	0-0	.991	10	105	192	C-53	-0.5
1999	Fla N	82	223	20	46	10	2	3	21	26-6	2	27	.206	.289	.309	56	-15	0-0	.989	7	139	144	C-78	-0.4
	†Atl N	6	8	0	0	0	0	0	0	0-0	0	0	.000	.000	.000	-99	-2	0-0	1.000	2	0	0	/C-4,1	-0.1
	Year	88	231	20	46	10	2	3	21	26-6	2	27	.199	.280	.299	51	-18	0-0	.990	9	135	140	C-82/1	-0.5
2000	KC A	43	142	13	40	4	0	3	17	8-1	0	11	.282	.320	.373	72	-6	1-0	.992	2	142	104	C-39/D	-0.1
2001	Ana A	53	148	9	33	4	2	2	16	3-0	0	15	.223	.235	.318	44	-13	0-0	.990	6	105	120	C-53	-0.4
2002	Ana A	35	88	8	17	1	0	0	8	6-1	0	6	.193	.245	.205	21	-10	0-0	.994	-0	71	82	C-32	-0.8
	Mil N	30	67	5	11	3	0	3	14	2-0	0	7	.164	.178	.343	39	-7	0-0	.992	1	139	112	C-20	-0.5
Total	9	646	1827	153	441	56	5	23	211	114-13	4	217	.241	.284	.315	56	-122	4-5	.989	31	109	121	C-595/1-2,D-2	-5.6

FABRIQUE, BUNNY Albert La Verne B 12.23.1887 Clinton, MI D 1.10.1960 Ann Arbor, MI BB/TR 5-8.5/150# d10.4

Year	Tm Lg	G	AB	R	H	2B	3B	HR	RBI	BB-IB	HP	SO	AVG	OBP	SLG	AOPS	ABR	SB-CS	FA	FR	Rng	Thr	G at Pos	BFW
1916	Bro N	2	2	0	0	0	0	0	0	0	0	1	.000	.000	.000	-97	0	0	1.000	0	91	374	/S-2	0.0
1917	Bro N	25	88	8	18	3	0	1	3	8	0	9	.205	.271	.273	65	-3	0	.874	-5	85	80	S-21	-0.8
Total	2	27	90	8	18	3	0	1	3	8	0	10	.200	.265	.267	62	-3	0	.878	-5	85	89	/S-23	-0.8

FAEDO, LENNY Leonardo Lago B 5.13.1960 Tampa, FL BR/TR 6/170# d9.6

Year	Tm Lg	G	AB	R	H	2B	3B	HR	RBI	BB-IB	HP	SO	AVG	OBP	SLG	AOPS	ABR	SB-CS	FA	FR	Rng	Thr	G at Pos	BFW
1980	Min A	5	8	1	2	1	0	0	0	0-0	0	0	.250	.250	.375	64	0	0-0	.818	-3	49	0	/S-5	-0.3
1981	Min A	12	41	3	8	0	1	0	6	1-0	0	5	.195	.209	.244	30	-4	0-0	.971	2	107	113	S-12	-0.1
1982	Min A	90	255	16	62	8	0	3	22	16-0	1	22	.243	.288	.310	63	-13	1-0	.967	-10	87	103	S-88/D	-1.4
1983	Min A	51	173	16	48	7	0	1	18	4-1	0	19	.277	.291	.335	70	-7	0-0	.954	-17	85	66	S-51	-1.9
1984	Min A	16	52	6	13	1	0	1	6	4-0	0	3	.250	.304	.327	71	-2	0-0	.968	-5	86	45	S-15/D	-0.5
Total	5	174	529	42	133	17	1	5	52	25-1	1	49	.251	.284	.316	64	-26	1-0	.961	-32	87	85	S-171/D-2	-4.2

FAGIN, FRED Frederick H. B Cincinnati, OH d6.25

Year	Tm Lg	G	AB	R	H	2B	3B	HR	RBI	BB-IB	HP	SO	AVG	OBP	SLG	AOPS	ABR	SB-CS	FA	FR	Rng	Thr	G at Pos	BFW
1895	StL N	1	3	0	1	0	0	0	2	0	0	0	.333	.333	.333	73	0	0	.636	-1	*74*	*172*	/C	-0.1

FAHEY, FRANK Francis Raymond B 1.22.1896 Milford, MA D 3.19.1954 Boston, MA BB/TR 6-1/190# d4.25 ▲

Year	Tm Lg	G	AB	R	H	2B	3B	HR	RBI	BB-IB	HP	SO	AVG	OBP	SLG	AOPS	ABR	SB-CS	FA	FR	Rng	Thr	G at Pos	BFW
1918	Phi A	10	17	2	3	1	0	0	1	0	0	3	.176	.176	.235	24	-2	0	1.000	-1	81	0	/O-5(4-1-0),P-3	-0.2

FAHEY, HOWARD Howard Simpson "Cap" or "Kid" B 6.24.1892 Medford, MA D 10.24.1971 Clearwater, FL BR/TR 5-7.5/145# d7.23

Year	Tm Lg	G	AB	R	H	2B	3B	HR	RBI	BB-IB	HP	SO	AVG	OBP	SLG	AOPS	ABR	SB-CS	FA	FR	Rng	Thr	G at Pos	BFW
1912	Phi A	5	8	0	0	0	0	0	0	0	0		.000	.000	.000	-99	-2	0	1.000	-1	0	1059	/3-2,2S	-0.3

FAHEY, BILL William Roger B 6.14.1950 Detroit, MI BL/TR 6/200# d9.26 C6

Year	Tm Lg	G	AB	R	H	2B	3B	HR	RBI	BB-IB	HP	SO	AVG	OBP	SLG	AOPS	ABR	SB-CS	FA	FR	Rng	Thr	G at Pos	BFW
1971	Was A	2	8	0	0	0	0	0	0	0-0	0	0	.000	.000	.000	-99	-2	0-0	.909	-0	85	186	/C-2	-0.3
1972	Tex A	39	119	8	20	2	0	1	10	12-0	1	23	.168	.250	.210	40	-9	4-0	.992	5	75	166	C-39	-0.2
1974	Tex A	6	16	1	4	0	0	0	0	0-0	0	1	.250	.250	.250	45	-1	0-0	1.000	-1	0	59	/C-6	-0.2
1975	Tex A	21	37	3	11	1	1	0	3	1-0	0	10	.297	.316	.378	96	0	0-0	.983	-2	71	64	C-21	-0.2
1976	Tex A	38	80	12	20	2	0	1	9	11-0	1	6	.250	.348	.313	92	0	1-0	.993	1	99	94	C-38	0.2
1977	Tex A	37	68	3	15	4	0	0	5	1-0	0	8	.221	.232	.279	38	-6	0-0	1.000	-6	72	47	C-34	-1.0
1979	SD N	73	209	14	60	8	1	3	19	21-5	0	17	.287	.348	.378	106	2	1-1	.994	-6	110	100	C-68	-0.1
1980	SD N	93	241	18	62	4	0	1	22	21-6	0	16	.257	.314	.286	74	-9	2-0	.977	-7	92	102	C-85	-1.3
1981	Det A	27	67	5	17	2	0	1	9	2-0	0	4	.254	.271	.328	71	-3	0-1	.981	1	93	95	C-27	-0.2

Year	Tm Lg	G	AB	R	H	2B	3B	HR	RBI	BB-IB	HP	SO	AVG	OBP	SLG	AOPS	ABR	SB-CS	FA	FR	Rng	Thr	G at Pos	BFW
1982	Det A	28	67	7	10	2	0	0	4	0-0	0	5	.149	.147	.179	-10	-10	1-0	1.000	2	103	158	C-28	-0.7
1983	Det A	19	22	4	6	1	0	0	2	5-1	0	3	.273	.407	.318	106	1	0-0	1.000	-3	630	0	C-18	-0.2
Total	11	383	934	75	225	26	2	7	83	74-12	2	93	.241	.296	.296	69	-37	9-2	.989	-15	109	103	C-366	-4.2
FAIN, FERRIS Ferris Roy "Burrhead" B 5.29.1921 San Antonio, TX D 10.18.2001 Georgetown, CA BL/TL 5-11/186# d4.15																								
1947	Phi A	136	461	70	134	28	6	7	71	95	2	34	.291	.414	.423	130	24	4-5	.985	-1	104	104	*1-132	1.9
1948	Phi A	145	520	81	146	27	6	7	88	113	3	37	.281	.412	.396	115	18	10-5	.989	8	**122**	105	*1-145	2.0
1949	Phi A	150	525	81	138	21	5	3	78	136	0	51	.263	.415	.339	104	12	8-1	.984	5	115	119	*1-150	1.3
1950	Phi A★	151	522	83	147	25	4	10	83	133	3	26	.282	.430	.402	116	22	8-5	.987	11	**132**	113	*1-151	2.5
1951	Phi A★	117	425	63	146	30	3	6	57	80	3	20	**.344**	.451	.471	146	33	0-3	.990	16	**159**	**119**	*1-108,O-11(1-0-10)	**4.3**
1952	Phi A☆	145	538	82	176	**43**	3	2	59	105	1	26	**.327**	**.438**	.429	133	32	3-5	.984	18	**148**	92	*1-144	**4.5**
1953	Chi A★	128	446	73	114	18	2	6	52	108	4	28	.256	.405	.345	101	8	3-2	.989	9	125	86	*1-127	0.9
1954	Chi A✱	65	235	30	71	10	1	5	51	40	1	14	.302	.399	.417	121	9	5-1	.987	-4	75	105	1-64	0.2
1955	Det A	58	140	23	37	8	0	2	23	52-2	0	12	.264	.459	.364	128	11	2-1	.988	-0	104	113	1-44	0.8
	Cle A	56	118	9	30	3	0	0	8	42-1	1	13	.254	.451	.280	97	3	3-0	.992	3	120	91	1-51	0.4
	Year	114	258	32	67	11	0	2	31	94-3	1	25	.260	.455	.326	113	14	5-1	.990	3	112	102	1-95	1.2
Total	9	1151	3930	595	1139	213	30	48	570	904-3	18	261	.290	.424	.396	120	172	46-28	.987	63	124	105	*1-1116/O-11(1-0-10)	18.8
FAIR, GEORGE George T. B 1.14.1856 Boston, MA D 2.12.1939 Roslindale, MA 5-7.5/140# d7.29																								
1876	NY N	1	4	0	0	0	0	0	0	0		0	.000	.000	.000	-99	-1		.750	-0	105	187	/2	-0.1
FAIREY, JIM James Burke B 9.22.1944 Orangeburg, SC BL/TL 5-10/190# d4.14																								
1968	LA N	99	156	17	31	3	3	1	10	9-0	0	32	.199	.241	.276	60	-9	1-1	.944	2	111	124	O-63(40-2-23)	-1.1
1969	Mon N	20	49	6	14	1	0	1	6	1-0	0	7	.286	.300	.367	86	-1	0-2	.913	-1	90	163	O-13(1-12-0)	-0.3
1970	Mon N	92	211	35	51	9	3	3	25	14-4	2	38	.242	.293	.355	74	-9	1-3	.978	-2	95	34	O-59(33-30-4)	-1.4
1971	Mon N	92	200	19	49	8	1	1	19	12-5	0	23	.245	.285	.310	69	-8	3-3	.968	3	96	231	O-58(56-2-1)	-0.9
1972	Mon N	86	141	9	33	7	0	1	15	10-2	0	21	.234	.285	.305	66	-6	1-3	.932	-2	85	56	O-37(20-1-18)	-1.2
1973	LA N	10	9	0	2	0	0	0	0	1-0	0	1	.222	.300	.222	49	-1	0-0	—	0			H	-0.1
Total	6	399	766	86	180	28	7	7	75	47-11	2	122	.235	.279	.317	69	-34	6-12	.957	-1	97	121	O-230(150-47-46)	-5.0
FAIRLY, RON Ronald Ray B 7.12.1938 Macon, GA BL/TL 5-10/181# d9.9 OF Total (212-LF 120-CF 727-RF)																								
1958	LA N	15	53	6	15	1	0	2	8	6-0	0	7	.283	.350	.415	100	0	0-0	.971	-2	94	0	O-15(4-11-1)	-0.2
1959	†LA N	118	244	27	58	12	1	4	23	31-2	1	29	.238	.324	.344	73	-8	0-4	.963	-1	84	190	O-88(7-23-62)	-1.4
1960	LA N	14	37	6	4	0	3	1	3	7-0	0	12	.108	.250	.351	59	-2	0-0	1.000	-0	87	122	O-13(5-0-8)	-0.3
1961	LA N	111	245	42	79	15	2	10	48	48-0	1	22	.322	.434	.522	140	17	0-0	.989	2	100	184	O-71(6-15-53),1-23	1.5
1962	LA N	147	460	80	128	15	7	14	71	75-6	3	59	.278	.379	.433	126	19	1-1	.989	-12	56	77	*1-120,O-48(4-5-42)	-0.1
1963	†LA N	152	490	62	133	21	0	12	77	58-7	1	69	.271	.347	.388	120	14	5-2	**.995**	-5	71	100	*1-119,O-45(16-22-10)	0.2
1964	LA N	150	454	62	116	19	5	10	74	65-6	2	59	.256	.349	.385	116	11	4-0	.987	0	100	96	*1-141	0.5
1965	†LA N	158	555	73	152	28	1	9	70	76-11	3	72	.274	.361	.377	117	16	2-0	.982	-8	90	68	*O-148(0-17-133),1-13	-0.2
1966	†LA N	117	351	53	101	20	0	14	61	52-4	2	38	.288	.380	.464	146	24	3-2	.974	-6	86	41	O-98(0-6-95),1-25	1.3
1967	LA N	153	486	45	107	19	0	10	55	54-9	1	51	.220	.295	.321	85	-9	1-4	.986	4	94	147	O-97(1-0-97),1-68	-1.7
1968	LA N	141	441	32	103	15	1	4	43	41-10	4	61	.234	.301	.299	89	-6	0-2	.989	3	94	169	*O-105(RF),1-36	-1.4
1969	LA N	30	64	3	14	3	2	0	8	9-1	0	6	.219	.315	.328	86	-1	0-0	.981	1	137	65	1-12,O-10(1-0-10)	-0.2
	Mon N	70	253	35	73	13	4	12	39	28-2	0	22	.289	.358	.514	142	13	1-0	.991	1	117	121	1-52,O-21(3-18-0)	1.0
	Year	100	317	38	87	16	6	12	47	37-3	0	28	.274	.349	.476	132	13	1-0	.989	1	121	111	1-64,O-31(4-18-10)	0.8
1970	Mon N	119	385	54	111	19	0	15	61	72-9	4	64	.288	.402	.455	130	20	10-2	.995	5	114	**117**	*1-118/O-4(2-2-0)	1.7
1971	Mon N	146	447	58	115	23	0	13	71	81-10	5	65	.257	.373	.396	119	15	1-3	.992	4	115	97	*1-135,O-10(10-1-0)	0.9
1972	Mon N	140	446	51	124	15	1	17	68	46-7	3	45	.278	.348	.430	118	11	3-4	.985	5	104	165	O-70(RF),1-68	0.7
1973	Mon N★	142	413	70	123	13	1	17	49	86-11	3	33	.298	.422	.458	139	27	2-2	.974	-4	84	56	*O-121(LF)/1-5	1.7
1974	Mon N	101	282	35	69	9	1	12	43	57-6	1	28	.245	.372	.411	113	7	2-1	.989	0	99	85	1-67,O-20(19-0-1)	0.1
1975	StL N	107	229	32	69	13	2	7	37	45-9	3	22	.301	.421	.467	142	16	0-1	.980	1	114	92	1-56,O-20(4-0-16)	1.2
1976	StL N	73	110	13	29	4	0	0	21	23-3	0	12	.264	.385	.300	97	1	0-0	.995	3	159	109	1-27	0.3
	Oak A	15	46	9	11	1	0	3	10	9-3	0	12	.239	.364	.457	145	3	0-0	1.000	0	97	88	1-15	0.2
1977	Tor A★	132	458	60	128	24	2	19	64	58-11	2	58	.279	.362	.465	122	15	0-4	.986	4	116	84	D-58,1-40,O-33(9-0-24)	1.2
1978	Cal A	91	235	23	51	5	0	10	40	25-2	1	31	.217	.289	.366	88	-4	0-1	.998	-3	72	91	1-78/D-5	-1.2
Total	21	2442	7184	931	1913	307	33	215	1044	1052-129	40	877	.266	.360	.408	117	199	35-33	.991	-8	98	97	*1-1218,*O-1037R/D-63	5.8
FALCH, ANTON Anton C. B 12.4.1860 Milwaukee, WI D 3.31.1936 Wauwatosa, WI 6-6/220# d9.30																								
1884	Mil U	5	18	0	2	0	0	0		0			.111	.111	.111	-60	-4		.600	-0	101	0	/O-3(LF),C-2	-0.4
FALK, BIBB Bibb August "Jockey" B 1.27.1899 Austin, TX D 6.8.1989 Austin, TX BL/TL 6/175# d9.17 M1 C2 b-Chet																								
1920	Chi A	7	17	1	5	1	1	0	2	0	0	5	.294	.294	.471	100	0	0-0	1.000	-0	93	0	/O-4(RF)	-0.1
1921	Chi A	152	585	62	167	31	11	5	82	37	2	69	.285	.330	.402	87	-14	4-4	.958	-13	89	48	*O-149(148-1-0)	-3.7
1922	Chi A	131	483	58	144	27	1	12	79	27	0	55	.298	.335	.433	99	-2	2-6	.963	-9	91	62	*O-129(126-2-1)	-2.2
1923	Chi A	87	274	44	84	18	6	5	38	25	1	12	.307	.367	.471	121	7	5-5	.951	-3	97	69	O-80(LF)	-0.2
1924	Chi A	138	526	77	185	37	8	6	99	47	1	21	.352	.406	.487	134	26	6-6	.970	8	96	**178**	*O-134(LF)	2.1
1925	Chi A	**154**	602	80	181	35	9	4	99	51	2	25	.301	.357	.409	99	-2	4-5	.959	-6	90	102	*O-153(LF)	-1.9
1926	Chi A	**155**	566	86	195	43	4	8	108	66	2	22	.345	.415	.477	137	33	9-10	**.992**	8	107	109	*O-155(LF)	2.7
1927	Chi A	145	535	76	175	35	6	9	83	52	4	19	.327	.391	.465	125	20	5-7	.978	**18**	**115**	146	*O-145(LF)	2.4
1928	Chi A	98	286	42	83	18	4	1	37	25	0	16	.290	.347	.392	95	-2	5-1	.972	2	100	125	O-78(LF)	-0.5
1929	Cle A	125	426	65	133	30	7	13	93	42	0	14	.312	.374	.507	120	12	4-4	.943	-4	89	123	*O-120(61-0-61)	-0.2
1930	Cle A	82	191	34	62	12	1	4	36	23	0	8	.325	.397	.461	113	4	2-0	.967	0	98	111	O-42(25-0-18)	0.2
1931	Cle A	79	161	30	49	13	1	2	28	17	0	13	.304	.371	.435	105	2	1-1	.949	-2	95	36	O-33(2-0-31)	-0.2
Total	12	1353	4652	655	1463	300	59	69	784	412	12	279	.314	.372	.449	113	84	47-49	.967	-1	97	106	*O-1222(1107-3-115)	-1.6
FALLON, CHARLIE Charles Augustus B 3.7.1881 New York, NY D 6.10.1960 Kings Park, NY BR/TR 5-6/?# d6.30																								
1905	NY A	1	0	0	0	0	0	0	0	0	0		—	—	—	—	0	0	—	0			R	0.0
FALLON, GEORGE George Decatur "Flash" B 7.8.1914 Jersey City, NJ D 10.25.1994 Lake Worth, FL BR/TR 5-9/155# d9.27 Mil 1945																								
1937	Bro N	4	8	0	2	1	0	0	0	1	0	0	.250	.333	.375	91	0	0	.895	-0	87	56	/2-4	0.0
1943	StL N	36	78	6	18	1	0	0	5	2	1	9	.231	.259	.244	44	-6	0	.968	9	122	133	2-36	0.4
1944	†StL N	69	141	16	28	6	0	1	9	16	1	11	.199	.285	.262	54	-8	1	.973	1	86	104	2-38,S-24/3-6	-0.5
1945	StL N	24	55	4	13	2	1	0	7	6	0	6	.236	.311	.309	71	-2	1	.948	-3	84	108	S-20/2-4	-0.4
Total	4	133	282	26	61	10	1	1	21	25	2	26	.216	.285	.270	56	-16	2	.966	6	103	112	/2-82,S-44,3-6	-0.5
FALSEY, PETE Peter James B 4.24.1891 New Haven, CT D 5.23.1976 Los Angeles, CA BL/TL 5-6.5/132# d7.16																								
1914	Pit N	3	1	0	0	0	0	0	0	0	0	1	.000	.000	.000	-99	0	0	—	0			H	0.0
FANEYTE, RIKKERT Rikkert B 5.31.1969 Amsterdam, Netherlands BR/TR 6-1/170# d8.29																								
1993	SF N	7	15	2	2	0	0	0	0	2-0	0	4	.133	.235	.133	2	-2	0-0	1.000	0	112	0	/O-6(1-5-0)	-0.2
1994	SF N	19	26	1	3	3	0	0	4	3-0	0	11	.115	.207	.231	15	-3	0-0	.900	0	122	0	/O-6(0-2-4)	-0.3
1995	SF N	46	86	7	17	4	1	0	4	11-0	0	27	.198	.289	.267	49	-6	1-0	.981	1	97	239	O-34(3-22-11)	-0.5
1996	Tex A	8	5	0	1	0	0	0	1	0-0	0	0	.200	.200	.200	1	-1	0-0	1.000	1	182	0	/O-6(2-4-0),D-2	0.0
Total	4	80	132	10	23	7	1	0	9	16-0	0	42	.174	.264	.242	35	-12	1-0	.976	2	108	167	/O-52(6-33-15),D-2	-1.0
FANNING, JIM William James B 9.14.1927 Chicago, IL BR/TR 5-11/180# d9.11 M3 C1																								
1954	Chi N	11	38	2	7	0	0	0	1	1	0	7	.184	.205	.184	2	-6	0-0	1.000	-1	_51_	_111_	C-11	-0.7
1955	Chi N	5	10	0	0	0	0	0	0	1-0	0	2	.000	.091	.000	-73	-3	0-0	1.000	1	_137_	_97_	/C-5	-0.1
1956	Chi N	1	4	0	1	0	0	0	0	0-0	0	0	.250	.250	.250	36	0	0-0	.800	0	_0_	_398_	/C	0.0
1957	Chi N	47	89	3	16	2	0	0	4	4-1	1	17	.180	.223	.202	16	-11	0-0	.981	1	_85_	_191_	C-35	-0.9
Total	4	64	141	5	24	2	0	0	5	6-1	1	26	.170	.209	.184	6	-20	0-0	.979	1	_80_	_167_	/C-52	-1.7
FANZONE, CARMEN Carmen Ronald B 8.30.1943 Detroit, MI BR/TR 6/200# d7.21																								
1970	Bos A	10	15	0	3	1	0	0	3	2-0	1	2	.200	.316	.267	63	-1	0-0	.750	-0	109	134	/3-5	-0.1
1971	Chi N	12	43	5	8	2	0	2	5	2-0	0	7	.186	.222	.372	57	-3	0-0	1.000	0	84	0	/O-6(5-0-1),3-3,1-2	-0.3
1972	Chi N	86	222	26	50	11	0	8	42	35-6	3	45	.225	.333	.383	95	0	2-3	.923	2	112	137	3-36,1-21,2-13/SO(LF)	0.0
1973	Chi N	64	150	22	41	7	0	6	22	20-1	0	38	.273	.357	.440	112	3	1-2	.922	-2	89	0	3-25,1-24/O-6(LF)	-0.1

Year	Tm Lg	G	AB	R	H	2B	3B	HR	RBI	BB-IB	HP	SO	AVG	OBP	SLG	AOPS	ABR	SB-CS	FA	FR	Rng	Thr	G at Pos	BFW
1974	Chi N	65	158	13	30	6	0	4	22	15-1	2	27	.190	.264	.304	57	-9	0-1	.885	-0	99	127	3-35,2-10/1-7,O(LF)	-1.1
Total	5	237	588	66	132	27	0	20	94	74-8	6	119	.224	.313	.372	86	-10	3-6	.896	0	104	101	3-104/1-54,2-23,O-14(13-0-1),S	-1.6
FARIES, PAUL Paul Tyrrell B 2.20.1965 Berkeley, CA BR/TR 5-10/165# d9.6																								
1990	SD N	14	37	4	7	1	0	0	2	4-0	1	7	.189	.279	.216	40	-3	0-1	1.000	2	94	83	/2-7,S-4,3	-0.1
1991	SD N	57	130	13	23	3	1	0	7	14-0	1	21	.177	.262	.215	35	-11	3-1	.988	6	115	129	2-36,3-12/S-8	-0.4
1992	SD N	10	11	3	5	1	0	0	1	1-0	0	2	.455	.500	.545	193	1	0-0	1.000	-1	94	115	/2-4,3-2,S	0.0
1993	SF N	15	36	6	8	2	1	0	4	1-0	0	4	.222	.237	.333	54	-3	2-0	1.000	-1	107	94	/2-7,S-4,3	-0.3
Total	4	96	214	26	43	7	2	0	14	20-0	2	34	.201	.273	.252	47	-16	5-2	.992	6	110	116	/2-54,S-17,3-16	-0.8
FARISS, MONTY Monty Ted B 10.13.1967 Cordell, OK BR/TR 6-4/180# d9.6																								
1991	Tex A	19	31	6	8	1	0	1	6	7-0	0	11	.258	.395	.387	119	1	0-0	1.000	3	190	0	/O-8(LF),2-4,D-4	0.4
1992	Tex A	67	166	13	36	7	1	3	21	17-0	2	51	.217	.297	.325	77	-5	0-2	1.000	-7	73	0	O-49(28-10-12),2-17/1D	-1.4
1993	Fla N	18	29	3	5	2	1	0	2	5-0	0	13	.172	.294	.310	59	-2	0-0	1.000	-0	110	0	/O-8(1-0-7)	-0.2
Total	3	104	226	22	49	10	2	4	29	29-0	2	75	.217	.311	.332	81	-6	0-2	1.000	-4	91	0	/O-65(37-10-19),2-21,D-8,1	-1.2
FARLEY, BOB Robert Jacob B 11.15.1937 Watsontown, PA BL/TL 6-2/200# d4.15																								
1961	SF N	13	20	3	2	0	0	0	1	3-0	0	5	.100	.217	.100	-13	-3	0-0	1.000	-0	83	0	/O-3(LF),1	-0.4
1962	Chi A	35	53	7	10	1	1	1	4	13-0	0	13	.189	.348	.302	77	-1	0-1	.989	-1	70	102	1-14	-0.3
	Det A	36	50	9	8	2	0	1	4	14-0	0	10	.160	.338	.260	63	-2	0-0	.857	-2	73	0	O-11(RF)/1-6	-0.4
	Year	71	103	16	18	3	1	2	8	27-0	0	23	.175	.344	.282	70	-3	0-1	.974	-2	70	98	1-20,O-11(RF)	-0.7
Total	2	84	123	19	20	3	1	2	9	30-0	0	28	.163	.325	.252	58	-6	0-1	.975	-3	67	103	/1-21,O-14(3-0-11)	-1.1
FARLEY, TOM Thomas T. B Chicago, IL d6.24																								
1884	Was AA	14	52	5	11	4	0	0		1	1		.212	.241	.288	81	-1		.867	1	74	194	O-14(LF)	0.0
FARMER, ALEX Alexander Johnson B 5.9.1880 New York, NY D 3.5.1920 New York, NY BR/TR 6/175# d9.1																								
1908	Bro N	12	30	1	5	1	0	0	2	1	0		.167	.194	.200	27	-3	0	.966	-0	*85*	*58*	C-11	-0.2
FARMER, JACK Floyd Haskell B 7.14.1892 Granville, TN D 5.21.1970 Columbia, LA BR/TR 6/180# d7.8																								
1916	Pit N	55	166	10	45	6	4	0	14	7	2	24	.271	.309	.355	103	0	1	.929	-9	88	50	2-31,O-15(8-0-7)/S-4,3	-1.1
1918	Cle A	7	9	1	2	0	0	0	1	0	1	3	.222	.300	.222	53	0	2	.429	-1	63	0	/O-3(2-0-1)	-0.2
Total	2	62	175	11	47	6	4	0	15	7	3	27	.269	.308	.349	100	0	3	.929	-11	88	50	/2-31,O-18(10-0-8),S-4,3	-1.3
FARMER, BILL William B 12.27.1870 BR/TR 5-11.5/187# d5.1																								
1888	Pit N	2	4	0	0	0	0	0	0	0	0	1	.000	.000	.000	-99	-1	0	.667	-0			/CO(RF)	-0.1
	Phi AA	3	12	0	2	0	0	0	1	0	0		.167	.167	.167	7	-1	0	.960	0			/C-3	-0.1
Total	1	5	16	0	2	0	0	0	1	0	0	1	.125	.125	.125	-20	-2	0	.903	0			/C-4,O(RF)	-0.2
FARRAR, SID Sidney Douglas B 8.10.1859 Paris Hill, ME D 5.7.1935 New York, NY TR 5-10/185# d5.1																								
1883	Phi N	**99**	377	41	88	19	8	0	29	4		37	.233	.241	.326	77	-9		.965	-0	96	69	*1-99	-1.6
1884	Phi N	111	428	62	105	16	6	1	45	9		25	.245	.261	.318	85	-7		.966	5	**131**	74	*1-111	-1.1
1885	Phi N	**111**	420	49	103	20	3	3	36	28		34	.245	.292	.329	103	2		.975	2	108	94	*1-111	-0.5
1886	Phi N	118	439	55	109	19	7	5	50	16		47	.248	.275	.358	90	-6	10	**.980**	3	99	75	*1-118	-1.3
1887	Phi N	116	443	83	125	20	9	4	72	42	10	29	.282	.358	.395	103	2	24	.977	3	108	90	*1-116	-0.5
1888	Phi N	**131**	508	53	124	24	7	1	53	31	**13**	38	.244	.304	.325	95	-2	21	.979	3	110	94	*1-131	-1.1
1889	Phi N	**130**	477	70	128	22	2	3	58	52	6	36	.268	.348	.342	86	-10	28	.978	-5	72	87	*1-130	-2.3
1890	Phi P	127	481	84	123	17	11	1	69	51	5	23	.256	.333	.343	79	-15	9	.973	-2	93	106	*1-127	-2.3
Total	8	943	3573	497	905	157	53	18	412	233	34	269	.253	.305	.342	90	-45	92	.974	8	102	87	1-943	-10.7
FARRELL, DUKE Charles Andrew B 8.31.1866 Oakdale, MA D 2.15.1925 Boston, MA BB/TR 6-1/208# d4.21 OF Total (48-LF 22-CF 39-RF)																								
1888	Chi N	64	241	34	56	6	3	3	19	4	0	41	.232	.245	.320	73	-8	8	.874	-8			C-33,O-31(10-2-19)/1	-1.4
1889	Chi N	101	407	66	107	19	7	11	75	41	1	21	.263	.332	.425	106	0	13	.910	-2			C-76,O-25(7-15-3)	0.4
1890	Chi P	117	451	79	131	21	12	2	84	42	1	28	.290	.352	.404	98	-3	8	.929	**30**	***115***	***127***	C-90,1-22,O-10(0-2-8)	2.6
1891	Bos AA	122	473	108	143	19	13	**12**	**110**	59	4	48	.302	.384	.474	148	28	21	.918	21	115	85	3-66,C-37,O-23(20-0-3)/1-4	**4.4**
1892	Pit N	**152**	605	96	130	10	13	8	77	46	5	53	.215	.276	.314	78	-19	20	.879	-9	96	97	*3-133,O-20(11-3-6)	-2.6
1893	Was N	124	511	84	144	13	13	4	75	47	5	12	.282	.348	.382	96	-4	11	.923	2	*77*	***161***	C-81,3-41/1-3	0.5
1894	†NY N	116	404	50	116	20	12	5	70	38	3	15	.287	.353	.433	89	-9	9	.925	26	*107*	***130***	*C-105/3-5,1-4	2.0
1895	NY N	90	312	38	90	16	9	1	58	38	3	18	.288	.371	.407	103	2	11	.941	2	*96*	*112*	C-62,3-24/1-2	0.8
1896	NY N	58	191	23	54	7	3	1	37	19	1	7	.283	.351	.366	92	-2	2	.954	-5	*94*	*107*	C-34,S-13/3-7	-0.3
	Was N	37	130	18	39	7	3	1	30	7	2	3	.300	.345	.423	102	0	2	1.000	-0	*88*	*130*	C-18,3-14	0.1
	Year	95	321	41	93	14	6	2	67	26	3	10	.290	.349	.389	96	-2	4	.970	-5	*92*	*115*	C-52,3-21,S-13	-0.2
1897	Was N	78	261	41	84	9	6	0	53	17	1		.322	.366	.402	103	1	8	.945	3	*80*	*149*	C-63/1	0.8
1898	Was N	99	338	47	106	12	6	1	53	34	4		.314	.383	.393	123	11	12	.929	-13	*65*	*145*	C-61,1-28	0.3
1899	Was N	5	12	2	4	1	0	0	1	2	0		.333	.429	.417	134	1	1	1.000	-0	*74*	*142*	/C-4	0.1
	Bro N	80	254	40	76	10	7	2	55	35	7		.299	.399	.417	121	9	6	.948	6	*91*	*115*	C-78	1.9
	Year	85	266	42	80	11	7	2	56	37	7		.301	.400	.417	122	10	7	.949	5	*90*	*116*	C-82	2.0
1900	†Bro N	76	273	33	75	11	5	0	39	11	3		.275	.310	.352	78	-9	3	.944	-4	*94*	*97*	C-74	-0.6
1901	Bro N	80	284	38	84	10	6	1	31	7	3		.296	.320	.384	101	-1	7	.979	-1	*80*	*129*	C-59,1-17	0.4
1902	Bro N	74	264	14	64	5	2	0	24	12	2		.242	.281	.277	71	-9	6	.976	-1	*84*	*124*	C-49,1-24	-0.6
1903	†Bos A	17	52	5	21	5	1	0	8	5	1		.404	.466	.538	190	6	1	.960	1	*118*	*114*	C-17	0.9
1904	Bos A	68	198	11	42	9	2	0	15	15	4		.212	.281	.278	73	-5	1	.958	-1	*128*	*91*	C-56	-0.1
1905	Bos A	7	21	2	6	1	0	0	2	1	0		.286	.318	.333	105	0	0	1.000	1	*146*	*119*	/C-7	0.2
Total	18	1565	5682	829	1572	211	123	52	916	480	50	246	.277	.338	.385	100	-11	150	.938	49	*85*	*112*	*C-1004,3-290,O-109L,1-106/S-13	9.8
FARRELL, DOC Edward Stephen B 12.26.1901 Johnson City, NY D 12.20.1966 Livingston, NJ BR/TR 5-8/160# d6.15																								
1925	NY N	27	56	6	12	1	0	0	4	4	0	6	.214	.267	.232	30	-6	0-1	.900	1	130	50	S-13/3-7,2	-0.4
1926	NY N	67	171	19	49	10	1	2	23	12	2	17	.287	.341	.392	98	0	4	.950	-8	86	86	S-53/2-3	-0.4
1927	NY N	42	142	13	55	10	1	3	34	12	2	11	.387	.442	.535	161	13	0	.919	-0	105	93	S-36/3-2	1.6
	Bos N	110	424	44	124	13	2	1	58	14	0	21	.292	.315	.340	82	-12	4	.931	-8	103	70	S-57,2-40,3-18	-1.2
	Year	152	566	57	179	23	3	4	92	26	2	32	.316	.348	.389	103	1	4	.926	-8	104	79	S-93,2-40,3-20	0.4
1928	Bos N	134	483	36	104	14	2	3	43	26	5	26	.215	.263	.271	42	-43	3	.933	-17	96	79	*S-132/2	-4.5
1929	Bos N	5	8	0	1	0	0	0	2	0	0	1	.125	.125	.125	-39	-2	0	—	-0	0	0	/2S	-0.2
	NY N	63	178	18	38	6	0	0	16	9	0	17	.213	.251	.247	24	-22	2	.925	2	109	193	3-28,2-25/S-4	-1.5
	Year	68	186	18	39	6	0	0	18	9	0	18	.210	.246	.242	22	-23	2	.925	2	109	193	3-28,2-26/S-5	-1.7
1930	StL N	23	61	3	13	1	1	0	6	4	0	2	.213	.262	.262	26	-8	1	.944	1	88	118	S-15/2-6,1	-0.5
	Chi N	46	113	21	33	6	0	1	16	9	0	5	.292	.344	.372	73	-5	0	.937	-1	101	87	S-38/2	-0.2
	Year	69	174	24	46	7	1	1	22	13	0	7	.264	.316	.333	56	-12	1	.938	-1	97	95	S-53/2-7,1	-0.7
1932	NY A	26	63	4	11	1	1	0	4	2	1	8	.175	.212	.222	13	-9	0-0	.963	-1	90	120	2-16/S-5,1-2,3	-0.8
1933	NY A	44	93	16	25	0	0	0	6	16	0	6	.269	.376	.269	78	-2	0-0	.947	-4	77	94	S-22,2-20	-0.4
1935	Bos A	4	7	1	2	1	0	0	1	1	0	0	.286	.375	.429	101	0	0-0	.917	-1	81	78	/2-4	0.0
Total	9	591	1799	181	467	63	8	10	213	109	10	120	.260	.306	.320	66	-96	14-1	.934	-36	97	82	S-376,2-118/3-56,1-3	-8.5
FARRELL, JACK John "Hartford Jack" B 1.2.1856 Hartford, CT D 11.15.1916 Hartford, CT d10.27																								
1874	Har NA	3	13	3	5	0	0	0	0	1		0	.385	.429	.385	155	1	0-0	1.000	-0	0	0	/O-3(CF)	0.1
FARRELL, JACK John A. "Moose" B 7.5.1857 Newark, NJ D 2.10.1914 Cedar Grove, NJ BR/TR 5-9/165# d5.1 M1																								
1879	Syr N	54	241	40	73	6	2	1	21	3		13	.303	.311	.357	135	9		.870	-19	93	65	2-54	-0.7
	Pro N	12	51	5	13	2	0	0	5	0		0	.255	.255	.294	82	-1		.915	5	117	169	2-12	0.4
	Year	66	292	45	86	8	2	1	26	3		13	.295	.302	.346	125	8		.879	-14	98	85	2-66	-0.3
1880	Pro N	80	339	46	92	12	5	3	36	10		6	.271	.292	.363	125	9		.887	-13	101	91	*2-80	0.0
1881	Pro N	84	345	69	82	16	5	5	36	29		23	.238	.297	.357	106	4		.881	-5	**103**	98	*2-82/O-3(CF),M	0.2
1882	Pro N	**84**	366	67	93	21	6	2	31	16		23	.254	.285	.361	106	3		.875	-6	105	118	*2-84	0.0
1883	Pro N	95	420	92	128	24	11	3	61	15		21	.305	.329	.436	126	12		**.924**	**25**	**117**	136	*2-95	**3.5**
1884	†Pro N	111	469	70	102	13	6	1	37	35		44	.217	.272	.277	74	-13		.922	-8	98	104	*2-109/3-3	-1.5
1885	Pro N	68	257	27	53	7	1	1	19	10		25	.206	.236	.253	60	-11		.900	-13	92	57	2-68	-2.1
1886	Phi N	17	60	7	11	0	1	0	3	3		11	.183	.222	.217	34	-5	1	.825	-5	112	32	2-17	-0.8

Year	Tm Lg	G	AB	R	H	2B	3B	HR	RBI	BB-IB	HP	SO	AVG	OBP	SLG	AOPS	ABR	SB-CS	FA	FR	Rng	Thr	G at Pos	BFW
	Was N	47	171	24	41	11	4	2	18	15		12	.240	.301	.386	116	4	12	.913	-2	100	59	2-47	0.3
	Year	64	231	31	52	11	5	2	21	18		23	.225	.281	.342	94	-1	13	.888	-7	103	51	2-64	-0.5
1887	Was N	87	339	40	75	14	9	0	41	20	1	12	.221	.267	.316	65	-16	31	.876	-4	97	91	S-48,2-40	-1.4
1888	Bal AA	103	398	72	81	19	5	4	36	26	2		.204	.256	.307	82	-8	29	.902	9	101	80	S-54,2-52	0.4
1889	Bal AA	42	157	25	33	3	0	1	26	15	2	15	.210	.287	.248	52	-10	14	.891	-6	88	85	S-42	-1.2
Total	11	884	3613	584	877	148	55	23	370	197	5	205	.243	.283	.333	94	-23	87	.899	-42	104	95	2-740,S-144/3-3,O-3(CF)	-2.9
FARRELL, JACK John J. B 6.16.1892 Chicago, IL D 3.24.1918 Chicago, IL BB/TR 5-8/145# d4.16																								
1914	Chi F	156	524	58	123	23	4	0	35	52	3	65	.235	.307	.294	68	-32	12	.954	-4	102	107	*2-155/S-3	-3.5
1915	Chi F	70	222	27	48	10	1	0	14	25	1	18	.216	.298	.270	64	-14	8	.941	-3	98	112	2-70/S	-1.7
Total	2	226	746	85	171	33	5	0	49	77	4	83	.229	.305	.287	67	-46	20	.950	-7	101	108	2-225/S-4	-5.2
FARRELL, JOHN John Sebastian B 12.4.1876 Covington, KY D 5.13.1921 Kansas City, MO BR/TR 5-10/160# d4.26																								
1901	Was A	135	555	100	151	32	11	3	63	52	1		.272	.336	.386	101	1	25	.915	9	106	134	2-72,O-62(CF)/3	0.7
1902	StL N	138	565	68	141	13	5	0	25	43	5		.250	.308	.290	88	-7	9	.947	**32**	**119**	**146**	*2-118,S-21	2.7
1903	StL N	130	519	83	141	25	8	1	32	48	2		.272	.336	.356	100	1	17	.927	24	**115**	**124**	*2-118,O-12(2-10-0)	2.4
1904	StL N	131	509	72	130	23	3	0	20	46	2		.255	.320	.312	100	1	16	.934	15	**109**	**143**	*2-130	1.8
1905	StL N	7	24	6	4	0	1	0	1	4	0		.167	.286	.250	62	-1	1	.892	-3	66	0	/2-7	-0.5
Total	5	541	2172	329	567	93	28	4	141	193	10		.261	.324	.335	97	-5	68	.932	77	112	135	2-445/O-74(2-72-0),S-21,3	7.1
FARRELL, JOE Joseph F. B 1857 Brooklyn, NY D 4.18.1893 Brooklyn, NY BR 5-6/160# d5.1																								
1882	Det N	69	283	34	70	12	2	1	24	4		20	.247	.258	.314	83	-6		.816	-15	75	153	3-42,2-18/S-9	-1.7
1883	Det N	**101**	444	58	108	13	5	0	36	5		29	.243	.252	.295	69	-17		.845	13	123	92	*3-101	-0.2
1884	Det N	110	461	59	104	10	5	3	41	14		66	.226	.248	.289	73	-14		.842	-4	97	83	*3-110/O(LF)	-1.5
1886	Bal AA	73	301	36	63	8	3	1	31	12	0		.209	.240	.266	60	-15	5	.870	-8	94	36	2-45,3-27/O(CF)	-1.8
Total	4	353	1489	187	345	43	15	5	132	35	0	115	.232	.249	.291	71	-52	5	.840	-14	104	94	3-280/2-63,S-9,O-2(1-1-0)	-5.2
FARRELL, KERBY Major Kerby B 9.3.1913 Leapwood, TN D 12.17.1975 Nashville, TN BL/TL 5-11/172# d4.24 M1 C6 ▲																								
1943	Bos N	85	280	11	75	14	1	0	21	16	0	15	.268	.307	.325	84	-6	1	.996	1	104	107	1-69/P-5	-1.0
1945	Chi A	103	396	44	102	11	3	0	34	24	0	18	.258	.300	.301	76	-13	4-9	.989	2	106	90	1-97	-2.0
Total	2	188	676	55	177	25	4	0	55	40	0	33	.262	.303	.311	80	-19	5-9	.992	2	105	97	1-166/P-5	-3.0
FARRELL, BILL William d5.3																								
1882	Phi AA	2	7	2	2	1	0	0	1	1			.286	.375	.429	160	1		—	-0	0	0	/O-2(0-1-1),C	0.0
1883	Bal AA	2	7	0	0	0	0	0		1			.000	.125	.000	-55	-1		.750	-1	88	203	/S-2	-0.1
Total	2	4	14	2	2	1	0	0	1	2			.143	.250	.214	52	0		.750	-1	88	203	/S-2,O-2(0-1-1),C	-0.1
FARROW, JOHN John Jacob B 11.8.1853 Verplanck, NY D 12.31.1914 Perth Amboy, NJ BL/TR d4.28																								
1873	Res NA	12	48	2	8	1	0	0	3	0		3	.167	.167	.188	5	-5	0-0	.686	-3			/C-9,O-4(RF),1S	-0.6
1874	Atl NA	27	122	16	26	3	0	0	10	1		1	.213	.220	.238	53	-5	0-0	.694	-1			C-16,2-12/O-3(0-2-1)	-0.6
1884	Bro AA	16	58	7	11	2	0	0		3	0		.190	.230	.224	48	-3		.915	-0			C-16	-0.2
Total	2 NA	39	170	18	34	4	0	0	13	1	0	4	.200	.205	.224	38	-10	0-0	.000	-4			/C-25,2-12,O-7(0-2-5),S1	-1.2
FASANO, SAL Salvatore Frank B 8.10.1971 Chicago, IL BR/TR 6-2/220# d4.3																								
1996	KC A	51	143	20	29	2	0	6	19	14-0	2	25	.203	.283	.343	57	-10	1-1	.984	7	138	87	C-51	0.0
1997	KC A	13	38	4	8	2	0	1	1	1-0	0	12	.211	.231	.342	46	-3	0-0	.982	-1	675	93	C-12/D	-0.4
1998	KC A	74	216	21	49	10	0	8	31	10-1	16	56	.227	.307	.384	77	-8	1-0	.996	1	203	83	C-70/1-5,3	-0.2
1999	KC A	23	60	11	14	2	0	5	16	7-0	7	17	.233	.373	.517	123	2	0-1	1.000	7	181	47	C-23	0.9
2000	†Oak A	52	126	21	27	6	0	7	19	14-0	3	47	.214	.306	.429	86	-3	0-0	.981	-1	106	103	C-52	-0.1
2001	Oak A	11	21	2	1	0	0	0	0	1-0	1	12	.048	.130	.048	-50	-5	0-0	.952	-1	158	102	/C-9,D	-0.5
	KC A	3	1	0	0	0	0	0	0	0-0	0	0	.000	.000	.000	-92	0	0-0	1.000	-0	0	0	/C-3	-0.1
	Year	14	22	2	1	0	0	0	0	1-0	1	12	.045	.125	.045	-51	-5	0-0	.955	-1	145	94	C-12/D	-0.6
	Col N	25	63	10	16	5	0	3	9	4-0	3	19	.254	.329	.476	85	-1	0-0	.982	7	179	110	C-25	0.7
2002	Ana A	2	1	0	0	0	0	0	0	0-0	0	1	.000	.000	.000	-99	0	0-0	1.000	2	42	1009	/C-2	0.1
Total	7	254	669	89	144	27	0	30	95	51-1	32	189	.215	.300	.390	74	-28	2-2	.988	20	187	91	C-247/1-5,D-2,3	0.4
FAUSETT, BUCK Robert Shaw "Leaky" B 4.8.1908 Sheridan, AR D 5.2.1994 College Station, TX BL/TR 5-10/170# d4.18 ▲																								
1944	Cin N	13	31	2	3	0	1	0	1	1	0	2	.097	.125	.161	-21	-5	0	1.000	2	136	96	/3-6,P-2	-0.3
FAUTSCH, JOE Joseph Roamon B 2.28.1887 Minneapolis, MN D 3.16.1971 New Hope, MN BR/TR 5-10/162# d4.24																								
1916	Chi A	1	1	0	0	0	0	0	0	0	0	0	.000	.000	.000	-99	0	0	—	0			H	0.0
FAZIO, ERNIE Ernest Joseph B 1.25.1942 Oakland, CA BR/TR 5-7/165# d7.3																								
1962	Hou N	12	12	3	1	0	0	0	1	2-0	0	5	.083	.214	.083	-18	-2	0-0	.783	-1	110	41	S-10	-0.3
1963	Hou N	102	228	31	42	10	3	2	5	27-1	1	70	.184	.273	.281	64	-10	4-4	.972	-14	85	54	2-84/S3	-2.2
1966	KC A	27	34	3	7	0	1	0	2	4-2	0	10	.206	.289	.265	62	-2	1-0	1.000	1	128	105	2-10/S-4	0.0
Total	3	141	274	37	50	10	4	2	8	33-3	1	85	.182	.273	.270	60	-14	5-4	.974	-14	89	58	/2-94,S-15,3	-2.5
FEBLES, CARLOS Carlos Manuel B 5.24.1976 ElSeibo, D.R. BR/TR 5-11/170# d9.14																								
1998	KC A	11	25	5	10	1	2	0	2	4-0	0	7	.400	.483	.600	175	3	2-1	1.000	-1	89	42	2-11	0.2
1999	KC A	123	453	71	116	22	9	10	53	47-0	9	91	.256	.336	.411	88	-9	20-4	.979	3	103	112	*2-122	0.3
2000	KC A	100	339	59	87	12	1	2	29	36-1	10	48	.257	.345	.316	67	-16	17-6	.978	-7	98	111	2-99	-1.5
2001	KC A	79	292	45	69	9	2	8	25	22-0	1	58	.236	.291	.363	66	-15	5-2	.981	-2	101	127	2-78	-1.2
2002	KC A	119	351	44	86	16	4	4	26	41-0	7	63	.245	.336	.348	74	-13	16-5	.971	-2	103	105	*2-116/S	-0.8
2003	KC A	74	196	31	46	5	0	0	11	13-0	5	30	.235	.299	.260	44	-16	8-2	.989	-10	97	82	2-67/SD	-2.1
Total	6	506	1656	255	414	65	18	24	146	163-1	32	297	.250	.328	.354	72	-66	68-20	.979	-19	101	108	2-493/D-4,S-2	-5.1
FEDEROFF, AL Alfred "Whitey" B 7.11.1924 Bairdford, PA BR/TR 5-10.5/165# d9.27																								
1951	Det A	2	4	0	0	0	0	0	0	0	0	0	.000	.000	.000	-99	-1	0-0	.889	0	148	0	/2	-0.1
1952	Det A	74	231	14	56	4	2	0	14	16	1	13	.242	.294	.277	59	-13	1-0	.976	3	108	90	2-70/S-7	-0.6
Total	2	76	235	14	56	4	2	0	14	16	1	13	.238	.290	.272	56	-14	1-0	.973	4	109	88	/2-71,S-7	-0.7
FEHRING, DUTCH William Paul "Bill" B 5.31.1912 Columbus, IN BB/TR 6/195# d6.25																								
1934	Chi A	1	1	0	0	0	0	0	0	0	0	1	.000	.000	.000	-97	0	0-0	1.000	0	*0*	*0*	/C	0.0
FEINBERG, EDDIE Edward Isadore "Itzzy" B 9.29.1917 Philadelphia, PA D 4.20.1986 Hollywood, FL BB/TR 5-9/165# d9.11																								
1938	Phi N	10	20	0	3	0	0	0	0	0	0	1	.150	.150	.150	-18	-3	0	.957	2	124	128	/S-4,O-2(1-0-2)	-0.1
1939	Phi N	6	18	2	4	1	0	0	0	2	0	0	.222	.300	.278	58	-1	0	.909	-3	64	92	/2-4,S	-0.3
Total	2	16	38	2	7	1	0	0	0	2	0	1	.184	.225	.211	20	-4	0	.957	-1	116	120	/S-5,2-4,O-2(1-0-2)	-0.4
FELDER, MIKE Michael Otis B 11.18.1961 Vallejo, CA BB/TR 5-8/160# d9.11																								
1985	Mil A	15	56	8	11	1	0	0	0	5-0	0	6	.196	.262	.214	33	-5	4-1	1.000	-1	84	111	O-14(CF)	-0.6
1986	Mil A	44	155	24	37	2	4	1	13	13-1	0	16	.239	.289	.323	67	-8	16-2	1.000	1	115	0	O-42(30-7-6)/D	-0.6
1987	Mil A	108	289	48	77	5	7	2	31	28-0	0	23	.266	.329	.353	79	-9	34-8	.975	9	120	149	O-99(80-22-0)/2D	0.1
1988	Mil A	50	81	14	14	1	0	0	5	0-0	1	11	.173	.183	.185	3	-11	8-2	.976	-1	104	0	O-28(12-11-5),D-16/2	-1.2
1989	Mil A	117	315	50	76	11	3	3	23	23-2	0	38	.241	.293	.324	74	-11	26-5	.985	6	108	158	O-93(30-34-38),D-11,2-10	-0.3
1990	Mil A	121	237	38	65	7	2	3	27	22-0	0	17	.274	.330	.359	95	-2	20-9	.972	7	111	173	*O-109(61-15-44)/23D	0.4
1991	SF N	132	348	51	92	10	6	0	18	30-2	1	31	.264	.325	.328	87	-7	21-6	.985	5	112	60	*O-107(45-38-44)/3-3,2	-0.1
1992	SF N	145	322	44	92	13	3	4	23	21-1	2	29	.286	.330	.382	108	3	14-4	.994	-4	94	52	*O-105(53-58-11)/2-3	-0.1
1993	Sea A	109	342	31	72	7	5	1	20	22-2	2	34	.211	.262	.269	43	-29	15-9	.987	0	89	190	O-95(89-7-0)/3-2,D-6	-3.1
1994	Hou N	58	117	10	28	2	2	0	13	4-0	0	12	.239	.264	.291	47	-10	3-0	.974	-1	83	136	O-32(8-6-21)	-1.1
Total	10	899	2262	318	564	59	32	14	173	168-8	6	217	.249	.301	.322	73	-89	161-46	.984	20	105	117	O-724(408-212-169)/D-38,2-17,3-6	-6.6
FELDERMAN, MARV Marvin Wilfred "Coonie" B 12.20.1915 Bellevue, IA D 8.6.2000 Riverside, CA BR/TR 6-1/187# d4.19 Mil 1943-45																								
1942	Chi N	3	6	0	1	0	0	0	0	1	0	4	.167	.286	.167	35	0	0	1.000	0	*60*	*198*	/C-2	0.0
FELIX, GUS August Guenther B 5.24.1895 Cincinnati, OH D 5.12.1960 Montgomery, AL BR/TR 6/180# d4.19																								
1923	Bos N	139	506	64	138	17	2	6	44	51	7	65	.273	.348	.350	88	-7	8-13	.950	-1	104	92	*O-123(121-6-0)/2-5,3-4	-2.0
1924	Bos N	59	204	25	43	7	1	1	10	18	0	16	.211	.275	.270	48	-15	0-3	.950	2	110	106	O-51(11-38-2)	-1.7

Year	Tm Lg	G	AB	R	H	2B	3B	HR	RBI	BB-IB	HP	SO	AVG	OBP	SLG	AOPS	ABR	SB-CS	FA	FR	Rng	Thr	G at Pos	BFW
1925	Bos N	121	459	60	141	25	7	2	66	30	5	34	.307	.356	.405	103	2	5-5	.972	10	111	134	*O-114(42-74-3)	0.4
1926	Bro N	134	432	64	121	21	7	3	53	51	3	32	.280	.360	.382	101	2	9	.956	-0	100	104	*O-125(53-74-0)	-0.5
1927	Bro N	130	445	43	118	21	8	0	57	39	2	47	.265	.327	.348	81	-12	6	.947	-5	90	117	*O-119(117-4-0)	-2.6
Total	5	583	2046	256	561	91	25	12	230	189	17	194	.274	.341	.361	89	-30	28-21	.957	5	102	111	O-532(344-196-5)/2-5,3-4	-6.4
FELIX, JUNIOR Junior Francisco (Sanchez) B 10.3.1967 Laguna Salada, D.R. BB/TR 5-11/165# d5.3																								
1989	†Tor A	110	415	62	107	14	8	9	46	33-2	3	101	.258	.315	.395	101	-1	18-12	.966	0	100	116	*O-107(0-24-86)/D-2	-0.3
1990	Tor A	127	463	73	122	23	7	15	65	45-0	2	99	.263	.328	.441	112	6	13-8	.966	-6	87	126	*O-125(0-28-99)/D	-0.3
1991	Cal A	66	230	32	65	10	2	2	26	11-0	3	55	.283	.321	.370	91	-3	7-5	.977	-9	81	32	O-65(0-63-2)	-1.2
1992	Cal A	139	509	63	125	22	5	9	72	33-5	2	128	.246	.289	.361	82	-14	8-8	.983	1	99	128	*O-128(0-125-4)/D-8	-1.5
1993	Fla N	57	214	25	51	11	1	7	22	10-1	1	50	.238	.276	.397	73	-9	2-1	.940	-4	90	79	O-52(0-3-50)	-1.5
1994	Det A	86	301	54	92	25	1	13	49	26-2	8	76	.306	.372	.525	129	13	1-6	.980	2	112	65	O-81(5-2-75)/D-2	0.8
Total	6	585	2132	309	562	105	24	55	280	158-10	19	509	.264	.317	.413	99	-8	49-40	.972	-15	95	101	O-558(5-245-316)/D-13	-4.0
FELIZ, PEDRO Pedro Julio B 4.27.1975 Azua, D.R. BR/TR 6-1/180# d9.5																								
2000	SF N	8	7	1	2	0	0	0	0	0-0	0	1	.286	.286	.286	49	-1	0-0	—	-1	0	0	/3-4	-0.1
2001	SF N	94	220	23	50	9	1	7	22	10-2	2	50	.227	.264	.373	68	-12	2-1	.908	-17	70	59	3-86/D	-2.8
2002	†SF N	67	146	14	37	4	1	2	13	6-1	0	27	.253	.281	.336	68	-8	0-0	.966	-1	93	150	3-44/SO(LF)	-0.9
2003	†SF N	95	235	31	58	9	3	16	48	10-0	1	53	.247	.278	.515	104	-1	2-2	.972	5	123	136	3-49,O-15(14-0-1),1-12	0.3
Total	4	264	608	69	147	22	5	25	83	26-3	3	131	.242	.274	.418	82	-22	4-3	.945	-13	89	102	3-183/O-16(15-0-1),1-12,SD	-3.5
FELLER, JACK Jack Leland B 12.10.1936 Adrian, MI BR/TR 5-10.5/185# d9.13																								
1958	Det A	1	0	0	0	0	0	0	0	0-0	0	0	—	—	—	—	0	0-0	1.000	0	*0*	*0*	/C	0.0
FELSCH, HAPPY Oscar Emil B 8.22.1891 Milwaukee, WI D 8.17.1964 Milwaukee, WI BR/TR 5-11/175# d4.14 Def 1918																								
1915	Chi A	121	427	65	106	18	11	3	53	51	4	59	.248	.334	.363	105	2	16-18	.959	-6	99	56	*O-118(34-73-10)	-1.4
1916	Chi A	146	546	73	164	24	12	7	70	31	3	67	.300	.341	.427	129	16	13	**.981**	1	102	94	*O-141(CF)	0.7
1917	†Chi A	152	575	75	177	17	10	6	102	33	6	52	.308	.352	.403	128	16	26	.985	15	**117**	107	*O-152(CF)	2.2
1918	Chi A	53	206	16	52	2	5	1	20	15	1	13	.252	.306	.325	90	-4	6	.957	5	120	94	O-53(CF)	-0.3
1919	†Chi A	135	502	68	138	34	11	7	86	40	6	35	.275	.336	.428	113	8	19	.968	17	107	**166**	*O-135(CF)	1.6
1920	Chi A	142	556	88	188	40	15	14	115	37	4	25	.338	.384	.540	143	31	8-13	.981	12	109	**136**	*O-142(CF)	3.0
Total	6	749	2812	385	825	135	64	38	446	207	24	251	.293	.347	.427	123	69	88-31	.975	44	108	112	O-741(34-696-10)	5.8
FELSKE, JOHN John Frederick B 5.30.1942 Chicago, IL BR/TR 6-3/195# d7.26 M3 C3																								
1968	Chi N	4	2	0	0	0	0	0	0	0-0	0	1	.000	.000	.000	-94	0	0-0	.833	0	*0*	*0*	/C-3	0.0
1972	Mil A	37	80	6	11	3	0	1	5	8-0	0	23	.138	.216	.213	28	-7	0-0	.972	-2	143	38	C-23/1-8	-1.0
1973	Mil A	13	22	1	3	0	1	0	4	1-0	0	11	.136	.167	.227	12	-3	0-0	1.000	-1	107	75	/C-7,1-6	-0.4
Total	3	54	104	7	14	3	1	1	9	9-0	0	35	.135	.202	.212	23	-10	0-0	.969	-3	*133*	*44*	/C-33,1-14	-1.4
FENNELLY, FRANK Francis John B 2.18.1860 Fall River, MA D 8.4.1920 Fall River, MA BR/TR 5-8/168# d5.1																								
1884	Was AA	62	257	52	75	17	7	2		20	0		.292	.343	.436	172	22		.863	13	117	78	S-60/2-4	3.3
	Cin AA	28	122	42	43	5	8	2		11	2		.352	.415	.574	209	14		.813	-6	95	172	S-28	0.8
	Year	90	379	94	118	22	15	4		31	2		.311	.367	.480	186	37		.849	7	110	109	S-88/2-4	4.1
1885	Cin AA	**112**	454	82	124	14	17	10	**89**	38	3		.273	.333	.445	142	20		.873	-12	95	**135**	*S-112	1.0
1886	Cin AA	132	497	113	124	13	17	6	72	60	**18**		.249	.351	.380	125	15	32	.848	11	**113**	**130**	*S-132	2.6
1887	Cin AA	134	526	133	140	15	16	8	97	82	4		.266	.369	.401	112	9	74	.855	-11	101	96	*S-134	0.2
1888	Cin AA	120	448	64	88	8	7	2	56	63	1		.196	.297	.259	75	-12	43	.858	11	112	140	*S-112/2-4,O-4(2-2-0)	0.3
	Phi AA	15	47	13	11	2	2	1	12	9	0		.234	.357	.426	151	3	5	.912	-1	91	121	S-15	0.3
	Year	135	495	77	99	10	9	3	68	72	1		.200	.303	.275	82	-9	48	**.863**	10	110	**138**	*S-127/2-4,O-4(2-2-0)	0.6
1889	Phi AA	**138**	513	70	132	20	5	1	64	65	3	78	.257	.344	.322	91	-3	15	.872	-20	95	106	*S-138	-1.6
1890	Bro AA	45	178	40	44	8	3	2	18	30	0		.247	.356	.360	115	4	6	.858	-5	103	56	S-38/3-7	0.1
Total	7	786	3042	609	781	102	82	34	408	378	31	78	.257	.345	.378	118	72	175	.860	-19	104	116	S-769/2-8,3-7,O-4(2-2-0)	7.0
FENWICK, BOBBY Robert Richard B 12.10.1946 Naha, Okinawa BR/TR 5-9/165# d4.26																								
1972	Hou N	36	50	7	9	3	0	0	4	3-1	0	13	.180	.226	.240	33	-4	0-1	.945	-1	100	174	2-17/S-4,3-2	-0.5
1973	StL N	5	6	0	1	0	0	0	1	0-0	0	2	.167	.167	.167	-7	-1	0-0	.750	-2	23	227	/2-3	-0.2
Total	2	41	56	7	10	3	0	0	5	3-1	0	15	.179	.220	.232	29	-5	0-1	.932	-2	91	180	/2-20,S-4,3-2	-0.7
FERGUSON, JOE Joseph Vance B 9.19.1946 San Francisco, CA BR/TR 6-2/200# d9.12 C6																								
1970	LA N	5	4	0	1	0	0	0	1	2-0	0	2	.250	.429	.250	112	0	0-0	1.000	0	63	0	/C-3	0.0
1971	LA N	36	102	13	22	3	0	2	7	12-1	1	15	.216	.304	.304	77	-3	1-0	.983	-2	110	84	C-35	-0.4
1972	LA N	8	24	2	7	3	0	1	5	2-0	0	4	.292	.346	.542	152	2	0-0	1.000	1	141	176	/C-7,O-2(RF)	0.3
1973	LA N	136	487	84	128	26	0	25	88	87-9	1	81	.263	.369	.470	139	29	1-1	**.996**	6	113	84	*C-122,O-20(5-1-14)	4.0
1974	†LA N	111	349	54	88	14	1	16	57	75-10	0	73	.252	.380	.436	134	19	2-2	.988	-1	125	103	C-82,O-32(RF)	2.1
1975	LA N	66	202	15	42	2	1	5	23	35-5	1	47	.208	.325	.302	79	-5	2-1	.994	2	133	107	C-35,O-34(2-0-32)	-0.4
1976	LA N	54	185	24	41	7	0	6	18	25-1	1	41	.222	.318	.357	93	-1	2-0	.966	-0	108	63	O-39(RF),C-17	-0.3
	StL N	71	189	22	38	8	4	4	21	32-3	1	40	.201	.317	.349	89	-2	4-2	.978	9	169	131	C-48,O-14(RF)	0.9
	Year	125	374	46	79	15	4	10	39	57-4	2	81	.211	.317	.353	91	-4	6-2	.975	9	142	123	C-65,O-53(RF)	0.6
1977	Hou N	132	421	59	108	21	3	16	61	85-7	0	79	.257	.379	.435	130	21	6-2	.985	-7	94	122	*C-122/1	2.0
1978	Hou N	51	150	20	31	5	0	7	22	37-6	1	30	.207	.363	.380	118	5	0-0	.994	0	98	104	C-51	0.8
	†LA N	67	198	20	47	11	0	7	28	34-5	1	41	.237	.350	.399	110	4	1-2	.984	-2	129	64	C-62/O-3(2-0-1)	0.4
	Year	118	348	40	78	16	0	14	50	71-11	2	71	.224	.356	.391	113	9	1-2	.989	-2	115	82	*C-113/O-3(2-0-1)	1.2
1979	LA N	122	363	54	95	14	0	20	69	70-6	2	68	.262	.380	.466	133	19	1-0	.981	-4	90	75	C-67,O-52(5-0-47)	1.6
1980	LA N	77	172	20	41	3	2	9	29	38-11	0	46	.238	.371	.436	128	8	2-2	.982	-2	83	56	C-66/O(RF)	0.8
1981	LA N	17	14	2	2	1	0	0	1	2-0	0	5	.143	.250	.214	34	-1	0-0	—	-0	0	0	/O(RF)	-0.1
	Cal A	12	30	5	7	1	0	1	5	9-0	0	8	.233	.400	.367	125	2	0-0	.976	-0	99	168	/C-8,O-4(3-0-1)	0.2
1982	Cal A	36	84	10	19	2	0	3	8	12-0	0	19	.226	.323	.357	87	-1	0-0	.993	4	76	154	C-32/O-2(RF)	0.4
1983	Cal A	12	27	3	2	0	0	0	2	5-0	0	8	.074	.219	.074	-15	-4	0-0	.968	-1	72	98	/C-9,O-3(1-0-2)	-0.6
Total	14	1013	3001	407	719	121	11	122	445	562-64	9	607	.240	.358	.409	117	92	22-12	.987	2	109	98	C-766,O-207(18-1-188)/1	11.7
FERGUSON, BOB Robert Vavasour B 1.31.1845 Brooklyn, NY D 5.3.1894 Brooklyn, NY BB/TR 5-9.5/149# d5.18 M16 U10 I OF Total (1-CF 5-RF)																								
1871	Mut NA	**33**	158	30	38	6	1	0	25	3		2	.241	.255	.291	62	-6	4-4	.774	4	**145**	148	*3-20,2-11/C-5,PM	-0.2
1872	Atl NA	**37**	164	33	46	3	0	0	19	3		0	.280	.293	.299	70	-8	4-2	.807	**34**	**195**	141	*3-37/CM	1.7
1873	Atl NA	51	228	36	59	3	5	0	25	4		8	.259	.272	.316	83	-3	1-2	.746	**28**	**164**	123	*3-50/P-4,M	1.6
1874	Atl NA	**56**	245	34	64	4	0	0	19	2		7	.261	.267	.278	85	-2	5-3	.760	2	120	13	*3-55/C-2,PM	-0.1
1875	Har NA	85	366	65	88	10	4	0	43	3		5	.240	.247	.290	82	-8	2-1	**.827**	9	91	106	*3-85/PM	-0.1
1876	Har N	**69**	310	48	82	8	5	0	32	2		11	.265	.269	.323	89	-5		.826	2	96	105	*3-69,M	0.0
1877	Har N	58	254	40	65	7	2	0	35	3		10	.256	.265	.299	86	-3		.841	17	**139**	102	*3-56/P-3,M	1.4
1878	Chi N	**61**	259	44	91	10	2	0	39	10		12	.351	**.375**	.405	147	13		.881	15	**124**	137	*S-57/2-4,CM	2.8
1879	Tro N	30	123	18	31	5	2	0	4	4		3	.252	.276	.325	104	1		.808	2	105	145	3-24/2-6,M	0.3
1880	Tro N	82	332	55	87	9	0	0	22	**24**		24	.262	.312	.289	100	0		.904	-5	94	105	*2-82,M	0.0
1881	Tro N	**85**	339	56	96	13	5	1	35	29		12	.283	.340	.360	114	6		.904	-13	91	108	*2-85,M	-0.3
1882	Tro N	81	319	44	82	15	2	0	32	23		21	.257	.307	.317	106	4		.914	-12	90	94	*2-79/S-2,M	-0.5
1883	Phi N	86	329	39	85	9	2	0	27	18		21	.258	.297	.298	89	-3		.862	-11	101	74	*2-86/PM	-1.0
1884	Pit AA	10	41	2	6	0	0	0		0	0		.146	.146	.146	-4	-5		.714	-3	0	0	/O-6(0-1-5),1-3,3M	-0.7
Total	5 NA	262	1161	198	295	26	10	0	131	15	0	22	.254	.264	.294	77	-27	16-12	.000	76	132	97	3-247/2-11,C-8,P-7	2.9
Total	9	562	2306	346	625	76	20	1	226	113	0	114	.271	.305	.323	102	8		.895	-7	94	95	2-342,3-150/S-59,O-6R,P-4,1-3,C	2.0
FERMIN, FELIX Felix Jose (Minaya) B 10.9.1963 Mao Valverde, D.R. BR/TR 5-11/170# d7.8																								
1987	Pit N	23	68	6	17	0	0	0	4	4-1	1	9	.250	.301	.250	48	-5	0-0	.980	2	103	113	S-23	-0.1
1988	Pit N	43	87	9	24	0	2	0	2	8-1	3	10	.276	.354	.322	98	0	3-1	.955	-7	86	86	S-43	-0.4
1989	Cle A	156	484	50	115	9	1	0	21	41-0	4	27	.238	.302	.260	59	-26	6-4	.967	12	110	91	*S-153/2-2	-0.2
1990	Cle A	148	414	47	106	13	2	1	40	26-0	0	22	.256	.297	.304	70	-17	3-3	.975	5	105	90	*S-147/2	-0.3
1991	Cle A	129	424	30	111	13	2	0	31	26-0	3	27	.262	.307	.302	69	-18	5-4	.980	2	100	91	*S-129	-0.7
1992	Cle A	79	215	27	58	7	2	0	13	18-1	1	10	.270	.326	.321	84	-5	0-0	.971	-6	93	114	S-55,3-17/2-7,1-2	-0.7
1993	Cle A	140	480	48	126	16	2	2	45	24-1	4	14	.262	.303	.317	67	-23	4-5	.960	-28	86	95	*S-140	-4.1

Year	Tm Lg	G	AB	R	H	2B	3B	HR	RBI	BB-IB	HP	SO	AVG	OBP	SLG	AOPS	ABR	SB-CS	FA	FR	Rng	Thr	G at Pos	BFW
1994	Sea A	101	379	52	120	21	0	1	35	11-0	4	22	.317	.338	.380	84	-9	4-4	.974	-6	80	86	S-77,2-25	-0.8
1995	†Sea A	73	200	21	39	6	0	0	15	6-0	4	6	.195	.232	.225	20	-24	2-0	.971	5	89	128	S-46,2-29	-1.4
1996	Chi N	11	16	4	2	1	0	0	1	2-0	0	0	.125	.222	.188	9	-2	0-0	.875	-3	59	57	/2-6,S-2	-0.5
Total	10	903	2767	294	718	86	11	4	207	166-4	24	147	.259	.305	.303	67	-129	27-21	.971	-24	97	95	S-815/2-70,3-17,1-2	-9.2

FERNANDES, ED Edward Paul B 3.11.1918 Oakland, CA D 11.27.1968 Hayward, CA BB/TR 5-9/185# d6.9 Mil 1945

Year	Tm Lg	G	AB	R	H	2B	3B	HR	RBI	BB-IB	HP	SO	AVG	OBP	SLG	AOPS	ABR	SB-CS	FA	FR	Rng	Thr	G at Pos	BFW
1940	Pit N	28	33	1	4	1	0	0	2	7	0	6	.121	.275	.152	21	-3	0	.981	-0	77	96	C-27	-0.3
1946	Chi A	14	32	4	8	2	0	0	4	8	0	7	.250	.400	.313	105	1	0-0	.922	-1	77	117	C-12	0.0
Total	2	42	65	5	12	3	0	0	6	15	0	13	.185	.338	.231	61	-2	0-0	.952	-1	77	106	/C-39	-0.3

FERNANDEZ, FRANK Frank B 4.16.1943 Staten Island, NY BR/TR 6-1/192# d9.12 Mil 1967

Year	Tm Lg	G	AB	R	H	2B	3B	HR	RBI	BB-IB	HP	SO	AVG	OBP	SLG	AOPS	ABR	SB-CS	FA	FR	Rng	Thr	G at Pos	BFW
1967	NY A	9	28	1	6	2	0	1	4	2-0	1	7	.214	.281	.393	104	0	1-1	1.000	1	0	49	/C-7,O-2(RF)	0.1
1968	NY A	51	135	15	23	6	1	7	30	35-2	0	50	.170	.341	.385	124	5	1-0	.989	4	104	123	C-45/O-4(RF)	1.3
1969	NY A	89	229	34	51	6	1	12	29	65-3	3	68	.223	.399	.415	133	14	1-3	.994	1	106	123	C-65,O-14(RF)	1.7
1970	Oak A	94	252	30	54	5	0	15	44	40-4	2	76	.214	.327	.413	106	2	1-0	.993	2	127	74	C-76/O(LF)	0.8
1971	Oak A	2	4	0	0	0	0	0	0	1-0	0	2	.000	.200	.000	-40	-1	0-0	1.000	-2	0	145	/C-2	-0.3
	Was A	18	30	0	3	0	0	0	4	4-0	0	10	.100	.194	.100	-12	-4	0-0	1.000	-1	73	311	/O-6(3-1-2),C	-0.6
	Oak A	2	5	1	1	1	0	0	1	0-0	0	1	.200	.200	.400	68	0	0-0	1.000	-2	0	145	/C	-0.3
	Year	22	39	1	4	1	0	0	5	5-0	0	13	.103	.196	.128	-4	-5	0-0	1.000	-5	73	311	/O-6(3-1-2),C-4	-1.2
	Chi N	17	41	11	7	1	0	4	4	17-0	0	15	.171	.414	.488	135	3	0-0	.980	1	112	168	C-16	0.5
1972	Chi N	3	3	0	0	0	0	0	0	0-0	0	2	.000	.000	.000	-90	-1	0-0	1.000	0	0	0	/C	-0.1
Total	6	285	727	92	145	21	2	39	116	164-9	6	231	.199	.350	.395	114	18	4-4	.992	3	106	106	C-214/O-27(4-1-22)	3.1

FERNANDEZ, NANNY Froilan B 10.25.1918 Wilmington, CA D 9.19.1996 Harbor City, CA BR/TR 5-9/170# d4.14 Mil 1943-45

Year	Tm Lg	G	AB	R	H	2B	3B	HR	RBI	BB-IB	HP	SO	AVG	OBP	SLG	AOPS	ABR	SB-CS	FA	FR	Rng	Thr	G at Pos	BFW
1942	Bos N	145	577	63	147	29	3	6	55	38	2	61	.255	.303	.347	92	-8	15	.914	2	102	83	3-98,O-44(42-3-0)	-0.5
1946	Bos N	115	372	37	95	15	2	2	42	30	1	44	.255	.313	.323	79	-10	1	.940	1	104	92	3-81,S-18,O-14(LF)	-1.1
1947	Bos N	83	209	16	43	4	0	2	21	22	0	20	.206	.281	.254	44	-17	2	.933	-9	95	79	S-62/O-8(RF),3-6	-2.3
1950	Pit N	65	198	23	51	11	0	6	27	19	1	17	.258	.326	.404	88	-4	2	.925	-3	99	57	3-52	-0.7
Total	4	408	1356	139	336	59	5	16	145	109	4	142	.248	.306	.334	80	-39	20	.925	-10	101	79	3-237/S-80,O-66(56-3-8)	-4.6

FERNANDEZ, CHICO Humberto (Perez) B 3.2.1932 Havana, Cuba BR/TR 6/170# d7.14

Year	Tm Lg	G	AB	R	H	2B	3B	HR	RBI	BB-IB	HP	SO	AVG	OBP	SLG	AOPS	ABR	SB-CS	FA	FR	Rng	Thr	G at Pos	BFW
1956	Bro N	34	66	11	15	2	0	1	9	3-1	0	10	.227	.261	.303	47	-5	2-3	.978	4	114	114	S-25	0.0
1957	Phi N	149	500	42	131	14	4	5	51	31-5	1	64	.262	.302	.336	75	-19	18-5	.960	-23	86	79	*S-149	-2.8
1958	Phi N	148	522	38	120	18	5	6	51	37-3	2	48	.230	.280	.318	60	-31	12-6	.975	-14	94	87	*S-148	-3.3
1959	Phi N	45	123	15	26	5	1	0	3	10-0	0	11	.211	.269	.268	43	-10	2-1	.958	-1	87	120	S-40/2-2	-0.8
1960	Det A	133	435	44	105	13	3	4	35	39-4	1	50	.241	.303	.313	66	-21	13-4	.947	-7	98	87	*S-130	-1.6
1961	Det A	133	435	41	108	15	4	3	40	36-4	0	45	.248	.305	.322	66	-21	8-5	.958	-12	94	91	*S-121/3-8	-2.3
1962	Det A	141	503	64	125	17	2	20	59	42-2	0	69	.249	.305	.410	88	-10	10-3	.960	-28	87	65	*S-138/3-2,1	-2.5
1963	Det A	15	49	3	7	1	0	0	2	6-0	0	11	.143	.236	.163	14	-6	0-1	.947	0	97	97	S-14	-0.5
	NY N	58	145	12	29	6	0	1	9	9-2	0	30	.200	.244	.262	46	-10	3-0	.944	-9	87	80	S-45/3-5,2-3	-1.7
Total	8	856	2778	270	666	91	19	40	259	213-21	4	338	.240	.292	.329	67	-133	68-28	.960	-89	92	84	S-810/3-15,2-5,1	-15.5

FERNANDEZ, JOSE Jose Mayobanex (Rojas) B 11.2.1974 LaVega, D.R. BR/TR 6-2/220# d7.3

Year	Tm Lg	G	AB	R	H	2B	3B	HR	RBI	BB-IB	HP	SO	AVG	OBP	SLG	AOPS	ABR	SB-CS	FA	FR	Rng	Thr	G at Pos	BFW
1999	Mon N	8	24	0	5	2	0	0	1	1-0	0	7	.208	.240	.292	35	-2	0-0	.889	0	101	0	/3-6	-0.2
2001	Ana A	13	25	1	2	1	0	0	0	2-0	0	10	.080	.148	.120	-27	-5	0-1	.000	-0	0	0	/1-2,3D	-0.5
Total	2	21	49	1	7	3	0	0	1	3-0	0	17	.143	.192	.204	3	-7	0-1	.889	-0	99	0	/D-7,3-7,1-2	-0.7

FERNANDEZ, CHICO Lorenzo Marto (Mosquera) B 4.23.1939 Havana, Cuba BR/TR 5-10/160# d4.20

Year	Tm Lg	G	AB	R	H	2B	3B	HR	RBI	BB-IB	HP	SO	AVG	OBP	SLG	AOPS	ABR	SB-CS	FA	FR	Rng	Thr	G at Pos	BFW
1968	Bal A	24	18	0	2	0	0	0	0	1-0	0	2	.111	.158	.111	-17	-3	0-0	.923	-1	94	161	/S-7,2-4	-0.3

FERNANDEZ, TONY Octavio Antonio (Castro) (born Fernando (Castro)) B 6.30.1962 San Pedro De Macoris, D.R. BB/TR 6-2/175# d9.2

Year	Tm Lg	G	AB	R	H	2B	3B	HR	RBI	BB-IB	HP	SO	AVG	OBP	SLG	AOPS	ABR	SB-CS	FA	FR	Rng	Thr	G at Pos	BFW
1983	Tor A	15	34	5	9	1	1	0	2	2-0	1	2	.265	.324	.353	81	-1	0-1	1.000	-3	65	111	S-13/D	-0.3
1984	Tor A	88	233	29	63	5	3	3	19	17-0	0	15	.270	.317	.356	84	-6	5-7	.974	14	107	115	S-73,3-10/D	1.3
1985	†Tor A	**161**	564	71	163	31	10	2	51	43-2	2	41	.289	.340	.390	97	-2	13-6	.962	9	104	118	*S-160	2.5
1986	Tor A★	**163**	687	91	213	33	9	10	65	27-0	4	52	.310	.338	.428	105	3	25-12	**.983**	3	98	105	*S-163	2.4
1987	Tor A★	146	578	90	186	29	8	5	67	51-3	5	48	.322	.379	.426	112	11	32-12	.979	16	98	115	*S-146	4.1
1988	Tor A	154	648	76	186	41	4	5	70	45-3	4	65	.287	.335	.386	101	2	15-5	.981	10	103	109	*S-154	2.4
1989	†Tor A★	140	573	64	147	25	9	11	64	29-1	3	51	.257	.291	.389	93	-8	22-6	**.992**	16	107	104	*S-140	2.2
1990	Tor A	161	635	84	175	27	**17**	4	66	71-4	7	70	.276	.352	.391	106	6	26-13	.989	9	101	96	*S-161	2.8
1991	SD N	145	558	81	152	27	5	4	38	55-0	0	74	.272	.337	.360	93	-4	23-9	.972	10	104	**115**	*S-145	1.9
1992	SD N★	155	622	84	171	32	4	4	37	56-4	4	62	.275	.337	.359	96	-2	20-20	.983	-18	90	80	*S-154	-1.2
1993	NY N	48	173	20	39	5	2	1	14	25-0	1	19	.225	.323	.295	69	-7	6-2	.975	3	104	100	S-48	0.0
	†Tor A	94	353	45	108	18	9	4	50	31-3	0	26	.306	.361	.442	114	6	15-8	.985	10	95	102	S-94	2.3
1994	Cin N	104	366	50	102	18	6	8	50	44-8	5	40	.279	.361	.426	106	4	12-7	**.991**	0	98	92	3-93/S-9,2-5	0.6
1995	†NY A	108	384	57	94	20	2	5	45	42-4	4	40	.245	.322	.346	76	-13	6-6	.976	-14	91	99	*S-103/2-4	-1.9
1997	†Cle A	120	409	55	117	21	1	11	44	22-0	2	47	.286	.323	.423	90	-7	6-6	.980	14	**105**	94	*2-109,S-10/D	1.1
1998	Tor A	138	486	71	156	36	2	9	72	45-5	11	53	.321	.387	.459	120	16	13-8	.975	-12	94	90	2-82,3-54/D	0.8
1999	Tor A★	142	485	73	159	41	0	6	75	77-11	10	62	.328	.427	.449	123	23	6-7	.939	-14	90	99	*3-132/D-9,2	0.8
2001	Mil N	28	64	6	18	0	0	1	3	7-0	0	9	.281	.352	.328	79	-2	1-2	.966	0	114	172	3-13	-0.2
	Tor A	48	59	5	18	4	0	1	12	1-0	1	8	.305	.323	.424	94	-1	0-1	—	0	0	0	D-13	-0.2
Total	17	2158	7911	1057	2276	414	92	94	844	690-48	64	784	.288	.347	.399	101	18	246-138	.980	51	100	105	*S-1573,3-302,2-201/D-26	21.4

FERRARA, AL Alfred John "The Bull" B 12.22.1939 Brooklyn, NY BR/TR 6-1/203# d7.30

Year	Tm Lg	G	AB	R	H	2B	3B	HR	RBI	BB-IB	HP	SO	AVG	OBP	SLG	AOPS	ABR	SB-CS	FA	FR	Rng	Thr	G at Pos	BFW
1963	LA N	21	44	2	7	0	0	1	1	6-0	1	9	.159	.275	.227	50	-3	0-0	.950	0	100	137	O-11(7-0-4)	-0.4
1965	LA N	41	81	5	17	2	1	1	10	9-0	1	20	.210	.297	.296	72	-3	0-0	.927	-2	99	0	O-27(10-0-19)	-0.6
1966	†LA N	63	115	15	31	4	0	5	23	9-0	3	35	.270	.333	.435	123	3	0-0	.956	-2	98	0	O-32(4-1-27)	0.0
1967	LA N	122	347	41	96	16	1	16	50	33-4	3	73	.277	.345	.467	142	18	0-1	.978	-6	92	18	O-94(27-0-71)	0.7
1968	LA N	2	7	0	1	0	0	0	0	0-0	0	2	.143	.143	.143	-15	-1	0-0	.500	-1	43	0	/O-2(LF)	-0.2
1969	SD N	138	366	39	95	22	1	14	56	45-5	7	69	.260	.349	.440	125	13	0-0	.958	-4	85	100	O-96(95-1-0)	0.5
1970	SD N	138	372	44	103	15	4	13	51	46-2	11	63	.277	.372	.444	123	13	0-0	.968	-8	83	33	O-96(LF)	0.0
1971	SD N	17	17	0	2	1	0	0	2	5-1	0	5	.118	.318	.176	47	-1	0-0	1.000	-1	29	0	/O-2(LF)	-0.2
	Cin N	32	33	2	6	0	0	1	5	3-0	1	10	.182	.270	.273	55	-2	0-0	1.000	0	137	0	/O-5(LF)	-0.2
	Year	49	50	2	8	1	0	1	7	8-1	1	15	.160	.288	.240	53	-3	0-0	1.000	-0	92	0	/O-7(LF)	-0.4
Total	8	574	1382	148	358	60	7	51	198	156-12	27	286	.259	.344	.423	120	37	0-1	.962	-21	89	46	O-365(248-2-121)	-0.4

FERRARO, MIKE Michael Dennis B 8.18.1944 Kingston, NY BR/TR 5-11/175# d9.6 M2 C13

Year	Tm Lg	G	AB	R	H	2B	3B	HR	RBI	BB-IB	HP	SO	AVG	OBP	SLG	AOPS	ABR	SB-CS	FA	FR	Rng	Thr	G at Pos	BFW
1966	NY A	10	28	4	5	0	0	0	0	3-0	1	3	.179	.281	.179	37	-2	0-0	.926	1	127	216	3-10	-0.1
1968	NY A	23	87	5	14	0	1	0	1	2-1	0	17	.161	.180	.184	11	-10	0-0	.975	4	134	77	3-22	-0.7
1969	Sea A	5	4	0	0	0	0	0	0	1-0	0	0	.000	.200	.000	-41	-1	0-0	—	0			H	-0.1
1972	Mil A	124	381	19	97	18	1	2	29	17-1	0	41	.255	.284	.323	83	-9	0-5	.950	-17	83	77	*3-115/S	-3.3
Total	4	162	500	28	116	18	2	2	30	23-2	1	61	.232	.265	.288	67	-22	0-5	.953	-12	94	85	3-147/S	-4.2

FERRELL, RICK Richard Benjamin B 10.12.1905 Durham, NC D 7.27.1995 Bloomfield Hills, MI BR/TR 5-10/160# d4.19 C8 HF1984 b-Wes

Year	Tm Lg	G	AB	R	H	2B	3B	HR	RBI	BB-IB	HP	SO	AVG	OBP	SLG	AOPS	ABR	SB-CS	FA	FR	Rng	Thr	G at Pos	BFW
1929	StL A	64	144	21	33	6	1	0	20	32	1	10	.229	.373	.285	69	-5	1-2	.962	1	136	108	C-45	-0.2
1930	StL A	101	314	43	84	18	4	1	41	46	1	10	.268	.363	.360	81	-8	1-4	.983	-4	117	**123**	*C-101	-0.6
1931	StL A	117	386	47	118	30	4	3	57	56	0	12	.306	.394	.427	112	9	2-3	.973	7	114	98	*C-108	2.0
1932	StL A	126	438	67	138	30	5	2	65	66	1	18	.315	.406	.420	108	9	5-5	.986	2	110	104	*C-120	1.6
1933	StL A	22	72	8	18	2	0	1	5	12	0	4	.250	.357	.319	76	-2	2-0	.991	2	131	108	C-21	0.2
	Bos A★	118	421	50	125	19	4	3	72	58	2	19	.297	.385	.382	105	5	2-2	.990	2	81	118	*C-116	1.4
	Year	140	493	58	143	21	4	4	77	70	2	23	.290	.381	.373	100	3	4-2	.990	4	89	116	*C-137	1.6
1934	Bos A☆	132	437	50	130	29	4	1	48	66	0	20	.297	.390	.389	95	-1	0-0	**.990**	5	100	79	*C-128	1.1
1935	Bos A☆	133	458	54	138	34	4	3	61	65	0	15	.301	.388	.413	100	3	5-8	.979	13	116	**142**	*C-131	2.1
1936	Bos A★	121	410	59	128	27	5	8	55	65	0	17	.312	.406	.461	108	7	0-1	.987	9	88	93	*C-121	2.0
1937	Bos A	18	65	8	20	2	0	1	4	15	0	4	.308	.438	.385	105	1	0-0	.990	1	113	88	C-18	0.3
	Was A☆	86	279	31	64	6	0	1	32	50	1	18	.229	.348	.262	59	-16	1-1	.987	-5	96	97	C-84	-1.4
	Year	104	344	39	84	8	0	2	36	65	1	22	.244	.366	.285	68	-14	1-1	.988	-4	99	95	*C-102	-1.1

Year	Tm Lg	G	AB	R	H	2B	3B	HR	RBI	BB-IB	HP	SO	AVG	OBP	SLG	AOPS	ABR	SB-CS	FA	FR	Rng	Thr	G at Pos	BFW
1938	Was A☆	135	411	55	120	24	5	1	58	75	0	17	.292	.401	.382	104	7	1-0	.981	-7	*109*	*93*	*C-131	0.8
1939	Was A	87	274	32	77	13	1	0	31	41	1	12	.281	.377	.336	90	-2	1-1	.976	-2	***145***	*81*	C-83	0.1
1940	Was A	103	326	35	89	18	2	0	28	47	0	15	.273	.365	.340	90	-3	1-1	.980	-5	*80*	*130*	C-99	-0.2
1941	Was A	21	66	8	18	5	0	0	13	15	0	4	.273	.407	.348	107	2	1-0	.980	-1	*91*	*131*	C-21	0.2
	StL A	100	321	30	81	14	3	2	23	52	0	22	.252	.357	.333	81	-7	2-1	.995	-4	*93*	*92*	C-98	-0.5
	Year	121	387	38	99	19	3	2	36	67	0	26	.256	.366	.336	85	-6	3-1	.992	-5	*93*	*99*	*C-119	-0.3
1942	StL A	99	273	20	61	6	1	0	26	33	0	13	.223	.307	.253	57	-15	0-1	.986	3	*87*	*91*	C-95	-0.7
1943	StL A	74	209	12	50	7	0	0	20	34	1	14	.239	.348	.273	81	-3	0-0	.987	3	*72*	*113*	C-70	0.5
1944	Was A☆	99	339	14	94	11	1	0	25	46	0	13	.277	.364	.316	99	2	2-1	.981	2	*87*	*93*	C-96	1.0
1945	Was A✶	91	286	33	76	12	1	1	38	43	2	13	.266	.366	.325	110	6	2-4	.990	-1	*110*	*81*	C-83	1.0
1947	Was A	37	99	10	30	11	0	0	12	14	0	7	.303	.389	.414	127	5	0-0	.994	2	*97*	*151*	C-37	0.8
Total	18	1884	6028	687	1692	324	45	28	734	931	10	277	.281	.378	.363	95	-6	29-35	.984	24	*102*	*104*	*C-1806	11.5

FERRELL, WES Wesley Cheek B 2.2.1908 Greensboro, NC D 12.9.1976 Sarasota, FL BR/TR 6-2/195# d9.9 b-Rick ▲

Year	Tm Lg	G	AB	R	H	2B	3B	HR	RBI	BB-IB	HP	SO	AVG	OBP	SLG	AOPS	ABR	SB-CS	FA	FR	Rng	Thr	G at Pos	BFW
1927	Cle A	1	0	0	0	0	0	0	0	0	0	0	—	—	—	—	0	0-0	—	-0	0	0	/P	0.0
1928	Cle A	2	4	0	1	0	1	0	0	0	0	0	.250	.250	.750	152	1	0-0	1.000	0	110	0	/P-2	0.0
1929	Cle A	47	93	12	22	5	3	1	12	6	0	28	.237	.283	.387	68	4	1-0	.973	3	121	106	P-43	0.0
1930	Cle A	53	118	19	35	8	3	0	14	12	0	15	.297	.362	.415	93	8	0-0	.967	-3	65	0	P-43	0.0
1931	Cle A	48	116	24	37	6	1	9	30	10	0	21	.319	.373	.621	149	17	0-0	.969	5	132	96	P-40	0.0
1932	Cle A	55	128	14	31	5	2	2	18	6	0	21	.242	.276	.359	59	4	0-0	.986	0	101	148	P-38	0.0
1933	Cle A☆	61	140	26	38	7	0	7	26	20	0	22	.271	.363	.471	114	3	0-0	**1.000**	2	111	183	P-28,O-13(LF)	0.1
1934	Bos A	34	78	12	22	4	0	4	17	7	0	15	.282	.341	.487	104	8	1-0	.969	-3	64	104	P-26	0.0
1935	Bos A	75	150	25	52	5	1	7	32	21	0	16	.347	.427	.533	138	20	0-0	.977	2	119	29	P-41	0.0
1936	Bos A	61	135	20	36	6	1	5	24	14	0	10	.267	.336	.437	84	11	0-0	.962	-3	76	67	P-39	0.0
1937	Bos A	18	33	7	12	2	0	1	9	7	0	3	.364	.475	.515	144	6	0-0	.964	2	152	570	P-12	0.0
	Was A☆	53	106	7	27	5	0	0	16	9	0	18	.255	.313	.302	58	6	0-0	.975	-1	86	0	P-25	0.0
	Year	71	139	14	39	7	0	1	25	16	0	21	.281	.355	.353	81	12	0-0	.971	1	103	148	P-37	0.0
1938	Was A	26	49	6	11	2	0	1	6	15	0	7	.224	.406	.327	92	7	0-0	.976	1	114	163	P-23	0.0
	NY A	5	12	1	2	1	0	0	1	1	0	4	.167	.231	.250	20	0	0-0	.917	1	159	884	/P-5	0.0
	Year	31	61	7	13	3	0	1	7	16	0	11	.213	.377	.311	79	7	0-0	.962	1	122	284	P-28	0.0
1939	NY A	3	8	0	1	1	0	0	1	0	0	2	.125	.125	.250	-6	0	0-0	1.000	0	124	0	/P-3	0.0
1940	Bro N	2	2	0	0	0	0	0	0	0	0	2	.000	.000	.000	-94	0	0	1.000	1	372	0	/P	0.0
1941	Bos N	4	4	2	2	0	0	1	2	1	0	1	.500	.600	1.250	430	2	0	1.000	-0	35	0	/P-4	0.0
Total	15	548	1176	175	329	57	12	38	208	129	0	185	.280	.351	.446	99	97	2-0	.975	5	101	104	P-374/O-13(LF)	0.1

FERRER, SERGIO Sergio (Marrero) B 1.29.1951 Santurce, P.R. BB/TR 5-7/145# d4.5

Year	Tm Lg	G	AB	R	H	2B	3B	HR	RBI	BB-IB	HP	SO	AVG	OBP	SLG	AOPS	ABR	SB-CS	FA	FR	Rng	Thr	G at Pos	BFW
1974	Min A	24	57	12	16	0	2	0	0	8-0	1	6	.281	.379	.351	107	1	3-2	.855	-7	79	68	S-20/2	-0.4
1975	Min A	32	81	14	20	3	1	0	2	3-0	1	11	.247	.279	.309	66	-4	3-4	.924	-1	119	133	S-18,2-10/D-2	-0.4
1978	NY N	37	33	8	7	0	1	0	1	4-0	1	7	.212	.316	.273	68	-1	1-0	.971	3	114	98	S-29/2-3,3-2	0.3
1979	NY N	32	7	7	0	0	0	0	0	2-0	0	3	.000	.222	.000	-35	-1	0-2	.833	-0	48	0	3-12/S-5,2-4	-0.2
Total	4	125	178	41	43	3	4	0	3	17-0	3	27	.242	.317	.303	76	-5	7-8	.922	-5	103	103	/S-72,2-18,3-14,D-2	-0.7

FERRIS, HOBE Albert Sayles B 12.7.1877 Providence, RI D 3.18.1938 Detroit, MI BR/TR 5-8/162# d4.26

Year	Tm Lg	G	AB	R	H	2B	3B	HR	RBI	BB-IB	HP	SO	AVG	OBP	SLG	AOPS	ABR	SB-CS	FA	FR	Rng	Thr	G at Pos	BFW
1901	Bos A	**138**	523	68	131	16	15	2	63	23	6		.250	.290	.350	78	-18	13	.930	7	103	**130**	*2-138/S	-0.8
1902	Bos A	134	499	57	122	16	14	8	63	21	1		.244	.276	.381	79	-18	11	.952	**24**	**114**	115	*2-134	0.7
1903	†Bos A	**141**	525	69	132	19	7	9	66	25	1		.251	.287	.366	90	-8	11	.950	14	105	111	*2-139/S-2	0.8
1904	Bos A	156	563	50	120	23	10	3	63	23	1		.213	.245	.306	70	-20	7	.962	-0	98	107	*2-156	-2.2
1905	Bos A	142	523	51	115	24	16	6	59	23	0		.220	.253	.361	93	-8	11	.960	15	**108**	111	*2-142	0.9
1906	Bos A	130	495	47	121	25	13	2	44	10	2		.244	.262	.360	94	-6	8	.960	8	104	97	*2-126/3-4	0.3
1907	Bos A	150	561	41	135	25	2	4	60	10	0		.241	.254	.314	82	-14	11	.967	8	102	94	*2-150	-0.6
1908	StL A	148	555	54	150	26	7	2	74	14	2		.270	.291	.353	108	3	6	**.952**	14	103	**168**	*3-148	2.3
1909	StL A	148	556	36	120	18	5	4	58	12	0		.216	.232	.288	69	-23	11	.937	7	103	103	*3-114,2-34	-1.5
Total	9	1287	4800	473	1146	192	89	40	550	161	13		.239	.265	.341	84	-112	89	.954	96	104	109	*2-1019,3-266/S-3	-0.1

FETZER, WILLY William McKinnon B 6.24.1884 Concord, NC D 5.3.1959 Butner, NC BL/TR 5-10.5/180# d9.4

Year	Tm Lg	G	AB	R	H	2B	3B	HR	RBI	BB-IB	HP	SO	AVG	OBP	SLG	AOPS	ABR	SB-CS	FA	FR	Rng	Thr	G at Pos	BFW
1906	Phi A	1	1	0	0	0	0	0	0	0	0		.000	.000	.000	-97	0	0	—	0			H	0.0

FEWSTER, CHICK Wilson Lloyd B 11.10.1895 Baltimore, MD D 4.16.1945 Baltimore, MD BR/TR 5-11/160# d9.19

Year	Tm Lg	G	AB	R	H	2B	3B	HR	RBI	BB-IB	HP	SO	AVG	OBP	SLG	AOPS	ABR	SB-CS	FA	FR	Rng	Thr	G at Pos	BFW
1917	NY A	11	36	2	8	0	0	0	1	5	0	5	.222	.317	.222	64	-1	1	.919	-0	98	114	2-11	-0.1
1918	NY A	5	2	1	1	0	0	0	0	0	0	0	.500	.500	.500	197	0	0	—	-0	0	0	/2-2	0.0
1919	NY A	81	244	38	69	9	3	1	15	34	7	36	.283	.386	.357	108	5	8	.946	4	81	236	O-41(0-13-28),S-24/2-4,3-2	0.8
1920	NY A	21	21	8	6	1	0	0	1	7	0	2	.286	.464	.333	110	1	0-1	.840	-1	91	66	/S-6,2-3	0.0
1921	†NY A	66	207	44	58	19	0	1	19	28	6	43	.280	.382	.386	94	0	4-4	.974	-1	88	118	O-43(7-35-1),2-15	-0.2
1922	NY A	44	132	20	32	4	1	1	9	16	0	23	.242	.324	.311	65	-7	2-4	.975	2	86	198	O-38(35-4-0)/2-2	-0.8
	Bos A	23	83	8	24	4	1	0	9	6	1	10	.289	.344	.361	85	-2	8-3	.959	2	113	78	3-23	0.2
	Year	67	215	28	56	8	2	1	18	22	1	33	.260	.332	.330	72	-9	10-7	.975	4	86	198	O-38(35-4-0),3-23/2-2	-0.6
1923	Bos A	90	284	32	67	10	1	0	15	39	3	35	.236	.334	.278	62	-14	7-14	.938	-10	99	74	2-49,S-37/3-3	-2.3
1924	Cle A	101	322	36	86	12	2	0	36	24	3	36	.267	.324	.317	65	-17	12-12	.961	-20	91	73	2-94/3-5	-3.5
1925	Cle A	93	294	39	73	16	1	1	38	36	0	25	.248	.330	.320	65	-15	6-9	.939	-11	93	83	2-83,3-10/O(RF)	-2.4
1926	Bro N	105	337	53	82	16	3	2	24	45	5	49	.243	.341	.326	82	-7	9	.953	-12	90	66	*2-103	-1.6
1927	Bro N	4	1	1	0	0	0	0	0	0	0	0	.000	.000	.000	-99	0	0	—	0			H	0.0
Total	11	644	1963	282	506	91	12	6	167	240	25	264	.258	.346	.326	77	-57	57-47	.945	-47	93	78	2-366,O-123(42-52-30)/S-67,3-43	-9.9

FIALA, NEIL Neil Stephen B 8.24.1956 St.Louis, MO BL/TR 6-1/185# d9.3

Year	Tm Lg	G	AB	R	H	2B	3B	HR	RBI	BB-IB	HP	SO	AVG	OBP	SLG	AOPS	ABR	SB-CS	FA	FR	Rng	Thr	G at Pos	BFW
1981	StL N	3	3	0	0	0	0	0	0	0-0	0	1	.000	.000	.000	-97	-1	0-0	—	0			/H	-0.1
	Cin N	2	2	1	1	0	0	0	1	0-0	0	1	.500	.500	.500	181	0	0-0	—	0			/H	0.0
	Year	5	5	1	1	0	0	0	1	0-0	0	2	.200	.200	.200	13	-1	0-0	—	0				-0.1

FICK, ROBERT Robert Charles John B 3.15.1974 Torrance, CA BL/TR 6-1/189# d9.19

Year	Tm Lg	G	AB	R	H	2B	3B	HR	RBI	BB-IB	HP	SO	AVG	OBP	SLG	AOPS	ABR	SB-CS	FA	FR	Rng	Thr	G at Pos	BFW
1998	Det A	7	22	6	8	1	0	3	7	2-0	0	7	.364	.417	.818	209	3	1-0	.950	0	89	124	/C-3,1D	0.3
1999	Det A	15	41	6	9	0	0	3	10	7-0	0	6	.220	.327	.439	94	-1	1-0	1.000	1	98	0	/C-4,D-8	0.1
2000	Det A	66	163	18	41	7	2	3	22	22-2	1	39	.252	.340	.374	84	-4	2-1	.984	-3	114	95	1-34,C-16,D-12	-0.8
2001	Det A	124	401	62	109	21	2	19	61	39-3	4	62	.272	.339	.476	118	10	0-3	.986	-4	80	61	C-78,1-26/O-8(RF),D-8	0.7
2002	Det A★	148	556	66	150	36	2	17	63	46-4	7	90	.270	.331	.433	108	6	0-1	.963	9	101	**234**	*O-140(RF)/D-6	0.8
2003	†Atl N	126	409	52	110	26	1	11	80	42-4	2	47	.269	.335	.418	96	-2	1-0	.987	-8	78	102	*1-115	-1.9
Total	6	486	1592	210	427	91	7	56	243	158-13	14	251	.268	.336	.440	106	12	5-5	.987	-5	85	95	1-176,O-148(RF),C-101/D-36	-0.8

FIELD, JIM James C. B 4.24.1863 Philadelphia, PA D 5.13.1953 Atlantic City, NJ 6-1/170# d6.2 ▲

Year	Tm Lg	G	AB	R	H	2B	3B	HR	RBI	BB-IB	HP	SO	AVG	OBP	SLG	AOPS	ABR	SB-CS	FA	FR	Rng	Thr	G at Pos	BFW
1883	Col AA	75	291	31	75	10	6	1		7			.258	.275	.344	107	3		.938	-7	47	115	*1-75	-0.9
1884	Col AA	105	417	74	97	9	7	4		23	12		.233	.292	.317	107	5		.958	-4	75	134	*1-105	-0.7
1885	Pit AA	56	209	28	50	9	1	1	15	13	7		.239	.306	.306	95	0		.965	-0	99	123	1-56	-0.5
	Bal AA	38	144	16	30	3	2	0	10	13	1		.208	.278	.257	71	-4		.963	1	129	71	1-38	-0.6
	Year	94	353	44	80	12	3	1	25	26	8		.227	.295	.286	85	-4		.964	1	111	102	1-94	-1.1
1890	Roc AA	52	188	30	38	7	5	4	25	21	8		.202	.309	.356	104	1	8	.964	-4	61	92	1-51/P-2	-0.7
1898	Was N	5	21	1	2	0	0	0	0	0	0		.095	.095	.095	-46	-4	1	.979	-0	86	0	/1-5	-0.4
Total	5	331	1270	180	292	38	21	10	50	77	28		.230	.289	.317	97	1	9	.956	-15	77	112	1-330/P-2	-3.8

FIELD, SAM Samuel Jay B 10.12.1848 Philadelphia, PA D 10.28.1904 Sinking Spring, PA BR/TR 5-9.5/182# d5.19

Year	Tm Lg	G	AB	R	H	2B	3B	HR	RBI	BB-IB	HP	SO	AVG	OBP	SLG	AOPS	ABR	SB-CS	FA	FR	Rng	Thr	G at Pos	BFW
1875	Cen NA	3	11	2	1	0	0	0	0	0		0	.091	.091	.091	-40	-1	0-0	.714	-1			/C-2,O(RF)	-0.2
	Was NA	5	16	0	5	0	0	0	1	0		1	.313	.313	.313	122	0	1-0	.731	-2			/C-4,O(RF)	-0.1
	Year	8	27	2	6	0	0	0	1	0		1	.222	.222	.222	58	-1	1-0	.723	-3			/C-6,O-2(RF)	-0.3
1876	Cin N	4	14	2	0	0	0	0	0	1		3	.000	.067	.000	-89	-3		.667	-3			/C-3,2-2	-0.5

FIELDER, CECIL Cecil Grant B 9.21.1963 Los Angeles, CA BR/TR 6-3/240# d7.20

Year	Tm Lg	G	AB	R	H	2B	3B	HR	RBI	BB-IB	HP	SO	AVG	OBP	SLG	AOPS	ABR	SB-CS	FA	FR	Rng	Thr	G at Pos	BFW
1985	†Tor A	30	74	6	23	4	0	4	16	6-0	0	16	.311	.358	.527	137	4	0-0	.979	0	117	144	1-25	0.3
1986	Tor A	34	83	7	13	2	0	4	13	6-0	1	27	.157	.222	.325	46	-7	0-0	1.000	-0	83	82	D-22/1-7,3-2,O(LF)	-0.8

Year	Tm Lg	G	AB	R	H	2B	3B	HR	RBI	BB-IB	HP	SO	AVG	OBP	SLG	AOPS	ABR	SB-CS	FA	FR	Rng	Thr	G at Pos	BFW
1987	Tor A	82	175	30	47	7	1	14	32	20-2	1	48	.269	.345	.560	132	8	0-1	1.000	-1	74	136	D-55,1-16/3-2	0.4
1988	Tor A	74	174	24	40	6	1	9	23	14-0	1	53	.230	.289	.431	99	-1	0-1	.991	0	113	92	D-50,1-17/3-3,2-2	-0.4
1990	Det A★	159	573	104	159	25	1	**51**	**132**	90-11	5	182	.277	.377	**.592**	167	51	0-1	.989	5	114	107	*1-143,D-15	4.5
1991	Det A★	**162**	624	102	163	25	0	**44**	**133**	78-12	6	151	.261	.347	.513	133	27	0-0	.993	0	105	101	*1-122,D-42	1.7
1992	Det A	155	594	80	145	22	0	35	**124**	73-8	2	151	.244	.325	.458	118	13	0-0	.991	4	118	100	*1-114,D-43	0.7
1993	Det A★	154	573	80	153	23	0	30	117	90-15	4	125	.267	.368	.464	124	21	0-1	.991	-0	103	88	*1-119,D-36	0.7
1994	Det A	109	425	67	110	16	2	28	90	50-4	2	110	.259	.337	.504	113	7	0-0	.993	16	**162**	85	*1-102/D-7	1.2
1995	Det A	136	494	70	120	18	1	31	82	75-8	5	116	.243	.346	.472	112	8	0-1	.993	7	139	95	1-77,D-58	0.4
1996	Det A	107	391	55	97	12	0	26	80	63-8	3	91	.248	.354	.478	109	5	2-0	.989	4	123	71	1-71,D-36	0.0
	†NY A	53	200	30	52	8	0	13	37	24-4	2	48	.260	.342	.495	109	2	0-0	1.000	-0	71	103	D-43/1-9	-0.2
	Year	160	591	85	149	20	0	39	117	87-12	5	139	.252	.350	.484	109	7	2-0	.990	4	117	75	1-80,D-79	-0.2
1997	†NY A	98	361	40	94	15	0	13	61	51-3	7	87	.260	.358	.410	102	2	0-0	1.000	1	130	129	D-87/1-8	-0.3
1998	Ana A	103	381	48	92	16	1	17	68	52-1	3	98	.241	.335	.423	95	-3	0-1	.997	-2	84	101	1-72,D-31	-1.3
	Cle A	14	35	1	5	1	0	0	0	1-0	1	13	.143	.189	.171	-5	-6	0-0	.933	0	121	51	D-10/1-3	-0.6
	Year	117	416	49	97	17	1	17	68	53-1	4	111	.233	.324	.401	87	-8	0-1	.995	-2	85	99	1-75,D-41	-1.9
Total	13	1470	5157	744	1313	200	7	319	1008	693-76	43	1316	.255	.345	.482	119	131	2-6	.992	33	117	97	1-905,D-535/3-7,2-2,O(LF)	6.3
FIELDS, BRUCE Bruce Alan B 10.6.1960 Cleveland, OH BL/TR 6/185# d9.3 C1																								
1986	Det A	16	43	4	12	1	1	0	6	1-0	0	6	.279	.283	.349	75	-2	1-1	.962	-1	102	0	O-14(LF)/D	-0.3
1988	Sea A	39	67	8	18	5	0	1	5	4-0	0	11	.269	.310	.388	90	-1	0-1	1.000	-2	79	0	O-23(14-1-8)/D-6	-0.3
1989	Sea A	3	3	2	1	1	0	0	0	0-0	0	1	.333	.333	.667	170	0	0-0	—	-0	0	0	/O(RF)	0.0
Total	3	58	113	14	31	7	1	1	11	5-0	0	18	.274	.300	.381	86	-3	1-2	.980	-2	89	0	/O-38(28-1-9),D-7	-0.6
FIELDS, GEORGE George W. B 7.1853 Waterbury, CT D 9.22.1933 Waterbury, CT d5.2																								
1872	Man NA	18	86	17	19	3	1	0	14	0		2	.221	.221	.279	56	-4	0-0	.629	-7	72	0	3-12/O-5(1-0-4),S	-0.8
FIELDS, JOCKO John Joseph B 10.20.1864 Cork, Ireland D 10.14.1950 Jersey City, NJ BR/TR 5-10/160# d5.31 OF Total (160-LF 20-CF 27-RF)																								
1887	Pit N	43	164	26	44	9	2	0	17	7	2	13	.268	.306	.348	88	-2	7	.933	-0	100	0	O-27(7-13-7),C-14/1-3,3P	-0.2
1888	Pit N	45	169	22	33	7	2	1	15	8	0	19	.195	.232	.278	68	-6	9	.887	-4	118	0	O-29(23-2-4),C-14/3-3	-0.9
1889	Pit N	75	289	41	90	22	5	2	43	29	1	30	.311	.376	.443	142	17	7	.860	-5	64	103	O-60(54-2-4),C-16	1.1
1890	Pit P	126	526	101	148	18	20	9	86	57	3	52	.281	.355	.443	123	16	24	.879	-11	137	104	0-80(76-3-1),2-30,C-15/S-4	0.4
1891	Pit N	23	75	10	18	3	0	0	5	10	1	13	.240	.337	.280	82	-1	1	.897	-2	*103*	*104*	C-15/S-8	-0.2
	Phi N	8	30	4	7	2	1	0	5	4	0	2	.233	.324	.367	98	0	0	.769	-4	*90*	*76*	/C-8	-0.3
	Year	31	105	14	25	5	1	0	10	14	1	15	.238	.333	.305	87	-1	1	.857	-6	*98*	*94*	C-23/S-8	-0.5
1892	NY N	21	66	8	18	4	2	0	5	9	1	10	.273	.368	.394	133	3	2	.917	-2	249	0	O-11(RF),C-10	0.1
Total	6	341	1319	212	358	65	32	12	176	124	8	139	.271	.338	.397	114	27	50	.883	-29	113	72	0-207L/C-92,2-30,S-12,3-4,1-3,P	-0.0
FIGGA, MIKE Michael Anthony B 7.31.1970 Tampa, FL BR/TR 6/200# d9.16																								
1997	NY A	2	4	0	0	0	0	0	0	0-0	0	3	.000	.000	.000	-99	-1	0-0	1.000	-0	0	0	/CD	-0.1
1998	NY A	1	4	1	1	0	0	0	0	0-0	0	1	.250	.250	.250	32	0	0-0	1.000	-0	0	0	/C	-0.1
1999	NY A	2	0	0	0	0	0	0	0	0-0	0	0	—	—	—	—	0	0-0	1.000	0	0	0	/C-2	0.0
	Bal A	41	86	12	19	4	0	1	5	2-0	0	27	.221	.236	.302	38	-8	0-2	.973	-4	81	79	C-41	-1.1
	Year	43	86	12	19	4	0	1	5	2-0	0	27	.221	.236	.302	38	-8	0-2	.973	-4	80	78	C-43	-1.1
Total	3	46	94	13	20	4	0	1	5	2-0	0	31	.213	.227	.287	32	-9	0-2	.975	-5	75	73	/C-45,D	-1.3
FIGGINS, CHONE Desmond Dechone B 1.22.1978 Leary, GA BB/TR 5-8/155# d8.25																								
2002	†Ana A	15	12	6	2	1	0	0	1	0-0	0	5	.167	.167	.250	9	-2	2-1	.941	-0	95	102	/2-8	-0.1
2003	Ana A	71	240	34	71	9	4	0	27	20-0	0	38	.296	.345	.367	93	-2	13-7	1.000	-3	104	52	O-47(3-44-0),2-14/S-8,D-3	-0.4
Total	2	86	252	40	73	10	4	0	28	20-0	0	43	.290	.337	.361	89	-4	15-8	1.000	-4	104	52	/O-47(3-44-0),2-22,S-8,D-3	-0.5
FIGUEROA, BIEN Bienvenido B 2.7.1964 Santo Domingo, D.R. BR/TR 5-10/170# d5.17																								
1992	StL N	12	11	1	2	1	0	0	4	1-0	0	2	.182	.250	.273	49	-1	0-0	.938	-1	81	0	/S-9,2-3	-0.1
FIGUEROA, JESUS Jesus Maria (Figueroa) B 2.20.1957 Santo Domingo, D.R. BL/TL 5-10/160# d4.22																								
1980	Chi N	115	198	20	50	5	0	1	11	14-0	2	16	.253	.308	.293	64	-9	2-1	.979	2	92	222	O-57(22-36-1)	-0.8
FIGUEROA, LUIS Luis R. B 2.16.1974 Bayamon, D.R. BB/TR 5-9/152# d6.27																								
2001	Pit N	4	2	0	0	0	0	0	0	0-0	0	0	.000	.000	.000	-98	-1	0-0	1.000	1	224	222	/2-3	0.0
FILE, SAM Samuel Lawrence B 5.18.1922 Chester, PA BR/TR 5-11/160# d9.10																								
1940	Phi N	7	13	0	1	0	0	0	1	0	0	2	.077	.077	.077	-60	-3	0	.850	0	126	99	/S-6,3	-0.3
FILIPOWICZ, STEVE Stephen Charles "Flip" B 6.28.1921 Donora, PA D 2.21.1975 Wilkes-Barre, PA BR/TR 5-8/195# d9.3																								
1944	NY N	15	41	10	8	2	1	0	7	3	0	7	.195	.250	.293	52	-3	0	1.000	-1	94	0	O-10(6-4-0)/C	-0.4
1945	NY N	35	112	14	23	5	0	2	16	4	1	13	.205	.239	.304	50	-8	0	.935	-3	80	57	O-31(27-2-2)	-1.3
1948	Cin N	7	26	0	9	0	1	0	3	2	0	1	.346	.393	.423	125	1	0	1.000	0	83	220	/O-7(LF)	0.0
Total	3	57	179	24	40	7	2	2	26	9	1	21	.223	.265	.318	61	-10	0	.961	-4	84	67	/O-48(40-6-2),C	-1.7
FIMPLE, JACK John Joseph B 2.10.1959 Darby, PA BR/TR 6-2/185# d7.30																								
1983	†LA N	54	148	16	37	8	1	2	22	11-0	0	39	.250	.300	.358	83	-4	1-0	.989	11	116	136	C-54	1.0
1984	LA N	12	26	2	5	1	0	0	3	1-0	0	6	.192	.214	.231	28	-3	0-0	.983	-1	83	153	C-12	-0.3
1986	LA N	13	13	2	1	0	0	0	2	6-1	0	6	.077	.350	.077	32	-1	0-0	1.000	0	133	107	/C-7,12	0.0
1987	Cal A	13	10	1	2	0	0	0	1	1-0	0	2	.200	.273	.200	29	-1	0-0	.913	-1	92	161	C-13	-0.1
Total	4	92	197	21	45	9	1	2	28	19-1	0	53	.228	.292	.315	70	-9	1-0	.986	10	111	138	/C-86,21	0.6
FINIGAN, JIM James Leroy B 8.19.1928 Quincy, IL D 5.16.1981 Quincy, IL BR/TR 5-11/175# d4.25																								
1954	Phi A☆	136	487	57	147	25	6	7	51	64	0	66	.302	.381	.421	120	15	2-8	.948	6	107	114	*3-136	1.8
1955	KC A★	150	545	72	139	30	7	9	68	61-6	3	49	.255	.333	.385	92	-7	1-3	.975	-5	95	93	2-90,3-59	-0.6
1956	KC A	91	250	29	54	7	2	2	21	30-1	1	28	.216	.298	.284	55	-16	3-1	.969	1	94	108	2-52,3-32	-1.2
1957	Det A	64	174	20	47	4	2	0	17	23-2	1	18	.270	.357	.316	84	-3	1-1	.954	-1	99	95	3-59/2-3	-0.4
1958	SF N	23	25	3	5	2	0	0	1	3-1	1	5	.200	.310	.280	59	-1	0-0	.917	-1	97	106	/2-8,3-4	-0.2
1959	Bal A	48	119	14	30	6	0	1	10	9-0	0	10	.252	.300	.328	75	-4	1-0	.959	1	104	79	3-42/2-6,S-2	-0.3
Total	6	512	1600	195	422	74	17	19	168	190-10	6	176	.264	.342	.367	92	-16	8-13	.948	0	108	105	3-332,2-159/S-2	-0.9
FINLEY, BOB Robert Edward B 11.25.1915 Ennis, TX D 1.2.1986 W.Covina, CA BR/TR 6-1/200# d7.4																								
1943	Phi N	28	81	9	21	2	0	1	7	4	0	10	.259	.294	.321	81	-2	0	.962	2	*89*	*160*	C-24	0.1
1944	Phi N	94	281	18	70	11	1	1	21	12	5	25	.249	.292	.306	71	-11	1	.967	-2	*103*	*89*	C-74	-0.9
Total	2	122	362	27	91	13	1	2	28	16	5	35	.251	.292	.309	73	-13	1	.966	-1	*100*	*106*	/C-98	-0.8
FINLEY, STEVE Steven Allen B 3.12.1965 Paducah, KY BL/TL 6-2/180# d4.3																								
1989	Bal A	81	217	35	54	5	2	2	25	15-1	1	30	.249	.298	.318	77	-7	17-3	.986	-2	102	24	O-76(14-23-41)/D-3	-0.8
1990	Bal A	142	464	46	119	16	4	3	37	32-3	2	53	.256	.304	.328	80	-13	22-9	.977	2	112	52	*O-133(21-44-73)/D-2	-1.2
1991	Hou N	159	596	84	170	28	10	8	54	42-5	2	65	.285	.331	.406	114	9	34-18	.985	2	99	151	*O-153(1-124-69)	1.0
1992	Hou N	**162**	607	84	177	29	13	5	55	58-6	3	63	.292	.355	.407	121	16	44-9	.993	1	104	92	*O-160(CF)	2.4
1993	Hou N	142	545	69	145	15	**13**	8	44	28-1	3	65	.266	.304	.385	87	-14	19-6	.988	3	98	**178**	*O-140(CF)	-0.7
1994	Hou N	94	373	64	103	16	5	11	33	28-0	2	52	.276	.329	.434	102	0	13-7	.982	1	96	184	O-92(CF)	0.2
1995	SD N	139	562	104	167	23	8	10	44	59-5	3	62	.297	.366	.420	111	9	36-12	.977	-5	93	113	*O-138(CF)	0.9
1996	†SD N	161	655	126	195	45	9	30	95	56-5	4	87	.298	.354	.531	138	34	22-8	.982	-2	101	84	*O-160(CF)	3.5
1997	SD N★	143	560	101	146	26	5	28	92	43-2	3	92	.261	.313	.475	112	6	15-3	.989	6	108	152	*O-140(CF)	1.5
1998	†SD N	159	619	92	154	40	6	14	67	45-0	3	103	.249	.301	.401	90	-11	12-3	.981	1	101	130	*O-157(CF)	-0.7
1999	†Ari N	156	590	100	156	32	10	34	103	63-7	3	94	.264	.336	.525	113	9	8-4	.995	-0	106	60	*O-155(CF)/D	1.0
2000	Ari N★	152	539	100	151	27	5	35	96	65-7	8	87	.280	.361	.544	122	17	12-6	.992	-2	99	117	*O-148(CF)/D-2	1.6
2001	†Ari N	140	495	66	136	27	4	14	73	47-9	1	67	.275	.337	.430	91	-6	11-7	.994	-1	103	89	*O-131(CF)/P	-0.6
2002	†Ari N	150	505	82	145	24	4	25	89	65-7	3	73	.287	.370	.499	120	13	16-4	.994	0	107	58	*O-144(CF)	1.6
2003	Ari N	147	516	82	148	24	**10**	22	70	57-4	6	94	.287	.363	.500	111	8	15-8	.982	-7	87	131	*O-140(CF)	0.3
Total	15	2127	7843	1235	2166	377	108	249	977	703-62	47	1087	.276	.337	.447	108	70	296-107	.987	-4	101	109	*O-2067(36-1896-183)/D-8,P	10.0

Year	Tm Lg	G	AB	R	H	2B	3B	HR	RBI	BB-IB	HP	SO	AVG	OBP	SLG	AOPS	ABR	SB-CS	FA	FR	Rng	Thr	G at Pos	BFW
FINLEY, BILL William James B 10.4.1863 New York, NY D 10.6.1912 Asbury Park, NJ 5-3/170# d7.12																								
1886	NY N	13	44	2	8	0	0	0	5	1		8	.182	.200	.182	17	-4	2	.800	-2	0	0	/O-8(0-7-1),C-8	-0.5
FINN, NEAL Cornelius Francis "Mickey" B 1.24.1904 Brooklyn, NY D 7.7.1933 Allentown, PA BR/TR 5-11/168# d4.21																								
1930	Bro N	87	273	42	76	13	0	3	30	26	4	18	.278	.350	.359	73	-11	3	.948	-5	92	138	2-81	-1.2
1931	Bro N	118	413	46	113	22	2	0	45	21	3	42	.274	.314	.337	75	-14	2	.975	0	97	93	*2-112	-0.7
1932	Bro N	65	189	22	45	5	2	0	14	11	1	15	.238	.284	.286	55	-12	2	.933	4	118	95	3-50/2-2,S	-0.7
1933	Phi N	51	169	15	40	4	1	0	13	10	2	14	.237	.287	.272	54	-10	2	.964	1	108	107	2-51	-0.7
Total	4	321	1044	125	274	44	5	3	102	68	10	89	.262	.314	.323	67	-47	9	.964	-1	98	111	2-246/3-50,S	-3.3
FINNEY, HAL Harold Wilson B 7.30.1905 Lafayette, AL D 12.20.1991 Lafayette, AL BR/TR 5-11/170# d6.24 b-Lou																								
1931	Pit N	10	26	2	8	1	0	0	2	0	1	1	.308	.333	.346	84	-1	1	1.000	0	*109*	*54*	/C-6	0.0
1932	Pit N	31	33	14	7	3	0	0	4	3	1	4	.212	.297	.303	63	-2	0	.971	1	*77*	*54*	C-11	0.0
1933	Pit N	56	133	17	31	4	1	1	18	3	0	19	.233	.250	.301	57	-8	0	.993	-2	*75*	*62*	C-47	-0.8
1934	Pit N	5	0	3	0	0	0	0	0	0	1	0	—	1.000	—	188	0	0	—	0	*0*	*0*	/C	0.0
1936	Pit N	21	35	3	0	0	0	0	3	0	0	8	.000	.000	.000	-98	-10	0	.956	0	*87*	*88*	C-14	-0.9
Total	5	123	227	39	46	8	1	1	27	6	3	32	.203	.233	.260	37	-21	1	.983	-0	*81*	*64*	/C-79	-1.7
FINNEY, LOU Louis Klopsche B 8.13.1910 Buffalo, AL D 4.22.1966 Lafayette, AL BL/TR 6/180# d9.12 Def 1943-45 b-Hal																								
1931	Phi A	9	24	7	9	0	1	0	3	6	1	1	.375	.516	.458	149	2	0-0	1.000	1	124	134	/O-8(RF)	0.3
1933	Phi A	74	240	26	64	12	2	3	32	13	1	17	.267	.307	.371	78	-8	1-3	.947	2	112	106	O-63(17-1-46)	-1.0
1934	Phi A	92	272	32	76	11	4	1	28	14	0	17	.279	.315	.360	77	-11	4-3	.943	-0	104	70	O-54(12-4-40),1-15	-1.4
1935	Phi A	109	410	45	112	11	6	0	31	18	2	18	.273	.307	.329	65	-23	7-2	.943	-1	102	82	O-76(5-0-72),1-18	-2.8
1936	Phi A	151	653	100	197	26	10	1	41	47	3	22	.302	.351	.377	81	-20	7-9	.990	-5	80	95	1-78,O-73(22-21-32)	-3.4
1937	Phi A	92	379	53	95	14	9	1	20	20	0	16	.251	.288	.343	59	-26	2-5	.989	-4	104	89	1-50,O-39(2-37-0)/2	-3.4
1938	Phi A	122	454	61	125	21	12	10	48	39	0	25	.275	.333	.441	94	-7	5-8	.990	-5	59	59	1-64,O-46(19-21-6)	-2.0
1939	Phi A	9	22	1	3	0	0	0	1	2	0	0	.136	.208	.136	-10	-4	0-0	1.000	0	112	0	/O-4(0-3-1)	-0.4
	Bos A	95	249	43	81	18	3	1	46	24	0	11	.325	.385	.434	105	2	2-5	.986	-5	60	101	1-32,O-24(3-16-5)	-0.7
	Year	104	271	44	84	18	3	1	47	26	0	11	.310	.370	.410	96	-1	2-5	.986	-5	60	101	1-32,O-28(3-19-6)	-1.1
1940	Bos A★	130	534	73	171	31	15	5	73	33	0	13	.320	.360	.463	107	4	5-2	.975	-1	100	167	O-69(RF),1-51	-0.5
1941	Bos A	127	497	83	143	24	10	4	53	38	1	17	.288	.340	.400	93	-6	2-5	.945	-4	98	80	O-92(1-0-91),1-24	-1.9
1942	Bos A	113	397	58	113	16	7	3	61	29	1	11	.285	.335	.383	98	-2	3-3	.976	-1	99	108	O-95(3-1-92)/1-2	-1.0
1944	Bos A	68	251	37	72	11	2	0	32	23	0	7	.287	.347	.347	100	0	1-0	.987	-5	65	101	1-59/O-2(1-0-1)	-0.8
1945	Bos A	2	2	0	0	0	0	0	0	0	0	1	.000	.000	.000	-98	-1	0-0	—	0			H	-0.1
	StL A	57	213	24	59	8	4	2	22	21	1	6	.277	.345	.380	105	1	0-0	.986	0	100	131	O-36(24-0-13),1-22/3	-0.2
	Year	59	215	24	59	8	4	2	22	21	1	7	.274	.342	.377	103	1	0-0	.986	0	100	131	O-36(24-0-13),1-22/3	-0.3
1946	StL A	16	30	0	9	0	0	0	3	2	0	4	.300	.344	.300	77	-1	0-0	.938	0	106	205	/O-7(4-0-3)	-0.1
1947	Phi N	4	4	0	0	0	0	0	0	0	0	0	.000	.000	.000	-99	-1	0	—	0			H	-0.1
Total	15	1270	4631	643	1329	203	85	31	494	329	10	186	.287	.336	.388	88	-101	39-45	.961	-26	102	95	O-688(113-104-479);1-415/32	-19.5
FIORE, MIKE Michael Gary Joseph B 10.11.1944 Brooklyn, NY BL/TL 6/185# d9.21																								
1968	Bal A	6	17	2	1	0	0	0	0	4-0	1	4	.059	.273	.059	5	-2	0-0	.943	-0	110	238	/1-5,O(LF)	-0.3
1969	KC A	107	339	53	93	14	1	12	35	84-4	2	63	.274	.420	.428	137	22	4-4	.988	12	159	75	1-91,O-13(3-8-2)	2.7
1970	KC A	25	72	6	13	2	0	0	4	13-0	0	24	.181	.306	.208	44	-5	1-1	.986	1	118	70	1-20	-0.6
	Bos A	41	50	5	7	0	0	0	4	8-1	0	4	.140	.254	.140	12	-6	0-0	1.000	0	133	45	1-17/O-2(1-0-1)	-0.7
	Year	66	122	11	20	2	0	0	8	21-1	0	28	.164	.285	.180	30	-11	1-1	.991	1	122	63	1-37/O-2(1-0-1)	-1.3
1971	Bos A	51	62	9	11	2	0	1	6	12-1	0	14	.177	.311	.258	58	-3	0-3	1.000	-0	91	105	1-12	-0.5
1972	StL N	17	10	0	1	0	0	0	1	2-0	0	3	.100	.250	.100	3	-1	0-0	1.000	-0	0	270	/1-6,O(RF)	-0.2
	SD N	7	6	0	0	0	0	0	0	1-1	0	3	.000	.143	.000	-61	-1	0-0	—	0			H	-0.1
	Year	24	16	0	1	0	0	0	1	3-1	0	6	.063	.211	.063	-20	-2	0-0	1.000	-0	0	270	/1-6,O(RF)	-0.3
Total	5	254	556	75	126	18	1	13	50	124-7	3	115	.227	.369	.333	97	4	5-8	.988	12	144	81	1-151/O-17(5-8-4)	0.3
FIROVA, DAN Daniel Michael B 10.16.1956 Refugio, TX BR/TR 6/185# d9.1																								
1981	Sea A	13	2	0	0	0	0	0	0	0-0	0	1	.000	.000	.000	-96	-1	0-0	1.000	-1	0	123	C-13	-0.1
1982	Sea A	3	5	0	0	0	0	0	0	0-0	0	0	.000	.000	.000	-97	-1	0-0	.900	0	0	0	/C-3	-0.1
1988	Cle A	1	0	0	0	0	0	0	0	0-0	0	0	—	—	—	—	0	0-0	—	-0	0	0	/C	0.0
Total	3	17	7	0	0	0	0	0	0	0-0	0	1	.000	.000	.000	-97	-2	0-0	.944	-1	0	75	/C-17	-0.2
FISCHER, WILLIAM William Charles B 3.2.1891 New York, NY D 9.4.1945 Richmond, VA BL/TR 6/174# d6.11																								
1913	Bro N	62	165	16	44	9	4	1	12	10	1	5	.267	.313	.388	97	-1	0-1	.974	-2	96	100	C-51	0.1
1914	Bro N	43	105	12	27	1	2	0	8	8	0	12	.257	.310	.305	81	-3	1	.958	0	*90*	*115*	C-30	0.0
1915	Chi F	105	292	30	96	15	4	4	50	24	2	19	.329	.384	.449	142	12	5	.972	-4	*115*	*94*	C-80	1.5
1916	Chi N	65	179	15	35	9	2	1	14	11	1	8	.196	.246	.285	57	-9	2	.973	0	101	111	C-56	-0.5
	Pit N	42	113	11	29	7	1	1	6	10	1	3	.257	.323	.363	109	2	1	.974	1	91	109	C-35	0.7
	Year	107	292	26	64	16	3	2	20	21	2	11	.219	.276	.315	76	-8	3	.973	1	97	110	C-91	0.2
1917	Pit N	95	245	25	70	9	2	3	25	27	1	19	.286	.359	.376	121	7	11	.961	-11	*71*	*99*	C-69/1-2	0.2
Total	5	412	1099	109	301	50	15	10	115	90	6	66	.274	.332	.374	107	8	20-1	.969	-15	*95*	*103*	C-321/1-2	2.0
FISCHLIN, MIKE Michael Thomas B 9.13.1955 Sacramento, CA BR/TR 6-1/165# d9.3																								
1977	Hou N	13	15	0	3	0	0	0	0	0-0	0	2	.200	.200	.200	8	-2	0-0	1.000	-1	111	37	S-12	-0.2
1978	Hou N	44	86	3	10	1	0	0	0	4-1	1	9	.116	.165	.128	-19	-14	1-0	.928	-9	75	66	S-41	-2.2
1980	Hou N	1	1	0	0	0	0	0	0	0-0	0	1	.000	.000	.000	-99	0	0-0	1.000	-0	0	0	/S	0.0
1981	Cle A	22	43	3	10	1	0	0	5	3-0	0	6	.233	.277	.256	57	-2	3-2	.955	-2	81	73	S-19/2	-0.3
1982	Cle A	112	276	34	74	12	1	0	21	34-0	2	36	.268	.351	.319	86	-4	9-5	.970	-8	97	80	*S-101/3-8,2-6,C	-0.2
1983	Cle A	95	225	31	47	5	2	2	23	26-0	2	32	.209	.294	.276	56	-13	9-2	.965	6	100	106	2-71,S-15/3-4,D	-0.2
1984	Cle A	85	133	17	30	4	2	1	14	12-0	0	20	.226	.290	.308	64	-7	2-2	.981	2	100	99	2-55,3-17,S-15	-0.2
1985	Cle A	73	60	12	12	4	1	0	2	5-0	0	7	.200	.262	.300	54	-4	0-1	.990	10	120	120	2-31,S-22/1-6,3-3,D-5	0.7
1986	NY A	71	102	9	21	2	0	0	3	8-0	0	29	.206	.261	.225	35	-9	0-1	.955	-4	103	87	S-42,2-27	-1.0
1987	Atl N	1	0	0	0	0	0	0	0	0-0	0	0	—	—	—	—	0	0-0	—	0			/R	0.0
Total	10	517	941	109	207	29	6	3	68	92-1	5	142	.220	.291	.273	57	-55	24-13	.959	-7	95	83	S-268,2-191/3-32,1-6,D-6,C	-3.6
FISHBURN, SAM Samuel E. B 5.15.1893 Haverhill, MA D 4.11.1965 Bethlehem, PA BR/TR 5-9/157# d5.30																								
1919	StL N	9	6	0	2	1	0	0	2	0	0	0	.333	.333	.500	158	0	0	1.000	0	0	0	/12	0.1
FISHEL, JOHN John Alan B 11.8.1962 Fullerton, CA BR/TR 5-11/185# d7.14																								
1988	Hou N	19	26	1	6	0	0	1	2	3-0	0	6	.231	.310	.346	92	0	0-0	1.000	-1	29	0	/O-6(5-0-2)	-0.2
FISHER, GUS August Harris B 10.21.1885 Pottsboro, TX D 4.8.1972 Portland, OR BL/TR 5-10/175# d4.18																								
1911	Cle A	70	203	20	53	6	3	0	12	7	5		.261	.302	.320	73	-8	6	.956	2	*92*	*118*	C-58/1	-0.1
1912	NY A	4	10	1	1	0	0	0	0	0	0		.100	.100	.100	-40	-2	0	1.000	1	*98*	*95*	/C-4	-0.1
Total	2	74	213	21	54	6	3	0	12	7	5		.254	.293	.310	68	-10	6	.958	2	*92*	*117*	/C-62,1	-0.2
FISHER, CHARLES Charles d6.15																								
1889	Lou AA	1	2	0	1	0	0	0	0	0	0	0	.500	.500	.500	189	0	0	—	-0	0	0	/O(LF)	0.0
FISHER, CHARLES Charles G. (born Charles G. Fish) B 3.10.1852 Boxford, MA D 2.18.1917 Eagle, AK BL/TR 5-8/143# d6.7																								
1884	KC U	10	40	3	8	2	0	0		0			.200	.200	.250	41	-4		.711	0	134	0	/3-9,S	-0.3
	CP U	1	3	1	2	0	0	0		1			.667	.750	.667	335	1		.500	-1	0	0	/3	0.0
	Year	11	43	4	10	2	0	0		1			.233	.250	.279	68	-3		.702	-1	123	0	3-10/S	-0.3
FISHER, SHOWBOAT George Aloys B 1.16.1899 Wesley, IA D 5.15.1994 St.Cloud, MN BL/TR 5-10/170# d4.24																								
1923	Was A	13	23	4	6	2	0	0	2	4	0	3	.261	.370	.348	95	0	0-0	.750	0	75	318	/O-5(RF)	0.0
1924	Was A	15	41	7	9	1	0	0	6	6	0	6	.220	.319	.244	48	-3	2-0	.933	-1	94	0	O-11(RF)	-0.4
1930	†StL N	92	254	49	95	18	6	8	61	25	1	21	.374	.432	.587	139	16	4	.962	-2	95	94	O-67(24-0-42)	0.9
1932	StL A	18	22	2	4	0	0	0	2	2	0	5	.182	.250	.182	13	-3	0-0	1.000	0	112	0	/O-5(LF)	-0.3
Total	4	138	340	62	114	21	6	8	71	37	1	35	.335	.402	.503	119	10	6-0	.946	-3	94	95	/O-88(29-0-58)	0.2

Year	Tm Lg	G	AB	R	H	2B	3B	HR	RBI	BB-IB	HP	SO	AVG	OBP	SLG	AOPS	ABR	SB-CS	FA	FR	Rng	Thr	G at Pos	BFW
FISHER, GEORGE George C. B Wilmington, DE BL d8.9																								
1884	Cle N	6	24	2	3	0	0	0	0	0		3	.125	.125	.125	-20	-3		.897	-2	76	88	/2-6,C	-0.5
	Wil U	8	29	0	2	0	0	0		0			.069	.069	.069	-56	-6		.818	-1	0	0	/O-6(0-6-1),S-2	-0.7
Total	1	14	53	2	5	0	0	0	0	0		3	.094	.094	.094	-40	-9		.818	-3	0	0	/O-6(0-6-1),2-6,S-2,C	-1.2
FISHER, HARRY Harry Devereux B 1.3.1926 Newbury, ON, CAN D 9.20.1981 Waterloo, ON, CAN BL/TR 6/180# d9.16 ▲																								
1951	Pit N	3	3	0	0	0	0	0	0	0	0	0	.000	.000	.000	-97	-1	0-0	—	0			H	-0.1
1952	Pit N	15	15	0	5	1	0	0	1	0	0	3	.333	.333	.400	100	1	0-0	1.000	-1	31	0	/P-8	0.0
Total	2	18	18	0	5	1	0	0	1	0	0	3	.278	.278	.333	66	0	0-0	1.000	-1	31	0	/P-8	-0.1
FISHER, RED John Gus B 6.22.1887 Pittsburgh, PA D 1.31.1940 Louisville, KY BL/TR 5-9/176# d4.25																								
1910	StL A	23	72	5	9	2	1	0	3	8	1		.125	.222	.181	28	-6	5	.935	-1	91	82	O-19(14-0-5)	-0.9
FISHER, NEWT Newton "Ike" B 6.28.1871 Nashville, TN D 2.28.1947 Norwood Park, IL BR/TR 5-9.5/171# d5.17 b-Bob																								
1898	Phi N	9	26	0	3	1	0	0	0	0	1		.115	.148	.154	-14	-4	1	.844	-1	_114_	_37_	/C-8,3	-0.4
FISHER, BOB Robert Taylor B 11.3.1886 Nashville, TN D 8.4.1963 Jacksonville, FL BR/TR 5-9.5/170# d6.3 b-Newt																								
1912	Bro N	82	257	27	60	10	3	0	26	14	0	32	.233	.273	.296	58	-16	7	.917	-11	94	83	S-74/23	-2.2
1913	Bro N	132	474	42	124	11	10	4	54	10	1	43	.262	.278	.352	77	-17	16-16	.923	-20	90	**128**	*S-131	-3.1
1914	Chi N	15	50	5	15	2	2	0	5	3	0	4	.300	.340	.420	126	1	2	.943	-1	105	61	S-15	0.2
1915	Chi N	147	568	70	163	22	5	5	53	30	3	51	.287	.326	.370	110	6	9-20	.933	-19	95	56	*S-145	-1.0
1916	Cin N	61	136	9	37	4	3	0	11	8	0	14	.272	.313	.346	104	0	7	.905	-8	91	72	S-29/2-6,O(LF)	-0.7
1918	StL N	63	246	36	78	11	3	2	20	15	0	11	.317	.356	.411	138	11	7	.979	16	119	121	2-63	3.0
1919	StL N	3	11	0	3	1	0	0	1	0	0	2	.273	.273	.364	96	0	0	.900	0	91	144	/2-3	0.0
Total	7	503	1742	189	480	61	26	11	170	80	4	157	.276	.309	.359	96	-15	48-36	.925	-42	93	86	S-394/2-73,O(LF)3	-3.8
FISHER, WILBUR Wilbur McCullough B 7.18.1894 Green Bottom, WV D 10.24.1960 Welch, WV BL/TR 6/174# d6.13																								
1916	Pit N	1	1	0	0	0	0	0	0	0	0	0	.000	.000	.000	-99	0	0	—	0			H	0.0
FISHER, CHEROKEE William Charles B 12.1845 Philadelphia, PA D 9.26.1912 New York, NY BR/TR 5-9/164# d5.6 I OF NA (5-LF 14-CF 66-RF)																								
1871	Rok NA	**25**	123	24	28	3	3	1	22	3		1	.228	.246	.325	65	-5	1-2	**.927**	4	**147**	**181**	*P-24/1-2,2	0.1
1872	Bal NA	46	225	39	52	10	3	1	36	2		5	.231	.238	.316	66	-10	1-1	.761	-5	113	176	P-19,O-19(0-3-17),3-18	-0.9
1873	Ath NA	51	253	50	66	4	3	1	37	4		5	.261	.272	.312	68	-12	2-2	.743	4	192	285	*O-46(1-2-43),P-13/2-3,1	-0.2
1874	Har NA	52	241	28	54	7	0	0	31	2		7	.224	.230	.253	52	-13	2-3	.833	-4	76	154	P-39,O-12(0-8-6)/3-7,S-2	-0.6
1875	Phi NA	41	177	26	41	3	1	0	11	1		6	.232	.236	.260	69	-6	4-3	.896	-3	71	34	P-41/O-5(4-1-0)	-0.1
1876	Cin N	35	129	12	32	1	0	0	4	0		8	.248	.248	.256	80	-2		.793	-3	75	0	P-28,O-11(0-7-4)/S1	-0.2
1877	Chi N	1	4	0	0	0	0	0	0	0		2	.000	.000	.000	-89	-1		.667	-0	127	0	/3	-0.1
1878	Pro N	1	3	0	0	0	0	0	0	0		0	.000	.000	.000	-99	0		1.000	0	54	0	/P	0.0
Total	5 NA	215	1019	167	241	27	10	3	137	12		24	.237	.245	.291	64	-46	10-11	.000	-4	91	110	P-136/O-82R,3-25,2-4,1-3,S-2	-1.7
Total	3	37	136	12	32	1	0	0	4	0		10	.235	.235	.243	68	-3		.803	-3	74	0	/P-29,O-11(0-7-4),31S	-0.3
FISK, CARLTON Carlton Ernest "Pudge" B 12.26.1947 Bellows Falls, VT BR/TR 6-2/220# d9.18 HF2000																								
1969	Bos A	2	5	0	0	0	0	0	0	0-0	0	2	.000	.000	.000	-95	-1	0-0	1.000	-1	0	0	/C	-0.3
1971	Bos A	14	48	7	15	2	1	2	6	1-0	0	10	.313	.327	.521	128	1	0-0	.975	-1	147	134	C-14	0.1
1972	Bos A★	131	457	74	134	28	**9**	22	61	52-6	4	83	.293	.370	.538	159	33	5-2	.984	6	105	95	*C-131	5.1
1973	Bos A★	135	508	65	125	21	0	26	71	37-2	10	99	.246	.309	.441	103	1	7-2	.983	11	134	72	*C-131/D-3	1.9
1974	Bos A✳	52	187	36	56	12	1	11	26	24-2	2	23	.299	.383	.551	156	14	5-1	.980	6	128	79	C-50/D-2	2.3
1975	†Bos A	79	263	47	87	14	4	10	52	27-4	2	32	.331	.395	.529	147	16	4-3	.979	5	138	76	C-71/D-6	2.4
1976	Bos A★	134	487	76	124	17	5	17	58	56-3	6	71	.255	.336	.415	107	4	12-5	.984	20	**129**	86	*C-133/D	3.3
1977	Bos A★	152	536	106	169	26	3	26	102	75-3	9	85	.315	.402	.521	135	29	7-6	.987	12	163	80	*C-151	4.6
1978	Bos A★	157	571	94	162	39	5	20	88	71-6	7	83	.284	.366	.475	123	19	7-2	.980	11	98	80	*C-154/O(LF)D	3.9
1979	Bos A	91	320	49	87	23	2	10	42	10-0	6	38	.272	.304	.450	96	-3	3-0	.982	-5	94	40	D-42,C-39/O(LF)	-0.6
1980	Bos A★	131	478	73	138	25	3	18	62	36-6	**13**	62	.289	.353	.467	117	11	11-5	.983	-5	99	78	*C-115/O-5(LF),1-3,3-3,D-5	1.2
1981	Chi A★	96	338	44	89	12	0	7	45	38-3	12	37	.263	.354	.361	110	6	3-2	.990	2	79	95	C-92/13O(LF)	1.3
1982	Chi A★	135	476	66	127	17	3	14	65	46-7	6	60	.267	.336	.403	103	2	17-2	.994	4	93	100	*C-133/1-2	1.5
1983	†Chi A	138	488	85	141	26	4	26	86	46-3	6	88	.289	.355	.518	133	21	9-6	.991	5	102	78	*C-133/D-2	3.1
1984	Chi A	102	359	54	83	20	1	21	43	26-4	5	60	.231	.289	.468	102	0	6-0	.987	-7	90	79	C-90/D-5	-0.2
1985	Chi A★	153	543	85	129	23	1	37	107	52-12	17	81	.238	.320	.488	114	10	17-9	.989	7	92	117	*C-130,D-28	2.1
1986	Chi A	125	457	42	101	11	0	14	63	22-2	6	92	.221	.263	.337	61	-26	2-4	.991	8	73	108	C-71,O-31(LF)/D-22	-1.8
1987	Chi A	135	454	68	116	22	1	23	71	39-8	8	72	.256	.321	.460	103	1	1-4	.990	12	116	89	*C-122/1-9,O-2(LF),D-7	1.5
1988	Chi A	76	253	37	70	8	1	19	50	37-9	5	40	.277	.377	.542	155	19	0-0	.995	-2	83	90	C-74	2.2
1989	Chi A	103	375	47	110	25	2	13	68	36-8	3	60	.293	.356	.475	137	18	1-0	**.993**	-6	103	98	C-90,D-13	1.7
1990	Chi A	137	452	65	129	21	0	18	65	61-8	7	73	.285	.378	.451	134	23	7-2	.994	12	99	117	*C-116,D-14	4.1
1991	Chi A★	134	460	42	111	25	0	18	74	32-4	7	86	.241	.299	.413	98	-3	1-2	.993	8	104	**132**	*C-106,D-13,1-12	0.9
1992	Chi A	62	188	12	43	4	1	3	21	23-5	1	38	.229	.313	.309	77	-6	3-0	.993	-2	86	109	C-54/D-2	-0.4
1993	Chi A	25	53	2	10	0	0	1	4	2-0	1	11	.189	.228	.245	29	-6	0-1	1.000	-6	44	37	C-25	-1.1
Total	24	2499	8756	1276	2356	421	47	376	1330	849-105	143	1386	.269	.341	.457	116	183	128-58	.988	96	107	91	*C-2226,D-166/O-41(LF),1-27,3-4	38.8
FISLER, WES Weston Dickson "Icicle" B 7.5.1841 Camden, NJ D 12.25.1922 Philadelphia, PA 5-6/137# d5.20																								
1871	Ath NA	**28**	147	43	41	8	2	0	16	3		2	.279	.293	.361	88	-2	6-3	**.972**	1	24	80	*1-26/2-2	0.0
1872	Ath NA	**47**	244	49	85	13	3	0	48	4		4	.348	.359	.426	140	11	3-0	.889	7	108	92	*2-47	1.1
1873	Ath NA	44	218	44	75	11	4	1	41	2		2	.344	.350	.445	125	5	3-1	.855	2	107	136	*2-36,1-10	0.3
1874	Ath NA	37	180	26	59	12	1	0	22	0		1	.328	.328	.406	123	4	2-0	.953	5	194	210	1-28/2-9,O(RF)	0.7
1875	Ath NA	58	268	54	74	13	3	0	31	4		4	.276	.287	.347	107	1	1-4	.958	2	66	145	1-46,O-10(0-1-9)/2-5	0.2
1876	Phi N	59	278	42	80	15	1	1	30	2		4	.288	.293	.360	117	5		.911	2	133	100	O-24(0-15-9),2-21,1-14/S	0.6
Total	5 NA	214	1057	216	334	57	13	1	158	13		13	.316	.324	.397	118	19	15-8	.000	16	92	142	1-110/2-99,O-11(0-1-10)	2.3
FITZBERGER, CHARLIE Charles Casper B 2.13.1904 Baltimore, MD D 1.25.1965 Baltimore, MD BL/TL 6-1.5/170# d9.11																								
1928	Bos N	7	7	0	2	0	0	0	0	0	0	3	.286	.286	.286	52	-1	0	—	0			H	-0.1
FITZGERALD, DENNIS Dennis S. B 3.1865 , England D 10.16.1936 New Haven, CT 5-10/160# d4.17																								
1890	Phi AA	2	8	0	2	0	0	0	0	0	0		.250	.250	.250	48	-1	0	.667	-2	67	0	/S-2	-0.2
FITZ GERALD, ED Edward Raymond B 5.21.1924 Santa Ynez, CA BR/TR 6/180# d4.19 C5																								
1948	Pit N	102	262	31	70	9	3	1	35	32	1	37	.267	.349	.336	84	-5	3	.961	-3	_104_	_100_	C-96	-0.3
1949	Pit N	75	160	16	42	7	0	2	18	8	1	27	.262	.302	.344	71	-7	1	.974	-2	_125_	_115_	C-56	-0.6
1950	Pit N	6	15	1	1	1	0	0	0	0	0	3	.067	.067	.133	-47	-3	0	.950	-0	_119_	_106_	/C-5	-0.3
1951	Pit N	55	97	8	22	6	0	0	13	7	1	10	.227	.286	.289	53	-6	1-1	.965	-1	_106_	_94_	C-38	-0.7
1952	Pit N	51	73	4	17	1	0	1	7	7	0	15	.233	.300	.288	62	-4	0-2	1.000	-1	_80_	_82_	C-18/3-2	-0.5
1953	Pit N	6	17	2	2	1	0	0	1	0	0	2	.118	.118	.176	-25	-3	0-0	1.000	-1	_49_	_173_	/C-5	-0.4
	Was A	88	288	23	72	13	0	3	39	19	1	34	.250	.299	.326	70	-13	2-1	.989	0	_103_	_79_	C-85	-0.8
1954	Was A	115	360	33	104	13	5	4	40	33	2	22	.289	.349	.386	108	3	0-1	.973	-14	_86_	_68_	*C-107	-0.6
1955	Was A	74	236	28	56	3	1	4	19	25-0	3	23	.237	.317	.309	73	-9	0-1	.982	-7	_83_	_115_	C-72	-1.3
1956	Was A	64	148	15	45	8	0	2	12	20-1	0	16	.304	.387	.399	108	3	0-0	.974	-2	_85_	_116_	C-50	0.3
1957	Was A	45	125	14	34	8	0	1	13	10-1	1	9	.272	.331	.360	90	-2	2-0	.963	-7	_69_	_111_	C-37	-0.7
1958	Was A	58	114	7	30	3	0	0	11	8-0	0	15	.263	.309	.289	68	-5	0-0	.970	-6	_54_	_52_	C-21/1-5	-1.0
1959	Was A	19	62	5	12	3	0	0	5	4-0	0	8	.194	.242	.242	34	-6	0-0	1.000	-0	_57_	_176_	C-16	-0.5
	Cle A	49	129	12	35	6	1	1	4	12-1	2	14	.271	.343	.357	96	0	0-0	.978	-1	_90_	_152_	C-45	0.1
	Year	68	191	17	47	9	1	1	9	16-1	2	22	.246	.311	.319	76	-6	0-0	.984	-1	_80_	_159_	C-61	-0.4
Total	12	807	2086	199	542	82	10	19	217	185-3	12	235	.260	.323	.336	80	-57	9-6	.975	-43	_92_	_100_	C-651/1-5,3-2	-7.3
FITZGERALD, HOWIE Howard Chumney "Lefty" B 5.16.1902 Eagle Lake, TX D 2.27.1959 Matthews, TX BL/TL 5-11.5/163# d9.17																								
1922	Chi N	10	24	3	8	1	0	0	4	3	0	2	.333	.407	.375	101	0	1-0	.818	-1	81	0	/O-6(RF)	-0.1
1924	Chi N	7	19	1	3	0	0	0	2	0	0	2	.158	.158	.158	-15	-3	0-0	1.000	-1	64	0	/O-5(0-1-4)	-0.4
1926	Bos A	31	97	11	25	2	0	0	8	5	0	7	.258	.294	.278	52	-7	1-4	.882	-3	66	99	O-23(21-0-2)	-1.3
Total	3	48	140	15	36	3	0	0	14	8	0	11	.257	.297	.279	52	-10	2-4	.878	-5	69	70	/O-34(21-1-12)	-1.8

Year	Tm Lg	G	AB	R	H	2B	3B	HR	RBI	BB-IB	HP	SO	AVG	OBP	SLG	AOPS	ABR	SB-CS	FA	FR	Rng	Thr	G at Pos	BFW
FITZGERALD, JUSTIN Justin Howard B 6.22.1890 San Mateo, CA D 1.18.1945 San Mateo, CA BL/TR 5-8/160# d6.20																								
1911	NY A	16	37	6	10	1	0	0	6	4	0		.270	.341	.297	74	-1	4	1.000	-1	73	94	/O-9(LF)	-0.2
1918	Phi N	66	133	21	39	8	0	0	6	13	1	6	.293	.361	.353	110	2	3	.966	-4	84	48	O-59(34-2-19)	-0.3
Total	2	82	170	27	49	9	0	0	12	17	1	6	.288	.356	.341	102	1	7	.971	-4	82	56	/O-68(43-2-19)	-0.5
FITZGERALD, MATTY Matthew William B 8.31.1880 Albany, NY D 9.22.1949 Albany, NY BR/TR 6/185# d9.15																								
1906	NY N	4	6	2	4	0	0	0	2	0	0		.667	.667	.667	309	1	1	1.000	0	*161*	*0*	/C-3	0.2
1907	NY N	7	15	1	2	1	0	0	1	0	0		.133	.133	.200	4	-2	0	.952	-1	*129*	*93*	/C-6	-0.2
Total	2	11	21	3	6	1	0	0	3	0	0		.286	.286	.333	91	-1	1	.967	-1	*138*	*66*	/C-9	0.0
FITZGERALD, MIKE Michael Patrick B 3.28.1964 Savannah, GA BR/TR 6-1/196# d6.23																								
1988	StL N	13	46	4	9	1	0	0	1	0-0	1	9	.196	.213	.217	23	-5	0-0	.990	-1	54	128	1-12	-0.8
FITZGERALD, MIKE Michael Roy B 7.13.1960 Long Beach, CA BR/TR 5-11/190# d9.13 OF Total (15-LF 15-RF)																								
1983	NY N	8	20	1	2	0	0	1	2	3-1	0	6	.100	.217	.250	29	-2	0-0	.957	1	52	195	/C-8	-0.1
1984	NY N	112	360	20	87	15	1	2	33	24-7	1	71	.242	.288	.306	69	-15	1-0	**.995**	7	100	99	*C-107	-0.4
1985	Mon N	108	295	25	61	7	1	5	34	38-12	2	55	.207	.297	.288	70	-12	5-3	.987	-7	75	81	*C-108	-1.6
1986	Mon N	73	209	20	59	13	1	6	37	27-6	1	34	.282	.364	.440	123	7	3-2	.993	-5	69	78	C-71	0.5
1987	Mon N	107	287	32	69	11	0	3	36	42-7	1	54	.240	.338	.310	71	-10	3-4	.981	-7	70	67	*C-104/12	-1.5
1988	Mon N	63	155	17	42	6	1	5	23	19-0	0	22	.271	.347	.419	115	3	2-2	.979	2	57	81	C-47/O-4(3-0-1)	0.7
1989	Mon N	100	290	33	69	18	2	7	42	35-3	2	61	.238	.322	.386	101	1	3-4	.984	-7	72	103	C-77/3-8,O-6(LF)	-0.3
1990	Mon N	111	313	36	76	18	1	9	41	60-2	2	60	.243	.365	.393	114	9	8-1	.990	-4	74	85	C-98/O-6(1-0-5)	1.2
1991	Mon N	71	198	17	40	5	2	4	28	22-4	0	35	.202	.278	.308	67	-9	4-2	.994	2	62	112	C-54/1-3,O-3(RF)	-0.5
1992	Cal A	95	189	19	40	2	0	6	17	22-0	0	34	.212	.294	.317	71	-8	2-2	.990	-7	93	96	C-74,O-11(5-0-6)/3-3,1-2,2D	-1.2
Total	10	848	2316	220	545	95	9	48	293	292-42	9	432	.235	.321	.346	87	-36	31-20	.988	-26	76	89	C-748/O-30L,3-11,1-6,2-2,D	-3.2
FITZGERALD, RAY Raymond Francis B 12.5.1904 Chicopee, MA D 9.6.1977 Westfield, MA BR/TR 5-9/168# d4.18																								
1931	Cin N	1	1	0	0	0	0	0	0	0	0	0	.000	.000	.000	-99	0	0	—	0			H	0.0
FITZMAURICE, SHAUN Shaun Earle B 8.25.1942 Worcester, MA BR/TR 6/180# d9.9																								
1966	NY N	9	13	2	2	0	0	0	0	2-0	0	6	.154	.267	.154	21	-1	1-0	1.000	1	114	379	/O-5(2-3-0)	0.0
FITZPATRICK, ED Edward Henry B 12.9.1889 Lewistown, PA D 10.23.1965 Bethlehem, PA BR/TR 5-8/165# d4.17 Mil 1918																								
1915	Bos N	105	303	54	67	19	3	0	24	43	14	36	.221	.344	.304	101	4	13-8	.967	-1	94	102	2-71,O-29(0-7-22)	0.3
1916	Bos N	83	216	17	46	8	0	1	18	15	5	26	.213	.280	.264	70	-7	5	.950	-10	81	97	2-46,O-28(2-3-23)	-2.0
1917	Bos N	63	178	20	45	8	4	0	17	12	5	22	.253	.318	.343	109	2	4	.929	-11	86	25	2-22,O-19(4-6-7),3-15	-1.0
Total	3	251	697	91	158	35	7	1	59	70	24	84	.227	.319	.301	94	-1	22-8	.956	-22	88	88	2-139/O-76(6-16-52),3-15	-2.7
FITZSIMMONS, TOM Thomas William B 4.6.1890 Oakland, CA D 12.20.1971 Oakland, CA BR/TR 6-1/190# d6.12																								
1919	Bro N	4	4	1	0	0	0	0	0	1	0	2	.000	.200	.000	-36	-1	0	.500	-1	36	0	/3-4	-0.2
FLACK, MAX Max John B 2.5.1890 Belleville, IL D 7.31.1975 Belleville, IL BL/TL 5-7/148# d4.16																								
1914	Chi F	134	502	66	124	15	3	2	39	51	6	48	.247	.324	.301	75	-25	37	.973	-2	98	85	*O-133(112-0-23)	-3.5
1915	Chi F	141	523	88	164	20	14	3	45	40	2	21	.314	.365	.423	129	10	37	.969	5	97	137	*O-138(61-0-81)	0.9
1916	Chi N	141	465	65	120	14	3	3	20	42	0	43	.258	.320	.320	87	-6	24-19	**.991**	3	91	138	*O-136(RF)	-1.3
1917	Chi N	131	447	65	111	18	7	0	21	51	0	34	.248	.325	.320	91	-3	17	.947	-2	97	97	*O-117(40-6-77)	-1.3
1918	†Chi N	123	478	74	123	17	10	4	41	56	6	19	.257	.343	.360	111	8	17	.978	-1	94	102	*O-121(RF)	0.0
1919	Chi N	116	469	71	138	20	4	6	35	34	3	13	.294	.346	.392	121	12	18	.986	-0	94	109	*O-116(RF)	0.6
1920	Chi N	135	520	85	157	30	6	4	49	52	7	15	.302	.373	.406	121	17	13-19	.967	-5	90	99	*O-132(0-1-131)	0.1
1921	Chi N	133	572	80	172	31	4	6	37	32	4	15	.301	.342	.400	96	-3	17-11	**.989**	-0	97	106	*O-130(RF)	-1.4
1922	Chi N	17	54	7	12	1	0	0	6	2	0	4	.222	.250	.241	27	-6	2-1	.933	-2	101	0	O-15(RF)	-0.8
	StL N	66	267	46	78	12	1	2	21	31	1	11	.292	.368	.367	95	-1	3-5	.968	-3	94	62	O-66(0-1-65)	-1.0
	Year	83	321	53	90	13	1	2	27	33	1	15	.280	.349	.346	83	-7	5-6	.961	-5	95	51	O-81(0-1-80)	-1.8
1923	StL N	128	505	82	147	16	9	3	28	41	3	16	.291	.348	.376	93	-5	7-8	.951	-5	100	58	*O-121(RF)	-2.0
1924	StL N	67	209	31	55	11	3	2	21	21	0	5	.263	.330	.373	90	-3	3-5	.971	2	99	162	O-52(RF)	-0.5
1925	StL N	79	241	23	60	7	8	0	28	21	0	9	.249	.309	.344	65	-13	5-3	.991	1	100	116	O-59(5-0-54)	-1.5
Total	12	1411	5252	783	1461	212	72	35	391	474	32	253	.278	.342	.366	99	-18	200-71	.972	-10	96	103	*O-1336(218-8-1122)	-11.7
FLAGER, WALLY Walter Leonard B 11.3.1921 Chicago Heights, IL D 12.16.1990 Keizer, OR BL/TR 5-11/160# d4.17																								
1945	Cin N	21	52	5	11	1	0	0	6	8	0	5	.212	.317	.231	55	-3	0	.933	-4	85	58	S-15	-0.6
	Phi N	49	168	21	42	4	1	2	15	17	1	15	.250	.323	.321	82	-4	1	.946	5	105	91	S-48/2	0.4
	Year	70	220	26	53	5	1	2	21	25	1	20	.241	.321	.300	75	-7	1	.943	0	101	84	S-63/2	-0.2
FLAGSTEAD, IRA Ira James "Pete" B 9.22.1893 Montague, MI D 3.13.1940 Olympia, WA BR/TR 5-9/165# d7.20 Mil 1918																								
1917	Det A	4	4	0	0	0	0	0	0	0	0	1	.000	.000	.000	-99	-1	0	—	-0	0	0	/O-2(RF)	-0.1
1919	Det A	97	287	43	95	22	3	5	41	35	7	39	.331	.416	.481	155	23	6	.951	1	93	127	O-83(RF)	2.0
1920	Det A	110	311	40	73	13	5	3	35	37	1	27	.235	.318	.338	76	-11	3-4	.967	3	105	113	O-82(1-6-75)	-1.3
1921	Det A	85	259	40	79	16	2	0	31	21	6	21	.305	.371	.382	93	-2	8-4	.903	-7	90	33	S-55,O-12(6-2-5)/2-8,3	-0.3
1922	Det A	44	91	21	28	5	3	3	8	14	2	16	.308	.411	.527	148	7	0-1	.967	0	96	132	O-32(8-9-15)	0.5
1923	Det A	1	1	0	0	0	0	0	0	0	0	0	.000	.000	.000	-99	0	0-0	—	0			H	0.0
	Bos A	109	382	55	119	23	4	8	53	37	5	26	.312	.380	.455	119	10	7-10	.965	14	101	213	*O-102(0-3-99)/S	1.3
	Year	110	383	55	119	23	4	8	53	37	5	26	.311	.379	.454	118	10	7-10	.965	14	101	213	*O-102(0-3-99)/S	1.3
1924	Bos A	149	560	106	172	35	7	5	43	77	11	41	.307	.401	.421	112	14	10-13	.975	-10	94	64	*O-144(0-143-1)	-0.4
1925	Bos A	148	572	84	160	38	2	6	61	63	5	30	.280	.356	.385	88	-9	5-6	.976	14	108	154	*O-144(CF)	-0.2
1926	Bos A	98	415	65	124	31	7	3	31	36	6	22	.299	.363	.429	110	6	4-6	.982	-2	96	133	O-98(CF)	-0.2
1927	Bos A	131	466	63	133	26	8	4	69	57	9	25	.285	.374	.401	103	4	12-2	**.986**	4	97	145	*O-129(0-128-1)	0.4
1928	Bos A	140	510	84	148	41	4	1	39	60	1	23	.290	.366	.392	101	3	12-9	.973	2	99	123	*O-135(CF)	-0.1
1929	Bos A	14	36	9	11	2	0	0	3	5	0	1	.306	.390	.361	97	0	1-3	.955	-1	97	0	O-13(13-1-0)	-0.2
	Was A	18	39	5	7	1	0	0	9	4	0	5	.179	.256	.205	20	-5	1-0	.971	3	103	353	O-11(1-10-0)	-0.2
	Year	32	75	14	18	3	0	0	12	9	0	6	.240	.321	.280	57	-5	2-3	.965	2	100	187	O-24(14-11-0)	-0.4
	Pit N	26	50	8	14	2	1	0	6	4	0	2	.280	.333	.360	70	-2	1	1.000	-0	103	0	/O-9(6-1-2)	-0.3
1930	Pit N	44	156	21	39	7	4	2	21	17	0	9	.250	.324	.385	70	-8	1	.961	-1	89	141	O-40(21-15-5)	-1.0
Total	13	1218	4139	644	1202	262	50	40	450	467	53	288	.290	.370	.407	103	29	71-58	.974	20	99	134	*O-1036(56-695-288)/S-56,2-8,3	-0.1
FLAHERTY, JOHN John Timothy B 10.21.1967 New York, NY BR/TR 6-1/195# d4.12																								
1992	Bos A	35	66	3	13	2	0	0	2	3-0	0	7	.197	.229	.227	27	-6	0-0	.982	-6	107	83	C-34	-1.2
1993	Bos A	13	25	3	3	2	0	0	2	2-0	1	6	.120	.214	.200	11	-3	0-0	1.000	-2	67	146	C-13	-0.5
1994	Det A	34	40	2	6	1	0	0	4	1-0	0	11	.150	.167	.175	-11	-7	0-1	1.000	0	69	111	C-33/D	-0.5
1995	Det A	112	354	39	86	22	1	11	40	18-0	3	47	.243	.284	.404	77	-13	0-0	.982	-12	88	80	*C-112	-1.7
1996	Det A	47	152	18	38	12	0	4	23	8-1	1	25	.250	.290	.408	75	-6	1-0	.981	-9	122	79	C-46	-1.2
	†SD N	72	264	22	80	12	0	9	41	9-1	2	36	.303	.327	.451	110	3	2-3	.990	-8	96	111	C-72	-0.1
1997	SD N	129	439	38	120	21	1	9	46	33-7	0	62	.273	.323	.387	92	-6	4-4	.987	-26	71	120	*C-124	-2.5
1998	TB A	91	304	21	63	11	0	3	24	22-0	1	46	.207	.261	.273	39	-28	0-5	.993	6	129	105	C-91	-1.7
1999	TB A	117	446	53	124	19	0	14	71	19-0	6	64	.278	.310	.415	84	-12	0-2	.993	7	95	**147**	*C-115/D	0.1
2000	TB A	109	394	36	103	15	0	10	39	20-2	0	57	.261	.296	.376	70	-20	0-0	.993	-3	76	111	*C-108	-1.5
2001	TB A	78	248	20	59	17	1	4	29	10-1	1	33	.238	.269	.363	66	-13	1-0	.986	-7	89	77	C-78	-1.5
2002	TB A	76	281	27	73	20	0	4	33	15-0	1	50	.260	.296	.374	79	-9	2-2	.992	-8	85	136	C-75	-1.1
2003	†NY A	40	105	16	28	8	0	4	14	4-1	0	19	.267	.297	.457	97	-1	0-0	.991	-6	93	116	C-40	-0.4
Total	12	953	3118	298	796	162	3	72	368	164-13	17	463	.255	.293	.378	75	-121	10-17	.989	-75	92	110	C-941/D-2	-13.8
FLAHERTY, MARTIN Martin J. B 9.24.1853 Worcester, MA D 6.10.1920 Providence, RI BL/TL d8.18																								
1881	Wor N	1	2	0	0	0	0	0	0	0		2	.000	.000	.000	-95	0		.000	-1	0	0	/O(1-1-0)	-0.1
FLAHERTY, PAT Patrick Henry B 1.31.1866 St.Louis, MO D 1.28.1946 Chicago, IL BR 5-9/166# d7.11																								
1894	Lou N	39	150	15	43	5	3	0	15	9	1	7	.287	.331	.360	71	-7	2	.852	-2	99	117	3-39	-0.6
FLAHERTY, PATSY Patrick Joseph B 6.29.1876 Mansfield, PA D 1.23.1968 Alexandria, LA BL/TL 5-8/165# d9.8 ▲																								
1899	Lou N	7	24	3	5	1	1	0	6	3	0		.208	.296	.333	73	-1	0	.692	-1	71	0	/P-5,O-2(RF)	-0.1

Year	Tm Lg	G	AB	R	H	2B	3B	HR	RBI	BB-IB	HP	SO	AVG	OBP	SLG	AOPS	ABR	SB-CS	FA	FR	Rng	Thr	G at Pos	BFW
1900	Pit N	4	9	0	1	0	0	0	0	1	0		.111	.200	.111	-13	-1	0	1.000	1	181	0	/P-4	0.0
1903	Chi A	40	102	7	14	4	0	0	5	5	0		.137	.178	.176	7	-3	4	.914	2	121	241	P-40	0.0
1904	Chi A	5	12	1	4	1	0	0	0	4	0		.333	.500	.417	199	3	0	.880	1	129	0	/P-5	0.0
	Pit N	36	104	9	22	3	4	2	19	8	0		.212	.268	.375	95	-1	0	.965	4	132	146	P-29/O-2(CF)	0.2
1905	Pit N	30	76	7	15	4	2	0	4	3	0		.197	.228	.303	56	-4	0	.894	2	133	69	P-27/O-2(0-1-1)	0.0
1907	Bos N	41	115	9	22	3	2	2	11	2	1		.191	.212	.304	62	-6	1	.907	3	126	**316**	P-27/O-8(6-0-2)	-0.1
1908	Bos N	32	86	8	12	0	2	0	5	6	0		.140	.196	.186	22	0	2	.961	2	114	152	P-31	0.0
1910	Phi N	2	2	0	1	0	0	0	0	0	0	0	.500	.500	.500	186	0	0	—	0	0	0	/PO(CF)	0.0
1911	Bos N	38	94	9	27	3	2	2	20	8	0	11	.287	.343	.426	106	0	2	.933	-3	74	82	O-19(1-11-7)/P-4	-0.3
Total	9	235	624	53	123	19	13	6	70	40	1	11	.197	.247	.298	63	-13	9	.921	10	124	173	P-173/O-34(7-15-12)	-0.3
FLAIR, AL Albert Dell "Broadway" B 7.24.1916 New Orleans, LA D 7.25.1988 New Orleans, LA BL/TL 6-4/195# d9.6 Mil 1942-45																								
1941	Bos A	10	30	3	6	2	1	0	2	1	0	1	.200	.226	.333	45	-3	1-1	1.000	-0	85	86	/1-8	-0.3
FLANAGAN, CHARLIE Charles James B 12.31.1891 Oakland, CA D 1.8.1930 San Francisco, CA BR/TR 6/175# d7.9																								
1913	StL A	4	3	0	0	0	0	0	0	1	0	0	.000	.250	.000	-26	0	0	—	-0	0	0	/3O(LF)	-0.1
FLANAGAN, ED Edward J. "Sleepy" B 9.15.1861 Lowell, MA D 11.10.1926 Lowell, MA 6-1/190# d4.16																								
1887	Phi AA	19	80	12	20	5	0	1	10	3	1		.250	.286	.350	77	-3	3	.948	-1	82	100	1-19	-0.4
1889	Lou AA	23	88	11	22	7	3	0	8	7	0	11	.250	.305	.398	101	0	1	.953	-1	116	71	1-23	-0.3
Total	2	42	168	23	42	12	3	1	18	10	1	11	.250	.296	.375	89	-3	4	.951	-2	101	84	/1-42	-0.7
FLANAGAN, STEAMER James Paul B 4.20.1881 Kingston, PA D 4.21.1947 Wilkes-Barre, PA BL/TL 6-1/185# d9.25																								
1905	Pit N	7	25	7	7	1	1	0	3	1	0		.280	.308	.400	108	0	3	1.000	0	0	0	/O-5(CF)	0.0
FLANNERY, JOHN John Michael B 1.25.1957 Long Beach, CA BR/TR 6-3/173# d9.2																								
1977	Chi A	7	2	1	0	0	0	0	0	1-0	0	1	.000	.333	.000	0	0	0-0	1.000	0	117	140	/S-4,3D	0.0
FLANNERY, TIM Timothy Earl B 9.29.1957 Tulsa, OK BL/TR 5-11/175# d9.3 C7																								
1979	SD N	22	65	2	10	0	1	0	4	4-1	2	5	.154	.222	.185	14	-8	0-0	.991	3	113	132	2-21	-0.4
1980	SD N	95	292	15	70	12	0	0	25	18-4	0	30	.240	.283	.281	62	-15	2-2	.988	3	105	110	2-53,3-41	-1.2
1981	SD N	37	67	4	17	4	1	0	6	2-1	0	4	.254	.268	.343	80	-2	1-0	.967	-4	78	196	3-15/2-7	-0.6
1982	SD N	122	379	40	100	11	7	0	30	30-10	2	32	.264	.317	.330	87	-7	1-0	.974	-19	92	83	*2-104/3-5,S-2	-2.1
1983	SD N	92	214	24	50	7	3	3	19	20-8	5	23	.234	.309	.336	83	-5	2-2	.969	6	114	197	3-52,2-21/S-7	0.1
1984	†SD N	86	128	24	35	3	3	2	10	12-1	3	17	.273	.347	.391	108	1	4-1	.944	-6	99	55	2-22,3-14,S-14	-0.3
1985	SD N	126	384	50	108	14	3	1	40	58-1	9	39	.281	.386	.341	107	7	2-5	.977	-19	89	106	*2-121/3	-0.8
1986	SD N	134	368	48	103	11	2	3	28	54-4	5	61	.280	.378	.345	103	4	3-6	.993	3	96	96	*2-108,3-23/S-8	1.1
1987	SD N	106	276	23	63	5	1	0	20	42-4	2	30	.228	.332	.254	61	-14	2-4	.986	-0	100	90	2-84/3-8,S-2	-1.2
1988	SD N	79	170	16	45	5	4	0	19	24-1	4	32	.265	.365	.341	107	3	3-2	.972	-5	93	121	3-51/2-2,S	-0.2
1989	SD N	73	130	9	30	5	0	0	8	13-0	0	20	.231	.299	.269	64	-6	2-0	.920	1	110	77	3-33/2	-0.5
Total	11	972	2473	255	631	77	25	9	209	277-35	32	293	.255	.335	.317	86	-42	22-22	.982	-38	96	95	2-544,3-243/S-34	-6.1
FLASKAMPER, ROY Raymond Harold "Flash" B 10.31.1901 St.Louis, MO D 2.3.1978 San Antonio, TX BB/TR 5-7/140# d8.16																								
1927	Chi A	26	95	12	21	5	0	0	6	3	2	8	.221	.260	.274	40	-9	0-0	.962	-1	96	80	S-25	-0.7
FLEET, FRANK Frank H. B 1848 New York, NY D 6.13.1900 New York, NY d10.18 I OF Total (1-LF 2-CF 1-RF)																								
1871	Mut NA	1	6	1	2	0	0	0	1	0	0		.333	.333	.333	101	0	0-0	1.000	1	322	0	/P	0.0
1872	Eck NA	13	53	9	12	1	0	0	6	0	2		.226	.226	.245	53	-2	1-0	.800	2	107	56	3-10/2-2,O-2(0-1-1)	0.0
1873	Res NA	22	89	11	23	3	0	0	10	1	3		.258	.267	.292	71	-2	0-2	.808	3	105	88	/S-9,2-8,P-3,3-3,1	-0.1
1874	Atl NA	22	97	18	22	0	0	0	10	1	1		.227	.235	.227	55	-4	1-0	.759	-5			C-13,2-11/O(LF)	-0.7
1875	StL NA	4	16	1	1	0	0	0	1	0	0		.063	.063	.063	-62	-2	0-0	.900	0	124	479	/P-3,3O(CF)	-0.1
	Atl NA	26	111	13	25	2	0	0	9	1	1		.225	.232	.243	75	-2	0-0	.719	-9			C-11,2-10/S-9,P-2,3	-1.0
	Year	30	127	14	26	2	0	0	10	1	1		.205	.211	.220	57	-4	0-0	.719	-8			C-11,2-10/S-9,P-5,3-2,O(CF)	-1.1
Total	5 NA	88	372	53	85	6	0	0	37	3	7		.228	.235	.245	61	-12	2-2	.000	-7			/2-31,C-24,S-18,3-15,P-9,O-4C,1	-1.9
FLEITAS, ANGEL Angel Felix Husta B 11.10.1914 Los Abreus, Cuba BR/TR 5-9/160# d7.5																								
1948	Was A	15	13	1	1	0	0	0	1	3	0	5	.077	.250	.077	-11	-2	0-2	.952	1	132	0	/S-7	-0.2
FLEMING, LES Leslie Harvey "Moe" B 8.7.1915 Singleton, TX D 3.5.1980 Cleveland, TX BL/TL 5-10/185# d4.22																								
1939	Det A	8	16	0	0	0	0	0	1	0	0	4	.000	.000	.000	-93	-5	0-0	1.000	0	113	0	/O-3(1-0-2)	-0.5
1941	Cle A	2	8	0	2	1	0	0	2	0	0	0	.250	.250	.375	67	0	0-0	1.000	-0	70	171	/1-2	-0.1
1942	Cle A	**156**	548	71	160	27	4	14	82	106	6	57	.292	.412	.432	146	40	6-8	**.993**	-7	84	116	*1-156	1.7
1945	Cle A	42	140	18	46	10	2	3	22	11	1	5	.329	.382	.493	160	10	0-0	.938	-1	102	68	O-33(RF)/1-5	0.8
1946	Cle A	99	306	40	85	17	5	8	42	50	2	42	.278	.383	.444	140	18	1-0	.984	3	113	87	1-80/O(RF)	1.8
1947	Cle A	103	281	39	68	14	2	4	43	53	0	42	.242	.362	.349	101	2	0-0	.989	3	115	123	1-77	0.3
1949	Pit N	24	31	0	8	0	2	0	7	6	1	2	.258	.395	.387	108	0	0	1.000	-1	0	105	/1-5	-0.1
Total	7	434	1330	168	369	69	15	29	199	226	10	152	.277	.386	.417	131	65	7-8	.990	-3	98	110	1-325/O-37(1-0-36)	3.9
FLEMING, TOM Thomas Vincent "Sleuth" B 11.20.1873 Philadelphia, PA D 12.26.1957 Boston, MA BL/TL 5-11/155# d9.19																								
1899	NY N	22	77	9	16	1	1	0	4	1	0		.208	.218	.247	28	-8	1	.909	1	177	0	O-22(CF)	-0.8
1902	Phi N	5	16	2	6	0	0	0	2	1	0		.375	.412	.375	143	1	0	1.000	1	396	0	/O-5(RF)	0.1
1904	Phi N	3	6	0	0	0	0	0	0	0	0		.000	.000	.000	-99	-1	0	1.000	1	994	0	/O(RF)	-0.1
Total	3	30	99	11	22	1	1	0	6	2	0		.222	.238	.253	39	-8	1	.920	2	242	0	/O-28(0-22-6)	-0.8
FLETCHER, ART Arthur B 1.5.1885 Collinsville, IL D 2.6.1950 Los Angeles, CA BR/TR 5-10.5/170# d4.15 M5 C19																								
1909	NY N	33	98	7	21	0	1	0	6	1	2		.214	.238	.235	46	-7	1	.893	-1	93	116	S-22/2-7,3-6	-0.7
1910	NY N	51	125	12	28	2	1	0	13	4	0	9	.224	.248	.256	47	-9	9	.895	-5	82	90	S-22,2-11,3-11	-1.4
1911	†NY N	112	326	73	104	17	8	1	37	30	14	27	.319	.400	.429	128	13	20	.926	5	102	88	S-74,3-21,2-13	2.4
1912	†NY N	129	419	64	118	17	9	1	57	16	14	29	.282	.330	.372	89	-8	16	.927	15	108	131	*S-126/2-2,3	1.5
1913	†NY N	136	538	76	160	20	9	4	71	24	**15**	35	.297	.345	.390	109	5	32-18	.932	-6	102	96	*S-136	1.0
1914	NY N	135	514	62	147	26	8	2	79	22	**13**	37	.286	.332	.379	115	8	15	.922	6	105	101	*S-135	2.5
1915	NY N	149	562	59	143	17	7	3	74	6	14	36	.254	.280	.326	88	-11	12-18	.936	**35**	**118**	127	*S-149	3.3
1916	NY N	133	500	53	143	23	8	3	66	13	**14**	36	.286	.323	.382	122	11	15	.940	22	**114**	105	*S-133	4.7
1917	†NY N	151	557	70	145	24	5	4	56	23	**19**	28	.260	.312	.343	104	3	12	**.956**	28	**114**	119	*S-151	4.5
1918	NY N	**124**	468	51	123	20	2	0	47	18	**15**	26	.263	.311	.314	93	-4	12	**.959**	**25**	**113**	116	*S-124	3.3
1919	NY N	127	488	54	135	20	5	3	54	9	7	28	.277	.300	.357	98	-3	6	.944	25	**119**	95	*S-127	3.4
1920	NY N	41	171	21	44	7	2	0	24	1	5	15	.257	.282	.322	74	-6	3-2	.914	1	112	94	S-41	-0.3
	Phi N	102	379	36	112	25	7	4	38	15	4	28	.296	.329	.430	112	5	4-6	.958	14	109	93	*S-102	2.6
	Year	143	550	57	156	32	9	4	62	16	9	43	.284	.315	.396	100	-1	7-8	.945	14	110	93	*S-143	2.3
1922	Phi N	110	396	46	111	20	5	7	53	21	5	14	.280	.325	.409	80	-12	3-2	.939	6	**111**	102	*S-106	0.4
Total	13	1533	5541	684	1534	238	77	32	675	203	141	348	.277	.319	.365	100	-15	160-46	.939	169	110	108	*S-1448/3-39,2-33	27.2
FLETCHER, DARRIN Darrin Glen B 10.3.1966 Elmhurst, IL BL/TR 6-1/199# d9.10 f-Tom																								
1989	LA N	5	8	1	4	0	0	1	2	1-0	0	0	.500	.556	.875	308	2	0-0	1.000	0	0	0	/C-5	0.3
1990	LA N	2	1	0	0	0	0	0	0	0-0	0	1	.000	.000	.000	-99	0	0-0	—	-0	0	0	/C	-0.1
	Phi N	9	22	3	3	1	0	0	1	1-0	0	5	.136	.174	.182	-2	-3	0-0	1.000	-1	59	0	/C-6	-0.4
	Year	11	23	3	3	1	0	0	1	1-0	0	6	.130	.167	.174	-6	-3	0-0	1.000	-2	58	0	/C-7	-0.5
1991	Phi N	46	136	5	31	8	0	1	12	5-0	0	15	.228	.255	.309	59	-8	0-1	.992	0	99	80	C-45	-0.6
1992	Mon N	83	222	13	54	10	2	2	26	14-3	2	28	.243	.289	.333	78	-7	0-2	.995	-7	63	109	C-69	-1.2
1993	Mon N	133	396	33	101	20	1	9	60	34-2	6	40	.255	.320	.379	84	-9	0-0	.988	-6	73	73	*C-127	-0.7
1994	Mon N★	94	285	28	74	18	1	10	57	25-4	3	23	.260	.314	.435	95	-2	0-0	.996	-8	79	79	C-81	-0.6
1995	Mon N	110	350	42	100	21	1	11	45	32-1	4	23	.286	.351	.446	105	3	0-1	.994	7	82	127	C-98	1.5
1996	Mon N	127	394	41	105	22	0	12	57	27-4	6	42	.266	.321	.414	90	-6	0-0	.992	-11	70	88	*C-112	-1.0
1997	Mon N	96	310	39	86	20	1	17	55	17-3	5	35	.277	.323	.513	116	6	1-1	.994	1	87	56	C-83	1.1
1998	Tor A	124	407	37	115	23	1	9	52	25-7	6	39	.283	.328	.410	92	-5	0-0	.991	6	75	92	*C-121/D	0.8
1999	Tor A	115	412	48	120	26	0	18	80	26-0	6	47	.291	.339	.485	106	3	0-0	.997	-15	85	87	*C-113	-0.4
2000	Tor A	122	416	43	133	19	1	20	58	20-3	5	45	.320	.355	.514	114	7	1-0	.994	-8	83	79	*C-117/D-2	0.6
2001	Tor A	134	416	36	94	20	0	11	56	24-4	6	43	.226	.274	.353	63	-23	0-1	.995	-7	109	90	*C-129/D	-2.2

Year	Tm Lg	G	AB	R	H	2B	3B	HR	RBI	BB-IB	HP	SO	AVG	OBP	SLG	AOPS	ABR	SB-CS	FA	FR	Rng	Thr	G at Pos	BFW
2002	Tor A	45	127	8	28	6	0	3	22	4-0	0	13	.220	.239	.339	51	-9	0-0	.995	-2	69	92	C-36/D-4	-0.9
Total	14	1245	3902	377	1048	214	8	124	583	255-31	49	399	.269	.318	.423	92	-51	2-6	.993	-51	82	87	*C-1143/D-8	-3.8
FLETCHER, ELBIE Elburt Preston B 3.18.1916 Milton, MA D 3.9.1994 Milton, MA BL/TL 6/180# d9.16 Mil 1944-45																								
1934	Bos N	8	4	4	2	0	0	0	0	0	0	2	.500	.500	.500	182	0	1	.875	-0	0	287	/1	0.0
1935	Bos N	39	148	12	35	7	1	1	9	7	0	13	.236	.271	.318	63	-8	1	.997	2	117	75	1-39	-0.9
1937	Bos N	148	539	56	133	22	4	1	38	56	3	64	.247	.321	.308	79	-15	3	.993	-1	101	110	*1-148	-3.0
1938	Bos N	147	529	71	144	24	7	6	48	60	4	40	.272	.351	.378	112	9	5	.990	8	**127**	93	*1-146	0.4
1939	Bos N	35	106	14	26	2	0	0	6	19	1	5	.245	.365	.264	77	-2	1	.986	-6	39	123	1-31	-1.1
	Pit N	102	370	49	112	23	4	12	71	48	2	28	.303	.386	.484	134	19	3	.993	-5	82	104	*1-101	0.5
	Year	137	476	63	138	25	4	12	77	67	3	33	.290	.381	.435	122	17	4	.991	-10	72	108	*1-132	-0.6
1940	Pit N	147	510	94	139	22	7	16	104	**119**	**9**	54	.273	**.418**	.437	137	34	5	.993	5	**111**	97	*1-147	2.5
1941	Pit N	151	521	95	150	29	13	11	74	**118**	2	54	.288	**.421**	.457	148	40	5	.991	10	**128**	93	*1-151	3.6
1942	Pit N	145	506	86	146	22	5	7	57	105	6	60	.289	**.417**	.393	134	29	0	.992	11	**131**	92	*1-144	2.8
1943	Pit N★	154	544	91	154	24	5	9	70	95	6	49	.283	.395	.395	124	22	1	**.996**	3	107	109	*1-154	1.8
1946	Pit N	148	532	72	136	25	8	4	66	111	0	37	.256	.384	.355	108	11	4	.995	2	104	78	*1-147	0.9
1947	Pit N	69	157	22	38	9	1	1	22	29	1	24	.242	.364	.331	83	-2	2	.986	-1	99	86	1-50	-0.4
1949	Bos N	122	413	57	108	19	3	11	51	84	8	65	.262	.396	.402	121	17	1	.991	1	**102**	99	*1-121	1.4
Total	12	1415	4879	723	1323	228	58	79	616	851	42	495	.271	.384	.390	118	154	32	.993	30	110	97	*1-1380	8.5
FLETCHER, GEORGE George Horace Elliott B 4.21.1845 Brooklyn, NY D 6.18.1879 Brooklyn, NY d6.21																								
1872	Eck NA	2	8	1	2	0	0	0	1	0		1	.250	.250	.250	64	0	0-0	.600	-0	0	0	/O-2(RF)	0.0
FLETCHER, FRANK Oliver Frank B 3.6.1891 Hildreth, IL D 10.7.1974 St.Petersburg, FL BR/TR 5-10/165# d7.14																								
1914	Phi N	1	1	0	0	0	0	0	0	0	0	1	.000	.000	.000	-94	0	0	—	0			H	0.0
FLETCHER, SCOTT Scott Brian B 7.30.1958 Fort Walton Beach, FL BR/TR 5-11/173# d4.25																								
1981	Chi N	19	46	6	10	4	0	0	1	2-0	0	4	.217	.250	.304	54	-3	0-0	.972	4	108	131	2-13/S-4,3	0.2
1982	Chi N	11	24	4	4	0	0	0	1	4-0	0	5	.167	.286	.167	29	-2	1-0	1.000	-1	100	70	S-11	-0.2
1983	†Chi A	114	262	42	62	16	5	3	31	29-0	2	22	.237	.315	.370	85	-5	5-1	.965	23	116	122	*S-100,2-12/3-7,D	2.7
1984	Chi A	149	456	46	114	13	3	3	35	46-2	8	46	.250	.328	.311	75	-14	10-4	.973	14	107	108	*S-134,2-28/3-3	1.4
1985	Chi A	119	301	38	77	8	1	2	31	35-0	0	47	.256	.332	.309	74	-10	5-5	.934	3	89	97	3-55,S-44,2-37/D-2	-0.4
1986	Tex A	147	530	82	159	34	5	3	50	47-0	4	59	.300	.360	.400	104	5	12-11	.973	6	101	102	*S-136,3-12,2-11/D	2.3
1987	Tex A	156	588	82	169	28	4	5	63	61-3	5	66	.287	.358	.374	95	-2	13-12	.966	12	100	105	*S-155	2.2
1988	Tex A	140	515	59	142	19	4	0	47	62-1	12	34	.276	.364	.328	94	-1	8-5	.983	10	104	101	*S-139	1.9
1989	Tex A	83	314	47	75	14	1	0	22	38-1	2	41	.239	.323	.290	73	-10	1-0	.960	-14	78	86	S-81/D	-1.8
	Chi A	59	232	30	63	11	1	1	21	26-0	1	19	.272	.344	.341	97	0	1-1	1.000	-5	102	103	2-53/S-8	-0.3
	Year	142	546	77	138	25	2	1	43	64-1	3	60	.253	.332	.311	83	-10	2-1	.957	-18	76	88	S-89,2-53/D	-2.1
1990	Chi A	151	509	54	123	18	3	4	56	45-3	3	63	.242	.304	.312	75	-17	1-3	.988	-6	96	**115**	*2-151	-2.1
1991	Chi A	90	248	14	51	10	1	1	28	17-0	3	26	.206	.262	.266	48	-18	0-2	.992	-9	86	105	2-86/3-4	-2.5
1992	Mil A	123	386	53	106	18	3	3	51	30-1	7	33	.275	.335	.360	98	-1	17-10	.992	10	107	119	*2-106,S-22/3	1.4
1993	Bos A	121	480	81	137	31	5	5	45	37-1	5	35	.285	.341	.402	94	-4	16-3	.982	13	111	95	*2-116/S-2,3D	1.7
1994	Bos A	63	185	31	42	9	1	3	11	16-1	2	14	.227	.296	.335	59	-11	8-1	.996	11	107	120	2-53/D-4	0.3
1995	Det A	67	182	19	42	10	1	1	17	19-0	3	27	.231	.312	.313	64	-9	1-0	1.000	5	107	131	2-63/S-3,1D	-0.2
Total	15	1612	5258	688	1376	243	38	34	510	514-13	57	541	.262	.332	.342	84	-102	99-58	.971	78	101	104	S-839,2-729/3-84,D-11,1	6.6
FLICK, ELMER Elmer Harrison B 1.11.1876 Bedford, OH D 1.9.1971 Bedford, OH BL/TR 5-9/168# d4.26 HF1963																								
1898	Phi N	134	453	84	137	16	13	8	81	86	15		.302	.430	.448	158	41	23	.931	6	114	89	*O-133(RF)	3.7
1899	Phi N	127	485	98	166	22	11	2	98	42	11		.342	.407	.445	138	27	31	.931	7	123	139	*O-125(RF)	2.5
1900	Phi N	138	545	106	200	32	16	11	**110**	56	16		.367	.441	.545	173	**56**	35	.914	1	119	110	*O-138(RF)	**4.5**
1901	Phi N	138	540	112	180	32	17	8	88	52	7		.333	.399	.500	157	39	30	.962	14	130	175	*O-138(1-0-137)	4.5
1902	Phi A	11	37	15	11	2	1	0	3	6	3		.297	.435	.405	128	2	4	.947	-0	70	0	O-11(RF)	0.1
	Cle A	110	424	70	126	19	11	2	61	47	3		.297	.371	.408	121	13	20	.929	-5	90	69	*O-110(RF)	0.3
	Year	121	461	85	137	21	12	2	64	53	6		.297	.377	.408	121	15	24	.930	-5	88	63	*O-121(RF)	0.4
1903	Cle A	**140**	523	81	155	23	16	2	51	51	8		.296	.368	.413	136	25	24	.955	-1	96	78	*O-140(6-0-134)	1.7
1904	Cle A	150	579	97	177	31	17	6	56	51	9		.306	.371	.449	160	40	**38**	.955	7	116	120	*O-145(0-6-139)/2-6	4.5
1905	Cle A	132	500	72	154	29	**18**	4	64	53	8		**.308**	.383	**.462**	**165**	**38**	35	.939	-2	121	91	*O-131(RF)/2	3.3
1906	Cle A	**157**	624	**98**	194	34	**22**	1	62	54	7		.311	.372	.441	156	40	**39**	.981	-11	70	111	*O-150(0-86-65)/2-8	2.4
1907	Cle A	147	549	80	166	15	**18**	3	58	64	11		.302	.386	.412	153	35	41	.956	-1	115	162	*O-147(1-23-122)	3.0
1908	Cle A	9	35	4	8	1	1	0	2	3	0		.229	.289	.314	96	0	0	1.000	-0	103	416	/O-9(RF)	-0.1
1909	Cle A	66	235	28	60	10	2	0	15	22	1		.255	.322	.315	97	0	9	.958	-2	56	63	O-61(1-12-48)	-0.6
1910	Cle A	24	68	5	18	2	1	1	7	10	0		.265	.359	.368	126	2	1	.955	-2	94	0	O-18(RF)	-0.1
Total	13	1483	5597	950	1752	268	164	48	756	597	99		.313	.389	.445	149	358	330	.947	11	107	113	*O-1456(9-127-1320)/2-15	29.7
FLICK, LEW Lewis Miller "Noisy" B 2.18.1915 Bristol, TN D 12.7.1990 Weber City, VA BL/TL 5-9/155# d9.28																								
1943	Phi A	1	5	2	3	0	0	0	0	0	0	0	.600	.600	.600	253	1	0-0	1.000	0	117	0	/O(RF)	0.1
1944	Phi A	19	35	1	4	0	0	0	2	1	0	2	.114	.139	.114	-28	-6	1-0	1.000	-1	89	0	/O-6(0-1-5)	-0.7
Total	2	20	40	3	7	0	0	0	2	1	0	2	.175	.195	.175	6	-5	1-0	1.000	-1	95	0	/O-7(0-1-6)	-0.6
FLINN, DON Don Raphael B 11.17.1892 Bluff Dale, TX D 3.9.1959 Waco, TX BR/TR 6-1/185# d9.2																								
1917	Pit N	14	37	1	11	1	1	0	1	1	0	6	.297	.316	.378	109	0	1	1.000	1	122	77	O-12(7-1-4)	0.1
FLINT, SILVER Frank Sylvester B 8.3.1855 Philadelphia, PA D 1.14.1892 Chicago, IL BR/TR 6/180# d5.4 M1																								
1875	RS NA	17	61	4	5	0	0	0	1	1		10	.082	.097	.082	-41	-8	2-0	.820	-3			C-16/O-2(1-0-1),3	-0.9
1878	Ind N	**63**	254	23	57	7	0	0	18	2		15	.224	.230	.252	67	-8		.908	-3			*C-59/O-9(5-0-4)	-0.9
1879	Chi N	79	324	46	92	22	6	1	41	6		44	.284	.297	.398	120	6		.915	5			*C-78/O(RF)M	1.2
1880	Chi N	74	284	30	46	10	4	0	17	5		32	.162	.176	.225	33	-20		**.934**	7			*C-67,O-13(0-4-10)	-1.1
1881	Chi N	80	306	46	95	18	0	1	34	6		39	.310	.324	.379	115	5		.938	-6			*C-80/O-8(RF),1	0.1
1882	Chi N	81	331	48	83	18	8	4	44	2		50	.251	.255	.390	99	-2		.935	-1			*C-81,O-10(RF)	0.4
1883	Chi N	85	332	57	88	23	4	0	32	3		69	.265	.272	.358	83	-8		.877	-2			*C-83,O-23(RF)	-0.3
1884	Chi N	73	279	35	57	5	2	9	45	7		57	.204	.224	.333	67	-12		.884	-5			C-73	-0.9
1885	†Chi N	68	249	27	52	8	2	1	17	2		52	.209	.215	.269	49	-15		**.927**	8			C-68/O(RF)	-0.2
1886	†Chi N	54	173	30	35	6	2	1	13	12		36	.202	.254	.277	54	-10	1	.893	9			C-54/1-3	0.3
1887	Chi N	49	187	22	50	8	6	3	21	4	0	28	.267	.283	.422	83	-6	7	.909	5			C-47/1-2	0.2
1888	Chi N	22	77	6	14	3	0	0	3	1	1	21	.182	.203	.221	33	-6	1	.926	1			C-22	-0.3
1889	Chi N	15	56	6	13	1	0	1	9	3	0	18	.232	.271	.304	58	-4	1	.903	-2			C-15	-0.4
Total	12	743	2852	376	682	129	34	21	294	53	1	461	.239	.253	.330	78	-80	10-0	.913	16			C-727/O-65(5-4-57),1-6	-1.9
FLOOD, CURT Curtis Charles B 1.18.1938 Houston, TX D 1.20.1997 Los Angeles, CA BR/TR 5-9/165# d9.9																								
1956	Cin N	5	1	0	0	0	0	0	0	0-0	0	1	.000	.000	.000	-94	0	0-0	—	0			H	0.0
1957	Cin N	3	3	2	1	0	0	1	1	0-0	0	0	.333	.333	1.333	299	1	0-0	—	-1	0	0	/3-2,2	0.0
1958	StL N	121	422	50	110	17	2	10	41	31-1	4	56	.261	.317	.382	81	-12	2-12	.978	13	112	189	*O-120(CF)/3	-0.8
1959	StL N	121	208	24	53	7	3	7	26	16-0	0	35	.255	.305	.418	86	-5	2-1	.967	-8	89	25	*O-106(2-103-1)/2	-1.6
1960	StL N	140	396	37	94	20	1	8	38	35-7	4	54	.237	.303	.354	73	-14	0-3	**.993**	2	106	85	*O-134(1-133-0)/3	-1.9
1961	StL N	132	335	53	108	15	5	2	21	35-2	3	33	.322	.391	.415	104	3	6-2	.984	4	99	176	*O-119(CF)	0.5
1962	StL N	151	635	99	188	30	5	12	70	42-0	10	57	.296	.346	.416	95	-3	8-6	.990	5	104	115	*O-151(CF)	-0.3
1963	StL N	158	662	112	200	34	9	5	63	42-3	2	57	.302	.345	.403	105	5	17-12	.988	7	109	115	*O-158(CF)	0.8
1964	†StL N★	**162**	679	97	**211**	25	3	5	46	43-1	5	53	.311	.356	.378	98	0	8-11	.988	3	109	96	*O-162(CF)	-0.4
1965	StL N	156	617	90	191	30	3	11	83	51-4	6	50	.310	.366	.421	111	11	9-3	.986	1	103	80	*O-151(CF)	0.8
1966	StL N★	160	626	64	167	21	5	10	78	26-0	4	50	.267	.298	.364	83	-15	14-7	**1.000**	2	109	46	*O-159(CF)	-1.8
1967	†StL N	134	514	68	172	24	1	5	50	37-1	2	46	.335	.378	.414	129	20	2-2	.988	4	**111**	57	*O-126(CF)	2.2
1968	†StL N★	150	618	71	186	17	4	5	60	33-2	5	58	.301	.339	.366	114	9	11-6	.983	9	111	116	*O-149(CF)	1.6
1969	StL N	153	606	80	173	31	3	4	57	48-1	7	57	.285	.344	.366	99	0	9-7	.989	7	107	150	*O-152(CF)	0.3
1971	Was A	13	35	4	7	0	0	0	2	5-0	0	2	.200	.300	.200	47	-2	0-1	.941	-2	76	0	O-10(CF)	-0.5
Total	15	1759	6357	851	1861	271	44	85	636	444-22	52	609	.293	.342	.389	99	-2	88-73	.987	47	106	105	*O-1697(3-1693-1)/3-4,2-2	-1.1

Year	Tm Lg	G	AB	R	H	2B	3B	HR	RBI	BB-IB	HP	SO	AVG	OBP	SLG	AOPS	ABR	SB-CS	FA	FR	Rng	Thr	G at Pos	BFW
FLOOD, TIM Timothy A. B 3.13.1877 Montgomery City, MO D 6.15.1929 St.Louis, MO BR/TR 5-9/160# d9.24																								
1899	StL N	10	31	0	9	0	0	0	3	4	0		.290	.371	.290	81	-1	1	.878	-1	107	97	2-10	-0.1
1902	Bro N	132	476	43	104	11	4	3	51	23	9		.218	.268	.277	68	-19	8	.942	-15	94	72	*2-132/O(LF)	-3.5
1903	Bro N	89	309	27	77	15	2	0	32	15	3		.249	.291	.311	73	-11	14	.924	-11	88	133	2-84/S-2,O(CF)	-2.0
Total	3	231	816	70	190	26	6	3	86	42	12		.233	.280	.290	70	-31	23	.933	-27	92	96	2-226/S-2,O-2(1-1-0)	-5.6
FLORA, KEVIN Kevin Scot B 6.10.1969 Fontana, CA BR/TR 6/180# d9.27																								
1991	Cal A	3	8	1	1	0	0	0	0	1-0	0	5	.125	.222	.125	-1	-1	1-0	.846	-2	40	56	/2-3	-0.3
1995	Cal A	2	1	1	0	0	0	0	0	0-0	0	1	.000	.000	.000	-99	0	0-0	—	0			/D	0.0
	Phi N	24	75	12	16	3	0	2	7	4-0	0	22	.213	.253	.333	53	-5	1-0	1.000	-1	85	105	O-20(5-15-0)	-0.6
Total	2	29	84	14	17	3	0	2	7	5-0	0	28	.202	.247	.310	46	-6	2-0	1.000	-3	85	105	/O-20(5-15-0),2-3,D	-0.9
FLORENCE, PAUL Paul Robert "Pep" B 4.22.1900 Chicago, IL D 5.28.1986 Gainesville, FL BB/TR 6-1/185# d5.22																								
1926	NY N	76	188	19	43	4	3	2	14	23	3	12	.229	.322	.314	73	-7	2	.937	-8	*85*	*90*	C-76	-1.1
FLORES, GIL Gilberto (Garcia) B 10.27.1952 Ponce, P.R. BR/TR 6/185# d5.8																								
1977	Cal A	104	342	41	95	19	4	1	26	23-2	1	39	.278	.325	.365	92	-4	12-10	.978	0	101	92	O-85(41-45-9)/D-8	-0.7
1978	NY N	11	29	8	8	0	1	0	1	3-0	0	5	.276	.344	.345	96	0	1-0	.944	-1	97	0	/O-8(1-6-2)	-0.1
1979	NY N	70	93	9	18	1	1	1	10	8-0	1	17	.194	.262	.258	45	-7	2-0	.976	1	117	75	O-32(0-6-28)	-0.7
Total	3	185	464	58	121	20	6	2	37	34-2	2	61	.261	.313	.343	82	-11	15-10	.976	0	103	83	O-125(42-57-39)/D-8	-1.5
FLORES, JOSE Jose Carlos B 6.28.1973 New York, NY BR/TR 5-11/180# d9.7																								
2002	Oak A	7	3	2	0	0	0	0	0	1-0	1	0	.000	.400	.000	20	0	1-1	—	-1	0	0	/2-2,S	-0.1
FLOWERS, DICKIE Charles Richard B 1850 Philadelphia, PA D 10.5.1892 Philadelphia, PA d6.3																								
1871	Tro NA	21	105	39	33	5	4	0	18	4		0	.314	.339	.438	120	2	8-2	.769	-2	95	**142**	*S-20/P2	0.1
1872	Ath NA	3	15	1	4	0	0	0	4	2		2	.267	.353	.267	93	0	0-0	.643	-1	85	0	/S-3	-0.1
Total	2 NA	24	120	40	37	5	4	0	22	6		2	.308	.341	.417	117	2	8-2	.000	-3	94	125	/S-23,2P	0.0
FLOWERS, JAKE D'Arcy Raymond B 3.16.1902 Cambridge, MD D 12.27.1962 Clearwater, FL BR/TR 5-11.5/170# d9.7 C9																								
1923	StL N	13	32	0	3	1	0	0	2	2	0	7	.094	.147	.125	-28	-6	1-2	.971	-1	118	28	/S-7,2-2,3-2	-0.6
1926	†StL N	40	74	13	20	1	0	3	9	5	1	9	.270	.325	.405	92	-1	1	.984	-1	115	67	2-11/1-3,S	-0.2
1927	Bro N	67	231	26	54	5	5	2	20	21	1	25	.234	.300	.325	67	-11	3	.944	-7	89	81	S-65/2	-1.1
1928	Bro N	103	339	51	93	11	6	2	44	47	2	30	.274	.366	.360	92	-3	10	.971	-2	91	81	2-94/S-6	-0.3
1929	Bro N	46	130	16	26	6	0	1	16	22	0	6	.200	.316	.269	47	-10	9	.962	-7	84	69	2-39	-1.5
1930	Bro N	89	253	37	81	18	3	2	50	21	0	18	.320	.372	.439	96	-1	5	.949	-6	93	108	2-65/O(RF)	-0.5
1931	Bro N	22	31	3	7	0	0	0	1	7	0	4	.226	.368	.226	64	-1	1	1.000	0	83	62	/2-6,S	0.0
	†StL N	45	137	19	34	11	1	2	19	9	0	6	.248	.295	.387	79	-4	7	.971	3	103	109	S-24,2-21/3	0.1
	Year	67	168	22	41	11	1	2	20	16	0	10	.244	.310	.357	77	-5	8	.991	4	100	117	2-27,S-25/3	0.1
1932	StL N	67	247	35	63	11	1	2	18	31	1	18	.255	.341	.332	79	-6	7	.980	-0	89	99	3-54/S-7,2-2	-0.4
1933	Bro N	78	210	28	49	11	2	2	22	24	0	15	.233	.312	.333	88	-3	13	.955	-9	85	61	S-36,2-19/3-8,O(RF)	-0.8
1934	Cin N	13	9	1	3	0	0	0	0	1	1	1	.333	.455	.333	117	0	1	—	0			H	0.0
Total	10	583	1693	229	433	75	18	16	201	190	6	139	.256	.333	.350	80	-46	58-2	.967	-29	93	85	2-260,S-147/3-65,1-3,O-2(RF)	-5.3
FLOYD, CLIFF Cornelius Clifford B 12.5.1972 Chicago, IL BL/TL 6-4/230# d9.18																								
1993	Mon N	10	31	3	7	0	0	1	2	0-0	0	9	.226	.226	.323	43	-3	0-0	1.000	-1	73	85	1-10	-0.4
1994	Mon N	100	334	43	94	19	4	4	41	24-0	3	63	.281	.332	.398	89	-5	10-3	.991	-1	90	93	1-77,O-26(17-0-9)	-1.2
1995	Mon N	29	69	6	9	1	0	1	8	7-0	1	22	.130	.221	.188	9	-9	3-0	.987	-0	118	111	1-18/O-4(2-1-1)	-1.0
1996	Mon N	117	227	29	55	15	4	6	26	30-1	5	52	.242	.340	.423	98	0	7-1	.960	-3	95	66	O-85(69-16-7)/1-2	-0.4
1997	†Fla N	61	137	23	32	9	1	6	19	24-0	2	33	.234	.354	.445	113	3	6-2	.970	2	106	222	O-38(24-9-6)/1-9	0.4
1998	Fla N	153	588	85	166	45	3	22	90	47-7	3	112	.282	.337	.481	118	15	27-14	.974	-2	92	103	*O-146(146-2-0)/D-3	0.8
1999	Fla N	69	251	37	76	19	1	11	49	30-5	2	47	.303	.379	.518	132	13	5-6	.952	-0	95	106	O-62(LF)/D-3	0.9
2000	Fla N	121	420	75	126	30	0	22	91	50-5	8	82	.300	.378	.529	134	23	24-3	.951	-4	87	112	*O-108(LF)/D	1.8
2001	Fla N★	149	555	123	176	44	4	31	103	59-19	10	101	.317	.390	.578	152	44	18-3	.972	3	104	87	*O-142(LF)/D-3	4.3
2002	Fla N	84	296	49	85	20	0	18	57	58-18	7	68	.287	.414	.537	159	27	10-5	.983	4	111	94	O-80(20-0-60)/D	2.6
	Mon N	15	53	7	11	2	0	3	4	3-1	1	10	.208	.263	.415	72	-3	1-0	.941	-1	57	248	O-13(LF)	-0.4
	Year	99	349	56	96	22	0	21	61	61-19	8	78	.275	.394	.519	145	23	11-5	.980	3	104	115	O-93(33-0-60)/D	2.2
	Bos A	47	171	30	54	21	0	7	18	15-0	2	28	.316	.374	.561	142	11	4-0	.977	-2	84	70	O-26(21-0-6),D-19	0.8
2003	NY N	108	365	57	106	25	2	18	68	51-2	3	66	.290	.376	.518	136	21	3-0	.971	4	104	153	O-95(LF)/D-9	2.1
Total	11	1063	3497	567	997	250	19	150	576	398-58	47	693	.285	.363	.496	125	137	118-37	.968	-2	97	109	O-825(719-28-89),1-116/D-39	10.3
FLOYD, BUBBA Leslie Roe B 6.23.1917 Dallas, TX D 12.15.2000 Dallas, TX BR/TR 5-11/160# d6.16																								
1944	Det A	3	9	1	4	1	0	0	0	1	0	0	.444	.500	.556	191	1	0-0	1.000	-0	119	0	/S-3	0.1
FLOYD, BOBBY Robert Nathan B 10.20.1943 Hawthorne, CA BR/TR 6/181# d9.18 C1																								
1968	Bal A	5	9	0	1	1	0	0	1	0-0	0	3	.111	.100	.222	-1	-1	0-0	1.000	1	105	190	/S-4	0.0
1969	Bal A	39	84	7	17	4	0	0	1	6-1	0	17	.202	.253	.250	41	-7	0-0	.984	5	123	152	2-15,S-15/3-9	0.1
1970	Bal A	3	2	0	0	0	0	0	0	0-0	0	2	.000	.000	.000	-99	-1	0-0	1.000	-2	0	0	/S-2,2	-0.2
	KC A	14	43	5	14	4	0	0	9	4-0	0	9	.326	.375	.419	121	1	0-1	.880	0	111	104	/S-8,3-6	0.2
	Year	17	45	5	14	4	0	0	9	4-0	0	11	.311	.360	.400	111	1	0-1	.882	-1	106	100	S-10/3-6,2	0.0
1971	KC A	31	66	8	10	3	0	0	2	7-0	0	21	.152	.233	.197	23	-7	0-0	.970	2	107	142	S-15/2-8,3	-0.3
1972	KC A	61	134	9	24	3	0	0	5	5-0	0	29	.179	.209	.201	23	-13	1-0	.967	-11	68	64	3-30,S-29/2-2	-2.6
1973	KC A	51	78	10	26	3	1	0	8	4-0	0	14	.333	.357	.397	107	1	1-1	1.000	-1	84	71	2-25,S-24	0.2
1974	KC A	10	9	1	1	0	0	0	0	2-0	0	4	.111	.273	.111	13	-1	0-0	1.000	1	138	0	/2-5,3-2,S	0.0
Total	7	214	425	40	93	18	1	0	26	28-1	0	99	.219	.264	.266	52	-28	2-2	.940	-5	100	111	/S-98,2-56,3-48	-2.6
FLUHRER, JOHN John Lister (a/k/a Wm. G. Morris 1 Game In 1915) B 1.3.1894 Adrian, MI D 7.17.1946 Columbus, OH BR/TR 5-9/165# d9.5																								
1915	Chi N	6	6	0	2	0	0	0	0	1	0	0	.333	.429	.333	132	0	1	.500	-0	65	0	/O-2(LF)	0.0
FLYNN, ED Edward J. B 1.25.1864 Chicago, IL D 8.29.1929 Chicago, IL BL 5-9/165# d5.5 b-George																								
1887	Cle AA	7	27	0	5	1	0	0	4	1	0		.185	.214	.222	22	-3	3	.786	-1	73	0	/3-6,O(RF)	-0.3
FLYNN, GEORGE George A. "Dibby" B 5.24.1871 Chicago, IL D 12.28.1901 Chicago, IL 5-9/150# d4.17 b-Ed																								
1896	Chi N	29	106	15	27	1	2	0	4	11	2	9	.255	.336	.302	66	-5	12	.878	-0	129	246	O-29(LF)	-0.7
FLYNN, JOHN John Anthony B 9.7.1883 Providence, RI D 3.23.1935 Providence, RI BR/TR 6-0.5/175# d4.22																								
1910	Pit N	96	332	32	91	10	2	6	52	30	1	47	.274	.336	.370	100	-1	6	.977	-3	93	107	1-93	-0.6
1911	Pit N	33	59	5	12	0	1	0	3	9	0	8	.203	.309	.237	52	-4	0	1.000	1	121	123	1-13/O(RF)	-0.3
1912	Was A	20	71	9	12	4	1	0	5	7	1		.169	.253	.254	45	-5	2	.974	1	131	102	1-20	-0.4
Total	3	149	462	46	115	14	4	6	60	46	2	55	.249	.320	.335	85	-10	8	.978	-1	102	108	1-126/O(RF)	-1.3
FLYNN, JOE Joseph Nicholas B 1.1862 Providence, RI D 12.22.1933 Providence, RI d4.18																								
1884	Phi U	52	209	38	52	9	4	4		11			.249	.286	.388	111	-4		.778	-12	90	175	O-43(2-0-41),C-10/1S	-1.3
	Bos U	9	31	4	7	2	0	0		2			.226	.273	.290	72	-2		.864	3			/C-7,O-4(1-2-2),1	0.1
	Year	61	240	42	59	11	4	4		13			.246	.285	.375	105	-6		.764	-9	111	157	O-47(3-2-43),C-17/1-2,S	-1.2
FLYNN, MIKE Michael J. B 3.15.1872 County Kildare, Ireland D 6.16.1941 Los Angeles, CA d8.31																								
1891	Bos AA	1	2	0	0	0	0	0	0	0	0	1	.000	.000	.000	-99	-1	0	1.000	1	*121*	*272*	/C	0.0
FLYNN, DOUG Robert Douglas B 4.18.1951 Lexington, KY BR/TR 5-11/165# d4.9																								
1975	Cin N	89	127	17	34	7	0	1	20	11-2	0	13	.268	.324	.346	85	-2	3-0	.962	-4	80	53	3-40,2-30,S-17	-0.3
1976	†Cin N	93	219	20	62	5	2	1	20	10-1	0	24	.283	.312	.338	83	-6	2-0	.988	-19	77	84	2-55,3-23,S-20	-2.1
1977	Cin N	36	32	0	8	1	1	0	5	0-0	0	6	.250	.242	.344	56	-2	0-0	1.000	1	116	0	3-25/2-9,S-4	-0.1
	NY N	90	282	14	54	6	1	0	14	11-2	0	23	.191	.220	.220	20	-33	1-3	.954	-16	78	75	S-65,2-29/3-2	-4.4
	Year	126	314	14	62	7	2	0	19	11-2	0	29	.197	.223	.232	24	-35	1-3	.956	-15	80	78	S-69,2-38,3-27	-4.5
1978	NY N	156	532	37	126	12	8	0	36	30-10	1	50	.237	.277	.289	61	-30	3-5	.986	-16	98	109	*2-128,S-60	-3.9
1979	NY N	157	555	35	135	19	5	4	61	17-7	0	46	.243	.265	.317	61	-33	0-3	.983	-8	93	104	*2-148,S-20	-3.4
1980	NY N	128	443	46	113	9	8	0	24	22-14	0	20	.255	.288	.312	70	-20	2-2	**.991**	-6	93	86	*2-128/S-3	-2.0

Year	Tm Lg	G	AB	R	H	2B	3B	HR	RBI	BB-IB	HP	SO	AVG	OBP	SLG	AOPS	ABR	SB-CS	FA	FR	Rng	Thr	G at Pos	BFW
1981	NY N	**105**	325	24	72	12	4	1	20	11-8	0	19	.222	.247	.292	53	-21	1-2	.987	14	104	100	*2-100/S-5	-0.3
1982	Tex A	88	270	13	57	6	2	0	19	4-0	0	14	.211	.221	.248	31	-27	6-2	.989	-2	97	81	2-55,S-35	-2.2
	Mon N	58	193	13	47	6	2	0	20	4-0	0	23	.244	.256	.295	54	-13	0-2	.983	-2	87	126	2-58	-1.3
1983	Mon N	143	452	44	107	18	4	0	26	19-8	0	38	.237	.267	.294	56	-28	2-1	.986	-13	93	94	*2-107,S-37	-3.5
1984	Mon N	124	366	23	89	12	1	0	17	12-6	0	41	.243	.267	.281	57	-22	0-0	.979	-19	93	102	2-88,S-34	-3.6
1985	Mon N	9	6	0	1	0	0	0	0	0-0	0	0	.167	.167	.167	-7	-1	0-0	1.000	-1	64	0	/2-6,S	-0.2
	Det A	32	51	2	13	2	1	0	2	0-0	0	3	.255	.250	.333	60	-3	0-0	.984	-0	90	186	2-20/S-8,3-4	-0.2
Total	11	1308	3853	288	918	115	39	7	284	151-58	1	320	.238	.266	.294	57	-241	20-20	.986	-92	94	100	2-961,S-309/3-94	-27.5
FLYNN, CLIPPER William B 4.29.1849 Lansingburg, NY D 11.11.1881 Lansingburg, NY TR 5-7/140# d5.9																								
1871	Tro NA	**29**	142	43	48	6	1	0	27	4		2	.338	.356	.394	114	2	3-3	.955	4	268	120	1-19/O-8(RF),23	0.5
1872	Oly NA	**9**	40	4	9	1	0	0	2	0		0	.225	.225	.250	48	-2	0-0	.900	-1	95	103	/1-9	-0.2
Total	2 NA	38	182	47	57	7	1	0	29	4		2	.313	.328	.363	101	0	3-3	.000	3	212	114	/1-28,O-8(RF),32	0.3
FOGARTY, JIM James G. B 2.12.1864 San Francisco, CA D 5.20.1891 Philadelphia, PA BR/TR 5-10.5/180# d5.1 M1 b-Joe I OF Total (312-CF 373-RF)																								
1884	Phi N	97	378	42	80	12	6	1	37	20		54	.212	.251	.283	71	-12		.915	3	75	105	*O-78(0-72-6),3-14/2-4,S-3,P	-1.0
1885	Phi N	**111**	427	49	99	13	3	0	39	30		37	.232	.282	.276	83	-7		.941	19	154	233	*O-88(CF),2-10/S-8,3-5	0.9
1886	Phi N	77	280	54	82	13	5	3	47	42		16	.293	.385	.407	140	15	30	.953	-5	74	181	0-60(0-1-59),2-13/S-3,3-3,P	0.9
1887	Phi N	126	495	113	129	26	12	8	50	**82**	10	44	.261	.376	.410	112	10	102	.920	29	**176**	**240**	*O-123(RF)/S-2,3-2,2P	3.2
1888	Phi N	121	454	72	107	14	6	1	35	53	7	66	.236	.325	.300	95	-1	58	.930	12	130	**241**	*O-117(RF)/3-5,S	1.0
1889	Phi N	128	499	107	129	15	17	3	54	65	7	60	.259	.352	.375	95	-6	**99**	**.961**	18	**171**	129	*O-128(CF)/P-4	0.7
1890	Phi P	91	347	71	83	17	6	4	58	59	9	50	.239	.364	.357	91	-3	36	.963	5	97	85	O-91(0-23-68)/3M	0.1
Total	7	751	2880	508	709	110	55	20	320	351	33	327	.246	.335	.343	98	-4	325	.940	81	133	177	0-685R/3-30,2-28,S-17,P-7	5.8
FOGARTY, JOE Joseph J. B San Francisco, CA 5-9/158# d9.18 b-Jim																								
1885	StL N	2	8	1	1	0	0	0	0	0		1	.125	.125	.125	-20	-1		1.000	-0	0	0	/O-2(LF)	-0.1
FOHL, LEE Leo Alexander B 11.28.1876 Lowell, OH D 10.30.1965 Cleveland, OH BL/TR 5-10/175# d8.29 M11 C1																								
1902	Pit N	1	3	0	0	0	0	0	1	0	0		.000	.000	.000	-97	-1	0	.875	0	*118*	*105*	/C	0.0
1903	Cin N	4	14	3	5	1	1	0	2	0	1		.357	.400	.571	158	1	0	.955	-0	*132*	*115*	/C-4	0.1
Total	2	5	17	3	5	1	1	0	3	0	1		.294	.333	.471	120	0	0	.933	-0	*129*	*113*	/C-5	0.1
FOILES, HANK Henry Lee B 6.10.1929 Richmond, VA BR/TR 6/195# d4.21																								
1953	Cin N	5	13	1	2	0	0	0	0	1	0	2	.154	.214	.154	-2	-2	0-0	.909	-0	*79*	*202*	/C-3	-0.2
	Cle A	7	7	2	1	0	0	0	0	1	0	1	.143	.250	.143	9	-1	0-0	.933	0	*72*	*297*	/C-7	-0.1
1955	Cle A	62	111	13	29	9	0	1	7	17-3	0	18	.261	.354	.369	93	0	0-0	.988	9	*123*	*133*	C-41	1.0
1956	Cle A	1	0	0	0	0	0	0	0	0-0	0	0	—	—	—	—	0	0-0	—	-0	*0*	*0*	/C	0.0
	Pit N	79	222	24	47	10	2	7	25	17-4	0	56	.212	.266	.369	71	-10	0-1	.988	1	*100*	*123*	C-73	-0.6
1957	Pit N★	109	281	32	76	10	4	9	36	37-5	0	53	.270	.352	.431	113	6	1-3	.981	-3	*109*	*74*	*C-109	0.7
1958	Pit N	104	264	31	54	10	2	8	30	45-10	1	53	.205	.322	.348	80	-7	0-1	.990	8	*117*	*99*	*C-103	0.5
1959	Pit N	53	80	10	18	3	0	3	4	7-2	0	16	.225	.287	.375	75	-3	0-0	1.000	4	*132*	*72*	C-51	0.2
1960	KC A	6	7	1	4	0	0	0	1	3-0	0	2	.571	.700	.571	246	2	0-0	.900	-0	*63*	*0*	/C-2	0.2
	Cle A	24	68	9	19	1	0	1	6	7-0	0	5	.279	.347	.338	89	-1	0-0	.982	0	*89*	*168*	C-22	0.0
	Det A	26	56	5	14	3	0	0	3	1-1	0	8	.250	.263	.304	51	-4	1-0	1.000	3	*105*	*134*	C-22	0.0
	Year	56	131	15	37	4	0	1	10	11-1	0	15	.282	.338	.336	83	-3	1-0	.987	2	*95*	*145*	C-46	0.2
1961	Bal A	43	124	18	34	6	0	6	19	12-1	0	27	.274	.336	.468	117	3	0-2	.995	3	*119*	*96*	C-38	0.6
1962	Cin N	43	131	17	36	6	1	7	25	13-3	0	39	.275	.340	.496	118	3	0-0	.981	0	*106*	*54*	C-41	0.5
1963	Cin N	1	3	0	0	0	0	0	0	1-1	0	0	.000	.250	.000	-21	0	1-0	1.000	-0	*0*	*0*	/C	0.0
	LA A	41	84	8	18	1	1	4	10	8-1	0	13	.214	.290	.393	95	-1	0-0	.974	2	75	171	C-30	0.2
1964	LA A	4	4	0	1	0	0	0	0	0-0	0	2	.250	.250	.250	44	0	0-0	—	0			H	0.0
Total	11	608	1455	171	353	59	10	46	166	170-31	2	295	.243	.321	.392	92	-15	3-7	.986	26	*109*	*103*	C-544	3.0
FOLEY, CURRY Charles Joseph B 1.14.1856 Milltown, Ireland D 10.20.1898 Boston, MA TL 5-10/160# d5.13 ▲																								
1879	Bos N	35	146	16	46	3	1	0	17	3		4	.315	.329	.349	121	3		.857	-5	77	0	P-21,O-17(0-2-15)/1-2	-0.2
1880	Bos N	80	332	44	97	13	2	2	31	8		14	.292	.309	.361	130	10		.953	-0	103	0	P-36,O-35(RF),1-25	0.5
1881	Buf N	**83**	375	58	96	20	2	1	25	7		27	.256	.270	.328	88	-5		.795	-4	99	215	O-55(3-4-50),1-27,P-10	-0.9
1882	Buf N	**84**	341	51	104	16	4	3	49	12		26	.305	.329	.402	131	11		.833	1	120	184	*O-84(0-1-84)/P	1.0
1883	Buf N	23	111	23	30	5	3	0	6	4		12	.270	.296	.369	98	0		.885	-2	39	0	O-23(1-21-1)/P	-0.3
Total	5	305	1305	192	373	57	12	6	128	34		83	.286	.304	.362	114	19		.819	-10	101	148	O-214(4-28-185)/P-69,1-54	0.1
FOLEY, MARV Marvis Edwin B 8.29.1953 Stanford, KY BL/TR 6/195# d9.11 C2																								
1978	Chi A	11	34	3	12	0	0	0	6	4-0	0	6	.353	.421	.353	119	1	0-1	.938	-3	45	86	C-10	-0.2
1979	Chi A	34	97	6	24	3	0	2	10	7-1	0	5	.247	.292	.340	72	-4	0-0	.993	-3	76	96	C-33	-0.6
1980	Chi A	68	137	14	29	5	0	4	15	9-3	2	22	.212	.263	.336	65	-7	0-0	.991	3	76	127	C-64/1-3	-0.2
1982	Chi A	27	36	1	4	0	0	0	1	6-1	0	4	.111	.238	.111	-0	-5	0-0	.980	1	78	183	C-15/3-2,1D	-0.4
1984	Tex A	63	115	13	25	2	0	6	19	15-1	1	24	.217	.306	.391	91	-2	0-0	.988	1	47	66	C-36/13D	0.0
Total	5	203	419	37	94	10	0	12	51	41-6	3	61	.224	.292	.334	73	-17	0-1	.986	-2	67	106	C-158/D-5,1-5,3-3	-1.4
FOLEY, RAY Raymond Kirwin B 6.23.1906 Naugatuck, CT D 3.22.1980 Vero Beach, FL BL/TR 5-11/173# d7.4																								
1928	NY N	2	1	1	0	0	0	0	0	1	0	1	.000	.500	.000	41	0	0	—	0			H	0.0
FOLEY, TOM Thomas J. B 1847 Chicago, IL D 1.4.1896 LaGrange, IL 5-9.5/157# d5.8																								
1871	Chi NA	18	84	18	22	3	1	0	13	3		2	.262	.287	.321	67	-4	1-4	.633	-5	58	0	O-16(2-9-5)/C-4,3	-0.7
FOLEY, TOM Thomas Michael B 9.9.1959 Columbus, GA BL/TR 6-1/180# d4.9 C2																								
1983	Cin N	68	98	7	20	4	1	0	9	13-2	0	17	.204	.297	.265	55	-6	1-0	.983	1	94	102	S-37/2-5	-0.2
1984	Cin N	106	277	26	70	8	3	5	27	24-7	0	36	.253	.310	.357	84	-6	3-2	.965	-9	91	73	S-83,2-10/3	-0.8
1985	Cin N	43	92	7	18	5	1	0	6	6-1	0	16	.196	.245	.272	42	-7	1-0	.983	3	91	119	2-18,S-15/3	-0.2
	Phi N	46	158	17	42	8	0	3	17	13-7	0	18	.266	.322	.373	91	-2	1-3	.981	0	95	97	S-45	0.2
	Year	89	250	24	60	13	1	3	23	19-8	0	34	.240	.294	.336	73	-9	2-3	.978	3	99	113	S-60,2-18/3	0.0
1986	Phi N	39	61	8	18	2	1	0	5	10-1	0	11	.295	.389	.361	106	1	2-0	.975	0	89	109	S-24/23	0.3
	Mon N	64	202	18	52	13	2	1	18	20-5	0	26	.257	.320	.356	88	-3	8-3	.965	-1	78	61	S-29,2-25,3-15	0.0
	Year	103	263	26	70	15	3	1	23	30-6	0	37	.266	.337	.357	92	-2	10-3	.970	-1	82	80	S-53,2-26,3-16	0.3
1987	Mon N	106	280	35	82	18	3	5	28	11-0	1	40	.293	.322	.432	95	-3	6-10	.963	-1	95	115	S-49,2-39/3-9	-0.1
1988	Mon N	127	377	33	100	21	3	5	43	30-10	1	49	.265	.319	.377	95	-2	2-7	.972	3	106	107	2-89,S-32/3-9	0.3
1989	Mon N	122	375	34	86	19	2	7	39	45-4	3	53	.229	.314	.347	88	-5	2-3	.988	16	109	105	*2-108,3-16,S-14/P	1.4
1990	Mon N	73	164	11	35	2	1	0	12	12-2	0	22	.213	.266	.238	42	-14	0-1	.987	-2	107	148	S-45,2-20/3-7,1	-1.4
1991	Mon N	86	168	12	35	11	1	0	15	14-4	1	30	.208	.269	.286	58	-9	2-0	.967	-2	91	90	S-43,1-31/3-6,2-2	-1.1
1992	Mon N	72	115	7	20	3	1	0	5	8-2	1	21	.174	.230	.217	29	-11	3-0	.967	1	106	99	S-33,2-13,1-12/3-4,O(LF)	-0.9
1993	Pit N	86	194	18	49	11	1	3	22	11-1	0	26	.253	.287	.366	75	-7	0-0	.993	3	82	109	2-35,1-12/3-7,S-6	-0.3
1994	Pit N	59	123	13	29	7	0	3	15	13-2	0	18	.236	.307	.366	74	-5	0-0	.986	8	113	172	2-17,3-14/S-8,1-3	0.4
1995	Mon N	11	24	2	5	2	0	0	2	2-0	0	4	.208	.269	.292	46	-2	1-0	1.000	1	109	47	/1-4,2-3	-0.1
Total	13	1108	2708	248	661	134	20	32	263	232-48	7	387	.244	.303	.344	78	-81	32-29	.972	18	96	104	S-463,2-385/3-90,1-63,O(LF)P	-2.5
FOLEY, WILL William Brown B 11.15.1855 Chicago, IL D 11.12.1916 Chicago, IL BR/TR 5-9.5/150# d8.23																								
1875	Chi NA	3	12	0	3	1	0	0	1	0		2	.250	.250	.333	100	0	0-0	.813	1	142	339	/3-3	0.1
1876	Cin N	58	221	19	50	3	2	0	9	0		14	.226	.226	.258	71	-5		.804	-1	113	85	3-46,C-20	-0.4
1877	Cin N	56	216	23	41	5	1	0	18	4		13	.190	.205	.222	39	-14		.836	7	117	113	*3-56	-0.5
1878	Mil N	56	229	33	62	8	5	0	22	7		14	.271	.292	.349	103	0		.812	-8	84	131	*3-53/C-7	-0.6
1879	Cin N	56	218	22	46	5	1	0	25	2		16	.211	.218	.243	55	-10		.820	3	97	239	3-29,O-25(RF)/2-3	-0.6
1881	Det N	5	15	0	2	0	0	0	1	2		3	.133	.235	.133	18	-1		.769	-1	66	508	/3-5	-0.2
1884	CP U	19	71	15	20	1	1	0		5			.282	.329	.324	99	-2		.804	-1	77	129	3-19	-0.3
Total	6	250	970	112	221	22	10	0	75	20		60	.228	.243	.271	70	-32		.817	-2	101	137	3-208/C-27,O-25(RF),2-3	-2.6
FOLI, TIM Timothy John B 12.8.1950 Culver City, CA BR/TR 6/179# d9.11 C10 OF Total (1-LF 2-CF)																								
1970	NY N	5	11	0	4	0	0	0	1	0-0	0	2	.364	.364	.364	95	0	0-0	1.000	2	191	0	/S-2,3-2	0.2
1971	NY N	97	288	32	65	12	2	0	24	18-4	1	50	.226	.272	.281	58	-16	5-0	.964	5	91	111	2-58,3-36,S-12/O(CF)	-0.7

Year	Tm Lg	G	AB	R	H	2B	3B	HR	RBI	BB-IB	HP	SO	AVG	OBP	SLG	AOPS	ABR	SB-CS	FA	FR	Rng	Thr	G at Pos	BFW
1972	Mon N	149	540	45	130	12	2	2	35	25-2	6	43	.241	.280	.281	59	-29	11-7	.966	18	106	104	*S-148/2	0.7
1973	Mon N	126	458	37	110	11	0	2	36	28-11	1	40	.240	.284	.277	55	-28	6-3	.960	18	107	108	*S-123/2-2,O(CF)	0.5
1974	Mon N	121	441	41	112	10	3	0	39	28-0	3	27	.254	.300	.290	63	-22	8-2	.971	**35**	**116**	128	*S-120/3	2.8
1975	Mon N	152	572	64	136	25	2	1	29	36-5	2	49	.238	.284	.294	58	-32	13-3	.973	11	104	110	*S-151/2	-0.2
1976	Mon N	149	546	41	144	36	1	6	54	16-1	0	33	.264	.281	.366	80	-15	6-5	.975	17	105	108	*S-146/3	1.9
1977	Mon N	13	57	2	10	5	1	0	3	0-0	0	4	.175	.172	.298	25	-6	0-0	1.000	1	98	77	S-13	-0.4
	SF N	104	368	30	84	17	3	4	27	11-1	0	16	.228	.247	.323	53	-26	2-4	.974	7	100	127	*S-102/23O(LF)	-1.0
	Year	117	425	32	94	22	4	4	30	11-1	0	20	.221	.238	.320	49	-32	2-4	.977	8	100	121	*S-115/23O(LF)	-1.4
1978	NY N	113	413	37	106	21	1	1	27	14-1	2	30	.257	.283	.320	71	-17	2-5	.966	-1	97	**130**	*S-112	-0.9
1979	NY N	3	7	0	0	0	0	0	0	0-0	0	0	.000	.000	.000	-99	-2	0-0	1.000	0	103	89	/S-3	-0.2
	†Pit N	133	525	70	153	23	1	1	65	28-0	9	14	.291	.335	.345	83	-12	6-5	.978	7	97	132	*S-132	0.9
	Year	136	532	70	153	23	1	1	65	28-0	9	14	.288	.330	.340	81	-13	6-5	**.978**	7	97	**131**	*S-135	0.7
1980	Pit N	127	495	61	131	22	0	3	38	19-1	**6**	23	.265	.296	.327	74	-18	11-7	**.981**	11	102	**125**	*S-125	0.7
1981	Pit N	86	316	32	78	12	2	0	20	17-0	1	10	.247	.285	.297	64	-15	7-7	.965	-4	99	103	S-81	-1.3
1982	†Cal A	150	480	46	121	14	2	3	56	14-1	2	22	.252	.273	.308	60	-27	2-4	**.985**	14	108	115	*S-139/2-8,3-2	0.0
1983	Cal A	88	330	29	83	10	0	2	29	5-1	1	18	.252	.263	.300	56	-21	2-3	.975	13	123	108	S-74,3-13	-0.1
1984	NY A	61	163	8	41	11	0	0	16	2-0	1	16	.252	.265	.319	63	-8	0-0	.950	7	92	132	S-28,2-21,3-10/1-2	0.1
1985	Pit N	19	37	1	7	0	0	0	2	4-1	0	2	.189	.268	.189	30	-3	0-0	.980	4	128	111	S-13	0.1
Total	16	1696	6047	576	1515	241	20	25	501	265-29	35	399	.251	.283	.309	64	-297	81-55	.973	165	105	116	*S-1524/2-92,3-66,O-3C,1-2	3.1

FONDY, DEE Dee Virgil B 10.31.1924 Slaton, TX D 8.19.1999 Redlands, CA BL/TL 6-3/196# d4.17

Year	Tm Lg	G	AB	R	H	2B	3B	HR	RBI	BB-IB	HP	SO	AVG	OBP	SLG	AOPS	ABR	SB-CS	FA	FR	Rng	Thr	G at Pos	BFW
1951	Chi N	49	170	23	46	7	2	3	20	11	1	20	.271	.319	.388	88	-3	5-6	.976	-3	89	95	1-44	-0.8
1952	Chi N	145	554	69	166	21	9	10	67	28	1	60	.300	.334	.424	108	3	13-11	.990	1	103	75	*1-143	-0.2
1953	Chi N	150	595	79	184	24	11	18	78	44	1	106	.309	.358	.477	113	10	10-7	.987	4	111	75	*1-149	0.4
1954	Chi N	141	568	77	162	30	4	9	49	35	1	84	.285	.326	.400	87	-11	20-5	.993	8	**120**	100	*1-138	-0.8
1955	Chi N	150	574	69	152	23	8	17	65	35-6	2	87	.265	.307	.422	92	-9	8-9	.991	1	103	102	*1-147	-1.8
1956	Chi N	137	543	52	146	22	9	9	46	20-5	0	74	.269	.290	.392	84	-14	9-7	.985	-4	92	88	*1-133	-2.7
1957	Chi N	11	51	3	16	3	1	0	2	0-0	0	9	.314	.314	.412	94	-1	1-2	.991	-1	67	100	1-11	-0.3
	Pit N	95	323	42	101	13	2	2	35	25-0	1	59	.313	.360	.384	104	2	11-5	.982	-4	92	100	1-73	-0.5
	Year	106	374	45	117	16	3	2	37	25-0	1	68	.313	.354	.388	103	2	12-7	.983	-5	89	100	1-84	-0.8
1958	Cin N	89	124	23	27	1	1	1	11	5-0	0	27	.218	.246	.266	34	-12	7-1	.987	2	158	113	1-36,O-22(7-0-15)	-1.0
Total	8	967	3502	437	1000	144	47	69	373	203-11	7	526	.286	.324	.413	95	-35	84-53	.988	5	104	90	1-874/O-22(7-0-15)	-7.7

FONSECA, LEW Lewis Albert B 1.21.1899 Oakland, CA D 11.26.1989 Ely, IA BR/TR 5-10.5/180# d4.13 M3 OF Total (99-LF 15-CF 5-RF)

Year	Tm Lg	G	AB	R	H	2B	3B	HR	RBI	BB-IB	HP	SO	AVG	OBP	SLG	AOPS	ABR	SB-CS	FA	FR	Rng	Thr	G at Pos	BFW
1921	Cin N	82	297	38	82	10	3	1	41	8	4	13	.276	.304	.340	74	-12	2-3	.961	-3	95	92	2-50,1-16,O-16(14-0-2)	-1.6
1922	Cin N	81	291	55	105	20	3	4	45	14	0	18	.361	.390	.491	128	12	7-8	.970	9	103	117	2-71	2.0
1923	Cin N	65	237	33	66	11	4	3	28	9	2	16	.278	.310	.397	87	-5	4-0	.957	6	107	102	2-45,1-14	0.2
1924	Cin N	20	57	5	13	2	1	0	9	4	0	4	.228	.279	.298	55	-4	1-0	1.000	-1	107	72	2-10/1-6	-0.4
1925	Phi N	126	467	78	149	30	5	7	60	21	3	42	.319	.352	.450	95	-4	6-2	.956	-7	98	76	2-69,1-55	-1.1
1927	Cle A	112	428	60	133	20	7	2	40	12	2	17	.311	.333	.404	90	-9	12-4	.973	-2	101	89	2-96,1-13	-0.7
1928	Cle A	75	263	38	86	19	4	3	36	13	1	17	.327	.361	.464	114	5	4-2	1.000	5	122	143	1-56,3-15/S-4,2	0.7
1929	Cle A	148	566	97	209	44	15	6	103	50	**7**	23	**.369**	.427	.532	140	35	19-11	.995	7	**118**	**109**	*1-147	3.0
1930	Cle A	40	129	20	36	9	2	0	17	7	0	7	.279	.316	.380	73	-5	1-0	.980	1	154	64	1-28/3-6	-0.5
1931	Cle A	26	108	21	40	9	1	1	14	8	1	7	.370	.419	.500	133	5	3-2	.993	0	98	80	1-26	0.3
	Chi A	121	465	65	139	26	5	2	71	32	3	22	.299	.348	.389	99	-1	4-4	.974	-9	96	62	O-95(80-15-0),2-21/1-2,3	-1.3
	Year	147	573	86	179	35	6	3	85	40	4	29	.312	.361	.410	106	5	7-6	.974	-9	96	62	O-95(80-15-0),1-28,2-21/3	-1.0
1932	Chi A	18	37	0	5	1	0	0	6	1	0	7	.135	.158	.162	-18	-7	0-0	1.000	1	92	362	/O-8(5-0-3),PM	-0.5
1933	Chi A	23	59	8	12	2	0	2	15	7	0	6	.203	.288	.339	68	-3	1-0	1.000	2	172	149	1-12,M	-0.2
Total	12	937	3404	518	1075	203	50	31	485	186	23	199	.316	.355	.432	103	7	64-36	.994	10	112	104	1-375,2-363,O-119L/3-22,S-4,P	-0.1

FONVILLE, CHAD Chad Everette B 3.5.1971 Jacksonville, NC BB/TR 5-6/155# d4.28

Year	Tm Lg	G	AB	R	H	2B	3B	HR	RBI	BB-IB	HP	SO	AVG	OBP	SLG	AOPS	ABR	SB-CS	FA	FR	Rng	Thr	G at Pos	BFW
1995	Mon N	14	12	2	4	0	0	0	0	0-0	0	3	.333	.333	.333	74	0	0-2	—	-0	0	0	/2-2	-0.2
	†LA N	88	308	41	85	6	1	0	16	23-1	1	39	.276	.328	.302	74	-12	20-5	.971	-1	102	74	S-38,2-36,O-11(10-2-0)	-0.6
	Year	102	320	43	89	6	1	0	16	23-1	1	42	.278	.328	.303	73	-13	20-7	.971	-2	95	70	2-38,S-38,O-11(10-2-0)	-0.8
1996	LA N	103	201	34	41	4	1	0	13	17-1	0	31	.204	.266	.234	36	-19	7-2	.964	-4	103	159	O-35(19-18-0),2-23,S-20/3-2	-2.1
1997	LA N	9	14	1	2	0	0	0	1	2-0	0	3	.143	.250	.143	7	-2	0-1	.833	-4	47	0	/2-3	-0.6
	Chi A	9	9	1	1	0	0	0	1	1-0	0	1	.111	.200	.111	-17	-2	2-0	1.000	-1	245	0	/O-3(1-2-0),2-2,S-2,D	-0.1
1999	Bos A	3	2	1	0	0	0	0	0	2-0	0	0	.000	.500	.000	41	0	1-0	.900	1	85	142	/2-2	0.1
Total	4	226	546	80	133	10	2	0	31	45-2	1	77	.244	.302	.269	57	-35	30-10	.964	-10	92	75	/2-68,S-60,O-49(30-22-0),3-2,D	-3.5

FOOTE, BARRY Barry Clifton B 2.16.1952 Smithfield, NC BR/TR 6-3/210# d9.14 C3

Year	Tm Lg	G	AB	R	H	2B	3B	HR	RBI	BB-IB	HP	SO	AVG	OBP	SLG	AOPS	ABR	SB-CS	FA	FR	Rng	Thr	G at Pos	BFW
1973	Mon N	6	6	0	4	0	1	0	1	0-0	0	0	.667	.667	1.000	343	2	0-0	—	0			H	0.2
1974	Mon N	125	420	44	110	23	4	11	60	35-11	3	74	.262	.315	.414	100	-1	2-1	.984	11	109	113	*C-122	1.6
1975	Mon N	118	387	25	75	16	1	7	30	17-6	1	48	.194	.229	.295	43	-31	0-1	.985	5	121	83	*C-115	-2.3
1976	Mon N	105	350	32	82	12	2	7	27	17-3	1	32	.234	.272	.340	70	-15	2-1	.989	7	112	123	C-96/3-2,1	-0.4
1977	Mon N	15	49	4	12	3	1	2	8	4-0	0	10	.245	.302	.469	106	0	0-0	.988	2	258	107	C-13	0.2
	Phi N	18	32	3	7	1	0	1	3	3-0	0	6	.219	.286	.344	65	-2	0-0	.980	-1	113	54	C-17	-0.2
	Year	33	81	7	19	4	1	3	11	7-0	0	16	.235	.295	.420	88	-2	0-0	.985	1	199	86	C-30	0.0
1978	†Phi N	39	57	4	9	0	0	1	4	1-0	0	11	.158	.172	.211	6	-7	0-0	1.000	1	362	57	C-31	-0.6
1979	Chi N	132	429	47	109	26	0	16	56	34-7	5	49	.254	.316	.427	92	-5	5-2	.979	3	115	104	*C-129	0.4
1980	Chi N	63	202	16	48	13	1	6	28	13-2	0	18	.238	.282	.401	83	-5	1-1	.992	5	121	114	C-55	0.3
1981	Chi N	9	22	0	0	0	0	0	1	3-0	0	7	.000	.115	.000	-61	-5	0-0	1.000	-0	267	116	/C-8	-0.5
	†NY A	40	125	12	26	4	0	6	10	8-0	0	21	.208	.256	.384	83	-3	0-0	.996	8	82	117	C-34/1D	0.6
1982	NY A	17	48	4	7	5	0	0	2	1-0	0	11	.146	.160	.250	12	-6	0-0	.973	-4	117	64	C-17	-0.9
Total	10	687	2127	191	489	103	10	57	230	136-29	10	287	.230	.277	.368	75	-78	10-6	.985	37	124	104	C-637/D-4,1-2,3-2	-1.6

FORAN, JIM James H. B 1848 , NY D 1.30.1928 Los Angeles, CA 5-6.5/159# d5.4

Year	Tm Lg	G	AB	R	H	2B	3B	HR	RBI	BB-IB	HP	SO	AVG	OBP	SLG	AOPS	ABR	SB-CS	FA	FR	Rng	Thr	G at Pos	BFW
1871	Kek NA	**19**	89	21	31	1	3	1	18	2		1	.348	.363	.461	132	3	1-0	.878	0	163	27	1-16/O-4(3-1-0)	0.2

FORBES, P.J. Patrick Joseph B 9.22.1967 Pittsburg, KS BR/TR 5-10/160# d7.21

Year	Tm Lg	G	AB	R	H	2B	3B	HR	RBI	BB-IB	HP	SO	AVG	OBP	SLG	AOPS	ABR	SB-CS	FA	FR	Rng	Thr	G at Pos	BFW
1998	Bal A	9	10	0	1	0	0	0	2	0-0	0	0	.100	.100	.100	-48	-2	0-0	1.000	1	131	135	/2-7,3S	-0.1
2001	Phi N	3	7	1	2	0	0	0	1	0-0	0	2	.286	.286	.286	50	-1	0-0	1.000	-0	74	0	/2	-0.1
Total	2	12	17	1	3	0	0	0	3	0-0	0	2	.176	.176	.176	-8	-3	0-0	1.000	0	114	95	/2-8,S3	-0.2

FORCE, DAVY David W. "Wee Davy" or "Tom Thumb" B 7.27.1849 New York, NY D 6.21.1918 Englewood, NJ BR/TR 5-4/130# d5.5 ▲

Year	Tm Lg	G	AB	R	H	2B	3B	HR	RBI	BB-IB	HP	SO	AVG	OBP	SLG	AOPS	ABR	SB-CS	FA	FR	Rng	Thr	G at Pos	BFW
1871	Oly NA	**32**	162	45	45	9	4	0	29	4		0	.278	.295	.383	98	1	8-0	**.844**	**18**	**136**	104	*S-31/3	1.2
1872	Tro NA	**25**	130	40	53	11	0	0	19	1		0	.408	.412	.492	174	11	2-2	.871	4	105	227	3-16/S-9	0.9
	Bal NA	19	95	29	41	2	2	0	14	1		0	.432	.438	.495	178	8	5-0	.846	4	100	0	3-19	0.8
	Year	44	225	69	94	13	2	0	33	2		0	.418	.423	.493	176	19	7-2	**.857**	7	102	107	3-35/S-9	1.7
1873	Bal NA	49	233	77	85	10	1	0	30	9		1	.365	.388	.416	140	12	1-0	**.830**	7	101	26	3-34,S-17/P-3	1.2
1874	Chi NA	**59**	294	61	92	9	0	0	26	3		1	.313	.320	.344	112	4	4-0	.802	9	111	100	*3-42,S-18/P	0.9
1875	Ath NA	**77**	386	78	120	22	5	0	49	7		5	.311	.323	.394	133	11	6-3	**.887**	11	100	**162**	*S-77/3-2	1.7
1876	Phi N	**60**	284	48	66	6	0	0	17	5		3	.232	.246	.254	67	-9		.898	20	122	75	*S-60/3-2	1.1
	NY N	1	3	0	0	0	0	0	0	0		0	.000	.000	.000	-99	-1		.833	0	105	0	/S	0.0
	Year	61	287	48	66	6	0	0	17	5		3	.230	.243	.251	66	-10		**.897**	20	**122**	74	S-61/3-2	1.1
1877	StL N	58	225	24	59	5	3	0	22	11		15	.262	.297	.311	97	0		**.914**	6	102	80	*S-50/3-8	0.7
1879	Buf N	**79**	316	36	66	5	2	0	8	13		37	.209	.240	.237	57	-15		**.929**	2	101	**164**	*S-78/3	-0.8
1880	Buf N	81	290	22	49	10	0	0	17	10		35	.169	.197	.203	35	-19		.939	26	121	108	2-53,S-30	1.1
1881	Buf N	75	278	21	50	9	1	0	15	11		29	.180	.211	.219	36	-20		.937	**25**	130	66	2-51,S-21/O-3(RF),3	0.8
1882	Buf N	73	278	39	67	10	1	1	28	12		17	.241	.272	.295	81	-6		**.908**	7	106	74	*S-61,3-11/2	0.3
1883	Buf N	96	378	40	82	11	3	0	35	12		39	.217	.241	.262	52	-22		.884	-9	96	103	*S-78,3-13/2-7	-2.5
1884	Buf N	106	403	47	83	13	3	0	36	27		41	.206	.256	.253	59	-19		**.898**	-4	97	91	*S-105/2	-1.8
1885	Buf N	71	253	20	57	6	1	0	15	13		19	.225	.263	.257	66	-10		.882	0	105	115	2-42,S-24/3-6	-0.6
1886	Was N	68	242	26	44	5	1	0	16	17		26	.182	.236	.211	39	-17	9	.909	18	124	119	S-56/2-8,3-4	0.3
Total	5 NA	261	1300	330	436	63	12	0	167	25		7	.335	.348	.402	132	47	26-5	.000	52	107	133	S-152,3-114/P-4	6.7

Year	Tm Lg	G	AB	R	H	2B	3B	HR	RBI	BB-IB	HP	SO	AVG	OBP	SLG	AOPS	ABR	SB-CS	FA	FR	Rng	Thr	G at Pos	BFW
Total	10	768	2950	323	623	80	15	1	209	131		261	.211	.245	.249	58	-138	9-0	.908	92	106	100	S-564,2-163/3-46,O-3(RF)	-1.4
FORD, CURT Curtis Glenn B 10.11.1960 Jackson, MS BL/TR 5-10/150# d6.22																								
1985	StL N	11	12	2	6	2	0	0	3	4-0	0	1	.500	.625	.667	264	3	1-0	.750	-1	71	0	/O-4(1-0-4)	0.3
1986	StL N	85	214	30	53	15	2	2	29	23-2	0	29	.248	.318	.364	89	-3	13-5	.975	4	105	169	O-64(24-0-40)	0.0
1987	†StL N	89	228	32	65	9	5	3	26	14-0	1	32	.285	.325	.408	92	-3	11-8	.981	7	136	48	O-75(15-2-61)	0.0
1988	StL N	91	128	11	25	6	0	1	18	8-1	0	26	.195	.239	.266	45	-9	6-1	.965	3	119	78	O-40(24-3-13)/1-7	-0.7
1989	Phi N	108	142	13	31	5	1	1	13	16-0	1	33	.218	.298	.289	70	-5	5-3	1.000	1	95	225	O-52(26-2-25)/12	-0.5
1990	Phi N	22	18	0	2	0	0	0	0	1-0	0	5	.111	.158	.111	-25	-3	0-0	1.000	0	162	0	/O-3(RF)	-0.3
Total	6	406	742	88	182	37	8	7	89	66-3	2	126	.245	.305	.345	80	-20	36-17	.977	14	116	118	O-238(90-7-146)/1-8,2	-1.2
FORD, DAN Darnell Glenn B 5.19.1952 Los Angeles, CA BR/TR 6-1/185# d4.12																								
1975	Min A	130	440	72	123	21	1	15	59	30-2	5	79	.280	.333	.434	114	7	6-7	.988	-11	88	40	*O-120(0-118-2)/D-3	-0.8
1976	Min A	145	514	87	137	24	7	20	86	36-2	10	118	.267	.323	.457	125	14	17-6	.968	-7	95	59	*O-139(1-0-139)/D-3	0.2
1977	Min A	144	453	66	121	25	7	11	60	41-3	10	79	.267	.338	.426	109	6	6-4	.964	-7	85	104	*O-137(1-3-135)/D-3	-0.7
1978	Min A	151	592	78	162	36	10	11	82	48-6	5	88	.274	.332	.424	109	7	7-7	.977	-15	88	59	*O-149(0-145-4)/D	-1.0
1979	†Cal A	142	569	100	165	26	5	21	101	40-0	3	86	.290	.333	.464	118	13	8-5	.977	6	113	99	*O-141(0-29-124)	1.2
1980	Cal A	65	226	22	63	11	0	7	26	19-1	2	45	.279	.339	.420	110	3	0-1	.940	-2	93	98	O-45(RF),D-15	-0.2
1981	Cal A	97	375	53	104	14	1	15	48	23-3	5	71	.277	.327	.440	119	8	2-2	.960	-7	94	42	O-97(RF)	-0.4
1982	Bal A	123	421	46	99	21	3	10	43	23-1	4	71	.235	.279	.371	78	-14	5-2	.975	5	116	76	*O-119(RF)/D	-1.4
1983	†Bal A	103	407	63	114	30	4	9	55	29-1	3	55	.280	.328	.440	113	7	9-2	.987	-2	107	26	*O-103(RF)	0.1
1984	Bal A	25	91	7	21	4	0	1	5	7-0	0	13	.231	.286	.308	66	-4	1-0	1.000	1	120	111	O-15(RF)/D-8	-0.3
1985	Bal A	28	75	4	14	2	0	1	1	7-0	0	17	.187	.256	.253	41	-6	0-1	—	0	0	0	D-28	-0.7
Total	11	1153	4163	598	1123	214	38	121	566	303-19	47	722	.270	.324	.427	109	41	61-37	.974	-38	98	67	*O-1065(2-295-783)/D-62	-4.0
FORD, ED Edward L. B 1862 Richmond, VA 5-9.5/160# d10.9																								
1884	Ric AA	2	5	0	0	0	0	0		0	0		.000	.000	.000	-99	-1		.556	1	116	0	/S1	-0.1
FORD, HOD Horace Hills B 7.23.1897 New Haven, CT D 1.29.1977 Winchester, MA BR/TR 5-10/165# d9.8																								
1919	Bos N	10	28	4	6	0	1	0	3	2	1	6	.214	.290	.286	77	-1	0	.946	2	133	122	/S-8,3-2	0.2
1920	Bos N	88	257	16	62	12	5	1	30	18	2	25	.241	.296	.339	86	-5	3-3	.972	11	117	73	2-59,S-18/1-4	0.8
1921	Bos N	152	555	50	155	29	5	2	61	36	4	49	.279	.328	.360	87	-10	2-11	**.973**	4	103	84	*2-119,S-33	-0.3
1922	Bos N	143	515	58	140	23	9	2	60	30	4	36	.272	.317	.363	78	-18	2-1	.953	-0	99	84	*S-115,2-28	-0.4
1923	Bos N	111	380	27	103	16	7	2	50	31	0	30	.271	.326	.366	86	-8	1-1	.970	-8	97	106	2-95,S-19	-1.1
1924	Phi N	145	530	58	144	27	5	3	53	27	1	40	.272	.308	.358	70	-22	1-9	.970	9	**106**	95	*2-145	-1.2
1925	Bro N	66	216	32	59	11	0	1	15	26	2	15	.273	.357	.338	81	-5	0-3	.966	2	97	88	S-66	0.2
1926	Cin N	57	197	14	55	6	1	0	18	14	3	12	.279	.336	.320	79	-5	1	.963	2	94	168	S-57	0.3
1927	Cin N	115	409	45	112	16	2	1	46	33	2	34	.274	.331	.330	80	-11	0	.952	-6	96	**129**	*S-104,2-12	-0.5
1928	Cin N	149	506	49	122	17	4	0	54	47	2	31	.241	.308	.291	58	-31	1	**.972**	15	102	**134**	*S-149	0.0
1929	Cin N	148	529	68	146	14	6	3	50	41	1	25	.276	.329	.342	70	-26	8	.953	8	100	**128**	*S-108,2-42	-0.5
1930	Cin N	132	424	36	98	16	7	1	34	24	0	28	.231	.272	.309	42	-41	2	.974	5	99	107	S-74,2-66	-2.5
1931	Cin N	84	175	18	40	8	1	0	13	13	1	13	.229	.286	.286	57	-11	0	.954	0	101	121	S-73/2-3,3	-0.7
1932	StL N	1	2	0	0	0	0	0	0	0	0	0	.000	.000	.000	-97	-1	0	.750	-0	45	235	/S	-0.1
	Bos N	40	95	9	26	5	2	0	6	6	1	9	.274	.324	.368	89	-2	0	.984	-1	96	118	2-20,S-16/3-2	-0.1
	Year	41	97	9	26	5	2	0	6	6	1	9	.268	.317	.361	85	-2	0	.984	-1	96	118	2-20,S-17/3-2	-0.2
1933	Bos N	5	15	0	1	0	0	0	1	3	0	1	.067	.222	.067	-16	-2	0	1.000	3	120	117	/S-5	0.1
Total	15	1446	4833	484	1269	200	55	16	494	351	24	354	.263	.316	.337	72	-199	21-28	.960	45	100	116	S-846,2-589/3-5,1-4	-5.8
FORD, LEW Jon Lewis B 8.12.1976 Beaumont, TX BR/TR 6/190# d5.29																								
2003	†Min A	34	73	16	24	7	1	3	15	8-0	1	9	.329	.402	.575	152	6	2-0	.923	-2	86	108	O-25(8-13-6)/D-4	0.4
FORD, TED Theodore Henry B 2.7.1947 Vineland, NJ BR/TR 5-10/180# d4.7																								
1970	Cle A	26	46	5	8	1	0	1	1	3-0	0	13	.174	.224	.261	32	-4	0-0	1.000	2	143	171	O-12(2-1-10)	-0.3
1971	Cle A	74	196	15	38	6	0	2	14	9-0	0	34	.194	.229	.255	34	-17	2-2	1.000	5	116	144	O-55(12-20-29)	-1.6
1972	Tex A	129	429	43	101	19	1	14	50	37-2	3	80	.235	.297	.382	107	2	4-3	.977	7	**113**	134	*O-119(16-0-104)	0.4
1973	Cle A	11	40	3	9	0	1	0	3	2-0	0	7	.225	.250	.275	50	-3	1-0	1.000	-4	27	0	O-10(0-6-5)	-0.7
Total	4	240	711	66	156	26	2	17	68	51-2	3	134	.219	.272	.333	76	-22	7-5	.985	10	110	131	O-196(30-27-148)	-2.2
FORDYCE, BROOK Brook Alexander B 5.7.1970 New London, CT BR/TR 6-1/185# d4.26																								
1995	NY N	4	2	1	1	1	0	0	0	1-0	0	0	.500	.667	1.000	343	1	0-0	—	0			/H	0.1
1996	Cin N	4	7	0	2	1	0	0	1	3-0	0	1	.286	.500	.429	147	1	0-0	1.000	-1	223	112	/C-4	0.0
1997	Cin N	47	96	7	20	5	0	1	8	8-1	0	15	.208	.267	.292	46	-8	2-0	.983	-5	59	73	C-30/D	-1.1
1998	Cin N	57	146	8	37	9	0	3	14	11-3	0	28	.253	.306	.377	77	-5	0-1	.978	-1	90	133	C-54	-0.3
1999	Chi A	105	333	36	99	25	1	9	49	21-0	3	48	.297	.343	.459	102	1	2-0	.987	-10	96	93	*C-103	-0.2
2000	Chi A	40	125	18	34	7	1	5	21	6-0	2	23	.272	.313	.464	93	-2	0-0	1.000	8	139	116	C-40	0.7
	Bal A	53	177	23	57	11	0	9	28	11-0	2	27	.322	.361	.537	132	8	0-0	.988	-8	68	50	C-52	0.3
	Year	93	302	41	91	18	1	14	49	17-0	4	50	.301	.341	.507	115	6	0-0	.993	0	97	77	C-92	1.0
2001	Bal A	95	292	30	61	18	0	5	19	21-1	3	56	.209	.268	.322	58	-18	1-2	.983	-13	64	93	C-95	-2.5
2002	Bal A	56	130	7	30	8	0	1	8	9-0	4	19	.231	.301	.315	68	-6	1-0	.986	-8	54	76	C-55	-1.1
2003	Bal A	108	348	28	95	12	2	6	31	19-1	1	44	.273	.311	.371	82	-10	2-3	.996	-8	79	83	*C-107	-1.1
Total	9	569	1656	158	436	97	4	39	179	110-6	15	261	.263	.313	.397	86	-38	8-6	.988	-45	81	89	C-540/D	-5.2
FORSTER, TOM Thomas W. B 5.1.1859 New York, NY D 7.17.1946 New York, NY BR/TR 5-9/153# d8.4																								
1882	Det N	21	76	5	7	0	0	0	2	5		12	.092	.148	.092	-21	-10		.830	-8	81	51	2-21	-1.7
1884	Pit AA	35	126	10	28	5	0	0		7	0		.222	.263	.262	73	-3		.897	4	110	93	S-28/3-6,2	0.2
1885	NY AA	57	213	28	47	7	2	0	18	17	1		.221	.281	.272	79	-4		.903	-5	95	95	2-52/O-5(3-2-0)	-0.7
1886	NY AA	67	251	33	49	3	2	1	20	20	3		.195	.263	.235	61	-10	9	.891	-4	101	97	2-62/O-4(2-2-0),S	-1.0
Total	4	180	666	76	131	15	4	1	40	49	4	12	.197	.256	.236	59	-27	9	.885	-13	96	88	2-136/S-29,O-9(5-4-0),3-6	-3.2
FORSYTHE, ED Edward James B 4.30.1887 Kingston, NY D 6.22.1956 Hoboken, NJ BR/TR 5-10/155# d10.2																								
1915	Bal F	1	3	0	0	0	0	0	0	1	0	0	.000	.250	.000	-26	-1	0	.667	-0	112	0	/3	-0.1
FOSS, GEORGE George Dueward "Deeby" B 6.13.1897 Register, GA D 11.10.1969 Brandon, FL BR/TR 5-10.5/170# d4.16																								
1921	Was A	4	7	0	0	0	0	0	0	0	0	1	.000	.000	.000	-99	-2	0-0	.750	-0	89	536	/3	-0.2
FOSSE, RAY Raymond Earl B 4.4.1947 Marion, IL BR/TR 6-2/215# d9.8																								
1967	Cle A	7	16	0	1	0	0	0	0	0-0	0	5	.063	.063	.063	-62	-3	0-0	1.000	2	75	275	/C-7	-0.1
1968	Cle A	1	0	0	0	0	0	0	0	0-0	0	0	—	—	—	—	0	0-0	1.000	-0	0	0	/C	0.0
1969	Cle A	37	116	11	20	3	0	2	9	8-1	1	29	.172	.230	.250	34	-11	1-0	.977	-3	48	142	C-37	-1.2
1970	Cle A★	120	450	62	138	17	1	18	61	39-5	1	55	.307	.361	.469	122	13	1-5	.989	8	139	137	*C-120	2.6
1971	Cle A∗	133	486	53	134	21	1	12	62	36-6	4	62	.276	.329	.397	97	-2	4-1	.988	3	96	112	*C-126/1-4	0.8
1972	Cle A	134	457	42	110	20	1	10	41	45-15	3	46	.241	.312	.354	95	-2	5-1	.985	7	108	90	*C-124/1-3	1.3
1973	†Oak A	143	492	37	126	23	2	7	52	25-4	1	62	.256	.291	.354	86	-11	2-2	.987	7	**171**	114	*C-141/D-2	0.2
1974	†Oak A	69	204	20	40	8	3	4	23	11-1	2	31	.196	.241	.324	66	-10	1-1	.973	1	101	86	C-68/D	-0.7
1975	†Oak A	82	136	14	19	3	2	0	12	8-0	1	19	.140	.192	.191	9	-17	0-1	.981	-3	85	69	C-82/12	-1.9
1976	Cle A	90	276	26	83	9	1	2	30	20-1	0	20	.301	.347	.362	109	3	1-2	.987	2	103	88	C-85/1-3,D	0.8
1977	Cle A	78	238	25	63	7	1	6	27	7-2	3	26	.265	.293	.378	84	-6	0-5	.983	3	66	128	C-77/1D	-0.2
	Sea A	11	34	3	12	3	0	0	5	2-0	0	2	.353	.389	.441	127	1	0-1	.968	-2	205	0	/C-8,D-2	-0.1
	Year	89	272	28	75	10	1	6	32	9-2	3	28	.276	.305	.386	90	-5	0-6	.982	1	78	117	C-85/D-3,1	-0.3
1979	Mil A	19	52	6	12	3	1	0	2	2-0	2	6	.231	.286	.327	65	-3	0-0	1.000	2	221	81	C-13/1D	-0.1
Total	12	924	2957	299	758	117	13	61	324	203-35	18	363	.256	.306	.367	90	-48	15-19	.985	27	115	109	C-889/1-13,D-12,2	1.4
FOSTER, POP Clarence Francis B 4.8.1878 New Haven, CT D 4.16.1944 Princeton, NJ BR/TR 5-8.5/?# d9.13																								
1898	NY N	32	112	10	30	6	1	0	9	0	0		.268	.268	.339	76	-4	0	.967	-3	39	0	O-21(17-0-4),3-10/S-2	-0.8
1899	NY N	84	301	48	89	9	7	3	57	20	4		.296	.348	.402	109	3	7	.949	-9	65	77	O-84(1-0-84)/S3	-0.9
1900	NY N	31	84	19	22	3	1	0	11	11	0		.262	.347	.321	89	-1	0	1.000	1	65	218	O-12(1-0-11)/S-7,2-5	0.0
1901	Was A	103	392	65	109	16	9	6	54	41	4		.278	.352	.411	113	7	10	.925	0	69	34	*O-102(LF)/S-2	0.1

Year	Tm Lg	G	AB	R	H	2B	3B	HR	RBI	BB-IB	HP	SO	AVG	OBP	SLG	AOPS	ABR	SB-CS	FA	FR	Rng	Thr	G at Pos	BFW
	Chi A	12	35	4	10	2	2	1	6	4	0		.286	.359	.543	152	2	0	.909	-1	111	0	/O-9(RF)	0.1
	Year	115	427	69	119	18	11	7	60	45	4		.279	.353	.422	116	9	10	.924	-0	72	32	*O-111(102-0-9)/S-2	0.2
Total	4	262	924	146	260	36	20	10	137	76	8		.281	.341	.396	107	7	17	.938	-11	66	55	O-228(121-0-108)/S-12,3-11,2-5	-1.5

FOSTER, EDDIE Edward Cunningham "Kid" B 2.13.1887 Chicago, IL D 1.15.1937 Washington, DC BR/TR 5-6.5/145# d4.14

Year	Tm Lg	G	AB	R	H	2B	3B	HR	RBI	BB-IB	HP	SO	AVG	OBP	SLG	AOPS	ABR	SB-CS	FA	FR	Rng	Thr	G at Pos	BFW
1910	NY A	30	83	5	11	2	0	0	1	8	1		.133	.217	.157	16	-8	2	.909	-2	99	88	S-22	-1.0
1912	Was A	**154**	618	98	176	34	9	2	70	53	4		.285	.345	.379	106	5	27	.920	10	**108**	105	*3-154	1.9
1913	Was A	106	409	56	101	11	5	1	41	36	1	31	.247	.309	.306	78	-12	22	.901	2	**106**	**146**	*3-105	-0.7
1914	Was A	**157**	616	82	174	16	10	2	50	60	2	47	.282	.348	.351	106	4	31-18	.929	-19	80	123	*3-157	-1.1
1915	Was A	154	618	75	170	25	10	0	52	48	2	30	.275	.329	.348	101	-1	20-6	.919	-7	98	124	3-79,2-75	-0.2
1916	Was A	158	606	75	153	18	9	1	44	68	4	26	.252	.332	.317	96	-3	23-16	.929	-17	78	88	3-84,2-72	-1.8
1917	Was A	143	554	66	130	16	8	0	43	46	0	23	.235	.293	.292	80	-15	11	.935	-6	98	116	3-86,2-57	-2.0
1918	Was A	129	519	70	147	13	3	0	29	41	3	20	.283	.339	.320	101	0	12	.936	-3	100	**133**	*3-127/2-2	0.1
1919	Was A	120	478	57	126	12	5	0	26	33	2	21	.264	.314	.310	76	-16	20	.946	7	109	85	*3-115	-0.7
1920	Bos A	117	386	48	100	17	6	0	41	42	3	17	.259	.336	.334	82	-10	10-4	.957	9	110	138	3-88,2-21	0.2
1921	Bos A	120	412	51	117	18	6	0	35	57	0	15	.284	.371	.357	89	-5	13-7	.943	-10	99	115	3-94,2-22	-0.8
1922	Bos A	48	109	11	23	3	0	0	3	9	1	10	.211	.277	.239	36	-10	1-1	.886	-7	83	44	3-28/S-3	-1.6
	StL A	37	144	29	44	4	0	0	12	20	1	8	.306	.394	.333	88	-1	3-1	.916	0	100	187	3-37	0.1
	Year	85	253	40	67	7	0	0	15	29	2	18	.265	.345	.292	67	-11	4-2	.905	-7	93	132	3-65/S-3	-1.5
1923	StL A	27	100	9	18	2	0	0	4	7	1	7	.180	.241	.200	16	-12	0-0	.961	-4	81	125	2-20/3-7	-1.6
Total	13	1500	5652	732	1490	191	71	6	451	528	25	255	.264	.329	.326	89	-84	195-53	.930	-48	98	119	*3-1161,2-269/S-25	-9.2

FOSTER, ELMER Elmer Ellsworth B 8.15.1861 Minneapolis, MN D 7.22.1946 Deephaven, MN BR/TL 5-10/178# d4.17

Year	Tm Lg	G	AB	R	H	2B	3B	HR	RBI	BB-IB	HP	SO	AVG	OBP	SLG	AOPS	ABR	SB-CS	FA	FR	Rng	Thr	G at Pos	BFW
1886	NY AA	35	125	16	23	0	1	0	7	7	2		.184	.239	.200	41	-8	3	.853	-4	108	41	2-21,O-14(9-5-0)	-1.0
1888	NY N	37	136	15	20	3	2	0	10	9	3	20	.147	.216	.199	33	-10	13	.852	-3	78	0	O-37(16-21-0)/3	-1.4
1889	NY N	2	4	2	0	0	0	0	0	3	0	1	.000	.429	.000	25	0	2	1.000	0	0	0	/O-2(CF)	0.0
1890	Chi N	27	105	20	26	4	2	5	23	9	3	21	.248	.325	.467	125	2	18	.986	2	46	0	O-27(CF)	0.3
1891	Chi N	4	16	3	3	0	0	1	1	1	0	2	.188	.235	.375	77	-1	1	.875	0	189	0	/O-4(CF)	-0.1
Total	5	105	386	56	72	7	5	6	41	29	8	44	.187	.258	.277	66	-17	37	.883	-5	73	0	/O-84(25-59-0),2-21,3	-2.2

FOSTER, GEORGE George Arthur B 12.1.1948 Tuscaloosa, AL BR/TR 6-1/185# d9.10

Year	Tm Lg	G	AB	R	H	2B	3B	HR	RBI	BB-IB	HP	SO	AVG	OBP	SLG	AOPS	ABR	SB-CS	FA	FR	Rng	Thr	G at Pos	BFW
1969	SF N	9	5	1	2	0	0	0	1	0-0	0	1	.400	.400	.400	127	0	0-0	1.000	-0	87	0	/O-8(RF)	0.0
1970	SF N	9	19	2	6	1	1	1	4	2-1	0	5	.316	.381	.632	168	2	0-0	1.000	-0	107	0	/O-7(6-0-1)	0.1
1971	SF N	36	105	11	28	5	0	3	8	6-1	0	27	.267	.304	.400	100	0	0-1	.980	-1	93	54	O-30(24-0-7)	-0.4
	Cin N	104	368	39	86	18	4	10	50	23-2	7	93	.234	.289	.386	92	-5	7-6	.986	5	103	133	*O-102(1-101-1)	-0.3
	Year	140	473	50	114	23	4	13	58	29-3	7	120	.241	.292	.389	94	-5	7-7	.985	4	101	116	*O-132(25-101-8)	-0.7
1972	†Cin N	59	145	15	29	4	1	2	12	5-1	1	44	.200	.230	.283	48	-11	2-1	.973	-2	100	36	O-47(2-1-44)	-1.5
1973	Cin N	17	39	6	11	3	0	4	9	4-0	0	7	.282	.349	.667	185	4	0-1	1.000	-0	81	148	O-13(1-11-5)	0.3
1974	Cin N	106	276	31	73	18	0	7	41	30-5	4	52	.264	.343	.406	111	5	3-2	.989	-1	102	39	O-98(6-45-69)	0.0
1975	†Cin N	134	463	71	139	24	4	23	78	40-11	3	73	.300	.356	.518	139	22	2-1	.990	10	112	118	*O-125(95-30-18)/1	2.7
1976	†Cin N★	144	562	86	172	21	9	29	**121**	52-4	4	89	.306	.364	.530	149	34	17-3	**.994**	5	106	89	*O-142(116-36-24)/1	3.6
1977	Cin N★	158	615	**124**	197	31	2	**52**	**149**	61-10	5	107	.320	.382	**.631**	165	**54**	6-4	.992	11	112	117	*O-158(136-32-1)	5.9
1978	Cin N★	158	604	97	170	26	7	**40**	**120**	70-16	7	138	.281	.360	.546	151	39	4-4	.971	-0	100	76	*O-157(154-11-0)	3.3
1979	†Cin N★	121	440	68	133	18	3	30	98	59-7	3	105	.302	.386	.561	155	33	0-2	.982	-2	93	78	*O-116(LF)	2.6
1980	Cin N	144	528	79	144	21	5	25	93	75-14	1	99	.273	.362	.473	132	23	1-0	.997	3	107	58	*O-141(LF)	2.1
1981	Cin N★	**108**	414	64	122	23	2	22	90	51-5	3	75	.295	.373	.519	150	27	4-0	.991	3	103	84	*O-108(LF)	2.7
1982	NY N	151	550	64	136	23	2	13	70	50-9	2	123	.247	.309	.367	90	-8	1-1	.974	6	105	106	*O-138(LF)	-0.8
1983	NY N	157	601	74	145	19	2	28	90	38-5	4	111	.241	.289	.419	95	-7	1-1	.988	3	98	97	*O-153(LF)	-1.2
1984	NY N	146	553	67	149	22	1	24	86	30-9	6	122	.269	.311	.443	112	6	2-2	.976	2	105	56	*O-141(LF)	0.2
1985	NY N	129	452	57	119	24	1	21	77	46-5	2	87	.263	.331	.460	123	13	0-1	.976	-5	87	81	*O-123(LF)	0.2
1986	NY N	72	233	28	53	6	1	13	38	21-1	0	53	.227	.289	.429	99	-2	1-1	.962	-2	87	102	O-62(LF)	-0.7
	Chi A	15	51	2	11	0	2	1	4	3-0	0	8	.216	.259	.353	63	-3	0-0	1.000	1	90	307	O-11(LF)/D-3	-0.3
Total	18	1977	7023	986	1925	307	47	348	1239	666-106	52	1419	.274	.338	.480	127	226	51-31	.984	33	102	88	*O-1880(1534-267-178)/D-3,1-2	18.5

FOSTER, LEO Leonard Norris B 2.2.1951 Covington, KY BR/TR 5-11/165# d7.9

Year	Tm Lg	G	AB	R	H	2B	3B	HR	RBI	BB-IB	HP	SO	AVG	OBP	SLG	AOPS	ABR	SB-CS	FA	FR	Rng	Thr	G at Pos	BFW
1971	Atl N	9	10	1	0	0	0	0	0	0-0	0	1	.000	.000	.000	-94	-3	0-0	.900	-0	114	141	/S-3	-0.3
1973	Atl N	3	6	1	1	1	0	0	0	0-0	0	2	.167	.167	.333	33	-1	0-0	1.000	-1	24	115	/S	-0.1
1974	Atl N	72	112	16	22	2	0	1	5	9-0	0	22	.196	.254	.241	38	-9	1-2	.977	-3	98	91	S-43,2-10/3-3,O(RF)	-1.0
1976	NY N	24	59	11	12	2	0	1	15	8-1	0	5	.203	.299	.288	71	-2	3-0	.920	-1	101	82	/3-9,S-7,2-3	-0.2
1977	NY N	36	75	6	17	3	0	0	6	5-0	1	14	.227	.284	.267	51	-5	3-1	.968	-3	79	83	2-20/S-8,3-2	-0.7
Total	5	144	262	35	52	8	0	2	26	22-1	1	44	.198	.262	.252	44	-20	7-3	.964	-9	97	90	/S-62,2-33,3-14,O(RF)	-2.3

FOSTER, REDDY Oscar E. B 8.1864 Richmond, VA D 12.19.1908 Richmond, VA d6.3

Year	Tm Lg	G	AB	R	H	2B	3B	HR	RBI	BB-IB	HP	SO	AVG	OBP	SLG	AOPS	ABR	SB-CS	FA	FR	Rng	Thr	G at Pos	BFW
1896	NY N	1	1	0	0	0	0	0	0	0	0	0	.000	.000	.000	-99	0	0	—	0			H	0.0

FOSTER, BOB Robert d6.18

Year	Tm Lg	G	AB	R	H	2B	3B	HR	RBI	BB-IB	HP	SO	AVG	OBP	SLG	AOPS	ABR	SB-CS	FA	FR	Rng	Thr	G at Pos	BFW
1884	Phi U	1	3	0	1	0	1	0		0			.333	.333	1.000	313	1		.625	-1			/C	-0.1
	Phi AA	4	11	4	2	0	0	0		3	0		.182	.357	.182	76	0		.885	-1			/C-4,O(RF)	-0.1
Total	1	5	14	4	3	0	1	0		3	0		.214	.353	.357	124	1		.824	-2			/C-5,O(RF)	-0.2

FOSTER, ROY Roy B 7.29.1945 Bixby, OK BR/TR 6/185# d4.7

Year	Tm Lg	G	AB	R	H	2B	3B	HR	RBI	BB-IB	HP	SO	AVG	OBP	SLG	AOPS	ABR	SB-CS	FA	FR	Rng	Thr	G at Pos	BFW
1970	Cle A	139	477	66	128	26	0	23	60	54-4	**12**	75	.268	.357	.468	120	14	3-3	.965	-6	88	79	*O-131(114-0-17)	0.0
1971	Cle A	125	396	51	97	21	1	18	45	35-2	6	48	.245	.314	.439	103	1	6-1	.968	0	94	142	*O-107(46-0-64)	-0.4
1972	Cle A	73	143	19	32	4	0	4	13	21-2	2	23	.224	.325	.336	96	0	0-2	.966	-2	87	82	O-45(15-0-31)	-0.5
Total	3	337	1016	136	257	51	1	45	118	110-8	20	146	.253	.336	.438	110	15	9-6	.967	-8	90	104	O-283(175-0-112)	-0.9

FOTHERGILL, BOB Robert Roy "Fats" B 8.16.1897 Massillon, OH D 3.20.1938 Detroit, MI BR/TR 5-10.5/230# d4.18

Year	Tm Lg	G	AB	R	H	2B	3B	HR	RBI	BB-IB	HP	SO	AVG	OBP	SLG	AOPS	ABR	SB-CS	FA	FR	Rng	Thr	G at Pos	BFW
1922	Det A	42	152	20	49	12	4	0	29	8	0	9	.322	.356	.454	113	3	1-5	.945	-5	73	53	O-38(2-10-26)	-0.7
1923	Det A	101	241	34	76	18	2	1	49	12	4	19	.315	.358	.419	106	2	5-4	.977	-2	99	61	O-68(45-20-3)	-0.4
1924	Det A	54	166	28	50	8	3	0	15	5	1	13	.301	.326	.386	84	-5	2-3	.968	-2	101	46	O-45(43-0-2)	-1.0
1925	Det A	71	204	38	72	14	0	2	28	6	2	3	.353	.377	.451	111	3	3-2	.977	3	109	112	O-59(40-16-4)	0.3
1926	Det A	110	387	63	142	31	7	3	73	33	3	23	.367	.421	.506	139	23	4-12	.961	-3	110	29	*O-103(76-19-9)	0.9
1927	Det A	143	527	93	189	38	9	9	114	47	2	31	.359	.413	.516	138	30	9-15	.961	-7	103	21	*O-137(LF)	0.8
1928	Det A	111	347	49	110	28	10	3	63	24	3	19	.317	.366	.481	119	9	8-3	.959	-4	96	69	O-90(70-0-20)	-0.1
1929	Det A	115	277	42	98	24	9	6	62	11	0	11	.354	.378	.570	140	15	3-1	.967	-1	109	38	O-59(39-0-20)	1.0
1930	Det A	55	143	14	37	9	3	2	14	6	0	10	.259	.289	.406	72	-7	1-1	.947	-2	92	45	O-38(32-0-6)	-1.0
	Chi A	52	135	10	40	9	0	0	24	4	2	8	.296	.326	.363	77	-5	0-0	.879	-2	95	85	O-31(8-0-22)	-0.8
	Year	107	278	24	77	18	3	2	38	10	2	18	.277	.307	.385	75	-11	1-1	.913	-4	93	64	O-69(40-0-28)	-1.8
1931	Chi A	108	312	25	88	9	4	3	56	17	2	17	.282	.323	.365	86	-8	2-2	.972	-1	109	33	O-74(48-0-26)	-1.2
1932	Chi A	116	346	36	102	24	1	7	50	27	1	10	.295	.348	.431	107	4	4-4	.952	-6	87	70	O-86(53-0-34)	-0.6
1933	Bos A	28	32	1	11	1	0	0	5	2	0	4	.344	.382	.375	102	0	0-0	1.000	-0	97	0	/O-4(1-0-3)	0.0
Total	12	1106	3269	453	1064	225	52	36	582	202	20	177	.325	.368	.459	115	64	42-52	.961	-31	101	49	O-832(594-65-175)	-2.8

FOURNIER, JACK John Frank B 9.28.1889 AuSable, MI D 9.5.1973 Tacoma, WA BL/TR 6/195# d4.13

Year	Tm Lg	G	AB	R	H	2B	3B	HR	RBI	BB-IB	HP	SO	AVG	OBP	SLG	AOPS	ABR	SB-CS	FA	FR	Rng	Thr	G at Pos	BFW
1912	Chi A	35	73	6	14	5	2	0	2	4	3		.192	.262	.315	67	-3	2	.988	3	172	55	1-17	-0.1
1913	Chi A	68	172	20	40	8	5	1	23	21	2	23	.233	.323	.355	99	0	9	.990	3	105	72	1-29,O-23(11-0-12)	0.1
1914	Chi A	109	379	44	118	14	9	6	44	31	3	44	.311	.368	.443	146	19	10-13	.978	4	127	69	1-97/O-6(3-1-2)	2.0
1915	Chi A	126	422	86	136	20	18	5	77	64	**15**	37	.322	.429	**.491**	170	38	21-16	.986	1	104	105	1-65,O-57(38-13-6)	3.6
1916	Chi A	105	313	36	75	13	9	3	44	36	5	40	.240	.328	.367	108	2	19	.976	-3	95	109	1-85/O(LF)	-0.3
1917	Chi A	1	1	0	0	0	0	0	0	0	0	1	.000	.000	.000	-98	0	0	—	0			H	0.0
1918	NY A	27	100	9	35	6	1	0	12	7	0	7	.350	.393	.430	145	5	7	.976	-3	74	137	1-27	0.2
1920	StL N	141	530	77	162	33	14	3	61	42	**12**	42	.306	.370	.438	136	26	26-20	.983	0	106	101	*1-138	2.2
1921	StL N	149	574	103	197	27	9	16	86	56	**8**	48	.343	.409	.505	144	38	20-22	.987	-4	89	89	*1-149	2.0
1922	StL N	128	404	64	119	23	9	10	61	40	7	21	.295	.368	.470	120	12	6-8	.982	2	115	82	*1-109/P	0.6
1923	Bro N	133	515	91	181	30	13	22	102	43	9	28	.351	.411	.588	165	47	11-4	.985	4	118	83	*1-133	**4.2**
1924	Bro N	**154**	563	93	188	25	4	**27**	116	83	10	46	.334	.428	.536	162	54	7-5	.985	7	117	83	*1-153	4.9

Year	Tm Lg	G	AB	R	H	2B	3B	HR	RBI	BB-IB	HP	SO	AVG	OBP	SLG	AOPS	ABR	SB-CS	FA	FR	Rng	Thr	G at Pos	BFW
1925	Bro N	145	545	99	191	21	16	22	130	**86**	8	39	.350	.446	.569	162	54	4-6	.989	3	105	85	*1-145	4.2
1926	Bro N	87	243	39	69	9	2	11	48	30	1	16	.284	.365	.473	126	9	0	.986	-2	84	40	1-64	0.3
1927	Bos N	122	374	55	106	18	2	10	53	44	6	16	.283	.368	.422	121	12	4	.989	-0	100	73	*1-102	0.5
Total	15	1530	5208	822	1631	252	113	136	859	587	89	408	.313	.392	.483	143	313	146-94	.984	16	107	85	*1-1313/O-87(53-14-20),P	24.4

FOUSER, BILL William C. B 10.1855 Philadelphia, PA D 3.1.1919 Philadelphia, PA d4.22

1876	Phi N	21	89	11	12	0	1	0	2	0		0	.135	.135	.157	-3	-10		.827	1	124	49	2-14/O-7(0-1-6),1	-0.7

FOUTZ, DAVE David Luther "Scissors" B 9.7.1856 Carroll Co., MD D 3.5.1897 Waverly, MD BR/TR 6-2/161# d7.29 M4 b-Frank ▲

1884	StL AA	33	119	17	27	4	0	0		8	0		.227	.276	.261	73	-3		.940	1	108	**728**	P-25,O-14(0-3-11)	-0.1
1885	†StL AA	65	238	42	59	6	4	0	34	11	0		.248	.281	.307	82	-6		.899	6	**150**	207	P-47,1-15/O-4(LF)	0.0
1886	†StL AA	102	414	66	116	18	9	3	59	9	1		.280	.297	.389	109	1	17	.949	2	86	86	P-59,O-34(RF),1-11	0.0
1887	†StL AA	102	423	79	151	26	13	4	108	23	2		.357	.393	.508	136	17	22	.899	-4	49	0	O-50(RF),P-40,1-15	0.4
1888	Bro AA	140	563	91	156	20	13	3	99	28	2		.277	.314	.375	121	11	35	.895	2	103	125	O-78(0-1-77),1-42,P-23	0.5
1889	†Bro AA	**138**	553	118	152	19	8	6	113	64	3	23	.275	.353	.371	106	5	43	.979	-3	70	95	*1-134,P-12	-0.9
1890	†Bro N	**129**	509	106	154	25	13	5	98	52	1	25	.303	.368	.432	133	20	42	.978	-1	98	114	*1-113,O-13(4-9-1)/P-5	0.7
1891	Bro N	130	521	87	134	26	8	2	73	40	2	25	.257	.313	.349	93	-5	48	.976	-3	85	75	*1-124/P-6,S	-1.7
1892	Bro N	61	220	33	41	5	3	1	26	14	0	14	.186	.235	.250	48	-14	19	.850	0	135	0	O-29(11-7-11),P-27/1-6	-1.0
1893	Bro N	**130**	557	91	137	20	10	7	67	32	0	34	.246	.287	.355	74	-25	39	.913	-7	75	36	O-77(66-11-0),1-54/P-6,M	-3.1
1894	Bro N	73	297	40	90	12	9	0	52	14	1	13	.303	.337	.404	84	-9	14	.976	-3	81	78	1-73/PM	-0.9
1895	Bro N	31	115	14	34	4	1	0	21	4	0	2	.296	.319	.348	78	-4	1	.879	-3	120	188	O-20(7-2-11)/1-8,M	-0.7
1896	Bro N	2	8	0	2	1	0	0	0	1	0	0	.250	.333	.375	92	0	0	1.000	1	1017	0	/O(RF)1M	0.0
Total	13	1136	4537	784	1253	186	91	31	750	300	12	136	.276	.323	.378	101	-12	280	.977	-13	81	94	1-596,O-320(92-33-196),P-251/S	-6.8

FOUTZ, FRANK Frank Hayes B 4.8.1877 Baltimore, MD D 12.25.1961 Lima, OH BR/TR 5-11/165# d4.26 b-Dave

1901	Bal A	20	72	13	17	4	1	2	14	8	1		.236	.321	.403	96	0	0	.959	-0	107	69	1-20	-0.1

FOWLER, BOOB Joseph Chester "Gink" B 11.11.1900 Waco, TX D 10.8.1988 Dallas, TX BL/TR 5-11.5/180# d5.6

1923	Cin N	11	33	9	11	0	1	1	6	1	0	3	.333	.353	.485	121	1	1-0	.847	-2	88	115	S-10	0.0
1924	Cin N	59	129	20	43	6	1	0	9	5	0	15	.333	.358	.395	103	1	2-2	.936	-4	96	87	S-32/2-4,3-2	-0.1
1925	Cin N	6	5	0	2	1	0	0	2	0	0	1	.400	.400	.600	155	0	0-0	—	0			H	0.0
1926	Bos A	2	8	1	1	0	0	0	1	0	0	0	.125	.125	.125	-36	-2	0-0	.800	-0	117	0	/3-2	-0.2
Total	4	78	175	30	57	7	2	1	18	6	0	19	.326	.348	.406	102	0	3-2	.910	-6	94	94	/S-42,3-4,2-4	-0.3

FOX, ANDY Andrew Junipero B 1.12.1971 Sacramento, CA BL/TR 6-4/205# d4.7 OF Total (23-LF 10-CF 46-RF)

1996	†NY A	113	189	26	37	4	0	3	13	20-0	1	28	.196	.276	.265	38	-19	11-3	.958	-3	87	71	2-72,3-31/S-9,O(RF)D	-1.6
1997	†NY A	22	31	13	7	1	0	0	1	7-0	0	9	.226	.368	.258	68	-1	2-1	1.000	4	132	124	3-11/2-5,S-2,O-2(RF),D-2	0.3
1998	Ari N	139	502	67	139	21	6	9	44	43-0	18	97	.277	.355	.396	98	-1	14-7	.982	-13	83	73	2-60,O-48(10-8-33),3-26,1-12	-1.3
1999	†Ari N	99	274	34	70	12	2	6	33	33-10	9	61	.255	.351	.380	85	-6	4-1	.958	-12	88	84	S-82,3-12	-1.1
2000	Ari N	31	86	10	18	4	0	1	10	4-1	0	16	.209	.244	.291	33	-9	2-1	.952	-3	81	101	3-20/O-6(1-1-4),1	-1.1
	Fla N	69	164	19	40	4	2	3	10	18-3	3	37	.244	.330	.348	75	-7	8-3	.932	3	111	68	S-33,O-14(9-0-5),3-12/2-2	-0.1
	Year	100	250	29	58	8	2	4	20	22-4	3	53	.232	.302	.328	60	-16	10-4	.932	1	111	68	S-33,3-32,O-20(10-1-9)/2-2,1	-1.2
2001	Fla N	54	81	8	15	0	1	3	7	15-1	2	17	.185	.327	.321	71	-4	1-0	.938	-2	94	122	S-12/3-9,2-2,O-2(1-1-0)	-0.4
2002	Fla N	133	435	55	109	14	5	4	41	49-6	10	94	.251	.338	.333	85	-11	31-7	.965	-6	90	101	*S-112/2-7,3-4,O(RF)	-0.4
2003	Fla N	70	108	12	21	5	1	0	8	7-0	4	29	.194	.269	.259	40	-10	1-2	.923	-6	80	92	2-15/S-9,3-5,1-2,O-2(LF)	-1.5
Total	8	730	1870	244	456	65	17	29	167	196-21	47	388	.244	.330	.343	77	-68	74-25	.956	-36	92	94	S-259,2-163,3-130/O-76R,1-15,D-5	-7.2

FOX, CHARLIE Charles Francis "Irish" B 10.7.1921 New York, NY BR/TR 5-11/180# d9.24 Mil 1943-45 M7 C5

1942	NY N	3	7	1	3	0	0	0	1	1	0	2	.429	.500	.429	172	1	0	1.000	-1	*67*	*0*	/C-3	0.0

FOX, ERIC Eric Hollis B 8.15.1963 Lemoore, CA BB/TL 5-10/180# d7.7

1992	†Oak A	51	143	24	34	5	2	3	13	13-0	0	29	.238	.299	.364	90	-2	3-4	.990	2	104	127	O-43(20-19-16)/D-4	-0.2
1993	Oak A	29	56	5	8	1	0	1	5	2-0	0	7	.143	.172	.214	3	-8	0-2	1.000	1	112	0	O-26(5-18-3)/D-2	-0.8
1994	Oak A	26	44	7	9	2	0	1	1	3-0	0	8	.205	.255	.318	51	-3	2-0	1.000	1	110	142	O-24(0-16-8)	-0.2
1995	Tex A	10	15	2	0	0	0	0	0	3-0	0	4	.000	.167	.000	-51	-3	0-0	1.000	0	117	0	/O-8(3-2-3),D	-0.3
Total	4	116	258	38	51	8	2	5	19	21-0	0	48	.198	.257	.302	55	-16	5-6	.995	4	108	91	O-101(28-55-30)/D-7	-1.5

FOX, PETE Ervin B 3.8.1909 Evansville, IN D 7.5.1966 Detroit, MI BR/TR 5-11/165# d4.12

1933	Det A	128	535	82	154	26	13	7	57	23	2	38	.288	.320	.424	94	-8	9-6	.978	-5	100	56	*O-124(0-116-8)	-1.6
1934	†Det A	128	516	101	147	31	2	2	45	49	4	53	.285	.351	.364	85	-11	25-10	.974	4	101	137	*O-121(0-11-110)	-1.1
1935	†Det A	131	517	116	166	38	8	15	73	45	6	52	.321	.382	.513	134	25	14-4	.988	-1	100	87	*O-125(0-6-123)	1.7
1936	Det A	73	220	46	67	12	1	4	26	34	3	23	.305	.405	.423	104	3	1-3	.968	-1	107	59	O-55(5-0-50)	-0.2
1937	Det A	148	628	116	208	39	8	12	82	41	0	43	.331	.372	.476	110	8	12-8	.976	-5	102	43	*O-143(11-27-106)	-0.4
1938	Det A	**155**	634	91	186	35	10	7	96	31	2	39	.293	.328	.413	80	-22	16-7	**.994**	-3	96	90	*O-155(1-0-154)	-3.0
1939	Det A	141	519	69	153	24	6	7	66	35	2	41	.295	.342	.405	84	-14	23-12	.970	8	**113**	126	*O-126(RF)	-1.1
1940	†Det A	93	350	49	101	17	4	5	48	21	0	30	.289	.329	.403	81	-10	7-7	.967	0	103	90	O-85(2-1-82)	-1.6
1941	Bos A	73	268	38	81	12	7	0	31	21	2	32	.302	.357	.399	98	-1	9-2	.977	-0	100	91	O-62(8-5-49)	-0.4
1942	Bos A	77	256	42	67	15	5	3	42	20	3	28	.262	.323	.395	98	-1	8-7	.966	-5	90	44	O-71(7-0-64)	-1.1
1943	Bos A	127	489	54	141	24	4	2	44	34	2	40	.288	.337	.366	104	2	22-8	.961	-4	95	104	*O-125(3-0-122)	-0.9
1944	Bos A☆	121	496	70	156	37	6	1	64	27	3	34	.315	.354	.419	122	13	10-5	.987	-1	98	88	*O-119(RF)	0.5
1945	Bos A	66	208	21	51	4	1	0	20	11	4	18	.245	.296	.274	64	-10	2-2	.989	-3	84	99	O-57(RF)	-1.8
Total	13	1461	5636	895	1678	314	75	65	694	392	33	471	.298	.347	.415	98	-26	158-81	.977	-15	100	87	*O-1368(37-166-1170)	-11.0

FOX, PADDY George B. B 12.1.1868 Pottstown, PA D 5.8.1914 Philadelphia, PA d7.13

1891	Lou AA	6	19	1	2	0	1	0	2	2	2	3	.105	.261	.211	36	-2	0	.929	-1	69	0	/3-6	-0.3
1899	Pit N	13	41	4	10	0	1	1	3	3	1		.244	.311	.366	86	-1	2	.971	2	153	204	/1-9,C-3	0.1
Total	2	19	60	5	12	0	2	1	5	5	3	3	.200	.294	.317	70	-3	2	.971	0	153	204	/1-9,3-6,C-3	-0.2

FOX, NELLIE Jacob Nelson B 12.25.1927 St.Thomas, PA D 12.1.1975 Baltimore, MD BL/TR 5-9/150# d6.8 C8 HF1997

1947	Phi A	7	3	2	0	0	0	0	0	1	0	0	.000	.250	.000	-26	0	0-0	1.000	-0	0	0	/2	-0.1
1948	Phi A	3	13	0	2	0	0	0	0	1	0	0	.154	.214	.154	-1	-2	1-0	.950	-2	53	36	/2-3	-0.3
1949	Phi A	88	247	42	63	6	2	0	21	32	6	9	.255	.354	.296	75	-8	2-2	.982	-1	97	117	2-77	-0.5
1950	Chi A	130	457	45	113	12	7	0	30	35	2	17	.247	.304	.304	58	-31	4-3	.974	4	102	97	*2-121	-2.0
1951	Chi A★	147	604	93	189	32	12	4	55	43	14	11	.313	.372	.425	118	14	9-12	.981	-9	96	103	*2-147	1.2
1952	Chi A☆	152	648	76	**192**	25	10	0	39	34	3	14	.296	.334	.366	94	-7	5-5	**.985**	9	98	105	*2-151	0.9
1953	Chi A★	154	624	92	178	31	8	3	72	49	7	18	.285	.344	.375	91	-7	4-5	.983	3	95	87	*2-154	0.6
1954	Chi A★	**155**	631	111	**201**	24	8	2	47	51	5	12	.319	.372	.391	106	6	16-9	**.989**	-2	96	99	*2-155	1.6
1955	Chi A★	154	636	100	198	28	7	6	59	38-1	**17**	15	.311	.364	.406	104	4	7-9	.974	**31**	**117**	100	*2-154	4.4
1956	Chi A★	**154**	649	109	192	20	10	4	52	44-1	10	14	.296	.347	.376	90	-10	8-4	**.986**	4	95	110	*2-154	0.6
1957	Chi A★	**155**	619	110	**196**	27	8	6	61	75-2	16	13	.317	.403	.415	124	24	5-6	.986	**25**	**110**	**132**	*2-155	6.1
1958	Chi A★	**155**	623	82	**187**	21	6	0	49	47-5	11	11	.300	.357	.353	99	0	5-6	.985	0	94	101	*2-155	1.1
1959	†Chi A★	**156**	624	84	191	34	6	2	70	71-8	7	13	.306	.380	.389	114	15	5-6	**.988**	-8	102	89	*2-156	1.8
1960	Chi A★	150	605	85	175	24	**10**	2	59	50-2	10	13	.289	.351	.372	97	-2	2-4	.985	17	**108**	112	*2-149	2.5
1961	Chi A★	159	606	67	152	11	5	2	51	59-3	9	12	.251	.323	.295	69	-27	2-3	.982	0	100	91	*2-159	-1.3
1962	Chi A	157	621	79	166	27	7	2	54	38-0	7	12	.267	.314	.343	78	-20	1-2	**.990**	4	102	96	*2-154	-0.3
1963	Chi A★	137	539	54	140	19	0	2	42	24-1	7	17	.260	.299	.306	72	-21	0-2	**.988**	-3	97	94	*2-134	-1.4
1964	Hou N	133	442	45	117	12	6	0	28	27-1	10	13	.265	.320	.319	86	-8	0-2	.977	-4	99	82	*2-115	-0.4
1965	Hou N	21	41	3	11	2	0	0	1	0-0	1	2	.268	.286	.317	75	-1	0-0	1.000	1	110	111	/3-6,1-2,2	-0.1
Total	19	2367	9232	1279	2663	355	112	35	790	719-24	142	216	.288	.348	.363	94	-81	76-80	.984	69	101	101	*2-2295/3-6,1-2	14.4

FOX, JACK John Paul B 5.21.1885 Reading, PA D 6.28.1963 Reading, PA BR/TR 5-10/185# d6.2

1908	Phi A	9	30	2	6	0	0	0	0	0	0		.200	.200	.200	28	-2	2	.923	-1	0	0	/O-8(0-1-7)	-0.4

FOX, BILL William Henry B 1.15.1872 Sturbridge, MA D 5.7.1946 Minneapolis, MN BB/TR 5-10/160# d8.20

1897	Was N	4	14	4	4	0	0	0	0	1	0		.286	.333	.286	65	-1	0	.700	-1	127	0	/S-2,2-2	-0.1
1901	Cin N	43	159	9	28	2	1	0	7	4	1		.176	.201	.201	18	-17	9	.948	4	106	115	2-43	-1.2
Total	2	47	173	13	32	2	1	0	7	5	1		.185	.212	.208	22	-18	9	.944	4	103	125	/2-45,S-2	-1.3

FOXX, JIMMIE James Emory "Beast" or "Double X" B 10.22.1907 Sudlersville, MD D 7.21.1967 Miami, FL BR/TR 6/195# d5.1 C1 HF1951 I OF Total (12-LF 9-RF)

Year	Tm Lg	G	AB	R	H	2B	3B	HR	RBI	BB-IB	HP	SO	AVG	OBP	SLG	AOPS	ABR	SB-CS	FA	FR	Rng	Thr	G at Pos	BFW
1925	Phi A	10	9	2	6	1	0	0	0	0	0	1	.667	.667	.778	249	2	0-0	—	0	*0*	*0*	/C	0.2
1926	Phi A	26	32	8	10	2	1	0	5	1	0	6	.313	.333	.438	95	0	1-0	1.000	1	*105*	*128*	C-12/O-3(RF)	0.1
1927	Phi A	61	130	23	42	6	5	3	20	14	1	11	.323	.393	.515	127	5	2-1	.975	-2	86	53	1-32/C-5	0.2
1928	Phi A	118	400	85	131	29	10	13	79	60	1	43	.327	.416	.548	147	29	3-9	.940	0	104	92	3-60,1-30,C-19	2.8
1929	†Phi A	149	517	123	183	23	9	33	118	103	2	70	.354	**.463**	.625	171	59	9-7	.995	-3	85	89	*1-142/3-8	4.3
1930	†Phi A	153	562	127	188	33	13	37	156	93	0	66	.335	.429	.637	159	51	7-7	.990	-1	91	87	*1-153	3.5
1931	†Phi A	139	515	93	150	32	10	30	120	73	1	84	.291	.380	.567	138	27	4-3	.993	-3	83	120	*1-112,3-26/O(LF)	1.3
1932	Phi A	**154**	585	**151**	213	33	9	**58**	**169**	116	0	96	.364	.469	**.749**	203	**91**	3-7	**.994**	-3	94	104	*1-141,3-13	**6.7**
1933	Phi A☆	149	573	125	204	37	9	**48**	**163**	96	1	93	**.356**	.449	**.703**	**199**	**82**	2-2	.990	7	**122**	78	*1-149/S	**6.9**
1934	Phi A★	150	539	120	180	28	6	44	130	**111**	1	75	.334	.449	.653	188	73	11-2	.993	4	**112**	107	*1-140/3-9	6.1
1935	Phi A★	147	535	118	185	33	7	**36**	115	114	0	99	.346	.461	**.636**	**182**	70	6-4	**.997**	4	113	97	*1-121,C-26/3-2	**5.9**
1936	Bos A★	**155**	585	130	198	32	8	41	143	105	1	119	.338	.440	.631	153	49	13-4	.991	1	106	95	*1-139,O-16(11-0-5)/3	3.3
1937	Bos A★	150	569	111	162	24	6	36	127	99	1	96	.285	.392	.538	127	23	10-8	**.994**	11	**129**	91	*1-150/C	1.8
1938	Bos A★	149	565	139	197	33	9	50	**175**	**119**	0	76	**.349**	**.462**	**.704**	**180**	**72**	5-4	.987	7	**123**	115	*1-149	**5.8**
1939	Bos A☆	124	467	130	168	31	10	**35**	105	89	2	72	.360	**.464**	**.694**	185	**62**	4-3	.992	8	125	98	*1-123/P	5.2
1940	Bos A★	144	515	106	153	30	4	36	119	101	0	87	.297	.412	.581	148	39	4-7	.990	0	132	101	1-95,C-42/3	3.0
1941	Bos A★	135	487	87	146	27	8	19	105	93	0	103	.300	.412	.505	138	30	2-5	.992	8	**125**	95	*1-124/3-5,O(RF)	2.3
1942	Bos A	30	100	18	27	4	0	5	14	18	2	15	.270	.392	.460	134	5	0-0	.996	6	174	127	1-27	0.9
	Chi N	70	205	25	42	8	0	3	19	22	0	55	.205	.282	.288	69	-8	1	.983	-4	78	80	1-52/C	-1.8
1944	Chi N	15	20	0	1	1	0	0	2	2	0	5	.050	.136	.100	-33	-4	0	1.000	1	163	0	/3-2,C	-0.2
1945	Phi N	89	224	30	60	11	1	7	38	23	0	39	.268	.336	.420	112	3	0	.988	-1	113	63	1-40,3-14/P-9	0.0
Total	20	2317	8134	1751	2646	458	125	534	1922	1452	13	1311	.325	.428	.609	161	760	87-73	.992	41	109	96	*1-1919,3-141,C-108/O-21L,P-10,S	58.3

FOY, JOE Joseph Anthony B 2.21.1943 New York, NY D 10.12.1989 Bronx, NY BR/TR 6/215# d4.13 OF Total (5-LF 13-CF 2-RF)

Year	Tm Lg	G	AB	R	H	2B	3B	HR	RBI	BB-IB	HP	SO	AVG	OBP	SLG	AOPS	ABR	SB-CS	FA	FR	Rng	Thr	G at Pos	BFW
1966	Bos A	151	554	97	145	23	8	15	63	91-2	2	80	.262	.364	.413	112	12	2-5	.953	5	104	104	*3-139,S-13	1.8
1967	†Bos A	130	446	70	112	22	4	16	49	46-1	3	87	.251	.325	.426	111	7	8-6	.921	-11	90	71	*3-118/O(RF)	-0.6
1968	Bos A	150	515	65	116	18	2	10	60	84-5	4	91	.225	.336	.326	96	1	26-8	.935	2	105	**132**	*3-147/O-3(LF)	0.6
1969	KC A	145	519	72	136	19	2	11	71	74-4	5	75	.262	.354	.370	104	5	37-15	.964	-12	89	89	*3-113,1-16,O-16(2-13-1)/S-5,2-3	-0.6
1970	NY N	99	322	39	76	12	0	6	37	68-5	4	58	.236	.373	.329	90	-1	22-13	.937	-1	94	123	3-97	-0.2
1971	Was A	41	128	12	30	8	0	0	11	27-0	0	14	.234	.363	.297	96	1	4-1	.960	4	105	158	3-37/2-3,S	0.6
Total	6	716	2484	355	615	102	16	58	291	390-17	18	405	.248	.351	.372	103	25	99-48	.943	-12	98	108	3-651/O-20C,S-19,1-16,2-6	1.6

FRANCO, JULIO Julio Cesar (born Julio Cesar Robles (Franco)) B 8.23.1958 Hato Mayor, D.R. BR/TR 6/190# d4.23 OF Total (4-LF 1-RF)

Year	Tm Lg	G	AB	R	H	2B	3B	HR	RBI	BB-IB	HP	SO	AVG	OBP	SLG	AOPS	ABR	SB-CS	FA	FR	Rng	Thr	G at Pos	BFW
1982	Phi N	16	29	3	8	1	0	0	3	2-1	0	4	.276	.323	.310	76	-1	0-2	1.000	-3	84	42	S-11/3-2	-0.4
1983	Cle A	149	560	68	153	24	8	8	80	27-1	2	50	.273	.306	.387	87	-11	32-12	.961	-3	97	95	*S-149	0.4
1984	Cle A	160	658	82	188	22	5	3	79	43-1	6	68	.286	.331	.348	88	-11	19-10	.955	3	101	114	*S-159/D	1.0
1985	Cle A	160	636	97	183	33	4	6	90	54-2	4	74	.288	.343	.381	100	1	13-9	.949	-15	98	94	*S-151/2-8,D	0.1
1986	Cle A	149	599	80	183	30	5	10	74	32-1	0	66	.306	.338	.422	108	6	10-7	.971	-3	104	90	*S-134,2-13/D-3	1.6
1987	Cle A	128	495	86	158	24	3	8	52	57-2	3	56	.319	.389	.428	117	14	32-9	.963	-18	92	76	*S-111/2-9,D-8	1.1
1988	Cle A	152	613	88	186	23	6	10	54	56-4	2	72	.303	.361	.409	113	11	25-11	.982	-2	102	87	*2-151/D	1.5
1989	Tex A★	150	548	80	173	31	5	13	92	66-11	1	69	.316	.386	.462	137	29	21-3	.980	-5	92	76	*2-140,D-10	3.1
1990	Tex A★	157	582	96	172	27	1	11	69	82-3	2	83	.296	.383	.402	120	19	31-10	.975	0	98	96	*2-152/D-3	2.7
1991	Tex A☆	146	589	108	201	27	3	15	78	65-8	3	78	**.341**	.408	.474	146	39	36-9	.979	-33	84	76	*2-146	1.5
1992	Tex A	35	107	19	25	7	0	2	8	15-2	0	17	.234	.328	.355	95	0	1-1	.906	-4	70	35	D-15/2-9,O-4(4-0-1)	-0.5
1993	Tex A	144	532	85	154	31	3	14	84	62-4	1	95	.289	.360	.438	119	15	9-3	—	0	0	0	*D-140	0.7
1994	Chi A	112	433	72	138	19	2	20	98	62-4	5	75	.319	.406	.510	138	27	8-1	.969	-1	79	91	D-99,1-14	1.8
1996	†Cle A	112	432	72	139	20	1	14	76	61-2	3	82	.322	.407	.470	122	17	8-8	.990	3	114	113	1-97,D-13	0.9
1997	Cle A	78	289	46	82	13	1	3	25	38-2	0	75	.284	.367	.367	89	-3	8-5	.983	6	111	106	D-42,2-35/1	0.2
	Mil A	42	141	22	34	3	0	4	19	31-2	1	41	.241	.373	.348	91	-1	7-1	.992	1	119	178	D-28,1-13	-0.2
	Year	120	430	68	116	16	1	7	44	69-4	1	116	.270	.369	.360	90	-4	15-6	.983	7	111	106	D-70,2-35,1-14	0.0
1999	TB A	1	1	0	0	0	0	0	0	0-0	0	1	.000	.000	.000	-99	0	0-0	1.000	0	0	0	/1	0.0
2001	†Atl N	25	90	13	27	4	0	3	11	10-1	1	20	.300	.376	.444	109	1	0-0	.995	1	121	127	1-23	0.1
2002	†Atl N	125	338	51	96	13	1	6	30	39-3	1	75	.284	.357	.382	98	-2	5-1	.990	3	123	127	1-95/D-2	-0.5
2003	†Atl N	103	197	28	58	12	2	5	31	25-5	0	43	.294	.372	.452	114	5	0-1	.998	1	107	120	1-75	0.1
Total	19	2144	7869	1196	2358	364	50	155	1053	827-59	35	1144	.300	.366	.418	112	155	265-103	.960	-67	98	95	S-715,2-663,D-366,1-319/O-4L,3-2	15.2

FRANCO, MATT Matthew Neil B 8.19.1969 Santa Monica, CA BL/TR 6-2/200# d9.6 OF Total (34-LF 6-RF)

Year	Tm Lg	G	AB	R	H	2B	3B	HR	RBI	BB-IB	HP	SO	AVG	OBP	SLG	AOPS	ABR	SB-CS	FA	FR	Rng	Thr	G at Pos	BFW
1995	Chi N	16	17	3	5	1	0	0	1	0-0	0	4	.294	.294	.353	71	-1	0-0	1.000	-1	64	0	/2-3,13	-0.2
1996	NY N	14	31	3	6	1	0	1	2	1-0	1	5	.194	.235	.323	50	-2	0-0	.824	-0	116	0	/3-8,1-2	-0.3
1997	NY N	112	163	21	45	5	0	5	21	13-4	0	23	.276	.330	.399	93	-2	1-0	.937	1	118	165	3-39,1-13/O(LF)D	-0.1
1998	NY N	103	161	20	44	7	2	1	13	23-6	1	26	.273	.366	.360	94	-1	0-1	1.000	-2	95	122	3-13,O-13(12-0-1),1-11/D-2	-0.4
1999	†NY N	122	132	18	31	5	0	4	21	28-3	0	21	.235	.366	.364	89	-1	0-0	1.000	2	157	212	1-19,O-19(15-0-3),3-12/P-2,D-4	0.0
2000	†NY N	101	134	9	32	4	0	2	14	21-3	0	22	.239	.340	.313	70	-6	0-0	.990	-1	109	104	1-28,3-22/O-3(LF),2D	-0.8
2002	†Atl N	81	205	25	65	15	4	6	30	27-2	0	31	.317	.395	.517	141	12	1-0	.990	0	113	91	1-51/O-4(LF)	0.8
2003	†Atl N	112	134	11	33	5	0	3	15	11-0	0	26	.246	.299	.351	70	-6	0-1	.977	-2	82	135	1-15/O-3(1-0-2),D-3	-0.9
Total	8	661	977	110	261	43	6	22	117	124-18	2	158	.267	.349	.391	95	-7	2-2	.990	-2	105	103	1-140/3-95,O-43L,D-12,2-4,P-2	-1.9

FRANCONA, TITO John Patsy B 11.4.1933 Aliquippa, PA BL/TL 5-11/190# d4.17 s-Terry

Year	Tm Lg	G	AB	R	H	2B	3B	HR	RBI	BB-IB	HP	SO	AVG	OBP	SLG	AOPS	ABR	SB-CS	FA	FR	Rng	Thr	G at Pos	BFW
1956	Bal A	139	445	62	115	16	4	9	57	51-4	1	60	.258	.334	.373	94	-5	11-5	.977	2	103	127	*O-122(1-41-97),1-21	-0.7
1957	Bal A	97	279	35	65	8	3	7	38	29-4	3	48	.233	.307	.358	88	-5	7-3	.992	-4	98	0	O-73(28-2-55)/1-4	-1.2
1958	Chi A	41	128	10	33	3	2	1	10	14-1	0	24	.258	.331	.336	86	-3	2-3	1.000	-1	85	121	O-35(7-0-32)	-0.5
	Det A	45	69	11	17	5	0	0	10	15-3	0	16	.246	.381	.319	88	0	0-0	1.000	-1	97	0	O-18(11-0-9)/1	-0.1
	Year	86	197	21	50	8	2	1	20	29-4	0	40	.254	.350	.330	86	-3	2-3	1.000	-2	88	87	O-53(18-0-41)/1	-0.6
1959	Cle A	122	399	68	145	17	2	20	79	35-3	3	42	.363	.414	.566	174	40	2-0	.972	-4	95	51	O-64(4-61-0),1-35	3.2
1960	Cle A	147	544	84	159	**36**	2	17	79	67-7	5	67	.292	.372	.460	128	23	4-1	.989	-0	100	43	*O-138(138-0-1),1-13	1.5
1961	Cle A☆	155	592	87	178	30	8	16	85	56-3	4	52	.301	.363	.459	122	18	2-1	.987	-1	106	48	*O-138(LF),1-14	0.8
1962	Cle A	158	621	82	169	28	5	14	70	47-3	7	74	.272	.327	.401	99	-2	3-2	.986	0	104	119	*1-158	-1.2
1963	Cle A	142	500	57	114	29	0	10	41	47-7	2	77	.228	.296	.346	80	-13	9-1	.986	-3	97	25	*O-122(121-0-1),1-11	-2.3
1964	Cle A	111	270	35	67	13	2	8	24	44-9	4	46	.248	.361	.400	113	6	1-3	.985	-5	80	71	O-69(1-1-68),1-17	-0.4
1965	StL N	81	174	15	45	6	2	5	19	17-0	0	30	.259	.323	.402	95	-1	0-0	.972	-4	89	0	O-34(1-0-34),1-13	-0.8
1966	StL N	83	156	14	33	4	1	4	17	7-1	1	27	.212	.250	.327	59	-9	0-0	.987	2	129	112	1-30/O-9(LF)	-1.0
1967	Phi N	27	73	7	15	1	0	0	3	7-1	0	10	.205	.272	.219	43	-5	0-1	1.000	1	121	104	1-24/O(RF)	-0.6
	Atl N	82	254	28	63	5	1	6	25	20-2	1	34	.248	.304	.346	87	-5	1-0	.991	0	96	86	1-56/O-6(5-0-1)	-0.8
	Year	109	327	35	78	6	1	6	28	27-3	1	44	.239	.297	.318	77	-10	1-1	.993	1	102	91	1-80/O-7(5-0-2)	-1.4
1968	Atl N	122	346	32	99	13	1	2	47	51-5	0	45	.286	.376	.347	118	11	3-0	.978	-6	98	57	O-65(LF),1-33	0.0
1969	Atl N	51	88	5	26	1	0	2	22	13-2	0	10	.295	.371	.375	114	2	0-1	.957	0	101	152	O-15(LF)/1-7	0.1
	Oak A	32	85	12	29	6	1	3	20	12-2	0	11	.341	.418	.541	175	9	0-0	.988	-3	47	76	1-19/O(LF)	0.5
1970	Oak A	32	33	2	8	0	0	1	6	6-1	1	6	.242	.375	.333	100	0	0-0	1.000	1	141	131	/1-6,O(LF)	0.1
	Mil A	52	65	4	15	3	0	0	4	6-1	0	15	.231	.296	.277	58	-4	1-0	1.000	1	125	149	1-13	-0.3
	Year	84	98	6	23	3	0	1	10	12-2	1	21	.235	.324	.296	73	-3	1-0	1.000	1	129	144	1-19/O(LF)	-0.2
Total	15	1719	5121	650	1395	224	34	125	656	544-59	32	694	.272	.343	.403	108	57	46-21	.984	-26	98	59	O-911(546-105-299),1-475	-3.7

FRANCONA, TERRY Terry Jon B 4.22.1959 Aberdeen, SD BL/TL 6-1/190# d8.19 M4 C3 f-Tito

Year	Tm Lg	G	AB	R	H	2B	3B	HR	RBI	BB-IB	HP	SO	AVG	OBP	SLG	AOPS	ABR	SB-CS	FA	FR	Rng	Thr	G at Pos	BFW
1981	†Mon N	34	95	11	26	0	1	1	8	5-1	1	6	.274	.317	.326	82	-3	1-0	1.000	1	86	243	O-26(24-0-2)/1	-0.2
1982	Mon N	46	131	14	42	3	0	0	9	8-0	0	11	.321	.360	.344	96	-1	2-3	.936	-5	77	0	O-33(30-1-3),1-16	-0.8
1983	Mon N	120	230	21	59	11	1	3	22	6-2	0	20	.257	.273	.352	73	-9	0-2	.978	0	106	102	O-51(13-3-37),1-47	-1.3
1984	Mon N	58	214	18	74	19	2	1	18	5-3	1	12	.346	.360	.467	138	10	0-0	.994	6	142	117	1-50/O-6(5-0-2)	1.3
1985	Mon N	107	281	19	75	15	1	2	31	12-4	1	12	.267	.299	.349	86	-6	5-5	.988	4	119	95	1-57,O-28(5-0-24)/3	-0.7
1986	Chi N	86	124	13	31	3	0	2	8	6-0	1	8	.250	.286	.323	64	-6	0-1	1.000	-1	110	0	O-30(20-2-10),1-23	-0.9
1987	Cin N	102	207	16	47	5	0	3	12	10-1	1	12	.227	.266	.295	46	-16	2-0	.995	6	153	116	1-57/O-8(2-0-6)	-1.3
1988	Cle A	62	212	24	66	8	0	1	12	5-1	0	18	.311	.324	.363	91	-3	0-0	.977	1	109	90	D-38/1-5,O-5(LF)	-0.4
1989	Mil A	90	233	26	54	10	1	3	23	8-3	0	20	.232	.255	.322	63	-12	2-1	.989	1	98	103	1-46,D-23,O-16(RF)/P	-1.6
1990	Mil A	3	4	1	0	0	0	0	0	0-0	0	0	.000	.000	.000	-99	-1	0-0	1.000	-0	0	121	/1-2,D	-0.1

Year	Tm Lg	G	AB	R	H	2B	3B	HR	RBI	BB-IB	HP	SO	AVG	OBP	SLG	AOPS	ABR	SB-CS	FA	FR	Rng	Thr	G at Pos	BFW
Total	10	708	1731	163	474	74	6	16	143	65-15	5	119	.274	.300	.351	81	-47	12-12	.992	13	121	107	1-304,O-203(104-6-100)/D-62,P3	-6.0
FRANK, CHARLIE Charles B 5.30.1870 Mobile, AL D 5.24.1922 Memphis, TN BL/TL 5-10/170# d8.18																								
1893	StL N	40	164	29	55	6	3	1	17	18	2	8	.335	.408	.427	122	5	8	.930	2	123	67	O-40(LF)	0.3
1894	StL N	80	319	52	89	12	7	4	42	44	3	13	.279	.372	.398	86	-7	14	.869	-4	80	124	O-77(77-0-1)/1-3,P-2	-1.4
Total	2	120	483	81	144	18	10	5	59	62	5	21	.298	.384	.408	97	-2	22	.889	-2	95	104	O-117(117-0-1)/1-3,P-2	-1.1
FRANK, FRED Frederick B 3.11.1874 Louisa, KY D 3.27.1950 Ashland, KY d9.27																								
1898	Cle N	17	53	3	11	1	1	0	3	4	1		.208	.276	.264	56	-3	1	.915	2	121	374	O-17(0-6-11)	-0.2
FRANK, MIKE Stephen Michael B 1.14.1974 Pomona, CA BL/TL 6-2/185# d6.19																								
1998	Cin N	28	89	14	20	6	0	0	7	7-0	0	12	.225	.278	.292	51	-6	0-0	1.000	1	112	70	O-28(1-25-2)	-0.5
FRANKLIN d9.27																								
1884	Was U	1	3	0	0	0	0	0		0			.000	.000	.000	-99	-1		1.000	0	0	0	/O(CF)	-0.1
FRANKLIN, MICAH Micah Ishanti B 4.25.1972 San Francisco, CA BB/TR 6/205# d5.13																								
1997	StL N	17	34	6	11	0	0	2	2	3-0	0	10	.324	.378	.500	129	1	0-0	1.000	-1	92	0	O-13(4-0-9)	0.0
FRANKLIN, MOE Murray Asher B 4.1.1914 Chicago, IL D 3.16.1978 Harbor City, CA BR/TR 6/175# d8.12 Mil 1943-45																								
1941	Det A	13	10	1	3	1	0	0	0	2	0	2	.300	.417	.400	106	0	0-0	.750	-1	77	167	/S-4,3	0.0
1942	Det A	48	154	24	40	7	0	2	16	7	2	5	.260	.301	.344	75	-5	0-0	.967	-3	88	73	S-32/2-7	-0.6
Total	2	61	164	25	43	8	0	2	16	9	2	7	.262	.309	.348	77	-5	0-0	.961	-4	88	76	/S-36,2-7,3	-0.6
FRANKS, HERMAN Herman Louis B 1.4.1914 Price, UT BL/TR 5-10.5/187# d4.27 Mil 1942-45 M7 C10																								
1939	StL N	17	17	1	1	0	0	0	3	3	0	3	.059	.200	.059	-26	-3	0	.973	2	*165*	*72*	C-13	-0.1
1940	Bro N	65	131	11	24	4	0	1	14	20	1	6	.183	.296	.237	46	-9	2	.990	6	*120*	*84*	C-43	-0.1
1941	†Bro N	57	139	10	28	7	0	1	11	14	0	13	.201	.275	.273	52	-9	0	.986	3	*152*	*85*	C-54/O(RF)	-0.3
1947	Phi A	8	15	2	3	0	1	0	1	4	0	4	.200	.368	.333	94	0	0-0	1.000	-0	*108*	*111*	/C-4	0.0
1948	Phi A	40	98	10	22	7	1	1	14	16	2	11	.224	.345	.347	84	-2	0-0	.977	1	*119*	*122*	C-27	0.1
1949	NY N	1	3	1	2	0	0	0	0	0	0	0	.667	.667	.667	259	1	0	1.000	0	*0*	*0*	/C	0.1
Total	6	188	403	35	80	18	2	3	43	57	3	37	.199	.302	.275	57	-22	2-0	.985	11	*132*	*93*	C-142/O(RF)	-0.3
FRAZIER, LOU Arthur Louis B 1.26.1965 St.Louis, MO BB/TR 6-2/175# d4.8																								
1993	Mon N	112	189	27	54	7	1	1	16	16-0	0	24	.286	.340	.349	82	-5	17-2	.986	-0	96	110	O-60(52-7-2)/1-8,2	-0.3
1994	Mon N	76	140	25	38	3	1	0	14	18-0	1	23	.271	.358	.307	75	-5	20-4	1.000	1	105	123	O-36(31-5-0)/2-6,1	-0.2
1995	Mon N	35	63	6	12	2	0	0	3	8-0	2	12	.190	.297	.222	39	-5	4-0	.973	1	123	0	O-25(10-11-5)/2	-0.4
	Tex A	49	99	19	21	2	0	0	8	7-0	2	20	.212	.278	.232	34	-10	9-1	.973	2	114	106	O-47(43-6-0)/D-2	-0.7
1996	Tex A	30	50	5	13	2	1	0	5	8-0	1	10	.260	.373	.340	78	-1	4-2	.971	2	112	349	O-15(12-3-0),D-13/2	-0.1
1998	Chi A	7	7	0	0	0	0	0	0	2-0	0	6	.000	.222	.000	-36	-1	4-0	1.000	0	111	0	/O-3(CF)	0.0
Total	5	309	548	82	138	16	3	1	46	59-0	6	95	.252	.330	.297	65	-27	58-9	.982	5	107	122	O-186(148-35-7)/D-15,2-9,1-9	-1.7
FRAZIER, JOE Joseph Filmore B 10.6.1922 Liberty, NC BL/TR 6/180# d8.31 M2																								
1947	Cle A	9	14	1	1	1	0	0	0	1	0	1	.071	.133	.143	-24	-2	0-0	.857	-0	105	0	/O-5(RF)	-0.3
1954	StL N	81	88	8	26	5	2	3	18	13	1	17	.295	.388	.500	129	4	0-0	.938	-1	96	0	O-11(2-0-8)/1	0.3
1955	StL N	58	70	12	14	1	0	4	9	6-0	1	12	.200	.269	.386	72	-3	0-0	1.000	-1	102	0	O-14(1-0-13)	-0.4
1956	StL N	14	19	1	4	2	0	1	4	3-0	0	3	.211	.318	.474	109	0	0-1	.800	-1	78	0	/O-3(RF)	-0.1
	Cin N	10	17	2	4	0	0	1	2	1-0	0	7	.235	.278	.412	77	-1	0-0	—	-0	0	0	/O-4(LF)	-0.1
	Year	24	36	3	8	2	0	2	6	4-0	0	10	.222	.300	.444	94	0	0-1	.800	-1	75	0	/O-7(4-0-3)	-0.2
	Bal A	45	74	7	19	6	0	1	12	11-2	1	6	.257	.356	.378	103	1	0-0	1.000	1	108	183	O-19(RF)	0.2
Total	4	217	282	31	68	15	2	10	45	35-2	3	46	.241	.328	.415	97	-1	0-1	.961	-1	101	73	/O-56(7-0-48),1	-0.4
FREDERICK, JOHNNY John Henry B 1.26.1902 Denver, CO D 6.18.1977 Tigard, OR BL/TL 5-11/165# d4.18																								
1929	Bro N	148	628	127	206	**52**	6	24	75	39	5	34	.328	.372	.545	126	24	6	.975	1	103	93	*O-143(CF)	1.7
1930	Bro N	142	616	120	206	44	11	17	76	46	3	34	.334	.383	.524	118	18	1	.990	4	103	103	*O-142(CF)	1.4
1931	Bro N	146	611	81	165	34	8	17	71	31	6	46	.270	.312	.435	99	-3	2	.965	-2	101	84	*O-145(CF)	-0.8
1932	Bro N	118	384	54	115	28	2	16	56	25	4	35	.299	.349	.508	130	16	1	.976	-4	94	74	O-88(1-47-39)	0.8
1933	Bro N	147	556	65	171	22	7	7	64	36	5	14	.308	.355	.410	123	16	9	.971	-5	97	67	*O-138(10-26-102)	0.4
1934	Bro N	104	307	51	91	20	1	4	35	33	3	13	.296	.370	.407	114	7	4	.957	2	88	193	O-77(22-0-55)/1	0.5
Total	6	805	3102	498	954	200	35	85	377	210	26	176	.308	.357	.477	118	78	23	.974	-4	99	95	O-733(33-503-196)/1	4.0
FREED, ED Edwin Charles B 8.22.1919 Centre Valley, PA D 11.15.2002 Rock Hill, SC BR/TR 5-6/165# d9.11 Mil 1943-45																								
1942	Phi N	13	33	3	10	3	1	0	1	4	0	3	.303	.378	.455	151	2	1	1.000	0	75	308	O-11(3-7-1)	0.2
FREED, ROGER Roger Vernon B 6.2.1946 Los Angeles, CA D 1.9.1996 Chino, CA BR/TR 6/190# d9.18																								
1970	Bal A	4	13	0	2	0	0	0	1	3-0	0	4	.154	.294	.154	32	-1	0-0	1.000	-0	52	264	/1-3,O(RF)	-0.2
1971	Phi N	118	348	23	77	12	1	6	37	44-3	3	86	.221	.312	.313	78	-9	0-3	.989	-4	97	57	*O-106(7-0-99)/C	-2.0
1972	Phi N	73	129	10	29	4	0	6	18	23-2	1	39	.225	.344	.395	108	2	0-1	.971	3	110	178	O-46(1-0-45)	0.3
1974	Cin N	6	6	1	2	0	0	1	3	1-0	0	1	.333	.429	.833	251	1	0-0	1.000	-0	0	0	/1	0.1
1976	Mon N	8	15	0	3	1	0	0	1	0-0	0	3	.200	.200	.267	30	-1	0-0	1.000	-0	54	40	/1-3,O(RF)	-0.2
1977	StL N	49	83	10	33	2	1	5	21	11-0	0	9	.398	.463	.627	194	11	0-0	1.000	-1	99	150	1-18/O-6(RF)	0.9
1978	StL N	52	92	3	22	6	0	2	20	8-0	0	17	.239	.297	.370	87	-2	1-0	.992	-1	121	134	1-15/O-6(3-0-3)	-0.3
1979	StL N	34	31	2	8	2	0	2	8	5-0	0	7	.258	.361	.516	135	2	0-0	.889	0	166	0	/1	0.2
Total	8	344	717	49	176	27	2	22	109	95-5	4	166	.245	.334	.381	101	3	1-4	.982	-3	97	80	O-166(11-0-156)/1-41,C	-1.2
FREEHAN, BILL William Ashley B 11.29.1941 Detroit, MI BR/TR 6-2/205# d9.26																								
1961	Det A	4	10	1	4	0	0	0	4	1-0	0	0	.400	.455	.400	127	0	0-0	1.000	1	*93*	*376*	/C-3	0.1
1963	Det A	100	300	37	73	12	2	9	36	39-4	2	56	.243	.331	.387	98	0	2-0	.995	3	149	107	C-73,1-19	0.6
1964	Det A☆	144	520	69	156	14	8	18	80	36-3	**8**	68	.300	.350	.462	123	15	5-1	.993	6	***215***	*101*	*C-141/1	3.0
1965	Det A★	130	431	45	101	15	0	10	43	39-5	7	63	.234	.306	.339	83	-9	4-2	.996	4	*139*	*91*	*C-129	0.1
1966	Det A★	136	492	47	115	22	0	12	46	40-9	3	72	.234	.294	.352	83	-10	5-2	**.996**	2	*134*	*68*	*C-132/1-5	-0.2
1967	Det A★	155	517	66	146	23	1	20	74	73-**15**	**20**	71	.282	.389	.447	143	32	1-2	.992	-4	101	79	*C-147,1-11	3.8
1968	†Det A★	155	540	73	142	24	2	25	84	65-4	**24**	64	.263	.366	.454	143	31	0-1	.994	10	107	96	*C-138,1-21/O(RF)	5.2
1969	Det A★	143	489	61	128	16	3	16	49	53-6	8	55	.262	.342	.405	104	3	1-2	.992	4	92	92	*C-120,1-20	1.1
1970	Det A★	117	395	44	95	17	3	16	52	52-5	4	48	.241	.332	.420	106	3	0-3	**.997**	-10	125	110	*C-114	-0.3
1971	Det A★	148	516	57	143	26	4	21	71	54-9	9	48	.277	.353	.465	126	18	2-7	.996	-12	99	89	*C-144/O(LF)	1.2
1972	†Det A★	111	374	51	98	18	2	10	56	48-0	6	51	.262	.354	.401	121	11	0-1	.989	4	85	114	*C-105/1	2.2
1973	Det A☆	110	380	33	89	10	1	6	29	40-2	11	30	.234	.323	.313	75	-11	0-0	**.995**	6	94	**128**	C-98/1-7,D-3	-0.1
1974	Det A	130	445	58	132	17	5	18	60	42-2	5	44	.297	.361	.479	136	20	2-0	.994	-8	97	81	1-65,C-63/D	1.1
1975	Det A☆	120	427	42	105	17	3	14	47	32-3	6	56	.246	.306	.398	94	-5	2-0	.991	-1	100	102	*C-113/1-5	-0.1
1976	Det A	71	237	22	64	10	1	5	27	12-0	1	27	.270	.303	.384	98	-1	0-0	.983	2	90	62	C-61/1-2,D-3	0.3
Total	15	1774	6073	706	1591	241	35	200	758	626-67	114	753	.262	.340	.412	111	97	24-21	.993	7	*117*	*98*	*C-1581,1-157/D-7,O-2(1-0-1)	18.0
FREEL, RYAN Ryan Paul B 3.8.1976 Jacksonville, FL BR/TR 5-10/185# d4.4																								
2001	Tor A	9	22	1	6	1	0	0	3	1-0	1	4	.273	.333	.318	71	-1	2-1	.969	1	123	112	/2-7,O(LF)	0.1
2003	Cin N	43	137	23	39	6	1	4	12	9-1	4	13	.285	.344	.431	103	0	9-4	1.000	-3	111	157	O-24(5-20-0),2-11/3-2	-0.1
Total	2	52	159	24	45	7	1	4	15	10-1	5	17	.283	.343	.415	98	-1	11-5	1.000	-2	110	156	/O-25(6-20-0),2-18,3-2	0.0
FREEMAN, JERRY Frank Ellsworth "Buck" B 12.26.1879 Placerville, CA D 9.30.1952 Los Angeles, CA BL/TR 6-2/220# d4.14																								
1908	Was A	154	531	45	134	15	5	1	45	36	3		.252	.304	.305	107	3	6	.975	-13	71	105	*1-154	-1.4
1909	Was A	19	48	2	8	0	1	0	3	4	1		.167	.245	.208	46	-3	3	.956	-2	86	159	1-14/O(LF)	-0.6
Total	2	173	579	47	142	15	6	1	48	40	4		.245	.299	.297	101	0	9	.974	-15	72	109	1-168/O(LF)	-2.0
FREEMAN, JOHN John Edward B 1.24.1901 Boston, MA D 4.14.1958 Washington, DC BR/TR 5-8/160# d6.17																								
1927	Bos A	4	2	0	0	0	0	0	0	0	0	0	.000	.000	.000	-99	-1	0-0	—	-0	0	0	/O-3(1-2-0)	-0.1
FREEMAN, BUCK John Frank B 10.30.1871 Catasauqua, PA D 6.25.1949 Wilkes-Barre, PA BL/TL 5-9/169# d6.27 ▲																								
1891	Was AA	5	18	1	4	1	0	0	1	2	0	2	.222	.300	.278	69	1	0	.769	-0	95	0	/P-5	0.0
1898	Was N	29	107	19	39	2	3	3	21	7	4		.364	.424	.523	171	9	2	.978	2	143	216	O-29(RF)	0.9

Year	Tm Lg	G	AB	R	H	2B	3B	HR	RBI	BB-IB	HP	SO	AVG	OBP	SLG	AOPS	ABR	SB-CS	FA	FR	Rng	Thr	G at Pos	BFW
1899	Was N	**155**	588	107	187	19	25	**25**	122	23	18		.318	.362	.563	154	36	21	.944	-10	62	44	*O-155(RF)/P-2	1.7
1900	Bos N	117	418	58	126	19	13	6	65	25	10		.301	.355	.452	109	3	10	.950	-6	28	38	O-91(16-3-72),1-19	-0.7
1901	Bos A	129	490	88	166	23	15	12	114	44	6		.339	.400	.520	157	37	17	.974	-5	84	**115**	*1-128/2O(RF)	2.7
1902	Bos A	**138**	564	75	174	38	19	11	**121**	32	6		.309	.352	.502	131	21	17	.944	-2	82	89	*O-138(RF)	1.2
1903	†Bos A	**141**	567	74	163	39	20	**13**	**104**	30	4		.287	.328	.496	137	23	5	.933	-7	83	56	*O-141(RF)	1.0
1904	Bos A	**157**	597	64	167	20	**19**	7	84	32	12		.280	.329	.412	126	16	7	.954	-7	80	102	*O-157(RF)	0.2
1905	Bos A	130	455	59	109	20	8	3	49	46	5		.240	.316	.338	106	4	8	.973	-11	72	82	1-66,O-57(0-1-56)/3-2	-1.1
1906	Bos A	121	392	42	98	18	9	1	30	28	1		.250	.302	.349	104	1	5	.989	4	157	121	O-65(0-3-62),1-43/3-4	0.2
1907	Bos A	4	12	1	2	0	0	1	2	3	0		.167	.333	.417	140	1	0	1.000	-0	0	0	/O-3(RF)	0.0
Total	11	1126	4208	588	1235	199	131	82	713	272	66	2	.293	.346	.462	131	152	92	.950	-42	75	73	O-837(16-7-814),1-256/P-7,3-6,2	6.1
FREEMAN, LA VEL La Vel Maurice B 2.18.1963 Oakland, CA BL/TL 5-9/170# d4.7																								
1989	Mil A	2	3	1	0	0	0	0	0	0-0	0	2	.000	.000	.000	-99	-1	0-0	—	0			/D-2	-0.1
FREESE, GENE Eugene Lewis "Augie" B 1.8.1934 Wheeling, WV BR/TR 5-11/175# d4.13 b-George																								
1955	Pit N	134	455	69	115	21	8	14	44	34-4	4	57	.253	.310	.426	94	-5	5-1	.943	-0	101	121	3-65,2-57	-0.1
1956	Pit N	65	207	17	43	9	0	3	14	16-3	3	45	.208	.273	.295	54	-13	2-1	.963	-3	95	32	3-47,2-26	-1.6
1957	Pit N	114	346	44	98	18	2	6	31	17-0	2	42	.283	.319	.399	95	-3	9-4	.924	-1	105	129	3-74,2-10,O-10(LF)	-0.4
1958	Pit N	17	18	1	3	0	0	1	2	1-0	0	2	.167	.211	.333	42	-2	0-0	.800	0	159	0	/3	-0.2
	StL N	62	191	28	49	11	1	6	16	10-0	0	32	.257	.294	.419	83	-5	1-1	.924	-18	66	54	S-28,2-14/3-3	-2.1
	Year	79	209	29	52	11	1	7	18	11-0	0	34	.249	.286	.411	80	-7	1-1	.924	-18	66	54	S-28,2-14/3-4	-2.3
1959	Phi N	132	400	60	107	14	5	23	70	43-4	5	61	.268	.343	.500	120	11	8-4	.916	-17	84	94	*3-109/2-6	-0.6
1960	Chi A	127	455	60	124	32	6	17	79	29-2	1	65	.273	.312	.481	114	7	10-6	.946	-2	105	**118**	*3-122	0.4
1961	†Cin N	152	575	78	159	27	2	26	87	27-5	0	78	.277	.307	.466	101	-2	8-2	.950	-15	90	83	*3-151/2	-1.6
1962	Cin N	18	42	2	6	1	0	0	1	6-2	0	8	.143	.250	.167	14	-5	0-0	1.000	-1	64	68	3-10	-0.7
1963	Cin N	66	217	20	53	9	1	6	26	17-2	2	42	.244	.303	.378	93	-2	4-2	.930	-4	89	97	3-62/O(RF)	-0.7
1964	Pit N	99	289	33	65	13	2	9	40	19-4	0	45	.225	.269	.377	81	-8	1-2	.920	-4	93	118	3-72	-1.4
1965	Pit N	43	80	6	21	4	0	0	8	6-1	2	18	.262	.326	.313	82	-2	0-2	.951	-1	95	43	3-19	-0.4
	Chi A	17	32	2	9	0	1	1	4	5-0	0	9	.281	.368	.438	140	2	0-0	.824	-2	78	91	/3-8	0.0
1966	Chi A	48	106	8	22	2	0	3	10	8-1	1	20	.208	.270	.311	71	-4	2-1	.894	2	126	126	3-34	-0.3
	Hou N	21	33	1	3	0	0	0	0	5-0	0	11	.091	.211	.091	-13	-5	1-0	.800	-1	93	0	/3-4,2-3,O(LF)	-0.6
Total	12	1115	3446	429	877	161	28	115	432	243-28	20	535	.254	.305	.418	94	-36	51-26	.934	-70	96	99	3-781,2-117/S-28,O-12(11-0-1)	-10.3
FREESE, GEORGE George Walter "Bud" B 9.12.1926 Wheeling, WV BR/TR 6/190# d4.29 C2 b-Gene																								
1953	Det A	1	1	0	0	0	0	0	0	0	0	0	.000	.000	.000	-99	0	0-0	—	0			H	0.0
1955	Pit N	51	179	17	46	8	2	3	22	17-2	2	18	.257	.327	.374	87	-3	1-1	.936	-7	88	31	3-50	-1.0
1961	Chi N	9	7	0	2	0	0	0	1	1-0	0	4	.286	.375	.286	78	0	0-0	—	0			H	0.0
Total	3	61	187	17	48	8	2	3	23	18-2	2	22	.257	.327	.369	86	-3	1-1	.936	-7	88	31	/3-50	-1.0
FREGOSI, JIM James Louis B 4.4.1942 San Francisco, CA BR/TR 6-1/190# d9.14 M15 OF Total (LF)																								
1961	LA A	11	27	7	6	0	0	0	3	1-0	0	4	.222	.250	.222	25	-3	0-0	.944	0	103	62	S-11	-0.2
1962	LA A	58	175	15	51	3	4	3	23	18-1	0	27	.291	.356	.406	108	2	2-1	.943	1	104	108	S-52	0.7
1963	LA A	154	592	83	170	29	12	9	50	36-3	0	104	.287	.325	.422	115	10	2-2	.964	8	106	102	*S-151	3.1
1964	LA A★	147	505	86	140	22	9	18	72	72-2	4	87	.277	.369	.463	145	32	8-3	.966	10	**108**	111	*S-137	**5.6**
1965	Cal A	161	602	66	167	19	7	15	64	54-4	4	107	.277	.337	.407	114	10	13-5	.968	7	103	102	*S-160	3.4
1966	Cal A★	**162**	611	78	154	32	7	13	67	67-1	2	89	.252	.325	.391	109	8	17-8	.959	15	**109**	**126**	*S-162/1	4.0
1967	Cal A★	151	590	75	171	23	6	9	56	49-2	5	77	.290	.349	.395	124	17	9-6	.965	-2	99	89	*S-151	3.1
1968	Cal A★	159	614	77	150	21	**13**	9	49	60-4	5	101	.244	.315	.365	110	6	9-4	.962	-12	95	108	*S-159	1.0
1969	Cal A★	161	580	78	151	22	6	12	47	93-7	1	86	.260	.361	.381	114	14	9-2	.972	-6	97	100	*S-160	2.9
1970	Cal A★	158	601	95	167	33	5	22	82	69-3	3	92	.278	.353	.459	127	22	0-2	.973	7	101	**117**	*S-150/1-6	4.7
1971	Cal A	107	347	31	81	15	1	5	33	39-6	5	61	.233	.317	.326	90	-4	2-1	.938	-3	108	76	S-74,1-18/O-7(LF)	0.0
1972	NY N	101	340	31	79	15	4	5	32	38-2	1	71	.232	.311	.344	88	-5	0-1	.935	-7	82	68	3-85/S-6,1-3	-1.4
1973	NY N	45	124	7	29	4	1	0	11	20-3	0	25	.234	.340	.282	75	-3	1-2	.906	-7	73	111	S-17,3-17/1-3,O(LF)	-1.0
	Tex A	45	157	25	42	6	2	6	16	12-0	1	31	.268	.318	.446	120	3	0-1	.937	-7	73	108	3-34,1-10/S-6	-0.4
1974	Tex A	78	230	31	60	5	0	12	34	22-4	0	41	.261	.324	.439	121	5	0-1	1.000	0	103	104	1-47,3-32	0.2
1975	Tex A	77	191	25	50	5	0	7	33	20-4	1	39	.262	.329	.398	107	2	0-1	.985	1	123	96	1-54,D-13/3-4	-0.1
1976	Tex A	58	133	17	31	7	0	2	12	23-1	0	33	.233	.342	.331	97	1	2-0	.995	-1	88	113	1-26,D-18/3-5	-0.2
1977	Tex A	13	28	4	7	1	0	1	5	3-0	0	4	.250	.313	.393	93	0	0-0	1.000	1	164	78	/1-5,D-3	0.0
	Pit N	36	56	10	16	1	1	3	16	13-1	0	10	.286	.408	.500	142	4	2-0	.981	-1	70	98	1-15/3	0.2
1978	Pit N	20	20	3	4	1	0	0	1	6-0	0	8	.200	.385	.250	77	0	0-0	.667	-1	87	0	/3-5,1-2,2	-0.1
Total	18	1902	6523	844	1726	264	78	151	706	715-48	32	1097	.265	.338	.398	114	121	76-40	.963	4	102	106	*S-1396,1-190,3-183/D-34,O-8L,2	25.5
FREIBURGER, VERN Vern Donald B 12.19.1923 Detroit, MI D 2.27.1990 Palm Springs, CA BR/TL 6-1/170# d9.6																								
1941	Cle A	2	8	0	1	0	0	0	1	0	0	2	.125	.125	.125	-35	-2	0-0	.947	1	223	120	/1-2	-0.1
FREIGAU, HOWARD Howard Earl "Ty" B 8.1.1902 Dayton, OH D 7.18.1932 Chattanooga, TN BR/TR 5-10.5/160# d9.13 OF Total (1-LF 1-CF)																								
1922	StL N	3	1	0	0	0	0	0	0	0	0	0	.000	.000	.000	-99	0	0-0	1.000	1	154	290	/S-2,3	0.0
1923	StL N	113	358	30	94	18	1	1	35	25	2	36	.263	.314	.327	71	-15	5-4	.929	-6	100	82	S-87,2-16/1-9,3O(LF)	-1.2
1924	StL N	98	376	35	101	17	6	2	39	19	1	24	.269	.306	.362	80	-12	10-3	.958	-2	92	132	3-98/S-2	-0.6
1925	StL N	9	26	2	4	0	0	0	0	2	0	1	.154	.214	.154	-4	-4	0-0	.936	1	111	133	/S-7,2	-0.2
	Chi N	117	476	77	146	22	10	8	71	30	1	31	.307	.349	.445	100	-1	10-6	.913	-4	103	114	3-96,S-17/1-7	0.2
	Year	126	502	79	150	22	10	8	71	32	1	32	.299	.342	.430	94	-6	10-6	.913	-3	103	114	3-96,S-24/1-7,2	0.0
1926	Chi N	140	508	51	137	27	7	3	51	43	0	42	.270	.327	.368	86	-10	6	**.966**	-2	95	97	*3-135/S-2,O(CF)	-0.4
1927	Chi N	30	86	12	20	5	0	0	10	9	1	10	.233	.313	.291	62	-4	0	.883	-1	107	82	3-30	-0.3
1928	Bro N	17	34	6	7	2	0	0	3	1	0	3	.206	.229	.265	29	-4	0	.810	-3	61	0	3-10/S	-0.6
	Bos N	52	109	11	28	8	1	1	17	9	1	14	.257	.319	.376	86	-2	1	.938	-8	82	58	S-14,2-11	-0.9
	Year	69	143	17	35	10	1	1	20	10	1	17	.245	.299	.350	72	-6	1	.938	-11	81	57	S-15,2-11,3-10	-1.5
Total	7	579	1974	224	537	99	25	15	226	138	6	161	.272	.322	.370	82	-52	32-13	.940	-24	96	108	3-371,S-132/2-28,1-16,O-2L	-4.0
FRENCH, CHARLIE Charles Calvin B 10.12.1883 Indianapolis, IN D 3.30.1962 Indianapolis, IN BL/TR 5-6/140# d5.23																								
1909	Bos A	51	167	15	42	3	1	0	13	15	3		.251	.324	.281	90	-1	8	.921	-5	103	106	2-28,S-23	-0.7
1910	Bos A	9	40	4	8	1	0	0	3	1	0		.200	.220	.225	38	-3	0	.889	-0	115	106	/2-8	-0.4
	Chi A	45	170	17	28	1	1	0	4	10	3		.165	.224	.182	29	-14	5	.930	-9	77	76	2-28,O-16(RF)	-2.7
	Year	54	210	21	36	2	1	0	7	11	3		.171	.223	.190	31	-17	5	.919	-9	87	84	2-36,O-16(RF)	-3.1
Total	2	105	377	36	78	5	2	0	20	26	6		.207	.269	.231	58	-18	13	.920	-15	93	93	/2-64,S-23,O-16(RF)	-3.8
FRENCH, PAT Frank Alexander B 9.22.1893 Dover, NH D 7.13.1969 Bath, ME BR/TR 6-1/180# d7.2																								
1917	Phi A	3	2	0	0	0	0	0	0	0	0	0	.000	.000	.000	-99	0	0	1.000	0	133	0	/O(RF)	-0.1
FRENCH, RAY Raymond Edward B 1.9.1895 Alameda, CA D 4.3.1978 Alameda, CA BR/TR 5-9.5/158# d9.17																								
1920	NY A	2	2	2	0	0	0	0	1	0	0	1	.000	.000	.000	-97	-1	0-0	.500	-1	0	0	/S	-0.1
1923	Bro N	43	73	14	16	2	1	0	7	4	1	7	.219	.269	.274	45	-6	0-0	.874	1	109	127	S-30	-0.2
1924	Chi A	37	112	13	20	4	0	0	11	10	0	13	.179	.246	.214	20	-14	3-1	.927	-2	113	64	S-28/2-3	-1.2
Total	3	82	187	29	36	6	1	0	19	14	1	21	.193	.252	.235	28	-21	3-1	.897	-1	110	92	/S-59,2-3	-1.5
FRENCH, JIM Richard James B 8.13.1941 Warren, OH BL/TR 5-7/182# d9.12																								
1965	Was A	13	37	4	11	0	0	1	7	9-1	0	5	.297	.435	.378	135	2	1-0	.974	-0	*109*	*146*	C-13	0.3
1966	Was A	10	24	0	5	1	0	0	3	4-0	0	5	.208	.321	.250	67	-1	0-1	.979	-1	*114*	*50*	C-10	-0.2
1967	Was A	6	16	0	1	0	0	0	1	3-1	0	4	.063	.211	.063	-16	-2	0-0	.968	-2	35	69	/C-6	-0.4
1968	Was A	59	165	9	32	5	0	1	10	19-0	1	19	.194	.277	.242	62	-7	1-2	.984	-1	84	146	C-53	-0.7
1969	Was A	63	158	14	29	6	3	2	13	41-6	0	15	.184	.348	.297	88	-1	1-0	.989	8	96	190	C-63	1.0
1970	Was A	69	166	20	35	3	1	1	13	38-2	0	23	.211	.358	.259	76	-3	0-1	.973	-4	137	139	C-62/O(LF)	-0.6
1971	Was A	14	41	6	6	2	0	0	4	7-0	0	7	.146	.271	.195	36	-3	0-2	.985	-1	144	110	C-14	-0.5
Total	7	234	607	53	119	17	4	5	51	121-10	1	78	.196	.328	.262	74	-15	3-6	.982	-1	*107*	*149*	C-221/O(LF)	-1.1
FRENCH, WALTER Walter Edward "Piggy" or "Fitz" B 7.12.1899 Moorestown, NJ D 5.13.1984 Mountain Home, AR BL/TR 5-7.5/155# d9.15																								
1923	Phi A	16	39	7	9	3	0	0	2	5	0	7	.231	.318	.308	64	-2	0-1	1.000	-1	83	108	O-10(CF)	-0.3

Year	Tm Lg	G	AB	R	H	2B	3B	HR	RBI	BB-IB	HP	SO	AVG	OBP	SLG	AOPS	ABR	SB-CS	FA	FR	Rng	Thr	G at Pos	BFW
1925	Phi A	67	100	20	37	9	0	0	14	1	0	9	.370	.376	.460	104	1	1-1	.971	1	101	179	O-19(3-0-16)	0.0
1926	Phi A	112	397	51	121	18	7	1	36	18	3	24	.305	.340	.393	86	-10	2-3	.971	0	98	107	O-99(0-1-98)	-1.8
1927	Phi A	109	326	48	99	10	5	0	41	16	1	14	.304	.338	.365	78	-11	9-1	.956	2	115	66	O-94(8-5-81)	-1.4
1928	Phi A	48	74	9	19	4	0	0	7	2	1	5	.257	.286	.311	55	-5	1-1	1.000	1	128	77	O-19(8-0-11)	-0.5
1929	†Phi A	45	45	7	12	1	0	1	9	2	0	3	.267	.298	.356	65	-3	0-0	1.000	0	120	0	O-10(6-1-3)	-0.3
Total	6	397	981	142	297	45	12	2	109	44	5	62	.303	.336	.379	81	-30	13-7	.968	4	106	93	O-251(25-17-209)	-4.3

FRENCH, BILL William B Baltimore, MD d4.14 ▲

Year	Tm Lg	G	AB	R	H	2B	3B	HR	RBI	BB-IB	HP	SO	AVG	OBP	SLG	AOPS	ABR	SB-CS	FA	FR	Rng	Thr	G at Pos	BFW
1873	Mar NA	5	18	3	4	0	0	0	1	0		0	.222	.222	.222	42	-1	0-0	.905	-0	0	0	/1-2,O-2(RF),P3	-0.1

FREY, LONNY Linus Reinhard "Junior" B 8.23.1910 St.Louis, MO BL/TR (BB 1933-38) 5-10/160# d8.29 Mil 1944-45

Year	Tm Lg	G	AB	R	H	2B	3B	HR	RBI	BB-IB	HP	SO	AVG	OBP	SLG	AOPS	ABR	SB-CS	FA	FR	Rng	Thr	G at Pos	BFW
1933	Bro N	34	135	25	43	5	3	0	12	13	0	13	.319	.378	.400	128	5	4	.896	-11	85	52	S-34	-0.3
1934	Bro N	125	490	77	139	24	5	8	57	52	5	54	.284	.358	.402	109	7	11	.945	10	107	**121**	*S-109,3-13	2.4
1935	Bro N	131	515	88	135	35	11	11	77	66	5	68	.262	.352	.437	113	11	6	.937	-1	101	103	*S-127/2-4	1.9
1936	Bro N	148	524	63	146	29	4	4	60	71	4	56	.279	.369	.372	99	3	7	.918	-32	89	70	*S-117,2-30/O(CF)	-1.8
1937	Chi N	78	198	33	55	9	3	1	22	33	0	15	.278	.381	.369	100	2	6	.938	-13	75	65	S-30,2-13/3-9,O-5(4-1-0)	-0.9
1938	Cin N	124	501	76	133	26	6	4	36	49	0	50	.265	.331	.365	94	-4	4	.964	-7	98	110	*2-121/S-3	-0.3
1939	†Cin N★	125	484	95	141	27	9	11	55	72	4	46	.291	.387	.452	124	19	5	.976	14	**105**	**106**	*2-124	4.0
1940	†Cin N	150	563	102	150	23	6	8	54	80	3	48	.266	.361	.371	101	4	**22**	.977	15	105	**132**	*2-150	2.8
1941	Cin N★	146	543	78	138	29	5	6	59	72	3	37	.254	.345	.359	98	0	16	**.970**	-4	98	111	*2-145	0.6
1942	Cin N	141	523	66	139	23	6	2	39	87	2	38	.266	.373	.344	111	11	9	.977	5	103	**119**	*2-140	2.7
1943	Cin N★	144	586	78	154	20	8	2	43	76	0	56	.263	.347	.334	99	1	7	**.985**	13	103	122	*2-144	2.3
1946	Cin N	111	333	46	82	10	3	3	24	63	1	31	.246	.368	.321	100	3	5	.963	1	103	107	2-65,O-28(3-13-12)	0.7
1947	Chi N	24	43	4	9	0	0	0	3	4	0	6	.209	.277	.209	32	-4	0	1.000	-1	95	77	/2-9	-0.5
	†NY A	24	28	10	5	2	0	0	2	10	1	1	.179	.410	.250	87	1	3-0	.923	1	114	158	/2-8	0.3
1948	NY A	1	0	1	0	0	0	0	0	0	0	0	—	—	—	—	0	0-0	—	0			R	0.0
	NY N	29	51	6	13	1	0	1	6	4	0	6	.255	.309	.333	73	-2	0	.920	-2	90	76	2-13	-0.3
Total	14	1535	5517	848	1482	263	69	61	549	752	28	525	.269	.359	.374	104	57	105-0	.973	-10	101	115	2-966,S-420/O-34(7-15-12),3-22	13.6

FRIAS, HANLEY Hanley (Acevedo) B 12.5.1973 Villa Altagracia, D.R. BB/TR 6/160# d6.21

Year	Tm Lg	G	AB	R	H	2B	3B	HR	RBI	BB-IB	HP	SO	AVG	OBP	SLG	AOPS	ABR	SB-CS	FA	FR	Rng	Thr	G at Pos	BFW
1997	Tex A	14	26	4	5	1	0	0	1	1-0	0	4	.192	.222	.231	18	-3	0-0	1.000	-5	50	38	S-12/2	-0.7
1998	Ari N	15	23	4	3	0	1	1	2	0-0	0	5	.130	.130	.348	20	-3	0-0	1.000	0	82	149	/2-3,3-2,S-2	-0.3
1999	†Ari N	69	150	27	41	3	2	1	16	29-2	0	18	.273	.391	.340	87	-2	4-3	.965	-9	83	73	S-53/2-8	-0.8
2000	Ari N	75	112	18	23	5	0	2	6	17-0	0	18	.205	.310	.304	54	-8	2-2	.938	-3	94	135	S-21,2-15/3-7	-0.9
Total	4	173	311	53	72	9	3	4	25	47-2	0	45	.232	.332	.318	65	-16	6-5	.962	-17	82	83	/S-88,2-27,3-9	-2.7

FRIAS, PEPE Jesus Maria (Andujar) B 7.14.1948 San Pedro De Macoris, D.R. BR/TR (BB 1976 (part), 1977-7) 5-10/159# d4.6

Year	Tm Lg	G	AB	R	H	2B	3B	HR	RBI	BB-IB	HP	SO	AVG	OBP	SLG	AOPS	ABR	SB-CS	FA	FR	Rng	Thr	G at Pos	BFW
1973	Mon N	100	225	19	52	10	1	0	22	10-2	1	24	.231	.266	.284	51	-15	1-3	.950	2	111	101	S-46,2-44/3-6,O(RF)	-0.8
1974	Mon N	75	112	12	24	4	1	0	7	7-3	0	10	.214	.258	.268	45	-8	1-0	.962	7	107	98	S-30,3-27,2-15/O-3(1-0-2)	0.2
1975	Mon N	51	64	4	8	2	0	0	4	3-0	0	13	.125	.162	.156	-10	-10	0-1	.938	-0	90	107	S-29,3-11/2-7	-0.8
1976	Mon N	76	113	7	28	5	0	0	8	4-3	0	14	.248	.271	.292	58	-6	1-1	.957	-2	95	105	2-35,S-35/3-4,O(CF)	-0.5
1977	Mon N	53	70	10	18	1	0	0	5	0-0	0	10	.257	.257	.271	43	-6	1-0	.978	0	110	138	2-16,S-14/3	-0.5
1978	Mon N	73	15	5	4	2	1	0	5	0-0	0	3	.267	.267	.533	120	0	0-0	1.000	-5	79	91	2-61/S-3	-0.4
1979	Atl N	140	475	41	123	18	4	1	44	20-5	2	36	.259	.290	.320	62	-25	3-2	.954	8	104	96	*S-137	-0.3
1980	Tex A	116	227	27	55	5	1	0	10	4-0	1	23	.242	.256	.273	47	-17	5-1	.947	-16	77	77	*S-106/3-7,2-2	-2.6
	LA N	14	9	1	2	1	0	0	0	0-0	0	0	.222	.222	.333	54	-1	0-0	.933	-1	82	106	S-11	-0.1
1981	LA N	25	36	6	9	1	0	0	3	1-1	1	3	.250	.282	.278	64	-2	0-0	.906	-8	63	41	S-15/2-6,3	-0.9
Total	9	723	1346	132	323	49	8	1	108	49-14	5	136	.240	.267	.290	52	-90	12-8	.951	-14	96	91	S-426,2-186/3-57,O-5(1-1-3)	-6.7

FRIBERG, BERNIE Bernard Albert (born Gustaf Bernhard Friberg) B 8.18.1899 Manchester, NH D 12.8.1958 Lynn, MA BR/TR 5-11/178# d8.20 OF Total (84-LF 52-CF 62-RF)

Year	Tm Lg	G	AB	R	H	2B	3B	HR	RBI	BB-IB	HP	SO	AVG	OBP	SLG	AOPS	ABR	SB-CS	FA	FR	Rng	Thr	G at Pos	BFW
1919	Chi N	8	20	0	4	1	0	0	1	0	0	2	.200	.200	.250	35	-2	0	1.000	-0	110	0	/O-7(2-5-0)	-0.2
1920	Chi N	50	114	11	24	5	1	0	7	6	0	20	.211	.250	.272	49	-8	2-2	.963	4	105	84	2-24,O-24(15-8-3)	-0.5
1922	Chi N	97	296	51	92	8	2	0	23	37	2	37	.311	.391	.351	91	-2	8-10	.972	0	87	147	O-74(8-11-55)/1-6,3-5,2-3	-0.8
1923	Chi N	146	547	91	174	27	11	12	88	45	2	49	.318	.372	.473	122	16	13-19	.955	10	105	**136**	*3-146	3.0
1924	Chi N	142	495	67	138	19	3	5	82	66	5	53	.279	.369	.360	95	0	19-27	.954	5	105	90	*3-142	0.9
1925	Chi N	44	152	12	39	5	3	1	16	14	2	22	.257	.327	.349	72	-7	0-1	.889	-3	93	119	3-26,O-12(LF)/1-6,S-2	-0.9
	Phi N	91	304	41	82	12	1	5	22	39	0	35	.270	.353	.365	77	-10	1-1	.965	-1	102	78	2-77,3-14/PC	-0.7
	Year	135	456	53	121	17	4	6	38	53	2	57	.265	.344	.360	75	-16	1-2	.965	-3	102	78	2-77,3-40,O-12(LF)/1-6,S-2,PC	-1.6
1926	Phi N	144	478	38	128	21	3	1	51	57	0	77	.268	.346	.331	79	-12	2	.976	22	107	94	*2-144	1.3
1927	Phi N	111	335	31	78	8	2	1	28	41	3	49	.233	.322	.278	61	-17	3	.959	20	**118**	**129**	*3-103/2-5	0.9
1928	Phi N	52	94	11	19	3	0	1	7	12	0	16	.202	.292	.266	45	-7	0	.908	0	95	109	S-31/3-5,2-3,O-3(2-1-0),1-2	-0.5
1929	Phi N	128	455	74	137	21	10	7	55	49	1	54	.301	.370	.437	93	-5	1	.923	-18	86	65	S-73,O-40(18-19-4)/2-8,1-2	-1.7
1930	Phi N	105	331	62	113	21	1	4	42	47	1	35	.341	.425	.447	104	5	1	.953	-1	102	77	2-44,O-35(27-8-0),S-12/3-8	0.3
1931	Phi N	103	353	33	92	19	5	1	26	33	0	25	.261	.324	.351	75	-12	1	.955	6	103	95	2-64,3-25/1-5,S-3	-0.1
1932	Phi N	61	154	17	37	8	2	0	14	19	0	23	.240	.324	.318	66	-7	0	.957	-5	98	77	2-56	-0.9
1933	Bos A	17	41	5	13	3	0	0	9	6	0	1	.317	.404	.390	112	1	0-0	.950	1	113	123	/2-6,3-5,S-2	0.2
Total	14	1299	4169	544	1170	181	44	38	471	471	16	498	.281	.356	.373	87	-67	51-60	.953	41	107	109	3-479,2-434,O-195L,S-123/1-21,CP	0.3

FRIDLEY, JIM James Riley "Big Jim" B 9.6.1924 Philippi, WV D 2.28.2003 Port Charlotte, FL BR/TR 6-2/205# d4.15

Year	Tm Lg	G	AB	R	H	2B	3B	HR	RBI	BB-IB	HP	SO	AVG	OBP	SLG	AOPS	ABR	SB-CS	FA	FR	Rng	Thr	G at Pos	BFW
1952	Cle A	62	175	23	44	2	0	4	16	14	1	40	.251	.311	.331	84	-5	3-3	.978	-1	97	98	O-54(37-0-20)	-0.9
1954	Bal A	85	240	25	59	8	5	4	36	21	2	41	.246	.311	.371	93	-4	0-1	.985	-2	99	25	O-67(64-0-3)	-1.0
1958	Cin N	5	9	2	2	2	0	0	1	0-0	0	2	.222	.222	.444	67	0	0-0	1.000	-0	49	0	/O-2(LF)	-0.1
Total	3	152	424	50	105	12	5	8	53	35-0	3	83	.248	.309	.356	89	-9	3-4	.982	-3	98	54	O-123(103-0-23)	-2.0

FRIEL, PAT Patrick Henry B 6.11.1860 Lewisburg, WV D 1.15.1924 Providence, RI BB 5-11/170# d7.13 b-Bill

Year	Tm Lg	G	AB	R	H	2B	3B	HR	RBI	BB-IB	HP	SO	AVG	OBP	SLG	AOPS	ABR	SB-CS	FA	FR	Rng	Thr	G at Pos	BFW
1890	Syr AA	62	261	51	65	8	2	3	21	17	3		.249	.302	.330	96	-1	34	.913	-4	72	87	O-62(13-0-49)	-0.5
1891	Phi AA	2	8	2	2	1	0	0	0	0	0	0	.250	.250	.375	78	0	0	1.000	-0	0	0	/O-2(RF)	0.0
Total	2	64	269	53	67	9	2	3	21	17	3	0	.249	.301	.331	96	-1	34	.914	-4	71	85	/O-64(13-0-51)	-0.5

FRIEL, BILL William Edward B 4.1.1876 Renovo, PA D 12.24.1959 St.Louis, MO BL/TR 5-10/165# d5.3 C1 U1 b-Pat OF Total (6-LF 27-CF 39-RF)

Year	Tm Lg	G	AB	R	H	2B	3B	HR	RBI	BB-IB	HP	SO	AVG	OBP	SLG	AOPS	ABR	SB-CS	FA	FR	Rng	Thr	G at Pos	BFW
1901	Mil A	106	376	51	100	13	7	4	35	23	1		.266	.310	.370	92	-5	15	.866	-6	107	119	3-61,O-29(5-23-1)/2-9,S-6	-0.9
1902	StL A	80	267	26	64	9	2	2	20	14	2		.240	.283	.311	65	-13	4	.921	-6	97	168	O-33(1-0-32),2-25,1-10/3-8,S-3,PC	-1.9
1903	StL A	97	351	46	80	11	8	0	25	23	2		.228	.279	.305	77	-10	4	.915	-11	92	69	2-63,3-24/O-9(0-4-6)	-2.1
Total	3	283	994	123	244	33	17	6	80	60	5		.245	.292	.331	80	-28	23	.924	-24	91	70	/2-97,3-93,O-71R,1-10,S-9,CP	-4.9

FRIEND, FRANK Frank B. (born Lawrence Lentz Freund) B 7.5.1875 Jeffersonville, IN D 11.5.1933 Jeffersonville, IN TR 5-10/180# d8.2

Year	Tm Lg	G	AB	R	H	2B	3B	HR	RBI	BB-IB	HP	SO	AVG	OBP	SLG	AOPS	ABR	SB-CS	FA	FR	Rng	Thr	G at Pos	BFW
1896	Lou N	2	5	1	1	0	0	0	0	1	0	1	.200	.333	.200	44	0	0	1.000	0	*76*	*149*	/C-2	0.0

FRIEND, OWEN Owen Lacey "Red" B 3.21.1927 Granite City, IL BR/TR 6-1/180# d10.2 Mil 1951 C1

Year	Tm Lg	G	AB	R	H	2B	3B	HR	RBI	BB-IB	HP	SO	AVG	OBP	SLG	AOPS	ABR	SB-CS	FA	FR	Rng	Thr	G at Pos	BFW
1949	StL A	2	8	1	3	0	0	0	1	0	0	0	.375	.375	.375	95	0	0-0	1.000	1	140	57	/2-2	0.1
1950	StL A	119	372	48	88	15	2	8	50	40	1	68	.237	.312	.352	67	-19	2-1	.961	-3	112	74	2-93,3-24/S-3	-1.6
1953	Det A	31	96	10	17	4	0	3	10	6	1	9	.177	.233	.313	47	-8	0-1	.947	-0	98	101	2-26	-0.6
	Cle A	34	68	7	16	2	0	2	13	5	0	16	.235	.288	.353	74	-3	0-0	1.000	5	115	152	2-19/S-8,3	0.3
	Year	65	164	17	33	6	0	5	23	11	1	25	.201	.256	.329	58	-11	0-1	.964	5	104	118	2-45/S-8,3	-0.3
1955	Bos A	14	42	3	11	3	0	0	2	4-0	0	11	.262	.326	.333	71	-2	0-0	.951	1	114	73	S-14/2	0.0
	Chi N	6	10	0	1	0	0	0	0	0-0	0	3	.100	.100	.100	-47	-2	0-0	1.000	-1	67	0	/3-2,S	-0.3
1956	Chi N	2	2	0	0	0	0	0	0	0-0	0	2	.000	.000	.000	-99	-1	0-0	—	0			H	-0.1
Total	5	208	598	69	136	24	2	13	76	55-0	2	109	.227	.295	.339	63	-35	2-2	.963	3	110	86	2-141/3-27,S-26	-2.2

FRIERSON, BUCK Robert Lawrence B 7.29.1917 Chicota, TX D 6.26.1996 Paris, TX BR/TR 6-3/195# d9.9

Year	Tm Lg	G	AB	R	H	2B	3B	HR	RBI	BB-IB	HP	SO	AVG	OBP	SLG	AOPS	ABR	SB-CS	FA	FR	Rng	Thr	G at Pos	BFW
1941	Cle A	5	11	2	3	1	0	0	2	1	0	1	.273	.333	.364	89	0	0-0	1.000	-0	57	0	/O-3(2-0-1)	-0.1

FRINK, FRED Frederick Ferdinand B 8.25.1911 Macon, GA D 5.19.1995 Miami Springs, FL BR/TR 6-1/180# d7.1

Year	Tm Lg	G	AB	R	H	2B	3B	HR	RBI	BB-IB	HP	SO	AVG	OBP	SLG	AOPS	ABR	SB-CS	FA	FR	Rng	Thr	G at Pos	BFW
1934	Phi N	2	0	0	0	0	0	0	0	0	0	0	—	—	—	—	0	0	—	-0	0	0	/O(CF)	0.0

FRISBEE, CHARLIE Charles Augustus "Bunt" B 2.2.1874 Dows, IA D 11.7.1954 Iowa Falls, IA BB/TR 5-9/175# d6.22

Year	Tm Lg	G	AB	R	H	2B	3B	HR	RBI	BB-IB	HP	SO	AVG	OBP	SLG	AOPS	ABR	SB-CS	FA	FR	Rng	Thr	G at Pos	BFW
1899	Bos N	42	152	22	50	4	2	0	20	9	2		.329	.374	.382	98	-1	10	.875	-2	155	73	O-40(0-36-4)	-0.4
1900	NY N	4	13	2	2	1	0	0	3	2	0		.154	.267	.231	40	-1	0	.400	-2	0	0	/O-4(RF)	-0.3

Year	Tm Lg	G	AB	R	H	2B	3B	HR	RBI	BB-IB	HP	SO	AVG	OBP	SLG	AOPS	ABR	SB-CS	FA	FR	Rng	Thr	G at Pos	BFW
Total	2	46	165	24	52	5	2	0	23	11	2		.315	.365	.370	94	-2	10	.849	-3	141	66	/O-44(0-36-8)	-0.7
FRISCH, FRANKIE Frank Francis "The Fordham Flash" B 9.9.1898 Bronx, NY D 3.12.1973 Wilmington, DE BB/TR 5-11/165# d6.14 M16 C1 HF1947																								
1919	NY N	54	190	21	43	3	2	2	24	4	0	14	.226	.242	.295	62	-10	15	.972	3	101	61	2-29,3-20/S	-0.7
1920	NY N	110	440	57	123	10	10	4	77	20	0	18	.280	.311	.375	97	-4	34-11	.967	10	**116**	**134**	*3-109/S-2	1.4
1921	†NY N	**153**	618	121	211	31	17	8	100	42	1	28	.341	.384	.485	128	24	**49**-13	.936	8	112	105	3-93,2-61	4.5
1922	†NY N	132	514	101	168	16	13	5	51	47	3	13	.327	.387	.438	111	9	31-17	.975	8	105	104	2-85,3-53/S	2.1
1923	†NY N	151	641	116	**223**	32	10	12	111	46	4	12	.348	.395	.485	133	30	29-12	**.973**	0	98	106	*2-135,3-17	3.5
1924	†NY N	145	603	**121**	198	33	15	7	69	56	2	24	.328	.387	.468	132	28	22-9	.972	**28**	**106**	117	*2-143,S-10/3-2	6.0
1925	NY N	120	502	89	166	26	6	11	48	32	3	14	.331	.374	.472	119	14	21-12	.931	4	111	49	3-46,2-42,S-39	2.4
1926	NY N	135	545	75	171	29	4	5	44	33	0	16	.314	.353	.409	106	4	23	.975	10	108	99	*2-127/3-7	1.7
1927	StL N	**153**	617	112	208	31	11	10	78	43	7	10	.337	.387	.472	125	22	**48**	**.979**	**49**	**120**	**124**	*2-153/S	**7.2**
1928	†StL N	141	547	107	164	29	9	10	86	64	1	17	.300	.374	.441	110	9	29	**.976**	-5	100	92	*2-139	0.8
1929	StL N	138	527	93	176	40	12	5	74	53	2	12	.334	.397	.484	116	14	24	.970	-6	94	89	*2-121,3-13/S	1.1
1930	†StL N	133	540	121	187	46	9	10	114	55	0	16	.346	.407	.520	118	18	15	.969	**22**	**108**	**106**	*2-123,3-10	3.9
1931	†StL N	131	518	96	161	24	4	4	82	45	2	13	.311	.368	.396	101	2	**28**	.974	11	103	113	*2-129	2.1
1932	StL N	115	486	59	142	26	2	3	60	25	0	13	.292	.327	.372	85	-10	18	.971	16	103	111	2-75,3-37/S-4	1.2
1933	StL N★	147	585	74	177	32	6	4	66	48	3	16	.303	.358	.398	110	9	18	.982	-6	90	88	*2-132,S-15,M	1.4
1934	†StL N★	140	550	74	168	30	6	3	75	45	1	10	.305	.359	.398	96	-2	11	.977	3	95	117	*2-115,3-25,M	0.9
1935	StL N☆	103	354	52	104	16	2	1	55	33	1	16	.294	.356	.359	89	-4	2	.982	-5	95	112	2-88/3-5,M	-0.4
1936	StL N	93	303	40	83	10	0	1	26	36	1	10	.274	.353	.317	82	-6	2	.965	-13	94	79	2-60,3-22/SM	-1.5
1937	StL N	17	32	3	7	2	0	0	4	1	0	0	.219	.242	.281	41	-3	0	1.000	-1	89	0	/2-5,M	-0.3
Total	19	2311	9112	1532	2880	466	138	105	1244	728	31	272	.316	.369	.432	110	144	419-74	.974	135	102	104	*2-1762,3-459/S-75	37.3
FRISK, EMIL John Emil B 10.15.1874 Kalkaska, MI D 1.27.1922 Seattle, WA BL/TR 6-1/190# d9.2 ▲																								
1899	Cin N	9	25	5	7	1	0	0	2	2	1		.280	.357	.320	85	1	0	.950	-0	87	0	/P-9	0.0
1901	Det A	20	48	10	15	3	0	1	7	3	1		.313	.365	.438	117	1	0	.851	2	168	0	P-11/O-2(0-1-1)	0.1
1905	StL A	124	429	58	112	11	6	3	36	42	11		.261	.342	.336	122	12	7	.923	-7	121	70	*O-115(RF)	0.0
1907	StL A	5	4	0	1	0	0	0	0	1	0		.250	.400	.250	108	0	0	—	0			H	0.0
Total	4	158	506	73	135	15	6	4	45	48	13		.267	.346	.344	119	14	7	.918	-5	119	69	O-117(0-1-116)/P-20	0.1
FRITZ, HARRY Harry Koch "Dutchman" B 9.30.1890 Philadelphia, PA D 11.4.1974 Columbus, OH BR/TR 5-8/170# d9.29																								
1913	Phi A	5	13	1	0	0	0	0	0	2	1	4	.000	.188	.000	-45	-2	0	.846	-1	71	0	/3-5	-0.3
1914	Chi F	65	174	16	37	5	1	0	13	18	3	18	.213	.297	.253	54	-14	2	.912	-6	89	152	3-46/S-9,2	-1.9
1915	Chi F	79	236	27	59	8	4	3	26	13	3	27	.250	.298	.356	89	-9	4	.964	-5	90	101	3-70/2-6,S	-1.3
Total	3	149	423	44	96	13	5	3	39	33	7	49	.227	.294	.303	70	-25	6	.941	-12	89	116	3-121/S-10,2-7	-3.5
FRITZ, LARRY Lawrence Joseph B 2.14.1949 E.Chicago, IN BL/TL 6-2/225# d5.30																								
1975	Phi N	1	1	0	0	0	0	0	0	0-0	0	0	.000	.000	.000	-96	0	0-0	—	0			H	0.0
FROBEL, DOUG Douglas Steven B 6.6.1959 Ottawa, ON, CAN BL/TR 6-4/196# d9.5																								
1982	Pit N	16	34	5	7	2	0	2	3	1-0	0	11	.206	.229	.441	81	-1	1-1	1.000	0	117	0	O-12(RF)	-0.2
1983	Pit N	32	60	10	17	4	1	3	11	4-0	0	17	.283	.328	.533	132	2	1-1	.964	-2	91	0	O-24(18-0-6)	0.0
1984	Pit N	126	276	33	56	9	3	12	28	24-2	2	84	.203	.271	.388	83	-8	7-5	.956	9	121	168	*O-112(RF)	-0.4
1985	Pit N	53	109	14	22	5	0	0	7	19-5	0	24	.202	.320	.248	62	-5	4-3	.941	-1	86	101	O-36(20-0-16)	-0.8
	Mon N	12	23	3	3	1	0	1	4	2-0	0	6	.130	.200	.304	42	-2	0-0	.923	-0	114	0	/O-6(1-2-3)	-0.2
	Year	65	132	17	25	6	0	1	11	21-5	0	30	.189	.301	.258	59	-7	4-3	.938	-2	90	86	O-42(21-2-19)	-1.0
1987	Cle A	29	40	5	4	0	0	2	5	5-1	0	13	.100	.196	.250	18	-5	0-0	1.000	-1	63	0	O-12(2-2-7)/D-5	-0.6
Total	5	268	542	70	109	21	4	20	58	55-8	2	155	.201	.276	.365	78	-19	13-10	.957	5	108	115	O-202(41-4-156)/D-5	-2.2
FROELICH, BEN William Palmer B 11.12.1887 Pittsburgh, PA D 9.1.1916 Pittsburgh, PA BR/TR d7.2																								
1909	Phi N	1	1	0	0	0	0	0	0	0	0		.000	.000	.000	-99	0	0	—	0	*0*	*0*	/C	0.0
FRY, JERRY Jerry Ray B 2.29.1956 Salinas, CA BR/TR 6/185# d9.4																								
1978	Mon N	4	9	0	0	0	0	0	0	1-0	0	5	.000	.100	.000	-71	-2	0-0	1.000	-1	27	0	/C-4	-0.3
FRYE, JEFF Jeffrey Dustin B 8.31.1966 Oakland, CA BR/TR 5-9/165# d7.9 OF Total (9-LF 8-CF 18-RF)																								
1992	Tex A	67	199	24	51	9	1	1	12	16-0	3	27	.256	.320	.327	85	-4	1-3	.978	2	101	94	2-67	-0.1
1994	Tex A	57	205	37	67	20	3	0	18	29-0	1	23	.327	.408	.454	124	9	6-1	.983	-6	95	87	2-54/3D	0.6
1995	Tex A	90	313	38	87	15	2	4	29	24-0	5	45	.278	.335	.377	84	-7	3-3	.975	7	106	102	2-83	0.3
1996	Bos A	105	419	74	120	27	2	4	41	54-0	5	57	.286	.372	.389	92	-3	18-4	.983	14	106	92	*2-100/O-5(2-1-2),S-3,D	1.7
1997	Bos A	127	404	56	126	36	2	3	51	27-1	2	44	.312	.352	.433	103	3	19-8	.991	8	99	114	2-80,3-18,0-13(5-5-3),D-11/S-3,1	1.5
1999	Bos A	41	114	14	32	3	0	1	12	14-1	1	11	.281	.362	.333	77	-3	2-2	.980	-6	77	63	2-26/3-7,S-2,D-2	-0.8
2000	Bos A	69	239	35	69	13	0	1	13	28-0	1	38	.289	.364	.356	81	-6	1-3	.991	-5	91	69	2-52,O-15(1-2-13)/3-3,D-3	-0.9
	Col N	37	87	14	31	6	0	0	3	8-0	1	16	.356	.412	.425	91	-1	4-0	.989	2	106	118	2-27/3	0.3
2001	Tor A	74	175	24	43	6	1	2	15	12-0	3	18	.246	.305	.326	65	-9	2-1	.995	3	104	117	2-47,3-27/S-2,O(LF)	-0.4
Total	8	667	2155	316	626	135	11	16	194	212-2	22	279	.290	.357	.386	91	-21	56-25	.984	18	100	96	2-536/3-57,O-34R,D-18,S-10,1	2.2
FRYMAN, TRAVIS David Travis B 3.25.1969 Lexington, KY BR/TR 6-1/194# d7.7																								
1990	Det A	66	232	32	69	11	1	9	27	17-0	1	51	.297	.348	.470	126	7	3-3	.915	1	109	142	3-48,S-17/D	0.9
1991	Det A	149	557	65	144	36	3	21	91	40-0	3	149	.259	.309	.447	106	3	12-5	.946	-20	86	77	3-85,S-71	-1.1
1992	Det A★	161	659	87	175	31	4	20	96	45-1	6	144	.266	.316	.416	104	1	8-4	.970	-1	107	98	*S-137,3-26	1.1
1993	Det A★	151	607	98	182	37	5	22	97	77-1	4	128	.300	.379	.486	133	29	9-4	.953	-5	106	112	S-81,3-69/D	3.1
1994	Det A★	114	464	66	122	34	5	18	85	45-1	5	128	.263	.326	.474	105	3	2-2	.955	-1	105	67	*3-114	0.2
1995	Det A	**144**	567	79	156	21	5	15	81	63-4	3	100	.275	.347	.409	97	-2	4-2	.969	**27**	**127**	137	*3-144	2.5
1996	Det A★	157	616	90	165	32	3	22	100	57-2	4	118	.268	.329	.437	93	-8	4-3	**.979**	23	**122**	94	*3-128,S-29	1.6
1997	Det A	154	595	90	163	27	3	22	102	46-5	5	113	.274	.326	.440	100	-2	16-3	**.978**	14	111	84	*3-153	1.6
1998	†Cle A	146	557	74	160	33	2	28	96	44-0	3	125	.287	.340	.504	113	9	10-8	.963	-3	98	94	*3-144/S-3,D-2	0.7
1999	†Cle A	85	322	45	82	16	2	10	48	25-1	1	57	.255	.309	.410	78	-12	2-1	.969	-1	99	88	3-85	-1.1
2000	Cle A★	155	574	93	184	38	4	22	106	73-2	1	111	.321	.392	.516	126	25	1-1	**.978**	-1	97	71	*3-154/1D	2.3
2001	†Cle A	98	334	34	88	15	0	3	38	30-1	3	63	.263	.327	.335	75	-11	1-2	.944	-10	78	88	3-96/SD	-2.1
2002	Cle A	118	397	42	86	14	3	11	55	40-1	2	82	.217	.292	.350	71	-18	0-0	.960	-6	93	**139**	*3-113	-2.1
Total	13	1698	6481	895	1776	345	40	223	1022	602-19	41	1369	.274	.336	.443	104	24	72-38	.965	17	103	95	*3-1359,S-339/D-7,1	7.6
FUENTES, MIKE Michael Jay B 7.11.1958 Miami, FL BR/TR 6-3/190# d9.2																								
1983	Mon N	6	4	1	1	0	0	0	0	0-0	0	2	.250	.250	.250	39	0	0-0	—	0			/H	-0.1
1984	Mon N	3	4	0	1	0	0	0	0	1-0	0	2	.250	.400	.250	90	0	0-0	1.000	0	221	0	/O(LF)	0.0
Total	2	9	8	1	2	0	0	0	0	1-0	0	4	.250	.333	.250	67	0	0-0	1.000	0	221	0	/O(LF)	-0.1
FUENTES, TITO Rigoberto (Peat) B 1.4.1944 Havana, Cuba BB/TR (BR 1965-67, 70 (part)) 5-11/175# d8.18																								
1965	SF N	26	72	12	15	1	0	0	1	5-1	1	14	.208	.269	.222	39	-6	0-1	.919	-6	89	59	S-18/2-7,3	-1.1
1966	SF N	133	541	63	141	21	3	9	40	9-1	3	57	.261	.276	.360	73	-21	6-3	.957	-13	95	100	S-76,2-60	-2.2
1967	SF N	133	344	27	72	12	1	5	29	27-9	0	61	.209	.266	.294	61	-18	4-3	.980	18	108	**128**	*2-130/S-5	1.0
1969	SF N	67	183	28	54	4	3	1	14	15-1	1	25	.295	.350	.366	103	1	2-4	.925	-4	109	145	3-36,S-30	-0.2
1970	SF N	123	435	49	116	13	7	2	32	36-3	3	52	.267	.323	.343	81	-12	4-5	.966	-0	105	87	2-78,S-36,3-24	-0.7
1971	†SF N	152	630	63	172	28	6	4	52	18-2	6	46	.273	.299	.356	86	-14	12-2	.973	2	101	108	*2-152	0.0
1972	SF N	152	572	64	151	33	6	7	53	39-3	3	56	.264	.310	.379	95	-4	16-5	.964	-16	95	92	*2-152	-0.9
1973	SF N	160	656	78	182	25	5	6	63	45-0	7	62	.277	.328	.358	87	-11	12-6	**.993**	-6	98	97	*2-160/3	-0.6
1974	SF N	108	390	33	97	15	2	0	22	22-0	3	32	.249	.293	.297	63	-20	7-3	.979	2	100	111	*2-103	-1.1
1975	SD N	146	565	57	158	21	3	4	43	25-2	3	51	.280	.309	.349	89	-11	8-8	.970	9	107	107	*2-142	0.7
1976	SD N	135	520	48	137	18	0	2	36	18-0	1	38	.263	.287	.310	76	-18	5-3	.971	11	108	108	*2-127	0.1
1977	Det A	151	615	83	190	19	10	5	51	38-1	2	61	.309	.348	.397	98	-2	4-4	.970	8	101	118	*2-151/D	1.3
1978	Oak A	13	43	5	6	1	0	0	2	1-0	0	6	.140	.159	.163	-10	-6	0-0	.944	-6	57	61	2-13	-1.3
Total	13	1499	5566	610	1491	211	46	45	438	298-23	33	561	.268	.307	.347	82	-142	80-47	.974	-0	101	104	*2-1275,S-165/3-62,D	-5.0
FUHRMAN, OLLIE Alfred George B 7.20.1896 Jordan, MN D 1.11.1969 Peoria, IL BB/TR 5-11/185# d4.13																								
1922	Phi A	6	6	1	2	1	0	0	0	0	0	0	.333	.333	.500	112	0	0-0	1.000	0	*59*	*0*	/C-4	0.0

Year	Tm Lg	G	AB	R	H	2B	3B	HR	RBI	BB-IB	HP	SO	AVG	OBP	SLG	AOPS	ABR	SB-CS	FA	FR	Rng	Thr	G at Pos	BFW
FULGHUM, DOT James Lavoisier B 7.4.1900 Valdosta, GA D 11.11.1967 Miami, FL BR/TR 5-8.5/165# d9.15																								
1921	Phi A	2	2	0	0	0	0	0	0	1	0	1	.000	.333	.000	-9	0	0-0	—	-0	0	0	/S	0.0
FULLER, NIG Charles F. B 3.30.1879 Toledo, OH D 11.12.1947 Toledo, OH BR/TR 5-11/165# d7.1																								
1902	Bro N	3	9	0	0	0	0	0	1	0	0		.000	.000	.000	-99	-2	0	1.000	-1	*66*	*47*	/C-3	-0.3
FULLER, FRANK Frank Edward "Rabbit" B 1.1.1893 Detroit, MI D 10.29.1965 Warren, MI BB/TR 5-7/150# d4.14																								
1915	Det A	14	32	6	5	0	0	0	2	9	0	7	.156	.341	.156	47	-2	2-3	.962	-3	93	41	/2-9,S	-0.6
1916	Det A	20	10	2	1	0	0	0	1	1	0	4	.100	.182	.100	-15	-1	3	.846	1	166	323	/2-8,S	-0.1
1923	Bos A	6	21	3	5	0	0	0	0	1	0	1	.238	.273	.238	35	-2	1-1	.952	0	100	50	/2-6	-0.2
Total	3	40	63	11	11	0	0	0	3	11	0	12	.175	.297	.175	35	-5	6-4	.938	-2	104	73	/2-23,S-2	-0.9
FULLER, HARRY Henry W. B 12.5.1862 Cincinnati, OH D 12.12.1895 Cincinnati, OH 5-8/160# d9.19 b-Shorty																								
1891	StL AA	1	2	0	0	0	0	0	0	0	0	1	.000	.000	.000	-87	0	0	.000	-1	0	0	/3	-0.1
FULLER, JIM James Hardy B 11.28.1950 Bethesda, MD BR/TR 6-3/215# d9.10																								
1973	Bal A	9	26	2	3	0	0	2	4	1-0	0	17	.115	.148	.346	36	-3	0-0	1.000	2	161	396	/O-5(RF),1-2,D	-0.1
1974	Bal A	64	189	17	42	11	0	7	28	8-2	3	68	.222	.265	.392	90	-3	1-0	.960	1	109	75	O-59(4-0-56)/1-4,D-2	-0.5
1977	Hou N	34	100	5	16	6	0	2	9	10-1	1	45	.160	.243	.280	44	-8	0-1	.983	4	102	285	O-27(26-0-1)/1	-0.6
Total	3	107	315	24	61	17	0	11	41	19-3	4	130	.194	.249	.352	70	-14	1-1	.969	7	109	160	/O-91(30-0-62),1-7,D-3	-1.2
FULLER, JOHN John Edward B 1.29.1950 Lynwood, CA BL/TL 6-2/180# d5.9																								
1974	Atl N	3	3	1	1	0	0	0	0	0-0	0	0	.333	.333	.333	83	0	0-0	1.000	0	337	0	/O(CF)	0.0
FULLER, VERN Vernon Gordon B 3.1.1944 Menomonie, WI BR/TR 6-1/170# d9.5																								
1964	Cle A	2	1	0	0	0	0	0	0	0-0	0	0	.000	.000	.000	-99	0	0-0	—	0			H	0.0
1966	Cle A	16	47	7	11	2	1	2	2	7-0	2	6	.234	.357	.447	129	2	0-0	1.000	-2	76	153	2-16	0.2
1967	Cle A	73	206	18	46	10	0	7	21	19-0	4	55	.223	.300	.374	98	0	2-3	.986	-3	92	114	2-64/S-2	0.2
1968	Cle A	97	244	14	59	8	2	0	18	24-2	4	49	.242	.316	.291	87	-3	2-2	.988	-18	83	79	2-73,3-23/S-4	-1.9
1969	Cle A	108	254	25	60	11	1	4	22	20-2	2	53	.236	.295	.335	74	-9	2-1	.978	6	94	101	*2-102/3-7	0.3
1970	Cle A	29	33	3	6	2	0	1	2	3-0	0	9	.182	.250	.333	57	-2	0-0	.919	-1	78	80	2-16/3-4,1	-0.3
Total	6	325	785	67	182	33	4	14	65	73-4	12	172	.232	.305	.338	87	-12	6-6	.982	-17	89	101	2-271/3-34,S-6,1	-1.5
FULLER, SHORTY William Benjamin B 10.10.1867 Cincinnati, OH D 4.11.1904 Cincinnati, OH BR/TR 5-6/157# d7.19 b-Harry																								
1888	Was N	49	170	11	31	5	2	0	12	10	1	14	.182	.232	.235	53	-9	6	.845	-2	103	101	S-47/2-2	-0.9
1889	StL AA	**140**	517	91	117	18	6	0	51	52	5	56	.226	.303	.284	60	-29	38	**.913**	-2	93	101	*S-140	-2.3
1890	StL AA	130	526	118	146	9	9	1	40	73	11		.278	.377	.335	96	-3	60	.870	-0	92	105	*S-130	0.1
1891	StL AA	135	576	105	122	14	7	2	61	67	4	28	.212	.298	.271	55	-37	42	.857	-4	96	111	*S-102,2-38	-3.2
1892	NY N	141	508	74	116	11	4	1	48	52	0	24	.228	.300	.272	74	-15	37	.888	3	94	88	*S-141	-0.5
1893	NY N	130	474	78	112	14	8	0	51	60	2	21	.236	.325	.300	66	-23	26	.911	9	103	91	*S-130	-0.6
1894	†NY N	95	377	82	104	14	4	2	47	52	2	16	.276	.367	.350	74	-15	32	.881	-11	91	108	*S-91/O-2(RF),3-2,2	-1.6
1895	NY N	126	458	82	103	11	3	0	32	64	2	34	.225	.323	.262	53	-30	15	.913	33	114	114	*S-126	0.8
1896	NY N	18	72	10	12	0	0	0	7	14	1	5	.167	.310	.167	28	-7	4	.874	0	100	103	S-18	-0.5
Total	9	964	3678	651	863	96	43	6	349	444	28	198	.235	.322	.289	67	-168	260	.890	26	98	102	S-925/2-41,3-2,O-2(RF)	-8.7
FULLIS, CHICK Charles Philip B 2.27.1904 Girardville, PA D 3.28.1946 Ashland, PA BR/TR 5-9/170# d4.13																								
1928	NY N	11	1	5	0	0	0	0	0	1	0	1	.000	.500	.000	41	0	0	—	0			H	0.0
1929	NY N	86	274	67	79	11	1	7	29	30	3	26	.288	.365	.412	92	-3	7	.962	-9	84	48	O-78(33-46-1)	-1.5
1930	NY N	13	6	2	0	0	0	0	0	0	0	1	.000	.000	.000	-99	-2	1	—	-0	0	0	/O-2(1-1-0)	-0.2
1931	NY N	89	302	61	99	15	2	3	28	23	4	13	.328	.383	.421	119	9	13	.988	-4	90	97	O-68(1-65-0)/2-9	0.3
1932	NY N	96	235	35	70	14	3	1	21	11	1	12	.298	.332	.396	97	-1	1	.990	-4	91	31	O-55(36-19-0)/2	-0.7
1933	Phi N	151	647	91	200	31	6	1	45	36	5	34	.309	.350	.380	96	-2	18	.977	2	100	140	*O-151(CF)/3	-0.3
1934	Phi N	28	102	8	23	6	0	0	12	10	1	4	.225	.301	.284	51	-7	2	.956	-2	89	65	O-27(24-3-0)	-0.9
	†StL N	69	199	21	52	9	1	0	26	14	0	11	.261	.310	.317	64	-10	4	.969	-2	99	57	O-56(8-48-0)	-1.3
	Year	97	301	29	75	15	1	0	38	24	1	15	.249	.307	.306	59	-17	6	.966	-3	96	59	O-83(32-51-0)	-2.2
1936	StL N	47	89	15	25	6	1	0	6	7	0	11	.281	.333	.371	90	-1	0	1.000	2	109	115	O-26(2-15-9)	0.0
Total	8	590	1855	305	548	92	14	12	167	132	14	113	.295	.347	.380	92	-17	46	.977	-16	95	91	O-463(105-348-10)/2-10,3	-4.6
FULLMER, BRAD Bradley Ryan B 1.17.1975 Chatsworth, CA BL/TR 6-1/185# d9.2																								
1997	Mon N	19	40	4	12	2	0	3	8	2-1	1	7	.300	.349	.575	137	2	0-0	.982	0	138	116	/1-8,O-2(LF)	0.1
1998	Mon N	140	505	58	138	44	2	13	73	39-4	2	70	.273	.327	.446	103	2	6-6	.985	-7	86	79	*1-137	-1.8
1999	Mon N	100	347	38	96	34	2	9	47	22-6	2	35	.277	.321	.464	99	-1	2-3	.991	-8	67	66	1-94	-1.8
2000	Tor A	133	482	76	142	29	1	32	104	30-3	6	68	.295	.340	.558	119	12	3-1	1.000	0	683	0	*D-129/1	0.4
2001	Tor A	146	522	71	143	31	2	18	83	38-8	6	88	.274	.326	.444	99	-1	5-2	1.000	0	158	131	*D-135/1	-0.9
2002	†Ana A	130	429	75	124	35	6	19	59	32-6	15	44	.289	.357	.531	133	20	10-3	.995	-3	51	122	D-94,1-29	0.9
2003	Ana A	63	206	32	63	9	2	9	35	26-4	2	31	.306	.387	.500	137	12	5-4	1.000	-0	92	123	D-41,1-19	0.7
Total	7	731	2531	354	718	184	15	103	409	189-32	34	343	.284	.339	.490	113	46	31-19	.989	-18	79	83	D-399,1-289/O-2(LF)	-2.4
FULMER, CHICK Charles John B 2.12.1851 Philadelphia, PA D 2.15.1940 Philadelphia, PA BR/TR 6/158# d8.23 U1 b-Washington																								
1871	Rok NA	16	63	11	17	1	3	0	3	5		1	.270	.324	.381	106	1	0-0	.770	2	110	107	S-16/1	0.1
1872	Mut NA	36	165	29	50	1	1	1	15	3		3	.303	.315	.339	108	2	1-1	.752	-5	75	81	3-22,S-14	-0.3
1873	Phi NA	49	236	42	66	11	3	1	38	2		4	.280	.286	.364	88	-4	3-1	.801	18	**123**	**144**	*S-49/P-2,C1	0.9
1874	Phi NA	57	258	49	72	3	2	0	37	2		5	.279	.285	.306	86	-5	0-2	.793	3	109	127	S-32,3-25	-0.3
1875	Phi NA	69	295	50	65	6	1	0	24	0		6	.220	.220	.247	60	-12	10-4	.835	-2	99	74	*S-53,3-17	-1.3
1876	Lou N	66	267	28	73	9	5	1	29	1		10	.273	.276	.356	93	-4		.861	-5	95	104	*S-66	-0.6
1879	Buf N	76	306	30	82	11	5	0	28	5		34	.268	.280	.337	100	-1		.905	18	110	**171**	*2-76	1.9
1880	Buf N	11	44	3	7	0	0	0	1	2		4	.159	.196	.159	21	-4		.882	-1	96	40	2-11	-0.4
1882	Cin AA	79	324	54	91	13	4	0	27	10			.281	.302	.346	112	3		**.897**	-16	85	81	*S-79	-0.9
1883	Cin AA	92	362	52	92	13	5	5	52	12			.254	.278	.359	98	-2		.863	-0	94	**155**	*S-92	0.1
1884	Cin AA	31	114	13	20	2	1	0	8	1	0		.175	.183	.211	27	-9		.786	-8	85	115	S-29/O-2(0-1-1),3	-1.6
	StL AA	1	5	0	0	0	0	0		0	0		.000	.000	.000	-97	-1		.778	-1	69	0	/2	-0.2
	Year	32	119	13	20	2	1	0	8	1	0		.168	.175	.202	22	-10		.786	-9	85	115	S-29/O-2(0-1-1),32	-1.8
Total	5 NA	227	1017	181	270	22	10	2	117	12	0	19	.265	.274	.313	84	-18	14-8	.000	16	109	118	S-164/3-64,P-2,1-2,C	-0.9
Total	6	356	1422	180	365	48	20	6	145	31	0	48	.257	.273	.331	92	-18		.867	-13	91	116	S-266/2-88,O-2(0-1-1),3	-1.7
FULMER, CHRIS Christopher B 7.4.1858 Tamaqua, PA D 11.9.1931 Tamaqua, PA BR/TR 5-8/165# d8.4																								
1884	Was U	48	181	39	50	9	0	0		11			.276	.318	.326	99	-5		.937	2			C-34,O-16(0-7-9)/1-5	-0.1
1886	Bal AA	80	270	54	66	9	3	1	30	48	2		.244	.363	.311	115	8	29	.949	-5			C-68,O-12(6-5-1)/P	0.8
1887	Bal AA	56	201	52	54	11	4	0	32	36	1		.269	.382	.363	115	7	35	.913	-7			C-48/O-8(LF)	0.3
1888	Bal AA	52	166	20	31	5	1	0	10	21	2		.187	.286	.229	67	-5	10	.903	-14			C-45/O-7(2-1-4)	-1.4
1889	Bal AA	16	58	11	15	3	1	0	13	6	1	12	.259	.338	.345	93	0	2	.938	-3	0	0	O-14(0-11-3)/C-2	-0.3
Total	5	252	876	176	216	37	9	1	85	122	6	12	.247	.343	.313	102	5	76	.929	-25			C-197/O-57(16-24-17),1-5,P	-0.7
FULMER, WASHINGTON Washington Fayette B 6.15.1840 Philadelphia, PA D 12.8.1907 Philadelphia, PA d7.19 b-Chick																								
1875	Atl NA	1	4	1	2	0	0	0	1	0		0	.500	.500	.500	285	1	0-0	.750	-0	0	0	/O(CF)	0.0
FULTZ, DAVE David Lewis B 5.29.1875 Staunton, VA D 10.29.1959 DeLand, FL BR/TR 5-11/170# d7.1 OF Total (34-LF 510-CF 10-RF)																								
1898	Phi N	19	55	7	10	2	2	0	5	6	0		.182	.262	.291	61	-3	1	.871	-1	59	244	O-14(8-3-3)/2-3,S	-0.5
1899	Phi N	2	5	0	2	0	0	0	0	0	0		.400	.400	.400	124	0	1	.750	-1	80	0	/2S	-0.1
	Bal N	57	210	31	62	3	2	0	18	13	2		.295	.342	.329	80	-6	17	.940	-7	0	0	O-31(14-14-3),3-20/2-2,1	-1.4
	Year	59	215	31	64	3	2	0	18	13	2		.298	.343	.330	81	-6	18	.940	-8	0	0	O-31(14-14-3),3-20/2-3,S1	-1.5
1901	Phi A	132	561	95	164	17	9	0	52	32	3		.292	.334	.355	87	-11	36	.935	-8	93	0	*O-106(11-95-0),2-18/S-9	-2.1
1902	Phi A	129	506	**109**	153	20	5	1	49	62	2		.302	.381	.368	104	5	44	.961	-9	120	33	*O-114(CF),2-16	-0.9
1903	NY A	79	295	39	66	12	1	0	25	25	5		.224	.295	.271	67	-11	29	.933	-2	131	97	O-77(1-73-3)/3-2	-1.7
1904	NY A	97	339	39	93	17	4	2	32	24	1		.274	.324	.366	113	5	17	.976	1	80	84	O-90(CF)	0.2
1905	NY A	129	422	49	98	13	3	0	42	39	7		.232	.308	.277	77	-10	44	.966	-7	30	65	*O-122(0-121-1)	-2.5
Total	7	644	2393	369	648	84	26	3	223	201	20		.271	.332	.331	89	-31	189	.952	-34	82	53	O-554C/2-40,3-22,S-11,1	-9.0

Year	Tm Lg	G	AB	R	H	2B	3B	HR	RBI	BB-IB	HP	SO	AVG	OBP	SLG	AOPS	ABR	SB-CS	FA	FR	Rng	Thr	G at Pos	BFW
FUNDERBURK, MARK Mark Clifford B 5.16.1957 Charlotte, NC BR/TR 6-4/226# d9.4																								
1981	Min A	8	15	2	3	1	0	0	2	2-0	0	1	.200	.278	.267	59	-1	0-0	1.000	-1	39	302	/O-6(LF),D	-0.2
1985	Min A	23	70	7	22	7	1	2	13	5-0	0	12	.314	.351	.529	132	3	0-1	1.000	-0	102	0	D-15/O-5(LF),1	0.2
Total	2	31	85	9	25	8	1	2	15	7-0	0	13	.294	.337	.482	120	2	0-1	1.000	-1	65	178	/D-16,O-11(LF),1	0.0
FUNK, LIZ Elias Calvin B 10.28.1904 LaCygne, KS D 1.16.1968 Norman, OK BL/TL 5-8.5/160# d4.26																								
1929	NY A	1	0	0	0	0	0	0	0	0	0	0	—	—	—	—	0	0-0	—	0			R	0.0
1930	Det A	140	527	74	145	26	11	4	65	29	5	39	.275	.319	.389	77	-20	12-6	.965	1	102	86	*O-129(0-128-1)	-2.2
1932	Chi A	122	440	59	114	21	5	2	40	43	0	19	.259	.325	.343	78	-14	17-15	.979	6	101	**156**	*O-120(4-115-1)	-1.2
1933	Chi A	10	9	1	2	0	0	0	0	1	0	0	.222	.300	.222	42	-1	0-0	—	-0	0	0	/O-2(1-1-0)	-0.1
Total	4	273	976	134	261	47	16	6	105	73	5	58	.267	.322	.367	77	-35	29-21	.972	7	101	119	O-251(5-244-2)	-3.5
FURCAL, RAFAEL Rafael B 8.24.1980 Loma De Cabrera, D.R. BB/TR 5-10/150# d4.4																								
2000	†Atl N	131	455	87	134	20	4	4	37	73-0	3	80	.295	.394	.382	98	2	40-14	.950	5	104	98	*S-110,2-31	1.8
2001	Atl N	79	324	39	89	19	0	4	30	24-1	1	56	.275	.321	.370	78	-10	22-6	.970	0	98	108	S-79	-0.1
2002	†Atl N	154	636	95	175	31	8	8	47	43-0	3	114	.275	.323	.387	89	-15	27-15	.963	10	105	**123**	*S-150/2-4	0.8
2003	†Atl N★	156	664	130	194	35	**10**	15	61	60-2	3	76	.292	.352	.443	106	5	25-2	.959	4	106	112	*S-155	2.6
Total	4	520	2079	351	592	105	22	31	175	200-3	10	326	.285	.348	.401	95	-18	114-37	.960	20	104	112	S-494/2-35	5.1
FURILLO, CARL Carl Anthony "Skoonj" or "The Reading Rifle" B 3.8.1922 Stony Creek Mills, PA D 1.21.1989 Stony Creek Mills, PA BR/TR 6/190# d4.16																								
1946	Bro N	117	335	29	95	18	6	3	35	31	1	20	.284	.346	.400	110	4	6	.984	9	**117**	102	*O-112(5-103-4)	1.0
1947	†Bro N	124	437	61	129	24	7	8	88	34	1	24	.295	.347	.437	103	1	7	.977	1	101	111	*O-121(28-93-2)	-0.2
1948	Bro N	108	364	55	108	20	4	4	44	43	2	32	.297	.374	.407	108	5	6	.983	7	106	**178**	*O-104(0-96-12)	0.9
1949	†Bro N	142	549	95	177	27	10	18	106	37	3	29	.322	.368	.506	127	19	4	.965	2	105	102	*O-142(RF)	1.6
1950	Bro N	153	620	99	189	30	6	18	106	41	5	40	.305	.353	.460	110	7	8	.971	0	93	**164**	*O-153(RF)	0.3
1951	Bro N	**158**	667	93	197	32	4	16	91	43	7	33	.295	.344	.427	104	3	8-7	.986	12	107	**165**	*O-157(RF)	1.0
1952	†Bro N☆	134	425	52	105	18	1	8	59	31	4	33	.247	.304	.351	80	-12	1-4	.988	2	103	111	*O-131(RF)	-1.5
1953	†Bro N☆	132	479	82	165	38	6	21	92	34	4	32	**.344**	.393	.580	146	32	1-1	.988	1	97	117	*O-131(RF)	2.7
1954	Bro N	150	547	56	161	23	1	19	96	49	5	35	.294	.356	.444	104	4	2-4	.972	4	111	79	*O-149(3-5-145)	0.1
1955	†Bro N	140	523	83	164	24	3	26	95	43-5	7	43	.314	.371	.520	130	23	4-5	.981	-3	96	87	*O-140(6-1-139)	1.3
1956	†Bro N	149	523	66	151	30	0	21	83	57-15	1	41	.289	.357	.467	111	10	1-1	.984	-7	89	82	*O-146(9-3-143)	-0.3
1957	Bro N	119	395	61	121	17	4	12	66	29-4	5	33	.306	.358	.461	108	5	0-2	.988	-5	87	100	*O-107(1-0-106)	-0.4
1958	LA N	122	411	54	119	19	3	18	83	35-2	2	28	.290	.343	.482	113	7	0-2	.975	-9	89	55	*O-119(1-7-116)	-0.7
1959	†LA N	50	93	8	27	4	0	0	13	7-2	0	11	.290	.333	.333	75	-3	0-0	.920	-3	77	0	O-25(RF)	-0.6
1960	LA N	8	10	1	2	0	1	0	1	0-0	0	2	.200	.200	.400	56	-1	0-0	1.000	-0	103	0	/O-2(RF)	-0.1
Total	15	1806	6378	895	1910	324	56	192	1058	514-28	47	436	.299	.355	.458	112	104	48-26	.979	11	100	111	*O-1739(53-308-1408)	5.1
FUSSELBACK, EDDIE Edward L. B 7.17.1856 Philadelphia, PA D 4.14.1926 Philadelphia, PA BR 5-6/156# d5.3 ▲																								
1882	StL AA	35	136	13	31	2	0	0		5			.228	.255	.243	66	-5		.853	2			C-19,O-15(4-0-11)/P-4	-0.1
1884	Bal U	68	303	60	86	16	3	1		3			.284	.291	.366	89	-13		.912	14			C-54/3-6,S-5,O-4(1-2-1)	0.5
1885	Phi AA	5	19	2	6	1	0	0	2	0	0		.316	.316	.368	109	0		.911	0			/C-5	0.1
1888	Lou AA	1	4	0	1	0	0	0	1	0	0		.250	.250	.250	62	0	0	1.000	1	769	0	/O(RF)	0.0
Total	4	109	462	75	124	19	3	1	3	8	0		.268	.281	.329	84	-18	0	.901	16			/C-78,O-20(5-2-13),3-6,S-5,P-4	0.5
FUSSELMAN, LES Lester Leroy B 3.7.1921 Pryor, OK D 5.21.1970 Cleveland, OH BR/TR 6-1/195# d4.16																								
1952	StL N	32	63	5	10	3	0	1	3	0	0	9	.159	.159	.254	13	-8	0-0	.991	2	*145*	*90*	C-32	-0.5
1953	StL N	11	8	1	2	1	0	0	0	0	0	0	.250	.250	.375	60	0	0-0	1.000	1	*91*	*181*	C-11	0.1
Total	2	43	71	6	12	4	0	1	3	0	0	9	.169	.169	.268	18	-8	0-0	.992	3	*137*	*104*	/C-43	-0.4
GABLER, BILL William Louis "Gabe" B 8.4.1930 St.Louis, MO BL/TR 6-1/190# d9.16																								
1958	Chi N	3	3	0	0	0	0	0	0	0-0	0	3	.000	.000	.000	-99	-1	0-0	—	0			H	-0.1
GABRIELSON, LEN Leonard Gary B 2.14.1940 Oakland, CA BL/TR 6-4/210# d9.9 f-Len																								
1960	Mil N	4	3	1	0	0	0	0	0	1-0	0	0	.000	.250	.000	-27	-1	0-0	—	-0	0	0	/O(LF)	-0.1
1963	Mil N	46	120	14	26	5	0	3	15	8-1	0	23	.217	.264	.333	72	-4	1-1	1.000	-1	106	0	O-22(18-6-1),1-16/3-3	-0.7
1964	Mil N	24	38	0	7	2	0	0	1	1-0	0	8	.184	.205	.237	24	-4	1-0	1.000	-1	51	193	1-12/O-2(RF)	-0.5
	Chi N	89	272	22	67	11	2	5	23	19-1	1	37	.246	.298	.357	80	-7	9-4	.984	0	98	107	O-68(1-12-58)/1-8	-1.1
	Year	113	310	22	74	13	2	5	24	20-1	1	45	.239	.287	.342	74	-11	10-4	.984	-1	98	105	O-70(1-12-60),1-20	-1.6
1965	Chi N	28	48	4	12	0	0	3	5	7-2	0	16	.250	.345	.438	116	1	0-2	1.000	-1	84	0	O-14(0-2-12)/1	-0.1
	SF N	88	269	36	81	6	5	4	26	26-5	2	48	.301	.365	.405	114	5	4-0	.975	1	97	80	O-77(70-0-9)/1-5	0.3
	Year	116	317	40	93	6	5	7	31	33-7	2	64	.293	.362	.410	114	6	4-2	.977	-0	96	71	O-91(70-2-21)/1-6	0.2
1966	SF N	94	240	27	52	7	0	4	16	21-3	0	51	.217	.278	.296	58	-13	0-1	.948	-4	84	30	O-67(61-0-9)/1-6	-2.2
1967	Cal A	11	12	2	1	0	0	0	2	2-0	0	4	.083	.214	.083	-9	-2	0-0	—	-0	0	0	/O(LF)	-0.2
	LA N	90	238	20	62	10	3	7	29	15-3	1	41	.261	.307	.416	114	3	3-1	.980	1	94	188	O-68(47-1-26)	0.2
1968	LA N	108	304	38	82	16	1	10	35	32-4	0	47	.270	.337	.428	140	15	1-1	.976	0	96	120	O-86(57-0-30)	1.1
1969	LA N	83	178	13	48	5	1	1	18	12-1	0	25	.270	.313	.326	86	-4	1-2	.981	-4	78	40	O-47(13-0-34)/1-2	-1.1
1970	LA N	43	42	1	8	2	0	0	6	1-0	0	15	.190	.205	.238	20	-5	0-0	1.000	0	82	0	/O-2(RF),1	-0.5
Total	9	708	1764	178	446	64	12	37	176	145-20	4	315	.253	.309	.366	94	-16	20-12	.977	-9	93	92	O-455(269-21-183)/1-51,3-3	-4.9
GABRIELSON, LEN Leonard Hilbourne B 9.8.1915 Oakland, CA D 11.14.2000 Stanford, CA BL/TL 6-3/210# d4.21 s-Len																								
1939	Phi N	5	18	3	4	0	0	0	1	2	0	3	.222	.300	.222	43	-1	0	.977	2	289	66	/1-5	0.0
GAEDEL, EDDIE Edward Carl (born Edward Carl Gaedele) B 6.8.1925 Chicago, IL D 6.18.1961 Chicago, IL BR/TL 3-7/ 65# d8.19																								
1951	StL A	1	0	0	0	0	0	0	0	1	0	0	—	1.000	—	182	0	0-0	—	0			H	0.0
GAETTI, GARY Gary Joseph B 8.19.1958 Centralia, IL BR/TR 6/200# d9.20 OF Total (13-LF 1-RF)																								
1981	Min A	9	26	4	5	0	0	2	3	0-0	0	6	.192	.192	.423	68	-1	0-0	1.000	2	125	76	/3-8,D	0.0
1982	Min A	145	508	59	117	25	4	25	84	37-2	3	107	.230	.280	.443	94	-6	0-4	.963	-6	93	115	*3-142/S-2,D	-1.6
1983	Min A	157	584	81	143	30	3	21	78	54-2	4	121	.245	.309	.414	95	-5	7-1	.967	9	103	**124**	*3-154/S-3,D	0.3
1984	Min A	**162**	588	55	154	29	4	5	65	44-1	4	81	.262	.315	.350	81	-15	11-5	.960	15	111	95	*3-154/O-8(LF),S-2	-0.2
1985	Min A	160	560	71	138	31	0	20	63	37-3	7	89	.246	.301	.409	87	-10	13-5	.962	18	**110**	113	*3-156/O-4(LF),1D	0.6
1986	Min A	157	596	91	171	34	1	34	108	52-4	6	108	.287	.347	.518	129	24	14-15	.956	17	**112**	**128**	*3-156/S-2,2O(LF)	3.5
1987	†Min A	154	584	95	150	36	2	31	109	37-7	3	92	.257	.303	.485	101	-1	10-7	.973	1	93	99	*3-150/D-2	-0.2
1988	Min A★	133	468	66	141	29	2	28	88	36-5	5	85	.301	.353	.551	146	28	7-4	.977	-1	88	132	*3-115/S-2,D-5	2.7
1989	Min A★	130	498	63	125	11	4	19	75	25-5	3	87	.251	.286	.404	88	-11	6-2	.973	9	102	110	*3-125/1-2,D-3	-0.1
1990	Min A	154	577	61	132	27	5	16	85	36-1	3	101	.229	.274	.376	76	-20	6-1	.959	9	**107**	**133**	*3-151/1-2,S-2	-1.0
1991	Cal A	152	586	58	144	22	1	18	66	33-3	8	104	.246	.293	.379	85	-14	5-5	.965	16	105	139	*3-152	0.2
1992	Cal A	130	456	41	103	13	2	12	48	21-4	6	79	.226	.267	.342	70	-21	3-1	.927	14	117	161	3-67,1-44,D-17	-1.0
1993	Cal A	20	50	3	9	2	0	0	4	5-0	0	12	.180	.250	.220	28	-5	1-0	.857	-1	92	213	/3-7,1-6,D-5	-0.6
	KC A	82	281	37	72	18	1	14	46	16-0	8	75	.256	.309	.477	103	0	0-3	.974	10	113	132	3-72,1-18/D	0.8
	Year	102	331	40	81	20	1	14	50	21-0	8	87	.245	.300	.438	92	-5	1-3	.970	9	112	135	3-79,1-24/D-6	0.2
1994	KC A	90	327	53	94	15	3	12	57	19-3	2	63	.287	.328	.462	97	-3	0-2	**.982**	10	113	121	3-85/1-9	0.7
1995	KC A	137	514	76	134	27	0	35	96	47-6	8	91	.261	.329	.518	115	10	3-3	.954	-1	101	104	*3-123,1-11/D-6	0.8
1996	†StL N	141	522	71	143	27	4	23	80	35-6	8	97	.274	.326	.473	110	5	2-2	.970	-15	90	83	*3-133,1-14	-0.9
1997	StL N	148	502	63	126	24	1	17	69	36-3	6	88	.251	.305	.404	86	-12	7-3	**.978**	6	107	115	*3-132,1-20/P	-0.5
1998	StL N	91	306	39	81	23	1	11	43	31-1	5	39	.265	.339	.454	108	4	1-1	.985	-3	102	105	3-83/1-3,P20(RF)	0.1
	†Chi N	37	128	21	41	11	0	8	27	12-1	5	23	.320	.397	.594	152	10	0-0	.979	2	109	33	3-36	1.2
	Year	128	434	60	122	34	1	19	70	43-2	10	62	.281	.356	.495	121	14	1-1	**.983**	-1	104	83	*3-119/1-3,P20(RF)	1.3
1999	Chi N	113	280	22	57	9	1	9	46	21-0	2	51	.204	.260	.339	52	-22	0-1	.962	3	112	72	3-81/1-8,SP	-1.8
2000	Bos A	5	10	0	0	0	0	0	1	0-0	0	3	.000	.000	.000	-97	-3	0-0	—	0			/D-5	-0.3
Total	20	2507	8951	1130	2280	443	39	360	1341	634-57	96	1602	.255	.308	.434	97	-68	96-65	.965	114	104	114	*3-2282,1-138/D-48,O-14L,S-14,P2	2.7
GAFFKE, FABIAN Fabian Sebastian B 8.5.1913 Milwaukee, WI D 2.8.1992 Milwaukee, WI BR/TR 5-10/185# d9.9																								
1936	Bos A	15	55	5	7	2	0	1	3	4	1	5	.127	.200	.218	3	-9	0-0	1.000	-0	94	87	O-15(5-0-10)	-0.9
1937	Bos A	54	184	32	53	10	4	6	34	15	0	25	.288	.342	.484	102	-1	1-2	.965	-1	96	81	O-50(16-1-33)	-0.5
1938	Bos A	15	10	2	1	0	0	0	1	3	0	2	.100	.308	.100	6	-1	0-0	—	0	0	0	/O-2(RF),C	-0.1
1939	Bos A	1	1	0	0	0	0	0	1	0	0	0	.000	.000	.000	-96	0	0-0	—	0			H	0.0

Year	Tm Lg	G	AB	R	H	2B	3B	HR	RBI	BB-IB	HP	SO	AVG	OBP	SLG	AOPS	ABR	SB-CS	FA	FR	Rng	Thr	G at Pos	BFW
1941	Cle A	4	4	0	1	0	0	0	0	2	0	2	.250	.500	.250	109	0	0-0	1.000	-0	84	0	/O-2(CF)	0.0
1942	Cle A	40	67	4	11	2	0	0	3	6	1	13	.164	.243	.194	25	-7	1-0	1.000	-0	111	0	O-16(5-1-10)	-0.8
Total	6	129	321	43	73	14	4	7	42	30	2	47	.227	.297	.361	67	-18	2-2	.979	-2	98	66	/O-85(26-4-55),C	-2.3
GAGLIANO, PHIL Philip Joseph B 12.27.1941 Memphis, TN BR/TR 6-1/185# d4.16 b-Ralph OF Total (34-LF 31-RF)																								
1963	StL N	10	5	1	2	0	0	0	1	1-0	0	1	.400	.500	.400	149	0	0-0	1.000	1	91	0	/2-3,3	0.1
1964	StL N	40	58	5	15	4	0	1	9	3-0	0	10	.259	.290	.379	81	-1	0-1	.918	1	124	105	2-12/O-2(1-0-1),13	0.0
1965	StL N	122	363	46	87	14	2	8	53	40-0	1	45	.240	.312	.355	81	-8	2-1	.960	-11	87	95	2-57,O-25(4-0-23),3-19	-1.7
1966	StL N	90	213	23	54	8	2	2	15	24-1	1	29	.254	.329	.338	86	-3	2-1	.982	-2	90	95	3-41/1-8,O-5(LF),2	-0.7
1967	†StL N	73	217	20	48	7	0	2	21	19-3	1	26	.221	.283	.281	64	-10	0-0	.972	-11	80	64	2-27,3-25/1-4,S-2	-2.1
1968	†StL N	53	105	13	24	4	2	0	13	7-0	1	12	.229	.281	.305	77	-3	0-0	.982	-1	96	90	2-17,3-10/O-5(4-0-1)	-0.4
1969	StL N	62	128	7	29	2	0	1	10	14-0	0	12	.227	.303	.266	60	-7	0-0	.989	-0	82	104	2-20/1-9,3-9,O-2(RF)	-0.7
1970	StL N	18	32	0	6	0	0	0	2	1-0	0	3	.188	.212	.188	8	-4	0-1	1.000	-2	47	119	/3-6,1-3,2-2	-0.6
	Chi N	26	40	5	6	0	0	0	5	5-0	0	5	.150	.244	.150	7	-5	0-0	1.000	-1	106	39	2-16/13	-0.6
	Year	44	72	5	12	0	0	0	7	6-0	0	8	.167	.231	.167	8	-9	0-1	.980	-3	108	50	2-18/3-7,1-4	-1.2
1971	Bos A	47	68	11	22	5	0	0	13	11-0	0	5	.324	.412	.397	123	3	0-0	1.000	-3	78	0	O-11(7-0-4)/2-7,3-4	0.0
1972	Bos A	52	82	9	21	4	1	0	10	10-0	0	13	.256	.333	.329	94	0	1-0	.962	1	144	475	O-12(LF)/3-5,2-4,1-2	0.1
1973	†Cin N	63	69	8	20	2	0	0	7	13-2	0	16	.290	.402	.319	108	2	0-0	.824	-2	79	103	/3-7,2-4,1O(LF)	0.0
1974	Cin N	46	31	2	2	0	0	0	0	15-1	0	7	.065	.370	.065	27	-2	0-0	1.000	-0	0	0	/2-2,13	-0.2
Total	12	702	1411	150	336	50	7	14	159	163-7	4	184	.238	.316	.313	77	-38	5-4	.969	-30	90	82	2-172,3-130/O-63L,1-30,S-2	-6.8
GAGLIANO, RALPH Ralph Michael B 10.8.1946 Memphis, TN BL/TR 5-11/170# d9.21 b-Phil																								
1965	Cle A	1	0	0	0	0	0	0	0	0-0	0	0	—	—	—	—	0	0-0	—	0			R	0.0
GAGNE, GREG Gregory Carpenter B 11.12.1961 Fall River, MA BR/TR 5-11/172# d6.5																								
1983	Min A	10	27	2	3	1	0	0	3	0-0	0	6	.111	.103	.148	-28	-5	0-0	.923	-8	49	33	S-10	-1.2
1984	Min A	2	1	0	0	0	0	0	0	0-0	0	0	.000	.000	.000	-96	0	0-0	—	0			/H	0.0
1985	Min A	114	293	37	66	15	3	2	23	20-0	3	57	.225	.279	.317	60	-16	10-4	.968	3	104	86	*S-106/D-5	-0.3
1986	Min A	156	472	63	118	22	6	12	54	30-0	6	108	.250	.301	.398	87	-10	12-10	.959	-14	92	101	*S-155/2-4	-0.9
1987	†Min A	137	437	68	116	28	7	10	40	25-0	4	84	.265	.310	.430	91	-7	6-6	.970	19	111	102	*S-136/O-4(0-3-1),2D	2.3
1988	Min A	149	461	70	109	20	6	14	48	27-2	7	110	.236	.288	.397	87	-9	15-7	.970	-12	93	94	*S-146/O-2(CF),23	-1.0
1989	Min A	149	460	69	125	29	7	9	48	17-0	2	80	.272	.298	.424	96	-4	11-4	.971	-9	95	76	*S-146/O(CF)	-0.2
1990	Min A	138	388	38	91	22	3	7	38	24-0	1	76	.235	.280	.361	73	-15	8-8	.976	-4	102	77	*S-135/O(CF)D	-1.1
1991	†Min A	139	408	52	108	23	3	8	42	26-0	3	72	.265	.310	.395	90	-6	11-9	.984	4	105	96	*S-137/D	0.7
1992	Min A	146	439	53	108	23	0	7	39	19-0	2	83	.246	.280	.346	72	-17	6-7	.973	19	**109**	106	*S-141	1.1
1993	KC A	159	540	66	151	32	3	10	57	33-1	0	93	.280	.319	.406	89	-9	10-12	**.986**	12	101	99	*S-159	1.2
1994	KC A	107	375	39	97	23	3	7	51	27-0	4	79	.259	.314	.392	78	-13	10-17	.977	13	106	102	*S-106	0.5
1995	KC A	120	430	58	110	25	4	6	49	38-2	2	60	.256	.316	.374	79	-14	3-5	.969	12	**115**	**119**	*S-118/D-2	0.6
1996	†LA N	128	428	48	109	13	2	10	55	50-11	2	93	.255	.333	.364	92	-5	4-2	.966	14	**106**	**113**	*S-127	1.8
1997	LA N	144	514	49	129	20	3	9	57	31-4	4	120	.251	.298	.354	76	-20	2-5	.971	-25	89	71	*S-143	-3.5
Total	15	1798	5673	712	1440	296	50	111	604	367-20	40	1121	.254	.302	.382	82	-150	108-96	.972	26	101	95	*S-1765/D-11,O-8(0-7-1),2-6,3	0.0
GAGNIER, ED Edward James B 4.16.1883 Paris, France D 9.13.1946 Detroit, MI BR/TR 5-9/170# d4.14																								
1914	Bro F	94	337	22	63	12	2	0	25	13	1	24	.187	.219	.234	24	-43	8	.933	-1	93	108	S-88/3-6	-3.9
1915	Bro F	20	50	8	13	1	0	0	4	10	1	5	.260	.393	.280	92	0	2	.930	2	117	114	S-13/2-6	0.2
	Buf F	1	2	0	0	0	0	0	0	0	0	0	.000	.000	.000	-98	-1	0	.800	-1	44	0	/2	-0.1
	Year	21	52	8	13	1	0	0	4	10	1	5	.250	.381	.269	85	-1	2	.930	1	117	114	S-13/2-7	0.1
Total	2	115	389	30	76	13	2	0	29	23	2	29	.195	.244	.239	33	-44	10	.933	1	96	109	S-101/2-7,3-6	-3.8
GAGNON, CHICK Harold Dennis B 9.27.1897 Millbury, MA D 4.30.1970 Wilmington, DE BR/TR 5-7.5/158# d6.27																								
1922	Det A	10	4	2	1	0	0	0	0	0	0	2	.250	.250	.250	32	0	0-0	—	-1	0	0	/S3	-0.1
1924	Was A	4	5	1	1	0	0	0	1	0	0	0	.200	.200	.200	3	-1	0-0	1.000	0	116	0	/S-2	0.0
Total	2	14	9	3	2	0	0	0	1	0	0	2	.222	.222	.222	16	-1	0-0	1.000	-1	97	0	/S-3,3	-0.1
GAINER, DEL Dellos Clinton "Sheriff" B 11.10.1886 Montrose, WV D 1.29.1947 Elkins, WV BR/TR 6/180# d10.2 Mil 1918																								
1909	Det A	2	5	0	1	0	0	0	0	0	0		.200	.200	.200	25	0	0	.929	-0	132	0	/1-2	-0.1
1911	Det A	70	248	32	75	11	4	2	25	20	5		.302	.366	.403	109	3	10	.975	-4	85	107	1-69	-0.2
1912	Det A	52	179	28	43	5	6	0	20	18	3		.240	.320	.335	90	-3	15	.986	-3	76	99	1-50/O(CF)	-0.7
1913	Det A	105	363	47	97	16	8	2	25	30	6	45	.267	.333	.372	108	3	10	.988	-5	82	95	*1-103	-0.5
1914	Det A	1	0	0	0	0	0	0	0	0	0	0	—	—	—	—	0	0	1.000	-0	0	0	/1	0.0
	Bos A	38	84	11	20	9	2	2	13	8	1	14	.238	.312	.464	133	3	2-2	.981	-2	91	44	1-18,2-11/O(CF)	0.1
	Year	39	84	11	20	9	2	2	13	8	1	14	.238	.312	.464	133	3	2-2	.982	-2	88	43	1-19,2-11/O(CF)	0.1
1915	†Bos A	82	200	30	59	5	8	1	29	21	3	31	.295	.371	.415	139	9	7-2	.988	2	114	99	1-56/O-6(0-5-1)	1.1
1916	†Bos A	56	142	14	36	6	0	3	18	10	0	24	.254	.303	.359	98	-1	5	.997	1	107	94	1-48/2-2	-0.1
1917	Bos A	52	172	28	53	10	2	2	19	15	3	21	.308	.374	.424	145	9	1	.989	-1	96	123	1-50	0.8
1919	Bos A	47	118	9	28	6	2	0	13	13	1	15	.237	.318	.322	85	-2	5	.978	-0	98	67	1-21,O-18(LF)	-0.4
1922	StL N	43	97	19	26	7	4	2	23	14	0	6	.268	.360	.485	122	3	0-2	.979	0	91	48	1-26,O-10(6-4-0)	0.1
Total	10	548	1608	218	438	75	36	14	185	149	22	156	.272	.342	.390	113	24	55-6	.985	-11	91	96	1-444/O-36(24-11-1),2-13	0.1
GAINER, JAY Johnathan Keith B 10.8.1966 Panama City, FL BL/TL 6/190# d5.14																								
1993	Col N	23	41	4	7	0	0	3	6	4-0	0	12	.171	.244	.390	57	-3	1-1	.982	-1	40	49	/1-7	-0.5
GAINES, JOE Arnesta Joe B 11.22.1936 Bryan, TX BR/TR 6-1/190# d6.29																								
1960	Cin N	11	15	2	3	0	0	0	1	0-0	0	1	.200	.200	.200	10	-2	0-0	1.000	0	120	0	/O-3(1-1-2)	-0.2
1961	Cin N	5	3	2	0	0	0	0	0	2-0	0	1	.000	.400	.000	18	0	0-0	.500	-0	56	0	/O-3(1-2-0)	-0.1
1962	Cin N	64	52	12	12	3	0	1	7	8-0	0	16	.231	.333	.346	80	-1	0-0	1.000	0	139	0	O-13(11-0-2)	-0.1
1963	Bal A	66	126	24	36	4	1	6	20	20-0	0	39	.286	.381	.476	145	8	2-1	.945	-2	93	0	O-39(34-4-2)	0.4
1964	Bal A	16	26	2	4	0	0	1	2	3-0	0	7	.154	.241	.269	42	-2	0-0	.846	-0	115	0	/O-5(LF)	-0.3
	Hou N	89	307	37	78	9	7	7	34	27-0	2	69	.254	.318	.397	106	2	8-2	.957	-3	96	69	O-81(1-0-81)	-0.6
1965	Hou N	100	229	21	52	8	1	6	31	18-0	3	59	.227	.290	.349	86	-5	4-1	.913	-5	89	30	O-65(26-0-39)	-1.3
1966	Hou N	11	13	4	1	1	0	0	0	3-0	0	5	.077	.250	.154	17	-1	0-0	.500	-1	39	0	/O-3(1-0-2)	-0.2
Total	7	362	771	104	186	25	9	21	95	81-0	5	197	.241	.316	.379	99	-1	14-4	.934	-11	94	40	O-212(80-7-128)	-2.4
GAINEY, TY Telmanch B 12.25.1960 Cheraw, SC BL/TR 6-1/190# d4.24																								
1985	Hou N	13	37	5	6	0	0	0	0	2-0	2	9	.162	.244	.162	16	-4	0-0	.913	-1	97	0	/O-9(0-8-1)	-0.6
1986	Hou N	26	50	6	15	3	1	1	6	6-0	0	19	.300	.375	.460	133	2	3-1	1.000	0	115	0	O-19(7-14-3)	0.3
1987	Hou N	18	24	1	3	0	0	0	1	2-0	0	9	.125	.192	.125	-14	-4	1-0	1.000	1	145	0	/O-6(LF)	-0.4
Total	3	57	111	12	24	3	1	1	7	10-0	2	37	.216	.293	.288	62	-6	4-1	.968	-0	113	0	/O-34(13-22-4)	-0.7
GALAN, AUGIE August John B 5.23.1912 Berkeley, CA D 12.28.1993 Fairfield, CA BB/TR (BL 1943 (part), 44-49) 6/175# d4.29 C1 OF Total (1000-LF 335-CF 38-RF)																								
1934	Chi N	66	192	31	50	6	2	5	22	16	0	15	.260	.317	.391	90	-3	4	.961	-5	86	79	2-43/3-3,S	-0.6
1935	†Chi N	**154**	646	**133**	203	41	11	12	79	87	4	53	.314	.399	.467	131	32	**22**	.978	4	102	106	*O-154(LF)	2.6
1936	Chi N★	145	575	74	152	26	4	8	81	67	3	50	.264	.344	.365	89	-7	16	.987	-0	99	86	*O-145(8-139-0)	-1.1
1937	Chi N	147	611	104	154	24	10	18	78	79	1	48	.252	.339	.412	99	-1	**23**	.980	8	110	84	*O-140(133-6-1)/2-8,S-2	-0.1
1938	†Chi N	110	395	52	113	16	9	6	69	49	2	17	.286	.368	.418	112	7	8	.987	3	98	127	*O-103(LF)	0.5
1939	Chi N	148	549	104	167	36	8	6	71	75	4	26	.304	.392	.432	119	18	8	.970	-3	98	68	*O-145(LF)	0.7
1940	Chi N	68	209	33	48	14	2	3	22	37	0	23	.230	.346	.359	96	0	9	.984	-0	95	149	O-54(31-24-0)/2-2	-0.2
1941	Chi N	65	120	18	25	3	0	1	13	22	0	10	.208	.331	.258	70	-4	0	.959	-2	85	113	O-31(17-11-4)	-0.7
	†Bro N	17	27	3	7	3	0	0	4	3	0	1	.259	.333	.370	94	0	0	1.000	1	99	279	/O-6(CF)	0.0
	Year	82	147	21	32	6	0	1	17	25	0	11	.218	.331	.279	74	-4	0	.967	-1	87	139	O-37(17-17-4)	-0.7
1942	Bro N	69	209	24	55	16	0	0	22	24	0	12	.263	.339	.340	97	0	2	.990	-2	97	51	O-55(20-26-10)/1-4,2-3	-0.4
1943	Bro N★	139	495	83	142	26	3	9	67	**103**	2	39	.287	.412	.406	136	30	6	.981	10	111	101	*O-124(28-97-0),1-13	3.6
1944	Bro N★	151	547	96	174	43	9	12	93	**101**	2	23	.318	.426	.495	162	51	4	.988	1	103	91	*O-147(126-25-2)/2-2	4.5
1945	Bro N	152	576	114	177	36	7	9	92	114	2	27	.307	.423	.441	142	40	13	.988	-7	78	108	1-66,O-49(LF),3-40	2.6
1946	Bro N	99	274	53	85	22	5	3	38	68	2	21	.310	.451	.460	157	26	8	.935	-5	96	94	O-60(LF),3-19,1-12	1.8
1947	Cin N	124	392	60	123	18	2	6	61	94	2	19	.314	**.449**	.416	132	26	0	.988	-3	102	24	*O-118(118-1-1)	1.4

Year	Tm Lg	G	AB	R	H	2B	3B	HR	RBI	BB-IB	HP	SO	AVG	OBP	SLG	AOPS	ABR	SB-CS	FA	FR	Rng	Thr	G at Pos	BFW
1948	Cin N	54	77	18	22	3	2	2	16	26	1	4	.286	.471	.455	157	9	0	.967	-1	96	0	O-18(1-0-17)	0.7
1949	NY N	22	17	0	1	1	0	0	2	5	0	3	.059	.273	.118	8	-2	0	1.000	-0	0	156	/1-3,O(RF)	-0.2
	Phi A	12	26	4	8	2	0	0	0	9	0	2	.308	.486	.385	136	2	0-0	1.000	-0	107	0	/O-9(7-0-2)	0.2
Total	16	1742	5937	1004	1706	336	74	100	830	979	25	393	.287	.390	.419	122	224	123-0	.981	-4	102	87	*O-1359L/1-98,3-62,2-58,S-3	15.3
GALARRAGA, ANDRES Andres Jose (born Padovani (Galarraga)) B 6.18.1961 Caracas, Venezuela BR/TR 6-3/235# d8.23																								
1985	Mon N	24	75	9	14	1	0	2	4	3-0	1	18	.187	.228	.280	44	-6	1-2	.995	4	166	93	1-23	-0.5
1986	Mon N	105	321	39	87	13	0	10	42	30-5	3	79	.271	.338	.405	105	2	6-5	.995	-11	57	88	*1-102	-1.6
1987	Mon N	147	551	72	168	40	3	13	90	41-13	**10**	127	.305	.361	.459	113	11	7-10	.993	-2	93	89	*1-146	-0.2
1988	Mon N★	157	609	99	**184**	**42**	8	29	92	39-9	10	153	.302	.352	.540	147	35	13-4	.991	-7	87	118	*1-156	2.0
1989	Mon N	152	572	76	147	30	1	23	85	48-10	**13**	158	.257	.327	.434	115	11	12-5	.992	-4	88	98	*1-147	-0.3
1990	Mon N	155	579	65	148	29	0	20	87	40-8	4	169	.256	.306	.409	99	-2	10-1	.993	-8	82	95	*1-154	-2.0
1991	Mon N	107	375	34	82	13	2	9	33	23-5	2	86	.219	.268	.336	70	-17	5-6	.991	3	112	101	*1-105	-2.3
1992	StL N	95	325	38	79	14	2	10	39	11-0	8	69	.243	.282	.391	92	-5	5-4	.991	-3	96	124	1-90	-1.5
1993	Col N★	120	470	71	174	35	4	22	98	24-12	6	73	**.370**	.403	.602	143	29	2-4	.990	7	122	85	*1-119	2.4
1994	Col N	103	417	77	133	21	0	31	85	19-8	8	93	.319	.356	.592	123	13	8-3	.992	-5	83	94	*1-103	-0.1
1995	†Col N	143	554	89	155	29	3	31	106	32-6	13	146	.280	.331	.511	92	-6	12-2	.991	3	111	107	*1-142	-1.4
1996	Col N	159	626	119	190	39	3	**47**	**150**	40-3	17	157	.304	.357	.601	120	17	18-8	.992	-2	99	108	*1-159/3	0.1
1997	Col N★	154	600	120	191	31	3	41	**140**	54-2	17	141	.318	.389	.585	123	21	15-8	.991	-5	98	**131**	*1-154	0.2
1998	†Atl N★	153	555	103	169	27	1	44	121	63-11	25	146	.305	.397	.595	157	47	7-6	.992	-7	79	108	*1-149/D-2	2.5
2000	†Atl N★	141	494	67	149	25	1	28	100	36-5	17	126	.302	.369	.526	122	16	3-5	.988	-8	79	106	*1-132/D	-0.4
2001	Tex A	72	243	33	57	16	0	10	34	18-1	9	68	.235	.310	.424	88	-4	1-0	.995	0	101	112	D-39,1-25	-0.9
	SF N	49	156	17	45	12	1	7	35	13-1	3	49	.288	.351	.513	130	7	0-3	.984	-5	58	130	1-41	-0.2
2002	Mon N	104	292	30	76	12	0	9	40	30-6	9	81	.260	.344	.394	91	-5	2-2	.981	2	116	87	1-89	-1.1
2003	†SF N	110	272	36	82	15	0	12	42	19-1	2	61	.301	.352	.489	119	7	1-3	.994	-4	74	116	1-69/D-2	-0.4
Total	18	2250	8086	1194	2330	444	32	398	1423	583-106	177	2000	.288	.347	.499	116	171	128-81	.991	-52	93	104	*1-2105/D-44,3	-5.7
GALATZER, MILT Milton B 5.4.1907 Chicago, IL D 1.29.1976 San Francisco, CA BL/TL 5-10/168# d6.25																								
1933	Cle A	57	160	19	38	2	1	1	17	23	0	21	.237	.333	.281	61	-9	2-3	.975	0	95	116	O-40(11-4-25)/1-5	-1.1
1934	Cle A	49	196	29	53	10	2	0	15	21	1	8	.270	.344	.342	76	-7	3-2	.980	1	93	179	O-49(3-0-46)	-0.8
1935	Cle A	93	259	45	78	9	3	0	19	35	2	8	.301	.389	.359	93	-1	4-5	.934	-4	88	118	O-81(8-18-56)	-1.0
1936	Cle A	49	97	12	23	4	1	0	6	13	1	8	.237	.333	.299	57	-7	1-2	.964	-0	98	92	O-42(6-9-27)/P1	-0.7
1939	Cin N	3	5	0	0	0	0	0	0	0	0	1	.000	.000	.000	-99	-1	0	1.000	-0	0	0	/1-2	-0.2
Total	5	251	717	105	192	25	7	1	57	92	4	46	.268	.354	.326	75	-25	10-12	.959	-3	92	131	O-212(28-31-154)/1-8,P	-3.8
GALLAGHER, AL Alan Mitchell Edward George Patrick Henry B 10.19.1945 San Francisco, CA BR/TR 6/180# d4.7																								
1970	SF N	109	282	31	75	15	2	4	28	30-4	0	37	.266	.335	.376	92	-3	2-1	.971	-4	92	83	3-91	-0.7
1971	†SF N	136	429	47	119	18	5	5	57	40-10	2	57	.277	.340	.378	105	3	2-1	.951	-7	93	99	*3-128	-0.5
1972	SF N	82	233	19	52	3	1	2	18	33-4	1	39	.223	.317	.270	69	-9	2-1	.974	-3	92	64	3-69	-1.3
1973	SF N	5	9	1	2	0	0	0	1	0-0	1	0	.222	.300	.222	45	-1	0-0	.833	-1	20	0	/3-5	-0.2
	Cal A	110	311	16	85	6	1	0	26	35-3	1	31	.273	.345	.299	91	-3	1-3	.961	1	99	77	3-98/2S	-0.3
Total	4	442	1264	114	333	42	9	11	130	138-21	5	164	.263	.335	.337	91	-13	7-6	.961	-15	94	83	3-391/S2	-3.0
GALLAGHER, SHORTY Charles William B 4.30.1872 Detroit, MI D 6.23.1924 Detroit, MI d8.13																								
1901	Cle A	2	4	0	0	0	0	0	0	0	0		.000	.000	.000	-99	-1	0	.667	-0	0	0	/O-2(RF)	-0.1
GALLAGHER, DAVE David Thomas B 9.20.1960 Trenton, NJ BR/TR 6/184# d4.12																								
1987	Cle A	15	36	2	4	1	1	0	1	2-0	0	5	.111	.158	.194	-7	-6	2-0	.972	1	106	180	O-14(CF)	-0.5
1988	Chi A	101	347	59	105	15	3	5	31	29-3	0	40	.303	.354	.406	113	6	5-4	1.000	-2	94	109	O-95(5-78-17)/D-2	0.3
1989	Chi A	**161**	601	74	160	22	2	1	46	46-1	2	79	.266	.320	.314	82	-14	5-6	.993	-1	99	93	*O-160(1-138-27)/D	-1.8
1990	Chi A	45	75	5	21	3	1	0	5	3-0	1	9	.280	.316	.347	87	-1	0-1	.981	-1	93	84	O-37(14-22-1)/D-4	-0.3
	Bal A	23	51	7	11	1	0	0	2	4-0	0	3	.216	.268	.235	45	-4	1-1	.980	4	136	202	O-20(17-2-1)/D-2	-0.1
	Year	68	126	12	32	4	1	0	7	7-0	1	12	.254	.296	.302	70	-5	1-2	.980	3	111	132	O-57(31-24-2)/D-6	-0.4
1991	Cal A	90	270	32	79	17	0	1	30	24-0	2	43	.293	.355	.367	100	1	2-4	1.000	3	98	185	O-87(7-61-23)/D-2	0.1
1992	NY N	98	175	20	42	11	1	1	21	19-0	1	16	.240	.307	.331	85	-3	4-5	.982	4	111	149	O-76(22-13-48)	-0.1
1993	NY N	99	201	34	55	12	2	6	28	20-1	0	18	.274	.338	.443	109	2	1-1	1.000	2	99	180	O-72(19-39-20)/1-9	0.3
1994	Atl N	89	152	27	34	5	0	2	14	22-2	1	17	.224	.326	.296	62	-8	0-2	.989	3	120	41	O-77(71-5-7)/1	-0.8
1995	Phi N	62	157	12	50	12	0	1	12	16-0	0	20	.318	.379	.414	109	3	0-0	1.000	-1	102	37	O-55(8-21-28)	0.1
	Cal A	11	16	1	3	1	0	0	0	2-0	0	1	.188	.278	.250	39	-1	0-0	1.000	1	113	483	/O-6(2-3-1),D	0.0
Total	9	794	2081	273	564	100	10	17	190	187-7	7	251	.271	.331	.353	90	-25	20-24	.993	13	102	120	O-699(166-396-173)/D-12,1-10	-2.8
GALLAGHER, JIM James E. B Findlay, OH D 3.29.1894 Scranton, PA d9.4																								
1886	Was N	1	5	1	1	0	0	0	0	0		2	.200	.200	.200	24	0	0	.875	0	140	0	/S	0.0
GALLAGHER, JOHN John Carroll B 2.18.1892 Pittsburgh, PA D 3.30.1952 Norfolk, VA BR/TR 5-10.5/156# d8.20																								
1915	Bal F	40	126	11	25	4	0	0	4	5	0	22	.198	.229	.230	28	-14	1	.945	-1	104	70	2-37/S-5,3	-1.6
GALLAGHER, JACKIE John Laurence B 1.28.1902 Providence, RI D 9.10.1984 Gladwyne, PA BL/TR 5-10/175# d8.24																								
1923	Cle A	1	1	0	1	0	0	0	0	0	0	0	1.000	1.000	1.000	428	0	0-0	—	-0	0	0	/O(LF)	0.0
GALLAGHER, JOE Joseph Emmett "Muscles" B 3.7.1914 Buffalo, NY D 2.25.1998 Houston, TX BR/TR 6-2/210# d4.20 Mil 1941-45																								
1939	NY A	14	41	8	10	0	1	2	9	3	1	8	.244	.311	.439	91	-1	1-0	1.000	0	97	138	O-12(RF)	-0.1
	StL A	71	266	41	75	17	2	9	40	17	1	42	.282	.327	.462	98	-2	0-1	.944	1	96	170	O-67(56-0-11)	-0.5
	Year	85	307	49	85	17	3	11	49	20	2	50	.277	.325	.459	97	-3	1-1	.950	1	96	166	O-79(56-0-23)	-0.6
1940	StL A	23	70	14	19	3	1	2	8	4	0	12	.271	.311	.429	88	-2	2-0	.966	-1	85	95	O-15(LF)	-0.3
	Bro N	57	110	10	29	6	1	3	16	2	1	14	.264	.283	.418	86	-3	1	.941	-1	93	75	O-20(3-0-17)	-0.5
Total	2	165	487	73	133	26	5	16	73	26	3	76	.273	.314	.446	93	-8	4-1	.950	-1	94	142	O-114(74-0-40)	-1.4
GALLAGHER, GIL Lawrence Kirby B 9.5.1896 Washington, DC D 1.6.1957 Washington, DC BB/TR 5-8/155# d9.13																								
1922	Bos N	7	22	1	1	1	0	0	2	1	0	7	.045	.087	.091	-57	-5	0-0	.893	-1	120	0	/S-6	-0.6
GALLAGHER, BOB Robert Collins B 7.7.1948 Newton, MA BL/TL 6-3/185# d5.17 gf-Shano Collins																								
1972	Bos A	7	5	0	0	0	0	0	0	0-0	0	3	.000	.000	.000	-95	-1	0-0	—	0			H	-0.1
1973	Hou N	71	148	16	39	3	1	2	10	3-1	0	27	.264	.275	.338	70	-7	0-1	1.000	2	125	44	O-42(15-12-16)/1	-0.6
1974	Hou N	102	87	13	15	2	0	0	3	12-1	1	23	.172	.280	.195	36	-7	1-0	.978	-1	102	0	O-62(5-4-53)/1-4	-0.9
1975	NY N	33	15	5	2	1	0	0	0	1-0	0	3	.133	.188	.200	8	-2	0-0	.900	0	151	0	O-16(10-1-5)	-0.2
Total	4	213	255	34	56	6	1	2	13	16-2	1	56	.220	.266	.275	52	-17	1-1	.985	2	118	24	O-120(30-17-74)/1-5	-1.8
GALLAGHER, WILLIAM William Howard B 2.4.1874 Boston, MA D 3.11.1950 Worcester, MA d8.19																								
1896	Phi N	14	49	9	15	2	0	0	6	10	1	0	.306	.433	.347	108	2	0	.894	-2	99	87	S-14	0.0
GALLAGHER, BILL William John B Philadelphia, PA TL d5.2 ▲																								
1883	Bal AA	16	61	9	10	3	1	0		3			.164	.203	.246	43	-4		.824	-1	135	508	/O-9(1-0-8),P-7,S-4	-0.3
	Phi N	2	8	1	0	0	0	0	0	0		4	.000	.000	.000	-99	-2		1.000	-0	0	0	/O-2(CF)	-0.2
1884	Phi U	3	11	1	1	0	0	0		0			.091	.091	.091	-48	-2		.800	-0	107	0	/P-3	0.0
Total	2	21	80	11	11	3	1	0	0	3		4	.138	.169	.200	16	-8		.850	-2	113	425	/O-11(1-2-8),P-10,S-4	-0.5
GALLE, STAN Stanley Joseph (born Stanley Joseph Galazewski) B 2.7.1919 Milwaukee, WI BR/TR 5-7/165# d4.14 Mil 1942-45																								
1942	Was A	13	18	3	2	0	0	0	1	1	0	0	.111	.158	.111	-24	-3	0-0	.857	-0	76	0	/3-3	-0.4
GALLEGO, MIKE Michael Anthony B 10.31.1960 Whittier, CA BR/TR 5-8/160# d4.11 C1																								
1985	Oak A	76	77	13	16	5	1	1	9	12-0	1	14	.208	.319	.338	87	-1	1-1	.991	-2	93	133	2-42,S-21,3-12	-0.1
1986	Oak A	20	37	2	10	2	0	0	4	1-0	0	6	.270	.289	.324	72	-1	0-2	.986	5	135	72	2-19/3-2,S	0.3
1987	Oak A	72	124	18	31	6	0	2	14	12-0	1	21	.250	.319	.347	83	-3	0-1	.968	7	116	160	2-31,3-24,S-17	0.6
1988	†Oak A	129	277	38	58	8	0	2	20	34-0	1	53	.209	.298	.260	60	-14	2-3	.993	-12	92	85	2-83,S-42,3-16	-2.3
1989	†Oak A	133	357	45	90	14	2	3	30	35-0	6	43	.252	.327	.328	89	-4	7-5	.967	10	102	136	S-94,2-41/3-3,D	1.2
1990	†Oak A	140	389	36	80	13	2	3	34	35-0	4	50	.206	.277	.272	57	-23	5-5	.990	-2	109	104	2-83,S-38,3-27/O(RF)D	-2.1
1991	Oak A	159	482	67	119	15	4	12	49	67-3	5	84	.247	.343	.369	103	4	6-9	.989	-15	99	81	*2-135,S-55	-0.7

Year	Tm Lg	G	AB	R	H	2B	3B	HR	RBI	BB-IB	HP	SO	AVG	OBP	SLG	AOPS	ABR	SB-CS	FA	FR	Rng	Thr	G at Pos	BFW
1992	NY A	53	173	24	44	7	1	3	14	20-0	4	22	.254	.343	.358	98	0	0-1	.990	1	98	101	2-40,S-14	0.3
1993	NY A	119	403	63	114	20	1	10	54	50-0	4	65	.283	.364	.412	113	9	3-2	.976	**26**	124	123	S-55,2-52,3-27/D	3.9
1994	NY A	89	306	39	73	17	1	6	41	38-1	4	46	.239	.327	.359	81	-8	0-1	.970	16	114	125	S-72,2-26	1.3
1995	Oak A	43	120	11	28	0	0	0	8	9-0	1	24	.233	.292	.233	41	-11	0-1	.960	-1	107	91	2-18,S-14,3-12	-1.0
1996	†StL N	51	143	12	30	2	0	0	4	12-1	1	31	.210	.276	.224	34	-14	0-0	.985	1	101	126	2-43/3-7,S	-1.0
1997	StL N	27	43	6	7	2	0	0	1	1-0	0	6	.163	.178	.209	2	-6	0-0	.962	3	110	99	2-11,S-10/3-7	-0.3
Total	13	1111	2931	374	700	111	12	42	282	326-5	32	465	.239	.320	.328	81	-72	24-31	.986	38	105	103	2-624,S-434,3-137/D-3,0(RF)	0.1
GALLIGAN, JIM James M. B 1862 Easton, PA D 7.17.1901 New York, NY 5-10/160# d9.2																								
1889	Lou AA	31	120	6	20	0	2	0	7	6	1	17	.167	.213	.200	18	-13	1	.915	1	112	62	O-31(LF)	-1.2
GALLOWAY, CHICK Clarence Edward B 8.4.1896 Clinton, SC D 11.7.1969 Clinton, SC BR/TR 5-8/160# d9.9																								
1919	Phi A	17	63	2	9	0	0	0	4	1	0	8	.143	.156	.143	-16	-10	0	.969	2	93	153	S-17	-0.8
1920	Phi A	98	298	28	60	9	3	0	18	22	1	22	.201	.259	.252	35	-29	2-2	.928	3	101	67	S-84/2-4,3-3	-2.0
1921	Phi A	131	465	42	123	28	5	3	47	29	2	43	.265	.310	.366	72	-21	12-7	.922	-25	91	98	*S-110,3-20/2	-3.1
1922	Phi A	**155**	571	83	185	26	9	6	69	39	1	39	.324	.368	.433	105	4	10-19	.952	6	100	95	*S-155	2.1
1923	Phi A	134	504	64	140	18	9	2	62	37	0	30	.278	.327	.361	80	-16	12-10	.944	2	99	105	*S-134	0.0
1924	Phi A	129	464	41	128	16	4	2	48	23	1	23	.276	.311	.341	67	-24	11-12	.952	-4	96	103	*S-129	-1.4
1925	Phi A	149	481	52	116	11	4	3	71	59	0	28	.241	.324	.299	55	-33	16-9	.954	-4	96	105	*S-148	-1.9
1926	Phi A	133	408	37	98	13	6	0	49	31	1	20	.240	.295	.301	53	-29	8-7	.935	-16	85	78	*S-133	-3.2
1927	Phi A	77	181	25	48	10	4	0	22	18	0	9	.265	.332	.365	76	-7	1-3	.946	-1	94	74	S-61/3-7	-0.3
1928	Det A	53	148	17	39	5	2	1	17	15	0	3	.264	.331	.345	77	-5	7-3	.914	-2	84	94	S-22,3-21/1O(LF)	-0.4
Total	10	1076	3583	391	946	136	46	17	407	274	6	225	.264	.317	.342	69	-170	79-72	.943	-39	95	95	S-993/3-51,2-5,O(LF)1	-11.0
GALLOWAY, JIM James Cato "Bad News" B 9.16.1887 Iredell, TX D 5.3.1950 Fort Worth, TX BB/TR 6-3/187# d8.24																								
1912	StL N	21	54	4	10	2	0	0	4	5	0	8	.185	.254	.222	32	-5	2	.971	2	116	91	2-16/S	-0.3
GALVIN, JIM James Joseph B 8.11.1907 Somerville, MA D 9.30.1969 Marietta, GA BR/TR 5-11.5/180# d9.27																								
1930	Bos A	2	2	0	0	0	0	0	0	0	0	0	.000	.000	.000	-99	-1	0-0	—	0			H	-0.1
GALVIN, JOHN John A. B 1842 Brooklyn, NY D 4.20.1904 Brooklyn, NY 5-7/178# d5.7																								
1872	Atl NA	1	4	0	0	0	0	0	0	0		0	.000	.000	.000	-85	-1	0-0	.200	-2	0	0	/2	-0.2
GAMBLE, JOHN John Robert B 2.10.1948 Reno, NV BR/TR 5-10/165# d9.7																								
1972	Det A	6	3	0	0	0	0	0	0	0-0	0	0	.000	.000	.000	-97	-1	0-0	1.000	0	77	0	/S	-0.1
1973	Det A	7	0	1	0	0	0	0	0	0-0	0	0	—	—	—	—	0	0-0	—	0			R	0.0
Total	2	13	3	1	0	0	0	0	0	0-0	0	0	.000	.000	.000	-97	-1	0-0	1.000	0	77	0	/S	-0.1
GAMBLE, LEE Lee Jesse B 6.28.1910 Renovo, PA D 10.5.1994 Punxsutawney, PA BL/TR 6-1/170# d9.15																								
1935	Cin N	2	4	2	2	1	0	0	2	1	0	0	.500	.600	.750	269	1	1	1.000	-0	101	0	/O-2(LF)	0.1
1938	Cin N	53	75	13	24	3	1	0	5	0	0	6	.320	.320	.387	96	-1	0	1.000	0	114	0	/O-9(LF)	-0.1
1939	†Cin N	72	221	24	59	7	2	0	14	9	0	14	.267	.296	.317	64	-12	5	.989	-3	78	150	O-56(55-1-0)	-1.8
1940	Cin N	38	42	12	6	1	0	0	0	0	0	1	.143	.143	.167	-15	-7	0	1.000	1	135	190	O-10(2-0-8)	-0.6
Total	4	165	342	51	91	12	3	0	21	10	0	21	.266	.287	.319	64	-19	6	.993	-2	88	134	/O-77(68-1-8)	-2.4
GAMBLE, OSCAR Oscar Charles B 12.20.1949 Ramer, AL BL/TR 5-11/165# d8.27																								
1969	Chi N	24	71	6	16	1	1	1	5	10-1	0	12	.225	.321	.310	69	-3	0-2	.913	-2	86	76	O-24(1-23-0)	-0.7
1970	Phi N	88	275	31	72	12	4	1	19	27-3	1	37	.262	.330	.345	84	-6	5-4	.956	-1	103	96	O-74(0-47-28)	-1.0
1971	Phi N	92	280	24	62	11	1	6	23	21-2	1	35	.221	.275	.332	72	-11	5-2	.970	-3	91	80	O-80(54-1-26)	-1.9
1972	Phi N	74	135	17	32	5	2	1	13	19-0	1	16	.237	.331	.326	86	-2	0-1	1.000	-0	98	93	O-35(RF)/1	-0.4
1973	Cle A	113	390	56	104	11	3	20	44	34-1	3	37	.267	.329	.464	120	8	3-4	.971	-1	107	46	D-70,O-37(2-1-35)	0.4
1974	Cle A	135	454	74	132	16	4	19	59	48-10	5	51	.291	.363	.469	140	23	5-6	1.000	0	89	138	*D-115,O-13(12-0-1)	1.9
1975	Cle A	121	348	60	91	16	3	15	45	53-4	2	39	.261	.361	.454	130	14	11-5	.987	1	93	144	O-82(81-0-1),D-29	1.1
1976	†NY A	110	340	43	79	13	1	17	57	38-4	4	38	.232	.317	.426	117	7	5-3	.981	2	98	139	*O-104(RF)/D	0.5
1977	Chi A	137	408	75	121	22	2	31	83	54-2	6	54	.297	.386	.588	162	35	1-2	.987	-4	87	35	D-79,O-49(5-7-38)	2.7
1978	SD N	126	375	46	103	15	3	7	47	51-11	6	45	.275	.366	.387	121	12	1-2	.979	2	95	154	*O-107(39-0-70)	1.0
1979	Tex A	64	161	27	54	6	0	8	32	37-11	1	15	.335	.458	.522	167	18	2-1	1.000	2	115	153	D-37,O-21(RF)	1.7
	NY A	36	113	21	44	4	1	11	32	13-1	0	13	.389	.452	.735	219	19	0-0	.943	0	96	164	O-27(25-2-0)/D-6	1.7
	Year	100	274	48	98	10	1	19	64	50-12	1	28	.358	.456	.609	188	36	2-1	.969	2	104	159	O-48(25-2-21),D-43	3.4
1980	†NY A	78	194	40	54	10	2	14	50	28-4	4	21	.278	.376	.567	159	16	2-0	1.000	-2	89	74	O-49(36-0-14),D-20	1.2
1981	†NY A	80	189	24	45	8	0	10	27	35-2	1	23	.238	.357	.439	131	9	0-2	1.000	1	121	0	O-43(16-0-27),D-33	0.7
1982	NY A	108	316	49	86	21	2	18	57	58-2	4	47	.272	.387	.522	151	25	6-3	1.000	5	111	332	D-74,O-29(1-0-28)	2.6
1983	NY A	74	180	26	47	10	2	7	26	25-1	3	23	.261	.361	.456	128	7	0-0	.942	0	113	49	O-32(2-0-30),D-21	0.6
1984	NY A	54	125	17	23	2	0	10	27	25-0	0	18	.184	.318	.440	112	2	1-0	1.000	-1	73	164	D-28,O-12(RF)	0.0
1985	Chi A	70	148	20	30	5	0	4	20	34-3	1	22	.203	.353	.318	83	-2	0-0	—	0	0	0	D-48	-0.3
Total	17	1584	4502	656	1195	188	31	200	666	610-62	43	546	.265	.356	.454	127	171	47-37	.977	1	98	113	O-818(274-81-469),D-561/1	11.8
GAMMONS, DAFF John Ashley B 3.17.1876 New Bedford, MA D 9.24.1963 E.Greenwich, RI BR/TR 5-11/170# d4.23																								
1901	Bos N	28	93	10	18	0	1	0	10	3	3		.194	.242	.215	30	-8	5	.880	-3	203	0	O-23(20-0-3)/2-2,3	-1.2
GANDIL, CHICK Arnold B 1.19.1887 St.Paul, MN D 12.13.1970 Calistoga, CA BR/TR 6-1.5/190# d4.14																								
1910	Chi A	77	275	21	53	7	3	2	21	24	4		.193	.267	.262	69	-10	12	.989	6	130	107	1-74/O-2(LF)	-0.6
1912	Was A	117	443	59	135	20	15	2	81	27	4		.305	.350	.431	122	10	19	**.990**	2	98	91	*1-117	0.9
1913	Was A	148	550	61	175	25	8	1	72	36	3	33	.318	.363	.398	120	13	22	.990	8	**115**	**123**	*1-145	1.8
1914	Was A	145	526	48	136	24	10	3	75	44	7	44	.259	.324	.359	101	0	30-19	.991	23	**156**	**126**	*1-145	2.1
1915	Was A	136	485	53	141	20	15	2	64	29	7	33	.291	.340	.406	121	9	20-13	.986	-1	96	105	*1-134	0.5
1916	Cle A	146	533	51	138	26	9	0	72	36	5	48	.259	.312	.341	91	-7	13	**.995**	8	**118**	99	*1-145	-0.3
1917	†Chi A	149	553	53	151	9	7	0	57	30	5	36	.273	.316	.315	91	-8	16	**.995**	-6	81	103	*1-149	-2.0
1918	Chi A	114	439	49	119	18	4	0	55	27	4	19	.271	.319	.330	95	-4	9	.992	-3	86	107	*1-114	-1.0
1919	†Chi A	115	441	54	128	24	7	1	60	20	3	20	.290	.325	.383	98	-3	10	**.997**	-4	79	124	*1-115	-1.0
Total	9	1147	4245	449	1176	173	78	11	557	273	42	233	.277	.327	.362	103	0	151-32	.992	35	107	110	*1-1138/O-2(LF)	0.4
GANDY, BOB Robert Brinkley "String" B 8.25.1893 Jacksonville, FL D 6.19.1945 Jacksonville, FL BL/TR 6-3/180# d10.5																								
1916	Phi N	1	2	0	0	0	0	0	0	0	0	1	.000	.000	.000	-97	0	0	1.000	0	124	0	/O(CF)	-0.1
GANLEY, BOB Robert Stephen B 4.23.1875 Lowell, MA D 10.9.1945 Lowell, MA BL/TL 5-7/156# d9.1																								
1905	Pit N	32	127	12	40	1	2	0	7	8	0		.315	.356	.354	109	1	3	1.000	-2	76	0	O-32(0-6-27)	-0.2
1906	Pit N	137	511	63	132	7	6	0	31	41	2		.258	.316	.295	87	-8	19	.965	-3	96	137	*O-134(0-12-122)	-1.9
1907	Was A	**154**	605	73	167	10	5	1	35	54	2		.276	.337	.314	117	13	40	.940	7	112	98	*O-154(62-13-78)	1.2
1908	Was A	150	549	61	131	19	9	1	36	45	2		.239	.299	.311	107	4	30	.964	4	74	21	*O-150(LF)	0.0
1909	Was A	19	63	5	16	3	0	0	5	1	0		.254	.266	.302	83	-1	4	1.000	-2	0	0	O-17(11-5-1)	-0.5
	Phi A	80	274	32	54	4	2	0	9	28	0		.197	.272	.226	56	-13	16	.980	4	90	98	O-77(CF)	-1.5
	Year	99	337	37	70	7	2	0	14	29	0		.208	.270	.240	61	-15	20	.982	2	77	84	O-94(11-82-1)	-2.0
Total	5	572	2129	246	540	44	24	2	123	177	6		.254	.313	.300	97	-4	112	.962	9	90	79	O-564(223-113-228)	-2.9
GANNON, BILLY William G. B 1876 New Haven, CT D 4.26.1927 Fort Worth, TX 5-9/170# d9.9																								
1901	Chi N	15	61	2	9	0	0	0	0	1	0		.148	.161	.148	-11	-9	5	1.000	-0	128	0	O-15(RF)	-1.0
GANT, RON Ronald Edwin B 3.2.1965 Victoria, TX BR/TR 6/192# d9.6 OF Total (1184-LF 299-CF 9-RF)																								
1987	Atl N	21	83	9	22	4	0	2	9	1-0	0	11	.265	.271	.386	69	-4	4-2	.972	2	104	131	2-20	-0.1
1988	Atl N	146	563	85	146	28	8	19	60	46-4	3	118	.259	.317	.439	110	6	19-10	.963	4	105	104	*2-122,3-22	1.5
1989	Atl N	75	260	26	46	8	3	9	25	20-0	1	63	.177	.237	.335	61	-15	9-6	.887	-1	102	99	3-53,O-14(2-14-0)	-1.7
1990	Atl N	152	575	107	174	34	3	32	84	50-0	1	86	.303	.357	.539	136	27	33-16	.978	-0	104	84	*O-146(38-113-3)	2.7
1991	†Atl N	154	561	101	141	35	3	32	105	71-8	5	104	.251	.338	.496	125	19	34-15	.983	-8	95	86	*O-148(CF)	1.2
1992	†Atl N★	153	544	74	141	22	6	17	80	45-5	7	101	.259	.321	.415	102	1	32-10	.986	-6	95	73	*O-147(138-23-0)	-0.6
1993	†Atl N	157	606	113	166	27	4	36	117	67-2	2	117	.274	.345	.510	125	20	26-9	.962	-13	89	42	*O-155(LF)	0.3
1995	†Cin N★	119	410	79	113	19	4	29	88	74-5	3	108	.276	.386	.554	146	29	23-8	.985	1	103	106	*O-117(LF)	2.7
1996	†StL N	122	419	74	103	14	2	30	82	73-5	3	98	.246	.359	.504	126	16	13-4	.978	1	106	61	*O-116(LF)	1.4

Year	Tm Lg	G	AB	R	H	2B	3B	HR	RBI	BB-IB	HP	SO	AVG	OBP	SLG	AOPS	ABR	SB-CS	FA	FR	Rng	Thr	G at Pos	BFW
1997	StL N	139	502	68	115	21	4	17	62	58-3	1	162	.229	.310	.388	82	-14	14-6	.977	1	105	49	*O-128(LF)/D	-1.7
1998	StL N	121	383	60	92	17	1	26	67	51-2	2	92	.240	.331	.493	115	7	8-0	.971	-4	89	63	*O-104(LF)	0.1
1999	Phi N	138	516	107	134	27	5	17	77	85-0	1	112	.260	.364	.430	98	-1	13-3	.993	4	102	87	*O-133(LF)/D-2	0.0
2000	Phi N	89	343	54	87	16	2	20	38	36-1	1	73	.254	.324	.487	101	-1	5-4	.968	4	116	80	O-84(LF)	0.0
	Ana A	34	82	15	19	3	1	6	16	20-0	0	18	.232	.379	.512	121	3	1-2	.977	2	127	103	O-21(LF),D-12	0.3
2001	Col N	59	171	31	44	8	2	8	22	24-2	0	56	.257	.345	.468	89	-3	3-1	.965	-1	102	67	O-51(LF)	-0.5
	†Oak A	34	81	15	21	5	1	2	13	11-0	0	24	.259	.344	.420	101	0	2-0	1.000	-3	24	0	D-20,O-11(LF)	-0.4
2002	SD N	102	309	58	81	14	1	18	59	36-1	2	59	.262	.338	.489	131	11	4-6	.980	4	108	137	O-80(78-1-5)/D-4	1.1
2003	Oak A	17	41	4	6	0	0	1	4	2-0	0	9	.146	.182	.220	6	-6	0-0	1.000	-1	81	0	/O-9(8-0-1),D-6	-0.7
Total	16	1832	6449	1080	1651	302	50	321	1008	770-38	32	1411	.256	.336	.468	111	95	243-102	.978	-15	100	74	*O-1464L,2-142/3-75,D-45	5.6
GANTENBEIN, JOE Joseph Steven "Sep" B 8.25.1916 San Francisco, CA D 8.2.1993 Novato, CA BL/TR 5-9/168# d4.20																								
1939	Phi A	111	348	47	101	14	4	4	36	32	2	22	.290	.353	.388	91	-5	1-5	.948	-28	84	51	2-76,3-14/S-5	-2.7
1940	Phi A	75	197	21	47	6	2	4	23	11	1	21	.239	.282	.350	64	-11	1-0	.930	-4	95	144	3-45/1-6,S-3,O(LF)	-1.3
Total	2	186	545	68	148	20	6	8	59	43	3	43	.272	.328	.374	82	-16	2-5	.948	-32	84	51	/2-76,3-59,S-8,1-6,O(LF)	-4.0
GANTNER, JIM James Elmer B 1.5.1953 Fond Du Lac, WI BL/TR 6/180# d9.3 C2																								
1976	Mil A	26	69	6	17	1	0	0	7	6-0	1	11	.246	.316	.261	71	-2	1-0	.982	-4	82	77	3-24/D-2	-0.6
1977	Mil A	14	47	4	14	1	0	1	2	2-0	0	5	.298	.327	.383	93	-1	2-1	.902	1	116	129	3-14	0.0
1978	Mil A	43	97	14	21	1	0	1	8	5-0	2	10	.216	.269	.258	49	-7	2-0	.980	2	114	96	2-21,3-15/1S	-0.4
1979	Mil A	70	208	29	59	10	3	2	22	16-1	2	17	.284	.336	.389	96	-1	3-5	.952	1	93	125	3-42,2-22/S-3,P	0.0
1980	Mil A	132	415	47	117	21	3	4	40	30-5	1	29	.282	.330	.376	97	-2	11-10	.938	-3	107	135	3-69,2-66/S	-0.3
1981	†Mil A	107	352	35	94	14	1	2	33	29-5	3	29	.267	.325	.330	95	-2	3-6	.984	15	111	**127**	*2-107	1.8
1982	†Mil A	132	447	48	132	17	2	4	43	26-3	2	36	.295	.335	.369	100	-1	6-3	.982	10	108	116	*2-131	1.7
1983	Mil A	161	603	85	170	23	8	11	74	38-5	6	46	.282	.329	.401	109	5	5-6	.984	8	106	110	*2-158	2.1
1984	Mil A	153	613	61	173	27	1	3	56	30-0	3	51	.282	.314	.344	87	-11	6-5	.985	10	100	107	*2-153	0.7
1985	Mil A	143	523	63	133	15	4	5	44	33-7	3	42	.254	.300	.327	73	-20	11-8	.988	6	107	103	*2-124,3-24/S	-0.9
1986	Mil A	139	497	58	136	25	1	7	38	26-2	6	50	.274	.313	.370	84	-11	13-7	.985	-2	94	100	*2-135/3-3,SD	-0.5
1987	Mil A	81	265	37	72	14	0	4	30	19-2	5	22	.272	.331	.370	84	-6	6-2	.984	2	113	112	2-57,3-38/D	-0.1
1988	Mil A	155	539	67	149	28	2	0	47	34-1	3	50	.276	.322	.336	84	-11	20-8	.986	-5	98	100	*2-154/3	-1.0
1989	Mil A	116	409	51	112	18	3	0	34	21-2	**10**	33	.274	.321	.333	86	-7	20-6	.987	18	110	**122**	*2-114/D-2	1.6
1990	Mil A	88	323	36	85	8	5	0	25	29-0	2	19	.263	.328	.319	82	-8	18-3	.982	-9	97	97	2-80/3-9	-1.2
1991	Mil A	140	526	63	149	27	4	2	47	27-5	3	34	.283	.320	.361	91	-7	4-6	.976	0	92	88	3-90,2-59	-0.7
1992	Mil A	101	256	22	63	12	1	1	18	12-2	0	17	.246	.278	.313	67	-12	6-2	.994	2	101	119	2-68,3-31/1-2,D-2	-0.8
Total	17	1801	6189	726	1696	262	38	47	568	383-40	52	501	.274	.319	.351	88	-104	137-78	.985	52	105	109	*2-1449,3-360/D-8,S-7,1-3,P	1.4
GANZEL, CHARLIE Charles William B 6.18.1862 Waterford, WI D 4.7.1914 Quincy, MA BR/TR 6/161# d9.27 b-John s-Babe OF Total (25-LF 5-CF 71-RF)																								
1884	StP U	7	23	2	5	0	0	0		0			.217	.217	.217	59	-2		.956	0			/C-6,O(CF)	-0.1
1885	Phi N	34	125	15	21	3	1	0	6	4		13	.168	.194	.208	31	-10		.888	0			C-33/O(CF)	-0.6
1886	Phi N	1	3	0	0	0	0	0	0	0		1	.000	.000	.000	-99	-1	0	.600	-1			/C	-0.2
	Det N	57	213	28	58	7	2	1	31	7		22	.272	.295	.338	89	-3	5	.911	3			C-45/O-7(LF),1-5	0.3
	Year	58	216	28	58	7	2	1	31	7		23	.269	.291	.333	87	-4	5	.903	2			C-46/O-7(LF),1-5	0.1
1887	†Det N	57	227	40	59	6	5	0	20	8	1	2	.260	.288	.330	69	-10	3	.913	7			C-51/O-4(LF),1-2,3	0.1
1888	Det N	95	386	45	96	13	5	1	46	14	1	15	.249	.277	.316	88	-6	12	.900	-1	102	62	2-49,C-28/3-9,O-5(RF),S-3,1	-0.2
1889	Bos N	73	275	30	73	3	5	1	43	15	2	11	.265	.308	.324	72	-12	13	.927	7			C-39,O-26(0-1-25)/1-7,S-6,3	-0.2
1890	Bos N	38	163	21	44	7	3	0	24	5	2	6	.270	.300	.350	83	-5	1	.958	8	127	92	C-22,O-15(1-0-14)/S-3,2	0.4
1891	Bos N	70	263	33	68	18	5	1	29	12	5	13	.259	.304	.376	87	-6	7	.956	12	128	90	C-59,O-13(5-1-7)	0.9
1892	†Bos N	54	198	25	53	9	3	0	25	18	1	12	.268	.332	.343	95	-1	7	.933	2	133	86	C-51/O-2(1-1-0),1	0.4
1893	Bos N	73	281	50	75	10	2	1	48	22	2	9	.267	.325	.327	68	-14	6	.952	3	130	92	C-40,O-23(6-0-18),1-10	-0.7
1894	Bos N	70	266	51	74	7	6	3	56	19	0	6	.278	.326	.383	65	-17	1	.897	0	120	91	C-59/1-7,O-3(1-0-2),S-2,2	-0.9
1895	Bos N	81	280	38	73	2	5	1	52	25	1	6	.261	.324	.314	60	-18	1	.963	20	129	83	C-77/S-2,1-2	0.7
1896	Bos N	47	179	28	47	2	0	1	18	9	2	5	.263	.305	.291	54	-12	2	.989	9	113	118	C-41/1-3,S-2	0.0
1897	Bos N	30	105	15	28	4	3	0	14	4	1		.267	.300	.362	70	-5	2	.942	5	153	89	C-27/1-2	0.2
Total	14	787	2987	421	774	91	45	10	412	162	18	121	.259	.301	.330	73	-122	60	.935	74	82	58	C-579,O-100R/2-51,1-40,S-18,3-11	0.1
GANZEL, BABE Foster Pirie B 5.22.1901 Malden, MA D 2.6.1978 Jacksonville, FL BR/TR 5-10.5/172# d9.19 f-Charlie																								
1927	Was A	13	48	7	21	4	2	1	13	7	0	3	.438	.509	.667	206	8	0-0	.944	-1	101	74	O-13(4-9-0)	0.6
1928	Was A	10	26	2	2	1	0	0	4	1	0	4	.077	.111	.115	-41	-5	0-0	1.000	0	92	200	/O-7(4-2-2)	-0.5
Total	2	23	74	9	23	5	2	1	17	8	0	7	.311	.378	.473	122	3	0-0	.957	-0	99	108	/O-20(8-11-2)	0.1
GANZEL, JOHN John Henry B 4.7.1874 Kalamazoo, MI D 1.14.1959 Orlando, FL BR/TR 6-0.5/195# d4.21 M2 b-Charlie																								
1898	Pit N	15	45	5	6	0	0	0	2	4	1		.133	.220	.133	2	-6	0	.963	-1	59	84	1-12	-0.7
1900	Chi N	78	284	29	78	14	4	4	32	10	7		.275	.316	.394	99	-1	5	.980	-4	77	94	1-78	-0.5
1901	NY N	138	526	42	113	13	3	2	66	20	9		.215	.256	.262	52	-33	6	**.986**	2	99	80	*1-138	-3.2
1903	NY A	129	476	62	132	25	7	3	71	30	12		.277	.336	.378	107	5	9	**.988**	7	117	110	*1-129	1.0
1904	NY A	130	465	50	121	16	10	6	48	24	9		.260	.309	.376	111	5	13	.988	-1	87	108	*1-118/2-9,S	0.2
1907	Cin N	145	531	61	135	20	**16**	2	64	29	3		.254	.297	.363	102	-1	9	.990	1	97	123	*1-143	-0.3
1908	Cin N	112	388	32	97	16	10	1	53	19	2		.250	.289	.351	107	1	6	**.990**	-2	91	109	*1-108,M	-0.3
Total	7	747	2715	281	682	104	50	18	336	136	43		.251	.298	.346	93	-30	48	.987	2	96	104	1-726/2-9,S	-3.8
GARAGIOLA, JOE Joseph Henry B 2.12.1926 St.Louis, MO BL/TR 6/190# d5.26																								
1946	†StL N	74	211	21	50	4	1	3	22	23	0	25	.237	.312	.308	73	-8	0	.990	0	148	71	C-70	-0.4
1947	StL N	77	183	20	47	10	2	5	25	40	3	14	.257	.398	.415	111	5	0	.987	2	127	64	C-74	1.0
1948	StL N	24	56	9	6	1	0	2	7	12	1	9	.107	.275	.232	36	-5	0	.990	3	352	107	C-23	-0.1
1949	StL N	81	241	25	63	14	0	3	26	31	1	19	.261	.348	.357	85	-4	0	.984	4	128	85	C-80	0.5
1950	StL N	34	88	8	28	6	1	2	20	10	0	7	.318	.388	.477	120	3	0	1.000	-1	142	71	C-30	0.3
1951	StL N	27	72	9	14	3	2	2	9	9	0	7	.194	.284	.375	75	-3	0-0	1.000	-1	121	44	C-23	-0.3
	Pit N	72	212	24	54	8	2	9	35	32	2	20	.255	.358	.439	110	3	4-1	.986	-5	96	79	C-61	0.2
	Year	99	284	33	68	11	4	11	44	41	2	27	.239	.339	.423	101	1	4-1	**.989**	-6	102	70	C-84	-0.1
1952	Pit N	118	344	35	94	15	4	8	54	50	2	24	.273	.369	.410	113	7	0-1	.978	-1	78	**126**	*C-105	1.1
1953	Pit N	27	73	9	17	5	0	2	14	10	2	11	.233	.341	.384	89	-1	1-0	.989	-3	66	97	C-22	-0.2
	Chi N	74	228	21	62	9	4	1	21	21	1	23	.272	.336	.360	80	-7	0-0	.988	-1	88	116	C-68	-0.4
	Year	101	301	30	79	14	4	3	35	31	3	34	.262	.337	.365	82	-7	1-0	.988	-3	83	112	C-90	-0.6
1954	Chi N	63	153	16	43	5	0	5	21	28	4	12	.281	.403	.412	112	4	0-0	.982	-7	56	95	C-55	0.0
	NY N	5	11	1	3	2	0	0	1	1	0	2	.273	.308	.455	102	0	0-0	1.000	-0	86	0	/C-3	0.0
	Year	68	164	17	46	7	0	5	22	29	4	14	.280	.397	.415	112	5	0-0	.983	-7	58	89	C-58	0.0
Total	9	676	1872	198	481	82	16	42	255	267	16	173	.257	.354	.385	96	-6	5-2	.986	-9	112	91	C-614	1.7
GARBARK, MIKE Nathaniel Michael (born Nathaniel Michael Garbach) B 2.3.1916 Houston, TX D 8.31.1994 Charlotte, NC BR/TR 6/200# d4.18 b-Bob																								
1944	NY A	89	299	23	78	9	4	1	33	25	1	27	.261	.320	.328	82	-7	0-1	.988	6	116	92	C-85	0.4
1945	NY A	60	176	23	38	5	3	1	26	23	1	12	.216	.310	.295	73	-6	0-1	.972	-1	76	156	C-59	-0.4
Total	2	149	475	46	116	14	7	2	59	48	2	39	.244	.316	.316	79	-13	0-2	.982	6	100	117	C-144	0.0
GARBARK, BOB Robert Michael (born Robert Michael Garbach) B 11.13.1909 Houston, TX D 8.15.1990 Meadville, PA BR/TR 5-11/178# d9.3 b-Mike																								
1934	Cle A	5	11	1	0	0	0	0	0	1	0	3	.000	.083	.000	-76	-3	0-0	1.000	-1	103	0	/C-5	-0.4
1935	Cle A	6	18	4	6	1	0	0	4	5	0	1	.333	.478	.389	124	1	0-0	1.000	1	138	109	/C-6	0.2
1937	Chi N	1	1	0	0	0	0	0	0	0	0	0	.000	.000	.000	-96	0	0	—	0			H	0.0
1938	Chi N	23	54	2	14	0	0	0	5	1	0	3	.259	.273	.259	46	-4	0	1.000	1	125	97	C-20/1	-0.3
1939	Chi N	24	21	1	3	0	0	0	0	0	0	3	.143	.143	.143	-23	-4	0	1.000	0	134	88	C-21	-0.3
1944	Phi A	18	23	2	6	2	0	0	2	1	0	0	.261	.292	.348	83	-1	0-0	1.000	-0	74	73	C-15	-0.1
1945	Bos A	68	199	21	52	6	0	0	17	18	2	10	.261	.329	.291	79	-5	0-1	.993	-2	108	83	C-67	-0.4
Total	7	145	327	31	81	9	0	0	28	26	2	17	.248	.307	.275	64	-16	0-1	.996	-2	112	85	C-134/1	-1.3
GARBEY, BARBARO Barbaro (Garbey) B 12.4.1956 Santiago De Cuba, Cuba BR/TR 5-10/170# d4.3 OF Total (25-LF 2-CF 16-RF)																								
1984	†Det A	110	327	45	94	17	1	5	52	17-2	2	35	.287	.325	.391	98	-1	6-7	.989	-3	112	134	1-65,3-20,D-17,O-10(8-1-1)/2-3	-0.9
1985	Det A	86	237	27	61	9	1	6	29	15-1	3	37	.257	.305	.380	88	-4	3-2	.991	-2	114	130	1-37,O-24(10-1-14),D-21/3	-0.9

Year	Tm Lg	G	AB	R	H	2B	3B	HR	RBI	BB-IB	HP	SO	AVG	OBP	SLG	AOPS	ABR	SB-CS	FA	FR	Rng	Thr	G at Pos	BFW
1988	Tex A	30	62	4	12	2	0	0	5	4-0	0	11	.194	.239	.226	31	-6	0-0	.900	1	90	0	/O-8(7-0-1),1-7,3-3,D-7	-0.5
Total	3	226	626	76	167	28	2	11	86	36-3	5	83	.267	.309	.371	88	-11	9-9	.990	-4	119	129	1-109/D-45,O-42L,3-24,2-3	-2.3
GARBOWSKI, ALEX Alexander B 6.25.1925 Yonkers, NY BR/TR 6-1/185# d4.16																								
1952	Det A	2	0	0	0	0	0	0	0	0	0	0	—	—	—	—	0	0-0	—	0			R	0.0
GARCIA, KIKO Alfonso Rafael B 10.14.1953 Martinez, CA BR/TR 5-11/180# d9.11																								
1976	Bal A	11	32	2	7	1	1	1	4	0-0	0	4	.219	.219	.406	86	-1	2-1	1.000	-0	94	137	S-11	0.0
1977	Bal A	65	131	20	29	6	0	2	10	6-0	0	31	.221	.255	.313	58	-8	2-3	.966	14	121	189	S-61/2-2	1.0
1978	Bal A	79	186	17	49	6	4	0	13	7-0	0	43	.263	.287	.339	81	-6	7-1	.945	8	111	122	S-74/2-3	0.9
1979	†Bal A	126	417	54	103	15	9	5	24	32-0	2	87	.247	.303	.362	82	-12	11-9	.955	-10	88	117	*S-113,2-25/3-2,O-2(LF)	-1.1
1980	Bal A	111	311	27	62	8	0	1	27	24-0	0	57	.199	.255	.235	36	-28	8-4	.974	5	97	105	S-96,2-27/O(LF)	-1.3
1981	†Hou N	48	136	9	37	6	1	0	15	10-3	1	16	.272	.324	.331	91	-2	2-2	.950	3	105	89	S-28,3-13/2-9	0.4
1982	Hou N	34	76	5	16	5	0	1	5	3-1	0	15	.211	.241	.316	59	-4	1-0	.946	3	110	137	S-21/3-2,2	0.1
1983	Phi N	84	118	22	34	7	1	2	9	9-2	1	20	.288	.344	.415	111	2	1-2	.970	8	102	86	2-52,S-22,3-10	1.2
1984	Phi N	57	60	6	14	2	0	0	5	4-1	0	11	.233	.281	.267	54	-4	0-0	.965	-1	102	30	S-30,3-23/2	-0.4
1985	Phi N	4	3	0	0	0	0	0	0	0-0	0	1	.000	.000	.000	-97	-1	0-0	1.000	-1	69	0	/S-3,3	-0.2
Total	10	619	1470	162	351	56	16	12	112	95-7	4	285	.239	.286	.323	70	-64	34-22	.961	29	101	119	S-459,2-120/3-51,O-3(LF)	0.6
GARCIA, AMAURY Amaury Miguel (Paula) B 5.20.1975 Santo Domingo, D.R. BR/TR 5-10/160# d7.5																								
1999	Fla N	10	24	6	6	0	1	2	2	3-0	0	11	.250	.333	.583	133	1	0-0	.932	3	142	114	/2-8	0.4
GARCIA, CARLOS Carlos Jesus (Guerrero) B 10.15.1967 Tachira, Venezuela BR/TR 6-1/185# d9.20																								
1990	Pit N	4	4	1	2	0	0	0	0	0-0	0	2	.500	.500	.500	183	0	0-0	1.000	0	136	201	/S-3	0.1
1991	Pit N	12	24	2	6	0	2	0	1	1-0	0	8	.250	.280	.417	95	-1	0-0	.947	0	105	155	/S-9,3-2,2	0.0
1992	†Pit N	22	39	4	8	1	0	0	4	0-0	0	9	.205	.195	.231	23	-4	0-0	.977	0	101	169	2-14/S-8	-0.4
1993	Pit N	141	546	77	147	25	5	12	47	31-2	9	67	.269	.316	.399	91	-8	18-11	.983	-20	90	99	*2-140/S-3	-2.1
1994	Pit N★	98	412	49	114	15	2	6	28	16-2	4	67	.277	.309	.367	75	-16	18-9	.978	18	**114**	**122**	2-98	0.7
1995	Pit N	104	367	41	108	24	2	6	50	25-5	2	55	.294	.340	.420	98	-1	8-4	.982	7	104	114	2-92,S-15	1.2
1996	Pit N	101	390	66	111	18	4	6	44	23-3	4	58	.285	.329	.397	89	-7	16-6	.985	7	110	81	2-77,S-19,3-14	0.5
1997	Tor A	103	350	29	77	18	2	3	23	15-0	2	60	.220	.253	.309	46	-29	11-3	.981	-10	91	89	2-96/S-5,3-4	-3.1
1998	Ana A	19	35	4	5	1	0	0	0	3-0	1	11	.143	.231	.171	7	-5	2-0	.978	2	109	133	2-11/S-5,D-3	-0.1
1999	SD N	6	11	1	2	0	0	0	0	1-0	0	3	.182	.250	.182	13	-2	0-0	.778	-1	67	0	/3-4,1	-0.2
Total	10	610	2178	274	580	102	17	33	197	115-12	22	340	.266	.307	.374	79	-73	73-33	.982	5	100	104	2-529/S-67,3-24,D-3,1	-3.4
GARCIA, DAMASO Damaso Domingo (Sanchez) B 2.7.1955 Moca, D.R. BR/TR 6/170# d6.24																								
1978	NY A	18	41	5	8	0	0	0	1	2-0	0	6	.195	.227	.195	22	-4	1-0	.959	-1	88	129	2-16/S-3	-0.4
1979	NY A	11	38	3	10	1	0	0	4	0-0	0	2	.263	.263	.289	50	-3	2-0	.902	-4	90	65	S-10/3	-0.5
1980	Tor A	140	543	50	151	30	7	4	46	12-2	3	55	.278	.296	.381	81	-16	13-13	.980	7	105	104	*2-138/D	-0.3
1981	Tor A	64	250	24	63	8	1	1	13	9-1	0	32	.252	.277	.304	64	-12	13-3	.972	-19	85	68	2-62/D	-2.8
1982	Tor A	147	597	89	185	32	3	5	42	21-1	5	44	.310	.338	.399	93	-6	54-20	.980	6	105	100	*2-141/D-4	1.3
1983	Tor A	131	525	84	161	23	6	3	38	24-3	2	34	.307	.336	.390	94	-4	31-17	.981	-14	90	85	*2-130	-1.1
1984	Tor A★	152	633	79	180	32	5	5	46	16-1	9	46	.284	.310	.374	86	-13	46-12	.980	-16	92	102	*2-149/D	-1.5
1985	†Tor A★	146	600	70	169	25	4	8	65	15-2	4	41	.282	.302	.377	83	-16	28-15	.981	-15	89	105	*2-143	-2.3
1986	Tor A	122	424	57	119	22	0	6	46	13-0	4	32	.281	.306	.375	83	-11	9-6	.985	-0	97	104	*2-106,D-11/1	-0.5
1988	Atl N	21	60	3	7	1	0	1	4	3-0	0	10	.117	.159	.183	-2	-8	1-0	.984	-3	91	59	2-13	-1.2
1989	Mon N	80	203	26	55	9	1	3	18	15-1	0	20	.271	.317	.369	96	-1	5-4	.972	7	113	97	2-62/3	0.7
Total	11	1032	3914	490	1108	183	27	36	323	130-11	27	322	.283	.309	.371	84	-94	203-90	.980	-54	96	97	2-960/D-18,S-13,3-2,1	-8.6
GARCIA, DANIEL Daniel Joseph B 4.12.1980 Riverside, CA BR/TR 6/180# d9.2																								
2003	NY N	19	56	5	12	2	0	2	6	2-0	3	11	.214	.274	.357	67	-3	0-0	.950	-2	96	83	2-17/O(LF)	-0.4
GARCIA, DANNY Daniel Raphael B 4.29.1954 Brooklyn, NY BL/TL 6-1/182# d4.26																								
1981	KC A	12	14	4	2	0	0	0	0	0-0	0	2	.143	.143	.143	-18	-2	0-0	1.000	-1	70	0	/O-6(1-0-5),1-2	-0.3
GARCIA, FREDDY Freddy Adrian (Felix) B 8.1.1972 LaRomana, D.R. BR/TR 6-2/190# d5.3																								
1995	Pit N	42	57	5	8	1	1	0	1	8-0	0	17	.140	.246	.193	17	-7	0-1	1.000	3	97	0	O-10(LF)/3-8	-0.4
1997	Pit N	20	40	4	6	1	0	3	5	2-0	0	17	.150	.190	.400	49	-3	0-0	.842	-3	60	70	3-10/1-2	-0.6
1998	Pit N	56	172	27	44	11	1	9	26	18-3	2	45	.256	.332	.488	111	3	0-2	.949	5	116	113	3-47/1-4	0.7
1999	Pit N	55	130	16	30	5	0	6	23	4-0	0	41	.231	.252	.408	64	-8	0-0	.977	-0	113	0	O-24(17-0-7)/3-9,D-2	-0.9
	Atl N	2	2	1	1	0	0	1	1	1-0	0	1	.500	.667	2.000	540	1	0-0	—	-0	0	0	/1O(LF)	0.1
	Year	57	132	17	31	5	0	7	24	5-0	0	42	.235	.261	.432	72	-7	0-0	.977	-1	110	0	O-25(18-0-7)/3-9,D-2,1	-0.8
Total	4	175	401	53	89	18	2	19	56	33-3	2	121	.222	.283	.419	79	-14	0-3	.938	5	112	132	/3-74,O-35(28-0-7),1-7,D-2	-1.1
GARCIA, GUILLERMO Guillermo Antonio (Morel) B 4.4.1972 Santiago, D.R. BR/TR 6-3/215# d7.19																								
1998	Cin N	12	36	3	7	2	0	2	4	2-0	0	13	.194	.237	.417	67	-2	0-0	.988	2	65	258	C-11	0.1
1999	Fla N	4	4	0	1	0	0	0	0	0-0	0	2	.250	.250	.250	29	0	0-0	1.000	0	0	0	C-3	0.0
Total	2	16	40	3	8	2	0	2	4	2-0	0	15	.200	.238	.400	63	-2	0-0	.988	2	62	246	/C-14	0.1
GARCIA, KARIM Gustavo Karim B 10.29.1975 Ciudad Obregon, Mexico BL/TL 6/200# d9.2																								
1995	LA N	13	20	1	4	0	0	0	0	0-0	0	4	.200	.200	.200	6	-3	0-0	1.000	2	92	1007	/O-5(2-0-3)	-0.1
1996	LA N	1	1	0	0	0	0	0	0	0-0	0	1	.000	.000	.000	-99	0	0-0	—	0			/H	0.0
1997	LA N	15	39	5	5	0	0	1	8	6-1	0	14	.128	.239	.205	21	-5	0-0	1.000	-1	72	0	O-12(12-0-2)	-0.6
1998	Ari N	113	333	39	74	10	8	9	43	18-1	0	78	.222	.260	.381	67	-19	5-4	.975	3	109	98	*O-103(0-7-100)	-2.0
1999	Det A	96	288	38	69	10	3	14	32	20-1	0	67	.240	.288	.441	82	-10	2-4	.958	2	102	137	O-81(35-0-55)/D-6	-1.2
2000	Det A	8	17	1	3	0	0	0	0	0-0	0	4	.176	.176	.176	-10	-3	0-0	1.000	-1	74	0	/O-7(RF),D	-0.4
	Bal A	8	16	0	0	0	0	0	0	0-0	0	6	.000	.000	.000	-99	-5	0-0	1.000	0	208	0	/O-2(LF),D-4	-0.5
	Year	16	33	1	3	0	0	0	0	0-0	0	10	.091	.091	.091	-56	-8	0-0	1.000	-1	85	0	/O-9(2-0-7),D-5	-0.9
2001	Cle A	20	45	8	14	3	0	5	9	3-0	1	13	.311	.360	.711	173	5	0-0	.905	0	59	485	O-18(6-0-13)/1-2	0.4
2002	NY A	2	5	1	1	0	0	0	0	0-0	0	1	.200	.200	.200	7	-1	0-0	1.000	0	44	0	/O-2(1-0-1)	-0.1
	Cle A	51	197	29	59	8	0	16	52	6-0	0	40	.299	.317	.584	136	8	0-3	.990	-1	99	66	O-51(1-3-48)	0.4
	Year	53	202	30	60	8	0	16	52	6-0	0	41	.297	.314	.574	132	8	0-3	.990	-1	98	65	O-53(2-3-49)	0.3
2003	Cle A	24	93	8	18	1	0	5	14	5-1	1	20	.194	.238	.366	59	-6	0-0	.905	-3	71	158	O-23(0-7-17)/D	-1.0
	†NY A	52	151	17	46	5	0	6	21	9-1	0	32	.305	.342	.457	111	2	0-2	.981	4	112	202	O-50(13-3-37)/D	0.3
	Year	76	244	25	64	6	0	11	35	14-2	1	52	.262	.302	.422	91	-4	0-2	.959	1	98	187	O-73(13-10-54)/D-2	-0.7
Total	9	403	1205	147	293	37	11	56	179	67-5	2	280	.243	.282	.432	85	-37	7-13	.969	4	99	141	0-354(72-20-283)/D-13,1-2	-4.8
GARCIA, JESSE Jesus Jesse B 9.24.1973 Corpus Christi, TX BR/TR 5-10/155# d4.5																								
1999	Bal A	17	29	6	6	0	0	2	2	2-0	0	3	.207	.258	.414	70	-2	0-0	1.000	-1	96	156	/S-7,2-6,3-2,D	-0.2
2000	Bal A	14	17	2	1	0	0	0	0	2-0	0	2	.059	.158	.059	-44	-4	0-0	1.000	2	162	114	/2-6,S-5	-0.1
2001	Atl N	22	5	3	1	0	0	0	0	0-0	0	1	.200	.200	.200	4	-1	6-2	1.000	-0	82	192	/2-4,S-2	0.0
2002	Atl N	39	61	6	12	1	0	0	5	0-0	0	14	.197	.197	.213	10	-8	0-1	.986	5	118	123	2-21/S-5,O-4(2-0-2)	-0.3
2003	†Atl N	13	10	6	4	0	1	0	2	0-0	0	1	.400	.400	.600	156	1	0-1	1.000	-0	95	100	/2-6,S-3,3-2	0.0
Total	5	105	122	23	24	1	1	2	9	4-0	0	21	.197	.222	.270	28	-14	6-4	.992	5	115	123	/2-43,S-22,O-4(2-0-2),3-4,D	-0.6
GARCIA, LEO Leonardo Antonio (Peralta) B 11.6.1962 Santiago, D.R. BL/TL 5-8/160# d4.6																								
1987	Cin N	31	30	8	6	0	0	1	2	4-0	0	8	.200	.286	.300	55	-2	3-1	1.000	0	121	0	O-14(0-13-1)	-0.1
1988	Cin N	23	28	2	4	1	0	0	0	4-1	0	5	.143	.250	.179	24	-3	0-1	1.000	0	103	0	/O-9(2-4-3)	-0.3
Total	2	54	58	10	10	1	0	1	2	8-1	0	13	.172	.269	.241	41	-5	3-2	1.000	0	113	0	/O-23(2-17-4)	-0.4
GARCIA, LUIS Luis Carlos B 9.22.1975 Hermosillo, Mexico BR/TR 6-3/200# d4.10																								
2002	Bal A	6	3	0	1	0	0	0	0	0-0	0	1	.333	.333	.333	82	0	0-0	1.000	0	132	0	/O-2(0-1-1)	0.0
GARCIA, LUIS Luis Rafael B 5.20.1975 San Francisco De Macoris, D.R. BR/TR 6/175# d4.5																								
1999	Det A	8	9	0	1	1	0	0	0	0-0	0	2	.111	.111	.222	-18	-2	0-0	1.000	-2	37	0	/S-7,2	-0.3
GARCIA, PEDRO Pedro Modesto (Delfi) B 4.17.1950 Guayama, P.R. BR/TR 5-10/175# d4.6																								
1973	Mil A	160	580	67	142	**32**	5	15	54	40-4	5	119	.245	.296	.395	96	-5	11-10	.970	-21	96	91	*2-160	-1.6

Year	Tm Lg	G	AB	R	H	2B	3B	HR	RBI	BB-IB	HP	SO	AVG	OBP	SLG	AOPS	ABR	SB-CS	FA	FR	Rng	Thr	G at Pos	BFW
1974	Mil A	141	452	46	90	15	4	12	54	26-4	5	67	.199	.248	.330	66	-22	8-5	.970	-9	96	101	*2-140	-2.3
1975	Mil A	98	302	40	68	15	2	6	38	18-1	2	59	.225	.271	.348	74	-11	12-6	.985	10	109	99	2-94/D	0.6
1976	Mil A	41	106	12	23	7	1	1	9	4-0	2	23	.217	.257	.330	73	-4	2-2	.971	-3	96	113	2-39	-0.5
	Det A	77	227	21	45	10	2	3	20	9-0	4	40	.198	.239	.300	56	-13	2-3	.958	8	108	110	2-77	-0.2
	Year	118	333	33	68	17	3	4	29	13-0	6	63	.204	.244	.309	61	-17	4-5	.962	5	104	111	*2-116	-0.7
1977	Tor A	41	130	10	27	10	1	0	9	5-0	3	21	.208	.254	.300	50	-9	0-0	.971	-3	94	91	2-34/D-4	-1.0
Total	5	558	1797	196	395	89	15	37	184	102-9	21	329	.220	.267	.348	75	-64	35-26	.971	-18	100	99	2-544/D-5	-5.0
GARCIA, CHICO Vinicio Uzcanga B 12.24.1924 Veracruz, Mexico BR/TR 5-8/170# d4.24																								
1954	Bal A	39	62	6	7	0	2	0	5	8	0	3	.113	.211	.177	9	-8	0-0	.962	2	93	115	2-24	-0.5
GARCIAPARRA, NOMAR Anthony Nomar B 7.23.1973 Whittier, CA BR/TR 6/165# d8.31																								
1996	Bos A	24	87	11	21	2	3	4	16	4-0	0	14	.241	.272	.471	82	-3	5-0	.988	-4	80	69	S-22/2D	-0.4
1997	Bos A★	153	684	122	**209**	44	**11**	30	98	35-2	6	92	.306	.342	.534	122	19	22-9	.971	3	103	106	*S-153	3.4
1998	†Bos A	143	604	111	195	37	8	35	122	33-1	8	62	.323	.362	.584	139	32	12-6	.962	-11	96	80	*S-143	3.0
1999	†Bos A★	135	532	103	190	42	4	27	104	51-7	8	39	**.357**	.418	.603	153	43	14-3	.972	-4	92	87	*S-134	4.7
2000	Bos A★	140	529	104	197	51	3	21	96	61-**20**	2	50	**.372**	.434	.599	155	47	5-2	.971	-3	100	77	*S-136/D	5.0
2001	Bos A	21	83	13	24	3	0	4	8	7-0	1	9	.289	.352	.470	113	1	0-1	.968	1	98	100	S-21	0.4
2002	Bos A★	156	635	101	197	**56**	5	24	120	41-4	6	63	.310	.352	.528	129	26	5-2	.965	19	109	103	*S-154	5.4
2003	†Bos A★	156	658	120	198	37	13	28	105	39-1	11	61	.301	.345	.524	123	20	19-5	.971	7	**106**	82	*S-156	3.9
Total	8	928	3812	685	1231	272	47	173	669	271-35	42	390	.323	.370	.555	134	185	82-28	.969	9	101	89	S-919/D-2,2	25.4
GARDELLA, AL Alfred Stephan B 1.11.1918 New York, NY BL/TL 5-10/172# d5.17 b-Danny																								
1945	NY N	16	26	2	2	0	0	0	1	4	1	3	.077	.226	.077	-14	-4	0	.961	-1	82	39	/1-9,O(CF)	-0.5
GARDELLA, DANNY Daniel Lewis B 2.26.1920 New York, NY BL/TL 5-7.5/160# d5.14 b-Al																								
1944	NY N	47	112	20	28	2	2	6	14	11	1	13	.250	.323	.464	120	2	0	.912	1	101	167	O-25(11-4-10)	0.1
1945	NY N	121	430	54	117	10	1	18	71	46	5	55	.272	.349	.426	113	7	2	.954	-4	89	87	O-94(85-0-9),1-15	-0.3
1950	StL N	1	1	0	0	0	0	0	0	0	0	0	.000	.000	.000	-95	0	0	—	0			H	0.0
Total	3	169	543	74	145	12	3	24	85	57	6	68	.267	.343	.433	114	9	2	.943	-3	92	105	O-119(96-4-19)/1-15	-0.2
GARDENHIRE, RON Ronald Clyde B 10.24.1957 Butzbach, W.Germany BR/TR 6/175# d9.1 M2 C11																								
1981	NY N	27	48	2	13	1	0	0	3	5-2	0	9	.271	.340	.292	82	-1	2-2	.969	0	99	84	S-18/2-6,3	0.1
1982	NY N	141	384	29	92	17	1	3	33	23-2	0	55	.240	.279	.313	67	-18	5-6	.956	7	105	92	*S-135/23	0.1
1983	NY N	17	32	1	2	0	0	0	1	1-0	0	4	.063	.091	.063	-57	-7	0-0	1.000	-1	101	66	S-15	-0.8
1984	NY N	74	207	20	51	7	1	1	10	9-1	0	43	.246	.276	.304	64	-10	6-1	.947	-1	88	67	S-49,2-18/3-7	-0.6
1985	NY N	26	39	5	7	2	1	0	2	8-0	0	11	.179	.319	.282	71	-1	0-0	.911	-1	110	71	S-13/2-5,3-2	-0.1
Total	5	285	710	57	165	27	3	4	49	46-5	0	122	.232	.277	.296	62	-37	13-9	.955	4	101	84	S-230/2-30,3-11	-1.3
GARDNER, ALEX Alexander B 4.28.1861 Toronto, ON, CAN D 6.18.1926 Danvers, MA d5.10																								
1884	Was AA	1	3	0	0	0	0	0		0	0		.000	.000	.000	-99	-1		.600	-2			/C	-0.2
GARDNER, ART Arthur Junior B 9.21.1952 Madden, MS BL/TL 5-11/175# d9.2																								
1975	Hou N	13	31	3	6	0	0	0	2	1-1	1	8	.194	.242	.194	24	-3	1-0	1.000	-0	98	0	/O-8(3-1-4)	-0.4
1977	Hou N	66	65	7	10	0	0	0	3	3-1	1	15	.154	.203	.154	-3	-10	0-0	1.000	1	102	110	O-26(14-9-4)	-1.0
1978	SF N	7	3	2	0	0	0	0	0	0-0	0	2	.000	.000	.000	-99	-1	0-1	—	0			H	-0.1
Total	3	86	99	12	16	0	0	0	5	4-2	2	25	.162	.210	.162	2	-14	1-1	1.000	1	101	72	/O-34(17-10-8)	-1.5
GARDNER, EARLE Earle McClurkin B 1.24.1884 Sparta, IL D 3.2.1943 Sparta, IL BR/TR 5-11/160# d9.18																								
1908	NY A	20	75	7	16	2	0	0	4	1	1		.213	.234	.240	53	-4	0	.947	1	96	184	2-20	-0.3
1909	NY A	22	85	12	28	4	0	0	15	3	0		.329	.352	.376	129	3	4	.945	-6	85	39	2-22	-0.4
1910	NY A	86	271	36	66	4	2	1	24	21	2		.244	.303	.284	79	-7	9	.936	0	97	145	2-70	-0.6
1911	NY A	102	357	36	94	13	2	0	39	20	5		.263	.312	.311	69	-15	14	.959	3	105	134	*2-101	-1.1
1912	NY A	43	160	14	45	3	1	0	26	5	0		.281	.303	.313	72	-6	11	.922	-7	90	70	2-43	-1.3
Total	5	273	948	105	249	26	5	1	108	50	8		.263	.305	.304	76	-29	38	.944	-8	98	122	2-256	-3.7
GARDNER, GID Frank Washington B 5.6.1859 Boston, MA D 8.1.1914 Cambridge, MA ?/165# d8.23 I OF Total (16-LF 36-CF 69-RF)																								
1879	Tro N	2	6	1	1	0	0	0	0	0		0	.167	.167	.167	11	0		.429	-1	68	0	/P-2	0.0
1880	Cle N	10	32	0	6	1	1	0	4	2		4	.188	.235	.281	76	-1		.850	-0	111	0	/P-9,O(CF)	0.0
1883	Bal AA	42	161	28	44	10	3	1		18			.273	.346	.391	133	7		.837	-3	72	0	O-35(CF)/2-4,3-3,P-2	0.2
1884	Bal AA	41	173	32	37	6	8	2		14	2		.214	.280	.376	108	1		.860	0	131	0	O-40(1-0-39)/1-2	0.1
	CP U	38	149	22	38	10	2	0		10			.255	.302	.349	97	-5		.872	-1	28	0	O-29(15-0-14)/3-8,P2	-0.6
	Bal U	1	4	0	1	0	0	0		0			.250	.250	.250	47	0		.714	-0	55	476	/S	-0.1
	Year	39	153	22	39	10	2	0		10			.255	.301	.346	96	-5		.872	-2	28	0	O-29(15-0-14)/3-8,P2S	-0.7
1885	Bal AA	44	170	22	37	5	4	0	17	12	0		.218	.269	.294	79	-4		.891	-1	105	85	2-39/O-5(RF),1P	-0.3
1887	Ind N	18	63	8	11	1	0	1	8	12	0	11	.175	.307	.238	55	-3	7	1.000	-2	67	0	O-11(RF)/2-7	-0.4
1888	Was N	1	3	0	1	0	0	0	0	1	0	1	.333	.500	.333	182	0	0	.750	0	107	263	/S	0.0
	Phi N	1	3	0	2	0	0	0	1	0	0	0	.667	.667	.667	309	1	0	1.000	-0	45	0	/2	0.0
	Was N	1	1	0	0	0	0	0	0	0	0	0	.000	.000	.000	-99	0	0	1.000	-0	0	0	/2	-0.1
	Year	3	7	0	3	0	0	0	1	1	0	1	.429	.500	.429	204	1	0	1.000	-1	27	0	/2-2,S	-0.1
Total	7	199	765	113	178	33	18	4	30	69	2	16	.233	.298	.339	99	-4	7	.855	-8	85	0	O-121R/2-53,P-15,3-11,1-3,S-2	-1.2
GARDNER, JEFF Jeffrey Scott B 2.4.1964 Newport Beach, CA BL/TR 5-11/165# d9.10																								
1991	NY N	13	37	3	6	0	0	0	1	4-0	0	6	.162	.238	.162	17	-4	0-0	.818	-3	91	55	/S-8,2-3	-0.7
1992	SD N	15	19	0	2	0	0	0	0	1-0	0	8	.105	.150	.105	-26	-3	0-0	1.000	2	136	100	2-11	-0.1
1993	SD N	140	404	53	106	21	7	1	24	45-0	1	69	.262	.337	.356	85	-8	2-6	.983	-11	92	73	*2-133/3S	-1.5
1994	Mon N	18	32	4	7	0	1	0	1	3-0	0	5	.219	.286	.281	48	-3	0-0	.714	-5	22	0	/3-9,2-4	-0.7
Total	4	186	492	60	121	21	8	1	26	53-0	1	88	.246	.319	.327	73	-18	2-6	.984	-16	94	73	2-151/3-10,S-9	-3.0
GARDNER, RAY Raymond Vincent B 10.25.1901 Frederick, MD D 5.3.1968 Frederick, MD BR/TR 5-8/145# d4.16																								
1929	Cle A	82	256	28	67	3	2	1	24	29	0	16	.262	.337	.301	63	-14	10-13	.952	11	108	107	S-82	0.3
1930	Cle A	33	13	7	1	0	0	0	1	0	0	0	.077	.077	.077	-59	-3	0-1	.861	3	165	39	S-22/2-5,3	0.0
Total	2	115	269	35	68	3	2	1	25	29	0	16	.253	.326	.290	57	-17	10-14	.945	15	111	104	S-104/2-5,3	0.3
GARDNER, BILLY William Frederick "Shotgun" B 7.19.1927 Waterford, CT BR/TR 6/180# d4.22 M6 C5																								
1954	NY N	62	108	10	23	5	0	1	7	6	1	19	.213	.261	.287	42	-9	0-1	.987	5	127	52	3-30,2-13/S-5	-0.4
1955	NY N	59	187	26	38	10	1	3	17	13-0	2	19	.203	.261	.316	52	-13	0-0	.940	-2	102	109	S-38,3-10/2-4	-1.2
1956	Bal A	144	515	53	119	16	2	11	50	29-1	7	53	.231	.281	.334	67	-28	5-5	.974	-10	**99**	84	*2-132,S-25/3-6	-2.8
1957	Bal A	**154**	644	79	169	**36**	3	6	55	53-2	8	67	.262	.325	.356	92	-7	10-7	**.987**	8	106	93	*2-148/S-9	1.2
1958	Bal A	151	560	32	126	28	2	3	33	34-4	3	53	.225	.271	.298	60	-31	2-3	.985	-15	92	107	*2-151,S-13	-3.7
1959	Bal A	140	401	34	87	13	2	6	27	38-9	1	61	.217	.284	.304	64	-20	2-1	.976	**23**	**112**	**127**	*2-139/S3	1.2
1960	Was A	145	592	71	152	26	5	9	56	43-0	6	76	.257	.313	.363	83	-15	0-4	.973	-3	103	92	*2-145,S-13	-0.8
1961	Min A	45	154	13	36	9	0	1	11	10-1	0	14	.234	.280	.312	55	-10	0-0	.973	-3	96	118	2-41/3-2	-0.9
	†NY A	41	99	11	21	5	0	1	2	6-0	3	18	.212	.278	.293	56	-6	0-0	.952	3	107	139	3-33/2-6	-0.4
	Year	86	253	24	57	14	0	2	13	16-1	3	32	.225	.279	.304	56	-16	0-0	.975	0	95	117	2-47,3-35	-1.3
1962	NY A	4	1	1	0	0	0	0	0	0-0	0	1	.000	.000	.000	-99	0	0-0	1.000	0	0	0	/23	0.0
	Bos A	53	199	22	54	9	2	0	12	10-0	1	39	.271	.310	.337	72	-8	0-1	.963	-6	91	88	2-38/3-7,S-4	-1.1
	Year	57	200	23	54	9	2	0	12	10-0	1	40	.270	.308	.335	71	-8	0-1	.963	-6	90	87	2-39/3-8,S-4	-1.1
1963	Bos A	36	84	4	16	2	1	0	1	4-1	1	19	.190	.236	.238	32	-8	0-0	.989	3	103	113	2-21/3-2	-0.3
Total	10	1034	3544	356	841	159	18	41	271	246-18	33	439	.237	.292	.327	70	-155	19-22	.978	3	101	100	2-839,S-108/3-92	-9.2
GARDNER, LARRY William Lawrence B 5.13.1886 Enosburg Falls, VT D 3.11.1976 St.George, VT BL/TR 5-8/165# d6.25																								
1908	Bos A	3	10	0	3	1	0	0	1	0	0		.300	.300	.400	124	0	0	.571	-2	44	0	/3-3	-0.2
1909	Bos A	19	37	7	11	1	2	0	5	4	1		.297	.381	.432	153	2	1	.800	-3	94	0	/3-8,S-5	0.0
1910	Bos A	113	413	56	117	12	10	2	36	41	4		.283	.354	.375	125	12	8	.944	-9	101	73	*2-113	0.4
1911	Bos A	138	492	80	140	17	8	4	44	64	5		.285	.373	.376	110	9	27	.962	23	113	31	3-72,2-62	3.3
1912	†Bos A	143	517	88	163	24	18	3	86	56	1		.315	.383	.449	131	20	25	.930	-1	99	88	*3-143	2.2
1913	Bos A	131	473	64	133	17	10	0	63	47	1	34	.281	.347	.359	104	2	18	.943	-15	89	72	*3-130	-0.9

Year	Tm Lg	G	AB	R	H	2B	3B	HR	RBI	BB-IB	HP	SO	AVG	OBP	SLG	AOPS	ABR	SB-CS	FA	FR	Rng	Thr	G at Pos	BFW
1914	Bos A	155	553	50	143	23	19	3	68	35	0	39	.259	.303	.385	107	0	16-23	.942	-1	103	96	*3-153	-0.1
1915	†Bos A	127	430	51	111	14	6	1	55	39	5	24	.258	.327	.326	98	-1	11-12	.933	-7	96	91	*3-127	-0.7
1916	†Bos A	148	493	47	152	19	7	2	62	48	2	27	.308	.372	.387	128	17	12	.953	-12	93	97	*3-147	0.9
1917	Bos A	146	501	53	133	23	7	1	61	54	3	37	.265	.341	.345	110	7	16	.937	-7	101	91	*3-146	0.5
1918	Phi A	127	463	50	132	22	6	1	52	43	0	22	.285	.346	.365	113	7	9	.964	13	**110**	126	*3-127	2.6
1919	Cle A	**139**	524	67	157	29	7	2	79	39	3	29	.300	.352	.393	103	2	7	.946	-5	101	106	*3-139	0.1
1920	†Cle A	**154**	597	72	185	31	11	3	118	53	1	25	.310	.367	.414	103	3	3-20	**.976**	-1	101	**133**	*3-154	0.0
1921	Cle A	153	586	101	187	32	14	3	120	65	4	16	.319	.391	.437	109	9	3-3	.950	1	101	84	*3-152	1.8
1922	Cle A	137	470	74	134	31	3	2	68	49	2	21	.285	.355	.377	90	-5	9-8	.951	-6	96	96	*3-128	-0.4
1923	Cle A	52	79	4	20	5	1	0	12	12	0	7	.253	.352	.342	83	-2	0-1	.962	3	135	79	3-19	0.2
1924	Cle A	38	50	3	10	0	0	0	4	5	0	1	.200	.273	.200	23	-6	0-1	.875	-2	127	248	/3-8,2-6	-0.8
Total	17	1923	6688	867	1931	301	129	27	934	654	32	282	.289	.355	.384	109	76	165-68	.948	-31	100	95	*3-1656,2-181/S-5	8.9
GARIBALDI, ART Arthur Edward B 8.21.1907 San Francisco, CA D 10.19.1967 Sacramento, CA BR/TR 5-8/165# d6.20																								
1936	StL N	71	232	30	64	12	0	1	20	16	0	30	.276	.323	.341	79	-7	3	.925	-7	83	42	3-46,2-24	-1.0
GARMS, DEBS Debs C. "Tex" B 6.26.1908 Bangs, TX D 12.16.1984 Glen Rose, TX BL/TR 5-8.5/165# d8.10																								
1932	StL A	34	134	20	38	7	1	1	8	17	0	7	.284	.364	.373	86	-2	4-3	.953	-1	92	114	O-33(0-32-1)	-0.4
1933	StL A	78	189	35	60	10	2	4	24	30	2	21	.317	.416	.455	123	8	2-5	.960	-0	93	131	O-47(28-17-3)	0.4
1934	StL A	91	232	25	68	14	4	0	31	27	2	19	.293	.372	.388	89	-3	0-0	.942	-3	99	44	O-56(42-1-13)	-0.9
1935	StL A	10	15	1	4	0	0	0	0	2	0	2	.267	.353	.267	59	-1	0-0	.800	-0	90	0	/O-2(RF)	-0.1
1937	Bos N	125	478	60	124	15	8	2	37	37	3	33	.259	.317	.337	85	-11	2	.977	-6	99	17	O-81(64-15-2),3-36	-2.0
1938	Bos N	117	428	62	135	19	1	0	47	34	4	22	.315	.371	.364	114	10	4	.985	-3	91	114	O-63(51-2-12),3-54/2	0.5
1939	Bos N	132	513	68	153	24	9	2	37	39	2	20	.298	.350	.392	107	4	2	.964	1	96	75	O-96(25-0-73),3-37	0.1
1940	Pit N	103	358	76	127	23	7	5	57	23	1	6	**.355**	.395	.500	147	22	3	.964	3	104	144	3-64,O-19(8-4-8)	2.6
1941	Pit N	83	220	25	58	9	3	3	42	22	0	12	.264	.331	.373	98	-1	0	.911	-6	86	22	3-29,O-24(23-0-1)	-0.8
1943	†StL N	90	249	26	64	10	2	0	22	13	2	8	.257	.299	.313	74	-9	1	.980	-4	106	69	O-47(18-0-29),3-23/S	-1.6
1944	†StL N	73	149	17	30	3	0	0	5	13	0	8	.201	.265	.221	37	-12	0	1.000	-4	96	0	O-23(3-2-18),3-21	-1.8
1945	StL N	74	146	23	49	7	2	0	18	31	0	3	.336	.452	.411	137	10	0	.956	-4	83	96	3-32,O-10(1-0-9)	0.6
Total	12	1010	3111	438	910	141	39	17	328	288	16	161	.293	.355	.379	103	15	18-8	.966	-28	96	75	O-501(263-73-171),3-296/S2	-3.4
GARNER, PHIL Philip Mason B 4.30.1949 Jefferson City, TN BR/TR 5-10/177# d9.10 M11 C3																								
1973	Oak A	9	5	0	0	0	0	0	0	0-0	0	3	.000	.000	.000	-99	-1	0-0	1.000	-1	45	198	/3-9	-0.3
1974	Oak A	30	28	4	5	1	0	0	1	1-0	0	5	.179	.207	.214	23	-3	1-1	.955	-2	83	65	3-19/S-8,2-3,D-2	-0.5
1975	†Oak A	160	488	46	120	21	5	6	54	30-1	5	65	.246	.295	.346	83	-12	4-6	.968	-2	102	98	*2-160/S	-0.6
1976	Oak A★	159	555	54	145	29	12	8	74	36-1	2	71	.261	.307	.400	111	5	35-13	.975	-10	98	92	*2-159	0.9
1977	Pit N	153	585	99	152	35	10	17	77	55-4	2	65	.260	.325	.441	101	0	32-9	.971	-3	103	185	*3-107,2-50,S-12	0.2
1978	Pit N	154	528	66	138	25	9	10	66	66-12	5	71	.261	.345	.400	104	4	27-14	.976	7	98	110	2-81,3-81/S-4	1.5
1979	†Pit N	150	549	76	161	32	8	11	59	55-15	3	74	.293	.359	.441	112	10	17-8	.981	1	102	122	2-83,3-78,S-14	1.7
1980	Pit N★	151	548	62	142	27	6	5	58	46-12	2	53	.259	.315	.358	87	-9	32-7	.976	16	106	124	*2-151/S	2.0
1981	Pit N★	56	181	22	46	6	2	1	20	21-1	0	21	.254	.327	.326	84	-3	4-6	.968	-8	89	94	2-50	-1.1
	†Hou N	31	113	13	27	3	1	0	6	15-1	0	11	.239	.326	.283	79	-3	6-2	.982	4	108	104	2-31	0.4
	Year	87	294	35	73	9	3	1	26	36-2	0	32	.248	.326	.310	82	-6	10-8	.973	-4	96	98	2-81	-0.7
1982	Hou N	155	588	65	161	33	8	13	83	40-4	3	92	.274	.320	.423	116	10	24-13	.980	1	98	112	*2-136,3-18	2.1
1983	Hou N	154	567	76	135	24	2	14	79	63-8	5	84	.238	.317	.362	94	-5	18-12	.945	3	106	93	*3-154	-0.5
1984	Hou N	128	374	60	104	17	6	4	45	43-2	4	63	.278	.355	.388	118	10	3-2	.979	19	115	140	3-82,2-35	3.1
1985	Hou N	135	463	65	124	23	10	6	51	34-3	2	72	.268	.317	.400	103	0	4-4	.932	-10	90	74	*3-123,2-15	-1.2
1986	†Hou N	107	313	43	83	14	3	9	41	30-2	1	45	.265	.329	.415	108	3	12-6	.896	-1	97	120	3-84/2-7	0.2
1987	Hou N	43	112	15	25	5	0	3	15	8-1	0	20	.223	.268	.348	66	-6	1-0	.976	1	92	63	3-36/2-2	-0.5
	LA N	70	126	14	24	4	0	2	8	20-7	0	24	.190	.299	.270	54	-8	5-1	.923	3	109	95	3-46,2-12/S-2	-0.4
	Year	113	238	29	49	9	0	5	23	28-8	0	44	.206	.285	.307	60	-14	6-1	.947	4	101	79	3-82,2-14/S-2	-0.9
1988	SF N	15	13	0	2	0	0	0	1	1-0	0	3	.154	.214	.154	8	-2	0-1	—	-0	0	0	/3-2	-0.3
Total	16	1860	6136	780	1594	299	82	109	738	564-74	34	842	.260	.323	.389	100	-10	225-105	.974	17	99	107	2-975,3-839/S-42,D-2	6.7
GARR, RALPH Ralph Allen "Road Runner" B 12.12.1945 Monroe, LA BL/TR 5-11/197# d9.3																								
1968	Atl N	11	7	3	2	0	0	0	0	1-0	0	0	.286	.375	.286	100	0	1-0	—	0			H	0.0
1969	Atl N	22	27	6	6	1	0	0	2	2-1	0	4	.222	.276	.259	50	-2	1-1	.857	-1	57	0	/O-7(LF)	-0.4
1970	Atl N	37	96	18	27	3	0	0	8	5-1	0	12	.281	.314	.313	65	-5	5-2	1.000	0	111	0	O-21(1-8-12)	-0.5
1971	Atl N	154	639	101	219	24	6	9	44	30-1	2	68	.343	.372	.441	122	18	30-14	.968	9	96	130	*O-153(LF)	2.0
1972	Atl N	134	554	87	180	22	0	12	53	25-2	6	41	.325	.359	.430	113	10	25-9	.962	-3	92	82	*O-131(70-13-59)	0.2
1973	Atl N	148	668	94	200	32	6	11	55	22-5	2	64	.299	.323	.415	96	-5	35-11	.968	-4	95	63	*O-148(21-0-127)	-1.4
1974	Atl N★	143	606	87	**214**	24	**17**	11	54	28-10	2	52	**.353**	.383	.503	141	29	26-16	.967	-5	92	79	*O-139(107-0-80)	1.7
1975	Atl N	151	625	74	174	26	**11**	6	31	44-**17**	3	50	.278	.327	.384	94	-7	14-9	.966	-1	96	100	*O-148(LF)	-1.7
1976	Chi A	136	527	63	158	22	6	4	36	17-2	2	41	.300	.322	.387	107	2	14-5	.978	-5	93	80	*O-125(35-41-57)/D-6	-0.8
1977	Chi A	134	543	78	163	29	7	10	54	27-4	0	44	.300	.333	.435	108	4	12-7	.987	0	96	115	*O-126(125-0-1)/D-2	-0.1
1978	Chi A	118	443	67	122	18	9	3	29	24-1	1	41	.275	.314	.377	93	-6	7-5	.959	-2	101	75	*O-109(LF)/D-9	-1.2
1979	Chi A	102	307	34	86	10	2	9	39	17-0	1	19	.280	.318	.414	96	-3	2-4	.951	-4	91	76	O-67(LF),D-17	-1.0
	Cal A	6	24	0	3	0	0	0	0	0-0	0	3	.125	.125	.125	-33	-5	0-0	—	0			/D-6	-0.5
	Year	108	331	34	89	10	2	9	39	17-0	1	22	.269	.305	.393	87	-7	2-4	.951	-4	91	76	O-67(LF),D-23	-1.5
1980	Cal A	21	42	5	8	1	0	0	3	4-2	0	6	.190	.261	.214	33	-4	0-0	.750	-0	129	0	/O-2(1-0-1),D-8	-0.4
Total	13	1317	5108	717	1562	212	64	75	408	246-46	19	445	.306	.339	.416	106	26	172-83	.968	-16	95	88	*O-1176(844-62-337)/D-48	-4.1
GARRETT, ADRIAN Henry Adrian "Pat" B 1.3.1943 Brooksville, FL BL/TR 6-3/185# d4.13 Mil 1971 C5 b-Wayne																								
1966	Atl N	4	3	0	0	0	0	0	0	0-0	0	2	.000	.000	.000	-99	-1	0-0	—	-0	0	0	/O(RF)	-0.1
1970	Chi N	3	3	0	0	0	0	0	0	0-0	0	3	.000	.000	.000	-89	-1	0-0	—	0			H	-0.1
1971	Oak A	14	21	1	3	0	0	1	2	5-1	0	7	.143	.308	.286	70	-1	0-0	1.000	0	121	0	/O-5(4-0-1)	-0.1
1972	Oak A	14	11	0	0	0	0	0	0	1-0	0	4	.000	.083	.000	-78	-2	0-0	1.000	0	117	0	/O-2(LF)	-0.3
1973	Chi N	36	54	7	12	0	0	3	8	4-1	0	18	.222	.267	.389	77	-2	1-0	1.000	0	94	0	/O-7(3-0-4),C-6	-0.2
1974	Chi N	10	8	0	0	0	0	0	0	1-0	0	1	.000	.111	.000	-64	-2	0-0	1.000	1	0	0	/C-3,1O(LF)	-0.1
1975	Chi N	16	21	1	2	0	0	1	6	1-0	0	8	.095	.130	.238	2	-3	0-0	1.000	1	211	163	/1-4	-0.2
	Cal A	37	107	17	28	5	0	6	18	14-0	0	28	.262	.344	.477	141	6	3-0	1.000	0	130	126	D-23,1-10/O-2(RF),C	0.5
1976	Cal A	29	48	4	6	3	0	0	3	5-0	0	16	.125	.204	.188	17	-5	0-0	.974	-3	84	34	C-15/1D	-0.9
Total	8	163	276	30	51	8	0	11	37	31-2	0	87	.185	.263	.333	71	-11	4-0	.959	-2	70	112	/D-27,C-25,O-18(10-0-8),1-16	-1.5
GARRETT, WAYNE Ronald Wayne B 12.3.1947 Brooksville, FL BL/TR 5-11/183# d4.12 Mil 1971 b-Adrian																								
1969	†NY N	124	400	38	87	11	3	1	39	40-3	3	75	.218	.290	.268	57	-23	4-2	.951	-11	85	97	3-72,2-47/S-9	-3.3
1970	NY N	114	366	74	93	17	4	12	45	81-6	2	60	.254	.390	.421	118	13	5-1	.944	-12	82	51	3-70,2-45/S	0.4
1971	NY N	56	202	20	43	2	0	1	11	28-2	1	31	.213	.310	.238	58	-10	1-3	.967	-2	94	94	3-53/2-9	-1.4
1972	NY N	111	298	41	69	13	3	2	29	70-3	0	58	.232	.374	.315	101	5	3-2	.960	1	98	113	3-82,2-22	0.7
1973	†NY N	140	504	76	129	20	3	16	58	72-4	1	74	.256	.348	.403	110	8	6-5	.942	4	103	**165**	*3-130/S-9,2-6	1.3
1974	NY N	151	522	55	117	14	3	13	53	89-7	2	96	.224	.337	.337	91	-4	4-6	.955	2	97	115	*3-144/S-9	-0.3
1975	NY N	107	274	49	73	8	3	6	34	50-4	1	45	.266	.379	.383	118	9	3-2	.966	8	101	193	3-94/S-3,2	1.6
1976	NY N	80	251	36	56	8	1	4	26	52-5	1	26	.223	.359	.311	97	2	7-5	.948	5	105	127	3-64,2-10/S	0.7
	Mon N	59	177	15	43	4	1	2	11	30-7	0	20	.243	.353	.311	86	-2	2-2	.982	6	108	91	2-54/3-2	0.7
	Year	139	428	51	99	12	2	6	37	82-12	1	46	.231	.356	.311	92	-1	9-7	.949	11	104	125	3-66,2-64/S	1.4
1977	Mon N	68	159	17	43	6	1	2	22	30-7	1	18	.270	.385	.358	105	3	2-2	1.000	3	112	28	3-49/2	0.5
1978	Mon N	49	69	6	12	0	0	1	2	8-1	0	10	.174	.260	.217	35	-6	0-0	.969	-1	97	104	3-13	-0.8
	StL N	33	63	11	21	4	0	1	10	11-1	0	16	.333	.432	.444	148	5	1-0	.927	-1	91	202	3-19	0.4
	Year	82	132	17	33	4	0	2	12	19-2	0	26	.250	.344	.326	89	-1	1-0	.945	-2	94	159	3-32	-0.4
Total	10	1092	3285	438	786	107	22	61	340	561-50	12	529	.239	.350	.341	95	0	38-30	.956	2	97	119	3-792,2-195/S-32	0.5
GARRIDO, GIL Gil Gonzalo B 6.26.1941 Panama City, Panama BR/TR 5-8/160# d4.24																								
1964	SF N	14	25	1	2	0	0	0	1	2-0	0	7	.080	.148	.080	-33	-4	1-0	.969	-1	114	70	S-14	-0.5
1968	Atl N	18	53	5	11	0	0	0	2	2-1	0	2	.208	.228	.208	34	-4	0-0	.987	2	107	151	S-17	-0.1
1969	†Atl N	82	227	18	50	5	1	0	10	16-3	0	11	.220	.272	.251	47	-16	0-0	.973	-19	87	83	S-81	-2.9

Year	Tm Lg	G	AB	R	H	2B	3B	HR	RBI	BB-IB	HP	SO	AVG	OBP	SLG	AOPS	ABR	SB-CS	FA	FR	Rng	Thr	G at Pos	BFW
1970	Atl N	101	367	38	97	5	4	1	19	15-3	0	16	.264	.290	.308	58	-23	0-2	.975	-4	100	84	S-80,2-26	-1.7
1971	Atl N	79	125	8	27	3	0	0	12	15-1	0	12	.216	.300	.240	51	-8	0-1	.961	-5	91	114	S-32,3-28,2-18	-0.9
1972	Atl N	40	75	11	20	1	0	0	7	11-1	1	6	.267	.368	.280	79	-1	1-1	.989	-1	108	81	2-21,S-10/3-3	-0.1
Total	6	334	872	81	207	14	5	1	51	61-9	1	54	.237	.286	.268	53	-56	2-4	.974	-27	94	92	S-234/2-65,3-31	-6.2
GARRIOTT, CECIL Virgil Cecil B 8.15.1916 Harristown, IL D 2.20.1990 Lake Elsinore, CA BL/TR 5-8/165# d9.4																								
1946	Chi N	6	5	1	0	0	0	0	0	0	1	2	.000	.167	.000	-52	-1	0	—	0			H	-0.1
GARRISON, FORD Robert Ford "Rocky" or "Snapper" B 8.29.1915 Greenville, SC D 6.6.2001 Largo, FL BR/TR 5-10.5/180# d4.22 Mil 1945 C1																								
1943	Bos A	36	129	13	36	5	1	1	11	5	0	14	.279	.306	.357	92	-2	0-1	.988	-0	100	76	O-32(26-6-0)	-0.5
1944	Bos A	13	49	5	12	3	0	0	2	6	0	4	.245	.327	.306	82	-1	0-0	.969	-0	114	0	O-12(RF)	-0.2
	Phi A	121	449	58	121	13	2	4	37	22	2	40	.269	.307	.334	84	-11	10-4	.987	5	114	63	*O-119(95-0-24)	-1.3
	Year	134	498	63	133	16	2	4	39	28	2	44	.267	.309	.331	84	-12	10-4	.985	5	114	56	*O-131(95-0-36)	-1.5
1945	Phi A	6	23	3	7	1	0	1	6	4	0	3	.304	.407	.478	157	2	1-0	1.000	0	93	202	/O-5(LF)	0.2
1946	Phi A	9	37	1	4	0	0	0	0	0	0	6	.108	.108	.108	-40	-7	0-0	1.000	-1	65	0	/O-8(LF)	-1.0
Total	4	185	687	80	180	22	3	6	56	37	2	67	.262	.302	.329	81	-19	11-5	.986	4	109	63	O-176(134-6-36)	-2.8
GARRISON, WEBSTER Webster Leotis B 8.24.1965 Marrero, LA BR/TR 5-11/170# d8.2																								
1996	Oak A	5	9	0	0	0	0	0	0	1-0	0	0	.000	.100	.000	-73	-2	0-0	.875	-1	67	66	/2-3,1	-0.3
GARRITY, HANK Francis Joseph B 2.4.1908 Boston, MA D 9.1.1962 Boston, MA BR/TR 6-1/185# d7.26																								
1931	Chi A	8	14	0	3	1	0	0	2	1	0	2	.214	.267	.286	48	-1	0-0	.941	-1	*61*	*142*	/C-7	-0.1
GARVEY, STEVE Steven Patrick B 12.22.1948 Tampa, FL BR/TR 5-10/192# d9.1																								
1969	LA N	3	3	0	1	0	0	0	0	0-0	0	1	.333	.333	.333	94	0	0-0	—	0			H	0.0
1970	LA N	34	93	8	25	5	0	1	6	6-0	0	17	.269	.310	.355	82	-2	1-1	.943	5	130	100	3-27/2	0.2
1971	LA N	81	225	27	51	12	1	7	26	21-2	0	33	.227	.290	.382	95	-2	1-2	.939	12	123	110	3-79	1.0
1972	LA N	96	294	36	79	14	2	9	30	19-3	1	36	.269	.312	.422	110	3	4-2	.902	8	112	155	3-85/1-3	1.1
1973	LA N	114	349	37	106	17	3	8	50	11-4	3	42	.304	.328	.438	116	6	0-2	.993	-7	62	108	1-76,O-10(8-0-2)	-0.8
1974	†LA N★	156	642	95	200	32	3	21	111	31-4	3	66	.312	.342	.469	132	23	5-4	.995	-12	64	95	*1-156	-0.2
1975	LA N★	160	659	85	210	38	6	18	95	33-6	3	66	.319	.351	.476	135	27	11-2	**.995**	-11	70	85	*1-160	0.4
1976	LA N★	**162**	631	85	200	37	4	13	80	50-11	1	69	.317	.363	.450	134	27	19-8	**.998**	-15	62	**110**	*1-162	0.0
1977	†LA N★	**162**	646	91	192	25	3	33	115	38-10	1	90	.297	.335	.498	121	16	9-6	**.995**	-16	57	122	*1-160	-1.0
1978	†LA N★	**162**	639	89	**202**	36	9	21	113	40-9	1	70	.316	.353	.499	138	29	10-5	.994	-8	77	103	*1-161	1.2
1979	LA N★	**162**	648	92	204	32	1	28	110	37-16	2	59	.315	.351	.497	131	26	3-6	.995	-3	89	78	*1-162	1.1
1980	LA N★	**163**	658	78	**200**	27	1	26	106	36-6	3	67	.304	.341	.467	126	20	6-11	.996	3	103	103	*1-162	1.0
1981	†LA N★	**110**	431	63	122	23	1	10	64	25-6	1	49	.283	.322	.411	111	5	3-5	**.999**	-4	78	106	*1-110	-0.8
1982	LA N	**162**	625	66	176	35	1	16	86	20-10	1	86	.282	.301	.418	103	0	5-3	.995	5	109	93	*1-158	-0.6
1983	SD N	100	388	76	114	22	0	14	59	29-11	3	39	.294	.344	.459	126	13	4-1	.994	-8	72	91	*1-100	-0.1
1984	†SD N★	161	617	72	175	27	2	8	86	24-3	1	64	.284	.307	.373	92	-9	1-2	**1.000**	-2	92	101	*1-159	-2.2
1985	SD N★	**162**	654	80	184	34	6	17	81	35-7	3	67	.281	.318	.430	110	6	0-0	.997	-8	83	109	*1-162	-1.3
1986	SD N	155	557	58	142	22	0	21	81	23-5	1	72	.255	.284	.408	91	-10	1-2	.994	-18	54	87	*1-148	-3.9
1987	SD N	27	76	5	16	2	0	1	9	1-0	1	10	.211	.231	.276	35	-7	0-0	1.000	-0	89	76	1-20	-0.9
Total	19	2332	8835	1143	2599	440	43	272	1308	479-113	29	1003	.294	.329	.446	117	171	83-62	.996	-79	78	99	*1-2059,3-191/O-10(8-0-2),2	-5.8
GASPAR, ROD Rodney Earl B 4.3.1946 Long Beach, CA BB/TR 5-11/165# d4.8																								
1969	†NY N	118	215	26	49	6	1	1	14	25-2	2	19	.228	.313	.279	66	-9	7-3	.983	8	99	308	O-91(22-16-64)	-0.4
1970	NY N	11	14	4	0	0	0	0	0	1-0	0	4	.000	.067	.000	-80	-4	1-0	1.000	1	138	0	/O-8(0-4-5)	-0.3
1971	SD N	16	17	1	2	0	0	0	2	3-0	0	3	.118	.250	.118	8	-2	0-1	1.000	0	42	0	/O-2(LF)	-0.3
1974	SD N	33	14	4	3	0	0	0	1	4-0	0	3	.214	.389	.214	75	0	0-0	1.000	1	143	0	/O-8(2-5-1),1-2	0.0
Total	4	178	260	35	54	6	1	1	17	33-2	2	29	.208	.301	.250	55	-15	8-4	.986	9	101	271	O-109(26-25-70)/1-2	-1.0
GASTALL, TOM Thomas Everett B 6.13.1932 Fall River, MA D 9.20.1956 Riviera Beach, MD BR/TR 6-2/187# d6.21																								
1955	Bal A	20	27	4	4	1	0	0	0	3-0	0	5	.148	.233	.185	15	-3	0-0	.967	-1	*77*	*0*	C-15	-0.4
1956	Bal A	32	56	3	11	2	0	0	4	3-0	1	8	.196	.246	.232	30	-6	0-0	1.000	1	*84*	*87*	C-20	-0.4
Total	2	52	83	7	15	3	0	0	4	6-0	1	13	.181	.242	.217	25	-9	0-0	.990	-0	*82*	*58*	/C-35	-0.8
GASTFIELD, ED Edward B 8.1.1865 Chicago, IL D 12.1.1899 Chicago, IL BR 5-9.5/155# d8.13																								
1884	Det N	23	82	6	6	1	0	0	2	2		34	.073	.095	.085	-45	-13		.827	4			C-19/O-2(RF),1-2	-0.7
1885	Det N	1	3	0	0	0	0	0	0	0		2	.000	.000	.000	-99	-1		.714	-1			/C	-0.1
	Chi N	1	3	0	0	0	0	0	0	0		1	.000	.000	.000	-88	-1		1.000	1			/C	0.0
	Year	2	6	0	0	0	0	0	0	0		3	.000	.000	.000	-93	-1		.889	0			/C-2	-0.1
Total	2	25	88	6	6	1	0	0	2	2		37	.068	.089	.080	-49	-15		.832	4			/C-21,1-2,O-2(RF)	-0.8
GASTON, ALEX Alexander Nathaniel B 3.12.1893 New York, NY D 2.8.1979 Santa Monica, CA BR/TR 5-9/170# d9.26 b-Milt																								
1920	NY N	4	10	2	1	0	0	0	1	1	0	2	.100	.182	.100	-18	-2	0-0	.917	-1	*107*	*52*	/C-3	-0.2
1921	NY N	20	22	1	5	1	1	0	3	1	0	9	.227	.261	.364	63	-1	0-0	.950	-0	*125*	*0*	C-11	-0.1
1922	NY N	16	26	1	5	0	0	0	1	0	0	3	.192	.192	.192	-1	-4	1-0	1.000	0	*119*	*32*	C-13	-0.3
1923	NY N	22	39	3	8	2	0	1	5	0	1	6	.205	.225	.333	46	-3	0-0	.957	0	*160*	*115*	C-21	-0.2
1926	Bos A	98	301	37	67	5	3	0	21	21	4	28	.223	.282	.259	43	-26	3-0	.981	-15	*62*	*86*	C-98	-3.4
1929	Bos A	55	116	14	26	5	2	2	9	6	0	8	.224	.262	.353	58	-8	1-0	.986	1	*103*	*126*	C-49	-0.5
Total	6	215	514	58	112	13	6	3	40	29	5	56	.218	.266	.284	45	-44	5-0	.979	-15	*83*	*91*	C-195	-4.7
GASTON, CITO Clarence Edwin B 3.17.1944 San Antonio, TX BR/TR 6-4/210# d9.14 M9 C10																								
1967	Atl N	9	25	1	3	0	1	0	1	0-0	0	5	.120	.120	.200	-10	-4	1-0	.800	-1	62	330	/O-7(0-6-1)	-0.5
1969	SD N	129	391	20	90	11	7	2	28	24-0	1	117	.230	.275	.309	67	-19	4-4	.959	2	100	**179**	*O-113(CF)	-2.2
1970	SD N★	146	584	92	186	26	9	29	93	41-2	2	142	.318	.364	.543	146	34	4-1	.975	-5	97	87	*O-142(1-142-0)	2.6
1971	SD N	141	518	57	118	13	9	17	61	24-1	2	121	.228	.264	.386	88	-13	1-0	.982	-7	81	101	*O-133(6-126-1)	-2.5
1972	SD N	111	379	30	102	14	0	7	44	22-2	2	76	.269	.313	.361	98	-2	0-2	.977	-1	90	149	O-94(18-7-73)	-1.0
1973	SD N	133	476	51	119	18	4	16	57	20-3	1	88	.250	.281	.405	96	-7	0-0	.947	0	89	153	*O-119(1-0-118)	-1.3
1974	SD N	106	267	19	57	11	0	6	33	16-2	1	51	.213	.259	.322	65	-14	0-0	.992	4	107	170	O-63(18-0-50)	-1.4
1975	Atl N	64	141	17	34	4	0	6	15	17-3	0	33	.241	.321	.397	95	-1	1-0	.974	-0	102	96	O-35(2-17-17)/1	-0.3
1976	Atl N	69	134	15	39	4	0	4	25	13-1	0	21	.291	.354	.410	109	2	1-0	.977	-2	85	58	O-28(25-0-3)/1-2	-0.1
1977	Atl N	56	85	6	23	4	0	3	21	5-0	0	19	.271	.301	.424	85	-2	1-0	1.000	0	90	0	/O-9(7-0-2),1-5	-0.2
1978	Atl N	60	118	5	27	1	0	1	9	3-0	0	20	.229	.244	.263	38	-10	0-0	.957	-1	114	0	O-29(13-1-17)/1-4	-1.3
	Pit N	2	2	1	1	0	0	0	0	0-0	0	0	.500	.500	.500	172	0	0-0	—	-0	0	0	/O(LF)	0.0
	Year	62	120	6	28	1	0	1	9	3-0	0	20	.233	.248	.267	41	-10	0-0	.957	-1	112	0	O-30(14-1-17)/1-4	-1.3
Total	11	1026	3120	314	799	106	30	91	387	185-14	9	693	.256	.298	.397	95	-36	13-7	.970	-10	93	125	O-773(92-412-282)/1-12	-8.2
GATES, BRENT Brent Robert B 3.14.1970 Grand Rapids, MI BB/TR 6-1/180# d5.5																								
1993	Oak A	139	535	64	155	29	2	7	69	56-4	4	75	.290	.357	.391	109	8	7-3	.981	-5	102	88	*2-139	1.0
1994	Oak A	64	233	29	66	11	1	2	24	21-1	1	32	.283	.337	.365	91	-3	3-0	.974	-11	86	72	2-63/1	-0.9
1995	Oak A	136	524	60	133	24	4	5	56	46-2	0	84	.254	.308	.344	75	-20	3-3	.982	11	107	91	*2-132/1D	-0.3
1996	Oak A	64	247	26	65	19	2	2	30	18-0	2	35	.263	.316	.381	77	-9	1-1	.973	-1	100	105	2-63	-0.6
1997	†Sea A	65	151	18	36	8	0	3	20	14-0	0	21	.238	.298	.351	71	-7	0-0	.934	-4	90	90	3-32,2-21/S-5,1O(LF)D	-0.9
1998	Min A	107	333	31	83	15	0	3	42	36-0	2	46	.249	.324	.321	68	-15	3-3	.961	-7	90	48	3-77,2-21/1SD	-1.9
1999	Min A	110	306	40	78	13	2	3	38	34-1	1	56	.255	.328	.340	69	-14	1-3	.972	-3	98	146	3-61,2-47/1-5,SD	-1.5
Total	7	685	2329	268	616	119	11	25	279	225-8	10	349	.264	.327	.357	82	-60	18-13	.980	-19	102	89	2-486,3-170/1-9,S-7,D-7,O(LF)	-5.1
GATES, JOE Joseph Daniel B 10.3.1954 Gary, IN BL/TR 5-7/175# d9.12																								
1978	Chi A	8	24	6	6	0	0	0	1	4-0	1	6	.250	.379	.250	80	0	1-0	.972	-1	109	73	/2-8	-0.1
1979	Chi A	16	16	5	1	0	1	0	1	2-0	0	3	.063	.167	.188	-5	-3	1-1	.966	1	126	88	/2-8,3D	-0.1
Total	2	24	40	11	7	0	1	0	2	6-0	1	9	.175	.298	.225	46	-3	2-1	.969	0	115	78	/2-16,D3	-0.2
GATES, MIKE Michael Grant B 9.20.1956 Culver City, CA BL/TR 6/165# d5.6																								
1981	Mon N	1	2	1	1	0	1	0	1	0-0	0	1	.500	.500	1.500	445	1	0-0	1.000	0	135	0	/2	0.1
1982	Mon N	36	121	16	28	2	3	0	8	9-0	0	19	.231	.280	.298	62	-7	0-0	1.000	-2	94	106	2-36	-0.7
Total	2	37	123	17	29	2	4	0	9	9-0	0	20	.236	.284	.317	68	-6	0-0	1.000	-2	94	105	/2-37	-0.6

Year	Tm Lg	G	AB	R	H	2B	3B	HR	RBI	BB-IB	HP	SO	AVG	OBP	SLG	AOPS	ABR	SB-CS	FA	FR	Rng	Thr	G at Pos	BFW
GATINS, FRANK Frank Anthony B 3.6.1871 Johnstown, PA D 11.8.1911 Johnstown, PA d9.21																								
1898	Was N	17	58	6	13	2	0	0	5	3	1		.224	.274	.259	53	-4	2	.790	-5	91	94	S-17	-0.7
1901	Bro N	50	197	21	45	7	2	1	21	5	2		.228	.255	.299	59	-11	6	.919	-8	69	104	3-46/S-5	-1.7
Total	2	67	255	27	58	9	2	1	26	8	3		.227	.259	.290	58	-15	8	.919	-12	69	104	/3-46,S-22	-2.4
GAUDET, JIM James Jennings B 6.3.1955 New Orleans, LA BR/TR 6/185# d9.10																								
1978	KC A	3	8	0	0	0	0	0	0	0-0	0	3	.000	.000	.000	-97	-2	0-0	.938	1	0	0	/C-3	-0.1
1979	KC A	3	6	0	1	0	0	0	0	0-0	0	0	.167	.167	.167	-10	-1	0-0	1.000	1	32	0	/C-3	0.0
Total	2	6	14	0	1	0	0	0	0	0-0	0	3	.071	.071	.071	-59	-3	0-0	.966	1	13	0	/C-6	-0.1
GAULE, MIKE Michael John B 8.4.1869 Baltimore, MD D 1.24.1918 Baltimore, MD BL/TL 6-2/?# d6.15																								
1889	Lou AA	1	2	0	0	0	0	0	0	0	0	1	.000	.000	.000	-99	-1	0	.000	-1	0	0	/O(CF)	-0.1
GAUTREAU, DOC Walter Paul "Punk" B 7.26.1901 Cambridge, MA D 8.23.1970 Salt Lake City, UT BR/TR 5-4/129# d6.22																								
1925	Phi A	4	7	0	0	0	0	0	0	0	0	3	.000	.000	.000	-94	-2	0-0	.933	1	109	85	/2-4	-0.1
	Bos N	68	279	45	73	13	3	0	23	35	1	13	.262	.346	.330	81	-7	11-7	.976	-9	94	93	2-68	-1.3
1926	Bos N	79	266	36	71	9	4	0	8	35	2	24	.267	.356	.331	94	-1	17	.942	-19	83	94	2-74	-1.8
1927	Bos N	87	236	38	58	12	2	0	20	25	1	20	.246	.321	.314	76	-7	11	.965	-6	98	61	2-57	-1.1
1928	Bos N	23	18	3	5	0	1	0	1	4	0	3	.278	.409	.389	116	1	1	.750	-1	89	206	/2-4,S	0.0
Total	4	261	806	122	207	34	10	0	52	99	4	63	.257	.341	.324	83	-16	40-7	.960	-34	91	85	2-207/S	-4.3
GAUTREAUX, SID Sidney Allen "Pudge" B 5.4.1912 Schriever, LA D 4.19.1980 Morgan City, LA BB/TR 5-8/190# d4.15																								
1936	Bro N	75	71	8	19	3	0	0	16	9	1	7	.268	.358	.310	80	-1	0	.963	-0	*78*	*73*	C-15	-0.1
1937	Bro N	11	10	0	1	1	0	0	2	1	0	1	.100	.182	.200	4	-1	0	—	0			H	-0.1
Total	2	86	81	8	20	4	0	0	18	10	1	8	.247	.337	.296	71	-2	0	.963	-0	*78*	*73*	/C-15	-0.2
GAVERN d6.15																								
1874	Atl NA	1	4	1	0	0	0	0	0	0		0	.000	.000	.000	-99	-1	0-0	.750	1	237	0	/2	0.0
GAZELLA, MIKE Michael B 10.13.1896 Olyphant, PA D 9.11.1978 Odessa, TX BR/TR 5-7.5/165# d7.2																								
1923	NY A	8	13	2	1	0	0	0	1	2	0	3	.077	.200	.077	-25	-2	0-0	1.000	-0	121	0	/S-4,2-2,3-2	-0.3
1926	†NY A	66	168	21	39	6	0	0	20	25	1	24	.232	.335	.268	60	-9	2-2	.913	-6	93	79	3-45,S-11	-1.1
1927	NY A	54	115	17	32	8	4	0	9	23	1	16	.278	.403	.417	117	4	4-1	.961	-6	82	95	3-44/S-6	0.0
1928	NY A	32	56	11	13	0	0	0	2	6	1	7	.232	.317	.232	48	-4	2-1	.969	-2	95	52	3-16/2-4,S-3	-0.5
Total	4	160	352	51	85	14	4	0	32	56	3	50	.241	.350	.304	73	-11	8-4	.940	-14	89	81	3-107/S-24,2-6	-1.9
GEAR, DALE Dale Dudley B 2.2.1872 Lone Elm, KS D 9.23.1951 Topeka, KS BR/TR 5-11/165# d8.15 ▲																								
1896	Cle N	4	15	5	6	1	1	0	3	1	0	1	.400	.438	.600	163	1	0	.857	-1	70	0	/P-3,1	0.0
1897	Cle N	7	24	3	4	1	0	0	2	3	1		.167	.286	.208	30	-2	2	.750	0	342	0	/O-6(CF)	-0.2
1901	Was A	58	199	17	47	9	2	0	20	4	0		.236	.251	.302	54	-13	2	.944	3	159	350	O-35(12-1-22),P-24	-0.7
Total	3	69	238	25	57	11	3	0	25	8	1	1	.239	.267	.311	59	-14	4	.900	2	191	290	/O-41(12-7-22),P-27,1	-0.9
GEARHART, GARY Lloyd William B 8.10.1923 New Lebanon, OH D 4.2.2001 Dayton, OH BR/TL 5-11/180# d4.18																								
1947	NY N	73	179	26	44	9	0	6	17	17	1	30	.246	.315	.397	87	-4	1	.961	-1	91	133	O-44(17-28-0)	-0.7
GEARY, HUCK Eugene Francis Joseph B 1.22.1917 Buffalo, NY D 1.27.1981 Cuba, NY BL/TR 5-10.5/170# d7.17 Mil 1944-45																								
1942	Pit N	9	22	3	5	0	0	0	2	2	0	3	.227	.292	.227	52	-1	0	.939	-1	77	142	/S-8	-0.2
1943	Pit N	46	166	17	25	4	0	1	13	18	0	6	.151	.234	.193	23	-16	3	.956	-3	94	102	S-46	-1.7
Total	2	55	188	20	30	4	0	1	15	20	0	9	.160	.240	.197	26	-17	3	.954	-3	92	107	/S-54	-1.9
GEDEON, ELMER Elmer John B 4.15.1917 Cleveland, OH D 4.20.1944 St.Pol, France BR/TR 6-4/196# d9.18																								
1939	Was A	5	15	1	3	0	0	0	1	2	0	5	.200	.294	.200	31	-2	0-0	1.000	0	127	0	/O-5(0-4-1)	-0.1
GEDEON, JOE Elmer Joseph B 12.5.1893 Sacramento, CA D 5.19.1941 San Francisco, CA BR/TR 6/167# d5.13																								
1913	Was A	29	71	3	13	1	3	0	6	1	1	6	.183	.205	.282	41	-6	3	.929	1	95	167	O-15(14-0-1)/3-7,2-2,S-2,P	-0.5
1914	Was A	4	2	0	0	0	0	0	1	0	1	1	.000	.333	.000	1	0	0	.667	-0	100	0	/O-4(0-1-3)	-0.1
1916	NY A	122	435	50	92	14	4	0	27	40	3	61	.211	.282	.262	62	-20	14	.955	-13	95	114	*2-122	-3.5
1917	NY A	33	117	15	28	7	0	0	8	7	1	13	.239	.288	.299	78	-3	4	.983	1	93	93	2-31	-0.2
1918	StL A	**123**	441	39	94	14	3	1	41	27	**8**	29	.213	.271	.265	64	-21	8	**.977**	16	**107**	86	*2-123	-0.3
1919	StL A	120	437	57	111	13	4	0	27	50	7	35	.254	.340	.302	79	-11	4	**.975**	-3	96	90	*2-118	-1.2
1920	StL A	153	606	95	177	33	6	0	61	55	4	36	.292	.355	.366	89	-9	1-3	.964	-27	88	102	*2-153	-3.3
Total	7	584	2109	259	515	82	20	1	171	180	25	181	.244	.311	.303	75	-70	34-3	.969	-26	96	98	2-549/O-19(14-1-4),3-7,S-2,P	-9.1
GEDMAN, RICH Richard Leo B 9.26.1959 Worcester, MA BL/TR 6/215# d9.7																								
1980	Bos A	9	24	2	5	0	0	0	1	0-0	0	5	.208	.208	.208	14	-3	0-0	.867	-0	66	0	/C-2,D-4	-0.3
1981	Bos A	62	205	22	59	15	0	5	26	9-1	1	31	.288	.317	.434	109	2	0-0	.990	-7	72	105	C-59	-0.2
1982	Bos A	92	289	30	72	17	2	4	26	10-2	2	37	.249	.279	.363	71	-12	0-1	.977	-7	80	82	C-86	-1.6
1983	Bos A	81	204	21	60	16	1	2	18	15-6	1	37	.294	.345	.412	100	1	0-1	.980	-5	60	66	C-68	-0.2
1984	Bos A	133	449	54	121	26	4	24	72	29-8	1	72	.269	.312	.506	118	9	0-0	.977	-5	91	**136**	*C-125	0.9
1985	Bos A★	144	498	66	147	30	5	18	80	50-11	3	79	.295	.362	.484	124	17	2-0	.983	13	125	**125**	*C-139	3.5
1986	†Bos A★	135	462	49	119	29	0	16	65	37-13	4	61	.258	.315	.424	100	0	1-0	.994	18	153	**126**	*C-134	2.2
1987	Bos A	52	151	11	31	8	0	1	13	10-2	0	24	.205	.250	.278	40	-13	0-0	.976	1	147	94	C-51	-1.0
1988	†Bos A	95	299	33	69	14	0	9	39	18-2	3	49	.231	.279	.368	77	-10	0-0	.992	4	118	117	C-93/D	-0.1
1989	Bos A	93	260	24	55	9	0	4	16	23-1	0	47	.212	.273	.292	57	-15	0-1	.981	-8	74	99	C-91	-1.9
1990	Bos A	10	15	3	3	0	0	0	0	5-0	1	6	.200	.429	.200	78	0	0-0	.970	-2	44	201	/C-9	-0.1
	Hou N	40	104	4	21	7	0	1	10	15-6	0	24	.202	.300	.298	68	-4	0-0	1.000	3	73	114	C-39	0.1
1991	StL N	46	94	7	10	1	0	3	8	4-0	0	15	.106	.140	.213	-1	-13	0-1	.976	6	76	91	C-43	-0.6
1992	StL N	41	105	5	23	4	0	1	8	11-1	0	22	.219	.291	.286	67	-5	0-0	.988	4	66	27	C-40	0.2
Total	13	1033	3159	331	795	176	12	88	382	236-53	16	509	.252	.304	.399	90	-46	3-4	.984	15	103	108	C-979/D-5	0.9
GEDNEY, COUNT Alfred W. B 5.10.1849 Brooklyn, NY D 3.26.1922 Hackensack, NJ 5-9/140# d4.27 ▲																								
1872	Tro NA	9	47	14	20	3	0	3	18	0		0	.426	.426	.681	232	7	1-0	.933	-1	0	0	/O-9(CF)	0.4
	Eck NA	18	71	5	13	1	0	0	6	0		3	.183	.183	.197	20	-5	2-2	.881	1	0	0	O-18(LF)	-0.3
	Year	27	118	19	33	4	0	3	24	0		3	.280	.280	.390	115	3	3-2	.892	0	0	0	O-27(18-9-0)	0.1
1873	Mut NA	**53**	225	41	60	5	5	1	24	6		4	.267	.286	.347	88	-4	1-0	.852	14	134	313	*O-53(LF)	0.9
1874	Ath NA	54	222	49	61	4	1	1	34	7		11	.275	.297	.315	89	-4	2-2	.822	0	44	188	*O-51(LF)/1-4	-0.2
1875	Mut NA	68	267	30	55	12	2	0	17	0		8	.206	.206	.266	60	-11	2-3	.843	11	70	91	*O-67(67-0-1)/P-2	0.2
Total	4 NA	202	832	139	209	25	8	5	99	13		26	.251	.263	.319	83	-17	8-7	.000	26	72	162	O-198(189-9-1)/1-4,P-2	1.0
GEER, BILLY William Henry Harrison (born George Harrison Geer) TR 5-8/160# d10.15																								
1874	Mut NA	2	8	0	2	0	0	0	1	0		0	.250	.250	.250	59	0	0-0	.889	2	482	1500	/O-2(1-1-0)	0.1
1875	NH NA	37	164	20	40	4	1	0	9	1		4	.244	.248	.280	96	1	2-2	.765	1	205	476	0-17(4-11-3),2-13/S-6,13	0.0
1878	Cin N	**61**	237	31	52	13	2	0	20	10		18	.219	.251	.291	86	-2		.867	-4	93	118	*S-60/2-2	-0.3
1880	Wor N	2	6	0	0	0	0	0	0	0		0	.000	.000	.000	-92	-1		1.000	-0	0	0	/O(RF)S	-0.1
1884	Phi U	9	36	7	9	2	1	0		4			.250	.325	.361	116	0		.772	0	121	52	/S-9	0.0
	Bro AA	107	391	68	82	15	7	0		38	1		.210	.281	.284	84	-5		.870	17	109	122	*S-107/P-2,2-2	1.3
1885	Lou AA	14	51	2	6	2	0	0	3	2	1		.118	.167	.157	3	-5		.872	-0	96	47	S-14	-0.5
Total	2 NA	39	172	20	42	4	1	0	10	1	0	4	.244	.249	.279	93	1	2-2	.000	2	244	620	/O-19(5-12-3),2-13,S-6,31	0.1
Total	4	193	721	108	149	32	10	0	23	54	2	18	.207	.264	.279	79	-13		.864	13	104	111	S-191/2-4,P-2,O(RF)	0.4
GEHRIG, LOU Henry Louis "The Iron Horse" B 6.19.1903 New York, NY D 6.2.1941 Riverdale, NY BL/TL 6/200# d6.15 HF1939																								
1923	NY A	13	26	6	11	4	1	1	9	2	0	5	.423	.464	.769	217	4	0-0	.933	-1	82	104	/1-9	0.3
1924	NY A	10	12	2	6	1	0	0	5	1	0	3	.500	.538	.583	190	2	0-0	1.000	0	138	0	/1-2,O(RF)	0.2
1925	NY A	126	437	73	129	23	10	20	68	46	2	49	.295	.365	.531	127	15	6-3	.989	-9	70	82	*1-114/O-6(2-0-4)	-0.2
1926	†NY A	**155**	572	135	179	47	**20**	16	112	105	1	73	.313	.420	.549	154	48	6-5	.991	-8	76	79	*1-155	2.7
1927	†NY A	**155**	584	149	218	**52**	18	47	**175**	109	3	84	.373	.474	.765	224	**109**	10-8	.992	-7	83	99	*1-155	8.4
1928	†NY A	**154**	562	139	210	**47**	13	27	**142**	95	4	69	.374	**.467**	.648	197	83	4-11	.989	-9	80	96	*1-154	5.9
1929	NY A	**154**	553	127	166	32	10	35	126	122	5	68	.300	.431	.584	170	63	4-3	.994	-4	87	108	*1-154	4.5

Year	Tm Lg	G	AB	R	H	2B	3B	HR	RBI	BB-IB	HP	SO	AVG	OBP	SLG	AOPS	ABR	SB-CS	FA	FR	Rng	Thr	G at Pos	BFW
1930	NY A	**154**	581	143	220	42	17	41	**174**	101	3	63	.379	.473	.721	207	99	12-14	.989	2	102	86	*1-153/O(LF)	**7.7**
1931	NY A	**155**	619	**163**	**211**	31	15	**46**	**184**	117	0	56	.341	.446	.662	199	91	17-12	.991	-10	68	101	*1-154/O(RF)	6.0
1932	†NY A	**156**	596	138	208	42	9	34	151	108	3	38	.349	.451	.621	184	79	4-11	.987	-6	80	83	*1-156	5.1
1933	NY A★	**152**	593	**138**	198	41	12	32	139	92	1	42	.334	.424	.605	181	70	9-13	.993	-3	81	85	*1-152	4.7
1934	NY A★	**154**	579	128	210	40	6	**49**	**165**	109	2	31	**.363**	**.465**	**.706**	**213**	**100**	9-5	.994	1	99	107	*1-153/S	**7.9**
1935	NY A★	**149**	535	**125**	176	26	10	30	119	**132**	5	38	.329	**.466**	.583	180	**72**	8-7	.990	0	100	89	*1-149	5.3
1936	†NY A★	**155**	579	**167**	205	37	7	**49**	152	**130**	7	46	.354	**.478**	**.696**	**193**	**91**	3-4	.994	1	98	99	*1-155	**6.6**
1937	†NY A★	**157**	569	138	200	37	9	37	159	**127**	4	49	.351	**.473**	.643	**177**	**74**	4-3	.989	-6	84	92	*1-157	4.8
1938	†NY A★	**157**	576	115	170	32	6	29	114	107	5	75	.295	.410	.523	133	32	6-1	.991	-1	97	**117**	*1-157	1.5
1939	NY A★	8	28	2	4	0	0	0	1	5	0	1	.143	.273	.143	9	-4	0-0	.971	-1	86	90	/1-8	-0.5
Total	17	2164	8001	1888	2721	534	163	493	1995	1508	45	790	.340	.447	.632	182	1028	102-100	.991	-59	86	95	*1-2137/O-9(3-0-6),S	70.9
GEHRINGER, CHARLIE Charles Leonard "The Mechanical Man" B 5.11.1903 Fowlerville, MI D1.21.1993 Bloomfield Hills, MI BL/TR 5-11/180# d9.22 Mil 1942-45 C1 HF1949																								
1924	Det A	5	13	2	6	0	0	0	1	0	0	2	.462	.462	.462	141	1	1-1	.967	2	139	90	/2-5	0.3
1925	Det A	8	18	3	3	0	0	0	0	2	0	0	.167	.250	.167	7	-3	0-1	1.000	3	151	199	/2-6	0.0
1926	Det A	123	459	62	127	19	17	1	48	30	1	42	.277	.322	.399	86	-12	9-7	.973	-6	94	89	*2-112/3-6	-1.5
1927	Det A	133	508	110	161	29	11	4	61	52	2	31	.317	.383	.441	112	9	17-8	.965	17	108	**110**	*2-121	2.9
1928	Det A	**154**	603	108	193	29	16	6	74	69	6	22	.320	.395	.451	120	19	15-9	.962	-0	99	103	*2-154	2.2
1929	Det A	**155**	634	**131**	**215**	**45**	**19**	13	106	64	6	19	.339	.405	.532	139	36	**27**-10	**.975**	-8	96	82	*2-154	3.3
1930	Det A	**154**	610	144	201	47	15	16	98	69	7	17	.330	.404	.534	133	32	19-15	**.979**	5	97	94	*2-154	3.6
1931	Det A	101	383	67	119	24	5	4	53	29	0	15	.311	.359	.431	103	1	13-4	.979	-4	91	102	2-78/1-9	0.3
1932	Det A	152	618	112	184	44	11	19	107	68	3	34	.298	.370	.497	118	16	9-8	.967	2	97	110	*2-152	2.4
1933	Det A★	**155**	628	103	204	42	6	12	105	68	3	27	.325	.393	.468	125	24	5-4	.981	5	102	117	*2-155	3.6
1934	†Det A★	**154**	601	**134**	**214**	50	7	11	127	99	3	25	.356	.450	.517	149	50	11-8	.981	7	103	101	*2-154	6.0
1935	†Det A★	150	610	123	201	32	8	19	108	79	3	16	.330	.409	.502	139	37	11-4	**.985**	2	99	104	*2-149	4.6
1936	Det A★	**154**	641	144	227	**60**	12	15	116	83	4	13	.354	.431	.555	141	44	4-1	**.974**	16	103	**116**	*2-154	6.1
1937	Det A★	144	564	133	209	40	1	14	96	90	1	25	**.371**	.458	.520	143	43	11-4	**.986**	-0	106	100	*2-142	4.8
1938	Det A★	152	568	133	174	32	5	20	107	113	4	21	.306	.425	.486	121	23	14-1	.976	1	100	107	*2-152	3.2
1939	Det A	118	406	86	132	29	6	16	86	68	1	16	.325	.423	.544	135	23	4-3	**.977**	4	100	101	*2-107	3.1
1940	†Det A	139	515	108	161	33	3	10	81	101	3	17	.313	.428	.447	116	18	10-0	.972	-19	89	77	*2-138	1.0
1941	Det A	127	436	65	96	19	4	3	46	95	3	26	.220	.363	.303	71	-15	1-2	**.982**	0	95	77	*2-116	-0.8
1942	Det A	45	45	6	12	0	0	1	7	7	0	4	.267	.365	.333	90	0	0-0	1.000	1	113	59	/2-3	0.0
Total	19	2323	8860	1774	2839	574	146	184	1427	1186	50	372	.320	.404	.480	123	346	181-90	.976	27	99	100	*2-2206/1-9,3-6	45.1
GEIER, PHIL Philip Louis "Little Phil" B 11.3.1875 Washington, DC D 9.25.1967 Spokane, WA BL/TR 5-7/145# d8.17 OF Total (14-LF 167-CF 98-RF)																								
1896	Phi N	17	56	12	13	0	1	0	6	6	1	7	.232	.317	.268	56	-4	3	.813	-1	84	0	O-12(2-0-10)/2-3,C-2	-0.4
1897	Phi N	92	316	51	88	6	2	1	35	56	3		.278	.392	.320	91	0	19	.932	-5	185	87	O-45(2-3-40),2-37/S-6,3-2	-0.4
1900	Cin N	30	113	18	29	1	4	0	10	7	1		.257	.306	.336	79	-4	3	.941	0	128	0	O-27(0-9-18)/3-2	-0.5
1901	Phi A	50	211	42	49	5	2	0	23	24	1		.232	.314	.275	61	-11	7	.934	-5	76	65	O-50(6-14-30)/S-2,3	-1.7
	Mil A	11	39	4	7	1	1	0	1	5	0		.179	.273	.256	50	-3	4	1.000	0	276	574	/O-8(CF),3-3	-0.3
	Year	61	250	46	56	6	3	0	24	29	1		.224	.307	.272	60	-13	11	.941	-5	96	116	O-58(6-22-30)/3-4,S-2	-2.0
1904	Bos N	149	580	70	141	17	2	1	27	56	4		.243	.314	.284	88	-6	18	.933	-4	120	198	*O-137(4-133-0)/3-7,2-5,S	-1.7
Total	5	349	1315	197	327	30	12	2	102	154	10	7	.249	.332	.294	81	-28	54	.932	-15	125	136	O-279C/2-45,3-15,S-9,C-2	-5.0
GEIGER, GARY Gary Merle B 4.4.1937 Sand Ridge, IL D 4.24.1996 Murphysboro, IL BL/TR 6/168# d4.15																								
1958	Cle A	91	195	28	45	3	1	1	6	27-0	3	43	.231	.330	.272	70	-7	2-2	.986	3	114	99	O-53(1-44-8)/3-2,P	-0.7
1959	Bos A	120	335	45	82	10	4	11	48	21-0	0	55	.245	.289	.397	83	-9	9-3	.989	1	100	100	O-95(46-61-1)	-1.2
1960	Bos A	77	245	32	74	13	3	9	33	23-0	3	38	.302	.369	.490	126	9	2-2	1.000	5	103	227	O-66(5-7-59)	1.1
1961	Bos A	140	499	82	116	21	6	18	64	87-4	4	91	.232	.349	.407	99	1	16-4	.988	3	102	**173**	*O-137(CF)	0.2
1962	Bos A	131	466	67	116	18	4	16	54	67-3	2	66	.249	.344	.408	99	0	18-11	.987	-1	100	136	*O-129(CF)	-0.5
1963	Bos A	121	399	67	105	13	5	16	44	36-2	3	63	.263	.327	.441	110	5	9-4	.984	8	115	196	O-95(2-89-4)/1-6	1.0
1964	Bos A	5	13	3	5	0	1	0	1	2-0	0	2	.385	.467	.538	170	1	0-0	1.000	-0	97	0	/O-4(0-1-3)	0.1
1965	Bos A	24	45	5	9	3	0	1	2	13-1	0	10	.200	.379	.333	98	1	3-0	.970	0	118	0	O-16(5-10-1)	0.1
1966	Atl N	78	126	23	33	5	3	4	10	21-1	1	29	.262	.367	.444	124	5	0-1	.982	2	90	275	O-49(5-33-15)	0.5
1967	Atl N	69	117	17	19	1	1	1	5	20-0	0	35	.162	.285	.214	45	-8	1-1	.980	-0	92	136	O-38(6-26-7)	-1.0
1969	Hou N	93	125	19	28	4	1	0	16	24-2	1	34	.224	.351	.272	79	-2	2-1	.968	1	103	153	O-65(47-5-14)	-0.3
1970	Hou N	5	4	0	1	0	0	0	0	0-0	0	0	.250	.250	.250	36	0	0-0	1.000	0	101	0	/O-2(RF)	0.0
Total	12	954	2569	388	633	91	29	77	283	341-13	17	466	.246	.337	.394	98	-4	62-29	.986	20	104	157	O-749(117-542-114)/1-6,3-2,P	-0.7
GEIS, BILL William J. (born William J. Geiss) B 7.15.1858 Chicago, IL D 9.18.1924 Chicago, IL 5-10/164# d5.1 b-Emil																								
1884	Det N	75	283	22	50	11	4	2	16	6		60	.177	.194	.265	46	-17		.862	-7	95	86	2-73/O(RF)1P	-1.9
GEISS, EMIL Emil August B 3.20.1867 Chicago, IL D 10.4.1911 Chicago, IL BR/TR 5-11/170# d5.18 b-Bill ▲																								
1887	Chi N	3	12	0	1	0	0	0	0	0	0	7	.083	.083	.083	-47	-2	0	.571	-1	58	0	/21P	-0.3
GELBERT, CHARLIE Charles Magnus B 1.26.1906 Scranton, PA D 1.13.1967 Easton, PA BR/TR 5-11/170# d4.16																								
1929	StL N	146	512	60	134	29	8	3	65	51	0	46	.262	.329	.367	71	-23	8	.948	8	101	100	*S-146	0.0
1930	†StL N	139	513	92	156	39	11	3	72	43	2	41	.304	.360	.441	89	-8	6	.947	5	97	104	*S-139	1.0
1931	†StL N	131	447	61	129	29	5	1	62	54	0	31	.289	.365	.383	97	1	7	.959	9	101	105	*S-130	1.9
1932	StL N	122	455	60	122	28	9	1	45	39	3	30	.268	.330	.376	87	-8	8	.945	-3	94	87	*S-122	-0.1
1935	StL N	62	168	24	49	7	2	2	21	17	0	18	.292	.357	.393	97	0	0	.978	3	103	187	3-37,S-21/2-3	0.5
1936	StL N	93	280	33	64	15	2	3	27	25	0	26	.229	.292	.329	67	-13	2	.965	4	110	153	3-60,S-28/2-8	-0.5
1937	Cin N	43	114	12	22	4	0	1	13	15	0	12	.193	.287	.254	51	-8	1	.968	-0	93	85	S-37/2-9,3	-0.5
	Det A	20	47	4	4	2	0	0	1	4	0	11	.085	.157	.128	-27	-9	0-0	.934	-1	102	101	S-16	-0.9
1939	Was A	68	188	36	48	7	5	3	29	30	1	11	.255	.361	.394	100	0	2-0	.970	-2	104	100	S-28,3-20/2	0.1
1940	Was A	22	54	7	20	7	1	0	7	4	1	3	.370	.424	.537	157	5	0-0	.920	-4	81	42	S-12/P-2,2	0.1
	Bos A	30	91	9	18	2	0	0	8	8	0	16	.198	.263	.220	25	-10	0-0	.926	3	122	97	3-29/S	-0.6
	Year	52	145	16	38	9	1	0	15	12	1	19	.262	.323	.338	72	-6	0-0	.926	-1	122	97	3-29,S-13/P-2,2	-0.5
Total	9	876	2869	398	766	169	43	17	350	290	7	245	.267	.336	.374	82	-73	34-0	.951	22	98	98	S-680,3-147/2-22,P-2	1.0
GENINS, FRANK C. Frank "Frenchy" B 11.2.1866 St.Louis, MO D 9.30.1922 St.Louis, MO TR d7.5 OF Total (21-LF 36-CF 13-RF)																								
1892	Cin N	35	110	12	20	4	0	0	7	12	0	12	.182	.262	.218	46	-7	7	.901	3	115	119	S-17,O-14(7-7-0)/3-4	-0.4
	StL N	15	51	5	10	1	0	0	4	1	0	11	.196	.212	.216	31	-4	3	.821	-6	75	94	S-14/O(RF)	-0.9
	Year	50	161	17	30	5	0	0	11	13	0	23	.186	.247	.217	42	-11	10	.868	-3	97	108	S-31,O-15(7-7-1)/3-4	-1.3
1895	Pit N	73	252	43	63	8	0	2	24	22	2	14	.250	.315	.306	64	-13	19	.931	-7	24	0	O-29(14-3-12),3-16,2-16/S-8,1-2	-1.7
1901	Cle A	26	101	15	23	5	0	0	9	8	0		.228	.284	.277	58	-5	3	.940	1	94	125	O-26(CF)	-0.5
Total	3	149	514	75	116	18	0	2	44	43	2	37	.226	.288	.272	56	-29	32	.934	-9	66	48	/O-70C,S-39,3-20,2-16,1-2	-3.5
GENOVESE, GEORGE George Michael B 2.22.1922 Staten Island, NY BL/TR 5-6.5/160# d4.29																								
1950	Was A	3	1	1	0	0	0	0	0	1	0	0	.000	.500	.000	39	0	0-0	—	0			H	0.0
GENTILE, JIM James Edward "Diamond Jim" B 6.3.1934 San Francisco, CA BL/TL 6-4/215# d9.10																								
1957	Bro N	4	6	1	1	0	0	1	1	1-0	0	1	.167	.286	.667	133	0	0-0	1.000	-0	0	292	/1-2	0.0
1958	LA N	12	30	0	4	1	0	0	4	4-1	0	6	.133	.235	.167	9	-4	0-0	.981	-1	48	145	/1-8	-0.5
1960	Bal A★	138	384	67	112	17	0	21	98	68-5	7	72	.292	.403	.500	146	28	0-0	.993	-7	74	109	*1-124	1.5
1961	Bal A★	148	486	96	147	25	2	46	141	96-5	11	106	.302	.423	.646	189	65	1-1	.989	1	101	119	*1-144	5.6
1962	Bal A★	152	545	80	137	21	1	33	87	77-**16**	7	100	.251	.346	.475	128	22	1-0	.988	5	111	104	*1-150	1.7
1963	Bal A	145	496	65	123	16	1	24	72	76-9	6	101	.248	.353	.429	123	17	1-0	**.995**	8	117	113	*1-143	1.8
1964	KC A	136	439	71	110	10	0	28	71	84-6	4	122	.251	.372	.465	128	20	0-0	.988	-1	100	82	*1-128	1.2
1965	KC A	38	118	14	29	5	0	10	22	9-1	1	26	.246	.305	.542	138	5	0-0	.981	-2	88	100	1-35	0.2
	Hou N	81	227	22	55	11	1	7	31	34-7	5	72	.242	.352	.392	118	7	0-0	.993	1	101	88	1-68	0.4
1966	Hou N	49	144	16	35	6	1	7	18	21-3	4	39	.243	.355	.444	129	6	0-0	.989	2	117	89	1-43	0.6
	Cle A	33	47	2	6	1	0	2	4	5-1	0	18	.128	.212	.277	39	-4	0-0	.944	-0	113	81	/1-9	-0.5
Total	9	936	2922	434	759	113	6	179	549	475-54	45	663	.260	.368	.486	137	162	3-1	.990	5	102	104	1-854	12.0

Year	Tm Lg	G	AB	R	H	2B	3B	HR	RBI	BB-IB	HP	SO	AVG	OBP	SLG	AOPS	ABR	SB-CS	FA	FR	Rng	Thr	G at Pos	BFW
GENTILE, SAM Samuel Christopher B 10.12.1916 Charlestown, MA D 5.4.1998 Everett, MA BL/TR 5-11/180# d4.24 Mil 1944-45																								
1943	Bos N	8	4	1	1	1	0	0	0	1	0	0	.250	.400	.500	162	0	0	—	0			H	0.0
GENTRY, HARVEY Harvey William B 5.27.1926 Winston-Salem, NC BL/TR 6/170# d4.14 b-Rufe																								
1954	NY N	5	4	0	1	0	0	0	1	1	0	0	.250	.400	.250	73	0	0-0	—	0			H	0.0
GEORGE, ALEX Alex Thomas M. B 9.27.1938 Kansas City, MO BL/TR 5-11.5/170# d9.16																								
1955	KC A	5	10	0	1	0	0	0	0	1-0	0	7	.100	.182	.100	-22	-2	0-0	.917	-1	62	55	/S-5	-0.3
GEORGE, GREEK Charles Peter B 12.25.1912 Waycross, GA D 8.15.1999 Metairie, LA BR/TR 6-2/200# d6.30																								
1935	Cle A	2	0	0	0	0	0	0	0	0	0	0	—	—	—	—	0	0-0	1.000	0	0	0	/C	0.0
1936	Cle A	23	77	3	15	3	0	0	5	9	0	16	.195	.279	.234	28	-9	0-0	.994	8	122	122	C-22	0.1
1938	Bro N	7	20	0	4	0	1	0	2	0	0	4	.200	.200	.300	35	-2	0	1.000	1	72	170	/C-7	-0.1
1941	Chi N	35	64	4	10	2	0	0	6	2	0	10	.156	.182	.188	4	-8	0	.973	1	91	102	C-18	-0.7
1945	Phi A	51	138	8	24	4	1	0	11	17	0	29	.174	.265	.217	41	-10	0-0	.972	-5	87	62	C-46	-1.4
Total	5	118	299	15	53	9	2	0	24	28	0	59	.177	.248	.221	29	-29	0-0	.983	5	97	94	/C-94	-2.1
GERAGHTY, BEN Benjamin Raymond B 7.19.1912 Jersey City, NJ D 6.18.1963 Jacksonville, FL BR/TR 5-11/175# d4.17																								
1936	Bro N	51	129	11	25	4	0	0	9	8	0	16	.194	.241	.225	26	-14	4	.922	-7	83	60	S-31/2-9,3-5	-1.8
1943	Bos N	8	1	2	0	0	0	0	0	0	0	0	.000	.000	.000	-99	0	0	1.000	0	139	0	/2S3	0.0
1944	Bos N	11	16	3	4	0	0	0	0	1	0	2	.250	.294	.250	52	-1	0	1.000	-1	131	0	/2-4,3-3	-0.2
Total	3	70	146	16	29	4	0	0	9	9	0	18	.199	.245	.226	28	-15	4	.922	-8	82	59	/S-32,2-14,3-9	-2.0
GERBER, CRAIG Craig Stuart B 1.8.1959 Chicago, IL BL/TR 6/175# d4.11																								
1985	Cal A	65	91	8	24	1	2	0	6	2-0	0	3	.264	.277	.319	64	-5	0-3	.970	9	128	145	S-53/3-9,2D	0.6
GERBER, WALLY Walter "Spooks" B 8.18.1891 Columbus, OH D 6.19.1951 Columbus, OH BR/TR 5-10/152# d9.23 Mil 1918																								
1914	Pit N	17	54	5	13	1	1	0	5	2	1	8	.241	.281	.296	75	-2	0	.921	1	115	122	S-17	0.0
1915	Pit N	56	144	8	28	2	0	0	7	9	2	16	.194	.252	.208	40	-10	6-1	.930	1	97	72	3-23,S-21/2-2	-0.7
1917	StL A	14	39	2	12	1	1	0	2	3	0	2	.308	.357	.385	131	1	1	.939	0	115	45	S-12/2-2	0.2
1918	StL A	56	171	10	41	4	0	0	10	19	0	11	.240	.316	.263	77	-4	2	.922	-10	95	88	S-56	-1.1
1919	StL A	**140**	462	43	105	14	6	1	37	49	5	36	.227	.308	.290	67	-20	1	.940	-9	99	82	*S-140	-2.0
1920	StL A	**154**	584	70	163	26	2	2	60	58	2	32	.279	.346	.341	80	-15	4-13	.939	7	**106**	104	*S-154	-0.1
1921	StL A	114	436	55	121	12	9	2	48	34	5	19	.278	.337	.360	73	-18	4-7	.943	-1	94	111	*S-113	-0.8
1922	StL A	153	604	81	161	22	8	1	51	52	1	34	.267	.326	.334	70	-27	6-4	.944	-1	94	**127**	*S-153	-1.1
1923	StL A	**154**	605	85	170	26	3	1	62	54	2	50	.281	.342	.339	75	-21	4-6	.950	7	97	111	*S-154	0.2
1924	StL A	148	496	61	135	20	4	0	55	43	9	34	.272	.341	.329	69	-22	4-5	.946	-6	94	107	*S-147	-1.3
1925	StL A	72	246	29	67	13	1	0	19	26	1	15	.272	.344	.333	69	-11	1-2	.949	5	104	94	S-71	0.0
1926	StL A	131	411	37	111	8	0	0	42	40	3	29	.270	.339	.290	62	-22	0-2	.944	2	99	**127**	*S-129	-0.8
1927	StL A	142	438	44	98	13	9	0	45	35	2	25	.224	.284	.295	49	-35	3-6	.946	9	102	110	*S-141/3	-1.2
1928	StL A	6	18	1	5	1	0	0	0	1	0	3	.278	.316	.333	69	-1	0-0	.783	-2	91	158	/S-6	-0.2
	Bos A	104	300	21	64	6	1	0	28	32	0	31	.213	.289	.240	41	-26	6-1	.955	27	124	94	*S-103	1.2
	Year	110	318	22	69	7	1	0	28	33	0	34	.217	.291	.245	43	-26	6-1	**.948**	**26**	**122**	97	*S-109	1.0
1929	Bos A	61	91	6	15	3	1	0	5	8	0	12	.165	.232	.220	17	-12	1-0	.937	5	102	38	S-30,2-22	-0.4
Total	15	1522	5099	558	1309	172	46	7	476	465	33	357	.257	.323	.313	67	-245	43-47	.943	36	100	106	*S-1447/2-26,3-24	-8.1
GEREN, BOB Robert Peter B 9.22.1961 San Diego, CA BR/TR 6-3/221# d5.17 C1																								
1988	NY A	10	10	0	1	0	0	0	0	2-0	0	3	.100	.250	.100	2	-1	0-0	1.000	-0	124	0	C-10	-0.1
1989	NY A	65	205	26	59	5	1	9	27	12-0	1	44	.288	.329	.454	120	4	0-0	.991	5	189	81	C-60/D-2	1.2
1990	NY A	110	277	21	59	7	0	8	31	13-1	5	73	.213	.259	.325	63	-15	0-0	.993	1	101	**142**	*C-107/D	-0.9
1991	NY A	64	128	7	28	3	0	2	12	9-0	0	31	.219	.270	.289	55	-8	0-1	.989	-3	87	98	C-63	-0.9
1993	SD N	58	145	8	31	6	0	3	6	13-4	0	28	.214	.278	.317	58	-9	0-0	.993	1	80	133	C-49/13	-0.5
Total	5	307	765	62	178	21	1	22	76	49-5	6	179	.233	.283	.349	74	-29	0-1	.992	3	116	115	C-289/D-3,31	-1.2
GERHARDT, JOE John Joseph "Move Up Joe" B 2.14.1855 Washington, DC D 3.11.1922 Middletown, NY BR/TR 6/160# d9.1 M2																								
1873	Was NA	13	57	6	12	3	0	0	9	0		6	.211	.211	.263	41	-4	0-1	.710	-4	91	123	S-13	-0.6
1874	Bal NA	14	61	10	19	0	1	0	6	0		0	.311	.311	.344	111	1	0-0	.750	1	125	94	S-14	0.1
1875	Mut NA	58	252	29	54	7	3	0	20	0		2	.214	.214	.266	62	-10	0-5	.753	0	109	67	3-47,2-13/SO(LF)	-1.2
1876	Lou N	65	292	33	76	10	3	2	18	3		5	.260	.268	.336	85	-7		.944	4	**133**	83	*1-54/2-5,S-3,O-2(LF),3-2	-0.5
1877	Lou N	59	250	41	76	6	5	1	35	5		8	.304	.318	.380	101	-2		.888	19	**121**	**150**	*2-57/O(CF)S1	1.7
1878	Cin N	60	259	46	77	7	2	0	28	7		14	.297	.316	.340	127	8		.906	6	102	118	*2-60	1.6
1879	Cin N	79	313	22	62	12	3	1	39	3		19	.198	.206	.265	57	-14		.908	4	94	100	2-55,3-16/1-8,S	-0.7
1881	Det N	80	297	35	72	13	6	0	36	7		31	.242	.260	.327	80	-7		.908	6	94	**153**	*2-79/3	0.2
1883	Lou AA	78	319	56	84	11	9	0		14			.263	.294	.354	116	7		.906	18	112	133	*2-78,M	2.4
1884	Lou AA	106	404	39	89	7	8	0	40	13	5		.220	.254	.277	76	-10		.920	23	113	**164**	*2-106	1.5
1885	NY N	**112**	399	43	62	12	2	0	33	24		47	.155	.203	.195	30	-30		.911	9	98	151	*2-112	-1.6
1886	NY N	123	426	44	81	11	7	0	40	22		63	.190	.230	.249	45	-29	8	.924	9	96	105	*2-123	-1.4
1887	NY N	1	4	0	0	0	0	0	0	0	0	0	.000	.000	.000	-99	-1	0	1.000	0	108	0	/3	-0.1
	NY AA	85	307	40	68	13	2	0	27	24	1		.221	.280	.277	58	-16	15	.896	9	104	116	2-84/3	-0.4
1890	Bro AA	99	369	34	75	10	4	2	40	30	4		.203	.270	.268	61	-19	9	.938	33	122	133	*2-99	1.5
	StL AA	37	125	15	32	0	0	1	11	9	3		.256	.321	.280	68	-6	5	.955	6	101	64	2-20,3-17,M	0.1
	Year	136	494	49	107	10	4	3	51	39	7		.217	.283	.271	63	-25	14	**.940**	**38**	**119**	**122**	*2-119,3-17	1.6
1891	Lou AA	2	6	0	0	0	0	0	0	1	0	0	.000	.143	.000	-59	-1	0	.833	-1	98	0	/2-2	-0.2
Total	3 NA	85	370	45	85	10	4	0	35	0	0	8	.230	.230	.278	67	-13	0-6	.753	-2	109	67	/3-47,S-28,2-13,O(LF)	-1.7
Total	12	986	3770	448	854	112	51	7	347	162	13	187	.227	.261	.289	72	-127	37-0	.913	144	105	131	2-880/1-63,3-38,S-5,O-3(2-1-0)	4.1
GERHART, KEN Harold Kenneth B 5.19.1961 Charleston, SC BR/TR 6/190# d9.14																								
1986	Bal A	20	69	4	16	2	0	1	7	4-0	0	18	.232	.267	.304	58	-4	0-1	.971	-2	84	0	O-20(6-14-0)	-0.7
1987	Bal A	92	284	41	69	10	2	14	34	17-0	1	53	.243	.286	.440	92	-5	9-2	.973	-4	93	64	O-91(53-42-0)	-0.9
1988	Bal A	103	262	27	51	10	1	9	23	21-0	2	57	.195	.256	.344	69	-12	7-3	.975	-2	97	75	O-93(30-57-10)/D-3	-1.4
Total	3	215	615	72	136	22	3	24	64	42-0	3	128	.221	.271	.384	79	-21	16-6	.974	-8	94	63	O-204(89-113-10)/D-3	-3.0
GERKEN, GEORGE George Herbert "Pickles" B 7.28.1903 Chicago, IL D 10.23.1977 Arcadia, CA BR/TR 5-11.5/175# d4.19																								
1927	Cle A	6	14	1	3	0	0	0	2	1	0	3	.214	.267	.214	26	-2	0-0	.917	0	105	250	/O-5(2-3-0)	-0.1
1928	Cle A	38	115	16	26	7	2	0	9	12	1	22	.226	.305	.322	64	-6	3-4	.940	-1	99	89	O-34(14-16-4)	-1.0
Total	2	44	129	17	29	7	2	0	11	13	1	25	.225	.301	.310	60	-8	3-4	.937	-1	100	106	/O-39(16-19-4)	-1.1
GERLACH, JOHNNY John Glenn B 5.11.1917 Shullsburg, WI D 8.28.1999 Madison, WI BR/TR 5-9/165# d9.3																								
1938	Chi A	9	25	2	7	0	0	0	1	4	0	2	.280	.379	.280	66	-1	0-0	.949	1	97	197	/S-8	0.0
1939	Chi A	3	2	0	2	0	0	0	0	0	0	0	1.000	1.000	1.000	402	1	0-0	1.000	0	140	0	/3	0.1
Total	2	12	27	2	9	0	0	0	1	4	0	2	.333	.419	.333	89	0	0-0	.949	1	97	197	/S-8,3	0.1
GERMAN, ESTEBAN Esteban (Guridi) B 1.26.1978 Haina, D.R. BR/TR 5-10/180# d5.21																								
2002	Oak A	9	35	4	7	0	0	0	0	4-0	1	11	.200	.300	.200	37	-3	1-0	.978	1	95	111	/2-8	-0.2
2003	Oak A	5	4	0	1	0	0	0	1	0-0	0	1	.250	.250	.250	32	0	0-0	1.000	1	149	110	/2-5	0.1
Total	2	14	39	4	8	0	0	0	1	4-0	1	12	.205	.295	.205	36	-3	1-0	.982	2	103	111	/2-13	-0.1
GERNERT, DICK Richard Edward B 9.28.1928 Reading, PA BR/TR 6-3/210# d4.16 C2																								
1952	Bos A	102	367	58	89	20	2	19	67	35	5	83	.243	.317	.463	107	2	4-1	.987	-1	97	113	1-99	-0.2
1953	Bos A	139	494	73	125	15	1	21	71	88	5	82	.253	.371	.415	106	7	0-7	.986	-2	97	107	*1-136	-0.6
1954	Bos A	14	23	2	6	2	0	0	1	6	0	4	.261	.414	.348	99	0	0-0	1.000	-1	31	110	/1-6	-0.1
1955	Bos A	7	20	6	4	2	0	0	1	1-0	0	5	.200	.238	.300	40	-2	0-0	.974	-0	105	54	/1-5	-0.2
1956	Bos A	106	306	53	89	11	0	16	68	56-1	2	57	.291	.399	.484	119	10	1-0	.985	4	81	146	O-50(LF),1-37	0.9
1957	Bos A	99	316	45	75	13	3	14	58	39-3	3	62	.237	.324	.430	99	-1	1-1	.989	-0	107	123	1-71,O-16(LF)	-0.6
1958	Bos A	122	431	59	102	19	1	20	69	59-4	2	78	.237	.330	.425	100	0	2-0	.991	7	**127**	103	*1-114	0.1
1959	Bos A	117	298	41	78	14	1	11	42	52-3	0	49	.262	.369	.426	113	7	1-2	.995	6	130	101	1-75,O-25(21-0-7)	0.8
1960	Chi N	52	96	8	24	3	0	0	11	10-0	0	19	.250	.321	.281	67	-4	1-0	.987	2	153	109	1-18/O-5(LF)	-0.3

Year	Tm Lg	G	AB	R	H	2B	3B	HR	RBI	BB-IB	HP	SO	AVG	OBP	SLG	AOPS	ABR	SB-CS	FA	FR	Rng	Thr	G at Pos	BFW
	Det A	21	50	6	15	4	0	1	5	4-0	0	5	.300	.352	.440	110	1	0-0	1.000	-1	62	152	1-13/O-6(LF)	-0.1
1961	Det A	6	5	1	1	0	0	1	1	1-0	0	2	.200	.333	.800	187	1	0-0	—	0			H	0.1
	†Cin N	40	63	4	19	1	0	0	7	7-1	0	9	.302	.361	.317	84	-1	0-0	.993	3	156	74	1-21	0.1
1962	Hou N	10	24	1	5	0	0	0	1	5-0	0	7	.208	.345	.208	57	-1	0-0	1.000	-1	42	161	/1-9	-0.3
Total	11	835	2493	357	632	104	8	103	402	363-12	17	462	.254	.351	.426	104	19	10-11	.990	16	112	109	1-604,O-102(98-0-7)	-0.4
GERONIMO, CESAR Cesar Francisco (Zorrilla) B 3.11.1948 ElSeibo, D.R. BL/TL 6-2/170# d4.16																								
1969	Hou N	28	8	8	2	1	0	0	0	0-0	0	3	.250	.250	.375	74	0	0-0	1.000	-0	45	0	/O-9(4-1-4)	-0.1
1970	Hou N	47	37	5	9	0	0	0	2	2-0	1	5	.243	.293	.243	49	-3	0-0	.920	0	129	0	O-26(12-5-10)	-0.3
1971	Hou N	94	82	13	18	2	2	1	6	5-0	0	31	.220	.264	.329	69	-4	2-2	.977	-1	76	50	O-64(47-3-15)	-0.7
1972	†Cin N	120	255	32	70	9	7	4	29	24-7	3	64	.275	.344	.412	121	6	2-7	.982	3	102	179	*O-106(0-21-91)	0.4
1973	†Cin N	139	324	35	68	14	3	4	33	23-3	3	74	.210	.266	.309	63	-17	5-5	.992	4	106	135	*O-130(0-104-26)	-1.8
1974	Cin N	150	474	73	133	17	8	7	54	46-11	2	96	.281	.345	.395	109	5	9-5	.987	11	113	169	*O-145(CF)	1.3
1975	†Cin N	148	501	69	129	25	5	6	53	48-8	4	97	.257	.327	.363	90	-7	13-5	.993	11	113	134	*O-148(CF)	0.2
1976	†Cin N	149	486	59	149	24	11	2	49	56-13	6	95	.307	.382	.414	124	17	22-5	.985	-2	107	45	*O-146(CF)	1.5
1977	Cin N	149	492	54	131	22	4	10	52	35-13	5	89	.266	.321	.388	88	-9	10-4	.992	7	113	102	*O-147(CF)	-0.3
1978	Cin N	122	296	28	67	15	1	5	27	43-10	3	67	.226	.329	.334	86	-4	8-3	.981	2	108	77	*O-115(CF)	-0.3
1979	†Cin N	123	356	38	85	17	4	4	38	37-11	2	56	.239	.312	.343	79	-10	1-1	.993	6	109	144	*O-118(CF)	-0.5
1980	Cin N	103	145	16	37	5	0	2	9	14-3	0	24	.255	.319	.331	82	-3	2-1	1.000	0	102	72	O-86(CF)	-0.4
1981	†KC A	59	118	14	29	0	2	2	13	11-2	0	16	.246	.305	.331	85	-3	6-1	.980	2	120	37	O-57(5-4-50)	-0.2
1982	KC A	53	119	14	32	6	3	4	23	8-2	0	16	.269	.305	.471	112	1	2-0	1.000	3	114	141	O-44(10-32-3)/D	0.4
1983	KC A	38	87	2	18	4	0	0	4	2-0	2	13	.207	.242	.253	36	-8	0-1	.986	3	132	106	O-35(9-3-26)	-0.6
Total	15	1522	3780	460	977	161	50	51	392	354-83	31	746	.258	.325	.368	93	-39	82-40	.988	48	109	113	*O-1376(87-1079-225)/D	-1.4
GERTENRICH, LOU Louis Wilhelm B 5.4.1875 Chicago, IL D 10.20.1933 Chicago, IL BR/TR 5-8/175# d9.15																								
1901	Mil A	2	3	1	1	0	0	0	0	0	0		.333	.333	.333	90	0	0	—	-0	0	0	/O(RF)	0.0
1903	Pit N	1	3	0	0	0	0	0	0	0	0		.000	.000	.000	-97	-1	0	1.000	0	0	0	/O(RF)	-0.1
Total	2	3	6	1	1	0	0	0	0	0	0		.167	.167	.167	-6	-1	0	1.000	-0	0	0	/O-2(RF)	-0.1
GERUT, JODY Joseph Diego B 9.18.1977 Elmhurst, IL BL/TL 6/190# d4.26																								
2003	Cle A	127	480	66	134	33	2	22	75	35-4	7	70	.279	.336	.494	119	13	4-5	.984	2	98	138	*O-113(36-14-63),D-11	0.8
GESSLER, DOC Harry Homer "Brownie" B 12.23.1880 Greensburg, PA D 12.24.1924 Greensburg, PA BL/TL 5-10/180# d4.23 M1																								
1903	Det A	29	105	9	25	5	4	0	12	3	2		.238	.273	.362	92	-1	1	.974	-1	40	153	O-28(RF)	-0.3
	Bro N	49	154	20	38	8	3	0	18	17	12		.247	.366	.338	104	2	9	.984	-2	71	74	O-43(0-2-41)	-0.1
1904	Bro N	104	341	41	99	18	4	2	28	30	4		.290	.355	.384	131	13	13	.920	3	144	64	O-88(14-72-2)/12	1.3
1905	Bro N	126	431	44	125	17	4	3	46	38	14		.290	.366	.369	129	18	26	.973	2	115	89	*1-107,O-12(1-1-10)	1.8
1906	Bro N	9	33	3	8	1	2	0	4	3	1		.242	.324	.394	134	1	3	.946	1	153	89	/1-9	0.2
	†Chi N	34	83	8	21	3	0	0	10	12	1		.253	.354	.289	95	0	4	1.000	1	193	0	O-21(0-19-2)/1	0.0
	Year	43	116	11	29	4	2	0	14	15	2		.250	.346	.319	104	1	7	1.000	1	193	0	O-21(0-19-2),1-10	0.2
1908	Bos A	128	435	55	134	13	14	3	63	51	11		.308	**.394**	.423	161	31	19	.950	-4	60	111	*O-126(RF)	2.4
1909	Bos A	111	396	57	115	24	1	0	46	31	8		.290	.354	.356	122	11	16	.933	1	138	34	*O-109(RF)	0.9
	Was A	17	54	10	13	2	1	0	8	12	3		.241	.406	.315	134	4	4	1.000	-0	54	226	O-16(RF)/1	0.3
	Year	128	450	67	128	26	2	0	54	43	11		.284	.361	.351	123	15	20	.940	1	128	58	*O-125(RF)/1	1.2
1910	Was A	145	487	58	126	17	12	2	50	62	**16**		.259	.361	.355	131	20	18	.953	-1	87	126	*O-144(RF)	1.4
1911	Was A	128	450	65	127	19	5	4	78	74	20		.282	.406	.373	120	19	29	.943	-8	78	96	*O-126(2-0-124)/1	0.4
Total	8	880	2969	370	831	127	50	14	363	333	92		.280	.370	.370	128	118	142	.945	-9	95	91	O-713(17-94-602),1-120/2	8.3
GETTIG, CHARLIE Charles Henry B 12.1870 Baltimore, MD D 4.11.1935 Baltimore, MD BR 5-10/172# d8.5 I OF Total (3-LF 1-CF 21-RF)																								
1896	NY N	6	9	3	3	1	0	0	0	0	0	0	.333	.333	.444	107	1	0	1.000	0	144	0	/P-4	0.0
1897	NY N	22	75	8	15	6	0	0	12	6	2		.200	.277	.280	49	-5	3	.556	-6	37	0	/3-7,2-6,O-3(LF),S-3,P-3	-1.0
1898	NY N	64	196	30	49	6	2	0	26	15	2		.250	.310	.301	78	-6	5	.833	-4	56	0	O-21(0-1-20),P-17,2-12/S-9,3-4,1-2,C	-0.8
1899	NY N	34	97	7	24	3	0	0	9	7	1		.247	.305	.278	63	-5	4	.833	-3	99	0	P-18/3-8,2-3,1-3,O(RF)	-0.4
Total	4	126	377	48	91	16	2	0	47	28	5	0	.241	.302	.294	68	-15	12	.879	-13	116	43	/P-42,O-25R,2-21,3-19,S-12,1-5,C	-2.2
GETTINGER, TOM Lewis Thomas Leyton (born Lewis Thomas Leyton Gittinger) B 12.11.1868 Frederick, MD D 7.26.1943 Pensacola, FL BL/TL 5-10/180# d9.21																								
1889	StL AA	4	16	2	7	0	0	1	2	2	0	1	.438	.500	.625	194	2	0	.750	-1	0	0	/O-4(1-3-0)	0.0
1890	StL AA	58	227	31	54	7	5	3	30	20	1		.238	.302	.352	81	-7	8	.886	-4	88	52	O-58(LF)	-1.1
1895	Lou N	63	260	28	70	11	5	2	32	8	2	15	.269	.296	.373	77	-10	6	.910	-4	54	42	O-63(0-34-29)/P-2	-1.4
Total	3	125	503	61	131	18	10	6	64	30	3	16	.260	.306	.372	82	-15	14	.897	-9	68	45	O-125(59-37-29)/P-2	-2.5
GETTMAN, JAKE Jacob John B 10.25.1876 Frank, Russia D 10.4.1956 Denver, CO BB/TL 5-11/185# d8.20																								
1897	Was N	36	143	28	45	7	3	3	29	7	3		.315	.359	.469	118	3	8	.981	-2	63	0	O-36(RF)	0.0
1898	Was N	142	567	75	157	16	5	5	47	29	6		.277	.319	.349	92	-8	32	.926	2	96	80	*O-139(6-19-114)/1-3	-1.2
1899	Was N	19	62	5	13	1	0	0	2	4	0		.210	.258	.226	33	-6	4	1.000	0	53	0	O-16(6-10-0)/1-2	-0.6
Total	3	197	772	108	215	24	8	8	78	40	9		.278	.322	.361	92	-11	44	.941	1	87	60	O-191(12-29-150)/1-5	-1.8
GETZ, GUS Gustave "Gee-Gee" B 8.3.1889 Pittsburgh, PA D 5.28.1969 Red Bank, NJ BR/TR 5-11/165# d8.15																								
1909	Bos N	40	148	6	33	2	0	0	9	1	0		.223	.228	.236	42	-11	2	.934	3	122	65	3-36/2-2,S-2	-0.8
1910	Bos N	54	144	14	28	0	1	0	7	6	1	10	.194	.232	.208	27	-14	2	.915	5	117	141	3-22,2-13/O-8(4-1-3),S-4	-1.0
1914	Bro N	55	210	13	52	8	1	0	20	2	0	15	.248	.255	.295	62	-11	9	.949	12	123	159	3-55	0.3
1915	Bro N	130	477	39	123	10	5	2	46	8	3	14	.258	.275	.312	76	-16	19-15	.951	6	**113**	77	*3-128/S-2	-0.8
1916	†Bro N	40	96	9	21	1	2	0	8	0	0	5	.219	.219	.271	49	-6	9	.913	-3	81	0	3-20/S-7,1-3	-1.0
1917	Cin N	7	14	2	4	0	0	0	3	3	0	0	.286	.412	.286	121	1	0	.875	-2	40	124	/2-4,3-3	-0.2
1918	Cle A	6	15	2	2	1	0	0	0	4	1	1	.133	.350	.200	60	0	0	.941	-0	98	0	/3-5	-0.1
	Pit N	7	10	0	2	0	0	0	0	0	0	1	.200	.200	.200	21	-1	0	.875	0	96	334	/3-2	-0.1
Total	7	339	1114	85	265	22	9	2	93	24	5	46	.238	.257	.279	60	-58	41-15	.942	21	114	93	3-271/2-19,S-15,O-8(4-1-3),1-3	-3.7
GEYGAN, CHAPPIE James Edward B 6.3.1903 Ironton, OH D 3.15.1966 Columbus, OH BR/TR 5-11/170# d7.16																								
1924	Bos A	33	82	7	21	5	2	0	4	4	2	16	.256	.307	.366	73	-4	0-2	.952	2	99	94	S-32	0.0
1925	Bos A	3	11	0	2	0	0	0	0	0	0	2	.182	.182	.182	-8	-2	0-0	.813	-2	69	55	/S-3	-0.3
1926	Bos A	4	10	0	3	0	0	0	0	1	0	1	.300	.364	.300	77	0	0-0	.800	-1	89	0	/3-3	-0.1
Total	3	40	103	7	26	5	2	0	4	5	2	19	.252	.300	.340	65	-6	0-2	.938	-0	96	90	/S-35,3-3	-0.4
GHARRITY, PATSY Edward Patrick B 3.13.1892 Parnell, IA D 10.10.1966 Beloit, WI BR/TR 5-10/170# d5.16 C7																								
1916	Was A	39	92	8	21	5	1	0	9	8	1	18	.228	.297	.304	81	-2	2	1.000	-2	103	107	C-16,1-16	-0.4
1917	Was A	76	176	15	50	5	0	0	18	14	0	18	.284	.337	.313	99	0	7	.980	1	116	84	1-46/C-5,O(RF)	0.0
1918	Was A	4	4	0	1	1	0	0	2	0	0	1	.250	.250	.500	129	0	0	—	0			H	0.0
1919	Was A	111	347	35	94	19	4	2	43	25	3	39	.271	.325	.366	95	-3	4	.969	-0	*88*	*98*	C-60,O-33(30-2-1)/1-7	0.0
1920	Was A	131	428	51	105	18	3	3	44	37	1	52	.245	.307	.322	69	-20	6-5	.965	-2	*89*	*126*	*C-121/1-7,O(LF)	-1.2
1921	Was A	121	387	62	120	19	8	7	55	45	3	44	.310	.386	.455	120	12	4-3	.977	6	***137***	*104*	*C-115	2.3
1922	Was A	96	273	40	70	16	6	5	45	36	4	30	.256	.351	.414	104	2	3-3	.981	5	*97*	***122***	C-87	1.1
1923	Was A	93	251	26	52	9	4	3	33	22	2	27	.207	.276	.311	57	-17	6-2	.986	1	*97*	*114*	C-35,1-33	-1.5
1929	Was A	3	2	0	0	0	0	0	0	1	0	2	.000	.333	.000	-7	0	0-0	—	0			H	0.0
1930	Was A	2	1	0	0	0	0	0	0	0	0	0	.000	.000	.000	-99	0	0-0	1.000	-0	0	0	/1	0.0
Total	10	676	1961	237	513	92	26	20	249	188	14	231	.262	.331	.366	90	-28	32-13	.974	8	*105*	*114*	C-439,1-110/O-35(31-2-2)	0.3
GIAMBI, JASON Jason Gilbert B 1.8.1971 W.Covina, CA BL/TR 6-2/200# d5.8 b-Jeremy																								
1995	Oak A	54	176	27	45	7	0	6	25	28-0	3	31	.256	.364	.398	105	2	2-1	.960	0	100	88	3-30,1-26/D-2	0.1
1996	Oak A	140	536	84	156	40	1	20	79	51-3	5	95	.291	.355	.481	112	10	0-1	.993	5	110	95	1-45,O-45(44-0-1),3-39,D-12	0.8
1997	Oak A	142	519	66	152	41	2	20	81	55-3	6	89	.293	.362	.495	124	20	0-1	.982	-2	80	124	O-68(LF),1-51,D-25	0.8
1998	Oak A	153	562	92	166	28	0	27	110	81-7	5	102	.295	.384	.489	130	27	2-2	.990	-11	76	100	*1-146/D-7	0.2
1999	Oak A	158	575	115	181	36	1	33	123	105-6	7	106	.315	.422	.553	154	52	1-1	.995	-16	53	103	*1-142,D-15/3	2.0
2000	†Oak A★	152	510	108	170	29	1	43	137	**137**-6	9	96	.333	**.476**	.647	**187**	**78**	2-0	.995	-8	74	101	*1-124,D-24	5.2
2001	†Oak A★	154	520	109	178	**47**	2	38	120	**129**-24	13	83	.342	**.477**	**.660**	**197**	**85**	2-0	.992	-4	89	107	*1-136,D-17	6.3
2002	†NY A★	155	560	120	176	34	1	41	122	109-4	15	112	.314	.435	.598	173	66	2-2	.995	-7	64	77	1-92,D-63	4.3
2003	†NY A★	156	535	97	134	25	0	41	107	**129**-9	**21**	140	.250	.412	.527	149	45	2-1	.995	-13	35	94	1-85,D-69	1.8

Year	Tm Lg	G	AB	R	H	2B	3B	HR	RBI	BB-IB	HP	SO	AVG	OBP	SLG	AOPS	ABR	SB-CS	FA	FR	Rng	Thr	G at Pos	BFW
Total	9	1264	4493	818	1358	287	8	269	904	824-62	84	854	.302	.415	.549	152	385	13-9	.993	-57	72	99	1-847,D-234,O-113(112-0-1)/3-70	21.5
GIAMBI, JEREMY Jeremy Dean B 9.30.1974 San Jose, CA BL/TL 6/185# d9.1 b-Jason																								
1998	KC A	18	58	6	13	4	0	2	8	11-0	0	9	.224	.343	.397	91	-1	0-1	1.000	-0	82	191	/O-9(LF),D-7	-0.1
1999	KC A	90	288	34	82	13	1	3	34	40-5	3	67	.285	.373	.368	89	-3	0-0	.991	-4	54	92	D-48,1-26/O-5(LF)	-1.2
2000	†Oak A	104	260	42	66	10	2	10	50	32-2	3	61	.254	.338	.423	95	-2	0-0	.966	-2	91	99	O-55(6-0-49),D-21,1-15	-0.8
2001	†Oak A	124	371	64	105	26	0	12	57	63-1	4	83	.283	.391	.450	121	15	0-1	.943	-9	62	38	D-60,O-47(11-0-37),1-10	-0.1
2002	Oak A	42	157	26	43	7	0	8	17	27-0	3	40	.274	.390	.471	127	7	0-0	.984	-4	84	0	O-40(LF)/D-2	0.2
	Phi N	82	156	32	38	10	0	12	28	52-2	1	54	.244	.435	.538	167	18	0-1	.989	-4	76	119	1-21,O-20(2-0-18)/D-8	1.1
2003	Bos A	50	127	15	25	5	0	5	15	26-0	2	42	.197	.342	.354	82	-3	1-0	.944	0	113	0	D-30,O-11(9-0-2)	-0.5
Total	6	510	1417	219	372	75	3	52	209	251-10	16	356	.263	.377	.430	110	31	1-3	.963	-23	81	48	0-187(82-0-106),D-176/1-72	-1.4
GIANNELLI, RAY Raymond John B 2.5.1966 Brooklyn, NY BL/TR 6/195# d5.4																								
1991	Tor A	9	24	2	4	1	0	0	0	5-0	0	9	.167	.310	.208	45	-2	1-0	.923	-2	78	149	/3-9	-0.4
1995	StL N	9	11	0	1	0	0	0	0	3-0	0	4	.091	.286	.091	5	-1	0-0	1.000	-0	0	123	/1-2,O-2(1-0-1)	-0.2
Total	2	18	35	2	5	1	0	0	0	8-0	0	13	.143	.302	.171	32	-3	1-0	.923	-3	78	149	/3-9,O-2(1-0-1),1-2	-0.6
GIANNINI, JOE Joseph Francis B 9.8.1888 San Francisco, CA D 9.26.1942 San Francisco, CA BL/TR 5-8/155# d8.7																								
1911	Bos A	1	2	0	1	1	0	0	0	0	0		.500	.500	1.000	317	1	0	.500	-1	108	0	/S	0.0
GIBBONS, JAY Jay Jonathan B 3.2.1977 Rochester, MI BL/TL 6/200# d4.6																								
2001	Bal A	73	225	27	53	10	0	15	36	17-0	4	39	.236	.301	.480	107	1	0-1	1.000	2	114	183	O-28(LF),D-28/1-7	0.0
2002	Bal A	136	490	71	121	29	1	28	69	45-3	2	66	.247	.311	.482	113	7	1-3	.994	-2	97	105	O-92(RF),1-30,D-12	-0.3
2003	Bal A	160	625	80	173	39	2	23	100	49-11	3	89	.277	.330	.456	109	8	0-1	.983	-2	97	95	*O-144(RF),1-13/D-5	-0.3
Total	3	369	1340	178	347	78	3	66	205	111-14	9	194	.259	.318	.469	110	16	1-5	.989	-2	99	107	0-264(28-0-236)/1-50,D-45	-0.6
GIBBONS, JOHN John Michael B 6.8.1962 Great Falls, MT BR/TR 5-11/187# d4.11 C2																								
1984	NY N	10	31	1	2	0	0	0	1	3-1	1	11	.065	.171	.065	-32	-6	0-0	.983	-1	85	144	/C-9	-0.7
1986	NY N	8	19	4	9	4	0	1	1	3-1	0	5	.474	.545	.842	285	5	0-0	1.000	-0	110	39	/C-8	0.5
Total	2	18	50	5	11	4	0	1	2	6-2	1	16	.220	.316	.360	90	-1	0-0	.990	-1	95	102	/C-17	-0.2
GIBBS, JAKE Jerry Dean B 11.7.1938 Grenada, MS BL/TR 6/185# d9.11																								
1962	NY A	2	0	2	0	0	0	0	0	0-0	0	0	—	—	—	—	0	0-0	—	-0	0	0	/3	0.0
1963	NY A	4	8	1	2	0	0	0	0	0-0	0	1	.250	.250	.250	41	-1	0-0	1.000	-1	0	0	/C	-0.2
1964	NY A	3	6	1	1	0	0	0	0	0-0	0	2	.167	.167	.167	-7	-1	0-0	1.000	0	*0*	*0*	/C-2	-0.1
1965	NY A	37	68	6	15	1	0	2	7	4-0	1	20	.221	.267	.324	70	-3	0-0	.991	1	*104*	*109*	C-21	-0.1
1966	NY A	62	182	19	47	6	0	3	20	19-2	0	16	.258	.327	.341	96	-1	5-2	.988	5	*141*	*96*	C-54	0.8
1967	NY A	116	374	33	87	7	1	4	25	28-1	4	57	.233	.291	.289	75	-12	7-6	.975	-1	97	**129**	C-99	-0.9
1968	NY A	124	423	31	90	12	3	3	29	27-5	6	68	.213	.270	.277	68	-17	9-8	.991	6	165	91	*C-121	-0.7
1969	NY A	71	219	18	49	9	2	0	18	23-9	0	30	.224	.294	.283	65	-10	3-4	.990	8	170	68	C-66	0.0
1970	NY A	49	153	23	46	9	2	8	26	7-1	1	14	.301	.331	.542	146	8	2-0	.987	2	171	62	C-44	1.2
1971	NY A	70	206	23	45	9	0	5	21	12-1	3	23	.218	.270	.335	76	-7	2-2	.988	-5	143	37	C-51	-1.1
Total	10	538	1639	157	382	53	8	25	146	120-19	15	231	.233	.289	.321	81	-44	28-22	.986	15	*143*	*88*	C-459/3	-1.1
GIBRALTER, STEVE Stephan Benson B 10.9.1972 Dallas, TX BR/TR 6/185# d6.1																								
1995	Cin N	4	3	0	1	0	0	0	0	0-0	0	0	.333	.333	.333	77	0	0-0	1.000	0	91	0	/O-2(CF)	0.0
1996	Cin N	2	2	0	0	0	0	0	0	0-0	0	2	.000	.000	.000	-99	-1	0-0	.000	-1	0	0	/O-2(1-1-0)	-0.1
Total	2	6	5	0	1	0	0	0	0	0-0	0	2	.200	.200	.200	6	-1	0-0	.500	-1	40	0	/O-4(1-3-0)	-0.1
GIBSON, CHARLIE Charles Ellsworth "Gibby" B 11.17.1879 Sharon, PA D 11.22.1954 Sharon, PA BR/TR 6/160# d9.23																								
1905	StL A	1	3	0	0	0	0	0	0	0	0		.000	.000	.000	-99	-1	0	1.000	-0	*75*	*166*	/C	-0.1
GIBSON, CHARLIE Charles Griffin B 11.21.1899 LaGrange, GA D 12.18.1990 LaGrange, GA BR/TR 5-8/160# d5.30																								
1924	Phi A	12	15	1	2	0	0	0	1	2	0	0	.133	.235	.133	-3	-2	0-0	.870	-1	*100*	*128*	C-12	-0.3
GIBSON, DERRICK Derrick Lamont B 2.5.1975 Winter Haven, FL BR/TR 6-2/244# d9.8																								
1998	Col N	7	21	4	9	1	0	0	2	1-0	1	4	.429	.478	.476	125	1	0-0	.929	1	100	523	/O-7(LF)	0.2
1999	Col N	10	28	2	5	1	0	2	6	0-0	1	7	.179	.207	.429	43	-3	0-0	.944	2	112	447	O-10(RF)	-0.1
Total	2	17	49	6	14	2	0	2	8	1-0	2	11	.286	.327	.449	78	-2	0-0	.938	3	106	482	/O-17(7-0-10)	0.1
GIBSON, FRANK Frank Gilbert B 9.27.1890 Omaha, NE D 4.27.1961 Austin, TX BB/TR (BL 1913) 6-0.5/172# d4.22																								
1913	Det A	23	57	8	8	1	0	0	2	3	1	9	.140	.197	.158	4	-7	2	.914	-6	*78*	*82*	C-19/O-2(RF)	-1.2
1921	Bos N	63	125	14	33	5	4	2	13	3	2	17	.264	.292	.416	90	-3	0-0	.979	1	*113*	*104*	C-41	0.0
1922	Bos N	66	164	15	49	7	2	3	20	10	0	27	.299	.339	.421	99	-1	4-1	.981	-0	*98*	*99*	C-29,1-20	0.0
1923	Bos N	41	50	13	15	1	0	0	5	7	0	7	.300	.386	.320	92	0	0-2	.923	-1	*89*	*64*	C-20	-0.2
1924	Bos N	90	229	25	71	15	6	1	30	10	1	23	.310	.342	.441	113	3	1-1	.972	-2	*83*	*118*	C-46,1-10/3-2	0.4
1925	Bos N	104	316	36	88	23	5	2	50	15	1	28	.278	.313	.402	89	-6	3-3	.968	-2	*113*	*85*	C-86/1-2	-0.2
1926	Bos N	24	47	3	16	4	0	0	7	4	0	6	.340	.392	.426	132	2	0	1.000	1	*85*	*151*	C-13	0.4
1927	Bos N	60	167	7	37	1	2	0	19	3	0	10	.222	.235	.251	33	-17	2	.965	-2	*100*	*125*	C-47	-1.7
Total	8	471	1155	121	317	57	19	8	146	55	5	127	.274	.310	.377	86	-29	12-7	.967	-11	*100*	*102*	C-301/1-32,3-2,O-2(RF)	-2.5
GIBSON, GEORGE George C. "Moon" B 7.22.1880 London, ON, CAN D 1.25.1967 London, ON, CAN BR/TR 5-11.5/190# d7.2 M7 C3																								
1905	Pit N	46	135	14	24	2	2	2	14	15	2		.178	.270	.267	59	-7	2	.966	4	*129*	*90*	C-44	0.1
1906	Pit N	81	259	8	46	6	1	0	20	16	0		.178	.225	.208	34	-20	1	.971	-1	*118*	*94*	C-81	-1.5
1907	Pit N	113	382	28	84	8	7	3	35	18	3		.220	.261	.301	75	-13	2	.972	7	***132***	*91*	*C-109/1	0.5
1908	Pit N	143	486	37	111	19	4	2	45	19	2		.228	.260	.296	78	-14	4	.973	-2	*124*	*71*	*C-140	-0.2
1909	†Pit N	150	510	42	135	25	9	2	52	44	2		.265	.326	.361	104	2	9	**.983**	17	***148***	*91*	*C-150	3.7
1910	Pit N	143	482	53	125	22	6	3	44	47	6	31	.259	.333	.349	93	-4	7	**.984**	10	*123*	*90*	*C-143	2.1
1911	Pit N	100	311	32	65	12	2	0	19	29	2	16	.209	.281	.260	50	-21	3	.979	6	*116*	*92*	C-98	-0.7
1912	Pit N	95	300	23	72	14	3	2	35	20	1	16	.240	.290	.327	69	-14	0	**.990**	2	***132***	*86*	C-94	-0.3
1913	Pit N	48	118	6	33	4	2	0	12	10	1	8	.280	.341	.347	101	0	2-1	.986	-5	84	58	C-48	-0.2
1914	Pit N	102	274	19	78	9	5	0	30	27	5	27	.285	.359	.354	117	7	4	.974	-4	*108*	*94*	*C-101	1.1
1915	Pit N	120	351	28	88	15	6	1	30	31	1	25	.251	.313	.336	98	-1	5-2	.965	2	*90*	*95*	*C-118	1.3
1916	Pit N	33	84	4	17	2	2	0	4	3	1	7	.202	.239	.274	57	-5	0	.989	3	94	118	C-29	0.1
1917	NY N	35	82	1	14	3	0	0	5	7	0	2	.171	.236	.207	38	-6	1	.986	1	*107*	*69*	C-35	-0.3
1918	NY N	4	2	0	1	1	0	0	0	0	0	0	.500	.500	1.000	360	1	0	1.000	-0	*56*	*230*	/C-4	0.1
Total	14	1213	3776	295	893	142	49	15	345	286	26	132	.236	.295	.312	81	-95	40-3	.977	39	*121*	*88*	*C-1194/1	5.8
GIBSON, RUSS John Russell B 5.6.1939 Fall River, MA BR/TR 6-1/195# d4.14																								
1967	†Bos A	49	138	8	28	7	0	1	15	12-3	0	31	.203	.263	.275	56	-7	0-0	1.000	-3	168	88	C-48	-0.9
1968	Bos A	76	231	15	52	11	1	3	20	8-1	0	38	.225	.247	.320	68	-9	1-2	.983	-2	82	104	C-74/1	-1.0
1969	Bos A	85	287	21	72	9	1	3	27	15-1	1	25	.251	.289	.321	67	-13	1-1	.979	-7	108	**122**	C-83	-1.8
1970	SF N	24	69	3	16	6	0	0	6	7-1	0	12	.232	.303	.319	67	-3	0-0	.971	-1	67	139	C-23	-0.3
1971	SF N	25	57	2	11	1	1	1	7	2-0	0	13	.193	.220	.298	46	-4	0-0	.965	-3	170	78	C-22	-0.7
1972	SF N	5	12	0	2	0	1	0	3	0-0	0	4	.167	.167	.333	38	-1	0-0	1.000	-2	30	87	/C-5	-0.3
Total	6	264	794	49	181	34	4	8	78	44-6	1	123	.228	.267	.311	64	-37	2-3	.983	-19	111	108	C-255/1	-5.0
GIBSON, KIRK Kirk Harold B 5.28.1957 Pontiac, MI BL/TL 6-3/215# d9.8 C1																								
1979	Det A	12	38	3	9	3	0	1	4	1-0	0	3	.237	.256	.395	70	-2	3-3	1.000	-2	75	0	O-10(7-1-2)	-0.4
1980	Det A	51	175	23	46	2	1	9	16	10-0	1	45	.263	.303	.440	100	-1	4-7	.992	-2	100	32	O-49(CF)/D	-0.5
1981	Det A	83	290	41	95	11	3	9	40	18-1	2	64	.328	.369	.479	138	13	17-5	.973	-4	97	23	O-67(8-26-37)/D-9	0.9
1982	Det A	69	266	34	74	16	2	8	35	25-2	1	41	.278	.341	.444	113	5	9-7	.994	-2	94	91	O-64(CF)/D-4	0.2
1983	Det A	128	401	60	91	12	9	15	51	53-3	4	96	.227	.320	.414	104	1	14-3	.975	-1	101	58	D-66,O-54(29-22-4)	-0.1
1984	†Det A	149	531	92	150	23	10	27	91	63-6	8	103	.282	.363	.516	142	30	29-9	.954	-11	90	48	*O-139(0-1-140)/D-6	1.5
1985	Det A	154	581	96	167	37	5	29	97	71-16	5	137	.287	.364	.518	141	34	30-4	.963	-12	95	10	*O-144(0-20-127)/D-8	2.0
1986	Det A	119	441	84	118	11	2	28	86	68-4	7	107	.268	.371	.492	134	22	34-6	.990	-12	83	25	*O-114(0-1-114)/D-4	0.9
1987	†Det A	128	487	95	135	25	3	24	79	71-8	5	117	.277	.372	.489	132	25	26-7	.974	1	104	74	*O-121(119-2-0)/D-4	2.2
1988	†LA N	150	542	106	157	28	1	25	76	73-14	7	120	.290	.377	.483	151	38	31-4	.964	3	107	67	*O-148(148-1-0)	4.4

Year	Tm Lg	G	AB	R	H	2B	3B	HR	RBI	BB-IB	HP	SO	AVG	OBP	SLG	AOPS	ABR	SB-CS	FA	FR	Rng	Thr	G at Pos	BFW
1989	LA N	71	253	35	54	8	2	9	28	35-5	2	55	.213	.312	.368	96	-1	12-3	.980	1	102	82	O-70(62-15-0)	-0.1
1990	LA N	89	315	59	82	20	0	8	38	39-0	3	65	.260	.345	.400	108	5	26-2	.995	0	103	94	O-81(11-70-0)	0.9
1991	KC A	132	462	81	109	17	6	16	55	69-3	6	103	.236	.341	.403	105	4	18-4	.976	-5	87	61	O-94(91-0-3),D-30	-0.2
1992	Pit N	16	56	6	11	0	0	2	5	3-0	0	12	.196	.237	.304	53	-4	3-1	1.000	-0	92	108	O-13(RF)	-0.4
1993	Det A	116	403	62	105	18	6	13	62	44-4	4	87	.261	.337	.432	106	3	15-6	.987	-1	103	0	D-76,O-32(2-30-0)	-0.1
1994	Det A	98	330	71	91	17	2	23	72	42-3	3	69	.276	.358	.548	130	14	4-5	.988	-1	93	145	D-56,O-38(0-23-15)	0.8
1995	Det A	70	227	37	59	12	2	9	35	33-3	3	61	.260	.358	.449	110	4	9-2	—	-0	0	0	D-63/O(RF)	0.1
Total	17	1635	5798	985	1553	260	54	255	870	718-72	61	1285	.268	.352	.463	123	190	284-78	.976	-47	96	55	*O-1239(477-325-456),D-327	12.1
GIBSON, WHITEY Leighton P. B 10.6.1868 Lancaster, PA D 10.12.1907 Talmage, PA TR 5-9/178# d5.2																								
1888	Phi AA	1	3	0	0	0	0	0	0	0	0		.000	.000	.000	-99	-1	0	1.000	1			/C	0.0
GIEBEL, JOE Joseph Henry B 11.30.1891 Washington, DC D 3.17.1981 Silver Spring, MD BR/TR 5-10.5/175# d9.30																								
1913	Phi A	1	3	0	1	0	0	0	0	0	0	1	.333	.333	.333	97	0	0	1.000	-0	107	0	/C	0.0
GIGON, NORM Norman Phillip B 5.12.1938 Teaneck, NJ BR/TR 6/195# d4.12																								
1967	Chi N	34	70	8	12	3	1	1	6	4-0	2	14	.171	.234	.286	47	-5	0-0	.982	-1	108	88	2-12/O-4(RF),3	-0.5
GIL, GERONIMO Geronimo B 8.7.1975 Oaxaca, Mexico BR/TR 6-2/195# d9.8																								
2001	Bal A	17	58	3	17	2	0	0	6	5-0	2	7	.293	.369	.328	91	0	0-0	.985	3	93	99	C-17	0.4
2002	Bal A	125	422	33	98	19	0	12	45	21-1	1	88	.232	.270	.363	70	-20	2-2	.995	1	106	115	*C-125	-1.1
2003	Bal A	54	169	22	40	4	0	3	16	12-0	3	34	.237	.299	.314	64	-9	0-0	.984	4	72	85	C-53	-0.2
Total	3	196	649	58	155	25	0	15	67	38-1	6	129	.239	.287	.347	70	-29	2-2	.991	8	96	106	C-195	-0.9
GIL, BENJI Romar Benjamin (Aguilar) B 10.6.1972 Tijuana, Mexico BR/TR 6-2/180# d4.5																								
1993	Tex A	22	57	3	7	0	0	0	2	5-0	0	22	.123	.194	.123	-13	-9	1-2	.954	4	123	76	S-22	-0.4
1995	Tex A	130	415	36	91	20	3	9	46	26-0	1	147	.219	.266	.347	57	-28	2-4	.974	18	110	113	*S-130	-0.1
1996	Tex A	5	5	0	2	0	0	0	1	1-0	0	1	.400	.500	.400	125	0	0-1	.923	0	107	0	/S-5	0.0
1997	Tex A	110	317	35	71	13	2	5	31	17-0	1	96	.224	.263	.325	50	-24	1-2	.963	18	117	108	*S-106/D-4	0.1
2000	Ana A	110	301	28	72	14	1	6	23	30-0	5	59	.239	.317	.352	68	-15	10-6	.957	-1	102	101	S-94/2-7,1-3,D-6	-0.8
2001	Ana A	104	260	33	77	15	4	8	39	14-0	0	57	.296	.330	.477	107	2	3-4	.945	5	101	101	S-44,2-21,1-18,D-14/O(CF)	0.8
2002	†Ana A	61	130	11	37	8	1	3	20	5-0	0	33	.285	.307	.431	94	-1	2-1	.990	3	98	90	2-26,S-14,1-10,D-10	0.2
2003	Ana A	62	125	12	24	5	1	1	9	4-1	0	33	.192	.214	.272	29	-13	5-1	.979	1	107	114	2-28,S-20/1-5,3-4,D-2	-0.9
Total	8	604	1610	158	381	75	12	32	171	102-1	7	448	.237	.283	.358	65	-88	24-21	.962	48	110	106	S-435/2-82,1-36,D-36,3-4,O(CF)	-1.1
GIL, GUS Tomas Gustavo (Guillen) B 4.19.1939 Caracas, Venezuela BR/TR 5-10/180# d4.11																								
1967	Cle A	51	96	11	11	4	0	0	5	9-0	1	18	.115	.198	.156	6	-11	0-0	1.000	-3	83	74	2-49/1	-1.3
1969	Sea A	92	221	20	49	7	0	0	17	16-0	0	28	.222	.272	.253	49	-15	2-0	.942	1	121	116	3-38,2-18,S-12	-1.3
1970	Mil A	64	119	12	22	4	0	1	12	21-4	0	12	.185	.303	.244	53	-7	2-0	.978	-5	71	66	2-38,3-14	-1.0
1971	Mil A	14	32	3	5	1	0	0	3	10-1	0	5	.156	.357	.188	59	-1	1-0	.977	1	109	58	/2-8,3-6	0.0
Total	4	221	468	46	87	16	0	1	37	56-5	1	63	.186	.272	.226	43	-34	5-0	.987	-5	84	69	2-113/3-58,S-12,1	-3.6
GILBERT, SHAWN Albert Shawn B 3.12.1965 Camden, NJ BR/TR 5-9/170# d6.4																								
1997	NY N	29	22	3	3	0	0	1	1	1-0	0	8	.136	.174	.273	15	-3	1-0	.875	-2	20	97	/2-8,S-6,3-3,O(LF)	-0.4
1998	NY N	3	3	1	0	0	0	0	0	0-0	0	1	.000	.000	.000	-99	-1	0-0	—	-0	0	0	/3	-0.1
	StL N	4	2	0	1	0	0	0	0	0-0	0	1	.500	.500	.500	166	0	1-0	1.000	-0	0	0	/2-2	0.0
	Year	7	5	1	1	0	0	0	0	0-0	0	2	.200	.200	.200	6	-1	1-0	1.000	-1	0	0	/2-2,3	-0.1
2000	LA N	15	20	5	3	1	0	1	3	2-0	0	7	.150	.227	.350	46	-2	0-0	.941	1	123	297	O-14(8-4-2)	-0.1
Total	3	51	47	9	7	1	0	2	4	3-0	0	17	.149	.200	.298	27	-6	2-0	.941	-1	118	285	/O-15(9-4-2),2-10,S-6,3-4	-0.6
GILBERT, ANDY Andrew B 7.18.1914 Bradenville, PA D 8.29.1992 Davis, CA BR/TR 6/203# d9.14 Mil 1943-45 C4																								
1942	Bos A	6	11	0	1	0	0	0	1	1	0	3	.091	.167	.091	-26	-2	0-0	1.000	-0	93	0	/O-5(CF)	-0.2
1946	Bos A	2	1	1	0	0	0	0	0	0	0	0	.000	.000	.000	-95	0	0-0	—	-0	0	0	/O(CF)	0.0
Total	2	8	12	1	1	0	0	0	1	1	0	3	.083	.154	.083	-31	-2	0-0	1.000	-0	89	0	/O-6(CF)	-0.2
GILBERT, CHARLIE Charles Mader B 7.8.1919 New Orleans, LA D 8.13.1983 New Orleans, LA BL/TL 5-9/165# d4.16 Mil 1944-45 b-Tookie f-Larry																								
1940	Bro N	57	142	23	35	9	1	2	8	8	0	13	.246	.287	.366	74	-5	0	.960	1	101	135	O-43(CF)	-0.6
1941	Chi N	39	86	11	24	2	1	0	12	11	0	6	.279	.361	.326	98	0	1	1.000	-1	106	0	O-22(0-21-1)	-0.1
1942	Chi N	74	179	18	33	6	3	0	7	25	0	24	.184	.284	.251	60	-9	1	.981	0	93	149	O-47(3-44-0)	-1.1
1943	Chi N	8	20	1	3	0	0	0	0	3	0	3	.150	.261	.150	20	-2	1	1.000	0	84	230	/O-6(3-3-0)	-0.2
1946	Chi N	15	13	2	1	0	0	0	1	1	0	4	.077	.143	.077	-38	-2	0	1.000	1	82	2356	/O-2(CF)	-0.2
	Phi N	88	260	34	63	5	2	1	17	25	2	18	.242	.314	.288	73	-9	3	1.000	5	108	138	O-69(8-16-46)	-0.7
	Year	103	273	36	64	5	2	1	18	26	2	22	.234	.306	.278	68	-12	3	1.000	6	108	153	O-71(8-18-46)	-0.9
1947	Phi N	83	152	20	36	5	2	2	10	13	1	14	.237	.301	.336	72	-7	1	.961	2	104	168	O-37(18-7-12)	-0.6
Total	6	364	852	109	195	27	9	5	55	86	3	82	.229	.302	.299	70	-34	7	.982	8	102	138	O-226(32-136-59)	-3.5
GILBERT, BUDDY Drew Edward B 7.26.1935 Knoxville, TN BL/TR 6-3/195# d9.9																								
1959	Cin N	7	20	4	3	0	0	2	2	3-0	0	4	.150	.261	.450	82	-1	0-0	1.000	0	125	0	/O-6(RF)	-0.1
GILBERT, TOOKIE Harold Joseph B 4.4.1929 New Orleans, LA D 6.23.1967 New Orleans, LA BL/TR 6-2.5/185# d5.5 b-Charlie f-Larry																								
1950	NY N	113	322	40	71	12	2	4	32	43	1	36	.220	.314	.307	64	-16	3	.988	0	102	105	*1-111	-1.9
1953	NY N	70	160	12	27	3	0	3	16	22	0	21	.169	.269	.244	34	-16	1-0	.995	-1	92	96	1-44	-1.8
Total	2	183	482	52	98	15	2	7	48	65	1	57	.203	.299	.286	54	-32	4-0	.991	-1	99	102	1-155	-3.7
GILBERT, HARRY Harry H. B 7.7.1868 Pottstown, PA D 12.23.1909 Pottstown, PA d6.23 b-John																								
1890	Pit N	2	8	1	2	0	0	0	0	0	0	3	.250	.250	.250	52	-1	0	1.000	-0	109	132	/2-2	-0.1
GILBERT, JOHN John B. B 1.8.1864 Pottstown, PA D 11.12.1903 Pottstown, PA d6.23 b-Harry																								
1890	Pit N	2	8	0	0	0	0	0	0	0	0	2	.000	.000	.000	-99	-2	0	1.000	-0	81	118	/S-2	-0.2
GILBERT, JACK John Robert "Jackrabbit" B 9.4.1875 Rhinecliff, NY D 7.7.1941 Albany, NY d9.11																								
1898	Was N	2	5	0	1	0	0	0	1	1	1		.200	.429	.200	82	0	1	.500	0	514	0	/O-2(0-1-1)	0.0
	NY N	1	4	0	1	0	0	0	0	0	0		.250	.250	.250	45	0	1	.500	-1	0	0	/O(RF)	-0.1
	Year	3	9	0	2	0	0	0	1	1	1		.222	.364	.222	70	0	2	.500	-1	280	0	/O-3(0-1-2)	-0.1
1904	Pit N	25	87	13	21	0	0	0	3	12	3		.241	.353	.241	82	-1	3	.857	-4	0	0	O-25(LF)	-0.7
Total	2	28	96	13	23	0	0	0	4	13	4		.240	.354	.240	81	-1	5	.821	-5	29	0	/O-28(25-1-2)	-0.8
GILBERT, LARRY Lawrence William B 12.3.1891 New Orleans, LA D 2.17.1965 New Orleans, LA BL/TL 5-9/158# d4.14 s-Charlie s-Tookie																								
1914	†Bos N	72	224	32	60	6	1	5	25	26	1	34	.268	.347	.371	114	4	3	.979	1	79	158	O-60(3-6-51)	0.2
1915	Bos N	45	106	11	16	4	0	0	4	11	0	13	.151	.231	.189	29	-9	4-1	.941	0	83	171	O-27(2-0-26)	-1.0
Total	2	117	330	43	76	10	1	5	29	37	1	47	.230	.310	.312	88	-5	7-1	.969	1	80	162	/O-87(5-6-77)	-0.8
GILBERT, MARK Mark David B 8.22.1956 Atlanta, GA BB/TR 6/175# d7.21																								
1985	Chi A	7	22	3	6	1	0	0	3	4-0	0	5	.273	.385	.318	92	0	0-0	1.000	-1	92	0	/O-7(2-5-1)	-0.1
GILBERT, PETE Peter B 9.6.1867 Baltic, CT D 1.1.1912 Springfield, MA TR 5-8/180# d9.6																								
1890	Bal AA	29	100	25	28	2	1	1	18	10	3		.280	.363	.350	105	1	12	.899	0	96	126	3-29	0.1
1891	Bal AA	**139**	513	81	118	15	7	3	72	37	28	77	.230	.317	.304	77	-16	31	.862	2	**105**	**151**	*3-139	-1.0
1892	Bal N	4	15	0	3	0	0	0	0	1	0	3	.200	.250	.200	35	-1	1	.889	1	147	0	/3-4	0.0
1894	Bro N	6	25	1	2	0	0	0	1	1	1	3	.080	.148	.080	-47	-6	2	.938	1	126	0	/2-3,3-3	-0.4
	Lou N	28	108	13	33	3	1	1	14	5	3	4	.306	.353	.380	82	-3	2	.742	-7	83	100	3-28	-0.7
	Year	34	133	14	35	3	1	1	15	6	4	7	.263	.315	.323	58	-9	4	.766	-6	86	126	3-31/2-3	-1.1
Total	4	206	761	120	184	20	9	5	105	54	35	87	.242	.321	.311	76	-25	48	.851	-3	101	141	3-203/2-3	-2.0
GILBERT, WALLY Walter John B 12.19.1900 Oscoda, MI D 9.7.1958 Duluth, MN BR/TR 6/180# d8.18																								
1928	Bro N	39	153	26	31	4	0	0	3	14	1	8	.203	.274	.229	33	-15	2	.965	0	101	103	3-39	-1.2
1929	Bro N	143	569	88	173	31	4	3	58	42	7	29	.304	.359	.388	87	-11	7	.956	9	104	77	*3-142	0.6
1930	Bro N	150	623	92	183	34	5	3	67	47	2	33	.294	.345	.379	76	-24	7	.944	9	110	**112**	*3-150	-0.5
1931	Bro N	145	552	60	147	25	6	0	46	39	6	38	.266	.322	.333	77	-18	3	.948	8	**107**	95	*3-145	-0.5

Year	Tm Lg	G	AB	R	H	2B	3B	HR	RBI	BB-IB	HP	SO	AVG	OBP	SLG	AOPS	ABR	SB-CS	FA	FR	Rng	Thr	G at Pos	BFW
1932	Cin N	114	420	35	90	18	2	1	40	20	1	23	.214	.252	.274	43	-35	2	.929	-7	102	92	*3-111	-3.7
Total	5	591	2317	301	624	112	17	7	214	162	17	131	.269	.322	.341	71	-103	21	.947	19	106	95	3-587	-5.3

GILBERT, BILLY William Oliver B 6.21.1876 Tullytown, PA D 8.8.1927 New York, NY BR/TR 5-4/153# d4.25

Year	Tm Lg	G	AB	R	H	2B	3B	HR	RBI	BB-IB	HP	SO	AVG	OBP	SLG	AOPS	ABR	SB-CS	FA	FR	Rng	Thr	G at Pos	BFW
1901	Mil A	127	492	77	133	14	7	0	43	31	5		.270	.320	.327	84	-10	19	.936	-3	98	113	*2-127	-1.1
1902	Bal A	129	445	74	109	12	3	2	38	45	9		.245	.327	.299	71	-16	38	.907	-3	94	114	*S-129	-1.4
1903	NY N	128	413	62	104	9	0	1	40	41	20		.252	.348	.281	77	-10	37	.935	6	98	107	*2-128	-0.2
1904	NY N	146	478	57	121	13	3	1	54	46	17		.253	.340	.299	94	-1	33	.946	6	101	122	*2-146	0.6
1905	†NY N	115	376	45	93	11	3	0	24	41	6		.247	.331	.293	84	-5	11	.947	20	105	**128**	*2-115	1.6
1906	NY N	104	307	44	71	6	1	1	27	42	9		.231	.341	.267	88	-2	22	.940	22	113	105	2-98	2.3
1908	StL N	89	276	12	59	7	0	0	10	20	3		.214	.274	.239	67	-10	6	.952	5	96	86	2-89	-0.4
1909	StL N	12	29	4	5	0	0	0	1	4	3		.172	.333	.172	61	-1	1	.922	-1	107	29	2-12	-0.1
Total	8	850	2816	375	695	72	17	5	237	270	72		.247	.328	.290	81	-55	167	.942	53	102	111	2-715,S-129	1.3

GILBREATH, ROD Rodney Joe B 9.24.1952 Laurel, MS BR/TR (BB 1975 (part)) 6-2/185# d6.17

Year	Tm Lg	G	AB	R	H	2B	3B	HR	RBI	BB-IB	HP	SO	AVG	OBP	SLG	AOPS	ABR	SB-CS	FA	FR	Rng	Thr	G at Pos	BFW
1972	Atl N	18	38	2	9	1	0	0	1	2-0	1	10	.237	.293	.263	54	-2	1-1	1.000	1	84	86	/2-7,3-4	-0.1
1973	Atl N	29	74	10	21	2	1	0	2	6-1	1	10	.284	.341	.338	84	-1	2-1	.960	-0	97	112	3-22	-0.2
1974	Atl N	3	6	2	2	0	0	0	0	2-0	0	0	.333	.500	.333	131	0	0-0	1.000	-0	95	83	/2-2	0.0
1975	Atl N	90	202	24	49	3	1	2	16	24-0	1	26	.243	.323	.297	71	-8	5-5	.980	0	97	97	2-52,3-10/S	-0.6
1976	Atl N	116	383	57	96	11	8	1	32	42-1	4	36	.251	.329	.329	83	-8	7-7	.975	6	101	110	*2-104/3-7,S	0.4
1977	Atl N	128	407	47	99	15	2	8	43	45-6	2	79	.243	.320	.349	71	-16	3-9	.978	-6	90	77	*2-122/3	-1.9
1978	Atl N	116	326	22	80	13	3	3	31	26-3	0	51	.245	.300	.331	69	-13	7-6	.968	-7	106	94	3-62,2-39	-2.2
Total	7	500	1436	164	356	45	15	14	125	147-11	9	212	.248	.320	.329	74	-48	25-29	.978	-6	94	89	2-326,3-106/S-2	-4.6

GILE, DON Donald Loren "Bear" B 4.19.1935 Modesto, CA BR/TR 6-6/220# d9.25

Year	Tm Lg	G	AB	R	H	2B	3B	HR	RBI	BB-IB	HP	SO	AVG	OBP	SLG	AOPS	ABR	SB-CS	FA	FR	Rng	Thr	G at Pos	BFW
1959	Bos A	3	10	1	2	1	0	0	1	0-0	1	2	.200	.250	.300	55	-1	0-0	1.000	-0	*100*	*0*	/C-3	-0.1
1960	Bos A	29	51	6	9	1	1	1	4	1-0	0	13	.176	.189	.294	29	-5	0-0	1.000	-1	*123*	*152*	C-15,1-11	-0.6
1961	Bos A	8	18	2	5	0	0	1	1	1-0	0	5	.278	.316	.444	98	0	0-0	.958	-1	57	72	/1-6,C	-0.1
1962	Bos A	18	41	3	2	0	0	1	3	3-0	1	15	.049	.133	.122	-30	-8	0-0	.990	-1	65	128	1-14	-1.0
Total	4	58	120	12	18	2	1	3	9	5-0	2	35	.150	.194	.258	21	-14	0-0	.982	-3	64	100	/1-31,C-19	-1.8

GILES, BRIAN Brian Jeffrey B 4.27.1960 Manhattan, KS BR/TR 6-1/165# d9.12

Year	Tm Lg	G	AB	R	H	2B	3B	HR	RBI	BB-IB	HP	SO	AVG	OBP	SLG	AOPS	ABR	SB-CS	FA	FR	Rng	Thr	G at Pos	BFW
1981	NY N	9	7	0	0	0	0	0	0	0-0	0	3	.000	.000	.000	-99	-2	0-0	1.000	1	110	277	/2-2,S-2	0.0
1982	NY N	45	138	14	29	5	0	3	10	12-1	0	29	.210	.270	.312	64	-7	6-1	.992	8	102	99	2-45/S-2	0.4
1983	NY N	145	400	39	98	15	0	2	27	36-1	2	77	.245	.308	.298	70	-16	17-10	.980	8	104	111	*2-140,S-12	-0.1
1985	Mil A	34	58	6	10	1	0	1	1	7-0	0	16	.172	.262	.241	39	-5	2-1	.963	1	98	70	S-20,2-13/D-2	-0.3
1986	Chi A	9	11	0	3	0	0	0	1	0-0	0	2	.273	.273	.273	48	-1	0-0	1.000	2	120	304	/2-7,S	0.2
1990	Sea A	45	95	15	22	6	0	4	11	15-0	0	24	.232	.336	.421	109	1	2-1	.978	3	92	134	S-37/2-2,3D	0.7
Total	6	287	709	74	162	27	0	10	50	70-2	2	151	.228	.298	.309	70	-30	27-13	.985	23	103	111	2-209/S-74,D-3,3	0.9

GILES, BRIAN Brian Stephen B 1.21.1971 ElCajon, CA BL/TL 5-11/195# d9.16 b-Marcus

Year	Tm Lg	G	AB	R	H	2B	3B	HR	RBI	BB-IB	HP	SO	AVG	OBP	SLG	AOPS	ABR	SB-CS	FA	FR	Rng	Thr	G at Pos	BFW
1995	Cle A	6	9	6	5	0	0	1	3	0-0	0	1	.556	.556	.889	265	2	0-0	1.000	1	91	1304	/O-3(RF),D	0.2
1996	†Cle A	51	121	26	43	14	1	5	27	19-4	0	13	.355	.434	.612	164	13	3-0	1.000	1	128	0	D-21,O-16(11-0-5)	1.1
1997	†Cle A	130	377	62	101	15	3	17	61	63-2	1	50	.268	.368	.459	112	8	13-3	.972	-1	96	113	*O-115(82-20-25)/D-9	0.5
1998	†Cle A	112	350	56	94	19	0	16	66	73-8	3	75	.269	.396	.460	119	13	10-5	.978	5	107	119	*O-101(95-3-6)/D-6	1.3
1999	Pit N	141	521	109	164	33	3	39	115	95-7	3	80	.315	.418	.614	159	50	6-2	.990	-6	93	104	*O-138(8-108-25)/D-3	4.1
2000	Pit N★	156	559	111	176	37	7	35	123	114-13	7	69	.315	.432	.594	158	55	6-0	.982	-2	93	145	*O-155(46-72-39)	4.8
2001	Pit N★	160	576	116	178	37	7	37	95	90-14	4	67	.309	.404	.590	150	45	13-6	.969	-7	96	69	*O-159(124-61-0)	3.4
2002	Pit N	153	497	95	148	37	5	38	103	135-24	7	74	.298	.450	.622	183	65	15-6	.973	-3	88	138	*O-151(151-3-0)	5.7
2003	Pit N	105	388	70	116	30	4	16	70	85-11	6	48	.299	.430	.521	144	31	0-3	.992	3	108	60	*O-105(99-16-0)	2.8
	SD N	29	104	23	31	4	2	4	18	20-1	2	10	.298	.414	.490	150	9	4-0	.966	1	105	116	O-29(LF)	0.9
	Year	134	492	93	147	34	6	20	88	105-12	8	58	.299	.427	.514	146	39	4-3	.987	4	107	72	*O-134(128-16-0)	3.7
Total	9	1043	3502	674	1056	226	32	208	681	694-84	33	487	.302	.417	.563	150	291	70-25	.979	-9	97	109	O-972(645-283-103)/D-40	24.8

GILES, MARCUS Marcus William B 5.18.1978 San Diego, CA BR/TR 5-8/180# d4.17 b-Brian

Year	Tm Lg	G	AB	R	H	2B	3B	HR	RBI	BB-IB	HP	SO	AVG	OBP	SLG	AOPS	ABR	SB-CS	FA	FR	Rng	Thr	G at Pos	BFW
2001	†Atl N	68	244	36	64	10	2	9	31	28-0	0	37	.262	.338	.430	95	-2	2-5	.978	-1	105	92	2-62	-0.1
2002	†Atl N	68	213	27	49	10	1	8	23	25-3	2	41	.230	.315	.399	89	-5	1-1	.977	4	107	117	2-52/3-8	0.2
2003	†Atl N✳	145	551	101	174	49	2	21	69	59-2	11	80	.316	.390	.526	137	32	14-4	.982	18	**120**	91	*2-139	5.7
Total	3	281	1008	164	287	69	5	38	123	112-5	13	158	.285	.362	.476	117	25	17-10	.980	21	114	96	2-253/3-8	5.8

GILHAM, GEORGE George Louis B 9.17.1899 Shamokin, PA D 4.25.1937 Lansdowne, PA BR/TR 5-11/164# d9.24

Year	Tm Lg	G	AB	R	H	2B	3B	HR	RBI	BB-IB	HP	SO	AVG	OBP	SLG	AOPS	ABR	SB-CS	FA	FR	Rng	Thr	G at Pos	BFW
1920	StL N	1	3	0	0	0	0	0	0	0	0	1	.000	.000	.000	-99	-1	0-0	.750	-1	*60*	*187*	/C	-0.2
1921	StL N	1	1	0	0	0	0	0	0	0	0	0	.000	.000	.000	-99	0	0-0	—	0			H	0.0
Total	2	2	4	0	0	0	0	0	0	0	0	1	.000	.000	.000	-99	-1	0-0	.750	-1	*60*	*187*	/C	-0.2

GILHOOLEY, FRANK Frank Patrick "Flash" B 6.10.1892 Toledo, OH D 7.11.1959 Toledo, OH BL/TR 5-8/155# d9.18

Year	Tm Lg	G	AB	R	H	2B	3B	HR	RBI	BB-IB	HP	SO	AVG	OBP	SLG	AOPS	ABR	SB-CS	FA	FR	Rng	Thr	G at Pos	BFW
1911	StL N	1	0	0	0	0	0	0	0	0	0	0	—	—	—	—	0	0	—	-0	0	0	/O(RF)	0.0
1912	StL N	13	49	5	11	0	0	0	2	3	0	8	.224	.269	.224	37	-4	0	1.000	-1	76	72	O-11(CF)	-0.6
1913	NY A	24	85	10	29	2	1	0	14	4	1	9	.341	.378	.388	124	2	6	.977	-0	112	56	O-24(RF)	0.1
1914	NY A	1	3	0	2	0	0	0	0	1	0	0	.667	.750	.667	327	1	0	—	0	0	0	/O(RF)	0.1
1915	NY A	1	4	0	0	0	0	0	0	0	0	1	.000	.000	.000	-99	-1	0	1.000	-0	81	0	/O(RF)	-0.1
1916	NY A	58	223	40	62	5	3	1	10	37	1	17	.278	.383	.341	115	6	16	.971	0	95	121	O-57(0-2-55)	0.3
1917	NY A	54	165	14	40	6	1	0	8	30	1	13	.242	.362	.291	99	2	6	.933	-1	102	81	O-46(RF)	-0.2
1918	NY A	112	427	59	118	13	5	1	23	53	1	24	.276	.358	.337	107	5	7	.961	1	101	98	*O-111(0-4-107)	0.0
1919	Bos A	48	112	14	27	4	0	0	1	12	0	8	.241	.315	.277	71	-4	2	.922	-1	92	120	O-33(30-2-1)	-0.6
Total	9	312	1068	142	289	30	10	2	58	140	4	80	.271	.357	.323	102	7	37	.957	-3	99	97	O-285(30-19-236)	-1.0

GILKEY, BERNARD Otis Bernard B 9.24.1966 St.Louis, MO BR/TR 6/190# d9.4

Year	Tm Lg	G	AB	R	H	2B	3B	HR	RBI	BB-IB	HP	SO	AVG	OBP	SLG	AOPS	ABR	SB-CS	FA	FR	Rng	Thr	G at Pos	BFW
1990	StL N	18	64	11	19	5	2	1	3	8-0	0	5	.297	.375	.484	134	3	6-1	.961	2	128	157	O-18(18-1-0)	0.6
1991	StL N	81	268	28	58	7	2	5	20	39-0	1	33	.216	.316	.313	78	-7	14-8	.994	6	109	146	O-74(LF)	-0.3
1992	StL N	131	384	56	116	19	4	7	43	39-1	1	52	.302	.364	.427	128	15	18-12	.978	7	108	192	*O-111(110-0-1)	2.0
1993	StL N	137	557	99	170	40	5	16	70	56-2	4	66	.305	.370	.481	129	24	15-10	.969	-3	84	**178**	*O-134(133-0-2)/1-3	1.5
1994	StL N	105	380	52	96	22	1	6	45	39-2	10	65	.253	.336	.363	84	-8	15-8	.983	-1	90	146	*O-102(LF)	-1.1
1995	StL N	121	480	73	143	33	4	17	69	42-3	5	70	.298	.358	.490	122	15	12-6	.986	3	100	138	*O-118(LF)	1.3
1996	NY N	153	571	108	181	44	3	30	117	73-7	4	125	.317	.393	.562	157	49	17-9	.982	18	112	**209**	*O-151(LF)	5.8
1997	NY N	145	518	85	129	31	1	18	78	70-1	6	111	.249	.338	.417	102	3	7-11	.989	6	94	181	*O-136(136-1-0)/D-2	0.1
1998	NY N	82	264	33	60	15	0	4	28	32-1	4	66	.227	.317	.330	72	-10	5-1	.992	4	95	201	O-77(76-1-4)	-0.8
	Ari N	29	101	8	25	0	0	1	5	11-0	1	14	.248	.327	.277	61	-6	4-2	.981	1	98	169	O-27(LF)	-0.5
	Year	111	365	41	85	15	0	5	33	43-1	5	80	.233	.320	.315	69	-16	9-3	.989	5	96	192	*O-104(103-1-4)	-1.3
1999	†Ari N	94	204	28	60	16	1	8	39	29-2	2	42	.294	.379	.500	122	8	2-2	.969	1	104	105	O-53(15-0-40)	0.6
2000	Ari N	38	73	6	8	1	0	2	6	7-2	0	16	.110	.185	.205	-1	-12	0-0	1.000	0	101	112	O-17(2-0-16)	-1.2
	Bos A	36	91	11	21	5	1	1	9	10-0	3	12	.231	.327	.341	67	-4	0-0	1.000	1	117	97	O-22(7-0-16)/D-8	-0.4
2001	Atl N	69	106	8	29	6	0	2	14	11-0	1	31	.274	.339	.387	88	-2	0-1	1.000	-1	104	0	O-36(28-0-8)/D	-0.3
Total	12	1239	4061	606	1115	244	24	118	546	466-21	42	708	.275	.352	.434	110	68	115-71	.983	45	100	166	*O-1076(997-3-87)/D-11,1-3	7.3

GILKS, BOB Robert James B 7.2.1864 Cincinnati, OH D 8.21.1944 Brunswick, GA BR/TR 5-8/178# d8.25 I OF Total (181-LF 56-CF 21-RF)

Year	Tm Lg	G	AB	R	H	2B	3B	HR	RBI	BB-IB	HP	SO	AVG	OBP	SLG	AOPS	ABR	SB-CS	FA	FR	Rng	Thr	G at Pos	BFW
1887	Cle AA	22	83	12	26	2	0	0	13	3	2		.313	.352	.337	96	0	5	.881	3	132	337	P-13/1-6,O-3(0-2-1),2	0.1
1888	Cle AA	119	484	59	111	14	4	1	63	7	3		.229	.245	.281	70	-17	16	.899	1	75	63	O-87(57-27-3),3-28/S-4,P-4,2	-1.7
1889	Cle N	53	210	17	50	5	2	0	18	7	3	20	.238	.273	.281	56	-13	6	1.000	1	104	0	O-29(2-26-1),S-13,1-10/2	-1.2
1890	Cle N	130	544	65	116	10	3	0	41	32	6	38	.213	.265	.243	49	-36	17	.941	3	97	43	*O-123(121-1-1)/P-4,S-3,2-2	-3.1
1893	Bal N	15	64	10	17	2	0	0	7	0	1	3	.266	.277	.297	52	-5	3	.969	3	203	182	O-15(1-0-15)	-0.2
Total	5	339	1385	163	320	33	9	1	142	49	15	61	.231	.265	.270	60	-71	47	.937	11	98	63	O-257L/3-28,P-21,S-20,1-16,2-5	-6.1

GILL, JIM James Clifford B 7.1866 D 4.10.1923 Beaver Falls, PA d6.27

Year	Tm Lg	G	AB	R	H	2B	3B	HR	RBI	BB-IB	HP	SO	AVG	OBP	SLG	AOPS	ABR	SB-CS	FA	FR	Rng	Thr	G at Pos	BFW
1889	StL AA	2	8	2	2	1	0	0	1	1	0	2	.250	.333	.375	90	0	1	1.000	-1	0	0	/O(CF)2	-0.1

Year	Tm Lg	G	AB	R	H	2B	3B	HR	RBI	BB-IB	HP	SO	AVG	OBP	SLG	AOPS	ABR	SB-CS	FA	FR	Rng	Thr	G at Pos	BFW
GILL, JOHNNY John Wesley "Patcheye" B 3.27.1905 Nashville, TN D 12.26.1984 Nashville, TN BL/TR 6-2/190# d8.28																								
1927	Cle A	21	60	8	13	3	0	1	4	7	2	13	.217	.319	.317	65	-3	1-1	1.000	0	84	153	O-17(14-3-0)	-0.4
1928	Cle A	2	2	0	0	0	0	0	0	0	0	1	.000	.000	.000	-99	-1	0-0	—	0			H	-0.1
1931	Was A	8	30	2	8	2	1	0	5	1	1	6	.267	.313	.400	86	-1	0-1	1.000	2	128	220	/O-8(RF)	0.1
1934	Was A	13	53	7	13	3	0	2	7	2	1	3	.245	.286	.415	82	-2	0-0	1.000	-1	103	0	O-13(2-0-11)	-0.3
1935	Chi N	3	3	2	1	1	0	0	1	0	0	1	.333	.333	.667	161	0	0	—	0			H	0.0
1936	Chi N	71	174	20	44	8	0	7	28	13	1	19	.253	.309	.420	92	-2	0	.938	-1	95	104	O-41(35-1-5)	-0.6
Total	6	118	322	39	79	17	1	10	45	23	5	43	.245	.306	.398	84	-9	1-2	.968	1	99	111	/O-79(51-4-24)	-1.3
GILL, WARREN Warren Darst "Doc" B 12.21.1878 Ladoga, IN D 11.26.1952 Laguna Beach, CA BR/TR 6-1/175# d8.26																								
1908	Pit N	27	76	10	17	0	1	0	14	11	6		.224	.366	.250	97	1	3	1.000	-3	47	103	1-25	-0.2
GILLEN, SAM Samuel (born Samuel Gilleland) B 1.1871 Pittsburgh, PA D 5.13.1905 Pittsburgh, PA 5-8/?# d8.19																								
1893	Pit N	3	6	0	0	0	0	0	0	0	0	1	.000	.000	.000	-99	-2	0	.750	-0	106	189	/S-3	-0.2
1897	Phi N	75	270	32	70	10	3	0	27	35	4		.259	.353	.319	80	-6	2	.896	-23	88	24	S-69/3-6	-2.2
Total	2	78	276	32	70	10	3	0	27	35	4	1	.254	.346	.312	76	-8	2	.892	-23	88	27	/S-72,3-6	-2.4
GILLEN, TOM Thomas J. B 5.18.1862 Philadelphia, PA D 1.26.1889 Philadelphia, PA 5-8/160# d4.18																								
1884	Phi U	29	116	5	18	2	0	0		1			.155	.162	.172	2	-18		.895	-5			C-27/O-3(LF)	-1.8
1886	Det N	2	10	2	4	0	0	0	4	0		1	.400	.400	.400	139	0	0	.889	-1			/C-2	0.0
Total	2	31	126	7	22	2	0	0	4	1		1	.175	.181	.190	14	-18	0	.895	-6			/C-29,O-3(LF)	-1.8
GILLENWATER, CARDEN Carden Edison B 5.13.1917 Riceville, TN D 5.10.2000 Largo, FL BR/TR 6-1/178# d9.22																								
1940	StL N	7	25	1	4	1	0	0	5	0	0	2	.160	.160	.200	-1	-3	0	1.000	-0	99	0	/O-7(5-2-0)	-0.4
1943	Bro N	8	17	1	3	0	0	0	2	2	0	3	.176	.263	.176	28	-2	0	1.000	0	73	328	/O-4(2-1-1)	-0.2
1945	Bos N	144	517	74	149	20	2	7	72	73	3	70	.288	.379	.375	110	10	13	.979	17	110	**194**	*O-140(CF)	2.2
1946	Bos N	99	224	30	51	10	1	1	14	39	0	27	.228	.342	.295	81	-4	3	.979	4	111	104	O-78(11-67-0)	-0.3
1948	Was A	77	221	23	54	10	4	3	21	39	0	36	.244	.358	.367	96	-1	4-2	.974	-1	101	75	O-67(1-65-1)	-0.3
Total	5	335	1004	129	261	41	7	11	114	153	3	138	.260	.359	.348	96	0	20-2	.979	19	108	145	O-296(19-275-2)	1.0
GILLESPIE, JOHN John W.L. BL/TR d10.1																								
1890	Buf P	1	3	0	0	0	0	0	0	0	0	2	.000	.000	.000	-99	-1	0	.250	-0	391	0	/O(RF)	-0.1
GILLESPIE, PAUL Paul Allen B 9.18.1920 Sugar Valley, GA D 8.11.1970 Anniston, AL BL/TR 6-3/195# d9.11																								
1942	Chi N	5	16	3	4	0	0	2	4	1	0	2	.250	.294	.625	172	1	0	1.000	-1	*119*	*99*	/C-4	0.1
1944	Chi N	9	26	2	7	1	0	1	2	3	0	3	.269	.345	.423	116	1	0	.903	-1	*101*	*200*	/C-7	0.0
1945	†Chi N	75	163	12	47	6	0	3	25	18	2	9	.288	.366	.380	110	3	2	.989	3	*145*	*86*	C-45/O(RF)	0.8
Total	3	89	205	17	58	7	0	6	31	22	2	14	.283	.358	.405	115	5	2	.978	1	*137*	*103*	/C-56,O(RF)	0.9
GILLESPIE, PETE Peter Patrick B 11.30.1851 Carbondale, PA D 5.5.1910 Carbondale, PA BL/TR 6-1.5/178# d5.1																								
1880	Tro N	82	346	50	84	20	5	2	24	17		35	.243	.278	.347	105	2		.905	6	72	136	*O-82(LF)	0.3
1881	Tro N	84	348	43	96	14	3	0	41	9		24	.276	.294	.333	92	-4		.933	3	70	145	*O-84(LF)	-0.6
1882	Tro N	74	298	46	82	5	4	2	33	9		14	.275	.296	.339	108	3		.827	-6	53	25	*O-74(LF)	-0.4
1883	NY N	**98**	411	64	129	23	12	1	62	9		27	.314	.329	.436	131	14		.897	6	50	169	*O-98(97-1-0)	1.6
1884	NY N	101	413	75	109	7	4	2	44	19		35	.264	.296	.315	90	-5		.893	-3	39	28	*O-101(100-0-1)	-1.0
1885	NY N	102	420	67	123	17	6	0	52	15		32	.293	.317	.362	121	9		**.942**	-4	63	93	*O-102(LF)	0.2
1886	NY N	97	396	65	108	13	8	0	58	16		30	.273	.301	.346	95	-3	17	.901	-12	31	0	*O-97(95-1-1)	-1.6
1887	NY N	76	295	40	78	9	3	3	37	12	5	21	.264	.304	.346	84	-6	37	.946	2	119	49	O-76(LF)/3	-0.5
Total	8	714	2927	450	809	108	45	10	351	106	5	218	.276	.303	.354	104	10	54	.903	-7	60	82	O-714(710-2-2)/3	-2.0
GILLIAM, JIM James William "Junior" B 10.17.1928 Nashville, TN D 10.8.1978 Inglewood, CA BB/TR 5-10.5/175# d4.14 C14 OF Total (207-LF 5-CF 26-RF)																								
1953	†Bro N	151	605	125	168	31	**17**	6	63	100	3	38	.278	.383	.415	106	8	21-14	.976	1	97	106	*2-149	1.9
1954	Bro N	146	607	107	171	28	8	13	52	76	2	30	.282	.361	.418	100	1	8-7	.977	-14	92	97	*2-143/O-4(4-0-2)	-0.3
1955	†Bro N	147	538	110	134	20	8	7	40	70-4	6	37	.249	.341	.355	83	-12	15-15	.968	-6	98	102	2-99,O-46(41-4-7)	-1.6
1956	†Bro N☆	153	594	102	178	23	8	6	43	95-6	4	39	.300	.399	.396	107	11	21-9	.981	10	107	103	*2-102,O-56(53-0-7)	2.6
1957	Bro N	149	617	89	154	26	4	2	37	64-0	4	31	.250	.323	.314	66	-27	26-10	**.986**	6	93	101	*2-148/O-2(LF)	-0.8
1958	LA N	147	555	81	145	25	5	2	43	78-1	0	22	.261	.352	.335	81	-13	18-11	.987	8	101	91	O-75(71-1-5),3-44,2-32	-0.8
1959	†LA N★	145	553	91	156	18	4	3	34	**96**-4	0	25	.282	.387	.345	91	-2	23-10	.958	-1	94	87	*3-132/2-8,O-3(3-0-1)	-0.2
1960	LA N	151	557	96	138	20	2	5	40	96-1	3	28	.248	.359	.318	82	-9	12-9	.960	11	**111**	106	*3-130,2-30	0.3
1961	LA N	144	439	74	107	26	3	4	32	79-2	0	34	.244	.358	.344	81	-9	8-4	.956	3	95	84	3-74,2-71,O-11(LF)	0.0
1962	LA N	160	588	83	159	24	1	4	43	93-0	2	35	.270	.370	.335	97	3	17-7	.981	-4	99	96	*2-113,3-90/O(1-0-1)	0.8
1963	†LA N	148	525	77	148	27	4	6	49	60-2	2	28	.282	.354	.383	122	17	19-5	.985	-1	97	99	*2-119,3-55	2.9
1964	LA N	116	334	44	76	8	3	2	27	42-2	3	21	.228	.318	.287	78	-9	4-4	.936	-17	87	68	3-86,2-25/O-2(RF)	-2.6
1965	†LA N	111	372	54	104	19	4	4	39	53-5	4	31	.280	.374	.384	123	14	9-5	.960	-10	85	123	3-80,O-22(21-0-1)/2-5	0.3
1966	†LA N	88	235	30	51	9	0	1	16	34-3	0	17	.217	.315	.268	70	-8	2-1	.953	-9	82	80	3-70/1-2,2-2	-1.8
Total	14	1956	7119	1163	1889	304	71	65	558	1036-30	33	416	.265	.360	.355	92	-35	203-111	.979	-24	96	98	*2-1046,3-761,O-222L/1-2	0.7
GILLIGAN, BARNEY Andrew Bernard B 1.3.1856 Cambridge, MA D 4.1.1934 Lynn, MA BR/TR 5-6.5/130# d9.25																								
1875	Atl NA	2	8	2	2	0	0	0	0	0		0	.250	.250	.250	85	0	0-0	1.000	-0			/CO(RF)	0.0
1879	Cle N	52	205	20	35	6	2	0	11	0		13	.171	.171	.220	28	-16		.870	-0			C-27,O-23(21-2-0)/S-2	-1.5
1880	Cle N	30	99	9	17	4	3	1	13	6		12	.172	.219	.303	77	-2		.969	6			C-23/O-4(CF),S-4	0.4
1881	Pro N	46	183	19	40	7	2	0	20	9		24	.219	.255	.279	69	-6		.930	-1			C-36,S-10/O(CF)	-0.6
1882	Pro N	56	201	32	45	7	6	0	26	4		26	.224	.239	.318	77	-5		.932	6			C-54/S-2	0.5
1883	Pro N	74	263	34	52	13	3	0	24	26		32	.198	.270	.270	63	-11		.900	9			*C-74	0.3
1884	†Pro N	82	294	47	72	13	2	1	38	35		41	.245	.325	.313	104	3		.928	13			*C-81/31	2.0
1885	Pro N	71	252	23	54	7	3	0	12	23		33	.214	.280	.266	80	-5		.872	-2			C-65/S-5,O(LF)2	-0.1
1886	Was N	81	273	23	52	9	2	0	17	39		35	.190	.292	.238	68	-8	6	.925	-6			C-71,O-14(1-6-7)/S3	-0.8
1887	Was N	28	90	7	18	2	0	1	6	5	0	18	.200	.242	.256	41	-7	2	.874	-3			C-26/S-3,O(CF)	-0.7
1888	Det N	1	5	1	1	0	0	0	0	0	0	1	.200	.200	.200	28	0	0	.875	0			/C	0.0
Total	10	521	1865	215	386	68	23	3	167	147	0	235	.207	.265	.273	71	-57	8-0	.912	21			C-458/O-44(23-14-7),S-27,3-2,21	-0.5
GILLIS, GRANT Grant B 1.24.1901 Grove Hill, AL D 2.4.1981 Thomasville, AL BR/TR 5-10/165# d9.19																								
1927	Was A	10	36	8	8	3	1	0	2	2	0	0	.222	.263	.361	61	-2	0-0	1.000	-1	82	131	S-10	-0.2
1928	Was A	24	87	13	22	5	1	0	10	4	3	5	.253	.309	.333	69	-4	0-1	.910	-7	79	52	S-16/2-5,3-3	-0.9
1929	Bos A	28	73	5	18	4	0	0	11	6	0	8	.247	.304	.301	58	-5	0-1	.956	-3	98	81	2-25	-0.7
Total	3	62	196	26	48	12	2	0	23	12	3	13	.245	.299	.327	63	-11	0-2	.948	-11	94	82	/2-30,S-26,3-3	-1.8
GILMAN, JIMMY James Joseph B 6.14.1870 D 12.21.1912 Cleveland, OH TR d7.10																								
1893	Cle N	2	7	1	2	0	0	0	1	0	0	2	.286	.286	.286	49	-1	0	.667	-1	88	0	/3-2	-0.1
GILMAN, PIT Pitkin Clark B 3.14.1864 Laporte, OH D 8.17.1950 Elyria, OH BL/TL ?/170# d9.18																								
1884	Cle N	2	10	0	1	0	0	0	0	0		3	.100	.100	.100	-36	-2		1.000	0	0	0	/O-2(LF)	-0.1
GILMORE, GROVER Ernest Grover B 11.1.1888 Chicago, IL D 11.25.1919 Sioux City, IA BL/TL 5-9.5/170# d4.18																								
1914	KC F	139	530	91	152	25	5	1	32	37	3	108	.287	.337	.358	93	-14	23	.973	-1	92	107	*O-132(0-10-122)	-2.3
1915	KC F	119	411	53	117	22	15	1	47	26	13	50	.285	.347	.418	120	3	19	.979	5	109	107	*O-119(RF)	0.2
Total	2	258	941	144	269	47	20	2	79	63	16	158	.286	.341	.385	105	-11	42	.976	4	100	107	O-251(0-10-241)	-2.1
GILMORE, JIM James B 5.1853 Baltimore, MD D 11.18.1928 Baltimore, MD d4.26																								
1875	Was NA	3	12	2	3	0	0	0	0	0		3	.250	.250	.250	77	0	0-0	.667	-1			/C-2,3O(RF)	-0.1
GILROY d9.7																								
1874	Chi NA	8	38	4	8	1	0	0	7	1		3	.211	.231	.237	50	-2	0-0	.816	-1			/C-8	-0.2
1875	Ath NA	2	6	0	1	0	0	0	0	0		0	.167	.167	.167	15	-1	0-0	.800	1			/CO(RF)	0.0
Total	2 NA	10	44	4	9	1	0	0	7	1		3	.205	.222	.227	45	-3	0-0	.000	0			/C-9,O(RF)	-0.2
GINN, TINSLEY Tinsley Rucker B 9.26.1891 Royston, GA D 8.30.1931 Atlanta, GA BL/TR 5-9/180# d6.27																								
1914	Cle A	2	1	0	0	0	0	0	0	0	0	0	.000	.000	.000	-96	0	0	—	0	0	0	/O-2	0.0

Year	Tm Lg	G	AB	R	H	2B	3B	HR	RBI	BB-IB	HP	SO	AVG	OBP	SLG	AOPS	ABR	SB-CS	FA	FR	Rng	Thr	G at Pos	BFW
GINSBERG, JOE Myron Nathan B 10.11.1926 New York, NY BL/TR 5-11/180# d9.15																								
1948	Det A	11	36	7	13	0	0	0	1	3	0	1	.361	.410	.361	103	0	0-0	.943	-1	*104*	*43*	C-11	0.0
1950	Det A	36	95	12	22	6	0	0	12	11	1	6	.232	.318	.295	56	-6	1-0	.981	-2	*147*	*68*	C-31	-0.6
1951	Det A	102	304	44	79	10	2	8	37	43	2	21	.260	.355	.385	100	0	0-2	.978	-4	*76*	*108*	C-95	0.1
1952	Det A	113	307	29	68	13	2	6	36	51	3	21	.221	.338	.336	87	-4	1-1	.984	-8	*97*	*86*	*C-101	-0.7
1953	Det A	18	53	6	16	2	0	0	3	10	1	1	.302	.422	.340	109	2	0-0	.988	-1	*83*	*187*	C-15	0.1
	Cle A	46	109	10	31	4	0	0	10	14	1	4	.284	.371	.321	91	-1	0-0	.966	-3	*91*	*52*	C-39	-0.2
	Year	64	162	16	47	6	0	0	13	24	2	5	.290	.388	.327	97	1	0-0	.974	-4	*88*	*97*	C-54	-0.1
1954	Cle A	3	2	0	1	0	1	0	1	0	1	0	.500	.667	1.500	473	1	0-0	1.000	0	*0*	*0*	/C	0.1
1956	KC A	71	195	15	48	8	1	1	12	23-3	0	17	.246	.323	.313	69	-8	1-1	.989	-1	*81*	*120*	C-57	-0.7
	Bal A	15	28	0	2	0	0	0	2	2-0	0	4	.071	.129	.071	-48	-6	0-0	1.000	-0	*83*	*89*	/C-8	-0.6
	Year	86	223	15	50	8	1	1	14	25-3	0	21	.224	.299	.283	56	-14	1-1	.990	-2	*81*	*117*	C-65	-1.3
1957	Bal A	85	175	15	48	8	2	1	18	18-1	2	19	.274	.342	.360	100	0	2-1	.986	-1	*116*	*100*	C-66	0.2
1958	Bal A	61	109	4	23	1	0	3	16	13-1	2	14	.211	.302	.303	72	-4	0-0	.994	3	*154*	*51*	C-39	0.0
1959	Bal A	65	166	14	30	2	0	1	14	21-3	0	13	.181	.268	.211	35	-15	1-0	.993	3	*143*	*159*	C-62	-0.9
1960	Bal A	14	30	3	8	1	0	0	6	6-1	0	1	.267	.389	.300	90	0	0-0	.940	-1	*117*	*52*	C-14	0.0
	Chi A	28	75	8	19	4	0	0	9	10-0	1	8	.253	.345	.307	80	-2	1-0	.993	3	*124*	*78*	C-25	0.3
	Year	42	105	11	27	5	0	0	15	16-1	1	9	.257	.358	.305	83	-2	1-0	.976	2	*122*	*70*	C-39	0.3
1961	Chi A	6	3	0	0	0	0	0	0	1-0	0	2	.000	.250	.000	-27	-1	0-0	1.000	0	*0*	*0*	/C-2	0.0
	Bos A	19	24	1	6	0	0	0	5	0-0	0	2	.250	.250	.250	33	-2	0-0	1.000	-0	*81*	*0*	/C-6	-0.3
	Year	25	27	1	6	0	0	0	5	1-0	0	4	.222	.250	.222	27	-3	0-0	1.000	-0	*70*	*0*	/C-8	-0.3
1962	NY N	2	5	0	0	0	0	0	0	0-0	0	1	.000	.000	.000	-98	-1	0-0	1.000	1	*78*	*256*	/C-2	-0.1
Total	13	695	1716	168	414	59	8	20	182	226-9	14	135	.241	.332	.320	79	-47	7-5	.983	-13	*104*	*98*	C-574	-3.3
GINTER, KEITH Keith Michael B 5.5.1976 Norwalk, CA BR/TR 5-10/190# d9.20																								
2000	Hou N	5	8	3	2	0	0	1	3	1-0	0	3	.250	.300	.625	128	0	0-0	1.000	-0	84	145	/2-2	0.0
2001	Hou N	1	1	0	0	0	0	0	0	0-0	0	0	.000	.000	.000	-95	0	0-0	—	0			/H	0.0
2002	Hou N	7	5	1	1	1	0	0	0	2-0	1	1	.200	.500	.400	139	1	0-0	.875	1	144	345	/3-4,S	0.2
	Mil N	21	76	6	18	8	0	1	8	15-0	0	14	.237	.363	.382	101	1	0-0	.961	-4	75	67	3-21	-0.3
	Year	28	81	7	19	9	0	1	8	17-0	1	15	.235	.374	.383	103	1	0-0	.949	-3	80	85	3-25/S	-0.1
2003	Mil N	127	358	51	92	15	2	14	44	37-1	17	87	.257	.352	.427	105	3	1-1	.991	-19	89	95	2-53,3-40/S-2,O-2(LF)	-1.3
Total	4	161	448	61	113	24	2	16	55	55-1	18	105	.252	.354	.422	105	5	1-1	.933	-21	75	87	/3-65,2-55,S-3,O-2(LF)	-1.4
GIONFRIDDO, AL Albert Francis B 3.8.1922 Dysart, PA D 3.14.2003 Solvana, CA BL/TL 5-6/165# d9.23																								
1944	Pit N	4	6	0	1	0	0	0	0	1	0	1	.167	.286	.167	28	-1	0	1.000	-0	94	0	/O(CF)	-0.1
1945	Pit N	122	409	74	116	18	9	2	42	60	1	22	.284	.377	.386	108	6	12	.964	-7	91	73	*O-106(13-82-11)	-0.5
1946	Pit N	64	102	11	26	2	2	0	10	14	0	5	.255	.345	.314	85	-2	1	.944	-0	101	99	O-33(8-13-12)	-0.3
1947	Pit N	1	1	0	0	0	0	0	0	0	0	0	.000	.000	.000	-97	0	0	—	0			H	0.0
	†Bro N	37	62	10	11	2	1	0	6	16	0	11	.177	.346	.242	57	-3	2	.938	-1	96	89	O-17(11-0-6)	-0.5
	Year	38	63	10	11	2	1	0	6	16	0	11	.175	.342	.238	54	-4	2	.938	-1	96	89	O-17(11-0-6)	-0.5
Total	4	228	580	95	154	22	12	2	58	91	1	39	.266	.366	.355	97	0	15	.959	-8	93	78	O-157(32-96-29)	-1.4
GIORDANO, TOMMY Thomas Arthur "T-Bone" (born Carmine Arthur Giordano) B 10.9.1925 Newark, NJ BR/TR 6/175# d9.11																								
1953	Phi A	11	40	6	7	2	0	2	5	5	0	6	.175	.267	.375	69	-2	0-1	.984	0	101	117	2-11	-0.1
GIOVANOLA, ED Edward Thomas B 3.4.1969 Los Gatos, CA BL/TR 5-10/170# d9.10																								
1995	Atl N	13	14	2	1	0	0	0	0	3-0	0	5	.071	.235	.071	-14	-2	0-0	1.000	-1	61	57	/2-7,3-3,S	-0.3
1996	Atl N	43	82	10	19	2	0	0	7	8-0	1	13	.232	.304	.256	48	-6	1-0	.983	1	89	112	S-25/3-6,2-5	-0.3
1997	Atl N	14	8	0	2	0	0	0	0	2-1	0	1	.250	.400	.250	73	0	0-0	1.000	-0	94	0	/3-8,2S	0.0
1998	SD N	92	139	19	32	3	3	1	9	22-0	0	22	.230	.335	.317	79	-4	1-2	.965	12	127	66	3-37,2-36/S	0.8
1999	SD N	56	58	10	11	0	1	0	3	9-0	0	8	.190	.294	.224	38	-6	2-0	.938	4	124	0	3-25,2-19/S-7,P	-0.1
Total	5	218	301	41	65	5	4	1	19	44-1	1	49	.216	.316	.269	57	-18	4-2	.964	15	119	66	/3-79,2-68,S-35,P	0.1
GIPSON, CHARLES Charles Wells B 12.16.1972 Orange, CA BR/TR 6-2/180# d3.31 OF Total (134-LF 55-CF 81-RF)																								
1998	Sea A	44	51	11	12	1	0	0	2	5-1	1	9	.235	.316	.255	51	-4	2-1	.973	2	121	229	O-36(14-11-13)/3-4	-0.2
1999	Sea A	55	80	16	18	5	2	0	9	6-0	1	13	.225	.287	.338	60	-5	3-4	.960	9	105	895	O-28(8-9-15),3-17/2-3,S-3,D-4	0.3
2000	†Sea A	59	29	7	9	1	1	0	3	4-0	0	9	.310	.394	.414	108	0	2-3	1.000	1	86	136	O-48(14-8-29)/3-5,S-5,D	0.0
2001	†Sea A	94	64	16	14	2	2	0	5	4-0	2	20	.219	.282	.313	61	-4	1-1	1.000	-1	94	82	O-65(41-14-11),D-11/3-9,S-6,2	-0.6
2002	Sea A	79	72	22	17	5	2	0	8	9-0	1	14	.236	.329	.361	87	-1	4-0	.971	2	114	121	O-73(57-5-13)/3-4	0.0
2003	NY A	18	10	3	2	0	0	0	2	1-0	0	2	.200	.273	.200	28	-1	2-1	1.000	-0	88	0	/O-8(CF),D-3	-0.1
Total	6	349	306	75	72	14	7	0	29	29-1	5	67	.235	.311	.327	69	-15	14-10	.980	11	105	204	O-258L/3-39,D-19,S-14,2-4	-0.6
GIRARDI, JOE Joseph Elliott B 10.14.1964 Peoria, IL BR/TR 5-11/195# d4.4																								
1989	†Chi N	59	157	15	39	10	0	1	14	11-5	2	26	.248	.304	.331	76	-4	2-1	.981	9	107	121	C-59	0.8
1990	Chi N	133	419	36	113	24	2	1	38	17-11	3	50	.270	.300	.344	72	-16	8-3	.985	-8	137	103	*C-133	-1.6
1991	Chi N	21	47	3	9	2	0	0	6	6-1	0	6	.191	.283	.234	45	-3	0-0	.972	1	92	96	C-21	-0.2
1992	Chi N	91	270	19	73	3	1	1	12	19-3	1	38	.270	.320	.300	75	-9	0-2	.991	-3	131	114	C-86	-0.9
1993	Col N	86	310	35	90	14	5	3	31	24-0	3	41	.290	.346	.397	85	-6	6-6	.989	-3	92	111	C-84	-0.4
1994	Col N	93	330	47	91	9	4	4	34	21-1	2	48	.276	.321	.364	67	-16	3-3	.992	8	98	118	C-93	-0.2
1995	†Col N	125	462	63	121	17	2	8	55	29-0	2	76	.262	.308	.359	59	-27	3-3	.988	-1	104	87	*C-122	-2.0
1996	†NY A	124	422	55	124	22	3	2	45	30-1	5	55	.294	.346	.374	83	-11	13-4	.996	2	78	99	*C-120/D-2	0.0
1997	†NY A	112	398	38	105	23	1	1	50	26-1	2	53	.264	.311	.334	69	-18	2-3	.994	12	106	104	*C-111/D	0.1
1998	†NY A	78	254	31	70	11	4	3	31	14-1	2	38	.276	.317	.386	85	-6	2-4	.995	12	97	79	C-78	0.9
1999	†NY A	65	209	23	50	16	1	2	27	10-0	0	26	.239	.271	.354	59	-13	3-1	.984	3	72	98	C-65	-0.5
2000	Chi N☆	106	363	47	101	15	1	6	40	32-3	3	61	.278	.339	.375	83	-10	1-0	.993	-10	96	134	*C-103	-1.3
2001	Chi N	78	229	22	58	10	1	3	25	21-4	0	50	.253	.315	.345	75	-9	0-1	1.000	-1	131	114	C-71	-0.6
2002	Chi N	90	234	19	53	10	1	1	13	16-3	0	35	.226	.275	.291	53	-17	1-0	.990	-6	91	103	C-88	-1.9
2003	StL N	16	23	1	3	0	0	0	1	3-0	0	4	.130	.231	.130	-3	-4	0-0	.958	-4	98	0	C-13	-0.8
Total	15	1277	4127	454	1100	186	26	36	422	279-34	25	607	.267	.315	.350	71	-169	44-31	.991	11	103	105	*C-1247/D-3	-8.6
GIULIANI, TONY Angelo John B 11.24.1912 St.Paul, MN BR/TR 5-11/175# d4.18																								
1936	StL A	71	198	17	43	3	0	0	13	11	0	13	.217	.258	.232	21	-25	0-0	.966	2	*109*	*47*	C-66	-1.8
1937	StL A	19	53	6	16	1	0	0	3	3	0	3	.302	.339	.321	67	-3	0-0	.986	-1	*90*	*95*	C-19	-0.3
1938	Was A	46	115	10	25	4	0	0	15	8	0	3	.217	.268	.252	33	-12	1-0	1.000	-1	*109*	*92*	C-46	-1.0
1939	Was A	54	172	20	43	6	2	0	18	4	0	7	.250	.267	.308	50	-14	0-1	.979	2	*151*	*85*	C-50	-0.9
1940	Bro N	1	1	0	0	0	0	0	0	0	0	1	.000	.000	.000	-94	0	0	1.000	-0	*0*	*0*	/C	0.0
1941	Bro N	3	2	0	0	0	0	0	0	0	0	0	.000	.000	.000	-96	-1	0	1.000	1	*0*	*0*	/C-3	0.0
1943	Was A	49	133	5	30	4	1	0	20	12	0	14	.226	.290	.271	67	-6	0-1	.962	-1	*119*	*81*	C-49	-0.6
Total	7	243	674	58	157	18	3	0	69	38	0	41	.233	.274	.269	42	-61	1-2	.976	1	*119*	*75*	C-234	-4.6
GLADD, JIM James Walter B 10.2.1922 Ft.Gibson, OK D 11.8.1977 Long Beach, CA BR/TR 6-2/190# d9.9																								
1946	NY N	4	11	0	1	0	0	0	0	1	0	4	.091	.167	.091	-26	-2	0	1.000	2	*89*	*74*	/C-4	0.0
GLADDEN, DAN Clinton Daniel B 7.7.1957 San Jose, CA BR/TR 5-11/180# d9.5																								
1983	SF N	18	63	6	14	2	0	1	9	5-0	0	11	.222	.275	.302	63	-3	4-3	1.000	2	125	0	O-18(0-17-1)	-0.2
1984	SF N	86	342	71	120	17	2	4	31	33-2	2	37	.351	.410	.447	146	22	31-16	.988	4	105	164	O-85(CF)	2.7
1985	SF N	142	502	64	122	15	8	7	41	40-1	7	78	.243	.307	.347	87	-10	32-15	.975	-7	97	41	*O-124(14-111-1)	-1.8
1986	SF N	102	351	55	97	16	1	4	29	39-3	5	59	.276	.357	.362	104	3	27-10	.987	5	113	141	O-89(CF)	1.0
1987	†Min A	121	438	69	109	21	2	8	38	38-2	3	72	.249	.312	.361	75	-15	25-9	.987	7	110	136	*O-111(105-8-2)/D-4	-1.0
1988	Min A	141	576	91	155	32	6	11	62	46-4	4	74	.269	.325	.403	100	0	28-8	.991	12	113	151	*O-140(LF)/23P	1.1
1989	Min A	121	461	69	136	23	3	8	46	23-3	5	53	.295	.331	.410	102	1	23-7	.966	4	110	122	*O-117(116-2-0)/PD	0.4
1990	Min A	136	534	64	147	27	6	5	40	26-2	6	67	.275	.314	.376	87	-10	25-9	.980	9	110	146	*O-133(133-1-0)/D-2	-0.3
1991	†Min A	126	461	65	114	14	9	6	52	36-1	5	60	.247	.306	.356	80	-14	15-9	.988	0	102	63	*O-126(LF)	-1.7
1992	Det A	113	417	57	106	20	1	7	42	30-0	2	64	.254	.304	.357	85	-9	4-2	.987	1	98	130	*O-108(95-17-0)/D-2	-1.0
1993	Det A	91	356	52	95	16	2	13	56	21-0	3	50	.267	.312	.433	99	-2	8-5	.986	4	104	173	O-86(69-18-0)/D-5	0.0
Total	11	1197	4501	663	1215	203	40	74	446	337-18	42	625	.270	.324	.382	94	-37	222-93	.984	40	107	122	*O-1137(798-349-4)/D-15,P-2,32	-0.8

Year	Tm Lg	G	AB	R	H	2B	3B	HR	RBI	BB-IB	HP	SO	AVG	OBP	SLG	AOPS	ABR	SB-CS	FA	FR	Rng	Thr	G at Pos	BFW
GLADMAN, BUCK James Henry B 11.1863 Washington, DC D 1.13.1890 Washington, DC d7.7																								
1883	Phi N	1	4	1	0	0	0	0	0	0		2	.000	.000	.000	-99	-1		1.000	-0	74	0	/3	-0.1
1884	Was AA	56	224	17	35	5	3	1		3	3		.156	.178	.219	33	-15		.796	-5	94	70	3-53/O-2(RF),S	-1.8
1886	Was N	44	152	17	21	5	3	1	15	12		30	.138	.201	.230	33	-12	5	.830	-2	92	154	3-44	-1.2
Total	3	101	380	35	56	10	6	2	15	15		32	.147	.186	.221	31	-28	5	.812	-7	93	105	/3-98,O-2(RF),S	-3.1
GLADU, ROLAND Roland Edouard B 5.10.1911 Montreal, PQ, CAN D 7.26.1994 Montreal, PQ, CAN BL/TR 5-8.5/185# d4.18																								
1944	Bos N	21	66	5	16	2	1	1	7	3	0	8	.242	.275	.348	72	-3	0	.891	-2	74	244	3-15/O-3(LF)	-0.5
GLANVILLE, DOUG Douglas Metunwa B 8.25.1970 Hackensack, NJ BR/TR 6-2/170# d6.9																								
1996	Chi N	49	83	10	20	5	1	1	10	3-0	0	11	.241	.264	.361	62	-5	2-0	.973	-0	97	95	O-35(19-9-8)	-0.5
1997	Chi N	146	474	79	142	22	5	4	35	24-0	1	46	.300	.333	.392	87	-9	19-11	.989	9	108	166	*O-138(120-30-1)	-0.3
1998	Phi N	158	678	106	189	28	7	8	49	42-1	6	89	.279	.325	.376	83	-18	23-6	.995	-1	97	142	*O-158(CF)	-1.4
1999	Phi N	150	628	101	204	38	6	11	73	48-1	6	82	.325	.376	.457	107	7	34-2	.980	6	107	163	*O-148(CF)	2.0
2000	Phi N	154	637	89	175	27	6	8	52	31-1	2	76	.275	.307	.374	71	-30	31-8	.990	4	108	103	*O-150(CF)	-2.0
2001	Phi N	153	634	74	166	24	3	14	55	19-1	4	91	.262	.285	.375	71	-30	28-6	.991	6	114	96	*O-150(CF)	-1.7
2002	Phi N	138	422	49	105	16	3	6	29	25-4	2	57	.249	.292	.344	73	-20	19-2	**1.000**	-5	89	123	*O-117(CF)	-2.0
2003	Tex A	52	195	22	53	5	0	4	14	6-1	0	25	.272	.294	.359	65	-10	4-0	1.000	-3	94	46	O-52(CF)	-1.1
	†Chi N	28	51	2	12	0	0	1	2	2-0	0	4	.235	.259	.294	46	-4	0-1	1.000	2	136	188	O-18(3-15-1)	-0.2
Total	8	1028	3802	532	1066	165	31	57	319	200-9	21	481	.280	.318	.385	81	-119	160-36	.990	19	104	127	O-966(142-829-10)	-7.2
GLASSCOCK, JACK John Wesley "Pebbly Jack" B 7.22.1859 Wheeling, WV D 2.24.1947 Wheeling, WV BR/TR 5-8/160# d5.1 M2																								
1879	Cle N	80	325	31	68	9	3	0	29	6		24	.209	.224	.255	58	-14		.919	-9	86	63	*2-66,3-14	-1.8
1880	Cle N	77	296	37	72	13	3	0	27	2		21	.243	.248	.307	89	-3		.891	5	100	114	*S-77	0.5
1881	Cle N	**85**	335	49	86	9	5	0	33	15		8	.257	.289	.313	94	-2		**.911**	9	**105**	123	*S-79/2-6	1.0
1882	Cle N	**84**	358	66	104	27	9	4	46	13		9	.291	.315	.450	147	19		.900	**24**	**118**	**174**	*S-83/3	**4.1**
1883	Cle N	96	383	67	110	19	6	0	46	13		23	.287	.311	.368	107	3		**.922**	18	**107**	119	*S-93/2-3	2.0
1884	Cle N	72	281	45	70	4	4	1	22	25		16	.249	.310	.302	91	-3		.893	26	125	96	S-69/2-3,P-2	2.2
	Cin U	38	172	48	72	9	5	2		8			.419	.444	.564	189	14		.889	1	104	81	S-36/2-2	1.4
1885	StL N	**111**	446	66	125	18	3	1	40	29		10	.280	.324	.341	123	13		**.917**	21	**112**	98	*S-110/2	3.5
1886	StL N	121	486	96	158	29	7	3	40	38		13	.325	.374	.432	154	34	38	**.906**	15	**107**	**124**	*S-120/O(RF)	4.6
1887	Ind N	122	483	91	142	18	7	0	40	41	10	8	.294	.361	.360	105	6	62	.906	**39**	**122**	135	*S-122/P	4.0
1888	Ind N	113	442	63	119	17	3	1	45	14	7	17	.269	.302	.328	99	-1	48	**.901**	14	**106**	110	*S-110/2-3,P	1.6
1889	Ind N	134	582	128	**205**	40	3	7	85	31	5	10	.352	.390	.467	136	27	57	**.915**	**38**	**118**	**129**	*S-132/2-2,PM	**5.8**
1890	NY N	124	512	91	**172**	32	9	1	66	41	9	8	**.336**	.395	.439	143	28	54	.910	23	101	102	*S-124	**4.8**
1891	NY N	97	369	46	89	12	6	0	55	36	5	11	.241	.317	.306	85	-6	29	.913	1	91	126	*S-97	-0.2
1892	StL N	139	566	83	151	27	5	3	72	44	7	19	.267	.327	.348	110	7	26	.916	6	102	87	*S-139,M	1.9
1893	StL N	48	195	32	56	8	1	1	26	25	5	3	.287	.382	.354	96	0	20	.907	-5	96	100	S-48	-0.2
	Pit N	66	293	49	100	7	11	1	74	17	4	4	.341	.385	.451	124	8	16	.934	10	103	153	S-66	1.8
	Year	114	488	81	156	15	12	2	100	42	9	7	.320	.384	.412	113	9	36	.923	5	100	131	*S-114	1.6
1894	Pit N	87	335	47	94	10	7	1	65	32	4	4	.281	.350	.361	73	-15	18	.933	3	99	121	S-86	-0.6
1895	Lou N	18	74	9	25	3	1	1	6	3	3	1	.338	.387	.446	122	3	1	.900	1	102	91	S-13/1-5	0.3
	Was N	25	100	20	23	2	0	0	10	7	3	3	.230	.300	.250	43	-8	3	.895	6	118	84	S-25	-0.1
	Year	43	174	29	48	5	1	1	16	10	6	4	.276	.337	.333	76	-6	4	.897	7	112	86	S-38/1-5	0.2
Total	17	1737	7033	1164	2041	313	98	27	827	440	62	212	.290	.337	.374	112	110	372	.910	246	108	117	*S-1629/2-86,3-15,1-5,P-5,O(RF)	36.6
GLAUS, TROY Troy B 8.3.1976 Newport Beach, CA BR/TR 6-5/220# d7.31																								
1998	Ana A	48	165	19	36	9	0	1	23	15-0	0	51	.218	.280	.291	50	-12	1-0	.941	0	102	99	3-48	-1.1
1999	Ana A	154	551	85	132	29	0	29	79	71-1	6	143	.240	.331	.450	98	-2	5-1	.954	-6	97	99	*3-153/D	-0.6
2000	Ana A★	159	563	120	160	37	1	**47**	102	112-6	2	163	.284	.404	.604	147	43	14-11	.933	12	**117**	115	*3-156/S-6,D-4	5.0
2001	Ana A★	161	588	100	147	38	2	41	108	107-7	6	158	.250	.367	.531	131	28	10-3	.953	-16	92	79	*3-159/S-2,D-2	1.5
2002	†Ana A	156	569	99	142	24	1	30	111	88-4	6	144	.250	.352	.453	113	12	10-3	.950	-2	100	128	*3-156/S-2	1.2
2003	Ana A★	91	319	53	79	17	2	16	50	46-4	1	73	.248	.343	.464	115	7	7-2	.923	-8	91	79	3-87/D-4	0.1
Total	6	769	2755	476	696	154	6	164	473	439-22	21	732	.253	.357	.491	118	76	47-20	.944	-20	100	102	3-759/D-11,S-10	6.1
GLAVIANO, TOMMY Thomas Giatano "Rabbit" B 10.26.1923 Sacramento, CA BR/TR 5-9/175# d4.19																								
1949	StL N	87	258	32	69	16	1	6	36	41	6	35	.267	.380	.407	106	4	0	.929	7	113	106	3-73/2-7	1.1
1950	StL N	115	410	92	117	29	2	11	44	90	6	74	.285	.421	.446	122	19	6	.935	2	106	71	*3-106/2-5,S	2.1
1951	StL N	54	104	20	19	4	0	1	4	26	2	18	.183	.356	.250	66	-4	3-0	.972	-2	87	0	O-17(2-14-1)/2-9	-0.5
1952	StL N	80	162	30	39	5	1	3	19	27	5	26	.241	.366	.340	97	1	0-0	.934	2	105	70	3-52/2	0.2
1953	Phi N	53	74	17	15	1	2	3	5	24	2	20	.203	.410	.392	111	3	2-0	.892	-2	82	82	3-14,2-12/S	0.1
Total	5	389	1008	191	259	55	6	24	108	208	21	173	.257	.395	.395	108	23	11-0	.931	6	107	82	3-245/2-34,O-17(2-14-1),S-2	3.0
GLAVINE, MIKE Michael Patrick B 1.24.1973 Concord, MA BL/TL 6-3/210# d9.14 b-Tom																								
2003	NY N	6	7	0	1	0	0	0	0	0-0	0	2	.143	.143	.143	-26	-1	0-0	1.000	0	157	109	/1-3	-0.1
GLEASON, HARRY Harry Gilbert B 3.28.1875 Camden, NJ D 10.21.1961 Camden, NJ BR/TR 5-6/160# d9.27 b-Kid																								
1901	Bos A	1	1	0	1	0	0	0	0	0	0		1.000	1.000	1.000	464	0	1	.667	0	195	1796	/3	0.1
1902	Bos A	71	240	30	54	5	5	2	25	10	3		.225	.265	.313	58	-15	6	.930	-3	98	174	3-35,O-23(8-15-0)/2-4	-1.7
1903	Bos A	6	13	3	2	1	0	0	2	0	0		.154	.154	.231	13	-1	0	.750	-1	92	0	/3-2	-0.2
1904	StL A	46	155	10	33	7	1	0	6	4	3		.213	.247	.271	68	-6	1	.908	-4	109	132	S-20,3-20/2-5,O(CF)	-1.0
1905	StL A	150	535	45	116	11	5	1	57	34	4		.217	.269	.262	72	-18	23	.911	-15	95	64	*3-144/2-7	-3.2
Total	5	274	944	88	206	24	11	3	90	48	10		.218	.263	.276	67	-40	31	.914	-22	95	99	3-202/O-24(8-16-0),S-20,2-16	-6.0
GLEASON, JACK John Day B 7.14.1854 St.Louis, MO D 9.4.1944 St.Louis, MO BR/TR ?/170# d10.2 b-Bill																								
1877	StL N	1	4	0	1	0	0	0	0	0		1	.250	.250	.250	61	0		—	-0	0	0	/O(CF)	0.0
1882	StL AA	78	331	53	84	10	1	2		**27**			.254	.310	.308	105	2		.768	3	**105**	**134**	*3-73/O-6(RF),2	0.6
1883	StL AA	9	34	2	8	0	0	0		4			.235	.316	.235	76	-1		.833	1	186	0	/O-9(LF),3	0.0
	Lou AA	84	355	69	106	11	4	2		25			.299	.345	.369	140	18		.795	-32	62	66	*3-83/S	-1.1
	Year	93	389	71	114	11	4	2		29			.293	.342	.357	134	17		.798	-31	64	65	3-84/O-9(LF),S	-1.1
1884	StL U	92	395	90	128	30	2	4		23			.324	.361	.441	137	8		.768	-4	**105**	**146**	*3-92	0.4
1885	StL N	2	7	0	1	0	0	0	0	0		1	.143	.143	.143	-8	-1		.857	-0	77	0	/3-2	-0.1
1886	Phi AA	77	299	39	56	8	7	1	31	16	11		.187	.255	.271	64	-13	8	.797	-6	98	162	3-77	-1.6
Total	6	343	1425	253	384	59	14	9	31	95	11	2	.269	.320	.349	112	13	8	.781	-39	93	125	3-328/O-16(9-1-6),S2	-1.8
GLEASON, ROY Roy William B 4.9.1943 Melrose Park, IL BB/TR 6-5.5/220# d9.3																								
1963	LA N	8	1	3	1	1	0	0	0	0-0	0	0	1.000	1.000	2.000	795	1	0-0	—	0			H	0.1
GLEASON, BILL William G. "Will" B 11.12.1858 St.Louis, MO D 7.21.1932 St.Louis, MO BR/TR 5-8/170# d5.2 U1 b-Jack																								
1882	StL AA	**79**	347	63	100	11	6	1		6			.288	.300	.363	118	5		.833	10	106	112	*S-79	1.6
1883	StL AA	**98**	425	81	122	21	9	2	42	15			.287	.311	.393	119	8		.871	-2	93	129	*S-98	0.7
1884	StL AA	**110**	472	97	127	21	7	1		27	12		.269	.325	.350	116	9		.867	-21	89	87	*S-110/3	-0.8
1885	†StL AA	**112**	472	79	119	9	5	3	53	29	**15**		.252	.316	.311	94	-3		.869	-42	80	63	*S-112	-3.8
1886	†StL AA	125	524	97	141	18	5	0	61	43	7		.269	.333	.323	101	1	19	.853	-30	86	113	*S-125	-2.2
1887	†StL AA	135	598	135	172	19	1	0	76	41	8		.288	.342	.323	78	-20	23	.875	-11	98	85	*S-135	-2.2
1888	Phi AA	123	499	55	112	10	2	0	61	12	9		.224	.256	.253	63	-21	27	.858	-14	94	118	*S-121/31	-2.9
1889	Lou AA	16	58	6	14	2	0	0	5	4	1	1	.241	.302	.276	66	-2	1	.822	-1	107	63	S-16	-0.3
Total	8	798	3395	613	907	111	35	7	298	177	52	1	.267	.313	.327	95	-23	70	.860	-110	92	99	S-796/3-2,1	-9.9
GLEASON, KID William J. B 10.26.1866 Camden, NJ D 1.2.1933 Philadelphia, PA BB/TR 5-7/158# d4.20 M5 C16 b-Harry I OF Total (14-LF 15-CF 13-RF)																								
1888	Phi N	24	83	4	17	2	0	0	5	3	0	16	.205	.233	.229	45	-5	3	.841	-3	72	112	P-24/O(RF)	-0.2
1889	Phi N	30	99	11	25	5	0	0	8	8	0	12	.253	.308	.303	65	-5	4	.862	-1	109	61	P-29/O-3(CF),2-2	-0.1
1890	Phi N	63	224	22	47	3	0	0	17	12	0	21	.210	.250	.223	37	-18	10	.937	-2	93	118	P-60/2-2	-0.2
1891	Phi N	65	214	31	53	5	2	0	17	20	2	17	.248	.318	.290	75	-7	6	.896	-6	85	64	P-53/O-9(1-8-0),S-4	-0.5
1892	StL N	66	233	35	50	4	2	3	25	34	0	23	.215	.315	.288	87	-3	7	.934	4	112	122	P-47,O-10(3-2-6)/2-9,1	0.1
1893	StL N	59	199	25	51	6	4	0	20	19	2	8	.256	.327	.327	74	-8	2	.907	-1	103	112	P-48,O-11(5-0-6)/S	-0.3
1894	StL N	9	28	3	7	0	1	0	1	2	0	1	.250	.300	.321	50	-3	0	.885	1	146	0	/P-8,1	0.0

Year	Tm Lg	G	AB	R	H	2B	3B	HR	RBI	BB-IB	HP	SO	AVG	OBP	SLG	AOPS	ABR	SB-CS	FA	FR	Rng	Thr	G at Pos	BFW
	†Bal N	26	86	22	30	5	1	0	17	7	0	2	.349	.398	.430	95	-1	1	.900	-2	65	91	P-21/1	-0.1
	Year	35	114	25	37	5	2	0	18	9	0	3	.325	.374	.404	85	-3	1	.894	-1	85	68	P-29/1-2	-0.1
1895	†Bal N	112	421	90	130	14	12	0	74	33	5	18	.309	.366	.399	95	-5	19	.899	-16	96	99	2-85,3-12/P-9,O-4(LF)	-1.3
1896	NY N	**133**	541	79	162	17	5	4	89	42	2	13	.299	.352	.372	93	-5	46	.938	7	101	72	*2-130/3-3,O(CF)	0.6
1897	NY N	132	543	86	172	16	4	1	106	27	3		.317	.353	.366	93	-6	44	.930	-3	95	98	*2-130/S-3	-0.2
1898	NY N	150	570	78	126	8	5	0	62	39	6		.221	.278	.253	54	-34	21	.938	18	104	94	*2-144/S-6	-0.9
1899	NY N	147	580	73	154	14	5	0	60	24	0		.266	.295	.307	67	-27	29	.946	29	**105**	93	*2-147	0.7
1900	NY N	111	420	60	104	11	3	1	29	17	2		.248	.280	.295	62	-23	23	.931	13	104	101	*2-111/S	-0.5
1901	Det A	**135**	547	82	150	16	12	3	75	41	2		.274	.327	.364	87	-11	32	.925	4	**107**	113	*2-135	-0.5
1902	Det A	118	441	42	109	11	4	1	38	25	3		.247	.292	.297	62	-23	17	.941	6	99	132	*2-118	-1.5
1903	Phi N	106	412	65	117	19	6	1	49	23	3		.284	.326	.367	101	-1	12	.959	-3	97	85	*2-102/O-4(CF)	-0.3
1904	Phi N	153	587	61	161	23	6	0	42	37	2		.274	.319	.334	106	4	17	.942	4	99	84	*2-152/3	1.0
1905	Phi N	**155**	608	95	150	17	7	1	50	45	3		.247	.302	.303	83	-13	16	.947	-11	95	99	*2-155	-2.3
1906	Phi N	135	494	47	112	17	2	0	34	36	1		.227	.281	.269	71	-17	17	.947	-26	92	90	*2-135	-4.8
1907	Phi N	36	126	11	18	3	0	0	6	7	2		.143	.200	.167	15	-12	3	.979	-2	88	90	2-26/1-4,S-4,O(CF)	-1.6
1908	Phi N	2	1	0	0	0	0	0	0	0	0		.000	.000	.000	-97	0	0	1.000	-0	99	0	/2O(LF)	0.0
1912	Chi A	1	2	0	1	0	0	0	0	0	0		.500	.500	.500	192	0	0	1.000	-0	83	0	/2	0.0
Total	22	1968	7459	1022	1946	216	81	15	824	501	38	131	.261	.311	.318	78	-223	329	.938	10	99	96	*2-1585,P-299/O-45C,S-19,3-16,1	-12.9
GLEASON, BILLY William Patrick B 9.6.1894 Chicago, IL D 1.9.1957 Holyoke, MA BR/TR 5-6.5/157# d9.25																								
1916	Pit N	1	2	0	0	0	0	0	0	0	0	0	.000	.000	.000	-99	0	0	1.000	-0	75	0	/2	-0.1
1917	Pit N	13	42	3	7	1	0	0	0	5	0	5	.167	.255	.190	36	-3	1	.978	-3	88	62	2-13	-0.7
1921	StL A	26	74	6	19	0	1	0	8	6	2	6	.257	.329	.284	54	-5	0-1	.960	-3	94	96	2-25	-0.8
Total	3	40	118	9	26	1	1	0	8	11	2	11	.220	.298	.246	47	-8	1-1	.966	-6	92	83	/2-39	-1.6
GLEESON, JIM James Joseph "Gee Gee" B 3.5.1912 Kansas City, MO D 5.1.1996 Kansas City, MO BB/TR 6-1/191# d4.25 C2																								
1936	Cle A	41	139	26	36	9	2	4	12	18	0	17	.259	.344	.439	91	-2	2-1	.958	-2	100	32	O-33(4-0-30)	-0.6
1939	Chi N	111	332	43	74	19	6	4	45	39	2	46	.223	.308	.352	76	-11	7	.957	-3	98	68	O-91(13-12-66)	-2.0
1940	Chi N	129	485	76	152	39	11	5	61	54	6	52	.313	.389	.470	139	27	4	.983	-1	92	139	*O-123(32-82-13)	2.1
1941	Cin N	102	301	47	70	10	0	3	34	45	4	30	.233	.340	.296	80	-6	7	.981	-5	98	16	O-84(22-15-50)	-1.6
1942	Cin N	9	20	3	4	0	0	0	2	2	1	2	.200	.304	.200	49	-1	0	.889	-0	77	238	/O-5(RF)	-0.2
Total	5	392	1277	195	336	77	19	16	154	158	13	147	.263	.350	.391	101	7	20-1	.972	-12	96	82	O-336(71-109-164)	-2.3
GLEICH, FRANK Frank Elmer "Inch" B 3.7.1894 Columbus, OH D 3.27.1949 Columbus, OH BL/TR 5-11/175# d9.17																								
1919	NY A	5	4	0	1	0	0	0	1	1	0	0	.250	.400	.250	84	0	0	.000	-1	0	0	/O-4(3-1-0)	-0.1
1920	NY A	24	41	6	5	0	0	0	3	6	0	10	.122	.234	.122	-4	-6	0-0	.864	-2	93	0	/O-15(9-4-2)	-0.8
Total	2	29	45	6	6	0	0	0	4	7	0	10	.133	.250	.133	4	-6	0-0	.826	-3	85	0	/O-19(12-5-2)	-0.9
GLENALVIN, BOB Robert J. (born Robert J. Dowling) B 1.17.1867 Indianapolis, IN D 3.24.1944 Detroit, MI TR 5-9/160# d7.12																								
1890	Chi N	66	250	43	67	10	3	4	26	19	7	31	.268	.337	.380	105	1	30	.928	-8	96	86	2-66	-0.4
1893	Chi N	16	61	11	21	3	1	0	12	7	0	3	.344	.412	.426	125	2	7	.928	-3	89	55	2-16	0.0
Total	2	82	311	54	88	13	4	4	38	26	7	34	.283	.352	.389	109	3	37	.928	-11	95	80	/2-82	-0.4
GLENN, ED Edward C. "Mouse" B 9.19.1860 Richmond, VA D 2.10.1892 Richmond, VA BR/TR 5-10/160# d8.5																								
1884	Ric AA	43	175	26	43	2	4	1		5	1		.246	.271	.320	93	-2		.833	5	64	150	O-43(LF)	0.2
1886	Pit AA	71	277	32	53	6	5	0	26	17	1		.191	.241	.249	54	-15	19	.865	-0	82	101	O-71(LF)	-1.6
1888	KC AA	3	8	0	0	0	0	0	0	0	2		.000	.200	.000	-32	-1	1	.857	-0	0	0	/O-3(LF)	-0.1
	Bos N	20	65	8	10	0	2	0	3	2	2	8	.154	.203	.215	33	-5	0	.957	1	55	283	O-19(LF)/3	-0.5
Total	3	137	525	66	106	8	11	1	29	24	6	8	.202	.245	.265	62	-23	20	.867	6	71	142	O-136(LF)/3	-2.0
GLENN, ED Edward D. B 10.1875 , OH D 12.6.1911 Ludlow, KY BR/TR d9.7																								
1898	Was N	1	4	0	0	0	0	0	0	0	0		.000	.000	.000	-99	-1	0	1.000	-0	86	0	/S	-0.1
	NY N	2	4	1	1	0	0	0	0	3	0		.250	.571	.250	142	1	1	.750	-1	47	0	/S-2	-0.1
	Year	3	8	1	1	0	0	0	0	3	0		.125	.364	.125	42	0	1	.857	-2	61	0	/S-3	-0.2
1902	Chi N	2	7	0	0	0	0	0	0	1	0		.000	.125	.000	-63	-1	0	1.000	-0	115	0	/S-2	-0.2
Total	2	5	15	1	1	0	0	0	0	4	0		.067	.263	.067	-2	-1	1	.923	-2	85	0	/S-5	-0.4
GLENN, HARRY Harry Melville "Husky" B 6.9.1890 Shelburn, IN D 10.12.1918 St.Paul, MN BR/TR 6-1/200# d4.14																								
1915	StL N	6	16	1	5	0	0	0	1	3	0	0	.313	.421	.313	123	1	0	.929	-1	*109*	*55*	/C-5	0.0
GLENN, JOHN John B 7.10.1928 Moultrie, GA BR/TR 6-3/180# d6.16																								
1960	StL N	32	31	4	8	0	1	0	5	0-0	0	9	.258	.250	.323	53	-2	0-0	1.000	0	119	0	O-28(19-5-4)	-0.3
GLENN, JOHN John W. B 1849 Rochester, NY D 11.10.1888 Sandy Hill, NY BR/TR 5-8.5/169# d5.13																								
1871	Oly NA	26	120	25	37	3	2	0	21	3		1	.308	.325	.367	104	1	1-1	.860	1	112	**443**	*O-26(1-0-25)	0.3
1872	Oly NA	**9**	39	6	6	0	0	0	3	1		0	.154	.175	.154	2	-4	0-1	.800	3	313	725	/O-9(LF)	-0.1
	Nat NA	1	4	0	2	0	0	0	0	0		0	.500	.500	.500	179	0	0-0	.667	-0	0	0	/O(CF)	0.0
	Year	10	43	6	8	0	0	0	3	1		0	.186	.205	.186	21	-4	0-1	.791	3	281	651	O-10(9-1-0)	-0.1
1873	Was NA	**39**	186	39	49	9	2	1	22	3		0	.263	.275	.349	87	-2	3-1	.915	-2	45	81	*1-39	-0.3
1874	Chi NA	55	237	33	67	9	0	0	32	5		4	.283	.298	.321	97	0	2-2	.918	0	135	81	1-37,O-19(2-1-17)	0.1
1875	Chi NA	**69**	308	46	75	8	0	0	27	3		6	.244	.251	.269	80	-6	10-2	.898	-3	37	69	O-44(39-7-1),1-29	-0.5
1876	Chi N	**66**	276	55	84	9	2	0	32	12		6	.304	.333	.351	115	3		.881	-1	54	60	*O-56(LF),1-15	-0.1
1877	Chi N	50	202	31	46	6	1	0	20	8		16	.228	.257	.267	58	-10		.948	1	99	83	O-36(36-0-1),1-14	-1.1
Total	5 NA	199	894	149	236	29	4	1	105	15		11	.264	.276	.309	87	-11	16-7	.000	-1	65	87	1-105/O-99(51-9-43)	-0.5
Total	2	116	478	86	130	15	3	0	52	20		22	.272	.301	.316	90	-7		.904	0	72	69	/O-92(92-0-1),1-29	-1.2
GLENN, JOE Joseph Charles "Gabby" (born Joseph Charles Gurzensky) B 11.19.1908 Dickson City, PA D 5.6.1985 Tunkhannock, PA BR/TR 5-11/175# d9.15																								
1932	NY A	6	16	0	2	0	0	0	0	1	1	5	.125	.222	.125	-8	-3	0-0	1.000	-1	*72*	*0*	/C-5	-0.3
1933	NY A	5	21	1	3	0	0	0	1	0	0	3	.143	.143	.143	-26	-4	0-0	1.000	-1	*155*	*0*	/C-5	-0.4
1935	NY A	17	43	7	10	4	0	0	6	4	0	1	.233	.298	.326	65	-2	0-0	.984	0	*146*	*99*	C-16	-0.1
1936	NY A	44	129	21	35	7	0	1	20	20	1	10	.271	.373	.349	82	-3	1-1	.970	2	*159*	*120*	C-44	0.2
1937	NY A	25	53	6	15	2	2	0	4	10	0	11	.283	.397	.396	100	0	0-0	.978	3	*143*	*116*	C-24	0.4
1938	NY A	41	123	10	32	7	2	0	25	10	0	14	.260	.316	.350	67	-7	1-0	.974	1	*129*	*69*	C-40	-0.4
1939	StL A	88	286	29	78	13	1	4	29	31	0	40	.273	.344	.367	80	-8	4-4	.968	-13	*75*	***140***	C-82	-1.6
1940	Bos A	22	47	3	6	1	0	0	4	5	0	7	.128	.212	.149	-5	-7	0-0	.961	-2	*107*	*83*	C-19	-0.8
Total	8	248	718	77	181	34	5	5	89	81	2	91	.252	.330	.334	69	-34	6-5	.972	-10	*114*	*110*	C-235	-3.0
GLOAD, ROSS Ross P. B 4.5.1976 Brooklyn, NY BL/TL 6-2/210# d8.30																								
2000	Chi N	18	31	4	6	0	1	1	3	3-0	0	10	.194	.257	.355	56	-2	0-0	1.000	-1	95	0	/O-8(7-0-1),1-2	-0.3
2002	Col N	26	31	4	8	1	0	1	4	3-0	0	7	.258	.324	.387	77	-1	0-0	1.000	1	202	47	/1-4,O-2(LF)	0.0
Total	2	44	62	8	14	1	1	2	7	6-0	0	17	.226	.290	.371	67	-3	0-0	1.000	1	87	284	/O-10(9-0-1),1-6	-0.3
GLOCKSON, NORM Norman Stanley B 6.15.1894 Blue Island, IL D 8.5.1955 Maywood, IL BR/TR 6-2/200# d9.16																								
1914	Cin N	7	12	0	0	0	0	0	0	1	0	6	.000	.077	.000	-74	-3	0	.923	-1	*102*	*92*	/C-7	-0.3
GLOSSOP, AL Alban B 7.12.1914 Christopher, IL D 7.2.1991 Walnut Creek, CA BB/TR 6/170# d9.23 Mil 1944-45																								
1939	NY N	10	32	3	6	0	0	1	3	4	0	2	.188	.278	.281	50	-2	0	.980	2	128	121	2-10	0.0
1940	NY N	27	91	16	19	3	0	4	8	10	1	16	.209	.294	.374	82	-2	1	.952	2	113	53	2-24	0.1
	Bos N	60	148	17	35	2	1	3	14	17	0	22	.236	.315	.324	81	-4	1	.938	4	120	112	2-18,3-18/S	0.2
	Year	87	239	33	54	5	1	7	22	27	1	38	.226	.307	.343	82	-6	2	.947	6	116	76	2-42,3-18/S	0.3
1942	Phi N	121	454	33	102	15	1	4	40	29	1	35	.225	.273	.289	68	-20	3	.961	10	103	104	*2-118/3	-0.3
1943	Bro N	87	217	28	37	9	0	3	21	28	1	27	.171	.268	.253	51	-13	0	.927	-9	103	92	S-33,2-24,3-17/O(RF)	-2.0
1946	Chi N	4	10	2	0	0	0	0	0	1	2	3	.000	.231	.000	-32	-2	0	1.000	-2	61	0	/2-2,S-2	-0.3
Total	5	309	952	99	199	29	2	15	86	89	5	105	.209	.280	.291	66	-43	5	.954	8	105	93	2-196/S-36,3-36,O(RF)	-2.3
GLYNN, BILL William Vincent B 7.30.1925 Sussex, NJ BL/TL 6/190# d9.16																								
1949	Phi N	8	10	0	2	0	0	0	1	0	0	3	.200	.200	.200	8	-1	0	1.000	0	159	0	/1	-0.1
1952	Cle A	44	92	15	25	5	0	2	7	5	0	16	.272	.309	.391	101	0	1-0	.973	-0	106	105	1-32	-0.1

Year	Tm Lg	G	AB	R	H	2B	3B	HR	RBI	BB-IB	HP	SO	AVG	OBP	SLG	AOPS	ABR	SB-CS	FA	FR	Rng	Thr	G at Pos	BFW
1953	Cle A	147	411	60	100	14	2	3	30	44	5	65	.243	.324	.309	74	-15	1-3	**.993**	3	108	**138**	*1-135/O-2(1-0-1)	-1.9
1954	†Cle A	111	171	19	43	3	2	5	18	12	0	21	.251	.297	.380	84	-5	3-2	.987	1	113	111	1-96/O(RF)	-0.7
Total	4	310	684	94	170	22	4	10	56	61	5	105	.249	.314	.336	79	-21	5-5	.989	4	109	126	1-264/O-3(1-0-2)	-2.8
GOCHNAUER, JOHN John Peter B 9.12.1875 Altoona, PA D 9.27.1929 Altoona, PA BR/TR 5-9/160# d9.29																								
1901	Bro N	3	11	1	4	0	0	0	2	1	0		.364	.417	.364	124	0	1	1.000	0	105	0	/S-3	0.0
1902	Cle A	127	459	45	85	16	4	0	37	38	0		.185	.247	.237	36	-40	7	.933	-5	103	109	*S-127	-3.9
1903	Cle A	134	438	48	81	16	4	0	48	48	0		.185	.265	.240	53	-23	10	.869	-23	97	101	*S-134	-4.4
Total	3	264	908	94	170	32	8	0	87	87	0		.187	.258	.240	45	-63	18	.901	-28	100	104	S-264	-8.3
GODAR, JOHN John Michael B 10.25.1864 Cincinnati, OH D 6.23.1949 Park Ridge, IL BR/TR 5-9/170# d7.8																								
1892	Bal N	5	14	2	3	0	0	0	1	2	1	1	.214	.353	.214	70	0	1	1.000	0	186	0	/O-5(RF)	0.0
GODBY, DANNY Danny Ray B 11.4.1946 Logan, WV BR/TR 6/185# d8.10																								
1974	StL N	13	13	2	2	0	0	0	1	3-1	0	4	.154	.294	.154	34	-1	0-0	1.000	1	152	520	/O-4(2-0-2)	0.0
GODDARD, JOE Joseph Harold B 7.23.1950 Beckley, WV BR/TR 5-11/181# d7.31																								
1972	SD N	12	35	0	7	2	0	0	2	5-0	0	9	.200	.300	.257	64	-1	0-0	.973	-5	38	88	C-12	-0.6
GODWIN, JOHN John Henry "Bunny" B 3.10.1877 E.Liverpool, OH D 5.5.1956 E.Liverpool, OH BR/TR 6/190# d8.14																								
1905	Bos A	15	43	4	14	1	0	0	10	3	3		.326	.408	.349	139	2	3	.950	-0	0	0	/O-7(5-2-0),2-5	0.2
1906	Bos A	66	193	11	36	2	1	0	15	6	1		.187	.215	.207	32	-15	6	.907	1	107	218	3-27,S-14,O-10(0-1-9)/2-3,1	-1.5
Total	2	81	236	15	50	3	1	0	25	9	4		.212	.253	.233	53	-13	9	.907	0	107	218	/3-27,O-17(5-3-9),S-14,2-8,1	-1.3
GOEBEL, ED Edwin B 9.1.1899 Brooklyn, NY D 8.12.1959 Brooklyn, NY BR/TR 5-11/170# d5.13																								
1922	Was A	37	59	13	16	1	0	1	3	8	0	16	.271	.358	.339	87	-1	1-1	1.000	1	120	70	O-16(2-1-13)	-0.1
GOECKEL, BILLY William John B 9.3.1871 Wilkes-Barre, PA D 11.1.1922 Philadelphia, PA BR/TL 5-11/162# d8.10																								
1899	Phi N	37	141	17	37	3	1	0	16	1	3		.262	.283	.298	61	-8	6	.978	-3	61	57	1-36	-1.0
GOFF, JERRY Jerry Leroy B 4.12.1964 San Rafael, CA BL/TR 6-3/207# d5.15																								
1990	Mon N	52	119	14	27	1	0	3	7	21-4	0	36	.227	.343	.311	84	-2	0-2	.963	-7	82	62	C-38/1-3,3-3	-0.8
1992	Mon N	3	3	0	0	0	0	0	0	0-0	0	3	.000	.000	.000	-99	-1	0-0	—	0			/H	-0.1
1993	Pit N	14	37	5	11	2	0	2	6	8-1	0	9	.297	.422	.514	149	3	0-0	.984	-2	129	98	C-14	0.2
1994	Pit N	8	25	0	2	0	0	0	1	0-0	0	11	.080	.080	.080	-57	-6	0-0	.950	-2	124	87	/C-7	-0.7
1995	Hou N	12	26	2	4	2	0	1	3	4-0	0	13	.154	.267	.346	64	-1	0-0	1.000	4	49	159	C-11	0.3
1996	Hou N	1	4	1	2	0	0	1	2	0-0	0	1	.500	.500	1.250	371	1	0-0	1.000	0	68	0	/C	0.2
Total	6	90	214	22	46	5	0	7	19	33-5	0	73	.215	.320	.336	80	-6	0-2	.974	-6	92	84	/C-71,3-3,1-3	-0.9
GOGGIN, CHUCK Charles Francis B 7.7.1945 Pompano Beach, FL BB/TR 5-11/175# d9.8																								
1972	Pit N	5	7	0	2	0	0	0	0	1-0	0	1	.286	.375	.286	92	0	0-0	1.000	-0	129	0	/2	0.0
1973	Pit N	1	1	1	1	0	0	0	0	0-0	0	0	1.000	1.000	1.000	468	0	0-0	1.000	0	0	0	/C	0.0
	Atl N	64	90	18	26	5	0	0	7	9-0	0	19	.289	.350	.344	88	-1	0-1	.938	-7	93	88	2-19/O-6(5-0-1),S-5,C	-0.7
	Year	65	91	19	27	5	0	0	7	9-0	0	19	.297	.356	.352	91	-1	0-1	.938	-7	93	88	2-19/O-6(5-0-1),S-5,C-2	-0.7
1974	Bos A	2	1	0	0	0	0	0	0	0-0	0	1	.000	.000	.000	-93	0	0-0	.667	0	158	601	/2-2	0.0
Total	3	72	99	19	29	5	0	0	7	10-0	0	21	.293	.355	.343	90	-1	0-1	.927	-7	99	101	/2-22,O-6(5-0-1),S-5,C-2	-0.7
GOLDEN, MIKE Michael Henry B 9.11.1851 Shirley, MA D 1.11.1929 Rockford, IL BR/TR 5-8/168# d5.5 ▲																								
1875	Wes NA	**13**	46	6	6	0	0	0	1	0		3	.130	.130	.130	-9	-4	0-0	.844	-1	76	0	P-13	0.0
	Chi NA	39	155	16	40	3	0	0	14	2		10	.258	.268	.277	89	-2	3-2	.833	0	120	133	O-27(25-0-2),P-14	0.0
	Year	52	201	22	46	3	0	0	15	2		13	.229	.236	.244	66	-7	3-2	.833	-1	81	0	P-27,O-27(25-0-2)	0.0
1878	Mil N	55	214	16	44	6	3	0	20	3		35	.206	.217	.262	53	-11		.831	-3	96	135	O-39(0-25-14),P-22/1	-1.1
GOLDMAN, JONAH Jonah John B 8.29.1906 New York, NY D 8.17.1980 Palm Beach, FL BR/TR 5-7/170# d9.22																								
1928	Cle A	7	21	1	5	1	0	0	2	3	0	0	.238	.333	.286	63	-1	0-0	.878	-1	111	45	/S-7	-0.1
1930	Cle A	111	306	32	74	18	0	1	44	28	3	25	.242	.312	.310	56	-20	3-5	.945	15	108	102	S-93,3-20	0.3
1931	Cle A	30	62	0	8	1	0	0	3	4	0	6	.129	.182	.145	-12	-10	1-1	.947	10	140	100	S-30	0.1
Total	3	148	389	33	87	20	0	1	49	35	3	31	.224	.293	.283	46	-31	4-6	.941	25	114	98	S-130/3-20	0.3
GOLDSBERRY, GORDON Gordon Frederick B 8.30.1927 Sacramento, CA D 2.23.1996 Lake Forest, CA BL/TL 6/170# d4.20																								
1949	Chi A	39	145	25	36	3	2	1	13	18	0	9	.248	.331	.317	74	-6	2-0	.990	-1	93	95	1-38	-0.7
1950	Chi A	82	127	19	34	8	2	2	25	26	0	18	.268	.392	.409	108	3	0-2	.989	5	167	128	1-40/O-3(1-0-2)	0.5
1951	Chi A	10	11	4	1	0	0	0	1	2	0	2	.091	.231	.091	-11	-2	0-0	1.000	1	225	144	/1-8	-0.1
1952	StL A	86	227	30	52	9	3	3	17	34	0	37	.229	.330	.335	83	-5	0-2	.983	-2	93	96	1-72/O-2(LF)	-1.0
Total	4	217	510	78	123	20	7	6	56	80	0	66	.241	.344	.343	85	-10	2-4	.987	3	112	104	1-158/O-5(3-0-2)	-1.3
GOLDSBY, WALT Walton Hugh B 12.31.1861 , LA D 1.11.1914 Dallas, TX BL d5.28																								
1884	StL AA	5	20	2	4	0	0	0	1	0	0		.200	.200	.200	30	-2		.800	-1	0	0	/O-5(1-4-0)	-0.3
	Was AA	6	24	4	9	0	0	0	3	1	0		.375	.400	.375	174	2		.909	1	182	0	/O-6(1-3-2)	0.2
	Ric AA	11	40	4	9	1	0	0	4	1	1		.225	.262	.250	69	-1		.737	0	117	687	O-11(2-6-3)	-0.1
	Year	22	84	10	22	1	0	0	8	2	1		.262	.287	.274	87	-1		.800	-0	104	306	O-22(4-13-5)	-0.2
1886	Was N	6	18	0	4	1	0	0	1	2		3	.222	.300	.278	83	0	0	.818	-1	0	0	/O-6(0-5-1)	-0.1
1888	Bal AA	45	165	13	39	1	1	0	14	8	4		.236	.288	.255	76	-4	17	.903	-3	47	0	O-45(LF)	-0.8
Total	3	73	267	23	65	3	1	0	23	12	5	3	.243	.289	.262	80	-5	17	.858	-4	62	96	/O-73(49-18-6)	-1.1
GOLDSMITH, WALLY Warren M. B 10.1848 Baltimore, MD D 9.16.1915 Washington, DC 5-7/146# d5.4																								
1871	Kek NA	**19**	88	8	18	1	0	0	12	4		2	.205	.239	.216	31	-8	0-0	.767	-10	70	36	S-14/3-8,C-2	-1.2
1872	Oly NA	**9**	41	4	10	2	0	0	5	0		0	.244	.244	.293	68	-1	0-0	.679	-2	80	72	/S-5,2-4	-0.2
1873	Mar NA	1	4	0	0	0	0	0	0	0		0	.000	.000	.000	-99	-1	0-0	.667	-1	118	0	/2	-0.1
1875	Wes NA	**13**	51	3	6	0	0	0	1	0		2	.118	.118	.118	-17	-6	0-0	.814	-1	90	172	3-13	-0.6
Total	4 NA	42	184	15	34	3	0	0	18	4		4	.185	.202	.201	24	-16	0-0	.000	-13	73	117	/3-21,S-19,2-5,C-2	-2.1
GOLDSTEIN, LONNIE Leslie Elmer B 5.13.1918 Austin, TX BL/TL 6-2.5/190# d9.11 Mil 1945-46																								
1943	Cin N	5	5	1	1	0	0	0	0	2	0	1	.200	.429	.200	85	0	0	1.000	-0	0	0	/1-2	0.0
1946	Cin N	6	5	1	0	0	0	0	0	1	0	1	.000	.167	.000	-53	-1	0	—	0			H	-0.1
Total	2	11	10	2	1	0	0	0	0	3	0	2	.100	.308	.100	20	-1	0	1.000	-0	0	0	/1-2	-0.1
GOLDY, PURNAL Purnal William B 11.28.1937 Camden, NJ BR/TR 6-5/200# d4.12																								
1962	Det A	20	70	8	16	1	1	3	12	0-0	1	12	.229	.236	.400	66	-4	0-0	.964	-0	99	123	O-15(RF)	-0.5
1963	Det A	9	8	1	2	0	0	0	0	0-0	0	4	.250	.250	.250	39	-1	0-0	—	0			H	-0.1
Total	2	29	78	9	18	1	1	3	12	0-0	1	16	.231	.237	.385	64	-5	0-0	.964	-0	99	123	/O-15(RF)	-0.6
GOLETZ, STAN Stanley "Stash" B 5.21.1918 Crescent, OH D 6.7.1997 Temple, TX BL/TL 6-3/200# d9.9 Mil 1942-45																								
1941	Chi A	5	5	0	3	0	0	0	0	0	0	2	.600	.600	.600	221	1	0-0	—	0			H	0.1
GOLIAT, MIKE Mike Mitchel B 11.5.1925 Yatesboro, PA BR/TR 6/180# d8.3																								
1949	Phi N	55	189	24	40	6	3	3	19	20	1	32	.212	.290	.323	66	-10	0	.969	-5	99	91	2-50/1-5	-1.2
1950	†Phi N	145	483	49	113	13	6	13	64	53	3	75	.234	.314	.366	80	-16	3	.972	-15	98	89	*2-145	-2.2
1951	Phi N	41	138	14	31	2	1	4	15	9	1	18	.225	.277	.341	66	-7	0-1	.968	-8	89	87	2-37/3-2	-1.4
	StL A	5	11	0	2	0	0	0	1	0	0	1	.182	.182	.182	-1	-2	0-0	1.000	0	101	97	/2-2	-0.1
1952	StL A	3	4	0	0	0	0	0	0	1	0	1	.000	.200	.000	-40	-1	0-0	1.000	1	103	287	/2-3	0.0
Total	4	249	825	87	186	21	10	20	99	83	5	127	.225	.300	.348	73	-36	3-1	.971	-27	97	90	2-237/1-5,3-2	-4.9
GOLVIN, WALT Walter George B 2.1.1894 Hershey, NE D 6.11.1973 Gardena, CA BL/TL 6/165# d4.15																								
1922	Chi N	2	2	0	0	0	0	0	1	0	0	0	.000	.000	.000	-98	-1	0-0	1.000	-0	0	0	/1-2	-0.1
GOMES, JONNY Jonny Johnson B 11.22.1980 Petaluma, CA BR/TR 6-1/200# d9.12																								
2003	TB A	8	15	1	2	1	0	0	0	0-0	1	6	.133	.188	.200	2	-2	0-0	—	0			/D-8	-0.3

Year	Tm Lg	G	AB	R	H	2B	3B	HR	RBI	BB-IB	HP	SO	AVG	OBP	SLG	AOPS	ABR	SB-CS	FA	FR	Rng	Thr	G at Pos	BFW
GOMEZ, ALEXIS Alexis Dejesus B 8.6.1978 Loma De Cabrera, D.R. BL/TL 6-2/180# d6.16																								
2002	KC A	5	10	0	2	0	0	0	0	0-0	0	2	.200	.200	.200	6	-1	0-0	1.000	1	115	909	/O-2(RF)	0.0
GOMEZ, CHRIS Christopher Cory B 6.16.1971 Los Angeles, CA BR/TR 6-1/183# d7.19																								
1993	Det A	46	128	11	32	7	1	0	11	9-0	1	17	.250	.304	.320	69	-6	2-2	.963	-1	104	105	S-29,2-17/D	-0.5
1994	Det A	84	296	32	76	19	0	8	53	33-0	3	64	.257	.336	.402	89	-4	5-3	.981	-24	84	58	S-57,2-30	-2.1
1995	Det A	123	431	49	96	20	2	11	50	41-0	3	96	.223	.292	.355	68	-21	4-1	.973	-2	104	92	S-97,2-31/D-2	-1.3
1996	Det A	48	128	21	31	5	0	1	16	18-0	1	20	.242	.340	.305	65	-6	1-1	.970	4	101	111	S-47	0.0
	†SD N	89	328	32	86	16	1	3	29	39-1	6	64	.262	.349	.345	90	-3	2-2	.967	-7	96	101	S-89	-0.4
1997	SD N	150	522	62	132	19	2	5	54	53-1	5	114	.253	.326	.326	77	-17	5-8	.978	-4	101	84	*S-150	-1.1
1998	†SD N	145	449	55	120	32	3	4	39	51-7	5	87	.267	.346	.379	99	1	1-3	**.980**	9	101	120	*S-143	1.9
1999	SD N	76	234	20	59	8	1	1	15	27-3	1	49	.252	.331	.308	69	-11	1-2	.961	1	98	115	S-75	-0.5
2000	SD N	33	54	4	12	0	0	0	3	7-0	0	5	.222	.306	.222	41	-5	0-0	.928	2	109	122	S-17/2-3	-0.2
2001	SD N	40	112	6	21	3	0	0	7	9-0	0	14	.188	.244	.214	23	-13	1-0	.937	-11	74	82	S-36/2-8	-2.2
	TB A	58	189	31	57	16	0	8	36	8-0	2	24	.302	.332	.513	121	6	3-0	.968	-11	85	80	S-58	0.0
2002	TB A	130	461	51	122	31	3	10	46	21-0	7	58	.265	.305	.410	90	-7	1-3	.980	-1	98	104	*S-130	0.0
2003	†Min A	58	175	14	44	9	3	1	15	7-1	0	13	.251	.279	.354	65	-9	2-1	.989	-7	96	89	2-23,3-18,S-17	-1.4
Total	11	1080	3507	388	888	185	16	52	374	323-13	34	625	.253	.320	.360	81	-95	28-26	.972	-54	97	97	S-945,2-112/3-18,D-3	-7.8
GOMEZ, CHILE Jose Luis (Gonzales) B 5.23.1909 Villa Union, Mexico D 12.1.1992 Nuevo Laredo, Mexico BR/TR 5-10/165# d7.27																								
1935	Phi N	67	222	24	51	3	0	0	16	17	0	34	.230	.285	.243	39	-19	2	.948	9	104	44	S-36,2-32	-0.5
1936	Phi N	108	332	24	77	4	1	0	28	14	1	32	.232	.265	.250	36	-30	0	.948	11	116	84	2-71,S-40	-1.3
1942	Was A	25	73	8	14	2	2	0	6	9	0	7	.192	.280	.274	57	-4	1-0	.973	-2	97	88	2-23/3	-0.5
Total	3	200	627	56	142	9	3	0	50	40	1	73	.226	.274	.250	39	-53	3-0	.954	18	114	103	2-126/S-76,3	-2.3
GOMEZ, LEO Leonardo (Velez) B 3.2.1966 Canovanas, P.R. BR/TR 6/208# d9.17																								
1990	Bal A	12	39	3	9	0	0	0	1	8-0	0	7	.231	.362	.231	71	-1	0-0	.886	-2	88	92	3-12	-0.3
1991	Bal A	118	391	40	91	17	2	16	45	40-0	2	82	.233	.302	.409	100	-1	1-1	.972	-13	89	99	*3-105,D-10/1-3	-1.4
1992	Bal A	137	468	62	124	24	0	17	64	63-4	8	78	.265	.356	.425	117	12	2-3	.951	-10	93	82	*3-137	0.2
1993	Bal A	71	244	30	48	7	0	10	25	32-1	3	60	.197	.295	.348	70	-11	0-1	.951	6	110	137	3-70/D	-0.4
1994	Bal A	84	285	46	78	20	0	15	56	41-0	3	55	.274	.366	.502	116	8	0-0	.975	-1	94	108	3-78/1D	0.7
1995	Bal A	53	127	16	30	5	0	4	12	18-1	2	23	.236	.336	.370	83	-3	0-1	.978	2	105	54	3-44/1-3,D-5	-0.1
1996	Chi N	136	362	44	86	19	0	17	56	53-0	7	94	.238	.344	.431	101	1	1-4	**.972**	-1	97	110	*3-124/1-8,S	0.0
Total	7	611	1916	241	466	92	2	79	259	255-6	25	399	.243	.336	.417	101	5	4-10	.962	-18	96	100	3-570/D-21,1-15,S	-1.3
GOMEZ, LUIS Luis (Sanchez) B 8.19.1951 Guadalajara, Mexico BR/TR 5-9/150# d4.28																								
1974	Min A	82	168	18	35	1	0	0	3	12-0	0	16	.208	.261	.214	37	-14	2-3	.960	6	103	103	S-74/2-2,D	-0.1
1975	Min A	89	72	7	10	0	0	0	5	4-0	0	12	.139	.182	.139	-7	-10	0-2	.975	-4	77	99	S-70/2-6,D-7	-1.2
1976	Min A	38	57	5	11	1	0	0	3	3-0	0	3	.193	.233	.211	30	-5	1-0	.988	1	96	146	S-24/2-8,3-4,O(CF)D	-0.2
1977	Min A	32	65	6	16	4	2	0	11	4-0	0	9	.246	.290	.369	79	-2	0-2	.983	2	102	70	2-19/S-7,3-4,O(CF)D	0.0
1978	Tor A	153	413	39	92	7	3	0	32	34-1	0	41	.223	.280	.254	51	-27	2-10	.976	-7	92	105	*S-153	-2.3
1979	Tor A	59	163	11	39	7	0	0	11	6-0	0	17	.239	.266	.282	48	-12	1-0	1.000	-1	82	202	3-22,2-20,S-15	-1.1
1980	Atl N	121	278	18	53	6	0	0	24	17-2	1	27	.191	.239	.212	26	-28	0-4	.968	0	105	101	*S-119	-2.0
1981	Atl N	35	35	4	7	0	0	0	1	6-0	0	4	.200	.317	.200	48	-2	0-1	.895	-7	77	42	S-21/3-9,2-3,P	-0.9
Total	8	609	1251	108	263	26	5	0	90	86-3	1	129	.210	.261	.239	40	-100	6-22	.970	-10	97	105	S-483/2-58,3-39,D-11,O-2(CF),P	-7.8
GOMEZ, PRESTON Pedro (Martinez) B 4.20.1923 Preston, Cuba BR/TR 5-11/170# d5.5 M7 C13																								
1944	Was A	8	7	2	2	1	0	0	2	0	0	4	.286	.286	.429	107	0	0-0	1.000	-1	0	0	/2-2,S-2	-0.1
GOMEZ, RANDY Randell Scott B 2.4.1957 San Mateo, CA BR/TR 5-10/185# d8.21																								
1984	SF N	14	30	0	5	1	0	0	0	8-0	0	3	.167	.342	.200	57	-1	0-0	.951	-2	42	49	C-14	-0.2
GONDER, JESSE Jesse Lemar B 1.20.1936 Monticello, AR BL/TR 5-10/190# d9.23																								
1960	NY A	7	7	1	2	0	0	1	3	1-0	0	1	.286	.333	.714	199	1	0-0	1.000	0	*0*	*0*	/C	0.1
1961	NY A	15	12	2	4	1	0	0	3	3-1	0	1	.333	.467	.417	146	1	0-0	—	0			H	0.1
1962	Cin N	4	4	0	0	0	0	0	0	0-0	0	3	.000	.000	.000	-97	-1	0-0	—	0			H	-0.1
1963	Cin N	31	32	5	10	2	0	3	5	1-0	0	12	.313	.333	.656	172	3	0-0	1.000	1	*104*	*131*	/C-7	0.4
	NY N	42	126	12	38	4	0	3	15	6-0	0	25	.302	.328	.405	110	1	1-2	.978	-7	*95*	*115*	C-31	-0.5
	Year	73	158	17	48	6	0	6	20	7-0	0	37	.304	.329	.456	122	4	1-2	.981	-7	*96*	*116*	C-38	-0.1
1964	NY N	131	341	28	92	11	1	7	35	29-5	2	65	.270	.329	.370	99	0	0-0	.979	-1	*83*	***171***	C-97	0.3
1965	NY N	53	105	6	25	4	0	4	9	11-4	0	20	.238	.308	.390	100	0	0-0	.992	-2	*75*	*150*	C-31	-0.1
	Mil N	31	53	2	8	2	0	1	5	4-0	0	9	.151	.211	.245	28	-5	0-0	.989	3	*100*	*175*	C-13	-0.2
	Year	84	158	8	33	6	0	5	14	15-4	0	29	.209	.276	.342	75	-5	0-0	.991	1	*83*	*158*	C-44	-0.3
1966	Pit N	59	160	13	36	3	1	7	16	12-7	2	39	.225	.287	.387	85	-4	0-0	.978	-2	*107*	*97*	C-52	-0.3
1967	Pit N	22	36	4	5	1	0	0	3	5-3	2	9	.139	.279	.167	30	-3	0-0	.971	-0	*114*	*154*	C-18	-0.3
Total	8	395	876	73	220	28	2	26	94	72-20	6	184	.251	.310	.377	94	-7	1-2	.981	-9	*91*	*143*	C-250	-0.6
GONZALES, DAN Daniel David B 9.30.1953 Whittier, CA BL/TR 6-1/195# d4.7																								
1979	Det A	7	18	1	4	1	0	0	2	0-0	0	2	.222	.222	.278	33	-2	1-0	1.000	-1	50	0	/O-3(RF),D	-0.2
1980	Det A	2	7	1	1	0	0	0	0	0-0	0	1	.143	.143	.143	-21	-1	0-0	.750	-0	148	0	/O(LF)D	-0.1
Total	2	9	25	2	5	1	0	0	2	0-0	0	3	.200	.200	.240	18	-3	1-0	.857	-1	73	0	/O-4(1-0-3),D-2	-0.3
GONZALES, LARRY Lawrence Christopher B 3.28.1967 West Covina, CA BR/TR 6-3/200# d6.13																								
1993	Cal A	2	2	0	1	0	0	0	1	1-0	0	0	.500	.667	.500	212	0	0-0	1.000	0	0	0	/C-2	0.1
GONZALES, RENE Rene Adrian B 9.3.1960 Austin, TX BR/TR 6-3/201# d7.27 OF Total (1-LF 2-RF)																								
1984	Mon N	29	30	5	7	1	0	0	2	2-0	1	5	.233	.303	.267	64	-1	0-0	.957	-4	77	76	S-27	-0.5
1986	Mon N	11	26	1	3	0	0	0	0	2-0	0	7	.115	.179	.115	-17	-4	0-2	1.000	-0	97	91	/S-6,3-5	-0.5
1987	Bal A	37	60	14	16	2	1	1	7	3-0	0	11	.267	.302	.383	82	-2	1-0	.963	3	105	62	3-29/2-6,S	0.1
1988	Bal A	92	237	13	51	6	0	2	15	13-0	3	32	.215	.263	.266	50	-16	2-0	.966	13	129	164	3-80,2-14/S-2,1O(RF)	-0.2
1989	Bal A	71	166	16	36	4	0	1	11	12-0	0	30	.217	.268	.259	51	-11	5-3	.978	-4	98	126	2-54,3-17/S	-1.4
1990	Bal A	67	103	13	22	3	1	1	12	12-0	0	14	.214	.296	.291	67	-5	1-2	.994	1	105	98	2-43,3-16/S-9,O(RF)	-0.3
1991	†Tor A	71	118	16	23	3	0	1	6	12-0	4	22	.195	.289	.246	48	-8	0-0	.973	0	84	88	S-36,3-26,2-11/1-2	-0.6
1992	Cal A	104	329	47	91	17	1	7	38	41-1	4	46	.277	.363	.398	113	7	7-4	.954	2	103	102	3-53,2-42,1-13/S-8	1.0
1993	Cal A	118	335	34	84	17	0	2	31	49-2	1	45	.251	.346	.319	78	-8	5-5	.956	0	102	151	3-79,1-31/S-5,2-4,P	-1.0
1994	Cle A	22	23	6	8	1	1	1	5	5-0	0	3	.348	.448	.609	173	3	2-0	.952	2	157	0	3-13/1-4,S-4,2	0.5
1995	Cal A	30	18	1	6	1	0	1	3	0-0	0	4	.333	.333	.556	127	1	0-0	1.000	-1	65	0	3-18/2-6,SD	0.0
1996	†Tex A	51	92	19	20	4	0	2	5	10-0	0	11	.217	.288	.326	54	-7	0-0	.989	4	74	106	1-23,3-15,S-10/2-5,O(LF)	-0.3
1997	Col N	2	2	0	1	0	0	0	1	0-0	0	0	.500	.500	.500	133	0	0-0	—	-0	0	0	/3	0.0
Total	13	705	1539	185	368	59	4	19	136	161-3	13	230	.239	.315	.320	75	-51	23-16	.957	16	113	129	3-352,2-186,S-110/1-74,O-3R,DP	-3.2
GONZALEZ, ALEX Alexander B 2.15.1977 Cagua, Venezuela BR/TR 6/170# d8.25																								
1998	Fla N	25	86	11	13	2	0	3	7	9-0	1	30	.151	.240	.279	38	-8	0-0	.978	-7	83	101	S-25	-1.3
1999	Fla N★	136	560	81	155	28	8	14	59	15-0	12	113	.277	.308	.430	90	-12	3-5	.955	-8	95	99	*S-135	-1.0
2000	Fla N	109	385	35	77	17	4	7	42	13-0	2	77	.200	.229	.319	38	-39	7-1	.957	1	104	100	*S-104	-2.8
2001	Fla N	145	515	57	129	36	1	9	48	30-6	10	107	.250	.303	.377	77	-18	2-2	.960	5	101	114	*S-142	-0.2
2002	Fla N	42	151	15	34	7	1	2	18	12-1	4	32	.225	.296	.325	70	-7	3-1	.984	3	99	120	S-42	-0.1
2003	†Fla N	150	528	52	135	33	6	18	77	33-13	13	106	.256	.313	.443	99	-3	0-4	.976	4	96	**117**	*S-150	1.1
Total	6	607	2225	251	543	123	20	53	251	112-20	42	465	.244	.291	.389	77	-87	15-13	.965	-1	98	109	S-598	-4.3
GONZALEZ, ALEX Alexander Scott B 4.8.1973 Miami, FL BR/TR 6/180# d4.4																								
1994	Tor A	15	53	7	8	3	1	0	1	4-0	1	17	.151	.224	.245	21	-6	3-0	.918	1	113	62	S-15	-0.3
1995	Tor A	111	367	51	89	19	4	10	42	44-1	1	114	.243	.322	.398	88	-7	4-4	.957	-29	77	68	S-97/3-9,D-3	-2.8
1996	Tor A	147	527	64	124	30	5	14	64	45-0	5	127	.235	.300	.391	74	-23	16-6	.973	**28**	**109**	126	*S-147	1.7
1997	Tor A	126	426	46	102	23	2	12	35	34-1	5	94	.239	.302	.387	78	-14	15-6	**.986**	7	97	102	*S-125	0.3
1998	Tor A	158	568	70	136	28	1	13	51	28-1	6	121	.239	.281	.361	66	-30	21-6	.976	-7	93	99	*S-158	-2.1
1999	Tor A	38	154	22	45	13	0	2	12	16-0	3	23	.292	.370	.416	98	0	4-2	.980	12	120	130	S-37/D	1.4

Year	Tm Lg	G	AB	R	H	2B	3B	HR	RBI	BB-IB	HP	SO	AVG	OBP	SLG	AOPS	ABR	SB-CS	FA	FR	Rng	Thr	G at Pos	BFW
2000	Tor A	141	527	68	133	31	2	15	69	43-0	4	113	.252	.313	.404	77	-19	4-4	.975	-8	97	102	*S-141	-1.5
2001	Tor A	154	636	79	161	25	5	17	76	43-0	7	149	.253	.303	.388	80	-20	18-11	.987	**33**	**118**	**122**	*S-154	2.4
2002	Chi N	142	513	58	127	27	5	18	61	46-7	3	136	.248	.312	.425	97	-6	5-3	.965	1	90	93	*S-142	0.6
2003	†Chi N	152	536	71	122	37	0	20	59	47-1	6	123	.228	.295	.409	83	-14	3-3	**.984**	26	104	109	*S-150	2.1
Total	10	1184	4307	536	1047	236	25	121	470	350-11	41	1017	.243	.304	.394	80	-139	93-45	.976	64	100	105	*S-1166/3-9,D-4	1.8
GONZALEZ, TONY Andres Antonio (Gonzalez) B 8.28.1936 Central Cunagua, Cuba BL/TR 5-9/170# d4.12																								
1960	Cin N	39	99	10	21	5	1	3	14	4-0	1	27	.212	.248	.374	67	-5	1-0	.957	-1	95	88	O-31(1-0-30)	-0.7
	Phi N	78	241	27	72	17	5	6	33	11-0	3	47	.299	.337	.485	122	7	2-2	.981	3	106	138	O-67(3-61-5)	0.6
	Year	117	340	37	93	22	6	9	47	15-0	4	74	.274	.311	.453	106	2	3-2	.975	2	103	123	O-98(4-61-35)	-0.1
1961	Phi N	126	426	58	118	16	8	12	58	49-7	6	66	.277	.358	.437	112	7	15-5	.984	-3	98	79	*O-118(1-86-34)	0.2
1962	Phi N	118	437	76	132	16	4	20	63	40-5	9	82	.302	.371	.494	134	21	17-8	**1.000**	1	99	105	*O-114(0-114-1)	1.9
1963	Phi N	155	555	78	170	36	12	4	66	53-5	8	68	.306	.372	.436	134	26	13-8	.986	-3	91	122	*O-151(56-107-9)	1.9
1964	Phi N	131	421	55	117	25	3	4	40	44-7	6	74	.278	.352	.380	108	7	0-5	**.996**	-1	104	73	*O-119(6-114-0)	0.1
1965	Phi N	108	370	48	109	19	1	13	41	31-3	3	52	.295	.351	.457	129	14	3-4	.983	-3	95	59	*O-104(53-60-2)	0.6
1966	Phi N	132	384	53	110	20	4	6	40	26-1	3	60	.286	.335	.406	105	3	2-6	.986	3	104	100	*O-121(73-47-4)	-0.1
1967	Phi N	149	508	74	172	23	9	9	59	47-14	5	58	.339	.396	.472	147	32	10-9	**.993**	5	106	119	*O-143(105-29-16)	3.1
1968	Phi N	121	416	45	110	13	4	3	38	40-3	7	42	.264	.335	.337	103	3	6-5	.979	-4	97	58	*O-117(19-98-4)	-0.6
1969	SD N	53	182	17	41	4	0	2	8	19-2	3	24	.225	.309	.280	69	-7	1-0	.975	4	127	71	O-49(40-11-3)	-0.6
	†Atl N	89	320	51	94	15	2	10	50	27-1	5	22	.294	.354	.447	124	10	3-1	.989	-1	105	21	O-82(35-49-0)	0.7
	Year	142	502	68	135	19	2	12	58	46-3	8	46	.269	.338	.386	104	3	4-1	.983	4	113	40	*O-131(75-60-3)	0.1
1970	Atl N	123	430	57	114	18	2	7	55	46-10	8	45	.265	.345	.365	86	-7	3-5	.987	-8	94	16	*O-119(3-116-0)	-2.0
	Cal A	26	92	9	28	2	0	1	12	2-0	1	11	.304	.326	.359	92	-1	3-2	.960	-2	86	137	O-24(0-23-1)	-0.4
1971	Cal A	111	314	32	77	9	2	3	38	28-5	3	28	.245	.310	.315	84	-7	0-1	.987	-3	94	81	O-88(67-18-9)	-1.6
Total	12	1559	5195	690	1485	238	57	103	615	467-63	71	706	.286	.350	.413	114	103	79-61	.987	-13	100	83	*O-1447(462-933-118)	3.1
GONZALEZ, DENNY Denio Mariano (Manzueta) B 7.22.1963 Sabana Grande De Boya, D.R. BR/TR 5-11/185# d8.6																								
1984	Pit N	26	82	9	15	3	1	0	4	7-1	0	21	.183	.247	.244	38	-7	1-1	1.000	-1	113	183	3-11,S-10/O-3(LF)	-0.8
1985	Pit N	35	124	11	28	4	0	4	12	13-2	0	27	.226	.299	.355	83	-3	2-4	.894	-5	72	85	3-21,O-13(LF)/2-6	-1.0
1987	Pit N	5	7	1	0	0	0	0	0	1-0	0	2	.000	.125	.000	-63	-2	0-0	1.000	-1	33	0	/S	-0.2
1988	Pit N	24	32	5	6	1	0	0	1	6-0	0	10	.188	.316	.219	57	-2	0-0	1.000	0	68	105	S-14/2-4,3-2	-0.1
1989	Cle A	8	17	3	5	1	0	0	1	0-0	1	4	.294	.333	.353	92	0	0-0	.000	-0	0	0	/3D	0.0
Total	5	98	262	29	54	9	1	4	18	27-3	1	64	.206	.283	.294	62	-14	3-5	.925	-7	87	118	/3-35,S-25,O-16(LF),2-10,D-6	-2.1
GONZALEZ, EUSEBIO Eusebio Miguel (Lopez) "Papo" B 7.13.1892 Havana, Cuba D 2.14.1976 Havana, Cuba BR/TR 5-10/165# d7.26																								
1918	Bos A	3	5	2	2	0	1	0	0	1	1	1	.400	.571	.800	319	1	0	1.000	-0	95	0	/S-2,3	0.1
GONZALEZ, FERNANDO Jose Fernando (Quinones) B 6.19.1950 Arecibo, P.R. BR/TR 5-10/170# d9.15																								
1972	Pit N	3	2	0	0	0	0	0	0	0-0	0	2	.000	.000	.000	-99	-1	0-0	.500	0	468	0	/3	0.0
1973	Pit N	37	49	5	11	0	1	1	5	1-0	1	11	.224	.255	.327	62	-3	0-0	.923	-1	77	0	/3-5	-0.4
1974	KC A	9	21	1	3	1	0	0	2	0-0	0	4	.143	.143	.190	-5	-3	1-0	1.000	0	71	97	/3-8,D	-0.3
	NY A	51	121	11	26	5	1	1	7	7-0	0	7	.215	.258	.298	60	-6	0-0	.982	-0	90	92	2-42/3-7,S-3	-0.5
	Year	60	142	12	29	6	1	1	9	7-0	0	11	.204	.242	.282	50	-9	1-0	.982	-0	90	92	2-42,3-15/S-3,D	-0.8
1977	Pit N	80	181	17	50	10	0	4	27	13-6	0	21	.276	.320	.398	90	-3	3-3	.972	-5	92	79	3-37,O-16(15-0-1)/2-6,S-2	-0.9
1978	Pit N	9	21	2	4	1	0	0	0	1-0	0	3	.190	.227	.238	29	-2	0-0	.923	-4	65	0	/2-4,3-3	-0.7
	SD N	101	320	27	80	10	2	2	29	18-3	0	32	.250	.286	.313	74	-12	4-4	.982	7	108	132	2-94	-0.2
	Year	110	341	29	84	11	2	2	29	19-3	0	35	.246	.282	.308	71	-15	4-4	.981	2	106	127	2-98/3-3	-0.9
1979	SD N	114	323	22	70	13	3	9	34	18-11	0	34	.217	.258	.359	71	-15	0-0	.976	-9	93	94	*2-103/3-3	-2.1
Total	6	404	1038	85	244	40	7	17	104	58-20	1	114	.235	.274	.336	71	-45	8-7	.979	-13	98	107	2-249/3-64,O-16(15-0-1),S-5,D	-5.1
GONZALEZ, JOSE Jose Rafael (Gutierrez) B 11.23.1964 Puerto Plata, D.R. BR/TR 6-2/196# d9.2																								
1985	LA N	23	11	6	3	2	0	0	0	1-0	0	3	.273	.333	.455	122	0	1-1	1.000	-0	99	0	O-18(5-6-8)	0.0
1986	LA N	57	93	15	20	5	1	2	6	7-0	0	29	.215	.270	.355	76	-3	4-3	.924	-3	102	0	O-57(0-49-8)	-0.7
1987	LA N	19	16	2	3	2	0	0	1	1-0	0	5	.188	.222	.313	45	-1	5-0	1.000	2	153	278	O-16(8-5-3)	0.2
1988	†LA N	37	24	7	2	1	0	0	0	2-0	0	10	.083	.154	.125	-20	-4	3-0	.938	-0	104	0	O-24(9-9-9)	-0.4
1989	LA N	95	261	31	70	11	2	3	18	23-5	0	53	.268	.326	.360	98	-1	9-3	.968	5	105	216	O-87(4-55-34)	0.4
1990	LA N	106	99	15	23	5	3	2	8	6-1	1	27	.232	.280	.404	89	-2	3-1	1.000	-0	99	53	O-81(43-18-25)	-0.3
1991	LA N	42	28	3	0	0	0	0	0	2-0	0	9	.000	.067	.000	-82	-7	0-0	1.000	1	127	0	O-27(12-1-15)	-0.7
	Pit N	16	20	2	2	0	0	1	3	0-0	0	6	.100	.095	.250	-5	-3	0-0	1.000	2	146	307	O-14(3-6-5)	-0.1
	Year	58	48	5	2	0	0	1	3	2-0	0	15	.042	.078	.104	-50	-10	0-0	1.000	2	135	124	O-41(15-7-20)	-0.8
	Cle A	33	69	10	11	2	1	1	4	11-0	1	27	.159	.284	.261	51	-5	8-0	.981	-0	103	66	O-32(5-10-17)	-0.6
1992	Cal A	33	55	4	10	2	0	0	2	7-1	0	20	.182	.270	.218	39	-4	0-1	1.000	-0	96	101	O-22(11-5-8)/D	-0.6
Total	8	461	676	95	144	30	7	9	42	60-7	2	186	.213	.277	.318	69	-30	33-9	.972	5	106	116	O-378(100-164-132)/D	-2.6
GONZALEZ, JUAN Juan Alberto (Vazquez) B 10.20.1969 Arecibo, P.R. BR/TR 6-3/210# d9.1																								
1989	Tex A	24	60	6	9	3	0	1	7	6-0	0	17	.150	.227	.250	34	-5	0-0	.964	0	112	0	O-24(1-24-0)	-0.6
1990	Tex A	25	90	11	26	7	1	4	12	2-0	2	18	.289	.316	.522	131	3	0-1	1.000	-1	93	0	O-16(1-12-4)/D-9	0.2
1991	Tex A	142	545	78	144	34	1	27	102	42-7	5	118	.264	.321	.479	121	14	4-4	.981	-2	97	82	*O-136(92-93-8)/D-4	0.8
1992	Tex A	155	584	77	152	24	2	**43**	109	35-1	5	143	.260	.304	.529	135	22	0-1	.975	2	103	111	*O-148(31-123-1)/D-4	2.2
1993	Tex A★	140	536	105	166	33	1	**46**	118	37-7	13	99	.310	.368	**.632**	170	50	4-1	.985	-1	105	66	*O-129(LF),D-10	4.2
1994	Tex A	107	422	57	116	18	4	19	85	30-10	7	66	.275	.330	.472	105	1	6-4	.991	3	103	117	*O-107(LF)	0.0
1995	Tex A	90	352	57	104	20	2	27	82	17-3	0	66	.295	.324	.594	131	13	0-0	1.000	0	70	347	D-83/O-5(LF)	0.7
1996	†Tex A	134	541	89	170	33	2	47	144	45-12	3	82	.314	.368	.643	142	32	2-0	.988	-8	81	85	*O-102(RF),D-32	1.6
1997	Tex A	133	533	87	158	24	3	42	131	33-7	3	107	.296	.335	.589	130	20	0-0	.971	1	96	143	D-69,O-64(RF)	1.2
1998	†Tex A★	154	606	110	193	**50**	2	45	**157**	46-9	6	126	.318	.366	.630	148	42	2-1	.982	-4	94	96	*O-116(RF),D-38	2.8
1999	†Tex A	144	562	114	183	36	1	39	128	51-7	4	105	.326	.378	.601	140	33	3-3	.983	-7	89	78	*O-131(RF),D-14	1.7
2000	Det A	115	461	69	133	30	2	22	67	32-3	2	84	.289	.337	.505	112	7	1-2	.992	-3	95	46	O-66(RF),D-48	-0.3
2001	†Cle A★	140	532	97	173	34	1	35	140	41-5	6	94	.325	.370	.590	148	37	1-0	.987	4	103	143	*O-119(RF),D-21	3.2
2002	Tex A	70	277	38	78	21	1	8	35	17-1	1	56	.282	.324	.451	98	-1	2-0	.992	5	100	247	O-62(RF)/D-8	0.1
2003	Tex A	82	327	49	96	17	1	24	70	14-1	4	73	.294	.329	.572	121	9	1-1	1.000	5	93	329	O-57(RF),D-24	0.8
Total	15	1655	6428	1044	1901	384	24	429	1387	448-73	61	1254	.296	.344	.563	133	277	26-18	.984	-5	97	112	*O-1282(366-252-730),D-364	18.6
GONZALEZ, JULIO Julio Cesar (Hernandez) B 12.25.1952 Caguas, P.R. BR/TR 5-11/165# d4.8																								
1977	Hou N	110	383	34	94	18	3	1	27	19-1	4	45	.245	.287	.316	68	-19	3-3	.921	-15	86	90	S-63,2-45	-2.6
1978	Hou N	78	223	24	52	3	1	1	16	8-1	1	31	.233	.263	.269	53	-15	6-1	.983	-13	89	83	2-54,S-17/3-4	-2.6
1979	Hou N	68	181	16	45	5	2	0	10	5-0	3	14	.249	.280	.298	62	-10	2-1	.987	4	104	97	2-32,S-21/3-9	-0.3
1980	Hou N	40	52	5	6	1	0	0	1	1-1	0	8	.115	.132	.135	-28	-9	1-0	1.000	1	89	152	S-16,3-11/2-2	-0.8
1981	StL N	20	22	2	7	1	0	1	3	1-0	0	3	.318	.348	.500	135	1	0-0	1.000	0	147	115	/S-5,2-4,3-2	0.1
1982	StL N	42	87	9	21	3	2	1	7	1-0	1	24	.241	.258	.356	70	-4	1-1	.907	-2	93	39	3-21/2-9,S	-0.7
1983	Det A	12	21	0	3	1	0	0	2	1-0	0	7	.143	.182	.190	3	-3	0-0	.889	0	129	36	/S-6,2-5,3	-0.2
Total	7	370	969	90	228	32	8	4	66	36-3	9	132	.235	.269	.297	59	-59	13-6	.976	-25	100	98	2-151,S-129/3-48	-7.1
GONZALEZ, LUIS Luis Emilio B 9.3.1967 Tampa, FL BL/TR 6-2/180# d9.4																								
1990	Hou N	12	21	1	4	2	0	0	0	2-1	0	5	.190	.261	.286	52	-1	0-0	1.000	2	170	218	/3-4,1-2	0.1
1991	Hou N	137	473	51	120	28	9	13	69	40-4	8	101	.254	.320	.433	117	10	10-7	.984	9	**114**	85	*O-133(LF)	1.5
1992	Hou N	122	387	40	94	19	3	10	55	24-3	2	52	.243	.289	.385	94	-5	7-7	.993	14	**129**	108	*O-111(LF)	0.5
1993	Hou N	154	540	82	162	34	3	15	72	47-7	10	83	.300	.361	.457	124	19	20-9	.978	15	**124**	95	*O-149(LF)	2.9
1994	Hou N	112	392	57	107	29	4	8	67	49-6	3	57	.273	.353	.429	110	7	15-13	.991	6	112	77	*O-111(LF)	0.7
1995	Hou N	56	209	35	54	10	4	6	35	18-3	3	30	.258	.322	.431	105	1	1-3	.980	-1	101	62	O-55(LF)	-0.3
	Chi N	77	262	34	76	19	4	7	34	39-5	3	33	.290	.384	.473	128	12	5-5	.978	8	126	111	O-76(74-6-0)	1.6
	Year	133	471	69	130	29	8	13	69	57-8	6	63	.276	.357	.454	118	13	6-8	.978	7	**115**	90	*O-131(129-6-0)	1.3
1996	Chi N	146	483	70	131	30	4	15	79	61-8	4	49	.271	.354	.443	107	6	9-6	.988	-0	96	79	*O-139(LF)/1-2	0.0
1997	†Hou N	152	550	78	142	31	2	10	68	71-7	5	67	.258	.345	.376	93	-4	10-7	.982	1	98	105	*O-146(LF)/1	-0.9
1998	Det A	154	547	84	146	35	5	23	71	57-7	8	62	.267	.340	.475	110	8	12-7	.988	-7	86	99	*O-132(132-3-0),D-19	-0.5
1999	†Ari N★	153	614	112	**206**	45	4	26	111	66-6	7	63	.336	.403	.549	138	37	9-5	.983	-1	97	107	*O-148(LF)/D-4	2.8
2000	Ari N	**162**	618	106	192	47	2	31	114	78-6	12	85	.311	.392	.544	131	32	2-4	.990	-2	103	42	*O-162(LF)	2.1

Year	Tm Lg	G	AB	R	H	2B	3B	HR	RBI	BB-IB	HP	SO	AVG	OBP	SLG	AOPS	ABR	SB-CS	FA	FR	Rng	Thr	G at Pos	BFW
2001	†Ari N★	**162**	609	128	198	36	7	57	142	100-24	14	83	.325	.429	.688	172	68	1-1	**1.000**	-0	100	77	*O-161(LF)	5.9
2002	Ari N★	148	524	90	151	19	3	28	103	97-8	5	76	.288	.400	.496	128	22	9-2	.985	-1	105	48	*O-146(LF)	1.7
2003	Ari N★	156	579	92	176	46	4	26	104	94-17	3	67	.304	.402	.532	129	28	5-3	.989	-2	92	100	*O-154(LF)	1.9
Total	14	1903	6808	1060	1959	430	58	275	1124	843-112	87	913	.288	.370	.489	123	240	115-79	.986	40	105	85	*O-1823(1821-9-0)/D-23,1-5,3-4	20.0
GONZALEZ, MIKE Miguel Angel (Cordero) B 9.24.1890 Havana, Cuba D 2.19.1977 Havana, Cuba BR/TR 6-1/200# d9.28 M2 C13																								
1912	Bos N	1	2	0	0	0	0	0	0	1	0	1	.000	.333	.000	-5	0	0	.875	0	135	278	/C	0.0
1914	Cin N	95	176	19	41	6	0	0	10	13	2	16	.233	.293	.267	65	-7	2	.954	6	100	**130**	C-83	0.4
1915	StL N	51	97	12	22	2	2	0	10	8	3	9	.227	.306	.289	80	-2	4-2	.992	4	118	88	C-32/1-8	0.4
1916	StL N	118	331	33	79	15	4	0	29	28	3	18	.239	.304	.308	89	-4	5	.981	4	82	119	C-93,1-13	0.8
1917	StL N	106	290	28	76	8	1	1	28	22	1	24	.262	.316	.307	94	-2	12	.977	2	119	118	C-68,1-18/O(RF)	0.6
1918	StL N	117	349	33	88	13	4	3	20	39	0	30	.252	.327	.338	107	4	14	.978	-6	82	109	*C-100/O-5(1-1-3),1-2	0.7
1919	NY N	58	158	18	30	6	0	0	8	20	3	9	.190	.293	.228	58	-7	3	.962	-3	102	76	C-52/1-4	-0.6
1920	NY N	11	13	1	3	0	0	0	0	3	0	1	.231	.375	.231	77	0	1-0	1.000	-0	120	94	/C-8	0.0
1921	NY N	13	24	3	9	1	0	0	0	1	0	0	.375	.400	.417	116	1	0-0	.981	-1	80	171	/1-6,C-2	0.0
1924	StL N	120	402	34	119	27	1	3	53	24	1	22	.296	.337	.391	96	-2	1-5	.986	-3	98	86	*C-119	0.1
1925	StL N	22	71	9	22	3	0	0	4	6	2	2	.310	.380	.352	86	-1	1-2	.982	3	134	75	C-22	0.3
	Chi N	70	197	26	52	13	1	3	18	13	2	15	.264	.316	.386	77	-7	2-1	.989	3	136	94	C-50/1-9	-0.1
	Year	92	268	35	74	16	1	3	22	19	4	17	.276	.333	.377	80	-8	3-3	.987	7	135	87	C-72/1-9	0.2
1926	Chi N	80	253	24	63	13	3	1	23	13	1	17	.249	.288	.336	67	-12	3	**.989**	9	173	82	C-78	0.2
1927	Chi N	39	108	15	26	4	1	1	15	10	1	8	.241	.311	.324	70	-5	1	.994	7	156	109	C-36	0.5
1928	Chi N	49	158	12	43	9	2	1	21	12	0	7	.272	.324	.373	83	-4	2	.983	8	178	95	C-45	0.7
1929	†Chi N	60	167	15	40	3	0	0	18	18	1	14	.240	.317	.257	44	-14	1	.992	6	127	103	C-60	-0.5
1931	StL N	15	19	1	2	0	0	0	3	0	0	3	.105	.105	.105	-42	-4	0	1.000	0	120	196	C-12	-0.4
1932	StL N	17	14	0	2	0	0	0	3	0	0	2	.143	.143	.143	-22	-2	0	1.000	1	51	244	/C-7	-0.2
Total	17	1042	2829	283	717	123	19	13	263	231	20	198	.253	.314	.324	81	-68	52-10	.980	40	117	101	C-868/1-60,O-6(1-1-4)	2.9
GONZALEZ, ORLANDO Orlando Eugene B 11.15.1951 Havana, Cuba BL/TL 6-2/180# d6.7																								
1976	Cle A	28	68	5	17	2	0	0	4	5-0	0	7	.250	.301	.279	72	-2	1-2	.992	-1	89	68	1-15/O-7(3-0-4),D-2	-0.5
1978	†Phi N	26	26	1	5	0	0	0	0	1-0	0	1	.192	.222	.192	17	-3	0-0	1.000	0	135	0	O-11(1-0-10)/1-3	-0.3
1980	Oak A	25	70	10	17	0	0	0	1	9-0	0	8	.243	.329	.243	64	-3	0-2	.990	1	113	85	1-11/O-2(LF),D-8	-0.4
Total	3	79	164	16	39	2	0	0	5	15-0	0	16	.238	.302	.250	59	-8	1-4	.991	1	98	74	/1-29,O-20(6-0-14),D-10	-1.2
GONZALEZ, PEDRO Pedro (Olivares) B 12.12.1937 San Pedro De Macoris, D.R. BR/TR 6/176# d4.11 OF Total (5-LF 19-RF)																								
1963	NY A	14	26	3	5	1	0	0	1	0-0	0	5	.192	.192	.231	18	-3	0-1	.963	-2	59	62	/2-7	-0.5
1964	†NY A	80	112	18	31	8	1	0	5	7-0	2	22	.277	.331	.366	92	-1	3-4	.992	2	161	124	1-31,O-20(5-0-15)/3-9,2-6	-0.1
1965	NY A	7	5	0	2	1	0	0	0	0-0	0	2	.400	.400	.600	181	1	0-0	—	0			H	0.1
	Cle A	116	400	38	101	14	3	5	39	18-7	3	57	.253	.288	.340	78	-13	7-4	.980	4	96	89	*2-112/O-3(RF),3-2	0.1
	Year	123	405	38	103	15	3	5	39	18-7	3	59	.254	.289	.343	79	-12	7-4	.980	4	96	89	*2-112/O-3(RF),3-2	0.2
1966	Cle A	110	352	21	82	9	2	2	17	15-1	2	54	.233	.268	.287	60	-19	8-5	.984	5	96	105	*2-104/3O(RF)	-0.6
1967	Cle A	80	189	19	43	6	0	1	8	12-0	1	36	.228	.275	.275	63	-9	4-6	.971	-5	91	101	2-64/1-4,3-4,S-3	-1.2
Total	5	407	1084	99	264	39	6	8	70	52-8	8	176	.244	.282	.313	70	-44	22-20	.980	4	94	96	2-293/1-35,O-24R,3-16,S-3	-2.2
GONZALEZ, RAUL Victor Raul B 12.27.1973 Santurce, P.R. BR/TR 5-8/190# d5.25																								
2000	Chi N	3	2	0	0	0	0	0	0	0-0	0	2	.000	.000	.000	-99	-1	0-0	—	-0	0	0	/O-2(LF)	-0.1
2001	Cin N	11	14	0	3	0	0	0	0	1-0	0	3	.214	.267	.214	26	-2	0-0	1.000	0	105	0	/O-2(LF)	-0.2
2002	Cin N	10	23	4	6	1	0	0	1	2-0	0	5	.261	.320	.304	67	-1	2-0	1.000	0	93	360	/O-6(1-5-0)	0.0
	NY N	30	81	9	21	2	0	3	11	4-0	0	17	.259	.291	.395	86	-3	2-2	1.000	1	112	92	O-24(11-13-4)	-0.2
	Year	40	104	13	27	3	0	3	12	6-0	0	22	.260	.297	.375	81	-4	4-2	1.000	1	108	147	O-30(12-18-4)	-0.2
2003	NY N	107	217	28	50	12	2	2	21	27-1	1	34	.230	.317	.332	72	-9	3-0	.993	5	120	116	O-88(45-25-40)	-0.5
Total	4	161	337	41	80	15	2	5	33	34-1	1	61	.237	.307	.338	72	-16	7-2	.995	6	116	122	O-122(61-43-44)	-1.0
GONZALEZ, WIKI Wiklenman Vicente B 5.17.1974 Aragua, Venezuela BR/TR 5-11/175# d8.14																								
1999	SD N	30	83	7	21	2	1	3	12	1-0	1	8	.253	.271	.410	75	-4	0-0	.992	3	417	155	C-17	0.0
2000	SD N	95	284	25	66	15	1	5	30	30-4	3	31	.232	.311	.345	71	-13	1-2	.991	2	102	115	C-87	-0.6
2001	SD N	64	160	16	44	6	0	8	27	11-1	4	28	.275	.335	.463	114	3	2-0	.989	-4	92	126	C-47/D	0.1
2002	SD N	56	164	16	36	8	1	1	20	27-3	1	24	.220	.330	.299	78	-5	0-0	.985	0	134	112	C-54	-0.2
2003	SD N	24	65	1	13	5	0	0	10	5-1	1	13	.200	.264	.277	47	-5	0-0	.993	-1	61	105	C-23/P	-0.5
Total	5	269	756	65	180	36	3	17	99	74-9	10	104	.238	.312	.361	80	-24	3-2	.989	1	132	119	C-228/PD	-1.2
GOOCH, CHARLIE Charles Furman B 6.5.1902 Smyrna, TN D 5.30.1982 Lanham, MD BR/TR 5-9/170# d4.18																								
1929	Was A	39	57	6	16	2	1	0	5	7	0	8	.281	.359	.351	83	-1	0-1	.970	-1	218	65	/1-7,3-7,S	-0.2
GOOCH, JOHNNY John Beverley B 11.9.1897 Smyrna, TN D 5.15.1975 Nashville, TN BB/TR 5-11/175# d9.9 C3																								
1921	Pit N	13	38	2	9	0	0	0	3	3	0	3	.237	.293	.237	41	-3	1-0	.985	2	149	106	C-13	0.0
1922	Pit N	105	353	45	116	15	3	1	42	39	5	15	.329	.403	.397	106	5	1-1	.970	-3	95	87	*C-103	0.9
1923	Pit N	66	202	16	56	10	2	1	20	17	1	13	.277	.336	.361	82	-5	2-1	.975	4	133	81	C-66	0.3
1924	Pit N	70	224	26	65	6	5	0	25	16	2	12	.290	.343	.362	88	-4	1-3	.988	1	142	71	C-69	0.0
1925	†Pit N	79	215	24	64	8	4	0	30	20	0	16	.298	.357	.372	81	-6	1-0	.968	1	125	73	C-76	-0.1
1926	Pit N	86	218	19	59	15	1	1	42	20	3	14	.271	.340	.362	85	-4	1	.980	0	119	72	C-80	0.1
1927	†Pit N	101	291	22	75	17	2	2	48	19	1	21	.258	.305	.351	70	-12	0	.974	5	133	74	C-91	-0.2
1928	Pit N	31	80	7	19	2	1	0	5	3	0	6	.237	.265	.287	43	-7	0	.957	1	81	119	C-31	-0.4
	Bro N	42	101	9	32	1	2	0	12	7	0	9	.317	.361	.366	92	-1	0	.969	-1	77	85	C-38	0.0
	Year	73	181	16	51	3	3	0	17	10	0	15	.282	.319	.331	70	-9	0	.964	0	79	102	C-69	-0.4
1929	Bro N	1	1	0	0	0	0	0	0	0	0	0	.000	.000	.000	-99	0	0	—	0			H	0.0
	Cin N	92	287	22	86	13	5	0	34	24	1	10	.300	.356	.380	86	-6	4	.975	5	108	117	C-86	0.4
	Year	93	288	22	86	13	5	0	34	24	1	10	.299	.355	.378	86	-6	4	.975	5	108	117	C-86	0.4
1930	Cin N	82	276	29	67	10	3	2	30	27	2	15	.243	.315	.322	57	-19	0	.955	-5	91	101	C-79	-1.7
1933	Bos A	37	77	6	14	1	1	0	2	11	0	7	.182	.284	.221	36	-7	0-0	.991	2	82	176	C-26	-0.4
Total	11	805	2363	227	662	98	29	7	293	206	15	141	.280	.342	.355	79	-69	11-5	.973	12	113	90	C-758	-1.1
GOOCH, LEE Lee Currin B 2.23.1890 Oxford, NC D 5.18.1966 Raleigh, NC BR/TR 6/190# d8.17																								
1915	Cle A	2	2	0	1	0	0	0	0	0	0	0	.500	.500	.500	196	0	0	—	0			H	0.0
1917	Phi A	17	59	4	17	2	0	1	8	4	0	10	.288	.333	.373	117	1	0	.893	-2	87	45	O-16(RF)	-0.2
Total	2	19	61	4	18	2	0	1	8	4	0	10	.295	.338	.377	120	1	0	.893	-2	87	45	/O-16(RF)	-0.2
GOOD, GENE Eugene J. B 12.13.1882 Roxbury, MA D 8.6.1947 Boston, MA BL/TR 5-6/130# d4.12																								
1906	Bos N	34	119	4	18	0	0	0	0	13	2		.151	.246	.151	25	-10	2	.873	-3	114	88	O-34(24-10-0)	-1.7
GOOD, WILBUR Wilbur David "Lefty" B 9.28.1885 Punxsutawney, PA D 12.30.1963 Brooksville, FL BL/TL 5-11.5/180# d8.18 ▲																								
1905	NY A	5	8	2	3	0	0	0	0	0	0		.375	.375	.375	124	1	0	.889	0	120	0	/P-5	0.0
1908	Cle A	46	154	23	43	1	3	1	14	13	4		.279	.351	.344	126	4	7	.845	-8	0	0	O-42(2-17-23)	-0.7
1909	Cle A	94	318	33	68	6	5	0	17	28	9		.214	.296	.264	74	-9	13	.953	2	119	90	O-80(RF)	-1.2
1910	Bos N	23	86	15	29	5	4	0	11	6	2	13	.337	.394	.488	150	5	5	.969	3	100	207	O-23(0-22-1)	0.7
1911	Bos N	43	165	21	44	9	3	0	15	12	0	22	.267	.316	.358	82	-4	3	.945	5	102	192	O-43(0-41-2)	-0.3
	Chi N	58	145	27	39	5	4	2	21	11	2	17	.269	.329	.400	103	0	10	.928	-4	90	56	O-40(3-34-3)	-0.7
	Year	101	310	48	83	14	7	2	36	23	2	39	.268	.322	.377	92	-4	13	.938	1	97	132	O-83(3-75-5)	-1.0
1912	Chi N	39	35	7	5	0	0	0	1	3	0	7	.143	.211	.143	-2	-5	3	1.000	1	112	229	O-10(5-4-1)	-0.4
1913	Chi N	49	91	11	23	3	2	1	12	11	1	16	.253	.340	.363	100	0	5-2	.974	-1	107	39	O-26(3-1-22)	-0.1
1914	Chi N	154	580	70	158	24	7	2	43	53	7	74	.272	.341	.348	105	5	31	.930	-0	99	106	*O-154(RF)	-0.4
1915	Chi N	128	498	66	126	18	9	2	27	34	5	65	.253	.307	.337	95	-4	19-17	.936	-1	101	98	*O-125(0-1-125)	-1.4
1916	Phi N	75	136	25	34	4	3	1	15	8	3	13	.250	.306	.346	96	-1	7	.983	0	98	101	O-46(9-1-36)	-0.3
1918	Chi A	35	148	24	37	9	4	0	11	11	3	16	.250	.315	.365	104	0	1	.982	3	120	77	O-35(1-33-1)	0.0
Total	11	749	2364	324	609	84	44	9	187	190	36	243	.258	.322	.342	98	-8	104-19	.942	-1	96	99	O-624(23-154-448)/P-5	-4.8
GOODENOUGH, BILL William B. B 1863 , NY D 5.24.1905 St.Louis, MO BL 6-1/170# d8.31																								
1893	StL N	10	31	4	5	1	0	0	2	3	3	4	.161	.297	.194	31	-3	2	.880	-1	69	0	O-10(CF)	-0.3

GOODFELLOW, MIKE Michael J. B 10.3.1866 Port Jervis, NY D 2.12.1920 Newark, NJ BR/TR 6/180# d6.13

Year	Tm Lg	G	AB	R	H	2B	3B	HR	RBI	BB-IB	HP	SO	AVG	OBP	SLG	AOPS	ABR	SB-CS	FA	FR	Rng	Thr	G at Pos	BFW
1887	StL AA	1	4	0	0	0	0	0	0	0	0		.000	.000	.000	-90	-1	0	.800	-0			/C	-0.1
1888	Cle AA	68	269	24	66	7	0	0	29	11	3		.245	.283	.271	80	-6	7	.863	-4	75	39	O-62(11-0-52)/C-4,1-3,S	-0.9
Total	2	69	273	24	66	7	0	0	29	11	3		.242	.279	.267	77	-7	7	.863	-4			/O-62(11-0-52),C-5,1-3,S	-1.0

GOODMAN, IVAL Ival Richard "Goodie" B 7.23.1908 Northview, MO D 11.25.1984 Cincinnati, OH BL/TR 5-11/170# d4.16

Year	Tm Lg	G	AB	R	H	2B	3B	HR	RBI	BB-IB	HP	SO	AVG	OBP	SLG	AOPS	ABR	SB-CS	FA	FR	Rng	Thr	G at Pos	BFW
1935	Cin N	148	592	86	159	23	**18**	12	72	35	4	50	.269	.314	.429	101	-3	14	.960	5	108	111	*O-146(2-0-144)	-0.7
1936	Cin N	136	489	81	139	15	**14**	17	71	38	**9**	53	.284	.347	.476	128	16	6	.972	-2	110	44	*O-120(1-1-118)	0.7
1937	Cin N	147	549	86	150	25	12	12	55	55	7	58	.273	.347	.428	115	11	10	.974	3	109	92	*O-141(7-1-133)	0.5
1938	Cin N★	145	568	103	166	27	10	30	92	53	**15**	51	.292	.368	.533	149	37	3	.988	3	108	77	*O-142(RF)	3.0
1939	†Cin N★	124	470	85	152	37	16	7	84	54	**7**	32	.323	.401	.515	144	30	2	.981	7	105	148	*O-123(RF)	2.9
1940	†Cin N	136	519	78	134	20	6	12	63	60	0	54	.258	.335	.389	98	-1	9	.970	-7	97	56	*O-135(RF)	-1.7
1941	Cin N	42	149	14	40	5	2	1	12	16	1	15	.268	.343	.349	95	-1	1	.966	-1	110	29	O-40(RF)	-0.5
1942	Cin N	87	226	21	55	18	1	0	15	24	1	32	.243	.319	.332	91	-2	0	.991	1	95	142	O-57(RF)	-0.5
1943	Chi N	80	225	31	72	10	5	3	45	24	2	20	.320	.390	.449	144	13	4	.968	-4	95	36	O-61(55-10-0)	0.6
1944	Chi N	62	141	24	37	8	1	1	16	23	3	15	.262	.377	.355	107	3	0	1.000	-3	89	0	O-35(23-14-0)	-0.2
Total	10	1107	3928	609	1104	188	85	95	525	382	49	380	.281	.352	.445	120	103	49	.975	1	105	82	O-1000(88-26-892)	4.1

GOODMAN, JAKE Jacob B 9.14.1853 Lancaster, PA D 3.9.1890 Reading, PA 6-1.5/?# d5.2

Year	Tm Lg	G	AB	R	H	2B	3B	HR	RBI	BB-IB	HP	SO	AVG	OBP	SLG	AOPS	ABR	SB-CS	FA	FR	Rng	Thr	G at Pos	BFW
1878	Mil N	60	252	28	62	4	3	1	27	7		33	.246	.266	.298	80	-6		.944	-4	71	52	*1-60	-1.2
1882	Pit AA	10	41	5	13	2	2	0		2			.317	.349	.463	180	3		.962	1	177	0	1-10	0.3
Total	2	70	293	33	75	6	5	1	27	9		33	.256	.278	.321	92	-3		.946	-3	85	45	/1-70	-0.9

GOODMAN, BILLY William Dale B 3.22.1926 Concord, NC D 10.1.1984 Sarasota, FL BL/TR 5-11/165# d4.19 C3 OF Total (68-LF 43-RF)

Year	Tm Lg	G	AB	R	H	2B	3B	HR	RBI	BB-IB	HP	SO	AVG	OBP	SLG	AOPS	ABR	SB-CS	FA	FR	Rng	Thr	G at Pos	BFW
1947	Bos A	12	11	1	2	0	0	0	1	1	0	2	.182	.250	.182	20	-1	0-0	1.000	0	146	0	/O(RF)	-0.1
1948	Bos A	127	445	65	138	27	2	1	66	74	5	44	.310	.414	.387	108	10	5-3	.993	-3	91	107	*1-117/2-2,3-2	0.3
1949	Bos A★	122	443	54	132	23	3	0	56	58	2	21	.298	.382	.363	91	-4	2-0	**.992**	-1	95	**121**	*1-117	-0.7
1950	Bos A	110	424	91	150	25	3	4	68	52	2	25	**.354**	.427	.455	115	12	2-4	.991	-2	99	55	O-45(LF),3-27,1-21/2-5,S	0.5
1951	Bos A	141	546	92	162	34	4	0	50	79	2	37	.297	.388	.374	97	1	7-4	.995	-2	72	102	1-62,2-44,O-38(2-0-36)/3	-0.1
1952	Bos A	138	513	79	157	27	3	4	56	48	4	23	.306	.370	.394	104	4	8-2	.975	**23**	**113**	118	*2-103,1-23/3-5,O-4(LF)	3.4
1953	Bos A★	128	514	73	161	33	5	2	41	57	2	11	.313	.384	.409	108	8	1-4	.974	-1	102	104	*2-112,1-20	1.3
1954	Bos A	127	489	71	148	25	4	1	36	51	2	15	.303	.370	.376	95	-2	3-3	.979	6	110	108	2-72,1-27,O-13(LF),3-12	0.7
1955	Bos A	149	599	100	176	31	2	0	52	99-1	3	44	.294	.394	.352	94	1	5-5	.969	-21	93	84	*2-143/1-5,O(RF)	-1.0
1956	Bos A	105	399	61	117	22	8	2	38	40-1	0	22	.293	.356	.404	90	-6	0-3	.966	-8	100	94	2-95	-0.8
1957	Bos A	18	16	1	1	1	0	0	0	2-0	0	1	.063	.167	.125	-18	-3	0-0	—	0			H	-0.3
	Bal A	73	263	36	81	10	3	3	33	21-1	3	18	.308	.362	.403	117	6	0-2	.961	-7	87	100	3-54/O-9(4-0-5),1-8,2-5,S-5	-0.2
	Year	91	279	37	82	11	3	3	33	23-1	3	19	.294	.351	.387	106	2	0-2	.961	-7	87	100	3-54/O-9(4-0-5),1-8,2-5,S-5	-0.5
1958	Chi A	116	425	41	127	15	5	0	40	37-1	2	21	.299	.355	.358	100	0	1-0	.954	-11	97	79	*3-111/1-3,2S	-1.1
1959	†Chi A	104	268	21	67	14	1	1	28	19-0	2	20	.250	.304	.321	73	-10	3-0	.950	-0	106	95	3-74/2-3	-1.0
1960	Chi A	30	77	5	18	4	0	0	6	12-1	0	8	.234	.337	.286	71	-3	0-0	.982	2	104	56	3-20/2-7	0.0
1961	Chi A	41	51	4	13	4	0	1	10	7-0	0	6	.255	.339	.392	98	0	0-0	.944	-1	104	87	/3-7,1-2,2	0.0
1962	Hou N	82	161	12	41	4	1	0	10	12-2	0	11	.255	.306	.292	66	-8	0-0	.972	-6	99	59	2-31,3-17/1	-1.3
Total	16	1623	5644	807	1691	299	44	19	591	669-7	29	329	.300	.376	.378	98	5	37-30	.972	-31	102	99	2-624,1-406,3-330,O-111L/S-7	-0.4

GOODSON, ED James Edward B 1.25.1948 Pulaski, VA BL/TR (BB 1975 (part)) 6-3/185# d9.5

Year	Tm Lg	G	AB	R	H	2B	3B	HR	RBI	BB-IB	HP	SO	AVG	OBP	SLG	AOPS	ABR	SB-CS	FA	FR	Rng	Thr	G at Pos	BFW
1970	SF N	7	11	1	3	0	0	0	0	0-0	0	2	.273	.273	.273	47	-1	0-0	.941	0	163	67	/1-2	-0.1
1971	SF N	20	42	4	8	1	0	0	1	2-0	0	4	.190	.227	.214	26	-4	0-0	1.000	0	106	39	1-14	-0.5
1972	SF N	58	150	15	42	1	1	6	30	8-2	1	12	.280	.319	.420	107	1	0-0	.991	2	132	32	1-42	0.0
1973	SF N	102	384	37	116	20	1	12	53	15-4	2	44	.302	.331	.453	111	4	0-1	.911	-8	97	76	3-93	-0.4
1974	SF N	98	298	25	81	15	0	6	48	18-6	3	22	.272	.320	.383	91	-4	1-0	.997	-2	73	100	1-73/3-8	-1.1
1975	SF N	39	121	10	25	7	0	1	8	7-2	0	14	.207	.248	.289	47	-9	0-1	.993	2	125	95	1-16,3-13	-0.9
	Atl N	47	76	5	16	2	0	1	8	2-0	0	8	.211	.228	.276	39	-7	0-0	.990	-0	100	88	1-13/3	-0.8
	Year	86	197	15	41	9	0	2	16	9-2	0	22	.208	.240	.284	44	-15	0-1	.992	2	115	92	1-29,3-14	-1.7
1976	LA N	83	118	8	27	4	0	3	17	8-2	0	19	.229	.273	.339	76	-4	0-0	.833	-4	93	85	3-16/1-3,O-2(LF),2	-0.8
1977	†LA N	61	66	3	11	1	0	1	5	3-2	0	10	.167	.203	.227	15	-8	0-1	1.000	0	94	203	1-13/3-4	-0.9
Total	8	515	1266	108	329	51	2	30	170	63-18	6	135	.260	.297	.374	84	-32	1-3	.994	-9	99	79	1-176,3-135/O-2(LF),2	-5.5

GOODWIN, PEP Claire Vernon B 12.19.1891 Pocatello, ID D 2.15.1972 Oakland, CA BL/TR 5-10.5/160# d4.16

Year	Tm Lg	G	AB	R	H	2B	3B	HR	RBI	BB-IB	HP	SO	AVG	OBP	SLG	AOPS	ABR	SB-CS	FA	FR	Rng	Thr	G at Pos	BFW
1914	KC F	112	374	38	88	15	6	1	32	27	2	23	.235	.290	.316	68	-24	4	.907	-7	111	89	S-67,3-40/1	-2.7
1915	KC F	81	229	22	54	5	1	0	16	15	3	23	.236	.291	.266	60	-16	6	.906	-5	97	82	S-42,2-23	-2.0
Total	2	193	603	60	142	20	7	1	48	42	5	46	.235	.291	.297	65	-40	10	.907	-12	106	86	S-109/3-40,2-23,1	-4.7

GOODWIN, CURTIS Curtis La Mar B 9.30.1972 Oakland, CA BL/TL 5-11/180# d6.2

Year	Tm Lg	G	AB	R	H	2B	3B	HR	RBI	BB-IB	HP	SO	AVG	OBP	SLG	AOPS	ABR	SB-CS	FA	FR	Rng	Thr	G at Pos	BFW
1995	Bal A	87	289	40	76	11	3	1	24	15-0	2	53	.263	.301	.332	64	-16	22-4	.990	-1	104	26	O-84(CF)/D-3	-1.2
1996	Cin N	49	136	20	31	3	0	0	5	19-0	0	34	.228	.323	.250	53	-9	15-6	.970	-4	85	0	O-42(9-28-6)	-1.1
1997	Cin N	85	265	27	67	11	0	1	12	24-0	1	53	.253	.316	.306	63	-14	22-13	1.000	4	116	82	O-71(32-41-1)	-1.0
1998	Col N	119	159	27	39	7	0	1	6	16-0	0	40	.245	.313	.308	53	-11	5-1	.983	1	112	35	O-91(14-74-7)	-0.9
1999	Chi N	89	157	15	38	6	1	0	9	13-1	0	38	.242	.298	.293	52	-12	2-4	.983	4	112	123	O-76(36-42-0)	-0.9
	Tor A	2	8	0	0	0	0	0	0	0-0	0	3	.000	.000	.000	-99	-2	0-0	1.000	1	142	821	/O-2(CF)	-0.1
Total	5	431	1014	129	251	38	4	3	56	87-1	3	221	.248	.307	.302	58	-64	66-28	.988	5	107	59	O-366(91-271-14)/D-3	-5.2

GOODWIN, DANNY Danny Kay B 9.2.1953 St.Louis, MO BL/TR 6-1/195# d9.3

Year	Tm Lg	G	AB	R	H	2B	3B	HR	RBI	BB-IB	HP	SO	AVG	OBP	SLG	AOPS	ABR	SB-CS	FA	FR	Rng	Thr	G at Pos	BFW
1975	Cal A	4	10	0	1	0	0	0	0	0-0	0	5	.100	.100	.100	-47	-2	0-0	—	0			/D-3	-0.2
1977	Cal A	35	91	5	19	6	1	1	8	5-1	0	19	.209	.250	.330	59	-5	0-0	—	0	0	0	D-23	-0.6
1978	Cal A	24	58	9	16	5	0	2	10	10-0	0	13	.276	.377	.466	143	4	0-0	—	0	0	0	D-15	0.3
1979	Min A	58	159	22	46	8	5	5	27	11-1	0	23	.289	.335	.497	117	3	0-0	1.000	-1	55	104	D-51/1-8	0.0
1980	Min A	55	115	12	23	5	0	1	11	17-0	0	32	.200	.301	.270	54	-7	0-0	1.000	0	109	74	D-38,1-13	-0.8
1981	Min A	59	151	18	34	6	1	2	17	16-2	0	32	.225	.298	.318	73	-5	3-1	.992	-2	76	76	1-40/O(LF)D	-1.0
1982	Oak A	17	52	6	11	2	1	2	8	2-0	0	13	.212	.236	.404	77	-2	0-0	—	0	0	0	D-15	-0.3
Total	7	252	636	72	150	32	8	13	81	61-4	0	137	.236	.301	.373	84	-14	3-1	.994	-3	80	79	D-150/1-61,O(LF)	-2.6

GOODWIN, TOM Thomas Jones B 7.27.1968 Fresno, CA BL/TR 6-1/170# d9.1

Year	Tm Lg	G	AB	R	H	2B	3B	HR	RBI	BB-IB	HP	SO	AVG	OBP	SLG	AOPS	ABR	SB-CS	FA	FR	Rng	Thr	G at Pos	BFW
1991	LA N	16	7	3	1	0	0	0	0	0-0	0	2	.143	.143	.143	-20	-1	1-1	1.000	1	167	0	/O-5(2-4-0)	-0.1
1992	LA N	57	73	15	17	1	1	0	3	6-0	0	10	.233	.291	.274	62	-4	7-3	1.000	1	92	0	O-45(35-9-2)	-0.6
1993	LA N	30	17	6	5	1	0	0	1	1-0	0	4	.294	.333	.353	89	0	1-2	1.000	-0	93	0	O-12(6-4-2)	-0.1
1994	KC A	2	2	0	0	0	0	0	0	0-0	0	1	.000	.000	.000	-96	-1	0-0	1.000	0	146	0	/O(RF)D	-0.1
1995	KC A	133	480	72	138	16	3	4	28	38-0	5	72	.287	.346	.358	83	-12	50-18	.990	-7	90	82	*O-130(37-95-1)/D-2	-1.4
1996	KC A	143	524	80	148	14	4	1	35	39-0	2	79	.282	.334	.330	69	-25	66-22	.984	-6	94	77	*O-136(75-81-0)/D-5	-2.4
1997	KC A	97	367	51	100	13	4	2	22	19-0	2	51	.272	.311	.346	70	-17	34-10	.996	-4	96	61	O-96(CF)	-1.6
	Tex A	53	207	39	49	13	2	0	17	25-1	1	37	.237	.319	.319	65	-10	16-6	.986	3	110	118	O-51(5-49-0)	-0.6
	Year	150	574	90	149	26	6	2	39	44-1	3	88	.260	.314	.336	68	-27	50-16	.992	-2	101	81	*O-147(5-145-0)	-2.2
1998	†Tex A	154	520	102	151	13	3	2	33	73-0	2	90	.290	.378	.338	85	-9	38-20	.992	4	109	61	*O-150(CF)/D	-0.2
1999	†Tex A	109	405	63	105	12	6	3	33	40-0	0	61	.259	.324	.341	67	-21	39-11	.989	-5	96	61	*O-107(CF)	-1.9
2000	Col N	91	317	65	86	8	8	5	47	50-2	1	76	.271	.368	.394	75	-12	39-7	.986	-1	107	62	O-88(CF)	-0.5
	LA N	56	211	29	53	3	1	1	11	18-0	0	41	.251	.310	.289	56	-15	16-3	1.000	3	114	65	O-55(10-48-0)	-0.9
	Year	147	528	94	139	11	9	6	58	68-2	1	117	.263	.346	.352	69	-25	55-10	.992	2	110	63	*O-143(10-136-0)	-1.4
2001	LA N	105	286	51	66	8	5	4	22	23-0	0	58	.231	.286	.336	65	-16	22-8	.994	-5	94	26	O-78(8-70-0)	-1.8
2002	†SF N	78	154	23	40	5	2	1	17	14-0	0	25	.260	.321	.338	81	-5	16-2	.990	3	129	0	O-53(28-22-7)	0.0
2003	†Chi N	87	171	26	49	10	0	1	12	11-0	0	33	.287	.328	.363	82	-5	19-5	1.000	-3	92	0	O-57(17-27-15)	-0.5
Total	13	1211	3741	625	1008	117	39	24	281	357-3	13	638	.269	.334	.341	73	-153	364-118	.991	-20	100	60	*O-1064(223-850-28)/D-9	-12.7

GOOLSBY, RAY Raymond Daniel "Ox" B 9.5.1919 Florala, AL D 11.13.1999 Apopka, FL BR/TR 6-1/185# d4.18

Year	Tm Lg	G	AB	R	H	2B	3B	HR	RBI	BB-IB	HP	SO	AVG	OBP	SLG	AOPS	ABR	SB-CS	FA	FR	Rng	Thr	G at Pos	BFW
1946	Was A	3	4	0	0	0	0	0	0	1	0	1	.000	.200	.000	-43	-1	0-0	1.000	-0	65	0	/O(LF)	-0.1

GOOSSEN, GREG Gregory Bryant B 12.14.1945 Los Angeles, CA BR/TR 6-1.5/210# d9.3

Year	Tm Lg	G	AB	R	H	2B	3B	HR	RBI	BB-IB	HP	SO	AVG	OBP	SLG	AOPS	ABR	SB-CS	FA	FR	Rng	Thr	G at Pos	BFW
1965	NY N	11	31	2	9	0	0	1	2	1-0	0	5	.290	.313	.387	99	0	0-0	.979	-1	95	0	/C-8	-0.1

Year	Tm Lg	G	AB	R	H	2B	3B	HR	RBI	BB-IB	HP	SO	AVG	OBP	SLG	AOPS	ABR	SB-CS	FA	FR	Rng	Thr	G at Pos	BFW
1966	NY N	13	32	1	6	2	0	1	5	1-0	1	11	.188	.235	.344	60	-2	0-0	1.000	-2	*79*	*48*	C-11	-0.4
1967	NY N	37	69	2	11	1	0	0	3	4-0	1	26	.159	.216	.174	13	-8	0-0	.973	-1	*78*	*84*	C-23	-0.9
1968	NY N	38	106	4	22	7	0	0	6	10-0	2	21	.208	.288	.274	69	-3	0-0	.992	2	129	92	1-31/C	-0.4
1969	Sea A	52	139	19	43	8	1	10	24	14-0	3	29	.309	.385	.597	174	13	1-1	.993	1	111	55	1-31/O-2(LF)	1.2
1970	Mil A	21	47	3	12	3	0	1	3	10-0	2	12	.255	.407	.383	118	2	0-0	.990	-2	57	77	1-15	0.0
	Was A	21	36	2	8	3	0	0	1	2-0	0	8	.222	.256	.306	59	-2	0-0	1.000	-0	51	0	/O-5(LF),1-2	-0.3
	Year	42	83	5	20	6	0	1	4	12-0	2	20	.241	.347	.349	96	0	0-0	.992	-2	81	101	1-17/O-5(LF)	-0.3
Total	6	193	460	33	111	24	1	13	44	42-0	9	112	.241	.316	.383	99	0	1-1	.992	-3	112	78	/1-79,C-43,O-7(LF)	-0.9
GORBOUS, GLEN Glen Edward B 7.8.1930 Drumheller, AL, CAN D 6.12.1990 Calgary, AL, CAN BL/TR 6-2/175# d4.11																								
1955	Cin N	8	18	2	6	3	0	0	4	3-0	0	1	.333	.429	.500	137	1	0-0	.857	-0	115	0	/O-5(LF)	0.1
	Phi N	91	224	25	53	9	1	4	23	21-3	0	17	.237	.301	.339	71	-9	0-3	.984	7	111	226	O-57(0-4-53)	-0.6
	Year	99	242	27	59	12	1	4	27	24-3	0	18	.244	.311	.351	77	-8	0-3	.971	6	111	207	O-62(5-4-53)	-0.5
1956	Phi N	15	33	1	6	0	0	0	1	0-0	0	1	.182	.182	.182	-2	-5	0-0	1.000	-1	84	0	/O-8(RF)	-0.6
1957	Phi N	3	2	1	1	1	0	0	1	1-0	0	0	.500	.667	1.000	351	1	0-0	—	0			H	0.1
Total	3	117	277	29	66	13	1	4	29	25-3	0	19	.238	.300	.336	70	-12	0-3	.973	6	109	190	/O-70(5-4-61)	-1.0
GORDON, JOE Joseph Lowell "Flash" B 2.18.1915 Los Angeles, CA D 4.14.1978 Sacramento, CA BR/TR 5-10/180# d4.18 Mil 1944-45 M5 C1																								
1938	†NY A	127	458	83	117	24	7	25	97	56	3	72	.255	.340	.502	109	3	11-3	.960	**21**	**116**	115	*2-126	3.0
1939	†NY A★	151	567	92	161	32	5	28	111	75	2	57	.284	.370	.506	124	19	11-10	.967	8	102	**135**	*2-151	3.3
1940	NY A★	**155**	616	112	173	32	10	30	103	52	3	57	.281	.340	.511	122	16	18-8	.975	14	105	116	*2-155	3.8
1941	†NY A★	**156**	588	104	162	26	7	24	87	72	4	80	.276	.358	.466	118	14	10-9	.958	9	102	**134**	*2-131,1-30	2.7
1942	†NY A★	147	538	88	173	29	4	18	103	79	1	95	.322	.409	.491	156	42	12-6	.966	6	98	**146**	*2-147	5.8
1943	†NY A☆	152	543	82	135	28	5	17	69	98	2	75	.249	.365	.413	126	21	4-7	.969	25	**107**	**117**	*2-152	5.6
1946	NY A★	112	376	35	79	15	0	11	47	49	4	72	.210	.308	.338	79	-10	2-5	.974	18	**109**	120	*2-108	1.3
1947	Cle A★	155	562	89	153	27	6	29	93	62	1	49	.272	.346	.496	136	24	7-3	.978	-6	101	106	*2-155	2.8
1948	†Cle A★	144	550	96	154	21	4	32	124	77	3	68	.280	.371	.507	136	26	5-2	.971	-8	100	103	*2-144/S-2	2.5
1949	Cle A★	148	541	74	136	18	3	20	84	83	4	33	.251	.355	.407	103	2	5-6	.980	-17	97	115	*2-145	-0.7
1950	Cle A	119	368	59	87	12	1	19	57	56	2	44	.236	.340	.429	99	-2	4-1	.969	-18	91	88	*2-105	-1.3
Total	11	1566	5707	914	1530	264	52	253	975	759	29	702	.268	.357	.466	121	155	89-60	.970	51	103	118	*2-1519/1-30,S-2	28.8
GORDON, KEITH Keith Bradley B 1.22.1969 Bethesda, MD BR/TR 6-1/205# d7.9																								
1993	Cin N	3	6	0	1	0	0	0	0	0-0	0	2	.167	.167	.167	-10	-1	0-0	1.000	-0	89	0	/O-2(LF)	-0.1
GORDON, MIKE Michael William B 9.11.1953 Leominster, MA BB/TR 6-3/215# d4.7																								
1977	Chi N	8	23	0	1	0	0	0	2	2-0	0	8	.043	.120	.043	-49	-5	0-0	.970	-3	55	38	/C-8	-0.8
1978	Chi N	4	5	0	1	0	0	0	0	3-1	1	2	.200	.556	.200	106	1	0-0	1.000	0	81	0	/C-4	0.1
Total	2	12	28	0	2	0	0	0	2	5-1	1	10	.071	.235	.071	-11	-4	0-0	.979	-3	62	28	/C-12	-0.7
GORDON, SID Sidney B 8.13.1917 Brooklyn, NY D 6.17.1975 New York, NY BR/TR 5-10/185# d9.11 Mil 1944-45																								
1941	NY N	9	31	4	8	1	1	0	4	6	0	1	.258	.378	.355	105	0	0	1.000	-1	97	0	/O-9(3-6-0)	0.0
1942	NY N	6	19	4	6	0	1	0	2	3	0	2	.316	.409	.421	142	1	0	.913	1	109	0	/3-6	0.2
1943	NY N	131	474	50	119	9	11	9	63	43	1	32	.251	.315	.373	98	-4	2	.941	2	106	117	3-53,1-41,O-28(LF)/2-3	-0.6
1946	NY N	135	450	64	132	15	4	5	45	60	3	27	.293	.380	.378	115	11	1	.995	1	95	91	*O-101(LF),3-30	0.4
1947	NY N	130	437	57	119	19	8	13	57	50	0	21	.272	.347	.442	107	4	2	.971	-1	96	142	*O-124(LF)/3-2	-0.6
1948	NY N☆	142	521	100	156	26	4	30	107	74	3	39	.299	.390	.537	148	35	8	**.948**	-3	97	99	*3-115,O-23(18-0-2)	3.0
1949	NY N★	141	489	87	139	26	2	26	90	95	3	37	.284	.404	.505	142	33	1	.958	-18	84	79	*3-123,O-15(3-0-12)/1	1.4
1950	Bos N	134	481	78	146	33	4	27	103	78	2	31	.304	.403	.557	160	44	2	.990	3	105	87	*O-123(LF),3-10	3.6
1951	Bos N	150	550	96	158	28	1	29	109	80	5	32	.287	.383	.500	146	37	2-0	.984	-5	101	38	*O-122(103-0-23),3-34	2.4
1952	Bos N	144	522	69	151	22	2	25	75	77	3	49	.289	.384	.483	144	33	0-4	**.996**	-1	98	88	*O-142(LF)/3-2	2.1
1953	Mil N	140	464	67	127	22	4	19	75	71	2	40	.274	.372	.461	123	18	1-1	.977	2	106	99	*O-137(LF)	1.2
1954	Pit N	131	363	38	111	12	0	12	49	67	0	24	.306	.405	.438	124	16	0-0	.977	2	100	165	O-73(8-0-66),3-40	1.5
1955	Pit N	16	47	2	8	1	0	0	1	2-0	0	6	.170	.204	.191	6	-6	0-0	1.000	2	132	238	/3-8,O-4(LF)	-0.5
	NY N	66	144	19	35	6	1	7	25	25-2	0	15	.243	.349	.444	110	3	0-0	1.000	6	110	121	3-31,O-17(12-0-5)	0.7
	Year	82	191	21	43	7	1	7	26	27-2	0	21	.225	.317	.382	86	-4	0-0	1.000	7	115	149	3-39,O-21(16-0-5)	0.2
Total	13	1475	4992	735	1415	220	43	202	805	731-2	22	356	.283	.377	.466	130	225	19-5	.985	-10	100	98	0-918(806-6-108),3-454/1-42,2-3	14.8
GORE, GEORGE George F. "Piano Legs" B 5.3.1857 Saccarappa, ME D 9.16.1933 Utica, NY BL/TR 5-11/195# d5.1 M1																								
1879	Chi N	63	266	43	70	17	4	0	32	8		30	.263	.285	.357	104	1		.872	-3	73	0	O-54(0-48-6)/1-9	-0.4
1880	Chi N	77	322	70	116	23	2	2	47	21		10	**.360**	**.399**	**.463**	**180**	**27**		.879	2	100	142	*O-74(0-73-1)/1-7	2.5
1881	Chi N	73	309	**86**	92	18	9	1	44	27		23	.298	.354	.424	137	13		.874	1	110	114	*O-72(CF)/31	1.0
1882	Chi N	**84**	367	**99**	117	15	7	3	51	**29**		19	.319	.369	.422	146	19		.842	3	122	143	*O-84(CF)	1.7
1883	Chi N	92	392	105	131	30	9	2	52	27		13	.334	.377	.472	144	20		.867	9	130	117	*O-92(CF)	2.2
1884	Chi N	103	422	104	134	18	4	5	34	**61**		26	.318	.404	.415	146	24		.868	-1	116	141	*O-103(0-103-1)	1.8
1885	†Chi N	109	441	115	138	21	13	5	57	68		25	.313	.405	.454	156	28		.884	-5	83	80	*O-109(1-108-0)	1.8
1886	†Chi N	118	444	150	135	20	12	6	63	**102**		30	.304	.434	.444	146	28	23	.876	-6	85	124	*O-118(0-115-3)	1.6
1887	NY N	111	459	95	133	16	5	1	49	42	7	18	.290	.358	.353	103	5	39	.889	0	103	210	*O-111(CF)	0.1
1888	†NY N	64	254	37	56	4	4	2	17	30	2	31	.220	.308	.291	93	-1	11	.836	-10	37	0	O-64(42-21-1)	-1.2
1889	†NY N	120	488	132	149	21	7	7	54	84	8	28	.305	.416	.420	134	26	28	.864	-8	92	122	*O-120(0-118-3)	1.2
1890	NY P	93	399	132	127	26	8	10	55	77	3	23	.318	.432	.499	136	22	28	.877	-13	62	87	O-93(52-33-10)	0.5
1891	NY N	130	528	103	150	22	7	2	48	74	7	34	.284	.379	.364	122	19	19	.909	-11	78	86	*O-130(1-127-3)	0.3
1892	NY N	53	193	47	49	11	2	0	11	49	3	16	.254	.412	.332	127	11	20	.932	-1	92	105	O-53(0-50-3)	0.7
	StL N	20	73	9	15	0	1	0	4	18	0	6	.205	.363	.233	85	0	2	.844	-2	97	0	O-20(CF),M	-0.3
	Year	73	266	56	64	11	3	0	15	67	3	22	.241	.359	.305	116	11	22	.908	-3	93	78	O-73(0-70-3)	0.4
Total	14	1310	5357	1327	1612	262	94	46	618	717	30	332	.301	.386	.411	134	242	170	.876	-44	93	109	*O-1297(96-1175-31)/1-17,3	13.5
GORINSKI, BOB Robert John B 1.7.1952 Latrobe, PA BR/TR 6-3/215# d4.10																								
1977	Min A	54	118	14	23	4	1	3	22	5-0	0	29	.195	.226	.322	49	-9	1-0	.936	-3	87	0	O-37(30-0-7)/D-9	-1.3
GORMAN, HERB Herbert Allen B 12.18.1924 San Francisco, CA D 4.5.1953 San Diego, CA BL/TL 5-11/180# d4.19																								
1952	StL N	1	1	0	0	0	0	0	0	0	0	0	.000	.000	.000	-99	0	0-0	—	0			H	0.0
GORMAN, HOWIE Howard Paul "Lefty" B 5.14.1913 Pittsburgh, PA D 4.29.1984 Harrisburg, PA BL/TL 6-2/160# d8.7																								
1937	Phi N	13	19	3	4	1	0	0	1	1	0	1	.211	.250	.263	37	-2	1	.500	-1	26	0	/O-7(RF)	-0.3
1938	Phi N	1	1	0	0	0	0	0	0	0	0	0	.000	.000	.000	-99	0	0	—	0			H	0.0
Total	2	14	20	3	4	1	0	0	1	1	0	1	.200	.238	.250	30	-2	1	.500	-1	26	0	/O-7(RF)	-0.3
GORMAN, JACK John F. "Stooping Jack" B 1859 St.Louis, MO D 9.9.1889 St.Louis, MO d7.1 ▲																								
1883	StL AA	1	4	0	0	0	0	0		0			.000	.000	.000	-95	-1		.667	0	349	0	/O(LF)	-0.1
1884	KC U	8	31	3	4	1	0	0		0			.129	.129	.161	-14	-5		.579	-1	60	0	/3-4,O-4(LF)	-0.6
	Pit AA	8	27	3	4	0	1	0		1	0		.148	.179	.222	30	-2		.750	-1	120	0	/P-3,O-3(0-1-2),3-2	-0.2
Total	2	17	62	6	8	1	1	0		1	0		.129	.143	.177	0	-8		.933	-2	128	301	/O-8(5-1-2),3-6,P-3	-0.9
GORMAN, TOM Thomas BL d6.10																								
1884	KC U	25	106	22	34	4	2	0		4			.321	.345	.396	143	3		.954	-1	56	70	1-24/O(LF)	-0.1
GORYL, JOHNNY John Albert B 10.21.1933 Cumberland, RI BR/TR 5-10/175# d9.20 M2 C13																								
1957	Chi N	9	38	7	8	2	0	0	1	5-0	1	9	.211	.318	.263	59	-2	0-1	.952	-0	90	243	/3-9	-0.3
1958	Chi N	83	219	27	53	9	3	4	14	27-2	2	34	.242	.331	.365	85	-4	0-1	.931	7	105	154	3-44,2-35	0.4
1959	Chi N	25	48	1	9	3	1	1	6	5-0	0	3	.188	.264	.354	63	-3	1-1	.973	1	127	23	2-11/3-4	-0.2
1962	Min A	37	26	6	5	0	1	2	2	2-0	0	6	.192	.250	.500	93	-1	0-0	.923	-1	260	109	/2-4,S	-0.1
1963	Min A	64	150	29	43	5	3	9	24	15-4	1	29	.287	.353	.540	144	8	0-0	.958	-8	87	87	2-34,3-11/S-7	0.4
1964	Min A	58	114	9	16	0	2	0	1	10-2	1	25	.140	.216	.175	10	-14	1-0	.975	-1	93	55	2-28,3-13	-1.4
Total	6	276	595	79	134	19	10	16	48	64-8	5	106	.225	.305	.371	83	-16	2-3	.960	-2	102	73	2-112/3-81,S-8	-1.2
GOSGER, JIM James Charles B 11.6.1942 Port Huron, MI BL/TL 5-11/185# d5.4																								
1963	Bos A	19	16	3	1	0	0	0	0	3-0	0	5	.063	.211	.063	-19	-3	0-0	.818	0	168	0	/O-4(0-2-2)	-0.3
1965	Bos A	81	324	45	83	15	4	9	35	29-1	2	61	.256	.318	.410	100	0	3-1	.975	3	112	100	O-81(0-61-22)	0.0

Year	Tm Lg	G	AB	R	H	2B	3B	HR	RBI	BB-IB	HP	SO	AVG	OBP	SLG	AOPS	ABR	SB-CS	FA	FR	Rng	Thr	G at Pos	BFW
1966	Bos A	40	126	16	32	4	0	5	17	15-0	0	20	.254	.333	.405	101	0	0-1	.985	-3	93	0	O-32(0-29-4)	-0.4
	KC A	88	272	34	61	14	1	5	27	37-1	2	53	.224	.321	.338	93	-1	5-3	.994	-0	102	64	O-77(47-33-1)	-0.5
	Year	128	398	50	93	18	1	10	44	52-1	2	73	.234	.325	.359	96	-1	5-4	.991	-3	99	45	*O-109(47-62-5)	-0.9
1967	KC A	134	356	31	86	14	5	5	36	53-8	0	69	.242	.337	.351	108	5	5-7	.981	4	112	97	*O-113(54-30-40)	0.3
1968	Oak A	88	150	7	27	1	1	0	5	17-8	0	21	.180	.262	.200	44	-10	4-0	1.000	5	112	176	O-64(39-26-4)	-0.7
1969	Sea A	39	55	4	6	2	1	1	1	6-0	0	11	.109	.197	.236	21	-6	2-1	1.000	1	113	112	O-26(1-24-1)	-0.6
	NY N	10	15	0	2	2	0	0	1	1-1	0	6	.133	.188	.267	25	-1	0-0	1.000	-0	78	0	/O-5(4-1-0)	-0.2
1970	Mon N	91	274	38	72	11	2	5	37	35-3	1	35	.263	.348	.372	93	-2	5-3	1.000	1	104	149	O-71(21-50-4),1-19	-0.4
1971	Mon N	51	102	7	16	2	2	0	8	9-0	1	17	.157	.230	.216	27	-10	1-1	.952	1	96	79	O-23(20-6-1)/1-6	-1.1
1973	NY N	38	92	9	22	2	0	0	10	9-2	0	16	.239	.304	.261	60	-5	0-1	1.000	-3	85	0	O-35(21-18-0)	-0.9
1974	NY N	26	33	3	3	0	0	0	0	3-1	0	2	.091	.167	.091	-27	-6	0-0	1.000	-2	68	0	O-24(9-11-4)	-0.9
Total	10	705	1815	197	411	67	16	30	177	217-25	6	316	.226	.309	.331	83	-39	25-18	.985	7	105	91	O-555(216-291-83)/1-25	-5.7

GOSLIN, GOOSE Leon Allen B 10.16.1900 Salem, NJ D 5.15.1971 Bridgeton, NJ BL/TR 5-11.5/185# d9.16 HF1968

Year	Tm Lg	G	AB	R	H	2B	3B	HR	RBI	BB-IB	HP	SO	AVG	OBP	SLG	AOPS	ABR	SB-CS	FA	FR	Rng	Thr	G at Pos	BFW
1921	Was A	14	50	8	13	1	1	1	6	6	1	5	.260	.351	.380	91	-1	0-0	1.000	1	123	55	O-14(1-0-14)	-0.1
1922	Was A	101	358	44	116	19	7	3	53	25	3	26	.324	.373	.441	117	8	4-4	.932	-3	103	70	O-92(88-0-5)	-0.2
1923	Was A	150	600	86	180	29	**18**	9	99	40	3	53	.300	.347	.453	115	9	7-2	.957	4	97	141	*O-149(LF)	0.1
1924	†Was A	154	579	100	199	30	17	12	**129**	68	9	29	.344	.421	.516	145	39	15-14	.960	4	111	74	*O-154(LF)	2.8
1925	†Was A	150	601	116	201	34	**20**	18	113	53	6	50	.334	.394	.547	140	33	27-8	.971	14	**112**	139	*O-150(140-20-0)	3.5
1926	Was A	147	568	105	201	26	15	17	108	63	7	38	.354	.425	.542	155	45	8-8	.964	12	107	168	*O-147(86-61-0)	4.4
1927	Was A	148	581	96	194	37	15	13	120	50	5	28	.334	.392	.516	136	29	21-6	.955	-2	106	51	*O-148(146-2-0)	1.6
1928	Was A	135	456	80	173	36	10	17	102	48	3	19	**.379**	.442	.614	176	51	16-3	.962	8	109	128	*O-125(125-0-2)	4.9
1929	Was A	145	553	82	159	28	7	18	91	66	2	33	.288	.366	.461	111	9	11-3	.968	-6	98	50	*O-142(LF)	-0.7
1930	Was A	47	188	34	51	11	5	7	38	19	2	19	.271	.344	.495	110	2	3-2	.937	-4	83	61	O-47(LF)	-0.5
	StL A	101	396	81	129	25	7	30	100	48	1	35	.326	.400	.652	156	32	14-9	.973	9	111	163	*O-101(LF)	2.9
	Year	148	584	115	180	36	12	37	138	67	3	54	.308	.382	.601	142	35	17-11	.964	5	103	133	*O-148(LF)	2.4
1931	StL A	151	591	114	194	42	10	24	105	80	4	41	.328	.412	.555	147	41	9-6	.960	2	101	127	*O-151(LF)	3.2
1932	StL A	150	572	88	171	28	9	17	104	92	2	35	.299	.398	.469	117	16	12-9	.951	5	102	139	*O-149(148-1-0)/3	1.1
1933	†Was A	132	549	97	163	35	10	10	64	42	1	32	.297	.348	.452	112	7	5-2	.965	5	100	140	*O-128(3-0-125)	0.4
1934	†Det A	151	614	106	187	38	7	13	100	65	2	38	.305	.373	.453	112	11	5-4	.953	0	98	124	*O-149(145-0-4)	0.2
1935	†Det A	147	590	88	172	34	6	9	109	56	2	31	.292	.355	.415	102	1	5-4	.965	0	108	51	*O-144(128-0-18)	-0.6
1936	Det A★	147	572	122	180	33	8	24	125	85	0	50	.315	.403	.526	127	25	14-4	.955	-4	95	93	*O-144(LF)	1.3
1937	Det A	79	181	30	43	11	1	4	35	35	2	18	.238	.367	.376	86	-3	0-1	.954	-2	97	65	O-40(39-0-1)/1	-0.7
1938	Was A	38	57	6	9	3	0	2	8	8	0	5	.158	.262	.316	47	-5	0-0	1.000	0	114	0	O-13(12-0-1)	-0.5
Total	18	2287	8656	1483	2735	500	173	248	1609	949	55	585	.316	.387	.500	128	349	176-89	.960	42	103	108	*O-2187(1949-84-170)/13	23.1

GOSS, HOWIE Howard Wayne B 11.1.1934 Wewoka, OK D 7.31.1996 Reno, NV BR/TR 6-4/204# d4.10

Year	Tm Lg	G	AB	R	H	2B	3B	HR	RBI	BB-IB	HP	SO	AVG	OBP	SLG	AOPS	ABR	SB-CS	FA	FR	Rng	Thr	G at Pos	BFW
1962	Pit N	89	111	19	27	6	0	2	10	9-0	1	36	.243	.306	.351	76	-4	5-2	.985	2	115	101	O-66(47-18-6)	-0.3
1963	Hou N	133	411	37	86	18	2	9	44	31-2	0	128	.209	.264	.328	74	-14	4-6	.993	6	**111**	100	*O-123(CF)	-1.5
Total	2	222	522	56	113	24	2	11	54	40-2	1	164	.216	.273	.333	75	-18	9-8	.991	8	112	100	O-189(47-141-6)	-1.8

GOSSETT, DICK John Star B 8.21.1891 Dennison, OH D 10.6.1962 Massillon, OH BR/TR 5-11/185# d4.30

Year	Tm Lg	G	AB	R	H	2B	3B	HR	RBI	BB-IB	HP	SO	AVG	OBP	SLG	AOPS	ABR	SB-CS	FA	FR	Rng	Thr	G at Pos	BFW
1913	NY A	39	105	9	17	2	0	0	9	10	3	22	.162	.254	.181	28	-9	1	.972	-6	*66*	*116*	C-38	-1.4
1914	NY A	10	21	3	3	0	0	0	1	5	1	5	.143	.333	.143	44	-1	0	.977	-1	*87*	*54*	C-10	-0.1
Total	2	49	126	12	20	2	0	0	10	15	4	27	.159	.269	.175	31	-10	1	.973	-7	*70*	*104*	/C-48	-1.5

GOTAY, JULIO Julio Enrique (Sanchez) B 6.9.1939 Fajardo, P.R. BR/TR 6/180# d8.6

Year	Tm Lg	G	AB	R	H	2B	3B	HR	RBI	BB-IB	HP	SO	AVG	OBP	SLG	AOPS	ABR	SB-CS	FA	FR	Rng	Thr	G at Pos	BFW
1960	StL N	3	8	1	3	0	0	0	0	0-0	0	2	.375	.375	.375	98	0	1-0	.750	-1	54	0	/S-2,3	-0.1
1961	StL N	10	45	5	11	4	0	0	5	3-1	0	5	.244	.292	.333	59	-2	0-0	.804	-4	82	89	S-10	-0.6
1962	StL N	127	369	47	94	12	1	2	27	27-6	6	47	.255	.316	.309	62	-19	7-3	.956	5	106	104	*S-120/2-8,O-2(LF),3	-0.4
1963	Pit N	4	2	0	1	0	0	0	0	0-0	0	0	.500	.500	.500	188	0	0-0	.667	-0	0	0	/2	0.0
1964	Pit N	3	2	1	1	0	0	0	0	1-0	0	0	.500	.667	.500	235	1	0-0	—	0			H	0.1
1965	Cal A	40	77	6	19	4	0	1	3	4-2	0	9	.247	.284	.338	78	-2	0-0	.961	3	135	94	2-23/3-9,S	0.2
1966	Hou N	4	5	0	0	0	0	0	0	0-0	0	0	.000	.000	.000	-99	-1	0-0	1.000	0	89	0	/3	-0.1
1967	Hou N	77	234	30	66	10	2	2	15	15-1	2	30	.282	.329	.368	103	1	1-1	.971	-2	95	95	2-30,S-20/3-3	0.3
1968	Hou N	75	165	9	41	3	0	1	11	4-0	1	21	.248	.271	.285	68	-7	1-2	.982	5	93	111	2-48/3	0.1
1969	Hou N	46	81	7	21	5	0	0	9	7-1	0	13	.259	.318	.321	81	-2	2-1	.987	5	108	138	2-16/3	0.4
Total	10	389	988	106	257	38	3	6	70	61-11	9	127	.260	.309	.323	75	-31	12-7	.944	9	103	98	S-153,2-126/3-17,O-2(LF)	-0.1

GOULD, CHARLIE Charles Harvey B 8.21.1847 Cincinnati, OH D 4.10.1917 Flushing, NY BR/TR 6/172# d5.5 M2

Year	Tm Lg	G	AB	R	H	2B	3B	HR	RBI	BB-IB	HP	SO	AVG	OBP	SLG	AOPS	ABR	SB-CS	FA	FR	Rng	Thr	G at Pos	BFW
1871	Bos NA	**31**	151	38	43	9	2	2	32	3		1	.285	.299	.411	98	-1	6-2	.906	-4	62	**160**	*1-30/O(RF)	-0.2
1872	Bos NA	45	212	40	54	9	**8**	0	32	2		3	.255	.262	.373	88	-5	0-0	.933	-0	**116**	**251**	*1-44/O-2(RF)	-0.3
1874	Bal NA	33	143	19	32	6	0	0	14	2		2	.224	.234	.266	60	-6	1-0	.951	0	68	86	1-32/C	-0.4
1875	NH NA	27	109	9	29	4	1	0	8	1		2	.266	.273	.321	121	3	0-1	.946	-4	58	69	1-26/CO(RF)M	0.0
1876	Cin N	61	258	27	65	7	0	0	11	6		11	.252	.269	.279	97	2		.939	1	122	114	*1-61/P-2,M	0.0
1877	Cin N	24	91	5	25	2	1	0	13	5		5	.275	.313	.319	112	2		.922	-1	124	99	1-24/O(LF)	0.0
Total	4 NA	136	615	106	158	28	11	2	86	8		8	.257	.266	.348	90	-9	7-3	.000	-7	81	154	1-132/O-4(RF),C-2	-0.9
Total	2	85	349	32	90	9	1	0	24	11		16	.258	.281	.289	101	4		.934	0	123	110	/1-85,P-2,O(LF)	0.0

GOULISH, NICK Nicholas Edward B 11.13.1917 Punxsutawney, PA D 5.15.1984 Youngstown, OH BL/TL 6-1/179# d4.19

Year	Tm Lg	G	AB	R	H	2B	3B	HR	RBI	BB-IB	HP	SO	AVG	OBP	SLG	AOPS	ABR	SB-CS	FA	FR	Rng	Thr	G at Pos	BFW
1944	Phi N	1	1	0	0	0	0	0	0	0	0	0	.000	.000	.000	-99	0	0	—	0			H	0.0
1945	Phi N	13	11	4	3	0	0	0	2	1	0	3	.273	.333	.273	72	0	0	1.000	-0	69	0	/O-2(1-0-1)	-0.1
Total	2	14	12	4	3	0	0	0	2	1	0	3	.250	.308	.250	58	0	0	1.000	-0	69	0	/O-2(1-0-1)	-0.1

GOUZZIE, CLAUDE Claude B 1873 , France D 9.21.1907 Denver, CO BR/TR 5-9/170# d7.22

Year	Tm Lg	G	AB	R	H	2B	3B	HR	RBI	BB-IB	HP	SO	AVG	OBP	SLG	AOPS	ABR	SB-CS	FA	FR	Rng	Thr	G at Pos	BFW
1903	StL A	1	1	0	0	0	0	0	0	0	0		.000	.000	.000	-99	0	0	1.000	0	149	0	/2	0.0

GOWDY, HANK Henry Morgan B 8.24.1889 Columbus, OH D 8.1.1966 Columbus, OH BR/TR 6-2/182# d9.13 Mil 1917-19 M1 C18

Year	Tm Lg	G	AB	R	H	2B	3B	HR	RBI	BB-IB	HP	SO	AVG	OBP	SLG	AOPS	ABR	SB-CS	FA	FR	Rng	Thr	G at Pos	BFW
1910	NY N	7	14	1	3	1	0	0	2	2	0	3	.214	.313	.286	75	0	1	.943	0	152	52	/1-5	0.0
1911	NY N	4	4	1	1	1	0	0	0	2	0	0	.250	.500	.500	175	1	0	1.000	-0	0	0	/1-2	0.0
	Bos N	29	97	9	28	4	2	0	16	4	1	19	.289	.324	.371	87	-2	2	.966	-2	88	56	1-26/C	-0.4
	Year	33	101	10	29	5	2	0	16	6	1	19	.287	.333	.376	92	-1	2	.969	-2	83	53	1-28/C	-0.4
1912	Bos N	44	96	16	26	6	1	3	10	16	2	13	.271	.386	.448	126	4	3	.926	-3	*91*	*108*	C-22/1-7	0.3
1913	Bos N	3	5	0	3	1	0	0	2	3	0	2	.600	.750	.800	336	2	0	1.000	-1	108	0	/C-2	0.2
1914	†Bos N	128	366	42	89	17	6	3	46	48	4	40	.243	.337	.347	104	3	14	.968	3	***133***	*93*	*C-115/1-9	1.6
1915	Bos N	118	316	27	78	15	3	2	30	41	3	34	.247	.339	.332	108	5	10-4	.974	6	***138***	*104*	*C-114	2.3
1916	Bos N	118	349	32	88	14	1	0	34	24	6	33	.252	.311	.307	94	-2	8	.980	15	**171**	93	*C-116	2.6
1917	Bos N	49	154	12	33	7	0	0	14	15	1	13	.214	.288	.260	73	-4	2	.969	1	*110*	*120*	C-49	0.1
1919	Bos N	78	219	18	61	8	1	1	22	19	1	16	.279	.339	.338	108	3	5	.977	4	*101*	*113*	C-74/1	1.3
1920	Bos N	80	214	14	52	11	2	0	18	20	2	15	.243	.314	.313	84	-4	6-1	.980	10	*114*	*130*	C-74	1.3
1921	Bos N	64	164	17	49	7	2	2	17	16	2	11	.299	.368	.402	110	3	2-0	.981	-0	*110*	*107*	C-53	0.6
1922	Bos N	92	221	23	70	11	1	1	27	24	3	13	.317	.391	.389	107	4	2-1	.971	-0	*99*	*131*	C-72/1	0.7
1923	Bos N	23	48	5	6	1	1	0	5	15	2	5	.125	.354	.188	48	-3	1-1	.982	-1	*80*	*98*	C-15	-0.3
	†NY N	53	122	13	40	6	3	1	18	21	0	9	.328	.427	.451	133	7	2-0	.986	-3	*149*	*59*	C-43	0.7
	Year	76	170	18	46	7	4	1	23	36	2	14	.271	.404	.376	109	5	3-1	.985	-4	*128*	*71*	C-58	0.4
1924	†NY N	87	191	25	62	9	1	4	37	26	2	11	.325	.411	.445	133	10	1-0	.982	1	*110*	*89*	C-78	1.6
1925	NY N	47	114	14	37	4	3	3	19	12	0	7	.325	.389	.491	128	5	0-0	1.000	1	*92*	*112*	C-41	0.7
1929	Bos N	10	16	1	7	0	0	0	3	0	0	2	.438	.438	.438	122	1	0	1.000	0	*101*	*68*	/C-9	0.1
1930	Bos N	16	25	0	5	1	0	0	2	3	1	1	.200	.310	.240	37	-2	0	.972	0	*100*	*85*	C-15	-0.2
Total	17	1050	2735	270	738	124	27	21	322	311	30	247	.270	.351	.358	105	31	59-7	.975	31	*124*	*104*	C-893/1-51	13.2

GRABARKEWITZ, BILLY Billy Cordell B 1.18.1946 Lockhart, TX BR/TR 5-10/170# d4.22

Year	Tm Lg	G	AB	R	H	2B	3B	HR	RBI	BB-IB	HP	SO	AVG	OBP	SLG	AOPS	ABR	SB-CS	FA	FR	Rng	Thr	G at Pos	BFW
1969	LA N	34	65	4	6	1	1	0	5	4-1	0	19	.092	.145	.138	-22	-11	1-0	.954	-6	87	46	S-18/3-6,2-3	-1.6
1970	LA N★	156	529	92	153	20	8	17	84	95-8	6	149	.289	.399	.454	135	30	19-9	.959	-10	103	116	3-97,S-50,2-20	2.6
1971	LA N	44	71	9	16	5	0	0	6	19-0	0	16	.225	.389	.296	102	2	1-2	1.000	4	110	127	2-13,3-10/S	0.7
1972	LA N	53	144	17	24	4	0	4	16	18-1	2	53	.167	.265	.278	57	-8	3-0	.902	-3	88	32	3-24,2-19/S-2	-1.0

Year	Tm Lg	G	AB	R	H	2B	3B	HR	RBI	BB-IB	HP	SO	AVG	OBP	SLG	AOPS	ABR	SB-CS	FA	FR	Rng	Thr	G at Pos	BFW
1973	Cal A	61	129	27	21	6	1	3	9	28-0	1	27	.163	.316	.295	79	-3	2-2	.965	-3	94	95	2-18,3-12/SO(LF)D	-0.5
	Phi N	25	66	12	19	2	0	2	7	12-0	0	18	.288	.397	.409	121	2	3-1	.960	3	105	134	2-20/3-3,O(RF)	0.6
1974	Phi N	34	30	7	4	0	0	1	2	5-0	0	10	.133	.257	.233	36	-3	3-1	1.000	-0	93	0	/O-5(LF),3	-0.3
	Chi N	53	125	21	31	3	2	1	12	21-2	1	28	.248	.358	.328	90	-1	1-2	.954	-2	100	34	2-45/S-7,3-6	-0.1
	Year	87	155	28	35	3	2	2	14	26-2	1	38	.226	.339	.310	80	-4	4-3	.954	-3	100	34	2-45/3-7,S-7,O-5(LF)	-0.4
1975	Oak A	6	2	0	0	0	0	0	0	0-0	0	1	.000	.000	.000	-99	-1	0-0	.833	0	107	0	/2-4,D	0.0
Total	7	466	1161	189	274	41	12	28	141	202-12	10	321	.236	.351	.364	101	7	33-17	.952	-17	101	105	3-159,2-142/S-79,O-7(6-0-1),D-6	0.4
GRABER, ROD Rodney Blaine B 6.20.1930 Massillon, OH BL/TL 5-11/175# d9.9																								
1958	Cle A	4	8	0	1	0	0	0	0	1-0	0	2	.125	.222	.125	-2	-1	0-0	1.000	0	119	0	/O-2(CF)	-0.1
GRABOWSKI, JASON Jason William B 5.24.1976 New Haven, CT BL/TR 6-3/200# d9.22																								
2002	Oak A	4	8	3	3	1	1	0	1	3-0	0	1	.375	.545	.750	239	2	0-0	1.000	-0	96	0	/O-4(LF)	0.1
2003	Oak A	8	8	0	0	0	0	0	0	1-0	0	5	.000	.111	.000	-66	-2	0-0	1.000	0	185	0	/O-3(RF),3D	-0.2
Total	2	12	16	3	3	1	1	0	1	4-0	0	6	.188	.350	.375	92	0	0-0	1.000	-0	114	0	/O-7(4-0-3),D3	-0.1
GRABOWSKI, JOHNNY John Patrick "Nig" B 1.7.1900 Ware, MA D 5.23.1946 Albany, NY BR/TR 5-10/185# d7.11																								
1924	Chi A	20	56	10	14	3	0	0	3	2	0	4	.250	.276	.304	51	-4	0-0	.972	1	*77*	*158*	C-19	-0.3
1925	Chi A	21	46	5	14	4	1	0	10	2	0	4	.304	.333	.435	99	0	0-1	.983	0	*172*	*85*	C-21	0.1
1926	Chi A	48	122	6	32	1	1	1	11	4	0	15	.262	.286	.311	58	-8	0-1	.973	-1	*129*	*91*	C-38/1	-0.8
1927	†NY A	70	195	29	54	2	4	0	25	20	2	15	.277	.350	.328	79	-6	0-0	.984	2	*104*	*67*	C-68	-0.1
1928	NY A	75	202	21	48	7	1	1	21	10	0	21	.238	.274	.297	51	-15	0-0	.987	0	*94*	*81*	C-75	-1.0
1929	NY A	22	59	4	12	1	0	0	2	3	0	6	.203	.242	.220	21	-7	1-0	.943	-1	*112*	*71*	C-22	-0.6
1931	Det A	40	136	9	32	7	1	1	14	6	0	19	.235	.268	.324	53	-10	0-0	.984	0	*76*	*123*	C-39	-0.7
Total	7	296	816	84	206	25	8	3	86	47	2	84	.252	.295	.314	60	-50	1-2	.979	1	*103*	*91*	C-282/1	-3.4
GRACE, JOE Joseph Laverne B 1.5.1914 Gorham, IL D 9.18.1969 Murphysboro, IL BL/TR 6-1/180# d9.24 Mil 1942-45																								
1938	StL A	12	47	7	16	1	0	0	4	2	0	3	.340	.367	.362	83	-1	0-1	.933	-1	75	126	O-12(RF)	-0.3
1939	StL A	74	207	35	63	11	2	3	22	19	0	24	.304	.363	.420	98	-1	3-2	.968	1	82	265	O-53(10-22-21)	-0.2
1940	StL A	80	229	45	59	14	2	5	25	26	1	23	.258	.336	.402	88	-4	2-2	.958	-2	89	153	O-51(3-0-48),C-12	-0.8
1941	StL A	115	362	53	112	17	4	6	60	57	5	31	.309	.410	.428	118	12	1-3	.983	0	95	157	O-88(RF)/C-9	0.6
1946	StL A	48	161	21	37	7	2	1	13	16	2	20	.230	.307	.317	71	-6	1-3	.967	1	99	159	O-43(RF)	-0.7
	Was A	77	321	39	97	17	4	2	31	24	4	19	.302	.358	.399	118	7	1-4	.959	-1	101	65	O-74(60-0-14)	-0.1
	Year	125	482	60	134	24	6	3	44	40	6	39	.278	.341	.371	101	0	2-7	.962	0	100	96	*O-117(60-0-57)	-0.8
1947	Was A	78	234	25	58	9	4	3	17	35	1	15	.248	.348	.359	99	0	1-2	.976	2	109	87	O-67(56-3-8)	-0.2
Total	6	484	1561	225	442	76	18	20	172	179	13	135	.283	.362	.393	102	7	9-17	.969	1	97	135	O-388(129-25-234)/C-21	-1.7
GRACE, MARK Mark Eugene B 6.28.1964 Winston-Salem, NC BL/TL 6-2/190# d5.2																								
1988	Chi N	134	486	65	144	23	4	7	57	60-5	0	43	.296	.371	.403	118	13	3-3	.987	-4	92	93	*1-133	-0.1
1989	†Chi N	142	510	74	160	28	3	13	79	80-13	0	42	.314	.405	.457	136	28	14-7	.996	12	**128**	95	*1-142	3.2
1990	Chi N	157	589	72	182	32	1	9	82	59-5	5	54	.309	.372	.413	109	10	15-6	.992	**25**	**156**	103	*1-153	2.6
1991	Chi N	**160**	619	87	169	28	5	8	58	70-7	3	53	.273	.346	.373	99	1	3-4	.995	17	**134**	95	*1-160	0.5
1992	Chi N	158	603	72	185	37	5	9	79	72-8	4	36	.307	.380	.430	127	24	6-1	.998	6	112	102	*1-157	2.1
1993	Chi N★	155	594	86	193	39	4	14	98	71-14	1	32	.325	.393	.475	135	32	8-4	.997	1	101	112	*1-154	1.9
1994	Chi N	106	403	55	120	23	3	6	44	48-5	0	41	.298	.370	.414	106	5	0-1	.993	-1	98	108	*1-103	-0.6
1995	Chi N★	143	552	97	180	**51**	3	16	92	65-9	2	46	.326	.395	.516	142	36	6-2	.995	1	102	81	*1-143	2.3
1996	Chi N	142	547	88	181	39	1	9	75	62-8	1	41	.331	.396	.455	122	20	2-3	.997	0	100	110	*1-141	0.7
1997	Chi N★	151	555	87	177	32	5	13	78	88-3	2	45	.319	.409	.465	127	26	2-4	.995	5	108	79	*1-148	1.5
1998	†Chi N	158	595	92	184	39	3	17	89	93-8	3	56	.309	.401	.471	125	26	4-7	.994	0	99	63	*1-156	1.0
1999	Chi N	161	593	107	183	44	5	16	91	83-4	2	44	.309	.390	.481	122	23	3-4	.994	-4	91	90	*1-160	0.3
2000	Chi N	143	510	75	143	41	1	11	82	95-11	6	28	.280	.394	.429	112	15	1-2	**.997**	5	109	87	*1-140	0.6
2001	†Ari N	145	476	66	142	31	2	15	78	67-6	4	36	.298	.386	.466	113	12	1-0	.995	-4	81	112	*1-135	-0.4
2002	†Ari N	124	298	43	75	19	0	7	48	46-6	1	30	.252	.351	.386	90	-4	2-0	.990	-5	71	101	1-98/P	-1.6
2003	Ari N	66	135	13	27	5	0	3	16	16-2	0	15	.200	.279	.304	49	-10	0-0	.993	-0	92	97	1-39/D	-1.3
Total	16	2245	8065	1179	2445	511	45	173	1146	1075-114	34	642	.303	.383	.442	118	257	70-48	.995	54	107	95	*1-2162/DP	12.7
GRACE, MIKE Michael Lee B 6.14.1956 Pontiac, MI BR/TR 6/175# d4.18																								
1978	Cin N	5	3	0	0	0	0	0	0	0-0	0	2	.000	.000	.000	-99	-1	0-0	1.000	0	219	0	/3-2	0.0
GRACE, EARL Robert Earl B 2.24.1907 Barlow, KY D 12.22.1980 Phoenix, AZ BL/TR 6/175# d4.23																								
1929	Chi N	27	80	7	20	1	0	2	17	9	1	7	.250	.333	.338	67	-4	0	1.000	3	*133*	*113*	C-27	0.0
1931	Chi N	7	9	2	1	0	0	0	1	4	0	1	.111	.385	.111	39	0	0	1.000	0	*78*	*0*	/C-2	0.0
	Pit N	47	150	8	42	6	1	1	20	13	0	5	.280	.337	.353	87	-3	0	.974	-1	*99*	*82*	C-45	-0.1
	Year	54	159	10	43	6	1	1	21	17	0	6	.270	.341	.340	84	-3	0	.976	-1	*98*	*78*	C-47	-0.1
1932	Pit N	115	390	41	107	17	5	8	55	14	3	23	.274	.305	.405	91	-7	0	**.998**	-3	*83*	*68*	*C-114	-0.3
1933	Pit N	93	291	22	84	13	1	3	44	26	1	23	.289	.349	.371	106	3	0	.980	-1	*78*	*72*	C-88	0.8
1934	Pit N	95	289	27	78	17	1	4	24	20	0	19	.270	.317	.377	83	-7	0	.982	-7	*67*	**12**	C-83/1	-0.9
1935	Pit N	77	224	19	59	8	1	3	29	32	0	17	.263	.355	.348	87	-3	1	.990	4	*83*	*103*	C-69	0.5
1936	Phi N	86	221	24	55	11	0	4	32	34	1	20	.249	.352	.353	82	-4	0	.976	-3	*94*	*71*	C-65	-0.4
1937	Phi N	80	223	19	47	10	1	6	29	33	0	15	.211	.313	.345	73	-8	0	.990	-2	*136*	*69*	C-64	-0.6
Total	8	627	1877	169	493	83	10	31	251	185	6	130	.263	.331	.367	86	-33	1	.987	-10	*91*	*65*	C-557/1	-1.0
GRADY, JOHN John J. B 6.18.1860 Lowell, MA D 7.15.1893 Lowell, MA 5-7/150# d5.10																								
1884	Alt U	9	36	5	11	3	0	0		2			.306	.342	.389	119	0		.909	-1	121	27	/1-8,O(CF)	-0.2
GRADY, MIKE Michael William B 12.23.1869 Kennett Square, PA D 12.3.1943 Kennett Square, PA BR/TR 5-11/190# d4.24 OF Total (14-LF 7-CF 29-RF)																								
1894	Phi N	61	190	45	69	13	8	0	40	14	7	13	.363	.427	.516	129	9	3	.878	-11	*91*	*82*	C-45,1-11/O-2(1-0-1)	0.1
1895	Phi N	46	123	21	40	3	1	1	23	14	3	8	.325	.407	.390	106	2	5	.926	-9	*93*	*37*	C-38/O-5(3-0-2),31	-0.4
1896	Phi N	72	242	49	77	20	7	1	44	16	9	19	.318	.382	.471	126	9	10	.942	-6	*104*	*104*	C-61/3-7	0.7
1897	Phi N	4	13	1	2	0	0	0	0	1	0		.154	.214	.154	-2	-2	0	1.000	0	*111*	*124*	/C-3	-0.1
	StL N	84	326	49	91	11	3	8	57	26	10		.279	.351	.405	101	0	7	.974	-1	105	106	1-84/O(RF)	0.0
	Year	88	339	50	93	11	3	8	57	27	10		.274	.346	.395	97	-2	7	.974	-0	105	106	1-84/C-3,O(RF)	-0.1
1898	NY N	93	287	64	85	19	5	3	49	38	11		.296	.399	.429	142	18	20	.944	-6	*91*	*109*	C-57,O-30(7-7-16)/1-7,S-3	1.4
1899	NY N	87	315	49	106	18	8	2	54	29	7		.337	.405	.463	143	19	20	.940	-8	*86*	*116*	C-44,3-35/O-4(RF),1-4	1.4
1900	NY N	83	251	36	55	8	4	0	27	34	8		.219	.331	.283	74	-7	9	.932	-4	*110*	*82*	C-41,1-12,S-11/3-7,O-5(RF),2-2	-0.7
1901	Was A	94	347	57	99	17	10	9	56	27	8		.285	.351	.470	128	12	14	.975	8	173	104	1-59,C-30/O-3(LF)	1.9
1904	StL N	101	323	44	101	15	11	5	43	31	2		.313	.376	.474	169	26	6	.955	-18	*81*	*65*	C-77,1-11/2-3,3	1.6
1905	StL N	100	311	41	89	20	7	4	41	33	3		.286	.360	.434	141	16	15	.956	-11	*84*	*85*	C-71,1-20	1.2
1906	StL N	97	280	33	70	11	3	3	27	48	5		.250	.369	.343	127	12	5	.983	-11	*72*	*97*	C-60,1-38	0.6
Total	11	922	3008	489	884	155	67	36	461	311	73	40	.294	.374	.426	127	114	114	.946	-74	*91*	*87*	C-527,1-247/3-51,O-50R,S-14,2-5	7.7
GRAFF, FRED Frederick Gottleib B 8.25.1889 Canton, OH D 10.4.1979 Chattanooga, TN BR/TR 5-10.5/164# d5.14																								
1913	StL A	4	5	1	2	1	0	0	2	3	0	3	.400	.625	.600	266	2	0	1.000	-0	109	363	/3-4	0.2
GRAFF, LOUIS Louis George "Chappie" B 7.25.1866 Philadelphia, PA D 4.16.1955 Bryn Mawr, PA TR d6.23																								
1890	Syr AA	1	5	0	2	1	0	0	3	0	0		.400	.400	.600	217	1	0	.333	-2	*75*	*0*	/C	-0.1
GRAFF, MILT Milton Edward B 12.30.1930 Jefferson Center, PA BL/TR 5-7.5/158# d4.16 C1																								
1957	KC A	56	155	16	28	4	3	0	10	15-0	2	10	.181	.260	.245	39	-13	2-5	.988	-1	102	105	2-53	-1.3
1958	KC A	5	1	0	0	0	0	0	0	0-0	0	0	.000	.000	.000	-98	0	0-0	1.000	-0	0	0	/2	0.0
Total	2	61	156	16	28	4	3	0	10	15-0	2	10	.179	.259	.244	38	-13	2-5	.988	-1	102	104	/2-54	-1.3
GRAFFANINO, TONY Anthony Joseph B 6.6.1972 Amityville, NY BR/TR 6-1/175# d4.19																								
1996	Atl N	22	46	7	8	1	1	0	2	4-0	1	13	.174	.250	.239	30	-5	0-0	.969	1	110	121	2-18	-0.3
1997	†Atl N	104	186	33	48	9	1	8	20	26-1	1	46	.258	.344	.446	105	2	6-4	.982	7	118	97	2-75/3-2,S-2,1	1.0
1998	†Atl N	105	289	32	61	14	1	5	22	24-0	2	68	.211	.275	.318	56	-19	1-4	.971	13	114	99	2-93/S-2,3	-0.4
1999	TB A	39	130	20	41	9	4	2	19	9-0	1	22	.315	.364	.492	115	3	3-2	.990	8	129	108	2-17,S-17/3	1.1
2000	TB A	13	20	8	6	1	0	0	1	1-0	1	2	.300	.364	.350	83	0	0-0	1.000	2	114	127	/2-6,3-3,S	0.2

Year	Tm Lg	G	AB	R	H	2B	3B	HR	RBI	BB-IB	HP	SO	AVG	OBP	SLG	AOPS	ABR	SB-CS	FA	FR	Rng	Thr	G at Pos	BFW
	†Chi A	57	148	25	40	5	1	2	16	21-0	1	25	.270	.363	.358	83	-3	7-4	.966	6	108	127	S-21,2-19,3-12/D-3	0.5
	Year	70	168	33	46	6	1	2	17	22-0	2	27	.274	.363	.357	83	-4	7-4	.973	8	124	119	2-25,S-22,3-15/D-3	0.7
2001	Chi A	74	145	23	44	9	0	2	15	16-0	1	29	.303	.370	.407	103	1	4-1	.923	4	106	28	3-38,2-20/S-5,O-3(LF),1D	0.7
2002	Chi A	70	229	35	60	12	4	6	31	22-1	2	38	.262	.329	.428	98	-1	2-1	.952	2	101	93	3-35,2-25/S-8	0.3
2003	Chi A	90	250	51	65	15	3	7	23	24-1	3	37	.260	.331	.428	98	-1	8-0	.968	9	106	105	S-36,2-29,3-20/1-2,D-3	1.2
Total	8	574	1443	234	373	75	15	32	149	147-3	13	280	.258	.330	.398	89	-23	31-16	.975	51	116	113	2-302,3-112/S-92,D-9,1-4,O-3(LF)	4.3
GRAHAM, MOONLIGHT Archibald Wright B 11.9.1876 Fayetteville, NC D 8.25.1965 Chisholm, MN BL/TR 5-10.5/170# d6.29																								
1905	NY N	1	0	0	0	0	0	0	0	0	0		—	—	—	—	0	0	—	0	0	0	/O(RF)	0.0
GRAHAM, SKINNY Arthur William B 8.12.1909 Somerville, MA D 7.10.1967 Cambridge, MA BL/TR 5-7/162# d9.14																								
1934	Bos A	13	47	7	11	2	1	0	3	6	0	13	.234	.321	.319	61	-3	2-2	1.000	-1	83	113	O-13(0-4-9)	-0.4
1935	Bos A	8	10	1	3	0	0	0	1	1	0	3	.300	.364	.300	69	0	1-0	1.000	-0	89	0	/O-2(RF)	0.0
Total	2	21	57	8	14	2	1	0	4	7	0	16	.246	.328	.316	62	-3	3-2	1.000	-1	84	103	/O-15(0-4-11)	-0.4
GRAHAM, BERNIE Bernard W. B 1860 Beloit, WI D 10.30.1886 Mobile, AL BL d7.11																								
1884	CP U	1	5	2	1	0	0	0		0			.200	.200	.200	22	-1		1.000	-0	0	0	/O(LF)	-0.1
	Bal U	41	167	21	45	11	0	0		2			.269	.278	.335	77	-9		.814	-1	94	115	O-40(0-25-15)/1	-1.1
	Year	42	172	23	46	11	0	0		2			.267	.276	.331	76	-10		.816	-2	92	112	O-41(1-25-15)/1	-1.2
GRAHAM, BERT Bert "B.G." B 4.3.1886 Tilton, IL D 6.19.1971 Cottonwood, AZ BB/TR 5-11.5/187# d9.9																								
1910	StL A	8	26	1	3	2	1	0	5	1	0		.115	.148	.269	32	-2	0	.964	1	146	0	/1-5,2-2	-0.1
GRAHAM, CHARLIE Charles Henry B 4.24.1878 Santa Clara, CA D 8.29.1948 San Francisco, CA BR/TR 6/190# d4.16																								
1906	Bos A	30	90	10	21	1	0	1	12	10	3		.233	.330	.278	91	0	1	.963	2	*88*	*128*	C-27	0.5
GRAHAM, DAN Daniel Jay B 7.19.1954 Ray, AZ BL/TR 6-1/205# d6.8																								
1979	Min A	2	4	0	0	0	0	0	0	0-0	0	0	.000	.000	.000	-96	-1	0-0	—	0			/D	-0.1
1980	Bal A	86	266	32	74	7	1	15	54	14-0	0	40	.278	.310	.481	116	4	0-0	.981	1	106	99	C-73/3-9,O(RF)D	0.8
1981	Bal A	55	142	7	25	3	0	2	11	13-1	0	32	.176	.244	.239	40	-11	0-0	.975	-3	93	153	C-40/3-4,D-6	-1.4
Total	3	143	412	39	99	10	1	17	65	27-1	0	72	.240	.284	.393	88	-8	0-0	.979	-2	102	116	C-113/3-13,D-9,O(RF)	-0.7
GRAHAM, TINY Dawson Francis B 9.9.1892 Nashville, TN D 12.29.1962 Nashville, TN BR/TR 6-2/185# d8.30																								
1914	Cin N	25	61	5	14	1	0	0	3	3	0	10	.230	.266	.246	51	-4	1	.961	-2	87	142	1-25	-0.6
GRAHAM, PEACHES George Frederick B 3.23.1877 Aledo, IL D 7.25.1939 Long Beach, CA BR/TR 5-9/180# d9.14 s-Jack																								
1902	Cle A	2	6	0	2	0	0	0	1	1	0		.333	.429	.333	118	0	0	1.000	0	123	0	/2	0.0
1903	Chi N	1	2	0	0	0	0	0	0	0	0		.000	.000	.000	-99	0	0	1.000	0	220	0	/P	0.0
1908	Bos N	75	215	22	59	5	0	0	22	23	6		.274	.361	.298	112	5	4	.955	-5	*91*	*99*	C-62/2-5	0.6
1909	Bos N	92	267	27	64	6	3	0	17	24	0		.240	.302	.285	79	-7	7	.948	-5	*83*	*113*	C-76/O-6(1-0-3),S3	-0.5
1910	Bos N	110	291	31	82	13	2	0	21	33	2	15	.282	.359	.340	100	1	5	.966	-10	*82*	*111*	C-87/3-2,1O(RF)	-0.1
1911	Bos N	33	88	7	24	6	1	0	12	14	0	5	.273	.373	.364	98	0	2	.912	-7	*75*	*97*	C-26	-0.4
	Chi N	36	71	6	17	3	0	0	8	11	3	8	.239	.365	.282	82	-1	2	.972	0	*149*	*89*	C-28	0.1
	Year	69	159	13	41	9	1	0	20	25	3	13	.258	.369	.327	92	0	4	.937	-7	*108*	*93*	C-54	-0.3
1912	Phi N	24	59	6	17	1	0	1	4	8	0	5	.288	.373	.356	94	0	1	.944	-2	*88*	*107*	C-19	-0.1
Total	7	373	999	99	265	34	6	1	85	114	11	33	.265	.347	.314	95	-2	21	.953	-29	*89*	*106*	C-298/O-7(1-0-4),2-6,3-3,1SP	-0.4
GRAHAM, BARNEY James B Philadelphia, PA d9.4																								
1889	Phi AA	4	18	0	3	0	0	0	0	0	0	0	.167	.167	.167	-5	-3	0	.933	1	155	151	/3-4	-0.1
GRAHAM, JACK John Bernard B 12.24.1916 Minneapolis, MN D 12.30.1998 Los Alamitos, CA BL/TL 6-2/200# d4.16 f-Peaches																								
1946	Bro N	2	5	0	1	0	0	0	0	0	0	0	.200	.200	.200	14	-1	0	1.000	0	104	0	/1-2	-0.1
	NY N	100	270	34	59	6	4	14	47	23	1	37	.219	.282	.426	99	-3	1	.949	-1	97	125	O-62(1-0-60)/1-7	-0.6
	Year	102	275	34	60	6	4	14	47	23	1	37	.218	.281	.422	97	-4	1	.949	-1	97	125	O-62(1-0-60)/1-9	-0.7
1949	StL A	137	500	71	119	22	1	24	79	61	4	62	.238	.326	.430	95	-6	0-1	.984	-6	88	77	*1-136	-1.7
Total	2	239	775	105	179	28	5	38	126	84	5	99	.231	.310	.427	96	-10	1-1	.985	-6	88	75	1-145/O-62(1-0-60)	-2.4
GRAHAM, LEE Lee Willard B 9.22.1959 Summerfield, FL BL/TL 5-10/170# d9.3																								
1983	Bos A	5	6	2	0	0	0	0	1	0-0	0	0	.000	.000	.000	-93	-2	0-1	1.000	1	125	923	/O-3(0-2-1)	-0.1
GRAHAM, ROY Roy Vincent B 2.22.1895 San Francisco, CA D 4.26.1933 Manila, Philippines BR/TR 5-10.5/175# d5.28																								
1922	Chi A	5	3	0	0	0	0	0	0	0	2	0	.000	.400	.000	12	0	0-0	1.000	-0	*0*	*0*	/C-3	0.0
1923	Chi A	36	82	3	16	2	0	0	6	9	2	6	.195	.290	.220	36	-7	0-0	.949	-5	*71*	*79*	C-33	-1.1
Total	2	41	85	3	16	2	0	0	6	9	4	6	.188	.296	.212	35	-7	0-0	.950	-5	*69*	*77*	/C-36	-1.1
GRAHAM, WAYNE Wayne Leon B 4.6.1937 Yoakum, TX BR/TR 6/200# d4.10																								
1963	Phi N	10	22	1	4	0	0	0	0	3-0	0	1	.182	.280	.182	36	-2	0-0	.857	-1	80	0	/O-6(LF)	-0.3
1964	NY N	20	33	1	3	1	0	0	0	0-0	0	5	.091	.091	.121	-42	-6	0-0	1.000	-1	81	0	3-11	-0.8
Total	2	30	55	2	7	1	0	0	0	3-0	0	6	.127	.172	.145	-9	-8	0-0	1.000	-2	81	0	/3-11,O-6(LF)	-1.1
GRAMMAS, ALEX Alexander Peter B 4.3.1926 Birmingham, AL BR/TR 6/178# d4.13 M3 C26																								
1954	StL N	142	401	57	106	17	4	2	29	40	5	29	.264	.335	.342	77	-13	6-1	.966	22	**113**	118	*S-142/3	2.1
1955	StL N	128	366	32	88	19	2	3	25	33-9	3	36	.240	.308	.328	69	-16	4-1	.968	4	98	102	*S-126	-0.1
1956	StL N	6	12	1	3	0	0	0	1	1-0	0	2	.250	.308	.250	52	-1	0-0	1.000	0	117	60	/S-5	0.0
	Cin N	77	140	17	34	11	0	0	16	16-1	1	18	.243	.323	.321	70	-5	0-1	.968	-0	101	117	3-58,S-12/2-5	-0.5
	Year	83	152	18	37	11	0	0	17	17-1	1	20	.243	.322	.316	69	-6	0-1	.968	0	101	117	3-58,S-17/2-5	-0.5
1957	Cin N	73	99	14	30	4	0	0	8	10-0	0	6	.303	.364	.343	86	-1	1-3	.966	-0	93	39	S-42,2-20/3-9	-0.1
1958	Cin N	105	216	25	47	8	0	0	12	34-1	2	24	.218	.329	.255	54	-13	2-2	.993	-2	100	116	S-61,3-38,2-14	-1.2
1959	StL N	131	368	43	99	14	2	3	30	38-6	1	26	.269	.337	.342	77	-11	3-3	.964	6	102	104	*S-130	0.5
1960	StL N	102	196	20	48	4	1	4	17	12-1	1	15	.245	.290	.337	66	-9	0-1	.972	13	100	75	S-46,2-38,3-13	0.7
1961	StL N	89	170	23	36	10	1	0	21	19-3	1	21	.212	.293	.282	49	-12	0-1	.960	10	108	104	S-65,2-18/3-3	0.3
1962	StL N	21	18	0	2	0	0	0	1	1-1	0	6	.111	.158	.111	-24	-3	0-0	.933	-0	108	65	S-16/2-2	-0.3
	Chi N	23	60	3	14	3	0	0	3	2-0	1	7	.233	.270	.283	47	-4	1-1	1.000	2	113	133	S-13/2-3,3	-0.1
	Year	44	78	3	16	3	0	0	4	3-1	1	13	.205	.244	.244	29	-8	1-1	.978	2	112	113	S-29/2-5,3	-0.4
1963	Chi N	16	27	1	5	0	0	0	0	0-0	0	3	.185	.185	.185	7	-3	0-0	.955	-2	85	34	S-13	-0.5
Total	10	913	2073	236	512	90	10	12	163	206-22	15	193	.247	.318	.317	67	-91	17-14	.968	54	104	104	S-671,3-123,2-100	0.8
GRANEY, JACK John Gladstone B 6.10.1886 St.Thomas, ON, CAN D 4.20.1978 Louisiana, MO BL/TL 5-9/180# d4.30																								
1908	Cle A	2	0	0	0	0	0	0	0	0	0		—	—	—	—	0	0	—	-0	0	0	/P-2	0.0
1910	Cle A	116	454	62	107	13	9	1	31	37	0		.236	.293	.311	88	-7	18	.949	-2	99	85	*O-114(53-43-18)	-1.8
1911	Cle A	146	527	84	142	25	5	1	45	66	11		.269	.363	.342	96	0	21	.927	3	105	104	*O-142(139-1-2)	-0.3
1912	Cle A	78	264	44	64	13	2	0	20	50	2		.242	.367	.307	90	0	9	.958	4	105	119	O-75(LF)	0.1
1913	Cle A	148	517	56	138	18	12	3	68	48	5	55	.267	.335	.366	102	0	27	.970	0	103	81	*O-148(144-0-4)	-0.7
1914	Cle A	130	460	63	122	17	10	1	39	67	3	46	.265	.362	.352	111	8	20-18	.935	5	118	86	*O-127(LF)	0.6
1915	Cle A	116	404	42	105	20	7	1	56	59	2	29	.260	.357	.351	110	7	12-15	.972	5	105	117	*O-115(107-1-8)	0.3
1916	Cle A	155	589	106	142	**41**	14	5	54	102	2	72	.241	.355	.384	115	14	10	.959	1	97	109	*O-154(LF)	0.9
1917	Cle A	146	535	87	122	29	7	3	35	**94**	4	49	.228	.348	.325	98	3	16	.959	-11	92	65	*O-145(LF)	-1.6
1918	Cle A	70	177	27	42	7	4	0	9	28	3	13	.237	.351	.322	94	0	3	.975	-4	94	37	O-45(44-0-1)	-0.6
1919	Cle A	128	461	79	108	22	8	1	30	**105**	3	39	.234	.380	.323	93	1	7	.961	3	108	98	*O-125(LF)	-0.1
1920	†Cle A	62	152	31	45	11	1	0	13	27	3	21	.296	.412	.382	108	4	4-2	.941	-1	97	82	O-47(44-2-1)	0.1
1921	Cle A	68	107	19	32	3	0	2	18	20	1	9	.299	.414	.383	103	2	1-1	.933	-3	98	0	O-32(17-11-5)	-0.2
1922	Cle A	37	58	6	9	0	0	0	2	9	1	12	.155	.279	.155	16	-7	0-0	.862	-1	96	75	O-13(2-4-7)	-0.9
Total	14	1402	4705	706	1178	219	79	18	420	712	40	345	.250	.354	.342	100	25	148-36	.953	-0	103	91	*O-1282(1176-62-46)/P-2	-4.2
GRANT, EDDIE Edward Leslie "Harvard Eddie" B 5.21.1883 Franklin, MA D 10.5.1918 Argonne Forest, France BL/TR 5-11.5/168# d8.4																								
1905	Cle A	2	8	1	3	0	0	0	0	0	0		.375	.375	.375	136	0	0	.833	-1	92	0	/2-2	-0.1
1907	Phi N	74	268	26	65	4	3	0	19	10	1		.243	.272	.280	74	-9	10	.916	-4	93	63	3-74	-1.2
1908	Phi N	147	598	69	146	13	8	0	32	35	3		.244	.289	.293	83	-12	27	.930	-2	99	**138**	*3-134,S-13	-1.2
1909	Phi N	**154**	631	75	170	18	4	1	37	35	3		.269	.311	.315	94	-6	28	.957	3	101	98	*3-154	0.1

Year	Tm Lg	G	AB	R	H	2B	3B	HR	RBI	BB-IB	HP	SO	AVG	OBP	SLG	AOPS	ABR	SB-CS	FA	FR	Rng	Thr	G at Pos	BFW
1910	Phi N	152	579	70	155	15	5	1	67	39	1	54	.268	.315	.316	81	-15	25	.935	-12	87	101	*3-152	-2.4
1911	Cin N	136	458	49	102	12	7	1	53	51	0	47	.223	.301	.286	67	-21	28	.953	-5	97	129	*3-122,S-11	-2.2
1912	Cin N	96	255	37	61	6	1	2	20	18	1	27	.239	.292	.294	62	-14	11	.948	0	103	92	S-56,3-15	-0.9
1913	Cin N	27	94	12	20	1	0	0	9	11	0	10	.213	.295	.223	49	-6	7-4	.929	-1	98	126	3-26	-0.6
	†NY N	27	20	8	4	1	0	0	1	2	0	2	.200	.273	.250	49	-1	1-1	1.000	3	269	0	/3-5,2-3,S	0.2
	Year	54	114	20	24	2	0	0	10	13	0	12	.211	.291	.228	49	-7	8-5	.940	2	114	114	3-31/2-3,S	-0.4
1914	NY N	88	282	34	78	7	1	0	29	23	1	21	.277	.333	.309	94	-2	11	.948	-3	108	115	3-52,S-21,2-16	-0.2
1915	NY N	87	192	18	40	2	1	0	10	9	1	20	.208	.248	.229	47	-13	5-6	.970	-2	90	70	3-35/2-9,1S	-1.7
Total	10	990	3385	399	844	79	30	5	277	233	11	181	.249	.300	.295	78	-99	153-11	.942	-21	97	108	3-769,S-103/2-30,1	-10.2
GRANT, JIMMY James Charles B 10.6.1918 Racine, WI D 7.8.1970 Rochester, MN BL/TR 5-8/166# d9.8																								
1942	Chi A	12	36	0	6	1	1	0	1	5	0	6	.167	.268	.250	47	-3	0-0	.944	0	93	164	3-10	-0.2
1943	Chi A	58	197	23	51	9	2	4	22	18	0	34	.259	.321	.386	106	1	4-3	.893	-2	109	113	3-51	-0.1
	Cle A	15	22	3	3	2	0	0	1	4	0	7	.136	.269	.227	49	-1	0-0	.941	1	142	0	/3-5	0.0
	Year	73	219	26	54	11	2	4	23	22	0	41	.247	.315	.370	101	0	4-3	.897	-1	112	104	3-56	-0.1
1944	Cle A	61	99	12	27	4	3	1	12	11	2	20	.273	.357	.404	122	3	1-0	.926	-4	98	47	2-20/3-4	0.0
Total	3	146	354	38	87	16	6	5	36	38	2	67	.246	.322	.367	101	0	5-3	.907	-4	108	110	/3-70,2-20	-0.3
GRANT, TOM Thomas Raymond B 5.28.1957 Worcester, MA BL/TR 6-2/190# d6.17																								
1983	Chi N	16	20	2	3	1	0	0	2	3-0	0	4	.150	.261	.200	28	-2	0-0	1.000	0	72	316	O-10(5-0-5)	-0.2
GRANTHAM, GEORGE George Farley "Boots" B 5.20.1900 Galena, KS D 3.16.1954 Kingman, AZ BL/TR 5-10/170# d9.20																								
1922	Chi N	7	23	3	4	1	1	0	3	1	0	3	.174	.208	.304	30	-3	2-0	1.000	-1	52	149	/3-5	-0.3
1923	Chi N	152	570	81	160	36	8	8	70	71	0	92	.281	.360	.414	104	5	43-28	.942	4	101	106	*2-150	1.2
1924	Chi N	127	469	85	148	19	6	12	60	55	2	63	.316	.390	.458	125	18	21-21	.941	-1	101	108	*2-118/3-6	1.8
1925	†Pit N	114	359	74	117	24	6	8	52	50	3	29	.326	.413	.493	122	14	14-4	.989	-4	82	123	*1-102	0.5
1926	Pit N	141	449	66	143	27	13	8	70	60	1	42	.318	.400	.490	131	21	6	.990	-2	92	106	*1-132	1.1
1927	†Pit N	151	531	96	162	33	11	8	66	74	6	39	.305	.396	.454	119	17	9	.953	-22	88	101	*2-124,1-29	-0.4
1928	Pit N	124	440	93	142	24	9	10	85	59	4	37	.323	.408	.486	128	19	9	.986	1	109	86	*1-119/23	1.3
1929	Pit N	110	349	85	107	23	10	12	90	93	1	38	.307	.454	.533	140	27	10	.967	0	96	125	2-76,O-19(LF),1-12	2.5
1930	Pit N	146	552	120	179	34	14	18	99	81	2	66	.324	.413	.534	126	25	5	.958	-12	101	82	*2-141/1-4	1.5
1931	Pit N	127	465	91	142	26	6	10	46	71	2	50	.305	.400	.452	130	23	5	.985	-22	63	100	1-78,2-51	-0.4
1932	Cin N	126	493	81	144	29	6	6	39	56	0	40	.292	.364	.412	112	10	4	.959	-25	95	70	*2-115,1-10	-0.9
1933	Cin N	87	260	32	53	14	3	4	28	38	2	21	.204	.310	.327	83	-5	4	.948	-8	95	93	2-72,1-12	-1.0
1934	NY N	32	29	5	7	2	0	1	4	8	0	6	.241	.405	.414	123	1	0	1.000	0	82	71	/1-4,3-2	0.1
Total	13	1444	4989	912	1508	292	93	105	712	717	23	526	.302	.392	.461	121	172	132-53	.949	-92	97	97	2-848,1-502/O-19(LF),3-14	7.0
GRASSO, MICKEY Newton Michael B 5.10.1920 Newark, NJ D 10.15.1975 Miami, FL BR/TR 6/195# d9.18																								
1946	NY N	7	22	1	3	0	0	0	1	0	0	3	.136	.136	.136	-22	-4	0	.967	0	*106*	*184*	/C-7	-0.3
1950	Was A	75	195	25	56	4	1	1	22	25	2	31	.287	.374	.333	86	-3	1-1	.942	-1	*74*	*138*	C-69	-0.1
1951	Was A	52	175	16	36	3	0	1	14	14	1	17	.206	.268	.240	39	-15	0-0	.967	-3	*102*	*108*	C-49	-1.6
1952	Was A	115	361	22	78	9	0	0	27	29	1	36	.216	.276	.241	46	-27	1-0	.970	4	*116*	*75*	*C-114	-1.7
1953	Was A	61	196	13	41	7	0	2	22	9	2	20	.209	.251	.276	43	-16	0-0	.984	2	*105*	*85*	C-59	-1.2
1954	†Cle A	4	6	1	2	0	0	1	1	1	1	1	.333	.500	.833	256	1	0-0	.833	-1	*68*	*191*	/C-4	0.1
1955	NY N	8	2	0	0	0	0	0	0	3-0	0	0	.000	.600	.000	77	0	0-0	.900	-0	*0*	*0*	/C-8	0.0
Total	7	322	957	78	216	23	1	5	87	81-0	7	108	.226	.291	.268	53	-64	2-1	.964	-0	*101*	*99*	C-310	-4.8
GRAULICH, LEW Lewis B Camden, NJ d9.17																								
1891	Phi N	7	26	2	8	0	0	0	3	1	0	2	.308	.333	.308	85	-1	0	.640	-3	*94*	*46*	/C-4,1-3	-0.3
GRAVES, FRANK Frank Norris B 11.2.1860 Cincinnati, OH BR 6/163# d5.10																								
1886	StL N	43	138	7	21	2	0	0	9	7		48	.152	.193	.167	11	-14	11	.885	0			C-41/O-3(CF),P	-1.0
GRAVES, JOE Joseph Ebenezer B 2.26.1906 Marblehead, MA D 12.22.1980 Salem, MA BR/TR 5-10/160# d9.26 b-Sid																								
1926	Chi N	2	5	0	0	0	0	0	0	0	0	1	.000	.000	.000	-99	-1	0	.250	-1	42	470	/3-2	-0.3
GRAVES, SID Samuel Sidney "Whitey" B 11.30.1901 Marblehead, MA D 12.26.1983 Biddeford, ME BR/TR 6/170# d7.23 b-Joe																								
1927	Bos N	7	20	5	5	1	1	0	2	0	0	1	.250	.250	.400	78	-1	1	.857	0	78	405	/O-5(CF)	-0.1
GRAY, GARY Gary George B 9.21.1952 New Orleans, LA BR/TR 6/203# d6.23																								
1977	Tex A	1	2	0	0	0	0	0	0	0-0	0	1	.000	.000	.000	-99	-1	0-0	—	-0	0	0	/O(LF)	-0.1
1978	Tex A	17	50	4	12	1	0	2	6	1-0	0	12	.240	.255	.380	76	-2	1-0	—	0	0	0	D-11	-0.2
1979	Tex A	16	42	4	10	0	0	0	1	2-0	0	8	.238	.273	.238	40	-4	1-1	—	0	0	0	D-13	-0.4
1980	Cle A	28	54	4	8	1	0	2	4	3-1	0	13	.148	.193	.278	27	-6	0-0	1.000	-0	148	50	/1-6,O-6(LF),D-9	-0.6
1981	Sea A	69	208	27	51	7	1	13	31	4-1	0	44	.245	.257	.476	104	-1	2-0	.993	-2	78	119	1-34,D-15/O-4(LF)	-0.5
1982	Sea A	80	269	26	69	14	2	7	29	24-0	2	59	.257	.322	.401	95	-2	1-1	.984	-3	82	77	1-60,D-14	-0.9
Total	6	211	625	65	150	23	3	24	71	34-2	2	137	.240	.281	.402	86	-16	5-2	.988	-6	82	91	1-100/D-62,O-11(LF)	-2.7
GRAY, REDDY James W. B 8.1863 Allegheny, PA D 1.31.1938 Allegheny, PA TR d10.9																								
1884	Pit AA	1	2	0	1	0	0	0		0	0		.500	.500	.500	230	0		.500	-0	138	0	/3	0.0
1890	Pit P	2	9	3	2	0	0	1	3	0	0	2	.222	.222	.556	114	0	0	.813	-1	67	0	/2-2	-0.1
	Pit N	1	3	0	0	0	0	0	0	0	0	1	.000	.000	.000	-99	-1	0	.571	-1	57	210	/S	-0.2
1893	Pit N	2	9	0	4	1	0	0	2	0	0	1	.444	.444	.556	168	1	0	.800	-2	20	0	/S-2	-0.1
Total	3	6	23	3	7	1	0	1	5	0	0	4	.304	.304	.478	119	0	0	.667	-4	35	86	/S-3,2-2,3	-0.4
GRAY, LORENZO Lorenzo B 3.4.1958 Mound Bayou, MS BR/TR 6-1/180# d7.8																								
1982	Chi A	17	28	4	8	1	0	0	0	2-0	0	4	.286	.333	.321	81	-1	1-0	.864	-3	59	122	3-16	-0.3
1983	Chi A	41	78	18	14	3	0	1	4	8-0	0	16	.179	.256	.256	40	-6	1-0	.940	-2	89	65	3-31/D-7	-0.9
Total	2	58	106	22	22	4	0	1	4	10-0	0	20	.208	.276	.274	50	-7	2-0	.921	-5	81	79	/3-47,D-7	-1.2
GRAY, MILT Milton Marshall B 2.21.1914 Louisville, KY D 6.30.1969 Quincy, FL BR/TR 6-1/170# d5.27																								
1937	Was A	2	6	0	0	0	0	0	0	0	0	1	.000	.000	.000	-99	-2	0-0	1.000	0	*84*	*0*	/C-2	-0.2
GRAY, PETE Peter J. (born Peter Wyshner) B 3.6.1915 Nanticoke, PA D 6.30.2002 Nanticoke, PA BL/TL 6-1/169# d4.17																								
1945	StL A	77	234	26	51	6	2	0	13	13	0	11	.218	.259	.261	49	-16	5-6	.959	2	117	59	O-61(35-29-0)	-1.9
GRAY, DICK Richard Benjamin B 7.11.1931 Jefferson, PA BR/TR 5-11/165# d4.15																								
1958	LA N	58	197	25	49	5	6	9	30	19-0	4	30	.249	.327	.472	105	1	1-1	.929	11	117	157	3-55	1.1
1959	LA N	21	52	8	8	1	0	2	4	6-0	0	12	.154	.241	.288	38	-5	0-0	1.000	0	105	133	3-11	-0.5
	StL N	36	51	9	16	1	0	1	6	6-1	0	8	.314	.386	.392	101	0	3-0	.958	-5	64	71	S-13/3-6,2-2,O(LF)	-0.3
	Year	57	103	17	24	2	0	3	10	12-1	0	20	.233	.313	.340	69	-4	3-0	.935	-4	98	103	3-17,S-13/2-2,O(LF)	-0.8
1960	StL N	9	5	1	0	0	0	0	1	2-0	0	2	.000	.250	.000	-13	-1	0-0	1.000	1	161	360	/2-4,3	0.0
Total	3	124	305	43	73	7	6	12	41	33-1	4	52	.239	.321	.420	91	-5	4-1	.930	7	114	146	/3-73,S-13,2-6,O(LF)	0.3
GRAY, STAN Stanley Oscar B 12.10.1888 Ladonia, TX D 10.11.1964 Snyder, TX BR/TR 6-0.5/184# d9.17																								
1912	Pit N	6	20	4	5	0	1	0	2	0	0	3	.250	.250	.350	64	-1	0	1.000	-1	0	94	/1-4	-0.2
GRAY, BILL William Tolan B 4.15.1871 Philadelphia, PA D 12.8.1932 Philadelphia, PA 5-11/175# d5.14 OF Total (8-LF 7-CF 9-RF)																								
1890	Phi N	34	128	20	31	8	4	0	21	6	2	3	.242	.287	.367	88	-3	5	1.000	-6	170	0	O-10(6-3-1)/3-8,2-8,C-7,1	-0.7
1891	Phi N	23	75	11	18	0	0	0	7	3	3	10	.240	.296	.240	55	-4	3	.804	-5	*92*	*66*	C-11,O-10(0-4-6)/S-3,3	-0.8
1895	Cin N	52	181	24	55	17	4	1	29	15	2	8	.304	.364	.459	107	2	4	.906	-3	97	162	3-27,2-16/S-5,C-5,O(LF)	0.0
1896	Cin N	46	121	15	25	2	1	0	17	19	0	11	.207	.314	.240	44	-10	6	.927	1	126	123	2-12,C-11/S-8,O-3(1-0-2),1-2,3	-0.6
1898	Pit N	137	528	56	121	17	5	0	67	28	12		.229	.283	.280	63	-26	5	.879	-21	88	86	*3-137	-4.2
Total	5	292	1033	126	250	44	14	1	141	71	19	32	.242	.303	.315	72	-41	23	.879	-34	87	97	3-174/2-36,C-34,O-24R,S-16,1-3	-6.3
GREBECK, CRAIG Craig Allen B 12.29.1964 Johnstown, PA BR/TR 5-7/148# d4.13 OF Total (4-LF 1-RF)																								
1990	Chi A	59	119	7	20	3	1	1	9	8-0	2	24	.168	.227	.235	32	-11	0-0	.987	1	112	65	3-35,S-16/2-6,D	-1.0
1991	Chi A	107	224	37	63	16	3	6	31	38-0	1	40	.281	.386	.460	137	13	1-3	.933	-3	108	151	3-49,2-36,S-26	1.1
1992	Chi A	88	287	24	77	21	2	3	35	30-0	3	34	.268	.341	.387	106	3	0-3	.980	2	111	89	S-85/3-7,O-2(1-0-1)	1.0

Year	Tm Lg	G	AB	R	H	2B	3B	HR	RBI	BB-IB	HP	SO	AVG	OBP	SLG	AOPS	ABR	SB-CS	FA	FR	Rng	Thr	G at Pos	BFW
1993	†Chi A	72	190	25	43	5	0	1	12	26-0	0	26	.226	.319	.268	61	-10	1-2	.983	10	106	111	S-46,2-16,3-14	0.3
1994	Chi A	35	97	17	30	5	0	0	5	12-0	1	5	.309	.391	.361	97	0	0-0	.982	-5	78	50	2-14,S-14/3-7	-0.2
1995	Chi A	53	154	19	40	12	0	1	18	21-0	3	23	.260	.360	.357	91	-1	0-0	.961	4	118	106	S-31,3-18/2-8	0.6
1996	Fla N	50	95	8	20	1	0	1	9	4-1	1	14	.211	.245	.253	34	-9	0-0	.985	5	100	160	2-29/S-2,3	-0.3
1997	Ana A	63	126	12	34	9	0	1	6	18-1	0	11	.270	.359	.365	90	-1	0-1	1.000	-5	94	124	2-26,S-20,3-15/O-3(LF),D-2	-0.4
1998	Tor A	102	301	33	77	17	2	2	27	29-0	4	42	.256	.327	.346	76	-10	2-2	.975	1	101	76	2-91/S-6,3-4	-0.4
1999	Tor A	34	113	18	41	7	0	0	10	15-0	2	13	.363	.443	.425	122	5	0-0	.959	-6	85	65	2-17,D-10/S-4,3-2	0.0
2000	Tor A	66	241	38	71	19	0	3	23	25-0	2	33	.295	.364	.411	93	-1	0-0	.968	4	109	87	2-56/S-8	0.5
2001	Bos A	23	41	1	2	1	0	0	2	2-0	0	9	.049	.093	.073	-55	-9	0-0	1.000	-3	87	47	S-23	-1.1
Total	12	752	1988	239	518	116	8	19	187	228-2	19	274	.261	.340	.356	86	-31	4-11	.981	7	101	93	2-299,S-281,3-152/D-13,O-5L	0.1

GREEN, SCARBOROUGH Bertrum Scarborough B 6.9.1974 Creve Coeur, MO BB/TR 5-10/170# d8.2

Year	Tm Lg	G	AB	R	H	2B	3B	HR	RBI	BB-IB	HP	SO	AVG	OBP	SLG	AOPS	ABR	SB-CS	FA	FR	Rng	Thr	G at Pos	BFW
1997	StL N	20	31	5	3	0	0	0	1	2-0	0	5	.097	.152	.097	-34	-6	0-0	.952	0	101	209	O-19(7-12-0)	-0.6
1999	Tex A	18	13	4	4	0	0	0	0	1-0	0	2	.308	.357	.308	69	-1	0-1	1.000	-0	84	0	/O-9(3-4-3),D-4	-0.1
2000	Tex A	79	124	21	29	1	1	0	9	10-0	0	26	.234	.291	.258	40	-12	10-6	1.000	8	114	393	O-65(3-41-23)/D-6	-0.4
Total	3	117	168	30	36	1	1	0	10	13-0	0	33	.214	.271	.232	30	-19	10-7	.993	8	110	333	/O-93(13-57-26),D-10	-1.1

GREEN, DAVID David Alejandro (Casaya) B 12.4.1960 Managua, Nicaragua BR/TR 6-3/170# d9.4

Year	Tm Lg	G	AB	R	H	2B	3B	HR	RBI	BB-IB	HP	SO	AVG	OBP	SLG	AOPS	ABR	SB-CS	FA	FR	Rng	Thr	G at Pos	BFW
1981	StL N	21	34	6	5	1	0	0	2	6-1	0	5	.147	.275	.176	29	-3	0-1	.970	0	103	126	O-18(CF)	-0.4
1982	†StL N	76	166	21	47	7	1	2	23	8-2	1	29	.283	.315	.373	92	-2	11-3	.991	1	102	134	O-68(7-46-19)	0.0
1983	StL N	146	422	52	120	14	10	8	69	26-1	1	76	.284	.325	.422	106	1	34-16	.970	-1	94	130	*O-136(20-19-100)	-0.3
1984	StL N	126	452	49	121	14	4	15	65	20-4	1	105	.268	.297	.416	102	-2	17-9	.991	-2	96	114	*1-117,O-14(0-6-8)	-1.1
1985	SF N	106	294	36	73	10	2	5	20	22-3	1	58	.248	.301	.347	85	-7	6-5	.987	-2	93	94	1-78,O-12(1-0-11)	-1.4
1987	StL N	14	30	4	8	2	1	1	1	2-0	0	5	.267	.313	.500	109	0	0-1	.882	0	104	206	O-10(1-0-9)/1-3	0.0
Total	6	489	1398	168	374	48	18	31	180	84-11	4	278	.268	.308	.394	97	-13	68-35	.972	-3	98	131	O-258(29-89-147),1-198	-3.2

GREEN, DANNY Edward B 11.6.1876 Burlington, NJ D 11.9.1914 Camden, NJ BL/TR d8.17

Year	Tm Lg	G	AB	R	H	2B	3B	HR	RBI	BB-IB	HP	SO	AVG	OBP	SLG	AOPS	ABR	SB-CS	FA	FR	Rng	Thr	G at Pos	BFW
1898	Chi N	47	188	26	59	4	3	4	27	7	1		.314	.342	.431	121	4	12	.970	4	148	331	O-47(8-2-37)	0.5
1899	Chi N	117	475	90	140	12	11	6	56	35	7		.295	.352	.404	110	5	18	.947	1	125	**261**	*O-115(9-0-106)	0.0
1900	Chi N	103	389	63	116	21	5	5	49	17	7		.298	.339	.416	112	5	28	.938	-0	73	56	*O-102(3-60-39)	-0.1
1901	Chi N	133	537	82	168	16	12	6	61	40	3		.313	.364	.421	132	21	31	.932	7	96	161	*O-133(CF)	2.1
1902	Chi A	129	481	77	150	16	11	0	62	53	7		.312	.388	.391	122	17	35	.942	-3	66	124	*O-129(18-2-110)	0.7
1903	Chi A	135	499	75	154	26	7	6	62	47	6		.309	.375	.425	146	30	29	.933	2	111	**216**	*O-133(RF)	2.7
1904	Chi A	147	536	83	142	16	10	2	62	63	9		.265	.352	.343	125	18	28	.964	1	81	133	*O-146(RF)	1.4
1905	Chi A	112	379	56	92	13	6	0	44	53	6		.243	.345	.309	112	8	11	.914	-8	83	138	*O-107(0-7-100)	-0.4
Total	8	923	3484	552	1021	124	65	29	423	315	46		.293	.359	.391	124	108	192	.941	3	94	167	O-912(38-204-671)	6.9

GREEN, PUMPSIE Elijah Jerry B 10.27.1933 Oakland, CA BB/TR 6/175# d7.21

Year	Tm Lg	G	AB	R	H	2B	3B	HR	RBI	BB-IB	HP	SO	AVG	OBP	SLG	AOPS	ABR	SB-CS	FA	FR	Rng	Thr	G at Pos	BFW
1959	Bos A	50	172	30	40	6	3	1	10	29-0	2	22	.233	.350	.320	81	-3	4-2	.972	4	106	115	2-45/S	0.4
1960	Bos A	133	260	36	63	10	3	3	21	44-2	1	47	.242	.350	.338	85	-4	3-4	.982	-9	92	66	2-69,S-41	-0.8
1961	Bos A	88	219	33	57	12	3	6	27	42-3	0	32	.260	.376	.425	112	5	4-2	.940	-2	104	95	S-57/2-7	0.8
1962	Bos A	56	91	12	21	2	1	2	11	11-0	0	18	.231	.308	.341	74	-3	1-0	.953	-6	83	83	2-18/S-5	-0.8
1963	NY N	17	54	8	15	1	2	1	5	12-0	0	13	.278	.409	.426	139	3	0-2	.857	-1	111	73	3-16	0.2
Total	5	344	796	119	196	31	12	13	74	138-5	3	132	.246	.357	.364	94	-2	12-10	.975	-13	98	93	2-139,S-104/3-16	-0.2

GREEN, GARY Gary Allan B 1.14.1962 Pittsburgh, PA BR/TR 6-3/175# d9.14 f-Fred

Year	Tm Lg	G	AB	R	H	2B	3B	HR	RBI	BB-IB	HP	SO	AVG	OBP	SLG	AOPS	ABR	SB-CS	FA	FR	Rng	Thr	G at Pos	BFW
1986	SD N	13	33	2	7	1	0	0	2	1-0	0	11	.212	.235	.242	33	-3	0-0	1.000	2	109	141	S-13	0.0
1989	SD N	15	27	4	7	3	0	0	0	1-0	0	1	.259	.286	.370	86	0	0-1	.921	2	133	189	S-11/3	0.2
1990	Tex A	62	88	10	19	3	0	0	8	6-0	0	18	.216	.263	.250	45	-7	1-1	.972	7	111	119	S-58	0.3
1991	Tex A	8	20	0	3	1	0	0	1	1-0	0	6	.150	.190	.200	8	-3	0-0	.968	1	112	124	/S-8	-0.1
1992	Cin N	8	12	3	4	1	0	0	0	0-0	0	2	.333	.333	.417	108	0	0-0	1.000	-3	32	0	/S-6,3	-0.3
Total	5	106	180	19	40	9	0	0	11	9-0	0	38	.222	.258	.272	49	-13	1-2	.970	9	109	126	/S-96,3-2	0.1

GREEN, GENE Gene Leroy B 6.26.1933 Los Angeles, CA D 5.23.1981 St.Louis, MO BR/TR 6-2/205# d9.10

Year	Tm Lg	G	AB	R	H	2B	3B	HR	RBI	BB-IB	HP	SO	AVG	OBP	SLG	AOPS	ABR	SB-CS	FA	FR	Rng	Thr	G at Pos	BFW
1957	StL N	6	15	0	3	1	0	0	2	0-0	0	3	.200	.188	.267	23	-2	0-0	1.000	-1	49	0	/O-3(RF)	-0.2
1958	StL N	137	442	47	124	18	3	13	55	37-4	1	48	.281	.333	.423	96	-3	2-1	.956	5	101	192	O-75(0-1-75),C-48	0.2
1959	StL N	30	74	8	14	6	0	1	3	5-1	0	18	.189	.241	.311	43	-6	0-0	.944	5	102	521	O-19(RF),C-11	-0.2
1960	Bal A	1	4	0	1	0	0	0	0	0-0	0	0	.250	.250	.250	36	0	0-0	1.000	1	0	2014	/O(RF)	0.0
1961	Was A	110	364	52	102	16	3	18	62	35-5	1	65	.280	.341	.489	122	10	0-2	.986	-15	*61*	*75*	C-79,O-21(RF)	-0.3
1962	Cle A	66	143	16	40	4	1	11	28	8-0	0	21	.280	.316	.552	133	5	0-0	.964	0	102	128	O-33(3-0-30)/1-2	0.4
1963	Cle A	43	78	4	16	3	0	2	7	4-0	2	22	.205	.259	.321	63	-4	0-0	1.000	-2	65	115	O-18(1-0-17)	-0.7
	Cin N	15	31	3	7	1	0	1	3	0-0	1	8	.226	.250	.355	70	-1	0-0	.932	-1	*80*	*114*	/C-8	-0.3
Total	7	408	1151	130	307	49	7	46	160	89-10	5	185	.267	.318	.441	101	-1	2-3	.963	-9	97	197	O-170(4-1-166),C-146/1-2	-1.1

GREEN, JIM James F. B 5.22.1854 Windham Co., CT D 12.12.1912 Cleveland, OH d7.19

Year	Tm Lg	G	AB	R	H	2B	3B	HR	RBI	BB-IB	HP	SO	AVG	OBP	SLG	AOPS	ABR	SB-CS	FA	FR	Rng	Thr	G at Pos	BFW
1884	Was U	10	36	4	5	1	0	0		0			.139	.139	.167	-8	-6		.818	0	119	0	/3-9,O(RF)	-0.5

GREEN, JOE Joseph Henry (a/k/a Joseph Henry Greene) B 9.17.1897 Philadelphia, PA D 2.4.1972 Bryn Mawr, PA BR/TR 6-2/170# d7.2

Year	Tm Lg	G	AB	R	H	2B	3B	HR	RBI	BB-IB	HP	SO	AVG	OBP	SLG	AOPS	ABR	SB-CS	FA	FR	Rng	Thr	G at Pos	BFW
1924	Phi A	1	1	0	0	0	0	0	0	0	0	0	.000	.000	.000	-99	0	0-0	—	0			H	0.0

GREEN, LENNY Leonard Charles B 1.6.1933 Detroit, MI BL/TL 5-11/170# d8.25

Year	Tm Lg	G	AB	R	H	2B	3B	HR	RBI	BB-IB	HP	SO	AVG	OBP	SLG	AOPS	ABR	SB-CS	FA	FR	Rng	Thr	G at Pos	BFW
1957	Bal A	19	33	2	6	1	1	1	5	1-0	0	4	.182	.206	.364	56	-2	0-1	.950	-1	101	0	O-15(3-12-2)	-0.4
1958	Bal A	69	91	10	21	4	0	0	4	9-0	0	10	.231	.297	.275	63	-4	0-2	.965	3	131	57	O-53(28-30-6)	-0.4
1959	Bal A	27	24	3	7	0	0	1	2	1-0	1	3	.292	.346	.417	111	0	0-0	1.000	1	90	625	O-23(20-0-5)	0.1
	Was A	88	190	29	46	6	1	2	15	20-0	0	15	.242	.314	.316	74	-7	9-5	.979	0	97	143	O-58(21-13-27)	-0.9
	Year	115	214	32	53	6	1	3	17	21-0	1	18	.248	.318	.327	78	-6	9-5	.981	1	96	191	O-81(41-13-32)	-0.8
1960	Was A	127	330	62	97	16	7	5	33	43-4	6	25	.294	.383	.430	121	11	21-8	.991	-1	103	72	*O-100(20-92-0)	0.8
1961	Min A	156	600	92	171	28	7	9	50	81-2	6	50	.285	.374	.400	102	4	17-11	.978	-5	102	33	*O-153(56-141-4)	-0.7
1962	Min A	158	619	97	168	33	3	14	63	88-2	8	36	.271	.367	.402	104	7	8-4	.995	0	100	94	*O-156(88-146-0)	0.1
1963	Min A	145	280	41	67	10	1	4	27	31-1	2	21	.239	.315	.325	80	-7	11-5	.988	-4	101	22	*O-119(15-118-0)	-1.4
1964	Min A	26	15	3	0	0	0	0	0	4-0	0	6	.000	.211	.000	-35	-3	0-1	1.000	0	100	0	/O-7(6-1-0)	-0.3
	LA A	39	92	13	23	2	0	2	4	10-0	1	8	.250	.327	.337	96	-1	2-0	.977	-1	91	76	O-23(11-13-0)	-0.2
	Bal A	14	21	0	4	0	0	0	1	7-1	0	3	.190	.393	.190	69	0	1-0	1.000	1	144	0	/O-8(2-6-0)	0.1
	Year	79	128	16	27	2	0	2	5	21-1	1	17	.211	.325	.273	72	-4	3-1	.985	-0	104	56	O-38(19-20-0)	-0.4
1965	Bos A	119	373	69	103	24	6	7	24	48-0	3	43	.276	.361	.429	117	10	8-2	.980	-1	104	51	O-95(12-86-0)	0.7
1966	Bos A	85	133	18	32	6	0	1	12	15-1	2	19	.241	.325	.308	76	-3	0-1	.978	-1	84	226	O-27(4-23-0)	-0.6
1967	Det A	58	151	22	42	8	1	1	13	9-0	0	17	.278	.317	.364	99	0	1-1	.983	-2	93	0	O-44(43-2-0)	-0.5
1968	Det A	6	4	0	1	0	0	0	0	1-1	0	0	.250	.400	.250	97	0	0-0	—	-0	0	0	/O-2(LF)	0.0
Total	12	1136	2956	461	788	138	27	47	253	368-12	29	260	.267	.351	.379	99	5	78-41	.984	-11	102	69	O-883(331-683-44)	-3.6

GREEN, DICK Richard Larry B 4.21.1941 Sioux City, IA BR/TR 5-10/180# d9.9

Year	Tm Lg	G	AB	R	H	2B	3B	HR	RBI	BB-IB	HP	SO	AVG	OBP	SLG	AOPS	ABR	SB-CS	FA	FR	Rng	Thr	G at Pos	BFW
1963	KC A	13	37	5	10	2	0	1	4	2-0	1	10	.270	.317	.405	98	0	0-0	.941	3	138	85	/S-6,2-4	0.3
1964	KC A	130	435	48	115	14	5	11	37	27-3	3	87	.264	.311	.395	92	-5	3-3	.990	13	112	82	*2-120	1.8
1965	KC A	133	474	64	110	15	1	15	55	50-1	3	110	.232	.308	.363	92	-5	0-2	.980	-10	100	86	*2-126	-0.6
1966	KC A	140	507	58	127	24	3	9	62	27-4	7	101	.250	.297	.363	92	-6	6-1	.979	-8	100	91	*2-137/3-2	-0.1
1967	KC A	122	349	26	69	12	4	5	37	30-1	0	68	.198	.260	.298	67	-15	6-3	.946	-4	86	60	3-59,2-50/1S	-1.6
1968	Oak A	76	202	19	47	6	0	6	18	21-3	1	41	.233	.307	.351	104	1	3-1	.974	7	107	113	2-61/C3	1.5
1969	Oak A	136	483	61	133	25	6	12	64	53-3	8	94	.275	.353	.427	123	16	2-3	**.986**	-4	99	111	*2-131	2.1
1970	Oak A	135	384	34	73	7	0	4	29	38-5	3	73	.190	.267	.240	43	-30	3-0	.978	-3	99	96	*2-127/3-5,C	-2.7
1971	†Oak A	144	475	58	116	14	1	12	49	51-14	3	83	.244	.320	.354	93	-5	1-1	.986	3	97	114	*2-143/S	0.9
1972	†Oak A	26	42	1	12	1	1	0	3	3-0	1	5	.286	.348	.357	116	1	0-1	.964	-1	105	95	2-26	0.1
1973	†Oak A	133	332	33	87	17	0	3	42	21-0	2	63	.262	.308	.340	88	-6	0-2	.988	-0	102	123	*2-133/S3	0.0
1974	†Oak A	100	287	20	61	8	2	2	22	22-0	0	50	.213	.269	.275	61	-15	2-3	.983	8	105	111	*2-100	-0.2
Total	12	1288	4007	427	960	145	23	80	422	345-34	32	785	.240	.303	.347	87	-69	26-20	.983	4	101	102	*2-1158/3-68,S-9,C-2,1	1.5

GREEN, SHAWN Shawn David B 11.10.1972 Des Plaines, IL BL/TL 6-4/190# d9.28

Year	Tm Lg	G	AB	R	H	2B	3B	HR	RBI	BB-IB	HP	SO	AVG	OBP	SLG	AOPS	ABR	SB-CS	FA	FR	Rng	Thr	G at Pos	BFW
1993	Tor A	3	6	0	0	0	0	0	0	0-0	0	1	.000	.000	.000	-99	-2	0-0	1.000	-0	62	0	/O-2(RF),D	-0.2

Year	Tm Lg	G	AB	R	H	2B	3B	HR	RBI	BB-IB	HP	SO	AVG	OBP	SLG	AOPS	ABR	SB-CS	FA	FR	Rng	Thr	G at Pos	BFW
1994	Tor A	14	33	1	3	1	0	0	1	1-0	0	8	.091	.118	.121	-38	-7	1-0	1.000	0	68	325	O-14(10-0-5)	-0.7
1995	Tor A	121	379	52	109	31	4	15	54	20-3	3	68	.288	.326	.509	115	7	1-2	.973	5	107	135	*O-109(RF)	0.5
1996	Tor A	132	422	52	118	32	3	11	45	33-3	8	75	.280	.342	.448	98	-1	5-1	.992	8	111	124	*O-127(0-2-127)/D	0.2
1997	Tor A	135	429	57	123	22	4	16	53	36-4	1	99	.287	.340	.469	109	4	14-3	.984	4	106	116	O-91(45-0-46),D-35	0.4
1998	Tor A	158	630	106	175	33	4	35	100	50-2	5	142	.278	.334	.510	115	12	35-12	.979	1	100	132	*O-157(0-32-128)	1.0
1999	Tor A★	153	614	134	190	**45**	0	42	123	66-4	11	117	.309	.384	.588	142	39	20-7	.997	5	112	47	*O-152(RF)	3.4
2000	LA N	**162**	610	98	164	44	4	24	99	90-9	8	121	.269	.367	.472	118	19	24-5	.980	-9	88	88	*O-161(0-1-161)	0.5
2001	LA N	161	619	121	184	31	4	49	125	72-10	5	107	.297	.372	.598	157	51	20-4	.982	-2	100	77	*O-159(0-2-159)/1	4.2
2002	LA N★	158	582	110	166	31	1	42	114	93-22	5	112	.285	.385	.558	160	48	8-5	.994	3	106	66	*O-156(RF)/D	4.3
2003	LA N	160	611	84	171	49	2	19	85	68-2	6	112	.280	.355	.460	118	17	6-2	.982	-7	88	91	*O-157(RF)/D-2	0.2
Total	11	1357	4935	815	1403	319	26	253	799	529-59	52	962	.284	.357	.513	126	187	134-41	.985	7	101	95	*O-1285(55-37-1202)/D-40,1	13.8
GREENBERG, HANK Henry Benjamin "Hammerin' Hank" B 1.1.1911 New York, NY D 9.4.1986 Beverly Hills, CA BR/TR 6-3.5/210# d9.14 Mil 1941-45 HF1956																								
1930	Det A	1	1	0	0	0	0	0	0	0	0	0	.000	.000	.000	-98	0	0-0	—	0			H	0.0
1933	Det A	117	449	59	135	33	3	12	87	46	1	78	.301	.367	.468	118	11	6-2	.988	1	103	**129**	*1-117	0.2
1934	†Det A	153	593	118	201	**63**	7	26	139	63	2	93	.339	.404	.600	156	49	9-5	.990	1	101	102	*1-153	3.3
1935	†Det A	**152**	619	121	203	46	16	**36**	**170**	87	0	91	.328	.411	.628	171	64	4-3	.992	6	**114**	**118**	*1-152	5.0
1936	Det A	12	46	10	16	6	2	1	16	9	0	6	.348	.455	.630	165	5	1-0	.992	1	136	135	1-12	0.4
1937	Det A☆	154	594	137	200	49	14	40	**183**	102	3	101	.337	.436	.668	171	65	8-3	.992	5	115	98	*1-154	5.1
1938	Det A✳	**155**	556	**144**	175	23	4	**58**	146	**119**	3	92	.315	.438	.683	167	58	7-5	.991	7	118	103	*1-155	4.5
1939	Det A★	138	500	112	156	42	7	33	112	91	2	95	.312	.420	.622	152	40	8-3	**.993**	-2	90	97	*1-136	2.4
1940	†Det A★	148	573	129	195	**50**	8	**41**	**150**	93	1	75	.340	.433	**.670**	166	**57**	6-3	.954	-1	95	133	*O-148(LF)	4.5
1941	Det A	19	67	12	18	5	1	2	12	16	0	12	.269	.410	.463	118	2	1-0	.914	-3	86	0	O-19(LF)	-0.1
1945	†Det A✳	78	270	47	84	20	2	13	60	42	0	40	.311	.404	.544	164	23	3-1	1.000	-5	89	48	O-72(LF)	1.5
1946	Det A	142	523	91	145	29	5	**44**	**127**	80	0	88	.277	.373	.604	160	41	5-1	.989	2	100	99	*1-140	3.9
1947	Pit N	125	402	71	100	13	2	25	74	**104**	4	73	.249	.408	.478	131	22	0	.992	1	104	86	*1-119	1.9
Total	13	1394	5193	1051	1628	379	71	331	1276	852	16	844	.313	.412	.605	157	437	58-26	.991	11	106	104	*1-1138,O-239(LF)	32.6
GREENE, ALTAR Altar Alphonse B 11.9.1954 Detroit, MI BL/TR 5-11/190# d7.23																								
1979	Det A	29	59	9	8	1	0	3	6	10-1	0	15	.136	.257	.305	50	-4	0-1	1.000	1	203	0	D-15/O-6(4-0-2)	-0.4
GREENE, CHARLIE Charles Patrick B 1.23.1971 Miami, FL BR/TR 6-1/170# d9.15																								
1996	NY N	2	1	0	0	0	0	0	0	0-0	0	0	.000	.000	.000	-99	0	0-0	1.000	0	0	0	/C	0.0
1997	Bal A	5	2	0	0	0	0	0	1	0-0	0	1	.000	.000	.000	-99	-1	0-0	1.000	0	0	0	/C-4	-0.1
1998	Bal A	13	21	1	4	1	0	0	0	0-0	0	8	.190	.190	.238	11	-3	0-0	1.000	3	499	45	C-13	0.1
1999	Mil N	32	42	4	8	1	0	0	1	5-0	0	11	.190	.271	.214	27	-5	0-0	.991	-1	70	82	C-31	-0.5
2000	Tor A	3	9	0	1	0	0	0	0	0-0	0	5	.111	.111	.111	-42	-2	0-0	1.000	-0	0	0	/C-3	-0.2
Total	5	55	75	5	13	2	0	0	2	5-0	0	25	.173	.222	.200	10	-11	0-0	.995	2	177	62	/C-52	-0.7
GREENE, JUNE Julius Foust B 6.25.1899 Ramseur, NC D 3.19.1974 Glendora, CA BL/TR 6-2.5/185# d4.20 ▲																								
1928	Phi N	11	6	0	3	0	0	0	0	3	0	1	.500	.667	.500	202	2	0	1.000	0	429	0	/P	0.0
1929	Phi N	21	19	1	4	1	0	0	0	2	0	4	.211	.286	.263	35	0	0	1.000	0	128	0	/P-5	0.0
Total	2	32	25	1	7	1	0	0	0	5	0	5	.280	.400	.320	79	2	0	1.000	1	166	0	/P-6	0.0
GREENE, KHALIL Khalil Tabit B 10.21.1979 Butler, PA BR/TR 5-11/210# d9.3																								
2003	SD N	20	65	8	14	4	1	2	6	4-0	1	19	.215	.271	.400	79	-2	0-1	.963	0	100	96	S-20	-0.1
GREENE, PADDY Patrick Joseph "Patsy" (a/k/a Patrick Foley In 1902) B 3.20.1875 Providence, RI D 10.20.1934 Providence, RI BR/TR 5-8/150# d9.10																								
1902	Phi N	19	65	6	11	1	0	0	1	2	1		.169	.206	.185	21	-6	2	.912	0	104	78	3-19	-0.6
1903	NY A	4	13	1	4	1	0	0	0	0	0		.308	.308	.385	100	0	0	1.000	1	191	0	/3-2,S	0.1
	Det A	1	3	0	0	0	0	0	0	0	0		.000	.000	.000	-99	-1	0	.750	-1	0	0	/3	-0.2
	Year	5	16	1	4	1	0	0	0	0	0		.250	.250	.313	65	-1	0	.933	0	135	0	/3-3,S	-0.1
Total	2	24	81	7	15	2	0	0	1	2	1		.185	.214	.210	30	-7	2	.916	1	109	64	/3-22,S	-0.7
GREENE, TODD Todd Anthony B 5.8.1971 Augusta, GA BR/TR 5-10/195# d7.30																								
1996	Cal A	29	79	9	15	1	0	2	9	4-0	1	11	.190	.238	.278	30	-9	2-0	1.000	0	83	142	C-26/D	-0.6
1997	Ana A	34	124	24	36	6	0	9	24	7-1	0	25	.290	.328	.556	126	4	2-0	1.000	-3	108	78	C-26/D-8	0.3
1998	Ana A	29	71	3	18	4	0	1	7	2-0	0	20	.254	.274	.352	61	-4	0-0	1.000	-2	68	0	O-12(LF)/1-3,D-4	-0.6
1999	Ana A	97	321	36	78	20	0	14	42	12-0	3	63	.243	.275	.436	79	-12	1-4	.974	-5	67	54	D-44,O-30(5-0-25),C-12	-2.0
2000	Tor A	34	85	11	20	2	0	5	10	5-0	0	18	.235	.278	.435	74	-4	0-0	1.000	-1	27	0	D-23/C-2,O(LF)	-0.6
2001	NY A	35	96	9	20	4	0	1	11	3-0	1	21	.208	.240	.281	36	-9	0-0	1.000	-6	46	78	C-34/D-2	-1.3
2002	Tex A	42	112	15	30	5	0	10	19	2-0	1	23	.268	.282	.580	116	2	0-0	.989	3	55	98	C-15,1-15/O(LF)D	0.4
2003	Tex A	62	205	25	47	10	1	10	20	2-0	2	47	.229	.243	.434	68	-10	0-0	.987	-8	72	160	C-51/1-2,D-3	-1.4
Total	8	362	1093	132	264	52	1	52	142	37-1	8	228	.242	.270	.434	77	-42	5-4	.994	-20	75	124	C-166/D-89,O-44(19-0-25),1-20	-5.8
GREENE, WILLIE Willie Louis B 9.23.1971 Milledgeville, GA BL/TR 5-11/184# d9.1 OF Total (26-LF 72-RF)																								
1992	Cin N	29	93	10	25	5	2	2	13	10-0	0	23	.269	.337	.430	114	2	0-2	.948	-2	83	155	3-25	-0.1
1993	Cin N	15	50	7	8	1	1	2	5	2-0	0	19	.160	.189	.340	39	-5	0-0	.978	2	105	145	S-10/3-5	-0.2
1994	Cin N	16	37	5	8	2	0	0	3	6-1	0	14	.216	.318	.270	58	-2	0-0	.958	-1	104	64	3-13/O(LF)	-0.3
1995	Cin N	8	19	1	2	0	0	0	0	3-0	0	7	.105	.227	.105	-9	-3	0-0	1.000	-0	106	113	/3-7	-0.3
1996	Cin N	115	287	48	70	5	5	19	63	36-6	0	88	.244	.327	.495	113	4	0-1	.927	10	121	129	3-74,O-10(9-0-1)/1-2,S	1.3
1997	Cin N	151	495	62	125	22	1	26	91	78-5	1	111	.253	.354	.459	110	8	6-0	.934	-11	90	43	*3-103,O-39(6-0-33)/1-7,S-3	-0.3
1998	Cin N	111	356	57	96	18	1	14	49	56-2	3	80	.270	.372	.444	113	8	6-3	.936	-2	93	161	3-76,O-28(9-0-22)/S-2,D	0.6
	Bal A	24	40	8	6	1	0	1	5	13-0	0	10	.150	.358	.250	63	-2	1-0	.941	-1	72	132	O-14(1-0-13)/D	-0.3
1999	Tor A	81	226	22	46	7	0	12	41	20-0	0	56	.204	.266	.394	65	-13	0-0	.917	-2	62	0	D-51/3-7,O-3(RF)	-1.8
2000	Chi N	105	299	34	60	15	2	10	37	36-2	2	69	.201	.289	.365	66	-17	4-0	.967	5	108	124	3-90	-0.9
Total	9	655	1902	254	446	76	12	86	307	260-16	6	477	.234	.326	.423	94	-20	17-6	.943	-1	100	107	3-400/O-95R,D-53,S-16,1-9	-2.3
GREENGRASS, JIM James Raymond B 10.24.1927 Addison, NY BR/TR 6-1/200# d9.9																								
1952	Cin N	18	68	10	21	2	1	5	24	7	0	12	.309	.373	.588	163	5	0-0	.965	-1	110	0	O-17(4-13-0)	0.4
1953	Cin N	154	606	86	173	22	7	20	100	47	3	83	.285	.340	.444	102	0	6-4	.983	3	110	80	*O-153(LF)	-0.6
1954	Cin N	139	542	79	152	27	4	27	95	41	0	81	.280	.329	.494	109	5	0-3	.968	3	105	101	*O-137(LF)	-0.2
1955	Cin N	13	39	1	4	2	0	0	1	9-0	0	9	.103	.271	.154	16	-5	0-0	1.000	1	125	111	O-11(LF)	-0.4
	Phi N	94	323	43	88	20	2	12	37	33-2	1	43	.272	.339	.458	112	6	0-2	.988	3	106	151	O-83(5-0-79)/3-2	0.4
	Year	107	362	44	92	22	2	12	38	42-2	1	52	.254	.331	.425	100	1	0-2	.990	4	108	146	O-94(16-0-79)/3-2	0.0
1956	Phi N	86	215	24	44	9	2	5	25	28-3	0	43	.205	.294	.335	71	-9	0-0	.991	-0	105	63	O-62(RF)	-1.1
Total	5	504	1793	243	482	82	16	69	282	165-5	4	271	.269	.330	.448	102	2	6-9	.980	8	108	94	O-463(310-13-141)/3-2	-1.5
GREENWELL, MIKE Michael Lewis B 7.18.1963 Louisville, KY BL/TR 6/200# d9.5																								
1985	Bos A	17	31	7	10	1	0	4	8	3-1	0	4	.323	.382	.742	191	4	1-0	1.000	-1	74	0	O-17(16-0-3)	0.2
1986	†Bos A	31	35	4	11	2	0	0	4	5-0	0	7	.314	.400	.371	111	1	0-0	1.000	2	153	257	O-15(8-0-7)/D-3	0.3
1987	Bos A	125	412	71	135	31	6	19	89	35-1	6	40	.328	.386	.570	146	27	5-4	.971	1	98	141	O-91(64-0-28),D-15/C	2.2
1988	†Bos A★	158	590	86	192	39	8	22	119	87-**18**	9	38	.325	.416	.531	158	49	16-8	.981	3	104	75	*O-147(143-0-8),D-11	4.8
1989	Bos A★	145	578	87	178	36	0	14	95	56-15	3	44	.308	.370	.443	121	18	13-5	.967	-10	76	136	*O-139(LF)/D-5	0.5
1990	†Bos A	159	610	71	181	30	6	14	73	65-12	4	43	.297	.367	.434	118	16	8-7	.977	-3	87	130	*O-159(LF)	0.7
1991	Bos A	147	544	76	163	26	6	9	83	43-6	3	35	.300	.350	.419	108	6	15-5	.989	0	96	120	*O-143(LF)/D	0.3
1992	Bos A	49	180	16	42	2	0	2	18	18-1	2	19	.233	.307	.278	62	-9	2-3	1.000	-1	102	36	O-41(LF)/D-6	-1.3
1993	Bos A	146	540	77	170	38	6	13	72	54-12	4	46	.315	.379	.480	122	18	5-4	.993	-1	98	77	*O-134(LF),D-10	1.0
1994	Bos A	95	327	60	88	25	1	11	45	38-6	4	26	.269	.348	.453	101	1	2-2	.993	0	86	175	O-84(LF)/D-6	-0.2
1995	†Bos A	120	481	67	143	25	4	15	76	38-4	2	35	.297	.349	.459	105	3	9-5	.972	-7	81	133	*O-118(LF)/D-2	-0.8
1996	Bos A	77	295	35	87	20	1	7	44	18-3	2	27	.295	.336	.441	93	-3	4-0	.973	3	96	188	O-76(75-1-1)	-0.2
Total	12	1269	4623	657	1400	275	38	130	726	460-79	39	364	.303	.368	.463	119	131	80-43	.981	-15	92	121	*O-1164(1124-1-47)/D-59,C	7.5
GREENWOOD, BILL William F. B 1857 Philadelphia, PA D 5.2.1902 Philadelphia, PA BB/TL 5-7.5/180# d9.16																								
1882	Phi AA	7	30	8	9	1	0	0	1	1			.300	.323	.333	114	0		.909	-1	0	0	/O-7(RF),2-2	-0.1
1884	Bro AA	92	385	52	83	8	3	3		10	1		.216	.237	.275	66	-15		.900	-9	103	96	*2-92/S	-1.9
1887	Bal AA	118	495	114	130	16	6	0	65	54	1		.263	.336	.319	88	-5	71	**.928**	10	102	69	*2-117/O(LF)	0.7

Year	Tm Lg	G	AB	R	H	2B	3B	HR	RBI	BB-IB	HP	SO	AVG	OBP	SLG	AOPS	ABR	SB-CS	FA	FR	Rng	Thr	G at Pos	BFW
1888	Bal AA	115	409	69	78	13	1	0	29	30	6		.191	.256	.227	57	-18	46	.913	-17	102	54	2-86,S-28/O(RF)	-3.0
1889	Col AA	118	414	62	93	7	10	3	49	58	5	71	.225	.327	.312	86	-6	37	.914	-2	95	84	*2-118	-0.3
1890	Roc AA	124	437	76	97	11	6	2	41	48	8		.222	.310	.288	83	-8	40	.921	1	100	114	*2-123/S	-0.2
Total	6	574	2170	381	490	56	26	8	185	201	21	71	.226	.298	.287	78	-52	194	.916	-18	100	85	2-538/S-30,O-9(1-0-8)	-4.8
GREER, BRIAN Brian Keith B 5.14.1959 Lynwood, CA BR/TR 6-3/210# d9.13																								
1977	SD N	1	1	0	0	0	0	0	0	0-0	0	1	.000	.000	.000	-99	0	0-0	—	0			H	0.0
1979	SD N	4	3	0	0	0	0	0	0	0-0	0	1	.000	.000	.000	-99	-1	0-0	1.000	-0	102	0	/O-4(CF)	-0.1
Total	2	5	4	0	0	0	0	0	0	0-0	0	2	.000	.000	.000	-99	-1	0-0	1.000	-0	102	0	/O-4(CF)	-0.1
GREER, ED Edward C. B 1865 Philadelphia, PA D 2.4.1890 Philadelphia, PA BR d6.24																								
1885	Bal AA	56	211	32	42	7	0	0	21	8	2		.199	.235	.232	49	-12		.908	-1	74	61	O-47(2-38-7),C-12	-1.2
1886	Bal AA	11	38	2	5	1	0	0	4	2	0		.132	.175	.158	5	-4	4	.875	-1	207	0	O-9(LF),C-2	-0.4
	Phi AA	71	264	33	51	5	3	1	20	8	2		.193	.223	.246	46	-17	12	.921	6	86	145	O-70(0-66-4)/C	-1.2
	Year	82	302	35	56	6	3	1	24	10	2		.185	.217	.235	41	-21	16	.919	6	96	133	O-79(9-66-4)/C-3	-1.6
1887	Phi AA	3	11	1	2	0	0	0	0	0	0		.182	.182	.182	2	-1	2	.857	0	238	0	/O-3(CF)	-0.1
	Bro AA	91	327	49	83	13	2	2	48	25	6		.254	.318	.324	79	-9	33	.921	2	64	35	O-76(LF),C-16	-0.6
	Year	94	338	50	85	13	2	2	48	25	6		.251	.314	.320	76	-11	35	.918	3	70	34	O-79(76-3-0),C-16	-0.7
Total	3	232	851	117	183	26	5	3	93	43	10		.215	.261	.268	58	-43	51	.916	7	80	76	O-205(87-107-11)/C-31	-3.5
GREER, RUSTY Thurman Clyde B 1.21.1969 Fort Rucker, AL BL/TL 6/190# d5.16																								
1994	Tex A	80	277	36	87	16	1	10	46	46-2	2	46	.314	.410	.487	132	15	0-0	.976	-4	101	41	O-73(11-23-53)/1-9	0.8
1995	Tex A	131	417	58	113	21	2	13	61	55-1	1	66	.271	.355	.424	100	1	3-1	.982	-2	95	121	*O-125(51-4-101)/1-3	-0.6
1996	†Tex A	139	542	96	180	41	6	18	100	62-4	3	86	.332	.397	.530	127	24	9-0	.984	2	105	62	*O-137(136-1-0)/1D	2.0
1997	Tex A	157	601	112	193	42	3	26	87	83-4	3	87	.321	.405	.531	135	33	9-5	.965	-1	101	93	*O-153(148-19-1)/D-2	2.6
1998	†Tex A	155	598	107	183	31	5	16	108	80-1	4	93	.306	.386	.455	115	15	2-4	.990	-1	100	66	*O-154(154-2-0)	0.7
1999	†Tex A	147	556	107	167	41	3	20	101	96-2	5	67	.300	.405	.493	123	23	2-2	.983	-6	97	32	*O-145(LF)/D	1.1
2000	Tex A	105	394	65	117	34	3	8	65	51-1	3	61	.297	.377	.459	110	8	4-1	.985	-4	99	51	O-97(LF)/D-2	0.1
2001	Tex A	62	245	38	67	23	0	7	29	27-1	1	32	.273	.342	.453	105	3	1-2	.962	-1	106	54	O-60(LF)/D	-0.1
2002	Tex A	51	199	24	59	9	2	1	17	19-0	0	17	.296	.356	.377	91	-2	1-0	.947	-5	71	0	O-26(22-0-6),D-22/1	-0.9
Total	9	1027	3829	643	1166	258	25	119	614	519-16	22	555	.305	.387	.478	118	120	31-15	.979	-21	99	65	O-970(824-49-161)/D-29,1-14	5.7
GREGG, TOMMY William Thomas B 7.29.1963 Boone, NC BL/TL 6-1/190# d9.14																								
1987	Pit N	10	8	3	2	1	0	0	0	0-0	0	2	.250	.250	.375	62	0	0-0	1.000	-0	83	0	/O-4(1-2-2)	-0.1
1988	Pit N	14	15	4	3	1	0	1	3	1-0	0	4	.200	.235	.467	103	0	0-1	1.000	-0	71	0	/O-6(5-0-1)	-0.1
	Atl N	11	29	1	10	3	0	0	4	2-1	0	2	.345	.387	.448	132	1	0-0	1.000	2	142	242	/O-7(5-3-0)	0.3
	Year	25	44	5	13	4	0	1	7	3-1	0	6	.295	.333	.455	125	1	0-1	1.000	2	122	174	O-13(10-3-1)	0.2
1989	Atl N	102	276	24	67	8	0	6	23	18-2	0	45	.243	.288	.337	76	-9	3-4	.967	-4	81	51	O-48(7-2-41),1-37	-1.9
1990	Atl N	124	239	18	63	13	1	5	32	20-4	1	39	.264	.322	.389	90	-3	4-3	.987	1	123	101	1-50,O-20(7-0-12)	-0.6
1991	†Atl N	72	107	13	20	8	1	1	4	12-2	1	24	.187	.275	.308	60	-5	2-2	1.000	0	91	0	O-14(9-0-5),1-13	-0.7
1992	Atl N	18	19	1	5	0	0	1	1	1-0	0	7	.263	.300	.421	96	0	1-0	1.000	1	188	0	/O-9(2-4-4)	0.1
1993	Cin N	10	12	1	2	0	0	0	1	0-0	0	0	.167	.154	.167	-10	-2	0-0	1.000	-1	50	0	/O-4(3-0-1)	-0.3
1995	Fla N	72	156	20	37	5	0	6	20	16-1	2	33	.237	.313	.385	83	-4	3-1	.984	-2	97	0	O-38(6-4-30)/1-2	-0.7
1997	†Atl N	13	19	1	5	2	0	0	0	1-0	0	2	.263	.300	.368	72	-1	1-1	1.000	-1	37	0	/O-6(5-0-1),1	-0.2
Total	9	446	880	86	214	41	2	20	88	71-10	4	158	.243	.301	.363	81	-23	14-12	.981	-4	92	32	O-156(50-15-97),1-103	-4.2
GREGORIO, TOM Thomas Andrew B 5.5.1977 Brooklyn, NY BR/TR 6-2/200# d9.5																								
2003	Ana A	12	19	1	3	0	0	0	2	1-0	1	8	.158	.238	.158	8	-3	0-0	.979	-0	121	129	C-12	-0.2
GREMMINGER, ED Lorenzo Edward "Battleship" B 3.30.1874 Canton, OH D 5.26.1942 Canton, OH BR/TR 6-1/200# d4.21																								
1895	Cle N	20	78	10	21	1	0	0	15	5	0	13	.269	.313	.282	51	-6	0	.873	-1	95	119	3-20	-0.5
1902	Bos N	140	522	55	134	20	12	1	65	39	5		.257	.314	.347	103	1	7	**.951**	2	94	83	*3-140	0.7
1903	Bos N	**140**	511	57	135	24	9	5	56	31	5		.264	.313	.376	100	-2	12	.935	16	106	132	*3-140	1.7
1904	Det A	83	309	18	66	13	3	1	28	14	4		.214	.257	.285	73	-9	3	.950	-13	78	38	3-83	-2.4
Total	4	383	1420	140	356	58	24	7	164	89	14	13	.251	.301	.340	92	-16	22	.940	4	95	93	3-383	-0.5
GREMP, BUDDY Lewis Edward B 8.5.1919 Denver, CO D 1.30.1995 Manteca, CA BR/TR 6-1/175# d9.13 Mil 1942-45																								
1940	Bos N	4	9	0	2	0	0	0	2	0	0	0	.222	.222	.222	24	-1	0	1.000	-0	80	117	/1-3	-0.1
1941	Bos N	37	75	7	18	3	0	0	10	5	0	3	.240	.287	.280	63	-4	0	.977	-3	59	115	1-21/2-6,C-3	-0.9
1942	Bos N	72	207	12	45	11	0	3	19	13	1	21	.217	.267	.314	71	-8	1	.991	1	108	10	1-62/3	-1.3
Total	3	113	291	19	65	14	0	3	31	18	1	24	.223	.271	.302	67	-13	1	.988	-3	96	38	/1-86,2-6,C-3,3	-2.3
GREY, REDDY Romer Carl (born Romer Carl Gray) B 4.8.1875 Zanesville, OH D 11.9.1934 Altadena, CA BL/TL 5-11/175# d5.28																								
1903	Pit N	1	3	1	1	0	0	0	1	1	0		.333	.500	.333	135	0	0	1.000	-0	0	0	/O(LF)	0.0
GRICH, BOBBY Robert Anthony B 1.15.1949 Muskegon, MI BR/TR 6-2/190# d6.29																								
1970	Bal A	30	95	11	20	1	3	0	8	9-0	0	21	.211	.279	.284	55	-6	1-1	.915	2	101	49	S-20/2-9,3	-0.2
1971	Bal A	7	30	7	9	0	0	1	6	5-0	0	8	.300	.400	.400	128	1	1-0	1.000	3	149	73	/S-5,2-2	0.5
1972	Bal A★	133	460	66	128	21	3	12	50	53-3	7	96	.278	.358	.415	127	17	13-6	.950	-6	97	126	S-81,2-45,1-16/3-8	2.5
1973	†Bal A	**162**	581	82	146	29	7	12	50	107-3	7	91	.251	.373	.387	116	17	17-9	**.995**	27	**114**	**129**	*2-162	5.5
1974	†Bal A★	160	582	92	153	29	6	19	82	90-6	**20**	117	.263	.376	.431	137	33	17-11	.979	16	**108**	**114**	*2-160	6.1
1975	Bal A	150	524	81	136	26	4	13	57	107-4	8	88	.260	.389	.399	133	30	14-10	.977	26	**111**	**133**	*2-150	6.5
1976	Bal A★	144	518	93	138	31	4	13	54	86-1	3	99	.266	.373	.417	140	30	14-6	.985	6	101	103	*2-140/3-2,D-2	**4.9**
1977	Cal A	52	181	24	44	6	0	7	23	37-4	1	40	.243	.369	.392	114	5	6-6	.983	-3	89	74	S-52	0.7
1978	Cal A	144	487	68	122	16	2	6	42	75-1	7	83	.251	.357	.329	98	2	4-3	.983	0	96	82	*2-144	1.0
1979	†Cal A★	153	534	78	157	30	5	30	101	59-10	2	84	.294	.365	.537	145	33	1-0	.984	-1	93	102	*2-153	3.9
1980	Cal A★	150	498	60	135	22	2	14	62	84-2	4	108	.271	.377	.408	119	17	3-7	.989	4	102	91	*2-146/1-3	2.7
1981	Cal A	100	352	56	107	14	2	**22**	61	40-4	4	71	.304	.378	**.543**	**164**	29	2-4	.983	18	**113**	122	*2-100	**5.2**
1982	†Cal A★	145	506	74	132	28	5	19	65	82-3	8	109	.261	.371	.449	124	20	3-3	.986	17	108	120	*2-142/D	4.3
1983	Cal A	120	387	65	113	17	0	16	62	76-2	7	62	.292	.414	.460	142	27	2-4	.969	18	**122**	106	*2-118/S	5.0
1984	Cal A	116	363	60	93	15	1	18	58	57-3	2	70	.256	.357	.452	124	13	2-5	.982	-3	99	120	2-91,1-25,3-21	1.2
1985	Cal A	144	479	74	116	17	3	13	53	81-3	3	77	.242	.355	.372	100	3	3-5	**.997**	12	110	**135**	*2-116,1-16,3-15/D-6	1.9
1986	†Cal A	98	313	42	84	18	0	9	30	39-1	3	54	.268	.354	.412	109	5	1-3	.980	-9	95	106	2-87,1-11/3-2	-0.1
Total	17	2008	6890	1033	1833	320	47	224	864	1087-50	86	1278	.266	.371	.424	125	276	104-83	.984	126	106	112	*2-1765,S-159/1-71,3-49,D-9	51.6
GRIESENBECK, TIM Carlos Phillipe Timothy B 12.10.1897 San Antonio, TX D 3.25.1953 San Antonio, TX BR/TR 5-10.5/190# d9.11																								
1920	StL N	5	3	1	1	0	0	0	0	0	0	0	.333	.333	.333	95	0	0-0	1.000	0	*0*	*0*	/C-3	0.0
GRIEVE, BEN Benjamin B 5.4.1976 Arlington, TX BL/TR 6-4/220# d9.3 f-Tom																								
1997	Oak A	24	93	12	29	6	0	3	24	13-1	1	25	.312	.402	.473	129	5	0-0	1.000	-2	78	63	O-24(RF)	0.1
1998	Oak A★	155	583	94	168	41	2	18	89	85-3	9	123	.288	.386	.458	122	22	2-2	.993	-10	88	64	*O-151(RF)/D-3	0.4
1999	Oak A	148	486	80	129	21	0	28	86	63-2	8	108	.265	.358	.481	117	12	4-0	.988	-2	96	77	*O-137(131-0-8)/D-4	0.6
2000	†Oak A	158	594	92	166	40	1	27	104	73-2	3	130	.279	.359	.487	115	14	3-0	.988	-10	84	73	*O-144(LF),D-12	-0.1
2001	TB A	154	542	72	143	30	2	11	72	87-2	8	159	.264	.372	.387	103	6	7-1	.984	0	106	55	*O-120(56-0-64),D-32	0.0
2002	TB A	136	482	62	121	30	0	19	64	69-5	8	121	.251	.353	.432	109	9	8-2	.988	0	103	79	*O-118(RF),D-16	0.3
2003	TB A	55	165	28	38	7	0	4	17	32-1	6	41	.230	.371	.345	93	0	0-0	.947	-0	86	175	D-37,O-10(RF)	-0.3
Total	7	830	2945	440	794	175	5	110	456	422-16	43	707	.270	.368	.444	113	68	24-5	.988	-24	94	71	O-704(331-0-375),D-104	1.0
GRIEVE, TOM Thomas Alan B 3.4.1948 Pittsfield, MA BR/TR 6-2/190# d7.5 s-Ben																								
1970	Was A	47	116	12	23	5	1	3	10	14-0	1	38	.198	.290	.336	76	-4	0-0	.939	-4	82	0	O-39(15-1-24)	-1.0
1972	Tex A	64	142	12	29	2	1	3	11	11-1	2	39	.204	.271	.296	72	-6	1-3	.985	1	89	216	O-49(45-3-5)	-0.8
1973	Tex A	66	123	22	38	6	0	7	21	7-0	1	25	.309	.348	.528	151	8	1-0	1.000	-3	92	0	O-59(34-10-19)/D	0.3
1974	Tex A	84	259	30	66	10	4	9	32	20-1	2	48	.255	.311	.429	114	4	0-0	1.000	3	99	232	D-40,O-38(31-0-7)/1	0.4
1975	Tex A	118	369	46	102	17	1	14	61	22-0	0	74	.276	.316	.442	113	5	0-2	.990	-4	83	73	O-63(46-2-16),D-45	-0.4
1976	Tex A	149	546	57	139	23	3	20	81	35-5	4	119	.255	.301	.418	108	3	4-1	.983	2	107	110	D-96,O-52(45-0-8)	0.1
1977	Tex A	79	236	24	53	9	0	7	30	13-1	3	57	.225	.273	.352	68	-11	1-0	.976	-3	76	136	O-60(30-0-32),D-13	-1.7
1978	NY N	54	101	5	21	3	0	2	8	9-0	0	23	.208	.273	.297	61	-6	0-1	.979	3	120	195	O-26(2-0-24)/1-2	-0.4

Year	Tm Lg	G	AB	R	H	2B	3B	HR	RBI	BB-IB	HP	SO	AVG	OBP	SLG	AOPS	ABR	SB-CS	FA	FR	Rng	Thr	G at Pos	BFW
1979	StL N	9	15	1	3	1	0	0	0	4-1	0	1	.200	.368	.267	76	0	0-0	.875	-1	89	0	/O-5(LF)	-0.1
Total	9	670	1907	209	474	76	10	65	254	135-9	13	424	.249	.301	.401	100	-7	7-7	.982	-4	91	113	O-391(253-16-135),D-195/1-3	-3.6
GRIFFEY, KEN George Kenneth Jr. "Junior" B 11.21.1969 Donora, PA BL/TL 6-3/205# d4.3 f-Ken																								
1989	Sea A	127	455	61	120	23	0	16	61	44-8	2	83	.264	.329	.420	107	4	16-7	.969	0	95	**184**	*O-127(CF)	0.4
1990	Sea A★	155	597	91	179	28	7	22	80	63-12	2	81	.300	.366	.481	134	27	16-11	.980	-11	87	108	*O-151(CF)/D-2	1.4
1991	Sea A★	154	548	76	179	42	1	22	100	71-21	1	82	.327	.399	.527	156	44	18-6	.989	3	96	202	*O-152(CF)/D	4.6
1992	Sea A★	142	565	83	174	39	4	27	103	44-15	5	67	.308	.361	.535	148	34	10-5	.997	-2	97	105	*O-137(CF)/D-3	3.2
1993	Sea A★	156	582	113	180	38	3	45	109	96-25	6	91	.309	.408	.617	170	60	17-9	.991	-7	89	109	*O-139(CF),D-19/1	5.1
1994	Sea A★	111	433	94	140	24	4	**40**	90	56-19	2	73	.323	.402	.674	168	43	11-3	.983	1	91	**239**	*O-103(0-103-1)/D-9	4.2
1995	†Sea A✳	72	260	52	67	7	0	17	42	52-6	0	53	.258	.379	.481	121	9	4-2	.990	6	115	157	O-70(CF)/D-2	1.5
1996	Sea A✳	140	545	125	165	26	2	49	140	78-13	7	104	.303	.392	.628	153	44	16-1	.990	5	109	122	*O-137(CF)/D-5	4.8
1997	†Sea A★	157	608	**125**	185	34	3	**56**	**147**	76-**23**	8	121	.304	.382	**.646**	165	57	15-4	.985	4	106	122	*O-153(1-153-0)/D-4	**6.0**
1998	Sea A★	**161**	633	120	180	33	3	**56**	146	76-11	7	121	.284	.365	.611	148	43	20-5	.988	8	108	120	*O-158(1-158-1)/1D	5.1
1999	Sea A★	160	606	123	173	26	3	**48**	134	91-**17**	7	108	.285	.384	.576	144	40	24-7	.978	-1	101	106	*O-158(CF)/D-6	4.0
2000	Cin N✳	145	520	100	141	22	3	40	118	94-17	9	117	.271	.387	.556	133	27	6-4	.987	2	106	103	*O-141(CF)	2.9
2001	Cin N	111	364	57	104	20	2	22	65	44-6	4	72	.286	.365	.533	124	13	2-0	.985	-10	89	20	O-90(CF)/D-2	0.4
2002	Cin N	70	197	17	52	8	0	8	23	28-6	3	39	.264	.358	.426	108	2	1-2	.971	-5	78	139	O-55(1-54-1)	-0.4
2003	Cin N	53	166	34	41	12	1	13	26	27-5	6	44	.247	.370	.566	143	11	1-0	.989	-2	89	129	O-43(CF)/D-3	0.9
Total	15	1914	7079	1271	2080	382	36	481	1384	940-204	69	1256	.294	.379	.562	145	458	177-66	.985	-10	98	130	*O-1814(3-1813-3)/D-59,1-2	44.1
GRIFFEY, KEN George Kenneth Sr. B 4.10.1950 Donora, PA BL/TL 6/200# d8.25 C9 s-Ken																								
1973	†Cin N	25	86	19	33	5	1	3	14	6-0	0	10	.384	.424	.570	182	9	4-2	1.000	-4	62	53	O-21(RF)	0.5
1974	Cin N	88	227	24	57	9	5	2	19	27-2	1	43	.251	.333	.361	96	-1	9-4	1.000	1	102	120	O-70(2-0-68)	-0.3
1975	†Cin N	132	463	95	141	15	9	4	46	67-2	1	67	.305	.391	.402	119	14	16-7	.967	-8	87	73	*O-119(RF)	0.1
1976	†Cin N★	148	562	111	189	28	9	6	74	62-0	1	65	.336	.401	.450	139	30	34-11	.979	-3	98	86	*O-144(RF)	2.5
1977	Cin N☆	154	585	117	186	35	8	12	57	69-2	0	84	.318	.389	.467	126	24	17-8	.990	4	108	91	*O-147(RF)	2.1
1978	Cin N	158	614	90	177	33	8	10	63	54-1	0	70	.288	.344	.417	112	9	23-5	.969	-1	101	108	*O-154(0-13-142)	0.5
1979	Cin N	95	380	62	120	27	4	8	32	36-3	1	39	.316	.374	.471	129	16	12-5	.984	-3	94	103	O-93(0-8-92)	0.9
1980	Cin N★	146	544	89	160	28	10	13	85	62-4	1	77	.294	.364	.454	128	21	23-1	.978	-3	106	43	*O-138(0-2-138)	1.6
1981	Cin N	101	396	65	123	21	6	2	34	39-6	1	42	.311	.370	.409	120	11	12-4	.989	5	109	123	O-99(CF)	1.8
1982	NY A	127	484	70	134	23	2	12	54	39-1	0	58	.277	.329	.407	103	2	10-4	.983	4	108	96	*O-125(0-26-102)	0.2
1983	NY A	118	458	60	140	21	3	11	46	34-3	2	45	.306	.355	.437	121	13	6-1	.992	1	98	99	*1-101/O-14(2-12-1),D-2	0.8
1984	NY A	120	399	44	109	20	1	7	56	29-2	1	32	.273	.321	.381	98	-1	2-2	.974	-0	105	124	O-82(38-35-9),1-27/D-2	-0.6
1985	NY A	127	438	68	120	28	4	10	69	41-4	0	51	.274	.331	.425	109	6	7-7	.970	5	109	128	*O-110(106-5-1)/1D	0.5
1986	NY A	59	198	33	60	7	0	9	26	15-0	1	24	.303	.349	.475	125	6	2-2	.971	2	103	167	O-51(50-2-1)/D-2	0.6
	Atl N	80	292	36	90	15	3	12	32	20-4	0	43	.308	.351	.503	126	9	12-7	.986	-2	96	20	O-77(LF)/1	0.4
1987	Atl N	122	399	65	114	24	1	14	64	46-11	1	54	.286	.358	.456	109	6	4-7	.995	-3	90	97	*O-107(107-1-0)/1-3	-0.3
1988	Atl N	69	193	21	48	5	0	2	19	17-2	0	26	.249	.307	.306	74	-6	1-3	.969	-3	79	83	O-42(41-0-2),1-11	-1.3
	Cin N	25	50	5	14	1	0	2	4	2-1	0	5	.280	.308	.420	103	0	0-0	.986	0	106	16	1-10	-0.1
	Year	94	243	26	62	6	0	4	23	19-3	0	31	.255	.307	.329	80	-6	1-3	.969	-3	79	83	O-42(41-0-2),1-21	-1.4
1989	Cin N	106	236	26	62	8	3	8	30	29-3	1	42	.263	.346	.424	115	5	4-2	.987	-6	79	74	O-58(58-0-1)/1-9	-0.3
1990	Cin N	46	63	6	13	2	0	1	8	2-0	1	5	.206	.235	.286	43	-5	2-1	.979	1	113	60	/1-9,O-6(5-0-1)	-0.5
	Sea A	21	77	13	29	2	0	3	18	10-0	0	3	.377	.443	.519	168	7	0-0	.963	-2	73	93	O-20(LF)	0.5
1991	Sea A	30	85	10	24	7	0	1	9	13-0	1	13	.282	.380	.400	117	3	0-0	1.000	-3	75	0	O-26(LF)/D	-0.1
Total	19	2097	7229	1129	2143	364	77	152	859	719-51	14	898	.296	.359	.431	118	178	200-83	.981	-17	99	91	*O-1703(532-203-989),1-172/D-14	9.5
GRIFFIN, ALFREDO Alfredo Claudino (born Baptist (Griffin)) B 10.6.1957 Santo Domingo, D.R. BB/TR 5-11/165# d9.4 C6																								
1976	Cle A	12	4	0	1	0	0	0	0	0-0	0	2	.250	.250	.250	47	0	0-1	.750	-1	51	0	/S-6,D-4	-0.2
1977	Cle A	14	41	5	6	1	0	0	3	3-0	0	5	.146	.205	.171	4	-6	2-2	.940	-3	86	86	S-13/D	-0.8
1978	Cle A	5	4	1	2	1	0	0	0	2-0	0	1	.500	.667	.750	301	1	0-0	.917	1	123	439	/S-2	0.3
1979	Tor A	153	624	81	179	22	10	2	31	40-0	5	59	.287	.333	.364	87	-12	21-16	.956	11	105	112	*S-153	1.3
1980	Tor A	155	653	63	166	26	**15**	2	41	24-2	4	58	.254	.283	.349	70	-30	18-23	.955	4	101	113	*S-155	-1.3
1981	Tor A	101	388	30	81	19	6	0	21	17-1	1	38	.209	.243	.289	50	-26	8-12	.937	-12	92	96	S-97/3-4,2	-3.2
1982	Tor A	**162**	539	57	130	20	8	1	48	22-0	0	48	.241	.269	.314	55	-34	10-8	.968	12	100	98	*S-162	-0.6
1983	Tor A	**162**	528	62	132	22	9	4	47	27-0	3	44	.250	.289	.348	71	-22	8-11	.965	-5	93	92	*S-157/2-5,D	-1.4
1984	Tor A★	140	419	53	101	8	2	4	30	4-0	1	33	.241	.248	.298	49	-30	11-3	.962	-17	86	99	*S-115,2-21/D-5	-3.4
1985	Oak A	**162**	614	75	166	18	7	2	64	20-1	0	50	.270	.290	.332	77	-22	24-9	.960	-10	97	85	*S-162	-1.4
1986	Oak A	**162**	594	74	169	23	6	4	51	35-6	2	52	.285	.323	.364	95	-6	33-16	.966	-8	95	83	*S-162	0.5
1987	Oak A	144	494	69	130	23	5	3	60	28-2	4	41	.263	.306	.348	79	-16	26-13	.963	9	100	91	*S-137/2	0.9
1988	†LA N	95	316	39	63	8	3	1	27	24-7	2	30	.199	.259	.253	49	-21	7-5	.965	5	101	94	S-93	-1.1
1989	LA N	136	506	49	125	27	2	0	29	29-2	0	57	.247	.287	.308	72	-19	10-7	.975	-3	93	113	*S-131	-1.4
1990	LA N	141	461	38	97	11	3	1	35	29-11	2	65	.210	.258	.254	43	-37	6-3	.959	12	104	95	*S-139	-1.6
1991	LA N	109	350	27	85	6	2	0	27	22-5	1	49	.243	.286	.271	60	-19	5-4	.961	21	**115**	89	*S-109	1.0
1992	†Tor A	63	150	21	35	7	0	0	10	9-0	0	19	.233	.273	.280	54	-9	3-1	.981	-4	93	55	S-48,2-16	-1.0
1993	†Tor A	46	95	15	20	3	0	0	3	3-0	0	13	.211	.235	.242	28	-10	0-0	.960	-2	70	74	S-20,2-11/3-6	-1.0
Total	18	1962	6780	759	1688	245	78	24	527	338-37	25	664	.249	.285	.319	67	-318	192-134	.961	9	98	96	*S-1861/2-55,D-11,3-10	-14.4
GRIFFIN, DOUG Douglas Lee B 6.4.1947 South Gate, CA BR/TR 6/170# d9.11																								
1970	Cal A	18	55	2	7	1	0	0	4	6-1	0	5	.127	.213	.145	1	-8	0-0	.964	-1	115	141	2-11/3-8	-0.9
1971	Bos A	125	483	51	118	23	2	3	27	31-3	2	45	.244	.291	.319	68	-20	11-5	.986	6	102	104	*2-124	-0.5
1972	Bos A	129	470	43	122	12	1	2	35	45-6	2	48	.260	.325	.302	83	-8	9-2	.978	-3	92	91	*2-129	-0.1
1973	Bos A	113	396	43	101	14	5	1	33	21-0	3	42	.255	.293	.323	71	-16	7-5	.990	-6	92	100	*2-113	-1.5
1974	Bos A	93	312	35	83	12	4	0	33	28-3	2	21	.266	.329	.330	85	-6	2-8	.979	-13	98	82	2-91/S	-1.6
1975	†Bos A	100	287	21	69	6	0	1	29	18-0	2	29	.240	.288	.272	55	-17	2-2	.967	-14	91	83	2-99/S	-2.7
1976	Bos A	49	127	14	24	2	0	0	4	9-0	1	14	.189	.248	.205	30	-11	2-1	.989	-12	84	62	2-44/D-2	-2.2
1977	Bos A	5	6	0	0	0	0	0	0	0-0	0	0	.000	.000	.000	-90	-2	0-0	1.000	-0	99	125	/2-3	-0.2
Total	8	632	2136	209	524	70	12	7	165	158-13	12	204	.245	.299	.299	68	-88	33-23	.981	-43	95	92	2-614/3-8,D-2,S-2	-9.7
GRIFFIN, PUG Francis Arthur B 4.24.1896 Lincoln, NE D 10.12.1951 Colorado Springs, CO BR/TR 5-11.5/187# d7.27																								
1917	Phi A	18	25	4	5	1	0	1	3	1	0	9	.200	.231	.360	81	-1	1	1.000	1	161	55	/1-3	0.0
1920	NY N	5	4	0	1	0	0	0	0	1	0	2	.250	.400	.250	90	0	0-0	1.000	-0	56	0	/O-2(0-1-1)	0.0
Total	2	23	29	4	6	1	0	1	3	2	0	11	.207	.258	.345	83	-1	1-0	1.000	0	161	55	/1-3,O-2(0-1-1)	0.0
GRIFFIN, IVY Ivy Moore B 11.16.1896 Thomasville, AL D 8.25.1957 Gainesville, FL BL/TR 5-11/180# d9.9																								
1919	Phi A	17	68	5	20	2	2	0	6	3	1	10	.294	.333	.382	99	0	0	.989	4	182	106	1-17	0.3
1920	Phi A	129	467	46	111	15	1	0	20	17	11	49	.238	.281	.274	47	-36	3-3	.990	5	118	101	*1-127/2-2	-3.4
1921	Phi A	39	103	14	33	4	2	0	13	5	3	6	.320	.369	.398	95	-1	1-2	.973	-2	82	69	1-27	-0.5
Total	3	185	638	65	164	21	5	0	39	25	15	65	.257	.301	.306	60	-37	4-5	.988	7	119	97	1-171/2-2	-3.6
GRIFFIN, MIKE Michael Joseph B 3.20.1865 Utica, NY D 4.10.1908 Utica, NY BL/TR 5-7/160# d4.16 M1																								
1887	Bal AA	136	532	142	160	32	13	3	94	55	8		.301	.375	.427	131	25	94	.924	-15	58	21	*O-136(1-135-0)	0.4
1888	Bal AA	**137**	542	103	139	21	11	0	46	55	5		.256	.331	.336	117	12	46	.938	5	123	117	*O-137(CF)	1.2
1889	Bal AA	137	531	**152**	148	21	14	4	48	91	3	29	.279	.387	.394	120	17	39	.910	-12	81	108	*O-109(CF),S-25/2-5	0.2
1890	Phi P	115	489	127	140	29	6	6	54	64	7	19	.286	.377	.407	107	6	30	**.954**	13	**148**	**223**	*O-115(4-100-13)	1.2
1891	Bro N	134	521	106	139	**36**	9	3	65	57	1	31	.267	.340	.388	113	9	65	**.960**	20	147	191	*O-134(2-132-0)	2.2
1892	Bro N	129	452	103	125	17	11	3	66	68	4	36	.277	.376	.383	134	22	49	**.986**	6	120	164	*O-127(0-126-1)/S-2	1.8
1893	Bro N	95	362	85	103	21	7	6	59	59	8	23	.285	.396	.431	126	16	30	**.965**	7	122	243	*O-93(CF)/2-2	1.4
1894	Bro N	108	406	123	145	29	4	5	76	78	4	14	.357	.465	.485	139	35	39	.966	4	77	113	*O-107(CF)	2.4
1895	Bro N	132	524	140	174	38	7	4	65	93	10	30	.332	.442	.454	143	44	27	**.969**	12	117	**287**	*O-132(CF)/S	3.8
1896	Bro N	122	493	101	152	27	9	4	51	48	9	25	.308	.380	.424	118	15	23	.961	1	46	23	*O-122(CF)	0.7
1897	Bro N	134	534	136	169	25	11	2	56	81	10		.316	.416	.416	127	27	16	.956	3	68	161	*O-134(CF)	1.8
1898	Bro N	134	537	88	161	18	6	2	40	60	8		.300	.379	.367	114	12	15	**.974**	6	107	154	*O-134(CF),M	0.9
Total	12	1513	5923	1406	1755	314	108	42	720	809	77	207	.296	.388	.407	124	240	473	.956	50	101	149	*O-1480(7-1461-14)/S-28,2-7	18.0

Year	Tm Lg	G	AB	R	H	2B	3B	HR	RBI	BB-IB	HP	SO	AVG	OBP	SLG	AOPS	ABR	SB-CS	FA	FR	Rng	Thr	G at Pos	BFW
GRIFFIN, THOMAS Thomas William B 1.1857 Titusville, PA D 4.17.1933 Rockford, IL d9.27																								
1884	Mil U	11	41	5	9	2	0	0		3			.220	.273	.268	119	0		.918	-2	31	0	1-11	-0.2
GRIFFIN, SANDY Tobias Charles B 10.24.1858 Fayetteville, NY D 6.4.1926 Syracuse, NY BR/TR 5-10/160# d5.26 M1																								
1884	NY N	16	62	7	11	2	0	0	6	1		19	.177	.190	.210	25	-5		.842	-2	78	227	O-16(0-5-11)	-0.6
1890	Roc AA	107	407	85	125	28	4	5	53	50	4		.307	.388	.432	153	30	21	.856	-21	38	25	*O-107(CF)/2	0.5
1891	Was AA	20	69	15	19	4	2	0	10	10	4	3	.275	.398	.391	132	4	2	.939	-2	35	138	O-20(CF),M	0.1
1893	StL N	23	92	9	18	1	1	0	9	16	0	2	.196	.315	.228	45	-7	2	.906	-2	50	0	O-23(LF)	-0.9
Total	4	166	630	116	173	35	7	5	78	77	8	24	.275	.361	.376	120	22	25	.873	-26	43	49	O-166(23-132-11)/2	-0.9
GRIFFITH, BERT Bartholomew Joseph "Buck" B 3.30.1896 St.Louis, MO D 5.5.1973 Bishop, CA BR/TR 5-11/185# d4.13 gf-Matt Williams																								
1922	Bro N	106	325	45	100	22	8	2	35	5	2	11	.308	.322	.443	96	-3	5-7	.981	0	102	77	O-77(0-8-69)/1-6	-1.0
1923	Bro N	79	248	23	73	8	4	2	37	13	1	16	.294	.332	.383	91	-4	1-2	.949	-5	96	19	O-62(51-9-3)	-1.3
1924	Was A	6	8	1	1	0	0	0	0	0	0	1	.125	.125	.125	-37	-2	0-0	1.000	0	165	0	/O-2(CF)	-0.1
Total	3	191	581	69	174	30	12	4	72	18	3	28	.299	.324	.413	92	-9	6-9	.968	-4	100	51	O-141(51-19-72)/1-6	-2.4
GRIFFITH, DERRELL Robert Derrell B 12.12.1943 Anadarko, OK BL/TR 6/168# d9.26																								
1963	LA N	1	2	0	0	0	0	0	0	0-0	0	0	.000	.000	.000	-99	-1	0-0	—	-0	0	0	/2	-0.1
1964	LA N	78	238	27	69	16	2	4	23	5-0	1	21	.290	.307	.424	112	3	5-1	.769	-11	83	61	3-35,O-29(6-0-23)	-1.0
1965	LA N	22	41	3	7	0	0	1	2	0-0	0	9	.171	.171	.244	16	-5	0-0	1.000	0	120	0	O-11(10-0-1)	-0.5
1966	LA N	23	15	3	1	0	0	0	2	2-2	0	3	.067	.176	.067	-32	-3	0-0	1.000	0	171	0	/O-7(5-1-2)	-0.3
Total	4	124	296	33	77	16	2	5	27	7-2	1	33	.260	.280	.378	90	-6	5-1	.970	-11	106	39	/O-47(21-1-26),3-35,2	-1.9
GRIFFITH, TOMMY Thomas Herman B 10.26.1889 Prospect, OH D 4.13.1967 Cincinnati, OH BL/TR 5-10/175# d8.28																								
1913	Bos N	37	127	16	32	4	1	1	12	9	0	8	.252	.301	.323	77	-4	1-7	.886	-0	93	152	O-35(RF)	-0.9
1914	Bos N	16	48	3	5	0	0	0	1	2	0	6	.104	.140	.104	-27	-8	0	.931	3	82	307	O-14(1-0-14)	-0.6
1915	Cin N	**160**	583	59	179	31	16	4	85	41	2	34	.307	.355	.436	136	24	6-24	.952	-14	85	60	*O-160(2-0-160)	-0.7
1916	Cin N	**155**	595	50	158	28	7	2	61	36	2	37	.266	.310	.346	104	2	16	.967	2	90	140	*O-155(RF)	-0.6
1917	Cin N	115	363	45	98	18	7	1	45	19	1	23	.270	.308	.366	111	4	5	.974	7	103	155	*O-100(RF)	0.6
1918	Cin N	118	427	47	113	10	4	2	48	39	0	30	.265	.326	.321	99	0	10	.969	3	107	104	*O-118(RF)	-0.3
1919	Bro N	125	484	65	136	18	4	6	57	23	1	32	.281	.315	.372	104	1	8	.954	-2	93	111	*O-125(RF)	-0.8
1920	†Bro N	93	334	41	87	9	4	2	30	15	0	18	.260	.292	.329	76	-11	3-3	.972	-7	86	68	O-92(RF)	-2.5
1921	Bro N	129	455	66	142	21	6	12	71	36	1	13	.312	.364	.464	113	9	3-3	.972	7	95	**169**	*O-124(RF)	0.6
1922	Bro N	99	329	44	104	17	8	4	49	23	0	10	.316	.361	.453	110	4	7-1	.952	2	101	120	O-82(RF)	0.0
1923	Bro N	131	481	70	141	21	9	8	66	50	1	19	.293	.361	.424	109	7	8-2	.927	-7	87	100	*O-127(RF)	-0.9
1924	Bro N	140	482	43	121	19	5	3	67	34	0	19	.251	.300	.330	71	-20	0-5	.965	-7	94	65	*O-139(RF)	-3.9
1925	Bro N	7	4	2	0	0	0	0	0	3	0	2	.000	.429	.000	20	0	1-0	1.000	0	145	0	/O-2(RF)	0.0
	Chi N	76	235	38	67	12	1	7	27	21	1	11	.285	.346	.434	97	-1	2-4	.937	-2	92	117	O-60(4-4-53)	-0.8
	Year	83	239	40	67	12	1	7	27	24	1	13	.280	.348	.427	96	-1	3-4	.938	-2	93	116	O-62(4-4-55)	-0.8
Total	13	1401	4947	589	1383	208	72	52	619	351	9	262	.280	.328	.382	102	7	70-49	.956	-15	93	112	*O-1333(7-4-1326)	-10.8
GRIGGS, ART Arthur Carle B 12.10.1883 Topeka, KS D 12.19.1938 Los Angeles, CA BR/TR 5-11/185# d5.2 OF Total (44-LF 2-CF 50-RF)																								
1909	StL A	108	364	38	102	17	5	0	43	24	3		.280	.330	.354	125	10	11	.982	-2	110	84	1-49,O-41(36-2-3)/2-8,S	0.5
1910	StL A	123	416	28	98	22	5	2	30	25	1		.236	.281	.327	96	-3	11	.878	-1	98	60	O-49(6-0-43),2-41,1-17/S-3,3-3	-0.7
1911	Cle A	27	68	7	17	3	2	1	7	5	0		.250	.301	.397	93	-1	1	.949	-1	104	76	2-11/O-4(1-0-3),3-3,1	-0.1
1912	Cle A	89	273	29	83	16	7	0	39	33	1		.304	.381	.414	123	9	10	.986	1	102	93	1-71	0.8
1914	Bro F	40	112	10	32	6	1	1	15	5	2	11	.286	.328	.384	94	-3	1	.980	-3	61	71	1-27/O(LF)	-0.6
1915	Bro F	27	38	4	11	1	0	1	2	3	2	7	.289	.372	.395	117	0	0	1.000	1	146	104	/1-5,O(RF)	0.1
1918	Det A	28	99	11	36	8	0	0	16	10	0	5	.364	.422	.444	168	9	2	.986	-3	55	64	1-25	0.6
Total	7	442	1370	127	379	73	20	5	152	105	9	23	.277	.332	.370	115	21	36	.983	-8	94	85	1-195/O-96R,2-60,3-6,S-4	0.6
GRIGSBY, DENVER Denver Clarence B 3.25.1901 Jackson, KY D 11.10.1973 Sapulpa, OK BL/TR 5-9/155# d8.29																								
1923	Chi N	24	72	8	21	5	2	0	5	7	1	5	.292	.363	.417	105	1	1-3	1.000	-1	102	47	O-22(6-1-16)	-0.2
1924	Chi N	124	411	58	123	18	2	3	48	31	6	47	.299	.357	.375	95	-1	10-19	.974	5	100	134	*O-121(108-5-8)	-1.0
1925	Chi N	51	137	20	35	5	0	0	20	19	0	12	.255	.346	.292	64	-7	1-1	.966	-0	96	115	O-39(21-15-3)	-0.9
Total	3	199	620	86	179	28	4	3	73	57	7	64	.289	.355	.361	89	-7	12-23	.975	4	99	120	O-182(135-21-27)	-2.1
GRIM, JOHN John Helm B 8.9.1867 Lebanon, KY D 7.28.1961 Indianapolis, IN BR/TR 6-2/175# d9.29 OF Total (2-LF 12-RF)																								
1888	Phi N	2	7	0	1	0	0	0	0	0	0	0	.143	.143	.143	-8	-1	0	—	-1	0	0	/O(RF)2	-0.2
1890	Roc AA	50	192	30	51	6	9	2	34	7	2		.266	.299	.422	121	3	14	.851	-5	78	122	S-21,C-15/3-8,2-4,O-3(RF),1-2,P	0.0
1891	Mil AA	29	119	14	28	5	1	1	14	2	0	5	.235	.248	.319	52	-9	1	.926	4	*120*	*76*	C-16,3-10/2-3	-0.3
1892	Lou N	97	370	40	90	16	4	1	36	13	6	24	.243	.280	.316	87	-7	18	.940	-9	*90*	*102*	C-69,1-11,2-10/O-8(1-0-7),S3	-0.9
1893	Lou N	99	415	68	111	19	8	3	54	12	9	10	.267	.303	.373	86	-10	15	.952	-5	*105*	*112*	*C-92/1-3,2-2,O(RF)S	-0.5
1894	Lou N	109	412	66	123	27	7	7	71	18	10	15	.299	.343	.449	96	-4	14	.927	10	*99*	*126*	C-78,2-24/1-7,3	1.1
1895	Bro N	94	333	55	93	17	5	0	45	13	7	9	.279	.320	.360	82	-9	10	.947	8	*132*	*114*	*C-92/O(LF)1	0.6
1896	Bro N	81	281	32	75	13	1	2	35	12	6	14	.267	.311	.342	76	-10	7	.939	-1	*105*	*103*	C-77/1-5	-0.3
1897	Bro N	80	290	26	72	10	1	0	25	1	3		.248	.259	.290	47	-23	3	.947	-1	*89*	***129***	C-77	-1.5
1898	Bro N	52	178	17	50	5	1	0	11	8	3		.281	.323	.320	85	-4	1	.950	-4	*93*	*102*	C-52	-0.3
1899	Bro N	15	47	3	13	1	0	0	7	1	2		.277	.320	.298	68	-2	0	.966	1	*89*	*112*	C-12	0.0
Total	11	708	2644	351	707	119	37	16	332	87	48	77	.267	.303	.359	82	-76	83	.943	-3	*104*	*112*	C-580/2-44,1-29,S-23,3-20,O-14R,P	-2.3
GRIMES, ROY Austin Roy "Bummer" B 9.11.1893 Bergholz, OH D 9.13.1954 Hanover Twsp., OH BR/TR 6-1/176# d7.5 twb-Ray																								
1920	NY N	26	57	5	9	1	0	0	3	3	0	8	.158	.200	.175	8	-7	1-1	.948	-2	106	48	2-21	-0.9
GRIMES, ED Edward Adelbert B 9.8.1905 Chicago, IL D 10.5.1974 Chicago, IL BR/TR 5-10/165# d4.19																								
1931	StL A	43	57	9	15	1	2	0	5	9	0	3	.263	.364	.351	86	-1	1-0	.892	-2	91	0	3-22/2-4,S-3	-0.2
1932	StL A	31	68	7	16	0	1	0	13	6	0	12	.235	.297	.265	44	-6	0-1	.891	1	119	148	3-18/2-2,S	-0.4
Total	2	74	125	16	31	1	3	0	18	15	0	15	.248	.329	.304	63	-7	1-1	.891	-1	107	86	/3-40,2-6,S-4	-0.6
GRIMES, OSCAR Oscar Ray Jr. B 4.13.1915 Minerva, OH D 5.19.1993 Westlake, OH BR/TR 5-11/178# d9.28 f-Ray																								
1938	Cle A	4	10	2	2	0	1	0	2	2	0	0	.200	.333	.400	85	0	0-0	1.000	-1	58	123	/2-2,1	-0.1
1939	Cle A	119	364	51	98	20	5	4	56	56	1	61	.269	.368	.385	96	-1	8-3	.968	-10	91	81	2-48,1-43,S-37/3-3	-0.8
1940	Cle A	11	13	3	0	0	0	0	0	0	0	5	.000	.000	.000	-99	-4	0-0	.958	1	164	132	/1-4,3	-0.3
1941	Cle A	77	244	28	58	9	3	4	24	39	1	47	.238	.345	.348	88	-4	4-0	.995	-4	75	104	1-62,2-13/3	-1.2
1942	Cle A	51	84	10	15	2	0	0	2	13	0	17	.179	.289	.202	42	-6	3-2	.944	-4	83	98	2-24/3-8,1S	-0.9
1943	NY A	9	20	4	3	0	0	0	1	3	0	7	.150	.261	.150	21	-2	0-0	1.000	0	105	224	/S-3,1	-0.2
1944	NY A	116	387	44	108	17	8	5	46	59	2	57	.279	.377	.403	119	11	6-0	.945	-11	90	79	3-97,S-20	0.4
1945	NY A*	142	480	64	127	19	7	4	45	97	6	73	.265	.395	.358	114	14	7-6	.937	7	105	**136**	*3-141/1	2.3
1946	NY A	14	39	1	8	1	0	0	4	1	0	7	.205	.225	.231	27	-4	0-1	.895	-1	72	75	/S-7,2-5	-0.5
	Phi A	59	191	28	50	5	0	1	20	27	1	29	.262	.356	.304	86	-2	2-0	.958	-9	85	99	2-43/3-6,S-4	-0.9
	Year	73	230	29	58	6	0	1	24	28	1	36	.252	.336	.291	76	-6	2-1	.957	-10	86	97	2-48,S-11/3-6	-1.4
Total	9	602	1832	235	469	73	24	18	200	297	11	303	.256	.363	.352	98	2	30-12	.940	-32	100	109	3-257,2-135,1-113/S-72	-2.2
GRIMES, RAY Oscar Ray Sr. B 9.11.1893 Bergholz, OH D 5.25.1953 Minerva, OH BR/TR 5-11/168# d9.24 twb-Roy s-Oscar																								
1920	Bos A	1	4	1	1	0	0	0	0	1	0	0	.250	.400	.250	78	0	0-0	1.000	-0	0	283	/1	0.0
1921	Chi N	147	530	91	170	38	6	6	79	70	6	55	.321	.406	.449	126	24	5-8	.993	-5	83	86	*1-147	0.8
1922	Chi N	138	509	99	180	45	12	14	99	75	6	33	.354	.442	.572	157	47	7-7	.987	-2	96	106	*1-138	3.2
1923	Chi N	64	216	32	71	7	2	2	36	24	2	17	.329	.401	.407	114	5	5-0	.991	-1	91	99	1-62	0.1
1924	Chi N	51	177	33	53	6	5	5	34	28	2	15	.299	.401	.475	132	9	4-2	.982	-8	42	95	1-50	-0.2
1926	Phi N	32	101	13	30	5	0	0	15	6	1	13	.297	.343	.347	82	-2	0	.981	0	112	121	1-28	-0.4
Total	6	433	1537	269	505	101	25	27	263	204	17	133	.329	.413	.480	132	83	21-17	.989	-16	85	98	1-426	3.5
GRIMM, CHARLIE Charles John "Jolly Cholly" B 8.28.1898 St.Louis, MO D 11.15.1983 Scottsdale, AZ BL/TL 5-11.5/173# d7.30 M19 C4																								
1916	Phi A	12	22	0	2	0	0	0	0	2	0	4	.091	.167	.091	-24	-3	0	.875	-1	91	0	/O-7(3-1-3)	-0.5
1918	StL N	50	141	11	31	7	0	0	12	6	2	15	.220	.262	.270	64	-6	2	.971	-3	65	115	1-42/O-2(RF),3	-1.2
1919	Pit N	14	44	6	14	1	3	0	6	2	0	4	.318	.348	.477	141	2	1	.968	-3	29	17	1-13	-0.1
1920	Pit N	148	533	38	121	13	7	2	54	30	4	40	.227	.273	.289	60	-28	7-8	**.995**	4	108	106	*1-148	-3.1

Year	Tm Lg	G	AB	R	H	2B	3B	HR	RBI	BB-IB	HP	SO	AVG	OBP	SLG	AOPS	ABR	SB-CS	FA	FR	Rng	Thr	G at Pos	BFW
1921	Pit N	151	562	62	154	21	17	7	71	31	2	38	.274	.314	.409	88	-12	6-8	.994	-7	78	94	*1-150	-3.0
1922	Pit N	154	593	64	173	28	13	0	76	43	3	15	.292	.343	.383	86	-13	6-10	.994	-3	84	94	*1-154	-2.7
1923	Pit N	152	563	78	194	29	13	7	99	41	0	43	.345	.389	.480	125	20	6-9	**.995**	3	103	**111**	*1-152	1.0
1924	Pit N	151	542	53	156	25	12	2	63	37	2	22	.288	.336	.389	92	-6	3-6	**.995**	-3	87	**121**	*1-151	-2.1
1925	Chi N	141	519	73	159	29	5	10	76	38	0	25	.306	.354	.439	100	0	4-3	.989	-0	99	**112**	*1-139	-0.9
1926	Chi N	147	524	58	145	30	6	8	82	49	3	25	.277	.342	.403	99	-1	3	.988	-6	81	119	*1-147	-1.6
1927	Chi N	147	543	68	169	29	6	2	74	45	3	21	.311	.367	.398	105	5	3	.990	2	105	96	*1-147	-0.3
1928	Chi N	147	547	67	161	25	5	5	62	39	1	20	.294	.342	.386	91	-8	7	**.993**	-2	86	122	*1-147	-1.9
1929	†Chi N	120	463	66	138	28	3	10	91	42	1	25	.298	.358	.436	95	-3	3	.992	-1	94	116	*1-120	-1.1
1930	Chi N	114	429	58	124	27	2	6	65	41	6	26	.289	.359	.403	83	-10	1	**.995**	0	96	99	*1-113	-1.6
1931	Chi N	146	531	65	176	33	11	4	66	53	1	29	.331	.393	.458	126	21	1	**.993**	1	99	85	*1-144	0.8
1932	†Chi N	149	570	66	175	42	2	7	80	35	2	22	.307	.349	.425	108	7	2	.993	9	119	**108**	*1-149,M	0.2
1933	Chi N	107	384	38	95	15	2	3	37	23	0	15	.247	.290	.320	74	-13	1	**.996**	9	125	119	*1-104,M	-1.5
1934	Chi N	75	267	24	79	8	1	5	47	16	1	12	.296	.338	.390	96	-2	1	.995	1	98	75	1-74,M	-0.8
1935	Chi N	2	8	0	0	0	0	0	0	0	0	1	.000	.000	.000	-99	-2	0	1.000	-0	65	236	/1-2,M	-0.3
1936	Chi N	39	132	13	33	4	0	1	16	5	0	8	.250	.277	.303	55	-9	0	1.000	5	150	128	1-35,M	-0.6
Total	20	2166	7917	908	2299	394	108	79	1077	578	31	410	.290	.341	.397	95	-61	57-44	.993	5	97	106	*1-2131/O-9(3-1-5),3	-21.3
GRIMSHAW, MYRON Myron Frederick B 11.30.1875 St.Johnsville, NY D 12.11.1936 Canajoharie, NY BB/TR 6-1/173# d4.25																								
1905	Bos A	85	285	39	68	8	2	4	35	21	1		.239	.293	.323	94	-2	4	.980	-5	74	126	1-74	-1.0
1906	Bos A	110	428	46	124	16	12	0	48	23	4		.290	.332	.383	124	10	5	.987	-2	90	83	*1-110	0.7
1907	Bos A	64	181	19	37	7	2	0	33	16	1		.204	.273	.265	72	-5	6	.980	-4	84	127	1-20,O-18(1-0-17)/S-2	-1.1
Total	3	259	894	104	229	31	16	4	116	60	6		.256	.307	.340	104	3	15	.984	-11	84	103	1-204/O-18(1-0-17),S-2	-1.4
GRISSOM, MARQUIS Marquis Deon B 4.17.1967 Atlanta, GA BR/TR 5-11/190# d8.22																								
1989	Mon N	26	74	16	19	2	0	1	2	12-0	0	21	.257	.360	.324	96	0	1-0	.943	-3	69	104	O-23(1-22-1)	-0.3
1990	Mon N	98	288	42	74	14	2	3	29	27-2	0	40	.257	.320	.351	88	-5	22-2	.988	0	100	106	O-87(18-35-40)	-0.2
1991	Mon N	148	558	73	149	23	9	6	39	34-0	1	89	.267	.310	.373	93	-7	**76**-17	.984	8	108	**194**	*O-138(3-125-11)	1.0
1992	Mon N	159	653	99	180	39	6	14	66	42-6	5	81	.276	.322	.418	110	7	**78**-13	.983	-7	97	78	*O-157(CF)	1.2
1993	Mon N★	157	630	104	188	27	2	19	95	52-6	3	76	.298	.351	.438	106	6	53-10	.984	0	102	97	*O-157(CF)	1.5
1994	Mon N★	110	475	96	137	25	4	11	45	41-4	1	66	.288	.344	.427	99	-1	36-6	.985	9	118	117	*O-109(CF)	1.5
1995	†Atl N	139	551	80	142	23	3	12	42	47-4	3	61	.258	.317	.376	80	-16	29-9	.994	3	104	132	*O-136(CF)	-0.8
1996	†Atl N	158	671	106	207	32	10	23	74	41-6	3	73	.308	.349	.489	112	10	28-11	.997	-3	94	127	*O-158(CF)	1.1
1997	†Cle A	144	558	74	146	27	6	12	66	43-1	6	89	.262	.317	.396	83	-15	22-13	.992	-2	99	97	*O-144(CF)	-1.4
1998	Mil N	142	542	57	147	28	1	10	60	24-2	2	78	.271	.304	.382	79	-18	13-8	.991	-2	100	95	*O-137(CF)	-1.9
1999	Mil N	154	603	92	161	27	1	20	83	49-4	0	109	.267	.320	.415	86	-15	24-6	.987	-8	100	12	*O-149(CF)	-1.8
2000	Mil N	146	595	67	145	18	2	14	62	39-2	0	99	.244	.288	.351	62	-37	20-10	.992	-12	95	33	*O-142(CF)	-4.4
2001	LA N	135	448	56	99	17	1	21	60	16-0	2	107	.221	.250	.404	71	-23	7-5	**1.000**	-3	94	100	*O-123(26-95-3)/D-2	-2.6
2002	LA N	111	343	57	95	21	4	17	60	22-2	2	68	.277	.321	.510	127	9	5-1	.978	-4	92	103	*O-102(36-72-2)	0.5
2003	†SF N	149	587	82	176	33	3	20	79	20-0	2	82	.300	.322	.468	107	3	11-3	.977	-6	101	38	*O-148(CF)	0.0
Total	15	1976	7576	1101	2065	356	54	203	862	509-39	30	1139	.273	.319	.414	93	-102	425-114	.987	-29	100	93	*O-1910(84-1786-57)/D-2	-6.6
GROAT, DICK Richard Morrow B 11.4.1930 Wilkinsburg, PA BR/TR 5-11.5/180# d6.19 Mil 1953																								
1952	Pit N	95	384	38	109	6	1	1	29	19	1	27	.284	.319	.313	74	-14	2-4	.952	5	99	91	S-94	-0.5
1955	Pit N	151	521	45	139	28	2	4	51	38-11	1	26	.267	.317	.351	78	-16	0-2	.961	17	105	106	*S-149	1.2
1956	Pit N	142	520	40	142	19	3	0	37	35-3	0	25	.273	.317	.321	74	-19	0-3	.954	7	104	82	*S-141/3-2	-0.1
1957	Pit N	125	501	58	158	30	5	7	54	27-1	3	28	.315	.350	.437	114	10	0-1	.968	4	106	94	*S-123/3-2	2.4
1958	Pit N	151	584	67	175	36	9	3	66	23-7	4	32	.300	.328	.408	97	-4	2-2	.975	9	102	**126**	*S-149	1.7
1959	Pit N★	147	593	74	163	22	7	5	51	32-2	2	35	.275	.312	.361	80	-18	0-2	.964	2	103	**110**	*S-145	-0.4
1960	†Pit N★	138	573	85	186	26	4	2	50	39-0	4	35	**.325**	.371	.394	109	8	0-2	.966	13	**109**	**123**	*S-136	3.3
1961	Pit N	148	596	71	164	25	6	6	55	40-0	1	44	.275	.320	.367	82	-16	0-4	.957	11	108	**125**	*S-144/3	0.6
1962	Pit N★	**161**	678	76	199	34	3	2	61	31-1	3	61	.294	.325	.361	85	-15	2-1	.956	16	104	**126**	*S-161	1.5
1963	StL N★	158	631	85	201	**43**	11	6	73	56-2	6	58	.319	.377	.450	126	24	3-1	.964	-14	95	101	*S-158	2.6
1964	†StL N★	161	636	70	186	35	6	1	70	44-3	0	42	.292	.335	.371	92	-5	2-3	.949	-11	101	101	*S-160	-0.3
1965	StL N	153	587	55	149	26	5	0	52	56-2	1	50	.254	.316	.315	73	-19	1-1	.962	-5	100	99	*S-148/3-2	-1.3
1966	Phi N	155	584	58	152	21	4	2	53	40-6	5	38	.260	.311	.320	77	-18	2-1	.974	15	106	97	*S-139,3-20/1	1.0
1967	Phi N	10	26	3	3	0	0	0	1	4-0	0	4	.115	.233	.115	3	-3	0-0	.947	1	108	129	/S-6	-0.2
	SF N	34	70	4	12	1	1	0	4	6-1	0	7	.171	.237	.214	30	-6	0-0	.912	-4	89	120	S-24/2	-1.0
	Year	44	96	7	15	1	1	0	5	10-1	0	11	.156	.236	.188	23	-10	0-0	.925	-3	95	123	S-30/2	-1.2
Total	14	1929	7484	829	2138	352	67	39	707	490-39	31	512	.286	.330	.366	89	-111	14-27	.961	66	103	107	*S-1877/3-27,21	10.5
GROH, HEINIE Henry Knight B 9.18.1889 Rochester, NY D 8.22.1968 Cincinnati, OH BR/TR 5-8/158# d4.12 M1 b-Lew																								
1912	NY N	27	48	8	13	2	1	0	3	8	0	7	.271	.375	.354	97	0	6	.887	0	103	124	2-12/S-7,3-6	0.1
1913	NY N	4	2	0	0	0	0	0	0	0	0	1	.000	.000	.000	-99	-1	0	1.000	0	0	0	/3-2,S	0.0
	Cin N	117	397	51	112	19	5	3	48	38	4	36	.282	.351	.378	109	5	24-17	.963	11	108	91	*2-113/S-4	1.8
	Year	121	399	51	112	19	5	3	48	38	4	37	.281	.349	.376	107	5	24-17	.963	11	108	91	*2-113/S-5,3-2	1.8
1914	Cin N	139	455	59	131	18	4	2	32	64	**13**	28	.288	.391	.358	120	15	24	.936	-5	100	108	*2-134/S-2	1.4
1915	Cin N	**160**	587	72	170	32	9	3	50	50	9	33	.290	.354	.390	123	17	12-17	.969	12	106	**183**	*3-131,2-29	3.3
1916	Cin N	149	553	85	149	24	14	2	28	**84**	4	34	.269	.370	.374	132	25	13	.957	14	109	**179**	*3-110,2-33/S-5	**4.8**
1917	Cin N	156	599	91	**182**	**39**	11	1	53	71	8	30	.304	**.385**	.411	150	40	15	**.966**	9	104	104	*3-154/2-2	5.8
1918	Cin N	126	493	**86**	158	**28**	3	1	37	54	7	24	.320	**.395**	.396	144	**30**	11	**.969**	5	93	**164**	*3-126,M	**4.1**
1919	†Cin N	122	448	79	139	17	11	5	63	56	4	26	.310	.392	.431	151	30	21	.971	-2	90	**147**	*3-121	3.4
1920	Cin N	145	550	86	164	28	12	0	49	60	8	29	.298	.375	.393	122	19	16-19	.969	-4	91	129	*3-144/S	1.7
1921	Cin N	97	357	54	118	19	6	0	48	36	4	17	.331	.398	.417	122	13	22-14	.950	3	100	164	3-97	2.1
1922	†NY N	115	426	63	113	21	3	3	51	53	5	21	.265	.353	.350	81	-10	5-6	**.965**	4	107	**169**	*3-110	0.0
1923	†NY N	123	465	91	135	22	5	4	48	60	6	22	.290	.379	.385	103	5	3-4	**.975**	4	105	96	*3-118	1.5
1924	†NY N	145	559	82	157	32	3	2	46	52	**11**	29	.281	.354	.360	94	-2	8-6	**.983**	7	112	103	*3-145	1.4
1925	NY N	25	65	7	15	4	0	0	4	6	0	3	.231	.296	.292	53	-4	0-0	.909	-4	68	46	3-16/2-2	-0.7
1926	NY N	12	35	2	8	2	0	0	3	2	0	3	.229	.270	.286	50	-2	0	.950	-0	99	88	/3-7	-0.2
1927	†Pit N	14	35	2	10	1	0	0	3	2	0	2	.286	.324	.314	67	-2	0	.958	0	100	0	3-12	-0.1
Total	16	1676	6074	918	1774	308	87	26	566	696	83	345	.292	.373	.384	119	178	180-83	.967	55	101	139	*3-1299,2-325/S-20	30.4
GROH, LEW Lewis Carl "Silver" B 10.16.1883 Rochester, NY D 10.20.1960 Rochester, NY BR/TR d8.2 b-Heinie																								
1919	Phi A	2	4	0	0	0	0	0	0	0	0	2	.000	.000	.000	-99	-1	0	1.000	-0	85	0	/3	-0.1
GROSKLOSS, HOWDY Howard Hoffman B 4.9.1907 Pittsburgh, PA BR/TR 5-9/176# d6.23																								
1930	Pit N	2	3	0	1	0	0	0	1	0	0	0	.333	.333	.333	62	0	0	.000	-1	0	0	/S	-0.1
1931	Pit N	53	161	13	45	7	2	0	20	11	0	16	.280	.326	.348	82	-4	1	.981	-2	97	145	2-39/S-3	-0.4
1932	Pit N	17	20	1	2	0	0	0	0	0	0	3	.100	.100	.100	-47	-4	0	.800	-1	60	0	/S	-0.5
Total	3	72	184	14	48	7	2	0	21	11	0	19	.261	.303	.321	68	-8	1	.981	-4	97	145	/2-39,S-5	-1.0
GROSS, EMIL Emil Michael B 3.3.1858 Chicago, IL D 8.24.1921 Eagle River, WI BR/TR 6/190# d8.13																								
1879	Pro N	30	132	31	46	9	5	0	24	4		8	.348	.368	.492	183	12		.897	-3			C-30	0.9
1880	Pro N	**87**	347	43	90	18	3	1	34	16		15	.259	.292	.337	116	7		.866	-18			*C-87	-0.8
1881	Pro N	51	182	15	50	9	4	1	24	13		11	.275	.323	.385	124	5		.893	-5			C-50/O(RF)	0.2
1883	Phi N	57	231	39	71	25	7	1	25	12		18	.307	.342	.489	163	19		.789	-23			C-55/O-2(1-1-0)	0.0
1884	CP U	23	95	13	34	6	2	4		6			.358	.396	.589	196	8		.860	-3			C-15/O-9(6-0-3)	0.6
Total	5	248	987	141	291	67	21	7	107	51		52	.295	.329	.427	146	51		.859	-50			C-237/O-12(7-1-4)	0.9
GROSS, TURKEY Ewell B 2.21.1896 Mesquite, TX D 1.11.1936 Dallas, TX BR/TR 6/165# d4.14																								
1925	Bos A	9	32	2	3	0	1	0	2	2	1	2	.094	.171	.156	-16	-6	0-0	.976	1	119	78	/S-9	-0.4
GROSS, GREG Gregory Eugene B 8.1.1952 York, PA BL/TL 5-11/175# d9.5 C3																								
1973	Hou N	14	39	5	9	2	1	0	1	4-0	0	4	.231	.302	.333	76	-1	2-1	1.000	0	52	199	/O-9(4-2-3)	-0.2
1974	Hou N	156	589	78	185	21	8	0	36	76-4	1	39	.314	.393	.377	121	20	12-20	.994	5	101	139	*O-151(56-0-143)	1.3
1975	Hou N	132	483	67	142	14	10	0	41	63-1	0	37	.294	.373	.364	114	10	2-2	.958	-0	91	158	*O-121(60-0-61)	0.3

Year	Tm Lg	G	AB	R	H	2B	3B	HR	RBI	BB-IB	HP	SO	AVG	OBP	SLG	AOPS	ABR	SB-CS	FA	FR	Rng	Thr	G at Pos	BFW
1976	Hou N	128	426	52	122	12	3	0	27	64-3	0	39	.286	.375	.329	112	10	2-6	.978	0	95	138	*O-115(RF)	0.3
1977	Chi N	115	239	43	77	10	4	5	32	33-4	0	19	.322	.397	.460	118	7	0-1	.991	-1	92	82	O-71(45-25-9)	0.4
1978	Chi N	124	347	34	92	12	7	1	39	33-5	0	19	.265	.323	.349	80	-9	3-1	.979	-5	87	104	*O-111(40-70-12)	-1.6
1979	Phi N	111	174	21	58	6	3	0	15	29-4	0	5	.333	.422	.402	124	8	5-2	.978	2	95	163	O-73(49-19-11)	0.8
1980	†Phi N	127	154	19	37	7	2	0	12	24-1	1	7	.240	.346	.312	80	-3	1-1	.973	-1	84	166	O-91(58-14-26)/1	-0.6
1981	†Phi N	83	102	14	23	6	1	0	7	15-4	0	5	.225	.319	.304	76	-3	2-2	.982	5	106	376	O-55(13-5-38)	0.1
1982	Phi N	119	134	14	40	4	0	0	10	19-3	0	8	.299	.386	.328	99	1	4-3	.983	2	108	172	O-71(50-12-19)	0.2
1983	†Phi N	136	245	25	74	12	3	0	29	34-4	1	16	.302	.385	.376	114	6	3-5	.991	-5	87	26	*O-110(77-27-25)/1	-0.2
1984	Phi N	112	202	19	65	9	1	0	16	24-3	1	11	.322	.393	.376	116	6	1-0	.986	4	130	101	O-48(30-1-20),1-28	0.8
1985	Phi N	93	169	21	44	5	2	0	14	32-1	0	9	.260	.374	.314	93	0	1-0	1.000	-0	77	166	O-52(46-0-9)/1-8	-0.2
1986	Phi N	87	101	11	25	5	0	0	8	21-7	1	11	.248	.379	.297	87	0	1-0	1.000	2	122	102	O-27(21-1-6)/1-5,P	0.1
1987	Phi N	114	133	14	38	4	1	1	12	25-4	1	12	.286	.395	.353	99	1	0-0	1.000	-3	75	61	O-50(49-0-1),1-11	-0.3
1988	Phi N	98	133	10	27	1	0	0	5	16-1	1	3	.203	.291	.211	46	-9	0-0	1.000	-1	87	138	O-37(20-0-19),1-14	-1.2
1989	Hou N	60	75	2	15	0	0	0	4	11-2	1	6	.200	.310	.200	51	-4	0-0	.929	-1	84	0	O-12(5-0-7)/1-6,P	-0.7
Total	17	1809	3745	449	1073	130	46	7	308	523-51	8	250	.287	.372	.351	103	40	39-44	.982	3	94	133	*O-1204(623-176-524)/1-74,P-2	-0.7
GROSS, WAYNE Wayne Dale B 1.14.1952 Riverside, CA BL/TR 6-2/210# d8.21																								
1976	Oak A	10	18	0	4	0	0	0	1	2-0	0	1	.222	.300	.222	57	-1	0-0	.966	-1	54	99	/1-3,O-2(RF),D-3	-0.2
1977	Oak A☆	146	485	66	113	21	1	22	63	86-6	5	84	.233	.352	.416	111	10	5-4	.932	-26	80	93	*3-145/1	-1.8
1978	Oak A	118	285	18	57	10	2	7	23	40-2	5	63	.200	.308	.323	82	-6	0-2	.917	-8	88	131	*3-106,1-15	-1.8
1979	Oak A	138	442	54	99	19	1	14	50	72-9	1	62	.224	.332	.367	94	-2	4-3	.943	-6	88	74	*3-120,1-18/O-2(LF)	-1.1
1980	Oak A	113	366	45	103	20	3	14	61	44-9	1	39	.281	.355	.467	134	18	5-3	.948	-17	78	79	3-99,1-10/D	-0.1
1981	†Oak A	82	243	29	50	7	1	10	31	34-0	2	28	.206	.304	.366	98	0	2-1	.946	-2	97	59	3-73/1-2,D	-0.4
1982	Oak A	129	386	43	97	14	0	9	41	53-0	2	50	.251	.342	.358	98	0	3-1	.970	-1	93	117	*3-108,1-16/D	-0.2
1983	Oak A	137	339	34	79	18	0	12	44	36-4	3	52	.233	.311	.392	98	-1	3-5	.996	-10	64	88	1-74,3-67/PD	-1.6
1984	Bal A	127	342	53	74	9	1	22	64	68-4	1	69	.216	.346	.442	119	10	1-2	.937	-0	108	75	*3-117/1-3,D	0.8
1985	Bal A	103	217	31	51	8	0	11	18	46-0	0	48	.235	.369	.424	120	8	1-1	.933	-0	98	137	3-67,D-10/1-9	0.6
1986	Oak A	3	2	0	0	0	0	0	0	1-0	0	0	.000	.333	.000	0	0	0-0	.000	-0	0	0	/3	-0.1
Total	11	1106	3125	373	727	126	9	121	396	482-34	20	496	.233	.337	.395	106	36	24-22	.941	-71	90	93	3-903,1-151/D-18,O-4(2-0-2),P	-5.9
GROSSART, GEORGE George Albert B 4.11.1880 Meadville, PA D 4.18.1902 Pittsburgh, PA d6.7																								
1901	Bos N	7	26	4	3	0	0	0	1	0	0		.115	.115	.115	-30	-4	0	1.000	0	0	0	/O-7(LF)	-0.5
GROTE, JERRY Gerald Wayne B 10.6.1942 San Antonio, TX BR/TR 5-10/190# d9.21																								
1963	Hou N	3	5	0	1	0	0	0	1	1-0	0	3	.200	.286	.200	61	0	0-0	1.000	-0	*69*	*0*	/C-3	-0.1
1964	Hou N	100	298	26	54	9	3	3	24	20-5	4	75	.181	.240	.262	44	-23	0-2	.985	1	*69*	*90*	C-98	-1.9
1966	NY N	120	317	26	75	12	2	3	31	40-8	3	81	.237	.327	.315	82	-6	4-3	.981	-3	*90*	*94*	*C-115/3-2	-0.5
1967	NY N	120	344	25	67	8	0	4	23	14-8	1	65	.195	.226	.253	38	-28	2-2	.990	-0	*81*	***131***	*C-119	-2.6
1968	NY N★	124	404	29	114	18	0	3	31	44-11	3	81	.282	.357	.349	112	8	1-5	.994	5	*100*	*111*	*C-115	1.9
1969	†NY N	113	365	38	92	12	3	6	40	32-5	1	59	.252	.313	.351	84	-8	2-1	.991	19	140	**138**	*C-112	1.6
1970	NY N	126	415	38	106	14	1	2	34	36-8	1	39	.255	.313	.308	68	-19	2-1	.991	15	155	85	*C-125	0.2
1971	NY N	125	403	35	109	25	0	2	35	40-4	2	47	.270	.339	.347	96	0	1-4	.990	3	101	64	*C-122	0.8
1972	NY N	64	205	15	43	5	1	3	21	26-8	3	27	.210	.304	.288	72	-7	1-0	.998	4	174	111	C-59/3-3,O(RF)	0.0
1973	†NY N	84	285	17	73	10	2	1	32	13-1	1	23	.256	.290	.316	69	-13	0-0	.995	10	130	76	C-81/3-2	0.1
1974	NY N★	97	319	25	82	8	1	5	36	33-4	2	33	.257	.326	.335	88	-5	0-1	.988	0	117	94	C-94	-0.1
1975	NY N	119	386	28	114	14	5	2	39	38-8	1	23	.295	.357	.373	109	4	0-1	**.995**	6	101	111	*C-111	1.5
1976	NY N	101	323	30	88	14	2	4	28	38-4	1	19	.272	.350	.365	110	5	1-2	.993	10	104	99	C-95/O-2(1-0-1)	2.0
1977	NY N	42	115	8	31	3	1	0	7	9-1	2	12	.270	.333	.313	78	-4	0-0	1.000	-3	87	87	C-28,3-11	-0.5
	†LA N	18	27	3	7	0	0	0	4	2-1	0	5	.259	.310	.259	55	-2	0-1	1.000	3	64	96	C-16/3-2	0.1
	Year	60	142	11	38	3	1	0	11	11-2	2	17	.268	.329	.303	73	-5	0-1	1.000	0	81	89	C-44,3-13	-0.4
1978	†LA N	41	70	5	19	5	0	0	9	10-1	0	5	.271	.354	.343	98	0	0-0	.985	4	80	28	C-32/3-7	0.6
1981	KC A	22	56	4	17	3	1	1	9	3-0	1	2	.304	.344	.446	129	2	1-0	1.000	-1	79	58	C-22	0.2
	LA N	2	2	0	0	0	0	0	0	0-0	0	1	.000	.000	.000	-99	-1	0-0	1.000	0	0	0	/C	0.0
Total	16	1421	4339	352	1092	160	22	39	404	399-77	26	600	.252	.316	.326	83	-97	15-23	.991	72	*110*	*98*	*C-1348/3-27,O-3(1-0-2)	3.3
GROTEWOLD, JEFF Jeffrey Scott B 12.8.1965 Madera, CA BL/TR 6/215# d4.12																								
1992	Phi N	72	65	7	13	2	0	3	5	9-0	1	16	.200	.307	.369	91	-1	0-0	1.000	-0	0	0	/C-2,O-2(LF),1	-0.1
1995	KC A	15	36	4	10	1	0	1	6	9-0	0	7	.278	.422	.389	111	1	0-0	.750	-0	0	257	D-11/1	0.0
Total	2	87	101	11	23	3	0	4	11	18-0	1	23	.228	.350	.376	99	0	0-0	.833	-0	0	171	/D-11,1-2,O-2(LF),C-2	-0.1
GROTH, JOHNNY John Thomas B 7.23.1926 Chicago, IL BR/TR 6/182# d9.5																								
1946	Det A	4	9	1	0	0	0	0	0	0	0	3	.000	.000	.000	-94	-2	0-0	1.000	-0	105	0	/O-4(CF)	-0.3
1947	Det A	2	4	1	1	0	0	0	0	2	0	1	.250	.500	.250	109	0	0-0	1.000	0	133	0	/O(LF)	0.0
1948	Det A	6	17	3	8	3	0	1	5	1	0	1	.471	.500	.824	242	3	0-0	.900	0	78	341	/O-4(CF)	0.3
1949	Det A	103	348	60	102	19	5	11	73	65	2	27	.293	.407	.471	132	18	3-7	.966	-2	95	122	O-99(CF)	1.0
1950	Det A	**157**	566	95	173	30	8	12	85	95	2	27	.306	.407	.451	116	16	1-5	.985	-18	84	65	*O-157(CF)	-0.7
1951	Det A	118	428	41	128	29	1	3	49	31	2	32	.299	.349	.393	100	0	1-1	**.993**	-5	90	109	*O-112(CF)	-0.8
1952	Det A	141	524	56	149	22	2	4	51	51	0	39	.284	.348	.357	96	-3	2-10	.986	-5	88	135	*O-139(2-137-0)	-1.5
1953	StL A	141	557	65	141	27	4	10	57	42	2	53	.253	.308	.370	81	-16	5-6	.991	12	109	146	*O-141(CF)	-1.2
1954	Chi A	125	422	41	116	20	0	7	60	42	2	37	.275	.341	.372	93	-4	3-9	.988	-1	102	66	*O-125(9-116-2)	-1.3
1955	Chi A	32	77	13	26	7	0	2	11	6-1	0	13	.338	.376	.506	135	4	1-0	1.000	1	107	79	O-26(CF)	0.4
	Was A	63	183	22	40	4	5	2	17	18-0	0	18	.219	.286	.328	69	-9	2-0	.984	-0	102	64	O-48(12-40-1)	-1.2
	Year	95	260	35	66	11	5	4	28	24-1	0	31	.254	.313	.381	89	-5	3-0	.989	0	104	69	O-74(12-66-1)	-0.8
1956	KC A	95	244	22	63	13	3	5	37	30-2	0	31	.258	.335	.398	94	-2	1-2	1.000	-1	86	168	O-84(13-56-18)	-0.7
1957	KC A	55	59	10	15	0	0	0	2	7-0	0	6	.254	.333	.254	62	-3	0-0	.974	-1	107	0	O-50(9-3-38)	-0.5
	Det A	38	103	11	30	10	0	0	16	6-0	1	7	.291	.333	.388	95	0	0-0	1.000	1	113	0	O-36(12-25-0)	-0.1
	Year	93	162	21	45	10	0	0	18	13-0	1	13	.278	.333	.340	83	-3	0-0	.991	-0	111	0	O-86(21-28-38)	-0.6
1958	Det A	88	146	24	41	5	2	2	11	13-0	0	19	.281	.340	.384	92	-2	0-1	.990	1	105	73	O-80(52-19-10)	-0.4
1959	Det A	55	102	12	24	7	1	1	10	7-0	0	14	.235	.284	.353	70	-4	0-0	.983	0	114	0	O-41(11-18-13)	-0.5
1960	Det A	25	19	3	7	1	0	0	2	3-0	0	1	.368	.455	.421	135	1	0-1	1.000	0	123	0	/O-8(0-7-1)	0.1
Total	15	1248	3808	480	1064	197	31	60	486	419-3	11	329	.279	.352	.395	99	-3	19-42	.987	-19	96	99	*O-1155(121-964-83)	-7.4
GROVER, ROY Roy Arthur B 1.17.1892 Snohomish, WA D 2.7.1978 Milwaukie, OR BR/TR 5-8/150# d9.13																								
1916	Phi A	20	77	8	21	1	2	0	7	6	0	10	.273	.325	.338	104	0	5	.952	-3	78	81	2-20	-0.3
1917	Phi A	141	482	45	108	15	7	0	34	43	3	53	.224	.292	.284	77	-14	12	.960	6	105	81	*2-139	-0.6
1919	Phi A	22	56	8	13	1	0	0	2	5	0	6	.232	.295	.250	53	-3	0	.915	-5	83	58	2-12/3-3	-0.9
	Was A	24	75	6	14	0	0	0	7	6	1	10	.187	.256	.187	25	-7	2	.947	-5	75	66	2-24	-1.3
	Year	46	131	14	27	1	0	0	9	11	1	16	.206	.273	.214	37	-11	2	.936	-10	78	63	2-36/3-3	-2.2
Total	3	207	690	67	156	17	9	0	50	60	4	79	.226	.292	.277	72	-24	19	.956	-7	98	78	2-195/3-3	-3.1
GRUBB, HARVEY Harvey Harrison B 9.18.1890 Lexington, NC D 1.25.1970 Corpus Christi, TX BR/TR 6/165# d9.27																								
1912	Cle A	1	0	0	0	0	0	0	0	0	1		—	1.000	—	187	0	0	1.000	0	0	0	/3	0.0
GRUBB, JOHNNY John Maywood B 8.4.1948 Richmond, VA BL/TR 6-3/188# d9.10 OF Total (389-LF 408-CF 280-RF)																								
1972	SD N	7	21	4	7	1	1	0	1	1-0	0	3	.333	.364	.476	147	1	0-1	1.000	0	124	0	/O-6(CF)	0.1
1973	SD N	113	389	52	121	22	3	8	37	37-2	2	50	.311	.373	.445	137	20	9-3	.988	1	98	181	*O-102(1-102-0)/3-2	1.9
1974	SD N★	140	444	53	127	20	4	8	42	46-2	4	47	.286	.355	.403	118	11	4-0	.976	5	113	112	*O-122(8-114-0)/3-2	1.4
1975	SD N	144	553	72	149	36	2	4	38	59-4	5	59	.269	.342	.363	103	4	2-7	.991	-13	90	33	*O-139(CF)	-1.6
1976	SD N	109	384	54	109	22	1	5	27	65-10	4	53	.284	.391	.385	132	21	1-2	.974	-7	95	44	O-98(63-15-30)/1-9,3-3	0.9
1977	Cle A	34	93	8	28	3	3	2	14	19-2	1	18	.301	.425	.462	146	7	0-3	1.000	0	94	109	O-28(27-0-1)/D-4	0.5
1978	Cle A	113	378	54	100	16	6	14	61	59-5	2	60	.265	.365	.450	130	16	5-1	.973	4	96	204	*O-110(108-0-6)	1.7
	Tex A	21	33	8	13	3	0	1	6	11-0	0	5	.394	.545	.576	215	6	1-1	1.000	1	88	382	O-13(8-0-5)/D-3	0.7
	Year	134	411	62	113	19	6	15	67	70-5	2	65	.275	.381	.460	137	23	6-2	.974	5	95	**216**	*O-123(116-0-11)/D-3	2.4
1979	Tex A	102	289	42	79	14	0	10	37	34-3	1	44	.273	.350	.426	110	5	2-4	.986	-0	89	164	O-82(38-29-25)/D-6	0.1
1980	Tex A	110	274	40	76	12	1	9	32	42-5	2	35	.277	.374	.427	124	11	2-3	.952	-4	86	124	O-77(19-3-60)/D-8	0.3
1981	Tex A	67	199	26	46	9	1	3	26	23-0	2	25	.231	.316	.332	92	-2	0-3	.990	-5	83	50	O-58(2-0-56)	-1.1

Year	Tm Lg	G	AB	R	H	2B	3B	HR	RBI	BB-IB	HP	SO	AVG	OBP	SLG	AOPS	ABR	SB-CS	FA	FR	Rng	Thr	G at Pos	BFW
1982	Tex A	103	308	35	86	13	3	3	26	39-2	6	37	.279	.368	.370	110	6	0-3	.965	-4	90	85	O-77(41-0-40),D-18	-0.3
1983	Det A	57	134	20	34	5	2	4	22	28-1	2	17	.254	.388	.410	124	6	0-0	1.000	-2	85	66	O-26(2-0-24),D-18	0.2
1984	†Det A	86	176	25	47	5	0	8	17	36-5	2	36	.267	.395	.432	130	9	1-0	1.000	-1	96	0	O-36(27-0-9),D-33	0.6
1985	Det A	78	155	19	38	7	1	5	25	24-0	1	25	.245	.342	.400	106	2	0-1	1.000	-1	95	0	D-33,O-18(14-0-4)	-0.1
1986	Det A	81	210	32	70	13	1	13	51	28-0	2	28	.333	.412	.590	171	22	0-1	1.000	1	106	122	D-52,O-19(10-0-10)	1.9
1987	†Det A	59	114	9	23	6	0	2	13	15-0	0	16	.202	.290	.307	63	-6	0-0	1.000	0	108	75	O-31(21-0-10),D-16/3	-0.7
Total	16	1424	4154	553	1153	207	29	99	475	566-41	36	558	.278	.366	.413	121	139	27-33	.981	-24	95	106	*O-1042C,D-191/1-9,3-8	6.5
GRUBE, FRANK Franklin Thomas "Hans" B 1.7.1905 Easton, PA D 7.2.1945 New York, NY BR/TR 5-9/190# d5.12																								
1931	Chi A	88	265	29	58	13	2	1	24	22	2	22	.219	.284	.294	55	-18	2-2	.977	-10	*65*	*87*	C-81	-2.2
1932	Chi A	93	277	36	78	16	2	0	31	33	2	13	.282	.362	.354	92	-2	6-1	.957	-5	*84*	*125*	C-92	0.0
1933	Chi A	85	256	23	59	13	0	0	23	38	2	20	.230	.334	.281	67	-10	1-1	.984	-9	*85*	*82*	C-83	-1.4
1934	StL A	65	170	22	49	10	0	0	11	24	1	11	.288	.379	.347	82	-3	2-1	.963	2	*99*	*81*	C-55	0.1
1935	StL A	3	6	3	2	1	0	0	0	0	0	1	.333	.333	.500	108	0	0-0	1.000	0	*64*	*0*	/C-3	0.0
	Chi A	9	19	1	7	2	0	0	6	3	0	2	.368	.455	.474	137	1	0-0	.944	1	*132*	*109*	/C-9	0.3
	Year	12	25	4	9	3	0	0	6	3	0	3	.360	.429	.480	131	1	0-0	.955	1	*119*	*88*	C-12	0.3
1936	Chi A	33	93	6	15	2	1	0	11	9	0	15	.161	.235	.204	9	-14	1-0	.991	3	*125*	*121*	C-32	-0.9
1941	StL A	18	39	1	6	2	0	0	1	2	0	4	.154	.195	.205	6	-5	0-0	.951	1	*121*	*183*	C-18	-0.4
Total	7	394	1125	121	274	59	5	1	107	131	7	88	.244	.326	.308	67	-51	12-5	.970	-18	*88*	*102*	C-373	-4.5
GRUBER, KELLY Kelly Wayne B 2.26.1962 Houston, TX BR/TR 6/185# d4.20 OF Total (8-LF 6-CF 25-RF)																								
1984	Tor A	15	16	1	1	0	0	1	2	0-0	0	5	.063	.063	.250	-18	-3	0-0	.933	2	180	0	3-12/O-2(RF),S	0.0
1985	Tor A	5	13	0	3	0	0	0	1	0-0	0	3	.231	.231	.231	26	-1	0-0	1.000	-0	101	0	/3-5,2	-0.2
1986	Tor A	87	143	20	28	4	1	5	15	5-0	0	27	.196	.220	.343	50	-11	2-5	.940	-2	112	64	3-42,2-14,D-14/O-9(4-2-3),S-5	-1.4
1987	Tor A	138	341	50	80	14	3	12	36	17-2	7	70	.235	.283	.399	77	-12	12-2	.948	-3	102	75	*3-119,S-21/2-7,O-2(CF),D	-1.3
1988	Tor A	158	569	75	158	33	5	16	81	38-1	7	92	.278	.328	.438	113	9	23-5	.971	26	**118**	125	*3-156/2-7,O-2(CF),SD	3.9
1989	†Tor A☆	135	545	83	158	24	4	18	73	30-0	3	60	.290	.328	.448	120	12	10-5	.945	16	119	76	*3-119,O-16(3-0-14)/SD	2.8
1990	Tor A★	150	592	92	162	36	6	31	118	48-2	8	94	.274	.330	.512	132	23	14-2	.955	-3	97	86	*3-145/O-6(RF),D	2.3
1991	†Tor A	113	429	58	108	18	2	20	65	31-5	6	70	.252	.308	.443	102	0	12-7	.962	5	101	80	*3-111/D-2	0.5
1992	†Tor A	120	446	42	102	16	3	11	43	26-3	4	72	.229	.275	.352	72	-18	7-7	.949	-1	93	52	*3-120	-2.1
1993	Cal A	18	65	10	18	3	0	3	9	2-0	1	11	.277	.309	.462	101	0	0-0	.938	5	128	106	3-17/O(LF)D	0.5
Total	10	939	3159	431	818	148	24	117	443	197-13	36	504	.259	.307	.432	102	-1	80-33	.955	46	106	84	3-846/O-38R,2-29,S-29,D-21	5.0
GRUDZIELANEK, MARK Mark James B 6.30.1970 Milwaukee, WI BR/TR 6-1/185# d4.28																								
1995	Mon N	78	269	27	66	12	2	1	20	14-4	7	47	.245	.300	.316	60	-15	8-3	.987	5	105	92	S-34,3-31,2-13	-0.6
1996	Mon N★	153	657	99	201	34	4	6	49	26-3	9	83	.306	.340	.397	92	-8	33-7	.959	-6	97	89	*S-153	0.3
1997	Mon N	156	649	76	177	**54**	3	4	51	23-0	10	76	.273	.307	.384	80	-19	25-9	.955	-3	98	110	*S-156	-0.7
1998	Mon N	105	396	51	109	15	1	8	41	21-1	9	50	.275	.323	.379	86	-9	11-5	.950	-8	96	89	*S-105	-0.8
	LA N	51	193	11	51	6	0	2	21	5-1	2	23	.264	.286	.326	66	-10	7-0	.962	13	116	113	S-51	0.8
	Year	156	589	62	160	21	1	10	62	26-2	11	73	.272	.311	.362	80	-19	18-5	.954	4	103	97	*S-156	0.0
1999	LA N	123	488	72	159	23	5	7	46	31-1	10	65	.326	.376	.436	112	9	6-6	.973	-10	94	95	*S-119	0.7
2000	LA N	148	617	101	172	35	6	7	49	45-0	9	81	.279	.335	.389	88	-12	12-3	.976	2	99	106	*2-148/S	-0.1
2001	LA N	133	539	83	146	21	3	13	55	28-0	11	83	.271	.317	.393	90	-10	4-4	.984	-6	95	96	*2-133	-0.9
2002	LA N	150	536	56	145	23	0	9	50	22-4	3	89	.271	.301	.364	83	-18	4-1	.989	-11	99	90	*2-147/D	-2.1
2003	†Chi N	121	481	73	151	38	1	3	38	30-0	11	64	.314	.366	.416	106	5	6-2	.986	17	97	123	*2-121	2.8
Total	9	1218	4825	649	1377	261	25	60	420	245-14	81	661	.285	.329	.387	89	-87	116-40	.961	-6	98	98	S-619,2-562/3-31,D	-0.6
GRYSKA, SIG Sigmund Stanley B 11.4.1914 Chicago, IL D 8.27.1994 Hines, IL BR/TR 5-11.5/173# d9.28																								
1938	StL A	7	21	3	10	2	1	0	4	3	0	3	.476	.542	.667	202	4	0-0	.912	-0	90	108	/S-7	0.3
1939	StL A	18	49	4	13	2	0	0	8	6	0	10	.265	.345	.306	66	-2	3-1	.873	-3	97	47	S-14	-0.4
Total	2	25	70	7	23	4	1	0	12	9	0	13	.329	.405	.414	107	2	3-1	.887	-3	95	68	/S-21	-0.1
GUBANICH, CREIGHTON Creighton Wade B 3.27.1972 Belleville, NJ BR/TR 6-3/200# d4.16																								
1999	Bos A	18	47	4	13	2	1	1	11	3-0	2	13	.277	.346	.426	93	-1	0-0	.979	-3	78	100	C-14/3D	-0.3
GUDAT, MARV Marvin John B 8.27.1903 Goliad, TX D 3.1.1954 Los Angeles, CA BL/TL 5-11/162# d5.21 ▲																								
1929	Cin N	9	10	0	2	0	0	0	0	0	0	0	.200	.200	.200	-1	0	0	.800	-1	66	0	/P-7	0.0
1932	†Chi N	60	94	15	24	4	1	1	15	16	1	10	.255	.369	.351	96	0	0	.933	-2	77	0	O-14(5-1-9)/1-8,P	-0.3
Total	2	69	104	15	26	4	1	1	15	16	1	10	.250	.355	.337	87	0	0	.933	-3	77	0	/O-14(5-1-9),1-8,P-8	-0.3
GUERRA, MIKE Fermin (Romero) B 10.11.1912 Havana, Cuba D 10.9.1992 Miami Beach, FL BR/TR 5-9/162# d9.19																								
1937	Was A	1	3	0	0	0	0	0	0	0	0	2	.000	.000	.000	-99	-1	0-0	.750	-0	*0*	*0*	/C	-0.1
1944	Was A	75	210	29	59	7	2	1	29	13	0	14	.281	.323	.348	96	-2	8-2	.960	-3	*82*	*75*	C-58/O(LF)	-0.1
1945	Was A	56	138	11	29	1	1	1	15	10	1	12	.210	.268	.254	57	-8	4-1	.990	3	*119*	*76*	C-38	-0.3
1946	Was A	41	83	3	21	2	1	0	4	5	0	6	.253	.295	.301	71	-4	1-0	.938	-2	*94*	*150*	C-27	-0.4
1947	Phi A	72	209	20	45	2	2	0	18	10	0	15	.215	.251	.244	37	-19	1-2	.964	3	*145*	*130*	C-62	-1.4
1948	Phi A	53	142	18	30	4	2	1	23	18	0	13	.211	.300	.289	57	-9	2-3	.973	-1	*120*	*95*	C-47	-0.8
1949	Phi A	98	298	41	79	14	1	3	31	37	0	26	.265	.346	.349	87	-5	3-0	.982	-3	*101*	***111***	C-95	-0.3
1950	Phi A	87	252	25	71	10	4	2	26	16	0	12	.282	.325	.377	81	-9	1-0	.990	-5	*87*	*78*	C-78	-0.9
1951	Bos A	10	32	1	5	0	0	0	2	6	0	5	.156	.289	.156	21	-3	1-0	1.000	-0	*116*	*39*	C-10	-0.3
	Was A	72	214	20	43	2	1	1	20	16	0	18	.201	.257	.234	34	-21	4-4	.977	-8	*95*	*89*	C-66	-2.6
	Year	82	246	21	48	2	1	1	22	22	0	23	.195	.261	.224	32	-24	5-4	.982	-8	*98*	*81*	C-76	-2.9
Total	9	565	1581	168	382	42	14	9	168	131	1	123	.242	.300	.303	65	-81	25-12	.975	-16	*104*	*96*	C-482/O(LF)	-7.2
GUERRERO, JUAN Juan Antonio B 2.1.1967 Los Llanos, D.R. BR/TR 5-11/160# d4.9																								
1992	Hou N	79	125	8	25	4	2	1	14	10-2	1	32	.200	.261	.288	59	-7	1-0	.980	-6	82	61	S-19,3-12/O-3(LF),2-2	-1.3
GUERRERO, MARIO Mario Miguel (Abud) B 9.28.1949 Santo Domingo, D.R. BR/TR 5-10/155# d4.8																								
1973	Bos A	66	219	19	51	5	2	0	11	10-0	2	21	.233	.272	.274	51	-14	2-2	.974	0	100	126	S-46,2-24	-0.9
1974	Bos A	93	284	18	70	6	2	0	23	13-0	2	22	.246	.282	.282	59	-15	3-1	.969	-3	99	99	S-93	-0.9
1975	StL N	64	184	17	44	9	0	0	11	10-1	2	7	.239	.281	.288	57	-11	0-0	.955	7	115	86	S-64	0.3
1976	Cal A	83	268	24	76	12	0	1	18	7-2	3	12	.284	.304	.340	96	-2	0-0	.973	-9	91	83	2-41,S-41/D-7	-0.5
1977	Cal A	86	244	17	69	8	2	1	28	4-1	0	16	.283	.292	.344	76	-9	0-0	.985	-1	95	91	S-31,D-19,2-12	-0.7
1978	Oak A	143	505	27	139	18	4	3	38	15-2	6	35	.275	.302	.345	87	-11	0-5	.958	-24	82	80	*S-142	-2.3
1979	Oak A	46	166	12	38	5	0	0	18	6-0	0	7	.229	.253	.259	42	-14	0-1	.952	-2	98	100	S-43	-1.1
1980	Oak A	116	381	32	91	16	2	2	23	19-2	1	32	.239	.273	.307	64	-20	3-3	.962	-36	80	71	*S-116	-4.5
Total	8	697	2251	166	578	79	12	7	170	84-8	16	152	.257	.285	.312	69	-96	8-12	.961	-67	91	87	S-576/2-77,D-26	-10.6
GUERRERO, PEDRO Pedro B 6.29.1956 San Pedro De Macoris, D.R. BR/TR 6/195# d9.22 OF Total (216-LF 108-CF 239-RF)																								
1978	LA N	5	8	3	5	0	1	0	1	0-0	0	0	.625	.625	.875	316	2	0-0	1.000	-0	77	0	/1-4	0.2
1979	LA N	25	62	7	15	2	0	2	9	1-1	0	14	.242	.250	.371	69	-3	2-0	1.000	-1	92	0	O-12(4-1-9)/1-8,3-3	-0.4
1980	LA N	75	183	27	59	9	1	7	31	12-3	0	31	.322	.359	.497	141	9	2-1	.987	-4	97	44	O-40(3-25-15),2-12/3-3,1-2	0.5
1981	†LA N★	98	347	46	104	17	2	12	48	34-3	2	57	.300	.365	.464	139	17	5-9	.974	1	97	66	O-75(0-8-70),3-21/1	1.4
1982	LA N	150	575	87	175	27	5	32	100	65-16	5	89	.304	.378	.536	157	44	22-5	.976	0	95	119	*O-137(0-44-105),3-24	4.3
1983	†LA N★	160	584	87	174	28	6	32	103	72-12	2	110	.298	.373	.531	150	39	23-7	.934	3	98	93	*3-157/1-2	4.3
1984	LA N	144	535	85	162	29	4	16	72	49-7	1	105	.303	.358	.462	132	22	9-8	.917	-7	93	100	3-76,O-58(1-20-38),1-16	1.1
1985	†LA N✳	137	487	99	156	22	2	33	87	83-14	6	68	.320	**.422**	**.577**	**183**	**57**	12-4	.974	4	98	129	O-81(71-10-1),3-44,1-12	**5.9**
1986	LA N	31	61	7	15	3	0	5	10	2-0	1	19	.246	.281	.541	131	2	0-0	1.000	-1	78	240	O-10(LF)/1-4	0.1
1987	LA N★	152	545	89	184	25	2	27	89	74-18	4	85	.338	.416	.539	156	46	9-7	.971	-2	85	87	*O-109(LF),1-40	3.6
1988	LA N	59	215	24	64	7	1	5	35	25-2	3	33	.298	.374	.409	130	9	2-1	.895	-6	84	32	3-45,1-15/O-2(1-0-1)	0.3
	StL N	44	149	16	40	7	1	5	30	21-7	2	26	.268	.358	.430	126	6	2-0	1.000	-1	95	74	1-37/O-7(LF)	0.3
	Year	103	364	40	104	14	2	10	65	46-9	5	59	.286	.367	.418	128	15	4-1	.998	-7	104	71	1-52,3-45/O-9(8-0-1)	0.6
1989	StL N★	162	570	60	177	**42**	1	17	117	79-13	4	84	.311	.391	.477	145	37	2-0	.990	-13	71	101	*1-160	1.5
1990	StL N	136	498	42	140	31	1	13	80	44-14	1	70	.281	.334	.426	109	6	1-1	.989	-8	83	86	*1-132	-1.1
1991	StL N	115	427	41	116	12	1	8	70	37-2	1	46	.272	.326	.361	94	-4	4-2	.985	-9	80	105	*1-112	-2.1
1992	StL N	43	146	10	32	6	1	1	16	11-3	0	25	.219	.270	.295	63	-7	2-2	.988	-7	29	93	1-28,O-10(LF)	-1.9

Year	Tm Lg	G	AB	R	H	2B	3B	HR	RBI	BB-IB	HP	SO	AVG	OBP	SLG	AOPS	ABR	SB-CS	FA	FR	Rng	Thr	G at Pos	BFW
Total	15	1536	5392	730	1618	267	29	215	898	609-115	32	862	.300	.370	.480	138	282	97-47	.988	-51	82	94	1-573,O-541R,3-373/2-12	18.0
GUERRERO, VLADIMIR Vladimir B 2.9.1976 Nizao Bani, D.R. BR/TR 6-2/158# d9.19 b-Wilton																								
1996	Mon N	9	27	2	5	0	0	1	1	0-0	0	3	.185	.185	.296	24	-3	0-0	1.000	-0	94	0	/O-8(0-1-7)	-0.4
1997	Mon N	90	325	44	98	22	2	11	40	19-2	7	39	.302	.350	.483	117	7	3-4	.929	1	97	165	O-85(0-1-84)	0.3
1998	Mon N	159	623	108	202	37	7	38	109	42-13	7	95	.324	.371	.589	150	43	11-9	.951	2	109	86	*O-157(RF)	3.5
1999	Mon N★	160	610	102	193	37	5	42	131	55-14	7	62	.316	.378	.600	147	41	14-7	.948	5	108	143	*O-160(RF)	3.6
2000	Mon N★	154	571	101	197	28	11	44	123	58-**23**	8	74	.345	.410	.664	162	52	9-10	.969	3	103	129	*O-151(RF)/D-2	4.3
2001	Mon N★	159	599	107	184	45	4	34	108	60-24	9	88	.307	.377	.566	137	34	37-16	.965	5	103	136	*O-158(RF)	3.2
2002	Mon N★	161	614	106	**206**	37	2	39	111	84-32	6	70	.336	.417	.593	154	48	40-20	.969	-1	95	130	*O-161(RF)	4.0
2003	Mon N	112	394	71	130	20	3	25	79	63-22	6	53	.330	.426	.586	148	30	9-5	.970	3	104	140	*O-112(RF)	2.6
Total	8	1004	3763	641	1215	226	34	234	702	381-130	50	484	.323	.390	.588	146	252	123-71	.959	17	103	129	O-992(0-2-990)/D-2	21.1
GUERRERO, WILTON Wilton B 10.24.1974 Don Gregorio, D.R. BB/TR (BR 1996) 5-11/145# d9.3 b-Vladimir OF Total (80-LF 19-CF 27-RF)																								
1996	LA N	5	2	1	0	0	0	0	0	0-0	0	2	.000	.000	.000	-99	-1	0-0	—	0			/H	-0.1
1997	LA N	111	357	39	104	10	9	4	32	8-1	0	52	.291	.305	.403	91	-8	6-5	.989	-18	88	50	2-90/S-5	-2.1
1998	LA N	64	180	21	51	4	3	0	7	4-0	1	33	.283	.299	.339	73	-8	5-2	.968	-5	84	91	2-32,S-14/O-7(6-1-0)	-1.0
	Mon N	52	222	29	63	10	6	2	20	10-0	0	30	.284	.313	.410	90	-4	3-0	.975	-10	88	74	2-52	-1.1
	Year	116	402	50	114	14	9	2	27	14-0	1	63	.284	.307	.378	83	-12	8-2	.972	-15	87	80	2-84,S-14/O-7(6-1-0)	-2.1
1999	Mon N	132	315	42	92	15	7	2	31	13-0	2	38	.292	.324	.403	85	-9	7-6	.931	-14	87	66	2-54,O-22(LF)/D-5	-2.1
2000	Mon N	127	288	30	77	7	2	2	23	19-0	0	41	.267	.312	.326	60	-18	8-1	.967	3	111	126	O-75(42-13-24)/2D	-1.5
2001	Cin N	60	142	16	48	5	1	1	8	3-0	0	17	.338	.352	.408	92	-2	5-2	.927	-5	84	108	S-16,2-11/O-6(LF),3-4,D	-0.5
2002	Cin N	59	78	9	19	1	1	0	4	6-0	0	13	.244	.298	.282	55	-6	2-1	1.000	0	121	118	2-10/S-7,3-3	-0.5
	Mon N	44	62	3	12	1	0	0	1	1-1	0	19	.194	.206	.210	11	-8	5-0	1.000	-2	100	362	O-12(4-5-3)/2-7,3-2	-0.9
	Year	103	140	12	31	2	1	0	5	7-1	0	32	.221	.259	.250	35	-14	7-1	1.000	-2	100	89	2-17,O-12(4-5-3)/S-7,3-5	-1.4
Total	7	654	1646	190	466	53	29	11	126	64-2	3	245	.283	.310	.371	77	-64	41-17	.974	-51	88	66	2-257,O-122L/S-42,D-12,3-9	-9.8
GUEVARA, GIOMAR Giomar Antonio (Diaz) B 10.23.1972 Miranda, Venezuela BB/TR 5-8/150# d9.19																								
1997	Sea A	5	4	0	0	0	0	0	0	0-0	0	2	.000	.000	.000	-99	-1	1-0	.875	1	166	0	/2-2,SD	0.0
1998	Sea A	11	13	4	3	2	0	0	0	4-0	1	4	.231	.444	.385	118	1	0-0	1.000	-0	124	116	/2-5,S-5	0.1
1999	Sea A	10	12	2	3	2	0	0	2	0-0	0	2	.250	.250	.417	68	-1	0-0	.870	-1	96	55	/S-9	-0.1
Total	3	26	29	6	6	4	0	0	2	4-0	1	8	.207	.324	.345	74	-1	1-0	.900	-1	85	57	/S-15,2-7,D-2	0.0
GUIEL, AARON Aaron Colin B 10.5.1972 Vancouver, BC, CAN BL/TR 5-10/190# d6.22																								
2002	KC A	70	240	30	56	13	0	4	38	19-1	4	61	.233	.296	.338	62	-13	1-5	.952	0	99	139	O-61(0-1-61)/D-2	-1.7
2003	KC A	99	354	63	98	30	0	15	52	27-0	13	63	.277	.346	.489	104	3	3-5	.985	6	105	177	O-89(1-1-87)/D-2	0.3
Total	2	169	594	93	154	43	0	19	90	46-1	17	124	.259	.326	.428	87	-10	4-10	.972	6	103	162	O-150(1-2-148)/D-4	-1.4
GUILLEN, CARLOS Carlos Alfonso B 9.30.1975 Maracay, Venezuela BB/TR 6-1/180# d9.6																								
1998	Sea A	10	39	9	13	1	1	0	5	3-0	0	9	.333	.381	.410	106	0	2-0	1.000	2	118	86	2-10	0.3
1999	Sea A	5	19	2	3	0	0	1	3	1-0	0	6	.158	.200	.316	30	-2	0-0	.938	2	130	58	/S-3,2-2	0.0
2000	†Sea A	90	288	45	74	15	2	7	42	28-0	2	53	.257	.324	.396	84	-7	1-3	.911	-5	96	63	3-68,S-23	-1.0
2001	Sea A	140	456	72	118	21	4	5	53	53-0	1	89	.259	.333	.355	88	-7	4-1	.980	-21	87	110	*S-137/D	-1.7
2002	Sea A	134	475	73	124	24	6	9	56	46-4	1	91	.261	.326	.394	94	-4	4-5	.966	-23	83	91	*S-130/D-3	-1.8
2003	Sea A	109	388	63	107	19	3	7	52	52-2	1	64	.276	.359	.394	103	3	4-4	.963	-11	82	137	S-76,3-32/D	-0.2
Total	6	488	1665	264	439	80	16	29	211	183-6	5	312	.264	.335	.383	92	-17	15-13	.969	-56	85	109	S-369,3-100/2-12,D-5	-4.4
GUILLEN, JOSE Jose Manuel B 5.17.1976 San Cristobal, D.R. BR/TR 5-11/165# d4.1																								
1997	Pit N	143	498	58	133	20	5	14	70	17-0	8	88	.267	.300	.412	83	-14	1-2	.963	-4	93	95	*O-136(0-4-134)	-2.5
1998	Pit N	153	573	60	153	38	2	14	84	21-0	6	100	.267	.298	.414	84	-14	3-5	.968	7	103	166	*O-151(0-2-149)	-1.6
1999	Pit N	40	120	18	32	6	0	1	18	10-1	0	21	.267	.321	.342	69	-6	1-0	.952	-1	98	51	O-37(RF)	-0.8
	TB A	47	168	24	41	10	0	2	13	10-1	7	36	.244	.312	.339	66	-9	0-0	.966	-1	88	156	O-47(RF)	-1.1
2000	TB A	105	316	40	80	16	5	10	41	18-1	13	65	.253	.320	.430	88	-7	3-1	.978	0	99	117	O-99(0-1-98)	-1.0
2001	TB A	41	135	14	37	5	0	3	11	6-2	3	26	.274	.317	.378	84	-3	2-3	.969	8	129	309	O-36(RF)/D-4	0.2
2002	Ari N	54	131	13	30	4	0	4	15	7-1	2	25	.229	.277	.351	62	-8	3-4	1.000	-0	95	106	O-37(2-2-34)	-1.1
	Cin N	31	109	12	27	3	0	4	16	7-0	1	18	.248	.299	.385	79	-4	1-1	.980	-0	87	169	O-27(4-0-26)/D	-0.6
	Year	85	240	25	57	7	0	8	31	14-1	3	43	.237	.287	.367	69	-12	4-5	.990	-1	91	135	O-64(6-2-60)/D	-1.7
2003	Cin N	91	315	52	106	21	1	23	63	17-1	9	63	.337	.385	.629	162	28	1-3	.957	7	114	181	O-78(22-1-63)	2.9
	†Oak A	45	170	25	45	7	1	8	23	7-1	5	32	.265	.311	.459	99	-1	0-0	.942	-7	75	0	O-44(10-4-33)/D	-0.9
Total	7	750	2535	316	684	130	14	83	354	120-8	54	474	.270	.315	.430	92	-38	15-19	.966	7	99	135	O-692(38-14-657)/D-6	-6.5
GUILLEN, OZZIE Oswaldo Jose (Barrios) B 1.20.1964 Oculare Del Tuy, Venezuela BL/TR 5-11/150# d4.9 C2																								
1985	Chi A	150	491	71	134	21	9	1	33	12-1	1	36	.273	.291	.358	74	-19	7-4	**.980**	4	95	93	*S-150	-0.1
1986	Chi A	159	547	58	137	19	4	2	47	12-1	1	52	.250	.265	.311	55	-35	8-4	.970	18	111	102	*S-157/D	-0.1
1987	Chi A	149	560	64	156	22	7	2	51	22-2	1	52	.279	.303	.354	73	-23	25-8	.975	19	112	**124**	*S-149	1.4
1988	Chi A✳	156	566	58	148	16	7	0	39	25-3	2	40	.261	.294	.314	71	-23	25-13	.977	**41**	**123**	111	*S-156	3.0
1989	Chi A	155	597	63	151	20	8	1	54	15-3	0	48	.253	.270	.318	67	-29	36-17	.973	18	109	102	*S-155	0.3
1990	Chi A★	160	516	61	144	21	4	1	58	26-8	1	37	.279	.312	.341	85	-11	13-17	.977	6	103	103	*S-159	0.3
1991	Chi A★	154	524	52	143	20	3	3	49	11-1	0	38	.273	.284	.340	75	-20	21-15	.970	0	101	103	*S-149	-1.0
1992	Chi A	12	40	5	8	4	0	0	7	1-0	0	5	.200	.214	.300	45	-3	1-0	1.000	1	106	90	S-12	-0.1
1993	†Chi A	134	457	44	128	23	4	4	50	10-0	0	41	.280	.292	.374	80	-15	5-4	.972	-10	95	103	*S-133	-1.4
1994	Chi A	100	365	46	105	9	5	1	39	14-2	0	35	.288	.311	.348	72	-17	5-4	.959	-22	82	82	S-99	-2.9
1995	Chi A	122	415	50	103	20	3	1	41	13-1	0	25	.248	.270	.318	55	-29	6-7	.976	-8	96	75	*S-120/D	-2.8
1996	Chi A	150	499	62	131	24	8	4	45	10-0	0	27	.263	.273	.367	64	-30	6-5	.981	-22	88	76	*S-146/O-2(LF)	-3.9
1997	Chi A	142	490	59	120	21	6	4	52	22-1	0	24	.245	.275	.337	62	-30	5-3	.974	-21	89	88	*S-139	-3.8
1998	Bal A	12	16	2	1	0	0	0	0	1-0	0	2	.063	.118	.063	-52	-4	0-1	.933	-0	113	48	/S-6,3	-0.4
	†Atl N	83	264	35	73	15	1	1	22	24-0	1	25	.277	.337	.352	82	-6	1-4	.977	-6	86	74	S-71/2-2,13	-0.8
1999	†Atl N	92	232	21	56	16	0	1	20	15-2	0	17	.241	.284	.323	54	-16	4-2	.965	-1	100	110	S-53/3-6,2	-1.3
2000	TB A	63	107	22	26	4	0	2	12	6-0	0	7	.243	.283	.336	57	-7	1-0	.948	1	108	85	S-42,3-11/1-5,2-2	-0.4
Total	16	1993	6686	773	1764	275	69	28	619	239-25	7	511	.264	.287	.338	69	-317	169-108	.974	17	101	97	*S-1896/3-19,1-6,2-5,O-2(LF),D-2	-14.0
GUINDON, BOBBY Robert Joseph B 9.4.1943 Brookline, MA BL/TL 6-2/185# d9.19																								
1964	Bos A	5	8	0	1	1	0	0	0	1-0	0	4	.125	.222	.250	30	-1	0-0	1.000	-0	0	0	/1O(LF)	-0.1
GUINEY, BEN Benjamin Franklin B 11.16.1858 Detroit, MI D 12.5.1930 Detroit, MI BB/TR 6/170# d9.4																								
1883	Det N	1	5	1	1	0	0	0	0	0		1	.200	.200	.200	23	0		.000	-1	0	0	/O(CF)	-0.1
1884	Det N	2	7	0	0	0	0	0	0	0		3	.000	.000	.000	-99	-2		.750	-1			/C-2	-0.2
Total	2	3	12	1	1	0	0	0	0	0		4	.083	.083	.083	-51	-2		.750	-2			/C-2,O(CF)	-0.3
GUINTINI, BEN Benjamin John B 1.13.1919 Los Banos, CA D 12.2.1998 Roseville, CA BR/TR 6-1.5/190# d4.21																								
1946	Pit N	2	3	0	0	0	0	0	0	0	0	0	.000	.000	.000	-98	-1	0	1.000	0	112	0	/O(RF)	-0.1
1950	Phi A	3	4	0	0	0	0	0	0	0	0	1	.000	.000	.000	-99	-1	0-0	1.000	1	0	2754	/O(LF)	-0.1
Total	2	5	7	0	0	0	0	0	0	0	0	1	.000	.000	.000	-99	-2	0-0	1.000	1	56	1377	/O-2(1-0-1)	-0.2
GUISTO, LOU Louis Joseph B 1.16.1895 Napa, CA D 10.15.1989 Napa, CA BR/TR 5-11/193# d9.10 Mil 1917-18																								
1916	Cle A	6	19	2	3	0	0	0	2	4	0	3	.158	.304	.158	37	-1	1	1.000	-0	85	88	/1-6	-0.2
1917	Cle A	73	200	9	37	4	2	0	29	25	2	18	.185	.282	.225	51	-11	3	.989	-1	93	144	1-59	-1.6
1921	Cle A	2	2	0	1	0	0	0	1	0	0	1	.500	.500	.500	153	0	0-0	1.000	0	337	0	/1	0.0
1922	Cle A	35	84	7	21	10	1	0	9	2	1	7	.250	.276	.393	72	-4	0-0	.995	1	108	103	1-24	-0.4
1923	Cle A	40	144	17	26	5	0	0	18	15	1	15	.181	.262	.215	27	-15	1-1	.988	1	116	104	1-40	-1.7
Total	5	156	449	35	88	19	3	0	59	46	4	44	.196	.277	.252	47	-31	5-1	.990	1	103	121	1-130	-3.9
GULAN, MIKE Michael Watts B 12.18.1970 Steubenville, OH BR/TR 6-1/192# d5.14																								
1997	StL N	5	9	2	0	0	0	0	1	1-0	0	5	.000	.100	.000	-72	-2	0-0	1.000	-0	39	428	/3-3	-0.3
2001	Fla N	6	6	1	0	0	0	0	0	2-0	0	2	.000	.250	.000	-28	-1	0-0	1.000	0	110	0	/3	-0.1
Total	2	11	15	3	0	0	0	0	1	3-0	0	7	.000	.167	.000	-53	-3	0-0	1.000	-0	69	245	/3-4	-0.4

Year	Tm Lg	G	AB	R	H	2B	3B	HR	RBI	BB-IB	HP	SO	AVG	OBP	SLG	AOPS	ABR	SB-CS	FA	FR	Rng	Thr	G at Pos	BFW
GULDEN, BRAD Bradley Lee B 6.10.1956 New Ulm, MN BL/TR 5-11/180# d9.22																								
1978	LA N	3	4	0	0	0	0	0	0	0-0	0	2	.000	.000	.000	-99	-1	0-0	1.000	1	0	0	/C-3	0.0
1979	NY A	40	92	10	15	4	0	0	6	9-0	0	16	.163	.238	.207	21	-10	0-1	.995	8	102	138	C-40	-0.1
1980	NY A	2	3	1	1	0	0	1	2	0-0	0	0	.333	.333	1.333	340	1	0-0	1.000	-0	0	0	/C-2	0.1
1981	Sea A	8	16	0	3	2	0	0	1	0-0	0	2	.188	.188	.313	40	-1	0-0	1.000	2	95	85	/C-6	0.1
1982	Mon N	5	6	1	0	0	0	0	0	1-0	0	1	.000	.143	.000	-56	-1	0-0	1.000	-0	23	233	/C-2	-0.1
1984	Cin N	107	292	31	66	8	2	4	33	33-2	2	35	.226	.307	.308	71	-11	2-2	.975	-2	87	111	*C-100	-1.0
1986	SF N	17	22	2	2	0	0	0	1	2-2	0	5	.091	.167	.091	-28	-4	0-0	1.000	0	120	62	C-10	-0.4
Total	7	182	435	45	87	14	2	5	43	45-4	2	61	.200	.277	.276	53	-27	2-3	.982	8	90	115	C-163	-1.4
GULLEY, TOM Thomas Jefferson B 12.25.1899 Garner, NC D 11.24.1966 St.Charles, AR BL/TR 5-11/178# d8.24																								
1923	Cle A	2	3	1	1	1	0	0	0	0	0	0	.333	.333	.667	159	0	0-0	1.000	-0	85	0	/O(CF)	0.0
1924	Cle A	8	20	4	3	0	1	0	1	3	0	2	.150	.261	.250	32	-2	0-0	.933	-0	118	0	/O-5(0-2-3)	-0.3
1926	Chi A	16	35	5	8	3	1	0	8	5	0	2	.229	.325	.371	84	-1	0-0	1.000	-0	113	0	O-12(RF)	-0.2
Total	3	26	58	10	12	4	2	0	9	8	0	4	.207	.303	.345	69	-3	0-0	.971	-1	114	0	/O-18(0-3-15)	-0.5
GULLIC, TED Tedd Jasper B 1.2.1907 Koshkonong, MO D 1.28.2000 West Plains, MO BR/TR 6-2/175# d4.15																								
1930	StL A	92	308	39	77	7	5	4	44	27	0	43	.250	.310	.344	64	-18	4-0	.967	0	85	153	O-82(RF)/1-3	-2.2
1933	StL A	104	304	34	74	18	3	5	35	15	1	38	.243	.281	.372	67	-15	3-1	.988	10	100	249	O-36(14-16-7),3-33,1-14	-0.6
Total	2	196	612	73	151	25	8	9	79	42	1	81	.247	.296	.358	65	-33	7-1	.975	10	89	180	O-118(14-16-89)/3-33,1-17	-2.8
GULLIVER, GLENN Glenn James B 10.15.1954 Detroit, MI BL/TR 5-11/175# d7.17																								
1982	Bal A	50	145	24	29	7	0	1	5	37-0	0	18	.200	.363	.269	77	-2	0-0	.970	2	106	74	3-50	-0.1
1983	Bal A	23	47	5	10	3	0	0	2	9-0	0	5	.213	.333	.277	73	-1	0-1	1.000	3	116	119	3-21	0.1
Total	2	73	192	29	39	10	0	1	7	46-0	0	23	.203	.356	.271	76	-3	0-1	.978	5	108	84	/3-71	0.0
GUNKLE, FRED Frederick William B 10.26.1857 Reading, PA D 12.21.1936 Long Beach, CA d5.17																								
1879	Cle N	1	3	1	0	0	0	0	0	0		1	.000	.000	.000	-99	-1		1.000	-2	0	0	/O(RF)C	-0.2
GUNNING, HY Hyland B 8.6.1888 Maplewood, NJ D 3.28.1975 Togus, ME BL/TR 6-1.5/189# d8.8																								
1911	Bos A	4	9	0	1	0	0	0	2	2	0		.111	.273	.111	9	-1	0	1.000	-1	0	0	/1-4	-0.2
GUNNING, TOM Thomas Francis B 3.4.1862 Newmarket, NH D 3.17.1931 Fall River, MA BR/TR 5-10/160# d7.26 U2																								
1884	Bos N	12	45	4	5	1	1	0	2	1		12	.111	.130	.178	-4	-5		.914	-3			C-12	-0.7
1885	Bos N	48	174	17	32	3	0	0	15	5		29	.184	.207	.201	34	-13		.877	-5			C-48	-1.3
1886	Bos N	27	98	15	22	2	1	0	7	3		19	.224	.248	.265	58	-5	3	.892	-7			C-27	-0.9
1887	Phi N	28	104	22	27	6	1	1	16	5	2	6	.260	.306	.365	81	-3	18	.895	5			C-28	0.4
1888	Phi AA	23	92	18	18	0	0	0	5	2	3		.196	.237	.196	40	-6	14	.894	-1			C-23	-0.5
1889	Phi AA	8	24	3	6	0	1	1	1	0	0	4	.250	.250	.458	101	0	3	.838	-1			/C-8	-0.1
Total	6	146	537	79	110	12	4	2	46	16	5	70	.205	.235	.253	50	-32	38	.887	-11			C-146	-3.1
GUNSON, JOE Joseph Brook B 3.23.1863 Philadelphia, PA D 11.15.1942 Philadelphia, PA BR/TR 5-6/160# d6.14																								
1884	Was U	45	166	15	23	2	0	0		3			.139	.154	.151	-8	-27		.915	6			C-33,O-18(0-10-9)	-1.7
1889	KC AA	34	122	15	24	3	1	0	12	3	2	17	.197	.228	.238	31	-12	2	.862	-6			C-32/O(LF)3	-1.3
1892	Bal N	89	314	35	67	10	5	0	32	16	7	17	.213	.267	.277	63	-15	2	.921	-4	*95*	*109*	C-67,O-20(10-3-7)/1-2,2	-1.3
1893	StL N	40	151	20	41	5	0	0	15	6	5	6	.272	.321	.305	66	-7	0	.927	2	*87*	*101*	C-35/O-5(1-0-4)	-0.2
	Cle N	21	73	11	19	1	0	0	9	6	0	0	.260	.316	.274	54	-5	0	.942	3	*114*	*111*	C-20	-0.1
	Year	61	224	31	60	6	0	0	24	12	5	6	.268	.320	.295	62	-12	0	.932	4	*96*	*105*	C-55/O-5(1-0-4)	-0.3
Total	4	229	826	96	174	21	6	0	68	34	14	40	.211	.254	.251	45	-66	4	.912	0	*64*	*72*	C-187/O-44(12-13-20),1-2,23	-4.6
GUST, ERNIE Ernest Herman Frank "Red" B 1.24.1888 Bay City, MI D 10.26.1945 Maupin, OR BR/TR 6/170# d8.17																								
1911	StL A	3	12	0	0	0	0	0	0	0	0		.000	.000	.000	-99	-3	0	.974	-0	94	123	/1-3	-0.4
GUSTINE, FRANKIE Frank William B 2.20.1920 Hoopeston, IL D 4.1.1991 Davenport, IA BR/TR 6/180# d9.13 C1																								
1939	Pit N	22	70	5	13	3	0	0	3	9	0	4	.186	.278	.229	38	-6	0	.896	2	125	74	3-22	-0.3
1940	Pit N	133	524	59	147	32	7	1	55	35	2	39	.281	.328	.374	94	-4	7	.941	-8	100	103	*2-130	-0.4
1941	Pit N	121	463	46	125	24	7	1	46	28	1	38	.270	.313	.359	89	-8	5	.954	-2	105	73	*2-104,3-15	-0.3
1942	Pit N	115	388	34	89	11	4	2	35	29	2	27	.229	.286	.294	68	-16	5	.954	-14	101	84	*2-108/S-2,3-2,C	-2.5
1943	Pit N	112	414	40	120	21	3	0	43	32	0	36	.290	.341	.355	98	-1	12	.938	-4	103	101	S-68,2-40/1	0.3
1944	Pit N	127	405	42	93	18	3	2	42	33	0	41	.230	.288	.304	64	-20	8	.938	-23	94	85	*S-116,2-11/3	-3.5
1945	Pit N	128	478	67	134	27	5	2	66	37	2	33	.280	.335	.370	92	-5	8	.930	-14	93	98	*S-104,2-29/C	-1.0
1946	Pit N★	131	495	60	128	23	6	8	52	40	3	52	.259	.318	.378	95	-5	2	.967	8	**108**	92	*2-113,S-13/3-7	1.0
1947	Pit N★	**156**	616	102	183	30	6	9	67	63	2	65	.297	.364	.409	102	3	5	.944	16	**110**	122	*3-156	1.8
1948	Pit N★	131	449	68	120	19	2	9	42	42	2	62	.267	.333	.379	90	-6	5	.947	**13**	**115**	114	*3-118	0.6
1949	Chi N	76	261	29	59	13	4	4	27	18	1	22	.226	.279	.352	70	-12	3	.931	0	98	106	3-55,2-16	-1.1
1950	StL A	9	19	1	3	1	0	0	2	3	0	8	.158	.273	.211	24	-2	0-1	.857	-1	70	219	/3-6	-0.3
Total	12	1261	4582	553	1214	222	47	38	480	369	15	427	.265	.322	.359	87	-82	60-1	.955	-27	103	90	2-551,3-382,S-303/C-2,1	-5.7
GUTH, BUCKY Charles Henry B 8.18.1947 Baltimore, MD BR/TR 6-1/180# d9.12																								
1972	Min A	3	3	1	0	0	0	0	0	0-0	0	0	.000	.000	.000	-95	-1	0-0	1.000	-0	125	0	/S	-0.1
GUTIERREZ, CESAR Cesar Dario "Cocoa" B 1.26.1943 Coro, Venezuela BR/TR 5-9/155# d4.16																								
1967	SF N	18	21	4	3	0	0	0	0	1-0	1	4	.143	.217	.143	5	-3	1-0	.946	1	99	118	S-15/2	-0.1
1969	SF N	15	23	4	5	1	0	0	0	6-1	0	2	.217	.379	.261	84	0	1-0	.882	-2	105	0	/3-7,S-4	-0.1
	Det A	17	49	5	12	1	0	0	0	5-0	0	3	.245	.315	.265	61	-2	1-2	.946	0	100	75	S-16	-0.1
1970	Det A	135	415	40	101	11	6	0	22	18-6	1	39	.243	.275	.299	58	-25	4-3	.957	-22	86	77	*S-135	-3.5
1971	Det A	38	37	8	7	0	0	0	4	0-0	1	3	.189	.211	.189	13	-4	0-0	.971	0	103	49	S-14/3-5,2-2	-0.3
Total	4	223	545	61	128	13	6	0	26	30-7	3	51	.235	.277	.281	55	-34	7-5	.955	-23	89	77	S-184/3-12,2-3	-4.1
GUTIERREZ, JACKIE Joaquin Fernando B 6.27.1960 Cartagena, Colombia BR/TR 5-11/175# d9.6																								
1983	Bos A	5	10	2	3	0	0	0	0	1-0	0	1	.300	.364	.300	79	0	0-1	.938	-1	61	50	/S-4	-0.1
1984	Bos A	151	449	55	118	12	3	2	29	15-0	0	49	.263	.284	.316	64	-23	12-5	.949	-25	84	68	*S-150	-3.4
1985	Bos A	103	275	33	60	5	2	2	21	12-0	0	37	.218	.250	.273	42	-23	10-2	.943	-3	98	85	S-99	-1.6
1986	Bal A	61	145	8	27	3	0	0	4	3-0	1	27	.186	.207	.207	14	-18	3-1	.990	-5	85	107	2-53/3-6,D	-2.0
1987	Bal A	3	1	0	0	0	0	0	0	0-0	0	0	.000	.000	.000	-99	0	0-0	—	-0	0	0	/23	-0.1
1988	Phi N	33	77	8	19	4	0	0	9	2-0	0	9	.247	.259	.299	61	-4	0-0	.919	-3	104	76	S-22,3-13	-0.6
Total	6	356	957	106	227	24	5	4	63	33-0	1	123	.237	.261	.285	50	-68	25-9	.945	-38	90	74	S-275/2-54,3-20,D	-7.8
GUTIERREZ, RICKY Ricardo B 5.23.1970 Miami, FL BR/TR 6-1/175# d4.13																								
1993	SD N	133	438	76	110	10	5	5	26	50-2	5	97	.251	.334	.331	78	-13	4-3	.971	-3	92	83	*S-117/2-6,O-5(3-0-2),3-4	-0.8
1994	SD N	90	275	27	66	11	2	1	28	32-1	2	54	.240	.321	.305	67	-13	2-6	.925	-11	91	77	S-78/2-7	-1.9
1995	Hou N	52	156	22	43	6	0	0	12	10-3	1	33	.276	.321	.314	74	-6	5-0	.956	-6	88	70	S-44/3-2	-0.8
1996	Hou N	89	218	28	62	8	1	1	15	23-3	3	42	.284	.359	.344	94	-1	6-1	.953	-9	85	90	S-74/3-6,2-5	-0.5
1997	†Hou N	102	303	33	79	14	4	3	34	21-2	3	50	.261	.315	.363	80	-10	5-2	.967	-3	97	116	S-64,3-22/2-9	-0.8
1998	†Hou N	141	491	55	128	24	3	2	46	54-5	6	84	.261	.337	.334	81	-12	13-7	.976	14	103	111	*S-141	1.2
1999	†Hou N	85	268	33	70	7	5	1	25	37-4	2	45	.261	.354	.336	77	-9	2-5	.971	-6	94	83	S-80/3	-1.0
2000	Chi N	125	449	73	124	19	2	11	56	66-0	7	58	.276	.375	.401	99	1	8-2	**.986**	-13	88	82	*S-121	-0.1
2001	Chi N	147	528	76	153	23	3	10	66	40-0	10	56	.290	.345	.402	99	-1	4-3	.971	-8	91	81	*S-144	0.3
2002	Cle A	94	353	38	97	13	0	4	38	20-0	7	48	.275	.325	.346	80	-10	0-1	.976	12	109	103	2-93/D	0.6
2003	Cle A	16	50	2	13	3	0	0	3	3-0	1	5	.260	.309	.320	70	-2	0-0	.929	-3	102	71	/S-9,3-7	-0.4
Total	11	1074	3529	463	945	138	25	38	349	356-20	47	572	.268	.340	.353	84	-76	49-30	.967	-36	93	88	S-872,2-120/3-42,O-5(3-0-2),D	-4.2
GUTTERIDGE, DON Donald Joseph B 6.19.1912 Pittsburg, KS BR/TR 5-10.5/165# d9.7 M2 C14																								
1936	StL N	23	91	13	29	3	4	3	16	1	0	14	.319	.326	.538	130	3	3	.967	0	94	109	3-23	0.3
1937	StL N	119	447	66	121	26	10	7	61	25	1	66	.271	.311	.421	95	-5	12	.978	0	93	**133**	*3-105/S-8	0.0
1938	StL N	142	552	61	141	21	15	9	64	29	0	49	.255	.293	.397	83	-15	14	.945	-7	98	132	3-73,S-68	-1.5
1939	StL N	148	524	71	141	27	4	7	54	27	3	70	.269	.309	.376	78	-17	5	.934	-19	79	107	*3-143/S-2	-3.2
1940	StL N	69	108	19	29	5	0	3	14	5	0	15	.269	.301	.398	86	-2	3	.877	-4	79	90	3-39	-0.6

Year	Tm Lg	G	AB	R	H	2B	3B	HR	RBI	BB-IB	HP	SO	AVG	OBP	SLG	AOPS	ABR	SB-CS	FA	FR	Rng	Thr	G at Pos	BFW
1942	StL A	147	616	90	157	27	11	1	50	59	0	54	.255	.320	.339	84	-14	16-13	.973	2	102	98	*2-145/3-2	-0.3
1943	StL A	132	538	77	147	35	6	1	36	50	0	46	.273	.335	.366	103	2	10-9	.958	-29	85	69	*2-132	-2.2
1944	†StL A	148	603	89	148	27	11	3	36	51	0	63	.245	.304	.342	80	-17	20-8	.957	-10	96	94	*2-146	-1.8
1945	StL A	143	543	72	129	24	3	2	49	43	1	46	.238	.295	.304	70	-21	9-6	.970	-17	91	83	*2-128,O-14(LF)	-3.4
1946	†Bos A	22	47	8	11	3	0	1	6	2	0	7	.234	.265	.362	70	-2	0-0	1.000	-1	125	136	/2-9,3-8	-0.3
1947	Bos A	54	131	20	22	2	0	2	5	17	0	13	.168	.264	.229	35	-12	3-1	.938	-2	96	85	2-20,3-19	-1.3
1948	Pit N	4	2	0	0	0	0	0	0	0	0	1	.000	.000	.000	-98	-1	0	—	0			H	-0.1
Total	12	1151	4202	586	1075	200	64	39	391	309	5	444	.256	.308	.362	84	-101	95-37	.964	-86	94	87	2-580,3-412/S-78,O-14(LF)	-14.4

GUZMAN, CRISTIAN Cristian B 3.21.1978 Santo Domingo, D.R. BB/TR 6/180# d4.6

Year	Tm Lg	G	AB	R	H	2B	3B	HR	RBI	BB-IB	HP	SO	AVG	OBP	SLG	AOPS	ABR	SB-CS	FA	FR	Rng	Thr	G at Pos	BFW
1999	Min A	131	420	47	95	12	3	1	26	22-0	3	90	.226	.267	.276	38	-40	9-7	.959	-5	100	101	*S-131	-3.4
2000	Min A	156	631	89	156	25	**20**	8	54	46-1	2	101	.247	.299	.388	70	-32	28-10	.967	-17	90	94	*S-151/D	-3.2
2001	Min A★	118	493	80	149	28	**14**	10	51	21-0	5	78	.302	.337	.477	108	4	25-8	.959	-10	100	85	*S-118	0.5
2002	†Min A	148	623	80	170	31	6	9	59	17-2	2	79	.273	.292	.385	78	-22	12-13	.981	-17	87	98	*S-147/D	-2.9
2003	†Min A	143	534	78	143	15	**14**	3	53	30-0	5	79	.268	.311	.365	77	-19	18-9	.980	-30	88	78	*S-141	-3.6
Total	5	696	2701	374	713	111	57	31	243	136-3	17	427	.264	.302	.382	75	-109	92-47	.969	-79	92	91	S-688/D-2	-12.6

GUZMAN, EDWARDS Edwards B 9.11.1976 Bayamon, P.R. BL/TR 5-11/205# d4.6

Year	Tm Lg	G	AB	R	H	2B	3B	HR	RBI	BB-IB	HP	SO	AVG	OBP	SLG	AOPS	ABR	SB-CS	FA	FR	Rng	Thr	G at Pos	BFW
1999	SF N	14	15	0	0	0	0	0	0	0-0	0	4	.000	.000	.000	-99	-5	0-0	1.000	1	150	0	/3-5,C	-0.4
2001	SF N	61	115	8	28	6	0	3	7	5-2	0	16	.243	.273	.374	71	-6	0-0	.990	-4	149	91	C-26/1-7,3-7,2-3,O-2(LF)	-0.8
2003	Mon N	52	146	15	35	5	0	1	14	5-2	0	17	.240	.263	.295	42	-13	0-0	.956	-5	95	81	3-28,1-13/C-4,D-3	-1.7
Total	3	127	276	23	63	11	0	4	21	10-4	0	37	.228	.253	.312	45	-24	0-0	.969	-7	100	84	/3-40,C-31,1-20,D-3,2-3,O-2(LF)	-2.9

GWOSDZ, DOUG Douglas Wayne "Eye Chart" B 6.20.1960 Houston, TX BR/TR 5-11/185# d8.17

Year	Tm Lg	G	AB	R	H	2B	3B	HR	RBI	BB-IB	HP	SO	AVG	OBP	SLG	AOPS	ABR	SB-CS	FA	FR	Rng	Thr	G at Pos	BFW
1981	SD N	16	24	1	4	2	0	0	3	3-2	0	6	.167	.241	.250	48	-2	0-0	1.000	2	328	130	C-13	0.1
1982	SD N	7	17	1	3	0	0	0	0	2-1	0	7	.176	.263	.176	27	-2	0-0	1.000	2	443	0	/C-7	0.1
1983	SD N	39	55	7	6	1	0	1	4	7-0	0	19	.109	.210	.182	10	-7	0-0	.971	-2	137	53	C-32	-0.9
1984	SD N	7	8	0	2	0	0	0	1	2-0	0	5	.250	.400	.250	86	0	0-0	.963	2	114	98	/C-6	0.2
Total	4	69	104	9	15	3	0	1	8	14-3	0	37	.144	.242	.202	27	-11	0-0	.981	4	228	67	/C-58	-0.5

GWYNN, TONY Anthony Keith B 5.9.1960 Los Angeles, CA BL/TL 5-11/199# d7.19 b-Chris

Year	Tm Lg	G	AB	R	H	2B	3B	HR	RBI	BB-IB	HP	SO	AVG	OBP	SLG	AOPS	ABR	SB-CS	FA	FR	Rng	Thr	G at Pos	BFW
1982	SD N	54	190	33	55	12	2	1	17	14-0	0	16	.289	.337	.389	109	2	8-3	.991	-2	100	29	O-52(23-28-13)	0.0
1983	SD N	86	304	34	94	12	2	1	37	23-5	0	21	.309	.355	.372	106	3	7-4	.994	4	102	153	O-81(26-6-54)	0.2
1984	†SD N★	158	606	88	**213**	21	10	5	71	59-13	2	23	**.351**	.410	.444	140	34	33-18	.989	9	112	103	*O-156(0-1-156)	3.6
1985	SD N★	154	622	90	197	29	5	6	46	45-4	2	33	.317	.364	.408	118	14	14-11	.989	11	112	129	*O-152(RF)	1.7
1986	SD N★	160	642	**107**	**211**	33	7	14	59	52-11	3	35	.329	.381	.467	136	31	37-9	.989	14	113	147	*O-160(RF)	4.2
1987	SD N★	157	589	119	**218**	36	13	7	54	82-26	3	35	**.370**	.447	.511	160	**55**	56-12	.981	4	104	123	*O-156(RF)	5.8
1988	SD N	133	521	64	163	22	5	7	70	51-13	0	40	**.313**	.373	.415	128	20	26-11	.982	-3	94	122	*O-133(0-32-102)	1.7
1989	SD N★	158	604	82	**203**	27	7	4	62	56-16	1	30	**.336**	.389	.424	133	27	40-16	.984	1	97	153	*O-157(0-86-73)	3.0
1990	SD N★	141	573	79	177	29	10	4	72	44-20	1	23	.309	.357	.415	112	9	17-8	.985	6	107	104	*O-141(RF)	1.1
1991	SD N★	134	530	69	168	27	11	4	62	34-8	0	19	.317	.355	.432	118	11	8-8	.990	5	108	78	*O-134(RF)	1.1
1992	SD N★	128	520	77	165	27	3	6	41	46-12	0	16	.317	.371	.415	121	15	3-6	.982	4	104	102	*O-127(RF)	1.4
1993	SD N★	122	489	70	175	41	3	7	59	36-11	1	19	.358	.398	.497	137	27	14-1	.981	2	107	90	*O-121(0-4-121)	2.5
1994	SD N★	110	419	79	**165**	35	1	12	64	48-16	2	19	**.394**	**.454**	.568	171	47	5-0	.985	-2	99	81	*O-106(0-1-105)	3.9
1995	SD N★	135	535	82	**197**	33	1	9	90	35-10	1	15	**.368**	.404	.484	139	31	17-5	.992	2	103	89	*O-133(RF)	2.7
1996	†SD N✳	116	451	67	159	27	2	3	50	39-12	1	17	**.353**	.400	.441	131	22	11-4	.989	-10	87	27	*O-111(RF)	0.7
1997	SD N★	149	592	97	**220**	49	2	17	119	43-12	3	28	**.372**	.409	.547	162	54	12-5	.983	-10	83	77	*O-143(RF)/D-3	3.6
1998	†SD N★	127	461	65	148	35	0	16	69	35-6	1	18	.321	.364	.501	137	24	3-1	.993	-11	75	74	*O-116(RF)/D-3	0.9
1999	SD N✳	111	411	59	139	27	0	10	62	29-5	2	14	.338	.381	.477	126	17	7-2	.993	-8	83	67	*O-104(RF)/D-2	0.5
2000	SD N	36	127	17	41	12	0	1	17	9-2	1	4	.323	.364	.441	112	3	0-1	1.000	-4	66	66	O-26(RF)/D-6	-0.2
2001	SD N☆	71	102	5	33	9	1	1	17	10-1	0	9	.324	.384	.461	128	5	1-0	1.000	-0	72	254	O-17(RF)/D	0.4
Total	20	2440	9288	1383	3141	543	85	135	1138	790-203	24	434	.338	.388	.459	133	451	319-125	.987	12	100	102	*O-2326(49-158-2144)/D-15	38.8

GWYNN, CHRIS Christopher Karlton B 10.13.1964 Los Angeles, CA BL/TL 6/210# d8.14 b-Tony

Year	Tm Lg	G	AB	R	H	2B	3B	HR	RBI	BB-IB	HP	SO	AVG	OBP	SLG	AOPS	ABR	SB-CS	FA	FR	Rng	Thr	G at Pos	BFW
1987	LA N	17	32	2	7	1	0	0	2	1-0	0	7	.219	.242	.250	32	-3	0-0	1.000	-1	83	0	O-10(LF)	-0.4
1988	LA N	12	11	1	2	0	0	0	0	1-0	0	2	.182	.250	.182	27	-1	0-0	—	-0	0	0	/O-4(LF)	-0.2
1989	LA N	32	68	8	16	4	1	0	7	2-0	0	9	.235	.254	.324	66	-3	1-0	1.000	-0	86	132	O-19(14-5-2)	-0.4
1990	LA N	101	141	19	40	2	1	5	22	7-2	0	28	.284	.311	.418	104	0	0-1	1.000	-2	80	64	O-44(32-5-8)	-0.3
1991	LA N	94	139	18	35	5	1	5	22	10-1	1	23	.252	.301	.410	102	0	1-0	1.000	-2	76	132	O-41(31-2-14)	-0.2
1992	KC A	34	84	10	24	3	2	1	7	3-0	0	10	.286	.303	.405	96	-1	0-0	1.000	-2	91	0	O-19(5-0-14)/D-2	-0.3
1993	KC A	103	287	36	86	14	4	1	25	24-5	1	34	.300	.354	.387	94	-2	0-1	.994	3	102	135	O-83(66-0-19)/1D	-0.3
1994	LA N	58	71	9	19	0	0	3	13	7-0	0	7	.268	.333	.394	95	-1	0-2	1.000	-1	75	0	O-20(19-0-1)	-0.3
1995	†LA N	67	84	8	18	3	2	1	10	6-1	1	23	.214	.272	.333	65	-5	0-0	1.000	0	109	0	O-17(12-0-5)/1-2	-0.5
1996	†SD N	81	90	8	16	4	0	1	10	10-0	0	28	.178	.260	.256	39	-8	0-0	1.000	-1	90	0	O-29(5-0-24)/1	-0.9
Total	10	599	1007	119	263	36	11	17	118	71-9	3	171	.261	.308	.369	85	-24	2-4	.997	-5	91	84	O-286(198-12-87)/D-7,1-4	-3.8

GYSELMAN, DICK Richard Renald B 4.6.1908 San Francisco, CA D 9.20.1990 Seattle, WA BR/TR 6-2/170# d4.20

Year	Tm Lg	G	AB	R	H	2B	3B	HR	RBI	BB-IB	HP	SO	AVG	OBP	SLG	AOPS	ABR	SB-CS	FA	FR	Rng	Thr	G at Pos	BFW
1933	Bos N	58	155	10	37	6	2	0	12	7	0	21	.239	.272	.303	70	-7	0	.926	2	110	72	3-42/2-5,S	-0.4
1934	Bos N	24	36	7	6	1	1	0	4	2	0	11	.167	.211	.250	25	-4	0	.739	-3	67	0	3-15/2-2	-0.7
Total	2	82	191	17	43	7	3	0	16	9	0	32	.225	.260	.293	61	-11	0	.901	-1	104	62	/3-57,2-7,S	-1.1

HAAD, YAMID Yamid Salcedo B 9.2.1977 Cartagena, Colombia BR/TR 6-2/204# d7.5

Year	Tm Lg	G	AB	R	H	2B	3B	HR	RBI	BB-IB	HP	SO	AVG	OBP	SLG	AOPS	ABR	SB-CS	FA	FR	Rng	Thr	G at Pos	BFW
1999	Pit N	1	1	0	0	0	0	0	0	0-0	0	0	.000	.000	.000	-99	0	0-0	—	0			/H	0.0

HAAS, BERT Berthold John B 2.8.1914 Naperville, IL D 6.23.1999 Tampa, FL BR/TR 5-11/180# d9.9 Mil 1944-45

Year	Tm Lg	G	AB	R	H	2B	3B	HR	RBI	BB-IB	HP	SO	AVG	OBP	SLG	AOPS	ABR	SB-CS	FA	FR	Rng	Thr	G at Pos	BFW
1937	Bro N	16	25	2	10	3	0	0	2	1	0	1	.400	.423	.520	152	2	0	1.000	-0	109	0	/O-4(RF),1-3	0.1
1938	Bro N	1	0	0	0	0	0	0	0	0	0	0	—	—	—	—	0	0	—	0			H	0.0
1942	Cin N	**154**	585	59	140	21	6	6	54	59	1	54	.239	.310	.326	86	-10	6	.925	-14	91	**125**	*3-146/1-6,O-2(LF)	-2.1
1943	Cin N	101	332	39	87	17	6	4	44	22	0	26	.262	.308	.386	101	-1	6	.993	6	169	142	1-44,3-23,O-18(CF)	0.3
1946	Cin N	140	535	57	141	24	7	3	50	33	3	42	.264	.310	.351	91	-9	22	.994	-2	93	**141**	*1-140/3-6	-1.7
1947	Cin N★	135	482	58	138	17	7	3	67	42	2	27	.286	.346	.369	91	-7	9	.956	-6	108	47	O-69(8-58-0),1-53	-1.7
1948	Phi N	95	333	35	94	9	2	4	34	36	1	25	.282	.354	.357	95	-2	8	.892	-7	85	101	3-54,1-35	-1.0
1949	Phi N	2	1	0	0	0	0	0	0	1	0	1	.000	.500	.000	47	0	0	—	0			H	0.0
	NY N	54	104	12	27	2	3	1	10	5	0	8	.260	.294	.365	76	-4	0	.983	-2	97	95	1-23,3-11	-0.7
	Year	56	105	12	27	2	3	1	10	6	0	9	.257	.297	.362	76	-4	0	.983	-2	97	95	1-23,3-11	-0.7
1951	Chi A	23	43	1	7	0	1	1	2	5	0	4	.163	.250	.279	44	-4	0-0	1.000	-0	99	80	/1-7,O-4(1-0-3),3	-0.4
Total	9	721	2440	263	644	93	32	22	263	204	7	188	.264	.323	.355	91	-35	51-0	.991	-26	95	120	1-311,3-241/O-97(11-76-7)	-7.2

HAAS, EDDIE George Edwin B 5.26.1935 Paducah, KY BL/TR 5-11/178# d9.8 M1 C5

Year	Tm Lg	G	AB	R	H	2B	3B	HR	RBI	BB-IB	HP	SO	AVG	OBP	SLG	AOPS	ABR	SB-CS	FA	FR	Rng	Thr	G at Pos	BFW
1957	Chi N	14	24	1	5	1	0	0	4	1-0	0	5	.208	.231	.250	32	-2	0-0	1.000	-1	65	0	/O-4(3-1-0)	-0.3
1958	Mil N	9	14	2	5	0	0	0	1	2-0	0	1	.357	.438	.357	124	1	0-0	1.000	-0	99	0	/O-3(0-2-1)	0.0
1960	Mil N	32	32	4	7	2	0	1	5	5-0	0	14	.219	.324	.375	98	0	0-0	1.000	-0	77	0	/O-2(1-0-1)	0.0
Total	3	55	70	7	17	3	0	1	10	8-0	0	20	.243	.316	.329	80	-1	0-0	1.000	-1	79	0	/O-9(4-3-2)	-0.3

HAAS, MULE George William B 10.15.1903 Montclair, NJ D 6.30.1974 New Orleans, LA BL/TR 6-1/175# d8.15 C7

Year	Tm Lg	G	AB	R	H	2B	3B	HR	RBI	BB-IB	HP	SO	AVG	OBP	SLG	AOPS	ABR	SB-CS	FA	FR	Rng	Thr	G at Pos	BFW
1925	Pit N	4	3	1	0	0	0	0	0	0	0	1	.000	.000	.000	-94	-1	0-0	1.000	0	142	0	/O-2(0-1-1)	-0.1
1928	Phi A	91	332	41	93	21	4	6	39	23	2	20	.280	.331	.422	94	-4	2-3	.974	-3	91	110	O-82(10-69-4)	-1.1
1929	†Phi A	139	578	115	181	41	9	16	82	34	4	38	.313	.356	.498	113	9	0-4	.982	-4	97	68	*O-139(1-139-0)	-0.2
1930	†Phi A	132	532	91	159	33	7	2	68	43	1	33	.299	.352	.398	86	-11	2-2	.976	7	106	121	*O-131(CF)	-0.8
1931	†Phi A	102	440	82	142	29	7	8	56	30	0	29	.323	.366	.475	113	7	0-0	.989	-1	98	75	*O-102(CF)	0.3
1932	Phi A	143	558	91	170	28	5	6	65	62	2	49	.305	.376	.405	99	0	1-0	.987	1	106	54	*O-137(0-108-29)	-0.3
1933	Chi A	146	585	97	168	33	4	1	51	65	2	41	.287	.360	.362	96	-1	0-5	.983	-10	90	85	*O-146(CF)	-1.5
1934	Chi A	106	351	54	94	16	3	2	22	47	0	22	.268	.354	.348	79	-10	1-0	.991	-5	92	72	O-89(0-85-4)	-1.6
1935	Chi A	92	327	44	95	22	1	2	40	37	0	17	.291	.363	.382	90	-4	4-1	.989	-1	102	58	O-84(0-22-64)	-0.8
1936	Chi A	119	408	75	116	26	2	0	46	64	1	29	.284	.383	.358	81	-10	1-1	.989	-5	91	79	O-96(2-1-94)/1-7	-1.8
1937	Chi A	54	111	8	23	3	3	0	15	16	1	10	.207	.313	.288	52	-8	1-0	.975	0	127	103	1-32/O-2(RF)	-1.0

Year	Tm Lg	G	AB	R	H	2B	3B	HR	RBI	BB-IB	HP	SO	AVG	OBP	SLG	AOPS	ABR	SB-CS	FA	FR	Rng	Thr	G at Pos	BFW
1938	Phi A	40	78	7	16	2	0	0	12	12	0	10	.205	.311	.231	39	-7	0-0	1.000	-1	100	128	O-12(0-5-7)/1-6	-0.8
Total	12	1168	4303	706	1257	254	45	43	496	433	13	299	.292	.359	.402	93	-40	12-16	.984	-20	97	80	*O-1022(13-809-205)/1-45	-9.7
HABERER, EMIL Emil Karl B 2.2.1878 Cincinnati, OH D 10.19.1951 Louisville, KY BR/TR 6-1/204# d7.9																								
1901	Cin N	6	18	2	3	0	1	0	1	3	0		.167	.286	.278	68	-1	0	.545	-2	84	0	/3-3,1-2	-0.2
1903	Cin N	5	13	1	1	0	0	0	0	2	0		.077	.200	.077	-18	-2	0	.933	-1	*92*	*53*	/C-4	-0.3
1909	Cin N	5	16	1	3	1	0	0	2	0	0		.188	.188	.250	36	-1	0	.895	-1	*81*	*59*	/C-4	-0.3
Total	3	16	47	4	7	1	1	0	3	5	0		.149	.231	.213	31	-4	0	.912	-4	*86*	*56*	/C-8,3-3,1-2	-0.8
HACH, IRV Irvin William "Major" B 6.6.1873 Louisville, KY D 8.13.1936 Louisville, KY BR/TR d7.1																								
1897	Lou N	16	51	5	11	2	0	0	3	5	3		.216	.322	.255	55	-3	1	.889	-2	97	88	/2-9,3-7	-0.3
HACK, STAN Stanley Camfield "Smiling Stan" B 12.6.1909 Sacramento, CA D 12.15.1979 Dixon, IL BL/TR 6/170# d4.12 M4 C3																								
1932	†Chi N	72	178	32	42	5	6	2	19	17	1	16	.236	.306	.365	80	-6	5	.913	-4	100	60	3-51	-0.8
1933	Chi N	20	60	10	21	3	1	1	2	8	3	3	.350	.451	.483	167	6	4	.983	4	113	320	3-17	1.1
1934	Chi N	111	402	54	116	16	6	1	21	45	2	42	.289	.363	.366	98	0	11	.949	8	107	77	*3-109	1.1
1935	†Chi N	124	427	75	133	23	9	4	64	65	3	17	.311	.406	.436	125	19	14	.942	5	**112**	**128**	*3-111/1-7	2.6
1936	Chi N	149	561	102	167	27	4	6	78	89	2	39	.298	.396	.392	110	13	17	.950	-13	87	82	*3-140,1-11	0.4
1937	Chi N	**154**	582	106	173	27	6	2	63	83	3	42	.297	.388	.375	104	7	16	.968	-11	89	129	*3-150/1-4	0.2
1938	†Chi N★	152	609	109	195	34	11	4	67	94	0	39	.320	.411	.432	128	29	**16**	.954	7	100	103	*3-152	4.0
1939	Chi N★	**156**	641	112	191	28	6	8	56	65	2	35	.298	.364	.398	103	4	**17**	.956	-8	91	54	*3-156	0.1
1940	Chi N	149	603	101	**191**	38	6	8	40	75	3	24	.317	.395	.439	132	30	21	.954	10	103	122	*3-148/1	4.5
1941	Chi N★	151	586	111	**186**	33	5	7	45	99	1	40	.317	.417	.427	143	39	10	.954	-14	92	78	*3-150/1	3.1
1942	Chi N	140	553	91	166	36	3	6	39	94	0	40	.300	.402	.409	143	36	9	**.965**	-12	92	75	*3-139	3.1
1943	Chi N★	144	533	78	154	24	4	3	35	82	0	27	.289	.384	.366	119	17	5	.960	-5	98	48	*3-136	1.4
1944	Chi N	98	383	65	108	16	1	3	32	53	0	21	.282	.369	.352	104	5	5	.939	5	108	55	3-75,1-18	1.0
1945	†Chi N✱	150	597	110	193	29	7	2	43	99	1	30	.323	.420	.405	133	33	12	**.975**	20	105	115	*3-146/1-5	**5.3**
1946	Chi N	92	323	55	92	13	4	0	26	83	0	32	.285	.431	.350	125	18	3	.968	-2	97	45	3-90	1.6
1947	Chi N	76	240	28	65	11	2	0	12	41	0	19	.271	.377	.333	94	0	0	.962	8	115	97	3-66	0.7
Total	16	1938	7278	1239	2193	363	81	57	642	1092	21	466	.301	.394	.397	120	250	165	.957	-3	98	90	*3-1836/1-47	29.4
HACKER, RICH Richard Warren B 10.6.1947 Belleville, IL BB/TR (BR 1971 (part)) 6/160# d7.2 C9																								
1971	Mon N	16	33	2	4	1	0	0	2	3-0	0	12	.121	.194	.152	-1	-4	0-0	.984	4	129	119	S-16	0.1
HACKETT, JIM James Joseph "Sunny Jim" B 10.1.1877 Jacksonville, IL D 3.28.1961 Douglas, MI BR/TR 6-2/185# d9.14 ▲																								
1902	StL N	6	21	2	6	1	0	0	4	2	0		.286	.348	.333	115	0	1	.833	-1	92	0	/P-4,O-2(RF)	-0.1
1903	StL N	99	351	24	80	13	8	0	36	19	2		.228	.272	.311	68	-16	2	.972	-6	78	132	1-89/P-7	-2.2
Total	2	105	372	26	86	14	8	0	40	21	2		.231	.276	.312	70	-16	3	.972	-7	78	132	/1-89,P-11,O-2(RF)	-2.3
HACKETT, MERT Mortimer Martin B 11.11.1859 Cambridge, MA D 2.22.1938 Cambridge, MA BR/TR 5-10.5/175# d5.2 b-Walter																								
1883	Bos N	46	179	20	42	8	6	2	24	1		48	.235	.239	.380	82	-5		.909	-2			C-44/O-4(0-3-1)	-0.3
1884	Bos N	72	268	28	55	13	2	1	20	2		66	.205	.211	.280	53	-14		.928	7			C-71/3	-0.1
1885	Bos N	34	115	9	21	7	1	0	4	2		28	.183	.197	.261	49	-6		.901	4			C-34	0.1
1886	KC N	62	230	18	50	8	3	3	25	4		59	.217	.231	.317	61	-12	1	.926	-13			C-52,O-13(0-6-7)	-1.9
1887	Ind N	42	147	12	35	6	3	2	10	7	2	24	.238	.282	.361	80	-4	4	.938	-6			C-40/O-2(1-0-1),1	-0.6
Total	5	256	939	87	203	42	15	8	83	16	2	225	.216	.231	.318	65	-41	5	.921	-10			C-241/O-19(1-9-9),13	-2.8
HACKETT, WALTER Walter Henry B 8.15.1857 Cambridge, MA D 10.2.1920 Cambridge, MA d4.17 b-Mert																								
1884	Bos U	103	415	71	101	19	0	1		7			.243	.256	.296	68	-28		**.855**	12	99	79	*S-103	-1.2
1885	Bos N	35	125	8	23	3	0	0	9	3		22	.184	.203	.208	34	-9		.893	-7	85	61	2-20,S-15	-1.5
Total	2	138	540	79	124	22	0	1	9	10		22	.230	.244	.276	61	-37		.852	4	97	81	S-118/2-20	-2.7
HADLEY, KENT Kent William B 12.17.1934 Pocatello, ID BL/TL 6-3/190# d9.14																								
1958	KC A	3	11	1	2	0	0	0	0	0-0	0	4	.182	.182	.182	0	-2	0-0	1.000	-1	0	45	/1-2	-0.2
1959	KC A	113	288	40	73	11	1	10	39	24-0	1	74	.253	.310	.403	93	-3	1-2	.989	-2	93	101	1-95	-1.0
1960	NY A	55	64	8	13	2	0	4	11	6-0	0	19	.203	.271	.422	90	-1	0-0	.991	-0	90	111	1-24	-0.2
Total	3	171	363	49	88	13	1	14	50	30-0	1	97	.242	.300	.399	90	-6	1-2	.989	-2	90	101	1-121	-1.4
HAEFFNER, BILL William Bernhard B 7.8.1894 Philadelphia, PA D 1.27.1982 Springfield, PA BR/TR 5-9/165# d6.29																								
1915	Phi A	3	4	0	1	0	0	0	0	0	0	1	.250	.250	.250	51	0	0	1.000	-1	*34*	*199*	/C-3	-0.1
1920	Pit N	54	175	8	34	4	1	0	14	8	0	14	.194	.230	.229	31	-16	1-1	.972	-3	*96*	*78*	C-52	-1.6
1928	NY N	2	1	0	0	0	0	0	0	0	0	0	.000	.000	.000	-99	0	0	.750	-0	*0*	*0*	/C-2	0.0
Total	3	59	180	8	35	4	1	0	14	8	0	15	.194	.229	.228	30	-16	1-1	.968	-4	*94*	*78*	/C-57	-1.7
HAFEY, CHICK Charles James B 2.12.1903 Berkeley, CA D 7.2.1973 Calistoga, CA BR/TR 6/185# d8.28 HF1971																								
1924	StL N	24	91	10	23	5	2	2	22	4	1	8	.253	.292	.418	90	-2	1-0	.927	0	99	133	O-24(16-7-1)	-0.3
1925	StL N	93	358	36	108	25	2	5	57	10	0	29	.302	.321	.425	87	-8	3-7	.955	1	107	90	O-88(25-5-58)	-1.4
1926	†StL N	78	225	30	61	19	2	4	38	11	2	36	.271	.311	.427	93	-2	2	.974	-0	99	96	O-64(28-0-36)	-0.7
1927	StL N	103	346	62	114	26	5	18	63	36	5	41	.329	.401	**.590**	157	28	12	.980	5	89	199	O-94(71-3-22)	2.5
1928	†StL N	138	520	101	175	46	6	27	111	40	2	53	.337	.386	.604	152	38	8	.965	-1	97	114	*O-133(117-0-16)	2.6
1929	StL N	134	517	101	175	47	9	29	125	45	2	42	.338	.394	.632	148	37	7	.966	2	105	93	*O-130(LF)	2.6
1930	†StL N	120	446	108	150	39	12	26	107	46	7	51	.336	.407	.652	146	32	12	.976	-2	89	147	*O-116(LF)	1.9
1931	†StL N	122	450	94	157	35	8	16	95	39	3	43	**.349**	**.404**	.569	153	34	11	.983	-5	93	66	*O-118(LF)	2.2
1932	Cin N	83	253	34	87	19	3	2	36	22	3	20	.344	.403	.466	137	15	4	.965	-0	98	133	O-65(LF)	1.1
1933	Cin N★	144	568	77	172	34	6	7	62	40	2	44	.303	.351	.421	121	16	3	.987	6	102	149	*O-144(59-85-0)	1.7
1934	Cin N	140	535	75	157	29	6	18	67	52	3	63	.293	.359	.471	123	18	4	.967	-1	104	68	*O-140(18-122-0)	1.2
1935	Cin N	15	59	10	20	6	1	1	9	4	2	5	.339	.400	.525	151	4	1	.912	-3	82	0	O-15(CF)	0.1
1937	Cin N	89	257	39	67	11	5	9	41	23	1	42	.261	.324	.447	113	3	2	.971	-2	93	107	O-64(20-44-0)	0.0
Total	13	1283	4625	777	1466	341	67	164	833	372	33	477	.317	.372	.526	133	213	70-7	.971	1	98	113	*O-1195(783-281-133)	13.5
HAFEY, BUD Daniel Albert B 8.6.1912 Berkeley, CA D 7.27.1986 Sacramento, CA BR/TR 6/185# d4.21 b-Tom																								
1935	Chi A	2	0	1	0	0	0	0	0	0	0	0	—	—	—	—	0	0-0	—	0			R	0.0
	Pit N	58	184	29	42	11	2	6	16	16	0	48	.228	.290	.408	83	-5	0	.970	3	110	128	O-47(1-36-10)	-0.3
1936	Pit N	39	118	19	25	6	1	4	13	10	0	27	.212	.273	.381	73	-5	0	.932	-1	97	126	O-29(0-18-10)	-0.7
1939	Cin N	6	13	1	2	1	0	0	1	1	0	4	.154	.214	.231	19	-1	1	1.000	-0	97	0	/O-4(LF)	-0.2
	Phi N	18	51	3	9	1	0	0	3	3	0	12	.176	.222	.196	14	-6	1	1.000	1	116	94	O-13(3-1-9)/P-2	-0.6
	Year	24	64	4	11	2	0	0	4	4	0	16	.172	.221	.203	15	-8	2	1.000	1	112	73	O-17(7-1-9)/P-2	-0.8
Total	3	123	366	53	78	19	3	10	33	30	0	91	.213	.273	.363	68	-17	2-0	.963	3	106	117	O-93(8-55-29),P-2	-1.8
HAFEY, TOM Thomas Francis "Heave-O" or "The Arm" B 7.12.1913 Berkeley, CA D 10.2.1996 ElCerrito, CA BR/TR 6-1/180# d7.21 b-Bud																								
1939	NY N	70	256	37	62	10	1	6	26	10	0	44	.242	.271	.359	67	-13	1	.960	-0	99	84	3-70	-1.1
1944	StL A	8	14	1	5	2	0	0	2	1	0	4	.357	.400	.500	148	1	0-0	1.000	0	117	0	/O-4(3-0-1),1	0.1
Total	2	78	270	38	67	12	1	6	28	11	0	48	.248	.278	.367	72	-12	1-0	.960	0	99	84	/3-70,O-4(3-0-1),1	-1.0
HAFNER, TRAVIS Travis Lee B 6.3.1977 Jamestown, ND BL/TR 6-3/240# d8.6																								
2002	Tex A	23	62	6	15	4	1	1	6	8-1	0	15	.242	.329	.387	85	-1	0-1	.909	0	188	0	D-13/1-3	-0.2
2003	Cle A	91	291	35	74	19	3	14	40	22-2	10	81	.254	.327	.485	114	6	2-1	.985	-3	77	152	D-43,1-42	-0.4
Total	2	114	353	41	89	23	4	15	46	30-3	10	96	.252	.327	.467	109	5	2-2	.983	-3	84	143	/D-56,1-45	-0.6
HAGUE, JOE Joe Clarence B 4.25.1944 Huntington, WV D 11.5.1994 San Antonio, TX BL/TL 6/198# d9.19																								
1968	StL N	7	17	2	4	0	0	1	1	2-0	0	2	.235	.316	.412	119	0	0-0	.800	-1	86	0	/O-3(RF),1-2	0.0
1969	StL N	40	100	8	17	2	1	2	8	12-1	0	23	.170	.259	.270	48	-7	0-2	.939	-1	110	0	O-17(1-0-16)/1-9	-1.1
1970	StL N	139	451	58	122	16	4	14	68	63-3	1	87	.271	.358	.417	106	4	2-1	.994	-3	97	103	1-82,O-52(6-0-47)	-0.6
1971	StL N	129	380	46	86	9	3	16	54	58-10	2	69	.226	.330	.392	100	1	0-3	.996	-1	107	97	1-91,O-36(RF)	-0.9
1972	StL N	27	76	8	18	5	1	3	11	17-2	0	18	.237	.368	.447	135	4	0-1	1.000	-1	78	99	1-22/O-3(RF)	0.2
	†Cin N	69	138	17	34	7	1	4	20	20-5	0	18	.246	.340	.399	116	3	1-1	1.000	1	74	99	1-22,O-19(RF)	0.2
	Year	96	214	25	52	12	2	7	31	37-7	0	36	.243	.350	.416	124	8	1-2	1.000	-0	76	99	1-44,O-22(RF)	0.4
1973	Cin N	19	33	2	5	2	0	0	1	5-0	0	5	.152	.256	.212	35	-3	1-0	1.000	-1	65	0	/O-5(RF),1-4	-0.4

Year	Tm Lg	G	AB	R	H	2B	3B	HR	RBI	BB-IB	HP	SO	AVG	OBP	SLG	AOPS	ABR	SB-CS	FA	FR	Rng	Thr	G at Pos	BFW
Total	6	430	1195	141	286	41	10	40	163	177-21	3	222	.239	.336	.391	101	2	4-8	.996	-6	97	98	1-232,O-135(7-0-129)	-2.6
HAGUE, BILL William L. (born William L. Haug) B 1852 Philadelphia, PA BR/TR 5-9/164# d5.4																								
1875	StL NA	62	260	24	57	2	0	0	22	2		9	.219	.225	.227	63	-8	3-4	.781	2	107	58	*3-62/1	-0.7
1876	Lou N	67	294	31	78	8	0	1	22	2		10	.265	.270	.303	77	-9		.754	-27	66	101	*3-67/S	-3.0
1877	Lou N	59	263	38	70	7	1	1	24	7		18	.266	.285	.312	75	-9		.843	-19	65	65	*3-59	-2.4
1878	Pro N	**62**	250	21	51	3	0	0	25	5		34	.204	.220	.216	44	-15		**.925**	19	**133**	64	*3-62	0.6
1879	Pro N	51	209	20	47	3	1	0	21	3		19	.225	.236	.249	61	-9		.822	4	114	35	3-51	-0.3
Total	4	239	1016	110	246	21	2	2	92	17		81	.242	.255	.273	66	-42		.843	-23	93	69	3-239/S	-5.1
HAHN, DON Donald Antone B 11.16.1948 San Francisco, CA BR/TR 6-1/185# d4.8																								
1969	Mon N	4	9	0	1	0	0	0	2	0-0	0	5	.111	.111	.111	-37	-2	0-0	1.000	0	60	728	/O-3(CF)	-0.2
1970	Mon N	82	149	22	38	8	0	0	8	27-1	2	27	.255	.374	.309	86	-1	4-2	.986	1	91	195	O-61(42-14-9)	-0.2
1971	NY N	98	178	16	42	5	1	1	11	21-1	1	32	.236	.317	.292	76	-5	2-3	.973	1	111	68	O-80(CF)	-0.7
1972	NY N	17	37	0	6	0	0	0	1	4-0	0	12	.162	.244	.162	18	-4	0-0	1.000	-2	49	0	O-10(0-1-9)	-0.7
1973	†NY N	93	262	22	60	10	0	2	21	22-2	0	43	.229	.285	.290	62	-14	2-1	.989	-2	106	45	O-87(4-83-2)	-1.8
1974	NY N	110	323	34	81	14	1	4	28	37-5	1	34	.251	.328	.337	88	-5	2-0	.987	-2	94	142	*O-106(0-104-2)	-0.9
1975	Phi N	9	5	0	0	0	0	0	0	0-0	0	2	.000	.000	.000	-96	-1	0-0	1.000	1	110	943	/O-7(1-4-2)	-0.1
	StL N	7	8	3	1	0	0	0	0	1-0	0	1	.125	.222	.125	-2	-1	0-0	1.000	-0	73	0	/O-4(1-2-1)	-0.2
	SD N	34	26	7	6	1	2	0	3	10-0	0	2	.231	.444	.423	151	3	1-0	1.000	1	104	142	O-26(17-11-0)	0.3
	Year	50	39	10	7	1	2	0	3	11-0	0	5	.179	.360	.308	89	0	1-0	1.000	1	99	212	O-37(19-17-3)	0.0
Total	7	454	997	104	235	38	4	7	74	122-9	4	158	.236	.319	.303	75	-30	11-6	.985	-2	99	113	O-384(65-302-25)	-4.5
HAHN, DICK Richard Frederick B 7.24.1916 Canton, OH D 11.5.1992 Orlando, FL BR/TR 5-11/176# d9.7																								
1940	Was A	1	3	0	0	0	0	0	0	0	0	0	.000	.000	.000	-99	-1	0-0	1.000	0	*0*	*543*	/C	-0.1
HAHN, ED William Edgar B 8.27.1875 Nevada, OH D 11.29.1941 Des Moines, IA BL/TR ?/160# d8.31																								
1905	NY A	43	160	32	51	5	0	0	11	25	5		.319	.426	.350	132	8	1	.957	1	99	85	O-43(20-10-13)	0.7
1906	NY A	11	22	2	2	1	0	0	1	3	2		.091	.259	.136	23	-2	2	1.000	-0	0	0	/O-7(3-4-0)	-0.2
	†Chi A	130	484	80	110	7	5	0	27	69	9		.227	.335	.262	90	-1	21	.949	-5	128	97	*O-130(55-0-75)	-1.4
	Year	141	506	82	112	8	5	0	28	72	11		.221	.331	.257	86	-4	23	.952	-5	123	93	*O-137(58-4-75)	-1.6
1907	Chi A	156	592	87	151	9	7	0	45	84	12		.255	.359	.294	112	14	17	**.990**	-4	121	143	*O-156(RF)	0.3
1908	Chi A	122	447	58	112	12	8	0	21	39	13		.251	.329	.313	111	7	11	.965	-12	29	62	*O-118(18-14-86)	-1.3
1909	Chi A	76	287	30	52	6	0	1	16	31	3		.181	.268	.213	54	-14	9	.990	-7	31	51	O-76(RF)	-2.8
1910	Chi A	15	53	2	6	2	0	0	1	7	0		.113	.217	.151	16	-5	0	.933	-2	83	0	O-15(RF)	-0.9
Total	6	553	2045	291	484	42	20	1	122	258	44		.237	.335	.278	97	7	61	.970	-29	86	92	O-545(96-28-421)	-5.6
HAIGH, ED Edward E. B 2.7.1867 Philadelphia, PA D 2.13.1953 Atlantic City, NJ d8.14																								
1892	StL N	1	4	0	1	0	0	0	0	0	0	2	.250	.250	.250	54	0	0	—	-0	0	0	/O(RF)	0.0
HAINES, HINKEY Henry Luther B 12.23.1898 Red Lion, PA D 1.9.1979 Sharon Hill, PA BR/TR 5-10/170# d4.20																								
1923	†NY A	28	25	9	4	2	0	0	3	4	0	5	.160	.276	.240	36	-2	3-1	1.000	1	133	151	O-14(2-8-4)	-0.1
HAIRSTON, JERRY Jerry Wayne Jr. B 5.29.1976 Naperville, IL BR/TR 5-10/172# d9.11 f-Jerry gf-Sammy																								
1998	Bal A	6	7	2	0	0	0	0	0	0-0	0	1	.000	.000	.000	-99	-2	0-0	.750	-2	38	89	/2-4	-0.3
1999	Bal A	50	175	26	47	12	1	4	17	11-0	3	24	.269	.323	.417	90	-3	9-4	1.000	8	101	140	2-50	0.7
2000	Bal A	49	180	27	46	5	0	5	19	21-0	6	22	.256	.353	.367	87	-3	8-5	.981	6	104	126	2-49	0.5
2001	Bal A	159	532	63	124	25	5	8	47	44-0	13	73	.233	.305	.344	75	-19	29-11	.976	4	101	94	*2-156	-0.5
2002	Bal A	122	426	55	114	25	3	5	32	34-0	7	55	.268	.329	.376	92	-4	21-6	.982	2	102	98	*2-119	0.6
2003	Bal A	58	218	25	59	12	2	2	21	23-0	6	25	.271	.353	.372	96	0	14-5	.980	1	96	104	2-48/D-9	0.4
Total	6	444	1538	198	390	79	11	24	136	133-0	35	200	.254	.325	.366	85	-31	81-31	.981	20	101	105	2-426/D-9	1.4
HAIRSTON, JERRY Jerry Wayne Sr. B 2.16.1952 Birmingham, AL BB/TR 5-10/180# d7.26 b-Johnny f-Sammy s-Jerry																								
1973	Chi A	60	210	25	57	11	1	0	23	33-0	1	30	.271	.371	.333	97	1	0-0	.944	1	105	136	O-33(LF),1-19/D-8	-0.1
1974	Chi A	45	109	8	25	7	0	0	8	13-0	0	18	.229	.311	.294	73	-3	0-2	.926	-3	70	81	O-22(19-0-3),D-10	-0.8
1975	Chi A	69	219	26	62	8	0	0	23	46-3	1	23	.283	.407	.320	107	6	1-0	.951	-1	95	136	O-59(57-0-3)/D-8	0.1
1976	Chi A	44	119	20	27	2	2	0	10	24-0	0	19	.227	.352	.277	87	-1	1-1	.973	-0	106	42	O-40(1-0-39)	-0.3
1977	Chi A	13	26	3	8	2	0	0	4	5-0	0	7	.308	.419	.385	121	1	0-0	1.000	0	97	203	O-11(6-6-0)	0.1
	Pit N	51	52	5	10	2	0	2	6	6-0	0	10	.192	.271	.346	64	-3	0-0	.923	-1	81	0	O-14(6-0-8)/2	-0.4
1981	Chi A	9	25	5	7	1	0	1	6	2-0	1	4	.280	.345	.440	131	1	0-0	.933	-0	106	0	/O-7(4-2-1)	0.1
1982	Chi A	85	90	11	21	5	0	5	18	9-0	0	15	.233	.294	.456	105	0	0-0	1.000	1	104	208	O-36(22-7-7)/D-2	0.1
1983	†Chi A	101	126	17	37	9	1	5	22	23-4	0	16	.294	.397	.500	141	8	0-1	.968	-2	84	88	O-32(19-11-3)/D-4	0.6
1984	Chi A	115	227	41	59	13	2	5	19	41-3	1	29	.260	.373	.401	110	5	2-1	.967	-2	90	106	O-37(22-13-3),D-20	0.2
1985	Chi A	95	140	9	34	8	0	2	20	29-3	2	18	.243	.371	.343	96	1	0-0	1.000	-0	88	0	D-29/O-5(LF)	0.0
1986	Chi A	101	225	32	61	15	0	5	26	26-3	1	26	.271	.348	.404	101	1	0-0	1.000	-2	61	83	D-29,1-19,O-11(9-0-2)	-0.2
1987	Chi A	66	126	14	29	8	0	5	20	25-2	1	25	.230	.357	.413	102	1	0-0	1.000	1	143	0	O-13(LF),D-13/1-7	0.1
1988	Chi A	2	2	0	0	0	0	0	0	0-0	0	0	.000	.000	.000	-99	-1	0-0	—	0			/H	-0.1
1989	Chi A	3	3	0	1	0	0	0	0	0-0	0	0	.333	.333	.333	91	0	0-0	—	0			/D-2	0.0
Total	14	859	1699	216	438	91	6	30	205	282-18	8	240	.258	.362	.371	103	17	4-5	.963	-6	97	107	O-320(216-39-69),D-125/1-45,2	-0.6
HAIRSTON, JOHNNY John Louis B 8.27.1944 Birmingham, AL BR/TR 6-2/200# d9.6 b-Jerry f-Sammy																								
1969	Chi N	3	4	0	1	0	0	0	0	0-0	0	2	.250	.250	.250	36	0	0-0	1.000	0	0	0	/CO(LF)	0.0
HAIRSTON, SAMMY Samuel Harding B 1.20.1920 Crawford, MS D 10.31.1997 Birmingham, AL BR/TR 5-10.5/187# d7.21 C1 s-Jerry s-Johnny gs-Jerry																								
1951	Chi A	4	5	1	2	1	0	0	1	2	0	0	.400	.571	.600	222	1	0-0	1.000	-0	*0*	*0*	/C-2	0.1
HAJDUK, CHET Chester B 7.21.1918 Chicago, IL BR/TR 6/195# d4.16																								
1941	Chi A	1	1	0	0	0	0	0	0	0	0	0	.000	.000	.000	-99	0	0-0	—	0			H	0.0
HAJEK, DAVE David Vincent B 10.14.1967 Roseville, CA BR/TR 5-10/165# d9.15																								
1995	Hou N	5	2	0	0	0	0	0	0	1-0	0	1	.000	.333	.000	-3	0	1-0	—	0			/H	0.0
1996	Hou N	8	10	3	3	1	0	0	0	2-0	0	0	.300	.417	.400	127	1	0-0	1.000	1	158	0	/3-3,2-2	0.1
Total	2	13	12	3	3	1	0	0	0	3-0	0	1	.250	.400	.333	104	1	1-0	1.000	1	158	0	/3-3,2-2	0.1
HALAS, GEORGE George Stanley B 2.2.1895 Chicago, IL D 10.31.1983 Chicago, IL BB/TR 6/164# d5.6																								
1919	NY A	12	22	0	2	0	0	0	0	0	0	8	.091	.091	.091	-49	-4	0	1.000	-0	101	0	/O-6(0-1-5)	-0.5
HALDEMAN, JOHN John Avery B 12.2.1855 Pewee Valley, KY D 9.17.1899 Louisville, KY BL/TR 5-10/175# d7.3																								
1877	Lou N	1	4	0	0	0	0	0	0	0		0	.000	.000	.000	-85	-1		.571	-1	116	0	/2	-0.2
HALE, ODELL Arvel Odell "Bad News" B 8.10.1908 Hosston, LA D 6.9.1980 ElDorado, AR BR/TR 5-10/175# d8.1																								
1931	Cle A	25	92	14	26	2	4	1	5	8	0	8	.283	.340	.424	94	-1	2-0	.918	-4	87	35	3-15,2-10/S	-0.3
1933	Cle A	98	351	49	97	19	8	10	64	30	0	37	.276	.333	.462	104	0	2-3	.954	-2	99	102	2-73,3-21	0.3
1934	Cle A	143	563	82	170	44	6	13	101	48	0	50	.302	.357	.471	110	7	8-12	.956	**26**	109	113	*2-137/3-5	3.6
1935	Cle A	150	589	80	179	37	11	16	101	52	1	55	.304	.361	.486	115	11	15-13	.938	6	109	87	*3-149/2	1.9
1936	Cle A	153	620	126	196	50	13	14	87	64	0	43	.316	.380	.506	116	14	8-5	.946	**17**	**108**	103	*3-148/2-3	3.2
1937	Cle A	154	561	74	150	32	4	6	82	56	1	41	.267	.335	.371	77	-20	9-6	.964	22	109	130	3-90,2-64	0.9
1938	Cle A	130	496	69	138	32	2	8	69	44	1	39	.278	.338	.399	86	-12	8-1	.963	-11	90	81	*2-127	-1.1
1939	Cle A	108	253	36	79	16	2	4	48	25	0	18	.312	.374	.439	111	4	4-5	.966	-11	85	83	2-73/3-2	-0.4
1940	Cle A	48	50	3	11	3	1	0	6	5	0	7	.220	.291	.320	60	-3	0-0	.700	-1	86	0	/3-3	-0.4
1941	Bos A	12	24	5	5	2	0	1	1	3	0	4	.208	.296	.417	85	-1	0-0	.857	-3	43	0	/3-6,2	-0.3
	NY N	41	102	13	20	3	0	0	9	18	0	13	.196	.317	.225	53	-6	1	.964	0	90	95	2-29	-0.4
Total	10	1062	3701	551	1071	240	51	73	573	353	3	315	.289	.352	.441	100	-7	57-45	.959	40	99	94	2-518,3-439/S	7.0
HALE, GEORGE George Wagner "Ducky" B 8.3.1894 Dexter, KS D 11.1.1945 Wichita, KS BR/TR 5-10/160# d8.24																								
1914	StL A	6	11	1	2	0	0	0	0	0	0	3	.182	.182	.182	10	-1	0	.895	-1	*97*	*184*	/C-6	-0.2
1916	StL A	4	1	0	0	0	0	0	0	0	1	1	.000	.500	.000	54	0	0	1.000	0	0	0	/C-3	0.0
1917	StL A	38	61	4	12	2	1	0	8	10	0	12	.197	.310	.262	78	-1	0	.927	-0	*92*	*121*	C-28	0.0
1918	StL A	12	30	0	4	1	0	0	1	1	0	5	.133	.161	.167	-1	-4	0	.981	1	*90*	*94*	C-11	-0.2

Year	Tm Lg	G	AB	R	H	2B	3B	HR	RBI	BB-IB	HP	SO	AVG	OBP	SLG	AOPS	ABR	SB-CS	FA	FR	Rng	Thr	G at Pos	BFW
Total	4	60	103	5	18	3	1	0	9	11	1	21	.175	.261	.223	49	-6	0	.940	0	*91*	*118*	/C-48	-0.4
HALE, JOHN John Steven B 8.5.1953 Fresno, CA BL/TR 6-2/195# d9.8																								
1974	LA N	4	4	2	4	1	0	0	2	0-0	0	0	1.000	1.000	1.250	549	2	0-0	—	-0	0	0	/O-3(RF)	0.2
1975	LA N	71	204	20	43	7	0	6	22	26-4	2	51	.211	.303	.333	81	-5	1-2	.977	-2	99	53	O-68(0-35-42)	-1.0
1976	LA N	44	91	4	14	2	1	0	8	16-1	2	14	.154	.291	.198	42	-6	4-1	.983	-1	86	132	O-37(0-11-27)	-0.9
1977	LA N	79	108	10	26	4	1	2	11	15-1	0	28	.241	.331	.352	84	-2	2-1	.986	-2	92	38	O-73(25-13-37)	-0.6
1978	Sea A	107	211	24	36	8	0	4	22	34-1	0	64	.171	.283	.265	56	-12	3-4	.988	-3	103	20	O-98(27-24-47)/D-3	-1.8
1979	Sea A	54	63	6	14	3	0	2	7	12-4	0	26	.222	.342	.365	91	0	0-0	1.000	-3	80	0	O-42(34-0-9)/D-2	-0.4
Total	6	359	681	66	137	25	2	14	72	103-11	4	183	.201	.307	.305	72	-23	10-8	.985	-11	95	45	O-321(86-83-165)/D-5	-4.5
HALE, BOB Robert Houston B 11.7.1933 Sarasota, FL BL/TL 5-10/195# d7.4																								
1955	Bal A	67	182	13	65	7	1	0	29	5-0	1	19	.357	.376	.407	119	4	0-2	.974	2	133	71	1-44	0.3
1956	Bal A	85	207	18	49	10	1	1	24	11-0	1	10	.237	.274	.309	60	-13	0-2	.975	-1	106	84	1-51	-1.6
1957	Bal A	42	44	2	11	0	0	0	7	2-1	0	2	.250	.265	.250	50	-3	0-0	1.000	-0	62	44	/1-5	-0.4
1958	Bal A	19	20	2	7	2	0	0	3	2-0	0	1	.350	.409	.450	144	1	0-0	1.000	1	373	253	/1-2	0.2
1959	Bal A	40	54	2	10	3	0	0	7	2-1	0	6	.185	.214	.241	25	-6	0-0	1.000	-1	59	117	/1-8	-0.7
1960	Cle A	70	70	2	21	7	0	0	12	3-1	0	6	.300	.312	.400	99	0	0-0	.944	0	186	45	/1-5	0.0
1961	Cle A	42	36	0	6	0	0	0	6	1-0	1	7	.167	.200	.167	2	-5	0-0	—	0			H	-0.5
	NY A	11	13	2	2	0	0	1	1	0-0	0	0	.154	.154	.385	41	-1	0-0	1.000	0	84	75	/1-5	-0.1
	Year	53	49	2	8	0	0	1	7	1-0	1	7	.163	.189	.224	12	-6	0-0	1.000	0	84	75	/1-5	-0.6
Total	7	376	626	41	171	29	2	2	89	26-3	3	51	.273	.299	.335	76	-23	0-4	.977	2	118	81	1-120	-2.8
HALE, SAMMY Samuel Douglas B 9.10.1896 Glen Rose, TX D 9.6.1974 Wheeler, TX BR/TR 5-8.5/160# d4.20																								
1920	Det A	76	116	13	34	3	3	1	14	5	0	15	.293	.322	.397	92	-2	2-0	.886	-1	110	97	3-16/O-4(CF),2	-0.2
1921	Det A	9	2	2	0	0	0	0	0	0	0	1	.000	.000	.000	-99	-1	0-1	—	0			H	-0.1
1923	Phi A	115	434	68	125	22	8	3	51	17	8	31	.288	.327	.396	89	-9	8-3	.916	-14	96	88	*3-107	-1.6
1924	Phi A	80	261	41	83	14	2	2	17	17	3	19	.318	.367	.410	99	-1	3-2	.948	-2	103	112	3-55/O-5(4-0-1),S	0.0
1925	Phi A	110	391	62	135	30	11	8	63	17	2	27	.345	.376	.540	122	11	7-4	.919	-4	97	113	3-96/2	1.2
1926	Phi A	111	327	49	92	22	9	4	43	13	1	36	.281	.311	.440	89	-7	1-4	.947	0	96	142	3-77/O(RF)	-0.4
1927	Phi A	131	501	77	157	24	8	5	81	32	3	32	.313	.358	.423	97	-4	11-3	.961	1	94	**189**	*3-128	0.6
1928	Phi A	88	314	38	97	20	9	4	58	9	3	21	.309	.334	.468	106	1	2-0	.932	8	111	126	3-79	1.4
1929	Phi A	101	379	51	105	14	3	1	40	12	2	18	.277	.303	.338	62	-22	6-2	.956	-6	94	79	3-99/2	-2.1
1930	StL A	62	190	21	52	8	1	2	25	8	0	18	.274	.303	.358	65	-11	1-1	.947	-1	101	68	3-47	-0.9
Total	10	883	2915	422	880	157	54	30	392	130	22	218	.302	.336	.424	93	-45	41-20	.939	-19	98	120	3-704/O-10(4-4-2),2-3,S	-2.1
HALE, CHIP Walter William B 12.2.1964 San Jose, CA BL/TR 5-11/191# d8.27																								
1989	Min A	28	67	6	14	3	0	0	4	1-0	0	6	.209	.214	.254	31	-6	0-0	.980	-2	115	108	2-16/3-9,D-2	-0.8
1990	Min A	1	2	0	0	0	0	0	2	0-0	0	1	.000	.000	.000	-94	-1	0-0	1.000	1	200	279	/2	0.1
1993	Min A	69	186	25	62	6	1	3	27	18-0	6	17	.333	.408	.425	124	7	2-1	.952	-1	104	98	2-21,3-19,D-19/1S	0.6
1994	Min A	67	118	13	31	9	0	1	11	16-1	1	14	.263	.350	.364	86	-2	0-2	.964	4	139	70	3-21,D-10/1-7,2-5,O(RF)	0.1
1995	Min A	69	103	10	27	4	0	2	18	11-1	0	20	.262	.333	.359	80	-3	0-0	1.000	-1	102	89	D-27/2-7,3-5,1-3	-0.5
1996	Min A	85	87	8	24	5	0	1	16	10-2	0	6	.276	.347	.368	81	-2	0-0	1.000	0	101	66	2-14,D-10/1-6,3-3,O-3(RF)	-0.2
1997	LA N	14	12	0	1	0	0	0	0	2-0	0	4	.083	.214	.083	-20	-2	0-0	1.000	-0	0	0	/3-2	-0.2
Total	7	333	575	62	159	27	1	7	78	58-4	7	68	.277	.346	.363	88	-9	2-3	.969	2	110	106	/D-68,2-64,3-59,1-17,O-4(RF),S	-0.9
HALEY, FRED Frederick B 6.18.1853 Wheeling, WV TR d6.22																								
1880	Tro N	2	7	0	0	0	0	0	0	1		2	.000	.125	.000	-51	-1		.750	-2			/C-2	-0.3
HALEY, RAY Raymond Timothy "Pat" B 1.23.1891 Danbury, IA D 10.8.1973 Bradenton, FL BR/TR 5-11/180# d4.21 Mil 1918-19																								
1915	Bos A	5	7	2	1	1	0	0	0	1	0	0	.143	.250	.286	62	0	0	1.000	0	*123*	*113*	/C-4	0.0
1916	Bos A	1	1	0	0	0	0	0	0	0	0	1	.000	.000	.000	-99	0	0	—	0			H	0.0
	Phi A	34	108	8	25	5	0	0	4	6	1	19	.231	.278	.278	70	-4	0	.982	-1	60	171	C-33	-0.2
	Year	35	109	8	25	5	0	0	4	6	1	20	.229	.276	.275	69	-4	0	.982	-1	60	171	C-33	-0.2
1917	Phi A	41	98	7	27	2	1	0	11	4	1	12	.276	.311	.316	93	-1	2	.947	-5	*72*	*91*	C-34	-0.5
Total	3	81	214	17	53	8	1	0	15	11	2	32	.248	.291	.294	80	-5	2	.970	-6	*67*	*136*	/C-71	-0.7
HALL, ALBERT Albert B 3.7.1958 Birmingham, AL BB/TR 5-11/155# d9.12																								
1981	Atl N	6	2	1	0	0	0	0	0	1-0	0	1	.000	.333	.000	1	0	0-0	—	-0	0	0	/O-2(1-0-1)	0.0
1982	Atl N	5	0	1	0	0	0	0	0	0-0	0	0	—	—	—	—	0	0-0	—	0			/R	0.0
1983	Atl N	10	8	2	0	0	0	0	0	2-0	0	2	.000	.200	.000	-37	-1	1-1	.750	-1	62	0	/O-4(4-1-0)	-0.3
1984	Atl N	87	142	25	37	6	1	1	9	10-0	0	18	.261	.309	.338	76	-4	6-4	.932	-0	92	148	O-66(48-2-17)	-0.7
1985	Atl N	54	47	5	7	0	1	0	3	9-1	0	12	.149	.286	.191	34	-4	1-1	.900	0	63	621	O-13(6-6-3)	-0.4
1986	Atl N	16	50	6	12	2	0	0	1	5-0	0	6	.240	.309	.280	60	-3	8-3	.900	-0	109	95	O-14(RF)	-0.3
1987	Atl N	92	292	54	83	20	4	3	24	38-3	2	36	.284	.369	.411	102	2	33-10	.981	-2	93	132	O-69(0-68-1)	0.3
1988	Atl N	85	231	27	57	7	1	1	15	21-1	2	35	.247	.314	.299	73	-7	15-10	.973	2	97	278	O-63(1-63-0)	-0.7
1989	Pit N	20	33	4	6	2	1	0	1	3-0	0	5	.182	.250	.303	59	-2	3-0	.909	-1	71	0	O-12(5-1-6)	-0.3
Total	9	375	805	125	202	37	8	5	53	89-5	4	115	.251	.328	.335	80	-19	67-29	.958	-3	93	182	O-243(65-141-42)	-2.4
HALL, AL Archibald W. B Worcester, MA D 2.10.1885 Warren, PA d5.1																								
1879	Tro N	67	306	30	79	7	3	0	14	3		13	.258	.265	.301	92	-2		.842	2	114	150	*O-67(2-63-2)	-0.3
1880	Cle N	3	8	1	1	0	0	0	0	0		0	.125	.125	.125	-15	-1		1.000	-1	0	0	/O-3(LF)	-0.2
Total	2	70	314	31	80	7	3	0	14	3		13	.255	.262	.296	90	-3		.843	1	111	146	/O-70(5-63-2)	-0.5
HALL, CHARLIE Charles Walter "Doc" B 8.24.1863 Toulon, IL D 6.24.1921 Tacoma, WA 5-10/158# d5.3																								
1887	NY AA	3	12	1	1	0	0	0	0	2	0		.083	.214	.083	-16	-2	1	1.000	-0	0	0	/O-3(CF)	-0.2
HALL, GEORGE George William B 3.29.1849 Stepney, England D 6.11.1923 Ridgewood, NY BL 5-7/142# d5.5																								
1871	Oly NA	**32**	136	31	40	3	3	2	17	8		0	.294	.333	.404	117	4	2-1	.913	6	81	0	*O-32(1-31-0)	0.6
1872	Bal NA	53	250	69	84	17	6	1	37	3		1	.336	.344	.464	140	10	8-1	.836	-3	71	191	*O-52(3-51-0)/1	0.6
1873	Bal NA	35	168	44	58	6	4	0	31	2		1	.345	.353	.429	132	6	0-0	.865	2	59	0	*O-35(CF)	0.6
1874	Bos NA	47	222	58	64	10	8	1	34	1		0	.288	.291	.419	118	3	2-0	.811	-3	73	174	*O-47(20-21-7)	0.1
1875	Ath NA	**77**	358	71	107	10	12	4	62	3		4	.299	.305	.427	136	10	8-5	.887	4	63	87	*O-77(74-0-3)/1	1.4
1876	Phi N	**60**	268	51	98	7	13	**5**	45	8		4	.366	.384	.545	208	29		.801	-2	68	109	*O-60(59-0-1)	2.0
1877	Lou N	**61**	269	53	87	15	8	0	26	12		19	.323	.352	.439	125	6		**.900**	-5	60	56	*O-61(LF)	-0.3
Total	5 NA	244	1134	273	353	46	33	8	181	17		6	.311	.321	.431	130	33	20-7	.000	6	68	102	O-243(98-138-10)/1-2	3.3
Total	2	121	537	104	185	22	21	5	71	20		23	.345	.368	.492	162	35		.837	-7	64	82	O-121(120-0-1)	1.7
HALL, IRV Irvin Gladstone B 10.7.1918 Alberton, MD BR/TR 5-10.5/160# d4.20																								
1943	Phi A	151	544	37	139	15	4	0	54	22	6	42	.256	.292	.298	73	-21	10-7	.948	-9	98	88	*S-148/23	-1.9
1944	Phi A	143	559	60	150	20	8	0	45	31	2	46	.268	.309	.333	85	-13	2-5	.980	-8	99	62	2-97,S-40/1-4	-1.4
1945	Phi A	151	616	62	161	17	5	0	50	35	6	42	.261	.307	.305	78	-18	3-10	.978	20	110	103	*2-151	0.8
1946	Phi A	63	185	19	46	6	2	0	19	9	1	18	.249	.287	.303	65	-9	1-1	.973	-5	92	66	2-40/S-7	-1.3
Total	4	508	1904	178	496	58	19	0	168	97	15	148	.261	.302	.311	77	-61	16-23	.977	-1	104	85	2-289,S-195/1-4,3	-3.8
HALL, JIM James D 1.30.1886 Brooklyn, NY d5.20																								
1872	Atl NA	13	57	9	18	0	1	0	6	1		1	.316	.328	.351	93	-1	0-0	.750	-4	90	105	2-13	-0.4
1874	Atl NA	2	9	0	1	0	0	0	0	0		0	.111	.111	.111	-32	-1	0-0	.857	-1	50	0	/2-2,O(RF)	-0.2
1875	Wes NA	1	3	0	1	0	1	0	1	0		0	.333	.333	1.000	327	1	0-0	.000	-1	0	0	/O(LF)	0.0
Total	3 NA	16	69	9	20	0	2	0	7	1		1	.290	.300	.348	89	-1	0-0	.000	-5	86	95	/2-15,O-2(1-0-1)	-0.6
HALL, JIMMIE Jimmie Randolph B 3.17.1938 Mt.Holly, NC BL/TR 6/175# d4.9																								
1963	Min A	156	497	88	129	21	5	33	80	63-4	0	101	.260	.342	.521	136	23	3-3	.982	10	113	151	*O-143(87-93-16)	2.8
1964	Min A★	149	510	61	144	20	3	25	75	44-3	1	112	.282	.338	.480	125	16	5-2	.985	9	112	148	*O-137(CF)	2.3
1965	†Min A★	148	522	81	149	25	4	20	86	51-6	1	79	.285	.347	.464	124	16	14-7	.976	-6	92	114	*O-141(6-140-6)	0.6
1966	Min A	120	356	52	85	7	4	20	47	33-5	0	66	.239	.302	.449	106	2	1-2	.978	2	103	110	*O-103(69-27-12)	-0.2
1967	Cal A	129	401	54	100	8	3	16	55	42-7	0	65	.249	.318	.404	117	8	4-1	.990	0	104	85	*O-120(2-6-116)	0.1
1968	Cal A	46	126	15	27	3	0	1	8	16-3	0	19	.214	.303	.262	75	-3	1-0	.981	-3	89	0	O-39(4-2-33)	-1.0

Year	Tm Lg	G	AB	R	H	2B	3B	HR	RBI	BB-IB	HP	SO	AVG	OBP	SLG	AOPS	ABR	SB-CS	FA	FR	Rng	Thr	G at Pos	BFW
	Cle A	53	111	4	22	4	0	1	8	10-3	0	19	.198	.264	.261	61	-5	1-0	.983	3	139	72	O-29(20-6-4)	-0.4
	Year	99	237	19	49	7	0	2	16	26-6	0	38	.207	.285	.262	68	-9	2-0	.982	0	109	29	O-68(24-8-37)	-1.4
1969	Cle A	4	10	1	0	0	0	0	0	2-1	0	3	.000	.167	.000	-48	-2	1-0	1.000	-0	86	0	/O-3(2-1-0)	-0.2
	NY A	80	212	21	50	8	5	3	26	19-1	0	34	.236	.296	.363	88	-5	8-3	.963	-6	84	29	O-50(9-19-22)/1-7	-1.3
	Year	84	222	22	50	8	5	3	26	21-2	0	37	.225	.290	.347	81	-7	9-3	.966	-6	84	27	O-53(11-20-22)/1-7	-1.5
	Chi N	11	24	1	5	1	0	0	1	1-0	0	5	.208	.240	.250	33	-2	0-0	1.000	-1	55	0	/O-5(1-4-0)	-0.4
1970	Chi N	28	32	2	3	1	0	0	1	4-1	0	12	.094	.194	.125	-11	-5	0-0	1.000	-0	100	0	/O-8(2-7-0)	-0.5
	Atl N	39	47	7	10	2	0	2	4	2-1	0	14	.213	.245	.383	62	-3	0-0	1.000	-0	85	128	O-28(19-1-8)	-0.4
	Year	67	79	9	13	3	0	2	5	6-2	0	26	.165	.224	.278	31	-8	0-0	1.000	-1	89	91	O-36(21-8-8)	-0.9
Total	8	963	2848	387	724	100	24	121	391	287-35	2	529	.254	.321	.434	112	40	38-18	.982	8	103	108	O-806(221-443-217)/1-7	1.4
HALL, JOE Joseph Geroy B 3.6.1966 Paducah, KY BR/TR 6/180# d4.5																								
1994	Chi A	17	28	6	11	3	0	1	5	2-0	1	4	.393	.452	.607	173	3	0-0	.917	-1	93	0	/O-9(7-0-2),D-2	0.2
1995	Det A	7	15	2	2	0	0	0	0	2-0	0	3	.133	.235	.133	-1	-2	0-0	1.000	1	135	369	/O-5(LF),D-2	-0.1
1997	Det A	2	4	1	2	1	0	0	3	0-0	0	0	.500	.500	.750	222	1	0-0	1.000	-0	60	0	/O(RF)	0.0
Total	3	26	47	9	15	4	0	1	8	4-0	1	7	.319	.385	.468	121	2	0-0	.960	0	106	132	/O-15(12-0-3),D-4	0.1
HALL, MEL Melvin B 9.16.1960 Lyons, NY BL/TL 6-1/205# d9.3																								
1981	Chi N	10	11	1	1	0	0	1	2	1-0	0	4	.091	.167	.364	45	-1	0-0	—	-1	0	0	/O-3(1-2-0)	-0.2
1982	Chi N	24	80	6	21	3	2	0	4	5-1	2	17	.262	.318	.350	86	-2	0-1	.939	-0	82	322	O-22(0-21-1)	-0.2
1983	Chi N	112	410	60	116	23	5	17	56	42-6	3	101	.283	.352	.488	125	14	6-6	.988	-4	89	153	*O-112(5-108-0)	0.8
1984	Chi N	48	150	25	42	11	3	4	22	12-3	0	23	.280	.329	.473	114	3	2-1	.961	0	94	190	O-46(5-5-40)	0.1
	Cle A	83	257	43	66	13	1	7	30	35-5	2	55	.257	.344	.397	104	3	1-1	.993	2	105	69	O-69(64-1-6)/D-9	0.1
1985	Cle A	23	66	7	21	6	0	0	12	8-0	0	12	.318	.387	.409	121	2	0-1	1.000	-3	65	0	O-15(15-0-1)/D-5	-0.1
1986	Cle A	140	442	68	131	29	2	18	77	33-8	2	65	.296	.346	.493	128	17	6-2	.972	-1	97	93	*O-126(123-0-14)/D-7	1.1
1987	Cle A	142	485	57	136	21	1	18	76	20-6	1	68	.280	.309	.439	95	-5	5-4	.989	6	118	40	*O-122(LF),D-14	-0.5
1988	Cle A	150	515	69	144	32	4	6	71	28-12	0	50	.280	.312	.392	95	-4	7-3	.967	-2	105	39	*O-141(135-7-3)/D-6	-1.0
1989	NY A	113	361	54	94	9	0	17	58	21-4	0	37	.260	.295	.427	104	0	0-0	.993	1	105	70	O-75(46-0-31),D-34	-0.3
1990	NY A	113	360	41	93	23	2	12	46	6-2	2	46	.258	.272	.433	95	-5	0-0	.973	-5	77	67	D-54,O-50(36-0-15)	-1.3
1991	NY A	141	492	67	140	23	2	19	80	26-6	3	40	.285	.321	.455	113	7	0-1	.987	0	97	111	*O-120(62-1-65),D-10	0.3
1992	NY A	152	583	67	163	36	3	15	81	29-4	1	53	.280	.310	.429	107	3	4-2	.990	1	99	109	*O-136(99-0-37),D-11	0.0
1996	SF N	25	25	3	3	0	0	0	5	1-0	0	4	.120	.148	.120	-28	-5	0-0	—	-1	0	0	/O-4(3-0-1)	-0.5
Total	13	1276	4237	568	1171	229	25	134	620	267-57	16	575	.276	.318	.437	107	27	31-22	.981	-6	99	94	*O-1041(716-145-214),D-150	-1.7
HALL, DICK Richard Wallace B 9.27.1930 St.Louis, MO BR/TR 6-6/200# d4.15 ▲																								
1952	Pit N	26	80	6	11	1	0	0	2	2	0	17	.138	.159	.150	-14	-12	0-1	.972	0	105	79	O-14(0-12-2)/3-5	-1.4
1953	Pit N	7	24	2	4	0	0	0	1	1	0	3	.167	.200	.167	-3	-4	1-1	.978	2	112	113	/2-7	-0.1
1954	Pit N	112	310	38	74	8	4	2	27	33	0	46	.239	.304	.310	64	-17	3-0	.956	3	113	75	*O-102(42-44-18)	-1.8
1955	Pit N	21	40	3	7	1	0	1	3	6-0	0	5	.175	.283	.275	50	-3	0-0	1.000	-2	39	0	P-15/O-3(1-3-0)	-0.1
1956	Pit N	33	29	5	10	0	0	0	1	5-0	0	7	.345	.441	.345	118	1	0-0	1.000	-1	58	0	P-19/1	0.0
1957	Pit N	10	1	0	0	0	0	0	0	0-0	0	1	.000	.000	.000	-99	0	0-0	—	-0	0	0	/P-8	0.0
1959	Pit N	2	2	0	0	0	0	0	0	0-0	0	0	.000	.000	.000	-99	0	0-0	1.000	-0	69	0	/P-2	0.0
1960	KC A	32	56	5	6	0	0	0	4	4-0	0	15	.107	.167	.107	-24	-2	1-0	.925	-1	97	46	P-29	0.0
1961	Bal A	30	36	4	5	0	0	0	1	3-0	0	13	.139	.205	.139	-6	0	0-0	.970	1	118	74	P-29	0.0
1962	Bal A	44	24	3	4	1	0	0	1	4-0	0	9	.167	.286	.208	38	1	0-0	1.000	-0	91	73	P-43	0.0
1963	Bal A	48	28	7	13	1	0	1	4	0-0	0	8	.464	.464	.607	205	6	0-0	1.000	1	121	99	P-47	0.0
1964	Bal A	45	16	1	2	0	0	0	3	1-0	0	3	.125	.176	.125	-14	0	0-0	1.000	-0	90	105	P-45	0.0
1965	Bal A	49	15	1	5	2	0	0	4	1-0	1	4	.333	.412	.467	146	3	0-0	.923	-1	51	217	P-48	0.0
1966	Bal A	32	12	0	2	0	0	0	2	0-0	1	5	.167	.231	.167	17	0	0-0	1.000	-0	95	0	P-32	0.0
1967	Phi N	48	14	1	1	0	0	0	0	0-0	0	5	.071	.071	.071	-58	-1	0-0	1.000	1	147	121	P-48	0.0
1968	Phi N	32	3	0	1	0	0	0	0	0-0	0	1	.333	.333	.333	101	0	0-0	1.000	-0	80	0	P-32	0.0
1969	†Bal A	39	7	1	2	0	0	0	2	1-0	0	1	.286	.375	.286	86	1	1-0	1.000	-1	61	296	P-39	0.0
1970	†Bal A	32	12	2	1	0	0	0	1	0-0	0	3	.083	.083	.083	-53	-1	0-0	1.000	-2	34	0	P-32	0.0
1971	†Bal A	27	5	0	2	1	0	0	0	0-0	0	1	.400	.400	.600	182	1	0-0	.800	-1	44	0	P-27	0.0
Total	19	669	714	79	150	15	4	4	56	61-0	2	147	.210	.271	.259	44	-27	6-2	.976	-3	85	77	P-495,O-119(43-59-20)/2-7,3-5,1	-3.4
HALL, BOB Robert Prill B 12.20.1878 Baltimore, MD D 12.1.1950 Wellesley, MA TR 5-10/158# d4.18 OF Total (24-LF 12-CF 8-RF)																								
1904	Phi N	46	163	11	26	4	0	0	17	14	0		.160	.226	.184	28	-13	5	.843	-9	92	98	3-20,S-15,1-11	-2.4
1905	NY N	1	3	1	1	0	0	0	0	0	0		.333	.333	.333	97	0	0	—	0	0	0	/O(RF)	0.0
	Bro N	56	203	21	48	4	1	2	15	11	1		.236	.279	.296	77	-6	8	.939	2	97	117	O-42(24-12-7)/2-7,1-3	-0.7
	Year	57	206	22	49	4	1	2	15	11	1		.238	.280	.296	77	-6	8	.939	2	97	117	O-43(24-12-8)/2-7,1-3	-0.7
Total	2	103	369	33	75	8	1	2	32	25	1		.203	.256	.247	55	-19	13	.939	-7	97	117	/O-43L,3-20,S-15,1-14,2-7	-3.1
HALL, RUSS Robert Russell B 9.29.1871 Shelbyville, KY D 7.1.1937 Los Angeles, CA TL 5-10/170# d4.15																								
1898	StL N	39	143	13	35	2	1	0	10	7	1		.245	.285	.273	59	-8	1	.835	-12	91	81	S-35/3-3,O(RF)	-1.7
1901	Cle A	1	4	2	2	0	0	0	0	0	0		.500	.500	.500	185	0	0	.500	-1	60	0	/S	-0.1
Total	2	40	147	15	37	2	1	0	10	7	1		.252	.290	.279	62	-8	1	.824	-13	90	79	/S-36,3-3,O(RF)	-1.8
HALL, TOBY Toby Jason B 10.21.1975 Tacoma, WA BR/TR 6-3/205# d9.15																								
2000	TB A	4	12	1	2	0	0	1	1	1-0	0	0	.167	.231	.417	60	-1	0-0	1.000	1	0	0	/C-4	0.0
2001	TB A	49	188	28	56	16	0	4	30	4-0	3	16	.298	.321	.447	101	0	2-2	.986	3	124	87	C-46	0.6
2002	TB A	85	330	37	85	19	1	6	42	17-3	1	27	.258	.293	.376	78	-11	0-1	.989	-5	112	114	C-83	-1.0
2003	TB A	130	463	50	117	23	0	12	47	23-4	7	40	.253	.295	.380	79	-15	0-1	.988	-2	151	115	*C-130	-0.8
Total	4	268	993	116	260	58	1	23	120	45-7	11	83	.262	.299	.392	83	-27	2-4	.988	-3	132	108	C-263	-1.2
HALL, BILL William B 12.28.1979 Tupelo, MS BR/TR 6/175# d9.1																								
2002	Mil N	19	36	3	7	1	1	1	5	3-0	0	13	.194	.256	.361	64	-2	0-1	.949	-3	77	74	S-13/3-2	-0.5
2003	Mil N	52	142	23	37	9	2	5	20	7-0	1	28	.261	.298	.458	96	-2	1-2	.956	-0	105	126	2-18,S-18/3	0.0
Total	2	71	178	26	44	10	3	6	25	10-0	1	41	.247	.289	.438	89	-4	1-3	.950	-3	87	81	/S-31,2-18,3-3	-0.5
HALL, BILL William Lemuel B 7.30.1928 Moultrie, GA D 1.1.1986 Moultrie, GA BL/TR 5-11/165# d4.18																								
1954	Pit N	5	7	0	0	0	0	0	0	0	0	0	.000	.000	.000	-99	-2	0-0	1.000	-0	*0*	*0*	/C	-0.2
1956	Pit N	1	3	0	0	0	0	0	0	0-0	0	1	.000	.000	.000	-99	-1	0-0	1.000	1	*0*	*0*	/C	0.0
1958	Pit N	51	116	15	33	6	0	1	15	15-8	0	13	.284	.366	.362	96	0	0-0	.982	5	*114*	*140*	C-51	0.7
Total	3	57	126	15	33	6	0	1	15	15-8	0	14	.262	.340	.333	81	-3	0-0	.983	6	*109*	*133*	/C-53	0.5
HALLER, TOM Thomas Frank B 6.23.1937 Lockport, IL BL/TR 6-4/195# d4.11 C3																								
1961	SF N	30	62	5	9	1	0	2	8	9-0	1	23	.145	.260	.258	41	-5	0-1	1.000	2	*88*	*80*	C-25	-0.3
1962	†SF N	99	272	53	71	13	1	18	55	51-1	4	59	.261	.384	.515	142	18	1-4	.992	-0	*126*	*71*	C-91	2.0
1963	SF N	98	298	32	76	8	1	14	44	34-5	2	45	.255	.332	.430	120	8	4-6	.994	-3	*101*	*77*	C-85/O-7(1-0-6)	0.8
1964	SF N	117	388	43	98	14	3	16	48	55-10	2	51	.253	.345	.428	115	9	4-2	.989	-1	*91*	*80*	*C-113/O-3(1-0-2)	1.5
1965	SF N	134	422	40	106	4	3	16	49	47-15	8	67	.251	.335	.389	101	1	0-0	.987	-0	*118*	*59*	*C-133	0.7
1966	SF N☆	142	471	74	113	19	2	27	67	53-11	6	74	.240	.323	.461	112	8	1-3	.991	-9	*94*	*74*	*C-136/1-4	0.5
1967	SF N★	141	455	54	114	23	5	14	49	62-9	4	61	.251	.344	.415	118	12	0-4	.997	-2	*100*	*93*	*C-136/O(RF)	1.7
1968	LA N★	144	474	37	135	27	5	4	53	46-13	2	76	.285	.345	.388	132	19	1-4	.994	19	*106*	*128*	*C-139	3.7
1969	LA N	134	445	46	117	18	3	6	39	48-13	2	58	.263	.337	.357	102	2	0-3	.992	-2	83	90	*C-132	0.4
1970	LA N	112	325	47	93	16	6	10	47	32-7	2	35	.286	.351	.465	123	10	3-0	.993	-6	76	77	*C-106	0.9
1971	LA N	84	202	23	54	5	0	5	32	25-8	2	30	.267	.346	.366	111	3	0-2	.978	2	75	104	C-67	0.8
1972	†Det A	59	121	7	25	5	2	2	13	15-4	0	14	.207	.292	.331	83	-2	0-1	1.000	3	120	93	C-36	0.2
Total	12	1294	3935	461	1011	153	31	134	504	477-96	35	593	.257	.340	.414	114	83	14-30	.992	-7	*98*	*86*	*C-1199/O-11(2-0-9),1-4	12.9
HALLIDAY, NEWT Newton Schurz B 6.18.1896 Chicago, IL D 4.6.1918 Great Lakes, IL BR/TR 6-1/175# d8.19																								
1916	Pit N	1	1	0	0	0	0	0	0	0	0	1	.000	.000	.000	-99	0	0	1.000	0	603	0	/1	0.0
HALLIGAN, JOCKO William E. B 12.8.1868 Avon, NY D 2.13.1945 Buffalo, NY BL 5-9/166# d5.13																								
1890	Buf P	57	211	28	53	9	2	3	33	20	1	19	.251	.319	.355	87	-3	7	.824	-7	137	52	O-43(1-5-37),C-16	-0.8
1891	Cin N	61	247	43	77	13	6	3	44	24	1	25	.312	.375	.449	139	12	5	.856	-5	59	58	O-61(RF)	0.5

Year	Tm Lg	G	AB	R	H	2B	3B	HR	RBI	BB-IB	HP	SO	AVG	OBP	SLG	AOPS	ABR	SB-CS	FA	FR	Rng	Thr	G at Pos	BFW
1892	Cin N	26	101	14	29	4	0	2	12	12	0	9	.287	.363	.386	128	4	3	.875	-1	94	114	O-26(RF)	0.1
	Bal N	46	178	38	48	4	7	2	43	30	2	24	.270	.381	.404	134	8	8	.861	-6	116	115	O-22(1-0-21),1-19/C-5	0.1
	Year	72	279	52	77	8	7	4	55	42	2	33	.276	.375	.398	132	12	11	.869	-7	104	114	O-48(1-0-47),1-19/C-5	0.2
Total	3	190	737	123	207	30	15	10	132	86	4	77	.281	.359	.403	121	21	23	.848	-20	94	73	O-152(2-5-145)/C-21,1-19	-0.1
HALLINAN, ED Edward S. B 8.23.1888 San Francisco, CA D 8.24.1940 San Francisco, CA BR/TR 5-9/168# d5.13																								
1911	StL A	52	169	13	35	3	1	0	14	14	0		.207	.268	.237	43	-13	4	.902	-5	94	164	S-34,2-15/3-3	-1.6
1912	StL A	28	86	11	19	2	0	0	1	5	1		.221	.272	.244	50	-6	3	.866	-5	87	166	S-26	-0.9
Total	2	80	255	24	54	5	1	0	15	19	1		.212	.269	.239	45	-19	7	.887	-10	91	165	/S-60,2-15,3-3	-2.5
HALLINAN, JIMMY James H. B 5.27.1849 , Ireland D 10.28.1879 Chicago, IL BL/TL 5-9/172# d7.26																								
1871	Kek NA	5	25	7	5	0	0	0	2	2		0	.200	.259	.200	34	-2	1-1	.475	-7	54	0	/S-5	-0.6
1875	Wes NA	**13**	51	12	14	2	1	0	3	0		1	.275	.275	.353	110	0	2-2	.742	-4	74	91	S-13	-0.4
	Mut NA	44	203	29	58	6	3	3	21	1		2	.286	.289	.389	127	4	2-2	.765	-11	89	36	S-43/3O(RF)	-0.7
	Year	57	254	41	72	8	4	3	24	1		3	.283	.286	.382	123	5	4-4	.761	-15	86	48	S-56/3O(RF)	-1.1
1876	NY N	54	240	45	67	7	6	2	36	2		4	.279	.285	.383	139	11		.764	-17	102	57	*S-50/2-4,O-2(RF)	-0.3
1877	Cin N	16	73	18	27	1	1	0	7	1		1	.370	.378	.411	167	6		.854	-5	69	111	2-16	0.1
	Chi N	19	89	17	25	4	1	0	11	4		2	.281	.312	.348	96	-1		.800	-1	30	177	O-19(RF)	-0.2
	Year	35	162	35	52	5	2	0	18	5		3	.321	.341	.377	124	4		.800	-7	30	177	O-19(RF),2-16	-0.1
1878	Chi N	16	67	14	19	3	0	0	2	5		6	.284	.333	.328	111	1		.789	-5	67	0	O-11(LF)/2-5	-0.4
	Ind N	3	12	0	3	2	0	0	1	0		2	.250	.250	.417	134	1		.667	-1	0	0	/O-3(2-1-0)	0.0
	Year	19	79	14	22	5	0	0	3	5		8	.278	.321	.342	114	2		.760	-5	53	0	O-14(13-1-0)/2-5	-0.4
Total	2 NA	62	279	48	77	8	4	3	26	3		3	.276	.284	.366	114	2	5-5	.000	-22	83	44	/S-61,O(RF)3	-1.7
Total	3	108	481	94	141	17	8	2	57	12		15	.293	.310	.374	129	18		.764	-17	102	57	/S-50,O-35(13-1-21),2-25	-0.8
HALLMAN, BILL William Harry B 3.15.1876 Philadelphia, PA D 4.23.1950 Philadelphia, PA BL/TL 5-8/165# d4.25																								
1901	Mil A	**139**	549	70	135	27	6	2	47	41	2		.246	.301	.328	78	-16	12	.905	-1	121	144	*O-139(49-15-75)	-2.1
1903	Chi A	63	207	29	43	7	4	0	18	31	3		.208	.320	.280	85	-2	11	.953	2	111	0	O-57(51-0-6)	-0.3
1906	Pit N	23	89	12	24	3	1	1	6	15	0		.270	.375	.360	124	3	3	.935	-1	107	0	O-23(8-15-0)	0.1
1907	Pit N	94	302	39	67	6	2	0	15	33	3		.222	.305	.255	74	-8	21	.966	-1	87	41	O-84(14-28-45)	-1.4
Total	4	319	1147	150	269	43	13	3	86	120	8		.235	.311	.303	82	-23	47	.933	-1	109	78	O-303(122-58-126)	-3.7
HALLMAN, BILL William Wilson B 3.31.1867 Pittsburgh, PA D 9.11.1920 Philadelphia, PA BR/TR 5-8/160# d4.23 M1 OF Total (3-LF 4-CF 35-RF)																								
1888	Phi N	18	63	5	13	4	1	0	6	1	0	12	.206	.219	.302	61	-3	1	.898	-4			C-10/2-4,O-3(LF),S3	-0.6
1889	Phi N	119	462	67	117	21	8	2	60	36	4	54	.253	.313	.346	77	-17	20	.895	3	98	98	*S-106,2-13/C	-0.9
1890	Phi P	84	356	59	95	16	7	1	37	33	5	24	.267	.338	.360	84	-9	6	.885	-3	100	397	O-34(0-3-32),C-26,2-14,3-10/S-2	-0.8
1891	Phi AA	141	587	112	166	21	13	6	69	38	5	56	.283	.332	.394	107	2	18	.930	-4	96	93	*2-141	0.2
1892	Phi N	138	586	106	171	27	10	2	84	32	6	52	.292	.335	.382	117	10	19	.936	-28	87	108	*2-138	-1.1
1893	Phi N	132	596	119	183	28	7	5	76	51	5	27	.307	.367	.403	104	3	22	.950	-13	97	97	*2-120,1-12	-0.4
1894	Phi N	122	519	111	162	19	9	0	69	37	5	15	.312	.364	.383	82	-15	37	.932	-19	87	114	*2-122	-2.2
1895	Phi N	124	539	94	169	26	5	1	91	34	4	20	.314	.359	.386	92	-7	16	.943	4	105	105	*2-122/S-3	0.2
1896	Phi N	120	469	82	150	21	3	2	83	45	2	23	.320	.382	.390	105	5	16	.945	4	100	116	*2-120/P	1.2
1897	Phi N	31	126	16	33	3	0	0	15	8	4		.262	.326	.286	64	-6	1	.958	-8	80	91	2-31	-1.1
	StL N	80	302	32	67	7	2	0	26	24	4		.222	.288	.258	46	-24	12	.940	5	104	117	2-78/1-3,M	-1.3
	Year	111	428	48	100	10	2	0	41	32	8		.234	.299	.266	51	-30	13	.945	-3	97	109	*2-109/1-3	-2.4
1898	Bro N	134	509	57	124	10	7	2	63	29	5		.244	.291	.303	70	-21	9	.944	-4	108	90	*2-124,3-10	-1.8
1901	Cle A	5	19	2	4	0	0	0	3	2	0		.211	.286	.211	41	-1	0	.815	-3	66	47	/S-5	-0.4
	Phi N	123	445	46	82	13	5	0	38	26	4		.184	.236	.236	36	-37	13	.971	-4	100	72	2-90,3-33	-3.9
1902	Phi N	73	254	14	63	8	4	0	35	14	0		.248	.287	.311	85	-5	9	.932	-1	104	32	3-72	-0.5
1903	Phi N	63	198	20	42	11	2	0	17	16	0		.212	.271	.288	61	-10	2	.932	-3	103	65	2-22,3-19/1-9,O-4(0-1-3),S-3	-1.2
Total	14	1507	6030	942	1641	235	83	21	772	426	53	<u>283</u>	.272	.326	.349	85	-135	201	.941	-79			*2-1139,3-145,S-120/O-41R,C1P	-14.6
HALPIN, JIM James Nathaniel B 10.4.1863 , England D 1.4.1893 Boston, MA d6.15																								
1882	Wor N	2	8	0	0	0	0	0	0	0		2	.000	.000	.000	-98	-2		.625	-1	53	0	/3-2	-0.3
1884	Was U	46	168	24	31	3	0	0		2			.185	.194	.202	21	-21		.809	-5	88	65	S-39/3-7	-2.3
1885	Det N	15	54	3	7	2	0	0	1	1		12	.130	.145	.167	1	-6		.846	-1	106	61	S-15	-0.6
Total	3	63	230	27	38	5	0	0	<u>1</u>	3		<u>14</u>	.165	.176	.187	12	-29		.821	-7	93	64	/S-54,3-9	-3.2
HALT, AL Alva William B 11.23.1890 Sandusky, OH D 1.22.1973 Sandusky, OH BR/TR 6/180# d5.29																								
1914	Bro F	80	261	26	61	6	2	3	25	13	0	39	.234	.270	.307	57	-21	11	.890	-10	88	110	S-71/2-3,O(CF)	-2.8
1915	Bro F	151	524	41	131	22	7	3	64	39	4	79	.250	.307	.336	81	-22	20	.930	6	**106**	**138**	*3-111,S-40	-1.1
1918	Cle A	26	69	9	12	2	0	0	1	9	0	12	.174	.269	.203	39	-5	4	.971	1	97	49	3-14/2-4,S-4,1-2	-0.4
Total	3	257	854	76	204	30	9	6	90	61	4	130	.239	.293	.316	70	-48	35	.933	-4	105	130	3-125,S-115/2-7,1-2,O(CF)	-4.3
HALTER, SHANE Shane David B 11.8.1969 LaPlata, MD BR/TR 5-10/160# d4.6 OF Total (28-LF 15-CF 24-RF)																								
1997	KC A	74	123	16	34	5	1	2	10	10-0	2	28	.276	.341	.382	86	-2	4-3	1.000	-4	92	96	O-32(10-9-17),2-18,3-12/S-5,D-4	-0.7
1998	KC A	86	204	17	45	12	0	2	13	12-0	1	38	.221	.265	.309	48	-16	2-5	.964	5	116	90	S-66/O-9(6-0-3),3-8,2-6,1P	-0.8
1999	NY N	7	0	0	0	0	0	0	0	0-0	0	0	—	—	—	—	0	0-0	—	-0	0	0	/O-2(0-1-1),S	0.0
2000	Det A	105	238	26	62	12	2	3	27	14-0	1	49	.261	.302	.366	71	-11	5-2	.937	8	104	184	3-55,1-29,S-17,2-10/O-8(2-5-3),C-2,P	-0.3
2001	Det A	136	450	53	128	32	7	12	65	37-2	7	100	.284	.344	.467	117	11	3-3	.924	14	129	102	3-74,S-62/1-8,D	2.8
2002	Det A	122	410	46	98	22	6	10	39	39-1	4	92	.239	.309	.395	91	-6	0-4	.962	4	113	69	S-81,3-30/O-8(LF),2-4,1D	0.3
2003	Det A	114	360	33	78	5	2	12	30	27-0	0	77	.217	.269	.342	65	-20	2-3	.985	8	125	154	3-50,S-27,2-24,1-12/O-2(LF),D-4	-1.0
Total	7	644	1785	191	445	88	18	41	184	139-3	15	384	.249	.306	.388	84	-44	16-20	.963	35	111	92	S-259,3-229/2-62,O-61L,1-51,DCP	0.3
HAM, RALPH Ralph A. B 3.1849 Troy, NY D 2.13.1905 Troy, NY 5-8/158# d5.6																								
1871	Rok NA	**25**	113	25	28	4	0	0	12	1		7	.248	.254	.283	57	-5	6-2	.723	-6	215	232	O-19(LF)/3-7,S-2	-0.7
HAMBURG, CHARLIE Charles M. (born Charles M. Hambrick) B 11.22.1863 Louisville, KY D 5.18.1931 Union, NJ 6/175# d4.18																								
1890	†Lou AA	133	485	93	132	22	2	3	77	69	6		.272	.370	.344	113	12	46	.946	-3	72	69	*O-133(LF)	0.4
HAMBY, JIM James Sanford "Cracker" B 7.29.1897 Wilkesboro, NC D 10.21.1991 Springfield, IL BR/TR 6/170# d9.20																								
1926	NY N	1	3	0	0	0	0	0	0	0	0	0	.000	.000	.000	-99	-1	0	.600	-1	*48*	*0*	/C	-0.2
1927	NY N	21	52	6	10	0	1	0	5	7	0	7	.192	.288	.231	40	-4	1	.904	-1	*119*	*151*	C-19	-0.4
Total	2	22	55	6	10	0	1	0	5	7	0	7	.182	.274	.218	33	-5	1	.885	-2	*115*	*142*	/C-20	-0.6
HAMELIN, BOB Robert James B 11.29.1967 Elizabeth, NJ BL/TL 6/235# d9.12																								
1993	KC A	16	49	2	11	3	0	2	5	6-0	0	15	.224	.309	.408	86	-1	0-0	.986	-1	90	88	1-15	-0.3
1994	KC A	101	312	64	88	25	1	24	65	56-3	1	62	.282	.388	.599	145	22	4-3	.992	0	106	57	D-70,1-24	1.4
1995	KC A	72	208	20	35	7	1	7	25	26-1	6	56	.168	.278	.313	53	-15	0-1	1.000	2	171	180	D-56/1-8	-1.7
1996	KC A	89	239	31	61	14	1	9	40	54-2	2	58	.255	.391	.435	110	6	5-2	.984	0	109	108	D-47,1-33	0.1
1997	Det A	110	318	47	86	15	0	18	52	48-3	1	72	.270	.366	.487	122	11	2-1	1.000	-1	38	31	D-95/1-7	0.3
1998	Mil N	109	146	15	32	6	0	7	22	16-1	1	30	.219	.295	.404	83	-4	0-1	.992	-5	35	93	1-51/D	-1.2
Total	6	497	1272	179	313	70	3	67	209	206-10	11	293	.246	.352	.464	109	19	11-8	.990	-5	87	92	D-269,1-138	-1.4
HAMILTON, DARRYL Darryl Quinn B 12.3.1964 Baton Rouge, LA BL/TR 6-1/180# d6.3																								
1988	Mil A	44	103	14	19	4	0	1	11	12-0	1	9	.184	.274	.252	49	-7	7-3	1.000	1	109	54	O-37(8-6-23)/D-3	-0.7
1990	Mil A	89	156	27	46	5	0	1	18	9-0	0	12	.295	.333	.346	91	-2	10-3	.992	3	123	32	O-72(41-6-25)/D-9	0.1
1991	Mil A	122	405	64	126	15	6	1	57	33-2	0	38	.311	.361	.385	110	5	16-6	.996	-5	95	45	*O-117(25-55-49)	-0.1
1992	Mil A	128	470	67	140	19	7	5	62	45-0	1	42	.298	.356	.400	115	9	41-14	**1.000**	2	100	121	*O-124(30-32-74)	1.2
1993	Mil A	135	520	74	161	21	1	9	48	45-5	3	62	.310	.367	.406	109	7	21-13	.992	11	**117**	117	*O-129(31-49-70)/D	1.4
1994	Mil A	36	141	23	37	10	1	1	13	15-1	0	17	.262	.331	.369	77	-5	3-0	1.000	-4	74	122	O-32(CF)/D-4	-0.7
1995	Mil A	112	398	54	108	20	6	5	44	47-3	3	35	.271	.350	.389	88	-7	11-1	.989	-2	99	78	*O-109(CF)/D-2	-0.5
1996	†Tex A	148	627	94	184	29	4	6	51	54-4	2	66	.293	.348	.381	81	-18	15-5	**1.000**	-6	103	22	*O-147(CF)	-1.9
1997	†SF N	125	460	78	124	23	3	5	43	61-1	0	61	.270	.354	.365	92	-4	15-10	.980	-8	96	19	*O-118(CF)	-1.1
1998	SF N	97	367	65	108	19	2	1	26	59-0	2	53	.294	.393	.365	108	8	9-8	1.000	-9	87	67	O-96(CF)	-0.1
	Col N	51	194	30	65	9	1	5	25	23-1	1	20	.335	.406	.469	107	3	4-1	.990	-4	91	33	O-48(CF)	0.0
	Year	148	561	95	173	28	3	6	51	82-1	3	73	.308	.398	.401	107	10	13-9	.997	-13	88	56	*O-144(CF)	-0.1

Year	Tm Lg	G	AB	R	H	2B	3B	HR	RBI	BB-IB	HP	SO	AVG	OBP	SLG	AOPS	ABR	SB-CS	FA	FR	Rng	Thr	G at Pos	BFW
1999	Col N	91	337	63	102	11	3	4	24	38-0	1	21	.303	.374	.389	74	-12	4-5	1.000	-2	105	23	O-82(CF)	-1.3
	†NY N	55	168	19	57	8	1	5	21	19-0	1	18	.339	.410	.488	130	8	2-3	1.000	-3	92	83	O-52(CF)	0.5
	Year	146	505	82	159	19	4	9	45	57-0	2	39	.315	.386	.422	90	-6	6-8	1.000	-4	100	45	*O-134(CF)	-0.8
2000	†NY N	43	105	20	29	4	1	1	6	14-0	0	20	.276	.358	.362	87	-2	2-0	1.000	-2	81	66	O-33(17-11-8)	-0.4
2001	NY N	52	126	15	27	7	1	1	5	19-3	2	20	.214	.322	.310	69	-5	3-1	1.000	1	103	99	O-37(24-11-3)	-0.5
Total	13	1328	4577	707	1333	204	37	51	454	493-20	17	494	.291	.360	.385	95	-22	163-73	.995	-27	100	63	*O-1233(176-854-252)/D-19	-4.1
HAMILTON, JEFF Jeffrey Robert B 3.19.1964 Flint, MI BR/TR 6-3/207# d6.28																								
1986	LA N	71	147	22	33	5	0	5	19	2-1	0	43	.224	.232	.361	66	-8	0-0	.968	5	105	90	3-66/S-2	-0.4
1987	LA N	35	83	5	18	3	0	0	1	7-2	1	22	.217	.286	.253	45	-6	0-1	.935	6	122	119	3-31/S	-0.1
1988	†LA N	111	309	34	73	14	2	6	33	10-1	4	51	.236	.268	.353	80	-9	0-2	.941	0	96	60	*3-105/S-2,1	-1.0
1989	LA N	151	548	45	134	35	1	12	56	20-5	3	71	.245	.272	.378	86	-12	0-0	.951	-1	88	**133**	*3-147/P2S	-1.4
1990	LA N	7	24	1	3	0	0	0	1	0-0	0	3	.125	.125	.125	-32	-4	0-0	1.000	1	108	234	/3-7	-0.4
1991	LA N	41	94	4	21	4	0	1	14	4-0	0	21	.223	.255	.298	56	-6	0-0	.928	0	101	56	3-33/S	-0.6
Total	6	416	1205	111	282	61	3	24	124	43-9	8	211	.234	.263	.349	74	-45	0-3	.948	11	96	104	3-389/S-7,2P1	-3.9
HAMILTON, TOM Thomas Ball "Ham" B 9.29.1925 Altoona, KS D 11.29.1973 Tyler, TX BL/TR 6-4/213# d9.4																								
1952	Phi A	9	10	1	2	1	0	0	1	1	0	1	.200	.273	.300	56	-1	0-0	1.000	-0	0	79	/1-5	-0.1
1953	Phi A	58	56	8	11	2	0	0	5	7	0	11	.196	.286	.232	40	-5	0-0	1.000	0	105	0	/1-7,O-2(RF)	-0.5
Total	2	67	66	9	13	3	0	0	6	8	0	12	.197	.284	.242	42	-6	0-0	1.000	-0	72	25	/1-12,O-2(RF)	-0.6
HAMILTON, BILLY William Robert "Sliding Billy" B 2.16.1866 Newark, NJ D 12.16.1940 Worcester, MA BL/TR 5-6/165# d7.31 HF1961																								
1888	KC AA	35	129	21	34	4	4	0	11	4	4		.264	.307	.357	106	0	19	.961	-0	82	0	O-35(3-0-32)	0.0
1889	KC AA	137	534	144	161	17	12	3	77	87	14	41	.301	.413	.395	123	20	**111**	.857	-8	75	93	*O-137(7-0-130)	0.9
1890	Phi N	123	496	133	161	13	9	2	49	83	9	37	.325	.430	.399	139	29	**102**	.882	3	107	88	*O-123(LF)	2.6
1891	Phi N	133	527	**141**	**179**	23	7	2	60	**102**	7	28	**.340**	**.453**	.421	151	42	**111**	.907	7	81	191	*O-133(LF)	**4.0**
1892	Phi N	139	554	132	183	21	7	3	53	81	8	29	.330	.423	.410	152	40	57	.919	12	112	149	*O-139(138-1-0)	3.7
1893	Phi N	82	355	110	135	22	7	5	44	63	13	7	.380	**.490**	.524	**169**	41	43	.937	1	55	196	O-82(19-63-0)	3.0
1894	Phi N	**132**	558	**198**	225	25	15	4	90	**128**	10	19	.403	**.522**	.523	156	**66**	**100**	.962	2	67	74	*O-132(CF)	**4.5**
1895	Phi N	123	517	**166**	201	22	6	7	74	**96**	7	30	.389	.490	.495	154	50	**97**	.913	-4	60	114	*O-123(3-120-0)	3.1
1896	Bos N	131	524	153	192	24	10	3	55	**110**	2	29	.366	**.478**	.468	141	39	83	.934	-13	44	46	*O-131(6-125-0)	1.6
1897	†Bos N	127	507	**152**	174	17	5	3	61	**105**	6		.343	.461	.414	124	26	66	.962	-6	55	0	*O-126(CF)	1.0
1898	Bos N	110	417	110	154	16	5	3	50	87	2		.369	**.480**	.453	**159**	39	54	.904	-17	53	64	*O-110(CF)	1.4
1899	Bos N	84	297	63	92	7	1	1	33	72	1		.310	.446	.350	109	9	19	.952	-4	88	68	O-81(2-78-1)	0.0
1900	Bos N	136	520	103	173	20	5	1	47	107	3		.333	.449	.396	119	21	32	.947	-0	76	130	*O-136(CF)	1.1
1901	Bos N	102	348	71	100	11	2	3	38	64	4		.287	.404	.356	111	9	20	.945	-0	56	138	O-99(0-98-1)	0.4
Total	14	1594	6283	1697	2164	242	95	40	742	1189	90	220	.344	.455	.432	139	431	914	.926	-28	73	101	*O-1587(434-989-164)	27.3
HAMLIN, KEN Kenneth Lee B 5.18.1935 Detroit, MI BR/TR 5-10/170# d6.17																								
1957	Pit N	2	1	0	0	0	0	0	0	0-0	0	0	.000	.000	.000	-99	0	0-0	1.000	-0	0	0	/S	0.0
1959	Pit N	3	8	1	1	0	0	0	0	2-0	0	1	.125	.300	.125	19	-1	0-0	1.000	-0	89	155	/S-3	-0.1
1960	KC A	140	428	51	96	10	2	2	24	44-1	1	48	.224	.297	.271	55	-27	1-1	.955	-34	88	72	*S-139	-5.3
1961	LA A	42	91	4	19	3	0	1	5	11-2	1	9	.209	.298	.275	49	-6	0-1	.963	8	108	128	S-39	0.4
1962	Was A	98	292	29	74	12	0	3	22	22-0	0	22	.253	.303	.325	70	-12	7-7	.963	-10	94	100	S-87/2-2	-1.7
1965	Was A	117	362	45	99	21	1	4	22	33-1	1	45	.273	.333	.370	102	2	8-2	.976	-18	87	75	2-77,S-47/3	-0.8
1966	Was A	66	158	13	34	7	1	1	16	13-1	0	21	.215	.267	.291	63	-7	1-0	.963	4	112	115	2-50/3	0.0
Total	7	468	1340	143	323	53	4	11	89	125-5	3	146	.241	.304	.311	71	-51	17-11	.959	-51	92	88	S-316,2-129/3-2	-7.5
HAMMOCK, ROB Robert Wade B 3.13.1977 Macon, GA BR/TR 5-11/180# d4.11																								
2003	Ari N	65	195	30	55	10	2	8	28	17-3	2	44	.282	.343	.477	102	0	3-2	.993	15	83	105	C-36,O-17(5-0-12),3-16/D	1.6
HAMMOND, STEVE Steven Benjamin B 5.9.1957 Atlanta, GA BL/TR 6-2/190# d6.28 b-Chris																								
1982	KC A	46	126	14	29	5	1	1	11	4-0	0	18	.230	.252	.310	54	-8	0-1	1.000	4	121	130	O-37(RF)/D	-0.7
HAMMOND, JACK Walter Charles "Wobby" B 2.26.1891 Amsterdam, NY D 3.4.1942 Kenosha, WI BR/TR 5-11/170# d4.15																								
1915	Cle A	35	84	9	18	2	1	0	4	1	0	19	.214	.224	.262	44	-6	0-1	.957	-5	87	80	2-19	-1.2
1922	Cle A	1	4	1	1	0	0	0	0	0	0	0	.250	.250	.250	30	0	0-0	.333	-1	41	0	/2	-0.2
	Pit N	9	11	3	3	0	0	0	0	1	0	0	.273	.333	.273	57	-1	0-0	1.000	0	83	156	/2-4	0.0
Total	2	45	99	13	22	2	1	0	4	2	0	19	.222	.238	.263	45	-7	0-1	.943	-6	85	86	/2-24	-1.4
HAMMONDS, JEFFREY Jeffrey Bryan B 3.5.1971 Plainfield, NJ BR/TR 6/195# d6.25																								
1993	Bal A	33	105	10	32	8	0	3	19	2-1	0	16	.305	.312	.467	104	0	4-0	.961	1	104	138	O-23(14-0-10)/D-8	0.1
1994	Bal A	68	250	45	74	18	2	8	31	17-1	2	39	.296	.339	.480	105	1	5-0	.962	2	110	103	O-66(9-0-58)	0.1
1995	Bal A	57	178	18	43	9	1	4	23	9-0	1	30	.242	.279	.371	67	-9	4-2	.989	0	109	36	O-46(RF)/D-5	-1.1
1996	Bal A	71	248	38	56	10	1	9	27	23-1	4	53	.226	.301	.383	72	-11	3-3	.980	-0	105	63	O-70(64-1-11)/D	-1.4
1997	†Bal A	118	397	71	105	19	3	21	55	32-1	3	73	.264	.323	.486	111	4	15-1	.980	1	107	66	*O-114(31-40-54)/D-4	0.6
1998	Bal A	63	171	36	46	12	1	6	28	26-1	3	38	.269	.369	.456	117	5	7-2	.980	-2	95	67	O-53(7-24-29)/D-7	0.3
	Cin N	26	86	14	26	4	1	0	11	13-0	0	18	.302	.390	.372	102	1	1-1	.985	3	117	207	O-25(CF)	0.4
1999	Cin N	123	262	43	73	13	0	17	41	27-0	1	64	.279	.347	.523	113	4	3-6	1.000	5	111	118	*O-106(46-21-53)	0.6
2000	Col N★	122	454	94	152	24	2	20	106	44-4	5	83	.335	.395	.529	105	5	14-7	.991	-4	89	109	*O-118(32-9-85)	-0.3
2001	Mil N	49	174	20	43	11	1	6	21	14-1	4	42	.247	.314	.425	92	-2	5-3	.982	-3	95	78	O-46(CF)	-0.5
2002	Mil N	128	448	47	115	26	5	9	41	52-0	2	86	.257	.332	.397	97	-4	4-5	.992	-7	94	42	*O-125(2-78-55)	-1.4
2003	Mil N	10	38	2	6	2	0	1	3	3-0	0	7	.158	.220	.289	32	-4	0-0	1.000	-1	91	0	O-10(RF)	-0.5
	†SF N	36	94	20	26	10	0	3	10	13-0	1	21	.277	.370	.479	123	4	1-0	1.000	-1	95	70	O-30(17-14-4)	0.3
	Year	46	132	22	32	12	0	4	13	16-0	1	28	.242	.329	.424	97	0	1-0	1.000	-1	94	50	O-40(17-14-14)	-0.2
Total	11	904	2905	458	797	166	17	107	416	275-10	26	570	.274	.339	.454	100	-6	66-30	.984	-5	101	81	O-832(222-258-415)/D-25	-2.8
HAMNER, GRANNY Granville Wilbur B 4.26.1927 Richmond, VA D 9.12.1993 Philadelphia, PA BR/TR 5-10/163# d9.14 Mil 1945 b-Garvin ▲																								
1944	Phi N	21	77	6	19	1	0	0	5	3	0	7	.247	.275	.260	53	-5	0	.933	5	132	131	S-21	0.2
1945	Phi N	14	41	3	7	2	0	0	6	1	0	3	.171	.190	.220	14	-5	0	.861	0	103	97	S-13	-0.4
1946	Phi N	2	7	0	1	0	0	0	0	0	0	3	.143	.143	.143	-19	-1	0	.857	-1	101	98	/S-2	-0.2
1947	Phi N	2	7	1	2	0	0	0	0	1	0	0	.286	.375	.286	81	0	0	1.000	0	94	80	/S-2	0.0
1948	Phi N	129	446	42	116	21	5	3	48	22	2	39	.260	.298	.350	76	-16	2	.967	-10	98	92	2-87,S-37/3-3	-2.0
1949	Phi N	**154**	662	83	174	32	5	6	53	25	0	47	.263	.290	.353	74	-27	6	.961	-3	104	**111**	*S-154	-2.0
1950	†Phi N	**157**	637	78	172	27	5	11	82	39	2	35	.270	.314	.380	83	-18	2	.944	-4	103	101	*S-157	-1.2
1951	Phi N	150	589	61	150	23	7	9	72	29	0	32	.255	.290	.363	76	-23	10-5	.958	-2	102	99	*S-150	-1.5
1952	Phi N★	151	596	74	164	30	5	17	87	27	0	51	.275	.307	.428	103	-1	7-3	.951	-2	106	113	*S-151	0.8
1953	Phi N★	154	609	90	168	30	8	21	92	32	1	28	.276	.313	.455	98	-5	2-1	.970	-6	108	108	2-93,S-71	0.1
1954	Phi N★	152	596	83	178	39	11	13	89	53	0	44	.299	.351	.466	112	10	1-2	.978	-20	94	95	*2-152/S	0.1
1955	Phi N	104	405	57	104	12	4	5	43	41-1	1	30	.257	.323	.343	79	-12	0-1	.960	-27	87	82	2-82,S-32	-3.2
1956	Phi N	122	401	42	90	24	3	4	42	30-5	0	42	.224	.276	.329	64	-21	2-0	.937	-13	95	102	*S-110,2-11/P-3	-2.5
1957	Phi N	133	502	59	114	19	5	10	62	34-3	0	42	.227	.274	.345	68	-24	3-1	.963	-33	82	72	*2-125/S-5,P	-4.9
1958	Phi N	35	133	18	40	7	3	2	18	8-0	0	16	.301	.340	.444	107	1	0-0	.984	-3	102	165	3-22,2-11/S-3	-0.1
1959	Phi N	21	64	10	19	4	0	2	6	5-1	0	5	.297	.348	.453	109	1	0-1	.947	-3	104	51	S-15/3	-0.1
	Cle A	27	67	4	11	1	1	1	3	1-0	0	8	.164	.174	.254	17	-8	0-0	.960	-2	81	62	S-10/2-7,3-5	-1.0
1962	KC A	3	0	0	0	0	0	0	0	0-0	0	0	—	—	—	—	0	0-0	1.000	0	157	0	/P-3	0.0
Total	17	1531	5839	711	1529	272	62	104	708	351-10	6	432	.262	.303	.383	84	-154	35-14	.946	-123	101	103	S-934,2-568/3-31,P-7	-17.9
HAMNER, GARVIN Wesley Garvin B 3.18.1924 Richmond, VA BR/TR 5-11/172# d4.17 b-Granny																								
1945	Phi N	32	101	12	20	3	0	0	5	7	0	9	.198	.250	.228	34	-9	2	.962	-4	103	75	2-21/S-9,3	-1.1
HAMPTON, IKE Isaac Bernard B 8.22.1951 Camden, SC BB/TR (BR 1978-79) 6-1/185# d9.12																								
1974	NY N	4	4	0	0	0	0	0	1	0-0	0	1	.000	.000	.000	-99	-1	0-0	1.000	-0	30	0	/C	-0.1
1975	Cal A	31	66	8	10	3	0	0	4	7-0	1	19	.152	.243	.197	28	-6	0-0	.947	-9	100	125	C-28/S-2,3	-1.5
1976	Cal A	3	2	0	0	0	0	0	0	0-0	0	0	.000	.000	.000	-99	-1	0-0	1.000	0	0	0	/C-2,S	0.0
1977	Cal A	52	44	5	13	1	0	3	9	2-0	1	10	.295	.340	.523	137	2	0-0	.968	-4	85	98	C-47/D-2	-0.1
1978	Cal A	19	14	2	3	0	1	1	4	2-0	0	7	.214	.313	.571	149	1	1-0	.905	-1	52	81	C-13/1D	0.0

Year	Tm Lg	G	AB	R	H	2B	3B	HR	RBI	BB-IB	HP	SO	AVG	OBP	SLG	AOPS	ABR	SB-CS	FA	FR	Rng	Thr	G at Pos	BFW
1979	Cal A	4	5	0	2	0	0	0	0	0-0	0	1	.400	.400	.400	121	0	0-0	1.000	0	211	0	/1-2	0.0
Total	6	113	135	15	28	4	1	4	18	11-0	2	38	.207	.275	.341	75	-5	1-0	.953	-14	89	110	/C-91,D-6,1-3,S-3,3	-1.7
HAMRIC, BERT Odbert Herman B 3.1.1928 Clarksburg, WV D 8.8.1984 Springboro, OH BL/TR 6/165# d4.24																								
1955	Bro N	2	1	0	0	0	0	0	0	0-0	0	1	.000	.000	.000	-97	0	0-0	—	0			H	0.0
1958	Bal A	8	8	0	1	0	0	0	0	0-0	0	6	.125	.125	.125	-33	-1	0-0	—	0			H	-0.2
Total	2	10	9	0	1	0	0	0	0	0-0	0	7	.111	.111	.111	-41	-1	0-0	.953	0				-0.2
HAMRICK, RAY Raymond Bernard B 8.1.1921 Nashville, TN BR/TR 5-11.5/160# d8.14 Mil 1944-46																								
1943	Phi N	44	160	12	32	3	1	0	9	8	0	28	.200	.238	.231	37	-14	0	.960	-8	96	53	2-31,S-12	-2.0
1944	Phi N	74	292	22	60	10	1	1	23	23	2	34	.205	.268	.257	50	-20	1	.948	13	114	122	S-74	0.0
Total	2	118	452	34	92	13	2	1	32	31	2	62	.204	.258	.248	46	-34	1	.946	6	111	111	/S-86,2-31	-2.0
HANCKEN, BUDDY Morris Medlock B 8.30.1914 Birmingham, AL BR/TR 6-1/175# d5.14 C5																								
1940	Phi A	1	0	0	0	0	0	0	0	0	0	0	—	—	—	—	0	0-0	1.000	-0	*0*	*0*	/C	0.0
HANCOCK, FRED Fred James B 3.28.1920 Allenport, PA D 3.12.1986 Clearwater, FL BR/TR 5-8/170# d4,26																								
1949	Chi A	39	52	7	7	2	1	0	9	8	1	9	.135	.262	.212	27	-6	0-1	.978	-2	83	140	S-27/3-3,O(RF)	-0.7
HANCOCK, GARRY Ronald Garry B 1.23.1954 Tampa, FL BL/TL 6/175# d7.16																								
1978	Bos A	38	80	10	18	3	0	0	4	1-0	0	12	.225	.232	.262	36	-7	0-0	1.000	2	105	355	O-19(4-5-10),D-13	-0.5
1980	Bos A	46	115	9	33	6	0	4	19	3-0	0	11	.287	.300	.443	97	-1	0-3	.963	-1	81	185	O-27(6-20-1),D-12	-0.4
1981	Bos A	26	45	4	7	3	0	0	3	2-1	0	4	.156	.191	.222	18	-5	0-0	1.000	1	74	566	/O-8(0-5-3),D-4	-0.4
1982	Bos A	11	14	3	0	0	0	0	0	1-0	0	1	.000	.067	.000	-75	-3	0-0	1.000	-1	58	0	/O-7(RF)	-0.4
1983	Oak A	101	256	29	70	7	3	8	30	5-4	1	13	.273	.289	.418	98	-3	2-0	.981	-1	107	115	O-67(26-1-40),1-27/D-9	-0.6
1984	Oak A	51	60	2	13	2	0	0	8	0-0	0	1	.217	.217	.250	31	-6	0-0	1.000	0	131	0	O-18(9-2-9)/1-4,PD	-0.6
Total	6	273	570	57	141	21	3	12	64	12-5	1	42	.247	.262	.358	71	-25	2-3	.982	1	98	177	O-146(45-33-70)/D-43,1-31,P	-2.9
HANDIBOE, MIKE Aloysius James "Coalyard Mike" B 7.21.1887 Washington, DC D 1.31.1953 Savannah, GA BL/TL 5-10/155# d9.8																								
1911	NY A	5	15	0	1	0	0	0	0	2	0		.067	.176	.067	-29	-3	0	1.000	-0	108	0	/O-4(2-0-2)	-0.3
HANDLEY, GENE Eugene Louis B 11.25.1914 Kennett, MO BR/TR 5-10.5/165# d4.16 b-Lee																								
1946	Phi A	89	251	31	63	8	5	0	21	22	0	25	.251	.311	.323	78	-8	8-3	.947	-16	80	71	2-68/3-4,S	-2.1
1947	Phi A	36	90	10	23	2	1	0	8	10	0	2	.256	.330	.300	74	-3	1-0	.973	-6	92	98	2-17,3-10/S	-0.8
Total	2	125	341	41	86	10	6	0	29	32	0	27	.252	.316	.317	77	-11	9-3	.952	-21	82	76	/2-85,3-14,S-2	-2.9
HANDLEY, LEE Lee Elmer "Jeep" B 7.31.1913 Clarion, IA D 4.8.1970 Pittsburgh, PA BR/TR 5-7/160# d4.15 b-Gene																								
1936	Cin N	24	78	10	24	1	0	2	8	7	0	16	.308	.365	.397	112	1	3	.926	-1	95	67	2-16/3-7	0.2
1937	Pit N	127	480	59	120	21	12	3	37	37	1	40	.250	.305	.363	81	-14	5	.950	-14	91	91	*2-126/3	-2.0
1938	Pit N	139	570	91	153	25	8	6	51	53	1	31	.268	.332	.372	93	-6	7	.948	11	**115**	115	*3-136	1.0
1939	Pit N	101	376	43	107	14	5	1	42	32	0	20	.285	.341	.356	89	-6	**17**	.936	-3	102	82	*3-100	-0.6
1940	Pit N	98	302	50	85	7	4	1	19	27	0	16	.281	.340	.341	89	-4	7	.925	0	101	99	3-80/2-2	-0.1
1941	Pit N	124	459	59	132	18	4	0	33	35	0	22	.288	.338	.344	93	-5	16	.947	1	105	92	*3-114	0.1
1944	Pit N	40	86	7	19	2	0	0	5	3	0	5	.221	.247	.244	37	-7	1	.947	1	92	101	2-19,3-11/S-3	-0.6
1945	Pit N	98	312	39	93	16	2	1	32	20	0	16	.298	.340	.372	94	-3	7	.947	11	116	95	3-79	0.9
1946	Pit N	116	416	43	99	8	7	1	28	29	1	20	.238	.289	.298	65	-21	4	.958	12	122	82	*3-102/2-3	-0.9
1947	Phi N	101	277	17	70	10	3	0	42	24	0	18	.253	.312	.310	68	-13	1	.975	0	101	62	3-83/2-3,S	-1.3
Total	10	968	3356	418	902	122	45	15	297	267	3	204	.269	.323	.345	84	-78	68	.949	18	110	92	3-713,2-169/S-4	-3.3
HANEBRINK, HARRY Harry Aloysius B 11.12.1927 St.Louis, MO D 9.9.1996 Bridgeton, MO BL/TR 6/165# d5.3																								
1953	Mil N	51	80	8	19	1	1	1	8	6	0	8	.237	.291	.313	61	-5	1-0	.979	2	106	149	2-21/3	-0.2
1957	Mil N	6	7	0	2	0	0	0	0	1-0	0	2	.286	.375	.286	87	0	0-0	1.000	0	181	0	/3-2	0.0
1958	†Mil N	63	133	14	25	3	0	4	10	13-2	2	9	.188	.270	.301	56	-9	0-1	.982	1	101	145	O-33(24-0-9)/3-7	-1.0
1959	Phi N	57	97	10	25	3	1	1	7	2-0	0	12	.258	.273	.340	61	-6	0-0	.889	-3	77	164	2-15/3-9,O(RF)	-0.9
Total	4	177	317	32	71	7	2	6	25	22-2	2	31	.224	.279	.315	60	-20	1-1	.959	-1	99	153	/2-36,O-34(24-0-10),3-19	-2.1
HANEY, FRED Fred Girard "Pudge" B 4.25.1898 Albuquerque, NM D 11.9.1977 Beverly Hills, CA BR/TR 5-6/170# d4.18 M10 C1																								
1922	Det A	81	213	41	75	7	4	0	25	32	1	14	.352	.439	.423	129	11	3-8	.937	3	114	130	3-53,1-11/S-2	1.3
1923	Det A	142	503	85	142	13	4	4	67	45	5	23	.282	.347	.348	85	-11	13-5	.955	-2	94	74	2-69,3-55,S-16	-0.5
1924	Det A	86	256	54	79	11	1	1	30	39	0	13	.309	.400	.371	101	2	7-4	.933	1	117	90	3-59/S-4,2-3	0.8
1925	Det A	114	398	84	111	15	3	0	40	66	2	29	.279	.384	.332	84	-6	11-1	.953	-1	99	107	*3-106	0.1
1926	Bos A	138	462	47	102	15	7	0	52	74	1	28	.221	.330	.284	63	-24	13-6	.957	8	**110**	113	*3-137	-0.7
1927	Bos A	47	116	23	32	4	1	3	12	25	0	14	.276	.404	.405	113	3	4-1	.936	-3	81	66	3-34/O(CF)	0.3
	Chi N	4	3	0	0	0	0	0	0	0	0	0	.000	.000	.000	-99	-1	0	—	0			H	-0.1
1929	StL N	10	26	4	3	1	1	0	2	1	1	2	.115	.179	.231	1	-4	0	.958	1	110	191	/3-6	-0.3
Total	7	622	1977	338	544	66	21	8	228	282	10	123	.275	.368	.342	87	-30	51-25	.949	7	106	110	3-450/2-72,S-22,1-11,O(CF)	0.9
HANEY, TODD Todd Michael B 7.30.1965 Waco, TX BR/TR 5-9/165# d9.9																								
1992	Mon N	7	10	0	3	1	0	0	1	0-0	0	0	.300	.300	.400	97	0	0-0	1.000	-1	93	80	/2-5	-0.1
1994	Chi N	17	37	6	6	0	0	1	2	3-0	1	3	.162	.238	.243	28	-4	2-1	.979	-0	95	139	2-11/3-3	-0.4
1995	Chi N	25	73	11	30	8	0	2	6	7-0	0	11	.411	.463	.603	182	9	0-0	.978	4	125	124	2-17/3-4	1.3
1996	Chi N	49	82	11	11	1	0	0	3	7-0	0	15	.134	.200	.146	-6	-13	1-0	.978	4	129	124	2-23/3-4,S-3	-0.7
1998	NY N	3	3	0	0	0	0	0	0	1-0	0	0	.000	.250	.000	-27	-1	0-0	—	-1	0	0	/2O(LF)	-0.1
Total	5	101	205	28	50	10	0	3	12	18-0	1	29	.244	.305	.337	70	-9	3-1	.979	7	118	124	/2-57,3-11,S-3,O(LF)	-0.0
HANEY, LARRY Wallace Larry B 11.19.1942 Charlottesville, VA BR/TR 6-2/195# d7.27 C14 s-Chris																								
1966	Bal A	20	56	3	9	1	0	1	3	1-0	1	15	.161	.190	.232	21	-6	0-0	.985	0	*93*	*91*	C-20	-0.5
1967	Bal A	58	164	13	44	11	0	3	20	6-0	0	28	.268	.294	.390	101	0	1-0	.991	-1	103	139	C-57	0.2
1968	Bal A	38	89	5	21	3	1	1	5	0-0	0	19	.236	.236	.326	69	-4	0-0	.994	1	89	186	C-32	-0.3
1969	Sea A	22	59	3	15	3	0	2	7	6-0	0	12	.254	.323	.407	105	0	1-1	.956	-3	50	89	C-20	-0.2
	Oak A	53	86	8	13	4	0	2	12	7-1	1	19	.151	.221	.267	38	-7	0-0	.994	-5	102	114	C-53	-1.1
	Year	75	145	11	28	7	0	4	19	13-1	1	31	.193	.262	.324	66	-7	1-1	.979	-8	84	105	C-73	-1.3
1970	Oak A	2	2	2	0	0	0	0	0	2-0	0	1	.000	.500	.000	51	0	0-0	1.000	-0	37	0	/C	0.0
1972	Oak A	5	4	0	0	0	0	0	0	0-0	0	1	.000	.000	.000	-99	-1	0-0	.800	-1	0	0	/C-4,2	-0.2
1973	Oak A	2	2	0	1	0	0	0	0	0-0	0	0	.500	.500	.500	192	0	0-0	1.000	0	0	0	/C-2	0.0
	StL N	2	1	0	0	0	0	0	0	0-0	0	1	.000	.000	.000	-99	0	0-0	1.000	-0	0	0	/C-2	0.0
1974	†Oak A	76	121	12	20	4	0	2	3	3-0	0	18	.165	.185	.248	25	-12	1-0	.992	2	152	94	C-73/3-3,1-2	-0.9
1975	Oak A	47	26	3	5	0	0	1	2	1-0	0	4	.192	.222	.308	50	-2	0-0	1.000	0	115	59	C-43/3-4	-0.1
1976	Oak A	88	177	12	40	2	0	0	10	13-0	1	26	.226	.280	.237	56	-10	0-1	.974	0	82	106	C-87	-0.7
1977	Mil A	63	127	7	29	2	0	0	10	5-0	0	30	.228	.254	.244	38	-11	0-0	.985	5	118	84	C-63	-0.4
1978	Mil A	4	5	0	1	0	0	0	1	0-0	0	1	.200	.200	.200	13	-1	0-0	1.000	-0	0	0	/C-4	-0.1
Total	12	480	919	68	198	30	1	12	73	44-1	3	175	.215	.252	.289	57	-54	3-2	.985	-2	*103*	*108*	C-461/3-7,1-2,2	-4.3
HANFORD, CHARLIE Charles Joseph B 6.3.1881 Tunstall, England D 7.19.1963 Trenton, NJ BR/TR 5-6.5/145# d4.13																								
1914	Buf F	**155**	597	83	174	28	13	12	90	32	4	81	.291	.332	.442	107	-6	37	.973	7	104	114	*O-155(CF)	-1.0
1915	Chi F	77	179	27	43	4	5	0	22	12	2	28	.240	.295	.318	77	-9	10	.971	-2	105	41	O-43(10-1-32)	-1.4
Total	2	232	776	110	217	32	18	12	112	44	6	109	.280	.323	.414	101	-15	47	.972	5	104	100	O-198(10-156-32)	-2.4
HANKINS, JAY Jay Nelson B 11.7.1935 St.Louis Co., MO BL/TR 5-7/170# d4.15																								
1961	KC A	76	173	23	32	0	3	3	6	8-0	1	17	.185	.225	.272	32	-18	2-0	.970	-2	102	35	O-65(23-31-14)	-2.1
1963	KC A	10	34	2	6	0	1	1	4	0-0	0	3	.176	.176	.324	35	-3	0-1	.952	1	126	245	/O-9(CF)	-0.3
Total	2	86	207	25	38	0	4	4	10	8-0	1	20	.184	.218	.280	32	-21	2-1	.967	-0	105	62	/O-74(23-40-14)	-2.4
HANKINSON, FRANK Frank Edward B 4.29.1856 New York, NY D 4.5.1911 Palisades Park, NJ BR/TR 5-11/168# d5.1 I OF Total (26-LF 8-CF 1-RF)																								
1878	Chi N	58	240	38	64	8	3	1	27	5		36	.267	.282	.338	96	-2		.875	8	110	**135**	*3-57/P	0.7
1879	Chi N	44	171	14	31	4	0	0	8	2		14	.181	.191	.205	29	-13		.933	7	139	105	P-26,O-14(10-4-0)/3-5	-0.1
1880	Cle N	69	263	32	55	7	4	1	19	1		23	.209	.212	.278	66	-9		.844	-10	77	127	*3-56,O-12(10-2-0)/P-4	-1.8
1881	Tro N	**85**	321	34	62	15	0	1	19	10		41	.193	.218	.249	44	-20		.907	5	99	**161**	*3-84/S	-1.1

Year	Tm Lg	G	AB	R	H	2B	3B	HR	RBI	BB-IB	HP	SO	AVG	OBP	SLG	AOPS	ABR	SB-CS	FA	FR	Rng	Thr	G at Pos	BFW
1883	NY N	94	337	40	74	13	6	2	30	19		38	.220	.261	.312	74	-10		.870	-2	93	75	*3-93/O(RF)	-0.9
1884	NY N	105	389	44	90	16	7	2	43	23		59	.231	.274	.324	85	-7		.871	1	94	61	*3-105/O(CF)	-0.4
1885	NY AA	94	362	43	81	12	2	2	44	12	1		.224	.251	.285	72	-11		**.906**	21	**123**	67	*3-94/P	1.0
1886	NY AA	136	522	66	126	14	5	2	63	49	0		.241	.306	.299	98	2	10	.873	27	**118**	**139**	*3-136	2.7
1887	NY AA	127	512	79	137	29	11	1	71	38	0		.268	.318	.373	97	-2	19	.864	9	**109**	120	*3-127	0.7
1888	KC AA	37	155	20	27	4	1	1	20	11	0		.174	.229	.232	45	-10	2	.947	-2	105	54	2-13/S-9,O-7(6-1-0),3-7,1-2	-1.0
Total	10	849	3272	410	747	122	39	13	344	170	1	211	.228	.267	.301	77	-82	31	.875	63	105	109	3-764/O-35L,P-32,2-13,S-10,1-2	-0.2
HANLON, NED Edward Hugh B 8.22.1857 Montville, CT D 4.14.1937 Baltimore, MD BL/TR 5-9.5/170# d5.1 M19 HF1996																								
1880	Cle N	73	280	30	69	10	3	0	32	11		30	.246	.275	.304	98	0		.804	-6	50	135	*O-69(67-2-0)/S-4	-1.0
1881	Det N	76	305	63	85	14	8	2	28	22		11	.279	.327	.397	122	7		.897	-6	77	134	*O-74(2-72-0)/S-2	-0.1
1882	Det N	82	347	68	80	18	6	5	38	26		25	.231	.284	.360	105	3		.887	10	100	**201**	*O-82(CF)/2	0.9
1883	Det N	100	413	65	100	13	2	1	40	34		44	.242	.300	.291	84	-6		.884	-2	63	172	*O-90(2-88-0),2-11	-0.9
1884	Det N	**114**	450	86	119	18	6	5	39	40		52	.264	.324	.364	124	15		.874	12	132	123	*O-114(CF)	2.1
1885	Det N	105	424	93	128	18	8	1	29	47		18	.302	.372	.389	146	23		.863	1	95	71	*O-105(CF)	2.0
1886	Det N	**126**	494	105	116	6	6	4	60	57		39	.235	.314	.296	83	-9	50	.929	-7	72	118	*O-126(CF)/2	-1.9
1887	†Det N	118	471	79	129	13	7	4	69	30	2	24	.274	.320	.357	84	-11	69	.904	1	86	110	*O-118(1-117-0)	-1.2
1888	Det N	109	459	64	122	6	8	5	39	15	4	32	.266	.295	.346	103	0	38	.919	-8	38	87	*O-109(CF)	-1.2
1889	Pit N	116	461	81	110	14	10	2	37	58	2	25	.239	.326	.325	91	-4	53	.919	-3	82	52	*O-116(CF),M	-0.9
1890	Pit P	118	472	106	131	16	6	1	44	80	6	24	.278	.389	.343	105	10	65	.911	-4	70	98	*O-118(CF),M	0.2
1891	Pit N	119	455	87	121	12	8	0	60	48	4	30	.266	.341	.327	97	-1	54	.881	-1	137	32	*O-119(39-80-0)/SM	-0.5
1892	Bal N	11	43	3	7	1	1	0	2	3	0	3	.163	.217	.233	35	-4	0	.786	-1	105	0	O-11(8-2-1),M	-0.5
Total	13	1267	5074	930	1317	159	79	30	517	471	18	357	.260	.325	.340	102	23	329	.891	-14	85	106	*O-1251(119-1130-1)/2-13,S-7	-3.0
HANLON, BILL William Joseph "Big Bill" B 6.24.1876 Los Angeles, CA D 11.23.1905 Los Angeles, CA BR 6/175# d4.16																								
1903	Chi N	8	21	4	2	0	0	0	2	6	0		.095	.296	.095	14	-2	1	.980	-0	86	54	/1-8	-0.2
HANNA, JOHN John B 11.3.1863 Philadelphia, PA D 11.7.1930 Philadelphia, PA d5.23																								
1884	Was AA	23	76	8	5	0	0	0		6	0		.066	.134	.066	-37	-11		.874	-0			C-18/O-6(1-1-4)	-0.9
	Ric AA	22	67	6	13	2	1	0		0	1		.194	.206	.254	50	-4		.924	3			C-21/S	0.1
	Year	45	143	14	18	2	1	0		6	1		.126	.167	.154	6	-14		.900	2			C-39/O-6(1-1-4),S	-0.8
HANNAH, TRUCK James Harrison B 6.5.1889 Larimore, ND D 4.27.1982 Fountain Valley, CA BR/TR 6-1/190# d4.15																								
1918	NY A	90	250	24	55	6	0	2	21	51	4	25	.220	.361	.268	88	0	5	.974	4	*121*	*99*	C-88	1.2
1919	NY A	75	227	14	54	8	3	1	20	22	3	19	.238	.313	.313	76	-7	0	**.984**	-6	*103*	*82*	C-73/1	-0.8
1920	NY A	79	259	24	64	11	1	2	25	24	1	35	.247	.313	.320	66	-13	2-0	.961	-2	*113*	*67*	C-78	-0.7
Total	3	244	736	62	173	25	4	5	66	97	8	79	.235	.331	.300	76	-20	7-0	.973	-5	*113*	*83*	C-239/1	-0.3
HANNIFAN, PAT Patrick James B 4.20.1866 Halifax, NS, CAN D 11.5.1908 Springfield, MA BB/TL d4.29																								
1897	Bro N	10	20	4	5	0	0	0	2	1	3		.250	.375	.250	71	-1	4	.867	0	302	774	/O-3(1-2-0),2-2	0.0
HANNIFIN, JACK John Joseph B 2.25.1883 Holyoke, MA D 10.27.1945 Northampton, MA BR/TR 5-11/167# d4.19																								
1906	Phi A	1	1	0	1	0	0	0	0	0	0		1.000	1.000	1.000	511	0	0	—	0			H	0.0
	NY N	10	30	4	6	0	1	0	3	2	0		.200	.250	.267	60	-2	1	.903	-0	98	107	/S-6,3-3,2	-0.2
1907	NY N	56	149	16	34	7	3	1	15	15	1		.228	.303	.336	97	-1	6	.996	-2	80	40	1-29,3-10/S-9,O-2(0-1-1)	-0.3
1908	NY N	1	2	0	0	0	0	0	0	0	0		.000	.000	.000	-95	0	0	—	-0	0	0	/O(RF)	-0.1
	Bos N	90	257	30	53	6	2	2	22	28	0		.206	.284	.268	78	-6	7	.930	5	113	342	3-35,2-22,S-15/O-7(2-1-2)	0.0
	Year	91	259	30	53	6	2	2	22	28	0		.205	.282	.266	77	-6	7	.930	5	113	342	3-35,2-22,S-15/O-8(2-1-3)	-0.1
Total	3	158	439	50	94	13	6	3	40	45	1		.214	.289	.292	84	-9	14	.937	2	106	302	/3-48,S-30,1-29,2-23,O-10(2-2-4)	-0.6
HANSEN, DAVE David Andrew B 11.24.1968 Long Beach, CA BL/TR 6/195# d9.16 OF Total (3-LF 2-RF)																								
1990	LA N	5	7	0	1	0	0	0	1	0-0	0	3	.143	.143	.143	-22	-1	0-0	.500	-1	48	0	/3-2	-0.2
1991	LA N	53	56	3	15	4	0	1	5	2-0	0	12	.268	.293	.393	93	-1	1-0	1.000	2	124	81	3-21/S	0.2
1992	LA N	132	341	30	73	11	0	6	22	34-3	1	49	.214	.286	.299	67	-15	0-2	**.968**	6	**107**	78	*3-108	-1.0
1993	LA N	84	105	13	38	3	0	4	30	21-3	0	13	.362	.465	.505	170	12	0-1	.927	0	106	42	3-18	1.2
1994	LA N	40	44	3	15	3	0	0	5	5-0	0	5	.341	.408	.409	122	2	0-0	.857	-1	84	0	/3-7	0.1
1995	†LA N	100	181	19	52	10	0	1	14	28-4	1	28	.287	.384	.359	107	4	0-0	.933	-4	85	91	3-58	0.0
1996	†LA N	80	104	7	23	1	0	0	6	11-1	0	22	.221	.293	.231	45	-8	0-0	.962	0	103	67	3-19/1-8	-0.9
1997	Chi N	90	151	19	47	8	2	3	21	31-1	1	32	.311	.429	.450	128	8	1-2	.922	-5	78	94	3-51/1-4,2	0.3
1999	LA N	100	107	14	27	8	1	2	17	26-0	2	20	.252	.404	.402	112	4	0-0	.982	-2	100	129	1-20,3-13/O-2(RF),D-2	0.2
2000	LA N	102	121	18	35	6	2	8	26	26-0	0	32	.289	.415	.570	155	11	0-1	.980	0	136	121	1-16,3-16/O-3(LF),D-5	1.0
2001	LA N	92	140	13	33	10	0	2	20	32-5	0	29	.236	.371	.350	97	1	0-1	.984	4	105	86	1-25,3-21/D	0.3
2002	LA N	96	120	15	35	6	0	2	17	14-3	0	22	.292	.363	.392	110	1	1-0	1.000	-0	85	40	1-27,3-11/D-4	0.0
2003	SD N	110	135	13	33	4	1	2	15	23-3	1	25	.244	.358	.333	90	-1	1-0	1.000	1	136	149	1-20,3-11/2D	-0.1
Total	13	1084	1612	167	427	74	6	31	199	253-23	6	292	.265	.365	.376	103	17	4-7	.945	-0	100	81	3-356,1-120/D-15,O-5L,2-2,S	1.1
HANSEN, DOUG Douglas William B 12.16.1928 Los Angeles, CA D 9.16.1999 Orem, UT BR/TR 6/180# d9.4																								
1951	Cle A	3	0	2	0	0	0	0	0	0	0	0	—	—	—	—	0	0-0	—	0			R	0.0
HANSEN, JED Jed Ramon B 8.19.1972 Tacoma, WA BR/TR 6-1/195# d7.29																								
1997	KC A	34	94	11	29	6	1	1	14	13-0	1	29	.309	.394	.426	112	2	3-2	.993	-2	99	90	2-31	0.2
1998	KC A	4	3	0	0	0	0	0	0	0-0	0	3	.000	.000	.000	-97	-1	0-0	1.000	-1	0	0	/2-2	-0.2
1999	KC A	49	79	16	16	1	0	3	5	10-0	0	32	.203	.289	.329	57	-5	0-1	.989	-1	79	130	2-21,S-10/3-4,O-2(CF),1D	-0.5
Total	3	87	176	27	45	7	1	4	19	23-0	1	64	.256	.342	.375	84	-4	3-3	.991	-3	90	105	/2-54,S-10,3-4,D-3,O-2(CF),1	-0.5
HANSEN, BOB Robert Joseph B 5.26.1948 Boston, MA BL/TL 6/195# d5.10																								
1974	Mil A	58	88	8	26	4	1	2	9	3-0	0	16	.295	.319	.432	115	1	2-1	1.000	-0	0	0	D-18/1-3	0.0
1976	Mil A	24	61	4	10	1	0	0	4	6-0	0	8	.164	.239	.180	24	-6	0-0	—	0	0	0	D-14/1	-0.7
Total	2	82	149	12	36	5	1	2	13	9-0	0	24	.242	.285	.329	78	-5	2-1	1.000	-0	0	0	/D-32,1-4	-0.7
HANSEN, RON Ronald Lavern B 4.5.1938 Oxford, NE BR/TR 6-3/200# d4.15 C9																								
1958	Bal A	12	19	1	0	0	0	0	1	0-0	1	7	.000	.048	.000	-90	-5	0-0	.943	-1	101	87	S-12	-0.6
1959	Bal A	2	4	0	0	0	0	0	0	1-0	0	1	.000	.200	.000	-41	-1	0-0	.889	0	124	107	/S-2	-0.1
1960	Bal A★	153	530	72	135	22	5	22	86	69-5	2	94	.255	.342	.440	111	8	3-3	.964	10	97	116	*S-153	3.1
1961	Bal A	155	533	51	132	13	2	12	51	66-2	1	96	.248	.329	.347	85	-11	1-3	.959	10	102	**131**	*S-149/2-7	1.1
1962	Bal A	71	196	12	34	7	0	3	17	30-3	2	36	.173	.289	.255	51	-13	0-1	.965	2	98	110	S-64	-0.7
1963	Chi A	144	482	55	109	17	2	13	67	78-2	0	74	.226	.330	.351	94	-2	1-1	.983	**28**	**115**	**122**	*S-144	3.9
1964	Chi A	158	575	85	150	25	3	20	68	73-7	6	73	.261	.347	.419	116	14	1-0	.975	14	107	**127**	*S-158	4.4
1965	Chi A	**162**	587	61	138	23	4	11	66	60-8	2	73	.235	.304	.344	91	-8	1-1	.969	13	**110**	114	*S-161/2	2.1
1966	Chi A	23	74	3	13	1	0	0	4	15-3	1	10	.176	.322	.189	55	-4	0-1	.946	1	101	131	S-23	-0.1
1967	Chi A	157	498	35	116	20	0	8	51	64-11	0	51	.233	.317	.321	94	-2	0-3	.964	2	106	**116**	*S-157	1.3
1968	Was A	86	275	28	51	12	0	8	28	35-5	2	49	.185	.281	.316	84	-5	0-0	.963	10	114	100	S-81/3-5	1.4
	Chi A	40	87	7	20	3	0	1	4	11-0	0	12	.230	.316	.299	86	-1	0-0	.959	2	125	114	3-29/S-7,2-2	0.2
	Year	126	362	35	71	15	0	9	32	46-5	2	61	.196	.290	.312	84	-6	0-0	.963	13	115	99	S-88,3-34/2-2	1.6
1969	Chi A	85	185	15	48	6	1	2	22	18-0	1	25	.259	.327	.335	82	-4	2-0	.967	1	101	106	2-26,1-21/S-8,3-7	-0.3
1970	NY A	59	91	13	27	4	0	4	14	19-0	1	9	.297	.420	.473	155	8	0-1	.983	0	106	88	S-15,3-11/2	1.0
1971	NY A	61	145	6	30	3	0	2	20	9-2	0	27	.207	.245	.269	51	-10	0-0	.918	-3	97	190	3-30/2-9,S-3	-1.3
1972	KC A	16	30	2	4	0	0	0	2	3-1	0	6	.133	.212	.133	4	-4	0-0	.944	4	134	54	/S-6,3-4,2	0.0
Total	15	1384	4311	446	1007	156	17	106	501	551-49	19	643	.234	.320	.351	92	-40	9-14	.968	93	106	117	*S-1143/3-86,2-47,1-21	15.4
HANSKI, DON Donald Thomas (born Donald Thomas Hanyzewski) B 2.27.1916 LaPorte, IN D 9.2.1957 Worth, IL BL/TL 5-11/180# d5.6 Mil 1945																								
1943	Chi A	9	21	1	5	1	0	0	2	0	0	5	.238	.238	.286	53	-1	0-1	.952	-0	105	135	/1-5,P	-0.2
1944	Chi A	2	1	0	0	0	0	0	0	0	0	0	.000	.000	.000	-99	0	0-0	—	-0	0	0	/P-2	0.0
Total	2	11	22	1	5	1	0	0	2	0	0	5	.227	.227	.273	46	-1	0-1	.952	-0	105	135	/1-5,P-3	-0.2
HANSON, HARRY Harry Francis B 1.17.1896 Elgin, IL D 10.5.1966 Savannah, GA BR/TR 5-11/?# d7.14																								
1913	NY A	1	2	0	0	0	0	0	0	0	0	0	.000	.000	.000	-99	-1	0	1.000	-0	*62*	*201*	/C	-0.1

Year	Tm Lg	G	AB	R	H	2B	3B	HR	RBI	BB-IB	HP	SO	AVG	OBP	SLG	AOPS	ABR	SB-CS	FA	FR	Rng	Thr	G at Pos	BFW
HAPPENNY, CLIFF John Clifford B 5.18.1901 Waltham, MA D 12.29.1988 Coral Springs, FL BR/TR 5-11/165# d7.2																								
1923	Chi A	32	86	7	19	5	0	0	10	3	1	13	.221	.256	.279	41	-8	0-0	.947	-1	124	133	2-19/S-9,3-2	-0.7
HARBRIDGE, BILL William Arthur "Yaller Bill" B 3.29.1855 Philadelphia, PA D 3.17.1924 Philadelphia, PA BL/TL ?/162# d5.15 OF Total (13-LF 112-CF 47-RF)																								
1875	Har NA	53	208	32	50	3	3	0	26	9		3	.240	.272	.284	89	-3	2-4	.871	2			C-31,O-13(RF),2-11/1-3,S	-0.2
1876	Har N	30	106	11	23	2	1	0	6	3		2	.217	.239	.255	59	-5		.799	1			C-24/O-6(0-2-4),1-2	-0.3
1877	Har N	41	167	18	37	5	2	0	8	3		6	.222	.235	.275	68	-5		.881	-6			C-32/O-5(0-3-2),2-4,3	-0.9
1878	Chi N	54	240	32	71	12	0	0	37	6		13	.296	.313	.346	109	2		.878	-6			*C-53/O-8(4-3-1)	-0.3
1879	Chi N	4	18	2	2	0	0	0	1	0		5	.111	.111	.111	-25	-2		.571	-1	125	0	/O-4(1-3-0)	-0.3
1880	Tro N	9	27	3	10	0	1	0	2	0		3	.370	.370	.444	166	2		.887	0			/C-9,O(0-1-1)	0.2
1882	Tro N	32	123	11	23	1	1	0	13	10		17	.187	.248	.211	52	-6		.836	-5	57	81	O-23(CF)/1-6,C-3	-1.1
1883	Phi N	73	280	32	62	12	3	0	21	24		20	.221	.283	.286	81	-4		.796	-12	72	50	O-44(8-36-0),S-11/2-9,C-7,3-5	-1.5
1884	Cin U	82	341	59	95	12	5	2		25			.279	.328	.361	101	-10		.906	4	**129**	79	*O-80(0-41-39)/S-3,1-2	-0.6
Total	8	325	1302	168	323	44	13	2	88	71		66	.248	.287	.306	86	-28		.849	-24			O-171C,C-128/S-14,2-13,1-10,3-6	-4.8
HARDESTY, SCOTT Scott Durbin B 1.26.1870 Bellville, OH D 10.29.1944 Fostoria, OH d8.17																								
1899	NY N	22	72	4	16	0	0	0	4	1	1		.222	.243	.222	29	-7	2	.895	4	117	118	S-20/1-2	-0.2
HARDGROVE, PAT William Henry B 5.10.1895 Palmyra, KS D 1.26.1973 Jackson, MS BR/TR 5-10/158# d6.8 Mil 1918																								
1918	Chi A	2	2	0	0	0	0	0	0	0	0	0	.000	.000	.000	-99	0	0	—	0			H	-0.1
HARDIE, LOU Louis W. B 8.24.1864 New York, NY D 3.5.1929 Oakland, CA BR 5-11/180# d5.22																								
1884	Phi N	3	8	0	3	2	0	0	0	0		2	.375	.375	.625	219	1		.857	-2			/C-3	-0.1
1886	Chi N	16	51	4	9	0	0	0	3	4		10	.176	.236	.176	24	-5	1	.964	0			C-13/O-2(RF),3	-0.3
1890	Bos N	47	185	17	42	8	0	3	17	18	0	36	.227	.296	.319	73	-7	4	.886	1	127	103	C-25,O-15(6-4-6)/3-7,S1	-0.4
1891	Bal AA	15	56	7	13	0	3	0	1	8	0	8	.232	.328	.339	90	-1	3	1.000	1	36	0	O-15(0-3-12)	0.0
Total	4	81	300	28	67	10	3	3	21	30	0	56	.223	.294	.307	71	-12	8	.910	-0	87	70	/C-41,O-32(6-7-20),3-8,1S	-0.8
HARDIN, BUD William Edgar B 6.14.1922 Shelby, NC D 7.28.1997 Rancho Santa Fe, CA BR/TR 5-10/165# d4.15																								
1952	Chi N	3	7	1	1	0	0	0	0	0	0	0	.143	.143	.143	-20	-1	0-0	1.000	-0	100	153	/S-2,2	-0.1
HARDING, ED Edward H. A. "Jumbo" B 1862 5-9.5/213# d10.5																								
1886	StL AA	1	3	0	1	1	0	0	1	0	0		.333	.333	.667	201	0	0	.889	1			/C	0.1
HARDTKE, JASON Jason Robert B 9.15.1971 Milwaukee, WI BB/TR 5-10/175# d9.8																								
1996	NY N	19	57	3	11	5	0	0	6	2-0	1	12	.193	.233	.281	36	-5	0-0	1.000	-3	85	102	2-18	-0.7
1997	NY N	30	56	9	15	2	0	2	8	4-1	1	6	.268	.323	.411	95	-1	1-1	.981	-6	70	93	2-21/3	-0.6
1998	Chi N	18	21	2	5	0	0	0	2	2-0	0	6	.238	.304	.238	44	-2	0-0	1.000	-0	101	0	/3-7,O(RF)D	-0.2
Total	3	67	134	14	31	7	0	2	16	8-1	2	24	.231	.283	.328	62	-8	1-1	.991	-9	78	98	/2-39,3-8,DO(RF)	-1.5
HARDY, CARROLL Carroll William B 5.18.1933 Sturgis, SD BR/TR 6/185# d4.15																								
1958	Cle A	27	49	10	10	3	0	1	6	6-0	1	14	.204	.298	.327	75	-1	1-2	1.000	2	114	270	O-17(0-16-1)	-0.1
1959	Cle A	32	53	12	11	1	0	0	2	3-0	0	7	.208	.250	.226	33	-5	1-1	1.000	1	133	0	O-15(1-14-0)	-0.4
1960	Cle A	29	18	7	2	1	0	0	1	2-0	0	2	.111	.200	.167	0	-3	0-0	1.000	1	184	0	O-17(4-9-5)	-0.1
	Bos A	73	145	26	34	5	2	2	15	17-0	0	40	.234	.313	.338	74	-5	3-2	.968	2	110	116	O-59(44-8-14)	-0.5
	Year	102	163	33	36	6	2	2	16	19-0	0	42	.221	.301	.319	67	-8	3-2	.973	4	117	105	O-76(48-17-19)	-0.6
1961	Bos A	85	281	46	74	20	2	3	36	26-0	2	53	.263	.330	.381	87	-5	4-2	.961	-0	94	156	O-76(20-38-21)	-0.8
1962	Bos A	115	362	52	78	13	5	8	36	54-1	2	68	.215	.318	.345	77	-11	3-7	.991	2	102	133	*O-105(3-45-64)	-1.7
1963	Hou N	15	44	5	10	3	0	0	3	3-0	0	7	.227	.277	.295	69	-2	1-0	.947	0	98	159	O-10(LF)	-0.2
1964	Hou N	46	157	13	29	1	1	2	12	8-0	2	30	.185	.232	.242	36	-14	0-0	.990	2	112	109	O-41(5-33-4)	-1.5
1967	Min A	11	8	1	3	0	0	1	2	1-0	0	1	.375	.444	.750	229	1	0-0	—	-0	0	0	/O-4(1-0-3)	0.1
Total	8	433	1117	172	251	47	10	17	113	120-1	7	222	.225	.302	.330	72	-45	13-14	.981	10	105	132	O-344(88-163-112)	-5.2
HARDY, JACK John Doolittle B 6.23.1877 Cleveland, OH D 10.20.1921 Cleveland, OH BR/TR 6/185# d8.29																								
1903	Cle A	5	19	1	3	1	0	0	1	1	0		.158	.200	.211	24	-2	1	1.000	-1	0	0	/O-5(RF)	-0.3
1907	Chi N	1	4	0	1	0	0	0	0	0	0		.250	.250	.250	53	0	0	.909	-0	158	76	/C	0.0
1909	Was A	10	24	3	4	0	0	0	4	1	0		.167	.200	.167	17	-2	0	.974	-1	83	32	/C-9,2	-0.4
1910	Was A	7	8	1	2	0	0	0	0	0	0		.250	.250	.250	59	0	0	.933	0	119	104	/C-4,O(LF)	0.0
Total	4	23	55	5	10	1	0	0	5	2	0		.182	.211	.200	28	-4	1	.953	-2	102	54	/C-14,O-6(1-0-5),2	-0.7
HARE, SHAWN Shawn Robert B 3.26.1967 St.Louis, MO BL/TL 6-2/190# d9.6																								
1991	Det A	9	19	0	1	1	0	0	0	2-0	0	1	.053	.143	.105	-30	-3	0-0	1.000	1	124	387	/O-6(RF),D-2	-0.3
1992	Det A	15	26	0	3	1	0	0	5	2-0	0	4	.115	.172	.154	-6	-4	0-0	1.000	0	104	0	/O-9(3-0-7),1-4	-0.4
1994	NY N	22	40	7	9	1	1	0	2	4-0	0	11	.225	.295	.300	56	-3	0-0	1.000	0	119	0	O-14(LF)	-0.3
1995	Tex A	18	24	2	6	1	0	0	2	4-0	0	6	.250	.357	.292	70	-1	0-0	1.000	0	86	283	/O-9(4-0-5),1D	-0.1
Total	4	64	109	9	19	4	1	0	9	12-0	0	22	.174	.254	.229	31	-11	0-0	1.000	2	109	117	/O-38(21-0-18),1-5,D-5	-1.1
HARGIS, GARY Gary Lynn B 11.2.1956 Minneapolis, MN BR/TR 5-11/165# d9.29																								
1979	Pit N	1	0	0	0	0	0	0	0	0-0	0	0	—	—	—	—	0	0-0	—	0			/R	0.0
HARGRAVE, BUBBLES Eugene Franklin B 7.15.1892 New Haven, IN D 2.23.1969 Cincinnati, OH BR/TR 5-10.5/174# d9.18 b-Pinky																								
1913	Chi N	3	3	0	1	0	0	0	1	0	0	0	.333	.333	.333	91	0	0	1.000	0	86	151	/C-2	0.0
1914	Chi N	23	36	3	8	2	0	0	2	0	0	4	.222	.222	.278	48	-2	2	.930	-3	82	61	C-16	-0.5
1915	Chi N	15	19	2	3	0	1	0	2	1	0	5	.158	.200	.263	40	-2	0	1.000	-0	79	147	/C-9	-0.2
1921	Cin N	93	263	28	76	17	8	1	38	12	3	15	.289	.327	.426	102	0	4-2	.973	-1	109	62	C-73	0.4
1922	Cin N	98	320	49	101	22	10	7	57	26	2	18	.316	.371	.512	128	12	7-4	.982	-2	114	76	C-87	1.5
1923	Cin N	118	378	54	126	23	9	10	78	44	**12**	22	.333	.419	.521	150	29	4-5	.988	4	106	110	*C-109	3.8
1924	Cin N	98	312	42	94	19	10	3	33	30	4	20	.301	.370	.455	122	10	2-2	.983	0	96	99	C-91	1.5
1925	Cin N	87	273	28	82	13	6	2	33	25	1	23	.300	.361	.414	100	0	4-3	.979	-7	75	73	C-84	-0.2
1926	Cin N	105	326	42	115	22	8	6	62	25	4	17	**.353**	.406	.525	153	24	2	.988	-7	109	62	C-93	2.2
1927	Cin N	102	305	36	94	18	3	0	35	31	2	18	.308	.376	.387	108	5	0	**.988**	-7	83	63	C-92	0.4
1928	Cin N	65	190	19	56	12	3	0	23	13	4	14	.295	.353	.389	95	-1	4	.991	2	103	99	C-57	0.4
1930	NY A	45	108	11	30	7	0	0	12	10	0	9	.278	.339	.343	77	-3	0-0	.992	-3	83	84	C-34	-0.5
Total	12	852	2533	314	786	155	58	29	376	217	32	165	.310	.372	.452	119	72	29-16	.983	-25	99	82	C-747	8.8
HARGRAVE, PINKY William McKinley B 1.31.1896 New Haven, IN D 10.3.1942 Ft.Wayne, IN BB/TR (BR 1923-26) 5-8.5/180# d5.18 b-Bubbles																								
1923	Was A	33	59	4	17	2	0	0	8	2	0	6	.288	.311	.322	70	-3	0-0	.917	-2	56	131	/3-8,C-5,O(LF)	-0.4
1924	Was A	24	33	3	5	1	0	0	5	1	0	4	.152	.176	.242	8	-5	0-0	1.000	-0	122	51	/C-8	-0.5
1925	Was A	5	6	0	3	0	0	0	0	1	0	2	.500	.571	.500	177	1	0-0	1.000	1	0	194	/C	0.1
	StL A	67	225	34	64	15	2	8	43	13	1	13	.284	.326	.476	97	-3	2-0	.981	-5	83	106	C-62	-0.3
	Year	72	231	34	67	15	2	8	43	14	1	15	.290	.333	.476	99	-2	2-0	.981	-5	81	108	C-63	-0.2
1926	StL A	92	235	20	66	16	3	7	37	10	3	38	.281	.319	.464	98	-2	3-0	.977	1	128	132	C-58	0.3
1928	Det A	121	320	38	88	13	5	10	63	32	1	28	.275	.343	.441	103	0	4-1	.977	-9	92	80	C-88	-0.3
1929	Det A	76	185	26	61	12	0	3	26	20	2	24	.330	.401	.443	117	6	2-2	.973	-4	72	129	C-48	0.4
1930	Det A	55	137	18	39	8	0	5	18	20	1	12	.285	.380	.453	108	2	2-0	.984	-4	67	74	C-40	0.1
	Was A	10	31	3	6	2	2	1	7	3	0	1	.194	.265	.484	85	-1	1-0	1.000	1	131	107	/C-9	0.1
	Year	65	168	21	45	10	2	6	25	23	1	13	.268	.359	.458	104	1	3-0	.987	-3	79	80	C-49	0.2
1931	Was A	40	80	6	26	8	0	1	19	9	0	12	.325	.393	.463	124	3	1-0	.978	-1	112	80	C-25	0.3
1932	Bos N	82	217	20	57	14	3	4	33	24	0	18	.263	.336	.410	103	1	1	.968	-0	139	100	C-73	0.5
1933	Bos N	45	73	5	13	0	0	0	6	5	1	7	.178	.241	.178	23	-7	1	.957	0	201	59	C-25	-0.7
Total	10	650	1601	177	445	91	16	39	265	140	9	165	.278	.339	.428	98	-8	17-3	.976	-24	105	99	C-442/3-8,O(LF)	-0.4
HARGREAVES, CHARLIE Charles Russell B 12.14.1896 Trenton, NJ D 5.9.1979 Neptune, NJ BR/TR 6/170# d6.27																								
1923	Bro N	20	57	5	16	0	0	0	4	1	0	2	.281	.293	.281	54	-4	0-0	.921	-3	75	75	C-15	-0.6
1924	Bro N	15	27	4	11	2	0	0	5	1	0	1	.407	.429	.481	148	2	0-1	1.000	-1	84	70	/C-9	0.1
1925	Bro N	45	83	9	23	3	1	0	13	6	0	1	.277	.326	.337	72	-4	1-1	.986	1	72	196	C-18/1-2	-0.2
1926	Bro N	85	208	14	52	13	2	2	23	19	1	10	.250	.316	.361	83	-5	1	.986	3	78	148	C-70	0.2
1927	Bro N	46	133	9	38	3	1	0	11	14	2	7	.286	.362	.323	85	-2	1	.985	1	78	125	C-44	0.2

Year	Tm Lg	G	AB	R	H	2B	3B	HR	RBI	BB-IB	HP	SO	AVG	OBP	SLG	AOPS	ABR	SB-CS	FA	FR	Rng	Thr	G at Pos	BFW
1928	Bro N	20	61	3	12	2	0	0	5	6	0	6	.197	.269	.230	32	-6	1	.979	1	*73*	*109*	C-20	-0.4
	Pit N	79	260	15	74	8	2	1	32	12	1	9	.285	.319	.342	70	-12	1	.962	-5	*80*	*105*	C-77	-1.1
	Year	99	321	18	86	10	2	1	37	18	1	15	.268	.309	.321	63	-18	2	.966	-4	*79*	*106*	C-97	-1.5
1929	Pit N	102	328	33	88	12	5	1	44	16	2	12	.268	.306	.345	60	-22	1	.981	4	*99*	*101*	*C-101	-1.1
1930	Pit N	11	31	4	7	1	0	0	2	2	0	1	.226	.273	.258	29	-4	0	1.000	4	*103*	*156*	C-11	0.1
Total	8	423	1188	96	321	44	11	4	139	77	6	49	.270	.318	.336	69	-57	6-2	.977	5	*85*	*119*	C-365/1-2	-2.8

HARGROVE, MIKE Dudley Michael B 10.26.1949 Perryton, TX BL/TL 6/195# d4.7 M13 C2

Year	Tm Lg	G	AB	R	H	2B	3B	HR	RBI	BB-IB	HP	SO	AVG	OBP	SLG	AOPS	ABR	SB-CS	FA	FR	Rng	Thr	G at Pos	BFW
1974	Tex A	131	415	57	134	18	6	4	66	49-4	4	42	.323	.395	.424	141	24	0-0	.987	8	140	84	1-91,D-32/O-6(LF)	2.5
1975	Tex A★	145	519	82	157	22	2	11	62	79-10	4	66	.303	.395	.416	132	26	4-3	.964	1	94	29	O-96(LF),1-48,D-12	1.8
1976	Tex A	151	541	80	155	30	1	7	58	**97**-13	6	64	.287	.397	.384	128	26	2-3	.984	0	106	89	*1-141/D-5	1.5
1977	Tex A	153	525	98	160	28	4	18	69	103-7	6	59	.305	.420	.476	143	38	2-5	.993	-3	92	117	*1-152	2.4
1978	Tex A	146	494	63	124	24	1	7	40	**107**-8	7	47	.251	.388	.346	109	13	2-5	.987	10	**132**	90	*1-140/D-4	1.4
1979	SD N	52	125	15	24	5	0	0	8	25-3	0	15	.192	.325	.232	59	-6	0-2	.986	-1	92	97	1-37	-1.0
	Cle A	100	338	60	110	21	4	10	56	63-2	5	40	.325	.433	.500	152	29	2-3	.993	-0	109	67	O-65(LF),1-28/D-7	2.3
1980	Cle A	**160**	589	86	179	22	2	11	85	111-10	8	36	.304	.415	.404	127	29	4-2	.993	-5	84	83	*1-160	1.5
1981	Cle A	94	322	43	102	21	0	2	49	60-5	5	16	.317	**.424**	.401	143	23	5-4	.989	5	121	81	1-88/D-4	2.4
1982	Cle A	160	591	67	160	26	1	4	65	101-3	3	58	.271	.377	.338	100	6	2-2	.996	8	115	83	*1-153/D-5	0.4
1983	Cle A	134	469	57	134	21	4	3	57	78-5	5	40	.286	.388	.367	107	9	0-6	.994	11	127	111	*1-131/D	0.9
1984	Cle A	133	352	44	94	14	2	2	44	53-3	0	38	.267	.361	.335	93	-1	0-2	.991	4	117	104	*1-124	-0.3
1985	Cle A	107	284	31	81	14	1	1	27	39-2	0	29	.285	.370	.352	100	2	1-0	.991	5	126	98	1-85	0.3
Total	12	1666	5564	783	1614	266	28	80	686	965-75	53	550	.290	.396	.391	121	218	24-37	.991	44	113	94	*1-1378,O-167(LF)/D-70	16.1

HARKNESS, TIM Thomas William B 12.23.1937 Lachine, PQ, CAN BL/TL 6-2/182# d9.12

Year	Tm Lg	G	AB	R	H	2B	3B	HR	RBI	BB-IB	HP	SO	AVG	OBP	SLG	AOPS	ABR	SB-CS	FA	FR	Rng	Thr	G at Pos	BFW
1961	LA N	5	8	4	4	2	0	0	0	3-0	0	1	.500	.636	.750	245	2	1-0	1.000	0	81	133	/1-2	0.2
1962	LA N	92	62	9	16	2	0	2	7	10-1	1	20	.258	.370	.387	110	1	1-0	1.000	0	101	138	1-59	0.1
1963	NY N	123	375	35	79	12	3	10	41	36-5	7	79	.211	.290	.339	80	-10	4-3	.986	17	166	86	*1-106	0.1
1964	NY N	39	117	11	33	2	1	2	13	9-1	1	18	.282	.336	.368	101	0	1-1	.993	3	146	138	1-32	0.2
Total	4	259	562	59	132	18	4	14	61	58-7	9	118	.235	.315	.356	90	-7	7-4	.989	20	155	101	1-199	0.6

HARLEY, DICK Richard Joseph B 9.25.1872 Philadelphia, PA D 4.3.1952 Philadelphia, PA BL/TR 5-10.5/165# d6.2

Year	Tm Lg	G	AB	R	H	2B	3B	HR	RBI	BB-IB	HP	SO	AVG	OBP	SLG	AOPS	ABR	SB-CS	FA	FR	Rng	Thr	G at Pos	BFW
1897	StL N	90	333	43	96	6	4	3	35	36	12		.288	.378	.357	97	0	23	.901	1	158	139	*O-90(1-89-0)	-0.4
1898	StL N	142	549	74	135	6	5	0	42	34	22		.246	.316	.275	68	-22	13	.926	8	129	60	*O-141(135-5-1)	-2.5
1899	Cle N	142	567	70	142	15	7	1	50	40	13		.250	.315	.307	76	-18	15	.924	8	128	94	*O-142(140-0-2)	-2.0
1900	Cin N	5	21	2	9	1	0	0	5	1	0		.429	.455	.476	161	2	4	1.000	-1	0	0	/O-5(LF)	0.1
1901	Cin N	133	535	69	146	13	2	4	27	31	9		.273	.323	.327	95	-3	37	.898	-4	118	43	*O-133(LF)	-1.5
1902	Det A	125	491	59	138	9	8	2	44	36	**12**		.281	.345	.344	90	-7	20	.930	1	96	31	*O-125(LF)	-1.2
1903	Chi N	104	386	72	89	9	1	0	33	45	11		.231	.328	.259	70	-13	27	.923	2	124	62	*O-103(RF)	-1.5
Total	7	741	2882	389	755	59	27	10	236	223	79		.262	.332	.312	83	-61	139	.918	14	123	68	O-739(539-94-106)	-9.0

HARLOW, LARRY Larry Duane B 11.13.1951 Colorado Springs, CO BL/TL 6-2/185# d9.20

Year	Tm Lg	G	AB	R	H	2B	3B	HR	RBI	BB-IB	HP	SO	AVG	OBP	SLG	AOPS	ABR	SB-CS	FA	FR	Rng	Thr	G at Pos	BFW
1975	Bal A	4	3	1	1	0	0	0	0	0-0	0	1	.333	.333	.333	95	0	0-0	1.000	-0	67	0	/O-4(2-2-0)	0.0
1977	Bal A	46	48	4	10	0	1	0	0	5-0	0	8	.208	.283	.250	50	-3	6-1	.887	-3	95	0	O-38(0-37-1)	-0.5
1978	Bal A	147	460	67	112	25	1	8	26	55-3	1	72	.243	.324	.354	97	-1	14-11	.979	-4	97	91	*O-138(0-135-3)/P	-0.6
1979	Bal A	38	41	5	11	1	0	0	1	7-0	0	4	.268	.375	.293	86	0	1-3	.970	-1	94	0	O-31(0-12-22)/D	-0.3
	†Cal A	62	159	22	37	8	2	0	14	25-0	2	34	.233	.344	.308	80	-3	1-3	.975	2	102	128	O-58(11-33-15)	-0.4
	Year	100	200	27	48	9	2	0	15	32-0	2	38	.240	.350	.305	81	-4	2-6	.974	1	100	98	O-89(11-45-37)/D	-0.7
1980	Cal A	109	301	47	83	13	4	4	27	48-1	1	61	.276	.376	.385	112	7	3-2	.976	13	123	179	O-94(5-32-59)/1D	1.7
1981	Cal A	43	82	13	17	1	0	0	4	16-0	0	25	.207	.337	.220	63	-3	1-1	.981	-2	91	56	O-39(21-7-13)	-0.6
Total	6	449	1094	159	271	48	8	12	72	156-4	4	205	.248	.343	.339	94	-3	26-21	.971	5	104	108	O-402(39-258-113)/D-2,1P	-0.7

HARMAN, BILL William Bell B 1.2.1919 Bridgewater, VA BR/TR 6-4/200# d6.17 Mil 1942 ▲

Year	Tm Lg	G	AB	R	H	2B	3B	HR	RBI	BB-IB	HP	SO	AVG	OBP	SLG	AOPS	ABR	SB-CS	FA	FR	Rng	Thr	G at Pos	BFW
1941	Phi N	15	14	1	1	0	0	0	0	0	0	3	.071	.071	.071	-62	-3	0	1.000	-1	75	0	/P-5,C-5	-0.2

HARMON, CHUCK Charles Byron B 4.23.1924 Washington, IN BR/TR 6-2/175# d4.17

Year	Tm Lg	G	AB	R	H	2B	3B	HR	RBI	BB-IB	HP	SO	AVG	OBP	SLG	AOPS	ABR	SB-CS	FA	FR	Rng	Thr	G at Pos	BFW
1954	Cin N	94	286	39	68	7	3	2	25	17	1	27	.238	.277	.304	52	-21	7-3	.961	4	103	164	3-67/1-3	-1.7
1955	Cin N	96	198	31	50	6	3	5	28	26-0	3	24	.253	.345	.389	90	-2	9-9	.935	2	91	63	3-39,O-32(32-2-0)/1-4	-0.3
1956	Cin N	13	4	2	0	0	0	0	0	0-0	0	0	.000	.000	.000	-94	-1	1-0	1.000	0	155	0	/O-6(1-1-4),1-2	-0.1
	StL N	20	15	2	0	0	0	0	0	2-0	0	2	.000	.118	.000	-65	-4	0-0	1.000	-1	102	0	O-11(3-4-5)/1-2,3	-0.4
	Year	33	19	4	0	0	0	0	0	2-0	0	2	.000	.095	.000	-70	-5	1-0	1.000	-0	117	0	O-17(4-5-9)/1-4,3	-0.5
1957	StL N	9	3	2	1	0	1	0	1	0-0	0	0	.333	.333	1.000	236	0	1-0	1.000	0	126	0	/O-8(0-1-7)	0.1
	Phi N	57	86	14	22	2	1	0	5	1-0	0	4	.256	.264	.302	53	-6	7-2	1.000	2	145	0	O-25(21-2-2)/3-5,1-2	-0.4
	Year	66	89	16	23	2	2	0	6	1-0	0	4	.258	.267	.326	60	-6	8-2	1.000	2	143	0	O-33(21-3-9)/3-5,1-2	-0.3
Total	4	289	592	90	141	15	8	7	59	46-0	4	57	.238	.294	.326	62	-34	25-14	.952	8	99	133	3-112/O-82(57-10-18),1-13	-2.8

HARMON, TERRY Terry Walter B 4.12.1944 Toledo, OH BR/TR 6-2/180# d7.23

Year	Tm Lg	G	AB	R	H	2B	3B	HR	RBI	BB-IB	HP	SO	AVG	OBP	SLG	AOPS	ABR	SB-CS	FA	FR	Rng	Thr	G at Pos	BFW
1967	Phi N	2	0	0	0	0	0	0	0	0-0	0	0	—	—	—	—	0	0-0	—	0			R	0.0
1969	Phi N	87	201	25	48	8	1	0	16	22-1	3	31	.239	.323	.289	74	-6	1-2	.968	7	105	130	S-38,2-19/3-2	0.6
1970	Phi N	71	129	16	32	2	4	0	7	12-1	1	22	.248	.315	.326	75	-5	6-3	.989	-10	76	72	S-35,2-14/3-2	-1.1
1971	Phi N	79	221	27	45	4	2	0	12	20-0	4	45	.204	.279	.240	49	-15	3-2	.986	4	111	111	2-58/S-9,3-3,1-2	-0.7
1972	Phi N	73	218	35	62	8	2	2	13	29-0	2	28	.284	.372	.367	108	4	3-2	.996	6	114	112	2-50,S-15/3-5	1.5
1973	Phi N	72	148	17	31	3	0	0	8	13-3	1	14	.209	.278	.230	41	-12	1-0	.988	-1	84	92	2-43,S-19/3	-1.0
1974	Phi N	27	15	5	2	0	0	0	0	3-0	0	3	.133	.278	.133	17	-2	0-0	1.000	-1	41	71	/S-7,2-5	-0.2
1975	Phi N	48	72	14	13	1	2	0	5	9-0	1	13	.181	.280	.250	46	-5	0-0	.989	-5	86	68	S-25/2-7,3	-0.8
1976	†Phi N	42	61	12	18	4	1	0	6	3-0	0	10	.295	.328	.393	101	0	3-0	.960	-3	85	64	S-19,2-13/3-5	-0.1
1977	Phi N	46	60	13	11	1	0	2	5	6-0	1	9	.183	.265	.300	50	-4	0-2	.982	3	132	175	2-28,S-16/3-3	-0.1
Total	10	547	1125	164	262	31	12	4	72	117-5	13	175	.233	.311	.292	69	-45	17-11	.989	1	106	107	2-237,S-183/3-22,1-2	-1.9

HARPER, BRIAN Brian David B 10.16.1959 Los Angeles, CA BR/TR 6-2/195# d9.29 OF Total (78-LF 38-RF)

Year	Tm Lg	G	AB	R	H	2B	3B	HR	RBI	BB-IB	HP	SO	AVG	OBP	SLG	AOPS	ABR	SB-CS	FA	FR	Rng	Thr	G at Pos	BFW
1979	Cal A	1	2	0	0	0	0	0	0	0-0	0	1	.000	.000	.000	-99	-1	0-0	—	0			/D	-0.1
1981	Cal A	4	11	1	3	0	0	0	1	0-0	0	0	.273	.250	.273	58	-1	1-0	.833	-0	125	0	/O-2(1-0-1),D	-0.1
1982	Pit N	20	29	4	8	1	0	2	4	1-1	0	4	.276	.300	.517	121	1	0-0	1.000	-0	104	0	/O-8(RF)	0.0
1983	Pit N	61	131	16	29	4	1	7	20	2-0	1	15	.221	.232	.427	79	-5	0-0	1.000	-3	82	0	O-35(33-0-2)/1	-0.9
1984	Pit N	46	112	4	29	4	0	2	11	5-0	2	11	.259	.300	.348	82	-3	0-0	.981	1	101	150	O-37(34-0-4)/C-2	-0.3
1985	†StL N	43	52	5	13	4	0	0	8	2-0	0	3	.250	.273	.327	69	-2	0-0	1.000	-1	109	0	O-13(7-0-6)/3-6,C-2,1	-0.3
1986	Det A	19	36	2	5	1	0	0	3	3-0	0	3	.139	.200	.167	3	-5	0-0	.929	0	100	0	O-11(RF)/C-2,1-2,D-6	-0.5
1987	Oak A	11	17	1	4	1	0	0	3	0-0	0	4	.235	.222	.294	42	-1	0-0	—	-0	0	0	/O(LF)D	-0.1
1988	Min A	60	166	15	49	11	1	3	20	10-1	3	12	.295	.344	.428	112	3	0-3	.991	-5	123	100	C-48/3-2,D-5	-0.1
1989	Min A	126	385	43	125	24	0	8	57	13-3	6	16	.325	.353	.449	118	9	2-4	.978	-4	112	96	*C-101,D-19/O-3(RF),1-2,3-2	0.8
1990	Min A	134	479	61	141	42	3	6	54	19-2	7	27	.294	.328	.432	105	3	3-2	.985	9	86	130	*C-120,D-11/3-3,1-2	1.8
1991	†Min A	123	441	54	137	28	1	10	69	14-3	6	22	.311	.336	.447	111	6	1-2	.988	-5	73	78	*C-119/1O(LF)D	0.7
1992	Min A	140	502	58	154	25	0	9	73	26-7	7	22	.307	.343	.410	109	5	0-1	.984	-3	79	108	*C-133/D-2	1.0
1993	Min A	147	530	52	161	26	1	12	73	29-9	9	29	.304	.347	.425	107	4	1-3	.988	-12	77	113	*C-134/D-7	0.0
1994	Mil A	64	251	23	73	15	0	4	32	9-1	3	18	.291	.318	.398	81	-7	0-2	.981	1	58	118	D-36,C-25/O-3(1-0-3)	-0.7
1995	Oak A	2	7	0	0	0	0	0	0	0-0	0	1	.000	.000	.000	-99	-2	0-0	1.000	-1	0	0	/C-2	-0.3
Total	16	1001	3151	339	931	186	7	63	428	133-27	44	188	.295	.329	.419	102	4	8-17	.985	-21	85	106	C-688,O-114L/D-97,3-13,1-9	0.9

HARPER, GEORGE George Washington B 6.24.1892 Arlington, KY D 8.18.1978 Magnolia, AR BL/TR 5-8/167# d4.15

Year	Tm Lg	G	AB	R	H	2B	3B	HR	RBI	BB-IB	HP	SO	AVG	OBP	SLG	AOPS	ABR	SB-CS	FA	FR	Rng	Thr	G at Pos	BFW
1916	Det A	44	56	4	9	1	0	0	3	5	0	8	.161	.230	.179	22	-5	0	.938	-2	86	0	O-14(2-4-8)	-0.8
1917	Det A	47	117	6	24	3	0	0	12	11	3	15	.205	.290	.231	59	-5	2	.980	-2	97	51	O-31(0-3-28)	-1.0
1918	Det A	69	227	19	55	5	2	0	16	18	1	14	.242	.301	.282	79	-6	3	.956	-3	104	54	O-64(0-1-63)	-1.4
1922	Cin N	128	430	67	146	22	8	2	68	35	6	22	.340	.397	.442	118	13	11-10	.955	-1	98	105	*O-109(1-5-103)	0.2
1923	Cin N	61	125	14	32	4	2	3	16	11	0	9	.256	.316	.392	88	-3	0-2	.967	-1	91	100	O-29(9-17-3)	-0.6
1924	Cin N	28	74	7	20	3	0	0	3	13	2	5	.270	.393	.311	92	0	1-3	.964	0	98	129	O-22(12-10-0)	-0.2
	Phi N	109	411	68	121	26	6	16	55	38	5	23	.294	.361	.504	115	9	10-11	.991	3	103	101	*O-109(0-3-107)	0.2
	Year	137	485	75	141	29	6	16	58	51	7	28	.291	.366	.474	113	10	11-14	.986	3	102	106	*O-131(12-13-107)	0.0

Year	Tm Lg	G	AB	R	H	2B	3B	HR	RBI	BB-IB	HP	SO	AVG	OBP	SLG	AOPS	ABR	SB-CS	FA	FR	Rng	Thr	G at Pos	BFW
1925	Phi N	132	495	86	173	35	7	18	97	28	6	32	.349	.391	.558	128	20	10-8	.971	4	103	117	*O-126(36-61-33)	1.5
1926	Phi N	56	194	32	61	6	5	7	38	16	0	7	.314	.367	.505	126	6	6	.942	-3	102	39	O-55(44-8-8)	0.0
1927	NY N	145	483	85	160	19	6	16	87	84	5	27	.331	.435	.495	149	38	7	.975	-2	101	75	*O-142(RF)	2.5
1928	NY N	19	57	11	13	1	0	2	7	10	1	4	.228	.353	.351	84	-1	1	.957	2	100	210	O-18(RF)	-0.1
	†StL N	99	272	41	83	8	2	17	58	51	2	15	.305	.418	.537	145	19	2	.988	2	90	157	O-84(RF)	1.5
	Year	118	329	52	96	9	2	19	65	61	3	19	.292	.407	.505	135	18	3	.982	4	92	167	*O-102(RF)	1.4
1929	Bos N	136	457	65	133	25	5	10	68	69	4	27	.291	.389	.433	108	8	5	.972	2	106	82	*O-130(119-1-10)	0.0
Total	11	1073	3398	505	1030	158	43	91	528	389	35	208	.303	.380	.455	118	93	58-34	.970	0	100	95	O-933(223-113-607)	1.8
HARPER, TERRY Terry Joe B 8.19.1955 Douglasville, GA BR/TR 6-4/195# d9.12																								
1980	Atl N	21	54	3	10	2	1	0	3	6-0	1	5	.185	.279	.259	49	-4	2-1	.968	-1	104	0	O-18(15-1-3)	-0.5
1981	Atl N	40	73	9	19	1	0	2	8	11-0	0	17	.260	.353	.356	100	0	5-1	.976	1	107	129	O-27(9-0-18)	0.1
1982	†Atl N	48	150	16	43	3	0	2	16	14-0	1	28	.287	.347	.347	92	-1	7-4	.987	1	98	133	O-41(29-1-16)	-0.2
1983	Atl N	80	201	19	53	13	1	3	26	20-0	1	43	.264	.332	.383	91	-2	6-5	.952	1	101	140	O-60(28-2-32)	-0.4
1984	Atl N	40	102	4	16	3	1	0	8	4-0	1	21	.157	.194	.206	12	-12	4-1	1.000	4	121	150	O-29(28-0-1)	-1.0
1985	Atl N	138	492	58	130	15	2	17	72	44-4	3	76	.264	.327	.407	98	-2	9-9	.978	-4	87	107	*O-131(129-0-2)	-1.2
1986	Atl N	106	265	26	68	12	0	8	30	29-2	1	39	.257	.330	.392	94	-2	3-6	.970	-5	74	110	O-83(66-0-25)	-1.2
1987	Det A	31	64	4	13	3	0	3	10	9-0	0	8	.203	.301	.391	85	-1	1-0	.952	-1	104	0	D-15,O-14(1-0-13)	-0.3
	Pit N	36	66	8	19	3	0	1	7	7-1	0	11	.288	.356	.379	94	0	0-1	1.000	-1	94	0	O-20(10-0-11)	-0.2
Total	8	540	1467	147	371	55	5	36	180	144-7	8	248	.253	.321	.371	88	-24	37-28	.976	-4	92	108	O-423(315-4-121)/D-15	-4.9
HARPER, TOMMY Tommy B 10.14.1940 Oak Grove, LA BR/TR 5-10/168# d4.9 C18 OF Total (683-LF 258-CF 348-RF)																								
1962	Cin N	6	23	1	4	0	0	0	1	2-0	0	6	.174	.240	.174	13	-3	1-0	.929	-1	70	105	/3-6	-0.4
1963	Cin N	129	408	67	106	12	3	10	37	44-1	3	72	.260	.335	.377	102	2	12-1	.983	2	108	84	*O-118(1-23-94)/3	-0.1
1964	Cin N	102	317	42	77	5	2	4	22	39-1	1	56	.243	.326	.309	78	-8	24-3	.994	4	110	79	O-92(88-4-0)/3-2	-0.5
1965	Cin N	159	646	**126**	166	28	3	18	64	78-0	5	127	.257	.340	.393	99	2	35-6	.983	3	109	73	*O-159(156-5-0)/3-2,2	0.1
1966	Cin N	149	553	85	154	22	5	5	31	57-4	3	85	.278	.348	.363	91	-5	29-10	.996	-1	102	52	*O-147(73-25-95)	-1.3
1967	Cin N	103	365	55	82	17	3	7	22	43-1	0	51	.225	.306	.345	77	-10	23-8	.995	4	112	82	*O-100(2-4-97)	-1.1
1968	Cle A	130	235	26	51	15	2	6	26	26-2	1	56	.217	.295	.374	104	1	11-7	.984	-4	99	0	*O-115(67-7-46)/2-2	-0.8
1969	Sea A	148	537	78	126	10	2	9	41	95-2	1	90	.235	.349	.311	88	-5	**73**-18	.959	-6	92	83	2-59,3-59,O-26(3-22-1)	0.1
1970	Mil A★	154	604	104	179	35	4	31	82	77-5	4	107	.296	.377	.522	145	38	38-16	.943	13	113	87	*3-128,2-22,O-13(8-5-2)	**5.5**
1971	Mil A	152	585	79	151	26	3	14	52	65-4	1	92	.258	.333	.385	104	3	25-3	.975	-6	97	40	O-90(77-13-2),3-70/2	-0.3
1972	Bos A	144	556	92	141	29	2	14	49	67-1	9	104	.254	.341	.388	111	10	25-7	.985	-6	99	46	*O-144(CF)	0.4
1973	Bos A	147	566	92	159	23	3	17	71	61-2	1	93	.281	.351	.422	111	8	**54**-14	.985	1	96	136	*O-143(139-5-0)/D	0.8
1974	Bos A	118	443	66	105	15	3	5	24	46-2	3	65	.237	.312	.318	77	-13	28-12	.982	-4	88	48	O-61(LF),D-51	-2.0
1975	Cal A	89	285	40	68	10	1	3	31	38-5	2	51	.239	.329	.312	89	-3	19-8	.992	-1	65	127	D-57,1-19/O-9(2-0-7)	-0.5
	†Oak A	34	69	11	22	4	0	2	7	5-0	1	9	.319	.373	.464	139	4	7-0	.963	-2	36	81	1-16/O-9(5-1-4),3-2,D-3	0.2
	Year	123	354	51	90	14	1	5	38	43-5	3	60	.254	.337	.342	99	1	26-8	.978	-3	51	105	D-60,1-35,O-18(7-1-11)/3-2	-0.3
1976	Bal A	46	77	8	18	5	0	1	7	10-0	0	16	.234	.318	.338	99	0	4-3	1.000	-0	0	0	D-27/1O(LF)	-0.1
Total	15	1810	6269	972	1609	256	36	146	567	753-30	35	1080	.257	.338	.379	100	21	408-116	.986	-4	103	69	*O-1227L,3-270,D-139/2-85,1-36	0.0
HARRAH, TOBY Colbert Dale B 10.26.1948 Sissonville, WV BR/TR 6/180# d9.5 M1 C8																								
1969	Was A	8	1	4	0	0	0	0	0	0-0	0	0	.000	.000	.000	-99	0	0-0	—	-0	0	0	/S	0.0
1971	Was A	127	383	45	88	11	3	2	22	40-3	0	48	.230	.300	.290	73	-14	10-9	.955	-4	98	108	*S-116/3-7	-0.7
1972	Tex A✳	116	374	47	97	14	3	1	31	34-1	0	31	.259	.316	.321	95	-2	16-7	.960	-8	95	91	*S-106	0.3
1973	Tex A	118	461	64	120	16	1	10	50	46-2	2	49	.260	.328	.364	100	0	10-3	.951	3	112	81	S-76,3-52	1.2
1974	Tex A	**161**	573	79	149	23	2	21	74	50-2	2	65	.260	.319	.417	114	9	15-14	.963	6	96	105	*S-158/3-3	3.3
1975	Tex A☆	151	522	81	153	24	1	20	93	98-3	1	71	.293	.403	.458	145	36	23-9	.963	17	112	101	*S-118,3-28,2-21	**6.8**
1976	Tex A★	155	584	64	152	21	1	15	67	91-5	3	59	.260	.360	.377	114	14	8-5	.955	2	101	92	*S-146/3-5,D-4	3.5
1977	Tex A	159	539	90	142	25	5	27	87	**109**-7	10	73	.263	.393	.479	136	32	27-5	.963	-21	89	72	*3-159/S	1.2
1978	Tex A	139	450	56	103	17	3	12	59	83-3	2	66	.229	.349	.360	100	3	31-8	.965	-2	91	93	3-91,S-49	0.9
1979	Cle A	149	527	99	147	25	1	20	77	89-2	8	60	.279	.389	.444	124	22	20-9	.940	-42	64	81	*3-127,S-33/D-9	-1.8
1980	Cle A	**160**	561	100	150	22	4	11	72	98-3	7	60	.267	.379	.380	109	12	17-2	.971	5	99	83	*3-156/S-2,D-3	1.7
1981	Cle A	**103**	361	64	105	12	4	5	44	57-8	1	44	.291	.382	.388	126	15	12-1	.949	-11	90	63	*3-101/S-3,D	0.5
1982	Cle A☆	**162**	602	100	183	29	4	25	78	84-7	12	52	.304	.398	.490	144	40	17-3	.971	-15	89	76	*3-159/2-3,S-2	2.5
1983	Cle A	138	526	81	140	23	1	9	53	75-1	7	49	.266	.363	.365	98	2	16-10	**.971**	-5	95	100	*3-137/2D	-0.5
1984	NY A	88	253	40	55	9	4	1	26	42-2	2	28	.217	.331	.296	79	-6	3-0	.968	1	97	140	3-74/2-4,O(RF)D	-0.5
1985	Tex A	126	396	65	107	18	1	9	44	113-2	4	60	.270	.432	.389	127	24	11-4	.989	-6	97	86	*2-122/S-2,D	2.5
1986	Tex A	95	289	36	63	18	2	7	41	44-0	2	53	.218	.322	.367	86	-5	2-5	.982	-14	84	83	2-93	-1.5
Total	17	2155	7402	1115	1954	307	40	195	918	1153-51	63	868	.264	.365	.395	114	182	238-94	.963	-94	90	83	*3-1099,S-813,2-244/D-21,O(RF)	19.4
HARRELL, JOHN John Robert B 11.27.1947 Long Beach, CA BR/TR 6-2/190# d10.1																								
1969	SF N	2	6	0	3	0	0	0	2	2-0	0	1	.500	.625	.500	223	1	0-0	1.000	-0	0	0	/C-2	0.1
HARRELL, BILLY William B 7.18.1928 Norristown, PA BR/TR 6-1.5/180# d9.2																								
1955	Cle A	13	19	2	8	0	0	0	1	3-0	0	3	.421	.500	.421	144	1	1-0	.926	-0	106	30	S-11	0.2
1957	Cle A	22	57	6	15	1	1	1	5	4-0	0	7	.263	.311	.368	86	-1	3-1	.893	-4	86	67	S-14/3-6,2	-0.4
1958	Cle A	101	229	36	50	4	0	7	19	15-2	2	36	.218	.271	.328	66	-12	12-2	.986	-5	111	151	3-46,S-45/2-7,O(RF)	-1.2
1961	Bos A	37	37	10	6	2	0	0	1	1-0	0	8	.162	.184	.216	6	-5	1-0	1.000	3	138	316	3-10/S-7,1-3	-0.1
Total	4	173	342	54	79	7	1	8	26	23-2	2	54	.231	.283	.327	68	-17	17-3	.933	-6	93	72	/S-77,3-62,2-8,1-3,O(RF)	-1.5
HARRELSON, BUD Derrel McKinley B 6.6.1944 Niles, CA BB/TR (BR 1965, 1975 (part)) 5-11/160# d9.2 M2 C7																								
1965	NY N	19	37	3	4	1	1	0	0	2-0	0	11	.108	.154	.189	-4	-5	0-0	.955	1	103	83	S-18	-0.4
1966	NY N	33	99	20	22	2	4	0	4	13-1	0	23	.222	.313	.323	79	-3	7-3	.993	5	109	149	S-29	0.6
1967	NY N	151	540	59	137	16	4	1	28	48-0	4	64	.254	.317	.304	80	-13	12-13	.958	14	106	102	*S-149	1.2
1968	NY N	111	402	38	88	7	3	0	14	29-2	1	68	.219	.273	.251	58	-21	4-5	.972	-5	91	103	*S-106	-2.0
1969	†NY N	123	395	42	98	11	6	0	24	54-7	2	54	.248	.341	.306	81	-8	1-3	.969	1	94	113	*S-119	0.6
1970	NY N★	157	564	72	137	18	8	1	42	95-4	3	74	.243	.351	.309	79	-13	23-4	.971	-26	80	97	*S-156	-1.7
1971	NY N★	142	547	55	138	16	6	0	32	53-0	2	59	.252	.319	.303	79	-15	28-7	.978	15	96	104	*S-140	2.2
1972	NY N	115	418	54	90	10	4	1	24	58-4	3	57	.215	.313	.266	68	-16	12-4	.970	-9	90	79	*S-115	-1.0
1973	†NY N	106	356	35	92	12	3	0	20	48-4	1	49	.258	.348	.309	85	-6	5-1	.979	-10	91	82	*S-103	-0.2
1974	NY N	106	331	48	75	10	0	1	13	71-1	2	39	.227	.366	.266	80	-4	9-4	.968	20	106	121	S-97	2.8
1975	NY N	34	73	5	16	2	0	0	3	12-2	0	13	.219	.329	.247	65	-3	0-0	.941	-2	86	129	S-34	-0.2
1976	NY N	118	359	34	84	12	4	1	26	63-5	2	56	.234	.351	.298	91	-1	9-3	.962	-11	87	73	*S-117	0.3
1977	NY N	107	269	25	48	6	2	1	12	27-1	1	28	.178	.255	.227	32	-26	5-4	.984	-2	92	92	S-98	-2.1
1978	Phi N	71	103	16	22	1	0	0	9	18-0	0	21	.214	.331	.223	57	-5	5-2	.972	12	127	199	2-43,S-15	1.0
1979	Phi N	53	71	7	20	6	0	0	7	13-0	1	14	.282	.395	.366	107	2	3-3	.990	1	97	103	2-25,S-17/3-9,O(LF)	0.4
1980	Tex A	87	180	26	49	6	0	1	9	29-0	0	23	.272	.373	.322	95	0	4-4	.952	11	104	119	S-87/2-2	1.7
Total	16	1533	4744	539	1120	136	45	7	267	633-31	22	653	.236	.327	.288	75	-137	127-60	.969	16	94	100	*S-1400/2-70,3-9,O(LF)	3.2
HARRELSON, KEN Kenneth Smith “Hawk” B 9.4.1941 Woodruff, SC BR/TR 6-2/190# d6.9																								
1963	KC A	79	226	16	52	10	1	6	23	23-3	0	58	.230	.299	.363	81	-6	1-1	.980	-7	65	89	1-34,O-28(LF)	-1.7
1964	KC A	49	139	15	27	5	0	7	12	13-0	0	34	.194	.263	.381	74	-5	0-1	.977	3	102	178	O-24(LF),1-15	-0.5
1965	KC A	150	483	61	115	17	3	23	66	66-3	1	112	.238	.329	.429	116	10	9-7	.992	-5	85	91	*1-125/O-4(3-0-1)	-0.3
1966	KC A	63	210	24	47	5	0	5	22	27-3	0	59	.224	.312	.319	85	-4	9-2	.985	2	118	87	1-58/O-3(3-0-1)	-0.4
	Was A	71	250	25	62	8	1	7	28	26-2	1	53	.248	.321	.372	100	0	4-1	.991	-3	84	100	1-70	-0.7
	Year	134	460	49	109	13	1	12	50	53-5	1	112	.237	.317	.348	93	-4	13-3	.989	-1	99	94	*1-128/O-3(3-0-1)	-1.1
1967	Was A	26	79	10	16	0	0	3	10	7-1	0	15	.203	.261	.316	75	-3	1-0	.996	0	110	108	1-23	-0.4
	KC A	61	174	23	53	11	0	6	30	17-1	0	17	.305	.361	.471	151	11	8-2	.992	-2	84	68	1-45	0.9
	†Bos A	23	80	9	16	4	1	3	14	5-2	0	12	.200	.247	.387	79	-2	1-1	.929	-3	74	77	O-23(RF)/1	-0.7
	Year	110	333	42	85	15	1	12	54	29-4	0	44	.255	.311	.414	115	6	10-3	.993	-4	93	81	1-69,O-23(RF)	-0.2
1968	Bos A★	150	535	79	147	17	4	35	**109**	69-9	2	90	.275	.356	.518	153	34	2-6	**1.000**	4	110	111	*O-132(RF),1-19	3.0
1969	Bos A	10	46	6	10	1	0	3	8	4-0	0	6	.217	.275	.435	92	-1	0-1	.991	1	138	145	1-10	-0.1
	Cle A	149	519	83	115	13	4	27	84	95-6	2	96	.222	.341	.418	109	7	17-8	.985	1	105	66	*O-144(7-0-137),1-16	0.1
	Year	159	565	89	125	14	4	30	92	99-6	2	102	.221	.336	.419	107	6	17-9	.985	2	105	66	*O-144(7-0-137),1-26	0.0

Year	Tm Lg	G	AB	R	H	2B	3B	HR	RBI	BB-IB	HP	SO	AVG	OBP	SLG	AOPS	ABR	SB-CS	FA	FR	Rng	Thr	G at Pos	BFW
1970	Cle A	17	39	3	11	1	0	1	1	6-0	0	4	.282	.378	.385	106	1	0-0	1.000	1	111	179	1-13	0.0
1971	Cle A	52	161	20	32	2	0	5	14	24-3	0	21	.199	.301	.304	66	-7	1-0	.988	-1	92	81	1-40/O-7(5-0-2)	-1.2
Total	9	900	2941	374	703	94	14	131	421	382-33	6	577	.239	.325	.414	109	35	53-30	.990	-8	94	94	1-469,O-365(70-0-296)	-2.0
HARRINGTON, ANDY Andrew Matthew B 2.12.1903 Mountain View, CA D 1.26.1979 Boise, ID BR/TR 5-11/170# d4.18																								
1925	Det A	1	1	0	0	0	0	0	0	0	0	0	.000	.000	.000	-99	0	0-0	—	0			H	0.0
HARRINGTON, MICKEY Charles Michael B 10.8.1934 Hattiesburg, MS BR/TR 6-4/205# d7.10																								
1963	Phi N	1	0	0	0	0	0	0	0	0-0	0	0	—	—	—	—	0	0-0	—	0			R	0.0
HARRINGTON, JERRY Jeremiah Peter B 8.12.1869 Keokuk, IA D 4.16.1913 Keokuk, IA BR/TR 5-11/220# d4.30																								
1890	Cin N	65	236	25	58	7	1	1	23	15	3	29	.246	.299	.297	74	-8	4	.957	11	*123*	*90*	C-65	0.7
1891	Cin N	92	333	25	76	10	5	2	41	19	1	34	.228	.272	.306	68	-15	4	.908	-8	*90*	*96*	C-92/3	-1.4
1892	Cin N	22	61	6	13	1	0	0	3	6	0	1	.213	.284	.230	56	-3	0	.989	2	*115*	*91*	C-22/1	0.0
1893	Lou N	10	36	4	4	1	0	0	6	3	0	9	.111	.179	.139	-16	-6	0	.853	-3	*101*	*72*	C-10	-0.7
Total	4	189	666	60	151	19	6	3	73	43	4	73	.227	.278	.287	64	-32	8	.932	1	*105*	*92*	C-189/13	-1.4
HARRINGTON, JOE Joseph C. B 12.21.1869 Fall River, MA D 9.13.1933 Fall River, MA BR/TR 5-8.5/162# d9.10																								
1895	Bos N	18	65	21	18	0	2	2	13	7	1	5	.277	.356	.431	95	-1	3	.912	-1	99	96	2-18	-0.1
1896	Bos N	54	199	26	40	5	3	1	25	19	1	17	.201	.274	.271	42	-18	2	.819	-6	104	107	3-49/S-4,2	-2.0
Total	2	72	264	47	58	5	5	3	38	26	2	22	.220	.295	.311	55	-19	5	.819	-8	104	107	/3-49,2-19,S-4	-2.1
HARRIS, CANDY Alonzo B 9.17.1947 Selma, AL BB/TR 6/160# d4.13																								
1967	Hou N	6	1	0	0	0	0	0	0	0-0	0	1	.000	.000	.000	-99	0	0-0	—	0			H	0.0
HARRIS, SPENCER Anthony Spencer B 8.12.1900 Duluth, MN D 7.3.1982 Minneapolis, MN BL/TL 5-9/145# d4.14																								
1925	Chi A	56	92	12	26	2	0	1	13	14	1	13	.283	.383	.337	89	-1	1-3	.957	-0	94	141	O-27(1-12-17)	-0.3
1926	Chi A	80	222	36	56	11	3	2	27	20	1	15	.252	.317	.356	78	-8	8-3	.949	-2	95	101	O-63(7-11-48)	-1.3
1929	Was A	6	14	1	3	1	0	0	1	0	0	3	.214	.214	.286	27	-2	1-0	1.000	-0	94	0	/O-4(CF)	-0.2
1930	Phi A	22	49	4	9	1	0	0	5	5	0	2	.184	.259	.204	18	-6	0-0	.958	1	97	242	O-13(10-1-2)	-0.6
Total	4	164	377	53	94	15	3	3	46	39	2	33	.249	.323	.329	70	-17	10-6	.954	-1	95	124	O-107(18-28-67)	-2.4
HARRIS, GAIL Boyd Gail B 10.15.1931 Abingdon, VA BL/TL 6/195# d6.3																								
1955	NY N	79	263	27	61	9	0	12	36	20-3	2	46	.232	.289	.403	82	-8	0-0	.982	-0	105	106	1-75	-1.2
1956	NY N	12	38	2	5	0	1	1	1	3-1	2	10	.132	.233	.263	33	-4	0-0	.975	0	113	128	1-11	-0.5
1957	NY N	90	225	28	54	7	3	9	31	16-2	6	28	.240	.305	.418	93	-3	1-0	.985	-2	96	119	1-61	-0.8
1958	Det A	134	451	63	123	18	8	20	83	36-3	4	60	.273	.328	.481	113	6	1-2	.986	2	108	88	*1-122	0.1
1959	Det A	114	349	39	77	4	3	9	39	29-3	6	49	.221	.290	.327	66	-17	0-1	.992	3	106	87	1-93	-2.0
1960	Det A	8	5	0	0	0	0	0	0	2-1	0	1	.000	.286	.000	-15	-1	0-0	1.000	0	149	112	/1-5	-0.1
Total	6	437	1331	159	320	38	15	51	190	106-13	20	194	.240	.304	.406	88	-27	2-3	.986	3	105	98	1-367	-4.5
HARRIS, CHARLIE Charles Jenkins B 10.21.1877 Macon, GA D 3.14.1963 Gainesville, FL BR/TR 5-8/200# d5.26																								
1899	Bal N	30	68	16	19	3	0	0	1	3	1		.279	.319	.324	73	-3	4	.872	-3	92	106	3-21/O-3(2-0-1),2-2,S	-0.5
HARRIS, DAVE David Stanley "Sheriff" B 7.14.1900 Summerfield, NC D 9.18.1973 Atlanta, GA BR/TR 5-11/170# d4.14																								
1925	Bos N	92	340	49	90	8	7	5	36	27	1	44	.265	.321	.374	84	-10	6-4	.962	7	110	142	O-90(87-4-0)	-0.9
1928	Bos N	7	17	2	2	1	0	0	0	2	0	6	.118	.211	.176	2	-2	0	.833	-1	105	0	/O-6(LF)	-0.3
1930	Chi A	33	86	16	21	2	1	5	13	7	1	22	.244	.309	.465	96	-1	0-0	1.000	-0	107	62	O-23(LF)/2	-0.3
	Was A	73	205	40	65	19	8	4	44	28	0	35	.317	.399	.546	137	12	6-3	.983	4	99	190	O-59(19-12-28)	1.1
	Year	106	291	56	86	21	9	9	57	35	1	57	.296	.373	.522	125	11	6-3	.988	4	101	152	O-82(42-12-28)/2	0.8
1931	Was A	77	231	49	72	14	8	5	50	49	1	38	.312	.434	.506	146	18	7-6	.950	-1	100	76	O-60(3-0-57)	1.2
1932	Was A	81	156	26	51	7	4	6	29	19	0	34	.327	.400	.538	143	10	4-4	.932	-0	100	127	O-34(7-8-20)	0.7
1933	†Was A	82	177	33	46	9	2	5	38	25	2	26	.260	.358	.418	106	2	3-1	.964	-3	103	31	O-45(4-11-32)/1-6,3-2	-0.2
1934	Was A	97	235	28	59	14	3	2	37	39	0	40	.251	.358	.362	89	-3	2-3	.973	2	99	169	O-64(15-1-49)/3-5	-0.4
Total	7	542	1447	243	406	74	33	32	247	196	5	245	.281	.368	.444	112	26	28-21	.963	8	103	122	O-381(164-36-186)/3-7,1-6,2	0.9
HARRIS, DONALD Donald B 11.12.1967 Waco, TX BR/TR 6-1/185# d9.4																								
1991	Tex A	18	8	4	3	0	0	1	2	1-0	0	3	.375	.444	.750	228	1	1-0	1.000	-0	88	0	O-12(2-7-5)/D-3	0.1
1992	Tex A	24	33	3	6	1	0	0	1	0-0	0	15	.182	.182	.212	10	-4	1-0	.974	2	125	150	O-24(5-15-5)	-0.2
1993	Tex A	40	76	10	15	2	0	1	8	5-0	1	18	.197	.253	.263	41	-7	0-1	.943	-2	78	213	O-38(1-27-11)/D-3	-0.9
Total	3	82	117	17	24	3	0	2	11	6-0	1	36	.205	.248	.282	46	-10	2-1	.959	-0	93	176	/O-74(8-49-21),D-6	-1.0
HARRIS, FRANK Frank W. B 11.2.1858 Pittsburgh, PA D 11.26.1939 E.Moline, IL BR/TR d4.17																								
1884	Alt U	24	95	10	25	2	1	0		3			.263	.286	.305	78	-5		.941	1	160	13	1-17/O-8(4-3-1)	-0.6
HARRIS, BILLY James William B 11.24.1943 Hamlet, NC BL/TR 6/175# d6.16																								
1968	Cle A	38	94	10	20	5	1	0	3	8-0	0	22	.213	.275	.287	71	-3	2-0	.970	2	119	90	2-27,3-10/S	0.1
1969	KC A	5	7	1	2	1	0	0	0	0-0	0	1	.286	.286	.429	97	0	0-0	1.000	0	213	0	/2	0.0
Total	2	43	101	11	22	6	1	0	3	8-0	0	23	.218	.275	.297	73	-3	2-0	.971	2	121	88	/2-28,3-10,S	0.1
HARRIS, JOHN John Thomas B 9.13.1954 Portland, OR BL/TL 6-3/205# d9.26																								
1979	Cal A	1	2	0	0	0	0	0	0	0-0	0	0	.000	.000	.000	-99	-1	0-0	1.000	-0	0	0	/1	-0.1
1980	Cal A	19	41	8	12	5	0	2	7	7-0	0	4	.293	.388	.561	163	4	0-1	1.000	-0	38	51	1-10/O-3(LF)	0.3
1981	Cal A	36	77	5	19	3	0	3	9	3-0	0	11	.247	.275	.403	93	-1	0-0	.976	-3	88	124	1-11,O-10(LF)/D	-0.5
Total	3	56	120	13	31	8	0	5	16	10-0	0	15	.258	.313	.450	115	2	0-1	.987	-3	61	85	/1-22,O-13(LF),D	-0.3
HARRIS, JOE Joseph "Moon" B 5.20.1891 Plum Borough, PA D 12.10.1959 Renton, PA BR/TR 5-9/170# d6.9 Mil 1918																								
1914	NY A	2	1	0	0	0	0	0	0	3	1	1	.000	.800	.000	143	1	0	1.000	-0	0	0	/1O(LF)	0.1
1917	Cle A	112	369	40	112	22	4	0	65	55	3	32	.304	.398	.385	129	16	11	.985	9	140	107	1-95/O-5(RF),3-2	2.5
1919	Cle A	62	184	30	69	16	1	1	46	33	1	21	.375	.472	.489	160	18	2	.988	2	122	92	1-46/S-4	2.0
1922	Bos A	119	408	53	129	30	9	6	54	30	1	15	.316	.364	.478	119	10	2-6	.953	6	102	139	O-83(71-0-12),1-21	0.6
1923	Bos A	142	483	82	162	28	11	13	76	52	5	27	.335	.406	.520	142	29	7-3	.968	-1	106	71	*O-132(LF)/1-9	1.7
1924	Bos A	133	491	82	148	36	9	3	77	81	5	25	.301	.406	.430	115	15	6-1	.993	5	111	104	*1-128/O-3(LF)	1.2
1925	Bos A	8	19	4	3	0	1	1	2	5	0	5	.158	.333	.421	90	0	0-0	1.000	-1	31	48	/1-6	-0.1
	†Was A	100	300	60	97	21	9	12	59	51	5	28	.323	.430	.573	156	27	6-3	.989	4	121	106	1-58,O-41(16-0-25)	2.3
	Year	108	319	64	100	21	10	13	61	56	5	33	.313	.424	.564	152	26	6-3	.990	3	113	101	1-64,O-41(16-0-25)	2.2
1926	Was A	92	257	43	79	13	9	5	55	37	5	9	.307	.405	.486	135	14	2-3	.994	-0	84	80	1-36,O-35(3-0-32)	0.8
1927	†Pit N	129	411	57	134	27	9	5	73	48	4	19	.326	.402	.472	125	16	0	.990	2	105	96	*1-116/O-3(LF)	1.0
1928	Pit N	16	23	2	9	2	1	0	2	4	1	2	.391	.500	.565	171	3	0	1.000	1	218	206	/1-6	0.4
	Bro N	55	89	8	21	6	1	1	8	14	0	4	.236	.340	.360	84	-2	0	.958	-1	76	164	O-16(6-0-10)	-0.3
	Year	71	112	10	30	8	2	1	10	18	1	6	.268	.374	.402	103	1	0	.958	1	76	164	O-16(6-0-10)/1-6	0.1
Total	10	970	3035	461	963	201	64	47	517	413	31	188	.317	.404	.472	131	147	36-16	.989	28	117	100	1-522,O-319(235-0-84)/S-4,3-2	12.2
HARRIS, LENNY Leonard Anthony B 10.28.1964 Miami, FL BL/TR 5-10/205# d9.7 OF Total (148-LF 3-CF 154-RF)																								
1988	Cin N	16	43	7	16	1	0	0	8	5-0	0	4	.372	.420	.395	135	2	4-1	1.000	1	127	0	3-10/2-6	0.4
1989	Cin N	61	188	17	42	4	0	2	11	9-0	1	20	.223	.263	.277	52	-12	10-6	.980	5	91	112	2-32,S-17,3-16	-0.6
	LA N	54	147	19	37	6	1	1	15	11-0	1	13	.252	.308	.327	83	-3	4-3	1.000	-5	76	94	O-21(20-0-1),2-14/3-8,S	-1.0
	Year	115	335	36	79	10	1	3	26	20-0	2	33	.236	.283	.299	66	-15	14-9	.975	-1	87	115	2-46,3-24,O-21(20-0-1),S-18	-1.6
1990	LA N	137	431	61	131	16	4	2	29	29-2	1	31	.304	.348	.374	102	1	15-10	.959	-0	101	109	3-94,2-44/O-2(0-1-1),S	0.1
1991	LA N	145	429	59	123	16	1	3	38	37-5	5	32	.287	.349	.350	100	1	12-3	.943	7	95	116	*3-113,2-27,S-20/O(LF)	1.1
1992	LA N	135	347	28	94	11	0	0	30	24-3	1	24	.271	.318	.303	78	-10	19-7	.963	17	108	99	2-81,3-33,O-15(7-0-8),S-10	1.1
1993	LA N	107	160	20	38	6	1	2	11	15-4	0	15	.237	.303	.325	72	-7	3-1	.987	-0	107	65	2-35,3-17/S-3,O-2(RF)	-0.5
1994	Cin N	66	100	13	31	3	1	0	14	5-0	0	13	.310	.340	.360	84	-2	7-2	.846	1	128	132	3-15/1-4,O-3(RF),2-2	0.0
1995	†Cin N	101	197	32	41	8	3	2	16	14-0	0	20	.208	.259	.310	50	-15	10-1	.939	7	145	114	3-24,1-23/O-8(4-0-4),2	-0.7
1996	Cin N	125	302	33	86	17	2	5	32	21-1	1	31	.285	.330	.404	93	-3	14-6	1.000	3	102	138	O-37(23-1-18),3-24,1-16/2-8	-0.2
1997	Cin N	120	238	32	65	13	1	3	28	18-1	2	18	.273	.327	.374	83	-6	4-3	.977	-2	88	58	O-42(26-0-17),2-20,3-13,1-11	-0.9
1998	Cin N	57	122	12	36	8	0	0	10	8-2	1	9	.295	.338	.361	85	-2	1-3	.929	0	100	153	O-32(13-0-20)/P	-0.4
	NY N	75	168	18	39	7	0	6	17	9-1	1	12	.232	.272	.381	71	-8	5-2	.988	2	112	119	O-65(21-1-53),3-10/2-2,1D	-0.7

Year	Tm Lg	G	AB	R	H	2B	3B	HR	RBI	BB-IB	HP	SO	AVG	OBP	SLG	AOPS	ABR	SB-CS	FA	FR	Rng	Thr	G at Pos	BFW
	Year	132	290	30	75	15	0	6	27	17-3	2	21	.259	.300	.372	77	-10	6-5	.968	2	108	131	O-97(34-1-73),3-10/2-2,P1D	-1.1
1999	Col N	91	158	15	47	12	0	0	13	6-0	0	6	.297	.323	.373	59	-9	1-1	.924	5	114	157	2-24,O-14(3-0-11)/3-2,D-2	-0.3
	†Ari N	19	29	2	11	1	0	1	7	0-0	0	1	.379	.367	.517	123	1	1-0	1.000	-0	65	352	/3-5,O-2(RF)	0.1
	Year	110	187	17	58	13	0	1	20	6-0	0	7	.310	.330	.396	68	-9	2-1	.924	5	114	157	2-24,O-16(3-0-13)/3-7,D-2	-0.2
2000	Ari N	36	85	9	16	1	1	1	13	3-1	0	5	.188	.209	.259	19	-11	5-0	.909	-3	80	33	3-20/O-3(RF)	-1.3
	†NY N	76	138	22	42	6	3	3	13	17-1	0	17	.304	.381	.457	115	3	8-1	.854	1	100	92	3-16,O-11(6-0-5),1-10/2-3,D	0.5
	Year	112	223	31	58	7	4	4	26	20-2	0	22	.260	.317	.381	78	-8	13-1	.880	-2	88	57	3-36,O-14(6-0-8),1-10/2-3,D	-0.8
2001	NY N	110	135	12	30	5	1	0	9	8-0	0	9	.222	.266	.274	42	-12	3-2	.875	-2	55	0	3-11/O-8(5-0-3),1-7,2D	-1.4
2002	Mil N	122	197	23	60	8	2	3	17	14-1	2	17	.305	.355	.411	106	1	4-1	1.000	0	112	0	O-16(LF),3-14,1-12/D-2	0.0
2003	Chi N	75	131	11	24	3	0	1	7	13-3	0	20	.183	.255	.229	29	-14	1-0	.948	-1	90	86	3-35/1-2,O-2(1-0-1)	-1.5
	†Fla N	13	14	3	4	0	0	0	1	3-0	0	1	.286	.412	.286	90	0	0-0	1.000	0	130	0	/O-4(2-0-2)	0.0
	Year	88	145	14	28	3	0	1	8	16-3	0	21	.193	.272	.234	35	-14	1-0	.948	-1	90	86	3-35/O-6(3-0-3),1-2	-1.5
Total	16	1741	3759	448	1013	152	21	35	339	269-25	16	318	.269	.319	.349	80	-105	131-53	.937	33	99	103	3-480,2-300,O-288R/1-86,S-52,DP	-6.2
HARRIS, NED Robert Ned B 7.9.1916 Ames, IA D 12.18.1976 W.Palm Beach, FL BL/TL 5-11/175# d4.20 Mil 1944-45																								
1941	Det A	26	61	11	13	3	1	1	4	6	0	13	.213	.284	.344	59	-4	1-0	1.000	-1	78	0	O-12(LF)	-0.5
1942	Det A	121	398	53	108	16	10	9	45	49	0	35	.271	.351	.430	110	5	5-4	.944	-7	88	73	*O-104(RF)	-0.9
1943	Det A	114	354	43	90	14	3	6	32	47	1	29	.254	.343	.362	99	0	6-8	.961	-3	96	87	O-96(4-6-86)	-1.2
1946	Det A	1	1	0	0	0	0	0	0	0	0	0	.000	.000	.000	-94	0	0-0	—	0			H	0.0
Total	4	262	814	107	211	33	14	16	81	102	1	77	.259	.342	.393	101	1	12-12	.955	-12	91	76	O-212(16-6-190)	-2.6
HARRIS, BUCKY Stanley Raymond B 11.8.1896 Port Jervis, NY D 11.8.1977 Bethesda, MD BR/TR 5-9.5/156# d8.28 M29 HF1975																								
1919	Was A	8	28	0	6	2	0	0	4	1	1	3	.214	.267	.286	56	-2	0	.925	-0	100	105	/2-8	-0.2
1920	Was A	136	506	76	152	26	6	1	68	41	**21**	36	.300	.377	.381	104	5	16-17	.958	-12	95	91	*2-134	-0.7
1921	Was A	**154**	584	82	169	22	8	0	54	54	**18**	39	.289	.367	.354	89	-8	29-9	.959	12	103	116	*2-154	1.2
1922	Was A	**154**	602	95	162	24	8	2	40	52	**14**	38	.269	.341	.346	84	-14	25-11	.970	**31**	**104**	**134**	*2-154	2.2
1923	Was A	145	532	60	150	21	13	2	70	50	13	29	.282	.358	.382	100	0	23-16	.961	19	103	**136**	*2-144/S	2.1
1924	†Was A	143	544	88	146	28	9	1	58	56	7	41	.268	.344	.358	84	-13	20-10	.968	-12	86	**136**	*2-143,M	-1.9
1925	†Was A	144	551	91	158	30	3	1	66	64	9	21	.287	.370	.358	87	-8	14-12	.970	5	94	**129**	*2-144,M	-0.1
1926	Was A	141	537	94	152	39	9	1	63	58	9	41	.283	.363	.395	100	1	16-11	.963	-11	93	90	*2-141,M	-0.6
1927	Was A	128	475	98	127	20	3	1	55	66	5	33	.267	.363	.328	81	-10	18-3	**.972**	2	97	94	*2-128,M	-0.2
1928	Was A	99	358	34	73	11	5	0	28	27	2	26	.204	.264	.263	39	-33	5-2	.970	11	104	110	2-96/3O(RF)M	-1.9
1929	Det A	7	11	3	1	0	0	0	0	2	0	2	.091	.231	.091	-14	-2	1-0	.900	-0	131	0	/2-4,SM	-0.2
1931	Det A	4	8	1	1	1	0	0	0	1	0	1	.125	.222	.250	23	-1	0-0	1.000	-0	96	79	/2-3,M	-0.1
Total	12	1263	4736	722	1297	224	64	9	506	472	99	310	.274	.352	.354	86	-85	167-91	.965	44	98	116	*2-1253/S-2,O(RF)3	-0.4
HARRIS, VIC Victor Lanier B 3.27.1950 Los Angeles, CA BB/TR 6/170# d7.21																								
1972	Tex A	61	186	8	26	5	1	0	10	12-1	0	39	.140	.192	.177	11	-21	7-3	.960	-9	91	76	2-58/S	-3.1
1973	Tex A	152	555	71	138	14	7	8	44	55-1	2	81	.249	.317	.342	90	-8	13-12	.977	-4	108	63	*O-113(2-111-7),3-25,2-18	-1.6
1974	Chi N	62	200	18	39	6	3	0	11	29-3	0	26	.195	.294	.255	53	-12	9-3	.943	-9	92	54	2-56	-1.8
1975	Chi N	51	56	6	10	0	0	0	5	6-0	0	7	.179	.254	.179	22	-6	0-0	.900	-0	76	0	O-11(9-2-0)/3-7,2-5	-0.7
1976	StL N	97	259	21	59	12	3	1	19	16-0	1	55	.228	.275	.309	65	-12	1-2	.945	-1	99	91	2-37,O-35(9-25-1),3-12/S	-1.3
1977	SF N	69	165	28	43	12	0	2	14	19-1	0	36	.261	.332	.370	90	-2	2-1	.973	-6	88	104	2-27,S-11/3-9,O-3(0-2-1)	-0.6
1978	SF N	53	100	8	15	4	0	1	11	11-1	0	24	.150	.230	.220	29	-10	0-0	.934	-4	96	59	S-22,2-10/O-6(4-2-1)	-1.3
1980	Mil A	34	89	8	19	4	1	1	7	12-0	0	13	.213	.304	.315	73	-3	4-1	.967	-1	106	52	O-31(4-5-22)/3-2,2	-0.5
Total	8	579	1610	168	349	57	15	13	121	160-7	3	281	.217	.287	.295	65	-74	36-22	.954	-33	93	77	2-212,O-199(28-147-32)/3-55,S-35	-10.9
HARRIS, WILLIE William Charles B 6.22.1978 Cairo, GA BL/TR 5-9/175# d9.2																								
2001	Bal A	9	24	3	3	1	0	0	0	0-0	0	7	.125	.125	.167	-25	-4	0-0	1.000	1	97	271	/O-8(CF)	-0.4
2002	Chi A	49	163	14	38	4	0	2	12	9-0	0	21	.233	.270	.294	50	-12	8-0	.985	5	100	90	2-38/O-6(CF)	-0.3
2003	Chi A	79	137	19	28	3	1	0	5	10-0	0	28	.204	.259	.241	33	-14	12-2	.977	3	110	229	O-61(CF),2-12	-0.8
Total	3	137	324	36	69	8	1	2	17	19-0	0	56	.213	.255	.262	38	-30	20-2	.984	8	114	257	/O-75(CF),2-50	-1.5
HARRISON, CHUCK Charles William B 4.25.1941 Abilene, TX BR/TR 5-10/190# d9.15																								
1965	Hou N	15	45	2	9	4	0	1	9	8-0	0	9	.200	.321	.356	97	0	0-0	.983	-0	96	98	1-12	-0.1
1966	Hou N	119	434	52	111	23	2	9	52	37-4	2	69	.256	.316	.380	100	0	2-0	.992	2	104	74	*1-114	-0.5
1967	Hou N	70	177	13	43	7	3	2	26	13-0	0	30	.243	.292	.350	87	-4	0-0	.987	-1	94	60	1-59	-0.8
1969	KC A	75	213	18	47	5	1	3	18	16-2	1	20	.221	.276	.296	60	-12	1-2	.993	1	104	64	1-55	-1.7
1971	KC A	49	143	9	31	4	0	2	21	11-2	0	19	.217	.266	.287	59	-8	0-0	.992	-0	99	100	1-39	-1.2
Total	5	328	1012	94	241	43	6	17	126	85-8	3	147	.238	.297	.343	83	-24	3-2	.991	2	101	74	1-279	-4.3
HARRISON, BEN Leo J. BR/TR d9.27																								
1901	Was A	1	2	0	0	0	0	0	0	1	0		.000	.333	.000	-2	0	0	—	-0	0	0	/O(LF)	0.0
HARRISON, RIT Washington Ritter B 9.16.1849 Waterbury, CT D 11.7.1888 Bridgeport, CT d5.20																								
1875	NH NA	1	4	0	2	1	0	0	1	0		0	.500	.500	.750	376	1	0-1	.333	-2			/CS	-0.1
HARSHANEY, SAM Samuel B 4.24.1910 Madison, IL D 2.1.2001 San Antonio, TX BR/TR 6/180# d9.28																								
1937	StL A	5	11	0	1	1	0	0	0	3	0	0	.091	.286	.182	20	-1	0-0	.905	-0	*94*	*181*	/C-4	-0.1
1938	StL A	11	24	2	7	0	0	0	0	3	0	2	.292	.370	.292	68	-1	0-0	.975	-1	*78*	*109*	C-10	-0.1
1939	StL A	42	145	15	35	2	0	0	15	9	1	8	.241	.290	.255	40	-13	0-1	.994	-3	*78*	*135*	C-36	-1.4
1940	StL A	3	1	0	0	0	0	0	0	1	0	0	.000	.500	.000	41	0	0-0	—	0	*0*	*0*	/C-2	0.0
Total	4	61	181	17	43	3	0	0	15	16	1	10	.238	.303	.254	43	-15	0-1	.983	-4	*79*	*135*	/C-52	-1.6
HART, BO Bodhi J. B 9.27.1976 Creswell, OR BR/TR 5-11/170# d6.19																								
2003	StL N	77	296	46	82	13	5	4	28	12-0	6	64	.277	.317	.395	88	-6	3-1	.989	-9	90	78	2-69/S-3	-1.1
HART, BURT James Burton B 6.28.1870 Brown Co., MN D 1.29.1921 Sacramento, CA BB 6-3/200# d6.6																								
1901	Bal A	58	206	33	64	3	5	0	23	20	4		.311	.383	.374	106	2	7	.976	-8	30	83	1-58	-0.6
HART, HUB James Henry B 2.2.1878 Everett, MA D 10.10.1960 Fort Wayne, IN BL/TR 5-11/170# d7.16																								
1905	Chi A	11	20	3	2	0	0	0	4	3	0		.100	.217	.100	2	-2	0	1.000	-1	*120*	*26*	/C-7	-0.3
1906	Chi A	17	37	1	6	0	0	0	0	2	0		.162	.205	.162	16	-4	0	.935	-2	*125*	*55*	C-15	-0.5
1907	Chi A	29	70	6	19	1	0	0	7	5	1		.271	.329	.286	100	0	1	.956	-3	*110*	*92*	C-25	-0.1
Total	3	57	127	10	27	1	0	0	11	10	1		.213	.275	.220	59	-6	1	.957	-5	*116*	*73*	/C-47	-0.9
HART, MIKE James Michael B 12.20.1951 Kalamazoo, MI BB/TR 6-3/185# d6.12																								
1980	Tex A	5	4	1	1	0	0	0	0	1-0	0	1	.250	.400	.250	85	0	0-0	1.000	-1	33	0	/O-2(CF)	0.0
HART, JIM RAY James Ray B 10.30.1941 Hookerton, NC BR/TR 5-11/185# d7.7																								
1963	SF N	7	20	1	4	1	0	0	2	3-1	2	6	.200	.360	.250	80	0	0-0	1.000	-0	73	106	/3-7	-0.1
1964	SF N	153	566	71	162	15	6	31	81	47-4	4	94	.286	.342	.498	132	22	5-2	.937	6	103	110	*3-149/O-6(1-0-5)	2.9
1965	SF N	160	591	91	177	30	6	23	96	47-3	2	75	.299	.349	.487	130	23	6-4	.919	-7	92	77	*3-144,O-15(14-0-1)	1.6
1966	SF N★	156	578	88	165	23	4	33	93	48-6	4	75	.285	.342	.510	130	23	2-5	.941	-4	104	98	*3-139,O-17(16-0-1)	1.7
1967	SF N	158	578	98	167	26	7	29	99	77-11	4	100	.289	.373	.509	153	41	1-1	.937	-13	94	72	3-89,O-72(LF)	2.6
1968	SF N	136	480	67	124	14	3	23	78	46-10	3	74	.258	.323	.444	130	16	3-1	.925	-11	81	99	3-72,O-65(LF)	0.3
1969	SF N	95	236	27	60	9	0	3	26	28-1	5	49	.254	.343	.331	92	-1	0-0	.943	-3	86	67	O-68(LF)/3-3	-0.8
1970	SF N	76	255	30	72	12	1	8	37	30-6	3	29	.282	.360	.431	114	6	0-0	.908	-13	76	22	3-56,O-18(LF)	-0.9
1971	†SF N	31	39	5	10	0	0	2	5	6-0	0	8	.256	.356	.410	118	1	0-1	.833	0	76	610	/3-3,O-3(LF)	0.1
1972	SF N	24	79	10	24	5	0	5	8	6-0	1	10	.304	.360	.557	155	5	0-1	.886	-8	56	61	3-20	-0.3
1973	SF N	5	3	0	0	0	0	0	1	3-0	0	1	.000	.429	.000	48	0	0-0	.600	0	269	0	/3	0.0
	NY A	114	339	29	86	13	2	13	52	36-7	0	45	.254	.324	.419	112	5	0-2	—	0	0	0	*D-106	0.1
1974	NY A	10	19	1	1	0	0	0	0	3-0	0	7	.053	.182	.053	-30	-3	0-0	—	0			/D-4	-0.4
Total	12	1125	3783	518	1052	148	29	170	578	380-49	28	573	.278	.345	.467	128	138	17-17	.929	-52	94	87	3-683,O-264(257-0-7),D-110	6.8
HART, JASON Jason Wyatt B 9.5.1977 Walnut Creek, CA BR/TR 6-4/237# d8.18																								
2002	Tex A	10	15	2	4	3	0	0	0	2-0	0	7	.267	.353	.467	110	0	0-0	1.000	-0	97	0	/O-7(LF),1-2	0.0

Year	Tm Lg	G	AB	R	H	2B	3B	HR	RBI	BB-IB	HP	SO	AVG	OBP	SLG	AOPS	ABR	SB-CS	FA	FR	Rng	Thr	G at Pos	BFW
HART, MIKE Michael Lawrence B 2.17.1958 Milwaukee, WI BL/TL 5-11/185# d5.8																								
1984	Min A	13	29	0	5	0	0	0	5	1-0	0	2	.172	.194	.172	4	-4	0-1	1.000	1	127	166	O-11(8-0-3)	-0.3
1987	Bal A	34	76	7	12	2	0	4	12	6-0	0	19	.158	.217	.342	47	-6	1-4	1.000	1	113	0	O-32(4-29-1)	-0.6
Total	2	47	105	7	17	2	0	4	17	7-0	0	21	.162	.211	.295	35	-10	1-5	1.000	3	117	42	/O-43(12-29-4)	-0.9
HART, TOM Thomas Henry "Bushy" B 6.15.1869 Canaan, NY D 9.17.1939 Gardner, MA 5-7/160# d4.15																								
1891	Was AA	8	24	1	3	0	0	0	2	2	0	1	.125	.192	.125	-9	-3	1	1.000	1	*81*	*203*	/C-5,O-3(CF)	-0.2
HART, BILL William Woodrow B 3.4.1913 Wiconisco, PA D 7.29.1968 Lykens, PA BR/TR 6/175# d9.18																								
1943	Bro N	8	19	0	3	0	0	0	1	1	0	2	.158	.200	.158	4	-2	0	1.000	2	127	112	/3-6,S	0.0
1944	Bro N	29	90	8	16	4	2	0	4	9	0	7	.178	.253	.267	47	-7	1	.941	-6	95	44	S-25/3-2	-1.1
1945	Bro N	58	161	27	37	6	2	3	27	14	0	21	.230	.291	.348	78	-6	7	.913	-5	78	111	3-39/S-8	-1.0
Total	3	95	270	35	56	10	4	3	32	24	0	30	.207	.272	.307	63	-15	8	.924	-9	83	111	/3-47,S-34	-2.1
HARTFORD, BRUCE Bruce Daniel B 5.14.1892 Chicago, IL D 5.25.1975 Los Angeles, CA BR/TR 6-0.5/190# d6.3																								
1914	Cle A	8	22	5	4	1	0	0	0	4	0	9	.182	.308	.227	59	-1	0	.913	-2	99	0	/S-8	-0.3
HARTJE, CHRIS Christian Henry B 3.25.1915 San Francisco, CA D 6.26.1946 Seattle, WA BR/TR 5-10.5/165# d9.9																								
1939	Bro N	9	16	2	5	1	0	0	5	1	0	0	.313	.353	.375	92	0	0	.909	-1	*90*	*0*	/C-8	-0.1
HARTLEY, GROVER Grover Allen "Slick" B 7.2.1888 Osgood, IN D 10.19.1964 Daytona Beach, FL BR/TR 5-11/175# d5.13 C10																								
1911	NY N	11	18	1	4	2	0	0	1	1	0	1	.222	.263	.333	64	-1	1	.962	2	*149*	*84*	C-10	0.2
1912	NY N	25	34	3	8	2	1	0	7	0	1	4	.235	.257	.353	64	-2	2	.960	2	*146*	*75*	C-25	0.1
1913	NY N	23	19	4	6	0	0	0	0	1	0	2	.316	.350	.316	90	0	4-1	.978	2	138	54	C-21/1	0.2
1914	StL F	86	212	24	61	13	2	1	25	12	1	26	.288	.329	.382	89	-6	4	.956	-8	*81*	*93*	C-32,2-13/1-9,3-3,O-2(CF)	-1.2
1915	StL F	120	394	47	108	21	6	1	50	42	8	21	.274	.356	.365	98	-5	10	.972	-4	*102*	*91*	*C-113/1	0.1
1916	StL A	89	222	19	50	8	0	0	12	30	3	24	.225	.325	.261	80	-4	4	.968	-3	85	84	C-75	-0.1
1917	StL A	19	13	2	3	0	0	0	0	2	0	1	.231	.333	.231	75	0	0	.875	0	*102*	*244*	/C-4,S3	0.0
1924	NY N	4	7	1	2	1	0	0	1	1	0	0	.286	.375	.429	118	0	1-0	1.000	-0	*112*	*100*	/C-3	0.1
1925	NY N	46	95	9	30	1	1	0	8	8	1	3	.316	.375	.347	89	-1	2-0	.974	3	*93*	*140*	C-37/1-8	0.3
1926	NY N	13	21	0	1	0	0	0	0	5	0	0	.048	.231	.048	-22	-4	0	1.000	0	*90*	*72*	C-13	-0.3
1927	Bos A	103	244	23	67	11	0	1	31	22	1	14	.275	.337	.332	76	-8	1-0	.967	-14	*60*	*70*	C-86	-1.7
1929	Cle A	24	33	2	9	0	1	0	8	2	0	1	.273	.314	.333	64	-2	0-0	1.000	-1	*85*	*0*	C-13	-0.3
1930	Cle A	1	4	0	3	0	0	0	1	0	0	0	.750	.750	.750	271	1	0-0	.750	-1	*46*	*0*	/C	0.1
1934	StL A	5	3	0	1	1	0	0	0	1	0	0	.333	.500	.667	183	0	0-0	1.000	0	*0*	*0*	/C-2	0.1
Total	14	569	1319	135	353	60	11	3	144	127	15	97	.268	.339	.337	85	-32	29-1	.968	-23	*90*	*86*	C-435/1-19,2-13,3-4,O-2(CF),S	-2.4
HARTLEY, CHICK Walter Scott B 8.22.1880 Philadelphia, PA D 7.18.1948 Philadelphia, PA BR/TR 5-8/180# d6.4																								
1902	NY N	1	4	0	0	0	0	0	0	0	0		.000	.000	.000	-99	-1	0	1.000	-0	0	0	/O(LF)	-0.1
HARTMAN, FRED Frederick Orrin "Dutch" B 4.25.1868 Allegheny, PA D 11.11.1938 McKeesport, PA BR/TR 5-8/170# d7.26																								
1894	Pit N	49	182	41	58	4	7	2	20	16	5	11	.319	.389	.451	103	0	12	.876	-2	99	77	3-49	-0.1
1897	StL N	125	519	67	158	21	8	2	67	26	10		.304	.350	.387	96	-4	18	.867	-1	106	83	*3-125	-0.2
1898	NY N	123	475	57	129	16	11	2	88	25	4		.272	.313	.364	97	-4	11	.882	8	107	87	*3-123	0.5
1899	NY N	51	177	25	42	3	5	1	17	12	10		.237	.322	.328	81	-5	2	.883	-2	94	132	3-51	-0.5
1901	Chi A	120	473	77	146	23	13	3	89	25	9		.309	.355	.431	120	12	31	.894	-6	98	96	*3-119	0.8
1902	StL N	114	416	30	90	10	3	0	52	14	5		.216	.251	.255	58	-21	14	.908	-4	102	59	*3-105/S-4,1-3	-2.4
Total	6	582	2242	297	623	77	47	10	333	118	43	11	.278	.326	.368	95	-22	88	.886	-7	102	86	3-572/S-4,1-3	-1.9
HARTMAN, J C J C B 4.15.1934 Cottonton, AL BR/TR 6/175# d7.21																								
1962	Hou N	51	148	11	33	5	0	0	5	4-0	1	16	.223	.248	.257	39	-13	1-1	.972	5	98	122	S-48	-0.5
1963	Hou N	39	90	2	11	1	0	0	3	2-1	1	13	.122	.151	.133	-19	-14	1-0	.950	-0	99	104	S-32	-1.3
Total	2	90	238	13	44	6	0	0	8	6-1	2	29	.185	.211	.210	18	-27	2-1	.964	5	98	115	/S-80	-1.8
HARTNETT, GABBY Charles Leo B 12.20.1900 Woonsocket, RI D 12.20.1972 Park Ridge, IL BR/TR 6-1/195# d4.12 M3 C3 HF1955																								
1922	Chi N	31	72	4	14	1	1	0	4	6	0	8	.194	.256	.236	27	-8	1-0	.982	4	*128*	*167*	C-27	-0.2
1923	Chi N	85	231	28	62	12	2	8	39	25	3	22	.268	.347	.442	107	2	4-0	.994	5	*118*	*75*	C-39,1-31	0.8
1924	Chi N	111	354	56	106	17	7	16	67	39	5	37	.299	.377	.523	137	19	10-2	.963	-1	***116***	*118*	*C-105	2.6
1925	Chi N	117	398	61	115	28	3	24	67	36	2	77	.289	.351	.555	126	14	1-5	.958	10	***143***	*124*	*C-110	2.8
1926	Chi N	93	284	35	78	25	3	8	41	32	2	37	.275	.352	.468	118	8	0	.978	9	***180***	*121*	C-88	2.2
1927	Chi N	127	449	56	132	32	5	10	80	44	3	42	.294	.361	.454	117	11	2	.973	9	***163***	*101*	*C-126	2.9
1928	Chi N	120	388	61	117	26	9	14	57	65	2	32	.302	.404	.523	143	26	3	**.989**	15	***184***	*112*	*C-118	4.7
1929	†Chi N	25	22	2	6	2	1	1	9	5	0	5	.273	.407	.591	144	2	1	1.000	0	*0*	*0*	/C	0.2
1930	Chi N	141	508	84	172	31	3	37	122	55	1	62	.339	.404	.630	144	35	0	**.989**	3	***131***	*89*	*C-136	4.1
1931	Chi N	116	380	53	107	32	1	8	70	52	1	48	.282	.370	.434	113	9	3	.981	4	*120*	*98*	*C-105	2.0
1932	†Chi N	121	406	52	110	25	3	12	52	51	1	59	.271	.354	.436	112	8	0	.982	10	***194***	*104*	*C-117/1	2.4
1933	Chi N★	140	490	55	135	21	4	16	88	37	0	51	.276	.326	.433	115	9	1	.989	11	*145*	*95*	*C-140	2.9
1934	Chi N★	130	438	58	131	21	1	22	90	37	3	46	.299	.358	.502	130	18	0	**.996**	11	***120***	***143***	*C-129	3.5
1935	†Chi N★	116	413	67	142	32	6	13	91	41	1	46	.344	.404	.545	152	31	1	.984	11	*109*	***135***	*C-110	4.7
1936	Chi N★	121	424	49	130	25	6	7	64	30	6	36	.307	.361	.443	113	8	0	**.991**	9	*121*	*106*	*C-114	2.2
1937	Chi N★	110	356	47	126	21	6	12	82	43	0	19	.354	.424	.548	156	28	0	**.996**	0	*121*	*102*	*C-103	3.4
1938	†Chi N☆	88	299	40	82	19	1	10	59	48	3	17	.274	.380	.445	123	11	1	**.995**	-0	*109*	*80*	C-83,M	1.6
1939	Chi N	97	306	36	85	18	2	12	59	37	1	32	.278	.358	.467	118	8	0	.992	-3	*134*	*109*	C-86,M	1.0
1940	Chi N	37	64	3	17	3	0	1	12	8	0	7	.266	.347	.359	97	0	0	.951	-0	*98*	*84*	C-22/1M	0.1
1941	NY N	64	150	20	45	5	0	5	26	12	1	14	.300	.356	.433	119	3	0	.994	-1	*114*	*68*	C-34	0.4
Total	20	1990	6432	867	1912	396	64	236	1179	703	35	697	.297	.370	.489	126	242	28-7	.984	106	*138*	*108*	*C-1793/1-33	44.3
HARTNETT, PAT Patrick J. "Happy" B 10.20.1863 Boston, MA D 4.10.1935 Boston, MA 6-1/175# d4.18																								
1890	StL AA	14	53	6	10	2	1	0	4	6	1		.189	.283	.264	54	-3	1	.954	-1	89	28	1-14	-0.5
HARTS, GREG Gregory Rudolph B 4.21.1950 Atlanta, GA BL/TL 6/168# d9.15																								
1973	NY N	3	2	0	1	0	0	0	0	0-0	0	0	.500	.500	.500	181	0	0-0	—	0			H	0.0
HARTSEL, TOPSY Tully Frederick B 6.26.1874 Polk, OH D 10.14.1944 Toledo, OH BL/TL 5-5/155# d9.14																								
1898	Lou N	22	71	11	23	0	0	0	9	11	1		.324	.422	.324	116	2	2	.931	-1	78	159	O-21(RF)	0.0
1899	Lou N	30	75	8	18	1	1	1	7	11	1		.240	.345	.320	83	-1	1	.927	-1	70	135	O-22(7-0-15)	-0.3
1900	Cin N	18	64	10	21	2	1	2	5	8	0		.328	.403	.484	148	4	7	.957	-4	0	0	O-18(LF)	0.0
1901	Chi N	**140**	558	111	187	25	16	7	54	74	1		.335	.414	.475	163	48	41	.951	-2	88	63	*O-140(131-0-9)	3.6
1902	Phi A	**137**	545	**109**	154	20	12	5	58	**87**	2		.283	.383	.391	110	11	**47**	.955	-1	100	55	*O-137(LF)	0.1
1903	Phi A	98	373	65	116	19	14	5	26	49	0		.311	.391	.477	152	25	13	.968	-4	59	0	O-96(94-2-0)	1.7
1904	Phi A	147	534	79	135	17	12	2	25	75	2		.253	.347	.341	112	10	19	.959	-3	94	50	*O-147(122-25-0)	-0.1
1905	†Phi A	150	538	88	148	22	8	0	28	**121**	1		.275	**.409**	.346	138	33	37	.939	-9	35	27	*O-149(134-15-0)	1.6
1906	Phi A	144	533	96	136	21	9	1	30	**88**	2		.255	.363	.334	115	14	31	.969	1	82	127	*O-144(LF)	0.7
1907	Phi A	143	507	93	142	23	6	3	29	**106**	0		.280	**.405**	.367	143	33	20	.967	-11	60	50	*O-143(LF)	1.5
1908	Phi A	129	460	73	112	16	6	4	29	**93**	0		.243	.371	.330	120	16	15	.960	-4	41	50	*O-129(LF)	0.6
1909	Phi A	83	267	30	72	4	4	1	18	48	0		.270	.381	.326	121	9	3	.966	-3	0	0	O-74(72-0-2)	0.2
1910	†Phi A	90	285	45	63	10	3	0	22	58	0		.221	.353	.277	99	3	11	.945	-2	94	86	O-83(LF)	-0.3
1911	Phi A	25	38	8	9	2	0	0	1	8	2		.237	.396	.289	94	1	0	.941	1	92	248	/O-9(LF)	0.1
Total	14	1356	4848	826	1336	182	92	31	341	837	12		.276	.384	.370	128	208	247	.956	-42	67	57	*O-1312(1223-42-47)	9.4
HARTSFIELD, ROY Roy Thomas "Spec" B 10.25.1925 Chattahoochee, GA BR/TR 5-9/165# d4.28 M3 C5																								
1950	Bos N	107	419	62	116	15	2	7	24	27	1	61	.277	.322	.372	88	-9	7	.949	-18	93	73	2-96	-2.1
1951	Bos N	120	450	63	122	11	2	6	31	41	1	73	.271	.333	.344	89	-7	7-2	.969	-5	92	97	*2-114	-0.6
1952	Bos N	38	107	13	28	4	3	0	4	5	0	12	.262	.295	.355	82	-3	0-0	.950	-6	94	54	2-29	-0.8
Total	3	265	976	138	266	30	7	13	59	73	2	146	.273	.324	.358	88	-19	14-2	.959	-28	93	82	2-239	-3.5
HARTUNG, CLINT Clinton Clarence "Floppy" or "The Hondo Hurricane" B 8.10.1922 Hondo, TX BR/TR 6-4/215# d4.15 ▲																								
1947	NY N	34	94	13	29	4	3	4	13	3	0	21	.309	.330	.543	127	3	0	1.000	-2	85	126	P-23/O-7(LF)	-0.1

Year	Tm Lg	G	AB	R	H	2B	3B	HR	RBI	BB-IB	HP	SO	AVG	OBP	SLG	AOPS	ABR	SB-CS	FA	FR	Rng	Thr	G at Pos	BFW
1948	NY N	43	56	5	10	1	1	0	3	7	0	24	.179	.270	.232	37	2	0	1.000	-0	102	60	P-36	0.0
1949	NY N	38	63	7	12	0	0	4	7	4	0	21	.190	.239	.381	64	4	0	.957	2	130	55	P-33	0.0
1950	NY N	32	43	7	13	2	1	3	10	1	0	13	.302	.318	.605	136	2	0	.939	2	197	0	P-20/O-2(1-0-1),1	0.1
1951	†NY N	21	44	4	9	1	0	0	2	1	0	9	.205	.222	.227	21	-5	0-0	1.000	-0	82	157	O-12(RF)	-0.5
1952	NY N	28	78	6	17	2	1	3	8	9	0	24	.218	.299	.385	88	-2	0-0	.932	0	94	156	O-24(3-0-22)	-0.2
Total	6	196	378	42	90	10	6	14	43	25	0	112	.238	.285	.407	84	4	0-0	.972	1	118	69	P-112/O-45(11-0-35),1	-0.7
HARTZELL, ROY Roy Allen B 7.6.1881 Golden, CO D 11.6.1961 Golden, CO BL/TR 5-8.5/155# d4.17 OF Total (213-LF 32-CF 307-RF)																								
1906	StL A	113	404	43	86	7	0	0	24	19	10		.213	.266	.230	58	-19	21	.889	-3	**101**	**122**	*3-103/S-6,2-2	-2.2
1907	StL A	60	220	20	52	3	5	0	13	11	4		.236	.285	.295	85	-4	7	.911	-1	96	130	3-38,2-12/S-2,O-2(RF)	-0.4
1908	StL A	115	422	41	112	5	6	2	32	19	3		.265	.302	.320	101	-1	24	.943	-2	164	208	O-82(0-4-78),S-18/3-7,2-4	-0.7
1909	StL A	152	595	64	161	12	5	0	32	29	7		.271	.312	.308	103	0	14	.940	6	188	193	O-85(RF),S-65/2	0.5
1910	StL A	151	542	52	118	13	5	2	30	49	6		.218	.290	.271	81	-12	18	.929	7	107	132	3-89,S-38,O-23(RF)	-0.2
1911	NY A	144	527	67	156	17	11	3	91	63	4		.296	.375	.387	106	5	22	.936	-12	87	103	*3-124,S-12/O-8(2-0-8)	-0.3
1912	NY A	125	416	50	113	10	11	1	38	64	1		.272	.370	.356	102	2	20	.906	-2	91	50	3-56,O-56(0-13-43),S-10/2-2	0.0
1913	NY A	141	490	60	127	18	1	0	38	67	4	40	.259	.353	.300	91	-2	26	.942	3	101	100	2-81,O-31(4-11-16),3-21/S-4	0.2
1914	NY A	137	481	55	112	15	9	1	32	68	6	38	.233	.335	.308	94	-2	22-25	.973	-2	100	80	*O-128(91-3-34)/2-5	-1.6
1915	NY A	119	387	39	97	11	2	3	60	57	3	37	.251	.351	.313	99	2	7-19	.963	-4	96	72	*O-107(105-0-2)/2-5,3-2	-1.3
1916	NY A	33	64	12	12	1	0	0	7	9	1	3	.188	.297	.203	49	-4	1	1.000	-1	95	50	O-28(11-1-16)	-0.6
Total	11	1290	4548	503	1146	112	55	12	397	455	49	118	.252	.327	.309	93	-35	182-44	.959	-10	123	126	O-550R,3-440,S-155,2-112	-6.6
HARVEL, LUTHER Luther Raymond "Red" B 9.30.1905 Cambria, IL D 4.10.1986 Kansas City, MO BR/TR 5-11/180# d7.31																								
1928	Cle A	40	136	12	30	6	1	0	12	4	4	17	.221	.264	.279	42	-12	1-1	.948	-1	92	153	O-39(CF)	-1.4
HARVEY, ZAZA Ervin King B 1.5.1879 Saratoga, CA D 6.3.1954 Santa Monica, CA BL/TL 6/190# d5.3 ▲																								
1900	Chi N	2	3	0	0	0	0	0	0	0	0		.000	.000	.000	-99	-1	0	1.000	-0	0	0	/P	0.0
1901	Chi A	17	40	11	10	3	1	0	3	2	1		.250	.302	.375	89	2	1	.930	2	133	248	P-16	0.0
	Cle A	45	170	21	60	5	5	1	24	9	2		.353	.392	.459	141	9	15	.890	2	121	276	O-45(21-0-24)	0.8
	Year	62	210	32	70	8	6	1	27	11	3		.333	.375	.443	131	8	16	.890	3	121	276	O-45(21-0-24),P-16	0.8
1902	Cle A	12	46	5	16	2	0	0	5	3	0		.348	.388	.391	121	1	1	1.000	1	136	340	O-12(RF)	0.1
Total	3	76	259	37	86	10	6	1	32	14	3		.332	.373	.429	127	11	17	.907	4	124	289	/O-57(21-0-36),P-17	0.9
HARVEY, KEN Kenneth Eugene B 3.1.1978 Los Angeles, CA BR/TR 6-2/240# d9.18																								
2001	KC A	4	12	1	3	1	0	0	2	0-0	0	4	.250	.250	.333	48	-1	0-1	1.000	-0	72	60	/1-3,D	-0.2
2003	KC A	135	485	50	129	30	0	13	64	29-4	5	94	.266	.313	.408	78	-15	2-3	.988	6	132	94	1-99,D-32	-2.0
Total	2	139	497	51	132	31	0	13	66	29-4	5	98	.266	.311	.406	77	-16	2-4	.988	6	131	93	1-102/D-33	-2.2
HASBROOK, ZIGGY Robert Lyndon "Ziggy" (born Robert Lyndon Hasbrouck" B 11.21.1893 Grundy Center, IA D 2.9.1976 Garland, TX BR/TR 6-1/180# d9.6																								
1916	Chi A	9	8	1	1	0	0	0	0	1	0	2	.125	.222	.125	4	-1	0	1.000	1	234	93	/1-7	0.0
1917	Chi A	2	1	1	0	0	0	0	0	0	0	0	.000	.000	.000	-98	0	0	1.000	0	205	763	/2	0.0
Total	2	11	9	2	1	0	0	0	0	1	0	2	.111	.200	.111	-6	-1	0	1.000	1	234	93	/1-7,2	0.0
HASELMAN, BILL William Joseph B 5.25.1966 Long Branch, NJ BR/TR 6-3/220# d9.3																								
1990	Tex A	7	13	0	2	0	0	0	3	1-0	0	5	.154	.214	.154	5	-2	0-0	1.000	1	0	0	/CD	-0.1
1992	Sea A	8	19	1	5	0	0	0	0	0-0	0	7	.263	.263	.263	48	-1	0-0	1.000	-1	280	142	/C-5,O-2(LF)	-0.2
1993	Sea A	58	137	21	35	8	0	5	16	12-0	1	19	.255	.316	.423	97	-1	2-1	.992	-3	67	77	C-49/O-2(RF),D-4	-0.1
1994	Sea A	38	83	11	16	7	1	1	8	3-0	1	11	.193	.230	.337	43	-7	1-0	.982	-3	72	113	C-33/O-2(RF),D-3	-0.8
1995	†Bos A	64	152	22	37	6	1	5	23	17-0	2	30	.243	.322	.395	84	-4	0-2	.989	4	103	101	C-48,D-11/13	0.2
1996	Bos A	77	237	33	65	13	1	8	34	19-3	1	52	.274	.331	.439	91	-4	4-2	.994	9	91	92	C-69/1-2,D-2	0.9
1997	Bos A	67	212	22	50	15	0	6	26	15-2	2	44	.236	.290	.392	75	-8	0-2	.983	-4	66	113	C-66	-0.8
1998	Tex A	40	105	11	33	6	0	6	17	3-0	0	17	.314	.327	.543	118	2	0-0	.995	-2	75	68	C-36/D-2	0.2
1999	Det A	48	143	13	39	8	0	4	14	10-1	0	26	.273	.320	.413	85	-4	2-0	.996	-1	113	83	C-39/D-9	-0.2
2000	Tex A	62	193	23	53	18	0	6	26	15-0	1	36	.275	.329	.461	96	-1	0-1	.989	-1	95	95	C-62	0.1
2001	Tex A	47	130	12	37	6	0	3	25	8-0	1	27	.285	.331	.400	88	-2	0-1	1.000	-6	82	128	C-47	-0.6
2002	Tex A	69	179	16	44	7	0	3	18	11-1	2	25	.246	.297	.335	64	-9	0-0	.991	-11	87	76	C-67/D-2	-1.6
2003	Bos A	4	3	0	0	0	0	0	0	0-0	0	1	.000	.000	.000	-98	-1	0-0	1.000	-0	13	0	/C-2,D-2	-0.1
Total	13	589	1606	185	416	94	3	47	210	114-7	11	300	.259	.311	.409	83	-42	9-9	.991	-17	87	95	C-524/D-38,O-6(2-0-4),1-3,3	-3.1
HASENMAYER, DON Donald Irvin B 4.4.1927 Roslyn, PA BR/TR 5-10.5/180# d5.2 Mil 1945																								
1945	Phi N	5	18	1	2	0	0	0	1	2	0	1	.111	.200	.111	-13	-3	0	.920	1	130	40	/2-4,3	-0.1
1946	Phi N	6	12	0	1	1	0	0	0	0	0	2	.083	.083	.167	-31	-2	0	1.000	1	128	449	/3-3	-0.1
Total	2	11	30	1	3	1	0	0	1	2	0	3	.100	.156	.133	-19	-5	0	1.000	3	142	295	/3-4,2-4	-0.2
HASLIN, MICKEY Michael Joseph (born Michael Joseph Haslinsky) B 10.31.1909 Wilkes-Barre, PA D 3.7.2002 Wilkes-Barre, PA BR/TR 5-8/165# d9.7																								
1933	Phi N	26	89	3	21	2	0	0	9	3	0	5	.236	.261	.258	43	-6	1	.956	-2	104	76	2-26	-0.8
1934	Phi N	72	166	28	44	8	2	1	11	16	0	13	.265	.330	.355	74	-6	1	.941	-3	100	115	3-26,2-21/S-4	-0.7
1935	Phi N	110	407	53	108	17	3	3	52	19	1	25	.265	.300	.344	66	-20	5	.931	-2	96	98	S-87,3-11/2-9	-1.4
1936	Phi N	16	64	6	22	1	1	0	6	3	0	5	.344	.373	.391	96	0	0	.938	-3	97	93	2-12/3-5	-0.3
	Bos N	36	104	14	29	1	2	2	11	5	0	9	.279	.312	.385	93	-2	0	.892	-3	65	0	3-17/2-7	-0.4
	Year	52	168	20	51	2	3	2	17	8	0	14	.304	.335	.387	95	-2	0	.854	-6	71	40	3-22,2-19	-0.7
1937	NY N	27	42	8	8	1	0	0	5	9	0	3	.190	.333	.214	51	-2	1	.920	5	148	96	/S-9,2-4,3-4	0.3
1938	NY N	31	102	13	33	3	0	3	15	4	2	4	.324	.361	.441	119	2	0	.902	-1	117	0	3-15,2-13	0.3
Total	6	318	974	125	265	33	8	9	109	59	3	64	.272	.316	.350	74	-34	8	.927	-9	100	99	S-100/2-92,3-78	-3.0
HASNEY, PETE Peter James B 5.26.1865 , England D 5.24.1908 Philadelphia, PA d9.13																								
1890	Phi AA	2	7	1	1	0	0	0	0	1	0		.143	.250	.143	16	-1	0	.000	-1	0	0	/O-2(RF)	-0.2
HASSAMAER, BILL William Louis "Roaring Bill" B 7.26.1864 St.Louis, MO D 5.29.1910 St.Louis, MO 6/180# d4.19 OF Total (3-LF 140-RF)																								
1894	Was N	118	494	106	159	33	17	4	90	41	1	20	.322	.375	.482	108	5	16	.916	3	104	144	O-68(3-0-65),3-31,2-14/S-4	0.5
1895	Was N	86	363	42	101	18	4	1	60	26	0	13	.278	.326	.358	77	-13	8	.964	-6	40	39	O-75(RF)/1-10,S3	-1.7
	Lou N	23	96	7	20	2	2	0	14	3	0	4	.208	.232	.271	31	-10	0	.980	3	153	86	1-21/2S	-0.6
	Year	109	459	49	121	20	6	1	74	29	0	17	.264	.307	.340	68	-23	8	.964	-3	40	39	O-75(RF),1-31/S-2,32	-2.3
1896	Lou N	30	106	8	26	5	0	2	14	14	0	7	.245	.333	.349	83	-2	1	.976	6	195	116	1-29	0.3
Total	3	257	1059	163	306	58	23	7	178	84	1	44	.289	.342	.407	89	-20	25	.938	6	71	90	O-143R/1-60,3-32,2-15,S-6	-1.5
HASSETT, BUDDY John Aloysius B 9.5.1911 New York, NY D 8.23.1997 Westwood, NJ BL/TL 5-11/180# d4.14 Mil 1943-46																								
1936	Bro N	**156**	635	79	197	29	11	3	82	35	4	17	.310	.350	.405	102	0	5	.983	5	**114**	71	*1-156	-0.9
1937	Bro N	137	556	71	169	31	6	1	53	20	5	19	.304	.334	.387	94	-5	13	.984	10	**129**	92	*1-131/O-7(1-6-1)	-0.8
1938	Bro N	115	335	49	98	11	6	0	40	32	1	19	.293	.356	.361	95	-2	3	.945	-2	102	0	O-71(71-0-2)/1-8	-0.8
1939	Bos N	147	590	72	182	15	3	2	60	29	1	14	.308	.342	.354	94	-7	13	.985	10	**139**	116	*1-123,O-23(RF)	-0.9
1940	Bos N	124	458	59	107	19	4	0	27	25	0	16	.234	.273	.293	59	-27	4	.979	9	146	119	1-98,O-13(RF)	-2.8
1941	Bos N	118	405	59	120	9	4	1	33	36	0	15	.296	.354	.346	102	1	10	.991	7	129	111	1-99	-0.1
1942	†NY A	132	538	80	153	16	6	5	48	32	0	16	.284	.325	.364	95	-6	5-5	.991	11	126	**137**	*1-132	-0.8
Total	7	929	3517	469	1026	130	40	12	343	209	11	116	.292	.333	.362	92	-46	53-5	.985	49	130	105	1-747,O-114(72-6-39)	-7.1
HASSEY, RON Ronald William B 2.27.1953 Tucson, AZ BL/TR 6-2/200# d4.23 C4																								
1978	Cle A	25	74	5	15	0	0	2	9	5-0	1	7	.203	.256	.284	54	-5	2-0	.993	4	94	91	C-24	0.0
1979	Cle A	75	223	20	64	14	0	4	32	19-2	0	19	.287	.339	.404	100	0	1-0	.992	3	76	82	C-68/1-2,D	0.6
1980	Cle A	130	390	43	124	18	4	8	65	49-3	1	51	.318	.390	.446	130	18	0-2	.993	-9	86	114	*C-113/1-3,D-7	1.2
1981	Cle A	61	190	8	44	4	0	1	25	17-0	2	11	.232	.297	.268	66	-8	0-1	.991	9	126	**155**	C-56/1-5,D	0.2
1982	Cle A	113	323	33	81	18	0	5	34	53-5	1	32	.251	.356	.353	97	1	3-2	.993	1	67	116	*C-105/1-2,D-2	0.6
1983	Cle A	117	341	48	92	21	0	6	42	38-2	2	35	.270	.342	.384	97	0	2-2	.995	2	106	95	*C-113/D	0.6
1984	Cle A	48	149	11	38	5	1	0	19	15-2	0	26	.255	.321	.302	73	-5	1-0	1.000	-3	80	83	C-44/1D	-0.6
	Chi N	19	33	5	11	0	0	2	5	4-1	0	6	.333	.405	.515	144	2	0-1	1.000	1	108	69	/C-6,1-4	0.3
1985	NY A	92	267	31	79	16	1	13	42	28-4	3	21	.296	.369	.509	141	15	0-0	.984	-3	80	64	C-69/1-2,D-2	1.5
1986	NY A	64	191	23	57	14	0	6	29	24-1	2	16	.298	.381	.466	131	9	1-1	.985	-9	102	76	C-51/D-3	0.2
	Chi A	49	150	22	53	11	1	3	20	22-2	1	11	.353	.437	.500	150	12	0-0	1.000	5	178	107	D-34,C-11	1.6

Year	Tm Lg	G	AB	R	H	2B	3B	HR	RBI	BB-IB	HP	SO	AVG	OBP	SLG	AOPS	ABR	SB-CS	FA	FR	Rng	Thr	G at Pos	BFW
	Year	113	341	45	110	25	1	9	49	46-3	3	27	.323	.406	.481	140	21	1-1	.988	-4	113	81	C-62,D-37	1.8
1987	Chi A	49	145	15	31	9	0	3	12	17-2	2	11	.214	.303	.338	69	-6	0-0	1.000	1	75	67	C-24,D-18	-0.5
1988	†Oak A	107	323	32	83	15	0	7	45	30-1	4	42	.257	.323	.368	98	0	2-0	.994	-3	134	75	C-91/D-9	0.2
1989	†Oak A	97	268	29	61	12	0	5	23	24-2	1	45	.228	.290	.328	78	-8	1-0	.991	1	92	99	C-78/1D	-0.3
1990	†Oak A	94	254	18	54	7	0	5	22	27-3	1	29	.213	.288	.299	68	-11	0-0	.997	5	178	63	C-59,D-15/1-3	-0.4
1991	Mon N	52	119	5	27	8	0	1	14	13-1	0	16	.227	.301	.319	76	-3	1-1	.989	-6	75	74	C-34	-0.8
Total	14	1192	3440	348	914	172	7	71	438	385-31	21	378	.266	.340	.382	100	11	14-10	.993	-3	100	93	C-946/D-96,1-23	4.4
HASSLER, JOE Joseph Frederick B 4.7.1905 Ft.Smith, AR D 9.4.1971 Duncan, OK BR/TR 6/165# d5.26																								
1928	Phi A	28	34	5	9	2	0	0	3	2	0	4	.265	.306	.324	64	-2	0-1	.879	-2	89	79	S-28	-0.3
1929	Phi A	4	4	1	0	0	0	0	0	0	0	2	.000	.000	.000	-97	-1	0-0	.600	-1	82	0	/S-2	-0.2
1930	StL A	5	8	3	2	0	0	0	1	0	0	1	.250	.250	.250	26	-1	0-0	1.000	1	126	312	/S-3	0.0
Total	3	37	46	9	11	2	0	0	4	2	0	7	.239	.271	.283	43	-4	0-1	.875	-2	93	100	/S-33	-0.5
HASSON, GENE Charles Eugene B 7.20.1915 Connellsville, PA BL/TL 6/197# d9.9																								
1937	Phi A	28	98	12	30	6	3	3	14	13	0	14	.306	.387	.520	129	4	0-0	1.000	-3	51	126	1-28	-0.1
1938	Phi A	19	69	10	19	6	2	1	12	12	0	7	.275	.383	.464	114	2	0-0	.958	-3	51	100	1-19	-0.3
Total	2	47	167	22	49	12	5	4	26	25	0	21	.293	.385	.497	123	6	0-0	.985	-6	51	116	/1-47	-0.4
HASTINGS, SCOTT Winfield Scott B 8.10.1847 Hillsboro, OH D 8.14.1907 Sawtelle, CA BR/TR 5-8/161# d5.6 M2																								
1871	Rok NA	**25**	118	27	30	6	4	0	20	2		4	.254	.267	.373	85	-2	11-2	.856	-1			*C-23/2-2,O-2(2-1-0),1M	0.0
1872	Cle NA	**22**	115	34	45	4	0	0	16	3		2	.391	.407	.426	165	10	5-1	.797	-7			C-12/O-8(0-3-5),2-6,M	0.2
	Bal NA	13	62	16	19	3	1	0	4	1		2	.306	.317	.387	111	0	0-1	.905	3			C-13/2-2,O(CF)	0.2
	Year	35	177	50	64	7	1	0	20	4		4	.362	.376	.412	145	10	5-2	.854	-4			C-25/O-9(0-4-5),2-8	0.4
1873	Bal NA	30	145	41	41	4	0	0	15	4		1	.283	.302	.310	83	-3	4-2	.901	0			C-19,O-12(CF)/2	-0.2
1874	Har NA	52	247	60	80	11	2	0	30	4		3	.324	.335	.385	124	6	10-5	.753	-10			C-39,O-26(0-12-14)/2S	-0.3
1875	Chi NA	65	287	43	73	9	0	0	30	9		14	.254	.277	.286	95	-1	13-11	.815	4			C-46,O-29(1-15-15)/2-3	0.3
1876	Lou N	67	283	36	73	6	1	0	21	5		11	.258	.271	.286	73	-10		.872	-9	102	203	*O-65(CF)/C-5	-1.9
1877	Cin N	20	71	7	10	1	0	0	3	3		6	.141	.176	.155	6	-7		.791	-7			C-20/O(CF)	-1.3
Total	5 NA	207	974	221	288	37	7	0	115	23		26	.296	.312	.348	108	10	43-22	.000	-10			C-152/O-78(3-44-34),2-15,S1	0.2
Total	2	87	354	43	83	7	1	0	24	8		17	.234	.251	.260	61	-17		.872	-16			/O-66(CF),C-25	-3.2
HATCHER, CHRIS Christopher Kenneth B 1.7.1969 Anaheim, CA BR/TR 6-3/220# d9.6																								
1998	KC A	8	15	0	1	0	0	0	1	1-0	0	7	.067	.125	.067	-47	-3	0-0	1.000	-1	82	0	/O-5(LF)	-0.4
HATCHER, MICKEY Michael Vaughn B 3.15.1955 Cleveland, OH BR/TR 6-2/200# d8.3 C7 OF Total (345-LF 88-CF 146-RF)																								
1979	LA N	33	93	9	25	4	1	1	5	7-0	1	12	.269	.327	.366	90	-1	1-3	.974	1	109	72	O-19(1-1-18),3-17	-0.2
1980	LA N	57	84	4	19	2	0	1	5	2-1	0	12	.226	.244	.286	48	-6	0-2	1.000	2	85	106	O-25(4-0-21),3-18	-0.6
1981	Min A	99	377	36	96	23	2	3	37	15-2	2	29	.255	.285	.350	77	-11	3-1	.992	-2	100	55	O-91(5-86-0)/1-7,3-2,D	-1.5
1982	Min A	84	277	23	69	13	2	3	26	8-1	0	27	.249	.269	.343	65	-14	0-2	.988	2	87	250	O-47(26-1-21),D-29/3-5	-1.6
1983	Min A	106	375	50	119	15	3	9	47	14-0	1	19	.317	.342	.445	111	5	2-0	.979	7	130	102	O-56(10-0-48),D-39/1-7,3	0.8
1984	Min A	152	576	61	174	35	5	5	69	37-3	2	34	.302	.342	.406	103	3	0-1	.974	8	115	155	*O-100(LF),D-37,1-17/3	0.4
1985	Min A	116	444	46	125	28	0	3	49	16-1	2	23	.282	.308	.365	79	-12	0-0	.991	5	112	102	O-97(96-0-1),D-11/1-4	-1.2
1986	Min A	115	317	40	88	13	3	3	32	19-2	0	26	.278	.315	.366	84	-8	2-1	.971	1	90	283	O-46(LF),D-28,1-22/3-3	-1.0
1987	LA N	101	287	27	81	19	1	7	42	20-4	1	19	.282	.328	.429	102	1	2-3	.929	4	104	105	3-49,1-37/O-7(1-0-6)	0.2
1988	†LA N	88	191	22	56	8	0	1	25	7-3	2	7	.293	.322	.351	97	-1	0-0	1.000	1	90	189	O-29(8-0-21),1-25/3-3	-0.2
1989	LA N	94	224	18	66	9	2	2	25	13-3	1	16	.295	.328	.379	106	1	1-2	.961	-0	93	252	O-48(39-0-10),3-16/1-5,P	-0.1
1990	LA N	85	132	12	28	3	1	0	13	6-1	1	22	.212	.248	.250	40	-11	0-0	1.000	-2	79	120	1-25,3-10,O-10(LF)	-1.5
Total	12	1130	3377	348	946	172	20	38	375	164-21	13	246	.280	.313	.377	89	-54	11-15	.983	26	105	139	O-575L,1-149,D-145,3-125/P	-6.5
HATCHER, BILLY William Augustus B 10.4.1960 Williams, AZ BR/TR 5-9/175# d9.10 C6																								
1984	Chi N	8	9	1	1	0	0	0	0	1-1	0	0	.111	.200	.111	-10	-1	2-0	1.000	0	55	682	/O-4(LF)	-0.1
1985	Chi N	53	163	24	40	12	1	2	10	8-0	3	12	.245	.290	.368	75	-5	2-4	.988	-3	86	79	O-44(16-27-3)	-1.0
1986	†Hou N	127	419	55	108	15	4	6	36	22-1	5	52	.258	.302	.356	83	-11	38-14	.983	0	99	115	*O-121(39-95-9)	-1.0
1987	Hou N	141	564	96	167	28	3	11	63	42-1	9	70	.296	.352	.415	107	6	53-9	.986	5	96	**204**	*O-140(51-94-6)	1.6
1988	Hou N	145	530	79	142	25	4	7	52	37-4	8	56	.268	.321	.370	103	2	32-13	.983	-1	100	86	*O-142(124-25-0)	-0.1
1989	Hou N	108	395	49	90	15	3	3	44	30-2	1	53	.228	.281	.304	71	-16	22-6	.991	0	107	18	*O-104(96-11-0)	-1.7
	Pit N	27	86	10	21	4	0	1	7	0-0	1	9	.244	.253	.326	67	-4	2-1	1.000	-4	62	0	O-20(2-10-9)	-0.9
	Year	135	481	59	111	19	3	4	51	30-2	2	62	.231	.277	.308	70	-20	24-7	.992	-4	100	15	*O-124(98-21-9)	-2.6
1990	†Cin N	139	504	68	139	28	5	5	25	33-5	6	42	.276	.327	.381	91	-6	30-10	**.997**	7	109	129	*O-131(76-69-0)	0.2
1991	Cin N	138	442	45	116	25	3	4	41	26-4	7	55	.262	.312	.360	86	-8	11-9	.981	0	107	66	*O-121(81-54-0)	-1.2
1992	Cin N	43	94	10	27	3	0	2	10	5-0	0	11	.287	.314	.383	97	-1	0-2	.967	-2	85	0	O-23(LF)	-0.4
	Bos A	75	315	37	75	16	2	1	23	17-1	3	41	.238	.283	.311	62	-16	4-6	.968	-4	91	103	O-75(63-13-0)	-2.4
1993	Bos A	136	508	71	146	24	3	9	57	28-4	11	46	.287	.336	.400	92	-6	14-7	.993	-11	86	87	*O-130(0-129-2)/2-2	-1.5
1994	Bos A	44	164	24	40	9	1	1	18	11-0	1	14	.244	.292	.329	58	-10	4-5	.968	0	104	98	O-43(RF)/D	-1.2
	Phi N	43	134	15	33	5	1	2	13	6-0	0	14	.246	.271	.343	60	-8	4-1	1.000	1	93	208	O-40(7-26-11)	-0.7
1995	Tex A	6	12	2	1	1	0	0	0	1-0	0	1	.083	.154	.167	-16	-2	0-0	1.000	1	119	388	/O-5(1-0-4),D	-0.1
Total	12	1233	4339	586	1146	210	30	54	399	267-23	55	476	.264	.312	.364	85	-86	218-87	.986	-8	98	105	*O-1143(583-553-87)/D-2,2-2	-10.5
HATFIELD, FRED Fred James B 3.18.1925 Lanett, AL D 5.22.1998 Tallahassee, FL BL/TR 6-1/171# d8.31 C2																								
1950	Bos A	10	12	3	3	0	0	0	2	3	0	1	.250	.400	.250	63	-1	0-0	1.000	2	152	320	/3-3	0.1
1951	Bos A	80	163	23	28	4	2	2	14	22	1	27	.172	.274	.258	40	-14	1-0	.959	14	139	170	3-49	0.0
1952	Bos A	19	25	6	8	1	1	1	3	4	1	2	.320	.433	.560	162	2	0-3	1.000	2	137	0	3-17	0.3
	Det A	112	441	42	104	12	2	2	25	35	6	52	.236	.301	.286	63	-22	2-2	.968	10	107	124	*3-107/S-9	-1.3
	Year	131	466	48	112	13	3	3	28	39	7	54	.240	.309	.300	69	-20	2-5	**.971**	12	109	116	*3-124/S-9	-1.0
1953	Det A	109	311	41	79	11	1	3	19	40	1	34	.254	.341	.325	81	-7	3-5	.978	5	110	99	3-54,2-28/S	-0.1
1954	Det A	81	218	31	64	12	0	2	25	28	5	24	.294	.385	.376	112	5	4-2	.972	-6	98	84	2-54,3-15	0.3
1955	Det A	122	413	51	96	15	3	8	33	61-6	5	49	.232	.337	.341	85	-8	3-2	.975	-5	103	109	2-92,3-16,S-14	-0.5
1956	Det A	8	12	2	3	0	0	0	2	2-0	1	1	.250	.400	.250	75	0	0-0	1.000	-1	83	48	/2-4	-0.1
	Chi A	106	321	46	84	9	1	7	33	37-3	8	36	.262	.349	.361	88	-5	1-0	.961	-0	101	124	*3-100/S-3	-0.5
	Year	114	333	48	87	9	1	7	35	39-3	9	37	.261	.351	.357	87	-5	1-0	.961	-1	101	124	*3-100/2-4,S-3	-0.6
1957	Chi A	69	114	14	23	3	0	0	8	15-1	5	20	.202	.316	.228	52	-7	1-0	.951	3	117	192	3-44	-0.4
1958	Cle A	3	8	0	1	0	0	0	1	1-0	0	1	.125	.222	.125	-2	-1	0-0	1.000	0	140	0	/3-2	-0.1
	Cin N	3	1	0	0	0	0	0	0	0-0	0	0	.000	.000	.000	-95	0	0-0	—	-0	0	0	/23	-0.1
Total	9	722	2039	259	493	67	10	25	165	248-10	33	247	.242	.332	.321	78	-58	15-14	.962	25	111	129	3-408,2-179/S-27	-2.4
HATFIELD, GIL Gilbert "Colonel" B 1.27.1855 Hoboken, NJ D 5.26.1921 Hoboken, NJ TR 5-9.5/168# d9.24 b-John ▲																								
1885	Buf N	11	30	1	4	0	1	0	0	0		11	.133	.133	.200	6	-3		.913	-0	112	0	/3-8,2-3	-0.3
1887	NY N	2	7	2	3	1	0	0	3	0	0	1	.429	.429	.571	184	1	0	1.000	0	76	0	/3-2	0.1
1888	†NY N	28	105	7	19	1	0	0	9	2	2	18	.181	.211	.190	29	-8	8	.813	-2	76	0	3-14,S-13/O(CF)2	-1.0
1889	NY N	32	125	21	23	2	0	1	12	9	2	15	.184	.250	.224	33	-12	9	.858	1	98	74	S-24/P-6,3-2	-0.7
1890	NY P	71	287	32	80	13	6	2	37	17	4	19	.279	.328	.387	83	-9	12	.836	-15	98	71	3-42,S-27/P-3,O(CF)	-1.8
1891	Was AA	134	500	83	128	11	8	1	48	50	9	39	.256	.335	.316	90	-5	43	.869	13	104	99	*S-105,3-27/P-4,O-3(1-0-2)	0.9
1893	Bro N	34	120	24	35	3	3	2	19	17	2	5	.292	.388	.417	119	4	9	.875	-6	84	33	3-34	-0.2
1895	Lou N	5	16	3	3	0	0	0	1	1	1	1	.188	.278	.188	23	-2	0	.889	-0	94	0	/3-3,S-2	-0.2
Total	8	317	1190	173	295	31	18	6	129	96	20	109	.248	.315	.319	79	-34	81	.850	-10	100	93	S-171,3-132/P-13,O-5(1-2-2),2-4	-3.2
HATFIELD, JOHN John Van Buskirk B 7.20.1847 , NJ D 2.20.1909 Long Island City, NY 5-10/165# d5.18 M2 b-Gil OF Total (83-LF 1-RF)																								
1871	Mut NA	**33**	168	41	43	3	2	0	22	4		0	.256	.273	.298	70	-5	10-3	.853	1	65	0	*O-24(LF)/2-7,3-2	-0.1
1872	Mut NA	**56**	288	76	93	15	2	1	47	9		6	.323	.343	.399	136	15	12-5	.847	4	102	151	*2-55/1M	1.1
1873	Mut NA	52	255	54	78	5	6	2	46	3		2	.306	.314	.396	110	2	2-0	.743	-9	79	91	*3-45,2-12/O(RF)M	-0.6
1874	Mut NA	63	292	47	66	12	1	0	29	7		12	.226	.244	.274	64	-11	4-0	.874	6	36	0	*O-58(LF)/3-7,P-3,1S	-0.2
1875	Mut NA	1	4	1	2	1	0	0	1	0		0	.500	.500	.750	312	1	0-0	1.000	0	0	0	/O(LF)	0.1
1876	NY N	1	4	0	1	0	0	0	1	0		0	.250	.250	.250	77	0		.833	-0	126	0	/2	0.0
Total	5 NA	205	1007	219	282	36	11	3	145	23		20	.280	.296	.347	98	2	28-8	.000	3	44	0	/O-84L,2-74,3-54,P-3,1-2,S	0.3

Year	Tm Lg	G	AB	R	H	2B	3B	HR	RBI	BB-IB	HP	SO	AVG	OBP	SLG	AOPS	ABR	SB-CS	FA	FR	Rng	Thr	G at Pos	BFW
HATTEBERG, SCOTT Scott Allen B 12.14.1969 Salem, OR BL/TR 6-1/185# d9.8																								
1995	Bos A	2	2	1	1	0	0	0	0	0-0	0	0	.500	.500	.500	156	0	0-0	1.000	1	0	0	/C-2	0.1
1996	Bos A	10	11	3	2	1	0	0	0	3-0	0	2	.182	.357	.273	61	-1	0-0	1.000	-0	43	89	C-10	0.0
1997	Bos A	114	350	46	97	23	1	10	44	40-2	2	70	.277	.354	.434	102	2	0-1	.983	-14	69	90	*C-106/D	-0.5
1998	†Bos A	112	359	46	99	23	1	12	43	43-3	5	58	.276	.359	.446	106	4	0-0	.993	8	94	114	*C-108	1.8
1999	†Bos A	30	80	12	22	5	0	1	11	18-0	1	14	.275	.410	.375	100	1	0-0	.993	1	51	105	C-23/D-6	0.3
2000	Bos A	92	230	21	61	15	0	8	36	38-3	0	39	.265	.367	.435	100	1	0-1	.981	-6	47	117	C-48,D-20/3	-0.4
2001	Bos A	94	278	34	68	19	0	3	25	33-0	4	26	.245	.332	.345	79	-7	1-1	.992	-22	43	60	C-72/D-8	-2.4
2002	†Oak A	136	492	58	138	22	4	15	61	68-1	6	56	.280	.374	.433	114	12	0-0	.994	9	147	120	1-91,D-42	1.0
2003	†Oak A	147	541	63	137	34	0	12	61	66-0	9	53	.253	.342	.383	91	-5	0-1	.992	2	105	102	*1-128,D-15	-1.6
Total	9	737	2343	284	625	142	6	61	281	309-9	27	318	.267	.357	.411	99	7	1-4	.989	-22	67	96	C-369,1-219/D-92,3	-1.7
HATTON, GRADY Grady Edgebert B 10.7.1922 Beaumont, TX BL/TR 5-9/175# d4.16 M3 C3																								
1946	Cin N	116	436	56	118	18	3	14	69	66	2	53	.271	.369	.422	129	18	6	.941	-16	92	**90**	*3-116/O-2(LF)	0.1
1947	Cin N	146	524	91	147	24	8	16	77	81	0	50	.281	.377	.448	119	16	7	.938	-8	93	72	*3-136	0.7
1948	Cin N	133	458	58	110	17	2	9	44	72	0	50	.240	.343	.345	90	-5	7	.932	4	100	103	*3-123/2-3,S-2,O(LF)	-0.2
1949	Cin N	137	537	71	141	38	5	11	69	62	3	48	.263	.342	.413	101	1	4	**.975**	-3	98	98	*3-136	-0.2
1950	Cin N	130	438	67	114	17	1	11	54	70	3	39	.260	.366	.379	96	0	6	.954	-1	93	76	*3-126/2S	-0.2
1951	Cin N	96	331	41	84	9	3	4	37	33	0	32	.254	.321	.335	76	-11	4-2	.972	5	101	126	3-87/O-2(LF)	-0.7
1952	Cin N☆	128	433	48	92	14	1	9	57	66	2	60	.212	.319	.312	76	-13	5-4	**.990**	-9	91	86	*2-120	-1.7
1953	Cin N	83	159	22	37	3	1	7	22	29	0	24	.233	.351	.396	94	-1	0-1	.991	-4	88	105	2-35,1-10/3-5	-0.4
1954	Cin N	1	1	0	0	0	0	0	0	0	0	0	.000	.000	.000	-97	0	0-0	—	0			H	0.0
	Chi A	13	30	3	5	1	0	0	3	5	0	3	.167	.278	.200	34	-3	1-0	1.000	-1	82	68	3-10/1-3	-0.3
	Bos A	99	302	40	85	12	3	5	33	58	2	25	.281	.399	.391	106	5	1-1	.966	6	111	116	3-93/1S	1.1
	Year	112	332	43	90	13	3	5	36	63	2	28	.271	.388	.373	100	3	2-1	**.969**	5	**108**	112	*3-103/1-4,S	0.8
1955	Bos A	126	380	48	93	11	4	4	49	76-3	0	28	.245	.367	.326	81	-7	0-1	.976	4	**107**	106	*3-111/2	-0.4
1956	Bos A	5	5	0	2	0	0	0	2	0-0	0	0	.400	.400	.400	100	0	0-0	—	0			H	0.0
	StL N	44	73	10	18	1	2	0	7	13-0	0	7	.247	.360	.315	84	-1	1-0	.951	-2	100	100	2-13/3	-0.2
	Bal A	27	61	4	9	1	0	1	3	13-1	0	6	.148	.297	.213	40	-5	0-0	1.000	-2	99	42	2-15,3-12	-0.7
1960	Chi N	28	38	3	13	0	0	0	7	2-1	1	5	.342	.381	.342	104	0	0-0	.931	-1	102	55	/2-8	0.0
Total	12	1312	4206	562	1068	166	33	91	533	646-5	13	430	.254	.354	.374	96	-6	42-9	.956	-29	98	95	3-956,2-196/1-14,O-5(LF),S-4	-3.1
HAUGER, ARTHUR John Arthur B 11.18.1893 Delhi, OH D 8.2.1944 Redwood City, CA BL/TR 5-11/168# d7.17																								
1912	Cle A	15	18	0	1	0	0	0	0	1	0		.056	.105	.056	-52	-4	0	1.000	-0	111	0	/O-5(1-2-2)	-0.4
HAUSER, ARNOLD Arnold George "Peewee" or "Stub" B 9.25.1888 Chicago, IL D 5.22.1966 Aurora, IL BR/TR 5-6/145# d4.21																								
1910	StL N	119	375	37	77	7	2	2	36	49	9	39	.205	.312	.251	67	-14	15	.931	-7	101	62	*S-117/3	-1.8
1911	StL N	136	515	61	124	11	8	3	46	26	7	67	.241	.286	.311	69	-24	24	.918	-13	98	93	*S-134/3-2	-2.9
1912	StL N	133	479	73	124	14	7	1	42	39	3	69	.259	.319	.324	78	-15	26	.934	8	**109**	96	*S-132	0.2
1913	StL N	22	45	3	13	0	3	0	9	2	2	2	.289	.347	.422	121	1	1-2	.848	-3	84	78	/S-8,2-4	-0.2
1915	Chi F	23	54	6	11	1	0	0	4	5	1	7	.204	.283	.222	46	-5	2	.851	-4	90	141	S-16/3-6	-0.8
Total	5	433	1468	180	349	33	20	6	137	121	22	184	.238	.305	.300	72	-57	68-2	.924	-17	102	87	S-407/3-9,2-4	-5.5
HAUSER, JOE Joseph John "Unser Choe" B 1.12.1899 Milwaukee, WI D 7.11.1997 Sheboygan, WI BL/TL 5-10.5/175# d4.18																								
1922	Phi A	111	368	61	119	21	5	9	43	30	2	37	.323	.378	.481	119	10	1-5	.986	-3	92	92	1-94	-0.1
1923	Phi A	146	537	93	165	21	9	17	94	69	12	52	.307	.398	.475	127	22	6-6	.990	-3	93	99	*1-146	0.8
1924	Phi A	149	562	97	162	31	8	27	115	56	5	52	.288	.358	.516	123	15	7-5	.993	-3	92	116	*1-146	0.3
1926	Phi A	91	229	31	44	10	0	8	36	39	1	35	.192	.312	.341	66	-11	1-1	.996	0	93	91	1-65	-1.5
1928	Phi A	95	300	61	78	19	5	16	59	52	0	45	.260	.369	.517	127	12	4-2	.986	-5	75	83	1-88	0.1
1929	Cle A	37	48	8	12	1	1	3	9	4	1	8	.250	.321	.500	104	0	0-0	.986	0	137	39	/1-8	0.0
Total	6	629	2044	351	580	103	28	80	356	250	21	229	.284	.368	.479	117	48	19-19	.990	-13	90	98	1-547	-0.4
HAUSMANN, GEORGE George John B 2.11.1916 St.Louis, MO BR/TR 5-5/145# d4.18																								
1944	NY N	131	466	70	124	20	4	1	30	40	0	25	.266	.324	.333	85	-9	3	.960	-1	98	90	*2-122	-0.4
1945	NY N	**154**	623	98	174	15	8	2	45	73	1	46	.279	.356	.339	92	-5	7	.968	2	103	76	*2-154	0.6
1949	NY N	16	47	5	6	0	1	0	3	7	0	6	.128	.241	.170	12	-6	0	.984	1	114	104	2-13	-0.5
Total	3	301	1136	173	304	35	13	3	78	120	1	77	.268	.338	.329	86	-20	10	.965	2	101	83	2-289	-0.3
HAUTZ, CHARLIE Charles A. B 2.5.1852 St.Louis, MO D 1.24.1929 St.Louis, MO BR 5-7/150# d5.4 U3																								
1875	RS NA	**19**	83	5	25	3	0	0	4	0		9	.301	.301	.337	134	3	5-1	.921	-1	80	74	1-19	0.3
1884	Pit AA	7	24	0	5	0	0	0		3	0		.208	.296	.208	68	-1		.980	1	64	121	/1-5,O-2(CF)	-0.1
HAWES, ROY Roy Lee B 7.5.1926 Shiloh, IL BL/TL 6-2/190# d9.23																								
1951	Was A	3	6	0	1	0	0	0	0	0	0	1	.167	.167	.167	-10	-1	0-0	1.000	-0	0	0	/1	-0.1
HAWES, BILL William Hildreth B 11.17.1853 Nashua, NH D 6.16.1940 Lowell, MA BR/TR 5-10/155# d5.1																								
1879	Bos N	38	155	19	31	3	3	0	9	2		13	.200	.210	.258	52	-8		.828	-2	141	279	O-34(1-7-26)/C-5	-0.9
1884	Cin U	79	349	80	97	7	4	4		5			.278	.288	.355	87	-17		.827	-7	51	0	O-58(22-9-28),1-21	-2.4
Total	2	117	504	99	128	10	7	4	9	7		13	.254	.264	.325	77	-25		.827	-9	84	103	/O-92(23-16-54),1-21,C-5	-3.3
HAWKES, THORNY Thorndike Proctor B 10.15.1852 Danvers, MA D 2.3.1929 Danvers, MA BR/TR 5-8/135# d5.1																								
1879	Tro N	64	250	24	52	6	1	0	20	4		14	.208	.220	.240	55	-11		.896	15	**116**	93	*2-64	0.6
1884	Was AA	38	151	16	42	4	2	0		4	0		.278	.297	.331	118	3		.917	1	96	53	2-38/O-2(CF)	0.5
Total	2	102	401	40	94	10	3	0	20	8	0	14	.234	.249	.274	79	-8		.903	15	109	79	2-102/O-2(CF)	1.1
HAWKS, CHICKEN Nelson Louis B 2.3.1896 San Francisco, CA D 5.26.1973 San Rafael, CA BL/TL 5-11/167# d4.14																								
1921	NY A	41	73	16	21	2	3	2	15	5	0	12	.288	.333	.479	103	0	0-1	.970	-1	105	0	O-15(5-10-0)	-0.2
1925	Phi N	105	320	52	103	15	5	5	45	32	2	33	.322	.387	.447	103	2	3-6	.986	-0	102	90	1-90	-0.4
Total	2	146	393	68	124	17	8	7	60	37	2	45	.316	.377	.453	103	2	3-7	.986	-1	102	90	/1-90,O-15(5-10-0)	-0.6
HAWORTH, HOWIE Homer Howard "Cully" B 8.27.1893 Newberg, OR D 1.28.1953 Troutdale, OR BL/TR 5-10.5/165# d8.14																								
1915	Cle A	7	7	0	1	0	0	0	1	2	0	2	.143	.333	.143	42	0	0	.917	-1	*107*	*64*	/C-5	-0.1
HAYDEN, JACK John Francis B 10.21.1880 Bryn Mawr, PA D 8.3.1942 Haverford, PA BL/TL 5-9/170# d4.26																								
1901	Phi A	51	211	35	56	6	4	0	17	18	0		.265	.323	.332	78	-6	4	.841	-4	168	0	O-50(30-4-16)	-1.2
1906	Bos A	85	322	22	80	6	4	1	14	17	3		.248	.292	.301	86	-6	6	.973	-3	61	41	O-85(RF)	-1.4
1908	Chi N	11	45	3	9	2	0	0	2	1	0		.200	.217	.244	45	-3	1	1.000	-1	0	0	O-11(RF)	-0.5
Total	3	147	578	60	145	14	8	1	33	36	3		.251	.298	.308	80	-15	11	.929	-8	91	24	O-146(30-4-112)	-3.1
HAYES, CHARLIE Charles Dewayne B 5.29.1965 Hattiesburg, MS BR/TR 6/207# d9.11 OF Total (4-LF 1-RF)																								
1988	SF N	7	11	0	1	0	0	0	0	0-0	0	3	.091	.091	.091	-50	-2	0-0	1.000	-1	98	0	/O-4(3-0-1),3-3	-0.3
1989	SF N	3	5	0	1	0	0	0	0	0-0	0	1	.200	.200	.200	15	-1	0-0	1.000	-1	39	0	/3-3	-0.1
	Phi N	84	299	26	77	15	1	8	43	11-1	0	49	.258	.281	.395	92	-4	3-1	.910	4	109	109	3-82	0.0
	Year	87	304	26	78	15	1	8	43	11-1	0	50	.257	.280	.391	91	-5	3-1	.911	4	108	107	3-85	-0.1
1990	Phi N	152	561	56	145	20	0	10	57	28-3	2	91	.258	.293	.348	77	-19	4-4	.957	19	**114**	**139**	*3-146/1-4,2	-0.1
1991	Phi N	142	460	34	106	23	1	12	53	16-3	1	75	.230	.257	.363	74	-18	3-3	.958	2	101	123	*3-138/S-2	-1.8
1992	NY A	142	509	52	131	19	2	18	66	28-0	3	100	.257	.297	.409	98	-4	3-5	.963	-9	93	117	*3-139/1-4	-1.5
1993	Col N	157	573	89	175	**45**	2	25	98	43-6	5	82	.305	.355	.522	114	12	11-6	.954	8	105	79	*3-154/S	2.1
1994	Col N	113	423	46	122	23	4	10	50	36-4	3	71	.288	.348	.433	88	-7	3-6	.944	6	109	95	*3-110	-0.1
1995	Phi N	141	529	58	146	30	3	11	85	50-2	4	88	.276	.340	.406	96	-3	5-1	.963	-5	91	114	*3-141	-0.5
1996	Pit N	128	459	51	114	21	2	10	62	36-4	0	78	.248	.301	.368	74	-18	6-0	.950	8	112	121	*3-124	-0.7
	†NY A	20	67	7	19	3	0	2	13	1-0	0	12	.284	.294	.418	77	-3	0-0	1.000	2	101	144	3-19	0.0
1997	†NY A	100	353	39	91	16	0	11	53	40-2	1	66	.258	.332	.397	91	-5	3-2	.947	-5	91	126	3-98/2-5	-0.8
1998	SF N	111	329	39	94	8	0	12	62	34-0	0	61	.286	.351	.419	108	3	2-1	.989	-3	87	89	3-46,1-45/D-2	-0.2
1999	SF N	95	264	33	54	9	1	6	48	33-0	1	41	.205	.292	.314	59	-18	3-1	.940	-9	85	36	3-55,1-20/O(LF)D	-2.6
2000	Mil N	121	370	46	93	17	0	9	46	57-4	1	84	.251	.348	.370	85	-8	1-1	.976	-5	100	62	3-59,1-57/D	-1.6
2001	Hou N	31	50	4	10	2	0	0	4	7-1	0	16	.200	.293	.240	40	-4	0-0	1.000	-0	82	149	3-11/1-2,D	-0.5

Year	Tm Lg	G	AB	R	H	2B	3B	HR	RBI	BB-IB	HP	SO	AVG	OBP	SLG	AOPS	ABR	SB-CS	FA	FR	Rng	Thr	G at Pos	BFW
Total	14	1547	5262	580	1379	251	16	144	740	420-30	21	918	.262	.316	.398	88	-99	47-31	.954	11	101	108	*3-1328,1-132/D-6,2-6,O-5L,S-3	-8.7
HAYES, FRANKIE Franklin Witman "Blimp" B 10.13.1914 Jamesburg, NJ D 6.22.1955 Point Pleasant, NJ BR/TR 6/185# d9.21																								
1933	Phi A	3	5	0	0	0	0	0	0	0	0	2	.000	.000	.000	-99	-1	0-0	.889	0	0	0	/C-3	-0.1
1934	Phi A	92	248	24	56	10	0	6	30	20	1	44	.226	.286	.339	63	-15	2-1	.955	-10	85	94	C-89	-1.9
1936	Phi A	144	505	59	137	25	2	10	67	46	2	58	.271	.335	.388	79	-18	3-5	.972	-25	69	101	*C-143	-3.1
1937	Phi A	60	188	24	49	11	1	10	38	29	0	34	.261	.359	.489	114	4	0-0	.971	-5	89	79	C-56	0.2
1938	Phi A	99	316	56	92	19	3	11	55	54	1	51	.291	.396	.475	120	11	2-3	.975	-14	75	94	C-90	0.1
1939	Phi A☆	124	431	66	122	28	5	20	83	40	3	55	.283	.348	.510	119	10	4-1	.978	-16	72	102	*C-114	0.2
1940	Phi A★	136	465	73	143	23	4	16	70	61	1	59	.308	.389	.477	126	19	9-3	.971	-14	64	78	*C-134/1-2	1.3
1941	Phi A★	126	439	66	123	27	4	12	63	62	0	56	.280	.369	.442	117	11	2-0	.983	-10	79	94	*C-123	0.9
1942	Phi A	21	63	8	15	4	0	0	5	9	0	8	.238	.333	.302	80	-1	1-1	1.000	-3	68	134	C-20	-0.4
	StL A	56	159	14	40	6	0	2	17	28	0	39	.252	.364	.327	94	0	0-0	.971	-6	79	74	C-51	-0.4
	Year	77	222	22	55	10	0	2	22	37	0	47	.248	.355	.320	90	-1	1-1	.979	-9	76	90	C-71	-0.8
1943	StL A	88	250	16	47	7	0	5	30	37	1	36	.188	.295	.276	66	-10	1-0	.983	-9	64	83	C-76/1	-1.6
1944	Phi A★	**155**	581	62	144	18	6	13	78	57	0	59	.248	.315	.367	96	-5	2-1	.982	-3	72	116	*C-155/1	0.1
1945	Phi A	32	110	12	25	2	1	3	14	18	0	14	.227	.336	.345	98	0	1-0	.994	1	91	134	C-32	0.3
	Cle A✳	119	385	39	91	15	6	6	43	53	4	52	.236	.335	.353	104	3	1-1	.988	5	84	86	*C-119	1.5
	Year	151	495	51	116	17	7	9	57	71	4	66	.234	.335	.352	103	3	2-1	.989	5	86	97	*C-151	1.8
1946	Cle A★	51	156	11	40	12	0	3	18	21	0	26	.256	.345	.391	112	3	1-3	.981	-1	121	69	C-50	0.4
	Chi A	53	179	15	38	6	0	2	16	29	0	33	.212	.322	.279	72	-6	1-1	.979	-1	83	111	C-52	-0.5
	Year	104	335	26	78	18	0	5	34	50	0	59	.233	.332	.331	90	-3	2-4	.980	-2	102	90	*C-102	-0.1
1947	Bos A	5	13	0	2	0	0	0	1	0	0	1	.154	.154	.154	-13	-2	0-0	.917	0	129	92	/C-4	-0.2
Total	14	1364	4493	545	1164	213	32	119	628	564	13	627	.259	.343	.400	100	3	30-20	.977	-112	77	95	*C-1311/1-4	-3.2
HAYES, JACKIE John J. B 6.27.1861 Brooklyn, NY TR 5-8/175# d5.2 OF Total (4-LF 75-CF 24-RF)																								
1882	Wor N	78	326	27	88	22	4	4	54	6		26	.270	.283	.399	113	5		.855	-11	101	59	*O-58(0-55-3),C-15/3-5,S	-0.6
1883	Pit AA	85	351	41	92	23	5	3		15			.262	.292	.382	120	9		.911	-16			C-62,O-18(0-15-3)/S-5,1-5,2	-0.2
1884	Pit AA	33	124	11	28	6	1	0		4	1		.226	.256	.290	79	-3		.912	-1			C-24/1-5,O-3(RF),2	-0.1
	Bro AA	16	51	4	12	3	0	0		3	0		.235	.278	.294	86	-1		.946	4			C-14/O-2(1-1-0)	0.4
	Year	49	175	15	40	9	1	0		7	1		.229	.262	.291	81	-3		.925	4			C-38/1-5,O-5(1-1-3),2	0.3
1885	Bro AA	42	137	10	18	3	0	0	10	5	3		.131	.179	.153	6	-14		.900	-4			C-42	-1.3
1886	Was N	26	89	8	17	3	0	3	9	4		23	.191	.226	.326	71	-3	0	.926	-2			C-14,O-12(1-4-7)/2	-0.4
1887	Bal AA	8	28	2	4	3	0	0	3	0	0		.143	.143	.250	9	-3	0	.250	-3	0	0	/O-4(2-0-2),3-3,C	-0.5
1890	Bro P	12	42	3	8	0	0	0	5	2	0	4	.190	.227	.190	11	-6	0	.867	-3	78	0	/O-6(RF),S-3,C-2,2	-0.7
Total	7	300	1148	106	267	63	10	10	81	39	4	53	.233	.260	.331	87	-16	0	.906	-34			C-174,O-103C/1-10,S-9,3-8,2-4	-3.4
HAYES, MIKE Michael B 1853 Cleveland, OH 5-7.5/170# d9.9																								
1876	NY N	5	21	1	3	0	2	0	2	0		0	.143	.143	.333	63	-1		.882	0	0	0	/O-5(LF)	-0.1
HAYES, JACKIE Minter Carney B 7.19.1906 Clanton, AL D 2.9.1983 Birmingham, AL BR/TR 5-10.5/165# d8.5																								
1927	Was A	10	29	2	7	0	0	0	2	1	0	2	.241	.267	.241	33	-3	0-0	.969	-0	103	30	/S-8,3	-0.2
1928	Was A	60	210	30	54	7	3	0	22	5	0	10	.257	.274	.319	56	-14	3-0	.974	7	102	120	2-41,S-15/3-2	-0.4
1929	Was A	123	424	52	117	20	3	2	57	24	1	29	.276	.316	.351	71	-19	4-5	.945	5	114	168	3-63,2-57/S-2	-0.9
1930	Was A	51	166	25	47	7	2	1	20	7	0	8	.283	.312	.367	71	-8	2-3	.981	4	103	133	2-29/3-9,1-8	-0.3
1931	Was A	38	108	11	24	2	1	0	8	6	0	4	.222	.263	.259	38	-10	2-0	.962	-4	81	72	2-19/3-8,S-3	-1.2
1932	Chi A	117	475	53	122	20	5	2	54	30	1	28	.257	.302	.333	69	-23	7-4	.967	2	106	114	2-97,S-10,3-10	-1.3
1933	Chi A	138	535	65	138	23	5	2	47	55	3	36	.258	.331	.331	79	-16	2-3	.981	6	**107**	104	*2-138	-0.1
1934	Chi A	62	226	19	58	9	1	1	31	23	0	20	.257	.325	.319	65	-12	3-2	.980	-10	93	77	2-61	-1.7
1935	Chi A	89	329	45	88	14	0	4	45	29	0	15	.267	.327	.347	72	-14	3-1	.966	-5	99	90	2-85	-1.2
1936	Chi A	108	417	53	130	34	3	5	84	35	1	25	.312	.366	.444	96	-3	4-2	.979	13	113	118	2-89,S-13/3-2	1.5
1937	Chi A	143	573	63	131	27	4	2	79	41	2	37	.229	.282	.300	47	-48	1-6	.984	23	**109**	**123**	*2-143	-1.6
1938	Chi A	62	238	40	78	21	2	1	20	24	0	6	.328	.389	.445	106	3	3-2	.976	-2	101	121	2-61	0.5
1939	Chi A	72	269	34	67	12	3	0	23	27	1	10	.249	.320	.316	62	-16	0-3	.974	3	101	125	2-69	-0.9
1940	Chi A	18	41	2	8	0	1	0	1	2	0	11	.195	.233	.244	23	-5	0-0	.981	-1	100	123	2-15	-0.5
Total	14	1091	4040	494	1069	196	33	20	493	309	9	241	.265	.318	.344	70	-188	34-31	.976	43	104	111	2-904/3-95,S-51,1-8	-8.3
HAYES, VON Von Francis B 8.31.1958 Stockton, CA BL/TR 6-5/185# d4.14 OF Total (207-LF 398-CF 555-RF)																								
1981	Cle A	43	109	21	28	8	2	1	17	14-1	2	10	.257	.346	.394	116	3	8-1	.939	1	111	236	D-21,O-13(12-0-1)/3-5	0.4
1982	Cle A	150	527	65	132	25	3	14	82	42-3	4	63	.250	.310	.389	91	-7	32-13	.981	5	111	95	*O-139(14-7-123)/3-5,1-4	-0.7
1983	†Phi N	124	351	45	93	9	5	6	32	36-7	3	55	.265	.337	.370	97	-1	20-12	.972	-2	95	130	*O-103(3-39-77)	-0.7
1984	Phi N	152	561	85	164	27	6	16	67	59-4	0	84	.292	.359	.447	124	18	48-13	.988	-4	101	24	*O-148(14-116-36)	1.8
1985	Phi N	152	570	76	150	30	4	13	70	61-6	0	99	.263	.332	.398	101	1	21-8	.984	8	111	98	*O-146(66-123-14)	0.8
1986	Phi N	158	610	**107**	186	**46**	2	19	98	74-9	1	77	.305	.379	.480	131	28	24-12	.990	3	102	99	*1-134,O-31(24-6-3)	2.3
1987	Phi N	158	556	84	154	36	5	21	84	121-12	0	77	.277	.404	.473	128	28	16-7	.990	-5	88	94	*1-144,O-32(5-29-3)	1.6
1988	Phi N	104	367	43	100	28	2	6	45	49-5	1	59	.272	.355	.409	118	11	20-9	.990	1	97	98	1-85,O-16(4-12-2)/3-3	0.7
1989	Phi N★	154	540	93	140	27	2	26	78	101-14	4	103	.259	.376	.461	139	32	28-7	.980	5	99	140	*O-128(0-13-124),1-30,3-10	3.7
1990	Phi N	129	467	70	122	14	3	17	73	87-16	4	81	.261	.375	.413	119	16	16-7	.979	-1	100	85	*O-127(45-4-81)	1.2
1991	Phi N	77	284	43	64	15	1	0	21	31-1	3	42	.225	.303	.285	69	-11	9-2	.990	6	121	72	O-72(20-49-6)	-0.5
1992	Cal A	94	307	35	69	17	1	4	29	37-4	0	54	.225	.305	.326	77	-9	11-6	.983	-2	101	19	O-85(RF)/1-4,D-5	-1.3
Total	12	1495	5249	767	1402	282	36	143	696	712-82	22	804	.267	.354	.416	113	109	253-97	.983	14	105	90	*O-1040R,1-401/D-26,3-23	9.3
HAYES, BILL William Ernest B 10.24.1957 Cheverly, MD BR/TR 6/195# d9.30 C1																								
1980	Chi N	4	9	0	2	1	0	0	0	0-0	0	3	.222	.222	.333	49	-1	0-0	1.000	-1	69	329	/C-3	-0.1
1981	Chi N	1	0	0	0	0	0	0	0	0-0	0	0	—	—	—	—	0	0-0	—	-0	0	0	/C	0.0
Total	2	5	9	0	2	1	0	0	0	0-0	0	3	.222	.222	.333	49	-1	0-0	1.000	-1	66	313	/C-4	-0.1
HAYWORTH, RED Myron Claude B 5.14.1916 High Point, NC BR/TR 6-1.5/200# d4.21 b-Ray																								
1944	†StL A	90	270	20	60	11	1	1	25	10	1	13	.222	.253	.281	50	-18	0-0	.967	-2	94	77	C-87	-1.6
1945	StL A	56	160	7	31	4	0	0	17	7	0	6	.194	.228	.219	28	-15	0-2	.992	2	108	69	C-55	-1.2
Total	2	146	430	27	91	15	1	1	42	17	1	19	.212	.243	.258	42	-33	0-2	.976	-0	99	74	C-142	-2.8
HAYWORTH, RAY Raymond Hall B 1.29.1904 High Point, NC D 9.25.2002 Salisbury, NC BR/TR 6/180# d6.27 C2 b-Red																								
1926	Det A	12	11	1	3	0	0	0	5	1	0	1	.273	.333	.273	59	-1	0-0	1.000	-1	115	0	/C-8	-0.1
1929	Det A	14	43	5	11	0	0	0	4	3	0	8	.256	.304	.256	45	-4	0-0	.951	-1	75	146	C-14	-0.4
1930	Det A	77	227	24	63	15	4	0	22	20	0	19	.278	.336	.379	79	-7	0-2	.977	-11	65	83	C-76	-1.3
1931	Det A	88	273	28	70	10	3	0	25	19	1	27	.256	.307	.315	62	-16	0-1	.973	-1	78	**125**	C-88	-1.1
1932	Det A	109	338	41	99	20	2	2	44	31	1	22	.293	.354	.382	87	-6	1-1	.991	3	92	102	*C-106	0.2
1933	Det A	134	425	37	104	14	3	1	45	35	0	28	.245	.302	.299	59	-26	0-0	.994	-6	61	**121**	*C-133	-2.3
1934	†Det A	54	167	20	49	5	2	0	27	16	0	22	.293	.355	.347	82	-5	0-2	.984	4	153	106	C-54	0.2
1935	Det A	51	175	22	54	14	2	0	22	9	0	14	.309	.342	.411	98	-1	0-0	.996	8	138	148	C-48	0.9
1936	Det A	81	250	31	60	10	0	1	30	39	2	18	.240	.347	.292	59	-15	0-0	**.988**	-4	123	73	C-81	-1.3
1937	Det A	30	78	9	21	2	0	1	8	14	2	15	.269	.394	.333	83	-1	0-0	.992	2	101	87	C-28	0.2
1938	Det A	8	19	1	4	0	0	0	5	3	0	4	.211	.318	.211	33	-2	1-0	.971	1	281	0	/C-7	0.0
	Bro N	5	4	0	0	0	0	0	0	1	0	1	.000	.200	.000	-40	-1	0	1.000	0	0	0	/C-3	-0.1
1939	Bro N	21	26	0	4	2	0	0	1	4	0	7	.154	.267	.231	34	-2	0	1.000	1	108	55	C-18	-0.1
	NY N	5	13	1	3	0	0	0	0	0	0	1	.231	.231	.231	24	-1	0	1.000	1	113	210	/C-5	0.0
	Year	26	39	1	7	2	0	0	1	4	0	8	.179	.256	.231	31	-4	0	1.000	2	110	105	C-23	-0.1
1942	StL A	1	1	0	1	0	0	0	0	0	0	0	1.000	1.000	1.000	456	0	0-0	—	0			H	0.0
1944	Bro N	7	10	1	0	0	0	0	0	2	0	1	.000	.167	.000	-51	-2	0	1.000	1	99	135	/C-6	-0.1
1945	Bro N	2	2	0	0	0	0	0	0	1	0	0	.000	.333	.000	-3	0	0	1.000	0	0	0	/C-2	0.0
Total	15	699	2062	221	546	92	16	5	238	198	6	188	.265	.331	.332	71	-90	2-6	.987	-3	95	106	C-677	-5.3
HAZEWOOD, DRUNGO Drungo La Rue B 9.2.1959 Mobile, AL BR/TR 6-3/210# d9.19																								
1980	Bal A	6	5	1	0	0	0	0	0	0-0	0	4	.000	.000	.000	-99	-1	0-0	1.000	-0	36	0	/O-3(RF)	-0.2

Year	Tm Lg	G	AB	R	H	2B	3B	HR	RBI	BB-IB	HP	SO	AVG	OBP	SLG	AOPS	ABR	SB-CS	FA	FR	Rng	Thr	G at Pos	BFW
HAZLE, BOB Robert Sidney "Hurricane" B 12.9.1930 Laurens, SC D 4.25.1992 Columbia, SC BL/TR 6/190# d9.8																								
1955	Cin N	6	13	0	3	0	0	0	0	0-0	0	3	.231	.231	.231	22	-1	0-0	1.000	1	149	333	/O-3(LF)	0.0
1957	†Mil N	41	134	26	54	12	0	7	27	18-4	1	15	.403	.477	.649	214	23	1-3	.906	-5	84	37	O-40(RF)	1.6
1958	Mil N	20	56	6	10	0	0	0	5	9-0	1	4	.179	.303	.179	34	-5	0-0	1.000	-1	106	0	O-20(RF)	-0.7
	Det A	43	58	5	14	2	0	2	5	5-0	0	13	.241	.302	.379	80	-2	0-0	1.000	-0	94	0	O-12(8-0-4)	-0.2
Total	3	110	261	37	81	14	0	9	37	32-4	2	35	.310	.390	.467	135	15	1-3	.951	-4	95	42	/O-75(11-0-64)	0.7
HAZLETON, DOC Willard Carpenter B 8.28.1876 Strafford, VT D 3.10.1941 Burlington, VT BR d4.17																								
1902	StL N	7	23	0	3	0	0	0	0	2	1		.130	.231	.130	12	-2	0	.973	0	109	209	/1-7	-0.3
HEALY, FRAN Francis Xavier B 9.6.1946 Holyoke, MA BR/TR 6-5/220# d9.3																								
1969	KC A	6	10	0	4	1	0	0	0	0-0	0	5	.400	.400	.500	149	1	0-0	1.000	0	124	0	/C-5	0.1
1971	SF N	47	93	10	26	3	0	2	11	15-0	0	24	.280	.380	.376	117	3	1-0	.966	-3	55	106	C-22	0.1
1972	SF N	45	99	12	15	4	0	1	8	13-2	1	24	.152	.257	.222	37	-8	0-1	.995	4	114	172	C-43	-0.3
1973	KC A	95	279	25	77	15	2	6	34	31-0	0	56	.276	.348	.409	104	2	3-4	.979	-1	117	112	C-92/D	0.4
1974	KC A	139	445	59	112	24	2	9	53	62-1	1	73	.252	.343	.375	101	3	16-8	.977	-8	86	90	*C-138	0.2
1975	KC A	56	188	16	48	5	2	2	18	14-1	0	19	.255	.307	.335	79	-6	4-3	.982	-3	109	64	C-51/D-4	-0.7
1976	KC A	8	24	2	3	0	0	0	1	4-0	0	10	.125	.250	.125	12	-3	2-0	1.000	1	71	117	/C-6,D	-0.1
	NY A	46	120	10	32	3	0	0	9	9-0	0	17	.267	.318	.292	80	-3	3-1	.983	2	289	94	C-31/D-9	0.1
	Year	54	144	12	35	3	0	0	10	13-0	0	27	.243	.306	.264	68	-6	5-1	.987	3	245	99	C-37,D-10	0.0
1977	NY A	27	67	10	15	5	0	0	7	6-0	0	13	.224	.288	.299	61	-3	1-0	.971	-3	114	62	C-26	-0.5
1978	NY A	1	1	0	0	0	0	0	0	0-0	0	1	.000	.000	.000	-99	0	0-0	—	-0	0	0	/C	-0.1
Total	9	470	1326	144	332	60	6	20	141	154-4	2	242	.250	.329	.350	90	-14	30-17	.980	-10	112	98	C-415/D-15	-0.8
HEALY, FRANCIS Francis Xavier Paul B 6.29.1910 Holyoke, MA D 2.12.1997 Springfield, MA BR/TR 5-9.5/175# d4.29																								
1930	NY N	7	2	2	0	0	0	0	0	0	0	0	.000	.000	.000	-99	-1	0	—	0	*0*	*0*	/C	-0.1
1931	NY N	6	7	1	1	0	0	0	0	0	0	0	.143	.143	.143	-24	-1	0	1.000	0	*0*	*0*	/C-4	-0.1
1932	NY N	14	32	5	8	2	0	0	4	2	0	8	.250	.294	.313	65	-2	0	.960	1	*113*	*110*	C-11	0.0
1934	StL N	15	13	1	4	1	0	0	1	0	0	2	.308	.308	.385	79	0	0	1.000	1	*0*	*0*	/C-2,3O(RF)	0.0
Total	4	42	54	9	13	3	0	0	5	2	0	10	.241	.268	.296	51	-4	0	.969	1	*91*	*89*	/C-18,O(RF)3	-0.2
HEALY, THOMAS Thomas Fitzgerald B 10.30.1895 Altoona, PA D 1.15.1974 Cleveland, OH BR/TR 6/172# d7.13																								
1915	Phi A	23	77	11	17	1	0	0	5	6	4	4	.221	.310	.234	65	-3	0-4	.933	4	116	107	3-17/S	0.0
1916	Phi A	6	23	4	6	1	1	0	2	1	1	2	.261	.320	.391	119	0	1	.947	0	100	77	/3-6	0.1
Total	2	29	100	15	23	2	1	0	7	7	5	6	.230	.313	.270	77	-3	1-4	.936	4	112	100	/3-23,S	0.1
HEARD, CHARLIE Charles B 1.30.1872 Philadelphia, PA D 2.20.1945 Philadelphia, PA BR/TR 6-2/190# d7.14 ▲																								
1890	Pit N	12	43	2	8	2	0	0	0	1	0	15	.186	.205	.233	31	-4	0	.600	-2	0	0	/O-6(1-0-5),P-6	-0.3
HEARN, ED Edward John B 8.23.1960 Stuart, FL BR/TR 6-3/215# d5.17																								
1986	NY N	49	136	16	36	5	0	4	10	12-0	0	19	.265	.322	.390	99	0	0-1	.987	-11	106	53	C-45	-1.1
1987	KC A	6	17	2	5	2	0	0	3	4-0	0	2	.294	.429	.412	121	1	0-0	1.000	-1	126	59	/C-5	0.0
1988	KC A	7	18	1	4	2	0	0	1	0-0	0	1	.222	.222	.333	53	-1	0-0	1.000	-1	99	0	/C-4,D-2	-0.2
Total	3	62	171	19	45	9	0	4	14	16-0	0	22	.263	.324	.386	97	0	0-1	.989	-14	108	50	/C-54,D-2	-1.3
HEARNE, ED Edmund B 9.17.1888 Ventura, CA D 9.8.1952 Sawtelle, CA BR/TR 5-9/160# d6.9																								
1910	Bos A	2	2	0	0	0	0	0	0	0	0		.000	.000	.000	-98	0	0	1.000	1	140	326	/S-2	0.0
HEARNE, HUGHIE Hugh Joseph B 4.18.1873 Troy, NY D 9.22.1932 Troy, NY BR/TR 5-8/182# d8.29																								
1901	Bro N	2	5	1	2	0	0	0	3	0	0		.400	.400	.400	129	0	0	1.000	-0	*70*	*179*	/C-2	0.0
1902	Bro N	66	231	22	65	10	0	0	28	16	3		.281	.336	.325	103	2	3	.966	-11	*78*	*89*	C-65	-0.4
1903	Bro N	26	57	8	16	3	2	0	4	3	1		.281	.328	.404	111	1	2	.960	-1	*76*	*137*	C-17/1-2	0.1
Total	3	94	293	31	83	13	2	0	35	19	4		.283	.335	.341	105	3	5	.965	-12	*77*	*100*	/C-84,1-2	-0.3
HEARRON, JEFF Jeffrey Vernon B 11.19.1961 Long Beach, CA BR/TR 6-1/195# d8.25																								
1985	†Tor A	4	7	0	1	0	0	0	0	0-0	0	2	.143	.143	.143	-21	-1	0-0	1.000	1	74	280	/C-4	0.0
1986	Tor A	12	23	2	5	1	0	0	4	3-0	0	7	.217	.308	.261	55	-1	0-0	.980	-1	102	38	C-12	-0.2
Total	2	16	30	2	6	1	0	0	4	3-0	0	9	.200	.273	.233	39	-2	0-0	.985	-0	96	94	/C-16	-0.2
HEATH, JEFF John Geoffrey B 4.1.1915 Ft.William, ON, CAN D 12.9.1975 Seattle, WA BL/TR 5-11.5/200# d9.13																								
1936	Cle A	12	41	6	14	3	3	1	8	3	0	4	.341	.386	.634	147	2	1-0	1.000	-1	61	151	O-12(10-2-0)	0.1
1937	Cle A	20	61	8	14	1	4	0	8	0	0	9	.230	.230	.377	50	-6	0-1	1.000	-1	105	0	O-14(2-0-12)	-0.7
1938	Cle A	126	502	104	172	31	**18**	21	112	33	0	55	.343	.383	.602	146	31	3-1	.974	0	106	58	*O-122(113-0-9)	2.2
1939	Cle A	121	431	64	126	31	7	14	69	41	0	64	.292	.354	.494	119	11	8-4	.964	4	109	95	*O-108(LF)	0.8
1940	Cle A	100	356	55	78	16	3	14	50	40	0	62	.219	.298	.399	81	-12	5-3	.971	2	104	93	O-90(LF)	-1.4
1941	Cle A★	151	585	89	199	32	**20**	24	123	50	4	69	.340	.396	.586	165	50	18-12	.949	-5	86	144	*O-151(25-0-126)	3.4
1942	Cle A	147	568	82	158	37	13	10	76	62	1	66	.278	.350	.442	130	21	9-9	.980	4	104	102	*O-146(145-0-2)	1.5
1943	Cle A★	118	424	58	116	22	6	18	79	63	1	58	.274	.369	.481	157	30	5-8	.968	-3	103	44	*O-111(107-3-4)	2.1
1944	Cle A✳	60	151	20	50	5	2	5	33	18	0	12	.331	.402	.490	160	12	0-1	.952	0	96	134	O-37(31-5-1)	1.0
1945	Cle A✳	102	370	60	113	16	7	15	61	56	1	39	.305	.398	.508	169	33	3-1	.973	-6	97	32	*O-101(LF)	2.2
1946	Was A	48	166	23	47	12	3	4	27	36	0	36	.283	.411	.464	153	14	0-4	.969	-2	92	97	O-47(LF)	0.8
	StL A	86	316	46	87	20	4	12	57	37	1	37	.275	.353	.478	124	10	0-2	.962	-2	94	103	O-83(LF)	0.3
	Year	134	482	69	134	32	7	16	84	73	1	73	.278	.374	.473	134	23	0-6	.965	-3	93	101	*O-130(LF)	1.1
1947	StL A	141	491	81	123	20	7	27	85	88	1	87	.251	.366	.485	133	22	2-1	.987	0	99	76	*O-140(LF)	1.2
1948	Bos N	115	364	64	116	26	5	20	76	51	1	46	.319	.404	.582	167	34	2	**.991**	1	103	76	*O-106(99-7-0)	2.8
1949	Bos N	36	111	17	34	7	0	9	23	15	0	26	.306	.389	.613	174	11	0	.983	-1	95	86	O-31(26-0-5)	0.9
Total	14	1383	4937	777	1447	279	102	194	887	593	10	670	.293	.370	.509	140	263	56-47	.972	-8	100	85	*O-1299(1127-17-159)	17.2
HEATH, KELLY Kelly Mark B 9.4.1957 Plattsburgh, NY BR/TR 5-7/155# d4.20																								
1982	KC A	1	1	0	0	0	0	0	0	0-0	0	0	.000	.000	.000	-99	0	0-0	1.000	1	212	436	/2	0.0
HEATH, MIKE Michael Thomas B 2.5.1955 Tampa, FL BR/TR 5-11/190# d6.3 OF Total (79-LF 1-CF 142-RF)																								
1978	†NY A	33	92	6	21	3	1	0	8	4-0	1	9	.228	.265	.283	56	-6	0-0	.970	1	164	54	C-33	-0.4
1979	Oak A	74	258	19	66	8	0	3	27	17-1	3	18	.256	.304	.322	75	-9	1-0	.978	-1	103	165	O-46(23-0-23),C-22/3-7,D-3	-1.1
1980	Oak A	92	305	27	74	10	2	1	33	16-2	0	28	.243	.280	.298	63	-16	3-3	.986	14	191	96	C-47,D-31/O-8(4-0-4)	-0.2
1981	†Oak A	84	301	26	71	7	1	8	30	13-1	1	36	.236	.269	.346	80	-9	3-3	.978	8	127	115	C-78/O-6(5-0-1)	0.2
1982	Oak A	101	318	43	77	18	4	3	39	27-3	0	36	.242	.298	.352	82	-8	8-3	.973	-6	114	117	C-90,O-10(9-0-2)/3-5	-1.0
1983	Oak A	96	345	45	97	17	0	6	33	18-4	1	59	.281	.318	.383	98	-2	3-4	.973	-1	105	98	C-80,O-24(1-0-23)/3-2,D-2	-0.1
1984	Oak A	140	475	49	118	21	5	13	64	26-2	1	72	.248	.287	.396	94	-6	7-4	.986	-5	93	118	*C-108,O-45(13-0-32)/3-2,S	-0.9
1985	Oak A	138	436	71	109	18	6	13	55	41-0	1	63	.250	.313	.408	104	1	7-7	.981	2	129	97	*C-112,O-35(16-0-24),3-13	0.5
1986	StL N	65	190	19	39	8	1	4	25	23-4	1	36	.205	.293	.321	70	-8	2-3	.967	-0	139	73	C-63/O-2(1-0-1)	-0.7
	Det A	30	98	11	26	3	0	4	11	4-0	0	17	.265	.291	.418	92	-2	4-1	.987	-2	128	57	C-29/3	-0.2
1987	†Det A	93	270	34	76	16	0	8	33	21-0	3	42	.281	.339	.430	107	3	1-5	.989	6	124	117	C-67,O-24(4-1-20)/1-4,3-4,S-2,2D	0.9
1988	Det A	86	219	24	54	7	2	5	18	18-0	1	32	.247	.307	.365	91	-3	1-0	.984	-1	141	63	C-75/O-9(RF)	0.0
1989	Det A	122	396	38	104	16	2	10	43	24-2	4	71	.263	.308	.389	98	-2	7-1	.986	2	95	124	*C-117/3-4,O-3(LF),D	0.7
1990	Det A	122	370	46	100	18	2	7	38	19-0	4	71	.270	.311	.386	94	-4	7-6	.980	-1	80	96	*C-117/O-3(RF),SD	0.0
1991	Atl N	49	139	4	29	3	1	1	12	7-5	1	26	.209	.250	.266	43	-11	0-0	.991	-4	69	121	C-45	-1.3
Total	14	1325	4212	462	1061	173	27	86	469	278-24	22	616	.252	.300	.367	87	-82	54-40	.981	11	115	103	*C-1083,O-215R/D-40,3-38,1-4,S2	-3.6
HEATH, MICKEY Minor Wilson B 10.30.1903 Toledo, OH D 7.30.1986 Dallas, TX BL/TL 6/175# d4.18																								
1931	Cin N	7	26	2	7	0	0	0	3	2	0	5	.269	.321	.269	64	-1	0	1.000	-0	87	128	/1-7	-0.2
1932	Cin N	39	134	14	27	1	3	0	15	20	1	23	.201	.310	.254	55	-8	0	.991	1	114	94	1-39	-1.1
Total	2	46	160	16	34	1	3	0	18	22	1	28	.213	.311	.256	57	-9	0	.992	1	110	99	/1-46	-1.3
HEATH, TOMMY Thomas George B 8.18.1913 Akron, CO D 2.26.1967 Los Gatos, CA BR/TR 5-10/185# d4.23																								
1935	StL A	47	93	10	22	3	0	0	9	20	0	13	.237	.372	.269	65	-4	0-0	.982	-0	*119*	*45*	C-37	-0.3
1937	StL A	17	43	4	10	0	2	1	3	10	0	3	.233	.377	.395	94	0	0-0	1.000	-1	*88*	*55*	C-14	0.0
1938	StL A	70	194	22	44	13	0	2	22	35	0	24	.227	.345	.325	69	-8	0-1	.986	3	*81*	*121*	C-65	-0.2

Year	Tm Lg	G	AB	R	H	2B	3B	HR	RBI	BB-IB	HP	SO	AVG	OBP	SLG	AOPS	ABR	SB-CS	FA	FR	Rng	Thr	G at Pos	BFW
Total	3	134	330	36	76	16	2	3	34	65	0	40	.230	.357	.318	71	-12	0-1	.987	2	*91*	*93*	C-116	-0.5
HEATH, BILL William Chris B 3.10.1939 Yuba City, CA BL/TR 5-8/175# d10.3																								
1965	Chi A	1	1	0	0	0	0	0	0	0-0	0	0	.000	.000	.000	-99	0	0-0	—	0			H	0.0
1966	Hou N	55	123	12	37	6	0	0	8	9-1	1	11	.301	.353	.350	103	1	1-0	.995	1	*100*	*121*	C-37	0.3
1967	Hou N	9	11	0	1	0	0	0	0	4-0	0	3	.091	.333	.091	28	-1	0-0	1.000	1	*119*	*117*	/C-5	0.0
	Det A	20	32	0	4	0	0	0	4	1-0	0	4	.125	.152	.125	-17	-5	0-0	1.000	0	29	0	/C-7	-0.5
1969	Chi N	27	32	1	5	0	1	0	1	12-2	0	4	.156	.378	.219	65	-1	0-0	.979	-0	100	153	/C-9	-0.1
Total	4	112	199	13	47	6	1	0	13	26-3	1	22	.236	.326	.276	73	-6	1-0	.993	1	*93*	*112*	/C-58	-0.3
HEATHCOTE, CLIFF Clifton Earl B 1.24.1898 Glen Rock, PA D 1.18.1939 York, PA BL/TL 5-10.5/160# d6.4																								
1918	StL N	88	348	37	90	12	3	4	32	20	1	40	.259	.301	.345	100	-1	12	.934	-8	97	50	O-87(3-84-0)	-1.7
1919	StL N	114	401	53	112	13	4	1	29	20	1	41	.279	.315	.339	103	0	27	.967	-2	101	80	*O-101(1-85-17)/1-2	-0.9
1920	StL N	133	489	55	139	18	8	3	56	25	1	31	.284	.320	.372	102	0	21-14	.964	10	105	**151**	*O-129(0-74-57)	0.2
1921	StL N	62	156	18	38	6	2	0	9	10	1	9	.244	.293	.308	61	-9	7-5	.926	-3	92	94	O-51(1-40-10)	-1.4
1922	StL N	34	98	11	24	5	2	0	14	9	1	4	.245	.315	.337	71	-4	0-2	.950	2	123	58	O-32(CF)	-0.4
	Chi N	76	243	37	68	8	7	1	34	18	0	15	.280	.330	.383	82	-7	5-2	.986	-2	98	65	O-60(0-21-40)	-1.2
	Year	110	341	48	92	13	9	1	48	27	1	19	.270	.325	.370	79	-11	5-4	.971	-0	106	63	O-92(0-53-40)	-1.6
1923	Chi N	117	393	48	98	14	3	1	27	25	2	22	.249	.298	.308	60	-23	32-17	.980	4	105	111	*O-112(1-0-111)	-2.6
1924	Chi N	113	392	66	121	19	7	0	30	28	1	28	.309	.356	.393	100	0	26-24	.979	-2	104	57	*O-111(1-20-90)	-1.2
1925	Chi N	109	380	57	100	14	5	5	39	39	7	26	.263	.343	.366	80	-11	15-11	.970	8	105	141	O-99(3-8-88)	-1.1
1926	Chi N	139	510	98	141	33	3	10	53	58	2	30	.276	.353	.412	104	4	18	**.985**	9	105	123	*O-133(13-13-110)	0.2
1927	Chi N	83	228	28	67	12	4	2	25	20	3	16	.294	.359	.408	105	2	6	.987	7	104	182	O-57(0-9-49)	0.5
1928	Chi N	67	137	26	39	8	0	3	18	17	0	12	.285	.364	.409	103	1	6	.973	1	93	172	O-39(7-13-20)	0.0
1929	†Chi N	82	224	45	70	17	0	2	31	25	1	17	.313	.384	.415	98	1	9	.985	1	107	70	O-52(1-6-45)	-0.3
1930	Chi N	70	150	30	39	10	1	9	18	18	1	15	.260	.343	.520	104	0	4	.986	0	100	111	O-35(0-3-32)	-0.1
1931	Cin N	90	252	24	65	15	6	0	28	32	0	16	.258	.342	.365	96	-1	3	.989	11	120	166	O-59(RF)	0.6
1932	Cin N	8	3	3	0	0	0	0	0	0	0	0	.000	.000	.000	-99	-1	0	—	0			H	-0.1
	Phi N	30	39	7	11	2	0	1	5	3	0	3	.282	.333	.410	88	-1	0	.962	-1	88	160	/1-7	-0.2
	Year	38	42	10	11	2	0	1	5	3	0	3	.262	.311	.381	78	-1	0	.962	-1	88	160	/1-7	-0.3
Total	15	1415	4443	643	1222	206	55	42	448	367	22	325	.275	.333	.375	92	-50	191-75	.971	35	104	109	*O-1157(31-408-728)/1-9	-9.7
HEBNER, RICHIE Richard Joseph B 11.26.1947 Boston, MA BL/TR 6-1/197# d9.23 C4 OF Total (5-LF 27-RF)																								
1968	Pit N	2	1	0	0	0	0	0	0	0-0	0	0	.000	.000	.000	-99	0	0-0	—	0			H	0.0
1969	Pit N	129	459	72	138	23	4	8	47	53-10	8	53	.301	.380	.420	127	19	4-1	.944	2	98	**147**	*3-124/1	2.2
1970	†Pit N	120	420	60	122	24	8	11	46	42-5	7	48	.290	.362	.464	123	14	2-3	.940	1	107	112	*3-117	1.3
1971	†Pit N	112	388	50	105	17	8	17	67	32-1	3	68	.271	.326	.487	130	13	2-2	.949	-4	93	126	*3-108	0.9
1972	†Pit N	124	427	63	128	24	4	19	72	52-7	6	54	.300	.378	.508	155	31	0-0	.969	-11	94	92	*3-121	2.1
1973	Pit N	144	509	73	138	28	1	25	74	56-12	4	60	.271	.346	.477	130	20	0-1	.939	-12	95	69	*3-139	0.8
1974	†Pit N	146	550	97	160	21	6	18	68	60-5	6	53	.291	.363	.449	132	23	0-3	.937	-13	93	123	*3-141	0.8
1975	†Pit N	128	472	65	116	16	4	15	57	43-6	10	48	.246	.319	.392	98	-2	0-1	.946	-16	88	83	*3-126	-2.0
1976	Pit N	132	434	60	108	21	3	8	51	47-2	4	39	.249	.325	.366	96	-2	1-3	.953	-13	92	76	*3-126	-1.8
1977	†Phi N	118	397	67	113	17	4	18	62	61-8	3	46	.285	.381	.484	125	16	7-8	.991	3	122	130	*1-103,3-13/2	1.1
1978	†Phi N	137	435	61	123	22	3	17	71	53-16	9	58	.283	.369	.464	131	19	4-7	.994	-2	82	**120**	*1-117,3-19/2	0.9
1979	NY N	136	473	54	127	25	2	10	79	59-6	8	59	.268	.354	.393	109	8	3-1	.940	-8	96	111	*3-134/1-6	-0.1
1980	Det A	104	341	48	99	10	7	12	82	38-3	2	45	.290	.360	.466	123	10	0-3	.998	-2	98	71	1-61,3-32/D-5	0.4
1981	Det A	78	226	19	51	8	2	5	28	27-5	2	28	.226	.311	.345	87	-4	1-2	.995	-4	76	81	1-61,D-11	-1.2
1982	Det A	68	179	25	49	6	0	8	18	25-2	0	21	.274	.361	.441	119	5	1-1	.990	2	122	64	1-40,D-20	0.4
	Pit N	25	70	6	21	2	0	2	12	5-0	0	3	.300	.347	.414	109	1	4-0	.964	-0	99	207	O-21(RF)/1-4,3	0.1
1983	Pit N	78	162	23	43	4	1	5	26	17-4	1	28	.265	.332	.395	100	0	8-3	.967	-9	68	20	3-40/1-7,O-7(2-0-5)	-0.9
1984	†Chi N	44	81	12	27	3	0	2	8	10-2	0	15	.333	.407	.444	127	3	1-0	.963	0	115	109	3-14/1-3,O-3(2-0-1)	0.4
1985	Chi N	83	120	10	26	2	0	3	22	7-1	1	15	.217	.266	.308	54	-8	0-1	.991	1	80	163	1-12/3-7,O(LF)	-0.9
Total	18	1908	6144	865	1694	273	57	203	890	687-95	74	741	.276	.352	.438	120	166	38-40	.946	-86	95	103	*3-1262,1-415/D-36,O-32R,2-2	4.5
HECHINGER, MIKE Michael Vincent B 2.14.1890 Chicago, IL D 8.13.1967 Chicago, IL BR/TR 6/175# d9.27																								
1912	Chi N	2	3	0	0	0	0	0	0	2	0	0	.000	.400	.000	14	0	0	1.000	0	*177*	*71*	/C-2	0.0
1913	Chi N	2	2	0	0	0	0	0	0	0	0	0	.000	.000	.000	-99	-1	0	—	0			H	-0.1
	Bro N	9	11	1	2	1	0	0	0	0	0	2	.182	.182	.273	28	-1	0	1.000	-1	78	81	/C-4	-0.2
	Year	11	13	1	2	1	0	0	0	0	0	2	.154	.154	.231	9	-2	0	1.000	-1	78	81	/C-4	-0.3
Total	2	13	16	1	2	1	0	0	0	2	0	2	.125	.222	.188	16	-2	0	1.000	-0	*130*	*76*	/C-6	-0.3
HECKER, GUY Guy Jackson B 4.3.1856 Youngsville, PA D 12.3.1938 Wooster, OH BR/TR 6/190# d5.2 M1 U1 ▲																								
1882	Lou AA	78	340	62	94	14	4	3		5			.276	.287	.368	126	9		.958	5	**132**	**163**	*1-66,P-13/O-2(CF)	0.5
1883	Lou AA	81	332	59	90	6	6	1		12			.271	.297	.334	111	5		.933	6	109	167	P-53,O-23(9-14-0),1-10	0.4
1884	Lou AA	78	316	53	94	14	8	4	42	10	2		.297	.323	.430	150	17		.951	5	108	128	*P-75/O-5(4-1-0)	0.3
1885	Lou AA	70	297	48	81	9	2	2	35	5	1		.273	.287	.337	97	-2		.927	4	122	53	P-53,1-17/O-3(LF)	0.0
1886	Lou AA	84	343	76	117	14	5	4	48	32	3		**.341**	.402	.446	157	22	25	.875	-3	101	229	P-49,1-22,O-17(6-0-11)	0.3
1887	Lou AA	91	370	89	118	21	6	4	50	31	6		.319	.381	.441	126	13	48	.954	-3	29	136	1-43,P-34,O-16(LF)	-0.1
1888	Lou AA	56	211	32	48	9	2	0	29	11	6		.227	.285	.289	86	-3	20	.936	-4	46	79	1-30,P-26/O(LF)	-0.8
1889	Lou AA	81	327	42	93	17	5	1	36	18	6	27	.284	.333	.376	104	1	17	.969	0	103	106	1-65,P-19/O(RF)	-0.4
1890	Pit N	86	340	43	77	13	9	0	38	19	9	17	.226	.285	.318	86	-7	13	.962	2	136	58	1-69,P-14/O-7(5-1-1),M	-0.8
Total	9	705	2876	504	812	117	47	19	278	143	33	44	.282	.324	.376	118	55	123	.934	13	111	118	P-336,1-322/O-75(44-18-13)	-0.6
HEEP, DANNY Daniel William B 7.3.1957 San Antonio, TX BL/TL 5-11/185# d8.31																								
1979	Hou N	14	14	0	2	0	0	0	2	1-1	0	4	.143	.176	.143	-5	-2	0-0	1.000	1	256	0	/O-2(LF)	-0.1
1980	†Hou N	33	87	6	24	8	0	0	6	8-0	1	9	.276	.340	.368	107	1	0-0	.990	-2	58	55	1-22	-0.3
1981	Hou N	33	96	6	24	3	0	0	11	10-2	0	11	.250	.321	.281	76	-3	0-0	.990	-2	61	80	1-22/O(RF)	-0.7
1982	Hou N	85	198	16	47	14	1	4	22	21-3	1	31	.237	.311	.379	100	0	0-2	1.000	-2	103	85	O-39(1-0-39),1-16	-0.6
1983	NY N	115	253	30	64	12	0	8	21	29-6	1	40	.253	.326	.395	102	1	3-3	1.000	-3	82	118	O-61(11-19-31),1-14	-0.6
1984	NY N	99	199	36	46	9	2	1	12	27-3	1	22	.231	.319	.312	81	-4	3-1	.967	2	118	36	O-48(25-0-23),1-10	-0.5
1985	NY N	95	271	26	76	17	0	7	42	27-1	1	27	.280	.341	.421	117	6	2-2	.977	-3	96	21	O-78(45-7-31)/1-4	0.0
1986	†NY N	86	195	24	55	8	2	5	33	30-5	1	31	.282	.379	.421	124	7	1-4	.988	-1	95	61	O-56(44-0-13)	0.3
1987	LA N	60	98	7	16	4	0	0	9	8-0	0	10	.163	.226	.204	16	-12	1-0	.962	1	91	219	O-22(17-0-6)/1-6	-1.2
1988	†LA N	95	149	14	36	2	0	0	11	22-0	1	13	.242	.341	.255	76	-4	2-0	1.000	2	122	97	O-32(17-0-16),1-12/P	-0.2
1989	Bos A	113	320	36	96	17	0	5	49	29-4	1	26	.300	.356	.400	107	4	0-1	.989	-5	83	51	O-75(17-0-59),1-19/D-9	-0.4
1990	†Bos A	41	69	3	12	1	1	0	8	7-0	1	14	.174	.256	.217	33	-6	0-0	1.000	1	121	178	O-14(1-0-13)/1-5,PD	-0.5
1991	Atl N	14	12	4	5	1	0	0	3	1-0	0	4	.417	.462	.500	161	1	0-1	1.000	-0	0	0	/1O(LF)	0.1
Total	13	883	1961	208	503	96	6	30	229	220-25	9	242	.257	.330	.357	95	-11	12-14	.986	-12	97	70	O-429(181-26-232),1-131/D-15,P-2	-4.7
HEFFERNAN, BERT Bertram Alexander B 3.3.1965 Centereach, NY BL/TR 5-10/185# d5.13																								
1992	Sea A	8	11	0	1	1	0	0	1	0-0	0	1	.091	.091	.182	-25	-2	0-0	1.000	-0	55	90	/C-5,D	-0.2
HEFFNER, DON Donald Henry "Jeep" B 2.8.1911 Rouzerville, PA D 8.1.1989 Pasadena, CA BR/TR 5-10/155# d4.17 M1 C8																								
1934	NY A	72	241	29	63	8	3	0	25	25	0	18	.261	.331	.320	73	-10	1-1	.971	-9	88	115	2-68	-1.4
1935	NY A	10	36	3	11	3	1	0	8	4	0	1	.306	.375	.444	118	1	0-0	.980	-1	93	89	2-10	0.1
1936	NY A	19	48	7	11	2	1	0	6	6	0	5	.229	.315	.313	57	-3	0-0	.971	2	123	138	/3-8,2-5,S-3	0.0
1937	NY A	60	201	23	50	6	5	0	21	19	0	19	.249	.314	.328	62	-13	1-4	.980	-6	78	116	2-38,S-13/3-3,1O(RF)	-1.6
1938	StL A	141	473	47	116	23	3	2	69	65	4	53	.245	.341	.319	67	-23	1-1	.971	-5	88	96	*2-141	-1.7
1939	StL A	110	375	45	100	10	2	1	35	48	0	39	.267	.350	.312	69	-16	1-7	.944	-0	105	68	S-73,2-32	-1.1
1940	StL A	126	487	52	115	23	2	3	53	39	2	37	.236	.295	.310	56	-32	5-5	**.977**	**16**	**111**	108	*2-125	-0.9
1941	StL A	110	399	48	93	14	2	0	17	38	2	27	.233	.303	.278	53	-27	5-6	.974	-0	105	81	*2-105	-2.1
1942	StL A	19	36	2	6	2	0	0	3	1	0	4	.167	.189	.222	15	-4	1-0	.906	0	108	31	/2-6,1-4	-0.4
1943	StL A	18	33	2	4	1	0	0	2	2	0	2	.121	.171	.152	-5	-4	0-0	.974	-1	81	80	2-13/1	-0.5
	Phi A	52	178	17	37	6	0	0	8	18	1	12	.208	.284	.242	55	-10	3-2	.978	-7	94	82	2-47/1	-1.6
	Year	70	211	19	41	7	0	0	10	20	1	14	.194	.267	.227	45	-14	3-2	.978	-8	92	82	2-60/1-2	-2.1
1944	Det A	6	19	0	4	1	0	0	1	5	0	1	.211	.375	.263	80	0	0-0	.962	0	98	122	/2-5	0.0

Year	Tm Lg	G	AB	R	H	2B	3B	HR	RBI	BB-IB	HP	SO	AVG	OBP	SLG	AOPS	ABR	SB-CS	FA	FR	Rng	Thr	G at Pos	BFW
Total	11	743	2526	275	610	99	19	6	248	270	9	218	.241	.317	.303	61	-141	18-26	.973	-11	97	97	2-595/S-89,3-11,1-7,O(RF)	-11.2
HEGAN, JIM James Edward B 8.3.1920 Lynn, MA D 6.17.1984 Swampscott, MA BR/TR 6-2/195# d9.9 Mil 1943-45 C21 s-Mike																								
1941	Cle A	16	47	4	15	2	0	1	5	4	0	7	.319	.373	.426	116	1	0-0	.973	0	*104*	*113*	C-16	0.2
1942	Cle A	68	170	10	33	5	0	0	11	11	0	31	.194	.243	.224	34	-15	1-3	.977	5	*118*	*88*	C-66	-0.8
1946	Cle A	88	271	29	64	11	5	0	17	17	1	44	.236	.284	.314	71	-12	1-4	.991	5	*123*	***121***	C-87	-0.3
1947	Cle A☆	135	378	38	94	14	5	4	42	41	1	49	.249	.324	.344	88	-7	3-1	.989	7	***174***	*86*	*C-133	0.8
1948	†Cle A	144	472	60	117	21	6	14	61	48	0	74	.248	.317	.407	94	-7	6-3	.990	22	***151***	*81*	*C-142	2.2
1949	Cle A☆	152	468	54	105	19	5	8	55	49	0	89	.224	.298	.338	69	-23	1-0	.990	13	***143***	*96*	*C-152	-0.2
1950	Cle A★	131	415	53	91	16	5	14	58	42	0	52	.219	.291	.383	74	-20	1-0	.993	21	***149***	*131*	*C-129	0.8
1951	Cle A★	133	416	60	99	17	5	6	43	38	0	72	.238	.302	.346	79	-14	0-3	.991	9	*97*	*82*	*C-129	0.1
1952	Cle A☆	112	333	39	75	17	2	4	41	29	0	47	.225	.287	.324	75	-12	0-2	.987	2	*97*	*96*	*C-107	-0.6
1953	Cle A	112	299	37	65	10	1	9	37	25	1	41	.217	.280	.348	71	-14	1-2	.976	-0	*95*	*76*	*C-106	-1.0
1954	†Cle A	139	423	56	99	12	7	11	40	34	0	48	.234	.289	.374	80	-14	0-1	**.994**	10	*114*	*90*	*C-137	0.2
1955	Cle A	116	304	30	67	5	2	9	40	34-5	0	33	.220	.293	.339	69	-15	0-1	**.997**	8	*114*	*69*	*C-111	-0.2
1956	Cle A	122	315	42	70	15	2	6	34	49-6	0	54	.222	.327	.340	75	-11	1-1	.985	9	*90*	*65*	*C-118	0.3
1957	Cle A	58	148	14	32	7	0	4	15	16-1	0	23	.216	.291	.345	74	-5	0-1	1.000	0	*79*	*58*	C-58	-0.3
1958	Det A	45	130	14	25	6	0	1	7	10-1	0	32	.192	.250	.262	38	-11	0-0	.996	2	*103*	*119*	C-45	-0.7
	Phi N	25	59	5	13	6	0	0	6	4-0	0	16	.220	.270	.322	57	-4	0-0	.991	1	*89*	*93*	C-25	-0.2
1959	Phi N	25	51	1	10	1	0	0	8	3-1	0	10	.196	.232	.216	22	-6	0-1	.990	1	*72*	*217*	C-25	-0.5
	SF N	21	30	0	4	1	0	0	0	1-0	0	10	.133	.161	.167	-13	-5	0-1	.975	2	*112*	*135*	C-21	-0.2
	Year	46	81	1	14	2	0	0	8	4-1	0	20	.173	.207	.198	10	-11	0-2	.983	3	*88*	*185*	C-46	-0.7
1960	Chi N	24	43	4	9	2	1	1	5	1-0	1	10	.209	.244	.372	67	-2	0-0	.977	0	*75*	*155*	C-22	-0.1
Total	17	1666	4772	550	1087	187	46	92	525	456-14	4	742	.228	.295	.344	74	-196	15-24	.990	118	*121*	*93*	*C-1629	-0.5
HEGAN, MIKE James Michael B 7.21.1942 Cleveland, OH BL/TL 6-1/190# d9.13 Mil 1967 f-Jim																								
1964	†NY A	5	5	0	0	0	0	0	0	1-0	0	2	.000	.167	.000	-48	-1	0-0	1.000	1	427	182	/1-2	0.0
1966	NY A	13	39	7	8	0	1	0	2	7-0	0	11	.205	.326	.256	73	-1	1-1	.991	0	107	67	1-13	-0.2
1967	NY A	68	118	12	16	4	1	1	3	20-1	1	40	.136	.266	.212	44	-8	7-1	1.000	-1	95	123	1-54,O-10(RF)	-1.2
1969	Sea A✳	95	267	54	78	9	6	8	37	62-1	1	61	.292	.427	.461	151	22	6-5	.955	3	100	159	O-64(2-1-61),1-19	2.0
1970	Mil A	148	476	70	116	21	2	11	52	67-3	1	116	.244	.336	.366	93	-3	9-7	.994	10	**127**	98	*1-139/O-8(2-0-6)	-0.3
1971	Mil A	46	122	19	27	4	1	4	11	26-2	0	19	.221	.356	.369	107	2	1-1	1.000	4	130	64	1-45	0.3
	†Oak A	65	55	5	13	3	0	0	3	5-0	0	13	.236	.300	.291	69	-2	1-0	1.000	0	113	112	1-47/O-2(1-0-1)	-0.3
	Year	111	177	24	40	7	1	4	14	31-2	0	32	.226	.340	.345	96	0	2-1	1.000	4	125	79	1-92/O-2(1-0-1)	0.0
1972	†Oak A	98	79	13	26	3	1	1	5	7-1	0	20	.329	.375	.430	150	5	1-0	1.000	1	90	150	1-64/O-3(RF)	0.4
1973	Oak A	75	71	8	13	2	0	1	5	5-1	0	17	.183	.237	.254	40	-6	0-0	.988	-3	37	87	1-56/O-3(2-0-1),D-3	-1.1
	NY A	37	131	12	36	3	2	6	14	7-1	0	34	.275	.309	.466	121	2	0-0	.992	1	114	82	1-37	0.1
	Year	112	202	20	49	5	2	7	19	12-2	0	51	.243	.284	.391	93	-3	0-0	.991	-2	88	84	1-93/O-3(2-0-1),D-3	-1.0
1974	NY A	18	53	3	12	2	0	2	9	5-0	2	9	.226	.317	.377	101	0	1-1	1.000	0	92	73	1-17	-0.1
	Mil A	89	190	21	45	7	1	7	32	33-4	0	34	.237	.347	.395	114	4	0-4	.991	-2	48	101	D-37,1-17,O-17(4-0-13)	-0.1
	Year	107	243	24	57	9	1	9	41	38-4	2	43	.235	.340	.391	111	5	1-5	.996	-2	70	87	D-37,1-34,O-17(4-0-13)	-0.2
1975	Mil A	93	203	19	51	11	0	5	22	31-3	0	42	.251	.347	.379	106	3	1-1	.984	1	95	44	O-42(33-0-9),1-27/D-5	0.0
1976	Mil A	80	218	30	54	4	3	5	31	25-1	1	54	.248	.324	.362	104	1	0-0	1.000	-0	103	0	D-40,O-20(5-0-15),1-10	-0.2
1977	Mil A	35	53	8	9	0	0	2	3	10-1	1	17	.170	.313	.283	64	-2	0-0	1.000	-0	68	0	/O-8(LF),1-6,D-7	-0.3
Total	12	965	2080	281	504	73	18	53	229	311-19	7	489	.242	.341	.371	103	16	28-21	.995	15	112	97	1-553,O-177(57-1-119)/D-92	-1.0
HEGMAN, BOB Robert Hilmer B 2.26.1958 Springfield, MN BR/TR 6-1/180# d8.8																								
1985	KC A	1	0	0	0	0	0	0	0	0-0	0	0	—	—	—	—	0	0-0	—	-0	0	0	/2	0.0
HEIDEMANN, JACK Jack Seale B 7.11.1949 Brenham, TX BR/TR 6/178# d5.2																								
1969	Cle A	3	3	0	0	0	0	0	0	0-0	1	2	.000	.250	.000	-24	0	0-0	1.000	0	118	0	/S-3	0.0
1970	Cle A	133	445	44	94	14	2	6	37	34-8	2	88	.211	.265	.292	52	-29	2-4	.961	-8	90	98	*S-132	-2.4
1971	Cle A	81	240	16	50	7	0	0	9	12-0	2	46	.208	.251	.237	36	-20	1-3	.977	-14	85	70	S-81	-2.9
1972	Cle A	10	20	0	3	0	0	0	0	2-0	1	3	.150	.261	.150	24	-2	0-0	.964	-2	80	73	S-10	-0.4
1974	Cle A	12	11	2	1	0	0	0	0	0-0	0	2	.091	.091	.091	-48	-2	0-0	1.000	-2	30	0	/3-6,S-4,12	-0.4
	StL N	47	70	8	19	1	0	0	3	5-0	0	10	.271	.320	.286	71	-3	0-0	.967	-9	68	71	S-45/3	-1.0
1975	NY N	61	145	12	31	4	2	1	16	17-3	0	28	.214	.291	.290	66	-7	1-0	.951	-9	75	70	S-44/3-4,2	-1.2
1976	NY N	5	12	0	1	0	0	0	0	0-0	0	0	.083	.083	.083	-56	-3	0-0	1.000	-1	69	87	/S-3,2	-0.3
	Mil A	69	146	11	32	1	0	2	10	7-0	0	24	.219	.253	.267	54	-9	1-3	.962	-8	68	35	3-40,2-24/D	-1.8
1977	Mil A	5	1	1	0	0	0	0	0	1-0	0	0	.000	.500	.000	50	0	0-0	1.000	1	292	1287	/2D	0.1
Total	8	426	1093	94	231	27	4	9	75	78-11	6	203	.211	.264	.268	49	-75	5-10	.965	-52	85	83	S-322/3-51,2-28,D-4,1	-10.3
HEIDRICK, EMMET R. Emmet "Snags" B 7.9.1876 Queenstown, PA D 1.20.1916 Clarion, PA BL/TR 6/185# d9.14																								
1898	Cle N	19	76	10	23	2	2	0	8	3	0		.303	.329	.382	105	0	3	.850	-0	195	181	O-19(1-12-7)	-0.1
1899	StL N	146	591	109	194	21	14	2	82	34	3		.328	.368	.421	114	9	55	.925	3	**153**	106	*O-145(0-2-143)	0.4
1900	StL N	85	339	51	102	6	8	2	45	18	1		.301	.338	.383	100	-2	22	.959	13	181	136	O-83(CF)	0.5
1901	StL N	118	502	94	170	24	12	6	67	21	1		.339	.366	.470	149	29	32	.945	-1	99	53	*O-118(CF)	2.1
1902	StL A	110	447	75	129	19	10	3	56	34	0		.289	.339	.396	105	2	17	.940	-3	109	142	*O-109(CF)/PS3	-0.6
1903	StL A	120	461	55	129	20	15	1	42	19	1		.280	.310	.395	113	6	19	.954	1	130	155	*O-119(CF)/C	0.1
1904	StL A	133	538	66	147	14	10	1	36	16	0		.273	.294	.342	107	2	35	.963	7	149	155	*O-130(CF)	0.2
1908	StL A	26	93	8	20	2	2	1	6	1	0		.215	.223	.312	73	-3	3	.957	-0	120	153	O-25(2-23-0)	-0.5
Total	8	757	3047	468	914	108	73	16	342	146	6		.300	.333	.399	114	43	186	.946	18	137	126	O-748(3-596-150)/C3SP	2.1
HEIFER, FRANK Franklin "Heck" B 1.18.1854 Reading, PA D 8.29.1893 Reading, PA 5-10.5/175# d6.3																								
1875	Bos NA	11	50	11	14	0	3	0	5	0		0	.280	.280	.400	129	1	0-0	.885	-2	0	56	/1-9,O-6(4-1-1),P-2	-0.1
HEILEMAN, CHINK John George B 8.10.1872 Cincinnati, OH D 7.19.1940 Cincinnati, OH BR/TR 5-8/155# d7.8																								
1901	Cin N	5	15	1	2	1	0	0	1	0	0		.133	.133	.200	-4	-2	0	.667	-1	73	487	/3-4,2	-0.3
HEILMANN, HARRY Harry Edwin "Slug" B 8.3.1894 San Francisco, CA D 7.9.1951 Southfield, MI BR/TR 6-1/195# d5.16 Mil 1918 C1 HF1952																								
1914	Det A	68	182	25	41	8	1	2	18	22	2	29	.225	.316	.313	86	-3	1-8	.870	-4	63	151	O-31(2-29-0),1-16/2-6	-1.2
1916	Det A	136	451	57	127	30	11	2	73	42	5	40	.282	.349	.410	124	12	9	.952	-10	80	98	O-77(5-6-66),1-30/2-9	-0.3
1917	Det A	150	556	57	156	22	11	5	86	41	3	54	.281	.333	.387	120	11	11	.960	-2	91	103	*O-123(0-28-95),1-27	0.2
1918	Det A	79	286	34	79	10	6	5	39	35	2	10	.276	.359	.406	136	12	13	.957	-3	88	115	O-40(RF),1-37/2-2	0.7
1919	Det A	**140**	537	74	172	30	15	8	93	37	2	41	.320	.366	.477	139	25	7	.979	-10	82	80	*1-140	1.2
1920	Det A	145	543	66	168	28	5	9	89	39	2	32	.309	.358	.429	111	7	3-7	.985	2	101	69	*1-122,O-22(RF)	0.3
1921	Det A	149	602	114	**237**	43	14	19	139	53	2	37	**.394**	.444	.606	167	61	2-6	.962	-11	94	51	*O-147(RF)/1-3	3.4
1922	Det A	118	455	92	162	27	10	21	92	58	3	28	.356	.432	.598	172	48	8-4	.948	-11	85	47	*O-115(RF)/1-5	2.7
1923	Det A	144	524	121	211	44	11	18	115	74	5	40	**.403**	.481	.632	195	76	9-7	.960	-1	104	74	*O-130(6-0-124),1-12	6.0
1924	Det A	153	570	107	197	**45**	16	10	114	78	4	41	.346	.428	.533	149	43	13-5	.970	7	97	150	*O-147(RF)/1-4	3.7
1925	Det A	150	573	97	225	40	11	13	134	67	1	27	**.393**	.457	.569	161	**55**	6-6	.970	-6	100	59	*O-148(RF)	3.4
1926	Det A	141	502	90	184	41	8	9	103	67	4	19	.367	.445	.534	153	42	6-7	.972	-0	94	126	*O-134(RF)	2.9
1927	Det A	141	505	106	201	50	9	14	120	72	2	16	**.398**	.475	.616	179	63	11-5	.966	-9	87	76	*O-135(RF)	4.1
1928	Det A	151	558	83	183	38	10	14	107	57	0	45	.328	.390	.507	132	26	7-3	.971	-1	92	131	*O-125(RF),1-25	1.4
1929	Det A	125	453	86	156	41	7	15	120	50	2	39	.344	.412	.565	148	34	5-6	.966	-6	95	71	*O-114(RF)/1-2	1.7
1930	Cin N	142	459	79	153	43	6	19	91	64	1	50	.333	.416	.577	144	35	2	.955	12	**120**	121	*O-106(RF),1-19	3.3
1932	Cin N	15	31	3	8	2	0	0	6	0	0	2	.258	.258	.323	57	-2	0	.981	-0	84	51	/1-6	-0.3
Total	17	2147	7787	1291	2660	542	151	183	1539	856	40	550	.342	.410	.520	148	545	113-64	.962	-52	94	95	*O-1594(13-63-1518),1-448/2-17	33.2
HEIM, VAL Val Raymond B 11.4.1920 Plymouth, WI BL/TR 5-11/170# d8.31 Mil 1942-45																								
1942	Chi A	13	45	6	9	1	1	0	7	5	1	3	.200	.294	.267	60	-2	1-0	.958	-1	94	0	O-12(9-0-3)	-0.4
HEINE, BUD William Henry B 9.22.1900 Elmira, NY D 9.2.1976 Ft.Lauderdale, FL BL/TR 5-8/145# d10.1																								
1921	NY N	1	2	0	0	0	0	0	0	0	0	0	.000	.000	.000	-99	-1	0-0	1.000	-0	106	0	/2	-0.1
HEINTZELMAN, TOM Thomas Kenneth B 11.3.1946 St.Charles, MO BR/TR 6-1/180# d8.12 f-Ken																								
1973	StL N	23	29	5	9	0	0	0	0	3-2	0	3	.310	.375	.310	92	0	0-0	1.000	0	107	120	/2-6	0.0

Year	Tm Lg	G	AB	R	H	2B	3B	HR	RBI	BB-IB	HP	SO	AVG	OBP	SLG	AOPS	ABR	SB-CS	FA	FR	Rng	Thr	G at Pos	BFW
1974	StL N	38	74	10	17	4	0	1	6	9-0	0	14	.230	.313	.324	79	-2	0-0	.978	-2	97	102	2-28/3-2,S	-0.3
1977	SF N	2	2	0	0	0	0	0	0	0-0	0	0	.000	.000	.000	-99	-1	0-0	—	0			H	-0.1
1978	SF N	27	35	2	8	1	0	2	6	2-0	0	5	.229	.270	.429	96	0	0-0	1.000	2	152	73	/2-5,3-3,1-2	0.2
Total	4	90	140	17	34	5	0	3	12	14-2	0	22	.243	.312	.343	84	-3	0-0	.984	0	104	102	/2-39,3-5,1-2,S	-0.2
HEINZMAN, JACK John Peter B 9.27.1863 New Albany, IN D 11.10.1914 Louisville, KY BR/TR d10.2																								
1886	Lou AA	1	5	1	0	0	0	0	0	0	0		.000	.000	.000	-95	-1	0	1.000	-0	0	0	/1	-0.1
HEISE, BOB Robert Lowell B 5.12.1947 San Antonio, TX BR/TR 6/175# d9.12																								
1967	NY N	16	62	7	20	4	0	0	3	3-0	0	1	.323	.354	.387	114	1	0-1	.973	-1	86	71	2-12/S-3,3-2	0.2
1968	NY N	6	23	3	5	0	0	0	1	1-0	0	1	.217	.250	.217	41	-2	0-0	.929	-3	50	176	/S-6,2	-0.5
1969	NY N	4	10	1	3	1	0	0	0	3-1	0	2	.300	.462	.400	140	1	0-0	1.000	-2	52	0	/S-3	-0.1
1970	SF N	67	154	15	36	5	1	1	22	5-0	0	13	.234	.256	.299	49	-12	0-1	.915	-3	112	107	S-33,2-28/3-2	-1.1
1971	SF N	13	11	2	0	0	0	0	0	0-0	0	1	.000	.000	.000	-99	-3	0-0	.833	-1	67	120	/S-3,3-2,2	-0.4
	Mil A	68	189	10	48	7	0	0	7	7-1	0	15	.254	.279	.291	63	-10	1-1	.961	4	110	142	S-51,3-11/2-3,O(LF)	0.0
1972	Mil A	95	271	23	72	10	1	0	12	12-1	2	14	.266	.301	.310	84	-6	1-1	.990	-5	97	98	2-49,3-24/S-9	-0.9
1973	Mil A	49	98	8	20	2	0	0	4	4-0	0	4	.204	.235	.224	31	-9	1-0	.956	-5	92	62	S-29/3-9,1-4,2-4,D-2	-1.2
1974	StL N	3	7	0	1	0	0	0	0	0-0	0	0	.143	.143	.143	-20	-1	0-0	1.000	2	141	159	/2-3	0.0
	Cal A	29	75	7	20	7	0	0	6	5-0	0	10	.267	.313	.360	99	0	0-1	1.000	2	107	102	2-17/3-6,S-3	0.3
1975	Bos A	63	126	12	27	3	0	0	21	4-0	2	6	.214	.246	.238	35	-11	0-0	.940	2	117	105	3-45,2-14/S-4,1	-0.9
1976	Bos A	32	56	5	15	2	0	0	5	1-0	1	2	.268	.293	.304	67	-2	0-1	.968	-1	91	57	3-22/S-9,2	-0.3
1977	KC A	54	62	11	16	2	1	0	5	2-0	1	8	.258	.292	.323	67	-3	0-1	1.000	2	94	132	2-21,S-21,3-12/1	0.0
Total	11	499	1144	104	283	43	3	1	86	47-3	6	77	.247	.280	.293	63	-57	3-7	.945	-9	101	112	S-174,2-154,3-135/1-6,D-2,O(LF)	-4.9
HEIST, AL Alfred Michael B 10.5.1927 Brooklyn, NY BR/TR 6-2/185# d7.17 C3																								
1960	Chi N	41	102	11	28	5	3	1	6	10-0	0	12	.275	.339	.412	106	1	3-1	.985	1	107	109	O-33(1-32-0)	0.1
1961	Chi N	109	321	48	82	14	3	7	37	39-0	1	51	.255	.337	.383	90	-4	3-3	.978	0	99	138	O-99(CF)	-0.7
1962	Hou N	27	72	4	16	1	0	0	3	3-0	1	9	.222	.263	.236	38	-6	0-0	.974	-1	90	89	O-23(CF)	-0.8
Total	3	177	495	63	126	20	6	8	46	52-0	2	72	.255	.327	.368	86	-9	6-4	.979	0	99	126	O-155(1-154-0)	-1.4
HEITMULLER, HEINIE William Frederick B 5.25.1883 San Francisco, CA D 10.8.1912 Los Angeles, CA BR/TR 6-2/215# d4.26																								
1909	Phi A	64	210	36	60	9	8	0	15	18	3		.286	.351	.405	136	8	7	.927	-0	54	132	O-61(54-7-0)	0.5
1910	Phi A	31	111	11	27	2	2	0	7	7	0		.243	.288	.297	84	-2	6	.981	-0	104	56	O-28(15-11-2)	-0.5
Total	2	95	321	47	87	11	10	0	22	25	3		.271	.330	.368	118	6	13	.943	-0	70	108	/O-89(69-18-2)	0.0
HELD, WOODIE Woodson George B 3.25.1932 Sacramento, CA BR/TR 5-11/180# d9.5 OF Total (113-LF 276-CF 111-RF)																								
1954	NY A	4	3	2	0	0	0	0	0	2	0	1	.000	.400	.000	17	0	0-0	1.000	-0	86	140	/S-4,3	0.0
1957	NY A	1	1	0	0	0	0	0	0	0-0	0	0	.000	.000	.000	-99	0	0-0	—	0			H	0.0
	KC A	92	326	48	78	14	3	20	50	37-1	3	81	.239	.321	.485	116	6	4-0	.996	9	110	180	O-92(CF)	1.2
	Year	93	327	48	78	14	3	20	50	37-1	3	81	.239	.320	.483	115	5	4-0	.996	9	110	180	O-92(CF)	1.2
1958	KC A	47	131	13	28	2	0	4	16	10-0	2	28	.214	.276	.321	64	-7	0-1	1.000	-1	96	55	O-41(CF)/3-4,S	-1.0
	Cle A	67	144	12	28	4	1	3	17	15-0	4	36	.194	.285	.299	63	-7	1-2	.966	1	114	173	O-43(7-37-0),S-14/3-4	-0.8
	Year	114	275	25	56	6	1	7	33	25-0	6	64	.204	.281	.309	64	-14	1-3	.982	-0	105	113	O-84(7-78-0),S-15/3-8	-1.8
1959	Cle A	143	525	82	132	19	3	29	71	46-1	2	118	.251	.313	.465	115	8	1-2	.962	-10	92	71	*S-103,3-40/O-6(CF),2-3	0.6
1960	Cle A	109	376	45	97	15	1	21	67	44-5	5	73	.258	.342	.471	122	11	0-1	.967	6	101	**118**	*S-109	2.6
1961	Cle A	146	509	67	136	23	5	23	78	69-11	3	111	.267	.354	.468	122	16	0-0	.960	-10	96	102	*S-144	1.8
1962	Cle A	139	466	55	116	12	2	19	58	73-5	11	107	.249	.362	.406	110	9	5-1	.956	-5	100	123	*S-133/3-5,O(CF)	1.5
1963	Cle A	133	416	61	103	19	4	17	61	61-10	8	96	.248	.352	.435	121	13	2-2	.982	2	103	95	2-96,O-35(12-12-12)/S-5,3-3	2.3
1964	Cle A	118	364	50	86	13	0	18	49	43-8	7	88	.236	.328	.420	107	4	1-0	.966	-1	103	115	2-52,O-41(5-19-18),3-30	0.5
1965	Was A	122	332	46	82	16	2	16	54	49-1	3	74	.247	.345	.452	128	13	0-0	.963	1	105	102	*O-106(57-43-50)/3-5,2-4,S-2	1.0
1966	Bal A	56	82	6	17	3	1	1	7	12-0	0	30	.207	.309	.305	78	-2	0-0	1.000	-2	88	250	O-10(LF)/2-5,S-3,3-3	-0.4
1967	Bal A	26	41	4	6	3	0	1	6	6-0	2	12	.146	.286	.293	72	-1	0-0	.974	1	102	150	/2-9,3-5,O-2(LF)	0.1
	Cal A	58	141	15	31	3	0	4	17	18-0	2	41	.220	.317	.326	94	-1	0-2	.979	-0	117	123	3-19,O-17(8-10-1),S-13/2-3	-0.1
	Year	84	182	19	37	6	0	5	23	24-0	4	53	.203	.310	.319	88	-2	0-2	.962	1	118	114	3-24,O-19(10-10-1),S-13,2-12	0.0
1968	Cal A	33	45	4	5	1	0	0	0	5-0	2	15	.111	.231	.133	13	-5	0-0	1.000	-3	118	0	/2-5,S-5,3-5,O-3(0-1-2)	-0.8
	Chi A	40	54	5	9	1	0	0	2	5-0	1	14	.167	.246	.185	33	-4	0-0	1.000	1	113	227	O-33(9-3-23)/3-5,2	-0.5
	Year	73	99	9	14	2	0	0	2	10-0	3	29	.141	.239	.162	24	-9	0-0	1.000	-2	112	212	O-36(9-4-25),3-10/2-6,S-5	-1.3
1969	Chi A	56	63	9	9	2	0	3	6	13-3	1	19	.143	.299	.317	69	-2	0-0	1.000	1	79	0	O-18(3-11-5)/S-3,3-3,2	-0.2
Total	14	1390	4019	524	963	150	22	179	559	508-45	56	944	.240	.331	.421	109	51	14-11	.960	-10	97	104	S-539,O-448C,2-179,3-132	7.8
HELF, HANK Henry Hartz B 8.26.1913 Austin, TX D 10.27.1984 Austin, TX BR/TR 6-1/196# d5.5 Mil 1944-45																								
1938	Cle A	6	13	1	1	0	0	0	1	1	0	1	.077	.143	.077	-44	-3	0-0	.947	0	*68*	*230*	/C-5	-0.2
1940	Cle A	1	1	0	0	0	0	0	0	0	0	0	.000	.000	.000	-99	0	0-0	1.000	-0	*0*	*0*	/C	0.0
1946	StL A	71	182	17	35	11	0	6	21	9	1	40	.192	.234	.352	59	-11	0-1	.965	3	*74*	*152*	C-69	-0.5
Total	3	78	196	18	36	11	0	6	22	10	1	41	.184	.227	.332	51	-14	0-1	.964	3	*73*	*156*	/C-75	-0.7
HELFAND, ERIC Eric James B 3.25.1969 Erie, PA BL/TR 6/195# d9.4																								
1993	Oak A	8	13	1	3	0	0	0	1	0-0	0	1	.231	.231	.231	26	-1	0-0	1.000	3	63	185	/C-5	0.2
1994	Oak A	7	6	1	1	0	0	0	1	0-0	0	1	.167	.167	.167	-15	-1	0-0	1.000	2	0	0	/C-6	0.1
1995	Oak A	38	86	9	14	2	1	0	7	11-0	1	25	.163	.265	.209	27	-9	0-0	.994	-4	88	97	C-36	-1.1
Total	3	53	105	11	18	2	1	0	9	11-0	1	27	.171	.256	.210	25	-11	0-0	.996	1	83	101	/C-47	-0.8
HELFRICH, TY Emory Wilbur B 10.9.1890 Pleasantville, NJ D 3.18.1955 Pleasantville, NJ BR/TR 5-10/178# d6.30																								
1915	Bro F	43	104	12	25	6	0	0	5	15	0	21	.240	.336	.298	80	-4	2	.912	-2	113	38	2-34/O(RF)	-0.5
HELLINGS B Philadelphia, PA d7.19																								
1875	Atl NA	1	4	0	1	0	0	0	0	0		0	.250	.250	.250	85	0	0-0	.750	-0	98	0	/2	0.0
HELLMAN, TONY Anthony Joseph B 1861 Cincinnati, OH D 3.29.1898 Cincinnati, OH 5-9/175# d10.10																								
1886	Bal AA	1	3	0	0	0	0	0	0	0	0		.000	.000	.000	-99	-1	0	1.000	0			/C	0.0
HELMS, TOMMY Tommy Vann B 5.5.1941 Charlotte, NC BR/TR 5-10/175# d9.23 M2 C9																								
1964	Cin N	2	1	0	0	0	0	0	0	0-0	0	1	.000	.000	.000	-97	0	0-0	—	0			H	0.0
1965	Cin N	21	42	4	16	2	2	0	6	3-1	0	7	.381	.435	.524	158	3	1-0	.973	-1	84	99	/S-8,3-2,2	0.3
1966	Cin N	138	542	72	154	23	1	9	49	24-2	2	31	.284	.315	.380	85	-10	3-4	.961	-9	86	70	*3-113,2-20	-2.0
1967	Cin N★	137	497	40	136	27	4	2	35	24-8	0	41	.274	.305	.356	80	-12	5-10	.978	-11	93	97	2-88,S-46	-1.6
1968	Cin N★	127	507	35	146	28	2	2	47	12-6	2	27	.288	.305	.363	94	-4	5-6	.979	2	99	98	*2-127/S-2,3	1.0
1969	Cin N	126	480	38	129	18	1	1	40	18-5	1	33	.269	.296	.317	68	-21	4-6	.975	-5	98	101	*2-125/S-4	-1.9
1970	†Cin N	150	575	42	136	21	1	1	45	21-4	0	33	.237	.262	.282	46	-45	2-2	**.983**	1	101	**116**	*2-148,S-12	-3.5
1971	Cin N	150	547	40	141	26	1	3	52	26-5	1	33	.258	.289	.325	76	-18	3-4	**.990**	**26**	**110**	**136**	*2-149	1.8
1972	Hou N	139	518	45	134	20	5	5	60	24-8	4	27	.259	.291	.346	84	-13	4-3	.979	**29**	108	**126**	*2-139	2.7
1973	Hou N	146	543	44	156	28	2	4	61	32-12	0	21	.287	.325	.368	93	-6	1-1	.988	2	103	105	*2-145	0.6
1974	Hou N	137	452	32	126	21	1	5	50	23-7	1	27	.279	.313	.363	93	-6	5-4	**.985**	11	105	126	*2-133	1.4
1975	Hou N	64	135	7	28	2	0	0	14	10-1	1	8	.207	.265	.222	40	-11	0-0	.988	4	119	89	2-42/3-3,S	-0.6
1976	Pit N	62	87	10	24	5	1	1	13	10-0	1	5	.276	.350	.391	111	2	0-0	.921	-1	103	188	3-22,2-11/S	0.1
1977	Pit N	15	12	0	0	0	0	0	0	0-0	0	3	.000	.000	.000	-97	-3	0-0	—	0			H	-0.4
	Bos A	21	59	5	16	2	0	1	5	4-1	1	4	.271	.328	.356	77	-2	0-0	1.000	-1	25	0	D-13/3-2,2	-0.4
Total	14	1435	4997	414	1342	223	21	34	477	231-60	15	301	.269	.300	.342	79	-146	33-40	.983	45	103	113	*2-1129,3-143/S-74,D-13	-2.5
HELMS, WES Wesley Ray B 5.12.1976 Gastonia, NC BR/TR 6-4/230# d9.5																								
1998	Atl N	7	13	2	4	1	0	1	2	0-0	0	4	.308	.308	.615	135	1	0-0	.750	-1	41	0	/3-4	-0.1
2000	Atl N	6	5	0	1	0	0	0	0	0-0	0	2	.200	.200	.200	1	-1	0-0	.833	1	161	472	/3-5	0.0
2001	Atl N	100	216	28	48	10	3	10	36	21-2	1	56	.222	.293	.435	83	-6	1-1	.991	0	94	105	1-77,3-17/O(LF)	-1.1
2002	†Atl N	85	210	20	51	16	0	6	22	11-2	3	57	.243	.283	.405	83	-7	1-1	.987	-3	133	130	1-45,3-24/O-9(5-0-4)	-1.3
2003	Mil N	134	476	56	124	21	0	23	67	43-3	10	131	.261	.330	.450	104	2	0-1	.945	-16	88	79	*3-130	-1.3
Total	5	332	920	106	228	48	3	40	127	75-7	14	250	.248	.310	.437	94	-11	2-3	.945	-20	87	74	3-180,1-122/O-10(6-0-4)	-3.8

Year	Tm Lg	G	AB	R	H	2B	3B	HR	RBI	BB-IB	HP	SO	AVG	OBP	SLG	AOPS	ABR	SB-CS	FA	FR	Rng	Thr	G at Pos	BFW
HELTON, TODD Todd Lynn B 8.20.1973 Knoxville, TN BL/TL 6-2/195# d8.2																								
1997	Col N	35	93	13	26	2	1	5	11	8-0	0	11	.280	.337	.484	91	-1	0-1	1.000	1	63	223	O-15(13-0-2)/1-8	-0.2
1998	Col N	152	530	78	167	37	1	25	97	53-5	6	54	.315	.380	.530	113	12	3-3	.995	16	**140**	**129**	*1-146	1.3
1999	Col N	159	578	114	185	39	5	35	113	68-6	6	77	.320	.395	.587	114	13	7-6	.993	3	107	109	*1-156	0.2
2000	Col N★	160	580	138	**216**	**59**	2	42	**147**	103-22	4	61	**.372**	**.463**	**.698**	152	51	5-3	.995	19	**145**	111	*1-160	5.1
2001	Col N★	159	587	132	197	54	2	49	146	98-15	5	104	.336	.432	.685	150	47	7-5	**.999**	13	**133**	108	*1-157	4.4
2002	Col N★	156	553	107	182	39	4	30	109	99-21	5	91	.329	.429	.577	145	38	5-1	.995	7	119	101	*1-156	3.1
2003	Col N★	160	583	135	209	49	5	33	117	111-21	2	72	.358	.458	.630	159	57	0-4	.993	20	**153**	102	*1-159	5.8
Total	7	981	3504	717	1182	279	20	219	740	540-90	28	470	.337	.425	.616	138	217	27-23	.995	79	133	110	1-942/O-15(13-0-2)	19.7
HELTZEL, HEINIE William Wade B 12.21.1913 York, PA D 5.1.1998 York, PA BR/TR 5-10/150# d7.27																								
1943	Bos N	29	86	6	13	3	0	0	5	7	0	13	.151	.215	.186	17	-9	0	.880	-1	116	85	3-29	-1.1
1944	Phi N	11	22	1	4	1	0	0	0	2	1	3	.182	.280	.227	45	-2	0	.919	-2	80	27	S-10	-0.3
Total	2	40	108	7	17	4	0	0	5	9	1	16	.157	.229	.194	23	-11	0	.880	-3	116	85	/3-29,S-10	-1.4
HEMINGWAY, ED Edson Marshall B 5.8.1893 Sheridan, MI D 7.5.1969 Grand Rapids, MI BB/TR 5-11.5/165# d9.17																								
1914	StL A	3	5	0	0	0	0	0	0	1	0	1	.000	.167	.000	-51	-1	1	1.000	-0	64	0	/3-3	-0.1
1917	NY N	7	25	3	8	1	1	0	1	2	0	1	.320	.370	.440	153	1	2	.958	1	110	205	/3-7	0.3
1918	Phi N	33	108	7	23	4	1	0	12	7	1	9	.213	.267	.269	59	-5	4	.955	-1	104	67	2-25/3-3,1	-0.6
Total	3	43	138	10	31	5	2	0	13	10	1	11	.225	.282	.290	71	-5	7	.955	0	104	67	/2-25,3-13,1	-0.4
HEMOND, SCOTT Scott Mathew B 11.18.1965 Taunton, MA BR/TR 6/205# d9.9 OF Total (8-LF 1-CF 3-RF)																								
1989	Oak A	4	0	2	0	0	0	0	0	0-0	0	0	—	—	—	—	0	0-0	—	0			R-3	0.0
1990	Oak A	7	13	0	2	0	0	0	1	0-0	0	5	.154	.154	.154	-14	-2	0-0	1.000	-1	70	0	/3-7,2	-0.4
1991	Oak A	23	23	4	5	0	0	0	0	1-0	0	7	.217	.250	.217	32	-2	1-2	.947	-1	216	88	/C-8,2-7,3-2,SD	-0.3
1992	Oak A	17	27	7	6	1	0	0	1	3-0	0	7	.222	.300	.259	61	-1	1-0	1.000	-1	65	150	/C-8,S-3,3-2,O-2(1-0-1),D	-0.2
	Chi A	8	13	1	3	1	0	0	1	1-0	0	6	.231	.267	.308	67	-1	0-0	1.000	0	73	1133	/O-2(LF),C3D	0.0
	Year	25	40	8	9	2	0	0	2	4-0	0	13	.225	.289	.275	63	-2	1-0	1.000	-1	64	147	/C-9,D-5,O-4(3-0-1),S-3,3-3	-0.2
1993	Oak A	91	215	31	55	16	0	6	26	32-0	1	55	.256	.353	.414	113	5	14-5	.991	-3	91	104	C-75/O-6(4-1-1),12D	0.8
1994	Oak A	91	198	23	44	11	0	3	20	16-0	0	51	.222	.280	.323	60	-12	7-6	1.000	-6	169	84	C-39,2-25,3-12/1-7,O-2(1-0-1),D-3	-1.5
1995	StL N	57	118	11	17	1	0	3	9	12-0	2	31	.144	.233	.229	23	-14	0-0	.985	0	98	186	C-38/2-6	-1.1
Total	7	298	607	79	132	30	0	12	58	65-0	3	162	.217	.295	.326	69	-27	23-13	.991	-11	111	119	C-169/2-40,3-24,D-15,O-12L,1-8,S-2	-2.7
HEMP, DUCKY William H. B 12.27.1867 St.Louis, MO D 3.6.1923 St.Louis, MO d10.6																								
1887	Lou AA	1	3	1	1	1	0	0	0	1	0		.333	.500	.667	219	1	0	.000	-1	0	0	/O(RF)	0.0
1890	Pit N	21	81	9	19	0	2	0	4	8	1	12	.235	.311	.284	83	-2	3	.867	1	155	343	O-21(2-14-5)	-0.1
	Syr AA	9	33	1	5	1	0	0	1	0	1		.152	.176	.182	6	-4	1	.947	3	302	635	/O-9(2-7-0)	-0.1
Total	2	31	117	11	25	2	2	0	5	9	2	12	.214	.281	.265	67	-5	4	.877	3	192	416	/O-31(4-21-6)	-0.2
HEMPHILL, BRET Bret Ryan B 12.17.1971 Santa Clara, CA BB/TR 6-3/200# d6.28																								
1999	Ana A	12	21	3	3	0	0	0	2	4-0	0	4	.143	.269	.143	12	-3	0-0	.955	-1	103	202	C-12	-0.3
HEMPHILL, CHARLIE Charles Judson "Eagle Eye" B 4.20.1876 Greenville, MI D 6.22.1953 Detroit, MI BL/TL 5-9/160# d6.27 b-Frank																								
1899	StL N	11	37	4	9	0	0	1	3	6	1		.243	.364	.324	87	0	0	.750	-2	140	274	O-10(CF)	-0.3
	Cle N	55	202	23	56	3	5	2	23	6	1		.277	.301	.371	91	-4	3	.859	-5	84	40	O-54(RF)	-1.1
	Year	66	239	27	65	3	5	3	26	12	2		.272	.312	.364	90	-5	3	.837	-7	93	79	O-64(0-10-54)	-1.4
1901	Bos A	136	545	71	142	10	10	3	62	39	2		.261	.312	.332	80	-16	11	.925	-5	124	114	*O-136(0-2-134)	-2.4
1902	Cle A	25	94	14	25	2	0	0	11	5	0		.266	.303	.287	67	-4	4	.860	-2	108	0	O-19(17-1-1)	-0.7
	StL A	103	416	67	132	14	11	6	58	44	0		.317	.383	.447	131	18	23	.952	-4	111	229	*O-101(1-31-71)/2-2	0.9
	Year	128	510	81	157	16	11	6	69	49	0		.308	.369	.418	120	14	27	.935	-6	110	190	*O-120(18-32-72)/2-2	0.2
1903	StL A	105	383	36	94	6	3	3	29	23	2		.245	.292	.300	80	-10	16	.961	2	150	144	*O-104(4-18-82)	-1.3
1904	StL A	114	438	47	112	13	2	2	45	35	0		.256	.311	.308	102	2	23	.926	-5	95	151	*O-108(6-26-76)/2	-1.0
1906	StL A	**154**	585	90	169	19	12	4	62	43	0		.289	.338	.383	131	19	33	.961	-5	84	25	*O-154(0-114-40)	0.8
1907	StL A	153	603	66	156	20	9	0	38	51	2		.259	.319	.322	105	3	14	.957	-7	60	44	*O-153(0-134-19)	-1.2
1908	NY A	142	505	62	150	12	9	0	44	59	3		.297	.374	.356	136	22	42	.937	-4	82	41	*O-142(4-130-8)	1.4
1909	NY A	73	181	23	44	5	1	0	10	32	0		.243	.357	.282	101	2	10	.976	1	117	82	O-45(13-32-0)	0.1
1910	NY A	102	351	45	84	9	4	0	21	55	5		.239	.350	.288	95	1	19	.971	-4	96	77	O-94(0-63-31)	-0.8
1911	NY A	69	201	32	57	4	2	1	15	37	1		.284	.397	.338	99	2	9	.952	-5	93	49	O-55(0-46-9)	-0.6
Total	11	1242	4541	580	1230	117	68	22	421	435	17		.271	.337	.341	106	35	207	.944	-44	98	90	*O-1175(45-607-525)/2-3	-6.2
HEMPHILL, FRANK Frank Vernon B 5.13.1878 Greenville, MI D 11.16.1950 Chicago, IL BR/TR 5-11/165# d4.17 b-Charlie																								
1906	Chi A	13	40	0	3	0	0	0	2	9	2		.075	.275	.075	11	-3	1	.970	-0	48	0	O-13(LF)	-0.5
1909	Was A	1	3	0	0	0	0	0	0	0	0		.000	.000	.000	-99	-1	0	1.000	0	0	0	/O(LF)	-0.1
Total	2	14	43	0	3	0	0	0	2	9	2		.070	.259	.070	5	-4	1	.971	-0	45	0	/O-14(LF)	-0.6
HEMSLEY, ROLLIE Ralston Burdett B 6.24.1907 Syracuse, OH D 7.31.1972 Washington, DC BR/TR 5-10/170# d4.13 Mil 1944-45 C3																								
1928	Pit N	50	133	14	36	2	3	0	18	4	0	10	.271	.292	.331	60	-8	1	.962	-1	79	105	C-49	-0.7
1929	Pit N	88	235	31	68	13	7	0	37	11	0	22	.289	.321	.404	77	-10	1	.954	5	98	114	C-80	0.0
1930	Pit N	104	324	45	82	19	6	2	45	22	0	21	.253	.301	.367	60	-22	3	.979	4	96	103	C-98	-1.0
1931	Pit N	10	35	3	6	3	0	0	1	3	0	3	.171	.237	.257	33	-3	0	1.000	0	96	62	/C-9	-0.3
	Chi N	66	204	28	63	17	4	3	31	17	0	30	.309	.362	.475	121	6	4	.975	4	125	113	C-53	1.3
	Year	76	239	31	69	20	4	3	32	20	0	33	.289	.344	.444	109	3	4	.978	4	120	105	C-62	1.0
1932	†Chi N	60	151	27	36	10	3	4	20	10	0	16	.238	.286	.424	89	-3	2	.974	3	195	73	C-47/O(CF)	0.2
1933	Cin N	49	116	9	22	8	0	0	7	6	0	8	.190	.230	.259	40	-9	0	.970	2	98	101	C-41	-0.5
	StL A	32	95	7	23	2	1	1	15	11	0	12	.242	.321	.316	65	-5	0-0	.965	-1	112	81	C-27	-0.4
1934	StL A	123	431	47	133	31	7	2	52	29	2	37	.309	.355	.427	93	-5	6-2	.973	23	106	**135**	*C-114/O-6(LF)	2.4
1935	StL A★	144	504	57	146	32	7	0	48	44	2	41	.290	.349	.381	85	-11	3-2	.979	11	118	86	*C-141	0.8
1936	StL A☆	116	377	43	99	24	2	2	39	46	0	30	.263	.343	.353	70	-17	2-3	.969	-5	98	66	*C-114	-1.5
1937	StL A	100	334	30	74	12	3	3	28	25	0	29	.222	.276	.302	45	-29	0-0	.969	-5	91	116	C-94/1-2	-2.7
1938	Cle A	66	203	27	60	11	3	2	28	23	0	14	.296	.367	.409	96	-1	1-1	.980	6	88	117	C-58	0.8
1939	Cle A☆	107	395	58	104	17	4	2	36	26	0	26	.263	.309	.342	69	-20	2-4	.984	7	111	101	*C-106	-0.7
1940	Cle A★	119	416	46	111	20	5	4	42	22	0	25	.267	.304	.368	75	-17	1-3	**.994**	12	**146**	104	*C-117	0.2
1941	Cle A	98	288	29	69	10	5	2	24	18	0	19	.240	.284	.330	65	-16	2-0	.980	1	114	91	C-96	-1.0
1942	Cin N	36	115	7	13	1	2	0	7	4	0	11	.113	.143	.157	-12	-17	0	.982	5	95	77	C-34	-1.0
	NY A	31	85	12	25	3	1	0	15	5	0	9	.294	.333	.353	95	-1	1-0	.991	3	192	82	C-29	0.3
1943	NY A	62	180	12	43	6	3	2	24	13	0	9	.239	.290	.339	83	-5	0-1	.981	3	176	97	C-52	0.1
1944	NY A★	81	284	23	76	12	5	2	26	9	0	13	.268	.290	.366	84	-7	0-2	.983	1	107	91	C-76	-0.3
1946	Phi N	49	139	7	31	4	1	0	11	9	0	10	.223	.270	.266	54	-9	0	.977	7	95	170	C-45	0.0
1947	Phi N	2	3	0	1	0	0	0	1	0	0	0	.333	.333	.333	80	0	0	1.000	0	0	0	/C-2	0.0
Total	19	1593	5047	562	1321	257	72	31	555	357	4	395	.262	.311	.360	74	-209	29-18	.978	82	114	101	*C-1482/O-7(6-1-0),1-2	-4.0
HEMUS, SOLLY Solomon Joseph B 4.17.1923 Phoenix, AZ BL/TR 5-9/175# d4.27 M3 C4																								
1949	StL N	20	33	8	11	1	0	0	2	7	0	3	.333	.450	.364	115	1	0	.981	1	105	72	2-16	0.3
1950	StL N	11	15	1	2	1	0	0	0	2	0	4	.133	.235	.200	15	-2	0	1.000	1	135	179	/3-5	-0.1
1951	StL N	120	420	68	118	18	9	2	32	75	4	31	.281	.395	.381	109	9	7-7	.965	12	**111**	108	*S-105,2-12	2.7
1952	StL N	151	570	**105**	153	28	8	15	52	96	**20**	55	.268	.392	.425	126	26	1-5	.960	5	101	111	*S-148/3-2	3.9
1953	StL N	154	585	110	163	32	11	14	61	86	**12**	40	.279	.382	.443	114	16	2-1	.964	9	105	96	*S-150/2-3	3.5
1954	StL N	124	214	43	65	15	3	2	27	55	5	27	.304	.453	.430	131	15	5-1	.944	-9	95	76	S-66,3-27,2-12	1.1
1955	StL N	96	206	36	50	10	2	5	21	27-0	2	22	.243	.335	.383	91	-2	1-1	.956	-3	95	100	3-43,2-10/S-2	-0.5
1956	StL N	8	5	1	1	0	0	0	2	1-0	1	0	.200	.429	.200	77	0	0-0	—	0			H	0.0
	Phi N	78	187	24	54	10	4	5	24	28-2	7	21	.289	.397	.465	134	11	1-1	.974	-18	74	61	2-49/3	-0.4
	Year	86	192	25	55	10	4	5	26	29-2	8	21	.286	.398	.458	133	11	1-1	.974	-18	74	61	2-49/3	-0.4
1957	Phi N	70	108	8	20	6	1	0	5	20-4	2	8	.185	.323	.259	61	-5	1-1	.980	-4	78	81	2-24	-0.8
1958	Phi N	105	334	53	95	14	3	8	36	51-6	**8**	34	.284	.390	.416	116	10	3-1	.969	-17	90	84	2-85/3	0.0
1959	StL N	24	17	2	4	2	0	0	1	8-0	1	2	.235	.500	.353	124	2	0-0	1.000	1	188	0	/23M	0.2
Total	11	961	2694	459	736	137	41	51	263	456-12	62	247	.273	.390	.411	115	81	21-18	.962	-21	104	102	S-471,2-212/3-80	9.9

Year	Tm Lg	G	AB	R	H	2B	3B	HR	RBI	BB-IB	HP	SO	AVG	OBP	SLG	AOPS	ABR	SB-CS	FA	FR	Rng	Thr	G at Pos	BFW
HENDERSON, DAVE David Lee B 7.21.1958 Merced, CA BR/TR 6-2/220# d4.9																								
1981	Sea A	59	126	17	21	3	0	6	13	16-1	1	24	.167	.264	.333	69	-5	2-1	1.000	3	101	150	O-58(2-33-31)	-0.4
1982	Sea A	104	324	47	82	17	1	14	48	36-2	0	67	.253	.327	.441	106	3	2-5	.985	5	100	179	*O-101(2-99-2)	0.5
1983	Sea A	137	484	50	130	24	5	17	55	28-3	1	93	.269	.306	.444	101	-1	9-3	.982	7	100	203	*O-133(0-80-56)/D-3	0.3
1984	Sea A	112	350	42	98	23	0	14	43	19-0	2	56	.280	.320	.466	116	7	5-5	.988	8	109	203	O-97(0-88-11),D-10	1.3
1985	Sea A	139	502	70	121	28	2	14	68	48-2	3	104	.241	.310	.388	90	-7	6-1	.986	-4	95	92	*O-138(1-126-27)	-1.3
1986	Sea A	103	337	51	93	19	4	14	44	37-4	2	95	.276	.350	.481	123	11	1-3	.979	5	105	208	O-80(0-51-31),D-22	1.2
	†Bos A	36	51	8	10	3	0	1	3	2-0	0	15	.196	.226	.314	45	-4	1-0	.981	3	126	256	O-32(CF)	-0.1
	Year	139	388	59	103	22	4	15	47	39-4	2	110	.265	.335	.459	113	7	2-3	.980	8	109	**216**	*O-112(0-83-31),D-22	1.1
1987	Bos A	75	184	30	43	10	0	8	25	22-0	0	48	.234	.313	.418	90	-3	1-1	.958	-2	101	0	O-64(5-29-30)/D	-0.6
	SF N	15	21	2	5	2	0	0	1	8-0	0	5	.238	.448	.333	117	1	2-0	1.000	0	78	319	/O-9(1-8-1)	0.2
1988	†Oak A	146	507	100	154	38	1	24	94	47-1	4	92	.304	.363	.525	152	35	2-4	.982	0	103	79	*O-143(1-142-0)	3.3
1989	†Oak A	152	579	77	145	24	3	15	80	54-1	3	131	.250	.315	.380	99	-1	8-5	.977	-5	99	63	*O-149(CF)/D-2	-0.8
1990	†Oak A	127	450	65	122	28	0	20	63	40-1	1	105	.271	.331	.467	126	15	3-1	.988	2	106	83	*O-116(1-110-5)/D-6	1.6
1991	Oak A★	150	572	86	158	33	0	25	85	58-3	4	113	.276	.346	.465	130	23	6-6	.997	2	101	139	*O-140(4-135-1)/2D	2.3
1992	Oak A	20	63	1	9	1	0	0	2	2-0	0	16	.143	.169	.159	-8	-9	0-0	.950	-2	73	0	O-12(0-9-3)/D-4	-1.2
1993	Oak A	107	382	37	84	19	0	20	53	32-0	0	113	.220	.275	.427	93	-6	0-3	.991	7	112	164	O-76(2-60-14),D-28	-0.2
1994	KC A	56	198	27	49	14	1	5	31	16-1	1	28	.247	.304	.404	78	-7	2-0	.962	-1	91	154	O-40(17-6-17),D-16	-0.9
Total	14	1538	5130	710	1324	286	17	197	708	465-19	22	1105	.258	.320	.436	108	52	50-38	.984	28	102	129	*O-1388(36-1157-229)/D-99,2	5.2
HENDERSON, KEN Kenneth Joseph B 6.15.1946 Carroll, IA BB/TR 6-2/180# d4.23																								
1965	SF N	63	73	10	14	1	1	0	7	9-4	0	19	.192	.277	.233	45	-5	1-1	.980	3	121	173	O-48(5-31-16)	-0.4
1966	SF N	11	29	4	9	1	1	1	1	2-0	1	3	.310	.375	.517	141	2	0-0	.917	-1	78	0	O-10(1-7-4)	0.0
1967	SF N	65	179	15	34	3	0	4	14	19-0	2	52	.190	.274	.274	58	-10	0-1	.947	-2	92	106	O-52(8-33-18)	-1.5
1968	SF N	3	3	1	1	0	0	0	0	2-0	0	1	.333	.600	.333	186	1	0-0	1.000	0	114	0	/O-2(1-1-0)	0.1
1969	SF N	113	374	42	84	14	4	6	44	42-2	5	64	.225	.308	.332	82	-9	6-4	.969	0	95	145	*O-111(64-5-57)/3-3	-1.5
1970	SF N	148	554	104	163	35	3	17	88	87-9	5	78	.294	.394	.460	130	27	20-3	.966	4	100	146	*O-146(113-25-35)	2.6
1971	†SF N	141	504	80	133	26	6	15	65	84-12	3	76	.264	.370	.429	128	22	18-3	.966	-3	104	33	*O-138(109-14-26)/1	1.5
1972	SF N	130	439	60	113	21	2	18	51	38-6	2	66	.257	.317	.437	112	6	14-7	.974	9	105	178	*O-123(95-26-2)	0.9
1973	Chi A	73	262	32	68	13	0	6	32	27-2	1	49	.260	.330	.378	96	-1	3-4	.972	-3	97	32	O-44(8-36-0),D-26	-0.7
1974	Chi A	162	602	76	176	35	5	20	95	66-9	2	112	.292	.360	.467	134	27	12-7	.987	-4	103	58	*O-162(CF)	2.0
1975	Chi A	140	513	65	129	20	3	9	53	74-14	4	65	.251	.347	.355	98	1	5-3	.990	1	107	71	*O-137(CF)/D	-0.1
1976	Atl N	133	435	52	114	19	0	13	61	62-7	1	68	.262	.352	.395	106	5	5-7	.987	-10	92	31	*O-122(0-20-115)	-1.3
1977	Tex A	75	244	23	63	14	0	5	23	18-4	3	37	.258	.317	.377	87	-4	2-1	.983	-6	91	0	O-65(0-8-61)/D-3	-1.3
1978	NY N	7	22	2	5	2	0	1	4	4-1	0	4	.227	.346	.455	127	1	0-1	1.000	-0	113	0	/O-7(RF)	0.0
	Cin N	64	144	10	24	6	1	3	19	23-3	0	32	.167	.278	.285	59	-8	0-0	1.000	-2	99	0	O-38(0-30-9)	-1.1
	Year	71	166	12	29	8	1	4	23	27-4	0	36	.175	.287	.307	67	-7	0-1	1.000	-2	101	0	O-45(0-30-16)	-1.1
1979	Cin N	10	13	1	3	1	0	0	2	0-0	0	2	.231	.231	.308	45	-1	0-0	1.000	-0	96	0	/O-2(1-0-1)	-0.1
	Chi N	62	81	11	19	2	0	2	8	15-1	1	16	.235	.361	.333	83	-1	0-0	.950	-2	83	0	O-23(14-9-0)	-0.4
	Year	72	94	12	22	3	0	2	10	15-1	1	18	.234	.345	.330	79	-2	0-0	.955	-2	84	0	O-25(15-9-1)	-0.5
1980	Chi N	44	82	7	16	3	0	2	9	17-3	0	19	.195	.333	.305	74	-2	0-0	.944	1	90	214	O-22(15-0-9)	-0.3
Total	16	1444	4553	595	1168	216	26	122	576	589-77	30	763	.257	.343	.396	106	51	86-42	.977	-15	100	84	*O-1252(434-544-360)/D-30,3-3,1	-1.6
HENDERSON, RICKEY Rickey Henley B 12.25.1958 Chicago, IL BR/TL 5-10/195# d6.24																								
1979	Oak A	89	351	49	96	13	3	1	26	34-0	2	39	.274	.338	.336	88	-5	33-11	.973	1	106	78	O-88(62-32-1)	-0.3
1980	Oak A★	158	591	111	179	22	4	9	53	117-7	5	54	.303	.420	.399	136	38	**100**-26	.984	14	111	121	*O-157(157-1-0)/D	5.7
1981	†Oak A	108	423	**89**	**135**	18	7	6	35	64-4	2	68	.319	.408	.437	152	31	**56**-22	.979	15	**128**	87	*O-107(107-1-0)	4.7
1982	Oak A★	149	536	119	143	24	4	10	51	**116**-1	2	94	.267	.398	.382	121	23	**130**-42	.977	4	112	21	*O-144(138-10-0)/D-4	3.4
1983	Oak A★	145	513	105	150	25	7	9	48	**103**-8	4	80	.292	.414	.421	139	34	**108**-19	.992	8	114	81	*O-142(138-10-0)/D	5.2
1984	Oak A★	142	502	113	147	27	4	16	58	86-1	5	81	.293	.399	.458	147	37	**66**-18	.969	8	116	74	*O-140(140-6-0)	4.7
1985	NY A★	143	547	**146**	172	28	5	24	72	99-1	3	65	.314	.419	.516	159	50	**80**-10	.980	10	**117**	79	*O-141(6-141-0)/D	**7.0**
1986	NY A★	153	608	**130**	160	31	5	28	74	89-2	2	81	.263	.358	.469	125	22	**87**-18	.986	4	110	50	*O-146(11-138-0)/D-5	3.6
1987	NY A★	95	358	78	104	17	3	17	37	80-1	2	52	.291	.423	.497	144	27	41-8	.980	5	120	79	O-69(34-39-0),D-24	3.4
1988	NY A★	140	554	118	169	30	2	6	50	82-1	3	54	.305	.394	.399	125	23	**93**-13	.965	4	110	86	*O-136(135-3-0)/D-3	3.9
1989	NY A	65	235	41	58	13	1	3	22	56-0	1	29	.247	.392	.349	112	8	25-8	.993	2	110	78	O-65(LF)	1.0
	†Oak A	85	306	72	90	13	2	9	35	70-5	2	39	.294	.425	.438	150	25	52-6	.985	4	112	62	O-82(LF)/D-3	3.6
	Year	150	541	**113**	148	26	3	12	57	**126**-5	3	68	.274	.411	.399	133	33	**77**-14	.988	6	111	69	*O-147(LF)/D-3	**4.6**
1990	†Oak A★	136	489	**119**	159	33	3	28	61	97-2	4	60	.325	**.439**	.577	**190**	**65**	**65**-10	.983	7	115	65	*O-118(LF),D-15	**7.8**
1991	Oak A★	134	470	105	126	17	1	18	57	98-7	7	73	.268	.400	.423	136	29	**58**-18	.970	7	105	160	*O-119(LF),D-10	3.8
1992	†Oak A	117	396	77	112	18	3	15	46	95-5	6	56	.283	.426	.457	156	37	48-11	.984	5	104	130	*O-108(LF)/D-6	4.6
1993	Oak A	90	318	77	104	19	1	17	47	85-6	2	46	.327	.469	.553	186	46	31-6	.974	6	115	110	O-74(LF),D-16	5.0
	†Tor A	44	163	37	35	3	1	4	12	35-1	2	19	.215	.356	.319	84	-3	22-2	.975	-4	85	39	O-44(LF)	-0.4
	Year	134	481	114	139	22	2	21	59	120-7	4	65	.289	.432	.474	150	42	53-8	.974	2	104	83	*O-118(LF),D-16	4.6
1994	Oak A	87	296	66	77	13	0	6	20	72-1	5	45	.260	.411	.365	112	11	22-7	.977	5	119	90	O-71(66-10-0),D-13	1.5
1995	Oak A	112	407	67	122	31	1	9	54	72-2	4	66	.300	.407	.447	130	23	32-10	.988	-2	92	87	O-90(LF),D-19	1.8
1996	†SD N	148	465	110	112	17	2	9	29	125-2	10	90	.241	.410	.344	108	15	37-15	.975	-5	96	40	*O-134(114-10-17)	0.8
1997	SD N	88	288	63	79	11	0	6	27	71-2	4	62	.274	.422	.375	120	14	29-4	.959	3	112	87	O-78(55-17-8)/D-2	1.9
	Ana A	32	115	21	21	3	0	2	7	26-0	2	23	.183	.343	.261	61	-6	16-4	1.000	-0	111	0	D-19,O-13(11-2-0)	-0.5
1998	Oak A	152	542	101	128	16	1	14	57	**118**-0	5	114	.236	.376	.347	92	-1	**66**-13	.988	2	110	34	*O-151(142-24-0)	0.6
1999	†NY N	121	438	89	138	30	0	12	42	82-1	2	82	.315	.423	.466	129	25	37-14	.988	-8	88	0	*O-116(LF)/D	1.5
2000	NY N	31	96	17	21	1	0	0	2	25-1	2	20	.219	.387	.229	65	-4	5-2	.946	-3	82	0	O-29(LF)	-0.7
	†Sea A	92	324	58	77	13	2	4	30	63-0	2	55	.238	.362	.327	80	-8	31-9	.984	-1	111	0	O-88(LF)	-0.7
2001	SD N	123	379	70	86	17	3	8	42	81-0	3	84	.227	.366	.351	96	1	25-7	.982	-3	90	80	*O-104(LF)/D	-0.2
2002	Bos A	72	179	40	40	6	1	5	16	38-0	4	47	.223	.369	.352	92	0	8-2	.946	-2	88	152	O-54(49-4-1)/D-5	-0.3
2003	LA N	30	72	7	15	1	0	2	5	11-0	1	16	.208	.321	.306	69	-3	3-0	.955	-1	73	108	O-18(LF)	-0.4
Total	25	3081	10961	2295	3055	510	66	297	1115	2190-61	98	1694	.279	.401	.419	128	554	1406-335	.979	84	108	73	*O-2826(2421-448-27),D-149	72.0
HENDERSON, STEVE Stephen Curtis B 11.18.1952 Houston, TX BR/TR 6-2/190# d6.16 C4																								
1977	NY N	99	350	67	104	16	6	12	65	43-2	1	79	.297	.372	.480	134	17	6-3	.980	4	111	68	O-97(LF)	1.6
1978	NY N	157	587	83	156	30	9	10	65	60-3	2	109	.266	.333	.399	108	6	13-7	.968	8	103	137	*O-155(LF)	0.8
1979	NY N	98	350	42	107	16	8	5	39	38-6	4	58	.306	.380	.440	128	14	13-5	.990	4	106	80	O-94(LF)	1.5
1980	NY N	143	513	75	149	17	8	8	58	62-3	3	90	.290	.368	.402	119	14	23-12	.981	7	113	71	*O-136(LF)	1.6
1981	Chi N	82	287	32	84	9	5	5	35	42-7	2	61	.293	.382	.411	121	9	5-7	.951	-3	98	58	O-77(LF)	0.2
1982	Chi N	92	257	23	60	12	4	2	29	22-3	0	64	.233	.293	.335	73	-9	6-5	.956	1	99	99	O-70(LF)	-1.2
1983	Sea A	121	436	50	128	32	3	10	54	44-2	0	82	.294	.356	.450	116	11	10-14	.970	0	85	192	*O-112(LF)/D-6	0.4
1984	Sea A	109	325	42	85	12	3	10	35	38-4	1	62	.262	.341	.409	108	4	2-4	.936	-2	91	131	O-53(LF),D-51	-0.2
1985	Oak A	85	193	25	58	8	3	3	31	18-0	0	34	.301	.358	.420	122	6	0-0	.953	-3	86	106	O-58(47-0-11)/D	0.1
1986	Oak A	11	26	2	2	1	0	0	3	0-0	0	5	.077	.074	.115	-52	-6	0-0	.800	-1	67	0	/O-7(LF),D	-0.7
1987	Oak A	46	114	14	33	7	0	3	9	12-1	0	19	.289	.357	.430	115	3	0-0	.943	-4	72	0	O-31(5-0-28)/D-9	-0.3
1988	Hou N	42	46	4	10	2	0	0	5	7-1	0	14	.217	.321	.261	72	-1	1-1	1.000	1	133	398	/O-8(4-0-4),1	-0.1
Total	12	1085	3484	459	976	162	49	68	428	386-32	13	677	.280	.352	.413	113	68	79-58	.968	12	100	104	O-898(856-0-43)/D-68,1	3.7
HENDRICK, GEORGE George Andrew B 10.18.1949 Los Angeles, CA BR/TR 6-3/195# d6.4 C4																								
1971	Oak A	42	114	8	27	4	1	0	8	3-0	0	20	.237	.254	.289	55	-7	0-1	.981	-2	86	56	O-36(18-16-10)	-1.2
1972	†Oak A	58	121	10	22	1	1	4	15	3-0	1	22	.182	.205	.306	54	-8	3-2	1.000	-2	97	0	O-41(5-28-12)	-1.3
1973	Cle A	113	440	64	118	18	0	21	61	25-1	2	71	.268	.308	.452	111	4	7-6	.988	-11	85	85	*O-110(0-107-3)	-1.0
1974	Cle A★	139	495	65	138	23	1	19	67	33-4	1	73	.279	.322	.444	121	11	6-4	.989	-5	96	91	*O-133(2-131-0)/D	0.3
1975	Cle A★	145	561	82	145	21	2	24	86	40-2	0	78	.258	.304	.431	107	2	6-7	.983	-9	97	36	*O-143(1-89-53)	-1.3
1976	Cle A	149	551	72	146	20	3	25	81	51-6	0	82	.265	.323	.448	127	17	4-4	.987	2	96	128	*O-146(136-13-3)/D-3	1.0
1977	SD N	152	541	75	168	25	2	23	81	61-8	2	74	.311	.381	.492	148	37	11-6	.983	8	109	115	*O-142(24-131-9)	4.2
1978	SD N	36	111	9	27	4	0	3	8	12-0	0	16	.243	.317	.360	96	-1	1-1	.986	-1	96	55	O-33(1-26-6)	-0.3
	StL N	102	382	55	110	27	1	17	67	28-1	2	44	.288	.337	.497	133	16	1-0	.996	-2	98	85	*O-101(2-87-12)	1.3
	Year	138	493	64	137	31	1	20	75	40-1	2	60	.278	.332	.467	126	16	2-1	.994	-3	98	78	*O-134(3-113-18)	1.0
1979	StL N	140	493	67	148	27	1	16	75	49-5	0	62	.300	.359	.456	121	15	2-3	.993	3	92	**177**	*O-138(0-14-124)	1.1

Year	Tm Lg	G	AB	R	H	2B	3B	HR	RBI	BB-IB	HP	SO	AVG	OBP	SLG	AOPS	ABR	SB-CS	FA	FR	Rng	Thr	G at Pos	BFW
1980	StL N★	150	572	73	173	33	2	25	109	32-9	4	67	.302	.342	.498	128	20	6-1	.994	-2	99	81	*O-149(0-54-121)	1.4
1981	StL N	101	394	67	112	19	3	18	61	41-7	4	44	.284	.356	.485	134	17	4-2	.983	-7	90	71	*O-101(0-51-59)	0.7
1982	†StL N	136	515	65	145	20	5	19	104	37-8	1	80	.282	.323	.450	115	9	3-2	.980	-8	93	61	*O-134(RF)	-0.6
1983	StL N☆	144	529	73	168	33	3	18	97	51-15	2	76	.318	.373	.493	140	29	3-4	.992	-1	117	99	1-92,O-51(RF)	1.9
1984	StL N	120	441	57	122	28	1	9	69	32-2	1	75	.277	.324	.406	108	4	0-2	.990	-6	85	115	*O-116(RF)/1	-0.9
1985	Pit N	69	256	23	59	15	0	2	25	18-1	0	42	.230	.278	.313	66	-12	1-0	.971	0	111	46	O-65(RF)	-1.6
	Cal A	16	41	5	5	1	0	2	6	4-1	0	8	.122	.196	.293	33	-4	0-0	1.000	-0	85	140	O-12(RF)/D	-0.5
1986	†Cal A	102	283	45	77	13	1	14	47	26-5	1	41	.272	.332	.473	119	7	1-1	.968	2	108	129	O-93(0-2-92)/1-7,D-4	0.5
1987	Cal A	65	162	14	39	10	0	5	25	14-1	0	18	.241	.301	.395	85	-3	0-0	.967	-4	84	42	O-45(37-0-11)/1-9,D-5	-0.9
1988	Cal A	69	127	12	31	1	0	3	19	7-1	1	20	.244	.283	.323	73	-5	0-1	.933	0	109	0	O-24(20-0-4),1-12/D-3	-0.6
Total	18	2048	7129	941	1980	343	27	267	1111	567-77	22	1013	.278	.329	.446	117	148	59-47	.985	-46	96	89	*O-1813(246-749-897),1-121/D-17	2.2
HENDRICK, HARVEY Harvey "Gink" B 11.9.1897 Mason, TN D 10.29.1941 Covington, TN BL/TR 6-2/190# d4.20 OF Total (128-LF 21-CF 86-RF)																								
1923	†NY A	37	66	9	18	3	1	3	12	2	0	8	.273	.294	.485	101	-1	3-0	.947	-0	78	179	O-13(11-2-0)	-0.1
1924	NY A	40	76	7	20	0	0	1	11	2	1	7	.263	.291	.303	53	-6	1-0	.975	1	117	60	O-17(15-0-2)	-0.6
1925	Cle A	25	28	2	8	1	2	0	9	3	0	5	.286	.355	.464	106	0	0-0	1.000	0	117	46	/1-3	0.0
1927	Bro N	128	458	55	142	18	11	4	50	24	4	40	.310	.350	.424	106	2	29	.969	-3	88	88	O-64(15-0-64),1-53/2	-0.8
1928	Bro N	126	425	83	135	15	10	11	59	54	2	34	.318	.397	.478	129	19	16	.913	0	103	115	3-91,O-17(6-11-0)	2.3
1929	Bro N	110	384	69	136	25	6	14	82	31	1	20	.354	.404	.560	139	23	14	.975	1	98	107	O-42(30-2-10),1-39/3-7,S-4	1.7
1930	Bro N	68	167	29	43	10	1	5	28	20	2	19	.257	.344	.419	84	-4	2	.947	0	96	164	O-42(36-6-0)/1-7	-0.6
1931	Bro N	1	1	0	0	0	0	0	0	0	0	0	.000	.000	.000	-99	0	0	—	0			H	0.0
	Cin N	137	530	74	167	32	9	1	75	53	2	40	.315	.379	.415	121	17	3	.987	-6	87	**121**	*1-137	-0.1
	Year	138	531	74	167	32	9	1	75	53	2	40	.315	.379	.414	120	16	3	.987	-6	87	**121**	*1-137	-0.1
1932	StL N	28	72	8	18	2	0	1	5	5	0	9	.250	.299	.319	64	-4	0	.862	-1	82	147	3-12/O-5(RF)	-0.5
	Cin N	94	398	56	120	30	3	4	40	23	1	29	.302	.341	.422	107	4	3	.986	-4	91	100	1-94	-0.9
	Year	122	470	64	138	32	3	5	45	28	1	38	.294	.335	.406	100	0	3	.986	-5	91	100	1-94,3-12/O-5(RF)	-1.4
1933	Chi N	69	189	30	55	13	3	4	23	13	3	17	.291	.346	.455	128	7	4	.983	-1	99	114	1-38/O-8(4-0-4),3	0.2
1934	Phi N	59	116	12	34	8	0	0	19	9	0	15	.293	.344	.362	79	-3	0	.962	-2	98	121	O-12(11-0-1)/1-7,3-7	-0.6
Total	11	922	2910	434	896	157	46	48	413	239	16	243	.308	.364	.443	113	54	75-0	.986	-15	95	106	1-378,O-220L,3-118/S-4,2	-0.0
HENDRICKS, ELLIE Elrod Jerome B 12.22.1940 Charlotte Amalie, V.I. BL/TR 6-1/175# d4.13 C26																								
1968	Bal A	79	183	19	37	8	1	7	23	19-2	1	51	.202	.279	.372	96	-1	0-0	.991	-1	88	99	C-53	0.0
1969	†Bal A	105	295	36	72	5	0	12	38	39-5	2	44	.244	.333	.383	100	0	0-1	**.998**	8	**156**	98	C-87/1-4	1.2
1970	†Bal A	106	322	32	78	9	0	12	41	33-4	4	44	.242	.317	.382	92	-4	1-0	.986	-2	142	97	C-95	-0.2
1971	†Bal A	101	316	33	79	14	1	9	42	39-5	2	38	.250	.334	.386	105	3	0-0	.985	-5	109	102	C-90/1-3	0.2
1972	Bal A	33	84	6	13	4	0	0	4	12-2	0	19	.155	.258	.202	38	-6	0-1	.986	1	163	136	C-28	-0.5
	Chi N	17	43	7	5	1	0	2	6	13-6	0	8	.116	.321	.279	65	-2	0-1	.978	2	75	101	C-16	0.0
1973	Bal A	41	101	9	18	5	1	3	15	10-4	1	22	.178	.257	.337	67	-5	0-0	.994	1	93	82	C-38/D	-0.2
1974	†Bal A	66	159	18	33	8	2	3	8	17-4	1	25	.208	.283	.340	83	-4	0-0	1.000	-6	95	82	C-54/1D	-0.8
1975	Bal A	85	223	32	48	8	2	8	38	34-5	1	40	.215	.319	.377	103	1	0-1	**.995**	1	109	99	C-83	0.5
1976	Bal A	28	79	2	11	1	0	1	4	7-1	0	13	.139	.209	.190	19	-8	0-1	.971	-7	66	77	C-27	-1.6
	†NY A	26	53	6	12	1	0	3	5	3-0	0	10	.226	.263	.415	99	0	0-0	1.000	-0	136	53	C-18	0.0
	Year	54	132	8	23	2	0	4	9	10-1	0	23	.174	.231	.280	52	-9	0-1	.982	-7	91	68	C-45	-1.6
1977	NY A	10	11	1	3	1	0	1	5	0-0	0	2	.273	.273	.636	140	1	0-0	1.000	-0	146	0	/C-6	0.0
1978	Bal A	13	18	4	6	1	0	1	1	3-2	0	3	.333	.429	.556	186	2	0-0	.955	0	104	81	/C-6,PD	0.3
1979	Bal A	1	1	0	0	0	0	0	0	0-0	0	0	.000	.000	.000	-99	0	0-0	.500	-1	11	0	/C	-0.1
Total	12	711	1888	205	415	66	7	62	230	229-40	12	319	.220	.306	.361	90	-23	1-5	.990	-10	118	96	C-602/1-8,D-3,P	-1.2
HENDRICKS, JACK John Charles B 4.9.1875 Joliet, IL D 5.13.1943 Chicago, IL BL/TL 5-11.5/160# d6.12 M7																								
1902	NY N	8	26	1	6	2	0	0	0	2	0		.231	.286	.308	84	0	2	.929	-0	92	0	/O-7(RF)	-0.1
	Chi N	2	7	0	4	0	1	0	0	0	0		.571	.571	.857	350	2	0	1.000	0	0	0	/O-2(RF)	0.2
	Year	10	33	1	10	2	1	0	0	2	0		.303	.343	.424	138	1	2	.950	-0	68	0	/O-9(RF)	0.1
1903	Was A	32	112	10	20	1	3	0	4	13	0		.179	.264	.241	51	-7	3	.891	-3	33	122	O-32(RF)	-1.1
Total	2	42	145	11	30	3	4	0	4	15	0		.207	.281	.283	70	-5	5	.909	-3	43	87	/O-41(RF)	-1.0
HENDRYX, TIM Timothy Green B 1.31.1891 LeRoy, IL D 8.14.1957 Corpus Christi, TX BR/TR 5-9/170# d9.4																								
1911	Cle A	4	7	0	2	0	0	0	0	0			.286	.286	.286	59	0	0	1.000	0	84	0	/3-3	0.0
1912	Cle A	23	70	9	17	2	4	1	14	8	1		.243	.329	.429	113	1	3	1.000	-1	99	34	O-22(CF)	-0.2
1915	NY A	13	40	4	8	2	0	0	1	4	1	2	.200	.289	.250	61	-2	0-3	.968	0	102	118	O-12(CF)	-0.3
1916	NY A	15	62	10	18	7	1	0	5	8	1	6	.290	.380	.435	142	4	4	1.000	-1	85	62	O-15(RF)	0.2
1917	NY A	125	393	43	98	14	7	5	44	62	5	45	.249	.359	.359	118	10	6	.955	2	104	111	*O-107(0-30-77)	0.6
1918	StL A	88	219	22	61	14	3	0	33	37	2	35	.279	.388	.370	133	11	5	.982	-4	94	52	O-65(28-20-18)	0.5
1920	Bos A	99	363	54	119	21	5	0	73	42	2	27	.328	.400	.413	121	13	7-9	.964	-12	87	48	O-98(CF)	-0.8
1921	Bos A	49	137	10	33	8	2	0	22	24	2	13	.241	.362	.328	79	-3	1-1	.958	-3	100	41	O-41(2-2-37)	-0.8
Total	8	416	1291	152	356	68	22	6	192	185	14	128	.276	.372	.376	115	34	26-13	.966	-19	96	70	O-360(30-184-147)/3-3	-0.8
HENGEL, DAVE David Lee B 12.18.1961 Oakland, CA BR/TR 6/185# d9.3																								
1986	Sea A	21	63	3	12	1	0	1	6	1-0	1	13	.190	.215	.254	27	-7	0-0	1.000	-1	63	215	D-11/O-8(6-0-2)	-0.8
1987	Sea A	10	19	2	6	0	0	1	4	0-0	0	4	.316	.316	.474	100	0	0-0	.875	-1	81	0	/O-7(2-0-7),D	-0.1
1988	Sea A	26	60	3	10	1	0	2	7	1-0	0	15	.167	.177	.283	27	-6	0-0	.952	-0	103	0	O-12(4-0-8),D-12	-0.7
1989	Cle A	12	25	2	3	1	0	0	1	2-0	0	4	.120	.185	.160	-2	-3	0-0	1.000	-1	71	199	/O-9(LF),D-3	-0.4
Total	4	69	167	10	31	3	0	4	18	4-0	1	36	.186	.208	.275	31	-16	0-0	.962	-2	81	108	/O-36(21-0-17),D-27	-2.0
HENGLE, MOXIE Emery J. B 10.7.1857 Chicago, IL D 12.11.1924 River Forest, IL BR 5-8/144# d4.20																								
1884	CP U	19	74	9	15	2	1	0		3			.203	.234	.257	49	-7		.840	-5	79	39	2-19	-1.0
	StP U	**9**	33	2	5	1	1	0		0			.152	.152	.242	32	-4		.923	3	106	106	/2-9	-0.1
	Year	28	107	11	20	3	2	0		3			.187	.209	.252	46	-10		.870	-2	87	59	2-28	-1.1
1885	Buf N	7	26	2	4	0	0	0	0	1		2	.154	.185	.154	10	-3		.864	-2	49	52	/2-5,O-3(0-2-1)	-0.4
Total	2	35	133	13	24	3	2	0	0	4		2	.180	.204	.233	38	-14		.869	-4	82	58	/2-33,O-3(0-2-1)	-1.5
HENLEY, GAIL Gail Curtice B 10.15.1928 Wichita, KS BL/TR 5-9/180# d4.13																								
1954	Pit N	14	30	7	9	1	0	1	2	4	0	4	.300	.382	.433	114	1	0-0	1.000	0	102	173	/O-9(1-0-8)	0.1
HENLEY, BOB Robert Clifton B 1.30.1973 Mobile, AL BR/TR 6-2/190# d7.19																								
1998	Mon N	41	115	16	35	8	1	3	18	11-0	3	26	.304	.377	.470	124	4	3-0	.995	-2	96	114	C-35	0.5
HENLINE, BUTCH Walter John B 12.20.1894 Ft.Wayne, IN D 10.9.1957 Sarasota, FL BR/TR 5-10/175# d4.13 U4																								
1921	NY N	1	1	0	0	0	0	0	0	0	0	1	.000	.000	.000	-99	0	0-0	—	0			H	0.0
	Phi N	33	111	8	34	2	0	0	8	2	0	6	.306	.319	.324	65	-5	1-0	.987	3	*81*	*142*	C-32	0.0
	Year	34	112	8	34	2	0	0	8	2	0	7	.304	.316	.321	64	-6	1-0	.987	3	*81*	*142*	C-32	0.0
1922	Phi N	125	430	57	136	20	4	14	64	36	8	33	.316	.380	.479	110	6	2-2	**.983**	-3	*82*	*99*	*C-119	1.1
1923	Phi N	111	330	45	107	14	3	7	46	37	9	33	.324	.407	.448	112	8	7-5	.978	-16	*76*	*95*	C-96/O(LF)	-0.2
1924	Phi N	115	289	41	82	18	4	5	35	27	8	15	.284	.361	.426	98	0	1-2	.973	-2	*90*	*106*	C-83/O-2(1-1-0)	0.3
1925	Phi N	93	263	43	80	12	5	8	48	24	8	16	.304	.380	.479	108	3	3-1	.956	-3	*103*	*96*	C-68/O(LF)	0.5
1926	Phi N	99	283	32	80	14	1	2	30	21	3	18	.283	.339	.360	84	-6	1	.970	-7	*81*	*87*	C-77/1-4,O-2(LF)	-0.9
1927	Bro N	67	177	12	47	10	3	1	18	17	2	10	.266	.337	.373	90	-2	1	.947	1	*78*	*146*	C-60	0.2
1928	Bro N	55	132	12	28	3	1	2	8	17	0	8	.212	.302	.295	58	-8	2	.976	-1	*76*	*97*	C-45	-0.7
1929	Bro N	27	62	5	15	2	0	1	7	9	0	9	.242	.338	.323	66	-3	0	.967	-1	*60*	*143*	C-21	-0.3
1930	Chi A	3	8	1	1	0	0	0	2	0	0	3	.125	.125	.125	-38	-2	0-0	1.000	0	*121*	*113*	/C-3	-0.1
1931	Chi A	11	15	2	1	1	0	0	2	2	0	4	.067	.176	.133	-19	-3	0-0	.889	-1	*80*	*81*	/C-4	-0.3
Total	11	740	2101	258	611	96	21	40	268	192	38	156	.291	.361	.414	96	-12	18-10	.971	-30	*83*	*106*	C-608/O-6(5-1-0),1-4	-0.4
HENNESSEY, LES Lester Baker B 12.12.1893 Lynn, MA D 11.20.1976 New York, NY BR/TR 6/190# d6.4																								
1913	Det A	14	22	2	3	0	0	0	0	3	0	6	.136	.240	.136	11	-2	2	.880	-2	98	0	2-10	-0.4
HENRICH, FRITZ Frank Wilde B 5.8.1899 Cincinnati, OH D 5.1.1959 Philadelphia, PA BL/TL 5-10/160# d4.19																								
1924	Phi N	36	90	4	19	4	0	0	4	2	0	12	.211	.228	.256	26	-9	0-0	.978	-1	92	92	O-32(12-14-10)	-1.1

Year	Tm Lg	G	AB	R	H	2B	3B	HR	RBI	BB-IB	HP	SO	AVG	OBP	SLG	AOPS	ABR	SB-CS	FA	FR	Rng	Thr	G at Pos	BFW
HENRICH, BOBBY Robert Edward B 12.24.1938 Lawrence, KS BR/TR 6-1/185# d5.3																								
1957	Cin N	29	10	8	2	0	0	0	1	1-0	0	4	.200	.250	.200	28	-1	0-0	.875	1	188	0	/S-7,O-6(4-2-0),3-2,2	0.0
1958	Cin N	5	3	2	0	0	0	0	0	0-0	0	2	.000	.000	.000	-95	-1	0-0	1.000	0	114	0	/S-2	-0.1
1959	Cin N	14	3	3	0	0	0	0	0	0-0	0	1	.000	.000	.000	-97	-1	0-0	1.000	-0	0	0	/S-5,3	-0.1
Total	3	48	16	13	2	0	0	0	1	1-0	0	7	.125	.167	.125	-17	-3	0-0	.929	1	138	0	/S-14,O-6(4-2-0),3-3,2	-0.2
HENRICH, TOMMY Thomas David "The Clutch" or "Old Reliable" B 2.20.1910 Massillon, OH BL/TL 6/180# d5.11 Mil 1942-45 C4																								
1937	NY A	67	206	39	66	14	5	8	42	35	0	17	.320	.419	.553	142	14	4-0	.970	-1	87	137	O-59(30-0-29)	1.0
1938	†NY A	131	471	109	127	24	7	22	91	92	2	32	.270	.391	.490	120	16	6-2	.984	-1	95	120	*O-130(RF)	0.7
1939	NY A	99	347	64	96	18	4	9	57	51	1	23	.277	.371	.429	106	4	7-0	.991	1	102	99	O-88(1-38-50)/1	0.2
1940	NY A	90	293	57	90	28	5	10	53	48	2	30	.307	.408	.539	149	23	1-2	.969	1	92	176	O-76(1-24-52)/1-2	1.9
1941	†NY A	144	538	106	149	27	5	31	85	81	5	40	.277	.377	.519	137	28	3-1	.980	-3	95	99	*O-139(0-19-121)	1.7
1942	NY A★	127	483	77	129	30	5	13	67	58	5	42	.267	.352	.431	122	14	4-4	.987	1	97	119	*O-119(RF)/1-7	0.6
1946	NY A	150	565	92	142	25	4	19	83	87	**7**	63	.251	.358	.411	113	12	5-2	.992	-0	103	100	*O-111(RF),1-41	0.7
1947	†NY A★	142	550	109	158	35	**13**	16	98	71	3	54	.287	.372	.485	139	28	3-2	.983	3	105	138	*O-132(0-8-125)/1-6	2.7
1948	NY A★	146	588	**138**	181	42	**14**	25	100	76	4	42	.308	.391	.554	151	41	2-3	.978	-1	102	108	*O-102(6-3-96),1-46	3.2
1949	†NY A☆	115	411	90	118	20	3	24	85	86	5	34	.287	.416	.526	148	31	2-2	.958	-5	94	89	O-61(RF),1-52	2.1
1950	NY A★	73	151	20	41	6	8	6	34	27	0	6	.272	.382	.536	137	8	0-1	.987	-4	38	79	1-34	0.2
Total	11	1284	4603	901	1297	269	73	183	795	712	34	383	.282	.382	.491	132	219	37-19	.981	-9	98	117	*O-1017(38-92-894),1-189	15.0
HENRIKSEN, OLAF Olaf "Swede" B 4.26.1888 Kirkerup, Denmark D 10.17.1962 Norwood, MA BL/TL 5-7.5/158# d8.11																								
1911	Bos A	27	93	17	34	2	1	0	8	14	0		.366	.449	.409	141	6	4	.953	0	113	80	O-25(5-0-20)	0.5
1912	†Bos A	44	56	20	18	3	1	0	8	14	0		.321	.457	.411	142	4	0	.909	-1	85	0	O-11(0-1-10)	0.2
1913	Bos A	31	40	8	15	1	0	0	2	7	0	5	.375	.468	.400	151	3	3	1.000	-0	102	0	/O-7(6-1-0)	0.3
1914	Bos A	63	95	16	25	2	1	1	5	22	1	12	.263	.407	.337	124	4	5-4	.947	-1	100	40	O-29(8-11-10)	0.2
1915	†Bos A	73	92	9	18	2	2	0	13	18	1	7	.196	.333	.261	80	-1	1-5	.967	1	101	105	O-25(9-4-12)	-0.3
1916	†Bos A	68	99	13	20	2	2	0	11	19	0	15	.202	.331	.263	78	-2	2	1.000	0	106	74	O-31(14-7-9)	-0.3
1917	Bos A	15	12	1	1	0	0	0	1	3	0	4	.083	.267	.083	7	-1	0	—	0			H	-0.1
Total	7	321	487	84	131	12	7	1	48	97	2	43	.269	.392	.329	112	13	15-9	.966	-2	104	64	O-128(42-24-61)	0.5
HENRY, SNAKE Frederick Marshall B 7.19.1895 Waynesville, NC D 10.12.1987 Wendell, NC BL/TL 6/170# d9.15																								
1922	Bos N	18	66	5	13	4	1	0	5	2	0	8	.197	.221	.288	32	-7	2-2	.995	1	130	52	1-18	-0.7
1923	Bos N	11	9	1	1	0	0	0	2	1	0	1	.111	.200	.111	-17	-2	0-0	—	0			H	-0.1
Total	2	29	75	6	14	4	1	0	7	3	0	9	.187	.218	.267	26	-9	2-2	.995	1	130	52	/1-18	-0.8
HENRY, GEORGE George Washington B 8.10.1863 Philadelphia, PA D 12.30.1934 Lynn, MA BR/TR 5-9/180# d4.27																								
1893	Cin N	21	83	11	23	3	0	0	13	11	2	12	.277	.375	.313	82	-2	2	.965	3	151	119	O-21(10-0-11)	0.0
HENRY, JOHN John Michael B 9.2.1863 Springfield, MA D 6.11.1939 Hartford, CT TL d8.13 ▲																								
1884	Cle N	9	26	2	4	0	0	0	0	0		12	.154	.154	.154	-3	-3		1.000	1	128	0	/P-5,O-4(RF)	0.0
1885	Bal AA	10	34	4	9	3	0	0	3	1	0		.265	.286	.353	102	0		.931	2	153	320	/P-9,O(LF)	0.1
1886	Was N	4	14	3	5	0	0	0	0	0		3	.357	.357	.357	127	1	0	.833	-0	52	0	/P-4	0.0
1890	NY N	37	144	19	35	6	0	0	16	7	1	12	.243	.283	.285	65	-7	12	.870	-3	61	71	O-37(34-1-3)	-0.9
Total	4	60	218	28	53	9	0	0	19	8	1	27	.243	.273	.284	66	-9	12	.867	-0	69	66	/O-42(35-1-7),P-18	-0.8
HENRY, JOHN John Park "Bull" B 12.26.1889 Amherst, MA D 11.24.1941 Fort Huachuca, AZ BR/TR 6/180# d7.8																								
1910	Was A	28	87	2	13	1	1	0	5	2	0		.149	.169	.184	11	-9	2	.989	3	*101*	*131*	C-18,1-10	-0.6
1911	Was A	85	261	24	53	5	0	0	21	25	0		.203	.273	.222	39	-21	8	.969	9	*106*	*118*	C-51,1-30	-0.9
1912	Was A	66	191	23	37	4	1	0	9	31	1		.194	.309	.225	53	-10	10	.977	13	*132*	*111*	C-65	0.8
1913	Was A	96	273	26	61	8	4	1	26	30	4	43	.223	.309	.293	75	-8	5	**.982**	7	*114*	*103*	C-96	0.6
1914	Was A	92	261	22	44	7	4	0	20	37	1	47	.169	.274	.226	49	-16	7-3	.980	5	*105*	*97*	C-92	-0.3
1915	Was A	95	277	20	61	9	2	1	22	36	6	28	.220	.323	.278	78	-6	10-2	.972	8	*114*	*92*	C-94	1.1
1916	Was A	117	305	28	76	12	3	0	46	49	6	40	.249	.364	.308	103	4	12	.981	-0	99	92	*C-116	1.4
1917	Was A	65	163	10	31	6	0	0	18	24	2	16	.190	.302	.227	62	-6	1	.988	1	*87*	*90*	C-59	-0.1
1918	Bos N	43	102	6	21	2	0	0	4	10	1	15	.206	.283	.225	58	-5	0	.964	-2	*96*	*102*	C-38	-0.4
Total	9	687	1920	161	397	54	15	2	171	244	21	189	.207	.303	.254	65	-77	55-5	.978	43	*107*	*100*	C-629/1-40	1.6
HENRY, RON Ronald Baxter B 8.7.1936 Chester, PA BR/TR 6-1/180# d4.15																								
1961	Min A	20	28	1	4	0	0	0	3	2-0	0	7	.143	.194	.143	-6	-4	0-0	1.000	-0	*135*	*146*	/C-5,1	-0.4
1964	Min A	22	41	4	5	1	1	2	5	2-0	0	17	.122	.163	.341	36	-4	0-0	.984	-0	*94*	*189*	C-13	-0.4
Total	2	42	69	5	9	1	1	2	8	4-0	0	24	.130	.176	.261	18	-8	0-0	.988	-0	*107*	*176*	/C-18,1	-0.8
HENSON, DREW Drew Daniel B 2.13.1980 San Diego, CA BR/TR 6-5/222# d9.5																								
2002	NY A	3	1	1	0	0	0	0	0	0-0	0	1	.000	.000	.000	-99	0	0-0	—	0			/D-2	0.0
2003	NY A	5	8	2	1	0	0	0	0	0-0	0	2	.125	.125	.125	-34	-2	0-0	1.000	0	80	0	/3-3	-0.1
Total	2	8	9	3	1	0	0	0	0	0-0	0	3	.111	.111	.111	-42	-2	0-0	1.000	0	80	0	/3-3,D-2	-0.1
HERMAN, BABE Floyd Caves B 6.26.1903 Buffalo, NY D 11.27.1987 Glendale, CA BL/TL 6-4/190# d4.14 C1																								
1926	Bro N	137	496	64	158	35	11	11	81	44	1	53	.319	.375	.500	136	24	8	.986	1	107	69	*1-101,O-35(6-0-29)	1.7
1927	Bro N	130	412	65	112	26	9	14	73	39	1	41	.272	.336	.481	116	8	4	.980	1	107	81	*1-105/O(LF)	0.2
1928	Bro N	134	486	64	165	37	6	12	91	38	2	36	.340	.390	.514	136	26	1	.937	-8	86	97	*O-127(RF)	0.8
1929	Bro N	146	569	105	217	42	13	21	113	55	0	45	.381	.436	.612	160	53	21	.941	-15	83	70	*O-141(RF)/1-2	2.4
1930	Bro N	153	614	143	241	48	11	35	130	66	4	56	.393	.455	.678	171	72	18	.978	-21	78	52	*O-153(RF)	3.4
1931	Bro N	151	610	93	191	43	16	18	97	50	0	65	.313	.365	.525	137	30	17	.960	-1	90	132	*O-150(RF)	1.9
1932	Cin N	148	577	87	188	38	**19**	16	87	60	0	45	.326	.389	.541	152	42	7	.969	13	**117**	113	*O-146(RF)	4.5
1933	Chi N	137	508	77	147	36	12	16	93	50	0	57	.289	.353	.502	142	27	6	.957	-6	92	96	*O-131(RF)	1.4
1934	Chi N	125	467	65	142	34	5	14	84	35	0	71	.304	.353	.488	125	16	1	.971	-11	84	68	*O-113(RF)/1-7	-0.2
1935	Pit N	26	81	8	19	8	1	0	7	3	1	10	.235	.271	.358	65	-4	0	.958	-2	79	110	O-15(LF)/1-3	-0.7
	Cin N	92	349	44	117	23	5	10	58	35	0	25	.335	.396	.516	147	24	5	.976	-0	98	95	O-76(LF),1-14	1.7
	Year	118	430	52	136	31	6	10	65	38	1	35	.316	.373	.486	131	19	5	.974	-3	95	97	O-91(LF),1-17	1.0
1936	Cin N	119	380	59	106	25	2	13	71	39	1	36	.279	.348	.458	123	12	4	.967	-3	99	47	O-92(91-0-1)/1-4	0.4
1937	Det A	17	20	2	6	3	0	0	3	1	1	6	.300	.364	.450	102	0	2-0	1.000	-0	93	0	/O-2(LF)	0.0
1945	Bro N	37	34	6	9	1	0	1	9	5	0	7	.265	.359	.382	107	0	0	—	-0	0	0	/O-3(RF)	0.0
Total	13	1552	5603	882	1818	399	110	181	997	520	11	553	.324	.383	.532	141	330	94-0	.961	-52	91	88	*O-1185(191-0-994),1-236	17.5
HERMAN, BILLY William Jennings Bryan B 7.7.1909 New Albany, IN D 9.5.1992 W.Palm Beach, FL BR/TR 5-11/180# d8.29 Mil 1944-45 M4 C16 HF1975																								
1931	Chi N	25	98	14	32	7	0	0	16	13	0	6	.327	.405	.398	115	3	2	.939	-2	90	93	2-25	0.3
1932	†Chi N	**154**	656	102	206	42	7	1	51	40	5	33	.314	.358	.404	105	6	14	.961	12	105	112	*2-154	2.8
1933	Chi N	153	619	82	173	35	2	0	44	45	4	34	.279	.332	.342	93	-4	5	.956	29	103	**129**	*2-153	3.7
1934	Chi N★	113	456	79	138	21	6	3	42	34	3	31	.303	.355	.395	102	2	6	.975	9	102	102	*2-111	1.7
1935	†Chi N★	**154**	666	113	**227**	**57**	6	7	83	42	3	29	.341	.383	.476	128	28	6	**.964**	16	103	**135**	*2-154	5.2
1936	Chi N★	153	632	101	211	57	7	5	93	59	1	30	.334	.392	.470	128	27	5	**.975**	17	97	128	*2-153	5.2
1937	Chi N★	138	564	106	189	35	11	8	65	56	1	22	.335	.396	.479	131	26	2	.954	15	103	115	*2-137	4.9
1938	†Chi N★	152	624	86	173	34	7	1	56	59	2	31	.277	.342	.359	90	-7	3	**.981**	22	103	120	*2-151	2.4
1939	Chi N★	**156**	623	111	191	34	**18**	7	70	66	5	31	.307	.378	.453	120	18	9	.967	-4	99	92	*2-156	2.4
1940	Chi N★	135	558	77	163	24	4	5	57	47	0	30	.292	.347	.376	101	1	1	.974	**20**	**107**	111	*2-135	3.0
1941	Chi N	11	36	4	7	0	1	0	0	9	0	5	.194	.356	.250	75	-1	0	.898	-3	67	81	2-11	-0.4
	†Bro N★	133	536	77	156	30	4	3	41	58	1	38	.291	.361	.379	104	5	1	.970	-26	89	92	*2-133	-1.4
	Year	144	572	81	163	30	5	3	41	67	1	43	.285	.361	.371	103	4	1	.964	-29	87	91	*2-144	-1.8
1942	Bro N★	**155**	571	76	146	34	2	2	65	72	0	52	.256	.339	.333	95	-1	6	.973	-10	90	117	*2-153/1-3	-0.2
1943	Bro N★	**153**	585	76	193	41	2	2	100	66	0	26	.330	.398	.417	135	30	4	.971	-17	88	88	*2-117,3-37	2.0
1946	Bro N	47	184	24	53	8	4	0	28	26	0	10	.288	.376	.375	112	4	2	.945	-2	98	180	3-29,2-16	0.3
	Bos N	75	252	32	77	23	1	3	22	43	1	13	.306	.409	.440	139	16	1	.956	-12	85	99	2-44,1-22/3-5	0.5
	Year	122	436	56	130	31	5	3	50	69	1	23	.298	.395	.413	128	19	3	.968	-14	85	88	2-60,3-34,1-22	0.8
1947	Pit N	15	47	3	10	4	0	0	6	2	0	7	.213	.245	.298	42	-4	0	1.000	-5	60	38	2-10/1-2,M	-0.8
Total	15	1922	7707	1163	2345	486	82	47	839	737	26	428	.304	.367	.407	112	149	67	.967	59	98	111	*2-1813/3-71,1-27	31.6

Year	Tm Lg	G	AB	R	H	2B	3B	HR	RBI	BB-IB	HP	SO	AVG	OBP	SLG	AOPS	ABR	SB-CS	FA	FR	Rng	Thr	G at Pos	BFW
HERMANN, AL Albert Bartel B 3.28.1899 Milltown, NJ D 8.20.1980 Lewes, DE BR/TR 6/180# d7.13																								
1923	Bos N	31	93	2	22	4	0	0	11	0	0	7	.237	.237	.280	37	-9	3-2	.957	-4	100	49	2-15/3-5,1-4	-1.2
1924	Bos N	1	1	0	0	0	0	0	0	0	0	1	.000	.000	.000	-99	0	0-0	—	0			H	0.0
Total	2	32	94	2	22	4	0	0	11	0	0	8	.234	.234	.277	36	-9	3-2	.957	-4	100	49	/2-15,3-5,1-4	-1.2
HERMANSEN, CHAD Chad Bruce B 9.10.1977 Salt Lake City, UT BR/TR 6-2/185# d9.7																								
1999	Pit N	19	60	5	14	3	0	1	1	7-1	1	19	.233	.324	.333	67	-3	2-2	1.000	-3	76	0	O-18(3-9-6)	-0.6
2000	Pit N	33	108	12	20	4	1	2	8	6-0	0	37	.185	.226	.296	31	-12	0-0	.979	-6	63	112	O-31(0-27-4)	-1.7
2001	Pit N	22	55	5	9	1	0	2	5	1-0	0	18	.164	.179	.291	18	-7	0-1	1.000	0	96	112	O-20(0-6-15)	-0.8
2002	Pit N	65	194	22	40	11	1	7	15	17-0	1	68	.206	.272	.381	72	-9	7-5	.982	-0	94	187	O-60(2-59-2)	-0.9
	Chi N	35	43	3	9	3	0	1	3	5-0	0	14	.209	.292	.349	72	-2	0-0	.895	-1	84	0	O-21(4-9-9)	-0.4
	Year	100	237	25	49	14	1	8	18	22-0	1	82	.207	.276	.376	73	-11	7-5	.970	-1	92	154	O-81(6-68-11)	-1.3
2003	LA N	11	25	2	4	1	0	0	2	2-0	0	9	.160	.222	.200	12	-3	0-0	1.000	-0	98	0	/O-6(LF)	-0.4
Total	5	185	485	49	96	23	2	13	34	38-1	2	165	.198	.258	.334	53	-36	9-8	.980	-10	84	111	O-156(15-110-36)	-4.8
HERMANSKI, GENE Eugene Victor B 5.11.1920 Pittsfield, MA BL/TR 5-11.5/185# d8.15 Mil 1943-45																								
1943	Bro N	18	60	6	18	2	1	0	12	11	1	7	.300	.417	.367	127	3	1	.976	2	102	238	O-17(11-0-6)	0.4
1946	Bro N	64	110	15	22	2	2	0	8	17	1	10	.200	.313	.255	61	-5	2	.938	-3	94	0	O-34(12-4-17)	-1.0
1947	†Bro N	79	189	36	52	7	1	7	39	28	3	7	.275	.377	.434	111	4	5	.982	2	100	138	O-66(64-1-3)	0.2
1948	Bro N	133	400	63	116	22	7	15	60	64	2	46	.290	.391	.493	133	20	15	.971	6	105	161	*O-119(6-0-113)	2.2
1949	†Bro N	87	224	48	67	12	3	8	42	47	5	21	.299	.431	.487	140	15	12	.980	2	102	128	O-77(64-0-17)	1.3
1950	Bro N	94	289	36	86	17	3	7	34	36	3	26	.298	.381	.450	115	7	2	.989	5	116	97	O-78(76-0-3)	0.7
1951	Bro N	31	80	8	20	4	0	1	5	10	0	12	.250	.333	.338	79	-2	0-2	.977	1	100	117	O-19(18-0-1)	-0.4
	Chi N	75	231	28	65	12	1	3	20	35	4	30	.281	.385	.381	105	4	3-0	.966	2	103	147	O-63(3-0-60)	0.4
	Year	106	311	36	85	16	1	4	25	45	4	42	.273	.372	.370	98	2	3-2	.969	3	102	140	O-82(21-0-61)	0.0
1952	Chi N	99	275	28	70	6	0	4	34	29	2	32	.255	.330	.320	80	-7	2-0	.981	4	112	110	O-76(3-0-73)	-0.5
1953	Chi N	18	40	1	6	1	0	0	1	4	0	7	.150	.227	.175	7	-6	1-0	1.000	-0	106	0	O-13(3-0-10)	-0.6
	Pit N	41	62	7	11	0	0	1	4	8	1	14	.177	.282	.226	35	-6	0-0	1.000	0	121	0	O-13(5-0-8)	-0.6
	Year	59	102	8	17	1	0	1	5	12	1	21	.167	.261	.206	24	-12	1-0	1.000	0	114	0	O-26(8-0-18)	-1.2
Total	9	739	1960	276	533	85	18	46	259	289	22	212	.272	.372	.404	107	27	43-2	.977	21	106	124	O-575(265-5-311)	2.1
HERMOSO, REMY Angel Remigio B 10.1.1946 Carabobo, Venezuela BR/TR 5-8/155# d9.14																								
1967	Atl N	11	26	3	8	0	0	0	0	2-0	0	4	.308	.357	.308	93	0	1-0	.952	-1	98	89	/S-9,2-2	0.0
1969	Mon N	28	74	6	12	0	0	0	3	5-0	1	10	.162	.225	.162	10	-9	3-1	.968	1	116	141	2-18/S-6	-0.7
1970	Mon N	4	1	1	0	0	0	0	0	0-0	0	0	.000	.000	.000	-99	0	0-0	1.000	0	301	0	/23	0.0
1974	Cle A	48	122	15	27	3	1	0	5	7-0	0	7	.221	.262	.262	52	-8	2-2	.967	3	113	102	2-45	-0.3
Total	4	91	223	25	47	3	1	0	8	14-0	1	21	.211	.259	.233	42	-17	6-3	.968	4	114	114	/2-66,S-15,3	-1.0
HERNANDEZ, ALEX Alexander (Vargas) B 5.28.1977 San Juan, P.R. BL/TL 6-4/190# d9.1																								
2000	Pit N	20	60	4	12	3	0	1	5	0-0	0	13	.200	.200	.300	24	-7	1-1	.992	-1	38	130	1-12/O-5(3-0-2)	-0.9
2001	Pit N	7	11	0	1	0	0	0	0	0-0	0	2	.091	.091	.091	-52	-3	0-0	1.000	0	62	633	/O-4(RF),1-2	-0.2
Total	2	27	71	4	13	3	0	1	5	0-0	0	15	.183	.183	.268	12	-10	1-1	.992	-1	37	136	/1-14,O-9(3-0-6)	-1.1
HERNANDEZ, CARLOS Carlos Alberto (Almeida) B 5.24.1967 San Felix, Venezuela BR/TR 5-11/218# d4.20																								
1990	LA N	10	20	2	4	1	0	0	1	0-0	0	2	.200	.200	.250	24	-2	0-0	1.000	0	537	185	C-10	-0.2
1991	LA N	15	14	1	3	1	0	0	1	0-0	1	5	.214	.250	.286	57	-1	1-0	.966	-0	121	113	C-13/3	0.0
1992	LA N	69	173	11	45	4	0	3	17	11-1	4	21	.260	.316	.335	87	-3	0-1	.979	-0	87	84	C-63	-0.1
1993	LA N	50	99	6	25	5	0	2	7	2-0	0	11	.253	.267	.364	71	-5	0-0	.966	1	92	79	C-43	-0.2
1994	LA N	32	64	6	14	2	0	2	6	1-0	0	14	.219	.231	.344	51	-5	0-0	1.000	1	80	136	C-27	-0.3
1995	LA N	45	94	3	14	1	0	2	8	7-0	1	25	.149	.216	.223	18	-12	0-0	.983	7	177	133	C-41	-0.3
1996	LA N	13	14	1	4	0	0	0	0	2-0	0	2	.286	.375	.286	84	0	0-0	1.000	1	282	88	/C-9	0.1
1997	SD N	50	134	15	42	7	1	3	14	3-0	0	27	.313	.328	.448	109	1	0-2	.989	1	83	192	C-44/1-4	0.3
1998	†SD N	129	390	34	102	15	0	9	52	16-2	9	54	.262	.305	.369	83	-11	2-2	.992	6	112	80	*C-122/1	0.2
2000	SD N	58	191	16	48	11	0	2	25	16-1	3	26	.251	.316	.340	72	-8	1-3	.987	-0	80	126	C-54/1	-0.6
	†StL N	17	51	7	14	4	0	1	10	5-0	1	9	.275	.345	.412	91	-1	1-0	.963	-2	46	174	C-16	-0.2
	Year	75	242	23	62	15	0	3	35	21-1	4	35	.256	.322	.355	76	-9	2-3	.982	-3	73	137	C-70/1	-0.8
Total	10	488	1244	102	315	51	1	24	141	63-4	19	196	.253	.298	.354	76	-47	5-8	.985	15	109	112	C-442/1-6,3	-1.3
HERNANDEZ, CARLOS Carlos Eduardo B 12.12.1975 Caracas, Venezuela BR/TR 5-9/175# d5.26																								
1999	Hou N	16	14	4	2	0	0	0	1	0-0	0	0	.143	.143	.143	-28	-3	3-1	1.000	2	191	238	/2-7,S-2	0.0
2000	Sea A	2	1	0	0	0	0	0	0	0-0	0	1	.000	.000	.000	-99	0	0-1	1.000	-0	0	0	/3-2	-0.1
Total	2	18	15	4	2	0	0	0	1	0-0	0	1	.133	.133	.133	-33	-3	3-2	1.000	2	191	238	/2-7,3-2,S-2	-0.1
HERNANDEZ, CESAR Cesar Dario (Perez) B 9.28.1966 Yamasa, D.R. BR/TR 6/160# d7.19																								
1992	Cin N	34	51	6	14	4	0	0	4	0-0	0	10	.275	.275	.353	74	-2	3-1	.952	1	95	442	O-18(12-6-1)	-0.1
1993	Cin N	27	24	3	2	0	0	0	1	1-0	0	8	.083	.120	.083	-44	-5	1-2	.970	4	155	394	O-23(17-7-0)	-0.2
Total	2	61	75	9	16	4	0	0	5	1-0	0	18	.213	.224	.267	35	-7	4-3	.963	5	124	419	/O-41(29-13-1)	-0.3
HERNANDEZ, ENZO Enzo Octavio B 2.12.1949 Valle De Guanape, Venezuela BR/TR 5-8/155# d4.17																								
1971	SD N	143	549	58	122	9	3	0	12	54-1	3	34	.222	.295	.250	60	-29	21-5	.955	-5	95	88	*S-143	-1.5
1972	SD N	114	329	33	64	11	2	1	15	22-6	0	25	.195	.243	.249	44	-25	24-3	.963	-7	97	88	*S-107/O-3(2-0-1)	-1.7
1973	SD N	70	247	26	55	2	1	0	9	17-0	0	14	.223	.273	.239	47	-19	15-4	.977	1	97	106	S-67	-0.9
1974	SD N	147	512	55	119	19	2	0	34	38-2	0	36	.232	.285	.277	60	-28	37-10	.966	-2	101	67	*S-145	-0.8
1975	SD N	116	344	37	75	12	2	0	19	26-0	2	25	.218	.275	.265	54	-22	20-4	.965	1	102	116	*S-111	-0.7
1976	SD N	113	340	31	87	13	3	1	24	32-4	0	16	.256	.319	.321	89	-5	12-7	.964	7	111	111	*S-101	1.4
1977	SD N	7	3	1	0	0	0	0	0	0-0	0	0	.000	.000	.000	-99	-1	0-0	1.000	0	101	0	/S-7	-0.1
1978	LA N	4	3	0	0	0	0	0	0	0-0	0	1	.000	.000	.000	-99	-1	0-0	—	-1	0	0	/S-2	-0.2
Total	8	714	2327	241	522	66	13	2	113	189-13	5	151	.224	.283	.266	59	-130	129-33	.964	-5	100	92	S-683/O-3(2-0-1)	-4.5
HERNANDEZ, JACKIE Jacinto (Zulueta) B 9.11.1940 Central Tinguaro, Cuba BR/TR 6/175# d9.14																								
1965	Cal A	6	6	2	2	1	0	0	1	0-0	0	1	.333	.333	.500	137	0	1-0	1.000	-1	152	0	/S-2,3	0.0
1966	Cal A	58	23	19	1	0	0	0	2	1-0	0	4	.043	.080	.043	-64	-5	1-1	.857	6	155	0	3-11/2-8,S-8,O-3(0-1-2)	0.2
1967	Min A	29	28	1	4	0	0	0	3	0-0	0	6	.143	.143	.143	-14	-4	0-0	.974	0	85	50	S-15,3-13	-0.3
1968	Min A	83	199	13	35	3	0	2	17	9-2	2	52	.176	.218	.221	32	-17	5-2	.927	4	100	127	S-79/1	-0.8
1969	KC A	145	504	54	112	14	2	4	40	38-1	2	111	.222	.278	.282	57	-30	17-7	.954	-13	89	76	*S-144	-2.7
1970	KC A	83	238	14	55	4	1	2	10	15-0	2	50	.231	.281	.282	56	-15	1-3	.951	-8	90	89	S-77	-1.6
1971	†Pit N	88	233	30	48	7	3	3	26	17-2	0	45	.206	.257	.300	59	-13	0-2	.950	7	112	101	S-75/3-9	0.1
1972	Pit N	72	176	12	33	7	1	1	14	9-1	0	43	.188	.227	.256	38	-15	0-0	.929	-1	102	106	S-68/3-4	-1.0
1973	Pit N	54	73	8	18	1	2	0	8	4-2	0	12	.247	.286	.315	68	-4	0-0	.940	-0	99	114	S-49	-0.1
Total	9	618	1480	153	308	37	9	12	121	93-8	6	324	.208	.256	.270	49	-103	25-15	.945	-6	97	95	S-517/3-38,2-8,O-3(0-1-2),1	-6.2
HERNANDEZ, JOSE Jose Antonio (Figueroa) B 7.14.1969 Rio Piedras, P.R. BR/TR 6-1/180# d8.9 OF Total (48-LF 48-CF 5-RF)																								
1991	Tex A	45	98	8	18	2	1	0	4	3-0	0	31	.184	.208	.224	20	-11	0-1	.975	3	110	75	S-44/3	-0.6
1992	Cle A	3	4	0	0	0	0	0	0	0-0	0	2	.000	.000	.000	-99	-1	0-0	.857	0	108	0	/S-3	-0.1
1994	Chi N	56	132	18	32	2	3	1	9	8-0	1	29	.242	.291	.326	61	-8	2-2	.938	3	87	0	3-28,S-21/2-8,O(CF)	-0.4
1995	Chi N	93	245	37	60	11	4	13	40	13-3	0	69	.245	.281	.482	99	-3	1-0	.961	3	99	115	S-43,2-29,3-20	0.4
1996	Chi N	131	331	52	80	14	1	10	41	24-4	1	97	.242	.293	.381	75	-13	4-0	.948	-6	95	109	S-87,3-43/2O(CF)	-1.2
1997	Chi N	121	183	33	50	8	5	7	26	14-2	0	42	.273	.323	.486	106	1	2-5	.922	-4	72	83	3-47,S-21,2-20/O-6(LF),1D	-0.3
1998	†Chi N	149	488	76	124	23	7	23	75	40-3	1	140	.254	.311	.471	99	-3	4-6	.958	7	106	38	3-72,O-54(31-31-2),S-45/1-3,2-2	0.5
1999	Chi N	99	342	57	93	12	2	15	43	40-3	5	101	.272	.357	.450	104	2	7-2	.971	6	110	103	S-92,O-20(6-14-2)/1	1.3
	†Atl N	48	166	22	42	8	0	4	19	12-3	0	44	.253	.302	.373	70	-8	4-1	.964	-1	100	110	S-45/1O(LF)	-0.5
	Year	147	508	79	135	20	2	19	62	52-6	5	145	.266	.339	.425	93	-6	11-3	.969	5	107	105	*S-137,O-21(7-14-2)/1-2	0.8
2000	Mil N	124	446	51	109	22	1	11	59	41-3	6	125	.244	.315	.372	75	-18	3-7	.950	8	107	137	3-95,S-37/O-2(LF)	-0.8
2001	Mil N	152	542	67	135	26	2	25	78	39-8	2	185	.249	.300	.443	91	-9	5-4	.972	-1	104	93	*S-150/O-2(1-1-0)	0.1
2002	Mil N★	152	525	72	151	24	2	24	73	52-5	4	188	.288	.356	.478	122	14	3-5	.973	17	107	108	*S-149	4.1
2003	Col N	69	257	33	61	6	1	8	27	27-0	0	95	.237	.308	.362	65	-13	1-1	.983	-5	93	104	S-69/1	-1.3

Year	Tm Lg	G	AB	R	H	2B	3B	HR	RBI	BB-IB	HP	SO	AVG	OBP	SLG	AOPS	ABR	SB-CS	FA	FR	Rng	Thr	G at Pos	BFW
	Chi N	23	69	6	13	3	1	2	9	3-0	0	26	.188	.222	.348	46	-6	0-0	.968	2	97	209	3-17/S-5,O-2(1-0-1),2	-0.4
	Pit N	58	193	19	43	9	1	3	21	16-0	1	56	.223	.282	.326	58	-12	1-0	.955	13	138	146	3-58	0.1
	Year	150	519	58	117	18	3	13	57	46-0	1	177	.225	.287	.347	61	-31	2-1	.957	10	130	159	3-75,S-74/O-2(1-0-1),12	-1.6
Total	12	1323	4021	551	1011	170	31	146	524	332-34	21	1230	.251	.310	.418	87	-88	37-34	.969	45	104	105	S-811,3-381/O-89L,2-61,1-7,D	0.9
HERNANDEZ, KEITH Keith B 10.20.1953 San Francisco, CA BL/TL 6/195# d8.30																								
1974	StL N	14	34	3	10	1	2	0	2	7-0	0	8	.294	.415	.441	141	2	0-0	.973	-2	18	112	/1-9	-0.1
1975	StL N	64	188	20	47	8	2	3	20	17-2	0	26	.250	.309	.362	84	-4	0-1	.996	1	105	80	1-56	-0.8
1976	StL N	129	374	54	108	21	5	7	46	49-5	3	53	.289	.376	.428	126	14	4-2	.990	16	**164**	101	*1-110	2.4
1977	StL N	161	560	90	163	41	4	15	91	79-11	1	88	.291	.379	.459	126	23	7-7	.992	4	112	**127**	*1-158	1.7
1978	StL N	159	542	90	138	32	4	11	64	82-11	2	68	.255	.351	.389	109	9	13-5	.994	-1	96	106	*1-158	0.1
1979	StL N★	161	610	**116**	210	**48**	11	11	105	80-5	1	78	**.344**	.417	.513	152	48	11-6	.995	15	**137**	119	*1-160	5.4
1980	StL N★	159	595	**111**	191	39	8	16	99	86-4	4	73	.321	**.408**	.494	147	41	14-8	.995	6	117	**120**	*1-157	3.9
1981	StL N	**103**	376	65	115	27	4	8	48	61-6	2	45	.306	.401	.463	142	24	12-5	.997	6	126	**130**	1-98/O-3(LF)	2.6
1982	†StL N	160	579	79	173	33	6	7	94	100-**19**	2	67	.299	.397	.413	128	27	19-11	.994	5	117	121	*1-158/O-4(2-0-2)	2.4
1983	StL N	55	218	34	62	15	4	3	26	24-5	0	30	.284	.352	.431	117	5	1-1	.991	3	123	135	1-54	0.4
	NY N	95	320	43	98	8	3	9	37	64-9	2	42	.306	.424	.434	140	21	8-4	.993	10	139	115	1-90	2.6
	Year	150	538	77	160	23	7	12	63	88-14	2	72	.297	.396	.433	131	26	9-5	.992	12	133	123	*1-144	3.0
1984	NY N★	154	550	83	171	31	0	15	94	97-12	1	89	.311	.409	.449	145	39	2-3	.994	17	**133**	104	*1-153	4.7
1985	NY N	158	593	87	183	34	4	10	91	77-15	2	59	.309	.384	.430	132	29	3-3	**.997**	13	**124**	94	*1-157	3.2
1986	†NY N★	149	551	94	171	34	1	13	83	**94**-9	4	69	.310	.413	.446	141	37	2-1	**.996**	18	138	108	*1-149	4.7
1987	NY N★	154	587	87	170	28	2	18	89	81-8	4	104	.290	.377	.436	122	21	0-2	.993	16	**134**	96	*1-154	2.7
1988	†NY N	95	348	43	96	16	0	11	55	31-3	1	57	.276	.333	.417	121	9	2-1	.998	9	125	110	1-93	1.2
1989	NY N	75	215	18	50	8	0	4	19	27-3	2	39	.233	.324	.326	90	-2	0-3	.991	-1	88	62	1-58	-0.9
1990	Cle A	43	130	7	26	2	0	1	8	14-3	1	17	.200	.283	.238	47	-9	0-0	.994	-2	80	87	1-42	-1.4
Total	17	2088	7370	1124	2182	426	60	162	1071	1070-130	32	1012	.296	.384	.436	129	334	98-63	.994	133	123	109	*1-2014/O-7(5-0-2)	34.8
HERNANDEZ, LEO Leonardo Jesus B 11.6.1959 Santa Lucia, Venezuela BR/TR 5-11/170# d9.19																								
1982	Bal A	2	2	0	0	0	0	0	0	0-0	0	2	.000	.000	.000	-99	-1	0-0	—	0			/H	-0.1
1983	Bal A	64	203	21	50	6	1	6	26	12-1	0	19	.246	.287	.374	82	-6	1-0	.922	-8	89	26	3-64	-1.5
1985	Bal A	12	21	0	1	0	0	0	0	0-0	0	4	.048	.048	.048	-76	-5	0-0	1.000	-0	0	0	/1O(LF)D	-0.6
1986	NY A	7	22	2	5	2	0	1	4	1-0	0	8	.227	.261	.455	91	0	0-0	1.000	-1	95	0	/3-7,2	-0.1
Total	4	85	248	23	56	8	1	7	30	13-1	0	33	.226	.263	.351	69	-12	1-0	.927	-9	90	24	/3-71,D-8,2O(LF)1	-2.3
HERNANDEZ, MICHEL Michel B 8.12.1978 LaHabana, Cuba BR/TR 6/210# d9.6																								
2003	NY A	5	4	0	1	0	0	0	0	1-0	0	1	.250	.400	.250	78	0	0-0	1.000	-0	81	0	/C-5	0.0
HERNANDEZ, PEDRO Pedro Julio (born Pedro Julio Montas (Hernandez)) B 4.4.1959 LaRomana, D.R. BR/TR 6-1/160# d9.8																								
1979	Tor A	3	0	1	0	0	0	0	0	0-0	0	0	—	—	—	—	0	0-0	—	0			/R-2	0.0
1982	Tor A	8	9	1	0	0	0	0	0	0-0	0	3	.000	.000	.000	-92	-2	0-0	—	-1	0	0	/3-2,O(LF)D	-0.3
Total	2	11	9	2	0	0	0	0	0	0-0	0	3	.000	.000	.000	-92	-2	0-0	.000	-1	0	0	/D-3,3-2,O(LF)	-0.3
HERNANDEZ, TOBY Rafael Tobias (Alvarado) B 11.30.1958 Calabozo, Venezuela BR/TR 6-1/160# d6.22																								
1984	Tor A	3	2	1	1	0	0	0	0	0-0	0	0	.500	.500	.500	171	0	0-0	1.000	-0	0	0	/C-3	0.0
HERNANDEZ, RAMON Ramon Jose (Marin) B 5.20.1976 Caracas, Venezuela BR/TR 6/203# d6.29																								
1999	Oak A	40	136	13	38	7	0	3	21	18-0	1	11	.279	.363	.397	99	0	1-0	.980	5	79	89	C-40	0.7
2000	†Oak A	143	419	52	101	19	0	14	62	38-1	7	64	.241	.311	.387	78	-15	1-0	.984	2	108	84	*C-142	-0.5
2001	†Oak A	136	453	55	115	25	0	15	60	37-3	6	68	.254	.316	.408	89	-7	1-1	.989	15	98	111	*C-135/1-2	1.6
2002	†Oak A	136	403	51	94	20	0	7	42	43-1	5	64	.233	.313	.335	73	-15	0-0	.992	11	156	91	*C-135	0.5
2003	†Oak A★	140	483	70	132	24	1	21	78	33-2	12	79	.273	.331	.458	105	3	0-0	.991	11	104	109	*C-139	2.2
Total	5	595	1894	241	480	95	1	60	263	169-7	31	286	.253	.322	.400	88	-34	3-1	.988	44	114	98	C-591/1-2	4.5
HERNANDEZ, RUDY Rodolfo (Acosta) B 10.18.1951 Empalme, Mexico BR/TR 5-9/150# d9.6																								
1972	Chi A	8	21	0	4	0	0	0	1	0-0	0	3	.190	.190	.190	13	-2	0-0	1.000	-0	91	92	/S-6	-0.2
HERNANDEZ, CHICO Salvador Jose (Ramos) B 1.3.1916 Havana, Cuba D 1.3.1986 Havana, Cuba BR/TR 6/195# d4.16																								
1942	Chi N	47	118	6	27	5	0	0	7	11	0	13	.229	.295	.271	69	-5	0	.975	-2	*108*	*88*	C-43	-0.5
1943	Chi N	43	126	10	34	4	0	0	9	9	1	9	.270	.324	.302	82	-3	0	.981	-2	*132*	*72*	C-41	-0.3
Total	2	90	244	16	61	9	0	0	16	20	1	22	.250	.309	.287	76	-8	0	.978	-4	*120*	*80*	/C-84	-0.8
HERNDON, LARRY Larry Darnell B 11.3.1953 Sunflower, MS BR/TR 6-3/195# d9.4 C7																								
1974	StL N	12	1	3	1	0	0	0	0	0-0	0	0	1.000	1.000	1.000	465	0	0-0	1.000	0	112	0	/O(CF)	0.0
1976	SF N	115	337	42	97	11	3	2	23	23-0	2	45	.288	.337	.356	94	-3	12-10	.967	-1	99	144	*O-110(CF)	-0.7
1977	SF N	49	109	13	26	4	3	1	5	5-1	1	20	.239	.278	.358	69	-5	4-2	.957	2	121	106	O-44(CF)	-0.3
1978	SF N	151	471	52	122	15	9	1	32	35-2	1	71	.259	.311	.335	84	-12	13-8	.974	-2	107	40	*O-149(CF)	-1.5
1979	SF N	132	354	35	91	14	5	7	36	29-5	1	70	.257	.313	.384	96	-3	8-6	.963	-1	97	147	*O-122(40-84-12)	-0.7
1980	SF N	139	493	54	127	17	11	8	49	19-1	1	91	.258	.284	.385	88	-11	8-8	.959	-5	95	91	*O-122(53-53-28)	-2.2
1981	SF N	96	364	48	105	15	8	5	41	20-2	1	55	.288	.325	.415	111	4	15-6	.977	4	110	97	O-93(82-7-10)	0.4
1982	Det A	157	614	92	179	21	13	23	88	38-3	1	92	.292	.332	.480	120	14	12-9	.983	0	94	113	*O-155(LF)/D-3	0.6
1983	Det A	153	603	88	182	28	9	20	92	46-6	3	95	.302	.351	.478	130	23	9-3	.951	-5	95	57	*O-133(LF),D-19	1.3
1984	†Det A	125	407	52	114	18	5	7	43	32-1	2	63	.280	.333	.400	103	2	6-2	.986	-4	87	97	*O-117(LF)/D-4	-0.6
1985	Det A	137	442	45	108	12	7	12	37	33-1	1	79	.244	.298	.385	86	-10	2-1	.976	3	104	88	*O-136(LF)	-1.3
1986	Det A	106	283	33	70	13	1	8	37	27-2	1	40	.247	.310	.385	90	-4	2-1	.988	-2	101	41	O-83(LF),D-18	-0.9
1987	†Det A	89	225	32	73	13	2	9	47	23-0	0	35	.324	.378	.520	144	14	1-0	.989	2	102	142	O-57(32-0-26),D-23	1.3
1988	Det A	76	174	16	39	5	0	4	20	23-0	1	37	.224	.313	.322	83	-4	0-1	1.000	0	108	0	D-53,O-15(LF)	-0.6
Total	14	1537	4877	605	1334	186	76	107	550	353-24	16	793	.274	.322	.409	103	5	92-57	.972	-8	99	92	*O-1337(847-448-76),D-120	-5.2
HERNON, TOM Thomas H. B 11.4.1866 E.Bridgewater, MA D 2.4.1902 New Bedford, MA BR/TR 5-7.5/156# d9.13																								
1897	Chi N	4	16	2	1	0	0	0	2	0			.063	.063	.063	-64	-4	1	1.000	-0	0	0	/O-4(LF)	-0.4
HERR, JOE Joseph B 3.1867 , MO BR/TR 5-9.5/179# d4.16																								
1887	Cle AA	11	44	6	12	2	0	0	6	6	0		.273	.360	.318	93	0	2	.729	-3	76	50	3-11	-0.2
1888	†StL AA	43	172	21	46	7	1	3	43	11	3		.267	.323	.372	110	1	9	.872	-6	80	75	S-28,O-11(4-4-3)/3-4	-0.4
1890	StL AA	12	41	5	9	2	1	0	1	5	3		.220	.347	.317	84	-1	2	.793	-5	45	40	/2-7,O-4(CF),3	-0.5
Total	3	66	257	32	67	11	2	3	50	22	6		.261	.333	.354	102	0	13	.872	-14	80	75	/S-28,3-16,O-15(4-8-3),2-7	-1.1
HERR, TOM Thomas Mitchell B 4.4.1956 Lancaster, PA BB/TR 6/185# d8.13																								
1979	StL N	14	10	4	2	0	0	0	1	2-0	0	2	.200	.333	.200	49	-1	1-0	1.000	1	108	147	/2-6	0.1
1980	StL N	76	222	29	55	12	5	0	15	16-5	1	21	.248	.299	.347	78	-7	9-2	.984	3	102	131	2-58,S-14	0.1
1981	StL N	**103**	411	50	110	14	9	0	46	39-3	1	30	.268	.329	.345	90	-5	23-7	**.992**	3	**113**	**118**	*2-103	0.7
1982	†StL N	135	493	83	131	19	4	0	36	57-2	2	56	.266	.341	.320	86	-7	25-12	.987	9	**110**	**130**	*2-128	1.0
1983	StL N	89	313	43	101	14	4	2	31	43-2	1	27	.323	.403	.412	127	14	6-8	.986	-2	103	115	2-86	1.5
1984	StL N	145	558	67	154	23	2	4	49	49-2	2	56	.276	.335	.346	94	-3	13-7	.992	9	105	**117**	*2-144	1.4
1985	†StL N★	159	596	97	180	38	3	8	110	80-5	2	55	.302	.379	.416	126	24	31-3	.985	-25	93	121	*2-158	1.4
1986	StL N	152	559	48	141	30	4	2	61	73-10	5	75	.252	.342	.331	88	-7	22-8	.988	-15	95	**141**	*2-152	-1.2
1987	†StL N	141	510	73	134	29	0	2	83	68-3	3	62	.263	.346	.331	81	-11	19-4	.989	-11	94	120	*2-137	-1.2
1988	StL N	15	50	4	13	0	0	1	3	11-3	0	4	.260	.393	.320	106	1	3-0	.984	-5	81	103	2-15	-0.3
	Min A	86	304	42	80	16	0	1	21	40-1	0	47	.263	.349	.326	88	-3	10-3	.988	-3	95	116	2-73/S-2,D-3	-0.3
1989	Phi N	151	561	65	161	25	6	2	37	54-2	3	63	.287	.352	.364	105	5	10-7	.990	11	107	94	*2-144	2.1
1990	Phi N	119	447	39	118	21	3	4	50	36-4	2	47	.264	.320	.351	85	-9	7-1	.991	0	98	130	*2-114	-0.5
	NY N	27	100	9	25	5	0	1	10	14-0	0	11	.250	.342	.330	86	-1	0-0	.979	-4	83	118	2-26	-0.5
	Year	146	547	48	143	26	3	5	60	50-4	2	58	.261	.324	.347	85	-10	7-1	**.989**	-4	95	**128**	*2-140	-1.0
1991	NY N	70	155	17	30	7	0	1	14	32-4	0	21	.194	.328	.258	68	-5	7-2	1.000	4	96	130	2-57/O(CF)	0.1
	SF N	32	60	6	15	1	1	0	7	13-1	0	7	.250	.384	.300	98	1	2-0	1.000	-4	83	66	2-15/3-3	-0.3
	Year	102	215	23	45	8	1	1	21	45-5	0	28	.209	.344	.270	77	-4	9-2	1.000	0	93	117	2-72/3-3,O(CF)	-0.2
Total	13	1514	5349	676	1450	254	41	28	574	627-47	22	584	.271	.347	.350	95	-14	188-64	.989	-29	100	121	*2-1416/S-16,3-3,D-3,O(CF)	4.1

HERRERA, JOSE Jose Concepcion (Ontiveros) "Loco" B 4.8.1942 San Lorenzo, Venezuela BR/TR 5-8/165# d6.3

Year	Tm Lg	G	AB	R	H	2B	3B	HR	RBI	BB-IB	HP	SO	AVG	OBP	SLG	AOPS	ABR	SB-CS	FA	FR	Rng	Thr	G at Pos	BFW
1967	Hou N	5	4	0	1	0	0	0	1	0-0	0	1	.250	.250	.250	45	0	0-0	—	0			H	0.0
1968	Hou N	27	100	9	24	5	0	0	7	4-0	0	12	.240	.269	.290	69	-4	0-2	.958	-2	82	85	O-17(5-0-12)/2-7	-0.8
1969	Mon N	47	126	7	36	5	0	2	12	3-0	0	14	.286	.302	.373	88	-2	1-2	.980	-2	90	127	O-31(20-13-0)/2-2,3	-0.6
1970	Mon N	1	1	0	0	0	0	0	0	0-0	0	1	.000	.000	.000	-99	0	0-0	—	0			H	0.0
Total	4	80	231	16	61	10	0	2	20	7-0	0	28	.264	.286	.333	79	-6	1-4	.973	-4	87	112	/O-48(25-13-12),2-9,3	-1.4

HERRERA, JOSE Jose Ramon (Catalino) B 8.30.1972 Santo Domingo, D.R. BL/TL 6/165# d8.12

Year	Tm Lg	G	AB	R	H	2B	3B	HR	RBI	BB-IB	HP	SO	AVG	OBP	SLG	AOPS	ABR	SB-CS	FA	FR	Rng	Thr	G at Pos	BFW
1995	Oak A	33	70	9	17	1	2	0	2	6-0	0	11	.243	.299	.314	64	-4	1-3	.956	1	98	231	O-25(0-22-5)/D-5	-0.4
1996	Oak A	108	320	44	86	15	1	6	30	20-1	3	59	.269	.318	.378	77	-12	8-2	.970	-0	110	35	*O-100(0-18-92)/D	-1.3
Total	2	141	390	53	103	16	3	6	32	26-1	3	70	.264	.314	.367	74	-16	9-5	.967	0	108	70	O-125(0-40-97)/D-6	-1.7

HERRERA, PANCHO Juan Francisco (Willavicencio) B 6.16.1934 Santiago De Cuba, Cuba BR/TR 6-3/220# d4.15

Year	Tm Lg	G	AB	R	H	2B	3B	HR	RBI	BB-IB	HP	SO	AVG	OBP	SLG	AOPS	ABR	SB-CS	FA	FR	Rng	Thr	G at Pos	BFW
1958	Phi N	29	63	5	17	3	0	1	6	7-0	1	15	.270	.347	.365	92	0	1-2	.980	0	88	101	3-16,1-11	-0.1
1960	Phi N	145	512	61	144	26	6	17	71	51-6	5	136	.281	.348	.455	119	14	2-3	.988	7	**117**	89	*1-134,2-17	1.4
1961	Phi N	126	400	56	103	17	2	13	51	55-4	4	120	.257	.351	.408	102	3	5-1	.993	5	**113**	101	*1-115	0.1
Total	3	300	975	122	264	46	8	31	128	113-10	10	271	.271	.349	.430	110	17	8-6	.990	11	116	95	1-260/2-17,3-16	1.4

HERRERA, MIKE Ramon B 12.19.1897 Havana, Cuba D 2.3.1978 Havana, Cuba BR/TR 5-6/147# d9.22

Year	Tm Lg	G	AB	R	H	2B	3B	HR	RBI	BB-IB	HP	SO	AVG	OBP	SLG	AOPS	ABR	SB-CS	FA	FR	Rng	Thr	G at Pos	BFW
1925	Bos A	10	39	2	15	0	0	0	8	2	0	2	.385	.415	.385	104	0	1-0	.958	2	128	45	2-10	0.3
1926	Bos A	74	237	20	61	14	1	0	19	15	1	13	.257	.304	.325	66	-12	0-5	.962	6	109	83	2-48,3-16/S-4	-0.5
Total	2	84	276	22	76	14	1	0	27	17	1	15	.275	.320	.333	72	-12	1-5	.961	8	112	76	/2-58,3-16,S-4	-0.2

HERRING, LEFTY Silas Clarke B 3.4.1880 Philadelphia, PA D 2.11.1965 Massapequa, NY BL/TL 5-11/160# d5.16

Year	Tm Lg	G	AB	R	H	2B	3B	HR	RBI	BB-IB	HP	SO	AVG	OBP	SLG	AOPS	ABR	SB-CS	FA	FR	Rng	Thr	G at Pos	BFW
1899	Was N	2	1	1	1	0	0	0	0	1	0		1.000	1.000	1.000	454	1	0	1.000	0	198	0	/P-2	0.0
1904	Was A	15	46	3	8	1	0	0	2	7	0		.174	.283	.196	54	-2	0	.991	1	162	125	1-10/O-5(CF)	-0.1
Total	2	17	47	4	9	1	0	0	2	8	0		.191	.309	.213	67	-1	0	.991	2	162	125	/1-10,O-5(CF),P-2	-0.1

HERRMANN, ED Edward Martin B 8.27.1946 San Diego, CA BL/TR 6-1/210# d9.1 gf-Marty

Year	Tm Lg	G	AB	R	H	2B	3B	HR	RBI	BB-IB	HP	SO	AVG	OBP	SLG	AOPS	ABR	SB-CS	FA	FR	Rng	Thr	G at Pos	BFW
1967	Chi A	2	3	1	2	1	0	0	1	1-1	0	0	.667	.750	1.000	429	1	0-0	1.000	1	0	337	/C-2	0.3
1969	Chi A	102	290	31	67	8	0	8	31	30-0	8	35	.231	.319	.341	81	-7	0-2	.983	-5	105	80	C-92	-0.9
1970	Chi A	96	297	42	84	9	0	19	52	31-3	3	41	.283	.356	.505	130	12	0-1	.988	0	60	105	C-88	1.6
1971	Chi A	101	294	32	63	6	0	11	35	44-12	2	48	.214	.317	.347	86	-5	2-0	.995	7	94	118	C-97	0.8
1972	Chi A	116	354	23	88	9	0	10	40	43-**19**	4	37	.249	.333	.359	105	3	0-0	.989	0	108	**143**	*C-112	0.9
1973	Chi A	119	379	42	85	17	1	10	39	31-3	7	55	.224	.291	.354	79	-11	2-4	.984	3	74	96	*C-114/D-2	-0.3
1974	Chi A*	107	367	32	95	13	1	10	39	16-6	0	49	.259	.288	.381	90	-6	1-0	.987	-1	105	105	*C-107	-0.2
1975	NY A	80	200	16	51	9	2	6	30	16-5	0	23	.255	.309	.410	104	0	0-0	.979	7	138	83	D-35,C-24	0.8
1976	Cal A	29	46	5	8	3	0	2	8	7-2	0	8	.174	.278	.370	96	0	0-0	.954	-8	55	105	C-27	-0.8
	Hou N	79	265	14	54	8	0	3	25	22-2	4	40	.204	.273	.268	60	-14	0-0	.987	-2	76	106	C-79	-1.4
1977	Hou N	56	158	7	46	7	0	1	17	15-1	1	18	.291	.352	.354	100	0	1-1	.990	4	73	81	C-49	0.6
1978	Hou N	16	36	1	4	1	0	0	0	3-1	0	3	.111	.179	.139	-11	-5	0-0	1.000	-3	76	73	C-14	-0.8
	Mon N	19	40	1	7	1	0	0	3	1-0	0	4	.175	.195	.200	11	-5	0-0	.977	-4	45	88	C-12	-0.9
	Year	35	76	2	11	2	0	0	3	4-1	0	7	.145	.188	.171	1	-10	0-0	.991	-6	62	80	C-26	-1.7
Total	11	922	2729	247	654	92	4	80	320	260-55	29	361	.240	.310	.364	91	-37	6-8	.987	2	88	106	C-817/D-37	-0.3

HERRNSTEIN, JOHN John Ellett B 3.31.1938 Hampton, VA BL/TL 6-3/215# d9.15

Year	Tm Lg	G	AB	R	H	2B	3B	HR	RBI	BB-IB	HP	SO	AVG	OBP	SLG	AOPS	ABR	SB-CS	FA	FR	Rng	Thr	G at Pos	BFW
1962	Phi N	6	5	0	1	0	0	0	1	1-0	0	3	.200	.333	.200	48	0	0-0	—	-0	0	0	/O(RF)	0.0
1963	Phi N	15	12	1	2	0	0	1	1	1-0	0	5	.167	.231	.417	83	0	0-0	1.000	-0	130	0	/O-2(LF),1	-0.1
1964	Phi N	125	303	38	71	12	4	6	25	22-0	2	67	.234	.288	.360	83	-7	1-2	.977	-7	102	0	O-69(63-4-3),1-68	-2.0
1965	Phi N	63	85	8	17	2	0	1	5	2-1	1	18	.200	.227	.259	37	-7	0-0	.984	1	96	129	1-18,O-14(11-2-1)	-0.8
1966	Phi N	4	10	0	1	0	0	0	1	0-0	0	7	.100	.100	.100	-44	-2	0-0	1.000	-0	100	0	/O-2(LF)	-0.2
	Chi N	9	17	3	3	0	0	0	0	3-0	0	8	.176	.300	.176	36	-1	0-0	.975	-1	0	93	/1-4,O(LF)	-0.3
	Atl N	17	18	2	4	0	0	0	1	0-0	0	7	.222	.222	.222	24	-2	0-0	1.000	0	131	0	/O-5(LF)	-0.2
	Year	30	45	5	8	0	0	0	2	3-0	0	22	.178	.229	.178	15	-5	0-0	1.000	-1	108	0	/O-8(LF),1-4	-0.7
Total	5	239	450	52	99	14	4	8	34	29-1	3	115	.220	.270	.322	67	-19	1-2	.983	-7	104	56	/O-94(84-6-5),1-91	-3.6

HERRSCHER, RICK Richard Franklin B 11.3.1936 St.Louis, MO BR/TR 6-2.5/187# d8.1

Year	Tm Lg	G	AB	R	H	2B	3B	HR	RBI	BB-IB	HP	SO	AVG	OBP	SLG	AOPS	ABR	SB-CS	FA	FR	Rng	Thr	G at Pos	BFW
1962	NY N	35	50	5	11	3	0	1	6	5-0	0	11	.220	.291	.340	68	-2	0-0	1.000	2	166	138	1-10/3-6,O-4(3-0-1),S-3	-0.1

HERSH, EARL Earl Walter B 5.21.1932 Ebbvale, MD BL/TL 6/205# d9.4

Year	Tm Lg	G	AB	R	H	2B	3B	HR	RBI	BB-IB	HP	SO	AVG	OBP	SLG	AOPS	ABR	SB-CS	FA	FR	Rng	Thr	G at Pos	BFW
1956	Mil N	7	13	0	3	3	0	0	0	0-0	0	5	.231	.231	.462	85	0	0-0	.000	-1	0	0	/O-2(LF)	-0.1

HERSHBERGER, MIKE Norman Michael B 10.9.1939 Massillon, OH BR/TR 5-10/175# d9.5

Year	Tm Lg	G	AB	R	H	2B	3B	HR	RBI	BB-IB	HP	SO	AVG	OBP	SLG	AOPS	ABR	SB-CS	FA	FR	Rng	Thr	G at Pos	BFW
1961	Chi A	15	55	9	17	3	0	0	5	2-0	0	2	.309	.333	.364	88	-1	1-1	1.000	0	92	241	O-13(1-9-3)	-0.1
1962	Chi A	148	427	54	112	14	2	4	46	37-0	3	36	.262	.324	.333	78	-13	10-6	.984	-1	100	112	*O-135(1-52-90)	-2.0
1963	Chi A	135	476	64	133	26	2	3	45	39-1	4	39	.279	.338	.361	98	0	9-3	.976	-1	94	**173**	*O-119(1-73-67)	-0.6
1964	Chi A	141	452	55	104	15	3	2	31	48-1	4	47	.230	.308	.290	70	-18	8-6	.984	-2	93	124	*O-134(0-64-85)	-2.8
1965	KC A	150	494	43	114	15	5	5	48	37-5	5	42	.231	.289	.312	72	-19	7-3	.988	6	101	170	*O-144(5-9-134)	-2.2
1966	KC A	146	538	55	136	27	7	2	57	47-3	3	37	.253	.313	.340	92	-5	13-5	.977	8	107	**165**	*O-143(12-3-130)	-0.6
1967	KC A	142	480	55	122	25	1	1	49	38-2	7	40	.254	.314	.317	91	-4	10-3	.982	8	101	219	*O-130(10-0-122)	-0.4
1968	Oak A	99	246	23	67	9	2	5	32	21-4	1	22	.272	.327	.386	123	6	8-3	.978	1	102	117	O-90(71-6-27)	0.5
1969	Oak A	51	129	11	26	2	0	1	10	10-0	0	15	.202	.259	.240	42	-10	1-2	.980	-4	81	0	O-35(16-8-13)	-1.8
1970	Mil A	49	98	7	23	5	0	1	6	10-0	0	8	.235	.306	.316	71	-4	1-2	.946	-2	81	65	O-35(RF)	-0.8
1971	Chi A	74	177	22	46	9	0	2	15	30-3	4	23	.260	.377	.345	103	3	6-2	.960	-6	84	34	O-59(0-58-2)	-0.5
Total	11	1150	3572	398	900	150	22	26	344	319-19	31	311	.252	.316	.328	85	-65	74-36	.980	8	98	145	*O-1037(117-282-708)	-11.3

HERSHBERGER, WILLARD Willard McKee "Bill" B 5.28.1910 Lemoncove, CA D 8.3.1940 Boston, MA BR/TR 5-10.5/167# d4.19

Year	Tm Lg	G	AB	R	H	2B	3B	HR	RBI	BB-IB	HP	SO	AVG	OBP	SLG	AOPS	ABR	SB-CS	FA	FR	Rng	Thr	G at Pos	BFW
1938	Cin N	49	105	12	29	3	1	0	12	5	1	6	.276	.315	.324	78	-3	1	.960	-1	*126*	*81*	C-39/2	-0.3
1939	†Cin N	63	174	23	60	9	2	0	32	9	2	4	.345	.384	.420	115	4	1	.987	-1	*109*	*99*	C-60	0.6
1940	Cin N	48	123	6	38	4	2	0	26	6	2	6	.309	.351	.374	99	0	0	.985	-1	*117*	*47*	C-37	0.0
Total	3	160	402	41	127	16	5	0	70	20	5	16	.316	.356	.381	101	1	2	.980	-3	*116*	*79*	C-136/2	0.3

HERTWECK, NEAL Neal Charles B 11.22.1931 St.Louis, MO BL/TL 6-1.5/175# d9.27

Year	Tm Lg	G	AB	R	H	2B	3B	HR	RBI	BB-IB	HP	SO	AVG	OBP	SLG	AOPS	ABR	SB-CS	FA	FR	Rng	Thr	G at Pos	BFW
1952	StL N	2	6	0	0	0	0	0	0	1	0	1	.000	.143	.000	-57	-1	0-0	1.000	-0	78	241	/1-2	-0.2

HERTZ, STEVE Stephen Allan B 2.26.1945 Fairfield, OH BR/TR 6-1/195# d4.21

Year	Tm Lg	G	AB	R	H	2B	3B	HR	RBI	BB-IB	HP	SO	AVG	OBP	SLG	AOPS	ABR	SB-CS	FA	FR	Rng	Thr	G at Pos	BFW
1964	Hou N	5	4	2	0	0	0	0	0	0-0	0	3	.000	.000	.000	-99	-1	0-0	1.000	-0	0	0	/3-2	-0.1

HERZOG, BUCK Charles Lincoln B 7.9.1885 Baltimore, MD D 9.4.1953 Baltimore, MD BR/TR 5-11/160# d4.17 M3 OF Total (28-LF 4-RF)

Year	Tm Lg	G	AB	R	H	2B	3B	HR	RBI	BB-IB	HP	SO	AVG	OBP	SLG	AOPS	ABR	SB-CS	FA	FR	Rng	Thr	G at Pos	BFW
1908	NY N	64	160	38	48	6	2	0	11	36	7		.300	.448	.363	152	13	16	.921	-0	107	189	2-42,S-12/3-4,O(LF)	1.6
1909	NY N	42	130	16	24	2	0	0	8	13	1		.185	.264	.200	43	-8	10	.914	-3	90	106	O-29(26-0-4)/2-6,3-4,S	-1.5
1910	Bos N	106	380	51	95	20	3	3	32	30	15	34	.250	.329	.342	92	-3	13	.915	8	**116**	111	*3-105	0.7
1911	Bos N	79	294	53	91	19	5	5	41	33	10	21	.310	.398	.459	129	12	26	.934	3	106	85	S-74/3-4	2.1
	†NY N	69	247	37	66	14	4	1	26	14	7	19	.267	.325	.368	91	-3	22	.926	7	110	83	3-65/2-3,S	0.6
	Year	148	541	90	157	33	9	6	67	47	17	40	.290	.365	.418	112	9	48	.935	10	106	85	S-75,3-69/2-3	2.7
1912	†NY N	140	482	72	127	20	9	2	47	57	7	34	.263	.350	.355	90	-6	37	.942	20	**117**	126	*3-140	1.8
1913	†NY N	96	290	46	83	15	3	3	31	22	6	12	.286	.349	.390	110	4	23-15	.947	2	97	205	3-84/2-2	0.8
1914	Cin N	138	498	54	140	14	8	1	40	42	9	27	.281	.348	.347	104	3	46	.939	33	113	118	*S-137/1-2,M	4.8
1915	Cin N	155	579	61	153	14	10	1	42	34	8	21	.264	.314	.328	93	-6	35-16	.945	30	108	**141**	*S-153/1-2,M	4.0
1916	Cin N	79	281	30	75	14	2	1	24	21	5	12	.267	.329	.342	109	4	15-12	.931	-4	94	99	S-65,3-12/O(LF)M	0.5
	NY N	77	280	40	73	10	4	0	25	22	5	24	.261	.326	.325	106	2	19-16	.978	12	105	117	2-44,3-27/S-9	1.8
	Year	156	561	70	148	24	6	1	49	43	10	36	.264	.327	.333	107	6	34-28	.926	8	97	105	S-74,2-44,3-39/O(LF)	2.3
1917	†NY N	114	417	69	98	10	8	2	31	31	13	36	.235	.308	.312	93	-3	12	.948	-9	95	**128**	*2-113	-1.1
1918	Bos N	118	473	57	108	12	6	0	26	29	5	28	.228	.280	.279	74	-15	10	.961	2	**104**	99	2-99,1-12/S-7	-1.2
1919	Bos N	73	275	27	77	8	5	1	25	13	6	11	.280	.327	.356	110	3	16	.953	-15	91	80	2-70/1	-1.2
	Chi N	52	193	15	53	4	4	0	17	10	8	7	.275	.336	.337	102	1	12	.987	-4	99	75	2-52	-0.3
	Year	125	468	42	130	12	9	1	42	23	**14**	18	.278	.331	.348	106	3	28	.967	-18	94	78	*2-122/1	-1.5

Year	Tm Lg	G	AB	R	H	2B	3B	HR	RBI	BB-IB	HP	SO	AVG	OBP	SLG	AOPS	ABR	SB-CS	FA	FR	Rng	Thr	G at Pos	BFW
1920	Chi N	91	305	39	59	9	2	0	19	20	8	21	.193	.261	.236	43	-22	8-9	.938	-4	93	87	2-59,3-28/1	-2.8
Total	13	1493	5284	705	1370	191	75	20	445	427	120	307	.259	.329	.335	96	-24	320-68	.954	80	98	108	2-490,3-473,S-459/O-31L,1-18	10.6
HERZOG, WHITEY Dorrel Norman Elvert B 11.9.1931 New Athens, IL BL/TL 5-11/182# d4.17 M18 C4																								
1956	Was A	117	421	49	103	13	7	4	35	35-0	0	74	.245	.302	.337	69	-21	8-5	.980	-4	93	125	*O-103(15-84-7)/1-5	-3.0
1957	Was A	36	78	7	13	3	0	0	4	13-0	2	12	.167	.301	.205	41	-6	1-2	.981	-1	101	0	O-28(2-26-0)	-0.9
1958	Was A	8	5	0	0	0	0	0	0	1-0	0	5	.000	.167	.000	-51	-1	0-0	1.000	0	138	0	/O-7(0-5-2)	-0.1
	KC A	88	96	11	23	1	2	0	9	16-1	0	21	.240	.345	.292	77	-3	0-3	.968	-0	127	0	O-37(29-7-1),1-22	-0.5
	Year	96	101	11	23	1	2	0	9	17-1	0	26	.228	.336	.277	71	-4	0-3	.972	0	128	0	O-44(29-12-3),1-22	-0.6
1959	KC A	38	123	25	36	7	1	1	9	34-0	0	23	.293	.446	.390	129	8	1-0	.963	0	107	95	O-34(1-13-20)/1	0.7
1960	KC A	83	252	43	67	10	2	8	38	40-2	0	32	.266	.364	.417	111	5	0-1	.985	-1	98	89	O-69(29-0-42)/1-2	0.1
1961	Bal A	113	323	39	94	11	6	5	35	50-1	1	41	.291	.387	.409	117	9	1-4	1.000	-6	89	32	O-98(27-0-73)	-0.3
1962	Bal A	99	263	34	70	13	1	7	35	41-1	3	36	.266	.369	.403	116	7	2-3	.978	1	103	102	O-70(13-1-59)	0.3
1963	Det A	52	53	5	8	2	1	0	7	11-3	1	17	.151	.303	.226	51	-3	0-0	.976	-1	31	55	/1-7,O-4(1-1-2)	-0.5
Total	8	634	1614	213	414	60	20	25	172	241-8	7	261	.257	.354	.365	96	-5	13-18	.982	-12	98	81	O-450(117-137-206)/1-37	-4.2
HESS, OTTO Otto C. B 10.10.1878 Bern, Switzerland D 2.25.1926 Tucson, AZ BL/TL 6-1/170# d8.3 ▲																								
1902	Cle A	7	14	2	1	0	0	0	1	2	0		.071	.188	.071	-27	-1	0	.870	1	124	0	/P-7	0.0
1904	Cle A	34	100	4	12	2	1	0	5	3	0		.120	.146	.160	-3	-12	0	.951	1	92	0	P-21,O-12(7-5-0)	-0.3
1905	Cle A	54	173	15	44	8	1	2	13	7	2		.254	.291	.347	101	0	2	.950	3	165	297	O-28(27-0-1),P-26	0.1
1906	Cle A	53	154	13	31	5	2	0	11	2	0		.201	.212	.260	48	-10	1	.949	-2	85	165	P-43/O-5(CF)	-0.1
1907	Cle A	19	30	4	4	0	0	0	0	4	2		.133	.278	.133	31	-2	1	.941	-1	90	0	P-17/O-2(LF)	0.0
1908	Cle A	9	14	0	0	0	0	0	0	1	0		.000	.067	.000	-78	-3	0	1.000	-0	140	0	/P-4,O-4(RF)	-0.3
1912	Bos N	33	94	10	23	4	4	0	10	0	0	26	.245	.245	.372	66	3	0	.951	-4	74	145	P-33	0.0
1913	Bos N	35	83	9	26	0	1	2	11	7	0	15	.313	.367	.410	119	8	0	.945	1	103	141	P-29	0.0
1914	Bos N	31	47	5	11	1	0	1	6	1	0	11	.234	.250	.319	69	-2	0	.947	1	140	293	P-14/1-5	0.0
1915	Bos N	5	5	1	2	1	0	0	1	0	0	2	.400	.400	.600	210	1	0	.800	-0	106	0	/P-4,1	0.0
Total	10	280	714	63	154	21	9	5	58	27	4	54	.216	.248	.291	63	-18	4	.941	1	94	105	P-198/O-51(36-10-5),1-6	-0.6
HESS, TOM Thomas (born Thomas Heslin) B 8.15.1875 Brooklyn, NY D 12.15.1945 Albany, NY d6.6																								
1892	Bal N	1	2	0	0	0	0	0	0	0	0	0	.000	.000	.000	-97	0	0	—	0	0	0	/C	0.0
HESSMAN, MIKE Michael Steven B 3.5.1978 Fountain Valley, CA BR/TR 6-5/210# d8.22																								
2003	Atl N	19	21	2	6	2	0	2	3	5-1	0	6	.286	.423	.667	178	3	0-0	.800	-1	123	0	/O-8(7-0-1),1-4,3-3	0.2
HETLING, GUS August Julius B 11.21.1885 St.Louis, MO D 10.13.1962 Wichita, KS BR/TR 5-10/165# d10.6																								
1906	Det A	2	7	0	1	0	0	0	0	0	0		.143	.143	.143	-10	-1	0	1.000	-0	59	0	/3-2	-0.1
HEUBEL, GEORGE George A. B 1849 Paterson, NJ D 1.22.1896 Philadelphia, PA 5-11.5/178# d5.20 U2																								
1871	Ath NA	17	75	18	23	4	2	0	13	2		0	.307	.325	.413	112	1	1-0	.758	0	160	0	O-16(RF)/1	0.2
1872	Oly NA	5	23	2	3	0	0	0	1	0		0	.130	.130	.130	-21	-3	0-0	.800	-1	0	0	/O-5(CF)	-0.3
1876	NY N	1	4	0	0	0	0	0	0	0		0	.000	.000	.000	-99	-1		.750	-0	0	0	/1	-0.1
Total	2 NA	22	98	20	26	4	2	0	14	2		0	.265	.280	.347	83	-2	1-0	.000	-0	124	0	/O-21(0-5-16),1	-0.1
HEVING, JOHNNIE John Aloysius B 4.29.1896 Covington, KY D 12.24.1968 Salisbury, NC BR/TR 6/175# d9.24 b-Joe																								
1920	StL A	1	1	0	0	0	0	0	0	0	0	0	.000	.000	.000	-97	0	0-0	—	0			H	0.0
1924	Bos A	45	109	15	31	5	1	0	11	10	0	7	.284	.345	.349	79	-3	0-0	.969	2	101	148	C-29	0.0
1925	Bos A	45	119	14	20	7	0	0	6	12	0	7	.168	.244	.227	20	-15	0-1	.958	-0	74	102	C-34	-1.2
1928	Bos A	82	158	11	41	7	2	0	11	11	0	10	.259	.308	.329	69	-7	1-1	.967	-5	78	107	C-62	-1.0
1929	Bos A	76	188	26	60	4	3	0	23	8	2	7	.319	.354	.372	89	-4	1-2	.988	4	110	123	C-55	0.4
1930	Bos A	75	220	15	61	5	3	0	17	11	0	14	.277	.312	.327	65	-12	2-0	.987	1	155	88	C-71	-0.7
1931	†Phi A	42	113	8	27	3	2	1	12	6	0	8	.239	.277	.327	55	-8	0-0	.993	3	126	65	C-40	-0.3
1932	Phi A	33	77	14	21	6	1	0	10	7	0	6	.273	.333	.377	81	-2	0-0	1.000	-0	110	34	C-28	-0.1
Total	8	399	985	103	261	37	12	1	90	65	2	59	.265	.312	.330	66	-51	4-4	.981	3	112	100	C-319	-2.9
HEYDON, MIKE Michael Edward "Ed" B 7.15.1874 , MO D 10.13.1913 Indianapolis, IN BL/TR 6/?# d10.12																								
1898	Bal N	3	9	2	1	0	0	0	1	2	1		.111	.333	.111	28	-1	0	.917	-0	95	131	/C-3	-0.1
1899	Was N	3	3	0	0	0	0	0	0	2	0		.000	.400	.000	14	0	0	.833	-0	85	147	/C-2	0.0
1901	StL N	16	43	2	9	1	1	1	6	5	0		.209	.292	.349	90	-1	2	.941	-2	97	69	C-13/O(CF)	-0.2
1904	Chi A	4	10	0	1	1	0	0	1	1	1		.100	.250	.200	45	0	0	1.000	1	153	123	/C-4	0.1
1905	Was A	77	245	20	47	7	4	1	26	21	2		.192	.261	.265	70	-9	5	.955	9	101	**113**	C-77	0.9
1906	Was A	49	145	14	23	7	1	0	10	14	1		.159	.237	.221	46	-9	2	.937	-6	80	124	C-49	-1.1
1907	Was A	62	164	14	30	3	0	0	9	25	3		.183	.302	.201	66	-4	3	.961	-9	85	92	C-57	-0.9
Total	7	214	619	52	111	19	6	2	53	70	8		.179	.271	.239	64	-24	12	.952	-7	92	108	C-205/O(CF)	-1.3
HIATT, JACK Jack E B 7.27.1942 Bakersfield, CA BR/TR 6-2/190# d9.7 C1																								
1964	LA A	9	16	2	6	0	0	0	2	2-0	0	3	.375	.444	.375	145	1	0-0	.889	-1	56	0	/C-3,1-2	0.0
1965	SF N	40	67	5	19	4	0	1	7	12-2	0	14	.284	.392	.388	118	2	0-0	.987	-1	106	99	C-21/1-7	0.1
1966	SF N	18	23	2	7	2	0	0	1	4-0	0	5	.304	.407	.391	120	1	0-0	.982	1	189	114	/1-7	0.2
1967	SF N	73	153	24	42	6	0	6	26	27-1	1	37	.275	.387	.431	136	8	0-0	.990	-2	90	109	1-36/C-3,O-2(LF)	0.5
1968	SF N	90	224	14	52	10	2	4	34	41-4	1	61	.232	.351	.348	111	5	0-0	.994	-0	77	104	C-58,1-10	0.8
1969	SF N	69	194	18	38	4	0	7	34	48-5	0	58	.196	.352	.325	93	0	0-0	.992	2	146	118	C-60/1-3	0.5
1970	Mon N	17	43	4	14	2	0	0	7	14-0	0	14	.326	.491	.372	135	4	0-0	.961	-3	45	0	C-12/1-2	0.1
	Chi N	66	178	19	43	12	1	2	22	31-2	0	48	.242	.352	.354	81	-4	0-0	.990	6	87	100	C-63/1-2	0.5
	Year	83	221	23	57	14	1	2	29	45-2	0	62	.258	.382	.357	91	0	0-0	.986	3	80	84	C-75/1-4	0.6
1971	Hou N	69	174	16	48	8	1	1	16	35-2	2	39	.276	.401	.351	118	7	0-1	.991	-2	87	90	C-65/1	0.7
1972	Hou N	10	25	2	5	3	0	0	0	5-2	0	5	.200	.333	.320	88	0	0-0	1.000	-4	76	87	C-10	-0.4
	Cal A	22	45	4	13	0	1	1	5	5-0	0	11	.289	.360	.400	133	2	0-0	1.000	-6	129	92	C-17	-0.4
Total	9	483	1142	110	287	51	5	22	154	224-18	4	295	.251	.374	.363	109	26	0-1	.990	-10	98	97	C-312/1-70,O-2(LF)	2.6
HIATT, PHIL Philip Farrell B 5.1.1969 Pensacola, FL BR/TR 6-3/200# d4.7																								
1993	KC A	81	238	30	52	12	1	7	36	16-0	7	82	.218	.285	.366	70	-11	6-3	.909	-3	98	55	3-70/D-9	-1.2
1995	KC A	52	113	11	23	6	0	4	12	9-0	0	37	.204	.262	.363	60	-7	1-0	.957	2	105	195	O-47(1-2-45)/D-2	-0.6
1996	Det A	7	21	3	4	0	1	0	1	2-0	0	11	.190	.261	.286	38	-2	0-0	1.000	1	135	161	/3-3,O-2(1-0-1),D	-0.1
2001	LA N	30	50	6	12	3	0	2	6	3-1	0	19	.240	.283	.420	85	-1	0-0	1.000	-3	49	64	3-17/1-6	-0.5
Total	4	170	422	50	91	21	2	13	55	30-1	7	149	.216	.278	.367	67	-21	7-3	.920	-3	93	60	/3-90,O-49(2-2-46),D-12,1-6	-2.4
HIBBS, JIM James Kerr B 9.10.1944 Klamath Falls, OR BR/TR 6/190# d4.12																								
1967	Cal A	3	3	0	0	0	0	0	0	0-0	0	2	.000	.000	.000	-99	-1	0-0	—	0			H	-0.1
HICKEY, EDDIE Edward A. B 8.18.1872 Cleveland, OH D 3.25.1941 Tacoma, WA d9.3																								
1901	Chi N	10	37	4	6	0	0	0	3	2	1		.162	.225	.162	14	-4	1	.743	-2	93	183	3-10	-0.6
HICKEY, MIKE Michael Francis B 12.25.1871 Chicopee, MA D 6.11.1918 Springfield, MA BR/TR 5-10.5/150# d9.14																								
1899	Bos N	1	3	0	1	0	0	0	0	0	0		.333	.333	.333	76	0	0	.889	0	139	0	/2	0.0
HICKMAN, CHARLIE Charles Taylor "Cheerful Charlie" or "Piano Legs" B 3.4.1876 Taylortown, PA D 4.19.1934 Morgantown, WV BR/TR 5-9/180# d9.8 ▲ OF Total (46-LF 3-CF 242-RF)																								
1897	†Bos N	2	3	1	2	0	0	1	2	0	0		.667	.667	1.667	476	2	0	1.000	0	55	1809	/P-2	0.0
1898	Bos N	19	58	4	15	2	0	0	7	1	1		.259	.283	.293	62	-3	0	1.000	-1	101	0	/O-7(6-1-0),1-6,P-6	-0.3
1899	Bos N	19	63	15	25	2	7	0	15	2	2		.397	.433	.651	178	6	1	.941	-3	72	235	P-11/O-7(6-1-0),1	0.0
1900	NY N	127	473	65	148	19	17	9	91	17	17		.313	.359	.482	137	21	10	.842	-4	99	105	*3-120/O-7(RF)	1.7
1901	NY N	112	406	44	113	20	6	4	62	15	7		.278	.315	.387	107	3	5	.904	-3	132	59	O-50(6-1-44),S-23,3-15/P-9,2-7,1-2	-0.1
1902	Bos A	28	108	13	32	5	2	3	16	3	4		.296	.339	.463	118	2	1	.939	-1	51	0	O-27(LF)	-0.1
	Cle A	102	426	61	161	31	11	8	94	12	3		.378	.399	.559	170	38	8	.966	-7	87	110	1-98/2-3,P	2.7
	Year	130	534	74	**193**	36	13	11	110	15	7		.361	.387	.539	159	39	9	.966	-8	87	110	1-98,O-27(LF)/2-3,P	2.6
1903	Cle A	131	522	64	154	31	11	12	97	17	6		.295	.325	.466	137	22	14	.972	-7	84	112	*1-125/2-7	1.3
1904	Cle A	86	337	34	97	22	10	4	45	13	2		.288	.318	.448	142	15	9	.943	1	112	56	2-45,1-40/O(LF)	1.6

Year	Tm Lg	G	AB	R	H	2B	3B	HR	RBI	BB-IB	HP	SO	AVG	OBP	SLG	AOPS	ABR	SB-CS	FA	FR	Rng	Thr	G at Pos	BFW
	Det A	42	144	18	35	6	6	2	22	11	0		.243	.297	.410	126	4	3	.970	-2	91	99	1-39	0.1
	Year	128	481	52	132	28	16	6	67	24	2		.274	.312	.437	137	18	12	.969	-2	89	100	1-79,2-45/O(LF)	1.7
1905	Det A	59	213	21	47	12	3	2	20	12	5		.221	.278	.333	93	-2	3	.940	3	136	238	O-47(RF),1-12	-0.2
	Was A	88	360	48	112	25	9	2	46	9	2		.311	.332	.447	152	19	3	.922	6	119	83	2-85/1-3	2.8
	Year	147	573	69	159	37	12	4	66	21	7		.277	.311	.405	129	16	6	.922	9	119	83	2-85,O-47(RF),1-15	2.6
1906	Was A	120	451	53	128	25	5	9	57	14	4		.284	.311	.421	135	16	9	.955	-1	100	70	O-95(RF),1-18/3-5,2	1.2
1907	Was A	60	198	20	55	9	3	1	23	14	4		.278	.338	.369	136	8	4	.965	-2	87	84	1-30,O-18(RF)/2-3,P	0.5
	Chi A	21	23	1	6	2	0	0	1	4	0		.261	.370	.348	134	1	0	.667	-1	0	0	/O-3(RF)	0.1
	Year	81	221	21	61	11	3	1	24	18	4		.276	.342	.367	135	9	4	.965	-2	87	84	1-30,O-21(RF)/2-3,P	0.6
1908	Cle A	65	197	16	46	6	1	2	16	9	1		.234	.271	.305	86	-3	2	.907	-1	150	121	O-28(RF),1-20/2	-0.6
Total	12	1081	3982	478	1176	217	91	59	614	153	58		.295	.331	.440	133	149	72	.968	-22	90	106	1-394,O-290R,2-152,3-140/P-30,S	10.7

HICKMAN, JIM David James B 5.19.1892 Johnson City, TN D 12.30.1958 Brooklyn, NY BR/TR 5-7.5/170# d9.17 Mil 1918

Year	Tm Lg	G	AB	R	H	2B	3B	HR	RBI	BB-IB	HP	SO	AVG	OBP	SLG	AOPS	ABR	SB-CS	FA	FR	Rng	Thr	G at Pos	BFW
1915	Bal F	20	81	7	17	4	1	1	7	4	1	14	.210	.256	.321	60	-6	5	.963	4	101	242	O-20(CF)	-0.4
1916	Bro N	9	5	3	1	0	0	0	0	2	0	0	.200	.429	.200	94	0	1	1.000	0	141	0	/O-3(2-1-0)	0.0
1917	Bro N	114	370	46	81	15	4	6	36	17	0	66	.219	.253	.330	76	-12	14	.942	6	99	169	*O-101(26-71-3)	-1.4
1918	Bro N	53	167	14	39	4	7	1	16	8	3	31	.234	.281	.359	95	-2	5	.914	-1	92	132	O-46(0-10-42)	-0.6
1919	Bro N	57	104	14	20	3	1	0	11	6	0	17	.192	.236	.240	43	-7	2	.962	1	107	95	O-29(4-6-22)	-0.9
Total	5	253	727	84	158	26	13	8	70	37	4	128	.217	.259	.322	74	-27	27	.941	9	99	158	O-199(32-108-67)	-3.3

HICKMAN, JIM James Lucius B 5.10.1937 Henning, TN BR/TR 6-4/205# d4.14

Year	Tm Lg	G	AB	R	H	2B	3B	HR	RBI	BB-IB	HP	SO	AVG	OBP	SLG	AOPS	ABR	SB-CS	FA	FR	Rng	Thr	G at Pos	BFW
1962	NY N	140	392	54	96	18	2	13	46	47-2	3	96	.245	.328	.401	94	-3	4-4	.971	1	106	85	*O-124(7-84-33)	-0.8
1963	NY N	146	494	53	113	21	6	17	51	44-1	1	120	.229	.291	.399	96	-4	0-5	.963	-1	92	110	O-82(19-42-22),3-59	-1.2
1964	NY N	139	409	48	105	14	1	11	57	36-4	2	90	.257	.319	.377	98	-1	0-1	.976	4	110	115	*O-113(39-89-19)/3	-0.2
1965	NY N	141	369	32	87	18	0	15	40	27-3	2	76	.236	.291	.407	98	-2	3-1	.965	-1	100	74	O-91(35-44-16),1-30,3-14	-0.8
1966	NY N	58	160	15	38	7	0	4	16	13-0	1	34	.237	.299	.356	83	-4	2-1	.986	4	99	207	O-45(16-8-23),1-17	-0.2
1967	LA N	65	98	7	16	6	1	0	10	14-1	0	28	.163	.268	.245	52	-6	1-1	1.000	2	111	129	O-37(13-13-12)/1-2,3-2,P	-0.6
1968	Chi N	75	188	22	42	6	3	5	23	18-2	1	38	.223	.290	.367	91	-2	1-1	.975	0	104	91	O-66(3-20-49)	-0.6
1969	Chi N	134	338	38	80	11	2	21	54	47-3	0	74	.237	.326	.467	107	3	2-1	.981	-5	89	85	*O-125(5-9-116)	-0.7
1970	Chi N★	149	514	102	162	33	4	32	115	93-8	1	99	.315	.419	.582	148	38	0-1	.974	6	97	165	O-79(2-53-28),1-74	3.6
1971	Chi N	117	383	50	98	13	2	19	60	50-7	3	61	.256	.342	.449	108	5	0-1	.982	-2	90	70	O-69(1-3-66),1-44	-0.4
1972	Chi N	115	368	65	100	15	2	17	64	52-3	2	64	.272	.364	.462	121	11	3-1	.992	7	153	110	1-77,O-27(1-0-26)	1.2
1973	Chi N	92	201	27	49	1	2	3	20	42-2	0	42	.244	.368	.313	86	-2	1-1	.988	-1	108	106	1-51,O-13(3-0-11)	-0.7
1974	StL N	50	60	5	16	0	0	2	4	8-0	0	10	.267	.353	.367	102	0	0-0	.986	1	153	220	1-14/3	0.1
Total	13	1421	3974	518	1002	163	25	159	560	491-36	16	832	.252	.335	.426	106	33	17-19	.976	16	99	101	O-871(144-365-421),1-309/3-77,P	-1.3

HICKS, BUDDY Clarence Walter B 2.15.1927 Belvedere, CA BB/TR 5-10/170# d4.17

Year	Tm Lg	G	AB	R	H	2B	3B	HR	RBI	BB-IB	HP	SO	AVG	OBP	SLG	AOPS	ABR	SB-CS	FA	FR	Rng	Thr	G at Pos	BFW
1956	Det A	26	47	5	10	2	0	0	5	3-0	0	2	.213	.260	.255	36	-4	0-1	1.000	-1	117	86	S-16/2-6,3	-0.4

HICKS, JIM James Edward B 5.18.1940 East Chicago, IN BR/TR 6-3/205# d10.2

Year	Tm Lg	G	AB	R	H	2B	3B	HR	RBI	BB-IB	HP	SO	AVG	OBP	SLG	AOPS	ABR	SB-CS	FA	FR	Rng	Thr	G at Pos	BFW
1964	Chi A	2	0	0	0	0	0	0	0	0-0	0	0	—	—	—	—	0	0-0	—	0			R	0.0
1965	Chi A	13	19	2	5	1	0	1	2	0-0	0	9	.263	.263	.474	112	0	0-0	.750	-1	63	0	/O-5(3-0-2)	-0.1
1966	Chi A	18	26	3	5	0	1	0	1	1-0	0	5	.192	.222	.269	43	-2	0-0	1.000	-0	117	0	O-10(2-0-8)/1-2	-0.3
1969	StL N	19	44	5	8	0	2	1	3	4-0	0	14	.182	.250	.341	64	-3	0-0	1.000	1	111	216	O-15(RF)	-0.2
	Cal A	37	48	6	4	0	0	3	8	13-1	0	18	.083	.274	.271	57	-3	0-1	1.000	-2	92	0	O-10(4-3-3)/1-8	-0.6
1970	Cal A	4	4	0	1	0	0	0	0	0-0	0	2	.250	.250	.250	40	0	0-0	—	0			H	0.0
Total	5	93	141	16	23	1	3	5	14	18-1	0	48	.163	.256	.319	64	-8	0-1	.981	-1	104	99	/O-40(9-3-28),1-10	-1.2

HICKS, NAT Nathan Woodhull B 4.19.1845 Hempstead, NY D 4.21.1907 Hoboken, NJ BR/TR 6-1/186# d4.22 M2

Year	Tm Lg	G	AB	R	H	2B	3B	HR	RBI	BB-IB	HP	SO	AVG	OBP	SLG	AOPS	ABR	SB-CS	FA	FR	Rng	Thr	G at Pos	BFW
1872	Mut NA	**56**	267	54	82	12	2	0	32	6		3	.307	.322	.367	119	8	3-0	.875	5			*C-54/O-3(RF)	0.9
1873	Mut NA	28	120	12	29	1	2	1	14	8		0	.242	.289	.308	78	-3	2-1	.778	2			C-28	-0.1
1874	Phi NA	**58**	266	51	73	8	1	0	30	5		4	.274	.288	.312	89	-4	3-2	.823	7			*C-57/O-4(CF),2M	0.3
1875	Mut NA	62	269	32	67	10	0	0	22	2		10	.249	.255	.286	83	-5	1-0	.819	5			*C-60/O-5(0-1-4),M	0.1
1876	NY N	45	188	20	44	4	1	0	15	3		4	.234	.246	.266	81	-2		.741	-6			C-45	-0.6
1877	Cin N	8	32	3	6	0	0	0	3	1		2	.188	.212	.188	30	-2		.868	0			/C-8	-0.2
Total	4 NA	204	922	149	251	31	5	1	98	21		17	.272	.288	.320	94	-4	9-3	.000	19			C-199/O-12(0-5-7),2	1.2
Total	2	53	220	23	50	4	1	0	18	4		6	.227	.241	.255	73	-4		.757	-6			/C-53	-0.8

HICKS, JOE William Joseph B 4.7.1933 Ivy, VA BL/TR 6/180# d9.18

Year	Tm Lg	G	AB	R	H	2B	3B	HR	RBI	BB-IB	HP	SO	AVG	OBP	SLG	AOPS	ABR	SB-CS	FA	FR	Rng	Thr	G at Pos	BFW
1959	Chi A	6	7	0	3	0	0	0	0	1-0	0	1	.429	.500	.429	160	1	0-1	1.000	1	83	951	/O-4(1-2-1)	0.1
1960	Chi A	36	47	3	9	1	0	0	2	6-0	1	3	.191	.291	.213	40	-4	0-1	1.000	-1	82	0	O-14(3-11-0)	-0.6
1961	Was A	12	29	2	5	0	0	1	1	0-0	0	4	.172	.172	.276	18	-4	0-1	1.000	1	109	201	/O-7(3-0-4)	-0.4
1962	Was A	102	174	20	39	4	2	6	14	15-0	0	34	.224	.286	.374	76	-7	3-1	.962	-1	104	57	O-42(5-22-16)	-0.9
1963	NY N	56	159	16	36	6	1	5	22	7-0	3	31	.226	.272	.371	82	-4	0-2	.966	-2	98	38	O-41(5-33-5)	-0.9
Total	5	212	416	41	92	11	3	12	39	29-0	4	73	.221	.278	.349	72	-18	3-6	.970	-2	99	71	O-108(17-68-26)	-2.7

HIDALGO, RICHARD Richard Jose B 7.2.1975 Caracas, Venezuela BR/TR 6-3/190# d9.1

Year	Tm Lg	G	AB	R	H	2B	3B	HR	RBI	BB-IB	HP	SO	AVG	OBP	SLG	AOPS	ABR	SB-CS	FA	FR	Rng	Thr	G at Pos	BFW
1997	†Hou N	19	62	8	19	5	0	2	6	4-0	1	18	.306	.358	.484	123	2	1-0	1.000	-3	77	0	O-19(1-17-1)	0.0
1998	†Hou N	74	211	31	64	15	0	7	35	17-0	2	37	.303	.355	.474	121	6	3-3	.978	0	103	85	O-72(9-57-14)	0.6
1999	Hou N	108	383	49	87	25	2	15	56	56-2	4	73	.227	.328	.420	90	-6	8-5	.991	9	101	238	*O-108(97-30-3)	0.0
2000	Hou N	153	558	118	175	42	3	44	122	56-3	21	110	.314	.391	.636	147	41	13-6	.984	14	**122**	77	*O-150(36-125-37)	5.0
2001	†Hou N	146	512	70	141	29	3	19	80	54-3	16	107	.275	.356	.455	104	4	3-5	.991	6	104	139	*O-144(23-128-37)	0.7
2002	Hou N	114	388	54	91	17	4	15	48	43-1	6	85	.235	.319	.415	91	-7	6-2	.995	3	108	90	*O-110(0-1-110)	-0.9
2003	Hou N	141	514	91	159	43	4	28	88	58-8	8	104	.309	.385	.572	140	31	9-7	.987	14	105	**249**	*O-137(RF)/D	3.7
Total	7	755	2628	421	736	176	16	130	435	288-17	58	534	.280	.359	.508	118	71	43-28	.988	44	107	147	O-740(166-358-339)/D	9.1

HIGBEE, MAHLON Mahlon Jesse B 8.16.1901 Louisville, KY D 4.7.1968 Depauw, IN BR/TR 5-11/165# d9.27

Year	Tm Lg	G	AB	R	H	2B	3B	HR	RBI	BB-IB	HP	SO	AVG	OBP	SLG	AOPS	ABR	SB-CS	FA	FR	Rng	Thr	G at Pos	BFW
1922	NY N	3	10	2	4	0	0	1	5	0	0	2	.400	.400	.700	177	1	0-0	1.000	-0	57	0	/O-3(2-0-1)	0.0

HIGBY d9.18

Year	Tm Lg	G	AB	R	H	2B	3B	HR	RBI	BB-IB	HP	SO	AVG	OBP	SLG	AOPS	ABR	SB-CS	FA	FR	Rng	Thr	G at Pos	BFW
1872	Atl NA	1	4	0	0	0	0	0	0	0		0	.000	.000	.000	-85	-1	0-0	.667	-0	0	0	/O(RF)	-0.1

HIGDON, BILL William Travis B 4.27.1924 Camp Hill, AL D 8.30.1986 Pascagoula, MS BL/TR 6-1/193# d9.10

Year	Tm Lg	G	AB	R	H	2B	3B	HR	RBI	BB-IB	HP	SO	AVG	OBP	SLG	AOPS	ABR	SB-CS	FA	FR	Rng	Thr	G at Pos	BFW
1949	Chi A	11	23	3	7	3	0	0	1	6	0	3	.304	.448	.435	139	2	1-0	1.000	-0	71	314	/O-6(CF)	0.2

HIGGINS, KEVIN Kevin Wayne B 1.22.1967 San Gabriel, CA BL/TR 5-11/170# d5.29

Year	Tm Lg	G	AB	R	H	2B	3B	HR	RBI	BB-IB	HP	SO	AVG	OBP	SLG	AOPS	ABR	SB-CS	FA	FR	Rng	Thr	G at Pos	BFW
1993	SD N	71	181	17	40	4	1	0	13	16-0	3	17	.221	.294	.254	48	-13	0-1	.983	2	82	98	C-59/3-4,1-3,O-3(1-0-2),2	-0.9

HIGGINS, MARK Mark Douglas B 7.9.1963 Miami, FL BR/TR 6-2/210# d9.7

Year	Tm Lg	G	AB	R	H	2B	3B	HR	RBI	BB-IB	HP	SO	AVG	OBP	SLG	AOPS	ABR	SB-CS	FA	FR	Rng	Thr	G at Pos	BFW
1989	Cle A	6	10	1	1	0	0	0	0	1-0	0	6	.100	.182	.100	-18	-2	0-0	1.000	0	146	39	/1-5	-0.1

HIGGINS, PINKY Michael Franklin "Mike" B 5.27.1909 Red Oak, TX D 3.21.1969 Dallas, TX BR/TR 6-1/185# d6.25 Mil 1945 M8

Year	Tm Lg	G	AB	R	H	2B	3B	HR	RBI	BB-IB	HP	SO	AVG	OBP	SLG	AOPS	ABR	SB-CS	FA	FR	Rng	Thr	G at Pos	BFW
1930	Phi A	14	24	1	6	2	0	0	0	4	0	5	.250	.357	.333	73	-1	0-0	1.000	-1	86	0	/3-5,2-2,S	-0.2
1933	Phi A	**152**	567	85	178	34	12	13	99	61	2	53	.314	.383	.485	127	22	2-7	.947	-6	96	80	*3-152	1.8
1934	Phi A☆	144	543	89	179	37	6	16	90	56	0	70	.330	.392	.508	136	28	9-2	.914	-15	89	116	*3-144	1.8
1935	Phi A	133	524	69	155	32	4	23	94	42	2	62	.296	.350	.504	120	12	6-2	.947	-12	87	75	*3-131	0.6
1936	Phi A★	146	550	89	159	32	2	12	80	67	0	61	.289	.366	.420	96	-3	7-4	.941	-11	94	93	*3-145	-0.9
1937	Bos A	153	570	88	172	33	5	9	106	76	1	51	.302	.385	.425	100	2	2-6	.935	-21	81	94	*3-152	-1.4
1938	Bos A	139	524	77	159	29	5	5	106	71	1	55	.303	.388	.406	95	-2	10-9	.914	-10	95	**112**	*3-138	-0.8
1939	Det A	132	489	57	135	23	2	8	76	56	2	41	.276	.353	.380	81	-13	7-4	.914	-8	92	90	*3-130	-1.5
1940	†Det A	131	480	70	130	24	3	13	76	61	3	31	.271	.357	.415	91	-6	4-2	.928	-7	91	66	*3-129	-0.8
1941	Det A	147	540	79	161	28	3	11	73	67	2	45	.298	.378	.422	101	2	5-4	.946	2	101	51	*3-145	0.9
1942	Det A	143	499	65	133	34	2	11	79	72	3	21	.267	.362	.409	108	7	3-7	.926	-15	87	92	*3-137	-0.5
1943	Det A	138	523	62	145	20	1	10	84	57	1	31	.277	.349	.377	104	4	2-5	.940	-10	88	88	*3-138	-0.7
1944	Det A★	148	543	79	161	32	4	7	76	81	4	34	.297	.392	.409	122	20	4-4	.954	-9	93	79	*3-146	1.2
1946	Det A	18	60	2	13	3	1	0	8	5	0	6	.217	.277	.300	58	-3	0-1	.949	-2	85	71	3-17	-0.6
	†Bos A	64	200	18	55	11	1	2	28	24	1	24	.275	.356	.370	97	0	0-2	.947	-1	99	125	3-59	-0.1
	Year	82	260	20	68	14	2	2	36	29	1	30	.262	.338	.354	88	-3	0-3	.947	-2	96	114	3-76	-0.7

Year	Tm Lg	G	AB	R	H	2B	3B	HR	RBI	BB-IB	HP	SO	AVG	OBP	SLG	AOPS	ABR	SB-CS	FA	FR	Rng	Thr	G at Pos	BFW
Total	14	1802	6636	930	1941	374	51	140	1075	800	22	590	.292	.370	.428	106	69	61-59	.935	-127	91	87	*3-1768/2-2,S	-1.2
HIGGINS, BOB Robert Stone B 9.23.1886 Fayetteville, TN D 5.25.1941 Chattanooga, TN BR/TR 5-8/176# d9.13																								
1909	Cle A	8	23	0	2	0	0	0	0	0	0		.087	.087	.087	-43	-4	0	1.000	2	*119*	*101*	/C-8	-0.1
1911	Bro N	4	10	1	3	0	0	0	2	1	0	0	.300	.364	.300	90	0	1	.933	-0	*98*	*85*	/C-2,3	0.0
1912	Bro N	1	2	0	0	0	0	0	0	0	0	1	.000	.000	.000	-99	-1	0	.750	-0	*73*	*0*	/C	-0.1
Total	3	13	35	1	5	0	0	0	2	1	0	1	.143	.167	.143	-6	-5	1	.970	2	*111*	*91*	/C-11,3	-0.2
HIGGINS, BILL William Edward B 9.8.1861 Wilmington, DE D 4.25.1919 Wilmington, DE TR 5-9/155# d8.9																								
1888	Bos N	14	54	5	10	1	0	0	4	1	0	3	.185	.200	.204	28	-4	1	.906	2	104	210	2-14	-0.2
1890	StL AA	67	258	39	65	6	2	0	35	24	0		.252	.316	.291	69	-11	7	.951	13	105	122	2-67	0.3
	Syr AA	1	4	1	1	1	0	0	1	0	0		.250	.250	.500	135	0	0	1.000	1	122	188	/2	0.1
	Year	68	262	40	66	7	2	0	36	24	0		.252	.315	.294	70	-11	7	.952	14	105	123	2-68	0.4
Total	2	82	316	45	76	8	2	0	40	25	0	3	.241	.296	.278	64	-15	8	.943	16	105	139	/2-82	0.2
HIGGINSON, BOBBY Robert Leigh B 8.18.1970 Philadelphia, PA BL/TR 5-11/180# d4.26																								
1995	Det A	131	410	61	92	17	5	14	43	62-3	5	107	.224	.329	.393	89	-7	6-4	.985	6	102	159	*O-123(65-0-67)/D-2	-0.6
1996	Det A	130	440	75	141	35	0	26	81	65-7	1	66	.320	.404	.577	146	33	6-3	.963	-3	93	112	*O-123(63-19-57)/D-4	2.3
1997	Det A	146	546	94	163	30	5	27	101	70-2	3	85	.299	.379	.520	133	27	12-7	.972	9	99	**217**	*O-143(104-2-57)/D-2	2.8
1998	Det A	157	612	92	174	37	4	25	85	63-2	6	101	.284	.355	.480	114	13	3-3	.982	3	97	159	*O-153(17-0-136)/D-2	0.7
1999	Det A	107	377	51	90	18	0	12	46	64-2	2	66	.239	.351	.382	87	-6	4-6	.983	-2	102	33	O-88(RF),D-17	-1.4
2000	Det A	154	597	104	179	44	4	30	102	74-6	2	99	.300	.377	.538	132	30	15-3	.979	10	99	**215**	*O-145(LF),D-10	3.2
2001	Det A	147	541	84	150	28	6	17	71	80-3	2	65	.277	.367	.445	120	18	20-12	.976	7	107	110	*O-142(LF)/D-5	1.8
2002	Det A	119	444	50	125	24	3	10	63	41-3	6	45	.282	.345	.417	109	6	12-5	.973	6	98	210	*O-117(LF)/D	0.8
2003	Det A	130	469	61	110	13	4	14	52	59-3	3	73	.235	.320	.369	89	-8	8-8	.981	-2	102	57	*O-118(0-1-117)/D-8	-1.6
Total	9	1221	4436	672	1224	246	31	175	644	578-31	30	707	.276	.360	.464	115	106	86-51	.977	32	100	148	*O-1152(653-22-522)/D-51	8.0
HIGH, ANDY Andrew Aird "Handy Andy" B 11.21.1897 Ava, IL D 2.22.1981 Sylvania, OH BL/TR 5-6/155# d4.12 C2 b-Charlie b-Hugh																								
1922	Bro N	153	579	82	164	27	10	6	65	59	4	26	.283	.354	.396	94	-5	3-12	.958	-3	102	106	*3-130,S-22/2	-0.1
1923	Bro N	123	426	51	115	23	9	3	37	47	1	13	.270	.344	.387	95	-2	4-1	.969	-4	97	90	3-80,S-45/2-5	0.4
1924	Bro N	144	582	98	191	26	13	6	61	57	2	16	.328	.390	.448	128	24	3-6	.964	-9	91	62	*2-133,S-17/3	1.8
1925	Bro N	44	115	11	23	4	1	0	6	14	0	5	.200	.287	.252	40	-10	0-1	.938	-4	87	86	2-11,3-11/S-3	-1.3
	Bos N	60	219	31	63	11	1	4	28	24	1	2	.288	.361	.402	104	2	3-5	.979	-5	94	72	3-60/2	-0.1
	Year	104	334	42	86	15	2	4	34	38	1	7	.257	.335	.350	80	-9	3-6	.963	-9	91	78	3-71,2-12/S-3	-1.4
1926	Bos N	130	476	55	141	17	10	2	66	39	1	9	.296	.351	.387	108	5	4	.962	-11	97	99	3-81,2-49	0.0
1927	Bos N	113	384	59	116	15	9	4	46	26	2	11	.302	.350	.419	114	6	4	.915	-19	76	61	3-89/2-8,S-2	-0.8
1928	†StL N	111	368	58	105	14	3	6	37	37	3	10	.285	.355	.389	93	-4	2	.935	-16	85	87	3-73,2-19	-1.4
1929	StL N	146	603	95	178	32	4	10	63	38	3	18	.295	.340	.411	84	-16	7	**.967**	-14	90	98	*3-123,2-22	-2.0
1930	†StL N	72	215	34	60	12	2	2	29	23	0	6	.279	.349	.381	74	-9	1	.990	-6	81	63	3-48/2-3	-1.1
1931	†StL N	63	131	20	35	6	1	0	19	24	2	4	.267	.389	.328	91	0	0	1.000	-2	85	176	3-23,2-19	-0.1
1932	Cin N	84	191	16	36	4	2	0	12	23	0	6	.188	.276	.230	39	-16	1	.950	-6	89	32	3-46,2-12	-2.1
1933	Cin N	24	43	4	9	2	0	1	6	5	0	1	.209	.292	.326	77	-1	0	.966	1	115	82	3-11/2-2	0.0
1934	Phi N	47	68	4	14	2	0	0	7	9	0	3	.206	.299	.235	40	-6	1	.906	-2	74	184	3-14/2-2	-0.7
Total	13	1314	4400	618	1250	195	65	44	482	425	19	130	.284	.350	.388	94	-32	33-25	.956	-100	91	90	3-790,2-287/S-89	-7.5
HIGH, CHARLIE Charles Edwin B 12.1.1898 Ava, IL D 9.11.1960 Oak Grove, OR BL/TR 5-9/170# d9.5 b-Andy b-Hugh																								
1919	Phi A	11	29	2	2	0	0	0	1	3	1	4	.069	.182	.069	-28	-5	2	.944	-0	97	81	/O-9(0-1-8)	-0.6
1920	Phi A	17	65	7	20	2	1	1	6	3	4	6	.308	.375	.415	108	1	0-2	.882	-1	84	128	O-17(0-2-15)	-0.2
Total	2	28	94	9	22	2	1	1	7	6	5	10	.234	.314	.309	68	-4	2-2	.904	-2	88	112	/O-26(0-3-23)	-0.8
HIGH, HUGH Hugh Jenken "Bunny" B 10.24.1887 Pottstown, PA D 11.16.1962 St.Louis, MO BL/TL 5-7.5/155# d4.11 b-Andy b-Charlie																								
1913	Det A	87	183	18	42	6	1	0	16	28	1	24	.230	.335	.273	80	-3	6	.982	2	105	108	O-52(3-43-7)	-0.5
1914	Det A	84	184	25	49	5	3	0	17	26	2	21	.266	.363	.326	104	2	7-6	.959	-6	88	31	O-53(13-39-1)	-0.8
1915	NY A	119	427	51	110	19	7	1	43	62	3	47	.258	.356	.342	109	7	22-13	**.981**	-5	97	60	*O-117(44-71-1)	-0.6
1916	NY A	116	377	44	99	13	4	1	28	47	3	44	.263	.349	.326	101	2	13	.950	-2	97	98	*O-110(107-2-1)	-0.5
1917	NY A	103	365	37	86	11	6	1	19	48	3	31	.236	.329	.307	93	-2	8	.986	-3	88	108	*O-100(99-1-0)	-1.1
1918	NY A	7	10	1	0	0	0	0	0	1	0	1	.000	.091	.000	-71	-2	0	1.000	1	103	257	/O-4(2-1-1)	-0.2
Total	6	516	1546	176	386	54	21	3	123	212	12	168	.250	.345	.318	98	4	56-19	.972	-14	95	85	O-436(268-157-11)	-3.7
HIGHAM, DICK Richard B 7.24.1851 Ipswich, England D 3.18.1905 Chicago, IL BL/TR 5-8.5/171# d6.1 M1 U2 OF NA (9-CF 93-RF)																								
1871	Mut NA	21	94	21	34	3	1	0	9	2		0	.362	.375	.415	139	6	3-2	.747	-5	93	86	2-12/O-8(RF),C	0.1
1872	Bal NA	50	245	72	84	10	1	2	37	2		3	.343	.348	.416	128	7	4-5	.847	-2			C-25,O-24(0-2-22)/2-5,3-2,1	0.4
1873	Mut NA	49	244	57	77	5	4	0	34	2		1	.316	.321	.369	105	1	2-2	.750	-9	34	202	O-19(0-1-18),2-18,C-17	-0.6
1874	Mut NA	**65**	333	58	87	14	3	1	38	4		0	.261	.270	.330	89	-5	5-3	**.852**	6			*C-48,O-33(0-3-31)/2M	0.3
1875	Chi NA	42	208	44	49	5	3	0	12	0		0	.236	.236	.288	80	-4	6-2	.821	-5			C-24,O-14(0-3-11),2-13	-0.8
	Mut NA	15	64	12	25	5	0	0	10	0		1	.391	.391	.469	187	5	0-0	.739	-4			/C-8,2-6,O-3(RF),1-2	0.1
	Year	57	272	56	74	10	3	0	22	0		1	.272	.272	.331	106	1	6-2	.802	-9			C-32,2-19,O-17(0-3-14)/1-2	-0.7
1876	Har N	67	312	59	102	**21**	2	0	35	2		7	.327	.331	.407	134	10		.869	1	**168**	62	*O-59(RF),C-13/S2	1.0
1878	Pro N	**62**	281	**60**	90	**22**	1	1	29	5		16	.320	.332	.416	145	14		.811	2	168	158	*O-62(RF)/C	1.5
1880	Tro N	1	5	1	1	0	0	0	0	0		0	.200	.200	.200	34	0		—	-1	0	0	/O(RF)C	-0.2
Total	5 NA	242	1188	264	356	42	12	3	140	10		5	.300	.306	.363	108	10	20-14	.000	-18			C-123,O-101R/2-55,1-3,3-2	-0.5
Total	3	130	598	120	193	43	3	1	64	7		23	.323	.331	.410	138	24		.834	2			O-122(RF)/C-15,2S	2.3
HILAND, JOHN John William B 9.1860 Baltic, RI D 4.10.1901 Philadelphia, PA BL/TL 5-8.5/165# d8.20																								
1885	Phi N	3	9	0	0	0	0	0	0	0		4	.000	.000	.000	-99	-2		.833	-1	59	0	/2-3	-0.3
HILDEBRAND d8.29																								
1902	Chi N	1	4	1	0	0	0	0	0	1	0		.000	.200	.000	-39	-1	0	1.000	-0	0	0	/O(RF)	-0.1
HILDEBRAND, GEORGE George Albert B 9.6.1878 San Francisco, CA D 5.30.1960 Reseda, CA BR/TR 5-8/170# d4.17 U22																								
1902	Bro N	11	41	3	9	1	0	0	5	3	1		.220	.289	.244	64	-2	0	1.000	2	135	0	O-11(LF)	0.0
HILDEBRAND, PALMER Palmer Marion "Pete" B 12.23.1884 Shauck, OH D 1.25.1960 N.Canton, OH BR/TR 5-10/170# d5.14																								
1913	StL N	26	55	3	9	2	0	0	1	1	2	10	.164	.207	.200	17	-6	1-2	.968	-1	81	103	C-22/O(LF)	-0.6
HILL, BELDEN Belden L. B 8.24.1864 Kewanee, IL D 10.22.1934 Cedar Rapids, IA BR/TR 6/?# d8.27																								
1890	Bal AA	9	30	3	5	2	0	0	2	3	3		.167	.306	.233	56	-1	6	.857	0	79	126	/3-9	-0.1
HILL, DONNIE Donald Earl B 11.12.1960 Pomona, CA BB/TR 5-10/160# d7.25 OF Total (RF)																								
1983	Oak A	53	158	20	42	7	0	2	15	4-0	0	21	.266	.280	.348	77	-5	1-1	.961	-3	95	80	S-53	-0.4
1984	Oak A	73	174	21	40	6	0	2	16	5-0	0	12	.230	.249	.299	55	-11	1-1	.949	-13	81	80	S-66/2-4,3-2,D-2	-2.0
1985	Oak A	123	393	45	112	13	2	3	48	23-2	0	33	.285	.321	.351	92	-5	9-4	.973	-29	90	68	*2-122	-2.7
1986	Oak A	108	339	37	96	16	2	4	29	23-1	0	38	.283	.329	.378	99	-1	5-2	.984	-9	92	74	2-68,3-33/S-2,D-3	-0.7
1987	Chi A	111	410	57	98	14	6	9	46	30-1	1	35	.239	.290	.368	72	-18	1-0	.987	-11	98	95	2-84,3-32/D	-2.4
1988	Chi A	83	221	17	48	6	1	2	20	26-1	0	32	.217	.296	.281	64	-10	3-1	.975	-3	96	108	2-59,3-12/D-5	-1.2
1990	Cal A	103	352	36	93	18	2	3	32	29-1	1	27	.264	.319	.352	90	-5	1-5	.990	10	115	125	2-60,S-24,3-21/1-3,PD	0.7
1991	Cal A	77	209	36	50	8	1	1	20	30-1	0	21	.239	.335	.301	77	-5	1-0	.971	10	103	111	2-39,S-29/1-3	0.7
1992	Min A	25	51	7	15	3	0	0	2	5-0	1	6	.294	.368	.353	100	0	0-0	.944	-0	118	97	S-10/2-7,3-5,O(RF)	0.1
Total	9	756	2307	276	594	91	14	26	228	175-7	3	225	.257	.308	.343	81	-60	22-11	.980	-50	97	90	2-443,S-184,3-105/D-12,1-6,OP	-7.9
HILL, GLENALLEN Glenallen B 3.22.1965 Santa Cruz, CA BR/TR 6-2/210# d9.1																								
1989	Tor A	19	52	4	15	0	0	1	7	3-0	0	12	.288	.327	.346	92	-1	2-1	.964	-1	92	0	O-16(3-0-13)/D-3	-0.2
1990	Tor A	84	260	47	60	11	3	12	32	18-0	0	62	.231	.281	.435	95	-3	8-3	.983	-1	95	99	O-60(27-1-34),D-20	-0.6
1991	Tor A	35	99	14	25	5	2	3	11	7-0	0	24	.253	.296	.434	97	-1	2-2	.967	0	119	0	D-16,O-13(9-0-4)	-0.2
	Cle A	37	122	15	32	3	0	5	14	16-0	0	30	.262	.345	.410	108	1	4-2	.978	1	115	0	O-33(12-26-1)/D	0.2
	Year	72	221	29	57	8	2	8	25	23-0	0	54	.258	.324	.421	103	1	6-4	.975	1	116	0	O-46(21-26-5),D-17	0.0
1992	Cle A	102	369	38	89	16	1	18	49	20-0	4	73	.241	.287	.436	102	-1	9-6	.956	-2	93	114	O-59(50-1-8),D-34	-0.7
1993	Cle A	66	174	19	39	7	2	5	25	11-1	1	50	.224	.268	.374	73	-8	7-3	.940	-3	93	44	O-39(9-0-30),D-18	-1.2

Year	Tm Lg	G	AB	R	H	2B	3B	HR	RBI	BB-IB	HP	SO	AVG	OBP	SLG	AOPS	ABR	SB-CS	FA	FR	Rng	Thr	G at Pos	BFW
	Chi N	31	87	14	30	7	0	10	22	6-0	0	21	.345	.387	.770	204	12	1-0	.957	2	117	145	O-21(18-0-4)	1.3
1994	Chi N	89	269	48	80	12	1	10	38	29-0	0	57	.297	.365	.461	115	6	19-6	.987	-3	97	0	O-78(31-44-7)	0.4
1995	SF N	132	497	71	131	29	4	24	86	39-4	1	98	.264	.317	.483	111	6	25-5	.959	-6	88	105	*O-125(0-1-124)	-0.3
1996	SF N	98	379	56	106	26	0	19	67	33-3	6	95	.280	.344	.499	125	13	6-3	.960	-6	86	92	O-98(RF)	0.3
1997	†SF N	128	398	47	104	28	4	11	64	19-0	4	87	.261	.297	.435	93	-6	7-4	.947	-6	95	31	O-97(RF)/D-7	-1.6
1998	Sea A	74	259	37	75	20	2	12	33	14-1	3	45	.290	.332	.521	118	6	1-1	.965	-3	98	58	O-71(LF)	0.1
	†Chi N	48	131	26	46	5	0	8	23	14-1	0	34	.351	.414	.573	151	10	0-0	.984	3	116	170	O-34(28-0-6)	1.1
1999	Chi N	99	253	43	76	9	1	20	55	22-1	0	61	.300	.353	.581	134	11	5-1	.955	-4	81	92	O-62(37-0-26)/D-4	0.6
2000	Chi N	64	168	23	44	4	1	11	29	10-2	0	43	.262	.303	.494	99	-2	0-1	.955	1	89	210	O-29(LF)/D-9	-0.2
	†NY A	40	132	22	44	5	0	16	29	9-0	1	33	.333	.378	.735	175	14	0-0	1.000	-0	107	0	D-24,O-12(LF)	1.1
2001	Ana A	16	66	4	9	0	0	1	2	0-0	0	20	.136	.136	.182	-17	-11	0-0	—	0	0	0	D-16	-1.2
Total	13	1162	3715	528	1005	187	21	186	586	270-13	20	845	.271	.321	.482	112	46	96-38	.964	-28	94	77	O-847(336-73-452),D-152	-1.1
HILL, HERMAN Herman Alexander B 10.12.1945 Tuskegee, AL D 12.14.1970 Valencia, Venezuela BL/TR 6-2/190# d9.2																								
1969	Min A	16	2	4	0	0	0	0	0	0-0	0	1	.000	.000	.000	-98	-1	1-2	—	-0	0	0	/O-2(CF)	-0.1
1970	Min A	27	22	8	2	0	0	0	0	0-0	0	6	.091	.091	.091	-49	-5	0-0	1.000	1	117	277	O-14(2-10-2)	-0.4
Total	2	43	24	12	2	0	0	0	0	0-0	0	7	.083	.083	.083	-53	-6	1-2	1.000	1	106	251	/O-16(2-12-2)	-0.5
HILL, HUGH Hugh Ellis B 7.21.1879 Ringgold, GA D 9.6.1958 Cincinnati, OH BL/TR 5-11.5/168# d5.1 b-Bill																								
1903	Cle A	1	1	0	0	0	0	0	0	0	0		.000	.000	.000	-99	0	0	—	0			H	0.0
1904	StL N	23	93	13	21	2	1	3	4	2	0		.226	.242	.366	91	-2	3	1.000	0	67	122	O-23(LF)	-0.3
Total	2	24	94	13	21	2	1	3	4	2	0		.223	.240	.362	89	-2	3	1.000	0	67	122	/O-23(LF)	-0.3
HILL, HUNTER Hunter Benjamin B 6.21.1879 Austin, TX D 2.22.1959 Austin, TX BR/TR d7.1																								
1903	StL A	86	317	30	77	11	3	0	25	8	1		.243	.264	.297	70	-12	2	.923	1	99	113	3-86	-1.0
1904	StL A	58	219	19	47	3	0	0	14	6	3		.215	.246	.228	54	-12	4	.826	-18	70	56	3-56/O(LF)	-3.3
	Was A	77	290	18	57	6	1	0	17	11	1		.197	.228	.224	44	-19	10	.895	-3	98	57	3-71/O-5(RF)	-2.3
	Year	135	509	37	104	9	1	0	31	17	4		.204	.236	.226	48	-31	14	.864	-21	85	57	*3-127/O-6(1-0-5)	-5.6
1905	Was A	104	374	37	78	12	1	1	24	32	4		.209	.278	.254	72	-11	10	.908	-1	100	109	*3-103	-1.0
Total	3	325	1200	104	259	32	5	1	80	57	9		.216	.257	.253	62	-54	26	.895	-21	94	89	3-316/O-6(1-0-5)	-7.6
HILL, JESSE Jesse Terrill B 1.20.1907 Yates, MO D 8.31.1993 Pasadena, CA BR/TR 5-9/165# d4.17																								
1935	NY A	107	392	69	115	20	3	4	33	42	0	32	.293	.362	.390	100	0	14-4	.951	2	102	117	O-94(LF)	-0.2
1936	Was A	85	233	50	71	19	5	0	34	29	1	23	.305	.384	.429	106	3	11-0	.967	-2	86	124	O-60(54-4-2)	0.1
1937	Was A	33	92	24	20	2	1	1	4	13	0	16	.217	.314	.293	57	-6	2-1	.986	1	122	0	O-21(3-18-0)	-0.5
	Phi A	70	242	32	71	12	3	1	37	31	0	20	.293	.374	.380	92	-2	16-3	.954	-3	98	69	O-68(3-65-0)	-0.4
	Year	103	334	56	91	14	4	2	41	44	0	36	.272	.357	.356	82	-8	18-4	.964	-2	104	51	O-89(6-83-0)	-0.9
Total	3	295	959	175	277	53	12	6	108	115	1	91	.289	.366	.388	95	-5	43-8	.959	-2	100	94	O-243(154-87-2)	-1.0
HILL, KOYIE Koyie Dolan B 3.9.1979 Tulsa, OK BB/TR 6/190# d9.5																								
2003	LA N	3	3	0	1	1	0	0	0	0-0	0	2	.333	.333	.667	161	0	0-0	—	0			/H	0.0
HILL, MARC Marc Kevin B 2.18.1952 Elsberry, MO BR/TR 6-3/210# d9.28 C2																								
1973	StL N	1	3	0	0	0	0	0	0	0-0	0	1	.000	.000	.000	-99	-1	0-0	1.000	-0	49	0	/C	-0.1
1974	StL N	10	21	2	5	1	0	0	2	4-1	0	5	.238	.360	.286	83	0	0-0	1.000	2	432	45	/C-9	0.2
1975	SF N	72	182	14	39	4	0	5	23	25-5	0	27	.214	.305	.319	71	-7	0-0	.994	3	89	137	C-60/3	-0.2
1976	SF N	54	131	11	24	5	0	3	15	10-2	1	19	.183	.243	.290	50	-9	0-1	.995	-0	108	73	C-49/1	-0.8
1977	SF N	108	320	28	80	10	0	9	50	34-6	0	34	.250	.316	.366	84	-7	0-1	.989	-1	94	102	*C-102	-0.4
1978	SF N	117	358	20	87	15	1	3	36	45-8	1	39	.243	.329	.316	84	-7	1-2	.986	1	99	109	*C-116/1-2	-0.2
1979	SF N	63	169	20	35	3	0	3	15	26-5	0	25	.207	.308	.278	67	-7	0-1	.991	-4	96	145	C-58/1	-0.9
1980	SF N	17	41	1	7	2	0	0	0	1-0	0	7	.171	.190	.220	14	-5	0-0	.972	-0	85	101	C-14	-0.5
	Sea A	29	70	8	16	2	1	2	9	3-0	0	10	.229	.260	.371	70	-3	0-0	.991	1	151	111	C-29	-0.2
1981	Chi A	16	6	0	0	0	0	0	0	0-0	0	1	.000	.000	.000	-99	-2	0-0	1.000	-1	0	91	C-14/13	-0.3
1982	Chi A	53	88	9	23	2	0	3	13	6-0	1	13	.261	.313	.386	92	-1	0-0	.993	1	102	114	C-49/13	0.1
1983	Chi A	58	133	11	30	6	0	1	11	9-2	0	24	.226	.275	.293	54	-8	0-1	.991	0	123	96	C-55/1D	-0.7
1984	Chi A	77	193	15	45	10	1	5	20	9-0	2	26	.233	.275	.373	74	-7	0-1	.991	-2	108	77	C-72/1-2	-0.7
1985	Chi A	40	75	5	10	2	0	0	4	12-0	0	9	.133	.253	.160	16	-9	0-0	.985	-0	101	56	C-37/3	-0.8
1986	Chi A	22	19	2	3	0	0	0	0	1-0	1	3	.158	.238	.158	10	-2	0-0	1.000	4	110	139	C-22	0.1
Total	14	737	1809	146	404	62	3	34	198	185-29	6	243	.223	.295	.317	69	-75	1-7	.990	2	106	104	C-687/1-9,3-4,D-2	-5.4
HILL, OLIVER Oliver Clinton B 10.16.1909 Powder Springs, GA D 9.20.1970 Decatur, GA BL/TR 5-11/178# d4.19																								
1939	Bos N	2	2	1	1	1	0	0	0	0	0	0	.500	.500	1.000	317	1	0	—	0			H	0.1
HILL, BOBBY William Robert B 4.3.1978 San Jose, CA BB/TR 5-10/180# d5.10																								
2002	Chi N	59	190	26	48	7	2	4	20	17-4	4	42	.253	.327	.374	89	-4	6-1	.991	-2	84	98	2-55/S	-0.3
2003	Chi N	5	4	0	1	0	0	0	0	1-0	0	2	.250	.400	.250	76	0	0-0	1.000	-1	0	0	/2-2	-0.1
	Pit N	1	3	1	1	0	0	0	0	1-0	0	0	.333	.500	.333	121	0	0-0	1.000	-0	96	0	/2	0.0
	Year	6	7	1	2	0	0	0	0	2-0	0	2	.286	.444	.286	97	0	0-0	1.000	-1	52	0	/2-3	-0.1
Total	2	65	197	27	50	7	2	4	20	19-4	4	44	.254	.332	.371	89	-4	6-1	.991	-4	83	95	/2-58,S	-0.4
HILLEBRAND, HOMER Homer Hiller Henry B 10.10.1879 Freeport, IL D 1.20.1974 Elsinore, CA BR/TL 5-8/165# d4.24 ▲																								
1905	Pit N	39	110	9	26	3	2	0	7	6	1		.236	.282	.300	72	-4	1	.978	-3	62	95	1-16,P-10/O-7(1-0-6),C-3	-0.6
1906	Pit N	7	21	1	5	1	0	0	3	1	0		.238	.273	.286	71	1	0	1.000	1	125	442	/P-7	0.0
1908	Pit N	1	0	0	0	0	0	0	0	0	0		—	—	—	—	0	0	—	-0	0	0	/P	0.0
Total	3	47	131	10	31	4	2	0	10	7	1		.237	.281	.298	71	-3	1	1.000	-2	92	204	/P-18,1-16,O-7(1-0-6),C-3	-0.6
HILLENBRAND, SHEA Shea Matthew B 7.27.1975 Mesa, AZ BR/TR 6-1/200# d4.2																								
2001	Bos A	139	468	52	123	20	2	12	49	13-3	7	61	.263	.291	.391	77	-17	3-4	.941	-2	92	78	*3-129/1-6,D	-1.8
2002	Bos A★	156	634	94	186	43	4	18	83	25-4	12	95	.293	.330	.459	105	4	4-2	.943	4	102	113	*3-156	0.9
2003	Bos A	49	185	20	56	17	0	3	38	7-1	4	26	.303	.335	.443	103	1	1-0	.958	-1	87	64	3-29,1-28/D-2	-0.1
	Ari N	85	330	40	88	18	1	17	59	17-3	2	44	.267	.302	.482	92	-5	0-0	.989	-5	76	75	1-56,3-34	-1.4
Total	3	429	1617	206	453	98	7	50	229	62-11	25	226	.280	.314	.442	94	-17	8-6	.941	-4	96	95	3-348/1-90,D-3	-2.4
HILLER, CHUCK Charles Joseph B 10.1.1934 Johnsburg, IL BL/TR 5-11/170# d4.11 C10																								
1961	SF N	70	240	38	57	12	1	2	12	32-0	1	30	.237	.328	.321	76	-7	4-4	.973	-13	86	78	2-67	-1.6
1962	†SF N	161	602	94	166	22	2	3	48	55-3	8	49	.276	.341	.334	84	-11	5-4	.964	-12	95	108	*2-161	-1.0
1963	SF N	111	417	44	93	10	2	6	33	20-0	2	23	.223	.261	.300	62	-21	3-2	.963	-17	93	77	*2-109	-3.3
1964	SF N	80	205	21	37	8	1	1	17	17-0	1	23	.180	.243	.244	38	-17	1-1	.977	1	101	102	2-60/3	-1.2
1965	SF N	7	7	1	1	0	0	1	1	0-0	0	1	.143	.143	.571	88	0	0-0	1.000	-0	72	0	/2-2	-0.1
	NY N	100	286	24	68	11	1	5	21	14-2	1	24	.238	.275	.336	74	-11	1-1	.959	-6	100	92	2-80/O-4(3-0-1),3-2	-1.2
	Year	107	293	25	69	11	1	6	22	14-2	1	25	.235	.272	.341	74	-11	1-1	.959	-6	100	91	2-82/O-4(3-0-1),3-2	-1.3
1966	NY N	108	254	25	71	8	2	2	14	15-0	5	22	.280	.332	.350	92	-3	0-0	.981	10	120	125	2-45,3-14/O-9(LF)	1.0
1967	NY N	25	54	0	5	3	0	0	3	2-0	0	11	.093	.125	.148	-22	-9	0-0	.968	2	111	119	2-14	-0.7
	Phi N	31	43	4	13	1	0	0	2	2-0	0	4	.302	.333	.326	88	-1	0-2	.947	-2	74	37	/2-6	-0.3
	Year	56	97	4	18	4	0	0	5	4-0	0	15	.186	.218	.227	27	-9	0-2	.963	-0	101	96	2-20	-1.0
1968	Pit N	11	13	2	5	1	0	0	1	0-0	0	0	.385	.385	.462	155	1	0-0	.857	-1	61	0	/2-2	0.0
Total	8	704	2121	253	516	76	9	20	152	157-5	18	187	.243	.299	.316	72	-79	14-14	.967	-38	97	95	2-546/3-17,O-13(12-0-1)	-8.4
HILLER, HOB Harvey Max B 5.12.1893 E.Mauch Chunk, PA D 12.27.1956 Lehighton, PA BR/TR 5-8/162# d4.22																								
1920	Bos A	17	29	4	5	1	1	0	2	2	0	5	.172	.226	.276	34	-3	0-3	.905	1	116	113	/3-6,S-5,2-2,O(RF)	-0.3
1921	Bos A	1	1	0	0	0	0	0	0	0	0	0	.000	.000	.000	-99	0	0-0	—	0			H	0.0
Total	2	18	30	4	5	1	1	0	2	2	0	5	.167	.219	.267	29	-3	0-3	.905	1	116	113	/3-6,S-5,2-2,O(RF)	-0.3
HILLEY, ED Edward Garfield "Whitey" B 6.17.1879 Cleveland, OH D 11.14.1956 Cleveland, OH BR/TR 5-10.5/170# d9.29																								
1903	Phi A	1	3	1	1	0	0	0	0	1	0		.333	.500	.333	147	0	0	.800	-0	35	655	/3	0.0
HILLIS, MACK Malcolm David B 7.23.1901 Cambridge, MA D 6.16.1961 Cambridge, MA BR/TR 5-10/165# d9.13																								
1924	NY A	1	1	1	0	0	0	0	0	0	0	0	.000	.000	.000	-99	0	0-0	—	-0	0	0	/2	0.0

Year	Tm Lg	G	AB	R	H	2B	3B	HR	RBI	BB-IB	HP	SO	AVG	OBP	SLG	AOPS	ABR	SB-CS	FA	FR	Rng	Thr	G at Pos	BFW
1928	Pit N	11	36	6	9	2	3	1	7	0	0	6	.250	.250	.556	101	-1	1	.973	-1	111	96	/2-8,3	-0.1
Total	2	12	37	7	9	2	3	1	7	0	0	6	.243	.243	.541	96	-1	1-0	.973	-1	109	94	/2-9,3	-0.1
HILLY, PAT William Edward (born William Edward Hilgerink) B 2.24.1887 Fostoria, OH D 7.25.1953 Eureka, MO BR/TR 5-11/180# d5.7																								
1914	Phi N	8	10	2	3	0	0	0	1	1	0	5	.300	.364	.300	92	0	0	1.000	0	138	0	/O-4(RF)	0.0
HILTON, DAVE John David B 9.15.1950 Uvalde, TX BR/TR 5-11/191# d9.10 C2																								
1972	SD N	13	47	2	10	2	1	0	5	3-0	0	6	.213	.260	.298	63	-3	1-0	.939	-3	73	43	3-13	-0.6
1973	SD N	70	234	21	46	9	0	5	16	19-6	1	35	.197	.260	.299	59	-14	2-1	.970	-10	94	120	3-47,2-23	-2.3
1974	SD N	74	217	17	52	8	2	1	12	13-1	0	28	.240	.281	.309	68	-10	3-5	.948	-5	91	117	3-55,2-15	-1.6
1975	SD N	4	8	0	0	0	0	0	0	0-0	0	0	.000	.000	.000	-99	-2	0-0	.900	1	142	0	/3-4	-0.2
Total	4	161	506	40	108	19	3	6	33	35-7	1	69	.213	.265	.298	61	-29	6-6	.954	-16	91	107	3-119/2-38	-4.7
HIMES, JACK John Herb B 9.22.1878 Bryan, OH D 12.16.1949 Joliet, IL BL/TR 6-2/180# d9.18																								
1905	StL N	12	41	3	6	0	0	0	0	1	0		.146	.167	.146	-7	-5	0	1.000	-0	74	0	O-11(1-0-11)	-0.7
1906	StL N	40	155	10	42	5	2	0	14	7	1		.271	.307	.329	102	0	4	.977	4	197	158	O-40(0-32-8)	0.2
Total	2	52	196	13	48	5	2	0	14	8	1		.245	.278	.291	79	-5	4	.981	4	172	126	/O-51(1-32-19)	-0.5
HINCH, A.J. Andrew Jay B 5.15.1974 Waverly, IA BR/TR 6-1/195# d4.1																								
1998	Oak A	120	337	34	78	10	0	9	35	30-0	4	89	.231	.296	.341	69	-16	3-0	.986	-8	112	99	*C-118	-1.5
1999	Oak A	76	205	26	44	4	1	7	24	11-0	2	41	.215	.260	.346	56	-15	6-2	.987	-10	101	73	C-73	-1.9
2000	Oak A	6	8	1	2	0	0	0	0	1-0	0	1	.250	.333	.250	52	-1	0-0	.900	-1	131	174	/C-5,D	-0.2
2001	KC A	45	121	10	19	3	0	6	15	8-1	3	26	.157	.226	.331	41	-11	1-1	.987	-1	125	62	C-43/D-2	-0.9
2002	KC A	72	197	25	49	7	1	7	27	18-0	3	35	.249	.321	.401	81	-6	3-3	.989	-5	80	62	C-68	-0.6
2003	Det A	27	74	7	15	3	1	3	11	3-0	2	18	.203	.247	.392	72	-3	0-0	.983	-7	54	59	C-27	-0.9
Total	6	346	942	103	207	27	3	32	112	71-1	14	210	.220	.281	.357	65	-52	13-6	.987	-32	100	78	C-334/D-3	-6.0
HINCHMAN, HARRY Harry Sibley B 8.4.1878 Philadelphia, PA D 1.19.1933 Toledo, OH BB/TR 5-11/165# d7.29 b-Bill																								
1907	Cle A	15	51	3	11	3	1	0	9	5	0		.216	.286	.314	90	0	2	.904	3	135	106	2-15	0.3
HINCHMAN, BILL William White B 4.4.1883 Philadelphia, PA D 2.20.1963 Columbus, OH BR/TR 5-11/190# d9.24 C1 b-Harry OF Total (330-LF 61-CF 357-RF)																								
1905	Cin N	17	51	10	13	4	1	0	10	13	1		.255	.415	.373	122	2	4	.905	-2	65	251	O-12(LF)/3-4,1	0.0
1906	Cin N	18	54	7	11	1	1	0	1	8	0		.204	.306	.259	73	-1	2	.963	1	153	415	O-16(8-0-8)	-0.2
1907	Cle A	152	514	62	117	19	9	1	50	47	**15**		.228	.311	.305	96	-1	15	.958	-1	99	73	*O-148(128-14-8)/1-4,2	-1.1
1908	Cle A	137	464	55	107	23	8	6	59	38	9		.231	.301	.353	112	6	9	.975	-9	146	45	O-75(23-1-51),S-51/1-4	-0.5
1909	Cle A	139	457	57	118	20	13	2	53	41	9		.258	.331	.372	117	9	22	.918	0	107	27	*O-131(87-38-6)/S-6	0.2
1915	Pit N	**156**	577	72	177	33	14	5	77	48	8	75	.307	.368	.438	146	32	17-17	.969	2	103	96	*O-156(6-0-151)	2.5
1916	Pit N	152	555	64	175	18	**16**	4	76	54	2	61	.315	.378	.427	146	30	10	.962	-5	107	54	*O-124(23-0-101),1-31	2.1
1917	Pit N	69	244	27	46	5	5	2	29	33	1	27	.189	.288	.275	71	-8	5	.945	-1	102	84	O-48(41-8-0),1-20	-1.3
1918	Pit N	50	111	10	26	5	2	0	13	15	2	8	.234	.336	.315	96	0	1	1.000	2	77	245	O-40(2-0-32)/1-3	0.1
1920	Pit N	18	16	0	3	0	0	0	1	1	1	3	.188	.278	.188	34	-1	0-0	—	0			H	-0.1
Total	10	908	3043	364	793	128	69	20	369	298	48	174	.261	.336	.368	118	68	85-17	.954	-13	108	79	O-750R/1-63,S-57,3-4,2	1.7
HINES, HUNKEY Henry Fred B 9.29.1867 Elgin, IL D 1.2.1928 Rockford, IL BR/TR 5-7/165# d5.16																								
1895	Bro N	2	8	3	2	0	0	0	1	2	0	0	.250	.400	.250	76	0	0	1.000	-0	0	0	/O-2(RF)	0.0
HINES, MIKE Michael P. B 9.1862 , Ireland D 3.14.1910 New Bedford, MA BR/TL 5-10/176# d5.1																								
1883	Bos N	63	231	38	52	13	1	0	16	7		36	.225	.248	.290	61	-11		.887	6			C-59/O-7(0-2-5)	0.1
1884	Bos N	35	132	16	23	3	0	0	3	3		24	.174	.193	.197	23	-12		.919	4			C-35	-0.4
1885	Bos N	14	56	11	13	4	0	0	4	4		5	.232	.283	.304	93	0		.857	-2	49	0	O-14(RF)	-0.2
	Bro AA	3	13	1	1	0	1	0	1	0	0		.077	.077	.231	-6	-2		1.000	-1			/C-3	-0.2
	Pro N	1	3	0	0	0	0	0	0	0		2	.000	.000	.000	-99	-1		.636	-1			/C	-0.1
1888	Bos N	4	16	3	2	0	1	0	2	2	0	0	.125	.222	.250	49	-1	0	1.000	-1	0	0	/O-3(2-0-1),C	-0.2
Total	4	120	451	69	91	20	3	0	26	16	0	67	.202	.229	.259	51	-27	0	.896	5			/C-99,O-24(2-2-20)	-1.0
HINES, PAUL Paul A. B 3.1.1852 Washington, DC D 7.10.1935 Hyattsville, MD BR/TR 5-9.5/173# d4.20 OF NA (41-LF 85-CF) OF Total (27-LF 1218-CF 7-RF)																								
1872	Nat NA	**11**	49	9	11	1	0	0	5	0		0	.224	.224	.245	38	-4	0-0	.862	-3	95	0	/1-9,3-2,C	-0.5
1873	Was NA	**39**	181	33	60	6	3	1	29	1		2	.331	.335	.414	125	6	0-1	.798	-0	79	0	*O-36(LF)/2-2,C	0.4
1874	Chi NA	**59**	271	47	80	10	2	0	34	4		4	.295	.305	.347	108	2	4-1	.877	3	73	157	*O-50(1-50-0),2-11/S-2	0.4
1875	Chi NA	**69**	308	45	101	14	4	0	36	1		0	.328	.330	.399	151	15	6-9	.889	7	108	258	O-39(4-35-0),2-30/CS	1.5
1876	Chi N	64	305	62	101	**21**	3	2	59	1		3	.331	.333	.439	139	11		**.923**	4	75	209	*O-64(CF)/2	1.1
1877	Chi N	**60**	261	44	73	11	7	0	23	1		8	.280	.282	.375	94	-3		.806	-10	45	66	*O-49(24-18-7),2-11	-1.3
1878	Pro N	**62**	257	42	92	13	4	**4**	**50**	2		10	.358	.363	**.486**	178	20		.849	1	95	161	*O-61(CF)/S	1.7
1879	Pro N	**85**	409	81	**146**	25	10	2	52	8		16	.357	.369	.482	181	**35**		.867	5	124	149	*O-85(CF)	3.2
1880	Pro N	85	374	64	115	20	2	3	35	13		17	.307	.331	.396	150	20		**.927**	3	91	**251**	*O-75(CF)/2-6,1-4	1.9
1881	Pro N	80	361	65	103	**27**	5	2	31	13		12	.285	.310	.404	125	11		.897	-2	69	65	*O-78(CF)/2-4,1	0.5
1882	Pro N	**84**	379	73	117	28	10	4	34	10		14	.309	.326	.467	151	21		.861	-2	86	117	*O-82(CF)/1-2	1.4
1883	Pro N	97	442	94	132	32	4	4	45	18		23	.299	.326	.416	120	11		.905	5	106	72	*O-89(CF)/1-9	1.1
1884	†Pro N	**114**	490	94	148	**36**	10	3	41	44		28	.302	.360	.435	151	31		.895	-3	87	174	*O-108(CF)/1-7,P	2.1
1885	Pro N	98	411	63	111	20	4	1	35	19		18	.270	.302	.345	112	6		.865	2	104	127	*O-92(CF)/1-4,S32	0.4
1886	Was N	121	487	80	152	30	8	9	56	35		21	.312	.358	.462	160	36	21	.899	0	108	33	*O-92(1-91-0),3-15,1-10/S-5,2-3	3.0
1887	Was N	123	478	83	147	32	5	10	72	48	8	24	.308	.380	.458	141	30	46	.886	-16	72	143	*O-109(CF)/1-7,2-5,S-4	0.9
1888	Ind N	133	513	84	144	26	3	4	58	41	8	45	.281	.343	.366	124	16	31	.912	-8	63	67	*O-125(CF)/1-6,S-2	0.3
1889	Ind N	121	486	77	148	27	1	6	72	49	5	22	.305	.374	.401	114	10	34	.964	3	121	108	*1-109,O-12(CF)	0.3
1890	Pit N	31	121	11	22	1	0	0	9	11	1	7	.182	.256	.190	34	-10	6	.973	2	219	69	1-17,O-14(CF)	-0.8
	Bos N	69	273	41	72	12	3	2	48	32	4	20	.264	.350	.352	97	-1	9	.881	-11	36	96	O-69(2-68-0)/1	-1.3
	Year	100	394	52	94	13	3	2	57	43	5	27	.239	.321	.302	80	-9	15	.871	-9	45	108	O-83(2-82-0),1-18	-2.1
1891	Was AA	54	206	25	58	7	5	0	31	21	10	16	.282	.376	.364	117	6	6	.856	-3	99	197	O-47(CF)/1-8	0.0
Total	4 NA	178	809	134	252	31	9	1	104	6	0	6	.311	.317	.376	122	19	10-11	.000	6	86	143	O-125C/2-43,1-9,S-3,C-3,3-2	1.8
Total	16	1481	6253	1083	1881	368	84	56	751	366	36	304	.301	.343	.413	133	250	153-0	.887	-29	86	125	*O-1251C,1-185/2-31,3-16,S-13,P	14.5
HINKLE, GORDIE Daniel Gordon B 4.3.1905 Toronto, OH D 3.19.1972 Houston, TX BR/TR 6/185# d4.19																								
1934	Bos A	27	75	7	13	6	1	0	9	7	0	23	.173	.244	.280	33	-8	0-0	.992	3	*110*	*73*	C-26	-0.3
HINSHAW, GEORGE George Addison B 10.23.1959 Los Angeles, CA BR/TR 6/185# d9.19																								
1982	SD N	6	15	1	4	0	0	0	1	3-1	0	5	.267	.389	.267	91	0	0-0	1.000	0	90	261	/O-6(1-0-5)	0.0
1983	SD N	7	16	1	7	1	0	0	4	0-0	0	4	.438	.438	.500	165	1	1-0	1.000	-1	60	0	/3-5	0.1
Total	2	13	31	2	11	1	0	0	5	3-1	0	9	.355	.412	.387	129	1	1-0	1.000	-1	90	261	/O-6(1-0-5),3-5	0.1
HINSKE, ERIC Eric Scott B 8.5.1977 Menasha, WI BL/TR 6-2/225# d4.1																								
2002	Tor A	151	566	99	158	38	2	24	84	77-5	2	138	.279	.365	.481	119	17	13-1	.946	-8	97	55	*3-148	1.3
2003	Tor A	124	449	74	109	45	3	12	63	59-1	1	104	.243	.329	.437	99	1	12-2	.930	-7	97	61	*3-124	-0.3
Total	2	275	1015	173	267	83	5	36	147	136-6	3	242	.263	.349	.461	110	18	25-3	.939	-15	97	58	3-272	1.0
HINSON, PAUL James Paul B 5.9.1904 Vanleer, TN D 9.23.1960 Muskogee, OK BR/TR 5-10/150# d4.19																								
1928	Bos A	3	0	1	0	0	0	0	0	0	0	0	—	—	—	—	0	0-0	—	0			R	0.0
HINTON, CHUCK Charles Edward B 5.3.1934 Rocky Mount, NC BR/TR 6-1/197# d5.14 OF Total (525-LF 201-CF 299-RF)																								
1961	Was A	106	339	51	88	13	5	6	34	40-1	1	81	.260	.337	.381	93	-3	22-5	.963	-1	96	86	O-92(72-2-20)	-0.7
1962	Was A	151	542	73	168	25	6	17	75	47-0	0	66	.310	.361	.472	124	18	28-10	.988	-2	92	99	*O-136(54-28-67),2-12/S	1.2
1963	Was A	150	566	80	152	20	12	15	55	64-2	1	79	.269	.340	.426	115	11	25-9	.989	1	111	91	*O-125(86-7-45),3-19/1-6,S-2	0.6
1964	Was A★	138	514	71	141	25	7	11	53	57-7	1	77	.274	.346	.414	112	9	17-6	.985	4	106	99	*O-131(131-1-1)/3-2	0.7
1965	Cle A	133	431	59	110	17	6	18	54	53-2	1	65	.255	.336	.448	120	11	17-3	.966	-5	93	135	O-72(33-43-4),1-40,2-23/3	0.7
1966	Cle A	123	348	46	89	9	3	12	50	35-2	1	66	.256	.323	.402	108	3	10-6	.973	1	105	119	*O-104(53-57-11)/1-6,2-2	0.0
1967	Cle A	147	498	55	122	19	3	10	37	43-5	1	100	.245	.304	.355	94	-4	6-8	.976	-1	103	64	*O-136(26-53-92)/2-5	-1.5
1968	Cal A	116	267	28	52	10	3	7	23	24-3	0	61	.195	.259	.333	82	-7	3-1	.987	4	148	112	1-48,O-37(10-6-23),3-13/2-9	-0.6
1969	Cle A	94	121	18	31	3	2	3	19	8-2	1	22	.256	.303	.388	91	-2	2-0	.941	-2	106	0	O-40(28-4-9),3-14	-0.5
1970	Cle A	107	195	24	62	4	0	9	29	25-1	0	34	.318	.392	.477	133	9	0-2	.994	-4	61	81	1-40,O-35(17-0-22)/C-4,2-3,3-2	0.2

Year	Tm Lg	G	AB	R	H	2B	3B	HR	RBI	BB-IB	HP	SO	AVG	OBP	SLG	AOPS	ABR	SB-CS	FA	FR	Rng	Thr	G at Pos	BFW
1971	Cle A	88	147	13	33	7	0	5	14	20-2	0	34	.224	.317	.374	87	-2	0-0	1.000	-4	75	166	1-20,O-20(15-0-5)/C-5	-0.8
Total	11	1353	3968	518	1048	152	47	113	443	416-27	7	685	.264	.332	.412	108	43	130-50	.979	-9	101	95	O-928L,1-160/2-54,3-51,C-9,S-3	-0.7
HINTON, JOHN John Robert "Red" B 6.20.1876 Pittsburgh, PA D 7.19.1920 Braddock, PA BR/TR 6/200# d6.3																								
1901	Bos N	4	13	0	1	0	0	0	0	2	0		.077	.200	.077	-17	-2	0	.750	-2	69	0	/3-4	-0.3
HINZO, TOMMY Thomas Lee B 6.18.1964 San Diego, CA BB/TR 5-10/170# d7.16																								
1987	Cle A	67	257	31	68	9	3	3	21	10-0	2	47	.265	.296	.358	72	-11	9-4	.973	1	110	96	2-67	-0.5
1989	Cle A	18	17	4	0	0	0	0	0	2-0	0	6	.000	.105	.000	-67	-4	1-2	.867	-4	64	42	/2-6,SD	-0.8
Total	2	85	274	35	68	9	3	3	21	12-0	2	53	.248	.284	.336	64	-15	10-6	.968	-2	107	93	/2-73,DS	-1.3
HISER, GENE Gene Taylor B 12.11.1948 Baltimore, MD BL/TL 5-11/175# d8.20																								
1971	Chi N	17	29	4	6	0	0	0	1	4-0	0	8	.207	.303	.207	41	-2	1-0	1.000	0	111	0	/O-9(0-4-5)	-0.2
1972	Chi N	32	46	2	9	0	0	0	4	6-0	0	8	.196	.288	.196	36	-4	1-0	1.000	1	95	250	O-15(4-2-9)	-0.3
1973	Chi N	100	109	15	19	3	0	1	6	11-1	1	17	.174	.254	.229	33	-10	4-5	.980	-4	81	0	O-64(25-22-18)	-1.7
1974	Chi N	12	17	2	4	1	0	0	1	0-0	0	3	.235	.235	.294	46	-1	0-0	1.000	0	107	0	/O-8(6-1-1)	-0.2
1975	Chi N	45	62	11	15	3	0	0	6	11-1	0	7	.242	.351	.290	77	-1	0-1	1.000	0	117	0	O-18(7-6-5)/1	-0.2
Total	5	206	263	34	53	7	0	1	18	32-2	1	43	.202	.289	.240	46	-18	6-6	.992	-3	95	46	O-114(42-35-38)/1	-2.6
HISLE, LARRY Larry Eugene B 5.5.1947 Portsmouth, OH BR/TR 6-2/195# d4.10 C4																								
1968	Phi N	7	11	1	4	1	0	0	1	1-0	0	4	.364	.417	.455	161	1	0-0	1.000	0	116	0	/O-6(CF)	0.1
1969	Phi N	145	482	75	128	23	5	20	56	48-8	5	152	.266	.338	.459	125	15	18-8	.977	7	111	137	*O-140(1-139-0)	2.0
1970	Phi N	126	405	52	83	22	4	10	44	53-2	3	139	.205	.299	.353	77	-13	5-5	.978	1	107	72	*O-121(0-86-36)	-1.7
1971	Phi N	36	76	7	15	3	0	0	3	6-1	0	22	.197	.256	.237	40	-6	1-0	.962	2	123	157	O-27(19-8-0)	-0.5
1973	Min A	143	545	88	148	25	6	15	64	64-2	4	128	.272	.351	.422	113	10	11-4	.975	1	102	110	*O-143(49-93-3)	0.7
1974	Min A	143	510	68	146	20	7	19	79	48-5	8	112	.286	.353	.465	131	20	12-6	.979	-5	97	44	*O-137(74-52-26)	0.9
1975	Min A	80	255	37	80	9	2	11	51	27-3	1	39	.314	.376	.494	144	15	17-3	.976	-3	93	49	O-58(37-26-9),D-14	1.1
1976	Min A	155	581	81	158	19	5	14	96	56-4	4	93	.272	.335	.394	112	9	31-18	.984	11	109	142	*O-154(135-5-18)	1.2
1977	Min A★	141	546	95	165	36	3	28	**119**	56-5	6	106	.302	.369	.533	146	35	21-10	.974	-6	90	110	*O-134(68-65-6)/D-6	2.6
1978	Mil A★	142	520	96	151	24	0	34	115	67-3	5	90	.290	.374	.533	153	37	10-6	.978	-5	87	100	O-87(67-22-1),D-51	2.7
1979	Mil A	26	96	18	27	7	0	3	14	11-2	0	19	.281	.352	.448	115	2	1-0	1.000	0	77	254	D-15,O-10(LF)	0.2
1980	Mil A	17	60	16	17	0	0	6	16	14-2	1	7	.283	.421	.583	180	7	1-1	—	0	0	0	D-17	0.6
1981	Mil A	27	87	11	20	4	0	4	11	6-0	2	17	.230	.289	.414	108	1	0-0	—	0	0	0	D-24	0.0
1982	Mil A	9	31	7	4	0	0	2	5	5-0	0	13	.129	.250	.323	60	-2	0-0	—	0			/D-8	-0.2
Total	14	1197	4205	652	1146	193	32	166	674	462-37	39	941	.273	.347	.452	123	131	128-61	.978	3	101	103	*O-1017(460-502-99),D-135	9.7
HITCHCOCK, JIM James Franklin B 6.28.1911 Inverness, AL D 6.23.1959 Montgomery, AL BR/TR 5-11/175# d8.24 b-Billy																								
1938	Bos N	28	76	2	13	0	0	0	7	2	0	11	.171	.192	.171	1	-11	1	.881	-4	93	109	S-24/3-2	-1.3
HITCHCOCK, BILLY William Clyde B 7.31.1916 Inverness, AL BR/TR 6-1.5/185# d4.14 Mil 1943-45 M5 C7 b-Jim																								
1942	Det A	85	280	27	59	8	1	0	29	26	1	21	.211	.280	.246	45	-20	2-2	.944	-3	93	86	S-80/3	-1.9
1946	Det A	3	3	0	0	0	0	0	0	1	0	0	.000	.250	.000	-25	0	0-0	1.000	0	122	0	/2	0.0
	Was A	98	354	27	75	8	3	0	25	26	1	52	.212	.268	.251	48	-26	2-4	.966	-10	94	78	S-53,3-46	-3.6
	Year	101	357	27	75	8	3	0	25	27	1	52	.210	.268	.249	48	-26	2-4	.966	-10	94	78	S-53,3-46/2	-3.6
1947	StL A	80	275	25	61	2	2	1	28	21	0	34	.222	.277	.255	47	-20	3-0	.977	6	101	97	2-46,3-17/S-7,1-5	-1.1
1948	Bos A	49	124	15	37	3	2	1	20	7	1	9	.298	.341	.379	87	-3	0-0	.951	3	109	114	2-15,3-15	0.1
1949	Bos A	55	147	22	30	6	1	0	9	17	1	11	.204	.291	.259	43	-12	2-3	.993	-5	75	95	1-29/2-8	-1.8
1950	Phi A	115	399	35	109	22	5	1	54	45	0	32	.273	.347	.361	83	-10	3-1	.967	-0	104	105	*2-107/S	-0.4
1951	Phi A	77	222	27	68	10	4	1	36	21	2	23	.306	.371	.401	107	2	2-0	.929	5	116	161	3-45,2-23/1	0.8
1952	Phi A	119	407	45	100	8	4	1	56	39	4	45	.246	.318	.292	66	-18	1-1	.942	-1	101	109	*3-104,1-13	-2.1
1953	Det A	22	38	8	8	0	0	0	0	3	0	3	.211	.268	.211	31	-4	0-0	.929	-0	103	50	3-12/2S	-0.4
Total	9	703	2249	231	547	67	22	5	257	206	10	230	.243	.310	.299	65	-111	15-11	.938	-4	105	111	3-240,2-201,S-142/1-48	-10.4
HOAG, MYRIL Myril Oliver B 3.9.1908 Davis, CA D 7.28.1971 High Springs, FL BR/TR 5-11/180# d4.15 Mil 1943																								
1931	NY A	44	28	6	4	2	0	0	3	1	0	8	.143	.172	.214	1	-4	0-0	1.000	2	162	337	O-23(11-2-10)/3	-0.3
1932	†NY A	46	54	18	20	5	0	1	7	7	0	13	.370	.443	.519	156	5	1-1	.962	2	97	371	O-35(27-2-9)/1	0.5
1934	NY A	97	251	45	67	8	2	3	34	21	0	21	.267	.324	.351	79	-9	1-3	.974	5	112	144	O-86(29-17-50)	-0.7
1935	NY A	48	110	13	28	4	1	1	13	12	0	19	.255	.328	.336	76	-4	4-2	.986	2	120	88	O-37(2-3-32)/3	-0.3
1936	NY A	45	156	23	47	9	4	3	34	7	3	16	.301	.343	.468	102	-1	3-1	.955	-2	95	64	O-39(2-26-12)	-0.3
1937	†NY A	106	362	48	109	19	8	3	46	33	3	33	.301	.364	.423	97	-2	4-7	.955	-2	96	96	O-99(24-9-70)	-1.0
1938	†NY A	85	267	28	74	14	3	0	48	25	2	31	.277	.344	.352	75	-10	4-3	.965	-2	94	91	O-70(31-13-28)	-1.4
1939	StL A★	129	482	58	142	23	4	10	75	24	1	35	.295	.329	.421	89	-10	9-5	.971	-2	89	**153**	*O-117(11-49-60)/P	-1.5
1940	StL A	76	191	20	50	11	0	3	26	13	0	30	.262	.309	.366	73	-8	2-0	.971	-1	85	132	O-46(1-1-44)	-1.0
1941	StL A	1	1	0	0	0	0	0	0	0	0	0	.000	.000	.000	-97	0	0-0	—	0			H	0.0
	Chi A	106	380	30	97	13	3	1	44	27	1	29	.255	.306	.313	65	-20	6-10	.957	-5	94	71	O-99(75-25-0)	-3.2
	Year	107	381	30	97	13	3	1	44	27	1	29	.255	.306	.312	65	-20	6-10	.957	-5	94	71	O-99(75-25-0)	-3.2
1942	Chi A	113	412	47	99	18	2	2	37	36	0	21	.240	.301	.308	73	-15	17-8	.972	2	98	146	*O-112(41-81-0)	-1.6
1944	Chi A	17	48	5	11	1	0	0	4	10	0	1	.229	.362	.250	77	-1	1-3	.969	-0	87	173	O-14(0-13-1)	-0.2
	Cle A	67	277	33	79	9	3	1	27	25	1	23	.285	.347	.350	103	1	6-4	.947	-5	87	131	O-66(CF)	-0.6
	Year	84	325	38	90	10	3	1	31	35	1	24	.277	.349	.335	99	0	7-7	.950	-5	87	137	O-80(0-79-1)	-0.8
1945	Cle A	40	128	10	27	5	3	0	3	11	1	18	.211	.279	.297	70	-5	1-2	.987	1	96	152	O-33(0-27-6)/P-2	-0.7
Total	13	1020	3147	384	854	141	33	28	401	252	12	298	.271	.328	.364	83	-83	59-49	.965	-7	96	123	O-876(254-334-322)/P-3,3-2,1	-12.3
HOAK, DON Donald Albert "Tiger" B 2.5.1928 Roulette, PA D 10.9.1969 Pittsburgh, PA BR/TR 6/175# d4.18 C1																								
1954	Bro N	88	261	41	64	9	5	7	26	25	4	39	.245	.318	.398	83	-7	8-3	.950	3	103	100	3-75	-0.3
1955	†Bro N	94	279	50	67	13	3	5	19	46-0	1	50	.240	.350	.362	87	-4	9-5	.960	15	120	112	3-78	1.1
1956	Chi N	121	424	51	91	18	4	5	37	41-0	1	46	.215	.283	.311	61	-23	8-3	.949	-13	80	87	*3-110	-3.7
1957	Cin N★	149	529	78	155	**39**	2	19	89	74-5	4	54	.293	.381	.482	122	20	8-15	**.971**	-1	93	**105**	*3-149/2	1.5
1958	Cin N	114	417	51	109	30	0	6	50	43-4	2	36	.261	.333	.376	83	-8	6-8	.964	1	99	133	*3-112/S	-1.0
1959	Pit N	**155**	564	60	166	29	3	8	65	71-4	4	75	.294	.374	.399	108	9	9-2	.961	8	106	128	*3-155	1.8
1960	†Pit N	**155**	553	97	156	24	9	16	79	74-9	1	74	.282	.366	.445	120	17	3-2	.948	3	106	135	*3-155	2.0
1961	Pit N	145	503	72	150	27	7	12	61	73-8	3	53	.298	.388	.451	122	19	4-2	.953	-4	95	107	*3-143	1.4
1962	Pit N	121	411	63	99	14	8	5	48	49-5	1	49	.241	.320	.350	81	-11	4-2	**.969**	-1	101	92	*3-116	-1.3
1963	Phi N	115	377	35	87	11	3	6	24	27-1	1	52	.231	.282	.324	75	-13	5-5	.958	8	108	88	*3-106	-0.6
1964	Phi N	6	4	0	0	0	0	0	0	0-0	0	2	.000	.000	.000	-99	-1	0-0	—	0			H	-0.1
Total	11	1263	4322	598	1144	214	44	89	498	523-36	22	530	.265	.345	.396	98	-2	64-47	.959	19	100	111	*3-1199/S2	0.8
HOBBS, BILL William Lee "Smokey" B 5.7.1893 Grants Lick, KY D 1.5.1945 Hamilton, OH BR/TR 5-9.5/155# d8.9																								
1913	Cin N	4	4	0	0	0	0	0	0	0	0	3	.000	.000	.000	-99	-1	0	1.000	0	199	0	/23	-0.1
1916	Cin N	6	11	1	2	1	0	0	1	2	0	0	.182	.308	.273	81	0	1	.947	4	160	127	/S-6	0.4
Total	2	10	15	1	2	1	0	0	1	2	0	3	.133	.235	.200	32	-1	1	.947	4	160	127	/S-6,32	0.3
HOBLITZEL, DICK Richard Carleton "Doc" (born Richard Carleton Hoblitzell) B 10.26.1888 Waverly, WV D 11.14.1962 Parkersburg, WV BL/TL 6/172# d9.5 Mil 1918-20																								
1908	Cin N	32	114	8	29	3	2	0	8	7	2		.254	.309	.316	102	0	2	.985	2	123	79	1-32	0.1
1909	Cin N	142	517	59	159	23	11	4	67	44	2		.308	.364	.418	144	25	17	.982	-3	95	111	*1-142	2.1
1910	Cin N	155	611	85	170	24	13	4	70	47	2	32	.278	.332	.380	112	7	28	.984	-7	80	71	*1-148/2-7	-0.3
1911	Cin N	158	622	81	180	19	13	11	91	42	8	44	.289	.342	.415	116	9	32	.990	2	102	92	*1-158	0.7
1912	Cin N	148	558	73	164	32	12	2	85	48	2	28	.294	.352	.405	110	7	23	.985	2	107	90	*1-147	0.5
1913	Cin N	137	502	59	143	23	7	3	62	35	2	26	.285	.334	.376	103	1	18-12	.988	-5	82	105	*1-134	-0.7
1914	Cin N	78	248	31	52	8	7	0	26	26	1	26	.210	.287	.298	72	-9	7	.988	-4	74	107	1-75	-1.7
	Bos A	69	229	31	73	10	3	0	33	19	6	21	.319	.386	.389	133	10	12-12	.979	-5	74	80	1-68	0.1
1915	†Bos A	124	399	54	113	15	12	2	61	38	4	26	.283	.351	.396	128	12	9-14	.987	-1	95	100	*1-117	0.6
1916	†Bos A	130	417	57	108	17	1	0	39	47	3	28	.259	.338	.305	93	-2	10	.989	-1	95	102	*1-126	-0.7
1917	Bos A	120	420	49	108	19	7	1	47	46	4	22	.257	.336	.343	108	5	12	.990	-8	73	97	*1-118	-0.7
1918	Bos A	25	69	4	11	1	0	0	4	8	2	3	.159	.266	.174	33	-5	3	.996	1	118	171	1-19	-0.5
Total	11	1318	4706	591	1310	194	88	27	593	407	38	256	.278	.341	.374	111	60	173-38	.987	-28	91	96	*1-1284/2-7	-0.5

Year	Tm Lg	G	AB	R	H	2B	3B	HR	RBI	BB-IB	HP	SO	AVG	OBP	SLG	AOPS	ABR	SB-CS	FA	FR	Rng	Thr	G at Pos	BFW
HOBSON, BUTCH Clell Lavern B 8.17.1951 Tuscaloosa, AL BR/TR 6-1/193# d9.7 M3																								
1975	Bos A	2	4	0	1	0	0	0	0	0-0	0	2	.250	.250	.250	38	0	0-0	1.000	0	131	0	/3	0.0
1976	Bos A	76	269	34	63	7	5	8	34	15-1	0	62	.234	.272	.387	82	-7	0-1	.936	-6	97	87	3-76	-1.5
1977	Bos A	159	593	77	157	33	5	30	112	27-4	4	162	.265	.300	.489	100	-2	5-4	.946	-18	88	92	*3-159	-2.3
1978	Bos A	147	512	65	128	26	2	17	80	50-3	0	122	.250	.312	.408	92	-5	1-0	.899	-8	98	98	*3-133,D-14	-1.6
1979	Bos A	146	528	74	138	26	7	28	93	30-2	0	78	.261	.298	.496	105	1	3-2	.935	-16	90	64	*3-142/2	-1.8
1980	Bos A	93	324	35	74	6	0	11	39	25-2	0	69	.228	.281	.349	69	-15	1-1	.910	1	107	46	3-57,D-36	-1.6
1981	Cal A	85	268	27	63	7	4	4	36	35-0	1	60	.235	.321	.336	91	-3	1-1	.929	-6	87	92	3-83/D-2	-1.1
1982	NY A	30	58	2	10	2	0	0	3	1-0	0	14	.172	.183	.207	8	-7	0-0	.951	-1	76	78	D-15,1-11	-0.9
Total	8	738	2556	314	634	107	23	98	397	183-12	5	569	.248	.297	.423	91	-38	11-9	.926	-53	93	83	3-651/D-67,1-11,2	-10.8
HOCK, ED Edward Francis B 3.27.1899 Franklin Furnace, OH D 11.21.1963 Portsmouth, OH BL/TL 5-10.5/165# d7.8																								
1920	StL N	1	0	0	0	0	0	0	0	0	0	0	—	—	—	—	0	0-0	—	-0	0	0	/O(LF)	0.0
1923	Cin N	2	0	0	0	0	0	0	0	0	0	0	—	—	—	—	0	0-0	—	0			R	0.0
1924	Cin N	16	10	7	1	0	0	0	0	0	1	2	.100	.182	.100	-23	-2	0-0	1.000	0	178	0	/O-2(1-2-0)	-0.1
Total	3	19	10	7	1	0	0	0	0	0	1	2	.100	.182	.100	-23	-2	0-0	1.000	0	164	0	/O-3(2-2-0)	-0.1
HOCKETT, ORIS Oris Leon "Brown" B 9.29.1909 Amboy, IN D 3.23.1969 Torrance, CA BL/TR 5-9/182# d9.4																								
1938	Bro N	21	70	8	23	5	1	1	8	4	0	9	.329	.365	.471	126	2	0	.893	-2	75	91	O-17(4-13-0)	0.0
1939	Bro N	9	13	3	3	0	0	0	1	1	0	1	.231	.286	.231	39	-1	0	1.000	1	41	1401	/O(LF)	-0.1
1941	Cle A	2	6	0	2	0	0	0	1	2	0	0	.333	.500	.333	131	1	0-0	1.000	-0	56	0	/O-2(CF)	0.0
1942	Cle A	148	601	85	150	22	7	7	48	45	3	45	.250	.305	.344	88	-13	12-12	.980	-3	94	109	*O-145(0-2-144)	-2.6
1943	Cle A	141	601	70	166	33	4	2	51	45	4	45	.276	.331	.354	107	4	13-18	.960	-4	95	113	*O-139(35-81-26)	-1.0
1944	Cle A☆	124	457	47	132	29	5	1	50	35	0	27	.289	.339	.381	110	5	8-9	.986	-6	96	58	*O-110(45-65-1)	-0.7
1945	Chi A	106	417	46	122	23	4	2	55	27	3	30	.293	.340	.381	112	6	10-9	.982	-2	98	79	*O-106(CF)	-0.1
Total	7	551	2165	259	598	112	21	13	214	159	10	157	.276	.329	.365	103	4	43-48	.974	-16	95	96	O-520(85-269-171)	-4.5
HOCKING, DENNY Dennis Lee B 4.2.1970 Torrance, CA BB/TR 5-10/176# d9.10 OF Total (65-LF 43-CF 97-RF)																								
1993	Min A	15	36	7	5	1	0	0	0	6-0	0	8	.139	.262	.167	18	-4	1-0	.971	-1	79	169	S-12/2	-0.4
1994	Min A	11	31	3	10	3	0	0	2	0-0	0	4	.323	.323	.419	89	0	2-0	1.000	-1	100	116	S-10	0.0
1995	Min A	9	25	4	5	0	2	0	3	2-1	0	2	.200	.259	.360	59	-2	1-0	.971	1	110	116	/S-6	0.0
1996	Min A	49	127	16	25	6	0	1	10	8-0	0	24	.197	.243	.268	29	-14	3-3	.985	1	99	183	O-33(RF)/S-6,2-2,1D	-1.4
1997	Min A	115	253	28	65	12	4	2	25	18-0	1	51	.257	.308	.360	73	-11	3-5	.975	5	99	130	S-44,3-39,O-20(7-2-12),2-15/1D	-0.4
1998	Min A	110	198	32	40	6	1	3	15	16-1	0	44	.202	.259	.288	42	-18	2-1	1.000	-6	99	88	2-47,S-28,O-24(17-1-7),3-11/1-2,D-2	-2.1
1999	Min A	136	386	47	103	18	2	7	41	22-1	3	54	.267	.307	.378	72	-17	11-7	.987	-9	84	87	S-61,2-56,O-38(17-11-13)/3-6,1-2	-2.0
2000	Min A	134	373	52	111	24	4	4	47	48-1	2	77	.298	.373	.416	97	0	7-5	1.000	-4	97	261	O-51(16-21-19),2-47,3-16,S-15,1-12/D	-0.3
2001	Min A	112	327	34	82	16	2	3	25	29-1	2	67	.251	.315	.339	71	-14	6-1	.983	-3	93	105	S-47,2-17,O-16(6-5-5),1-11/3-6,D-9	-1.2
2002	†Min A	102	260	28	65	13	0	2	25	24-0	1	44	.250	.310	.323	70	-11	0-2	.963	-15	91	82	2-56,S-25,3-16/1-6,O-5(0-1-4)	-2.3
2003	†Min A	83	188	22	45	10	2	3	22	15-0	0	37	.239	.291	.362	72	-8	0-1	1.000	-1	80	93	2-25,3-24,S-17,1-10/O-8(2-2-4),D-2	-0.7
Total	11	876	2204	273	556	109	17	25	215	188-5	7	412	.252	.310	.351	70	-99	36-25	.980	-32	90	100	S-271,2-266,O-195R,3-118/1-45,D	-10.8
HODAPP, JOHNNY Urban John B 9.26.1905 Cincinnati, OH D 6.14.1980 Cincinnati, OH BR/TR 6/185# d8.19																								
1925	Cle A	37	130	12	31	5	1	0	14	11	0	7	.238	.298	.292	50	-10	2-3	.960	2	109	98	3-37	-0.6
1926	Cle A	3	5	0	1	0	0	0	0	0	0	1	.200	.200	.200	5	-1	0-0	.750	-1	73	0	/3-3	-0.1
1927	Cle A	79	240	25	73	15	3	5	40	14	0	23	.304	.343	.454	105	1	2-2	.935	1	108	120	3-67/1-4	0.4
1928	Cle A	116	449	51	145	31	6	2	73	20	0	20	.323	.352	.432	104	2	2-1	.944	2	109	102	*3-101,1-13	0.9
1929	Cle A	90	294	30	96	12	7	4	51	15	1	14	.327	.361	.456	105	1	3-3	.977	8	115	68	2-72	1.0
1930	Cle A	**154**	635	111	**225**	**51**	8	9	121	32	1	29	.354	.386	.502	119	18	6-5	.970	10	106	97	*2-154	2.9
1931	Cle A	122	468	71	138	19	4	2	56	27	2	23	.295	.336	.365	80	-14	1-5	.969	15	110	95	*2-121	0.6
1932	Cle A	7	16	2	2	1	0	0	0	0	0	2	.125	.125	.188	-19	-3	0-0	1.000	-1	97	0	/2-7	-0.3
	Chi A	68	176	21	40	8	0	3	20	11	0	3	.227	.273	.324	58	-12	1-0	.967	-5	94	0	O-31(29-0-2)/2-5,3-4	-1.6
	Year	75	192	23	42	9	0	3	20	11	0	5	.219	.261	.313	51	-15	1-0	.967	-6	94	0	O-31(29-0-2),2-12/3-4	-1.9
1933	Bos A	115	413	55	129	27	5	3	54	33	1	14	.312	.365	.424	109	6	1-1	.960	-0	99	100	*2-101,1-10	1.1
Total	9	791	2826	378	880	169	34	28	429	163	5	136	.311	.350	.425	98	-12	18-20	.967	32	106	92	2-460,3-212/O-31(29-0-2),1-27	4.3
HODERLEIN, MEL Melvin Anthony B 6.26.1923 Mt.Carmel, OH D 5.21.2001 Mt.Carmel, OH BB/TR 5-10/185# d8.16																								
1951	Bos A	9	14	1	5	1	1	0	1	6	0	2	.357	.550	.571	185	2	0-1	1.000	0	87	217	/2-3,3-3	0.2
1952	Was A	72	208	16	56	8	2	0	17	18	2	22	.269	.333	.327	87	-4	2-0	.978	-6	97	100	2-58	-0.7
1953	Was A	23	47	5	9	0	0	0	5	6	0	9	.191	.283	.191	31	-5	0-0	.953	-2	96	97	2-11/S-2	-0.5
1954	Was A	14	25	0	4	1	0	0	1	1	0	4	.160	.192	.200	8	-3	0-0	.939	0	106	123	/S-6,2-5	-0.3
Total	4	118	294	22	74	10	3	0	24	31	2	37	.252	.327	.306	78	-10	2-1	.973	-8	97	103	/2-77,S-8,3-3	-1.3
HODES, CHARLIE Charles B 1848 New York, NY D 2.14.1875 Brooklyn, NY TR 5-11.5/175# d5.8 OF Total (20-CF 6-RF)																								
1871	Chi NA	**28**	130	32	36	4	1	2	25	7		0	.277	.314	.369	86	-4	3-0	.796	3			*C-20,3-10/O-4(0-3-1),S	0.0
1872	Tro NA	13	62	17	15	3	0	0	10	1		0	.242	.254	.290	66	-2	0-0	.759	-0	108	0	/S-5,O-4(CF),C-3,3	-0.2
1874	Atl NA	21	81	8	12	3	0	0	7	0		2	.148	.148	.185	7	-7	0-0	.825	-4	40	0	O-18(0-13-5)/C-3,2-3,1	-0.9
Total	3 NA	62	273	57	63	10	1	2	42	8		2	.231	.253	.297	63	-13	3-0	.000	-2			/O-26C,C-26,3-11,S-6,2-3,1	-1.1
HODGE, GOMER Harold Morris B 4.3.1944 Rutherfordton, NC BB/TR 6-2/185# d4.6																								
1971	Cle A	80	83	3	17	3	0	1	9	4-1	2	19	.205	.256	.277	47	-6	0-0	1.000	-1	63	132	/1-3,3-3,2-2	-0.7
HODGES, BERT Edward Burton B 5.25.1917 Knoxville, TN D 1.8.2001 Knoxville, TN BL/TR 5-11/170# d4.14																								
1942	Phi N	8	11	0	2	0	0	0	0	1	0	0	.182	.250	.182	29	-1	0	1.000	-0	91	0	/3-2	-0.1
HODGES, GIL Gilbert Raymond (born B 4.4.1924 Princeton, IN D 4.2.1972 West Palm Beach, FL BR/TR 6-1.5/200# d10.3 Mil 1944-45 M9 OF Total (53-LF 1-CF 25-RF)																								
1943	Bro N	1	2	0	0	0	0	0	0	1	0	2	.000	.333	.000	0	0	1	.600	-0	82	438	/3	-0.1
1947	†Bro N	28	77	9	12	3	1	1	7	14	0	19	.156	.286	.260	44	-6	0	.958	-1	*97*	*153*	C-24	-0.6
1948	Bro N	134	481	48	120	18	5	11	70	43	0	61	.249	.311	.376	82	-13	7	.986	-2	92	114	1-96,C-38	-1.6
1949	†Bro N★	**156**	596	94	170	23	4	23	115	66	4	64	.285	.360	.453	112	10	10	**.995**	-4	82	**114**	*1-156	0.0
1950	Bro N☆	153	561	98	159	26	2	32	113	73	1	73	.283	.367	.508	125	20	6	**.994**	-1	92	**114**	*1-153	1.4
1951	Bro N★	**158**	582	118	156	25	3	40	103	93	5	99	.268	.374	.527	137	31	9-7	.992	7	**111**	**120**	*1-158	3.2
1952	†Bro N☆	153	508	87	129	27	1	32	102	107	2	90	.254	.386	.500	142	33	2-4	.992	4	106	114	*1-153	3.1
1953	†Bro N★	141	520	101	157	22	7	31	122	75	3	84	.302	.393	.550	139	31	1-4	.993	7	115	108	*1-127,O-24(18-0-6)	2.7
1954	Bro N★	**154**	579	106	176	23	5	42	130	74	1	84	.304	.373	.579	142	35	3-3	.995	7	109	94	*1-154	3.1
1955	†Bro N★	150	546	75	158	24	5	27	102	80-3	3	91	.289	.377	.500	128	24	2-1	.991	2	106	112	*1-139,O-16(9-1-6)	1.8
1956	†Bro N	153	550	86	146	29	4	32	87	76-10	0	91	.265	.354	.507	119	16	3-3	.992	0	104	112	*1-138,O-30(22-0-8)/C	0.7
1957	Bro N★	150	579	94	173	28	7	27	98	63-6	2	91	.299	.366	.511	122	19	5-3	.990	3	103	99	*1-150/3-2,2	1.3
1958	LA N	141	475	68	123	15	1	22	64	52-3	0	87	.259	.330	.434	98	-2	8-2	.992	3	100	**130**	*1-122,3-15/O-9(4-0-5),C	-0.4
1959	†LA N	124	413	57	114	19	2	25	80	58-6	3	92	.276	.367	.513	123	14	3-2	**.992**	0	91	88	*1-113/3-4	0.9
1960	LA N	101	197	22	39	8	1	8	30	26-1	1	37	.198	.291	.371	76	-7	0-1	.995	1	100	114	1-92,3-10	-0.9
1961	LA N	109	215	25	52	4	0	8	31	24-1	0	43	.242	.313	.372	76	-8	3-1	.998	1	91	88	*1-100	-1.0
1962	NY N	54	127	15	32	1	0	9	17	15-1	0	27	.252	.331	.472	111	2	0-0	.986	3	138	73	1-47	0.2
1963	NY N	11	22	2	5	0	0	0	3	3-0	0	2	.227	.320	.227	60	-1	0-0	1.000	2	188	131	1-10	0.0
Total	18	2071	7030	1105	1921	295	48	370	1274	943-31	25	1137	.273	.359	.487	119	198	63-31	.992	32	102	109	*1-1908/O-79L,C-64,3-32,2	13.8
HODGES, RON Ronald Wray B 6.22.1949 Rocky Mount, VA BL/TR 6-1/185# d6.13																								
1973	†NY N	45	127	5	33	2	0	1	18	11-2	0	19	.260	.314	.299	73	-5	0-1	.992	2	156	86	C-40	-0.1
1974	NY N	59	136	16	30	4	0	4	14	19-3	0	11	.221	.310	.338	84	-3	0-0	.953	-7	81	63	C-44	-0.8
1975	NY N	9	34	3	7	1	0	2	4	1-0	0	6	.206	.229	.412	79	-1	0-0	1.000	-1	79	137	/C-9	-0.2
1976	NY N	56	155	21	35	6	0	4	24	27-2	0	16	.226	.339	.342	100	1	2-0	.976	-8	119	72	C-52	-0.5
1977	NY N	66	117	6	31	4	0	1	5	9-1	0	17	.265	.317	.325	76	-4	0-2	.992	-2	82	122	C-27	-0.6
1978	NY N	47	102	4	26	4	1	0	7	10-0	1	11	.255	.322	.314	83	-2	1-2	.982	3	82	152	C-30	0.1
1979	NY N	59	86	4	14	4	0	0	5	19-3	0	16	.163	.311	.209	47	-5	0-0	.980	-0	99	137	C-22	-0.5
1980	NY N	36	42	4	10	2	0	0	5	10-1	0	13	.238	.377	.286	92	0	1-1	.982	2	88	196	/C-9	0.3
1981	NY N	35	43	5	13	2	0	1	6	5-2	0	8	.302	.375	.419	127	2	1-0	1.000	-2	56	102	/C-7	0.1
1982	NY N	80	228	26	56	12	1	5	27	41-6	0	40	.246	.358	.373	106	4	4-3	.980	0	96	100	C-74	0.7

Year	Tm Lg	G	AB	R	H	2B	3B	HR	RBI	BB-IB	HP	SO	AVG	OBP	SLG	AOPS	ABR	SB-CS	FA	FR	Rng	Thr	G at Pos	BFW
1983	NY N	110	250	20	65	12	0	0	21	49-6	2	42	.260	.383	.308	95	2	0-3	.971	-9	86	93	C-96	-0.4
1984	NY N	64	106	5	22	3	0	1	11	23-0	1	18	.208	.351	.264	77	-2	1-1	.979	-1	81	97	C-35	-0.2
Total	12	666	1426	119	342	56	2	19	147	224-26	4	217	.240	.342	.322	88	-13	10-13	.978	-22	97	99	C-445	-2.1
HODGIN, RALPH Elmer Ralph B 2.10.1916 Greensboro, NC BL/TR 5-10/170# d4.19 Mil 1945																								
1939	Bos N	32	48	4	10	1	0	0	4	3	0	4	.208	.255	.229	33	-5	0	1.000	-0	108	0	/O-9(2-0-7)	-0.5
1943	Chi A	117	407	52	128	22	8	1	50	20	6	24	.314	.356	.415	125	11	3-5	.945	-2	111	70	3-56,O-42(17-0-25)	0.7
1944	Chi A	121	465	56	137	25	7	1	51	21	6	14	.295	.333	.385	106	2	3-1	.942	7	112	143	3-82,O-33(LF)	0.9
1946	Chi A	87	258	32	65	10	1	0	25	19	2	6	.252	.308	.298	73	-10	0-1	.983	-2	93	73	O-57(49-0-8)	-1.7
1947	Chi A	59	180	26	53	10	3	1	24	13	3	4	.294	.352	.400	113	3	1-0	.990	0	103	66	O-41(40-0-1)	0.0
1948	Chi A	114	331	28	88	11	5	1	34	21	0	11	.266	.310	.338	75	-14	0-3	.970	3	102	146	O-79(39-2-40)	-1.6
Total	6	530	1689	198	481	79	24	4	188	97	17	63	.285	.330	.367	98	-13	7-10	.985	6	102	86	O-261(180-2-81),3-138	-2.2
HODGSON, PAUL Paul Joseph Denis B 4.14.1960 Montreal, PQ, CAN BR/TR 6-2/190# d8.31																								
1980	Tor A	20	41	5	9	0	1	1	5	3-0	0	12	.220	.273	.341	64	-2	0-1	1.000	-1	80	126	O-11(10-1-0)/D-3	-0.4
HOELSKOETTER, ART Arthur "Holley" or "Hoss" (a/k/a Arthur H. Hostetter) B 9.30.1882 St.Louis, MO D 8.3.1954 St.Louis, MO BR/TR 6-2/?# d9.10 I OF Total (1-LF 7-CF 13-RF)																								
1905	StL N	24	83	7	20	2	1	0	5	3	0		.241	.267	.289	68	-4	1	.972	1	108	128	3-20/2-3,P	-0.2
1906	StL N	94	317	21	71	6	3	0	14	4	2		.224	.238	.262	58	-17	2	.943	-0	110	113	3-53,S-16,P-12,O-12(1-1-11)/2	-1.6
1907	StL N	119	397	21	98	6	3	2	28	27	2		.247	.298	.292	88	-6	5	.927	2	109	96	2-73,1-27/C-8,O-8(0-6-2),P-2,3-2	-0.4
1908	StL N	62	155	10	36	7	1	0	6	6	1		.232	.265	.290	81	-4	1	.948	-6	67	112	C-41/3-2,12	-0.6
Total	4	299	952	59	225	21	8	2	53	40	5		.236	.271	.282	75	-31	9	.924	-2	106	94	/2-78,3-77,C-49,1-28,O-20R,S-16,P	-2.8
HOEY, JACK John Bernard B 11.10.1881 Watertown, MA D 11.14.1947 Waterbury, CT BL/TL 5-9/185# d6.27																								
1906	Bos A	94	361	27	88	8	4	0	24	14	1		.244	.274	.288	76	-11	10	.915	-7	59	0	O-94(LF)	-2.6
1907	Bos A	39	96	7	21	2	1	0	8	1	0		.219	.227	.260	56	-5	2	.857	-4	0	0	O-21(17-4-0)	-1.1
1908	Bos A	13	43	5	7	0	0	0	3	0	0		.163	.163	.163	6	-5	1	1.000	1	189	0	O-11(RF)	-0.5
Total	3	146	500	39	116	10	5	0	35	15	1		.232	.256	.272	66	-21	13	.913	-10	60	0	O-126(111-4-11)	-4.2
HOFFERTH, STEW Stewart Edward B 1.27.1913 Logansport, IN D 3.7.1994 Valparaiso, IN BR/TR 6-2/195# d4.19																								
1944	Bos N	66	180	14	36	8	0	1	26	11	0	5	.200	.246	.261	41	-14	0	.984	-1	63	112	C-47	-1.3
1945	Bos N	50	170	13	40	2	0	3	15	14	1	11	.235	.297	.300	66	-8	1	.980	4	102	140	C-45	-0.1
1946	Bos N	20	58	3	12	1	1	0	10	3	0	6	.207	.246	.259	43	-5	0	1.000	-1	78	48	C-15	-0.6
Total	3	136	408	30	88	11	1	4	51	28	1	22	.216	.268	.277	52	-27	1	.985	2	82	115	C-107	-2.0
HOFFMAN, DUTCH Clarence Casper "Red" B 1.28.1904 Freeburg, IL D 12.6.1962 Belleville, IL BR/TR 6/175# d4.23																								
1929	Chi A	107	337	27	87	16	5	3	37	24	0	28	.258	.307	.362	73	-15	6-3	.984	-0	106	45	O-88(2-74-12)	-1.8
HOFFMAN, DANNY Daniel John B 3.2.1880 Canton, CT D 3.14.1922 Manchester, CT BL/TL 5-9/175# d4.20																								
1903	Phi A	74	248	29	61	5	7	2	22	6	1		.246	.267	.347	79	-7	7	.950	-0	57	0	O-62(43-0-19)/P	-1.2
1904	Phi A	53	204	31	61	7	5	3	24	5	4		.299	.329	.426	131	6	9	.936	-0	87	70	O-51(14-14-23)	0.4
1905	†Phi A	120	459	66	120	10	10	1	35	33	1		.261	.312	.333	103	0	**46**	.942	-3	93	141	*O-118(14-102-2)	-1.0
1906	Phi A	7	22	4	5	0	0	0	0	3	0		.227	.320	.227	70	-1	1	1.000	1	240	0	O-7(CF)	0.0
	NY A	100	320	34	82	10	6	0	23	27	2		.256	.318	.325	92	-3	32	.938	-3	67	46	O-98(CF)	-1.1
	Year	107	342	38	87	10	6	0	23	30	2		.254	.318	.319	91	-3	33	.943	-3	80	43	*O-105(CF)	-1.1
1907	NY A	136	517	81	131	10	3	5	46	42	13		.253	.325	.313	96	-1	30	.953	4	116	90	*O-135(CF)	-0.4
1908	StL A	99	363	41	91	9	7	1	25	23	5		.251	.304	.322	103	1	17	.962	9	168	270	O-99(6-46-47)	0.6
1909	StL A	110	387	44	104	6	7	2	26	41	7		.269	.349	.336	125	12	24	.968	1	75	194	*O-110(0-109-1)	1.0
1910	StL A	106	380	20	90	11	5	0	27	34	4		.237	.306	.292	93	-3	16	.960	-2	97	92	*O-106(0-102-4)	-1.1
1911	StL A	24	81	11	17	3	2	0	7	12	2		.210	.326	.296	77	-2	3	.908	2	113	145	O-23(CF)	-0.2
Total	9	829	2981	361	762	71	52	14	235	226	39		.256	.316	.328	101	2	185	.951	8	100	122	O-809(77-636-96)/P	-3.0
HOFFMAN, TEX Edward Adolph B 11.30.1893 San Antonio, TX D 5.19.1947 New Orleans, LA BL/TR 5-9/195# d7.11																								
1915	Cle A	9	13	1	2	0	0	0	2	1	0	5	.154	.214	.154	10	-1	0	.750	-1	59	0	/3-3	-0.3
HOFFMAN, GLENN Glenn Edward B 7.7.1958 Orange, CA BR/TR 6-2/190# d4.12 M1 C4 b-Trevor																								
1980	Bos A	114	312	37	89	15	4	4	42	19-2	2	41	.285	.326	.397	94	-3	2-4	.946	-3	103	85	*3-110/S-5,2-2	-0.8
1981	Bos A	78	242	28	56	10	0	1	20	12-0	1	25	.231	.271	.285	57	-13	0-1	.960	3	102	108	S-78/3	-0.4
1982	Bos A	150	469	53	98	23	2	7	49	30-5	5	69	.209	.262	.311	54	-30	0-4	.972	16	104	112	*S-150	-0.1
1983	Bos A	143	473	56	123	24	1	4	41	30-1	2	76	.260	.306	.340	73	-17	1-1	.962	-6	96	93	*S-143	-0.9
1984	Bos A	64	74	8	14	4	0	0	4	5-0	0	10	.189	.241	.243	33	-7	0-1	.957	-3	88	99	S-56/3-4,2-2	-0.8
1985	Bos A	96	279	40	77	17	2	6	34	25-0	5	40	.276	.343	.416	103	2	2-2	.975	5	99	115	S-93/2-3,3-3	1.4
1986	Bos A	12	23	1	5	2	0	0	1	2-0	0	3	.217	.269	.304	59	-1	0-0	.923	-3	53	72	S-11/3	-0.3
1987	Bos A	21	55	5	11	3	0	0	6	3-0	2	9	.200	.267	.255	38	-5	0-0	.984	2	122	103	S-16/3-3,2-2	-0.1
	LA N	40	132	10	29	5	0	0	10	7-1	2	23	.220	.270	.258	42	-11	0-1	.966	-1	90	87	S-40	-0.9
1989	Cal A	48	104	9	22	3	0	1	3	3-0	1	13	.212	.241	.269	44	-8	0-2	.982	-1	92	101	S-23,3-18/2-4,1D	-0.8
Total	9	766	2163	247	524	106	9	23	210	136-9	20	309	.242	.291	.331	68	-93	5-16	.966	9	99	103	S-615,3-140/2-13,D1	-3.7
HOFFMAN, IZZY Harry C. B 1.5.1875 Bridgeport, NJ D 11.13.1942 Philadelphia, PA BL/TL 5-9/160# d4.14																								
1904	Was A	10	30	1	3	1	0	0	1	2	0		.100	.156	.133	-8	-4	0	1.000	1	110	365	/O-9(CF)	-0.4
1907	Bos N	19	86	17	24	3	1	0	3	6	0		.279	.326	.337	108	1	2	.897	-2	143	133	O-19(3-1-16)	-0.2
Total	2	29	116	18	27	4	1	0	4	8	0		.233	.282	.284	79	-3	2	.939	-1	133	201	/O-28(3-10-16)	-0.6
HOFFMAN, JOHN John Edward "Pork Chop" B 10.31.1943 Aberdeen, SD D 12.27.2001 Seattle, WA BL/TR 6/190# d7.30																								
1964	Hou N	6	15	1	1	0	0	0	0	1-0	0	7	.067	.125	.067	-47	-3	0-0	1.000	-1	70	0	/C-5	-0.4
1965	Hou N	2	6	1	2	0	0	0	1	0-0	0	3	.333	.333	.333	95	0	0-0	1.000	-1	59	0	/C-2	-0.1
Total	2	8	21	2	3	0	0	0	1	1-0	0	10	.143	.182	.143	-8	-3	0-0	1.000	-2	67	0	/C-7	-0.5
HOFFMAN, LARRY Lawrence Charles B 7.18.1878 Chicago, IL D 12.29.1948 Chicago, IL BR/TR d7.4																								
1901	Chi N	6	22	2	7	1	0	0	6	0	1		.318	.348	.364	110	0	1	.800	-1	75	0	/3-5,2	-0.1
HOFFMAN, HICKEY Otto Charles B 10.27.1856 Cleveland, OH D 10.27.1915 Peoria, IL d5.10																								
1879	Cle N	2	6	0	0	0	0	0	0	0		3	.000	.000	.000	-99	-1		.857	0			/C-2,O(RF)	-0.1
HOFFMAN, RAY Raymond Lamont B 6.14.1917 Detroit, MI BL/TR 6-0.5/175# d8.30																								
1942	Was A	7	19	2	1	0	0	0	2	1	0	1	.053	.100	.053	-57	-4	0-0	.815	1	135	0	/3-6	-0.4
HOFFMEISTER, JESSE Jesse H. B Toledo, OH TR d7.24																								
1897	Pit N	48	188	33	58	6	9	3	36	8	0		.309	.337	.484	120	3	6	.792	-10	82	129	3-48	-0.5
HOFMAN, SOLLY Arthur Frederick "Circus Solly" B 10.29.1882 St.Louis, MO D 3.10.1956 St.Louis, MO BR/TR 6/160# d7.28 OF Total (77-LF 557-CF 79-RF)																								
1903	Pit N	3	2	1	0	0	0	0	0	0	0		.000	.000	.000	-97	-1	0	—	-0	0	0	/O-2(1-1-0)	-0.1
1904	Chi N	7	26	7	7	0	0	1	4	1	0		.269	.296	.385	110	0	2	1.000	0	296	560	/O-6(1-3-2),S	0.0
1905	Chi N	86	287	43	68	14	4	1	38	20	1		.237	.289	.324	79	-8	15	.955	2	99	81	2-59/1-9,S-9,3-3,O-3(0-2-1)	-0.6
1906	†Chi N	64	195	30	50	2	3	2	20	20	0		.256	.326	.328	98	-1	13	.976	-1	84	205	O-23(1-17-6),1-21/S-9,2-4,3-4	-0.2
1907	Chi N	134	470	67	126	11	3	1	36	41	1		.268	.328	.311	94	-3	29	.938	-3	126	170	O-69(12-23-35),S-42,1-18/3-4,2-3	-0.9
1908	†Chi N	120	411	55	100	15	5	2	42	33	6		.243	.309	.319	96	-1	15	.955	-3	128	65	O-50(0-50-2),1-37,2-22/3-9	-0.9
1909	Chi N	153	527	60	150	21	4	2	58	53	1		.285	.351	.351	115	10	20	.965	-2	71	115	*O-153(0-143-11)	0.1
1910	†Chi N	136	477	83	155	24	16	3	86	65	0	34	.325	.406	.461	154	33	29	.975	-0	97	124	*O-110(0-110-1),1-24/3	2.8
1911	Chi N	143	512	66	129	17	2	2	70	66	3	40	.252	.341	.305	81	-11	30	.968	-11	89	67	*O-107(2-107-0),1-36	-3.0
1912	Chi N	36	125	28	34	11	0	0	18	22	1	13	.272	.385	.360	105	2	5	.987	2	99	158	O-27(CF)/1-9	0.2
	Pit N	17	53	7	15	4	1	0	2	5	0	6	.283	.345	.396	104	0	0	1.000	2	113	133	O-15(CF)	0.1
	Year	53	178	35	49	15	1	0	20	27	1	19	.275	.374	.371	105	3	5	.991	3	104	150	O-42(CF)/1-9	0.3
1913	Pit N	28	83	11	19	5	2	0	7	8	0	6	.229	.297	.337	84	-2	3-3	.964	0	101	101	O-24(0-23-2)	-0.3
1914	Bro F	147	515	65	148	25	12	5	83	54	2	41	.287	.357	.412	110	-1	34	.951	-1	96	92	*2-108,1-22,O-21(10-10-1)/S	-0.2
1915	Buf F	109	346	29	81	10	6	0	27	30	0	28	.234	.295	.298	66	-21	12	.961	3	91	157	O-82(46-20-18),1-11/3-4,2-2,S	-2.5
1916	NY A	6	27	0	8	1	1	0	2	1	0	1	.296	.321	.407	116	0	1	1.000	1	107	206	/O-6(CF)	0.1
	Chi N	5	16	2	5	2	1	0	2	2	0	2	.313	.389	.563	172	1	0	1.000	0	89	234	/O-4(LF)	0.2
Total	14	1194	4072	554	1095	162	60	19	495	421	15	171	.269	.340	.352	102	-3	208-3	.967	-10	98	128	O-702C,2-198,1-187/S-63,3-25	-5.2

Year	Tm Lg	G	AB	R	H	2B	3B	HR	RBI	BB-IB	HP	SO	AVG	OBP	SLG	AOPS	ABR	SB-CS	FA	FR	Rng	Thr	G at Pos	BFW
HOFMAN, BOBBY Robert George B 10.5.1925 St.Louis, MO D 4.5.1994 Chesterfield, MO BR/TR 5-11/175# d4.19 C10																								
1949	NY N	19	48	4	10	0	0	0	3	5	1	6	.208	.296	.208	38	-4	0	.939	0	119	103	2-16	-0.3
1952	NY N	32	63	11	18	2	2	2	4	8	1	10	.286	.375	.476	134	3	0-0	.964	-0	104	93	2-21/3-2,1	0.4
1953	NY N	74	169	21	45	7	2	12	34	12	0	23	.266	.315	.544	117	3	1-1	.918	0	98	117	3-23,2-17	0.4
1954	NY N	71	125	12	28	5	0	8	30	17	1	15	.224	.317	.456	99	0	0-0	.994	-5	51	140	1-21,2-10/3-8	-0.5
1955	NY N	96	207	32	55	7	2	10	28	22-2	1	31	.266	.336	.464	110	3	0-2	1.000	-3	69	101	1-24,C-19,2-19/3-5	-0.1
1956	NY N	47	56	1	10	1	0	0	2	6-0	1	8	.179	.270	.196	28	-6	0-0	1.000	0	135	0	/C-7,3-7,1-3,2-2	-0.5
1957	NY N	2	2	0	0	0	0	0	0	0-0	0	1	.000	.000	.000	-99	-1	0-0	—	0			H	-0.1
Total	7	341	670	81	166	22	6	32	101	70-2	5	94	.248	.322	.442	100	-2	1-3	.969	-7	104	93	/2-85,1-49,3-45,C-26	-0.7
HOFMANN, FRED Fred "Bootnose" B 6.10.1894 St.Louis, MO D 11.19.1964 St.Helena, CA BR/TR 5-11.5/175# d9.26 C13																								
1919	NY A	1	1	0	0	0	0	0	0	0	0	0	.000	.000	.000	-99	0	0	1.000	0	0	446	/C	0.0
1920	NY A	15	24	3	7	0	0	0	1	1	1	2	.292	.346	.292	68	-1	0-0	.905	-2	84	33	C-14	-0.3
1921	NY A	23	62	7	11	1	1	1	5	5	1	13	.177	.250	.274	33	-7	0-0	.952	-1	110	81	C-18/1	-0.6
1922	NY A	37	91	13	27	5	3	2	10	9	0	12	.297	.360	.484	116	2	0-0	.962	-2	133	60	C-29	0.1
1923	†NY A	72	238	24	69	10	4	3	26	18	4	27	.290	.350	.403	96	-2	2-1	.979	-3	124	55	C-70	0.0
1924	NY A	62	166	17	29	6	1	1	11	12	2	15	.175	.239	.241	24	-20	2-1	.991	2	111	112	C-54	-1.4
1925	NY A	3	2	0	0	0	0	0	0	0	0	0	.000	.000	.000	-99	-1	0-0	1.000	0	0	930	/C	-0.1
1927	Bos A	87	217	20	59	19	1	0	24	21	2	26	.272	.342	.369	86	-4	2-0	.943	-10	66	77	C-81	-0.8
1928	Bos A	78	199	14	45	8	1	0	16	11	1	25	.226	.270	.276	45	-16	0-1	.982	-1	82	135	C-71	-1.3
Total	9	378	1000	98	247	49	11	7	93	77	11	120	.247	.308	.339	68	-49	6-3	.969	-16	98	89	C-339/1	-4.4
HOGAN, HARRY Harry S. B 11.1.1875 Syracuse, NY D 1.24.1934 Syracuse, NY d8.13																								
1901	Cle A	1	4	0	0	0	0	0	0	0	0		.000	.000	.000	-99	-1	0	—	-0	0	0	/O(RF)	-0.1
HOGAN, SHANTY James Francis B 3.21.1906 Somerville, MA D 4.7.1967 Boston, MA BR/TR 6-1/240# d6.23																								
1925	Bos N	9	21	2	6	1	1	0	3	1	0	3	.286	.318	.429	97	0	0-0	1.000	-0	98	0	/O-5(2-0-3)	-0.1
1926	Bos N	4	14	1	4	1	1	0	5	0	0	0	.286	.286	.500	119	0	0	.852	-1	76	113	/C-4	0.0
1927	Bos N	71	229	24	66	17	1	3	32	9	3	23	.288	.324	.410	104	1	2	.985	1	99	128	C-61	0.6
1928	NY N	131	411	48	137	25	2	10	71	42	8	25	.333	.406	.477	129	19	0	.978	-3	140	56	*C-124	2.3
1929	NY N	102	317	19	95	13	0	5	45	25	6	22	.300	.362	.388	86	-6	1	.979	1	**139**	52	C-93	0.0
1930	NY N	122	389	60	132	26	2	13	75	21	3	24	.339	.378	.517	116	10	2	.982	-2	103	89	C-96	1.3
1931	NY N	123	396	42	119	17	1	12	65	29	4	29	.301	.354	.439	115	8	1	**.996**	5	**144**	88	*C-113	1.9
1932	NY N	140	502	36	144	18	2	8	77	26	1	22	.287	.323	.378	90	-8	0	.983	-5	98	93	*C-136	-0.5
1933	Bos N	96	328	15	83	7	0	3	30	13	3	9	.253	.288	.302	75	-12	0	**.997**	2	**188**	89	C-95	-0.4
1934	Bos N	92	279	20	73	5	2	4	34	16	6	13	.262	.316	.337	81	-8	0	.986	-1	111	125	C-90	-0.4
1935	Bos N	59	163	9	49	8	0	2	25	21	4	8	.301	.394	.387	120	6	0	.990	-5	88	79	C-56	0.5
1936	Was A	19	65	8	21	4	0	1	7	11	0	2	.323	.421	.431	117	2	0-1	.989	1	91	81	C-19	0.4
1937	Was A	21	66	4	10	4	0	0	5	6	0	8	.152	.222	.212	10	-9	0-1	.979	1	97	170	C-21	-0.7
Total	13	989	3180	288	939	146	12	61	474	220	38	188	.295	.348	.406	101	3	6-2	.985	-6	124	89	C-908/O-5(2-0-3)	4.9
HOGAN, KENNY Kenneth Sylvester B 10.9.1902 Cleveland, OH D 1.2.1980 Cleveland, OH BL/TR 5-9/145# d10.2																								
1921	Cin N	1	2	0	0	0	0	0	0	0	0	1	.000	.000	.000	-99	-1	0-0	—	-0	0	0	/O(CF)	-0.1
1923	Cle A	1	0	0	0	0	0	0	0	0	0	0	—	—	—	—	0	0-0	—	0			R	0.0
1924	Cle A	2	1	0	0	0	0	0	0	0	0	0	.000	.000	.000	-99	0	0-0	—	0			H	0.0
Total	3	4	3	0	0	0	0	0	0	0	0	1	.000	.000	.000	-99	-1	0-0	.000	-0	0	0	/O(CF)	-0.1
HOGAN, MARTY Martin F. B 10.25.1869 Wensbury, England D 8.15.1923 Youngstown, OH BR/TR 5-8/145# d8.6																								
1894	Cin N	6	23	4	3	0	0	0	3	1	0	4	.130	.167	.130	-27	-5	2	.846	-0	109	0	/O-6(RF)	-0.4
	StL N	29	100	11	28	3	4	0	13	3	1	13	.280	.308	.390	67	-6	7	.887	1	121	517	O-29(1-1-28)	-0.5
	Year	35	123	15	31	3	4	0	16	4	1	17	.252	.281	.341	49	-11	9	.879	1	119	423	O-35(1-1-34)	-0.9
1895	StL N	5	18	2	3	1	0	0	2	3	0	0	.167	.286	.222	33	-2	2	.833	0	235	0	/O-5(CF)	-0.1
Total	2	40	141	17	34	4	4	0	18	7	1	17	.241	.282	.326	47	-13	11	.869	1	137	355	/O-40(1-6-34)	-1.0
HOGAN, EDDIE Robert Edward B 4.6.1862 St.Louis, MO D 1.22.1932 Yucaipa, CA BR 5-7/153# d7.5																								
1882	StL AA	1	3	1	1	0	0	0		0			.333	.333	.333	121	0		.333	-1	38	0	/P	0.0
1884	Mil U	11	37	6	3	1	0	0		7			.081	.227	.108	9	-4		.806	8	600	738	O-11(RF)	0.3
1887	NY AA	32	120	22	24	6	1	0	5	30	3		.200	.373	.267	84	0	12	.750	-6	108	88	O-29(1-2-26)/S-4,3	-0.5
1888	Cle AA	78	269	60	61	16	6	0	24	50	10		.227	.368	.331	128	13	30	.896	-4	65	34	O-78(26-0-52)	0.8
Total	4	122	429	89	89	23	7	0	29	87	13		.207	.357	.294	108	9	42	.844	-2	106	87	O-118(27-2-89)/S-4,3P	0.6
HOGAN, WILLIE William Henry B 9.14.1884 N.San Juan, CA D 9.28.1974 San Jose, CA BR/TR 5-10/175# d4.12 b-George																								
1911	Phi A	7	19	1	2	1	0	0	2	0	0		.105	.105	.158	-27	-3	0	.900	1	89	297	/O-6(LF)	-0.3
	StL A	123	443	53	115	17	8	2	62	43	2		.260	.328	.348	92	-5	18	.929	11	116	133	*O-117(115-0-2)/1-5	0.1
	Year	130	462	54	117	18	8	2	64	43	2		.253	.320	.340	87	-8	18	.928	12	**115**	139	*O-123(121-0-2)/1-5	-0.2
1912	StL A	108	360	32	77	10	2	1	36	34	1		.214	.284	.261	58	-20	17	.972	10	118	108	*O-100(91-5-4)	-1.4
Total	2	238	822	86	194	28	10	3	100	77	3		.236	.304	.305	75	-28	35	.947	22	116	125	O-223(212-5-6)/1-5	-1.6
HOGG, WILLY Wilbert George "Sonny" B 4.21.1913 Detroit, MI D 11.5.1973 Detroit, MI BR/TR 5-11.5/162# d6.1																								
1934	Bro N	2	1	0	0	0	0	0	0	0	0	0	.000	.000	.000	-99	0	0	—	-0	0	0	/3	0.0
HOGRIEVER, GEORGE George C. B 3.17.1869 Cincinnati, OH D 1.26.1961 Appleton, WI BR/TR 5-8/160# d4.24																								
1895	Cin N	69	239	61	65	8	7	2	34	36	3	17	.272	.374	.389	93	-2	41	.934	0	100	134	O-66(10-48-8)/2-3	-0.5
1901	Mil A	54	221	25	52	10	2	0	16	30	1		.235	.329	.299	79	-5	7	.901	-2	36	51	O-54(49-5-0)	-1.0
Total	2	123	460	86	117	18	9	2	50	66	4	17	.254	.353	.346	87	-7	48	.920	-2	68	93	O-120(59-53-8)/2-3	-1.5
HOHMAN, BILL William Henry B 11.27.1903 Brooklyn, MD D 10.29.1968 Baltimore, MD BR/TR 6/178# d8.24																								
1927	Phi N	7	18	1	5	0	0	0	0	2	0	3	.278	.350	.278	69	-1	0	.917	0	102	226	/O-6(LF)	-0.1
HOHNHORST, EDDIE Edward Hicks B 1.31.1885 Covington, KY D 3.28.1916 Covington, KY BL/TL 6-1/175# d9.10																								
1910	Cle A	18	63	8	20	3	1	0	6	4	0		.317	.358	.397	135	2	3	.972	-1	77	117	1-18	0.1
1912	Cle A	15	54	5	11	1	0	0	2	2	0		.204	.232	.222	29	-5	5	.963	-1	90	120	1-15	-0.7
Total	2	33	117	13	31	4	1	0	8	6	0		.265	.301	.316	83	-3	8	.968	-2	83	118	/1-33	-0.6
HOILES, CHRIS Christopher Allen B 3.20.1965 Bowling Green, OH BR/TR 6/213# d4.25																								
1989	Bal A	6	9	0	1	1	0	0	1	1-0	0	3	.111	.200	.222	19	-1	0-0	1.000	1	0	0	/C-3,D-3	0.0
1990	Bal A	23	63	7	12	3	0	1	6	5-1	0	12	.190	.250	.286	51	-4	0-0	1.000	-1	90	214	/C-7,1-6,D-7	-0.6
1991	Bal A	107	341	36	83	15	0	11	31	29-1	1	61	.243	.304	.384	93	-4	0-2	**.998**	-7	112	93	C-89,D-13/1-2	-0.8
1992	Bal A	96	310	49	85	10	1	20	40	55-2	2	60	.274	.384	.506	145	20	0-2	.994	-9	80	63	C-95/D	1.6
1993	Bal A	126	419	80	130	28	0	29	82	69-4	9	94	.310	.416	.585	160	38	1-1	.993	10	122	102	*C-124/D-2	5.3
1994	Bal A	99	332	45	82	10	0	19	53	63-2	5	73	.247	.371	.449	106	4	2-0	.989	12	133	77	C-98	2.1
1995	Bal A	114	352	53	88	15	1	19	58	67-3	4	80	.250	.373	.460	114	9	1-0	**.996**	3	101	110	*C-107/D-6	1.7
1996	†Bal A	127	407	64	105	13	0	25	73	57-1	9	97	.258	.356	.474	110	6	0-1	.992	-10	79	86	*C-126/1	0.3
1997	†Bal A	99	320	45	83	15	0	12	49	51-3	10	86	.259	.375	.419	111	7	1-0	**1.000**	-2	78	72	C-87/1-4,3D	1.0
1998	Bal A	97	267	36	70	12	0	15	56	38-0	4	50	.262	.358	.476	117	7	0-1	**.995**	-4	55	112	C-83/1-6,D-6	0.7
Total	10	894	2820	415	739	122	2	151	449	435-17	44	616	.262	.366	.467	119	82	5-7	.994	-8	96	90	C-819/D-46,1-19,3	11.3
HOLBERT, AARON Aaron Keith B 1.9.1973 Torrance, CA BR/TR 6/160# d4.14 b-Ray																								
1996	StL N	1	3	0	0	0	0	0	0	0-0	0	0	.000	.000	.000	-99	-1	0-0	1.000	-1	62	0	/2	-0.1
HOLBERT, RAY Ray Arthur B 9.25.1970 Torrance, CA BR/TR 6/170# d5.2 b-Aaron																								
1994	SD N	5	5	1	1	0	0	0	0	0-0	0	4	.200	.200	.200	5	-1	0-0	—	-0	0	0	/S	-0.1
1995	SD N	63	73	11	13	2	1	2	5	8-1	2	20	.178	.277	.315	58	-5	4-0	.940	0	103	113	S-30/2-7,O(RF)	-0.2
1998	Atl N	8	15	2	2	0	0	0	1	2-0	0	4	.133	.222	.133	0	-2	0-0	.952	1	112	132	/S-7	-0.1
	Mon N	2	5	0	0	0	0	0	0	0-0	0	1	.000	.000	.000	-99	-1	0-0	1.000	-0	102	0	/2	-0.2
	Year	10	20	2	2	0	0	0	1	2-0	0	5	.100	.174	.100	-23	-4	0-0	.952	1	112	132	/S-7,2	-0.3
1999	KC A	34	100	14	28	3	0	0	5	8-0	0	20	.280	.330	.310	64	-5	7-4	.987	-7	81	111	S-22,2-11/3	-1.0
2000	KC A	3	4	0	1	0	0	0	0	0-0	0	2	.250	.250	.250	26	0	0-0	1.000	1	94	402	/23S	0.0

Year	Tm Lg	G	AB	R	H	2B	3B	HR	RBI	BB-IB	HP	SO	AVG	OBP	SLG	AOPS	ABR	SB-CS	FA	FR	Rng	Thr	G at Pos	BFW
Total	5	115	202	28	45	5	1	2	11	18-1	2	51	.223	.290	.287	51	-14	11-4	.962	-6	94	116	/S-61,2-20,3-2,O(RF)	-1.6

HOLBERT, BILL William Henry B 3.14.1855 Baltimore, MD D 3.20.1935 Laurel, MD BR/TR ?/197# d9.5 M1 U1 OF Total (12-LF 19-CF 38-RF)

Year	Tm Lg	G	AB	R	H	2B	3B	HR	RBI	BB-IB	HP	SO	AVG	OBP	SLG	AOPS	ABR	SB-CS	FA	FR	Rng	Thr	G at Pos	BFW
1876	Lou N	12	43	3	11	0	0	0	5	0		3	.256	.256	.256	60	-2		.843	6			C-12	0.3
1878	Mil N	45	173	10	32	2	0	0	12	3		14	.185	.199	.197	28	-13		.818	5	229	76	O-30(RF),C-21	-0.7
1879	Syr N	59	229	11	46	0	0	0	21	1		20	.201	.204	.201	39	-14		.897	-0			*C-56/O-4(0-3-1),M	-1.2
	Tro N	4	15	1	4	0	0	0	2	0		1	.267	.267	.267	82	0		.893	1			/C-4	0.0
	Year	63	244	12	50	0	0	0	23	1		21	.205	.208	.205	41	-15		.897	1			C-60/O-4(0-3-1)	-1.2
1880	Tro N	60	212	18	40	5	1	0	8	9		18	.189	.222	.222	48	-11		.911	11			*C-58/O-3(RF)	0.2
1881	Tro N	46	180	16	49	3	0	0	14	3		13	.272	.284	.289	77	-5		.918	7			C-43/O-3(RF)	0.3
1882	Tro N	71	251	24	46	5	0	0	23	11		22	.183	.218	.203	38	-17		.892	15			*C-58,3-12/O-3(CF)	0.3
1883	NY AA	73	299	26	71	9	1	0		1			.237	.240	.274	62	-13		.920	**33**			*C-68/O-5(CF),2	2.2
1884	†NY AA	65	255	28	53	5	0	0		7	2		.208	.235	.227	53	-13		.920	21			C-59/O-5(4-0-1),S	1.2
1885	NY AA	56	202	13	35	3	0	0	13	8	0		.173	.205	.188	26	-17		.900	11			C-39,O-13(8-5-0)/3-5	-0.3
1886	NY AA	48	171	8	35	4	2	0	13	6	0		.205	.232	.251	56	-9	4	.922	16			C-45/O-3(CF),S	0.9
1887	NY AA	69	255	20	58	4	3	0	32	7	0		.227	.248	.267	46	-19	12	.894	2			C-60/1-8,S-2,2	-1.0
1888	Bro AA	15	50	4	6	1	0	0	1	2	1		.120	.170	.140	-0	-6	0	.926	1			C-15	-0.3
Total	12	623	2335	182	486	41	7	0	144	58	3	91	.208	.228	.232	47	-139	16	.907	128			C-538/O-69R,3-17,1-8,S-4,2-2	1.9

HOLBROOK, SAMMY James Marbury B 7.17.1910 Meridian, MS D 4.10.1991 Jackson, MS BR/TR 5-11/189# d4.25

Year	Tm Lg	G	AB	R	H	2B	3B	HR	RBI	BB-IB	HP	SO	AVG	OBP	SLG	AOPS	ABR	SB-CS	FA	FR	Rng	Thr	G at Pos	BFW
1935	Was A	52	135	20	35	2	2	2	25	30	4	16	.259	.408	.348	101	2	0-0	.952	-12	*77*	*47*	C-47	-0.7

HOLDEN, JOE Joseph Francis "Socks" B 6.4.1913 St.Clair, PA D 5.10.1996 St.Clair, PA BL/TR 5-8/175# d6.14

Year	Tm Lg	G	AB	R	H	2B	3B	HR	RBI	BB-IB	HP	SO	AVG	OBP	SLG	AOPS	ABR	SB-CS	FA	FR	Rng	Thr	G at Pos	BFW
1934	Phi N	10	14	1	1	0	0	0	0	0	0	2	.071	.071	.071	-54	-3	0	1.000	1	*98*	*282*	/C-6	-0.1
1935	Phi N	6	9	0	1	0	0	0	0	0	0	3	.111	.111	.111	-36	-2	1	1.000	-0	*0*	*0*	/C-4	-0.2
1936	Phi N	1	1	0	0	0	0	0	0	0	0	0	.000	.000	.000	-91	0	0	—	0			H	0.0
Total	3	17	24	1	2	0	0	0	0	0	0	5	.083	.083	.083	-49	-5	1	1.000	1	*68*	*197*	/C-10	-0.3

HOLDEN, BILL William Paul B 9.7.1889 Birmingham, AL D 9.14.1971 Pensacola, FL BR/TR 6/170# d9.11

Year	Tm Lg	G	AB	R	H	2B	3B	HR	RBI	BB-IB	HP	SO	AVG	OBP	SLG	AOPS	ABR	SB-CS	FA	FR	Rng	Thr	G at Pos	BFW
1913	NY A	18	53	6	16	3	1	0	8	8	0	5	.302	.393	.396	131	2	0	.977	2	102	192	O-16(CF)	0.4
1914	NY A	50	165	12	30	3	2	0	12	16	0	26	.182	.254	.224	44	-12	2-4	.981	-1	106	52	O-45(3-37-6)	-1.8
	Cin N	11	28	2	6	0	0	0	1	3	0	5	.214	.290	.214	49	-2	0	1.000	-0	86	112	O-10(7-3-1)	-0.2
Total	2	79	246	20	52	6	3	0	21	27	0	36	.211	.289	.260	64	-12	2-4	.981	1	103	93	/O-71(10-56-7)	-1.6

HOLDSWORTH, JIM James "Long Jim" B 7.14.1850 New York, NY D 3.22.1918 New York, NY BR/TR d5.14

Year	Tm Lg	G	AB	R	H	2B	3B	HR	RBI	BB-IB	HP	SO	AVG	OBP	SLG	AOPS	ABR	SB-CS	FA	FR	Rng	Thr	G at Pos	BFW
1872	Cle NA	**22**	110	19	33	5	0	0	11	1		2	.300	.306	.345	106	1	3-2	.765	-2	78	200	S-22	-0.1
	Eck NA	3	11	1	3	1	0	0	0	0		0	.273	.273	.364	111	0	0-0	.833	1	123	0	/S-3	0.1
	Year	25	121	20	36	6	0	0	11	1		2	.298	.303	.347	106	2	3-2	.774	-0	84	175	S-25	0.0
1873	Mut NA	**53**	232	46	75	4	8	0	28	0		4	.323	.323	.409	117	4	1-0	.770	-14	75	92	*S-53	-0.9
1874	Phi NA	57	285	60	97	8	9	0	37	1		0	.340	.343	.432	142	11	1-2	.694	-22	60	119	3-31,S-21/O-6(0-3-3),2-2,1	-1.0
1875	Mut NA	**71**	324	45	92	12	1	0	23	1		3	.284	.286	.327	107	1	3-3	.780	-4	148	128	O-45(0-43-2),S-26	-0.3
1876	NY N	52	241	23	64	3	2	0	19	1		2	.266	.269	.295	101	1		.902	-1	118	46	*O-49(CF)/2-3	-0.2
1877	Har N	55	260	26	66	5	2	0	20	2		8	.254	.260	.288	81	-5		.833	-4	108	62	*O-55(CF)	-1.0
1882	Tro N	1	3	0	0	0	0	0	0	0		1	.000	.000	.000	-99	-1		1.000	1	443	0	/O(CF)	0.0
1884	Ind AA	5	18	1	2	0	0	0		2	0		.111	.200	.111	4	-2		.929	1	103	613	/O-5(CF)	-0.1
Total	4 NA	206	962	171	300	30	18	0	99	3	0	9	.312	.314	.380	120	17	8-7	.000	-40	81	117	S-125/O-51(0-46-5),3-31,2-2,1	-2.2
Total	4	113	522	50	132	8	4	0	39	5	0	11	.253	.260	.284	85	-7		.875	-3	115	78	O-110(CF)/2-3	-1.3

HOLKE, WALTER Walter Henry "Union Man" B 12.25.1892 St.Louis, MO D 10.12.1954 St.Louis, MO BB/TL 6-1.5/185# d10.6 Def 1918 C1

Year	Tm Lg	G	AB	R	H	2B	3B	HR	RBI	BB-IB	HP	SO	AVG	OBP	SLG	AOPS	ABR	SB-CS	FA	FR	Rng	Thr	G at Pos	BFW
1914	NY N	2	6	0	2	0	0	0	0	0	0	0	.333	.333	.333	102	0	0	.950	0	210	120	/1-2	0.0
1916	NY N	34	111	16	39	4	2	0	13	6	1	16	.351	.390	.423	158	7	10	.997	-0	85	92	1-34	0.7
1917	†NY N	153	527	55	146	12	7	2	55	34	5	54	.277	.327	.338	107	4	13	.989	-6	83	**121**	*1-153	-0.6
1918	NY N	88	326	38	82	17	4	1	27	10	1	26	.252	.276	.337	88	-6	10	.990	5	**120**	107	1-88	-0.3
1919	Bos N	137	518	48	151	14	6	0	48	21	5	25	.292	.325	.342	105	2	19	.993	6	115	108	*1-136	0.5
1920	Bos N	144	551	53	162	15	11	3	64	28	1	31	.294	.329	.377	107	3	4-11	.991	-3	92	91	*1-143	-0.7
1921	Bos N	150	579	60	151	15	10	3	63	17	2	41	.261	.284	.337	67	-30	8-11	**.997**	2	100	94	*1-150	-4.0
1922	Bos N	105	395	35	115	9	4	0	46	14	1	23	.291	.317	.334	71	-18	6-8	.993	-4	81	81	*1-105	-2.8
1923	Phi N	147	562	64	175	31	4	7	70	16	0	37	.311	.330	.418	86	-12	7-9	.991	-2	93	103	*1-146/P	-2.3
1924	Phi N	148	563	60	169	23	6	6	64	25	0	33	.300	.330	.394	83	-14	3-8	.993	4	109	96	*1-148	-2.2
1925	Phi N	39	86	11	21	5	0	1	17	3	0	6	.244	.270	.337	50	-7	0-0	.994	1	126	103	1-23	-0.6
	Cin N	65	232	24	65	8	4	1	20	17	0	12	.280	.329	.362	78	-8	1-3	.997	1	103	128	1-65	-1.1
	Year	104	318	35	86	13	4	2	37	20	0	18	.270	.314	.355	69	-15	1-3	.996	3	108	123	1-88	-1.7
Total	11	1212	4456	464	1278	153	58	24	487	191	16	304	.287	.318	.363	89	-79	81-50	.993	5	99	102	*1-1193/P	-13.4

HOLLAHAN, BILL William James "Happy" B 11.22.1896 New York, NY D 11.27.1965 New York, NY BR/TR 5-8/165# d9.27

Year	Tm Lg	G	AB	R	H	2B	3B	HR	RBI	BB-IB	HP	SO	AVG	OBP	SLG	AOPS	ABR	SB-CS	FA	FR	Rng	Thr	G at Pos	BFW
1920	Was A	3	4	0	1	0	0	0	1	1	0	2	.250	.400	.250	77	0	1-0	1.000	-0	54	0	/3-3	0.0

HOLLAND, DUTCH Robert Clyde B 10.12.1903 Middlesex, NC D 6.16.1967 Lumberton, NC BR/TR 6-1/190# d8.16

Year	Tm Lg	G	AB	R	H	2B	3B	HR	RBI	BB-IB	HP	SO	AVG	OBP	SLG	AOPS	ABR	SB-CS	FA	FR	Rng	Thr	G at Pos	BFW
1932	Bos N	39	156	15	46	11	1	1	18	12	0	20	.295	.345	.397	103	1	0	.990	-0	97	108	O-39(LF)	-0.2
1933	Bos N	13	31	3	8	3	0	0	3	3	0	8	.258	.324	.355	102	0	1	.867	-1	88	0	/O-7(LF)	-0.1
1934	Cle A	50	128	19	32	12	1	2	13	13	0	11	.250	.319	.406	85	-3	0-0	.957	-2	85	48	O-31(15-0-16)	-0.7
Total	3	102	315	37	86	26	2	3	34	28	0	39	.273	.332	.397	95	-2	1-0	.969	-4	92	78	/O-77(61-0-16)	-1.0

HOLLAND, WILL Willard A. B 1862 Georgetown, DE D 7.19.1930 Philadelphia, PA 5-10/180# d7.10

Year	Tm Lg	G	AB	R	H	2B	3B	HR	RBI	BB-IB	HP	SO	AVG	OBP	SLG	AOPS	ABR	SB-CS	FA	FR	Rng	Thr	G at Pos	BFW
1889	Bal AA	40	143	13	27	1	2	0	16	9	2	28	.189	.247	.224	34	-13	4	.853	-11	85	73	S-39/O(LF)	-1.9

HOLLANDSWORTH, TODD Todd Mathew B 4.20.1973 Dayton, OH BL/TL 6-2/195# d4.25

Year	Tm Lg	G	AB	R	H	2B	3B	HR	RBI	BB-IB	HP	SO	AVG	OBP	SLG	AOPS	ABR	SB-CS	FA	FR	Rng	Thr	G at Pos	BFW
1995	†LA N	41	103	16	24	2	0	5	13	10-2	1	29	.233	.304	.398	92	-2	2-1	.938	-1	96	65	O-37(9-25-3)	-0.3
1996	†LA N	149	478	64	139	26	4	12	59	41-1	2	93	.291	.348	.437	115	10	21-6	.978	-2	94	100	*O-142(122-18-9)	0.6
1997	LA N	106	296	39	73	20	2	4	31	17-2	0	60	.247	.286	.368	76	-12	5-5	.984	6	125	45	O-99(80-30-4)	-0.8
1998	LA N	55	175	23	47	6	4	3	20	9-0	1	42	.269	.308	.400	90	-4	4-3	.957	-1	105	36	O-51(48-10-1)	-0.6
1999	LA N	92	261	39	74	12	2	9	32	24-1	1	61	.284	.345	.448	105	1	5-2	.984	1	104	68	O-67(27-34-9),1-13	0.1
2000	LA N	81	261	42	61	12	0	8	24	30-2	1	61	.234	.314	.372	77	-10	11-4	.987	1	98	163	O-77(9-68-1)	-0.7
	Col N	56	167	39	54	8	0	11	23	11-1	0	38	.323	.365	.569	105	1	7-3	.988	1	87	223	O-48(31-4-18)	0.1
	Year	137	428	81	115	20	0	19	47	41-3	1	99	.269	.333	.449	89	-8	18-7	.987	2	93	188	*O-125(40-72-19)	-0.6
2001	Col N	33	117	21	43	15	1	6	19	8-2	0	20	.368	.408	.667	140	7	5-0	.981	-1	90	111	O-31(25-12-5)	0.6
2002	Col N	95	298	39	88	21	1	11	48	26-4	1	71	.295	.352	.483	105	1	7-8	.973	-0	94	140	O-90(74-1-20)	-0.4
	Tex A	39	132	16	34	6	0	5	19	14-0	0	27	.258	.327	.417	92	-2	1-0	1.000	-3	89	0	O-38(25-16-4)	-0.5
2003	†Fla N	93	228	32	58	23	3	3	20	22-4	0	55	.254	.317	.421	95	-2	2-3	.983	3	111	143	O-64(61-0-3)/D	-0.1
Total	9	840	2516	370	695	151	17	77	308	212-19	7	557	.276	.333	.442	100	-12	70-35	.979	4	100	104	O-744(511-218-77)/1-13,D	-2.0

HOLLE, GARY Gary Charles B 8.11.1954 Albany, NY BR/TL 6-6/210# d6.2

Year	Tm Lg	G	AB	R	H	2B	3B	HR	RBI	BB-IB	HP	SO	AVG	OBP	SLG	AOPS	ABR	SB-CS	FA	FR	Rng	Thr	G at Pos	BFW
1979	Tex A	5	6	0	1	1	0	0	0	1-0	0	0	.167	.286	.333	67	0	0-0	1.000	-0	0	128	/1	-0.1

HOLLIDAY, BUG James Wear B 2.8.1867 St.Louis, MO D 2.15.1910 Cincinnati, OH BR/TR 5-11/151# d4.17 U1 OF Total (211-LF 598-CF 92-RF)

Year	Tm Lg	G	AB	R	H	2B	3B	HR	RBI	BB-IB	HP	SO	AVG	OBP	SLG	AOPS	ABR	SB-CS	FA	FR	Rng	Thr	G at Pos	BFW
1889	Cin AA	135	563	107	181	28	7	**19**	104	43	2	59	.321	.372	.497	142	28	46	.923	-9	112	107	*O-135(CF)	1.2
1890	Cin N	131	518	93	140	18	14	4	75	49	7	36	.270	.341	.382	111	6	50	.948	-5	89	118	*O-131(CF)	-0.3
1891	Cin N	111	442	74	141	21	10	9	84	37	3	28	.319	.376	.473	145	24	30	.939	-8	78	107	*O-111(49-62-0)	1.1
1892	Cin N	152	602	114	177	23	16	**13**	91	57	1	39	.294	.356	.450	145	31	43	.933	-5	82	119	*O-152(1-78-77)/P	1.5
1893	Cin N	126	500	108	155	24	10	5	89	73	3	22	.310	.401	.428	117	14	32	.944	-12	67	90	*O-125(1-125-0)/1	-0.5
1894	Cin N	123	521	126	196	24	8	13	123	41	2	20	.376	.424	.528	124	19	33	.912	1	107	116	*O-121(111-5-8)/1	0.7
1895	Cin N	32	127	25	38	9	2	0	20	10	0	3	.299	.350	.402	90	-2	6	.940	-2	74	109	O-32(5-27-0)	-0.5
1896	Cin N	29	84	17	27	4	0	0	8	9	1	4	.321	.394	.369	95	0	1	.925	-2	45	0	O-16(10-3-3)/1-5,SP	-0.3
1897	Cin N	61	195	50	61	9	4	2	20	27	1		.313	.399	.431	112	4	6	.940	-4	37	0	O-42(32-6-4)/S-4,2-3,1-3	-0.2
1898	Cin N	30	106	21	25	2	1	0	7	14	0		.236	.325	.274	67	-4	5	.969	-1	28	118	O-28(2-26-0)	-0.7
Total	10	930	3658	735	1141	162	72	65	621	360	20	211	.312	.377	.449	125	120	252	.934	-47	84	103	O-893C/1-10,S-5,2-3,P-2	2.0

Year	Tm Lg	G	AB	R	H	2B	3B	HR	RBI	BB-IB	HP	SO	AVG	OBP	SLG	AOPS	ABR	SB-CS	FA	FR	Rng	Thr	G at Pos	BFW
HOLLINGSHEAD, HOLLY John Samuel (a/k/a Samuel John Holly) B 1.17.1853 Washington, DC D 10.6.1926 Washington, DC d4.20 M2 U1																								
1872	Nat NA	9	44	12	14	1	1	0	6	1		0	.318	.333	.386	103	-1	0-0	.778	-4	70	45	/2-9	-0.3
1873	Was NA	30	136	25	35	2	2	0	22	0		5	.257	.257	.301	68	-5	0-0	.824	2	119	0	O-30(CF)/2-2	-0.2
1875	Was NA	19	81	8	20	1	1	0	5	1		2	.247	.256	.284	91	-1	2-1	.826	2	202	126	O-19(4-13-3),M	0.2
Total	3 NA	58	261	45	69	4	4	0	33	2		7	.264	.270	.310	81	-7	2-1	.000	1	150	47	/O-49(4-43-3),2-11	-0.3
HOLLINS, DAMON Damon Jamall B 6.12.1974 Fairfield, CA BR/TL 5-11/180# d4.24																								
1998	Atl N	3	6	0	1	0	0	0	0	0-0	0	1	.167	.167	.167	-12	-1	0-0	1.000	-0	67	0	/O-3(2-0-1)	-0.1
	LA N	5	9	1	2	0	0	0	2	0-0	0	2	.222	.222	.222	18	-1	0-1	1.000	-0	103	0	/O-4(1-0-3)	-0.2
	Year	8	15	1	3	0	0	0	2	0-0	0	3	.200	.200	.200	6	-2	0-1	1.000	-0	89	0	/O-7(3-0-4)	-0.3
HOLLINS, DAVE David Michael B 5.25.1966 Buffalo, NY BB/TR 6-1/207# d4.12																								
1990	Phi N	72	114	14	21	0	0	5	15	10-3	1	28	.184	.252	.316	57	-7	0-0	.932	-3	86	0	3-30/1	-1.1
1991	Phi N	56	151	18	45	10	2	6	21	17-1	3	26	.298	.378	.510	150	10	1-1	.922	-2	94	37	3-36/1-6	0.8
1992	Phi N	156	586	104	158	28	4	27	93	76-4	**19**	110	.270	.369	.469	137	31	9-6	.954	-18	84	83	*3-156/1	1.4
1993	†Phi N★	143	543	104	148	30	4	18	93	85-5	5	109	.273	.372	.442	120	18	2-3	.914	-29	79	40	*3-143	-1.0
1994	Phi N	44	162	28	36	7	1	4	26	23-0	4	32	.222	.328	.352	77	-5	1-0	.887	-13	61	31	3-43/O(RF)	-1.7
1995	Phi N	65	205	46	47	12	2	7	25	53-4	5	38	.229	.393	.410	113	7	1-1	.988	-6	67	109	1-61	-0.5
	Bos A	5	13	2	2	0	0	0	1	4-0	0	7	.154	.353	.154	37	-1	0-0	1.000	0	111	0	/O-2(RF),D-3	-0.1
1996	Min A	121	422	71	102	26	0	13	53	71-5	10	102	.242	.364	.396	91	-4	6-4	.953	0	102	82	*3-116/SD	-0.2
	Sea A	28	94	17	33	3	0	3	25	13-2	3	15	.351	.438	.479	134	6	0-2	.961	2	105	122	3-28/1	0.7
	Year	149	516	88	135	29	0	16	78	84-7	13	117	.262	.377	.411	98	2	6-6	.955	2	103	90	*3-144/D-3,S1	0.5
1997	Ana A	149	572	101	165	29	2	16	85	62-2	8	124	.288	.363	.430	107	7	16-6	.922	-8	94	76	*3-135,1-14	0.0
1998	Ana A	101	363	60	88	16	2	11	39	44-2	7	69	.242	.334	.388	87	-7	11-3	.929	-2	94	99	3-91/1-7,D-2	-0.7
1999	Tor A	27	99	12	22	5	0	2	6	5-0	0	22	.222	.260	.333	49	-8	0-0	—	0	0	0	D-23	-0.9
2001	Cle A	2	5	0	1	0	0	0	0	1-0	0	2	.200	.333	.200	45	0	0-0	—	0			/D-2	0.0
2002	Phi N	14	17	1	2	0	0	0	0	0-0	1	3	.118	.167	.118	-23	-3	0-1	1.000	-0	45	106	/1-5	-0.4
Total	12	983	3346	578	870	166	17	112	482	464-28	66	687	.260	.358	.420	107	44	47-27	.933	-80	89	70	3-778/1-96,D-33,O-3(RF),S	-3.7
HOLLMIG, STAN Stanley Ernest "Hondo" B 1.2.1926 Fredericksburg, TX D 12.4.1981 San Antonio, TX BR/TR 6-2.5/190# d4.19																								
1949	Phi N	81	251	28	64	11	6	2	26	20	2	43	.255	.315	.371	85	-6	1	.958	-4	88	87	O-66(RF)	-1.2
1950	Phi N	11	12	1	3	2	0	0	1	0	0	3	.250	.250	.417	73	0	0	1.000	0	127	0	/O-3(2-0-1)	0.0
1951	Phi N	2	2	0	0	0	0	0	0	0	0	0	.000	.000	.000	-99	-1	0-0	—	0			H	-0.1
Total	3	94	265	29	67	13	6	2	27	20	2	46	.253	.310	.370	84	-7	1-0	.959	-4	89	85	/O-69(2-0-67)	-1.3
HOLLOCHER, CHARLIE Charles Jacob B 6.11.1896 St.Louis, MO D 8.14.1940 Frontenac, MO BL/TR 5-7/154# d4.16																								
1918	†Chi N	**131**	509	72	**161**	23	6	2	38	47	4	30	.316	.379	.397	133	22	26	.929	-22	90	75	*S-131	1.0
1919	Chi N	115	430	51	116	14	5	3	26	44	7	19	.270	.347	.347	108	6	16	.941	6	105	107	*S-115	2.2
1920	Chi N	80	301	53	96	17	2	0	22	41	3	15	.319	.406	.389	126	13	20-14	.954	9	102	89	S-80	2.9
1921	Chi N	140	558	71	161	28	8	3	37	43	2	13	.289	.342	.384	91	-6	5-16	**.963**	6	105	95	*S-137	1.0
1922	Chi N	152	592	90	201	37	8	3	69	58	5	5	.340	.403	.444	116	17	19-29	**.965**	-6	98	101	*S-152	2.0
1923	Chi N	66	260	46	89	14	2	1	28	26	4	5	.342	.410	.423	120	9	9-10	.963	-4	96	96	S-65	1.0
1924	Chi N	76	286	28	70	12	4	2	21	18	1	7	.245	.292	.336	67	-14	4-11	.969	2	102	93	S-71	-0.7
Total	7	760	2936	411	894	145	35	14	241	277	26	94	.304	.370	.392	110	47	99-80	.954	-9	100	94	S-751	9.4
HOLLY, ED Edward William (born Edward William Ruthlavy) B 7.6.1879 Chicago, IL D 11.27.1973 Williamsport, PA BR/TR 5-10/165# d7.18																								
1906	StL N	10	34	1	2	0	0	0	7	5	0		.059	.179	.059	-27	-5	0	.939	-2	73	214	S-10	-0.7
1907	StL N	150	545	55	125	18	3	1	40	36	5		.229	.283	.279	79	-14	16	.927	9	105	86	*S-147/2-3	0.0
1914	Pit F	100	350	28	86	9	4	0	26	17	0	52	.246	.281	.294	57	-28	14	.942	-3	95	87	S-94/O-2(1-0-1),2	-2.5
1915	Pit F	16	42	8	11	2	0	0	5	5	1	6	.262	.354	.310	88	-1	3	.865	-4	77	106	S-11/3-3	-0.5
Total	4	276	971	92	224	29	7	1	78	63	6	58	.231	.282	.278	67	-48	33	.931	1	99	92	S-262/2-4,3-3,O-2(1-0-1)	-3.7
HOLM, WATTIE Roscoe Albert B 12.28.1901 Peterson, IA D 5.19.1950 Everly, IA BR/TR 5-9.5/160# d4.15																								
1924	StL N	81	293	40	86	10	4	0	23	8	2	16	.294	.317	.355	81	-9	1-4	.988	1	101	140	O-64(1-63-0)/C-9,3-4	-1.1
1925	StL N	13	58	10	12	1	1	0	2	3	0	1	.207	.246	.259	28	-6	1-0	.976	1	127	50	O-13(3-0-11)	-0.6
1926	†StL N	55	144	18	41	5	1	0	21	18	0	14	.285	.364	.333	85	-2	3	.962	-2	102	25	O-39(26-0-13)	-0.7
1927	StL N	110	419	55	120	27	8	3	66	24	1	29	.286	.327	.411	93	-5	4	.967	-8	93	31	O-97(55-25-18)/3-9	-1.9
1928	†StL N	102	386	61	107	24	6	3	47	32	1	17	.277	.334	.394	88	-7	1	.918	-17	81	61	3-83/O-7(RF)	-1.8
1929	StL N	64	176	21	41	5	6	0	14	12	0	8	.233	.282	.330	50	-15	1	.944	2	116	90	O-44(6-4-34)/3	-1.5
1932	StL N	11	17	2	3	1	0	0	1	3	1	1	.176	.333	.235	55	-1	0	1.000	-0	110	0	/O-4(2-0-2)	-0.1
Total	7	436	1493	207	410	73	26	6	174	100	5	86	.275	.322	.370	81	-45	11-4	.970	-22	103	65	O-268(93-92-85)/3-97,C-9	-7.7
HOLM, BILLY William Frederick Henry B 7.21.1912 Chicago, IL D 7.27.1977 East Chicago, IN BR/TR 5-10.5/168# d9.24																								
1943	Chi N	7	15	0	1	0	0	0	0	2	0	4	.067	.176	.067	-29	-2	0	1.000	1	*152*	*83*	/C-7	-0.2
1944	Chi N	54	132	10	18	2	0	0	6	16	1	19	.136	.235	.152	10	-16	1	.979	-2	*97*	*92*	C-50	-1.6
1945	Bos A	58	135	12	25	2	1	0	9	23	3	17	.185	.317	.215	54	-7	1-1	.980	-3	*105*	*113*	C-57	-0.8
Total	3	119	282	22	44	4	1	0	15	41	4	40	.156	.272	.177	30	-25	2-1	.981	-4	*104*	*102*	C-114	-2.6
HOLMAN, GARY Gary Richard B 1.25.1944 Long Beach, CA BL/TL 6-1/200# d6.26																								
1968	Was A	75	85	10	25	5	1	0	7	13-1	0	15	.294	.388	.376	137	4	0-0	1.000	2	112	44	1-33,O-10(3-0-8)	0.6
1969	Was A	41	31	1	5	1	0	0	2	4-0	0	7	.161	.257	.194	29	-3	0-0	1.000	-1	0	58	1-11/O-3(1-0-2)	-0.4
Total	2	116	116	11	30	6	1	0	9	17-1	0	22	.259	.353	.328	107	1	0-0	1.000	1	90	47	/1-44,O-13(4-0-10)	0.2
HOLMES, FRED Frederick C. B 7.1.1878 Chicago, IL D 2.13.1956 Norwood Park, IL BR/TR d8.23																								
1903	NY A	1	0	0	0	0	0	0	0	1	0		—	1.000	—	207	0	0	.833	-0	0	0	/1	0.0
1904	Chi N	1	3	1	1	1	0	0	0	0	0		.333	.333	.667	206	0	0	1.000	0	*99*	*118*	/C	0.0
Total	2	2	3	1	1	1	0	0	0	1	0		.333	.500	.667	255	0	0	1.000	-0	*99*	*118*	/C1	0.0
HOLMES, DUCKY Howard Elbert B 7.8.1883 Dayton, OH D 9.18.1945 Dayton, OH BR/TR 5-10/160# d4.18 U1																								
1906	StL N	9	27	2	5	0	0	0	2	2	1		.185	.267	.185	43	-2	0	.979	-1	*78*	*91*	/C-9	-0.2
HOLMES, DUCKY James William B 1.28.1869 Des Moines, IA D 8.6.1932 Truro, IA BL/TR 5-6/170# d8.8 ▮ OF Total (564-LF 37-CF 285-RF)																								
1895	Lou N	40	161	33	60	10	2	3	20	12	3	9	.373	.426	.516	152	13	9	.780	-6	180	99	O-29(0-3-26)/S-8,3-4,P-2	0.5
1896	Lou N	47	141	22	38	3	2	0	18	13	7	5	.270	.360	.319	83	-3	8	.790	-7	140	80	O-33(0-26-7)/P-2,S2	-0.9
1897	Lou N	2	4	0	0	0	0	0	0	1	0		.000	.200	.000	-46	-1	0	1.000	1	101	420	/S	0.0
	NY N	80	310	52	82	8	6	1	45	18	4		.265	.313	.339	74	-13	30	.905	-9	78	92	O-78(LF)/S	-2.5
	Year	82	314	52	82	8	6	1	45	19	4		.261	.312	.334	73	-13	30	.905	-8	78	92	O-78(LF)/S-2	-2.5
1898	StL N	23	101	9	24	1	1	0	0	2	1		.238	.260	.267	50	-7	4	.900	1	183	367	O-22(11-2-9)	-0.7
	Bal N	113	442	54	126	10	9	1	64	23	9		.285	.333	.355	96	-4	25	.935	2	79	116	*O-113(LF)	-1.1
	Year	136	543	63	150	11	10	1	64	25	10		.276	.320	.339	87	-11	29	.930	3	96	**158**	*O-135(124-2-9)	-1.8
1899	Bal N	138	553	80	177	31	7	4	66	39	15		.320	.381	.423	114	11	50	.927	7	113	92	*O-138(137-0-1)	0.5
1901	Det A	131	537	90	158	28	10	4	62	37	6		.294	.347	.406	103	2	35	.907	-2	107	129	*O-131(2-0-131)	-0.5
1902	Det A	92	362	50	93	15	4	2	33	28	5		.257	.319	.337	80	-9	16	.950	4	131	195	O-92(1-0-91)	-0.9
1903	Was A	21	71	13	16	3	1	1	8	5	1		.225	.286	.338	85	-1	10	.912	1	302	0	O-14(0-3-11)/3-4,2-2	-0.1
	Chi A	86	344	53	96	7	5	0	18	25	4		.279	.335	.328	104	2	25	.965	3	156	0	O-82(LF)/3-3	0.1
	Year	107	415	66	112	10	6	1	26	30	5		.270	.327	.330	101	1	35	.956	4	**179**	0	O-96(82-3-11)/3-7,2-2	0.0
1904	Chi A	68	251	42	78	11	9	1	19	14	3		.311	.354	.438	156	15	13	.975	1	110	174	O-63(53-2-8)	1.3
1905	Chi A	92	328	42	66	15	2	0	22	19	6		.201	.258	.259	67	-12	11	.936	-4	105	48	O-89(87-1-1)	-2.4
Total	10	933	3605	540	1014	142	58	17	375	236	64	14	.281	.336	.367	99	-7	236	.924	-7	117	110	O-884L/3-11,S-11,P-4,2-3	-6.7
HOLMES, TOMMY Thomas Francis "Kelly" B 3.29.1917 Brooklyn, NY BL/TL 5-10/180# d4.14 M2																								
1942	Bos N	141	558	56	155	24	4	4	41	64	1	10	.278	.353	.357	110	8	2	.990	5	105	117	*O-140(0-137-3)	1.1
1943	Bos N	152	629	75	170	33	10	5	41	58	2	20	.270	.334	.378	107	5	7	.993	-2	94	114	*O-152(2-149-1)	-0.2
1944	Bos N	**155**	631	93	195	42	6	13	73	61	2	11	.309	.372	.456	127	23	4	.991	-2	97	95	*O-155(2-154-0)	1.7
1945	Bos N✶	**154**	636	125	**224**	**47**	6	**28**	117	70	4	9	.352	.420	**.577**	**175**	**64**	15	.983	-2	98	89	*O-154(32-2-121)	5.1
1946	Bos N	149	568	80	176	35	6	6	79	58	3	14	.310	.377	.424	126	20	7	.987	5	104	115	*O-146(RF)	2.2
1947	Bos N	150	618	90	**191**	33	3	9	53	44	5	16	.309	.360	.416	108	7	3	.989	6	109	90	*O-147(RF)	0.7

Year	Tm Lg	G	AB	R	H	2B	3B	HR	RBI	BB-IB	HP	SO	AVG	OBP	SLG	AOPS	ABR	SB-CS	FA	FR	Rng	Thr	G at Pos	BFW
1948	†Bos N★	139	585	85	190	35	7	6	61	46	1	20	.325	.375	.439	122	18	1	.983	-2	99	74	*O-137(RF)	1.1
1949	Bos N	117	380	47	101	20	4	8	59	39	2	6	.266	.337	.403	103	1	1	.987	6	**112**	114	*O-103(RF)	0.4
1950	Bos N	105	322	44	96	20	1	9	51	33	4	8	.298	.370	.450	122	11	0	1.000	1	104	100	O-88(RF)	0.9
1951	Bos N	27	29	1	5	2	0	0	5	3	0	4	.172	.250	.241	35	-3	0-0	1.000	-0	65	0	/O-3(2-0-1),M	-0.3
1952	†Bro N	31	36	2	4	1	0	0	1	4	0	4	.111	.200	.139	-4	-5	0-0	1.000	0	89	300	/O-6(RF)	-0.5
Total	11	1320	4992	698	1507	292	47	88	581	480	24	122	.302	.366	.432	122	149	40-0	.989	16	102	101	*O-1231(38-442-753)	12.2
HOLT, RED James Emmett Madison B 7.25.1894 Dayton, TN D 2.2.1961 Birmingham, AL BL/TL 5-11/175# d9.5																								
1925	Phi A	27	88	13	24	7	0	1	8	12	0	9	.273	.360	.386	84	-2	0-0	.986	-0	98	103	1-25	-0.3
HOLT, JIM James William B 5.27.1944 Graham, NC BL/TR 6/195# d4.17																								
1968	Min A	70	106	9	22	2	1	0	8	4-2	0	20	.208	.236	.245	44	-7	0-1	.973	-1	85	145	O-38(23-2-14)/1	-1.1
1969	Min A	12	14	3	5	0	0	1	2	0-0	0	4	.357	.357	.571	153	1	0-0	1.000	-1	44	0	/O-5(1-0-4),1	0.0
1970	†Min A	142	319	37	85	9	3	3	40	17-3	0	32	.266	.300	.342	77	-11	3-1	.995	2	111	36	*O-130(76-52-4)/1-2	-1.4
1971	Min A	126	340	35	88	11	3	1	29	16-4	1	28	.259	.292	.318	71	-14	5-1	.986	0	104	75	*O-106(12-86-12)/1-3	-1.7
1972	Min A	10	27	6	12	1	0	1	6	0-0	0	1	.444	.429	.593	197	3	0-0	.917	0	92	236	/O-7(2-0-5),1	0.3
1973	Min A	132	441	52	131	25	3	11	58	29-4	2	43	.297	.341	.442	115	8	0-3	.990	5	105	94	*O-102(80-3-21),1-33	0.5
1974	Min A	79	197	24	50	11	0	0	16	14-2	1	16	.254	.302	.310	75	-6	0-0	.996	5	137	128	1-67/O-5(2-0-3)	-0.5
	†Oak A	30	42	1	6	0	0	0	0	1-0	1	9	.143	.182	.143	-6	-6	0-0	1.000	1	143	81	1-17/D-3	-0.6
	Year	109	239	25	56	11	0	0	16	15-2	2	25	.234	.282	.280	63	-11	0-0	.996	6	138	122	1-84/O-5(2-0-3),D-3	-1.1
1975	†Oak A	102	123	7	27	3	0	2	16	11-2	2	11	.220	.292	.293	68	-5	0-0	.991	0	117	102	1-52/O-2(LF),CD	-0.7
1976	Oak A	4	7	0	2	2	0	0	2	1-0	0	2	.286	.375	.571	182	1	0-0	—	0			/D-2	0.1
Total	9	707	1616	174	428	64	10	19	177	93-17	7	166	.265	.305	.352	84	-36	8-6	.988	12	104	76	O-395(198-143-63),1-177/D-9,C	-5.1
HOLT, ROGER Roger Boyd B 4.8.1956 Daytona Beach, FL BB/TR 5-11/165# d10.4																								
1980	NY A	2	6	0	1	0	0	0	1	1-0	0	2	.167	.286	.167	28	-1	0-0	1.000	1	150	0	/2-2	0.0
HONAN, MARTY Martin Weldon B 5.29.1869 Chicago, IL D 8.20.1908 Chicago, IL d10.3																								
1890	Chi N	1	3	0	0	0	0	0	1	0	0	2	.000	.000	.000	-96	-1	0	.857	-1	*105*	*0*	/C	-0.1
1891	Chi N	5	12	1	2	0	1	0	3	1	0	3	.167	.231	.333	64	-1	0	.963	1	*141*	*170*	/C-5	0.1
Total	2	6	15	1	2	0	1	0	4	1	0	5	.133	.188	.267	32	-2	0	.941	0	*133*	*134*	/C-6	0.0
HOOD, ABIE Albie Larrison B 1.31.1903 Sanford, NC D 10.14.1988 Chesapeake, VA BL/TR 5-7/152# d7.15																								
1925	Bos N	5	21	2	6	2	0	1	2	1	0	0	.286	.318	.524	122	1	0-0	.920	-3	64	68	/2-5	-0.2
HOOD, WALLY Wallace James Sr. B 2.9.1895 Whittier, CA D 5.2.1965 Hollywood, CA BR/TR 5-11.5/160# d4.15 s-Wally																								
1920	Bro N	7	14	4	2	1	0	0	1	4	0	4	.143	.333	.214	58	0	2-0	.944	1	125	126	/O-5(0-2-3)	0.0
	Pit N	2	1	1	0	0	0	0	0	1	0	0	.000	.500	.000	50	0	1-0	—	0			H	0.0
	Year	9	15	5	2	1	0	0	1	5	0	4	.133	.350	.200	59	0	3-0	.944	1	125	126	/O-5(0-2-3)	0.0
1921	Bro N	56	65	16	17	1	2	1	4	9	1	14	.262	.360	.385	94	0	2-2	.957	-1	99	0	O-20(3-9-7)	-0.3
1922	Bro N	2	0	2	0	0	0	0	0	0	0	0	—	—	—	—	0	0-0	—	0			R	0.0
Total	3	67	80	23	19	2	2	1	5	14	1	18	.237	.358	.350	88	0	5-2	.951	-1	109	48	/O-25(3-11-10)	-0.3
HOOKS, ALEX Alexander Marcus B 8.29.1906 Edgewood, TX D 6.19.1993 Edgewood, TX BL/TL 6-1/183# d4.17																								
1935	Phi A	15	44	4	10	3	0	0	4	3	0	10	.227	.277	.295	48	-3	0-0	1.000	0	93	127	1-10	-0.4
HOOPER, HARRY Harry Bartholomew B 8.24.1887 Bell Station, CA D 12.18.1974 Santa Cruz, CA BL/TR 5-10/168# d4.16 HF1971																								
1909	Bos A	81	255	29	72	3	4	0	12	16	5		.282	.337	.325	107	2	15	.952	4	149	143	O-74(62-4-8)	0.3
1910	Bos A	155	584	81	156	9	10	2	27	62	8		.267	.346	.327	108	7	40	.938	9	107	139	*O-155(9-4-142)	0.9
1911	Bos A	130	524	93	163	20	6	4	45	73	4		.311	.399	.395	123	20	38	.954	6	105	131	*O-130(RF)	1.8
1912	†Bos A	147	590	98	143	20	12	2	53	66	7		.242	.326	.327	83	-13	29	.964	1	100	105	*O-147(RF)	-2.0
1913	Bos A	148	586	100	169	29	12	4	40	60	5	51	.288	.359	.399	119	14	26	.968	8	110	114	*O-147(1-9-137)/P	1.4
1914	Bos A	142	530	85	137	23	15	1	41	58	4	47	.258	.336	.364	110	6	19-14	.973	10	113	128	*O-140(0-1-139)	0.9
1915	†Bos A	149	566	90	133	20	13	2	51	89	3	36	.235	.342	.327	103	4	22-20	.972	9	**111**	125	*O-149(RF)	0.3
1916	†Bos A	151	575	75	156	20	11	1	37	80	1	35	.271	.361	.350	113	11	27-11	.966	5	111	104	*O-151(RF)	1.1
1917	Bos A	151	559	89	143	21	11	3	45	80	6	40	.256	.355	.349	116	13	21	.971	-4	94	94	*O-151(RF)	0.1
1918	†Bos A	**126**	474	81	137	26	13	1	44	75	4	25	.289	.391	.405	142	27	24	.963	-0	100	94	*O-126(RF)	2.2
1919	Bos A	128	491	76	131	25	6	3	49	79	5	28	.267	.374	.360	113	13	23	.979	6	110	102	*O-128(RF)	1.2
1920	Bos A	139	536	91	167	30	17	7	53	88	2	27	.312	.411	.470	139	33	16-18	.963	5	106	116	*O-139(2-0-137)	2.7
1921	Chi A	108	419	74	137	26	5	8	58	55	1	21	.327	.406	.470	125	17	13-7	.975	-3	95	83	*O-108(RF)	0.6
1922	Chi A	152	602	111	183	35	8	11	80	68	5	33	.304	.379	.444	114	14	16-12	.962	5	106	112	*O-149(RF)	0.5
1923	Chi A	145	576	87	166	32	4	10	65	68	7	22	.288	.370	.410	106	7	18-18	.960	-6	95	77	*O-143(RF)	-1.3
1924	Chi A	130	476	107	156	27	8	10	62	65	4	26	.328	.413	.481	134	26	16-13	.986	10	112	128	*O-123(RF)	2.4
1925	Chi A	127	442	62	117	23	5	6	55	54	5	21	.265	.351	.380	90	-6	12-8	.976	4	102	127	*O-124(RF)	-1.1
Total	17	2309	8785	1429	2466	389	160	75	817	1136	76	412	.281	.368	.387	114	195	375-121	.966	68	106	112	*O-2284(74-18-2192)/P	12.0
HOOPER, MIKE Michael H. B 2.7.1850 Baltimore, MD D 12.2.1917 Baltimore, MD 5-6/165# d6.27																								
1873	Mar NA	3	14	3	3	1	0	0	2	0		0	.214	.214	.286	62	0	0-0	.833	-2	0	0	/O-2(LF),C	-0.1
HOOVER, CHARLIE Charles E. B 9.21.1865 Mound City, IL BL/TR 5-8/170# d10.9																								
1888	KC AA	3	10	0	3	0	0	0	1	0	0		.300	.300	.300	87	0	0	.857	-0			/C-3	0.0
1889	KC AA	71	258	44	64	2	5	1	25	29	2	38	.248	.329	.306	77	-9	9	.916	-4			C-66/3-4,O-3(LF)	-0.6
Total	2	74	268	44	67	2	5	1	26	29	2	38	.250	.328	.306	77	-9	9	.913	-4			/C-69,3-4,O-3(LF)	-0.6
HOOVER, PAUL Paul Chester B 4.14.1976 Columbus, OH BR/TR 6-1/210# d9.8																								
2001	TB A	3	4	1	1	0	0	0	0	0-0	0	1	.250	.250	.250	33	0	0-0	1.000	-1	82	0	/C-2	-0.1
2002	TB A	5	17	1	3	0	0	0	2	0-0	0	5	.176	.176	.176	-6	-3	0-0	1.000	-2	52	308	/C-4	-0.5
Total	2	8	21	2	4	0	0	0	2	0-0	0	6	.190	.190	.190	2	-3	0-0	1.000	-3	59	238	/C-6	-0.6
HOOVER, JOE Robert Joseph B 4.15.1915 Brawley, CA D 9.2.1965 Los Angeles, CA BR/TR 5-11/175# d4.21																								
1943	Det A	144	575	78	140	15	8	4	38	36	1	101	.243	.289	.318	72	-22	6-5	.944	-8	90	94	*S-144	-2.1
1944	Det A	120	441	67	104	20	2	0	29	35	6	66	.236	.301	.290	66	-19	7-10	.932	15	102	**131**	*S-119/2	0.4
1945	†Det A	74	222	33	57	10	5	1	17	21	1	35	.257	.324	.360	92	-2	6-2	.944	-4	89	102	S-68	-0.2
Total	3	338	1238	178	301	45	15	5	84	92	8	202	.243	.300	.316	73	-43	19-17	.939	3	94	109	S-331/2	-1.9
HOOVER, BUSTER William James B 4.12.1863 Philadelphia, PA D 4.16.1924 Jersey City, NJ BR/TR 6-1/178# d4.17																								
1884	Phi U	63	275	76	100	20	8	0		12			.364	.390	.495	180	19		.780	0	141	112	O-37(LF),S-15/1-6,2-6,3	1.6
	Phi N	10	42	6	8	1	0	1	4	4		9	.190	.261	.286	75	-1		.929	-1	59	0	O-10(6-4-0)	-0.2
1886	Bal AA	40	157	25	34	2	6	0	10	16	2		.217	.297	.306	91	-2	15	.839	-3	43	0	O-40(CF)	-0.5
1892	Cin N	14	51	7	9	0	0	0	2	5	0	4	.176	.250	.176	30	-4	1	.966	1	129	417	O-14(12-1-2)	-0.4
Total	3	127	525	114	151	23	14	1	16	37	2	13	.288	.337	.390	129	12	16	.840	-2	92	100	O-101(55-45-2)/S-15,2-6,1-6,3	0.5
HOPKINS, DON Donald B 1.9.1952 West Point, MS BL/TR 6/175# d4.8																								
1975	†Oak A	82	6	25	1	0	0	0	0	2-0	0	0	.167	.375	.167	59	0	21-9	1.000	0	113	0	D-20/O-5(1-2-2),R	0.1
1976	Oak A	3	0	0	0	0	0	0	0	0-0	0	0	—	—	—	—	0	0-1	—	0			H-2	0.0
Total	2	85	6	25	1	0	0	0	0	2-0	0	0	.167	.375	.167	59	0	21-10	1.000	0	113	0	/D-20,O-5(1-2-2)	0.1
HOPKINS, GAIL Gail Eason B 2.19.1943 Tulsa, OK BL/TR 5-10/200# d6.29																								
1968	Chi A	29	37	4	8	2	0	0	2	6-1	0	3	.216	.326	.270	81	-1	0-0	1.000	-1	32	79	/1-7	-0.2
1969	Chi A	124	373	52	99	13	3	8	46	50-1	1	28	.265	.351	.381	100	1	2-1	.994	-2	91	103	*1-101	-0.8
1970	Chi A	116	287	32	82	8	1	6	29	28-5	1	19	.286	.346	.383	99	0	0-0	.987	-1	101	115	1-77/C-8	-0.6
1971	KC A	103	295	35	82	16	1	9	47	37-9	4	13	.278	.364	.431	126	11	3-1	.990	2	114	118	1-83	0.8
1972	KC A	53	71	1	15	2	0	0	5	7-1	0	4	.211	.282	.239	56	-4	0-0	.990	-2	34	86	1-13/3	-0.7
1973	KC A	74	138	17	34	6	1	2	16	29-2	2	15	.246	.380	.348	100	2	1-2	1.000	0	101	68	D-36,1-10	0.0
1974	LA N	15	18	1	4	0	0	0	0	3-2	0	1	.222	.333	.222	60	-1	0-0	1.000	1	0	0	/C-2,1-2	0.0
Total	7	514	1219	142	324	47	6	25	145	160-21	8	83	.266	.352	.376	103	8	6-4	.991	-2	98	108	1-293/D-36,C-10,3	-1.5
HOPKINS, BUCK John Winton "Sis" B 1.3.1883 Grafton, VA D 10.2.1929 Phoebus, VA BL/TL 5-10/165# d7.22																								
1907	StL N	15	44	7	6	3	0	0	3	10	3		.136	.333	.205	71	0	2	.875	-3	0	0	O-15(CF)	-0.5

Year	Tm Lg	G	AB	R	H	2B	3B	HR	RBI	BB-IB	HP	SO	AVG	OBP	SLG	AOPS	ABR	SB-CS	FA	FR	Rng	Thr	G at Pos	BFW
HOPKINS, MARTY Meredith Hilliard B 2.22.1907 Wolfe City, TX D 11.20.1963 Dallas, TX BR/TR 5-11/175# d4.17																								
1934	Phi N	10	25	6	3	2	0	0	3	7	0	5	.120	.313	.200	36	-2	0	1.000	-0	93	189	/3-9	-0.2
	Chi A	67	210	22	45	7	0	2	28	42	1	26	.214	.348	.276	61	-11	0-3	.957	5	116	32	3-63	-0.5
1935	Chi A	59	144	20	32	3	0	2	17	36	0	23	.222	.378	.285	72	-4	1-0	.960	-4	102	83	3-49/2-5	-0.7
Total	2	136	379	48	80	12	0	4	48	85	1	54	.211	.357	.274	63	-17	1-3	.960	0	110	61	3-121/2-5	-1.4
HOPKINS, MIKE Michael Joseph "Skinner" B 11.1.1872 Glasgow, Scotland D 2.5.1952 Pittsburgh, PA BR/TR 5-8/160# d8.24																								
1902	Pit N	1	2	0	2	1	0	0	0	0	0		1.000	1.000	1.500	648	1	0	1.000	0	*0*	*189*	/C	0.1
HOPP, JOHNNY John Leonard "Hippity" B 7.18.1916 Hastings, NE D 6.1.2003 Scottsbluff, NE BL/TL 5-10/175# d9.18 C2																								
1939	StL N	6	4	1	2	1	0	0	2	1	0	1	.500	.600	.750	246	1	0	1.000	0	342	258	/1-2	0.1
1940	StL N	80	152	24	41	7	4	1	14	9	1	21	.270	.315	.388	88	-3	3	.967	2	125	44	O-39(12-27-0),1-10	-0.2
1941	StL N	134	445	83	135	25	11	4	50	50	3	63	.303	.378	.436	121	13	15	.982	-1	107	60	O-91(58-23-10),1-39	0.5
1942	†StL N	95	314	41	81	16	7	3	37	36	0	40	.258	.334	.382	102	1	14	.983	-4	85	116	1-88	-1.2
1943	†StL N	91	241	33	54	10	2	2	25	24	1	22	.224	.297	.307	71	-9	8	.950	1	113	23	O-52(40-12-0),1-27	-1.3
1944	†StL N	139	527	106	177	35	9	11	72	58	2	47	.336	.404	.499	150	36	15	**.997**	-8	98	19	*O-131(1-130-0)/1-6	2.5
1945	StL N	124	446	67	129	22	8	3	44	49	3	24	.289	.363	.395	108	5	14	.980	2	**113**	56	*O-104(2-26-89),1-15	0.1
1946	Bos N★	129	445	71	148	23	8	3	48	34	5	34	.333	.386	.440	133	19	21	.981	-2	94	96	1-68,O-58(1-57-0)	1.4
1947	Bos N	134	430	74	124	20	2	2	32	58	2	30	.288	.376	.358	98	1	13	.980	-6	100	25	*O-125(0-123-2)	-0.7
1948	Pit N	120	392	64	109	15	12	1	31	40	0	25	.278	.345	.385	95	-3	5	1.000	-3	95	52	O-80(1-71-8),1-25	-0.9
1949	Pit N	20	55	5	12	3	1	0	3	7	0	3	.218	.306	.309	64	-3	0	.929	-1	88	166	/O-7(2-0-5),1-6	-0.4
	Bro N	8	14	0	0	0	0	0	0	0	0	3	.000	.000	.000	-96	-4	0	1.000	1	105	393	/O-4(1-0-3),1-2	-0.3
	Pit N	85	316	50	106	11	4	5	36	30	0	26	.335	.393	.443	121	9	9	.994	-0	113	79	1-71/O-9(2-0-7)	0.7
	Year	113	385	55	118	14	5	5	39	37	0	32	.306	.367	.408	105	3	9	.990	0	102	110	1-79,O-20(5-0-15)	-0.0
1950	Pit N	106	318	51	108	24	5	8	47	43	1	17	.340	.420	.522	141	21	7	.990	-4	75	98	1-70/O-7(2-2-3)	1.4
	†NY A	19	27	9	9	2	1	1	8	8	0	1	.333	.486	.593	180	4	0-1	1.000	0	71	23	1-12/O-6(LF)	0.3
1951	†NY A	46	63	10	13	1	0	2	4	9	0	11	.206	.306	.317	71	-3	2-0	.992	-2	55	83	1-25	-0.4
1952	NY A	15	25	4	4	0	0	0	2	2	1	3	.160	.250	.160	17	-3	2-0	1.000	1	119	156	1-12	-0.2
	Det A	42	46	5	10	1	0	0	3	6	0	7	.217	.308	.239	53	-3	0-0	1.000	-0	91	0	/O-4(LF),1	-0.3
	Year	57	71	9	14	1	0	0	5	8	1	10	.197	.287	.211	41	-6	2-0	1.000	0	115	150	1-13/O-4(LF)	-0.5
Total	14	1393	4260	698	1262	216	74	46	458	464	19	378	.296	.368	.414	113	79	128-1	.985	-23	104	44	O-717(132-471-127),1-479	1.1
HORAN, SHAGS Joseph Patrick B 9.6.1895 St.Louis, MO D 2.13.1969 Torrance, CA BR/TR 5-10/170# d7.14																								
1924	NY A	22	31	4	9	1	0	0	7	1	0	5	.290	.313	.323	64	-2	0-0	1.000	0	89	156	O-14(4-1-9)	-0.2
HORN, SAM Samuel Lee B 11.2.1963 Dallas, TX BL/TL 6-5/250# d7.25																								
1987	Bos A	46	158	31	44	7	0	14	34	17-0	2	55	.278	.356	.589	141	9	0-1	—	0	0	0	D-40	0.7
1988	Bos A	24	61	4	9	0	0	2	8	11-3	0	20	.148	.274	.246	46	-4	0-0	—	0	0	0	D-16	-0.5
1989	Bos A	33	54	1	8	2	0	0	4	8-1	0	16	.148	.258	.185	25	-5	0-0	1.000	-0	0	0	D-14/1-2	-0.6
1990	Bal A	79	246	30	61	13	0	14	45	32-1	0	62	.248	.332	.472	127	9	0-0	.970	-1	93	95	D-63,1-10	0.6
1991	Bal A	121	317	45	74	16	0	23	61	41-4	3	99	.233	.326	.502	131	13	0-0	—	0	0	0	*D-102	0.9
1992	Bal A	63	162	13	38	10	1	5	19	21-2	1	60	.235	.324	.401	100	0	0-0	—	0	0	0	D-46	-0.1
1993	Cle A	12	33	8	15	1	0	4	8	1-0	1	5	.455	.472	.848	252	7	0-0	—	0	0	0	D-11	0.6
1995	Tex A	11	9	0	1	0	0	0	0	1-0	0	6	.111	.200	.111	-16	-2	0-0	—	0			/D	-0.2
Total	8	389	1040	132	250	49	1	62	179	132-11	7	323	.240	.328	.468	118	27	0-1	.972	-1	88	90	D-293/1-12	1.4
HORNER, BOB James Robert B 8.6.1957 Junction City, KS BR/TR 6-1/210# d6.16																								
1978	Atl N	89	323	50	86	17	1	23	63	24-2	2	42	.266	.313	.539	123	8	0-0	.956	10	110	108	3-89	1.8
1979	Atl N	121	487	66	153	15	1	33	98	22-6	3	74	.314	.346	.552	132	19	0-2	.930	-7	96	74	3-82,1-45	0.8
1980	Atl N	124	463	81	124	14	1	35	89	27-3	1	50	.268	.307	.529	126	13	3-1	.935	11	**115**	124	*3-121/1	2.3
1981	Atl N	79	300	42	83	10	0	15	42	32-3	1	39	.277	.345	.460	125	9	2-3	.938	-11	89	50	3-79	-0.4
1982	†Atl N★	140	499	85	130	24	0	32	97	66-3	4	75	.261	.350	.501	131	21	3-5	.970	-14	86	92	*3-137	0.4
1983	Atl N	104	386	75	117	25	1	20	68	50-2	1	63	.303	.383	.528	140	22	4-2	.958	-10	83	113	*3-104/1	1.1
1984	Atl N	32	113	15	31	8	0	3	19	14-2	0	17	.274	.349	.425	110	2	0-0	.965	2	108	121	3-32	0.3
1985	Atl N	130	483	61	129	25	3	27	89	50-4	1	57	.267	.333	.499	123	14	1-1	1.000	-8	93	134	1-87,3-40	0.0
1986	Atl N	141	517	70	141	22	0	27	87	52-8	2	72	.273	.336	.472	116	10	1-4	.995	0	98	**123**	*1-139	0.1
1988	StL N	60	206	15	53	9	1	3	33	32-6	1	23	.257	.348	.354	105	3	0-0	.990	1	106	98	1-57	-0.1
Total	10	1020	3777	560	1047	169	8	218	685	369-39	16	512	.277	.340	.499	125	121	14-18	.946	-27	96	97	3-684,1-330	6.3
HORNSBY, ROGERS Rogers "Rajah" B 4.27.1896 Winters, TX D 1.5.1963 Chicago, IL BR/TR 5-11/175# d9.10 M14 C3 HF1942 OF Total (6-LF 1-CF 13-RF)																								
1915	StL N	18	57	5	14	2	0	0	4	2	0	6	.246	.271	.281	67	-2	0-2	.922	-2	82	163	S-18	-0.4
1916	StL N	139	495	63	155	17	15	6	65	40	4	63	.313	.369	.444	150	28	17	.928	-0	112	56	3-83,S-45,1-15/2	3.7
1917	StL N	145	523	86	171	24	**17**	8	66	45	4	34	.327	.385	**.484**	**170**	**42**	17	.939	19	112	**129**	*S-144	**7.8**
1918	StL N	115	416	51	117	19	11	5	60	40	3	43	.281	.349	.416	138	18	8	.933	9	**113**	113	*S-109/O-3(0-1-2)	3.8
1919	StL N	**138**	512	68	163	15	9	8	71	48	7	41	.318	.384	.430	**154**	**34**	17	.933	9	106	106	3-72,S-37,2-25/1-5	**5.1**
1920	StL N	149	589	96	**218**	**44**	20	9	**94**	60	3	50	**.370**	**.431**	**.559**	**190**	**69**	12-15	.962	7	**104**	94	*2-149	**7.9**
1921	StL N	**154**	592	**131**	**235**	**44**	**18**	21	**126**	60	7	48	**.397**	**.458**	**.639**	**191**	**79**	13-13	.969	-2	100	87	*2-142/O-6(LF),S-3,3-3,1	**7.7**
1922	StL N	**154**	623	**141**	**250**	**46**	14	**42**	**152**	65	1	50	**.401**	**.459**	**.722**	**210**	**100**	17-12	**.967**	-7	90	95	*2-154	**8.9**
1923	StL N	107	424	89	163	32	10	17	83	55	3	29	**.384**	**.459**	**.627**	**188**	**56**	3-7	.962	-16	92	86	2-96,1-10	3.8
1924	StL N	143	536	**121**	**227**	**43**	14	25	94	**89**	2	32	**.424**	**.507**	**.696**	**223**	**99**	5-12	.965	-3	100	105	*2-143	**9.3**
1925	StL N	138	504	133	203	41	10	**39**	**143**	83	2	39	**.403**	**.489**	**.756**	**208**	**85**	5-3	.954	-14	91	122	*2-136,M	**6.8**
1926	†StL N	134	527	96	167	34	5	11	93	61	0	39	.317	.388	.463	123	19	3	.962	-31	94	100	*2-134,M	-0.8
1927	NY N	**155**	568	**133**	205	32	9	26	125	**86**	4	38	.361	**.448**	.586	**176**	**64**	9	.972	2	107	106	*2-155,M	6.8
1928	Bos N	140	486	99	188	42	7	21	94	**107**	1	41	**.387**	**.498**	**.632**	**204**	**83**	5	.973	-23	97	85	*2-140,M	**6.1**
1929	†Chi N	**156**	602	**156**	229	47	8	39	149	87	1	65	.380	.459	**.679**	**178**	**76**	2	.973	-3	103	112	*2-156	**6.8**
1930	Chi N	42	104	15	32	5	1	2	18	12	1	12	.308	.385	.433	96	0	0	.916	-3	99	104	2-25,M	-0.2
1931	Chi N	100	357	64	118	37	1	16	90	56	0	23	.331	.421	.574	162	34	1	.951	-8	103	58	2-69,3-26,M	3.0
1932	Chi N	19	58	10	13	2	0	1	7	10	2	4	.224	.357	.310	82	-1	0	1.000	-4	86	0	O-10(RF)/3-6,M	-0.5
1933	StL N	46	83	9	27	6	0	2	21	12	2	6	.325	.423	.470	147	6	1	.967	-3	86	90	2-17	0.4
	StL A	11	9	2	3	1	0	1	2	2	0	1	.333	.455	.778	208	1	0-0	—	0			HM	0.1
1934	StL A	24	23	2	7	2	0	1	11	7	1	4	.304	.484	.522	147	2	0-0	1.000	0	123	397	/3O(RF)M	0.2
1935	StL A	10	24	1	5	3	0	0	3	3	0	6	.208	.296	.333	60	-1	0-0	1.000	-0	50	31	/1-3,2-2,3M	-0.2
1936	StL A	2	5	1	2	0	0	0	2	1	0	0	.400	.500	.400	121	0	0-0	1.000	-0	0	0	/1M	0.0
1937	StL A	20	56	7	18	3	0	1	11	7	0	5	.321	.397	.429	107	1	0-0	.947	-3	93	90	2-17,M	-0.1
Total	23	2259	8173	1579	2930	541	169	301	1584	1038	48	679	.358	.434	.577	176	892	135-64	.965	-77	99	98	*2-1561,S-356,3-192/1-35,O-20R	86.0
HORNUNG, JOE Michael Joseph "Ubbo Ubbo" B 6.12.1857 Carthage, NY D 10.30.1931 Howard Beach, NY BR/TR 5-8.5/164# d5.1 U2 OF Total (1051-LF 1-CF 5-RF)																								
1879	Buf N	78	319	46	85	18	7	0	38	2		27	.266	.271	.367	105	1		.844	-1	69	57	*O-77(76-0-1)/1	-0.4
1880	Buf N	**85**	342	47	91	8	11	1	42	8		29	.266	.283	.363	115	4		.874	1	77	62	*O-67(LF),1-18/2-5,P	0.0
1881	Bos N	**83**	324	39	78	12	8	2	25	5		25	.241	.252	.346	90	-4		**.948**	12	86	149	*O-83(83-1-0)	0.2
1882	Bos N	**85**	388	67	117	14	11	1	50	2		25	.302	.305	.402	124	9		**.932**	12	75	114	*O-84(LF)/1	1.7
1883	Bos N	**98**	446	**107**	124	25	13	8	66	8		54	.278	.291	.446	117	7		**.936**	7	67	96	*O-98(LF)/3	1.0
1884	Bos N	115	518	119	139	27	10	7	51	17		80	.268	.292	.400	116	8		.916	2	60	33	*O-110(LF)/1-6	0.6
1885	Bos N	25	109	14	22	4	1	1	7	1		20	.202	.209	.284	61	-5		.919	-2	23	0	O-25(LF)	-0.7
1886	Bos N	94	424	67	109	12	2	2	40	10		62	.257	.274	.309	79	-11	16	**.948**	5	62	33	*O-94(LF)	-0.8
1887	Bos N	98	437	85	118	10	6	5	49	17	3	28	.270	.302	.355	81	-13	41	**.935**	12	128	87	*O-98(LF)	-0.3
1888	Bos N	107	431	61	103	11	7	3	53	16	2	39	.239	.269	.318	84	-9	29	.947	-7	57	0	*O-107(106-0-1)	-1.8
1889	Bal AA	135	533	73	122	13	9	1	78	22	7	72	.229	.269	.293	59	-32	34	.913	12	126	179	*O-134(134-0-1)/3	-2.0
1890	NY N	120	513	62	122	18	5	0	65	12	2	37	.238	.258	.292	60	-29	39	.931	-1	94	109	O-77(76-0-2),1-36/3-5,S-2	-3.1
Total	12	1123	4784	787	1230	172	90	31	564	120	14	498	.257	.277	.350	90	-74	159	.922	51	82	83	*O-1054L/1-62,3-7,2-5,S-2,P	-5.6
HORTON, TONY Anthony Darrin B 12.6.1944 Santa Monica, CA BR/TR 6-3/210# d7.31																								
1964	Bos A	36	126	9	28	5	0	1	8	3-0	0	20	.222	.238	.286	44	-10	0-0	1.000	0	103	188	O-24(LF)/1-8	-1.2
1965	Bos A	60	163	23	48	8	1	7	23	18-1	0	36	.294	.361	.485	131	7	0-2	.980	-1	93	94	1-44	0.3
1966	Bos A	6	22	0	3	0	0	0	2	0-0	0	5	.136	.136	.136	-19	-3	0-0	1.000	1	131	157	/1-6	-0.4
1967	Bos A	21	39	2	12	3	0	0	9	0-0	0	5	.308	.300	.385	96	0	0-0	.929	-1	95	97	/1-6	-0.2

Year	Tm Lg	G	AB	R	H	2B	3B	HR	RBI	BB-IB	HP	SO	AVG	OBP	SLG	AOPS	ABR	SB-CS	FA	FR	Rng	Thr	G at Pos	BFW
	Cle A	106	363	35	102	13	4	10	44	18-3	4	52	.281	.321	.421	117	6	3-0	.991	-5	74	95	1-94	-0.4
	Year	127	402	37	114	16	4	10	53	18-3	4	57	.284	.319	.418	114	6	3-0	.987	-6	75	95	*1-100	-0.6
1968	Cle A	133	477	57	119	29	3	14	59	34-5	3	56	.249	.302	.411	117	9	3-1	.992	-4	79	93	*1-128	-0.4
1969	Cle A	159	625	77	174	25	4	27	93	37-3	2	91	.278	.319	.461	113	7	3-3	.989	2	101	95	*1-157	-0.4
1970	Cle A	115	413	48	111	19	3	17	59	30-5	4	54	.269	.321	.453	107	3	3-2	.994	4	106	116	*1-112	-0.3
Total	7	636	2228	251	597	102	15	76	297	140-17	13	319	.268	.313	.430	109	19	12-8	.990	-6	91	99	1-555/O-24(LF)	-3.0
HORTON, WILLIE Willie Watterson B 10.18.1942 Arno, VA BR/TR 5-11/209# d9.10 C2																								
1963	Det A	15	43	6	14	2	1	1	4	0-0	0	8	.326	.326	.488	120	1	2-0	1.000	-1	78	0	/O-9(8-0-1)	0.0
1964	Det A	25	80	6	13	1	3	1	10	11-2	1	20	.162	.272	.287	55	-5	0-0	.943	-1	100	0	O-23(20-0-3)	-0.8
1965	Det A★	143	512	69	140	20	2	29	104	48-9	6	101	.273	.340	.490	132	21	5-9	.988	3	104	85	*O-141(111-0-34)/3	1.4
1966	Det A	146	526	72	138	22	6	27	100	44-4	3	103	.262	.321	.481	125	15	1-1	.979	-5	94	47	*O-137(129-0-20)	0.2
1967	Det A	122	401	47	110	20	3	19	67	36-0	4	80	.274	.338	.481	137	18	0-0	.971	1	99	79	*O-110(109-0-1)	1.4
1968	†Det A★	143	512	68	146	20	2	36	85	49-8	8	110	.285	.352	.543	165	39	0-3	.973	-6	88	70	*O-139(LF)	2.8
1969	Det A	141	508	66	133	17	1	28	91	52-10	3	93	.262	.332	.465	116	10	3-3	.972	5	112	78	*O-136(135-0-3)	0.7
1970	Det A★	96	371	53	113	18	2	17	69	28-6	2	43	.305	.354	.501	133	16	0-1	.982	3	96	172	O-96(96-0-2)	1.3
1971	Det A	119	450	64	130	25	1	22	72	37-8	7	75	.289	.349	.496	133	19	1-5	.963	-7	85	113	*O-118(106-0-29)	0.4
1972	†Det A	108	333	44	77	9	5	11	36	27-5	3	47	.231	.293	.387	99	-2	0-0	1.000	-4	86	96	O-98(81-0-30)	-1.2
1973	Det A★	111	411	42	130	19	3	17	53	23-5	7	57	.316	.362	.501	132	17	1-4	.942	-9	89	31	*O-107(LF)/D	0.1
1974	Det A	72	238	32	71	8	1	15	47	21-3	3	36	.298	.361	.529	149	14	0-1	.947	-4	91	48	O-64(LF)/D	0.6
1975	Det A	159	615	62	169	13	1	25	92	44-11	0	109	.275	.319	.421	104	1	1-2	—	0	0	0	*D-159	-0.4
1976	Det A	114	401	40	105	17	0	14	56	49-7	2	63	.262	.342	.409	116	9	0-0	—	0	0	0	*D-105	0.6
1977	Det A	1	4	0	1	0	0	0	0	0-0	0	0	.250	.250	.250	35	0	0-0	1.000	-0	49	0	/O(LF)	-0.1
	Tex A	139	519	55	150	23	3	15	75	42-5	0	117	.289	.337	.432	108	6	2-3	.938	-1	89	0	*D-128,O-10(LF)	0.0
	Year	140	523	55	151	23	3	15	75	42-5	0	117	.289	.337	.430	108	5	2-3	.941	-1	85	0	*D-128,O-11(LF)	-0.1
1978	Cle A	50	169	15	42	7	0	5	22	15-4	1	25	.249	.314	.379	95	-1	3-0	—	0	0	0	D-48	-0.2
	Oak A	32	102	11	32	8	0	3	19	9-2	0	15	.314	.369	.480	145	6	0-1	.333	-0	104	0	D-27/O(LF)	0.5
	Tor A	33	122	12	25	6	0	3	19	4-0	0	29	.205	.228	.328	54	-8	0-0	—	0	0	0	D-30	-0.9
	Year	115	393	38	99	21	0	11	60	28-6	1	69	.252	.303	.389	95	-3	3-1	.697	-0	104	0	*D-105/O(LF)	-0.6
1979	Sea A	162	646	77	180	19	5	29	106	42-4	4	112	.279	.326	.458	107	4	1-1	—	0	0	0	*D-162	-0.1
1980	Sea A	97	335	32	74	10	1	8	36	39-2	4	70	.221	.306	.328	74	-12	0-4	—	0	0	0	D-92	-1.6
Total	18	2028	7298	873	1993	284	40	325	1163	620-95	58	1313	.273	.332	.457	119	168	20-38	.972	-26	95	79	*O-1190(1117-0-123),D-753/3	4.7
HOSEY, DWAYNE Dwayne Samuel B 3.11.1967 Sharon, PA BB/TR 5-10/175# d9.1																								
1995	†Bos A	24	68	20	23	8	1	3	7	8-0	0	16	.338	.408	.618	157	6	6-0	1.000	0	103	111	O-21(2-19-1)/D	0.7
1996	Bos A	28	78	13	17	2	2	1	3	7-0	0	17	.218	.282	.333	54	-6	6-3	.984	3	121	156	O-26(7-20-0)/D-2	-0.3
Total	2	52	146	33	40	10	3	4	10	15-0	0	33	.274	.342	.466	102	0	12-3	.991	3	113	136	/O-47(9-39-1),D-3	0.4
HOSEY, STEVE Steven Bernard B 4.2.1969 Oakland, CA BR/TR 6-3/215# d8.29																								
1992	SF N	21	56	6	14	1	0	1	6	0-0	0	15	.250	.241	.321	64	-3	1-1	.960	-2	81	0	O-18(RF)	-0.6
1993	SF N	3	2	0	1	1	0	0	1	1-0	0	1	.500	.667	1.000	350	1	0-0	—	-0	0	0	/O(RF)	0.1
Total	2	24	58	6	15	2	0	1	7	1-0	0	16	.259	.262	.345	77	-2	1-1	.960	-2	80	0	/O-19(RF)	-0.5
HOSLEY, TIM Timothy Kenneth B 5.10.1947 Spartanburg, SC BR/TR 5-10/195# d9.8																								
1970	Det A	7	12	1	2	0	0	1	2	0-0	0	6	.167	.154	.417	55	-1	0-0	1.000	1	135	348	/C-4	0.0
1971	Det A	7	16	2	3	0	0	2	6	0-0	0	1	.188	.188	.563	102	0	0-0	1.000	0	126	0	/C-4,1	0.0
1973	Oak A	13	14	3	3	0	0	0	2	2-0	0	3	.214	.313	.214	53	-1	0-0	.952	-1	0	68	C-13	-0.1
1974	Oak A	11	7	3	2	0	0	0	1	1-0	0	2	.286	.333	.286	99	0	0-0	1.000	1	87	0	/C-8,1	0.1
1975	Chi N	62	141	22	36	7	0	6	20	27-3	2	25	.255	.382	.433	120	5	1-1	.968	0	107	90	C-53	0.7
1976	Oak A	37	55	4	9	2	0	1	4	8-0	0	12	.164	.270	.255	56	-3	0-0	.968	0	78	58	C-37	-0.2
	Chi N	1	1	0	0	0	0	0	0	0-0	0	0	.000	.000	.000	-92	0	0-0	—	0			H	0.0
1977	Oak A	39	78	5	15	0	0	1	10	16-0	1	13	.192	.333	.231	59	-4	0-0	.955	2	69	100	C-19,D-12/1-3	-0.2
1978	Oak A	13	23	1	7	2	0	0	3	1-0	1	6	.304	.360	.391	117	1	0-0	.962	0	66	131	/C-6,D	0.1
1981	Oak A	18	21	2	2	0	0	1	5	2-0	0	5	.095	.174	.238	19	-2	0-0	.750	-0	0	0	/1D	-0.3
Total	9	208	368	43	79	11	0	12	53	57-3	4	73	.215	.324	.342	87	-5	1-1	.968	3	89	91	C-144/D-17,1-6	0.1
HOSTETLER, CHUCK Charles Cloyd B 9.22.1903 McClellandtown, PA D 2.18.1971 Fort Collins, CO BL/TR 6/175# d4.18																								
1944	Det A	90	265	42	79	9	2	0	20	21	0	31	.298	.350	.347	94	-2	4-4	.985	-1	96	109	O-65(1-4-61)	-0.7
1945	†Det A	42	44	3	7	3	0	0	2	7	0	8	.159	.275	.227	43	-3	0-0	.889	-1	82	0	/O-8(6-1-1)	-0.4
Total	2	132	309	45	86	12	2	0	22	28	0	39	.278	.338	.330	87	-5	4-4	.979	-1	95	102	/O-73(7-5-62)	-1.1
HOSTETLER, DAVE David Alan B 3.27.1956 Pasadena, CA BR/TR 6-4/215# d9.15																								
1981	Mon N	5	6	1	3	0	0	1	1	0-0	0	2	.500	.500	1.000	314	2	0-0	1.000	-0	0	303	/1-2	0.1
1982	Tex A	113	418	53	97	12	3	22	67	42-3	1	113	.232	.300	.433	105	1	2-2	.990	-9	70	105	*1-109/D-3	-1.5
1983	Tex A	94	304	31	67	9	2	11	46	42-1	5	103	.220	.323	.372	93	-2	0-2	1.000	-0	0	0	D-88/1-2	-0.6
1984	Tex A	37	82	7	18	2	1	3	10	13-0	0	27	.220	.326	.378	91	-1	0-0	1.000	0	104	102	1-14,D-13	-0.2
1988	Pit N	6	8	0	2	0	0	0	0	0-0	0	3	.250	.250	.250	45	-1	0-0	.944	0	241	0	/1-4,C	-0.1
Total	5	255	818	92	187	23	6	37	124	97-4	6	248	.229	.313	.407	100	-1	2-4	.990	-10	73	104	1-131,D-104/C	-2.3
HOTALING, PETE Peter James "Monkey" B 12.16.1856 Mohawk, NY D 7.3.1928 Cleveland, OH BL/TR (BR 1880 (1 game)) 5-8/166# d5.1																								
1879	Cin N	**81**	369	64	103	20	9	1	27	12		17	.279	.302	.390	133	14		.843	0	107	116	*O-69(0-67-2)/C-8,2-6,3-3	1.1
1880	Cle N	78	325	40	78	17	8	0	41	10		30	.240	.263	.342	105	2		.896	-5	76	131	*O-78(2-76-0)/C-2	-0.7
1881	Wor N	77	317	51	98	15	3	1	35	18		12	.309	.346	.385	123	8		.862	-4	107	61	*O-74(2-72-1)/C-3	0.1
1882	Bos N	84	378	64	98	16	5	0	28	16		21	.259	.289	.328	97	-1		.865	0	84	139	*O-84(0-84-1)	-0.3
1883	Cle N	**100**	417	54	108	20	8	0	30	12		31	.259	.280	.345	90	-5		.829	-2	101	149	*O-100(CF)	-0.9
1884	Cle N	102	408	69	99	16	6	3	27	28		50	.243	.291	.333	93	-4		.849	-1	113	144	*O-102(3-99-0)/2	-0.7
1885	Bro AA	94	370	73	95	9	5	1	34	49	4		.257	.350	.316	111	7		.893	-1	107	105	*O-94(CF)	0.3
1887	Cle AA	126	505	108	151	28	13	3	94	53	7		.299	.373	.424	126	19	43	.903	-1	112	94	*O-126(CF)	1.2
1888	Cle AA	98	403	67	101	7	6	0	55	26	7		.251	.307	.298	97	-1	35	.878	-10	64	187	*O-98(CF)	-1.3
Total	9	840	3492	590	931	148	63	9	371	224	18	161	.267	.314	.353	108	39	78	.869	-23	97	126	O-825(7-816-4)/C-13,2-7,3-3	-1.2
HOTTMAN, KEN Kenneth Roger B 5.7.1948 Stockton, CA BR/TR 5-11/190# d9.11																								
1971	Chi A	6	16	1	2	0	0	0	0	1-0	0	2	.125	.176	.125	-13	-2	0-0	1.000	-1	65	0	/O-5(LF)	-0.4
HOUCK, SADIE Sargent Perry B 3.1856 Washington, DC D 5.26.1919 Washington, DC BR/TR 5-7/151# d5.1																								
1879	Bos N	80	356	69	95	24	9	2	49	4		11	.267	.275	.402	117	6		.814	-10	144	168	O-47(1-5-42),S-33	-0.2
1880	Bos N	12	47	2	7	0	0	0	2	0		6	.149	.149	.149	1	-5		.786	-2	35	0	O-12(0-2-10)	-0.6
	Pro N	49	184	27	37	7	7	1	22	3		6	.201	.214	.332	85	-3		.873	-1	82	0	O-49(38-12-2)	-0.7
	Year	61	231	29	44	7	7	1	24	3		12	.190	.201	.294	68	-8		.855	-3	73	0	O-61(38-14-12)	-1.3
1881	Det N	75	308	43	86	16	6	1	36	6		6	.279	.293	.380	106	1		.868	1	97	**166**	*S-75	0.5
1883	Det N	**101**	416	52	105	18	12	0	40	9		18	.252	.268	.353	91	-5		.852	4	103	122	*S-101	0.2
1884	Phi AA	**108**	472	93	140	19	14	0		7	8		.297	.318	.396	124	10		**.893**	22	**112**	117	*S-108/2	3.2
1885	Phi AA	93	388	74	99	10	9	0	54	10	7		.255	.286	.327	88	-7		.863	19	114	117	*S-93	1.3
1886	Bal AA	61	260	29	50	8	1	0	17	4	4		.192	.216	.231	41	-18	25	.849	-6	86	25	S-55/2-5,O(CF)	-2.0
	Was N	52	195	14	42	3	0	0	14	2		28	.215	.223	.231	41	-14	4	.858	2	107	59	S-51/2	-1.0
1887	NY AA	10	33	3	5	1	0	0	0	3	1		.152	.243	.182	20	-3	2	.831	2	137	106	S-10/2	-0.1
Total	8	641	2659	406	666	106	58	4	234	48	20	75	.250	.269	.338	91	-38	31	.863	31	104	111	S-526,O-109(39-20-54)/2-8	0.6
HOUK, RALPH Ralph George "Major" B 8.9.1919 Lawrence, KS BR/TR 5-11/193# d4.26 M20 C4																								
1947	†NY A	41	92	7	25	3	1	0	12	11	1	5	.272	.356	.326	91	-1	0-0	.987	0	*88*	*81*	C-41	0.1
1948	NY A	14	29	3	8	2	0	0	3	0	0	0	.276	.276	.345	65	-2	0-0	1.000	3	*132*	*146*	C-14	0.1
1949	NY A	5	7	0	4	0	0	0	1	0	0	1	.571	.571	.571	203	1	0-0	.889	-1	*49*	*0*	/C-5	0.0
1950	NY A	10	9	0	1	1	0	0	1	0	0	2	.111	.111	.222	-17	-2	0-0	.929	0	*0*	*0*	/C-9	-0.1
1951	NY A	3	5	0	1	0	0	0	2	0	0	1	.200	.200	.200	9	-1	0-0	1.000	-0	*0*	*447*	/C-3	-0.1
1952	†NY A	9	6	0	2	0	0	0	0	1	0	0	.333	.429	.333	121	0	0-0	.917	0	*0*	*0*	/C-9	0.1
1953	NY A	8	9	2	2	0	0	0	1	0	0	1	.222	.222	.222	21	-1	0-0	1.000	0	*0*	*0*	/C-8	-0.1

Year	Tm Lg	G	AB	R	H	2B	3B	HR	RBI	BB-IB	HP	SO	AVG	OBP	SLG	AOPS	ABR	SB-CS	FA	FR	Rng	Thr	G at Pos	BFW
1954	NY A	1	1	0	0	0	0	0	0	0	0	0	.000	.000	.000	-99	0	0-0	—	0			H	0.0
Total	8	91	158	12	43	6	1	0	20	12	1	10	.272	.327	.323	79	-6	0-0	.981	2	*81*	*87*	/C-89	0.0
HOUSE, FRANK Henry Franklin "Pig" B 2.18.1930 Bessemer, AL BL/TR 6-2/190# d7.21 Mil 1952																								
1950	Det A	5	5	1	2	1	0	0	0	0	0	1	.400	.400	.600	148	0	0-0	1.000	0	*0*	*0*	/C-5	0.0
1951	Det A	18	41	3	9	2	0	1	4	6	0	2	.220	.319	.341	78	-1	1-1	.957	-0	*74*	*152*	C-18	-0.1
1954	Det A	114	352	35	88	12	1	9	38	31	1	34	.250	.307	.366	87	-7	2-1	.992	2	*131*	*121*	*C-107	-0.1
1955	Det A	102	328	37	85	11	1	15	53	22-4	3	25	.259	.308	.436	102	-2	0-0	.987	-1	*100*	*115*	C-93	0.2
1956	Det A	94	321	44	77	6	2	10	44	21-0	3	19	.240	.290	.364	72	-15	1-1	.986	-3	*133*	*101*	C-88	-1.3
1957	Det A	106	348	31	90	9	0	7	36	35-13	1	26	.259	.327	.345	82	-8	1-1	.997	8	***147***	*80*	C-97	0.4
1958	KC A	76	202	16	51	6	3	4	24	12-2	1	13	.252	.295	.371	81	-6	1-0	.992	-4	*122*	*84*	C-55	-0.7
1959	KC A	98	347	32	82	14	3	1	30	20-6	2	23	.236	.282	.303	59	-20	0-3	.982	-4	*105*	*65*	C-95	-2.1
1960	Cin N	23	28	0	5	2	0	0	3	0-0	0	2	.179	.179	.250	16	-3	0-0	1.000	1	*141*	*111*	/C-8	-0.2
1961	Det A	17	22	3	5	1	1	0	3	4-0	0	2	.227	.333	.364	87	0	0-0	.974	-1	*106*	*82*	C-14	-0.1
Total	10	653	1994	202	494	64	11	47	235	151-25	11	147	.248	.302	.362	80	-62	6-7	.988	-3	*122*	*96*	C-580	-4.0
HOUSE, J.R. James Rodger B 11.11.1979 Charleston, WV BR/TR 5-10/202# d9.27																								
2003	Pit N	1	1	0	1	0	0	0	0	0-0	0	0	1.000	1.000	1.000	416	0	0-0	—	0			/H	0.0
HOUSEHOLDER, CHARLIE Charles F. B 1856 Harrisburg, PA D 12.26.1908 Harrisburg, PA BR/TR 5-7/150# d4.20																								
1884	CP U	83	310	32	74	12	5	1		12			.239	.267	.319	77	-18		.796	-4	78	107	3-41,O-40(LF)/S-3,P-2	-2.0
HOUSEHOLDER, CHARLIE Charles W. B 2.8.1854 Philadelphia, PA D 9.3.1913 Philadelphia, PA BL/TL 5-11/158# d5.2																								
1882	Bal AA	**74**	307	42	78	10	7	1		4			.254	.264	.342	111	4		.971	3	111	83	*1-74/C-3	0.0
1884	Bro AA	76	273	28	66	15	3	3		12	2		.242	.279	.352	104	1		.959	-4	132	87	1-40,C-31/O-6(2-2-1),2	-0.4
Total	2	150	580	70	144	25	10	4		16	2		.248	.271	.347	108	5		.967	-1	118	84	1-114/C-34,O-6(2-2-1),2	-0.4
HOUSEHOLDER, ED Edward H. B 10.12.1869 Pittsburgh, PA D 7.3.1924 Los Angeles, CA BL/TL 5-9.5/180# d4.17																								
1903	Bro N	12	43	5	9	0	0	0	9	2	0		.209	.244	.209	31	-4	3	.967	1	60	250	O-12(CF)	-0.4
HOUSEHOLDER, PAUL Paul Wesley B 9.4.1958 Columbus, OH BB/TR 6/180# d8.26																								
1980	Cin N	20	45	3	11	1	1	0	7	1-0	0	13	.244	.261	.311	59	-3	1-0	1.000	0	81	234	O-14(0-1-13)	-0.3
1981	Cin N	23	69	12	19	4	0	2	9	10-0	0	16	.275	.367	.420	121	2	3-1	1.000	-1	95	77	O-19(1-6-13)	0.1
1982	Cin N	138	417	40	88	11	5	9	34	30-5	2	77	.211	.265	.326	64	-22	17-11	.992	8	106	**182**	*O-131(0-9-123)	-2.1
1983	Cin N	123	380	40	97	24	4	6	43	44-5	2	60	.255	.335	.387	96	-1	12-12	**.991**	2	109	80	*O-112(6-36-80)	-0.5
1984	Cin N	14	12	3	1	1	0	0	0	3-1	0	3	.083	.267	.167	23	-1	1-1	1.000	1	121	670	O-10(3-1-6)	0.0
	StL N	13	14	1	2	0	0	0	0	0-0	0	3	.143	.143	.143	-20	-2	0-0	1.000	-1	64	0	/O-8(4-1-4)	-0.3
	Year	27	26	4	3	1	0	0	0	3-1	0	6	.115	.207	.154	3	-3	1-1	1.000	1	92	327	O-18(7-2-10)	-0.3
1985	Mil A	95	299	41	77	15	0	11	34	27-0	1	60	.258	.320	.418	101	0	1-2	.986	2	105	90	O-91(7-32-59)/D-3	-0.2
1986	Mil A	26	78	4	17	3	1	1	16	7-0	1	16	.218	.284	.321	64	-4	1-2	1.000	-1	89	87	O-22(12-5-8)/D-3	-0.6
1987	Hou N	14	12	2	1	1	0	0	1	4-0	0	2	.083	.313	.167	33	-1	0-0	1.000	-1	64	0	/O-7(0-6-1)	-0.1
Total	8	466	1326	146	313	60	11	29	144	126-11	6	250	.236	.304	.363	83	-32	36-29	.991	10	104	123	O-414(33-97-307)/D-6	-4.0
HOUSEMAN, JOHN John Franklin B 1.10.1870 , Netherlands D 11.4.1922 Chicago, IL ?/160# d9.11																								
1894	Chi N	4	15	5	6	3	1	0	4	5	1	3	.400	.571	.733	201	3	2	.950	1	107	129	/S-3,2	0.3
1897	StL N	80	278	34	68	6	6	0	21	28	7		.245	.329	.309	70	-12	16	.918	-1	102	61	2-41,O-33(7-7-19)/S-5,3-3	-1.0
Total	2	84	293	39	74	9	7	0	25	33	8	3	.253	.344	.331	79	-9	18	.916	-0	102	69	/2-42,O-33(7-7-19),S-8,3-3	-0.7
HOUSER, BEN Benjamin Franklin B 11.30.1883 Shenandoah, PA D 1.15.1952 Augusta, ME BL/TL 6-1/185# d5.2																								
1910	Phi A	34	69	9	13	3	2	0	7	7	0		.188	.263	.290	74	-2	0	1.000	-0	72	142	1-26	-0.3
1911	Bos N	20	71	11	18	1	0	1	9	8	0	6	.254	.329	.310	73	-2	2	.988	1	112	111	1-20	-0.2
1912	Bos N	108	332	38	95	17	3	8	52	22	1	29	.286	.332	.428	105	1	1	.986	-3	84	103	1-83	-0.4
Total	3	162	472	58	126	21	5	9	68	37	1	35	.267	.322	.390	96	-3	3	.989	-3	86	110	1-129	-0.9
HOUSIE, WAYNE Wayne Tyrone B 5.20.1965 Hampton, VA BB/TR 5-9/165# d9.17																								
1991	Bos A	11	8	2	2	1	0	0	0	1-0	0	3	.250	.333	.375	91	0	1-0	1.000	-1	58	0	/O-4(CF),D-2	0.0
1993	NY N	18	16	2	3	1	0	0	1	1-0	0	1	.188	.235	.250	30	-2	0-0	—	-0	0	0	/O-2(RF)	-0.2
Total	2	29	24	4	5	2	0	0	1	2-0	0	4	.208	.269	.292	51	-2	1-0	1.000	-1	45	0	/O-6(0-4-2),D-2	-0.2
HOUSTON, TYLER Tyler Sam B 1.17.1971 Las Vegas, NV BL/TR 6-2/210# d4.3 OF Total (1-LF 1-RF)																								
1996	Atl N	33	27	3	6	2	1	1	8	1-0	0	9	.222	.250	.481	83	-1	0-0	1.000	-0	59	55	1-11	-0.1
	Chi N	46	115	18	39	7	0	2	19	8-1	0	18	.339	.382	.452	116	3	3-2	.986	-5	66	101	C-27/3-9,2-2,1O(LF)	0.0
	Year	79	142	21	45	9	1	3	27	9-1	0	27	.317	.358	.458	109	2	3-2	.986	-5	66	101	C-27,1-12/3-9,2-2,O(LF)	-0.1
1997	Chi N	72	196	15	51	10	0	2	28	9-1	0	35	.260	.290	.342	64	-11	1-0	.986	-1	71	69	C-41,3-12/1-2,2S	-0.9
1998	†Chi N	95	255	26	65	7	1	9	33	13-1	0	53	.255	.290	.396	76	-10	2-2	.993	-3	78	91	C-63,3-12/1-7	-1.0
1999	Chi N	100	249	26	58	9	1	9	27	28-4	0	67	.233	.309	.386	76	-10	1-1	.901	-10	88	83	3-63,C-18/1-2,O(RF)	-1.8
	Cle A	13	27	2	4	1	0	1	3	3-0	0	11	.148	.233	.296	32	-3	0-0	1.000	-0	102	101	3-10/C	-0.3
2000	Mil N	101	284	30	71	15	0	18	43	17-3	0	72	.250	.292	.493	95	-4	2-1	.982	2	99	116	1-35,3-28,C-23	-0.3
2001	Mil N	75	235	36	68	7	0	12	38	18-1	1	62	.289	.343	.472	110	3	0-0	.928	-2	102	107	3-62/1-3	0.1
2002	Mil N	76	255	25	77	15	2	7	33	14-3	4	41	.302	.347	.459	115	4	1-0	.947	-13	79	58	3-72/1	-0.8
	LA N	35	65	9	13	5	1	0	7	2-0	0	21	.200	.224	.308	43	-6	0-0	.981	-2	50	115	1-12/3-2	-0.8
	Year	111	320	34	90	20	3	7	40	16-3	4	62	.281	.323	.428	102	-2	1-0	.943	-15	80	57	3-74,1-13	-1.6
2003	Phi N	54	97	7	27	6	0	2	14	6-1	0	19	.278	.320	.402	93	-1	0-0	.936	-1	92	0	3-21/1	-0.2
Total	8	700	1805	197	479	84	6	63	253	119-15	5	408	.265	.312	.423	89	-36	10-6	.930	-36	94	81	3-291,C-173/1-75,2-3,O-2L,S	-6.1
HOUTZ, LEFTY Fred Fritz B 9.4.1875 Connersville, IN D 2.15.1959 St.Marys, OH BL/TL 5-10/170# d7.23																								
1899	Cin N	5	17	1	4	0	1	0	0	4	0		.235	.381	.353	100	0	1	1.000	3	399	773	/O-5(1-4-0)	0.3
HOVLEY, STEVE Stephen Eugene B 12.18.1944 Ventura, CA BL/TL 5-10/188# d6.26																								
1969	Sea A	91	329	41	91	14	3	3	20	30-3	1	34	.277	.338	.365	98	-1	10-4	.989	4	106	136	O-84(3-35-49)	0.0
1970	Mil A	40	135	17	38	9	0	0	16	17-1	1	11	.281	.366	.348	97	0	5-1	.958	-0	110	45	O-38(0-4-38)	-0.1
	Oak A	72	100	8	19	1	0	0	1	5-1	0	11	.190	.229	.200	20	-11	3-0	1.000	1	113	66	O-42(10-26-7)	-1.1
	Year	112	235	25	57	10	0	0	17	22-2	1	22	.243	.310	.285	67	-10	8-1	.977	1	111	54	O-80(10-30-45)	-1.2
1971	Oak A	24	27	3	3	2	0	0	3	7-0	1	9	.111	.306	.185	45	-1	2-0	1.000	1	129	285	O-11(4-3-4)	0.0
1972	KC A	105	196	24	53	5	1	3	24	24-2	1	29	.270	.351	.352	111	3	3-3	.982	3	102	184	O-68(5-25-39)	0.4
1973	KC A	104	232	29	59	8	1	2	24	33-2	0	34	.254	.346	.323	83	-4	6-4	.975	1	103	113	O-79(4-25-53),D-15	-0.6
Total	5	436	1019	122	263	39	5	8	88	116-9	4	128	.258	.335	.330	88	-14	29-12	.982	10	106	125	O-322(26-118-190)/D-15	-1.4
HOWARD, CHRIS Christopher Hugh B 2.27.1966 San Diego, CA BR/TR 6-2/200# d9.15																								
1991	Sea A	9	6	1	1	1	0	0	0	1-0	0	2	.167	.286	.333	71	0	0-0	1.000	-1	218	265	/C-9	-0.1
1993	Sea A	4	1	0	0	0	0	0	0	0-0	0	0	.000	.000	.000	-99	0	0-0	1.000	-0	19	0	/C-4	-0.1
1994	Sea A	9	25	2	5	1	0	0	2	1-0	1	6	.200	.250	.240	29	-3	0-0	1.000	-0	0	86	/C-9	-0.2
Total	3	22	32	3	6	2	0	0	2	2-0	1	8	.188	.250	.250	33	-3	0-0	1.000	-2	67	136	/C-22	-0.4
HOWARD, DAVE David Austin "Del" B 5.1.1889 Washington, DC D 1.26.1956 Dallas, TX BR/TR 5-11/165# d5.8																								
1912	Was A	1	0	1	0	0	0	0	0	0	0		—	—	—	—	0	0	—	0			R	0.0
1915	Bro F	24	36	5	8	1	0	0	1	1	0	8	.222	.243	.250	39	-4	0	.925	1	134	0	2-12/O-2(0-1-1),S3	-0.2
Total	2	25	36	6	8	1	0	0	1	1	0	8	.222	.243	.250	39	-4	0	.925	1	134	0	/2-12,O-2(0-1-1),3S	-0.2
HOWARD, DAVID David Wayne B 2.26.1967 Sarasota, FL BB/TR 6/175# d4.14 f-Bruce OF Total (20-LF 25-CF 28-RF)																								
1991	KC A	94	236	20	51	7	0	1	17	16-0	1	45	.216	.267	.258	46	-17	3-2	.962	6	111	80	S-63,2-26/3O(RF)D	-0.7
1992	KC A	74	219	19	49	6	2	1	18	15-0	0	43	.224	.271	.283	55	-14	3-4	.976	1	97	116	S-74/O-2(CF)	-0.8
1993	KC A	15	24	5	8	0	1	0	2	2-0	0	5	.333	.370	.417	109	0	1-0	.927	1	114	46	/2-7,S-3,3-2,O(CF)	0.1
1994	KC A	46	83	9	19	4	0	1	13	11-0	0	23	.229	.309	.313	61	-5	3-2	1.000	5	118	43	3-25,S-15/2-3,O(LF)PD	0.2
1995	KC A	95	255	23	62	13	4	0	19	24-1	1	41	.243	.310	.325	65	-13	6-1	.994	12	105	102	2-41,S-33,O-30(11-16-8)/1D	0.2
1996	KC A	143	420	51	92	14	5	4	48	40-0	4	74	.219	.291	.305	52	-32	5-6	**.982**	13	**109**	**136**	*S-135/2-3,1-2,O(CF)	-0.9
1997	KC A	80	162	24	39	8	1	1	13	10-1	1	31	.241	.287	.321	58	-10	2-2	.973	5	102	138	2-34,O-23(5-2-17)/S-9,3-7,D-5	-0.4
1998	StL N	46	102	15	25	1	1	2	12	12-2	0	22	.245	.322	.333	74	-4	0-0	1.000	-0	120	52	2-19,S-16,3-14/O-2(0-2-1)	-0.3

Year	Tm Lg	G	AB	R	H	2B	3B	HR	RBI	BB-IB	HP	SO	AVG	OBP	SLG	AOPS	ABR	SB-CS	FA	FR	Rng	Thr	G at Pos	BFW
1999	StL N	52	82	3	17	4	0	1	6	7-3	2	27	.207	.286	.293	47	-7	0-2	.966	-2	91	44	S-13/1-9,2-9,O-5(3-1-1),3-4	-0.9
Total	9	645	1583	169	362	57	14	11	148	137-7	9	311	.229	.291	.303	57	-102	23-19	.976	41	108	116	S-361,2-142/O-66R,3-53,1-12,D-9,P	-3.5
HOWARD, DOUG Douglas Lynn B 2.6.1948 Salt Lake City, UT BR/TR 6-3/185# d9.6																								
1972	Cal A	11	38	4	10	1	0	0	2	1-0	1	3	.263	.300	.289	81	-1	0-0	1.000	-1	63	373	/O-8(LF),13	-0.2
1973	Cal A	8	21	2	2	0	0	0	1	1-0	0	6	.095	.130	.095	-37	-4	0-0	1.000	-0	81	0	/O-6(LF),13	-0.5
1974	Cal A	22	39	5	9	0	1	0	5	2-0	0	1	.231	.268	.282	62	-2	1-0	1.000	-1	59	0	/O-8(2-6-0),1-5,D-3	-0.3
1975	StL N	17	29	1	6	0	0	1	1	0-0	0	7	.207	.207	.310	41	-3	0-0	1.000	1	172	115	/1-7	-0.2
1976	Cle A	39	90	7	19	4	0	0	13	3-2	1	13	.211	.237	.256	47	-6	1-1	.991	1	110	96	1-32/O-2(RF),D-4	-0.8
Total	5	97	217	19	46	5	1	1	22	7-2	2	30	.212	.239	.258	46	-16	2-1	.994	0	118	99	/1-46,O-24(16-6-2),D-7,3-2	-2.0
HOWARD, ELSTON Elston Gene B 2.23.1929 St.Louis, MO D 12.14.1980 New York, NY BR/TR 6-2/200# d4.14 C11																								
1955	†NY A	97	279	33	81	8	7	10	43	20-5	1	36	.290	.336	.477	120	5	0-0	.978	5	98	191	O-75(62-0-15)/C-9	0.7
1956	†NY A	98	290	35	76	8	3	5	34	21-6	1	30	.262	.312	.362	81	-9	0-1	.990	0	94	51	O-65(62-0-5),C-26	-1.1
1957	†NY A☆	110	356	33	90	13	4	8	44	16-6	0	43	.253	.283	.379	81	-11	2-5	.961	-3	66	177	O-71(69-0-2),C-32/1-2	-1.8
1958	†NY A☆	103	376	45	118	19	5	11	66	22-6	0	60	.314	.348	.479	131	14	1-1	.997	0	_98_	_119_	C-67,O-24(17-0-8)/1-5	1.6
1959	NY A☆	125	443	59	121	24	6	18	73	20-4	3	57	.273	.306	.476	116	7	0-1	.985	-2	86	96	1-50,C-43,O-28(18-0-10)	0.2
1960	†NY A★	107	323	29	79	11	3	6	39	28-7	0	43	.245	.298	.353	82	-9	3-0	.987	3	_128_	_110_	C-91/O(LF)	-0.1
1961	†NY A★	129	446	64	155	17	5	21	77	28-6	3	65	.348	.387	.549	156	33	0-3	.993	7	**_146_**	_90_	*C-111/1-9	4.3
1962	†NY A★	136	494	63	138	23	5	21	91	31-1	1	76	.279	.318	.474	115	8	1-1	.995	3	**_169_**	_85_	*C-129	1.7
1963	†NY A★	135	487	75	140	21	6	28	85	35-4	6	68	.287	.342	.528	141	25	0-0	.994	2	**203**	71	*C-132	3.4
1964	†NY A★	150	550	63	172	27	3	15	84	48-12	5	73	.313	.371	.455	127	21	1-1	**.998**	8	_169_	_81_	*C-146	3.8
1965	NY A☆	110	391	38	91	15	1	9	45	24-3	1	65	.233	.278	.345	77	-13	0-0	.991	-2	_107_	_83_	C-95/1-5,O(LF)	-1.1
1966	NY A	126	410	38	105	19	2	6	35	37-9	1	65	.256	.317	.356	97	-1	0-0	.985	2	_136_	_76_	*C-100,1-13	0.6
1967	NY A	66	199	13	39	6	0	3	17	12-3	2	36	.196	.247	.271	56	-11	0-0	.984	0	104	79	C-48/1	-1.0
	†Bos A	42	116	9	17	3	0	1	11	9-3	1	24	.147	.211	.198	21	-11	0-0	.996	3	110	73	C-41	-0.8
	Year	108	315	22	56	9	0	4	28	21-6	3	60	.178	.233	.244	42	-23	0-0	.990	3	107	76	C-89/1	-1.8
1968	Bos A	71	203	22	49	4	0	5	18	22-7	1	45	.241	.317	.335	92	-2	1-1	.995	-6	73	83	C-68	-0.5
Total	14	1605	5363	619	1471	218	50	167	762	373-82	26	786	.274	.322	.427	108	46	9-14	.993	21	_141_	_88_	*C-1138,O-265(230-0-40)/1-85	9.9
HOWARD, FRANK Frank Oliver "Hondo" or "The Capital Punisher" B 8.8.1936 Columbus, OH BR/TR 6-7/255# d9.10 M2 C19																								
1958	LA N	8	29	3	7	1	0	1	2	1-0	0	11	.241	.267	.379	66	-1	0-0	1.000	0	90	178	/O-8(3-0-5)	-0.2
1959	LA N	9	21	2	3	0	1	1	6	2-0	0	9	.143	.217	.381	52	-2	0-0	1.000	-0	101	0	/O-6(4-0-2)	-0.2
1960	LA N	117	448	54	120	15	2	23	77	32-1	3	108	.268	.320	.464	105	2	0-1	.984	-4	92	85	*O-115(22-0-94)/1-4	-0.7
1961	LA N	92	267	36	79	10	2	15	45	21-3	1	50	.296	.347	.517	116	6	0-1	.934	-2	86	134	O-65(20-0-46)/1-7	-0.1
1962	LA N	141	493	80	146	25	6	31	119	39-10	1	108	.296	.346	.560	148	31	1-0	.972	4	91	**195**	*O-131(9-0-128)	2.6
1963	†LA N	123	417	58	114	16	1	28	64	33-4	4	116	.273	.330	.518	151	26	1-2	.960	-5	100	49	*O-111(6-0-107)	1.4
1964	LA N	134	433	60	98	13	2	24	69	51-10	0	113	.226	.303	.432	114	7	1-0	.979	-6	97	25	*O-122(RF)	-0.7
1965	Was A	149	516	53	149	22	6	21	84	55-2	2	112	.289	.358	.477	138	25	0-0	.981	-3	92	67	*O-138(138-0-5)	1.6
1966	Was A	146	493	52	137	19	4	18	71	53-6	1	104	.278	.348	.442	127	17	1-1	.982	0	101	65	*O-135(LF)	1.1
1967	Was A	149	519	71	133	20	2	36	89	60-7	5	155	.256	.338	.511	154	34	0-1	.986	-6	88	55	*O-141(141-0-3)/1-4	2.3
1968	Was A★	158	598	79	164	28	3	**44**	106	54-12	6	141	.274	.338	**.552**	**172**	49	0-0	.955	-1	83	161	*O-107(LF),1-55	4.5
1969	Was A★	161	592	111	175	17	2	48	111	102-19	5	96	.296	.402	.574	180	65	1-0	.974	-16	73	36	*O-114(108-0-6),1-70	4.0
1970	Was A★	161	566	90	160	15	1	**44**	**126**	**132-29**	2	125	.283	.416	.546	173	62	1-2	.973	-9	83	83	*O-120(114-0-6),1-48	4.4
1971	Was A★	153	549	60	153	25	2	26	83	77-**20**	2	121	.279	.367	.474	146	34	1-0	.993	5	79	119	*O-100(95-0-5),1-68	3.1
1972	Tex A	95	287	28	70	9	0	9	31	42-8	1	55	.244	.341	.369	117	7	1-0	.981	-6	83	77	1-66,O-21(20-0-1)	-0.5
	Det A	14	33	1	8	1	0	1	7	4-0	0	8	.242	.324	.364	101	0	0-0	.952	0	121	84	1-10/O(LF)	0.0
	Year	109	320	29	78	10	0	10	38	46-8	1	63	.244	.340	.369	115	7	1-0	.978	-6	88	78	1-76,O-22(21-0-1)	-0.5
1973	Det A	85	227	26	58	9	1	12	29	24-4	0	28	.256	.327	.463	113	3	0-1	.923	-0	0	0	D-76/1-2	0.0
Total	16	1895	6488	864	1774	245	35	382	1119	782-135	33	1460	.273	.352	.499	143	365	8-9	.975	-49	89	86	*O-1435(923-0-530),1-334/D-76	22.6
HOWARD, DEL George Elmer B 12.24.1877 Kenney, IL D 12.24.1956 Seattle, WA BL/TR 6/180# d4.15 b-Ivan OF Total (137-LF 34-CF 85-RF)																								
1905	Pit N	123	435	56	127	18	5	2	63	27	8		.292	.345	.370	110	6	19	.978	-5	85	133	1-90,O-28(1-0-27)/P	-0.2
1906	Bos N	147	545	46	142	19	8	1	54	26	10		.261	.306	.330	101	-1	17	.911	-12	128	106	O-87(LF),2-45,S-14/1-2	-1.9
1907	Bos N	50	187	20	51	4	2	1	13	11	5		.273	.330	.332	108	1	11	.969	-1	140	131	O-45(LF)/2-3	-0.2
	†Chi N	51	148	10	34	2	2	0	13	6	2		.230	.269	.270	65	-6	3	.972	-3	88	132	1-33/O-8(0-3-6)	-1.1
	Year	101	335	30	85	6	4	1	26	17	7		.254	.304	.304	88	-5	14	.961	-4	121	113	O-53(45-3-6),1-33/2-3	-1.3
1908	†Chi N	96	315	42	88	7	3	1	26	23	5		.279	.338	.330	109	3	11	.965	-3	101	46	O-81(4-31-52)/1-5	-0.3
1909	Chi N	69	203	25	40	4	2	1	24	18	6		.197	.282	.251	64	-8	6	.980	-0	101	120	1-57	-1.1
Total	5	536	1833	199	482	54	22	6	193	111	36		.263	.318	.326	98	-5	67	.946	-23	115	77	O-249L,1-187/2-48,S-14,P	-4.8
HOWARD, IVAN Ivan Chester B 10.12.1882 Kenney, IL D 3.30.1967 Medford, OR BB/TR 5-10/170# d4.25 b-Del																								
1914	StL A	81	209	21	51	6	2	0	20	28	3	42	.244	.342	.292	94	0	14-10	.936	-4	93	75	3-34,1-28/O-3(1-1-1),S	-0.5
1915	StL A	113	324	43	90	10	7	2	43	43	3	48	.278	.368	.370	126	11	29-12	.992	8	132	93	1-48,3-23,O-17(5-1-11)/2-2,S-2	2.0
1916	Cle A	81	246	20	46	11	5	0	23	30	9	34	.187	.298	.272	68	-9	9	.970	6	116	62	2-65/1-7	-0.2
1917	Cle A	27	39	7	4	0	0	0	0	3	0	5	.103	.167	.103	-17	-5	1	.833	-0	86	414	/3-6,2-4,O-4(CF)	-0.7
Total	4	302	818	91	191	27	14	2	86	104	15	129	.233	.331	.308	92	-3	53-22	.990	9	125	68	/1-83,2-71,3-63,O-24(6-6-12),S-3	0.6
HOWARD, LARRY Lawrence Rayford B 6.6.1945 Columbus, OH BR/TR 6-3/200# d8.9																								
1970	Hou N	31	88	11	27	6	0	2	16	10-3	0	23	.307	.378	.443	124	3	0-0	.993	-2	192	120	C-26/1-2,O(RF)	0.2
1971	Hou N	24	64	6	15	3	0	2	14	3-0	0	17	.234	.265	.375	83	-2	0-1	.992	3	149	122	C-22	0.2
1972	Hou N	54	157	16	35	7	0	2	13	17-3	0	30	.223	.299	.306	74	-5	0-0	.980	-6	79	80	C-53/O(LF)	-1.0
1973	Hou N	20	48	3	8	3	0	0	4	5-2	0	12	.167	.245	.229	32	-4	0-0	.989	-1	99	152	C-20	-0.5
	Atl N	4	8	0	1	0	0	0	0	2-0	0	3	.125	.300	.125	20	-1	0-0	1.000	-0	88	0	/C-2	-0.1
	Year	24	56	3	9	3	0	0	4	7-2	0	15	.161	.254	.214	31	-5	0-0	.990	-2	98	135	C-22	-0.6
Total	4	133	365	36	86	19	0	6	47	37-8	0	85	.236	.305	.337	81	-9	0-1	.986	-6	118	104	C-123/O-2(1-0-1),1-2	-1.2
HOWARD, MATT Matthew Christopher B 9.22.1967 Fall River, MA BR/TR 5-10/170# d5.17																								
1996	NY A	35	54	9	11	1	0	1	9	2-0	0	8	.204	.228	.278	28	-6	1-0	.976	-8	72	54	2-30/3-6	-1.2
HOWARD, MIKE Michael Fredric B 4.2.1958 Seattle, WA BB/TR 6-2/185# d9.12																								
1981	NY N	14	24	4	4	1	0	0	3	4-0	0	6	.167	.276	.208	43	-2	2-0	.952	1	114	313	O-14(6-1-7)	0.0
1982	NY N	33	39	5	7	0	0	1	3	6-0	1	7	.179	.298	.256	59	-2	2-0	1.000	2	111	272	O-22(9-7-8)/2-3	0.0
1983	NY N	1	3	0	1	0	0	0	1	0-0	0	1	.333	.333	.333	86	0	0-0	—	-1	0	0	/O(RF)	-0.1
Total	3	48	66	9	12	1	0	1	7	10-0	1	14	.182	.291	.242	54	-4	4-0	.980	3	106	274	/O-37(15-8-16),2-3	-0.1
HOWARD, PAUL Paul Joseph "Del" B 5.20.1884 Boston, MA D 8.29.1968 Miami, FL BR/TR 5-8/170# d9.16																								
1909	Bos A	6	15	2	3	1	0	0	2	3	1		.200	.368	.267	99	0	0	1.000	-0	228	0	/O-6(4-0-2)	0.0
HOWARD, STEVE Steven Bernard B 12.7.1963 Oakland, CA BR/TR 6-2/205# d6.16																								
1990	Oak A	21	52	5	12	4	0	0	1	4-1	0	17	.231	.286	.308	69	-2	0-0	.933	-2	71	0	O-14(4-3-8)/D-7	-0.4
HOWARD, THOMAS Thomas Sylvester B 12.11.1964 Middletown, OH BB/TR (BL 1996-98) 6-2/205# d7.3																								
1990	SD N	20	44	4	12	2	0	0	0	0-0	0	11	.273	.273	.318	61	-2	0-1	.950	-1	92	0	O-13(9-2-2)	-0.4
1991	SD N	106	281	30	70	12	3	4	22	24-4	1	57	.249	.309	.356	84	-6	10-7	.995	4	113	92	O-86(34-41-14)	-0.4
1992	SD N	5	3	1	1	0	0	0	0	0-0	0	0	.333	.333	.333	88	0	0-0	—	0			/H	0.0
	Cle A	117	358	36	99	15	2	2	32	17-1	0	60	.277	.308	.346	85	-8	15-8	.990	-2	96	90	O-97(68-22-13)/D-2	-1.2
1993	Cle A	74	178	26	42	7	0	3	23	12-0	0	42	.236	.278	.326	64	-10	5-1	.977	2	106	129	O-47(9-11-28)/D-7	-0.8
	Cin N	38	141	22	39	8	3	4	13	12-0	0	21	.277	.331	.461	110	2	5-6	.987	2	103	180	O-37(27-12-0)	0.2
1994	Cin N	83	178	24	47	11	0	5	24	10-1	0	30	.264	.302	.410	85	-4	4-2	.965	1	106	83	O-57(41-7-12)	-0.5
1995	†Cin N	113	281	42	85	15	2	3	26	20-1	1	37	.302	.350	.402	98	-1	17-8	.985	-0	102	58	O-82(36-39-14)	-0.1
1996	Cin N	121	360	50	98	19	10	6	42	17-3	3	51	.272	.307	.431	93	-6	6-5	.982	1	97	146	*O-103(51-40-32)	-0.7
1997	†Hou N	107	255	24	63	16	1	3	22	26-1	3	48	.247	.323	.353	80	-7	1-2	1.000	0	93	163	O-62(10-41-18)	-0.8
1998	LA N	47	76	9	14	4	0	2	4	3-0	0	15	.184	.215	.316	40	-7	1-0	1.000	1	102	207	O-29(11-13-6)/D	-0.6
1999	StL N	98	195	16	57	10	0	6	28	17-0	2	26	.292	.353	.436	98	-1	1-1	.987	-2	100	0	O-48(3-0-45)/D	-0.4
2000	StL N	86	133	13	28	4	1	6	28	7-0	1	34	.211	.255	.391	60	-9	1-0	.960	-2	75	101	O-27(6-0-22)/1D	-1.1
Total	11	1015	2483	297	655	123	22	44	264	165-10	11	432	.264	.311	.384	85	-59	66-41	.986	4	100	106	O-688(305-228-206)/D-14,1	-6.8

Year	Tm Lg	G	AB	R	H	2B	3B	HR	RBI	BB-IB	HP	SO	AVG	OBP	SLG	AOPS	ABR	SB-CS	FA	FR	Rng	Thr	G at Pos	BFW
HOWARD, WILBUR Wilbur Leon B 1.8.1949 Lowell, NC BB/TR 6-2/175# d9.4																								
1973	Mil A	16	39	3	8	0	0	0	1	2-1	0	10	.205	.244	.205	28	-4	0-1	.969	2	135	268	O-12(5-0-7)/D	-0.2
1974	Hou N	64	111	19	24	4	0	2	5	5-0	0	18	.216	.250	.306	57	-7	4-5	1.000	2	103	137	O-50(43-4-3)	-0.8
1975	Hou N	121	392	62	111	16	8	0	21	21-3	3	67	.283	.324	.365	98	-3	32-11	.995	2	101	112	O-95(53-34-12)	-0.2
1976	Hou N	94	191	26	42	7	2	1	18	7-1	0	28	.220	.245	.293	58	-12	7-5	.961	1	107	65	O-63(37-11-20)/2-2	-1.5
1977	Hou N	87	187	22	48	6	0	2	13	5-1	0	30	.257	.276	.321	65	-10	11-1	.990	2	109	68	O-62(46-15-4)/2-4	-0.7
1978	Hou N	84	148	17	34	4	1	1	13	5-0	3	22	.230	.268	.291	61	-8	6-2	1.000	-3	78	103	O-38(30-5-4)/C-3,2	-1.2
Total	6	466	1068	149	267	37	11	6	71	45-6	6	175	.250	.283	.322	73	-44	60-25	.987	7	103	105	O-320(214-69-50)/2-7,C-3,D	-4.6
HOWARTH, JIM James Eugene B 3.7.1947 Biloxi, MS BL/TL 5-11/175# d9.5																								
1971	SF N	7	13	3	3	1	0	0	2	3-0	0	3	.231	.375	.308	97	0	0-0	1.000	0	144	0	/O-6(2-1-3)	0.0
1972	SF N	74	119	16	28	4	0	1	7	16-1	0	18	.235	.326	.294	76	-3	3-2	1.000	-1	97	0	O-25(8-17-0)/1-4	-0.6
1973	SF N	65	90	8	18	1	1	0	7	7-0	0	8	.200	.258	.233	36	-8	0-0	1.000	0	102	79	O-33(5-21-7)/1	-0.9
1974	SF N	6	4	0	0	0	0	0	0	0-0	0	0	.000	.000	.000	-96	-1	0-0	—	-0	0	0	/O(LF)	-0.1
Total	4	152	226	27	49	6	1	1	16	26-1	0	29	.217	.298	.265	58	-12	3-2	1.000	-1	103	36	/O-65(16-39-10),1-5	-1.6
HOWE, ART Arthur Henry B 12.15.1946 Pittsburgh, PA BR/TR 6-2/190# d7.10 M13 C5																								
1974	†Pit N	29	74	10	18	4	1	1	5	9-0	0	13	.243	.321	.365	96	0	0-0	.937	1	110	216	3-20/S-2	0.0
1975	Pit N	63	146	13	25	9	0	1	10	15-3	0	15	.171	.248	.253	40	-12	1-0	.938	-4	102	61	3-42/S-3	-1.6
1976	Hou N	21	29	0	4	1	0	0	0	6-1	0	6	.138	.286	.172	35	-2	0-0	.938	0	90	99	/3-8,2-2	-0.2
1977	Hou N	125	413	44	109	23	7	8	58	41-6	5	60	.264	.336	.412	110	5	0-1	.985	-1	101	89	2-96,3-19,S-11	0.9
1978	Hou N	119	420	46	123	33	3	7	55	34-3	1	41	.293	.343	.436	127	15	2-3	.977	-9	92	81	*2-107,3-11/1	1.1
1979	Hou N	118	355	32	88	15	2	6	33	36-5	1	37	.248	.316	.352	88	-6	3-1	.991	11	106	96	2-68,3-59/1-3	0.8
1980	†Hou N	110	321	34	91	12	5	10	46	34-6	1	29	.283	.350	.445	132	13	1-0	.986	-1	108	98	1-77,3-25/S-5,2-3	0.8
1981	†Hou N	103	361	43	107	22	4	3	36	41-7	0	23	.296	.365	.404	125	13	1-3	.966	5	107	118	3-98/1-2	1.7
1982	Hou N	110	365	29	87	15	1	5	38	41-15	1	45	.238	.315	.326	87	-6	2-0	.972	8	111	118	3-72,1-35	-0.1
1984	StL N	89	139	17	30	5	0	2	12	18-1	0	18	.216	.300	.295	71	-5	0-2	.979	3	117	121	3-45,1-11/2-8,S-5	-0.3
1985	StL N	4	3	0	0	0	0	0	0	0-0	0	0	.000	.000	.000	-99	-1	0-0	1.000	1	0	572	/13	0.0
Total	11	891	2626	268	682	139	23	43	293	275-47	9	287	.260	.329	.379	103	14	10-10	.965	14	106	108	3-400,2-284,1-130/S-26	3.1
HOWE, SHORTY John B New York, NY d6.17																								
1890	NY N	19	64	4	11	0	0	0	4	3	1	2	.172	.221	.172	15	-7	3	.887	2	111	44	2-18/3	-0.4
1893	NY N	1	5	1	3	0	0	0	2	0	0	0	.600	.600	.600	218	1	1	.400	-1	69	0	/3	0.0
Total	2	20	69	5	14	0	0	0	6	3	1	2	.203	.247	.203	30	-6	4	.887	0	111	44	/2-18,3-2	-0.4
HOWELL, DIXIE Homer Elliott B 4.24.1920 Louisville, KY D 10.5.1990 Binghamton, NY BR/TR 5-11/195# d5.6																								
1947	Pit N	76	214	23	59	11	0	4	25	27	0	34	.276	.357	.383	94	-1	1	.974	-4	*91*	*85*	C-74	-0.1
1949	Cin N	64	172	17	42	6	1	2	18	8	2	21	.244	.286	.326	63	-10	0	.987	3	*117*	*138*	C-56	-0.4
1950	Cin N	82	224	30	50	9	1	2	22	32	2	31	.223	.326	.299	65	-11	0	.986	-5	*74*	*83*	C-81	-1.1
1951	Cin N	77	207	22	52	6	1	2	18	15	0	34	.251	.302	.319	66	-10	0-2	.987	0	*80*	*87*	C-73	-0.7
1952	Cin N	17	37	4	7	1	1	2	4	3	0	9	.189	.250	.432	86	-1	0-0	.981	1	*83*	*165*	C-16	0.0
1953	Bro N	1	1	0	0	0	0	0	0	0	0	1	.000	.000	.000	-98	0	0-0	—	0			H	0.0
1955	Bro N	16	42	2	11	4	0	0	5	1-0	0	7	.262	.273	.357	66	-2	0-0	.981	-1	*128*	*50*	C-13	-0.2
1956	Bro N	7	13	0	3	2	0	0	1	1-1	0	3	.231	.267	.385	72	0	0-0	1.000	-0	*104*	*0*	/C-6	0.0
Total	8	340	910	98	224	39	4	12	93	87-1	4	140	.246	.314	.337	73	-35	1-2	.984	-5	*90*	*95*	C-319	-2.5
HOWELL, JACK Jack Robert B 8.18.1961 Tucson, AZ BL/TR 6/201# d5.20 OF Total (88-LF 1-CF 23-RF)																								
1985	Cal A	43	137	19	27	4	0	5	18	16-2	0	33	.197	.279	.336	68	-6	1-1	.931	-2	98	132	3-42	-0.9
1986	†Cal A	63	151	26	41	14	2	4	21	19-0	0	28	.272	.349	.470	123	5	2-0	.977	-1	95	77	3-39/O-8(7-0-1),D-2	0.4
1987	Cal A	138	449	64	110	18	5	23	64	57-4	2	118	.245	.331	.461	111	7	4-3	.987	2	97	76	O-89(78-0-15),3-48,2-13	0.4
1988	Cal A	154	500	59	127	32	2	16	63	46-8	6	130	.254	.323	.422	110	7	2-6	.953	-12	96	74	*3-152/O-2(1-1-0)	-0.7
1989	Cal A	144	474	56	108	19	4	20	52	52-9	3	125	.228	.308	.411	103	1	0-3	**.974**	23	**121**	**123**	*3-142/O-4(1-0-3)	2.3
1990	Cal A	105	316	35	72	19	1	8	33	46-5	1	61	.228	.326	.370	97	0	3-0	.939	-0	99	102	*3-102/1S	0.0
1991	Cal A	32	81	11	17	2	0	2	7	11-0	0	11	.210	.304	.309	70	-3	1-1	.968	5	132	62	2-12/3-8,O-5(1-0-4),1-3,D	0.1
	SD N	58	160	24	33	3	1	6	16	18-1	0	33	.206	.287	.350	76	-6	0-0	.985	6	114	106	3-54	0.0
1996	Cal A	66	126	20	34	4	1	8	21	10-0	0	30	.270	.324	.508	106	0	0-1	.884	-2	97	111	3-43/1-2,2D	-0.1
1997	Ana A	77	174	25	45	7	0	14	34	13-2	0	36	.259	.305	.540	117	3	1-0	.976	-2	80	134	3-24,D-22,1-12	0.0
1998	Hou N	24	38	4	11	5	0	1	7	4-0	0	12	.289	.357	.500	126	2	0-0	1.000	1	145	66	1-10/3-2	0.2
1999	Hou N	37	33	2	7	2	0	1	1	8-0	0	9	.212	.366	.364	87	0	0-0	1.000	1	179	307	/1-5,3-3,D-2	0.0
Total	11	941	2639	345	632	129	16	108	337	300-31	12	626	.239	.318	.423	103	10	14-15	.958	19	105	107	3-659,O-108L/1-33,D-31,2-26,S	1.7
HOWELL, RED Murray Donald "Porky" B 1.29.1909 Atlanta, GA D 10.1.1950 Travelers Rest, SC BR/TR 6/215# d4.24																								
1941	Cle A	11	7	0	2	0	0	0	2	4	0	2	.286	.545	.286	132	1	0-0	—	0			H	0.1
HOWELL, PAT Patrick O'Neal B 8.31.1968 Mobile, AL BB/TR 5-11/155# d7.10																								
1992	NY N	31	75	9	14	1	0	0	1	2-0	1	15	.187	.218	.200	19	-8	4-2	1.000	2	129	0	O-28(CF)	-0.7
HOWELL, ROY Roy Lee B 12.18.1953 Lompoc, CA BL/TR 6-1/190# d9.9																								
1974	Tex A	13	44	2	11	1	0	1	3	2-0	0	10	.250	.283	.341	81	-1	0-0	.906	-1	105	41	3-12	-0.2
1975	Tex A	125	383	43	96	15	2	10	51	39-6	3	79	.251	.322	.379	99	-1	2-2	.933	-2	100	**159**	*3-115/D-5	-0.3
1976	Tex A	140	491	55	124	28	2	8	53	30-8	1	106	.253	.295	.367	92	-6	1-0	.926	-6	98	95	*3-130/D-8	-1.3
1977	Tex A	7	17	0	0	0	0	0	0	2-0	0	4	.000	.105	.000	-68	-4	0-0	1.000	-0	135	0	/O-2(LF),13D	-0.5
	Tor A	96	364	41	115	17	1	10	44	42-2	1	76	.316	.386	.451	126	15	4-1	.953	-4	94	67	3-87/D-8	1.0
	Year	103	381	41	115	17	1	10	44	44-2	1	80	.302	.374	.430	117	11	4-1	.954	-4	94	67	3-88,D-10/O-2(LF),1	0.5
1978	Tor A★	140	551	67	149	28	3	8	61	44-3	1	78	.270	.325	.376	95	-4	0-1	.950	8	106	97	*3-131/O-5(RF),D	0.2
1979	Tor A	138	511	60	126	28	4	15	72	42-4	6	91	.247	.310	.405	90	-8	1-4	.952	4	105	103	*3-133/D-4	-0.7
1980	Tor A	142	528	51	142	28	9	10	57	50-8	5	92	.269	.335	.413	100	0	0-0	.958	-14	92	79	*3-138/D-2	-1.6
1981	†Mil A	76	244	37	58	13	1	6	33	23-4	2	39	.238	.306	.373	101	0	0-0	.958	-4	93	97	3-53,D-13/1-3,O(RF)	-0.6
1982	†Mil A	98	300	31	78	11	2	4	38	21-2	0	39	.260	.305	.350	86	-6	0-2	.933	-0	117	43	D-84/1-4,O-2(RF)	-1.0
1983	Mil A	69	194	23	54	9	6	4	25	15-0	0	29	.278	.330	.448	121	5	1-3	.960	1	284	217	D-54/1-2	0.3
1984	Mil A	68	164	12	38	5	1	4	17	8-1	4	32	.232	.284	.348	77	-6	0-1	.907	0	107	110	3-46/1-4,D-8	-0.7
Total	11	1112	3791	422	991	183	31	80	454	318-38	23	675	.261	.321	.389	97	-16	9-14	.944	-18	99	99	3-846,D-189/1-14,O-10(2-0-8)	-5.4
HOWERTON, BILL William Ray "Hopalong" B 12.12.1921 Lompoc, CA BL/TR 5-11/185# d9.11																								
1949	StL N	9	13	1	4	1	0	0	1	0	0	2	.308	.308	.385	81	0	0	.900	0	123	0	/O-6(2-3-1)	-0.1
1950	StL N	110	313	50	88	20	8	10	59	47	0	60	.281	.375	.492	120	10	0	.969	-5	96	31	O-94(32-54-11)	0.1
1951	StL N	24	65	10	17	4	1	1	4	10	0	12	.262	.360	.400	104	1	0-1	.949	1	106	132	O-17(3-0-14)	0.0
	Pit N	80	219	29	60	12	2	11	37	26	0	44	.274	.351	.498	122	7	1-0	.950	-6	83	76	O-53(4-38-11)/3-4	0.0
	Year	104	284	39	77	16	3	12	41	36	0	56	.271	.353	.475	118	7	1-1	.950	-5	89	91	O-70(7-38-25)/3-4	0.0
1952	Pit N	13	25	3	8	1	1	0	4	6	0	5	.320	.452	.440	144	2	0-0	.900	-2	92	0	/O-5(0-2-3),3	0.0
	NY N	11	15	2	1	1	0	0	1	3	0	2	.067	.222	.133	1	-2	0-0	1.000	-0	99	0	/O-3(0-1-2)	-0.2
	Year	24	40	5	9	2	1	0	5	9	0	7	.225	.367	.325	92	0	0-0	.938	-2	95	0	/O-8(0-3-5),3	-0.2
Total	4	247	650	95	178	39	12	22	106	92	0	125	.274	.364	.472	117	18	1-1	.958	-12	94	53	O-178(41-98-42)/3-5	-0.2
HOWITT, DANN Dann Paul John B 2.13.1964 Battle Creek, MI BL/TR 6-5/205# d9.15																								
1989	Oak A	3	3	0	0	0	0	0	0	0-0	0	2	.000	.000	.000	-99	-1	0-0	1.000	-0	0	0	/1O(RF)	-0.1
1990	Oak A	14	22	3	3	0	1	0	1	3-0	0	12	.136	.240	.227	33	-2	0-0	1.000	1	207	0	O-11(RF)/1-5,3	-0.1
1991	Oak A	21	42	5	7	1	0	1	3	1-0	0	12	.167	.182	.262	24	-5	0-0	1.000	1	126	0	O-20(5-7-10)/1	-0.4
1992	Oak A	22	48	1	6	0	0	1	2	5-1	0	4	.125	.208	.188	12	-6	0-0	.951	3	109	311	O-19(4-5-12)/1-4,D	-0.4
	Sea A	13	37	6	10	4	1	1	8	3-0	0	5	.270	.302	.514	131	1	1-1	1.000	1	107	135	O-11(10-0-1)	0.1
	Year	35	85	7	16	4	1	2	10	8-1	0	9	.188	.250	.329	66	-4	1-1	.970	3	108	235	O-30(14-5-13)/1-4,D	-0.3
1993	Sea A	32	76	6	16	3	1	2	8	4-0	0	18	.211	.250	.355	60	-5	0-0	1.000	1	110	85	O-29(16-6-12)/D-2	-0.5
1994	Chi A	10	14	4	5	3	0	0	0	1-0	0	7	.357	.400	.571	149	1	0-0	1.000	-0	82	0	/O-7(1-1-5),1-4	0.1
Total	6	115	242	25	47	11	3	5	22	17-1	0	60	.194	.243	.326	57	-17	1-1	.987	5	116	126	/O-98(36-19-52),1-15,D-3,3	-1.3
HOWLEY, DAN Daniel Philip "Howling Dan" or "Dapper Dan" B 10.16.1885 Weymouth, MA D 3.10.1944 Weymouth, MA BR/TR 6/187# d5.15 M6 C3																								
1913	Phi N	26	32	5	4	2	0	0	2	4	0	4	.125	.222	.188	17	-3	3	.954	1	111	52	C-22	-0.1

Year	Tm Lg	G	AB	R	H	2B	3B	HR	RBI	BB-IB	HP	SO	AVG	OBP	SLG	AOPS	ABR	SB-CS	FA	FR	Rng	Thr	G at Pos	BFW
HOWSER, DICK Richard Dalton B 5.14.1936 Miami, FL D 6.17.1987 Kansas City, MO BR/TR 5-8/155# d4.11 M8 C10																								
1961	KC A★	158	611	108	171	29	6	3	45	92-0	5	38	.280	.377	.362	97	2	37-9	.950	-14	95	79	*S-157	0.6
1962	KC A	83	286	53	68	8	3	6	34	38-0	1	8	.238	.326	.350	79	-8	19-2	.962	-4	96	80	S-72	-0.2
1963	KC A	15	41	4	8	0	0	0	1	7-1	0	3	.195	.313	.195	44	-3	0-0	.957	-2	81	100	S-10	-0.4
	Cle A	49	162	25	40	5	0	1	10	22-0	0	18	.247	.333	.296	80	-4	9-3	.950	-11	76	66	S-44	-1.0
	Year	64	203	29	48	5	0	1	11	29-1	0	21	.236	.329	.276	72	-7	9-3	.951	-13	77	73	S-54	-1.4
1964	Cle A	162	637	101	163	23	4	3	52	76-1	2	39	.256	.335	.319	84	-11	20-7	.974	0	95	98	*S-162	0.5
1965	Cle A	107	307	47	72	8	2	1	6	57-0	1	25	.235	.354	.283	83	-4	17-4	.977	-2	89	92	S-73,2-17	0.4
1966	Cle A	67	140	18	32	9	1	2	4	15-0	0	23	.229	.299	.350	87	-2	2-4	.986	-4	97	86	2-26,S-26	-0.4
1967	NY A	63	149	18	40	6	0	0	10	25-0	2	15	.268	.381	.309	110	4	1-4	.990	-5	87	122	2-22,3-12/S-3	-0.1
1968	NY A	85	150	24	23	2	1	0	3	35-0	2	17	.153	.321	.180	57	-6	0-1	.982	7	133	118	2-29/3-2,S	0.4
Total	8	789	2483	398	617	90	17	16	165	367-2	13	186	.248	.346	.318	86	-32	105-34	.963	-34	93	86	S-548/2-94,3-14	-0.2
HOY, DUMMY William Ellsworth B 5.23.1862 Houcktown, OH D 12.15.1961 Cincinnati, OH BL/TR 5-6/160# d4.20																								
1888	Was N	**136**	503	77	138	10	8	2	29	69	11	48	.274	.374	.338	137	27	**82**	.897	7	117	148	*O-136(0-136-1)	2.9
1889	Was N	**127**	507	98	139	11	6	0	39	75	6	30	.274	.374	.320	101	5	35	.890	-4	121	80	*O-127(1-126-0)	-0.3
1890	Buf P	122	493	107	147	17	8	1	53	94	8	36	.298	.418	.371	122	25	39	.912	4	104	172	*O-122(CF)/2	2.0
1891	StL AA	**139**	559	134	163	13	5	5	64	**117**	12	25	.292	.424	.360	108	10	59	.911	-2	107	62	*O-139(CF)	0.3
1892	Was N	152	593	108	167	19	8	3	75	86	4	23	.282	.376	.356	125	23	60	.884	21	128	106	*O-152(3-150-0)	3.5
1893	Was N	**130**	564	106	138	12	6	0	45	66	13	9	.245	.337	.287	68	-23	48	.892	-4	119	148	*O-130(CF)	-2.9
1894	Cin N	128	503	118	153	23	13	5	71	90	12	19	.304	.421	.431	102	5	28	.895	0	138	55	*O-128(CF)	-0.2
1895	Cin N	107	429	93	119	21	12	3	55	52	6	8	.277	.363	.403	94	-4	50	.883	-5	86	163	*O-107(62-41-4)	-1.4
1896	Cin N	121	443	120	132	23	7	4	57	65	13	13	.298	.403	.409	107	7	50	.946	3	83	77	*O-120(CF)	0.2
1897	Cin N	128	497	87	145	24	6	2	42	54	12		.292	.375	.376	92	-4	37	.934	5	55	147	*O-128(CF)	-0.6
1898	Lou N	148	582	104	177	15	16	6	66	49	9		.304	.367	.416	126	18	37	.946	2	92	119	*O-148(CF)	1.0
1899	Lou N	155	636	117	194	17	13	5	49	62	10		.305	.376	.396	112	11	33	.928	-11	87	128	*O-155(CF)	-0.9
1901	Chi A	132	527	112	155	28	11	2	60	**86**	**14**		.294	.407	.400	128	27	27	.958	-3	92	164	*O-132(CF)	1.6
1902	Cin N	72	279	48	81	15	2	2	20	41	4		.290	.389	.380	125	11	11	.933	-5	43	42	O-72(CF)	0.3
Total	14	1797	7115	1429	2048	248	121	40	725	1006	134	211	.288	.386	.374	110	138	596	.915	10	99	117	*O-1796(66-1727-5)/2	5.5
HRBEK, KENT Kent Alan B 5.21.1960 Minneapolis, MN BL/TR 6-4/235# d8.24																								
1981	Min A	24	67	5	16	5	0	1	7	5-1	1	9	.239	.301	.358	84	-1	0-0	1.000	-2	49	126	1-13/D-8	-0.4
1982	Min A★	140	532	82	160	21	4	23	92	54-12	0	80	.301	.363	.485	128	20	3-1	.993	1	100	102	*1-138/D-2	1.3
1983	Min A	141	515	75	153	41	5	16	84	57-5	3	71	.297	.366	.489	130	22	4-6	.990	-1	100	97	*1-137/D-2	1.2
1984	Min A	149	559	80	174	31	3	27	107	65-15	4	87	.311	.383	.522	142	33	1-1	.990	-4	92	94	*1-148/D	2.0
1985	Min A	158	593	78	165	31	2	21	93	67-12	2	87	.278	.351	.444	110	9	1-1	.995	1	102	91	*1-156/D-2	0.1
1986	Min A	149	550	85	147	27	1	29	91	71-9	6	81	.267	.353	.478	122	18	2-2	.992	-1	95	110	*1-147/D	0.7
1987	†Min A	143	477	85	136	20	1	34	90	84-12	0	60	.285	.389	.545	140	29	5-2	.996	-10	69	103	*1-137/D	1.1
1988	Min A	143	510	75	159	31	0	25	76	67-7	0	54	.312	.387	.520	149	35	0-3	.997	-5	78	109	*1-105,D-37	2.0
1989	Min A	109	375	59	102	17	0	25	84	53-4	1	35	.272	.360	.517	136	18	3-0	.995	3	109	89	1-89,D-18	1.5
1990	Min A	143	492	61	141	26	0	22	79	69-8	7	45	.287	.377	.474	129	22	5-2	**.997**	3	103	98	*1-120,D-20/3	1.6
1991	†Min A	132	462	72	131	20	1	20	89	67-4	0	48	.284	.373	.461	124	16	4-4	.994	3	108	111	*1-128	0.9
1992	Min A	112	394	52	96	20	0	15	58	71-9	0	56	.244	.357	.409	111	8	5-2	.997	1	99	91	*1-104/D-8	0.2
1993	Min A	123	392	60	95	11	1	25	83	71-6	1	57	.242	.357	.467	120	12	4-2	.995	2	107	103	*1-115/D-2	0.4
1994	Min A	81	274	34	74	11	0	10	53	37-6	1	28	.270	.353	.420	100	0	0-0	.997	-1	96	85	1-72/D-4	-0.6
Total	14	1747	6192	903	1749	312	18	293	1086	838-110	26	798	.282	.367	.481	127	241	37-26	.994	-10	96	100	*1-1609,D-106/3	12.0
HRINIAK, WALT Walter John B 5.22.1943 Natick, MA BL/TR 5-11/180# d9.10 C21																								
1968	Atl N	9	26	0	9	0	0	0	3	0-0	0	3	.346	.346	.346	108	0	0-0	.967	1	*112*	*0*	/C-9	0.1
1969	Atl N	7	7	0	1	0	0	0	0	2-0	0	1	.143	.333	.143	38	0	0-0	1.000	0	0	0	/C-6	0.0
	SD N	31	66	4	15	0	0	0	1	8-1	2	11	.227	.329	.227	61	-3	0-0	.981	-2	72	64	C-19	-0.4
	Year	38	73	4	16	0	0	0	1	10-1	2	12	.219	.329	.219	58	-4	0-0	.982	-2	65	58	C-25	-0.4
Total	2	47	99	4	25	0	0	0	4	10-1	2	15	.253	.333	.253	71	-3	0-0	.977	-1	*80*	*40*	/C-34	-0.3
HUBBARD, AL Allen (a/k/a Al West For 1 Game In 1883) B 12.9.1860 Westfield, MA D 12.14.1930 Newton, MA d9.13																								
1883	Phi AA	2	6	2	2	0	0	0	2	1			.333	.429	.333	136	0		.750	-1	45	0	/SC	0.0
HUBBARD, GLENN Glenn Dee B 9.25.1957 Hahn Air Force Base, W.Germany BR/TR 5-7/180# d7.14 C5																								
1978	Atl N	44	163	15	42	4	0	2	13	10-1	2	20	.258	.309	.319	68	-7	2-1	.979	2	101	107	2-44	-0.2
1979	Atl N	97	325	34	75	12	0	3	29	27-2	1	43	.231	.290	.295	56	-19	0-6	.968	-0	100	95	2-91	-1.7
1980	Atl N	117	431	55	107	21	3	9	43	49-2	0	69	.248	.322	.374	91	-4	7-5	.978	21	**113**	**130**	*2-117	2.4
1981	Atl N	99	361	39	85	13	5	6	33	33-2	2	59	.235	.302	.349	82	-9	4-2	.991	-4	105	82	2-98	-0.8
1982	†Atl N	145	532	75	132	25	1	9	59	59-5	3	62	.248	.324	.350	86	-9	4-3	.983	19	109	125	*2-144	1.8
1983	Atl N★	148	517	65	136	24	6	12	70	55-2	4	71	.263	.334	.402	97	-1	3-8	.985	25	110	112	*2-148	3.0
1984	Atl N	120	397	53	93	27	2	9	43	55-6	4	61	.234	.331	.380	93	-2	4-1	.988	14	111	107	*2-117	2.0
1985	Atl N	142	439	51	102	21	0	5	39	56-2	4	54	.232	.321	.314	75	-13	4-3	.989	**60**	**131**	**131**	*2-140	5.6
1986	Atl N	143	408	42	94	16	1	4	36	66-14	4	74	.230	.340	.304	76	-11	3-2	.976	**40**	**118**	138	*2-142	3.7
1987	Atl N	141	443	69	117	33	2	5	38	77-17	6	57	.264	.378	.381	98	3	1-1	.986	**28**	**118**	123	*2-139	3.8
1988	†Oak A	105	294	35	75	12	2	3	33	33-0	3	50	.255	.334	.340	93	-2	1-3	.987	1	99	104	*2-104/D	0.1
1989	Oak A	53	131	12	26	6	0	3	12	19-0	0	20	.198	.296	.313	76	-4	2-0	.968	7	109	142	2-48/D-3	0.5
Total	12	1354	4441	545	1084	214	22	70	448	539-53	33	640	.244	.328	.349	85	-78	35-35	.983	212	112	117	*2-1332/D-4	20.2
HUBBARD, MIKE Michael Wayne B 2.16.1971 Lynchburg, VA BR/TR 6-1/180# d7.13																								
1995	Chi N	15	23	2	4	0	0	0	1	2-0	0	2	.174	.240	.174	12	-3	0-0	.971	-3	80	98	/C-9	-0.6
1996	Chi N	21	38	1	4	0	0	1	4	0-0	0	15	.105	.103	.184	-25	-7	0-0	1.000	1	623	41	C-14	-0.6
1997	Chi N	29	64	4	13	0	0	1	2	2-1	0	21	.203	.227	.250	24	-7	0-0	.992	1	89	70	C-20/3	-0.5
1998	Mon N	32	55	3	8	1	0	1	3	0-0	1	17	.145	.161	.218	-2	-8	0-0	1.000	-6	32	129	C-24/2	-1.3
2000	Atl N	2	1	0	0	0	0	0	0	0-0	0	1	.000	.000	.000	-99	0	0-0	1.000	0	0	0	/C	0.0
2001	Tex A	5	11	1	3	1	0	1	1	0-0	0	4	.273	.273	.636	125	0	0-0	1.000	-2	40	99	/C-5	-0.1
Total	6	104	192	11	32	2	0	4	11	4-1	1	60	.167	.187	.240	11	-25	0-0	.994	-9	158	88	/C-73,23	-3.1
HUBBARD, TRENIDAD Trenidad Aviel (born B 5.11.1964 Chicago, IL BR/TR 5-8/180# d7.7																								
1994	Col N	18	25	3	7	1	1	1	3	3-0	0	4	.280	.357	.520	107	0	0-0	1.000	-1	53	0	/O-5(2-3-0)	-0.1
1995	†Col N	24	58	13	18	4	0	3	9	8-0	0	6	.310	.394	.534	110	1	2-1	1.000	-2	57	146	O-16(4-14-0)	-0.1
1996	Col N	45	60	12	13	5	1	1	12	9-0	1	22	.217	.329	.383	70	-2	2-0	1.000	1	121	0	O-19(3-16-0)	-0.1
	SF N	10	29	3	6	0	1	1	2	2-0	0	5	.207	.258	.379	68	-2	0-0	1.000	2	134	229	/O-9(8-1-0)	0.0
	Year	55	89	15	19	5	2	2	14	11-0	1	27	.213	.307	.382	68	-4	2-0	1.000	2	126	93	O-28(11-17-0)	-0.1
1997	Cle A	7	12	3	3	1	0	0	0	1-0	0	3	.250	.308	.333	65	-1	2-0	1.000	-1	44	0	/O-6(5-1-0)	-0.1
1998	LA N	94	208	29	62	9	1	7	18	18-0	3	46	.298	.358	.452	120	6	9-5	.991	-1	97	90	O-81(34-46-4)/3	0.4
1999	LA N	82	105	23	33	5	0	1	13	13-1	0	24	.314	.387	.390	104	1	4-3	.980	-1	97	76	O-51(29-19-3)/C2	0.0
2000	Atl N	61	81	15	15	2	1	1	6	11-0	1	20	.185	.290	.272	43	-7	2-1	1.000	-1	89	68	O-44(36-0-10)	-0.9
	Bal A	31	27	3	5	0	1	0	0	0-0	0	3	.185	.185	.259	11	-4	2-1	.929	-1	73	188	O-24(11-0-14)/D-6	-0.4
2001	KC A	5	12	2	3	0	1	0	0	0-0	0	2	.250	.250	.417	66	-1	0-0	1.000	-1	38	0	/O-3(0-2-1)	-0.1
2002	SD N	89	129	16	27	5	0	1	7	14-0	0	28	.209	.285	.271	56	-9	9-6	.981	-1	91	129	O-57(16-16-26)/3-6,2-4,D	-1.1
2003	Chi N	10	16	2	4	1	0	0	2	4-0	1	3	.250	.429	.313	99	0	1-0	1.000	-1	69	0	/O-4(0-4-1)	0.0
Total	10	476	762	124	196	33	7	16	72	83-1	6	166	.257	.333	.382	86	-18	33-17	.989	-7	91	93	O-319(148-122-59)/D-7,3-7,2-5,C	-2.5
HUBBS, KEN Kenneth Douglas B 12.23.1941 Riverside, CA D 2.13.1964 Provo, UT BR/TR 6-2/175# d9.10																								
1961	Chi N	10	28	4	5	1	1	1	2	0-0	0	8	.179	.179	.393	46	-2	0-0	1.000	-1	95	49	/2-8	-0.3
1962	Chi N	160	661	90	172	24	9	5	49	35-0	3	129	.260	.299	.346	71	-29	3-7	.983	1	106	92	*2-159	-1.6
1963	Chi N	154	566	54	133	19	3	8	47	39-2	2	93	.235	.285	.322	71	-21	8-9	.974	21	117	112	*2-152	1.3
Total	3	324	1255	148	310	44	13	14	98	74-2	5	230	.247	.290	.336	70	-52	11-16	.979	21	111	101	2-319	-0.6
HUBER, CLARENCE Clarence Bill "Gilly" B 10.27.1896 Tyler, TX D 2.22.1965 Laredo, TX BR/TR 5-10/165# d9.17																								
1920	Det A	11	42	4	9	2	1	0	5	0	0	5	.214	.214	.310	39	-4	0-0	.907	1	103	0	3-11	-0.3
1921	Det A	1	0	0	0	0	0	0	0	0	0	0	—	—	—	—	0	0-0	1.000	-0	0	0	/3	0.0

Year	Tm Lg	G	AB	R	H	2B	3B	HR	RBI	BB-IB	HP	SO	AVG	OBP	SLG	AOPS	ABR	SB-CS	FA	FR	Rng	Thr	G at Pos	BFW
1925	Phi N	124	436	46	124	28	5	5	54	17	0	33	.284	.311	.406	75	-17	3-5	.947	-9	94	72	*3-120	-1.9
1926	Phi N	118	376	45	92	17	7	1	34	42	2	29	.245	.324	.335	74	-13	9	.956	9	111	110	*3-115	0.2
Total	4	254	854	95	225	47	13	6	93	59	2	67	.263	.313	.370	73	-34	12-5	.948	1	102	85	3-247	-2.0
HUBER, OTTO Otto B 3.12.1914 Garfield, NJ D 4.9.1989 Passaic, NJ BR/TR 5-10/165# d6.10																								
1939	Bos N	11	22	2	6	1	0	0	3	0	0	1	.273	.273	.318	63	-1	0	1.000	-0	99	0	/2-4,3-4	-0.1
HUCKABY, KEN Kenneth Paul B 1.27.1971 San Leandro, CA BR/TR 6-1/205# d10.6																								
2001	Ari N	1	1	0	0	0	0	0	0	0-0	0	1	.000	.000	.000	-94	0	0-0	1.000	0	0	0	/C	0.0
2002	Tor A	88	273	29	67	6	1	3	22	9-1	0	44	.245	.270	.308	51	-20	0-0	.989	0	115	97	C-88	-1.4
2003	Tor A	5	11	1	2	1	0	0	2	0-0	0	2	.182	.182	.273	17	-1	0-0	1.000	-0	35	0	/C-4	-0.1
Total	3	94	285	30	69	7	1	3	24	9-1	0	47	.242	.265	.305	49	-21	0-0	.989	0	111	93	/C-93	-1.5
HUDGENS, DAVE David Mark B 12.5.1956 Oroville, CA BL/TL 6-2/210# d9.4 C1																								
1983	Oak A	6	7	0	1	0	0	0	0	0-0	0	3	.143	.143	.143	-22	-1	0-0	1.000	-0	0	0	/1-3,D	-0.1
HUDGENS, JIMMY James Price B 8.24.1902 Newburg, MO D 8.26.1955 St.Louis, MO BL/TR 6/180# d9.14																								
1923	StL N	6	12	2	3	1	0	0	0	3	0	3	.250	.400	.333	97	0	0-0	1.000	-0	210	0	/1-3,2	0.0
1925	Cin N	3	7	0	3	1	1	0	0	1	0	1	.429	.500	.857	245	2	0-0	1.000	-0	71	103	/1-3	0.1
1926	Cin N	17	20	2	5	1	0	0	1	1	0	0	.250	.286	.300	59	-1	0	1.000	0	129	50	/1-6	-0.1
Total	3	26	39	4	11	3	1	0	1	5	0	4	.282	.364	.410	107	1	0-0	1.000	-0	138	50	/1-12,2	0.0
HUDLER, REX Rex Allen B 9.2.1960 Tempe, AZ BR/TR 6/180# d9.9 OF Total (124-LF 65-CF 64-RF)																								
1984	NY A	9	7	2	1	1	0	0	0	1-0	1	5	.143	.333	.286	76	0	0-0	1.000	-2	72	44	/2-9	-0.2
1985	NY A	20	51	4	8	0	1	0	1	1-0	0	9	.157	.173	.196	1	-7	0-1	.977	4	115	124	2-16/1S	-0.3
1986	Bal A	14	1	1	0	0	0	0	0	0-0	0	0	.000	.000	.000	-99	0	1-0	.800	-2	36	0	2-13/3	-0.2
1988	Mon N	77	216	38	59	14	2	4	14	10-6	0	34	.273	.303	.412	100	-1	29-7	.978	-5	103	120	2-41,S-27/O-4(2-0-2)	0.1
1989	Mon N	92	155	21	38	7	0	6	13	6-2	1	23	.245	.278	.406	92	-2	15-4	.958	-5	99	113	2-38,O-23(14-5-4),S-18	-0.5
1990	Mon N	4	3	1	1	0	0	0	0	0-0	0	1	.333	.333	.333	87	0	0-0	—	0			/H	0.0
	StL N	89	217	30	61	11	2	7	22	12-1	2	31	.281	.323	.447	110	2	18-10	.979	5	108	108	O-45(17-3-27),2-10/1-6,3-6,S	0.6
	Year	93	220	31	62	11	2	7	22	12-1	2	32	.282	.323	.445	109	2	18-10	.979	5	108	108	O-45(17-3-27),2-10/1-6,3-6,S	0.6
1991	StL N	101	207	21	47	10	2	1	15	10-1	0	29	.227	.260	.309	60	-12	12-8	.981	0	99	154	O-58(28-21-10),1-12/2-5	-1.3
1992	StL N	61	98	17	24	4	0	3	5	2-0	1	23	.245	.265	.378	83	-3	2-6	.957	-1	108	89	2-16,O-12(5-1-7)/1-8	-0.6
1994	Cal A	56	124	17	37	8	0	8	20	6-0	0	28	.298	.326	.556	122	3	2-2	.971	3	109	149	2-22,O-18(LF)/3-4,1D	0.6
1995	Cal A	84	223	30	59	16	0	6	27	10-1	5	48	.265	.310	.417	88	-4	13-0	.986	4	104	126	2-52,O-22(18-4-1)/1-2,D-3	0.4
1996	Cal A	92	302	60	94	20	3	16	40	9-0	3	54	.311	.337	.556	120	8	14-5	.982	-5	91	106	2-53,O-21(8-14-0)/1-7,D-8	0.5
1997	Phi N	50	122	17	27	4	0	5	10	6-1	1	28	.221	.264	.377	65	-7	1-0	.962	1	104	76	O-35(11-16-8)/2-6	-0.6
1998	Phi N	25	41	2	5	1	0	0	2	4-0	0	12	.122	.200	.146	-7	-6	0-0	1.000	1	145	0	/O-9(3-1-5),1	-0.6
Total	13	774	1767	261	461	96	10	56	169	77-12	14	325	.261	.296	.422	91	-29	107-43	.975	-1	102	115	2-281,O-247L/S-47,1-38,D-15,3-11	-2.1
HUDSON, JOHNNY John Wilson "Mr. Chips" B 6.30.1912 Bryan, TX D 11.7.1970 Bryan, TX BR/TR 5-10/160# d6.20																								
1936	Bro N	6	12	1	2	0	0	0	0	2	0	1	.167	.286	.167	24	-1	0	.889	-2	68	49	/S-4,2	-0.3
1937	Bro N	13	27	3	5	4	0	0	2	3	0	9	.185	.267	.333	61	-1	0	.867	-3	83	49	S-11/2	-0.4
1938	Bro N	135	498	59	130	21	5	2	37	39	0	76	.261	.315	.335	77	-16	7	.963	-0	99	100	*2-132/S-3	-0.8
1939	Bro N	109	343	46	87	17	3	2	32	30	2	36	.254	.317	.338	74	-13	5	.959	-13	93	105	S-50,2-45/3	-2.0
1940	Bro N	85	179	13	39	4	3	0	19	9	0	26	.218	.255	.274	43	-14	2	.921	-4	97	67	S-38,2-27/3	-1.6
1941	Chi N	50	99	8	20	4	0	0	6	3	0	15	.202	.225	.242	33	-9	3	.907	-1	83	97	S-17,2-13,3-10	-0.9
1945	NY N	28	11	8	0	0	0	0	0	1	0	1	.000	.083	.000	-75	-3	0	.875	1	112	406	/3-5,2-2	-0.2
Total	7	426	1169	138	283	50	11	4	96	87	2	164	.242	.296	.314	65	-57	17	.962	-23	99	99	2-221,S-123/3-17	-6.2
HUDSON, ORLANDO Orlando Thill B 12.12.1977 Darlington, SC BB/TR 6/175# d7.24																								
2002	Tor A	54	192	20	53	10	5	4	23	11-0	2	27	.276	.319	.443	97	-2	0-1	.986	9	104	139	2-52	1.0
2003	Tor A	142	474	54	127	21	6	9	57	39-1	5	87	.268	.328	.395	89	-8	5-4	.984	**45**	**123**	112	*2-139	4.0
Total	2	196	666	74	180	31	11	13	80	50-1	7	114	.270	.326	.408	91	-10	5-5	.985	54	118	120	2-191	5.0
HUELSMAN, FRANK Frank Elmer B 6.5.1874 St.Louis, MO D 6.9.1959 Affton, MO BR/TR 6-2/210# d10.3																								
1897	StL N	2	7	0	2	1	0	0	0	0	0		.286	.286	.429	89	0	0	.000	-1	0	0	/O-2(LF)	-0.1
1904	Chi A	3	6	0	1	1	0	0	0	0	0		.167	.167	.333	58	0	0	.000	-1	0	0	/O(CF)	-0.1
	Det A	4	18	1	6	1	0	0	4	1	0		.333	.368	.389	144	1	1	1.000	-0	0	0	/O-4(LF)	0.0
	Chi A	1	1	0	0	0	0	0	0	0	0		.000	.000	.000	-99	0	0	—	0			H	0.0
	StL A	20	68	6	15	2	1	0	1	6	2		.221	.303	.279	90	0	0	1.000	-2	0	0	O-18(RF)	-0.3
	Was A	84	303	21	75	19	4	2	30	24	5		.248	.313	.356	113	5	6	.960	-1	80	76	O-84(82-2-0)	0.0
	Year	112	396	28	97	23	5	2	35	31	7		.245	.311	.343	110	5	7	.960	-4	65	62	*O-107(86-3-18)	-0.4
1905	Was A	121	421	48	114	28	8	3	62	31	8		.271	.333	.397	136	17	11	.929	-7	56	67	*O-116(115-0-1)	0.4
Total	3	235	824	76	213	52	13	5	97	62	15		.258	.322	.371	123	23	18	.941	-12	60	64	O-225(203-3-19)	-0.1
HUFF, AUBREY Aubrey Lewis B 12.20.1976 Marion, OH BL/TR 6-4/220# d8.2																								
2000	TB A	39	122	12	35	7	0	4	14	5-1	1	18	.287	.318	.443	91	-2	0-0	.939	-2	94	52	3-37	-0.4
2001	TB A	111	411	42	102	25	1	8	45	23-2	0	72	.248	.288	.372	73	-17	1-3	.918	-4	95	104	3-73,D-20,1-19	-2.3
2002	TB A	113	454	67	142	25	0	23	59	37-7	1	55	.313	.364	.520	134	22	4-1	.987	-4	70	98	D-53,1-45,3-14	1.0
2003	TB A	**162**	636	91	198	47	3	34	107	53-17	8	80	.311	.367	.555	142	39	2-3	.970	-7	96	87	*O-102(RF),D-33,1-22/3-8	2.1
Total	4	425	1623	212	477	104	4	69	225	118-27	10	225	.294	.343	.490	119	42	7-7	.920	-17	93	86	3-132,D-106,O-102(RF)/1-86	0.4
HUFF, MIKE Michael Kale B 8.11.1963 Honolulu, HI BR/TR 6-1/190# d8.7																								
1989	LA N	12	25	4	5	1	0	1	2	3-0	1	6	.200	.310	.360	93	0	0-1	1.000	0	122	0	/O-9(7-1-2)	0.0
1991	Cle A	51	146	28	35	6	1	2	10	25-0	4	30	.240	.364	.336	95	0	11-2	.990	-1	97	145	O-48(8-39-5)/2-2	0.0
	Chi A	51	97	14	26	4	1	1	15	12-2	2	18	.268	.357	.361	103	1	3-2	.986	-1	104	48	O-48(9-14-35)/2-2,D-2	-0.1
	Year	102	243	42	61	10	2	3	25	37-2	6	48	.251	.361	.346	98	1	14-4	.988	-2	100	102	O-96(17-53-40)/2-4,D-2	-0.1
1992	Chi A	60	115	13	24	5	0	0	8	10-1	1	24	.209	.273	.252	50	-8	1-2	1.000	-0	99	89	O-56(10-3-45)/D	-1.0
1993	Chi A	43	44	4	8	2	0	1	6	9-0	1	15	.182	.321	.295	72	-1	1-0	1.000	-1	98	0	O-43(31-8-7)	-0.2
1994	Tor A	80	207	31	63	15	3	3	25	27-2	3	27	.304	.392	.449	116	6	2-1	.992	2	106	111	O-76(57-19-8)	0.6
1995	Tor A	61	138	14	32	9	1	1	9	22-0	1	21	.232	.337	.333	77	-4	1-1	.980	1	105	133	O-55(9-33-15)	-0.3
1996	Tor A	11	29	5	5	0	1	0	0	1-0	0	5	.172	.200	.241	11	-4	0-0	1.000	-1	104	0	/O-9(1-4-4),3-3	-0.5
Total	7	369	801	113	198	42	7	9	75	109-5	13	146	.247	.344	.351	88	-10	19-9	.991	-0	103	94	O-344(132-121-121)/2-4,3-3,D-3	-1.5
HUFFMAN, BEN Bennie F B 7.18.1914 Rileyville, VA BL/TR 5-11.5/175# d4.23																								
1937	StL A	76	176	18	48	9	0	1	24	10	3	7	.273	.323	.341	67	-9	1-0	.970	-6	*84*	*77*	C-42	-1.2
HUG, ED Edward Ambrose B 7.14.1880 Fayetteville, OH D 5.11.1953 Cincinnati, OH BR/TR d7.6																								
1903	Bro N	1	0	0	0	0	0	0	0	1	0		—	1.000	—	199	0	0	—	0	*0*	*0*	/C	0.0
HUGGINS, MILLER Miller James "Hug" or "Mighty Mite" B 3.27.1879 Cincinnati, OH D 9.25.1929 New York, NY BB/TR 5-6.5/140# d4.15 M17 HF1964																								
1904	Cin N	140	491	96	129	12	7	2	30	88	2		.263	.377	.328	108	9	13	.945	-2	101	78	*2-140	0.9
1905	Cin N	149	564	117	154	11	8	1	38	**103**	7		.273	.392	.326	103	8	27	.945	**37**	**116**	108	*2-149	4.7
1906	Cin N	146	545	81	159	11	7	0	26	71	3		.292	.376	.338	118	14	41	.948	22	**107**	128	*2-146	4.0
1907	Cin N	**156**	561	64	139	12	4	1	31	**83**	1		.248	.346	.289	95	1	28	.961	4	99	**134**	*2-156	0.6
1908	Cin N	135	498	65	119	14	5	0	23	58	2		.239	.321	.287	97	0	30	.959	6	102	116	*2-135	0.8
1909	Cin N	57	159	18	34	3	1	0	6	28	1		.214	.335	.245	81	-2	11	.933	4	113	130	2-31,3-15	0.3
1910	StL N	151	547	101	145	15	6	1	36	**116**	6	46	.265	.399	.320	114	19	34	.963	6	107	81	*2-151	2.7
1911	StL N	138	509	106	133	19	2	1	24	96	6	52	.261	.385	.312	99	6	37	.961	11	**111**	100	*2-136	1.9
1912	StL N	120	431	82	131	15	4	0	29	87	1	31	.304	.422	.357	117	17	35	.943	-7	99	96	*2-114	1.1
1913	StL N	121	382	74	109	12	0	0	27	92	7	49	.285	**.432**	.317	117	18	23-19	**.977**	4	102	91	*2-113,M	2.3
1914	StL N	148	509	85	134	17	4	1	24	**105**	7	63	.263	.396	.318	115	18	32	.964	-8	98	109	*2-147,M	1.3
1915	StL N	107	353	57	85	5	2	2	24	74	3	68	.241	.377	.283	101	6	13-12	.957	6	**111**	110	*2-105,M	1.3
1916	StL N	18	9	2	3	0	0	0	0	2	1	3	.333	.500	.333	159	1	0	1.000	2	149	0	/2-7,M	0.4
Total	13	1586	5558	948	1474	146	50	9	318	1003	47	312	.265	.382	.314	107	115	324-31	.956	84	105	105	*2-1530/3-15	22.3

Year	Tm Lg	G	AB	R	H	2B	3B	HR	RBI	BB-IB	HP	SO	AVG	OBP	SLG	AOPS	ABR	SB-CS	FA	FR	Rng	Thr	G at Pos	BFW
HUGHES, JOE Joseph Thompson B 2.21.1880 Pardoe, PA D 3.13.1951 Cleveland, OH BR/TR 5-10/165# d8.30																								
1902	Chi N	1	3	0	0	0	0	0	0	0	0		.000	.000	.000	-99	-1	0	—	-0	0	0	/O(RF)	-0.1
HUGHES, KEITH Keith Wills B 9.12.1963 Bryn Mawr, PA BL/TL 6-3/210# d5.19																								
1987	NY A	4	4	0	0	0	0	0	0	0-0	0	2	.000	.000	.000	-99	-1	0-0	—	0			/H	-0.1
	Phi N	37	76	8	20	2	0	0	10	7-0	1	11	.263	.333	.289	65	-4	0-0	.963	-2	88	0	O-19(13-0-6)	-0.6
1988	Bal A	41	108	10	21	4	2	2	14	16-1	0	27	.194	.294	.324	76	-3	1-0	.969	1	95	220	O-31(RF)/D	-0.3
1990	NY N	8	9	0	0	0	0	0	0	0-0	0	4	.000	.000	.000	-99	-2	0-0	1.000	0	185	0	/O-5(4-1-0)	-0.2
1993	Cin N	3	4	0	0	0	0	0	0	0-0	0	0	.000	.000	.000	-99	-1	0-0	—	-0	0	0	/O-2(LF)	-0.1
Total	4	93	201	18	41	6	2	2	24	23-1	1	44	.204	.286	.284	57	-11	1-0	.969	-0	95	138	/O-57(19-1-37),D	-1.3
HUGHES, BOBBY Robert E. B 3.10.1971 Burbank, CA BR/TR 6-4/237# d4.2																								
1998	Mil N	85	218	28	50	7	2	9	29	16-1	1	54	.229	.284	.404	78	-8	1-2	.995	-2	81	74	C-72/O-3(RF)	-0.6
1999	Mil N	48	101	10	26	2	0	3	8	5-0	0	28	.257	.292	.366	66	-6	0-0	.988	-2	105	103	C-44/D	-0.6
Total	2	133	319	38	76	9	2	12	37	21-1	1	82	.238	.287	.392	74	-14	1-2	.993	-4	88	83	C-116/O-3(RF),D	-1.2
HUGHES, ROY Roy John "Jeep" or "Sage" B 1.11.1911 Cincinnati, OH D 3.5.1995 Asheville, NC BR/TR 5-10.5/167# d4.16																								
1935	Cle A	82	266	40	78	15	3	0	14	18	1	17	.293	.340	.372	83	-7	13-3	.987	1	106	99	2-40,S-29/3	0.0
1936	Cle A	152	638	112	188	35	9	0	63	57	4	40	.295	.356	.378	81	-19	20-9	.973	7	95	96	*2-152	-0.2
1937	Cle A	104	346	57	96	12	6	1	40	40	0	22	.277	.352	.355	78	-11	11-6	.939	11	103	59	3-58,2-32	0.4
1938	StL A	58	96	16	27	3	0	2	13	12	0	11	.281	.361	.375	85	-2	3-0	.957	3	98	105	2-21/3-5,S-2	0.2
1939	StL A	17	23	6	2	0	0	0	1	4	0	4	.087	.222	.087	-18	-4	0-0	1.000	1	108	129	/2-6,S	-0.3
	Phi N	65	237	22	54	5	1	1	16	21	0	18	.228	.291	.270	53	-16	4	.984	-4	92	64	2-65	-1.6
1940	Phi N	1	0	0	0	0	0	0	0	0	0	0	—	—	—	—	0	0	1.000	-0	0	0	/2	0.0
1944	Chi N	126	478	86	137	16	6	1	28	35	1	30	.287	.337	.351	94	-4	16	.951	14	111	163	3-66,S-52	1.4
1945	†Chi N	69	222	34	58	8	1	0	8	16	0	18	.261	.311	.306	73	-8	6	.931	-2	93	130	S-36,2-21/3-9,1-2	-0.7
1946	Phi N	89	276	23	65	11	1	0	22	19	1	15	.236	.287	.283	64	-14	7	.942	-8	93	82	S-34,3-31/2-7,1	-2.1
Total	9	763	2582	396	705	105	27	5	205	222	7	175	.273	.332	.340	78	-85	80-18	.980	22	97	91	2-345,3-170,S-154/1-3	-2.9
HUGHES, TERRY Terry Wayne B 5.13.1949 Spartanburg, SC BR/TR 6-1/185# d9.2																								
1970	Chi N	2	3	0	1	0	0	0	0	0-0	0	0	.333	.333	.333	71	0	0-0	—	-0	0	0	/3O(RF)	-0.1
1973	StL N	11	14	1	3	1	0	0	1	1-0	0	4	.214	.267	.286	53	-1	0-0	1.000	-0	110	277	/3-5,1	-0.1
1974	Bos A	41	69	5	14	2	0	1	6	6-0	2	18	.203	.282	.275	58	-4	0-0	.958	-1	90	105	3-36/D	-0.5
Total	3	54	86	6	18	3	0	1	7	7-0	2	22	.209	.281	.279	58	-5	0-0	.961	-1	91	118	/3-42,D1O(RF)	-0.7
HUGHES, TOM Thomas Franklin B 8.6.1907 Emmet, AR D 8.10.1989 Beaumont, TX BL/TR 6-1/190# d9.9																								
1930	Det A	17	59	8	22	2	3	0	5	4	0	8	.373	.413	.508	130	2	0-1	.897	-2	83	0	O-16(4-12-0)	-0.1
HUGHES, BILL William R. B 11.25.1866 Blandinsville, IL D 8.25.1943 Santa Ana, CA BL/TL d9.28 ▲																								
1884	Was U	14	49	5	6	0	0	0		2			.122	.157	.122	-15	-8		.955	-0	82	33	/1-9,O-6(0-1-5)	-0.9
1885	Phi AA	4	16	3	3	1	1	0	1	1	1		.188	.278	.375	99	0		1.000	-0	0	0	/O-2(RF),P-2	0.0
Total	2	18	65	8	9	1	1	0	1	3	1		.138	.188	.185	15	-8		.955	-1	82	33	/1-9,O-8(0-1-7),P-2	-0.9
HUHN, EMIL Emil Hugo "Hap" B 3.10.1892 North Vernon, IN D 9.5.1925 Camden, SC BR/TR 6/180# d4.10																								
1915	New F	124	415	34	94	18	1	1	41	28	2	40	.227	.279	.282	61	-29	13	.985	-1	93	121	*1-101,C-16	-3.4
1916	Cin N	37	94	4	24	3	2	0	3	2	0	11	.255	.271	.330	86	-2	0	.989	-0	82	105	C-18,1-14/O(RF)	-0.2
1917	Cin N	23	51	2	10	1	2	0	3	2	0	5	.196	.226	.294	62	-3	1	.969	-1	*88*	*110*	C-15/1	-0.3
Total	3	184	560	40	128	22	5	1	47	32	2	56	.229	.273	.291	65	-34	14	.986	-3	95	119	1-116/C-49,O(RF)	-3.9
HULEN, BILLY William Franklin B 3.12.1870 Dixon, CA D 10.2.1947 Santa Rosa, CA BL/TL 5-8/148# d5.2																								
1896	Phi N	88	339	87	90	18	7	0	38	55	0	20	.265	.368	.360	93	-1	23	.874	-19	85	101	S-73,O-12(CF)/2-2	-1.5
1899	Was N	19	68	10	10	1	0	0	3	10	0		.147	.256	.162	16	-8	5	.902	-1	111	26	S-19	-0.7
Total	2	107	407	97	100	19	7	0	41	65	0	20	.246	.350	.327	81	-9	28	.880	-20	90	86	/S-92,O-12(CF),2-2	-2.2
HULETT, TIM Timothy Craig B 1.12.1960 Springfield, IL BR/TR 6/195# d9.15																								
1983	Chi A	6	5	0	1	0	0	0	0	0-0	0	0	.200	.200	.200	10	-1	1-0	.875	-1	76	56	/2-6	-0.1
1984	Chi A	8	7	1	0	0	0	0	0	1-0	0	4	.000	.125	.000	-59	-2	1-0	1.000	3	116	0	/3-4,2-3	0.2
1985	Chi A	141	395	52	106	19	4	5	37	30-1	4	81	.268	.324	.375	88	-6	6-4	.924	3	103	118	*3-115,2-28/O(LF)	-0.4
1986	Chi A	150	520	53	120	16	5	17	44	21-0	1	91	.231	.260	.379	70	-25	4-1	.951	2	96	72	3-89,2-66	-2.0
1987	Chi A	68	240	20	52	10	0	7	28	10-1	0	41	.217	.246	.346	54	-17	0-2	.953	-1	103	136	3-61/2-8	-1.8
1989	Bal A	33	97	12	27	5	0	3	18	10-0	0	17	.278	.343	.423	119	3	0-0	.976	-1	99	92	2-23,3-11	0.2
1990	Bal A	53	153	16	39	7	1	3	16	15-0	0	41	.255	.321	.373	97	-1	1-0	.961	9	135	101	3-24,2-16/D-8	0.9
1991	Bal A	79	206	29	42	9	0	7	18	13-0	1	49	.204	.255	.350	68	-10	0-1	.976	-5	99	125	3-39,2-26,D-15/S	-1.6
1992	Bal A	57	142	11	41	7	2	2	21	10-1	1	31	.289	.340	.408	106	1	0-1	.935	11	147	168	3-27,D-13,2-10/S-5	1.1
1993	Bal A	85	260	40	78	15	0	2	23	23-1	3	56	.300	.361	.381	96	0	1-2	.963	15	126	202	3-75/S-8,2-4,D-2	1.4
1994	Bal A	36	92	11	21	2	1	2	15	12-0	0	24	.228	.314	.337	66	-5	0-0	.992	13	127	187	2-23/3-9,S-6	0.8
1995	StL N	4	11	0	2	0	0	0	0	0-0	0	3	.182	.182	.182	-4	-2	0-0	.941	3	227	274	/2-2,S	0.1
Total	12	720	2128	245	529	90	13	48	220	145-4	10	438	.249	.298	.371	80	-65	14-11	.947	51	109	125	3-454,2-215/D-38,S-21,O(LF)	-1.2
HULSE, DAVID David Lindsey B 2.25.1968 San Angelo, TX BL/TL 5-11/170# d8.11																								
1992	Tex A	32	92	14	28	4	0	0	2	3-0	0	18	.304	.326	.348	92	-1	3-1	.984	-2	96	0	O-31(0-29-2)/D	-0.3
1993	Tex A	114	407	71	118	9	10	1	29	26-1	1	57	.290	.333	.369	92	-6	29-9	.988	-5	95	56	*O-112(CF)/D-2	-0.6
1994	Tex A	77	310	58	79	8	4	1	19	21-0	2	53	.255	.305	.316	61	-19	18-2	.978	-8	90	0	O-76(CF)/D	-2.1
1995	Mil A	119	339	46	85	11	6	3	47	18-2	0	60	.251	.285	.345	61	-21	15-3	.984	-10	84	34	*O-115(67-52-17)	-2.9
1996	Mil A	81	117	18	26	3	0	0	6	8-0	0	16	.222	.272	.248	32	-12	4-1	.990	0	105	42	O-68(24-37-11)/D-4	-1.1
Total	5	423	1265	207	336	35	20	5	103	76-3	3	204	.266	.307	.337	69	-59	69-16	.985	-24	92	31	O-402(91-306-30)/D-8	-7.0
HULSWITT, RUDY Rudolph Edward B 2.23.1877 Newport, KY D 1.16.1950 Louisville, KY BR/TR 5-8.5/165# d6.16 C3																								
1899	Lou N	1	0	0	0	0	0	0	0	0	0		—	—	—	—	0	0	.333	-2	42	0	/S	-0.1
1902	Phi N	128	497	59	135	11	7	0	38	30	2		.272	.316	.322	97	-3	12	.917	8	97	78	*S-125/3-3	1.0
1903	Phi N	138	519	56	128	22	9	1	58	28	2		.247	.288	.329	78	-17	10	.906	-1	98	83	*S-138	-1.2
1904	Phi N	113	406	36	99	11	4	1	36	16	2		.244	.276	.298	80	-11	8	.912	-11	89	95	*S-113	-1.9
1908	Cin N	119	386	27	88	5	7	1	28	30	2		.228	.287	.285	85	-7	7	.936	-8	95	100	*S-118/2	-1.3
1909	StL N	82	289	21	81	8	3	0	29	19	2		.280	.329	.329	111	3	7	.930	-7	96	61	S-65,2-12	-0.2
1910	StL N	63	133	9	33	7	2	0	14	13	1	10	.248	.320	.331	93	-1	5	.854	-10	93	33	S-30/2-2	-1.1
Total	7	644	2230	208	564	64	32	3	203	136	11	10	.253	.299	.314	89	-36	49	.915	-30	95	83	S-590/2-15,3-3	-4.8
HUMMEL, JOHN John Edwin "Silent John" B 4.4.1883 Bloomsburg, PA D 5.18.1959 Springfield, MA BR/TR 5-11/160# d9.12 OF Total (145-LF 26-CF 125-RF)																								
1905	Bro N	30	109	19	29	3	4	0	7	9	0		.266	.322	.367	114	1	6	.962	2	100	120	2-30	0.4
1906	Bro N	97	286	20	57	6	4	1	21	36	0		.199	.289	.259	77	-7	10	.953	2	102	151	2-50,O-21(15-1-4),1-15	-0.7
1907	Bro N	107	342	41	80	12	3	3	31	26	3		.234	.294	.313	98	-2	8	.951	9	115	102	2-44,O-33(22-3-9),1-12/S-8	0.6
1908	Bro N	**154**	594	51	143	11	12	4	41	34	2		.241	.284	.320	97	-5	20	.973	12	172	284	O-95(92-4-2),2-43/S-9,1-8	0.2
1909	Bro N	146	542	54	152	15	9	4	52	22	2		.280	.311	.363	113	4	16	.987	-11	50	77	1-54,2-38,S-36,O-17(0-6-11)	-0.8
1910	Bro N	153	578	67	141	21	13	5	74	57	2	81	.244	.314	.351	97	-4	21	**.965**	-18	94	96	*2-153	-2.3
1911	Bro N	137	477	54	129	21	11	5	58	67	0	66	.270	.360	.392	115	10	16	**.972**	-4	96	105	*2-127/1-4,S-2	0.8
1912	Bro N	122	411	55	116	21	7	5	54	49	0	55	.282	.359	.404	113	8	7	.969	-5	98	73	2-58,O-44(RF),1-11	0.2
1913	Bro N	67	198	20	48	7	7	2	24	13	1	23	.242	.292	.379	88	-4	4-1	.938	1	97	195	O-28(3-0-25),S-17/1-6,2-3	-0.3
1914	Bro N	73	208	25	55	8	9	0	20	16	0	25	.264	.317	.389	107	1	5	.982	-1	91	68	1-36,O-19(5-4-11)/2S	-0.2
1915	Bro N	53	100	6	23	2	3	0	8	6	0	11	.230	.274	.310	75	-3	1-1	1.000	-2	105	0	O-21(2-1-18),1-11/S	-0.7
1918	NY A	22	61	9	18	1	2	0	4	11	1	8	.295	.411	.377	135	3	5	.960	-3	91	0	O-15(6-7-1)/1-3,2	0.0
Total	12	1161	3906	421	991	128	84	29	394	346	11	269	.254	.316	.352	103	2	119-2	.963	-17	99	98	2-548,O-293L,1-160/S-74	-2.8
HUMMEL, TIM Timothy Robert B 11.18.1978 Goshen, NY BR/TR 6-2/190# d8.26																								
2003	Cin N	26	84	9	19	5	0	2	10	8-0	0	13	.226	.290	.357	70	-4	0-0	.894	-3	90	0	3-20/S-2,2	-0.7
HUMPHREY, AL Albert B 2.28.1886 Ashtabula, OH D 5.13.1961 Ashtabula, OH BL/TR 5-11/180# d9.1																								
1911	Bro N	8	27	4	5	0	0	0	0	3	0	7	.185	.267	.185	29	-3	0	.923	-1	82	0	/O-8(0-7-1)	-0.5

Year	Tm Lg	G	AB	R	H	2B	3B	HR	RBI	BB-IB	HP	SO	AVG	OBP	SLG	AOPS	ABR	SB-CS	FA	FR	Rng	Thr	G at Pos	BFW
HUMPHREY, TERRY Terryal Gene B 8.4.1949 Chickasha, OK BR/TR 6-3/190# d9.5																								
1971	Mon N	9	26	1	5	1	0	0	1	0-0	0	4	.192	.192	.231	19	-3	0-0	.981	1	64	179	/C-9	-0.1
1972	Mon N	69	215	13	40	8	0	1	9	16-4	2	38	.186	.248	.237	38	-17	4-1	.986	-5	123	161	C-65	-2.1
1973	Mon N	43	90	5	15	2	0	1	9	5-0	0	16	.167	.206	.222	19	-10	0-1	1.000	3	177	150	C-35	-0.6
1974	Mon N	20	52	3	10	3	0	0	3	4-0	0	9	.192	.246	.250	38	-4	0-0	.990	5	84	299	C-17	0.1
1975	Det A	18	41	0	10	0	0	0	1	2-0	0	6	.244	.279	.244	47	-3	0-0	1.000	-3	66	86	C-18	-0.6
1976	Cal A	71	196	17	48	10	0	1	19	13-0	5	30	.245	.306	.311	87	-3	0-1	.980	-2	73	127	C-71	-0.3
1977	Cal A	123	304	17	69	11	0	2	34	21-0	4	58	.227	.283	.283	58	-18	1-1	.989	2	78	**138**	*C-123	-1.1
1978	Cal A	53	114	11	25	4	1	1	9	6-0	2	12	.219	.264	.298	62	-6	0-1	.978	0	69	89	C-52/23	-0.5
1979	Cal A	9	17	2	1	0	0	0	0	1-0	0	2	.059	.111	.059	-55	-4	0-0	.983	3	47	126	/C-9	-0.1
Total	9	415	1055	69	223	39	1	6	85	68-4	13	175	.211	.265	.267	51	-68	5-5	.986	3	91	141	C-399/32	-5.3
HUMPHREYS, MIKE Michael Butler B 4.10.1967 Dallas, TX BR/TR 6/185# d7.29																								
1991	NY A	25	40	9	8	0	0	0	3	9-0	0	7	.200	.347	.200	55	-2	2-0	1.000	-1	90	0	/O-9(8-0-2),3-6,D-7	-0.3
1992	NY A	4	10	0	1	0	0	0	0	0-0	0	1	.100	.100	.100	-44	-2	0-0	1.000	1	189	847	/O-2(LF),D	-0.1
1993	NY A	25	35	6	6	2	1	1	6	4-0	0	11	.171	.250	.371	69	-2	2-1	1.000	-2	69	0	O-21(11-5-7)/D-3	-0.4
Total	3	54	85	15	15	2	1	1	9	13-0	0	19	.176	.283	.259	51	-6	4-1	1.000	-2	88	91	/O-32(21-5-9),D-11,3-6	-0.8
HUMPHRIES, JOHN John Henry B 11.12.1861 N.Gower, ON, CAN D 11.29.1933 Salinas, CA BL/TL 6/185# d7.7																								
1883	NY N	29	107	5	12	1	0	0	4	1		22	.112	.120	.121	-26	-16		.815	-4			C-20,O-12(0-1-11)	-1.7
1884	Was AA	49	193	23	34	2	0	0		9	1		.176	.217	.187	37	-12		.890	-6			C-35,O-12(1-3-8)/1-4	-1.5
	NY N	20	64	6	6	0	0	0	2	9		19	.094	.205	.094	-2	-7		.896	7			C-20	0.1
Total	2	98	364	34	52	3	0	0	6	19		41	.143	.188	.151	9	-35		.876	-4			/C-75,O-24(1-4-19),1-4	-3.1
HUNDLEY, RANDY Cecil Randolph B 6.1.1942 Martinsville, VA BR/TR 6/175# d9.27 C1 s-Todd																								
1964	SF N	2	1	1	0	0	0	0	0	0-0	0	1	.000	.000	.000	-98	0	0-0	—	-0	*0*	*0*	/C-2	-0.1
1965	SF N	6	15	0	1	0	0	0	0	0-0	0	4	.067	.067	.067	-61	-3	0-0	1.000	3	*116*	*301*	/C-6	0.0
1966	Chi N	149	526	50	124	22	3	19	63	35-3	3	113	.236	.285	.397	87	-10	1-3	.986	-12	*95*	*118*	*C-149	-1.6
1967	Chi N	152	539	68	144	25	3	14	60	44-6	2	75	.267	.322	.403	102	2	2-4	.996	-7	*122*	*77*	*C-152	0.1
1968	Chi N	160	553	41	125	18	4	7	65	39-6	4	69	.226	.280	.311	73	-18	1-0	.995	-5	***143***	*105*	*C-160	-1.7
1969	Chi N★	151	522	67	133	15	1	18	64	61-7	3	90	.255	.334	.391	91	-5	2-3	.992	17	125	123	*C-151	1.9
1970	Chi N	73	250	13	61	5	0	7	36	16-0	0	52	.244	.288	.348	62	-14	0-1	.990	6	177	99	C-73	-0.5
1971	Chi N	9	21	1	7	1	0	0	2	0-0	0	2	.333	.333	.381	89	0	0-0	.979	3	109	172	/C-8	0.3
1972	Chi N	114	357	23	78	12	0	5	30	22-10	0	62	.218	.261	.294	53	-22	1-0	**.995**	6	87	87	*C-113	-1.2
1973	Chi N	124	368	35	83	11	1	10	43	30-8	0	51	.226	.283	.342	68	-17	5-6	.993	16	120	105	*C-122	0.3
1974	Min A	32	88	2	17	2	0	0	3	4-0	0	12	.193	.228	.216	27	-8	0-0	.965	1	80	204	C-28	-0.7
1975	SD N	74	180	7	37	5	1	2	14	19-1	1	29	.206	.284	.278	60	-10	0-0	.970	1	100	100	C-51	-0.7
1976	Chi N	13	18	3	3	2	0	0	1	1-0	0	4	.167	.200	.278	35	-2	0-0	.923	-0	48	88	/C-9	-0.2
1977	Chi N	2	4	0	0	0	0	0	0	0-0	0	1	.000	.000	.000	-90	-1	0-0	1.000	0	102	0	/C-2	-0.1
Total	14	1061	3442	311	813	118	13	82	381	271-41	13	565	.236	.292	.350	76	-108	12-17	.990	27	*119*	*106*	*C-1026	-4.2
HUNDLEY, TODD Todd Randolph B 5.27.1969 Martinsville, VA BB/TR (BL 1999 (part), 2000 (part)) 5-11/185# d5.18 f-Randy																								
1990	NY N	36	67	8	14	6	0	0	2	6-0	0	18	.209	.274	.299	58	-4	0-0	.988	-1	109	49	C-36	-0.4
1991	NY N	21	60	5	8	0	1	1	7	6-0	1	14	.133	.221	.217	25	-6	0-0	1.000	-5	88	101	C-20	-1.1
1992	NY N	123	358	32	75	17	0	7	32	19-4	4	76	.209	.256	.316	62	-19	3-0	.996	1	89	86	*C-121	-1.2
1993	NY N	130	417	40	95	17	2	11	53	23-7	2	62	.228	.269	.357	68	-21	1-1	.988	-4	81	89	*C-123	-1.8
1994	NY N	91	291	45	69	10	1	16	42	25-4	3	73	.237	.303	.443	93	-5	2-1	.990	-1	128	88	C-82	0.0
1995	NY N	90	275	39	77	11	0	15	51	42-5	5	64	.280	.382	.484	131	14	1-0	.987	-4	123	70	C-89	1.5
1996	NY N★	153	540	85	140	32	1	41	112	79-15	3	146	.259	.356	.550	141	32	1-3	.992	-2	116	72	*C-150	3.8
1997	NY N✳	132	417	78	114	21	2	30	86	83-16	3	116	.273	.394	.549	150	33	2-3	.987	-10	113	62	*C-122/D	2.9
1998	NY N	53	124	8	20	4	0	3	12	16-0	1	55	.161	.261	.266	40	-11	1-1	.898	1	92	124	O-34(LF)/C-2	-1.1
1999	LA N	114	376	49	78	14	0	24	55	44-3	4	113	.207	.295	.436	87	-10	3-0	.979	-10	68	107	*C-108	-1.2
2000	LA N	90	299	49	85	16	0	24	70	45-6	2	69	.284	.375	.579	147	21	0-1	.979	-12	64	106	C-84/D	1.4
2001	Chi N	79	246	23	46	10	0	12	31	25-0	3	89	.187	.268	.374	67	-13	0-0	.993	-3	69	73	C-70	-1.2
2002	Chi N	92	266	32	56	8	0	16	35	32-3	3	80	.211	.301	.421	93	-5	0-0	.984	6	71	105	C-79/D	0.5
2003	LA N	21	33	2	6	1	0	2	11	8-0	0	13	.182	.341	.394	97	0	0-1	.981	-2	72	123	C-10	-0.2
Total	14	1225	3769	495	883	167	7	202	599	453-63	34	988	.234	.320	.443	103	6	14-11	.988	-46	94	85	*C-1096/O-34(LF),D-3	1.9
HUNGLING, BERNIE Bernard Herman "Bud" B 3.5.1896 Dayton, OH D 3.30.1968 Dayton, OH BR/TR 6-2/180# d4.14																								
1922	Bro N	39	102	9	23	1	2	1	13	6	0	20	.225	.269	.304	48	-8	2-0	.968	-1	*77*	*86*	C-36	-0.7
1923	Bro N	2	4	0	0	0	0	0	0	0	0	2	.000	.000	.000	-99	-1	0-1	.667	-1	*47*	*0*	/C	-0.2
1930	StL A	10	31	4	10	2	0	0	2	5	0	3	.323	.417	.387	102	0	0-1	1.000	-2	*92*	*39*	C-10	-0.1
Total	3	51	137	13	33	3	2	1	15	11	0	25	.241	.297	.314	57	-9	2-2	.968	-4	*80*	*75*	/C-47	-1.0
HUNNEFIELD, BILL William Fenton "Wild Bill" B 1.5.1899 Dedham, MA D 8.28.1976 Nantucket, MA BB/TR 5-10/165# d4.17																								
1926	Chi A	131	470	81	129	26	4	3	48	37	1	28	.274	.329	.366	84	-12	24-9	.931	-5	97	94	S-98,3-17,2-15	-0.3
1927	Chi A	112	365	45	104	25	1	2	36	25	1	24	.285	.332	.375	85	-8	15-13	.933	-17	93	97	S-79,2-17/3	-1.7
1928	Chi A	94	333	42	98	8	3	2	24	26	3	24	.294	.351	.354	87	-6	16-6	.967	-10	94	99	2-82/S-3,3	-1.2
1929	Chi A	47	127	13	23	5	0	0	9	7	0	3	.181	.224	.220	15	-16	5-2	.969	-2	101	107	2-29/3-4,S-2	-1.6
1930	Chi A	31	81	11	22	2	0	1	5	4	1	10	.272	.314	.333	67	-4	1-1	.932	-6	74	88	S-22/1	-0.8
1931	Cle A	21	71	13	17	4	1	0	4	9	0	4	.239	.325	.324	67	-3	3-1	.853	-6	84	73	S-21/2	-0.7
	Bos N	11	21	2	6	0	0	0	1	0	0	2	.286	.286	.286	56	-1	0	.864	1	118	0	/3-5,2-4	-0.1
	NY N	64	196	23	53	5	0	1	17	9	0	16	.270	.302	.311	67	-10	3	.951	-2	96	96	2-56/S-5	-0.9
	Year	75	217	25	59	5	0	1	18	9	0	18	.272	.301	.309	66	-11	3	.951	-2	97	95	2-60/3-5,S-5	-1.0
Total	6	511	1664	230	452	75	9	9	144	117	6	111	.272	.322	.344	76	-60	67-32	.925	-48	93	92	S-230,2-204/3-28,1	-7.3
HUNT, RANDY James Randall B 1.3.1960 Prattville, AL BR/TR 6/185# d6.4																								
1985	StL N	14	19	1	3	0	0	0	1	0-0	0	5	.158	.158	.158	-12	-3	0-1	1.000	-0	149	0	C-13	-0.3
1986	Mon N	21	48	4	10	0	0	2	5	5-2	0	16	.208	.283	.333	70	-2	0-0	.960	2	77	84	C-21	0.0
Total	2	35	67	5	13	0	0	2	6	5-2	0	21	.194	.250	.284	48	-5	0-1	.967	1	96	62	/C-34	-0.3
HUNT, KEN Kenneth Lawrence B 7.13.1934 Grand Forks, ND D 6.8.1997 Gardena, CA BR/TR 6-1/205# d9.10																								
1959	NY A	6	12	2	4	1	0	0	1	0-0	0	3	.333	.308	.417	108	0	0-0	1.000	0	121	0	/O-5(RF)	0.0
1960	NY A	25	22	4	6	2	0	0	1	4-0	1	4	.273	.407	.364	117	1	0-0	.957	0	121	0	O-24(17-5-2)	0.1
1961	LA A	149	479	70	122	29	3	25	84	49-1	4	120	.255	.325	.484	103	1	8-2	.950	-8	93	86	*O-134(8-108-23)/2	-1.0
1962	LA A	13	11	4	2	0	0	1	1	1-0	0	5	.182	.250	.455	88	0	1-0	.867	-1	0	0	/1-3	-0.1
1963	LA A	59	142	17	26	6	1	5	16	15-2	0	49	.183	.261	.345	72	-6	0-1	.972	-2	93	38	O-50(22-2-27)	-1.1
	Was A	7	20	1	4	0	0	1	4	2-1	0	6	.200	.273	.350	73	-1	0-0	1.000	-0	112	0	/O-5(1-3-1)	-0.1
	Year	66	162	18	30	6	1	6	20	17-3	0	55	.185	.263	.346	73	-6	0-1	.976	-2	95	34	O-55(23-5-28)	-1.2
1964	Was A	51	96	9	13	4	0	1	4	14-0	0	35	.135	.243	.208	28	-9	0-1	1.000	1	111	54	O-37(4-33-0)	-1.0
Total	6	310	782	107	177	42	4	33	111	85-4	5	222	.226	.303	.417	89	-14	9-4	.964	-9	97	66	O-255(52-151-58)/1-3,2	-3.2
HUNT, JOEL Oliver Joel "Jodie" B 10.11.1905 Texico, NM D 7.24.1978 Teague, TX BR/TR 5-10/165# d4.27																								
1931	StL N	4	1	2	0	0	0	0	0	0	0	1	.000	.000	.000	-96	0	0	—	-0	0	0	/O(RF)	0.0
1932	StL N	12	21	0	4	1	0	0	3	4	0	3	.190	.320	.238	51	-1	0	1.000	0	124	0	/O-5(RF)	-0.1
Total	2	16	22	2	4	1	0	0	3	4	0	4	.182	.308	.227	45	-1	0	1.000	0	121	0	/O-6(RF)	-0.1
HUNT, DICK Richard M. B 1847 , NY D 11.20.1895 Brooklyn, NY 5-9/145# d5.7																								
1872	Eck NA	11	46	10	15	1	1	0	4	1		0	.326	.340	.391	146	3	0-1	.583	-1	257	0	/O-9(0-1-8),2-2	0.2
HUNT, RON Ronald Kenneth B 2.23.1941 St.Louis, MO BR/TR 6/186# d4.16																								
1963	NY N	143	533	64	145	28	4	10	42	40-0	13	50	.272	.334	.396	109	7	5-4	.967	6	105	91	*2-142/3	2.7
1964	NY N★	127	475	59	144	19	6	6	42	29-4	11	30	.303	.357	.406	117	11	6-2	.979	-0	103	107	*2-109,3-12	2.1
1965	NY N	57	196	21	47	12	1	1	10	14-2	6	19	.240	.309	.327	82	-4	2-7	.979	-2	102	58	2-46/3-6	-0.5
1966	NY N★	132	479	63	138	19	2	3	33	41-2	11	34	.288	.356	.355	101	3	8-10	.970	9	110	96	*2-123/S3	2.1
1967	LA N	110	388	44	102	17	3	3	33	39-3	10	24	.263	.344	.345	107	5	2-1	.980	-10	92	91	2-90/3-8	0.3
1968	SF N	148	529	79	132	19	0	2	28	78-2	**25**	41	.250	.371	.297	103	9	6-6	.972	-13	100	81	*2-147	0.9

Year	Tm Lg	G	AB	R	H	2B	3B	HR	RBI	BB-IB	HP	SO	AVG	OBP	SLG	AOPS	ABR	SB-CS	FA	FR	Rng	Thr	G at Pos	BFW
1969	SF N	128	478	72	125	23	3	3	41	51-0	**25**	47	.262	.361	.341	100	4	9-2	.979	-7	106	91	*2-125/3	0.7
1970	SF N	117	367	70	103	17	1	6	41	44-1	**26**	29	.281	.394	.381	111	9	1-2	.968	-22	82	75	2-85,3-16	-0.8
1971	Mon N	152	520	89	145	20	3	5	38	58-1	**50**	41	.279	.402	.358	116	18	5-7	.979	-8	97	78	*2-133,3-19	1.8
1972	Mon N	129	443	56	112	20	0	0	18	51-4	**26**	29	.253	.363	.298	88	-2	9-2	.982	9	105	84	*2-122/3-5	1.7
1973	Mon N	113	401	61	124	14	0	0	18	52-3	**24**	19	.309	.418	.344	110	11	10-7	.982	-7	94	79	*2-102,3-14	1.0
1974	Mon N	115	403	66	108	15	0	0	26	55-0	14	17	.268	.375	.305	87	-3	2-5	.941	-3	103	104	3-75,2-31/S	-0.6
	StL N	12	23	1	4	0	0	0	0	3-0	2	2	.174	.321	.174	42	-2	0-0	1.000	-0	100	104	/2-5	-0.2
	Year	127	426	67	112	15	0	0	26	58-0	**16**	19	.263	.372	.298	85	-4	2-5	.941	-3	103	104	3-75,2-36/S	-0.8
Total	12	1483	5235	745	1429	223	23	39	370	555-22	243	382	.273	.368	.347	104	66	65-55	.976	-48	100	87	*2-1260,3-158/S-2	11.2
HUNTER, BRIAN Brian Lee B 3.5.1971 Portland, OR BR/TR 6-4/180# d6.27																								
1994	Hou N	6	24	2	6	1	0	0	0	1-0	0	6	.250	.280	.292	52	-2	2-1	.938	0	92	300	/O-6(CF)	-0.1
1995	Hou N	78	321	52	97	14	5	2	28	21-0	2	52	.302	.346	.396	103	1	24-7	.955	4	106	204	O-74(CF)	0.8
1996	Hou N	132	526	74	145	27	2	5	35	17-0	2	92	.276	.297	.363	80	-17	35-9	.960	3	102	184	*O-127(CF)	-0.8
1997	Det A	**162**	658	112	177	29	7	4	45	66-1	1	121	.269	.334	.353	81	-18	**74**-18	.990	-5	97	95	*O-162(CF)	-1.0
1998	Det A	142	595	67	151	29	3	4	36	36-0	2	94	.254	.298	.333	64	-33	42-12	.988	5	105	124	*O-139(CF)	-2.0
1999	Det A	18	55	8	13	2	1	0	0	5-0	1	11	.236	.311	.309	59	-3	0-3	1.000	2	120	100	O-18(CF)	-0.3
	Sea A	121	484	71	112	11	5	4	34	32-0	1	80	.231	.277	.300	49	-39	44-5	.985	8	111	189	*O-121(119-19-0)	-2.5
	Year	139	539	79	125	13	6	4	34	37-0	2	91	.232	.280	.301	50	-43	**44**-8	.988	10	112	**178**	*O-139(119-37-0)	-2.8
2000	Col N	72	200	36	55	4	1	1	13	21-0	1	31	.275	.347	.320	56	-13	15-3	.981	-0	96	103	O-63(27-34-12)	-1.1
	Cin N	32	40	11	9	1	0	0	1	6-0	0	9	.225	.319	.250	47	-3	5-0	.971	3	115	558	O-25(9-16-0)	0.1
	Year	104	240	47	64	5	1	1	14	27-0	1	40	.267	.342	.308	56	-16	20-3	.979	3	100	192	O-88(36-50-12)	-1.0
2001	Phi N	83	145	22	40	6	0	2	16	16-0	0	25	.276	.344	.359	86	-3	14-3	1.000	3	110	161	O-41(22-18-5)/D	0.1
2002	Hou N	98	201	32	54	16	3	3	20	16-0	2	39	.269	.329	.423	95	-2	5-0	1.000	2	105	150	O-88(CF)	0.1
2003	Hou N	56	98	13	23	6	1	0	13	6-0	1	21	.235	.278	.316	54	-7	0-0	.944	-2	80	85	O-32(5-14-15)	-0.9
Total	10	1000	3347	500	882	146	28	25	241	243-1	13	581	.264	.313	.346	72	-139	260-61	.980	22	103	152	O-896(182-715-32)/D	-7.6
HUNTER, BRIAN Brian Ronald B 3.4.1968 Torrance, CA BR/TL 6/195# d5.31																								
1991	†Atl N	97	271	32	68	16	1	12	50	17-0	1	48	.251	.296	.450	101	0	0-2	.988	-1	102	97	1-85/O-6(5-0-1)	-0.7
1992	†Atl N	102	238	34	57	13	2	14	41	21-3	0	50	.239	.292	.487	113	3	1-2	.997	5	118	81	1-92/O-6(1-0-5)	0.3
1993	Atl N	37	80	4	11	3	1	0	8	2-1	0	15	.138	.153	.200	-5	-12	0-0	.994	0	99	143	1-29/O-2(RF)	-1.4
1994	Pit N	76	233	28	53	15	1	11	47	15-2	0	55	.227	.270	.442	82	-7	0-0	.991	1	113	115	1-59/O-5(LF)	-1.1
	Cin N	9	23	6	7	1	0	4	10	2-0	0	1	.304	.346	.870	209	3	0-0	1.000	0	114	0	/O-5(1-0-4),1	0.3
	Year	85	256	34	60	16	1	15	57	17-2	0	56	.234	.277	.480	93	-4	0-0	.991	1	113	113	1-60,O-10(6-0-4)	-0.8
1995	Cin N	40	79	9	17	6	0	1	9	11-1	1	21	.215	.312	.329	72	-3	2-1	.983	1	105	160	1-23/O-4(3-0-1)	-0.4
1996	Sea A	75	198	21	53	10	0	7	28	15-2	4	43	.268	.327	.424	89	-4	0-1	.991	-0	43	85	1-41,O-29(29-0-2)/D-2	-0.7
1998	StL N	62	112	11	23	9	1	4	13	7-0	1	23	.205	.258	.411	73	-5	1-1	.938	1	115	152	O-25(16-0-11),1-10/D	-0.5
1999	†Atl N	114	181	28	45	12	1	6	30	31-1	4	40	.249	.367	.425	101	1	0-1	.991	2	115	100	*1-101/O-8(LF)	-0.2
2000	Atl N	2	2	1	1	0	0	1	1	0-0	0	0	.500	.500	2.000	490	1	0-0	—	0			/H	0.1
	Phi N	85	138	13	29	5	0	7	22	20-1	0	39	.210	.310	.399	77	-5	0-1	.994	1	106	64	1-40/O-9(6-0-3),D	-0.7
	Year	87	140	14	30	5	0	8	23	20-1	0	39	.214	.313	.421	82	-4	0-1	.994	1	106	64	1-40/O-9(6-0-3),D	-0.6
Total	9	699	1555	187	364	90	7	67	259	141-11	11	335	.234	.298	.430	90	-28	4-9	.991	10	104	99	1-481/O-99(74-0-29),D-4	-5.0
HUNTER, EDDIE Edison Franklin B 2.6.1905 Bellevue, KY D 3.14.1967 Colerain, OH BR/TR 5-7.5/150# d8.5																								
1933	Cin N	1	0	0	0	0	0	0	0	0	0	0	—	—	—	—	0	0	—	-0	0	0	/3	0.0
HUNTER, NEWT Frederick Creighton B 1.5.1880 Chillicothe, OH D 10.26.1963 Columbus, OH BR/TR 6/180# d4.12 C5																								
1911	Pit N	65	209	35	53	10	6	2	24	25	4	43	.254	.345	.388	101	0	9	.989	-2	81	159	1-61	-0.3
HUNTER, GEORGE George Henry B 7.8.1887 Buffalo, NY D 1.11.1968 Harrisburg, PA BB/TL 5-8.5/165# d5.4 twb-Bill ▲																								
1909	Bro N	44	123	8	28	7	0	0	8	9	1		.228	.286	.285	80	-3	1	.871	-2	40	165	O-23(4-1-18),P-16	-0.5
1910	Bro N	1	0	0	0	0	0	0	0	0	0	0	—	—	—	—	0	0	—	-0	0	0	/O(RF)	0.0
Total	2	45	123	8	28	7	0	0	8	9	1	0	.228	.286	.285	80	-3	1	.871	-2	40	164	/O-24(4-1-19),P-16	-0.5
HUNTER, BILLY Gordon William B 6.4.1928 Punxsutawney, PA BR/TR 6/180# d4.14 M2 C14																								
1953	StL A★	**154**	567	50	124	18	1	1	37	24	2	45	.219	.253	.259	38	-51	3-1	.970	14	108	91	*S-152	-2.4
1954	Bal A	125	411	28	100	9	5	2	27	21	2	38	.243	.281	.304	66	-22	5-4	.948	0	96	96	*S-124	-1.3
1955	NY A	98	255	14	58	7	1	3	20	15-2	0	18	.227	.269	.298	54	-18	9-2	.958	-1	100	123	S-98	-1.0
1956	NY A	39	75	8	21	3	4	0	11	2-0	0	4	.280	.299	.427	93	-2	0-1	1.000	7	102	164	S-32/3-4	0.6
1957	KC A	116	319	39	61	10	4	8	29	27-2	3	43	.191	.259	.323	58	-20	1-2	.974	-6	105	100	2-64,S-35,3-17	-2.1
1958	KC A	22	58	6	9	1	1	2	11	5-0	0	7	.155	.222	.310	44	-5	1-1	.933	-1	105	60	S-12/2-8,3	-0.5
	Cle A	76	190	21	37	10	2	0	9	17-1	1	37	.195	.263	.268	48	-13	4-1	.948	-7	88	110	S-75/3-2	-1.5
	Year	98	248	27	46	11	3	2	20	22-1	1	44	.185	.254	.278	47	-18	5-2	.946	-8	90	103	S-87/2-8,3-3	-2.0
Total	6	630	1875	166	410	58	18	16	144	111-5	8	192	.219	.264	.294	53	-131	23-12	.958	6	100	103	S-528/2-72,3-24	-8.2
HUNTER, BUDDY Harold James B 8.9.1947 Omaha, NE BR/TR 5-10/170# d7.1																								
1971	Bos A	8	9	2	2	1	0	0	0	2-0	0	1	.222	.364	.333	92	0	0-0	1.000	-1	97	42	/2-6	-0.1
1973	Bos A	13	7	3	3	1	0	0	2	3-0	1	1	.429	.636	.571	229	2	0-0	1.000	1	50	604	/3-3,2-2,D	0.3
1975	Bos A	1	1	0	0	0	0	0	0	0-0	0	0	.000	.000	.000	-92	0	0-0	.750	-0	61	264	/2	0.0
Total	3	22	17	5	5	2	0	0	2	5-0	1	2	.294	.478	.412	144	2	0-0	.968	-0	103	122	/2-9,3-3,D	0.2
HUNTER, HERB Herbert Harrison B 12.25.1896 Boston, MA D 7.25.1970 Orlando, FL BL/TR 6-0.5/165# d4.29																								
1916	NY N	21	28	3	7	0	0	1	4	0	0	5	.250	.250	.357	90	-1	0	1.000	-0	71	0	/3-6,1-2	-0.1
	Chi N	2	4	0	0	0	0	0	0	0	0	0	.000	.000	.000	-90	-1	0	.750	-0	110	0	/3	-0.1
	Year	23	32	3	7	0	0	1	4	0	0	5	.219	.219	.313	65	-2	0	.941	-0	79	0	/3-7,1-2	-0.2
1917	Chi N	3	3	0	0	0	0	0	0	0	0	0	.000	.000	.000	-93	-1	0	1.000	-0	0	0	/23	-0.1
1920	Bos A	4	12	2	1	0	0	0	0	1	0	1	.083	.154	.083	-38	-2	0-0	.857	-0	70	234	/O-4(3-1-0)	-0.3
1921	StL N	9	2	3	0	0	0	0	0	1	0	0	.000	.333	.000	-4	0	0-3	1.000	-0	0	632	/1	-0.1
Total	4	39	49	8	8	0	0	1	4	2	0	6	.163	.196	.224	24	-5	0-3	.905	-1	86	0	/3-8,O-4(3-1-0),1-3,2	-0.7
HUNTER, LEM Robert Lemuel B 1.16.1863 Warren, OH D 11.9.1956 W.Lafayette, OH d9.1																								
1883	Cle N	1	4	1	1	0	0	0	0	0		2	.250	.250	.250	53	0		—	-0	0	0	/O(RF)P	0.0
HUNTER, TORII Torii Kedar B 7.18.1975 Pine Bluff, AR BR/TR 6-2/205# d8.22																								
1997	Min A	1	0	0	0	0	0	0	0	0-0	0	0	—	—	—	—	0	0-0	—	0			/R	0.0
1998	Min A	6	17	0	4	1	0	0	2	2-0	0	6	.235	.316	.294	59	-1	0-1	1.000	-1	59	0	/O-6(CF)	-0.3
1999	Min A	135	384	52	98	17	2	9	35	26-1	6	72	.255	.309	.380	73	-16	10-6	.997	2	104	98	*O-130(16-107-14)	-1.3
2000	Min A	99	336	44	94	14	7	5	44	18-2	2	68	.280	.318	.408	79	-12	4-3	.989	11	113	257	O-99(1-98-0)	0.0
2001	Min A	148	564	82	147	32	5	27	92	29-0	8	125	.261	.306	.479	100	-2	9-6	.992	19	**121**	164	*O-147(CF)	1.7
2002	†Min A★	148	561	89	162	37	4	29	94	35-3	5	118	.289	.334	.524	123	17	23-8	.992	-2	99	94	*O-146(CF)/D	1.8
2003	†Min A	154	581	83	145	31	4	26	102	50-7	5	106	.250	.312	.451	98	-3	6-7	.991	3	107	73	*O-151(CF)/D-3	0.0
Total	7	691	2443	350	650	132	22	96	369	160-13	26	495	.266	.316	.456	97	-17	52-31	.992	32	108	129	O-679(17-655-14)/D-4	1.9
HUNTER, BILL William Ellsworth B 7.8.1887 Buffalo, NY D 4.10.1934 Buffalo, NY BL/TL 5-7.5/155# d8.6 twb-George																								
1912	Cle A	21	55	6	9	2	0	0	2	10	1		.164	.303	.200	43	-4	0	1.000	-1	100	44	O-16(CF)	-0.5
HUNTER, BILL William F. B 1855 St.Thomas, ON, CAN 5-7.5/160# d5.2																								
1884	Lou AA	2	7	1	1	0	0	0		0	0		.143	.143	.143	-7	-1		.667	-2			/C-2	-0.2
HUNTZ, STEVE Stephen Michael B 12.3.1945 Cleveland, OH BB/TR 6-1/204# d9.19																								
1967	StL N	3	6	1	1	0	0	0	0	1-0	0	2	.167	.286	.167	33	0	0-0	1.000	-1	58	0	/2-2	-0.1
1969	StL N	71	139	13	27	4	0	3	13	27-7	0	34	.194	.325	.288	73	-4	0-0	.945	-4	93	113	S-52,2-12/3-6	-0.4
1970	SD N	106	352	54	77	8	0	11	37	66-1	1	69	.219	.341	.335	86	-5	0-3	.958	6	115	109	S-57,3-51	0.5
1971	Chi A	35	86	10	18	3	1	2	6	7-0	0	9	.209	.266	.337	69	-4	1-0	1.000	-2	95	83	2-14/S-7,3-6	-0.4
1975	SD N	22	53	3	8	4	0	0	4	7-2	0	8	.151	.250	.226	35	-5	0-0	.939	2	116	257	3-16/2-2	-0.3
Total	5	237	636	81	131	19	1	16	60	108-10	1	122	.206	.320	.314	76	-18	1-3	.955	1	106	111	S-116/3-79,2-30	-0.7

Year	Tm Lg	G	AB	R	H	2B	3B	HR	RBI	BB-IB	HP	SO	AVG	OBP	SLG	AOPS	ABR	SB-CS	FA	FR	Rng	Thr	G at Pos	BFW
HUPPERT, DAVE David Blain B 4.17.1957 South Gate, CA BR/TR 6-1/190# d9.15																								
1983	Bal A	2	0	0	0	0	0	0	0	0-0	0	0	—	—	—	—	0	0-0	1.000	0	0	0	/C-2	0.0
1985	Mil A	15	21	1	1	0	0	0	0	2-0	0	7	.048	.130	.048	-49	-4	0-0	.960	-1	78	74	C-15	-0.5
Total	2	17	21	1	1	0	0	0	0	2-0	0	7	.048	.130	.048	-49	-4	0-0	.962	-0	74	70	/C-17	-0.5
HURDLE, CLINT Clinton Merrick B 7.30.1957 Big Rapids, MI BL/TR 6-3/195# d9.18 M2 C6 OF Total (97-LF 238-RF)																								
1977	KC A	9	26	5	8	0	0	2	7	2-0	0	7	.308	.357	.538	139	1	0-0	1.000	0	121	0	/O-9(RF)	0.1
1978	†KC A	133	417	48	110	25	5	7	56	56-1	1	84	.264	.348	.398	108	6	1-3	.958	-5	93	102	O-78(41-0-42),1-52/3D	-0.6
1979	KC A	59	171	16	41	10	3	3	30	28-4	1	24	.240	.343	.386	96	0	0-1	.968	-2	96	60	O-50(30-0-20)/3D	-0.4
1980	†KC A	130	395	50	116	31	2	10	60	34-5	2	61	.294	.349	.458	119	11	0-0	.960	-2	99	91	*O-126(RF)	0.3
1981	†KC A	28	76	12	25	3	1	4	15	13-3	0	10	.329	.427	.553	182	8	0-0	1.000	2	119	57	O-28(2-0-26)	0.9
1982	Cin N	19	34	2	7	1	0	0	1	2-2	1	6	.206	.270	.235	42	-3	0-1	.950	1	90	258	O-17(17-0-1)	-0.3
1983	NY N	13	33	3	6	2	0	0	2	2-0	0	10	.182	.229	.242	31	-3	0-0	.800	-1	123	181	/3-9,O(RF)	-0.4
1985	NY N	43	82	7	16	4	0	3	7	13-3	1	20	.195	.313	.354	88	-1	0-1	1.000	-3	84	105	C-17,O-10(2-0-8)	-0.5
1986	StL N	78	154	18	30	5	1	3	15	26-0	1	38	.195	.311	.299	71	-6	0-0	.994	1	102	139	1-39,O-10(5-0-5)/C-5,3-4	-0.7
1987	NY N	3	3	1	1	0	0	0	0	0-0	0	1	.333	.333	.333	82	0	0-0	1.000	-0	0	0	/1	0.0
Total	10	515	1391	162	360	81	12	32	193	176-18	7	261	.259	.341	.403	106	13	1-6	.965	-9	98	90	O-329R/1-92,C-22,3-15,D-5	-1.6
HURLEY, JERRY Jeremiah B 4.1875 New York, NY D 12.27.1919 New York, NY BR/TR d9.23																								
1901	Cin N	9	21	1	1	0	0	0	0	1	1		.048	.130	.048	-51	-4	1	.938	-0	120	74	/C-7	-0.4
1907	Bro N	1	2	0	0	0	0	0	0	1	0		.000	.333	.000	5	0	0	1.000	-0	107	113	/C	0.0
Total	2	10	23	1	1	0	0	0	0	2	1		.043	.154	.043	-44	-4	1	.943	-0	118	79	/C-8	-0.4
HURLEY, JERRY Jeremiah Joseph B 6.15.1863 Boston, MA D 9.17.1950 Boston, MA BR/TR 6/190# d5.1																								
1889	Bos N	1	4	0	0	0	0	0	0	0	0	0	.000	.000	.000	-94	-1	0	—	-1	0	0	/O(RF)C	-0.1
1890	Pit P	8	22	5	6	1	0	0	2	2	0	5	.273	.333	.318	81	0	0	.906	-0	102	50	/C-7,O(LF)	0.0
1891	Cin AA	24	66	10	14	3	2	0	6	12	0	13	.212	.333	.318	80	-2	2	.862	-4	89	51	C-24/O(RF)1	-0.3
Total	3	33	92	15	20	4	2	0	8	14	0	18	.217	.321	.304	73	-3	2	.870	-4	88	48	/C-32,O-3(1-0-2),1	-0.4
HURLEY, DICK William H. B 1847 Honesdale, PA 5-7/160# d4.18																								
1872	Oly NA	2	7	0	0	0	0	0	0	0		1	.000	.000	.000	-99	-2	0-0	.667	-0	0	0	/O-2(RF)	-0.1
HURST, DON Frank O'Donnell B 8.12.1905 Maysville, KY D 12.6.1952 Los Angeles, CA BL/TL 6/215# d5.13																								
1928	Phi N	107	396	73	113	23	4	19	64	68	1	40	.285	.391	.508	129	18	3	.989	5	119	87	*1-104	1.5
1929	Phi N	**154**	589	100	179	29	4	31	125	80	3	36	.304	.390	.525	117	15	10	.985	5	117	88	*1-154	0.9
1930	Phi N	119	391	78	128	19	3	17	78	46	2	22	.327	.401	.522	113	9	6	.984	-2	103	91	1-96/O-7(CF)	0.1
1931	Phi N	137	489	63	149	37	5	11	91	64	1	28	.305	.386	.468	119	16	8	.986	11	**139**	90	*1-135	1.4
1932	Phi N	150	579	109	196	41	4	24	**143**	65	7	27	.339	.412	.547	139	34	10	**.993**	-2	92	81	*1-150	1.8
1933	Phi N	147	550	58	147	27	8	8	76	48	1	32	.267	.327	.389	92	-5	3	.985	8	**128**	106	*1-142	-1.1
1934	Phi N	40	130	16	34	9	0	2	21	12	0	7	.262	.324	.377	77	-4	1	.994	-1	84	113	1-34	-0.8
	Chi N	51	151	13	30	5	0	3	12	8	0	18	.199	.239	.291	42	-13	0	.986	-3	72	131	1-48	-2.0
	Year	91	281	29	64	14	0	5	33	20	0	25	.228	.279	.331	60	-16	1	.990	-4	77	123	1-82	-2.8
Total	7	905	3275	510	976	190	28	115	610	391	15	210	.298	.375	.478	113	70	41	.987	21	113	93	1-863/O-7(CF)	1.8
HURST, JIMMY Jimmy O'Neal B 3.1.1972 Tuscaloosa, AL BR/TR 6-6/225# d9.10																								
1997	Det A	13	17	1	3	1	0	1	1	2-0	0	6	.176	.263	.412	73	-1	0-0	1.000	-0	97	0	O-12(1-1-10)/D	-0.1
HUSKEY, BUTCH Robert Leon B 11.10.1971 Anadarko, OK BR/TR 6-3/244# d9.8																								
1993	NY N	13	41	2	6	1	0	0	3	1-1	0	13	.146	.159	.171	-10	-6	0-0	.923	1	113	104	3-13	-0.6
1995	NY N	28	90	8	17	1	0	3	11	10-0	0	16	.189	.267	.300	52	-7	1-0	.925	3	124	52	3-27/O(LF)	-0.3
1996	NY N	118	414	43	115	16	2	15	60	27-3	0	77	.278	.319	.435	102	-1	1-2	.984	-4	85	104	1-75,O-40(RF)/3-6	-1.3
1997	NY N	142	471	61	135	26	2	24	81	25-5	1	84	.287	.319	.503	117	9	8-5	.968	1	110	97	O-92(30-0-72),1-22,3-15/D-4	0.4
1998	NY N	113	369	43	93	18	0	13	59	26-3	1	66	.252	.300	.407	86	-9	7-6	.978	0	96	131	*O-103(RF)/D	-1.4
1999	Sea A	74	262	44	76	9	0	15	49	27-0	0	45	.290	.353	.496	117	6	3-1	1.000	-1	109	32	O-53(30-0-24)/1-10,3D	0.2
	†Bos A	45	124	18	33	6	0	7	28	7-1	0	20	.266	.305	.484	94	-2	0-0	1.000	-0	61	449	D-37/O-4(2-0-2),3-2	-0.4
	Year	119	386	62	109	15	0	22	77	34-1	0	65	.282	.338	.492	109	4	3-1	1.000	-1	106	60	O-57(32-0-26),D-44,1-10/3-3	-0.2
2000	Min A	64	215	22	48	13	0	5	27	25-1	2	49	.223	.306	.353	65	-12	0-2	.975	2	123	196	D-39,O-15(RF)/1-9	-1.3
	Col N	45	92	18	32	8	0	4	18	16-1	0	14	.348	.432	.565	122	4	1-1	1.000	0	103	88	O-23(15-0-8)/1-8	0.3
Total	7	642	2078	259	555	98	4	86	336	164-15	4	384	.267	.318	.442	97	-18	21-17	.976	3	104	104	O-331(78-0-264),1-124/D-88,3-64	-4.4
HUSON, JEFF Jeffrey Kent B 8.15.1964 Scottsdale, AZ BL/TR 6-3/180# d9.2 OF Total (10-LF 3-CF 3-RF)																								
1988	Mon N	20	42	7	13	2	0	0	3	4-2	0	3	.310	.370	.357	105	0	2-1	.932	-1	102	76	S-15/2-2,3O(CF)	0.0
1989	Mon N	32	74	1	12	5	0	0	2	6-3	0	6	.162	.225	.230	30	-7	3-0	.886	1	99	96	S-20/2-9,3	-0.4
1990	Tex A	145	396	57	95	12	2	0	28	46-0	2	54	.240	.320	.280	70	-15	12-4	.960	6	97	**117**	*S-119,3-36,2-12	-0.1
1991	Tex A	119	268	36	57	8	3	2	26	39-0	0	32	.213	.312	.287	68	-11	8-3	.965	1	103	72	*S-116/2-2,3	-0.3
1992	Tex A	123	318	49	83	14	3	4	24	41-2	1	43	.261	.342	.362	102	2	18-6	.968	-3	99	113	S-82,2-47/O-2(CF),D	0.6
1993	Tex A	23	45	3	6	1	1	0	2	0-0	0	10	.133	.133	.200	-12	-7	0-0	.909	3	129	143	S-12/2-5,3-2,D-2	-0.4
1995	Bal A	66	161	24	40	4	2	1	19	15-1	1	20	.248	.315	.317	64	-9	5-4	1.000	-0	95	127	3-33,2-21/SD	-0.7
1996	Bal A	17	28	5	9	1	0	0	2	1-0	0	3	.321	.333	.357	78	-1	0-0	.973	0	86	133	2-12/3-3,O(RF)	0.0
1997	Mil A	84	143	12	29	3	0	0	11	5-0	2	15	.203	.238	.224	22	-17	3-0	.989	-3	91	86	2-32,1-21/O-9(8-0-1),3-2,D-4	-1.8
1998	Sea A	31	49	8	8	1	0	1	4	5-0	0	6	.163	.241	.245	27	-5	1-1	1.000	-4	60	84	/2-8,3-8,1-7,SO(RF)D	-1.0
1999	Ana A	97	225	21	59	7	1	0	18	16-0	0	27	.262	.307	.302	58	-15	10-1	.993	-3	105	98	2-41,S-22/3-9,1-8,O-2(LF),D-7	-1.3
2000	Chi N	70	130	19	28	7	1	0	11	13-1	0	9	.215	.287	.285	46	-11	2-1	1.000	-3	83	52	3-18,2-17,S-17/1	-1.2
Total	12	827	1879	242	439	65	13	8	150	191-9	6	228	.234	.304	.295	64	-96	64-21	.956	-7	100	98	S-405,2-208,3-114/1-37,D-18,OL	-6.6
HUSTA, CARL Carl Lawrence "Sox" B 4.8.1902 Egg Harbor City, NJ D 11.6.1951 Kingston, NY BR/TR 5-11/176# d9.24																								
1925	Phi A	6	22	2	3	0	0	0	2	2	0	3	.136	.208	.136	-11	-4	0-0	.976	1	100	96	/S-6	-0.2
HUSTON, HARRY Harry Emanuel Kress B 10.14.1883 Bellefontaine, OH D 10.13.1969 Blackwell, OK BR/TR 5-9/168# d9.3																								
1906	Phi N	2	4	0	0	0	0	0	0	1	0		.000	.200	.000	-37	-1	0	1.000	0	75	81	/C-2	-0.1
HUSTON, WARREN Warren Llewellyn B 10.31.1913 Newtonville, MA D 8.30.1999 Wareham, MA BR/TR 6/170# d6.24																								
1937	Phi A	38	54	5	7	3	0	0	3	2	0	9	.130	.161	.185	-13	-10	0-1	.918	4	117	153	2-16,S-15/3-2	-0.5
1944	Bos N	33	55	7	11	1	0	0	1	8	1	5	.200	.313	.218	49	-3	0	.979	2	121	45	3-20/2-5,S-4	-0.1
Total	2	71	109	12	18	4	0	0	4	10	1	14	.165	.242	.202	19	-13	0-1	.964	6	124	106	/3-22,2-21,S-19	-0.6
HUTCHESON, JOE Joseph Johnson "Slug" or "Poodles" B 2.5.1905 Springtown, TX D 2.23.1993 Tyler, TX BL/TR 6-2/200# d7.8																								
1933	Bro N	55	184	19	43	4	1	6	21	15	1	13	.234	.295	.364	91	-3	1	.989	2	92	194	O-45(RF)	-0.3
HUTCHINSON, ED Edwin Forrest B 5.19.1867 Pittsburgh, PA D 7.19.1934 Colfax, CA BL/TR 5-11/175# d6.17																								
1890	Chi N	4	17	0	1	1	0	0	0	0	0	0	.059	.059	.118	-47	-3	0	1.000	3	227	164	/2-4	0.0
HUTSON, ROY Roy Lee B 2.27.1902 Luray, MO D 5.20.1957 LaMesa, CA BL/TR 5-9/165# d9.20																								
1925	Bro N	7	8	1	4	0	0	0	1	1	0	1	.500	.556	.500	177	1	0-0	1.000	0	114	0	/O-4(3-0-1)	0.1
HUTTO, JIM James Neamon B 10.17.1947 Norfolk, VA BR/TR 5-11/195# d4.17																								
1970	Phi N	57	92	7	17	2	0	3	12	5-0	0	20	.185	.222	.304	42	-8	0-0	1.000	0	102	197	O-22(16-0-6),1-12/C-5,3	-0.9
1975	Bal A	4	5	0	0	0	0	0	0	0-0	0	2	.000	.000	.000	-99	-1	0-0	1.000	-1	34	0	/C-3	-0.2
Total	2	61	97	7	17	2	0	3	12	5-0	0	22	.175	.212	.289	35	-9	0-0	1.000	-1	102	197	/O-22(16-0-6),1-12,C-8,3	-1.1
HUTTON, TOM Thomas George B 4.20.1946 Los Angeles, CA BL/TL 5-11/180# d9.16																								
1966	LA N	3	2	0	0	0	0	0	0	0-0	0	0	.000	.000	.000	-99	-1	0-0	1.000	-0	0	0	/1-3	-0.1
1969	LA N	16	48	2	13	0	0	0	4	5-0	0	7	.271	.340	.271	78	-1	0-0	.993	4	217	88	1-16	0.2
1972	Phi N	134	381	40	99	16	2	4	38	56-4	0	24	.260	.354	.344	97	1	5-8	.992	4	106	90	1-87,O-48(5-4-39)	-0.5
1973	Phi N	106	247	31	65	11	0	5	29	32-6	0	31	.263	.346	.368	96	0	3-1	.998	4	122	117	1-71	-0.1
1974	Phi N	96	208	32	50	6	3	4	33	30-8	0	13	.240	.331	.356	90	-3	2-2	.996	-2	87	108	1-39,O-33(LF)	-0.9
1975	Phi N	113	165	24	41	6	0	3	24	27-1	0	10	.248	.352	.339	90	-1	2-5	.994	5	148	132	1-71,O-12(RF)	-0.1
1976	†Phi N	95	124	15	25	5	1	1	13	27-0	0	11	.202	.342	.282	77	-2	1-2	1.000	3	125	92	1-72/O(RF)	-0.3

Year	Tm Lg	G	AB	R	H	2B	3B	HR	RBI	BB-IB	HP	SO	AVG	OBP	SLG	AOPS	ABR	SB-CS	FA	FR	Rng	Thr	G at Pos	BFW
1977	†Phi N	107	81	12	25	3	0	2	11	12-3	0	10	.309	.394	.420	114	2	1-1	.993	2	183	102	1-73/O-9(7-0-2)	0.3
1978	Tor A	64	173	19	44	9	0	2	9	19-0	0	11	.254	.328	.341	87	-3	1-2	1.000	-2	91	63	O-55(32-0-23)/1-9	-0.8
	Mon N	39	59	4	12	3	0	0	5	10-2	0	5	.203	.319	.254	63	-3	0-0	1.000	-2	51	89	1-17/O-5(3-1-1)	-0.5
1979	Mon N	86	83	14	21	2	1	1	13	10-0	0	7	.253	.333	.337	84	-2	0-0	1.000	3	221	64	1-25/O-9(RF)	0.0
1980	Mon N	62	55	2	12	2	0	0	5	4-0	0	10	.218	.267	.255	47	-4	0-0	1.000	-1	71	182	/1-7,O-4(1-0-3),P	-0.5
1981	Mon N	31	29	1	3	0	0	0	2	2-0	0	1	.103	.161	.103	-23	-5	0-0	1.000	0	90	90	/1-9,O-2(1-0-1)	-0.5
Total	12	952	1655	196	410	63	7	22	186	234-24	0	140	.248	.339	.334	87	-22	15-21	.995	17	126	103	1-499,O-178(82-5-91)/P	-3.8
HYATT, HAM Robert Hamilton B 11.1.1884 Buncombe Co., NC D 9.11.1963 Liberty Lake, WA BL/TR 6-1/185# d4.15																								
1909	†Pit N	49	67	9	20	3	4	0	7	3	0		.299	.329	.463	134	2	1	.933	3	583	592	/O-6(5-0-1),1-2	0.5
1910	Pit N	74	175	19	46	5	6	1	30	8	3	14	.263	.306	.377	94	-3	3	.986	-0	95	99	1-38/O-4(0-3-1)	-0.4
1912	Pit N	46	97	13	28	3	1	0	22	6	0	8	.289	.330	.340	85	-2	2	.955	-2	83	48	O-15(0-1-14)/1-3	-0.5
1913	Pit N	63	81	8	27	6	2	4	16	3	2	8	.333	.372	.605	184	8	0	1.000	-0	42	46	/1-5,O-5(1-0-5)	0.8
1914	Pit N	74	79	2	17	3	1	1	15	7	2	14	.215	.295	.316	86	-1	1	.980	-2	0	39	/1-7,C	-0.3
1915	StL N	106	295	23	79	8	9	2	46	28	3	24	.268	.337	.376	116	5	3-3	.991	-4	69	98	1-64,O-25(0-1-26)	-0.2
1918	NY A	53	131	11	30	8	0	2	10	8	0	8	.229	.273	.336	82	-3	1	1.000	0	94	99	O-25(21-2-2)/1-5	-0.5
Total	7	465	925	85	247	36	23	10	146	63	10	76	.267	.321	.388	108	6	11-3	.989	-5	76	102	1-124/O-80(27-7-49),C	-0.6
HYERS, TIM Timothy James B 10.3.1971 Atlanta, GA BL/TL 6-1/185# d4.4																								
1994	SD N	52	118	13	30	3	0	0	7	9-0	0	15	.254	.307	.280	56	-8	3-0	.986	0	103	82	1-41/O-2(RF)	-1.0
1995	SD N	6	5	0	0	0	0	0	0	0-0	0	1	.000	.000	.000	-99	-1	0-0	1.000	0	1166	0	/1	-0.1
1996	Det A	17	26	1	2	1	0	0	0	4-2	0	5	.077	.200	.115	-18	-5	0-0	1.000	-1	36	145	/1-9,O(LF)D	-0.5
1999	Fla N	58	81	8	18	4	1	2	12	14-0	0	11	.222	.333	.370	84	-2	0-0	1.000	-1	92	0	O-15(12-0-4),1-14/D	-0.4
Total	4	133	230	22	50	8	1	2	19	27-2	0	32	.217	.298	.287	54	-16	3-0	.990	-1	91	90	/1-65,O-18(13-0-6),D-3	-2.0
HYNES, PAT Patrick J. B 3.12.1884 St.Louis, MO D 3.12.1907 St.Louis, MO TL d9.27 ▲																								
1903	StL N	1	3	0	0	0	0	0	0	0	0		.000	.000	.000	-99	0	0	.500	-1	0	0	/P	0.0
1904	StL A	66	254	23	60	7	3	0	15	3	1		.236	.248	.287	74	-9	3	.901	-9	16	0	O-63(RF)/P-5	-2.2
Total	2	67	257	23	60	7	3	0	15	3	1		.233	.245	.284	71	-9	3	.901	-9	16	0	/O-63(RF),P-6	-2.2
HYZDU, ADAM Adam Davis B 12.6.1971 San Jose, CA BR/TR 6-2/210# d9.8																								
2000	Pit N	12	18	2	7	2	0	1	4	0-0	0	4	.389	.389	.667	161	2	0-0	1.000	-0	92	0	/O-5(1-0-4)	0.1
2001	Pit N	51	72	7	15	1	0	5	9	4-0	1	18	.208	.260	.431	72	-4	0-1	1.000	-0	96	0	O-27(8-1-18)/1-4	-0.5
2002	Pit N	59	155	24	36	6	0	11	34	21-0	1	44	.232	.324	.484	113	2	0-0	1.000	-2	90	82	O-50(10-36-13)/1	-0.1
2003	Pit N	51	63	16	13	5	0	1	8	10-0	1	21	.206	.320	.333	71	-2	0-0	1.000	0	98	103	O-34(3-20-11)	-0.3
Total	4	173	308	49	71	14	0	18	55	35-0	3	87	.231	.312	.451	97	-2	0-1	1.000	-3	93	68	O-116(22-57-46)/1-5	-0.8
IBANEZ, RAUL Raul Javier B 6.2.1972 New York, NY BL/TR 6-2/210# d8.1																								
1996	Sea A	4	5	0	0	0	0	0	0	0-0	1	1	.000	.167	.000	-53	-1	0-0	—	0			/D-2	-0.1
1997	Sea A	11	26	3	4	0	1	1	4	0-0	0	6	.154	.154	.346	26	-3	0-0	1.000	-1	76	0	/O-8(2-0-6),D	-0.4
1998	Sea A	37	98	12	25	7	1	2	12	5-0	0	22	.255	.291	.408	79	-3	0-0	1.000	-2	63	155	O-17(6-0-12),1-16/D	-0.7
1999	Sea A	87	209	23	54	7	0	9	27	17-1	0	32	.258	.313	.421	87	-5	5-1	.988	1	120	42	O-57(22-0-39),1-21/CD	-0.6
2000	†Sea A	92	140	21	32	8	0	2	15	14-1	1	25	.229	.301	.329	62	-8	2-0	.978	0	111	40	O-76(35-0-44)/1-3,D-4	-0.8
2001	KC A	104	279	44	78	11	5	13	54	32-2	0	51	.280	.353	.495	111	4	0-2	.967	-1	87	147	O-42(17-2-24),D-33,1-10/3	-0.2
2002	KC A	137	497	70	146	37	6	24	103	40-5	2	76	.294	.346	.537	117	12	5-3	.989	-3	87	101	O-55(42-0-16),1-49,D-36	0.0
2003	KC A	157	608	95	179	33	5	18	90	49-5	3	81	.294	.345	.454	97	-3	8-4	.988	1	95	115	*O-131(128-0-5),1-22,D-12	-0.8
Total	8	629	1862	268	518	103	18	69	305	157-14	7	294	.278	.334	.464	99	-7	20-10	.985	-3	96	97	O-386(252-2-146),1-121/D-90,3C	-3.6
INCAVIGLIA, PETE Peter Joseph B 4.2.1964 Pebble Beach, CA BR/TR 6-1/230# d4.8																								
1986	Tex A	153	540	82	135	21	2	30	88	55-2	4	185	.250	.320	.463	108	5	3-2	.921	-11	80	88	*O-114(1-0-112),D-36	-1.2
1987	Tex A	139	509	85	138	26	4	27	80	48-1	1	168	.271	.332	.497	116	11	9-3	.945	-6	89	99	*O-132(LF)/D-6	0.1
1988	Tex A	116	418	59	104	19	3	22	54	39-3	7	153	.249	.321	.467	116	8	6-4	.989	3	92	229	O-93(LF),D-21	0.7
1989	Tex A	133	453	48	107	27	4	21	81	32-0	6	136	.236	.293	.453	106	2	5-7	.973	-3	93	108	*O-125(120-10-0)/D-5	-0.6
1990	Tex A	153	529	59	123	27	0	24	85	45-5	9	146	.233	.302	.420	100	-1	3-4	.974	2	98	138	*O-145(135-27-1)/D-2	-0.4
1991	Det A	97	337	38	72	12	1	11	38	36-0	1	92	.214	.290	.353	76	-11	1-3	.973	1	101	134	O-54(50-0-4),D-41	-1.4
1992	Hou N	113	349	31	93	22	1	11	44	25-2	3	99	.266	.319	.430	116	6	2-2	.970	6	108	163	O-98(57-0-48)	1.0
1993	†Phi N	116	368	60	101	16	3	24	89	21-1	6	82	.274	.318	.530	126	11	1-1	.971	-2	100	63	O-97(89-0-8)	0.5
1994	Phi N	80	244	28	56	10	1	13	32	16-3	1	71	.230	.278	.439	82	-8	1-0	.979	-3	89	60	O-63(LF)	-1.3
1996	Phi N	99	269	33	63	7	2	16	42	30-2	3	82	.234	.318	.454	99	-1	2-0	.969	-3	86	116	O-71(70-0-2)	-0.6
	†Bal A	12	33	4	10	2	0	2	8	0-0	1	7	.303	.314	.545	115	1	0-0	1.000	0	85	275	/O-7(LF),D-4	0.1
1997	Bal A	48	138	18	34	4	0	5	12	11-2	3	43	.246	.314	.384	84	-4	0-0	.952	-1	95	0	D-26,O-18(4-0-14)	-0.6
	NY A	5	16	1	4	0	0	0	0	0-0	0	3	.250	.250	.250	31	-2	0-0	—	0			/D-5	-0.2
	Year	53	154	19	38	4	0	5	12	11-2	3	46	.247	.308	.370	79	-5	0-0	.952	-1	95	0	D-31,O-18(4-0-14)	-0.8
1998	Det A	7	14	0	1	0	0	0	0	1-0	0	6	.071	.133	.071	-44	-3	0-0	—	-0	0	0	/O(LF)D	-0.3
	†Hou N	13	16	0	2	1	0	0	2	1-0	0	4	.125	.176	.188	-4	-2	0-0	1.000	-0	92	0	/O-3(LF)	-0.3
Total	12	1284	4233	546	1043	194	21	206	655	360-21	45	1277	.246	.310	.448	104	12	33-26	.966	-17	93	120	*O-1021(825-37-189),D-150	-4.5
INFANTE, ALEXIS Fermin Alexis (Carpio) B 12.4.1961 Barquisimeto, Venezuela BR/TR 5-10/175# d9.27																								
1987	Tor A	1	0	0	0	0	0	0	0	0-0	0	0	—	—	—	—	0	0-0	—	0			/R	0.0
1988	Tor A	19	15	7	3	0	0	0	0	2-0	0	4	.200	.294	.200	41	-1	0-0	.909	-2	66	0	/3-9,S-2,D-7	-0.3
1989	Tor A	20	12	1	2	0	0	0	0	0-0	0	1	.167	.167	.167	-6	-2	1-0	1.000	-1	90	100	/S-9,3-4,2D	-0.2
1990	Atl N	20	28	3	1	1	0	0	0	0-0	1	7	.036	.069	.071	-58	-6	0-0	.964	1	98	105	2-10/3-4,S-3	-0.5
Total	4	60	55	11	6	1	0	0	0	2-0	1	12	.109	.155	.127	-20	-9	1-0	.933	-2	80	0	/3-17,S-14,2-11,D-11	-1.0
INFANTE, OMAR Omar R. B 12.26.1981 Puerto La Cruz, Venezuela BR/TR 6/150# d9.7																								
2002	Det A	18	72	4	24	3	0	1	6	3-0	0	10	.333	.360	.417	112	1	0-1	.935	2	118	91	S-16/2-2	0.4
2003	Det A	69	221	24	49	6	1	0	8	18-0	0	37	.222	.278	.258	47	-17	6-3	.962	16	125	124	S-63/3-4,2-2	0.4
Total	2	87	293	28	73	9	1	1	14	21-0	0	47	.249	.297	.297	63	-16	6-4	.957	18	124	117	/S-79,3-4,2-4	0.8
INGE, BRANDON Charles Brandon B 5.19.1977 Lynchburg, VA BR/TR 5-11/185# d4.3																								
2001	Det A	79	189	13	34	11	0	0	15	9-0	0	41	.180	.215	.238	21	-22	1-4	.989	2	145	140	C-79	-1.6
2002	Det A	95	321	27	65	15	3	7	24	24-0	4	101	.202	.266	.333	62	-19	1-3	.998	-2	117	72	C-94/D	-1.5
2003	Det A	104	330	32	67	15	3	8	30	24-0	5	79	.203	.265	.339	63	-19	4-4	.996	4	77	**180**	*C-104	-0.9
Total	3	278	840	72	166	41	6	15	69	57-0	9	221	.198	.254	.314	53	-60	6-11	.995	4	108	131	C-277/D	-4.0
INGERTON, SCOTTY William John B 4.19.1886 Peninsula, OH D 6.15.1956 Cleveland, OH BR/TR 6-1/172# d4.12																								
1911	Bos N	136	521	63	130	24	4	5	61	39	2	68	.250	.304	.340	74	-19	6	.942	13	104	58	3-58,O-43(43-0-2),1-17,2-11/S-4	-0.7
INGRAHAM, CHARLIE Charles W. B 4.8.1860 , IL D 2.18.1906 Chicago, IL 5-11/170# d7.4																								
1883	Bal AA	1	4	0	1	0	0	0		0			.250	.250	.250	60	0		.833	-1			/C	-0.1
INGRAM, GAREY Garey Lamar B 7.25.1970 Columbus, GA BR/TR 5-11/180# d5.15																								
1994	LA N	26	78	10	22	1	0	3	8	7-3	0	22	.282	.341	.410	101	0	0-0	.982	1	100	104	2-23	0.2
1995	LA N	44	55	5	11	2	0	0	3	9-0	0	8	.200	.313	.236	52	-4	3-0	.750	-0	100	0	3-12/2-7,O-4(LF)	-0.3
1997	LA N	12	9	2	4	0	0	0	1	1-0	0	3	.444	.500	.444	162	1	1-0	1.000	-0	87	0	/O-7(6-1-0)	0.1
Total	3	82	142	17	37	3	0	3	12	17-3	0	33	.261	.340	.345	87	-3	4-0	.985	1	100	109	/2-30,3-12,O-11(10-1-0)	-0.0
INGRAM, MEL Melvin David B 7.4.1904 Asheville, NC D 10.28.1979 Medford, OR BR/TR 5-11.5/175# d7.24																								
1929	Pit N	3	0	1	0	0	0	0	0	0	0	0	—	—	—	—	0	0	—	0			R	0.0
INGRAM, RICCARDO Riccardo Benay B 9.10.1966 Douglas, GA BR/TR 6/205# d6.26																								
1994	Det A	12	23	3	5	0	0	0	2	1-0	0	2	.217	.240	.217	22	-3	0-1	1.000	0	94	224	/O-8(7-1-0),D	-0.3
1995	Min A	4	8	0	1	0	0	0	1	2-0	0	1	.125	.300	.125	16	-1	0-0	—	0			/D-3	-0.1
Total	2	16	31	3	6	0	0	0	3	3-0	0	3	.194	.257	.194	21	-4	0-1	1.000	0	94	224	/O-8(7-1-0),D-4	-0.4
IORG, DANE Dane Charles B 5.11.1950 Eureka, CA BL/TR 6/180# d4.9 b-Garth OF Total (223-LF 124-RF)																								
1977	Phi N	12	30	3	5	1	0	0	2	1-0	0	3	.167	.194	.200	6	-4	0-0	.986	-0	95	108	/1-9	-0.5
	StL N	30	32	2	10	1	0	0	4	5-0	0	4	.313	.395	.344	105	1	0-1	.875	-0	107	0	/O-7(4-0-3)	0.0

Year	Tm Lg	G	AB	R	H	2B	3B	HR	RBI	BB-IB	HP	SO	AVG	OBP	SLG	AOPS	ABR	SB-CS	FA	FR	Rng	Thr	G at Pos	BFW
	Year	42	62	5	15	2	0	0	6	6-0	0	7	.242	.304	.274	58	-4	0-1	.986	-0	95	108	/1-9,O-7(4-0-3)	-0.5
1978	StL N	35	85	6	23	4	1	0	4	4-1	0	10	.271	.300	.341	81	-2	0-0	1.000	2	93	326	O-25(8-0-18)	-0.1
1979	StL N	79	179	12	52	11	1	1	21	12-1	1	28	.291	.337	.380	95	-1	1-2	.964	-3	81	78	O-39(22-0-20),1-10	-0.6
1980	StL N	105	251	33	76	23	1	3	36	20-2	0	34	.303	.349	.438	116	6	1-1	.991	-3	96	45	O-63(49-0-14)/1-5,3	0.0
1981	StL N	75	217	23	71	11	2	2	39	7-0	0	9	.327	.344	.424	115	4	2-0	.963	-6	82	0	O-57(46-0-14)/1-8,3-2	-0.5
1982	†StL N	102	238	17	70	14	1	0	34	23-3	0	23	.294	.352	.361	100	1	0-1	.971	-1	99	50	O-63(47-0-17),1-10/3-2	-0.3
1983	StL N	58	116	6	31	9	1	0	11	10-2	1	11	.267	.321	.362	92	-1	1-0	.974	-1	115	0	O-22(10-0-13),1-11	-0.3
1984	StL N	15	28	3	4	2	0	0	3	2-1	0	6	.143	.200	.214	17	-3	0-0	1.000	1	47	159	/1-6,O-5(3-0-2)	-0.3
	†KC A	78	235	27	60	16	2	5	30	13-3	0	15	.255	.287	.404	90	-3	0-1	.995	-2	86	109	1-43,O-22(18-0-4)/3D	-0.9
1985	†KC A	64	130	7	29	9	1	1	21	8-2	0	16	.223	.268	.331	63	-7	0-1	1.000	-3	90	0	O-32(13-0-19)/1-2,3D	-1.0
1986	SD N	90	106	10	24	2	1	2	11	2-0	0	21	.226	.239	.321	55	-7	0-0	1.000	-3	31	84	1-10/3-6,O-3(LF),P-2	-1.1
Total	10	743	1647	149	455	103	11	14	216	107-15	2	180	.276	.317	.378	92	-16	5-7	.977	-18	95	57	O-338L,1-114/3-13,D-7,P-2	-5.6
IORG, GARTH Garth Ray B 10.12.1954 Arcata, CA BR/TR 5-11/170# d4.9 C2 b-Dane OF Total (13-LF 1-CF)																								
1978	Tor A	19	49	3	8	0	0	0	3	3-0	1	4	.163	.218	.163	11	-6	0-0	.966	2	108	124	2-18	-0.3
1980	Tor A	80	222	24	55	10	1	2	14	12-0	0	39	.248	.286	.329	65	-11	2-1	.988	11	118	137	2-32,3-20,O-14(13-1-0),1-11/SD	0.1
1981	Tor A	70	215	17	52	11	0	0	10	7-1	1	31	.242	.269	.293	58	-12	2-3	.963	0	107	92	2-46,3-17/S-2,1D	-1.0
1982	Tor A	129	417	45	119	20	5	1	36	12-2	4	38	.285	.307	.365	78	-13	3-2	.946	1	103	84	*3-100,2-30/D	-1.2
1983	Tor A	122	375	40	103	22	5	2	39	13-3	1	45	.275	.298	.376	80	-11	7-0	.976	-6	108	69	3-85,2-39/S	-1.4
1984	Tor A	121	247	24	56	10	3	1	25	5-0	1	16	.227	.244	.304	49	-18	1-3	.945	0	97	**127**	*3-112/2-7,S-2,D	-2.0
1985	†Tor A	131	288	33	90	22	1	7	37	21-3	0	26	.313	.358	.469	122	9	3-6	.951	-2	108	114	*3-104,2-23	0.5
1986	Tor A	137	327	30	85	19	1	3	44	20-0	1	47	.260	.303	.352	76	-11	3-0	.955	-19	99	68	3-90,2-52/S-2	-2.8
1987	Tor A	122	310	35	65	11	0	4	30	21-0	2	52	.210	.262	.284	45	-25	2-2	.982	-13	90	71	2-91,3-28/D-5	-3.3
Total	9	931	2450	251	633	125	16	20	238	114-9	11	298	.258	.292	.347	72	-98	23-17	.955	-25	105	101	3-556,2-338/O-14L,1-12,D-10,S-8	-11.4
IOTT, HAPPY Frederick "Happy Jack" or "Biddo" (born Frederick Hoyot) B 7.7.1876 Houlton, ME D 2.17.1941 Island Falls, ME BR/TR 5-10/175# d9.16																								
1903	Cle A	3	10	1	2	0	0	0	0	2	0		.200	.333	.200	64	0	1	.875	-0	0	0	/O-3(CF)	-0.1
IRELAN, HAL Harold "Grump" B 8.5.1890 Burnettsville, IN D 7.16.1944 Carmel, IN BB/TR 5-7/165# d4.23																								
1914	Phi N	67	165	16	39	8	0	1	16	21	1	22	.236	.326	.303	82	-3	3	.909	4	112	67	2-44/S-3,1-2,3-2	0.2
IRELAND, TIM Timothy Neal B 3.14.1953 Oakland, CA BR/TR (BB 1981) 6/180# d9.20																								
1981	KC A	4	0	1	0	0	0	0	0	0-0	0	0	—	—	—	—	0	0-1	1.000	-0	0	0	/1-4	-0.1
1982	KC A	7	7	2	1	0	0	0	0	1-0	0	1	.143	.250	.143	11	-1	0-0	1.000	-0	145	119	/2-4,O-2(RF),3	-0.1
Total	2	11	7	3	1	0	0	0	0	1-0	0	1	.143	.250	.143	11	-1	0-1	1.000	-0	145	119	/2-4,1-4,O-2(RF),3	-0.2
IRWIN, ED William Edward B 1882 Philadelphia, PA D 2.5.1916 Philadelphia, PA BR/TR d5.18																								
1912	Det A	1	3	0	2	0	2	0	0		0		.667	.667	2.000	675	2	0	.500	-1	72	0	/3	0.1
IRVIN, MONTE Monford B 2.25.1919 Columbia, AL BR/TR 6-1/195# d7.8 HF1973																								
1949	NY N	36	76	7	17	3	2	0	7	17	0	11	.224	.366	.316	84	-1	0	1.000	1	89	379	O-10(RF)/1-5,3-5	0.0
1950	NY N	110	374	61	112	19	5	15	66	52	5	41	.299	.392	.497	131	18	3	.979	3	126	136	1-59,O-49(20-0-30)/3	1.7
1951	†NY N	151	558	94	174	19	11	24	**121**	89	9	44	.312	.415	.514	147	40	12-2	.996	5	94	94	*O-112(89-0-27),1-39	3.7
1952	NY N✳	46	126	10	39	2	1	4	21	10	1	11	.310	.365	.437	120	3	0-1	1.000	-1	83	147	O-32(30-1-1)	0.0
1953	NY N	124	444	72	146	21	5	21	97	55	3	34	.329	.406	.541	142	28	2-0	.973	4	109	107	*O-113(102-0-13)	2.5
1954	†NY N	135	432	62	113	13	3	19	64	70	2	23	.262	.363	.438	108	6	7-4	.976	2	106	86	*O-128(126-0-2)/13	0.0
1955	NY N	51	150	16	38	7	1	1	17	17-0	3	15	.253	.337	.333	80	-4	3-0	.961	2	108	121	O-45(44-0-4)	-0.4
1956	Chi N	111	339	44	92	13	3	15	50	41-5	0	41	.271	.346	.460	118	8	1-0	.991	8	125	108	O-96(LF)	1.1
Total	8	764	2499	366	731	97	31	99	443	351-5	23	220	.293	.383	.475	126	98	28-7	.983	24	106	102	O-585(507-1-87),1-104/3-7	8.6
IRWIN, ARTHUR Arthur Albert "Doc" or "Sandy" B 2.14.1858 Toronto, ON, CAN D 7.16.1921 , At Sea Atlantic Ocean N.Y. To Boston BL/TR 5-8.5/158# d5.1 M8 U1 b-John																								
1880	Wor N	**85**	352	53	91	19	4	1	35	11		27	.259	.281	.344	102	0		.895	**29**	**126**	134	*S-82/3-3,C	3.2
1881	Wor N	50	206	27	55	8	2	0	24	7		4	.267	.291	.325	88	-3		.851	-7	97	65	S-50	-0.8
1882	Wor N	**84**	333	30	73	12	4	0	30	14		34	.219	.251	.279	68	-12		.837	17	131	93	3-51,S-33	0.6
1883	Pro N	**98**	406	67	116	22	7	0	44	12		38	.286	.306	.374	103	1		.856	-8	98	**127**	*S-94/2-4	-0.4
1884	†Pro N	102	404	73	97	14	3	2	44	28		52	.240	.289	.304	89	-4		.881	-10	96	109	*S-102/P	-1.0
1885	Pro N	59	218	16	39	2	1	0	14	14		29	.179	.228	.197	40	-14		.875	2	109	94	S-58/32	-0.9
1886	Phi N	101	373	51	87	6	6	0	34	35		39	.233	.299	.282	77	-10	24	.891	1	102	82	*S-100/3	-0.6
1887	Phi N	100	374	65	95	14	8	2	56	48	3	26	.254	.344	.350	88	-6	19	.892	-14	87	96	*S-100	-1.4
1888	Phi N	125	448	51	98	12	4	0	28	33	3	56	.219	.277	.263	69	-15	19	.900	10	102	95	*S-122/2-3	-0.1
1889	Phi N	18	73	9	16	5	0	0	10	6	0	6	.219	.278	.288	54	-5	6	.845	-3	90	101	S-18	-0.7
	Was N	85	313	49	73	10	5	0	32	42	1	37	.233	.326	.297	80	-8	9	.895	12	107	108	S-85/P2M	0.6
	Year	103	386	58	89	15	5	0	42	48	1	43	.231	.317	.295	74	-13	15	.888	8	104	107	*S-103/P2	-0.1
1890	Bos P	96	354	60	92	17	1	0	45	57	1	29	.260	.364	.314	77	-10	16	.878	2	**106**	115	*S-96	-0.4
1891	Bos AA	6	17	1	2	0	0	0	0	2	2	1	.118	.286	.118	16	-2	0	.778	-1	90	330	/S-6,M	-0.2
1894	Phi N	1	0	0	0	0	0	0	0	0	0	0	—	—	—	—	0	0	—	-0	0	0	/SM	0.0
Total	13	1010	3871	552	934	141	45	5	396	309	10	378	.241	.299	.305	81	-88	93	.881	30	103	106	S-947/3-56,2-9,P-2,C	-2.1
IRWIN, CHARLIE Charles Edwin B 2.15.1869 Clinton, IL D 9.21.1925 Chicago, IL BL/TR 5-10/160# d9.3																								
1893	Chi N	21	82	14	25	6	2	0	13	10	2	1	.305	.394	.427	120	3	4	.910	2	94	112	S-21	0.4
1894	Chi N	130	504	85	149	25	9	8	100	64	10	23	.296	.386	.429	91	-8	35	.819	-4	93	130	3-68,S-62	-0.6
1895	Chi N	3	10	4	2	0	0	0	0	2	0	1	.200	.333	.200	37	-1	0	.900	-1	84	113	/S-3	-0.1
1896	Cin N	127	476	77	141	16	6	1	67	26	4	17	.296	.338	.361	79	-16	31	**.931**	7	98	**162**	*3-127	-0.6
1897	Cin N	**134**	505	89	146	26	6	0	74	47	9		.289	.360	.364	86	-10	27	.940	-6	90	117	*3-134	-1.1
1898	Cin N	136	501	77	120	14	5	3	55	31	10		.240	.297	.305	68	-22	18	.940	12	105	104	*3-136	-0.8
1899	Cin N	90	314	42	73	4	8	1	52	26	2		.232	.295	.306	64	-17	26	.909	-10	84	47	3-78/S-6,2-3,1	-2.3
1900	Cin N	87	333	59	91	15	6	1	44	14	6		.273	.314	.363	89	-6	9	.931	-8	91	137	3-61,S-16/O-6(1-0-5),2-3	-1.1
1901	Cin N	67	260	25	62	12	2	0	25	14	3		.238	.285	.300	75	-8	13	.893	4	105	126	3-67	-0.3
	Bro N	65	242	25	52	13	2	0	20	14	4		.215	.269	.285	59	-12	4	.956	-4	82	68	3-65	-1.4
	Year	132	502	50	114	25	4	0	45	28	7		.227	.277	.293	67	-21	17	.921	-0	94	97	*3-132	-1.7
1902	Bro N	131	458	59	125	14	0	2	43	39	12		.273	.346	.317	104	4	13	.927	-9	89	136	*3-130/S	-0.1
Total	10	991	3685	556	986	145	46	16	493	287	62	42	.268	.331	.345	82	-93	180	.921	-16	94	118	3-866,S-109/O-6(1-0-5),2-6,1	-8.0
IRWIN, JOHN John B 7.21.1861 Toronto, ON, CAN D 2.28.1934 Boston, MA BL/TR 5-10/168# d5.31 b-Arthur																								
1882	Wor N	1	4	0	0	0	0	0	0	0		2	.000	.000	.000	-98	-1		.636	-1	0	171	/1	-0.2
1884	Bos U	105	432	81	101	22	6	1		15			.234	.260	.319	76	-26		.780	4	103	73	*3-105	-1.8
1886	Phi AA	3	13	4	3	1	0	0	1	0	0		.231	.231	.308	67	-1	0	.714	-1	58	0	/S-2,3	-0.1
1887	Was N	8	31	6	11	2	0	2	3	3	1	6	.355	.429	.613	198	4	6	.875	-2	77	67	/S-5,3-4	0.3
1888	Was N	37	126	14	28	5	2	0	8	5	2	18	.222	.263	.294	83	-2	15	.860	-2	102	58	S-27,3-10	-0.3
1889	Was N	58	228	42	66	11	4	0	25	25	4	14	.289	.370	.373	115	6	10	.868	1	104	116	3-58	0.7
1890	Buf P	77	308	62	72	11	4	0	34	43	4	19	.234	.335	.295	75	-8	18	.883	8	106	105	3-64,1-12/2	0.0
1891	Bos AA	19	72	6	16	2	2	0	15	6	0	9	.222	.282	.306	69	-3	6	.882	-0	166	0	O-17(9-0-9)/3-2,S	-0.3
	Lou AA	14	55	7	15	1	1	0	7	5	1	6	.273	.344	.327	93	0	1	.795	-5	77	47	3-14	-0.4
	Year	33	127	13	31	3	3	0	22	11	1	15	.244	.309	.315	80	-4	7	.882	-5	166	0	O-17(9-0-9),3-16/S	-0.7
Total	8	322	1269	222	312	55	19	3	93	102	12	74	.246	.308	.326	87	-31	56	.829	4	101	88	3-258/S-35,O-17(9-0-9),1-13,2	-2.1
IRWIN, TOMMY Thomas Andrew B 12.20.1912 Altoona, PA D 4.25.1996 Altoona, PA BR/TR 5-11/165# d10.1																								
1938	Cle A	3	9	1	1	0	0	0	0	3	0	1	.111	.333	.111	16	-1	0-0	1.000	0	110	121	/S-3	-0.1
IRWIN, WALT Walter Kingsley B 9.23.1897 Henrietta, PA D 8.18.1976 Spring Lake, MI BR/TR 5-10.5/170# d4.24																								
1921	StL N	4	1	1	0	0	0	0	0	0	0	1	.000	.000	.000	-99	0	0-0	—	0			H	0.0
ISALES, ORLANDO Orlando (Pizarro) B 12.22.1959 Santurce, P.R. BR/TR 5-9/175# d9.11																								
1980	Phi N	3	5	1	2	0	1	0	3	1-0	0	0	.400	.500	.800	244	1	0-0	1.000	-0	105	0	/O-2(RF)	0.1
ISBELL, FRANK William Frank "Bald Eagle" B 8.21.1875 Delevan, NY D 7.15.1941 Wichita, KS BL/TR 5-11/190# d5.1 I OF Total (15-LF 33-CF 54-RF)																								
1898	Chi N	45	159	17	37	4	0	0	8	3	1		.233	.252	.258	46	-12	3	.956	-4	103	0	0-28(4-12-11),P-13/3-3,2-3,S-2	-1.3
1901	Chi A	**137**	556	93	143	15	8	3	70	36	7		.257	.311	.329	79	-16	**52**	.980	13	**139**	109	*1-137/2-2,PS3	-0.5

Year	Tm Lg	G	AB	R	H	2B	3B	HR	RBI	BB-IB	HP	SO	AVG	OBP	SLG	AOPS	ABR	SB-CS	FA	FR	Rng	Thr	G at Pos	BFW
1902	Chi A	137	515	62	130	14	4	4	59	14	3		.252	.276	.318	68	-24	38	.986	10	**125**	**128**	*1-133/S-4,PC	-1.6
1903	Chi A	**138**	546	52	132	25	9	2	59	12	6		.242	.266	.332	82	-13	26	.984	4	122	99	*1-117,3-19/2-2,SO(RF)	-1.1
1904	Chi A	96	314	27	66	10	3	1	34	16	3		.210	.255	.271	69	-11	19	.986	-1	137	102	1-57,2-27/O-5(RF),S-4	-1.4
1905	Chi A	94	341	55	101	21	11	2	45	15	5		.296	.335	.440	151	18	15	.964	1	100	198	2-43,O-41(2-5-34)/1-9,S-2	1.8
1906	†Chi A	143	549	71	153	18	11	0	57	30	7		.279	.324	.352	115	8	37	.949	-18	97	93	*2-132,O-14(4-7-3)/PC	-1.0
1907	Chi A	125	486	60	118	19	7	0	41	22	4		.243	.281	.311	92	-6	22	.957	9	106	114	*2-119/O-5(LF),PS	0.4
1908	Chi A	84	320	31	79	15	3	1	49	19	4		.247	.297	.322	103	1	18	.990	0	111	114	1-65,2-18	0.0
1909	Chi A	120	433	33	97	17	6	0	33	23	1		.224	.265	.291	79	-12	23	.994	2	105	106	*1-101/O-9(CF),2-5	-1.4
Total	10	1119	4219	501	1056	158	62	13	455	190	41		.250	.289	.326	89	-67	253	.986	16	126	111	1-619,2-351,O-103R/3-23,P-17,SC	-6.1
IVIE, MIKE Michael Wilson B 8.8.1952 Atlanta, GA BR/TR 6-3/205# d9.4																								
1971	SD N	6	17	0	8	0	0	0	3	1-1	1	1	.471	.526	.471	198	2	0-0	1.000	-2	33	95	/C-6	0.1
1974	SD N	12	34	1	3	0	0	1	3	2-0	0	8	.088	.139	.176	-13	-5	0-0	.986	-0	85	105	1-11	-0.7
1975	SD N	111	377	36	94	16	2	8	46	20-2	4	63	.249	.291	.366	88	-8	4-4	.989	-4	122	117	1-78,3-61/C	-1.8
1976	SD N	140	405	51	118	19	5	7	70	30-8	5	41	.291	.345	.415	126	13	6-6	.995	1	105	100	*1-135/C-2,3-2	0.4
1977	SD N	134	489	66	133	29	2	9	66	39-4	2	57	.272	.326	.395	104	2	3-2	.992	-4	99	91	*1-105,3-25	-0.9
1978	SF N	117	318	34	98	14	3	11	55	27-6	2	45	.308	.363	.475	139	16	3-0	.995	-8	54	77	1-76,O-22(LF)	0.4
1979	SF N	133	402	58	115	18	3	27	89	47-7	1	80	.286	.359	.547	155	29	5-1	.995	-2	89	77	1-98,O-24(LF)/3-4,2	2.2
1980	SF N	79	286	21	69	16	1	4	25	19-2	0	40	.241	.288	.346	78	-9	1-2	.993	-5	72	79	1-72	-2.0
1981	SF N	7	17	1	5	2	0	0	3	0-0	0	1	.294	.278	.412	100	0	0-0	1.000	1	150	63	/1-5	0.0
	Hou N	19	42	2	10	3	0	0	6	2-0	0	11	.238	.267	.310	68	-2	0-1	.989	2	172	78	1-10	-0.1
	Year	26	59	3	15	5	0	0	9	2-0	0	12	.254	.270	.339	78	-2	0-1	.992	3	165	74	1-15	-0.1
1982	Hou N	7	6	0	2	0	0	0	0	1-0	0	0	.333	.429	.333	125	0	0-0	—	0			/H	0.0
	Det A	80	259	35	60	12	1	14	38	24-3	2	51	.232	.299	.448	102	0	0-0	—	0	0	0	D-79	-0.2
1983	Det A	12	42	4	9	4	0	0	7	2-1	0	4	.214	.244	.310	54	-3	0-0	1.000	-0	82	76	1-12	-0.4
Total	11	857	2694	309	724	133	17	81	411	214-34	17	402	.269	.324	.421	112	35	22-16	.993	-22	93	89	1-602/3-92,D-79,O-46(LF),C-9,2	-3.0
IZQUIERDO, HANK Enrique Roberto (Valdes) B 3.20.1931 Matanzas, Cuba BR/TR 5-11/175# d8.9																								
1967	Min A	16	26	4	7	2	0	0	2	1-0	0	2	.269	.296	.346	83	-1	0-0	.986	2	125	115	C-16	0.2
IZTURIS, CESAR Cesar D. B 2.10.1980 Barquisimeto, Venezuela BB/TR 5-9/175# d6.23																								
2001	Tor A	46	134	19	36	6	2	2	9	2-0	0	15	.269	.279	.388	72	-6	8-1	.988	1	108	103	2-41/S-6	-0.2
2002	LA N	135	439	43	102	24	2	1	31	14-1	0	39	.232	.253	.303	52	-34	7-7	.979	-12	91	103	*S-128/2D	-3.8
2003	LA N	158	558	47	140	21	6	1	40	25-8	0	70	.251	.282	.315	59	-36	10-5	.977	18	104	106	*S-158	-0.6
Total	3	339	1131	109	278	51	10	4	80	41-9	0	124	.246	.270	.319	58	-76	25-13	.977	6	98	105	S-292/2-42,D	-4.6
JABLONSKI, RAY Raymond Leo "Jabbo" B 12.17.1926 Chicago, IL D 11.25.1985 Chicago, IL BR/TR 5-10/183# d4.14																								
1953	StL N	**157**	604	64	162	23	5	21	112	34	1	61	.268	.308	.427	89	-12	2-2	.932	-18	93	86	*3-157	-3.0
1954	StL N★	152	611	80	181	33	3	12	104	49	2	42	.296	.345	.419	99	-1	9-4	.925	-10	**99**	90	*3-149/1	-1.1
1955	Cin N	74	221	28	53	9	0	9	28	13-1	3	35	.240	.289	.403	77	-8	0-1	.872	-6	84	64	3-28,O-28(LF)	-1.5
1956	Cin N	130	407	42	104	25	1	15	66	37-6	7	57	.256	.324	.432	96	-1	2-4	.970	-20	80	59	*3-127/2	-2.3
1957	NY N	107	305	37	88	15	1	9	57	31-2	0	47	.289	.346	.433	110	5	0-2	.941	2	111	134	3-70/1-6,O(LF)	0.5
1958	SF N	82	230	28	53	15	1	12	46	17-2	2	50	.230	.287	.461	97	-2	2-0	.946	-8	87	20	3-57	-1.0
1959	StL N	60	87	11	22	4	0	3	14	8-0	0	19	.253	.313	.402	84	-2	1-0	.900	-2	93	106	3-19/S	-0.4
	KC A	25	65	4	17	1	0	2	8	3-0	0	11	.262	.294	.369	79	-2	0-0	.947	-2	85	121	3-17	-0.4
1960	KC A	21	32	3	7	1	0	0	3	4-0	0	8	.219	.297	.250	52	-2	0-0	.944	0	118	0	/3-6	-0.2
Total	8	808	2562	297	687	126	11	83	438	196-11	15	330	.268	.320	.423	94	-25	16-13	.936	-63	93	80	3-630/O-29(LF),1-7,S2	-9.4
JACKLITSCH, FRED Frederick Lawrence B 5.24.1876 Brooklyn, NY D 7.18.1937 Brooklyn, NY BR/TR 5-9/180# d6.6																								
1900	Phi N	5	11	0	2	1	0	0	3	0	0		.182	.182	.273	25	-1	0	1.000	-1	*68*	*61*	/C-3	-0.2
1901	Phi N	33	120	14	30	4	3	0	24	12	2		.250	.328	.333	90	-1	2	.971	-0	*98*	*107*	C-30/3	0.2
1902	Phi N	38	114	8	23	4	0	0	8	9	3		.202	.278	.237	59	-5	2	.927	-9	*75*	*96*	C-29/O(CF)	-1.2
1903	Bro N	60	176	31	47	8	3	1	21	33	2		.267	.389	.364	118	6	4	.975	-13	*65*	*112*	C-53/2O(CF)	-0.1
1904	Bro N	26	77	8	18	3	1	0	8	7	3		.234	.322	.299	94	0	7	.957	-6	85	129	1-11/2-8,C-5	-0.6
1905	NY A	1	3	1	0	0	0	0	1	1	0		.000	.250	.000	-17	0	0	1.000	-0	*119*	*105*	/C	0.0
1907	Phi N	73	202	19	43	7	0	0	17	27	2		.213	.312	.248	76	-4	7	.984	13	*123*	*113*	C-58/1-6,O(RF)	1.6
1908	Phi N	37	86	6	19	3	0	0	7	14	1		.221	.337	.256	87	0	3	.976	5	*134*	*104*	C-30	0.8
1909	Phi N	20	32	6	10	1	1	0	1	10	0		.313	.476	.406	173	4	1	.964	-1	*101*	*84*	C-11/2	0.4
1910	Phi N	25	51	7	10	3	0	0	2	5	0	9	.196	.268	.255	51	-3	0	.989	2	*105*	*119*	C-13/1-2,23	0.0
1914	Bal F	122	337	40	93	21	4	2	48	52	2	66	.276	.376	.380	103	-1	7	**.988**	4	*110*	*102*	*C-118	1.3
1915	Bal F	49	135	20	32	9	0	2	13	31	2	25	.237	.387	.348	104	1	2	.992	-4	*101*	*83*	C-45/S	0.0
1917	Bos N	1	0	0	0	0	0	0	0	0	0	0	—	—	—	—	0	0	1.000	-0	*0*	*0*	/C	0.0
Total	13	490	1344	160	327	64	12	5	153	201	17	100	.243	.349	.320	95	-4	35	.978	-11	*103*	*103*	C-397/1-19,2-11,O-3(0-2-1),3-2,S	2.2
JACKSON, CHARLIE Charles Herbert "Lefty" B 2.7.1894 Granite City, IL D 5.27.1968 Radford, VA BL/TL 5-9/150# d8.20 Mil 1918																								
1915	Chi A	1	1	0	0	0	0	0	0	0	0	1	.000	.000	.000	-97	0	0	—	0			H	0.0
1917	Pit N	41	121	7	29	3	2	0	1	10	1	22	.240	.303	.298	82	-2	4	.986	2	106	122	O-36(20-1-15)	-0.3
Total	2	42	122	7	29	3	2	0	1	10	1	23	.238	.301	.295	80	-2	4	.986	2	106	122	/O-36(20-1-15)	-0.3
JACKSON, CHUCK Charles Leo B 3.19.1963 Seattle, WA BR/TR 6- /185# d5.26																								
1987	Hou N	35	71	3	15	3	0	1	6	7-0	0	19	.211	.282	.296	55	-5	1-1	.957	3	137	177	3-16,O-13(1-12-0)/S	-0.2
1988	Hou N	46	83	7	19	5	1	1	8	7-4	0	16	.229	.286	.349	86	-2	1-1	.908	1	107	170	3-32/S-3,O-3(0-1-2)	-0.1
1994	Tex A	1	2	0	0	0	0	0	0	0-0	0	0	.000	.000	.000	-99	-1	0-0	—	-0	0	0	/3	-0.1
Total	3	82	156	10	34	8	1	2	14	14-4	0	35	.218	.281	.321	69	-8	2-2	.928	3	117	171	/3-49,O-16(1-13-2),S-4	-0.4
JACKSON, DAMIAN Damian Jacques B 8.16.1973 Los Angeles, CA BR/TR 5-10/160# d9.12 OF Total (35-LF 21-CF 14-RF)																								
1996	Cle A	5	10	2	3	2	0	0	1	1-0	0	4	.300	.364	.500	116	0	0-0	1.000	3	191	266	/S-5	0.3
1997	Cle A	8	9	2	1	0	0	0	0	0-0	1	1	.111	.200	.111	-15	-2	1-0	1.000	-0	91	111	/S-5,2	-0.1
	Cin N	12	27	6	6	2	1	1	2	4-1	0	7	.222	.323	.481	106	0	1-1	1.000	0	93	68	/S-6,2-3	0.1
1998	Cin N	13	38	4	12	5	0	0	7	6-0	0	4	.316	.400	.447	124	2	2-0	.972	-1	87	60	S-10/O-3(0-3-1)	0.2
1999	SD N	133	388	56	87	20	2	9	39	53-3	3	105	.224	.320	.356	77	-14	34-10	.940	7	105	110	*S-100,2-21/O-3(2-0-1)	0.5
2000	SD N	138	470	68	120	27	6	6	37	62-2	3	108	.255	.345	.377	89	-8	28-6	.955	13	115	100	S-88,2-36,O-17(LF)	1.6
2001	SD N	122	440	67	106	21	6	4	38	44-2	6	128	.241	.316	.343	78	-15	23-6	.986	0	99	98	*2-118/S-3,O-2(CF)	-0.6
2002	Det A	81	245	31	63	20	1	1	25	21-0	3	36	.257	.320	.359	86	-4	12-3	.981	-7	96	99	2-56/S-6,O-6(3-3-0),3-2,D-5	-0.6
2003	†Bos A	109	161	34	42	7	0	1	13	8-0	0	28	.261	.294	.323	62	-9	16-8	.960	-1	106	54	2-38,O-38(13-13-12),S-18/3-3,1-2,D-9	-0.8
Total	8	621	1788	270	440	104	16	22	162	199-8	16	421	.246	.325	.359	81	-50	117-34	.981	14	99	98	2-273,S-241/O-69L,D-14,3-5,1-2	0.6
JACKSON, DARRIN Darrin Jay B 8.22.1962 Los Angeles, CA BR/TR 6/185# d6.17																								
1985	Chi N	5	11	0	1	0	0	0	0	0-0	0	3	.091	.091	.091	-44	-2	0-0	1.000	-1	82	0	/O-4(CF)	-0.3
1987	Chi N	7	5	2	4	1	0	0	0	0-0	0	0	.800	.800	1.000	359	2	0-0	1.000	-0	46	0	/O-5(2-3-0)	0.2
1988	Chi N	100	188	29	50	11	3	6	20	5-1	1	28	.266	.287	.452	105	0	4-1	.983	0	104	45	O-74(11-46-20)	0.0
1989	Chi N	45	83	7	19	4	0	1	8	6-1	0	17	.229	.281	.313	65	-4	1-2	.970	4	124	231	O-39(10-9-20)	-0.1
	SD N	25	87	10	18	3	0	3	12	7-4	0	17	.207	.260	.345	73	-3	0-2	.954	-0	95	154	O-24(CF)	-0.5
	Year	70	170	17	37	7	0	4	20	13-5	0	34	.218	.270	.329	68	-7	1-4	.962	3	109	191	O-63(10-33-20)	-0.6
1990	SD N	58	113	10	29	3	0	3	9	5-1	0	24	.257	.286	.363	77	-4	3-0	.985	-1	99	68	O-39(4-30-5)	-0.4
1991	SD N	122	359	51	94	12	1	21	49	27-2	2	66	.262	.315	.476	117	6	5-3	.992	2	113	39	O-98(21-79-0)/P	0.7
1992	SD N	155	587	72	146	23	5	17	70	26-4	4	106	.249	.283	.392	88	-12	14-3	.996	14	108	205	*O-153(5-152-2)	0.4
1993	Tor A	46	176	15	38	8	0	5	19	8-0	0	53	.216	.250	.347	58	-11	0-2	.989	-4	88	63	O-46(0-10-37)	-1.7
	NY N	31	87	4	17	1	0	1	7	2-0	0	22	.195	.211	.241	22	-10	0-0	1.000	2	98	301	O-26(10-16-0)	-0.8
1994	Chi A	104	369	43	115	17	3	10	51	27-3	3	56	.312	.362	.455	111	6	7-1	.996	3	117	31	*O-102(0-16-92)	0.5
1997	Min A	49	130	19	33	2	1	3	21	4-0	0	21	.254	.272	.354	62	-8	2-0	.990	2	101	216	O-44(CF)	-0.5
	Mil A	26	81	7	22	7	0	2	15	2-0	0	10	.272	.289	.432	84	-2	2-1	1.000	3	117	155	O-26(21-9-3)	0.0
	Year	75	211	26	55	9	1	5	36	6-0	0	31	.261	.279	.384	70	-10	4-1	.994	4	107	193	O-70(21-53-3)	-0.5
1998	Mil N	114	204	20	49	13	1	4	20	9-0	1	37	.240	.276	.373	68	-10	1-1	.982	-1	95	89	O-94(55-43-5)/D-2	-1.2
1999	Chi A	73	149	22	41	9	1	4	16	3-0	0	20	.275	.288	.430	80	-5	4-1	.972	3	118	82	O-64(46-25-3)/D-3	-0.2
Total	12	960	2629	311	676	114	15	80	317	131-16	11	480	.257	.293	.403	87	-57	43-17	.989	27	107	117	O-838(185-510-187)/D-5,P	-3.9

Year	Tm Lg	G	AB	R	H	2B	3B	HR	RBI	BB-IB	HP	SO	AVG	OBP	SLG	AOPS	ABR	SB-CS	FA	FR	Rng	Thr	G at Pos	BFW
JACKSON, GEORGE George Christopher "Hickory" B 10.14.1882 Springfield, MO D 11.25.1972 Cleburne, TX BR/TR 6-0.5/180# d8.2																								
1911	Bos N	39	147	28	51	11	2	0	25	12	2	21	.347	.404	.449	128	6	12	.929	-2	98	75	O-39(38-1-0)	0.3
1912	Bos N	110	397	55	104	13	5	4	48	38	10	72	.262	.342	.350	88	-6	22	.943	1	96	119	*O-107(96-11-0)	-1.0
1913	Bos N	3	10	2	3	0	0	0	0	0	0	2	.300	.300	.300	70	0	0	.875	0	90	254	/O-3(CF)	0.0
Total	3	152	554	85	158	24	7	4	73	50	12	95	.285	.357	.375	98	0	34	.938	-1	96	111	O-149(134-15-0)	-0.7
JACKSON, HENRY Henry Everett B 6.23.1861 Union City, IN D 9.14.1932 Chicago, IL BR/TR 6-2/185# d9.13																								
1887	Ind N	10	38	1	10	1	0	0	3	0	0	12	.263	.263	.289	55	-2	2	.933	-1	82	112	1-10	-0.4
JACKSON, JIM James Benner B 11.28.1877 Philadelphia, PA D 10.9.1955 Philadelphia, PA BR/TR (BL 1906 (1 game)) 5-6.5/165# d4.26																								
1901	Bal A	99	364	42	91	17	3	2	50	20	1		.250	.291	.330	69	-16	11	**.971**	2	32	34	O-96(35-59-2)	-1.7
1902	NY N	37	116	14	21	5	1	0	15	16	0		.181	.280	.241	62	-5	6	.899	-2	88	0	O-36(32-2-2)	-0.9
1905	Cle A	109	426	60	109	12	4	2	31	34	4		.256	.317	.317	100	0	15	.951	4	135	115	*O-106(104-0-2)/3-3	-0.2
1906	Cle A	105	374	44	80	13	2	0	38	38	2		.214	.290	.259	73	-10	25	.975	-7	37	75	*O-104(103-1-0)	-2.6
Total	4	350	1280	160	301	47	10	4	134	108	7		.235	.298	.297	79	-31	57	.959	-2	71	69	O-342(274-62-6)/3-3	-5.4
JACKSON, JOE Joseph Jefferson "Shoeless Joe" B 7.16.1889 Pickens Co., SC D 12.5.1951 Greenville, SC BL/TR 6-1/200# d8.25 Def 1918																								
1908	Phi A	5	23	0	3	0	0	0	3	0	0		.130	.130	.130	-14	-3	0	.875	-0	221	0	/O-5(CF)	-0.4
1909	Phi A	5	17	3	3	0	0	0	3	1	0		.176	.222	.176	26	-1	0	.833	-1	0	0	/O-4(3-1-0)	-0.3
1910	Cle A	20	75	15	29	2	5	1	11	8	0		.387	.446	.587	220	10	4	.977	-0	103	67	O-20(0-15-5)	0.9
1911	Cle A	147	571	126	233	45	19	7	83	56	8		.408	**.468**	.590	192	71	41	.958	5	98	129	*O-147(0-47-100)	6.5
1912	Cle A	154	572	121	**226**	44	**26**	3	90	54	12		.395	.458	.579	190	67	35	.950	14	**118**	144	*O-150(0-19-131)	7.1
1913	Cle A	148	528	109	**197**	**39**	17	7	71	80	5	26	.373	.460	**.551**	190	**63**	26	.930	1	95	126	*O-148(RF)	5.9
1914	Cle A	122	453	61	153	22	13	3	53	41	5	34	.338	.399	.464	153	29	22-15	.967	2	107	91	*O-119(0-31-88)	2.6
1915	Cle A	83	303	42	99	16	9	3	45	28	3	11	.327	.389	.469	154	19	10-10	.961	-2	100	113	O-50(5-0-44),1-30	1.4
	Chi A	45	158	21	43	4	5	2	36	24	3	12	.272	.378	.399	129	6	6-10	.947	-2	89	101	O-45(19-26-0)	-0.1
	Year	128	461	63	142	20	14	5	81	52	6	23	.308	.385	.445	145	25	16-20	.953	-4	94	107	O-95(24-26-44),1-30	1.3
1916	Chi A	**155**	592	91	202	40	**21**	3	78	46	5	25	.341	.393	.495	165	44	24-14	.975	-4	94	84	*O-155(131-1-23)	3.6
1917	†Chi A	146	538	91	162	20	17	5	75	57	7	25	.301	.375	.429	142	27	13	.984	6	111	84	*O-145(134-0-11)	2.8
1918	Chi A	17	65	9	23	2	2	1	20	8	0	1	.354	.425	.492	175	6	3	1.000	-0	109	45	O-17(14-0-3)	0.5
1919	†Chi A	139	516	79	181	31	14	7	96	60	4	10	.351	.422	.506	159	42	9	.967	-3	92	105	*O-139(133-0-6)	3.3
1920	Chi A	146	570	105	218	42	**20**	12	121	56	7	14	.382	.444	.589	172	59	9-12	.965	-3	101	71	*O-145(LF)	4.5
Total	13	1332	4981	873	1772	307	168	54	785	519	59	158	.356	.423	.517	169	439	202-61	.962	13	101	102	*O-1289(584-145-559)/1-30	38.3
JACKSON, KEN Kenneth Bernard B 8.21.1963 Shreveport, LA BR/TR 5-9/170# d9.12																								
1987	Phi N	8	16	1	4	2	0	0	2	1-1	1	4	.250	.333	.375	85	0	0-0	.955	-1	94	33	/S-8	-0.1
JACKSON, LOU Louis Clarence B 7.26.1935 Riverton, LA D 5.27.1969 Tokyo, Japan BL/TR 5-10/168# d7.23																								
1958	Chi N	24	35	5	6	2	1	1	6	1-0	0	9	.171	.194	.371	46	-3	0-1	1.000	-1	84	0	O-12(4-4-6)	-0.4
1959	Chi N	6	4	2	1	0	0	0	1	0-0	0	2	.250	.250	.250	34	0	0-0	—	0			H	0.0
1964	Bal A	4	8	0	3	0	0	0	0	0-0	0	2	.375	.375	.375	110	0	0-0	1.000	0	143	0	/O(LF)	0.0
Total	3	34	47	7	10	2	1	1	7	1-0	0	13	.213	.229	.362	55	-3	0-1	1.000	-0	98	0	/O-13(5-4-6)	-0.4
JACKSON, RANDY Ransom Joseph "Handsome Ransom" B 2.10.1926 Little Rock, AR BR/TR 6-1.5/180# d5.2																								
1950	Chi N	34	111	13	25	4	3	3	6	7	0	25	.225	.271	.396	74	-5	4	.911	-4	95	48	3-27	-0.9
1951	Chi N	145	557	78	153	24	6	16	76	47	1	44	.275	.332	.425	101	-1	14-3	.956	7	103	86	*3-143	0.8
1952	Chi N	116	379	44	88	8	5	9	34	27	1	42	.232	.285	.351	75	-15	6-5	.958	-2	104	79	*3-104/O(LF)	-1.8
1953	Chi N	139	498	61	142	22	8	19	66	42	0	61	.285	.341	.476	108	4	8-4	.949	4	104	79	*3-133	0.7
1954	Chi N★	126	484	77	132	17	6	19	67	44	2	55	.273	.333	.450	102	0	2-1	.955	-4	**99**	85	*3-124	-0.5
1955	Chi N★	138	499	73	132	13	7	21	70	58-6	1	58	.265	.340	.445	107	4	0-2	.949	-12	92	102	*3-134	-0.8
1956	†Bro N	101	307	37	84	15	7	8	53	28-3	2	38	.274	.333	.446	101	0	2-1	.993	22	129	164	3-80	2.2
1957	Bro N	48	131	7	26	1	0	2	16	9-0	0	20	.198	.246	.252	32	-13	0-0	.976	0	93	144	3-34	-1.3
1958	LA N	35	65	8	12	3	0	1	4	5-1	0	10	.185	.243	.277	36	-6	0-0	.964	5	137	207	3-17	-0.1
	Cle A	29	91	7	22	3	1	4	13	3-0	0	18	.242	.266	.429	90	-2	0-0	.901	1	112	77	3-24	-0.1
1959	Cle A	3	7	0	1	0	0	0	0	0-0	0	1	.143	.143	.143	-22	-1	0-0	1.000	-0	82	0	/3-2	-0.2
	Chi N	41	74	7	18	5	1	1	10	11-1	0	10	.243	.341	.378	92	0	0-0	.941	-2	86	76	3-22/O(LF)	-0.2
Total	10	955	3203	412	835	115	44	103	415	281-11	7	382	.261	.320	.421	94	-35	36-16	.955	16	103	96	3-844/O-2(LF)	-2.2
JACKSON, REGGIE Reginald Martinez B 5.18.1946 Wyncote, PA BL/TL 6/200# d6.9 HF1993																								
1967	KC A	35	118	13	21	4	4	1	6	10-0	5	46	.178	.269	.305	72	-4	1-1	.933	-3	90	45	O-34(19-3-14)	-1.0
1968	Oak A	154	553	82	138	13	6	29	74	50-5	5	171	.250	.316	.452	138	22	14-4	.959	6	108	169	*O-151(1-9-147)	2.3
1969	Oak A★	152	549	**123**	151	36	3	47	118	114-**20**	12	142	.275	.410	**.608**	**190**	**71**	13-5	.964	-2	99	116	*O-150(0-10-144)	6.4
1970	Oak A	149	426	57	101	21	2	23	66	75-11	8	135	.237	.359	.458	129	19	26-17	.956	-3	100	97	*O-142(0-49-113)	1.1
1971	†Oak A★	150	567	87	157	29	3	32	80	63-5	6	161	.277	.352	.508	145	32	16-10	.977	6	103	156	*O-145(0-3-145)	3.3
1972	†Oak A★	135	499	72	132	25	2	25	75	59-7	8	125	.265	.350	.473	152	32	9-8	.971	-8	95	54	*O-135(0-92-43)	2.0
1973	†Oak A★	151	539	**99**	158	28	2	**32**	**117**	76-11	7	111	.293	.383	**.531**	**165**	**48**	22-8	.971	-1	106	42	*O-145(0-1-144)/D-3	4.2
1974	†Oak A★	148	506	90	146	25	1	29	93	86-**20**	4	105	.289	.391	.514	**171**	50	25-5	.968	6	115	83	*O-127(0-3-126),D-19	5.4
1975	†Oak A★	157	593	91	150	39	3	**36**	104	67-5	3	133	.253	.329	.511	138	28	17-8	.965	5	109	107	*O-147(RF)/D-9	2.7
1976	Bal A	134	498	84	138	27	2	27	91	54-7	4	108	.277	.351	**.502**	**158**	35	28-7	.964	1	104	87	*O-121(0-16-111),D-11	3.5
1977	†NY A★	146	525	93	150	39	2	32	110	74-4	3	129	.286	.375	.550	151	39	17-3	.949	-4	97	80	*O-127(RF),D-18	3.0
1978	†NY A✳	139	511	82	140	13	5	27	97	58-2	9	133	.274	.356	.477	136	24	14-11	.986	-3	97	77	*O-104(RF),D-35	1.4
1979	NY A★	131	465	78	138	24	2	29	89	65-3	2	107	.297	.382	.544	151	34	9-8	.986	1	104	74	*O-125(RF)/D-3	2.6
1980	†NY A★	143	514	94	154	22	4	**41**	111	83-15	2	122	.300	.398	.597	172	52	1-2	.962	-4	96	45	O-94(RF),D-46	4.0
1981	†NY A★	94	334	33	79	17	1	15	54	46-2	1	82	.237	.330	.428	119	9	0-3	.974	-2	93	73	O-61(RF),D-33	0.2
1982	†Cal A★	153	530	92	146	17	1	**39**	101	85-12	2	156	.275	.375	.532	147	35	4-5	.972	-17	75	64	*O-139(RF)/D-5	1.0
1983	Cal A✳	116	397	43	77	14	1	14	49	52-5	4	140	.194	.290	.340	74	-14	0-2	.986	-4	74	121	D-62,O-47(RF)	-2.3
1984	Cal A★	143	525	67	117	17	2	25	81	55-7	3	141	.223	.300	.406	94	-6	8-4	1.000	-0	107	0	*D-134/O-3(RF)	-1.0
1985	Cal A	143	460	64	116	27	0	27	85	78-12	1	138	.252	.360	.487	130	21	1-2	.944	-8	75	120	O-81(RF),D-52	0.8
1986	†Cal A	132	419	65	101	12	2	18	58	92-11	3	115	.241	.379	.408	116	13	1-1	.833	1	99	698	*D-121/O-4(RF)	1.0
1987	Oak A	115	336	42	74	14	1	15	43	33-0	4	97	.220	.297	.402	89	-6	2-1	1.000	-2	83	0	D-79,O-20(RF)	-1.1
Total	21	2820	9864	1551	2584	463	49	563	1702	1375-164	96	2597	.262	.356	.490	140	534	228-115	.967	-34	99	92	*O-2102(20-186-1939),D-630	39.5
JACKSON, SONNY Roland Thomas B 7.9.1944 Washington, DC BL/TR 5-9/155# d9.27 C8																								
1963	Hou N	1	3	0	0	0	0	0	0	0-0	0	1	.000	.000	.000	-99	-1	0-0	.833	0	170	0	/S	-0.1
1964	Hou N	9	23	3	8	1	0	0	1	2-0	0	3	.348	.400	.391	131	1	1-0	.870	-2	81	35	/S-7	-0.1
1965	Hou N	10	23	1	3	0	0	0	0	1-0	0	1	.130	.167	.130	-16	-4	1-1	.969	-1	78	78	/S-8,3	-0.5
1966	Hou N	150	596	80	174	6	5	3	25	42-0	3	53	.292	.341	.334	95	-4	49-14	.951	-5	97	80	*S-150	1.0
1967	Hou N	129	520	67	123	18	3	0	25	36-1	0	45	.237	.285	.283	66	-24	22-9	.943	-7	94	81	*S-128	-1.9
1968	Atl N	105	358	37	81	8	2	1	19	25-6	3	35	.226	.282	.268	66	-15	16-6	.952	-12	101	70	S-99	-2.0
1969	†Atl N	98	318	41	76	3	5	1	27	35-2	2	33	.239	.317	.289	71	-12	12-7	.961	-9	93	100	S-97	-1.1
1970	Atl N	103	328	60	85	14	3	0	20	45-1	1	27	.259	.347	.320	76	-9	11-4	.933	-13	92	83	S-87	-1.2
1971	Atl N	149	547	58	141	20	5	2	25	35-1	1	45	.258	.302	.324	73	-19	7-6	.980	-7	85	87	*O-145(CF)	-3.3
1972	Atl N	60	126	20	30	6	3	0	8	7-0	0	9	.238	.278	.333	67	-6	1-0	.976	4	117	101	S-17,O-10(0-9-1)/3-6	0.0
1973	Atl N	117	206	29	43	5	2	0	12	22-0	1	13	.209	.283	.252	47	-14	6-3	.981	-1	94	56	O-56(48-4-4),S-36	-1.4
1974	Atl N	5	7	0	3	0	0	0	0	0-0	0	0	.429	.429	.429	134	0	0-1	1.000	0	131	0	/O(RF)	0.0
Total	12	936	3055	396	767	81	28	7	162	250-11	11	265	.251	.308	.303	73	-107	126-51	.949	-54	96	81	S-630,O-212(48-158-6)/3-7	-10.6
JACKSON, RON Ronald Harris B 10.22.1933 Kalamazoo, MI BR/TR 6-7/225# d6.15																								
1954	Chi A	40	93	10	26	4	0	4	10	6	2	20	.280	.333	.452	111	1	2-1	.988	-3	55	74	1-35	-0.3
1955	Chi A	40	74	10	15	1	1	2	7	8-2	0	22	.203	.277	.324	61	-5	1-0	.988	-1	77	93	1-29	-0.7
1956	Chi A	22	56	7	12	3	0	1	4	10-1	0	13	.214	.333	.321	73	-2	1-0	1.000	1	114	116	1-19	-0.2
1957	Chi A	13	60	4	19	3	0	2	8	1-1	0	12	.317	.328	.467	114	1	0-0	.992	-1	62	87	1-13	-0.1
1958	Chi A	61	146	19	34	4	0	7	21	18-0	2	46	.233	.323	.404	101	0	2-0	.997	-2	76	98	1-38	-0.3
1959	Chi A	10	14	3	3	1	0	1	2	1-0	1	0	.214	.313	.500	121	0	0-0	1.000	-0	53	127	/1-5	0.0
1960	Bos A	10	31	1	7	2	0	0	0	1-0	0	6	.226	.250	.290	44	-2	0-0	.973	-0	97	134	/1-9	-0.3
Total	7	196	474	54	116	18	1	17	52	45-4	5	119	.245	.315	.395	92	-7	6-1	.992	-7	76	96	1-148	-1.9

Year	Tm Lg	G	AB	R	H	2B	3B	HR	RBI	BB-IB	HP	SO	AVG	OBP	SLG	AOPS	ABR	SB-CS	FA	FR	Rng	Thr	G at Pos	BFW
JACKSON, RON Ronnie Damien B 5.9.1953 Birmingham, AL BR/TR 6/205# d9.12 C6 OF Total (51-LF 1-CF 4-RF)																								
1975	Cal A	13	39	2	9	2	0	0	2	2-0	0	10	.231	.268	.282	60	-2	1-1	.947	0	97	160	/O-9(LF),3-3,D	-0.3
1976	Cal A	127	410	44	93	18	3	8	40	30-1	7	58	.227	.289	.344	91	-5	5-4	.950	4	100	109	*3-114/2-7,O-4(3-0-1),D-6	-0.3
1977	Cal A	106	292	38	71	15	2	8	28	24-2	1	42	.243	.301	.390	91	-4	3-2	.990	2	121	99	1-43,3-30,D-20/O-3(LF),S	-0.5
1978	Cal A	105	387	49	115	18	6	6	57	16-1	9	31	.297	.337	.421	117	8	2-3	.994	-5	116	86	1-75,3-31/O(RF)D	-0.3
1979	Min A	159	583	85	158	40	5	14	68	51-5	9	59	.271	.337	.429	102	2	3-1	.994	13	**128**	**125**	*1-157/S3O(LF)	0.5
1980	Min A	131	396	48	105	29	3	5	42	28-5	3	41	.265	.316	.391	87	-7	1-8	.991	4	**124**	121	*1-119,O-15(14-1-0)/3-2,D	-1.2
1981	Min A	54	175	17	46	9	0	4	28	10-0	1	15	.263	.305	.383	91	-2	2-2	.988	0	109	80	1-36/O-7(6-0-1),3-3,D-6	-0.5
	Det A	31	95	12	27	8	1	1	12	8-0	0	11	.284	.337	.421	114	2	4-1	1.000	-0	90	103	1-29	0.1
	Year	85	270	29	73	17	1	5	40	18-0	1	26	.270	.316	.396	99	0	6-3	.993	-0	101	89	1-65/O-7(6-0-1),D-6,3-3	-0.4
1982	†Cal A	53	142	15	47	6	0	2	19	10-0	2	12	.331	.381	.415	119	4	0-1	.994	-2	89	140	1-37/3-9	0.0
1983	Cal A	102	348	41	80	16	1	8	39	27-2	3	33	.230	.291	.351	76	-12	2-2	.957	2	110	103	3-38,1-35,D-16,O-15(14-0-1)	-1.4
1984	Cal A	33	91	5	15	2	1	0	5	7-1	0	13	.165	.222	.209	21	-10	0-0	.990	-1	90	103	1-21/3-9,O(LF)	-1.3
	Bal A	12	28	0	8	2	0	0	2	0-0	0	4	.286	.286	.357	78	-1	0-2	.960	2	94	344	3-10	0.0
	Year	45	119	5	23	4	1	0	7	7-1	0	17	.193	.236	.244	34	-11	0-2	.990	0	90	103	1-21,3-19/O(LF)	-1.3
Total	10	926	2986	356	774	165	22	56	342	213-17	35	329	.259	.314	.385	94	-27	23-27	.993	18	116	112	1-552,3-250/O-56L,D-51,2-7,S-2	-5.2
JACKSON, RYAN Ryan Dewitte B 11.15.1971 Orlando, FL BL/TL 6-2/195# d3.31																								
1998	Fla N	111	260	26	65	15	1	5	31	20-0	1	73	.250	.305	.373	82	-7	1-1	.973	-5	82	90	1-44,O-32(10-0-23)/D-5	-1.6
1999	Sea A	32	68	4	16	3	0	0	10	6-0	1	19	.235	.299	.279	52	-5	3-3	.989	-0	97	94	1-29/O(LF)	-0.7
2001	Det A	79	118	19	25	4	2	2	11	5-0	1	26	.212	.250	.331	54	-9	3-1	1.000	-2	128	114	1-35,O-34(19-0-15)/D-5	-1.2
2002	Det A	4	6	0	2	1	1	0	0	1-0	0	2	.333	.429	.833	238	1	0-0	1.000	-0	73	0	/O-3(2-1-0)	0.1
Total	4	226	452	49	108	23	4	7	52	32-0	3	120	.239	.292	.354	72	-20	7-5	.983	-7	95	96	1-108/O-70(32-1-38),D-10	-3.4
JACKSON, SAM Samuel B 3.24.1849 Ripon, England D 8.4.1930 Clifton Springs, NY BR/TR 5-5.5/160# d5.16																								
1871	Bos NA	16	76	17	17	5	3	0	11	1		4	.224	.234	.368	68	-3	0-1	.818	-1	110	22	2-14/SO(CF)	-0.4
1872	Atl NA	4	12	0	2	0	0	0	0	0		0	.167	.167	.167	2	-2	0-0	.667	-1	317	0	/O-3(LF),23	-0.2
Total	2 NA	20	88	17	19	5	3	0	11	1		4	.216	.225	.341	58	-5	0-1	.000	-2	108	22	/2-15,O-4(3-1-0),3S	-0.6
JACKSON, TRAVIS Travis Calvin "Stonewall" B 11.2.1903 Waldo, AR D 7.27.1987 Waldo, AR BR/TR 5-10.5/160# d9.27 C4 HF1982																								
1922	NY N	3	8	1	0	0	0	0	0	0	0	2	.000	.000	.000	-99	-2	0-0	.909	0	120	113	/S-3	-0.2
1923	†NY N	96	327	45	90	12	7	4	37	22	0	40	.275	.321	.391	88	-7	3-3	.943	3	112	86	S-60,3-31/2	0.3
1924	†NY N	151	596	81	180	26	8	11	76	21	0	56	.302	.326	.428	103	0	6-7	.937	0	102	107	*S-151	1.5
1925	NY N	112	411	51	117	15	2	9	59	24	2	43	.285	.327	.397	87	-9	8-3	.942	2	99	95	*S-110	0.5
1926	NY N	111	385	64	126	24	8	8	51	20	1	26	.327	.362	.494	130	15	2	.962	-1	97	111	*S-108/O(RF)	2.5
1927	NY N	127	469	67	149	29	4	14	98	32	1	30	.318	.363	.486	126	16	8	.952	26	**113**	116	*S-124/3-2	5.4
1928	NY N	150	537	73	145	35	6	14	77	56	0	46	.270	.339	.436	101	0	8	.952	28	**111**	125	*S-149	4.2
1929	NY N	149	551	92	162	21	12	21	94	64	0	56	.294	.367	.490	111	7	10	**.969**	15	107	123	*S-149	3.5
1930	NY N	116	431	70	146	27	8	13	82	32	1	25	.339	.386	.529	121	14	6	.956	9	**109**	91	*S-115	3.1
1931	NY N	145	555	65	172	26	10	5	71	36	1	23	.310	.353	.420	110	6	13	**.970**	10	102	88	*S-145	2.6
1932	NY N	52	195	23	50	17	1	4	38	13	2	16	.256	.310	.415	95	-1	1	.925	-4	95	98	S-52	-0.1
1933	†NY N	53	122	11	30	5	0	0	12	8	0	11	.246	.292	.287	67	-5	2	.890	2	96	175	S-21,3-21	-0.1
1934	NY N★	137	523	75	140	26	7	16	101	37	0	71	.268	.316	.436	102	-1	1	.945	10	**109**	87	*S-130/3-9	1.8
1935	NY N	128	511	74	154	20	12	9	80	29	1	64	.301	.340	.440	110	5	3	.947	-9	92	70	*3-128	0.1
1936	†NY N	126	465	41	107	8	1	7	53	18	1	56	.230	.260	.297	50	-34	0	.952	-2	101	61	*3-116/S-9	-3.1
Total	15	1656	6086	833	1768	291	86	135	929	412	10	565	.291	.337	.433	102	4	71-13	.952	90	105	105	*S-1326,3-307/O(RF)2	22.0
JACKSON, BO Vincent Edward B 11.30.1962 Bessemer, AL BR/TR 6-1/225# d9.2																								
1986	KC A	25	82	9	17	2	1	2	9	7-0	2	34	.207	.286	.329	66	-4	3-1	.886	-3	67	133	O-23(RF)/D	-0.8
1987	KC A	116	396	46	93	17	2	22	53	30-0	5	158	.235	.296	.455	93	-5	10-4	.955	-7	82	132	*O-113(95-21-3)/D	-1.6
1988	KC A	124	439	63	108	16	4	25	68	25-6	1	146	.246	.287	.472	108	2	27-6	.973	3	100	162	*O-121(103-5-15)/D-2	0.5
1989	KC A★	135	515	86	132	15	6	32	105	39-8	3	172	.256	.310	.495	125	13	26-9	.967	4	100	172	*O-110(110-1-0),D-24	1.6
1990	KC A	111	405	74	110	16	1	28	78	44-2	2	128	.272	.342	.523	142	21	15-9	.952	2	102	154	O-97(36-61-0),D-10	2.2
1991	Chi A	23	71	8	16	4	0	3	14	12-1	0	25	.225	.333	.408	108	1	0-1	—	0	0	0	D-21	0.0
1993	†Chi A	85	284	32	66	9	0	16	45	23-1	0	106	.232	.289	.433	94	-4	0-2	.989	4	108	190	O-47(28-0-19),D-36	-0.5
1994	Cal A	75	201	23	56	7	0	13	43	20-2	1	72	.279	.344	.507	115	4	1-0	.964	-0	104	110	O-46(43-0-3)/D-9	0.2
Total	8	694	2393	341	598	86	14	141	415	200-20	14	841	.250	.309	.474	112	28	82-32	.962	2	96	154	O-557(415-88-63),D-104	1.6
JACKSON, BILL William Riley B 4.4.1881 Pittsburgh, PA D 9.24.1958 Peoria, IL BL/TL 5-11.5/160# d4.30																								
1914	Chi F	26	25	2	1	0	0	0	1	3	0	5	.040	.143	.040	-52	-6	0	.917	1	152	178	/O-6(2-2-2),1-4	-0.6
1915	Chi F	50	98	15	16	1	0	1	12	14	0	15	.163	.268	.204	36	-10	3	.983	0	109	71	1-36/O(CF)	-1.2
Total	2	76	123	17	17	1	0	1	13	17	0	20	.138	.243	.171	18	-16	3	.984	1	105	76	/1-40,O-7(2-3-2)	-1.8
JACOBS, JAKE Lamar Gary B 6.9.1937 Youngstown, OH BR/TR 6/175# d9.13																								
1960	Was A	6	2	0	0	0	0	0	0	0-0	0	0	.000	.000	.000	-99	-1	0-0	—	0			H	-0.1
1961	Min A	4	8	0	2	0	0	0	0	0-0	0	2	.250	.250	.250	32	-1	0-0	1.000	-0	67	0	/O-3(CF)	-0.1
Total	2	10	10	0	2	0	0	0	0	0-0	0	2	.200	.200	.200	7	-2	0-0	1.000	-0	67	0	/O-3(CF)	-0.2
JACOBS, MIKE Morris Elmore B 12.1877 Louisville, KY D 3.21.1949 Louisville, KY d7.16																								
1902	Chi N	5	19	1	4	0	0	0	2	0	0		.211	.211	.211	31	-2	0	.880	-1	87	66	/S-5	-0.3
JACOBS, OTTO Otto Albert B 4.19.1889 Chicago, IL D 11.19.1955 Chicago, IL BR/TR 5-9/180# d6.13																								
1918	Chi A	29	73	4	15	3	1	0	3	5	0	8	.205	.256	.274	59	-4	0	.955	-2	*119*	*83*	C-21	-0.5
JACOBS, RAY Raymond Frederick B 1.2.1902 Salt Lake City, UT D 4.5.1952 Los Angeles, CA BR/TR 6/160# d4.20																								
1928	Chi N	2	2	0	0	0	0	0	0	0	0	1	.000	.000	.000	-99	-1	0	—	0			H	-0.1
JACOBS, SPOOK Robert Forrest Vandergrift B 11.4.1925 Cheswold, DE BR/TR 5-8.5/155# d4.13																								
1954	Phi A	132	508	63	131	11	1	0	26	60	0	22	.258	.336	.283	71	-19	17-3	.974	-16	88	91	*2-131	-2.4
1955	KC A	13	23	7	6	0	0	0	1	3-0	1	0	.261	.370	.261	71	-1	1-2	1.000	-2	78	109	/2-7	-0.2
1956	KC A	32	97	13	21	3	0	0	5	15-1	0	5	.216	.321	.247	52	-6	4-1	.968	-2	92	116	2-31	-0.5
	Pit N	11	37	4	6	2	0	0	1	2-0	1	5	.162	.225	.216	20	-4	0-2	.926	-3	79	71	2-11	-0.8
Total	3	188	665	87	164	16	1	0	33	80-1	2	32	.247	.329	.274	65	-30	22-8	.971	-22	88	94	2-180	-3.9
JACOBSON, MERWIN Merwin John William "Jake" B 3.7.1894 New Britain, CT D 1.13.1978 Baltimore, MD BL/TL 5-11.5/165# d9.8																								
1915	NY N	8	24	0	2	0	0	0	0	1	0	5	.083	.120	.083	-40	-4	0	.909	0	90	164	/O-5(0-2-3)	-0.5
1916	Chi N	4	13	2	3	0	0	0	0	1	0	4	.231	.286	.231	54	-1	2	1.000	-0	120	0	/O-4(RF)	-0.1
1926	Bro N	110	288	41	71	9	2	0	23	36	0	24	.247	.330	.292	70	-11	5	.975	-0	106	61	O-86(2-53-32)	-1.6
1927	Bro N	11	6	4	0	0	0	0	1	0	0	1	.000	.000	.000	-99	-2	0	1.000	0	142	0	/O-3(RF)	-0.2
Total	4	133	331	47	76	9	2	0	24	38	0	34	.230	.309	.269	59	-18	7	.973	-0	106	64	/O-98(2-55-42)	-2.4
JACOBSON, BABY DOLL William Chester B 8.16.1890 Cable, IL D 1.16.1977 Orion, IL BR/TR 6-3/215# d4.14 Mil 1918																								
1915	Det A	37	65	5	14	6	2	0	4	5	1	14	.215	.282	.369	90	-1	0-2	.983	-1	69	103	1-10/O-7(3-5-0)	-0.3
	StL A	34	115	13	24	6	1	1	9	10	4	26	.209	.295	.304	82	-2	3-3	.981	-1	105	55	O-32(3-3-26)	-0.6
	Year	71	180	18	38	12	3	1	13	15	5	40	.211	.290	.328	84	-4	3-5	.984	-1	104	70	O-39(6-8-26),1-10	-0.9
1917	StL A	148	529	53	131	23	7	4	55	31	4	67	.248	.294	.340	97	-4	10	.975	3	108	95	*O-131(0-54-77),1-11	-1.1
1919	StL A	120	455	70	147	31	8	4	51	24	4	47	.323	.362	.453	125	14	9	.949	-3	107	61	*O-106(17-73-16)/1-8	0.4
1920	StL A	**154**	609	97	216	34	14	9	122	46	2	37	.355	.402	.501	134	29	11-7	.979	10	116	94	*O-154(0-120-34)/1	2.7
1921	StL A	151	599	90	211	38	14	5	90	42	3	30	.352	.398	.487	118	16	8-8	.982	-1	107	39	*O-142(0-141-1),1-10	0.7
1922	StL A	145	555	88	176	22	16	9	102	46	9	36	.317	.379	.463	114	11	19-6	.969	-1	108	62	*O-137(11-125-1)/1-7	0.5
1923	StL A	147	592	76	183	29	6	8	81	29	2	27	.309	.343	.419	95	-7	6-6	.974	4	111	61	*O-146(CF)	-1.0
1924	StL A	152	579	103	184	41	12	19	97	35	4	45	.318	.361	.528	120	13	6-8	.986	10	**119**	48	*O-152(CF)	1.4
1925	StL A	142	540	103	184	30	9	15	76	45	1	26	.341	.392	.513	122	16	8-11	.965	-4	90	120	*O-139(CF)	0.4
1926	StL A	50	182	18	52	15	1	2	21	9	0	14	.286	.319	.412	86	-4	1-2	.964	-5	94	47	O-50(CF)	-1.1
	Bos A	98	394	44	120	36	1	6	69	22	2	22	.305	.344	.447	109	4	4-1	.980	-11	85	68	O-98(6-57-36)	-1.2
	Year	148	576	62	172	51	2	8	90	31	2	36	.299	.337	.436	101	-1	5-3	.975	-16	88	62	*O-148(6-107-36)	-2.3
1927	Bos A	45	155	11	38	9	3	0	24	5	2	12	.245	.278	.342	61	-10	1-0	.979	-0	99	94	O-39(LF)	-1.2

Year	Tm Lg	G	AB	R	H	2B	3B	HR	RBI	BB-IB	HP	SO	AVG	OBP	SLG	AOPS	ABR	SB-CS	FA	FR	Rng	Thr	G at Pos	BFW
	Cle A	32	103	13	26	5	0	0	13	6	1	4	.252	.300	.301	56	-7	0-0	.932	-2	104	33	O-31(CF)	-1.0
	Phi A	17	35	3	8	3	0	1	5	0	0	3	.229	.229	.400	57	-2	0-0	1.000	-1	69	0	O-14(9-2-3)	-0.4
	Year	94	293	27	72	17	3	1	42	11	3	19	.246	.280	.334	59	-19	1-0	.959	-3	99	63	O-84(48-33-3)	-2.6
Total	11	1472	5507	787	1714	328	94	83	819	355	39	410	.311	.357	.450	111	66	86-54	.973	-3	106	71	*O-1378(88-1098-194)/1-47	-1.8
JACOBY, BROOK Brook Wallace B 11.23.1959 Philadelphia, PA BR/TR 5-11/195# d9.13																								
1981	Atl N	11	10	0	2	0	0	0	1	0-0	0	3	.200	.200	.200	13	-1	0-0	1.000	2	229	695	/3-3	0.0
1983	Atl N	4	8	0	0	0	0	0	0	0-0	0	1	.000	.000	.000	-93	-2	0-0	1.000	-1	63	0	/3-2	-0.3
1984	Cle A	126	439	64	116	19	3	7	40	32-0	3	73	.264	.314	.369	88	-7	3-2	.951	-23	81	71	*3-126/S	-3.3
1985	Cle A	161	606	72	166	26	3	20	87	48-3	0	120	.274	.324	.426	105	3	2-3	.958	-8	98	78	*3-161/2	-0.8
1986	Cle A★	158	583	83	168	30	4	17	80	56-5	0	137	.288	.350	.441	116	13	2-1	.941	-12	100	79	*3-158	-0.2
1987	Cle A	155	540	73	162	26	4	32	69	75-2	3	73	.300	.387	.541	142	34	2-3	.946	-5	94	65	*3-144/1-7,D-4	2.4
1988	Cle A	152	552	59	133	25	0	9	49	48-2	1	101	.241	.300	.335	76	-17	2-3	.975	2	103	91	*3-151	-1.6
1989	Cle A	147	519	49	141	26	5	13	64	62-3	3	90	.272	.348	.416	114	11	2-5	.955	-14	92	64	*3-144/D-3	-0.5
1990	Cle A★	155	553	77	162	24	4	14	75	63-6	2	58	.293	.365	.427	122	17	1-4	.981	-15	90	86	3-99,1-78	-0.4
1991	Cle A	66	231	14	54	9	1	4	24	16-2	2	32	.234	.289	.333	71	-9	0-1	.988	1	95	63	1-55,3-15	-1.3
	Oak A	56	188	14	40	12	0	0	20	11-1	1	22	.213	.255	.277	51	-12	2-0	.982	-6	78	92	3-52/1-3	-1.9
	Year	122	419	28	94	21	1	4	44	27-3	3	54	.224	.274	.308	63	-22	2-1	.987	-6	85	97	3-67,1-58	-3.2
1992	Cle A	120	291	30	76	7	0	4	36	28-2	1	54	.261	.324	.326	85	-6	0-3	.957	-1	105	115	*3-111,1-10	-0.8
Total	11	1311	4520	535	1220	204	24	120	545	439-26	16	764	.270	.334	.405	104	24	16-25	.958	-82	95	80	*3-1166,1-153/D-7,2S	-8.7
JACOBY, HARRY Harry B Philadelphia, PA D 6.12.1900 Philadelphia, PA d5.2																								
1882	Bal AA	31	121	17	21	1	1	1		7			.174	.219	.223	53	-5		.776	7	112	83	3-19,O-13(RF)	0.2
1885	Bal AA	11	43	4	6	2	0	0	1	2	0		.140	.178	.186	15	-4		.896	-5	75	46	2-11	-0.8
Total	2	42	164	21	27	3	1	1	1	9	0		.165	.208	.213	43	-9		.776	3	112	83	/3-19,O-13(RF),2-11	-0.6
JAHA, JOHN John Emil B 5.27.1966 Portland, OR BR/TR 6-1/205# d7.9																								
1992	Mil A	47	133	17	30	3	1	2	10	12-1	2	30	.226	.291	.308	72	-5	10-0	1.000	-1	89	87	1-38/O(LF)D	-0.7
1993	Mil A	153	515	78	136	21	0	19	70	51-4	8	109	.264	.337	.416	103	2	13-9	.992	7	121	92	*1-150/23	-0.5
1994	Mil A	84	291	45	70	14	0	12	39	32-3	10	75	.241	.332	.412	88	-5	3-3	.989	-2	96	103	1-73,D-11	-1.4
1995	Mil A	88	316	59	99	20	2	20	65	36-0	4	66	.313	.389	.579	140	19	2-1	.997	2	113	122	1-81/D-6	1.3
1996	Mil A	148	543	108	163	28	1	34	118	85-1	5	118	.300	.398	.543	130	27	3-1	.992	1	108	113	1-85,D-63	1.4
1997	Mil A	46	162	25	40	7	0	11	26	25-1	3	40	.247	.354	.494	118	5	1-0	.992	-1	82	125	1-27,D-20	0.0
1998	Mil N	73	216	29	45	6	1	7	38	49-3	6	66	.208	.366	.343	89	-2	1-3	.994	-5	64	134	1-57/D-8	-1.3
1999	Oak A★	142	457	93	126	23	0	35	111	101-2	9	129	.276	.414	.556	151	40	2-0	1.000	1	153	79	*D-121/1-8	3.0
2000	Oak A	33	97	14	17	1	0	1	5	33-0	3	38	.175	.398	.216	63	-3	1-0	—	0	0	0	D-30	-0.5
2001	Oak A	12	45	2	4	3	0	0	8	6-0	0	15	.089	.192	.156	-6	-7	0-0	—	0	0	0	D-12	-0.8
Total	10	826	2775	470	730	126	5	141	490	430-15	50	686	.263	.369	.465	115	71	36-17	.993	1	104	107	1-519,D-279/320(LF)	0.5
JAHN, ART Arthur Charles B 12.2.1895 Struble, IA D 1.9.1948 Little Rock, AR BR/TR 6/180# d7.2																								
1925	Chi N	58	226	30	68	10	8	0	37	11	1	20	.301	.336	.416	90	-4	2-2	.985	0	98	91	O-58(LF)	-0.9
1928	NY N	10	29	7	8	1	0	1	7	2	0	5	.276	.323	.414	91	0	0	1.000	1	108	148	/O-8(7-1-0)	-0.1
	Phi N	36	94	8	21	4	0	0	11	4	2	11	.223	.270	.266	39	-8	0	.978	-1	97	48	O-29(2-0-27)	-1.1
	Year	46	123	15	29	5	0	1	18	6	2	16	.236	.282	.301	51	-9	0	.985	-0	100	77	O-37(9-1-27)	-1.2
Total	2	104	349	45	97	15	8	1	55	17	3	36	.278	.317	.375	76	-12	2-2	.985	-0	99	86	/O-95(67-1-27)	-2.1
JAMES, ART Arthur B 8.2.1952 Detroit, MI BL/TL 6/170# d4.10																								
1975	Det A	11	40	2	9	2	0	0	1	1-0	0	3	.225	.244	.275	44	-3	1-2	1.000	2	149	0	O-11(0-4-7)	-0.2
JAMES, BERT Berton Hulon "Jesse" B 7.7.1886 Coopertown, TN D 1.2.1959 Adairville, KY BL/TR 5-11/175# d9.18																								
1909	StL N	6	21	1	6	0	0	0	0	4	0		.286	.400	.286	120	1	1	.909	0	119	477	/O-6(RF)	0.1
JAMES, CHARLIE Charles Wesley B 12.22.1937 St.Louis, MO BR/TR 6-1/195# d8.2																								
1960	StL N	43	50	5	9	1	0	2	5	1-0	0	12	.180	.196	.320	35	-5	0-0	.917	-0	98	111	O-37(23-7-9)	-0.5
1961	StL N	108	349	43	89	19	2	4	44	15-1	3	59	.255	.288	.355	64	-18	2-2	.962	-2	103	44	O-90(39-4-56)	-2.5
1962	StL N	129	388	50	107	13	4	8	59	10-1	4	58	.276	.301	.392	77	-13	3-4	.988	-4	91	87	*O-116(17-1-104)	-2.5
1963	StL N	116	347	34	93	14	2	10	45	10-0	2	64	.268	.291	.406	91	-5	2-1	.994	5	117	71	*O-101(82-1-25)	-0.5
1964	†StL N	88	233	24	52	9	1	5	17	11-1	1	58	.223	.261	.335	61	-12	0-0	.963	-1	95	96	O-60(46-0-14)	-1.6
1965	Cin N	26	39	2	8	0	0	0	2	1-0	0	9	.205	.225	.205	21	-4	0-0	.909	-0	107	0	/O-7(3-0-4)	-0.5
Total	6	510	1406	158	358	56	9	29	172	48-3	10	260	.255	.283	.369	71	-57	7-7	.976	-2	102	73	O-411(210-13-212)	-8.1
JAMES, CLEO Cleo Joel B 8.31.1940 Clarksdale, MS BR/TR 5-10/176# d4.15																								
1968	LA N	10	10	2	2	1	0	0	0	0-0	0	6	.200	.200	.300	52	-1	0-0	1.000	0	160	0	/O-2(LF)	-0.1
1970	Chi N	100	176	33	37	7	2	3	14	17-5	5	24	.210	.298	.324	59	-10	5-0	1.000	0	95	159	O-90(5-83-2)	-1.0
1971	Chi N	54	150	25	43	7	0	2	13	10-0	6	16	.287	.353	.373	93	-1	6-2	.979	1	97	170	O-48(1-35-14)/3-2	-0.1
1973	Chi N	44	45	9	5	0	0	0	0	1-0	0	6	.111	.130	.111	-30	-8	5-0	.960	1	103	154	O-22(14-8-1)	-0.7
Total	4	208	381	69	87	15	2	5	27	28-5	11	52	.228	.299	.318	63	-20	16-2	.988	2	97	161	O-162(22-126-17)/3-2	-1.9
JAMES, DION Dion B 11.9.1962 Philadelphia, PA BL/TL 6-1/170# d9.16																								
1983	Mil A	11	20	1	2	0	0	0	1	2-0	0	2	.100	.182	.100	-22	-3	1-0	1.000	-0	78	220	/O-9(4-8-1),D-2	-0.4
1984	Mil A	128	387	52	114	19	5	1	30	32-1	3	41	.295	.351	.377	106	4	10-10	.989	3	106	104	*O-118(2-30-93)	0.1
1985	Mil A	18	49	5	11	1	0	0	3	6-0	0	6	.224	.309	.245	54	-3	0-0	1.000	-3	67	0	O-11(CF)/D-3	-0.6
1987	Atl N	134	494	80	154	37	6	10	61	70-2	2	63	.312	.397	.472	124	20	10-8	**.996**	-8	92	55	*O-126(29-99-0)	1.0
1988	Atl N	132	386	46	99	17	5	3	30	58-5	1	59	.256	.353	.350	98	1	9-9	.987	-4	93	82	*O-120(86-49-3)	-0.7
1989	Atl N	63	170	15	44	7	0	1	11	25-2	1	23	.259	.355	.318	92	-1	1-3	1.000	1	106	0	O-46(26-1-23)/1-8	-0.2
	Cle A	71	245	26	75	11	0	4	29	24-4	0	26	.306	.368	.400	114	5	1-4	.976	1	115	52	O-37(26-10-0),D-27/1-2	0.3
1990	Cle A	87	248	28	68	15	2	1	22	27-3	1	23	.274	.347	.363	99	1	5-3	.996	-4	87	84	1-35,O-33(24-8-0),D-10	-0.6
1992	NY A	67	145	24	38	8	0	3	17	22-0	1	15	.262	.359	.379	109	3	1-0	1.000	-4	77	44	O-46(8-12-27)/D-5	-0.2
1993	NY A	115	343	62	114	21	2	7	36	31-1	2	31	.332	.390	.466	134	17	0-0	.966	-8	82	82	*O-103(91-14-1)/1D	0.6
1995	†NY A	85	209	22	60	6	1	2	26	20-2	0	16	.287	.346	.354	85	-5	4-1	.968	-2	77	0	O-29(23-0-6),D-27/1-6	-0.9
1996	NY A	6	12	1	2	0	0	0	0	1-0	0	2	.167	.231	.167	3	-2	1-0	1.000	-1	56	0	/O-4(3-0-1),D	-0.2
Total	11	917	2708	362	781	142	21	32	266	318-20	11	307	.288	.364	.392	107	37	43-38	.986	-29	93	64	O-682(322-242-155)/D-76,1-52	-1.8
JAMES, CHRIS Donald Chris B 10.4.1962 Rusk, TX BR/TR 6-1/190# d4.23 OF Total (322-LF 51-CF 229-RF)																								
1986	Phi N	16	46	5	13	3	0	1	5	1-0	0	13	.283	.298	.413	91	-1	0-0	1.000	-1	90	0	O-11(4-7-0)	-0.2
1987	Phi N	115	358	48	105	20	6	17	54	27-0	2	67	.293	.344	.525	123	10	3-1	.990	2	109	78	*O-108(96-16-5)	0.9
1988	Phi N	150	566	57	137	24	1	19	66	31-2	3	73	.242	.283	.389	90	-9	7-4	.989	-2	110	124	*O-116(8-27-101)/3-31	-1.5
1989	Phi N	45	179	14	37	4	0	2	19	4-0	0	23	.207	.223	.263	39	-15	3-1	.985	-2	89	155	O-37(LF),3-11	-2.0
	SD N	87	303	41	80	13	2	11	46	22-2	1	45	.264	.314	.429	111	3	2-1	.987	1	101	75	O-79(50-0-29)/3-6	0.2
	Year	132	482	55	117	17	2	13	65	26-2	1	68	.243	.281	.367	84	-12	5-2	.986	-1	97	101	*O-116(87-0-29),3-17	-1.8
1990	Cle A	140	528	62	158	32	4	12	70	31-4	4	71	.299	.341	.443	119	12	4-3	1.000	0	95	124	*D-124,O-14(12-1-1)	0.8
1991	Cle A	115	437	31	104	16	2	5	41	18-2	4	61	.238	.273	.318	63	-23	3-4	1.000	1	103	86	D-60,O-39(25-0-18),1-15	-2.8
1992	SF N	111	248	25	60	10	4	5	32	14-2	2	45	.242	.285	.375	91	-4	2-3	.974	2	109	82	O-62(60-0-2)	-0.5
1993	Hou N	65	129	19	33	10	1	6	19	15-2	1	34	.256	.333	.488	122	4	2-0	.958	4	121	195	O-34(16-0-18)	0.7
	Tex A	8	31	5	11	1	0	3	7	3-0	0	6	.355	.412	.677	195	4	0-0	1.000	-0	105	0	/O-7(4-0-4)	0.3
1994	Tex A	52	133	28	34	8	4	7	19	20-0	3	38	.256	.361	.534	128	6	0-0	1.000	-2	87	75	O-48(1-0-47)	0.1
1995	KC A	26	58	6	18	3	0	2	7	6-0	1	10	.310	.373	.466	118	2	1-0	1.000	0	130	0	D-14/O-5(LF)	0.1
	Bos A	16	24	2	4	1	0	0	1	1-0	0	4	.167	.200	.208	6	-3	0-0	1.000	1	141	0	/O-8(4-0-4),D-6	-0.3
	Year	42	82	8	22	4	0	2	8	7-0	1	14	.268	.326	.390	86	-2	1-0	1.000	1	137	0	D-20,O-13(9-0-4)	-0.2
Total	10	946	3040	343	794	145	24	90	386	193-14	21	490	.261	.307	.413	99	-14	27-17	.987	3	105	98	O-568L,D-204/3-48,1-15	-4.2
JAMES, SKIP Philip Robert B 10.21.1949 Elmhurst, IL BL/TL 6/185# d9.12																								
1977	SF N	10	15	3	4	1	0	0	3	2-0	0	3	.267	.353	.333	86	0	0-0	1.000	1	134	53	/1-9	0.0
1978	SF N	41	21	5	2	1	0	0	3	4-0	0	5	.095	.240	.143	10	-2	1-0	1.000	1	143	92	1-27	-0.2
Total	2	51	36	8	6	2	0	0	6	6-0	0	8	.167	.286	.222	42	-2	1-0	1.000	1	139	77	/1-36	-0.2

Year	Tm Lg	G	AB	R	H	2B	3B	HR	RBI	BB-IB	HP	SO	AVG	OBP	SLG	AOPS	ABR	SB-CS	FA	FR	Rng	Thr	G at Pos	BFW
JAMES, BERNIE Robert Byrne B 9.2.1905 Angleton, TX D 8.1.1994 San Antonio, TX BB/TR 5-9.5/150# d5.6																								
1929	Bos N	46	101	12	31	3	2	0	9	9	1	13	.307	.369	.376	89	-2	3	.940	-7	74	75	2-32/O(CF)	-0.7
1930	Bos N	8	11	1	2	1	0	0	1	0	0	1	.182	.182	.273	8	-2	0	.941	0	118	53	/2-7	-0.1
1933	NY N	60	125	22	28	2	1	1	10	8	0	12	.224	.271	.280	58	-7	5	.948	1	105	78	2-26/S-6,3-5	-0.4
Total	3	114	237	35	61	6	3	1	20	17	1	26	.257	.310	.321	70	-11	8	.944	-5	91	75	/2-65,S-6,3-5,O(CF)	-1.2
JAMIESON, CHARLIE Charles Devine "Cuckoo" B 2.7.1893 Paterson, NJ D 10.27.1969 Paterson, NJ BL/TL 5-8.5/165# d9.20 ▲																								
1915	Was A	17	68	9	19	3	2	0	7	6	0	9	.279	.338	.382	113	1	0	1.000	3	111	232	O-17(LF)	0.3
1916	Was A	64	145	16	36	4	0	0	13	18	0	18	.248	.331	.276	83	-2	5	.913	0	105	105	O-41(24-2-15)/1-4,P	-0.4
1917	Was A	20	35	4	6	2	0	0	2	6	0	5	.171	.293	.229	60	-1	0	.875	-1	104	0	/O-9(LF),P	-0.3
	Phi A	85	345	41	92	6	2	0	27	37	2	36	.267	.341	.296	96	-1	8	.937	-4	86	104	O-83(RF)	-1.1
	Year	105	380	45	98	8	2	0	29	43	2	41	.258	.336	.289	92	-2	8	.930	-5	87	96	O-92(9-0-83)/P	-1.4
1918	Phi A	110	416	50	84	11	2	0	11	54	2	30	.202	.297	.238	61	-18	11	.970	-2	94	101	*O-102(0-1-101)/P-5	-2.9
1919	Cle A	26	17	3	6	2	1	0	2	0	0	2	.353	.353	.588	153	1	2	.750	-0	58	0	/P-4,O-3(0-2-1)	0.0
1920	†Cle A	108	370	69	118	17	7	1	40	41	1	26	.319	.388	.411	108	5	2-9	.966	2	100	122	O-98(93-5-0)/1-4	0.1
1921	Cle A	140	536	94	166	33	10	1	46	67	1	27	.310	.387	.414	103	5	8-4	.974	3	100	108	*O-137(125-19-0)	-0.2
1922	Cle A	145	567	87	183	29	11	3	57	54	6	22	.323	.388	.429	112	11	15-9	.978	3	100	107	*O-144(141-2-1)/P-2	0.3
1923	Cle A	152	644	130	**222**	36	12	2	51	80	6	37	.345	.422	.447	129	31	18-14	.974	5	109	95	*O-152(LF)	2.2
1924	Cle A	143	594	98	213	34	8	3	54	47	2	15	.359	.407	.458	121	19	21-12	.974	2	106	72	*O-139(LF)	1.0
1925	Cle A	138	557	109	165	24	5	4	42	72	3	26	.296	.380	.379	92	-5	14-18	.955	5	108	101	*O-135(LF)	-1.3
1926	Cle A	143	555	89	166	33	7	2	45	53	1	22	.299	.361	.395	96	-3	9-7	.960	2	100	108	*O-143(LF)	-1.2
1927	Cle A	127	489	73	151	23	6	0	36	64	5	14	.309	.394	.380	101	4	7-9	.969	4	106	96	*O-127(LF)	-0.4
1928	Cle A	112	433	63	133	18	4	1	37	56	1	20	.307	.388	.374	100	2	3-12	.984	16	111	**195**	*O-111(LF)	0.6
1929	Cle A	102	364	56	106	22	1	0	26	50	1	12	.291	.378	.357	87	-4	2-13	.980	-3	93	84	O-93(LF)	-1.8
1930	Cle A	103	366	64	110	22	1	1	52	36	3	20	.301	.368	.374	85	-7	5-2	.955	-4	90	106	O-95(93-2-0)	-1.5
1931	Cle A	28	43	7	13	2	1	0	4	5	0	1	.302	.375	.395	97	0	1-1	.833	-1	82	0	/O-7(6-1-0)	-0.2
1932	Cle A	16	16	0	1	1	0	0	0	2	1	3	.063	.211	.125	-10	-3	0-0	1.000	1	87	739	/O-2(RF)	-0.2
Total	18	1779	6560	1062	1990	322	80	18	552	748	35	345	.303	.378	.385	101	35	131-110	.967	29	101	108	*O-1638(1408-34-203)/P-13,1-8	-7.0
JANOWICZ, VIC Victor Felix B 2.26.1930 Elyria, OH D 2.27.1996 Columbus, OH BR/TR 5-9/185# d5.31																								
1953	Pit N	42	123	10	31	3	1	2	8	5	1	31	.252	.287	.341	63	-7	0-1	.937	-9	*59*	*111*	C-35	-1.5
1954	Pit N	41	73	10	11	3	0	0	2	7	1	23	.151	.235	.192	13	-9	0-0	.904	0	106	98	3-18/O(LF)	-1.0
Total	2	83	196	20	42	6	1	2	10	12	2	54	.214	.267	.286	44	-16	0-1	.937	-9	*59*	*111*	/C-35,3-18,O(LF)	-2.5
JANSEN, RAY Raymond William B 1.16.1889 St.Louis, MO D 3.19.1934 St.Louis, MO BR/TR 5-11/155# d9.30																								
1910	StL A	1	5	0	4	0	0	0	0	0	0		.800	.800	.800	428	2	0	.700	-0	122	0	/3	0.2
JANTZEN, HEINIE Walter C. B 4.9.1890 Chicago, IL D 4.1.1948 Hines, IL BR/TR 5-11.5/170# d6.29																								
1912	StL A	31	119	10	22	0	1	1	8	4	1		.185	.218	.227	28	-12	3	1.000	3	111	132	O-31(RF)	-1.1
JANVRIN, HAL Harold Chandler "Childe Harold" B 8.27.1892 Haverhill, MA D 3.1.1962 Boston, MA BR/TR 5-11.5/168# d7.9 Mil 1918 OF Total (17-LF 4-CF 1-RF)																								
1911	Bos A	9	27	2	4	1	0	0	1	3	1		.148	.258	.185	25	-3	0	.733	-2	75	0	/3-5,1-4	-0.5
1913	Bos A	87	276	18	57	5	1	3	25	23	2	27	.207	.272	.264	56	-16	17	.923	-10	97	49	S-48,3-19/2-8,1-6	-2.4
1914	Bos A	145	492	65	117	18	6	1	51	38	3	50	.238	.296	.305	81	-12	29-20	.919	-18	89	78	2-59,1-57,S-20/3-6	-3.4
1915	†Bos A	99	316	41	85	9	1	0	37	14	8	27	.269	.317	.304	88	-5	8-14	.917	-17	90	73	S-64,3-20/2-8	-2.2
1916	†Bos A	117	310	32	69	11	4	0	26	32	2	32	.223	.299	.284	75	-9	6	.921	-12	81	130	S-59,2-39/1-4,3-4	-2.0
1917	Bos A	55	127	21	25	3	0	0	8	11	1	13	.197	.266	.220	49	-8	2	.940	-0	107	137	2-38,S-10/1	-0.8
1919	Was A	61	208	17	37	4	1	1	13	19	2	17	.178	.253	.221	34	-18	8	.927	-22	75	65	2-56/S-2	-4.3
	StL N	7	14	1	3	1	0	0	1	2	0	2	.214	.313	.286	86	0	0	1.000	-1	38	0	/2-2,S3	-0.1
1920	StL N	87	270	33	74	8	4	1	28	17	0	19	.274	.317	.344	93	-3	5-6	.926	-1	82	120	S-27,1-25,O-20(16-4-0)/2-6	-0.5
1921	StL N	18	32	5	9	1	0	0	5	1	0	0	.281	.303	.313	65	-2	1-0	.968	0	94	126	/1-9,2	-0.2
	Bro N	44	92	8	18	4	0	0	14	7	0	6	.196	.253	.239	30	-9	3-1	.922	-4	91	46	S-17,2-10/1-8,3-5,O(RF)	-1.2
	Year	62	124	13	27	5	0	0	19	8	0	6	.218	.265	.258	38	-11	4-1	.922	-4	81	65	1-17,S-17,2-11/3-5,O(RF)	-1.4
1922	Bro N	30	57	7	17	3	1	0	1	4	0	4	.298	.344	.386	89	-1	0-0	.889	-3	111	60	2-15/S-4,3-2,1O(LF)	-0.3
Total	10	759	2221	250	515	68	18	6	210	171	19	197	.232	.292	.287	70	-86	79-41	.907	-90	87	92	S-252,2-242,1-115/3-62,O-22L	-17.9
JARVIS, ROY Leroy Gilbert B 6.27.1926 Shawnee, OK D 1.13.1990 Oklahoma City, OK BR/TR 5-9/160# d4.30 Mil 1944-46																								
1944	Bro N	1	1	0	0	0	0	0	0	0	0	1	.000	.000	.000	-99	0	0	1.000	-0	*0*	*0*	/C	0.0
1946	Pit N	2	4	0	1	0	0	0	0	1	0	1	.250	.400	.250	84	0	0	.800	-1	*44*	*0*	/C	-0.1
1947	Pit N	18	45	4	7	1	0	1	4	6	0	5	.156	.255	.244	32	-4	0	.967	-1	*94*	*100*	C-15	-0.4
Total	3	21	50	4	8	1	0	1	4	7	0	7	.160	.263	.240	34	-4	0	.955	-1	*88*	*90*	/C-17	-0.5
JATA, PAUL Paul B 9.4.1949 Astoria, NY BR/TR 6-1/190# d4.19																								
1972	Det A	32	74	8	17	2	0	0	3	7-0	0	14	.230	.296	.257	64	-3	0-1	.991	0	104	72	1-12,O-10(5-0-5)/C	-0.5
JAVIER, AL Ignacio Alfredo (born Wilkes (Javier)) B 2.4.1954 San Pedro De Macoris, D.R. BR/TR 5-11/170# d9.9																								
1976	Hou N	8	24	1	5	0	0	0	0	2-1	0	5	.208	.269	.208	41	-2	0-0	1.000	-1	57	0	/O-7(4-0-4)	-0.4
JAVIER, JULIAN Manuel Julian (Liranzo) B 8.9.1936 San Francisco De Macoris, D.R. BR/TR 6-1/175# d5.28 s-Stan																								
1960	StL N	119	451	55	107	19	8	4	21	21-1	1	72	.237	.273	.341	62	-25	19-4	.962	10	105	98	*2-119	-0.3
1961	StL N	113	445	58	124	14	3	2	41	30-1	2	51	.279	.326	.337	70	-19	11-4	.966	2	105	101	*2-113	-0.6
1962	StL N	155	598	97	157	25	5	7	39	47-0	1	73	.263	.316	.356	73	-22	26-9	.977	-1	100	107	*2-151/S-4	-0.7
1963	StL N★	161	609	82	160	27	9	9	46	24-1	6	86	.263	.296	.381	86	-12	18-10	.969	-12	94	99	*2-161	-1.0
1964	†StL N	155	535	66	129	19	5	12	65	30-7	1	82	.241	.282	.363	74	-19	9-7	.966	2	99	114	*2-154	-0.5
1965	StL N	77	229	34	52	6	4	2	23	8-2	3	44	.227	.260	.314	56	-14	5-5	.975	-2	100	105	2-69	-1.2
1966	StL N	147	460	52	105	13	5	7	31	26-2	1	63	.228	.269	.324	64	-23	11-5	.981	4	104	114	*2-145	-0.8
1967	†StL N	140	520	68	146	16	3	14	64	25-3	1	92	.281	.314	.404	106	2	6-7	.965	-21	92	86	*2-138	-0.9
1968	†StL N★	139	519	54	135	25	4	4	52	24-2	1	61	.260	.291	.347	93	-6	10-3	.976	-19	90	91	*2-139	-1.4
1969	StL N	143	493	59	139	28	2	10	42	40-11	1	74	.282	.336	.408	107	5	8-4	.967	-19	98	86	*2-141	-0.5
1970	StL N	139	513	62	129	16	3	2	42	24-6	1	70	.251	.284	.306	58	-32	6-4	.980	16	**113**	92	*2-137	-0.7
1971	StL N	90	259	32	67	6	4	3	28	9-3	2	33	.259	.286	.347	76	-9	5-1	.978	-4	95	90	2-80/3	-0.8
1972	†Cin N	44	91	3	19	2	0	2	12	6-0	0	11	.209	.255	.297	61	-5	1-0	.896	-3	94	154	3-19/2-5,1	-0.9
Total	13	1622	5722	722	1469	216	55	78	506	314-39	21	812	.257	.296	.355	78	-179	135-63	.972	-45	99	99	*2-1552/3-20,S-4,1	-10.3
JAVIER, STAN Stanley Julian Antonio (De Javier) B 1.9.1964 San Francisco De Macoris, D.R. BB/TR 6/185# d4.15 f-Julian OF Total (465-LF 691-CF 492-RF)																								
1984	NY A	7	7	1	1	0	0	0	0	0-0	0	1	.143	.143	.143	-22	-1	0-0	1.000	-1	53	0	/O-5(0-3-3)	-0.2
1986	Oak A	59	114	13	23	8	0	0	8	16-0	1	27	.202	.305	.272	63	-5	8-0	1.000	3	120	50	O-51(3-49-0)/D-2	0.0
1987	Oak A	81	151	22	28	3	1	2	9	19-3	0	33	.185	.276	.258	46	-12	3-2	.983	2	105	138	O-71(8-52-15)/1-6,D	-1.1
1988	†Oak A	125	397	49	102	13	3	2	35	32-1	2	63	.257	.313	.320	81	-10	20-1	.980	2	102	108	*O-115(69-45-29)/1-4,D-2	-0.7
1989	†Oak A	112	310	42	77	12	3	1	28	31-1	1	45	.248	.317	.316	82	-7	12-2	.991	5	113	65	*O-107(23-28-72)/12	-0.3
1990	Oak A	19	33	4	8	0	2	0	3	3-0	0	6	.242	.306	.364	90	-1	0-0	1.000	1	130	0	O-13(4-4-5)/D-2	0.0
	LA N	104	276	56	84	9	4	3	24	37-2	0	44	.304	.384	.399	120	9	15-7	1.000	6	123	51	O-87(9-70-12)	1.4
1991	LA N	121	176	21	36	5	3	1	11	16-0	0	36	.205	.268	.284	57	-10	7-1	.986	-1	95	43	O-69(49-7-18)/1-2	-1.2
1992	LA N	56	58	6	11	3	0	1	5	6-2	1	11	.190	.277	.293	63	-3	1-2	1.000	-1	83	0	O-27(15-2-11)	-0.5
	Phi N	74	276	36	72	14	1	0	24	31-0	2	43	.261	.338	.319	88	-3	17-1	.986	11	127	189	O-74(27-49-1)	1.1
	Year	130	334	42	83	17	1	1	29	37-2	3	54	.249	.327	.314	84	-6	18-3	.987	10	121	165	*O-101(42-51-12)	0.6
1993	Cal A	92	237	33	69	10	4	3	28	27-1	1	33	.291	.362	.405	104	1	12-2	.981	-4	96	66	O-64(36-16-16),1-12/2-2,D	-0.2
1994	Oak A	109	419	75	114	23	0	10	44	49-1	2	76	.272	.349	.399	101	2	24-7	.986	1	104	55	*O-108(12-102-1)/13	0.6
1995	Oak A	130	442	81	123	20	2	8	56	49-3	4	63	.278	.353	.387	98	0	36-5	**1.000**	9	**118**	49	*O-124(32-101-1)/3	1.3
1996	SF N	71	274	44	74	25	0	2	22	25-0	2	51	.270	.336	.383	93	-2	14-2	.984	4	119	53	O-71(0-53-18)	0.4
1997	†SF N	142	440	69	126	16	4	8	50	56-1	5	70	.286	.368	.395	104	4	25-3	.977	0	112	28	*O-130(5-46-94)/1-3	0.5
1998	SF N	135	417	63	121	13	5	4	49	65-4	1	63	.290	.385	.374	108	7	21-5	.986	-7	98	0	*O-121(6-29-95)	-0.1
1999	SF N	112	333	49	92	15	1	3	30	29-4	1	55	.276	.335	.354	81	-10	13-6	.976	-1	98	76	O-94(51-3-42)	-1.3
	†Hou N	20	64	12	21	4	1	0	4	9-0	0	8	.328	.405	.422	113	2	3-1	1.000	-0	94	106	O-18(7-6-10)/D	0.1
	Year	132	397	61	113	19	2	3	34	38-4	1	63	.285	.347	.365	86	-8	16-7	.980	-1	97	81	*O-112(58-9-52)/D	-1.2
2000	†Sea A	105	342	61	94	18	5	5	40	42-2	0	64	.275	.351	.401	94	-3	4-3	.993	-4	85	124	O-88(47-13-38)/1-3,D-4	-0.9

Year	Tm Lg	G	AB	R	H	2B	3B	HR	RBI	BB-IB	HP	SO	AVG	OBP	SLG	AOPS	ABR	SB-CS	FA	FR	Rng	Thr	G at Pos	BFW
2001	†Sea A	89	281	44	82	14	1	4	33	36-1	2	47	.292	.375	.391	109	5	11-1	.993	-1	105	25	O-76(62-13-11)/1-6,D-2	0.4
Total	17	1763	5047	781	1358	225	40	57	503	578-26	25	839	.269	.345	.363	93	-37	246-51	.988	23	107	66	*O-1513C/1-38,D-15,2-3,3-2	-0.7
JEANES, TEX Ernest Lee B 12.19.1900 Maypearl, TX D 4.5.1973 Longview, TX BR/TR 6/176# d4.20																								
1921	Cle A	5	3	2	2	1	0	0	4	1	0	0	.667	.750	1.000	338	1	0-0	1.000	1	49	854	/O-5(1-2-1)	0.2
1922	Cle A	1	1	0	0	0	0	0	0	1	0	0	.000	.500	.000	39	0	0-0	—	-0	0	0	/PO(LF)	0.0
1925	Was A	15	19	2	5	1	0	1	4	3	0	2	.263	.364	.474	113	0	1-0	1.000	-1	90	0	O-13(1-10-2)	0.0
1926	Was A	21	30	6	7	2	0	0	3	0	0	3	.233	.233	.300	39	-3	0-0	1.000	0	133	0	O-14(3-10-1)	-0.3
1927	NY N	11	20	5	6	0	0	0	0	2	0	2	.300	.364	.300	79	-1	0	1.000	1	123	166	/O-6(4-0-2),P	0.0
Total	5	53	73	15	20	4	0	1	11	7	0	7	.274	.338	.370	85	-3	1-0	1.000	1	114	102	/O-39(10-22-6),P-2	-0.1
JEFFCOAT, HAL Harold Bentley B 9.6.1924 W.Columbia, SC BR/TR 5-10.5/185# d4.20 b-George ▲																								
1948	Chi N	134	473	53	132	16	4	4	42	24	1	68	.279	.315	.355	85	-12	8	.976	3	102	146	*O-119(CF)	-1.2
1949	Chi N	108	363	43	89	18	6	2	26	20	1	48	.245	.286	.344	70	-17	12	.963	0	97	148	*O-101(1-68-32)	-1.9
1950	Chi N	66	179	21	42	13	1	2	18	6	0	23	.235	.259	.352	60	-11	7	.967	0	91	177	O-53(12-11-31)	-1.2
1951	Chi N	113	278	44	76	20	2	4	27	16	1	23	.273	.315	.403	90	-4	8-4	.989	5	102	175	O-87(14-39-34)	-0.1
1952	Chi N	102	297	29	65	17	2	4	30	15	1	40	.219	.259	.330	61	-16	7-2	.996	10	108	209	O-95(CF)	-0.8
1953	Chi N	106	183	22	43	3	1	4	22	21	0	26	.235	.314	.328	66	-9	5-0	.973	5	113	116	*O-100(2-99-0)	-0.6
1954	Chi N	56	31	13	8	2	1	1	6	1	0	7	.258	.265	.484	94	-1	2-0	.889	0	112	69	P-43/O-3(CF)	0.0
1955	Chi N	52	23	3	4	0	0	1	1	2-0	0	9	.174	.240	.304	43	1	0-0	.903	1	144	85	P-50	0.0
1956	Cin N	49	54	5	8	2	0	0	5	3-0	0	20	.148	.193	.185	2	-1	0-1	.969	3	**148**	178	P-38	0.0
1957	Cin N	53	69	13	14	3	1	4	11	5-0	1	20	.203	.267	.449	82	6	0-0	.958	-1	90	202	P-37	0.0
1958	Cin N	50	9	2	5	0	0	0	0	1-0	0	2	.556	.600	.556	198	1	0-0	1.000	2	158	219	P-49/O(CF)	0.1
1959	Cin N	17	1	1	1	1	0	0	0	0-0	0	0	1.000	1.000	2.000	655	1	0-0	1.000	0	57	378	P-17	0.0
	StL N	12	3	0	0	0	0	0	0	0-0	0	3	.000	.000	.000	-94	0	0-0	1.000	-0	104	0	P-11	0.0
	Year	29	4	1	1	1	0	0	0	0-0	0	3	.250	.250	.500	90	0	0-0	1.000	-0	78	208	P-28	0.0
Total	12	918	1963	249	487	95	18	26	188	114-0	5	289	.248	.291	.355	73	-62	49-7	.978	29	102	160	O-559(29-435-97),P-245	-5.7
JEFFERIES, GREGG Gregory Scott B 8.1.1967 Burlingame, CA BB/TR 5-10/185# d9.6 OF Total (LF)																								
1987	NY N	6	6	0	3	1	0	0	2	0-0	0	0	.500	.500	.667	217	1	0-0	—	0			/H	0.1
1988	†NY N	29	109	19	35	8	2	6	17	8-0	0	10	.321	.364	.596	181	11	5-1	.979	-2	81	181	3-20,2-10	1.0
1989	NY N	141	508	72	131	28	2	12	56	39-8	5	46	.258	.314	.392	107	4	21-6	.975	-26	78	66	*2-123,3-20	-1.8
1990	NY N	153	604	96	171	**40**	3	15	68	46-2	5	40	.283	.337	.434	111	9	11-2	.976	-1	88	86	*2-118,3-34	1.3
1991	NY N	136	486	59	132	19	2	9	62	47-2	2	38	.272	.336	.374	101	1	26-5	.982	-15	87	42	2-77,3-51	-0.9
1992	KC A	152	604	66	172	36	3	10	75	43-4	1	29	.285	.329	.404	103	2	19-9	.939	2	106	87	*3-146/2D	0.5
1993	StL N★	142	544	89	186	24	3	16	83	62-7	2	32	.342	.408	.485	142	34	46-9	.993	-7	84	110	*1-140/2	2.1
1994	StL N★	103	397	52	129	27	1	12	55	45-12	1	26	.325	.391	.489	131	20	12-5	.993	-7	77	111	*1-102	0.4
1995	Phi N	114	480	69	147	31	2	11	56	35-5	0	26	.306	.349	.448	109	6	9-5	.994	-5	76	112	1-59,O-55(LF)	-0.7
1996	Phi N	104	404	59	118	17	3	7	51	36-6	1	21	.292	.348	.401	97	-2	20-6	.998	5	108	94	1-53,O-51(LF)	-0.1
1997	Phi N	130	476	68	122	25	3	11	48	53-7	2	27	.256	.333	.391	89	-8	12-6	.986	1	101	69	*O-124(LF)	-1.0
1998	Phi N	125	483	65	142	22	3	8	48	29-4	1	27	.294	.331	.402	91	-7	11-3	.994	-4	82	100	*O-121(LF)	-1.3
	Ana A	19	72	7	25	6	0	1	10	0-0	0	5	.347	.347	.472	110	1	1-0	1.000	0	113	0	O-15(LF)/1-3	0.1
1999	Det A	70	205	22	41	8	0	6	18	13-1	4	11	.200	.258	.327	49	-17	3-4	1.000	0	239	41	D-45/1-3,2-2,O-2(LF)	-1.9
2000	Det A	41	142	18	39	8	0	2	14	16-1	0	10	.275	.344	.373	85	-3	0-2	.994	-3	122	116	1-20,2-14/3-6,O(LF)D	-0.7
Total	14	1465	5520	761	1593	300	27	126	663	472-59	24	348	.289	.344	.421	107	52	196-63	.994	-62	87	108	1-380,O-369L,2-346,3-277/D-48	-2.9
JEFFERSON, REGGIE Reginald Jirod B 9.25.1968 Tallahassee, FL BL/TL (BB 1991-93) 6-4/215# d5.18																								
1991	Cin N	5	7	1	1	0	0	1	1	1-0	0	2	.143	.250	.571	120	0	0-0	1.000	0	113	346	/1-2	0.0
	Cle A	26	101	10	20	3	0	2	12	3-0	0	22	.198	.219	.287	39	-9	0-0	.993	2	133	122	1-26	-0.8
1992	Cle A	24	89	8	30	6	2	1	6	1-0	1	17	.337	.352	.483	134	3	0-0	.993	0	110	66	1-15/D-7	0.3
1993	Cle A	113	366	35	91	11	2	10	34	28-7	5	78	.249	.310	.372	83	-10	1-3	.976	-0	111	87	D-88,1-15	-1.8
1994	Sea A	63	162	24	53	11	0	8	32	17-5	1	32	.327	.392	.543	136	9	0-0	.981	1	156	143	D-32,1-13/O-2(LF)	0.7
1995	†Bos A	46	121	21	35	8	0	5	26	9-1	0	24	.289	.333	.479	106	1	0-0	1.000	1	152	127	D-32/1-7,O-2(LF)	-0.1
1996	Bos A	122	386	67	134	30	4	19	74	25-5	3	89	.347	.388	.593	141	24	0-0	.969	0	89	44	D-49,O-45(LF),1-16	1.6
1997	Bos A	136	489	74	156	33	1	13	67	24-5	7	93	.319	.358	.470	112	9	1-2	.975	-1	81	108	*D-119,1-12	-0.1
1998	Bos A	62	196	24	60	16	1	8	31	21-2	1	40	.306	.374	.520	127	8	0-0	.953	0	124	57	D-48/1-7	0.4
1999	Bos A	83	206	21	57	13	1	5	17	17-0	2	54	.277	.338	.422	90	-3	0-0	1.000	0	278	0	D-58/1-2	-0.6
Total	9	680	2123	285	637	131	11	72	300	146-25	20	451	.300	.349	.474	111	32	2-5	.986	5	129	100	D-433,1-115/O-49(LF)	-0.4
JEFFERSON, STAN Stanley B 12.4.1962 New York, NY BB/TR 5-11/175# d9.7																								
1986	NY N	14	24	6	5	1	0	1	3	2-0	1	8	.208	.296	.375	86	0	0-0	1.000	-0	98	0	/O-7(1-7-0)	-0.1
1987	SD N	116	422	59	97	8	7	8	29	39-2	2	92	.230	.296	.339	71	-20	34-11	.987	-0	103	50	*O-107(61-83-0)	-1.9
1988	SD N	49	111	16	16	1	2	1	4	9-0	1	22	.144	.211	.216	25	-11	5-1	1.000	-3	84	0	O-38(10-27-0)	-1.6
1989	NY A	10	12	1	1	0	0	0	1	0-0	0	4	.083	.083	.083	-54	-2	1-1	1.000	-1	53	0	/O-7(0-2-6),D	-0.3
	Bal A	35	127	19	33	7	0	4	20	4-0	1	22	.260	.284	.409	97	-1	9-3	.988	2	106	125	O-32(1-8-26)/D-2	0.1
	Year	45	139	20	34	7	0	4	21	4-0	1	26	.245	.267	.381	84	-4	10-4	.988	1	102	116	O-39(1-10-32)/D-3	-0.2
1990	Bal A	10	19	1	0	0	0	0	0	2-0	0	8	.000	.095	.000	-74	-5	1-0	1.000	-1	93	0	/O-5(0-3-5),D	-0.5
	Cle A	49	98	21	27	8	0	2	10	8-0	2	18	.276	.333	.418	112	2	8-4	.985	2	103	247	O-34(23-11-1)/D-5	0.4
	Year	59	117	22	27	8	0	2	10	10-0	2	26	.231	.295	.350	83	-3	9-4	.987	2	102	212	O-39(23-14-6)/D-6	-0.1
1991	Cin N	13	19	2	1	0	0	0	0	1-0	0	3	.053	.100	.053	-54	-4	2-0	1.000	-1	56	0	/O-5(4-1-1)	-0.5
Total	6	296	832	125	180	25	9	16	67	65-2	7	177	.216	.276	.326	66	-41	60-20	.990	-2	99	76	O-235(100-142-39)/D-9	-4.4
JEFFRIES, IRV Irvine Franklin B 9.10.1905 Louisville, KY D 6.8.1982 Louisville, KY BR/TR 5-10/175# d4.30																								
1930	Chi A	40	97	14	23	3	0	2	11	3	2	2	.237	.275	.330	54	-7	1-2	.976	-1	97	135	3-20,S-13	-0.6
1931	Chi A	79	223	29	50	10	0	2	16	14	0	9	.224	.270	.296	52	-16	3-0	.949	1	102	42	3-61/2-6,S-5,O(CF)	-1.2
1934	Phi N	56	175	28	43	6	0	4	19	15	0	10	.246	.305	.349	66	-8	2	.962	3	101	147	2-52/3	-0.2
Total	3	175	495	71	116	19	0	8	46	32	2	21	.234	.284	.321	58	-31	6-2	.955	3	100	60	/3-82,2-58,S-18,O(CF)	-2.0
JELIC, CHRIS Christopher John B 12.16.1963 Bethlehem, PA BR/TR 5-11/180# d9.30																								
1990	NY N	4	11	2	1	0	0	1	1	0-0	0	3	.091	.091	.364	19	-1	0-0	1.000	-1	22	0	/O-4(LF)	-0.2
JELINCICH, FRANK Frank Anthony "Jelly" B 9.3.1919 San Jose, CA D 6.27.1992 Rochester, MN BR/TR 6-2/198# d9.6 Mil 1942-45																								
1941	Chi N	4	8	0	1	0	0	0	2	1	0	2	.125	.222	.125	-1	-1	0	1.000	-0	45	0	/O-2(LF)	-0.1
JELKS, GREG Gregory Dion B 8.16.1961 Cherokee, AL BR/TR 6-2/190# d8.20																								
1987	Phi N	10	11	2	1	1	0	0	0	3-0	0	4	.091	.286	.182	26	-1	0-0	.750	-0	67	0	/3-4,1-2,O(LF)	-0.2
JELTZ, STEVE Larry Steven B 5.28.1959 Paris, France BB/TR (BR 1983-85) 5-11/180# d7.17 OF Total (2-LF 2-CF 11-RF)																								
1983	Phi N	13	8	0	1	0	1	0	1	1-0	0	2	.125	.222	.375	63	-1	0-0	1.000	-1	43	201	/2-4,S-2,3-2	-0.1
1984	Phi N	28	68	7	14	0	1	1	7	7-1	0	11	.206	.276	.279	57	-4	2-1	.992	7	123	61	S-27/3	0.5
1985	Phi N	89	196	17	37	4	1	0	12	26-4	0	55	.189	.283	.219	41	-15	1-1	.958	-3	98	87	S-86	-1.1
1986	Phi N	145	439	44	96	11	4	0	36	65-9	1	97	.219	.320	.262	60	-22	6-3	.967	-5	100	100	*S-141	-1.3
1987	Phi N	114	293	37	68	9	6	0	12	39-4	1	54	.232	.324	.304	66	-14	1-2	.971	-6	91	97	*S-114/O(LF)	-1.1
1988	Phi N	148	379	39	71	11	4	0	27	59-8	0	58	.187	.295	.237	54	-21	3-0	.976	-4	97	93	*S-148	-1.6
1989	Phi N	116	263	28	64	7	3	4	25	45-6	1	44	.243	.356	.338	99	1	4-2	.985	3	90	59	S-63,3-30,2-23/O(CF)	0.9
1990	KC A	74	103	11	16	4	0	0	10	6-0	0	21	.155	.200	.194	11	-12	1-1	.977	-0	99	92	2-34,S-23,O-13(1-1-11)/3-3,D-3	-1.2
Total	8	727	1749	183	367	46	20	5	130	248-32	3	342	.210	.308	.268	61	-88	18-10	.971	-9	97	90	S-604/2-61,3-36,O-15R,D-3	-5.0
JENKINS, GEOFF Geoffrey Scott B 7.21.1974 Olympia, WA BL/TR 6-1/205# d4.24																								
1998	Mil N	84	262	33	60	12	1	9	28	20-4	2	61	.229	.288	.385	75	-10	1-3	.968	0	92	134	O-81(81-0-1)	-1.4
1999	Mil N	135	447	70	140	43	3	21	82	35-7	7	87	.313	.371	.564	134	23	5-1	.974	11	109	187	*O-128(LF)	2.8
2000	Mil N	135	512	100	155	36	4	34	94	33-6	15	135	.303	.360	.588	137	27	11-1	.975	7	101	145	*O-131(LF)	2.9
2001	Mil N	105	397	60	105	21	1	20	63	36-7	8	120	.264	.334	.474	109	5	4-2	.986	6	107	115	*O-104(LF)	0.7
2002	Mil N	67	243	35	59	17	1	10	29	22-1	6	60	.243	.320	.444	103	0	1-2	.992	4	103	172	O-66(LF)	0.1
2003	Mil N☆	124	487	81	144	30	2	28	95	58-10	6	120	.296	.375	.538	138	28	0-0	**1.000**	3	97	142	*O-123(LF)/D	2.4
Total	6	650	2348	379	663	159	12	122	391	204-35	44	583	.282	.349	.516	122	73	22-9	.983	30	102	149	O-633(633-0-1)/D	7.5

Year	Tm Lg	G	AB	R	H	2B	3B	HR	RBI	BB-IB	HP	SO	AVG	OBP	SLG	AOPS	ABR	SB-CS	FA	FR	Rng	Thr	G at Pos	BFW
JENKINS, JOHN John Robert B 7.7.1896 Bosworth, MO D 8.3.1968 Columbia, MO BR/TR 5-8/160# d8.5																								
1922	Chi A	5	3	0	0	0	0	0	1	0	0	2	.000	.000	.000	-99	-1	0-0	.000	-1	0	0	/2S	-0.1
JENKINS, JOE Joseph Daniel B 10.12.1890 Shelbyville, TN D 6.21.1974 Fresno, CA BR/TR 5-11/170# d4.30 Mil 1918																								
1914	StL A	19	32	0	4	1	1	0	0	1	0	11	.125	.152	.219	12	-4	2	.931	-3	*79*	*34*	/C-9	-0.6
1917	Chi A	10	9	0	1	0	0	0	2	0	0	5	.111	.111	.111	-32	-1	0	—	0	*0*	*0*	/C	-0.2
1919	Chi A	11	19	0	3	1	0	0	1	1	0	1	.158	.200	.211	15	-2	1	.824	-1	*121*	*102*	/C-4	-0.3
Total	3	40	60	0	8	2	1	0	3	2	0	17	.133	.161	.200	6	-7	3	.891	-4	*93*	*58*	/C-14	-1.1
JENKINS, TOM Thomas Griffith "Tut" B 4.10.1898 Camden, AL D 5.3.1979 Weymouth, MA BL/TR 6-1.5/174# d9.15																								
1925	Bos A	15	64	9	19	2	1	0	5	3	1	4	.297	.338	.359	77	-2	0-0	.938	-2	94	0	O-15(LF)	-0.5
1926	Bos A	21	50	3	9	1	1	0	6	3	0	7	.180	.226	.240	22	-6	0-0	1.000	-1	96	0	O-13(12-1-0)	-0.8
	Phi A	6	23	3	4	2	0	0	0	0	0	2	.174	.174	.261	12	-3	0-0	1.000	0	115	0	/O-6(5-0-1)	-0.4
	Year	27	73	6	13	3	1	0	6	3	0	9	.178	.211	.247	19	-9	0-0	1.000	-1	102	0	O-19(17-1-1)	-1.2
1929	StL A	21	22	1	4	0	1	0	0	4	0	8	.182	.308	.273	49	-2	0-0	1.000	-0	66	0	/O-3(0-1-2)	-0.2
1930	StL A	2	8	1	2	1	1	0	3	0	0	1	.250	.250	.625	110	0	0-0	1.000	-0	98	0	/O-2(RF)	0.0
1931	StL A	81	230	20	61	7	2	3	25	17	0	25	.265	.316	.352	73	-10	1-3	.952	-2	89	119	O-58(RF)	-1.4
1932	StL A	25	62	5	20	1	0	0	5	1	0	6	.323	.333	.339	70	-3	0-0	.939	1	111	197	O-12(RF)	-0.2
Total	6	171	459	42	119	14	6	3	44	28	1	53	.259	.303	.336	64	-26	1-3	.958	-4	95	86	O-109(32-2-75)	-3.5
JENNINGS, ALAMAZOO Alfred Gorden B 11.30.1850 Newport, KY D 11.2.1894 Cincinnati, OH d8.15 U2																								
1878	Mil N	1	2	0	0	0	0	0	0	1		0	.000	.333	.000	16	0		.429	-2			/C	-0.2
JENNINGS, HUGHIE Hugh Ambrose "Ee-Yah" B 4.2.1869 Pittston, PA D 2.1.1928 Scranton, PA BR/TR 5-8.5/165# d6.1 M16 C5 HF1945																								
1891	Lou AA	88	351	51	103	10	8	1	58	17	9	35	.293	.342	.376	107	1	12	.891	6	100	118	S-68,1-17/3-3	0.7
1892	Lou N	152	594	65	133	16	4	2	61	30	9	30	.224	.272	.274	71	-21	28	.907	15	105	111	*S-152	0.1
1893	Lou N	23	88	6	12	3	0	0	9	3	1	3	.136	.174	.170	-9	-14	0	.899	4	109	102	S-23	-0.8
	Bal N	16	55	6	14	0	0	1	6	4	3	3	.255	.339	.309	71	-2	0	.886	-3	79	70	S-15/O(RF)	-0.4
	Year	39	143	12	26	3	0	1	15	7	4	6	.182	.240	.224	25	-16	0	.895	1	98	91	S-38/O(RF)	-1.2
1894	†Bal N	128	501	134	168	28	16	4	109	37	**27**	17	.335	.411	.479	109	7	37	**.928**	**33**	112	129	*S-128	3.5
1895	†Bal N	**131**	529	159	204	41	7	4	125	24	**32**	17	.386	.444	.512	142	35	53	**.940**	**37**	102	**147**	*S-131	**6.3**
1896	†Bal N	130	521	125	209	27	9	0	121	19	**51**	11	.401	.472	.488	151	43	70	**.928**	31	107	**138**	*S-130	**6.7**
1897	†Bal N	117	439	133	156	26	9	2	79	42	**46**		.355	.463	.469	146	36	60	**.933**	23	105	128	*S-116	**5.5**
1898	Bal N	143	534	135	175	25	11	1	87	78	**46**		.328	.454	.421	149	44	28	.929	3	96	97	*S-115,2-27/O(RF)	**4.9**
1899	Bro N	16	41	7	7	0	2	0	6	9	2		.171	.346	.268	68	-2	4	.825	-5	64	80	S-11/1-4	-0.5
	Bal N	2	8	2	3	0	2	0	2	0	0		.375	.375	.875	227	1	0	1.000	-0	93	0	/2-2	0.1
	Bro N	51	175	35	57	3	8	0	34	13	17		.326	.424	.434	133	9	14	.987	-0	239	68	1-46/2S	0.8
	Year	69	224	44	67	3	12	0	42	22	19		.299	.408	.420	124	8	18	.985	-5	110	90	1-50,S-12/2-3	0.4
1900	†Bro N	115	441	61	120	18	6	1	69	31	20		.272	.348	.347	87	-7	31	.982	5	119	111	*1-112/2-2	-0.2
1901	Phi N	82	302	38	79	21	2	1	39	25	12		.262	.342	.354	100	2	13	.979	-3	85	57	1-80/2S	-0.3
1902	Phi N	78	290	32	79	13	4	1	32	14	11		.272	.330	.355	111	4	8	.983	2	118	81	1-69/S-5,2-4	0.5
1903	Bro N	6	17	2	4	0	0	0	1	1	1		.235	.316	.235	60	-1	1	1.000	-0	0	0	/O-4(1-0-3)	-0.1
1907	Det A	1	4	0	1	1	0	0	0	0	0		.250	.250	.500	133	0	0	.750	-1	99	0	/2SM	-0.1
1909	Det A	2	4	1	2	0	0	0	2	0	0		.500	.500	.500	207	0	0	1.000	0	182	477	/1-2,M	0.1
1910	Det A	1	0	0	0	0	0	0	0	0	0		—	—	—	—	0	0	—	0			/RM	0.0
1912	Det A	1	1	0	0	0	0	0	0	0	0		.000	.000	.000	-99	0	0	—	0			/HM	0.0
1918	Det A	1	0	0	0	0	0	0	0	0	0	0	—	—	—	—	0	0	1.000	-0	0	0	/1M	0.0
Total	18	1284	4895	992	1526	232	88	18	840	347	287	<u>116</u>	.312	.391	.406	118	135	359	.922	146	103	122	S-897,1-331/2-38,O-6(1-0-5),3-3	26.8
JENNINGS, DOUG James Douglas B 9.30.1964 Atlanta, GA BL/TL 5-10/170# d4.8																								
1988	Oak A	71	101	9	21	6	0	1	15	21-1	2	28	.208	.346	.297	88	0	0-1	1.000	-0	107	119	O-23(16-0-7),1-14/D-2	-0.2
1989	Oak A	4	4	0	0	0	0	0	0	0-0	0	2	.000	.000	.000	-99	-1	0-0	1.000	-0	76	0	/O-3(LF)	-0.1
1990	†Oak A	64	156	19	30	7	2	2	14	17-0	2	48	.192	.275	.301	65	-7	0-3	.984	-3	90	46	O-45(33-0-15)/1-4,D-8	-1.3
1991	Oak A	8	9	0	1	0	0	0	0	2-0	0	2	.111	.273	.111	11	-1	0-1	1.000	1	151	0	/O-6(LF)	-0.1
1993	Chi N	42	52	8	13	3	1	2	8	3-0	2	10	.250	.316	.462	107	0	0-0	1.000	-1	41	153	1-10	-0.1
Total	5	189	322	36	65	16	3	5	37	43-1	6	90	.202	.302	.317	76	-9	0-5	.991	-4	98	63	/O-77(58-0-22),1-28,D-10	-1.8
JENNINGS, ROBIN Robin Christopher B 4.11.1972 Singapore, Singapore BL/TL 6-2/205# d4.18																								
1996	Chi N	31	58	7	13	5	0	0	4	3-0	1	9	.224	.274	.310	52	-4	1-0	1.000	1	109	319	O-11(RF)	-0.3
1997	Chi N	9	18	1	3	1	0	0	2	0-0	0	2	.167	.158	.222	1	-3	0-0	1.000	-1	72	0	/O-5(4-2-0)	-0.3
1999	Chi N	5	5	0	1	0	0	0	0	0-0	0	2	.200	.200	.200	2	-1	0-0	—	0			/H	-0.1
2001	Oak A	20	52	4	13	3	0	0	4	2-0	0	6	.250	.273	.308	54	-3	0-0	1.000	-1	67	154	O-13(3-0-12)/1-6,D-2	-0.5
	Col N	1	3	0	0	0	0	0	0	0-0	0	1	.000	.000	.000	-82	-1	0-0	.000	-1	0	0	/O(LF)	-0.1
	Cin N	27	77	10	22	5	2	3	14	5-1	0	11	.286	.329	.519	110	1	0-0	.893	1	89	233	O-15(RF)/1-8	0.0
	Year	28	80	10	22	5	2	3	14	5-1	0	12	.275	.318	.500	102	0	0-0	.862	0	83	217	O-16(1-0-15)/1-8	-0.1
Total	4	93	213	22	52	14	2	3	24	10-1	1	31	.244	.279	.371	67	-11	1-0	.942	0	84	204	/O-45(8-2-38),1-14,D-2	-1.3
JENNINGS, BILL William Lee B 9.28.1925 St.Louis, MO BR/TR 6-2/175# d7.19																								
1951	StL A	64	195	20	35	10	2	0	13	26	0	42	.179	.276	.251	42	-16	1-0	.953	-8	91	74	S-64	-2.0
JENSEN, WOODY Forrest Docenus B 8.11.1907 Bremerton, WA D 10.5.2001 Wichita, KS BL/TL 5-10.5/160# d4.20																								
1931	Pit N	73	267	43	65	5	4	3	17	10	2	18	.243	.276	.326	62	-16	4	.974	3	116	51	O-67(64-3-0)	-1.7
1932	Pit N	7	5	2	0	0	0	0	0	0	0	2	.000	.000	.000	-99	-1	0	—	-0	0	0	/O(LF)	-0.1
1933	Pit N	70	196	29	58	7	3	0	15	8	2	2	.296	.330	.362	98	-1	1	.980	-1	106	30	O-40(LF)	-0.4
1934	Pit N	88	283	34	82	13	4	0	27	4	2	13	.290	.304	.364	76	-10	2	.993	-0	107	23	O-66(46-17-4)	-1.3
1935	Pit N	143	627	97	203	28	7	8	62	15	4	14	.324	.344	.429	103	1	9	.977	-6	93	59	*O-140(138-0-2)	-1.3
1936	Pit N	153	696	98	197	34	10	10	58	16	6	19	.283	.305	.404	87	-15	2	.975	-2	104	52	*O-153(152-1-0)	-2.5
1937	Pit N	124	509	77	142	23	9	5	45	15	1	29	.279	.301	.389	86	-12	2	.963	-2	103	58	*O-120(88-32-0)	-2.0
1938	Pit N	68	125	12	25	4	0	0	10	1	1	3	.200	.213	.232	22	-14	0	.900	-4	85	0	O-38(15-21-2)	-1.9
1939	Pit N	12	12	0	2	0	0	0	1	0	0	0	.167	.167	.167	-10	-2	0	1.000	1	0	1636	/O-3(0-1-2)	-0.1
Total	9	738	2720	392	774	114	37	26	235	69	18	100	.285	.307	.382	84	-70	20	.972	-12	102	50	O-628(544-75-10)	-11.3
JENSEN, JACKIE Jack Eugene B 3.9.1927 San Francisco, CA D 7.14.1982 Charlottesville, VA BR/TR 5-11/190# d4.18																								
1950	†NY A	45	70	13	12	2	2	1	5	7	0	8	.171	.247	.300	41	-7	4-0	.947	0	120	0	O-23(17-0-7)	-0.7
1951	NY A	56	168	30	50	8	1	8	25	18	1	18	.298	.369	.500	138	8	8-2	.974	2	101	158	O-48(21-27-1)	0.9
1952	NY A	7	19	3	2	1	1	0	2	4	0	4	.105	.261	.263	49	-1	1-0	1.000	-1	77	0	/O-5(CF)	-0.2
	Was A★	144	570	80	163	29	5	10	80	63	3	40	.286	.360	.407	117	13	17-6	.977	3	102	135	*O-143(0-7-142)	1.4
	Year	151	589	83	165	30	6	10	82	67	3	44	.280	.357	.402	115	12	18-6	.978	2	101	132	*O-148(0-12-142)	1.2
1953	Was A	147	552	87	147	32	8	10	84	73	5	51	.266	.357	.408	109	8	18-8	.983	-8	95	65	*O-146(0-1-145)	-0.5
1954	Bos A	152	580	92	160	25	7	25	117	79	2	52	.276	.359	.472	115	12	**22**-7	.986	-11	88	90	*O-151(8-106-44)	-0.3
1955	Bos A★	152	574	95	158	27	6	26	**116**	89-8	3	63	.275	.369	.479	118	15	16-7	.977	-4	96	90	*O-150(RF)	0.6
1956	Bos A	151	578	80	182	23	**11**	20	97	89-5	1	43	.315	.405	.497	123	20	11-3	.962	-5	93	108	*O-151(RF)	1.1
1957	Bos A	145	544	82	153	29	2	23	103	75-3	2	66	.281	.367	.469	121	17	8-5	.960	1	97	149	*O-144(4-0-143)	1.3
1958	Bos A★	154	548	83	157	31	0	35	**122**	99-7	3	65	.286	.396	.535	144	37	9-4	.981	-3	95	102	*O-153(2-0-153)	3.0
1959	Bos A	148	535	101	148	31	0	28	**112**	88-3	0	67	.277	.372	.492	131	25	20-5	.982	8	113	141	*O-146(0-7-142)	3.1
1961	Bos A	137	498	64	131	21	2	13	66	66-2	3	69	.263	.350	.392	96	-1	9-8	.986	7	105	136	*O-131(2-0-129)	-0.5
Total	11	1438	5236	810	1463	259	45	199	929	750-<u>28</u>	23	546	.279	.369	.460	119	146	143-55	.977	-10	98	112	*O-1391(54-153-1207)	9.2
JENSEN, MARCUS Marcus Christian B 12.14.1972 Oakland, CA BB/TR 6-4/195# d4.14																								
1996	SF N	9	19	4	4	1	0	0	4	8-0	0	7	.211	.444	.263	96	1	0-0	.955	1	154	166	/C-7	0.2
1997	SF N	30	74	5	11	2	0	1	3	7-1	0	23	.149	.222	.216	16	-9	0-0	.983	-7	113	134	C-28	-1.5
	Det A	8	11	1	2	0	0	0	1	1-0	0	5	.182	.250	.182	15	-1	0-0	.964	0	0	0	/C-8	-0.1
1998	Mil N	2	2	0	0	0	0	0	0	0-0	0	2	.000	.000	.000	-99	-1	0-0	1.000	0	0	0	/C	-0.1
1999	StL N	16	34	5	8	5	0	1	1	6-1	0	12	.235	.350	.471	105	0	0-0	.988	3	185	130	C-14	0.4
2000	Min A	52	139	16	29	7	1	3	14	24-0	0	36	.209	.325	.338	66	-7	0-1	.993	1	153	81	C-49/D	-0.3
2001	Bos A	1	4	0	1	0	0	0	0	0-0	0	1	.250	.250	.250	32	0	0-0	1.000	1	0	321	/C	0.1

Year	Tm Lg	G	AB	R	H	2B	3B	HR	RBI	BB-IB	HP	SO	AVG	OBP	SLG	AOPS	ABR	SB-CS	FA	FR	Rng	Thr	G at Pos	BFW
	Tex A	11	25	0	4	1	0	0	2	0-0	0	9	.160	.160	.200	-6	-4	0-0	1.000	-2	70	97	C-11	-0.6
	Year	12	29	0	5	1	0	0	2	0-0	0	10	.172	.172	.207	-1	-4	0-0	1.000	-1	61	127	C-12	-0.5
2002	Mil N	16	35	2	4	0	0	1	4	4-2	0	11	.114	.200	.200	9	-5	0-0	.976	2	155	175	C-15	-0.3
Total	7	145	343	33	63	16	1	6	29	50-4	0	106	.184	.287	.289	49	-26	0-1	.985	-1	135	113	C-134/D	-2.2
JESSEE, DAN Daniel Edward B 2.22.1901 Olive Hill, KY D 4.30.1970 Venice, FL BL/TR 5-10/165# d8.14																								
1929	Cle A	1	0	0	0	0	0	0	0	0	0	0	—	—	—	—	0	0-0	—	0			R	0.0
JESTADT, GARRY Garry Arthur B 3.19.1947 Chicago, IL BR/TR 6-2/188# d9.17																								
1969	Mon N	6	6	1	0	0	0	0	1	0-0	0	0	.000	.000	.000	-99	-2	0-0	.667	-1	0	0	/S	-0.2
1971	Chi N	3	3	0	0	0	0	0	0	0-0	0	0	.000	.000	.000	-87	-1	0-0	—	-0	0	0	/3	-0.1
	SD N	75	189	17	55	13	0	0	13	11-0	0	24	.291	.328	.360	102	1	1-3	.935	2	129	65	3-49,2-23/S	0.3
	Year	78	192	17	55	13	0	0	13	11-0	0	24	.286	.324	.354	98	0	1-3	.935	1	128	64	3-50,2-23/S	0.2
1972	SD N	92	256	15	63	5	1	6	22	13-2	0	21	.246	.281	.344	83	-7	0-0	.944	-17	80	80	2-48,3-25/S-3	-2.3
Total	3	176	454	33	118	18	1	6	36	24-2	0	45	.260	.296	.344	87	-9	1-3	.942	-16	111	81	/3-75,2-71,S-5	-2.3
JETER, DEREK Derek Sanderson B 6.26.1974 Pequannock, NJ BR/TR 6-3/175# d5.29																								
1995	NY A	15	48	5	12	4	1	0	7	3-0	0	11	.250	.294	.375	73	-2	0-0	.962	-4	83	81	S-15	-0.4
1996	†NY A	157	582	104	183	25	6	10	78	48-1	9	102	.314	.370	.430	103	3	14-7	.969	-2	96	80	*S-157	1.3
1997	†NY A	159	654	116	190	31	7	10	70	74-0	10	125	.291	.370	.405	103	5	23-12	.975	-6	96	88	*S-159	1.2
1998	†NY A★	149	626	**127**	203	25	8	19	84	57-1	5	119	.324	.384	.481	128	26	30-6	.986	-22	88	97	*S-148	1.8
1999	†NY A★	158	627	134	**219**	37	9	24	102	91-5	12	116	.349	.438	.552	153	55	19-8	.978	-32	83	83	*S-158	3.4
2000	†NY A★	148	593	119	201	31	4	15	73	68-4	12	99	.339	.416	.481	128	28	22-4	.961	-36	79	80	*S-148	0.7
2001	†NY A★	150	614	110	191	35	3	21	74	56-3	10	99	.311	.377	.480	122	21	27-3	.974	-27	81	78	*S-150	1.0
2002	†NY A★	157	644	124	191	26	0	18	75	73-2	7	114	.297	.373	.421	112	13	32-3	.977	-40	80	73	*S-156/D	-0.9
2003	†NY A	119	482	87	156	25	3	10	52	43-2	13	88	.324	.393	.450	124	19	11-5	.968	-31	80	70	*S-118	-0.2
Total	9	1212	4870	926	1546	239	41	127	615	513-18	78	873	.317	.389	.462	121	168	178-48	.973	-199	86	81	*S-1209/D	7.9
JETER, JOHNNY John B 10.24.1944 Shreveport, LA BR/TR 6-1/180# d6.14 s-Shawn																								
1969	Pit N	28	29	7	9	1	1	1	6	3-1	0	15	.310	.375	.517	151	2	1-1	1.000	-0	79	186	O-20(16-1-4)	0.1
1970	†Pit N	85	126	27	30	3	2	2	12	13-1	1	34	.238	.314	.341	77	-4	9-5	1.000	-1	90	96	O-56(35-10-11)	-0.6
1971	SD N	18	75	8	24	4	0	1	3	2-0	0	16	.320	.338	.413	120	2	2-0	.967	2	87	66	O-17(CF)	0.4
1972	SD N	110	326	25	72	4	3	7	21	18-4	2	92	.221	.266	.316	70	-15	11-5	.987	-1	109	20	O-91(CF)	-1.9
1973	Chi A	89	300	38	72	14	4	7	26	9-0	0	74	.240	.260	.383	77	-11	4-3	.955	-3	97	63	O-72(19-27-29)/D-3	-1.8
1974	Cle A	6	17	3	6	1	0	0	1	1-0	0	6	.353	.389	.412	132	1	1-2	.833	-1	57	0	/O-6(5-1-0)	-0.1
Total	6	336	873	108	213	27	10	18	69	46-6	3	237	.244	.283	.360	82	-25	28-16	.975	-4	98	55	O-262(75-147-44)/D-3	-3.9
JETER, SHAWN Shawn Darrell B 6.28.1966 Shreveport, LA BL/TR 6-2/185# d6.13 f-Johnny																								
1992	Chi A	13	18	1	2	0	0	0	0	0-0	0	7	.111	.111	.111	-38	-3	0-0	.909	-0	114	0	/O-8(1-1-6),D-3	-0.4
JETHROE, SAM Samuel "Jet" B 1.20.1918 E.St.Louis, IL D 6.16.2001 Erie, PA BB/TR 6-1/178# d4.18																								
1950	Bos N	141	582	100	159	28	8	18	58	52	5	93	.273	.338	.442	110	7	**35**	.969	3	98	148	*O-141(CF)	0.6
1951	Bos N	148	572	101	160	29	10	18	65	57	11	88	.280	.356	.460	127	21	**35**-5	.974	-2	94	142	*O-140(13-127-2)	2.0
1952	Bos N	151	608	79	141	23	7	13	58	68	9	112	.232	.318	.357	90	-8	28-9	.970	-4	102	66	*O-151(1-150-0)	-1.4
1954	Pit N	2	1	0	0	0	0	0	0	0	0	0	.000	.000	.000	-99	0	0-0	1.000	0	153	0	/O(RF)	0.0
Total	4	442	1763	280	460	80	25	49	181	177	25	293	.261	.337	.418	108	20	98-14	.971	-3	98	117	O-433(14-418-3)	1.2
JEWETT, NAT Nathan W. B 12.25.1842 New York, NY D 2.23.1914 Bronx, NY 5-6/137# d7.4																								
1872	Eck NA	2	8	1	1	0	0	0	0	0		0	.125	.125	.125	-27	-1	0-0	.700	-2			/C-2	-0.2
JIMENEZ, HOUSTON Alfonso (Gonzales) B 10.30.1957 Navojoa, Mexico BR/TR 5-8/144# d6.13																								
1983	Min A	36	86	5	15	5	1	0	9	4-0	0	11	.174	.207	.256	27	-9	0-1	.969	-1	97	110	S-36	-0.7
1984	Min A	108	298	28	60	11	1	0	19	15-0	0	34	.201	.238	.245	33	-27	0-1	.959	-12	94	104	*S-107	-3.1
1987	Pit N	5	6	0	0	0	0	0	0	1-0	0	2	.000	.143	.000	-58	-1	0-0	1.000	1	0	0	/2-2,S-2	0.0
1988	Cle A	9	21	1	1	0	0	0	1	0-0	0	2	.048	.048	.048	-71	-5	0-0	.973	5	173	84	/2-7,S-2	0.0
Total	4	158	411	34	76	16	2	0	29	20-0	0	49	.185	.221	.234	25	-42	0-2	.962	-7	96	107	S-147/2-9	-3.8
JIMENEZ, D'ANGELO D'Angelo B 12.21.1977 Santo Domingo, D.R. BB/TR 6/160# d9.15																								
1999	NY A	7	20	3	8	2	0	0	4	3-0	0	4	.400	.478	.500	152	2	0-0	1.000	-0	101	295	/3-6,2	0.1
2001	SD N	86	308	45	85	19	0	3	33	39-4	0	68	.276	.355	.367	96	0	2-3	.948	4	107	91	S-85	0.9
2002	SD N	87	321	39	77	11	4	3	33	34-1	0	63	.240	.311	.327	79	-12	4-2	.975	17	110	123	2-54,3-32/P	0.8
	Chi A	27	108	22	31	4	3	1	11	16-0	1	10	.287	.384	.407	109	2	2-1	.988	5	109	147	2-17,S-10/3	0.8
2003	Chi A	73	271	35	69	11	5	7	26	32-1	0	46	.255	.332	.410	94	-3	4-3	.977	-6	90	99	2-68/3-2	-0.6
	Cin N	73	290	34	84	13	2	7	31	34-0	2	43	.290	.365	.421	107	4	7-4	.990	-2	99	105	2-73/3-2	0.6
Total	4	353	1318	178	354	60	14	21	138	158-6	3	234	.269	.346	.383	96	-7	19-13	.982	17	99	110	2-213/S-95,3-43,P	2.6
JIMENEZ, ELVIO Felix Elvio (Rivera) B 1.6.1940 San Pedro De Macoris, D.R. BR/TR 5-9/170# d10.4 b-Manny																								
1964	NY A	1	6	0	2	0	0	0	0	0-0	0	0	.333	.333	.333	85	0	0-0	1.000	0	110	0	/O(LF)	0.0
JIMENEZ, MANNY Manuel Emilio (Rivera) B 11.19.1938 San Pedro De Macoris, D.R. BL/TR 6-1/195# d4.11 b-Elvio																								
1962	KC A	139	479	48	144	24	2	11	69	31-3	11	34	.301	.354	.428	105	4	0-1	.985	-6	81	108	*O-122(116-0-6)	-0.9
1963	KC A	60	157	12	44	9	0	0	15	16-2	5	14	.280	.361	.338	93	0	0-1	.960	2	91	233	O-40(33-0-8)	-0.1
1964	KC A	95	204	19	46	7	0	12	38	15-1	5	24	.225	.293	.436	97	-1	0-0	.939	-1	87	152	O-49(46-0-4)	-0.5
1966	KC A	13	35	1	4	0	1	0	1	6-0	0	4	.114	.244	.171	22	-4	0-0	.909	-1	64	212	O-12(8-0-4)	-0.5
1967	Pit N	50	56	3	14	2	0	2	10	1-0	1	4	.250	.276	.393	89	-1	0-0	1.000	-0	86	0	/O-6(LF)	-0.2
1968	Pit N	66	66	7	20	1	1	1	11	6-0	5	15	.303	.403	.394	142	4	0-0	.857	-1	87	0	/O-5(LF)	0.4
1969	Chi N	6	6	0	1	0	0	0	0	0-0	0	2	.167	.167	.167	-6	-1	0-0	—	0			H	-0.1
Total	7	429	1003	90	273	43	4	26	144	75-6	27	97	.272	.337	.401	100	1	0-2	.966	-6	84	140	O-234(214-0-22)	-1.9
JOHNS, KEITH Robert Keith B 7.19.1971 Callahan, FL BR/TR 6-1/175# d5.23																								
1998	Bos A	2	0	0	0	0	0	0	0	1-0	0	0	—	1.000	—	188	0	0-0	1.000	0	150	755	/2D	0.1
JOHNS, TOMMY Thomas Pearce B 9.7.1851 Baltimore, MD D 4.13.1927 Baltimore, MD d5.14																								
1873	Mar NA	1	4	0	0	0	0	0	0	0		0	.000	.000	.000	-99	-1	0-0	.000	-1	0	0	/O(LF)	-0.1
JOHNS, PETE William R. B 1.17.1889 Cleveland, OH D 8.9.1964 Cleveland, OH BR/TR 5-10/165# d8.25																								
1915	Chi A	28	100	7	21	2	1	0	11	8	1	11	.210	.275	.250	56	-6	2-7	.943	0	102	112	3-28	-0.7
1918	StL A	46	89	5	16	1	1	0	11	4	0	6	.180	.215	.213	30	-8	0	.990	-1	177	60	1-10/S-4,3-4,O-4(1-3-0),2-2	-1.0
Total	2	74	189	12	37	3	2	0	22	12	1	17	.196	.248	.233	44	-14	2-7	.929	-0	100	105	/3-32,1-10,O-4(1-3-0),S-4,2-2	-1.7
JOHNSON, ABBIE Albert L. B 1875 Chicago, IL D 11.28.1960 Detroit, MI 5-9.5/165# d9.1																								
1896	Lou N	25	87	10	20	2	1	0	14	4	0	6	.230	.264	.276	44	-7	0	.937	-3	87	84	2-25	-0.8
1897	Lou N	49	165	16	40	6	1	0	23	13	1		.242	.302	.291	59	-10	2	.882	-9	92	67	2-34,S-12	-1.4
Total	2	74	252	26	60	8	2	0	37	17	1	6	.238	.289	.286	54	-17	2	.904	-12	90	74	/2-59,S-12	-2.2
JOHNSON, ALEX Alexander B 12.7.1942 Helena, AR BR/TR 6/205# d7.25																								
1964	Phi N	43	109	18	33	7	1	4	18	6-1	1	26	.303	.345	.495	135	5	1-2	.980	0	103	58	O-35(34-0-1)	0.3
1965	Phi N	97	262	27	77	9	3	8	28	15-3	2	60	.294	.337	.443	120	6	4-4	.966	-0	102	88	O-82(76-9-1)	0.2
1966	StL N	25	86	7	16	0	1	2	6	5-1	0	18	.186	.231	.279	41	-7	1-1	.962	-1	74	160	O-22(LF)	-1.0
1967	StL N	81	175	20	39	9	2	1	12	9-0	3	26	.223	.271	.314	68	-7	6-3	.970	5	112	228	O-57(5-6-48)	-0.5
1968	Cin N	149	603	79	188	32	6	2	58	26-4	3	71	.312	.342	.395	114	10	16-6	.947	-1	103	87	*O-140(140-0-1)	0.3
1969	Cin N	139	523	86	165	18	4	17	88	25-1	9	69	.315	.350	.463	122	14	11-8	.927	-2	101	71	*O-132(LF)	0.5
1970	Cal A★	156	614	85	202	26	6	14	86	35-9	7	68	**.329**	.370	.459	133	25	17-2	.959	-0	98	112	*O-156(155-0-1)	2.0
1971	Cal A	65	242	19	63	8	0	2	21	15-3	2	34	.260	.308	.318	84	-6	5-2	.926	-7	76	81	O-61(LF)	-1.7
1972	Cle A	108	356	31	85	10	1	8	37	22-10	1	40	.239	.283	.340	83	-9	6-8	.955	-5	88	59	O-95(LF)	-2.4
1973	Tex A	158	624	62	179	26	3	8	68	32-5	2	82	.287	.322	.377	101	-1	10-5	.987	1	94	148	*D-116,O-41(40-1-0)	-0.5
1974	Tex A	114	453	57	132	14	3	4	41	28-4	4	59	.291	.338	.362	104	2	20-9	.956	4	108	114	O-81(LF),D-32	0.2
	NY A	10	28	3	6	1	0	1	2	0-0	0	3	.214	.214	.357	63	-2	0-0	—	-0	0	0	/O(LF)D	-0.2
	Year	124	481	60	138	15	3	5	43	28-4	4	62	.287	.331	.362	102	0	20-9	.956	4	107	113	O-82(LF),D-36	0.0

Year	Tm Lg	G	AB	R	H	2B	3B	HR	RBI	BB-IB	HP	SO	AVG	OBP	SLG	AOPS	ABR	SB-CS	FA	FR	Rng	Thr	G at Pos	BFW
1975	NY A	52	119	15	31	5	1	1	15	7-1	0	21	.261	.297	.345	84	-3	2-3	1.000	-1	83	0	D-28/O-7(5-0-2)	-0.5
1976	Det A	125	429	41	115	15	2	6	45	19-1	2	49	.268	.298	.354	88	-7	14-10	.954	-5	90	111	O-90(LF),D-19	-1.9
Total	13	1322	4623	550	1331	180	33	78	525	244-43	36	626	.288	.326	.392	105	20	113-63	.953	-11	97	100	O-1000(937-16-54),D-199	-5.2

JOHNSON, TONY Anthony Clair B 6.23.1956 Memphis, TN BR/TR 6-3/195# d9.28

Year	Tm Lg	G	AB	R	H	2B	3B	HR	RBI	BB-IB	HP	SO	AVG	OBP	SLG	AOPS	ABR	SB-CS	FA	FR	Rng	Thr	G at Pos	BFW
1981	Mon N	2	1	0	0	0	0	0	0	0-0	0	0	.000	.000	.000	-99	0	0-0	—	-0	0	0	/O(LF)	0.0
1982	Tor A	70	98	17	23	2	1	3	14	11-1	0	26	.235	.309	.367	79	-3	3-13	.979	2	108	176	O-28(25-2-2),D-28	-0.7
Total	2	72	99	17	23	2	1	3	14	11-1	0	26	.232	.306	.364	77	-3	3-13	.979	2	107	175	/O-29(26-2-2),D-28	-0.7

JOHNSON, BOB Bobby Earl B 7.31.1959 Dallas, TX BR/TR 6-3/195# d9.1

Year	Tm Lg	G	AB	R	H	2B	3B	HR	RBI	BB-IB	HP	SO	AVG	OBP	SLG	AOPS	ABR	SB-CS	FA	FR	Rng	Thr	G at Pos	BFW
1981	Tex A	6	18	2	5	0	0	2	4	1-0	0	3	.278	.316	.611	171	1	0-0	1.000	-0	118	0	/C-5,1	0.1
1982	Tex A	20	56	4	7	2	0	2	7	3-0	1	22	.125	.183	.268	23	-6	0-1	1.000	0	146	122	C-14/1-3	-0.6
1983	Tex A	72	175	18	37	6	1	5	16	16-0	1	55	.211	.280	.343	72	-7	3-0	1.000	4	137	75	C-62,1-10	-0.1
Total	3	98	249	24	49	8	1	9	27	20-0	2	80	.197	.261	.345	68	-12	3-1	1.000	4	138	81	/C-81,1-14	-0.6

JOHNSON, BRIAN Brian David B 1.8.1968 Oakland, CA BR/TR 6-2/210# d4.5

Year	Tm Lg	G	AB	R	H	2B	3B	HR	RBI	BB-IB	HP	SO	AVG	OBP	SLG	AOPS	ABR	SB-CS	FA	FR	Rng	Thr	G at Pos	BFW
1994	SD N	36	93	7	23	4	1	3	16	5-0	0	21	.247	.283	.409	81	-3	0-0	1.000	3	66	178	C-24/1-5	0.1
1995	SD N	68	207	20	52	9	0	3	29	11-2	1	39	.251	.287	.338	68	-10	0-0	.993	2	111	87	C-55/1-2	-0.5
1996	†SD N	82	243	18	66	13	1	8	35	4-2	4	36	.272	.290	.432	94	-3	0-0	.989	-3	95	88	C-66/13	-0.2
1997	Det A	45	139	13	33	6	1	2	18	5-1	0	19	.237	.262	.338	56	-10	1-0	.987	-10	80	66	C-43/D-2	-1.6
	†SF N	56	179	19	50	7	2	11	27	14-7	2	26	.279	.333	.525	125	5	0-1	.995	3	127	101	C-55/1-2	1.1
1998	SF N	99	308	34	73	8	1	13	34	28-4	5	67	.237	.310	.396	90	-6	0-2	.994	-3	132	81	C-95/O(LF)	-0.4
1999	Cin N	45	117	12	27	7	0	5	18	9-0	0	31	.231	.286	.419	73	-5	0-0	.995	4	147	82	C-39	0.1
2000	KC A	37	125	9	26	6	0	4	18	4-0	0	28	.208	.229	.352	44	-11	0-0	.991	-2	68	90	C-37	-1.0
2001	LA N	3	4	0	1	0	0	0	1	0-0	0	1	.250	.250	.250	32	0	0-0	1.000	-0	0	0	/C-2	0.0
Total	8	471	1415	132	351	60	6	49	196	80-16	12	268	.248	.291	.403	82	-43	1-3	.993	-5	108	91	C-416/1-10,D-2,O(LF)3	-2.4

JOHNSON, CALEB Caleb Clark B 5.23.1844 Fulton, IL D 3.7.1925 Sterling, IL d5.20

Year	Tm Lg	G	AB	R	H	2B	3B	HR	RBI	BB-IB	HP	SO	AVG	OBP	SLG	AOPS	ABR	SB-CS	FA	FR	Rng	Thr	G at Pos	BFW
1871	Cle NA	16	67	10	15	1	0	0	7	0		1	.224	.224	.239	35	-5	1-0	.736	-4	81	88	2-10/O-6(RF)	-0.6

JOHNSON, CHARLIE Charles Cleveland "Home Run" B 3.12.1885 Slatington, PA D 8.28.1940 Marcus Hook, PA BL/TL 5-9/150# d9.21

Year	Tm Lg	G	AB	R	H	2B	3B	HR	RBI	BB-IB	HP	SO	AVG	OBP	SLG	AOPS	ABR	SB-CS	FA	FR	Rng	Thr	G at Pos	BFW
1908	Phi N	6	16	2	4	0	1	0	2	1	1		.250	.333	.375	122	0	0	1.000	-0	0	0	/O-4(1-3-0)	0.0

JOHNSON, CHARLES Charles Edward B 7.20.1971 Fort Pierce, FL BR/TR 6-2/215# d5.6

Year	Tm Lg	G	AB	R	H	2B	3B	HR	RBI	BB-IB	HP	SO	AVG	OBP	SLG	AOPS	ABR	SB-CS	FA	FR	Rng	Thr	G at Pos	BFW
1994	Fla N	4	11	5	5	1	0	1	4	1-0	0	4	.455	.462	.818	229	2	0-0	1.000	1	0	106	/C-4	0.3
1995	Fla N	97	315	40	79	15	1	11	39	46-2	4	71	.251	.351	.410	100	1	0-2	.992	3	145	122	C-97	1.0
1996	Fla N	120	386	34	84	13	1	13	37	40-6	2	91	.218	.292	.358	73	-16	1-0	**.995**	19	**203**	114	*C-120	1.0
1997	†Fla N★	124	416	43	104	26	1	19	63	60-6	3	109	.250	.347	.454	113	9	0-2	**1.000**	13	153	**128**	*C-123	2.9
1998	Fla N	31	113	13	25	5	0	7	23	16-0	0	30	.221	.315	.451	105	0	0-1	.990	-6	112	80	C-31	-0.4
	LA N	102	346	31	75	13	0	12	35	29-1	1	99	.217	.279	.358	70	-17	0-1	.992	5	154	107	*C-100	-0.5
	Year	133	459	44	100	18	0	19	58	45-1	1	129	.218	.289	.381	79	-16	0-2	.992	-1	144	101	*C-131	-0.9
1999	Bal A	135	426	58	107	19	1	16	54	55-2	4	107	.251	.340	.413	95	-3	0-0	.994	5	128	97	*C-135	0.9
2000	Bal A	84	286	52	84	16	0	21	55	32-0	0	69	.294	.364	.570	138	16	2-0	.994	-8	119	72	C-83/D	1.2
	†Chi A	44	135	24	44	8	0	10	36	20-0	1	37	.326	.411	.607	153	11	0-0	.987	-7	144	97	C-43	0.6
	Year	128	421	76	128	24	0	31	91	52-0	1	106	.304	.379	.582	143	27	2-0	.992	-16	127	80	*C-126/D	1.8
2001	Fla N★	128	451	51	117	32	0	18	75	38-2	4	133	.259	.321	.450	100	0	0-0	.996	4	128	110	*C-125	1.1
2002	Fla N	83	244	18	53	19	0	6	36	31-7	0	61	.217	.301	.369	83	-7	0-0	.994	0	106	**135**	C-82	-0.2
2003	Col N	108	356	49	82	20	0	20	61	49-2	1	84	.230	.320	.455	88	-6	1-3	.993	-5	143	114	*C-107	-0.5
Total	10	1060	3485	418	859	187	4	154	518	417-28	20	895	.246	.328	.435	99	-10	4-9	.994	24	143	110	*C-1050/D	7.4

JOHNSON, CLIFF Clifford B 7.22.1947 San Antonio, TX BR/TR 6-4/225# d9.13

Year	Tm Lg	G	AB	R	H	2B	3B	HR	RBI	BB-IB	HP	SO	AVG	OBP	SLG	AOPS	ABR	SB-CS	FA	FR	Rng	Thr	G at Pos	BFW
1972	Hou N	5	4	0	1	0	0	0	0	2-0	0	0	.250	.500	.250	121	0	0-0	1.000	1	0	0	/C	0.1
1973	Hou N	7	20	6	6	2	0	2	6	1-0	1	7	.300	.364	.700	189	2	0-0	1.000	-0	68	169	/1-5	0.2
1974	Hou N	83	171	26	39	4	1	10	29	33-1	3	45	.228	.357	.439	129	7	0-1	.978	-3	66	82	C-28,1-21	0.4
1975	Hou N	122	340	52	94	16	1	20	65	46-5	5	64	.276	.370	.506	152	24	1-0	.991	-14	70	84	1-47,C-41/O(LF)	0.9
1976	Hou N	108	318	36	72	21	2	10	49	62-6	4	59	.226	.359	.399	126	14	0-0	.977	-14	54	104	C-66,O-20(LF),1-16	0.1
1977	Hou N	51	144	22	43	8	0	10	23	23-2	4	30	.299	.409	.563	173	16	0-1	.946	1	85	205	O-34(33-0-4),1-10	1.5
	†NY A	56	142	24	42	8	0	12	31	20-0	6	23	.296	.405	.606	173	15	0-1	1.000	2	721	108	D-25,C-15,1-11	1.6
1978	†NY A	76	174	20	32	9	1	6	19	30-5	1	32	.184	.307	.351	87	-3	0-0	.975	-5	101	72	D-39,C-22/1	-0.8
1979	NY A	28	64	11	17	6	0	2	6	10-4	0	7	.266	.360	.453	122	2	0-0	1.000	-1	92	99	D-22/C-4	0.1
	Cle A	72	240	37	65	10	0	18	61	24-1	5	39	.271	.343	.538	135	11	2-0	—	-0	0	0	D-62/C	0.9
	Year	100	304	48	82	16	0	20	67	34-5	5	46	.270	.347	.520	132	14	2-0	1.000	-1	85	91	D-84/C-5	1.0
1980	Cle A	54	174	25	40	3	1	6	28	25-5	0	30	.230	.320	.362	88	-3	0-1	—	0	0	0	D-45	-0.4
	Chi N	68	196	28	46	8	0	10	34	29-5	1	35	.235	.335	.429	104	2	0-0	.992	-6	53	90	1-46/O-3(LF),C	-0.8
1981	†Oak A	84	273	40	71	8	0	17	59	28-2	3	60	.260	.329	.476	138	13	5-3	1.000	-1	24	41	D-68/1-9	0.9
1982	Oak A	73	214	19	51	10	0	7	31	26-2	2	41	.238	.324	.383	98	0	1-2	.987	1	134	88	D-48,1-11	-0.2
1983	Tor A	142	407	59	108	23	1	22	76	67-8	5	69	.265	.373	.489	128	18	0-1	1.000	0	98	106	*D-130/1-6	1.3
1984	Tor A	127	359	51	109	23	1	16	61	50-4	3	62	.304	.390	.507	142	22	0-1	1.000	-1	0	0	*D-109/1-2	1.8
1985	Tex A	82	296	31	76	17	1	12	56	31-2	3	44	.257	.330	.443	109	4	0-0	—	0	0	0	D-82	0.1
	†Tor A	24	73	4	20	0	0	1	10	9-0	0	15	.274	.349	.315	83	-2	0-0	.947	-1	57	225	D-21/1-3	-0.3
	Year	106	369	35	96	17	1	13	66	40-2	3	59	.260	.334	.417	104	2	0-0	.947	-1	57	225	*D-103/1-3	-0.2
1986	Tor A	107	336	48	84	12	1	15	55	52-1	4	57	.250	.355	.426	109	5	0-1	1.000	0	124	244	D-95/1	0.2
Total	15	1369	3945	539	1016	188	10	196	699	568-53	50	719	.258	.355	.459	125	147	9-12	.993	-40	72	97	D-746,1-189,C-179/O-58(57-0-4)	7.6

JOHNSON, DARRELL Darrell Dean B 8.25.1928 Horace, NE BR/TR 6-1/180# d4.20 M8 C8

Year	Tm Lg	G	AB	R	H	2B	3B	HR	RBI	BB-IB	HP	SO	AVG	OBP	SLG	AOPS	ABR	SB-CS	FA	FR	Rng	Thr	G at Pos	BFW
1952	StL A	29	78	9	22	2	1	0	9	11	0	4	.282	.371	.333	94	0	0-0	.990	1	*103*	*137*	C-22	0.2
	Chi A	22	37	3	4	0	0	0	1	5	0	9	.108	.214	.108	-8	-5	1-0	.955	2	*89*	*125*	C-21	-0.3
	Year	51	115	12	26	2	1	0	10	16	0	13	.226	.321	.261	62	-6	1-0	.974	2	*98*	*132*	C-43	-0.1
1957	NY A	21	46	4	10	1	0	1	8	3-0	1	10	.217	.275	.304	61	-3	0-0	1.000	3	*115*	*176*	C-20	0.1
1958	NY A	5	16	1	4	0	0	0	0	0-0	0	2	.250	.250	.250	39	-1	0-0	1.000	1	*108*	*229*	/C-4	-0.1
1960	StL N	8	2	0	0	0	0	0	0	1-0	0	0	.000	.333	.000	1	0	0-0	1.000	1	*0*	*0*	/C-8	0.1
1961	Phi N	21	61	4	14	1	0	0	3	3-0	1	8	.230	.277	.246	41	-5	0-0	.982	1	*95*	*167*	C-21	-0.3
	†Cin N	20	54	3	17	2	0	1	6	1-0	0	2	.315	.321	.407	92	-1	0-0	1.000	2	*83*	*159*	C-20	0.2
	Year	41	115	7	31	3	0	1	9	4-0	1	10	.270	.298	.322	65	-6	0-0	.991	3	*89*	*163*	C-41	-0.1
1962	Cin N	2	4	0	0	0	0	0	0	2-1	0	0	.000	.333	.000	-2	0	0-0	1.000	1	*100*	*194*	/C-2	0.1
	Bal A	6	22	0	4	0	0	0	1	0-0	0	4	.182	.182	.182	-2	-3	0-0	1.000	-1	*62*	*107*	/C-6	-0.4
Total	6	134	320	24	75	6	1	2	28	26-1	2	39	.234	.294	.278	57	-18	1-0	.988	10	*94*	*152*	C-124	-0.4

JOHNSON, DAVEY David Allen B 1.30.1943 Orlando, FL BR/TR 6-1/180# d4.13 M14

Year	Tm Lg	G	AB	R	H	2B	3B	HR	RBI	BB-IB	HP	SO	AVG	OBP	SLG	AOPS	ABR	SB-CS	FA	FR	Rng	Thr	G at Pos	BFW
1965	Bal A	20	47	5	8	3	0	0	1	5-0	0	6	.170	.245	.234	38	-4	3-0	.929	2	115	61	/3-9,2-3,S-2	-0.1
1966	†Bal A	131	501	47	129	20	3	7	56	31-3	1	64	.257	.298	.351	88	-8	3-4	.971	-3	98	95	*2-126/S-3	0.0
1967	Bal A	148	510	62	126	30	3	10	64	59-10	4	82	.247	.325	.376	109	7	4-5	.981	-2	96	97	*2-144/3-3	1.8
1968	Bal A★	145	504	50	122	24	4	9	56	44-5	5	80	.242	.308	.359	102	1	7-3	.978	-5	99	103	*2-127,S-34	1.1
1969	†Bal A✶	142	511	52	143	34	1	7	57	57-2	3	52	.280	.351	.391	108	7	3-4	.984	-2	98	118	*2-142/S-2	1.5
1970	†Bal A★	149	530	68	149	27	1	10	53	66-8	0	68	.281	.360	.392	106	7	2-1	.990	1	98	118	*2-149/S-2	1.8
1971	†Bal A	142	510	67	144	26	1	18	72	51-5	5	55	.282	.351	.443	125	17	3-1	.984	4	100	**125**	*2-140	3.2
1972	Bal A	118	376	31	83	22	3	5	32	52-8	4	68	.221	.320	.335	93	-1	1-1	**.990**	10	103	**127**	*2-116	1.8
1973	Atl N★	157	559	84	151	25	0	43	99	81-9	9	93	.270	.370	.546	140	31	5-3	.966	-17	94	97	*2-156	2.6
1974	Atl N	136	454	56	114	18	0	15	62	75-6	3	59	.251	.358	.390	105	6	1-2	.993	-4	116	113	1-73,2-71	0.0
1975	Atl N	1	1	0	1	1	0	0	1	0-0	0	0	1.000	1.000	2.000	691	1	0-0	—	0			H	0.1
1977	†Phi N	78	156	23	50	9	1	8	36	23-1	2	20	.321	.408	.545	148	12	1-1	1.000	0	79	112	1-43/2-9,3-6	1.0
1978	Phi N	44	89	14	17	2	0	2	14	10-0	2	19	.191	.284	.281	59	-5	0-0	.930	-3	92	105	2-15/3-9,1-7	-0.8
	Chi N	24	49	5	15	1	1	2	6	5-0	2	9	.306	.393	.490	130	2	0-0	.839	-1	108	57	3-12	0.1
	Year	68	138	19	32	3	1	4	20	15-0	4	28	.232	.323	.355	86	-3	0-0	.844	-4	94	35	3-21,2-15/1-7	-0.7
Total	13	1435	4797	564	1252	242	18	136	609	559-57	40	675	.261	.340	.404	110	73	33-25	.980	-19	98	111	*2-1198,1-123/S-43,3-39	14.1

Year	Tm Lg	G	AB	R	H	2B	3B	HR	RBI	BB-IB	HP	SO	AVG	OBP	SLG	AOPS	ABR	SB-CS	FA	FR	Rng	Thr	G at Pos	BFW
JOHNSON, DERON Deron Roger B 7.17.1938 San Diego, CA D 4.23.1992 Poway, CA BR/TR 6-2/209# d9.20 C12 OF Total (216-LF 1-CF 32-RF)																								
1960	NY A	6	4	0	2	1	0	0	0	0-0	0	0	.500	.500	.750	247	1	0-0	.750	-0	143	0	/3-5	0.1
1961	NY A	13	19	1	2	0	0	0	2	2-0	0	5	.105	.182	.105	-20	-3	0-0	1.000	2	154	0	/3-8	-0.2
	KC A	83	283	31	61	11	3	8	42	14-1	1	44	.216	.252	.360	61	-17	0-1	.948	3	94	141	O-59(28-1-30),3-19/1-3	-1.8
	Year	96	302	32	63	11	3	8	44	16-1	1	49	.209	.247	.344	57	-20	0-1	.948	5	94	141	O-59(28-1-30),3-27/1-3	-2.0
1962	KC A	17	19	1	2	1	0	0	0	3-0	0	8	.105	.227	.158	6	-3	0-0	1.000	-1	0	0	/1-2,3-2,O-2(RF)	-0.3
1964	Cin N	140	477	63	130	24	4	21	79	37-0	2	98	.273	.326	.472	118	11	4-3	.990	4	107	99	*1-131,O-10(LF)/3	0.7
1965	Cin N	159	616	92	177	30	7	32	**130**	52-9	2	97	.287	.340	.515	129	23	0-4	.948	-12	85	96	*3-159	0.9
1966	Cin N	142	505	75	130	25	3	24	81	39-5	2	87	.257	.309	.461	103	2	1-2	.980	-3	100	72	*O-106(LF),1-71,3-18	-0.9
1967	Cin N	108	361	39	81	18	1	13	53	22-2	2	104	.224	.270	.388	78	-10	0-1	.997	-4	87	84	1-81,3-24	-2.1
1968	Atl N	127	342	29	71	11	1	8	33	35-2	3	79	.208	.285	.316	81	-8	0-1	.996	-3	88	122	1-97,3-21	-1.8
1969	Phi N	138	475	51	121	19	4	17	80	60-4	0	111	.255	.333	.419	114	9	4-2	1.000	-10	79	28	O-72(LF),3-50,1-18	-0.7
1970	Phi N	159	574	66	147	28	3	27	93	72-7	0	132	.256	.338	.456	114	11	0-0	.995	-10	71	83	*1-154/3-3	-1.1
1971	Phi N	158	582	74	154	29	0	34	95	72-8	2	146	.265	.347	.490	135	27	0-1	.995	-4	100	**111**	*1-136,3-22	1.2
1972	Phi N	96	230	19	49	4	1	9	31	26-4	3	69	.213	.298	.357	84	-5	0-1	.982	-3	82	98	1-62	-1.4
1973	Phi N	12	36	3	6	2	0	1	5	5-0	1	10	.167	.279	.306	62	-2	0-0	.976	-0	101	137	1-10	-0.3
	†Oak A	131	464	61	114	14	2	19	81	59-7	1	116	.246	.330	.407	113	8	0-1	.994	-2	51	124	*D-107,1-23	0.1
1974	Oak A	50	174	16	34	1	2	7	23	11-2	0	37	.195	.239	.345	72	-8	1-0	.991	-2	66	70	1-28,D-23	-1.3
	Mil A	49	152	14	23	3	0	6	18	21-2	0	41	.151	.253	.289	56	-9	1-0	.833	-0	144	300	D-46/1-2	-1.1
	Bos A	11	25	0	3	0	0	0	2	0-0	0	6	.120	.115	.120	-29	-4	0-0	—	0			/D-8	-0.5
	Year	110	351	30	60	4	2	13	43	32-4	0	84	.171	.237	.305	57	-21	2-0	.983	-2	69	80	D-77,1-30	-2.9
1975	Chi A	148	555	66	129	25	1	18	72	48-0	1	117	.232	.292	.378	88	-10	0-1	.994	-2	80	82	D-93,1-55	-2.0
	Bos A	3	10	2	6	0	0	1	3	2-0	0	0	.600	.667	.900	313	3	0-0	1.000	-1	0	134	/1-2,D	0.2
	Year	151	565	68	135	25	1	19	75	50-0	1	117	.239	.300	.388	92	-7	0-1	.994	-3	77	84	D-94,1-57	-1.8
1976	Bos A	15	38	3	5	1	1	0	0	5-1	0	11	.132	.233	.211	27	-4	0-0	1.000	-1	40	110	/1-5,D-9	-0.5
Total	16	1765	5941	706	1447	247	33	245	923	585-54	20	1318	.244	.311	.420	102	12	11-18	.993	-49	85	97	1-880,3-332,D-287,O-249L	-12.8
JOHNSON, DON Donald Spore "Pep" B 12.7.1911 Chicago, IL D 4.6.2000 Laguna Beach, CA BR/TR 6/170# d9.26 f-Ernie																								
1943	Chi N	10	42	5	8	2	0	0	1	2	0	4	.190	.227	.238	35	-4	0	.957	2	105	126	2-10	-0.1
1944	Chi N☆	154	608	50	169	37	1	2	71	28	1	48	.278	.311	.352	87	-11	8	.947	-1	100	94	*2-154	-0.4
1945	†Chi N✱	138	557	94	168	23	2	2	58	32	3	34	.302	.343	.361	98	-2	9	.975	15	108	111	*2-138	2.0
1946	Chi N	83	314	37	76	10	1	1	19	26	3	39	.242	.306	.290	71	-12	6	.981	-9	96	72	2-83	-1.8
1947	Chi N	120	402	33	104	17	2	3	26	24	1	45	.259	.302	.333	71	-18	2	.970	-2	100	91	*2-108/3-6	-1.4
1948	Chi N	6	12	0	3	0	0	0	0	0	0	1	.250	.250	.250	37	-1	1	1.000	-1	53	235	/2-2,3-2	-0.2
Total	6	511	1935	219	528	89	6	8	175	112	8	171	.273	.315	.337	83	-48	26	.966	4	102	95	2-495/3-8	-1.9
JOHNSON, ED Edwin Cyril B 3.31.1899 Morganfield, KY D 7.3.1975 Morganfield, KY BL/TR 5-9/160# d9.26																								
1920	Was A	4	13	1	3	0	0	0	2	3	0	2	.231	.375	.231	65	0	0-0	.625	-2	66	0	/O-4(RF)	-0.2
JOHNSON, ELMER Elmer Ellsworth "Hickory" B 6.12.1884 Beard, IN D 10.31.1966 Hollywood, FL BR/TR 5-9/185# d4.24																								
1914	NY N	11	12	0	2	1	0	0	0	1	0	3	.167	.231	.250	44	-1	0	.947	-1	*119*	*70*	C-11	-0.1
JOHNSON, ERIK Erik Anthony B 10.11.1965 Oakland, CA BR/TR 5-11/175# d7.8																								
1993	SF N	4	5	1	2	2	0	0	0	0-0	0	1	.400	.400	.800	219	1	0-0	1.000	-1	0	0	/2-2,3S	0.0
1994	SF N	5	13	0	2	0	0	0	0	0-0	0	4	.154	.154	.154	-20	-2	0-0	1.000	0	95	317	/2-2,S	-0.2
Total	2	9	18	1	4	2	0	0	0	0-0	0	5	.222	.222	.333	45	-1	0-0	1.000	-0	78	259	/2-4,S-2,3	-0.2
JOHNSON, ERNIE Ernest Rudolph B 4.29.1888 Chicago, IL D 5.1.1952 Monrovia, CA BL/TR 5-9/151# d8.5 s-Don																								
1912	Chi A	21	42	7	11	0	1	0	5	1	0		.262	.279	.310	70	-2	0	.984	2	112	91	S-16	0.1
1915	StL F	152	512	58	123	18	10	7	67	46	2	35	.240	.305	.355	81	-21	32	.942	16	102	117	*S-152	0.6
1916	StL A	74	236	29	54	9	3	0	19	30	3	23	.229	.323	.292	89	-2	13	.936	-3	106	90	S-60,3-12	-0.1
1917	StL A	80	199	28	49	6	2	2	20	12	2	16	.246	.296	.327	93	-3	13	.924	9	105	51	S-39,2-18,3-14	1.0
1918	StL A	29	34	7	9	1	0	0	0	0	1	2	.265	.286	.294	77	-1	4	.821	-2	100	47	S-11/3	-0.3
1921	Chi A	142	613	93	181	28	7	1	51	29	1	24	.295	.328	.369	78	-21	22-13	.947	21	**112**	115	*S-141	1.4
1922	Chi A	144	603	85	153	17	3	0	56	40	4	30	.254	.304	.292	56	-39	21-18	.952	-1	101	103	*S-141	-2.5
1923	Chi A	12	53	5	10	2	0	0	1	3	1	5	.189	.246	.226	25	-6	2-1	.922	-2	89	137	S-12	-0.6
	†NY A	19	38	6	17	1	1	1	8	1	0	1	.447	.462	.605	176	4	0-0	.977	-1	80	97	S-15/3	0.3
	Year	31	91	11	27	3	1	1	9	4	1	6	.297	.333	.385	88	-2	2-1	.944	-3	85	121	S-27/3	-0.3
1924	NY A	64	119	24	42	4	8	3	12	11	1	7	.353	.412	.597	158	9	1-6	.955	-1	102	94	2-27/S-9,3-2	0.7
1925	NY A	76	170	30	48	5	1	5	17	8	0	10	.282	.315	.412	85	-5	6-3	.955	-8	95	100	2-34,S-28/3-2	-1.0
Total	10	813	2619	372	697	91	36	19	256	181	15	153	.266	.317	.350	80	-87	114-41	.944	31	103	105	S-624/2-79,3-32	-0.4
JOHNSON, FRANK Frank Herbert B 7.22.1942 ElPaso, TX BR/TR 6-1/155# d9.7 OF Total (51-LF 10-CF 14-RF)																								
1966	SF N	15	32	2	7	0	0	0	0	2-0	0	7	.219	.265	.219	35	-3	0-1	1.000	-1	97	0	O-13(8-2-7)	-0.4
1967	SF N	8	10	3	3	0	0	0	0	1-0	0	2	.300	.364	.300	93	0	0-0	.889	-0	123	0	/O-3(2-1-1)	0.0
1968	SF N	67	174	11	33	2	0	1	7	12-2	1	23	.190	.246	.218	40	-13	1-0	.944	-1	99	69	3-36/O-8(4-5-0),S-5,2-3	-1.6
1969	SF N	7	10	2	1	0	0	0	0	0-0	0	1	.100	.100	.100	-45	-2	0-0	1.000	0	115	0	/O-7(5-1-1)	-0.2
1970	SF N	67	161	25	44	1	2	3	31	19-3	2	18	.273	.357	.360	94	-1	1-1	.979	-0	100	110	O-33(29-1-4),1-27	-0.4
1971	SF N	32	49	4	4	1	0	0	5	3-0	0	9	.082	.132	.102	-33	-9	0-0	.975	-2	28	73	/1-9,O-4(3-0-1)	-1.3
Total	6	196	436	47	92	4	2	4	43	37-5	3	60	.211	.277	.257	52	-28	2-2	.979	-4	101	55	/O-68L,1-36,3-36,S-5,2-3	-3.9
JOHNSON, GARY Gerald Clyde B 10.29.1975 Palo Alto, CA BL/TL 6-3/210# d4.26																								
2003	Ana A	5	8	1	3	1	0	0	0	1-0	0	1	.375	.444	.500	155	1	0-1	1.000	0	139	0	/O-4(2-0-2)	0.1
JOHNSON, HOWARD Howard Michael B 11.29.1960 Clearwater, FL BB/TR 5-11/178# d4.14 OF Total (99-LF 86-CF 36-RF)																								
1982	Det A	54	155	23	49	5	0	4	14	16-1	1	30	.316	.384	.426	122	5	7-4	.901	-7	70	111	3-33,D-10/O-9(3-1-5)	-0.3
1983	Det A	27	66	11	14	0	0	3	5	7-0	1	10	.212	.297	.348	79	-2	0-0	.851	-1	101	67	3-21/D-2	-0.4
1984	†Det A	116	355	43	88	14	1	12	50	40-1	1	67	.248	.324	.394	99	0	10-6	.944	-11	87	101	*3-108/S-9,10(1-1-0)D	-1.3
1985	NY N	126	389	38	94	18	4	11	46	34-10	0	78	.242	.300	.393	96	-4	6-4	.941	-10	85	131	*3-113/S-7,O(LF)	-1.6
1986	†NY N	88	220	30	54	14	0	10	39	31-8	1	64	.245	.341	.445	119	6	8-1	.903	-2	106	191	3-45,S-34/O(LF)	0.7
1987	NY N	157	554	93	147	22	1	36	99	83-18	5	113	.265	.364	.504	135	28	32-10	.938	-16	91	70	*3-140,S-38/O-2(LF)	1.6
1988	†NY N	148	495	85	114	21	1	24	68	86-25	3	104	.230	.343	.422	126	19	23-7	.951	-13	83	95	*3-131/S-52	1.2
1989	NY N★	153	571	**104**	164	41	3	36	101	77-8	1	126	.287	.369	.559	171	53	41-8	.910	-40	69	75	*3-143,S-31	2.3
1990	NY N	154	590	89	144	37	3	23	90	69-12	0	100	.244	.319	.434	107	5	34-8	.913	2	92	92	3-92,S-73	1.7
1991	NY N★	156	564	108	146	34	4	**38**	**117**	78-12	1	120	.259	.342	.535	147	34	30-16	.927	-3	89	70	*3-104,O-30(RF),S-28	3.4
1992	NY N	100	350	48	78	19	0	7	43	55-5	2	79	.223	.329	.337	91	-2	22-5	.981	-9	88	58	O-98(16-84-1)	-1.0
1993	NY N	72	235	32	56	8	2	7	26	43-3	0	43	.238	.354	.379	98	0	6-4	.944	2	104	105	3-67	0.3
1994	Col N	93	227	30	48	10	2	10	40	39-2	0	73	.211	.323	.405	77	-8	11-3	.979	-1	95	66	O-62(LF)/1	-0.9
1995	Chi N	87	169	26	33	4	1	7	22	34-0	1	46	.195	.330	.355	83	-4	1-1	.926	-4	98	86	3-34,O-13(LF)/2-8,1-3,S	-0.8
Total	14	1531	4940	760	1229	247	22	228	760	692-105	17	1053	.249	.340	.446	118	130	231-77	.929	-114	87	94	*3-1031,S-273,O-217L/D-16,2-8,1	4.9
JOHNSON, SPUD John Ralph B 1860, , CAN BL/TL 5-9/175# d4.18																								
1889	Col AA	116	459	91	130	14	10	2	79	39	12	47	.283	.355	.370	112	8	34	.879	-4	108	76	O-69(RF),3-44/1-2,S	0.4
1890	Col AA	135	538	106	186	23	18	1	**113**	48	10		.346	.409	.461	168	46	43	.926	-13	55	24	*O-135(96-0-39)	2.7
1891	Cle N	80	327	49	84	8	3	1	46	22	8	23	.257	.319	.309	80	-9	16	.872	-4	84	46	O-79(RF)/1	-1.3
Total	3	331	1324	246	400	45	31	4	238	109	30	70	.302	.368	.392	125	45	93	.899	-21	75	42	O-283(96-0-187)/3-44,1-3,S	1.8
JOHNSON, KEITH Keith B 4.17.1971 Hanford, CA BR/TR 5-11/200# d4.17																								
2000	Ana A	6	4	2	2	0	0	0	0	2-0	0	0	.500	.667	.500	197	1	0-0	1.000	1	0	0	/1-3,2-2,S	0.2
JOHNSON, LANCE Kenneth Lance B 7.6.1963 Cincinnati, OH BL/TL 5-11/160# d7.10																								
1987	†StL N	33	59	4	13	2	1	0	7	4-1	0	6	.220	.270	.288	47	-5	6-1	.931	-2	89	0	O-25(3-6-17)	-0.6
1988	Chi A	33	124	11	23	4	1	0	6	6-0	0	11	.185	.223	.234	28	-12	6-2	.970	-5	76	71	O-31(CF)/D	-1.7
1989	Chi A	50	180	28	54	8	2	0	16	17-0	0	24	.300	.360	.367	108	2	16-3	.983	1	119	0	O-45(42-8-0)/D	0.5
1990	Chi A	151	541	76	154	18	9	1	51	33-2	1	45	.285	.325	.357	93	-7	36-22	.973	-3	100	72	*O-148(6-148-0)/D	-1.1
1991	Chi A	159	588	72	161	14	**13**	0	49	26-2	1	58	.274	.304	.342	81	-18	26-11	.995	6	105	136	*O-157(0-157-2)	-1.2
1992	Chi A	157	567	67	158	15	**12**	3	47	34-4	1	33	.279	.318	.363	92	-8	41-14	.987	-1	98	121	*O-157(CF)	-0.7

Year	Tm Lg	G	AB	R	H	2B	3B	HR	RBI	BB-IB	HP	SO	AVG	OBP	SLG	AOPS	ABR	SB-CS	FA	FR	Rng	Thr	G at Pos	BFW
1993	†Chi A	147	540	75	168	18	**14**	0	47	36-1	0	33	.311	.354	.396	104	1	35-7	.980	9	114	90	*O-146(CF)	1.6
1994	Chi A	106	412	56	114	11	**14**	3	54	26-5	2	23	.277	.321	.393	85	-12	26-6	**1.000**	7	119	19	*O-103(CF)/D	0.0
1995	Chi A	142	607	98	**186**	18	12	10	57	32-2	1	31	.306	.341	.425	103	-1	40-6	.991	-1	98	119	*O-140(CF)/D	0.6
1996	NY N★	160	682	117	**227**	31	**21**	9	69	33-8	1	40	.333	.362	.479	126	22	50-12	.971	3	105	111	*O-157(CF)	3.2
1997	NY N	72	265	43	82	10	6	1	24	33-2	0	21	.309	.385	.404	111	5	15-10	.975	-1	100	125	O-66(CF)	0.5
	Chi N	39	145	17	44	6	2	4	15	9-1	0	10	.303	.342	.455	105	0	5-2	.963	-1	109	0	O-39(CF)/D	0.0
	Year	111	410	60	126	16	8	5	39	42-3	0	31	.307	.370	.422	109	5	20-12	.971	-2	103	83	*O-105(CF)/D	0.5
1998	†Chi N	85	304	51	85	8	4	2	21	26-1	0	22	.280	.335	.352	79	-10	10-6	.975	-4	91	112	O-78(CF)	-1.3
1999	Chi N	95	335	46	87	11	6	1	21	37-0	0	20	.260	.332	.337	71	-15	13-3	.988	6	115	132	O-91(CF)	-0.6
2000	NY A	18	30	6	9	1	0	0	2	0-0	0	7	.300	.300	.333	61	-2	2-0	1.000	-1	51	0	/O-4(2-0-2),D-2	-0.2
Total	14	1447	5379	767	1565	175	117	34	486	352-29	7	384	.291	.334	.386	95	-60	327-105	.983	13	104	96	*O-1387(53-1327-21)/D-8	-1.0
JOHNSON, LAMAR Lamar B 9.2.1950 Bessemer, AL BR/TR 6-2/225# d5.18 C9																								
1974	Chi A	10	29	1	10	0	0	0	2	0-0	0	3	.345	.333	.345	97	0	0-0	1.000	-0	67	159	/1-7,D-3	-0.1
1975	Chi A	8	30	2	6	3	0	1	1	1-0	0	5	.200	.226	.400	73	-1	0-0	.960	-1	63	82	/1-6,D-2	-0.2
1976	Chi A	82	222	29	71	11	1	4	33	19-1	2	37	.320	.372	.432	136	10	2-1	.983	-1	100	87	D-35,1-34/O(LF)	0.7
1977	Chi A	118	374	52	113	12	5	18	65	24-3	0	53	.302	.342	.505	128	13	1-1	.990	2	113	86	D-68,1-45	1.0
1978	Chi A	148	498	52	136	23	2	8	72	43-2	2	46	.273	.329	.376	98	-1	6-5	.992	4	114	91	*1-108,D-36	-0.5
1979	Chi A	133	479	60	148	29	1	12	74	41-1	2	56	.309	.363	.449	118	13	8-2	.987	4	124	81	1-94,D-37	1.1
1980	Chi A	147	541	51	150	26	3	13	81	47-5	0	53	.277	.331	.409	103	2	2-3	.990	5	129	102	1-80,D-66	0.0
1981	Chi A	41	134	10	37	7	0	1	15	5-1	0	14	.276	.298	.351	89	-2	0-2	.989	-1	81	121	1-36/D-2	-0.6
1982	Tex A	105	324	37	84	11	0	7	38	31-0	1	40	.259	.326	.358	92	-3	3-5	.982	-2	56	59	D-77,1-12	-0.9
Total	9	792	2631	294	755	122	12	64	381	211-13	7	307	.287	.338	.415	109	31	22-19	.989	9	112	92	1-422,D-326/O(LF)	0.5
JOHNSON, LARRY Larry Doby B 8.17.1950 Cleveland, OH BR/TR 6/185# d10.3																								
1972	Cle A	1	2	0	1	0	0	0	0	0-0	0	1	.500	.500	.500	192	0	0-0	1.000	0	0	0	/C	0.1
1974	Cle A	1	0	1	0	0	0	0	0	0-0	0	0	—	—	—	—	0	0-0	—	0			R	0.0
1975	Mon N	1	3	0	1	1	0	0	1	1-0	0	1	.333	.500	.667	212	1	0-0	1.000	-0	54	0	/C	0.0
1976	Mon N	6	13	0	2	1	0	0	0	0-0	0	2	.154	.154	.231	8	-2	0-0	1.000	-0	57	70	/C-5	-0.2
1978	Chi A	3	8	0	1	0	0	0	0	1-0	0	4	.125	.222	.125	0	-1	0-0	.857	-1	27	414	/C-2,D	-0.2
Total	5	12	26	1	5	2	0	0	1	2-0	0	8	.192	.250	.269	46	-2	0-0	.975	-1	47	120	/C-9,D	-0.3
JOHNSON, LOU Louis Brown "Slick" B 9.22.1934 Lexington, KY BR/TR 5-11/175# d4.17																								
1960	Chi N	34	68	6	14	2	1	0	1	5-1	1	19	.206	.270	.265	48	-5	3-1	1.000	3	114	240	O-25(8-4-13)	-0.3
1961	LA A	1	0	0	0	0	0	0	0	0-0	0	0	—	—	—	—	0	0-0	—	-0	0	0	/O(LF)	0.0
1962	Mil N	61	117	22	33	4	5	2	13	11-0	1	27	.282	.349	.453	116	2	6-1	1.000	1	108	50	O-55(38-20-1)	0.2
1965	†LA N	131	468	57	121	24	1	12	58	24-8	16	81	.259	.315	.391	105	3	15-6	.985	-2	99	44	*O-128(124-11-3)	-0.5
1966	†LA N	152	526	71	143	20	2	17	73	21-4	**14**	75	.272	.316	.414	110	6	8-10	.985	2	104	84	*O-148(104-2-65)	-0.3
1967	LA N	104	330	39	89	14	1	11	41	24-5	7	52	.270	.330	.418	124	10	4-3	.976	1	101	124	O-91(81-1-11)	0.6
1968	Chi N	62	205	14	50	14	3	1	14	6-2	7	23	.244	.289	.356	87	-3	3-1	.970	-4	98	0	O-57(1-0-56)	-1.2
	Cle A	65	202	25	52	11	1	5	23	9-2	4	24	.257	.298	.396	112	2	6-1	.989	2	101	166	O-57(41-0-20)	0.3
1969	Cal A	67	133	10	27	8	0	0	9	10-1	3	19	.203	.272	.263	53	-8	5-1	.935	-0	102	86	O-44(23-0-23)	-1.0
Total	8	677	2049	244	529	97	14	48	232	110-23	53	320	.258	.311	.389	103	7	50-24	.981	2	102	84	O-606(421-38-192)	-2.2
JOHNSON, MARK Mark Landon B 9.12.1975 Wheat Ridge, CO BL/TR 6/185# d9.14																								
1998	Chi A	7	23	2	2	0	2	0	1	1-0	0	8	.087	.125	.261	-3	-4	0-0	1.000	0	219	99	/C-7	-0.3
1999	Chi A	73	207	27	47	11	0	4	16	36-0	2	58	.227	.344	.338	76	-7	3-1	.993	2	117	92	C-72/D-2	0.0
2000	Chi A	75	213	29	48	11	0	3	23	27-0	1	40	.225	.315	.319	60	-13	3-2	.992	6	103	161	C-74/D	-0.2
2001	Chi A	61	173	21	43	6	1	5	18	23-1	2	31	.249	.338	.382	88	-3	2-1	.992	3	126	103	C-61	0.4
2002	Chi A	86	263	31	55	8	1	4	18	30-1	3	52	.209	.297	.293	57	-16	0-0	.994	-3	105	116	C-85	-1.3
2003	Oak A	13	27	3	3	1	0	0	3	3-0	1	4	.111	.219	.148	2	-4	0-0	1.000	2	108	85	C-13	-0.2
Total	6	315	906	113	198	37	4	16	79	120-2	9	193	.219	.314	.321	65	-47	8-4	.993	9	114	117	C-312/D-3	-1.6
JOHNSON, MARK Mark Patrick B 10.17.1967 Worcester, MA BL/TL 6-4/230# d4.26																								
1995	Pit N	79	221	32	46	6	1	13	28	37-2	2	66	.208	.326	.421	94	-2	5-2	.986	-4	82	101	1-70	-1.2
1996	Pit N	127	343	55	94	24	0	13	47	44-3	5	64	.274	.361	.458	112	7	6-4	.994	6	126	92	*1-100/O(LF)	0.5
1997	Pit N	78	219	30	47	10	0	4	29	43-1	2	78	.215	.345	.315	74	-7	1-1	.992	1	106	102	1-63/D	-1.1
1998	Ana A	10	14	1	1	0	0	0	0	0-0	0	6	.071	.071	.071	-62	-3	0-0	1.000	-0	78	121	/1-5,D-2	-0.4
2000	NY N	21	22	2	4	0	0	1	6	5-0	0	9	.182	.333	.318	69	-1	0-0	1.000	1	0	113	/1-4,O(LF)D	-0.1
2001	NY N	71	118	17	30	6	1	6	23	16-1	0	31	.254	.338	.475	114	2	0-2	.991	-3	93	110	1-21,O-19(12-0-7)/D-3	-0.3
2002	NY N	42	51	5	7	4	0	1	4	9-0	0	18	.137	.267	.275	47	-4	0-0	.989	-0	97	84	1-15/O(LF)	-0.5
Total	7	428	988	142	229	50	2	38	137	154-7	9	272	.232	.338	.402	93	-8	12-9	.991	-0	105	98	1-278/O-22(15-0-7),D-7	-3.1
JOHNSON, NICK Nicholas Robert B 9.19.1978 Sacramento, CA BL/TL 6-3/224# d8.21																								
2001	NY A	23	67	6	13	2	0	2	8	7-0	4	15	.194	.308	.313	64	-3	0-0	1.000	-1	67	44	1-15/D-6	-0.5
2002	†NY A	129	378	56	92	15	0	15	58	48-5	12	98	.243	.347	.402	99	1	1-3	.988	2	114	95	1-78,D-50/O-2(LF)	-0.7
2003	†NY A	96	324	60	92	19	0	14	47	70-4	8	57	.284	.422	.472	138	23	5-2	.991	-2	87	92	1-60,D-34	1.3
Total	3	248	769	122	197	36	0	31	113	125-9	24	170	.256	.376	.424	113	21	6-5	.990	-1	98	89	1-153/D-90,O-2(LF)	0.1
JOHNSON, OTIS Otis L. B 11.5.1883 Fowler, IN D 11.9.1915 Johnson City, NY BB/TR 5-9/185# d4.12																								
1911	NY A	71	209	21	49	9	6	3	36	39	3		.234	.363	.378	100	1	12	.907	-8	94	116	S-47,2-15/3-3	-0.4
JOHNSON, PAUL Paul Oscar B 9.2.1896 N.Grosvenor Dale, CT D 2.14.1973 McAllen, TX BR/TR 5-8/160# d9.13																								
1920	Phi A	18	72	6	15	0	0	0	5	4	0	8	.208	.250	.208	22	-8	1-1	.933	-2	76	97	O-18(13-4-1)	-1.1
1921	Phi A	48	127	17	40	6	2	1	10	9	0	17	.315	.360	.417	97	-1	0-2	.969	-3	91	28	O-32(6-24-2)	-0.6
Total	2	66	199	23	55	6	2	1	15	13	0	25	.276	.321	.342	71	-9	1-3	.958	-5	86	53	/O-50(19-28-3)	-1.7
JOHNSON, RANDY Randall Glenn B 6.10.1956 Escondido, CA BR/TR 6-1/190# d4.27																								
1982	Atl N	27	46	5	11	5	0	0	6	6-1	2	4	.239	.345	.348	93	0	0-1	.955	2	123	102	2-13/3-4	0.2
1983	Atl N	86	144	22	36	3	0	1	17	20-3	1	27	.250	.345	.292	73	-5	1-3	.991	8	110	204	3-53/2-4	0.2
1984	Atl N	91	294	28	82	13	0	5	30	21-6	1	21	.279	.329	.374	91	-3	4-7	.939	6	117	110	3-81	0.0
Total	3	204	484	55	129	21	0	6	53	47-10	4	52	.267	.336	.347	85	-8	5-11	.956	16	115	136	3-138/2-17	0.4
JOHNSON, RANDY Randall Stuart B 8.15.1958 Miami, FL BL/TL 6-2/195# d7.5																								
1980	Chi A	12	20	0	4	0	0	0	3	2-0	1	4	.200	.280	.200	41	-2	0-0	—	-0	0	0	/1O(LF)D	-0.2
1982	Min A	89	234	26	58	10	0	10	33	30-2	0	46	.248	.325	.419	102	1	0-0	1.000	-0	71	0	D-67/O-2(RF)	-0.1
Total	2	101	254	26	62	10	0	10	36	32-2	1	50	.244	.321	.402	98	-1	0-0	1.000	-0	85	0	/D-71,O-3(1-0-2),1	-0.3
JOHNSON, REED Reed Cameron B 12.8.1976 Riverside, CA BR/TR 5-10/180# d4.17																								
2003	Tor A	114	412	79	121	21	2	10	52	20-1	20	67	.294	.353	.427	104	3	5-3	.977	-7	82	104	*O-111(53-5-71)	-0.9
JOHNSON, FOOTER Richard Allan "Treads" B 2.15.1932 Dayton, OH BL/TL 5-11/175# d6.15																								
1958	Chi N	8	5	1	0	0	0	0	0	0-0	0	1	.000	.000	.000	-99	-1	0-0	—	0			H	-0.1
JOHNSON, BOB Robert Lee "Indian Bob" B 11.26.1905 Pryor, OK D 7.6.1982 Tacoma, WA BR/TR 6/180# d4.12 b-Roy OF Total (1592-LF 162-CF 24-RF)																								
1933	Phi A	142	535	103	155	44	4	21	93	85	0	74	.290	.387	.505	133	28	8-3	.952	-0	97	111	*O-142(127-1-15)	1.9
1934	Phi A	141	547	111	168	26	6	34	92	58	1	60	.307	.375	.563	144	32	12-8	.967	9	107	147	*O-139(LF)	3.0
1935	Phi A★	147	582	103	174	29	5	28	109	78	2	76	.299	.384	.510	130	26	2-4	.946	4	106	107	*O-147(LF)	1.9
1936	Phi A	153	566	91	165	29	14	25	121	88	2	71	.292	.389	.525	126	22	6-6	.962	5	108	114	*O-131(131-1-0),2-22/1	1.7
1937	Phi A	138	477	91	146	32	6	25	108	98	1	65	.306	.425	.556	148	38	9-7	.976	10	111	135	*O-133(129-6-0)/2-2	3.6
1938	Phi A★	152	563	114	176	27	9	30	113	87	2	73	.313	.406	.552	142	36	9-8	.963	8	106	**158**	*O-150(29-122-0)/2-3,3	3.5
1939	Phi A☆	150	544	115	184	30	9	23	114	99	0	59	.338	.440	.553	156	49	15-5	.967	9	108	145	*O-150(138-14-0)/2	4.8
1940	Phi A☆	138	512	93	137	25	4	31	103	83	4	64	.268	.374	.514	130	23	8-2	.962	6	102	**149**	*O-136(116-13-8)	2.1
1941	Phi A	149	552	98	152	30	8	22	107	95	3	75	.275	.385	.478	130	26	6-4	.990	7	105	161	*O-122(118-4-0),1-28	2.2
1942	Phi A★	149	550	78	160	35	7	13	80	82	1	61	.291	.384	.451	135	28	3-2	.963	5	102	157	*O-149(148-0-1)	2.5
1943	Was A★	117	438	65	116	22	8	7	63	64	3	50	.265	.362	.400	127	16	11-5	.996	8	106	153	O-88(LF),3-19,1-10	2.0
1944	Bos A★	144	525	106	170	40	8	17	106	95	4	67	.324	**.431**	.528	**175**	**57**	2-7	.977	5	91	**203**	*O-142(LF)	5.3

Year	Tm Lg	G	AB	R	H	2B	3B	HR	RBI	BB-IB	HP	SO	AVG	OBP	SLG	AOPS	ABR	SB-CS	FA	FR	Rng	Thr	G at Pos	BFW
1945	Bos A✶	143	529	71	148	27	7	12	74	63	1	56	.280	.358	.425	124	16	5-3	.975	4	101	122	*O-140(140-1-0)	1.2
Total	13	1863	6920	1239	2051	396	95	288	1283	1075	24	851	.296	.393	.506	139	397	96-64	.968	79	104	143	*O-1769L/1-39,2-28,3-20	35.7
JOHNSON, BOB Robert Wallace B 3.4.1936 Omaha, NE BR/TR 5-10/175# d4.19																								
1960	KC A	76	146	12	30	4	0	1	9	19-1	1	23	.205	.301	.253	51	-10	2-0	.947	4	101	96	S-30,2-27,3-11	-0.2
1961	Was A	61	224	27	66	13	1	6	28	19-2	1	26	.295	.350	.442	113	4	4-2	.956	0	105	86	S-57/2-2,3-2	0.9
1962	Was A	135	466	58	134	20	2	12	43	32-1	1	50	.288	.334	.416	102	0	9-6	.944	-7	98	94	3-72,S-50/2-3,O(LF)	-0.3
1963	Bal A	82	254	34	75	10	0	8	32	18-0	2	35	.295	.347	.429	120	7	5-1	.987	2	106	122	2-50/1-8,S-7,3-5	1.4
1964	Bal A	93	210	18	52	8	2	3	29	9-1	1	37	.248	.281	.348	74	-8	0-0	.964	-5	82	66	S-18,1-15,2-15/30(LF)	-1.2
1965	Bal A	87	273	36	66	13	2	5	27	15-2	1	34	.242	.282	.359	80	-8	1-0	.996	-8	75	84	1-34,S-23,3-13/2-5	-1.6
1966	Bal A	71	157	13	34	5	0	1	10	12-1	1	24	.217	.276	.268	58	-8	0-1	.966	-0	109	111	2-20,1-17/3-3	-0.9
1967	Bal A	4	3	1	1	0	0	0	0	1-0	0	1	.333	.500	.333	152	0	0-0	—	0			H	0.0
	NY N	90	230	26	80	8	3	5	27	12-0	0	29	.348	.377	.474	145	13	1-1	.987	-4	91	103	2-39,1-23,S-14/3	1.1
1968	Cin N	16	15	2	4	0	0	0	1	1-0	0	2	.267	.313	.267	71	-1	0-0	.500	-1	92	0	/S-2,1	-0.2
	Atl N	59	187	15	49	5	1	0	11	10-3	0	20	.262	.298	.299	80	-5	0-0	.948	2	107	106	3-48/2-4	-0.3
	Year	75	202	17	53	5	1	0	12	11-3	0	22	.262	.299	.297	79	-5	0-0	.948	1	107	106	3-48/2-4,S-2,1	-0.5
1969	StL N	19	29	1	6	0	0	1	2	2-0	0	4	.207	.258	.310	58	-2	0-0	.833	-1	91	157	/3-4,1	-0.2
	Oak A	51	67	5	23	1	0	1	9	3-1	1	4	.343	.375	.403	125	2	0-0	1.000	0	125	176	/1-7,2-2	0.2
1970	Oak A	30	46	6	8	1	0	1	2	3-0	1	2	.174	.235	.261	39	-4	2-1	.952	1	137	86	/3-6,1	-0.3
Total	11	874	2307	254	628	88	11	44	230	156-12	10	291	.272	.320	.377	95	-20	24-12	.956	-16	98	80	S-201,2-167,3-166,1-107/O-2(LF)	-1.6
JOHNSON, RON Ronald David B 3.23.1956 Long Beach, CA BR/TR 6-3/215# d9.12																								
1982	KC A	8	14	2	4	2	0	0	0	4-0	0	3	.286	.444	.429	141	1	0-0	.976	-0	74	80	/1-7	0.0
1983	KC A	9	27	2	7	0	0	0	1	3-0	0	1	.259	.333	.259	66	-1	0-0	.971	-1	64	134	/1-7,C-2	-0.3
1984	Mon N	5	5	0	1	0	0	0	1	0-0	0	2	.200	.200	.200	13	-1	0-0	1.000	-0	0	0	/1-2,O(RF)	-0.1
Total	3	22	46	4	12	2	0	0	2	7-0	0	6	.261	.358	.304	85	-1	0-0	.974	-2	64	107	/1-16,C-2,O(RF)	-0.4
JOHNSON, RONDIN Rondin Allen B 12.16.1958 Bremerton, WA BB/TR 5-10/160# d9.3																								
1986	KC A	11	31	1	8	0	1	0	2	0-0	0	3	.258	.258	.323	56	-2	0-0	1.000	3	135	94	2-11	0.1
JOHNSON, RONTREZ Rontrez Demon B 12.8.1976 Marshall, TX BR/TR 5-10/180# d3.31																								
2003	KC A	8	3	3	1	0	0	0	0	0-0	0	2	.333	.333	.333	68	0	0-0	.000	-1	0	0	/O-6(CF),D-2	-0.1
JOHNSON, ROY Roy Cleveland B 2.23.1903 Pryor, OK D 9.10.1973 Tacoma, WA BL/TR 5-9/175# d4.18 b-Bob																								
1929	Det A	148	640	128	201	**45**	14	10	69	67	0	60	.314	.379	.475	118	17	20-16	.928	6	103	153	*O-146(91-37-23)	1.1
1930	Det A	125	462	84	127	30	13	2	35	40	0	46	.275	.333	.409	85	-11	17-10	.936	5	106	**153**	*O-118(7-2-110)	-1.4
1931	Det A	151	621	107	173	37	**19**	8	55	72	2	51	.279	.355	.438	104	3	33-21	.960	11	105	**165**	*O-150(0-5-148)	0.4
1932	Det A	49	195	33	49	14	2	3	22	20	1	26	.251	.324	.390	81	-6	7-2	.929	-1	103	78	O-48(RF)	-0.8
	Bos A	94	349	70	104	24	4	11	47	44	1	41	.298	.378	.484	125	14	13-4	.930	-8	86	85	O-85(14-16-56)	0.2
	Year	143	544	103	153	38	6	14	69	64	2	67	.281	.359	.450	109	7	20-6	.930	-9	92	82	*O-133(14-16-104)	-0.6
1933	Bos A	133	483	88	151	30	7	10	95	55	4	36	.313	.387	.466	126	19	13-10	.922	1	104	116	*O-125(26-10-95)	1.1
1934	Bos A	143	569	85	182	43	10	7	119	54	0	36	.320	.379	.467	109	8	11-5	.948	-5	92	102	*O-137(LF)	-0.4
1935	Bos A	145	553	70	174	33	9	3	66	74	3	34	.315	.398	.423	105	7	11-12	.944	2	91	184	*O-142(LF)	0.0
1936	†NY A	63	147	21	39	8	2	1	19	21	1	14	.265	.361	.367	83	-4	3-1	.944	-0	105	74	O-33(28-0-3)	-0.5
1937	NY A	12	51	5	15	3	0	0	6	3	0	2	.294	.333	.353	73	-2	1-0	.840	-2	85	0	O-12(LF)	-0.4
	Bos N	85	260	24	72	8	3	3	22	38	0	29	.277	.369	.365	110	5	5	.965	-1	98	105	O-63(LF)/3	0.0
1938	Bos N	7	29	2	5	0	0	0	1	1	0	5	.172	.200	.172	4	-4	1	.769	-2	67	0	/O-7(LF)	-0.7
Total	10	1155	4359	717	1292	275	83	58	556	489	12	380	.296	.369	.437	107	46	135-81	.938	6	99	131	*O-1066(527-70-483)/3	-1.4
JOHNSON, ROY Roy Edward B 6.27.1959 Parkin, AR BL/TL 6-4/205# d7.3																								
1982	Mon N	17	32	2	7	2	0	0	2	1-0	0	6	.219	.235	.281	45	-2	0-0	1.000	-0	108	0	O-11(0-9-3)	-0.3
1984	Mon N	16	33	2	5	2	0	1	2	7-0	0	10	.152	.300	.303	73	-1	1-0	.938	-1	87	0	O-10(9-0-1)	-0.2
1985	Mon N	3	5	0	0	0	0	0	0	0-0	0	3	.000	.000	.000	-99	-1	0-0	—	-1	0	0	/O-3(0-1-2)	-0.2
Total	3	36	70	4	12	4	0	1	4	8-0	0	19	.171	.253	.271	49	-4	1-0	.971	-2	90	0	/O-24(9-10-6)	-0.7
JOHNSON, STAN Stanley Lucius B 2.12.1937 Dallas, TX BL/TL 5-10/180# d9.18																								
1960	Chi A	5	6	1	1	0	0	1	1	0-0	0	1	.167	.167	.667	116	0	0-1	1.000	-0	84	0	/O-2(LF)	0.0
1961	KC A	3	3	1	0	0	0	0	0	2-0	0	1	.000	.400	.000	17	0	0-0	—	-0	0	0	/O-2(RF)	0.0
Total	2	8	9	2	1	0	0	1	1	2-0	0	2	.111	.273	.444	89	0	0-1	1.000	-0	70	0	/O-4(2-0-2)	0.0
JOHNSON, TIM Timothy Evald B 7.22.1949 Grand Forks, ND BL/TR 6-1/170# d4.24 M1 C4 OF Total (LF)																								
1973	Mil A	136	465	39	99	10	2	0	32	29-2	1	93	.213	.259	.243	44	-36	6-3	.962	-13	94	100	*S-135	-3.4
1974	Mil A	93	245	25	60	7	7	0	25	11-1	1	48	.245	.278	.331	76	-9	4-3	.970	-1	106	94	S-64,2-26/30(LF)D	-0.2
1975	Mil A	38	85	6	12	1	0	0	2	6-0	0	17	.141	.198	.153	0	-11	3-0	1.000	-4	105	91	2-11,3-11,S-10/1-2,D-3	-1.4
1976	Mil A	105	273	25	75	4	3	0	14	19-0	2	32	.275	.327	.311	89	-4	4-1	.980	-14	93	76	*2-100,3-17/1S	-1.3
1977	Mil A	30	33	5	2	1	0	0	2	5-1	0	10	.061	.179	.091	-22	-6	1-0	.929	-2	18	0	2-10/S-6,3-4,O(LF)D	-0.6
1978	Mil A	3	3	1	0	0	0	0	0	2-0	0	0	.000	.400	.000	22	0	0-0	1.000	-2	0	0	/S-2	-0.2
	Tor A	68	79	9	19	2	0	0	3	8-0	1	16	.241	.315	.266	65	-3	0-1	.975	1	95	57	S-49,2-13	-0.1
	Year	71	82	10	19	2	0	0	3	10-0	1	16	.232	.319	.256	63	-4	0-1	.975	-2	89	53	S-51,2-13	-0.3
1979	Tor A	43	86	6	16	2	1	0	6	8-0	0	15	.186	.255	.233	32	-8	0-1	.958	3	87	138	2-25/3-9,1-7	-0.5
Total	7	516	1269	116	283	27	13	0	84	88-4	5	231	.223	.274	.265	55	-77	18-9	.965	-31	97	95	S-267,2-185/3-42,1-10,D-8,O-2L	-7.7
JOHNSON, WALLACE Wallace Darnell B 12.25.1956 Gary, IN BB/TR 5-11/185# d9.8 C5																								
1981	†Mon N	11	9	1	2	0	1	0	3	1-1	0	1	.222	.300	.444	108	0	1-1	1.000	0	135	388	/2	0.0
1982	Mon N	36	57	5	11	0	2	0	2	5-0	0	5	.193	.258	.263	45	-4	4-1	.952	-2	71	90	2-13	-0.6
1983	Mon N	3	2	1	1	0	0	0	0	1-0	0	0	.500	.667	.500	229	1	1-0	—	0			/H	0.1
	SF N	7	8	0	1	0	0	0	1	0-0	0	0	.125	.125	.125	-32	-1	0-0	1.000	0	73	168	/2	-0.1
	Year	10	10	1	2	0	0	0	1	1-0	0	0	.200	.273	.200	34	-1	1-0	1.000	0	73	168	/2	0.0
1984	Mon N	17	24	3	5	0	0	0	4	5-0	0	4	.208	.345	.208	61	-1	0-0	.968	0	134	126	/1-4	-0.1
1986	Mon N	61	127	13	36	3	1	1	10	7-0	0	9	.283	.321	.346	85	-3	6-3	.991	-0	98	89	1-27	-0.4
1987	Mon N	75	85	7	21	5	0	1	14	7-0	0	6	.247	.298	.341	69	-4	5-0	.972	-1	44	91	/1-9	-0.4
1988	Mon N	86	94	7	29	5	1	0	3	12-1	0	15	.309	.387	.383	116	3	0-2	.989	1	116	49	1-13/2	0.2
1989	Mon N	85	114	9	31	3	1	2	17	7-0	0	12	.272	.309	.368	93	-1	1-0	.972	-1	77	92	1-18	-0.4
1990	Mon N	47	49	6	8	1	0	1	5	7-2	1	6	.163	.281	.245	48	-3	1-0	1.000	-1	0	285	/1-7	-0.5
Total	9	428	569	52	145	17	6	5	59	52-4	1	58	.255	.316	.332	81	-13	19-7	.983	-5	86	98	/1-78,2-16	-2.2
JOHNSON, BILL William F. "Sleepy Bill" B 9.1862 , NJ D 7.17.1942 Chester, PA BL/TL ?/140# d6.27																								
1884	Phi U	1	4	0	0	0	0	0		0			.000	.000	.000	-99	-1		—	-0	0	0	/O(LF)	-0.1
1887	Ind N	11	42	3	8	0	0	0	3	0	1	6	.190	.209	.190	12	-5	5	.765	-1	120	0	O-11(RF)	-0.5
1890	Bal AA	24	95	15	28	2	3	0	6	7	1		.295	.350	.379	110	1	8	.865	3	151	347	O-24(RF)	0.3
1891	Bal AA	129	480	101	130	13	14	2	79	89	4	55	.271	.389	.369	116	13	32	.877	3	120	103	*O-129(60-24-46)	1.1
1892	Bal N	4	15	2	2	0	0	0	2	2	0	0	.133	.235	.133	12	-2	0	.667	-1	0	0	/O-4(1-0-3)	-0.3
Total	5	169	636	121	168	15	17	2	90	98	6	61	.264	.368	.351	105	6	45	.867	3	121	128	O-169(62-24-84)	0.5
JOHNSON, BILL William Lawrence B 10.18.1892 Chicago, IL D 11.15.1950 Los Angeles, CA BL/TR 5-11/170# d9.22																								
1916	Phi A	4	15	1	4	1	0	0	1	0	0	4	.267	.267	.333	84	0	0	1.000	-1	70	0	/O-4(CF)	-0.1
1917	Phi A	48	109	7	19	2	2	1	8	8	1	14	.174	.237	.257	51	-7	4	.900	-2	70	142	O-30(2-1-27)	-1.1
Total	2	52	124	8	23	3	2	1	9	8	1	18	.185	.241	.266	55	-7	4	.909	-2	70	129	/O-34(2-5-27)	-1.2
JOHNSON, BILLY William Russell "Bull" B 8.30.1918 Montclair, NJ BR/TR 5-10/180# d4.22 Mil 1944-46																								
1943	†NY A	**155**	592	70	166	24	6	5	94	53	4	30	.280	.344	.367	107	5	3-5	.966	13	106	120	*3-155	2.0
1946	NY A	85	296	51	77	14	5	4	35	31	2	42	.260	.334	.382	98	-1	1-0	.955	5	108	97	3-74	0.5
1947	†NY A★	132	494	67	141	19	8	10	95	44	6	43	.285	.351	.417	114	8	1-2	.952	-17	81	54	*3-132	-1.1
1948	NY A	127	446	59	131	20	6	12	64	41	4	30	.294	.358	.446	114	7	0-0	.947	3	94	122	*3-118	0.9
1949	†NY A	113	329	48	82	11	3	8	56	48	2	44	.249	.348	.374	91	-5	1-0	.951	-3	93	95	3-81,1-21/2	-0.8
1950	†NY A	108	327	44	85	16	2	6	40	42	1	30	.260	.346	.376	87	-6	1-0	.958	-3	94	113	*3-100/1-5	-0.9
1951	NY A	15	40	5	12	3	0	0	4	7	0	0	.300	.404	.375	116	1	0-1	.960	-2	83	0	3-13	-0.1

Year	Tm Lg	G	AB	R	H	2B	3B	HR	RBI	BB-IB	HP	SO	AVG	OBP	SLG	AOPS	ABR	SB-CS	FA	FR	Rng	Thr	G at Pos	BFW
	StL N	124	442	52	116	23	1	14	64	46	6	49	.262	.340	.414	101	1	5-3	**.976**	10	**115**	**106**	*3-124	1.0
1952	StL N	94	282	23	71	10	2	2	34	34	3	21	.252	.339	.323	84	-5	1-0	.951	4	112	79	3-89	-0.2
1953	StL N	11	5	0	1	1	0	0	1	1	0	1	.200	.333	.400	90	0	0-0	1.000	1	172	206	3-11	0.1
Total	9	964	3253	419	882	141	33	61	487	347	28	290	.271	.346	.391	102	5	13-11	.959	10	100	98	3-897/1-26,2	1.4
JOHNSON, RUSS William Russell B 2.22.1973 Baton Rouge, LA BR/TR 5-10/185# d4.8																								
1997	†Hou N	21	60	7	18	1	0	2	9	6-0	0	14	.300	.364	.417	108	1	1-1	.963	-2	93	99	3-14/2-3	-0.1
1998	Hou N	8	13	2	3	1	0	0	0	1-0	1	5	.231	.333	.308	72	0	1-0	1.000	1	174	0	/3-5,2	0.1
1999	†Hou N	83	156	24	44	10	0	5	23	20-0	0	31	.282	.358	.442	104	1	2-3	.944	7	109	201	3-36,2-15/S-2	0.8
2000	Hou N	26	45	4	8	0	0	0	3	2-0	0	10	.178	.213	.178	-0	-7	1-1	1.000	-4	67	71	/S-5,3-4,2-3	-1.0
	TB A	74	185	28	47	8	0	2	17	25-0	1	30	.254	.344	.330	73	-7	4-1	.967	9	135	108	3-49,2-18,S-11	0.3
2001	TB A	85	248	32	73	19	2	4	33	34-0	1	57	.294	.380	.435	116	7	2-2	.922	-4	91	116	3-36,2-33/S-6,D-2	0.5
2002	TB A	45	111	15	24	5	0	1	12	16-1	1	22	.216	.320	.288	65	-5	5-2	.984	-5	75	99	3-27/S-2,2D	-0.9
Total	6	342	818	112	217	44	2	14	97	104-1	4	169	.265	.349	.375	89	-10	16-10	.956	2	104	122	3-171/2-74,S-26,D-7	-0.3
JOHNSTON, GREG Gregory Bernard B 2.12.1955 Los Angeles, CA BL/TL 6/175# d7.27																								
1979	SF N	42	74	5	15	2	0	1	7	2-0	0	17	.203	.224	.270	37	-7	0-0	.966	1	118	110	O-17(13-1-5)	-0.7
1980	Min A	14	27	3	5	3	0	0	1	2-0	0	4	.185	.233	.296	43	-2	0-0	1.000	-0	106	0	O-14(CF)	-0.2
1981	Min A	7	16	2	2	0	0	0	0	2-0	0	5	.125	.222	.125	2	-2	0-0	1.000	0	76	307	/O-6(CF)	-0.2
Total	3	63	117	10	22	5	0	1	8	6-0	0	26	.188	.226	.256	33	-11	0-0	.985	1	105	115	/O-37(13-21-5)	-1.1
JOHNSTON, JIMMY James Harle B 12.10.1889 Cleveland, TN D 2.14.1967 Chattanooga, TN BR/TR 5-10/160# d5.3 C1 b-Doc OF Total (72-LF 112-CF 177-RF)																								
1911	Chi A	1	2	0	0	0	0	0	2	0	0		.000	.000	.000	-99	-1	0	1.000	-0	100	0	/O(CF)	-0.1
1914	Chi N	50	101	9	23	3	2	1	8	4	1	9	.228	.264	.327	76	-4	3	.929	4	119	246	O-28(2-22-4)/2-4	-0.1
1916	†Bro N	118	425	58	107	13	8	1	26	35	3	38	.252	.313	.327	94	-3	22-19	.964	4	104	119	*O-106(8-45-55)	-0.9
1917	Bro N	103	330	33	89	10	4	0	25	23	2	28	.270	.321	.324	96	-2	16	.958	0	103	90	O-66(37-24-5),1-14/S-4,2-3,3-3	-0.6
1918	Bro N	123	484	54	136	16	8	0	27	33	1	31	.281	.328	.347	106	3	22	.956	4	98	121	O-96(20-5-75),1-21/3-4,2	0.2
1919	Bro N	117	405	56	114	11	4	1	23	29	3	26	.281	.334	.336	100	0	11	.960	-2	105	84	2-87,O-14(1-8-6)/1-2,S	-0.1
1920	†Bro N	**155**	635	87	185	17	12	1	52	43	2	23	.291	.338	.361	98	-2	19-15	.934	-7	96	88	*3-146/O-7(RF),S-3	-0.7
1921	Bro N	**152**	624	104	203	41	14	5	56	45	1	26	.325	.372	.460	115	14	28-16	.935	7	103	**120**	*3-150/S-3	3.0
1922	Bro N	138	567	110	181	20	7	4	49	38	2	17	.319	.364	.400	98	-2	18-9	.947	0	97	105	2-62,S-50,3-26	0.8
1923	Bro N	151	625	111	203	29	11	4	60	53	0	15	.325	.378	.426	115	14	16-13	.948	14	99	92	2-84,S-52,3-14	3.5
1924	Bro N	86	315	51	94	11	2	2	29	27	1	10	.298	.356	.365	97	-1	5-6	.939	-4	93	80	S-63,3-10/1-4,O(RF)	0.1
1925	Bro N	123	431	63	128	13	3	2	43	45	4	15	.297	.369	.355	88	-6	7-5	.886	-20	75	66	3-81,O-20(2-0-18)/1-8,S-2	-2.2
1926	Bos N	23	57	7	14	1	0	1	5	10	0	3	.246	.358	.316	91	0	2	.865	-3	89	128	3-14/2-2,O(LF)	-0.2
	NY N	37	69	11	16	0	0	0	5	6	0	5	.232	.293	.232	43	-5	0	1.000	-2	60	0	O-14(1-7-6)	-0.8
	Year	60	126	18	30	1	0	1	10	16	0	8	.238	.324	.270	64	-6	2	1.000	-5	62	0	O-15(2-7-6),3-14/2-2	-1.0
Total	13	1377	5070	754	1493	185	75	22	410	391	20	246	.294	.347	.374	100	5	169-83	.926	-4	93	88	3-448,O-354R,2-243,S-178/1-49	1.9
JOHNSTON, JOHNNY John Thomas B 3.28.1890 Longview, TX D 3.7.1940 San Diego, CA BL/TR 5-11/172# d4.10																								
1913	StL A	111	380	37	85	14	4	2	27	42	4	51	.224	.308	.297	79	-9	11	.965	10	107	152	*O-107(LF)	-0.5
JOHNSTON, REX Rex David B 11.8.1937 Colton, CA BB/TR 6-1.5/202# d4.15																								
1964	Pit N	14	7	1	0	0	0	0	0	3-1	0	0	.000	.300	.000	-7	-1	0-0	1.000	0	99	0	/O-8(6-2-0)	-0.1
JOHNSTON, DICK Richard Frederick B 4.6.1863 Kingston, NY D 4.4.1934 Detroit, MI BR/TR 5-8/155# d8.12																								
1884	Ric AA	39	146	23	41	5	5	2		2	0		.281	.291	.425	132	4		.865	8	143	254	O-37(CF)/S-2	1.0
1885	Bos N	26	111	17	26	6	3	1	23	0		15	.234	.234	.369	96	-1		.842	1	174	306	O-26(CF)	0.0
1886	Bos N	109	413	48	99	18	9	1	57	3		70	.240	.245	.334	77	-13	11	.892	14	133	117	*O-109(CF)	-0.3
1887	Bos N	**127**	507	87	131	13	20	5	77	16	0	35	.258	.281	.393	84	-14	52	.933	23	151	209	*O-127(CF)	0.3
1888	Bos N	135	585	102	173	31	**18**	12	68	15	1	33	.296	.314	.472	144	26	35	.898	4	131	67	*O-135(CF)	2.5
1889	Bos N	132	539	80	123	16	4	5	67	41	2	60	.228	.285	.301	60	-32	34	.917	-8	87	139	*O-132(CF)	-3.9
1890	Bos P	2	9	0	1	0	0	0	0	0	0	1	.111	.111	.111	-38	-2	0	.800	0	313	0	/O-2(CF)	-0.1
	NY P	77	306	37	74	9	7	1	43	18	2	25	.242	.288	.327	59	-20	7	.897	-0	123	106	O-76(12-62-2)/S-2	-1.9
	Year	79	315	37	75	9	7	1	43	18	2	26	.238	.284	.321	56	-22	7	.894	0	127	104	O-78(12-64-2)/S-2	-2.0
1891	Cin AA	99	376	59	83	11	2	6	51	38	5	44	.221	.301	.309	69	-17	12	.895	-2	115	102	*O-99(0-99-1)	-2.0
Total	8	746	2992	453	751	109	68	33	386	133	10	283	.251	.285	.366	86	-69	151	.903	40	126	137	O-743(12-729-3)/S-4	-4.4
JOHNSTON, DOC Wheeler Roger B 9.9.1887 Cleveland, TN D 2.17.1961 Chattanooga, TN BL/TL 6/170# d10.3 b-Jimmy																								
1909	Cin N	3	10	1	0	0	0	0	1	0	0		.000	.000	.000	-99	-2	0	1.000	0	142	0	/1-3	-0.2
1912	Cle A	43	164	22	46	7	4	1	11	11	0		.280	.326	.390	101	-1	8	.991	-1	76	142	1-41	-0.3
1913	Cle A	133	530	74	135	19	12	2	39	35	7	65	.255	.309	.347	89	-9	19	.989	-1	92	105	*1-133	-1.4
1914	Cle A	104	340	43	83	15	1	0	23	28	5	46	.244	.311	.294	79	-8	14-9	.987	-7	65	86	1-90/O-2(CF)	-1.9
1915	Pit N	147	543	71	144	19	12	5	64	38	13	40	.265	.328	.372	113	8	26-17	.991	-12	61	84	*1-147	-0.9
1916	Pit N	114	404	33	86	10	10	0	39	20	7	42	.213	.262	.287	68	-16	17	.987	-3	87	71	*1-110	-2.5
1918	Cle A	74	273	30	62	12	2	0	25	26	3	19	.227	.301	.286	70	-9	12	.989	-3	83	58	1-73	-1.6
1919	Cle A	102	331	42	101	17	3	1	33	25	3	18	.305	.359	.384	102	1	21	.984	-4	89	117	1-98	-0.5
1920	†Cle A	147	535	68	156	24	10	2	71	28	5	32	.292	.333	.385	87	-11	13-7	.992	-1	95	105	*1-147	-1.5
1921	Cle A	118	384	53	114	20	7	2	46	29	4	15	.297	.353	.401	90	-6	2-9	.988	-2	95	110	*1-116	-1.6
1922	Phi A	71	260	41	65	11	7	1	29	24	1	15	.250	.316	.358	73	-11	7-6	.990	-5	74	73	1-65	-2.0
Total	11	1056	3774	478	992	154	68	14	381	264	48	292	.263	.319	.351	88	-64	139-48	.989	-37	83	94	*1-1023/O-2(CF)	-14.4
JOHNSTON, FRED Wilfred Ivy B 7.9.1899 Charlotte, NC D 7.14.1959 Tyler, TX BR/TR 5-11.5/170# d6.29																								
1924	Bro N	4	4	1	1	0	0	0	0	0	0	1	.250	.250	.250	35	0	0-0	.667	-0	123	0	/23	-0.1
JOHNSTONE, JAY John William B 11.20.1945 Manchester, CT BL/TR 6-1/175# d7.30 OF Total (258-LF 521-CF 572-RF)																								
1966	Cal A	61	254	35	67	12	4	3	17	11-1	1	36	.264	.297	.378	95	-3	3-3	.975	-3	93	50	O-61(41-12-13)	-1.0
1967	Cal A	79	230	18	48	7	1	2	10	5-0	1	37	.209	.226	.274	49	-16	3-2	.973	3	119	95	O-63(0-62-1)	-1.6
1968	Cal A	41	115	11	30	4	1	0	3	7-0	0	15	.261	.303	.313	90	-2	2-1	.984	2	100	233	O-29(1-21-7)	-0.1
1969	Cal A	148	540	64	146	20	5	10	59	38-5	5	75	.270	.321	.381	102	-1	3-9	.983	3	104	139	*O-144(CF)	-0.3
1970	Cal A	119	320	34	76	10	5	11	39	24-6	1	53	.237	.290	.403	93	-5	1-0	.981	-1	99	124	*O-100(2-88-10)	-0.8
1971	Chi A	124	388	53	101	14	1	16	40	38-4	3	50	.260	.329	.425	109	4	10-5	.968	-2	95	136	*O-119(11-92-23)	0.0
1972	Chi A	113	261	27	49	9	0	4	17	25-2	0	42	.188	.259	.268	56	-14	2-1	.988	-2	94	109	O-97(13-85-6)	-2.1
1973	Oak A	23	28	1	3	1	0	0	3	2-0	0	4	.107	.167	.143	-13	-4	0-1	1.000	1	204	0	/O-7(3-1-3),2-2,D-4	-0.4
1974	Phi N	64	200	30	59	10	4	6	30	24-4	0	28	.295	.371	.475	130	8	5-5	.968	-2	88	109	O-59(31-1-40)	0.2
1975	Phi N	122	350	50	115	19	2	7	54	42-7	0	39	.329	.397	.454	132	16	7-3	.976	3	95	181	*O-101(0-3-100)	1.6
1976	†Phi N	129	440	62	140	38	4	5	53	41-5	2	39	.318	.373	.457	132	20	5-5	.982	8	121	88	*O-122(2-0-120)/1-6	2.3
1977	†Phi N	112	363	64	103	18	4	15	59	38-3	2	38	.284	.349	.479	116	8	3-7	1.000	4	103	146	O-91(4-0-87),1-19	0.5
1978	Phi N	35	56	3	10	2	0	0	4	6-0	0	9	.179	.258	.214	33	-5	0-2	.988	0	161	173	/1-8,O-7(3-0-4)	-0.7
	†NY A	36	65	6	17	0	0	1	6	4-0	3	10	.262	.329	.308	83	-1	0-1	1.000	-0	110	0	O-22(8-0-14)/D-5	-0.3
1979	NY A	23	48	7	10	1	0	1	7	2-0	0	7	.208	.240	.292	44	-4	1-0	1.000	1	127	0	O-19(14-4-1)/D-3	-0.4
	SD N	75	201	10	59	8	2	0	32	18-3	0	21	.294	.348	.353	99	0	1-3	.985	-0	80	142	O-45(35-7-4),1-22	-0.4
1980	LA N	109	251	31	77	15	2	2	20	24-1	2	29	.307	.372	.406	119	7	3-2	.965	3	101	202	O-61(5-0-57)	0.8
1981	†LA N	61	83	8	17	3	0	3	6	7-0	0	13	.205	.267	.349	76	-3	0-1	.957	1	93	334	O-16(8-0-8)/1-2	-0.3
1982	LA N	21	13	1	1	1	0	0	2	5-1	0	2	.077	.316	.154	41	-1	0-0	—	0			H	-0.1
	Chi N	98	269	39	67	13	1	10	43	40-8	0	41	.249	.343	.416	109	4	0-2	.982	4	106	140	O-86(34-0-58)	0.4
	Year	119	282	40	68	14	1	10	45	45-9	0	43	.241	.341	.404	107	4	0-2	.982	4	106	140	O-86(34-0-58)	0.3
1983	Chi N	86	140	16	36	7	0	6	22	20-6	3	24	.257	.362	.436	115	3	1-1	.935	-1	90	127	O-44(36-0-8)	0.1
1984	Chi N	52	73	8	21	2	2	0	3	7-4	0	18	.288	.350	.370	94	-1	0-0	1.000	-2	64	0	O-15(7-1-8)	-0.3
1985	†LA N	17	15	0	2	1	0	0	2	1-1	0	2	.133	.188	.200	9	-2	0-0	—	0			H	-0.2
Total	20	1748	4703	578	1254	215	38	102	531	429-61	22	632	.267	.329	.394	103	8	50-54	.979	21	101	128	*O-1308R/1-57,D-12,2-2	-3.1
JOK, STAN Stanley Edward "Tucker" B 5.3.1926 Buffalo, NY D 3.6.1972 Buffalo, NY BR/TR 6/190# d4.13																								
1954	Phi N	3	3	0	0	0	0	0	0	0	0	2	.000	.000	.000	-99	-1	0-0	—	0			H	-0.1
	Chi A	3	12	1	2	0	0	0	2	1	0	2	.167	.231	.167	10	-2	0-0	1.000	0	101	180	/3-3	-0.1
1955	Chi A	6	4	3	1	0	0	1	2	1-0	0	1	.250	.333	1.000	260	1	0-0	.857	-0	112	0	/3-3,O(LF)	0.1

Year	Tm Lg	G	AB	R	H	2B	3B	HR	RBI	BB-IB	HP	SO	AVG	OBP	SLG	AOPS	ABR	SB-CS	FA	FR	Rng	Thr	G at Pos	BFW
Total	2	12	19	4	3	0	0	1	4	2-0	0	5	.158	.227	.316	47	-2	0-0	.941	0	105	116	/3-6,O(LF)	-0.1
JOLLEY, SMEAD Smead Powell "Guinea" or "Smudge" B 1.14.1902 Wesson, AR D 11.17.1991 Alameda, CA BL/TR 6-3.5/210# d4.17																								
1930	Chi A	152	616	76	193	38	12	16	114	28	3	52	.313	.346	.492	114	10	3-1	.950	-0	93	146	*O-151(68-0-83)	-0.1
1931	Chi A	54	110	5	33	11	0	3	28	7	2	4	.300	.353	.482	125	4	0-0	.857	-3	76	60	O-23(8-0-15)	0.0
1932	Chi A	12	42	3	15	3	0	0	7	3	1	0	.357	.413	.429	127	2	1-0	.923	-1	63	158	O-11(7-0-4)	0.1
	Bos A	137	531	57	164	27	5	18	99	27	2	29	.309	.345	.480	115	8	0-5	.943	-3	90	131	*O-126(120-0-6)/C-5	-0.3
	Year	149	573	60	179	30	5	18	106	30	3	29	.312	.350	.476	116	10	1-5	.942	-4	88	133	*O-137(127-0-10)/C-5	-0.2
1933	Bos A	118	411	47	116	32	4	9	65	24	2	20	.282	.325	.445	103	1	1-1	.955	-0	92	132	*O-102(87-0-15)	-0.5
Total	4	473	1710	188	521	111	21	46	313	89	10	105	.305	.343	.475	112	25	5-7	.944	-8	90	134	O-413(290-0-123)/C-5	-0.8
JONES B Johnstown, PA d7.14																								
1884	Was AA	4	17	2	5	0	0	0		1	0		.294	.333	.294	120	0		1.000	0	0	0	/O-4(LF)	0.0
JONES d4.30																								
1885	NY AA	1	4	0	1	0	0	0	0	0	0		.250	.250	.250	61	0		1.000	1	156	0	/3	0.1
JONES, ANDRUW Andruw Rudolf B 4.23.1977 Willemstad, Curacao BR/TR 6-1/170# d8.15																								
1996	†Atl N	31	106	11	23	7	1	5	13	7-0	0	29	.217	.265	.443	78	-4	3-0	.975	6	141	256	O-29(0-12-20)	0.2
1997	†Atl N	153	399	60	92	18	1	18	70	56-2	4	107	.231	.329	.416	92	-5	20-11	.977	17	**126**	**202**	*O-147(2-57-95)	1.0
1998	†Atl N	159	582	89	158	33	8	31	90	40-8	4	129	.271	.321	.515	116	10	27-4	.995	20	118	**215**	*O-159(CF)	3.5
1999	†Atl N	**162**	592	97	163	35	5	26	84	76-11	9	103	.275	.365	.483	113	12	24-12	.981	17	**122**	145	*O-162(CF)	3.0
2000	†Atl N★	161	656	122	199	36	6	36	104	59-0	9	100	.303	.366	.541	126	24	21-6	.996	5	110	91	*O-161(CF)	3.1
2001	†Atl N	161	625	104	157	25	2	34	104	56-3	3	142	.251	.312	.461	95	-7	11-4	.987	11	**117**	111	*O-161(CF)	0.7
2002	†Atl N★	154	560	91	148	34	0	35	94	83-4	10	135	.264	.366	.512	132	24	8-3	.993	-1	106	56	*O-154(CF)/D	2.5
2003	†Atl N★	156	595	101	165	28	2	36	116	53-2	5	125	.277	.338	.513	119	14	4-3	.993	2	105	93	*O-155(CF)	1.7
Total	8	1137	4115	675	1105	216	25	221	675	430-30	44	870	.269	.341	.494	113	68	118-43	.989	77	115	130	*O-1128(2-1021-115)/D	15.7
JONES, CHARLIE Charles Claude "Casey" B 6.2.1876 Butler, PA D 4.2.1947 Two Harbors, MN BR/TR 6-1/165# d5.2																								
1901	Bos A	10	41	6	6	2	0	0	6	1	0		.146	.167	.195	0	-6	2	.929	-2	0	0	O-10(0-8-2)	-0.7
1904	Chi A	5	17	2	4	0	1	0	1	1	0		.235	.278	.353	103	0	0	1.000	1	411	0	/O-5(CF)	0.1
1905	Was A	142	544	68	113	18	4	2	41	31	3		.208	.254	.267	68	-21	24	.971	14	153	161	*O-142(CF)	-1.5
1906	Was A	131	497	56	120	11	11	3	42	24	5		.241	.283	.326	95	-5	34	.961	5	124	181	*O-128(CF)/2	-0.7
1907	Was A	121	437	48	116	14	10	0	37	22	2		.265	.304	.343	115	5	26	.967	-2	43	58	*O-111(12-90-8)/2-5,1-4,S-2	-0.2
1908	StL A	74	263	37	61	11	2	0	17	14	3		.232	.279	.289	84	-5	14	.963	2	182	107	O-72(0-70-2)	-0.7
Total	6	483	1799	217	420	56	28	5	144	93	13		.233	.276	.304	87	-32	100	.966	17	122	130	O-468(12-443-12)/2-6,1-4,S-2	-3.7
JONES, CHARLIE Charles F. B 10.24.1861 New York, NY D 9.15.1922 New York, NY d6.28																								
1884	Bro AA	25	90	10	16	1	0	0		5	0		.178	.221	.189	35	-6		.871	-5	94	75	2-13,3-11/O-2(1-0-1)	-1.0
JONES, CHARLEY Charles Wesley "Baby" (born Benjamin Wesley Rippay) B 4.30.1850 Alamance Co., NC BR/TR 5-11.5/202# d5.4 U2																								
1875	Wes NA	12	47	4	13	2	4	0	10	0		5	.277	.277	.489	152	2	1-1	.800	-2	103	0	O-12(LF)	0.1
	Har NA	1	4	1	0	0	0	0	0	0		1	.000	.000	.000	-95	-1	0-0	.667	-0	0	0	/O(CF)	-0.1
	Year	13	51	5	13	2	4	0	10	0		6	.255	.255	.451	133	1	1-1	.778	-2	93	0	O-13(12-1-0)	0.0
1876	Cin N	64	276	40	79	17	4	4	38	7		17	.286	.304	.420	162	21		.857	1	99	69	*O-64(10-53-1)	1.6
1877	Cin N	17	69	16	21	3	3	1	10	4		8	.304	.342	.478	175	6		.920	1	95	70	1-10/O-8(5-3-0)	0.5
	Chi N	2	8	1	3	1	0	0	2	1		0	.375	.444	.500	176	1		1.000	1	251	0	/O-2(CF)	0.1
	Cin N	38	163	36	51	8	7	1	26	10		17	.313	.353	.466	175	15		.838	10	136	0	O-38(LF)	2.0
	Year	57	240	53	75	12	10	2	38	15		25	.313	.353	.471	175	22		.845	12	163	102	O-48(43-5-0),1-10	**2.6**
1878	Cin N	**61**	261	50	81	11	7	3	39	4		17	.310	.321	.441	163	18		.896	4	53	42	*O-61(51-10-0)	1.7
1879	Bos N	83	355	**85**	112	22	10	**9**	**62**	**29**		38	.315	.367	.510	182	32		**.933**	13	109	54	*O-83(LF)	3.6
1880	Bos N	66	280	44	84	15	3	5	37	11		27	.300	.326	.429	159	17		.826	-4	71	98	*O-66(66-1-0)	0.9
1883	Cin AA	90	391	84	115	15	12	10	80	20			.294	.328	.471	146	18		.876	-0	69	58	*O-90(16-75-0)	1.3
1884	Cin AA	**112**	472	117	148	19	17	7	71	37	10		.314	**.376**	.470	166	34		.887	-1	52	0	*O-112(63-51-0)	2.7
1885	Cin AA	**112**	487	108	157	19	17	5	35	21	9		.322	.362	.462	156	29		.891	11	114	161	*O-112(LF)	3.3
1886	Cin AA	127	500	87	135	22	10	6	68	61	6		.270	.356	.390	130	18	3	.879	2	107	24	*O-127(LF)	1.5
1887	Cin AA	41	153	28	48	7	4	2	40	19	3		.314	.400	.451	134	7	7	.900	1	106	151	O-41(41-1-0)	0.6
	NY AA	62	247	30	63	11	3	3	29	12	6		.255	.306	.360	89	-4	8	.917	4	182	246	O-62(6-50-7)/P-2,1	-0.1
	Year	103	400	58	111	18	7	5	69	31	9		.278	.343	.395	107	4	15	.910	5	**152**	**208**	*O-103(47-51-7)/P-2,1	0.5
1888	KC AA	6	25	2	4	0	1	0	5	1	0		.160	.192	.240	36	-2	1	.750	-1	98	0	/O-6(LF)	-0.3
Total	11	881	3687	728	1101	170	98	56	542	237	34	124	.299	.347	.443	150	210	19-0	.882	43	98	79	O-872(624-246-8)/1-11,P-2	19.4
JONES, CHRIS Christopher Carlos B 12.16.1965 Utica, NY BR/TR 6-2/205# d4.21																								
1991	Cin N	52	89	14	26	1	2	2	6	2-0	0	31	.292	.304	.416	98	-1	2-1	1.000	-1	82	99	O-26(18-3-9)	-0.3
1992	Hou N	54	63	7	12	2	1	1	4	7-0	0	21	.190	.271	.302	65	-3	3-0	.931	-3	77	0	O-43(17-5-25)	-0.6
1993	Col N	86	209	29	57	11	4	6	31	10-1	0	48	.273	.305	.450	85	-5	9-4	.983	-2	92	71	O-70(16-52-4)	-0.7
1994	Col N	21	40	6	12	2	1	0	2	2-1	0	14	.300	.333	.400	77	-1	0-1	.941	-2	70	0	O-14(4-13-0)	-0.3
1995	NY N	79	182	33	51	6	2	8	31	13-1	1	45	.280	.327	.467	111	2	2-1	.976	2	111	117	O-52(25-0-28)/1-5	0.2
1996	NY N	89	149	22	36	7	0	4	18	12-1	2	42	.242	.307	.369	81	-4	1-0	.957	-2	104	0	O-66(17-8-44)/1-5	-0.7
1997	SD N	92	152	24	37	9	0	7	25	16-0	2	45	.243	.322	.441	105	1	7-2	.951	1	97	176	O-61(24-19-25)	0.1
1998	Ari N	20	31	3	6	1	0	0	3	3-0	0	9	.194	.265	.226	31	-3	0-0	1.000	-0	107	0	/O-8(1-0-7)	-0.3
	SF N	43	90	14	17	2	1	2	10	8-0	0	28	.189	.250	.300	48	-7	2-1	.941	-2	84	77	O-29(5-0-24)/D-2	-1.0
	Year	63	121	17	23	3	1	2	13	11-0	0	37	.190	.254	.281	43	-11	2-1	.956	-2	89	61	O-37(6-0-31)/D-2	-1.3
2000	Mil N	12	16	3	3	2	0	0	1	1-0	0	4	.188	.235	.313	37	-2	0-0	1.000	0	157	0	/O-2(RF)	-0.1
Total	9	548	1021	155	257	43	11	30	131	74-4	5	287	.252	.303	.404	86	-23	26-10	.967	-8	95	77	O-371(127-100-168)/1-10,D-2	-3.7
JONES, CHRIS Christopher Dale B 7.13.1957 Los Angeles, CA BL/TL 6/183# d6.8																								
1985	Hou N	31	25	0	5	0	0	0	1	3-0	0	7	.200	.286	.200	39	-2	0-0	1.000	1	161	0	O-15(2-9-4)	-0.1
1986	SF N	3	1	0	0	0	0	0	0	0-0	0	0	.000	.000	.000	-99	0	1-0	—	0			/H	0.0
Total	2	34	26	0	5	0	0	0	1	3-0	0	7	.192	.276	.192	34	-2	1-0	1.000	1	161	0	/O-15(2-9-4)	-0.1
JONES, CLARENCE Clarence Woodrow B 11.7.1941 Zanesville, OH BL/TL 6-2/185# d4.20 C15																								
1967	Chi N	53	135	13	34	7	0	2	16	14-3	0	33	.252	.314	.348	88	-2	0-0	.978	-3	92	0	O-31(2-0-29),1-13	-0.8
1968	Chi N	5	2	0	0	0	0	0	0	2-0	0	1	.000	.500	.000	56	0	0-0	1.000	-0	0	0	/1	0.0
Total	2	58	137	13	34	7	0	2	16	16-3	0	34	.248	.318	.343	88	-2	0-0	.978	-3	92	0	/O-31(2-0-29),1-14	-0.8
JONES, CLEON Cleon Joseph B 8.4.1942 Plateau, AL BR/TL 6/200# d9.14																								
1963	NY N	6	15	1	2	0	0	0	1	0-0	0	4	.133	.133	.133	-23	-2	0-0	1.000	-0	88	0	/O-5(1-5-0)	-0.3
1965	NY N	30	74	2	11	1	0	1	9	2-0	0	23	.149	.171	.203	5	-10	1-0	1.000	0	94	189	O-23(2-18-3)	-1.0
1966	NY N	139	495	74	136	16	4	8	57	30-2	3	62	.275	.318	.372	94	-5	16-8	.979	-3	95	106	*O-129(3-107-35)	-1.3
1967	NY N	129	411	46	101	10	5	5	30	19-6	4	57	.246	.282	.331	77	-14	12-2	.977	-3	96	80	*O-115(20-86-21)	-2.0
1968	NY N	147	509	63	151	29	4	14	55	31-3	5	98	.297	.341	.452	136	22	23-12	.963	-2	101	83	*O-139(117-28-18)	1.6
1969	†NY N★	137	483	92	164	25	4	12	75	64-10	7	60	.340	.422	.482	150	36	16-8	.991	5	112	62	*O-122(121-1-0),1-15	3.4
1970	NY N	134	506	71	140	25	8	10	63	57-2	5	87	.277	.352	.417	106	5	12-3	.981	6	110	109	*O-130(125-6-1)	0.5
1971	NY N	136	505	63	161	24	6	14	69	53-6	2	87	.319	.382	.473	144	30	6-5	.981	3	**112**	51	*O-132(132-1-0)	2.6
1972	NY N	106	375	39	92	15	1	5	52	30-4	4	83	.245	.305	.331	84	-8	1-6	.986	1	94	152	O-84(71-5-14),1-20	-1.6
1973	†NY N	92	339	48	88	13	0	11	48	28-6	3	51	.260	.315	.395	99	-1	1-1	.967	-2	95	98	O-92(73-13-8)	-0.9
1974	NY N	124	461	62	130	23	1	13	60	38-3	6	79	.282	.343	.421	115	9	3-3	.970	0	101	99	*O-120(117-3-3)	0.2
1975	NY N	21	50	2	12	1	0	0	2	3-0	0	6	.240	.283	.260	54	-3	0-0	1.000	-2	50	0	O-12(LF)	-0.6
1976	Chi A	12	40	2	8	1	0	0	3	5-0	1	5	.200	.304	.225	56	-2	0-0	1.000	-2	49	0	/O-8(LF),D-3	-0.5
Total	13	1213	4263	565	1196	183	33	93	524	360-42	40	702	.281	.339	.404	111	57	91-48	.978	2	101	91	*O-1111(802-273-103)/1-35,D-3	0.1
JONES, COBE Coburn Dyas B 8.21.1907 Denver, CO D 6.3.1969 Denver, CO BB/TR 5-7/155# d9.27																								
1928	Pit N	1	2	0	1	0	0	0	0	0	0	0	.500	.500	.500	156	0	0	1.000	-0	89	0	/S	0.0
1929	Pit N	25	63	6	16	5	1	0	4	1	0	5	.254	.266	.365	53	-5	1	.919	-6	69	80	S-15	-0.9
Total	2	26	65	6	17	5	1	0	4	1	0	5	.262	.273	.369	56	-5	1	.921	-6	70	78	/S-16	-0.9

Year	Tm Lg	G	AB	R	H	2B	3B	HR	RBI	BB-IB	HP	SO	AVG	OBP	SLG	AOPS	ABR	SB-CS	FA	FR	Rng	Thr	G at Pos	BFW
JONES, DARRYL Darryl Lee B 6.5.1951 Meadville, PA BR/TR 5-10/175# d6.6 b-Lynn																								
1979	NY A	18	47	6	12	5	1	0	6	2-0	0	7	.255	.286	.404	86	-1	0-0	1.000	0	103	0	D-15/O-2(1-0-1)	-0.1
JONES, DAVY David Jefferson "Kangaroo" B 6.30.1880 Cambria, WI D 3.30.1972 Mankato, MN BL/TR 5-10/165# d9.15																								
1901	Mil A	14	52	12	9	0	0	3	5	11	1		.173	.328	.346	91	0	4	.911	0	0	0	O-14(LF)	-0.1
1902	StL A	15	49	4	11	1	1	0	3	6	0		.224	.309	.286	67	-2	5	.973	3	212	662	O-15(RF)	0.0
	Chi N	64	243	41	74	12	3	0	14	38	0		.305	.399	.379	144	15	12	.955	-4	32	45	O-64(0-47-17)	0.9
1903	Chi N	130	497	64	140	18	3	1	62	53	1		.282	.352	.336	99	1	15	.970	1	82	79	*O-130(0-97-33)	-0.3
1904	Chi N	98	336	44	82	11	5	3	39	41	2		.244	.330	.333	105	3	14	.932	-9	68	0	O-97(0-1-97)	-1.1
1906	Det A	84	323	41	84	12	2	0	24	41	2		.260	.347	.310	103	3	21	.981	3	96	122	O-83(0-82-1)	0.2
1907	†Det A	126	491	101	134	10	6	0	27	60	4		.273	.357	.318	111	9	30	.971	13	92	52	*O-125(121-4-0)	1.6
1908	†Det A	56	121	17	25	2	1	0	10	13	0		.207	.284	.240	68	-4	11	.960	2	139	196	O-32(4-26-2)	-0.4
1909	†Det A	69	204	44	57	2	2	0	10	28	1		.279	.369	.309	110	4	12	.982	-2	56	65	O-57(42-13-2)	-0.1
1910	Det A	113	377	77	100	6	6	0	24	51	6		.265	.362	.313	105	4	25	.956	2	104	97	*O-101(95-6-0)	0.0
1911	Det A	98	341	78	93	10	0	0	19	41	2		.273	.354	.302	80	-7	25	.950	1	96	108	O-92(LF)	-1.0
1912	Det A	99	316	54	93	5	2	0	24	38	0		.294	.370	.323	102	2	16	.962	-0	88	122	O-81(72-5-4)	-0.2
1913	Chi A	12	21	2	6	0	0	0	0	9	0	0	.286	.500	.286	132	2	1	.867	-0	79	197	/O-9(LF)	0.2
1914	Pit F	97	352	58	96	9	8	2	24	42	3	16	.273	.355	.361	96	-7	15	.970	6	123	73	O-93(LF)	-0.6
1915	Pit F	14	49	6	16	0	1	0	4	6	0	0	.327	.400	.367	118	1	1	.926	-1	102	60	O-13(LF)	-0.1
Total	14	1089	3772	643	1020	98	40	9	289	478	22	16	.270	.356	.325	102	24	207	.962	15	89	89	*O-1006(555-281-171)	-1.0
JONES, DAX Dax Xenos B 8.4.1970 Pittsburgh, PA BR/TR 6/170# d7.11																								
1996	SF N	34	58	7	10	0	2	1	7	8-0	0	12	.172	.269	.293	51	-5	2-2	1.000	2	124	117	O-33(0-29-4)	-0.3
JONES, FIELDER Fielder Allison B 8.13.1871 Shinglehouse, PA D 3.13.1934 Portland, OR BL/TR 5-11/180# d4.18 M10																								
1896	Bro N	104	395	82	140	10	8	3	46	48	2	15	.354	.427	.443	137	24	18	.928	-4	70	167	*O-103(RF)	1.3
1897	Bro N	135	548	134	172	15	10	1	49	61	9		.314	.392	.383	111	12	48	.941	3	113	**210**	*O-135(2-0-133)	0.7
1898	Bro N	146	596	89	181	15	9	1	69	46	8		.304	.362	.364	108	7	36	.946	-8	84	142	*O-144(0-4-144)/S-2	-0.7
1899	Bro N	102	365	75	104	8	2	2	38	54	9		.285	.390	.334	97	2	18	.946	-5	74	52	O-96(2-89-6)	-0.8
1900	†Bro N	136	552	106	171	26	4	4	54	57	9		.310	.383	.393	108	8	33	.957	-1	82	61	*O-136(CF)	-0.1
1901	Chi A	133	521	120	162	16	3	2	65	84	6		.311	.412	.365	120	21	38	.937	-2	112	134	*O-133(0-5-128)	1.2
1902	Chi A	135	532	98	171	16	5	0	54	57	3		.321	.390	.370	117	15	33	.972	10	142	**322**	*O-135(CF)	1.8
1903	Chi A	136	530	71	152	18	5	0	45	47	3		.287	.348	.340	112	10	21	**.985**	-1	73	78	*O-136(CF)	0.2
1904	Chi A	149	547	72	133	14	5	3	42	53	5		.243	.316	.303	100	2	25	.977	2	92	104	*O-149(CF),M	-0.3
1905	Chi A	153	568	91	139	17	12	2	38	73	4		.245	.335	.327	115	12	20	.970	7	129	153	*O-153(CF),M	1.3
1906	†Chi A	144	496	77	114	22	4	2	34	83	5		.230	.346	.302	106	9	26	**.988**	3	125	143	*O-144(CF),M	0.6
1907	Chi A	154	559	72	146	18	1	0	47	67	5		.261	.345	.297	109	10	17	.973	-1	91	143	*O-154(CF),M	0.1
1908	Chi A	149	529	92	134	11	7	1	50	86	8		.253	.366	.306	121	18	26	.968	-4	101	125	*O-149(CF),M	0.8
1914	StL F	5	3	0	1	0	0	0	0	1	0	0	.333	.500	.333	123	0	0	—	0			HM	0.0
1915	StL F	7	6	1	0	0	0	0	0	0	0	0	.000	.000	.000	-95	-2	0	1.000	-0	82	0	/O-3(0-1-2),M	-0.2
Total	15	1788	6747	1180	1920	206	75	21	631	817	76	15	.285	.368	.347	112	148	359	.964	0	100	142	*O-1770(4-1255-516)/S-2	5.9
JONES, FRANK Frank M. B 8.25.1858 Princeton, IL D 2.4.1936 Marietta, OH BL d7.2																								
1884	Det N	2	8	0	1	0	0	0	0	0	1		.125	.125	.125	-22	-1		.667	-1	83	0	/SO(RF)	-0.2
JONES, DEACON Grover William B 4.18.1934 White Plains, NY BL/TR 5-10/185# d9.8 C11																								
1962	Chi A	18	28	3	9	2	0	0	8	4-2	0	6	.321	.394	.393	117	1	0-0	.962	-0	101	69	/1-6	0.0
1963	Chi A	17	16	4	3	0	1	1	2	2-1	1	2	.188	.316	.500	127	0	0-0	1.000	0	144	529	/1	0.1
1966	Chi A	5	5	0	2	0	0	0	0	0-0	0	0	.400	.400	.400	140	0	0-0	—	0			H	0.0
Total	3	40	49	7	14	2	1	1	10	6-3	1	8	.286	.368	.429	122	1	0-0	.966	-0	108	142	/1-7	0.1
JONES, HAL Harold Marion B 4.9.1936 Louisiana, MO BR/TR 6-2/194# d4.25																								
1961	Cle A	12	35	2	6	0	0	2	4	2-0	0	12	.171	.216	.343	48	-3	0-0	.974	-2	47	163	1-10	-0.5
1962	Cle A	5	16	2	5	1	0	0	1	0-0	1	4	.313	.353	.375	99	0	0-0	.969	0	111	34	/1-4	0.0
Total	2	17	51	4	11	1	0	2	5	2-0	1	16	.216	.259	.353	64	-3	0-0	.973	-2	66	125	/1-14	-0.5
JONES, HENRY Henry Monroe B 5.10.1857 , NY D 5.31.1955 Manistee, MI BB 5-6/149# d8.20																								
1884	Det N	34	127	24	28	3	1	0	3	16		18	.220	.308	.260	86	-1		.897	-1	95	45	2-16,O-11(RF)/S-7	-0.1
JONES, HOWIE Howard "Cotton" (born, Howard Painter) B 3.1.1897 Irwin, PA D 7.15.1972 Jeannette, PA BL/TL 5-11/165# d9.5																								
1921	StL N	3	2	0	0	0	0	0	0	0	0	1	.000	.000	.000	-99	-1	0-0	—	-0	0	0	/O(LF)	-0.1
JONES, JACQUE Jacque Dewayne B 4.25.1975 San Diego, CA BL/TL 5-10/175# d6.9																								
1999	Min A	95	322	54	93	24	2	9	44	17-1	4	63	.289	.329	.460	96	-2	3-4	.980	9	117	175	O-93(1-82-19)	0.5
2000	Min A	154	523	66	149	26	5	19	76	26-4	0	111	.285	.319	.463	91	-10	7-5	.994	7	112	119	*O-147(90-63-1)	-0.5
2001	Min A	149	475	57	131	25	0	14	49	39-2	3	92	.276	.335	.417	94	-4	12-9	.983	4	108	100	*O-140(137-2-2)/D-5	-0.5
2002	†Min A	149	577	96	173	37	2	27	85	37-2	2	129	.300	.341	.511	122	17	6-7	.986	13	119	136	*O-143(LF)/D-3	2.3
2003	†Min A	136	517	76	157	33	1	16	69	21-2	4	105	.304	.333	.464	107	5	13-1	.977	-0	108	34	*O-101(90-0-11),D-29	0.1
Total	5	683	2414	349	703	145	10	85	323	140-11	13	500	.291	.332	.465	103	6	41-26	.985	34	113	112	O-624(461-147-33)/D-37	1.9
JONES, DALTON James Dalton B 12.10.1943 McComb, MS BL/TR 6-1/180# d4.17 OF Total (12-LF 8-RF)																								
1964	Bos A	118	374	37	86	16	4	6	39	22-2	1	38	.230	.274	.342	67	-17	6-3	.959	-8	86	74	2-85/S3	-2.0
1965	Bos A	112	367	41	99	13	5	5	37	28-0	2	45	.270	.325	.373	92	-4	8-1	.930	-1	104	83	3-81/2-8	-0.4
1966	Bos A	115	252	26	59	11	5	4	23	22-4	3	27	.234	.303	.365	83	-6	1-2	.962	-12	81	73	2-70/3-3	-1.5
1967	†Bos A	89	159	18	46	6	2	3	25	11-3	0	23	.289	.333	.409	110	2	0-1	.912	-3	114	120	3-30,2-19/1	-0.1
1968	Bos A	111	354	38	83	13	0	5	29	17-0	1	53	.234	.271	.314	72	-12	1-1	.996	-10	85	120	1-56,2-26/3-8	-2.8
1969	Bos A	111	336	50	74	18	3	3	33	39-3	2	36	.220	.303	.318	71	-13	1-1	.992	-2	105	91	1-81/3-9,2	-2.2
1970	Det A	89	191	29	42	7	0	6	21	33-4	1	33	.220	.333	.351	90	-2	1-1	.985	-4	90	90	2-35,3-18,1-10	-0.5
1971	Det A	83	138	15	35	5	0	5	11	9-1	1	21	.254	.304	.399	94	-1	1-3	1.000	-5	72	0	O-16(10-0-8),3-13/1-3,2	-0.9
1972	Det A	7	7	0	0	0	0	0	0	0-0	0	2	.000	.000	.000	-97	-2	0-0	—	0			H	-0.2
	Tex A	72	151	14	24	2	0	4	19	10-1	0	31	.159	.207	.252	39	-12	1-0	.979	-4	76	68	3-23,2-17/1-7,O-2(LF)	-1.8
	Year	79	158	14	24	2	0	4	19	10-1	0	33	.152	.199	.241	33	-14	1-0	.979	-4	76	68	3-23,2-17/1-7,O-2(LF)	-2.0
Total	9	907	2329	268	548	91	19	41	237	191-18	11	309	.235	.295	.343	79	-67	20-13	.967	-50	84	76	2-262,3-186,1-158/O-18L,S	-12.4
JONES, JAKE James Murrell B 11.23.1920 Epps, LA D 12.13.2000 Delhi, LA BR/TR 6-3/197# d9.20 Mil 1942-45																								
1941	Chi A	3	11	0	0	0	0	0	0	0	0	4	.000	.000	.000	-99	-3	0-0	1.000	-1	0	0	/1-3	-0.4
1942	Chi A	7	20	2	3	1	0	0	0	2	0	2	.150	.227	.200	21	-2	1-0	.961	-1	60	51	/1-5	-0.3
1946	Chi A	24	79	10	21	5	1	3	13	2	0	13	.266	.284	.468	112	0	0-0	.986	-3	40	108	1-20	-0.4
1947	Chi A	45	171	15	41	7	1	3	20	13	1	25	.240	.297	.345	81	-5	1-0	.988	-1	100	115	1-43	-0.7
	Bos A	109	404	50	95	14	3	16	76	41	3	60	.235	.310	.403	91	-6	5-4	.991	-3	91	108	*1-109	-1.4
	Year	154	575	65	136	21	4	19	96	54	4	85	.237	.306	.386	88	-11	6-4	**.990**	-3	94	**110**	*1-152	-2.1
1948	Bos A	36	105	3	21	4	0	1	8	11	0	26	.200	.276	.267	43	-9	1-0	.993	2	122	114	1-31	-0.8
Total	5	224	790	80	181	31	5	23	117	69	4	130	.229	.294	.368	80	-25	8-4	.989	-6	91	108	1-211	-4.0
JONES, JIM James Tilford "Sheriff" B 12.25.1876 London, KY D 5.6.1953 London, KY BR/TR 5-10/162# d6.29 ▲																								
1897	Lou N	2	4	2	1	1	0	0	0	1	0		.250	.400	.500	141	1	0	—	-0	0	0	/P	0.0
1901	NY N	21	91	10	19	4	3	0	5	4	1		.209	.250	.319	67	-4	2	.900	-0	137	124	O-20(RF)/P	-0.5
1902	NY N	67	249	16	59	11	1	0	19	13	0		.237	.275	.289	75	-8	7	.897	-2	94	82	O-67(49-3-15)	-1.5
Total	3	90	344	28	79	16	4	0	24	18	1		.230	.270	.299	74	-11	9	.898	-3	105	92	/O-87(49-3-35),P-2	-2.0
JONES, JASON Jason D. B 10.17.1976 Marietta, GA BB/TR 6-3/210# d7.23																								
2003	Tex A	40	107	11	23	6	0	3	11	10-0	3	21	.215	.298	.355	66	-5	0-1	.978	1	97	241	O-27(14-0-13)/1-3,D-6	-0.5
JONES, JEFF Jeffrey Raymond B 10.22.1957 Philadelphia, PA BR/TR 6-2/200# d4.4																								
1983	Cin N	16	44	6	10	3	0	0	5	11-0	1	13	.227	.379	.295	90	0	2-0	1.000	0	109	109	O-13(8-0-5)/1	0.1
JONES, BINKY John Joseph B 7.11.1899 St.Louis, MO D 5.13.1961 St.Louis, MO BR/TR 5-9/154# d4.15																								
1924	Bro N	10	37	0	4	1	0	0	2	0	0	3	.108	.108	.135	-36	-7	0-0	.898	-1	90	109	S-10	-0.8

JONES, JOHN John William "Skins" B 5.13.1901 Coatesville, PA D 11.3.1956 Baltimore, MD BL/TL 5-11/185# d9.26

Year	Tm Lg	G	AB	R	H	2B	3B	HR	RBI	BB-IB	HP	SO	AVG	OBP	SLG	AOPS	ABR	SB-CS	FA	FR	Rng	Thr	G at Pos	BFW
1923	Phi A	1	4	0	1	0	0	0	1	0	0	1	.250	.250	.250	31	0	0-0	1.000	-0	105	0	/O(CF)	-0.1
1932	Phi A	4	6	0	1	0	0	0	0	0	0	3	.167	.167	.167	-13	-1	0-0	1.000	-0	89	0	/O(RF)	-0.1
Total	2	5	10	0	2	0	0	0	1	0	0	4	.200	.200	.200	4	-1	0-0	1.000	-0	101	0	/O-2(0-1-1)	-0.2

JONES, CHIPPER Larry Wayne B 4.24.1972 DeLand, FL BB/TR 6-3/185# d9.11

Year	Tm Lg	G	AB	R	H	2B	3B	HR	RBI	BB-IB	HP	SO	AVG	OBP	SLG	AOPS	ABR	SB-CS	FA	FR	Rng	Thr	G at Pos	BFW
1993	Atl N	8	3	2	2	1	0	0	0	1-0	0	1	.667	.750	1.000	360	1	0-0	1.000	-1	48	0	/S-3	0.1
1995	†Atl N	140	524	87	139	22	3	23	86	73-1	0	99	.265	.353	.450	107	6	8-4	.931	1	97	104	*3-123,O-20(15-0-5)	0.7
1996	†Atl N★	157	598	114	185	32	5	30	110	87-0	0	88	.309	.393	.530	134	32	14-1	.947	-30	75	52	*3-118,S-38/O(RF)	0.9
1997	†Atl N★	157	597	100	176	41	3	21	111	76-8	0	88	.295	.371	.479	119	18	20-5	.955	-25	81	76	*3-152/O-5(3-0-3)	-0.3
1998	†Atl N★	160	601	123	188	29	5	34	107	96-1	1	93	.313	.404	.547	148	45	16-6	.971	-5	89	111	*3-158	4.2
1999	†Atl N	157	567	116	181	41	1	45	110	126-18	2	94	.319	.441	.633	169	66	25-3	.950	-34	76	42	*3-156/S	3.5
2000	†Atl N★	156	579	118	180	38	1	36	111	95-10	2	64	.311	.404	.566	143	41	14-7	.944	-4	100	91	*3-152/S-6	3.7
2001	†Atl N★	159	572	113	189	33	5	38	102	98-20	2	82	.330	.427	.605	160	55	9-10	.945	-25	83	51	*3-149/O-8(LF),D	2.9
2002	†Atl N	158	548	90	179	35	1	26	100	107-23	2	89	.327	.435	.536	158	49	8-2	.975	-6	94	81	*O-152(LF)	3.8
2003	†Atl N	153	555	103	169	33	2	27	106	94-13	1	83	.305	.402	.517	139	35	2-2	.968	-14	74	97	*O-149(LF)/D	1.4
Total	10	1405	5144	966	1588	305	26	280	943	853-94	10	781	.309	.404	.541	142	348	116-40	.949	-142	86	75	*3-1008,O-335(327-0-9)/S-48,D-2	20.9

JONES, LEVIN Levin B Baltimore, MD d5.14

Year	Tm Lg	G	AB	R	H	2B	3B	HR	RBI	BB-IB	HP	SO	AVG	OBP	SLG	AOPS	ABR	SB-CS	FA	FR	Rng	Thr	G at Pos	BFW
1873	Mar NA	1	4	0	3	0	0	0	1	0		0	.750	.750	.750	452	2	0-0	.800	-0	0	0	/O(CF)	0.1
1874	Bal NA	2	7	0	1	0	0	0	1	0		0	.143	.143	.143	-8	-1	0-0	.875	-0			/CO(RF)	-0.1
Total	2 NA	3	11	0	4	0	0	0	2	0		0	.364	.364	.364	140	1	0-0	.000	-1			/O-2(0-1-1),C	0.0

JONES, LYNN Lynn Morris B 1.1.1953 Meadville, PA BR/TR 5-9/175# d4.13 C3 b-Darryl

Year	Tm Lg	G	AB	R	H	2B	3B	HR	RBI	BB-IB	HP	SO	AVG	OBP	SLG	AOPS	ABR	SB-CS	FA	FR	Rng	Thr	G at Pos	BFW
1979	Det A	95	213	33	63	8	0	4	26	17-0	1	22	.296	.349	.390	96	-1	9-6	.980	-0	102	73	O-84(20-42-25)/D-6	-0.3
1980	Det A	30	55	9	14	2	2	0	6	10-0	0	5	.255	.364	.364	99	0	1-0	1.000	1	125	0	O-17(4-4-9)/D-6	0.1
1981	Det A	71	174	19	45	5	0	2	19	18-1	1	10	.259	.328	.322	86	-3	1-2	.989	-1	88	146	O-60(9-0-52)/D-4	-0.7
1982	Det A	58	139	15	31	3	1	0	14	7-0	0	14	.223	.259	.259	43	-11	0-2	1.000	1	102	103	O-56(5-2-49)/D	-1.3
1983	Det A	49	64	9	17	1	2	0	6	3-0	0	6	.266	.299	.344	78	-2	1-0	.968	1	102	198	O-31(9-1-22)/D-6	-0.2
1984	†KC A	47	103	11	31	6	0	1	10	4-0	1	9	.301	.330	.388	98	0	1-3	.962	-4	81	0	O-45(13-7-29)	-0.7
1985	†KC A	110	152	12	32	7	0	0	9	8-0	3	15	.211	.261	.257	43	-12	0-1	.983	-1	100	60	*O-100(57-21-32)/D-2	-1.5
1986	KC A	67	47	1	6	2	0	0	1	6-0	0	5	.128	.226	.170	10	-6	0-0	.971	-3	82	0	O-62(37-8-19)/2D	-0.9
Total	8	527	947	109	239	34	5	7	91	73-1	6	86	.252	.308	.321	73	-35	13-14	.983	-6	96	78	O-455(154-85-237)/D-28,2	-5.5

JONES, MACK Mack "Mack The Knife" B 11.6.1938 Atlanta, GA BL/TR 6-1/180# d7.13

Year	Tm Lg	G	AB	R	H	2B	3B	HR	RBI	BB-IB	HP	SO	AVG	OBP	SLG	AOPS	ABR	SB-CS	FA	FR	Rng	Thr	G at Pos	BFW
1961	Mil N	28	104	13	24	3	2	0	12	12-2	2	28	.231	.322	.298	70	-4	4-4	1.000	-3	74	108	O-26(CF)	-0.9
1962	Mil N	91	333	51	85	17	4	10	36	44-3	7	100	.255	.354	.420	110	6	5-1	.973	-6	92	43	O-91(0-9-85)	-0.5
1963	Mil N	93	228	36	50	11	4	3	22	26-5	7	59	.219	.317	.342	91	-2	8-4	.978	-3	101	25	O-80(12-69-0)	-0.7
1965	Mil N	143	504	78	132	18	7	31	75	29-1	9	122	.262	.313	.510	127	15	8-2	.980	-5	97	30	*O-133(31-119-0)	0.7
1966	Atl N	118	417	60	110	14	1	23	66	39-4	8	85	.264	.335	.468	120	11	16-10	.981	-5	102	13	*O-112(1-112-3)/1	0.3
1967	Atl N	140	454	72	115	23	4	17	50	64-4	9	108	.253	.355	.434	127	18	10-6	.985	-2	96	99	*O-126(26-100-0)	1.2
1968	Cin N	103	234	40	59	9	1	10	34	28-3	5	46	.252	.341	.427	123	7	2-3	.988	-4	86	33	O-60(24-34-3)	0.1
1969	Mon N	135	455	73	123	23	5	22	79	67-8	15	110	.270	.379	.488	142	28	6-7	.959	2	105	88	*O-129(125-5-0)	2.2
1970	Mon N	108	271	51	65	11	3	14	32	59-0	13	74	.240	.398	.458	129	14	5-3	.968	-2	96	59	O-87(85-2-0)	0.8
1971	Mon N	43	91	11	15	3	0	3	9	15-1	2	24	.165	.296	.297	68	-3	1-0	.952	0	101	76	O-27(LF)	-0.5
Total	10	1002	3091	485	778	132	31	133	415	383-31	77	756	.252	.347	.444	120	90	65-40	.976	-28	97	55	O-871(331-476-91)/1	2.7

JONES, RED Morris E. B 11.2.1911 Timpson, TX D 6.30.1974 Lincoln, CA BL/TR 6-3/190# d4.16

Year	Tm Lg	G	AB	R	H	2B	3B	HR	RBI	BB-IB	HP	SO	AVG	OBP	SLG	AOPS	ABR	SB-CS	FA	FR	Rng	Thr	G at Pos	BFW
1940	StL N	12	11	0	1	0	0	0	1	1	0	2	.091	.167	.091	-26	-2	0	1.000	0	139	0	/O(LF)	-0.2

JONES, RICKY Ricky Miron B 6.4.1958 Tupelo, MS BR/TR 6-3/186# d9.3

Year	Tm Lg	G	AB	R	H	2B	3B	HR	RBI	BB-IB	HP	SO	AVG	OBP	SLG	AOPS	ABR	SB-CS	FA	FR	Rng	Thr	G at Pos	BFW
1986	Bal A	16	33	2	6	2	0	0	4	6-0	0	8	.182	.308	.242	53	-2	0-0	1.000	4	124	105	2-11/3-6	0.3

JONES, BOB Robert Oliver B 10.11.1949 Elkton, MD BL/TL 6-2/195# d10.1 C1

Year	Tm Lg	G	AB	R	H	2B	3B	HR	RBI	BB-IB	HP	SO	AVG	OBP	SLG	AOPS	ABR	SB-CS	FA	FR	Rng	Thr	G at Pos	BFW
1974	Tex A	2	5	0	0	0	0	0	0	0-0	0	1	.000	.000	.000	-99	-1	0-0	1.000	0	143	0	/O-2(LF)	-0.1
1975	Tex A	9	11	2	1	0	0	0	0	3-0	0	3	.091	.286	.091	11	-1	0-0	1.000	0	123	0	/O-5(3-1-1),D	-0.1
1976	Cal A	78	166	22	35	6	0	6	17	14-3	1	30	.211	.273	.355	90	-3	3-0	.990	1	91	182	O-62(17-25-21)/D-2	-0.4
1977	Cal A	14	17	3	3	0	0	1	3	4-0	0	5	.176	.318	.353	91	0	0-0	—	0			/D-6	0.0
1981	Tex A	10	34	4	9	1	0	3	7	1-0	0	7	.265	.286	.559	146	2	0-1	1.000	3	106	601	O-10(1-0-9)	0.4
1983	Tex A	41	72	5	16	4	0	1	11	5-1	2	17	.222	.284	.319	69	-3	0-2	1.000	0	124	0	O-11(6-0-5),D-11/1	-0.4
1984	Tex A	64	143	14	37	4	0	4	22	10-1	1	19	.259	.308	.371	85	-3	1-1	1.000	-0	103	155	O-22(11-0-11),1-15/D-4	-0.5
1985	Tex A	83	134	14	30	2	0	5	23	11-1	1	30	.224	.284	.351	73	-5	1-0	1.000	-3	81	0	O-30(8-1-22),D-10/1-4	-0.9
1986	Tex A	13	21	1	2	0	0	0	3	2-0	0	5	.095	.174	.095	-24	-4	0-0	.909	-1	100	0	/O-9(5-0-4),1-2	-0.5
Total	9	314	603	65	133	17	0	20	86	50-6	5	117	.221	.282	.348	78	-18	5-4	.992	1	97	152	O-151(53-27-73)/D-34,1-22	-2.5

JONES, BOB Robert Walter "Ducky" B 12.2.1889 Clayton, CA D 8.30.1964 San Diego, CA BL/TR 6/170# d4.11

Year	Tm Lg	G	AB	R	H	2B	3B	HR	RBI	BB-IB	HP	SO	AVG	OBP	SLG	AOPS	ABR	SB-CS	FA	FR	Rng	Thr	G at Pos	BFW
1917	Det A	46	77	16	12	1	2	0	2	4	0	8	.156	.198	.221	28	-7	3	.938	-1	114	19	2-18/3-8	-0.9
1918	Det A	74	287	43	79	14	4	0	21	17	2	16	.275	.320	.352	107	1	7	.947	-5	93	48	3-63/1-6,O	-0.2
1919	Det A	127	439	37	114	18	6	1	57	34	1	39	.260	.314	.335	84	-10	11	.944	-22	85	71	*3-127	-3.0
1920	Det A	81	265	35	66	6	3	1	18	22	1	13	.249	.309	.306	65	-14	3-4	.942	0	100	65	3-67/2-5,S	-1.2
1921	Det A	141	554	82	168	23	9	1	72	37	1	24	.303	.348	.383	87	-12	8-9	.950	9	**106**	45	*3-141	0.4
1922	Det A	124	455	65	117	10	6	3	44	36	2	18	.257	.314	.325	69	-22	8-5	**.962**	10	**105**	95	*3-119	-0.4
1923	Det A	100	372	51	93	15	4	1	40	29	1	13	.250	.306	.320	66	-19	7-6	.954	7	107	100	3-97	-0.7
1924	Det A	110	393	52	107	27	4	0	47	20	0	20	.272	.308	.361	73	-17	1-5	.956	-2	100	76	*3-106	-1.4
1925	Det A	50	148	18	35	6	0	0	15	9	0	5	.236	.280	.277	42	-13	1-1	.985	6	119	66	3-46	-0.5
Total	9	853	2990	399	791	120	38	7	316	208	8	156	.265	.314	.337	75	-113	49-30	.953	3	101	72	3-774/2-23,1-6,SO	-7.9

JONES, RON Ronald Glen B 6.11.1964 Seguin, TX BL/TR 5-10/195# d8.26

Year	Tm Lg	G	AB	R	H	2B	3B	HR	RBI	BB-IB	HP	SO	AVG	OBP	SLG	AOPS	ABR	SB-CS	FA	FR	Rng	Thr	G at Pos	BFW
1988	Phi N	33	124	15	36	6	1	8	26	2-0	0	14	.290	.295	.548	136	5	0-0	1.000	2	115	65	O-32(RF)	0.6
1989	Phi N	12	31	7	9	0	0	2	4	9-1	0	1	.290	.450	.484	167	3	1-0	1.000	2	142	191	O-12(3-0-10)	0.6
1990	Phi N	24	58	5	16	2	0	3	7	9-0	0	9	.276	.373	.466	130	3	0-1	1.000	-1	82	94	O-16(8-0-8)	0.1
1991	Phi N	28	26	0	4	2	0	0	3	2-0	0	9	.154	.214	.231	25	-3	0-0	—	0			H	-0.4
Total	4	97	239	27	65	10	1	13	40	22-1	0	33	.272	.330	.485	128	8	1-1	1.000	3	111	95	/O-60(11-0-50)	0.9

JONES, ROSS Ross A. B 1.14.1960 Miami, FL BR/TR 6-2/185# d4.2

Year	Tm Lg	G	AB	R	H	2B	3B	HR	RBI	BB-IB	HP	SO	AVG	OBP	SLG	AOPS	ABR	SB-CS	FA	FR	Rng	Thr	G at Pos	BFW
1984	NY N	17	10	2	1	1	0	0	1	3-0	0	4	.100	.308	.200	46	-1	0-0	.833	-1	90	92	/S-6,23	-0.1
1986	Sea A	11	21	0	2	0	0	0	0	0-0	0	4	.095	.095	.095	-48	-4	0-1	1.000	-0	79	53	/S-4,2-3,3-2,D	-0.5
1987	KC A	39	114	10	29	4	2	0	10	5-0	1	15	.254	.285	.325	62	-7	1-0	.974	1	112	65	S-36/2-3	-0.2
Total	3	67	145	12	32	5	2	0	11	8-0	1	23	.221	.261	.283	46	-12	1-1	.971	-0	109	65	/S-46,2-7,3-3,D	-0.8

JONES, RUPPERT Ruppert Sanderson B 3.12.1955 Dallas, TX BL/TL 5-10/175# d8.1

Year	Tm Lg	G	AB	R	H	2B	3B	HR	RBI	BB-IB	HP	SO	AVG	OBP	SLG	AOPS	ABR	SB-CS	FA	FR	Rng	Thr	G at Pos	BFW
1976	KC A	28	51	9	11	1	1	1	7	3-0	0	16	.216	.259	.333	72	-2	0-2	1.000	-1	87	0	O-17(2-7-9)/D-3	-0.5
1977	Sea A★	160	597	85	157	26	8	24	76	55-3	2	120	.263	.324	.454	111	8	13-9	.981	9	114	99	*O-155(CF)/D-4	1.6
1978	Sea A	129	472	48	111	24	3	6	46	55-2	0	85	.235	.312	.337	84	-9	22-6	.985	6	107	116	*O-128(CF)	-0.2
1979	Sea A	**162**	622	109	166	29	9	21	78	85-4	3	78	.267	.356	.444	113	12	33-12	.989	4	102	121	*O-161(CF)	1.8
1980	NY A	83	328	38	73	11	3	9	42	34-3	3	50	.223	.299	.357	81	-9	18-8	.988	2	108	70	O-82(CF)	-0.7
1981	SD N	105	397	53	99	34	1	4	39	43-2	0	66	.249	.318	.370	104	3	7-9	.993	3	103	119	*O-104(CF)	0.3
1982	SD N★	116	424	69	120	20	2	12	61	62-11	1	90	.283	.373	.425	130	19	18-15	.984	-2	105	42	*O-114(CF)	1.5
1983	SD N	133	335	42	78	12	3	12	49	35-4	0	58	.233	.305	.394	96	-3	11-11	.981	1	106	67	*O-111(CF)/1-5	-0.5
1984	†Det A	79	215	26	61	12	1	12	37	21-0	0	47	.284	.346	.516	136	10	2-4	1.000	5	112	104	O-73(61-24-0)/D-2	1.2
1985	Cal A	125	389	66	90	17	2	21	67	57-2	0	82	.231	.328	.447	111	6	7-4	.995	11	112	255	O-73(31-18-31),D-43	1.3
1986	†Cal A	126	393	73	90	21	3	17	49	64-5	3	87	.229	.339	.427	109	6	10-3	.981	-6	93	68	*O-121(28-10-96)	-0.4
1987	Cal A	85	192	25	47	8	2	8	28	20-2	0	38	.245	.316	.432	99	-1	2-1	.965	-3	91	34	O-66(52-3-21)/D-3	-0.6
Total	12	1331	4415	643	1103	215	38	147	579	534-38	12	817	.250	.330	.416	106	40	143-84	.986	28	105	99	*O-1205(174-917-157)/D-55,1-5	4.8

JONES, JACK Ryerson L. "Ri" or "Angel Sleeves" B Cincinnati, OH BR/TR d8.13

Year	Tm Lg	G	AB	R	H	2B	3B	HR	RBI	BB-IB	HP	SO	AVG	OBP	SLG	AOPS	ABR	SB-CS	FA	FR	Rng	Thr	G at Pos	BFW
1883	Lou AA	2	7	1	0	0	0	0		0			.000	.000	.000	-99	-2		.500	-1	0	0	/O-2(CF),S	-0.2

Year	Tm Lg	G	AB	R	H	2B	3B	HR	RBI	BB-IB	HP	SO	AVG	OBP	SLG	AOPS	ABR	SB-CS	FA	FR	Rng	Thr	G at Pos	BFW
1884	Cin U	69	272	36	71	5	1	2		12			.261	.292	.309	76	-16		.858	-1	109	146	S-41,2-19,3-10	-1.4
Total	2	71	279	37	71	5	1	2		12			.254	.285	.301	73	-18		.857	-2	109	143	/S-42,2-19,3-10,O-2(CF)	-1.6
JONES, TERRY Terry Lee B 2.15.1971 Birmingham, AL BB/TR 5-10/160# d9.9																								
1996	Col N	12	10	6	3	0	0	0	1	0-0	0	3	.300	.273	.300	48	-1	0-0	1.000	-0	91	0	/O-4(CF)	-0.1
1998	Mon N	60	212	30	46	7	2	1	15	21-1	0	46	.217	.288	.283	52	-15	16-4	.988	5	121	113	O-60(CF)	-0.7
1999	Mon N	17	63	4	17	1	1	0	3	3-0	0	14	.270	.303	.317	59	-4	1-2	1.000	3	134	235	O-17(5-12-0)	-0.1
2000	Mon N	108	168	30	42	8	2	0	13	10-1	0	32	.250	.292	.321	53	-12	7-2	.970	3	111	163	O-78(55-26-7)	-0.9
2001	Mon N	30	77	8	20	5	0	0	2	2-0	0	11	.260	.278	.325	54	-5	3-0	.977	2	109	195	O-22(10-13-2)	-0.3
Total	5	227	530	78	128	21	5	1	34	36-2	0	106	.242	.289	.306	53	-37	27-8	.984	13	117	151	O-181(70-115-9)	-2.1
JONES, TOM Thomas B 1.22.1877 Honesdale, PA D 6.19.1923 Danville, PA BR/TR 6-1/195# d8.25																								
1902	Bal A	37	159	22	45	8	4	0	14	2	0		.283	.292	.384	83	-5	1	.955	-2	110	94	1-37/2	-0.6
1904	StL A	**156**	625	53	152	15	10	2	68	15	8		.243	.270	.309	88	-11	16	.988	1	107	87	*1-134,2-23/O-4(RF)	-1.5
1905	StL A	135	504	44	122	16	2	0	48	30	4		.242	.290	.282	86	-8	19	.985	7	**119**	92	*1-135	-0.4
1906	StL A	144	539	51	136	22	6	0	30	24	5		.252	.290	.315	94	-5	27	.985	11	**129**	101	*1-143	0.4
1907	StL A	**155**	549	52	137	17	3	0	34	34	4		.250	.298	.291	88	-7	24	.983	2	106	101	*1-155	-0.9
1908	StL A	**155**	549	43	135	14	2	1	50	30	4		.246	.290	.284	86	-9	18	.986	-2	93	118	*1-155	-1.5
1909	StL A	97	337	30	84	9	3	0	29	18	6		.249	.299	.294	94	-3	13	.989	7	121	120	1-95/3-2	0.3
	†Det A	44	153	13	43	9	0	0	18	5	3		.281	.317	.340	103	0	9	.984	3	131	104	1-44	0.3
	Year	141	490	43	127	18	3	0	47	23	9		.259	.305	.308	97	-2	22	.988	9	124	115	*1-139/3-2	0.6
1910	Det A	135	432	32	110	12	4	1	45	35	10		.255	.325	.308	92	-3	22	.985	-4	89	81	*1-135	-1.1
Total	8	1058	3847	340	964	122	34	4	336	193	44		.251	.294	.303	90	-51	149	.984	22	109	100	*1-1033/2-24,O-4(RF),3-2	-5.0
JONES, TRACY Tracy Donald B 3.31.1961 Hawthorne, CA BR/TR 6-3/220# d4.7																								
1986	Cin N	46	86	16	30	3	0	2	10	9-1	0	5	.349	.406	.453	132	4	7-1	1.000	2	125	82	O-24(23-3-0)/1-2	0.6
1987	Cin N	117	359	53	104	17	3	10	44	23-0	3	40	.290	.333	.437	99	-1	31-8	.990	0	109	36	O-95(56-34-17)	0.0
1988	Cin N	37	83	9	19	1	0	1	9	8-2	1	6	.229	.304	.277	65	-4	9-0	.955	-0	105	0	O-25(3-0-23)	-0.3
	Mon N	53	141	20	47	5	1	2	15	12-1	1	12	.333	.390	.426	128	5	9-6	1.000	-4	73	99	O-43(26-9-15)	0.1
	Year	90	224	29	66	6	1	3	24	20-3	2	18	.295	.358	.371	105	2	18-6	.980	-4	85	63	O-68(29-9-38)	-0.2
1989	SF N	40	97	5	18	4	0	0	12	5-3	1	14	.186	.233	.227	33	-9	2-1	1.000	-4	69	0	O-30(9-5-22)	-1.5
	Det A	46	158	17	41	10	0	3	26	16-1	1	16	.259	.326	.380	102	1	1-1	.986	-1	102	0	O-36(34-0-3)/D-8	-0.2
1990	Det A	50	118	15	27	4	1	4	9	6-0	3	13	.229	.283	.381	84	-3	1-1	.952	1	91	237	O-27(LF),D-20	-0.4
	Sea A	25	86	8	26	4	0	2	15	3-0	2	12	.302	.341	.419	110	1	0-1	1.000	-1	92	0	O-18(18-1-0)/D-5	-0.1
	Year	75	204	23	53	8	1	6	24	9-0	5	25	.260	.307	.397	95	-2	1-2	.973	-1	91	126	O-45(45-1-0),D-25	-0.5
1991	Sea A	79	175	30	44	8	1	3	24	18-2	1	22	.251	.321	.360	89	-2	2-0	1.000	-0	108	0	D-37,O-36(35-0-3)	-0.4
Total	6	493	1303	173	356	56	6	27	164	100-10	13	140	.273	.329	.388	96	-8	62-19	.988	-9	98	46	O-334(231-52-83)/D-70,1-2	-2.2
JONES, NIPPY Vernal Leroy B 6.29.1925 Los Angeles, CA D 10.3.1995 Sacramento, CA BR/TR 6-1/185# d6.8																								
1946	†StL N	16	12	3	4	0	0	0	1	2	0	2	.333	.429	.333	113	0	0	.800	0	127	319	/2-3	0.1
1947	StL N	23	73	6	18	4	0	1	5	2	0	10	.247	.267	.342	58	-5	0	.935	-2	103	57	2-13/O-2(RF)	-0.6
1948	StL N	132	481	58	122	21	9	10	81	36	1	45	.254	.307	.397	84	-12	2	.986	-8	78	107	*1-128	-2.5
1949	StL N	110	380	51	114	20	2	8	62	16	1	20	.300	.330	.426	97	-3	1	.984	-7	74	113	1-98	-1.3
1950	StL N	13	26	0	6	1	0	0	6	3	0	1	.231	.310	.269	52	-2	0	.983	-0	79	147	/1-8	-0.2
1951	StL N	80	300	20	79	12	0	3	41	9	1	13	.263	.287	.333	66	-15	1-2	.991	-0	100	115	1-71	-1.8
1952	Phi N	8	30	3	5	0	0	1	5	0	0	4	.167	.167	.267	19	-4	0-0	.976	0	123	125	/1-8	-0.4
1957	†Mil N	30	79	5	21	2	1	2	8	3-1	0	7	.266	.293	.392	88	-2	0-0	.994	0	103	90	1-20/O(RF)	-0.3
Total	8	412	1381	146	369	60	12	25	209	71-1	3	102	.267	.304	.382	81	-43	4-2	.987	-17	84	111	1-333/2-16,O-3(RF)	-7.0
JONES, BILL William B Syracuse, NY d5.17																								
1882	Bal AA	4	15	1	1	0	0	0		0			.067	.067	.067	-59	-2		1.000	1	248	0	/O-2(0-1-1),C-2	-0.2
1884	Phi U	4	14	2	2	0	0	0		1			.143	.200	.143	6	-2		.862	-1			/C-4,O(RF)	-0.3
Total	2	8	29	3	3	0	0	0		1			.103	.133	.103	-25	-4		.857	-1			/C-6,O-3(0-1-2)	-0.5
JONES, BILL William Dennis "Midget" B 4.8.1887 Hartland, NB, CAN D 10.10.1946 Boston, MA BL/TR 5-6.5/157# d6.20																								
1911	Bos N	24	51	6	11	2	1	0	3	15	0	7	.216	.394	.294	87	0	1	.867	-1	97	127	O-18(CF)	-0.2
1912	Bos N	3	2	0	1	0	0	0	2	0	0	1	.500	.500	.500	171	0	0	—	0			H	0.0
Total	2	27	53	6	12	2	1	0	5	15	0	8	.226	.397	.302	89	0	1	.867	-1	97	127	/O-18(CF)	-0.2
JONES, TEX William Roderick B 8.4.1885 Marion, KS D 2.26.1938 Wichita, KS BR/TR 6/192# d4.13																								
1911	Chi A	9	31	4	6	1	0	0	4	3	0		.194	.265	.226	39	-3	1	1.000	3	198	153	/1-9	0.0
JONES, TIM William Timothy B 12.1.1962 Sumter, SC BL/TR 5-10/175# d7.26																								
1988	StL N	31	52	2	14	0	0	0	3	4-0	0	10	.269	.321	.269	70	-2	4-1	.955	3	110	121	/S-9,2-8,3	0.2
1989	StL N	42	75	11	22	6	0	0	7	7-1	1	8	.293	.353	.373	107	1	1-0	1.000	-3	102	58	2-12,S-12/3-5,CO(LF)	-0.1
1990	StL N	67	128	9	28	7	1	1	12	12-1	1	20	.219	.291	.313	66	-6	3-4	.944	-0	110	96	S-29,2-19/3-6,P	-0.5
1991	StL N	16	24	1	4	2	0	0	2	2-1	0	6	.167	.222	.250	35	-2	0-1	1.000	-5	70	95	S-14/2-4	-0.7
1992	StL N	67	145	9	29	4	0	0	3	11-1	0	29	.200	.256	.228	39	-12	5-2	.972	-9	85	126	S-34,2-28/3-2,O(CF)	-1.9
1993	StL N	29	61	13	16	6	0	0	1	9-0	1	8	.262	.366	.361	97	0	2-2	.976	2	120	94	S-21/2-7	0.3
Total	6	252	485	45	113	25	1	1	28	45-4	3	81	.233	.300	.295	68	-21	15-10	.964	-13	98	98	S-119/2-78,3-14,O-2(1-1-0),PC	-2.7
JONES, WILLIE Willie Edward "Puddin' Head" B 8.16.1925 Dillon, SC D 10.18.1983 Cincinnati, OH BR/TR 6-1/192# d9.10																								
1947	Phi N	18	62	5	14	0	1	0	10	7	0	0	.226	.304	.258	53	-4	2	.909	1	110	90	3-17	-0.4
1948	Phi N	17	60	9	20	2	0	2	9	3	0	5	.333	.365	.467	126	2	0	.926	1	95	34	3-17	0.3
1949	Phi N	149	532	71	130	35	1	19	77	65	1	66	.244	.328	.421	102	2	3	.948	-6	98	63	*3-145	-0.5
1950	†Phi N★	**157**	610	100	163	28	6	25	88	61	3	40	.267	.337	.456	108	5	5	.954	-5	95	95	*3-157	0.0
1951	Phi N★	148	564	79	161	28	5	22	81	60	4	47	.285	.358	.470	123	18	6-2	.966	-8	91	95	*3-147	1.0
1952	Phi N	147	541	60	135	12	3	18	72	53	6	36	.250	.323	.383	96	-4	5-3	**.969**	5	97	**135**	*3-147	0.1
1953	Phi N	149	481	61	108	16	2	19	70	85	1	45	.225	.342	.385	90	-6	1-1	**.975**	1	93	**124**	*3-147	-0.5
1954	Phi N	142	535	64	145	28	3	12	56	61	0	54	.271	.342	.402	94	-4	4-1	**.968**	2	96	95	*3-141	-0.2
1955	Phi N	146	516	65	133	20	3	16	81	77-5	3	51	.258	.352	.401	103	4	6-2	**.960**	-7	84	86	*3-146	-0.3
1956	Phi N	149	520	88	144	20	4	17	78	92-6	1	49	.277	.383	.429	121	19	5-4	**.973**	-1	89	91	*3-149	1.8
1957	Phi N	133	440	58	96	19	2	9	47	61-3	0	41	.218	.310	.332	76	-14	1-0	.966	-7	83	87	*3-126	-2.2
1958	Phi N	118	398	52	108	15	1	14	60	49-4	2	45	.271	.351	.420	105	4	1-2	**.967**	-14	82	60	*3-110/1	-1.1
1959	Phi N	47	160	23	43	9	1	7	24	19-2	0	14	.269	.343	.469	113	3	0-0	.975	-2	93	72	3-46	0.1
	Cle A	11	18	1	4	1	0	0	1	1-0	0	3	.222	.263	.278	51	-1	0-0	.929	1	125	295	/3-4	0.0
	Cin N	72	233	33	58	12	1	7	31	28-1	1	26	.249	.330	.399	91	-3	0-2	.966	-3	84	86	3-68	-0.6
1960	Cin N	79	149	16	40	7	0	3	27	31-3	0	16	.268	.388	.376	110	4	1-0	.962	-2	90	86	3-46/2	0.2
1961	Cin N	9	7	1	0	0	0	0	0	2-0	0	3	.000	.222	.000	-34	-1	0-0	.000	-1	0	0	/3	-0.2
Total	15	1691	5826	786	1502	252	33	190	812	755-24	22	541	.258	.343	.410	102	24	40-17	.963	-44	91	93	*3-1614/21	-2.5
JONNARD, BUBBER Clarence James B 11.23.1897 Nashville, TN D 8.23.1977 New York, NY BR/TR 6-1/185# d10.1 C6 twb-Claude																								
1920	Chi A	2	5	0	0	0	0	0	0	0	0	1	.000	.000	.000	-99	-1	0-0	.857	-0	*0*	*142*	/C	-0.1
1922	Pit N	10	21	4	5	0	1	0	2	2	0	4	.238	.304	.333	64	-1	0-0	.974	1	*124*	*85*	C-10	0.0
1926	Phi N	19	34	3	4	1	0	0	2	3	0	4	.118	.189	.147	-8	-5	0	.949	-1	*89*	*116*	C-15	-0.5
1927	Phi N	53	143	18	42	6	0	0	14	7	0	7	.294	.327	.336	77	-5	0	.967	-7	*82*	*82*	C-41	-1.0
1929	StL N	18	31	1	3	0	0	0	2	0	0	6	.097	.097	.097	-51	-8	0	.957	1	*128*	*81*	C-18	-0.6
1935	Phi N	1	1	0	0	0	0	0	0	0	0	1	.000	.000	.000	-91	0	0	1.000	-0	*0*	*0*	/C	0.0
Total	6	103	235	26	54	7	1	0	20	12	0	23	.230	.267	.268	41	-20	0-0	.960	-6	*93*	*88*	/C-86	-2.2
JOOST, EDDIE Edwin David B 6.5.1916 San Francisco, CA BR/TR 6/175# d9.11 Def 1944 M1																								
1936	Cin N	13	26	1	4	1	0	0	1	2	0	5	.154	.214	.192	11	-3	0	.947	-0	114	127	/S-7,2-5	-0.3
1937	Cin N	6	12	0	1	0	0	0	0	0	0	0	.083	.083	.083	-57	-3	0	.875	-0	110	83	/2-6	-0.3
1939	Cin N	42	143	23	36	6	3	0	14	12	0	15	.252	.310	.336	73	-6	1	.957	-2	92	104	2-32/S-6	-0.6
1940	†Cin N	88	278	24	60	7	2	1	24	32	2	40	.216	.301	.266	57	-16	4	.960	-2	98	117	S-78/2-7,3-4	-1.2
1941	Cin N	152	537	67	136	25	4	4	40	69	2	59	.253	.340	.337	91	-5	9	.942	-8	93	105	*S-147/2-4,1-2,3	-0.2
1942	Cin N	142	562	65	126	30	3	6	41	62	5	57	.224	.307	.320	84	-11	9	.933	-15	94	109	*S-130,2-15	-1.5

Year	Tm Lg	G	AB	R	H	2B	3B	HR	RBI	BB-IB	HP	SO	AVG	OBP	SLG	AOPS	ABR	SB-CS	FA	FR	Rng	Thr	G at Pos	BFW
1943	Bos N	124	421	34	78	16	3	2	20	68	0	80	.185	.299	.252	61	-19	5	.945	3	122	125	3-67,2-60/S-4	-1.3
1945	Bos N	35	141	16	35	7	1	0	9	13	0	7	.248	.312	.312	73	-5	0	.945	-7	80	92	2-19,3-16	-1.1
1947	Phi A	151	540	76	111	22	3	13	64	114	4	110	.206	.348	.330	87	-5	6-6	.956	-0	98	97	*S-151	0.3
1948	Phi A	135	509	99	127	22	2	16	55	119	1	87	.250	.393	.395	110	12	2-4	.973	7	98	113	*S-135	2.6
1949	Phi A★	144	525	128	138	25	3	23	81	149	4	80	.263	.429	.453	138	38	2-1	.969	7	99	**110**	*S-144	5.1
1950	Phi A	131	476	79	111	12	3	18	58	103	3	68	.233	.373	.384	96	-1	5-1	.956	-5	98	109	*S-131	0.3
1951	Phi A	140	553	107	160	28	5	19	78	106	6	70	.289	.409	.461	132	29	10-8	.974	7	100	112	*S-140	4.3
1952	Phi A☆	146	540	94	132	26	3	20	75	122	5	94	.244	.388	.415	116	17	5-8	.962	-5	100	87	*S-146	2.0
1953	Phi A	51	177	39	44	6	0	6	15	45	0	24	.249	.401	.384	109	5	3-2	.958	-8	90	92	S-51	0.1
1954	Phi A	19	47	7	17	3	0	1	9	10	0	10	.362	.474	.489	163	5	0-1	.963	-1	92	65	/S-9,3-5,2M	0.4
1955	Bos A	55	119	15	23	2	0	5	17	17-2	1	21	.193	.299	.336	65	-6	0-0	.932	1	112	144	S-20,2-17/3-2	-0.3
Total	17	1574	5606	874	1339	238	35	134	601	1043-2	33	827	.239	.361	.366	99	26	61-31	.958	-28	97	106	*S-1299,2-166/3-95,1-2	8.3
JORDAN, DUTCH Adolf Otto B 1.5.1880 Pittsburgh, PA D 12.23.1972 W.Allegheny, PA BR/TR 5-10/185# d4.25																								
1903	Bro N	78	267	27	63	11	1	0	21	19	1		.236	.289	.285	66	-12	9	.928	-12	91	73	2-54,3-18/O-4(1-0-3),1	-2.3
1904	Bro N	87	252	21	45	10	2	0	19	13	2		.179	.225	.234	43	-17	7	.958	-19	82	77	2-70,3-11/1-4	-3.8
Total	2	165	519	48	108	21	3	0	40	32	3		.208	.258	.260	55	-29	16	.945	-31	86	75	2-124/3-29,1-5,O-4(1-0-3)	-6.1
JORDAN, BUCK Baxter Byerly B 1.16.1907 Cooleemee, NC D 3.18.1993 Salisbury, NC BL/TR 6/170# d9.15																								
1927	NY N	5	5	0	1	0	0	0	0	0	0	3	.200	.200	.200	7	-1	0	—	0			H	-0.1
1929	NY N	2	2	1	1	1	0	0	0	0	0	0	.500	.500	1.000	262	1	0	1.000	-0	0	592	/1	0.0
1931	Was A	9	18	3	4	2	0	0	1	1	0	3	.222	.263	.333	56	-1	0-0	.978	-1	0	95	/1-7	-0.2
1932	Bos N	49	212	27	68	12	3	2	29	4	0	5	.321	.333	.434	109	2	1	.991	-2	89	115	1-49	-0.5
1933	Bos N	152	588	77	168	29	9	4	46	34	2	22	.286	.327	.386	112	8	4	.991	-3	93	104	*1-150	-1.0
1934	Bos N	124	489	68	152	26	9	2	58	35	1	19	.311	.358	.413	114	10	3	.989	-3	92	93	*1-117	-0.5
1935	Bos N	130	470	62	131	24	5	5	35	19	0	17	.279	.307	.383	91	-7	3	.983	2	112	79	1-95/3-8,O-2(RF)	-1.4
1936	Bos N	138	555	81	179	27	5	3	66	45	2	22	.323	.375	.405	118	15	2	.993	1	104	**129**	*1-136	0.3
1937	Bos N	8	8	1	2	0	0	0	0	0	0	0	.250	.250	.250	40	-1	0	—	0			H	-0.1
	Cin N	98	316	45	89	14	3	1	28	25	0	14	.282	.334	.354	92	-4	6	.989	-1	96	91	1-76	-1.1
	Year	106	324	46	91	14	3	1	28	25	0	14	.281	.332	.352	91	-4	6	.989	-1	96	91	1-76	-1.2
1938	Cin N	9	7	0	2	0	0	0	0	2	0	0	.286	.444	.286	107	0	0	—	0			H	0.0
	Phi N	87	310	31	93	18	1	0	18	17	0	4	.300	.336	.365	95	-2	1	.973	0	98	126	3-58,1-17	-0.2
	Year	96	317	31	95	18	1	0	18	19	0	4	.300	.339	.363	96	-2	1	.973	0	98	126	3-58,1-17	-0.2
Total	10	811	2980	396	890	153	35	17	281	182	5	109	.299	.340	.391	106	20	20-0	.990	-8	98	102	1-648/3-66,O-2(RF)	-4.8
JORDAN, BRIAN Brian O'Neal B 3.29.1967 Baltimore, MD BR/TR 6-1/205# d4.8																								
1992	StL N	55	193	17	40	9	4	5	22	10-1	1	48	.207	.250	.373	77	-7	7-2	.991	-1	92	133	O-53(27-9-21)	-1.0
1993	StL N	67	223	33	69	10	6	10	44	12-0	4	35	.309	.351	.543	139	11	6-6	.973	-1	96	101	O-65(23-37-12)	0.8
1994	StL N	53	178	14	46	8	2	5	15	16-0	1	40	.258	.320	.410	91	-3	4-3	.991	5	114	165	O-46(18-9-22)/1	0.0
1995	StL N	131	490	83	145	20	4	22	81	22-4	11	79	.296	.339	.488	116	9	24-9	.996	2	107	45	*O-126(0-13-116)	0.7
1996	†StL N	140	513	82	159	36	1	17	104	29-4	7	84	.310	.349	.483	120	14	22-5	.994	11	**120**	103	*O-136(0-13-128)/1	2.1
1997	StL N	47	145	17	34	5	0	0	10	10-1	6	21	.234	.311	.269	54	-10	6-1	1.000	1	112	84	O-44(0-14-30)	-0.8
1998	StL N	150	564	100	178	34	7	25	91	40-1	9	66	.316	.368	.534	135	28	17-5	.970	2	102	118	*O-141(0-33-123)/3D	2.6
1999	†Atl N★	153	576	100	163	28	4	23	115	51-2	9	81	.283	.346	.465	104	2	13-8	.990	2	101	94	*O-150(RF)	-0.3
2000	†Atl N	133	489	71	129	26	0	17	77	38-1	5	80	.264	.320	.421	86	-12	10-2	.990	6	111	87	*O-130(RF)	-1.0
2001	†Atl N	148	560	82	165	32	3	25	97	31-3	6	88	.295	.334	.496	110	7	3-2	.991	10	112	117	*O-144(0-1-144)/D-2	0.9
2002	LA N	128	471	65	134	27	3	18	80	34-3	6	86	.285	.338	.469	122	11	2-2	.982	2	99	134	*O-125(121-0-4)/D-3	0.8
2003	LA N	66	224	28	67	9	0	6	28	23-3	4	30	.299	.372	.420	113	5	1-1	.990	-3	91	59	O-62(54-14-3)/D-2	0.0
Total	12	1271	4626	692	1329	244	34	173	764	316-23	69	738	.287	.339	.467	110	55	115-46	.988	35	106	101	*O-1222(243-143-883)/D-10,1-2,3	4.8
JORDAN, SLATS Clarence Veasey B 9.26.1879 Baltimore, MD D 12.7.1953 Catonsville, MD BL/TL 6-1/190# d9.28																								
1901	Bal A	1	3	0	0	0	0	0	0	0	0		.000	.000	.000	-96	-1	0	.867	-1	0	0	/1	-0.1
1902	Bal A	1	4	0	0	0	0	0	0	0	0		.000	.000	.000	-96	-1	0	—	-0	0	0	/O(RF)	-0.1
Total	2	2	7	0	0	0	0	0	0	0	0		.000	.000	.000	-96	-2	0	.000	-1	0	0	/O(RF)1	-0.2
JORDAN, JIMMY James William "Lord" B 1.13.1908 Tucapau, SC D 12.4.1957 Gastonia, NC BR/TR 5-9/157# d4.20																								
1933	Bro N	70	211	16	54	12	1	0	17	4	0	6	.256	.270	.322	71	-8	3	.969	6	113	77	S-51,2-11	0.2
1934	Bro N	97	369	34	98	17	2	0	43	9	1	32	.266	.285	.322	66	-19	1	.956	-6	102	52	S-51,2-41/3-9	-1.9
1935	Bro N	94	295	26	82	7	0	0	30	9	1	17	.278	.302	.302	64	-15	3	.983	19	121	103	2-46,S-28/3-5	0.8
1936	Bro N	115	398	26	93	15	1	2	28	15	0	21	.234	.262	.291	48	-30	1	.970	-17	86	78	2-98/S-9,3-6	-4.0
Total	4	376	1273	102	327	51	4	2	118	37	2	76	.257	.279	.308	60	-72	8	.969	2	98	93	2-196,S-139/3-20	-4.9
JORDAN, KEVIN Kevin Wayne B 10.9.1969 San Francisco, CA BR/TR 6-1/185# d8.8																								
1995	Phi N	24	54	6	10	1	0	2	6	2-1	1	9	.185	.228	.315	41	-5	0-0	.984	5	127	139	/2-9,3	0.1
1996	Phi N	43	131	15	37	10	0	3	12	5-0	1	20	.282	.309	.427	92	-2	2-1	1.000	1	68	93	1-30/2-7,3	-0.3
1997	Phi N	84	177	19	47	8	0	6	30	3-0	0	26	.266	.273	.412	78	-7	0-1	.987	-4	59	73	1-25,3-12/2-6,D	-1.3
1998	Phi N	112	250	23	69	13	0	2	27	8-1	2	30	.276	.303	.352	71	-11	0-0	1.000	2	100	103	1-24,2-22/3-6,D-8	-1.0
1999	Phi N	120	347	36	99	17	3	4	51	24-1	6	34	.285	.339	.386	81	-10	0-0	.943	7	96	115	3-62,2-33,1-13	-0.2
2000	Phi N	109	337	30	74	16	2	5	36	17-0	1	41	.220	.257	.323	46	-29	0-1	.988	-4	101	70	2-47,3-39/1-9	-3.1
2001	Phi N	68	113	9	27	5	0	1	13	14-2	0	21	.239	.323	.310	67	-5	0-0	.948	-2	43	67	1-10,2-10,3-10	-0.7
Total	7	560	1409	138	363	70	5	23	175	73-5	11	181	.258	.297	.363	69	-69	2-3	.977	4	110	104	2-134,3-131,1-111/D-9	-6.5
JORDAN, MIKE Michael Henry "Mitty" B 2.7.1863 Lawrence, MA D 9.25.1940 Lawrence, MA 5-7.5/155# d8.21																								
1890	Pit N	37	125	8	12	1	0	0	6	15	3	19	.096	.210	.104	-9	-16	5	.947	4	161	0	O-37(29-8-0)	-1.2
JORDAN, RICKY Paul Scott B 5.26.1965 Richmond, CA BR/TR 6-3/209# d7.17																								
1988	Phi N	69	273	41	84	15	1	11	43	7-2	0	39	.308	.324	.491	128	9	1-1	.992	-4	75	74	1-69	-0.1
1989	Phi N	144	523	63	149	22	3	12	75	23-5	5	62	.285	.317	.407	107	3	4-3	.993	-9	71	100	*1-140	-1.7
1990	Phi N	92	324	32	78	21	0	5	44	13-6	5	39	.241	.277	.352	73	-12	2-0	.995	-7	68	114	1-84	-2.6
1991	Phi N	101	301	38	82	21	3	9	49	14-2	2	49	.272	.304	.452	113	4	0-2	.987	-6	75	75	1-72	-0.8
1992	Phi N	94	276	33	84	19	0	4	34	5-0	0	44	.304	.313	.417	106	1	3-0	.995	-5	74	91	1-54,O-11(LF)	-0.7
1993	†Phi N	90	159	21	46	4	1	5	18	8-1	1	32	.289	.324	.421	100	-1	0-0	.990	-5	23	100	1-33	-0.8
1994	Phi N	72	220	29	62	14	2	8	37	6-1	1	32	.282	.303	.473	96	-2	0-0	.993	-7	45	108	1-49	-1.4
1996	Sea A	15	28	4	7	0	0	1	4	1-0	1	6	.250	.290	.357	65	-2	0-0	1.000	-1	32	114	/1-9,D-2	-0.3
Total	8	677	2104	261	592	116	10	55	304	77-17	15	303	.281	.308	.424	103	0	10-6	.993	-44	66	95	1-510/O-11(LF),D-2	-8.4
JORDAN, SCOTT Scott Allan B 5.27.1963 Waco, TX BR/TR 6/175# d9.2																								
1988	Cle A	7	9	0	1	0	0	0	1	0-0	0	3	.111	.111	.111	-37	-2	0-0	1.000	0	109	0	/O-6(0-5-1)	-0.2
JORDAN, TOM Thomas Jefferson B 9.5.1919 Lawton, OK BR/TR 6-1.5/195# d9.4																								
1944	Chi A	14	45	2	12	1	1	0	3	1	0	0	.267	.283	.333	77	-2	0-0	.947	-1	*130*	*94*	C-14	-0.2
1946	Chi A	10	15	1	4	2	1	0	0	0	0	1	.267	.267	.533	124	0	0-0	1.000	0	*65*	*0*	/C-2	0.1
	Cle A	14	35	2	7	1	0	1	3	3	0	1	.200	.263	.314	65	-2	1-1	.974	-3	*86*	*141*	C-13	-0.5
	Year	24	50	3	11	3	1	1	3	3	0	2	.220	.264	.380	83	-2	1-1	.980	-3	*82*	*111*	C-15	-0.4
1948	StL A	1	1	0	0	0	0	0	0	0	0	0	.000	.000	.000	-97	0	0-0	—	0			H	0.0
Total	3	39	96	5	23	4	2	1	6	4	0	2	.240	.270	.354	78	-4	1-1	.963	-4	*108*	*102*	/C-29	-0.6
JORDAN, TIM Timothy Joseph B 2.14.1879 New York, NY D 9.13.1949 Bronx, NY BL/TL 6-1/170# d8.10																								
1901	Was A	6	20	2	4	1	0	0	2	3	0		.200	.304	.250	56	-1	0	.941	-1	66	61	/1-6	-0.2
1903	NY A	2	8	2	1	0	0	0	0	0	0		.125	.125	.125	-23	-1	0	.889	-1	0	327	/1-2	-0.2
1906	Bro N	129	450	67	118	20	8	**12**	78	59	3		.262	.352	.422	153	28	16	.978	-9	79	71	*1-126	1.8
1907	Bro N	147	485	43	133	15	8	4	53	74	1		.274	.371	.363	141	26	10	.980	-6	89	97	*1-143	2.0
1908	Bro N	148	515	58	127	18	5	**12**	60	59	3		.247	.328	.371	128	17	9	.982	-15	61	81	*1-146	-0.1
1909	Bro N	103	330	47	90	20	3	3	36	59	2		.273	.386	.379	142	20	13	.983	-9	57	75	1-95	1.1
1910	Bro N	5	5	1	1	0	0	1	3	0	0	2	.200	.200	.800	195	0	0	—	0			H	0.0
Total	7	540	1813	220	474	74	24	32	232	254	9	2	.261	.355	.382	139	89	48	.980	-40	72	83	1-518	4.4

Year	Tm Lg	G	AB	R	H	2B	3B	HR	RBI	BB-IB	HP	SO	AVG	OBP	SLG	AOPS	ABR	SB-CS	FA	FR	Rng	Thr	G at Pos	BFW
JORGENS, ART Arndt Ludwig B 5.18.1905 Modum, Norway D 3.1.1980 Evanston, IL BR/TR 5-9/160# d4.26 b-Orville																								
1929	NY A	18	34	6	11	3	0	0	4	6	0	7	.324	.425	.412	125	2	0-4	.979	-0	*103*	*74*	C-15	0.1
1930	NY A	16	30	7	11	3	0	0	1	2	0	4	.367	.406	.467	126	1	0-0	.960	-1	*104*	*101*	C-16	0.1
1931	NY A	46	100	12	27	1	2	0	14	9	0	3	.270	.330	.320	76	-4	0-1	.962	-3	*104*	*66*	C-40	-0.5
1932	NY A	56	151	13	33	7	1	2	19	14	0	11	.219	.285	.318	59	-10	0-0	.967	-1	*107*	*80*	C-56	-0.8
1933	NY A	21	50	9	11	3	0	2	13	12	0	3	.220	.371	.400	111	1	1-0	.982	1	*185*	*22*	C-19	0.4
1934	NY A	58	183	14	38	6	1	0	20	23	0	24	.208	.296	.251	45	-15	2-0	.984	3	*109*	*69*	C-56	-0.8
1935	NY A	36	84	6	20	2	0	0	8	12	0	10	.238	.333	.262	59	-5	0-0	1.000	4	*134*	*77*	C-33	0.1
1936	NY A	31	66	5	18	3	1	0	5	2	0	3	.273	.294	.348	60	-5	0-0	.990	2	*150*	*92*	C-30	-0.1
1937	NY A	13	23	3	3	1	0	0	3	2	0	5	.130	.200	.174	-5	-4	0-0	1.000	0	*121*	*69*	C-11	-0.3
1938	NY A	9	17	3	4	2	0	0	2	3	0	3	.235	.350	.353	77	0	0-0	.923	0	*105*	*142*	/C-8	0.0
1939	NY A	3	0	1	0	0	0	0	0	0	0	0	—	—	—	—	0	0-0	1.000	0	*0*	*0*	/C-2	0.0
Total	11	307	738	79	176	31	5	4	89	85	0	73	.238	.317	.310	66	-39	3-5	.978	7	*120*	*73*	C-286	-1.8
JORGENSEN, PINKY Carl B 11.21.1914 Laton, CA D 5.2.1996 Santa Cruz, CA BR/TR 6-1/195# d9.14																								
1937	Cin N	6	14	1	4	0	0	0	1	1	0	2	.286	.333	.286	73	-1	0	.875	0	80	362	/O-4(LF)	-0.1
JORGENSEN, SPIDER John Donald B 11.3.1919 Folsom, CA D 11.6.2003 Rancho Cucamonga, CA BL/TR 5-9/155# d4.15																								
1947	†Bro N	129	441	57	121	29	8	5	67	58	1	45	.274	.360	.410	100	1	4	.949	-3	98	**123**	*3-128	-0.2
1948	Bro N	31	90	15	27	6	2	1	13	16	1	13	.300	.411	.444	127	4	1	.887	-6	74	82	3-24	-0.1
1949	†Bro N	53	134	15	36	5	1	1	14	23	0	13	.269	.376	.343	90	-1	0	.946	-2	90	84	3-36	-0.3
1950	Bro N	2	2	0	0	0	0	0	1	1	0	0	.000	.333	.000	-4	0	0	1.000	-0	104	0	/3	0.0
	NY N	24	37	5	5	0	0	0	4	5	0	2	.135	.238	.135	1	-5	0	.913	0	110	85	/3-5	-0.5
	Year	26	39	5	5	0	0	0	5	6	0	2	.128	.244	.128	1	-6	0	.917	0	110	79	/3-6	-0.5
1951	NY N	28	51	5	12	0	0	2	8	3	1	2	.235	.291	.353	72	-2	0-0	1.000	-1	95	0	O-11(RF)/3	-0.3
Total	5	267	755	97	201	40	11	9	107	106	3	75	.266	.359	.384	95	-3	5-0	.940	-11	94	109	3-195/O-11(RF)	-1.4
JORGENSEN, MIKE Michael B 8.16.1948 Passaic, NJ BL/TL 6/195# d9.10 M1																								
1968	NY N	8	14	0	2	1	0	0	0	0-0	0	4	.143	.143	.214	6	-2	0-0	1.000	-0	51	139	/1-4	-0.2
1970	NY N	76	87	15	17	3	1	3	4	10-1	0	23	.195	.278	.356	69	-4	2-2	.992	2	112	77	1-50,O-10(0-9-1)	-0.4
1971	NY N	45	118	16	26	1	1	5	11	11-1	3	24	.220	.303	.373	92	-2	1-2	.951	-2	95	0	O-31(4-25-4)/1	-0.5
1972	Mon N	113	372	48	86	12	3	13	47	53-7	4	75	.231	.332	.384	102	2	12-13	.995	-1	115	104	1-76,O-28(2-26-0)	-0.9
1973	Mon N	138	413	49	95	16	2	9	47	64-4	3	49	.230	.336	.344	86	-6	16-7	**.995**	4	**112**	93	*1-123,O-11(9-2-0)	-1.0
1974	Mon N	131	287	45	89	16	1	11	59	70-5	2	39	.310	.444	.488	153	25	3-5	.998	6	121	98	1-91,O-29(28-1-0)	2.5
1975	Mon N	144	445	58	116	18	0	18	67	79-8	7	75	.261	.378	.422	117	14	3-3	.994	5	**114**	114	*1-133/O-6(5-1-0)	0.9
1976	Mon N	125	343	36	87	13	0	6	23	52-9	0	48	.254	.349	.344	94	-1	7-1	.989	3	136	104	1-81,O-41(25-0-16)	-0.4
1977	Mon N	19	20	3	4	1	0	0	0	3-0	0	4	.200	.304	.250	52	-1	0-0	1.000	1	283	61	/1-5	0.0
	Oak A	66	203	18	50	4	1	8	32	25-2	2	44	.246	.329	.394	99	0	3-2	.989	2	121	77	1-48,O-20(6-1-13)/D-2	-0.1
1978	Tex A	96	97	20	19	3	0	1	9	18-1	0	10	.196	.319	.258	65	-4	3-1	.994	5	144	94	1-78/O-9(2-4-4),D	-0.1
1979	Tex A	90	157	21	35	7	0	6	16	14-1	2	29	.223	.293	.382	82	-4	0-2	.988	3	129	103	1-60,O-20(4-7-9)/D-2	-0.4
1980	NY N	119	321	43	82	11	0	7	43	46-6	0	55	.255	.349	.355	100	1	0-3	.995	-1	88	70	1-72,O-31(9-0-22)	-0.7
1981	NY N	86	122	8	25	5	2	3	15	12-1	0	24	.205	.270	.352	79	-4	4-0	.991	1	88	76	1-40,O-19(4-0-15)	-0.5
1982	NY N	120	114	16	29	6	0	2	14	21-3	0	24	.254	.370	.360	106	2	2-0	.991	-2	57	140	1-56,O-16(1-0-15)	-0.1
1983	NY N	38	24	5	6	3	0	1	3	2-0	1	4	.250	.333	.500	129	1	0-1	1.000	-0	92	143	1-19	0.0
	Atl N	57	48	5	12	1	0	1	8	8-0	0	8	.250	.351	.333	86	-1	0-0	1.000	0	89	169	1-19/O-6(LF)	-0.1
	Year	95	72	10	18	4	0	2	11	10-0	1	12	.250	.345	.389	100	0	0-1	1.000	0	90	156	1-38/O-6(LF)	-0.1
1984	Atl N	31	26	4	7	1	0	0	5	3-1	0	6	.269	.333	.308	79	-1	0-1	1.000	-1	0	0	/1-8,O-4(1-0-3)	-0.2
	StL N	59	98	5	24	4	2	1	12	10-1	0	17	.245	.315	.357	91	-1	0-0	.991	1	123	164	1-39	-0.2
	Year	90	124	9	31	5	2	1	17	13-2	0	23	.250	.319	.347	87	-2	0-1	.992	1	115	153	1-47/O-4(1-0-3)	-0.4
1985	†StL N	72	112	14	22	6	0	0	11	31-0	1	27	.196	.375	.250	79	-1	2-1	.994	-2	78	133	1-49/O-2(LF)	-0.5
Total	17	1633	3421	429	833	132	13	95	426	532-51	25	589	.243	.347	.373	100	13	58-44	.994	23	114	102	*1-1052,O-283(108-76-102)/D-5	-2.9
JORGENSEN, TERRY Terry Allen B 9.2.1966 Kewaunee, WI BR/TR 6-4/208# d9.10																								
1989	Min A	10	23	1	4	1	0	0	2	4-0	0	5	.174	.296	.217	44	-2	0-0	.958	1	120	223	/3-9	0.0
1992	Min A	22	58	5	18	1	0	0	5	3-0	1	11	.310	.349	.328	89	-1	1-2	1.000	3	111	127	1-13/3-9,S-2	0.1
1993	Min A	59	152	15	34	7	0	1	12	10-0	0	21	.224	.270	.289	51	-11	1-0	.982	6	115	113	3-45/1-9,S-6	-0.4
Total	3	91	233	21	56	9	0	1	19	17-0	1	37	.240	.292	.292	60	-14	2-2	.975	10	117	152	/3-63,1-22,S-8	-0.3
JOSE, FELIX Domingo Felix Andujar (born Andujar (Jose)) B 5.2.1965 Santo Domingo, D.R. BB/TR 6-1/190# d9.2																								
1988	Oak A	8	6	2	2	1	0	0	1	0-0	0	1	.333	.333	.500	135	0	1-0	1.000	1	235	0	/O-6(1-0-5)	0.1
1989	Oak A	20	57	3	11	2	0	0	5	4-0	0	13	.193	.246	.228	36	-5	0-1	.974	1	109	174	O-19(4-0-16)	-0.5
1990	Oak A	101	341	42	90	12	0	8	39	16-0	5	65	.264	.306	.370	92	-5	8-2	.977	3	111	87	O-92(26-24-53)/D-7	-0.3
	StL N	25	85	12	23	4	1	3	13	8-0	0	16	.271	.333	.447	112	1	4-4	1.000	-2	90	0	O-23(1-2-21)	-0.2
1991	StL N★	154	568	69	173	40	6	8	77	50-8	2	113	.305	.360	.438	123	18	20-12	.990	-2	90	130	*O-153(RF)	1.2
1992	StL N	131	509	62	150	22	3	14	75	40-8	1	100	.295	.347	.432	123	14	28-12	.979	3	102	119	*O-127(RF)	1.6
1993	KC A	149	499	64	126	24	3	6	43	36-5	1	95	.253	.303	.349	71	-21	31-13	.972	-8	91	66	*O-144(0-10-136)/D	-3.2
1994	KC A	99	366	56	111	28	1	11	55	35-6	0	75	.303	.362	.475	110	6	10-12	.980	-3	96	94	O-98(RF)	-0.4
1995	KC A	9	30	2	4	1	0	0	1	2-0	0	9	.133	.188	.167	-7	-5	0-0	1.000	2	108	417	/O-7(RF)	-0.4
2000	NY A	20	29	4	7	0	0	1	5	2-0	0	9	.241	.281	.345	60	-2	0-1	.929	-0	103	0	O-14(6-0-8)/D-2	-0.3
2002	Ari N	13	19	5	5	0	0	2	4	4-0	0	8	.263	.360	.579	142	1	0-0	1.000	-1	70	0	/O-5(1-0-4)	0.0
2003	Ari N	18	18	1	6	1	0	1	6	6-1	0	3	.333	.500	.556	159	2	0-0	—	-0	0	0	/O(RF)D	0.2
Total	11	747	2527	322	708	135	14	54	324	203-28	9	507	.280	.334	.409	102	4	102-57	.980	-6	97	101	O-689(39-36-629)/D-11	-2.2
JOSEPH, RICK Ricardo Emelindo (Harrigan) B 8.24.1939 San Pedro De Macoris, D.R. D 9.8.1979 Santiago, D.R. BR/TR 6-1/195# d6.18																								
1964	KC A	17	54	3	12	2	0	0	1	3-0	0	11	.222	.263	.259	45	-4	0-1	.981	-2	82	133	1-12/3-3	-0.7
1967	Phi N	17	41	4	9	2	0	1	5	4-0	0	10	.220	.289	.341	79	-1	0-0	1.000	1	141	88	1-13	-0.1
1968	Phi N	66	155	20	34	5	0	3	12	16-2	1	35	.219	.295	.310	82	-3	0-1	.992	1	96	91	1-30,3-14/O(LF)	-0.5
1969	Phi N	99	264	35	72	15	0	6	37	22-2	1	57	.273	.329	.398	106	2	2-1	.956	-2	95	111	3-58,1-17/2	-0.1
1970	Phi N	71	119	7	27	2	1	3	10	6-1	0	28	.227	.264	.336	61	-7	0-0	.917	-6	71	0	O-12(LF),1-10/3-9	-1.5
Total	5	270	633	69	154	26	1	13	65	51-5	2	141	.243	.300	.349	85	-13	2-3	.933	-8	90	133	/3-84,1-82,O-13(LF),2	-2.9
JOSEPHSON, DUANE Duane Charles B 6.3.1942 New Hampton, IA D 1.30.1997 New Hampton, IA BR/TR 6/195# d9.15																								
1965	Chi A	4	9	2	1	0	0	0	0	2-0	0	4	.111	.273	.111	14	-1	0-0	1.000	1	*130*	*0*	/C-4	0.0
1966	Chi A	11	38	3	9	1	0	0	3	3-0	0	3	.237	.293	.263	65	-2	0-0	.974	1	*85*	*151*	C-11	0.0
1967	Chi A	62	189	11	45	5	1	1	9	6-0	0	24	.238	.262	.291	65	-9	0-3	1.000	-4	103	102	C-59	-1.3
1968	Chi A★	128	434	35	107	16	6	6	45	18-2	6	52	.247	.284	.353	92	-6	2-4	.990	16	95	118	*C-122	1.7
1969	Chi A	52	162	19	39	6	2	1	20	13-0	1	17	.241	.296	.321	71	-7	0-0	.984	-2	80	111	C-47	-0.7
1970	Chi A	96	285	28	90	12	1	4	41	24-2	3	28	.316	.370	.407	111	5	0-1	.985	-9	76	77	C-84	-0.1
1971	Bos A	91	306	38	75	14	1	10	39	22-4	0	35	.245	.294	.395	88	-5	2-0	.989	-2	99	55	C-87	-0.3
1972	Bos A	26	82	11	22	4	1	1	7	4-0	1	11	.268	.310	.378	99	0	0-2	.980	-4	95	58	1-16/C-6	-0.7
Total	8	470	1505	147	388	58	12	23	164	92-8	11	174	.258	.303	.358	89	-25	4-10	.989	-3	*94*	*93*	C-420/1-16	-1.4
JOSHUA, VON Von Everett B 5.1.1948 Oakland, CA BL/TL 5-10/170# d9.2 C4																								
1969	LA N	14	8	2	2	0	0	0	0	0-0	0	2	.250	.250	.250	43	-1	1-0	.800	-1	74	0	/O-8(7-0-2)	-0.1
1970	LA N	72	109	23	29	1	3	1	8	6-2	0	24	.266	.302	.358	80	-4	2-2	.941	-0	104	61	O-41(21-10-16)	-0.6
1971	LA N	11	7	2	0	0	0	0	0	0-0	0	1	.000	.000	.000	-99	-2	0-0	1.000	1	317	0	/O-5(4-1-0)	-0.1
1973	LA N	75	159	19	40	4	1	2	17	8-2	1	29	.252	.288	.327	74	-6	7-2	.984	-3	82	77	O-46(42-1-4)	-1.1
1974	†LA N	81	124	11	29	5	1	1	16	7-5	1	17	.234	.276	.315	69	-6	3-2	.943	-5	67	0	O-35(12-17-6)	-1.2
1975	SF N	129	507	75	161	25	10	7	43	32-0	1	75	.318	.359	.448	118	11	20-10	**.993**	1	98	141	*O-117(CF)	1.0
1976	SF N	42	156	13	41	5	2	0	2	4-2	0	20	.263	.280	.321	68	-7	1-3	.948	-5	76	133	O-35(3-33-0)	-1.5
	Mil A	107	423	44	113	13	5	5	28	18-3	0	58	.267	.295	.357	93	-6	8-10	.982	2	99	131	*O-105(26-82-0)/D	-1.0
1977	Mil A	144	536	58	140	25	7	9	49	21-4	0	74	.261	.286	.384	82	-15	12-9	.970	-11	90	86	*O-140(CF)	-2.8
1979	LA N	94	142	22	40	7	1	3	14	7-1	0	23	.282	.315	.408	97	-1	1-1	.967	-0	103	95	O-46(11-10-28)	-0.3
1980	SD N	53	63	8	15	2	1	2	7	5-1	0	15	.238	.294	.397	97	-1	0-1	1.000	0	120	0	O-12(3-8-1)/1-2	-0.1
Total	10	822	2234	277	610	87	31	30	184	108-20	3	338	.273	.306	.380	91	-38	55-40	.975	-20	93	104	O-590(129-419-57)/1-2,D	-7.8

Year	Tm Lg	G	AB	R	H	2B	3B	HR	RBI	BB-IB	HP	SO	AVG	OBP	SLG	AOPS	ABR	SB-CS	FA	FR	Rng	Thr	G at Pos	BFW
JOURDAN, TED Theodore Charles B 9.5.1895 New Orleans, LA D 9.23.1961 New Orleans, LA BL/TL 6-0/175# d9.18 Mil 1918																								
1916	Chi A	3	2	0	0	0	0	0	0	1	0	1	.000	.333	.000	1	0	2	—	0			H	0.0
1917	Chi A	17	34	2	5	0	1	0	2	1	0	3	.147	.171	.206	15	-4	0	.973	-0	101	47	1-14	-0.5
1918	Chi A	7	10	1	1	0	0	0	1	0	0	0	.100	.100	.100	-39	-2	0	1.000	-0	0	0	/1-2	-0.2
1920	Chi A	48	150	16	36	5	2	0	8	17	5	17	.240	.337	.300	70	-6	3-2	.982	-4	71	163	1-40	-1.0
Total	4	75	196	19	42	5	3	0	11	19	5	21	.214	.300	.270	56	-12	5-2	.981	-4	74	140	/1-56	-1.7
JOY, POP Aloysius C. B 6.11.1860 Washington, DC D 6.28.1937 Washington, DC d6.3																								
1884	Was U	36	130	12	28	0	0	0		2			.215	.227	.215	36	-14		.966	0	69	112	1-36	-1.5
JOYCE, GEORGE George W. B 1847 Washington, DC D 11.9.1895 Washington, DC d8.14																								
1886	Was N	1	0	0	0	0	0	0	0	0		0	—	—	—	—	0	0	—	-0	0	0	/O(CF)	0.0
JOYCE, BILL William Michael "Scrappy Bill" B 9.21.1865 St.Louis, MO D 5.8.1941 St.Louis, MO BL/TR 5-11/185# d4.19 M3																								
1890	Bro P	**133**	489	121	123	18	18	1	78	**123**	12	77	.252	.413	.368	103	7	43	.811	-13	97	90	*3-133	-0.3
1891	Bos AA	65	243	76	75	9	15	3	51	63	5	27	.309	.460	.506	179	29	36	.849	-0	104	124	3-64/1	2.5
1892	Bro N	97	372	89	91	15	12	6	45	82	8	55	.245	.392	.398	144	25	23	.862	-20	76	56	3-94/O-3(LF)	0.6
1894	Was N	99	355	103	126	25	14	17	89	87	12	33	.355	.496	.648	179	52	21	.866	4	100	126	*3-99	4.3
1895	Was N	127	479	110	149	26	13	17	97	**96**	14	56	.311	.440	.526	150	41	29	.846	-4	93	78	*3-127	3.1
1896	Was N	81	310	85	97	16	10	8	51	67	12	20	.313	.452	.506	152	28	32	.888	-5	108	76	3-48,2-33	2.1
	NY N	49	165	36	61	9	2	5	43	34	10	14	.370	.502	.539	180	24	13	.883	2	102	55	3-49,M	2.2
	Year	130	475	121	158	25	12	**13**	94	101	22	34	.333	.470	.518	162	52	45	.885	-3	105	65	3-97,2-33	4.3
1897	NY N	110	389	111	118	15	13	3	64	81	17		.303	.444	.432	135	27	35	.851	-6	90	124	*3-107/1-2,M	1.9
1898	NY N	145	508	91	131	20	9	10	91	88	18		.258	.386	.392	127	23	34	.966	8	**142**	91	*1-130,3-14/2-2,M	2.9
Total	8	906	3310	822	971	153	106	70	609	721	108	282	.293	.435	.467	144	256	266	.851	-35	95	91	3-735,1-133/2-35,O-3(LF)	19.3
JOYNER, WALLY Wallace Keith B 6.16.1962 Atlanta, GA BL/TL 6-2/203# d4.8																								
1986	†Cal A★	154	593	82	172	27	3	22	100	57-8	2	58	.290	.348	.457	120	16	5-2	.989	6	113	**113**	*1-152	1.3
1987	Cal A	149	564	100	161	33	1	34	117	72-12	5	64	.285	.366	.528	140	33	8-2	.993	-8	83	**114**	*1-149	1.6
1988	Cal A	158	597	81	176	31	2	13	85	55-14	5	51	.295	.356	.419	120	17	8-2	.995	10	122	107	*1-156	1.7
1989	Cal A	159	593	78	167	30	2	16	79	46-7	6	58	.282	.335	.420	115	11	3-2	**.997**	-3	90	**114**	*1-159	-0.4
1990	Cal A	83	310	35	83	15	0	8	41	41-4	1	34	.268	.350	.394	111	6	2-1	.995	4	116	104	1-83	0.4
1991	Cal A	143	551	79	166	34	3	21	96	52-4	1	66	.301	.360	.488	133	25	2-0	.994	6	112	108	*1-141	2.0
1992	KC A	149	572	66	154	36	2	9	66	55-4	4	50	.269	.336	.386	100	1	11-5	.993	13	**131**	**113**	*1-145/D-4	0.4
1993	KC A	141	497	83	145	36	3	15	65	66-13	3	67	.292	.375	.467	119	15	5-9	.994	19	**145**	102	*1-140	1.8
1994	KC A	97	363	52	113	20	3	8	57	47-3	0	43	.311	.386	.449	111	7	3-2	.991	2	108	100	1-86,D-11	0.0
1995	KC A	131	465	69	144	28	0	12	83	69-10	2	65	.310	.394	.447	119	16	3-2	**.998**	11	**132**	116	*1-126/D-2	1.4
1996	†SD N	121	433	59	120	29	1	8	65	69-8	3	71	.277	.377	.404	114	12	5-3	**.997**	1	100	96	*1-119	0.2
1997	SD N	135	455	59	149	29	2	13	83	51-5	2	51	.327	.390	.486	140	28	3-5	**.996**	0	100	80	*1-131	1.5
1998	†SD N	131	439	58	131	30	1	12	80	51-8	1	44	.298	.370	.453	125	17	1-2	.993	-1	93	114	*1-127	0.4
1999	SD N	110	323	34	80	14	2	5	43	58-6	2	54	.248	.363	.350	89	-3	0-1	.995	4	112	122	*1-105/D	-0.8
2000	†Atl N	119	224	24	63	12	0	5	32	31-3	1	31	.281	.365	.402	95	-1	0-0	.992	2	119	110	1-55/D-7	-0.3
2001	Ana A	53	148	14	36	5	1	3	14	13-0	0	18	.243	.304	.351	70	-7	1-1	.997	-1	90	108	1-39/D-9	-1.0
Total	16	2033	7127	973	2060	409	26	204	1106	833-109	38	825	.289	.362	.440	117	193	60-39	.994	63	111	108	*1-1913/D-34	10.2
JUDE, FRANK Frank B 1884 Libby, MN D 5.4.1961 Brownsville, TX BR/TR 5-7/150# d7.9																								
1906	Cin N	80	308	31	64	6	4	1	31	16	6		.208	.261	.263	61	-15	7	.965	-0	152	44	O-80(RF)	-2.1
JUDGE, JOE Joseph Ignatius B 5.25.1894 Brooklyn, NY D 3.11.1963 Washington, DC BL/TL 5-8.5/155# d9.20 C2																								
1915	Was A	12	41	7	17	2	0	0	9	4	3	6	.415	.500	.463	185	5	2-3	.990	-0	82	149	1-10/O-2(RF)	0.4
1916	Was A	103	336	42	74	10	8	0	28	54	3	44	.220	.333	.298	91	-2	18	.986	4	112	94	*1-103	-0.1
1917	Was A	102	393	62	112	15	15	2	30	50	2	40	.285	.369	.415	141	19	17	.988	-1	95	103	*1-100	1.7
1918	Was A	**130**	502	56	131	23	7	1	46	49	4	32	.261	.332	.341	105	3	20	.985	0	102	94	*1-130	0.0
1919	Was A	135	521	83	150	33	12	2	31	81	2	35	.288	.386	.409	124	20	23	.988	-4	87	92	*1-133	1.4
1920	Was A	126	493	103	164	19	15	5	51	65	5	34	.333	.416	.462	136	27	12-12	.992	-7	76	88	*1-124	1.5
1921	Was A	153	622	87	187	26	11	7	72	68	3	35	.301	.372	.412	105	5	21-6	.996	-3	90	105	*1-152	-0.5
1922	Was A	148	591	84	174	32	15	10	81	50	6	20	.294	.355	.450	114	10	5-15	.996	5	107	**122**	*1-147	0.1
1923	Was A	113	405	56	127	24	6	2	63	58	5	20	.314	.406	.417	123	17	11-7	**.993**	8	**126**	**131**	*1-112	1.7
1924	†Was A	140	516	71	167	38	9	3	79	53	6	21	.324	.393	.450	121	17	13-8	.994	-2	89	**118**	*1-140	0.5
1925	†Was A	112	376	65	118	31	5	8	66	55	3	21	.314	.406	.487	128	18	7-12	**.993**	3	106	**117**	*1-109	1.1
1926	Was A	134	453	70	132	25	11	7	92	53	1	25	.291	.367	.442	113	8	7-5	.994	9	125	96	*1-128	0.8
1927	Was A	137	522	68	161	29	11	2	71	45	2	22	.308	.366	.418	104	3	10-5	**.996**	-6	77	80	*1-136	-1.1
1928	Was A	153	542	78	166	31	10	3	93	80	1	19	.306	.396	.417	115	15	16-4	.996	1	99	**106**	*1-149	0.8
1929	Was A	143	543	83	171	35	8	6	71	73	1	33	.315	.397	.442	115	15	12-5	**.996**	3	105	103	*1-142	0.9
1930	Was A	126	442	83	144	29	11	10	80	60	3	29	.326	.410	.509	131	22	13-6	**.998**	2	101	**111**	*1-117	1.6
1931	Was A	35	74	11	21	3	0	0	9	8	0	8	.284	.354	.324	79	-2	0-0	.994	1	115	78	1-15	-0.3
1932	Was A	82	291	45	75	16	3	3	29	37	1	19	.258	.343	.364	84	-6	3-3	.997	1	102	123	1-78	-1.1
1933	Bro N	42	112	7	24	2	1	0	9	7	0	10	.214	.261	.250	48	-8	1	.989	0	100	110	1-28	-1.1
	Bos A	35	108	20	32	8	1	0	22	13	0	4	.296	.372	.389	103	1	2-1	1.000	0	89	95	1-29	-0.2
1934	Bos A	10	15	3	5	2	0	0	2	2	0	1	.333	.412	.467	118	1	0-0	1.000	-0	82	49	/1-2	0.0
Total	20	2171	7898	1184	2352	433	159	71	1034	965	51	478	.298	.378	.420	115	188	213-92	.993	15	99	104	*1-2084/O-2(RF)	8.1
JUDNICH, WALLY Walter Franklin B 1.24.1916 San Francisco, CA D 7.10.1971 Glendale, CA BL/TL 6-1/205# d4.16 Mil 1943-45																								
1940	StL A	137	519	97	157	27	7	24	89	54	0	71	.303	.368	.520	125	18	8-5	**.989**	-5	96	68	*O-133(CF)	0.9
1941	StL A	146	546	90	155	40	6	14	83	80	2	45	.284	.377	.456	116	14	5-5	.980	2	102	95	*O-140(CF)	1.1
1942	StL A	132	457	78	143	22	6	17	82	74	4	41	.313	.413	.499	153	35	3-2	**.991**	-6	97	43	*O-122(CF)	2.6
1946	StL A	142	511	60	134	23	4	15	72	60	0	54	.262	.340	.411	104	3	0-4	**.995**	5	110	63	*O-137(6-131-1)	0.2
1947	StL A	144	500	58	129	24	3	18	64	60	0	62	.258	.338	.426	109	5	2-5	.989	-6	84	100	*1-129,O-15(0-14-1)	-0.7
1948	†Cle A	79	218	36	56	13	3	2	29	56	1	23	.257	.411	.372	112	7	2-3	.970	-5	85	121	O-49(0-35-14),1-20	0.0
1949	Pit N	10	35	5	8	1	0	0	1	1	0	2	.229	.250	.257	35	-3	0	1.000	0	112	0	/O-8(CF)	-0.3
Total	7	790	2786	424	782	150	29	90	420	385	7	298	.281	.369	.452	119	79	20-24	.988	-14	100	71	O-604(6-583-16),1-149	3.8
JUDY, LYLE Lyle Leroy "Punch" B 11.15.1913 Lawrenceville, IL D 1.15.1991 Ormond Beach, FL BR/TR 5-10/150# d9.17																								
1935	StL N	8	11	2	0	0	0	0	0	2	0	2	.000	.154	.000	-53	-2	2	1.000	0	80	142	/2-5	-0.2
JUELICH, RED John Samuel B 9.20.1916 St.Louis, MO D 12.25.1970 St.Louis, MO BR/TR 5-11.5/170# d5.30																								
1939	Pit N	17	46	5	11	0	2	0	4	2	0	4	.239	.271	.326	61	-3	0	.935	-3	84	81	2-10/3-2	-0.6
JUMONVILLE, GEORGE George Benedict B 5.16.1917 Mobile, AL D 12.12.1996 Mobile, AL BR/TR 6/175# d9.13																								
1940	Phi N	11	34	0	3	0	0	0	0	1	1	6	.088	.139	.088	-38	-7	0	.952	-2	79	58	S-10/3	-0.9
1941	Phi N	6	7	1	3	0	0	1	2	0	0	0	.429	.429	.857	266	1	0	1.000	0	178	0	/2S	0.2
Total	2	17	41	1	6	0	0	1	2	1	1	6	.146	.186	.220	12	-6	0	.953	-2	81	56	/S-11,23	-0.7
JURAK, ED Edward James B 10.24.1957 Los Angeles, CA BR/TR 6-2/185# d6.30 OF Total (2-LF 1-CF 1-RF)																								
1982	Bos A	12	21	3	7	0	0	0	7	2-0	0	4	.333	.375	.333	96	0	0-0	.923	1	127	76	3-11/O(CF)	0.1
1983	Bos A	75	159	19	44	8	4	0	18	18-1	1	25	.277	.350	.377	95	-1	1-2	.943	5	104	100	S-38,1-19,3-12/2D	0.4
1984	Bos A	47	66	6	16	3	1	1	7	12-0	0	12	.242	.359	.364	96	0	0-2	1.000	2	158	104	1-19,2-14/3-9,S-2	0.1
1985	Bos A	26	13	4	3	0	0	0	0	1-0	0	3	.231	.286	.231	42	-1	0-0	.833	1	119	0	/3-7,S-3,10(LF)D	0.0
1988	Oak A	3	1	1	0	0	0	0	0	0-0	0	0	.000	.000	.000	-99	0	0-0	—	-0	0	0	/3D	0.0
1989	SF N	30	42	2	10	0	0	0	1	5-0	0	5	.238	.319	.238	63	-2	0-0	.875	-1	97	143	/S-6,3-5,2-4,O-2(1-0-1),1	-0.3
Total	6	193	302	35	80	11	5	1	33	38-1	1	49	.265	.346	.344	88	-4	1-4	.941	7	103	98	/S-49,3-45,1-40,2-19,D-8,O-4L	0.3
JURGES, BILLY William Frederick B 5.9.1908 Bronx, NY D 3.3.1997 Clearwater, FL BR/TR 5-11/175# d5.4 M2 C6																								
1931	Chi N	88	293	34	59	15	5	0	23	25	0	41	.201	.264	.287	47	-22	2	.963	9	122	121	3-54,2-33/S-3	-1.0
1932	†Chi N	115	396	40	100	24	4	2	52	19	1	26	.253	.288	.348	71	-17	1	**.964**	**30**	**119**	116	*S-108/3-5	2.1
1933	Chi N	143	487	49	131	17	6	5	50	26	5	39	.269	.313	.359	92	-6	3	.958	23	**108**	114	*S-143	2.8
1934	Chi N	100	358	43	88	15	2	8	33	19	3	34	.246	.289	.366	76	-13	1	.966	-1	98	107	S-98	-0.6

Year	Tm Lg	G	AB	R	H	2B	3B	HR	RBI	BB-IB	HP	SO	AVG	OBP	SLG	AOPS	ABR	SB-CS	FA	FR	Rng	Thr	G at Pos	BFW
1935	†Chi N	146	519	69	125	33	1	1	59	42	5	39	.241	.304	.314	66	-24	3	**.964**	**25**	**107**	**132**	*S-146	1.2
1936	Chi N	118	429	51	120	25	1	1	42	23	3	25	.280	.321	.350	79	-12	4	.960	14	104	120	*S-116	1.0
1937	Chi N☆	129	450	53	134	18	10	1	65	42	6	41	.298	.365	.389	101	1	2	**.975**	-13	91	97	*S-128	-0.3
1938	†Chi N	137	465	53	114	18	3	1	47	58	5	53	.245	.335	.303	75	-14	3	.953	-5	97	100	*S-136	-0.9
1939	NY N☆	138	543	84	155	21	11	6	63	47	6	34	.285	.349	.398	99	-1	3	**.965**	**20**	**107**	102	*S-137	2.8
1940	NY N✱	63	214	23	54	3	3	2	36	25	6	14	.252	.347	.322	85	-4	2	.967	3	100	100	S-63	0.4
1941	NY N	134	471	50	138	25	2	5	61	47	3	36	.293	.361	.386	108	6	0	.957	6	**107**	105	*S-134	2.3
1942	NY N	127	464	45	119	7	1	2	30	43	3	42	.256	.324	.289	79	-12	1	.978	6	103	95	*S-124	0.4
1943	NY N	136	481	46	110	8	2	4	29	53	4	38	.229	.310	.279	70	-18	2	.955	4	96	69	S-99,3-28	-0.6
1944	NY N	85	246	28	52	2	1	1	23	23	0	20	.211	.279	.240	47	-17	4	.961	5	115	75	3-61,S-10/2	-1.1
1945	NY N	61	176	22	57	3	1	3	24	24	0	11	.324	.405	.403	123	6	2	.937	2	110	38	3-44/S-8	0.9
1946	Chi N	82	221	26	49	9	2	0	17	43	1	28	.222	.351	.281	82	-3	3	.976	-1	103	68	S-73/3-7,2-2	0.0
1947	Chi N	14	40	5	8	2	0	1	2	9	0	9	.200	.347	.325	83	-1	0	.925	-1	103	137	S-14	-0.1
Total	17	1816	6253	721	1613	245	55	43	656	568	51	530	.258	.325	.335	82	-151	36	.964	126	103	104	*S-1540,3-199/2-36	9.3

JUST, JOE Joseph Erwin (born Joseph Erwin Juszczak) B 1.8.1916 Milwaukee, WI BR/TR 5-11/185# d5.13

Year	Tm Lg	G	AB	R	H	2B	3B	HR	RBI	BB-IB	HP	SO	AVG	OBP	SLG	AOPS	ABR	SB-CS	FA	FR	Rng	Thr	G at Pos	BFW
1944	Cin N	11	11	0	2	0	0	0	0	0	1	2	.182	.250	.182	24	-1	0	.923	-0	*95*	*0*	C-10	-0.1
1945	Cin N	14	34	2	5	0	0	0	2	4	0	7	.147	.237	.147	8	-4	0	.947	-1	*84*	*73*	C-14	-0.5
Total	2	25	45	2	7	0	0	0	2	4	1	9	.156	.240	.156	12	-5	0	.941	-1	*87*	*56*	/C-24	-0.6

JUSTICE, DAVID David Christopher B 4.14.1966 Cincinnati, OH BL/TL 6-3/200# d5.24

Year	Tm Lg	G	AB	R	H	2B	3B	HR	RBI	BB-IB	HP	SO	AVG	OBP	SLG	AOPS	ABR	SB-CS	FA	FR	Rng	Thr	G at Pos	BFW
1989	Atl N	16	51	7	12	3	0	1	3	3-1	1	9	.235	.291	.353	81	-1	2-1	1.000	-2	80	0	O-16(3-0-13)	-0.4
1990	Atl N	127	439	76	124	23	2	28	78	64-4	0	92	.282	.373	.535	139	24	11-6	.981	-3	89	92	1-69,O-61(RF)	1.5
1991	†Atl N	109	396	67	109	25	1	21	87	65-9	3	81	.275	.377	.503	138	22	8-8	.968	-1	93	109	*O-106(RF)	1.7
1992	†Atl N	144	484	78	124	19	5	21	72	79-8	2	85	.256	.359	.446	121	15	2-4	.976	7	112	85	*O-140(RF)	1.8
1993	†Atl N★	157	585	90	158	15	4	40	120	78-12	3	90	.270	.357	.515	129	23	3-5	.985	-0	102	74	*O-157(RF)	1.4
1994	Atl N★	104	352	61	110	16	2	19	59	69-5	2	45	.313	.427	.531	145	27	2-4	.947	-2	100	83	*O-102(RF)	1.8
1995	†Atl N	120	411	73	104	17	2	24	78	73-5	2	68	.253	.365	.479	118	12	4-2	.984	3	104	97	*O-120(RF)	0.9
1996	Atl N	40	140	23	45	9	0	6	25	21-1	1	22	.321	.409	.514	135	8	1-1	1.000	4	118	115	O-40(RF)	0.9
1997	†Cle A✱	139	495	84	163	31	1	33	101	80-11	0	79	.329	.418	.596	156	43	3-5	.984	-6	81	64	O-78(74-0-5),D-61	2.7
1998	†Cle A	146	540	94	151	39	2	21	88	76-7	0	98	.280	.363	.476	114	13	9-3	1.000	-1	95	0	*D-123,O-21(19-0-2)	0.3
1999	†Cle A	133	429	75	123	18	0	21	88	94-11	2	90	.287	.413	.476	121	18	1-3	.977	-2	89	119	O-93(79-0-15),D-34	0.8
2000	Cle A	68	249	46	66	14	1	21	58	38-2	0	49	.265	.361	.582	131	11	1-1	.977	-2	95	72	O-47(25-2-23),D-20	0.6
	†NY A	78	275	43	84	17	0	20	60	39-1	1	42	.305	.391	.585	145	19	1-0	.985	6	116	177	O-60(43-1-25),D-18	1.9
	Year	146	524	89	150	31	1	41	118	77-3	1	91	.286	.377	.584	138	30	2-1	.982	4	106	129	*O-107(68-3-48),D-38	2.5
2001	†NY A	111	381	58	92	16	1	18	51	54-5	0	83	.241	.333	.430	99	-1	1-2	.981	4	121	308	D-85,O-25(16-0-11)	-0.4
2002	†Oak A	118	398	54	106	18	3	11	49	70-3	1	66	.266	.376	.410	109	8	4-1	.985	-3	92	74	O-75(53-0-23),D-37	0.0
Total	14	1610	5625	929	1571	280	24	305	1017	903-85	18	999	.279	.378	.500	127	241	53-46	.978	1	100	95	*O-1141(312-3-842),D-378/1-69	15.5

JUTZE, SKIP Alfred Henry B 5.28.1946 Bayside, NY BR/TR 5-11/195# d9.1

Year	Tm Lg	G	AB	R	H	2B	3B	HR	RBI	BB-IB	HP	SO	AVG	OBP	SLG	AOPS	ABR	SB-CS	FA	FR	Rng	Thr	G at Pos	BFW
1972	StL N	21	71	1	17	2	0	0	5	1-0	0	16	.239	.247	.268	48	-5	0-1	.964	0	135	242	C-17	-0.5
1973	Hou N	90	278	18	62	6	0	0	18	19-5	1	37	.223	.273	.245	45	-21	0-1	.984	-8	93	92	C-86	-2.7
1974	Hou N	8	13	0	3	0	0	0	1	1-0	0	1	.231	.267	.231	48	-1	0-0	1.000	-2	105	196	/C-7	-0.3
1975	Hou N	51	93	9	21	2	0	0	6	2-0	0	4	.226	.242	.247	39	-8	1-0	.988	-6	82	49	C-47	-1.3
1976	Hou N	42	92	7	14	2	3	0	6	4-0	0	16	.152	.186	.239	22	-10	0-0	.986	-3	76	108	C-42	-1.3
1977	Sea A	42	109	10	24	2	0	3	15	7-1	0	12	.220	.267	.321	60	-6	0-4	.984	-5	61	107	C-40	-1.1
Total	6	254	656	45	141	14	3	3	51	34-6	1	86	.215	.253	.259	44	-51	1-6	.983	-24	87	106	C-239	-7.2

KADING, JACK John Frederick B 11.17.1884 Waukesha, WI D 6.2.1964 Chicago, IL BR/TR 6-3/190# d9.12

Year	Tm Lg	G	AB	R	H	2B	3B	HR	RBI	BB-IB	HP	SO	AVG	OBP	SLG	AOPS	ABR	SB-CS	FA	FR	Rng	Thr	G at Pos	BFW
1910	Pit N	8	23	5	7	2	1	0	4	4	0	5	.304	.407	.478	149	2	0	1.000	1	166	124	/1-8	0.3
1914	Chi F	3	3	0	0	0	0	0	0	0	0	0	.000	.000	.000	-99	-1	0	—	0			H	-0.1
Total	2	11	26	5	7	2	1	0	4	4	0	5	.269	.367	.423	123	1	0	1.000	1	166	124	/1-8	0.2

KAFORA, JAKE Frank Jacob "Tomatoes" B 10.16.1888 Chicago, IL D 3.23.1928 Chicago, IL BR/TR 6/180# d10.5

Year	Tm Lg	G	AB	R	H	2B	3B	HR	RBI	BB-IB	HP	SO	AVG	OBP	SLG	AOPS	ABR	SB-CS	FA	FR	Rng	Thr	G at Pos	BFW
1913	Pit N	1	1	1	0	0	0	0	0	0	1	1	.000	.500	.000	52	0	0	1.000	-0	43	0	/C	0.0
1914	Pit N	21	23	2	3	0	0	0	0	0	2	6	.130	.200	.130	-1	-3	0	1.000	-1	*98*	*55*	C-17	-0.3
Total	2	22	24	3	3	0	0	0	0	0	3	7	.125	.222	.125	4	-3	0	1.000	-1	*95*	*52*	/C-18	-0.3

KAHDOT, IKE Isaac Leonard "Chief" B 10.22.1901 Georgetown, OK D 3.31.1999 Oklahoma City, OK BR/TR 5-5.5/145# d9.5

Year	Tm Lg	G	AB	R	H	2B	3B	HR	RBI	BB-IB	HP	SO	AVG	OBP	SLG	AOPS	ABR	SB-CS	FA	FR	Rng	Thr	G at Pos	BFW
1922	Cle A	4	2	0	0	0	0	0	0	0	0	1	.000	.000	.000	-99	-1	0-0	1.000	0	160	0	/3-2	0.0

KAHL, NICK Nicholas Alexander B 4.10.1879 Coulterville, IL D 7.13.1959 Sparta, IL BR/TR 5-9/185# d5.2

Year	Tm Lg	G	AB	R	H	2B	3B	HR	RBI	BB-IB	HP	SO	AVG	OBP	SLG	AOPS	ABR	SB-CS	FA	FR	Rng	Thr	G at Pos	BFW
1905	Cle A	40	135	16	29	4	1	0	21	4	2		.215	.248	.259	60	-6	1	.940	-3	106	37	2-32/SO(CF)	-1.1

KAHLE, BOB Robert Wayne B 11.23.1915 New Castle, IN D 12.16.1988 Inglewood, CA BR/TR 6/170# d4.21

Year	Tm Lg	G	AB	R	H	2B	3B	HR	RBI	BB-IB	HP	SO	AVG	OBP	SLG	AOPS	ABR	SB-CS	FA	FR	Rng	Thr	G at Pos	BFW
1938	Bos N	8	3	2	1	0	0	0	0	0	0	0	.333	.333	.333	93	0	0	—	0			H	0.0

KAHN, OWEN Owen Earle "Jack" B 6.5.1905 Richmond, VA D 1.17.1981 Richmond, VA BR/TR 5-11/160# d5.24

Year	Tm Lg	G	AB	R	H	2B	3B	HR	RBI	BB-IB	HP	SO	AVG	OBP	SLG	AOPS	ABR	SB-CS	FA	FR	Rng	Thr	G at Pos	BFW
1930	Bos N	1	0	1	0	0	0	0	0	0	0	0	—	—	—	—	0	0	—	0			R	0.0

KAHOE, MIKE Michael Joseph B 9.3.1873 Yellow Springs, OH D 5.14.1949 Akron, OH BR/TR 6/185# d9.22

Year	Tm Lg	G	AB	R	H	2B	3B	HR	RBI	BB-IB	HP	SO	AVG	OBP	SLG	AOPS	ABR	SB-CS	FA	FR	Rng	Thr	G at Pos	BFW
1895	Cin N	3	4	0	0	0	0	0	0	0	0	0	.000	.000	.000	-96	-1	0	1.000	-0	*122*	*0*	/C-3	-0.1
1899	Cin N	14	42	2	7	1	1	0	4	0	0		.167	.167	.238	10	-5	1	.957	2	*131*	*117*	C-13	-0.2
1900	Cin N	52	175	18	33	3	3	1	9	4	2		.189	.215	.257	31	-17	3	.963	5	*117*	*98*	C-51/S	-0.8
1901	Cin N	4	13	0	4	0	0	0	0	1	0		.308	.357	.308	100	0	0	1.000	-1	*98*	*64*	/C-4	-0.1
	Chi N	67	237	21	53	12	2	1	21	8	0		.224	.249	.304	62	-12	5	.974	4	*95*	*99*	C-63/1-6	-0.2
	Year	71	250	21	57	12	2	1	21	9	0		.228	.255	.304	64	-12	5	.974	3	*95*	*97*	C-67/1-6	-0.3
1902	Chi N	7	18	0	4	1	0	0	2	0	0		.222	.222	.278	56	-1	0	.875	-1	*114*	*81*	/C-4,3-2,S	-0.1
	StL A	55	197	21	48	9	2	2	28	6	1		.244	.270	.340	69	-9	4	.967	0	*115*	*80*	C-53	-0.3
1903	StL A	77	244	26	46	7	5	0	23	11	1		.189	.227	.258	46	-16	1	.971	2	*119*	*79*	C-71/O-2(0-1-1)	-0.8
1904	StL A	72	236	9	51	6	1	0	12	8	0		.216	.242	.250	59	-11	4	.968	-3	*95*	*113*	C-69	-0.9
1905	Phi N	16	51	2	13	2	0	0	4	1	0		.255	.269	.294	70	-2	1	.975	1	*116*	*98*	C-15	0.1
1907	Chi N	5	10	0	4	0	0	0	1	0	0		.400	.400	.400	142	0	0	1.000	-1	*79*	*76*	/C-3,1	0.0
	Was A	17	47	3	9	1	0	0	1	0	0		.191	.191	.213	31	-4	0	.976	-1	*90*	*130*	C-15	-0.4
1908	Was A	17	27	1	5	1	0	0	0	0	0		.185	.185	.222	35	-2	0	.983	2	*129*	*62*	C-11	0.1
1909	Was A	4	8	0	1	0	0	0	0	0	0		.125	.125	.125	-22	-1	2	.867	-1	*92*	*131*	/C-3	-0.2
Total	11	410	1309	103	278	43	14	4	105	39	4	0	.212	.237	.276	52	-81	21	.968	9	*108*	*95*	C-378/1-7,O-2(0-1-1),3-2,S-2	-3.9

KAISER, AL Alfred Edward "Deerfoot" B 8.3.1886 Cincinnati, OH D 4.11.1969 Cincinnati, OH BR/TR 5-9/165# d4.18

Year	Tm Lg	G	AB	R	H	2B	3B	HR	RBI	BB-IB	HP	SO	AVG	OBP	SLG	AOPS	ABR	SB-CS	FA	FR	Rng	Thr	G at Pos	BFW
1911	Chi N	26	84	16	21	0	5	0	7	7	0	12	.250	.308	.369	89	-2	6	.905	-3	74	99	O-22(1-21-0)	-0.7
	Bos N	66	197	20	40	5	2	2	15	10	2	26	.203	.249	.279	44	-16	4	.922	-1	99	86	O-58(35-21-2)	-2.0
	Year	92	281	36	61	5	7	2	22	17	2	38	.217	.267	.306	57	-18	10	.918	-4	92	90	O-80(36-42-2)	-2.7
1912	Bos N	4	13	0	0	0	0	0	0	0	0	3	.000	.000	.000	-98	-4	0	.900	0	94	167	/O-4(LF)	-0.4
1914	Ind F	59	187	22	43	10	0	1	16	17	2	41	.230	.301	.299	58	-13	6	.918	-3	112	42	O-50(40-10-0)/1	-2.0
Total	3	155	481	58	104	15	7	3	38	34	4	82	.216	.274	.295	53	-35	16	.917	-7	100	73	O-134(80-52-2)/1	-5.1

KALAHAN, JOHN John Joseph B 9.30.1878 Philadelphia, PA D 6.20.1952 Philadelphia, PA BR/TR 6/165# d9.29

Year	Tm Lg	G	AB	R	H	2B	3B	HR	RBI	BB-IB	HP	SO	AVG	OBP	SLG	AOPS	ABR	SB-CS	FA	FR	Rng	Thr	G at Pos	BFW
1903	Phi A	1	5	0	0	0	0	0	0	0	0		.000	.000	.000	-96	-1	0	1.000	-0	*106*	*118*	/C	-0.2

KALBFUS, CHARLIE Charles Henry "Skinny" B 12.28.1864 Washington, DC D 11.18.1941 Washington, DC BR/TR 5-11/145# d4.18

Year	Tm Lg	G	AB	R	H	2B	3B	HR	RBI	BB-IB	HP	SO	AVG	OBP	SLG	AOPS	ABR	SB-CS	FA	FR	Rng	Thr	G at Pos	BFW
1884	Was U	1	5	1	1	0	0	0		0			.200	.200	.200	22	-1		—	0	0	0	/O(RF)	-0.1

KALIN, FRANK Frank Bruno "Fats" (born Frank Bruno Kalinkiewicz) B 10.3.1917 Steubenville, OH D 1.12.1975 Weirton, WV BR/TR 6/200# d9.25 Mil 1943-45

Year	Tm Lg	G	AB	R	H	2B	3B	HR	RBI	BB-IB	HP	SO	AVG	OBP	SLG	AOPS	ABR	SB-CS	FA	FR	Rng	Thr	G at Pos	BFW
1940	Pit N	3	3	0	0	0	0	0	1	2	0	0	.000	.400	.000	19	0	0	.667	-1	67	0	/O-2(1-0-1)	-0.1
1943	Chi A	4	4	0	0	0	0	0	0	0	0	0	.000	.000	.000	-99	-1	0-0	—	0			H	-0.1
Total	2	7	7	0	0	0	0	0	1	2	0	0	.000	.222	.000	-34	-1	0-0	.667	-1	67	0	/O-2(1-0-1)	-0.2

Year	Tm Lg	G	AB	R	H	2B	3B	HR	RBI	BB-IB	HP	SO	AVG	OBP	SLG	AOPS	ABR	SB-CS	FA	FR	Rng	Thr	G at Pos	BFW
KALINE, AL Albert William B 12.19.1934 Baltimore, MD BR/TR 6-2/180# d6.25 HF1980 OF Total (16-LF 484-CF 2040-RF)																								
1953	Det A	30	28	9	7	0	0	1	2	1	1	5	.250	.300	.357	78	-1	1-0	1.000	0	92	239	O-20(5-11-4)	-0.1
1954	Det A	138	504	42	139	18	3	4	43	22	0	45	.276	.305	.347	80	-16	9-5	.971	7	108	157	*O-135(RF)	-1.4
1955	Det A★	152	588	121	**200**	24	8	27	102	82-12	5	57	**.340**	.421	.546	163	54	6-8	.979	3	103	115	*O-152(RF)	4.9
1956	Det A★	153	617	96	194	32	10	27	128	70-4	1	55	.314	.383	.530	139	33	7-1	.984	**12**	110	**156**	*O-153(1-12-142)	3.9
1957	Det A★	149	577	83	170	29	4	23	90	43-7	3	38	.295	.343	.478	120	14	11-9	.985	5	108	113	*O-145(5-21-137)	1.3
1958	Det A★	146	543	84	170	34	7	16	85	54-6	2	47	.313	.374	.490	127	21	7-4	.994	20	**119**	**192**	*O-145(RF)	3.7
1959	Det A★	136	511	86	167	19	2	27	94	72-**12**	4	42	.327	.410	**.530**	149	37	10-4	.989	2	110	44	*O-136(0-122-15)	3.3
1960	Det A★	147	551	77	153	29	4	15	68	65-3	3	47	.278	.354	.426	108	7	19-4	.987	-5	101	56	*O-142(CF)	-0.2
1961	Det A★	153	586	116	190	**41**	7	19	82	66-2	4	42	.324	.393	.515	138	33	14-1	.990	10	**118**	78	*O-147(1-22-141)/3	3.5
1962	Det A★	100	398	78	121	16	6	29	94	47-3	1	39	.304	.376	.593	152	28	4-0	.983	8	116	134	*O-100(RF)	2.9
1963	Det A★	145	551	89	172	24	3	27	101	54-**12**	4	48	.312	.375	.514	142	31	6-4	.992	-5	98	54	*O-140(0-2-140)	1.8
1964	Det A✳	146	525	77	154	31	5	17	68	75-6	3	51	.293	.383	.469	134	27	4-1	.990	6	**117**	73	*O-136(RF)	2.5
1965	Det A★	125	399	72	112	18	2	18	72	72-11	0	49	.281	.388	.471	142	25	6-0	.985	-6	95	38	*O-112(0-62-51)/3	1.6
1966	Det A★	142	479	85	138	29	1	29	88	81-7	5	66	.288	.392	.534	161	42	5-5	**.993**	2	106	96	*O-136(0-86-53)	3.9
1967	Det A✳	131	458	94	141	28	2	25	78	83-10	1	47	.308	.411	.541	176	47	8-2	.983	7	107	182	*O-130(0-1-130)	5.1
1968	†Det A	102	327	49	94	14	1	10	53	55-7	3	39	.287	.392	.428	145	21	6-4	.978	0	115	26	O-74(4-0-75),1-22	1.7
1969	Det A	131	456	74	124	17	0	21	69	54-4	1	61	.272	.346	.447	117	10	1-2	.966	-0	101	109	*O-118(RF)/1-9	0.3
1970	Det A	131	467	64	130	24	4	16	71	77-5	1	49	.278	.377	.450	127	20	2-2	.988	4	111	60	O-91(RF),1-52	1.6
1971	Det A★	133	405	69	119	19	2	15	54	82-9	7	57	.294	.416	.462	144	29	4-6	**1.000**	-2	96	82	*O-129(0-3-128)/1-5	2.1
1972	†Det A	106	278	46	87	11	2	10	32	28-5	2	33	.313	.374	.475	148	17	1-0	.991	-1	91	110	O-84(RF),1-11	1.4
1973	Det A	91	310	40	79	13	0	10	45	29-4	3	28	.255	.320	.394	95	-2	4-1	1.000	-1	108	31	O-63(RF),1-36	-0.8
1974	Det A★	147	558	71	146	28	2	13	64	65-2	1	75	.262	.337	.389	105	5	2-2	—	0	0	0	*D-146	0.1
Total	22	2834	10116	1622	3007	498	75	399	1583	1277-131	55	1020	.297	.376	.480	134	482	137-65	.986	67	107	100	*O-2488R,D-146,1-135/3-2	43.1
KAMM, WILLIE William Edward B 2.2.1900 San Francisco, CA D 12.21.1988 Belmont, CA BR/TR 5-10.5/170# d4.18																								
1923	Chi A	149	544	57	159	39	9	6	87	62	1	82	.292	.366	.430	110	8	18-13	.960	8	106	104	*3-149	2.4
1924	Chi A	147	528	58	134	28	6	6	93	64	2	59	.254	.337	.364	83	-13	10-9	**.971**	9	105	119	*3-146	0.4
1925	Chi A	152	509	82	142	32	4	6	83	**90**	4	36	.279	.391	.393	105	8	11-13	**.957**	-0	102	108	*3-152	1.5
1926	Chi A	143	480	63	141	24	10	0	62	77	4	24	.294	.396	.385	108	9	12-4	**.978**	16	**110**	72	*3-142	3.4
1927	Chi A	148	540	85	146	32	13	0	59	70	0	18	.270	.354	.378	92	-5	8-9	**.972**	3	96	75	*3-146	0.5
1928	Chi A	**155**	552	70	170	30	12	1	84	73	2	22	.308	.391	.411	112	13	17-9	**.977**	-0	89	113	*3-155	2.2
1929	Chi A	147	523	72	140	33	6	3	63	75	3	23	.268	.363	.371	90	-5	12-5	**.978**	4	98	97	*3-145	0.9
1930	Chi A	112	331	49	89	21	6	3	47	51	1	20	.269	.368	.396	97	0	5-4	.939	13	**111**	97	*3-106	1.7
1931	Chi A	18	59	9	15	4	1	0	9	7	0	6	.254	.333	.356	86	-1	1-1	.938	1	94	119	3-18	0.0
	Cle A	114	410	68	121	31	4	0	66	64	1	13	.295	.392	.390	100	3	13-9	.947	4	100	139	*3-114	1.1
	Year	132	469	77	136	35	5	0	75	71	1	19	.290	.384	.386	99	3	14-10	**.945**	5	**99**	**136**	*3-132	1.1
1932	Cle A	148	524	76	150	34	9	3	83	75	3	36	.286	.379	.403	96	-1	6-3	.967	9	**110**	84	*3-148	1.3
1933	Cle A	133	447	59	126	17	2	1	47	54	0	27	.282	.359	.336	81	-10	6-3	**.984**	3	99	79	*3-131	-0.2
1934	Cle A	121	386	52	104	23	3	0	42	62	1	38	.269	.372	.345	84	-6	7-1	**.978**	9	109	107	*3-118	0.7
1935	Cle A	6	18	2	6	0	0	0	1	0	0	1	.333	.333	.333	72	-1	0-1	.875	-1	69	0	/3-4	-0.2
Total	13	1693	5851	802	1643	348	85	29	826	824	22	405	.281	.372	.384	97	-1	126-84	.967	77	102	99	*3-1674	15.7
KAMPOURIS, ALEX Alexis William B 11.13.1912 Sacramento, CA D 5.29.1993 Sacramento, CA BR/TR 5-8/155# d7.31 Mil 1944-45																								
1934	Cin N	19	66	6	13	1	0	0	3	3	2	18	.197	.254	.212	27	-7	2	.946	-1	105	73	2-16	-0.7
1935	Cin N	148	499	46	123	26	5	7	62	32	2	84	.246	.295	.361	77	-17	8	.957	-3	95	115	*2-141/S-6	-1.0
1936	Cin N	122	355	43	85	10	4	5	46	24	1	46	.239	.289	.332	72	-16	3	.969	22	**115**	115	*2-119/O(LF)	1.3
1937	Cin N	146	458	62	114	21	4	17	71	60	5	65	.249	.342	.424	112	8	2	.961	9	100	97	*2-146	2.6
1938	Cin N	21	74	13	19	1	0	2	7	10	1	13	.257	.353	.351	97	0	0	.973	0	104	94	2-21	0.1
	NY N	82	268	35	66	9	1	5	37	27	1	50	.246	.318	.343	81	-7	0	.972	13	108	120	2-79	1.1
	Year	103	342	48	85	10	1	7	44	37	2	63	.249	.325	.345	84	-7	0	.972	13	107	115	*2-100	1.2
1939	NY N	74	201	23	50	12	2	5	29	30	1	41	.249	.349	.403	101	1	0	.973	11	111	97	2-62,3-11	1.5
1941	Bro N	16	51	8	16	4	2	2	9	11	1	8	.314	.444	.588	181	6	0	.987	-1	102	91	2-15	0.6
1942	Bro N	10	21	3	5	2	1	0	3	0	0	4	.238	.238	.429	92	0	0	.970	1	99	167	/2-9	0.1
1943	Bro N	19	44	9	10	4	1	0	4	17	1	6	.227	.452	.364	136	4	0	.946	-3	86	73	2-18	0.2
	Was A	51	145	24	30	4	0	2	13	30	5	25	.207	.361	.276	91	0	7-1	.936	-2	92	204	3-33,2-10/O(RF)	0.0
Total	9	708	2182	272	531	94	20	45	284	244	20	360	.243	.325	.367	91	-28	22-1	.964	47	103	105	2-636/3-44,S-6,O-2(1-0-1)	5.8
KANE, FRANK Francis Thomas "Sugar" (a/k/a Frank Thomas Kiley In 1915) B 3.9.1895 Whitman, MA D 12.2.1962 Brockton, MA BL/TR 5-11.5/175# d9.13																								
1915	Bro F	3	10	2	2	0	1	0	2	0	0	0	.200	.200	.400	67	-1	0	1.000	1	107	304	/O-2(LF)	0.0
1919	NY A	1	1	0	0	0	0	0	0	0	0	0	.000	.000	.000	-99	0	0	—	0			H	0.0
Total	2	4	11	2	2	0	1	0	2	0	0	0	.182	.182	.364	52	-1	0	1.000	1	107	304	/O-2(LF)	0.0
KANE, JIM James Joseph "Shamus" B 11.27.1881 Scranton, PA D 10.2.1947 Omaha, NE BL/TL 6-2/225# d4.21																								
1908	Pit N	55	145	16	35	3	3	0	22	12	0		.241	.299	.303	93	-1	5	.966	-2	98	118	1-40	-0.5
KANE, JOHN John Francis B 9.24.1882 Chicago, IL D 1.28.1934 St.Anthony, ID BR/TR 5-6/138# d4.11																								
1907	Cin N	79	262	40	65	9	4	3	19	22	8		.248	.325	.347	106	2	20	.959	-2	98	0	O-42(38-0-4),3-25/S-6,2-2	-0.2
1908	Cin N	130	455	61	97	11	7	3	23	43	13		.213	.299	.288	90	-4	30	**.981**	2	96	53	*O-127(0-120-7)/2	-0.9
1909	Chi N	20	45	6	4	1	0	0	5	2	1		.089	.146	.111	-20	-6	1	.917	2	238	0	/O-8(6-1-1),S-3,3-3,2-2	-0.5
1910	†Chi N	32	62	11	15	0	0	1	12	9	0	10	.242	.338	.290	84	-1	2	1.000	-2	100	0	O-18(9-9-1)/2-6,3-4,S-2	-0.4
Total	4	261	824	118	181	21	11	7	59	76	22	10	.220	.303	.297	89	-9	53	.975	-0	101	36	O-195(53-130-13)/3-32,2-11,S-11	-2.0
KANE, JOHN John Francis B 2.19.1900 Chicago, IL D 7.25.1956 Chicago, IL BB/TR 5-10.5/162# d9.3																								
1925	Chi A	14	56	6	10	1	0	0	3	0	1	3	.179	.193	.196	-1	-9	0-0	.935	1	116	125	/S-8,2-6	-0.7
KANE, TOM Thomas Joseph "Sugar" B 12.15.1906 Chicago, IL D 11.26.1973 Chicago, IL BR/TR 5-10.5/160# d8.3																								
1938	Bos N	2	2	0	0	0	0	0	0	2	0	0	.000	.500	.000	53	0	0	1.000	-1	67	0	/2-2	0.0
KANE, JERRY William Jeremiah B 4.1869 Baltimore, MD D 6.16.1949 E.St.Louis, IL BR/TR 6/175# d5.2																								
1890	StL AA	8	25	3	5	0	0	0	2	2	0		.200	.259	.200	31	-2	0	.907	-1	57	46	/1-5,C-4	-0.3
KANEHL, ROD Roderick Edwin "Hot Rod" B 4.1.1934 Wichita, KS BR/TR 6-1/180# d4.15 OF Total (42-LF 56-CF 7-RF)																								
1962	NY N	133	351	52	87	10	2	4	27	23-2	1	36	.248	.296	.322	65	-18	8-6	.944	7	107	118	2-62,3-30,O-20(10-7-3)/1-3,S-2	-0.6
1963	NY N	109	191	26	46	6	0	1	9	5-0	2	26	.241	.268	.288	59	-10	6-3	.974	0	106	232	O-58(30-26-4),3-13,2-12/1-3	-1.2
1964	NY N	98	254	25	59	7	1	1	11	7-0	1	18	.232	.256	.280	52	-17	3-1	.988	12	110	88	2-34,O-25(2-23-0),3-19/1-2	-0.4
Total	3	340	796	103	192	23	3	6	47	35-2	4	80	.241	.277	.300	60	-45	17-10	.950	19	105	106	2-108,O-103C/3-62,1-8,S-2	-2.2
KAPLER, GABE Gabriel Stefan B 8.31.1975 Hollywood, CA BR/TR 6-2/190# d9.20																								
1998	Det A	7	25	3	5	0	1	0	0	1-0	0	4	.200	.231	.280	32	-3	2-0	1.000	-1	73	0	/O-6(RF),D	-0.4
1999	Det A	130	416	60	102	22	4	18	49	42-0	2	74	.245	.315	.447	92	-7	11-5	.981	-2	101	52	*O-128(0-114-32)/D-2	-0.8
2000	Tex A	116	444	59	134	32	1	14	66	42-2	0	57	.302	.360	.473	108	6	8-4	.969	3	109	77	*O-116(0-84-40)	0.7
2001	Tex A	134	483	77	129	29	1	17	72	61-2	3	70	.267	.348	.437	103	3	23-6	.997	0	101	105	*O-133(CF)/D	0.7
2002	Tex A	72	196	25	51	12	1	0	17	8-0	0	30	.260	.285	.332	61	-11	5-2	.977	5	106	241	O-64(31-23-18)/1D	-0.7
	Col N	40	119	12	37	4	3	2	17	8-0	1	23	.311	.359	.445	98	-1	6-2	1.000	2	106	152	O-38(15-1-23)	0.0
2003	Col N	39	67	10	15	2	0	0	4	8-1	0	18	.224	.307	.254	42	-5	2-0	.970	2	94	304	O-29(15-2-13)	-0.4
	†Bos A	68	158	29	46	11	1	4	23	14-0	0	23	.291	.349	.449	106	2	4-2	.932	-2	82	199	O-61(25-8-30)/1	-0.2
Total	6	606	1908	275	519	112	12	55	248	184-5	6	299	.272	.335	.430	94	-16	61-21	.979	6	101	115	O-575(86-365-162)/D-5,1-2	-1.1
KAPPEL, HEINIE Henry B 9.1863 Philadelphia, PA D 8.27.1905 Philadelphia, PA BR/TR 5-8/160# d5.22 b-Joe																								
1887	Cin AA	23	78	11	22	3	2	0	15	2	1		.282	.309	.372	87	-2	3	.667	-2	93	74	/3-9,O-7(2-0-5),2-6,S	-0.3
1888	Cin AA	36	143	18	37	4	4	1	15	2	1		.259	.274	.364	98	-1	20	.790	-11	93	95	S-25,2-10/3	-1.0
1889	Col AA	46	173	25	47	7	5	3	21	21	1	28	.272	.354	.422	127	6	10	.791	-1	94	45	S-23,3-23	0.5
Total	3	105	394	54	106	14	11	4	51	25	3	28	.269	.318	.391	109	3	33	.796	-14	94	68	/S-49,3-33,2-16,O-7(2-0-5)	-0.8
KAPPEL, JOE Joseph B 4.27.1857 Philadelphia, PA D 7.8.1929 Philadelphia, PA BR 5-11/175# d5.26 b-Heinie																								
1884	Phi N	4	15	1	1	0	0	0	0	0		2	.067	.067	.067	-61	-3		.727	-4			/C-4	-0.6

Year	Tm Lg	G	AB	R	H	2B	3B	HR	RBI	BB-IB	HP	SO	AVG	OBP	SLG	AOPS	ABR	SB-CS	FA	FR	Rng	Thr	G at Pos	BFW
1890	Phi AA	56	208	29	50	8	1	1	22	20	1		.240	.310	.303	81	-5	12	.851	-4	146	0	O-23(11-8-5),S-18,3-11/C-3,2-2	-0.7
Total	2	60	223	30	51	8	1	1	22	20	1	2	.229	.295	.287	73	-8	12	.851	-7			/O-23(11-8-5),S-18,3-11,C-7,2-2	-1.3
KARKOVICE, RON Ronald Joseph B 8.8.1963 Union, NJ BR/TR 6-1/215# d8.17																								
1986	Chi A	37	97	13	24	7	0	4	13	9-0	1	37	.247	.315	.443	101	0	1-0	.996	8	87	132	C-37	1.0
1987	Chi A	39	85	7	6	0	0	2	7	7-0	2	40	.071	.160	.141	-19	-15	3-0	.982	6	444	100	C-37/D	-0.7
1988	Chi A	46	115	10	20	4	0	3	9	7-0	1	30	.174	.228	.287	43	-9	4-2	.995	6	169	121	C-46	-0.1
1989	Chi A	71	182	21	48	9	2	3	24	10-0	2	56	.264	.306	.385	97	-1	0-0	.986	12	152	135	C-68/D-2	1.4
1990	Chi A	68	183	30	45	10	0	6	20	16-1	1	52	.246	.308	.399	99	-1	2-0	.994	3	193	102	C-64/D-2	0.7
1991	Chi A	75	167	25	41	13	0	5	22	15-1	1	42	.246	.310	.413	101	0	0-0	.988	6	129	115	C-69/O(LF)	0.9
1992	Chi A	123	342	39	81	12	1	13	50	30-1	3	89	.237	.302	.392	95	-4	10-4	.990	0	109	85	*C-119/O(RF)	0.4
1993	†Chi A	128	403	60	92	17	1	20	54	29-1	6	126	.228	.287	.424	91	-7	2-2	.994	19	**166**	124	*C-127	1.9
1994	Chi A	77	207	33	44	9	1	11	29	36-2	0	68	.213	.325	.425	94	-2	0-3	.993	-1	141	70	C-76	0.1
1995	Chi A	113	323	44	70	14	1	13	51	39-0	5	84	.217	.306	.387	84	-8	2-3	.991	-4	95	123	*C-113	-0.6
1996	Chi A	111	355	44	78	22	0	10	38	24-2	1	93	.220	.270	.366	62	-22	0-0	.993	11	133	118	*C-111	-0.4
1997	Chi A	51	138	10	25	3	0	6	18	11-0	3	32	.181	.248	.333	55	-10	0-0	.996	-4	120	72	C-51	-1.1
Total	12	939	2597	336	574	120	6	96	335	233-8	26	749	.221	.289	.383	81	-79	24-14	.992	62	147	109	C-918/D-5,O-2(1-0-1)	3.5
KARLON, BILL William John "Hank" B 1.21.1909 Palmer, MA D 12.7.1964 Ware, MA BR/TR 6-1/190# d4.28																								
1930	NY A	2	5	0	0	0	0	0	0	0	0	1	.000	.000	.000	-99	-2	0-0	1.000	-0	74	0	/O(LF)	-0.2
KAROW, MARTY Martin Gregory (born Martin Gregory Karowsky) B 7.18.1904 Braddock, PA D 4.27.1986 Bryan, TX BR/TR 5-10.5/170# d6.21																								
1927	Bos A	6	10	0	2	1	0	0	0	0	0	2	.200	.200	.300	29	-1	0-0	1.000	0	95	318	/S-3,3-2	0.0
KARROS, ERIC Eric Peter B 11.4.1967 Hackensack, NJ BR/TR 6-4/216# d9.1																								
1991	LA N	14	14	0	1	1	0	0	1	1-0	0	6	.071	.133	.143	-23	-2	0-0	1.000	-0	74	225	1-10	-0.3
1992	LA N	149	545	63	140	30	1	20	88	37-3	2	103	.257	.304	.426	107	3	2-4	.993	8	**116**	93	*1-143	0.0
1993	LA N	158	619	74	153	27	2	23	80	34-1	2	82	.247	.287	.409	89	-13	0-1	.992	9	118	97	*1-157	-1.9
1994	LA N	111	406	51	108	21	1	14	46	29-1	2	53	.266	.310	.426	98	-2	2-0	.991	13	139	96	*1-109	0.1
1995	†LA N	143	551	83	164	29	3	32	105	61-4	4	115	.298	.369	.535	149	38	4-4	.995	0	96	94	*1-143	2.3
1996	†LA N	154	608	84	158	29	1	34	111	53-2	1	121	.260	.316	.479	116	11	8-0	.990	1	102	109	*1-154	-0.1
1997	LA N	**162**	628	86	167	28	0	31	104	61-2	2	116	.266	.329	.459	113	10	15-7	.992	-2	95	74	*1-162	-0.6
1998	LA N	139	507	59	150	20	1	23	87	47-1	3	93	.296	.355	.475	124	17	7-2	.991	5	111	115	*1-136/D-2	0.9
1999	LA N	153	578	74	176	40	0	34	112	53-0	2	119	.304	.362	.550	135	29	8-5	.991	9	126	93	*1-151	2.3
2000	LA N	155	584	84	146	29	0	31	106	63-2	4	122	.250	.321	.459	102	-1	4-3	.995	14	129	103	*1-153/D	-0.1
2001	LA N	121	438	42	103	22	0	15	63	41-2	3	101	.235	.303	.388	84	-12	3-1	.996	-2	90	93	*1-119	-2.4
2002	LA N	142	524	52	142	26	1	13	73	37-1	6	74	.271	.323	.399	100	-4	4-2	**.997**	11	**131**	97	*1-142	-0.6
2003	†Chi N	114	336	37	96	16	1	12	40	28-1	0	46	.286	.340	.446	105	2	1-1	.992	-2	83	117	1-97	-0.8
Total	13	1715	6338	789	1704	318	11	282	1016	545-20	31	1151	.269	.326	.456	111	76	58-30	.993	66	112	98	*1-1676/D-3	-1.2
KARST, JOHN John Gottlieb "King" B 10.15.1893 Philadelphia, PA D 5.21.1976 Cape May Court House, NJ BL/TR 5-11.5/175# d10.6																								
1915	Bro N	1	0	0	0	0	0	0	0	0	0	0	—	—	—	—	0	0	1.000	0	149	2105	/3	0.0
KASKO, EDDIE Edward Michael B 6.27.1932 Linden, NJ BR/TR 6/180# d4.18 M4																								
1957	StL N	134	479	59	131	16	5	1	35	33-7	0	53	.273	.319	.334	75	-17	6-1	.961	-0	**106**	102	*3-120,S-13/2	-1.6
1958	StL N	104	259	20	57	8	1	2	22	21-6	0	25	.220	.277	.282	47	-20	1-2	.961	-1	97	103	S-77,2-12/3	-1.6
1959	Cin N	118	329	39	93	14	1	2	31	14-5	0	38	.283	.309	.350	74	-12	2-2	.976	10	105	117	S-84,3-31/2-2	0.4
1960	Cin N	126	479	56	140	21	1	6	51	46-0	6	37	.292	.359	.378	101	2	9-9	.966	1	109	132	3-86,2-33,S-15	0.5
1961	†Cin N★	126	469	64	127	22	1	2	27	32-1	4	36	.271	.320	.335	74	-17	4-3	.964	-16	88	87	*S-112,3-12/2-6	-2.3
1962	Cin N	134	533	74	148	26	2	4	41	35-1	5	44	.278	.326	.356	81	-13	3-3	.941	-8	94	88	*3-114,S-21	-2.1
1963	Cin N	76	199	25	48	9	0	3	10	21-4	0	29	.241	.311	.332	83	-4	0-2	.959	-1	88	82	3-48,S-15/2	-0.5
1964	Hou N	133	448	45	109	16	1	0	22	37-8	1	52	.243	.302	.283	70	-17	4-6	**.978**	15	109	106	*S-128/3-2	0.7
1965	Hou N	68	215	18	53	7	1	1	10	11-1	4	20	.247	.296	.302	74	-8	1-3	.976	-7	92	81	S-59/3-2	-1.2
1966	Bos A	58	136	11	29	7	0	1	12	15-0	0	19	.213	.291	.287	61	-6	1-0	.976	5	117	70	S-20,3-10/2-8	0.1
Total	10	1077	3546	411	935	146	13	22	261	265-33	20	353	.264	.317	.331	76	-112	31-31	.971	-2	99	100	S-544,3-426/2-63	-7.6
KATA, MATT Matthew John B 3.14.1978 Avon Lakes, OH BB/TR 6-1/180# d6.15																								
2003	Ari N	78	288	42	74	16	5	7	29	25-0	1	53	.257	.315	.420	82	-8	3-2	.988	2	95	88	2-52,3-23/S-6	-0.3
KATT, RAY Raymond Frederick B 5.9.1927 New Braunfels, TX D 10.19.1999 New Braunfels, TX BR/TR 6-2/200# d9.16 C3																								
1952	NY N	9	27	4	6	0	0	0	1	1	0	5	.222	.250	.222	32	-3	0-0	1.000	1	249	53	/C-8	-0.1
1953	NY N	8	29	2	5	1	0	0	1	1	0	3	.172	.200	.207	6	-4	0-0	.975	-0	112	141	/C-8	-0.4
1954	NY N	86	200	26	51	7	1	9	33	19	0	29	.255	.314	.435	94	-3	1-0	.973	-3	146	89	C-82	-0.2
1955	NY N	124	326	27	70	7	2	7	28	22-4	2	38	.215	.268	.313	54	-23	0-0	.987	-5	115	89	*C-122	-2.3
1956	NY N	37	101	10	23	4	0	7	14	6-1	1	16	.228	.278	.475	98	-1	0-1	.978	1	117	125	C-37	0.1
	StL N	47	158	11	41	4	0	6	20	6-1	1	24	.259	.289	.399	83	-4	0-1	.984	-2	94	61	C-47	-0.5
	Year	84	259	21	64	8	0	13	34	12-2	2	40	.247	.285	.429	89	-5	0-2	.982	-1	103	87	C-84	-0.4
1957	NY N	72	165	11	38	3	1	2	17	15-1	2	35	.230	.294	.297	62	-9	1-0	.981	-3	128	101	C-68	-0.9
1958	StL N	19	41	1	7	1	0	1	4	4-0	0	6	.171	.239	.268	34	-4	0-0	.971	-1	69	51	C-14	-0.4
1959	StL N	15	24	0	7	2	0	0	2	0-0	0	8	.292	.292	.375	71	-1	0-0	.976	-0	106	81	C-14	-0.1
Total	8	417	1071	92	248	29	4	32	120	74-7	6	164	.232	.282	.356	69	-52	2-2	.981	-12	121	89	C-400	-4.8
KAUFF, BENNY Benjamin Michael B 1.5.1890 Pomeroy, OH D 11.17.1961 Columbus, OH BL/TL 5-8/157# d4.20 Mil 1918																								
1912	NY A	5	11	4	3	0	0	0	2	3	0		.273	.429	.273	96	0	1	1.000	-1	76	0	/O-4(CF)	0.0
1914	Ind F	154	571	**120**	**211**	**44**	13	8	95	72	8	55	**.370**	**.447**	.534	150	37	**75**	.953	9	107	123	*O-154(33-54-68)	3.7
1915	Bro F	136	483	92	165	23	11	12	83	85	6	50	**.342**	**.446**	**.509**	**170**	**43**	**55**	.959	11	103	**161**	*O-136(CF)	**4.7**
1916	NY N	154	552	71	146	22	15	9	74	68	3	65	.264	.348	.408	139	26	40-26	.962	-4	91	117	*O-154(CF)	1.2
1917	†NY N	153	559	89	172	22	4	5	68	59	5	54	.308	.379	.388	140	29	30	.976	-11	96	57	*O-153(3-150-0)	0.9
1918	NY N	67	270	41	85	19	4	2	39	16	1	30	.315	.355	.437	144	14	9	.952	-5	83	118	O-67(CF)	0.5
1919	NY N	135	491	73	136	27	7	10	67	39	3	45	.277	.334	.422	128	16	21	.950	-6	92	103	*O-134(CF)	0.1
1920	NY N	55	157	31	43	12	3	3	26	25	2	14	.274	.380	.446	138	9	3-7	.960	-6	76	120	O-51(CF)	-0.2
Total	8	859	3094	521	961	169	57	49	454	367	28	313	.311	.389	.450	146	174	234-33	.960	-12	95	112	O-853(36-750-68)	10.9
KAUFFMAN, DICK Howard Richard B 6.22.1888 E.Lewisburg, PA D 4.16.1948 Mifflinburg, PA BB/TR 6-3/190# d9.17																								
1914	StL A	7	15	1	4	1	0	0	2	0	0	3	.267	.267	.333	83	0	0	.967	-1	0	0	/1-7	-0.2
1915	StL A	37	124	9	32	8	2	0	14	5	2	27	.258	.298	.355	99	-1	0-3	.984	-1	90	135	1-32/O(RF)	-0.4
Total	2	44	139	10	36	9	2	0	16	5	2	30	.259	.295	.353	97	-1	0-3	.982	-2	81	121	/1-39,O(RF)	-0.6
KAUFMANN, TONY Anthony Charles B 12.16.1900 Chicago, IL D 6.4.1982 Elgin, IL BR/TR 5-11/165# d9.23 C4 ▲																								
1921	Chi N	2	5	0	2	1	0	0	0	0	0	1	.400	.400	.600	161	1	0-0	1.000	-1	29	0	/P-2	0.0
1922	Chi N	38	45	4	9	2	1	1	4	2	0	14	.200	.234	.356	49	1	0-0	.933	-1	79	0	P-37	0.0
1923	Chi N	33	74	10	16	2	0	2	10	7	0	17	.216	.284	.324	60	3	0-0	.962	-1	85	124	P-33	0.0
1924	Chi N	35	76	6	24	5	0	1	14	3	0	10	.316	.342	.421	102	6	0-0	.981	-2	75	123	P-34	0.0
1925	Chi N	31	78	8	15	7	0	2	13	2	0	17	.192	.213	.359	42	2	0-0	.981	-0	93	210	P-31	0.0
1926	Chi N	30	60	9	15	2	0	1	7	2	0	10	.250	.274	.333	62	2	1	**1.000**	-2	81	87	P-26	0.0
1927	Chi N	9	16	2	5	0	0	1	6	4	0	4	.313	.450	.500	154	3	0	1.000	2	155	176	/P-9	0.0
	Phi N	8	7	1	1	0	0	1	2	0	0	1	.143	.143	.571	83	0	0	1.000	-0	72	0	/P-5,O(LF)	0.0
	StL N	1	0	0	0	0	0	0	0	0	0	0	—	—	—	—	0	0	—	0	0	0	/P	0.0
	Year	18	23	3	6	0	0	2	8	4	0	5	.261	.370	.522	136	1	0	1.000	1	133	130	P-15/O(LF)	0.0
1928	StL N	5	0	0	0	0	0	0	0	0	0	0	—	—	—	—	0	0	1.000	-0	86	0	/P-4	0.0
1929	NY N	39	32	18	1	0	0	0	1	6	0	4	.031	.184	.031	-43	-7	3	.964	1	131	0	O-16(4-8-4)	-0.7
1930	StL N	2	3	1	1	0	0	0	0	1	0	1	.333	.500	.333	103	0	0	1.000	-0	50	0	/P-2	0.0
1931	StL N	20	18	1	2	0	0	0	0	1	0	3	.111	.158	.111	-26	-3	0	.929	-0	107	0	P-15/O(LF)	0.0
1935	StL N	7	0	2	0	0	0	0	0	0	0	0	—	—	—	—	0	0	1.000	0	119	0	/P-3	0.0
Total	12	260	414	62	91	19	1	9	57	28	0	82	.220	.269	.336	57	8	4-0	.972	-5	86	107	P-202/O-18(6-8-4)	-0.7

Year	Tm Lg	G	AB	R	H	2B	3B	HR	RBI	BB-IB	HP	SO	AVG	OBP	SLG	AOPS	ABR	SB-CS	FA	FR	Rng	Thr	G at Pos	BFW
KAVANAGH, CHARLIE Charles Hugh "Silk" B 6.9.1893 Chicago, IL D 9.6.1973 Reedsburg, WI BR/TR 5-9/165# d6.11																								
1914	Chi A	6	5	0	1	0	0	0	0	0	1	2	.200	.333	.200	62	0	0	—	0			H	0.0
KAVANAGH, LEO Leo Daniel B 8.9.1894 Chicago, IL D 8.10.1950 Chicago, IL BR/TR 5-9/180# d4.22																								
1914	Chi F	5	11	0	3	0	0	0	1	1	0	0	.273	.333	.273	70	-1	0	1.000	-0	76	123	/S-5	-0.1
KAVANAGH, MARTY Martin Joseph B 6.13.1891 Harrison, NJ D 7.28.1960 Eloise, MI BR/TR 6/187# d4.18																								
1914	Det A	128	439	60	109	21	6	4	35	41	4	42	.248	.318	.351	98	-1	16-14	.929	-11	102	79	*2-115/1-4	-1.3
1915	Det A	113	332	55	98	14	13	4	49	42	2	44	.295	.378	.452	141	16	8-8	.987	-11	88	70	1-44,2-42/S-2,O-2(LF),3	0.3
1916	Det A	58	78	6	11	4	0	0	5	9	1	15	.141	.239	.192	29	-7	0	1.000	-1	98	69	O-11(1-0-10)/2-2,3	-0.9
	Cle A	19	44	4	11	2	1	1	10	2	0	5	.250	.283	.409	102	0	0	.894	-1	123	55	/2-9,13	-0.1
	Year	77	122	10	22	6	1	1	15	11	1	20	.180	.254	.270	55	-7	0	1.000	-2	98	69	O-11(1-0-10),2-11/3-2,1	-1.0
1917	Cle A	14	14	1	0	0	0	0	0	3	0	2	.000	.176	.000	-43	-2	0	1.000	0	48	408	/O-2(CF)	-0.2
1918	Cle A	13	38	4	8	2	0	0	6	7	1	7	.211	.348	.263	77	-1	1	.967	-1	68	107	1-12	-0.3
	StL N	12	44	6	8	1	0	1	8	3	0	1	.182	.234	.273	56	-2	1	1.000	-2	95	0	/O-8(RF),2-4	-0.5
	Det A	13	44	2	12	3	0	0	9	11	0	6	.273	.418	.341	135	3	0	.964	-2	73	76	1-12	0.1
Total	5	370	1033	138	257	47	20	10	122	118	8	122	.249	.330	.362	104	6	26-22	.926	-28	101	71	2-172/1-73,O-23(3-2-18),3-3,S-2	-2.9
KAVANAUGH d9.11																								
1872	Eck NA	5	23	3	6	1	0	0	4	0		0	.261	.261	.304	86	0	0-0	.921	-0	0	0	/1-4,O-2(RF)	0.0
KAY, BILL Walter Brocton "King Bill" B 2.14.1878 New Castle, VA D 12.3.1945 Roanoke, VA BL/TR 6-2/180# d8.12																								
1907	Was A	25	60	8	20	1	1	0	7	0	0		.333	.333	.383	139	2	0	1.000	1	74	0	O-12(0-1-11)	0.2
KAZAK, EDDIE Edward Terrance (born Edward Terrance Tkaczuk) B 7.18.1920 Steubenville, OH D 12.15.1999 Austin, TX BR/TR 6/175# d9.29																								
1948	StL N	6	22	1	6	3	0	0	2	0	0	2	.273	.273	.409	78	-1	0	.900	-0	92	221	/3-6	-0.1
1949	StL N★	92	326	43	99	15	3	6	42	29	1	17	.304	.362	.423	105	2	0	.926	-2	103	132	3-80/2-5	0.0
1950	StL N	93	207	21	53	2	2	5	23	18	1	19	.256	.319	.357	74	-8	0	.936	1	107	83	3-48	-0.8
1951	StL N	11	33	2	6	2	0	0	4	5	0	5	.182	.289	.242	44	-2	0-0	.933	-1	85	46	3-10	-0.4
1952	StL N	3	2	1	0	0	0	0	0	0	0	0	.000	.000	.000	-99	-1	0-0	1.000	0	143	0	/3	-0.1
	Cin N	13	15	1	1	0	1	0	0	0	0	2	.067	.067	.200	-29	-3	0-0	.667	-1	54	0	/3-3,1	-0.4
	Year	16	17	2	1	0	1	0	0	0	0	2	.059	.059	.176	-37	-3	0-0	.750	-1	78	0	/3-4,1	-0.5
Total	5	218	605	69	165	22	6	11	71	52	2	45	.273	.332	.383	87	-13	0-0	.927	-4	102	114	3-148/2-5,1	-1.8
KAZANSKI, TED Theodore Stanley B 1.25.1934 Hamtramck, MI BR/TR 6-1/175# d6.25																								
1953	Phi N	95	360	39	78	17	5	2	27	26	3	53	.217	.275	.308	52	-26	1-1	.949	-18	85	93	S-95	-3.5
1954	Phi N	39	104	7	14	2	0	1	8	4	0	14	.135	.164	.183	-9	-17	0-1	.945	-4	95	111	S-38	-2.0
1955	Phi N	9	12	1	1	0	0	1	1	1-0	0	1	.083	.154	.333	25	-1	0-0	1.000	0	94	77	/S-4,3-4	-0.1
1956	Phi N	117	379	35	80	11	1	4	34	20-6	1	41	.211	.251	.277	43	-31	0-2	.979	-16	88	97	*2-116/S	-4.2
1957	Phi N	62	185	15	49	7	1	3	11	17-1	0	20	.265	.327	.362	88	-3	1-1	.968	-2	88	194	3-36,2-22/S-3	-0.5
1958	Phi N	95	289	21	66	12	2	3	35	22-2	4	34	.228	.291	.315	62	-16	2-3	.988	-13	89	100	2-59,S-22,3-16	-2.6
Total	6	417	1329	118	288	49	9	14	116	90-9	8	163	.217	.269	.299	51	-94	4-8	.981	-53	89	99	2-197,S-163/3-56	-12.9
KEARNEY, BOB Robert Henry B 10.3.1956 San Antonio, TX BR/TR 6/190# d9.25																								
1979	SF N	2	0	0	0	0	0	0	0	1-0	0	0	—	1.000	—	211	0	0-0	—	-0	0	0	/C	0.0
1981	Oak A	1	0	0	0	0	0	0	0	0-0	0	0	—	—	—	—	0	0-0	—	-0	0	0	/C	0.0
1982	Oak A	22	71	7	12	3	0	0	5	3-0	2	10	.169	.218	.211	21	-8	0-0	.970	4	102	132	C-22	-0.3
1983	Oak A	108	298	33	76	11	0	8	32	21-1	4	50	.255	.312	.372	93	-3	1-4	.982	2	116	105	*C-101/D-3	0.1
1984	Sea A	133	431	39	97	24	1	7	43	18-0	2	72	.225	.257	.334	64	-22	7-5	.988	7	106	118	*C-133	-1.0
1985	Sea A	108	305	24	74	14	1	6	27	11-1	4	59	.243	.277	.354	71	-13	1-1	**.995**	5	114	119	*C-108	-0.4
1986	Sea A	81	204	23	49	10	0	6	25	12-1	0	35	.240	.281	.377	77	-7	0-2	.989	13	89	175	C-79	0.8
1987	Sea A	24	47	5	8	4	1	0	1	1-0	0	9	.170	.188	.298	25	-5	0-0	.981	5	270	103	C-24	0.0
Total	8	479	1356	131	316	66	3	27	133	67-3	12	235	.233	.274	.346	70	-58	9-12	.987	34	113	124	C-469/D-3	-0.8
KEARNS, AUSTIN Austin Ryan B 5.20.1980 Lexington, KY BR/TR 6-3/220# d4.17																								
2002	Cin N	107	372	66	117	24	3	13	56	54-3	6	81	.315	.407	.500	138	21	6-3	.983	5	111	117	*O-103(13-6-95)	2.2
2003	Cin N	82	292	39	77	11	0	15	58	41-1	5	68	.264	.364	.455	114	7	5-2	.990	4	113	100	O-80(0-40-51)	0.9
Total	2	189	664	105	194	35	3	28	114	95-4	11	149	.292	.388	.480	128	28	11-5	.986	10	112	109	O-183(13-46-146)	3.1
KEARNS, TEDDY Edward Joseph B 1.1.1900 Trenton, NJ D 12.21.1949 Trenton, NJ BR/TR 5-11/180# d10.1																								
1920	Phi A	1	1	0	0	0	0	0	0	0	0	0	.000	.000	.000	-99	0	0-0	—	0			H	0.0
1924	Chi N	4	16	0	4	0	1	0	1	1	0	1	.250	.294	.375	77	-1	0-0	1.000	0	96	98	/1-4	-0.1
1925	Chi N	3	2	0	1	0	0	0	0	0	0	0	.500	.500	.500	154	0	0-0	1.000	-0	0	265	/1-3	0.0
Total	3	8	19	0	5	0	1	0	1	1	0	1	.263	.300	.368	76	-1	0-0	1.000	0	86	116	/1-7	-0.1
KEARNS, TOM Thomas J. "Dasher" B 11.9.1859 Rochester, NY D 12.7.1938 Buffalo, NY BR/TR 5-7/160# d8.26																								
1880	Buf N	2	7	0	0	0	0	0	0	0		0	.000	.000	.000	-98	-1		.667	-2			/C-2	-0.4
1882	Det N	4	13	2	4	2	0	0	1	0		4	.308	.308	.462	143	1		.733	-2	86	0	/2-4	-0.1
1884	Det N	21	79	9	16	0	1	0	7	2		10	.203	.222	.228	45	-5		.810	-8	80	58	2-21	-1.1
Total	3	27	99	11	20	2	1	0	8	2		14	.202	.218	.242	48	-5		.801	-12			/2-25,C-2	-1.6
KEARSE, EDDIE Edward Paul "Truck" B 2.23.1916 San Francisco, CA D 7.15.1968 Eureka, CA BR/TR 6-1/195# d6.13																								
1942	NY A	11	26	2	5	0	0	0	2	3	0	1	.192	.276	.192	34	-2	1-0	1.000	2	*184*	*143*	C-11	0.1
KEATING, CHICK Walter Francis B 8.8.1891 Philadelphia, PA D 7.13.1959 Philadelphia, PA BR/TR 5-9.5/155# d9.26																								
1913	Chi N	2	5	1	1	1	0	0	0	0	0	1	.200	.200	.400	69	0	0	1.000	-1	26	0	/S-2	-0.1
1914	Chi N	20	30	3	3	0	1	0	0	6	0	9	.100	.250	.167	25	-3	0	.951	-0	97	72	S-14	-0.3
1915	Chi N	4	8	1	0	0	0	0	0	0	0	3	.000	.000	.000	-99	-2	1	.750	-1	82	0	/S-2	-0.3
1926	Phi N	4	2	0	0	0	0	0	0	0	0	0	.000	.000	.000	-95	-1	0	1.000	-1	86	0	/2-2,S-2,3	-0.1
Total	4	30	45	5	4	1	1	0	0	6	0	13	.089	.196	.156	4	-6	1	.903	-3	86	50	/S-20,2-2,3	-0.8
KEATLEY, GREG Gregory Steven B 9.12.1953 Princeton, WV BR/TR 6-2/200# d9.27																								
1981	KC A	2	0	0	0	0	0	0	0	0-0	0	0	—	—	—	—	0	0-0	1.000	0	0	0	/C-2	0.0
KEEDY, PAT Charles Patrick B 1.10.1958 Birmingham, AL BR/TR 6-4/205# d9.10																								
1985	Cal A	3	4	1	2	1	0	1	1	0-0	0	0	.500	.500	1.500	424	2	0-1	—	-1	0	0	/3-2,O(LF)	0.1
1987	Chi A	17	41	6	7	1	0	2	2	2-0	0	14	.171	.209	.341	42	-4	1-0	.943	4	131	113	3-11/1-2,2SO(LF)D	0.0
1989	Cle A	9	14	3	3	2	0	0	1	2-0	0	5	.214	.313	.357	87	0	0-0	1.000	1	85	0	/O-3(LF),3-2,1SD	0.1
Total	3	29	59	10	12	4	0	3	4	4-0	0	19	.203	.254	.424	77	-2	1-1	.929	5	140	154	/3-15,O-5(LF),1-3,D-2,S-2,2	0.2
KEELER, WILLIE William Henry "Wee Willie" (born William Henry O'Kelleher) B 3.3.1872 Brooklyn, NY D 1.1.1923 Brooklyn, NY BL/TL 5-4.5/140# d9.30 HF1939																								
1892	NY N	14	53	7	17	3	0	0	6	3	1	3	.321	.368	.377	128	2	5	.878	-2	77	52	3-14	0.0
1893	NY N	7	24	5	8	2	1	1	7	5	0	1	.333	.448	.625	183	3	3	.667	-3	0	0	/O-3(CF),2-2,S-2	0.0
	Bro N	20	80	14	25	1	1	1	9	4	1	4	.313	.353	.387	101	0	2	.833	-2	96	83	3-12/O-8(LF)	-0.2
	Year	27	104	19	33	3	2	2	16	9	1	5	.317	.377	.442	121	3	5	.833	-5	96	83	3-12,O-11(8-3-0)/2-2,S-2	-0.2
1894	†Bal N	**129**	590	165	219	27	22	5	94	40	18	6	.371	.427	.517	121	19	32	.938	2	116	81	*O-128(RF)/2	1.1
1895	†Bal N	**131**	565	162	213	24	15	4	78	37	14	12	.377	.429	.494	134	28	47	.964	10	107	126	*O-131(RF)	2.5
1896	†Bal N	126	544	153	210	22	13	4	82	37	7	9	.386	.432	.496	142	33	67	.969	3	109	142	*O-126(2-0-124)	2.5
1897	†Bal N	129	564	145	**239**	27	19	0	74	35	7		**.424**	.464	.539	164	52	64	.970	-2	65	61	*O-129(RF)	3.7
1898	Bal N	129	561	126	**216**	7	2	1	44	31	3		**.385**	.420	.410	136	26	28	.961	-1	78	53	*O-128(RF)/3	1.7
1899	Bro N	141	570	**140**	216	12	13	1	61	37	9		.379	.425	.451	137	29	45	.979	-0	102	74	*O-141(RF)	2.0
1900	†Bro N	136	563	106	**204**	13	12	4	68	30	7		.362	.402	.449	127	19	41	.940	6	121	82	*O-136(RF)/2	1.6
1901	Bro N	136	595	123	202	18	12	2	43	21	7		.339	.369	.420	125	17	23	**.985**	-2	111	99	*O-125(RF),3-10/2-3	0.9
1902	Bro N	133	559	86	186	20	5	0	38	21	7		.333	.365	.386	131	19	19	**.978**	0	78	119	*O-133(RF)	1.4
1903	NY A	132	512	95	160	14	7	0	32	32	13		.313	.368	.367	114	10	24	.935	-8	74	120	*O-128(0-5-123)/3-4	-0.4
1904	NY A	143	543	78	186	14	8	2	40	35	7		.343	.390	.409	146	28	21	.935	-3	103	**188**	*O-142(RF)	2.1
1905	NY A	149	560	81	169	14	4	4	38	43	5		.302	.357	.363	115	10	19	.968	1	116	29	*O-137(3-0-134),2-12/3-3	0.6
1906	NY A	152	592	96	180	8	3	2	33	40	5		.304	.353	.338	106	4	23	.987	-2	83	75	*O-152(1-0-151)	-0.5

Year	Tm Lg	G	AB	R	H	2B	3B	HR	RBI	BB-IB	HP	SO	AVG	OBP	SLG	AOPS	ABR	SB-CS	FA	FR	Rng	Thr	G at Pos	BFW
1907	NY A	107	423	50	99	5	2	0	17	15	3		.234	.265	.255	61	-19	7	.969	-2	96	145	*O-107(RF)	-2.9
1908	NY A	91	323	38	85	3	1	1	14	31	5		.263	.337	.288	102	2	14	.936	-1	90	65	O-88(2-0-86)	-0.3
1909	NY A	99	360	44	95	7	5	1	32	24	10		.264	.327	.319	104	2	10	.968	-6	74	69	O-95(RF)	-0.9
1910	NY N	19	10	5	3	0	0	0	0	3	0	1	.300	.462	.300	123	1	1	1.000	-0	84	0	/O-2(1-1-0)	0.1
Total	19	2123	8591	1719	2932	241	145	33	810	524	129	36	.341	.388	.415	125	285	495	.960	-12	96	96	*O-2039(17-9-2013)/3-44,2-19,S-2	15.0
KEELY, BOB Robert William B 8.22.1909 St.Louis, MO D 5.20.2001 Arlington, TX BR/TR 6/175# d7.25 C12																								
1944	StL N	1	0	0	0	0	0	0	0	0	0	0	—	—	—	—	0	0	1.000	0	*0*	*0*	/C	0.0
1945	StL N	1	1	0	0	0	0	0	0	0	0	0	.000	.000	.000	-98	0	0	1.000	-0	*0*	*0*	/C	0.0
Total	2	2	1	0	0	0	0	0	0	0	0	0	.000	.000	.000	-98	0	0	1.000	-0	*0*	*0*	/C-2	0.0
KEEN, BILL William Brown "Buster" B 8.16.1892 Oglethorpe, GA D 7.16.1947 South Point, OH BR/TR 6/181# d8.8																								
1911	Pit N	6	7	0	0	0	0	0	0	1	0	4	.000	.125	.000	-61	-2	0	1.000	-0	0	0	/1	-0.2
KEENAN, JIM James William B 2.10.1858 New Haven, CT D 9.21.1926 Cincinnati, OH BR/TR 5-10/186# d5.17 ▮ OF Total (1-CF 12-RF)																								
1875	NH NA	5	13	1	1	0	0	0	0	0		0	.077	.077	.077	-53	-2	0-0	.800	-4			/C-3,3-2,O(LF)	-0.5
1880	Buf N	2	7	1	1	0	0	0	0	1		1	.143	.250	.143	36	0		.947	2			/C-2	0.1
1882	Pit AA	25	96	10	21	7	0	1		1			.219	.227	.323	87	-1		.906	-0			C-22/O-3(0-1-2),S	0.1
1884	Ind AA	68	249	36	73	14	4	3		16	3		.293	.343	.418	151	15		.923	-2			C-59/1-6,O-2(RF),SP	1.6
1885	Cin AA	36	132	16	35	2	2	1	15	8	0		.265	.307	.333	100	0		.926	0			C-33/1-4,P	0.2
1886	Cin AA	44	148	31	40	4	3	3	24	18	2		.270	.357	.399	132	6	0	.915	0			C-30/O-7(RF),3-5,1-4,P-2	0.7
1887	Cin AA	47	174	19	44	4	1	0	17	11	1		.253	.301	.287	63	-9	7	.934	8			C-38,1-11	0.1
1888	Cin AA	85	313	38	73	9	8	1	40	22	5		.233	.294	.323	93	-4	9	.946	3			C-69,1-16	0.3
1889	Cin AA	87	300	52	86	10	11	6	60	48	6	35	.287	.395	.453	137	15	18	.962	4			C-66,1-21/3	1.9
1890	Cin N	54	202	21	28	4	2	3	19	19	1	36	.139	.216	.223	28	-19	5	.950	9	*124*	*105*	C-50/1-2,O(RF)3	-0.5
1891	Cin N	75	252	30	51	7	5	4	33	33	3	39	.202	.302	.317	80	-7	2	.974	-4	133	89	1-41,C-34/3	-1.1
Total	10	523	1873	254	452	61	36	22	208	177	21	111	.241	.314	.348	99	-4	41-0	.935	18	*23*	*19*	C-403,1-105/O-13R,3-8,P-4,S-2	3.4
KEERL, GEORGE George Henry B 4.10.1847 Baltimore, MD D 9.9.1923 Menominee, MI BR/TR 5-7/145# d5.4																								
1875	Chi NA	6	23	2	3	0	0	0	3	0		2	.130	.130	.130	-9	-2	0-0	.815	-2	98	0	/2-6	-0.4
KEESEY, JIM James Ward B 10.27.1902 Perryville, MD D 9.5.1951 Boise, ID BR/TR 6-0.5/170# d9.6																								
1925	Phi A	5	5	1	2	0	0	0	1	0	0	2	.400	.400	.400	97	0	0-0	1.000	-0	0	0	/1-2	0.0
1930	Phi A	11	12	2	3	1	0	0	2	1	0	2	.250	.308	.333	60	-1	0-0	.909	-0	0	233	/1-3	-0.1
Total	2	16	17	3	5	1	0	0	3	1	0	4	.294	.333	.353	71	-1	0-0	.923	-1	0	179	/1-5	-0.1
KEISTER, BILL William Hoffman "Wagon Tongue" B 8.17.1874 Baltimore, MD D 8.19.1924 Baltimore, MD BL/TR 5-5.5/168# d5.20																								
1896	Bal N	15	58	8	14	3	0	0	5	3	2	5	.241	.302	.293	56	-4	4	.923	-4	80	47	/2-8,3-6	-0.6
1898	Bos N	10	30	5	5	2	0	0	4	0	0		.167	.167	.233	14	-3	0	1.000	2	111	170	/S-4,2-4,O(RF)	-0.2
1899	Bal N	136	523	96	172	22	16	3	73	16	16		.329	.368	.449	117	10	33	.895	-21	95	79	S-90,2-46/O(LF)	-0.4
1900	StL N	126	497	78	149	26	10	1	72	25	11		.300	.347	.398	106	4	32	.927	-23	97	59	*2-116/S-7,3-3	-1.2
1901	Bal A	115	442	78	145	20	**21**	2	93	18	8		.328	.365	.482	128	14	24	.851	-21	93	71	*S-112	-0.3
1902	Was A	119	483	82	145	33	9	9	90	14	7		.300	.329	.462	117	9	27	.912	-3	108	172	O-65(0-12-53),2-40,3-14/S-2	0.4
1903	Phi N	100	400	53	128	27	7	3	63	14	6		.320	.352	.445	131	14	11	.940	5	167	30	*O-100(RF)	1.4
Total	7	621	2433	400	758	133	63	18	400	90	50	5	.312	.349	.440	116	44	131	.870	-64	94	74	S-215,2-214,O-167(1-12-154)/3-23	-0.9
KELIHER, MICKEY Maurice Michael B 1.11.1890 Washington, DC D 9.7.1930 Washington, DC BL/TL 6/175# d9.10																								
1911	Pit N	3	7	0	0	0	0	0	0	0	0	5	.000	.000	.000	-96	-2	0	.875	0	142	164	/1-3	-0.2
1912	Pit N	2	0	1	0	0	0	0	0	0	0	0	—	—	—	—	0	0	—	0			R	0.0
Total	2	5	7	1	0	0	0	0	0	0	0	5	.000	.000	.000	-96	-2	0	.875	0	142	164	/1-3	-0.2
KELL, SKEETER Everett Lee B 10.11.1929 Swifton, AR BR/TR 5-9/160# d4.19 b-George																								
1952	Phi A	75	213	24	47	8	3	0	17	14	2	18	.221	.275	.286	53	-14	5-1	.963	-6	101	79	2-68	-1.6
KELL, GEORGE George Clyde B 8.23.1922 Swifton, AR BR/TR 5-9/175# d9.28 HF1983 b-Skeeter																								
1943	Phi A	1	5	1	1	0	1	0	1	0	0	0	.200	.200	.600	131	0	0-0	1.000	0	116	0	/3	0.0
1944	Phi A	139	514	51	138	15	3	0	44	22	1	23	.268	.300	.309	75	-18	5-2	.958	-2	95	103	*3-139	-1.9
1945	Phi A	147	567	50	154	30	3	4	56	27	1	15	.272	.306	.356	92	-8	2-0	**.964**	22	**114**	106	*3-147	1.7
1946	Phi A	26	87	3	26	6	1	0	11	10	1	6	.299	.378	.391	116	2	0-0	.979	4	107	80	3-26	0.6
	Det A	105	434	67	142	19	9	4	41	30	0	14	.327	.371	.440	119	10	3-2	.984	1	93	102	*3-105/1	1.1
	Year	131	521	70	168	25	10	4	52	40	1	20	.322	.372	.432	118	12	3-2	**.983**	5	**96**	**98**	*3-131/1	1.7
1947	Det A★	152	588	75	188	29	5	5	93	61	3	16	.320	.387	.412	118	16	9-11	.962	16	**110**	93	*3-152	3.1
1948	Det A☆	92	368	47	112	24	3	2	44	33	5	15	.304	.369	.402	102	2	2-2	.969	-7	82	92	3-92	-0.6
1949	Det A★	134	522	97	179	38	9	3	59	71	3	13	**.343**	.424	.467	136	29	7-5	.975	-3	97	76	*3-134	2.5
1950	Det A★	**157**	641	114	**218**	**56**	6	8	101	66	1	18	.340	.403	.484	122	23	3-3	**.982**	-2	99	96	*3-157	1.9
1951	Det A★	147	598	92	**191**	**36**	3	2	59	61	4	18	.319	.386	.400	112	12	10-3	**.960**	7	**103**	109	*3-147	2.0
1952	Det A	39	152	11	45	8	0	1	17	15	0	13	.296	.359	.368	102	1	0-1	.959	-1	96	79	3-39	0.0
	Bos A✳	75	276	41	88	15	2	6	40	31	1	10	.319	.390	.453	124	10	0-1	.959	-5	93	83	3-73	0.5
	Year	114	428	52	133	23	2	7	57	46	1	23	.311	.379	.423	117	11	0-2	.959	-5	94	82	*3-112	0.5
1953	Bos A★	134	460	68	141	41	2	12	73	52	5	22	.307	.383	.483	126	18	5-2	**.972**	-12	90	83	*3-124/O-7(LF)	0.6
1954	Bos A	26	93	15	24	3	0	0	10	15	0	3	.258	.361	.290	72	-3	0-0	.920	-3	89	96	3-25	-0.6
	Chi A✳	71	233	25	66	10	0	5	48	18	0	12	.283	.323	.391	95	-2	1-1	.996	-7	41	111	1-32,3-31/O-2(2-0-1)	-1.1
	Year	97	326	40	90	13	0	5	58	33	0	15	.276	.334	.362	88	-5	1-1	.936	-10	90	96	3-56,1-32/O-2(2-0-1)	-1.7
1955	Chi A	128	429	44	134	24	1	8	81	51-2	6	36	.312	.389	.429	118	13	2-2	**.976**	-15	85	46	*3-105,1-24/O(LF)	-0.3
1956	Chi A	21	80	7	25	5	0	1	11	8-0	0	6	.313	.371	.412	106	1	0-0	1.000	-2	81	0	3-18/1-4	-0.2
	Bal A★	102	345	45	90	17	2	8	37	25-3	3	31	.261	.313	.391	93	-5	0-1	.974	-3	91	105	3-97/1-2,2	-0.9
	Year	123	425	52	115	22	2	9	48	33-3	3	37	.271	.324	.395	96	-4	0-1	**.978**	-6	89	89	*3-115/1-6,2	-1.1
1957	Bal A★	99	310	28	92	9	0	9	44	25-2	2	16	.297	.352	.413	116	6	2-0	.979	-4	92	134	3-80,1-22	0.1
Total	15	1795	6702	881	2054	385	50	78	870	621-7	36	287	.306	.367	.414	111	107	51-36	.969	-16	97	93	*3-1692/1-85,O-10(10-0-1),2	8.5
KELLEHER, DUKE Albert Aloysius B 9.30.1893 New York, NY D 9.28.1947 Staten Island, NY TR d8.18																								
1916	NY N	1	0	0	0	0	0	0	0	0	0	0	—	—	—	—	0	0	—	-0	0	0	/C	0.0
KELLEHER, FRANKIE Francis Eugene B 8.22.1916 San Francisco, CA D 4.13.1979 Stockton, CA BR/TR 6-1/195# d7.18 Mil 1944-45																								
1942	Cin N	38	110	13	20	3	1	3	12	16	0	20	.182	.286	.309	74	-4	0	.986	-1	100	47	O-30(LF)	-0.6
1943	Cin N	9	10	1	0	0	0	0	0	2	0	0	.000	.167	.000	-51	-2	0	1.000	-0	94	0	/O(RF)	-0.2
Total	2	47	120	14	20	3	1	3	12	18	0	20	.167	.275	.283	64	-6	0	.986	-1	100	45	/O-31(30-0-1)	-0.8
KELLEHER, JOHN John Patrick B 9.13.1893 Brookline, MA D 8.21.1960 Brighton, MA BR/TR 5-11/150# d7.31																								
1912	StL N	8	12	0	4	1	0	0	1	0	0	2	.333	.333	.417	107	0	0	1.000	0	109	360	/3-3	0.1
1916	Bro N	2	3	0	0	0	0	0	0	0	0	0	.000	.000	.000	-97	-1	0	1.000	-1	54	0	/S3	-0.2
1921	Chi N	95	301	31	93	11	7	4	47	16	1	16	.309	.346	.432	104	1	2-5	.947	3	108	103	3-37,2-27,1-11,S-11/O(LF)	0.6
1922	Chi N	63	193	23	50	7	1	0	20	15	1	14	.259	.316	.306	60	-11	5-7	.932	2	110	123	3-46/S-7,1-4	-0.7
1923	Chi N	66	193	27	59	10	0	6	21	14	0	9	.306	.353	.451	110	3	2-4	.975	-7	86	74	1-22,S-14,3-11/2-6	-0.4
1924	Bos N	1	1	0	0	0	0	0	0	0	0	1	.000	.000	.000	-99	0	0-0	—	0			H	0.0
Total	6	235	703	81	206	29	8	10	89	45	2	42	.293	.337	.400	92	-8	9-16	.924	-2	106	117	/3-98,1-37,2-33,S-33,O(LF)	-0.6
KELLEHER, MICK Michael Dennis B 7.25.1947 Seattle, WA BR/TR 5-9/176# d9.1 C2																								
1972	StL N	23	63	5	10	2	1	0	1	6-0	0	15	.159	.232	.222	30	-6	0-0	.984	3	92	107	S-23	0.0
1973	StL N	43	38	4	7	2	0	0	2	4-1	1	11	.184	.279	.237	44	-3	0-0	.955	-1	97	91	S-42	-0.2
1974	Hou N	19	57	4	9	0	0	0	2	5-0	0	10	.158	.226	.158	9	-7	1-1	.944	3	122	105	S-18	-0.2
1975	StL N	7	4	0	0	0	0	0	0	0-0	0	1	.000	.000	.000	-97	-1	0-0	.909	1	129	94	/S-7	0.0
1976	Chi N	124	337	28	77	12	1	0	22	15-3	2	32	.228	.264	.270	48	-23	0-4	.980	5	106	97	*S-101,3-22/2-5	-0.9
1977	Chi N	63	122	14	28	5	2	0	11	9-2	1	12	.230	.288	.303	53	-8	0-0	.976	6	116	94	2-40,S-14/3	0.0
1978	Chi N	68	95	8	24	1	0	0	6	7-0	0	11	.253	.304	.263	53	-6	4-1	1.000	8	129	110	3-37,2-17,S-10	0.4
1979	Chi N	73	142	14	36	4	1	0	10	7-0	2	9	.254	.296	.296	57	-8	2-0	.966	13	106	108	3-32,2-29,S-14	0.7
1980	Chi N	105	96	12	14	1	1	0	4	9-1	0	17	.146	.217	.177	11	-12	1-3	.974	5	109	98	2-57,3-31,S-17	-0.6

Year	Tm Lg	G	AB	R	H	2B	3B	HR	RBI	BB-IB	HP	SO	AVG	OBP	SLG	AOPS	ABR	SB-CS	FA	FR	Rng	Thr	G at Pos	BFW
1981	Det A	61	77	10	17	4	0	0	6	7-0	0	10	.221	.282	.273	59	-4	0-0	.930	-1	82	68	3-39,2-11/S-9	-0.5
1982	Det A	2	1	0	0	0	0	0	0	0-0	0	0	.000	.000	.000	-99	0	0-0	1.000	0	285	0	/23	0.0
	Cal A	34	49	9	8	1	0	0	1	5-0	1	5	.163	.255	.184	23	-5	1-1	.965	1	100	81	S-28/3-6	-0.2
	Year	36	50	9	8	1	0	0	1	5-0	1	5	.160	.250	.180	20	-5	1-1	.965	1	100	81	S-28/3-7,2	-0.2
Total	11	622	1081	108	230	32	6	0	65	74-7	7	133	.213	.266	.253	43	-83	9-10	.976	43	105	95	S-283,3-169,2-160	-1.5
KELLER, CHARLIE Charles Ernest "King Kong" B 9.12.1916 Middletown, MD D 5.23.1990 Frederick, MD BL/TR 5-10/190# d4.22 Mer 1944-45 C2 b-Hal																								
1939	†NY A	111	398	87	133	21	6	11	83	81	0	49	.334	.447	.500	144	31	6-3	.969	-4	96	64	*O-105(47-0-58)	1.9
1940	NY A★	138	500	102	143	18	15	21	93	**106**	0	65	.286	.411	.508	142	34	8-2	.967	-3	104	44	*O-136(65-0-71)	2.3
1941	†NY A★	140	507	102	151	24	10	33	122	102	1	65	.298	.416	.580	163	48	6-4	.980	2	108	59	*O-137(LF)	4.0
1942	†NY A	152	544	106	159	24	9	26	108	114	2	61	.292	.417	.513	164	50	14-2	.985	-2	98	83	*O-152(LF)	4.2
1943	†NY A✶	141	512	97	139	15	11	31	86	**106**	0	60	.271	.396	.525	**167**	**45**	7-5	.994	2	105	70	*O-141(LF)	4.0
1945	NY A	44	163	26	49	7	4	10	34	31	0	21	.301	.412	.577	178	16	0-2	1.000	3	112	97	O-44(LF)	1.6
1946	NY A★	150	538	98	148	29	10	30	101	113	4	101	.275	.405	.533	158	46	1-4	.979	-3	101	40	*O-149(LF)	3.1
1947	NY A✶	45	151	36	36	6	1	13	36	41	1	18	.238	.404	.550	165	15	0-0	.967	-1	97	75	O-43(LF)	1.1
1948	NY A	83	247	41	66	15	2	6	44	41	0	25	.267	.372	.417	111	5	1-1	.977	-4	97	23	O-66(LF)	-0.4
1949	NY A	60	116	17	29	4	1	3	16	25	2	15	.250	.392	.379	104	2	2-0	.976	-3	83	0	O-31(LF)	-0.3
1950	Det A	50	51	7	16	1	3	2	16	13	0	6	.314	.453	.569	155	5	0-0	1.000	-0	101	0	/O-6(1-0-5)	0.4
1951	Det A	54	62	6	16	2	0	3	21	11	0	12	.258	.370	.435	117	2	0-0	1.000	1	127	0	/O-8(4-0-4)	0.2
1952	NY A	2	1	0	0	0	0	0	0	0	0	1	.000	.000	.000	-99	0	0-0	—	-0	0	0	/O(LF)	0.0
Total	13	1170	3790	725	1085	166	72	189	760	784	10	499	.286	.410	.518	152	299	45-23	.980	-12	102	58	*O-1019(881-0-138)	22.1
KELLER, HAL Harold Kefauver B 7.7.1927 Middletown, MD BL/TR 6-1/200# d9.13 b-Charlie																								
1949	Was A	3	3	1	1	0	0	0	0	0	0	0	.333	.333	.333	78	0	0-0	—	0			H	0.0
1950	Was A	11	28	1	6	3	0	1	5	2	0	2	.214	.267	.429	79	-1	0-0	1.000	-1	*71*	*0*	/C-8	-0.2
1952	Was A	11	23	2	4	2	0	0	0	1	0	1	.174	.208	.261	31	-2	0-0	.967	-0	*93*	*62*	C-11	-0.2
Total	3	25	54	4	11	5	0	1	5	3	0	3	.204	.246	.352	60	-3	0-0	.982	-1	*82*	*30*	/C-19	-0.4
KELLERT, FRANK Frank William B 7.6.1924 Oklahoma City, OK D 11.19.1976 Oklahoma City, OK BR/TR 6-2.5/185# d4.18																								
1953	StL A	2	4	0	0	0	0	0	0	0	0	0	.000	.000	.000	-98	-1	0-0	1.000	-0	0	0	/1	-0.1
1954	Bal A	10	34	3	7	2	0	0	1	5	0	4	.206	.308	.265	62	-2	0-0	1.000	-1	33	75	/1-9	-0.4
1955	†Bro N	39	80	12	26	4	2	4	19	9-0	0	10	.325	.385	.575	149	6	0-1	.983	-0	97	64	1-22	0.4
1956	Chi N	71	129	10	24	3	1	4	17	12-1	0	22	.186	.254	.318	54	-9	0-0	.991	2	122	100	1-27	-0.9
Total	4	122	247	25	57	9	3	8	37	26-1	0	36	.231	.301	.389	85	-6	0-1	.990	-0	97	82	/1-59	-1.0
KELLETT, RED Donald Stafford B 7.15.1909 Brooklyn, NY D 11.3.1970 Ft.Lauderdale, FL BR/TR 6/185# d7.2																								
1934	Bos A	9	9	0	0	0	0	0	0	1	0	5	.000	.100	.000	-68	-2	0-0	.778	-0	103	0	/S-4,2-2,3	-0.2
KELLEY, JOE Joseph James B 12.9.1871 Cambridge, MA D 8.14.1943 Baltimore, MD BR/TR 5-11/190# d7.27 M5 C1 HF1971 OF Total (1131-LF 328-CF 8-RF)																								
1891	Bos N	12	45	7	11	1	1	0	3	2	0	7	.244	.277	.311	63	-2	0	.852	-0	104	0	O-12(12-1-0)	-0.3
1892	Pit N	56	205	26	49	7	7	0	28	17	0	21	.239	.297	.341	93	-3	8	.919	0	148	212	O-56(CF)	-0.6
	Bal N	10	33	3	7	0	0	0	4	4	1	7	.212	.316	.212	59	-1	2	.824	-2	0	0	O-10(CF)	-0.4
	Year	66	238	29	56	7	7	0	32	21	1	28	.235	.300	.324	88	-4	10	.908	-2	130	186	O-66(CF)	-1.0
1893	Bal N	125	502	120	153	27	16	9	76	77	4	44	.305	.401	.476	131	22	33	.940	6	104	85	*O-125(18-107-1)	1.6
1894	†Bal N	**129**	507	165	199	48	20	6	111	107	5	36	.393	.502	.602	158	55	46	.951	2	74	60	*O-129(LF)	3.4
1895	†Bal N	**131**	518	148	189	26	19	10	134	77	10	29	.365	.456	.546	154	44	54	.946	1	101	125	*O-131(130-1-0)	2.6
1896	†Bal N	131	519	148	189	31	19	8	100	91	12	19	.364	.469	.543	164	54	**87**	.958	-0	105	69	*O-131(129-0-2)	3.5
1897	†Bal N	131	505	113	183	31	9	5	118	70	7		.362	.447	.489	147	39	44	.959	-0	84	93	*O-130(LF)/S-3,3-2	2.3
1898	Bal N	124	464	71	149	18	15	2	110	56	3		.321	.398	.438	137	23	24	.969	2	111	118	*O-122(39-83-0)/3-2	1.5
1899	Bro N	143	538	108	175	21	14	6	93	70	7		.325	.410	.450	133	26	31	.977	10	120	124	*O-143(LF)	2.1
1900	†Bro N	121	454	90	145	23	17	6	91	53	6		.319	.398	.485	135	21	26	.959	1	115	71	O-77(LF),1-32,3-13	1.4
1901	Bro N	120	492	77	151	22	12	4	65	40	3		.307	.363	.425	124	15	18	.975	7	126	107	*1-115/3-5	1.9
1902	Bal A	60	222	50	69	17	7	1	34	34	1		.311	.405	.464	134	12	12	.973	0	119	146	O-48(1-47-0)/3-8,1-5	0.9
	Cin N	40	156	24	50	9	2	1	12	15	0		.321	.380	.423	135	7	3	.971	4	183	178	O-20(18-2-0),2-10/3-9,S-2,M	1.1
1903	Cin N	105	383	85	121	22	4	3	45	51	4		.316	.402	.418	120	12	18	.947	-4	90	0	O-67(61-6-0),S-12,2-11/3-8,1-6,M	0.5
1904	Cin N	123	449	75	126	21	13	0	63	49	6		.281	.359	.385	119	11	15	.988	0	99	105	*1-117/O-6(0-3-3),2M	1.0
1905	Cin N	90	321	43	89	7	6	1	37	27	7		.277	.346	.346	96	-1	8	.974	-2	99	0	O-85(84-0-1)/1-2,M	-0.9
1906	Cin N	129	465	43	106	19	11	1	53	44	4		.228	.300	.323	90	-6	9	.966	-4	87	136	*O-122(LF)/1-3,S3	-1.9
1908	Bos N	73	228	25	59	8	2	2	17	27	2		.259	.342	.338	119	6	5	.938	-0	93	75	O-51(38-12-1),1-11,M	0.3
Total	17	1853	7006	1421	2220	358	194	65	1194	911	82	163	.317	.402	.451	132	334	443	.955	20	102	93	*O-1465L,1-291/3-48,2-22,S-18	20.0
KELLEY, MIKE Michael Joseph B 12.2.1875 Templeton, MA D 6.6.1955 Minneapolis, MN BR/TR 6/210# d7.15																								
1899	Lou N	76	282	48	68	11	2	3	33	21	6		.241	.307	.326	74	-10	10	.974	-0	104	88	1-76	-1.0
KELLIHER, FRANK Francis Mortimer "Yucka" B 5.23.1899 Somerville, MA D 3.4.1956 Somerville, MA BL/TL 5-9.5/175# d9.19																								
1919	Was A	1	1	0	0	0	0	0	0	0	0	0	.000	.000	.000	-99	0	0	—	0			H	0.0
KELLOGG, NATE Nathaniel Monroe B 9.28.1858 Rochester, IA D 1915 5-9/175# d8.27																								
1885	Det N	5	17	4	2	1	0	0	0	1		5	.118	.167	.176	11	-2		.783	-2	75	65	/S-5	-0.3
KELLOGG, BILL William Dearstyne B 5.25.1884 Albany, NY D 12.12.1971 Baltimore, MD BR/TR 5-10/153# d4.14																								
1914	Cin N	71	126	14	22	0	1	0	7	14	1	28	.175	.262	.190	34	-10	7	.988	-1	87	104	1-38,2-11/O-2(CF),3	-1.3
KELLY, RED Albert Michael B 11.15.1884 Union, IL D 2.4.1961 Zephyrhills, FL BR/TR 5-11.5/165# d6.18																								
1910	Chi A	14	45	6	7	0	1	0	1	7	2		.156	.296	.200	58	-2	0	1.000	-0	103	58	O-14(RF)	-0.3
KELLY, CHARLIE Charles H. d6.14																								
1883	Phi N	2	7	1	1	0	1	0	0	0		3	.143	.143	.429	71	0		.700	-0	93	270	/3-2	-0.1
1886	Phi AA	1	3	0	0	0	0	0	0	0	0		.000	.000	.000	-99	-1	0	.333	-1	68	0	/S	-0.2
Total	2	3	10	1	1	0	1	0	0	0	0	3	.100	.100	.300	19	-1	0	.700	-2	93	270	/3-2,S	-0.3
KELLY, PAT Dale Patrick B 8.27.1955 Santa Maria, CA BR/TR 6-3/210# d5.28																								
1980	Tor A	3	7	0	2	0	0	0	0	0-0	0	4	.286	.286	.286	55	0	0-0	1.000	1	0	0	/C-3	0.1
KELLY, GEORGE George Lange "Highpockets" B 9.10.1895 San Francisco, CA D 10.13.1984 Burlingame, CA BR/TR 6-4/190# d8.18 Mil 1918 C11 HF1973 b-Ren OF Total (27-LF 16-CF 19-RF)																								
1915	NY N	17	38	2	6	0	0	1	4	1	0	9	.158	.179	.237	27	-4	0-1	.983	0	96	31	/1-9,O-4(CF)	-0.5
1916	NY N	49	76	4	12	2	1	0	3	6	0	24	.158	.220	.211	34	-6	1	.981	-2	38	73	1-13,O-12(0-2-5)/3	-0.9
1917	NY N	11	7	0	0	0	0	0	0	0	0	3	.000	.000	.000	-99	-2	0	1.000	1	66	1005	/O-4(3-0-1),P12	-0.1
	Pit N	8	23	2	2	0	1	0	0	1	0	9	.087	.125	.174	-9	-3	0	.971	-1	58	73	/1-8	-0.5
	Year	19	30	2	2	0	1	0	0	1	0	12	.067	.097	.133	-30	-5	0	.972	-0	56	98	/1-9,O-4(3-0-1),P2	-0.6
1919	NY N	32	107	12	31	6	2	1	14	3	1	15	.290	.315	.411	119	2	1	.994	-3	61	108	1-32	-0.1
1920	NY N	**155**	590	69	157	22	11	11	**94**	41	6	92	.266	.320	.397	106	3	6-16	.994	4	109	**120**	*1-155	-0.1
1921	†NY N	149	587	95	181	42	9	**23**	122	40	3	73	.308	.356	.528	131	24	4-12	.990	12	**138**	**136**	*1-149	2.2
1922	†NY N	151	592	96	194	33	8	17	107	30	3	65	.328	.363	.497	119	14	12-3	.993	9	**129**	122	*1-151	1.4
1923	†NY N	145	560	82	172	23	5	16	103	47	1	64	.307	.362	.452	115	11	14-7	.993	-6	78	102	*1-145	-0.3
1924	†NY N	144	571	91	185	37	9	21	**136**	38	5	52	.324	.371	.531	143	33	7-2	.993	-3	89	108	*1-125,O-14(5-9-0)/2-5,3	2.2
1925	NY N	147	586	87	181	29	3	20	99	35	2	54	.309	.350	.471	112	9	5-2	.981	16	107	113	*2-108,1-25,O-17(8-0-9)	2.4
1926	NY N	136	499	70	151	24	4	13	80	36	2	52	.303	.352	.445	115	9	4	**.993**	7	118	101	*1-114,2-18	0.9
1927	Cin N	61	222	27	60	16	4	5	21	11	1	23	.270	.308	.446	103	0	1	.992	-1	117	138	1-49,2-13/O-2(LF)	-0.4
1928	Cin N	116	402	46	119	33	7	3	58	28	2	35	.296	.345	.435	104	2	2	.991	8	141	133	1-99,O-13(9-0-4)	0.3
1929	Cin N	147	577	73	169	45	9	5	103	33	1	61	.293	.332	.428	91	-9	7	.993	5	112	111	*1-147	-1.3
1930	Cin N	51	188	18	54	10	1	5	35	7	0	20	.287	.313	.431	81	-6	1	.993	2	111	95	1-50	-0.7
	Chi N	39	166	22	55	6	1	3	19	7	1	16	.331	.362	.434	91	-3	0	.998	3	120	79	1-39	-0.2
	Year	90	354	40	109	16	2	8	54	14	1	36	.308	.336	.432	86	-9	1	.995	4	115	88	1-89	-0.9
1932	Bro N	64	202	23	49	9	1	4	22	22	0	27	.243	.317	.356	82	-5	0	.984	-2	95	100	1-62/O(CF)	-1.2
Total	16	1622	5993	819	1778	337	76	148	1020	386	28	694	.297	.342	.452	110	69	65-43	.992	49	111	113	*1-1373,2-145/O-67L,3-2,P	3.1

Year	Tm Lg	G	AB	R	H	2B	3B	HR	RBI	BB-IB	HP	SO	AVG	OBP	SLG	AOPS	ABR	SB-CS	FA	FR	Rng	Thr	G at Pos	BFW
KELLY, PAT Harold Patrick B 7.30.1944 Philadelphia, PA BL/TL 6-1/185# d9.6 Mil 1967																								
1967	Min A	8	1	1	0	0	0	0	0	0-0	0	1	.000	.000	.000	-93	0	0-0	—	0			H	0.0
1968	Min A	12	35	2	4	2	0	1	2	3-0	1	10	.114	.205	.257	37	-3	0-2	.955	1	114	183	O-10(2-5-4)	-0.4
1969	KC A	112	417	61	110	20	4	8	32	49-3	5	70	.264	.348	.388	105	4	40-13	.980	7	110	157	*O-107(2-44-63)	1.1
1970	KC A	136	452	56	106	16	1	6	38	76-3	2	105	.235	.347	.314	84	-7	34-16	.963	7	118	103	*O-118(1-3-115)	-0.5
1971	Chi A	67	213	32	62	6	3	3	22	36-4	1	29	.291	.394	.390	119	7	14-9	.991	3	97	198	O-61(0-1-61)	0.7
1972	Chi A	119	402	57	105	14	7	5	24	55-1	4	69	.261	.355	.368	113	8	32-9	.968	-3	89	111	*O-109(RF)	0.4
1973	Chi A★	144	550	77	154	24	5	1	44	65-1	2	91	.280	.355	.347	96	0	22-15	.978	-2	96	100	*O-141(0-3-138)/D	-1.0
1974	Chi A	122	424	60	119	16	3	4	21	46-0	2	58	.281	.354	.361	103	3	18-11	.976	-4	83	56	D-67,O-53(1-0-52)	-0.5
1975	Chi A	133	471	73	129	21	7	9	45	58-2	2	69	.274	.353	.406	113	9	18-10	**.991**	-1	103	45	*O-115(RF),D-14	0.2
1976	Chi A	107	311	42	79	20	3	5	34	45-1	3	45	.254	.349	.386	116	8	15-7	.950	-2	87	67	D-63,O-26(14-0-12)	0.5
1977	Bal A	120	360	50	92	13	0	10	49	53-6	4	75	.256	.353	.375	106	5	25-7	.984	-7	95	27	*O-109(91-1-33)/D	-0.3
1978	Bal A	100	274	38	75	12	1	11	40	34-1	2	58	.274	.357	.445	133	12	10-8	.969	-6	86	64	O-80(73-1-7)/D-2	0.3
1979	†Bal A	68	153	25	44	11	0	9	25	20-1	1	25	.288	.367	.536	147	11	4-5	1.000	-2	90	0	O-24(23-0-1),D-18	0.6
1980	Bal A	89	200	38	52	10	1	3	26	34-0	0	54	.260	.363	.365	102	2	16-2	1.000	0	88	205	O-36(34-2-0),D-30	0.3
1981	Cle A	48	75	8	16	4	0	1	16	14-2	0	9	.213	.333	.307	88	0	2-4	1.000	0	113	0	D-18/O-8(3-0-5)	-0.2
Total	15	1385	4338	620	1147	189	35	76	418	588-25	29	768	.264	.354	.377	107	59	250-118	.978	-9	99	96	O-997(244-60-715),D-214	1.2
KELLY, JIM James Robert (Also Played Under Real Name Of Robert John Taggert In 1918) B 2.1.1884 Bloomfield, NJ D 4.10.1961 Kingsport, TN BL/TR 5-10.5/180# d4.26																								
1914	Pit N	32	44	4	10	2	1	0	3	2	0	3	.227	.261	.318	75	-2	0	1.000	0	114	105	/O-7(1-0-6)	-0.2
1915	Pit F	148	524	68	154	12	17	4	50	35	2	46	.294	.340	.405	110	-4	38	.952	13	**117**	138	*O-148(14-4-133)	0.2
1918	Bos N	35	146	19	48	1	4	0	4	9	2	9	.329	.376	.390	140	6	4	.955	-1	109	49	O-35(LF)	0.5
Total	3	215	714	91	212	15	22	4	57	46	4	58	.297	.343	.396	114	0	42	.954	13	115	119	O-190(50-4-139)	0.5
KELLY, TOM Jay Thomas B 8.15.1950 Graceville, MN BL/TL 5-11/188# d5.11 M16 C4																								
1975	Min A	49	127	11	23	5	0	1	11	15-0	0	22	.181	.262	.244	45	-9	0-0	.985	1	105	85	1-43/O-2(1-0-1)	-1.2
KELLY, JOHN John B. B 3.13.1879 Clifton Heights, PA D 3.19.1944 Baltimore, MD 5-9/165# d4.11																								
1907	StL N	53	197	12	37	5	0	0	6	13	2		.188	.245	.213	45	-12	7	.968	-3	92	0	O-52(0-16-36)	-2.0
KELLY, JOHN John Francis "Honest John" or "Father" B 3.3.1859 Paterson, NJ D 4.13.1908 Paterson, NJ BR/TR 6/185# d6.7																								
1879	Cle N	1	4	0	1	0	0	0	0	0		0	.250	.250	.250	66	0		.571	-1			/C1	-0.1
1882	Cle N	30	104	6	14	2	0	0	5	1		24	.135	.143	.154	-5	-12		.800	-13			C-30	-2.1
1883	Bal AA	48	202	18	46	9	2	0		3			.228	.239	.292	68	-7		.803	-16			C-38,O-13(0-1-12)	-1.9
	Phi N	1	3	0	0	0	0	0	0	0		2	.000	.000	.000	-99	-1		1.000	1	484	0	/O(CF)	0.0
1884	Cin U	38	142	23	40	5	1	1		6			.282	.311	.352	93	-5		.865	-3			C-37/O-2(0-1-1)	-0.5
	Was U	4	14	1	5	1	0	0		0			.357	.357	.429	142	0		.967	1			/C-3,O(RF)	0.1
	Year	42	156	24	45	6	1	1		6			.288	.315	.359	97	-5		.874	-2			C-40/O-3(0-1-2)	-0.4
Total	4	122	469	48	106	17	3	1	5	10		26	.226	.242	.281	63	-25		.831	-31			C-109/O-17(0-3-14),1	-4.5
KELLY, KICK John O. "Diamond John" B 10.31.1856 New York, NY D 3.27.1926 Malba, NY 6-0.5/185# d5.1 M2 U4																								
1879	Syr N	10	36	4	4	1	0	0	2	0		6	.111	.111	.139	-20	-4		.827	-2			/C-8,1-2	-0.6
	Tro N	6	22	1	5	0	0	0	0	0		1	.227	.227	.227	54	-1		.789	-2			/C-3,O-2(RF),3	-0.3
	Year	16	58	5	9	1	0	0	2	0		7	.155	.155	.172	9	-5		.817	-4			C-11/1-2,O-2(RF),3	-0.9
KELLY, JOE Joseph Henry B 9.23.1886 Weir City, KS D 8.16.1977 St.Joseph, MO BR/TR 5-10/175# d4.14 Mil 1918																								
1914	Pit N	141	508	47	113	19	9	1	48	39	4	59	.222	.283	.301	77	-16	21	.946	-3	100	90	*O-139(CF)	-3.0
1916	Chi N	54	169	18	43	7	1	2	15	9	1	16	.254	.296	.343	87	-3	10	.953	-1	102	76	O-46(16-25-6)	-0.7
1917	Bos N	116	445	41	99	9	8	3	36	26	2	45	.222	.268	.299	78	-13	21	.946	6	112	104	*O-116(87-29-0)	-1.5
1918	Bos N	47	155	20	36	2	4	0	15	6	1	12	.232	.265	.297	74	-6	12	.933	-1	102	82	O-45(22-18-0)	-1.0
1919	Bos N	18	64	3	9	1	0	0	3	0	1	11	.141	.154	.156	-7	-8	2	.943	0	94	146	O-16(LF)	-1.0
Total	5	376	1341	129	300	38	22	6	117	80	9	143	.224	.272	.298	75	-46	66	.945	1	104	95	O-362(141-211-6)	-7.2
KELLY, JOE Joseph James B 4.23.1900 New York, NY D 11.24.1967 Lynbrook, NY BL/TL 6/180# d4.13																								
1926	Chi N	65	176	16	59	15	3	0	32	7	0	11	.335	.361	.455	117	4	0	.953	-3	85	81	O-39(25-0-14)	-0.2
1928	Chi N	32	52	3	11	1	0	1	7	1	2	3	.212	.255	.288	42	-5	0	.974	-0	112	101	1-10	-0.5
Total	2	97	228	19	70	16	3	1	39	8	2	14	.307	.336	.417	100	-1	0	.953	-3	85	81	/O-39(25-0-14),1-10	-0.7
KELLY, KENNY Kenneth Alphonso B 1.26.1979 Plant City, FL BR/TR 6-3/180# d9.7																								
2000	TB A	2	1	0	0	0	0	0	0	0-0	0	0	.000	.000	.000	-99	0	0-0	—	0			/D	0.0
KELLY, KING Michael Joseph B 12.31.1857 Troy, NY D 11.8.1894 Boston, MA BR/TR 5-10/170# d5.1 M3 HF1945 ▲ OF Total (2-LF 8-CF 742-RF)																								
1878	Cin N	60	237	29	67	7	1	0	27	7		7	.283	.303	.321	116	5		.765	8	**199**	118	*O-47(RF),C-17/3-2	1.3
1879	Cin N	77	345	78	120	20	12	2	47	8		14	.348	.363	.493	**188**	32		.832	10	128	73	3-33,O-29(0-2-27),C-21/2	**3.9**
1880	Chi N	84	344	72	100	17	9	1	60	12		22	.291	.315	.401	133	11		.779	-1	**203**	41	*O-64(RF),C-17,3-14/S2P	1.0
1881	Chi N	82	353	84	114	**27**	3	2	55	16		14	.323	.352	.433	139	16		.841	2	170	79	*O-72(RF),C-11/3-8	1.7
1882	Chi N	**84**	377	81	115	**37**	4	1	55	10		27	.305	.323	.432	133	14		.810	2	90	87	S-42,O-38(RF),C-12/3-3,1	1.5
1883	Chi N	**98**	428	92	109	28	10	3	61	16		35	.255	.282	.388	93	-5		.813	5	**218**	**174**	*O-82(RF),C-38/2-3,3-2,P	0.1
1884	Chi N	108	452	**120**	160	28	5	13	95	46		24	.354	**.414**	.524	178	**41**		.794	-5	232	45	O-63(RF),C-28,S-12,3-10/1-2,P-2,2	3.3
1885	†Chi N	107	438	**124**	126	24	7	9	75	46		24	.288	.355	.436	136	17		.867	3	208	117	O-69(0-1-69),C-37/2-6,3-2,1-2	2.1
1886	†Chi N	118	451	**155**	175	32	11	4	79	83		33	**.388**	**.483**	.534	182	48	53	.811	7	210	64	O-56(0-1-55),C-53/1-9,3-8,2-6,S-5	**5.2**
1887	Bos N	116	484	120	156	34	11	8	63	55	1	40	.322	.393	.488	141	29	84	.856	-14	105	100	O-61(1-0-61),2-30,C-24/P-3,S-2,3-2,M	1.5
1888	Bos N	107	440	85	140	22	11	9	71	31	4	39	.318	.368	.480	164	31	56	.905	0			C-76,O-34(RF)	3.7
1889	Bos N	125	507	120	149	**41**	5	9	78	65	2	40	.294	.376	.448	122	15	68	.848	-6	112	109	*O-113(RF),C-23	0.9
1890	Bos P	89	340	83	111	18	6	4	66	52	2	22	.326	.419	.450	124	12	51	.915	6	*154*	*104*	C-56,S-27/O-6(0-2-4),1-4,3-2,PM	1.8
1891	Cin AA	82	283	56	84	15	7	1	53	51	2	28	.297	.408	.410	124	10	22	.904	8	*88*	*156*	C-66/3-8,O-7(0-2-5),2-6,1-5,P-3,SM	1.9
	Bos AA	4	15	2	4	0	0	1	4	0	0	2	.267	.267	.467	111	0	1	.950	0	*136*	*91*	/C-4	0.0
	Year	86	298	58	88	15	7	2	57	51	2	30	.295	.402	.413	123	10	23	**.906**	8	*91*	***152***	C-70/3-8,O-7(0-2-5),2-6,1-5,P-3,S	1.9
	Bos N	16	52	7	12	1	0	0	5	6	1	10	.231	.322	.250	60	-3	6	.844	-2	*125*	*82*	C-11/O-6(RF)	-0.4
1892	†Bos N	78	281	40	53	7	0	2	41	39	0	32	.189	.287	.235	53	-15	24	.912	6	*133*	*107*	C-72/O-2(1-0-1),3-2,1-2,P	-0.2
1893	NY N	20	67	9	18	1	0	0	15	6	0	5	.269	.329	.284	63	-4	3	.895	-3	*98*	*136*	C-17/O(RF)	-0.4
Total	16	1455	5894	1357	1813	359	102	69	950	549	12	418	.308	.368	.438	136	254	368	.820	27	179	104	O-750R,C-583/3-96,S-90,2-54,1P	28.9
KELLY, MIKE Michael Raymond B 6.2.1970 Los Angeles, CA BR/TR 6-4/195# d4.5																								
1994	Atl N	30	77	14	21	10	1	2	9	2-0	1	17	.273	.300	.506	103	0	0-1	.962	-3	71	0	O-25(19-6-1)	-0.4
1995	Atl N	97	137	26	26	6	1	3	17	11-0	2	49	.190	.258	.314	49	-11	7-3	.940	-4	90	0	O-83(58-8-17)	-1.5
1996	Cin N	19	49	5	9	4	0	1	7	9-0	2	11	.184	.333	.327	75	-1	4-0	.972	1	110	128	O-17(6-10-1)	0.0
1997	Cin N	73	140	27	41	13	2	6	19	10-0	0	30	.293	.338	.543	125	5	6-1	.978	4	138	89	O-59(17-11-31)/D	0.9
1998	TB A	106	279	39	67	11	2	10	33	22-1	0	80	.240	.295	.401	78	-10	13-6	1.000	-1	96	84	O-93(43-0-51)/D-6	-1.3
1999	Col N	2	2	0	1	1	0	0	1	0-0	0	0	.500	.500	1.000	210	0	0-0	—	-0	0	0	/O(RF)	0.0
Total	6	327	684	111	165	45	6	22	86	54-1	5	187	.241	.300	.421	85	-17	30-11	.978	-3	101	61	O-278(143-35-102)/D-7	-2.3
KELLY, PAT Patrick Franklin B 10.14.1967 Philadelphia, PA BR/TR 6/182# d5.20																								
1991	NY A	96	298	35	72	12	4	3	23	15-0	5	52	.242	.287	.339	73	-12	12-1	.926	3	102	93	3-80,2-19	-0.6
1992	NY A	106	318	38	72	22	2	7	27	25-1	10	72	.226	.301	.374	89	-5	8-5	.978	-4	100	92	*2-101/D	-0.6
1993	NY A	127	406	49	111	24	1	7	51	24-0	5	68	.273	.317	.389	93	-4	14-11	.978	11	110	108	*2-125	1.1
1994	NY A	93	286	35	80	21	2	3	41	19-1	5	51	.280	.330	.399	92	-3	6-5	.978	5	107	**127**	2-93	0.5
1995	†NY A	89	270	32	64	12	1	4	29	23-0	5	65	.237	.307	.333	68	-13	8-3	.983	6	105	100	2-87/D	-0.2
1996	NY A	13	21	4	3	0	0	0	2	2-0	0	9	.143	.217	.143	-6	-4	0-1	.970	2	137	69	2-10/D-3	-0.2
1997	NY A	67	120	25	29	6	1	2	10	14-1	1	37	.242	.324	.358	79	-4	8-1	.981	0	100	123	2-48,D-16	-0.1
1998	StL N	53	153	18	33	5	0	4	14	13-0	2	48	.216	.284	.327	61	-9	5-1	.964	-1	108	77	2-41/O-3(LF),S-2	-0.7
1999	Tor A	37	116	17	31	7	0	6	20	10-0	0	23	.267	.318	.483	101	0	0-1	.962	-4	97	76	2-35/D-2	-0.2
Total	9	681	1988	253	495	109	11	36	217	145-3	33	425	.249	.307	.369	82	-54	61-29	.977	18	105	105	2-559/3-80,D-23,O-3(LF),S-2	-1.0
KELLY, SPEED Robert Brown B 8.19.1884 Bryan, OH D 5.6.1949 Goshen, IN BR/TR 6-2/185# d7.13																								
1909	Was A	17	42	3	6	2	1	0	1	3	0		.143	.200	.238	40	-3	1	.852	-1	99	207	3-10/2-3,O(CF)	-0.4

Year	Tm Lg	G	AB	R	H	2B	3B	HR	RBI	BB-IB	HP	SO	AVG	OBP	SLG	AOPS	ABR	SB-CS	FA	FR	Rng	Thr	G at Pos	BFW
KELLY, ROBERTO Roberto Conrado (Gray) "Bobby" B 10.1.1964 Panama City, Panama BR/TR 6-2/192# d7.29																								
1987	NY A	23	52	12	14	3	0	1	7	5-0	0	15	.269	.328	.385	91	-1	9-3	.955	0	112	0	O-17(0-16-1)/D-2	0.0
1988	NY A	38	77	9	19	4	1	1	7	3-0	0	15	.247	.272	.364	78	-3	5-2	.986	2	114	95	O-30(1-28-2)/D-3	-0.1
1989	NY A	137	441	65	133	18	3	9	48	41-3	6	89	.302	.369	.417	123	14	35-12	.984	-0	99	124	*O-137(CF)	1.6
1990	NY A	**162**	641	85	183	32	4	15	61	33-0	4	148	.285	.323	.418	106	3	42-17	.988	-2	103	60	*O-160(11-151-0)/D	0.3
1991	NY A	126	486	68	130	22	2	20	69	45-2	5	77	.267	.333	.444	114	8	32-9	.986	-4	91	121	*O-125(52-73-0)	0.5
1992	NY A★	152	580	81	158	31	2	10	66	41-4	4	96	.272	.322	.384	99	-2	28-5	.983	2	103	91	*O-146(47-99-0)	0.2
1993	Cin N★	78	320	44	102	17	3	9	35	17-0	2	43	.319	.354	.475	120	8	21-5	.995	0	102	77	O-77(CF)	1.2
1994	Cin N	47	179	29	54	8	0	3	21	11-1	3	35	.302	.351	.397	96	-1	9-8	.992	1	108	83	O-47(CF)	0.0
	Atl N	63	255	44	73	15	3	6	24	24-0	0	36	.286	.345	.439	101	0	10-3	.985	-4	88	94	O-63(CF)	-0.2
	Year	110	434	73	127	23	3	9	45	35-1	3	71	.293	.347	.422	99	-1	19-11	.988	-3	96	89	*O-110(CF)	-0.2
1995	Mon N	24	95	11	26	4	0	1	9	7-1	2	14	.274	.337	.347	78	-3	4-3	1.000	-3	75	78	O-24(CF)	-0.6
	†LA N	112	409	47	114	19	2	6	48	15-5	4	65	.279	.306	.379	89	-9	15-7	.969	-8	88	34	*O-110(61-48-2)	-1.7
	Year	136	504	58	140	23	2	7	57	22-6	6	79	.278	.312	.373	87	-11	19-10	.974	-11	86	42	*O-134(61-72-2)	-2.3
1996	Min A	98	322	41	104	17	4	6	47	23-0	7	53	.323	.375	.457	109	5	10-2	.990	-2	101	67	O-93(6-40-54)/D-2	0.2
1997	Min A	75	247	39	71	19	2	5	37	17-0	2	50	.287	.336	.441	100	0	7-4	1.000	-3	94	30	O-59(1-1-57),D-12	-0.6
	†Sea A	30	121	19	36	7	0	7	22	5-0	1	17	.298	.328	.529	121	3	2-1	1.000	-0	107	60	O-29(28-1-0)/D	0.2
	Year	105	368	58	107	26	2	12	59	22-0	3	67	.291	.333	.470	107	3	9-5	1.000	-3	99	41	O-88(29-2-57),D-13	-0.4
1998	†Tex A	75	257	48	83	7	3	16	46	8-0	3	46	.323	.349	.560	127	8	0-2	.976	6	118	133	O-71(14-41-31)/D-2	1.1
1999	†Tex A	87	290	41	87	17	1	8	37	21-0	5	57	.300	.355	.448	99	0	6-1	.981	-3	94	80	O-85(18-37-37)	-0.4
2000	NY A	10	25	4	3	1	0	1	1	1-0	1	6	.120	.185	.280	16	-3	0-0	1.000	-0	112	0	O-10(7-3-0)	-0.3
Total	14	1337	4797	687	1390	241	30	124	585	317-16	49	862	.290	.337	.430	106	27	235-84	.985	-18	99	82	*O-1283(246-886-184)/D-23	1.4
KELLY, VAN Van Howard B 3.18.1946 Charlotte, NC BL/TR 5-11/180# d6.13																								
1969	SD N	73	209	16	51	7	1	3	15	12-2	0	24	.244	.285	.330	75	-8	0-1	.971	-2	103	117	3-49,2-10	-1.0
1970	SD N	38	89	9	15	3	0	1	9	15-0	0	21	.169	.288	.236	44	-7	0-1	.971	2	104	46	3-27/2	-0.6
Total	2	111	298	25	66	10	1	4	24	27-2	0	45	.221	.286	.302	65	-15	0-2	.971	-0	103	94	/3-76,2-11	-1.6
KELLY, BILL William Henry "Big Bill" B 12.28.1898 Syracuse, NY D 4.8.1990 Syracuse, NY BR/TR 6/190# d9.6																								
1920	Phi A	9	13	0	3	1	0	0	0	0	0	2	.231	.231	.308	41	-1	0-0	1.000	0	111	0	/1-2	-0.1
1928	Phi N	23	71	6	12	1	1	0	5	7	0	20	.169	.244	.211	19	-9	0	.991	1	119	88	1-23	-0.9
Total	2	32	84	6	15	2	1	0	5	7	0	22	.179	.242	.226	22	-10	0-0	.992	1	119	83	/1-25	-1.0
KELLY, BILL William J. B New York, NY d5.4																								
1871	Kek NA	18	67	16	15	1	1	0	7	6		1	.224	.288	.269	60	-3	0-0	.833	0	47	241	O-18(1-4-14)	-0.1
KELLY, BILLY William Joseph B 5.1.1886 Baltimore, MD D 6.3.1940 Detroit, MI BR/TR 6-0.5/183# d5.2																								
1910	StL N	2	2	1	0	0	0	0	0	1	0	0	.000	.333	.000	-1	0	0	—	-0	*0*	*0*	/C	0.0
1911	Pit N	6	8	0	1	0	0	0	0	0	0	2	.125	.125	.125	-29	-1	0	1.000	1	*173*	*0*	/C	-0.1
1912	Pit N	48	132	20	42	3	2	1	11	2	0	16	.318	.328	.394	99	-1	8	.990	-4	*124*	*66*	C-39	-0.2
1913	Pit N	48	82	11	22	2	2	0	9	2	2	12	.268	.302	.341	87	-2	1-1	.960	1	98	81	C-40	0.1
Total	4	104	224	32	65	5	4	1	20	5	2	30	.290	.312	.362	89	-4	9-1	.977	-3	*114*	*71*	/C-81	-0.2
KELSEY, BILLY George William B 8.24.1881 Covington, OH D 4.25.1968 Springfield, OH BR/TR 5-10/150# d10.4																								
1907	Pit N	2	5	1	2	0	0	0	0	0	0		.400	.400	.400	149	0	0	1.000	-0	*142*	*85*	/C-2	0.0
KELTNER, KEN Kenneth Frederick "Butch" B 10.31.1916 Milwaukee, WI D 12.12.1991 New Berlin, WI BR/TR 6/190# d10.2 Mil 1945																								
1937	Cle A	1	1	0	0	0	0	0	1	0	0	0	.000	.000	.000	-99	0	0-0	1.000	0	144	0	/3	0.0
1938	Cle A	149	576	86	159	31	9	26	113	33	3	75	.276	.319	.497	103	-3	4-3	.956	-10	90	69	*3-149	-0.7
1939	Cle A	**154**	587	84	191	35	11	13	97	51	0	41	.325	.379	.489	125	20	6-6	**.974**	5	94	**138**	*3-154	2.8
1940	Cle A★	149	543	67	138	24	10	15	77	51	3	56	.254	.322	.418	93	-8	10-5	.953	-6	89	105	*3-148	-0.8
1941	Cle A★	149	581	83	156	31	13	23	84	51	2	56	.269	.330	.485	119	11	2-2	**.971**	20	**108**	**129**	*3-149	3.5
1942	Cle A★	152	624	72	179	34	4	6	78	20	3	36	.287	.312	.383	101	-3	4-3	**.945**	11	**111**	**135**	*3-151	1.4
1943	Cle A★	110	427	47	111	31	3	4	39	36	0	20	.260	.317	.375	109	4	2-2	.969	3	104	120	*3-107	0.9
1944	Cle A★	149	573	74	169	41	9	13	91	53	0	29	.295	.355	.466	139	27	4-3	.968	12	109	120	*3-149	4.2
1946	Cle A★	116	398	47	96	17	1	13	45	30	0	38	.241	.294	.387	95	-5	0-3	.965	-2	92	77	*3-112	-0.8
1947	Cle A	151	541	49	139	29	3	11	76	59	1	45	.257	.331	.383	101	0	5-4	.972	-5	95	116	*3-150	-0.5
1948	†Cle A★	153	558	91	166	24	4	31	119	89	1	52	.297	.395	.522	146	37	2-1	.969	-2	106	105	*3-153	3.3
1949	Cle A	80	246	35	57	9	2	8	30	38	0	26	.232	.335	.382	91	-4	0-1	.980	-1	108	75	3-69	-0.5
1950	Bos A	13	28	2	9	2	0	0	2	3	0	6	.321	.387	.393	91	0	0-0	.947	-1	80	0	/3-8,1	-0.1
Total	13	1526	5683	737	1570	308	69	163	852	514	13	480	.276	.338	.441	113	76	39-33	.965	26	100	110	*3-1500/1	12.7
KELTON, DAVE David Wayne B 12.17.1979 Dothan, AL BR/TR 6-3/200# d6.8																								
2003	Chi N	10	12	1	2	1	0	0	1	0-0	0	5	.167	.167	.250	7	-2	0-0	1.000	0	160	0	/O-2(LF)	-0.1
KELTY, JOHN John James "Chief" B 3.10.1871 Jersey City, NJ D 4.13.1929 Jersey City, NJ 5-10/175# d4.19																								
1890	Pit N	59	207	24	49	10	2	1	27	22	4	42	.237	.322	.319	98	1	10	.898	-1	65	40	O-59(LF)	-0.1
KEMMER, BILL William Edward (born William Edward Kemmerer) B 11.15.1873 , PA D 6.8.1945 Washington, DC BR/TR 6-2/195# d6.3																								
1895	Lou N	11	38	5	7	0	0	1	3	2	0	4	.184	.225	.263	27	-4	0	.809	1	113	189	/3-9,1-2	-0.3
KEMMLER, RUDY Rudolph (born Rudolph Kemler) B 1860 Chicago, IL D 6.20.1909 Chicago, IL BR/TR 5-11/206# d7.26																								
1879	Pro N	2	7	0	1	0	0	0	0	0		1	.143	.143	.143	-6	-1		.833	1			/C-2	0.0
1881	Cle N	1	3	0	0	0	0	0	0	0		1	.000	.000	.000	-99	-1		1.000	1			/C	0.0
1882	Cin AA	3	11	0	1	1	0	0		0			.091	.091	.182	-10	-1		.909	-0			/C-3,O(RF)	-0.1
	Pit AA	24	99	7	25	4	0	0		1			.253	.260	.293	90	-1		.920	3			C-23/O(RF)	0.4
	Year	27	110	7	26	5	0	0		1			.236	.243	.282	79	-2		.919	2			C-26/O-2(RF)	0.3
1883	Col AA	84	318	27	66	6	2	0		13			.208	.239	.239	59	-13		.872	-8			*C-82/O-2(CF)	-1.2
1884	Col AA	61	211	28	42	3	3	0		15	0		.199	.252	.242	67	-6		.906	-12			C-58/1-2,O(LF)	-1.3
1885	Pit AA	18	64	2	13	2	1	0	5	2	1		.203	.239	.266	60	-3		.870	-3			C-18	-0.4
1886	StL AA	35	123	13	17	2	0	0	6	8	1		.138	.197	.154	10	-13	0	.914	4			C-32/1-3	-0.6
1889	Col AA	8	26	2	3	0	0	0	0	3	0	3	.115	.207	.115	-8	-4	0	.930	1			/C-8	-0.2
Total	8	236	862	79	168	18	6	0	11	42	2	5	.195	.234	.230	52	-43	0	.894	-15			C-227/1-5,O-5(1-2-2)	-3.4
KEMP, STEVE Steven F B 8.7.1954 San Angelo, TX BL/TL 6/195# d4.7																								
1977	Det A	151	552	75	142	29	4	18	88	71-0	5	93	.257	.343	.422	103	4	3-3	.981	-10	84	89	*O-148(LF)	-1.3
1978	Det A	159	582	75	161	18	4	15	79	97-3	1	87	.277	.379	.399	116	16	2-3	.977	-2	93	100	*O-157(LF)	0.7
1979	Det A★	134	490	88	156	26	3	26	105	68-2	2	70	.318	.398	.543	148	35	5-6	.976	-0	92	135	*O-120(117-0-3),D-11	2.7
1980	Det A	135	508	88	149	23	3	21	101	69-3	4	64	.293	.376	.474	130	23	5-1	.995	2	106	61	O-85(LF),D-46	2.0
1981	Det A	105	372	52	103	18	4	9	49	70-5	1	48	.277	.389	.419	129	18	9-3	.986	-2	99	60	O-92(LF),D-12	1.3
1982	Chi A	160	580	91	166	23	1	19	98	89-8	3	83	.286	.381	.428	123	22	7-7	.976	-12	86	64	*O-154(LF)/D-2	0.2
1983	NY A	109	373	53	90	17	3	12	49	41-3	2	37	.241	.318	.399	100	0	1-0	.987	3	109	69	*O-101(25-0-86)/D-2	-0.2
1984	NY A	94	313	37	91	12	1	7	41	40-0	1	54	.291	.369	.403	119	10	4-1	.972	-5	93	40	O-75(LF),D-12	0.2
1985	Pit N	92	236	19	59	13	2	2	21	25-1	0	54	.250	.317	.347	88	-3	1-0	1.000	0	105	26	O-63(LF)	-0.6
1986	Pit N	13	16	1	3	0	0	1	1	4-0	0	6	.188	.350	.375	98	0	1-0	1.000	1	183	0	/O-4(LF)	0.1
1988	Tex A	16	36	2	8	0	0	0	2	2-0	0	9	.222	.256	.222	36	-3	1-0	1.000	-0	91	0	/O-5(5-0-1),1D	-0.3
Total	11	1168	4058	581	1128	179	25	130	634	576-25	19	605	.278	.367	.431	119	122	39-24	.982	-25	95	78	*O-1004(925-0-90)/D-92,1	4.8
KENDALL, FRED Fred Lyn B 1.31.1949 Torrance, CA BR/TR 6-1/190# d9.8 C6 s-Jason																								
1969	SD N	10	26	2	4	0	0	0	0	2-0	0	5	.154	.214	.154	5	-3	0-0	1.000	0	150	103	/C-9	-0.3
1970	SD N	4	9	0	0	0	0	0	1	0-0	0	0	.000	.000	.000	-99	-3	0-0	1.000	-1	93	0	/C-2,1O(LF)	-0.4
1971	SD N	49	111	2	19	1	0	1	7	7-3	0	16	.171	.220	.207	23	-12	1-0	1.000	0	62	91	C-39/13	-1.1
1972	SD N	91	273	18	59	3	4	6	18	11-3	1	42	.216	.247	.322	66	-15	0-0	.995	1	85	99	C-82/1	-1.1
1973	SD N	145	507	39	143	22	3	10	59	30-4	1	35	.282	.320	.396	107	3	3-1	.984	-10	100	100	*C-138	0.0
1974	SD N	141	424	32	98	15	2	8	45	49-7	0	33	.231	.308	.333	84	-10	0-1	.983	-19	77	104	*C-133	-2.4
1975	SD N	103	286	16	57	12	1	0	24	26-5	0	28	.199	.265	.248	46	-21	0-1	.977	-10	74	126	C-85	-2.9
1976	SD N	146	456	30	112	17	0	2	39	36-4	3	42	.246	.302	.296	77	-14	1-1	.994	-12	114	90	*C-146	-2.1

Year	Tm Lg	G	AB	R	H	2B	3B	HR	RBI	BB-IB	HP	SO	AVG	OBP	SLG	AOPS	ABR	SB-CS	FA	FR	Rng	Thr	G at Pos	BFW
1977	Cle A	103	317	18	79	13	1	3	39	16-1	1	27	.249	.283	.325	69	-14	0-1	.991	-22	68	74	*C-102/D	-3.3
1978	Bos A	20	41	3	8	1	0	0	4	1-0	0	2	.195	.205	.220	20	-4	0-0	1.000	0	134	102	1-13/C-5,D	-0.5
1979	SD N	46	102	8	17	2	0	1	6	11-2	0	7	.167	.248	.216	29	-10	0-0	.977	1	92	133	C-40/1-2	-0.9
1980	SD N	19	24	2	7	0	0	0	2	0-0	0	3	.292	.292	.292	67	-1	0-0	.938	-1	85	83	C-14/1	-0.2
Total	12	877	2576	170	603	86	11	31	244	189-29	6	240	.234	.285	.312	72	-104	5-5	.987	-72	88	99	C-795/1-19,D-2,30(LF)	-15.2

KENDALL, JASON Jason Daniel B 6.26.1974 San Diego, CA BR/TR 6/180# d4.1 f-Fred

Year	Tm Lg	G	AB	R	H	2B	3B	HR	RBI	BB-IB	HP	SO	AVG	OBP	SLG	AOPS	ABR	SB-CS	FA	FR	Rng	Thr	G at Pos	BFW
1996	Pit N★	130	414	54	124	23	5	3	42	35-11	15	30	.300	.372	.401	102	3	5-2	.980	-6	69	110	*C-129	0.5
1997	Pit N	144	486	71	143	36	4	8	49	49-2	31	53	.294	.391	.434	115	14	18-6	.990	18	110	112	*C-142	4.3
1998	Pit N★	149	535	95	175	36	3	12	75	51-3	**31**	51	.327	.411	.473	132	29	26-5	.992	8	103	79	*C-144	4.9
1999	Pit N	78	280	61	93	20	3	8	41	38-3	12	32	.332	.428	.511	138	19	22-3	.988	13	142	132	C-75	3.8
2000	Pit N★	152	579	112	185	33	6	14	58	79-3	15	79	.320	.412	.470	124	25	22-12	.991	3	102	92	*C-147	3.6
2001	Pit N	157	606	84	161	22	2	10	53	44-4	20	48	.266	.335	.358	78	-19	13-14	.985	-11	94	85	*C-133,O-27(18-0-10)	-2.4
2002	Pit N	145	545	59	154	25	3	3	44	49-1	9	29	.283	.350	.356	90	-10	15-8	.990	-3	100	109	*C-143	-0.3
2003	Pit N	150	587	84	191	29	3	6	58	49-3	25	40	.325	.399	.416	111	13	8-7	.989	-14	114	71	*C-146	0.8
Total	8	1105	4032	620	1226	224	29	64	420	394-30	158	362	.304	.385	.422	109	74	129-57	.988	9	103	96	*C-1059/O-27(18-0-10)	15.2

KENDERS, AL Albert Daniel George B 4.4.1937 Barrington, NJ BR/TR 6/185# d8.14

Year	Tm Lg	G	AB	R	H	2B	3B	HR	RBI	BB-IB	HP	SO	AVG	OBP	SLG	AOPS	ABR	SB-CS	FA	FR	Rng	Thr	G at Pos	BFW
1961	Phi N	10	23	0	4	1	0	0	1	1-0	0	0	.174	.208	.217	13	-3	0-0	1.000	-1	*70*	*152*	C-10	-0.4

KENNA, EDDIE Edward Aloysius "Scrap Iron" B 9.30.1897 San Francisco, CA D 8.21.1972 San Francisco, CA BR/TR 5-7.5/150# d6.2

Year	Tm Lg	G	AB	R	H	2B	3B	HR	RBI	BB-IB	HP	SO	AVG	OBP	SLG	AOPS	ABR	SB-CS	FA	FR	Rng	Thr	G at Pos	BFW
1928	Was A	41	118	14	35	4	2	1	20	14	1	8	.297	.376	.390	102	1	1-5	.942	-1	*116*	*108*	C-33	0.0

KENNEDY, ADAM Adam Thomas B 1.10.1976 Riverside, CA BL/TR 6-1/180# d8.21

Year	Tm Lg	G	AB	R	H	2B	3B	HR	RBI	BB-IB	HP	SO	AVG	OBP	SLG	AOPS	ABR	SB-CS	FA	FR	Rng	Thr	G at Pos	BFW
1999	StL N	33	102	12	26	10	1	1	16	3-0	2	8	.255	.284	.402	72	-4	0-1	.971	-2	91	78	2-29	-0.6
2000	Ana A	156	598	82	159	33	11	9	72	28-5	3	73	.266	.300	.403	74	-26	22-8	.976	-13	96	100	*2-155	-2.7
2001	Ana A	137	478	48	129	25	3	6	40	27-3	11	71	.270	.318	.372	81	-13	12-7	.984	2	107	81	*2-131/D-5	-0.5
2002	†Ana A	144	474	65	148	32	6	7	52	19-1	7	80	.312	.345	.449	110	6	17-4	.983	9	101	**120**	*2-139/O(CF)D	2.3
2003	Ana A	143	449	71	121	17	1	13	49	45-4	9	73	.269	.344	.399	100	1	22-9	**.990**	-3	97	96	*2-140/D	0.6
Total	5	613	2101	278	583	117	22	36	229	122-13	32	305	.277	.323	.406	89	-36	73-29	.982	-7	100	98	2-594/D-7,O(CF)	-0.9

KENNEDY, ED Edward B 4.1.1856 Carbondale, PA D 5.20.1905 New York, NY 5-6/150# d5.1

Year	Tm Lg	G	AB	R	H	2B	3B	HR	RBI	BB-IB	HP	SO	AVG	OBP	SLG	AOPS	ABR	SB-CS	FA	FR	Rng	Thr	G at Pos	BFW
1883	NY AA	94	356	57	78	6	7	2		17			.219	.255	.292	72	-12		.884	-8	54	0	*O-94(LF)	-1.9
1884	†NY AA	103	378	49	72	6	2	1		16	1		.190	.225	.225	49	-21		.915	7	68	165	*O-100(99-1-0)/S2C	-1.5
1885	NY AA	96	349	35	71	8	4	2	21	12	4		.203	.238	.266	62	-15		.841	2	94	32	*O-96(95-1-0)	-1.4
1886	Bro AA	6	22	1	4	0	0	0	2	2	0		.182	.250	.182	36	-2	1	.909	-0	0	0	/O-6(3-4-0)	-0.2
Total	4	299	1105	142	225	20	13	5	23	47	5		.204	.239	.259	60	-50	1	.878	1	71	66	O-296(291-6-0)/C2S	-5.0

KENNEDY, JIM James Earl B 11.1.1946 Tulsa, OK BL/TR 5-9/160# d6.14 b-Junior

Year	Tm Lg	G	AB	R	H	2B	3B	HR	RBI	BB-IB	HP	SO	AVG	OBP	SLG	AOPS	ABR	SB-CS	FA	FR	Rng	Thr	G at Pos	BFW
1970	StL N	12	24	1	3	0	0	0	0	0-0	0	0	.125	.125	.125	-32	-5	0-0	.909	-1	88	80	/S-7,2-5	-0.5

KENNEDY, JOHN John Edward B 5.29.1941 Chicago, IL BR/TR 6/185# d9.5 Mil 1968

Year	Tm Lg	G	AB	R	H	2B	3B	HR	RBI	BB-IB	HP	SO	AVG	OBP	SLG	AOPS	ABR	SB-CS	FA	FR	Rng	Thr	G at Pos	BFW
1962	Was A	14	42	6	11	0	1	1	2	2-0	0	7	.262	.295	.381	81	-1	0-1	.974	-1	106	80	/S-9,3-2	-0.2
1963	Was A	36	62	3	11	1	1	0	4	6-0	1	22	.177	.261	.226	38	-5	2-0	.954	3	125	109	3-26/S-2	-0.2
1964	Was A	148	482	55	111	16	4	7	35	29-2	5	119	.230	.280	.324	68	-22	3-3	.941	6	109	88	*3-106,S-49/2-2	-1.4
1965	†LA N	104	105	12	18	3	0	1	5	8-1	2	33	.171	.243	.229	36	-9	1-0	.971	4	99	117	3-95/S-5	-0.5
1966	†LA N	125	274	15	55	9	2	3	24	10-1	5	64	.201	.241	.281	49	-20	1-2	.965	6	108	106	3-87,S-28,2-15	-1.2
1967	NY A	78	179	22	35	4	0	1	17	17-0	1	35	.196	.265	.235	52	-11	2-1	.915	-4	103	99	S-36,3-34/2-2	-1.3
1969	Sea A	61	128	18	30	3	1	4	14	14-1	1	25	.234	.315	.367	92	-2	4-0	.916	-1	86	99	S-33,3-23	0.0
1970	Mil A	25	55	8	14	2	0	2	6	5-0	0	9	.255	.317	.400	96	0	0-1	.921	-7	73	70	2-16/3-5,S-4,1	-0.7
	Bos A	43	129	15	33	7	1	4	17	6-1	1	14	.256	.292	.419	88	-2	0-0	.960	3	110	66	3-33/2-2	0.1
	Year	68	184	23	47	9	1	6	23	11-1	1	23	.255	.299	.413	91	-3	0-1	.962	-4	111	95	3-38,2-18/S-4,1	-0.6
1971	Bos A	74	272	41	75	12	5	5	22	14-0	4	42	.276	.320	.412	99	-1	1-1	.974	-15	89	73	2-37,S-33/3-5	-1.1
1972	Bos A	71	212	22	52	11	1	2	22	18-4	3	40	.245	.311	.335	88	-3	0-1	.962	-7	100	128	2-32,S-27,3-11	-0.6
1973	Bos A	67	155	17	28	9	1	1	16	12-0	2	45	.181	.246	.271	44	-12	0-0	.980	-1	93	129	2-31,3-24/D-9	-1.1
1974	Bos A	10	15	3	2	0	0	1	1	1-0	0	6	.133	.188	.333	44	-1	0-0	.778	-2	85	139	/2-6,3-4	-0.3
Total	12	856	2110	237	475	77	17	32	185	142-10	25	461	.225	.281	.323	70	-89	14-10	.953	-16	105	95	3-455,S-226,2-143/D-9,1	-8.5

KENNEDY, JOHN John Irvin B 10.12.1926 Jacksonville, FL D 4.27.1998 Jacksonville, FL BR/TR 5-10/175# d4.22

Year	Tm Lg	G	AB	R	H	2B	3B	HR	RBI	BB-IB	HP	SO	AVG	OBP	SLG	AOPS	ABR	SB-CS	FA	FR	Rng	Thr	G at Pos	BFW
1957	Phi N	5	2	1	0	0	0	0	0	0-0	0	1	.000	.000	.000	-99	-1	0-0	.500	0	113	1294	/3-2	-0.1

KENNEDY, JUNIOR Junior Raymond B 8.9.1950 Fort Gibson, OK BR/TR 6/185# d8.9 b-Jim

Year	Tm Lg	G	AB	R	H	2B	3B	HR	RBI	BB-IB	HP	SO	AVG	OBP	SLG	AOPS	ABR	SB-CS	FA	FR	Rng	Thr	G at Pos	BFW
1974	Cin N	22	19	2	3	0	0	0	0	6-1	0	4	.158	.360	.158	49	-1	0-0	.909	-4	64	30	2-17/3-5	-0.5
1978	Cin N	89	157	22	40	2	2	0	11	31-2	1	28	.255	.381	.293	91	0	4-1	.979	-2	99	93	2-71/3-4	0.1
1979	Cin N	83	220	29	60	7	0	1	17	28-0	0	31	.273	.355	.318	85	-4	4-3	.980	-4	100	94	2-59/S-5,3-4	-0.4
1980	Cin N	104	337	31	88	16	3	1	34	36-6	0	34	.261	.325	.335	87	-5	3-1	.988	1	102	91	*2-103	0.1
1981	Cin N	27	44	5	11	1	0	0	5	1-0	0	5	.250	.255	.273	52	-3	0-0	.980	-1	87	142	2-16/3-5	-0.3
1982	Chi N	105	242	22	53	3	1	2	25	21-1	0	34	.219	.278	.264	52	-16	1-4	.978	-2	106	87	2-71,S-28/3-7	-1.5
1983	Chi N	17	22	3	3	0	0	0	3	1-0	0	6	.136	.167	.136	-12	-3	0-0	1.000	-0	110	90	/2-7,3-4,S	-0.4
Total	7	447	1041	114	258	29	6	4	95	124-10	1	142	.248	.325	.299	75	-32	12-9	.982	-11	101	92	2-344/S-34,3-29	-2.9

KENNEDY, DOC Michael Joseph B 8.11.1853 Brooklyn, NY D 5.23.1920 Grove, NY BR/TR 5-9.5/185# d5.1

Year	Tm Lg	G	AB	R	H	2B	3B	HR	RBI	BB-IB	HP	SO	AVG	OBP	SLG	AOPS	ABR	SB-CS	FA	FR	Rng	Thr	G at Pos	BFW
1879	Cle N	49	193	19	56	8	2	1	18	2		10	.290	.297	.368	119	4		.891	3			C-46/1-4	0.7
1880	Cle N	66	250	26	50	10	1	0	18	5		12	.200	.216	.248	58	-10		.899	-2			*C-65/O-2(1-1-0)	-1.0
1881	Cle N	39	150	19	47	7	1	0	15	5		13	.313	.335	.373	129	5		.920	2			C-35/O-3(2-1-0),3	0.7
1882	Cle N	1	3	0	1	0	0	0	0	1		0	.333	.500	.333	180	0		.857	2			/C	0.2
1883	Buf N	5	19	3	6	0	0	0	2	2		2	.316	.381	.316	113	0		.583	-2	0	0	/O-4(1-3-0),1	-0.2
Total	5	160	615	67	160	25	4	1	53	15		37	.260	.278	.319	98	-1		.901	4			C-147/O-9(4-5-0),1-5,3	0.4

KENNEDY, RAY Raymond Lincoln B 5.19.1895 Pittsburgh, PA D 1.18.1969 Casselberry, FL BR/TR 5-9/165# d9.8

Year	Tm Lg	G	AB	R	H	2B	3B	HR	RBI	BB-IB	HP	SO	AVG	OBP	SLG	AOPS	ABR	SB-CS	FA	FR	Rng	Thr	G at Pos	BFW
1916	StL A	1	1	0	0	0	0	0	0	0	0	0	.000	.000	.000	-99	0	0	—	0			H	0.0

KENNEDY, BOB Robert Daniel B 8.18.1920 Chicago, IL BR/TR 6-2/193# d9.14 Mil 1942-45, 1952 M4 C5 s-Terry

Year	Tm Lg	G	AB	R	H	2B	3B	HR	RBI	BB-IB	HP	SO	AVG	OBP	SLG	AOPS	ABR	SB-CS	FA	FR	Rng	Thr	G at Pos	BFW
1939	Chi A	3	8	0	2	0	0	0	1	0	0	0	.250	.250	.250	27	-1	0-0	.750	-1	90	0	/3-2	-0.1
1940	Chi A	154	606	74	153	23	3	3	52	42	0	58	.252	.301	.315	59	-37	3-7	.938	-5	97	94	*3-154	-3.7
1941	Chi A	76	257	16	53	9	3	1	29	17	0	23	.206	.255	.276	41	-23	5-3	.934	0	102	100	3-71	-2.0
1942	Chi A	113	412	37	95	18	5	0	38	22	0	41	.231	.270	.299	61	-23	11-7	.956	7	110	101	3-96,O-16(13-0-3)	-1.5
1946	Chi A	113	411	43	106	13	5	5	34	24	1	42	.258	.300	.350	85	-11	6-8	.965	4	95	194	O-75(59-12-4),3-29	-1.4
1947	Chi A	115	428	47	112	19	3	6	48	18	0	38	.262	.291	.362	84	-12	3-4	.968	-4	93	103	*O-106(14-1-91)/3	-2.1
1948	Chi A	30	113	4	28	8	1	0	14	4	0	17	.248	.274	.336	64	-6	0-2	.970	0	97	141	O-30(25-0-5)	-0.9
	†Cle A	66	73	10	22	3	2	0	5	4	0	6	.301	.338	.397	98	-1	0-0	1.000	2	107	173	O-50(2-0-48)/2-2,1	0.0
	Year	96	186	14	50	11	3	0	19	8	0	23	.269	.299	.360	77	-7	0-2	.981	2	101	152	O-80(27-0-53)/2-2,1	-0.9
1949	Cle A	121	424	49	117	23	5	9	57	37	0	40	.276	.334	.417	100	-2	5-5	.990	4	100	131	O-98(1-0-98),3-21	-0.2
1950	Cle A	146	540	79	157	27	5	9	54	53	1	31	.291	.355	.409	99	-2	3-4	.987	2	102	108	*O-144(0-10-138)	-0.5
1951	Cle A	108	321	30	79	15	4	7	29	34	1	33	.246	.320	.383	95	-3	4-2	.968	2	101	143	*O-106(1-0-105)	-0.4
1952	Cle A	22	40	6	12	3	1	0	12	9	0	5	.300	.429	.425	148	3	1-0	1.000	2	120	0	O-13(1-5-8)/3-3	0.5
1953	Cle A	100	161	22	38	5	0	3	22	19	1	11	.236	.320	.323	76	-5	0-2	1.000	0	107	57	O-89(42-2-52)	-0.8
1954	Cle A	1	0	0	0	0	0	0	0	0	0	0	—	—	—	—	0	0-0	—	-0	0	0	/O(LF)	0.0
	Bal A	106	323	37	81	13	2	6	45	28	0	43	.251	.306	.359	90	-6	2-1	.938	-4	95	73	3-71,O-21(12-0-9)	-1.1
	Year	107	323	37	81	13	2	6	45	28	0	43	.251	.306	.359	90	-6	2-1	.938	-4	95	73	3-71,O-22(13-0-9)	-1.1
1955	Bal A	26	70	10	10	1	0	0	5	10-0	0	10	.143	.250	.157	12	-9	0-1	1.000	-0	111	0	O-14(RF)/1-6,3	-1.0
	Chi A	83	214	28	65	10	2	9	43	16-0	0	16	.304	.352	.495	122	6	0-2	.938	-6	85	132	3-55,O-20(4-0-16)/1-3	-0.2
	Year	109	284	38	75	11	2	9	48	26-0	0	26	.264	.326	.412	97	-2	0-3	.938	-7	85	131	3-56,O-34(4-0-30)/1-9	-1.2
1956	Chi A	8	13	0	1	0	0	0	0	2-0	0	4	.077	.200	.077	-24	-2	0-0	1.000	-0	53	393	/3-6	-0.3
	Det A	70	177	17	41	5	0	4	22	24-2	2	19	.232	.328	.328	74	-6	2-2	.931	-3	111	113	O-30(21-0-9),3-27	-1.0
	Year	78	190	17	42	5	0	4	22	26-2	2	23	.221	.320	.311	67	-9	2-2	.909	-3	76	92	3-33,O-30(21-0-9)	-1.3
1957	Chi A	4	2	0	0	0	0	0	0	0-0	0	1	.000	.000	.000	-99	-1	0-0	—	0			H	-0.1

Year	Tm Lg	G	AB	R	H	2B	3B	HR	RBI	BB-IB	HP	SO	AVG	OBP	SLG	AOPS	ABR	SB-CS	FA	FR	Rng	Thr	G at Pos	BFW
	Bro N	19	31	5	4	1	0	1	4	1-0	0	5	.129	.156	.258	8	-4	0-0	1.000	-1	79	0	/O-9(8-0-1),3-3	-0.6
Total	16	1484	4624	514	1176	196	41	63	514	364-2	6	443	.254	.309	.355	80	-145	45-50	.978	-3	100	117	O-822(204-30-601),3-540/1-10,2-2	-17.4
KENNEDY, SNAPPER Sherman Montgomery B 11.1.1878 Conneaut, OH D 8.15.1945 Pasadena, TX BB/TR 5-10/165# d5.1																								
1902	Chi N	1	5	0	0	0	0	0	0	0	0		.000	.000	.000	-99	-1	0	1.000	-0	0	0	/O(CF)	-0.2
KENNEDY, TERRY Terrence Edward B 6.4.1956 Euclid, OH BL/TR 6-3/220# d9.4 f-Bob																								
1978	StL N	10	29	0	5	0	0	0	2	4-2	0	3	.172	.273	.172	27	-3	0-0	.980	-0	130	65	C-10	-0.3
1979	StL N	33	109	11	31	7	0	2	17	6-2	0	20	.284	.319	.404	96	-1	0-0	.993	-5	85	67	C-32	-0.5
1980	StL N	84	248	28	63	12	3	4	34	28-3	0	34	.254	.325	.375	93	-2	0-0	.967	-4	76	78	C-41,O-28(LF)	-0.5
1981	SD N★	101	382	32	115	24	1	2	41	22-6	2	53	.301	.341	.385	114	7	0-2	.964	-7	96	121	*C-100	0.3
1982	SD N	153	562	75	166	42	1	21	97	26-9	5	91	.295	.328	.486	133	23	1-0	.990	-11	121	65	*C-139,1-12	1.8
1983	SD N☆	149	549	47	156	27	2	17	98	51-15	2	89	.284	.342	.434	119	14	1-3	.986	-7	92	101	*C-143/1-4	1.2
1984	†SD N	148	530	54	127	16	1	14	57	33-8	2	99	.240	.284	.353	79	-17	1-2	.982	-9	119	71	*C-147	-2.1
1985	SD N★	143	532	54	139	27	1	10	74	31-10	0	102	.261	.301	.372	89	-9	0-0	.986	6	113	110	*C-140/1-5	0.3
1986	SD N	141	432	46	114	22	1	12	57	37-7	2	74	.264	.324	.403	102	0	0-3	.990	1	104	95	*C-123	0.6
1987	Bal A★	143	512	51	128	13	1	18	62	35-6	1	112	.250	.299	.385	82	-15	1-0	.993	-10	95	106	*C-142	-1.8
1988	Bal A	85	265	20	60	10	0	3	16	15-0	1	53	.226	.269	.298	61	-14	0-0	.994	-13	78	112	C-79	-2.4
1989	†SF N	125	355	19	85	15	0	5	34	35-7	0	56	.239	.306	.324	83	-8	1-3	.986	3	128	101	*C-121/1-2	0.0
1990	SF N	107	303	25	84	22	0	2	26	31-7	0	38	.277	.342	.370	100	1	1-2	.991	-11	122	78	*C-103	-0.6
1991	SF N	69	171	12	40	7	1	3	13	11-4	1	31	.234	.283	.339	77	-6	0-0	.978	-3	87	190	C-58/1-2	-0.6
Total	14	1491	4979	474	1313	244	12	113	628	365-86	16	855	.264	.314	.386	97	-30	6-15	.985	-71	105	97	*C-1378/O-28(LF),1-25	-4.6
KENNEDY, ED William Edward B 4.5.1861 Bellevue, KY D 12.22.1912 Cheyenne, WY BR/TR 5-7/160# d5.17																								
1884	Cin U	13	48	6	10	1	1	0		1			.208	.224	.271	46	-5		.857	0	97	143	/3-8,S-4,O(RF)	-0.4
KENNEY, JERRY Gerald T B 6.30.1945 St.Louis, MO BL/TR 6-1/170# d9.5 Mil 1968																								
1967	NY A	20	58	4	18	2	0	1	5	10-0	0	8	.310	.412	.397	145	4	2-1	.952	-2	98	51	S-18	0.3
1969	NY A	130	447	49	115	14	2	2	34	48-2	1	36	.257	.328	.311	83	-9	25-14	.975	14	122	133	3-83,O-31(CF),S-10	0.5
1970	NY A	140	404	46	78	10	7	4	35	52-2	0	44	.193	.284	.282	60	-23	20-6	.960	16	**122**	80	*3-135/2-2	-0.5
1971	NY A	120	325	50	85	10	3	0	20	56-3	1	38	.262	.368	.311	101	3	9-8	.953	10	119	111	*3-109/S-5,1	1.3
1972	NY A	50	119	16	25	2	0	0	7	16-2	0	13	.210	.304	.227	62	-5	3-0	.969	3	112	136	S-45/3	-0.3
1973	Cle A	5	16	0	4	0	1	0	2	2-0	0	0	.250	.316	.375	97	0	0-0	1.000	-1	94	31	/2-5	-0.1
Total	6	465	1369	165	325	38	13	7	103	184-9	2	139	.237	.326	.299	82	-30	59-29	.962	40	121	104	3-328/S-78,O-31(CF),2-7,1	1.8
KENNEY, JOHN John d5.2																								
1872	Atl NA	5	19	0	0	0	0	0	1	0		1	.000	.000	.000	-85	-4	0-0	.692	-2	76	125	/2-3,O-3(2-0-1)	-0.5
KENT, JEFF Jeffrey Franklin B 3.7.1968 Bellflower, CA BR/TR 6-1/185# d4.12																								
1992	Tor A	65	192	36	46	13	1	8	35	20-0	6	47	.240	.324	.443	110	3	2-1	.915	-3	87	43	3-49,2-17/1-3	0.0
	NY N	37	113	16	27	8	1	3	15	7-0	1	29	.239	.289	.407	97	-1	0-2	.980	1	95	99	2-34/3S	0.1
1993	NY N	140	496	65	134	24	0	21	80	30-2	8	88	.270	.320	.446	104	2	4-4	.969	-20	90	92	*2-127,3-12/S-2	-1.2
1994	NY N	107	415	53	121	24	5	14	68	23-3	10	84	.292	.341	.475	112	6	1-4	.976	-6	101	114	*2-107	0.5
1995	NY N	125	472	65	131	22	3	20	65	29-3	8	89	.278	.327	.464	110	5	3-3	.984	-8	100	94	*2-122	0.3
1996	NY N	89	335	45	97	20	1	9	39	21-1	1	56	.290	.331	.436	106	2	4-3	.925	11	116	132	3-89	1.4
	†Cle A	39	102	16	27	7	0	3	16	10-0	1	22	.265	.328	.422	90	-1	2-1	.992	1	93	116	1-20/2-9,3-6,D-5	-0.1
1997	†SF N	155	580	90	145	38	2	29	121	48-6	13	133	.250	.316	.472	108	5	11-3	.979	19	110	116	*2-148,1-13	3.0
1998	SF N	137	526	94	156	37	3	31	128	48-4	9	110	.297	.359	.555	146	34	9-4	.972	5	**108**	103	*2-134/1	4.5
1999	SF N★	138	511	86	148	40	2	23	101	61-3	5	112	.290	.366	.511	129	23	13-6	.984	-9	93	107	*2-133/1	2.0
2000	†SF N★	159	587	114	196	41	7	33	125	90-6	9	107	.334	.424	.596	168	65	12-9	.986	1	103	104	*2-150,1-16	6.6
2001	SF N★	159	607	84	181	49	6	22	106	65-4	11	96	.298	.369	.507	135	33	7-6	.987	8	**110**	110	*2-140,1-30	4.4
2002	†SF N	152	623	102	195	42	2	37	108	52-3	4	101	.313	.368	.565	152	42	5-1	.978	2	102	**125**	*2-149/1-9	5.0
2003	Hou N	130	505	77	150	39	1	22	93	39-2	5	85	.297	.351	.509	116	12	6-2	.983	1	96	100	*2-128	2.0
Total	12	1632	6064	943	1754	404	34	275	1100	543-37	91	1159	.289	.352	.503	126	230	79-49	.980	4	102	106	*2-1398,3-157/1-93,D-5,S-3	28.5
KENWORTHY, DICK Richard Lee B 4.1.1941 Red Oak, IA BR/TR 5-9/170# d9.8																								
1962	Chi A	3	4	0	0	0	0	0	0	0-0	0	3	.000	.000	.000	-99	-1	0-0	1.000	1	182	396	/2-2	0.0
1964	Chi A	2	2	0	0	0	0	0	0	0-0	0	1	.000	.000	.000	-99	-1	0-0	—	0			H	-0.1
1965	Chi A	3	1	0	0	0	0	0	0	1-0	1	0	.000	.667	.000	113	0	0-0	—	0			H	0.0
1966	Chi A	9	25	1	5	0	0	0	0	0-0	0	0	.200	.200	.200	16	-3	0-0	.875	-1	88	0	/3-6	-0.5
1967	Chi A	50	97	9	22	4	1	4	11	4-0	1	17	.227	.262	.412	101	-1	0-2	.971	-2	100	28	3-35	-0.4
1968	Chi A	58	122	2	27	2	0	0	2	5-0	0	21	.221	.252	.238	49	-8	0-1	.938	-1	111	56	3-38	-1.1
Total	6	125	251	12	54	6	1	4	13	10-0	2	42	.215	.250	.295	63	-14	0-3	.948	-4	105	41	/3-79,2-2	-2.1
KENWORTHY, BILL William Jennings "Duke" B 7.4.1886 Cambridge, OH D 9.21.1950 Eureka, CA BR/TR 5-7/165# d8.28																								
1912	Was A	12	38	6	9	1	0	0	2	2	1		.237	.293	.263	59	-2	3	1.000	1	80	263	O-12(7-5-0)	-0.2
1914	KC F	146	545	93	173	40	14	15	91	36	**11**	44	.317	.372	.525	148	26	37	.952	22	100	**143**	*2-145	5.1
1915	KC F	122	396	59	118	30	7	3	52	28	7	32	.298	.355	.432	126	7	20	.936	-4	97	93	*2-108/O-7(RF)	0.5
1917	StL A	5	10	1	1	0	0	0	1	1	0	1	.100	.182	.100	-14	-1	1	.889	1	118	226	/2-4	-0.1
Total	4	285	989	159	301	71	21	18	146	67	19	77	.304	.360	.473	135	30	61	.945	20	99	123	2-257/O-19(7-5-7)	5.3
KEOUGH, JOE Joseph William B 1.7.1946 Pomona, CA BL/TL 6/185# d8.7 b-Marty																								
1968	Oak A	34	98	7	21	2	1	2	18	8-0	0	11	.214	.274	.316	82	-2	1-0	.962	1	106	126	O-29(28-0-1)/1	-0.3
1969	KC A	70	166	17	31	2	0	0	7	13-0	2	13	.187	.254	.199	28	-16	5-2	1.000	-0	104	73	O-49(3-26-21)/1	-1.9
1970	KC A	57	183	28	59	6	2	4	21	23-3	0	18	.322	.396	.443	132	8	1-1	.985	0	102	91	O-34(18-1-15),1-18	0.5
1971	KC A	110	351	34	87	14	2	3	30	35-5	1	26	.248	.316	.325	83	-8	0-6	.982	-6	88	63	*O-100(1-7-93)	-2.2
1972	KC A	56	64	8	14	2	0	0	5	8-1	2	7	.219	.324	.250	73	-2	2-0	1.000	-1	58	125	O-16(9-2-5)	-0.4
1973	Chi A	5	1	1	0	0	0	0	0	0-0	0	0	.000	.000	.000	-97	0	0-0	—	0			H	0.0
Total	6	332	863	95	212	26	5	9	81	87-9	5	75	.246	.317	.319	82	-20	9-9	.984	-7	94	81	O-228(59-36-135)/1-20	-4.3
KEOUGH, MARTY Richard Martin B 4.14.1934 Oakland, CA BL/TL 6/180# d4.21 b-Joe s-Matt																								
1956	Bos A	3	2	1	0	0	0	0	1	1-0	0	0	.000	.333	.000	-5	0	0-0	—	0			H	0.0
1957	Bos A	9	17	1	1	0	0	0	0	4-0	0	3	.059	.238	.059	-14	-3	0-0	1.000	0	116	0	/O-7(0-2-5)	-0.3
1958	Bos A	68	118	21	26	3	3	1	9	7-0	0	29	.220	.262	.322	57	-7	1-1	.974	-3	86	0	O-25(1-21-3)/1-2	-1.2
1959	Bos A	96	251	40	61	13	5	7	27	26-0	3	40	.243	.320	.418	97	-1	3-1	.993	1	100	126	O-69(CF)/1-3	-0.3
1960	Bos A	38	105	15	26	6	1	1	9	8-1	0	8	.248	.296	.352	73	-4	2-2	1.000	1	96	198	O-29(1-28-0)	-0.5
	Cle A	65	149	19	37	5	0	3	11	9-0	1	23	.248	.294	.342	74	-6	2-3	.986	-1	99	104	O-42(2-25-16)	-0.8
	Year	103	254	34	63	11	1	4	20	17-1	1	31	.248	.295	.346	74	-10	4-5	.992	0	98	146	O-71(3-53-16)	-1.3
1961	Was A	135	390	57	97	18	9	9	34	32-1	2	60	.249	.307	.410	92	-6	12-5	.978	1	103	100	*O-100(63-25-18),1-10	-1.0
1962	Cin N	111	230	34	64	8	2	7	27	21-4	4	31	.278	.346	.422	102	1	3-1	.968	3	103	63	O-71(48-17-10),1-29	0.1
1963	Cin N	95	172	21	39	8	2	6	21	25-4	4	37	.227	.337	.401	109	3	1-4	.992	2	124	116	1-46,O-28(4-3-22)	0.1
1964	Cin N	109	276	29	71	9	1	9	28	22-1	1	58	.257	.314	.395	95	-2	1-2	.991	-1	97	93	O-81(1-11-71)/1-4	-0.8
1965	Cin N	62	43	14	5	0	0	0	3	3-0	1	14	.116	.191	.116	-10	-6	0-0	.988	0	103	67	1-32/O-4(3-0-1)	-0.7
1966	Atl N	17	17	1	1	0	0	0	1	1-0	0	6	.059	.111	.059	-50	-3	0-0	1.000	-1	0	0	/1-4,O-3(2-0-1)	-0.5
	Chi N	33	26	3	6	1	0	0	5	5-0	1	9	.231	.375	.269	82	0	1-0	1.000	-0	90	0	/O-5(2-2-1)	0.0
	Year	50	43	4	7	1	0	0	6	6-0	1	15	.163	.280	.186	32	-4	1-0	.667	-1	64	0	/O-8(4-2-2),1-4	-0.5
Total	11	841	1796	256	434	71	23	43	176	164-11	17	318	.242	.309	.379	86	-34	26-19	.984	2	100	94	O-464(127-203-148),1-130	-5.9
KERINS, JOHN John Nelson B 7.15.1858 Indianapolis, IN D 9.8.1919 Louisville, KY BR/TR 5-10/177# d5.1 M2 U3 OF Total (13-LF 9-CF 49-RF)																								
1884	Ind AA	94	364	58	78	10	3	6		6	1		.214	.229	.308	76	-10		**.972**	6	**142**	47	*1-87/C-5,O-5(0-2-3),3	-1.0
1885	Lou AA	**112**	456	65	111	9	16	3	51	20	4		.243	.281	.353	100	-2		.947	3	111	100	*1-96,C-19/O-3(RF),3	-0.5
1886	Lou AA	120	487	113	131	19	9	4	50	66	3		.269	.360	.370	122	13	26	.933	**28**			C-65,1-47/O-7(2-2-3),S	3.7
1887	Lou AA	112	476	101	140	18	19	5	57	38	2		.294	.349	.443	118	8	49	.970	14	78	79	1-74,C-35/O-5(1-1-3)	1.6
1888	Lou AA	83	319	38	75	11	4	2	41	25	3		.235	.297	.313	98	0	16	.844	-4	29	64	0-47(10-2-35),C-33/1-4,3-2,2M	-0.2
1889	Lou AA	2	9	2	3	1	0	0	3	0	0	1	.333	.333	.444	123	0	0	.500	-1	0	0	/O-2(RF),C	0.0
	Bal AA	16	53	7	15	2	0	0	12	2	1	4	.283	.321	.321	82	-1	2	.981	-1	131	28	/1-9,C-4,O-2(CF),S	-0.2
	Year	18	62	9	18	3	0	0	15	2	1	5	.290	.323	.339	87	-1	2	.981	-2	131	28	/1-9,C-5,O-4(0-2-2),S	-0.2

Year	Tm Lg	G	AB	R	H	2B	3B	HR	RBI	BB-IB	HP	SO	AVG	OBP	SLG	AOPS	ABR	SB-CS	FA	FR	Rng	Thr	G at Pos	BFW
1890	StL AA	18	63	8	8	2	0	0	3	8	0		.127	.225	.159	12	-7	2	.968	1	148	143	1-17/CM	-0.7
Total	7	557	2227	392	561	72	51	20	<u>217</u>	165	14	<u>5</u>	.252	.308	.357	102	1	95	.963	47			1-334,C-163/O-71R,3-4,S-2,2	2.7
KERLIN, ORIE Orie Milton "Cy" B 1.23.1891 Summerfield, LA D 10.29.1974 Shreveport, LA BL/TR 5-7/149# d6.6																								
1915	Pit F	3	1	0	0	0	0	0	0	0	0	0	.000	.000	.000	-99	0	0	—	-0	*0*	*0*	/C-3	0.0
KERN, BILL William George B 2.28.1933 Coplay, PA BR/TR 6-2/184# d9.19																								
1962	KC A	8	16	1	4	0	0	1	1	0-0	0	3	.250	.250	.438	77	-1	0-0	1.000	1	56	1312	/O-3(LF)	0.0
KERNAN, JOE Joseph B Baltimore, MD d4.14																								
1873	Mar NA	2	8	1	3	0	0	0	1	0		0	.375	.375	.375	161	1	0-0	.700	0	126	0	/2O(CF)	0.0
KERNEK, GEORGE George Boyd B 1.12.1940 Holdenville, OK BL/TL 6-3/170# d9.5																								
1965	StL N	10	31	6	9	3	1	0	3	2-0	0	4	.290	.333	.452	109	0	0-0	.972	-0	104	160	/1-7	0.0
1966	StL N	20	50	5	12	0	1	0	3	4-0	1	9	.240	.309	.280	65	-2	1-0	.984	0	105	143	1-16	-0.3
Total	2	30	81	11	21	3	2	0	6	6-0	1	13	.259	.318	.346	82	-2	1-0	.980	-0	105	149	/1-23	-0.3
KERNS, RUSS Russell Eldon B 11.10.1920 Fremont, OH D 8.21.2000 Placerville, CA BL/TR 6/188# d8.18																								
1945	Det A	1	1	0	0	0	0	0	0	0	0	0	.000	.000	.000	-94	0	0-0	—	0			H	0.0
KERR, JOHN John Francis B 11.26.1898 San Francisco, CA D 10.19.1993 Long Beach, CA BR/TR (BB 1923-24) 5-8/158# d5.1 C1																								
1923	Det A	19	42	4	9	1	0	0	1	4	0	5	.214	.283	.238	39	-4	0-0	.877	1	120	81	S-15	-0.2
1924	Det A	17	11	3	3	0	0	0	1	0	0	0	.273	.273	.273	42	-1	0-0	—	0	0	0	/3-3,O-2	-0.1
1929	Chi A	127	419	50	108	20	4	1	39	31	1	24	.258	.310	.332	66	-22	9-8	.971	17	**113**	110	*2-122/S	-0.2
1930	Chi A	70	266	37	77	11	6	3	27	21	4	23	.289	.351	.410	95	-2	4-2	.980	-1	100	100	2-52,S-20	0.0
1931	Chi A	128	444	51	119	17	2	2	50	35	2	22	.268	.324	.329	77	-15	9-3	.968	1	102	103	*2-117/3-7,S	-0.6
1932	Was A	51	132	14	36	6	1	0	15	13	0	3	.273	.338	.333	75	-5	3-2	.954	-2	96	81	2-17,S-14/3-8	-0.5
1933	†Was A	28	40	5	8	0	0	0	0	3	0	2	.200	.256	.200	22	-5	0-0	.966	1	112	84	2-16/3	-0.3
1934	Was A	31	103	8	28	4	0	0	12	8	0	13	.272	.324	.311	67	-5	1-1	.971	4	131	116	3-17,2-13	0.0
Total	8	471	1457	172	388	59	13	6	145	115	7	92	.266	.323	.337	73	-59	26-16	.970	21	105	103	2-337/S-51,3-36,O-2	-1.9
KERR, DOC John Jonas B 1.17.1882 Dellroy, OH D 6.9.1937 Baltimore, MD BB/TR 5-10.5/190# d4.22																								
1914	Pit F	42	71	3	17	4	2	1	7	10	0	13	.239	.333	.394	99	-1	0	.970	0	*105*	*111*	C-18	0.0
	Bal F	14	34	4	9	1	1	0	1	1	0	6	.265	.286	.353	71	-2	1	.979	2	*137*	*81*	C-13/1	0.1
	Year	56	105	7	26	5	3	1	8	11	0	19	.248	.319	.381	90	-3	1	.974	3	*118*	*98*	C-31/1	0.1
1915	Bal F	3	6	1	2	0	0	0	0	1	0	0	.333	.429	.333	112	0	0	1.000	-1	*83*	*75*	/C-2,1	-0.1
Total	2	59	111	8	28	5	3	1	8	12	0	19	.252	.325	.378	91	-3	1	.975	2	*117*	*97*	/C-33,1-2	0.0
KERR, BUDDY John Joseph B 11.6.1922 Astoria, NY BR/TR 6-2/180# d9.8																								
1943	NY N	27	98	14	28	3	0	2	12	8	2	5	.286	.352	.378	110	1	1	.955	3	103	57	S-27	0.6
1944	NY N	150	548	68	146	31	4	9	63	37	3	32	.266	.316	.387	97	-3	14	.954	**19**	**106**	90	*S-149	2.8
1945	NY N	149	546	53	136	20	3	4	40	41	2	34	.249	.304	.319	72	-21	5	.964	**30**	**111**	101	*S-148	2.1
1946	NY N	145	497	50	124	20	3	6	40	53	2	31	.249	.324	.338	87	-8	7	**.982**	8	101	83	*S-126,3-18	0.8
1947	NY N	138	547	73	157	23	5	7	49	36	0	49	.287	.331	.386	89	-10	2	.977	12	**106**	88	*S-138	1.1
1948	NY N★	144	496	41	119	16	4	0	46	56	0	36	.240	.317	.288	64	-24	9	.967	4	106	88	*S-143	-1.1
1949	NY N	90	220	16	46	4	0	0	19	21	2	23	.209	.284	.227	39	-19	0	.959	3	106	85	S-89	-1.1
1950	Bos N	155	507	45	115	24	6	2	46	50	0	50	.227	.296	.310	64	-27	0	.965	2	100	96	*S-155	-1.6
1951	Bos N	69	172	18	32	4	0	1	18	22	1	20	.186	.282	.227	41	-14	0-0	.969	7	107	86	S-63/2-5	-0.3
Total	9	1067	3631	378	903	145	25	31	333	324	12	280	.249	.312	.328	76	-125	38-<u>0</u>	.967	89	105	90	*S-1038/3-18,2-5	3.3
KERR, MEL John Melville B 5.22.1903 Souris, MB, CAN D 8.9.1980 Vero Beach, FL BL/TL 5-11.5/155# d9.16																								
1925	Chi N	1	0	1	0	0	0	0	0	0	0	0	—	—	—	—	0	0-0	—	0			R	0.0
KERWIN, DAN Daniel Patrick (born Daniel Patrick Kervin) B 7.9.1879 Philadelphia, PA D 7.13.1960 Philadelphia, PA BL/TL 5-9/164# d9.27																								
1903	Cin N	2	6	1	4	1	0	0	1	2	1		.667	.778	.833	323	2	0	.500	-1	0	0	/O-2(LF)	0.1
KESSINGER, DON Donald Eulon B 7.17.1942 Forrest City, AR BB/TR (BR 1964-65) 6-1/175# d9.7 M1 s-Keith																								
1964	Chi N	4	12	1	2	0	0	0	0	0-0	0	1	.167	.167	.167	-6	-2	0-0	1.000	-0	101	73	/S-4	-0.2
1965	Chi N	106	309	19	62	4	3	0	14	20-1	2	44	.201	.252	.233	37	-26	1-2	.948	13	114	114	*S-105	-0.6
1966	Chi N	150	533	50	146	8	2	1	43	26-5	0	46	.274	.306	.302	70	-22	13-7	.951	-15	101	75	*S-148	-2.5
1967	Chi N	145	580	61	134	10	7	0	42	33-1	4	80	.231	.275	.272	55	-34	6-13	.973	-4	102	97	*S-143	-3.2
1968	Chi N★	160	655	63	157	14	7	1	32	38-1	2	86	.240	.283	.287	67	-26	9-9	.962	**24**	111	111	*S-159	1.1
1969	Chi N★	158	664	109	181	38	6	4	53	61-4	1	70	.273	.332	.366	85	-11	11-8	**.976**	**25**	109	112	*S-157	3.3
1970	Chi N★	154	631	100	168	21	14	1	39	66-6	2	59	.266	.337	.349	75	-22	12-6	.972	12	103	98	*S-154	0.9
1971	Chi N★	155	617	77	159	18	6	2	38	52-6	3	54	.258	.318	.316	70	-23	15-8	.966	11	103	103	*S-154	0.7
1972	Chi N★	149	577	77	158	20	6	1	39	67-8	2	44	.274	.351	.334	87	-8	8-7	.965	17	**110**	106	*S-146	2.8
1973	Chi N	160	577	52	151	22	3	0	43	57-18	0	44	.262	.327	.310	72	-20	6-6	.964	**27**	**110**	114	*S-158	2.6
1974	Chi N★	153	599	83	155	20	7	1	42	62-7	4	54	.259	.332	.321	80	-15	7-7	.958	7	103	91	*S-150	0.9
1975	Chi N	154	601	77	146	26	10	0	46	68-2	1	47	.243	.317	.319	75	-20	4-7	.967	7	102	112	*S-140,3-13	0.2
1976	StL N	145	502	55	120	22	6	1	40	61-5	1	51	.239	.320	.313	80	-12	3-0	.969	-2	98	**120**	*S-113,2-31/3-2	0.2
1977	StL N	59	134	14	32	4	0	0	7	14-1	0	26	.239	.309	.269	58	-8	0-0	.978	4	98	155	S-26,2-24/3-4	-0.1
	Chi A	39	119	12	28	3	2	0	11	13-2	0	7	.235	.308	.294	66	-6	2-1	.959	-6	69	104	S-21,2-13/3-9	-0.9
1978	Chi A	131	431	35	110	18	1	1	31	36-1	0	34	.255	.312	.309	75	-14	2-4	.974	-18	91	85	*S-123/2-9	-2.2
1979	Chi A	56	110	14	22	6	0	1	7	10-1	0	12	.200	.264	.282	48	-8	1-0	.988	-9	84	65	S-54/12M	-1.2
Total	16	2078	7651	899	1931	254	80	14	527	684-69	22	759	.252	.314	.312	72	-277	100-85	.966	93	104	102	*S-1955/2-78,3-28,1	1.8
KESSINGER, KEITH Robert Keith B 2.19.1967 Forrest City, AR BB/TR 6-2/185# d9.15 f-Don																								
1993	Cin N	11	27	4	7	1	0	1	3	4-0	0	4	.259	.344	.407	103	0	0-0	.935	-2	91	100	S-11	-0.1
KESSLER, HENRY Henry "Lucky" B 1847 Brooklyn, NY D 1.9.1900 Franklin, PA BR/TR 5-10/144# d8.4																								
1873	Atl NA	1	5	0	1	0	0	0	1	0		0	.200	.200	.200	21	0	0-0	.882	0	355	0	/1	0.0
1874	Atl NA	14	56	8	17	1	0	0	4	0		2	.304	.304	.321	114	1	0-0	.737	-4			/C-9,2-4,O-4(2-2-0),3	-0.2
1875	Atl NA	25	105	17	26	2	0	0	7	1		2	.248	.255	.267	93	0	0-2	.794	-3	107	29	S-18/O-7(0-4-3),C-3,12	-0.3
1876	Cin N	59	248	26	64	5	0	0	11	7		10	.258	.278	.278	100	2		.788	-8	85	106	S-46,O-16(0-2-14)	-0.3
1877	Cin N	6	20	0	2	0	0	0	0	2		1	.100	.182	.100	-10	-2		.500	-5			/C-5,1	-0.7
Total	3 NA	40	166	25	44	3	0	0	12	1		4	.265	.269	.283	98	1	0-2	.794	-7			/S-18,C-12,O-11(2-6-3),2-5,1-2,3	-0.5
Total	2	65	268	26	66	5	0	0	11	9		11	.246	.271	.265	91	0		.794	-13			/S-46,O-16(0-2-14),C-5,1	-1.0
KETCHUM, FRED Frederick L. B 7.27.1875 Elmira, NY D 3.12.1908 Cortland, NY BL/TR 5-8/157# d9.12																								
1899	Lou N	15	61	13	18	1	0	0	5	0	1		.295	.306	.311	70	-3	2	1.000	-2	0	0	O-15(4-1-10)	-0.5
1901	Phi A	5	22	5	5	0	0	0	2	0	0		.227	.227	.227	25	-2	0	.875	-1	0	0	/O-5(LF)	-0.3
Total	2	20	83	18	23	1	0	0	7	0	1		.277	.286	.289	58	-5	2	.960	-3	0	0	/O-20(9-1-10)	-0.8
KETTER, PHIL Philip (born Philip Ketterer) B 4.13.1884 St.Louis, MO D 4.9.1965 St.Louis, MO TR d5.23																								
1912	StL A	2	6	1	2	0	0	0	0	0	0		.333	.333	.333	94	0	0	1.000	-1	*68*	*121*	/C-2	-0.1
KHALIFA, SAMMY Sam B 12.5.1963 Fontana, CA BR/TR 5-11/170# d6.25																								
1985	Pit N	95	320	30	76	14	3	2	31	34-8	0	56	.237	.307	.319	77	-10	5-2	.967	9	106	75	S-95	1.0
1986	Pit N	64	151	8	28	6	0	0	4	19-6	0	28	.185	.276	.225	39	-12	0-2	.961	6	112	87	S-60/2-6	-0.2
1987	Pit N	5	17	1	3	0	0	0	2	0-0	0	2	.176	.176	.176	-6	-3	0-0	.917	-4	43	37	/S-5	-0.7
Total	3	164	488	39	107	20	3	2	37	53-14	0	86	.219	.294	.285	62	-25	5-4	.964	11	106	78	S-160/2-6	0.1
KIBBIE, HOD Horace Kent B 7.18.1903 Ft.Worth, TX D 10.19.1975 Ft.Worth, TX BR/TR 5-10/150# d6.13																								
1925	Bos N	11	41	5	11	2	0	0	2	5	0	6	.268	.348	.317	78	-1	0-0	.904	-2	95	38	/2-8,S-3	-0.2
KIBBLE, JACK John Westly "Happy" B 1.2.1892 Seatonville, IL D 12.13.1969 Roundup, MT BB/TR 5-9.5/154# d9.10																								
1912	Cle A	5	8	1	0	0	0	0	0	0	1		.000	.111	.000	-65	-2	0	1.000	2	171	721	/3-4,2	0.1
KIEFER, STEVE Steven George B 10.18.1960 Chicago, IL BR/TR 6-1/180# d9.3 b-Mark																								
1984	Oak A	23	40	7	7	1	2	0	2	2-0	0	10	.175	.209	.300	43	-3	2-1	.904	-4	92	61	S-17/3-2,D-3	-0.6

Year	Tm Lg	G	AB	R	H	2B	3B	HR	RBI	BB-IB	HP	SO	AVG	OBP	SLG	AOPS	ABR	SB-CS	FA	FR	Rng	Thr	G at Pos	BFW
1985	Oak A	40	66	8	13	1	1	1	10	1-0	0	18	.197	.203	.288	37	-6	0-0	.881	-4	88	119	3-34/D-2	-1.0
1986	Mil A	2	6	0	0	0	0	0	0	0-0	0	4	.000	.000	.000	-97	-2	0-0	1.000	2	155	175	/S-2	0.1
1987	Mil A	28	99	17	20	4	0	5	17	7-0	1	28	.202	.257	.394	69	-5	0-0	.966	-4	84	62	3-26/2-4	-0.8
1988	Mil A	7	10	2	3	1	0	1	1	2-0	1	3	.300	.462	.700	219	2	0-0	1.000	0	151	206	/2-4,3-4	0.2
1989	NY A	5	8	0	1	0	0	0	0	0-0	0	5	.125	.125	.125	-30	-1	0-0	1.000	-1	24	0	/3-5	-0.3
Total	6	105	229	34	44	7	3	7	30	12-0	2	68	.192	.234	.341	56	-15	2-1	.920	-10	82	80	/3-71,S-19,2-8,D-5	-2.4
KIELTY, BOBBY Robert Michael B 8.5.1976 Fontana, CA BB/TR 6-1/215# d4.10																								
2001	Min A	37	104	8	26	8	0	2	14	8-2	1	25	.250	.297	.385	80	-3	3-0	.956	-1	95	107	O-34(11-11-17)/D	-0.4
2002	†Min A	112	289	49	84	14	3	12	46	52-4	5	66	.291	.405	.484	134	17	4-1	1.000	0	102	95	O-82(9-34-50)/D-11,1-5	1.4
2003	Min A	75	238	40	60	13	0	9	32	42-2	3	56	.252	.370	.420	107	4	6-2	.972	-2	94	50	O-36(1-2-33),D-32	-0.1
	Tor A	62	189	31	44	13	1	4	25	29-4	4	36	.233	.342	.376	89	-2	2-1	.989	-3	87	69	O-60(3-1-56)/1-3	-0.7
	Year	137	427	71	104	26	1	13	57	71-6	7	92	.244	.358	.400	99	2	8-3	.981	-5	90	61	O-96(4-3-89),D-32/1-3	-0.8
Total	3	286	820	128	214	48	4	27	117	131-12	13	183	.261	.367	.428	109	16	15-4	.985	-5	95	81	O-212(24-48-156)/D-44,1-8	0.2
KIENZLE, BILL William H. B Philadelphia, PA BL/TL d9.15																								
1882	Phi AA	9	33	8	11	3	2	0	9	5			.333	.421	.545	210	4		.842	-1	47	0	/O-9(CF)	0.2
1884	Phi U	**67**	299	76	76	13	8	0		21			.254	.303	.351	106	-7		.772	-5	107	62	O-67(CF)	-1.3
Total	2	76	332	84	87	16	10	0	9	26			.262	.316	.370	116	-3		.781	-7	100	55	/O-76(CF)	-1.1
KIESCHNICK, BROOKS Michael Brooks B 6.6.1972 Robstown, TX BL/TR 6-4/225# d4.3 ▲																								
1996	Chi N	25	29	6	10	2	0	1	6	3-0	0	8	.345	.406	.517	138	2	0-0	.833	-1	68	0	/O-8(4-0-5)	0.1
1997	Chi N	39	90	9	18	2	0	4	12	12-0	0	21	.200	.294	.356	67	-5	1-0	.952	0	104	76	O-27(26-0-1)	-0.5
2000	Cin N	14	12	0	0	0	0	0	0	1-0	0	5	.000	.077	.000	-77	-3	0-0	1.000	0	0	0	/1	-0.3
2001	Col N	35	42	5	10	2	1	3	9	3-0	0	13	.238	.289	.548	89	-1	0-0	.818	-1	106	0	O-12(8-0-4)/1	-0.2
2003	Mil N	70	70	12	21	1	0	7	12	6-0	0	13	.300	.355	.614	149	4	0-0	1.000	0	145	346	P-42/O-3(LF),D-4	0.1
Total	5	183	243	32	59	7	1	15	39	25-0	0	60	.243	.313	.465	95	-3	1-0	.903	-1	94	48	/O-50(41-0-10),P-42,D-4,1-2	-0.8
KILDUFF, PETE Peter John B 4.4.1893 Weir City, KS D 2.14.1930 Pittsburg, KS BR/TR 5-7/155# d4.18 Mil 1918																								
1917	NY N	31	78	12	16	3	0	1	12	4	1	11	.205	.253	.282	66	-3	2	.954	-1	97	160	2-21/S-5,3	-0.5
	Chi N	56	202	23	56	9	5	0	15	12	2	19	.277	.324	.371	105	1	11	.920	-14	76	83	S-51/2-5	-1.1
	Year	87	280	35	72	12	5	1	27	16	3	30	.257	.304	.346	95	-2	13	.917	-15	77	79	S-56,2-26/3	-1.6
1918	Chi N	30	93	7	19	2	2	0	13	7	1	7	.204	.267	.269	62	-4	1	.935	-4	82	162	2-30	-0.8
1919	Chi N	31	88	5	24	4	2	0	8	10	2	5	.273	.360	.364	117	2	1	.974	-3	105	129	3-14/2-8,S-7	0.1
	Bro N	32	73	9	22	3	1	0	8	12	1	11	.301	.407	.370	132	4	5	.862	-4	91	134	3-26/2	0.1
	Year	63	161	14	46	7	3	0	16	22	3	16	.286	.382	.366	124	6	6	.903	-7	96	132	3-40/2-9,S-7	0.2
1920	†Bro N	141	478	62	130	26	8	0	58	58	0	43	.272	.351	.360	101	3	2-9	.967	7	101	**111**	*2-134/3-5	1.1
1921	Bro N	107	372	45	107	15	10	3	45	31	1	36	.288	.344	.406	94	-3	6-6	.963	12	**106**	107	*2-105/3	1.0
Total	5	428	1384	163	374	62	28	4	159	134	8	132	.270	.338	.364	98	0	28-15	.963	-7	101	117	2-304/S-63,3-47	-0.1
KILEY, JOHN John Frederick B 7.1.1859 Dedham, MA D 12.18.1940 Norwood, MA BL/TL 5-7/147# d5.1																								
1884	Was AA	14	56	9	12	2	2	0		3	1		.214	.267	.321	103	0		.571	-3	36	0	O-14(13-1-1)	-0.3
1891	Bos N	1	2	0	0	0	0	0	0	1	1	1	.000	.500	.000	45	0	0	1.000	0	121	0	/P	0.0
Total	2	15	58	9	12	2	2	0	0	4	2	1	.207	.281	.310	102	0	0	.571	-3	36	0	/O-14(13-1-1),P	-0.3
KILHULLEN, PAT Joseph Isadore B 8.10.1890 Carbondale, PA D 11.2.1922 Oakland, CA BR/TR 5-9/175# d6.10																								
1914	Pit N	1	1	0	0	0	0	0	0	0	0	0	.000	.000	.000	-99	0	0	—	-0	*0*	*0*	/C	0.0
KILLEBREW, HARMON Harmon Clayton "Killer" B 6.29.1936 Payette, ID BR/TR 5-11/213# d6.23 HF1984 OF Total (470-LF 1-RF)																								
1954	Was A	9	13	1	4	1	0	0	3	2	0	3	.308	.400	.385	122	1	0-0	1.000	-1	47	0	/2-3	0.0
1955	Was A	38	80	12	16	1	0	4	7	9-0	0	31	.200	.281	.363	76	-3	0-0	.935	2	112	67	3-23/2-3	-0.1
1956	Was A	44	99	10	22	2	0	5	13	10-0	0	39	.222	.291	.394	80	-3	0-0	.951	-0	106	72	3-20/2-4	-0.4
1957	Was A	9	31	4	9	2	0	2	5	2-0	0	8	.290	.333	.548	139	1	0-0	.947	-0	116	141	/3-7,2	0.1
1958	Was A	13	31	2	6	0	0	0	2	0-0	1	12	.194	.212	.194	15	-4	0-0	1.000	-0	92	63	/3-9	-0.4
1959	Was A★	153	546	98	132	20	2	**42**	105	90-1	7	116	.242	.354	.516	137	28	3-2	.938	-3	105	65	*3-150/O-4(LF)	2.4
1960	Was A	124	442	84	122	19	1	31	80	71-3	1	106	.276	.375	.534	145	28	1-0	.987	-10	73	109	1-71,3-65	1.5
1961	Min A★	150	541	94	156	20	7	46	122	107-6	3	109	.288	.405	.606	159	47	1-2	.987	-8	86	92	*1-119,3-45/O-2(LF)	3.0
1962	Min A	155	552	85	134	21	1	**48**	**126**	106-6	4	142	.243	.366	.545	137	30	1-2	.967	-4	93	68	*O-151(LF)/1-4	1.8
1963	Min A★	142	515	88	133	18	0	**45**	96	72-4	3	105	.258	.349	**.555**	147	32	0-0	.987	-1	93	80	*O-137(LF)	2.4
1964	Min A★	158	577	95	156	11	1	**49**	111	93-5	**8**	135	.270	.377	.548	153	43	0-0	.971	-10	89	13	*O-157(157-0-1)	2.5
1965	†Min A★	113	401	78	108	16	1	25	75	72-12	4	69	.269	.384	.501	144	25	0-0	.988	-7	78	119	1-72,3-44/O(LF)	1.5
1966	Min A★	**162**	569	89	160	27	1	39	110	**103-18**	2	98	.281	.391	.538	155	44	0-2	.951	-13	90	67	*3-107,1-42,O-18(LF)	2.8
1967	Min A★	163	547	105	147	24	1	**44**	113	**131-15**	3	111	.269	.408	.558	170	54	1-0	.992	-6	84	93	*1-160/3-3	4.2
1968	Min A★	100	295	40	62	7	2	17	40	70-9	2	70	.210	.361	.420	131	14	0-0	.994	5	128	95	1-77,3-11	1.6
1969	†Min A★	**162**	555	106	153	20	2	**49**	**140**	**145-20**	5	84	.276	**.427**	.584	177	64	8-2	.929	-14	97	67	*3-105,1-80	4.7
1970	†Min A★	157	527	96	143	20	1	41	113	128-23	2	84	.271	.411	.546	161	49	0-3	.948	-25	79	59	*3-138,1-28	2.2
1971	Min A★	147	500	61	127	19	1	28	**119**	**114**-14	0	96	.254	.386	.464	137	30	3-2	.997	-12	109	74	1-90,3-64	1.2
1972	Min A	139	433	53	100	13	2	26	74	94-12	1	91	.231	.367	.450	136	23	0-1	.992	11	**140**	92	*1-130	2.7
1973	Min A	69	248	29	60	9	1	5	32	41-2	1	59	.242	.352	.347	94	-1	0-0	.998	5	130	93	1-57/D-9	0.0
1974	Min A	122	333	28	74	7	0	13	54	45-6	0	61	.222	.312	.360	91	-4	0-0	.992	2	131	93	D-57,1-33	-0.5
1975	KC A	106	312	25	62	13	0	14	44	54-4	1	70	.199	.317	.375	93	-2	1-2	1.000	-1	0	126	D-92/1-6	-0.6
Total	22	2435	8147	1283	2086	290	24	573	1584	1559-160	48	1699	.256	.376	.509	142	496	19-18	.992	-90	97	96	1-969,3-791,O-470L,D-158/2-11	32.6
KILLEFER, RED Wade Hampton B 4.13.1885 Bloomingdale, MI D 9.4.1958 Los Angeles, CA BR/TR 5-9/175# d9.16 b-Bill OF Total (135-LF 135-CF 27-RF)																								
1907	Det A	1	4	0	0	0	0	0	0	0	0		.000	.000	.000	-97	-1	0	1.000	0	0	0	/O(RF)	-0.1
1908	Det A	28	75	9	16	1	0	0	11	3	1		.213	.253	.227	54	-4	4	.956	-5	90	171	2-16/S-7,3-4	-1.0
1909	Det A	23	61	6	17	2	2	1	4	3	3		.279	.343	.426	137	2	2	.912	-1	115	53	2-17/O(RF)	0.1
	Was A	40	121	11	21	1	0	0	5	13	2		.174	.265	.182	43	-7	4	.957	-4	36	0	O-24(6-17-1)/3-6,C-3,2-3,S	-1.4
	Year	63	182	17	38	3	2	1	9	16	5		.209	.291	.264	76	-5	6	.957	-5	36	0	O-25(6-17-2),2-20/3-6,C-3,S	-1.3
1910	Was A	106	345	35	79	17	1	0	24	29	**16**		.229	.318	.284	93	0	17	.940	-4	97	94	2-88,O-12(6-0-6)	-0.5
1914	Cin N	42	141	16	39	6	1	0	12	20	5	18	.277	.386	.333	111	3	11	.968	-4	80	103	O-37(1-18-18)/2-5,3	-0.3
1915	Cin N	155	555	75	151	25	11	1	41	38	**19**	33	.272	.340	.362	110	8	12-18	.970	1	102	93	*O-150(79-73-0)/1-2	-0.4
1916	Cin N	70	234	29	57	9	1	1	18	21	8	8	.244	.327	.303	96	0	7	.966	-0	102	83	O-68(43-27-0)	-0.4
	NY N	2	1	0	1	0	0	0	1	1	0	0	1.000	1.000	1.000	544	1	0	—	0			H	0.1
	Year	72	235	29	58	9	1	1	19	22	8	8	.247	.332	.306	99	1	7	.966	-0	102	83	O-68(43-27-0)	-0.3
Total	7	467	1537	181	381	61	16	3	116	128	54	59	.248	.328	.314	98	2	57-18	.965	-18	93	88	O-293L,2-129/3-11,S-8,C-3,1-2	-3.9
KILLEFER, BILL William Lavier "Reindeer Bill" B 10.10.1887 Bloomingdale, MI D 7.3.1960 Elsmere, DE BR/TR 5-10.5/170# d9.13 M9 C6 b-Red																								
1909	StL A	11	29	0	4	0	0	0	1	0	0		.138	.138	.138	-14	-4	2	.905	0	*99*	*166*	C-11	-0.3
1910	StL A	74	193	14	24	2	2	0	7	12	2		.124	.184	.155	7	-21	0	.938	3	*89*	*124*	C-73	-1.3
1911	Phi N	6	16	3	3	0	0	0	2	0	0	2	.188	.188	.188	5	-2	0	.975	1	*91*	*137*	/C-6	-0.1
1912	Phi N	85	268	18	60	6	3	1	21	4	2	14	.224	.241	.280	40	-24	6	.973	11	*92*	*118*	C-85	-0.6
1913	Phi N	120	360	25	88	14	3	0	24	4	1	17	.244	.255	.300	56	-22	2-4	.988	8	111	**117**	*C-118/1	-0.5
1914	Phi N	98	299	27	70	10	1	0	27	8	3	17	.234	.261	.274	56	-17	3	.978	4	*77*	*117*	C-90	-0.5
1915	†Phi N	105	320	26	76	9	2	0	24	18	4	14	.237	.287	.278	70	-12	5-3	.972	10	*117*	*97*	*C-104	0.8
1916	Phi N	97	286	22	62	5	4	3	27	8	3	14	.217	.246	.294	63	-14	2	**.985**	-1	111	92	C-91	-0.8
1917	Phi N	125	409	28	112	12	0	0	31	15	4	21	.274	.306	.303	84	-8	4	**.984**	11	*119*	*89*	*C-120/O(LF)	1.5
1918	†Chi N	104	331	30	77	10	3	0	22	17	3	10	.233	.276	.281	68	-13	5	.982	7	*110*	*95*	*C-104	0.4
1919	Chi N	103	315	17	90	10	2	0	22	15	2	8	.286	.322	.330	96	-2	5	**.987**	14	*107*	*95*	*C-100	2.3
1920	Chi N	62	191	16	42	7	1	0	16	8	8	5	.220	.280	.267	56	-10	2-2	.977	12	*114*	*117*	C-61	0.8
1921	Chi N	45	133	11	43	1	0	0	16	4	3	4	.323	.357	.331	83	-3	3-3	.964	-1	*98*	*103*	C-42,M	-0.2
Total	13	1035	3150	237	751	86	21	4	240	113	35	126	.238	.273	.283	63	-152	39-12	.976	79	*105*	*105*	*C-1005/O(LF)1	1.5
KIMBALL, GENE Eugene Boynton B 8.31.1850 Rochester, NY D 8.2.1882 Rochester, NY 5-10/160# d5.4																								
1871	Cle NA	**29**	131	18	25	1	0	0	9	3		2	.191	.209	.198	19	-13	5-1	.743	-7	83	59	2-17/O-9(2-1-7),S-6,3-2	-1.3

Year	Tm Lg	G	AB	R	H	2B	3B	HR	RBI	BB-IB	HP	SO	AVG	OBP	SLG	AOPS	ABR	SB-CS	FA	FR	Rng	Thr	G at Pos	BFW
KIMBLE, DICK Richard Lewis B 7.27.1915 Buchtel, OH D 5.7.2001 Toledo, OH BL/TR 5-9/160# d8.20																								
1945	Was A	20	49	5	12	1	1	0	1	5	0	2	.245	.315	.306	88	-1	0-0	.950	-3	96	69	S-15	-0.3
KIMM, BRUCE Bruce Edward B 6.29.1951 Cedar Rapids, IA BR/TR 5-11/175# d5.4 M1 C12																								
1976	Det A	63	152	13	40	8	0	1	6	15-0	0	20	.263	.329	.336	91	-1	4-3	.970	2	113	139	C-61/D-2	0.3
1977	Det A	14	25	2	2	1	0	0	1	0-0	1	4	.080	.115	.120	-34	-5	0-1	.958	-1	110	85	C-12/D-2	-0.6
1979	Chi N	9	11	0	1	0	0	0	0	0-0	0	0	.091	.091	.091	-46	-2	0-1	.969	1	69	72	/C-9	-0.2
1980	Chi A	100	251	20	61	10	1	0	19	17-0	0	26	.243	.290	.291	60	-14	1-3	.985	-3	107	84	C-98	-1.4
Total	4	186	439	35	104	19	1	1	26	32-0	1	50	.237	.290	.292	62	-22	5-8	.977	-1	108	104	C-180/D-4	-1.9
KIMMICK, WALLY Walter Lyons B 5.30.1897 Turtle Creek, PA D 7.24.1989 Boswell, PA BR/TR 5-11/174# d9.13																								
1919	StL N	2	1	1	0	0	0	0	0	1	0	0	.000	.500	.000	61	0	1	1.000	0	130	0	/S	0.0
1921	Cin N	3	6	0	1	0	0	0	1	0	0	1	.167	.167	.167	-12	-1	0-0	.667	-0	94	359	/3-2	-0.1
1922	Cin N	39	89	11	22	2	1	0	12	3	0	12	.247	.272	.292	46	-7	0-0	.965	2	109	109	S-30/2-3,3	-0.3
1923	Cin N	29	80	11	18	2	1	0	6	5	0	15	.225	.271	.275	45	-7	3-0	.972	6	127	78	2-17/3-4,S	0.1
1925	Phi N	70	141	16	43	3	2	1	10	22	0	26	.305	.399	.376	91	-1	0-3	.904	-3	106	51	S-28,3-21,2-13	-0.2
1926	Phi N	20	28	0	6	2	1	0	2	3	0	7	.214	.290	.357	70	-1	0	1.000	-2	0	0	/1-5,S-4,3-4,2	-0.3
Total	6	163	345	39	90	9	5	1	31	34	0	61	.261	.327	.325	67	-17	4-3	.933	3	107	84	/S-64,2-34,3-32,1-5	-0.8
KINDALL, JERRY Gerald Donald "Slim" B 5.27.1935 St.Paul, MN BR/TR (BB 1960 (part)) 6-2.5/175# d7.1																								
1956	Chi N	32	55	7	9	1	1	0	0	6-1	0	17	.164	.246	.218	27	-6	1-0	.956	0	102	101	S-18	-0.4
1957	Chi N	72	181	18	29	3	0	6	12	8-0	0	48	.160	.196	.276	25	-20	1-0	.920	-5	96	46	2-28,3-19/S-9	-2.4
1958	Chi N	3	6	0	1	1	0	0	0	0-0	0	3	.167	.167	.333	29	-1	0-0	1.000	1	104	154	/2-3	0.0
1960	Chi N	89	246	17	59	16	2	2	23	5-3	0	52	.240	.253	.346	63	-13	4-3	.966	10	119	103	2-82/S-2	0.2
1961	Chi N	96	310	37	75	22	3	9	44	18-0	2	89	.242	.288	.419	84	-8	2-2	.950	1	97	105	2-50,S-47	-0.1
1962	Cle A	154	530	51	123	21	1	13	55	45-9	0	107	.232	.290	.349	74	-21	4-3	.978	19	**111**	111	*2-154	1.2
1963	Cle A	86	234	27	48	4	1	5	20	18-0	2	71	.205	.266	.295	58	-14	3-1	.958	-6	85	68	S-46,2-37/1-4	-1.4
1964	Cle A	23	25	5	9	1	0	2	2	2-0	0	7	.360	.407	.640	188	3	0-0	.989	2	202	101	1-23	0.5
	Min A	62	128	8	19	2	0	1	6	7-1	1	44	.148	.199	.188	8	-16	0-0	.969	1	106	80	2-51/S-7,1	-1.3
	Year	85	153	13	28	3	0	3	8	9-1	1	51	.183	.233	.261	37	-13	0-0	.969	3	106	80	2-51,1-24/S-7	-0.8
1965	Min A	125	342	41	67	12	1	6	36	36-3	3	97	.196	.274	.289	59	-18	2-2	.963	-2	100	106	*2-106,3-10/S-7	-1.3
Total	9	742	2057	211	439	83	9	44	198	145-17	8	535	.213	.266	.327	62	-114	17-11	.967	21	107	101	2-511,S-136/3-29,1-28	-5.0
KINER, RALPH Ralph McPherran B 10.27.1922 Santa Rita, NM BR/TR 6-2/195# d4.16 HF1975																								
1946	Pit N	144	502	63	124	17	3	**23**	81	74	1	109	.247	.345	.430	116	10	3	.969	-5	102	47	*O-140(64-76-0)	-0.1
1947	Pit N	152	565	118	177	23	4	**51**	127	98	2	81	.313	.417	**.639**	**172**	**58**	1	.983	8	**115**	69	*O-152(LF)	**5.3**
1948	Pit N★	**156**	555	104	147	19	5	**40**	123	112	3	61	.265	.391	.533	145	37	1	.975	3	**111**	47	*O-154(LF)	2.7
1949	Pit N★	152	549	116	170	19	5	**54**	**127**	**117**	1	61	.310	.432	**.658**	**183**	**67**	6	.979	-3	94	95	*O-152(LF)	**5.1**
1950	Pit N★	150	547	112	149	21	6	**47**	118	122	3	79	.272	.408	.590	154	45	2	.965	-5	89	115	*O-150(LF)	2.8
1951	Pit N★	151	531	**124**	164	31	6	**42**	109	**137**	2	57	.309	**.452**	**.627**	182	69	2-1	.967	-9	94	82	O-94(LF),1-58	5.0
1952	Pit N☆	149	516	90	126	17	2	**37**	87	**110**	7	77	.244	.384	.500	140	31	3-0	.970	-10	85	81	*O-149(LF)	1.1
1953	Pit N	41	148	27	40	6	1	7	29	25	2	21	.270	.383	.466	121	5	1-0	1.000	1	93	154	O-41(LF)	0.4
	Chi N★	117	414	73	117	14	2	28	87	75	1	67	.283	.394	.529	135	23	1-1	.964	-5	98	65	*O-116(LF)	1.1
	Year	158	562	100	157	20	3	35	116	100	3	88	.279	.391	.512	131	28	2-1	.973	-4	97	88	*O-157(LF)	1.5
1954	Chi N	147	557	88	159	36	5	22	73	76	2	90	.285	.371	.487	121	18	2-0	.971	1	105	67	*O-147(LF)	1.0
1955	Cle A	113	321	56	78	13	0	18	54	65-1	0	46	.243	.367	.452	116	8	0-0	.986	-6	90	32	O-87(LF)	-0.2
Total	10	1472	5205	971	1451	216	39	369	1015	1011-1	24	749	.279	.398	.548	148	371	22-2	.974	-30	99	74	*O-1382(1306-76-0)/1-58	24.2
KING, CHICK Charles Gilbert B 11.10.1930 Paris, TN BR/TR 6-2/190# d8.27																								
1954	Det A	11	28	4	6	0	1	0	3	3	0	8	.214	.290	.286	59	-2	0-0	.958	1	105	138	/O-7(CF)	-0.2
1955	Det A	7	21	3	5	0	0	0	0	1-0	0	2	.238	.273	.238	39	-2	0-0	.923	-1	100	0	/O-6(LF)	-0.3
1956	Det A	6	9	0	2	0	0	0	0	1-0	0	4	.222	.300	.222	40	-1	0-0	.800	-0	109	0	/O-3(LF)	-0.1
1958	Chi N	8	8	1	2	0	0	0	1	3-1	0	1	.250	.455	.250	95	0	0-0	1.000	-0	95	0	/O-7(CF)	0.0
1959	Chi N	7	3	3	0	0	0	0	0	0-0	0	1	.000	.000	.000	-99	-1	0-0	1.000	0	118	0	/O(CF)	-0.1
	StL N	5	7	0	3	0	0	0	1	0-0	0	2	.429	.375	.429	121	0	0-0	1.000	0	124	0	/O-4(1-3-0)	0.0
	Year	12	10	3	3	0	0	0	1	0-0	0	3	.300	.273	.300	59	-1	0-0	1.000	0	123	0	/O-5(1-4-0)	-0.1
Total	5	44	76	11	18	0	1	0	5	8-1	0	18	.237	.306	.263	56	-6	0-0	.947	-0	106	51	/O-28(10-18-0)	-0.7
KING, LEE Edward Lee B 3.28.1894 Waltham, MA D 9.7.1938 Newton Center, MA BR/TR 5-10/160# d6.24 Mil 1918																								
1916	Phi A	42	144	13	27	1	2	0	8	7	1	15	.188	.230	.222	38	-12	4	1.000	-5	81	53	O-22(21-2-1),S-11/3-5,2-2	-1.9
1919	Bos N	2	1	0	0	0	0	0	0	0	0	0	.000	.000	.000	-99	0	0	—	0			H	0.0
Total	2	44	145	13	27	1	2	0	8	7	1	15	.186	.229	.221	37	-12	4	1.000	-5	81	53	/O-22(21-2-1),S-11,3-5,2-2	-1.9
KING, HAL Harold B 2.1.1944 Oviedo, FL BL/TR 6-1/200# d9.6																								
1967	Hou N	15	44	2	11	1	2	0	6	2-0	0	9	.250	.283	.364	87	-1	0-0	1.000	-1	*81*	*138*	C-11	-0.2
1968	Hou N	27	55	4	8	2	1	0	2	7-0	0	16	.145	.242	.218	40	-4	0-0	.968	-3	*66*	*82*	C-19	-0.7
1970	Atl N	89	204	29	53	8	0	11	30	32-6	2	41	.260	.364	.461	113	4	1-0	.985	-8	80	73	C-62	-0.1
1971	Atl N	86	198	14	41	9	0	5	19	29-5	4	43	.207	.320	.328	79	-4	0-0	.983	-2	146	90	C-60	-0.4
1972	Tex A	50	122	12	22	5	0	4	12	25-1	3	35	.180	.333	.320	99	1	0-0	.970	-5	106	90	C-38	-0.3
1973	†Cin N	35	43	5	8	0	0	4	10	6-0	0	10	.186	.286	.465	110	0	0-0	1.000	-1	131	0	/C-9	-0.1
1974	Cin N	20	17	1	3	1	0	0	3	3-0	0	4	.176	.300	.235	52	-1	0-0	1.000	-0	0	199	/C-5	-0.1
Total	7	322	683	67	146	26	3	24	82	104-12	9	158	.214	.325	.366	93	-5	1-0	.982	-21	*106*	*85*	C-204	-1.9
KING, JIM James Hubert B 8.27.1932 Elkins, AR BL/TR 6/185# d4.17																								
1955	Chi N	113	301	43	77	12	3	11	45	24-1	2	39	.256	.312	.425	95	-3	2-1	.990	7	111	141	O-93(17-0-76)	0.0
1956	Chi N	118	317	32	79	13	2	15	54	30-5	1	40	.249	.313	.445	103	1	1-2	.990	10	123	189	O-82(69-0-14)	0.6
1957	StL N	22	35	1	11	0	0	0	2	4-2	0	2	.314	.385	.314	89	0	0-0	1.000	-1	70	0	O-8(1-3-4)	-0.1
1958	SF N	34	56	8	12	2	1	2	8	10-1	0	8	.214	.343	.393	96	0	0-1	1.000	-1	92	0	O-15(9-0-6)	-0.2
1961	Was A	110	263	43	71	12	1	11	46	38-3	2	45	.270	.363	.449	118	8	4-0	.980	2	100	131	O-91(25-0-67)/C	0.6
1962	Was A	132	333	39	81	15	0	11	35	55-9	3	37	.243	.353	.387	101	2	4-2	.979	4	101	167	*O-101(20-0-81)	0.0
1963	Was A	136	459	61	106	16	5	24	62	45-3	1	43	.231	.300	.444	106	2	3-0	.987	2	95	164	*O-123(2-0-122)	-0.4
1964	Was A	134	415	46	100	15	1	18	56	55-7	5	65	.241	.335	.412	108	5	3-1	.973	8	**117**	141	*O-121(RF)	0.6
1965	Was A	120	258	46	55	10	2	14	49	44-2	5	50	.213	.337	.430	119	7	1-0	.993	3	101	155	O-88(1-0-87)	0.5
1966	Was A	117	310	41	77	14	2	10	30	38-2	0	41	.248	.330	.403	111	5	4-0	.987	-0	101	88	O-85(RF)	0.0
1967	Was A	47	100	10	21	2	2	1	12	15-0	3	13	.210	.328	.300	91	-1	1-1	.962	-1	111	0	O-31(RF)/C	-0.4
	Chi A	23	50	2	6	1	0	0	2	4-0	0	16	.120	.185	.140	-3	-6	0-0	1.000	-1	83	0	O-12(1-0-12)	-0.9
	Cle A	19	21	2	3	0	0	0	0	1-0	0	2	.143	.182	.143	-3	-3	0-0	1.000	-0	54	0	/O(RF)	-0.3
	Year	89	171	14	30	3	2	1	14	20-0	3	31	.175	.272	.234	53	-10	1-1	.971	-3	101	0	O-44(1-0-44)/C	-1.6
Total	11	1125	2918	374	699	112	19	117	401	363-35	23	401	.240	.326	.411	104	17	23-8	.984	30	106	138	O-851(145-3-707)/C-2	0.0
KING, JEFF Jeffrey Wayne B 12.26.1964 Marion, IN BR/TR 6-1/180# d6.2 OF Total (RF)																								
1989	Pit N	75	215	31	42	13	3	5	19	20-1	2	34	.195	.266	.353	80	-6	4-2	.995	-1	79	112	1-46,3-13/2-7,S	-1.1
1990	†Pit N	127	371	46	91	17	1	14	53	21-1	1	50	.245	.283	.410	93	-5	3-3	.938	6	**114**	117	*3-115/1	0.0
1991	Pit N	33	109	16	26	1	1	4	18	14-3	1	15	.239	.328	.376	100	0	3-1	.975	-4	93	0	3-33	-0.4
1992	†Pit N	130	480	56	111	21	2	14	65	27-3	2	56	.231	.272	.371	82	-13	4-6	.953	-2	109	137	3-73,1-32,2-32/S-6,0(RF)	-1.9
1993	Pit N	158	611	82	180	35	3	9	98	59-4	4	54	.295	.356	.406	105	6	8-6	.964	14	**113**	108	*3-156/2-2,S-2	2.1
1994	Pit N	94	339	36	89	23	0	5	42	30-1	0	38	.263	.316	.375	80	-9	3-2	.955	7	106	**182**	3-91/2	-0.1
1995	Pit N	122	445	61	118	27	2	18	87	55-5	1	63	.265	.342	.456	108	5	7-4	.942	-2	102	100	3-84,1-35/2-8,S-2	0.1
1996	Pit N	155	591	91	160	36	4	30	111	70-3	2	95	.271	.346	.497	117	14	15-1	.997	3	89	93	1-92,2-71,3-17	1.5
1997	KC A	155	543	84	129	30	1	28	112	89-4	2	96	.238	.341	.451	104	4	16-5	**.996**	21	**155**	**110**	*1-150/D-2	1.2
1998	KC A	131	486	83	128	17	1	24	93	42-1	2	73	.263	.319	.451	96	-4	10-2	.995	6	120	110	*1-112,D-16/3-4	-0.8
1999	KC A	21	72	14	17	2	0	3	11	15-1	3	10	.236	.385	.389	97	0	2-0	.990	1	127	110	1-20/D	0.0
Total	11	1201	4262	600	1091	222	18	154	709	442-27	20	584	.256	.324	.425	99	-8	75-32	.953	48	109	119	3-586,1-488,2-121/D-19,S-11,O	0.6
KING, LEE Lee B 12.26.1892 Hundred, WV D 9.16.1967 Shinnston, WV BR/TR 5-8/160# d9.20																								
1916	Pit N	8	18	0	2	0	0	0	1	0	0	7	.111	.111	.111	-31	-3	0	.714	-1	57	211	/O-8(2-0-4)	-0.4

Year	Tm Lg	G	AB	R	H	2B	3B	HR	RBI	BB-IB	HP	SO	AVG	OBP	SLG	AOPS	ABR	SB-CS	FA	FR	Rng	Thr	G at Pos	BFW
1917	Pit N	111	381	32	95	14	5	1	35	15	2	58	.249	.281	.320	82	-9	8	.968	8	112	121	*O-102(7-0-95)	-0.8
1918	Pit N	36	112	9	26	3	2	1	11	11	0	15	.232	.301	.321	87	-2	3	.909	-5	88	0	O-36(32-0-4)	-0.9
1919	NY N	21	20	5	2	1	0	0	1	1	0	6	.100	.143	.150	-12	-3	0	.667	-1	52	0	/O-7(2-1-3)	-0.4
1920	NY N	93	261	32	72	11	4	7	42	21	2	38	.276	.335	.429	120	6	3-7	.951	-16	73	61	O-84(0-83-1)	-1.9
1921	NY N	39	94	17	21	4	2	0	7	13	1	6	.223	.324	.309	68	-4	0-2	.921	-0	86	164	O-35(0-24-12)/1	-0.6
	Phi N	64	216	25	58	19	4	4	32	8	1	37	.269	.298	.449	88	-4	1-4	.911	-2	94	114	O-57(55-1-2)	-1.2
	Year	103	310	42	79	23	6	4	39	21	2	43	.255	.306	.406	83	-8	1-6	.914	-2	92	129	O-92(55-25-14)/1	-1.8
1922	Phi N	19	53	8	12	5	1	2	13	8	0	6	.226	.328	.472	95	0	0-0	.946	-1	102	54	O-15(11-4-0)	-0.2
	†NY N	20	34	6	6	3	0	0	2	5	0	2	.176	.282	.265	41	-3	1-0	1.000	-0	77	61	/1-5,O-5(0-1-4)	-0.3
	Year	39	87	14	18	8	1	2	15	13	0	8	.207	.310	.391	76	-3	1-0	.961	-1	107	40	O-20(11-5-4)/1-5	-0.5
Total	7	411	1189	134	294	60	18	15	144	82	6	175	.247	.299	.366	87	-22	16-13	.940	-17	93	92	O-349(109-114-125)/1-6	-6.7
KING, LYNN Lynn Paul "Dig" B 11.28.1907 Villisca, IA D 5.11.1972 Atlantic, IA BL/TR 5-9/165# d9.21																								
1935	StL N	8	22	6	4	0	0	0	0	4	0	1	.182	.308	.182	34	-2	2	1.000	1	130	0	/O-6(CF)	-0.1
1936	StL N	78	100	12	19	2	1	0	10	9	0	14	.190	.257	.230	32	-10	2	.984	2	128	55	O-34(7-12-15)	-0.8
1939	StL N	89	85	10	20	2	0	0	11	15	0	3	.235	.350	.259	62	-4	2	.982	2	132	78	O-44(14-29-1)	-0.2
Total	3	175	207	28	43	4	1	0	21	28	0	18	.208	.302	.237	45	-16	6	.986	5	130	54	/O-84(21-47-16)	-1.1
KING, MART Marshal Ney B 12.1849 Troy, NY D 10.19.1911 Troy, NY TR 5-9.5/176# d5.8																								
1871	Chi NA	20	101	23	21	1	0	2	16	8		1	.208	.266	.277	51	-7	5-0	.786	-2	0	0	O-11(1-10-0)/C-9,S-3,3	-0.6
1872	Tro NA	3	11	0	0	0	0	0	1	0		1	.000	.000	.000	-99	-3	0-0	.857	-0	0	0	/O-3(CF)	-0.2
Total	2 NA	23	112	23	21	1	0	2	17	8		2	.188	.242	.250	39	-10	5-0	.000	-2	0	0	/O-14(1-13-0),C-9,S-3,3	-0.8
KING, SAM Samuel Warren B 5.17.1852 Peabody, MA D 8.11.1922 Peabody, MA BL/TL 6/?# d5.1																								
1884	Was AA	12	45	3	8	2	0	0		1	1		.178	.213	.222	48	-2		.912	-1	96	85	1-12	-0.4
KING, STEVE Stephen F. B 1842 Troy, NY D 7.8.1895 Troy, NY 5-9/175# d5.9																								
1871	Tro NA	**29**	144	45	57	10	6	0	34	1		1	.396	.400	.549	167	12	3-3	.833	3	182	0	*O-29(LF)	1.0
1872	Tro NA	**25**	128	33	39	8	0	0	20	1		2	.305	.310	.367	106	1	1-1	.776	1	183	203	O-25(LF)	0.2
Total	2 NA	54	272	78	96	18	6	0	54	2		3	.353	.358	.463	139	13	4-4	.000	4	182	96	/O-54(LF)	1.2
KINGDON, WES Westcott William B 7.4.1900 Los Angeles, CA D 4.19.1975 Capistrano, CA BR/TR 5-8/148# d6.12																								
1932	Was A	18	34	10	11	3	1	0	3	5	0	2	.324	.410	.471	129	2	0-0	.929	-1	92	122	/3-8,S-4	0.1
KINGERY, MIKE Michael Scott B 3.29.1961 St.James, MN BL/TL 6/180# d7.7																								
1986	KC A	62	209	25	54	8	5	3	14	12-2	0	30	.258	.296	.388	83	-6	7-3	.973	-1	88	166	O-59(1-13-51)	-0.8
1987	Sea A	120	354	38	99	25	4	9	52	27-0	2	43	.280	.329	.449	100	0	7-9	.992	14	118	219	*O-114(0-6-111)/D-4	0.7
1988	Sea A	57	123	21	25	6	0	1	9	19-1	1	23	.203	.313	.276	64	-5	3-1	.989	3	106	174	O-44(9-24-13),1-10	-0.3
1989	Sea A	31	76	14	17	3	0	2	6	7-0	0	14	.224	.286	.342	75	-3	1-1	1.000	3	137	0	O-23(2-20-1)	0.0
1990	SF N	105	207	24	61	7	1	0	24	12-0	1	19	.295	.335	.338	89	-3	6-1	.978	4	107	175	O-95(15-9-74)	0.0
1991	SF N	91	110	13	20	2	2	0	8	15-1	0	21	.182	.280	.236	48	-8	1-0	.975	-0	113	0	O-38(14-2-22)/1-6	-0.9
1992	Oak A	12	28	3	3	0	0	0	1	1-0	0	3	.107	.138	.107	-32	-5	0-0	1.000	-1	78	0	O-10(2-6-2)	-0.6
1994	Col N	105	301	56	105	27	8	4	41	30-2	2	26	.349	.402	.532	123	11	5-7	.979	-1	96	111	O-98(20-77-2)/1	0.8
1995	†Col N	119	350	66	94	18	4	8	37	45-1	0	40	.269	.351	.411	78	-10	13-5	.979	-8	86	84	*O-108(CF)/1-5	-1.6
1996	Pit N	117	276	32	68	12	2	3	27	23-2	1	29	.246	.304	.337	68	-13	2-1	.985	-3	93	59	O-83(5-64-16)	-1.6
Total	10	819	2034	292	546	108	26	30	219	191-9	7	248	.268	.330	.391	86	-42	45-28	.984	9	101	128	O-672(68-329-292)/1-22,D-4	-4.3
KINGMAN, DAVE David Arthur B 12.21.1948 Pendleton, OR BR/TR 6-6/210# d7.30 OF Total (508-LF 144-RF)																								
1971	†SF N	41	115	17	32	10	2	6	24	9-0	1	35	.278	.328	.557	151	7	5-0	.981	-3	78	67	1-20,O-14(7-0-7)	0.3
1972	SF N	135	472	65	106	17	4	29	83	51-2	4	140	.225	.303	.462	114	7	16-6	.932	4	120	104	3-59,1-56,O-22(LF)	0.7
1973	SF N	112	305	54	62	10	1	24	55	41-3	2	122	.203	.300	.479	109	2	8-5	.910	3	114	64	3-60,1-46/P-2	0.2
1974	SF N	121	350	41	78	18	2	18	55	37-2	3	125	.223	.302	.440	101	-1	8-8	.983	1	128	110	1-91,3-21/O-2(RF)	-0.7
1975	NY N	134	502	65	116	22	1	36	88	34-5	4	153	.231	.284	.494	119	7	7-5	.958	4	108	61	O-71(68-0-3),1-58,3-12	0.3
1976	NY N★	123	474	70	113	14	1	37	86	28-4	5	135	.238	.286	.506	130	13	7-4	.959	1	99	119	*O-111(5-0-106),1-16	0.8
1977	NY N	58	211	22	44	7	0	9	28	13-3	3	66	.209	.263	.370	71	-10	3-2	.974	-1	104	0	O-45(26-0-20),1-17	-1.4
	SD N	56	168	16	40	9	0	11	39	12-1	2	48	.238	.292	.488	119	3	2-3	.964	3	100	171	O-28(LF),1-13/3-2	0.3
	Year	114	379	38	84	16	0	20	67	25-4	5	114	.222	.276	.422	92	-7	5-5	.970	2	102	69	O-73(54-0-20),1-30/3-2	-1.1
	Cal A	10	36	4	7	2	0	2	4	1-0	1	16	.194	.237	.417	77	-1	0-0	.974	-1	94	77	/1-8,O-2(LF)	-0.2
	NY A	8	24	5	6	2	0	4	7	2-0	1	13	.250	.333	.833	208	3	0-1	—	0			/D-6	0.3
	Year	18	60	9	13	4	0	6	11	3-0	2	29	.217	.277	.583	131	2	0-1	.974	-1	141	56	/1-8,D-6,O-2(LF)	0.1
1978	Chi N	119	395	65	105	17	4	28	79	39-8	6	111	.266	.336	.542	128	13	3-4	.978	-3	89	98	*O-100(LF)/1-6	0.6
1979	Chi N✳	145	532	97	153	19	5	**48**	115	45-7	4	131	.288	.343	**.613**	143	28	4-2	.954	-0	93	111	*O-139(LF)	2.3
1980	Chi N★	81	255	31	71	8	0	18	57	21-3	0	44	.278	.329	.522	126	8	2-2	.941	2	93	194	O-61(63-0-1)/1-2	0.7
1981	NY N	100	353	40	78	11	3	22	59	55-7	1	105	.221	.326	.456	122	10	6-0	.974	-5	92	100	1-56,O-48(LF)	0.1
1982	NY N	149	535	80	109	9	1	**37**	99	59-9	4	156	.204	.285	.432	99	-4	4-0	.986	-14	71	79	*1-143	-2.6
1983	NY N	100	248	25	49	7	0	13	29	22-1	1	57	.198	.265	.383	79	-9	2-1	.994	-5	76	109	1-50/O-5(RF)	-1.7
1984	Oak A	147	549	68	147	23	1	35	118	44-8	6	119	.268	.321	.505	136	24	2-1	1.000	-2	34	41	*D-139/1-9	1.8
1985	Oak A	158	592	66	141	16	0	30	91	62-6	2	114	.238	.309	.417	105	3	3-2	1.000	-1	22	55	*D-149/1-9	-0.3
1986	Oak A	144	561	70	118	19	0	35	94	33-3	3	126	.210	.255	.431	90	-12	3-3	.895	-1	0	129	*D-140/1-3	-1.7
Total	16	1941	6677	901	1575	240	25	442	1210	608-72	53	1816	.236	.302	.478	115	91	85-49	.957	-18	96	100	O-648L,1-603,D-434,3-154/P-2	-0.2
KINGMAN, HARRY Henry Lees B 4.3.1892 Tientsin, China D 12.27.1982 Oakland, CA BL/TL 6-1.5/165# d7.1																								
1914	NY A	4	3	0	0	0	0	0	0	1	0	2	.000	.250	.000	-24	0	0	1.000	-0	0	0	/1	-0.1
KINGSALE, EUGENE Eugene Humphrey B 8.20.1976 Solito, Aruba BB/TR 6-3/170# d9.3																								
1996	Bal A	3	0	0	0	0	0	0	0	0-0	0	0	—	—	—	—	0	0-0	1.000	0	226	0	/O-2(CF)	0.0
1998	Bal A	11	2	1	0	0	0	0	0	0-0	0	1	.000	.000	.000	-99	-1	0-0	1.000	0	99	0	/O-4(CF)	-0.1
1999	Bal A	28	85	9	21	2	0	0	7	5-0	2	13	.247	.301	.271	50	-6	1-3	.980	-3	80	68	O-24(CF)/D-2	-1.0
2000	Bal A	26	88	13	21	2	1	0	9	2-0	0	14	.239	.253	.284	38	-9	1-2	.954	1	105	179	O-24(CF)/D	-0.8
2001	Bal A	3	4	0	0	0	0	0	0	0-0	0	2	.000	.000	.000	-99	-1	1-1	1.000	-0	38	0	/O(CF)	-0.2
	Sea A	10	15	4	5	0	0	0	1	2-0	1	2	.333	.444	.333	116	1	2-0	1.000	0	117	0	/O-9(5-1-3)	0.1
	Year	13	19	4	5	0	0	0	1	2-0	1	4	.263	.364	.263	73	-1	3-1	1.000	-0	103	0	O-10(5-2-3)	-0.1
2002	Sea A	2	3	0	2	0	0	0	0	0-0	0	0	.667	.667	.667	266	1	0-0	1.000	0	129	0	/O-2(0-1-1)	0.1
	SD N	89	216	27	60	10	3	2	28	20-0	3	47	.278	.346	.380	104	0	9-2	.985	4	116	116	O-82(26-17-50)	0.3
2003	Det A	39	120	11	25	3	1	1	8	10-0	0	17	.208	.265	.275	48	-9	1-3	.985	-4	84	0	O-30(8-23-0)/D-4	-1.4
Total	7	211	533	65	134	17	5	3	53	39-0	6	96	.251	.307	.319	70	-24	15-11	.979	-3	101	86	O-178(39-97-54)/D-7	-3.0
KINKADE, MIKE Michael A. B 5.6.1973 Livonia, MI BR/TR 6-1/210# d9.8 OF Total (83-LF 14-RF)																								
1998	NY N	3	2	2	0	0	0	0	0	0-0	0	0	.000	.000	.000	-99	-1	0-0	—	-0	0	0	/3	-0.1
1999	NY N	28	46	3	9	2	1	2	6	3-0	2	9	.196	.275	.413	73	-2	1-0	1.000	-0	77	168	O-17(12-0-8)/3-3,C1	-0.3
2000	NY N	2	2	0	0	0	0	0	0	0-0	0	1	.000	.000	.000	-99	-1	0-0	—	-0	0	0	/O(RF)	-0.1
	Bal A	3	7	0	3	1	0	0	1	0-0	1	0	.429	.500	.571	179	1	0-0	1.000	0	0	0	/1D	0.1
2001	Bal A	61	160	19	44	5	0	4	16	14-0	3	31	.275	.345	.381	96	-1	2-1	.962	-1	95	63	O-32(29-0-3),3-10,D-10/1-3,C-2	-0.3
2002	LA N	37	50	7	19	5	0	2	11	4-0	6	10	.380	.483	.600	201	8	1-0	1.000	-1	128	74	1-11/O-8(LF)	0.7
2003	LA N	88	162	25	35	7	0	5	14	13-2	16	38	.216	.335	.352	84	-3	1-3	.914	-3	70	0	O-36(34-0-2),1-13/3-2,D	-0.9
Total	6	222	429	56	110	20	1	13	48	34-2	28	89	.256	.350	.399	101	1	5-4	.953	-6	78	48	/O-94L,1-29,3-16,D-13,C-3	-0.9
KINLOCK, WALT Walter B 1874 Providence, RI D 2.15.1931 New York, NY d8.1																								
1895	StL N	1	3	0	1	0	0	0	0	0	0	2	.333	.333	.333	73	0	0	1.000	0	46	608	/3	0.0
KINSELLA, BOB Robert Francis "Red" B 1.5.1899 Springfield, IL D 12.30.1951 Los Angeles, CA BL/TR 5-9.5/165# d9.20																								
1919	NY N	3	9	1	2	0	0	0	0	0	0	3	.222	.222	.222	34	-1	1	.500	-1	32	0	/O-3(2-0-1)	-0.2
1920	NY N	1	3	0	1	0	0	0	1	0	0	2	.333	.333	.333	93	0	0-0	.500	-0	66	0	/O(RF)	-0.1
Total	2	4	12	1	3	0	0	0	1	0	0	5	.250	.250	.250	49	-1	1-0	.500	-1	43	0	/O-4(2-0-2)	-0.3
KINSLER, WILLIAM William H. B 11.9.1867 New York, NY D 8.10.1963 Miami Beach, FL d6.8																								
1893	NY N	1	3	1	0	0	0	0	0	1	0	1	.000	.250	.000	-31	-1	0	1.000	-0	0	0	/O(RF)	-0.1

Year	Tm Lg	G	AB	R	H	2B	3B	HR	RBI	BB-IB	HP	SO	AVG	OBP	SLG	AOPS	ABR	SB-CS	FA	FR	Rng	Thr	G at Pos	BFW
KINSLOW, TOM Thomas F. B 1.12.1866 Washington, DC D 2.22.1901 Washington, DC BR/TR 5-10/160# d6.4																								
1886	Was N	3	8	1	2	0	0	0	1	0		1	.250	.250	.250	57	0	0	1.000	-0			/C-3	0.0
1887	NY AA	2	6	0	0	0	0	0	0	0	0		.000	.000	.000	-99	-2	0	1.000	0			/C-2	-0.1
1890	Bro P	64	242	30	64	11	6	4	46	10	2	22	.264	.299	.409	83	-8	2	.909	14	*128*	*93*	C-64	0.9
1891	Bro N	61	228	22	54	6	0	0	33	9	0	22	.237	.266	.263	55	-14	3	.922	-6	*97*	*82*	C-61	-1.3
1892	Bro N	66	246	37	75	6	11	2	40	13	1	17	.305	.342	.443	142	10	4	.933	2	*104*	*112*	C-66	1.7
1893	Bro N	78	312	38	76	8	4	4	45	11	1	13	.244	.272	.333	63	-19	4	.932	-1	*99*	*94*	C-76/O-2(RF)	-1.1
1894	Bro N	62	223	39	68	5	6	2	41	20	0	11	.305	.362	.408	92	-3	4	.907	-10	*90*	*79*	C-61/1	-0.7
1895	Pit N	19	62	10	14	2	0	0	5	2	0	2	.226	.250	.258	33	-6	1	.962	-3	*87*	*66*	C-18	-0.6
1896	Lou N	8	25	4	7	0	1	0	7	1	0	5	.280	.308	.360	78	-1	0	.810	-2	*76*	*60*	/C-5,1	-0.2
1898	Was N	3	9	0	1	0	0	0	0	0	0		.111	.111	.111	-36	-2	0	.800	-1	*72*	*172*	/C-3,1	-0.2
	StL N	14	53	5	15	2	1	0	4	1	1		.283	.309	.358	89	-1	0	.925	-1	*74*	*120*	C-14	-0.1
	Year	17	62	5	16	2	1	0	4	1	1		.258	.281	.323	72	-3	0	.909	-2	*74*	*127*	C-17/1	-0.3
Total	10	380	1414	186	376	40	29	12	222	67	5	93	.266	.301	.361	81	-46	18	.923	-9	*101*	*92*	C-373/1-3,O-2(RF)	-1.7
KINZIE, WALT Walter Harris B 3.1858 Chicago, IL D 11.5.1909 Chicago, IL BR/TR 5-10.5/161# d7.17																								
1882	Det N	13	53	5	5	0	1	0	2	0		8	.094	.094	.132	-28	-8		.852	-2	96	28	S-13	-0.9
1884	Chi N	19	82	4	13	3	0	2	8	0		13	.159	.159	.268	29	-7		.831	-2	97	112	S-17/3-2	-0.7
	StL AA	2	9	0	1	0	0	0		0	0		.111	.111	.111	-26	-1		.727	-2	62	0	/2-2	-0.3
Total	2	34	144	9	19	3	1	2	10	0	0	21	.132	.132	.208	6	-16		.840	-6	97	75	/S-30,2-2,3-2	-1.9
KIPPERT, ED Edward August "Kickapoo" B 1.3.1880 Detroit, MI D 6.3.1960 Detroit, MI BR/TR 5-10.5/180# d4.14																								
1914	Cin N	2	2	0	0	0	0	0	0	0	0	0	.000	.000	.000	-97	0	0	1.000	-0	71	0	/O-2(1-1-0)	-0.1
KIRBY, JIM James Herschel B 5.5.1923 Nashville, TN BR/TR 5-11/175# d5.1																								
1949	Chi N	3	2	0	1	0	0	0	0	0	0	0	.500	.500	.500	174	0	0	—	0			H	0.0
KIRBY, LA RUE La Rue B 12.30.1889 Eureka, MI D 6.10.1961 Lansing, MI BB/TR 6/185# d8.7 ▲																								
1912	NY N	3	5	1	1	1	0	0	0	0	0	0	.200	.200	.400	60	0	0	1.000	0	109	0	/P-3	0.0
1914	StL F	52	195	21	48	6	3	2	18	14	2	30	.246	.303	.338	71	-11	5	.973	2	103	107	O-50(0-49-1)	-1.4
1915	StL F	61	178	15	38	7	2	0	16	17	0	31	.213	.282	.275	54	-13	3	.969	-0	93	128	O-52(9-40-4)/P	-1.7
Total	3	116	378	37	87	14	5	2	34	31	2	61	.230	.292	.310	63	-24	8	.971	2	98	117	O-102(9-89-5)/P-4	-3.1
KIRBY, WAYNE Wayne Leonard B 1.22.1964 Williamsburg, VA BL/TR 5-10/185# d9.12																								
1991	Cle A	21	43	4	9	2	0	0	5	2-0	0	6	.209	.239	.256	38	-4	1-2	1.000	2	133	95	O-21(5-1-17)	-0.3
1992	Cle A	21	18	9	3	1	0	1	1	3-0	0	2	.167	.286	.389	89	0	0-3	1.000	0	205	0	/O-2(1-0-1),D-4	-0.1
1993	Cle A	131	458	71	123	19	5	6	60	37-2	3	58	.269	.323	.371	88	-9	17-5	.983	14	110	**227**	*O-123(2-15-113)/D-5	0.2
1994	Cle A	78	191	33	56	6	0	5	23	13-0	1	30	.293	.341	.403	91	-3	11-4	.959	-4	92	56	O-68(8-6-55)/D-2	-0.7
1995	†Cle A	101	188	29	39	10	2	1	14	13-0	1	32	.207	.260	.298	45	-16	10-3	.990	-1	93	81	O-68(1-34-35)/D-7	-1.6
1996	Cle A	27	16	3	4	1	0	0	1	2-0	0	2	.250	.333	.313	65	-1	0-1	1.000	-1	80	0	O-18(2-5-11)	-0.2
	†LA N	65	188	23	51	10	1	1	11	17-1	1	17	.271	.333	.351	88	-3	4-2	.969	-2	91	87	O-53(8-47-0)	-0.5
1997	LA N	46	65	6	11	2	0	0	4	10-0	0	12	.169	.280	.200	31	-7	0-0	1.000	2	121	136	O-26(9-16-2)	-0.5
1998	NY N	26	31	5	6	0	1	0	0	1-0	0	9	.194	.219	.258	25	-4	1-1	1.000	1	115	239	O-19(3-4-12)	-0.3
Total	8	516	1198	183	302	51	9	14	119	98-3	6	168	.252	.309	.345	75	-47	44-21	.981	11	103	140	O-398(39-128-246)/D-18	-4.0
KIRK, TOM Thomas Daniel B 9.27.1927 Philadelphia, PA D 8.1.1974 Philadelphia, PA BL/TL 5-10.5/182# d6.24																								
1947	Phi A	1	1	0	0	0	0	0	0	0	0	0	.000	.000	.000	-98	0	0-0	—	0			H	0.0
KIRKE, JAY Judson Fabian B 6.16.1888 Fleischmanns, NY D 8.31.1968 New Orleans, LA BL/TR 6/195# d9.28 OF Total (102-LF 2-CF 38-RF)																								
1910	Det A	8	25	3	5	1	0	0	3	1	0		.200	.231	.240	44	-2	1	.917	-2	86	39	/2-7,O(LF)	-0.4
1911	Bos N	20	89	9	32	5	5	0	12	2	1	6	.360	.380	.528	142	4	3	.929	-1	94	110	O-14(LF)/1-3,2S3	0.3
1912	Bos N	103	359	53	115	11	4	4	62	9	1	46	.320	.339	.407	102	-1	7	.903	-0	82	211	O-72(62-0-10),3-14/S-2,1	-0.4
1913	Bos N	18	38	3	9	2	0	0	3	1	2	6	.237	.293	.289	65	-2	0-1	.923	2	93	344	O-13(3-2-8)	0.0
1914	Cle A	67	242	18	66	10	2	1	25	7	1	30	.273	.296	.343	89	-5	5-10	.974	1	113	57	O-42(22-0-20),1-18	-0.9
1915	Cle A	87	339	35	105	19	2	2	40	14	5	21	.310	.346	.395	120	7	5-6	.986	-1	97	79	1-87	0.3
1918	NY N	17	56	1	14	1	0	0	3	1	0	3	.250	.263	.268	63	-3	0	.978	1	121	86	1-16	-0.3
Total	7	320	1148	122	346	49	13	7	148	35	10	112	.301	.328	.385	103	-2	21-17	.927	0	93	165	O-142L,1-125/3-15,2-8,S-3	-1.4
KIRKLAND, WILLIE Willie Charles B 2.17.1934 Siluria, AL BL/TR 6-1/206# d4.15																								
1958	SF N	122	418	48	108	25	6	14	56	43-7	5	69	.258	.332	.447	107	4	3-2	.961	-0	95	137	*O-115(5-0-112)	0.0
1959	SF N	126	463	64	126	22	3	22	68	42-3	3	84	.272	.335	.475	116	9	5-3	.969	-2	98	89	*O-117(13-0-109)	0.3
1960	SF N	146	515	59	130	21	10	21	65	44-8	4	86	.252	.315	.454	115	8	12-7	.978	2	98	125	*O-143(3-0-143)	0.5
1961	Cle A	146	525	84	136	22	5	27	95	48-4	1	77	.259	.318	.474	113	7	7-0	.974	5	105	112	*O-138(RF)	0.4
1962	Cle A	137	419	56	84	9	1	21	72	43-3	0	62	.200	.272	.377	76	-17	9-1	.972	6	109	170	*O-125(0-12-121)	-1.6
1963	Cle A	127	427	51	98	13	2	15	47	45-5	1	99	.230	.303	.375	90	-6	8-2	.984	3	103	159	*O-112(5-64-45)	-0.8
1964	Bal A	66	150	14	30	5	0	3	22	17-4	1	26	.200	.281	.293	62	-8	3-2	.989	5	109	266	O-58(2-10-48)	-0.5
	Was A	32	102	8	22	6	0	5	13	6-0	0	30	.216	.259	.422	86	-2	0-0	.907	-2	94	0	O-27(12-1-15)	-0.6
	Year	98	252	22	52	11	0	8	35	23-4	1	56	.206	.272	.345	72	-10	3-2	.964	3	104	173	O-85(14-11-63)	-1.1
1965	Was A	123	312	38	72	9	1	14	54	19-1	0	65	.231	.270	.401	91	-5	3-2	.987	1	106	62	O-92(32-5-67)	-1.1
1966	Was A	124	163	21	31	2	1	6	17	16-3	0	50	.190	.261	.325	68	-7	2-0	.983	1	102	159	O-68(50-0-19)	-0.8
Total	9	1149	3494	443	837	134	29	148	509	323-38	15	648	.240	.304	.422	99	-17	52-19	.974	19	102	129	O-995(122-92-817)	-4.2
KIRKPATRICK, ED Edgar Leon B 10.8.1944 Spokane, WA BL/TR 5-11.5/195# d9.13 OF Total (236-LF 62-CF 291-RF)																								
1962	LA A	3	6	0	0	0	0	0	0	0-0	0	2	.000	.000	.000	-99	-2	0-0	1.000	0	*0*	*0*	/C	-0.1
1963	LA A	34	77	4	15	5	0	2	7	6-0	1	19	.195	.259	.338	71	-3	1-0	.986	1	30	143	C-14,O-10(LF)	-0.2
1964	LA A	75	219	20	53	13	3	2	22	23-6	2	30	.242	.315	.356	97	-1	2-2	.969	-2	89	104	O-63(63-0-1)	-0.6
1965	Cal A	19	73	8	19	5	0	3	8	3-0	0	9	.260	.289	.452	110	1	1-2	.969	0	85	254	O-19(RF)	-0.1
1966	Cal A	117	312	31	60	7	4	9	44	51-8	5	67	.192	.313	.327	87	-4	7-4	.994	-3	93	77	*O-102(17-0-86)/1-3	-1.4
1967	Cal A	3	8	0	0	0	0	0	0	0-0	0	2	.000	.000	.000	-99	-2	0-0	1.000	-1	0	0	/C-2,O(LF)	-0.3
1968	Cal A	89	161	23	37	4	0	1	15	25-2	1	32	.230	.332	.273	90	-1	1-3	.982	-1	92	104	O-45(12-1-34)/C-4,1-2	-0.6
1969	KC A	120	315	40	81	11	4	14	49	43-4	3	42	.257	.348	.451	122	9	3-5	.995	7	119	139	O-82(29-24-32)/C-8,1-2,3-2,2	1.3
1970	KC A	134	424	59	97	17	2	18	62	55-8	1	65	.229	.319	.406	98	-1	4-4	.978	-2	79	**163**	C-89,O-19(8-3-8),1-16	-0.2
1971	KC A	120	365	46	80	12	1	9	46	48-8	2	60	.219	.308	.332	83	-7	3-4	.992	6	112	62	O-61(30-16-18),C-59	-0.2
1972	KC A	113	364	43	100	15	1	9	43	51-9	3	50	.275	.365	.396	128	14	3-5	.991	-3	85	98	*C-108/1	1.7
1973	KC A	126	429	61	113	24	3	6	45	46-6	1	48	.263	.333	.375	93	-1	3-7	.990	-0	96	43	*O-108(27-11-72),C-14/D-8	-1.0
1974	†Pit N	116	271	32	67	9	0	6	38	51-13	2	30	.247	.367	.347	105	4	1-2	.993	-1	99	122	1-59,O-14(0-2-12)/C-6	-0.2
1975	†Pit N	89	144	15	34	5	0	5	16	18-2	0	22	.236	.319	.375	93	-1	1-0	1.000	-0	99	82	1-28,O-14(8-0-6)	-0.3
1976	Pit N	83	146	14	34	9	0	0	16	14-2	0	15	.233	.294	.295	69	-6	1-0	.990	0	114	90	1-25/O-9(3-4-2),3	-0.8
1977	Pit N	21	28	5	4	2	0	1	4	8-0	0	6	.143	.324	.321	75	-1	1-0	.972	0	107	145	1-10/O-2(1-1-0),3	-0.1
	Tex A	20	48	2	9	1	0	0	3	4-1	0	11	.188	.250	.208	26	-5	2-0	1.000	1	148	0	/O-6(5-0-1),1-3,CD	-0.4
	Mil A	29	77	8	21	4	0	0	6	10-1	1	8	.273	.364	.325	89	-1	0-1	.973	-1	103	0	O-22(LF)/3D	-0.3
	Year	49	125	10	30	5	0	0	9	14-2	1	19	.240	.321	.280	65	-5	2-1	.980	-1	112	0	O-28(27-0-1)/D-8,1-3,C3	-0.7
Total	16	1311	3467	411	824	143	18	85	424	456-70	22	518	.238	.327	.363	97	-10	34-39	.989	1	100	80	O-577R,C-306,1-149/D-16,3-5,2	-3.8
KIRKPATRICK, ENOS Enos Claire B 12.9.1884 Pittsburgh, PA D 4.14.1964 Pittsburgh, PA BR/TR 5-10/175# d8.24																								
1912	Bro N	32	94	13	18	1	1	0	6	9	1	15	.191	.269	.223	37	-8	5	.968	5	129	85	3-29/S-3	-0.3
1913	Bro N	48	89	13	22	4	1	1	5	3	2	18	.247	.287	.348	79	-3	5-1	.897	-2	71	51	S-10/1-8,2-6,3-4	-0.4
1914	Bal F	55	174	22	44	7	2	2	16	18	2	30	.253	.330	.351	83	-7	10	.932	-1	80	25	3-36,S-11/O-3(2-0-1),1	-0.6
1915	Bal F	68	171	22	41	8	2	0	19	24	1	15	.240	.337	.310	80	-6	12	.911	-3	94	72	3-28,2-21/1-5,S-5	-0.9
Total	4	203	528	70	125	20	6	3	46	54	6	78	.237	.315	.314	74	-24	32-1	.936	-1	101	59	/3-97,S-29,2-27,1-14,O-3(2-0-1)	-2.2
KIRRENE, JOE Joseph John B 10.4.1931 San Francisco, CA BR/TR 6-2/195# d10.1 Mil 1952																								
1950	Chi A	1	4	0	1	0	0	0	0	0	0	1	.250	.250	.250	29	0	0-0	1.000	-0	59	0	/3	-0.1
1954	Chi A	9	23	4	7	1	0	0	4	5	1	2	.304	.448	.348	116	1	1-0	.947	-1	77	173	/3-9	0.0
Total	2	10	27	4	8	1	0	0	4	5	1	3	.296	.424	.333	105	1	1-0	.952	-1	75	154	/3-10	-0.1

Year	Tm Lg	G	AB	R	H	2B	3B	HR	RBI	BB-IB	HP	SO	AVG	OBP	SLG	AOPS	ABR	SB-CS	FA	FR	Rng	Thr	G at Pos	BFW
KISH, ERNIE Ernest Alexander B 2.6.1918 Washington, DC D 12.21.1993 Kirtland, OH BL/TR 5-9.5/170# d7.29																								
1945	Phi A	43	110	10	27	5	1	0	10	9	3	9	.245	.320	.309	83	-2	0-3	.932	-2	85	118	O-30(13-8-11)	-0.7
KISSINGER, BILL William Francis "Shang" B 8.15.1871 Dayton, KY D 4.20.1929 Cincinnati, OH BR/TR 5-11/185# d5.30 ▲																								
1895	Bal N	2	5	1	1	0	0	0	0	0	0	1	.200	.200	.200	3	0	0	1.000	-0	80	0	/P-2	0.0
	StL N	33	97	8	24	6	1	0	8	0	0	11	.247	.247	.330	49	-8	1	.975	-3	97	87	P-24/S-4,O-4(1-0-3),3	-0.4
	Year	35	102	9	25	6	1	0	8	0	0	12	.245	.245	.324	46	-9	1	**.976**	-3	96	81	P-26/S-4,O-4(1-0-3),3	-0.4
1896	StL N	23	73	8	22	4	0	0	12	0	0	4	.301	.301	.356	76	-3	0	.906	0	127	155	P-20/O-3(LF),3	-0.1
1897	StL N	14	39	7	13	3	2	0	6	3	0		.333	.381	.513	138	2	0	.786	-1	0	0	/O-7(6-1-0),P-7	0.0
Total	3	72	214	24	60	13	3	0	26	3	0	16	.280	.290	.369	73	-9	1	.935	-4	111	105	/P-53,O-14(10-1-3),S-4,3-2	-0.5
KITSOS, CHRIS Christopher Anestos B 2.11.1928 New York, NY BB/TR 5-9/165# d4.21																								
1954	Chi N	1	0	0	0	0	0	0	0	0	0	0	—	—	—	—	0	0-0	1.000	0	191	0	/S	0.0
KITTLE, RON Ronald Dale B 1.5.1958 Gary, IN BR/TR 6-4/220# d9.2																								
1982	Chi A	20	29	3	7	2	0	1	7	3-0	0	12	.241	.313	.414	97	0	0-0	1.000	-1	43	0	/O-5(RF),D-3	-0.1
1983	†Chi A★	145	520	75	132	19	3	35	100	39-8	8	150	.254	.314	.504	117	10	8-3	.964	-13	83	67	*O-139(LF)/D-2	-0.8
1984	Chi A	139	466	67	100	15	0	32	74	49-5	6	137	.215	.295	.453	100	-2	3-6	.972	-1	87	166	*O-124(LF)/D-7	-1.0
1985	Chi A	116	379	51	87	12	0	26	58	31-1	5	92	.230	.295	.467	101	-1	1-4	.989	-2	92	67	O-57(LF),D-57	-0.8
1986	Chi A	86	296	34	63	11	0	17	48	28-0	3	87	.213	.282	.422	87	-6	2-1	1.000	1	93	244	D-62,O-20(LF)	-0.7
	NY A	30	80	8	19	2	0	4	12	7-1	0	23	.237	.292	.412	92	-1	2-0	1.000	0	106	0	D-24/O(LF)	-0.1
	Year	116	376	42	82	13	0	21	60	35-1	3	110	.218	.284	.420	89	-7	4-1	.973	1	94	232	D-86,O-21(LF)	-0.8
1987	NY A	59	159	21	44	5	0	12	28	10-1	1	36	.277	.318	.535	123	4	0-1	1.000	1	198	1409	D-49/O-2(LF)	0.4
1988	Cle A	75	225	31	58	8	0	18	43	16-1	8	65	.258	.323	.533	134	9	0-0	—	0	0	0	D-63	0.7
1989	Chi A	51	169	26	51	10	0	11	37	22-1	1	42	.302	.378	.556	166	15	0-1	.982	-2	67	132	1-27,D-17/O-5(LF)	1.1
1990	Chi A	83	277	29	68	14	0	16	43	24-2	3	77	.245	.311	.469	118	6	0-0	.987	-4	38	115	D-54,1-25	-0.1
	Bal A	22	61	4	10	2	0	2	3	2-0	1	14	.164	.203	.295	39	-5	0-0	1.000	-1	42	37	D-13/1-5	-0.7
	Year	105	338	33	78	16	0	18	46	26-2	4	91	.231	.293	.438	104	0	0-0	.989	-4	39	104	D-67,1-30	-0.8
1991	Chi A	17	47	7	9	0	0	2	7	5-0	2	9	.191	.291	.319	72	-2	0-0	.982	-1	75	89	1-15	-0.4
Total	10	843	2708	356	648	100	3	176	460	236-20	38	744	.239	.306	.473	110	27	16-16	.974	-21	87	121	0-353(348-0-5),D-351/1-72	-2.5
KITTRIDGE, MALACHI Malachi Jeddidah "Jeddidah" B 10.12.1869 Clinton, MA D 6.23.1928 Gary, IN BR/TR 5-7/170# d4.19 M1																								
1890	Chi N	96	333	46	67	8	3	3	35	39	1	53	.201	.287	.270	60	-17	7	.944	5	*112*	*95*	*C-96	-0.4
1891	Chi N	79	296	26	62	8	5	2	27	17	0	28	.209	.252	.291	58	-17	4	.940	5	***132***	*91*	C-79	-0.5
1892	Chi N	69	229	19	41	5	0	0	10	11	0	27	.179	.217	.201	26	-21	2	.945	8	*105*	*100*	C-69	-0.6
1893	Chi N	70	255	32	59	9	5	2	30	17	0	15	.231	.279	.329	62	-15	3	.939	4	*90*	*116*	C-70	-0.4
1894	Chi N	51	168	36	53	8	2	0	23	26	0	20	.315	.407	.387	87	-3	2	.925	-5	*80*	*71*	C-51	-0.3
1895	Chi N	60	212	30	48	6	3	3	29	16	1	9	.226	.284	.325	53	-16	6	.976	0	*95*	*84*	C-59	-0.9
1896	Chi N	65	215	17	48	4	1	1	19	14	1	14	.223	.274	.265	41	-19	6	.962	-0	*93*	*90*	C-64/P	-1.2
1897	Chi N	79	262	25	53	5	5	1	30	22	0		.202	.264	.271	40	-24	9	.952	-1	*87*	*99*	C-79	-1.6
1898	Lou N	86	287	27	70	8	5	1	31	15	0		.244	.281	.317	72	-12	9	.944	-13	*81*	*103*	C-86	-1.6
1899	Lou N	46	131	11	26	2	1	0	13	26	1		.198	.335	.229	56	-7	3	.975	6	*116*	*110*	C-44	0.3
	Was N	44	133	14	20	3	0	0	11	10	1		.150	.215	.173	7	-17	2	.949	-4	*78*	*118*	C-43	-1.6
	Year	90	264	25	46	5	1	0	24	36	2		.174	.278	.201	32	-24	5	.962	3	*98*	*114*	C-87	-1.3
1901	Bos N	114	381	24	96	14	0	2	40	32	1		.252	.312	.304	72	-13	2	**.984**	17	***130***	*97*	*C-113	1.5
1902	Bos N	80	255	18	60	7	0	2	30	24	1		.235	.304	.286	81	-5	4	.981	6	*110*	*97*	C-72	0.9
1903	Bos N	32	99	10	21	2	0	0	6	11	0		.212	.291	.232	52	-6	1	.981	4	*98*	*85*	C-30	0.1
	Was A	60	192	8	41	4	1	0	16	10	0		.214	.252	.245	49	-12	1	.978	-8	*74*	*118*	C-60	-1.5
1904	Was A	81	265	11	64	7	0	0	24	8	1		.242	.266	.268	70	-9	2	.982	-5	*73*	***118***	C-79,M	-0.7
1905	Was A	77	238	16	39	8	0	0	14	15	0		.164	.213	.197	32	-18	1	.978	7	*96*	*112*	C-76	-0.5
1906	Was A	22	68	5	13	0	0	0	3	1	0		.191	.203	.191	25	-6	0	.946	-3	*81*	*72*	C-22	-0.8
	Cle A	5	10	0	1	0	0	0	0	0	0		.100	.100	.100	-38	-2	0	.938	-1	*118*	*35*	/C-5	-0.2
	Year	27	78	5	14	0	0	0	3	1	0		.179	.190	.179	16	-8	0	.945	-4	*86*	*67*	C-27	-1.0
Total	16	1216	4029	375	882	108	31	17	391	314	8	166	.219	.277	.274	56	-239	64	.961	22	*99*	*100*	*C-1197/P	-10.0
KLASSEN, DANNY Daniel Victor B 9.22.1975 Leamington, ON, CAN BR/TR 6/175# d7.4																								
1998	Ari N	29	108	12	21	2	1	3	8	9-0	1	33	.194	.263	.315	51	-8	1-1	.964	-3	97	95	2-29	-1.0
1999	Ari N	1	1	0	1	0	0	0	0	0-0	0	0	1.000	1.000	1.000	406	0	0-0	—	0			/H	0.0
2000	Ari N	29	76	13	18	3	0	2	8	8-0	1	24	.237	.318	.355	68	-4	1-1	.962	-2	93	115	3-25/S-3	-0.5
2002	Ari N	4	3	0	1	0	0	0	0	0-0	0	1	.333	.333	.333	73	0	0-0	1.000	-0	146	0	/3-2,S	0.0
2003	Det A	22	73	9	18	3	1	1	7	4-0	0	26	.247	.286	.356	74	-3	0-1	1.000	4	105	131	3-13/2-4,S-3	0.1
Total	5	85	261	34	59	8	2	6	23	21-0	2	84	.226	.289	.341	64	-15	2-3	.978	-1	98	120	/3-40,2-33,S-7	-1.4
KLAUS, BOBBY Robert Francis B 12.27.1937 Spring Grove, IL BR/TR 5-10/170# d4.21 b-Billy																								
1964	Cin N	40	93	10	17	5	1	2	6	4-0	0	13	.183	.212	.323	48	-7	1-0	.972	1	96	95	2-18,3-11/S-3	-0.5
	NY N	56	209	25	51	8	3	2	11	25-0	0	30	.244	.325	.340	90	-2	3-4	.986	-0	111	68	2-25,3-28/S-5	-0.1
	Year	96	302	35	68	13	4	4	17	29-0	0	43	.225	.291	.334	76	-10	4-4	.981	0	106	77	2-43,3-39/S-8	-0.6
1965	NY N	119	288	30	55	12	0	2	12	45-0	1	49	.191	.302	.253	61	-13	1-6	.968	11	111	117	2-72,S-28,3-25	0.2
Total	2	215	590	65	123	25	4	6	29	74-0	1	92	.208	.297	.295	69	-22	5-10	.973	12	109	101	2-115/3-64,S-36	-0.4
KLAUS, BILLY William Joseph B 12.9.1928 Spring Grove, IL BL/TR 5-10/165# d4.16 b-Bobby																								
1952	Bos N	7	4	3	0	0	0	0	0	1	0	1	.000	.200	.000	-42	-1	0-0	.500	-1	0	0	/S-4	-0.2
1953	Mil N	2	2	1	0	0	0	0	1	0	0	0	.000	.000	.000	-99	-1	0-0	—	0			H	-0.1
1955	Bos A	135	541	83	153	26	2	7	60	60-0	0	44	.283	.351	.377	89	-7	6-0	.955	-3	104	72	*S-126/3-8	0.1
1956	Bos A	135	520	91	141	29	5	7	59	90-0	1	43	.271	.378	.387	92	-3	1-0	.945	2	**113**	79	*3-106,S-26	0.1
1957	Bos A	127	477	76	120	18	4	10	42	55-0	0	53	.252	.326	.369	85	-9	2-0	.961	19	**113**	111	*S-118	2.0
1958	Bos A	61	88	5	14	4	0	1	7	5-0	0	16	.159	.204	.239	20	-10	0-0	.883	-4	94	23	S-27	-1.4
1959	Bal A	104	321	33	80	11	0	3	25	51-1	0	38	.249	.350	.312	86	-4	2-4	.970	-8	97	71	S-59,3-49/2	-0.9
1960	Bal A	46	43	8	9	2	0	1	6	9-0	0	9	.209	.346	.326	84	-1	0-0	.960	6	124	154	2-30,S-12/3-2	0.6
1961	Was A	91	251	26	57	8	2	7	30	30-3	2	34	.227	.311	.359	81	-7	2-2	.961	2	116	31	3-51,S-18/2O(LF)	-0.5
1962	Phi N	102	248	30	51	8	2	4	20	29-3	1	43	.206	.290	.302	61	-14	1-1	.983	-3	94	52	3-53,S-30,2-11	-1.5
1963	Phi N	11	18	1	1	0	0	0	0	1-0	0	4	.056	.105	.056	-53	-4	0-0	1.000	-1	67	0	/S-5,3-3	-0.4
Total	11	821	2513	357	626	106	15	40	250	331-7	4	285	.249	.335	.351	82	-61	14-7	.955	8	105	84	S-425,3-272/2-43,O(LF)	-2.2
KLEE, OLLIE Ollie Chester "Babe" B 5.20.1900 Piqua, OH D 2.9.1977 Toledo, OH BL/TL 5-9.5/160# d8.10																								
1925	Cin N	3	1	0	0	0	0	0	0	0	0	1	.000	.000	.000	-99	0	0-0	—	-0	0	0	/O(CF)	0.0
KLEIN, CHUCK Charles Herbert B 10.7.1904 Indianapolis, IN D 3.28.1958 Indianapolis, IN BL/TR 6/185# d7.30 C4 HF1980																								
1928	Phi N	64	253	41	91	14	4	11	34	14	1	22	.360	.396	.577	146	16	0	.978	-0	95	109	O-63(RF)	1.0
1929	Phi N	149	616	126	219	45	6	**43**	145	54	0	61	.356	.407	.657	149	45	5	.966	-1	96	117	*O-149(0-25-123)	3.0
1930	Phi N	**156**	648	**158**	250	**59**	8	40	170	54	4	50	.386	.436	.687	155	58	4	.960	21	102	**217**	*O-156(RF)	**5.7**
1931	Phi N	148	594	**121**	200	34	10	**31**	**121**	59	1	49	.337	.398	**.584**	149	40	7	.971	-2	94	121	*O-148(90-17-43)	3.0
1932	Phi N	**154**	650	**152**	**226**	50	15	**38**	137	60	1	49	.348	.404	**.646**	158	53	**20**	.960	7	96	**179**	*O-154(RF)	4.9
1933	Phi N★	**152**	606	101	**223**	**44**	7	**28**	**120**	56	1	36	**.368**	**.422**	**.602**	168	**55**	15	.986	8	103	142	*O-152(0-1-152)	**5.6**
1934	Chi N★	115	435	78	131	27	2	20	80	47	2	38	.301	.372	.510	136	23	3	.962	-3	97	76	*O-110(97-1-15)	1.3
1935	†Chi N	119	434	71	127	14	4	21	73	41	1	42	.293	.355	.488	123	13	4	.958	-3	94	94	*O-111(RF)	0.3
1936	Chi N	29	109	19	32	5	0	5	18	16	0	14	.294	.384	.477	128	5	0	.917	-1	104	89	O-29(RF)	0.2
	Phi N	117	492	83	152	30	7	20	86	33	0	45	.309	.352	.520	120	12	6	.930	-3	96	105	*O-117(2-0-115)	0.2
	Year	146	601	102	184	35	7	25	104	49	0	59	.306	.358	.512	122	17	6	.927	-4	98	102	*O-146(2-0-144)	0.4
1937	Phi N	115	406	74	132	20	2	15	57	39	1	21	.325	.386	.495	127	16	3	.949	-2	94	120	*O-102(29-0-75)	0.8
1938	Phi N	129	458	53	113	22	2	8	61	38	0	30	.247	.304	.356	83	-11	7	.960	0	106	81	*O-119(3-0-118)	-1.8
1939	Phi N	25	47	8	9	2	1	1	9	10	0	4	.191	.333	.340	84	-1	1	1.000	0	100	108	O-11(RF)/1	-0.1
	Pit N	85	270	37	81	16	4	11	47	26	0	17	.300	.361	.511	134	12	1	.951	-3	96	75	O-66(30-0-37)	0.5
	Year	110	317	45	90	18	5	12	56	36	0	21	.284	.357	.486	127	11	2	.958	-3	97	79	O-77(30-0-48)/1	0.4
1940	Phi N	116	354	39	77	16	2	7	37	44	0	30	.218	.304	.333	79	-10	2	.984	-0	106	58	O-96(6-0-90)	-1.6
1941	Phi N	50	73	6	9	0	0	1	3	10	0	6	.123	.229	.164	12	-9	0	.958	-0	101	106	O-14(2-0-12)	-1.0

Year	Tm Lg	G	AB	R	H	2B	3B	HR	RBI	BB-IB	HP	SO	AVG	OBP	SLG	AOPS	ABR	SB-CS	FA	FR	Rng	Thr	G at Pos	BFW
1942	Phi N	14	14	0	1	0	0	0	0	0	0	2	.071	.071	.071	-61	-3	0	—	0			H	-0.3
1943	Phi N	12	20	0	2	0	0	0	3	0	0	3	.100	.100	.100	-44	-4	1	.000	-1	0	0	/O-2(LF)	-0.5
1944	Phi N	4	7	1	1	0	0	0	0	0	0	2	.143	.143	.143	-20	-1	0	1.000	0	141	0	/O(RF)	-0.1
Total	17	1753	6486	1168	2076	398	74	300	1201	601	12	521	.320	.379	.543	135	309	79	.962	17	98	122	*O-1600(261-44-1305)/1	21.1
KLEIN, LOU Louis Frank B 10.22.1918 New Orleans, LA D 6.20.1976 Metairie, LA BR/TR 5-11/170# d4.21 Mil 1944-45 M3 C6																								
1943	†StL N	154	627	91	180	28	14	7	62	50	2	70	.287	.342	.410	112	8	9	.973	-4	98	**141**	*2-126,S-51	1.4
1945	StL N	19	57	12	13	4	1	1	6	14	1	9	.228	.389	.386	113	2	0	.929	-1	81	110	/S-7,O-7(4-0-3),3-4,2-2	0.1
1946	StL N	23	93	12	18	3	0	1	4	9	0	7	.194	.265	.258	47	-7	1	.975	-1	93	140	2-23	-0.7
1949	StL N	58	114	25	25	6	0	2	12	22	2	20	.219	.355	.325	80	-2	0	.890	-2	111	68	S-21/2-9,3-7	-0.3
1951	Cle A	2	2	0	0	0	0	0	0	0	0	1	.000	.000	.000	-99	-1	0-0	—	0			H	-0.1
	Phi A	49	144	22	33	7	0	5	17	10	0	12	.229	.279	.382	76	-6	0-0	.975	0	106	117	2-42	-0.3
	Year	51	146	22	33	7	0	5	17	10	0	13	.226	.276	.377	74	-6	0-0	.975	0	106	117	2-42	-0.4
Total	5	305	1037	162	269	48	15	16	101	105	5	119	.259	.330	.381	97	-6	10-0	.975	-8	99	135	2-202/S-79,3-11,O-7(4-0-3)	0.1
KLEINOW, RED John Peter B 7.20.1879 Milwaukee, WI D 10.9.1929 New York, NY BR/TR 5-10/165# d5.3																								
1904	NY A	68	209	12	43	8	4	0	16	15	0		.206	.259	.282	68	-8	4	.966	-4	*88*	*104*	C-62/3-2,O(RF)	-0.7
1905	NY A	88	253	23	56	6	3	1	24	20	2		.221	.284	.281	71	-8	7	.978	-3	*111*	*99*	C-83/1-3	-0.5
1906	NY A	96	268	30	59	9	3	0	31	24	1		.220	.287	.276	69	-9	8	.974	1	*103*	*103*	C-95/1	0.0
1907	NY A	90	269	30	71	6	4	0	26	24	1		.264	.327	.316	97	-1	5	.970	-2	*90*	*100*	C-86/1	0.6
1908	NY A	96	279	16	47	3	2	1	13	22	3		.168	.237	.204	43	-17	5	.973	-9	*78*	*117*	C-89/2-2	-2.1
1909	NY A	78	206	24	47	11	4	0	15	25	1		.228	.315	.320	100	1	7	.966	-3	*90*	*95*	C-77	0.5
1910	NY A	6	12	2	5	0	0	0	2	1	0		.417	.462	.417	166	1	2	1.000	0	*108*	*86*	/C-5	0.2
	Bos A	50	147	9	22	1	0	1	8	20	0		.150	.251	.177	34	-11	3	.968	1	*110*	*84*	C-49	-0.5
	Year	56	159	11	27	1	0	1	10	21	0		.170	.267	.195	44	-10	5	.970	1	*110*	*84*	C-54	-0.3
1911	Bos A	8	14	0	3	0	0	0	0	2	0		.214	.313	.214	48	-1	1	1.000	0	*98*	*125*	/C-8	0.0
	Phi N	4	8	0	1	1	0	0	0	0	0	1	.125	.125	.250	4	-1	0	1.000	0	*95*	*88*	/C-4	-0.1
Total	8	584	1665	146	354	45	20	3	135	153	8	1	.213	.282	.269	71	-54	42	.972	-19	*95*	*101*	C-558/1-5,2-2,3-2,O(RF)	-2.6
KLESKO, RYAN Ryan Anthony B 6.12.1971 Westminster, CA BL/TL 6-3/220# d9.12																								
1992	Atl N	13	14	0	0	0	0	0	1	0-0	1	5	.000	.067	.000	-75	-3	0-0	1.000	-1	0	134	/1-5	-0.4
1993	Atl N	22	17	3	6	1	0	2	5	3-1	0	4	.353	.450	.765	216	3	0-0	1.000	-0	0	0	/1-3,O-2(LF)	0.2
1994	Atl N	92	245	42	68	13	3	17	47	26-3	1	48	.278	.344	.563	130	10	1-0	.921	-7	72	96	O-74(LF)/1-6	0.0
1995	†Atl N	107	329	48	102	25	2	23	70	47-10	2	72	.310	.396	.608	156	27	5-4	.942	-10	79	40	*O-102(LF)/1-4	1.3
1996	†Atl N	153	528	90	149	21	4	34	93	68-10	2	129	.282	.364	.530	126	19	6-3	.975	-9	82	78	*O-144(LF)/1-2	0.4
1997	†Atl N	143	467	67	122	23	6	24	84	48-5	4	130	.261	.334	.490	110	6	4-4	.969	-9	89	40	*O-130(LF),1-22	-0.9
1998	†Atl N	129	427	69	117	29	1	18	70	56-5	3	66	.274	.359	.473	117	12	5-3	.994	-3	81	139	*O-120(LF)/1-7	0.4
1999	†Atl N	133	404	55	120	28	2	21	80	53-8	2	69	.297	.376	.532	128	18	5-2	.989	-8	81	85	1-75,O-53(LF)/D	0.3
2000	SD N	145	494	88	140	33	2	26	92	91-9	1	81	.283	.393	.516	137	31	23-7	.992	-1	101	99	*1-136/O-4(2-0-2)	2.0
2001	SD N★	146	538	105	154	34	6	30	113	88-7	3	89	.286	.384	.539	150	42	23-4	.991	-5	88	83	*1-145	2.6
2002	SD N	146	540	90	162	39	1	29	95	76-11	4	86	.300	.388	.537	159	45	6-2	.993	-3	100	93	*1-112,O-31(RF)/D	3.0
2003	SD N	121	397	47	100	18	0	21	67	65-5	3	83	.252	.354	.456	122	14	2-5	.994	6	119	75	*1-111/D	0.9
Total	12	1350	4400	704	1240	264	27	245	817	621-74	26	862	.282	.370	.521	133	224	80-34	.971	-51	81	73	O-660(627-0-33),1-628/D-3	9.8
KLEVEN, JAY Jay Allen B 12.2.1949 Oakland, CA BR/TR 6-2/190# d6.20																								
1976	NY N	2	5	0	1	0	0	0	2	0-0	0	1	.200	.200	.200	15	-1	0-0	1.000	0	0	0	/C-2	0.0
KLIMCHOCK, LOU Louis Stephen B 10.15.1939 Hostetter, PA BL/TR 5-11/180# d9.27																								
1958	KC A	2	10	2	2	0	0	1	1	0-0	0	1	.200	.200	.500	84	0	0-0	1.000	-0	114	67	/2-2	-0.1
1959	KC A	17	66	10	18	1	0	4	13	1-0	0	6	.273	.284	.470	101	0	0-0	.949	-2	97	98	2-16	-0.1
1960	KC A	10	10	0	3	0	0	0	0	0-0	0	0	.300	.300	.300	62	-1	0-0	—	-0	0	0	/2	-0.1
1961	KC A	57	121	8	26	4	1	1	16	5-0	0	13	.215	.244	.289	42	-10	0-0	.976	-4	57	42	1-11/O-7(4-0-3),3-6,2	-1.5
1962	Mil N	8	8	0	0	0	0	0	0	0-0	0	2	.000	.000	.000	-99	-2	0-0	—	0			H	-0.2
1963	Was A	9	14	1	2	0	0	0	2	0-0	0	1	.143	.143	.143	-20	-2	0-0	1.000	0	140	63	/2-3	-0.2
	Mil N	24	46	6	9	1	0	0	1	0-0	0	12	.196	.196	.217	19	-5	0-1	.988	0	118	185	1-12	-0.6
1964	Mil N	10	21	3	7	2	0	0	2	1-0	0	2	.333	.364	.429	121	1	0-0	1.000	-2	59	0	/3-4,2-2	-0.1
1965	Mil N	34	39	3	3	0	0	0	3	2-0	0	8	.077	.119	.077	-42	-7	0-0	.923	1	224	0	/1-4	-0.8
1966	NY N	5	5	0	0	0	0	0	0	0-0	0	3	.000	.000	.000	-99	-1	0-0	—	0			H	-0.1
1968	Cle A	11	15	0	2	0	0	0	3	1-1	0	0	.133	.176	.133	-2	-2	0-0	.500	-2	41	0	/3-4,12	-0.5
1969	Cle A	90	258	26	74	13	2	6	26	18-3	0	14	.287	.331	.422	107	2	0-0	.934	-13	78	67	3-56,2-21/C	-1.1
1970	Cle A	41	56	5	9	0	0	1	2	3-1	1	9	.161	.213	.214	18	-6	0-0	1.000	-2	41	124	/1-5,2-5	-0.9
Total	12	318	669	64	155	21	3	13	69	31-5	1	71	.232	.264	.330	63	-33	0-1	.906	-24	75	56	/3-70,2-52,1-33,O-7(4-0-3),C	-6.3
KLINE, BOBBY John Robert B 1.27.1929 St.Petersburg, FL BR/TR 6/179# d4.11																								
1955	Was A	77	140	12	31	5	0	0	9	11-0	2	27	.221	.288	.257	50	-10	0-0	.943	7	107	108	S-69/2-4,3-3,P	0.1
KLING, JOHNNY John "Noisy" B 2.25.1875 Kansas City, MO D 1.31.1947 Kansas City, MO BR/TR 5-9.5/160# d9.11 M1 b-Bill																								
1900	Chi N	15	51	8	15	3	1	0	7	2	0		.294	.321	.392	100	0	0	.901	-2	*94*	*85*	C-15	-0.1
1901	Chi N	74	256	26	70	6	3	0	21	9	1		.273	.301	.320	83	-6	8	.952	-9	*87*	*101*	C-69/1O(RF)	-0.9
1902	Chi N	115	436	50	126	19	3	0	59	29	0		.289	.333	.346	113	7	25	.974	8	*107*	*107*	*C-113/S	2.7
1903	Chi N	132	491	67	146	29	13	3	68	22	2		.297	.330	.428	118	9	23	.969	8	*116*	*106*	*C-132	2.8
1904	Chi N	123	452	41	110	18	0	2	46	16	1		.243	.271	.296	75	-14	7	.974	-4	*120*	*99*	*C-104,O-10(9-0-1)/1-6	-0.9
1905	Chi N	111	380	26	83	8	6	1	52	28	0		.218	.272	.279	62	-19	13	.966	6	*115*	*95*	*C-106/O-4(RF),1	-0.2
1906	†Chi N	107	343	45	107	15	8	2	46	23	1		.312	.357	.420	134	12	14	**.982**	14	***163***	*101*	C-96/O-3(RF)	3.9
1907	†Chi N	104	334	44	95	15	8	1	43	27	2		.284	.342	.386	120	7	9	**.987**	9	*114*	*91*	C-98/1-2	2.9
1908	†Chi N	126	424	51	117	23	5	4	59	21	3		.276	.315	.382	117	7	16	.979	2	*108*	*108*	*C-117/O-6(1-1-4),1-2	2.4
1910	†Chi N	91	297	31	80	17	2	2	32	37	2	27	.269	.354	.360	109	5	3	.979	5	***135***	*88*	C-86	1.9
1911	Chi N	27	80	8	14	3	2	1	5	8	0	14	.175	.250	.300	54	-5	1	.969	5	*170*	*93*	C-25	0.2
	Bos N	75	241	32	54	8	1	2	24	30	0	29	.224	.310	.290	63	-12	0	.951	-12	*75*	*115*	C-71/3	-1.8
	Year	102	321	40	68	11	3	3	29	38	0	43	.212	.295	.293	61	-17	1	.956	-6	*100*	*109*	C-96/3	-1.6
1912	Bos N	81	252	26	80	10	3	2	30	15	0	30	.317	.356	.405	106	1	3	.958	-0	*94*	*107*	C-74,M	0.7
1913	Cin N	80	209	20	57	7	6	0	23	14	0	14	.273	.318	.364	95	-2	2-1	.975	4	108	107	C-63	0.8
Total	13	1261	4246	475	1154	181	61	20	515	281	12	114	.272	.319	.357	100	-10	124-1	.971	36	*115*	*101*	*C-1169/O-24(10-1-13),1-12,3S	14.4
KLING, RUDY Rudolph A. B 3.23.1870 St.Louis, MO D 3.14.1937 St.Louis, MO BR/TR 5-10/178# d9.21																								
1902	StL N	4	10	1	2	0	0	0	0	4	0		.200	.429	.200	99	0	1	.842	-2	63	151	/S-4	-0.1
KLINGER, JOE Joseph John B 8.2.1902 Canonsburg, PA D 7.31.1960 Little Rock, AR BR/TR 6/190# d9.13																								
1927	NY N	3	5	0	2	0	0	0	0	0	0	2	.400	.400	.400	115	0	0	1.000	0	141	0	/O(LF)	0.0
1930	Chi A	4	8	0	3	0	0	0	1	0	0	0	.375	.375	.375	94	0	0-0	1.000	-1	*0*	*0*	/C-2,1-2	-0.1
Total	2	7	13	0	5	0	0	0	1	0	0	2	.385	.385	.385	102	0	0-0	1.000	-0	0	178	/1-2,C-2,O(LF)	-0.1
KLOZA, NAP John Clarence B 9.7.1903 , Poland D 6.11.1962 Milwaukee, WI BR/TR 5-11/180# d8.16																								
1931	StL A	3	7	1	1	0	0	0	0	1	0	4	.143	.250	.143	5	-1	0-0	1.000	0	33	682	/O-3(RF)	-0.1
1932	StL A	19	13	4	2	0	1	0	2	4	0	4	.154	.353	.308	69	-1	0-0	1.000	0	115	0	/O-3(1-2-0)	-0.1
Total	2	22	20	5	3	0	1	0	2	5	0	8	.150	.320	.250	48	-2	0-0	1.000	0	59	467	/O-6(1-2-3)	-0.2
KLUGMANN, JOE Josie B 3.26.1895 St.Louis, MO D 7.18.1951 Moberly, MO BR/TR 5-11/175# d9.23																								
1921	Chi N	6	21	3	6	0	0	0	2	1	1	2	.286	.348	.286	69	-1	0-1	.969	-0	90	37	/2-5	-0.1
1922	Chi N	2	2	0	0	0	0	0	0	0	0	0	.000	.000	.000	-98	-1	0-0	1.000	1	129	274	/2-2	0.0
1924	Bro N	31	79	7	13	2	1	0	3	2	0	9	.165	.185	.215	7	-11	0-0	.929	-3	85	107	2-28/S	-1.3
1925	Cle A	38	85	12	28	9	2	0	12	8	0	4	.329	.387	.482	119	2	3-1	.959	-3	100	79	2-29/1-4,3-2	0.0
Total	4	77	187	22	47	11	3	0	17	11	1	15	.251	.296	.342	67	-11	3-2	.947	-5	93	90	/2-64,1-4,3-2,S	-1.4
KLUMPP, ELMER Elmer Edward B 8.26.1906 St.Louis, MO D 10.18.1996 Menomonee Falls, WI BR/TR 6/184# d4.17																								
1934	Was A	12	15	2	2	0	0	0	0	0	1	1	.133	.188	.133	-17	-3	0-0	.889	-1	*194*	*94*	C-11	-0.3
1937	Bro N	5	11	0	1	0	0	0	2	1	0	4	.091	.167	.091	-28	-2	0	1.000	1	*98*	*0*	/C-3	-0.1

Year	Tm Lg	G	AB	R	H	2B	3B	HR	RBI	BB-IB	HP	SO	AVG	OBP	SLG	AOPS	ABR	SB-CS	FA	FR	Rng	Thr	G at Pos	BFW
Total	2	17	26	2	3	0	0	0	2	1	1	5	.115	.179	.115	-21	-5	0-0	.943	-1	156	57	/C-14	-0.4
KLUSMAN, BILLY William F. B 3.24.1865 Cincinnati, OH D 6.24.1907 Cincinnati, OH BR/TR 5-10.5/185# d6.21																								
1888	Bos N	28	107	9	18	4	0	2	11	5	0	13	.168	.205	.262	47	-6	3	.914	-6	89	62	2-28	-1.1
1890	StL AA	15	65	9	18	4	1	1	11	1	0		.277	.288	.415	94	-1	1	.896	-1	116	55	2-15	-0.1
Total	2	43	172	18	36	8	1	3	22	6	0	13	.209	.236	.320	66	-7	4	.908	-6	98	60	/2-43	-1.2
KLUSZEWSKI, TED Theodore Bernard "Big Klu" B 9.10.1924 Argo, IL D 3.29.1988 Cincinnati, OH BL/TL 6-2/225# d4.18 C9																								
1947	Cin N	9	10	1	1	0	0	0	2	1	0	2	.100	.182	.100	-23	-2	0	1.000	-0	0	115	/1-2	-0.2
1948	Cin N	113	379	49	104	23	4	12	57	18	0	32	.274	.307	.451	107	1	1	.990	2	106	80	1-98	0.0
1949	Cin N	136	531	63	164	26	2	8	68	19	0	24	.309	.333	.411	97	-4	3	.989	-6	84	97	*1-134	-1.4
1950	Cin N	134	538	76	165	37	0	25	111	33	1	28	.307	.348	.515	123	16	3	.987	-12	66	83	*1-131	0.0
1951	Cin N	154	607	74	157	35	2	13	77	35	2	33	.259	.301	.387	83	-16	6-2	**.997**	-7	80	81	*1-154	-2.8
1952	Cin N	135	497	62	159	24	11	16	86	47	4	28	.320	.383	.509	146	30	3-3	**.993**	-8	76	97	*1-133	1.8
1953	Cin N★	149	570	97	180	25	0	40	108	55	4	34	.316	.380	.570	142	35	2-0	**.995**	-15	62	**115**	*1-147	1.2
1954	Cin N★	149	573	104	187	28	3	**49**	**141**	78	3	35	.326	.407	.642	165	54	0-2	**.996**	-2	94	**117**	*1-149	4.2
1955	Cin N★	153	612	116	**192**	25	0	47	113	66-**25**	4	40	.314	.382	.585	144	39	1-1	**.995**	-8	81	**118**	*1-153	2.1
1956	Cin N★	138	517	91	156	14	1	35	102	49-22	3	31	.302	.362	.536	130	21	1-0	.990	-5	90	101	*1-131	0.9
1957	Cin N	69	127	12	34	7	0	6	21	5-3	1	5	.268	.301	.465	95	-1	0-0	.989	-0	101	66	1-23	-0.2
1958	Pit N	100	301	29	88	13	4	4	37	26-6	1	16	.292	.348	.402	101	1	0-0	.994	-5	73	102	1-72	-0.9
1959	Pit N	60	122	11	32	10	1	2	17	5-1	0	14	.262	.291	.410	85	-3	0-0	1.000	-0	90	93	1-20	-0.4
	†Chi A	31	101	11	30	2	1	2	10	9-3	0	10	.297	.351	.396	107	1	0-1	1.000	-2	62	64	1-29	-0.3
1960	Chi A	81	181	20	53	9	0	5	39	22-5	0	10	.293	.364	.425	116	4	0-1	.997	-1	83	117	1-39	0.1
1961	LA A	107	263	32	64	12	0	15	39	24-5	0	23	.243	.303	.460	91	-4	0-0	.989	-6	65	95	1-66	-1.3
Total	15	1718	5929	848	1766	290	29	279	1028	492-70	23	365	.298	.353	.498	122	172	20-10	.993	-75	80	99	*1-1481	2.8
KLUTTS, MICKEY Gene Ellis B 9.20.1954 Montebello, CA BR/TR 5-11/189# d7.7																								
1976	NY A	2	3	0	0	0	0	0	0	0-0	0	1	.000	.000	.000	-99	-1	0-0	.875	-0	83	0	/S-2	-0.1
1977	NY A	5	15	3	4	1	0	1	4	2-0	1	1	.267	.389	.533	150	1	0-1	1.000	2	168	155	/3-4,S	0.3
1978	NY A	1	2	1	2	1	0	0	0	0-0	0	0	1.000	1.000	1.500	608	2	0-0	.750	0	92	555	/3	0.2
1979	Oak A	24	73	3	14	2	1	1	4	7-0	0	20	.192	.262	.288	51	-5	0-1	.882	-3	105	60	S-10/2-8,3-6,D-2	-0.8
1980	Oak A	75	197	20	53	14	0	4	21	13-1	0	41	.269	.313	.401	102	0	1-4	.947	-7	92	35	3-62/S-8,2-7,D	-0.7
1981	†Oak A	15	46	9	17	0	0	5	11	2-1	0	9	.370	.396	.696	220	6	0-0	.957	-3	69	51	3-14	0.3
1982	Oak A	55	157	10	28	8	0	0	14	9-0	0	18	.178	.222	.229	26	-16	0-0	.946	-3	94	63	3-49	-2.0
1983	Tor A	22	43	3	11	0	0	3	5	1-1	1	11	.256	.289	.465	98	0	0-1	1.000	-4	57	94	3-17/D-2	-0.5
Total	8	199	536	49	129	26	1	14	59	34-3	3	101	.241	.289	.371	84	-13	1-7	.948	-18	91	57	3-153/S-21,2-15,D-5	-3.3
KLUTTZ, CLYDE Clyde Franklin B 12.12.1917 Rockwell, NC D 5.12.1979 Salisbury, NC BR/TR 6/198# d4.20																								
1942	Bos N	72	210	21	56	10	1	1	31	7	1	13	.267	.294	.338	86	-5	0	.979	-3	75	92	C-57	-0.4
1943	Bos N	66	207	13	51	7	0	0	20	15	0	9	.246	.297	.280	68	-9	0	.973	-3	58	158	C-55	-0.9
1944	Bos N	81	229	20	64	12	2	2	19	13	0	14	.279	.318	.376	91	-3	0	.980	1	64	155	C-58	0.1
1945	Bos N	25	81	9	24	4	1	0	10	2	0	6	.296	.313	.370	89	-2	0	.987	0	106	123	C-19	0.0
	NY N	73	222	25	62	14	0	4	21	15	2	10	.279	.331	.396	100	0	1	.978	-1	161	115	C-57	0.2
	Year	98	303	34	86	18	1	4	31	17	2	16	.284	.326	.389	97	-2	1	.981	-1	146	117	C-76	0.2
1946	NY N	5	8	0	3	0	0	0	1	0	0	1	.375	.375	.375	112	0	0	.857	-1	49	0	/C-2	0.0
	StL N	52	136	8	36	7	0	0	14	10	0	10	.265	.315	.316	76	-4	0	.980	3	149	105	C-49	0.1
	Year	57	144	8	39	7	0	0	15	10	0	11	.271	.318	.319	78	-4	0	.976	2	146	102	C-51	0.1
1947	Pit N	73	232	26	70	9	2	6	42	17	2	18	.302	.355	.435	106	1	1	.987	2	91	150	C-69	0.7
1948	Pit N	94	271	26	60	12	2	4	20	20	0	19	.221	.275	.325	61	-16	3	.978	2	104	**156**	C-91	-0.9
1951	StL A	4	4	2	2	1	0	0	1	1	0	0	.500	.600	.750	256	1	0-0	1.000	0	0	509	/C	0.1
	Was A	53	159	15	49	9	0	1	22	20	1	8	.308	.389	.384	111	4	0-0	.968	-6	96	65	C-46	0.0
	Year	57	163	17	51	10	0	1	23	21	1	8	.313	.395	.393	115	5	0-0	.968	-6	94	73	C-47	0.1
1952	Was A	58	144	7	33	5	0	1	11	12	1	11	.229	.293	.285	63	-7	0-0	.979	1	107	88	C-52	-0.5
Total	9	656	1903	172	510	90	8	19	212	132	7	119	.268	.318	.354	86	-40	5-0	.978	-5	98	126	C-556	-1.5
KMAK, JOE Joseph Robert B 5.3.1963 Napa, CA BR/TR 6/185# d4.6																								
1993	Mil A	51	110	9	24	5	0	0	7	14-0	2	13	.218	.317	.264	59	-6	6-2	1.000	-2	88	114	C-50	-0.5
1995	Chi N	19	53	7	13	3	0	1	6	6-0	1	12	.245	.328	.358	84	-1	0-0	1.000	-3	118	91	C-18/3	-0.3
Total	2	70	163	16	37	8	0	1	13	20-0	3	25	.227	.321	.294	67	-7	6-2	1.000	-5	97	107	/C-68,3	-0.8
KNABE, OTTO Franz Otto "Dutch" B 6.12.1884 Carrick, PA D 5.17.1961 Philadelphia, PA BR/TR 5-8/175# d10.3 M2																								
1905	Pit N	3	10	0	3	1	0	0	2	3			.300	.462	.400	154	1	0	.786	0	130	247	/3-3	0.1
1907	Phi N	129	444	67	113	16	9	1	34	52	5		.255	.339	.338	114	8	18	.960	2	95	129	*2-121/O-5(1-0-3)	1.2
1908	Phi N	151	555	63	121	26	8	0	27	49	7		.218	.290	.294	84	-9	27	.969	10	**104**	102	*2-151	0.2
1909	Phi N	113	402	40	94	13	3	0	34	35	8		.234	.308	.281	82	-8	9	.938	5	101	105	*2-110/O(LF)	-0.2
1910	Phi N	137	510	73	133	18	6	1	44	47	3	42	.261	.327	.325	87	-8	15	.954	14	97	119	*2-136	0.7
1911	Phi N	142	528	99	125	15	6	1	42	94	0	35	.237	.352	.294	80	-10	23	.950	2	100	88	*2-142	-0.6
1912	Phi N	126	426	56	120	11	4	0	46	55	2	20	.282	.366	.326	85	-7	16	.952	2	101	93	*2-123	-0.4
1913	Phi N	148	571	70	150	25	7	2	53	45	3	26	.263	.320	.342	85	-11	14-18	.959	6	106	97	*2-148	-0.6
1914	Bal F	147	469	45	106	26	2	2	42	53	2	28	.226	.307	.303	65	-29	10	.956	2	99	98	*2-144,M	-2.6
1915	Bal F	103	320	38	81	16	2	1	25	37	2	16	.253	.334	.325	83	-10	7	.975	5	98	129	2-94/O(RF)M	-0.4
1916	Pit N	28	89	4	17	3	1	0	9	6	2	6	.191	.258	.247	55	-5	1	.962	-3	103	27	2-28	-0.9
	Chi N	51	145	17	40	8	0	0	7	9	2	18	.276	.327	.331	92	-1	3	.939	3	113	113	2-42/S3O(RF)	0.4
	Year	79	234	21	57	11	1	0	16	15	4	24	.244	.300	.299	79	-5	4	.948	0	109	77	2-70/S3O(RF)	-0.5
Total	11	1278	4469	572	1103	178	48	8	365	485	36	191	.247	.325	.313	84	-89	143-18	.957	47	101	104	*2-1239/O-8(2-0-5),3-4,S	-3.1
KNAUPP, COTTON Henry Antone B 8.13.1889 San Antonio, TX D 7.6.1967 New Orleans, LA BR/TR 5-9/165# d8.30																								
1910	Cle A	18	59	3	14	3	1	0	11	8	1		.237	.338	.322	105	1	1	.884	-7	91	81	S-18	-0.6
1911	Cle A	13	39	2	4	1	0	0	0	0	0		.103	.103	.128	-35	-7	3	.964	2	118	57	S-13	-0.5
Total	2	31	98	5	18	4	1	0	11	8	1		.184	.252	.245	48	-6	4	.913	-6	100	73	/S-31	-1.1
KNICELY, ALAN Alan Lee B 5.19.1955 Harrisonburg, VA BR/TR 6-0.5/194# d8.12																								
1979	Hou N	7	6	0	0	0	0	0	0	2-0	0	3	.000	.250	.000	-27	-1	0-0	1.000	-1	0	0	/C-3,3	-0.2
1980	Hou N	1	1	0	0	0	0	0	0	0-0	0	1	.000	.000	.000	-99	0	0-0	—	0			/H	0.0
1981	Hou N	3	7	2	4	0	0	2	2	0-0	0	1	.571	.571	1.429	477	3	0-0	1.000	1	0	0	/C-2,O(LF)	0.4
1982	Hou N	59	133	10	25	2	0	2	12	14-3	1	30	.188	.270	.248	50	-9	0-1	.977	0	119	91	C-23,O-16(1-0-15)/3	-1.0
1983	Cin N	59	98	11	22	3	0	2	10	16-3	0	28	.224	.333	.316	78	-2	0-2	1.000	0	82	113	C-31/O-8(3-0-5),1-2	-0.3
1984	Cin N	10	29	0	4	0	0	0	0	5	3-0	0	6	.138	.200	.138	2	-4	0-0	.984	-2	92	76	/1-8,C	-0.6
1985	Cin N	48	158	17	40	9	0	5	26	16-2	1	34	.253	.322	.405	98	0	0-0	.968	-9	73	75	C-46	-0.8
	Phi N	7	7	0	0	0	0	0	0	0-0	0	4	.000	.000	.000	-97	-2	0-0	1.000	-0	0	335	/1	-0.2
	Year	55	165	17	40	9	0	5	26	16-2	1	38	.242	.310	.388	91	-2	0-0	.968	-10	73	75	C-46/1	-1.0
1986	StL N	34	82	8	16	3	0	1	6	17-0	0	21	.195	.330	.268	68	-3	1-1	.995	-0	104	125	1-29/C-2	-0.5
Total	8	228	521	48	111	17	0	12	61	68-8	2	128	.213	.303	.315	73	-18	1-4	.979	-10	83	84	C-108/1-40,O-25(5-0-20),3-2	-3.2
KNICKERBOCKER, AUSTIN Austin Jay B 10.15.1918 Bangall, NY D 2.18.1997 Clinton Corners, NY BR/TR 5-11/185# d4.19																								
1947	Phi A	21	48	8	12	3	2	0	2	3	0	4	.250	.294	.396	89	-1	0-1	.943	1	117	110	O-14(2-2-10)	-0.1
KNICKERBOCKER, BILL William Hart B 12.29.1911 Los Angeles, CA D 9.8.1963 Sebastopol, CA BR/TR 5-11/170# d4.12																								
1933	Cle A	80	279	20	63	16	3	2	32	11	0	30	.226	.255	.326	51	-21	1-4	.939	2	104	97	S-80	-1.4
1934	Cle A	146	593	82	188	32	5	4	67	25	2	40	.317	.347	.408	93	-8	6-6	.962	-7	96	**114**	*S-146	-0.5
1935	Cle A	132	540	77	161	34	5	0	55	27	0	31	.298	.332	.380	82	-15	2-12	.956	9	108	105	*S-128	-0.1
1936	Cle A	155	618	81	182	35	3	8	73	56	1	30	.294	.354	.400	85	-15	5-14	.952	-1	98	92	*S-155	-0.7
1937	StL A	121	491	53	128	29	5	4	61	30	0	32	.261	.303	.365	67	-26	3-2	.958	-9	103	73	*S-115/2-6	-2.5
1938	NY A	46	128	15	32	8	3	1	21	11	0	10	.250	.309	.383	73	-6	0-0	.982	1	96	117	2-34/S-3	-0.3
1939	NY A	6	13	2	2	1	0	0	1	0	0	0	.154	.154	.231	-3	-2	0-0	1.000	1	111	97	/2-2,S-2	-0.1
1940	NY A	45	124	17	30	8	1	1	10	14	3	8	.242	.333	.347	80	-3	1-1	.985	-0	103	147	S-19,3-17	-0.2

Year	Tm Lg	G	AB	R	H	2B	3B	HR	RBI	BB-IB	HP	SO	AVG	OBP	SLG	AOPS	ABR	SB-CS	FA	FR	Rng	Thr	G at Pos	BFW
1941	Chi A	89	343	51	84	23	2	7	29	41	2	27	.245	.329	.385	89	-5	6-5	.970	-13	90	113	2-88	-1.3
1942	Phi A	87	289	25	73	12	0	1	19	29	1	30	.253	.323	.304	77	-8	1-2	.964	-10	93	85	2-81/S	-1.4
Total	10	907	3418	423	943	198	27	28	368	244	9	238	.276	.326	.374	79	-109	25-46	.955	-28	101	98	S-649,2-211/3-17	-8.5
KNIGHT, LON Alonzo P. B 6.16.1853 Philadelphia, PA D 4.23.1932 Philadelphia, PA BR/TR 5-11.5/165# d9.4 M2 U3 ▲ OF Total (7-CF 473-RF)																								
1875	Ath NA	13	47	5	6	2	0	0	2	0		2	.128	.128	.170	2	-5	2-0	.875	-0	112	113	P-13/S	-0.1
1876	Phi N	55	240	32	60	9	3	0	24	2		2	.250	.256	.313	89	-3		.804	-6	92	56	P-34,1-13/O-9(0-3-6),2-6	-0.6
1880	Wor N	49	201	31	48	11	3	0	21	5		8	.239	.257	.323	88	-3		.863	2	181	49	O-49(RF)	0.0
1881	Det N	83	340	67	92	16	3	1	52	23		21	.271	.317	.344	104	2		.890	0	98	**184**	*O-82(RF)/21	0.2
1882	Det N	**86**	347	39	72	12	6	0	24	16		21	.207	.242	.277	66	-13		.867	-1	130	50	*O-84(RF)/1-2	-1.4
1883	Phi AA	97	429	98	108	23	9	1	53	21			.252	.287	.354	96	-3		.858	-1	120	235	*O-93(RF)/3-3,2-2,M	-0.4
1884	Phi AA	**108**	484	94	131	18	12	1		10	1		.271	.287	.364	104	0		.911	11	176	**198**	*O-108(RF)/P-2,1M	0.9
1885	Phi AA	29	119	17	25	1	1	0	14	9	1		.210	.271	.235	58	-6		.921	4	174	295	O-29(RF)/P	-0.2
	Pro N	25	81	8	13	1	0	0	8	11		17	.160	.261	.173	44	-4		.957	3	144	353	O-25(0-4-22)/P	-0.2
Total	7	532	2241	386	549	91	37	3	196	97		69	.245	.277	.323	89	-30		.887	11	140	170	O-479R/P-38,1-17,2-9,3-3	-1.7
KNIGHT, RAY Charles Ray B 12.28.1952 Albany, GA BR/TR 6-2/190# d9.10 M3 C5 OF Total (9-LF 1-RF)																								
1974	Cin N	14	11	1	2	1	0	0	2	1-0	0	2	.182	.250	.273	47	-1	0-0	1.000	-1	78	0	3-14	-0.2
1977	Cin N	80	92	8	24	5	1	1	13	9-1	0	16	.261	.324	.370	85	-2	1-1	.941	-1	96	120	3-37,2-17/O-5(LF),S-3	-0.3
1978	Cin N	83	65	7	13	3	0	1	4	3-0	0	13	.200	.235	.292	47	-5	0-0	.868	-0	115	35	3-60/2-4,O-3(2-0-1),1S	-0.6
1979	†Cin N	150	551	64	175	37	4	10	79	38-4	3	57	.318	.360	.454	121	16	4-4	.962	-10	92	101	*3-149	0.4
1980	Cin N★	162	618	71	163	39	7	14	78	36-9	4	62	.264	.307	.417	101	-1	1-2	.969	-11	89	80	*3-162	-1.6
1981	Cin N	106	386	43	100	23	1	6	34	33-3	4	51	.259	.322	.370	95	-2	2-4	.957	-7	88	110	*3-105	-1.3
1982	Hou N★	158	609	72	179	36	6	6	70	48-9	5	58	.294	.344	.402	119	15	2-5	.990	2	78	111	1-96,3-67	1.0
1983	Hou N	145	507	43	154	36	4	9	70	42-9	4	62	.304	.355	.444	130	21	0-3	.993	-11	73	**128**	*1-143	0.0
1984	Hou N	88	278	15	62	10	0	2	29	14-1	1	30	.223	.259	.281	57	-17	0-3	.946	-6	89	77	3-54,1-24	-2.8
	NY N	27	93	13	26	4	0	1	6	7-1	1	13	.280	.337	.355	96	0	0-0	.962	-5	73	92	3-27/1-3	-0.6
	Year	115	371	28	88	14	0	3	35	21-2	2	43	.237	.279	.299	67	-17	0-3	.951	-11	83	82	3-81,1-27	-3.4
1985	NY N	90	271	22	59	12	0	6	36	13-1	1	32	.218	.252	.328	64	-14	1-1	.958	-9	81	46	3-73/2-2,1	-2.6
1986	†NY N	137	486	51	145	24	2	11	76	40-2	4	63	.298	.351	.424	118	12	2-1	.948	-19	81	86	*3-132/1	-1.0
1987	Bal A	150	563	46	144	24	0	14	65	39-3	6	90	.256	.310	.373	82	-15	0-0	.956	12	**113**	113	*3-130,D-14/1-6	-0.5
1988	Det A	105	299	34	65	12	2	3	33	20-0	3	30	.217	.271	.301	63	-15	1-1	.991	-4	84	95	1-64,D-25,3-11/O-2(LF)	-2.4
Total	13	1495	4829	490	1311	266	27	84	595	343-43	36	579	.271	.321	.390	99	-8	14-25	.957	-70	92	96	*3-1021,1-339/D-39,2-23,O-10L,S	-12.5
KNIGHT, JOHN John Wesley "Schoolboy" B 10.6.1885 Philadelphia, PA D 12.19.1965 Walnut Creek, CA BR/TR 6-2.5/180# d4.14																								
1905	Phi A	88	325	28	66	12	1	3	29	9	1		.203	.227	.274	58	-17	4	.895	-26	79	39	S-79/3-4	-4.5
1906	Phi A	74	253	29	49	7	2	3	20	19	0		.194	.250	.273	62	-11	6	.922	2	102	98	3-67/2-7	-0.8
1907	Phi A	40	139	6	29	7	1	0	12	10	2		.209	.272	.273	72	-4	1	.862	-3	90	115	3-40	-0.6
	Bos A	98	360	31	78	9	3	2	29	19	0		.217	.256	.275	70	-13	8	.924	3	104	136	3-92/2-4	-0.8
	Year	138	499	37	107	16	4	2	41	29	2		.214	.260	.275	71	-17	9	**.906**	-0	100	**130**	*3-132/2-4	-1.4
1909	NY A	116	360	46	85	8	5	0	40	37	2		.236	.311	.286	88	-4	15	.901	-4	97	81	S-76,1-19,2-17/3-3	-0.7
1910	NY A	117	414	58	129	25	4	3	45	34	6		.312	.372	.413	138	19	23	.929	-2	97	143	S-79,1-23/2-7,3-4,O(RF)	2.1
1911	NY A	132	470	69	126	16	7	3	62	42	11		.268	.342	.351	88	-8	18	.907	-6	89	99	S-82,1-27,2-21/3	-0.8
1912	Was A	32	93	10	15	2	1	0	9	16	0		.161	.284	.204	40	-7	4	.926	-5	71	107	2-27/1-5	-1.2
1913	NY A	70	250	24	59	10	0	0	24	25	2	27	.236	.310	.276	72	-8	7	.980	8	148	95	1-50,2-21	-0.1
Total	8	767	2664	301	636	96	24	14	270	211	24	27	.239	.300	.309	84	-53	86	.909	-33	90	91	S-316,3-211,1-124,2-104/O(RF)	-7.4
KNIGHT, JOE Joseph William "Quiet Joe" B 9.28.1859 Port Stanley, ON, CAN D 10.16.1938 Lynhurst, ON, CAN BL/TL 5-11/185# d5.16 ▲																								
1884	Phi N	6	24	2	6	3	0	0	2	0		2	.250	.250	.375	98	1		.789	-0	115	0	/P-6	0.0
1890	Cin N	127	481	67	150	26	8	4	67	38	4	31	.312	.367	.424	131	18	17	.925	-6	51	0	*O-127(LF)	0.8
Total	2	133	505	69	156	29	8	4	69	38	4	33	.309	.362	.422	130	19	17	.925	-7	51	0	O-127(LF)/P-6	0.8
KNISELY, PETE Peter Cole B 8.11.1887 Waynesburg, PA D 7.1.1948 Brownsville, PA BR/TR 5-9/185# d9.4																								
1912	Cin N	21	67	10	22	7	3	0	7	4	1	5	.328	.375	.522	148	4	3	.939	-1	92	207	O-13(CF)/2-3,S	0.2
1913	Chi N	2	2	0	0	0	0	0	0	0	0	1	.000	.000	.000	-99	-1	0	—	0			H	-0.1
1914	Chi N	37	69	5	9	0	1	0	5	5	1	6	.130	.200	.159	7	-8	0	.975	2	116	130	O-17(10-1-6)	-0.8
1915	Chi N	64	134	12	33	9	0	0	17	15	2	18	.246	.331	.313	95	0	1-2	.940	-3	98	109	O-33(8-9-16)/2-9	-0.5
Total	4	124	272	27	64	16	4	0	29	24	4	30	.235	.307	.324	86	-5	4-2	.951	-2	102	138	/O-63(18-23-22),2-12,S	-1.2
KNOBLAUCH, CHUCK Edward Charles B 7.7.1968 Houston, TX BR/TR 5-9/181# d4.9																								
1991	†Min A	151	565	78	159	24	6	1	50	59-0	4	40	.281	.351	.350	91	-5	25-5	.975	2	107	104	*2-148/S-2	0.4
1992	Min A★	155	600	104	178	19	6	2	56	88-1	5	60	.297	.384	.358	108	10	34-13	.992	-8	96	107	*2-154/SD	1.0
1993	Min A	153	602	82	167	27	4	2	41	65-1	9	44	.277	.354	.346	89	-7	29-11	.988	-2	100	98	*2-148/S-6,O(CF)	0.1
1994	Min A★	109	445	85	139	**45**	3	5	51	41-2	10	56	.312	.381	.461	116	13	35-6	.994	-21	91	84	*2-109/S	0.3
1995	Min A	136	538	107	179	34	8	11	63	78-3	10	95	.333	.424	.487	137	33	46-18	.985	-9	98	94	*2-136/S-2	3.3
1996	Min A★	153	578	140	197	35	**14**	13	72	98-6	19	74	.341	.448	.517	142	44	45-14	**.988**	-17	93	94	*2-151/D-2	3.6
1997	Min A★	156	611	117	178	26	10	9	58	84-6	17	84	.291	.390	.411	108	11	62-10	.985	-7	101	105	*2-154/SD	2.0
1998	†NY A	150	603	117	160	25	4	17	64	76-1	**18**	70	.265	.361	.405	104	6	31-12	.981	1	100	106	*2-149/D	1.5
1999	†NY A	150	603	120	176	36	4	18	68	83-0	21	57	.292	.393	.454	118	20	28-9	.963	-20	94	68	*2-150	1.0
2000	†NY A	102	400	75	113	22	2	5	26	46-0	8	45	.283	.366	.385	92	-3	15-7	.958	-13	86	82	2-82,D-20	-1.2
2001	†NY A	137	521	66	130	20	3	9	44	58-1	14	73	.250	.339	.351	82	-12	38-9	.989	-2	89	133	*O-108(LF),D-24	-1.4
2002	KC A	80	300	41	63	9	0	6	22	28-1	4	32	.210	.284	.300	50	-22	19-3	.980	-0	96	115	O-74(LF)/D-2	-2.1
Total	12	1632	6366	1132	1839	322	64	98	615	804-22	139	730	.289	.378	.406	106	88	407-117	.982	-96	97	95	*2-1381,O-183(182-1-0)/D-51,S-13	8.5
KNODE, MIKE Kenneth Thomson B 11.8.1895 Westminster, MD D 12.20.1980 South Bend, IN BR/TR 5-10/160# d6.28 b-Ray																								
1920	StL N	42	65	11	15	1	1	0	12	5	2	6	.231	.306	.277	71	-2	0-1	.824	-1	85	102	/O-9(2-0-7),2-4,S-2,3-2	-0.4
KNODE, RAY Robert Troxell "Bob" B 1.28.1901 Westminster, MD D 4.13.1982 Battle Creek, MI BL/TL 5-10/160# d6.30 b-Mike																								
1923	Cle A	22	38	7	11	0	0	2	4	2	0	4	.289	.325	.447	102	0	1-0	.992	0	105	100	1-21	-0.1
1924	Cle A	11	37	6	9	1	0	0	4	3	0	0	.243	.300	.270	47	-3	2-1	.992	1	130	141	1-10	-0.3
1925	Cle A	45	108	13	27	5	0	0	11	10	0	4	.250	.314	.296	55	-7	3-3	.990	1	107	120	1-34	-0.8
1926	Cle A	31	24	6	8	1	1	0	2	2	0	3	.333	.385	.458	118	1	0-0	.984	0	148	97	1-11	0.1
Total	4	109	207	32	55	7	1	2	21	17	0	11	.266	.321	.338	69	-9	6-4	.990	2	114	118	/1-76	-1.1
KNOLL, PUNCH Charles Elmer B 10.7.1881 Evansville, IN D 2.8.1960 Evansville, IN BR/TR 5-7.5/170# d4.27																								
1905	Was A	79	244	24	52	10	5	0	29	9	2		.213	.247	.295	75	-8	3	.927	-1	75	63	O-63(10-0-53)/C-5,1-2	-1.3
KNOOP, BOBBY Robert Frank B 10.18.1938 Sioux City, IA BR/TR 6-1/170# d4.13 M1 C21																								
1964	LA A	**162**	486	42	105	8	1	7	38	46-6	5	109	.216	.289	.280	66	-23	3-2	.978	**33**	**117**	121	*2-161	2.5
1965	Cal A	142	465	47	125	24	4	7	43	31-5	0	101	.269	.313	.383	99	-1	3-2	.971	18	**115**	104	*2-142	3.0
1966	Cal A★	161	590	54	137	18	**11**	17	72	43-8	1	144	.232	.282	.386	94	-8	1-5	**.981**	21	**113**	**128**	*2-161	2.7
1967	Cal A	159	511	51	125	18	5	9	38	44-13	1	136	.245	.305	.352	98	-2	2-2	.986	9	102	107	*2-159	2.1
1968	Cal A	152	494	48	123	20	4	3	39	35-6	3	128	.249	.301	.324	93	-5	3-2	.981	19	110	**114**	*2-151	3.0
1969	Cal A	27	71	5	14	1	0	1	6	13-1	0	16	.197	.318	.254	66	-3	1-3	.977	2	99	95	2-27	0.0
	Chi A	104	345	34	79	14	1	6	41	35-3	2	68	.229	.301	.328	73	-12	2-0	.985	31	123	113	*2-104	2.6
	Year	131	416	39	93	15	1	7	47	48-4	2	84	.224	.304	.315	72	-15	3-3	**.984**	**33**	**118**	110	*2-131	2.6
1970	Chi A	130	402	34	92	13	2	5	36	34-4	2	79	.229	.290	.308	63	-20	0-1	.984	27	**123**	120	*2-126	1.5
1971	KC A	72	161	14	33	8	1	1	11	15-1	0	36	.205	.270	.286	59	-9	1-0	.968	-8	95	103	2-52/3	-1.4
1972	KC A	44	97	8	23	5	0	0	7	9-1	0	16	.237	.299	.289	77	-3	0-0	.972	4	113	145	2-33/3-4	0.3
Total	9	1153	3622	337	856	129	29	56	331	305-48	14	833	.236	.296	.334	83	-86	16-17	.980	156	113	115	*2-1116/3-5	16.3
KNORR, RANDY Randy Duane B 11.12.1968 San Gabriel, CA BR/TR 6-2/215# d9.5																								
1991	Tor A	3	1	0	0	0	0	0	0	1-0	0	1	.000	.500	.000	49	0	0-0	1.000	1	0	0	/C-3	0.1
1992	Tor A	8	19	1	5	0	0	1	2	1-1	0	5	.263	.300	.421	96	0	0-0	1.000	1	392	147	/C-8	0.1
1993	†Tor A	39	101	11	25	3	2	4	20	9-0	0	29	.248	.309	.436	97	-1	0-0	1.000	-3	67	98	C-39	-0.2
1994	Tor A	40	124	20	30	2	0	7	19	10-0	1	35	.242	.301	.427	86	-3	0-0	.993	-2	72	89	C-40	-0.3
1995	Tor A	45	132	18	28	8	0	3	16	11-0	0	28	.212	.273	.341	59	-8	0-0	.971	-6	66	83	C-45	-1.1

Year	Tm Lg	G	AB	R	H	2B	3B	HR	RBI	BB-IB	HP	SO	AVG	OBP	SLG	AOPS	ABR	SB-CS	FA	FR	Rng	Thr	G at Pos	BFW
1996	Hou N	37	87	7	17	5	0	1	7	5-2	1	18	.195	.245	.287	44	-7	0-1	1.000	5	160	116	C-33	-0.1
1997	Hou N	4	8	1	3	0	0	1	1	0-0	0	2	.375	.375	.750	193	1	0-0	1.000	1	85	251	/C-3,1-2	0.2
1998	Fla N	15	49	4	10	4	1	2	11	1-0	0	10	.204	.216	.449	74	-2	0-0	.989	-4	59	79	C-15	-0.5
1999	Hou N	13	30	2	5	1	0	0	0	1-0	0	8	.167	.194	.200	-0	-5	0-0	1.000	-1	66	0	C-11	-0.5
2000	Tex A	15	34	5	10	2	0	2	2	0-0	0	3	.294	.294	.529	101	0	0-0	.985	-1	90	150	C-15	-0.1
2001	Mon N	34	91	13	20	2	0	3	10	8-0	1	22	.220	.287	.341	61	-6	0-0	.989	-7	48	89	C-27	-1.1
Total	11	253	676	82	153	27	3	24	88	47-3	3	161	.226	.278	.382	71	-31	0-1	.990	-15	87	94	C-239/1-2	-3.5
KNOTHE, GEORGE George Bertram B 1.12.1898 Bayonne, NJ D 7.3.1981 Toms River, NJ BR/TR 5-10/165# d4.25 b-Fritz																								
1932	Phi N	6	12	2	1	1	0	0	0	0	0	0	.083	.083	.167	-31	-2	0	.923	-1	98	120	/2-5	-0.3
KNOTHE, FRITZ Wilfred Edgar B 5.1.1903 Passaic, NJ D 3.27.1963 Passaic, NJ BR/TR 5-10.5/180# d4.12 b-George																								
1932	Bos N	89	344	45	82	19	1	1	36	39	1	37	.238	.318	.308	72	-12	5	.947	-6	98	45	3-87	-1.5
1933	Bos N	44	158	15	36	5	2	1	6	13	1	25	.228	.291	.304	76	-5	1	.978	-3	91	148	3-33/S-9	-0.7
	Phi N	41	113	10	17	2	0	0	11	6	0	19	.150	.193	.168	3	-14	2	.949	9	127	151	3-32/2-4	-0.4
	Year	85	271	25	53	7	2	1	17	19	1	44	.196	.251	.247	42	-21	3	.961	5	110	150	3-65/S-9,2-4	-1.1
Total	2	174	615	70	135	26	3	2	53	58	2	81	.220	.289	.281	59	-31	8	.953	-1	103	88	3-152/S-9,2-4	-2.6
KNOTTS, JOE Joseph Steven B 3.3.1884 Greensboro, PA D 9.15.1950 Philadelphia, PA BR/TR 5-9/170# d9.18																								
1907	Bos N	3	8	0	0	0	0	0	0	1	0		.000	.111	.000	-65	-2	0	1.000	-0	*77*	*118*	/C-3	-0.2
KNOUFF, ED Edward "Fred" B 6.1868 Philadelphia, PA D 9.14.1900 Philadelphia, PA BR/TR ?/210# d7.1 ▲																								
1885	Phi AA	14	48	5	9	0	0	0	2	2	0		.188	.220	.188	28	-4		.867	1	126	442	P-14/O(RF)	0.0
1886	Bal AA	1	3	0	0	0	0	0	0	0	1		.000	.250	.000	-20	0	0	1.000	1	324	0	/P	0.0
1887	Bal AA	9	31	4	9	0	0	0	3	1	0		.290	.313	.290	73	-1	1	.889	0	109	356	/P-9,O-3(2-0-1)	0.0
	StL AA	15	56	4	10	1	2	0	6	1	1		.179	.207	.268	29	-6	1	.800	-2	0	0	/O-9(0-4-5),P-6	-0.5
	Year	24	87	8	19	1	2	0	9	2	1		.218	.244	.276	43	-7	2	.897	-2	96	412	P-15,O-12(2-4-6)	-0.5
1888	StL AA	9	31	1	3	0	0	0	1	3	1		.097	.200	.097	-3	-2	1	.842	-2	62	0	/P-9	0.0
	Cle AA	2	6	0	1	1	0	0	0	1	0		.167	.286	.333	101	0	0	1.000	1	252	0	/P-2,2	0.0
	Year	11	37	1	4	1	0	0	1	4	1		.108	.214	.135	12	-4	1	.880	-1	81	0	P-11/2	0.0
1889	Phi AA	3	12	2	3	1	0	0	2	1	0	1	.250	.308	.333	84	0	1	1.000	-1	40	0	/P-3	0.0
Total	5	53	187	16	35	3	2	0	14	9	3	1	.187	.236	.225	35	-13	4	.891	-2	103	272	/P-44,O-13(2-4-7),2	-0.5
KNOWDELL, JAKE Jacob Augustus B 7.27.1840 Brooklyn, NY 5-7.5/148# d6.20																								
1874	Atl NA	24	86	8	12	1	1	0	3	1		3	.140	.149	.174	4	-8	1-0	.824	-2			C-21/O-4(LF)	-0.8
1875	Atl NA	43	163	17	32	2	0	0	9	1		3	.196	.201	.209	49	-7	0-1	.781	-10			C-33,S-11/O-4(0-3-1),2	-1.5
1878	Mil N	4	14	2	3	1	0	0	2	0		3	.214	.214	.286	59	-1		.875	-2			/C-2,O(RF)S	-0.3
Total	2 NA	67	249	25	44	3	1	0	12	2		6	.177	.183	.197	32	-15	1-1	.000	-12			/C-54,S-11,O-8(4-3-1),2	-2.3
KNOWLES, JIMMY James "Darby" B 9.1856 Toronto, ON, CAN D 2.11.1912 Jersey City, NJ 5-9/160# d5.2																								
1884	Pit AA	46	182	19	42	5	7	0		5	2		.231	.259	.335	94	-2		.961	-0	95	80	1-46	-0.6
	Bro AA	41	153	19	36	5	1	1		3	1		.235	.255	.301	80	-3		.953	1	176	122	1-30,3-11	-0.5
	Year	87	335	38	78	10	8	1		8	3		.233	.257	.319	87	-5		.958	0	127	97	1-76,3-11	-1.1
1886	Was N	115	443	43	94	16	11	3	35	15		73	.212	.238	.318	73	-15	20	.899	21	113	103	2-62,3-53	0.9
1887	NY AA	16	60	12	15	1	1	0	6	1	0		.250	.262	.300	59	-4	6	.934	-2	85	60	2-16/3	-0.4
1890	Roc AA	123	491	83	138	12	8	5	84	59	1		.281	.359	.369	124	16	55	.881	7	111	99	*3-123	2.2
1892	NY N	16	59	9	9	1	0	0	7	6	0	8	.153	.231	.169	22	-5	2	.792	-4	81	92	3-15/S	-0.8
Total	5	357	1388	185	334	40	28	9	132	89	4	81	.241	.288	.329	92	-13	83	.861	23	109	101	3-203/2-78,1-76,S	0.8
KNOX, ANDY Andrew Jackson "Dasher" B 1.6.1864 Philadelphia, PA D 9.14.1940 Philadelphia, PA BR/TR d9.19																								
1890	Phi AA	21	75	6	19	3	0	0	8	9	0		.253	.333	.293	85	-1	5	.963	-2	63	65	1-21	-0.4
KNOX, CLIFF Clifford Hiram "Bud" B 1.7.1902 Coalville, IA D 9.24.1965 Oskaloosa, IA BB/TR 5-11.5/178# d7.1																								
1924	Pit N	6	18	1	4	0	0	0	2	2	0	0	.222	.300	.222	41	-1	0-0	.917	1	*191*	*133*	/C-6	0.0
KNOX, JOHN John Clinton B 7.26.1948 Newark, NJ BL/TR 6/170# d8.1																								
1972	†Det A	14	13	1	1	1	0	0	0	1-0	0	2	.077	.143	.154	-11	-2	0-0	1.000	3	226	281	/2-4	0.1
1973	Det A	12	32	1	9	1	0	0	3	3-0	0	3	.281	.343	.313	80	-1	1-1	1.000	-3	74	52	/2-9	-0.4
1974	Det A	55	88	11	27	1	1	0	6	6-0	0	13	.307	.351	.341	96	0	5-4	.956	-2	92	117	2-33/3D	-0.1
1975	Det A	43	86	8	23	1	0	0	2	10-0	0	9	.267	.344	.279	74	-3	1-2	.980	-3	101	67	2-23/3-3,D-3	-0.5
Total	4	124	219	21	60	4	1	0	11	20-0	0	27	.274	.335	.301	79	-6	7-7	.973	-5	97	93	/2-69,D-5,3-4	-0.9
KOBACK, NICK Nicholas Nicholie B 7.19.1935 Hartford, CT BR/TR 6/187# d7.29																								
1953	Pit N	7	16	1	2	0	1	0	0	1	0	4	.125	.176	.250	10	-2	0-0	1.000	-2	*44*	*192*	/C-6	-0.4
1954	Pit N	4	10	0	0	0	0	0	0	0	0	8	.000	.000	.000	-99	-3	0-0	1.000	-0	*79*	*0*	/C-4	-0.3
1955	Pit N	5	7	0	2	0	0	0	0	0-0	0	1	.286	.286	.286	53	0	0-0	1.000	0	*0*	*401*	/C-2	0.0
Total	3	16	33	1	4	0	1	0	0	1-0	0	13	.121	.147	.182	-15	-5	0-0	1.000	-2	*51*	*147*	/C-12	-0.7
KOCH, BARNEY Barnett B 3.23.1923 Campbell, NE D 6.6.1987 Tacoma, WA BR/TR 5-8/140# d7.23																								
1944	Bro N	33	96	11	21	2	0	0	1	3	0	9	.219	.242	.240	37	-8	0	.956	-5	87	59	2-29/S	-1.2
KOCHER, BRAD Bradley Wilson B 1.16.1888 White Haven, PA D 1.13.1965 White Haven, PA BR/TR 5-11/188# d4.24																								
1912	Det A	29	63	5	13	3	1	0	9	2	0		.206	.231	.286	49	-5	0	.904	-6	*81*	*107*	C-24	-0.9
1915	NY N	4	11	3	5	0	1	0	2	0	0	1	.455	.455	.636	243	2	0	1.000	-1	*85*	*140*	/C-3	0.1
1916	NY N	34	65	1	7	2	0	0	1	2	0	10	.108	.134	.138	-17	-9	0	.978	-4	101	48	C-30	-1.3
Total	3	67	139	9	25	5	2	0	12	4	0	11	.180	.203	.245	34	-12	0	.943	-10	*90*	*83*	/C-57	-2.1
KOEGEL, PETE Peter John B 7.31.1947 Mineola, NY BR/TR 6-6.5/230# d9.1																								
1970	Mil A	7	8	2	2	0	0	1	1	1-0	0	3	.250	.333	.625	157	1	0-0	1.000	-0	60	0	/O(LF)	0.0
1971	Mil A	2	3	0	0	0	0	0	0	2-0	0	2	.000	.400	.000	22	0	0-0	1.000	-0	0	0	/1	0.0
	Phi N	12	26	1	6	1	0	0	3	2-0	0	7	.231	.286	.269	58	-1	0-0	1.000	-1	53	87	/C-7,O(LF)	-0.3
1972	Phi N	41	49	3	7	2	0	0	1	6-0	0	16	.143	.236	.184	20	-5	0-0	1.000	-1	81	81	/1-8,C-5,3-4,O-2(RF)	-0.7
Total	3	62	86	6	15	3	0	1	5	11-0	0	28	.174	.268	.244	45	-5	0-0	.971	-3	49	68	/C-12,1-9,3-4,O-4(2-0-2)	-1.0
KOEHLER, BEN Benard James B 1.26.1877 Schoerndorn, Germany D 5.21.1961 South Bend, IN BR/TR 5-10.5/175# d4.23																								
1905	StL A	142	536	55	127	14	6	2	47	32	4		.237	.285	.297	89	-8	22	.969	1	**170**	**336**	*O-124(CF),1-12/2-6	-1.5
1906	StL A	66	186	27	41	1	1	0	15	24	4		.220	.322	.237	79	-3	9	.957	-2	142	363	O-52(1-34-17)/2-7,S3	-0.7
Total	2	208	722	82	168	15	7	2	62	56	8		.233	.295	.281	87	-11	31	.966	-1	163	343	O-176(1-158-17)/2-13,1-12,3S	-2.2
KOEHLER, PIP Horace Levering B 1.16.1902 Gilbert, PA D 12.8.1986 Tacoma, WA BR/TR 5-10/165# d4.22																								
1925	NY N	12	2	1	0	0	0	0	0	0	0	1	.000	.000	.000	-99	-1	0-0	1.000	0	178	0	/O-3(1-0-2)	0.0
KOELLING, BRIAN Brian Wayne B 6.11.1969 Cincinnati, OH BR/TR 6-1/185# d8.21																								
1993	Cin N	7	15	2	1	0	0	0	0	0-0	1	2	.067	.125	.067	-47	-3	0-0	.941	-0	146	58	/2-3,S-2	-0.3
KOENECKE, LEN Leonard George B 1.18.1904 Baraboo, WI D 9.17.1935 Toronto, ON, CAN BL/TR 5-11/180# d4.12																								
1932	NY N	42	137	33	35	5	0	4	14	11	2	13	.255	.320	.380	89	-2	3	.924	-4	87	0	O-35(LF)	-0.8
1934	Bro N	123	460	79	147	31	7	14	73	70	1	38	.320	.411	.509	152	37	8	**.994**	0	102	72	*O-121(CF)	3.3
1935	Bro N	100	325	43	92	13	2	4	27	43	1	45	.283	.369	.372	102	3	0	.966	-4	101	42	O-91(16-68-7)	-0.4
Total	3	265	922	155	274	49	9	22	114	124	4	96	.297	.383	.441	125	38	11	.976	-8	100	51	O-247(51-189-7)	2.1
KOENIG, MARK Mark Anthony B 7.19.1904 San Francisco, CA D 4.22.1993 Willows, CA BB/TR 6/180# d9.8 ▲																								
1925	NY A	28	110	14	23	6	1	0	4	5	0	4	.209	.243	.282	34	-12	0-1	.944	-2	95	99	S-28	-1.0
1926	†NY A	147	617	93	167	26	8	5	62	43	1	37	.271	.319	.363	79	-22	4-3	.931	2	101	90	*S-141	-0.4
1927	†NY A	123	526	99	150	20	11	3	62	25	2	21	.285	.320	.382	84	-15	3-2	.936	12	**109**	**121**	*S-122	1.0
1928	†NY A	132	533	89	170	19	10	4	63	32	2	19	.319	.360	.415	106	3	3-5	.923	-19	89	98	*S-125	-0.3
1929	NY A	116	373	44	109	27	5	3	41	23	1	17	.292	.335	.416	99	-2	1-1	.911	-9	96	97	S-61,3-37/2	-0.2
1930	NY A	21	74	9	17	5	0	0	9	6	1	5	.230	.296	.297	53	-5	0-0	.905	1	105	120	S-19	-0.2
	Det A	76	267	37	64	9	2	1	16	20	1	15	.240	.295	.300	50	-21	2-0	.922	-8	92	98	S-70/P-2,3-2,O(RF)	-1.9

Year	Tm Lg	G	AB	R	H	2B	3B	HR	RBI	BB-IB	HP	SO	AVG	OBP	SLG	AOPS	ABR	SB-CS	FA	FR	Rng	Thr	G at Pos	BFW
	Year	97	341	46	81	14	2	1	25	26	2	20	.238	.295	.299	51	-26	2-0	.918	-8	95	103	S-89/P-2,3-2,O(RF)	-2.1
1931	Det A	106	364	33	92	24	4	1	39	14	1	12	.253	.282	.349	63	-21	8-2	.955	-19	88	83	2-55,S-35/P-3	-3.1
1932	†Chi N	33	102	15	36	5	1	3	11	3	1	5	.353	.377	.510	137	5	0	.932	8	120	133	S-31	1.4
1933	Chi N	80	218	32	62	12	1	3	25	15	0	9	.284	.330	.390	105	2	5	.922	3	100	173	3-37,S-26/2-2	0.7
1934	Cin N	151	633	60	172	26	6	1	67	15	0	24	.272	.289	.336	68	-30	5	.930	-3	104	92	3-64,S-58,2-26/1-4	-2.4
1935	NY N	107	396	40	112	12	0	3	37	13	0	18	.283	.306	.336	74	-15	0	.968	-4	105	64	2-64,S-21,3-15	-1.3
1936	†NY N	42	58	7	16	4	0	1	7	8	1	4	.276	.373	.397	109	1	0	.905	-1	121	97	S-10/2-8,3-3	0.1
Total	12	1162	4271	572	1190	195	49	28	443	222	11	190	.279	.316	.367	81	-132	31-14	.927	-39	100	103	S-747,3-158,2-156/P-5,1-4,O(RF)	-7.6
KOHLER, HENRY Henry C. B 5.5.1852 Baltimore, MD D 8.27.1934 Baltimore, MD d7.12																								
1871	Kek NA	3	12	0	2	1	0	0	1	0		0	.167	.167	.250	17	-1	0-0	—	-1			/C-2,1-2,3	-0.1
1873	Mar NA	**6**	25	2	3	0	0	0	1	0		1	.120	.120	.120	-37	-4	0-0	.686	-3	48	0	/3-6,C1O(CF)	-0.5
1874	Bal NA	2	4	0	0	0	0	0	0	0		0	.000	.000	.000	-99	-1	0-0	.714	-1	426	0	/1	-0.1
Total	3 NA	11	41	2	5	1	0	0	2	0		1	.122	.122	.146	-24	-6	0-0	.000	-5			/3-7,1-4,C-3,O(CF)	-0.7
KOKOS, DICK Richard Jerome (born Richard Jerome Kokoszka) B 2.28.1928 Chicago, IL D 4.9.1986 Chicago, IL BL/TL 5-8.5/170# d7.8 Mil 1951																								
1948	StL A	71	258	40	77	15	3	4	40	28	3	32	.298	.374	.426	110	4	4-3	.964	0	92	166	O-71(RF)	0.2
1949	StL A	143	501	80	131	28	1	23	77	66	3	91	.261	.351	.459	109	5	3-5	.981	7	109	124	*O-138(RF)	0.6
1950	StL A	143	490	77	128	27	5	18	67	88	1	73	.261	.375	.447	106	5	8-8	.970	3	**110**	70	*O-127(81-0-50)	-0.1
1953	StL A	107	299	41	72	12	0	13	38	56	0	53	.241	.361	.411	106	4	0-5	.963	-2	97	82	O-83(61-0-22)	-0.4
1954	Bal A	11	10	1	2	0	0	1	1	4	0	3	.200	.429	.500	166	1	0-0	1.000	0	112	0	/O(LF)	0.1
Total	5	475	1558	239	410	82	9	59	223	242	7	252	.263	.365	.441	108	19	15-21	.971	9	104	105	O-420(143-0-281)	0.4
KOLB, GARY Gary Alan B 3.13.1940 Rock Falls, IL BL/TR 6/195# d9.7																								
1960	StL N	9	3	1	0	0	0	0	0	0-0	0	0	.000	.000	.000	-92	-1	0-0	1.000	0	196	0	/O-2(1-1-1)	-0.1
1962	StL N	6	14	1	5	0	0	0	0	1-0	0	3	.357	.400	.357	96	0	0-0	1.000	-0	108	0	/O-6(1-0-5)	-0.1
1963	StL N	75	96	23	26	1	5	3	10	22-0	0	26	.271	.403	.479	141	6	2-1	.981	0	112	54	O-58(25-0-35)/C3	0.5
1964	Mil N	36	64	7	12	1	0	0	2	6-1	0	10	.188	.257	.203	31	-6	3-2	1.000	-2	113	0	O-14(5-3-7)/3-7,2-6,C-2	-0.9
1965	Mil N	24	27	3	7	0	0	0	1	1-0	0	6	.259	.286	.259	54	-2	0-0	1.000	0	127	0	O-13(9-3-2)	-0.2
	NY N	40	90	8	15	2	0	1	7	3-0	0	28	.167	.191	.222	17	-10	3-0	.976	2	94	322	O-29(10-10-9)/13	-1.0
	Year	64	117	11	22	2	0	1	8	4-0	0	34	.188	.213	.231	26	-12	3-0	.981	2	100	259	O-42(19-13-11)/13	-1.2
1968	Pit N	74	119	16	26	4	1	2	6	11-2	0	17	.218	.285	.319	82	-3	2-1	.900	-1	97	132	O-25(6-1-18),C-10/3-4,2	-0.5
1969	Pit N	29	37	4	3	1	0	0	3	2-0	0	14	.081	.128	.108	-34	-7	0-0	1.000	-1	100	0	/C-7	-0.8
Total	7	293	450	63	94	9	6	6	29	46-3	0	104	.209	.281	.296	65	-23	10-4	.965	-2	106	127	O-147(57-18-77)/C-20,3-13,2-7,1	-3.1
KOLLOWAY, DON Donald Martin “Butch” or “Cab” B 8.4.1918 Posen, IL D 6.30.1994 Blue Island, IL BR/TR 6-3/200# d9.16 Mil 1943-45																								
1940	Chi A	10	40	5	9	1	0	0	3	0	0	3	.225	.225	.250	23	-5	1-0	.922	-2	94	115	2-10	-0.6
1941	Chi A	71	280	33	76	8	3	3	24	6	2	12	.271	.292	.354	71	-13	11-4	.955	-8	106	64	2-62/1-4	-1.6
1942	Chi A	147	601	72	164	**40**	4	3	60	30	3	39	.273	.311	.368	92	-8	16-14	.966	-4	99	108	*2-116,1-33	-0.9
1943	Chi A	85	348	29	75	14	4	1	33	9	0	30	.216	.235	.287	53	-23	11-7	.968	1	97	118	2-85	-1.9
1946	Chi A	123	482	45	135	23	4	3	53	9	0	29	.280	.293	.363	86	-12	14-6	.972	5	110	119	2-90,3-31	-0.1
1947	Chi A	124	485	49	135	25	4	2	35	17	0	34	.278	.303	.359	87	-11	11-4	.962	6	109	104	2-99,1-11/3-8	0.1
1948	Chi A	119	417	60	114	14	4	6	38	18	0	18	.273	.303	.369	81	-14	2-4	.966	11	109	94	2-83,3-18	0.0
1949	Chi A	4	4	0	0	0	0	0	0	0	0	1	.000	.000	.000	-99	-1	0-0	—	-0	0	0	/3-2	-0.1
	Det A	126	483	71	142	19	3	2	47	49	2	25	.294	.361	.358	91	-6	7-7	.956	-16	86	98	2-62,1-57/3-7	-2.1
	Year	130	487	71	142	19	3	2	47	49	2	26	.292	.359	.355	89	-8	7-7	.956	-16	86	98	2-62,1-57/3-9	-2.2
1950	Det A	125	467	55	135	20	4	6	62	29	0	28	.289	.331	.388	81	-15	1-3	.989	2	107	**120**	*1-118/2	-1.7
1951	Det A	78	212	28	54	7	0	1	17	15	1	12	.255	.307	.302	65	-11	2-3	.992	6	139	106	1-59	-0.7
1952	Det A	65	173	19	42	9	0	2	21	7	2	19	.243	.280	.329	69	-8	0-2	.979	1	132	51	1-32/2-8	-0.8
1953	Phi A	2	1	0	0	0	0	0	0	0	0	1	.000	.000	.000	-96	0	0-0	—	-0	0	0	/3	0.0
Total	12	1079	3993	466	1081	180	30	29	393	189	10	251	.271	.305	.353	80	-127	76-54	.964	2	103	103	2-616,1-314/3-67	-10.4
KOLSETH, KARL Karl Dickey “Koley” B 12.25.1892 Cambridge, MA D 5.3.1956 Cumberland, MD BL/TR 6/182# d9.30																								
1915	Bal F	6	23	1	6	1	1	0	1	1	0	0	.261	.292	.391	89	-1	0	.915	-2	57	132	/1-6	-0.3
KOMMERS, FRED Frederick Raymond “Bugs” B 3.31.1886 Chicago, IL D 6.14.1943 Chicago, IL BL/TR 6/175# d6.25																								
1913	Pit N	40	155	14	36	5	4	0	22	10	0	29	.232	.279	.316	73	-6	1-6	.979	-3	103	18	O-40(CF)	-1.4
1914	StL F	76	244	33	75	9	8	3	41	24	3	33	.307	.376	.447	117	2	7	.908	-1	97	121	O-67(3-36-28)	-0.2
	Bal F	16	42	5	9	1	0	1	1	7	1	10	.214	.340	.310	75	-2	0	.938	-2	86	0	O-12(11-1-0)	-0.4
	Year	92	286	38	84	10	8	4	42	31	4	43	.294	.371	.427	111	0	7	.911	-2	95	103	O-79(14-37-28)	-0.6
Total	2	132	441	52	120	15	12	4	64	41	4	72	.272	.340	.388	99	-6	8-6	.938	-5	98	73	O-119(14-77-28)	-2.0
KOMMINSK, BRAD Brad Lynn B 4.4.1961 Lima, OH BR/TR 6-2/205# d8.14																								
1983	Atl N	19	36	2	8	2	0	0	4	5-0	0	7	.222	.317	.278	62	-2	0-0	.944	-0	90	148	O-13(1-0-12)	-0.3
1984	Atl N	90	301	37	61	10	0	8	36	29-0	2	77	.203	.276	.316	62	-15	18-8	.993	-6	87	35	O-80(28-2-50)	-2.6
1985	Atl N	106	300	52	68	12	3	4	21	38-1	1	71	.227	.314	.327	75	-9	10-8	.959	-1	107	36	O-92(28-1-63)	-1.6
1986	Atl N	5	5	1	2	0	0	0	1	0-0	0	1	.400	.400	.400	115	0	0-1	1.000	-0	95	0	/3-2,O-2(RF)	-0.1
1987	Mil A	7	15	0	1	0	0	0	0	1-0	0	7	.067	.125	.067	-46	-3	1-0	1.000	0	142	0	/O-5(RF),D	-0.3
1989	Cle A	71	198	27	47	8	2	8	33	24-0	1	55	.237	.319	.419	106	1	8-2	.995	4	113	90	O-68(2-66-2)	0.6
1990	SF N	8	5	2	1	0	0	0	0	1-0	0	2	.200	.333	.200	52	0	0-0	1.000	-1	58	0	/O-7(2-2-3)	-0.1
	Bal A	46	101	18	24	4	0	3	8	14-1	2	29	.238	.342	.366	101	1	1-1	1.000	0	100	101	O-40(6-12-26)/D-2	0.0
1991	Oak A	24	25	1	3	1	0	0	2	2-0	0	9	.120	.185	.160	-4	-4	1-0	1.000	-0	88	178	O-22(7-8-8)	-0.4
Total	8	376	986	140	215	37	5	23	105	114-2	6	258	.218	.301	.336	75	-31	39-20	.984	-4	101	63	O-329(74-91-171)/D-3,3-2	-4.8
KONERKO, PAUL Paul Henry B 3.5.1976 Providence, RI BR/TR 6-3/205# d9.8																								
1997	LA N	6	7	0	1	0	0	0	0	1-0	0	2	.143	.250	.143	7	-1	0-0	1.000	-1	0	605	/13	-0.2
1998	LA N	49	144	14	31	1	0	4	16	10-0	2	30	.215	.272	.306	56	-10	0-1	.995	1	107	54	1-23,3-11,O-11(LF)	-1.2
	Cin N	26	73	7	16	3	0	3	13	6-0	1	10	.219	.284	.384	74	-3	0-0	1.000	1	110	0	/3-9,1-7,O-7(LF),D-3	-0.3
	Year	75	217	21	47	4	0	7	29	16-0	3	40	.217	.276	.332	62	-13	0-1	.996	1	118	48	1-30,3-20,O-18(LF)/D-3	-1.5
1999	Chi A	142	513	71	151	31	4	24	81	45-0	2	68	.294	.352	.511	117	12	1-0	.995	3	113	87	1-92,D-46/3	0.3
2000	†Chi A	143	524	84	156	31	1	21	97	47-0	10	72	.298	.363	.481	111	9	1-0	.991	-7	89	109	*1-122/3-7,D-7	-0.8
2001	Chi A	156	582	92	164	35	0	32	99	54-6	9	89	.282	.349	.507	118	16	1-0	.994	-3	95	101	*1-144,D-11	-0.1
2002	Chi A★	151	570	81	173	30	0	27	104	44-2	9	72	.304	.359	.498	124	19	0-0	.993	-5	85	102	*1-140/D-7	0.1
2003	Chi A	137	444	49	104	19	0	18	65	43-7	4	50	.234	.305	.399	84	-11	0-0	**.998**	5	112	**120**	*1-119,D-14	-1.6
Total	7	810	2857	398	796	150	5	129	475	250-15	37	393	.279	.342	.470	108	31	3-1	.994	-6	98	102	1-648/D-88,3-29,O-18(LF)	-3.8
KONETCHY, ED Edward Joseph “Big Ed” B 9.3.1885 LaCrosse, WI D 5.27.1947 Ft.Worth, TX BR/TR 6-2.5/195# d6.29 ▲																								
1907	StL N	91	331	34	83	11	9	2	30	26	6		.251	.317	.356	115	5	13	.975	4	125	94	1-91	0.8
1908	StL N	**154**	545	46	135	19	12	5	50	38	10		.248	.309	.354	117	9	16	.986	11	**128**	85	*1-154	2.0
1909	StL N	152	576	88	165	23	14	4	80	65	7		.286	.366	.396	145	31	25	.985	5	**117**	87	*1-152	3.6
1910	StL N	144	520	87	157	23	16	3	78	78	4	59	.302	.397	.425	145	32	18	**.991**	9	123	90	*1-144/P	**3.9**
1911	StL N	**158**	571	90	165	**38**	13	6	88	81	7	63	.289	.384	.433	132	27	27	**.991**	-6	79	91	*1-158	1.7
1912	StL N	143	538	81	169	26	13	8	82	62	4	66	.314	.389	.455	134	25	25	.991	6	114	92	*1-142/O(LF)	2.6
1913	StL N	140	504	75	139	18	17	8	68	53	7	41	.276	.353	.427	124	15	27-25	**.995**	8	**119**	92	*1-140/P	1.7
1914	Pit N	154	563	56	140	23	9	4	51	32	2	48	.249	.291	.343	92	-8	20	**.995**	5	109	94	*1-154	-0.8
1915	Pit F	152	576	79	181	31	18	10	93	41	3	52	.314	.363	.483	138	18	27	**.994**	0	95	103	*1-152	1.5
1916	Bos N	**158**	566	76	147	29	13	3	70	43	7	46	.260	.320	.373	117	11	13	.990	9	**124**	**121**	*1-158	1.8
1917	Bos N	130	474	56	129	19	13	2	54	36	5	40	.272	.330	.380	125	13	16	**.994**	2	99	82	*1-129	1.3
1918	Bos N	119	437	33	103	15	5	2	56	32	2	35	.236	.291	.307	86	-8	5	**.992**	-2	85	102	*1-112/O-6(1-4-1),P	-1.4
1919	Bro N	132	486	46	145	24	9	1	47	29	3	39	.298	.342	.391	117	10	14	**.994**	6	114	86	*1-132	1.4
1920	†Bro N	131	497	62	153	22	12	5	63	33	1	18	.308	.352	.431	120	12	3-2	.990	0	99	85	*1-130	0.9
1921	Bro N	55	197	25	53	6	5	3	23	19	1	21	.269	.336	.396	90	-3	3-3	.987	-1	93	104	1-54	-0.8
	Phi N	72	268	38	86	17	4	8	59	21	4	17	.321	.379	.504	122	9	3-0	.986	5	139	70	1-71	1.0
	Year	127	465	63	139	23	9	11	82	40	5	38	.299	.361	.458	109	6	6-3	.986	4	119	85	*1-125	0.2
Total	15	2085	7649	972	2150	344	182	74	992	689	73	545	.281	.346	.403	122	198	255-30	.990	60	110	93	*1-2073/O-7(2-4-1),P-3	21.2

Year	Tm Lg	G	AB	R	H	2B	3B	HR	RBI	BB-IB	HP	SO	AVG	OBP	SLG	AOPS	ABR	SB-CS	FA	FR	Rng	Thr	G at Pos	BFW
KONNICK, MIKE Michael Aloysius B 1.13.1889 Glen Lyon, PA D 7.9.1971 Wilkes-Barre, PA BR/TR 5-9/180# d10.3																								
1909	Cin N	2	5	0	2	1	0	0	1	0	0		.400	.400	.600	211	1	0	1.000	-0	*82*	*73*	/C-2	0.0
1910	Cin N	1	3	0	0	0	0	0	0	1	0	0	.000	.250	.000	-27	0	0	1.000	-0	72	0	/S	-0.1
Total	2	3	8	0	2	1	0	0	1	1	0	0	.250	.333	.375	117	1	0	1.000	-1	*82*	*73*	/C-2,S	-0.1
KONOPKA, BRUCE Bruno Bruce B 9.16.1919 Hammond, IN D 9.27.1996 Denver, CO BL/TL 6-2/190# d6.7 Mil 1943-45																								
1942	Phi A	5	10	2	3	0	0	0	1	1	0	0	.300	.364	.300	88	0	0-0	1.000	-0	68	110	/1-3	0.0
1943	Phi A	2	2	0	0	0	0	0	0	0	0	1	.000	.000	.000	-99	-1	0-0	—	0			H	-0.1
1946	Phi A	38	93	7	22	4	1	0	9	4	0	8	.237	.268	.301	59	-5	0-0	.994	2	129	75	1-20/O(LF)	-0.5
Total	3	45	105	9	25	4	1	0	10	5	0	9	.238	.273	.295	59	-6	0-0	.995	2	123	78	/1-23,O(LF)	-0.6
KOONCE, GRAY Graham Clinton B 5.15.1975 ElCajon, CA BL/TL 6-4/220# d9.20																								
2003	Oak A	6	8	0	1	1	0	0	0	0-0	0	6	.125	.125	.250	-4	-1	0-0	1.000	1	216	169	/1-5	-0.1
KOONS, HARRY Henry M. B 1863 Philadelphia, PA BR/TR 5-8/174# d4.17																								
1884	Alt U	21	78	8	18	2	1	0		2			.231	.250	.282	60	-6		.866	5	126	39	3-21/C	-0.1
	CP U	1	3	0	0	0	0	0		0			.000	.000	.000	-99	-1		—	-0	0	0	/3	-0.1
	Year	22	81	8	18	2	1	0		2			.222	.241	.272	54	-7		.866	5	125	39	3-22/C	-0.2
KOPACZ, GEORGE George Felix "Sonny" B 2.26.1941 Chicago, IL BL/TL 6-1/195# d9.18																								
1966	Atl N	6	9	1	0	0	0	0	0	1-0	0	5	.000	.100	.000	-68	-2	0-0	.909	-1	0	0	/1-2	-0.3
1970	Pit N	10	16	1	3	0	0	0	0	0-0	0	5	.188	.188	.188	1	-2	0-0	1.000	-1	0	99	/1-3	-0.3
Total	2	16	25	2	3	0	0	0	0	1-0	0	10	.120	.154	.120	-25	-4	0-0	.964	-1	0	63	/1-5	-0.6
KOPF, WALLY Walter Henry B 7.10.1899 Stonington, CT D 4.30.1979 Hamilton Co., OH BB/TR 5-11/168# d10.1 b-Larry																								
1921	NY N	2	3	0	1	0	0	0	0	1	0	1	.333	.500	.333	125	0	0-0	1.000	1	222	435	/3-2	0.1
KOPF, LARRY William Lorenz (a/k/a Fred Brady In 1913) B 11.3.1890 Bristol, CT D 10.15.1986 Anderson Twp., OH BB/TR 5-9/160# d9.2 Def 1918 b-Wally																								
1913	Cle A	6	10	2	3	1	0	0	1	0	0	0	.300	.300	.400	102	0	0	.923	1	146	150	/2-4,3	0.2
1914	Phi A	37	69	8	13	2	2	0	12	8	3	14	.188	.300	.275	76	-2	6	.899	-3	85	62	S-13/3-8,2-5	-0.2
1915	Phi A	118	386	39	87	10	2	1	33	41	9	45	.225	.314	.269	77	-10	5-9	.920	-7	92	71	S-74,3-42/2-2	-1.4
1916	Cin N	11	40	2	11	2	0	0	5	1	0	8	.275	.293	.325	92	0	1	.942	-1	103	89	S-11	-0.1
1917	Cin N	148	573	81	146	19	8	2	26	28	6	48	.255	.297	.326	95	-5	17	.916	-9	100	88	*S-145	-0.4
1919	†Cin N	135	503	51	136	18	5	0	58	28	3	27	.270	.313	.326	95	-4	18	.943	-35	86	75	*S-135	-3.3
1920	Cin N	126	458	56	112	15	6	0	59	35	5	24	.245	.305	.303	76	-14	14-13	.929	-33	85	90	*S-123/2-2,3-2,O(CF)	-4.3
1921	Cin N	107	367	36	80	8	3	1	25	43	6	20	.218	.310	.264	56	-22	3-14	.947	-17	93	81	S-93/2-4,3-3,O(LF)	-3.3
1922	Bos N	126	466	59	124	6	3	1	37	45	1	22	.266	.332	.298	67	-22	8-9	.944	-12	93	82	2-78,S-33,3-13	-2.8
1923	Bos N	39	138	15	38	3	1	0	10	13	0	6	.275	.338	.312	75	-5	0-3	.905	-5	99	110	S-37/2-4	-0.7
Total	10	853	3010	349	750	84	30	5	266	242	33	214	.249	.312	.302	78	-84	72-48	.928	-120	92	84	S-664/2-99,3-69,O-2(1-1-0)	-16.3
KOPP, MERLIN Merlin Henry "Manny" B 1.2.1892 Toledo, OH D 5.6.1960 Sacramento, CA BB/TR (BR 1915) 5-8/158# d8.2 Mil 1918																								
1915	Was A	16	32	2	8	0	0	0	0	5	0	7	.250	.351	.250	79	-1	1	.933	-1	109	0	/O-9(8-0-1)	-0.1
1918	Phi A	96	363	60	85	7	7	0	18	42	4	55	.234	.320	.292	84	-7	22	.972	10	108	149	O-96(LF)	-0.2
1919	Phi A	75	235	34	53	2	4	1	12	42	2	43	.226	.348	.281	77	-6	16	.924	-3	95	101	O-65(58-7-0)	-1.2
Total	3	187	630	96	146	9	11	1	30	89	6	105	.232	.332	.286	81	-14	39	.953	7	103	125	O-170(162-7-1)	-1.5
KOPPE, JOE Joseph (born B 10.19.1930 Detroit, MI BR/TR 5-10/165# d8.9																								
1958	Mil N	16	9	3	4	0	0	0	0	1-0	0	1	.444	.500	.444	167	1	0-0	.833	2	192	284	/S-3	0.3
1959	Phi N	126	422	68	110	18	7	7	28	41-0	2	80	.261	.327	.386	88	-7	7-7	.954	8	104	101	*S-113,2-11	0.9
1960	Phi N	58	170	13	29	6	1	1	13	23-3	1	47	.171	.272	.235	41	-14	3-2	.956	-10	87	73	S-55/3-2	-2.1
1961	Phi N	6	3	1	0	0	0	0	0	0-0	0	0	.000	.000	.000	-99	-1	0-0	.800	-0	84	186	/S-5	-0.1
	LA A	91	338	46	85	12	2	5	40	45-0	1	77	.251	.339	.343	75	-11	3-3	.947	1	102	91	S-88/2-3,3	-0.3
1962	LA A	128	375	47	85	16	0	4	40	73-3	2	84	.227	.352	.301	81	-6	2-1	.957	3	108	85	*S-118/2-5,3-4	0.7
1963	LA A	76	143	11	30	4	1	1	12	9-1	1	30	.210	.258	.273	53	-9	0-0	.962	4	116	66	S-19,3-18,2-14/O-3(RF)	-0.4
1964	LA A	54	113	10	29	4	1	0	6	14-1	0	16	.257	.339	.310	91	-1	0-0	.945	8	127	114	S-31,2-13/3-3	1.0
1965	Cal A	23	33	3	7	1	0	1	2	3-1	0	10	.212	.278	.333	75	-1	1-0	.979	5	158	90	2-10/S-4,3-4	0.5
Total	8	578	1606	202	379	61	12	19	141	209-9	7	345	.236	.324	.324	76	-49	16-13	.952	21	105	92	S-436/2-56,3-32,O-3(RF)	0.5
KOPSHAW, GEORGE George Karl B 7.5.1895 Passaic, NJ D 12.26.1934 Lynchburg, VA BR/TR 5-11.5/176# d8.4																								
1923	StL N	2	5	1	1	1	0	0	0	0	0	1	.200	.200	.400	56	0	0-0	1.000	-1	*54*	*0*	/C	-0.1
KORCHECK, STEVE Stephen Joseph "Hoss" B 8.11.1932 McClellandtown, PA BR/TR 6-1/205# d9.6 Mil 1956																								
1954	Was A	2	7	0	1	0	0	0	0	0	0	2	.143	.143	.143	-23	-1	0-0	.857	-1	*50*	*0*	/C-2	-0.2
1955	Was A	13	36	3	10	2	0	0	2	0-0	1	5	.278	.297	.333	73	-1	0-0	1.000	0	*86*	*207*	C-12	-0.1
1958	Was A	21	51	6	4	2	1	0	1	1-1	0	16	.078	.096	.157	-32	-9	0-0	.975	-1	*64*	*144*	C-20	-1.0
1959	Was A	22	51	3	8	2	0	0	4	5-0	0	13	.157	.228	.196	19	-6	0-0	.974	2	*72*	*93*	C-22	-0.3
Total	4	58	145	12	23	6	1	0	7	6-1	1	36	.159	.196	.214	13	-17	0-0	.976	1	*72*	*131*	/C-56	-1.6
KORES, ART Arthur Emil "Dutch" B 7.22.1886 Milwaukee, WI D 3.26.1974 Milwaukee, WI BR/TR 5-9/167# d7.24																								
1915	StL F	60	201	18	47	9	2	1	22	21	0	13	.234	.306	.313	71	-11	6	.960	16	127	141	3-60	0.8
KOSCO, ANDY Andrew John B 10.5.1941 Youngstown, OH BR/TR 6-3/207# d8.13																								
1965	Min A	23	55	3	13	4	0	1	6	1-0	0	15	.236	.241	.364	69	-2	0-0	1.000	2	97	477	O-14(RF)/1-2	-0.2
1966	Min A	57	158	11	35	5	0	2	13	7-1	0	31	.222	.251	.291	53	-10	0-1	.986	0	107	93	O-40(31-7-5)/1-5	-1.3
1967	Min A	9	28	4	4	1	0	0	4	2-0	0	4	.143	.200	.179	12	-3	0-0	.923	-0	107	0	/O-7(RF)	-0.4
1968	NY A	131	466	47	112	19	1	15	59	16-2	3	71	.240	.268	.382	99	-3	2-2	.960	-1	97	166	O-95(1-0-94),1-28	-1.4
1969	LA N	120	424	51	105	13	2	19	74	21-2	1	66	.248	.282	.422	103	-2	0-1	.981	-4	88	88	*O-109(38-0-76)/1-3	-1.3
1970	LA N	74	224	21	51	12	0	8	27	1-0	0	40	.228	.230	.388	66	-12	1-1	.981	-1	102	55	O-58(3-0-55)/1	-1.6
1971	Mil A	98	264	27	60	6	2	10	39	24-5	0	57	.227	.291	.379	90	-5	1-3	.988	-1	118	87	O-45(26-0-19),1-29,3-12	-1.1
1972	Cal A	49	142	15	34	4	2	6	13	5-1	1	23	.239	.267	.423	110	0	1-0	.985	1	108	86	O-36(24-0-13)	-0.1
	Bos A	17	47	5	10	2	1	3	6	2-0	1	9	.213	.260	.489	113	0	0-0	1.000	-0	90	115	O-12(LF)	0.0
	Year	66	189	20	44	6	3	9	19	7-1	2	32	.233	.265	.439	111	1	1-0	.988	1	103	94	O-48(36-0-13)	-0.1
1973	†Cin N	47	118	17	33	7	0	9	21	13-6	0	26	.280	.346	.568	159	9	0-0	1.000	-4	82	39	O-36(1-7-28)/1	0.4
1974	Cin N	33	37	3	7	2	0	0	5	7-1	0	8	.189	.311	.243	59	-2	0-0	.846	-2	65	0	/3-8,O(RF)	-0.4
Total	10	658	1963	204	464	75	8	73	267	99-18	6	350	.236	.273	.394	92	-30	5-8	.979	-10	98	107	O-453(136-14-312)/1-69,3-20	-7.4
KOSHOREK, CLEM Clement John "Scooter" B 6.20.1925 Royal Oak, MI D 9.8.1991 Royal Oak, MI BR/TR 5-4.5/165# d4.15																								
1952	Pit N	98	322	27	84	17	0	0	15	26	2	39	.261	.320	.314	74	-10	4-7	.949	4	117	124	S-33,2-27,3-26	-0.5
1953	Pit N	1	1	0	0	0	0	0	0	0	0	1	.000	.000	.000	-99	0	0-0	—	0			H	0.0
Total	2	99	323	27	84	17	0	0	15	26	2	40	.260	.319	.313	74	-10	4-7	.949	4	117	124	/S-33,2-27,3-26	-0.5
KOSKIE, COREY Cordel Leonard B 6.28.1973 Anola, MB, CAN BL/TR 6-3/215# d9.9																								
1998	Min A	11	29	2	4	0	0	1	2	2-0	0	10	.138	.194	.241	12	-4	0-0	.941	-2	68	82	3-10	-0.6
1999	Min A	117	342	42	106	21	0	11	58	40-4	5	72	.310	.387	.468	114	8	4-4	.962	0	109	72	3-79,O-25(RF),D-12	0.7
2000	Min A	146	474	79	142	32	4	9	65	77-7	4	104	.300	.400	.441	109	10	5-4	.966	-5	90	113	*3-139/D	0.6
2001	Min A	153	562	100	155	37	2	26	103	68-9	12	118	.276	.362	.488	119	17	27-6	.964	-1	103	79	*3-150/D-2	2.1
2002	†Min A	140	490	71	131	37	3	15	69	72-4	9	127	.267	.368	.447	115	14	10-11	.969	4	101	76	*3-138/D	1.7
2003	†Min A	131	469	76	137	29	2	14	69	77-5	7	113	.292	.393	.452	123	20	11-5	.973	-6	96	73	*3-131	1.5
Total	6	698	2366	370	675	156	11	76	366	336-29	37	544	.285	.379	.457	115	65	57-30	.967	-9	99	84	3-647/O-25(RF),D-16	6.0
KOSLOFSKI, KEVIN Kevin Craig B 9.24.1966 Decatur, IL BL/TR 5-8/165# d6.28																								
1992	KC A	55	133	20	33	0	2	3	13	12-0	1	23	.248	.313	.346	83	-4	2-1	.991	4	110	190	O-52(15-18-23)	0.0
1993	KC A	15	26	4	7	0	0	1	2	4-0	1	5	.269	.387	.385	102	0	0-1	1.000	3	123	459	O-13(3-4-7)/D	0.2
1994	KC A	2	4	2	1	0	0	0	0	2-1	0	1	.250	.500	.250	97	0	0-0	.750	0	75	1130	/O-2(0-1-1)	0.0
1996	Mil A	25	42	5	9	3	2	0	6	4-1	1	12	.214	.298	.381	67	-2	0-0	.972	-0	106	0	O-22(6-14-2)/D	-0.2
Total	4	97	205	31	50	3	4	4	21	22-2	3	41	.244	.325	.356	83	-6	2-2	.983	7	110	202	/O-89(24-37-33),D-2	0.0

Year	Tm Lg	G	AB	R	H	2B	3B	HR	RBI	BB-IB	HP	SO	AVG	OBP	SLG	AOPS	ABR	SB-CS	FA	FR	Rng	Thr	G at Pos	BFW
KOSMAN, MIKE Michael Thomas B 12.10.1917 Hamtramck, MI D 12.10.2002 Lafayette, IN BR/TR 5-9/160# d4.20																								
1944	Cin N	1	0	0	0	0	0	0	0	0	0	0	—	—	—	—	0	0	—	0			R	0.0
KOSTER, FRED Frederick Charles "Fritz" B 12.21.1905 Louisville, KY D 4.24.1979 St.Matthews, KY BL/TL 5-10.5/165# d4.27																								
1931	Phi N	76	151	21	34	2	2	0	8	14	0	21	.225	.291	.265	47	-11	4	.923	0	102	120	O-41(6-14-22)	-1.3
KOSTRO, FRANK Frank Jerry B 8.4.1937 Windber, PA BR/TR 6-2/190# d9.2																								
1962	Det A	16	41	5	11	3	0	0	3	1-0	0	6	.268	.279	.341	66	-2	0-0	.967	0	101	114	3-11	-0.2
1963	Det A	31	52	4	12	1	0	0	0	9-0	0	13	.231	.344	.250	67	-2	0-0	.929	0	121	0	/3-6,1-3,O-3(1-0-2)	-0.2
	LA A	43	99	6	22	2	1	2	10	6-0	0	17	.222	.264	.323	68	-5	0-0	.960	-2	85	154	3-19/1-5,O-3(1-0-2)	-0.7
	Year	74	151	10	34	3	1	2	10	15-0	0	30	.225	.293	.298	68	-7	0-0	.953	-2	93	120	3-25/1-8,O-6(2-0-4)	-0.9
1964	Min A	59	103	10	28	5	0	3	12	4-0	1	21	.272	.303	.408	96	-1	0-0	.912	-2	93	51	3-12/2-7,O-2(LF),1	-0.3
1965	Min A	20	31	2	5	2	0	0	1	4-0	0	5	.161	.250	.226	37	-2	0-0	.923	-1	98	141	/2-7,3-6,O-2(1-0-1)	-0.3
1967	Min A	32	31	4	10	0	0	0	2	3-0	0	2	.323	.382	.323	102	0	0-0	1.000	-1	28	0	/O-3(2-0-1),3	-0.1
1968	Min A	63	108	9	26	4	1	0	9	6-1	0	20	.241	.274	.296	71	-4	0-0	1.000	0	101	192	O-24(14-0-10)/1-5	-0.5
1969	Min A	2	2	0	0	0	0	0	0	0-0	0	1	.000	.000	.000	-98	-1	0-0	—	0			H	-0.1
Total	7	266	467	40	114	17	2	5	37	33-1	1	85	.244	.291	.321	74	-17	0-0	.926	-4	95	132	/3-55,O-37(21-0-16),2-14,1-14	-2.4
KOTSAY, MARK Mark Steven B 12.2.1975 Whittier, CA BL/TL 6/180# d7.11																								
1997	Fla N	14	52	5	10	1	1	0	4	4-0	0	7	.192	.250	.250	33	-5	3-0	1.000	2	108	331	O-14(CF)	-0.3
1998	Fla N	154	578	72	161	25	7	11	68	34-2	1	61	.279	.318	.403	93	-8	10-5	.984	19	118	211	*O-145(0-46-107)/1-3	0.6
1999	Fla N	148	495	57	134	23	9	8	50	29-5	0	50	.271	.306	.402	83	-15	7-6	.981	13	107	**246**	*O-129(RF),1-19	-1.0
2000	Fla N	152	530	87	158	31	5	12	57	42-2	0	46	.298	.347	.443	103	2	19-9	.990	11	111	173	*O-142(0-9-139)/1-2	0.7
2001	SD N	119	406	67	118	29	1	10	58	48-1	2	58	.291	.366	.441	118	12	13-5	.986	4	115	72	*O-111(1-106-5)	1.7
2002	SD N	153	578	82	169	27	7	17	61	59-0	3	89	.292	.359	.452	127	18	11-9	.989	5	106	144	*O-147(CF)	2.4
2003	SD N	128	482	64	128	28	4	7	38	56-3	1	82	.266	.343	.384	98	-1	6-3	.991	14	**116**	200	*O-126(CF)	1.4
Total	7	868	3121	434	878	164	34	65	336	272-13	7	393	.281	.338	.418	103	3	69-37	.987	66	112	179	O-814(1-448-380)/1-24	5.5
KOWITZ, BRIAN Brian Mark B 8.7.1969 Baltimore, MD BL/TL 5-10/180# d6.4																								
1995	Atl N	10	24	3	4	1	0	0	3	2-0	1	5	.167	.259	.208	24	-3	0-1	1.000	-1	53	0	/O-8(2-1-5)	-0.5
KOY, ERNIE Ernest Anyz "Chief" B 9.17.1909 Sealy, TX BR/TR 6/200# d4.19 Mil 1943-45																								
1938	Bro N	142	521	78	156	29	13	11	76	38	4	76	.299	.352	.468	121	13	15	.984	-0	104	66	*O-135(54-64-18)/3	0.8
1939	Bro N	125	425	57	118	37	5	8	67	39	0	64	.278	.338	.445	105	3	11	.962	0	106	56	*O-114(110-3-3)	-0.3
1940	Bro N	24	48	9	11	2	1	1	8	3	0	3	.229	.275	.375	73	-2	1	1.000	-0	105	0	O-19(11-5-2)	-0.3
	StL N	93	348	44	108	19	5	8	52	28	4	59	.310	.368	.463	121	10	12	.970	-3	99	30	O-91(LF)	0.2
	Year	117	396	53	119	21	6	9	60	31	4	62	.301	.357	.452	115	8	13	.973	-4	100	27	*O-110(102-5-2)	-0.1
1941	StL N	13	40	5	8	1	0	2	4	1	0	8	.200	.220	.375	61	-2	0	1.000	-0	98	0	O-12(LF)	-0.3
	Cin N	67	204	24	51	11	2	2	27	14	1	22	.250	.301	.353	84	-5	1	.990	-2	90	89	O-49(42-1-6)	-0.9
	Year	80	244	29	59	12	2	4	31	15	1	30	.242	.288	.357	80	-7	1	.991	-2	91	76	O-61(54-1-6)	-1.2
1942	Cin N	3	2	0	0	0	0	0	0	0	0	2	.000	.000	.000	-99	-1	0	—	0			H	-0.1
	Phi N	91	258	21	63	9	3	4	26	14	0	50	.244	.283	.349	89	-5	0	.981	-1	100	73	O-78(28-52-4)	-1.0
	Year	94	260	21	63	9	3	4	26	14	0	52	.242	.281	.346	87	-6	0	.981	-1	100	73	O-78(28-52-4)	-1.1
Total	5	558	1846	238	515	108	29	36	260	137	9	284	.279	.332	.427	107	11	40	.977	-7	101	57	O-498(348-125-33)/3	-1.9
KOZAR, AL Albert Kenneth B 7.5.1921 McKees Rocks, PA BR/TR 5-9.5/173# d4.19																								
1948	Was A	150	577	61	144	25	8	1	58	66	0	52	.250	.327	.326	76	-20	4-2	.967	-21	98	74	*2-149	-3.2
1949	Was A	105	350	46	94	15	2	4	31	25	2	23	.269	.321	.357	81	-11	2-1	.977	-8	94	75	*2-102	-1.4
1950	Was A	20	55	7	11	1	0	0	3	5	0	8	.200	.267	.218	27	-6	0-0	.962	-0	113	69	2-15	-0.5
	Chi A	10	10	4	3	0	0	1	2	0	0	3	.300	.300	.600	129	0	0-0	1.000	1	154	190	/2-4,3	0.2
	Year	30	65	11	14	1	0	1	5	5	0	11	.215	.271	.277	42	-6	0-0	.968	1	118	84	2-19/3	-0.3
Total	3	285	992	118	252	41	10	6	94	96	2	86	.254	.321	.334	76	-37	6-3	.971	-27	98	75	2-270/3	-4.9
KRACHER, JOE Joseph Peter "Jug" B 11.4.1915 Philadelphia, PA D 12.24.1981 San Angelo, TX BR/TR 5-11/185# d9.17																								
1939	Phi N	5	5	1	1	0	0	0	2	0	1	.200	.429	.200	76	0	0	1.000	-1	*0*	*0*	/C-2	0.0	
KRAFT, CLARENCE Clarence Otto "Big Boy" B 6.9.1887 Evansville, IN D 3.26.1958 Fort Worth, TX BR/TR 6/190# d5.1																								
1914	Bos N	3	3	0	1	0	0	0	0	0	0	1	.333	.333	.333	99	0	0	1.000	-0	0	0	/1	0.0
KRANEPOOL, ED Edward Emil B 11.8.1944 New York, NY BL/TL 6-3/215# d9.22																								
1962	NY N	3	6	0	1	1	0	0	0	0-0	0	1	.167	.167	.333	30	-1	0-0	1.000	1	345	0	/1-3	0.0
1963	NY N	86	273	22	57	12	2	2	14	18-0	0	50	.209	.256	.289	56	-15	4-2	.954	-0	90	132	O-55(6-0-50),1-20	-2.2
1964	NY N	119	420	47	108	19	4	10	45	32-2	2	50	.257	.310	.393	100	-1	0-1	.991	2	114	91	*1-104/O-6(0-1-5)	-0.6
1965	NY N☆	153	525	44	133	24	4	10	53	39-7	2	71	.253	.303	.371	94	-5	1-4	.992	0	102	99	*1-147	-1.6
1966	NY N	146	464	51	118	15	2	16	57	41-9	3	66	.254	.316	.399	100	0	1-1	.992	4	**114**	99	*1-132,O-11(LF)	-0.5
1967	NY N	141	469	37	126	17	1	10	54	37-15	1	51	.269	.321	.373	100	0	0-4	.992	3	108	101	*1-139	-0.7
1968	NY N	127	373	29	86	13	1	3	20	19-5	2	39	.231	.271	.295	70	-14	0-3	.994	4	112	104	*1-113/O-2(LF)	-2.1
1969	†NY N	112	353	36	84	9	2	11	49	37-7	0	32	.238	.307	.368	88	-6	3-2	.993	2	106	110	*1-106/O-2(LF)	-1.3
1970	NY N	43	47	2	8	0	0	0	3	5-0	0	2	.170	.250	.170	15	-6	0-0	1.000	-0	74	113	/1-8	-0.7
1971	NY N	122	421	61	118	20	4	14	58	38-6	1	33	.280	.340	.447	123	12	0-4	**.998**	-1	88	83	*1-108,O-11(6-0-5)	0.1
1972	NY N	122	327	28	88	15	1	8	34	34-13	1	35	.269	.336	.394	111	5	1-0	.996	0	96	95	*1-108/O(RF)	-0.2
1973	†NY N	100	284	28	68	12	2	1	35	30-4	0	28	.239	.310	.306	73	-10	1-0	.998	1	104	108	1-51,O-32(31-0-1)	-1.5
1974	NY N	94	217	20	65	11	1	4	24	18-0	0	14	.300	.350	.415	116	4	1-0	.977	-4	80	50	O-33(32-0-1),1-24	-0.3
1975	NY N	106	325	42	105	16	0	4	43	27-6	0	21	.323	.370	.409	123	10	1-1	.997	0	94	82	1-82/O-4(LF)	0.4
1976	NY N	123	415	47	121	17	1	10	49	35-4	0	38	.292	.344	.410	121	11	1-0	.996	-4	70	88	1-86,O-31(23-0-8)	-0.1
1977	NY N	108	281	28	79	17	0	10	40	23-7	0	20	.281	.330	.448	113	5	1-4	.984	2	99	0	O-42(10-0-32),1-41	0.2
1978	NY N	66	81	7	17	2	0	3	19	8-2	1	12	.210	.280	.346	79	-2	0-0	1.000	-0	68	0	O-12(3-0-9)/1-3	-0.4
1979	NY N	82	155	7	36	5	0	2	17	13-2	1	18	.232	.287	.303	66	-7	0-1	1.000	1	119	84	1-29/O-8(2-0-6)	-0.9
Total	18	1853	5436	536	1418	225	25	118	614	454-89	14	581	.261	.316	.377	97	-20	15-27	.994	10	104	96	*1-1304,O-250(132-1-118)	-12.4
KRAUSE, CHARLIE Charles B 10.2.1873 Detroit, MI D 3.30.1948 Eloise, MI TR d7.27																								
1901	Cin N	1	4	0	1	0	0	0	0	0	0		.250	.250	.250	48	0	0	—	-0	0	0	/2	0.0
KRAVITZ, DANNY Daniel "Dusty" or "Beak" B 12.21.1930 Lopez, PA BL/TR 5-11/195# d4.17																								
1956	Pit N	32	68	6	18	2	2	2	10	5-1	0	9	.265	.311	.441	103	0	1-1	.944	-0	*116*	*115*	C-26/3-2	0.0
1957	Pit N	19	41	2	6	1	0	0	4	2-0	0	10	.146	.186	.171	-3	-6	0-0	1.000	1	*112*	*192*	C-15	-0.5
1958	Pit N	45	100	9	24	3	2	1	5	11-5	0	10	.240	.313	.340	76	-4	0-0	.967	-2	*105*	*134*	C-37	-0.5
1959	Pit N	52	162	18	41	9	1	3	21	5-1	0	14	.253	.274	.377	72	-7	0-1	.986	-2	*105*	*102*	C-45	-0.7
1960	Pit N	8	6	0	0	0	0	0	0	1-0	0	2	.000	.143	.000	-57	-1	0-0	1.000	0	*0*	*0*	/C	-0.1
	KC A	59	175	17	41	7	2	4	14	11-1	0	19	.234	.280	.366	73	-7	0-0	.971	-5	*70*	*56*	C-47	-1.0
Total	5	215	552	52	130	22	7	10	54	35-8	0	64	.236	.280	.355	70	-25	1-2	.973	-8	*96*	*102*	C-171/3-2	-2.8
KREEVICH, MIKE Michael Andreas B 6.10.1908 Mt.Olive, IL D 4.25.1994 Pana, IL BR/TR 5-7.5/168# d9.7																								
1931	Chi N	5	12	0	2	0	0	0	0	0	0	6	.167	.167	.167	-10	-2	1	1.000	0	77	371	/O-4(1-1-2)	-0.2
1935	Chi A	6	23	3	10	2	0	0	2	1	0	0	.435	.458	.522	149	2	1-1	1.000	-2	44	0	/3-6	0.0
1936	Chi A	137	550	99	169	32	11	5	69	61	2	46	.307	.378	.433	96	-3	10-5	.964	-2	92	136	*O-133(17-65-57)	-0.9
1937	Chi A	144	583	94	176	29	**16**	12	73	43	0	45	.302	.350	.468	104	1	10-1	**.988**	4	103	96	*O-138(6-138-1)	0.2
1938	Chi A★	129	489	73	145	26	12	6	73	55	3	23	.297	.371	.436	99	-1	13-5	.975	-1	105	55	*O-127(0-127-1)	-0.4
1939	Chi A	145	541	85	175	30	8	5	77	59	0	40	.323	.390	.436	108	8	23-10	.975	9	105	146	*O-139(CF)/3-4	1.4
1940	Chi A	144	582	86	154	27	10	8	55	34	0	49	.265	.305	.387	77	-22	15-7	.982	7	107	109	*O-144(CF)	-1.7
1941	Chi A	121	436	44	101	16	8	0	37	35	0	26	.232	.289	.305	58	-28	17-5	**.994**	-2	98	74	*O-113(CF)	-3.0
1942	Phi A	116	444	57	113	19	1	1	30	47	0	31	.255	.326	.309	79	-11	7-9	.981	-0	106	49	*O-107(CF)	-1.6
1943	StL A	60	161	24	41	6	0	0	10	26	0	13	.255	.358	.292	89	-1	4-1	.993	5	112	132	O-51(3-47-1)	0.3
1944	†StL A	105	402	55	121	15	6	5	44	27	2	24	.301	.348	.405	108	4	3-3	.986	-3	102	42	*O-100(0-93-7)	-0.3
1945	StL A	84	295	34	70	11	1	2	21	37	0	27	.237	.322	.302	78	-8	4-1	.991	2	112	46	O-81(CF)	-0.8
	Was A	45	158	22	44	8	2	1	23	21	0	9	.278	.363	.373	124	5	7-5	.971	-2	96	62	O-40(CF)	0.2
	Year	129	453	56	114	19	3	3	44	58	0	36	.252	.337	.327	92	-3	11-6	.985	0	107	51	*O-121(CF)	-0.6

Year	Tm Lg	G	AB	R	H	2B	3B	HR	RBI	BB-IB	HP	SO	AVG	OBP	SLG	AOPS	ABR	SB-CS	FA	FR	Rng	Thr	G at Pos	BFW
Total	12	1241	4676	676	1321	221	75	45	514	446	7	339	.283	.346	.391	92	-56	115-53	.982	15	103	90	*O-1177(27-1095-69)/3-10	-6.8
KREHMEYER, CHARLIE Charles L. B 7.5.1863 St.Louis, MO D 2.10.1926 St.Louis, MO BL/TL 5-11/179# d7.8																								
1884	StL AA	21	70	3	16	0	1	0	5	2	0		.229	.250	.257	64	-3		.619	-3	87	0	O-15(5-9-1)/C-7,1	-0.6
1885	Lou AA	7	31	4	7	1	1	0	5	1	0		.226	.250	.323	80	-1		.909	-2			/C-4,O-2(1-0-1),1	-0.2
	StL N	1	3	0	0	0	0	0	0	0		2	.000	.000	.000	-99	-1		.429	-2			/C	-0.3
Total	2	29	104	7	23	1	2	0	10	3		2	.221	.243	.269	64	-5		.571	-7			/O-17(6-9-2),C-12,1-2	-1.1
KREITNER, MICKEY Albert Joseph B 10.9.1922 Nashville, TN D 3.6.2003 Nashville, TN BR/TR 6-3/190# d9.28																								
1943	Chi N	3	8	0	3	0	0	0	2	1	0	2	.375	.444	.375	140	0	0	1.000	-0	*67*	*0*	/C-3	0.0
1944	Chi N	39	85	3	13	2	0	0	1	8	1	16	.153	.234	.176	17	-9	0	.992	-0	*93*	*109*	C-39	-0.8
Total	2	42	93	3	16	2	0	0	3	9	1	18	.172	.252	.194	27	-9	0	.992	-0	*91*	*100*	/C-42	-0.8
KREITZ, RALPH Ralph Wesley "Red" B 11.13.1885 Plum Creek, NE D 7.20.1941 Portland, OR BR/TR 5-9.5/175# d8.1																								
1911	Chi A	7	17	0	4	1	0	0	0	2	0		.235	.316	.294	73	-1	0	1.000	-1	*127*	*58*	/C-7	-0.1
KREMERS, JIMMY James Edward B 10.8.1965 Little Rock, AR BL/TR 6-3/205# d6.5																								
1990	Atl N	29	73	7	8	1	1	1	2	6-1	0	27	.110	.177	.192	1	-10	0-0	.992	-5	77	69	C-27	-1.5
KRENCHICKI, WAYNE Wayne Richard B 9.17.1954 Trenton, NJ BL/TR 6-1/180# d6.15																								
1979	Bal A	16	21	1	4	1	0	0	0	0-0	0	0	.190	.190	.238	15	-3	0-0	.875	-2	71	0	/3-7,2-6	-0.5
1980	Bal A	9	14	1	2	0	0	0	0	1-0	0	3	.143	.200	.143	-4	-2	0-0	1.000	-0	73	91	/S-6,2D	-0.2
1981	Bal A	33	56	7	12	4	0	0	6	4-0	0	9	.214	.267	.286	59	-3	0-0	.964	1	119	109	S-16/2-7,3-6,D	-0.1
1982	Cin N	94	187	19	53	6	1	2	21	13-1	0	23	.283	.324	.358	91	-2	5-3	.955	4	106	96	3-70/2-9	0.1
1983	Cin N	51	77	6	21	2	0	0	11	8-2	1	4	.273	.345	.299	78	-2	0-0	.980	-1	103	85	3-39/2	-0.3
	Det A	59	133	18	37	7	0	1	16	11-0	1	27	.278	.333	.353	93	-1	0-0	.934	0	87	124	3-48/2-6,S-6,1-3	-0.1
1984	Cin N	97	181	18	54	9	2	6	22	19-3	0	23	.298	.358	.470	127	7	0-1	.967	2	111	71	3-62/1-3,2-3	0.8
1985	Cin N	90	173	16	47	9	0	4	25	28-4	0	20	.272	.369	.393	109	3	0-0	.967	1	97	128	3-52/2-3	0.4
1986	Mon N	101	221	21	53	6	2	2	23	22-3	0	32	.240	.306	.312	72	-9	2-4	.991	3	91	86	1-41,3-24/2O(LF)	-0.9
Total	8	550	1063	107	283	44	5	15	124	106-13	2	141	.266	.330	.359	92	-12	7-8	.955	8	102	102	3-308/1-47,2-37,S-28,D-2,O(LF)	-0.8
KRESS, CHUCK Charles Steven B 12.9.1921 Philadelphia, PA BL/TL 6/190# d4.16																								
1947	Cin N	11	27	4	4	0	0	0	0	6	0	4	.148	.303	.148	23	-3	0	.983	1	157	85	/1-8	-0.2
1949	Cin N	27	29	3	6	3	0	0	3	3	0	5	.207	.281	.310	58	-2	0	.974	-0	100	103	1-16	-0.2
	Chi A	97	353	45	98	17	6	1	44	39	0	44	.278	.349	.368	93	-4	6-7	.994	1	102	105	1-95	-0.7
1950	Chi A	3	8	0	0	0	0	0	0	0	0	2	.000	.000	.000	-99	-2	0-0	1.000	-0	78	94	/1-2	-0.3
1954	Det A	24	37	4	7	0	1	0	3	1	0	4	.189	.211	.243	24	-4	0-1	.971	-0	121	74	/1-7,O(RF)	-0.5
	Bro N	13	12	1	1	0	0	0	2	0	0	0	.083	.083	.083	-55	-3	0-0	.500	-0	0	505	/1	-0.3
Total	4	175	466	57	116	20	7	1	52	49	0	59	.249	.320	.328	74	-18	6-8	.990	1	106	103	1-129/O(RF)	-2.2
KRESS, RED Ralph B 1.2.1905 Columbia, CA D 11.29.1962 Los Angeles, CA BR/TR 5-11.5/165# d9.24 C15 ▲ OF Total (22-LF 103-RF)																								
1927	StL A	7	23	3	7	2	1	1	3	3	0	3	.304	.385	.609	150	2	0-0	.974	1	114	91	/S-7	0.3
1928	StL A	150	560	78	153	26	10	3	81	48	1	70	.273	.332	.371	82	-15	4-4	.929	-17	91	118	*S-150	-1.6
1929	StL A	147	557	82	170	38	4	9	107	52	1	54	.305	.366	.436	102	2	5-8	**.946**	2	100	**113**	*S-146	1.7
1930	StL A	**154**	614	94	192	43	8	16	112	50	2	56	.313	.366	.487	110	9	3-12	.938	-11	95	111	*S-123,3-31	1.0
1931	StL A	150	605	87	188	46	8	16	114	46	1	48	.311	.360	.493	118	14	3-16	.936	-5	94	86	3-84,O-40(RF),S-38,1-10	0.4
1932	StL A	14	52	2	9	0	1	2	9	4	0	6	.173	.232	.327	41	-5	1-1	.909	1	95	193	3-14	-0.4
	Chi A	135	515	83	147	42	4	9	57	47	1	36	.285	.346	.435	108	6	6-3	.956	11	94	214	O-64(16-0-49),S-53,3-19/1	1.6
	Year	149	567	85	156	42	5	11	66	51	1	42	.275	.336	.425	101	0	7-4	.956	12	94	214	O-64(16-0-49),S-53,3-33/1	1.2
1933	Chi A	129	467	47	116	20	5	10	78	37	0	40	.248	.304	.377	83	-14	4-4	.978	-5	99	96	*1-111/O-8(RF)	-2.9
1934	Chi A	8	14	3	4	0	0	0	1	3	0	3	.286	.412	.286	80	0	0-0	1.000	-2	28	0	/2-3	-0.2
	Was A	56	171	18	39	4	3	4	24	17	0	19	.228	.298	.357	71	-9	3-0	.993	-0	74	64	1-30,O-10(6-0-4)/2-6,S3	-1.0
	Year	64	185	21	43	4	3	4	25	20	0	22	.232	.307	.351	72	-9	3-0	.993	-3	74	64	1-30,O-10(6-0-4)/2-9,S3	-1.2
1935	Was A	84	252	32	75	13	4	2	42	25	0	16	.298	.361	.405	101	0	3-3	.964	11	112	137	S-53/1-5,P-3,O-2(RF),2	1.3
1936	Was A	109	391	51	111	20	6	8	51	39	0	25	.284	.349	.427	96	-4	6-0	.927	4	101	121	S-64,2-33/1-5	0.6
1938	StL A	150	566	74	171	33	3	7	79	69	0	47	.302	.378	.408	97	-1	5-4	**.965**	-12	86	90	*S-150	-0.2
1939	StL A	13	43	5	12	1	0	0	8	6	0	2	.279	.367	.302	72	-2	1-0	.933	-1	84	123	S-13	-0.2
	Det A	51	157	19	38	7	0	1	22	17	0	16	.242	.316	.306	55	-10	2-1	.959	1	93	104	S-25,2-16/3-4	-0.6
	Year	64	200	24	50	8	0	1	30	23	0	18	.250	.327	.305	59	-12	3-1	.951	-1	90	110	S-38,2-16/3-4	-0.8
1940	Det A	33	99	13	22	3	1	1	11	10	0	12	.222	.294	.303	50	-7	0-0	.924	5	109	29	3-17,S-12	-0.1
1946	NY N	1	1	0	0	0	0	0	0	1	0	0	.000	.500	.000	48	0	0	1.000	1	377	1785	/P	0.0
Total	14	1391	5087	691	1454	298	58	89	799	474	6	453	.286	.347	.420	96	-34	46-56	.944	-19	96	110	S-835,3-170,1-162,O-124R/2-59,P	-0.3
KREUTER, CHAD Chadden Michael B 8.26.1964 Greenbrae, CA BB/TR (BR 1989 (part), 90) 6-2/195# d9.14																								
1988	Tex A	16	51	3	14	2	1	1	5	7-0	0	13	.275	.362	.412	113	1	0-0	.990	1	77	118	C-16	0.3
1989	Tex A	87	158	16	24	3	0	5	9	27-0	0	40	.152	.274	.266	52	-10	0-1	.992	-1	65	73	C-85	-0.8
1990	Tex A	22	22	2	1	1	0	0	2	8-0	0	9	.045	.290	.091	14	-2	0-0	.977	-4	100	94	C-20/D	-0.6
1991	Tex A	3	4	0	0	0	0	0	0	0-0	0	1	.000	.000	.000	-99	-1	0-0	1.000	0	0	0	/C	-0.1
1992	Det A	67	190	22	48	9	0	2	16	20-1	0	38	.253	.321	.332	83	-4	0-1	.983	3	158	112	C-62/D	0.2
1993	Det A	119	374	59	107	23	3	15	51	49-4	3	92	.286	.371	.484	129	16	2-1	.988	1	121	116	*C-112/1D	2.3
1994	Det A	65	170	17	38	8	0	1	19	28-0	0	36	.224	.327	.288	62	-9	0-1	.987	1	143	123	C-64/1O(LF)	-0.4
1995	Sea A	26	75	12	17	5	0	1	8	5-0	2	22	.227	.293	.333	62	-4	0-0	.976	2	99	122	C-23	-0.1
1996	Chi A	46	114	14	25	8	0	3	18	13-0	2	29	.219	.308	.368	74	-4	0-0	.990	1	78	146	C-38/1-2	-0.1
1997	Chi A	19	37	6	8	2	1	1	3	8-0	0	9	.216	.356	.405	102	0	0-1	.984	-0	120	69	C-13/1-2	0.0
	Ana A	70	218	19	51	7	1	4	18	21-0	0	57	.234	.301	.330	65	-12	0-2	.994	6	134	122	C-67/D-2	-0.2
	Year	89	255	25	59	9	2	5	21	29-0	0	66	.231	.310	.341	70	-11	0-3	.992	5	132	115	C-80/1-2,D-2	-0.2
1998	Chi A	93	245	26	62	9	1	2	33	32-1	3	45	.253	.345	.322	78	-7	1-0	.985	-5	107	99	C-91	-0.6
	Ana A	3	7	1	1	1	0	0	0	1-0	0	4	.143	.250	.286	39	-1	0-0	.882	-2	48	116	/C-3	-0.2
	Year	96	252	27	63	10	1	2	33	33-1	3	49	.250	.343	.321	77	-8	1-0	.981	-6	105	100	C-94	-0.8
1999	KC A	107	324	31	73	15	0	5	35	34-1	6	65	.225	.309	.318	59	-20	0-0	.994	-7	81	130	*C-101/D	-1.9
2000	LA N	80	212	32	56	13	0	6	28	54-0	2	48	.264	.416	.410	118	9	1-0	.994	5	194	100	C-78	1.8
2001	LA N	73	191	21	41	11	1	6	17	41-2	1	52	.215	.355	.377	97	1	0-0	1.000	6	123	97	C-70/D	1.0
2002	LA N	41	95	8	25	5	0	2	12	10-4	1	31	.263	.333	.379	99	-1	1-0	.986	-0	95	131	C-41	0.1
2003	Tex A	7	18	0	2	1	0	0	0	3-0	0	2	.111	.238	.167	9	-2	0-0	1.000	-2	64	0	/C-7	-0.4
Total	16	944	2505	289	593	123	8	54	274	361-13	20	593	.237	.335	.357	84	-50	5-7	.990	5	117	110	C-892/D-8,1-6,O(LF)	0.3
KRICHELL, PAUL Paul Bernard B 12.19.1882 New York, NY D 6.4.1957 Bronx, NY BR/TR 5-7/150# d5.12																								
1911	StL A	28	82	6	19	3	0	0	8	4	1		.232	.276	.268	54	-5	2	.943	-3	*75*	*105*	C-25	-0.7
1912	StL A	59	161	19	35	6	0	0	8	19	1		.217	.304	.255	62	-7	2	.959	-3	*88*	*88*	C-59	-0.5
Total	2	87	243	25	54	9	0	0	16	23	2		.222	.295	.259	60	-12	4	.955	-6	*84*	*93*	/C-84	-1.2
KRIEG, BILL William Frederick B 1.29.1859 Petersburg, IL D 3.25.1930 Chillicothe, IL BR/TR 5-8/180# d4.20																								
1884	CP U	71	279	35	69	15	4	0		11			.247	.276	.330	83	-14		.932	9			C-52,O-20(13-6-2)/S1	-0.1
1885	Chi N	1	3	0	0	0	0	0	0	0		2	.000	.000	.000	-88	-1		.800	1	344	0	/O(RF)	0.0
	Bro AA	17	60	7	9	4	0	1	5	2	0		.150	.177	.267	39	-4		.910	-3			C-12/1-5	-0.6
1886	Was N	27	98	11	25	6	3	1	15	3		12	.255	.277	.408	115	2	2	.975	-1	57	55	1-27	-0.1
1887	Was N	25	95	9	24	4	1	2	17	7	1	5	.253	.311	.379	97	0	2	.973	-1	96	62	1-16/O-9(7-2-0)	-0.2
Total	4	141	535	62	127	29	8	4	37	23	1	19	.237	.270	.344	85	-17	4	.929	5			/C-64,1-49,O-30(20-8-3),S	-1.0
KRONER, JOHN John Harold B 11.13.1908 St.Louis, MO D 8.26.1968 St.Louis, MO BR/TR 6/185# d9.29																								
1935	Bos A	2	4	1	1	0	0	0	0	1	0	1	.250	.400	.250	67	0	0-0	1.000	-0	65	0	/3-2	0.0
1936	Bos A	84	298	40	87	17	8	4	62	26	0	24	.292	.349	.443	89	-6	2-3	.964	-4	101	79	2-38,3-28,S-18/O(RF)	-0.6
1937	Cle A	86	283	29	67	14	1	2	26	22	0	25	.237	.292	.314	52	-21	1-1	.969	3	99	105	2-64,3-11	-1.3
1938	Cle A	51	117	13	29	16	0	1	17	19	0	6	.248	.353	.410	92	-1	0-1	.974	6	102	130	2-31/1-7,3-3,S	0.6
Total	4	223	702	83	184	47	9	7	105	68	0	56	.262	.327	.385	75	-28	3-5	.968	5	100	103	2-133/3-44,S-19,1-7,O(RF)	-1.3

Year	Tm Lg	G	AB	R	H	2B	3B	HR	RBI	BB-IB	HP	SO	AVG	OBP	SLG	AOPS	ABR	SB-CS	FA	FR	Rng	Thr	G at Pos	BFW
KRSNICH, MIKE Michael B 9.24.1931 W.Allis, WI BR/TR 6-1/190# d4.23 b-Rocky																								
1960	Mil N	4	9	0	3	1	0	0	2	0-0	0	0	.333	.333	.444	120	0	0-0	1.000	0	120	0	/O-3(LF)	0.0
1962	Mil N	11	12	0	1	1	0	0	2	0-0	0	4	.083	.083	.167	-36	-2	0-0	1.000	0	101	0	/O-3(LF),13	-0.2
Total	2	15	21	0	4	2	0	0	4	0-0	0	4	.190	.190	.286	28	-2	0-0	1.000	0	113	0	/O-6(LF),31	-0.2
KRSNICH, ROCKY Rocco Peter B 8.5.1927 W.Allis, WI BR/TR 6-1/174# d9.13 b-Mike																								
1949	Chi A	16	55	7	12	3	1	1	9	6	0	4	.218	.295	.364	76	-2	0-1	.935	2	116	104	3-16	-0.1
1952	Chi A	40	91	11	21	7	2	1	15	12	1	9	.231	.327	.385	97	0	0-0	.959	6	114	92	3-37	0.6
1953	Chi A	64	129	9	26	8	0	1	14	12	0	11	.202	.270	.287	49	-9	0-2	.929	4	122	80	3-57	-0.6
Total	3	120	275	27	59	18	3	3	38	30	1	24	.215	.294	.335	70	-11	0-3	.942	12	118	89	3-110	-0.1
KRUEGER, OTTO Arthur William "Oom Paul" B 9.17.1876 Chicago, IL D 2.20.1961 St.Louis, MO BR/TR 5-7/165# d9.16																								
1899	Cle N	13	44	4	10	1	0	0	2	8	1		.227	.358	.250	73	-1	1	.763	-2	83	113	/3-9,S-2,2-2	-0.2
1900	StL N	12	35	8	14	3	2	1	3	10	1		.400	.543	.686	240	8	0	.852	-6	79	45	2-12	0.3
1901	StL N	**142**	520	77	143	16	12	2	79	50	13		.275	.353	.363	114	11	19	.881	-10	98	73	*3-142	0.5
1902	StL N	128	467	55	124	7	8	0	46	29	3		.266	.313	.315	98	-2	14	.897	3	**112**	114	*S-107,3-18	0.4
1903	Pit N	80	256	42	63	6	8	1	28	21	8		.246	.323	.344	87	-5	5	.884	-1	97	171	S-29,O-28(LF),3-13/2-3	-0.7
1904	Pit N	86	268	34	52	6	2	1	26	29	4		.194	.282	.243	61	-11	8	.905	-3	113	78	O-33(23-0-10),S-32,3-10	-1.6
1905	Phi N	46	114	10	21	1	1	0	12	13	1		.184	.273	.211	47	-7	1	.930	-5	92	119	S-23/O-6(0-3-3),3	-1.3
Total	7	507	1704	230	427	40	33	5	196	160	31		.251	.326	.322	94	-7	48	.902	-24	107	117	S-193,3-193/O-67(51-3-13),2-17	-2.6
KRUEGER, ERNIE Ernest George B 12.27.1890 Chicago, IL D 4.22.1976 Waukegan, IL BR/TR 5-10.5/185# d8.4 Mil 1918																								
1913	Cle A	5	6	0	0	0	0	0	0	0	0	2	.000	.000	.000	-97	-2	0	1.000	0	*78*	*159*	/C-4	-0.2
1915	NY A	10	29	3	5	1	0	0	0	0	1	5	.172	.200	.207	22	-3	0-1	.905	-3	*83*	*80*	/C-8	-0.6
1917	NY N	8	10	0	0	0	0	0	0	0	0	4	.000	.000	.000	-99	-2	0	.857	-1	*70*	*0*	/C-5	-0.4
	Bro N	31	81	10	22	2	2	1	6	5	2	7	.272	.330	.383	115	1	1	.979	1	*103*	*87*	C-23	0.4
	Year	39	91	10	22	2	2	1	6	5	2	11	.242	.296	.341	94	-1	1	.973	-1	*101*	*81*	C-28	0.0
1918	Bro N	30	87	4	25	4	2	0	7	4	0	9	.287	.319	.379	113	1	2	.986	3	*92*	*128*	C-23	0.7
1919	Bro N	80	226	24	56	7	4	5	36	19	2	25	.248	.312	.381	105	1	4	.963	0	*91*	*104*	C-66	0.8
1920	†Bro N	52	146	21	42	4	2	1	17	16	0	13	.288	.358	.363	104	1	2-0	.959	-3	*95*	*103*	C-46	0.2
1921	Bro N	65	163	18	43	11	4	3	20	14	0	12	.264	.322	.436	95	-1	2-2	.969	-2	*85*	*73*	C-52	0.0
1925	Cin N	37	88	7	27	4	0	1	7	6	0	8	.307	.351	.386	90	-1	1-2	.946	-3	*74*	*69*	C-30	-0.3
Total	8	318	836	87	220	33	14	11	93	64	5	85	.263	.319	.376	97	-5	12-5	.964	-8	*90*	*94*	C-257	0.6
KRUG, CHRIS Everett Ben B 12.25.1939 Los Angeles, CA BR/TR 6-4/200# d5.30 C1																								
1965	Chi N	60	169	16	34	5	0	5	24	13-2	1	52	.201	.258	.320	61	-9	0-1	.980	-0	*96*	*98*	C-58	-0.7
1966	Chi N	11	28	1	6	1	0	0	1	1-0	0	8	.214	.241	.250	36	-2	0-0	1.000	2	*119*	*124*	C-10	0.0
1969	SD N	8	17	0	1	0	0	0	0	1-0	0	6	.059	.111	.059	-53	-4	0-0	.938	-1	106	145	/C-7	-0.4
Total	3	79	214	17	41	6	0	5	25	15-2	1	66	.192	.245	.290	50	-15	0-1	.980	1	*100*	*105*	/C-75	-1.1
KRUG, GENE Gary Eugene B 2.12.1955 Garden City, KS BL/TL 6-4/225# d4.29																								
1981	Chi N	7	5	0	2	0	0	0	0	1-0	0	1	.400	.500	.400	151	0	0-0	—	0			/H	0.0
KRUG, HENRY Henry Charles B 12.4.1876 San Francisco, CA D 1.14.1908 San Francisco, CA BR/TR d7.26																								
1902	Phi N	53	198	20	45	3	3	0	14	7	2		.227	.261	.273	65	-9	2	.947	-4	108	98	O-28(LF),2-13/S-9,3-6	-1.5
KRUG, MARTY Martin John B 9.10.1888 Koblenz, Germany D 6.27.1966 Glendale, CA BR/TR 5-9/165# d5.29																								
1912	Bos A	20	39	6	12	2	1	0	7	5	0		.308	.386	.410	122	1	2	.895	-1	83	141	/S-11,2-4	0.0
1922	Chi N	127	450	67	124	23	4	4	60	43	3	43	.276	.343	.371	82	-11	7-9	.937	-7	93	111	*3-104,2-23/S	-1.1
Total	2	147	489	73	136	25	5	4	67	48	3	43	.278	.346	.374	85	-10	9-9	.937	-8	93	111	3-104/2-27,S-12	-1.1
KRUGER, ART Arthur T. B 3.16.1881 San Antonio, TX D 11.28.1949 Hondo, CA BR/TR 6/185# d4.11																								
1907	Cin N	100	317	25	74	10	9	0	28	18	5		.233	.285	.322	87	-6	10	.972	2	88	96	O-96(26-70-1)	-1.0
1910	Cle A	47	168	14	26	4	2	0	10	15	3		.155	.237	.202	37	-12	10	.947	2	99	126	O-47(LF)	-1.5
	Bos N	1	1	0	0	0	0	0	0	0	0	0	.000	.000	.000	-96	0	0	—	0			H	0.0
	Cle A	15	55	5	12	2	1	0	4	5	1		.218	.295	.291	82	-1	2	.974	1	99	126	O-15(LF)	-0.1
1914	KC F	122	441	45	114	24	7	4	47	23	1	59	.259	.297	.372	85	-19	11	.963	-2	99	83	*O-120(7-113-0)	-3.1
1915	KC F	80	240	24	57	9	2	2	26	12	1	29	.237	.277	.317	70	-15	5	.984	1	101	94	O-66(33-3-30)	-1.9
Total	4	365	1222	113	283	49	21	6	115	73	11	88	.232	.281	.321	76	-53	38	.968	3	98	95	O-344(128-186-31)	-7.6
KRUK, JOHN John Martin B 2.9.1961 Charleston, WV BL/TL 5-10/204# d4.7																								
1986	SD N	122	278	33	86	16	2	4	38	45-0	0	58	.309	.403	.424	132	14	2-4	.981	-2	90	98	O-74(70-0-6)/1-9	0.9
1987	SD N	138	447	72	140	14	2	20	91	73-15	0	93	.313	.406	.488	142	29	18-10	.996	2	107	99	*1-101,O-29(LF)	2.4
1988	SD N	120	378	54	91	17	1	9	44	80-12	0	68	.241	.369	.362	114	11	5-3	.995	-2	77	114	1-63,O-55(29-0-26)	0.3
1989	SD N	31	76	7	14	0	0	3	6	17-0	0	14	.184	.333	.303	83	-1	0-0	.962	2	103	231	O-27(2-0-25)	-0.1
	Phi N	81	281	46	93	13	6	5	38	27-2	0	39	.331	.386	.473	146	16	3-0	.983	-3	85	136	O-72(63-0-12)/1-7	1.3
	Year	112	357	53	107	13	6	8	44	44-2	0	53	.300	.374	.437	132	15	3-0	.977	-1	90	161	O-99(65-0-37)/1-7	1.2
1990	Phi N	142	443	52	129	25	8	7	67	69-16	0	70	.291	.386	.431	125	18	10-5	.986	-2	89	35	O-87(68-0-21),1-61	1.1
1991	Phi N☆	152	538	84	158	27	6	21	92	67-16	1	100	.294	.367	.483	141	30	7-0	.997	-3	74	81	*1-102,O-52(36-11-6)	2.0
1992	Phi N★	144	507	86	164	30	4	10	70	92-8	1	88	.323	.423	.458	151	40	3-5	.993	-11	73	93	*1-121,O-35(6-0-29)	2.1
1993	†Phi N★	150	535	100	169	33	5	14	85	111-10	0	87	.316	.430	.475	145	42	6-2	.993	-10	70	72	*1-144	1.9
1994	Phi N	75	255	35	77	17	0	5	38	42-4	0	51	.302	.395	.427	113	7	4-1	.995	-0	97	81	1-69	0.1
1995	Chi A	45	159	13	49	7	0	2	23	26-0	0	33	.308	.399	.390	113	5	0-1	.909	-0	0	118	D-42/1	0.1
Total	10	1200	3897	582	1170	199	34	100	592	649-83	2	701	.300	.397	.446	134	211	58-31	.995	-31	85	88	1-678,O-431(303-11-125)/D-42	12.1
KRYHOSKI, DICK Richard David B 3.24.1925 Leonia, NJ BL/TL 6-2/200# d4.19																								
1949	NY A	54	177	18	52	10	3	1	27	9	2	17	.294	.335	.401	94	-2	2-4	.983	-1	96	82	1-51	-0.5
1950	Det A	53	169	20	37	10	0	4	19	8	1	11	.219	.258	.349	53	-13	0-1	.991	-1	94	110	1-47	-1.5
1951	Det A	119	421	58	121	19	4	12	57	28	2	29	.287	.335	.437	107	2	1-2	.991	3	110	91	*1-112	0.1
1952	StL A	111	342	38	83	13	1	11	42	23	3	42	.243	.296	.383	86	-8	2-0	.989	-4	85	102	1-86	-1.5
1953	StL A	104	338	35	94	18	4	16	50	26	2	33	.278	.333	.497	119	7	0-5	.992	5	120	90	1-88	0.6
1954	Bal A	100	300	32	78	13	2	1	34	19	2	24	.260	.305	.327	80	-9	0-0	.992	2	105	80	1-69	-1.2
1955	KC A	28	47	2	10	2	0	0	2	6-0	0	7	.213	.302	.255	50	-3	0-1	.988	0	107	81	1-14	-0.4
Total	7	569	1794	203	475	85	14	45	231	119-0	12	163	.265	.314	.403	93	-26	5-13	.990	5	103	92	1-467	-4.4
KUBEK, TONY Anthony Christopher B 10.12.1936 Milwaukee, WI BL/TR 6-3/191# d4.20 OF Total (80-LF 46-CF 31-RF)																								
1957	†NY A	127	431	56	128	21	3	3	39	24-3	3	48	.297	.335	.381	98	-2	6-6	.938	-2	81	68	O-50(29-23-0),S-41,3-38/2	-0.5
1958	†NY A☆	138	559	66	148	21	1	2	48	25-3	1	57	.265	.295	.317	72	-23	5-4	.961	**20**	**110**	**112**	*S-134/O-3(0-1-2),12	0.9
1959	NY A★	132	512	67	143	25	7	6	51	24-3	1	46	.279	.313	.391	95	-5	3-3	.968	2	102	97	S-67,O-53(22-15-26),3-17/2	0.1
1960	†NY A	147	568	77	155	25	3	14	62	31-5	3	42	.273	.312	.401	98	-5	3-0	.968	8	108	101	*S-136,O-29(22-6-1)	1.4
1961	†NY A★	153	617	84	170	38	6	8	46	27-1	1	60	.276	.306	.395	91	-10	1-3	.959	14	104	129	*S-145	1.5
1962	†NY A	45	169	28	53	6	1	4	17	12-0	0	17	.314	.357	.432	115	3	2-1	.954	1	103	120	S-35/O-6(LF)	0.7
1963	†NY A	135	557	72	143	21	3	7	44	28-6	2	68	.257	.294	.343	79	-17	4-2	.980	8	102	113	*S-132/O(CF)	0.3
1964	NY A	106	415	46	95	16	3	8	31	26-3	1	55	.229	.275	.340	69	-18	4-1	.978	3	105	96	S-99	-0.6
1965	NY A	109	339	26	74	5	3	5	35	20-0	0	48	.218	.258	.295	58	-20	1-3	.964	-3	98	113	S-93/O-3(1-0-2),1	-1.7
Total	9	1092	4167	522	1109	178	30	57	373	217-24	13	441	.266	.303	.364	85	-97	29-23	.967	52	104	111	S-882,O-145L/3-55,2-3,1-2	2.1
KUBIAK, TED Theodore Rodger B 5.12.1942 New Brunswick, NJ BB/TR 6/175# d4.14 Mil 1968																								
1967	KC A	53	102	6	16	2	1	0	5	12-0	0	20	.157	.243	.196	33	-9	0-0	.984	-3	96	61	S-20,2-10/3-5	-1.1
1968	Oak A	48	120	10	30	5	2	0	8	8-1	2	18	.250	.305	.325	96	-1	1-1	.929	-5	86	81	2-24,S-12	-0.4
1969	Oak A	92	305	38	76	9	1	2	27	25-2	1	35	.249	.304	.305	75	-10	2-0	.976	2	100	103	S-42,2-33	-0.1
1970	Mil A	158	540	63	136	9	6	4	41	72-16	0	51	.252	.340	.313	81	-13	4-9	.989	-12	90	105	2-91,S-73	-1.4
1971	Mil A	89	260	26	59	6	5	3	17	41-3	0	31	.227	.330	.323	87	-4	0-5	.971	-4	88	75	2-48,S-39	-0.3
	StL N	32	72	8	18	3	2	1	10	11-3	0	12	.250	.345	.389	105	1	1-0	.959	-5	82	68	S-17,2-14	-0.2
1972	Tex A	46	116	5	26	3	0	0	7	12-3	1	12	.224	.300	.250	69	-4	0-1	.990	-4	91	84	2-25,S-15/3	-0.7
	†Oak A	51	94	14	17	4	1	0	8	9-0	0	11	.181	.250	.245	51	-6	0-0	.988	1	104	112	2-49/3	-0.3
	Year	97	210	19	43	7	1	0	15	21-3	1	23	.205	.278	.248	61	-10	0-1	.989	-3	99	101	2-74,S-15/3-2	-1.0

Year	Tm Lg	G	AB	R	H	2B	3B	HR	RBI	BB-IB	HP	SO	AVG	OBP	SLG	AOPS	ABR	SB-CS	FA	FR	Rng	Thr	G at Pos	BFW
1973	†Oak A	106	182	15	40	6	1	3	17	12-1	0	19	.220	.267	.313	67	-9	1-1	.973	3	111	102	2-83,S-26/3-2	-0.1
1974	Oak A	99	220	22	46	3	0	0	18	18-0	0	15	.209	.268	.223	46	-16	1-1	.995	-10	96	101	2-71,S-19,3-14/D-2	-2.2
1975	Oak A	20	28	2	7	1	0	0	4	2-0	0	2	.250	.300	.286	68	-1	0-0	1.000	-0	83	106	/S-7,3-7,2-6	-0.1
	SD N	87	196	13	44	5	0	0	14	24-5	0	18	.224	.308	.250	60	-10	3-1	.954	-3	105	104	3-64,2-11/1	-1.3
1976	SD N	96	212	16	50	5	2	0	26	25-2	0	28	.236	.314	.278	76	-6	0-3	.971	-7	99	124	3-27,2-25/S-6,1	-1.3
Total	10	977	2447	238	565	61	21	13	202	271-36	4	272	.231	.307	.289	73	-88	13-22	.981	-46	95	93	2-490,S-276,3-121/1-2,D-2	-9.5

KUBISZYN, JACK John Henry B 12.19.1936 Buffalo, NY BR/TR 5-11/170# d4.23

Year	Tm Lg	G	AB	R	H	2B	3B	HR	RBI	BB-IB	HP	SO	AVG	OBP	SLG	AOPS	ABR	SB-CS	FA	FR	Rng	Thr	G at Pos	BFW
1961	Cle A	25	42	4	9	0	0	0	0	2-0	0	5	.214	.250	.214	26	-5	0-0	1.000	1	114	0	/3-8,S-7,2-2	-0.3
1962	Cle A	25	59	3	10	2	0	1	2	5-0	0	7	.169	.231	.254	32	-6	0-0	.964	1	104	137	S-18/3	-0.3
Total	2	50	101	7	19	2	0	1	2	7-0	0	12	.188	.239	.238	30	-11	0-0	.969	3	104	145	/S-25,3-9,2-2	-0.6

KUBSKI, GIL Gilbert Thomas B 10.12.1954 Longview, TX BL/TR 6-3/185# d9.2

Year	Tm Lg	G	AB	R	H	2B	3B	HR	RBI	BB-IB	HP	SO	AVG	OBP	SLG	AOPS	ABR	SB-CS	FA	FR	Rng	Thr	G at Pos	BFW
1980	Cal A	22	63	11	16	3	0	0	6	6-0	0	10	.254	.319	.302	73	-2	1-1	1.000	2	111	164	O-20(1-0-19)	-0.2

KUCZEK, STEVE Stanislaw Leo B 12.28.1924 Amsterdam, NY BR/TR 6/160# d9.29

Year	Tm Lg	G	AB	R	H	2B	3B	HR	RBI	BB-IB	HP	SO	AVG	OBP	SLG	AOPS	ABR	SB-CS	FA	FR	Rng	Thr	G at Pos	BFW
1949	Bos N	1	1	0	1	1	0	0	0		0	0	1.000	1.000	2.000	723	1	0	—	0			H	0.1

KUEHNE, BILL William J. (born William J. Knelme) B 10.24.1858 Leipzig, Germany D 10.27.1921 Sulphur Springs, OH BR/TR 5-8/185# d5.1 OF Total (33-LF 9-CF 30-RF)

Year	Tm Lg	G	AB	R	H	2B	3B	HR	RBI	BB-IB	HP	SO	AVG	OBP	SLG	AOPS	ABR	SB-CS	FA	FR	Rng	Thr	G at Pos	BFW
1883	Col AA	95	374	38	85	8	14	1		2			.227	.231	.332	86	-6		.833	-3	99	138	*3-69,2-18/S-7,O-3(1-2-0)	-0.6
1884	Col AA	**110**	415	48	98	13	16	5		9	1		.236	.254	.381	113	5		.881	11	110	123	*3-110	1.7
1885	Pit AA	104	411	54	93	9	19	0	43	15	2		.226	.257	.341	89	-7		.865	-5	98	107	*3-97/S-7	-0.9
1886	Pit AA	117	481	73	98	16	17	1	48	19	2		.204	.237	.314	72	-18	26	.899	1	126	0	O-54(24-5-24),3-47,1-18	-1.7
1887	Pit N	102	402	68	120	18	15	1	41	14	1	39	.299	.324	.425	115	7	17	.883	-13	101	101	*S-91/3-4,1-4,O-3(0-1-2)	-0.3
1888	Pit N	**138**	524	60	123	22	11	3	62	9	2	68	.235	.250	.336	94	-5	34	.910	1	111	98	3-75,S-63	-0.1
1889	Pit N	97	390	43	96	20	5	5	57	9	0	36	.246	.263	.362	82	-12	15	.885	-2	100	109	3-75,O-13(8-1-4)/2-5,S-2,1-2	-1.1
1890	Pit P	126	528	66	126	21	12	5	73	28	0	37	.239	.277	.352	74	-22	21	.850	7	**111**	88	*3-126	-1.1
1891	Col AA	68	261	32	56	9	0	2	22	10	0	22	.215	.244	.272	50	-18	21	.885	0	101	144	3-68	-1.4
	Lou AA	39	152	25	41	3	1	1	17	7	1	13	.270	.306	.322	81	-5	9	.896	-1	99	107	3-39	-0.4
	Year	107	413	57	97	12	1	3	39	17	1	35	.235	.267	.291	62	-22	30	.889	-0	100	130	*3-107	-1.8
1892	Lou N	76	287	22	48	4	5	0	36	13	0	36	.167	.203	.216	29	-26	6	.874	-4	95	141	3-76	-2.7
	StL N	6	24	1	4	1	0	0	0	0	1	3	.167	.200	.208	25	-2	1	.895	-0	98	0	/3-5,S	-0.2
	Cin N	6	24	3	5	1	0	1	4	1	1	5	.208	.240	.375	87	-1	0	.941	0	107	356	/3-4,2-2	0.0
	StL N	1	4	0	0	0	0	0	0	0	0	1	.000	.000	.000	-99	-1	0	1.000	1	98	0	/3	0.0
	Year	89	339	26	57	6	5	1	40	14	1	45	.168	.203	.224	32	-29	7	.880	-3	97	154	3-86/2-2,S	-2.9
Total	10	1085	4277	533	993	145	115	25	403	136	10	260	.232	.258	.337	82	-111	150	.875	-5	104	115	3-796,S-171/O-73L,2-25,1-24	-8.8

KUENN, HARVEY Harvey Edward B 12.4.1930 W.Allis, WI D 2.28.1988 Peoria, AZ BR/TR 6-2/190# d9.6 M3 C12 OF Total (354-LF 163-CF 343-RF)

Year	Tm Lg	G	AB	R	H	2B	3B	HR	RBI	BB-IB	HP	SO	AVG	OBP	SLG	AOPS	ABR	SB-CS	FA	FR	Rng	Thr	G at Pos	BFW
1952	Det A	19	80	2	26	2	2	0	8	2	1	1	.325	.349	.400	107	0	2-1	.962	1	96	91	S-19	0.3
1953	Det A★	155	679	94	**209**	33	7	2	48	50	1	31	.308	.356	.386	101	1	6-5	.973	-24	89	68	*S-155	-1.0
1954	Det A☆	**155**	656	81	**201**	28	6	5	48	29	1	13	.306	.335	.390	100	-2	9-9	.966	5	104	86	*S-155	1.5
1955	Det A★	145	620	101	190	**38**	5	8	62	40-3	1	27	.306	.347	.423	109	7	8-3	.956	-26	88	95	*S-141	-0.6
1956	Det A★	146	591	96	**196**	32	7	12	88	55-3	3	34	.332	.387	.470	126	23	9-5	**.968**	-14	92	90	*S-141/O(LF)	1.9
1957	Det A★	151	624	74	173	30	6	9	44	47-4	0	28	.277	.327	.388	92	-7	5-8	.955	-46	80	95	*S-136,3-17/1	-4.6
1958	Det A☆	139	561	73	179	**39**	3	8	54	51-8	0	34	.319	.373	.442	116	14	5-10	.984	4	106	116	*O-138(CF)	0.9
1959	Det A★	139	561	99	**198**	**42**	7	9	71	48-1	1	37	**.353**	.402	.501	140	32	7-2	.988	-2	102	82	*O-137(0-23-116)	2.6
1960	Cle A★	126	474	65	146	24	0	9	54	55-6	1	25	.308	.379	.416	119	14	3-0	.966	-1	102	93	*O-119(2-2-117)/3-5	0.9
1961	SF N	131	471	60	125	22	4	5	46	47-2	1	34	.265	.329	.361	87	-8	5-4	.988	-5	97	120	O-93(67-0-31),3-32/S	-1.9
1962	†SF N	130	487	73	148	23	5	10	68	49-3	1	37	.304	.365	.433	116	12	3-6	.970	-5	99	45	*O-105(99-0-10),3-30	0.0
1963	SF N	120	417	61	121	13	2	6	31	44-3	2	38	.290	.358	.374	113	8	2-1	.975	-16	85	116	O-64(45-0-27),3-53	-1.2
1964	SF N	111	351	42	92	16	2	4	22	35-4	1	32	.262	.329	.353	91	-3	0-1	.952	-7	78	41	O-88(65-0-36),1-11/3-2	-1.6
1965	SF N	23	59	4	14	0	0	0	6	10-0	1	3	.237	.352	.237	69	-2	3-1	1.000	0	82	0	O-14(12-0-2)/1-7	-0.3
	Chi N	54	120	11	26	5	0	0	6	22-1	0	13	.217	.336	.258	69	-4	1-0	.975	-0	83	211	O-35(31-0-4)/1	-0.6
	Year	77	179	15	40	5	0	0	12	32-1	1	16	.223	.341	.251	69	-6	4-1	.981	-0	83	149	O-49(43-0-6)/1-8	-0.9
1966	Chi N	3	3	0	1	0	0	0	0	0-0	0	1	.333	.333	.333	85	0	0-0	—	0	0	0	/O(LF)	0.0
	Phi N	86	159	15	47	9	0	0	15	10-1	0	16	.296	.333	.352	92	-1	0-0	1.000	-3	100	0	O-31(LF),1-13/3	-0.6
	Year	89	162	15	48	9	0	0	15	10-1	0	17	.296	.333	.352	92	-1	0-0	1.000	-3	99	0	O-32(LF),1-13/3	-0.6
Total	15	1833	6913	951	2092	356	56	87	671	594-39	15	404	.303	.357	.408	108	84	68-56	.978	-140	97	90	O-826L,S-748,3-140/1-33	-4.3

KUHEL, JOE Joseph Anthony B 6.25.1906 Cleveland, OH D 2.26.1984 Kansas City, KS BL/TL 6/180# d7.31 M2

Year	Tm Lg	G	AB	R	H	2B	3B	HR	RBI	BB-IB	HP	SO	AVG	OBP	SLG	AOPS	ABR	SB-CS	FA	FR	Rng	Thr	G at Pos	BFW
1930	Was A	18	63	9	18	3	3	0	17	5	1	6	.286	.348	.429	95	-1	1-0	.981	-1	87	84	1-16	-0.2
1931	Was A	139	524	70	141	34	8	8	85	47	5	45	.269	.335	.410	94	-5	7-5	.991	-6	77	**121**	*1-139	-2.3
1932	Was A	101	347	52	101	21	5	4	52	32	1	19	.291	.353	.415	99	0	5-2	.994	-2	89	98	1-85	-0.9
1933	†Was A	**153**	602	89	194	34	10	11	107	59	2	48	.322	.385	.467	126	22	17-8	**.996**	-6	76	115	*1-153	0.2
1934	Was A	63	263	49	76	12	3	3	25	30	1	14	.289	.364	.392	99	0	2-7	.994	-4	72	116	1-63	-1.1
1935	Was A	151	633	99	165	25	9	2	74	78	4	44	.261	.345	.338	80	-18	5-4	.991	1	104	109	*1-151	-3.0
1936	Was A	149	588	107	189	42	8	16	118	64	4	30	.321	.392	.502	126	24	15-7	.993	-2	92	110	*1-149	0.8
1937	Was A	136	547	73	155	24	11	6	61	63	0	39	.283	.357	.400	95	-5	6-3	.993	3	109	116	*1-136	-1.4
1938	Chi A	117	412	67	110	27	4	8	51	72	0	35	.267	.376	.410	95	-2	9-7	.988	-8	79	95	*1-111	-1.9
1939	Chi A	139	546	107	164	24	9	15	56	64	2	51	.300	.376	.460	110	8	18-5	.992	-4	89	107	*1-136	-0.6
1940	Chi A	**155**	603	111	169	28	8	27	94	87	3	59	.280	.374	.488	120	18	12-5	.988	-5	91	93	*1-155	0.0
1941	Chi A	153	600	99	150	39	5	12	63	70	3	55	.250	.331	.392	92	-7	20-5	.994	0	100	94	*1-151	-1.8
1942	Chi A	115	413	60	103	14	4	4	52	60	2	22	.249	.347	.332	94	-2	22-9	.991	-3	91	103	*1-112	-1.4
1943	Chi A	153	531	55	113	21	1	5	46	76	7	45	.213	.319	.284	77	-13	14-8	.995	2	103	107	*1-153	-2.0
1944	Was A	139	518	90	144	26	7	4	51	68	2	40	.278	.364	.378	117	14	11-6	.987	-1	98	94	*1-138	0.6
1945	Was A	142	533	73	152	29	13	2	75	79	1	31	.285	.378	.400	137	28	10-5	.989	-6	87	91	*1-141	1.5
1946	Was A	14	20	2	3	0	0	0	2	5	0	2	.150	.320	.150	36	-1	0-0	1.000	0	125	61	/1-5	-0.1
	Chi A	64	238	24	65	9	3	4	20	21	1	24	.273	.335	.387	105	1	4-4	.994	-1	95	122	1-63	-0.3
	Year	78	258	26	68	9	3	4	22	26	1	26	.264	.333	.368	100	0	4-4	.994	-1	97	119	1-68	-0.4
1947	Chi A	3	3	0	0	0	0	0	0	0	0	3	.000	.000	.000	-99	-1	0-0	—	0			H	-0.1
Total	18	2104	7984	1236	2212	412	111	131	1049	980	39	612	.277	.359	.406	104	60	178-90	.992	-42	92	105	*1-2057	-14.0

KUHN, KENNY Kenneth Harold B 3.20.1937 Louisville, KY BL/TR 5-10.5/175# d7.7

Year	Tm Lg	G	AB	R	H	2B	3B	HR	RBI	BB-IB	HP	SO	AVG	OBP	SLG	AOPS	ABR	SB-CS	FA	FR	Rng	Thr	G at Pos	BFW
1955	Cle A	4	6	0	2	0	0	0	0	1-0	0	0	.333	.429	.333	103	0	1-0	1.000	-1	72	0	/S-4	0.0
1956	Cle A	27	22	7	6	1	0	0	2	0-0	0	4	.273	.273	.318	54	-2	0-1	1.000	1	92	127	S-17/2-5	-0.1
1957	Cle A	40	53	5	9	0	0	0	5	4-0	0	9	.170	.228	.170	10	-7	0-0	.974	-3	62	35	2-14/3-2,S	-0.9
Total	3	71	81	12	17	1	0	0	7	5-0	0	13	.210	.256	.222	30	-9	1-1	.963	-3	82	83	/S-22,2-19,3-2	-1.0

KUHN, WALT Walter Charles "Red" B 2.2.1884 Fresno, CA D 6.14.1935 Fresno, CA BR/TR 5-7/162# d4.18

Year	Tm Lg	G	AB	R	H	2B	3B	HR	RBI	BB-IB	HP	SO	AVG	OBP	SLG	AOPS	ABR	SB-CS	FA	FR	Rng	Thr	G at Pos	BFW
1912	Chi A	76	178	16	36	7	0	0	10	20	1		.202	.286	.242	53	-10	4	.966	5	*102*	*103*	C-75/2	0.0
1913	Chi A	26	50	5	8	1	0	0	5	13	0	8	.160	.333	.180	52	-2	1	.980	0	*124*	*89*	C-24	0.0
1914	Chi A	17	40	4	11	1	0	0	0	8	0	11	.275	.396	.300	111	1	2-3	.987	1	*121*	*85*	C-16	0.3
Total	3	119	268	25	55	9	0	0	15	41	1	19	.205	.313	.239	62	-11	7-3	.971	7	*109*	*98*	C-115/2	0.3

KUHNS, CHARLIE Charles B. B 10.27.1877 Freeport, PA D 7.15.1922 Pittsburgh, PA 5-9/160# d6.4

Year	Tm Lg	G	AB	R	H	2B	3B	HR	RBI	BB-IB	HP	SO	AVG	OBP	SLG	AOPS	ABR	SB-CS	FA	FR	Rng	Thr	G at Pos	BFW
1897	Pit N	1	3	0	0	0	0	0	0	1	0		.000	.250	.000	-32	-1	0	.667	-0	120	0	/3	-0.1
1899	Bos N	7	18	2	5	0	0	0	3	2	0		.278	.350	.278	67	-1	0	.813	-1	95	214	/S-3,3-3	-0.2
Total	2	8	21	2	5	0	0	0	3	3	0		.238	.333	.238	53	-2	0	.733	-1	112	0	/3-4,S-3	-0.3

KUIPER, DUANE Duane Eugene B 6.19.1950 Racine, WI BL/TR 6/175# d9.9

Year	Tm Lg	G	AB	R	H	2B	3B	HR	RBI	BB-IB	HP	SO	AVG	OBP	SLG	AOPS	ABR	SB-CS	FA	FR	Rng	Thr	G at Pos	BFW
1974	Cle A	10	22	7	11	2	0	0	4	2-0	0	2	.500	.542	.591	228	4	1-1	1.000	1	115	73	/2-8	0.5
1975	Cle A	90	346	42	101	11	1	0	25	30-0	8	26	.292	.362	.329	97	0	19-18	.972	-14	90	107	2-87/D	-1.0
1976	Cle A	135	506	47	133	13	6	0	37	30-2	1	42	.263	.303	.312	82	-13	10-17	**.987**	17	99	115	*2-128/1-5,D-2	0.9
1977	Cle A	148	610	62	169	15	8	1	50	37-1	7	55	.277	.324	.333	83	-15	11-11	.985	-3	95	105	*2-148	-1.1
1978	Cle A	149	547	52	155	18	6	0	43	19-1	4	35	.283	.311	.338	84	-13	4-9	.979	-12	93	89	*2-149	-2.0
1979	Cle A	140	479	46	122	9	5	0	39	37-7	4	27	.255	.313	.294	65	-24	4-9	**.988**	-5	92	88	*2-140	-2.3

Year	Tm Lg	G	AB	R	H	2B	3B	HR	RBI	BB-IB	HP	SO	AVG	OBP	SLG	AOPS	ABR	SB-CS	FA	FR	Rng	Thr	G at Pos	BFW
1980	Cle A	42	149	10	42	5	0	0	9	13-3	0	8	.282	.337	.315	80	-4	0-1	.995	-5	88	90	2-42	-0.6
1981	Cle A	72	206	15	53	6	0	0	14	8-2	0	13	.257	.284	.286	66	-9	1-1	.983	-11	90	53	2-72	-1.8
1982	SF N	107	218	26	61	9	1	0	17	32-0	2	24	.280	.375	.330	100	2	2-2	.978	-8	90	85	2-51	-0.4
1983	SF N	72	176	14	44	2	2	0	14	27-6	2	13	.250	.353	.284	82	-3	0-1	.988	-13	87	49	2-64	-1.4
1984	SF N	83	115	8	23	1	0	0	11	12-5	0	10	.200	.273	.209	39	-9	0-1	.969	4	109	99	2-31/1	-0.5
1985	SF N	9	5	0	3	0	0	0	0	1-0	0	0	.600	.667	.600	270	1	0-0	—	0			/H	0.1
Total	12	1057	3379	329	917	91	29	1	263	248-27	28	255	.271	.325	.316	81	-83	52-71	.983	-49	93	92	2-920/1-6,D-3	-9.6
KUNKEL, JEFF Jeffrey William B 3.25.1962 W.Palm Beach, FL BR/TR 6-2/180# d7.23 f-Bill OF Total (14-LF 30-CF 5-RF)																								
1984	Tex A	50	142	13	29	2	3	3	7	2-0	1	35	.204	.218	.324	47	-11	4-3	.922	-1	96	85	S-48/D	-0.8
1985	Tex A	2	4	1	1	0	0	0	0	0-0	0	3	.250	.250	.250	37	0	0-0	1.000	1	192	171	/S-2	0.1
1986	Tex A	8	13	3	3	0	0	1	2	0-0	0	2	.231	.231	.462	81	0	0-0	.769	-4	53	0	/S-5,D	-0.4
1987	Tex A	15	32	1	7	0	0	1	2	0-0	1	10	.219	.242	.313	46	-3	0-1	.955	1	103	140	2-10/3-3,O-3(1-2-0),1SD	-0.2
1988	Tex A	55	154	14	35	8	3	2	15	4-1	1	35	.227	.250	.357	67	-8	0-1	.949	4	111	101	2-28,S-19,3-10/O-6(4-2-0),PD	-0.3
1989	Tex A	108	293	39	79	21	2	8	29	20-0	3	75	.270	.323	.437	110	4	3-2	.936	-5	92	60	S-59,O-30(5-24-3)/2-8,3-4,PD	0.2
1990	Tex A	99	200	17	34	11	1	3	17	11-0	2	66	.170	.221	.280	39	-17	2-1	.958	5	103	101	S-67,3-15,2-13/O-5(1-2-2),D	-0.8
1992	Chi N	20	29	0	4	2	0	0	1	0-0	0	8	.138	.138	.207	-3	-4	0-0	1.000	2	172	90	/S-6,2-3,O-3(LF)	-0.2
Total	8	357	867	88	192	44	9	18	73	37-1	8	234	.221	.259	.355	69	-39	9-8	.940	3	97	80	S-207/2-62,O-47C,3-32,D-12,P-2,1-2.4	
KUNTZ, RUSTY Russell Jay B 2.4.1955 Orange, CA BR/TR 6-3/190# d9.1 C9																								
1979	Chi A	5	11	0	1	0	0	0	0	2-0	0	6	.091	.231	.091	-9	-2	0-0	1.000	2	183	444	/O-5(1-1-3)	0.0
1980	Chi A	36	62	5	14	4	0	0	3	5-0	0	13	.226	.284	.290	58	-3	1-0	.979	1	106	145	O-34(19-9-6)	-0.3
1981	Chi A	67	55	15	14	2	0	0	4	6-0	1	8	.255	.339	.291	85	-1	1-0	1.000	0	111	0	O-51(28-13-13)/D-5	-0.1
1982	Chi A	21	26	4	5	1	0	0	3	2-0	0	8	.192	.250	.231	33	-2	0-0	1.000	-1	83	0	O-21(1-20-1)	-0.4
1983	Chi A	28	42	6	11	1	0	0	1	6-0	0	13	.262	.354	.286	76	-1	1-0	.976	-1	103	0	O-27(2-25-0)/D	-0.2
	Min A	31	100	13	19	3	0	3	5	12-0	0	28	.190	.274	.310	59	-6	0-0	.986	-0	90	172	O-30(0-27-3)	-0.6
	Year	59	142	19	30	4	0	3	6	18-0	0	41	.211	.298	.303	64	-7	1-0	.982	-1	95	112	O-57(2-52-3)/D	-0.8
1984	†Det A	84	140	32	40	12	0	2	22	25-1	1	28	.286	.393	.414	126	7	2-2	.987	-4	84	80	O-67(12-22-37),D-10	0.1
1985	Det A	5	5	0	0	0	0	0	0	2-0	0	2	.000	.286	.000	-13	-1	0-1	.000	-0	0	0	/1D	-0.1
Total	7	277	441	75	104	23	0	5	38	60-1	2	106	.236	.328	.322	81	-9	5-3	.988	-3	97	89	O-235(63-117-63)/D-19,1	-1.6
KUROWSKI, WHITEY George John B 4.19.1918 Reading, PA D 12.9.1999 Sinking Spring, PA BR/TR 5-11/193# d9.23																								
1941	StL N	5	9	1	3	2	0	0	2	0	1	2	.333	.400	.556	157	1	0	1.000	-0	75	0	/3-4	0.0
1942	†StL N	115	366	51	93	17	3	9	42	33	6	60	.254	.326	.391	102	0	7	.944	6	101	119	*3-104/SO(LF)	1.1
1943	†StL N☆	139	522	69	150	24	8	13	70	31	2	54	.287	.330	.439	116	8	3	.952	-4	89	135	*3-137/S-2	0.6
1944	†StL N★	149	555	95	150	25	7	20	87	58	2	40	.270	.341	.449	119	13	2	**.965**	-1	92	95	*3-146/2-9,S	1.4
1945	StL N✳	133	511	84	165	27	3	21	102	45	5	45	.323	.383	.511	144	29	1	.964	-4	90	**130**	*3-131/S-6	2.6
1946	†StL N★	142	519	76	156	32	5	14	89	72	5	47	.301	.391	.462	136	26	2	**.966**	-3	91	88	*3-138	2.4
1947	StL N★	146	513	108	159	27	6	27	104	87	**10**	56	.310	.420	.544	148	38	4	.954	-15	88	71	*3-141	2.2
1948	StL N	77	220	34	47	8	0	2	33	42	5	28	.214	.352	.277	68	-8	0	.939	-7	85	79	3-65	-1.5
1949	StL N	10	14	0	2	0	0	0	0	1	0	0	.143	.200	.143	-6	-2	0	1.000	-0	57	0	/3-2	-0.2
Total	9	916	3229	518	925	162	32	106	529	369	36	332	.286	.366	.455	124	105	19	.957	-29	91	103	3-868/S-10,2-9,O(LF)	8.6
KUSICK, CRAIG Craig Robert B 9.30.1948 Milwaukee, WI BR/TR 6-3/232# d9.8																								
1973	Min A	15	48	4	12	2	0	0	4	7-0	1	9	.250	.357	.292	81	-1	0-0	.989	-1	75	81	1-11/O-2(LF),D-2	-0.3
1974	Min A	76	201	36	48	7	1	8	26	35-1	1	36	.239	.353	.403	114	5	0-0	.996	3	112	85	1-75	0.3
1975	Min A	57	156	14	37	8	0	6	27	21-1	5	23	.237	.346	.404	110	3	0-0	.990	1	102	121	1-51	0.0
1976	Min A	109	266	33	69	13	0	11	36	35-0	1	44	.259	.344	.432	125	9	5-1	.977	2	160	127	D-79,1-23	0.9
1977	Min A	115	268	34	68	12	0	12	45	49-5	3	60	.254	.370	.433	121	10	3-1	.972	-2	71	74	D-85,1-23	0.5
1978	Min A	77	191	23	33	3	2	4	20	37-2	1	38	.173	.305	.272	64	-8	3-2	.987	2	145	76	D-35,1-27/O-9(LF)	-1.0
1979	Min A	24	54	8	13	4	0	3	6	3-0	0	11	.241	.281	.481	97	0	0-0	1.000	0	100	151	D-12/1-8	-0.1
	Tor A	24	54	3	11	1	0	2	7	7-0	1	7	.204	.302	.333	72	-2	0-0	.978	1	129	88	1-20/PD	-0.2
	Year	48	108	11	24	5	0	5	13	10-0	1	18	.222	.292	.407	85	-3	0-0	.983	1	123	101	1-28,D-13/P	-0.3
Total	7	497	1238	155	291	50	3	46	171	194-9	13	228	.235	.342	.392	106	16	11-4	.988	6	113	96	1-238,D-214/O-11(LF),P	0.1
KUSNYER, ART Arthur William B 12.19.1945 Akron, OH BR/TR 6-2/198# d9.21 C22																								
1970	Chi A	4	10	0	1	0	0	0	0	0-0	0	4	.100	.100	.100	-43	-2	0-0	.941	0	20	152	/C-3	-0.2
1971	Cal A	6	13	0	2	0	0	0	0	0-0	0	3	.154	.154	.154	-14	-2	0-0	.958	-1	93	332	/C-6	-0.3
1972	Cal A	64	179	13	37	2	1	2	13	16-3	1	33	.207	.276	.263	64	-8	0-0	.975	-4	69	95	C-63	-1.1
1973	Cal A	41	64	5	8	2	0	0	3	2-0	0	12	.125	.149	.156	-14	-10	0-1	.979	-4	98	77	C-41	-1.3
1976	Mil A	15	34	2	4	1	0	0	3	1-1	1	5	.118	.167	.147	-8	-5	1-0	.938	-2	117	87	C-14	-0.7
1978	KC A	9	13	1	3	1	0	1	2	2-0	0	4	.231	.333	.538	138	1	0-0	.946	2	56	110	/C-9	0.3
Total	6	139	313	21	55	6	1	3	21	21-4	2	61	.176	.231	.230	37	-26	1-1	.970	-9	80	102	C-136	-3.3
KUSTUS, JOE Joseph J. "Jul" B 9.5.1882 Detroit, MI D 4.27.1916 Eloise, MI BR/TR 5-10/?# d4.17																								
1909	Bro N	53	173	12	25	5	0	1	11	11	2		.145	.204	.191	23	-16	9	.951	0	87	61	O-50(1-18-31)	-2.0
KUTCHER, RANDY Randy Scott B 4.20.1960 Anchorage, AK BR/TR 5-11/175# d6.19 OF Total (26-LF 78-CF 52-RF)																								
1986	SF N	71	186	28	44	9	1	7	16	11-0	0	41	.237	.279	.409	92	-3	6-5	.990	-2	115	138	O-51(7-44-1),S-13/3-4,2-3	-0.6
1987	SF N	14	16	7	3	1	1	0	1	1-0	0	5	.188	.235	.375	61	-1	1-0	1.000	1	147	0	/O-6(1-4-1),2-2,3-2,S	0.0
1988	Bos A	19	12	2	2	1	0	0	0	0-0	0	2	.167	.167	.250	14	-1	0-1	1.000	1	92	548	/O-7(5-0-2),3-2,D-7	-0.1
1989	Bos A	77	160	28	36	10	3	2	18	11-0	0	46	.225	.273	.363	74	-6	3-0	.982	1	116	0	O-57(11-21-25)/3-6,CD	-0.5
1990	†Bos A	63	74	18	17	4	1	1	5	13-0	0	18	.230	.345	.351	91	-1	3-3	1.000	3	114	0	O-34(2-9-23),3-11/2-5,D-5	0.2
Total	5	244	448	83	102	25	6	10	40	36-0	0	112	.228	.285	.377	82	-12	13-9	.989	4	115	69	O-155C/3-25,D-18,S-14,2-10,C	-1.0
KUTINA, JOE Joseph Peter B 1.16.1885 Chicago, IL D 4.13.1945 Chicago, IL BR/TR 6-2/205# d9.6																								
1911	StL A	26	101	12	26	6	2	3	15	2	1		.257	.279	.446	105	0	2	.981	-1	92	127	1-26	-0.2
1912	StL A	69	205	18	42	9	3	1	18	13	3		.205	.262	.293	61	-11	0	.985	-2	79	109	1-51/O(LF)	-1.5
Total	2	95	306	30	68	15	5	4	33	15	4		.222	.268	.343	76	-11	2	.984	-3	83	115	/1-77,O(LF)	-1.7
KVASNAK, AL Alexander B 1.11.1921 Sagamore, PA D 9.26.2002 Arcadia, CA BR/TR 6-1/170# d4.15 Mil 1942-45																								
1942	Was A	5	11	3	2	0	0	0	0	2	0	1	.182	.308	.182	40	-1	0-0	1.000	0	109	0	/O-3(1-0-2)	-0.1
KYLE, ANDY Andrew Ewing B 10.29.1889 Toronto, ON, CAN D 9.6.1971 Toronto, ON, CAN BL/TL 5-8/160# d9.7																								
1912	Cin N	9	21	3	7	1	0	0	4	4	0	2	.333	.440	.381	129	1	0-0	1.000	1	112	112	/O-7(2-5-0)	0.1
LAABS, CHET Chester Peter B 4.30.1912 Milwaukee, WI D 1.26.1983 Warren, MI BR/TR 5-8/175# d5.5 Def 1944 Mil 1945																								
1937	Det A	72	242	31	58	13	5	8	37	24	0	66	.240	.308	.434	83	-8	6-2	.971	-5	92	39	O-62(22-40-0)	-1.3
1938	Det A	64	211	26	50	7	3	7	37	15	0	52	.237	.288	.398	66	-13	3-2	.971	0	102	91	O-53(22-32-0)	-1.3
1939	Det A	5	16	1	5	1	1	0	2	2	0	0	.313	.389	.500	117	0	0-0	.933	1	112	283	/O-5(LF)	0.1
	StL A	95	317	52	95	20	5	10	62	33	1	62	.300	.368	.489	115	6	4-1	.972	-2	96	107	O-79(3-70-6)	0.3
	Year	100	333	53	100	21	6	10	64	35	1	62	.300	.369	.489	115	7	4-1	.969	-1	97	119	O-84(8-70-6)	0.4
1940	StL A	105	218	32	59	11	5	10	40	34	1	59	.271	.372	.505	122	7	3-3	.969	-1	99	77	O-63(25-29-10)	0.3
1941	StL A	118	392	64	109	23	6	15	59	51	0	59	.278	.361	.482	117	9	5-2	.982	-1	102	66	*O-100(21-15-64)	0.3
1942	StL A	144	520	90	143	21	7	27	99	88	0	88	.275	.380	.498	144	30	0-3	.970	-3	92	124	*O-139(36-25-80)	1.9
1943	StL A★	151	580	83	145	27	7	17	85	73	4	105	.250	.338	.409	115	11	5-7	.976	5	101	136	*O-150(125-24-6)	0.6
1944	†StL A	66	201	28	47	10	2	5	23	29	0	33	.234	.330	.378	96	-1	3-1	1.000	1	101	76	O-55(38-0-18)	-0.3
1945	StL A	35	109	15	26	4	3	1	8	16	3	17	.239	.352	.358	101	1	0-0	.986	-0	107	37	O-35(34-2-2)	-0.2
1946	StL A	80	264	40	69	13	0	16	52	20	1	50	.261	.316	.492	117	5	3-1	.987	2	111	83	O-72(6-0-66)	0.5
1947	Phi A	15	32	5	7	1	0	1	5	4	0	4	.219	.306	.344	79	-1	0-0	1.000	1	105	199	/O-7(6-0-1)	-0.1
Total	11	950	3102	467	813	151	44	117	509	389	10	595	.262	.346	.452	113	46	32-22	.977	-3	100	98	O-820(343-237-253)	0.8
LABOY, COCO Jose Alberto B 7.3.1939 Ponce, P.R. BR/TR 5-10/170# d4.8																								
1969	Mon N	157	562	53	145	29	1	18	83	40-2	4	96	.258	.308	.409	100	-1	0-2	.944	5	104	94	*3-156	0.3
1970	Mon N	137	432	37	86	26	1	5	53	31-5	2	81	.199	.254	.299	48	-32	0-2	.946	-7	90	81	*3-132/2-3	-4.1
1971	Mon N	76	151	10	38	4	0	1	14	11-0	0	19	.252	.302	.298	70	-6	0-1	.937	-2	93	54	3-65/2-2	-0.9
1972	Mon N	28	69	6	18	2	0	3	14	10-3	0	16	.261	.350	.420	117	2	0-0	.980	-3	90	61	3-24/2-3,S-2	-0.2

Year	Tm Lg	G	AB	R	H	2B	3B	HR	RBI	BB-IB	HP	SO	AVG	OBP	SLG	AOPS	ABR	SB-CS	FA	FR	Rng	Thr	G at Pos	BFW
1973	Mon N	22	33	2	4	1	0	1	2	5-1	0	8	.121	.237	.242	32	-3	0-0	.889	-1	88	87	3-20/2	-0.4
Total	5	420	1247	108	291	62	2	28	166	97-11	6	220	.233	.289	.354	77	-40	0-5	.944	-8	97	83	3-397/2-9,S-2	-5.3
LaCHANCE, CANDY George Joseph B 2.15.1870 Putnam, CT D 8.18.1932 Waterville, CT BB/TR 6-1/183# d8.15																								
1893	Bro N	11	35	1	6	1	0	0	6	2	1	12	.171	.237	.200	17	-4	0	.654	-4	*104*	*73*	/C-6,O-5(4-0-1)	-0.7
1894	Bro N	69	261	48	83	13	8	5	52	16	1	32	.318	.360	.487	110	3	20	.979	-8	52	72	1-56,C-11/O-3(RF)	-0.3
1895	Bro N	128	541	102	170	23	9	8	111	29	8	48	.314	.358	.434	113	9	37	.983	-6	78	98	*1-126/O-3(RF)	0.2
1896	Bro N	89	348	60	99	10	13	7	58	23	1	32	.284	.331	.448	110	2	17	.986	-4	77	115	*1-89	-0.1
1897	Bro N	126	520	86	160	28	16	4	90	15	5		.308	.333	.446	111	4	26	.978	-4	90	110	*1-126	0.0
1898	Bro N	136	526	62	130	23	7	5	65	31	8		.247	.299	.346	85	-12	23	.988	-16	56	116	1-74,S-48,O-13(11-2-0)	-2.5
1899	Bal N	125	472	65	145	23	10	1	75	21	10		.307	.350	.405	101	-1	31	.984	-7	65	102	*1-125	-0.7
1901	Cle A	133	548	81	166	22	9	1	75	7	2		.303	.314	.381	96	-5	11	.979	-3	85	89	*1-133	-0.9
1902	Bos A	**138**	541	60	151	13	4	6	56	18	5		.279	.309	.351	80	-16	8	.983	-12	59	106	*1-138	-2.9
1903	†Bos A	**141**	522	60	134	22	6	1	53	28	7		.257	.303	.328	85	-9	12	.984	-11	64	107	*1-141	-2.5
1904	Bos A	**157**	573	55	130	19	5	1	47	23	7		.227	.265	.283	69	-20	7	**.992**	-14	59	**111**	*1-157	-4.2
1905	Bos A	12	41	1	6	1	0	0	5	6	0		.146	.255	.171	36	-3	0	.988	-1	80	117	1-12	-0.4
Total	12	1265	4928	681	1380	198	87	39	693	219	55	<u>124</u>	.280	.318	.379	93	-52	192	.984	-90	69	104	*1-1177/S-48,O-24(15-2-7),C-17	-15.0
LACHEMANN, RENE Rene George B 5.4.1945 Los Angeles, CA BR/TR 6/198# d5.4 M8 C15 b-Marcel																								
1965	KC A	92	216	20	49	7	1	9	29	12-3	0	57	.227	.264	.394	87	-5	0-0	.980	-3	*70*	*76*	C-75	-0.5
1966	KC A	7	5	0	1	1	0	0	0	0-0	0	1	.200	.200	.400	70	0	0-0	1.000	0	*58*	*264*	/C-6	0.0
1968	Oak A	19	60	3	9	1	0	0	4	1-0	1	11	.150	.177	.167	5	-7	0-0	.967	-7	59	46	C-16	-1.6
Total	3	118	281	23	59	9	1	9	33	13-3	1	69	.210	.245	.345	70	-12	0-0	.978	-9	*67*	*73*	/C-97	-2.1
LaCOCK, PETE Ralph Pierre B 1.17.1952 Burbank, CA BL/TL 6-3/210# d9.6																								
1972	Chi N	5	6	3	3	0	0	0	4	0-0	0	1	.500	.429	.500	167	0	1-0	1.000	-0	68	0	/O-3(RF)	0.0
1973	Chi N	11	16	1	4	1	0	0	3	1-0	0	2	.250	.294	.313	63	-1	0-0	1.000	1	97	401	/O-5(RF)	0.0
1974	Chi N	35	110	9	20	4	1	1	8	12-2	1	16	.182	.268	.264	47	-8	0-0	.974	2	114	170	O-22(RF),1-11	-0.8
1975	Chi N	106	249	30	57	8	1	6	30	37-7	0	27	.229	.324	.341	82	-5	0-2	.988	3	136	95	1-53,O-26(11-0-15)	-0.8
1976	Chi N	106	244	34	54	9	2	8	28	42-6	1	37	.221	.337	.373	93	-1	1-4	.975	-4	85	117	1-54,O-19(7-0-12)	-1.2
1977	†KC A	88	218	25	66	12	1	3	29	15-1	1	25	.303	.345	.408	105	2	2-1	.990	2	122	98	1-29,D-26,O-12(8-1-3)	0.2
1978	†KC A	118	322	44	95	21	2	5	48	21-2	0	27	.295	.335	.419	109	4	1-0	.993	-6	74	104	*1-106	-0.7
1979	KC A	132	408	54	113	25	4	3	56	37-7	1	26	.277	.334	.380	92	-4	2-1	**.997**	2	107	95	*1-108,D-16	-0.8
1980	†KC A	114	156	14	32	6	0	1	18	17-1	1	10	.205	.284	.263	51	-10	1-0	.997	-1	117	109	1-86,O-29(26-0-5)	-1.4
Total	9	715	1729	214	444	86	11	27	224	182-26	5	171	.257	.326	.366	89	-23	8-8	.991	-0	102	100	1-447,O-116(52-1-65)/D-42	-5.5
LACY, LEE Leondaus B 4.10.1948 Longview, TX BR/TR 6-1/175# d6.30 OF Total (417-LF 77-CF 594-RF)																								
1972	LA N	60	243	34	63	7	3	0	12	19-0	0	37	.259	.312	.313	80	-7	5-3	.973	-2	104	113	2-58	-0.5
1973	LA N	57	135	14	28	2	0	0	8	15-1	0	34	.207	.287	.222	45	-10	2-3	.965	-5	90	112	2-41	-1.4
1974	†LA N	48	78	13	22	6	0	0	8	2-0	0	14	.282	.293	.359	87	-2	2-0	.968	-2	99	75	2-34/3	-0.2
1975	LA N	101	306	44	96	11	5	7	40	22-1	0	29	.314	.356	.451	129	11	5-9	.935	-7	77	63	2-43,O-43(37-3-8)/S	0.1
1976	Atl N	50	180	25	49	4	2	3	20	6-1	1	12	.272	.299	.367	83	-5	2-2	.969	-11	80	88	2-44/O-5(1-4-1),3	-1.4
	LA N	53	158	17	42	7	1	0	14	16-2	0	13	.266	.330	.323	88	-2	1-2	.979	-1	102	38	O-37(5-23-10)/3-3,2-2	-0.5
	Year	103	338	42	91	11	3	3	34	22-3	1	25	.269	.314	.346	86	-7	3-4	.970	-12	79	85	2-46,O-42(6-27-11)/3-4	-1.9
1977	†LA N	75	169	28	45	7	0	6	21	10-0	0	21	.266	.306	.414	92	-3	4-0	1.000	-2	60	0	O-32(18-0-18),2-22,3-12	-0.3
1978	†LA N	103	245	29	64	16	4	13	40	27-4	1	30	.261	.335	.518	136	11	7-4	.971	-4	99	70	O-44(17-0-27),2-24/3-9,S	0.7
1979	†Pit N	84	182	17	45	9	3	5	15	22-2	1	36	.247	.327	.412	97	-1	6-1	.973	-3	94	102	O-41(LF)/2-5	-0.4
1980	Pit N	109	278	45	93	20	4	7	33	28-3	2	33	.335	.394	.511	150	19	18-9	.984	9	120	130	O-88(86-3-0)/3-3	2.7
1981	Pit N	78	213	31	57	11	4	2	10	11-2	1	29	.268	.307	.385	92	-3	24-3	.977	5	115	153	O-63(34-1-29)/3	0.5
1982	Pit N	121	359	66	112	16	3	5	31	32-4	1	57	.312	.369	.415	116	8	40-15	.965	1	105	106	*O-113(40-17-71)/3-2	0.9
1983	Pit N	108	288	40	87	12	3	4	13	22-2	0	36	.302	.352	.406	107	2	31-13	1.000	4	120	44	O-98(59-24-28)	0.7
1984	Pit N	138	474	66	152	26	3	12	70	32-2	0	61	.321	.362	.464	131	19	21-11	**.996**	13	115	171	*O-127(78-0-88)/2-2	2.8
1985	Bal A	121	492	69	144	22	4	9	48	39-0	2	95	.293	.343	.409	109	6	10-3	.984	1	100	117	*O-115(0-1-115)/D-5	0.2
1986	Bal A	130	491	77	141	18	0	11	47	37-2	0	71	.287	.334	.391	99	-1	4-6	.992	3	104	101	*O-120(RF)/D-3	-0.5
1987	Bal A	87	258	35	63	13	3	7	28	32-0	0	49	.244	.326	.399	94	-2	3-2	.973	5	100	228	O-80(1-1-79)/D-4	-0.1
Total	16	1523	4549	650	1303	207	42	91	458	372-26	9	657	.286	.339	.410	108	40	185-86	.983	5	107	124	*O-1006R,2-275/3-32,D-12,S-2	3.3
LACY, GUY Osceola Guy B 6.12.1897 Cleveland, TN D 11.19.1953 Cleveland, TN BR/TR 5-11.5/170# d5.7																								
1926	Cle A	13	24	2	4	0	0	1	2	2	1	2	.167	.259	.292	43	-2	0-0	.976	-0	104	83	2-11/3-2	-0.2
LADD, HI Arthur Clifford B 2.9.1870 Willimantic, CT D 5.7.1948 Cranston, RI BL/TR 6-4/180# d7.12																								
1898	Pit N	1	1	0	0	0	0	0	0	0	0		.000	.000	.000	-99	0	0	—	0			H	0.0
	Bos N	1	4	1	1	0	0	0	0	0	0		.250	.250	.250	41	0	0	1.000	0	0	0	/O(LF)	0.0
	Year	2	5	1	1	0	0	0	0	0	0		.200	.200	.200	14	-1	0	1.000	0	0	0	/O(LF)	0.0
LADEW, STEVE Stephen B St.Louis, MO d9.27																								
1889	KC AA	2	4	0	0	0	0	0	0	0	0	3	.000	.000	.000	-95	-1	0	1.000	0	0	0	/O(LF)P	-0.1
LAFATA, JOE Joseph Joseph B 8.3.1921 Detroit, MI BL/TL 6/163# d4.17																								
1947	NY N	62	95	13	21	1	0	2	18	15	1	18	.221	.333	.295	68	-4	1	.974	1	93	241	O-19(20-1-0)/1-2	-0.5
1948	NY N	1	1	0	0	0	0	0	0	0	0	1	.000	.000	.000	-99	0	0	—	0			H	0.0
1949	NY N	64	140	18	33	2	2	3	16	9	0	23	.236	.282	.343	67	-7	1	.984	-4	51	97	1-47	-1.3
Total	3	127	236	31	54	3	2	5	34	24	1	42	.229	.303	.322	67	-11	2	.985	-4	49	101	/1-49,O-19(20-1-0)	-1.8
LAFFERTY, FLIP Frank Bernard B 5.4.1854 Scranton, PA D 2.8.1910 Wilmington, DE TR d9.15 ▲																								
1876	Phi N	1	3	0	0	0	0	0	0	0		0	.000	.000	.000	-99	-1		.750	0	141	1747	/P	0.0
1877	Lou N	4	17	2	1	1	0	0	0	0		4	.059	.059	.118	-39	-3		.750	-1	0	0	/O-4(CF)	-0.3
Total	2	5	20	2	1	1	0	0	0	0		4	.050	.050	.100	-46	-4		.750	-1	0	0	/O-4(CF),P	-0.3
LaFOREST, TY Byron Joseph (born Biron Joseph La Forest) B 4.18.1917 Edmundston, NB, CAN D 5.5.1947 Arlington, MA BR/TR 5-9/165# d8.4																								
1945	Bos A	52	204	25	51	7	4	2	16	10	0	35	.250	.285	.353	83	-6	4-4	.966	4	111	121	3-45/O-5(3-0-2)	-0.2
LaFOREST, PETE Pierre Luc B 1.27.1978 Hull, PQ, CAN BL/TR 6-2/200# d9.2																								
2003	TB A	19	48	0	8	2	0	0	6	1-0	1	14	.167	.196	.208	8	-6	0-0	1.000	-1	29	0	D-12/C-4	-0.8
LaFRANCOIS, ROGER Roger Victor B 8.2.1954 Norwich, CT BL/TR 6-2/215# d5.27																								
1982	Bos A	8	10	1	4	1	0	0	1	0-0	0	0	.400	.400	.500	137	1	0-0	1.000	0	0	0	/C-8	0.1
LAGA, MIKE Michael Russell B 6.14.1960 Ridgewood, NJ BL/TL 6-2/210# d9.1																								
1982	Det A	27	88	6	23	9	0	3	11	4-0	0	23	.261	.293	.466	104	0	1-0	.994	-3	33	127	1-19/D-8	-0.4
1983	Det A	12	21	2	4	0	0	0	2	1-0	0	9	.190	.227	.190	17	-2	0-0	1.000	0	97	180	/1-5,D-6	-0.3
1984	Det A	9	11	1	6	0	0	0	1	1-0	0	2	.545	.583	.545	216	2	0-0	1.000	0	100	101	/1-4,D-4	0.2
1985	Det A	9	36	3	6	1	0	2	6	0-0	0	9	.167	.167	.361	40	-3	0-0	.974	1	163	123	/1-4,D-5	-0.3
1986	Det A	15	45	6	9	1	0	3	8	5-1	0	13	.200	.280	.422	88	-1	0-0	1.000	-1	80	111	1-12/D-2	-0.2
	StL N	18	46	7	10	4	0	3	8	5-1	1	18	.217	.308	.500	120	1	0-0	1.000	2	169	105	1-16	0.3
1987	StL N	17	29	4	4	1	0	1	4	2-1	0	7	.138	.182	.276	22	-3	0-0	.973	1	143	170	1-12	-0.3
1988	StL N	41	100	5	13	0	0	1	4	2-0	0	21	.130	.147	.160	-12	-15	0-0	1.000	-0	91	133	1-37	-1.9
1989	SF N	17	20	1	4	1	0	1	7	1-0	0	6	.200	.238	.400	82	-1	0-0	1.000	-0	62	0	/1-4	-0.1
1990	SF N	23	27	4	5	1	0	2	4	1-0	1	7	.185	.241	.444	88	-1	0-0	1.000	1	132	114	1-10	-0.1
Total	9	188	423	39	84	18	0	16	55	22-3	2	115	.199	.241	.355	63	-23	1-0	.996	-0	98	124	1-123/D-25	-3.1
LAHOUD, JOE Joseph Michael B 4.14.1947 Danbury, CT BL/TL 6/202# d4.10																								
1968	Bos A	29	78	5	15	1	0	1	6	16-0	0	16	.192	.330	.244	71	-2	0-2	.926	-3	61	162	O-25(3-1-22)	-0.8
1969	Bos A	101	218	32	41	5	0	9	21	40-0	1	43	.188	.317	.335	78	-6	2-1	.979	-3	89	73	O-66(24-12-33)/1	-1.2
1970	Bos A	17	49	6	12	1	0	2	5	7-1	0	6	.245	.339	.388	93	0	0-0	.963	2	109	401	O-13(9-0-5)	0.1
1971	Bos A	107	256	39	55	9	3	14	32	40-3	4	45	.215	.330	.438	108	3	2-2	.993	3	109	91	O-69(7-0-63)	0.2
1972	Mil A	111	316	35	75	9	3	12	34	45-7	0	54	.237	.331	.399	119	8	3-4	.974	-1	109	30	O-97(38-0-63)	0.1
1973	Mil A	96	225	29	46	9	0	5	26	27-1	5	36	.204	.302	.311	75	-7	5-5	1.000	4	130	87	D-41,O-40(2-0-39)	-0.7

Year	Tm Lg	G	AB	R	H	2B	3B	HR	RBI	BB-IB	HP	SO	AVG	OBP	SLG	AOPS	ABR	SB-CS	FA	FR	Rng	Thr	G at Pos	BFW
1974	Cal A	127	325	46	88	16	3	13	44	47-3	3	57	.271	.367	.458	145	20	4-5	.976	1	99	105	*O-106(70-0-39),D-10	1.5
1975	Cal A	76	192	21	41	6	2	6	33	48-2	1	33	.214	.372	.359	116	7	2-1	1.000	-1	91	54	D-35,O-29(7-0-22)	0.3
1976	Cal A	42	96	8	17	4	0	0	4	18-2	2	16	.177	.319	.219	63	-3	0-0	.962	-0	114	0	O-26(21-1-6)/D-3	-0.5
	Tex A	38	89	10	20	3	1	1	5	10-1	0	16	.225	.303	.315	79	-2	1-0	1.000	-0	65	0	D-22/O-5(4-0-1)	-0.3
	Year	80	185	18	37	7	1	1	9	28-3	2	32	.200	.312	.265	72	-6	1-0	.964	-1	110	0	O-31(25-1-7),D-25	-0.8
1977	†KC A	34	65	8	17	5	0	2	8	11-1	0	16	.262	.364	.431	116	2	1-0	.952	0	83	247	O-15(13-0-2)/D-4	0.2
1978	KC A	13	16	0	2	0	0	0	0	0-0	0	1	.125	.125	.125	-29	-3	0-0	—	-0	0	0	/O(RF)D	-0.3
Total	11	791	1925	239	429	68	12	65	218	309-21	16	339	.223	.334	.372	103	17	20-20	.979	1	102	88	O-492(198-14-296),D-116/1	-1.4

LAIRD, GERALD Gerald Lee B 11.13.1979 Westminster, CA BR/TR 6-2/190# d4.30

Year	Tm Lg	G	AB	R	H	2B	3B	HR	RBI	BB-IB	HP	SO	AVG	OBP	SLG	AOPS	ABR	SB-CS	FA	FR	Rng	Thr	G at Pos	BFW
2003	Tex A	19	44	9	12	2	1	1	4	5-0	1	11	.273	.360	.432	99	0	0-0	.986	-2	178	98	C-16	-0.1

LAJESKIE, DICK Richard Edward B 1.8.1926 Passaic, NJ D 8.15.1976 Ramsey, NJ BR/TR 5-11/175# d9.10

Year	Tm Lg	G	AB	R	H	2B	3B	HR	RBI	BB-IB	HP	SO	AVG	OBP	SLG	AOPS	ABR	SB-CS	FA	FR	Rng	Thr	G at Pos	BFW
1946	NY N	6	10	3	2	0	0	0	0	3	1	2	.200	.429	.200	81	0	0	.964	3	179	42	/2-4	0.3

LAJOIE, NAP Napoleon "Larry" B 9.5.1874 Woonsocket, RI D 2.7.1959 Daytona Beach, FL BR/TR 6-1/195# d8.12 M5 HF1937 OF Total (4-LF 5-CF 18-RF)

Year	Tm Lg	G	AB	R	H	2B	3B	HR	RBI	BB-IB	HP	SO	AVG	OBP	SLG	AOPS	ABR	SB-CS	FA	FR	Rng	Thr	G at Pos	BFW
1896	Phi N	39	175	36	57	12	7	4	42	1	0	11	.326	.330	.543	129	5	7	.995	-3	53	107	1-39	0.2
1897	Phi N	127	545	107	197	40	23	9	127	15	12		.361	.392	**.569**	156	39	20	.984	-6	61	77	*1-108,O-19(2-0-18)/3-2	2.7
1898	Phi N	147	608	113	197	**43**	11	6	**127**	21	7		.324	.354	.461	139	27	25	.949	0	90	101	*2-146/1	3.2
1899	Phi N	77	312	70	118	19	9	6	70	12	10		.378	.419	.554	172	29	13	.954	14	103	145	2-67/O-5(CF)	4.1
1900	Phi N	102	451	95	152	33	12	7	92	10	8		.337	.362	.510	140	22	22	**.954**	22	**114**	**152**	*2-102/3	4.4
1901	Phi A	131	544	**145**	**232**	**48**	14	**14**	**125**	24	13		**.426**	**.463**	**.643**	**196**	**69**	27	**.960**	22	99	111	*2-119,S-12	**8.1**
1902	Phi A	1	4	0	1	0	0	0	1	0	0		.250	.250	.250	37	0	1	1.000	-0	98	0	/2	0.0
	Cle A	86	348	81	132	35	5	7	64	19	6		.379	.421	.569	180	38	19	.974	23	105	133	2-86	5.6
	Year	87	352	81	133	35	5	7	65	19	6		.378	.419	.565	178	37	20	.974	23	105	132	2-87	**5.6**
1903	Cle A	125	485	90	167	41	11	7	93	24	3		**.344**	.379	**.518**	**170**	**41**	21	.955	**39**	111	**146**	*2-122/13	**8.1**
1904	Cle A	140	553	92	**208**	**49**	15	5	**102**	27	8		**.376**	**.413**	**.546**	**204**	**64**	29	.962	2	90	155	2-95,S-44/1-2	**7.4**
1905	Cle A	65	249	29	82	12	2	2	41	17	2		.329	.377	.418	150	14	11	.991	8	105	165	2-59/1-5,M	2.4
1906	Cle A	152	602	88	**214**	**48**	9	0	91	30	6		.355	.392	.465	170	48	20	**.973**	21	**108**	**188**	*2-130,3-15/S-7,M	**7.6**
1907	Cle A	137	509	53	152	30	6	2	63	30	6		.299	.345	.393	134	19	24	**.969**	**45**	**120**	**211**	*2-128/1-9,M	**7.0**
1908	Cle A	**157**	581	77	168	32	6	2	74	47	9		.289	.352	.375	136	24	15	**.964**	**47**	**114**	**178**	*2-156/1M	**8.0**
1909	Cle A	128	469	56	152	33	7	1	47	35	6		.324	.378	.431	149	27	13	.959	**23**	110	**135**	*2-120/1-8,M	5.7
1910	Cle A	159	591	94	**227**	**51**	7	4	76	60	5		.384	.445	.514	198	**69**	26	.966	13	102	110	*2-149,1-10	**8.9**
1911	Cle A	90	315	36	115	20	1	2	60	26	4		.365	.420	.454	142	19	13	.990	-5	61	88	1-41,2-37	1.3
1912	Cle A	117	448	66	165	34	4	0	90	28	7		.368	.414	.462	146	27	18	.959	9	97	147	2-97,1-20	3.6
1913	Cle A	137	465	66	156	25	2	1	68	33	15	17	.335	.398	.404	131	20	17	**.970**	15	102	136	*2-126	3.8
1914	Cle A	121	419	37	108	14	3	0	50	32	2	15	.258	.313	.305	83	-9	14-15	.959	8	96	152	2-80,1-31	-0.3
1915	Phi A	129	490	40	137	24	5	1	61	11	4	16	.280	.301	.355	100	-4	10-6	.962	17	104	118	*2-110,S-10/1-5,3-2	1.7
1916	Phi A	113	426	33	105	14	4	2	35	14	1	26	.246	.272	.312	79	-14	15	.973	**27**	**107**	119	*2-105/1-5,O-2(LF)	1.6
Total	21	2480	9589	1504	3242	657	163	82	1599	516	134	85	.338	.380	.466	150	574	380-21	.963	339	104	144	*2-2035,1-286/S-73,O-26R,3-21	95.1

LAKE, EDDIE Edward Erving "Sparky" B 3.18.1916 Antioch, CA D 6.7.1995 Castro Valley, CA BR/TR 5-7/160# d9.26 ▲

Year	Tm Lg	G	AB	R	H	2B	3B	HR	RBI	BB-IB	HP	SO	AVG	OBP	SLG	AOPS	ABR	SB-CS	FA	FR	Rng	Thr	G at Pos	BFW
1939	StL N	2	4	0	1	0	0	0	0	1	0	0	.250	.400	.250	74	0	0	.857	-1	66	112	/S-2	-0.1
1940	StL N	32	66	12	14	3	0	2	7	12	1	17	.212	.342	.348	86	-1	1	.957	-4	87	47	2-17/S-6	-0.4
1941	StL N	45	76	9	8	2	0	0	0	15	0	22	.105	.253	.132	10	-9	3	.903	1	79	141	S-15,3-15/2-5	-0.7
1943	Bos A	75	216	26	43	10	0	3	16	47	1	35	.199	.345	.287	84	-2	3-6	.961	3	107	103	S-63	0.5
1944	Bos A	57	126	21	26	5	0	0	8	23	0	22	.206	.329	.246	66	-4	5-2	.927	-1	97	125	S-41/P-6,2-3,3	-0.3
1945	Bos A	133	473	81	132	27	1	11	51	106	1	37	.279	**.412**	.410	136	29	9-7	.948	24	**112**	**128**	*S-130/2	6.5
1946	Det A	**155**	587	105	149	24	1	8	31	103	4	69	.254	.369	.339	93	-1	15-9	.947	-21	88	99	*S-155	-1.3
1947	Det A	**158**	602	96	127	19	6	12	46	120	1	54	.211	.343	.322	83	-10	11-10	.943	-29	90	86	*S-158	-3.2
1948	Det A	64	198	51	52	6	0	2	18	57	0	20	.263	.427	.323	99	4	3-3	.972	-3	96	95	2-45,3-17	0.3
1949	Det A	94	240	38	47	9	1	1	15	61	0	33	.196	.359	.254	63	-10	2-8	.959	-7	98	103	S-38,2-19,3-18	-1.6
1950	Det A	20	7	3	0	0	0	0	1	1	0	3	.000	.125	.000	-64	-2	0-0	—	-0	0	0	/S3	-0.2
Total	11	835	2595	442	599	105	9	39	193	546	8	312	.231	.366	.323	91	-6	52-45	.947	-38	97	104	S-609/2-90,3-52,P-6	-0.5

LAKE, FRED Frederick Lovett B 10.16.1866 Nova Scotia, , CAN D 11.24.1931 Boston, MA BR/TR 5-10/170# d5.7 M3

Year	Tm Lg	G	AB	R	H	2B	3B	HR	RBI	BB-IB	HP	SO	AVG	OBP	SLG	AOPS	ABR	SB-CS	FA	FR	Rng	Thr	G at Pos	BFW
1891	Bos N	5	7	1	1	0	0	0	0	2	0	4	.143	.333	.143	36	0	0	1.000	1	*162*	*106*	/C-4,O(RF)	0.0
1894	Lou N	16	42	8	12	2	0	1	10	11	4	6	.286	.474	.405	122	3	2	.864	-3	80	226	/2-6,S-5,C-5	0.1
1897	†Bos N	19	62	2	15	4	0	0	5	1	0		.242	.254	.306	45	-5	2	.970	2	*150*	*93*	C-18	-0.2
1898	Pit N	5	13	1	1	0	0	0	1	2	0		.077	.200	.077	-20	-2	0	1.000	-0	64	165	/1-3	-0.2
1910	Bos N	3	1	0	0	0	0	0	0	1	0	0	.000	.500	.000	46	0	0	—	0			HM	0.0
Total	5	48	125	12	29	6	0	1	16	17	4	10	.232	.342	.304	68	-4	4	.930	-1	*137*	*90*	/C-27,2-6,S-5,1-3,O(RF)	-0.3

LAKE, STEVE Steven Michael B 3.14.1957 Inglewood, CA BR/TR 6-1/190# d4.9

Year	Tm Lg	G	AB	R	H	2B	3B	HR	RBI	BB-IB	HP	SO	AVG	OBP	SLG	AOPS	ABR	SB-CS	FA	FR	Rng	Thr	G at Pos	BFW
1983	Chi N	38	85	9	22	4	1	1	7	2-2	1	6	.259	.284	.365	75	-3	0-0	1.000	2	101	164	C-32	0.0
1984	†Chi N	25	54	4	12	4	0	2	7	0-0	1	7	.222	.232	.407	71	-2	0-0	.955	-1	151	164	C-24	-0.2
1985	Chi N	58	119	5	18	2	0	1	11	3-1	1	21	.151	.177	.193	4	-15	1-0	.995	3	179	152	C-55	-1.2
1986	Chi N	10	19	4	8	1	0	0	4	1-1	0	2	.421	.450	.474	144	1	0-0	1.000	-1	64	126	C-10	0.0
	StL N	26	49	4	12	1	0	2	10	2-0	0	5	.245	.275	.388	81	-2	0-0	.976	2	253	144	C-26	0.1
	Year	36	68	8	20	2	0	2	14	3-1	0	7	.294	.324	.412	100	0	0-0	.983	1	201	139	C-36	0.1
1987	†StL N	74	179	19	45	7	2	2	19	10-4	0	18	.251	.289	.346	67	-9	0-0	.996	-2	169	101	C-59	-0.8
1988	StL N	36	54	5	15	3	0	1	4	3-0	2	15	.278	.339	.389	107	1	0-0	.983	-1	117	126	C-19	0.1
1989	Phi N	58	155	9	39	5	1	2	14	12-4	0	20	.252	.304	.335	83	-4	0-0	.990	7	127	162	C-55	0.7
1990	Phi N	29	80	4	20	2	0	0	6	3-1	1	12	.250	.286	.275	55	-5	0-0	.993	5	294	130	C-28	0.1
1991	Phi N	58	158	12	36	4	1	1	11	2-1	0	26	.228	.237	.285	47	-12	0-0	.993	-2	116	81	C-58	-1.2
1992	Phi N	20	53	3	13	2	0	1	2	1-0	0	8	.245	.255	.340	69	-2	0-0	.975	-3	80	72	C-17	-0.5
1993	Chi N	44	120	11	27	6	0	5	13	4-3	0	19	.225	.250	.400	72	-5	0-0	.985	-0	260	100	C-41	-0.4
Total	11	476	1125	89	267	41	5	18	108	43-17	6	159	.237	.268	.331	64	-57	1-0	.989	9	166	124	C-424	-3.3

LAKEMAN, AL Albert Wesley "Moose" B 12.31.1918 Cincinnati, OH D 5.25.1976 Spartanburg, SC BR/TR 6-2/195# d4.19 C5

Year	Tm Lg	G	AB	R	H	2B	3B	HR	RBI	BB-IB	HP	SO	AVG	OBP	SLG	AOPS	ABR	SB-CS	FA	FR	Rng	Thr	G at Pos	BFW
1942	Cin N	20	38	0	6	1	0	0	2	3	1	10	.158	.238	.184	24	-4	0	.970	1	*99*	*120*	C-17	-0.2
1943	Cin N	22	55	5	14	2	1	0	6	3	0	11	.255	.293	.327	80	-2	0	1.000	0	*108*	*88*	C-21	-0.1
1944	Cin N	1	1	0	0	0	0	0	0	0	0	1	.000	.000	.000	-99	0	0	—	0			H	0.0
1945	Cin N	76	258	22	66	9	4	8	31	17	1	45	.256	.304	.415	101	-2	0	.963	-8	*84*	*73*	C-74	-0.5
1946	Cin N	23	30	0	4	0	0	0	4	2	0	7	.133	.188	.133	-9	-4	0	1.000	-0	*119*	*110*	/C-6	-0.5
1947	Cin N	2	2	0	0	0	0	0	0	0	0	1	.000	.000	.000	-99	-1	0	—	0			H	-0.1
	Phi N	55	182	11	29	3	0	6	19	5	1	39	.159	.186	.275	22	-22	0	.995	-3	82	77	1-29,C-23	-2.5
	Year	57	184	11	29	3	0	6	19	5	1	40	.158	.184	.272	20	-23	0	.995	-3	82	77	1-29,C-23	-2.6
1948	Phi N	32	68	2	11	2	0	1	4	5	0	22	.162	.219	.235	23	-8	0	1.000	-2	*61*	*55*	C-22/P	-0.8
1949	Bos N	3	6	0	1	0	0	0	0	1	0	0	.167	.286	.167	26	-1	0	1.000	0	180	130	/1-2	0.0
1954	Det A	5	6	0	0	0	0	0	0	0	0	1	.000	.000	.000	-99	-2	0-0	1.000	0	*0*	*0*	/C-4	-0.1
Total	9	239	646	40	131	17	5	15	66	36	3	137	.203	.248	.314	55	-46	0-0	.974	-11	*84*	*76*	C-167/1-31,P	-4.8

LAKER, TIM Timothy John B 11.27.1969 Encino, CA BR/TR 6-3/195# d8.18

Year	Tm Lg	G	AB	R	H	2B	3B	HR	RBI	BB-IB	HP	SO	AVG	OBP	SLG	AOPS	ABR	SB-CS	FA	FR	Rng	Thr	G at Pos	BFW
1992	Mon N	28	46	8	10	3	0	0	4	2-0	0	14	.217	.250	.283	51	-3	1-1	.991	2	83	37	C-28	-0.1
1993	Mon N	43	86	3	17	2	1	0	7	2-0	1	16	.198	.222	.244	24	-9	2-0	.987	-3	65	67	C-43	-1.1
1995	Mon N	64	141	17	33	8	1	3	20	14-4	1	38	.234	.306	.369	75	-5	0-1	.977	-5	81	100	C-61	-0.7
1997	Bal A	7	14	0	0	0	0	0	1	2-0	0	9	.000	.118	.000	-66	-4	0-0	.966	-2	51	67	/C-7	-0.5
1998	TB A	3	5	1	1	0	0	0	0	1-0	0	1	.200	.333	.200	43	0	0-1	1.000	-0	0	0	/C-2,D	-0.1
	Pit N	14	24	2	9	1	0	1	2	1-0	0	3	.375	.385	.542	143	1	0-0	1.000	-1	42	157	/1-4,C	0.1
1999	Pit N	6	9	0	3	0	0	0	0	0-0	0	2	.333	.333	.333	70	0	0-0	1.000	0	77	0	/C-2	0.0
2001	Cle A	16	33	5	6	0	0	1	5	6-0	0	8	.182	.308	.273	54	-2	0-0	.988	-1	47	69	C-14/P	-0.2
2003	Cle A	52	162	17	39	11	0	3	21	9-1	0	38	.241	.281	.364	71	-7	2-2	.983	-1	110	106	C-50/D-2	-0.5
Total	8	233	520	53	118	25	2	8	60	37-5	2	129	.227	.279	.329	61	-29	5-5	.983	-11	83	85	C-208/1-4,D-3,P	-3.1

Year	Tm Lg	G	AB	R	H	2B	3B	HR	RBI	BB-IB	HP	SO	AVG	OBP	SLG	AOPS	ABR	SB-CS	FA	FR	Rng	Thr	G at Pos	BFW
LALLY, DAN Daniel J. B 8.12.1867 Jersey City, NJ D 4.14.1936 Milwaukee, WI BR/TR 5-11.5/210# d8.19																								
1891	Pit N	41	143	24	32	6	2	1	17	16	4	20	.224	.319	.315	87	-2	0	.839	-4	39	0	O-41(0-4-37)	-0.5
1897	StL N	88	359	57	102	16	5	2	42	9	7		.284	.315	.373	83	-10	12	.896	-0	70	68	O-85(83-1-1)/1-3	-1.6
Total	2	129	502	81	134	22	7	3	59	25	11	20	.267	.316	.357	84	-12	12	.885	-4	62	49	O-126(83-5-38)/1-3	-2.1
LAMANNO, RAY Raymond Simond B 11.17.1919 Oakland, CA D 2.9.1994 Berkeley, CA BR/TR 6/185# d9.11 Mil 1943-45																								
1941	Cin N	1	0	0	0	0	0	0	0	0	1	0	—	1.000	—	197	0	0	1.000	-0	*0*	*0*	/C	0.0
1942	Cin N	111	371	40	98	12	2	12	43	31	2	54	.264	.324	.404	113	5	0	.978	-6	*97*	*105*	*C-104	0.5
1946	Cin N★	85	239	18	58	12	0	1	30	11	3	26	.243	.285	.305	70	-10	0	.974	3	*121*	*114*	C-61	-0.5
1947	Cin N	118	413	33	106	21	3	5	50	28	2	39	.257	.307	.358	77	-15	0	.986	6	*100*	*113*	*C-109	-0.3
1948	Cin N	127	385	31	93	12	0	0	27	48	2	32	.242	.329	.273	67	-16	2	.978	-13	*71*	*71*	*C-125	-2.3
Total	5	442	1408	122	355	57	5	18	150	118	10	151	.252	.314	.338	82	-36	2	.980	-11	*94*	*98*	C-400	-2.6
LAMAR, BILL William Harmong "Good Time Bill" B 3.21.1897 Rockville, MD D 5.24.1970 Rockport, MA BL/TR 6-1/185# d9.19 Mil 1918																								
1917	NY A	11	41	2	10	0	0	0	3	0	0	2	.244	.244	.244	48	-3	1	1.000	-1	98	55	O-11(10-1-0)	-0.5
1918	NY A	28	110	12	25	3	0	0	2	6	0	2	.227	.267	.255	56	-6	2	.884	-3	88	73	O-27(8-17-2)	-1.3
1919	NY A	11	16	1	3	1	0	0	0	2	0	1	.188	.278	.250	48	-1	1	1.000	-1	79	0	/O-3(0-1-2),1	-0.2
	Bos A	48	148	18	43	5	1	0	14	5	0	9	.291	.314	.338	88	-3	3	.922	-2	80	154	O-36(6-29-1)	-0.7
	Year	59	164	19	46	6	1	0	14	7	0	10	.280	.310	.329	83	-4	4	.926	-2	80	143	O-39(6-30-3)/1	-0.9
1920	†Bro N	24	44	5	12	4	0	0	4	0	0	1	.273	.273	.364	79	-1	0-0	1.000	-0	81	109	O-12(0-6-6)	-0.2
1921	Bro N	3	3	2	1	0	0	0	0	0	0	0	.333	.333	.333	74	0	0-0	—	-0	0	0	/O(CF)	0.0
1924	Phi A	87	367	68	121	22	5	7	48	18	0	21	.330	.361	.474	113	5	8-8	.971	2	96	136	O-87(LF)	-0.1
1925	Phi A	138	568	85	202	39	8	3	77	21	0	17	.356	.379	.468	107	5	2-6	.953	1	98	118	*O-131(LF)	-0.6
1926	Phi A	116	419	62	119	17	6	5	50	18	1	15	.284	.315	.389	78	-15	4-5	.954	-2	96	102	*O-107(LF)	-2.6
1927	Phi A	84	324	48	97	23	3	4	47	16	1	10	.299	.334	.426	91	-5	4-8	.952	-5	84	109	O-79(76-3-0)	-1.8
Total	9	550	2040	303	633	114	23	19	245	86	2	78	.310	.339	.417	94	-24	25-27	.952	-10	93	114	O-494(425-58-11)/1	-8.0
LAMB, DAVID David Christian B 6.6.1975 West Hills, CA BB/TR 6-2/165# d4.12																								
1999	TB A	55	124	18	28	5	1	1	13	10-0	0	18	.226	.284	.306	50	-10	0-1	.945	3	100	142	S-35,2-15/D-3	-0.4
2000	NY N	7	5	1	1	0	0	0	0	1-0	0	1	.200	.333	.200	41	0	0-0	1.000	-1	140	0	/3-3,2-2,S-2	-0.1
2002	†Min A	7	10	0	1	0	0	0	0	0-0	0	2	.100	.100	.100	-46	-2	0-0	1.000	-1	31	147	/S-4,2-2,3	-0.2
Total	3	69	139	19	30	5	1	1	13	11-0	0	21	.216	.273	.288	43	-12	0-1	.949	2	95	136	/S-41,2-19,3-4,D-3	-0.7
LAMB, LYMAN Laymon Raymond B 3.17.1895 Lincoln, NE D 10.5.1955 Fayetteville, AR BR/TR 5-7/150# d9.14																								
1920	StL A	9	24	4	9	2	0	0	4	0	0	7	.375	.375	.458	116	1	2-0	1.000	-1	97	0	/O-7(5-2-0)	0.0
1921	StL A	45	134	18	34	9	2	1	17	4	1	12	.254	.281	.373	62	-8	0-0	.942	-4	94	0	3-25/2-7,O-6(2-0-4)	-1.0
Total	2	54	158	22	43	11	2	1	21	4	1	19	.272	.294	.386	70	-7	2-0	.942	-4	94	0	/3-25,O-13(7-2-4),2-7	-1.0
LAMB, MIKE Michael Robert B 8.9.1975 West Covina, CA BL/TR 6-1/185# d4.23 OF Total (14-LF 5-RF)																								
2000	Tex A	138	493	65	137	25	2	6	47	34-6	4	60	.278	.328	.373	76	-18	0-2	.913	-11	89	91	*3-135/D-2	-2.6
2001	Tex A	76	284	42	87	18	0	4	35	14-1	5	27	.306	.348	.412	96	-1	2-1	.914	-5	95	102	3-74	-0.5
2002	Tex A	115	314	54	89	13	0	9	33	33-5	3	48	.283	.354	.411	98	0	0-0	.987	-0	115	104	1-52,D-21,O-16(12-0-5),3-14/C-3,2	-0.5
2003	Tex A	28	38	3	5	0	0	0	2	2-0	1	7	.132	.190	.132	-10	-6	1-0	1.000	-0	209	0	/1-5,O-2(LF),3D	-0.6
Total	4	357	1129	164	318	56	2	19	117	83-12	13	142	.282	.336	.385	84	-25	3-3	.914	-17	91	89	3-224/1-57,D-29,O-18L,C-3,2	-4.2
LAMERS, PETE Pierre B 12.1873 New York, NY D 10.24.1931 Brooklyn, NY TR 5-10/170# d9.10																								
1902	Chi N	2	9	2	2	0	0	0	0	0	0		.222	.222	.222	38	-1	0	.857	-0	*131*	*95*	/C-2	-0.1
1907	Cin N	1	2	0	0	0	0	0	0	0	0		.000	.000	.000	-96	0	0	1.000	-0	*39*	*309*	/C	-0.1
Total	2	3	11	2	2	0	0	0	0	0	0		.182	.182	.182	13	-1	0	.867	-0	*119*	*123*	/C-3	-0.2
LAMONT, GENE Gene William B 12.25.1946 Rockford, IL BL/TR 6-1/195# d9.2 M8 C10																								
1970	Det A	15	44	3	13	3	1	1	4	2-0	1	9	.295	.340	.477	122	1	0-0	1.000	-0	83	135	C-15	0.2
1971	Det A	7	15	2	1	0	0	0	1	0-0	0	5	.067	.067	.067	-60	-3	0-0	.952	1	215	76	/C-7	-0.2
1972	Det A	1	0	0	0	0	0	0	0	0-0	0	0	—	—	—	—	0	0-0	1.000	0	0	0	/C	0.0
1974	Det A	60	92	9	20	4	0	3	8	7-0	0	19	.217	.273	.359	78	-3	0-0	.974	1	95	112	C-60	-0.1
1975	Det A	4	8	1	3	1	0	0	1	0-0	0	2	.375	.375	.500	139	0	1-0	.944	1	38	110	/C-4	0.1
Total	5	87	159	15	37	8	1	4	14	9-0	1	35	.233	.278	.371	80	-5	1-0	.977	2	100	114	/C-87	0.0
LaMOTTE, BOBBY Robert Eugene B 2.15.1898 Savannah, GA D 11.2.1970 Chatham, GA BR/TR 5-11/160# d9.1																								
1920	Was A	4	3	0	0	0	0	0	0	1	0	1	.000	.250	.000	-31	-1	0-0	.750	0	139	0	/S3	0.0
1921	Was A	16	41	5	8	0	0	0	2	5	0	0	.195	.283	.195	25	-5	0-0	.940	1	118	19	S-12	-0.3
1922	Was A	68	214	22	54	10	2	1	23	15	2	21	.252	.307	.332	70	-10	6-1	.954	5	106	87	3-62/S-6	0.0
1925	StL A	97	356	61	97	20	4	2	51	34	1	22	.272	.338	.368	75	-14	5-5	.926	-0	96	114	S-93/3-3	-0.4
1926	StL A	36	79	11	16	4	3	0	9	11	0	6	.203	.300	.329	61	-5	0-0	.919	-2	97	110	S-30/3	-0.4
Total	5	221	693	99	175	34	9	3	85	66	3	50	.253	.320	.341	69	-35	11-6	.927	3	97	100	S-142/3-67	-1.1
LAMPARD, KEITH Christopher Keith B 12.20.1945 Warrington, England BL/TR 6-2/197# d9.15																								
1969	Hou N	9	12	2	3	0	0	1	2	0-0	0	3	.250	.250	.500	108	0	0-0	1.000	1	180	1408	/O(LF)	0.1
1970	Hou N	53	72	8	17	8	1	0	5	5-0	1	24	.236	.295	.375	82	-2	0-0	1.000	2	119	294	O-16(13-0-4)/1-2	-0.1
Total	2	62	84	10	20	8	1	1	7	5-0	1	27	.238	.289	.393	85	-2	0-0	1.000	3	125	403	/O-17(14-0-4),1-2	0.0
LAMPKIN, TOM Thomas Michael B 3.4.1964 Cincinnati, OH BL/TR 5-11/185# d9.10																								
1988	Cle A	4	4	0	0	0	0	0	0	1-0	0	0	.000	.200	.000	-38	-1	0-0	1.000	-1	0	0	/C-3	-0.1
1990	SD N	26	63	4	14	0	1	1	4	4-1	0	9	.222	.269	.302	56	-4	0-1	.971	-0	115	149	C-20	-0.4
1991	SD N	38	58	4	11	3	1	0	3	3-0	0	9	.190	.230	.276	40	-5	0-0	1.000	-1	76	82	C-11	-0.5
1992	SD N	9	17	3	4	0	0	0	0	6-0	1	1	.235	.458	.235	100	1	2-0	1.000	-1	116	93	/C-7,O(LF)	0.0
1993	Mil A	73	162	22	32	8	0	4	25	20-3	0	26	.198	.280	.321	64	-8	7-3	.978	-0	107	78	C-60/O-3(2-0-1),D	-0.5
1995	SF N	65	76	8	21	2	0	1	9	9-1	1	8	.276	.360	.342	89	-1	2-0	1.000	3	332	141	C-17/O-6(LF)	0.3
1996	SF N	66	177	26	41	8	0	6	29	20-2	5	22	.232	.324	.379	89	-3	1-5	.992	15	222	122	C-53	1.3
1997	StL N	108	229	28	56	8	1	7	22	28-5	4	30	.245	.335	.380	88	-4	2-1	.989	-6	85	99	C-86	-0.5
1998	StL N	93	216	25	50	12	1	6	28	24-5	7	32	.231	.328	.380	86	-4	3-2	.986	-4	111	82	C-62/O-5(4-0-1),1-2	-0.5
1999	Sea A	76	206	29	60	11	2	9	34	13-1	5	32	.291	.345	.495	115	4	1-3	.985	-4	107	160	C-56/O-2(LF),D-2	0.3
2000	Sea A	36	103	15	26	6	1	7	23	9-1	3	17	.252	.325	.534	118	2	0-0	.987	-2	81	134	C-28/D-3	0.2
2001	†Sea A	79	204	28	46	10	0	5	22	18-1	7	41	.225	.309	.348	78	-6	1-0	.995	3	153	58	C-71/O(RF)D	0.0
2002	SD N	104	281	32	61	10	1	10	37	38-7	3	59	.217	.313	.367	91	-6	4-2	.992	-7	121	84	C-94	-0.7
Total	13	777	1796	224	422	78	8	56	236	193-27	36	286	.235	.319	.381	87	-35	23-17	.989	-5	126	100	C-568/O-18(15-0-3),D-7,1-2	-1.1
LANCELLOTTI, RICK Richard Anthony B 7.5.1956 Providence, RI BL/TL 6-3/195# d8.27																								
1982	SD N	17	39	2	7	2	0	0	4	2-0	0	8	.179	.220	.231	28	-4	0-0	1.000	-1	48	156	/1-7,O-3(2-0-1)	-0.6
1986	SF N	15	18	2	4	0	0	2	6	0-0	0	7	.222	.222	.556	113	0	0-0	1.000	1	0	0	/1O(RF)	0.0
1990	Bos A	4	8	0	0	0	0	0	1	0-0	0	3	.000	.000	.000	-96	-2	0-0	1.000	0	146	186	/1-2	-0.2
Total	3	36	65	4	11	2	0	2	11	2-0	0	18	.169	.191	.292	35	-6	0-0	1.000	-0	68	158	/1-10,O-4(2-0-2)	-0.8
LAND, GROVER Grover Cleveland B 9.22.1884 Frankfort, KY D 7.22.1958 Phoenix, AZ BR/TR 6/190# d9.2 C7																								
1908	Cle A	8	16	1	3	0	0	0	2	0	0		.188	.188	.188	22	-1	0	.955	-0	*149*	*54*	/C-8	-0.2
1909	Cle A	1	4	0	2	0	0	0	1	0	0		.500	.500	.500	207	0	0	1.000	0	*142*	*85*	/C	0.1
1910	Cle A	34	111	4	23	0	0	0	7	2	1		.207	.228	.207	36	-9	1	.982	0	*91*	*95*	C-33	-0.6
1911	Cle A	35	107	5	15	1	2	0	10	3	0		.140	.164	.187	-2	-15	2	.961	-1	*87*	*119*	C-34/1	-1.4
1913	Cle A	17	47	3	11	1	0	0	9	4	2	1	.234	.321	.255	67	-2	1	.924	1	*122*	*96*	C-17	0.1
1914	Bro F	102	335	24	92	6	2	0	29	12	3	23	.275	.306	.304	67	-21	7	.970	-7	*86*	*107*	C-97	-2.1
1915	Bro F	96	290	25	75	13	2	0	22	6	2	20	.259	.279	.317	68	-18	3	.960	-10	*81*	*112*	C-81	-2.2
Total	7	293	910	62	221	21	6	0	80	27	8	44	.243	.271	.279	55	-66	14	.964	-17	*89*	*107*	C-271/1	-6.3
LAND, DOC William Gilbert (born Doc Burrell Land) B 5.14.1903 Binnsville, MS D 4.14.1986 Livingston, AL BL/TL 5-11/165# d10.6																								
1929	Was A	1	3	0	0	0	0	0	0	1	0	0	.000	.250	.000	-30	-1	0-0	1.000	-0	54	0	/O(CF)	-0.1
LANDENBERGER, KEN Kenneth Henry "Red" B 7.29.1928 Lyndhurst, OH D 7.28.1960 Cleveland, OH BL/TL 6-3/200# d9.20																								
1952	Chi A	2	5	0	1	0	0	0	0	0	0	2	.200	.200	.200	11	-1	0-0	1.000	0	135	0	/1	-0.1

Year	Tm Lg	G	AB	R	H	2B	3B	HR	RBI	BB-IB	HP	SO	AVG	OBP	SLG	AOPS	ABR	SB-CS	FA	FR	Rng	Thr	G at Pos	BFW
LANDESTOY, RAFAEL Rafael Silvialdo (Santana) B 5.28.1953 Bani, D.R. BB/TR (BR 1977) 5-10/165# d8.27 C3 OF Total (12-LF 4-CF 7-RF)																								
1977	†LA N	15	18	6	5	0	0	0	0	3-0	0	2	.278	.381	.278	80	0	2-0	1.000	-1	129	110	/2-8,S-3	-0.1
1978	Hou N	59	218	18	58	5	1	0	9	8-0	0	23	.266	.292	.298	70	-10	7-4	.980	-5	92	68	S-50/O-3(1-2-0),2-2	-1.0
1979	Hou N	129	282	33	76	9	6	0	30	29-5	1	24	.270	.338	.344	92	-3	13-4	.971	-6	95	112	*2-114/S-3	-0.3
1980	†Hou N	149	393	42	97	13	8	1	27	31-2	3	37	.247	.306	.328	84	-10	23-12	.991	-3	84	111	2-94,S-65/3-3	-0.4
1981	Hou N	35	74	6	11	1	1	0	4	16-4	0	9	.149	.300	.189	43	-5	4-1	.966	-6	82	82	2-31	-0.9
	Cin N	12	11	2	2	0	0	0	1	1-0	0	0	.182	.250	.182	24	-1	1-0	1.000	-1	29	0	/2-3	-0.2
	Year	47	85	8	13	1	1	0	5	17-4	0	9	.153	.294	.188	40	-6	5-1	.967	-6	80	79	2-34	-1.1
1982	Cin N	73	111	11	21	3	0	1	9	8-1	1	14	.189	.250	.243	38	-9	2-0	1.000	5	120	326	3-21,2-16/O-3(LF),S-2	-0.4
1983	Cin N	7	5	0	0	0	0	0	0	0-0	0	0	.000	.000	.000	-97	-1	0-0	1.000	-1	0	272	/1-2,3O(LF)	-0.2
	†LA N	64	64	6	11	1	1	1	1	3-0	0	8	.172	.209	.266	31	-6	0-2	1.000	3	104	142	2-14,3-10,O-10(6-1-3)/S	-0.4
	Year	71	69	6	11	1	1	1	1	3-0	0	8	.159	.194	.246	21	-8	0-2	1.000	2	104	142	2-14,3-11,O-11(7-1-3)/1-2,S	-0.6
1984	LA N	53	54	10	10	0	0	1	2	1-0	0	6	.185	.200	.241	24	-6	2-1	.886	-2	85	99	2-14,3-11/O-5(1-1-4)	-0.8
Total	8	596	1230	134	291	32	17	4	83	100-12	5	123	.237	.296	.300	70	-51	54-24	.976	-16	90	107	2-296,S-124/3-46,O-22L,1-2	-4.7
LANDIS, JIM James Henry B 3.9.1934 Fresno, CA BR/TR 6-1/180# d4.16																								
1957	Chi A	96	274	38	58	11	3	2	16	45-2	3	61	.212	.329	.296	72	-9	14-4	.985	5	109	137	O-90(11-38-44)	-0.6
1958	Chi A	142	523	72	145	23	7	15	64	52-1	8	80	.277	.351	.434	117	12	19-7	.986	-3	96	113	*O-142(CF)	0.4
1959	†Chi A	149	515	78	140	26	7	5	60	78-5	8	68	.272	.370	.379	109	10	20-9	.993	7	109	96	*O-148(CF)	1.1
1960	Chi A	148	494	89	125	25	6	10	49	80-4	9	84	.253	.365	.389	106	7	23-6	.985	4	103	146	*O-147(CF)	0.7
1961	Chi A	140	534	87	151	18	8	22	85	65-0	4	71	.283	.362	.470	123	17	19-5	.988	8	112	119	*O-139(CF)	2.3
1962	Chi A★	149	534	82	122	21	6	15	61	80-3	9	105	.228	.337	.375	92	-4	19-7	.995	4	115	31	*O-144(CF)	-0.3
1963	Chi A	133	396	56	89	6	6	13	45	47-4	6	75	.225	.316	.369	93	-4	8-6	**.993**	1	109	91	*O-124(CF)	-0.7
1964	Chi A	106	298	30	62	8	4	1	18	36-1	6	64	.208	.305	.272	64	-14	5-0	.995	-3	91	114	*O-101(CF)	-1.9
1965	KC A	118	364	46	87	15	1	3	36	57-1	3	84	.239	.346	.310	90	-2	8-3	.985	1	115	0	*O-108(0-108-1)	-0.4
1966	Cle A	85	158	23	35	5	1	3	14	20-1	2	25	.222	.317	.323	84	-3	2-1	1.000	-1	108	0	O-61(18-37-17)	-0.6
1967	Det A	25	48	4	10	0	0	2	4	7-0	0	12	.208	.304	.333	87	-1	0-2	.952	1	105	316	O-12(6-1-6)	-0.1
	Bos A	5	7	1	1	0	0	1	1	1-0	0	3	.143	.250	.571	126	0	0-0	1.000	0	132	0	/O-5(RF)	0.0
	Year	30	55	5	11	0	0	3	5	8-0	0	15	.200	.297	.364	92	-1	0-2	.960	1	109	266	O-17(6-1-11)	-0.1
	Hou N	50	143	19	36	11	1	1	14	20-0	1	35	.252	.341	.364	107	2	2-1	1.000	2	84	272	O-44(28-3-14)	0.2
Total	11	1346	4288	625	1061	169	50	93	467	588-22	59	767	.247	.344	.375	100	11	139-51	.989	25	106	99	*O-1265(63-1132-87)	0.1
LANDREAUX, KEN Kenneth Francis B 12.22.1954 Los Angeles, CA BL/TR 5-10/165# d9.11																								
1977	Cal A	23	76	6	19	5	1	0	5	5-1	0	15	.250	.296	.342	76	-3	1-1	.970	4	114	358	O-22(CF)	0.1
1978	Cal A	93	260	37	58	7	5	5	23	20-4	2	20	.223	.284	.346	79	-8	7-3	.986	1	97	137	O-83(32-23-35)/D	-1.0
1979	Min A	151	564	81	172	27	5	15	83	37-4	4	57	.305	.347	.450	110	7	10-3	.981	-15	81	99	*O-147(49-98-0)	-0.9
1980	Min A★	129	484	56	136	23	11	7	62	39-4	2	42	.281	.334	.417	98	-2	8-6	.976	-14	79	93	*O-120(54-68-0)/D-6	-1.9
1981	†LA N	99	390	48	98	16	4	7	41	25-3	1	42	.251	.297	.367	91	-6	18-4	**1.000**	-9	86	62	O-95(CF)	-1.5
1982	LA N	129	461	71	131	23	7	7	50	39-2	4	54	.284	.341	.410	113	8	31-10	.986	-5	100	44	*O-117(1-116-0)	0.6
1983	†LA N	141	481	63	135	25	3	17	66	34-5	2	52	.281	.328	.451	115	8	30-11	.990	-3	98	68	*O-137(7-131-2)	0.7
1984	LA N	134	438	39	110	11	5	11	47	29-3	1	35	.251	.295	.374	89	-8	10-9	.986	-15	79	46	*O-129(9-105-18)	-2.8
1985	†LA N	147	482	70	129	26	2	12	50	33-2	1	37	.268	.311	.405	103	1	15-5	.975	-8	94	55	*O-140(11-126-4)	-0.7
1986	LA N	103	283	34	74	13	2	4	29	22-3	1	39	.261	.313	.364	94	-3	10-5	.955	-2	98	128	O-85(20-69-1)	-0.5
1987	LA N	115	182	17	37	4	0	6	23	16-2	1	28	.203	.269	.324	58	-12	5-3	.951	1	96	190	O-63(15-6-45)	-1.2
Total	11	1264	4101	522	1099	180	45	91	479	299-33	19	421	.268	.317	.400	99	-18	145-60	.981	-63	90	87	*O-1138(198-859-105)/D-7	-9.1
LANDRITH, HOBIE Hobert Neal B 3.16.1930 Decatur, IL BL/TR 5-10/170# d7.30 C1																								
1950	Cin N	4	14	1	3	0	0	0	1	2	0	1	.214	.313	.214	41	-1	0	1.000	-1	*107*	*118*	/C-4	-0.2
1951	Cin N	4	13	3	5	1	0	0	0	1	0	1	.385	.429	.462	137	1	0-0	1.000	1	*82*	*99*	/C-4	0.2
1952	Cin N	15	50	1	13	4	0	0	4	0	0	4	.260	.260	.340	65	-2	0-1	1.000	0	*101*	*101*	C-14	-0.2
1953	Cin N	52	154	15	37	3	1	3	16	12	1	8	.240	.299	.331	64	-9	2-0	.985	0	*134*	*53*	C-47	-0.6
1954	Cin N	48	81	12	16	0	0	5	14	18	0	9	.198	.340	.383	86	-1	1-0	.986	2	*181*	*116*	C-42	0.2
1955	Cin N	43	87	9	22	3	0	4	7	10-1	0	14	.253	.330	.425	93	-1	0-1	1.000	3	*117*	*131*	C-27	0.2
1956	Chi N	111	312	22	69	10	3	4	32	39-15	1	38	.221	.307	.311	69	-13	0-2	.975	-2	*75*	***136***	C-99	-1.2
1957	StL N	75	214	18	52	6	0	3	26	25-1	0	27	.243	.318	.313	70	-8	1-2	.987	3	*110*	*95*	C-67	-0.3
1958	StL N	70	144	9	31	4	0	3	13	26-4	0	21	.215	.335	.306	68	-6	0-1	.992	-0	*67*	*88*	C-45	-0.4
1959	SF N	109	283	30	71	14	0	3	29	43-7	0	23	.251	.345	.332	85	-4	0-4	.992	6	*101*	*95*	*C-109	0.5
1960	SF N	71	190	18	46	10	0	1	20	23-2	0	11	.242	.321	.311	79	-5	1-1	.966	-5	*76*	*66*	C-70	-0.7
1961	SF N	43	71	11	17	4	0	2	10	12-3	0	7	.239	.337	.380	97	0	0-0	.985	1	*85*	*96*	C-30	0.2
1962	NY N	23	45	6	13	3	0	1	7	8-0	0	3	.289	.389	.422	118	2	0-0	.968	-2	*89*	*56*	C-21	0.0
	Bal A	60	167	18	37	4	1	4	17	19-1	1	9	.222	.302	.329	75	-6	0-0	.982	1	*73*	*182*	C-60	-0.2
1963	Bal A	2	1	0	0	0	0	0	0	0-0	0	0	.000	.000	.000	-99	0	0-0	1.000	0	0	0	/C	0.0
	Was A	42	103	6	18	3	0	1	7	15-1	0	12	.175	.280	.233	46	-7	0-0	.978	0	70	185	C-37	-0.6
	Year	44	104	6	18	3	0	1	7	15-1	0	12	.173	.277	.231	44	-7	0-0	.978	0	70	184	C-38	-0.6
Total	14	772	1929	179	450	69	5	34	203	253-35	3	188	.233	.320	.327	76	-60	5-12	.983	7	*95*	*109*	C-677	-3.1
LANDRUM, CED Cedric Bernard B 9.3.1963 Butler, AL BL/TR 5-7/167# d5.28																								
1991	Chi N	56	86	28	20	2	1	0	6	10-0	0	18	.233	.313	.279	65	-4	27-5	.968	-1	104	0	O-44(25-18-8)	-0.1
1993	NY N	22	19	2	5	1	0	0	1	0-0	0	5	.263	.263	.316	55	-1	0-0	—	-0	0	0	/O-3(LF)	-0.1
Total	2	78	105	30	25	3	1	0	7	10-0	0	23	.238	.304	.286	63	-5	27-5	.968	-1	102	0	/O-47(28-18-8)	-0.2
LANDRUM, DON Donald Leroy B 2.16.1936 Santa Rosa, CA D 1.9.2003 Pittsburg, CA BL/TR 6/180# d9.28																								
1957	Phi N	2	7	1	1	1	0	0	0	2-0	0	1	.143	.333	.286	71	0	0-0	1.000	1	162	0	/O-2(CF)	0.0
1960	StL N	13	49	7	12	0	1	2	3	4-0	1	6	.245	.315	.408	88	-1	3-0	1.000	0	107	93	O-13(2-13-3)	-0.1
1961	StL N	28	66	5	11	2	0	1	3	5-0	0	14	.167	.225	.242	22	-7	1-0	1.000	1	101	206	O-25(6-20-4)/2	-0.7
1962	StL N	32	35	11	11	0	0	0	3	4-1	0	2	.314	.375	.314	82	-1	2-0	1.000	-0	101	0	O-26(16-4-7)	-0.1
	Chi N	83	238	29	67	5	2	1	15	30-0	3	31	.282	.369	.332	87	-3	9-2	.969	-2	97	72	O-59(1-41-18)	-0.6
	Year	115	273	40	78	5	2	1	18	34-1	3	33	.286	.370	.330	85	-4	11-2	.973	-2	98	61	O-85(17-45-25)	-0.7
1963	Chi N	84	227	27	55	4	1	1	10	13-1	4	42	.242	.294	.282	64	-10	6-3	.972	-5	83	86	O-57(0-55-3)	-1.9
1964	Chi N	11	11	2	0	0	0	0	0	1-0	0	2	.000	.083	.000	-71	-3	0-0	1.000	1	48	1645	/O(CF)	-0.2
1965	Chi N	131	425	60	96	20	4	6	34	36-3	10	84	.226	.300	.334	77	-12	14-8	.988	-4	99	47	*O-115(3-111-1)	-2.0
1966	SF N	72	102	9	19	4	0	1	7	9-0	1	18	.186	.259	.255	42	-8	1-1	.968	4	106	320	O-54(38-14-3)	-0.6
Total	8	456	1160	151	272	36	8	12	75	104-5	19	200	.234	.307	.310	69	-45	36-14	.982	-4	97	100	O-352(66-261-39)/2	-6.2
LANDRUM, JESSE Jesse Glenn B 7.31.1912 Crockett, TX D 6.27.1983 Beaumont, TX BR/TR 5-11.5/175# d4.26																								
1938	Chi A	4	6	0	0	0	0	0	1	0	0	2	.000	.000	.000	-98	-2	0-0	1.000	-0	109	156	/2-3	-0.2
LANDRUM, TITO Terry Lee B 10.25.1954 Joplin, MO BR/TR 5-11/175# d7.23																								
1980	StL N	35	77	6	19	2	2	0	7	6-0	1	17	.247	.306	.325	75	-3	3-2	.976	-1	93	65	O-29(17-8-6)	-0.5
1981	StL N	81	119	13	31	5	4	0	10	6-0	1	14	.261	.297	.370	87	-3	4-2	1.000	2	94	190	O-67(43-6-24)	-0.2
1982	StL N	79	72	12	20	3	0	2	14	8-0	1	18	.278	.358	.403	111	1	0-1	1.000	2	111	124	O-56(24-6-29)	0.2
1983	StL N	6	5	0	1	0	1	0	0	1-0	0	2	.200	.333	.600	154	0	1-0	1.000	-0	72	0	/O-5(4-0-1)	0.0
	†Bal A	26	42	8	13	2	0	1	4	1-0	0	11	.310	.318	.429	108	0	0-2	1.000	2	140	0	O-26(11-4-15)	0.1
1984	StL N	105	173	21	47	9	1	3	26	10-1	0	27	.272	.306	.387	98	-1	3-4	.979	-3	90	30	O-88(55-20-25)	-0.7
1985	†StL N	85	161	21	45	8	2	4	21	19-1	0	30	.280	.356	.429	119	4	1-4	1.000	1	108	65	O-73(10-0-67)	0.2
1986	StL N	96	205	24	43	7	1	2	17	20-2	1	41	.210	.279	.283	57	-12	3-1	.993	7	123	135	O-78(9-4-70)	-0.8
1987	StL N	30	50	5	10	1	0	0	6	7-2	0	14	.200	.298	.220	39	-4	1-1	1.000	3	148	114	O-23(2-7-17)/1	-0.2
	LA N	51	67	8	16	3	0	1	4	3-0	1	16	.239	.282	.328	63	-4	1-1	.971	1	124	107	O-31(19-0-14)	-0.3
	Year	81	117	13	26	4	0	1	10	10-2	1	30	.222	.289	.282	53	-8	2-2	.987	4	136	110	O-54(21-7-31)/1	-0.5
1988	Bal A	13	24	2	3	0	1	0	2	4-0	0	6	.125	.250	.208	31	-2	0-0	1.000	-1	90	0	O-12(5-0-8)/D	-0.3
Total	9	607	995	120	248	40	12	13	111	85-6	5	196	.249	.309	.353	84	-24	17-18	.992	13	109	93	O-488(199-55-276)/D1	-2.5
LANE, CHAPPY George M. B Pittsburgh, PA BR ?/165# d5.16																								
1882	Pit AA	57	214	26	38	8	2	3		5			.178	.196	.276	60	-8		.974	5	111	108	1-43,O-13(0-12-1)/C-2	-0.7
1884	Tol AA	57	215	26	49	9	5	1		2	2		.228	.242	.330	82	-5		.948	2	125	79	1-46/O-9(5-0-4),3-2,C	-0.7
Total	2	114	429	52	87	17	7	4		7	2		.203	.219	.303	72	-13		.961	7	118	93	/1-89,O-22(5-12-5),C-3,3-2	-1.4

Year	Tm Lg	G	AB	R	H	2B	3B	HR	RBI	BB-IB	HP	SO	AVG	OBP	SLG	AOPS	ABR	SB-CS	FA	FR	Rng	Thr	G at Pos	BFW
LANE, HUNTER James Hunter "Dodo" B 7.20.1900 Pulaski, TN D 9.12.1994 Memphis, TN BR/TR 5-11/165# d5.13																								
1924	Bos N	7	15	0	1	0	0	0	0	1	0	1	.067	.125	.067	-49	-3	0-0	.909	-1	62	0	/3-4,2	-0.4
LANE, JASON Jason Dean B 12.22.1976 Santa Rosa, CA BR/TL 6-2/220# d5.10																								
2002	Hou N	44	69	12	20	3	1	4	10	10-1	0	12	.290	.375	.536	135	3	1-1	.980	3	118	226	O-38(11-1-27)	0.5
2003	Hou N	18	27	5	8	2	0	4	10	0-0	0	2	.296	.296	.815	168	2	0-0	1.000	-1	68	0	O-10(3-6-2)	0.1
Total	2	62	96	17	28	5	1	8	20	10-1	0	14	.292	.355	.615	145	5	1-1	.983	2	109	183	/O-48(14-7-29)	0.6
LANE, MARVIN Marvin B 1.18.1950 Sandersville, GA BR/TR 5-11/180# d9.4																								
1971	Det A	8	14	0	2	0	0	0	1	1-0	0	3	.143	.200	.143	-1	-2	0-0	1.000	-0	90	0	/O-6(3-0-3)	-0.3
1972	Det A	8	6	2	0	0	0	0	0	0-0	0	2	.000	.000	.000	-97	-1	0-0	1.000	-0	96	0	/O-3(1-1-1)	-0.2
1973	Det A	6	8	2	2	0	0	1	2	2-0	0	2	.250	.400	.625	173	1	0-0	1.000	0	147	0	/O-4(3-0-3)	0.1
1974	Det A	50	103	16	24	4	1	2	9	19-1	0	24	.233	.352	.350	99	1	2-0	.986	1	105	127	O-46(40-2-6)/D	0.0
1976	Det A	18	48	3	9	1	0	0	5	6-0	0	11	.188	.273	.208	42	-3	0-0	.960	-1	84	116	O-15(10-5-0)	-0.5
Total	5	90	179	23	37	5	1	3	17	28-1	0	42	.207	.313	.296	74	-4	2-0	.983	0	101	106	/O-74(57-8-13),D	-0.9
LANE, DICK Richard Harrison B 6.28.1927 Highland Park, MI BR/TR 5-11/178# d6.20																								
1949	Chi A	12	42	4	5	0	0	0	4	5	0	3	.119	.213	.119	-11	-7	0-1	1.000	1	103	245	O-11(LF)	-0.7
LANG, DON Donald Charles B 3.15.1915 Selma, CA BR/TR 6/175# d7.4																								
1938	Cin N	21	50	5	13	3	1	1	11	2	0	7	.260	.288	.420	95	-1	0	.976	1	106	155	3-15/2S	0.1
1948	StL N	117	323	30	87	14	1	4	31	47	1	38	.269	.364	.356	90	-3	2	.964	4	106	97	3-95/2-2	0.1
Total	2	138	373	35	100	17	2	5	42	49	1	45	.268	.355	.365	91	-4	2	.966	5	106	104	3-110/2-3,S	0.2
LANGE, BILL William Alexander "Little Eva" B 6.6.1871 San Francisco, CA D 7.23.1950 San Francisco, CA BR/TR 6-1.5/190# d4.27 OF Total (15-LF 702-CF 2-RF)																								
1893	Chi N	117	469	92	132	8	7	8	88	52	4	20	.281	.358	.380	98	-2	47	.888	-5	93	70	2-57,O-40(14-27-0)/3-8,S-7,C-7	-0.5
1894	Chi N	113	449	86	146	17	9	6	91	56	2	18	.325	.402	.443	98	-2	66	.912	4	136	207	*O-111(1-108-2)/S-2,3	-0.3
1895	Chi N	123	478	120	186	27	16	10	98	55	4	24	.389	.456	.575	155	39	67	.924	7	152	140	*O-123(CF)	3.1
1896	Chi N	122	469	114	153	21	16	4	92	65	5	24	.326	.414	.465	126	19	84	.932	6	103	66	*O-121(CF)/C	1.5
1897	Chi N	118	479	119	163	24	14	5	83	48	5		.340	.406	.480	129	19	**73**	.946	1	102	116	*O-118(CF)	1.1
1898	Chi N	113	442	79	141	16	11	5	69	36	5		.319	.377	.439	134	18	22	.970	6	120	113	*O-111(CF)/1-2	1.6
1899	Chi N	107	416	81	135	21	7	1	58	38	1		.325	.382	.416	122	13	41	.976	7	146	281	O-94(CF),1-14	1.3
Total	7	813	3202	691	1056	134	80	39	579	350	26	86	.330	.400	.458	123	104	400	.942	26	125	144	O-718C/2-57,1-16,S-9,3-9,C-8	7.8
LANGERHANS, RYAN Ryan David B 2.20.1980 San Antonio, TX BL/TL 6-3/195# d4.28																								
2002	Atl N	1	1	0	0	0	0	0	0	0-0	0	0	.000	.000	.000	-99	0	0-0	—	-0	0	0	/O(LF)	0.0
2003	Atl N	16	15	2	4	0	0	0	0	0-0	0	6	.267	.267	.267	40	-1	0-0	1.000	1	109	305	O-14(3-4-9)	-0.1
Total	2	17	16	2	4	0	0	0	0	0-0	0	6	.250	.250	.250	31	-1	0-0	1.000	1	104	292	/O-15(4-4-9)	-0.1
LANGFORD, SAM Elton B 5.21.1901 Briggs, TX D 7.31.1993 Plainview, TX BL/TR 6/180# d4.13																								
1926	Bos A	1	1	1	0	0	0	0	0	0	0	0	.000	.000	.000	-99	0	0-0	—	0			H	0.0
1927	Cle A	20	67	10	18	5	0	1	7	5	3	7	.269	.347	.388	90	-1	0-1	1.000	-1	91	58	O-20(1-18-1)	-0.3
1928	Cle A	110	427	50	118	17	8	4	50	21	1	35	.276	.312	.382	81	-14	3-8	.972	-8	93	46	*O-107(32-76-0)	-2.9
Total	3	131	495	61	136	22	8	5	57	26	4	42	.275	.316	.382	81	-15	3-9	.976	-10	93	48	O-127(33-94-1)	-3.2
LANGSFORD, BOB Robert William (born Robert Hugo Lankswert) B 8.5.1865 Louisville, KY D 1.10.1907 Louisville, KY BL/TL 5-7/168# d6.18																								
1899	Lou N	1	4	0	0	0	0	0	0	0	0		.000	.000	.000	-99	-1	0	1.000	-0	63	0	/S	-0.1
LANIER, HAL Harold Clifton B 7.4.1942 Denton, NC BR/TR (BB 1967 (part), 68-70) 6-2/180# d6.18 M3 C7 f-Max																								
1964	SF N	98	383	40	105	16	3	2	28	5-0	0	44	.274	.283	.347	75	-14	2-1	.979	6	104	85	2-98/S-3	0.1
1965	SF N	159	522	41	118	15	9	0	39	21-4	0	67	.226	.256	.289	52	-35	2-1	.976	-7	97	86	*2-158/S	-3.0
1966	SF N	149	459	37	106	14	2	3	37	16-7	0	49	.231	.256	.290	50	-31	1-0	.991	16	107	114	*2-112,S-41	-0.4
1967	SF N	151	525	37	112	16	3	0	42	16-2	2	61	.213	.239	.255	42	-41	2-2	.974	21	**111**	109	*S-137,2-34	-0.7
1968	SF N	151	486	37	100	14	1	0	27	12-0	0	57	.206	.222	.239	39	-37	2-2	**.979**	12	102	93	*S-150	-1.4
1969	SF N	150	495	37	113	9	1	0	35	25-5	0	68	.228	.263	.251	46	-37	0-1	.969	24	**116**	118	*S-150	0.4
1970	SF N	134	438	33	101	13	1	2	41	21-4	0	41	.231	.265	.279	47	-34	1-2	.967	8	101	103	*S-130/2-4,1-2	-1.2
1971	†SF N	109	206	21	48	8	0	1	13	15-3	0	26	.233	.283	.286	63	-10	0-0	.957	-5	83	76	3-83,2-13/S-8,1-3	-1.6
1972	NY A	60	103	5	22	3	0	0	6	2-0	1	13	.214	.234	.243	44	-7	1-2	.973	1	107	148	3-47/S-9,2-3	-0.7
1973	NY A	35	86	9	18	3	0	0	5	3-0	1	10	.209	.244	.244	39	-7	0-0	.960	-2	99	107	S-26/2-8,3	-0.6
Total	10	1196	3703	297	843	111	20	8	273	136-25	4	436	.228	.255	.275	50	-253	11-11	.971	74	107	105	S-655,2-430,3-131/1-5	-9.1
LANIER, RIMP Lorenzo B 10.19.1948 Tuskegee, AL BL/TR 5-8/150# d9.11																								
1971	Pit N	6	4	0	0	0	0	0	0	0-0	1	1	.000	.200	.000	-39	-1	0-0	—	0			H	-0.1
LANKFORD, RAY Raymond Lewis B 6.5.1967 Los Angeles, CA BL/TL 5-11/198# d8.21																								
1990	StL N	39	126	12	36	10	1	3	12	13-0	0	27	.286	.353	.452	119	4	8-2	.989	1	113	57	O-35(CF)	0.5
1991	StL N	151	566	83	142	23	**15**	9	69	41-1	1	114	.251	.301	.392	93	-8	44-20	.984	0	107	89	*O-149(CF)	-0.6
1992	StL N	153	598	87	175	40	6	20	86	72-6	5	147	.293	.371	.480	144	36	42-24	.996	-4	102	53	*O-153(CF)	3.4
1993	StL N	127	407	64	97	17	3	7	45	81-7	3	111	.238	.366	.346	95	1	14-14	.978	-4	97	93	*O-121(CF)	-0.4
1994	StL N	109	416	89	111	25	5	19	57	58-3	4	113	.267	.359	.488	121	13	11-10	.978	-2	99	87	*O-104(CF)	1.1
1995	StL N	132	483	81	134	35	2	25	82	63-6	2	110	.277	.360	.513	128	20	24-8	.990	-2	98	100	*O-129(CF)	2.2
1996	†StL N	149	545	100	150	36	8	21	86	79-10	3	133	.275	.366	.486	125	21	35-7	**.997**	4	105	122	*O-144(CF)	3.1
1997	StL N★	133	465	94	137	36	3	31	98	95-10	0	125	.295	.411	.585	160	44	21-11	.971	-6	99	64	*O-131(CF)	3.9
1998	StL N	154	533	94	156	37	1	31	105	86-5	3	151	.293	.391	.540	144	37	26-5	.986	-5	98	77	*O-145(CF)/D	3.6
1999	StL N	122	422	77	129	32	1	15	63	49-3	3	110	.306	.380	.493	119	13	14-4	.987	3	106	92	*O-106(105-2-0)/D	1.3
2000	†StL N	128	392	73	99	16	3	26	65	70-1	4	148	.253	.367	.508	119	11	5-6	.973	-4	90	63	*O-117(116-2-0)/D	0.2
2001	StL N	91	264	38	62	18	3	15	39	44-8	2	105	.235	.345	.496	116	7	4-2	.966	-1	96	98	O-85(LF)	0.3
	SD N	40	125	20	36	10	1	4	19	18-1	2	40	.288	.386	.480	134	7	6-0	.985	-2	92	49	O-38(21-16-2)	0.6
	Year	131	389	58	98	28	4	19	58	62-9	4	145	.252	.358	.491	121	13	10-2	.971	-3	95	83	*O-123(106-16-2)	0.9
2002	SD N	81	205	20	46	7	1	6	26	30-3	2	61	.224	.326	.356	92	-3	2-2	.953	2	105	131	O-59(59-3-0)/D	-0.4
Total	13	1609	5547	932	1510	342	53	232	852	799-64	34	1495	.272	.364	.478	124	203	256-115	.983	-19	100	85	*O-1516(386-1134-2)/D-4	18.8
LANNING, RED Lester Alfred B 5.13.1895 Harvard, IL D 6.13.1962 Bristol, CT BL/TL 5-9/165# d6.20 ▲																								
1916	Phi A	19	33	5	6	2	0	0	1	10	0	9	.182	.372	.242	89	0	0	.909	-1	82	0	/O-9(7-0-6),P-6	-0.1
LANSFORD, CARNEY Carney Ray B 2.7.1957 San Jose, CA BR/TR 6-2/195# d4.8 C2 b-Jody																								
1978	Cal A	121	453	63	133	23	2	8	52	31-2	4	67	.294	.339	.406	115	8	20-9	.942	-21	75	80	*3-117/S-2,D	-1.4
1979	†Cal A	157	654	114	188	30	5	19	79	39-2	3	115	.287	.329	.436	108	6	20-8	**.983**	-15	82	93	*3-157	-1.0
1980	Cal A	151	602	87	157	27	3	15	80	50-2	0	93	.261	.312	.390	95	-5	14-5	.955	-20	79	88	*3-150	-2.6
1981	Bos A	102	399	61	134	23	3	4	52	34-3	2	28	**.336**	.389	.439	131	17	15-10	.951	-2	97	104	3-86,D-16	1.3
1982	Bos A	128	482	65	145	28	4	11	63	46-2	2	48	.301	.359	.444	114	10	9-4	.968	-15	86	77	*3-114,D-13	-0.6
1983	Oak A	80	299	43	92	16	2	10	45	22-4	3	33	.308	.357	.475	136	14	3-8	.957	-6	94	105	3-78/S	0.5
1984	Oak A	151	597	70	179	31	5	14	74	40-6	3	62	.300	.342	.439	124	18	9-3	.957	-2	97	90	*3-151	1.5
1985	Oak A	98	401	51	111	18	2	13	46	18-1	4	27	.277	.311	.429	109	3	2-3	.976	-27	64	59	3-97	-2.6
1986	Oak A	151	591	80	168	16	4	19	72	39-2	5	51	.284	.332	.421	112	8	16-7	.982	-18	85	78	*3-100,1-60/2D	-1.3
1987	Oak A	151	554	89	160	27	4	19	76	60-11	9	44	.289	.366	.455	125	21	27-8	**.980**	3	100	60	*3-142,1-17/D-4	2.3
1988	†Oak A★	150	556	80	155	20	2	7	57	35-4	7	35	.279	.327	.360	96	-3	29-8	**.979**	-12	87	72	*3-143/1-9,2D	-1.2
1989	†Oak A	148	551	81	185	28	2	2	52	51-2	9	25	.336	.398	.405	132	26	37-15	.957	-20	77	55	*3-136,1-15/D-3	0.8
1990	†Oak A	134	507	58	136	15	1	3	50	45-4	6	50	.268	.333	.320	88	-8	16-14	**.970**	-9	89	116	*3-126/1-5,D-5	-1.9
1991	Oak A	5	16	0	1	0	0	0	1	0-0	0	2	.063	.063	.063	-69	-4	0-0	1.000	-2	53	0	/3-4,D	-0.6
1992	†Oak A	135	496	65	130	30	1	7	75	43-0	7	39	.262	.325	.369	101	1	7-2	.965	-20	79	52	*3-119,1-18/SD	-1.9
Total	15	1862	7158	1007	2074	332	40	151	874	553-45	64	719	.290	.343	.411	112	112	224-104	.966	-186	85	80	*3-1720,1-124/D-49,S-4,2-2	-8.7
LANSFORD, JODY Joseph Dale B 1.15.1961 San Jose, CA BR/TR 6-5/225# d7.31 b-Carney																								
1982	SD N	13	22	6	4	0	0	0	3	6-0	0	4	.182	.345	.182	58	-1	0-1	.986	-1	74	208	/1-9	-0.2
1983	SD N	12	8	1	2	0	0	1	2	0-0	0	3	.250	.250	.625	140	0	0-0	1.000	0	98	88	/1-8	0.0
Total	2	25	30	7	6	0	0	1	5	6-0	0	7	.200	.324	.300	82	-1	0-1	.988	-1	79	185	/1-17	-0.2

Year	Tm Lg	G	AB	R	H	2B	3B	HR	RBI	BB-IB	HP	SO	AVG	OBP	SLG	AOPS	ABR	SB-CS	FA	FR	Rng	Thr	G at Pos	BFW
LANSING, MIKE Michael Thomas B 4.3.1968 Rawlins, WY BR/TR 6/180# d4.7																								
1993	Mon N	141	491	64	141	29	1	3	45	46-2	5	56	.287	.352	.369	90	-5	23-5	.942	10	118	171	3-81,S-51,2-25	1.3
1994	Mon N	106	394	44	105	21	2	5	35	30-3	7	37	.266	.328	.368	81	-11	12-8	.983	1	93	111	2-82,3-27,S-12	-0.6
1995	Mon N	127	467	47	119	30	2	10	62	28-2	3	65	.255	.299	.392	78	-15	27-4	.991	15	107	97	*2-127/S-2	1.0
1996	Mon N	159	641	99	183	40	2	11	53	44-1	10	85	.285	.341	.406	94	-5	23-8	.985	-2	93	93	*2-159/S-2	0.3
1997	Mon N	144	572	86	161	45	2	20	70	45-2	5	92	.281	.338	.472	110	8	11-5	.987	-3	96	111	*2-144	1.2
1998	Col N	153	584	73	161	39	2	12	66	39-4	5	88	.276	.325	.411	76	-19	10-3	.987	6	100	114	*2-153/3	-0.5
1999	Col N	35	145	24	45	9	0	4	15	7-0	1	22	.310	.344	.455	79	-4	2-0	.990	8	103	154	2-35	0.5
2000	Col N	90	365	62	94	14	6	11	47	31-1	0	49	.258	.315	.419	67	-19	8-2	.983	-7	94	101	2-88	-2.0
	Bos A	49	139	10	27	4	0	0	13	7-1	0	26	.194	.230	.223	16	-18	0-0	1.000	-6	89	47	2-49/3	-2.1
2001	Bos A	106	352	45	88	23	0	8	34	22-1	1	50	.250	.294	.384	76	-12	3-3	.966	-4	89	84	S-76,2-31	-1.0
Total	9	1110	4150	554	1124	254	17	84	440	299-17	37	570	.271	.324	.401	82	-100	119-38	.986	17	97	103	2-893,S-143,3-110	-1.9
LAPAN, PETE Peter Nelson B 6.25.1891 Easthampton, MA D 1.5.1953 Norwalk, CA BR/TR 5-7/165# d9.16																								
1922	Was A	11	34	7	11	1	0	1	6	3	0	4	.324	.378	.441	119	1	1-0	.958	0	*106*	*119*	C-11	0.2
1923	Was A	2	2	0	0	0	0	0	0	0	0	0	.000	.000	.000	-99	-1	0-0	—	0			H	-0.1
Total	2	13	36	7	11	1	0	1	6	3	0	4	.306	.359	.417	107	0	1-0	.958	0	*106*	*119*	/C-11	0.1
LaPOINTE, RALPH Ralph Robert B 1.8.1922 Winooski, VT D 9.13.1967 Burlington, VT BR/TR 5-11/185# d4.15																								
1947	Phi N	56	211	33	65	7	0	1	15	17	1	15	.308	.362	.355	95	-1	8	.956	-5	100	81	S-54	-0.3
1948	StL N	87	222	27	50	3	0	0	15	18	0	19	.225	.283	.239	40	-18	1	.965	5	101	107	2-44,S-25/3	-1.0
Total	2	143	433	60	115	10	0	1	30	35	1	34	.266	.322	.296	66	-19	9	.955	-0	102	96	/S-79,2-44,3	-1.3
LaPORTE, FRANK Frank Breyfogle "Pot" B 2.6.1880 Uhrichsville, OH D 9.25.1939 Newcomerstown, OH BR/TR 5-8/175# d9.29																								
1905	NY A	11	40	4	16	1	0	1	12	1	0		.400	.415	.500	170	3	1	.918	-2	90	145	2-11	0.1
1906	NY A	123	454	60	120	23	9	2	54	22	1		.264	.300	.368	99	-2	10	.904	-4	94	106	*3-114/2-5,O(LF)	-0.3
1907	NY A	130	470	56	127	20	11	0	48	27	5		.270	.317	.360	107	3	10	.896	-6	95	58	3-64,O-63(14-13-36)/1	-0.5
1908	Bos A	62	156	14	37	1	3	0	15	12	1		.237	.296	.282	86	-3	3	.950	6	126	80	2-27,3-12/O-5(0-2-3)	0.4
	NY A	39	145	7	38	3	4	1	15	8	0		.262	.301	.359	113	1	3	.934	-2	99	111	2-26,O-11(3-0-8)	-0.1
	Year	101	301	21	75	4	7	1	30	20	1		.249	.298	.319	98	-1	6	.942	4	112	96	2-53,O-16(3-2-11),3-12	0.3
1909	NY A	89	309	35	92	19	3	0	31	18	2		.298	.340	.379	126	9	5	.938	-16	89	99	2-83	-0.7
1910	NY A	124	432	43	114	14	6	2	67	33	3		.264	.321	.338	100	0	16	.959	-4	106	83	2-79,O-23(17-1-5),3-15	-0.5
1911	StL A	136	507	71	159	37	12	2	82	34	4		.314	.361	.446	130	19	4	.950	-3	**105**	**120**	*2-133/3-3	1.8
1912	StL A	80	266	32	83	11	4	1	38	20	3		.312	.367	.395	122	7	7	.944	2	102	154	2-39,O-32(RF)	0.8
	Was A	40	136	13	42	9	1	0	17	12	0		.309	.365	.390	115	3	3	.939	-0	107	84	2-37	0.3
	Year	120	402	45	125	20	5	1	55	32	3		.311	.366	.393	120	10	10	.941	1	105	119	2-76,O-32(RF)	1.1
1913	Was A	79	242	25	61	5	4	0	18	17	3	16	.252	.309	.306	78	-7	10	.952	4	108	142	3-46,2-13,O-12(4-0-8)	-0.3
1914	Ind F	133	505	86	157	27	12	4	**107**	36	4	36	.311	.361	.436	105	-3	15	.956	4	100	124	*2-132	0.2
1915	New F	148	550	55	139	28	9	3	56	48	1	33	.253	.314	.353	93	-15	14	.960	-1	99	**117**	*2-146	-1.5
Total	11	1194	4212	501	1185	198	78	16	560	288	27	85	.281	.331	.377	107	15	101	.952	-22	101	114	2-731,3-254,O-147(39-16-92)/1	-0.3
LAPP, JACK John Walker B 9.10.1884 Frazer, PA D 2.6.1920 Philadelphia, PA BL/TR 5-8/160# d9.11																								
1908	Phi A	13	35	4	5	0	1	0	1	5	1		.143	.268	.200	49	-2	0	.947	-3	*67*	*109*	C-13	-0.5
1909	Phi A	21	56	8	19	3	1	0	10	3	0		.339	.373	.429	150	3	1	.938	1	*130*	*99*	C-19	0.7
1910	†Phi A	71	192	18	45	4	3	0	17	20	1		.234	.310	.286	88	-2	0	.980	7	*112*	*89*	C-63	1.1
1911	†Phi A	68	167	35	59	10	3	1	26	24	0		.353	.435	.467	154	13	4	.972	-1	*112*	*68*	C-57/1-4	1.6
1912	Phi A	91	281	26	82	15	6	1	35	19	0		.292	.337	.399	114	4	3	.958	-4	***127***	*88*	C-83	0.7
1913	†Phi A	82	238	23	54	4	4	1	20	37	2	26	.227	.336	.290	85	-3	1	.968	-8	*105*	*100*	C-78/1	-0.6
1914	†Phi A	69	199	22	46	7	2	0	19	31	1	14	.231	.338	.286	91	-1	1-4	.977	-6	*86*	*96*	C-67	-0.3
1915	Phi A	112	312	26	85	16	5	2	31	30	2	29	.272	.340	.375	118	6	5-2	.967	-14	*60*	*116*	C-89,1-12	-0.1
1916	Chi A	40	101	6	21	0	1	0	7	8	0	10	.208	.266	.228	48	-7	1	.989	3	147	115	C-34	-0.2
Total	9	567	1581	168	416	59	26	5	166	177	7	79	.263	.340	.343	105	11	16-6	.969	-25	*103*	*96*	C-503/1-17	2.4
LARKER, NORM Norman Howard John B 12.27.1930 Beaver Meadows, PA BL/TL 6/200# d4.15																								
1958	LA N	99	253	32	70	16	5	4	29	29-0	3	21	.277	.352	.427	103	2	1-1	.985	-0	96	120	O-43(41-0-2),1-35	-0.2
1959	†LA N	108	311	37	90	14	1	8	49	26-1	2	25	.289	.344	.418	96	-1	0-1	.990	5	114	120	1-55,O-30(22-0-8)	-0.2
1960	LA N★	133	440	56	142	26	3	5	78	36-2	1	24	.323	.368	.430	112	9	1-0	.993	4	104	100	*1-119/O-2(LF)	0.7
1961	LA N	97	282	29	76	16	1	5	38	24-7	1	22	.270	.326	.387	82	-7	0-0	.995	2	99	105	1-86/O(RF)	-0.9
1962	Hou N	147	506	58	133	19	5	9	63	70-7	7	47	.263	.358	.374	105	6	1-1	.991	5	109	93	*1-135/O-6(LF)	0.2
1963	Mil N	64	147	15	26	6	0	1	14	24-2	2	24	.177	.297	.238	58	-7	0-2	.992	4	149	89	1-42	-0.6
	SF N	19	14	0	1	0	0	0	0	2-0	0	2	.071	.188	.071	-22	-2	0-0	.929	-0	116	156	1-11	-0.3
	Year	83	161	15	27	6	0	1	14	26-2	2	26	.168	.288	.224	51	-9	0-2	.987	4	147	93	1-53	-0.9
Total	6	667	1953	227	538	97	15	32	271	211-19	16	165	.275	.347	.390	97	0	3-5	.991	19	109	100	1-483/O-82(71-0-11)	-1.3
LARKIN d5.29																								
1884	Was U	17	70	11	17	0	0	0		4			.243	.284	.243	63	-5		.726	-4	52	113	3-17	-0.8
LARKIN, BARRY Barry Louis B 4.28.1964 Cincinnati, OH BR/TR 6/190# d8.13 b-Stephen																								
1986	Cin N	41	159	27	45	4	3	3	19	9-1	0	21	.283	.320	.403	94	-2	8-0	.976	3	113	104	S-36/2-3	0.6
1987	Cin N	125	439	64	107	16	2	12	43	36-3	5	52	.244	.306	.371	76	-16	21-6	.965	-2	102	110	*S-119	-0.4
1988	Cin N★	151	588	91	174	32	5	12	56	41-3	8	24	.296	.347	.429	118	14	40-7	.960	9	105	90	*S-148	4.2
1989	Cin N☆	97	325	47	111	14	4	4	36	20-5	2	23	.342	.375	.446	132	13	10-5	.976	20	118	76	S-82	4.1
1990	†Cin N★	158	614	85	185	25	6	7	67	49-3	7	49	.301	.358	.396	103	3	30-5	.977	21	107	110	*S-156	4.1
1991	Cin N★	123	464	88	140	27	4	20	69	55-1	3	64	.302	.378	.506	141	26	24-6	.976	23	107	109	*S-119	**6.2**
1992	Cin N	140	533	76	162	32	6	12	78	63-8	4	58	.304	.377	.454	132	24	15-4	.983	15	102	94	*S-140	5.5
1993	Cin N★	100	384	57	121	20	3	8	51	51-6	1	33	.315	.394	.445	125	16	14-1	.965	3	98	95	S-99	2.8
1994	Cin N✳	110	427	78	119	23	5	9	52	64-3	0	58	.279	.369	.419	107	6	26-2	.980	2	95	97	*S-110	2.1
1995	†Cin N★	131	496	98	158	29	6	15	66	61-2	3	49	.319	.394	.492	133	25	51-5	.980	-12	90	105	*S-130	3.2
1996	Cin N★	152	517	117	154	32	4	33	89	96-3	7	52	.298	.410	.567	155	45	36-10	.975	4	99	89	*S-151	6.2
1997	Cin N✳	73	224	34	71	17	3	4	20	47-6	3	24	.317	.440	.473	138	16	14-3	.980	-1	100	98	S-63/D-2	2.1
1998	Cin N	145	538	93	166	34	10	17	72	79-5	2	69	.309	.397	.504	134	29	26-3	.979	-18	88	94	*S-145	2.6
1999	Cin N★	161	583	108	171	30	4	12	75	93-5	2	57	.293	.390	.420	103	6	30-8	.978	-21	90	89	*S-161	0.1
2000	Cin N★	102	396	71	124	26	5	11	41	48-0	1	31	.313	.389	.487	117	11	14-6	.973	-16	91	72	*S-102/D	0.4
2001	Cin N	45	156	29	40	12	0	2	17	27-2	2	25	.256	.373	.372	90	-1	3-2	.951	-4	98	92	S-44	-0.2
2002	Cin N	145	507	72	124	37	2	7	47	44-9	3	57	.245	.305	.367	78	-18	13-4	.979	2	105	108	*S-135	-0.5
2003	Cin N	70	241	39	68	16	1	2	18	22-0	1	32	.282	.345	.382	91	-3	2-0	.962	-4	103	99	S-60	-0.2
Total	18	2069	7591	1274	2240	426	73	190	916	905-65	54	778	.295	.371	.446	116	194	377-77	.974	23	100	96	*S-2000/D-3,2-3	42.9
LARKIN, ED Edward Francis B 7.1.1885 Wyalusing, PA D 3.28.1934 Wyalusing, PA BR/TR 5-8/?# d10.2																								
1909	Phi A	2	6	0	1	0	0	0	1	1	0		.167	.286	.167	42	0	0	.769	-1	*111*	*54*	/C-2	-0.2
LARKIN, GENE Eugene Thomas B 10.24.1962 Flushing, NY BB/TR 6-3/205# d5.21 OF Total (7-LF 193-RF)																								
1987	†Min A	85	233	23	62	11	2	4	28	25-3	2	31	.266	.340	.382	89	-3	1-4	.989	-2	66	72	D-40,1-26	-0.9
1988	Min A	149	505	56	135	30	2	8	70	68-8	**15**	55	.267	.368	.382	108	9	3-2	.994	-5	69	98	D-86,1-60	-0.2
1989	Min A	136	446	61	119	25	1	6	46	54-6	9	57	.267	.353	.368	98	1	5-2	.992	-4	76	90	1-67,D-41,O-32(1-0-31)	-0.8
1990	Min A	119	401	46	108	26	4	5	42	42-2	5	55	.269	.343	.392	99	1	5-3	1.000	-2	87	161	O-47(RF),D-43,1-28	-0.6
1991	†Min A	98	255	34	73	14	1	2	19	30-3	1	21	.286	.361	.373	99	1	2-3	.968	-5	79	37	O-47(2-0-48),1-39/23D	-0.7
1992	Min A	115	337	38	83	18	1	6	42	28-6	4	43	.246	.308	.359	85	-7	7-2	.992	-2	91	124	1-55,O-43(RF)/D-4	-1.3
1993	Min A	56	144	17	38	7	1	1	19	21-3	2	16	.264	.357	.347	92	-1	0-1	1.000	-4	74	65	O-28(4-0-25),1-18/3-2,D-3	-0.7
Total	7	758	2321	275	618	131	12	32	266	268-31	38	278	.266	.348	.374	97	1	23-17	.992	-23	78	102	1-293,D-221,O-197R/3-3,2	-5.2
LARKIN, TERRY Frank S. D 9.16.1894 Brooklyn, NY BR/TR d5.20 ▲																								
1876	NY N	1	4	0	0	0	0	0	0	0		0	.000	.000	.000	-99	-1		.500	-0	141	0	/P	0.0
1877	Har N	58	228	28	52	6	5	1	18	5		23	.228	.245	.311	83	-4		.885	-1	100	0	*P-56/3-2,2	-0.1
1878	Chi N	58	226	33	65	9	4	0	32	**17**		17	.288	.337	.363	122	6		.858	-4	86	0	*P-56/O(LF)3	-0.2
1879	Chi N	60	228	26	50	12	2	0	18	8		24	.219	.246	.289	71	-7		.918	-7	74	47	*P-58/O-3(2-1-0)	-0.3

Year	Tm Lg	G	AB	R	H	2B	3B	HR	RBI	BB-IB	HP	SO	AVG	OBP	SLG	AOPS	ABR	SB-CS	FA	FR	Rng	Thr	G at Pos	BFW
1880	Tro N	6	20	1	3	1	0	0	1	3		4	.150	.261	.200	56	-1		1.000	0	105	684	/P-5,O-2(0-1-1),S	0.0
1884	Ric AA	40	139	17	28	1	4	0		9	3		.201	.265	.266	75	-4		.907	4	109	79	2-40	0.1
Total	6	223	845	105	198	29	15	1	69	42	3	68	.234	.273	.308	88	-11		.884	-8	87	32	P-176/2-41,O-6(3-2-1),3-3,S	-0.5
LARKIN, HENRY Henry E. "Ted" B 1.12.1860 Reading, PA D 1.31.1942 Reading, PA BR/TR 5-10/175# d5.1 M1																								
1884	Phi AA	85	326	59	90	21	9	3	37	15	8		.276	.324	.423	133	11		.856	-6	47	0	*O-85(30-55-0)/2-2	0.3
1885	Phi AA	108	453	114	149	**37**	14	8	88	26	6		.329	.373	.525	171	36		.882	9	120	**239**	*O-108(48-61-0)	3.7
1886	Phi AA	**139**	565	133	180	**36**	16	2	74	59	7		.319	**.390**	.450	161	41	32	.866	5	91	44	*O-139(LF)	3.7
1887	Phi AA	126	497	105	154	22	12	3	88	48	8		.310	.380	.421	123	16	37	.895	2	93	0	O-93(86-7-0),1-23,2-10	1.1
1888	Phi AA	135	546	92	147	28	12	7	101	33	13		.269	.326	.403	134	20	20	.967	-8	80	87	*1-122,2-14	0.2
1889	Phi AA	133	516	105	164	23	12	3	74	83	16	41	.318	.428	.426	145	37	11	.973	-5	79	118	*1-131/32	1.8
1890	Cle P	125	506	93	167	32	15	5	112	65	12	18	.330	.419	.482	153	43	5	.978	-8	64	78	*1-125/O(CF)M	1.9
1891	Phi AA	133	526	94	147	27	14	10	93	66	15	56	.279	.376	.441	133	23	2	.974	-7	73	92	*1-111,O-23(5-0-18)	0.5
1892	Was N	119	464	76	130	13	7	8	96	39	8	21	.280	.346	.390	126	14	21	.969	2	116	115	*1-117/O-2(RF)	1.4
1893	Was N	81	319	54	101	20	3	4	73	50	8	5	.317	.422	.436	132	18	1	.963	-9	64	80	1-81	0.7
Total	10	1184	4718	925	1429	259	114	53	836	484	101	141	.303	.380	.440	142	259	129	.971	-23	80	96	1-710,O-451(308-124-20)/2-27,3	15.3
LARKIN, STEPHEN Stephen Karari B 7.24.1973 Cincinnati, OH BL/TL 6/190# d9.27 b-Barry																								
1998	Cin N	1	3	0	1	0	0	0	0	0-0	0	1	.333	.333	.333	75	0	0-0	1.000	-0	0	0	/1	0.0
LARMORE, BOB Robert McKahan "Red" B 12.6.1896 Anderson, IN D 1.15.1964 St.Louis, MO BR/TR 5-10.5/185# d5.14																								
1918	StL N	4	7	0	2	0	0	0	1	0	0	2	.286	.286	.286	77	0	0	.778	-1	85	0	/S-2	-0.1
LaROCCA, GREG Gregory Mark B 11.10.1972 Oswego, NY BR/TR 5-11/185# d9.7																								
2000	SD N	13	27	1	6	2	0	0	2	1-0	0	4	.222	.250	.296	40	-3	0-0	1.000	-4	54	0	/3-8,S-4,2-2	-0.6
2002	Cle A	21	52	12	14	3	1	0	4	6-0	2	6	.269	.367	.365	97	0	1-0	.800	-4	62	43	3-15/2-3,D	-0.4
2003	Cle A	5	9	3	3	1	0	0	0	1-0	0	1	.333	.400	.444	127	0	0-0	1.000	1	156	0	/3-2	0.1
Total	3	39	88	16	23	6	1	0	6	8-0	2	11	.261	.337	.352	83	-3	1-0	.857	-8	71	31	/3-25,2-5,S-4,D	-0.9
LaROQUE, SAM Samuel H. J. B 2.26.1864 St.Mathias, PQ, CAN TR 5-11/190# d7.30																								
1888	Det N	2	9	1	4	0	0	0	2	1	0	1	.444	.500	.444	201	1	0	.789	-1	86	300	/2-2	0.1
1890	Pit N	111	434	59	105	20	4	1	40	35	12	29	.242	.316	.313	95	-1	27	.925	-9	102	81	2-78,S-31/1-2,O(LF)	-0.5
1891	Pit N	1	4	0	0	0	0	0	0	0	0	1	.000	.000	.000	-99	-1	0	.714	-0	97	0	/3	-0.1
	Lou AA	10	35	6	11	2	1	1	8	5	2	8	.314	.429	.514	172	4	1	.875	-4	71	92	2-10/1	0.0
Total	3	124	482	66	120	22	5	2	50	41	14	39	.249	.326	.328	101	3	28	.916	-14	98	89	/2-90,S-31,1-3,3O(LF)	-0.5
LaROSE, VIC Victor Raymond B 12.23.1944 Los Angeles, CA BR/TR 5-11/180# d9.13																								
1968	Chi N	4	2	0	0	0	0	0	0	0-0	1	1	.000	.333	.000	6	0	0-0	1.000	0	103	0	/2-2,S-2	0.0
LaROSS, HARRY Harry Raymond "Spike" B 1.2.1888 Easton, PA D 3.22.1954 Chicago, IL BR/TR 5-11.5/170# d6.24																								
1914	Cin N	22	48	7	11	1	0	0	5	2	0	10	.229	.260	.250	50	-3	4	.739	-2	63	143	O-20(10-10-0)	-0.7
LARSEN, SWEDE Erling Adeli B 11.15.1913 Jersey City, NJ BR/TR 5-11/170# d6.17																								
1936	Bos N	3	1	0	0	0	0	0	0	0	0	0	.000	.000	.000	-99	0	0	1.000	-0	0	0	/2-2	-0.1
LARSON, BRANDON Brandon John B 5.24.1976 San Angelo, TX BR/TR 6/210# d5.4																								
2001	Cin N	14	33	2	4	2	0	0	1	2-0	0	10	.121	.171	.182	-8	-5	0-0	.939	2	131	125	/3-9	-0.3
2002	Cin N	23	51	8	14	2	0	4	13	6-1	1	10	.275	.362	.549	136	2	1-0	1.000	0	100	0	/O-9(LF),3-5,1-2	0.3
2003	Cin N	32	89	6	9	1	0	1	9	13-0	0	31	.101	.212	.146	-3	-14	2-2	.943	5	117	168	3-24/O-3(LF)	-1.0
Total	3	69	173	16	27	5	0	5	23	21-1	1	51	.156	.249	.272	37	-17	3-2	.948	7	121	177	/3-38,O-12(LF),1-2	-1.0
LaRUE, JASON Michael Jason B 3.19.1974 Houston, TX BR/TR 5-11/200# d6.15																								
1999	Cin N	36	90	12	19	7	0	3	10	11-1	2	32	.211	.311	.389	73	-4	4-1	.990	3	154	120	C-35	0.2
2000	Cin N	31	98	12	23	3	0	5	12	5-2	4	19	.235	.299	.418	77	-4	0-0	.991	6	148	60	C-31	0.4
2001	Cin N	121	364	39	86	21	2	12	43	27-4	9	106	.236	.303	.404	78	-13	3-3	.991	13	194	**161**	*C-107/3-3,O-2(LF),1	0.6
2002	Cin N	113	353	42	88	17	1	12	52	27-6	13	117	.249	.324	.405	92	-6	1-2	.994	2	**171**	103	*C-110	0.2
2003	Cin N	118	379	52	87	23	1	16	50	33-4	20	111	.230	.321	.422	94	-3	3-3	.984	-8	115	70	*C-114/1O(LF)	-0.5
Total	5	419	1284	157	303	71	4	48	167	103-17	48	385	.236	.315	.410	86	-30	11-9	.990	16	157	106	C-397/O-3(LF),3-3,1-2	0.9
LaRUSSA, TONY Anthony B 10.4.1944 Tampa, FL BR/TR 6-1/190# d5.10 M25 C1																								
1963	KC A	34	44	4	11	1	1	0	1	7-0	0	12	.250	.346	.318	85	-1	0-0	.957	-5	65	98	S-14/2-3	-0.5
1968	Oak A	5	3	0	1	0	0	0	0	0-0	0	0	.333	.333	.333	108	0	0-0	—	0			H	0.0
1969	Oak A	8	8	0	0	0	0	0	0	0-0	0	1	.000	.000	.000	-99	-2	0-0	—	0			H	-0.2
1970	Oak A	52	106	6	21	4	1	0	6	15-1	1	19	.198	.301	.255	57	-6	0-0	.969	-0	100	115	2-44	-0.4
1971	Oak A	23	8	3	0	0	0	0	0	0-0	0	4	.000	.000	.000	-99	-2	0-0	.833	-0	27	122	/2-7,S-4,3-2	-0.2
	Atl N	9	7	1	2	0	0	0	0	1-0	0	1	.286	.375	.286	84	0	0-0	.933	-1	64	138	/2-9	-0.1
1973	Chi N	1	0	1	0	0	0	0	0	0-0	0	0	—	—	—	—	0	0-0	—	0			R	0.0
Total	6	132	176	15	35	5	2	0	7	23-1	1	37	.199	.292	.250	54	-11	0-0	.963	-7	92	116	/2-63,S-18,3-2	-1.4
LARY, LYN Lynford Hobart "Broadway" B 1.28.1906 Armona, CA D 1.9.1973 Downey, CA BR/TR 6/165# d5.11																								
1929	NY A	80	236	48	73	9	2	5	26	24	3	15	.309	.380	.428	115	6	4-1	.943	2	104	115	3-55,S-14/2-2	1.2
1930	NY A	117	464	93	134	20	8	3	52	45	4	40	.289	.357	.386	92	-5	14-2	.940	-4	97	84	*S-113	0.5
1931	NY A	**155**	610	100	171	35	9	10	107	88	6	54	.280	.376	.416	115	16	13-10	.946	4	98	97	*S-155	2.9
1932	NY A	91	280	56	65	14	4	3	39	52	3	28	.232	.358	.343	87	-3	9-3	.941	-1	94	86	S-80/1-5,2-2,3-2,O(LF)	0.2
1933	NY A	52	127	25	28	3	3	0	13	28	0	17	.220	.361	.291	79	-3	2-1	.938	0	89	106	3-28,S-16/1-3,O(LF)	-0.1
1934	NY A	1	0	0	0	0	0	0	0	1	0	0	—	1.000	—	189	0	0-0	.800	-0	0	288	/1	0.0
	Bos A	129	419	58	101	20	4	2	54	66	0	51	.241	.344	.322	68	-19	12-5	**.965**	-7	95	80	*S-129	-1.4
	Year	130	419	58	101	20	4	2	54	67	0	51	.241	.346	.322	68	-18	12-5	.965	-7	95	80	*S-129/1	-1.4
1935	Was A	39	103	8	20	4	0	0	7	12	0	10	.194	.278	.233	35	-10	3-0	.953	-3	91	71	S-30	-1.0
	StL A	93	371	78	107	25	7	2	35	64	2	43	.288	.396	.410	104	5	25-4	.962	10	100	100	S-93	2.4
	Year	132	474	86	127	29	7	2	42	76	2	53	.268	.371	.371	90	-4	28-4	.960	6	98	94	*S-123	1.4
1936	StL A	**155**	619	112	179	30	6	2	52	117	2	54	.289	.404	.367	89	-5	**37**-9	.956	-2	101	77	*S-155	0.8
1937	Cle A	**156**	644	110	187	46	7	8	77	88	3	64	.290	.378	.421	100	3	18-8	.963	8	99	95	*S-156	2.1
1938	Cle A	141	568	94	152	36	4	3	51	88	0	65	.268	.366	.361	84	-11	23-6	.964	-2	93	91	*S-141	0.0
1939	Cle A	3	2	0	0	0	0	0	0	0	0	1	.000	.000	.000	-99	-1	0-0	.000	-1	0	0	/S-2	-0.1
	Bro N	29	31	7	5	1	1	0	1	12	1	6	.161	.409	.258	80	0	1	.947	-1	84	130	S-12/3-7	0.0
	StL N	34	75	11	14	3	0	0	9	16	0	15	.187	.330	.227	49	-5	1	.961	-4	90	58	S-30/3-3	-0.7
	Year	63	106	18	19	4	1	0	10	28	1	21	.179	.356	.236	59	-5	2	.958	-5	89	73	S-42,3-10	-0.7
1940	StL A	27	54	5	3	1	1	0	3	4	1	7	.056	.136	.111	-35	-11	0-0	.952	0	101	95	S-12/2	-1.0
Total	12	1302	4603	805	1239	247	56	38	526	705	25	470	.269	.369	.372	90	-43	162-49	.956	-0	97	88	*S-1138/3-95,1-9,2-5,O-2(LF)	5.8
LASSETTER, DON Donald O'Neal B 3.27.1933 Newnan, GA BR/TR 6-3/200# d9.21																								
1957	StL N	4	13	2	2	0	1	0	0	1-0	0	3	.154	.214	.308	37	-1	0-0	1.000	-0	101	0	/O-3(LF)	-0.2
LATHAM, CHRIS Christopher Joseph B 5.26.1973 Coeur D'Alene, ID BB/TR 6/195# d4.12																								
1997	Min A	15	22	4	4	1	0	0	1	0-0	0	8	.182	.182	.227	6	-3	0-0	.917	-1	89	0	O-10(0-8-3)	-0.4
1998	Min A	34	94	14	15	1	0	1	5	13-0	0	36	.160	.262	.202	23	-11	4-2	.972	0	110	56	O-32(13-15-5)	-1.1
1999	Min A	14	22	1	2	0	0	0	3	0-0	0	13	.091	.083	.091	-52	-5	0-0	1.000	-1	80	0	O-14(6-5-4)	-0.6
2001	Tor A	43	73	12	20	3	1	2	10	10-1	1	28	.274	.369	.425	106	1	4-1	1.000	3	122	162	O-31(15-2-14)	0.3
2003	NY A	4	2	3	2	0	0	0	0	0-0	0	0	1.000	1.000	1.000	437	1	1-0	1.000	0	193	0	/O-2(0-1-1)	0.1
Total	5	110	213	34	43	5	1	3	19	23-1	1	85	.202	.280	.277	46	-17	9-3	.980	1	109	78	/O-89(34-31-27)	-1.7
LATHAM, JUICE George Warren "Jumbo" B 9.6.1852 Utica, NY D 5.26.1914 Utica, NY BR/TR 5-8/164# d4.19 M2																								
1875	Bos NA	16	78	23	21	4	0	0	13	0		2	.269	.269	.321	100	0	0-0	.927	0	154	206	1-16	0.1
	NH NA	20	76	6	15	1	0	0	5	0		4	.197	.197	.211	48	-3	6-0	.954	2	219	113	1-14/S-4,3-3,M	0.0
	Year	36	154	29	36	5	0	0	18	0		6	.234	.234	.266	78	-3	6-0	.941	2	184	163	1-30/S-4,3-3	0.1
1877	Lou N	59	278	42	81	10	6	0	22	5		6	.291	.304	.371	94	-4		.950	2	127	113	*1-59	-0.4
1882	Phi AA	74	323	47	92	10	2	0	38	10			.285	.306	.328	107	1		**.972**	-0	64	89	*1-74,M	-0.5

Year	Tm Lg	G	AB	R	H	2B	3B	HR	RBI	BB-IB	HP	SO	AVG	OBP	SLG	AOPS	ABR	SB-CS	FA	FR	Rng	Thr	G at Pos	BFW
1883	Lou AA	88	368	60	92	7	6	0		12			.250	.274	.302	92	-2		.955	-1	110	132	*1-67,2-14/S-9	-0.8
1884	Lou AA	77	308	31	52	3	3	0	23	8	3		.169	.197	.198	31	-23		.961	3	121	**160**	*1-76/3	-2.5
Total	4	298	1277	180	317	30	17	0	83	35	3	6	.248	.270	.298	83	-28		.960	3	104	124	1-276/2-14,S-9,3	-4.2

LATHAM, ARLIE Walter Arlington "The Freshest Man On Earth" B 3.15.1860 W.Lebanon, NH D 11.29.1952 Garden City, NY BR/TR 5-8/150# d7.5 M1 C2 U2 OF Total (2-LF 11-RF)

Year	Tm Lg	G	AB	R	H	2B	3B	HR	RBI	BB-IB	HP	SO	AVG	OBP	SLG	AOPS	ABR	SB-CS	FA	FR	Rng	Thr	G at Pos	BFW
1880	Buf N	22	79	9	10	3	1	0	3	1		8	.127	.138	.190	10	-7		.887	-0	104	32	S-12,O-10(RF)/C	-0.7
1883	StL AA	**98**	406	86	96	12	7	0		18			.236	.269	.300	79	-10		.866	21	125	**162**	*3-98/C	1.1
1884	StL AA	**110**	474	115	130	17	12	1		18	6		.274	.309	.367	116	7		.864	**37**	**148**	**138**	*3-110/C	4.1
1885	†StL AA	110	485	84	100	15	3	1	35	18	5		.206	.242	.256	55	-25		.875	0	104	118	*3-109/C-2	-2.1
1886	†StL AA	134	578	**152**	174	23	8	1	47	55	6		.301	.368	.374	127	18	60	.827	-0	106	132	*3-133/2	1.8
1887	†StL AA	136	627	163	198	35	10	2	83	45	5		.316	.366	.413	106	2	129	.877	0	106	92	*3-132/2-5,C-2	0.4
1888	†StL AA	133	570	119	151	19	5	2	31	43	8		.265	.325	.326	98	-2	**109**	.882	3	101	123	*3-133/S	0.2
1889	StL AA	118	512	110	126	13	3	4	49	42	11	30	.246	.317	.307	69	-23	69	.883	9	100	117	*3-116/2-3	-1.0
1890	Chi P	52	214	47	49	7	2	1	20	22	3	22	.229	.310	.294	59	-13	32	.880	1	102	105	3-52	-0.8
	Cin N	41	164	35	41	6	2	0	15	23	1	18	.250	.346	.311	92	-1	20	.853	3	115	158	3-41/O(RF)	0.2
1891	Cin N	135	533	119	145	20	10	7	53	74	11	35	.272	.372	.386	120	16	87	.879	21	**122**	125	*3-135/C	3.4
1892	Cin N	152	622	111	148	20	4	0	44	60	5	55	.238	.310	.283	81	-13	66	.883	-6	103	122	*3-142/2-9,O(LF)	-1.5
1893	Cin N	127	531	101	150	18	6	2	49	62	10	20	.282	.368	.350	89	-7	57	.892	-13	94	99	*3-127	-1.5
1894	Cin N	131	534	132	167	23	6	4	60	61	9	24	.313	.392	.401	88	-9	62	.861	-12	97	93	*3-129/2-2	-1.4
1895	Cin N	112	460	93	143	14	6	2	69	42	5	25	.311	.375	.380	91	-6	48	.861	-13	92	85	*3-108/1-3,2	-1.4
1896	StL N	8	35	3	7	0	0	0	5	4	0	3	.200	.282	.200	29	-3	2	.744	-2	80	137	/3-8,M	-0.5
1899	Was N	6	6	1	1	0	0	0	0	1	0		.167	.286	.167	26	-1	0	1.000	0	0	0	/O(LF)2	-0.1
1909	NY N	4	2	1	0	0	0	0	0	0	0		.000	.000	.000	-99	0	1	1.000	0	217	0	/2-2	0.0
Total	17	1629	6832	1481	1836	245	85	27	563	589	85	240	.269	.334	.341	91	-77	742	.870	48	108	118	*3-1573/2-24,O-13R,S-13,C-8,1-3	0.2

LATHERS, CHICK Charles Ten Eyck B 10.22.1888 Detroit, MI D 7.26.1971 Petoskey, MI BL/TR 6/180# d5.1

Year	Tm Lg	G	AB	R	H	2B	3B	HR	RBI	BB-IB	HP	SO	AVG	OBP	SLG	AOPS	ABR	SB-CS	FA	FR	Rng	Thr	G at Pos	BFW
1910	Det A	41	82	4	19	2	0	0	3	8	0		.232	.300	.256	70	-3	0	.926	2	128	162	3-14/2-7,S-4	0.0
1911	Det A	29	45	5	10	1	0	0	4	5	1		.222	.314	.244	54	-3	0	.867	-2	115	101	/2-9,3-8,S-4,1-3	-0.4
Total	2	70	127	9	29	3	0	0	7	13	1		.228	.305	.252	64	-6	0	.933	0	131	111	/3-22,2-16,S-8,1-3	-0.4

LATIMER, TACKS Clifford Wesley B 11.30.1877 Loveland, OH D 4.24.1936 Loveland, OH BR/TR 6/160# d10.1

Year	Tm Lg	G	AB	R	H	2B	3B	HR	RBI	BB-IB	HP	SO	AVG	OBP	SLG	AOPS	ABR	SB-CS	FA	FR	Rng	Thr	G at Pos	BFW
1898	NY N	5	17	1	5	1	0	0	1	0	0		.294	.294	.353	88	0	0	.889	-1	*89*	*168*	/C-4,O-2(RF)	-0.1
1899	Lou N	9	29	3	8	1	0	0	4	2	0		.276	.323	.310	74	-1	1	.980	2	*113*	*84*	/C-8,1	0.1
1900	Pit N	4	12	1	4	1	0	0	2	0	0		.333	.333	.417	106	0	0	.947	-0	*126*	*99*	/C-4	0.0
1901	Bal A	1	4	0	1	0	0	0	0	0	0		.250	.250	.250	37	0	0	1.000	-0	*133*	*0*	/C	0.0
1902	Bro N	8	24	0	1	0	0	0	0	0	0		.042	.042	.042	-74	-5	0	.947	-1	*81*	*136*	/C-8	-0.6
Total	5	27	86	5	19	3	0	0	7	2	0		.221	.239	.256	41	-6	1	.949	-0	*104*	*110*	/C-25,O-2(RF),1	-0.6

LAU, CHARLIE Charles Richard B 4.12.1933 Romulus, MI D 3.18.1984 Key Colony Beach, FL BL/TR 6/190# d9.12 C15

Year	Tm Lg	G	AB	R	H	2B	3B	HR	RBI	BB-IB	HP	SO	AVG	OBP	SLG	AOPS	ABR	SB-CS	FA	FR	Rng	Thr	G at Pos	BFW
1956	Det A	3	9	1	2	0	0	0	0	0-0	0	1	.222	.222	.222	18	-1	0-0	1.000	0	*0*	*0*	/C-3	-0.1
1958	Det A	30	68	8	10	1	2	0	6	12-2	2	15	.147	.293	.221	41	-5	0-0	.985	1	*98*	*105*	C-27	-0.3
1959	Det A	2	6	0	1	0	0	0	0	0-0	0	2	.167	.167	.167	-8	-1	0-0	1.000	1	*0*	*0*	/C-2	0.0
1960	Mil N	21	53	4	10	2	0	0	2	6-1	0	10	.189	.271	.226	41	-4	0-0	1.000	3	*199*	*105*	C-16	-0.1
1961	Mil N	28	82	3	17	5	0	0	5	14-3	1	11	.207	.323	.268	65	-3	1-1	.968	-2	*127*	*72*	C-25	-0.4
	Bal A	17	47	3	8	0	0	1	4	1-1	0	3	.170	.188	.234	12	-6	0-0	.990	3	*123*	*78*	C-17	-0.3
1962	Bal A	81	197	21	58	11	2	6	37	7-1	1	11	.294	.319	.462	115	3	1-0	.996	-5	*69*	*87*	C-56	0.0
1963	Bal A	29	48	4	9	2	0	0	6	1-0	0	5	.188	.204	.229	22	-5	0-0	.964	1	115	85	/C-8	-0.4
	KC A	62	187	15	55	11	0	3	26	14-3	0	17	.294	.340	.401	102	1	1-0	.982	-11	59	101	C-50	-0.8
	Year	91	235	19	64	13	0	3	32	15-3	0	22	.272	.313	.366	88	-4	1-0	.979	-10	66	99	C-58	-1.2
1964	KC A	43	118	11	32	7	1	2	9	10-1	0	18	.271	.326	.398	98	0	0-0	.990	-6	*55*	*73*	C-35	-0.5
	Bal A	62	158	16	41	15	1	1	14	17-5	1	27	.259	.333	.386	100	1	0-0	.992	-2	*78*	*71*	C-47	0.1
	Year	105	276	27	73	22	2	3	23	27-6	1	45	.264	.330	.391	99	1	0-0	.991	-8	*68*	*72*	C-82	-0.4
1965	Bal A	68	132	15	39	5	2	2	18	17-5	0	18	.295	.371	.409	120	4	0-0	.989	-4	*96*	*78*	C-35	0.2
1966	Bal A	18	12	1	6	2	1	0	5	4-0	0	1	.500	.588	.833	320	4	0-0	—	0			H	0.4
1967	Bal A	11	8	0	1	1	0	0	3	2-1	0	2	.125	.273	.250	65	0	0-0	—	0			H	0.0
	Atl N	52	45	3	9	1	0	1	5	4-1	0	9	.200	.265	.289	59	-2	0-0	—	0			H	-0.3
Total	11	527	1170	105	298	63	9	16	140	109-24	5	150	.255	.318	.365	89	-14	3-1	.988	-22	*87*	*84*	C-321	-2.5

LAUDER, BILLY William B 2.23.1874 New York, NY D 5.20.1933 Norwalk, CT BR/TR 5-10/160# d6.25 C1

Year	Tm Lg	G	AB	R	H	2B	3B	HR	RBI	BB-IB	HP	SO	AVG	OBP	SLG	AOPS	ABR	SB-CS	FA	FR	Rng	Thr	G at Pos	BFW
1898	Phi N	97	361	42	95	14	7	2	67	19	0		.263	.300	.357	92	-5	6	.866	-19	82	42	3-97	-2.1
1899	Phi N	151	583	74	156	17	6	3	90	34	2		.268	.310	.333	79	-18	15	.893	-14	91	104	*3-151	-2.7
1901	Phi A	2	8	1	1	0	0	0	0	0	0		.125	.125	.125	-29	-1	0	.833	0	111	0	/3-2	-0.1
1902	NY N	127	490	42	115	20	1	0	43	10	0		.235	.250	.280	64	-22	19	.908	2	97	106	*3-123/O-4(2-0-2)	-1.8
1903	NY N	108	395	52	111	13	0	0	53	14	1		.281	.307	.314	74	-14	19	.908	-8	90	99	*3-108	-1.8
Total	5	485	1837	211	478	64	14	5	253	77	3		.260	.291	.318	76	-60	59	.894	-38	91	90	3-481/O-4(2-0-2)	-8.5

LAUDNER, TIM Timothy Jon B 6.7.1958 Mason City, IA BR/TR 6-3/212# d8.28

Year	Tm Lg	G	AB	R	H	2B	3B	HR	RBI	BB-IB	HP	SO	AVG	OBP	SLG	AOPS	ABR	SB-CS	FA	FR	Rng	Thr	G at Pos	BFW
1981	Min A	14	43	4	7	2	0	2	5	3-1	1	17	.163	.234	.349	62	-2	0-0	1.000	-0	108	51	C-12/D-2	-0.2
1982	Min A	93	306	37	78	19	1	7	33	34-2	0	74	.255	.328	.392	95	-2	0-2	.976	-13	74	107	C-93	-1.1
1983	Min A	62	168	20	31	9	0	6	18	15-0	0	49	.185	.250	.345	60	-9	0-0	.986	-2	67	96	C-57/D-4	-0.9
1984	Min A	87	262	31	54	16	1	10	35	18-0	1	78	.206	.258	.389	73	-10	0-0	.978	9	137	126	C-81/D-2	0.3
1985	Min A	72	164	16	39	5	0	7	19	12-0	1	45	.238	.292	.396	82	-4	0-1	.969	-6	110	94	C-68/1	-0.8
1986	Min A	76	193	21	47	10	0	10	29	24-0	3	56	.244	.333	.451	109	3	1-0	.984	-13	115	67	C-68	-0.7
1987	†Min A	113	288	30	55	7	1	16	43	23-0	1	80	.191	.252	.389	65	-16	1-0	.987	-3	92	79	*C-101/1-7,D-2	-1.5
1988	Min A★	117	375	38	94	18	1	13	54	36-0	1	89	.251	.316	.408	99	-1	0-0	.992	5	88	84	*C-109/1-3,D-4	1.0
1989	Min A	100	239	24	53	11	1	6	27	25-0	0	65	.222	.293	.351	76	-8	1-0	.991	-2	86	111	C-68,D-19,1-11	-0.7
Total	9	734	2038	221	458	97	5	77	263	190-3	8	553	.225	.292	.391	83	-49	3-3	.984	-24	96	95	C-657/D-33,1-22	-4.6

LAUER, CHUCK John Charles B 4.5.1865 Pittsburgh, PA D 5.14.1915 Buffalo, NY TR d7.17 ▲

Year	Tm Lg	G	AB	R	H	2B	3B	HR	RBI	BB-IB	HP	SO	AVG	OBP	SLG	AOPS	ABR	SB-CS	FA	FR	Rng	Thr	G at Pos	BFW
1884	Pit AA	13	44	5	5	0	0	0		0	0		.114	.114	.114	-26	-6		.938	-1	60	0	O-10(0-2-8)/P-3,1	-0.5
1889	Pit N	4	16	2	3	0	0	0	1	0	0	5	.188	.188	.188	5	-2	0	.815	0			/C-3,O(LF)	-0.1
1890	Chi N	2	8	1	2	1	0	0	2	0	0	0	.250	.250	.375	78	0	0	.833	-1	*103*	*100*	/C-2	-0.1
Total	3	19	68	8	10	1	0	0	3	0	0	5	.147	.147	.162	-5	-8	0	.944	-1	55	0	/O-11(1-2-8),C-5,P-3,1	-0.7

LAUGHLIN, BEN Benjamin d4.28

Year	Tm Lg	G	AB	R	H	2B	3B	HR	RBI	BB-IB	HP	SO	AVG	OBP	SLG	AOPS	ABR	SB-CS	FA	FR	Rng	Thr	G at Pos	BFW
1873	Res NA	12	51	3	12	0	0	0	5	0		1	.235	.235	.235	44	-3	0-0	.698	-3	105	108	2-12	-0.5

LAUTERBORN, BILL William Bernard B 6.9.1879 Hornell, NY D 4.19.1965 Andover, NY BR/TR 5-6/140# d9.20

Year	Tm Lg	G	AB	R	H	2B	3B	HR	RBI	BB-IB	HP	SO	AVG	OBP	SLG	AOPS	ABR	SB-CS	FA	FR	Rng	Thr	G at Pos	BFW
1904	Bos N	20	69	7	19	2	0	0	2	1	0		.275	.286	.304	85	-1	1	.943	-2	99	29	2-20	-0.3
1905	Bos N	67	200	11	37	1	1	0	9	12	2		.185	.238	.200	32	-17	1	.843	-10	91	0	3-29,2-23/S-3,O-2(CF)	-2.7
Total	2	87	269	18	56	3	1	0	11	13	2		.208	.250	.227	45	-18	2	.929	-11	101	33	/2-43,3-29,S-3,O-2(CF)	-3.0

LAVAGETTO, COOKIE Harry Arthur B 12.1.1912 Oakland, CA D 8.10.1990 Orinda, CA BR/TR 6/170# d4.17 Mil 1942-45 M5 C12

Year	Tm Lg	G	AB	R	H	2B	3B	HR	RBI	BB-IB	HP	SO	AVG	OBP	SLG	AOPS	ABR	SB-CS	FA	FR	Rng	Thr	G at Pos	BFW
1934	Pit N	87	304	41	67	16	3	3	46	32	0	39	.220	.295	.322	64	-16	6	.961	-12	89	83	2-83	-2.2
1935	Pit N	78	231	27	67	9	4	0	19	18	0	15	.290	.341	.364	87	-4	1	.951	-9	92	49	2-42,3-15	-1.0
1936	Pit N	60	197	21	48	15	2	2	26	15	1	13	.244	.300	.371	78	-6	0	.951	-4	94	123	2-37,3-13/S	-0.8
1937	Bro N	149	503	64	142	26	6	8	70	74	1	41	.282	.375	.406	110	10	13	.949	-7	93	92	*2-100,3-45	1.1
1938	Bro N☆	137	487	68	133	34	6	6	79	68	2	31	.273	.364	.405	109	8	15	.929	-8	91	114	*3-132/2-4	0.5
1939	Bro N☆	153	587	93	176	28	5	10	87	78	5	30	.300	.387	.416	112	13	14	.948	-5	96	113	*3-149	1.3
1940	Bro N★	118	448	56	115	21	3	4	43	70	3	32	.257	.361	.344	90	-3	4	.932	-14	84	74	*3-116	-1.3
1941	†Bro N★	132	441	75	122	24	7	1	78	80	0	21	.277	.388	.370	109	9	7	.938	-18	87	87	*3-120	-0.5
1946	Bro N	88	242	36	57	9	1	3	27	38	0	17	.236	.339	.318	86	-3	3	.927	-4	91	118	3-67	-0.8
1947	†Bro N	41	69	6	18	1	0	3	11	12	0	5	.261	.370	.406	102	0	0	.961	1	100	116	3-18/1-3	0.2
Total	10	1043	3509	487	945	183	37	40	486	485	12	244	.269	.360	.377	98	8	63	.936	-79	91	99	3-675,2-266/1-3,S	-3.5

LaVALLIERE, MIKE Michael Eugene B 8.18.1960 Charlotte, NC BL/TR (BB 1987 (2 gameS)) 5-9/190# d9.9

Year	Tm Lg	G	AB	R	H	2B	3B	HR	RBI	BB-IB	HP	SO	AVG	OBP	SLG	AOPS	ABR	SB-CS	FA	FR	Rng	Thr	G at Pos	BFW
1984	Phi N	6	7	0	0	0	0	0	0	2-0	0	2	.000	.222	.000	-32	-1	0-0	1.000	1	0	90	/C-6	0.0

Year	Tm Lg	G	AB	R	H	2B	3B	HR	RBI	BB-IB	HP	SO	AVG	OBP	SLG	AOPS	ABR	SB-CS	FA	FR	Rng	Thr	G at Pos	BFW
1985	StL N	12	34	2	5	1	0	0	6	7-0	0	3	.147	.273	.176	34	-3	0-0	1.000	-0	159	54	C-12	-0.3
1986	StL N	110	303	18	71	10	2	3	30	36-5	1	37	.234	.318	.310	74	-10	0-1	.988	8	**167**	84	*C-108	0.2
1987	Pit N	121	340	33	102	19	0	1	36	43-9	1	32	.300	.377	.365	98	1	0-0	.992	18	**136**	**148**	*C-112	2.3
1988	Pit N	120	352	24	92	18	0	2	47	50-10	2	34	.261	.353	.330	99	2	3-2	.987	7	111	123	*C-114	1.7
1989	Pit N	68	190	15	60	10	0	2	23	29-7	0	24	.316	.406	.400	136	11	0-2	.991	-10	69	66	C-65	0.3
1990	†Pit N	96	279	27	72	15	0	3	31	44-8	2	20	.258	.362	.344	99	2	0-3	.990	5	114	113	C-95	1.1
1991	†Pit N	108	336	25	97	11	2	3	41	33-4	2	27	.289	.351	.360	103	2	2-1	**.998**	-3	91	95	*C-105	0.5
1992	†Pit N	95	293	22	75	13	1	2	29	44-14	1	21	.256	.350	.328	95	0	0-3	.994	-1	98	133	C-92/3	0.3
1993	Pit N	1	5	0	1	0	0	0	0	0-0	0	0	.200	.200	.200	7	-1	0-0	1.000	1	77	0	/C	0.0
	†Chi A	37	97	6	25	2	0	0	8	4-0	0	14	.258	.282	.278	54	-7	0-1	1.000	5	250	213	C-37	0.0
1994	Chi A	59	139	6	39	4	0	1	24	20-0	1	15	.281	.368	.331	86	-2	0-2	.991	3	77	116	C-57	0.3
1995	Chi A	46	98	7	24	6	0	1	19	9-0	0	15	.245	.303	.337	71	-4	0-0	.996	5	140	182	C-46	0.3
Total	12	879	2473	185	663	109	5	18	294	321-57	10	244	.268	.351	.338	94	-10	5-15	.992	39	119	117	C-850/3	6.7

LAVAN, DOC John Leonard (born John Leonard Laven) B 10.28.1890 Grand Rapids, MI D 5.29.1952 Detroit, MI BR/TR 5-8.5/151# d6.22

Year	Tm Lg	G	AB	R	H	2B	3B	HR	RBI	BB-IB	HP	SO	AVG	OBP	SLG	AOPS	ABR	SB-CS	FA	FR	Rng	Thr	G at Pos	BFW
1913	StL A	46	149	8	21	2	1	0	4	10	3	46	.141	.210	.168	11	-17	3	.899	-5	101	132	S-46	-2.1
	Phi A	5	14	1	1	0	1	0	1	0	0	0	.071	.071	.214	-17	-2	0	1.000	0	107	0	/S-5	-0.2
	Year	51	163	9	22	2	2	0	5	10	3	46	.135	.199	.172	9	-19	3	.906	-5	101	122	S-51	-2.3
1914	StL A	75	239	21	63	7	4	1	21	17	2	39	.264	.318	.339	101	-1	6-12	.916	-14	89	60	S-74	-1.4
1915	StL A	157	514	44	112	17	7	1	48	42	3	83	.218	.281	.284	72	-19	13-19	.913	9	104	**139**	*S-157	-0.4
1916	StL A	110	343	32	81	13	1	0	19	32	2	38	.236	.305	.280	80	-8	7	.950	26	**121**	**140**	*S-106	2.7
1917	StL A	118	355	19	85	8	5	0	30	19	3	34	.239	.284	.290	78	-11	5	.923	13	107	**135**	*S-110/2-7	1.0
1918	Was A	117	464	44	129	17	2	0	45	14	2	21	.278	.302	.323	90	-8	12	.917	-18	91	96	*S-117/O(CF)	-2.0
1919	StL N	100	356	25	86	12	2	1	25	11	0	30	.242	.264	.295	72	-13	4	.929	9	105	110	S-99	0.3
1920	StL N	142	516	52	149	21	10	1	63	19	3	38	.289	.318	.374	102	-1	11-14	.942	10	103	108	*S-138	1.8
1921	StL N	150	560	58	145	23	11	2	82	23	2	30	.259	.291	.350	70	-26	7-7	.950	**21**	104	110	*S-150	1.0
1922	StL N	89	264	24	60	8	1	0	27	13	3	10	.227	.271	.265	41	-24	3-1	.937	5	102	92	S-82/3-5	-1.0
1923	StL N	50	111	10	22	6	0	1	12	9	1	7	.198	.264	.279	44	-9	0-3	.924	-2	99	119	S-40/3-4,1-3,2	-0.8
1924	StL N	4	6	0	0	0	0	0	0	0	0	0	.000	.000	.000	-99	-2	0-0	1.000	1	124	0	/2-2,S-2	-0.1
Total	12	1163	3891	338	954	134	45	7	377	209	24	376	.245	.288	.308	75	-141	71-56	.930	54	103	114	*S-1126/2-10,3-9,1-3,O(CF)	-1.2

LaVIGNE, ART Arthur David B 1.26.1885 Worcester, MA D 7.18.1950 Worcester, MA BR/TR 5-10/162# d4.24

Year	Tm Lg	G	AB	R	H	2B	3B	HR	RBI	BB-IB	HP	SO	AVG	OBP	SLG	AOPS	ABR	SB-CS	FA	FR	Rng	Thr	G at Pos	BFW
1914	Buf F	51	90	10	14	2	0	0	4	7	0	25	.156	.216	.178	8	-13	0	.967	4	*125*	*112*	C-34/1-3	-0.7

LAVIN, JOHNNY John B Troy, NY 5-11/175# d9.10

Year	Tm Lg	G	AB	R	H	2B	3B	HR	RBI	BB-IB	HP	SO	AVG	OBP	SLG	AOPS	ABR	SB-CS	FA	FR	Rng	Thr	G at Pos	BFW
1884	StL AA	16	52	9	11	2	0	0		3	1		.212	.268	.250	68	-2		.750	-2	41	0	O-16(0-15-1)	-0.4

LAW, RUDY Rudy Karl B 10.7.1956 Waco, TX BL/TL 6-1/165# d9.12

Year	Tm Lg	G	AB	R	H	2B	3B	HR	RBI	BB-IB	HP	SO	AVG	OBP	SLG	AOPS	ABR	SB-CS	FA	FR	Rng	Thr	G at Pos	BFW
1978	LA N	11	12	2	3	0	0	0	1	1-0	0	2	.250	.308	.250	58	-1	3-1	1.000	-1	49	0	/O-6(3-3-0)	-0.1
1980	LA N	128	388	55	101	5	4	1	23	23-1	3	27	.260	.306	.302	72	-16	40-13	.988	-1	98	97	*O-106(5-102-0)	-1.4
1982	Chi A	121	336	55	107	15	8	3	32	23-0	0	41	.318	.361	.438	118	8	36-10	.973	-2	102	38	O-94(4-90-0)/D-3	0.9
1983	†Chi A	141	501	95	142	20	7	3	34	42-2	2	36	.283	.340	.369	92	-5	77-12	**.994**	-5	94	69	*O-132(CF)/D-3	0.1
1984	Chi A	136	487	68	122	14	7	6	37	39-6	3	42	.251	.309	.345	77	-15	29-17	.985	-5	97	62	*O-130(10-122-0)	-2.2
1985	Chi A	125	390	62	101	21	6	4	36	27-0	3	40	.259	.311	.374	84	-9	29-6	.987	5	108	116	*O-120(104-32-0)/D-3	-0.3
1986	KC A	87	307	42	80	26	5	1	36	29-0	2	22	.261	.327	.388	92	-3	14-6	.987	-4	94	40	O-77(54-3-36)/D-2	-0.9
Total	7	749	2421	379	656	101	37	18	199	184-9	13	210	.271	.325	.366	88	-41	228-65	.986	-14	98	72	O-665(180-484-36)/D-11	-3.9

LAW, VANCE Vance Aaron B 10.1.1956 Boise, ID BR/TR 6-2/190# d6.1 f-Vern OF Total (6-LF 7-CF 2-RF)

Year	Tm Lg	G	AB	R	H	2B	3B	HR	RBI	BB-IB	HP	SO	AVG	OBP	SLG	AOPS	ABR	SB-CS	FA	FR	Rng	Thr	G at Pos	BFW
1980	Pit N	25	74	11	17	2	2	0	3	3-0	0	7	.230	.260	.311	58	-5	2-0	.964	-2	93	79	2-11/S-8,3	-0.5
1981	Pit N	30	67	1	9	0	1	0	3	2-0	0	15	.134	.157	.164	-8	-10	1-1	1.000	-1	99	99	2-19/S-7,3-2	-1.0
1982	Chi A	114	359	40	101	20	1	5	54	26-1	1	46	.281	.327	.384	96	-2	4-2	.953	3	102	96	S-85,3-39,2-10/O(LF)	0.9
1983	†Chi A	145	408	55	99	21	5	4	42	51-1	1	56	.243	.325	.348	83	-8	3-1	.966	9	104	106	*3-139/2-3,S-2,O(CF)D	-0.1
1984	Chi A	151	481	60	121	18	2	17	59	41-2	1	75	.252	.309	.403	92	-6	4-1	.955	-16	87	112	*3-137,2-22/O-5(CF),S-4	-2.3
1985	Mon N	147	519	75	138	30	6	10	52	86-0	2	96	.266	.369	.405	124	20	6-5	.985	4	100	111	*2-126,1-20,3-11/O(RF)	3.1
1986	Mon N	112	360	37	81	17	2	5	44	37-1	1	66	.225	.298	.325	73	-14	3-5	.993	10	105	97	2-94,1-20,3-13/P-3,O(RF)	-0.1
1987	Mon N	133	436	52	119	27	1	12	56	51-5	0	62	.273	.347	.422	100	1	8-5	.980	-12	96	83	*2-106,3-22,1-17/P-3	-0.7
1988	Chi N★	151	556	73	163	29	2	11	78	55-4	3	79	.293	.358	.412	116	13	1-4	.953	-10	92	83	*3-150/O(LF)	0.2
1989	†Chi N	130	408	38	96	22	3	7	42	38-0	0	73	.235	.296	.355	81	-10	2-2	.949	-16	82	74	*3-119/O(LF)	-2.8
1991	Oak A	74	134	11	28	7	1	0	9	18-0	0	27	.209	.303	.276	65	-6	0-0	.951	-7	78	82	3-67/S-3,O-3(LF),1P	-1.3
Total	11	1212	3802	453	972	193	26	71	442	408-14	9	602	.256	.326	.376	94	-27	34-26	.956	-38	92	93	3-700,2-391,S-109/1-58,O-14C,PD	-4.6

LAWING, GARLAND Garland Frederick "Knobby" B 8.29.1919 Gastonia, NC D 9.27.1996 Murrells Inlet, SC BR/TR 6-1/180# d5.29

Year	Tm Lg	G	AB	R	H	2B	3B	HR	RBI	BB-IB	HP	SO	AVG	OBP	SLG	AOPS	ABR	SB-CS	FA	FR	Rng	Thr	G at Pos	BFW
1946	Cin N	2	3	0	0	0	0	0	0	0	0	2	.000	.000	.000	-99	-1	0	—	-0	0	0	/O(CF)	-0.1
	NY N	8	12	2	2	0	0	0	0	0	0	3	.167	.167	.167	-5	-2	0	1.000	-0	109	0	/O-4(3-0-1)	-0.2
	Year	10	15	2	2	0	0	0	0	0	0	5	.133	.133	.133	-24	-3	0	1.000	-0	105	0	/O-5(3-1-1)	-0.3

LAWLESS, TOM Thomas James B 12.19.1956 Erie, PA BR/TR 5-11/170# d7.15 OF Total (14-LF 12-RF)

Year	Tm Lg	G	AB	R	H	2B	3B	HR	RBI	BB-IB	HP	SO	AVG	OBP	SLG	AOPS	ABR	SB-CS	FA	FR	Rng	Thr	G at Pos	BFW
1982	Cin N	49	165	19	35	6	0	0	4	9-0	0	30	.212	.253	.248	40	-13	16-5	.978	6	104	134	2-47	-0.3
1984	Cin N	43	80	10	20	2	0	1	2	8-1	0	12	.250	.318	.313	74	-3	6-3	1.000	-5	75	49	2-23/3-6	-0.7
	Mon N	11	17	1	3	1	0	0	0	0-0	0	4	.176	.176	.235	15	-2	1-0	1.000	-2	80	69	/2-9	-0.3
	Year	54	97	11	23	3	0	1	2	8-1	0	16	.237	.295	.299	66	-4	7-3	1.000	-7	76	54	2-32/3-6	-1.0
1985	†StL N	47	58	8	12	3	1	0	8	5-0	0	4	.207	.270	.293	58	-3	2-1	.971	1	137	145	3-13,2-11	-0.2
1986	StL N	46	39	5	11	1	0	0	3	2-0	0	8	.282	.310	.308	74	-1	8-1	.875	-1	86	125	3-12/2-7,O(LF)	-0.1
1987	†StL N	19	25	5	2	1	0	0	0	3-0	0	5	.080	.179	.120	-19	-4	2-0	1.000	0	142	132	/2-7,3-3,O(RF)	-0.4
1988	StL N	54	65	9	10	2	1	1	3	7-0	0	9	.154	.236	.262	42	-5	6-0	1.000	-1	81	47	3-24/O-6(4-0-2),2-5,1	-0.5
1989	Tor A	59	70	20	16	1	0	0	3	7-0	0	12	.229	.295	.243	55	-4	12-1	1.000	-1	95	0	O-16(7-0-9),3-12,D-12/2-7,C	-0.4
1990	Tor A	15	12	1	1	0	0	0	1	0-0	0	1	.083	.083	.083	-52	-2	0-2	.800	1	88	0	/3-4,O-2(LF),2D	-0.2
Total	8	343	531	78	110	17	2	2	24	41-1	0	85	.207	.263	.258	46	-37	53-13	.988	-2	98	108	2-117/3-74,O-26L,D-17,C1	-3.1

LAWLOR, MIKE Michael H. B 3.11.1854 Troy, NY D 8.3.1918 Troy, NY TR 6/180# d5.27

Year	Tm Lg	G	AB	R	H	2B	3B	HR	RBI	BB-IB	HP	SO	AVG	OBP	SLG	AOPS	ABR	SB-CS	FA	FR	Rng	Thr	G at Pos	BFW
1880	Tro N	4	9	1	1	0	0	0	0	1		1	.111	.200	.111	8	-1		.867	-0			/C-4	-0.1
1884	Was U	2	7	0	0	0	0	0		0			.000	.000	.000	-99	-2		1.000	1			/C-2	-0.1
Total	2	6	16	1	1	0	0	0	0	1		1	.063	.118	.063	-39	-3		.920	1			/C-6	-0.2

LAWRENCE, JIM James Ross B 2.12.1939 Hamilton, ON, CAN BL/TR 6-1/185# d5.30

Year	Tm Lg	G	AB	R	H	2B	3B	HR	RBI	BB-IB	HP	SO	AVG	OBP	SLG	AOPS	ABR	SB-CS	FA	FR	Rng	Thr	G at Pos	BFW
1963	Cle A	2	0	0	0	0	0	0	0	0-0	0	0	—	—	—	—	0	0-0	.750	-1	4	0	/C-2	-0.1

LAWRENCE, JOE Joseph Dudley B 2.13.1977 Lake Charles, LA BR/TR 6-2/190# d4.8

Year	Tm Lg	G	AB	R	H	2B	3B	HR	RBI	BB-IB	HP	SO	AVG	OBP	SLG	AOPS	ABR	SB-CS	FA	FR	Rng	Thr	G at Pos	BFW
2002	Tor A	55	150	16	27	4	0	2	15	16-0	2	38	.180	.262	.247	37	-14	2-1	.967	-7	97	64	2-49/D	-1.8

LAWRENCE, BILL William Henry B 3.11.1906 San Mateo, CA D 6.15.1997 Redwood City, CA BR/TR 6-4/194# d4.13

Year	Tm Lg	G	AB	R	H	2B	3B	HR	RBI	BB-IB	HP	SO	AVG	OBP	SLG	AOPS	ABR	SB-CS	FA	FR	Rng	Thr	G at Pos	BFW
1932	Det A	25	46	10	10	1	0	0	3	5	0	5	.217	.294	.239	38	-4	0-2	1.000	3	124	189	O-15(0-8-7)	-0.3

LAWRY, OTIS Otis Carroll "Rabbit" B 11.1.1893 Fairfield, ME D 10.23.1965 China, ME BL/TR 5-8/133# d6.28 Mil 1918

Year	Tm Lg	G	AB	R	H	2B	3B	HR	RBI	BB-IB	HP	SO	AVG	OBP	SLG	AOPS	ABR	SB-CS	FA	FR	Rng	Thr	G at Pos	BFW
1916	Phi A	41	123	10	25	0	0	0	4	9	1	21	.203	.263	.203	42	-9	4	.905	-4	101	67	2-29/O-5(3-2-0)	-1.4
1917	Phi A	30	55	7	9	1	0	0	1	2	0	9	.164	.193	.182	15	-6	1	.921	-2	97	36	2-17/O(LF)	-0.9
Total	2	71	178	17	34	1	0	0	5	11	1	30	.191	.242	.197	34	-15	5	.911	-6	100	57	/2-46,O-6(4-2-0)	-2.3

LAWTON, MARCUS Marcus Dwayne B 8.18.1965 Gulfport, MS BB/TR 6-1/160# d8.11 b-Matt

Year	Tm Lg	G	AB	R	H	2B	3B	HR	RBI	BB-IB	HP	SO	AVG	OBP	SLG	AOPS	ABR	SB-CS	FA	FR	Rng	Thr	G at Pos	BFW
1989	NY A	10	14	1	3	0	0	0	0	0-0	0	3	.214	.214	.214	21	-2	1-0	.818	-0	116	0	/O-8(7-0-1),D	-0.2

LAWTON, MATT Matthew B 11.3.1971 Gulfport, MS BL/TR 5-9/180# d9.5 b-Marcus

Year	Tm Lg	G	AB	R	H	2B	3B	HR	RBI	BB-IB	HP	SO	AVG	OBP	SLG	AOPS	ABR	SB-CS	FA	FR	Rng	Thr	G at Pos	BFW
1995	Min A	21	60	11	19	4	1	1	12	7-0	3	11	.317	.414	.467	128	3	1-1	.972	-1	90	112	O-19(1-12-8)/D	0.2
1996	Min A	79	252	34	65	7	1	6	42	28-1	4	28	.258	.339	.365	78	-9	4-4	.985	9	133	85	O-75(1-18-60)/D	-0.2
1997	Min A	142	460	74	114	29	3	14	60	76-3	10	81	.248	.366	.415	102	4	7-4	.976	1	101	109	*O-138(58-24-66)	0.0
1998	Min A	152	557	91	155	36	6	21	77	86-6	15	64	.278	.387	.478	122	21	16-8	.990	14	**119**	112	*O-151(12-47-100)	2.9
1999	Min A	118	406	58	105	18	0	7	54	57-7	6	42	.259	.353	.355	80	-11	26-4	.982	-3	102	41	*O-109(10-6-103)/D-6	-1.3
2000	Min A★	156	561	84	171	44	2	13	88	91-8	7	63	.305	.405	.460	115	18	23-7	.983	-4	100	45	*O-143(67-3-83)/D-9	0.9

Year	Tm Lg	G	AB	R	H	2B	3B	HR	RBI	BB-IB	HP	SO	AVG	OBP	SLG	AOPS	ABR	SB-CS	FA	FR	Rng	Thr	G at Pos	BFW
2001	Min A	103	376	71	110	25	0	10	51	63-6	3	46	.293	.396	.439	118	13	19-6	.980	-1	106	33	O-94(RF)/D-7	0.9
	NY N	48	183	24	45	11	1	3	13	22-0	8	34	.246	.352	.366	91	-2	10-2	1.000	-0	103	33	O-48(RF)	-0.3
2002	Cle A	114	416	71	98	19	2	15	57	59-0	8	34	.236	.342	.399	98	0	8-9	.975	5	114	97	*O-108(23-0-85)/D-3	-0.1
2003	Cle A	99	374	57	93	19	0	15	53	47-0	7	47	.249	.343	.420	103	3	10-3	.993	-4	89	87	O-74(62-0-13),D-21	-0.4
Total	9	1032	3645	575	975	212	16	105	507	536-31	71	450	.267	.370	.421	104	40	124-48	.984	17	107	76	O-959(234-110-660)/D-48	2.6
LAYDEN, GENE Eugene Francis B 3.14.1894 Pittsburgh, PA D 12.12.1984 Pittsburgh, PA BL/TL 5-10/160# d7.29																								
1915	NY A	3	7	2	2	0	0	0	0	0	0	1	.286	.286	.286	71	0	0-1	.750	-0	94	0	/O-2(CF)	-0.1
LAYDEN, PETE Peter John B 12.30.1919 Dallas, TX D 7.18.1982 Edna, TX BR/TR 5-11/185# d4.20																								
1948	StL A	41	104	11	26	2	1	0	4	6	1	10	.250	.297	.288	55	-7	4-2	.973	1	99	146	O-30(1-24-5)	-0.7
LAYNE, HERMAN Herman B 2.13.1901 New Haven, WV D 8.27.1973 Gallipolis, OH BR/TR 5-11/165# d4.16																								
1927	Pit N	11	6	3	0	0	0	0	0	1	0	0	.000	.143	.000	-55	-1	0	.000	-1	0	0	/O-2(1-1-0)	-0.2
LAYNE, HILLIS Ivoria Hillis "Tony" B 2.23.1918 Whitwell, TN BL/TR 6/170# d9.16 Mil 1942-43																								
1941	Was A	13	50	8	14	2	0	0	6	4	0	5	.280	.333	.320	77	-2	1-1	.953	-0	108	39	3-13	-0.1
1944	Was A	33	87	6	17	2	0	0	8	6	2	10	.195	.263	.218	40	-7	2-0	.949	1	106	32	3-18/2-3	-0.5
1945	Was A	61	147	23	44	5	4	1	14	10	2	7	.299	.352	.408	132	5	0-1	.956	-3	88	57	3-33	0.2
Total	3	107	284	37	75	9	4	1	28	20	4	22	.264	.321	.335	92	-4	3-2	.953	-2	97	46	/3-64,2-3	-0.4
LAYTON, LES Lester Lee B 11.18.1921 Nardin, OK BR/TR 6/165# d4.24																								
1948	NY N	63	91	14	21	4	4	2	12	6	1	21	.231	.286	.429	90	-2	1	.951	0	112	84	O-20(12-3-3)	-0.2
LAZOR, JOHNNY John Paul B 9.9.1912 Taylor, WA D 12.9.2002 Renton, WA BL/TR 5-9.5/180# d4.22																								
1943	Bos A	83	208	21	47	10	2	0	13	21	0	25	.226	.297	.293	72	-7	5-6	.979	3	102	153	O-63(51-7-8)	-1.0
1944	Bos A	16	24	0	2	1	0	0	0	1	0	0	.083	.120	.125	-30	-4	0-0	1.000	1	85	694	/O-6(1-0-5),C	-0.4
1945	Bos A	101	335	35	104	19	2	5	45	18	0	17	.310	.346	.424	120	7	3-2	.961	-6	88	76	O-81(12-0-73)	-0.5
1946	Bos A	23	29	1	4	0	0	1	4	2	0	11	.138	.194	.241	20	-3	0-0	1.000	-0	95	0	/O-7(3-0-4)	-0.4
Total	4	223	596	57	157	30	4	6	62	42	0	53	.263	.312	.357	92	-7	8-8	.971	-3	94	123	O-157(67-7-90)/C	-2.3
LAZZERI, TONY Anthony Michael "Poosh 'Em Up Tony" B 12.6.1903 San Francisco, CA D 8.6.1946 San Francisco, CA BR/TR 5-11.5/170# d4.13 C1 HF1991																								
1926	†NY A	**155**	589	79	162	28	14	18	114	54	2	96	.275	.338	.462	109	3	16-7	.961	-18	95	90	*2-149/S-5,3	-0.8
1927	†NY A	153	570	92	176	29	8	18	102	69	0	82	.309	.383	.482	127	22	22-14	.971	8	**111**	104	*2-113,S-38/3-9	3.5
1928	†NY A	116	404	62	134	30	11	10	82	43	1	50	.332	.397	.535	148	28	15-5	.956	-7	97	92	*2-110	2.4
1929	NY A	147	545	101	193	37	11	18	106	68	4	45	.354	.429	.561	164	54	9-10	.969	1	97	112	*2-147	5.2
1930	NY A	143	571	109	173	34	15	9	121	60	3	62	.303	.372	.462	115	13	4-4	.971	2	99	79	2-77,3-60/S-8,10(LF)	2.0
1931	NY A	135	484	67	129	27	7	8	83	79	1	80	.267	.371	.401	109	9	18-9	.958	-4	100	96	2-90,3-39	1.2
1932	†NY A	142	510	79	153	28	16	15	113	82	2	64	.300	.399	.506	140	32	11-11	.978	4	91	84	*2-134/3-5	3.9
1933	NY A☆	139	523	94	154	22	12	18	104	73	2	62	.294	.383	.486	137	28	15-7	.968	-12	88	80	*2-138	2.4
1934	NY A	123	438	59	117	24	6	14	67	71	0	64	.267	.369	.445	117	12	11-1	.976	-15	91	91	2-92,3-30	0.5
1935	NY A	130	477	72	130	18	6	13	83	63	3	75	.273	.361	.417	107	5	11-5	.970	-21	85	103	*2-118/S-9	-0.7
1936	†NY A	150	537	82	154	29	6	14	109	97	1	65	.287	.397	.441	110	12	8-5	.968	-37	84	92	*2-148/S-2	-1.4
1937	†NY A	126	446	56	109	21	3	14	70	71	0	76	.244	.348	.399	87	-9	7-1	.966	-9	101	84	*2-125	-0.8
1938	†Chi N	54	120	21	32	5	0	5	23	22	0	30	.267	.380	.433	120	4	0	.946	-5	88	94	S-25/3-7,2-4,O(LF)	0.1
1939	Bro N	14	39	6	11	2	0	3	6	10	2	7	.282	.451	.564	165	4	1	.914	-2	97	124	2-11/3-2	0.4
	NY N	13	44	7	13	0	0	1	8	7	0	6	.295	.392	.364	103	0	0	.889	-2	86	45	3-13	-0.1
	Year	27	83	13	24	2	0	4	14	17	2	13	.289	.422	.458	133	5	1	.897	-4	87	42	3-15,2-11	0.3
Total	14	1740	6297	986	1840	334	115	178	1191	869	21	864	.292	.380	.467	122	217	148-79	.967	-115	94	93	*2-1456,3-166/S-87,O-2(LF),1	17.8
LEACH, FREDDY Frederick B 11.23.1897 Springfield, MO D 12.10.1981 Hagerman, ID BL/TR 5-11/183# d5.24																								
1923	Phi N	52	104	5	27	4	0	1	16	3	0	14	.260	.280	.327	54	-7	1-2	.950	-2	97	0	O-26(17-9-1)	-1.0
1924	Phi N	8	28	6	13	2	1	2	7	2	0	1	.464	.500	.821	221	5	0-0	1.000	-0	67	172	/O-7(LF)	0.4
1925	Phi N	65	292	47	91	15	4	5	28	5	0	21	.312	.323	.442	86	-7	1-2	.952	-5	97	32	O-65(CF)	-1.5
1926	Phi N	129	492	73	162	29	7	11	71	16	1	33	.329	.352	.484	117	10	6	.979	6	105	126	*O-123(48-84-8)	0.9
1927	Phi N	140	536	69	164	30	4	12	83	21	8	32	.306	.342	.444	108	4	2	.981	16	107	**182**	*O-140(18-123-5)	1.4
1928	Phi N	145	588	83	179	36	11	13	96	30	4	30	.304	.342	.469	107	3	4	.978	7	108	109	*O-120(93-22-7),1-25	0.0
1929	NY N	113	411	74	119	22	6	8	47	17	4	14	.290	.324	.431	85	-11	10	.974	-12	78	32	O-95(94-0-1)	-2.8
1930	NY N	126	544	90	178	19	13	13	71	22	7	25	.327	.361	.482	104	1	3	.978	-5	85	125	*O-124(LF)	-1.2
1931	NY N	129	515	75	159	30	5	6	61	29	2	9	.309	.348	.421	109	5	4	.976	-1	100	98	*O-125(LF)	-0.2
1932	Bos N	84	223	21	55	9	2	1	29	18	1	10	.247	.306	.318	71	-9	1	.977	-2	100	43	O-50(8-22-21)	-1.4
Total	10	991	3733	543	1147	196	53	72	509	163	27	189	.307	.341	.446	101	-6	32-4	.975	3	98	104	O-875(534-325-43)/1-25	-5.4
LEACH, JALAL Jalal Donnell B 3.14.1969 San Francisco, CA BL/TL 6-2/200# d9.5																								
2001	SF N	8	10	0	1	0	0	0	1	2-0	0	3	.100	.250	.100	-5	-2	0-0	1.000	-1	35	0	/O-3(1-0-2)	-0.2
LEACH, RICK Richard Max B 5.4.1957 Ann Arbor, MI BL/TL 6/195# d4.30																								
1981	Det A	54	83	9	16	3	1	1	11	16-1	0	15	.193	.320	.289	75	-2	0-1	1.000	-1	132	122	1-32,O-15(RF)/D-2	-0.5
1982	Det A	82	218	23	52	7	2	3	12	21-2	0	29	.239	.303	.330	74	-8	4-0	.995	-3	88	98	1-56,O-14(4-0-10)/D-4	-1.3
1983	Det A	99	242	22	60	17	0	3	26	19-1	1	21	.248	.305	.355	83	-5	2-2	.994	2	113	87	1-73,O-13(2-0-11)/D-3	-0.8
1984	Tor A	65	88	11	23	6	2	0	7	8-0	0	14	.261	.320	.375	89	-1	0-0	1.000	3	93	132	O-23(5-1-17),1-15/PD	0.0
1985	Tor A	16	35	2	7	0	1	0	1	3-1	0	9	.200	.263	.257	42	-3	0-0	.987	0	106	141	1-10/O-4(1-0-3)	-0.3
1986	Tor A	110	246	35	76	14	1	5	39	13-3	0	24	.309	.335	.435	108	2	0-0	.978	-4	79	0	D-42,O-39(19-0-20)/1-7	-0.5
1987	Tor A	98	195	26	55	13	1	3	25	25-2	3	25	.282	.371	.405	104	2	0-1	.981	-2	95	53	O-43(21-0-22),D-30/1-5	-0.2
1988	Tor A	87	199	21	55	13	1	0	23	18-3	0	27	.276	.336	.352	93	-1	0-1	1.000	2	107	51	O-49(14-0-36),D-25/1-4	-0.2
1989	Tex A	110	239	32	65	14	1	1	23	32-7	1	33	.272	.358	.351	100	1	2-1	.951	-1	96	59	D-44,O-41(37-0-3)/1-4	-0.2
1990	SF N	78	174	24	51	13	0	2	16	21-0	1	20	.293	.372	.402	117	5	0-2	.989	2	109	109	O-52(13-0-40)/1-7	0.5
Total	10	799	1719	205	460	100	10	18	183	176-20	6	217	.268	.335	.369	94	-10	8-8	.983	-3	95	59	O-293(116-1-177),1-213,D-156/P	-3.5
LEACH, TOMMY Thomas William B 11.4.1877 French Creek, NY D 9.29.1969 Haines City, FL BR/TR 5-6.5/150# d9.28 OF Total (74-LF 996-CF 13-RF)																								
1898	Lou N	3	10	0	1	0	0	0	0	0	0		.100	.100	.100	-43	-2	0	.727	-1	116	0	/3-3,2	-0.2
1899	Lou N	106	406	75	117	10	6	5	57	37	1		.288	.349	.379	100	-1	19	.908	-5	105	108	3-80,S-25/2-2	-0.3
1900	†Pit N	51	160	20	34	1	2	1	16	21	0		.213	.304	.262	57	-9	8	.864	0	97	110	3-31/S-8,2-7,O-4(2-0-2)	-0.7
1901	Pit N	98	374	64	114	12	13	2	44	20	4		.305	.347	.422	119	7	16	.903	10	112	105	3-92/S-4	1.9
1902	Pit N	135	514	97	143	14	**22**	**6**	85	45	4		.278	.341	.426	132	17	25	.926	12	112	66	*3-134	3.4
1903	†Pit N	127	507	97	151	16	17	7	87	40	2		.298	.352	.438	121	11	22	.879	4	**111**	129	*3-127	1.8
1904	Pit N	146	579	92	149	15	12	2	56	45	5		.257	.316	.335	98	-2	23	.907	**36**	**128**	115	*3-146	4.0
1905	Pit N	131	499	71	128	10	14	2	53	37	1		.257	.309	.345	92	-6	17	.988	9	117	92	O-71(16-51-6),3-58/2-2,S-2	0.1
1906	Pit N	133	476	66	136	10	7	1	39	33	1		.286	.333	.342	106	2	21	.929	-2	103	58	3-65,O-60(15-44-1)/S	-0.1
1907	Pit N	149	547	102	166	19	12	4	43	40	1		.303	.352	.404	135	20	43	.980	5	96	136	*O-111(2-109-0),3-33/S-6,2	2.4
1908	Pit N	152	583	93	151	24	16	5	41	54	2		.259	.324	.381	125	15	24	.937	-7	96	109	*3-150/O-2(CF)	1.5
1909	†Pit N	151	587	**126**	153	29	8	6	43	66	2		.261	.337	.368	110	7	27	.969	-5	59	75	*O-138(CF),3-13	-0.4
1910	Pit N	135	529	83	143	24	5	4	52	38	0	62	.270	.319	.357	92	-7	18	.966	4	**113**	76	*O-131(CF)/S-2,2	-1.0
1911	Pit N	108	386	60	92	12	6	3	43	46	2	50	.238	.323	.324	78	-11	19	.987	4	111	126	O-89(1-89-0),S-13/3	-1.2
1912	Pit N	28	97	24	29	4	2	0	19	12	0	9	.299	.376	.381	109	1	6	.986	2	109	103	O-24(CF)	0.2
	Chi N	82	265	50	64	10	3	2	32	55	3	20	.242	.378	.325	93	1	14	.975	-0	100	93	O-73(CF)/3-4	-0.5
	Year	110	362	74	93	14	5	2	51	67	3	29	.257	.377	.340	98	2	20	.978	2	102	95	O-97(CF)/3-4	-0.3
1913	Chi N	131	456	**99**	131	23	10	6	32	77	1	44	.287	.391	.421	132	22	21-10	**.990**	-0	99	93	*O-121(3-118-0)/3-2	1.6
1914	Chi N	153	577	80	152	24	9	7	46	79	1	50	.263	.353	.373	116	13	16	.968	3	108	103	*O-136(CF),3-16	0.8
1915	Cin N	107	335	42	75	7	5	0	17	56	2	38	.224	.338	.275	85	-3	20-14	.959	-2	98	85	O-96(17-81-0)	-1.3
1918	Pit N	30	72	14	14	2	3	0	5	19	0	5	.194	.363	.306	101	1	2	.952	-1	95	128	O-23(18-0-4)/S-3	0.0
Total	19	2156	7959	1355	2143	266	172	63	810	820	32	278	.269	.340	.370	108	76	361-24	.975	68	98	91	*O-1079C,3-955/S-64,2-14	12.0
LEAHY, DAN Daniel C. B 8.8.1870 Knoxville, TN D 12.30.1903 Knoxville, TN 5-9/155# d9.2																								
1896	Phi N	2	6	0	2	1	0	0	1	1	0	2	.333	.429	.500	146	0	0	.857	0	121	0	/S-2	0.1
LEAHY, TOM Thomas Joseph B 6.2.1869 New Haven, CT D 6.11.1951 New Haven, CT BR/TR 5-7.5/168# d5.18																								
1897	Pit N	24	92	10	24	3	3	0	12	7	1		.261	.320	.359	82	-3	3	.935	-4	52	0	O-13(7-4-2)/C-6,3-6	-0.6

Year	Tm Lg	G	AB	R	H	2B	3B	HR	RBI	BB-IB	HP	SO	AVG	OBP	SLG	AOPS	ABR	SB-CS	FA	FR	Rng	Thr	G at Pos	BFW
	Was N	19	52	12	20	2	1	0	7	9	7		.385	.529	.462	164	7	6	.727	-1	237	0	O-10(2-8-0)/3-5,2-3,C	0.5
	Year	43	144	22	44	5	4	0	19	16	8		.306	.405	.396	115	4	9	.881	-5	108	0	O-23(9-12-2),3-11/C-7,2-3	-0.1
1898	Was N	15	55	10	10	2	0	0	5	8	1		.182	.297	.218	48	-3	6	.913	0	99	51	3-12/2-3	-0.2
1901	Mil A	33	99	18	24	6	2	0	10	11	5		.242	.348	.343	97	0	3	.941	-6	*70*	*106*	C-28/O-2(RF),2	-0.2
	Phi A	5	15	1	5	1	0	0	1	1	0		.333	.375	.400	110	0	0	1.000	-0	0	0	/O-2(LF),CS	0.0
	Year	38	114	19	29	7	2	0	11	12	5		.254	.351	.351	99	1	3	.944	-6	*74*	*109*	C-29/O-4(2-0-2),2S	-0.2
1905	StL N	35	97	3	22	1	3	0	7	8	0		.227	.286	.299	77	-3	0	.946	-7	*79*	*92*	C-29	-0.8
Total	4	131	410	54	105	15	9	0	42	44	14		.256	.348	.337	93	-2	18	.942	-17	*77*	*98*	/C-65,O-27(11-12-4),3-23,2-7,S	-1.3
LEAR, FRED Frederick Francis "King" B 4.7.1894 New York, NY D 10.13.1955 E.Orange, NJ BR/TR 6-0.5/180# d6.7																								
1915	Phi A	2	2	0	0	0	0	0	0	0	0	2	.000	.000	.000	-99	-1	0	.600	-1	0	0	/3-2	-0.1
1918	Chi N	2	1	0	0	0	0	0	0	1	0	0	.000	.500	.000	56	0	0	—	0			H	0.0
1919	Chi N	40	76	8	17	3	1	1	11	8	1	11	.224	.306	.329	90	-1	2	.990	-3	40	94	/1-9,2-9,S-3	-0.4
1920	NY N	31	87	12	22	0	1	1	7	8	1	15	.253	.323	.310	83	-2	0-2	.951	-1	101	163	3-24/2	-0.3
Total	4	75	166	20	39	3	2	2	18	17	2	28	.235	.314	.313	84	-4	2-2	.924	-4	96	155	/3-26,2-10,1-9,S-3	-0.8
LEARD, BILL William Wallace "Wild Bill" B 10.14.1885 Oneida, NY D 1.15.1970 San Francisco, CA BR/TR 5-10/155# d7.21																								
1917	Bro N	3	3	0	0	0	0	0	0	0	0	1	.000	.000	.000	-97	-1	0	—	-0	0	0	/2	-0.1
LEARY, JACK John J. B 1858 New Haven, CT TL 5-11/186# d8.21 ▲ OF Total (4-LF 15-CF 21-RF)																								
1880	Bos N	1	3	1	0	0	0	0	0	1		0	.000	.250	.000	-7	0		1.000	1	940	0	/O(RF)P	0.0
1881	Det N	3	11	2	3	1	1	0	4	1		1	.273	.333	.545	165	1		.833	-0	145	0	/O-2(0-1-1),P-2	0.0
1882	Pit AA	60	257	32	75	7	3	1		5			.292	.305	.354	128	7		.759	-9	93	33	3-33,O-27(0-8-19)/P-3,12	-0.2
	Bal AA	4	18	3	4	1	0	0		0			.222	.222	.278	73	0		.900	-0	105	0	/P-3,O(CF)	0.0
	Year	64	275	35	79	8	3	1		5			.287	.300	.349	124	7		.759	-9	93	33	3-33,O-28(0-9-19)/P-6,12	-0.2
1883	Lou AA	40	165	16	31	1	3	3		2			.188	.198	.285	58	-8		.816	-4	91	121	S-40	-0.9
	Bal AA	3	11	1	2	0	2	0		0			.182	.182	.545	122	0		.727	-1	69	228	/2-3	-0.1
	Year	43	176	17	33	1	5	3		2			.188	.197	.301	62	-8		.816	-5	91	121	S-40/2-3	-1.0
1884	Alt U	8	33	1	3	0	0	0		1			.091	.118	.091	-35	-7		.692	-2	0	0	/O-6(4-2-0),P-3,3	-0.6
	CP U	10	40	0	7	1	0	0		0			.175	.175	.200	13	-5		.840	-2	83	0	/2-4,3-3,O-3(CF),P-2	-0.6
	Year	18	73	1	10	1	0	0		1			.137	.149	.151	-9	-12		.625	-4	78	0	/O-9(4-5-0),P-5,3-4,2-4	-1.2
Total	5	129	538	56	125	11	9	4	4	10		1	.232	.246	.309	84	-12		.816	-17	91	121	/S-40,O-40R,3-37,P-14,2-8,1	-2.4
LEARY, JOHN John Louis "Jack" B 5.2.1891 Waltham, MA D 8.18.1961 Waltham, MA BR/TR 5-11.5/180# d4.14																								
1914	StL A	144	533	35	141	28	7	0	45	10	3	71	.265	.282	.343	91	-9	9-15	.987	-3	94	99	*1-130,C-15	-2.0
1915	StL A	75	227	19	55	10	0	0	15	5	3	36	.242	.268	.286	69	-10	2-4	.985	-2	118	164	1-53,C-11	-1.4
Total	2	219	760	54	196	38	7	0	60	15	6	107	.258	.278	.326	85	-19	11-19	.987	-5	100	116	1-183/C-26	-3.4
LEATHERS, HAL Harold Langford "Chuck" B 12.2.1898 Selma, CA D 4.12.1977 Modesto, CA BL/TR 5-8/152# d9.13																								
1920	Chi N	9	23	3	7	1	0	1	0	1	0	1	.304	.333	.478	129	1	1-0	.825	-2	89	0	/S-6,2-3	0.0
LEBER, EMIL Emil Bohmiel B 5.15.1881 Cleveland, OH D 11.6.1924 Cleveland, OH BR/TR 5-11/170# d9.2																								
1905	Cle A	2	6	1	0	0	0	0	0	1	0		.000	.143	.000	-53	-1	0	1.000	0	137	0	/3-2	-0.1
LeBOURVEAU, BEVO De Witt Wiley B 8.24.1894 Dana, CA D 12.10.1947 Nevada City, CA BL/TR 5-11/175# d9.9																								
1919	Phi N	17	63	4	17	0	0	0	0	10	0	8	.270	.370	.270	88	0	2	1.000	2	82	275	O-15(15-0-2)	0.1
1920	Phi N	84	261	29	67	7	2	3	12	11	3	36	.257	.295	.333	76	-8	9-6	.949	3	91	195	O-72(51-17-4)	-1.0
1921	Phi N	93	281	42	83	12	5	6	35	29	0	51	.295	.361	.438	102	1	4-5	.911	-6	89	76	O-76(27-1-48)	-1.1
1922	Phi N	74	167	24	45	8	3	2	20	24	2	29	.269	.368	.389	87	-3	0-3	.920	-3	92	81	O-42(33-4-5)	-0.9
1929	Phi A	12	16	1	5	0	1	0	2	5	0	1	.313	.476	.438	132	1	0-1	1.000	0	116	0	/O-3(0-2-1)	0.1
Total	5	280	788	100	217	27	11	11	69	79	5	125	.275	.345	.379	91	-9	15-15	.935	-4	90	134	O-208(126-24-60)	-2.8
LeCROY, MATT Matthew Hanks B 12.13.1975 Belton, SC BR/TR 6-2/225# d4.3																								
2000	Min A	56	167	18	29	10	0	5	17	17-2	2	38	.174	.254	.323	44	-15	0-0	.988	2	124	76	C-49/1-3,D-3	-0.9
2001	Min A	15	40	6	17	5	0	3	12	0-0	1	8	.425	.429	.775	206	6	0-1	1.000	0	72	338	/C-3,1-2,D-9	0.5
2002	†Min A	63	181	19	47	11	1	7	27	13-1	0	38	.260	.306	.448	97	-1	0-2	.976	-1	31	205	D-41/1-8,C-6	-0.6
2003	†Min A	107	345	39	99	19	0	17	64	25-1	4	82	.287	.342	.490	115	7	0-1	.980	-8	71	95	D-64,C-22,1-17	-0.6
Total	4	241	733	82	192	45	1	32	120	55-4	7	166	.262	.317	.457	98	-3	0-4	.987	-7	104	81	D-117/C-80,1-30	-1.6
LEDEE, RICKY Ricardo Alberto B 11.22.1973 Ponce, P.R. BL/TL 6-2/190# d6.14																								
1998	†NY A	42	79	13	19	5	2	1	12	7-0	0	29	.241	.299	.392	82	-2	3-1	.981	1	95	263	O-42(36-3-4)	-0.2
1999	†NY A	88	250	45	69	13	5	9	40	28-5	0	73	.276	.346	.476	109	3	4-3	.942	-1	107	71	O-77(69-6-3)/D-5	0.0
2000	NY A	62	191	23	46	11	1	7	31	26-2	1	39	.241	.332	.419	90	-3	7-3	.979	-1	101	37	O-49(46-4-1),D-10	-0.6
	Cle A	17	63	13	14	2	1	2	8	8-0	0	9	.222	.310	.381	72	-3	0-0	1.000	1	119	99	O-17(12-0-6)	-0.2
	Tex A	58	213	23	50	6	3	4	38	25-2	1	50	.235	.317	.347	67	-11	6-3	.977	-1	110	0	O-57(20-3-42)	-1.3
	Year	137	467	59	110	19	5	13	77	59-4	2	98	.236	.322	.381	77	-17	13-6	.981	-1	108	28	*O-123(78-7-49),D-10	-2.1
2001	Tex A	78	242	33	56	21	1	2	36	23-0	3	58	.231	.303	.351	70	-10	3-3	.979	-2	102	24	O-72(6-10-60)	-1.5
2002	Phi N	96	203	33	46	13	1	8	23	35-0	1	50	.227	.342	.419	108	2	1-2	1.000	-2	98	0	O-51(10-40-5)	-0.1
2003	Phi N	121	255	37	63	15	2	13	46	34-5	0	59	.247	.334	.475	115	5	0-0	1.000	-3	80	156	O-71(29-42-1)/D-2	0.2
Total	6	562	1496	220	363	86	16	46	234	186-14	6	367	.243	.327	.414	92	-19	24-15	.978	-8	101	67	O-436(228-108-122)/D-17	-3.7
LEDESMA, AARON Aaron David B 6.3.1971 Union City, CA BR/TR 6-2/200# d7.2																								
1995	NY N	21	33	4	8	0	0	0	3	6-1	0	7	.242	.359	.242	64	-1	0-0	.875	-1	113	0	3-10/1-2,S-2	-0.2
1997	Bal A	43	88	24	31	5	1	2	11	13-0	1	9	.352	.437	.500	149	7	1-0	.973	-3	87	79	2-22,3-11/1-5,S-4	0.5
1998	TB A	95	299	30	97	16	3	0	29	9-1	1	51	.324	.344	.398	91	-4	9-7	.971	16	110	154	S-58,2-19/3-7,1-2,D-6	1.5
1999	TB A	93	294	32	78	15	0	0	30	14-1	3	35	.265	.305	.316	58	-18	1-1	.978	12	95	99	S-50,3-26,2-17/1-4,D	-0.2
2000	Col N	32	40	4	9	2	0	0	3	2-0	1	9	.225	.279	.275	32	-4	0-0	1.000	0	58	0	/3-5,1-3	-0.4
Total	5	284	754	94	223	38	4	2	76	44-3	6	111	.296	.338	.365	80	-20	11-8	.974	24	102	126	S-114/3-59,2-58,1-16,D-7	1.2
LEDWITH, MIKE Michael B Brooklyn, NY D 1.2.1929 Bronx, NY d8.19																								
1874	Atl NA	1	4	1	1	0	0	0	1	0		0	.250	.250	.250	69	0	0-0	.600	-1			/C	-0.1
LEE, CARLOS Carlos (Noriel) B 6.20.1976 Aguadulce, Panama BR/TR 6-2/200# d5.7																								
1999	Chi A	127	492	66	144	32	2	16	84	13-0	4	72	.293	.312	.463	95	-5	4-2	.981	-2	103	47	*O-105(LF),D-16/1-5	-1.1
2000	†Chi A	152	572	107	172	29	2	24	92	38-1	3	94	.301	.345	.484	106	4	13-4	.990	-4	92	113	*O-149(LF)/D-2	-0.4
2001	Chi A	150	558	75	150	33	3	24	84	38-2	6	85	.269	.321	.468	101	0	17-7	.969	-1	97	117	*O-130(LF),D-17	-0.5
2002	Chi A	140	492	82	130	26	2	26	80	75-4	2	73	.264	.359	.484	121	16	1-4	.996	-2	93	103	*O-137(LF)/D-2	0.7
2003	Chi A	158	623	100	181	35	1	31	113	37-2	4	91	.291	.331	.499	115	12	18-4	.978	1	103	89	*O-156(LF)/D	0.9
Total	5	727	2737	430	777	155	10	121	453	201-9	19	415	.284	.334	.480	108	27	53-21	.983	-7	97	96	O-677(LF)/D-38,1-5	-0.4
LEE, CLIFF Clifford Walker B 8.4.1896 Lexington, NE D 8.25.1980 Denver, CO BR/TR 6-1/175# d5.15																								
1919	Pit N	42	112	5	22	2	4	0	2	6	0	8	.196	.237	.286	55	-7	2	.962	-6	*116*	*54*	C-28/O-6(2-2-2)	-1.2
1920	Pit N	37	76	9	18	2	2	0	8	4	0	14	.237	.275	.316	67	-3	0-1	.974	0	*93*	*124*	C-19/O-2(1-1-0)	-0.3
1921	Phi N	88	286	31	88	14	4	4	29	13	0	34	.308	.338	.427	94	-3	5-2	.987	-5	79	101	1-48,O-27(2-1-24)/C-2	-1.2
1922	Phi N	122	422	65	136	29	6	17	77	32	1	43	.322	.371	.540	121	12	2-3	.967	-4	92	92	O-89(83-0-6),1-18/3	-0.1
1923	Phi N	107	355	54	114	20	4	11	47	20	0	39	.321	.357	.493	110	4	3-3	.959	-2	98	58	O-83(54-0-32),1-16	-0.5
1924	Phi N	21	56	4	14	3	2	1	7	2	0	5	.250	.276	.429	77	-2	0-1	1.000	1	116	82	O-13(RF)/1-4	-0.3
	Cin N	6	6	1	2	1	0	0	2	0	0	2	.333	.333	.500	122	0	0-0	—	-0	0	0	/O(RF)	0.0
	Year	27	62	5	16	4	2	1	9	2	0	7	.258	.281	.435	82	-2	0-1	1.000	0	115	81	O-14(RF)/1-4	-0.3
1925	Cle A	77	230	43	74	15	6	4	42	21	0	33	.322	.378	.491	118	6	2-1	.951	1	105	113	O-70(0-15-56)	0.3
1926	Cle A	21	40	4	7	1	0	1	2	6	0	8	.175	.283	.275	45	-3	0-0	1.000	0	121	0	/O-9(6-1-2),C-3	-0.4
Total	8	521	1583	216	475	87	28	38	216	104	1	186	.300	.344	.462	103	4	14-11	.960	-15	99	80	O-300(148-20-136)/1-86,C-52,3	-3.7
LEE, DEREK Derek Gerald B 7.28.1966 Chicago, IL BL/TR 6-1/200# d6.27																								
1993	Min A	15	33	3	5	1	0	0	4	1-0	0	4	.152	.176	.182	-4	-5	0-0	1.000	-1	83	0	O-13(9-0-4)	-0.6
LEE, DERREK Derrek Leon B 9.6.1975 Sacramento, CA BR/TR 6-5/205# d4.28																								
1997	SD N	22	54	9	14	3	0	1	4	9-0	0	24	.259	.365	.370	101	0	0-0	1.000	1	119	95	1-21	0.0

Year	Tm Lg	G	AB	R	H	2B	3B	HR	RBI	BB-IB	HP	SO	AVG	OBP	SLG	AOPS	ABR	SB-CS	FA	FR	Rng	Thr	G at Pos	BFW
1998	Fla N	141	454	62	106	29	1	17	74	47-1	10	120	.233	.318	.414	96	-3	5-2	.993	10	132	103	*1-132	-0.4
1999	Fla N	70	218	21	45	9	1	5	20	17-1	0	70	.206	.263	.326	51	-18	2-1	.994	3	119	89	1-66	-1.9
2000	Fla N	158	477	70	134	18	3	28	70	63-6	4	123	.281	.368	.507	124	17	0-3	.993	6	117	96	*1-147	0.9
2001	Fla N	158	561	83	158	37	4	21	75	50-1	8	126	.282	.346	.474	114	11	4-2	.994	6	115	**116**	*1-156	0.4
2002	Fla N	**162**	581	95	157	35	7	27	86	98-8	5	164	.270	.378	.494	137	30	19-9	.992	5	113	96	*1-162	2.1
2003	†Fla N	155	539	91	146	31	2	31	92	88-7	10	131	.271	.379	.508	136	31	21-8	.996	2	101	**104**	*1-155	1.9
Total	7	866	2884	431	760	162	18	130	421	372-24	37	758	.264	.353	.467	117	68	51-25	.994	33	115	102	1-839	3.0
LEE, DUD Ernest Dudley (a/k/a Ernest Dudley In 1920-21) B 8.22.1899 Denver, CO D 1.7.1971 Denver, CO BL/TR 5-9/150# d10.3																								
1920	StL A	1	2	2	2	0	0	0	1	0	0	0	1.000	1.000	1.000	418	1	1-0	.333	-1	47	0	/S	0.0
1921	StL A	72	180	18	30	4	2	0	11	14	2	34	.167	.235	.211	14	-24	1-1	.922	-1	94	63	S-31,2-30/3-3	-2.0
1924	Bos A	94	288	36	73	9	4	0	29	40	3	17	.253	.350	.313	72	-11	8-4	.937	-6	92	96	S-90	-0.7
1925	Bos A	84	255	22	57	7	3	0	19	34	0	19	.224	.315	.275	51	-19	2-3	.924	13	109	127	S-84	0.1
1926	Bos A	2	7	2	1	0	0	0	0	0	1	0	.143	.250	.143	4	-1	0-0	1.000	-0	64	112	/S-2	-0.1
Total	5	253	732	80	163	20	9	0	60	88	6	70	.223	.311	.275	50	-54	12-8	.928	4	99	103	S-208/2-30,3-3	-2.7
LEE, HAL Harold Burnham "Sheriff" B 2.15.1905 Ludlow, MS D 9.4.1989 Pascagoula, MS BR/TR 5-11/180# d4.19																								
1930	Bro N	22	37	5	6	0	0	1	4	4	0	5	.162	.244	.243	19	-5	0	1.000	0	112	0	O-12(10-0-1)	-0.5
1931	Phi N	44	131	13	29	10	0	2	12	10	1	18	.221	.282	.344	62	-7	0	.967	1	110	45	O-38(26-11-2)	-0.8
1932	Phi N	149	595	76	180	42	10	18	85	36	1	45	.303	.343	.497	110	8	6	.965	9	114	114	*O-148(136-12-0)	0.9
1933	Phi N	46	167	25	48	12	2	0	12	18	1	13	.287	.360	.383	100	1	1	.981	1	100	141	O-45(LF)	0.0
	Bos N	88	312	32	69	15	9	1	28	18	1	26	.221	.266	.337	77	-11	1	.977	2	106	84	O-87(85-2-0)	-1.5
	Year	134	479	57	117	27	11	1	40	36	2	39	.244	.300	.353	87	-9	2	.978	3	104	103	*O-132(130-2-0)	-1.5
1934	Bos N	139	521	70	152	23	6	8	79	47	2	43	.292	.353	.405	111	8	3	.985	3	114	54	*O-128(LF)/2-4	0.3
1935	Bos N	112	422	49	128	18	6	0	39	18	1	25	.303	.333	.374	98	-3	0	.962	6	116	86	*O-110(98-0-12)	-0.2
1936	Bos N	152	565	46	143	24	7	3	64	52	2	50	.253	.318	.336	82	-15	4	.973	-8	96	43	*O-150(LF)	-3.0
Total	7	752	2750	316	755	144	40	33	323	203	9	225	.275	.326	.392	95	-24	15	.973	14	108	77	O-718(678-25-15)/2-4	-4.8
LEE, LEONIDAS Leonidas Pyrrhus (born Leonidas Pyrrhus Funkhouser) B 12.13.1860 St.Louis, MO D 6.11.1912 Hendersonville, NC d7.17																								
1877	StL N	4	18	0	5	1	0	0	0	0		1	.278	.278	.333	97	0		.667	-2	0	0	/O-4(1-2-1),S	-0.2
LEE, LERON Leron B 3.4.1948 Bakersfield, CA BL/TR 6/196# d9.5																								
1969	StL N	7	23	3	5	1	0	0	0	3-0	0	8	.217	.308	.261	60	-1	0-0	1.000	-0	60	230	/O-7(4-0-3)	-0.2
1970	StL N	121	264	28	60	13	1	6	23	24-4	1	66	.227	.290	.352	71	-11	5-1	.969	-2	98	68	O-77(1-0-76)	-1.5
1971	StL N	25	28	3	5	1	0	1	2	4-0	0	12	.179	.281	.321	68	-1	0-1	.800	-1	55	0	/O-8(5-0-4)	-0.3
	SD N	79	256	29	70	20	2	4	21	18-4	0	45	.273	.321	.414	115	4	4-5	.920	-5	66	128	O-68(LF)	-0.5
	Year	104	284	32	75	21	2	5	23	22-4	0	57	.264	.317	.405	108	3	4-6	.914	-6	65	121	O-76(73-0-4)	-0.8
1972	SD N	101	370	50	111	23	7	12	47	29-4	3	58	.300	.353	.497	151	23	2-5	.975	3	105	93	O-96(96-0-1)	2.0
1973	SD N	118	333	36	79	7	2	3	30	33-3	1	61	.237	.306	.297	74	-12	4-0	.970	2	100	126	O-84(72-0-14)	-1.4
1974	Cle A	79	232	18	54	13	0	5	25	15-2	0	42	.233	.279	.353	82	-6	3-2	.958	4	108	121	O-62(60-0-2)/D-2	-0.6
1975	Cle A	13	23	3	3	1	0	0	0	2-0	1	5	.130	.231	.174	16	-3	1-0	1.000	0	113	0	/O-5(LF),D-3	-0.3
	LA N	48	43	2	11	4	0	0	2	3-1	0	9	.256	.298	.349	85	-1	0-0	1.000	-0	40	0	/O-4(LF)	-0.1
1976	LA N	23	45	1	6	0	1	0	2	2-1	0	9	.133	.170	.178	-1	-6	0-0	1.000	-2	71	0	O-10(RF)	-0.9
Total	8	614	1617	173	404	83	13	31	152	133-19	6	315	.250	.307	.375	95	-14	19-14	.962	-1	94	104	O-421(315-0-110)/D-5	-3.8
LEE, MANUEL Manuel Lora "Manny" (born B 6.17.1965 San Pedro De Macoris, D.R. BB/TR 5-9/161# d4.10																								
1985	†Tor A	64	40	9	8	0	0	0	0	2-0	0	9	.200	.238	.200	21	-4	1-4	.971	1	98	97	2-38/S-8,3-5,D-8	-0.4
1986	Tor A	35	78	8	16	0	1	1	7	4-0	0	10	.205	.241	.269	39	-7	0-1	.990	-2	110	71	2-29/S-5/3-2	-0.8
1987	Tor A	56	121	14	31	2	3	1	11	6-0	0	13	.256	.289	.347	67	-6	2-0	.966	6	107	130	2-27,S-26/D	0.3
1988	Tor A	116	381	38	111	16	3	2	38	26-1	0	64	.291	.333	.365	96	-2	3-3	.988	8	102	106	2-98,S-23/3-8,D-2	0.9
1989	†Tor A	99	300	27	78	9	2	3	34	20-1	0	60	.260	.305	.333	82	-8	4-2	.985	-5	85	114	2-40,S-28,3-17,D-13/O(RF)	-1.0
1990	Tor A	117	391	45	95	12	4	6	41	26-0	0	90	.243	.288	.340	74	-15	3-1	**.993**	-12	89	93	*2-112/S-9	-2.4
1991	†Tor A	138	445	41	104	18	3	0	29	24-0	2	107	.234	.274	.288	54	-28	7-2	.967	-20	91	68	*S-138	-3.8
1992	†Tor A	128	396	49	104	10	1	3	39	50-0	0	73	.263	.343	.316	83	-8	6-2	.987	-11	89	88	*S-128	-0.9
1993	Tex A	73	205	31	45	3	1	1	12	22-3	2	39	.220	.300	.259	54	-13	2-4	.968	1	104	83	S-72/D	-0.8
1994	Tex A	95	335	41	93	18	2	2	38	21-0	0	66	.278	.319	.361	76	-12	3-1	.967	-1	105	95	S-85,2-13	-0.6
1995	StL N	1	1	1	1	0	0	0	0	0-0	0	0	1.000	1.000	1.000	431	0	0-0	.800	0	206	0	/2	0.1
Total	11	922	2693	304	686	88	20	19	249	201-5	4	531	.255	.305	.323	73	-103	31-20	.972	-35	96	85	S-522,2-358/3-32,D-25,O(RF)	-9.4
LEE, TERRY Terry James B 3.13.1962 San Francisco, CA BR/TR 6-5/215# d9.3																								
1990	Cin N	12	19	1	4	1	0	0	3	2-0	0	2	.211	.273	.263	50	-1	0-0	1.000	0	113	40	/1-6	-0.1
1991	Cin N	3	6	0	0	0	0	0	0	0-0	0	2	.000	.000	.000	-96	-2	0-0	1.000	1	413	0	/1-2	0.0
Total	2	15	25	1	4	1	0	0	3	2-0	0	4	.160	.214	.200	17	-3	0-0	1.000	1	193	29	/1-8	-0.1
LEE, TRAVIS Travis Reynolds B 5.26.1975 San Diego, CA BL/TL 6-3/205# d3.31																								
1998	Ari N	146	562	71	151	20	2	22	72	67-5	0	123	.269	.346	.429	103	2	8-1	.998	-2	96	92	*1-146	-1.3
1999	Ari N	120	375	57	89	16	2	9	50	58-4	0	50	.237	.337	.363	77	-13	17-3	**.997**	2	105	90	*1-114/O-2(RF)	-1.6
2000	Ari N	72	224	34	52	13	0	8	40	25-1	0	46	.232	.308	.397	75	-9	5-1	.983	5	125	105	O-55(0-2-54),1-23	-0.7
	Phi N	56	180	19	43	11	1	1	14	40-0	2	33	.239	.381	.328	81	-3	3-0	1.000	2	126	121	1-47,O-10(LF)	-0.4
	Year	128	404	53	95	24	1	9	54	65-1	2	79	.235	.342	.366	78	-12	8-1	.996	7	117	128	1-70,O-65(10-2-54)	-1.1
2001	Phi N	157	555	75	143	34	2	20	90	71-5	4	109	.258	.341	.434	103	3	3-4	.996	-7	81	101	*1-156	-1.9
2002	Phi N	153	536	55	142	26	2	13	70	54-10	0	104	.265	.331	.394	98	-5	5-3	.996	-6	83	103	*1-148	-2.4
2003	TB A	145	542	75	149	37	3	19	70	64-4	0	97	.275	.348	.459	114	12	6-2	.998	0	99	93	*1-142/D-2	-0.1
Total	6	849	2974	386	769	157	12	92	406	379-29	6	562	.259	.341	.412	97	-13	47-14	.997	-6	94	99	1-776/O-67(10-2-56),D-2	-8.4
LEE, BILLY William Joseph B 1.9.1892 Bayonne, NJ D 1.6.1984 West Hazleton, PA BR/TR 5-9/165# d4.15																								
1915	StL A	18	59	2	11	1	0	0	4	6	0	5	.186	.262	.203	41	-4	1-1	1.000	2	121	100	O-15(7-6-2)/3	-0.4
1916	StL A	7	11	1	2	0	0	0	0	1	0	1	.182	.250	.182	31	-1	0	1.000	-0	105	0	/O-4(0-2-2)	-0.1
Total	2	25	70	3	13	1	0	0	4	7	0	6	.186	.260	.200	39	-5	1-1	1.000	2	119	87	/O-19(7-8-4),3	-0.5
LEE, WATTY Wyatt Arnold B 8.12.1879 Lynch Station, VA D 3.6.1936 Washington, DC BL/TL 5-10.5/171# d4.30 ▲																								
1901	Was A	43	129	15	33	6	3	0	12	7	2		.256	.304	.349	82	-3	0	.948	1	108	120	P-36/O-7(2-1-4)	0.0
1902	Was A	109	391	61	100	21	5	4	45	33	3		.256	.319	.366	89	-6	8	.916	2	118	40	O-96(22-20-54),P-13	-0.8
1903	Was A	75	231	17	48	8	4	0	13	18	0		.208	.265	.277	62	-11	5	.930	5	110	136	O-47(0-10-37),P-22	-0.6
1904	Pit N	8	12	1	4	0	1	0	0	0	0		.333	.333	.500	152	1	0	.889	-0	111	0	/P-5	0.0
Total	4	235	763	94	185	35	13	4	70	58	5		.242	.300	.338	80	-19	13	.917	8	117	72	O-150(24-31-95)/P-76	-1.4
LEEK, GENE Eugene Harold B 7.15.1936 San Diego, CA BR/TR 6/185# d4.22																								
1959	Cle A	13	36	7	8	3	0	1	5	2-0	0	7	.222	.263	.389	80	-1	0-0	.955	-2	87	0	3-13/S	-0.3
1961	LA A	57	199	16	45	9	1	5	20	7-0	2	54	.226	.260	.357	57	-13	0-1	.958	11	118	98	3-49/S-7,O(LF)	-0.2
1962	LA A	7	14	0	2	0	0	0	0	0-0	0	6	.143	.143	.143	-24	-2	0-0	1.000	-0	70	182	/3-4	-0.3
Total	3	77	249	23	55	12	1	6	25	9-0	2	67	.221	.254	.349	55	-16	0-1	.959	9	112	90	/3-66,S-8,O(LF)	-0.8
LEEPER, DAVE David Dale B 10.30.1959 Santa Ana, CA BL/TL 5-11/170# d9.10																								
1984	KC A	4	6	1	0	0	0	0	0	0-0	0	1	.000	.000	.000	-99	-2	0-0	1.000	0	134	0	/O-2(LF),D	-0.2
1985	KC A	15	34	1	3	0	0	0	4	1-0	0	3	.088	.114	.088	-43	-7	0-0	.929	-1	86	0	/O-8(2-0-6)	-0.8
Total	2	19	40	2	3	0	0	0	4	1-0	0	4	.075	.098	.075	-52	-9	0-0	.944	-1	94	0	/O-10(4-0-6),D	-1.0
LEES, GEORGE George Edward B 2.2.1895 Bethlehem, PA D 1.2.1980 Harrisburg, PA BR/TR 5-9/150# d5.7																								
1921	Chi A	20	42	3	9	2	0	0	4	0	0	3	.214	.214	.262	21	-5	0-1	.951	-2	*84*	*75*	C-16	-0.6
LEFEBVRE, JIM James Kenneth B 1.7.1942 Inglewood, CA BB/TR 6/185# d4.12 M6 C11																								
1965	†LA N	157	544	57	136	21	4	12	69	71-7	2	92	.250	.337	.369	106	6	3-5	.970	-2	100	104	*2-156	1.8
1966	†LA N★	152	544	69	149	23	3	24	74	48-6	3	72	.274	.333	.460	129	20	1-1	.980	0	103	87	*2-119,3-40	3.1
1967	LA N	136	494	51	129	18	5	8	50	44-11	3	64	.261	.322	.366	106	3	1-5	.955	2	106	78	3-92,2-34/1-5	0.7
1968	LA N	84	286	23	69	12	1	5	31	26-4	1	55	.241	.304	.343	102	1	0-0	.978	-5	90	90	2-62,3-16/O-5(LF),1-3	0.0
1969	LA N	95	275	29	65	15	2	4	44	48-10	1	37	.236	.349	.349	104	4	2-1	.985	1	116	107	3-44,2-37/1-6	0.6
1970	LA N	109	314	33	79	15	1	4	44	29-2	1	42	.252	.314	.344	81	-9	1-1	.988	-9	94	84	2-70,3-21/1	-1.4

Year	Tm Lg	G	AB	R	H	2B	3B	HR	RBI	BB-IB	HP	SO	AVG	OBP	SLG	AOPS	ABR	SB-CS	FA	FR	Rng	Thr	G at Pos	BFW
1971	LA N	119	388	40	95	14	2	12	68	39-6	2	55	.245	.314	.384	104	1	0-2	.988	-6	92	109	*2-102/3-7	0.1
1972	LA N	70	169	11	34	8	0	5	24	17-6	0	30	.201	.271	.337	75	-6	0-0	.987	-0	105	124	2-33,3-11	-0.4
Total	8	922	3014	313	756	126	18	74	404	322-52	13	447	.251	.323	.378	105	20	8-15	.979	-19	98	98	2-613,3-231/1-15,O-5(LF)	4.5
LEFEBVRE, JOE Joseph Henry B 2.22.1956 Concord, NH BL/TR 5-10/175# d5.22 C2																								
1980	†NY A	74	150	26	34	1	1	8	21	27-3	0	30	.227	.345	.407	107	2	0-0	.975	-4	81	88	O-71(20-3-52)	-0.4
1981	SD N	86	246	31	63	13	4	8	31	35-7	2	33	.256	.352	.439	133	11	6-4	.994	4	111	95	O-84(0-2-83)	1.2
1982	SD N	102	239	25	57	9	0	4	21	18-2	1	50	.238	.292	.326	78	-8	0-0	.972	-2	98	115	3-39,O-36(18-2-18)/C-3	-1.2
1983	SD N	18	20	1	5	0	0	0	1	2-0	0	3	.250	.318	.250	61	-1	0-0	1.000	1	23	611	/O-6(RF),3-4,C-2	-0.1
	†Phi N	101	258	34	80	20	8	8	38	31-6	3	46	.310	.388	.543	158	20	5-3	.990	-4	90	103	O-74(22-0-58)/3-9,C-3	1.4
	Year	119	278	35	85	20	8	8	39	33-6	3	49	.306	.383	.522	151	20	5-3	.990	-3	87	123	O-80(22-0-64),3-13/C-5	1.3
1984	Phi N	52	160	22	40	9	0	3	18	23-4	2	37	.250	.348	.363	99	1	0-2	.966	0	101	133	O-47(16-0-34)/3	-0.2
1986	Phi N	14	18	0	2	0	0	0	0	3-0	0	5	.111	.238	.111	-1	-2	0-0	1.000	-0	95	0	/O-3(RF)	-0.3
Total	6	447	1091	139	281	52	13	31	130	139-22	8	204	.258	.344	.414	115	23	11-9	.986	-5	95	102	O-321(76-7-254)/3-53,C-8	0.4
LEFEBVRE, BILL Wilfred Henry "Lefty" B 11.11.1915 Natick, RI BL/TL 5-11.5/180# d6.10 Mil 1945 ▲																								
1938	Bos A	1	1	1	1	0	0	1	1	0	0	0	1.000	1.000	4.000	1048	1	0-0	—	-0	0	0	/P	0.0
1939	Bos A	7	10	3	3	0	0	0	1	2	0	2	.300	.417	.300	83	1	0-0	1.000	-1	45	0	/P-5	0.0
1943	Was A	7	14	0	4	3	0	0	1	1	0	0	.286	.333	.500	148	2	0-0	1.000	-0	92	249	/P-6	0.0
1944	Was A	60	62	4	16	2	2	0	8	12	0	9	.258	.378	.355	115	2	0-0	.933	-0	99	209	P-24/1-2	0.0
Total	4	75	87	8	24	5	2	1	11	15	0	11	.276	.382	.414	129	6	0-0	.960	-1	84	171	/P-36,1-2	0.0
LEFEVRE, AL Alfred Modesto B 9.16.1898 New York, NY D 1.21.1982 Glen Cove, NY BR/TR 5-10.5/160# d6.28																								
1920	NY N	17	27	5	4	0	1	0	0	0	0	13	.148	.148	.222	5	-3	0-0	1.000	3	142	115	/S-9,2-6,3	-0.1
LEFLER, WADE Wade Hampton B 6.5.1896 Cooleemee, NC D 3.6.1981 Hickory, NC BL/TR 5-11/162# d4.16																								
1924	Bos N	1	1	0	0	0	0	0	0	0	0	1	.000	.000	.000	-99	0	0-0	—	0			H	0.0
	Was A	5	8	0	5	3	0	0	4	0	0	0	.625	.625	1.000	325	3	0-0	1.000	0	121	0	/O(RF)	0.2
Total	1	6	9	0	5	3	0	0	4	0	0	1	.556	.556	.889	279	3	0-0	1.000	0	121	0	/O(RF)	0.2
LeFLORE, RON Ronald B 6.16.1948 Detroit, MI BR/TR 6/200# d8.1																								
1974	Det A	59	254	37	66	8	1	2	13	13-0	3	58	.260	.301	.323	78	-8	23-9	.935	-2	92	181	O-59(CF)	-1.0
1975	Det A	136	550	66	142	13	6	8	37	33-1	2	139	.258	.302	.347	80	-16	28-20	.973	-3	94	144	*O-134(CF)	-2.5
1976	Det A★	135	544	93	172	23	8	4	39	51-2	2	111	.316	.376	.410	125	18	58-20	.973	5	104	142	*O-132(CF)/D	2.6
1977	Det A	154	652	100	212	30	10	16	57	37-1	4	121	.325	.363	.475	121	17	39-19	.972	-12	88	107	*O-152(CF)	0.6
1978	Det A	155	666	**126**	198	30	3	12	62	65-7	4	104	.297	.361	.405	113	13	**68**-16	.976	-5	98	85	*O-155(CF)	1.6
1979	Det A	148	600	110	180	22	10	9	57	52-2	0	95	.300	.355	.415	104	3	78-14	.990	0	101	85	*O-113(CF),D-34	1.3
1980	Mon N	139	521	95	134	21	11	4	39	62-1	1	99	.257	.337	.363	95	-3	**97**-19	.957	2	96	153	*O-130(LF)	0.9
1981	Chi A	82	337	46	83	10	4	0	24	28-0	1	70	.246	.304	.300	77	-10	36-11	.960	-2	96	110	O-82(76-7-0)	-1.2
1982	Chi A	91	334	58	96	15	4	4	25	22-1	0	91	.287	.331	.392	98	-1	28-14	.939	-5	88	140	O-83(2-81-0)/D-2	-0.6
Total	9	1099	4458	731	1283	172	57	59	353	363-15	17	888	.288	.342	.392	103	13	455-142	.968	-22	96	123	*O-1040(208-833-0)/D-37	1.7
LEGETT, LOU Louis Alfred "Doc" B 6.1.1901 New Orleans, LA D 3.6.1988 New Orleans, LA BR/TR 5-10/166# d5.8																								
1929	Bos N	39	81	7	13	2	0	0	6	3	0	18	.160	.190	.185	-7	-14	2	.914	-1	*108*	*128*	C-28	-1.3
1933	Bos A	8	5	1	1	1	0	0	1	0	0	0	.200	.200	.400	56	0	0-0	1.000	0	*0*	*0*	/C-2	0.0
1934	Bos A	19	38	4	11	0	0	0	1	2	0	4	.289	.325	.289	56	-3	0-0	.977	0	*91*	*88*	C-17	-0.2
1935	Bos A	2	0	1	0	0	0	0	0	0	0	0	—	—	—	—	0	0-0	—	0			R	0.0
Total	4	68	124	13	25	3	0	0	8	5	0	22	.202	.233	.226	16	-17	2-0	.938	-1	*101*	*113*	/C-47	-1.5
LEGG, GREG Gregory Lynn B 4.21.1960 San Jose, CA BR/TR 6-1/185# d4.18																								
1986	Phi N	11	20	2	9	1	0	0	1	0-0	0	3	.450	.450	.500	156	1	0-0	.941	1	143	167	/2-4,S	0.3
1987	Phi N	3	2	1	0	0	0	0	0	0-0	0	0	.000	.000	.000	-97	-1	0-0	1.000	0	158	674	/2S3	0.0
Total	2	14	22	3	9	1	0	0	1	0-0	0	3	.409	.409	.455	132	0	0-0	.952	1	144	205	/2-5,S-2,3	0.3
LEHANE, MIKE Michael Patrick B 4.15.1865 New York, NY BR 6-1.5/180# d4.26																								
1884	Was U	3	12	1	4	2	0	0		0			.333	.333	.500	154	1		.688	-1	104	0	/S-3,O(LF)3	0.0
1890	Col AA	**140**	512	54	108	19	5	0	56	43	3		.211	.276	.268	65	-22	13	**.982**	10	**131**	**127**	*1-140	-2.2
1891	Col AA	137	511	59	110	12	7	1	52	34	3	77	.215	.268	.272	58	-29	16	**.981**	7	**125**	**128**	*1-137	-3.0
Total	3	280	1035	114	222	33	12	1	108	77	6	77	.214	.273	.272	62	-50	29	.982	16	128	127	1-277/S-3,3O(LF)	-5.2
LEHNER, PAUL Paul Eugene "Peanuts" or "Gulliver" B 7.1.1920 Dolomite, AL D 12.27.1967 Birmingham, AL BL/TL 5-9/165# d9.10																								
1946	StL A	16	45	6	10	1	2	0	5	1	0	5	.222	.239	.333	56	-3	0-0	.941	-1	71	178	O-12(0-11-1)	-0.5
1947	StL A	135	483	59	120	25	9	7	48	28	3	29	.248	.294	.381	85	-12	5-5	.980	-8	97	12	*O-127(2-125-0)	-2.6
1948	StL A	103	333	23	92	15	4	2	46	30	0	19	.276	.336	.363	84	-8	0-2	.974	-5	94	59	O-89(CF)/1-2	-1.6
1949	StL A	104	297	25	68	13	0	3	37	16	1	20	.229	.271	.303	50	-23	0-2	.987	1	114	25	O-56(12-35-10),1-18	-2.5
1950	Phi A	114	427	48	132	17	5	9	52	32	0	33	.309	.357	.436	104	1	1-1	.981	4	105	119	*O-101(80-7-15)	-0.2
1951	Phi A	9	28	1	4	1	0	0	1	1	0	1	.143	.172	.179	-5	-4	0-0	1.000	1	103	183	/O-6(LF)	-0.4
	Chi A	23	72	9	15	3	1	0	3	10	0	4	.208	.305	.278	60	-4	0-0	.980	1	97	171	O-20(8-13-9)	-0.4
	StL A	21	67	2	9	5	0	1	2	6	0	5	.134	.205	.254	23	-7	0-1	1.000	-1	105	0	O-18(1-17-0)	-0.9
	Cle A	12	13	2	3	0	0	0	1	1	0	2	.231	.286	.231	43	-1	0-0	1.000	-0	78	0	/O(LF)	-0.1
	Year	65	180	14	31	9	1	1	7	18	0	12	.172	.247	.250	35	-17	0-1	.991	0	101	109	O-45(16-30-9)	-1.8
1952	Bos A	3	3	0	2	0	0	0	2	2	0	0	.667	.800	.667	288	1	0-0	1.000	0	131	0	/O-2(RF)	0.1
Total	7	540	1768	175	455	80	21	22	197	127	4	118	.257	.309	.364	78	-60	6-11	.981	-8	101	63	O-432(110-297-37)/1-20	-9.1
LEHR, CLARENCE Clarence Emanuel "King" B 5.16.1886 Escanaba, MI D 1.31.1948 Highland Park, MI BR/TR 5-11/165# d5.18																								
1911	Phi N	23	27	2	4	0	0	0	2	0	0	7	.148	.148	.148	-17	-4	0	1.000	1	85	0	/O-5(1-1-3),2-4,S-4	-0.4
LEIBER, HANK Henry Edward B 1.17.1911 Phoenix, AZ D 11.8.1993 Tucson, AZ BR/TR 6-1.5/205# d4.16 ▲																								
1933	NY N	6	10	1	2	0	0	0	0	0	0	2	.200	.200	.200	15	-1	0	1.000	1	88	804	/O(LF)	-0.1
1934	NY N	63	187	17	45	5	3	2	25	4	0	13	.241	.257	.332	58	-12	1	.971	-3	86	94	O-51(2-49-0)	-1.7
1935	NY N	154	613	110	203	37	4	22	107	48	**10**	29	.331	.389	.512	143	37	0	.965	-22	83	38	*O-154(CF)	1.1
1936	†NY N	101	337	44	94	19	7	9	67	37	1	41	.279	.352	.457	118	8	1	.961	-8	77	150	O-86(7-78-1)/1	-0.2
1937	†NY N	51	184	24	54	7	3	4	32	15	0	27	.293	.347	.429	108	2	1	.988	-6	80	30	O-46(1-42-3)	-0.5
1938	NY N★	98	360	50	97	18	4	12	65	31	0	45	.269	.327	.442	109	3	0	.974	-9	84	81	O-89(2-86-4)	-0.8
1939	Chi N	112	365	65	113	16	1	24	88	59	4	42	.310	.411	.556	155	30	1	.977	-2	101	63	O-98(CF)	2.5
1940	Chi N✳	117	440	68	133	24	2	17	86	45	3	68	.302	.371	.482	136	22	1	.985	-6	85	101	*O-103(0-53-52),1-12	1.1
1941	Chi N✳	53	162	20	35	5	0	7	25	16	1	25	.216	.291	.377	90	-3	0	.964	-2	94	53	O-29(23-2-5),1-15	-0.8
1942	NY N	58	147	11	32	6	0	4	23	19	2	27	.218	.315	.340	91	-1	0	.990	-0	103	58	O-41(1-40-0)/P	-0.3
Total	10	813	2805	410	808	137	24	101	518	274	21	319	.288	.356	.462	122	85	5	.973	-58	87	77	O-698(37-602-65)/1-28,P	0.3
LEIBOLD, NEMO Harry Loran B 2.17.1892 Butler, IN D 2.4.1977 Detroit, MI BL/TR 5-6.5/157# d4.12																								
1913	Cle A	93	286	37	74	11	6	0	12	21	0	43	.259	.309	.339	87	-6	16	.945	-2	93	109	O-74(4-66-2)	-1.3
1914	Cle A	115	402	46	106	13	3	0	32	54	2	56	.264	.354	.311	96	0	12-14	.931	4	99	**159**	*O-107(0-90-17)	-0.5
1915	Cle A	57	207	28	53	5	4	0	4	24	2	16	.256	.339	.319	95	-1	5-3	.969	5	113	124	O-52(CF)	0.0
	Chi A	36	74	10	17	1	0	0	11	15	0	11	.230	.360	.243	78	-1	1-3	1.000	3	114	157	O-22(10-12-0)	0.0
	Year	93	281	38	70	6	4	0	15	39	2	27	.249	.345	.299	91	-2	6-6	.978	8	113	134	O-74(10-64-0)	0.0
1916	Chi A	45	82	5	20	1	2	0	13	7	0	7	.244	.303	.305	82	-2	7	1.000	-1	95	48	O-24(2-16-6)	-0.4
1917	†Chi A	125	428	59	101	12	6	0	29	74	1	34	.236	.350	.292	94	0	27	.961	3	104	117	*O-122(16-4-102)	-0.2
1918	Chi A	116	440	57	110	14	7	0	31	63	0	32	.250	.344	.314	97	0	15	.979	7	111	104	*O-114(95-7-12)	0.2
1919	†Chi A	122	434	81	131	18	2	0	26	72	2	30	.302	.404	.353	113	12	17	.928	8	103	162	*O-122(7-1-114)	1.4
1920	Chi A	108	413	61	91	16	3	1	28	55	3	30	.220	.316	.281	59	-23	7-15	.977	6	102	130	*O-105(3-4-98)	-2.6
1921	Bos A	123	467	88	143	26	6	0	31	41	1	27	.306	.363	.388	94	-3	13-7	.949	-1	98	100	*O-117(0-107-10)	-0.9
1922	Bos A	81	271	42	70	8	1	1	18	41	2	14	.258	.360	.306	76	-8	1-6	.966	2	100	126	O-71(1-66-4)	-1.1
1923	Bos A	12	18	1	2	0	0	0	0	1	0	2	.111	.158	.111	-28	-3	0-1	.909	0	88	218	O-10(CF)	-0.4
	Was A	95	315	68	96	13	4	1	22	53	2	16	.305	.408	.381	114	10	7-6	.980	-2	88	137	O-84(CF)	0.4
	Year	107	333	69	98	13	4	1	22	54	2	18	.294	.396	.366	106	6	7-7	.977	-2	88	141	O-94(CF)	0.0
1924	†Was A	84	246	41	72	6	4	0	20	42	1	10	.293	.398	.350	97	1	7-5	.994	1	102	114	O-70(4-52-14)	-0.1

Year	Tm Lg	G	AB	R	H	2B	3B	HR	RBI	BB-IB	HP	SO	AVG	OBP	SLG	AOPS	ABR	SB-CS	FA	FR	Rng	Thr	G at Pos	BFW
1925	†Was A	56	84	14	23	1	1	0	7	8	0	7	.274	.337	.310	66	-4	1-0	.972	0	97	144	O-26(2-22-2)/3	-0.4
Total	13	1268	4167	638	1109	145	49	3	284	571	16	335	.266	.357	.327	91	-28	136-60	.961	35	101	126	*O-1120(144-593-381)/3	-5.9
LEIFER, ELMER Elmer Edwin B 5.23.1893 Clarington, OH D 9.26.1948 Everett, WA BL/TR 5-9.5/170# d9.7																								
1921	Chi A	9	10	0	3	0	0	0	1	0	0	4	.300	.300	.300	54	-1	0-0	1.000	-0	67	0	/3O(LF)	-0.1
LEIGHTON, JOHN John Atkinson B 10.4.1861 Peabody, MA D 10.31.1956 Lynn, MA 5-11/170# d7.12																								
1890	Syr AA	7	27	6	8	2	0	0	0	3	0		.296	.367	.370	131	1	2	.938	-0	0	0	/O-7(CF)	0.1
LEINHAUSER, BILL William Charles B 11.4.1893 Philadelphia, PA D 4.14.1978 Elkins Park, PA BR/TR 5-10/150# d5.18																								
1912	Det A	1	4	0	0	0	0	0	0	0	0		.000	.000	.000	-99	-1	0	1.000	1	0	0	/O	0.0
LEIP, ED Edgar Ellsworth B 11.29.1910 Trenton, NJ D 11.24.1983 Zephyrhills, FL BR/TR 5-9/160# d9.16 Mil 1942-45																								
1939	Was A	9	32	4	11	1	0	0	2	2	0	4	.344	.382	.375	102	0	0-1	.951	-0	110	102	/2-8	0.0
1940	Pit N	3	5	2	1	0	0	0	0	0	0	0	.200	.200	.200	11	-1	0	1.000	-0	81	183	/2-2	-0.1
1941	Pit N	15	25	1	5	0	2	0	3	1	0	2	.200	.231	.360	65	-2	1	.889	0	120	84	/2-7,3	-0.1
1942	Pit N	3	0	0	0	0	0	0	0	0	0	0	—	—	—	—	0	0	—	0			R	0.0
Total	4	30	62	7	17	1	2	0	5	3	0	6	.274	.308	.355	80	-3	1-1	.931	0	111	101	/2-17,3	-0.2
LEIUS, SCOTT Scott Thomas B 9.24.1965 Yonkers, NY BR/TR 6-3/195# d9.3																								
1990	Min A	14	25	4	6	1	0	1	4	2-0	0	2	.240	.296	.400	87	0	0-0	1.000	2	96	174	S-12/3	0.2
1991	†Min A	109	199	35	57	7	2	5	20	30-1	0	35	.286	.378	.417	115	5	5-5	.953	2	101	88	3-79,S-19/O-2(CF)	0.7
1992	Min A	129	409	50	102	18	2	2	35	34-0	1	61	.249	.309	.318	73	-14	6-5	.955	-0	105	63	*3-125,S-10	-1.5
1993	Min A	10	18	4	3	0	0	0	2	2-0	0	4	.167	.227	.167	14	-2	0-0	.947	2	126	153	/S-9	0.0
1994	Min A	97	350	57	86	16	1	14	49	37-0	1	58	.246	.318	.417	88	-7	2-4	.969	-1	103	87	3-95/S-2	-0.7
1995	Min A	117	372	51	92	16	5	4	45	49-3	2	54	.247	.335	.349	79	-11	2-1	.945	-4	99	144	*3-112/S-7,D-3	-1.3
1996	Cle A	27	43	3	6	4	0	1	3	2-0	0	8	.140	.178	.302	18	-6	0-0	1.000	-1	76	0	/3-8,1-7,2-6,D	-0.6
1998	KC A	17	46	2	8	0	0	0	4	1-0	0	6	.174	.191	.174	-4	-7	0-0	.867	-1	91	118	3-15/S-2,D	-0.8
1999	KC A	37	74	8	15	1	0	1	10	4-0	1	8	.203	.244	.257	30	-8	1-0	.971	1	140	188	1-13,3-10/S-2,2D	-0.7
Total	9	557	1536	214	375	63	10	28	172	161-4	5	236	.244	.316	.353	77	-50	16-15	.954	1	102	98	3-445/S-63,1-20,D-11,2-7,O-2(CF)	-4.7
LEJA, FRANK Frank John B 2.7.1936 Holyoke, MA D 5.3.1991 Boston, MA BL/TL 6-4/205# d5.1																								
1954	NY A	12	5	2	1	0	0	0	0	0	0	1	.200	.200	.200	10	-1	0-0	1.000	-0	0	0	/1-6	-0.1
1955	NY A	7	2	1	0	0	0	0	0	0-0	0	1	.000	.000	.000	-99	-1	0-0	1.000	-0	0	507	/1-2	-0.1
1962	LA A	7	16	0	0	0	0	0	0	1-0	0	6	.000	.059	.000	-85	-4	0-0	.953	-0	102	113	/1-4	-0.5
Total	3	26	23	3	1	0	0	0	0	1-0	0	8	.043	.083	.043	-67	-6	0-0	.958	-1	92	127	/1-12	-0.7
LeJEUNE, LARRY Sheldon Aldenbert B 7.22.1885 Chicago, IL D 4.21.1952 Eloise, MI BR/TR 6/185# d5.10																								
1911	Bro N	6	19	2	3	0	0	0	2	2	0	8	.158	.238	.158	12	-2	2	.818	-1	82	0	/O-6(CF)	-0.4
1915	Pit N	18	65	4	11	0	1	0	2	2	1	7	.169	.206	.200	23	-6	4-3	.940	2	105	192	O-18(CF)	-0.7
Total	2	24	84	6	14	0	1	0	4	4	1	15	.167	.213	.190	21	-8	6-3	.918	1	100	151	/O-24(CF)	-1.1
LeJOHN, DON Donald Everett B 5.13.1934 Daisytown, PA BR/TR 5-10/175# d6.30																								
1965	†LA N	34	78	2	20	2	0	0	7	5-0	0	13	.256	.301	.282	70	-3	0-1	.959	-0	103	81	3-26	-0.4
LELIVELT, JACK John Frank B 11.14.1885 Chicago, IL D 1.20.1941 Seattle, WA BL/TL 5-11.5/175# d6.24 b-Bill																								
1909	Was A	91	318	25	93	8	6	0	24	19	1		.292	.334	.355	124	7	8	.970	6	116	104	O-91(41-35-15)	0.9
1910	Was A	110	347	40	92	10	3	0	33	40	1		.265	.343	.311	110	5	20	.964	6	112	126	O-86(80-5-1)/1-7	0.8
1911	Was A	72	225	29	72	12	4	0	22	22	2		.320	.386	.409	124	8	7	.939	2	93	134	O-49(36-0-13)/1-7	0.7
1912	NY A	36	149	12	54	6	7	2	23	4	1		.362	.383	.537	153	9	7	.963	-2	95	77	O-36(CF)	0.4
1913	NY A	18	28	2	6	0	1	0	4	2	0	2	.214	.267	.286	61	-2	1	1.000	1	110	128	/O-5(CF)	-0.2
	Cle A	23	23	0	9	2	0	0	7	0	0	3	.391	.391	.478	150	1	1	—	-0	0	0	/O(CF)	0.1
	Year	41	51	2	15	2	1	0	11	2	0	5	.294	.321	.373	101	0	2	1.000	0	108	125	/O-6(CF)	-0.1
1914	Cle A	34	64	6	21	5	1	0	13	2	0	10	.328	.348	.438	131	2	2-3	.933	-1	87	0	O-13(0-7-6)/1	-0.1
Total	6	384	1154	114	347	43	22	2	126	89	5	15	.301	.353	.381	124	30	46-3	.962	11	107	110	O-281(157-88-35)/1-15	2.6
LeMASTER, JOHNNIE Johnnie Lee B 6.19.1954 Portsmouth, OH BR/TR 6-2/167# d9.2																								
1975	SF N	22	74	4	14	4	0	2	9	4-0	1	15	.189	.241	.324	53	-5	2-1	.967	-3	93	92	S-22	-0.5
1976	SF N	33	100	9	21	3	2	0	9	2-0	0	21	.210	.223	.280	42	-8	2-0	.937	7	122	95	S-31	0.3
1977	SF N	68	134	13	20	5	1	0	8	13-3	0	27	.149	.223	.201	15	-16	2-1	.934	-3	103	66	S-54/3-2	-1.5
1978	SF N	101	272	23	64	18	3	1	14	21-1	1	45	.235	.293	.335	78	-8	6-6	.966	-7	96	87	S-96/2-2	-0.7
1979	SF N	108	343	42	87	11	2	3	29	23-1	2	55	.254	.304	.324	77	-12	9-5	.959	-1	96	88	*S-106	-0.3
1980	SF N	135	405	33	87	16	6	3	31	25-5	0	57	.215	.257	.306	59	-24	0-1	.957	-15	93	74	*S-134	-2.9
1981	SF N	104	324	27	82	9	1	0	28	24-7	1	46	.253	.306	.287	70	-13	3-7	.964	-10	94	92	*S-103	-1.6
1982	SF N	130	436	34	94	14	1	2	30	31-10	0	78	.216	.267	.266	50	-30	13-4	.963	-12	95	86	*S-130	-2.8
1983	SF N	141	534	81	128	16	1	6	30	60-3	2	96	.240	.317	.307	77	-16	39-19	.964	-12	97	71	*S-139	-1.3
1984	SF N	132	451	46	98	13	2	4	32	31-5	0	97	.217	.265	.282	56	-27	17-5	.964	5	104	89	*S-129	-0.9
1985	SF N	12	16	1	0	0	0	0	0	1-0	0	5	.000	.059	.000	-86	-4	0-0	.955	-3	49	29	S-10	-0.7
	Cle A	11	20	0	3	0	0	0	2	0-0	0	6	.150	.150	.150	-18	-3	0-1	.949	-0	83	137	S-10	-0.3
	Pit N	22	58	4	9	0	0	1	6	5-2	0	12	.155	.222	.207	21	-6	1-0	.983	10	129	108	S-21	0.6
1987	Oak A	20	24	3	2	0	0	0	1	1-0	0	4	.083	.120	.083	-48	-5	0-1	1.000	0	133	445	/3-8,S-7,2-5,D	-0.5
Total	12	1039	3191	320	709	109	19	22	229	241-37	7	564	.222	.277	.289	60	-177	94-51	.961	-44	98	84	S-992/3-10,2-7,D	-13.1
LEMBO, STEVE Stephen Neal B 11.13.1926 Brooklyn, NY D 12.4.1989 Flushing, NY BR/TR 6-1/185# d9.16																								
1950	Bro N	5	6	0	1	0	0	0	0	1	0	0	.167	.286	.167	22	-1	0	1.000	2	*0*	*196*	/C-5	0.1
1952	Bro N	2	5	0	1	0	0	0	1	0	0	1	.200	.200	.200	11	-1	0-0	1.000	0	*0*	*0*	/C-2	0.0
Total	2	7	11	0	2	0	0	0	1	1	0	1	.182	.250	.182	18	-2	0-0	1.000	2	*0*	*125*	/C-7	0.1
LEMKE, MARK Mark Alan B 8.13.1965 Utica, NY BB/TR 5-9/167# d9.17																								
1988	Atl N	16	58	8	13	4	0	0	2	4-0	0	5	.224	.274	.293	60	-3	0-2	.970	1	100	98	2-16	-0.3
1989	Atl N	14	55	4	10	2	1	2	10	5-0	0	7	.182	.250	.364	72	-2	0-1	1.000	-1	97	88	2-14	-0.4
1990	Atl N	102	239	22	54	13	0	0	21	21-3	0	22	.226	.286	.280	54	-14	0-1	.989	19	120	145	3-45,2-44/S	0.5
1991	†Atl N	136	269	36	63	11	2	2	23	29-2	0	27	.234	.305	.312	71	-10	1-2	.978	9	110	115	*2-110,3-15	0.0
1992	†Atl N	155	427	38	97	7	4	6	26	50-11	0	39	.227	.307	.304	70	-17	0-3	.984	-13	96	81	*2-145,3-13	-3.0
1993	†Atl N	151	493	52	124	19	2	7	49	65-13	0	50	.252	.335	.341	82	-11	1-2	.982	18	105	123	*2-150	1.4
1994	Atl N	104	350	40	103	15	0	3	31	38-12	0	37	.294	.363	.363	88	-5	0-3	**.994**	9	101	95	*2-103	0.8
1995	†Atl N	116	399	42	101	16	5	5	38	44-4	0	40	.253	.325	.356	78	-13	2-2	.990	-1	100	94	*2-115	-0.9
1996	†Atl N	135	498	64	127	17	0	5	37	53-1	0	48	.255	.323	.319	68	-23	5-2	.977	11	**113**	93	*2-133	-0.4
1997	Atl N	109	351	33	86	17	1	2	26	33-2	0	51	.245	.306	.316	63	-19	2-0	.980	17	114	122	*2-104	0.3
1998	Bos A	31	91	10	17	4	0	0	7	6-0	0	15	.187	.232	.231	22	-11	0-1	1.000	-7	86	91	2-31	-1.6
Total	11	1069	3230	349	795	125	15	32	270	348-48	0	341	.246	.317	.324	71	-128	11-19	.984	61	105	102	2-965/3-73,S	-3.6
LEMON, CHET Chester Earl B 2.12.1955 Jackson, MS BR/TR 6/195# d9.9																								
1975	Chi A	9	35	2	9	2	0	0	1	2-0	0	6	.257	.297	.314	72	-1	1-0	.923	-3	57	0	/3-6,O(CF)D	-0.4
1976	Chi A	132	451	46	111	15	5	4	38	28-0	7	65	.246	.298	.328	83	-10	13-7	.992	8	108	136	*O-131(1-130-0)	-0.6
1977	Chi A	150	553	99	151	38	4	19	67	52-1	11	88	.273	.343	.459	118	15	8-7	.978	23	**132**	114	*O-149(CF)	3.5
1978	Chi A★	105	357	51	107	24	6	13	55	39-2	8	46	.300	.377	.510	147	23	5-9	.983	11	120	137	O-95(0-84-12),D-10	3.1
1979	Chi A★	148	556	79	177	**44**	2	17	86	56-6	**13**	68	.318	.391	.496	138	33	7-11	.977	-0	101	101	*O-147(CF)/D	2.8
1980	Chi A	147	514	76	150	32	6	11	51	71-6	12	56	.292	.388	.442	128	24	6-6	.981	-5	93	117	*O-139(CF)/2D	1.6
1981	Chi A	94	328	50	99	23	6	9	50	33-0	**13**	48	.302	.384	.491	155	24	5-8	.984	-2	103	38	O-93(CF)	2.0
1982	Det A	125	436	75	116	20	1	19	52	56-2	**15**	69	.266	.368	.447	122	15	1-4	.984	-3	93	128	*O-121(0-29-93)/D	0.6
1983	Det A	145	491	78	125	21	5	24	69	54-1	**20**	70	.255	.350	.464	126	18	0-7	.988	1	104	68	*O-145(CF)	1.5
1984	†Det A★	141	509	77	146	34	6	20	76	51-9	7	83	.287	.357	.495	135	24	5-5	.995	4	110	65	*O-140(CF)/D	2.7
1985	Det A	145	517	69	137	28	4	18	68	45-3	10	93	.265	.334	.439	111	8	0-2	.990	-0	105	65	*O-144(CF)	0.6
1986	Det A	126	403	45	101	21	3	12	53	39-3	8	53	.251	.326	.407	99	0	2-1	.985	-0	101	95	*O-124(CF)	-0.1
1987	†Det A	146	470	75	130	30	3	20	75	70-1	8	82	.277	.376	.481	132	24	0-0	.992	-1	100	66	*O-145(CF)	2.1
1988	Det A	144	512	67	135	29	4	17	64	59-6	7	65	.264	.346	.436	123	16	1-2	.974	-1	99	92	*O-144(RF)	1.0
1989	Det A	127	414	45	98	19	2	7	47	46-3	8	71	.237	.323	.343	90	-4	1-5	.985	-7	86	75	*O-111(RF),D-13	-1.7

Year	Tm Lg	G	AB	R	H	2B	3B	HR	RBI	BB-IB	HP	SO	AVG	OBP	SLG	AOPS	ABR	SB-CS	FA	FR	Rng	Thr	G at Pos	BFW
1990	Det A	104	322	39	83	16	4	5	32	48-3	4	61	.258	.359	.379	106	4	3-2	.973	4	111	107	O-96(0-3-94)/D-6	0.6
Total	16	1988	6868	973	1875	396	61	215	884	749-46	151	1024	.273	.355	.442	121	213	58-76	.984	26	104	93	*O-1925(1-1473-454)/D-40,3-6,2	19.3
LEMON, JIM James Robert B 3.23.1928 Covington, VA BR/TR 6-4/200# d8.20 M1 C7																								
1950	Cle A	12	34	4	6	1	0	1	1	3	0	12	.176	.243	.294	38	-3	0-0	.824	-1	74	168	O-10(LF)	-0.5
1953	Cle A	16	46	5	8	1	0	1	5	3	0	15	.174	.224	.261	32	-5	0-0	.913	-1	90	130	O-11(LF)/1-2	-0.7
1954	Was A	37	128	12	30	2	3	2	13	9	0	34	.234	.283	.344	76	-5	0-0	.951	-4	88	0	O-33(1-0-32)	-1.1
1955	Was A	10	25	3	5	2	0	1	3	3-0	0	4	.200	.286	.400	88	-1	0-0	.923	-1	102	0	/O-6(1-0-5)	-0.1
1956	Was A	146	538	77	146	21	**11**	27	96	65-2	2	138	.271	.349	.502	123	15	2-4	.963	4	107	104	*O-141(12-0-130)	1.3
1957	Was A	137	518	58	147	23	6	17	64	49-3	3	94	.284	.345	.450	118	12	1-7	.971	-6	99	42	*O-131(RF)/1-3	-0.1
1958	Was A	142	501	65	123	15	9	26	75	50-3	1	120	.246	.314	.467	114	7	2-4	.978	-1	103	72	*O-137(2-0-135)	0.0
1959	Was A	147	531	73	148	18	3	33	100	46-0	1	99	.279	.334	.510	130	19	5-2	.969	-2	102	46	*O-142(117-0-25)	1.0
1960	Was A★	148	528	81	142	10	1	38	100	67-**8**	7	114	.269	.354	.508	133	23	2-0	.960	-3	90	115	*O-145(LF)	1.3
1961	Min A	129	423	57	109	26	1	14	52	44-2	4	98	.258	.329	.423	95	-2	1-1	.940	-0	101	98	*O-120(120-0-1)	-0.8
1962	Min A	12	17	1	3	0	0	1	5	3-0	0	4	.176	.286	.353	72	-1	0-0	1.000	-0	33	0	/O-3(2-0-1)	-0.1
1963	Min A	7	17	0	2	0	0	0	1	1-0	0	5	.118	.167	.118	-18	-3	0-0	.800	-1	60	0	/O-4(LF)	-0.4
	Phi N	31	59	6	16	2	0	2	6	8-1	0	18	.271	.353	.407	121	2	0-0	.963	-0	111	0	O-18(16-0-4)	0.1
	Chi A	36	80	4	16	0	1	1	8	12-0	0	32	.200	.304	.262	62	-4	0-0	.979	-2	61	144	1-25	-0.8
Total	12	1010	3445	446	901	121	35	164	529	363-19	18	787	.262	.332	.460	114	54	13-18	.961	-18	99	75	O-901(441-0-464)/1-30	-0.9
LEMON, BOB Robert Granville B 9.22.1920 San Bernardino, CA D 1.11.2000 Long Beach, CA BL/TR 6/185# d9.9 Mil 1943-45 M8 C6 HF1976 ▲																								
1941	Cle A	5	4	0	1	0	0	0	0	0	0	1	.250	.250	.250	34	0	0-0	1.000	0	103	0	/3	0.0
1942	Cle A	5	5	0	0	0	0	0	0	0	0	3	.000	.000	.000	-99	-1	0-0	.500	-0	107	0	/3	-0.2
1946	Cle A	55	89	9	16	3	0	1	4	7	0	18	.180	.240	.247	39	-8	0-1	.976	5	173	484	P-32,O-12(CF)	-0.2
1947	Cle A	47	56	11	18	4	3	2	5	6	0	9	.321	.387	.607	179	5	0-0	.983	4	**170**	242	P-37/O-2(0-1-1)	0.2
1948	†Cle A☆	52	119	20	34	9	0	5	21	8	0	23	.286	.331	.487	119	13	0-0	.965	8	**166**	238	P-43	0.0
1949	Cle A☆	46	108	17	29	6	2	7	19	10	0	20	.269	.331	.556	135	15	0-0	.963	6	137	137	P-37	0.0
1950	Cle A★	72	136	21	37	9	1	6	26	13	1	25	.272	.340	.485	113	17	0-0	.957	5	131	158	P-44	0.0
1951	Cle A★	56	102	11	21	4	1	3	13	9	0	22	.206	.270	.353	72	4	0-0	.976	4	132	138	P-42	0.0
1952	Cle A★	54	124	14	28	5	0	2	9	4	0	21	.226	.250	.315	60	6	0-0	.982	6	149	186	P-42	0.0
1953	Cle A☆	51	112	12	26	9	1	2	17	7	0	20	.232	.277	.384	79	8	2-0	.972	8	**159**	**466**	P-41	0.0
1954	†Cle A★	40	98	11	21	4	1	2	10	6	0	24	.214	.257	.337	61	5	0-0	.963	4	131	263	P-36	0.0
1955	Cle A	49	78	11	19	0	0	1	9	13-0	0	16	.244	.344	.282	69	5	0-0	.983	2	121	144	P-35	0.0
1956	Cle A	43	93	8	18	0	0	5	12	9-0	1	21	.194	.272	.355	63	4	0-0	.934	4	148	186	P-39	0.0
1957	Cle A	25	46	2	3	1	0	1	1	0-0	0	14	.065	.065	.152	-43	-3	0-0	1.000	3	159	265	P-21	0.0
1958	Cle A	15	13	1	3	0	0	0	1	1-0	0	4	.231	.286	.231	45	0	0-0	1.000	1	172	256	P-11	0.0
Total	15	615	1183	148	274	54	9	37	147	93-0	2	241	.232	.288	.386	82	70	2-1	.969	59	146	228	P-460/O-14(0-13-1),3-2	-0.2
LENHARDT, DON Donald Eugene "Footsie" B 10.4.1922 Alton, IL BR/TR 6-3/190# d4.18 C4																								
1950	StL A	139	480	75	131	22	6	22	81	90	2	94	.273	.390	.481	118	14	3-2	.988	-9	73	87	1-86,O-39(LF),3-10	-0.1
1951	StL A	31	103	9	27	3	0	5	18	6	0	13	.262	.303	.437	95	-1	1-0	.982	-2	97	0	O-27(LF)/1	-0.5
	Chi A	64	199	23	53	9	1	10	45	24	2	25	.266	.351	.472	124	6	1-1	.983	-2	98	50	O-53(LF)/1-2	0.0
	Year	95	302	32	80	12	1	15	63	30	2	38	.265	.335	.460	114	4	2-1	.983	-3	98	34	O-80(LF)/1-3	-0.5
1952	Bos A	30	105	18	31	4	0	7	24	15	0	18	.295	.383	.533	142	6	0-1	.981	-2	94	0	O-27(LF)	0.2
	Det A	45	144	18	27	2	1	3	13	28	0	18	.188	.320	.278	67	-6	0-1	.989	3	102	191	O-43(LF)	-0.7
	StL A	18	48	5	13	4	1	1	5	4	0	8	.271	.327	.458	114	1	0-0	1.000	1	110	0	O-11(10-1-0)/1-2	0.0
	Year	93	297	41	71	10	2	11	42	47	0	44	.239	.343	.397	102	1	0-2	.988	2	100	103	O-81(80-1-0)/1-2	-0.5
1953	StL A	97	303	37	96	15	0	10	35	41	1	41	.317	.400	.465	131	14	1-2	.969	1	96	143	O-77(72-0-5)/3-6	1.0
1954	Bal A	13	33	2	5	1	0	0	1	3	0	9	.152	.222	.182	12	-4	0-0	1.000	0	84	0	/O-7(LF),1-2	-0.5
	Bos A	44	66	5	18	4	0	3	17	3	1	9	.273	.310	.470	101	0	0-0	1.000	-1	87	0	O-13(LF)/3	-0.1
	Year	57	99	7	23	5	0	3	18	6	1	18	.232	.280	.374	74	-4	0-0	1.000	-0	86	0	O-20(LF)/1-2,3	-0.6
Total	5	481	1481	192	401	64	9	61	239	214	6	235	.271	.365	.450	114	30	6-7	.980	-11	97	82	O-297(291-1-5)/1-93,3-17	-0.7
LENNON, PATRICK Patrick Orlando B 4.27.1968 Whiteville, NC BR/TR 6-2/200# d9.15																								
1991	Sea A	9	8	2	1	1	0	0	1	3-0	0	1	.125	.364	.250	73	0	0-0	1.000	0	438	0	/O(LF)D	0.0
1992	Sea A	1	2	0	0	0	0	0	0	0-0	0	0	.000	.000	.000	-99	-1	0-0	1.000	-0	0	314	/1	-0.1
1996	KC A	14	30	5	7	3	0	0	1	7-0	0	10	.233	.378	.333	82	0	0-0	.947	-0	105	0	O-11(LF)/D	-0.1
1997	Oak A	56	116	14	34	6	1	1	14	15-0	0	35	.293	.374	.388	101	1	0-1	.948	-1	110	0	O-36(23-1-12),D-17	-0.2
1998	Tor A	2	4	1	2	2	0	0	0	0-0	0	1	.500	.500	1.000	276	1	0-0	1.000	0	172	0	/O-2(RF)	0.1
1999	Tor A	9	29	3	6	2	0	1	6	2-0	1	12	.207	.281	.379	65	-2	0-0	1.000	2	159	204	/O-8(5-0-4)	0.0
Total	6	91	189	25	50	14	1	2	22	27-0	1	59	.265	.359	.381	93	-1	0-1	.962	2	121	37	/O-58(40-1-18),D-23,1	-0.3
LENNON, BOB Robert Albert "Arch" B 9.15.1928 Brooklyn, NY BL/TL 6/200# d9.9																								
1954	NY N	3	3	0	0	0	0	0	0	0	0	0	.000	.000	.000	-99	-1	0-0	—	0			H	-0.1
1956	NY N	26	55	3	10	1	0	0	1	4-1	0	17	.182	.233	.200	19	-6	0-0	.885	-1	79	174	O-21(5-1-18)	-0.8
1957	Chi N	9	21	2	3	1	0	1	3	1-0	0	9	.143	.182	.333	35	-2	0-0	1.000	-1	53	0	/O-4(CF)	-0.3
Total	3	38	79	5	13	2	0	1	4	5-1	0	26	.165	.212	.228	19	-9	0-0	.900	-2	74	143	/O-25(5-5-18)	-1.2
LENNON, BILL William H. B 1848 Brooklyn, NY 5-7/145# d5.4 M1 U2																								
1871	Kek NA	12	48	5	11	3	0	0	5	1		0	.229	.245	.292	52	-3	1-0	.887	-2			C-12/S-2,O(RF)M	-0.3
1872	Nat NA	**11**	54	11	11	1	0	0	6	0		0	.204	.204	.222	26	-5	0-0	.765	-5			C-11/1	-0.7
1873	Mar NA	5	19	2	4	0	0	0	2	0		0	.211	.211	.211	33	-1	0-0	.942	-1	0	0	/1-4,C3	-0.2
Total	3 NA	28	121	18	26	4	0	0	13	1		0	.215	.221	.248	38	-9	1-0	.000	-9			/C-24,1-5,S-2,30(RF)	-1.2
LENNOX, ED James Edgar "Eggie" B 11.3.1885 Camden, NJ D 10.26.1939 Camden, NJ BR/TR 5-10/174# d8.8																								
1906	Phi A	6	17	1	1	1	0	0	0	1	0		.059	.111	.118	-28	-2	0	.909	3	145	0	/3-6	0.1
1909	Bro N	126	435	33	114	18	9	2	44	47	2		.262	.337	.359	120	10	11	**.959**	-3	88	115	*3-121	1.1
1910	Bro N	110	367	19	95	19	4	3	32	36	5	39	.259	.333	.357	104	2	7	.950	-16	78	97	*3-100	-1.2
1912	Chi N	27	81	13	19	4	1	1	16	12	2	10	.235	.347	.346	90	-1	1	.934	-3	84	38	3-24	-0.3
1914	Pit F	124	430	71	134	25	10	11	84	71	4	38	.312	.414	.493	148	25	19	.954	-17	87	65	*3-123	1.2
1915	Pit F	55	53	1	16	3	1	1	9	7	0	12	.302	.383	.453	136	2	0	1.000	1	135	0	/3-3	0.3
Total	6	448	1383	138	379	70	25	18	185	174	13	99	.274	.361	.400	122	36	38	.953	-35	86	87	3-377	1.2
LENTINE, JIM James Matthew B 7.16.1954 Los Angeles, CA BR/TR 6/175# d9.3																								
1978	StL N	8	11	1	2	0	0	0	1	0-0	1	0	.182	.250	.182	23	-1	1-0	1.000	-0	72	0	/O-3(2-0-1)	-0.2
1979	StL N	11	23	2	9	1	0	0	1	3-0	0	6	.391	.462	.435	145	2	0-1	1.000	1	99	221	/O-8(3-2-3)	0.2
1980	StL N	9	10	1	1	0	0	0	1	0-0	0	2	.100	.100	.100	-43	-2	0-0	1.000	-0	79	0	/O-6(5-1-0)	-0.2
	Det A	67	161	19	42	8	1	1	17	28-1	2	30	.261	.377	.342	96	1	2-1	.963	2	102	156	O-55(40-10-6)/D-9	0.1
Total	3	95	205	23	54	9	1	1	20	31-1	3	38	.263	.368	.332	92	0	3-2	.969	2	99	148	/O-72(50-13-10),D-9	-0.1
LEON, EDDIE Eduardo Antonio B 8.11.1946 Tucson, AZ BR/TR 6/175# d9.9																								
1968	Cle A	6	1	0	0	0	0	0	0	0-0	0	1	.000	.000	.000	-99	0	0-0	1.000	1	114	406	/S-6	0.1
1969	Cle A	64	213	20	51	6	0	3	19	19-3	0	37	.239	.300	.310	69	-9	2-2	.952	-1	94	110	S-64	-0.2
1970	Cle A	152	549	58	136	20	4	10	56	47-2	2	89	.248	.308	.353	78	-17	1-2	.982	17	100	111	*2-141,S-23/3	1.1
1971	Cle A	131	429	35	112	12	2	4	35	34-5	1	69	.261	.317	.326	76	-13	3-5	.983	0	95	93	*2-107,S-24	-0.6
1972	Cle A	89	225	14	45	2	1	4	16	20-1	1	47	.200	.265	.271	59	-12	0-2	.993	2	108	95	2-36,S-35	-0.6
1973	Chi A	127	399	37	91	10	3	3	30	34-0	3	103	.228	.291	.291	63	-20	1-5	.972	-6	95	95	*S-122/2-3	-1.4
1974	Chi A	31	46	1	5	1	0	0	3	2-0	0	12	.109	.143	.130	-20	-7	0-0	.962	4	101	126	S-21/2-7,3-2,D	-0.2
1975	NY A	1	0	0	0	0	0	0	0	0-0	0	0	—	—	—	—	0	0-0	—	-0	0	0	/S	0.0
Total	8	601	1862	165	440	51	10	24	159	156-11	7	358	.236	.296	.313	69	-78	7-16	.963	17	97	108	S-296,2-294/3-3,D	-1.8
LEON, JOSE Jose Geraldo (Vega) B 12.8.1976 Cayey, P.R. BR/TR 6/175# d6.16																								
2002	Bal A	36	89	8	22	2	0	3	10	3-0	1	20	.247	.280	.371	75	-4	1-0	1.000	0	92	132	1-17,3-12/O-2(LF),D-2	-0.4
2003	Bal A	21	54	6	13	1	0	0	0	3-0	2	18	.241	.305	.259	53	-4	0-0	.963	0	103	196	3-10/1-7,D-3	-0.4
Total	2	57	143	14	35	3	0	3	10	6-0	3	38	.245	.289	.329	66	-8	1-0	.995	1	81	137	/1-24,3-22,D-5,O-2(LF)	-0.8

Year	Tm Lg	G	AB	R	H	2B	3B	HR	RBI	BB-IB	HP	SO	AVG	OBP	SLG	AOPS	ABR	SB-CS	FA	FR	Rng	Thr	G at Pos	BFW
LEONARD d9.12																								
1892	StL N	1	0	0	0	0	0	0	0	1	0	0	—	1.000	—	219	0	1	—	-0	0	0	/O(RF)	0.0
LEONARD, ANDY Andrew Jackson B 6.1.1846 County Cavan, Ireland D 8.21.1903 Boston, MA BR/TR 5-7/168# d5.5 OF NA (218-LF 1-RF)																								
1871	Oly NA	31	148	33	43	8	3	0	30	3		1	.291	.305	.385	102	1	14-3	.863	-2	98	105	2-19,O-11(LF)/S	0.1
1872	Bos NA	46	241	57	84	7	1	2	42	0		2	.349	.349	.411	126	6	8-5	.828	-4	176	0	*O-38(LF)/3-6,2-4,S	0.2
1873	Bos NA	58	300	81	96	13	6	0	60	2		0	.320	.325	.403	106	0	27-9	.750	1	**259**	84	*O-45(45-0-1),2-12/1-2,S	0.3
1874	Bos NA	**71**	339	68	106	18	4	0	50	2		2	.313	.317	.389	119	6	11-3	.807	0	81	80	*O-51(LF),2-11,S-11	0.6
1875	Bos NA	80	396	87	127	14	6	1	74	2		6	.321	.324	.394	143	15	14-8	.806	-2	101	0	*O-73(LF)/S-3,3-3,2-2	1.4
1876	Bos N	64	303	53	85	10	2	0	27	4		6	.281	.290	.327	103	1		.925	2	109	157	O-35(LF),2-30	0.2
1877	Bos N	58	272	46	78	5	0	0	27	5		5	.287	.300	.305	88	-4		.875	-3	68	186	O-37(LF),S-21	-0.8
1878	Bos N	**60**	262	41	68	8	5	0	16	3		19	.260	.268	.328	88	-4		.777	-7	51	45	*O-60(LF)	-1.4
1880	Cin N	33	133	15	28	3	0	1	17	8		11	.211	.255	.256	75	-3		.833	-7	90	69	S-23,3-10	-0.8
Total	5 NA	286	1424	326	456	60	20	3	256	9		11	.320	.324	.397	121	28	74-28	.000	-6	149	37	O-218L/2-48,S-17,3-9,1-2	2.6
Total	4	215	970	155	259	26	7	1	87	20		41	.267	.282	.311	91	-10		.856	-14	70	114	O-132(LF)/S-44,2-30,3-10	-2.8
LEONARD, JEFFREY Jeffrey B 9.22.1955 Philadelphia, PA BR/TR 6-2/200# d9.2																								
1977	LA N	11	10	1	3	0	1	0	2	1-0	0	4	.300	.364	.500	130	0	0-0	1.000	0	123	0	O-10(6-0-4)	0.0
1978	Hou N	8	26	2	10	2	0	0	4	1-0	0	2	.385	.407	.462	154	2	0-1	1.000	1	112	199	/O-8(4-2-2)	0.2
1979	Hou N	134	411	47	119	15	5	0	47	46-7	2	68	.290	.360	.350	102	2	23-10	.959	-6	98	65	*O-123(4-22-100)	-0.8
1980	†Hou N	88	216	29	46	7	5	3	20	19-2	0	46	.213	.274	.333	75	-8	4-1	.979	0	100	161	O-56(3-9-44),1-11	-1.1
1981	Hou N	7	18	1	3	1	1	0	3	0-0	0	4	.167	.158	.333	41	-2	1-0	1.000	-1	63	0	/1-2,O-2(RF)	-0.2
	SF N	37	127	20	39	11	3	4	26	12-3	1	21	.307	.371	.535	158	9	4-2	1.000	1	114	91	O-28(8-19-4)/1-5	1.0
	Year	44	145	21	42	12	4	4	29	12-3	1	25	.290	.346	.510	145	8	5-2	1.000	1	112	85	O-30(8-19-6)/1-7	0.8
1982	SF N	80	278	32	72	16	1	9	49	19-2	2	65	.259	.306	.421	103	1	18-5	.958	-7	90	36	O-74(56-17-2)/1	-0.7
1983	SF N	139	516	74	144	17	7	21	87	35-2	1	116	.279	.323	.461	120	10	26-7	.975	4	96	171	*O-136(127-12-2)	1.3
1984	SF N	136	514	76	155	27	2	21	86	47-3	0	123	.302	.357	.484	140	26	17-7	.970	-0	92	135	*O-131(116-18-4)	2.3
1985	SF N	133	507	49	122	20	3	17	62	21-5	1	107	.241	.272	.393	88	-12	11-6	.977	-3	92	115	*O-126(125-3-0)	-2.1
1986	SF N	89	341	48	95	11	3	6	42	20-1	3	62	.279	.322	.381	99	-2	16-3	.970	-1	95	69	O-87(LF)	-0.5
1987	†SF N★	131	503	70	141	29	4	19	63	21-6	2	68	.280	.309	.467	108	3	16-7	.966	-7	84	85	*O-127(127-1-0)	-0.8
1988	SF N	44	160	12	41	8	1	2	20	9-1	0	24	.256	.292	.356	90	-2	7-5	.987	-4	90	0	O-43(LF)	-0.8
	Mil A	94	374	45	88	19	0	8	44	16-1	3	68	.235	.270	.350	72	-15	10-4	.985	-2	98	73	O-91(LF)/D-2	-1.9
1989	Sea A★	150	566	69	144	20	1	24	93	38-2	5	125	.254	.301	.420	100	-2	6-1	.982	1	105	137	*D-123,O-26(25-0-1)	-0.5
1990	Sea A	134	478	39	120	20	0	10	75	37-6	3	97	.251	.305	.356	84	-10	4-2	.983	-9	80	0	O-79(74-0-6),D-48	-2.4
Total	14	1415	5045	614	1342	223	37	144	723	342-41	23	1000	.266	.312	.411	103	0	163-61	.974	-31	93	93	*O-1147(896-103-171),D-173/1-19-7.0	
LEONARD, JOE Joseph Howard B 11.15.1894 W.Chicago, IL D 5.1.1920 Washington, DC BL/TR 5-7.5/156# d5.7 Mil 1918																								
1914	Pit N	53	126	17	25	2	2	0	4	12	0	21	.198	.268	.246	56	-7	4	.909	-6	88	53	3-38/S	-1.3
1916	Cle A	3	2	1	0	0	0	0	0	0	0	1	.000	.000	.000	-94	0	0	1.000	0	102	0	/2	0.0
	Was A	42	168	20	46	7	0	0	14	22	0	23	.274	.358	.315	103	2	4	.952	-7	75	78	3-42	-0.4
	Year	45	170	21	46	7	0	0	14	22	0	24	.271	.354	.312	101	1	4	.952	-7	75	78	3-42/2	-0.4
1917	Was A	99	297	30	57	6	7	0	23	45	2	40	.192	.302	.259	72	-9	6	.925	-2	89	158	3-68,1-19/SO(RF)	-1.1
1919	Was A	71	198	26	51	8	3	2	20	20	1	28	.258	.329	.359	94	-2	3	.944	-7	80	96	2-28,3-25/1-4,O(LF)	-0.8
1920	Was A	1	0	0	0	0	0	0	0	0	0	0	—	—	—	—	0	0-0	—	0			R	0.0
Total	5	269	791	94	179	23	12	2	61	99	3	113	.226	.315	.293	82	-16	17-0	.937	-21	85	114	3-173/2-29,1-23,O-2(1-0-1),S-2	-3.6
LEONARD, MARK Mark David B 8.14.1964 Mountain View, CA BL/TR 6/195# d7.21																								
1990	SF N	11	17	3	3	1	0	1	2	3-0	0	8	.176	.300	.412	97	0	0-0	1.000	0	112	0	/O-7(2-0-5)	0.0
1991	SF N	64	129	14	31	7	1	2	14	12-1	1	25	.240	.306	.357	90	-2	0-1	1.000	-4	74	0	O-34(24-0-12)	-0.7
1992	SF N	55	128	13	30	7	0	4	16	16-0	3	31	.234	.331	.383	108	2	0-1	.984	1	98	132	O-37(33-0-4)	0.1
1993	Bal A	10	15	1	1	1	0	0	3	3-0	0	7	.067	.190	.133	-2	-2	0-0	.833	0	133	0	/O-4(LF),D-3	-0.2
1994	SF N	14	11	2	4	1	1	0	2	3-0	0	2	.364	.500	.636	203	2	0-0	1.000	0	111	0	/O-2(LF)	0.2
1995	SF N	14	21	4	4	1	0	1	4	5-1	0	2	.190	.346	.381	94	0	0-0	1.000	-0	99	0	/O-6(1-0-5)	0.0
Total	6	168	321	37	73	18	2	8	41	42-2	4	75	.227	.319	.371	97	0	0-2	.985	-3	90	59	/O-90(66-0-26),D-3	-0.6
LEOVICH, JOHN John Joseph B 5.5.1918 Portland, OR D 2.3.2000 Lincoln City, OR BR/TR 6-0.5/200# d5.1																								
1941	Phi A	1	2	0	1	1	0	0	0	0	0	0	.500	.500	1.000	296	1	0-0	—	-0	*0*	*0*	/C	0.0
LEPCIO, TED Thaddeus Stanley B 7.28.1930 Utica, NY BR/TR 5-10/177# d4.15																								
1952	Bos A	84	274	34	72	17	2	5	26	24	3	41	.263	.329	.394	93	-2	3-3	.972	8	113	98	2-57,3-25/S	0.8
1953	Bos A	66	161	17	38	4	2	4	11	17	1	24	.236	.313	.360	77	-6	0-0	.981	11	121	126	2-34,S-20,3-11	0.8
1954	Bos A	116	398	42	102	19	4	8	45	42	3	62	.256	.328	.384	86	-7	3-4	.971	8	107	94	2-80,3-24,S-14	0.7
1955	Bos A	51	134	19	31	9	0	6	15	12-0	4	36	.231	.313	.433	91	-2	1-1	.943	3	107	78	3-45	0.1
1956	Bos A	83	284	34	74	10	0	15	51	30-1	3	77	.261	.335	.454	96	-2	1-3	.966	3	103	105	2-57,3-22	0.3
1957	Bos A	79	232	24	56	10	2	9	37	29-1	1	61	.241	.328	.418	97	-1	0-0	.976	5	110	122	2-68	0.9
1958	Bos A	50	136	10	27	3	0	6	14	12-1	1	47	.199	.268	.353	65	-7	0-1	.980	-2	99	90	2-40	-0.6
1959	Bos A	3	3	1	1	1	0	0	1	0-0	0	2	.333	.333	.667	160	0	0-0	1.000	0	158	0	/2	0.0
	Det A	76	215	25	60	8	0	7	24	17-2	0	49	.279	.332	.414	98	-1	2-0	.951	-2	95	92	S-35,2-24,3-11	0.1
	Year	79	218	26	61	9	0	7	25	17-2	0	51	.280	.332	.417	99	0	2-0	.951	-2	95	92	S-35,2-25,3-11	0.1
1960	Phi N	69	141	16	32	7	0	2	8	17-1	2	41	.227	.315	.319	75	-4	0-3	.942	-4	93	33	3-50,S-14/2-5	-0.9
1961	Chi A	5	2	0	0	0	0	0	0	1-1	0	0	.000	.333	.000	-2	0	0-0	.000	-0	0	0	/3	-0.1
	Min A	47	112	11	19	3	1	7	19	8-0	1	31	.170	.230	.402	62	-7	1-0	.919	0	80	81	3-35,2-22/S-6	-0.5
	Year	52	114	11	19	3	1	7	19	9-1	1	31	.167	.232	.395	62	-7	1-0	.895	-0	78	79	3-36,2-22/S-6	-0.6
Total	10	729	2092	233	512	91	11	69	251	209-7	19	471	.245	.318	.398	87	-39	11-15	.972	28	107	107	2-388,3-224/S-90	1.6
LePINE, PETE Louis Joseph B 9.5.1876 Montreal, PQ, CAN D 12.3.1949 Woonsocket, RI BL/TL 5-10/142# d7.21																								
1902	Det A	30	96	8	20	3	2	1	19	8	1		.208	.276	.313	62	-5	1	1.000	1	115	274	O-19(RF)/1-8	-0.5
LEPPERT, DON Don Eugene "Tiger" B 11.20.1930 Memphis, TN BL/TR 5-8/175# d4.11																								
1955	Bal A	40	70	6	8	0	1	0	2	9-0	0	10	.114	.213	.143	-2	-10	1-1	.937	-7	72	72	2-35	-1.7
LEPPERT, DON Donald George B 10.19.1931 Indianapolis, IN BR/TR 6-2/220# d6.18 C18																								
1961	Pit N	22	60	6	16	2	1	3	5	1-0	0	11	.267	.279	.483	97	-1	0-0	.968	0	*160*	*133*	C-21	0.0
1962	Pit N	45	139	14	37	6	1	3	18	12-2	1	21	.266	.327	.388	92	-2	0-1	.989	2	*95*	*79*	C-44	0.2
1963	Was A☆	73	211	20	50	11	0	6	24	20-2	1	29	.237	.305	.374	90	-3	0-0	.984	-5	93	34	C-60	-0.5
1964	Was A	50	122	6	19	3	0	3	12	11-1	0	32	.156	.224	.254	33	-11	0-0	.990	0	*103*	*113*	C-43	-1.0
Total	4	190	532	46	122	22	2	15	59	44-5	2	93	.229	.289	.363	78	-17	0-1	.985	-2	*103*	*76*	C-168	-1.3
LERCHEN, DUTCH Bertram Roe B 4.4.1889 Detroit, MI D 1.7.1962 Detroit, MI BR/TR 5-8/160# d8.14																								
1910	Bos A	6	15	1	0	0	0	0	0	1	0		.000	.063	.000	-78	-3	0	.929	-2	37	87	/S-6	-0.6
LERCHEN, GEORGE George Edward B 12.1.1922 Detroit, MI BB/TR (BL 1953) 5-11/175# d4.15																								
1952	Det A	14	32	1	5	1	0	1	3	7	0	10	.156	.308	.281	64	-1	1-0	1.000	-1	97	0	/O-7(0-3-4)	-0.2
1953	Cin N	22	17	2	5	1	0	0	2	5	0	6	.294	.455	.353	113	1	0-0	1.000	0	102	0	/O(CF)	0.1
Total	2	36	49	3	10	2	0	1	5	12	0	16	.204	.361	.306	82	0	1-0	1.000	-1	97	0	/O-8(0-4-4)	-0.1
LERIAN, WALT Walter Irvin "Peck" B 2.10.1903 Baltimore, MD D 10.22.1929 Baltimore, MD BR/TR 5-11/170# d4.16																								
1928	Phi N	96	239	28	65	16	2	2	25	41	3	29	.272	.385	.381	97	1	1	.977	-5	*75*	*126*	C-74	0.1
1929	Phi N	105	273	28	61	13	2	6	25	53	2	37	.223	.354	.352	71	-12	0	**.986**	-2	*92*	*119*	*C-103	-0.7
Total	2	201	512	56	126	29	4	8	50	94	5	66	.246	.368	.365	83	-11	1	.982	-8	*84*	*122*	C-177	-0.6
LESHER, BRIAN Brian Herbert B 3.5.1971 Wilrijk, Belgium BR/TL 6-5/205# d8.25																								
1996	Oak A	26	82	11	19	3	0	5	16	5-0	1	17	.232	.281	.451	84	-3	0-0	.977	-1	89	129	O-25(14-0-14)/1	-0.4
1997	Oak A	46	131	17	30	4	1	4	16	9-0	0	30	.229	.275	.366	68	-7	4-1	.958	2	106	152	O-32(31-0-3)/1-3,D-3	-0.6
1998	Oak A	7	7	0	1	1	0	0	1	0-0	0	3	.143	.143	.286	8	-1	0-0	1.000	2	108	1788	/O-4(LF),1	0.1
2000	Sea A	5	5	1	4	1	1	0	3	1-0	0	0	.800	.833	1.400	466	3	1-0	1.000	0	154	0	/1-4	0.3
2002	Tor A	24	38	2	5	1	0	0	2	4-0	0	15	.132	.209	.158	1	-5	0-0	1.000	1	122	24	1-12/O-5(3-0-2),D-3	-0.5

Year	Tm Lg	G	AB	R	H	2B	3B	HR	RBI	BB-IB	HP	SO	AVG	OBP	SLG	AOPS	ABR	SB-CS	FA	FR	Rng	Thr	G at Pos	BFW
Total	5	108	263	31	59	10	2	9	38	19-0	1	65	.224	.275	.380	69	-13	5-1	.970	4	102	186	/O-66(52-0-19),1-21,D-6	-1.1
LESLIE, ROY Roy Reid B 8.23.1894 Bailey, TX D 4.9.1972 Sherman, TX BR/TR 6-1/175# d9.6																								
1917	Chi N	7	19	1	4	0	0	0	1	1	0	5	.211	.250	.211	39	-1	1	.969	-0	102	90	/1-6	-0.2
1919	StL N	12	24	2	5	1	0	0	4	4	0	3	.208	.321	.250	78	0	0	.957	-0	111	142	/1-9	-0.1
1922	Phi N	141	513	44	139	23	2	6	50	37	0	49	.271	.320	.359	68	-24	3-7	.990	-5	86	102	*1-139	-3.8
Total	3	160	556	47	148	24	2	6	55	42	0	57	.266	.318	.349	68	-25	4-7	.988	-5	88	103	1-154	-4.1
LESLIE, SAM Samuel Andrew "Sambo" B 7.26.1905 Moss Point, MS D 1.21.1979 Pascagoula, MS BL/TL 6/192# d10.6																								
1929	NY N	1	1	0	0	0	0	0	1	0	0	0	.000	.000	.000	-99	0	0	1.000	-0	85	0	/O(LF)	0.0
1930	NY N	2	2	0	1	0	0	0	0	0	0	1	.500	.500	.500	146	0	0	—	0			H	0.0
1931	NY N	53	53	11	16	4	0	3	5	1	0	2	.302	.315	.547	131	2	3	1.000	0	110	0	/1-6	0.2
1932	NY N	77	75	5	22	4	0	1	15	2	2	5	.293	.329	.387	94	-1	0	1.000	-0	0	0	/1-2	-0.1
1933	NY N	40	137	21	44	12	3	3	27	12	1	9	.321	.380	.518	157	10	0	.990	-0	95	111	1-35	0.7
	Bro N	96	364	41	104	11	4	5	46	23	7	14	.286	.340	.379	110	4	1	.982	-6	81	57	1-95	-1.1
	Year	136	501	62	148	23	7	8	73	35	8	23	.295	.351	.417	123	15	1	.984	-6	85	72	*1-130	-0.4
1934	Bro N	146	546	75	181	29	6	9	102	69	3	34	.332	.409	.456	138	33	5	.993	5	112	93	*1-138	2.4
1935	Bro N	142	520	72	160	30	7	5	93	55	5	19	.308	.379	.421	117	15	4	.989	0	101	108	*1-138	0.3
1936	†NY N	117	417	49	123	19	5	6	54	23	2	16	.295	.335	.408	100	-1	0	.991	1	104	110	1-99	-1.0
1937	†NY N	72	191	25	59	7	2	3	30	20	2	12	.309	.380	.414	114	4	1	.990	4	128	142	1-44	0.4
1938	NY N	76	154	12	39	7	1	1	16	11	1	6	.253	.307	.331	75	-5	0	.988	-2	76	91	1-32	-1.0
Total	10	822	2460	311	749	123	28	36	389	216	23	118	.304	.366	.421	117	61	14	.989	0	101	98	1-589/O(LF)	0.8
LETCHAS, CHARLIE Charlie B 10.3.1915 Thomasville, GA D 3.14.1995 Tampa, FL BR/TR 5-10/150# d9.16 Mil 1945-46																								
1939	Phi N	12	44	2	10	2	0	1	3	1	0	2	.227	.244	.341	57	-3	0	.933	-1	97	117	/2-12	-0.3
1941	Was A	2	8	0	1	0	0	0	1	1	0	1	.125	.222	.125	-6	-1	0-0	.800	-1	121	74	/2-2	-0.2
1944	Phi N	116	396	29	94	8	0	0	33	32	2	27	.237	.298	.258	59	-21	0	.968	4	101	146	2-47,3-32,S-29	-1.3
1946	Phi N	6	13	1	3	0	0	0	0	1	0	1	.231	.286	.231	49	-1	0	1.000	0	89	204	/2-4	0.0
Total	4	136	461	32	108	10	0	1	37	35	2	31	.234	.291	.262	58	-26	0-0	.959	3	100	142	/2-65,3-32,S-29	-1.8
LETCHER, TOM Frederick Thomas B 1.1868 Bryan, OH BL 6/?# d9.27																								
1891	Mil AA	6	21	3	4	1	0	0	2	0	0	1	.190	.190	.238	19	-2	1	.857	1	241	1241	/O-6(1-0-5)	-0.1
LEUTZ d5.7																								
1872	Eck NA	4	12	2	1	0	0	0	0	0		0	.083	.083	.083	-57	-2	0-0	.733	-3			/C-4	-0.4
LEVAN, JESSE Jesse Roy B 7.15.1926 Reading, PA D 11.30.1998 Reading, PA BL/TR 6/172# d9.27																								
1947	Phi N	2	9	3	4	0	0	0	1	0	0	0	.444	.444	.444	142	0	0	1.000	-0	60	0	/O-2(LF)	0.0
1954	Was A	7	10	1	3	0	0	0	0	0	0	0	.300	.300	.300	68	-1	0-0	—	-0	0	0	/3-4,1	-0.1
1955	Was A	16	16	1	3	0	0	1	4	0-0	0	2	.188	.188	.375	51	-1	0-0	—	0			H	-0.1
Total	3	25	35	5	10	0	0	1	5	0-0	0	2	.286	.286	.371	80	-2	0-0	.000	-0	0	0	/3-4,O-2(LF),1	-0.2
LEVEY, JIM James Julius B 9.13.1906 Pittsburgh, PA D 3.14.1970 Dallas, TX BB/TR (BR 1930-31) 5-10.5/154# d9.17																								
1930	StL A	8	37	7	9	2	0	0	3	3	0	2	.243	.300	.297	50	-3	0-0	.958	1	102	117	/S-8	-0.1
1931	StL A	139	498	53	104	19	2	5	38	35	2	83	.209	.264	.285	43	-43	13-8	.920	-12	96	**114**	*S-139	-4.2
1932	StL A	152	568	59	159	30	8	4	63	21	4	48	.280	.310	.382	74	-24	6-4	.939	-19	94	83	*S-152	-3.0
1933	StL A	141	529	43	103	10	4	2	36	26	3	68	.195	.237	.240	25	-59	4-6	.945	-6	97	89	*S-138	-5.4
Total	4	440	1632	162	375	61	14	11	140	85	9	201	.230	.272	.305	48	-129	23-18	.936	-36	96	95	S-437	-12.7
LEVIS, CHARLIE Charles H. B 6.21.1860 St.Louis, MO D 10.16.1926 St.Louis, MO BR d4.17																								
1884	Bal U	87	373	59	85	11	4	5		3			.228	.234	.319	60	-31		.955	-0	89	100	*1-87	-3.5
	Was U	1	3	0	0	0	0	0		0			.000	.000	.000	-99	-1		1.000	0	0	0	/1	-0.1
	Year	88	376	59	85	11	4	5		3			.226	.232	.316	59	-31		.955	-0	88	99	1-88	-3.6
	Ind AA	3	10	0	2	0	0	0		0	0		.200	.200	.200	32	-1		1.000	0	128	86	/1-3	-0.1
1885	Bal AA	1	4	2	1	0	0	0	0	0	1		.250	.400	.250	110	0		.889	-0	0	0	/1	0.0
Total	2	92	390	61	88	11	4	5	0	3	1		.226	.234	.313	59	-33		.956	-0	88	97	/1-92	-3.7
LEVIS, JESSE Jesse B 4.14.1968 Philadelphia, PA BL/TR 5-9/180# d4.24																								
1992	Cle A	28	43	2	12	4	0	1	3	0-0	0	5	.279	.279	.442	101	0	0-0	.985	-0	104	54	C-21/D	0.0
1993	Cle A	31	63	7	11	2	0	0	4	2-0	0	10	.175	.197	.206	9	-8	0-0	.991	0	89	103	C-29	-0.6
1994	Cle A	1	1	0	1	0	0	0	0	0-0	0	0	1.000	1.000	1.000	417	0	0-0	—	0			/H	0.0
1995	Cle A	12	18	1	6	2	0	0	3	1-0	0	0	.333	.333	.444	109	0	0-0	1.000	-1	50	168	C-12	0.0
1996	Mil A	104	233	27	55	6	1	1	21	38-0	2	15	.236	.348	.283	60	-13	0-0	**.998**	9	106	83	C-90/D-6	0.0
1997	Mil A	99	200	19	57	7	0	1	19	24-0	1	17	.285	.361	.335	83	-4	1-0	.994	0	90	82	C-78/D-8	-0.1
1998	Mil N	22	37	4	13	0	0	0	4	7-2	2	6	.351	.468	.351	123	2	1-0	1.000	2	89	36	C-14	0.4
1999	Cle A	10	26	0	4	0	0	0	3	1-0	1	6	.154	.214	.154	-4	-4	0-0	1.000	-0	93	42	/C-9	-0.4
2001	Mil N	12	33	6	8	2	0	0	3	3-0	0	7	.242	.306	.303	60	-2	0-0	.984	-2	87	38	C-11	-0.3
Total	9	319	654	66	167	23	1	3	60	76-2	6	66	.255	.336	.307	68	-29	2-0	.995	8	95	79	C-264/D-15	-1.0
LEVY, ED Edward Clarence (born Edward Clarence Whitner) B 10.28.1916 Birmingham, AL BR/TR 6-5.5/190# d4.16																								
1940	Phi N	1	1	0	0	0	0	0	0	0	0	0	.000	.000	.000	-99	0	0	—	0			H	0.0
1942	NY A	13	41	5	5	0	0	0	3	4	0	5	.122	.200	.122	-9	-6	1-0	.992	1	132	142	1-13	-0.6
1944	NY A	40	153	12	37	11	2	4	29	6	0	19	.242	.270	.418	92	-3	1-1	.962	-2	96	67	O-36(LF)	-0.7
Total	3	54	195	17	42	11	2	4	32	10	0	24	.215	.254	.354	70	-9	2-1	.962	-0	96	67	/O-36(LF),1-13	-1.3
LEWIS, ALLAN Allan Sydney "The Panamanian Express" B 12.12.1941 Colon, Panama BB/TR 6/170# d4.11																								
1967	KC A	34	6	7	1	0	0	0	0	0-0	0	3	.167	.167	.167	-1	-1	14-5	—	0			H	0.1
1968	Oak A	26	4	9	1	0	0	0	0	1-0	0	0	.250	.400	.250	105	0	8-4	—	-0	0	0	/O(LF)	0.0
1969	Oak A	12	1	2	0	0	0	0	0	0-0	0	0	.000	.000	.000	-99	0	0-0	—	0			H	0.0
1970	Oak A	25	8	8	2	0	0	1	1	0-0	0	0	.250	.250	.625	139	0	7-1	1.000	-0	63	0	/O-2(LF)	0.1
1972	†Oak A	24	10	5	2	1	0	0	2	0-0	0	1	.200	.200	.300	50	-1	8-3	.900	0	143	0	/O-6(5-0-1)	0.0
1973	†Oak A	35	0	16	0	0	0	0	0	0-0	0	0	—	—	—	—	0	7-4	1.000	0	456	0	/O(LF)D	0.0
Total	6	156	29	47	6	1	0	1	3	1-0	0	4	.207	.233	.345	69	-2	44-17	.923	0	116	0	/O-10(9-0-1),D-6	0.2
LEWIS, DARREN Darren Joel B 8.28.1967 Berkeley, CA BR/TR 6/189# d8.21																								
1990	Oak A	25	35	4	8	0	0	0	1	7-0	1	4	.229	.372	.229	75	-1	2-0	1.000	0	107	0	O-23(3-16-5)/D-2	0.0
1991	SF N	72	222	41	55	5	3	1	15	36-0	2	30	.248	.358	.311	93	-1	13-7	1.000	2	113	62	O-68(CF)	0.1
1992	SF N	100	320	38	74	8	1	1	18	29-0	1	46	.231	.295	.272	66	-15	28-8	1.000	-0	104	63	O-94(CF)	-1.3
1993	SF N	136	522	84	132	17	7	2	48	30-0	7	40	.253	.302	.324	70	-24	46-15	**1.000**	3	106	62	*O-131(CF)	-1.5
1994	SF N	114	451	70	116	15	**9**	4	29	53-0	4	50	.257	.340	.357	86	-9	30-13	.993	-3	97	79	*O-113(CF)	-0.9
1995	SF N	74	309	47	78	10	3	1	16	17-0	6	37	.252	.303	.314	65	-16	21-7	.995	2	110	48	O-73(CF)	-1.1
	†Cin N	58	163	19	40	3	0	0	8	17-0	2	20	.245	.324	.264	58	-10	11-11	.992	3	116	126	O-57(CF)	-0.7
	Year	132	472	66	118	13	3	1	24	34-0	8	57	.250	.311	.297	63	-26	32-18	.994	5	112	77	*O-130(CF)	-1.8
1996	Chi A	141	337	55	77	12	2	4	53	45-1	3	40	.228	.321	.312	65	-18	21-5	.990	-6	104	0	*O-138(1-137-0)	-1.8
1997	Chi A	81	77	15	18	1	0	0	5	11-0	0	14	.234	.330	.247	56	-5	11-4	1.000	4	127	70	O-64(CF)/D-6	0.0
	LA N	26	77	7	23	3	1	1	10	6-0	0	17	.299	.349	.403	104	0	3-2	.980	2	124	75	O-25(23-2-1)	0.1
1998	†Bos A	155	585	95	157	25	3	8	63	70-0	8	94	.268	.352	.362	85	-11	29-12	.992	2	108	61	*O-152(4-109-55)/D	-0.8
1999	†Bos A	135	470	63	113	14	6	2	40	45-0	5	52	.240	.311	.309	58	-31	16-10	.994	1	107	50	*O-130(0-88-51)/D-2	-2.9
2000	Bos A	97	270	44	65	12	0	2	17	22-0	3	34	.241	.305	.307	54	-19	10-5	.981	-3	90	112	O-89(18-41-37)/D-5	-2.2
2001	Bos A	82	164	18	46	9	1	1	12	8-0	3	25	.280	.326	.366	81	-4	5-5	1.000	3	106	143	O-69(27-21-29)/D-6	-0.4
2002	Chi N	58	79	7	19	3	1	0	7	7-0	3	11	.241	.326	.304	72	-4	1-3	1.000	3	119	192	O-47(22-18-9)	-0.2
Total	13	1354	4081	607	1021	137	37	27	342	403-1	48	514	.250	.323	.322	72	-168	247-107	.994	11	106	67	*O-1273(98-1032-187)/D-22	-13.6
LEWIS, FRED Frederick Miller B 10.13.1858 Buffalo, NY D 6.5.1945 Utica, NY BB/TR 5-10.5/194# d7.2																								
1881	Bos N	27	114	17	25	6	0	0	9	7		5	.219	.264	.272	72	-3		.837	-3	82	90	O-27(0-3-24)	-0.6
1883	Phi N	38	160	21	40	7	0	0	18	4		13	.250	.268	.294	78	-4		.814	-1	91	55	O-38(CF)	-0.5
	StL AA	49	209	37	63	8	4	1	33	1			.301	.305	.392	116	3		.848	-3	61	0	O-49(CF)	-0.2
1884	StL AA	73	300	59	97	25	3	0		16	4		.323	.366	.427	152	18		.853	-1	100	46	O-73(CF)	1.3

Year	Tm Lg	G	AB	R	H	2B	3B	HR	RBI	BB-IB	HP	SO	AVG	OBP	SLG	AOPS	ABR	SB-CS	FA	FR	Rng	Thr	G at Pos	BFW
	StL U	8	30	6	9	1	0	0		3			.300	.364	.333	109	0		.909	-1	0	0	/O-8(CF)	-0.2
1885	StL N	45	181	12	53	9	0	1	27	9		10	.293	.326	.359	130	6		.957	7	216	173	O-45(9-37-0)	1.1
1886	Cin AA	77	324	72	103	14	6	2	32	20	4		.318	.365	.417	140	14	8	.884	-4	88	41	O-76(CF)/3	0.6
Total	5	317	1318	224	390	70	13	4	119	60	8	28	.296	.330	.378	124	34	8	.866	-6	102	59	O-316(9-284-24)/3	1.5
LEWIS, DUFFY George Edward B 4.18.1888 San Francisco, CA D 6.17.1979 Salem, NH BL/TL 5-10.5/165# d4.16 Mil 1918 C5																								
1910	Bos A	151	541	64	153	29	7	8	68	32	4		.283	.328	.407	127	15	10	.944	12	106	147	*O-149(LF)	1.9
1911	Bos A	130	469	64	144	32	4	7	86	25	10		.307	.355	.437	122	13	11	.939	5	93	145	*O-125(LF)	1.2
1912	†Bos A	**154**	581	85	165	36	9	6	109	52	3		.284	.346	.408	110	7	9	.947	6	103	121	*O-154(LF)	0.6
1913	Bos A	149	551	54	164	31	12	0	90	30	2	55	.298	.336	.397	112	6	12	.960	11	105	**159**	*O-142(LF)/P3	1.1
1914	Bos A	146	510	53	142	37	9	2	79	57	5	41	.278	.357	.398	127	18	22-31	.952	-3	92	105	*O-142(LF)	0.3
1915	†Bos A	152	557	69	162	31	7	2	76	45	4	63	.291	.348	.382	122	14	14-7	.952	-6	93	80	*O-152(LF)	0.2
1916	†Bos A	152	563	56	151	29	5	1	56	33	4	56	.268	.313	.343	97	-4	16	.970	-3	98	80	*O-151(136-15-0)	-1.6
1917	Bos A	150	553	55	167	29	9	1	65	29	5	54	.302	.342	.392	125	14	8	.972	5	108	96	*O-150(LF)	1.4
1919	NY A	**141**	559	67	152	23	4	7	89	17	0	42	.272	.293	.365	84	-15	8	.985	-8	86	86	*O-141(LF)	-3.1
1920	NY A	107	365	34	99	8	1	4	61	24	2	32	.271	.320	.332	70	-16	2-8	.961	-1	93	114	O-99(98-0-1)	-2.3
1921	Was A	27	102	11	19	4	1	0	14	8	1	10	.186	.252	.245	29	-11	1-1	.980	-1	88	96	O-27(26-0-1)	-1.4
Total	11	1459	5351	612	1518	289	68	38	793	352	40	353	.284	.333	.384	108	41	113-47	.959	16	98	112	*O-1432(1415-15-2)/3P	-1.7
LEWIS, JACK John David B 2.14.1884 Pittsburgh, PA D 2.25.1956 Steubenville, OH BR/TR 5-8/158# d9.16																								
1911	Bos A	18	59	7	16	0	0	0	6	7	2		.271	.368	.271	80	-1	2	.931	0	106	88	2-18	-0.1
1914	Pit F	117	394	32	92	14	5	1	48	17	6	46	.234	.276	.302	58	-31	9	.949	3	103	77	*2-115/S	-2.8
1915	Pit F	82	231	24	61	6	5	0	26	8	1	31	.264	.292	.333	76	-12	7	.962	-0	102	107	2-45,S-11/O-6(RF),1-5,3	-1.2
Total	3	217	684	63	169	20	10	1	80	32	9	77	.247	.290	.310	66	-44	18	.951	2	103	86	2-178/S-12,O-6(RF),1-5,3	-4.1
LEWIS, BUDDY John Kelly B 8.10.1916 Gastonia, NC BL/TR 6-1/175# d9.16 Mil 1942-45																								
1935	Was A	8	28	0	3	0	0	0	2	0	0	5	.107	.107	.107	-46	-6	0-0	.941	0	111	129	/3-6	-0.6
1936	Was A	143	601	100	175	21	13	6	67	47	4	46	.291	.347	.399	89	-14	6-6	.933	6	**108**	105	*3-139	-0.3
1937	Was A	156	668	107	210	32	6	10	79	52	3	44	.314	.367	.425	104	3	11-5	.938	-20	91	99	*3-156	-1.0
1938	Was A★	151	656	122	194	35	9	12	91	58	1	35	.296	.354	.431	103	1	17-9	.912	-5	103	109	*3-151	0.2
1939	Was A	140	536	87	171	23	**16**	10	75	72	2	27	.319	.402	.478	134	28	10-9	.933	11	**114**	117	*3-134	3.9
1940	Was A	148	600	101	190	38	10	6	63	74	1	36	.317	.393	.443	124	24	15-10	.960	1	96	127	*O-112(RF),3-36	1.8
1941	Was A	149	569	97	169	29	11	9	72	82	0	30	.297	.386	.434	122	20	10-7	.972	3	116	169	O-96(RF),3-49	1.7
1945	Was A	69	258	42	86	14	7	2	37	37	3	15	.333	.423	.465	172	25	1-2	.981	3	107	113	O-69(RF)	2.4
1946	Was A	150	582	82	170	28	13	7	45	59	2	26	.292	.359	.421	125	18	5-3	.970	2	101	119	*O-145(8-1-137)	1.6
1947	Was A★	140	506	67	132	15	4	6	48	51	1	27	.261	.330	.342	89	-8	6-6	.968	0	101	118	*O-130(RF)	-1.3
1949	Was A	95	257	25	63	14	4	3	28	41	3	12	.245	.355	.366	93	-2	2-2	.979	2	114	69	O-67(RF)	-0.3
Total	11	1349	5261	830	1563	249	93	71	607	573	20	303	.297	.368	.420	112	89	83-59	.927	4	102	109	3-671,O-619(8-1-611)	8.1
LEWIS, JOHNNY Johnny Joe B 8.10.1939 Greenville, AL BL/TR 6-1/189# d4.14 C9																								
1964	StL N	40	94	10	22	2	2	2	7	13-1	0	23	.234	.324	.362	86	-2	2-2	.966	1	102	139	O-36(2-0-34)	-0.3
1965	NY N	148	477	64	117	15	3	15	45	59-4	3	117	.245	.331	.384	105	4	4-7	.975	2	95	156	*O-142(0-48-101)	-0.4
1966	NY N	65	166	21	32	6	1	5	20	21-0	0	43	.193	.282	.331	72	-6	2-0	.988	-1	98	67	O-49(11-8-31)	-1.0
1967	NY N	13	34	2	4	1	0	0	2	2-0	0	11	.118	.167	.147	-10	-5	0-0	1.000	1	105	177	O-10(2-0-9)	-0.5
Total	4	266	771	97	175	24	6	22	74	95-5	3	194	.227	.313	.359	90	-9	8-9	.977	2	97	137	O-237(15-56-175)	-2.2
LEWIS, MARK Mark David B 11.30.1969 Hamilton, OH BR/TR 6-1/190# d4.26																								
1991	Cle A	84	314	29	83	15	1	0	30	15-0	0	45	.264	.293	.318	70	-13	2-2	.966	-12	95	84	2-50,S-36	-2.2
1992	Cle A	122	413	44	109	21	0	5	30	25-1	3	69	.264	.308	.351	87	-8	4-5	.954	-11	95	93	*S-121/3	-1.2
1993	Cle A	14	52	6	13	2	0	1	5	0-0	0	7	.250	.250	.346	59	-3	3-0	.964	-3	82	116	S-13	-0.4
1994	Cle A	20	73	6	15	5	0	1	8	2-0	0	13	.205	.227	.315	38	-7	1-0	.902	-5	92	50	S-13/3-6,2	-1.0
1995	†Cin N	81	171	25	58	13	1	3	30	21-2	0	33	.339	.407	.480	135	10	0-3	.968	-1	105	56	3-72/2-2,S-2	0.8
1996	Det A	145	545	69	147	30	3	11	55	42-0	5	109	.270	.326	.396	82	-16	6-1	.987	-9	98	81	*2-144/D	-1.5
1997	†SF N	118	341	50	91	14	6	10	42	23-2	4	62	.267	.318	.431	97	-3	3-2	.945	-15	84	93	3-69,2-29/D	-1.7
1998	Phi N	142	518	52	129	21	2	9	54	48-2	3	111	.249	.312	.349	74	-20	3-3	.978	7	106	83	*2-140	-0.6
1999	Cin N	88	173	18	44	16	0	6	28	7-1	0	24	.254	.280	.451	80	-6	0-0	.938	-8	78	129	3-52/2-2	-1.2
2000	Cin N	11	19	1	2	1	0	0	3	1-0	0	3	.105	.150	.158	-22	-4	0-0	.909	1	134	0	/3-5	-0.3
	Bal A	71	163	19	44	17	0	2	21	12-0	1	31	.270	.322	.411	89	-3	7-2	.857	-6	91	52	3-29,2-21,S-14/D-4	-0.5
2001	Cle A	6	13	1	1	0	0	0	0	0-0	0	4	.077	.077	.077	-58	-3	0-0	.889	0	123	225	/3-4,2-3	-0.3
Total	11	902	2795	320	736	155	13	48	306	196-8	16	511	.263	.312	.380	82	-76	29-18	.977	-62	100	83	2-392,3-238,S-199/D-6	-10.1
LEWIS, PHIL Philip B 10.8.1884 Pittsburgh, PA D 8.8.1959 Port Wentworth, GA BR/TR 6/195# d4.14																								
1905	Bro N	118	433	32	110	9	2	3	33	16	1		.254	.282	.305	81	-12	16	.904	-3	97	120	*S-118	-1.2
1906	Bro N	136	452	40	110	8	4	0	37	43	0		.243	.309	.279	90	-5	14	.922	-20	98	80	*S-135	-2.3
1907	Bro N	136	475	52	118	11	1	0	30	23	2		.248	.286	.276	83	-11	16	.938	-23	90	80	*S-136	-3.4
1908	Bro N	118	415	22	91	5	6	1	30	13	0		.219	.243	.267	66	-19	9	.943	-2	96	94	*S-116	-2.0
Total	4	508	1775	146	429	33	13	4	130	95	3		.242	.281	.282	80	-47	55	.926	-48	95	93	S-505	-8.9
LEWIS, BILL William Henry "Buddy" B 10.15.1904 Ripley, TN D 10.24.1977 Memphis, TN BR/TR 5-9/165# d6.3																								
1933	StL N	15	35	8	14	1	0	1	8	2	0	3	.400	.432	.514	161	3	0	1.000	0	*79*	*99*	/C-8	0.4
1935	Bos N	6	4	1	0	0	0	0	0	1	0	1	.000	.200	.000	-45	-1	0	—	-0	*0*	*0*	/C	-0.1
1936	Bos N	29	62	11	19	2	0	0	3	12	0	7	.306	.419	.339	113	2	0	.967	-2	*134*	*65*	C-21	0.1
Total	3	50	101	20	33	3	0	1	11	15	0	11	.327	.414	.386	124	4	0	.981	-2	*114*	*77*	/C-30	0.4
LEYRITZ, JIM James Joseph B 12.27.1963 Lakewood, OH BR/TR 6/195# d6.8 OF Total (25-LF 30-RF)																								
1990	NY A	92	303	28	78	13	1	5	25	27-1	7	51	.257	.331	.356	92	-3	2-3	.929	-14	76	40	3-69,O-14(10-0-4),C-11	-1.7
1991	NY A	32	77	8	14	3	0	0	4	13-0	0	15	.182	.300	.221	46	-5	0-1	.909	-5	65	64	3-18/C-5,1-3,D	-1.0
1992	NY A	63	144	17	37	6	0	7	26	14-1	6	22	.257	.341	.444	121	4	0-1	.990	3	70	188	D-31,C-18/1-2,3-2,O-2(RF),2	0.6
1993	NY A	95	259	43	80	14	0	14	53	37-3	8	59	.309	.410	.525	155	22	0-0	.993	-2	79	106	1-29,O-28(6-0-23),D-21,C-12	1.5
1994	NY A	75	249	47	66	12	0	17	58	35-1	6	61	.265	.365	.518	130	12	0-0	1.000	-1	153	47	C-37,D-25,1-10	0.9
1995	†NY A	77	264	37	71	12	0	7	37	37-2	8	73	.269	.374	.394	102	2	1-1	.993	-5	70	77	C-46,1-18,D-15	-0.2
1996	†NY A	88	265	23	70	10	0	7	40	30-3	9	68	.264	.355	.381	87	-4	2-0	.995	-2	106	87	C-55,3-13,D-12/1-5,O-3(LF),2-2	-0.3
1997	Ana A	84	294	47	81	7	0	11	50	37-2	3	56	.276	.357	.412	102	1	1-1	1.000	4	100	172	C-58,1-15,D-13	0.7
	Tex A	37	85	11	24	4	0	0	14	23-0	3	22	.282	.446	.329	102	2	1-0	.984	-2	62	184	C-11/1-9,D-9	0.1
	Year	121	379	58	105	11	0	11	64	60-2	6	78	.277	.379	.393	102	3	2-1	.998	2	94	174	C-69,1-24,D-22	0.8
1998	Bos A	52	129	17	37	6	0	8	24	21-1	2	34	.287	.385	.519	132	7	0-0	1.000	0	34	0	D-39/C1	0.4
	†SD N	62	143	17	38	10	0	4	18	21-0	7	40	.266	.384	.420	121	6	0-0	.987	-1	117	37	C-24,1-20/3O(LF)	0.5
1999	SD N	50	134	17	32	5	0	8	21	15-1	4	37	.239	.331	.455	105	1	0-0	.994	1	54	86	C-24,1-19/3	0.1
	†NY A	31	66	8	15	4	1	0	5	13-1	0	17	.227	.354	.318	74	-2	0-0	.986	1	191	102	D-14/1-9,C3	-0.2
2000	NY A	24	55	2	12	0	0	1	4	7-0	1	14	.218	.317	.273	52	-4	0-0	1.000	-1	53	0	D-15/C-2,1	-0.5
	LA N	41	60	3	12	1	0	1	8	7-0	1	12	.200	.294	.267	46	-5	0-0	1.000	-2	80	108	/1-8,O-6(5-0-1),C-3	-0.7
Total	11	903	2527	325	667	107	2	90	387	337-16	65	581	.264	.362	.415	106	34	7-7	.995	-24	104	101	C-308,D-195,1-149,3-105/O-54R,2	0.2
LEZCANO, CARLOS Carlos Manuel (Rubio) B 9.30.1955 Arecibo, P.R. BR/TR 6-2/185# d4.10																								
1980	Chi N	42	88	15	18	4	1	3	12	11-0	1	29	.205	.294	.375	81	-2	1-2	.948	-1	98	158	O-39(CF)	-0.4
1981	Chi N	7	14	1	1	0	0	0	2	0-0	0	4	.071	.071	.071	-57	-3	0-0	1.000	0	118	0	/O-5(1-0-4)	-0.3
Total	2	49	102	16	19	4	1	3	14	11-0	1	33	.186	.267	.333	64	-5	1-2	.952	-1	100	142	/O-44(1-39-4)	-0.7
LEZCANO, SIXTO Sixto Joaquin (Curras) B 11.28.1953 Arecibo, P.R. BR/TR 5-11/175# d9.10																								
1974	Mil A	15	54	5	13	2	0	2	9	4-0	0	9	.241	.283	.389	95	-1	1-1	.972	2	101	245	O-15(RF)	0.0
1975	Mil A	134	429	55	106	19	3	11	43	46-1	4	93	.247	.324	.382	99	-1	5-5	.977	-3	98	95	*O-129(0-2-128)/D-2	-1.1
1976	Mil A	145	513	53	146	19	5	7	56	51-2	2	112	.285	.348	.382	117	11	14-10	.973	6	**111**	94	*O-142(64-17-66)/D-3	1.0
1977	Mil A	109	400	50	109	21	4	21	49	52-1	2	78	.273	.358	.503	132	18	6-5	.988	9	111	142	*O-108(RF)	2.0
1978	Mil A	132	442	62	129	21	4	15	61	64-6	1	83	.292	.377	.459	135	23	3-3	.979	5	95	184	*O-127(RF)/D-3	2.1
1979	Mil A	138	473	84	152	29	3	28	101	77-5	3	74	.321	.414	.573	165	46	4-3	.986	-4	94	93	*O-135(RF)/D	3.4
1980	Mil A	112	411	51	94	19	3	18	55	39-3	3	75	.229	.298	.421	98	-2	1-1	.983	1	101	94	*O-108(RF)/D-4	-0.7

Year	Tm Lg	G	AB	R	H	2B	3B	HR	RBI	BB-IB	HP	SO	AVG	OBP	SLG	AOPS	ABR	SB-CS	FA	FR	Rng	Thr	G at Pos	BFW
1981	StL N	72	214	26	57	8	2	5	28	40-2	0	40	.266	.376	.393	117	6	0-1	.973	-6	79	87	O-65(32-0-34)	-0.3
1982	SD N	138	470	73	136	26	6	16	84	78-10	2	69	.289	.388	.472	149	34	2-1	.990	9	104	161	*O-134(RF)	3.7
1983	SD N	97	317	41	74	11	2	8	49	47-3	1	66	.233	.331	.356	95	-2	0-0	.968	2	101	128	O-91(RF)	-0.5
	†Phi N	18	39	8	11	1	0	0	7	5-0	0	9	.282	.364	.308	89	0	1-0	1.000	1	97	300	O-15(2-1-13)	0.0
	Year	115	356	49	85	12	2	8	56	52-3	1	75	.239	.334	.351	94	-2	1-0	.971	3	101	146	*O-106(2-1-104)	-0.5
1984	Phi N	109	256	36	71	6	2	14	40	38-1	0	43	.277	.371	.480	135	12	0-1	.981	3	118	67	O-87(4-0-83)	1.2
1985	Pit N	72	116	16	24	2	0	3	9	35-3	1	17	.207	.392	.302	98	2	0-0	.967	-0	99	92	O-40(25-0-16)	0.0
Total	12	1291	4134	560	1122	184	34	148	591	576-37	19	768	.271	.360	.440	125	146	37-31	.980	24	101	120	*O-1196(127-20-1058)/D-13	10.8
LIBBY, STEVE Stephen Augustus B 12.8.1853 Scarborough, ME D 3.31.1935 Milford, CT 6-1.5/168# d5.10																								
1879	Buf N	1	2	0	0	0	0	0	0	0		1	.000	.000	.000	-98	0		1.000	0	0	0	/1	0.0
LIBKE, AL Albert Walter B 9.12.1918 Tacoma, WA D 3.7.2003 Wenatchee, WA BL/TR 6-4/215# d4.19 ▲																								
1945	Cin N	130	449	41	127	23	5	4	53	34	2	62	.283	.336	.383	102	0	6	.963	1	96	131	*O-108(27-0-82)/P-4,1-2	-0.6
1946	Cin N	124	431	32	109	22	1	5	42	43	1	50	.253	.322	.343	92	-5	0	.972	-4	86	121	*O-115(RF)/P	-1.3
Total	2	254	880	73	236	45	6	9	95	77	3	112	.268	.329	.364	97	-5	6	.967	-4	91	126	O-223(27-0-197)/P-5,1-2	-1.9
LIBRAN, FRANKIE Francisco (Rosas) B 5.6.1948 Mayaguez, P.R. BR/TR 6/168# d9.3																								
1969	SD N	10	10	1	1	1	0	0	1	1-0	0	2	.100	.182	.200	7	-1	0-0	1.000	-2	85	41	/S-9	-0.2
LICKERT, JOHN John Wilbur B 4.4.1960 Pittsburgh, PA BR/TR 5-11/175# d9.19																								
1981	Bos A	1	0	0	0	0	0	0	0	0-0	0	0	—	—	—	—	0	0-0	1.000	0	0	0	/C	0.0
LIDDELL, DAVE David Alexander (born B 6.15.1966 Los Angeles, CA BR/TR 6/190# d6.3																								
1990	NY N	1	1	1	1	0	0	0	0	0-0	0	0	1.000	1.000	1.000	453	0	0-0	1.000	0	0	0	/C	0.0
LIEBERTHAL, MIKE Michael Scott B 1.18.1972 Glendale, CA BR/TR 6/170# d6.30																								
1994	Phi N	24	79	6	21	3	1	1	5	3-0	1	5	.266	.301	.367	71	-4	0-0	.969	-5	106	29	C-22	-0.7
1995	Phi N	16	47	1	12	2	0	0	4	5-0	0	5	.255	.327	.298	66	-2	0-0	.991	0	71	89	C-14	-0.1
1996	Phi N	50	166	21	42	8	0	7	23	10-0	2	30	.253	.297	.428	89	-3	0-0	.990	5	154	93	C-43	0.4
1997	Phi N	134	455	59	112	27	1	20	77	44-1	4	76	.246	.314	.442	97	-3	3-4	.988	4	126	93	*C-129/D	0.8
1998	Phi N	86	313	39	80	15	3	8	45	17-1	7	44	.256	.304	.399	83	-8	2-1	.988	6	**151**	78	C-83	0.3
1999	Phi N★	145	510	84	153	33	1	31	96	44-7	11	86	.300	.363	.551	125	19	0-0	**.997**	4	153	73	*C-143	3.0
2000	Phi N★	108	389	55	108	30	0	15	71	40-3	6	53	.278	.352	.470	105	3	2-0	.993	1	140	98	*C-106	1.1
2001	Phi N	34	121	21	28	8	0	2	11	12-2	3	21	.231	.316	.347	73	-5	0-0	.992	4	189	56	C-33	0.1
2002	Phi N	130	476	46	133	29	2	15	52	38-2	14	58	.279	.349	.443	116	9	0-1	.993	-8	143	82	*C-129	0.8
2003	Phi N	131	508	68	159	30	1	13	81	38-2	12	59	.313	.373	.453	122	17	0-0	.990	-12	77	64	*C-131	1.3
Total	10	858	3064	400	848	185	9	112	465	251-18	60	437	.277	.340	.453	106	23	7-6	.991	-1	132	79	C-833/D	7.0
LIEFER, JEFF Jeffrey David B 8.17.1974 Fontana, CA BL/TR 6-3/195# d4.7																								
1999	Chi A	45	113	8	28	7	1	0	14	8-0	0	28	.248	.295	.327	59	-7	2-0	1.000	2	106	114	O-17(14-0-3),1-15/D-7	-0.6
2000	Chi A	5	11	0	2	0	0	0	0	0-0	0	4	.182	.182	.182	-7	-2	0-0	1.000	-0	51	0	/O-5(RF),1	-0.2
2001	Chi A	83	254	36	65	13	0	18	39	20-1	2	69	.256	.313	.520	111	3	0-1	1.000	-7	73	90	O-38(35-0-4),1-15,3-15,D-10	-0.7
2002	Chi A	76	204	28	47	8	0	7	26	19-2	0	60	.230	.295	.373	75	-8	0-0	1.000	-3	94	58	O-36(24-0-12),1-31/D-6	-1.3
2003	Mon N	35	88	6	17	3	0	3	18	3-0	0	26	.193	.217	.330	37	-8	0-1	.980	-3	56	125	1-21	-1.3
	TB A	9	25	4	3	1	0	1	3	3-1	0	13	.120	.214	.280	29	-3	0-0	.929	-0	89	0	/3-6,O(LF)D	-0.3
Total	5	253	695	82	162	32	1	29	100	53-4	2	200	.233	.287	.407	78	-25	2-2	1.000	-10	87	80	/O-97(74-0-24),1-83,D-25,3-21	-4.4
LIESE, FRED Frederick Richard B 10.7.1885 , WI D 6.30.1967 Los Angeles, CA BL/TL 5-8/150# d4.14																								
1910	Bos N	5	4	0	0	0	0	0	0	1	0	2	.000	.200	.000	-39	-1	0	—	0			H	-0.1
LILLARD, GENE Robert Eugene B 11.12.1913 Santa Barbara, CA D 4.12.1991 Goleta, CA BR/TR 5-10.5/178# d5.8 b-Bill ▲																								
1936	Chi N	19	34	6	7	1	0	0	2	3	0	8	.206	.270	.235	36	-3	0	.947	-1	81	98	/S-4,3-3	-0.4
1939	Chi N	23	10	3	1	0	0	0	0	6	0	3	.100	.438	.100	51	1	0	1.000	0	98	0	P-20	0.0
1940	StL N	2	0	0	0	0	0	0	0	0	0	0	—	—	—	—	0	0	1.000	0	99	0	/P-2	0.0
Total	3	44	44	9	8	1	0	0	2	9	0	11	.182	.321	.205	43	-2	0	1.000	-1	98	0	/P-22,S-4,3-3	-0.4
LILLARD, BILL William Beverly B 1.10.1918 Goleta, CA BR/TR 5-10/170# d9.11 b-Gene																								
1939	Phi A	7	19	4	6	1	0	0	1	3	0	1	.316	.409	.368	102	0	0-0	.974	2	128	70	/S-7	0.2
1940	Phi A	73	206	26	49	8	2	1	21	28	1	28	.238	.332	.311	69	-9	0-1	.921	-13	90	72	S-69/2	-1.7
Total	2	80	225	30	55	9	2	1	22	31	1	29	.244	.339	.316	72	-9	0-1	.927	-12	94	72	/S-76,2	-1.5
LILLIE, JIM James J. "Grasshopper" (born James J. Lilly) B 7.27.1861 New Haven, CT D 11.9.1890 Kansas City, MO d5.17 ▲ OF Total (147-LF 38-CF 204-RF)																								
1883	Buf N	50	201	25	47	7	3	1	29	1		31	.234	.238	.313	64	-9		.835	-6	82	132	O-47(12-34-1)/P-3,C-2,S32	-1.4
1884	Buf N	**114**	471	68	105	12	5	3	53	5		71	.223	.231	.289	60	-23		.852	16	**180**	**197**	*O-114(RF)/P-2	-0.7
1885	Buf N	**112**	430	49	107	13	3	2	30	6		39	.249	.259	.307	80	-11		.862	2	112	121	*O-112(21-4-89)/S-3,1	-1.0
1886	KC N	114	416	37	73	9	0	0	22	11		80	.175	.197	.197	19	-41	13	.884	11	132	75	*O-114(LF)/P	-3.0
Total	4	390	1518	179	332	41	11	6	134	23		221	.219	.230	.272	54	-84	13	.863	23	135	131	O-387R/P-6,S-4,C-2,123	-6.1
LILLIS, BOB Robert Perry B 6.2.1930 Altadena, CA BR/TR 5-11/160# d8.30 M4 C22																								
1958	LA N	20	69	10	27	3	1	1	5	4-0	1	2	.391	.421	.507	143	4	1-2	.964	-0	99	81	S-19	0.5
1959	LA N	30	48	7	11	2	0	0	2	3-1	0	4	.229	.275	.271	43	-4	0-0	.919	3	113	113	S-20	0.1
1960	LA N	48	60	6	16	4	0	0	6	2-1	0	6	.267	.290	.333	66	-3	2-0	.982	9	116	167	S-23,3-14/2	0.8
1961	LA N	19	9	0	1	0	0	0	1	1-0	0	1	.111	.200	.111	-13	-1	0-0	1.000	-0	127	0	3-12/2S	-0.1
	StL N	86	230	24	50	4	0	0	21	7-2	2	13	.217	.245	.235	26	-24	3-3	.928	0	101	65	S-56,2-24	-1.9
	Year	105	239	24	51	4	0	0	22	8-2	2	14	.213	.243	.230	25	-26	3-3	.924	0	100	65	S-57,2-25,3-12	-2.0
1962	Hou N	129	457	38	114	12	4	1	30	28-1	0	23	.249	.292	.300	64	-24	7-3	.972	10	101	92	S-99,2-33/3-9	-0.4
1963	Hou N	147	469	31	93	13	1	1	19	15-1	4	35	.198	.229	.237	37	-39	3-4	.957	-5	98	78	*S-124,2-19/3-6	-3.7
1964	Hou N	109	332	31	89	11	2	0	17	11-1	0	10	.268	.291	.313	75	-12	4-9	.995	2	101	88	2-52,S-43,3-12	-0.6
1965	Hou N	124	408	34	90	12	1	0	20	20-6	6	10	.221	.267	.255	51	-27	2-2	.968	-12	91	81	*S-104/3-9,2-6	-3.2
1966	Hou N	68	164	14	38	6	0	0	11	7-0	0	4	.232	.260	.268	52	-11	1-1	.951	-9	73	77	2-35,S-18/3-6	-1.7
1967	Hou N	37	82	3	20	1	0	0	5	1-0	0	8	.244	.253	.256	48	-6	0-1	.947	1	112	72	S-23/2-3,3-2	-0.4
Total	10	817	2328	198	549	68	9	3	137	99-13	13	116	.236	.270	.277	54	-147	23-25	.959	-0	99	85	S-530,2-174/3-70	-10.6
LIMMER, LOU Louis B 3.10.1925 New York, NY BL/TL 6-2/190# d4.22																								
1951	Phi A	94	214	25	34	9	1	5	30	28	0	40	.159	.256	.280	44	-18	1-0	.988	3	124	113	1-58	-1.6
1954	Phi A	115	316	41	73	10	3	14	32	35	0	37	.231	.305	.415	96	-3	2-3	.988	3	115	84	1-79	-0.6
Total	2	209	530	66	107	19	4	19	62	63	0	77	.202	.285	.360	75	-21	3-3	.988	5	119	95	1-137	-2.2
LINARES, RUFINO Rufino (born Rufino De La Cruz (Linares)) B 2.28.1951 San Pedro De Macoris, D.R. D 5.16.1998 San Pedro De Macoris, D.R. BR/TR 6/170# d4.10																								
1981	Atl N	78	253	27	67	9	2	5	25	9-2	0	28	.265	.289	.375	85	-6	8-4	.963	3	107	119	O-60(LF)	-0.6
1982	Atl N	77	191	28	57	7	1	2	17	7-0	1	29	.298	.325	.377	92	-2	5-2	1.000	3	104	113	O-53(51-0-4)	-0.1
1984	Atl N	34	58	4	12	3	0	1	10	6-0	0	12	.207	.273	.310	62	-3	0-0	.958	1	101	241	O-13(12-0-1)	-0.2
1985	Cal A	18	43	7	11	2	0	3	11	2-0	0	5	.256	.283	.512	114	1	2-0	1.000	0	140	0	D-14/O-2(RF)	0.1
Total	4	207	545	66	147	21	3	11	63	24-2	1	74	.270	.299	.380	88	-10	15-6	.977	7	105	128	O-128(123-0-7)/D-14	-0.8
LIND, CARL Henry Carl "Hooks" B 9.19.1903 New Orleans, LA D 8.4.1946 New York, NY BR/TR 6/160# d9.14																								
1927	Cle A	12	37	2	5	0	0	0	1	5	1	7	.135	.256	.135	4	-5	1-0	.969	1	120	92	2-11/S	-0.3
1928	Cle A	154	650	102	191	42	4	1	54	36	0	48	.294	.331	.375	84	-15	8-3	.960	5	101	**114**	*2-154	-0.5
1929	Cle A	66	225	19	54	8	1	0	13	13	0	17	.240	.282	.284	44	-19	0-2	.957	10	101	158	2-64/3	-0.7
1930	Cle A	24	69	8	17	3	0	0	6	3	0	7	.246	.278	.290	43	-6	0-1	.940	8	127	142	S-22/2-2	0.3
Total	4	256	981	131	267	53	5	1	74	57	1	79	.272	.313	.339	69	-45	9-6	.960	24	102	125	2-231/S-23,3	-1.2
LIND, JACK Jackson Hugh B 6.8.1946 Denver, CO BB/TR 6/170# d9.10 C4																								
1974	Mil A	9	17	4	4	2	0	0	1	3-0	0	2	.235	.350	.353	103	0	0-0	1.000	-2	73	85	/S-5,2-4	-0.1
1975	Mil A	17	20	1	1	0	0	0	0	2-0	0	12	.050	.136	.050	-45	-4	1-0	.919	1	136	52	/S-9,3-6,1	-0.2
Total	2	26	37	5	5	2	0	0	1	5-0	0	14	.135	.238	.189	23	-4	1-0	.943	-1	111	65	/S-14,3-6,2-4,1	-0.3

Year	Tm Lg	G	AB	R	H	2B	3B	HR	RBI	BB-IB	HP	SO	AVG	OBP	SLG	AOPS	ABR	SB-CS	FA	FR	Rng	Thr	G at Pos	BFW
LIND, JOSE Jose (Salgado) "Chico" B 5.1.1964 Toa Baja, P.R. BR/TR 5-11/175# d8.28																								
1987	Pit N	35	143	21	46	8	4	0	11	8-1	0	12	.322	.358	.434	108	1	2-1	.995	6	127	55	2-35	0.9
1988	Pit N	154	611	82	160	24	4	2	49	42-0	0	75	.262	.308	.324	83	-14	15-4	.987	1	104	84	*2-153	-0.8
1989	Pit N	153	578	52	134	21	3	2	48	39-7	2	64	.232	.280	.289	66	-26	15-1	.976	-10	101	95	*2-151	-3.2
1990	†Pit N	152	514	46	134	28	5	1	48	35-19	1	52	.261	.305	.340	82	-13	8-0	.991	20	111	103	*2-152	1.2
1991	†Pit N	150	502	53	133	16	6	3	54	30-10	2	56	.265	.306	.339	83	-12	7-4	.989	**26**	**112**	111	*2-149	1.8
1992	†Pit N	135	468	38	110	14	1	0	39	26-12	1	29	.235	.275	.269	56	-28	3-1	**.992**	9	109	100	*2-134	-1.6
1993	KC A	136	431	33	107	13	2	0	37	13-0	2	36	.248	.271	.288	48	-32	3-2	**.994**	-10	92	88	*2-136	-3.5
1994	KC A	85	290	34	78	16	2	1	31	16-1	0	34	.269	.306	.348	66	-15	9-5	.988	-9	95	86	2-84/D	-1.8
1995	KC A	29	97	4	26	3	0	0	6	3-0	0	8	.268	.290	.299	53	-7	0-1	.992	-4	91	95	2-29	-1.0
	Cal A	15	43	5	7	2	0	0	1	3-0	0	4	.163	.217	.209	12	-6	0-0	1.000	1	105	114	2-15	-0.4
	Year	44	140	9	33	5	0	0	7	6-0	0	12	.236	.267	.271	40	-13	0-1	.995	-3	96	101	2-44	-1.4
Total	9	1044	3677	368	935	145	27	9	324	215-50	8	370	.254	.295	.316	70	-152	62-19	.988	29	105	95	*2-1038/D	-8.4
LINDBECK, EM Emerit Desmond B 8.27.1935 Kewanee, IL BL/TR 6/185# d4.22																								
1960	Det A	2	1	0	0	0	0	0	0	1-0	0	0	.000	.500	.000	46	0	0-0	—	0			H	0.0
LINDELL, JOHNNY John Harlan B 8.30.1916 Greeley, CO D 8.27.1985 Newport Beach, CA BR/TR 6-4.5/217# d4.18 Mil 1945 ▲																								
1941	NY A	1	1	0	0	0	0	0	0	0	0	0	.000	.000	.000	-99	0	0-0	—	0			H	0.0
1942	NY A	27	24	1	6	1	0	0	4	0	0	5	.250	.250	.292	53	1	0-0	.923	-0	66	279	P-23	0.0
1943	†NY A☆	122	441	53	108	17	**12**	4	51	51	4	55	.245	.329	.365	102	0	2-5	.966	-2	96	123	*O-122(3-55-66)	-0.9
1944	NY A	149	594	91	178	33	**16**	18	103	44	3	56	.300	.351	.500	137	25	5-4	.986	4	110	61	*O-149(2-148-0)	2.5
1945	NY A	41	159	26	45	6	3	1	20	17	3	10	.283	.363	.377	110	2	2-1	.982	-1	102	59	O-41(CF)	0.0
1946	NY A	102	332	41	86	10	5	10	40	32	2	47	.259	.328	.410	104	0	4-1	.982	-1	98	141	O-74(5-31-39),1-14	-0.3
1947	†NY A	127	476	66	131	18	7	11	67	32	1	70	.275	.322	.412	104	0	1-2	.978	6	**112**	72	*O-118(102-10-11)	-0.4
1948	NY A	88	309	58	98	17	2	13	55	35	0	50	.317	.387	.511	139	16	0-0	.994	2	99	125	O-79(72-1-7)	1.2
1949	†NY A	78	211	33	51	10	0	6	27	35	0	27	.242	.350	.374	92	-2	3-0	.983	-1	96	102	O-65(63-3-1)	-0.6
1950	NY A	7	21	2	4	0	0	0	2	4	0	2	.190	.320	.190	34	-2	0-0	.857	-1	70	0	/O-6(LF)	-0.3
	StL N	36	113	16	21	5	2	5	16	15	1	24	.186	.287	.398	74	-5	0	.984	-1	96	45	O-33(29-4-0)	-0.8
1953	Pit N	58	91	11	26	6	1	4	15	16	2	15	.286	.404	.505	136	6	0-0	.962	2	139	74	P-27/1-2	0.1
	Phi N	11	18	3	7	1	0	0	2	6	0	2	.389	.542	.444	162	2	0-0	1.000	-1	76	0	/P-5,O-2(RF)	0.0
	Year	69	109	14	33	7	1	4	17	22	2	17	.303	.429	.495	141	8	0-0	.964	1	132	65	P-32/1-2,O-2(RF)	0.1
1954	Phi N	7	5	0	1	0	0	0	2	2	0	3	.200	.429	.200	70	0	0-0	—	0			H	0.0
Total	12	854	2795	401	762	124	48	72	404	289	16	366	.273	.344	.429	113	43	17-13	.980	6	103	92	O-689(282-293-126)/P-55,1-16	0.5
LINDEMAN, JIM James William B 1.10.1962 Evanston, IL BR/TR 6-1/200# d9.3																								
1986	StL N	19	55	7	14	1	0	1	6	2-0	0	10	.255	.276	.327	68	-3	1-1	.992	0	116	90	1-17/3O(LF)	-0.4
1987	†StL N	75	207	20	43	13	0	8	28	11-0	3	56	.208	.253	.386	67	-11	3-1	.976	2	99	141	O-49(1-0-48),1-20	-1.2
1988	StL N	17	43	3	9	1	0	2	7	2-0	0	9	.209	.244	.372	74	-2	0-0	.941	-0	95	0	O-12(4-0-8)/1-3	-0.3
1989	StL N	73	45	8	5	1	0	0	2	3-0	0	18	.111	.163	.133	-13	-7	0-0	.989	1	118	141	1-42/O-5(3-0-2)	-0.7
1990	Det A	12	32	5	7	1	0	2	8	2-0	0	13	.219	.265	.438	92	-1	0-0	1.000	-0	0	0	D-10/1O(RF)	-0.1
1991	Phi N	65	95	13	32	5	0	0	12	13-1	0	14	.337	.413	.389	129	5	0-1	1.000	-2	81	85	O-30(14-6-10)/1	0.2
1992	Phi N	29	39	6	10	1	0	1	6	3-0	0	11	.256	.310	.359	89	-1	0-0	1.000	-1	72	0	/O-9(4-0-7)	-0.2
1993	Hou N	9	23	2	8	3	0	0	0	0-0	0	7	.348	.348	.478	123	1	0-0	1.000	1	131	162	/1-9	0.1
1994	NY N	52	137	18	37	8	1	7	20	6-2	1	35	.270	.308	.496	106	0	0-0	.948	-2	95	51	O-33(21-0-14)/1-4	-0.3
Total	9	351	676	82	165	34	1	21	89	42-3	4	173	.244	.289	.391	83	-19	4-3	.970	-2	93	85	O-140(48-6-90)/1-97,D-10,3	-2.9
LINDEMANN, BOB John Frederick Mann B 6.5.1881 Philadelphia, PA D 12.19.1951 Williamsport, PA BB/TR 6/175# d8.28																								
1901	Phi A	3	9	0	1	0	0	0	0	0	0		.111	.111	.111	-37	-2	0	.600	-0	294	0	/O-3(RF)	-0.2
LINDEN, TODD Todd Anthony B 6.30.1980 Edmonds, WA BB/TR 6-3/210# d8.18																								
2003	SF N	18	38	2	8	1	0	1	6	1-0	0	8	.211	.231	.316	42	-3	0-0	.929	-1	82	0	O-13(9-0-6)	-0.5
LINDEN, WALT Walter Charles B 3.27.1924 Chicago, IL BR/TR 6-1/190# d4.30																								
1950	Bos N	3	5	0	2	1	0	0	0	1	0	0	.400	.500	.600	201	1	0	1.000	-0	*0*	*0*	/C-3	0.1
LINDSAY, CHRIS Christian Haller "Pinky" or "The Crab" B 7.24.1878 Beaver County, PA D 1.25.1941 Cleveland, OH BR/TR 6/190# d7.6																								
1905	Det A	88	329	38	88	14	1	0	31	18	5		.267	.315	.316	100	0	10	.978	0	102	106	1-88	-0.1
1906	Det A	141	499	59	112	16	2	0	33	45	3		.224	.293	.265	73	-14	18	.977	-7	86	98	*1-122,2-17/3	-2.6
Total	2	229	828	97	200	30	3	0	64	63	8		.242	.301	.285	83	-14	28	.978	-7	93	101	1-210/2-17,3	-2.7
LINDSAY, BILL William Gibbons B 2.24.1881 Madison, NC D 7.14.1963 Greensboro, NC BL/TR 5-10.5/165# d6.21																								
1911	Cle A	19	66	6	16	2	0	0	5	1	1		.242	.265	.273	49	-5	2	.883	1	123	43	3-15/2	-0.3
LINDSEY, DOUG Michael Douglas B 9.22.1967 Austin, TX BR/TR 6-2/200# d10.6																								
1991	Phi N	1	3	0	0	0	0	0	0	0-0	0	3	.000	.000	.000	-99	-1	0-0	1.000	0	0	0	/C	-0.1
1993	Phi N	2	2	0	1	0	0	0	0	0-0	0	1	.500	.500	.500	171	0	0-0	1.000	0	0	0	/C-2	0.0
	Chi A	2	1	0	0	0	0	0	0	0-0	0	0	.000	.000	.000	-99	0	0-0	1.000	0	0	0	/C-2	0.0
Total	2	5	6	0	1	0	0	0	0	0-0	0	4	.167	.167	.167	-8	-1	0-0	1.000	0	0	0	/C-5	-0.1
LINDSEY, ROD Rodney Lee B 1.28.1976 Opelika, AL BR/TR 5-8/175# d9.2																								
2000	Det A	11	3	6	1	1	0	0	0	0-0	1	1	.333	.500	.667	197	1	2-1	1.000	-1	48	0	/O-7(2-4-2)	0.0
LINDSEY, BILL William Donald B 4.12.1960 Staten Island, NY BR/TR 6-3/195# d7.18																								
1987	Chi A	9	16	2	3	0	0	0	1	0-0	0	3	.188	.176	.188	-0	-2	0-0	1.000	1	226	196	/C-9	-0.1
LINDSTROM, CHUCK Charles William B 9.7.1936 Chicago, IL BR/TR 5-11/175# d9.28 f-Freddie																								
1958	Chi A	1	1	1	1	0	1	0	1	1-0	0	0	1.000	1.000	3.000	975	1	0-0	1.000	-0	*0*	*0*	/C	0.1
LINDSTROM, FREDDIE Frederick Charles (born Frederick Anthony Lindstrom) B 11.21.1905 Chicago, IL D 10.4.1981 Chicago, IL BR/TR 5-11/170# d4.15 HF1976 s-Chuck																								
1924	†NY N	52	79	19	20	3	1	0	4	6	1	10	.253	.314	.316	71	-3	3-1	.911	3	122	134	2-23,3-11	0.1
1925	NY N	104	356	43	102	15	12	4	33	22	2	20	.287	.332	.430	97	-4	5-9	.957	-3	88	58	3-96/2S	-0.3
1926	NY N	140	543	90	164	19	9	9	76	39	2	21	.302	.351	.420	108	5	11	.962	-1	97	103	*3-138/O(RF)	1.2
1927	NY N	138	562	107	172	36	8	7	58	40	2	40	.306	.354	.436	111	8	10	.968	2	107	85	3-87,O-51(LF)	1.2
1928	NY N	153	646	99	**231**	39	9	14	107	25	2	21	.358	.383	.511	131	27	15	**.958**	15	**112**	**132**	*3-153	4.9
1929	NY N	130	549	99	175	23	6	15	91	30	0	28	.319	.354	.464	101	-1	10	.966	6	104	**140**	*3-128	1.1
1930	NY N	148	609	127	231	39	7	22	106	48	0	33	.379	.425	.575	142	42	15	.953	4	103	96	*3-148	4.7
1931	NY N	78	303	38	91	12	6	5	36	26	0	12	.300	.356	.429	113	5	5	.975	-7	96	45	O-73(RF)/2-4	-0.6
1932	NY N	144	595	83	161	26	5	15	92	27	1	28	.271	.303	.407	91	-10	6	.982	-5	88	156	*O-128(CF),3-15	-1.8
1933	Pit N	138	538	70	167	39	10	5	55	33	0	22	.310	.350	.448	127	18	1	.988	6	**112**	73	*O-130(20-111-0)	2.1
1934	Pit N	97	383	59	111	24	4	4	49	23	2	21	.290	.333	.405	94	-3	1	.990	1	97	127	O-92(LF)	-0.7
1935	†Chi N	90	342	49	94	22	4	3	62	10	1	13	.275	.297	.389	82	-9	1	.979	-5	95	113	O-50(CF),3-33	-1.4
1936	Bro N	26	106	12	28	4	0	0	10	5	0	7	.264	.297	.302	61	-6	1	.982	1	95	214	O-26(24-2-0)	-0.6
Total	13	1438	5611	895	1747	301	81	103	779	334	13	276	.311	.351	.449	110	69	84-10	.959	17	101	108	3-809,O-551(187-291-74)/2-28,S	9.9
LINHART, CARL Carl James B 12.14.1929 Zborov, Czechoslovakia BL/TR 5-11/184# d8.2																								
1952	Det A	3	2	0	0	0	0	0	0	0	0	0	.000	.000	.000	-99	-1	0-0	—	0			H	-0.1
LINIAK, COLE Cole Edward B 8.23.1976 Encinitas, CA BR/TR 6-1/180# d9.3																								
1999	Chi N	12	29	3	7	2	0	0	2	1-0	0	4	.241	.267	.310	46	-2	0-1	1.000	-3	52	73	3-10	-0.5
2000	Chi N	3	3	0	0	0	0	0	0	0-0	0	2	.000	.000	.000	-99	-1	0-0	—	0			/H	-0.1
Total	2	15	32	3	7	2	0	0	2	1-0	0	6	.219	.242	.281	32	-3	0-1	1.000	-3	52	73	/3-10	-0.6
LINTON, BOB Claud Clarence B 4.18.1903 Emerson, AR D 4.3.1980 Destin, FL BL/TR 6/185# d4.26																								
1929	Pit N	17	18	0	2	0	0	0	1	1	0	2	.111	.158	.111	-31	-4	0	1.000	0	*125*	*220*	/C-8	-0.3
LINTZ, LARRY Larry B 10.10.1949 Martinez, CA BB/TR 5-9/150# d7.14																								
1973	Mon N	52	116	20	29	1	0	0	3	17-0	1	18	.250	.351	.259	69	-4	12-4	.945	-2	109	86	2-34,S-15	-0.2
1974	Mon N	113	319	60	76	10	1	0	20	44-0	2	50	.238	.334	.276	68	-12	50-7	.961	-7	98	77	2-67,S-31/3	-0.3

Year	Tm Lg	G	AB	R	H	2B	3B	HR	RBI	BB-IB	HP	SO	AVG	OBP	SLG	AOPS	ABR	SB-CS	FA	FR	Rng	Thr	G at Pos	BFW
1975	Mon N	46	132	18	26	0	0	0	3	23-0	0	18	.197	.316	.197	43	-9	17-9	.970	-4	95	69	2-39/S-2	-1.1
	StL N	27	18	6	5	1	0	0	1	3-0	0	2	.278	.381	.333	96	0	4-0	.889	2	98	0	/2-6,S-6	0.3
	Year	73	150	24	31	1	0	0	4	26-0	0	20	.207	.324	.213	49	-9	21-9	.963	-3	95	63	2-45/S-8	-0.8
1976	Oak A	68	1	21	0	0	0	0	0	2-0	0	0	.000	.667	.000	111	0	31-11	1.000	-1	66	0	D-19/2-5,O-3(1-0-2)	0.2
1977	Oak A	41	30	11	4	1	0	0	0	8-1	1	13	.133	.333	.167	42	-2	13-5	1.000	-1	94	106	2-28/S-2,3D	-0.1
1978	Cle A	3	0	1	0	0	0	0	0	0-0	0	0	—	—	—	—	0	1-2	—	0			R	-0.1
Total	6	350	616	137	140	13	1	0	27	97-1	4	101	.227	.336	.252	63	-27	128-38	.962	-13	99	77	2-179/S-56,D-24,O-3(1-0-2),3-2	-1.3
LINZ, PHIL Philip Francis B 6.4.1939 Baltimore, MD BR/TR 6-1/180# d4.13																								
1962	NY A	71	129	28	37	8	0	1	14	6-2	0	17	.287	.316	.372	88	-2	6-2	.937	-4	89	76	S-21/3-8,2-5,O-2(RF)	-0.4
1963	†NY A	72	186	22	50	9	0	2	12	15-0	2	18	.269	.328	.349	91	-2	1-6	.963	0	113	118	S-22,3-13,O-12(2-5-5)/2-6	-0.2
1964	†NY A	112	368	63	92	21	3	5	25	43-2	2	61	.250	.332	.364	92	-3	3-4	.952	8	117	125	S-55,3-41/2-5,O-3(1-2-0)	0.9
1965	NY A	99	285	37	59	12	1	2	16	30-1	0	33	.207	.281	.277	60	-15	2-1	.954	4	104	76	S-71/3-4,O-4(RF),2	-0.5
1966	Phi N	40	70	4	14	3	0	0	6	2-0	0	14	.200	.222	.243	29	-7	0-0	.971	0	96	97	3-14/S-6,2-3	-0.7
1967	Phi N	23	18	4	4	2	0	1	5	2-0	0	1	.222	.300	.500	124	1	0-0	.833	-1	50	0	/S-7,3	0.0
	NY N	24	58	8	12	2	0	0	1	4-0	1	10	.207	.270	.241	48	-4	0-0	.964	-2	85	101	2-11/S-8,3O(LF)	-0.4
	Year	47	76	12	16	4	0	1	6	6-0	1	11	.211	.277	.303	66	-3	0-0	.963	-3	79	31	S-15,2-11/3-2,O(LF)	-0.4
1968	NY N	78	258	19	54	7	0	0	17	10-0	2	41	.209	.243	.236	45	-18	1-0	.968	-9	90	101	2-71	-2.4
Total	7	519	1372	185	322	64	4	11	96	112-5	7	195	.235	.295	.311	72	-50	13-13	.952	-3	107	96	S-190,2-102/3-82,O-22(4-7-11)	-3.7
LIPON, JOHNNY John Joseph "Skids" B 11.10.1922 Martins Ferry, OH D 8.17.1998 Houston, TX BR/TR 6/175# d8.16 Mil 1943-45 M1 C4																								
1942	Det A	34	131	5	25	2	0	0	9	7	0	7	.191	.232	.206	22	-14	1-3	.945	3	98	107	S-34	-0.9
1946	Det A	14	20	4	6	0	0	0	1	5	0	3	.300	.440	.300	103	0	0-0	.933	1	87	160	/S-8,3	0.1
1948	Det A	121	458	65	133	18	8	5	52	68	2	22	.290	.384	.397	105	5	4-4	.970	-10	94	76	*S-117/23	0.1
1949	Det A	127	439	57	110	14	6	3	59	75	2	24	.251	.362	.330	84	-9	2-4	.965	0	99	107	*S-120	-0.2
1950	Det A	147	601	104	176	27	6	2	63	81	1	26	.293	.378	.368	89	-8	9-6	.958	9	106	**120**	*S-147	0.9
1951	Det A	129	487	56	129	15	1	0	38	49	2	27	.265	.335	.300	72	-18	7-6	.949	-11	98	87	*S-125	-2.1
1952	Det A	39	136	17	30	4	2	0	12	16	0	6	.221	.303	.279	62	-7	3-1	.978	-2	92	49	S-39	-0.7
	Bos A	79	234	25	48	8	1	0	18	32	0	20	.205	.301	.248	50	-15	1-1	.982	12	113	121	*S-69/3-7	0.1
	Year	118	370	42	78	12	3	0	30	48	0	26	.211	.301	.259	54	-22	4-2	**.981**	10	**105**	95	*S-108/3-7	-0.6
1953	Bos A	60	145	18	31	7	0	0	13	14	0	16	.214	.283	.262	46	-11	1-0	.951	2	105	86	S-58	-0.5
	StL A	7	9	0	2	0	0	0	1	0	0	1	.222	.222	.222	20	-1	0-0	1.000	-1	148	0	/3-6,2	-0.2
	Year	67	154	18	33	7	0	0	14	14	0	17	.214	.280	.260	44	-12	1-0	.951	1	105	86	S-58/3-6,2	-0.7
1954	Cin N	1	1	0	0	0	0	0	0	0	0	0	.000	.000	.000	-97	0	0-0	—	0			H	0.0
Total	9	758	2661	351	690	95	24	10	266	347	7	152	.259	.346	.324	77	-78	28-25	.961	2	101	98	S-717/3-15,2-2	-3.4
LIPSCOMB, NIG Gerard B 2.24.1911 Rutherfordton, NC D 2.27.1978 Huntersville, NC BR/TR 6/175# d4.23 ▲																								
1937	StL A	36	96	11	31	9	1	0	8	11	1	10	.323	.398	.438	110	2	0-0	.963	-0	97	130	2-27/P-3,3	0.3
LIPSKI, BOB Robert Peter B 7.7.1938 Scranton, PA BL/TR 6-1/180# d4.28																								
1963	Cle A	2	1	0	0	0	0	0	0	0-0	0	1	.000	.000	.000	-99	0	0-0	1.000	0	0	0	/C-2	0.0
LIRIANO, NELSON Nelson Arturo (Bonilla) B 6.3.1964 Puerto Plata, D.R. BB/TR 5-10/172# d8.25																								
1987	Tor A	37	158	29	38	6	2	2	10	16-2	0	22	.241	.310	.342	71	-7	13-2	.995	3	99	120	2-37	0.0
1988	Tor A	99	276	36	73	6	2	3	23	11-0	2	40	.264	.297	.333	76	-10	12-5	.961	-14	90	104	2-80,D-11/3	-2.1
1989	†Tor A	132	418	51	110	26	3	5	53	43-0	2	51	.263	.331	.376	102	2	16-7	.980	-14	95	97	*2-122/D-5	-0.8
1990	Tor A	50	170	16	36	7	2	1	15	16-0	1	20	.212	.282	.294	61	-9	3-5	.983	-8	93	84	2-49	-1.7
	Min A	53	185	30	47	5	7	0	13	22-0	0	24	.254	.332	.357	87	-3	5-2	.968	-9	95	83	2-50/SD	-1.1
	Year	103	355	46	83	12	9	1	28	38-0	1	44	.234	.308	.327	75	-12	8-7	.975	-16	94	84	2-99/D-2,S	-2.8
1991	KC A	10	22	5	9	0	0	0	1	0-0	0	2	.409	.409	.409	127	1	0-1	1.000	1	116	69	2-10	0.1
1993	Col N	48	151	28	46	6	3	2	15	18-2	0	22	.305	.376	.424	98	0	6-4	.975	-8	87	69	S-35,2-16/3	-0.5
1994	Col N	87	255	39	65	17	5	3	31	42-5	0	44	.255	.357	.396	83	-5	0-2	.973	-8	96	81	2-79/S-3,3-2	-1.0
1995	Pit N	107	259	29	74	12	1	5	38	24-3	2	34	.286	.347	.398	95	-2	2-2	.981	-11	86	84	2-67/3-5,S	-0.9
1996	Pit N	112	217	23	58	14	2	3	30	14-2	0	22	.267	.308	.392	82	-6	2-0	.984	-2	105	79	2-36/3-9,S-5	-0.5
1997	LA N	76	88	10	20	6	0	1	11	6-1	0	12	.227	.274	.330	63	-5	0-0	.949	-4	76	103	2-17/1-2,3S	-0.8
1998	Col N	12	17	0	0	0	0	0	0	0-0	0	7	.000	.000	.000	-82	-4	0-0	1.000	-2	43	90	/2-3,S	-0.6
Total	11	823	2216	296	576	105	27	25	240	212-15	7	300	.260	.324	.366	84	-48	59-30	.976	-73	94	92	2-566/S-47,3-19,D-18,1-2	-9.9
LIS, JOE Joseph Anthony B 8.15.1946 Somerville, NJ BR/TR 6/195# d9.5																								
1970	Phi N	13	37	1	7	2	0	1	4	5-0	0	11	.189	.286	.324	65	-2	0-0	.947	0	121	0	/O-9(LF)	-0.2
1971	Phi N	59	123	16	26	6	0	6	10	16-0	2	43	.211	.308	.407	102	0	0-1	.978	-2	77	102	O-35(LF)	-0.4
1972	Phi N	62	140	13	34	6	0	6	18	30-1	1	34	.243	.380	.414	122	6	0-1	.996	2	97	90	1-30,O-14(8-0-6)	0.5
1973	Min A	103	253	37	62	11	1	9	25	28-1	3	66	.245	.325	.403	101	0	0-1	.987	-1	99	93	1-96/D	-0.6
1974	Min A	24	41	5	8	0	0	0	3	5-0	1	12	.195	.298	.195	43	-3	0-0	.992	-1	78	83	1-18	-0.5
	Cle A	57	109	15	22	3	0	6	16	14-1	0	30	.202	.293	.394	97	-1	1-0	1.000	-2	81	85	1-31/3-9,O(LF)D	-0.4
	Year	81	150	20	30	3	0	6	19	19-1	1	42	.200	.294	.340	82	-4	1-0	.997	-3	80	84	1-49/3-9,D-9,O(LF)	-0.9
1975	Cle A	9	13	4	4	2	0	2	8	3-0	1	3	.308	.444	.923	286	3	0-0	1.000	-0	62	51	/1-8,D	0.3
1976	Cle A	20	51	4	16	1	0	2	7	8-0	0	8	.314	.400	.451	153	4	0-0	1.000	-1	72	79	1-17/D	0.2
1977	Sea A	9	13	1	3	0	0	0	1	1-0	0	2	.231	.286	.231	43	-1	0-0	1.000	-1	55	136	/1-4,C	-0.2
Total	8	356	780	96	182	31	1	32	92	110-3	8	209	.233	.332	.399	105	6	1-3	.992	-5	90	89	1-204/O-59(53-0-6),D-12,3-9,C	-1.3
LISI, RICK Riccardo Patrick Emilio B 3.17.1956 Halifax, NS, CAN BR/TR 6/175# d5.9																								
1981	Tex A	9	16	6	5	0	0	0	1	4-0	0	0	.313	.450	.313	130	1	0-1	1.000	-1	79	0	/O-8(0-2-6)	0.0
LISTACH, PAT Patrick Alan B 9.12.1967 Natchitoches, LA BB/TR 5-9/170# d4.8																								
1992	Mil A	149	579	93	168	19	6	1	47	55-0	1	124	.290	.352	.349	99	0	54-18	.966	2	104	107	*S-148/2O(CF)	1.8
1993	Mil A	98	356	50	87	15	1	3	30	37-0	3	70	.244	.319	.317	73	-13	18-9	.975	-10	100	92	S-95/O-6(CF)	-1.4
1994	Mil A	16	54	8	16	3	0	0	2	3-0	0	8	.296	.333	.352	74	-2	2-1	.958	2	122	113	S-16	0.1
1995	Mil A	101	334	35	73	8	2	0	25	25-0	2	61	.219	.276	.254	37	-31	13-3	1.000	11	112	118	2-59,S-36,O-11(1-10-1)/3-2	-1.3
1996	Mil A	87	317	51	76	16	2	1	33	36-0	1	51	.240	.317	.312	58	-20	25-5	.982	-7	97	154	O-68(2-66-0),2-12/S-7	-2.0
1997	Hou N	52	132	13	24	2	2	0	6	11-2	1	24	.182	.247	.227	27	-15	4-2	.951	-10	85	75	S-31/O-6(1-4-1)	-2.3
Total	6	503	1772	250	444	63	13	5	143	167-2	8	338	.251	.316	.309	68	-81	116-38	.967	-13	103	103	S-333/O-92(4-87-2),2-72,3-2	-5.1
LISTER, PETE Morris Elmer B 7.21.1881 Savanna, IL D 3.27.1947 St.Petersburg, FL BR/TR d9.14																								
1907	Cle A	22	65	5	18	2	0	0	4	3	1		.277	.319	.308	99	0	2	.974	-1	83	141	1-22	-0.2
LITTLE, SCOTT Dennis Scott B 1.19.1963 E.St.Louis, IL BR/TR 6/198# d7.27																								
1989	Pit N	3	4	0	1	0	0	0	0	0-0	0	1	.250	.250	.250	45	0	0-0	1.000	1	84	3020	/O(RF)	0.1
LITTLE, HARRY Harry A. B St.Louis, MO TR d7.16																								
1877	StL N	3	12	2	2	0	0	0	0	1		6	.167	.231	.167	29	-1		1.000	-0	0	0	/O-3(CF)	-0.1
	Lou N	1	3	0	0	0	0	0	0	1		1	.000	.250	.000	-13	0		.857	0	145	0	/2	0.0
	Year	4	15	2	2	0	0	0	0	2		7	.133	.235	.133	19	-1		1.000	-0	0	0	/O-3(CF),2	-0.1
LITTLE, MARK Mark Travis B 7.11.1972 Edwardsville, IL BR/TR 6/195# d9.12																								
1998	StL N	7	12	0	1	0	0	0	0	2-0	0	5	.083	.214	.083	-18	-2	1-0	1.000	0	128	0	/O-7(3-0-4)	-0.2
2001	Col N	51	85	18	29	6	0	3	13	1-1	4	20	.341	.378	.518	105	1	5-2	1.000	3	102	303	O-29(14-14-6)	0.3
2002	Col N	61	105	20	21	5	2	0	5	13-0	4	28	.200	.311	.286	53	-7	2-1	.970	3	118	130	O-36(16-11-16)	-0.5
	NY N	3	3	0	0	0	0	0	0	0-0	0	1	.000	.000	.000	-99	-1	0-1	—	-0	0	0	/O(RF)	-0.1
	†Ari N	15	22	8	6	0	1	0	2	2-0	4	5	.273	.429	.364	106	0	0-0	1.000	0	113	0	O-12(4-2-7)	0.0
	Year	79	130	28	27	5	3	0	7	15-0	8	34	.208	.327	.292	60	-8	2-2	.975	2	116	101	O-49(20-13-24)	-0.6
Total	3	137	227	46	57	11	3	3	20	18-1	12	59	.251	.339	.366	74	-9	8-4	.985	5	113	155	/O-85(37-27-34)	-0.5
LITTLE, BRYAN Richard Bryan "Twig" B 10.8.1959 Houston, TX BB/TR 5-10/160# d7.29 C3																								
1982	Mon N	29	42	6	9	0	0	0	3	4-0	0	6	.214	.277	.214	40	-3	2-1	1.000	-5	72	23	2-16,S-10	-0.8
1983	Mon N	106	350	48	91	15	3	1	36	50-1	2	22	.260	.352	.329	91	-2	4-5	.968	-18	79	83	S-66,2-51	-1.3
1984	Mon N	85	266	31	65	11	1	0	9	34-0	1	19	.244	.332	.293	81	-6	2-3	.982	-7	93	109	2-77/S-2	-1.0
1985	Chi A	73	188	35	47	9	1	2	27	26-0	3	21	.250	.345	.340	87	-2	0-1	.989	6	107	92	2-68/3-2,S	0.6

Year	Tm Lg	G	AB	R	H	2B	3B	HR	RBI	BB-IB	HP	SO	AVG	OBP	SLG	AOPS	ABR	SB-CS	FA	FR	Rng	Thr	G at Pos	BFW
1986	Chi A	20	35	3	6	1	0	0	2	4-0	0	4	.171	.256	.200	25	-4	0-0	1.000	2	102	67	2-12/S-7,3	-0.1
	NY A	14	41	3	8	1	0	0	0	2-0	0	7	.195	.233	.220	24	-4	0-0	.975	4	120	114	2-14	0.1
	Year	34	76	6	14	2	0	0	2	6-0	0	11	.184	.244	.211	25	-8	0-0	.983	6	114	97	2-26/S-7,3	0.0
Total	5	327	922	126	226	37	5	3	77	120-1	6	79	.245	.333	.306	80	-21	8-10	.987	-18	99	92	2-238/S-86,3-3	-2.5
LITTLE, JACK William Arthur B 3.12.1891 Mart, TX D 7.27.1961 Dallas, TX BR/TR 5-11/175# d7.2																								
1912	NY A	3	12	2	3	0	0	0	0	1	1		.250	.357	.250	70	0	2	1.000	0	85	217	/O-3(CF)	0.0
LITTLEJOHN, DENNIS Dennis Gerald B 10.4.1954 Santa Monica, CA BR/TR 6-2/200# d7.9																								
1978	SF N	2	0	0	0	0	0	0	0	0-0	0	0	—	—	—	—	0	0-0	—	-0	0	0	/C-2	0.0
1979	SF N	63	193	15	38	6	1	1	13	21-4	0	46	.197	.272	.254	49	-14	0-0	.986	-2	69	129	C-63	-1.3
1980	SF N	13	29	2	7	1	0	0	2	7-1	0	7	.241	.368	.276	91	0	0-0	.983	2	108	103	C-10	0.2
Total	3	78	222	17	45	7	1	1	15	28-5	0	53	.203	.286	.257	55	-14	0-0	.985	-0	74	125	/C-75	-1.1
LITTLETON, LARRY Larry Marvin B 4.3.1954 Charlotte, NC BR/TR 6-1/185# d4.12																								
1981	Cle A	26	23	2	0	0	0	0	1	3-0	0	6	.000	.111	.000	-65	-5	0-0	1.000	-2	57	0	O-24(19-6-1)	-0.8
LITTON, GREG Jon Gregory B 7.13.1964 New Orleans, LA BR/TR 6/190# d5.2 OF Total (42-LF 50-RF)																								
1989	†SF N	71	143	12	36	5	3	4	17	7-0	1	29	.252	.291	.413	102	-1	0-2	.953	-2	103	30	3-34,2-15/S-9,O-6(4-0-2),C-2	-0.4
1990	SF N	93	204	17	50	9	1	1	24	11-0	1	45	.245	.284	.314	68	-9	1-0	.985	3	89	257	O-56(14-0-42),2-18/S-7,3-5	-0.7
1991	SF N	59	127	13	23	7	1	1	15	11-0	1	25	.181	.250	.276	50	-9	0-2	.989	3	158	150	1-15,2-15,3-11/S-9,O-6(2-0-4),CP	-0.7
1992	SF N	68	140	9	32	5	0	4	15	11-0	0	33	.229	.285	.350	84	-4	0-1	.992	-1	98	124	2-31,3-10/1-8,S-3,O(LF)	-0.5
1993	Sea A	72	174	25	52	17	0	3	25	18-2	1	30	.299	.366	.448	116	5	0-1	1.000	1	83	327	O-22(21-0-2),2-17,1-13,D-12/3-7,S-5	0.4
1994	Bos A	11	21	2	2	0	0	0	1	0-0	0	5	.095	.091	.095	-48	-5	0-0	1.000	0	76	0	/2-4,1-3,3-2,D	-0.4
Total	6	374	809	78	195	43	5	13	97	58-2	4	167	.241	.293	.355	81	-23	1-6	.997	4	90	118	2-100/O-91R,3-69,1-39,S-33,DCP	-2.3
LITTRELL, JACK Jack Napier B 1.22.1929 Louisville, KY BR/TR 6/179# d4.19																								
1952	Phi A	4	2	0	0	0	0	0	0	1	0	2	.000	.333	.000	-2	0	0-0	1.000	0	150	345	/S-2,3	0.0
1954	Phi A	9	30	7	9	2	0	1	3	6	0	3	.300	.417	.467	141	2	1-0	.976	-1	84	123	/S-9	0.2
1955	KC A	37	70	7	14	0	1	0	1	4-0	0	12	.200	.243	.229	27	-8	0-0	.947	-1	93	77	S-22/1-6,2-4	-0.8
1957	Chi N	61	153	8	29	4	2	1	13	9-1	0	43	.190	.233	.261	34	-15	0-0	.944	-3	95	75	S-47/2-6,3-5	-1.4
Total	4	111	255	22	52	6	3	2	17	20-1	0	60	.204	.261	.275	45	-21	1-0	.949	-5	94	83	/S-80,2-10,1-6,3-6	-2.0
LITWHILER, DANNY Daniel Webster B 8.31.1916 Ringtown, PA BR/TR 5-10.5/198# d4.25 Mil 1945-46 C1																								
1940	Phi N	36	142	10	49	2	2	5	17	3	1	13	.345	.363	.493	139	6	1	.986	2	103	152	O-34(2-3-31)	0.6
1941	Phi N	151	590	72	180	29	6	18	66	39	2	43	.305	.350	.466	134	23	1	.964	13	**118**	113	*O-150(148-0-2)	2.8
1942	Phi N★	**151**	591	59	160	25	9	9	56	27	7	42	.271	.310	.389	109	3	2	**1.000**	-3	95	83	*O-151(130-0-24)	-0.9
1943	Phi N	36	139	23	36	6	0	5	17	11	0	14	.259	.313	.410	113	2	1	.989	4	113	142	O-34(LF)	0.3
	†StL N	80	258	40	72	14	3	7	31	19	2	31	.279	.333	.438	117	5	1	1.000	3	107	115	O-70(LF)	0.4
	Year	116	397	63	108	20	3	12	48	30	2	45	.272	.326	.428	115	6	2	.996	7	109	125	*O-104(LF)	0.7
1944	†StL N	140	492	53	130	25	5	15	82	37	**10**	56	.264	.328	.427	109	5	2	.974	-2	104	60	*O-136(LF)	-0.5
1946	StL N	6	5	0	0	0	0	0	0	1	0	1	.000	.167	.000	-49	-1	0	—	0			H	-0.1
	Bos N	79	247	29	72	12	2	8	38	19	2	23	.291	.347	.453	125	7	1	.985	-1	105	39	O-65(LF)/3-2	0.2
	Year	85	252	29	72	12	2	8	38	20	2	24	.286	.343	.444	121	6	1	.985	-1	105	39	O-65(LF)/3-2	0.1
1947	Bos N	91	226	38	59	5	2	7	31	25	1	43	.261	.337	.394	96	-2	1	.976	-1	101	49	O-66(64-0-1)	-0.7
1948	Bos N	13	33	0	9	2	0	0	6	4	2	2	.273	.385	.333	97	0	0	1.000	1	114	128	/O-8(LF)	0.0
	Cin N	106	338	51	93	19	2	14	44	48	0	41	.275	.365	.467	128	14	1	.988	3	105	51	O-83(5-1-77),3-15	1.4
	Year	119	371	51	102	21	2	14	50	52	2	43	.275	.367	.456	125	14	1	.990	4	106	59	O-91(13-1-77),3-15	1.4
1949	Cin N	102	292	35	85	18	1	11	48	44	0	42	.291	.384	.473	127	12	0	.987	0	101	94	O-82(11-1-71)/3-3	1.0
1950	Cin N	54	112	15	29	4	0	6	12	20	0	21	.259	.371	.455	116	3	0	.958	-1	105	0	O-29(8-0-21)	0.1
1951	Cin N	12	29	3	8	1	0	2	3	2	0	5	.276	.323	.517	120	1	0-0	.933	-1	103	0	/O-7(RF)	0.0
Total	11	1057	3494	428	982	162	32	107	451	299	27	377	.281	.342	.438	119	78	11-0	.982	17	105	83	O-915(681-5-234)/3-20	4.6
LIVINGSTON, PADDY Patrick Joseph B 1.14.1880 Cleveland, OH D 9.19.1977 Cleveland, OH BR/TR 5-8/197# d9.2 C1																								
1901	Cle A	1	2	0	0	0	0	0	0	0	1		.000	.333	.000	-2	0	0	1.000	-0	*79*	*159*	/C	0.0
1906	Cin N	50	139	8	22	1	4	0	8	12	7		.158	.259	.223	48	-8	0	.960	2	*101*	*108*	C-47	-0.2
1909	Phi A	64	175	15	41	6	4	0	15	15	8		.234	.323	.314	99	0	4	.969	10	*125*	*121*	C-64	1.8
1910	Phi A	37	120	11	25	4	3	0	9	6	3		.208	.264	.292	75	-4	2	.968	4	*111*	*112*	C-37	0.4
1911	Phi A	27	71	9	17	4	0	0	8	7	1		.239	.316	.296	72	-2	1	.977	3	*121*	*106*	C-26	0.3
1912	Cle A	20	47	5	11	2	1	0	3	1	2		.234	.280	.319	69	-2	0	.976	1	*93*	*91*	C-14	-0.1
1917	StL N	7	20	0	4	0	0	0	2	0	0	1	.200	.200	.200	23	-2	2	1.000	0	*120*	*81*	/C-6	-0.1
Total	7	206	574	48	120	17	12	0	45	41	22	1	.209	.287	.280	73	-18	9	.969	19	*113*	*111*	C-195	2.1
LIVINGSTON, MICKEY Thompson Orville B 11.15.1914 Newberry, SC D 4.3.1983 Newberry, SC BR/TR 6-1.5/185# d9.17 Mil 1944																								
1938	Was A	2	4	0	3	2	0	0	1	0	0	1	.750	.750	1.250	421	2	0-0	.667	-1	*0*	*0*	/C-2	0.1
1941	Phi N	95	207	16	42	6	1	0	18	20	1	38	.203	.276	.242	49	-14	2	.974	-3	*75*	*94*	C-71/1	-1.4
1942	Phi N	89	239	20	49	6	1	2	22	25	1	20	.205	.283	.264	64	-11	0	.987	-7	*67*	*97*	C-78/1-6	-1.6
1943	Phi N	84	265	25	66	9	2	3	18	19	2	18	.249	.304	.332	87	-5	1	.988	1	*94*	*109*	C-84/1-2	0.0
	Chi N	36	111	11	29	5	1	4	16	12	0	8	.261	.333	.432	122	3	1	1.000	-1	*122*	*59*	C-31/1-4	0.4
	Year	120	376	36	95	14	3	7	34	31	2	26	.253	.313	.362	98	-2	2	**.991**	0	*102*	*95*	*C-115/1-6	0.4
1945	†Chi N	71	224	19	57	4	2	2	23	19	4	6	.254	.324	.317	80	-6	2	.990	3	*153*	*70*	C-68/1	0.1
1946	Chi N	66	176	14	45	14	0	2	20	20	2	19	.256	.338	.369	103	1	0	.981	-1	*111*	*78*	C-56	0.3
1947	Chi N	19	33	2	7	2	0	0	3	1	0	5	.212	.235	.273	36	-3	0	1.000	-0	*86*	*0*	/C-7	-0.3
	NY N	5	6	0	1	0	0	0	0	1	0	2	.167	.286	.167	23	-1	0	.800	-0	*0*	*0*	/C	-0.1
	Year	24	39	2	8	2	0	0	3	2	0	7	.205	.244	.256	34	-4	0	.970	-0	*74*	*0*	/C-8	-0.4
1948	NY N	45	99	9	21	4	1	2	12	21	0	11	.212	.350	.333	85	-1	1	.980	-0	*111*	*54*	C-42	0.0
1949	NY N	19	57	6	17	2	0	4	12	2	1	8	.298	.333	.544	132	2	0	.985	-1	*85*	*61*	C-19	0.2
	Bos N	28	64	6	15	2	1	0	6	3	2	5	.234	.290	.297	61	-4	0	.977	0	*100*	*104*	C-22	-0.3
	Year	47	121	12	32	4	1	4	18	5	3	13	.264	.310	.413	95	-1	0	.980	-1	*93*	*84*	C-41	-0.1
1951	Bro N	2	5	0	2	0	0	0	2	1	0	0	.400	.500	.400	142	0	0-0	1.000	0	*0*	*364*	/C-2	0.0
Total	10	561	1490	128	354	56	9	19	153	144	13	141	.238	.310	.326	82	-37	7-0	.984	-10	*100*	*85*	C-483/1-14	-2.6
LIVINGSTONE, SCOTT Scott Louis B 7.15.1965 Dallas, TX BL/TR 6/198# d7.19																								
1991	Det A	44	127	19	37	5	0	2	11	10-0	0	25	.291	.341	.378	98	0	2-1	.980	-3	89	80	3-43	-0.4
1992	Det A	117	354	43	100	21	0	4	46	21-1	0	36	.282	.319	.376	95	-3	1-3	.962	-4	100	86	*3-112	-0.7
1993	Det A	98	304	39	89	10	2	2	39	19-1	0	32	.293	.328	.359	87	-6	1-3	.955	-10	85	58	3-62,D-32	-1.8
1994	Det A	15	23	0	5	1	0	0	1	1-0	0	4	.217	.250	.261	32	-2	0-0	1.000	0	0	142	/1-5,3D	-0.2
	SD N	57	180	11	49	12	1	2	10	6-0	0	22	.272	.294	.383	78	-6	2-2	.942	-0	100	89	3-50	-0.6
1995	SD N	99	196	26	66	15	0	5	32	15-1	0	22	.337	.380	.490	133	10	2-1	.991	-1	67	94	1-43,3-13/2-4	0.5
1996	†SD N	102	172	20	51	4	1	2	20	9-0	0	22	.297	.331	.366	89	-3	0-1	.993	-1	87	130	1-22,3-16	-0.6
1997	SD N	23	26	1	4	1	0	0	3	2-0	0	1	.154	.214	.192	8	-4	0-0	.750	1	154	0	/3-3,1-2,2	-0.3
	StL N	42	41	3	7	1	0	0	3	1-0	0	10	.171	.182	.195	1	-6	1-0	1.000	-1	47	0	/3-2,O(RF)D	-0.6
	Year	65	67	4	11	2	0	0	6	3-0	0	11	.164	.194	.194	4	-10	1-0	.778	0	111	0	/3-5,1-2,2O(RF)D	-0.9
1998	Mon N	76	110	1	23	6	0	0	12	5-2	0	15	.209	.237	.264	34	-11	1-1	.938	0	113	0	3-17/1-3,D-5	-1.1
Total	8	673	1533	163	431	76	4	17	177	89-5	0	189	.281	.317	.369	86	-31	10-12	.958	-19	97	74	3-319/1-75,D-43,2-5,O(RF)	-5.8
LIZOTTE, ABEL Abel B 4.13.1870 Lewiston, ME D 12.4.1926 Wilkes-Barre, PA 5-8/174# d9.17																								
1896	Pit N	7	29	3	3	0	0	0	3	2	0	2	.103	.161	.103	-31	-6	1	.952	1	163	72	/1-7	-0.4
LLENAS, WINSTON Winston Enriquillo (Davila) B 9.23.1943 Santiago, D.R. BR/TR 5-10/165# d8.15 C1																								
1968	Cal A	16	39	5	5	1	0	0	1	2-0	1	5	.128	.190	.154	6	-4	0-0	.800	-2	85	0	/3-9	-0.8
1969	Cal A	34	47	4	8	2	0	0	0	2-0	0	10	.170	.204	.213	18	-5	0-0	.929	-1	93	88	/3-9	-0.7
1972	Cal A	44	64	3	17	3	0	0	7	3-0	0	8	.266	.290	.313	87	-1	0-0	.950	-1	95	137	3-10/2-2,O-2(LF)	-0.2
1973	Cal A	78	130	16	35	1	0	1	25	10-0	1	16	.269	.317	.300	84	-3	0-0	1.000	2	77	38	2-20,3-11/O-4(LF),D-4	-0.1
1974	Cal A	72	138	16	36	6	0	2	17	11-1	0	19	.261	.301	.348	96	-1	0-0	1.000	-1	91	82	O-32(25-0-7),2-15,D-10/3-2	-0.2
1975	Cal A	56	113	6	21	4	0	0	11	10-0	0	11	.186	.250	.221	37	-9	0-1	1.000	4	111	94	2-12,O-10(9-0-1)/1-6,3-3,D-6	-0.6
Total	6	300	531	50	122	17	0	3	61	38-1	2	69	.230	.277	.279	66	-23	0-1	1.000	1	89	62	/2-49,O-48(40-0-8),3-44,D-20,1-6	-2.6

Year	Tm Lg	G	AB	R	H	2B	3B	HR	RBI	BB-IB	HP	SO	AVG	OBP	SLG	AOPS	ABR	SB-CS	FA	FR	Rng	Thr	G at Pos	BFW
LOAN, MIKE William Joseph B 9.27.1894 Philadelphia, PA D 11.21.1966 Springfield, PA BR/TR 5-11/185# d9.18																								
1912	Phi N	1	2	1	1	0	0	0	0	0	0	0	.500	.500	.500	163	0	0	1.000	-0	*44*	*0*	/C	0.0
LOANE, BOB Robert Kenneth B 8.5.1914 Berkeley, CA D 12.11.2002 Monterey, CA BR/TR 6/190# d7.29																								
1939	Was A	3	9	2	0	0	0	0	1	4	0	4	.000	.308	.000	-16	-1	0-0	.909	1	89	715	/O-3(CF)	0.0
1940	Bos N	13	22	4	5	3	0	0	1	2	0	5	.227	.292	.364	84	0	2	1.000	2	114	364	O-10(2-8-0)	0.1
Total	2	16	31	6	5	3	0	0	2	6	0	9	.161	.297	.258	54	-1	2-0	.969	3	106	478	/O-13(2-11-0)	0.1
LOBERT, FRANK Frank John B 11.26.1883 Williamsport, PA D 5.29.1932 Pittsburgh, PA BR/TR 6/180# d6.6 b-Hans																								
1914	Bal F	11	30	3	6	0	1	0	2	0	0	0	.200	.200	.267	26	-4	0	.870	-2	31	96	/3-7,2	-0.6
LOBERT, HANS John Bernard "Honus" B 10.18.1881 Wilmington, DE D 9.14.1968 Philadelphia, PA BR/TR 5-9/170# d9.21 M2 C11 b-Frank																								
1903	Pit N	5	13	1	1	1	0	0	0	1	0		.077	.143	.154	-15	-2	1	.778	-1	86	0	/3-3,2S	-0.3
1905	Chi N	14	46	7	9	2	0	0	1	3	1		.196	.260	.239	47	-3	4	.918	-1	90	137	3-13/O(CF)	-0.4
1906	Cin N	79	268	39	83	5	5	0	19	19	5		.310	.366	.366	123	7	20	.959	-7	99	98	3-35,S-31,2-10/O(CF)	0.2
1907	Cin N	148	537	61	132	9	12	1	41	37	4		.246	.299	.313	88	-9	30	.941	-16	89	111	*S-142/3-5	-2.3
1908	Cin N	**155**	570	71	167	17	18	4	63	46	2		.293	.348	.407	145	27	47	.921	-21	91	89	3-99,S-35,O-21(LF)	1.0
1909	Cin N	122	425	50	90	13	5	4	52	48	8		.212	.304	.294	86	-6	30	.921	-13	84	104	*3-122	-1.8
1910	Cin N	93	314	43	97	6	6	3	40	30	0	9	.309	.369	.395	128	10	41	.932	1	99	85	3-90	1.4
1911	Phi N	147	541	94	154	20	9	9	72	66	5	31	.285	.368	.405	115	11	40	.954	-18	78	62	*3-147	-0.2
1912	Phi N	65	257	37	84	12	5	2	33	19	0	13	.327	.373	.436	113	4	13	.976	-8	76	38	3-64	-0.2
1913	Phi N	150	573	98	172	28	11	7	55	42	5	34	.300	.353	.424	117	12	41-21	**.974**	-16	83	67	*3-145/S-3,2	0.2
1914	Phi N	135	505	83	139	24	5	1	52	49	3	32	.275	.343	.349	99	1	31	**.943**	-23	68	52	*3-133/S-2	-2.1
1915	NY N	106	386	46	97	18	4	0	38	25	4	24	.251	.304	.319	94	-3	14-15	.950	-4	95	65	*3-103	-0.7
1916	NY N	48	76	6	17	3	2	0	11	5	0	8	.224	.272	.316	84	-2	2	.961	2	115	97	3-20	0.0
1917	NY N	50	52	4	10	1	0	1	5	5	1	5	.192	.276	.269	70	-2	2	.906	1	114	167	3-21	-0.1
Total	14	1317	4563	640	1252	159	82	32	482	395	38	156	.274	.337	.366	109	45	316-36	.944	-123	85	74	3-1000,S-214/O-23(21-2-0),2-12	-5.3
LOCHHEAD, HARRY Robert Henry B 3.29.1876 Stockton, CA D 8.22.1909 Stockton, CA BR/TR 5-11/172# d4.16																								
1899	Cle N	148	541	52	129	7	1	1	43	21	10		.238	.280	.261	52	-36	23	.909	12	104	78	*S-146/2P	-1.5
1901	Det A	1	4	2	2	0	0	0	0	0	1		.500	.600	.500	198	1	0	.857	-0	108	0	/S	0.0
	Phi A	9	34	3	3	0	0	0	2	3	0		.088	.162	.088	-28	-6	0	.757	-6	71	33	/S-9	-1.1
	Year	10	38	5	5	0	0	0	2	3	1		.132	.214	.132	-3	-5	0	.773	-6	76	29	S-10	-1.1
Total	2	158	579	57	134	7	1	1	45	24	11		.231	.275	.252	48	-41	23	.903	6	102	75	S-156/P2	-2.6
LOCK, DON Don Wilson B 7.27.1936 Wichita, KS BR/TR 6-2/202# d7.17																								
1962	Was A	71	225	30	57	6	2	12	37	30-0	0	63	.253	.336	.458	114	4	4-5	.973	1	104	49	O-67(67-1-0)	0.0
1963	Was A	149	531	71	134	20	1	27	82	70-3	2	151	.252	.338	.446	119	14	7-3	.980	6	109	144	*O-146(10-135-9)	1.6
1964	Was A	152	512	73	127	17	4	28	80	79-3	1	137	.248	.346	.461	124	17	4-2	.987	9	103	179	*O-149(0-135-25)	2.2
1965	Was A	143	418	52	90	15	1	16	39	57-4	5	115	.215	.315	.371	96	-1	1-3	.969	2	107	121	*O-136(CF)	-0.4
1966	Was A	138	386	52	90	13	1	16	48	57-5	2	126	.233	.333	.396	110	6	2-6	.977	8	**118**	122	*O-129(0-126-4)	1.0
1967	Phi N	112	313	46	79	13	1	14	51	43-4	5	98	.252	.349	.435	123	10	9-5	.973	2	97	180	O-97(1-96-1)	1.0
1968	Phi N	99	248	27	52	7	2	8	34	26-0	0	64	.210	.283	.351	90	-3	3-4	.955	-2	105	43	O-78(8-46-27)	-1.0
1969	Phi N	4	4	0	0	0	0	0	0	0-0	0	1	.000	.000	.000	-99	-1	0-0	—	-0	0	0	/O(LF)	-0.1
	Bos A	53	58	8	13	1	0	1	2	11-0	0	21	.224	.348	.293	77	-1	0-1	1.000	-1	89	0	O-28(15-9-4)/1-4	-0.3
Total	8	921	2695	359	642	92	12	122	373	373-19	15	776	.238	.331	.417	111	45	30-29	.976	24	106	128	O-831(102-684-70)/1-4	4.0
LOCKE, MARSHALL Marshall Pinkney Wilder B 3.12.1857 Ashland, OH D 3.6.1940 Ashland, OH d7.5																								
1884	Ind AA	7	29	5	7	0	1	0	5	0	0		.241	.241	.310	81	-1		.800	-1	87	0	/O-7(0-3-4)	-0.1
LOCKHART, KEITH Keith Virgil B 11.10.1964 Whittier, CA BL/TR 5-10/170# d4.5																								
1994	SD N	27	43	4	9	0	0	2	6	4-0	1	10	.209	.286	.349	68	-2	1-0	1.000	1	56	0	3-13/2-5,SO(RF)	-0.1
1995	KC A	94	274	41	88	19	3	6	33	14-2	4	21	.321	.355	.478	115	6	8-1	.974	4	109	134	2-61,3-17,D-14	1.2
1996	KC A	138	433	49	118	33	3	7	55	30-4	2	40	.273	.319	.411	84	-11	11-6	.975	-5	106	121	2-84,3-55/D	-1.1
1997	†Atl N	96	147	25	41	5	3	6	32	14-0	1	17	.279	.337	.476	110	2	0-0	.983	-2	100	124	2-20,3-11/D-4	0.0
1998	†Atl N	109	366	50	94	21	0	9	37	29-0	1	37	.257	.311	.388	83	-9	2-2	.984	6	109	117	2-97/3D	0.1
1999	†Atl N	108	161	20	42	3	1	1	21	19-0	1	21	.261	.337	.311	67	-8	3-1	1.000	-1	111	97	2-25,3-10/D-4	-0.8
2000	†Atl N	113	275	32	73	12	3	2	32	29-7	0	31	.265	.331	.353	74	-11	4-1	.979	3	111	90	2-74,3-18	-0.4
2001	†Atl N	104	178	17	39	6	0	3	12	16-1	2	22	.219	.289	.303	53	-13	1-2	1.000	-6	89	98	2-47/3-4	-1.7
2002	†Atl N	128	296	34	64	13	3	5	32	27-9	1	50	.216	.282	.331	64	-18	0-1	.979	5	116	101	2-89/3	-0.9
2003	SD N	62	95	18	23	5	1	3	8	13-0	1	19	.242	.339	.411	104	1	0-1	.986	-3	75	78	2-27/3-3	-0.2
Total	10	979	2268	290	591	117	17	44	268	195-23	14	268	.261	.319	.385	82	-63	30-15	.981	3	107	109	2-529,3-133/D-25,O(RF)S	-3.9
LOCKLEAR, GENE Gene B 7.19.1949 Lumberton, NC BL/TR 5-10/165# d4.5																								
1973	Cin N	29	26	6	5	0	0	0	0	2-0	1	5	.192	.276	.192	34	-2	0-0	1.000	-1	71	0	/O-5(1-0-4)	-0.3
	SD N	67	154	20	37	6	1	3	25	21-1	0	22	.240	.330	.351	97	0	9-4	.952	2	103	78	O-37(LF)	0.0
	Year	96	180	26	42	6	1	3	25	23-1	1	27	.233	.322	.328	87	-3	9-4	.954	1	101	72	O-42(38-0-4)	-0.3
1974	SD N	39	74	7	20	3	2	1	3	4-0	0	12	.270	.308	.405	103	0	0-1	1.000	0	97	121	O-12(8-0-4)	-0.1
1975	SD N	100	237	31	76	11	1	5	27	22-4	1	26	.321	.378	.439	135	11	4-2	.970	-0	97	106	O-51(50-0-2)	0.9
1976	SD N	43	67	9	15	3	0	0	8	4-1	0	15	.224	.264	.269	57	-4	0-0	.952	-1	103	0	O-11(LF)	-0.5
	NY A	13	32	2	7	1	0	0	1	2-0	0	7	.219	.265	.250	52	-2	0-0	1.000	-1	70	0	/O-3(LF),D-6	-0.3
1977	NY A	1	5	1	3	0	0	0	2	0-0	0	0	.600	.600	.600	231	1	0-0	.667	-0	111	0	/O(LF)	0.1
Total	5	292	595	76	163	24	4	9	66	55-6	2	87	.274	.335	.373	105	4	13-7	.962	0	98	83	O-120(111-0-10)/D-6	-0.2
LOCKLIN, STU Stuart Carlton B 7.22.1928 Appleton, WI BL/TL 6-1.5/190# d6.23																								
1955	Cle A	16	18	4	3	1	0	0	0	3-0	0	4	.167	.286	.222	37	-2	0-0	1.000	-0	65	0	/O-7(0-4-3)	-0.2
1956	Cle A	9	6	0	1	0	0	0	0	0-0	0	1	.167	.167	.167	-12	-1	0-0	1.000	0	151	0	/O(RF)	-0.1
Total	2	25	24	4	4	1	0	0	0	3-0	0	5	.167	.259	.208	26	-3	0-0	1.000	-0	77	0	/O-8(0-4-4)	-0.3
LOCKMAN, WHITEY Carroll Walter B 7.25.1926 Lowell, NC BL/TR 6-1/175# d7.5 Mil 1945-46 M3 C7																								
1945	NY N	32	129	16	44	9	0	3	18	13	2	10	.341	.410	.481	145	8	1	.961	-4	87	40	O-32(CF)	0.4
1947	NY N	2	2	0	1	0	0	0	1	0	0	0	.500	.500	.500	165	0	0	—	0			H	0.0
1948	NY N	146	584	117	167	24	10	18	59	68	1	63	.286	.361	.454	119	14	8	.987	-3	102	52	*O-144(53-91-0)	0.5
1949	NY N	151	617	97	186	32	7	11	65	62	3	31	.301	.368	.429	113	12	12	.973	1	104	78	*O-151(LF)	0.2
1950	NY N	129	532	72	157	28	5	6	52	42	2	29	.295	.349	.400	96	-3	1	.978	4	103	109	*O-128(123-6-0)	-0.9
1951	†NY N	153	614	85	173	27	7	12	73	50	3	32	.282	.339	.407	99	-2	4-5	.986	0	104	111	*1-119,O-34(LF)	-0.9
1952	NY N★	**154**	606	99	176	17	4	13	58	67	2	52	.290	.363	.396	110	9	2-4	.992	2	105	115	*1-154	0.5
1953	NY N	150	607	85	179	22	4	9	61	52	0	36	.295	.351	.389	91	-8	3-4	.989	5	114	88	*1-120,O-30(0-3-28)	-1.1
1954	†NY N	148	570	73	143	17	3	16	60	59	0	31	.251	.318	.375	80	-17	2-2	.987	-7	85	97	*1-145/O-2(1-1-0)	-3.3
1955	NY N	147	576	76	157	19	0	15	49	39-2	3	34	.273	.320	.384	86	-12	3-3	.983	-4	105	68	O-81(79-2-1),1-68	-2.5
1956	NY N	48	169	13	46	7	1	1	10	16-2	0	17	.272	.333	.343	83	-4	0-2	.960	-2	95	122	O-39(38-1-1)/1-7	-0.9
	StL N	70	193	14	48	0	2	0	10	18-4	0	8	.249	.311	.269	59	-11	2-2	.955	-5	94	56	O-57(32-23-8)/1-2	-2.0
	Year	118	362	27	94	7	3	1	20	34-6	0	25	.260	.322	.304	70	-15	2-4	.957	-7	94	85	O-96(70-24-9)/1-9	-2.9
1957	NY N	133	456	51	113	9	4	7	30	39-3	2	19	.248	.308	.331	73	-18	5-5	.991	-4	97	112	*1-102,O-27(22-3-4)	-3.1
1958	SF N	92	122	15	29	5	0	2	7	13-4	0	8	.238	.311	.328	71	-5	0-0	1.000	-4	105	0	O-25(23-0-4),2-15/1-7	-0.9
1959	Bal A	38	69	7	15	1	1	0	2	8-0	0	4	.217	.299	.261	56	-4	0-0	.992	-3	38	128	1-22/2-5,O(RF)	-0.7
	Cin N	52	84	10	22	5	1	0	7	4-0	0	6	.262	.292	.345	68	-4	0-0	.971	0	131	101	1-20/2-6,3O(CF)	-0.4
1960	Cin N	21	10	6	2	0	0	1	1	2-0	1	3	.200	.385	.500	138	1	0-0	1.000	-0	0	444	/1-5	0.0
Total	15	1666	5940	836	1658	222	49	114	563	552-15	19	383	.279	.342	.391	95	-44	43-27	.989	-22	96	104	1-771,O-752(556-163-47)/2-26,3	-15.1
LOCKWOOD, SKIP Claude Edward B 8.17.1946 Boston, MA BR/TR 6/190# d4.23 ▲																								
1965	KC A	42	33	4	4	0	0	0	0	7-0	1	11	.121	.293	.121	23	-3	0-0	1.000	1	72	172	/3-7	-0.2
1969	Sea A	6	7	0	0	0	0	0	0	0-0	0	2	.000	.000	.000	-99	-1	0-0	1.000	0	145	330	/P-6	0.0
1970	Mil A	27	53	2	12	1	0	1	2	1-0	0	11	.226	.236	.302	48	2	0-0	.970	-2	71	56	P-27	0.0
1971	Mil A	36	62	2	5	1	0	1	4	5-0	0	20	.081	.149	.145	-17	-1	0-0	**1.000**	-3	54	98	P-33	0.0
1972	Mil A	31	53	3	7	0	0	0	0	3-0	1	12	.132	.193	.132	-2	-1	0-1	.958	-3	49	50	P-29	0.0
1973	Mil A	37	0	0	0	0	0	0	0	0-0	0	0	—	—	—	—	0	0-0	.944	-0	98	56	P-37	0.0

Year	Tm Lg	G	AB	R	H	2B	3B	HR	RBI	BB-IB	HP	SO	AVG	OBP	SLG	AOPS	ABR	SB-CS	FA	FR	Rng	Thr	G at Pos	BFW
1974	Cal A	37	0	0	0	0	0	0	0	0-0	0	0	—	—	—	—	0	0-0	1.000	-0	93	116	P-37	0.0
1975	NY N	24	6	0	1	0	0	0	1	0-0	0	0	.167	.167	.167	-8	0	0-0	.800	-1	42	0	P-24	0.0
1976	NY N	56	18	2	6	1	0	0	2	2-0	0	3	.333	.400	.389	132	3	0-1	.867	-0	78	139	P-56	0.0
1977	NY N	63	15	1	3	0	0	0	1	0-0	0	1	.200	.200	.200	8	0	0-0	.875	-2	38	0	P-63	0.0
1978	NY N	57	11	1	2	1	0	1	1	0-0	0	5	.182	.182	.545	100	1	0-0	.900	-2	35	106	P-57	0.0
1979	NY N	28	2	0	0	0	0	0	0	0-0	0	1	.000	.000	.000	-99	0	0-0	.800	-1	50	220	P-27	0.0
1980	Bos A	24	0	0	0	0	0	0	0	0-0	0	0	—	—	—	—	0	0-0	1.000	-1	44	0	P-24	0.0
Total	13	468	260	15	40	4	0	3	11	18-0	2	66	.154	.214	.204	19	0	0-2	.947	-13	64	78	P-420/3-7	-0.2
LOCKWOOD, MILO Milo Hathaway B 4.7.1858 Solon, OH D 10.9.1897 Economy, PA 5-10/160# d4.17 ▲																								
1884	Was U	20	67	9	14	1	0	0		8			.209	.293	.224	61	-5		.773	1	46	283	O-11(1-7-3),P-11/3-3	-0.2
LODIGIANI, DARIO Dario Antonio B 6.6.1916 San Francisco, CA BR/TR 5-8/150# d4.18 Mil 1943-45 C2																								
1938	Phi A	93	325	36	91	15	1	6	44	34	7	25	.280	.361	.388	90	-5	3-0	.953	-6	98	77	2-80,3-13	-0.4
1939	Phi A	121	393	46	102	22	4	6	44	42	4	18	.260	.337	.382	85	-9	2-0	.944	-3	104	43	3-89,2-28	-0.6
1940	Phi A	1	1	0	0	0	0	0	0	0	0	0	.000	.000	.000	-99	0	0-0	—	0			H	0.0
1941	Chi A	87	322	39	77	19	2	4	40	31	5	19	.239	.316	.348	76	-11	0-4	.962	4	99	146	3-86	-0.5
1942	Chi A	59	168	9	47	7	0	0	15	18	1	10	.280	.353	.321	92	-1	3-4	.944	4	117	55	3-43/2-7	0.4
1946	Chi A	44	155	12	38	8	0	0	13	16	2	14	.245	.324	.297	77	-4	4-0	.935	-3	99	45	3-44	-0.7
Total	6	405	1364	142	355	71	7	16	156	141	19	86	.260	.338	.358	84	-30	12-8	.947	-4	103	82	3-275,2-115	-1.8
LoDUCA, PAUL Paul Anthony B 4.12.1972 Brooklyn, NY BR/TR 5-10/193# d6.21																								
1998	LA N	6	14	2	4	1	0	0	1	0-0	0	1	.286	.286	.357	72	-1	0-0	1.000	0	83	259	/C-4	0.0
1999	LA N	36	95	11	22	1	0	3	11	10-4	2	9	.232	.312	.337	70	-5	1-2	.990	0	103	119	C-34	-0.3
2000	LA N	34	65	6	16	2	0	2	8	6-0	0	8	.246	.301	.369	75	-3	0-2	.992	4	117	206	C-20/O-8(7-0-2),3	0.2
2001	LA N	125	460	71	147	28	0	25	90	39-2	6	30	.320	.374	.543	146	31	2-4	.991	-8	105	123	C-99,1-33/O-5(4-0-1),D	2.5
2002	LA N	149	580	74	163	38	1	10	64	34-2	10	31	.281	.330	.402	102	-2	3-1	.992	1	83	116	*C-137,1-18/O-9(LF)	0.8
2003	LA N★	147	568	64	155	34	2	7	52	44-6	10	54	.273	.335	.377	91	-8	0-2	.987	**32**	74	**207**	*C-123,1-22/O-6(LF)	2.9
Total	6	497	1782	228	507	104	3	47	226	133-14	28	133	.285	.341	.425	107	12	6-11	.990	30	88	151	C-417/1-73,O-28(26-0-3),D3	6.1
LOEPP, GEORGE George Herbert B 9.11.1901 Detroit, MI D 9.4.1967 Los Angeles, CA BR/TR 5-11/170# d8.29																								
1928	Bos A	15	51	6	9	3	1	0	3	5	0	12	.176	.250	.275	38	-5	0-0	.949	0	103	128	O-14(1-10-6)	-0.5
1930	Was A	50	134	23	37	7	1	0	14	20	3	9	.276	.382	.343	85	-2	0-4	.958	-1	97	109	O-48(12-34-3)	-0.5
Total	2	65	185	29	46	10	2	0	17	25	3	21	.249	.347	.324	73	-7	0-4	.956	-0	99	114	/O-62(13-44-9)	-1.0
LOFTON, JAMES James O'Neal B 3.6.1974 Los Angeles, CA BB/TR 5-10/170# d9.19																								
2001	Bos A	8	26	1	5	1	0	0	1	1-0	0	4	.192	.214	.231	20	-3	2-1	.920	-1	84	78	/S-7	-0.4
LOFTON, KENNY Kenneth B 5.31.1967 E.Chicago, IN BL/TL 6/180# d9.14																								
1991	Hou N	20	74	9	15	1	0	0	0	5-0	0	19	.203	.253	.216	35	-7	2-1	.977	-0	101	107	O-20(CF)	-0.7
1992	Cle A	148	576	96	164	15	8	5	42	68-3	2	54	.285	.362	.365	106	6	**66**-12	.982	7	104	170	*O-143(CF)	2.2
1993	Cle A	148	569	116	185	28	8	1	42	81-6	1	83	.325	.408	.408	121	21	**70**-14	.979	5	105	138	*O-146(CF)	3.7
1994	Cle A★	112	459	105	**160**	32	9	12	57	52-5	2	56	.349	.412	.536	143	31	**60**-12	.993	1	91	214	*O-112(CF)	3.8
1995	†Cle A★	118	481	93	149	22	**13**	7	53	40-6	1	49	.310	.362	.453	110	6	**54**-15	.970	-5	86	197	*O-114(CF)/D-2	0.8
1996	†Cle A★	154	662	132	210	35	4	14	67	61-3	0	82	.317	.372	.446	107	8	**75**-17	.975	-5	95	138	*O-152(CF)	1.4
1997	†Atl N✳	122	493	90	164	20	6	5	48	64-5	2	83	.333	.409	.428	118	16	27-20	.983	1	108	88	*O-122(CF)	1.6
1998	†Cle A★	154	600	101	169	31	6	12	64	87-1	2	80	.282	.371	.413	101	4	54-10	.978	-4	86	**199**	*O-154(CF)	0.9
1999	†Cle A★	120	465	110	140	28	6	7	39	79-2	6	84	.301	.405	.432	110	11	25-6	.989	-3	91	159	*O-119(CF)/D	1.2
2000	Cle A	137	543	107	151	23	5	15	73	79-3	4	72	.278	.369	.422	99	1	30-7	.989	3	109	64	*O-135(CF)/D	0.8
2001	†Cle A	133	517	91	135	21	4	14	66	47-1	2	69	.261	.322	.398	88	-9	16-8	.981	-2	105	45	*O-130(CF)	-0.9
2002	Chi A	93	352	68	91	20	6	8	42	49-0	0	51	.259	.348	.418	101	1	22-8	1.000	0	103	67	O-92(CF)	0.4
	†SF N	46	180	30	48	10	3	3	9	23-0	1	22	.267	.353	.406	107	1	7-3	1.000	3	113	126	O-44(CF)	0.5
2003	Pit N	84	339	58	94	19	4	9	26	28-1	2	29	.277	.333	.437	98	-2	18-5	1.000	1	101	107	O-81(CF)	0.2
	†Chi N	56	208	39	68	13	4	3	20	18-2	2	22	.327	.381	.471	124	8	12-4	.974	-1	99	116	O-55(CF)	0.8
	Year	140	547	97	162	32	8	12	46	46-3	4	51	.296	.352	.450	108	6	30-9	.991	-0	100	111	*O-136(CF)	1.0
Total	13	1645	6518	1245	1943	318	86	115	648	781-38	27	855	.298	.373	.426	108	96	538-142	.984	-0	99	134	*O-1619(CF)/D-4	16.7
LOFTUS, DICK Richard Joseph B 3.7.1901 Concord, MA D 1.21.1972 Concord, MA BL/TR 6/155# d4.20																								
1924	Bro N	46	81	18	22	6	0	0	8	7	0	2	.272	.330	.346	84	-2	1-0	1.000	1	111	49	O-29(6-14-9)/1	-0.2
1925	Bro N	51	131	16	31	6	0	0	13	5	2	5	.237	.275	.282	44	-11	2-0	.977	2	114	83	O-38(3-0-35)	-1.1
Total	2	97	212	34	53	12	0	0	21	12	2	7	.250	.296	.307	59	-13	3-0	.985	2	113	71	/O-67(9-14-44),1	-1.3
LOFTUS, TOM Thomas Joseph B 11.15.1856 St.Louis, MO D 4.16.1910 Dubuque, IA BR ?/168# d8.17 M9																								
1877	StL N	3	11	2	2	0	0	0	0	0		1	.182	.182	.182	16	-1		.778	1	434	0	/O-3(1-0-2)	0.0
1883	StL AA	6	22	1	4	0	0	0		2			.182	.250	.182	39	-1		.882	-1	0	0	/O-6(CF)	-0.2
Total	2	9	33	3	6	0	0	0	0	2		1	.182	.229	.182	32	-2		.846	1	148	0	/O-9(1-6-2)	-0.2
LOGAN, JOHNNY John "Yatcha" B 3.23.1927 Endicott, NY BR/TR 5-11/175# d4.17																								
1951	Bos N	62	169	14	37	7	1	0	16	18	1	13	.219	.298	.272	59	-10	0-0	.958	2	102	91	S-58	-0.5
1952	Bos N	117	456	56	129	21	3	4	42	31	4	33	.283	.334	.368	98	-2	1-2	**.972**	13	**107**	99	*S-117	1.8
1953	Mil N	150	611	100	167	27	8	11	73	41	7	33	.273	.326	.398	93	-7	2-2	**.975**	21	105	**115**	*S-150	2.5
1954	Mil N	**154**	560	66	154	17	7	8	66	51	6	51	.275	.339	.373	92	-7	2-0	**.969**	13	103	107	*S-154	1.9
1955	Mil N★	**154**	595	95	177	**37**	5	13	83	58-1	4	58	.297	.360	.442	118	17	3-3	.963	5	108	97	*S-154	3.4
1956	Mil N	148	545	69	153	27	5	15	46	46-2	5	49	.281	.340	.431	113	10	3-0	.968	4	107	106	*S-148	2.7
1957	†Mil N☆	129	494	59	135	19	7	10	49	31-2	4	49	.273	.319	.401	100	-2	5-0	.960	22	**113**	112	*S-129	3.2
1958	†Mil N★	145	530	54	120	20	0	11	53	40-1	5	57	.226	.286	.326	68	-26	1-2	.959	15	**109**	110	*S-144	0.0
1959	Mil N☆	138	470	59	137	17	0	13	50	57-9	3	45	.291	.369	.411	118	14	1-3	.975	-2	101	97	*S-138	2.3
1960	Mil N	136	482	52	118	14	4	7	42	43-6	2	40	.245	.309	.334	82	-13	1-1	.956	-1	103	97	*S-136	-0.2
1961	Mil N	18	19	0	2	1	0	0	1	1-0	0	3	.105	.150	.158	-19	-3	0-0	1.000	0	125	203	/S-2	-0.3
	Pit N	27	52	5	12	4	0	0	5	4-0	0	8	.231	.286	.308	57	-3	0-0	1.000	1	115	217	/3-7,S-6	-0.2
	Year	45	71	5	14	5	0	0	6	5-0	0	11	.197	.250	.268	38	-6	0-0	.964	1	104	109	/S-8,3-7	-0.5
1962	Pit N	44	80	7	24	3	0	1	12	7-0	0	6	.300	.348	.375	96	0	0-0	.980	1	110	165	3-19	0.1
1963	Pit N	81	181	15	42	2	1	0	9	23-5	2	27	.232	.325	.254	69	-6	0-0	.920	2	105	119	S-44/3-4	-0.2
Total	13	1503	5244	651	1407	216	41	93	547	451-26	43	472	.268	.330	.378	95	-38	19-13	.965	94	106	104	*S-1380/3-30	16.5
LOHMAN, PETE George F. B 10.21.1864 Washington Co., MN D 11.21.1928 Los Angeles, CA d5.11																								
1891	Was AA	32	109	18	21	1	4	1	11	16	1	17	.193	.302	.303	77	-4	1	.914	-3	*87*	*86*	C-21/O-8(1-1-6),3-4,S2	-0.4
LOHR, HOWARD Howard Sylvester B 6.3.1892 Philadelphia, PA D 6.9.1977 Philadelphia, PA BR/TR 6/165# d6.17																								
1914	Cin N	18	47	6	10	1	1	0	7	0	0	8	.213	.213	.277	44	-4	2	.926	-1	89	68	O-17(0-17-1)	-0.6
1916	Cle A	3	7	0	1	0	0	0	1	0	0	1	.143	.143	.143	-13	-1	1	1.000	-0	104	0	/O-3(RF)	-0.1
Total	2	21	54	6	11	1	1	0	8	0	0	9	.204	.204	.259	36	-5	3	.933	-1	91	59	/O-20(0-17-4)	-0.7
LOHRKE, JACK Jack Wayne "Lucky" B 2.25.1924 Los Angeles, CA BR/TR 6/180# d4.18																								
1947	NY N	112	329	44	79	12	4	11	35	46	2	29	.240	.337	.401	95	-3	3	.939	-2	94	108	*3-111	-0.5
1948	NY N	97	280	35	70	15	1	5	31	30	0	30	.250	.323	.364	85	-6	3	.898	-4	94	64	3-50,2-36	-0.8
1949	NY N	55	180	32	48	11	4	5	22	16	2	12	.267	.333	.456	110	2	3	.969	1	135	36	2-23,3-19,S-15	0.5
1950	NY N	30	43	4	8	0	0	0	4	4	0	8	.186	.255	.186	18	-5	0	.958	0	101	145	3-16/2	-0.5
1951	†NY N	23	40	3	8	0	0	1	3	10	0	2	.200	.360	.275	73	-1	0-0	.943	-1	103	84	3-17/S	-0.2
1952	Phi N	25	29	4	6	0	0	0	1	4	0	3	.207	.303	.207	44	-2	0-0	1.000	1	113	123	/S-5,3-3,2	-0.1
1953	Phi N	12	13	3	2	0	0	0	0	1	0	2	.154	.214	.154	-2	-2	0-0	.750	0	178	0	/2-2,S-2,3	-0.2
Total	7	354	914	125	221	38	9	22	96	111	4	86	.242	.327	.375	87	-17	9-0	.928	-5	94	96	3-217/2-63,S-23	-1.8
LOIS, ALBERTO Alberto (born B 5.6.1956 Hato Mayor, D.R. BR/TR 5-9/175# d9.8																								
1978	Pit N	3	4	0	1	0	1	0	0	0-0	0	1	.250	.250	.750	163	0	0-0	1.000	0	160	0	/O-2(2-1-0)	0.0
1979	Pit N	11	0	6	0	0	0	0	0	0-0	0	0	—	—	—	—	0	1-1	—	0			/R	0.0
Total	2	14	4	6	1	0	1	0	0	0-0	0	1	.250	.250	.750	163	0	1-1	1.000	0	160	0	/O-2(2-1-0)	0.0

Year	Tm Lg	G	AB	R	H	2B	3B	HR	RBI	BB-IB	HP	SO	AVG	OBP	SLG	AOPS	ABR	SB-CS	FA	FR	Rng	Thr	G at Pos	BFW
LOLICH, RON Ronald John B 9.19.1946 Portland, OR BR/TR 6-1/185# d7.18																								
1971	Chi A	2	8	0	1	1	0	0	0	0-0	0	2	.125	.125	.250	4	-1	0-0	1.000	-1	29	0	/O-2(RF)	-0.2
1972	Cle A	24	80	4	15	1	0	2	8	4-1	0	20	.188	.224	.275	47	-6	0-0	1.000	-1	97	64	O-22(4-0-19)	-0.8
1973	Cle A	61	140	16	32	7	0	2	15	7-0	0	27	.229	.265	.321	63	-7	0-2	.909	-2	80	121	O-32(5-0-27),D-12	-1.2
Total	3	87	228	20	48	9	0	4	23	11-1	0	49	.211	.246	.303	56	-14	0-2	.953	-4	86	91	/O-56(9-0-48),D-12	-2.2
LOLLAR, SHERM John Sherman B 8.23.1924 Durham, AR D 9.24.1977 Springfield, MO BR/TR 6-1/185# d4.20 C5																								
1946	Cle A	28	62	7	15	6	0	1	9	5	0	9	.242	.299	.387	97	0	0-1	.990	-2	106	114	C-24	-0.1
1947	†NY A	11	32	4	7	0	1	1	6	1	0	5	.219	.242	.375	71	-2	0-1	1.000	0	89	44	/C-9	-0.1
1948	NY A	22	38	0	8	0	0	0	4	1	0	6	.211	.231	.211	18	-5	0-0	.976	1	109	118	C-10	-0.4
1949	StL A	109	284	28	74	9	1	8	49	32	2	22	.261	.340	.384	88	-6	0-1	.988	-2	98	107	C-93	-0.4
1950	StL A☆	126	396	55	111	22	3	13	65	64	8	25	.280	.391	.449	110	8	2-0	.981	-4	93	**152**	*C-109	0.9
1951	StL A	98	310	44	78	21	0	8	44	43	4	26	.252	.350	.397	99	0	1-0	**.995**	-3	91	**138**	C-85/3	0.2
1952	Chi A	132	375	35	90	15	0	13	50	54	12	34	.240	.354	.384	104	4	1-0	.989	-3	71	80	*C-120	0.7
1953	Chi A	113	334	46	96	19	0	8	54	47	8	29	.287	.388	.416	114	9	1-0	**.994**	1	85	106	*C-107/1	1.5
1954	Chi A☆	107	316	31	77	13	0	7	34	37	7	28	.244	.334	.351	85	-5	0-1	.993	2	113	107	C-93	0.0
1955	Chi A☆	138	426	67	111	13	1	16	61	68-12	10	34	.261	.374	.408	108	7	2-2	.995	12	119	84	*C-136	2.5
1956	Chi A★	136	450	55	132	28	2	11	75	53-4	16	34	.293	.383	.438	116	13	2-0	**.993**	3	**145**	67	*C-132	2.1
1957	Chi A	101	351	33	90	11	2	11	70	35-2	13	24	.256	.342	.393	101	1	2-0	.998	0	98	87	C-96	0.7
1958	Chi A☆	127	421	53	115	16	0	20	84	57-3	8	37	.273	.367	.454	128	18	2-1	.987	2	97	94	*C-116	2.5
1959	†Chi A★	140	505	63	134	22	3	22	84	55-6	9	49	.265	.345	.451	119	13	4-3	.993	7	80	101	*C-122,1-24	2.5
1960	Chi A★	129	421	43	106	23	0	7	46	42-3	8	39	.252	.326	.356	87	-7	2-0	**.995**	3	99	120	*C-123	0.3
1961	Chi A	116	337	38	95	10	1	7	41	37-10	6	22	.282	.360	.380	100	1	0-0	**.998**	-4	106	119	*C-107	0.2
1962	Chi A	84	220	17	59	12	0	2	26	32-9	3	23	.268	.369	.350	95	0	1-0	.991	-6	72	103	C-66	-0.2
1963	Chi A	35	73	4	17	4	0	0	6	8-0	1	7	.233	.317	.288	72	-2	0-0	.981	-2	118	172	C-23/1-2	-0.3
Total	18	1752	5351	623	1415	244	14	155	808	671-49	115	453	.264	.357	.402	104	47	20-10	.992	6	100	104	*C-1571/1-27,3	12.6
LOMAN, DOUG Douglas Edward B 5.9.1958 Bakersfield, CA BL/TL 5-11/185# d9.3																								
1984	Mil A	23	76	13	21	4	0	2	12	15-2	1	7	.276	.402	.408	130	4	0-2	.967	3	108	249	O-23(21-0-4)	0.5
1985	Mil A	24	66	10	14	3	2	0	7	1-0	0	12	.212	.221	.318	47	-5	0-0	1.000	3	100	344	O-20(0-8-15)	-0.3
Total	2	47	142	23	35	7	2	2	19	16-2	1	19	.246	.325	.366	93	-1	0-2	.981	6	105	290	/O-43(21-8-19)	0.2
LOMASNEY, STEVE Steven James B 8.29.1977 Melrose, MA BR/TR 6/185# d10.3																								
1999	Bos A	1	2	0	0	0	0	0	0	0-0	0	2	.000	.000	.000	-97	-1	0-0	1.000	2	0	1103	/C	0.1
LOMBARD, GEORGE George Paul B 9.14.1975 Atlanta, GA BL/TR 6/208# d9.4																								
1998	Atl N	6	6	2	2	0	0	1	1	0-0	0	1	.333	.333	.833	194	1	1-0	1.000	-0	87	0	/O-2(RF)	0.1
1999	Atl N	6	6	1	2	0	0	0	0	1-0	0	2	.333	.429	.333	96	0	2-0	1.000	0	129	0	/O-4(2-0-2)	0.0
2000	Atl N	27	39	8	4	0	0	0	2	1-0	1	14	.103	.146	.103	-36	-8	4-0	1.000	0	93	170	O-15(5-0-11)	-0.7
2002	Det A	72	241	34	58	11	3	5	13	20-1	1	78	.241	.300	.373	83	-7	13-2	.982	-2	100	54	O-69(29-40-1)/D-2	-0.7
2003	TB A	13	37	8	8	1	0	1	4	0-0	1	6	.216	.237	.324	47	-3	1-0	.964	1	121	160	O-13(3-0-11)	-0.2
Total	5	124	329	53	74	12	3	7	20	22-1	3	101	.225	.279	.343	66	-17	21-2	.981	-0	102	78	O-103(39-40-27)/D-2	-1.5
LOMBARDI, ERNIE Ernesto Natali "Schnozz" or "Bocci" B 4.6.1908 Oakland, CA D 9.26.1977 Santa Cruz, CA BR/TR 6-3/230# d4.15 HF1986																								
1931	Bro N	73	182	20	54	7	1	4	23	12	0	12	.297	.340	.412	102	0	1	.984	1	105	80	C-50	0.4
1932	Cin N	118	413	43	125	22	9	11	68	41	4	19	.303	.371	.479	131	18	0	.963	-9	91	115	*C-110	1.6
1933	Cin N	107	350	30	99	21	1	4	47	16	4	17	.283	.322	.383	102	1	2	.972	-9	94	94	C-95	-0.3
1934	Cin N	132	417	42	127	19	4	9	62	16	3	22	.305	.335	.434	107	2	0	.989	-3	99	105	*C-111	0.6
1935	Cin N	120	332	36	114	23	3	12	64	16	3	6	.343	.379	.539	148	22	0	.983	-4	88	121	C-82	2.2
1936	Cin N☆	121	387	42	129	23	2	12	68	19	7	16	.333	.375	.496	142	22	1	.962	-9	96	94	*C-105	1.8
1937	Cin N☆	120	368	41	123	22	1	9	59	14	2	17	.334	.362	.473	132	15	1	.973	-12	74	109	C-90	0.8
1938	Cin N★	129	489	60	167	30	1	19	95	40	0	14	**.342**	.391	.524	154	35	0	.985	-2	**127**	102	*C-123	4.1
1939	†Cin N★	130	450	43	129	26	2	20	85	35	3	19	.287	.342	.487	120	11	0	.984	1	113	111	*C-120	1.9
1940	†Cin N★	109	376	50	120	22	0	14	74	31	7	14	.319	.382	.489	137	20	0	.989	-1	113	60	*C-101	2.5
1941	Cin N	117	398	33	105	12	1	10	60	36	0	14	.264	.325	.374	96	-3	1	.983	-4	77	117	*C-116	0.0
1942	Bos N★	105	309	32	102	14	0	11	46	37	1	12	**.330**	.403	.482	162	25	1	.980	-12	76	92	C-85	1.8
1943	NY N★	104	295	19	90	7	0	10	51	16	3	11	.305	.347	.431	123	7	1	.971	-10	80	88	C-73	0.2
1944	NY N	117	373	37	95	13	0	10	58	33	1	25	.255	.317	.370	93	-4	0	.968	-9	105	90	*C-100	-0.8
1945	NY N✳	115	368	46	113	7	1	19	70	43	5	11	.307	.387	.486	140	19	0	.983	3	**160**	88	C-96	2.8
1946	NY N	88	238	19	69	4	1	12	39	18	3	24	.290	.347	.466	129	8	0	.978	-0	87	110	C-63	1.1
1947	NY N	48	110	8	31	5	0	4	21	7	0	9	.282	.325	.436	100	0	0	.980	-1	163	96	C-24	-0.1
Total	17	1853	5855	601	1792	277	27	190	990	430	46	262	.306	.358	.460	126	198	8	.979	-79	102	99	*C-1544	20.6
LOMBARDI, PHIL Phillip Arden B 2.20.1963 Abilene, TX BR/TR 6-2/200# d4.26																								
1986	NY A	20	36	6	10	3	0	2	6	4-0	1	7	.278	.366	.528	141	2	0-0	.867	0	100	255	/O-8(LF),C-3	0.2
1987	NY A	5	8	0	1	0	0	0	0	0-0	0	2	.125	.125	.125	-34	-2	0-0	1.000	1	61	367	/C-3	-0.1
1989	NY N	18	48	4	11	1	0	1	3	5-0	0	8	.229	.302	.313	80	-1	0-0	.980	-2	56	22	C-16/1	-0.3
Total	3	43	92	10	22	4	0	3	9	9-0	1	17	.239	.314	.380	95	-1	0-0	.975	-1	56	38	/C-22,O-8(LF),1	-0.2
LOMBARDOZZI, STEVE Stephen Paul B 4.26.1960 Malden, MA BR/TR 6/175# d7.12																								
1985	Min A	28	54	10	20	4	1	0	6	6-0	0	6	.370	.426	.481	142	3	3-2	.982	5	130	117	2-26	0.9
1986	Min A	156	453	53	103	20	5	8	33	52-2	1	76	.227	.308	.347	76	-15	3-1	**.991**	7	102	106	*2-155	0.0
1987	†Min A	136	432	51	103	19	3	8	38	33-1	4	66	.238	.298	.352	69	-20	5-1	.977	-2	97	94	*2-133	-1.4
1988	Min A	103	287	34	60	15	2	3	27	35-2	2	48	.209	.295	.307	68	-12	2-5	.986	-9	95	94	2-90,S-12/3-5	-1.9
1989	Hou N	21	37	5	8	3	1	1	3	4-1	0	9	.216	.293	.432	109	0	0-0	.922	-4	82	77	2-18/3	-0.4
1990	Hou N	2	1	0	0	0	0	0	0	1-0	0	1	.000	.500	.000	52	0	0-0	—	0			/H	0.0
Total	6	446	1264	153	294	61	12	20	107	131-6	7	206	.233	.307	.347	76	-44	13-9	.983	-2	100	99	2-422/S-12,3-6	-2.8
LONERGAN, WALTER Walter E. B 9.22.1885 Boston, MA D 1.23.1958 Lexington, MA BR/TR 5-7/156# d8.17																								
1911	Bos A	10	26	2	7	0	0	0	1	1	0		.269	.296	.269	59	-2	1	.935	-1	80	104	/2-7,S3	-0.2
LONG d8.29																								
1888	Lou AA	1	2	0	0	0	0	0	0	1	0		.000	.333	.000	11	0	0	—	0	0	0	/O(RF)	0.0
LONG, DAN Daniel W. B 8.27.1867 Boston, MA D 4.30.1929 Sausalito, CA d8.27																								
1890	Bal AA	21	77	19	12	0	0	0	2	14	2		.156	.301	.156	33	-6	16	.939	0	159	0	O-21(CF)	-0.6
LONG, HERMAN Herman C. "Germany" or "Flying Dutchman" B 4.13.1866 Chicago, IL D 9.17.1909 Denver, CO BL/TR 5-8.5/160# d4.17																								
1889	KC AA	136	574	137	158	32	6	3	60	64	10	63	.275	.358	.368	101	1	89	.874	31	108	110	*S-128/2-8,O(LF)	3.1
1890	Bos N	101	431	95	108	15	3	8	52	40	4	34	.251	.320	.355	90	-7	49	.898	7	100	121	*S-101	0.2
1891	Bos N	139	577	129	163	21	12	9	75	80	8	51	.282	.377	.407	115	10	60	.902	15	95	**143**	*S-139	2.6
1892	†Bos N	151	646	115	181	33	6	6	78	44	8	36	.280	.334	.378	105	2	57	.889	15	105	**145**	*S-141,O-12(11-1-0)/3	2.2
1893	Bos N	128	552	**149**	159	22	6	6	58	73	5	32	.288	.376	.382	94	-5	38	.883	16	110	**144**	*S-123/2-5	1.4
1894	Bos N	104	475	136	154	28	11	12	79	35	4	17	.324	.375	.505	103	-1	24	.885	1	105	125	*S-98/O-5(LF),2-3	0.3
1895	Bos N	125	540	109	170	23	10	9	75	31	3	13	.315	.355	.444	98	-5	36	.892	-13	94	100	*S-123/2-2	-1.0
1896	Bos N	120	502	106	173	26	8	6	101	26	5	16	.345	.383	.464	116	10	38	.897	9	103	110	*S-120	2.1
1897	†Bos N	107	450	89	145	32	7	3	69	23	2		.322	.358	.444	105	1	22	.905	-3	97	109	*S-107/O(LF)	0.3
1898	Bos N	144	589	99	156	21	10	6	99	39	0		.265	.311	.365	89	-12	20	.923	-1	97	124	*S-142/2-2	-0.5
1899	Bos N	145	578	91	153	30	8	6	100	45	3		.265	.321	.375	83	-16	20	.929	-15	87	**138**	*S-143/1-2	-2.1
1900	Bos N	125	486	80	127	19	4	**12**	66	44	2		.261	.325	.391	86	-11	26	.937	-8	99	71	*S-125	-1.1
1901	Bos N	138	518	54	112	14	6	3	68	25	1		.216	.254	.284	51	-34	20	**.946**	-7	97	112	*S-138	-3.6
1902	Bos N	120	437	40	101	11	0	2	44	31	1		.231	.284	.270	70	-15	24	**.946**	20	103	123	*S-107,2-13	0.9
1903	NY A	22	80	6	15	3	0	0	8	2	0		.188	.207	.225	28	-7	3	.889	-4	87	83	S-22	-1.1
	Det A	69	239	21	53	12	0	0	23	10	1		.222	.256	.272	60	-11	11	.879	-1	88	89	S-38,2-31	-1.2
	Year	91	319	27	68	15	0	0	31	12	1		.213	.244	.260	52	-18	14	.883	-5	88	87	S-60,2-31	-2.3
1904	Phi N	1	4	0	1	0	0	0	0	0	0		.250	.250	.250	56	0	0	.889	0	102	0	/2	0.0
Total	16	1875	7678	1456	2129	342	97	91	1055	612	57	262	.277	.335	.383	93	-100	537	.906	63	99	119	*S-1795/2-65,O-19(18-1-0),1-2,3	2.5

Year	Tm Lg	G	AB	R	H	2B	3B	HR	RBI	BB-IB	HP	SO	AVG	OBP	SLG	AOPS	ABR	SB-CS	FA	FR	Rng	Thr	G at Pos	BFW
LONG, JIMMIE James Albert B 6.29.1898 Ft.Dodge, IA D 9.14.1970 Ft.Dodge, IA BR/TR 5-11/160# d9.12																								
1922	Chi A	3	3	0	0	0	0	0	0	1	0	0	.000	.250	.000	-30	-1	0-0	1.000	-0	*0*	*0*	/C-2	-0.1
LONG, JIM James M. B 11.15.1862 Louisville, KY D 12.12.1932 Louisville, KY 5-10/160# d8.9																								
1891	Lou AA	6	25	5	6	0	0	0	4	3	2	6	.240	.367	.240	75	0	1	.857	1	186	435	/O-6(4-2-0)	0.0
1893	Bal N	55	226	31	48	8	1	2	25	16	4	27	.212	.276	.283	48	-18	23	.893	-1	86	48	O-55(LF)	-1.9
Total	2	61	251	36	54	8	1	2	29	19	6	33	.215	.286	.279	51	-18	24	.890	0	96	86	/O-61(59-2-0)	-1.9
LONG, JEOFF Jeoffrey Keith B 10.9.1941 Covington, KY BR/TR 6-1/200# d7.31																								
1963	StL N	5	5	0	1	0	0	0	0	0-0	0	1	.200	.200	.200	14	-1	0-0	—	0			H	-0.1
1964	StL N	28	43	5	10	1	0	1	4	6-0	1	18	.233	.340	.326	81	-1	0-0	.833	-2	75	0	/O-4(RF),1-3	-0.3
	Chi A	23	35	0	5	0	0	0	5	4-0	0	15	.143	.225	.143	7	-4	0-0	1.000	0	187	128	/1-5,O-5(LF)	-0.5
Total	2	56	83	5	16	1	0	1	9	10-0	1	34	.193	.284	.241	48	-6	0-0	.750	-2	74	0	/O-9(5-0-4),1-8	-0.9
LONG, DALE Richard Dale B 2.6.1926 Springfield, MO D 1.27.1991 Palm Coast, FL BL/TL 6-4/210# d4.21 C1																								
1951	Pit N	10	12	1	2	0	0	1	1	0	0	3	.167	.167	.417	50	-1	0-0	1.000	-0	0	0	/1	-0.1
	StL A	34	105	11	25	5	1	2	11	10	1	22	.238	.310	.362	79	-3	0-0	.988	-1	96	74	1-28/O(LF)	-0.5
1955	Pit N	131	419	59	122	19	**13**	16	79	48-6	1	72	.291	.362	.513	132	18	0-1	.988	6	120	105	*1-119	1.7
1956	Pit N★	148	517	64	136	20	7	27	91	54-11	0	85	.263	.326	.485	119	12	1-0	.982	-4	94	80	*1-138	0.0
1957	Pit N	7	22	0	4	1	0	0	5	4-0	0	10	.182	.296	.227	48	-1	0-0	1.000	0	105	116	/1-7	-0.2
	Chi N	123	397	55	121	19	0	21	62	52-4	1	63	.305	.383	.511	141	24	1-1	.995	-2	87	88	*1-104	1.6
	Year	130	419	55	125	20	0	21	67	56-4	1	73	.298	.378	.496	136	23	1-1	.995	-2	88	90	*1-111	1.4
1958	Chi N	142	480	68	130	26	4	20	75	66-9	2	64	.271	.357	.467	119	14	2-0	.992	-2	92	101	*1-137/C-2	0.5
1959	Chi N	110	296	34	70	10	3	14	37	31-2	0	53	.236	.306	.432	96	-3	0-0	.985	-4	90	105	1-85	-1.1
1960	SF N	37	54	4	9	0	0	3	6	7-1	0	7	.167	.262	.333	66	-3	0-0	1.000	0	106	78	1-10	-0.3
	†NY A	26	41	6	15	3	1	3	10	5-1	0	6	.366	.435	.707	216	7	0-0	.988	-1	75	42	1-11	0.5
1961	Was A	123	377	52	94	20	4	17	49	39-5	1	41	.249	.317	.459	107	3	0-0	.983	-5	89	107	1-95	-0.8
1962	Was A	67	191	17	46	8	0	4	24	18-0	1	22	.241	.307	.346	77	-6	5-1	.996	-0	96	114	1-51	-0.9
	†NY A	41	94	12	28	4	0	4	17	18-0	0	9	.298	.404	.468	140	6	1-0	.992	1	111	102	1-31	0.6
	Year	108	285	29	74	12	0	8	41	36-0	1	31	.260	.340	.386	98	0	6-1	.995	1	101	110	1-82	-0.3
1963	NY A	14	15	1	3	0	0	0	0	1-0	0	3	.200	.250	.200	28	-1	0-0	.917	-0	0	136	/1-2	-0.2
Total	10	1013	3020	384	805	135	33	132	467	353-39	7	460	.267	.341	.464	116	66	10-3	.988	-12	96	96	1-819/C-2,O(LF)	0.8
LONG, RYAN Ryan Marcus B 2.3.1973 Houston, TX BR/TR 6-2/215# d7.16																								
1997	KC A	6	9	2	2	0	0	0	2	0-0	1	3	.222	.300	.222	38	-1	0-0	1.000	1	157	0	/O-5(1-0-4),D	0.0
LONG, TERRENCE Terrence Deon B 2.29.1976 Montgomery, AL BL/TL 6-1/190# d4.14																								
1999	NY N	3	3	0	0	0	0	0	0	0-0	0	2	.000	.000	.000	-99	-1	0-0	—	0			/H	-0.1
2000	†Oak A	138	584	104	168	34	4	18	80	43-1	1	77	.288	.336	.452	100	-2	5-0	.971	-11	94	29	*O-137(CF)	-0.9
2001	†Oak A	**162**	629	90	178	37	4	12	85	52-8	0	103	.283	.335	.412	96	-4	9-3	.980	-10	92	51	*O-162(62-74-28)	-1.6
2002	†Oak A	**162**	587	71	141	32	4	16	67	48-6	2	96	.240	.298	.390	81	-17	3-6	.980	-13	90	58	*O-162(CF)	-2.8
2003	†Oak A	140	486	64	119	22	2	14	61	31-4	3	67	.245	.293	.385	76	-18	4-1	.984	-7	94	40	*O-137(75-0-74)/D	-2.9
Total	5	605	2289	329	606	125	14	60	293	174-19	6	345	.265	.317	.410	89	-42	21-10	.978	-41	92	46	O-598(137-373-102)/D	-8.3
LONG, TOM Thomas Augustus B 6.1.1890 Mitchum, AL D 6.15.1972 Mobile, AL BR/TR 5-10.5/165# d9.11																								
1911	Was A	14	48	1	11	3	0	0	5	1	0		.229	.245	.292	50	-3	4	.875	-2	78	56	O-13(4-0-9)	-0.6
1912	Was A	1	1	0	0	0	0	0	0	0	0		.000	.000	.000	-99	0	0	—	0			H	0.0
1915	StL N	140	507	61	149	21	**25**	2	61	31	4	50	.294	.339	.446	137	19	19-15	.927	-3	95	118	*O-136(2-51-87)	0.8
1916	StL N	119	403	37	118	11	10	1	33	10	1	43	.293	.312	.377	112	3	21-14	.945	-5	85	108	*O-106(3-12-94)	-0.8
1917	StL N	144	530	49	123	12	14	3	41	37	2	44	.232	.285	.325	89	-9	21	.919	-19	75	54	*O-137(30-0-109)	-3.9
Total	5	418	1489	148	401	47	49	6	140	79	7	137	.269	.309	.379	110	10	65-29	.928	-28	85	91	O-392(39-63-299)	-4.5
LONGMIRE, TONY Anthony Eugene B 8.12.1968 Vallejo, CA BL/TR 6-1/197# d9.3																								
1993	†Phi N	11	13	1	3	0	0	0	1	0-0	0	1	.231	.231	.231	24	-1	0-0	1.000	0	166	0	/O-2(LF)	-0.1
1994	Phi N	69	139	10	33	11	0	0	17	10-1	1	27	.237	.289	.317	58	-8	2-1	.941	-1	85	159	O-32(13-0-21)	-1.0
1995	Phi N	59	104	21	37	7	0	3	19	11-1	1	19	.356	.419	.510	143	7	1-1	1.000	1	103	186	O-23(19-2-2)	0.7
Total	3	139	256	32	73	18	0	3	37	21-2	2	47	.285	.340	.391	91	-2	3-2	.967	1	94	165	/O-57(34-2-23)	-0.4
LONNETT, JOE Joseph Paul B 2.7.1927 Beaver Falls, PA BR/TR 5-10/180# d4.22 C14																								
1956	Phi N	16	22	2	4	0	0	0	0	2-0	0	7	.182	.250	.182	19	-3	0-0	1.000	-0	*64*	*117*	/C-7	-0.3
1957	Phi N	67	160	12	27	5	0	5	15	22-1	1	39	.169	.272	.294	54	-10	0-0	.997	2	*70*	*71*	C-65	-0.7
1958	Phi N	17	50	0	7	2	0	0	2	2-0	0	11	.140	.167	.180	-6	-8	0-0	.988	1	*85*	*117*	C-15	-0.7
1959	Phi N	43	93	8	16	1	0	1	10	14-2	1	17	.172	.284	.215	36	-8	0-1	.983	-5	*73*	*33*	C-43	-1.2
Total	4	143	325	22	54	8	0	6	27	40-3	2	74	.166	.259	.246	37	-29	0-1	.992	-3	*73*	*68*	C-130	-2.9
LOOK, BRUCE Bruce Michael B 6.9.1943 Lansing, MI BL/TR 5-11/183# d4.17 b-Dean																								
1968	Min A	59	118	7	29	4	0	0	9	20-3	0	24	.246	.353	.280	90	0	0-1	.996	1	*81*	*89*	C-41	0.2
LOOK, DEAN Dean Zachary B 7.23.1937 Lansing, MI BR/TR 5-11/185# d9.22 b-Bruce																								
1961	Chi A	3	6	0	0	0	0	0	0	0-0	0	1	.000	.000	.000	-99	-2	0-0	1.000	-0	76	0	/O(LF)	-0.2
LOPATA, STAN Stanley Edward "Stash" B 9.12.1925 Delray, MI BR/TR 6-2/210# d9.19																								
1948	Phi N	6	15	2	2	1	0	0	2	0	0	4	.133	.133	.200	-11	-2	0	1.000	0	*59*	*126*	/C-4	-0.2
1949	Phi N	83	240	31	65	9	2	8	27	21	0	44	.271	.330	.425	104	0	1	.973	-2	*86*	*75*	C-58	0.1
1950	†Phi N	58	129	10	27	2	2	1	11	22	0	25	.209	.325	.279	61	-7	1	.974	1	*104*	*66*	C-51	-0.4
1951	Phi N	3	5	0	0	0	0	0	0	0	0	0	.000	.000	.000	-99	-1	0-0	1.000	0	*0*	*0*	/C	-0.1
1952	Phi N	57	179	25	49	9	1	4	27	36	0	33	.274	.395	.402	123	8	1-1	.987	4	*101*	*80*	C-55	1.4
1953	Phi N	81	234	34	56	12	3	8	31	28	0	39	.239	.321	.419	91	-3	3-1	.987	2	*114*	*71*	C-80	0.3
1954	Phi N	86	259	42	75	14	5	14	42	33	1	37	.290	.369	.544	136	13	1-3	.989	6	*123*	*74*	C-75/1	2.2
1955	Phi N★	99	303	49	82	9	3	22	58	58-6	2	62	.271	.388	.538	146	21	4-1	.995	7	*109*	*86*	C-66,1-24	3.0
1956	Phi N☆	146	535	96	143	33	7	32	95	75-10	1	93	.267	.353	.535	138	30	5-2	.982	-19	*74*	*54*	*C-102,1-39	1.4
1957	Phi N	116	388	50	92	18	2	18	67	56-7	1	81	.237	.331	.433	108	5	2-2	.988	-8	*68*	*72*	*C-108	0.2
1958	Phi N	86	258	36	64	9	0	9	33	60-9	2	63	.248	.391	.388	109	7	0-1	.987	-8	*85*	*69*	C-80	0.2
1959	Mil N	25	48	0	5	0	0	0	4	3-0	0	13	.104	.157	.104	-31	-9	0-0	1.000	-2	*148*	*0*	C-11/1-2	-1.1
1960	Mil N	7	8	0	1	0	0	0	0	1-0	0	3	.125	.222	.125	-2	-1	0-0	.944	0	*0*	*0*	/C-4	-0.1
Total	13	853	2601	375	661	116	25	116	397	393-32	7	497	.254	.351	.452	115	61	18-11	.986	-19	*93*	*70*	C-695/1-66	6.9
LOPES, DAVEY David Earl B 5.3.1945 E.Providence, RI BR/TR 5-9/170# d9.22 M3 C13 OF Total (86-LF 98-CF 66-RF)																								
1972	LA N	11	42	6	9	4	0	0	1	7-0	0	6	.214	.327	.310	84	-1	4-0	.964	-2	91	77	2-11	-0.1
1973	LA N	142	535	77	147	13	5	6	37	62-6	5	77	.275	.352	.351	101	2	36-16	.984	-2	101	**115**	*2-135/O-5(0-2-3),S-2,3	1.2
1974	†LA N	145	530	95	141	26	3	10	35	66-3	4	71	.266	.350	.383	110	8	59-18	.965	-12	93	93	*2-143	1.2
1975	LA N	155	618	108	162	24	6	8	41	91-3	2	93	.262	.358	.359	104	6	**77**-12	.979	-17	92	78	*2-137,O-24(0-23-1),S-14	1.1
1976	LA N	117	427	72	103	17	7	4	20	56-1	4	49	.241	.333	.342	94	-2	**63**-10	.964	-17	94	96	*2-100,O-19(CF)	-0.3
1977	†LA N	134	502	85	142	19	5	11	53	73-3	2	69	.283	.372	.406	110	10	47-12	.979	13	108	108	*2-130	3.6
1978	†LA N★	151	587	93	163	25	4	17	58	71-3	0	70	.278	.355	.421	117	14	45-4	.974	12	106	111	*2-147/O-2(CF)	4.3
1979	LA N★	153	582	109	154	20	6	28	73	97-4	4	88	.265	.372	.464	129	25	44-4	.981	-31	84	83	*2-152	1.1
1980	LA N★	141	553	79	139	15	3	10	49	58-2	1	71	.251	.321	.344	88	-9	23-7	.980	-5	98	106	*2-140	-0.4
1981	†LA N★	58	214	35	44	2	0	5	17	22-1	3	35	.206	.289	.285	66	-10	20-2	.993	-3	99	97	2-55	-0.1
1982	Oak A	128	450	58	109	19	3	11	42	40-1	1	51	.242	.304	.371	89	-8	28-12	.977	-16	92	91	*2-125/O-6(CF)	-1.5
1983	Oak A	147	494	64	137	13	4	17	67	51-7	2	61	.277	.341	.423	118	11	22-4	.983	-25	85	96	*2-123,D-12/O-7(0-2-5),3-5	-0.5
1984	Oak A	72	230	32	59	11	1	9	36	31-1	1	36	.257	.343	.430	122	7	12-0	.965	-4	100	179	O-42(3-8-31),2-17/3-5,D-9	0.6
	†Chi N	16	17	5	4	1	0	0	0	6-0	0	5	.235	.435	.294	99	0	3-0	1.000	-1	123	0	/O-9(2-1-6),2-2	0.0
1985	Chi N	99	275	52	78	11	0	11	44	46-1	0	37	.284	.383	.444	118	9	47-4	.991	-6	83	44	O-79(46-25-17)/3-4,2	0.9
1986	Chi N	59	157	38	47	8	2	6	22	31-0	2	16	.299	.419	.490	140	10	17-6	.902	2	110	66	3-32,O-22(21-0-2)	1.3
	†Hou N	37	98	11	23	2	1	1	13	12-0	0	9	.235	.315	.306	75	-3	8-2	1.000	3	121	270	O-19(9-10-1)/3-5	0.0
	Year	96	255	49	70	10	3	7	35	43-0	2	25	.275	.381	.420	117	7	25-8	1.000	5	121	156	O-41(30-10-3),3-37	1.3
1987	Hou N	47	43	4	10	2	0	1	6	13-2	0	8	.233	.411	.349	108	1	2-1	.857	-1	73	0	/O-5(LF)	0.1

Year	Tm Lg	G	AB	R	H	2B	3B	HR	RBI	BB-IB	HP	SO	AVG	OBP	SLG	AOPS	ABR	SB-CS	FA	FR	Rng	Thr	G at Pos	BFW
Total	16	1812	6354	1023	1671	232	50	155	614	833-38	31	852	.263	.349	.388	107	70	557-114	.977	-107	95	97	*2-1418,O-239C/3-52,D-21,S-16	12.5
LOPEZ, AL Alfonso Ramon B 8.20.1908 Tampa, FL BR/TR 5-11/165# d9.27 M17 HF1977																								
1928	Bro N	3	12	0	0	0	0	0	0	0	0	0	.000	.000	.000	-99	-4	0	1.000	-1	*111*	*0*	/C-3	-0.4
1930	Bro N	128	421	60	130	20	4	6	57	33	2	35	.309	.362	.418	89	-7	3	.983	9	*104*	*101*	*C-126	0.8
1931	Bro N	111	360	38	97	13	4	0	40	28	1	33	.269	.324	.328	76	-12	1	.977	-5	*102*	*113*	*C-105	-1.1
1932	Bro N	126	404	44	111	18	6	1	43	34	0	35	.275	.331	.356	87	-7	3	.976	-4	*95*	*124*	*C-125	-0.3
1933	Bro N	126	372	39	112	11	4	3	41	21	0	39	.301	.338	.376	108	3	10	.991	14	*96*	***129***	*C-124/2	2.5
1934	Bro N★	140	439	58	120	23	2	7	54	49	2	44	.273	.349	.383	101	2	2	.982	-7	*93*	*109*	*C-137/2-2,3-2	0.2
1935	Bro N	128	379	50	95	12	4	3	39	35	1	36	.251	.316	.327	75	-13	2	.980	6	*115*	*99*	*C-126	0.0
1936	Bos N	128	426	46	103	12	5	7	50	41	2	41	.242	.311	.343	81	-12	1	.975	8	***145***	*108*	*C-127/1	0.4
1937	Bos N	105	334	31	68	11	1	3	38	35	1	57	.204	.281	.269	55	-21	3	.984	11	***191***	*93*	*C-102	-0.3
1938	Bos N	71	236	19	63	6	1	1	14	11	2	24	.267	.305	.314	78	-8	5	.989	4	*169*	*98*	C-71	0.1
1939	Bos N	131	412	32	104	22	1	8	49	40	0	45	.252	.319	.369	91	-6	1	.986	4	***147***	*107*	*C-129	0.6
1940	Bos N	36	119	20	35	3	1	2	17	6	0	8	.294	.328	.387	102	0	1	.987	2	*100*	*152*	C-36	0.3
	Pit N	59	174	15	45	6	2	1	24	13	0	13	.259	.310	.333	78	-5	5	.992	1	*72*	*99*	C-59	-0.2
	Year	95	293	35	80	9	3	3	41	19	0	21	.273	.317	.355	87	-6	6	**.990**	2	*83*	*120*	C-95	0.1
1941	Pit N★	114	317	33	84	9	1	5	43	31	0	23	.265	.330	.347	91	-4	0	.980	1	*106*	*91*	*C-114	0.3
1942	Pit N	103	289	17	74	8	2	1	26	34	2	17	.256	.338	.308	88	-4	0	**.995**	5	*88*	*102*	C-99	0.7
1943	Pit N	118	372	40	98	9	4	1	39	44	0	25	.263	.341	.317	88	-5	2	**.991**	11	*137*	*104*	*C-116/3	1.4
1944	Pit N	115	331	27	76	12	1	1	34	34	1	24	.230	.303	.281	62	-16	4	**.984**	6	*100*	*118*	*C-115	-0.4
1945	Pit N	91	243	22	53	8	0	0	18	35	0	12	.218	.317	.251	57	-13	1	.992	3	*82*	*94*	C-91	-0.5
1946	Pit N	56	150	13	46	2	0	1	12	23	0	14	.307	.399	.340	108	3	1	.985	-1	*68*	*125*	C-56	0.5
1947	Cle A	61	126	9	33	1	0	0	14	9	0	13	.262	.311	.270	64	-6	1-1	1.000	2	*167*	*152*	C-57	-0.3
Total	19	1950	5916	613	1547	206	43	51	652	556	14	538	.261	.326	.337	83	-135	46-1	.985	69	*116*	*109*	*C-1918/3-3,2-3,1	4.3
LOPEZ, ART Arturo (Rodriguez) B 5.8.1937 Mayaguez, P.R. BL/TL 5-9/170# d4.12																								
1965	NY A	38	49	5	7	0	0	0	0	1-0	0	6	.143	.160	.143	-13	-7	0-0	.958	0	123	0	O-16(3-0-14)	-0.9
LOPEZ, CARLOS Carlos Antonio (Morales) B 9.27.1950 Mazatlan, Mexico BR/TR 6/190# d9.17																								
1976	Cal A	9	10	1	0	0	0	0	0	2-0	0	3	.000	.167	.000	-52	-2	2-0	1.000	-1	59	0	/O-4(1-0-4),D	-0.3
1977	Sea A	99	297	39	84	18	1	8	34	14-1	3	61	.283	.319	.431	104	1	16-4	.972	5	103	198	O-90(0-7-87)/D-2	0.5
1978	Bal A	129	193	21	46	6	0	4	20	9-1	1	34	.238	.273	.332	75	-7	5-7	.988	5	102	166	*O-114(0-41-91)/D	-0.7
Total	3	237	500	61	130	24	1	12	54	25-2	4	98	.260	.298	.384	90	-8	23-11	.979	9	102	180	O-208(1-48-182)/D-4	-0.5
LOPEZ, FELIPE Felipe B 5.12.1980 Bayamon, P.R. BB/TR 6/175# d8.3																								
2001	Tor A	49	177	21	46	5	4	5	23	12-1	0	39	.260	.304	.418	86	-4	4-3	.940	1	114	74	3-47/S-3	-0.3
2002	Tor A	85	282	35	64	15	3	8	34	23-1	1	90	.227	.287	.387	74	-11	5-4	.975	-8	94	98	S-79/3-2,D	-1.3
2003	Cin N	59	197	28	42	7	2	2	13	28-1	1	59	.213	.313	.299	62	-11	8-5	.928	-12	101	65	S-50/3-8,2-3	-1.9
Total	3	193	656	84	152	27	9	15	70	63-3	2	188	.232	.299	.369	74	-26	17-12	.955	-20	96	85	S-132/3-57,2-3,D	-3.5
LOPEZ, HECTOR Hector Headley (Swainson) B 7.9.1929 Colon, Panama BR/TR 5-11/182# d5.12 OF Total (477-LF 21-CF 172-RF)																								
1955	KC A	128	483	50	140	15	2	15	68	33-1	3	58	.290	.337	.422	103	0	1-4	.936	10	116	122	3-93,2-36	1.1
1956	KC A	151	561	91	153	27	3	18	69	63-3	3	73	.273	.347	.428	104	3	4-5	.940	3	105	89	*3-121,O-20(CF)/2-8,S-4	0.4
1957	KC A	121	391	51	115	19	4	11	35	41-5	0	66	.294	.357	.448	118	10	1-6	.937	3	106	100	*3-111/2-4,O-3(2-0-1)	1.1
1958	KC A	151	564	84	147	28	4	17	73	49-2	2	61	.261	.317	.415	99	-1	2-2	.974	2	107	105	2-96,3-55/SO(LF)	0.7
1959	KC A	35	135	22	38	10	3	6	24	8-0	1	23	.281	.324	.533	129	5	1-0	.933	-8	83	66	2-33	-0.1
	NY A	112	406	60	115	16	2	16	69	28-1	6	54	.283	.336	.451	119	9	3-1	.926	-5	98	115	3-76,O-35(LF)	0.2
	Year	147	541	82	153	26	5	22	93	36-1	7	77	.283	.333	.471	122	14	4-1	.926	-13	98	115	3-76,O-35(LF),2-33	0.1
1960	†NY A	131	408	66	116	14	6	9	42	46-0	4	64	.284	.361	.414	116	9	1-1	.976	-1	96	114	*O-106(93-0-17)/2-5,3	0.3
1961	†NY A	93	243	27	54	7	2	3	22	24-1	1	38	.222	.292	.305	64	-13	1-0	.977	3	102	147	O-72(65-0-9)	-1.4
1962	†NY A	106	335	45	92	19	1	6	48	33-2	0	53	.275	.338	.391	99	0	0-1	.984	1	103	59	O-84(64-0-21)/23	-0.5
1963	†NY A	130	433	54	108	13	4	14	52	35-5	0	71	.249	.304	.395	95	-4	1-2	.957	-2	86	138	*O-124(104-0-21)/2	-1.4
1964	†NY A	127	285	34	74	9	3	10	34	24-2	1	54	.260	.317	.418	101	0	1-1	.971	-3	94	47	*O-103(80-1-31)/3	-0.9
1965	NY A	111	283	25	74	12	2	7	39	26-2	1	61	.261	.322	.392	104	1	0-0	.942	-6	83	75	O-75(20-0-55)/1-2	-0.9
1966	NY A	54	117	14	25	4	1	4	16	8-0	1	20	.214	.268	.368	84	-3	0-0	.936	-2	92	64	O-29(13-0-17)	-0.6
Total	12	1450	4644	623	1251	193	37	136	591	418-24	23	696	.269	.330	.415	104	16	16-23	.967	-4	93	98	O-652L,3-459,2-184/S-5,1-2	-2.0
LOPEZ, JAVY Javier (Torres) B 11.5.1970 Ponce, P.R. BR/TR 6-3/185# d9.18																								
1992	†Atl N	9	16	3	6	2	0	0	2	0-0	0	1	.375	.375	.500	137	1	0-0	1.000	-1	46	57	/C-9	0.0
1993	Atl N	8	16	1	6	1	1	1	2	0-0	1	2	.375	.412	.750	201	2	0-0	.975	2	104	138	/C-7	0.4
1994	Atl N	80	277	27	68	9	0	13	35	17-0	5	61	.245	.299	.419	83	-8	0-2	.995	-0	80	83	C-75	-0.4
1995	†Atl N	100	333	37	105	11	4	14	51	14-0	2	57	.315	.344	.498	116	6	0-1	.988	2	113	60	C-93	1.3
1996	†Atl N	138	489	56	138	19	1	23	69	28-5	3	84	.282	.322	.466	100	-2	1-6	.994	20	104	91	*C-135	2.4
1997	†Atl N★	123	414	52	122	28	1	23	68	40-10	5	82	.295	.361	.534	129	17	1-1	.993	7	117	85	*C-117	3.1
1998	†Atl N★	133	489	73	139	21	1	34	106	30-1	6	85	.284	.328	.540	125	15	5-3	**.995**	24	146	76	*C-128/D	4.5
1999	Atl N	65	246	34	78	18	1	11	45	20-2	3	41	.317	.375	.533	126	10	0-3	.991	2	90	89	C-60/D-4	1.3
2000	†Atl N	134	481	60	138	21	1	24	89	35-3	4	80	.287	.337	.484	105	2	0-0	.993	1	105	67	*C-132	1.0
2001	†Atl N	128	438	45	117	16	1	17	66	28-3	10	82	.267	.322	.425	90	-7	1-0	.989	4	101	97	*C-127	0.5
2002	†Atl N	109	347	31	81	15	0	11	52	26-8	8	63	.233	.299	.372	78	-13	0-1	.986	13	100	132	*C-103	0.6
2003	†Atl N★	129	457	89	150	29	3	43	109	33-5	4	90	.328	.378	.687	170	44	0-1	.994	5	109	89	*C-120/D-3	5.4
Total	12	1156	4003	508	1148	190	14	214	694	271-37	51	728	.287	.337	.502	114	67	8-18	.992	79	108	87	*C-1106/D-8	20.1
LOPEZ, LUIS Luis B 10.5.1973 Brooklyn, NY BR/TR 6/205# d4.29																								
2001	Tor A	41	119	10	29	4	0	3	10	8-1	0	16	.244	.291	.353	67	-6	0-0	.936	1	113	87	3-28/1-5,D-4	-0.4
LOPEZ, LUIS Luis Antonio B 9.1.1964 Brooklyn, NY BR/TR 6-1/190# d9.14																								
1990	LA N	6	6	0	0	0	0	0	0	0-0	0	2	.000	.000	.000	-99	-2	0-0	1.000	-0	0	333	/1	-0.2
1991	Cle A	35	82	7	18	4	1	0	7	4-1	1	7	.220	.261	.293	54	-5	0-0	1.000	-1	86	138	C-12,1-10/3O(LF)D	-0.7
Total	2	41	88	7	18	4	1	0	7	4-1	1	9	.205	.245	.273	43	-7	0-0	1.000	-2	86	138	/C-12,1-11,D-6,O(LF)3	-0.9
LOPEZ, LUIS Luis Manuel (Santos) B 9.4.1970 Cidra, P.R. BB/TR 5-11/175# d9.7																								
1993	SD N	17	43	1	5	1	0	0	1	0-0	0	8	.116	.114	.140	-31	-8	0-0	.983	-2	90	65	2-15	-1.0
1994	SD N	77	235	29	65	16	1	2	20	15-2	3	39	.277	.325	.379	86	-5	3-2	.941	1	104	89	S-43,2-29/3-5	0.0
1996	†SD N	63	139	10	25	3	0	2	11	9-1	1	35	.180	.233	.245	28	-15	0-0	.981	-7	92	76	S-35,2-22/3-2	-1.9
1997	NY N	78	178	19	48	12	1	1	19	12-2	4	42	.270	.330	.365	85	-4	2-4	.966	9	113	117	S-45,2-20/3-4	0.7
1998	NY N	117	266	37	67	13	2	2	22	20-3	4	60	.252	.312	.338	73	-11	2-2	.975	-3	93	81	2-50,S-39,3-11/O-9(8-0-1)	-1.1
1999	NY N	68	104	11	22	4	0	2	13	12-0	3	33	.212	.308	.308	59	-7	1-1	.971	-1	106	93	S-33,2-16/3-9	-0.5
2000	Mil N	78	201	24	53	14	0	6	27	9-1	5	35	.264	.309	.423	85	-5	1-2	.959	-1	100	120	S-45,2-22/3-6	-0.3
2001	Mil N	92	222	22	60	8	3	4	18	14-2	5	44	.270	.326	.387	86	-5	0-1	.922	0	93	150	3-46,S-17,2-15	-0.4
2002	Mil N	6	8	1	0	0	0	0	1	2-0	0	1	.000	.200	.000	-40	-2	0-0	1.000	-2	22	0	/S-4	-0.3
	Bal A	52	109	10	23	6	0	2	9	3-0	0	20	.211	.232	.321	47	-9	1-0	.967	-6	114	60	S-22,2-12/1D	-1.2
Total	9	648	1505	164	368	77	7	21	141	96-11	25	317	.245	.299	.347	70	-71	10-12	.959	-11	101	101	S-283,2-201/3-83,O-9(8-0-1),D1	-6.0
LOPEZ, MENDY Mendy (Aude) B 10.15.1974 Pimentel, D.R. BR/TR 6-2/190# d6.3																								
1998	KC A	74	206	18	50	10	2	1	15	12-0	1	40	.243	.286	.325	58	-13	5-2	.955	12	115	123	S-72/3-2	0.4
1999	KC A	7	20	2	8	0	1	0	3	0-0	1	5	.400	.429	.500	133	1	0-0	1.000	-1	96	120	/2-6,S	0.0
2000	Fla N	4	3	0	0	0	0	0	0	1-0	0	1	.000	.250	.000	-31	-1	0-0	—	0			/H	-0.1
2001	Hou N	10	15	3	4	0	0	1	3	2-0	1	4	.267	.389	.467	114	0	0-0	1.000	-1	44	0	/2-3,3-2	-0.1
	Pit N	22	43	5	10	3	1	0	4	4-1	0	16	.233	.292	.349	65	-2	0-0	.970	2	101	89	/2-9,S-6,3-4	0.0
	Year	32	58	8	14	3	1	1	7	6-1	1	20	.241	.318	.379	78	-2	0-0	.975	1	90	72	2-12/3-6,S-6	-0.1
2002	Pit N	3	3	0	0	0	0	0	0	0-0	0	3	.000	.000	.000	-99	-1	0-0	—	0			/H	-0.1
2003	KC A	52	94	13	26	5	1	3	11	4-0	0	28	.277	.306	.447	84	-2	2-0	1.000	-2	206	50	1-17,3-13,2-11/S-4,O-3(1-0-2)	-0.3
Total	6	172	384	41	98	18	5	5	36	23-1	3	97	.255	.301	.367	70	-18	7-2	.956	10	117	126	/S-83,2-29,3-21,1-17,O-3(1-0-2)	-0.2
LORD, BRIS Bristol Robotham "The Human Eyeball" B 9.21.1883 Upland, PA D 11.13.1964 Prince Frederick, MD BR/TR 5-9/185# d4.21																								
1905	†Phi A	66	238	38	57	14	0	0	13	14	1		.239	.285	.298	83	-4	3	.963	1	142	216	O-61(4-38-19)	-0.6

Year	Tm Lg	G	AB	R	H	2B	3B	HR	RBI	BB-IB	HP	SO	AVG	OBP	SLG	AOPS	ABR	SB-CS	FA	FR	Rng	Thr	G at Pos	BFW
1906	Phi A	118	434	50	101	13	7	1	44	27	2		.233	.281	.302	80	-11	12	.941	-3	91	130	*O-115(5-103-7)	-2.2
1907	Phi A	57	170	12	31	3	0	1	11	14	1		.182	.249	.218	48	-10	2	.951	-2	88	0	O-53(10-40-4)/P	-1.6
1909	Cle A	69	249	26	67	7	3	1	25	8	1		.269	.295	.333	94	-3	10	.992	7	154	215	O-67(48-3-16)	0.0
1910	Cle A	58	210	23	46	8	7	0	17	12	2		.219	.268	.324	84	-5	4	.958	4	90	184	O-56(24-0-32)	-0.4
	†Phi A	70	279	54	78	13	11	1	20	23	1		.280	.337	.416	137	11	6	.980	1	112	61	O-70(64-4-2)	0.8
	Year	128	489	77	124	21	18	1	37	35	3		.254	.307	.376	114	5	10	.972	5	103	112	*O-126(88-4-34)	0.4
1911	†Phi A	134	574	92	178	37	11	3	55	35	5		.310	.355	.429	120	14	15	.963	3	109	78	*O-132(122-1-9)	1.0
1912	Phi A	97	378	63	90	12	9	0	25	34	5		.238	.309	.317	82	-9	15	.942	-2	92	105	O-97(19-0-78)	-1.6
1913	Bos N	73	235	22	59	12	1	6	26	8	0	22	.251	.276	.387	86	-5	7-6	.914	-6	85	59	O-62(25-3-35)	-1.6
Total	8	742	2767	380	707	119	49	13	236	175	18	22	.256	.304	.348	95	-22	74-6	.957	2	106	113	O-713(321-192-202)/P	-6.2
LORD, HARRY Harry Donald B 3.8.1882 Porter, ME D 8.9.1948 Westbrook, ME BL/TR 5-10.5/165# d9.25 M1																								
1907	Bos A	10	38	4	6	1	0	0	3	1	0		.158	.179	.184	16	-4	1	.919	0	106	0	3-10	-0.4
1908	Bos A	145	560	61	145	15	6	2	37	22	8		.259	.297	.318	97	-3	23	.902	-8	94	83	*3-144	-0.9
1909	Bos A	136	534	89	168	12	7	0	31	20	8		.315	.349	.363	122	12	36	.929	-10	95	59	*3-134	0.7
1910	Bos A	77	288	25	72	5	5	1	32	14	4		.250	.294	.313	88	-5	17	.927	-5	92	105	3-70/S	-0.9
	Chi A	44	165	26	49	6	3	0	10	14	0		.297	.352	.370	132	6	17	.952	-5	85	76	3-44	0.2
	Year	121	453	51	121	11	8	1	42	28	4		.267	.315	.333	103	0	34	.935	-10	89	94	*3-114/S	-0.7
1911	Chi A	141	561	103	180	18	18	3	61	32	6		.321	.364	.433	126	16	43	.941	-19	80	117	*3-138	0.1
1912	Chi A	151	570	81	152	19	12	5	54	52	5		.267	.333	.368	104	2	30	.895	-25	79	77	*3-106,O-45(32-4-9)	-2.2
1913	Chi A	150	547	62	144	18	12	1	42	45	7	39	.263	.327	.346	98	-3	24	.924	-29	81	70	*3-150	-3.0
1914	Chi A	21	69	8	13	1	1	1	3	5	0	3	.188	.243	.275	57	-4	2-2	.933	-2	101	0	3-19/O(LF)	-0.7
1915	Buf F	97	359	50	97	12	6	1	21	21	0	15	.270	.311	.345	83	-15	15	.946	-8	94	100	3-92/O(RF)M	-2.2
Total	9	972	3691	509	1026	107	70	14	294	226	38	57	.278	.326	.356	104	2	208-2	.924	-111	88	82	3-907/O-47(33-4-10),S	-9.3
LORD, CARLTON William Carlton B 1.7.1900 Philadelphia, PA D 8.15.1947 Chester, PA BR/TR 5-11/170# d7.12																								
1923	Phi N	17	47	3	11	2	0	0	2	2	0	3	.234	.265	.277	39	-4	0-1	.833	-2	100	40	3-14	-0.5
LORETTA, MARK Mark David B 8.14.1971 Santa Monica, CA BR/TR 6/175# d9.4 OF Total (LF)																								
1995	Mil A	19	50	13	13	3	0	1	3	4-0	1	7	.260	.327	.380	79	-2	1-1	.979	-3	100	64	S-13/2-4,D	-0.3
1996	Mil A	73	154	20	43	3	0	1	13	14-0	0	15	.279	.339	.318	65	-8	2-1	.989	-2	107	91	2-28,3-23,S-21	-0.7
1997	Mil A	132	418	56	120	17	5	5	47	47-2	2	60	.287	.354	.388	95	-2	5-5	.980	5	105	148	2-63,S-44,1-19,3-15/D	0.6
1998	Mil N	140	434	55	137	29	0	6	54	42-1	7	47	.316	.382	.424	112	10	9-6	.992	6	79	119	1-70,S-56,3-22,2-13/O(LF)	1.6
1999	Mil N	153	587	93	170	34	5	5	67	52-1	10	59	.290	.354	.390	90	-8	4-1	.986	-4	92	92	S-74,1-66,2-17,3-14	-1.0
2000	Mil N	91	352	49	99	21	1	7	40	37-2	1	38	.281	.350	.406	92	-4	0-3	.995	-1	107	95	S-90/2	0.1
2001	Mil N	102	384	40	111	14	2	2	29	28-0	7	46	.289	.346	.352	84	-9	1-2	.992	2	104	98	2-52,3-39/S-9,PD	-0.4
2002	Mil N	86	217	23	58	14	0	2	19	23-1	5	32	.267	.350	.359	92	-3	0-0	.991	-7	88	67	3-47,S-12/1-5,2-3	-0.8
	Hou N	21	66	10	28	4	0	2	8	9-0	0	5	.424	.481	.576	177	8	1-1	.944	-1	66	58	3-10/S-6,2-3,D	0.7
	Year	107	283	33	86	18	0	4	27	32-1	5	37	.304	.381	.410	113	6	1-1	.984	-7	84	65	3-57,S-18/2-6,1-5,D	-0.1
2003	SD N	154	589	74	185	28	4	13	72	54-2	3	62	.314	.372	.441	123	20	5-4	**.990**	-6	97	84	*2-150/S-3	2.1
Total	9	971	3251	433	964	167	17	44	352	310-9	36	371	.297	.361	.399	99	2	28-24	.987	-9	102	102	2-334,S-328,3-170,1-160/D-7,PO	1.9
LOUCKS, SCOTT Scott Gregory B 11.11.1956 Anchorage, AK BR/TR 6/178# d9.1																								
1980	Hou N	8	3	4	1	0	0	0	0	0-0	0	2	.333	.333	.333	94	0	0-0	1.000	-0	52	0	/O-4(0-2-2)	0.0
1981	Hou N	10	7	2	4	0	0	0	0	1-0	0	3	.571	.625	.571	254	2	1-0	1.000	-0	91	0	/O-5(CF)	0.2
1982	Hou N	44	49	6	11	2	0	0	3	3-0	0	17	.224	.269	.265	54	-3	4-1	.978	3	114	343	O-37(CF)	0.0
1983	Hou N	7	14	2	3	0	0	0	0	1-0	0	4	.214	.267	.214	37	-1	2-2	1.000	1	127	533	/O-6(1-5-0)	0.0
1985	Pit N	4	7	1	2	2	0	0	1	2-0	0	2	.286	.444	.571	184	1	0-0	1.000	-0	63	0	/O-4(3-0-1)	0.1
Total	5	73	80	15	21	4	0	0	4	7-0	0	28	.262	.322	.313	83	-1	7-3	.985	3	108	304	/O-56(4-49-3)	0.3
LOUDEN, BALDY William P. B 8.27.1885 Piedmont, WV D 12.8.1935 Piedmont, WV BR/TR 5-11/175# d9.13																								
1907	NY A	4	9	4	1	0	0	0	0	2	0		.111	.273	.111	21	-1	1	.750	-0	111	0	/3-3	-0.1
1912	Det A	122	403	57	97	12	4	1	36	58	11		.241	.352	.298	89	-2	27	.951	18	126	81	2-87,3-26/S-5	1.8
1913	Det A	76	191	28	46	4	5	0	23	24	6	22	.241	.344	.314	94	-1	6	.906	1	106	67	2-30,3-26/S-6,O-5(0-1-4)	0.1
1914	Buf F	126	431	73	135	11	4	6	63	52	3	41	.313	.391	.399	113	3	35	.931	-19	81	83	*S-115	-0.8
1915	Buf F	141	469	67	132	18	5	4	48	64	4	45	.281	.372	.367	106	0	30	.978	12	104	100	2-88,S-27,3-19	1.7
1916	Cin N	134	439	38	96	16	4	1	32	54	6	54	.219	.313	.280	85	-6	12	**.968**	17	111	107	*2-108,S-23	1.6
Total	6	603	1942	267	507	61	22	12	202	254	30	162	.261	.355	.334	98	-7	111	.961	28	113	94	2-313,S-176/3-74,O-5(0-1-4)	4.3
LOUDENSLAGER, CHARLIE Charles Edward B 5.21.1881 Baltimore, MD D 10.31.1933 Baltimore, MD TR 5-9/186# d4.15																								
1904	Bro N	1	2	0	0	0	0	0	0	0	0		.000	.000	.000	-99	0	0	1.000	-0	70	0	/2	-0.1
LOUGHLIN, BILL William H. B Baltimore, MD d5.9																								
1883	Bal AA	1	5	0	2	0	0	0		0			.400	.400	.400	154	0		—	-0	0	0	/O(RF)	0.0
LOUGHRAN, THOMAS Thomas B New York, NY d6.6																								
1884	NY N	9	29	4	3	1	1	0	3	7		11	.103	.278	.207	54	-1		.857	-2			/C-9,O(RF)	-0.3
LOVELACE, TOM Thomas Rivers B 10.19.1897 Wolfe City, TX D 7.12.1979 Dallas, TX BR/TR 5-11/170# d9.23																								
1922	Pit N	1	1	0	0	0	0	0	0	0	0	0	.000	.000	.000	-99	0	0-0	—	0			H	0.0
LOVETT, LEN Leonard Walker B 7.17.1852 Lancaster Co., PA D 11.18.1922 Newark, DE BR/TR d8.4 ▲																								
1873	Res NA	1	5	1	2	0	0	0	1	0		0	.400	.400	.400	150	1	0-0	.500	-0	68	0	/P	0.0
1875	Cen NA	6	21	2	5	1	0	0	2	1		5	.238	.273	.286	103	0	0-0	.700	-0	136	0	/O-6(1-0-5)	0.0
Total	2 NA	7	26	3	7	1	0	0	3	1		5	.269	.296	.308	113	1	0-0	.700	-1	136	0	/O-6(1-0-5),P	0.0
LOVETT, MEM Merritt Marwood B 6.15.1912 Chicago, IL D 9.19.1995 Downers Grove, IL BR/TR 5-9.5/165# d9.4																								
1933	Chi A	1	1	0	0	0	0	0	0	0	0	0	.000	.000	.000	-99	0	0-0	—	0			H	0.0
LOVIGLIO, JAY John Paul B 5.30.1956 Freeport, NY BR/TR 5-9/160# d9.2																								
1980	Phi N	16	5	7	0	0	0	0	0	1-0	0	0	.000	.167	.000	-47	-1	1-2	1.000	-1	60	0	/2	-0.2
1981	Chi A	14	15	5	4	0	0	0	2	1-0	0	1	.267	.313	.267	70	-1	2-2	.786	0	100	347	/3-4,2-3,D-2	-0.1
1982	Chi A	15	31	5	6	0	0	0	2	1-0	0	4	.194	.219	.194	14	-4	2-1	.964	1	107	72	2-13/D-2	-0.3
1983	Chi N	1	1	0	0	0	0	0	0	0-0	0	1	.000	.000	.000	-95	0	0-0	—	0			/H	0.0
Total	4	46	52	17	10	0	0	0	4	3-0	0	6	.192	.236	.192	21	-6	5-5	.971	0	99	57	/2-17,D-4,3-4	-0.6
LOVITTO, JOE Joseph B 1.6.1951 San Pedro, CA D 5.19.2001 Arlington, TX BB/TR 6/185# d4.15																								
1972	Tex A	117	330	23	74	9	1	1	19	37-2	2	54	.224	.306	.267	75	-10	13-11	.976	4	109	114	*O-103(8-77-23)	-1.1
1973	Tex A	26	44	3	6	1	0	0	0	5-0	0	7	.136	.224	.159	10	-5	1-0	.898	0	80	109	3-20/O-3(0-2-1)	-0.5
1974	Tex A	113	283	27	63	9	3	2	26	25-4	0	36	.223	.285	.297	69	-11	6-8	.972	-5	92	119	*O-107(0-105-2)/1-5	-2.2
1975	Tex A	50	106	17	22	3	0	1	8	13-1	0	16	.208	.289	.264	59	-6	2-2	.985	-1	89	150	O-38(18-25-0)/1-2,CD	-0.8
Total	4	306	763	70	165	22	4	4	53	80-7	2	113	.216	.291	.271	67	-32	22-21	.975	-2	99	120	O-251(26-209-26)/3-20,1-7,D-2,C	-4.6
LOVULLO, TOREY Salvatore Anthony B 7.25.1965 Santa Monica, CA BB/TR 6/180# d9.10 OF Total (1-LF 2-RF)																								
1988	Det A	12	21	2	8	1	1	1	2	1-0	0	2	.381	.409	.667	204	3	0-0	1.000	-0	101	53	/2-9,3-3	0.3
1989	Det A	29	87	8	10	2	0	1	4	14-0	0	20	.115	.233	.172	18	-9	0-0	1.000	-1	37	81	1-18,3-11	-1.2
1991	NY A	22	51	0	9	2	0	0	2	5-1	0	7	.176	.250	.216	30	-5	0-0	.940	1	106	33	3-22	-0.4
1993	Cal A	116	367	42	92	20	0	6	30	36-1	1	49	.251	.318	.354	78	-11	7-6	.981	-0	98	121	2-91,3-14/S-9,O-2(RF),1	-0.7
1994	Sea A	36	72	9	16	5	0	2	7	9-1	0	13	.222	.309	.375	74	-3	1-0	1.000	2	113	87	2-20/3-5,D-2	0.0
1996	Oak A	65	82	15	18	4	0	3	9	11-0	2	17	.220	.323	.378	79	-3	1-2	1.000	-1	94	160	1-42,3-11/2-2,SO(LF)D	-0.5
1998	Cle A	6	19	1	4	1	0	0	1	1-0	0	2	.211	.250	.263	33	-2	0-0	.947	0	112	111	/2-5,3	-0.2
1999	Phi N	17	38	3	8	0	0	2	5	3-0	0	11	.211	.268	.368	57	-3	0-0	1.000	-0	219	109	/1-6,2-6	-0.3
Total	8	303	737	80	165	35	1	15	60	80-3	3	121	.224	.301	.335	69	-33	9-8	.984	0	99	109	2-133/1-67,3-67,S-10,D-6,O-3R	-3.0
LOW, FLETCHER Fletcher B 4.7.1893 Essex, MA D 6.6.1973 Hanover, NH BR/TR 5-10.5/175# d10.7																								
1915	Bos N	1	4	1	1	0	1	0	1	0	0	0	.250	.250	.750	207	0	0	1.000	-0	50	0	/3	0.0
LOWE, CHARLIE Charles B Baltimore, MD d9.24																								
1872	Atl NA	7	31	2	5	0	0	0	3	0		2	.161	.161	.161	-0	-4	0-0	.827	-1	88	30	/2-7	-0.4

Year	Tm Lg	G	AB	R	H	2B	3B	HR	RBI	BB-IB	HP	SO	AVG	OBP	SLG	AOPS	ABR	SB-CS	FA	FR	Rng	Thr	G at Pos	BFW
LOWE, DICK Richard Alvern B 1.28.1854 Evansville, WI D 6.28.1922 Janesville, WI d6.26																								
1884	Det N	1	3	0	1	0	0	0	0	0		1	.333	.333	.333	117	0		.125	-3			/C	-0.3
LOWE, BOBBY Robert Lincoln "Link" B 7.10.1865 Pittsburgh, PA D 12.8.1951 Detroit, MI BR/TR 5-10/150# d4.19 M1 OF Total (173-LF 56-CF 11-RF)																								
1890	Bos N	52	207	35	58	13	2	2	21	26	2	32	.280	.366	.391	112	3	15	.951	-7	88	14	S-24,O-15(3-11-1),3-12	-0.3
1891	Bos N	125	497	92	129	19	5	6	74	53	9	54	.260	.342	.354	92	-6	43	.927	-5	99	82	*O-107(64-38-5),2-17/S-2,3P	-1.2
1892	†Bos N	124	475	79	115	16	7	3	57	37	8	47	.242	.308	.324	83	-11	36	.928	11	118	73	O-90(87-3-0),3-14,S-13,2-10	-0.6
1893	Bos N	126	526	130	157	19	5	14	89	55	4	29	.298	.369	.433	105	1	22	.936	1	104	111	*2-121/S-5	0.6
1894	Bos N	**133**	613	158	212	34	11	17	115	50	6	25	.346	.401	.520	112	9	23	.927	-7	98	106	*2-130/S-2,3	0.6
1895	Bos N	100	417	102	124	12	7	7	62	40	8	16	.297	.370	.410	94	-5	24	.954	10	106	**126**	*2-100	0.8
1896	Bos N	73	306	59	98	11	4	2	48	20	4	12	.320	.370	.402	98	-2	15	.965	18	117	104	2-73	1.6
1897	†Bos N	123	499	87	154	24	8	5	106	32	4		.309	.355	.419	98	-3	16	.952	-9	101	84	*2-123	-0.6
1898	Bos N	147	559	65	152	11	7	4	94	29	3		.272	.311	.338	82	-16	12	.958	12	100	124	*2-145/S-2	0.3
1899	Bos N	152	559	81	152	5	9	4	88	35	1		.272	.316	.335	72	-24	17	.954	-1	99	129	*2-148/S-4	-1.7
1900	Bos N	127	474	65	132	11	5	3	71	26	5		.278	.323	.342	74	-18	15	.951	-9	93	78	*2-127	-2.0
1901	Bos N	129	491	47	125	11	1	3	47	17	3		.255	.284	.299	63	-24	22	.912	-6	88	**110**	*3-111,2-18	-2.6
1902	Chi N	121	480	44	119	13	3	0	35	12	5		.248	.274	.287	75	-15	17	.956	18	111	136	*2-119/3-2	0.3
1903	Chi N	32	105	14	28	5	3	0	15	4	4		.267	.319	.371	99	-1	5	.948	2	118	125	2-22/1-6,3	0.2
1904	Pit N	1	1	0	0	0	0	0	0	0	0		.000	.000	.000	-97	0	0	—	0			H	0.0
	Det A	140	506	47	105	14	6	0	40	17	2		.208	.236	.259	58	-25	15	.964	0	98	103	*2-140,M	-2.7
1905	Det A	58	181	17	35	7	2	0	9	13	2		.193	.255	.254	61	-8	3	.980	2	196	0	O-24(17-3-4),3-22/2-6,S-4,1	-0.8
1906	Det A	41	145	11	30	3	0	1	12	4	1		.207	.233	.248	49	-9	3	.915	4	114	14	S-19,2-17/3-5	-0.4
1907	Det A	17	37	2	9	2	0	0	5	4	0		.243	.317	.297	93	0	0	.870	-2	101	0	3-10/O-4(2-1-1),S-2	-0.2
Total	18	1821	7078	1135	1934	230	85	71	988	474	71	215	.273	.325	.360	86	-154	303	.951	33	102	109	*2-1316,O-240L,3-179/S-77,1-7,P	-8.7
LOWELL, MIKE Michael Averett B 2.24.1974 San Juan, P.R. BR/TR 6-4/195# d9.13																								
1998	NY A	8	15	1	4	0	0	0	0	0-0	0	1	.267	.267	.267	41	-1	0-0	1.000	-1	66	182	/3-7	-0.2
1999	Fla N	97	308	32	78	15	0	12	47	26-1	5	69	.253	.317	.419	91	-5	0-0	.981	-3	97	82	3-83	-0.7
2000	Fla N	140	508	73	137	38	0	22	91	54-4	9	75	.270	.344	.474	111	8	4-0	.968	4	102	74	*3-136	1.4
2001	Fla N	146	551	65	156	37	0	18	100	43-3	10	79	.283	.340	.448	107	6	1-2	.976	10	103	**138**	*3-144	1.6
2002	Fla N★	160	597	88	165	44	0	24	92	65-5	4	92	.276	.346	.471	122	17	4-3	.969	1	94	109	*3-159	1.9
2003	†Fla N★	130	492	76	136	27	1	32	105	56-6	3	78	.276	.350	.530	132	22	3-1	**.973**	-3	93	119	*3-128/D-2	2.0
Total	6	681	2471	335	676	161	1	108	435	244-19	31	394	.274	.341	.471	114	47	12-6	.973	6	98	107	3-657/D-2	6.0
LOWENSTEIN, JOHN John Lee B 1.27.1947 Wolf Point, MT BL/TR 6/175# d9.2 OF Total (687-LF 49-CF 201-RF)																								
1970	Cle A	17	43	5	11	3	1	1	6	1-0	0	9	.256	.273	.442	89	-1	1-0	1.000	4	146	96	2-10/3-2,O-2(LF),S	0.4
1971	Cle A	58	140	15	26	5	0	4	9	16-1	0	28	.186	.269	.307	58	-8	1-5	.986	0	87	93	2-29,O-18(7-5-8)/S-3	-0.8
1972	Cle A	68	151	16	32	8	1	6	21	20-0	0	43	.212	.304	.397	104	1	2-4	1.000	3	91	219	O-58(27-3-29)/1-2	0.0
1973	Cle A	98	305	42	89	16	1	6	40	23-0	0	41	.292	.338	.410	109	3	5-3	.931	1	70	166	O-51(12-4-36),2-25/3-8,1D	0.3
1974	Cle A	140	508	65	123	14	2	8	48	53-2	2	85	.242	.313	.325	85	-9	36-17	.986	5	99	89	*O-100(88-8-7),3-28,1-12/2-4	-0.8
1975	Cle A	91	265	37	64	5	1	12	33	28-2	0	28	.242	.313	.404	102	0	15-10	.983	-4	82	77	O-36(19-3-17),D-31/3-8,2-2	-0.7
1976	Cle A	93	229	33	47	8	2	2	14	25-3	0	35	.205	.283	.284	67	-9	11-8	.972	-1	90	203	O-61(13-19-29),D-11/1-9	-1.5
1977	Cle A	81	149	24	36	6	1	4	12	21-1	0	29	.242	.335	.376	97	0	1-8	1.000	-1	100	46	O-39(18-5-17),D-19/1	-0.5
1978	Tex A	77	176	28	39	8	3	5	21	37-2	2	29	.222	.363	.386	110	4	16-3	.926	-2	92	51	3-25,D-21,O-16(14-0-2)	0.3
1979	†Bal A	97	197	33	50	8	2	11	34	30-3	1	37	.254	.351	.482	128	8	16-4	.992	4	116	106	O-72(44-1-41)/13D	1.1
1980	Bal A	104	196	38	61	8	0	4	27	32-1	0	29	.311	.403	.413	127	9	7-3	.992	1	106	69	O-91(88-0-3)/D-3	0.8
1981	Bal A	83	189	19	47	7	0	6	20	22-1	1	32	.249	.329	.381	105	1	7-6	.990	-4	86	77	O-73(67-0-10)/D-4	-0.6
1982	Bal A	122	322	69	103	15	2	24	66	54-10	1	59	.320	.415	.602	177	36	7-6	**1.000**	-2	102	35	*O-111(110-0-2)	2.9
1983	†Bal A	122	310	52	87	13	2	15	60	49-1	1	55	.281	.374	.481	138	17	2-1	.982	-4	86	120	*O-107(106-1-0)/2D	1.0
1984	Bal A	105	270	34	64	13	0	8	28	33-3	1	54	.237	.319	.374	94	-2	1-0	.971	-3	85	137	O-67(LF),D-22/1-2	-0.7
1985	Bal A	12	26	0	2	0	0	0	2	2-0	0	3	.077	.138	.077	-39	-5	0-0	1.000	0	129	0	/O-4(LF),D-6	-0.5
Total	16	1368	3476	510	881	137	18	116	441	446-30	9	596	.253	.337	.403	108	45	128-78	.984	-2	94	108	O-906L,D-125/3-72,2-71,1-28,S-4	0.7
LOWERY, TERRELL Quenton Terrell B 10.25.1970 Oakland, CA BR/TR 6-3/180# d9.13																								
1997	Chi N	9	14	2	4	0	0	0	0	3-0	0	3	.286	.412	.286	85	0	1-0	1.000	2	106	921	/O-6(5-2-0)	0.2
1998	Chi N	24	15	2	3	1	0	0	1	3-0	0	7	.200	.333	.267	58	-1	0-0	.929	-1	101	0	O-22(2-20-0)	-0.1
1999	TB A	66	185	25	48	15	1	2	17	19-0	1	53	.259	.330	.384	81	-5	0-2	.971	-2	87	133	O-60(29-36-1)	-0.8
2000	SF N	24	34	13	15	4	0	1	5	7-0	1	8	.441	.548	.647	216	7	1-0	.917	-1	72	0	O-20(13-0-8)/D	0.5
Total	4	123	248	42	70	20	1	3	23	32-0	2	71	.282	.367	.407	98	1	2-2	.964	-2	87	147	O-108(49-58-9)/D	-0.2
LOWREY, PEANUTS Harry Lee B 8.27.1917 Culver City, CA D 7.2.1986 Inglewood, CA BR/TR 5-8.5/170# d4.14 Mil 1944 C17 OF Total (548-LF 387-CF 62-RF)																								
1942	Chi N	27	58	4	11	0	0	1	4	4	0	4	.190	.242	.241	43	-4	0	.978	2	112	143	O-19(7-15-0)	-0.4
1943	Chi N	130	480	59	140	25	12	1	63	35	0	24	.292	.340	.400	115	7	13	.982	6	106	121	*O-113(CF),S-16/2-3	1.2
1945	†Chi N	143	523	72	148	22	7	7	89	48	0	27	.283	.343	.392	106	3	11	.987	4	95	176	*O-138(125-14-0)/S-2	0.0
1946	Chi N★	144	540	75	139	24	5	4	54	56	1	22	.257	.328	.343	92	-6	10	.979	2	100	127	*O-126(73-60-0),3-20	-1.2
1947	Chi N	115	448	56	126	17	5	5	37	38	1	26	.281	.339	.375	93	-5	2	.945	10	117	132	3-91,O-25(18-6-1)/2-6	0.3
1948	Chi N	129	435	47	128	12	3	2	54	34	1	31	.294	.347	.349	93	-5	2	.983	-0	98	119	*O-103(63-43-0)/3-9,2-2,S	-1.0
1949	Chi N	38	111	18	30	5	0	2	10	9	0	8	.270	.325	.369	88	-2	3	.966	-2	95	46	O-31(28-3-1)/3	-0.6
	Cin N	89	309	48	85	16	2	2	25	37	1	11	.275	.354	.359	91	-3	1	.995	6	112	102	O-78(77-1-0)	-0.3
	Year	127	420	66	115	21	2	4	35	46	1	19	.274	.347	.362	90	-5	4	.989	4	108	88	*O-109(105-4-1)/3	-0.9
1950	Cin N	91	264	34	60	14	0	1	11	36	0	7	.227	.320	.292	62	-14	0	.987	2	107	81	O-72(66-2-6)/2	-1.6
	StL N	17	56	10	15	0	0	1	4	6	1	1	.268	.349	.321	74	-2	0	1.000	1	96	85	/2-6,3-5,O-4(3-1-0)	-0.1
	Year	108	320	44	75	14	0	2	15	42	1	8	.234	.325	.297	64	-16	0	.982	3	106	78	O-76(69-3-6)/2-7,3-5	-1.7
1951	StL N	114	370	52	112	19	5	5	40	35	2	12	.303	.366	.422	111	6	0-1	.983	-8	92	75	O-85(13-74-0),3-11/2-3	-0.5
1952	StL N	132	374	48	107	18	2	1	48	34	4	13	.286	.352	.353	96	-1	3-2	.978	-5	96	42	*O-106(63-35-6)/3-6	-1.1
1953	StL N	104	182	26	49	9	2	5	27	15	0	21	.269	.325	.423	93	-2	1-0	1.000	-3	87	56	O-38(3-10-25),2-10/3	-0.5
1954	StL N	74	61	6	7	1	2	0	5	9	0	9	.115	.222	.197	12	-8	0-0	1.000	-0	104	0	O-12(3-1-9)	-0.8
1955	Phi N	54	106	9	20	4	0	0	8	7-0	0	10	.189	.237	.226	25	-12	2-0	.973	-1	95	73	O-28(6-9-14)/2-2,1	-1.3
Total	13	1401	4317	564	1177	186	45	37	479	403-0	11	226	.273	.336	.362	92	-48	48-3	.983	13	100	108	O-978L,3-144/2-33,S-19,1	-7.9
LOWRY, DWIGHT Dwight (born B 10.23.1957 Lumberton, NC D 7.10.1997 Jamestown, NY BL/TR 6-3/210# d4.3																								
1984	Det A	32	45	8	11	2	0	2	7	3-0	0	11	.244	.292	.422	95	0	0-0	1.000	1	107	83	C-31	0.1
1986	Det A	56	150	21	46	4	0	3	18	17-0	4	19	.307	.392	.393	115	4	0-0	.992	-5	97	72	C-55/1O(RF)	0.1
1987	Det A	13	25	0	5	2	0	0	1	0-0	0	6	.200	.200	.280	27	-3	0-0	1.000	-2	63	45	C-12/1	-0.4
1988	Min A	7	7	0	0	0	0	0	0	0-0	0	2	.000	.000	.000	-97	-2	0-0	1.000	0	26	214	/C-5	-0.2
Total	4	108	227	29	62	8	0	5	26	20-0	4	38	.273	.343	.374	96	-1	0-0	.995	-6	94	75	C-103/1-2,O(RF)	-0.4
LOWRY, JOHN John D. B Baltimore, MD d6.26																								
1875	Was NA	6	22	2	3	0	0	0	0	1		0	.136	.174	.136	10	-2	0-1	.727	-1	0	0	/O-6(CF)	-0.3
LOZADO, WILLIE William B 5.12.1959 New York, NY BR/TR 6/166# d7.16																								
1984	Mil A	43	107	15	29	8	2	1	20	12-0	0	23	.271	.339	.411	113	2	0-3	.925	-4	90	121	3-36/S-6,2D	-0.3
LUBRATICH, STEVE Steven George B 5.1.1955 Oakland, CA BR/TR 6/170# d9.27																								
1981	Cal A	7	21	2	3	1	0	0	1	0-0	0	2	.143	.143	.190	-5	-3	1-0	1.000	2	139	185	/3-6	-0.1
1983	Cal A	57	156	12	34	9	0	0	7	4-0	0	17	.218	.236	.276	41	-13	0-1	.949	9	105	130	S-23,3-22,2-14	-0.2
Total	2	64	177	14	37	10	0	0	8	4-0	0	19	.209	.225	.266	36	-16	1-1	.988	10	134	143	/3-28,S-23,2-14	-0.3
LUBY, HUGH Hugh Max "Hal" B 6.13.1913 Blackfoot, ID D 5.4.1986 Eugene, OR BR/TR 5-10/185# d9.10 Mil 1945																								
1936	Phi A	9	38	3	7	1	0	0	3	0	1	7	.184	.205	.211	3	-6	2-0	.880	-3	98	48	/2-9	-0.8
1944	NY N	111	323	30	82	10	2	2	35	52	4	15	.254	.364	.316	93	0	2	.943	13	107	129	3-65,2-45/1	1.5
Total	2	120	361	33	89	11	2	2	38	52	5	22	.247	.349	.305	83	-6	4-0	.943	9	107	129	/3-65,2-54,1	0.7
LUCADELLO, JOHNNY John B 2.22.1919 Thurber, TX D 10.30.2001 San Antonio, TX BB/TR 5-11/160# d9.24 Mil 1942-45																								
1938	StL A	7	20	1	3	1	0	0	0	0	0	0	.150	.150	.200	-13	-4	0-0	.909	-1	64	0	/3-6	-0.4
1939	StL A	9	30	0	7	2	0	0	4	2	0	4	.233	.281	.300	48	-2	0-0	.912	-3	75	58	/2-7	-0.5
1940	StL A	17	63	15	20	4	2	2	10	6	2	4	.317	.394	.540	137	3	1-0	.968	1	107	116	2-16	0.5

Year	Tm Lg	G	AB	R	H	2B	3B	HR	RBI	BB-IB	HP	SO	AVG	OBP	SLG	AOPS	ABR	SB-CS	FA	FR	Rng	Thr	G at Pos	BFW
1941	StL A	107	351	58	98	22	4	2	31	48	0	23	.279	.366	.382	95	-1	5-2	.962	-13	98	87	2-70,S-12/3-6,O(LF)	-0.9
1946	StL A	87	210	21	52	7	1	1	15	36	0	20	.248	.358	.305	82	-3	0-1	.942	-5	98	52	3-37,2-19	-0.8
1947	NY A	12	12	0	1	0	0	0	0	1	0	5	.083	.154	.083	-33	-2	0-0	1.000	-1	0	0	/2-5	-0.3
Total	6	239	686	95	181	36	7	5	60	93	2	56	.264	.353	.359	88	-9	6-3	.965	-22	94	88	2-117/3-49,S-12,O(LF)	-2.4
LUCAS, RED Charles Fred "The Nashville Narcissus" B 4.28.1902 Columbia, TN D 7.9.1986 Nashville, TN BL/TR 5-9.5/170# d4.19 ▲																								
1923	NY N	3	2	0	0	0	0	0	0	0	0	1	.000	.000	.000	-99	0	0-0	1.000	1	257	0	/P-3	0.0
1924	Bos N	33	33	5	11	1	0	0	5	1	0	4	.333	.353	.364	96	0	0-0	1.000	1	107	95	P-27/3-2	0.0
1925	Bos N	6	20	1	3	0	0	0	2	2	0	4	.150	.227	.150	-2	-3	0-0	.968	-0	109	122	/2-6	-0.3
1926	Cin N	66	76	15	23	4	4	0	14	10	0	13	.303	.384	.461	130	3	0	1.000	-1	94	52	P-39/2	-0.1
1927	Cin N	80	150	14	47	5	2	0	28	12	1	10	.313	.368	.373	102	1	0	.983	-4	97	84	P-37/2-5,S-3,O(LF)	-0.3
1928	Cin N	39	73	8	23	2	1	0	7	4	0	6	.315	.351	.370	90	6	0	**1.000**	-0	95	137	P-27	0.0
1929	Cin N	76	140	15	41	6	0	0	13	13	0	15	.293	.353	.336	75	12	1	.949	0	105	89	P-32	0.0
1930	Cin N	80	113	18	38	4	1	2	19	17	0	4	.336	.423	.442	115	16	0	**1.000**	-3	70	69	P-33	0.0
1931	Cin N	97	153	15	43	4	0	0	17	12	0	9	.281	.333	.307	78	12	0	.984	1	108	88	P-29	0.0
1932	Cin N	76	150	13	43	11	2	0	19	10	1	9	.287	.335	.387	97	15	0	.973	-0	98	126	P-31	0.0
1933	Cin N	75	122	14	35	6	1	1	15	12	1	6	.287	.356	.377	111	13	0	**1.000**	0	107	198	P-29	0.0
1934	Pit N	68	105	11	23	5	1	0	8	6	0	16	.219	.261	.286	45	3	1	.939	-3	67	98	P-29	0.0
1935	Pit N	47	66	6	21	6	0	0	10	7	1	11	.318	.392	.409	112	8	0	.968	-1	87	77	P-20	0.0
1936	Pit N	69	108	11	26	4	1	0	14	8	0	17	.241	.293	.296	58	4	0	.976	-1	88	175	P-27	0.0
1937	Pit N	59	82	8	22	3	0	0	17	7	0	6	.268	.326	.305	72	5	0	1.000	-2	70	76	P-20	0.0
1938	Pit N	33	46	1	5	0	0	0	2	3	0	2	.109	.163	.109	-24	-2	0	1.000	-1	82	98	P-13	0.0
Total	16	907	1439	155	404	61	13	3	190	124	4	133	.281	.340	.347	84	93	2-0	.981	-14	93	107	P-396/2-12,S-3,3-2,O(LF)	-0.7
LUCAS, FRED Frederick Warrington "Fritz" B 1.19.1903 Vineland, NJ D 3.11.1987 Cambridge, MD BR/TR 5-10/165# d7.15																								
1935	Phi N	20	34	1	9	0	0	0	2	3	0	6	.265	.324	.265	55	-2	0	.944	-0	105	0	O-10(4-3-3)	-0.3
LUCAS, JOHNNY John Charles "Buster" B 2.10.1903 Glen Carbon, IL D 10.31.1970 Maryville, IL BR/TL 5-10/186# d4.15																								
1931	Bos A	3	2	0	0	0	0	0	0	0	0	1	.000	.000	.000	-99	-1	0-0	—	-0	0	0	/O-2(1-1-0)	-0.1
1932	Bos A	1	1	0	0	0	0	0	0	0	0	0	.000	.000	.000	-99	0	0-0	—	0			H	0.0
Total	2	4	3	0	0	0	0	0	0	0	0	1	.000	.000	.000	-99	-1	0-0	.000	-0	0	0	/O-2(1-1-0)	-0.1
LUCE, FRANK Frank Edward B 12.6.1896 Spencer, OH D 2.3.1942 Milwaukee, WI BL/TR 5-11/180# d9.17																								
1923	Pit N	9	12	2	6	0	0	0	3	2	0	2	.500	.571	.500	181	2	2-1	1.000	-0	89	0	/O-5(3-1-1)	0.1
LUDERUS, FRED Frederick William B 9.12.1885 Milwaukee, WI D 1.5.1961 Three Lakes, WI BL/TR 5-11.5/185# d9.23																								
1909	Chi N	11	37	8	11	1	1	1	9	3	1		.297	.366	.459	152	2	0	.950	-2	67	88	1-11	0.0
1910	Chi N	24	54	5	11	1	1	0	3	4	0	3	.204	.259	.259	52	-4	0	.975	-1	88	93	1-17	-0.5
	Phi N	21	68	10	20	5	2	0	14	9	1	5	.294	.385	.426	132	3	2	.985	1	111	135	1-19	0.3
	Year	45	122	15	31	6	3	0	17	13	1	8	.254	.331	.352	98	0	2	.981	-0	101	117	1-36	-0.2
1911	Phi N	146	551	69	166	24	11	16	99	40	4	76	.301	.353	.472	128	17	6	.985	-2	92	102	*1-146	1.2
1912	Phi N	148	572	77	147	31	5	10	69	44	7	65	.257	.318	.381	85	-13	8	.990	10	**128**	96	*1-146	-0.6
1913	Phi N	155	588	67	154	32	7	18	86	34	2	51	.262	.304	.432	105	1	5-8	.984	1	104	90	*1-155	-0.4
1914	Phi N	121	443	55	110	16	5	12	55	33	5	31	.248	.308	.388	100	-1	2	.975	1	**114**	72	*1-121	-0.3
1915	†Phi N	141	499	55	157	36	7	7	62	42	7	36	.315	.376	.457	150	31	9-7	.993	10	**129**	107	*1-141	4.0
1916	Phi N	146	508	52	143	26	3	5	53	41	5	32	.281	.341	.374	115	10	8	.982	-2	99	109	*1-146	0.6
1917	Phi N	**154**	522	57	136	24	4	5	72	65	6	35	.261	.349	.351	110	10	5	.991	4	109	102	*1-154	1.1
1918	Phi N	**125**	468	54	135	23	2	5	67	42	3	33	.288	.351	.378	115	10	4	.988	6	119	95	*1-125	1.4
1919	Phi N	**138**	509	60	149	30	6	5	49	54	4	48	.293	.365	.405	123	16	6	.985	9	**131**	92	*1-138	2.4
1920	Phi N	16	32	1	5	2	0	0	4	3	0	6	.156	.229	.219	28	-3	0-1	.983	0	114	143	/1-7	-0.4
Total	12	1346	4851	570	1344	251	54	84	642	414	45	421	.277	.340	.403	113	79	55-16	.986	37	113	97	*1-1326	8.8
LUDWICK, RYAN Ryan Andrew B 7.13.1978 Satellite Beach, FL BR/TL 6-3/203# d6.5																								
2002	Tex A	23	81	10	19	6	0	1	9	7-0	0	24	.235	.295	.346	66	-4	2-1	1.000	-3	75	0	O-22(2-21-1)	-0.7
2003	Tex A	8	26	3	4	1	0	0	0	4-0	0	9	.154	.267	.192	22	-3	0-0	1.000	-0	98	0	/O-8(4-0-6)	-0.4
	Cle A	39	136	14	36	7	1	7	26	8-1	0	39	.265	.306	.485	107	1	2-0	1.000	1	108	105	O-32(13-0-19)/D-4	0.1
	Year	47	162	17	40	8	1	7	26	12-1	0	48	.247	.299	.438	92	-2	2-0	1.000	1	106	83	O-40(17-0-25)/D-4	-0.3
Total	2	70	243	27	59	14	1	8	35	19-1	0	72	.243	.298	.407	83	-6	4-1	1.000	-3	95	54	/O-62(19-21-26),D-4	-1.0
LUDWIG, BILL William Lawrence B 5.27.1882 Louisville, KY D 9.5.1947 Louisville, KY BR/TR d4.16																								
1908	StL N	66	187	15	34	2	2	0	8	16	0		.182	.246	.214	50	-11	3	.952	-10	*65*	*127*	C-62	-1.8
LUEBBE, ROY Roy John B 9.17.1900 Parkersburg, IA D 8.21.1985 Papillion, NE BB/TR 6/175# d8.22																								
1925	NY A	8	15	1	0	0	0	0	3	2	0	6	.000	.118	.000	-69	-4	0-0	1.000	1	*103*	*81*	/C-8	-0.3
LUFF, HENRY Henry T. B 9.14.1856 Philadelphia, PA D 10.11.1916 Philadelphia, PA 5-11/175# d4.21 ▲																								
1875	NH NA	38	166	15	45	10	3	2	18	0		5	.271	.271	.404	150	10	3-3	.689	-5	99	161	3-30,P-10/O-4(0-1-3),S	0.2
1882	Det N	3	11	1	3	2	0	0	1	0		0	.273	.273	.455	129	0		.667	-2	90	231	/2-3,O(CF)	-0.1
	Cin AA	28	120	16	28	2	2	0	6	2			.233	.246	.283	74	-4		.922	-2	95	112	1-27/O(RF)	-0.8
1883	Lou AA	6	23	1	4	0	0	0	2	0			.174	.174	.174	13	-2		.868	-1	0	65	/1-4,O-2(0-1-1)	-0.3
1884	Phi U	26	111	9	30	4	2	0		4			.270	.296	.342	100	-3		.733	-4	57	0	O-12(11-0-1)/1-6,3-5,2-3	-0.7
	KC U	5	19	0	1	0	0	0		1			.053	.100	.053	-60	-4		.444	-3	82	0	/3-4,O-4(3-1-1)	-0.7
	Year	31	130	9	31	4	2	0		5			.238	.267	.300	78	-7		.706	-7	51	0	O-16(14-1-2)/3-9,1-6,2-3	-1.4
Total	3	68	284	27	66	8	4	0	9	7		0	.232	.251	.289	73	-13		.911	-12	107	108	/1-37,O-20(14-3-4),3-9,2-6	-2.6
LUGO, JULIO Julio Cesar B 11.16.1975 Barahona, D.R. BR/TR 6/165# d4.15																								
2000	Hou N	116	420	78	119	22	5	10	40	37-0	4	93	.283	.346	.431	90	-7	22-9	.951	-9	93	84	S-60,2-45/O-6(3-1-2)	-0.7
2001	†Hou N	140	513	93	135	20	3	10	37	46-0	5	116	.263	.326	.372	77	-18	12-11	.964	15	106	101	*S-133/O-8(6-0-2),2-2	0.6
2002	Hou N	88	322	45	84	15	1	8	35	28-3	2	74	.261	.322	.388	86	-8	9-3	.976	-10	88	62	S-84	-1.1
2003	Hou N	22	65	6	16	3	0	0	2	9-1	0	12	.246	.338	.292	64	-3	2-1	.966	-1	95	83	S-22	-0.2
	TB A	117	433	58	119	13	4	15	53	35-0	4	88	.275	.333	.427	101	-1	10-3	.970	3	104	93	*S-117	1.2
Total	4	483	1753	280	473	73	13	43	167	155-4	15	383	.270	.332	.400	87	-37	55-27	.966	-2	99	87	S-416/2-47,O-14(9-1-4)	-0.2
LUKACHYK, ROB Robert James B 7.24.1968 Jersey City, NJ BL/TR 6/185# d7.5																								
1996	Mon N	2	2	0	0	0	0	0	0	0-0	0	1	.000	.000	.000	-98	-1	0-0	—	0			/H	-0.1
LUKE, MATT Matthew Clifford B 2.26.1971 Long Beach, CA BL/TL 6-5/220# d4.3																								
1996	NY A	1	0	1	0	0	0	0	0	0-0	0	0	—	—	—	—	0	0-0	—	0			/R	0.0
1998	LA N	33	77	10	22	7	0	3	11	3-0	0	18	.286	.313	.494	115	1	0-0	.958	-13	23	62	O-15(13-0-2),1-12	-1.4
	Cle A	2	2	0	0	0	0	0	0	0-0	0	0	.000	.000	.000	-97	-1	0-0	—	0			/H	-0.1
	LA N	69	160	24	34	5	1	9	23	14-2	1	42	.213	.278	.425	87	-4	2-1	1.000	-3	23	62	O-48(36-0-12)/1-6	-1.0
1999	Ana A	18	30	4	9	0	0	3	6	2-0	0	10	.300	.344	.600	135	1	0-0	1.000	1	101	0	/O-6(2-0-4),1-4	0.2
Total	3	123	269	39	65	12	1	15	40	19-2	1	70	.242	.293	.461	99	-3	2-1	.991	-15	55	90	/O-69(51-0-18),1-22	-2.3
LUKON, EDDIE Edward Paul "Mongoose" B 8.5.1920 Burgettstown, PA D 11.7.1996 Canonsburg, PA BL/TL 5-10/168# d8.6 Mil 1943-45																								
1941	Cin N	23	86	6	23	3	0	0	3	6	0	6	.267	.315	.302	74	-3	1	.980	1	110	103	O-22(RF)	-0.4
1945	Cin N	2	8	1	1	0	0	0	0	0	0	1	.125	.125	.125	-31	-1	0	1.000	0	126	0	/O-2(CF)	-0.1
1946	Cin N	102	312	31	78	8	8	12	34	26	1	29	.250	.310	.442	116	3	3	.985	-3	97	59	O-83(72-0-11)	-0.6
1947	Cin N	86	200	26	41	6	1	11	33	28	1	36	.205	.306	.410	89	-4	0	1.000	1	99	101	O-55(33-0-25)	-0.6
Total	4	213	606	64	143	17	9	23	70	60	2	72	.236	.307	.408	99	-5	4	.989	-2	100	77	O-162(105-2-58)	-1.7
LUM, MIKE Michael Ken-Wai B 10.27.1945 Honolulu, HI BL/TL 6/180# d9.12 C3																								
1967	Atl N	9	26	1	6	0	0	0	1	1-0	0	4	.231	.259	.231	42	-2	0-1	.944	1	105	263	/O-6(CF)	-0.2
1968	Atl N	122	232	22	52	7	3	3	21	14-2	4	35	.224	.277	.319	79	-6	3-5	.976	4	107	166	O-95(74-7-21)	-0.8
1969	†Atl N	121	168	20	45	8	0	1	22	16-4	0	18	.268	.326	.333	86	-3	0-0	.992	7	134	70	O-89(56-16-21)	0.2
1970	Atl N	123	291	25	74	17	2	7	28	17-0	5	43	.254	.306	.399	83	-8	3-2	.988	5	120	67	O-98(36-33-35)	-0.6
1971	Atl N	145	454	56	122	14	1	13	55	47-5	5	43	.269	.340	.390	101	1	0-3	.990	9	106	106	*O-125(10-17-104)/1	0.4
1972	Atl N	123	369	40	84	14	2	9	38	50-4	3	52	.228	.323	.350	84	-7	1-4	.976	6	**117**	55	*O-109(30-20-62)/1-2	-0.7

Year	Tm Lg	G	AB	R	H	2B	3B	HR	RBI	BB-IB	HP	SO	AVG	OBP	SLG	AOPS	ABR	SB-CS	FA	FR	Rng	Thr	G at Pos	BFW
1973	Atl N	138	513	74	151	26	6	16	82	41-7	6	89	.294	.351	.462	116	11	2-5	.991	-1	79	95	1-84,O-64(48-2-14)	-0.1
1974	Atl N	106	361	50	84	11	2	11	50	45-12	2	49	.233	.319	.366	88	-6	0-2	.994	-6	75	117	1-60,O-50(24-9-25)	-2.0
1975	Atl N	124	364	32	83	8	2	8	36	39-7	0	38	.228	.302	.327	72	-14	2-4	.992	-3	90	83	1-60,O-38(1-32-5)	-2.5
1976	†Cin N	84	136	15	31	5	1	3	20	22-1	1	24	.228	.331	.346	93	-1	0-1	1.000	-4	80	0	O-38(33-2-5)	-0.7
1977	Cin N	81	125	14	20	1	0	5	16	9-1	1	33	.160	.221	.288	35	-12	2-0	1.000	-1	108	0	O-24(12-1-11)/1-8	-1.4
1978	Cin N	86	146	15	39	7	1	6	23	22-4	0	18	.267	.361	.452	126	6	0-0	.987	3	97	305	O-43(10-26-9)/1-7	0.8
1979	Atl N	111	217	27	54	6	0	6	27	18-1	0	34	.249	.304	.359	75	-8	0-2	.998	1	106	100	1-51/O-3(LF)	-1.0
1980	Atl N	93	83	7	17	3	0	0	5	18-3	0	19	.205	.343	.241	65	-3	0-0	1.000	0	105	0	O-19(LF),1-10	-0.3
1981	Atl N	10	11	1	1	0	0	0	0	2-1	0	2	.091	.231	.091	-6	-2	0-0	1.000	0	157	0	/O(LF)	-0.1
	Chi N	41	58	5	14	1	0	2	7	5-2	1	5	.241	.308	.362	87	-1	0-0	.923	-2	64	0	O-14(12-0-3)/1	-0.4
	Year	51	69	6	15	1	0	2	7	7-3	1	7	.217	.295	.319	72	-3	0-0	.938	-2	72	0	O-15(13-0-3)/1	-0.5
Total	15	1517	3554	404	877	128	20	90	431	366-54	28	506	.247	.319	.370	89	-55	13-29	.986	20	109	80	O-816(369-171-315),1-284	-9.4

LUMLEY, HARRY Harry G "Judge" B 9.29.1880 Forest City, PA D 5.22.1938 Binghamton, NY BL/TL 5-10/183# d4.14 M1

1904	Bro N	150	577	79	161	23	**18**	**9**	78	41	4		.279	.331	.428	137	22	30	.955	4	141	144	*O-150(RF)	2.1
1905	Bro N	130	505	50	148	19	10	7	47	36	0		.293	.340	.412	134	19	22	.912	-0	128	88	*O-129(RF)	1.4
1906	Bro N	133	484	72	157	23	12	9	61	48	1		.324	.386	**.477**	**184**	**45**	35	.949	2	81	126	*O-131(RF)	4.5
1907	Bro N	127	454	47	121	23	11	9	66	31	2		.267	.316	.425	144	19	18	.959	-2	95	178	*O-118(RF)	1.4
1908	Bro N	127	440	36	95	13	12	4	39	29	1		.216	.266	.327	93	-6	4	.955	-3	93	177	*O-116(RF)	-1.7
1909	Bro N	55	172	13	43	8	3	0	14	16	0		.250	.314	.331	104	1	1	.948	2	123	57	O-52(RF),M	0.0
1910	Bro N	8	21	3	3	0	0	0	0	3	1	6	.143	.280	.143	25	-2	0	.833	-1	80	0	/O-4(RF)	-0.3
Total	7	730	2653	300	728	109	66	38	305	204	9	6	.274	.328	.408	135	98	110	.946	1	110	134	O-700(RF)	7.4

LUMPE, JERRY Jerry Dean B 6.2.1933 Lincoln, MO BL/TR 6-2/185# d4.17 C1

1956	NY A	20	62	12	16	3	0	0	4	5-2	0	11	.258	.313	.306	66	-3	1-1	.916	1	105	135	S-17/3	0.0
1957	†NY A	40	103	15	35	6	2	0	11	9-0	0	13	.340	.389	.437	128	4	2-2	.956	-1	92	142	3-30/S-6	0.3
1958	†NY A	81	232	34	59	8	4	3	32	23-2	1	21	.254	.319	.362	92	-3	1-2	.943	4	106	114	3-65/S-5	0.1
1959	NY A	18	45	2	10	0	0	0	2	6-5	0	7	.222	.314	.222	52	-3	0-0	1.000	2	126	182	3-12/S-4,2	0.0
	KC A	108	403	47	98	11	5	3	28	41-1	0	32	.243	.313	.318	72	-15	2-1	.986	-1	105	102	2-61,S-56/3-4	-0.8
	Year	126	448	49	108	11	5	3	30	47-6	0	39	.241	.313	.308	70	-18	2-1	.987	2	105	104	2-62,S-60,3-16	-0.8
1960	KC A	146	574	69	156	19	3	8	53	48-1	0	49	.272	.326	.357	85	-13	1-1	.982	-1	99	97	*2-134,S-15	-0.3
1961	KC A	148	569	81	167	29	9	3	54	48-0	2	39	.293	.348	.392	96	-3	1-0	.979	19	**110**	93	*2-147	2.9
1962	KC A	156	641	89	193	34	10	10	83	44-0	0	38	.301	.341	.432	103	2	0-2	.986	-5	98	91	*2-156/S-2	0.9
1963	KC A	157	595	75	161	26	7	5	59	58-3	0	44	.271	.333	.363	91	-6	3-2	.988	3	102	93	*2-155	1.0
1964	Det A☆	158	624	75	160	21	6	6	46	50-3	2	61	.256	.312	.338	80	-17	2-1	.983	-19	91	93	*2-158	-2.4
1965	Det A	145	502	72	129	15	3	4	39	56-1	3	34	.257	.333	.323	87	-7	7-0	.985	-14	90	87	*2-139	-0.9
1966	Det A	113	385	30	89	14	3	1	26	24-1	0	44	.231	.275	.291	62	-19	0-3	.991	-3	93	91	2-95	-1.7
1967	Det A	81	177	19	41	4	0	4	17	16-2	0	18	.232	.295	.322	80	-4	0-0	.963	1	108	75	2-54/3-6	0.0
Total	12	1371	4912	620	1314	190	52	47	454	428-21	8	411	.268	.325	.356	87	-87	20-15	.984	-14	99	92	*2-1100,3-118,S-105	-0.9

LUNAR, FERNANDO Fernando Jose B 5.25.1977 Cantaura, Venezuela BR/TR 6-1/195# d5.8

2000	Atl N	22	54	5	10	1	0	0	5	3-1	3	15	.185	.267	.204	21	-7	0-2	.993	4	60	109	C-22	-0.2
	Bal A	9	16	0	2	0	0	0	1	0-0	1	4	.125	.176	.125	-23	-3	0-0	1.000	3	0	177	/C-9	0.0
2001	Bal A	64	167	8	41	7	0	0	16	7-0	3	32	.246	.287	.287	55	-11	0-0	.987	-3	97	124	C-64	-1.0
2002	Bal A	2	0	0	0	0	0	0	0	0-0	0	0	—	—	—	—	0	0-0	1.000	0	0	0	/C-2	0.0
Total	3	97	237	13	53	8	0	0	22	10-1	7	51	.224	.275	.257	42	-21	0-2	.990	4	82	124	/C-97	-1.2

LUND, DON Donald Andrew B 5.18.1923 Detroit, MI BR/TR 6/200# d7.3 C2

1945	Bro N	4	3	0	0	0	0	0	0	1	0	1	.000	.250	.000	-27	0	0	—	0			H	0.0
1947	Bro N	11	20	5	6	2	0	2	5	3	0	7	.300	.391	.700	178	2	0	1.000	0	118	0	/O-5(LF)	0.2
1948	Bro N	27	69	9	13	4	0	1	5	5	0	16	.188	.243	.290	42	-6	1	.977	1	105	136	O-25(17-0-8)	-0.6
	StL A	63	161	21	40	7	4	3	25	10	3	17	.248	.305	.398	84	-5	0-0	1.000	-0	95	115	O-45(21-0-25)	-0.7
1949	Det A	2	2	0	0	0	0	0	0	0	0	1	.000	.000	.000	-99	-1	0-0	—	0			H	-0.1
1952	Det A	8	23	1	7	0	0	0	1	3	0	3	.304	.385	.304	93	0	0-1	1.000	0	99	220	/O-7(RF)	0.0
1953	Det A	131	421	51	108	21	4	9	47	39	2	65	.257	.323	.390	93	-5	3-3	.980	5	109	118	*O-123(37-29-69)	-0.6
1954	Det A	35	54	4	7	2	0	0	3	4	0	3	.130	.186	.167	-2	-8	1-0	.971	0	107	99	O-31(19-3-11)	-0.8
Total	7	281	753	91	181	36	8	15	86	65	5	113	.240	.305	.369	81	-23	5-4	.983	7	106	118	O-236(99-32-120)	-2.6

LUND, GORDY Gordon Thomas B 2.23.1941 Iron Mountain, MI BR/TR 5-11/170# d8.1

1967	Cle A	3	8	1	2	1	0	0	0	0-0	0	2	.250	.250	.375	82	0	0-0	.667	-2	51	182	/S-2	-0.2
1969	Sea A	20	38	4	10	0	0	0	1	5-1	0	7	.263	.349	.263	75	-1	1-1	.927	-2	99	88	S-17/23	-0.2
Total	2	23	46	5	12	1	0	0	1	5-1	0	9	.261	.333	.283	76	-1	1-1	.902	-4	92	101	/S-19,32	-0.4

LUNDSTEDT, TOM Thomas Robert B 4.10.1949 Davenport, IA BB/TR 6-4/195# d8.31

1973	Chi N	4	5	0	0	0	0	0	0	0-0	0	1	.000	.000	.000	-93	-1	0-0	1.000	-0	45	0	/C-4	-0.2
1974	Chi N	22	32	1	3	0	0	0	0	5-0	0	7	.094	.216	.094	-11	-5	0-0	.987	-1	81	59	C-22	-0.6
1975	Min A	18	28	2	3	0	0	0	1	4-1	0	5	.107	.219	.107	-5	-4	0-0	1.000	-2	51	59	C-14/D-2	-0.5
Total	3	44	65	3	6	0	0	0	1	9-1	0	13	.092	.203	.092	-15	-10	0-0	.993	-3	67	54	/C-40,D-2	-1.3

LUNSFORD, TREY James Lewis B 5.25.1979 Odessa, TX BR/TR 6-1/195# d9.12

2002	SF N	3	3	0	2	1	0	0	1	0-0	0	1	.667	.667	1.000	354	1	0-0	.800	-1	46	0	/C-3	0.0
2003	SF N	1	1	0	0	0	0	0	0	0-0	0	0	.000	.000	.000	-99	0	0-0	—	-0	0	0	/C	-0.1
Total	2	4	4	0	2	1	0	0	1	0-0	0	1	.500	.500	.750	236	1	0-0	.800	-1	40	0	/C-4	-0.1

LUNTE, HARRY Harry August B 9.15.1892 St.Louis, MO D 7.27.1965 St.Louis, MO BR/TR 5-11.5/165# d5.19

1919	Cle A	26	77	2	15	2	0	0	2	1	1	7	.195	.215	.221	21	-8	0	.935	-1	105	69	S-24	-0.8
1920	†Cle A	23	71	6	14	0	0	0	7	5	0	6	.197	.250	.197	19	-8	0-1	.979	4	121	115	S-21/2-2	-0.4
Total	2	49	148	8	29	2	0	0	9	6	1	13	.196	.232	.209	20	-16	0-1	.955	3	112	90	/S-45,2-2	-1.2

LUPIEN, TONY Ulysses John B 4.23.1917 Chelmsford, MA BL/TL 5-10.5/185# d9.12 Mil 1945

1940	Bos A	10	19	5	9	3	2	0	4	1	0	1	.474	.500	.842	232	4	0-0	1.000	-0	79	109	/1-8	0.3
1942	Bos A	128	463	63	130	25	7	3	70	50	0	20	.281	.351	.384	103	2	10-12	.992	-7	79	102	*1-121	-1.8
1943	Bos A	154	608	65	155	21	9	4	47	54	1	23	.255	.317	.339	90	-9	16-9	.993	3	108	105	*1-153	-1.5
1944	Phi N	153	597	82	169	23	9	5	52	56	2	29	.283	.347	.377	107	5	18	.992	2	104	95	*1-151	-0.1
1945	Phi N	15	54	1	17	1	0	0	3	6	0	0	.315	.383	.333	103	0	2	1.000	3	163	89	1-15	0.2
1948	Chi A	**154**	617	69	152	19	3	6	54	74	0	38	.246	.327	.316	74	-23	11-7	.993	-4	91	99	*1-154	-3.2
Total	6	614	2358	285	632	92	30	18	230	241	3	111	.268	.337	.355	94	-21	57-28	.993	-3	98	100	1-602	-6.1

LUPLOW, AL Alvin David B 3.13.1939 Saginaw, MI BL/TR 5-11/180# d9.16

1961	Cle A	5	18	0	1	0	0	0	0	2-0	0	6	.056	.150	.056	-44	-4	0-0	1.000	1	93	534	/O-5(1-0-4)	-0.3
1962	Cle A	97	318	54	88	15	3	14	45	36-0	6	44	.277	.359	.475	127	12	1-0	.960	-0	100	84	O-86(70-0-24)	0.7
1963	Cle A	100	295	34	69	6	2	7	27	33-2	3	62	.234	.316	.339	85	-6	4-4	.994	5	110	137	O-85(14-0-73)	-0.7
1964	Cle A	19	18	1	2	0	0	0	1	1-0	0	8	.111	.158	.111	-24	-3	0-0	1.000	0	129	0	/O-5(0-1-4)	-0.3
1965	Cle A	53	45	3	6	2	0	1	4	3-0	0	14	.133	.188	.244	22	-5	0-1	1.000	0	115	0	/O-6(2-1-3)	-0.6
1966	NY N	111	334	31	84	9	1	7	31	38-3	2	46	.251	.331	.347	91	-3	2-6	.987	-4	92	67	*O-101(16-24-71)	-1.5
1967	NY N	41	112	11	23	1	0	3	9	8-1	1	19	.205	.260	.295	61	-6	0-0	.966	-1	99	56	O-33(6-16-16)	-0.9
	Pit N	55	103	13	19	1	0	1	8	6-0	1	14	.184	.232	.223	32	-9	1-0	.961	3	108	260	O-25(15-2-8)	-0.8
	Year	96	215	24	42	2	0	4	17	14-1	2	33	.195	.247	.260	47	-15	1-0	.963	2	103	148	O-58(21-18-24)	-1.7
Total	7	481	1243	147	292	34	6	33	125	127-6	13	213	.235	.311	.352	85	-24	8-11	.977	4	101	110	O-346(124-44-203)	-4.4

LUSADER, SCOTT Scott Edward B 9.30.1964 Chicago, IL BL/TL 5-10/165# d9.1

1987	Det A	23	47	8	15	3	1	1	8	5-1	0	7	.319	.377	.489	135	2	1-0	.967	-1	98	0	O-22(6-3-16)/D	0.1
1988	Det A	16	16	3	1	0	0	1	3	1-0	0	4	.063	.111	.250	-0	-2	0-0	1.000	-0	98	0	/O-4(2-2-2),D-6	-0.3
1989	Det A	40	103	15	26	4	0	1	8	9-0	0	21	.252	.310	.320	81	-3	3-0	.933	-2	99	0	O-33(4-8-24)/D	-0.5
1990	Det A	45	87	13	21	2	0	2	16	12-0	0	8	.241	.324	.333	86	-1	0-0	.982	-2	90	51	O-42(12-5-27)/D-2	-0.4
1991	NY A	11	7	2	1	0	0	0	1	1-0	0	3	.143	.250	.143	12	-1	0-1	1.000	-0	86	0	/O-4(1-3-0),D	-0.1
Total	5	135	260	41	64	9	1	5	36	28-1	0	43	.246	.313	.346	86	-5	4-1	.961	-6	95	20	O-105(25-21-69)/D-11	-1.2

Year	Tm Lg	G	AB	R	H	2B	3B	HR	RBI	BB-IB	HP	SO	AVG	OBP	SLG	AOPS	ABR	SB-CS	FA	FR	Rng	Thr	G at Pos	BFW
LUSH, ERNIE Ernest Benjamin B 10.31.1884 Bridgeport, CT D 2.26.1937 Detroit, MI BR/TL d7.20 b-Billy																								
1910	StL N	1	4	0	0	0	0	0	0	1	0	1	.000	.200	.000	-42	-1	0	1.000	-0	55	0	/O(CF)	-0.1
LUSH, JOHNNY John Charles B 10.8.1885 Williamsport, PA D 11.18.1946 Beverly Hills, CA BL/TL 5-9.5/165# d4.22 ▲																								
1904	Phi N	106	369	39	102	22	3	2	42	27	6		.276	.336	.369	122	10	12	.950	-8	71	94	1-62,O-33(RF)/P-7	-0.1
1905	Phi N	6	16	3	5	0	0	0	1	1	1		.313	.389	.313	114	0	0	.667	-1	0	0	/O-3(0-2-1),P-2	-0.1
1906	Phi N	76	212	28	56	7	1	0	15	14	0		.264	.310	.307	92	-2	6	.907	4	111	76	P-37,O-22(0-6-16)/1-2	0.1
1907	Phi N	17	40	5	8	1	1	0	5	1	0		.200	.220	.275	56	-2	1	1.000	-0	114	386	/P-8,O-4(0-3-1)	-0.2
	StL N	27	82	6	23	2	3	0	5	5	0		.280	.322	.378	123	2	4	.917	-1	88	141	P-20/O-7(0-3-4)	-0.1
	Year	44	122	11	31	3	4	0	10	6	0		.254	.289	.344	101	-1	5	.941	-1	95	210	P-28,O-11(0-6-5)	-0.3
1908	StL N	45	89	7	15	2	0	0	2	7	0		.169	.229	.191	36	1	1	.926	0	102	0	P-38	0.0
1909	StL N	45	92	11	22	5	0	0	14	6	1		.239	.293	.293	87	-1	2	.945	-1	98	0	P-34/O-3(RF)	-0.1
1910	StL N	47	93	8	21	1	3	0	10	8	0	11	.226	.287	.301	74	4	2	.928	-2	89	86	P-36	0.0
Total	7	369	993	107	252	40	11	2	94	69	8	11	.254	.307	.322	98	12	28	.926	-9	101	75	P-182/O-72(0-14-58),1-64	-0.5
LUSH, BILLY William Lucas B 11.10.1873 Bridgeport, CT D 8.28.1951 Hawthorne, NY BB/TR 5-7/165# d9.3 b-Ernie																								
1895	Was N	5	18	2	6	0	0	0	2	2	0	1	.333	.400	.333	91	0	0	.692	-2	0	0	/O-5(4-0-1)	-0.2
1896	Was N	97	352	74	87	9	11	4	45	66	2	49	.247	.369	.369	95	-1	28	.885	-1	153	115	*O-91(10-14-68)/2-3	-0.5
1897	Was N	3	12	1	0	0	0	0	0	2	0		.000	.143	.000	-61	-3	0	1.000	0	208	0	/O-3(RF)	-0.2
1901	Bos N	7	27	2	5	1	1	0	3	3	0		.185	.267	.296	58	-2	0	.960	2	188	406	/O-7(CF)	0.0
1902	Bos N	120	413	68	92	8	1	2	19	76	2		.223	.346	.262	87	-1	30	.952	9	152	127	*O-116(10-104-2)/3	0.2
1903	Det A	119	423	71	116	18	14	1	33	70	1		.274	.379	.390	135	22	14	.968	8	138	125	*O-101(89-0-12),3-12/2-3,S-3	2.5
1904	Cle A	138	477	76	123	13	8	1	50	72	3		.258	.359	.325	118	14	12	.959	2	71	101	*O-138(125-13-0)	0.9
Total	7	489	1722	294	429	49	35	8	152	291	8	50	.249	.360	.332	107	29	84	.943	19	124	119	O-461(238-138-86)/3-13,2-6,S-3	2.7
LUSKEY, CHARLIE Charles Melton B 4.6.1876 Washington, DC D 12.20.1962 Bethesda, MD BR/TR 5-7/165# d9.12																								
1901	Was A	11	41	8	8	3	1	0	3	2	0		.195	.233	.317	52	-3	0	.818	-2	88	0	/O-8(LF),C-3	-0.4
LUTENBERG, LUKE Charles William B 10.4.1864 Quincy, IL D 12.24.1938 Quincy, IL BR/TR 6-2/225# d7.7																								
1894	Lou N	70	255	43	49	10	4	0	23	23	9	21	.192	.282	.263	34	-28	4	.977	2	104	124	1-68/2-2	-2.0
LUTTRELL, LYLE Lyle Kenneth B 2.22.1930 Bloomington, IL D 7.11.1984 Chattanooga, TN BR/TR 6/180# d5.15																								
1956	Was A	38	122	17	23	5	3	2	9	8-0	3	19	.189	.254	.328	53	-9	5-1	.939	-5	91	71	S-37	-1.0
1957	Was A	19	45	4	9	4	0	0	5	3-0	0	8	.200	.250	.289	47	-3	0-0	.927	-3	80	60	S-17	-0.6
Total	2	57	167	21	32	9	3	2	14	11-0	3	27	.192	.253	.317	52	-12	5-1	.936	-8	88	68	/S-54	-1.6
LUTZ, RED Louis William B 12.17.1898 Cincinnati, OH D 2.22.1984 Cincinnati, OH BR/TR 5-10/170# d5.31																								
1922	Cin N	1	1	0	1	1	0	0	0	0	0	0	1.000	1.000	2.000	669	1	0-0	—	0	*0*	*0*	/C	0.1
LUTZ, JOE Rollin Joseph B 2.18.1925 Keokuk, IA BL/TL 6/195# d4.17 C3																								
1951	StL A	14	36	7	6	0	1	0	2	6	0	9	.167	.286	.222	38	-3	0-0	1.000	-1	60	85	1-11	-0.4
LUTZKE, RUBE Walter John B 11.17.1897 Milwaukee, WI D 3.6.1938 Granville, WI BR/TR 5-11/175# d4.18																								
1923	Cle A	143	511	71	131	20	6	3	65	59	4	57	.256	.338	.337	78	-16	9-6	.939	16	**113**	89	*3-141/S-2	0.9
1924	Cle A	106	341	37	83	18	3	0	42	38	5	46	.243	.328	.314	65	-17	4-0	.947	17	**113**	**140**	*3-103/2-3	0.6
1925	Cle A	81	238	31	52	9	0	1	16	26	0	29	.218	.295	.269	44	-21	2-4	.936	0	108	77	3-69,2-10	-1.7
1926	Cle A	142	475	42	124	28	6	0	59	34	2	35	.261	.313	.345	71	-21	6-3	.960	-3	99	**124**	*3-142	-1.4
1927	Cle A	100	311	35	78	12	3	0	41	22	3	29	.251	.307	.309	60	-19	2-1	.938	4	105	124	3-98	-0.9
Total	5	572	1876	216	468	87	18	4	223	179	14	196	.249	.319	.321	66	-94	23-14	.945	34	107	113	3-553/2-13,S-2	-2.5
LUULOA, KEITH Keith H. M. B 12.24.1974 Honolulu, HI BR/TR 6/185# d5.17																								
2000	Ana A	6	18	3	6	0	0	0	0	1-0	0	1	.333	.368	.333	78	-1	0-0	.833	-2	42	60	/S-4,2-3	-0.2
LUZINSKI, GREG Gregory Michael B 11.22.1950 Chicago, IL BR/TR 6-1/225# d9.9 C4																								
1970	Phi N	8	12	0	2	0	0	0	0	3-0	0	5	.167	.333	.167	39	-1	0-1	1.000	1	170	46	/1-3	-0.1
1971	Phi N	28	100	13	30	8	0	3	15	12-0	2	32	.300	.386	.470	141	6	2-0	.996	6	189	70	1-28	1.1
1972	Phi N	150	563	66	158	33	5	18	68	42-4	3	114	.281	.332	.453	119	13	0-4	.960	-1	99	93	*O-145(145-0-1)/1-2	0.1
1973	Phi N	161	610	76	174	26	4	29	97	51-9	7	135	.285	.346	.484	125	19	3-3	**.993**	-7	87	67	*O-159(LF)	0.3
1974	Phi N	85	302	29	82	14	1	7	48	29-3	0	76	.272	.330	.394	99	0	3-0	.981	5	100	189	O-82(LF)	0.1
1975	Phi N★	161	596	85	179	35	3	34	**120**	89-**17**	8	151	.300	.394	.540	152	44	3-6	.966	-12	83	84	*O-159(LF)	2.2
1976	†Phi N★	149	533	74	162	28	1	21	95	50-2	**11**	107	.304	.369	.478	137	26	1-2	.964	-9	84	91	*O-144(LF)	1.0
1977	†Phi N★	149	554	99	171	35	3	39	130	80-14	3	140	.309	.394	.594	155	45	3-2	.964	-10	78	118	*O-148(LF)	2.9
1978	†Phi N★	155	540	85	143	32	2	35	101	100-15	11	135	.265	.388	.526	152	42	8-7	.984	-11	85	58	*O-154(LF)	2.5
1979	Phi N	137	452	47	114	23	1	18	81	56-5	**10**	103	.252	.343	.427	107	5	3-3	.946	-16	73	35	*O-125(LF)	-1.6
1980	†Phi N	106	368	44	84	19	1	19	56	60-5	**6**	100	.228	.342	.440	112	7	3-0	.993	-14	74	28	*O-105(LF)	-1.0
1981	Chi A	104	378	55	100	15	1	21	62	58-1	3	80	.265	.365	.476	144	23	0-0	—	0	0	0	*D-103	2.0
1982	Chi A	159	583	87	170	37	1	18	102	89-11	6	120	.292	.386	.451	130	29	1-1	—	0	0	0	*D-156	2.4
1983	†Chi A	144	502	73	128	26	1	32	95	70-6	11	117	.255	.352	.502	129	21	2-1	1.000	0	122	98	*D-139/1-2	1.7
1984	Chi A	125	412	47	98	13	0	13	58	56-3	3	80	.238	.329	.364	89	-5	5-1	—	0	0	0	*D-114	-0.8
Total	15	1821	6505	880	1795	344	24	307	1128	845-95	84	1495	.276	.363	.478	129	274	37-31	.972	-66	85	82	*O-1221(1221-0-1),D-512/1-35	12.8
LYDEN, MITCH Mitchell Scott B 12.14.1964 Portland, OR BR/TR 6-3/225# d6.16																								
1993	Fla N	6	10	2	3	0	0	1	1	0-0	0	3	.300	.300	.600	127	0	0-0	1.000	-1	93	0	/C-2	-0.1
LYDY, SCOTT Donald Scott B 10.26.1968 Mesa, AZ BR/TR 6-5/195# d5.18																								
1993	Oak A	41	102	11	23	5	0	2	7	8-0	1	39	.225	.288	.333	71	-4	2-0	.958	-0	100	101	O-38(17-5-16)/D-2	-0.5
LYNCH, JERRY Gerald Thomas B 7.17.1930 Bay City, MI BL/TR 6-1/189# d4.15																								
1954	Pit N	98	284	27	68	4	5	8	36	20	1	43	.239	.290	.373	73	-13	2-2	.965	3	95	201	O-83(46-4-36)	-1.4
1955	Pit N	88	282	43	80	18	6	5	28	22-4	0	33	.284	.331	.443	106	2	2-2	.950	1	85	224	O-71(40-0-32)/C-2	0.0
1956	Pit N	19	19	1	3	0	1	0	0	1-0	0	4	.158	.200	.263	24	-2	0-0	1.000	0	166	0	/O(LF)	-0.2
1957	Cin N	67	124	11	32	4	1	4	13	6-1	0	18	.258	.290	.403	79	-4	0-0	1.000	-1	108	0	O-24(1-0-22)/C-2	-0.5
1958	Cin N	122	420	58	131	20	5	16	68	18-1	0	54	.312	.338	.498	112	6	1-4	.970	-5	92	67	*O-101(1-0-101)	-0.3
1959	Cin N	117	379	49	102	16	3	17	58	29-1	1	50	.269	.320	.462	103	1	2-0	.979	1	103	70	O-98(97-0-1)	-0.3
1960	Cin N	102	159	23	46	8	2	6	27	16-3	1	25	.289	.356	.478	124	5	0-0	.913	-2	94	51	O-32(31-0-1)	0.2
1961	†Cin N	96	181	33	57	13	2	13	50	27-6	1	25	.315	.407	.624	166	18	2-2	.948	-2	87	74	O-44(42-0-2)	1.3
1962	Cin N	114	288	41	81	15	4	12	57	24-4	1	38	.281	.335	.486	115	5	3-3	.970	0	86	169	O-73(70-0-3)	0.2
1963	Cin N	22	32	5	8	3	0	2	9	1-0	1	5	.250	.294	.531	129	1	0-0	1.000	-0	84	0	/O-7(4-0-3)	0.1
	Pit N	88	237	26	63	6	3	10	36	22-2	1	28	.266	.328	.443	120	6	0-1	.960	-5	76	59	O-64(LF)	-0.3
	Year	110	269	31	71	9	3	12	45	23-2	2	33	.264	.324	.454	121	7	0-1	.962	-6	77	55	O-71(68-0-3)	-0.2
1964	Pit N	114	297	35	81	14	2	16	66	26-3	1	57	.273	.328	.495	130	11	0-1	.983	-9	63	0	O-78(77-0-1)	-0.1
1965	Pit N	73	121	7	34	1	0	5	16	8-3	1	26	.281	.328	.413	108	1	0-2	.903	-1	85	94	O-26(23-0-3)	-0.2
1966	Pit N	64	56	5	12	1	0	1	6	4-1	0	10	.214	.267	.286	54	-4	0-0	1.000	0	179	0	/O-4(LF)	-0.3
Total	13	1184	2879	364	798	123	34	115	470	224-29	9	416	.277	.329	.463	110	33	12-17	.964	-20	89	101	O-706(501-4-205)/C-4	-1.8
LYNCH, HENRY Henry W. B 4.8.1866 Worcester, MA D 11.23.1925 Worcester, MA BB 5-7/143# d9.21																								
1893	Chi N	4	14	0	3	2	0	0	2	1	0	1	.214	.267	.357	66	-1	0	.833	-1	0	0	/O-4(RF)	-0.1
LYNCH, DANNY Matt Dan "Dummy" B 2.7.1926 Dallas, TX D 6.30.1978 Plano, TX BR/TR 5-11/174# d9.14																								
1948	Chi N	7	7	3	2	0	0	1	1	1	0	1	.286	.375	.714	197	1	0	1.000	0	160	0	/2	0.1
LYNCH, MIKE Michael Joseph B 9.10.1875 St.Paul, MN D 4.1.1947 Jennings Lodge, OR TR 5-10/155# d4.24																								
1902	Chi N	7	28	4	4	0	0	0	0	2	0		.143	.200	.143	6	-3	0	.929	-0	117	0	/O-7(CF)	-0.4
LYNCH, TOM Thomas James B 4.3.1860 Bennington, VT D 3.28.1955 Cohoes, NY BL/TR 5-10.5/170# d8.18 U12																								
1884	Wil U	16	58	6	16	3	1	0		5			.276	.333	.362	108	-1		.846	-0			/C-8,O-8(LF),1	-0.1
	Phi N	13	48	7	15	4	2	0	3	4		5	.313	.365	.479	171	4		.860	-0			/C-7,O-7(1-6-0)	0.4
1885	Phi N	13	53	7	10	3	0	0	1	10		3	.189	.317	.245	86	0		.838	2	171	268	O-13(9-4-0)	0.1
Total	2	42	159	20	41	10	3	0	4	19		8	.258	.337	.358	119	3		.887	1			/O-28(18-10-0),C-15,1	0.4

Year	Tm Lg	G	AB	R	H	2B	3B	HR	RBI	BB-IB	HP	SO	AVG	OBP	SLG	AOPS	ABR	SB-CS	FA	FR	Rng	Thr	G at Pos	BFW
LYNCH, WALT Walter Edward "Jabber" B 4.15.1897 Buffalo, NY D 12.21.1976 Daytona Beach, FL TR 6/176# d7.8																								
1922	Bos A	3	2	1	1	0	0	0	0	0	0	0	.500	.500	.500	163	0	0-0	1.000	0	*0*	*0*	/C-3	0.0
LYNN, BYRD Byrd "Birdie" B 3.13.1889 Unionville, IL D 2.5.1940 Napa, CA BR/TR 5-11/165# d4.16																								
1916	Chi A	31	40	4	9	1	0	0	3	4	1	7	.225	.311	.250	68	-1	2	.952	4	219	259	C-13	0.4
1917	†Chi A	35	72	7	16	2	0	0	5	7	1	11	.222	.300	.250	67	-3	1	.959	1	*145*	*55*	C-29	0.0
1918	Chi A	5	8	0	2	0	0	0	0	2	0	1	.250	.400	.250	95	0	0	1.000	-1	*95*	*132*	/C-4	0.0
1919	†Chi A	29	66	4	15	4	0	0	4	4	0	9	.227	.271	.288	57	-4	0	.982	1	*121*	*94*	C-28	-0.1
1920	Chi A	16	25	0	8	2	1	0	3	1	0	3	.320	.346	.480	117	0	0-0	1.000	-0	*133*	*78*	C-14	0.1
Total	5	116	211	15	50	9	1	0	15	18	2	31	.237	.303	.289	72	-8	3-0	.969	5	*147*	*107*	/C-88	0.4
LYNN, FRED Fredric Michael B 2.3.1952 Chicago, IL BL/TL 6-1/190# d9.5																								
1974	Bos A	15	43	5	18	2	2	2	10	6-2	1	6	.419	.490	.698	226	7	0-0	1.000	-1	70	238	O-12(6-4-2)/D	0.6
1975	†Bos A★	145	528	**103**	175	**47**	7	21	105	62-10	3	90	.331	.401	**.566**	158	42	10-5	.983	2	105	107	*O-144(CF)	4.1
1976	Bos A★	132	507	76	159	32	8	10	65	48-2	1	67	.314	.367	.467	130	19	14-9	.984	4	102	134	*O-128(0-127-1)/D-5	2.0
1977	Bos A★	129	497	81	129	29	5	18	76	51-2	3	63	.260	.327	.447	98	-1	2-3	.994	-2	100	78	*O-125(CF)/D	-0.5
1978	Bos A★	150	541	75	161	33	3	22	82	75-11	1	50	.298	.380	.492	131	24	3-6	.984	-6	94	107	*O-149(CF)	1.6
1979	Bos A★	147	531	116	177	42	1	39	122	82-4	4	79	**.333**	**.423**	**.637**	**173**	**57**	2-2	.987	-0	99	107	*O-143(CF)/D	5.3
1980	Bos A★	110	415	67	125	32	3	12	61	58-3	0	39	.301	.383	.480	129	19	12-0	.994	2	99	143	*O-110(CF)	2.3
1981	Cal A★	76	256	28	56	8	1	5	31	38-4	3	42	.219	.322	.316	86	-3	1-2	.978	-3	95	96	O-69(CF)	-0.8
1982	†Cal A★	138	472	89	141	38	1	21	86	58-4	3	72	.299	.374	.517	143	30	7-8	.991	-10	89	68	*O-133(CF)	1.8
1983	Cal A★	117	437	56	119	20	3	22	74	55-10	2	83	.272	.352	.483	130	18	2-2	.993	-11	82	105	*O-113(CF)/D-2	0.5
1984	Cal A	142	517	84	140	28	4	23	79	77-8	2	97	.271	.366	.474	132	24	2-2	.982	0	96	132	*O-140(0-62-112)	1.9
1985	Bal A	124	448	59	118	12	1	23	68	53-6	1	100	.263	.339	.449	118	11	7-3	.994	-5	95	77	*O-123(CF)	0.5
1986	Bal A	112	397	67	114	13	1	23	67	53-1	2	59	.287	.371	.499	137	21	2-2	.984	-10	88	36	*O-107(CF)/D	1.0
1987	Bal A	111	396	49	100	24	0	23	60	39-6	1	72	.253	.320	.487	113	7	3-7	.991	-7	90	46	*O-101(CF)/D-8	-0.2
1988	Bal A	87	301	37	76	13	1	18	37	28-1	0	66	.252	.312	.482	123	8	2-2	.991	-0	105	25	O-83(0-64-21)/D-2	0.7
	Det A	27	90	9	20	1	0	7	19	5-0	1	16	.222	.265	.467	106	0	0-0	1.000	1	96	178	O-22(19-3-0)/D-3	0.0
	Year	114	391	46	96	14	1	25	56	33-1	1	82	.246	.302	.478	120	8	2-2	.992	0	103	56	*O-105(19-67-21)/D-5	0.7
1989	Det A	117	353	44	85	11	1	11	46	47-1	1	71	.241	.328	.371	100	1	1-1	.992	1	97	140	O-68(LF),D-46	-0.2
1990	SD N	90	196	18	47	3	1	6	23	22-2	1	44	.240	.315	.357	85	-4	2-0	1.000	-4	89	29	O-55(42-6-8)	-0.9
Total	17	1969	6925	1063	1960	388	43	306	1111	857-77	30	1116	.283	.360	.484	129	280	72-54	.988	-49	95	95	*O-1825(135-1584-144)/D-70	19.7
LYNN, JERRY Jerome Edward B 4.14.1916 Scranton, PA D 9.25.1972 Scranton, PA BR/TR 5-10/164# d9.19																								
1937	Was A	1	3	0	2	1	0	0	0	0	0	0	.667	.667	1.000	329	1	0-0	1.000	0	93	275	/2	0.1
LYON, RUSS Russell Mayo B 6.26.1913 Ball Ground, GA D 12.24.1975 Charleston, SC BR/TR 6-1/230# d4.21																								
1944	Cle A	7	11	1	2	0	0	0	0	1	0	1	.182	.250	.182	25	-1	0-0	.909	0	*95*	*175*	/C-3	-0.1
LYONS, BARRY Barry Stephen B 6.3.1960 Biloxi, MS BR/TR 6-1/202# d4.19																								
1986	NY N	6	9	1	0	0	0	0	2	1-1	0	2	.000	.100	.000	-72	-2	0-0	.941	-2	36	0	/C-3	-0.4
1987	NY N	53	130	15	33	4	1	4	24	8-1	2	24	.254	.301	.392	88	-3	0-0	.984	-6	85	79	C-49	-0.8
1988	NY N	50	91	5	21	7	1	0	11	3-0	0	12	.231	.253	.330	70	-4	0-0	.979	-4	78	108	C-32/1	-0.7
1989	NY N	79	235	15	58	13	0	3	27	11-1	2	28	.247	.283	.340	82	-6	0-1	.980	-1	86	87	C-76	-0.3
1990	NY N	24	80	8	19	0	0	2	7	2-0	1	9	.237	.265	.313	58	-5	0-0	.980	-1	56	84	C-23	-0.5
	LA N	3	5	1	1	0	0	1	2	0-0	0	1	.200	.200	.800	166	0	0-0	1.000	-0	0	0	/C-2	0.0
	Year	27	85	9	20	0	0	3	9	2-0	1	10	.235	.261	.341	65	-5	0-0	.980	-1	55	82	C-25	-0.5
1991	LA N	9	9	0	0	0	0	0	0	0-0	0	2	.000	.000	.000	-99	-2	0-0	1.000	1	153	0	/C-6	-0.2
	Cal A	2	5	0	1	0	0	0	0	0-0	0	0	.200	.200	.200	11	-1	0-0	1.000	0	142	0	/1-2	-0.1
1995	Chi A	27	64	8	17	2	0	5	16	4-0	0	14	.266	.304	.531	119	1	0-0	.987	1	41	215	C-16/1-4,D-6	0.2
Total	7	253	628	53	150	26	2	15	89	29-3	5	92	.239	.275	.358	78	-22	0-1	.981	-12	77	93	C-207/1-7,D-6	-2.8
LYONS, DENNY Dennis Patrick Aloysius B 3.12.1866 Cincinnati, OH D 1.2.1929 W.Covington, KY BR/TR 5-10/185# d9.18																								
1885	Pro N	4	16	3	2	1	0	0	1	0		3	.125	.125	.188	-0	-2		.824	-0	95	0	/3-4	-0.2
1886	Phi AA	32	123	22	26	3	1	0	11	8	4		.211	.281	.252	67	-5	7	.807	-5	89	22	3-32	-0.8
1887	Phi AA	**137**	570	128	209	43	14	6	102	47	6		.367	.421	.523	162	48	73	.866	-5	78	**144**	*3-137	3.6
1888	Phi AA	111	456	93	135	22	5	6	83	41	7		.296	.363	.406	147	25	39	.878	-12	82	76	*3-111	1.4
1889	Phi AA	131	510	135	168	36	4	9	82	79	7	44	.329	.426	.469	157	43	10	.860	9	107	**125**	*3-130/1	4.5
1890	Phi AA	88	339	79	120	29	5	7	73	57	10		.354	**.461**	**.531**	**193**	44	21	.909	10	105	93	3-88	4.7
1891	StL AA	120	451	124	142	24	3	11	84	88	18	58	.315	.445	.455	137	25	9	.871	-5	93	87	*3-120	1.9
1892	NY N	108	389	71	100	16	7	8	51	59	3	37	.257	.359	.396	130	16	11	.871	-7	86	77	*3-108	1.0
1893	Pit N	**131**	490	103	150	19	16	3	105	97	9	29	.306	.430	.429	131	28	19	.918	4	99	102	*3-131	2.7
1894	Pit N	72	257	52	82	14	4	4	51	43	4	13	.319	.424	.451	112	8	14	.897	4	102	90	3-72	0.9
1895	StL N	34	132	24	39	6	0	2	25	15	3	7	.295	.380	.386	99	1	3	.889	-5	71	37	3-34	-0.3
1896	Pit N	118	436	77	134	25	6	4	71	67	5	25	.307	.406	.420	123	19	13	.893	-16	81	86	*3-116	0.4
1897	Pit N	37	131	22	27	6	4	2	17	22	6		.206	.346	.359	90	-1	5	.989	-1	76	73	1-35/3-2	-0.2
Total	13	1123	4300	933	1334	244	69	62	756	623	82	216	.310	.407	.442	138	249	224	.882	-30	91	95	*3-1085/1-36	19.6
LYONS, ED Edward Hoyte "Mouse" B 5.12.1923 Winston-Salem, NC BR/TR 5-9/165# d9.15 C1																								
1947	Was A	7	26	2	4	0	0	0	0	2	0	2	.154	.214	.154	3	-3	0-0	1.000	3	127	123	/2-7	0.0
LYONS, HARRY Harry Pratt B 3.25.1866 Chester, PA D 6.29.1912 Mauricetown, NJ BR/TR 5-10.5/157# d8.29																								
1887	Phi N	1	4	0	0	0	0	0	0	1	0	0	.000	.200	.000	-38	-1	0	.500	-1	0	0	/O(LF)	-0.1
	†StL AA	2	8	2	1	0	0	0	1	0	0		.125	.125	.125	-27	-1	2	1.000	1	178	280	/2O(RF)	-0.1
1888	†StL AA	123	499	66	97	10	5	4	63	20	3		.194	.230	.259	51	-30	36	.891	5	163	115	*O-122(0-112-10)/3-2,S2	-2.7
1889	NY N	5	20	1	2	0	1	0	2	2	0	0	.100	.182	.200	7	-3	0	1.000	-1	0	0	/O-5(0-1-4)	-0.3
1890	Roc AA	**133**	584	83	152	11	11	3	58	27	1		.260	.294	.332	91	-10	47	.921	10	113	79	*O-132(130-0-2)/3-2,CP	-0.2
1892	NY N	96	411	67	98	5	2	0	53	33	1	29	.238	.297	.260	70	-15	25	.910	-3	99	28	O-96(10-86-0)	-2.3
1893	NY N	47	187	27	51	5	2	0	21	14	0	6	.273	.323	.321	71	-8	10	.917	-1	104	166	O-47(1-46-0)	-1.0
Total	6	407	1713	246	401	31	21	7	198	97	5	35	.234	.277	.289	69	-68	120	.908	11	122	87	O-404(142-245-17)/3-4,2-2,PCS	-6.7
LYONS, PAT Patrick Jerry B 3.1860 , , CAN D 1.20.1914 Springfield, OH TR d7.21																								
1890	Cle N	11	38	2	2	1	0	0	1	4	0	4	.053	.143	.079	-36	-7	0	.839	-5	84	44	2-11	-1.0
LYONS, STEVE Stephen John B 6.3.1960 Tacoma, WA BL/TR 6-3/195# d4.15 OF Total (59-LF 237-CF 43-RF)																								
1985	Bos A	133	371	52	98	14	3	5	30	32-0	1	64	.264	.322	.358	83	-8	12-9	.973	-6	96	64	*O-114(2-111-2)/3SD	-1.6
1986	Bos A	59	124	20	31	7	2	1	14	12-2	0	23	.250	.312	.363	84	-3	2-3	.972	2	106	158	O-55(CF)	-0.2
	Chi A	42	123	10	25	2	1	0	6	7-0	1	24	.203	.248	.236	33	-12	2-3	.987	1	105	96	O-35(22-6-7)/3-3,1D	-1.3
	Year	101	247	30	56	9	3	1	20	19-2	1	47	.227	.280	.300	58	-15	4-6	.978	2	106	129	O-90(22-61-7)/3-3,1D	-1.5
1987	Chi A	76	193	26	54	11	1	1	19	12-0	0	37	.280	.320	.363	79	-6	3-1	.971	7	114	132	3-51,O-15(6-8-2)/2D	0.0
1988	Chi A	146	472	59	127	28	3	5	45	32-1	1	59	.269	.313	.373	93	-5	1-2	.927	8	113	**190**	*3-128,O-14(0-8-6)/2-4,C-2,1	0.3
1989	Chi A	140	443	51	117	21	3	2	50	35-3	1	68	.264	.317	.339	88	-7	9-6	.982	2	101	109	2-70,1-40,3-28,O-20(10-1-9)/S-3,CD	-0.6
1990	Chi A	94	146	22	28	6	1	1	11	10-1	1	41	.192	.245	.267	45	-11	1-0	.991	0	105	123	1-61,2-15/O-7(2-3-3),3-5,SDP	-1.3
1991	Bos A	87	212	15	51	10	1	4	17	11-2	0	35	.241	.277	.354	70	-9	10-3	1.000	2	106	0	O-45(8-36-3),2-16,3-12/1-2,SDP	-0.6
1992	Atl N	11	14	0	1	0	1	0	1	0-0	0	4	.071	.071	.214	-21	-2	0-0	1.000	0	86	0	/O-6(2-0-4),2-2	-0.3
	Mon N	16	13	2	3	0	0	0	1	1-0	0	3	.231	.286	.231	48	-1	1-2	1.000	0	76	0	/O-8(7-1-0),1	-0.1
	Year	27	27	2	4	0	1	0	2	1-0	0	7	.148	.179	.222	13	-3	1-2	1.000	-0	81	0	O-14(9-1-4)/2-2,1	-0.4
	Bos A	21	28	3	7	0	1	0	2	2-0	0	1	.250	.300	.321	69	-1	0-1	1.000	1	140	67	/1-8,O-5(0-2-3),2D	-0.1
1993	Bos A	28	23	4	3	1	0	0	0	2-0	0	5	.130	.200	.174	1	-3	1-2	1.000	1	85	0	O-10(0-6-4)/2-9,C13D	-0.3
Total	9	853	2162	264	545	100	17	19	196	156-9	5	364	.252	.301	.340	77	-68	42-32	.979	17	102	81	O-334C,3-229,2-118,1-115/DSCP	-6.1
LYONS, TERRY Terence Hilbert B 12.14.1908 New Holland, OH D 9.9.1959 Dayton, OH BR/TR 6-0.5/165# d4.19																								
1929	Phi N	1	0	0	0	0	0	0	0	0	0	0	—	—	—	—	0	0	—	0	0	0	/1	0.0
LYONS, BILL William Allen B 4.26.1958 Alton, IL BR/TR 6-1/175# d7.20																								
1983	StL N	42	60	3	10	1	1	0	3	1-0	0	11	.167	.180	.217	10	-8	3-2	.985	-2	107	90	2-23/3-8,S-2	-1.0
1984	StL N	46	73	13	16	3	0	0	3	9-1	0	13	.219	.305	.260	62	-3	3-1	.991	6	110	163	2-25,S-11/3-3	0.4

Year	Tm Lg	G	AB	R	H	2B	3B	HR	RBI	BB-IB	HP	SO	AVG	OBP	SLG	AOPS	ABR	SB-CS	FA	FR	Rng	Thr	G at Pos	BFW
Total	2	88	133	16	26	4	1	0	6	10-1	0	24	.195	.252	.241	39	-11	6-3	.989	4	109	134	/2-48,S-13,3-11	-0.6
LYTLE, DAD Edward Benson "Pop" B 3.10.1862 Racine, WI D 12.21.1950 Long Beach, CA BR/TR 5-11/160# d8.11																								
1890	Chi N	1	4	1	0	0	0	0	0	0	0	1	.000	.000	.000	-96	-1	0	1.000	1	370	0	/O(RF)	0.0
	Pit N	15	55	2	8	1	0	0	0	8	0	9	.145	.254	.164	25	-5	0	.837	-5	89	0	/2-8,O-7(0-4-3)	-0.8
	Year	16	59	3	8	1	0	0	0	8	0	10	.136	.239	.153	16	-6	0	.824	-4	80	0	/O-8(0-4-4),2-8	-0.8
LYTTLE, JIM James Lawrence B 5.20.1946 Hamilton, OH BL/TR 6/186# d5.17																								
1969	NY A	28	83	7	15	4	0	0	4	4-0	0	19	.181	.218	.229	26	-8	1-2	.983	1	98	196	O-28(CF)	-0.9
1970	NY A	87	126	20	39	7	1	3	14	10-1	0	26	.310	.355	.452	129	5	3-6	.989	1	109	72	O-70(2-4-64)	0.2
1971	NY A	49	86	7	17	5	0	1	7	8-2	1	18	.198	.271	.291	64	-4	0-2	1.000	-0	100	65	O-29(3-6-20)	-0.7
1972	Chi A	44	82	8	19	5	2	0	5	1-0	0	28	.232	.241	.341	70	-3	0-1	1.000	-1	87	93	O-21(0-16-5)	-0.6
1973	Mon N	49	116	12	30	5	1	4	19	9-2	0	14	.259	.305	.422	98	-1	0-2	.974	4	104	164	O-36(29-7-0)	0.1
1974	Mon N	25	9	1	3	0	0	0	2	1-1	0	3	.333	.364	.333	101	0	0-0	1.000	1	88	433	O-18(14-5-0)	0.0
1975	Mon N	44	55	7	15	4	0	0	6	13-3	0	6	.273	.406	.345	107	2	0-1	1.000	-1	66	144	O-16(5-8-3)	0.0
1976	Mon N	42	85	6	23	4	1	1	8	7-1	0	13	.271	.326	.376	95	-1	0-0	.977	2	101	199	O-29(12-0-20)	0.0
	LA N	23	68	3	15	3	0	0	5	8-4	0	12	.221	.303	.265	63	-3	0-1	1.000	4	104	441	O-18(1-17-1)	0.0
	Year	65	153	9	38	7	1	1	13	15-5	0	25	.248	.315	.327	81	-4	0-1	.990	6	102	313	O-47(13-17-21)	0.0
Total	8	391	710	71	176	37	5	9	70	61-14	1	139	.248	.305	.352	86	-13	4-15	.988	8	100	164	O-265(66-91-113)	-1.9
MAAS, KEVIN Kevin Christian B 1.20.1965 Castro Valley, CA BL/TL 6-3/209# d6.29																								
1990	NY A	79	254	42	64	9	0	21	41	43-10	3	76	.252	.367	.535	149	17	1-2	.983	-2	95	92	1-57,D-18	1.0
1991	NY A	148	500	69	110	14	1	23	63	83-3	4	128	.220	.333	.390	100	1	5-1	.983	-1	92	71	*D-109,1-36	-0.6
1992	NY A	98	286	35	71	12	0	11	35	25-4	0	63	.248	.305	.406	99	-1	3-1	.986	-3	37	83	D-62,1-22	-0.7
1993	NY A	59	151	20	31	4	0	9	25	24-2	1	32	.205	.316	.411	97	-1	1-1	.984	-1	70	144	D-31,1-17	-0.5
1995	Min A	22	57	5	11	4	0	1	5	7-2	0	11	.193	.281	.316	55	-4	0-0	.936	-2	25	82	D-12/1-8	-0.7
Total	5	406	1248	171	287	43	1	65	169	182-21	8	310	.230	.329	.422	107	12	10-5	.982	-9	82	89	D-232,1-140	-1.5
MABRY, JOHN John Steven B 10.17.1970 Wilmington, DE BL/TR 6-4/195# d4.23 OF Total (122-LF 10-CF 305-RF)																								
1994	StL N	6	23	2	7	3	0	0	3	2-0	0	4	.304	.360	.435	108	0	0-0	1.000	1	145	0	/O-6(RF)	0.1
1995	StL N	129	388	35	119	21	1	5	41	24-5	2	45	.307	.347	.405	99	-1	0-3	.994	5	118	124	1-73,O-39(11-0-29)	-0.4
1996	†StL N	151	543	63	161	30	2	13	74	37-11	3	84	.297	.342	.431	104	3	3-2	.994	-10	78	103	*1-146,O-14(1-0-13)	-2.0
1997	StL N	116	388	40	110	19	0	5	36	39-9	3	77	.284	.352	.371	91	-4	0-1	1.000	-3	86	165	O-78(4-6-71),1-49/3	-1.4
1998	StL N	142	377	41	94	22	0	9	46	30-6	1	76	.249	.305	.379	80	-11	0-2	.971	-5	98	205	O-80(46-0-37),3-38,1-16	-2.0
1999	Sea A	87	262	34	64	14	0	9	33	20-1	0	60	.244	.297	.401	78	-10	2-1	.989	5	113	251	O-43(7-2-35),3-24,1-20/D	-0.7
2000	Sea A	48	103	18	25	5	0	1	7	10-0	2	31	.243	.322	.320	65	-5	0-1	.862	-5	71	122	3-22,O-19(7-0-12)/1-3,PD	-1.0
	SD N	48	123	17	28	8	0	7	25	5-0	0	38	.228	.256	.463	83	-4	0-0	.980	-1	94	60	O-32(2-0-30)/1-2	-0.6
2001	StL N	5	7	0	0	0	0	0	0	0-0	0	2	.000	.000	.000	-99	-2	0-0	1.000	-0	0	192	/1-2,O-2(RF)	-0.3
	Fla N	82	147	14	32	7	0	6	20	13-1	5	44	.218	.299	.388	80	-5	1-0	.958	-2	82	111	O-39(3-2-34)/1PD	-0.8
	Year	87	154	14	32	7	0	6	20	13-1	5	46	.208	.287	.370	72	-7	1-0	.958	-2	80	109	O-41(3-2-36)/1-3,PD	-1.1
2002	Phi N	21	21	1	6	0	0	0	3	1-1	0	5	.286	.304	.286	67	-1	0-0	1.000	0	194	0	/1O(RF)	-0.1
	†Oak A	89	193	27	53	13	1	11	40	14-1	1	37	.275	.322	.523	121	5	1-1	.978	2	106	40	O-53(33-0-21),1-50	0.3
2003	Sea A	64	104	12	22	6	0	3	16	15-2	3	21	.212	.328	.356	83	-2	0-0	.957	1	86	140	O-22(8-0-14),D-12/1-9	-0.3
Total	10	988	2679	304	721	148	4	69	344	210-37	20	524	.269	.325	.405	91	-37	7-11	.984	-12	96	144	O-428R,1-372/3-85,D-19,P-2	-9.2
MacDONALD, HARVEY Harvey Forsyth B 5.18.1898 New York, NY D 10.4.1965 Manoa, PA BL/TL 5-11/170# d6.12																								
1928	Phi N	13	16	0	4	0	0	0	2	2	0	3	.250	.333	.250	53	-1	0	1.000	-0	94	0	/O-2(RF)	-0.1
MACEY B Columbus, OH d10.2																								
1890	Phi AA	1	1	0	0	0	0	0	0	0	0		.000	.000	.000	-99	0	0	1.000	-1	*56*	*0*	/C	-0.1
MACFARLANE, MIKE Michael Andrew B 4.12.1964 Stockton, CA BR/TR 6-1/205# d7.23																								
1987	KC A	8	19	0	4	1	0	0	3	2-0	0	2	.211	.286	.263	46	-1	0-0	1.000	-1	120	184	/C-8	-0.2
1988	KC A	70	211	25	56	15	0	4	26	21-2	1	37	.265	.332	.393	102	1	0-0	.994	-12	90	75	C-68	-0.8
1989	KC A	69	157	13	35	6	0	2	19	7-0	2	27	.223	.263	.299	59	-9	0-0	.996	5	153	98	C-59/D-4	-0.2
1990	KC A	124	400	37	102	24	4	6	58	25-2	7	69	.255	.306	.380	94	-4	1-0	.991	-12	100	40	*C-112/D-5	-1.0
1991	KC A	84	267	34	74	18	2	13	41	17-0	6	52	.277	.330	.506	128	9	1-0	.993	-0	197	80	C-69/D-4	1.3
1992	KC A	129	402	51	94	28	3	17	48	30-2	**15**	89	.234	.310	.445	107	3	1-5	.993	3	102	78	*C-104,D-13	1.0
1993	KC A	117	388	55	106	27	0	20	67	40-2	16	83	.273	.360	.497	122	13	2-5	.985	12	101	**136**	*C-114	2.9
1994	KC A	92	314	53	80	17	3	14	47	35-1	**18**	71	.255	.359	.462	106	3	1-0	.993	6	80	82	C-81/D-8	1.3
1995	†Bos A	115	364	45	82	18	1	15	51	38-0	14	78	.225	.319	.404	85	-9	2-1	.993	2	125	99	*C-111/D-3	0.1
1996	KC A	112	379	58	104	24	2	19	54	31-5	7	57	.274	.339	.499	109	4	3-3	.993	-1	144	100	C-99/D-9	0.8
1997	KC A	82	257	34	61	14	2	8	35	24-3	6	47	.237	.316	.401	84	-6	0-2	.991	-7	192	46	C-81	-0.9
1998	KC A	3	11	1	1	0	0	0	0	0-0	0	2	.091	.091	.091	-51	-2	0-0	1.000	0	201	214	/C-3	-0.2
	Oak A	78	207	28	52	12	0	7	34	12-0	4	34	.251	.301	.411	86	-5	1-0	.989	4	119	72	C-70	0.3
	Year	81	218	29	53	12	0	7	34	12-0	4	36	.243	.291	.394	79	-7	1-0	.990	4	123	79	C-73	0.1
1999	Oak A	81	226	24	55	17	0	4	31	13-0	1	52	.243	.282	.372	69	-11	0-0	.997	2	110	129	C-79/D	-0.4
Total	13	1164	3602	458	906	221	17	129	514	295-17	97	700	.252	.322	.430	98	-14	12-16	.992	-0	123	87	*C-1058/D-47	4.0
MacGAMWELL, ED Edward M. B 1.10.1879 Buffalo, NY D 5.26.1924 Albany, NY BL/TL d4.14																								
1905	Bro N	4	16	0	4	0	0	0	0	1	0		.250	.294	.250	68	-1	0	.951	-1	74	0	/1-4	-0.1
MACHA, KEN Kenneth Edward B 9.29.1950 Monroeville, PA BR/TR 6-2/217# d9.14 M1 C13 b-Mike																								
1974	Pit N	5	5	1	3	1	0	0	1	0-0	0	0	.600	.600	.800	300	1	0-0	1.000	0	0	0	/C	0.2
1977	Pit N	35	95	2	26	4	0	0	11	6-0	0	17	.274	.317	.316	68	-4	1-1	.964	-6	73	0	3-17,1-11/O-4(3-0-1)	-1.2
1978	Pit N	29	52	5	11	1	1	0	5	12-1	0	10	.212	.354	.269	75	-1	2-0	.970	-4	65	120	3-21	-0.6
1979	Mon N	25	36	8	10	3	1	0	4	2-1	1	9	.278	.333	.417	104	0	0-0	1.000	1	99	70	3-13/1-2,O-2(RF),C	0.1
1980	Mon N	49	107	10	31	5	1	1	8	11-1	1	17	.290	.361	.383	108	1	0-2	.910	-6	78	73	3-33/1-2,CO(RF)	-0.7
1981	Tor A	37	85	4	17	2	0	0	6	8-0	0	15	.200	.266	.224	41	-6	1-1	.892	-1	108	78	3-19,1-16/CD	-0.9
Total	6	180	380	30	98	16	3	1	35	39-3	2	68	.258	.329	.324	80	-9	4-4	.938	-18	82	70	3-103/1-31,O-7(3-0-4),C-4,D-2	-3.1
MACHA, MIKE Michael William B 2.17.1954 Victoria, TX BR/TR 5-11/180# d4.20 b-Ken																								
1979	Atl N	6	13	2	2	0	0	0	1	1-0	0	5	.154	.214	.154	2	-2	0-0	.769	0	152	0	/3-3	-0.1
1980	Tor A	5	8	0	0	0	0	0	0	0-0	0	1	.000	.000	.000	-96	-2	0-0	.778	1	146	265	/3-2,C	-0.2
Total	2	11	21	2	2	0	0	0	1	1-0	0	6	.095	.136	.095	-33	-4	0-0	.773	1	150	102	/3-5,C	-0.3
MACHADO, ANDERSON Anderson Javier B 1.25.1981 Caracas, Venezuela BB/TR 5-11/165# d9.27																								
2003	Phi N	1	0	0	0	0	0	0	0	0-0	0	0	—	—	—	—	0	1-0	—	0			/R	0.0
MACHADO, ROBERT Robert Alexis B 6.3.1973 Caracas, Venezuela BR/TR 6-1/205# d7.24																								
1996	Chi A	4	6	1	4	1	0	0	2	0-0	0	0	.667	.667	.833	290	2	0-0	1.000	-2	65	176	/C-4	0.0
1997	Chi A	10	15	1	3	0	1	0	2	1-0	0	6	.200	.250	.333	53	-1	0-0	1.000	0	58	237	C-10	-0.1
1998	Chi A	34	111	14	23	6	0	3	15	7-0	0	22	.207	.254	.342	55	-8	0-0	.981	-2	95	113	C-34	-0.7
1999	Mon N	17	22	3	4	1	0	0	0	2-0	0	6	.182	.250	.227	23	-3	0-0	1.000	-0	0	55	C-17	-0.2
2000	Sea A	8	14	2	3	0	0	1	1	1-0	0	4	.214	.267	.429	74	-1	0-0	1.000	2	246	0	/C-8	0.2
2001	Chi N	52	135	13	30	10	0	2	13	7-3	1	26	.222	.266	.341	58	-9	0-0	.997	1	77	125	C-47	-0.5
2002	Chi N	22	58	5	16	4	0	1	5	5-0	0	11	.276	.333	.397	96	-1	0-0	.985	2	92	231	C-21/1	0.3
	Mil N	51	153	14	39	10	1	2	17	12-4	1	30	.255	.310	.373	84	-4	0-0	.987	-1	78	122	C-48/1-2	-0.3
	Year	73	211	19	55	14	1	3	22	17-4	1	41	.261	.316	.379	87	-5	0-0	.987	1	82	151	C-69/1-3	0.0
2003	Bal A	18	49	8	13	1	0	1	3	6-0	0	12	.265	.345	.347	87	-1	0-0	.990	0	62	200	C-18	0.1
Total	8	216	563	61	135	33	2	10	58	41-7	2	117	.240	.293	.359	72	-26	0-0	.990	1	82	137	C-207/1-3	-1.2
MACHEMER, DAVE David Ritchie B 5.24.1951 St.Joseph, MO BR/TR 5-11.5/180# d6.21																								
1978	Cal A	10	22	6	6	1	0	1	2	2-0	0	1	.273	.333	.455	124	1	0-1	1.000	-4	76	0	/2-5,3-3,S	-0.3
1979	Det A	19	26	8	5	1	0	0	2	3-0	0	2	.192	.276	.231	37	-2	0-3	.972	-1	84	111	2-11/O(LF)D	-0.4
Total	2	29	48	14	11	2	0	1	4	5-0	0	3	.229	.302	.333	74	-1	0-4	.978	-5	82	80	/2-16,3-3,DO(LF)S	-0.7

Year	Tm Lg	G	AB	R	H	2B	3B	HR	RBI	BB-IB	HP	SO	AVG	OBP	SLG	AOPS	ABR	SB-CS	FA	FR	Rng	Thr	G at Pos	BFW
MACIAS, JOSE Jose Prado (Salazar) B 1.25.1972 Panama City, Panama BB/TR 5-10/173# d5.12 OF Total (44-LF 96-CF 15-RF)																								
1999	Det A	5	4	2	1	0	0	1	2	0-0	0	1	.250	.250	1.000	198	0	0-0	1.000	1	216	0	/2	0.1
2000	Det A	73	173	25	44	3	5	2	24	18-0	1	24	.254	.328	.364	77	-7	2-0	.976	-2	106	106	2-39,3-26/O-3(0-1-2),SD	-0.6
2001	Det A	137	488	62	131	24	6	8	51	32-0	3	54	.268	.316	.391	89	-9	21-6	.955	12	120	146	3-89,O-29(3-22-4),2-18/D-2	0.7
2002	Det A	33	107	10	25	4	0	0	6	8-0	1	13	.234	.291	.271	55	-7	3-2	.964	-1	129	49	2-17,O-10(0-9-1)/3-8	-0.7
	Mon N	90	231	33	59	17	1	7	33	13-0	1	44	.255	.294	.429	84	-6	5-6	.978	6	111	230	O-49(CF),3-22/2-6,S-4	0.0
2003	Mon N	111	272	31	65	15	2	4	22	11-1	2	45	.239	.273	.353	56	-18	4-3	.977	-0	97	157	O-62(41-15-8),3-25/2-4,D	-1.9
Total	5	449	1275	163	325	63	14	22	138	82-1	8	181	.255	.302	.378	77	-47	35-17	.950	16	112	101	3-170,O-153C/2-85,S-5,D-4	-2.4
MACK, CONNIE Cornelius Alexander "The Tall Tactician" (b Cornelius Alexander McGillicuddy) B12.22.1862 E.Brookfield, MA D2.8.1956 Philadelphia, PA BR/TR 6-1/150# d9.11 M53 HF1937 s-Earle																								
1886	Was N	10	36	4	13	2	1	0	5	0		2	.361	.361	.472	164	3	0	.957	5			C-10	0.7
1887	Was N	82	314	35	63	6	1	0	20	8	3	17	.201	.228	.226	28	-30	26	.906	1			C-76/O-5(2-2-1),2-2	-1.9
1888	Was N	85	300	49	56	5	6	3	29	17	8	18	.187	.249	.273	71	-9	31	.916	10			C-79/O-4(2-0-2),S1	0.6
1889	Was N	98	386	51	113	16	1	0	42	15	8	12	.293	.333	.339	94	-4	26	.891	7			C-45,O-34(1-0-33),1-22	0.4
1890	Buf P	123	503	95	134	15	12	0	53	47	**20**	13	.266	.353	.344	94	-1	16	.925	-22	*81*	*104*	*C-112/O-9(0-1-8),1-5	-1.2
1891	Pit N	75	280	43	60	10	0	0	29	19	9	11	.214	.286	.250	58	-14	4	.926	8	*104*	*97*	C-72/1-3	0.0
1892	Pit N	97	346	39	84	9	4	1	31	21	6	22	.243	.298	.301	81	-9	11	**.951**	23	*113*	*134*	C-92/O-3(1-0-2),1	2.1
1893	Pit N	37	133	22	38	3	1	0	15	10	5	9	.286	.358	.323	83	-3	4	.941	4	*98*	*117*	C-37	0.4
1894	Pit N	70	231	33	57	7	1	1	21	21	4	14	.247	.320	.299	50	-19	8	.948	2	*102*	*96*	C-70,M	-0.8
1895	Pit N	14	49	12	15	2	0	0	4	7	1	1	.306	.404	.347	100	1	1	.962	-2	*88*	*93*	C-12/1M	0.0
1896	Pit N	33	120	9	26	4	1	0	16	5	0	8	.217	.248	.267	37	-11	0	.974	0	112	87	1-28/C-5,M	-0.9
Total	11	724	2698	392	659	79	28	5	265	170	64	127	.244	.305	.300	72	-96	127	.927	35	*64*	*71*	C-610/1-61,O-55(6-3-46),2-2,S	-0.6
MACK, DENNY Dennis Joseph (born Dennis Joseph McGee) B 1851 Easton, PA D 4.10.1888 Wilkes-Barre, PA BR/TR 5-7/164# d5.6 M1 U2 ▲																								
1871	Rok NA	**25**	122	34	30	7	1	0	17	8		7	.246	.292	.320	79	-2	12-0	.936	1	**162**	104	*1-24/P-3,SO(LF)	0.1
1872	Ath NA	**47**	205	68	59	9	1	0	34	**23**		9	.288	.360	.341	116	6	9-5	.948	-1	349	87	1-26,S-21	0.3
1873	Phi NA	48	205	55	60	5	0	0	19	15		9	.293	.341	.317	93	-2	6-2	.938	3	86	109	*1-42/O-5(1-1-3),S-3,2	0.2
1874	Phi NA	56	246	48	51	8	4	0	22	2		3	.207	.214	.272	53	-13	4-0	.900	-4	77	159	*1-56	-1.2
1876	StL N	48	180	32	39	5	0	1	7	11		5	.217	.262	.261	79	-3		.886	-5	89	106	S-41/2-5,O-2(1-1-0)	-0.6
1880	Buf N	17	59	5	12	0	0	0	3	5		7	.203	.266	.203	60	-2		.940	1	99	72	S-16/2	-0.1
1882	Lou AA	72	264	41	48	3	1	0		16			.182	.229	.201	49	-13		.898	2	100	85	S-49,2-24/O-5(1-3-1),M	-0.8
1883	Pit AA	60	224	26	44	5	3	0		13			.196	.241	.246	59	-9		.844	5	112	83	S-38,1-25/2	-0.4
Total	4 NA	176	778	205	200	29	6	0	92	48		28	.257	.300	.310	85	-11	31-7	.000	-2	143	123	1-148/S-25,O-6(2-1-3),P-3,2	-0.6
Total	4	197	727	104	143	13	4	1	10	45		12	.197	.244	.230	60	-27		.886	2	100	89	S-144/2-31,1-25,O-7(2-4-1)	-1.9
MACK, EARLE Earle Thaddeus (born Earle Thaddeus McGillicuddy) B 2.1.1890 Spencer, MA D 2.4.1967 Upper Darby Township, PA BL/TR 5-8/140# d10.5 M2 C27 f-Connie																								
1910	Phi A	1	4	0	2	0	1	0	0	0	0		.500	.500	1.000	372	1	0	1.000	-0	*118*	*105*	/C	0.1
1911	Phi A	2	4	0	0	0	0	0	0	0	0		.000	.000	.000	-99	-1	0	—	-0	0	0	/3-2	-0.1
1914	Phi A	2	8	0	0	0	0	0	1	0	0	0	.000	.000	.000	-99	-2	1	1.000	0	83	0	/1-2	-0.2
Total	3	5	16	0	2	0	1	0	1	0	0	0	.125	.125	.250	11	-2	1	1.000	-0	83	0	/1-2,3-2,C	-0.2
MACK, REDDY Joseph (born Joseph McNamara) B 5.2.1866 , Ireland D 12.30.1916 Newport, KY 5-8/182# d9.16																								
1885	Lou AA	11	41	7	10	1	0	0	5	2	1		.244	.295	.268	79	-1		.885	1	103	193	2-11	0.1
1886	Lou AA	137	483	82	118	23	11	1	56	68	4		.244	.342	.344	109	6	13	.900	6	103	99	*2-137	1.5
1887	Lou AA	128	478	117	147	23	8	1	69	83	5		.308	.415	.395	124	21	22	.912	1	99	91	*2-128	2.1
1888	Lou AA	112	446	77	97	13	5	3	34	52	15		.217	.320	.289	98	2	18	.907	5	103	81	*2-112	1.1
1889	Bal AA	136	519	84	125	24	7	1	87	60	8	69	.241	.329	.320	84	-10	23	.897	-7	93	112	*2-135/O(CF)	-1.0
1890	Bal AA	26	95	14	27	3	5	0	11	10	3		.284	.370	.421	127	3	7	.932	3	109	67	2-26	0.6
Total	6	550	2062	381	524	87	36	6	262	275	36	69	.254	.352	.340	104	21	83	.905	9	100	97	2-549/O(CF)	4.4
MACK, JOE Joseph John (born Joseph John Maciarz) B 1.4.1912 Chicago, IL D 12.19.1998 Atlanta, GA BB/TL 5-11.5/185# d4.17																								
1945	Bos N	66	260	30	60	13	1	3	44	34	0	39	.231	.320	.323	79	-7	1	.991	-0	102	92	1-65	-1.1
MACK, QUINN Quinn David B 9.11.1965 Los Angeles, CA BL/TL 5-10/185# d6.16 b-Shane																								
1994	Sea A	5	21	1	5	3	0	0	2	1-0	0	3	.238	.273	.381	65	-1	2-0	1.000	-0	84	0	/O-4(3-1-0),D	-0.1
MACK, RAY Raymond James (born Raymond James Mlckovsky) B 8.31.1916 Cleveland, OH D 5.7.1969 Bucyrus, OH BR/TR 6/200# d9.9 Mil 1945																								
1938	Cle A	2	6	2	2	0	1	0	2	0	0	1	.333	.333	.667	147	0	0-0	1.000	1	102	0	/2-2	0.1
1939	Cle A	36	112	12	17	4	1	1	6	12	1	19	.152	.240	.232	22	-14	0-2	.976	1	94	131	2-34/3	-1.1
1940	Cle A★	146	530	60	150	21	5	12	69	51	0	77	.283	.346	.409	98	-3	4-2	.965	-5	94	**117**	*2-146	0.2
1941	Cle A	145	500	54	114	22	4	9	44	54	0	69	.228	.303	.342	74	-20	8-4	.970	-2	93	114	*2-145	-1.2
1942	Cle A	143	481	43	108	14	6	2	45	41	2	51	.225	.288	.291	67	-23	9-3	.969	-1	**104**	117	*2-143	-1.4
1943	Cle A	**153**	545	56	120	25	2	7	62	47	2	61	.220	.285	.312	79	-16	8-3	.967	-4	98	116	*2-153	-1.2
1944	Cle A	83	284	24	66	15	3	0	29	28	0	45	.232	.301	.306	77	-9	4-1	.951	2	103	117	2-83	-0.1
1946	Cle A	61	171	13	35	6	2	1	9	23	0	27	.205	.299	.281	67	-8	2-2	.970	-3	93	103	2-61	-0.8
1947	NY A	1	0	0	0	0	0	0	0	0	0	0	—	—	—	—	0	0-0	—	0			R	0.0
	Chi N	21	78	9	17	6	0	2	12	5	1	15	.218	.274	.372	73	-3	0	.965	4	118	92	2-21	0.2
Total	9	791	2707	273	629	113	24	34	278	261	6	365	.232	.301	.330	76	-96	35-17	.966	-7	98	115	2-788/3	-5.3
MACK, SHANE Shane Lee B 12.7.1963 Los Angeles, CA BR/TR 6/190# d5.25 b-Quinn																								
1987	SD N	105	238	28	57	11	3	4	25	18-0	3	47	.239	.299	.361	77	-8	4-6	.982	-1	108	28	O-91(0-90-2)	-1.1
1988	SD N	56	119	13	29	3	0	0	12	14-0	3	21	.244	.336	.269	78	-3	5-1	.983	4	111	214	O-55(9-46-6)	0.2
1990	Min A	125	313	50	102	10	4	8	44	29-1	5	69	.326	.392	.460	129	12	13-4	.988	8	114	145	*O-109(23-43-51)/D-4	2.0
1991	†Min A	143	442	79	137	27	8	18	74	34-1	6	79	.310	.363	.529	139	22	13-9	.977	3	110	76	*O-140(48-36-81)/D	2.1
1992	Min A	156	600	101	189	31	6	16	75	64-1	**15**	106	.315	.394	.467	136	31	26-14	.988	-1	101	88	*O-155(150-9-4)	2.6
1993	Min A	128	503	66	139	30	4	10	61	41-1	4	76	.276	.335	.412	99	-1	15-5	.986	9	114	107	*O-128(64-67-2)	0.8
1994	Min A	81	303	55	101	21	2	15	61	32-1	6	51	.333	.402	.564	147	22	4-1	.990	4	120	39	O-75(66-24-0)/D-4	2.2
1997	Bos A	60	130	13	41	7	0	3	17	9-1	3	24	.315	.368	.438	109	2	2-1	1.000	-5	83	0	O-45(3-43-0)/D-5	-0.2
1998	Oak A	3	2	1	0	0	0	0	0	0-0	0	0	.000	.000	.000	-99	-1	0-0	—	0			/H	-0.1
	KC A	66	207	30	58	15	1	6	29	15-0	6	36	.280	.345	.449	102	1	8-2	.982	-2	91	54	O-32(30-0-3),D-21	-0.2
	Year	69	209	31	58	15	1	6	29	15-0	6	36	.278	.342	.445	101	0	8-2	.982	-2	91	54	O-32(30-0-3),D-21	-0.3
Total	9	923	2857	436	853	155	28	80	398	256-6	51	509	.299	.364	.456	120	77	90-43	.985	19	108	87	O-830(393-358-149)/D-35	8.3
MACKANIN, PETE Peter B 8.1.1951 Chicago, IL BR/TR 6-2/190# d7.3 C5 OF Total (4-LF 1-RF)																								
1973	Tex A	44	90	3	9	2	0	0	2	4-0	1	26	.100	.146	.122	-24	-15	0-0	.947	-5	95	75	S-33,3-10	-1.7
1974	Tex A	2	6	0	1	0	1	0	0	0-0	0	2	.167	.167	.500	88	0	0-0	1.000	2	151	293	/S-2	0.2
1975	Mon N	130	448	59	101	19	6	12	44	31-4	2	99	.225	.276	.375	77	-16	11-5	.966	14	111	115	*2-127/S3	0.7
1976	Mon N	114	380	36	85	15	2	8	33	15-1	2	66	.224	.256	.337	65	-19	6-2	.965	3	105	90	*2-100/3-8,S-3,O(LF)	-1.0
1977	Mon N	55	85	9	19	2	2	1	6	4-1	0	17	.224	.258	.329	58	-6	3-1	1.000	2	89	96	/2-9,S-8,3-5,O-4(3-0-1)	-0.2
1978	Phi N	5	8	0	2	0	0	0	1	0-0	0	4	.250	.250	.250	40	-1	0-0	1.000	0	190	0	/13	0.0
1979	Phi N	13	9	2	1	0	0	1	2	1-0	0	2	.111	.200	.444	69	-1	0-0	1.000	2	231	0	/2-2,S-2,3-2	0.1
1980	Min A	108	319	31	85	18	0	4	35	14-2	0	34	.266	.296	.361	74	-12	6-2	.968	5	108	111	2-71,S-30/1-4,3-3,D-5	0.0
1981	Min A	77	225	21	52	7	1	4	18	7-2	1	40	.231	.256	.324	63	-12	1-2	.980	-5	110	80	2-31,S-28,1-10/3-4,D-6	-1.5
Total	9	548	1570	161	355	63	12	30	141	76-10	6	290	.226	.263	.339	65	-82	27-12	.968	19	108	103	2-340,S-107/3-34,1-15,D-11,O-5L	-3.4
MacKENZIE, ERIC Eric Hugh B 8.29.1932 Glendon, AL, CAN BL/TR 6/185# d4.23																								
1955	KC A	1	1	0	0	0	0	0	0	0-0	0	0	.000	.000	.000	-99	0	0-0	—	0	*0*	*0*	/C	0.0
MacKENZIE, GORDON Henry Gordon B 7.9.1937 St.Petersburg, FL BR/TR 5-11/175# d8.13 C7																								
1961	KC A	11	24	1	3	0	0	0	1	1-0	0	6	.125	.160	.125	-22	-4	0-0	1.000	0	*86*	*104*	/C-7	-0.4
MACKIEWICZ, FELIX Felix Thaddeus B 11.20.1917 Chicago, IL D 12.20.1993 Olivette, MO BR/TR 6-2/195# d9.7																								
1941	Phi A	5	14	3	4	0	1	0	0	1	0	0	.286	.333	.429	103	0	0-0	1.000	-0	86	0	/O-3(0-1-2)	-0.1
1942	Phi A	6	14	3	3	2	0	0	2	0	0	4	.214	.214	.357	59	-1	0-0	1.000	1	94	526	/O-3(0-2-1)	0.0
1943	Phi A	9	16	1	1	0	0	0	0	2	0	8	.063	.167	.063	-32	-3	0-0	1.000	0	123	0	/O-3(0-2-1)	-0.3
1945	Cle A	120	359	42	98	14	7	2	37	44	2	41	.273	.356	.368	115	7	5-5	.987	7	109	131	*O-112(CF)	1.2
1946	Cle A	78	258	35	67	15	4	0	16	16	1	32	.260	.305	.349	88	-5	5-1	.983	-0	105	48	O-72(0-71-1)	-0.7

Year	Tm Lg	G	AB	R	H	2B	3B	HR	RBI	BB-IB	HP	SO	AVG	OBP	SLG	AOPS	ABR	SB-CS	FA	FR	Rng	Thr	G at Pos	BFW
1947	Cle A	2	5	0	0	0	0	0	0	0	0	2	.000	.000	.000	-99	-1	0-0	1.000	0	119	0	/O-2(CF)	-0.1
	Was A	3	6	1	1	1	0	0	0	0	0	1	.167	.167	.333	38	-1	0-0	1.000	-0	85	0	/O-3(CF)	-0.1
	Year	5	11	1	1	1	0	0	0	0	0	3	.091	.091	.182	-26	-2	0-0	1.000	-0	103	0	/O-5(CF)	-0.2
Total	6	223	672	85	174	32	12	2	55	63	3	88	.259	.325	.351	97	-4	10-6	.986	7	107	100	O-198(0-193-5)	-0.1
MACKO, STEVE Steven Joseph B 9.6.1954 Burlington, IA D 11.15.1981 Arlington, TX BL/TR 5-10/160# d8.18																								
1979	Chi N	19	40	2	9	1	0	0	3	4-0	0	8	.225	.295	.250	46	-3	0-0	1.000	3	93	80	2-10/3-4	0.0
1980	Chi N	6	20	2	6	2	0	0	2	0-0	0	3	.300	.300	.400	87	0	0-0	1.000	1	149	227	/S-3,3-2,2	0.1
Total	2	25	60	4	15	3	0	0	5	4-0	0	11	.250	.297	.300	59	-3	0-0	1.000	4	85	70	/2-11,3-6,S-3	0.1
MACKOWIAK, ROB Robert William B 6.20.1976 Oak Lawn, IL BL/TR 5-10/168# d5.19																								
2001	Pit N	83	214	30	57	15	2	4	21	15-5	3	52	.266	.319	.411	86	-4	4-3	.986	2	94	121	O-46(10-0-40),2-21/3-2,1	-0.3
2002	Pit N	136	385	57	94	22	0	16	48	42-5	7	120	.244	.328	.426	100	-2	9-3	.988	1	86	139	*O-106(2-42-76),3-26/2-3	-0.3
2003	Pit N	77	174	20	47	4	4	6	19	15-2	4	53	.270	.342	.443	101	0	6-0	1.000	-4	93	0	O-30(8-8-14),3-19,2-15	-0.3
Total	3	296	773	107	198	41	6	26	88	72-12	14	225	.256	.329	.426	96	-6	19-6	.989	-2	89	118	O-182(20-50-130)/3-47,2-39,1	-0.9
MACLIN, LONNIE Lonnie Lee B 2.17.1967 Clayton, MO BL/TL 5-11/185# d9.7																								
1993	StL N	12	13	2	1	0	0	0	1	0-0	0	5	.077	.071	.077	-60	-3	1-0	1.000	-1	64	0	/O-5(LF)	-0.3
MACON, MAX Max Cullen B 10.14.1915 Pensacola, FL D 8.5.1989 Jupiter, FL BL/TL 6-3/175# d4.21 Mil 1945-46 ▲																								
1938	StL N	46	36	5	11	0	0	0	3	2	0	4	.306	.342	.306	75	-1	0	.946	1	123	120	P-38/O(RF)	0.0
1940	Bro N	2	1	0	1	0	0	0	0	0	0	0	1.000	1.000	1.000	427	0	0	—	-0	0	0	/P-2	0.0
1942	Bro N	26	43	4	12	2	1	0	1	2	0	4	.279	.311	.372	98	3	1	.960	-0	83	0	P-14	0.0
1943	Bro N	45	55	7	9	0	0	0	6	0	0	1	.164	.164	.164	-5	-8	1	1.000	0	121	174	P-25/1-3	-0.1
1944	Bos N	106	366	38	100	15	3	3	36	12	0	23	.273	.296	.355	79	-11	7	.977	-2	106	115	1-72,O-22(21-2-0)/P	-1.8
1947	Bos N	1	1	0	0	0	0	0	0	0	0	0	.000	.000	.000	-99	0	0	1.000	0	267	0	/P	0.0
Total	6	226	502	54	133	17	4	3	46	16	0	32	.265	.288	.333	72	-17	9	.965	-1	112	97	/P-81,1-75,O-23(21-2-1)	-1.9
MacPHEE, WADDY Walter Scott B 12.23.1899 Brooklyn, NY D 1.20.1980 Charlotte, NC BR/TR 5-8/140# d9.27																								
1922	NY N	2	7	2	2	0	1	0	0	1	0	0	.286	.375	.571	140	0	0-0	.889	0	116	0	/3-2	0.1
MACULLAR, JIMMY James F. "Little Mac" B 1.16.1855 Boston, MA D 4.8.1924 Baltimore, MD BR/TL 5-6/155# d5.5 M1 U1																								
1879	Syr N	64	246	24	52	9	0	0	13	3		27	.211	.221	.248	61	-9		.865	-4	93	100	S-37,O-26(CF)/2-4,3M	-1.2
1882	Cin AA	79	299	44	70	6	6	0	22	14			.234	.268	.294	85	-5		.922	-4	68	122	*O-79(CF)	-1.1
1883	Cin AA	14	48	4	8	2	0	0	4	4			.167	.231	.208	40	-3		.900	-2	53	0	O-14(2-6-7)/S	-0.4
1884	Bal AA	107	360	73	73	16	6	4		36	8		.203	.290	.314	93	-1		.866	-2	93	87	*S-107	0.0
1885	Bal AA	100	320	52	61	7	6	3	26	49	4		.191	.306	.278	87	-2		.877	-0	94	90	*S-98/O-2(RF),P	0.1
1886	Bal AA	85	268	49	55	7	1	0	26	49	2		.205	.332	.239	82	-2	23	.852	-8	81	81	S-82/O-2(CF),2P	-0.6
Total	6	449	1541	246	319	47	19	7	91	155	14	27	.207	.285	.276	83	-22	23	.865	-19	90	88	S-325,O-123(2-113-9)/2-5,P-2,3	-3.2
MADDEN, GENE Eugene B 6.5.1890 Elm Grove, WV D 4.6.1949 Utica, NY BL/TR 5-10/155# d4.20																								
1916	Pit N	1	1	0	0	0	0	0	0	0	0	0	.000	.000	.000	-99	0	0	—	0			H	0.0
MADDEN, FRANK Francis A. "Red" B 10.17.1892 Pittsburgh, PA D 4.30.1952 Pittsburgh, PA d7.4																								
1914	Pit F	2	2	0	1	0	0	0	1	0	0	0	.500	.500	.500	174	0	0	—	-0	*0*	*0*	/C	0.0
MADDEN, BUNNY Thomas Francis B 9.14.1882 Boston, MA D 1.20.1954 Cambridge, MA BR/TR 5-10/190# d6.3																								
1909	Bos A	10	17	0	4	0	0	0	1	0	0		.235	.235	.235	48	-1	0	.941	1	*141*	*86*	/C-7	0.0
1910	Bos A	14	35	4	13	3	0	0	4	3	1		.371	.436	.457	175	3	0	.938	-3	*102*	*65*	C-12	0.2
1911	Bos A	4	15	2	3	0	0	0	2	2	0		.200	.294	.200	39	-1	0	1.000	-1	*82*	*50*	/C-4	-0.2
	Phi N	28	76	4	21	1	1	0	4	0	0	13	.276	.276	.316	65	-4	0	.924	-1	*94*	*110*	C-22	-0.3
Total	3	56	143	10	41	4	1	0	11	5	1	13	.287	.315	.329	87	-3	0	.935	-4	*101*	*90*	/C-45	-0.3
MADDEN, TOMMY Thomas Joseph B 7.31.1883 Philadelphia, PA D 7.26.1930 Philadelphia, PA BL/TL 5-11/160# d9.10																								
1906	Bos N	4	15	1	4	0	0	0	0	1	0		.267	.313	.267	83	0	0	1.000	0	243	0	/O-4(LF)	-0.1
1910	NY A	1	1	0	0	0	0	0	0	0	0		.000	.000	.000	-95	0	0	—	0			H	0.0
Total	2	5	16	1	4	0	0	0	0	1	0		.250	.294	.250	71	0	0	1.000	0	243	0	/O-4(LF)	-0.1
MADDERN, CLARENCE Clarence James B 9.26.1921 Bisbee, AZ D 8.9.1986 Tucson, AZ BR/TR 6-1/185# d9.19																								
1946	Chi N	3	3	0	0	0	0	0	0	0	1	0	.000	.250	.000	-27	0	0	1.000	0	149	0	/O-2(LF)	0.0
1948	Chi N	80	214	16	54	12	1	4	27	10	5	25	.252	.301	.374	85	-5	0	.981	1	95	154	O-55(48-0-10)	-0.8
1949	Chi N	10	9	1	3	0	0	1	2	2	0	0	.333	.455	.667	202	1	0	1.000	0	352	0	/1	0.2
1951	Cle A	11	12	0	2	0	0	0	0	0	0	1	.167	.167	.167	-10	-2	0-0	.667	-0	86	0	/O(LF)	-0.2
Total	4	104	238	17	59	12	1	5	29	12	6	26	.248	.301	.370	84	-6	0-0	.973	1	96	147	/O-58(51-0-10),1	-0.8
MADDOX, ELLIOTT Elliott B 12.21.1947 East Orange, NJ BR/TR 5-11/181# d4.7 OF Total (77-LF 472-CF 189-RF)																								
1970	Det A	109	258	30	64	13	4	3	24	30-1	3	42	.248	.332	.364	92	-3	2-3	.919	3	103	101	3-40,O-37(28-1-9),S-19/2	-0.1
1971	Was A	128	258	38	56	8	2	1	18	51-3	0	42	.217	.344	.275	83	-4	10-4	.990	8	116	154	*O-103(12-84-10),3-12	0.3
1972	Tex A	98	294	40	74	7	2	0	10	49-4	2	53	.252	.361	.289	100	3	20-10	.990	3	102	126	O-94(11-70-14)	0.4
1973	Tex A	100	172	24	41	1	0	1	17	29-2	3	28	.238	.356	.262	80	-3	5-4	.981	5	107	176	O-89(22-58-11)/3-7,D	0.0
1974	NY A	137	466	75	141	26	2	3	45	69-4	4	48	.303	.395	.386	128	22	6-5	.986	9	103	**202**	*O-135(1-112-25)/2-2,3	2.8
1975	NY A	55	218	36	67	10	3	1	23	21-0	7	24	.307	.382	.394	123	8	9-3	1.000	4	110	131	O-55(CF)/2	1.1
1976	†NY A	18	46	4	10	2	0	0	3	4-1	0	3	.217	.275	.261	60	-2	0-1	1.000	0	80	248	O-13(0-6-7)/D-2	-0.3
1977	Bal A	49	107	14	28	7	0	2	9	13-0	4	9	.262	.357	.383	110	2	2-2	.990	1	119	0	O-45(1-44-0)/3	0.3
1978	NY N	119	389	43	100	18	2	2	39	71-1	2	38	.257	.370	.329	102	5	2-11	.988	4	115	152	O-79(0-13-72),3-43/1	0.3
1979	NY N	86	224	21	60	13	0	1	12	20-0	3	27	.268	.335	.339	88	-3	3-2	.985	4	116	126	O-65(2-26-40),3-11	-0.1
1980	NY N	130	411	35	101	16	1	4	34	52-5	**6**	44	.246	.336	.319	87	-5	1-9	.956	3	96	106	*3-115/O-4(0-3-1),1-2	-0.8
Total	11	1029	2843	360	742	121	16	18	234	409-21	34	358	.261	.358	.334	100	20	60-54	.989	44	109	149	O-719C,3-230/S-19,2-4,1-3,D-3	3.9
MADDOX, GARRY Garry Lee B 9.1.1949 Cincinnati, OH BR/TR 6-3/184# d4.25																								
1972	SF N	125	458	62	122	26	7	12	58	14-3	4	97	.266	.293	.432	103	-1	13-6	.979	-1	101	94	*O-121(20-96-6)	-0.5
1973	SF N	144	587	81	187	30	10	11	76	24-2	6	73	.319	.350	.460	118	13	24-10	.969	-4	107	44	*O-140(CF)	0.7
1974	SF N	135	538	74	153	31	3	8	50	29-3	3	64	.284	.322	.398	97	-3	21-9	.986	-3	105	37	*O-131(CF)	-0.8
1975	SF N	17	52	4	7	1	0	1	4	6-1	1	3	.135	.237	.212	24	-5	1-1	1.000	2	106	346	O-13(CF)	-0.4
	Phi N	99	374	50	109	25	8	4	46	36-5	5	54	.291	.359	.433	115	8	24-3	.983	13	121	169	O-97(CF)	2.3
	Year	116	426	54	116	26	8	5	50	42-6	6	57	.272	.344	.406	104	3	25-4	.985	15	**119**	**192**	*O-110(CF)	1.9
1976	†Phi N	146	531	75	175	37	6	6	68	42-8	4	59	.330	.377	.456	133	24	29-12	.989	14	**123**	114	*O-144(CF)	3.8
1977	†Phi N	139	571	85	167	27	10	14	74	24-8	4	58	.292	.323	.448	101	-1	22-6	.977	3	111	77	*O-138(CF)	0.3
1978	†Phi N	155	598	62	172	34	3	11	68	39-11	2	89	.288	.332	.410	106	4	33-7	.983	6	112	81	*O-154(CF)	1.4
1979	Phi N	148	548	70	154	28	6	13	61	17-5	4	71	.281	.304	.425	95	-6	26-13	.996	17	**123**	130	*O-140(CF)	1.1
1980	†Phi N	143	549	59	142	31	3	11	73	18-5	0	52	.259	.278	.386	80	-16	25-5	.976	1	107	71	*O-143(CF)	-1.3
1981	†Phi N	94	323	37	85	7	1	5	40	17-1	1	42	.263	.295	.337	78	-10	9-4	.977	8	115	139	O-94(CF)	-0.3
1982	Phi N	119	412	39	117	27	2	8	61	12-0	0	32	.284	.303	.417	98	-2	7-5	**.992**	3	104	135	*O-111(CF)	-0.1
1983	†Phi N	97	324	27	89	14	2	4	32	17-5	1	31	.275	.312	.367	89	-6	7-6	.977	-2	105	26	O-95(CF)	-0.9
1984	Phi N	77	241	29	68	11	0	5	19	13-1	0	29	.282	.316	.390	97	-2	3-2	1.000	3	110	93	O-69(CF)	0.0
1985	Phi N	105	218	22	52	8	1	4	23	13-2	1	26	.239	.281	.339	72	-9	4-2	.980	-0	104	88	O-94(CF)	-1.0
1986	Phi N	6	7	1	3	0	0	0	1	2-0	0	1	.429	.556	.429	169	1	0-1	1.000	-1	25	0	/O-3(CF)	0.0
Total	15	1749	6331	777	1802	337	62	117	754	323-60	36	781	.285	.320	.413	100	-11	248-92	.983	59	111	93	*O-1687(20-1660-6)	4.3
MADDOX, JERRY Jerry Glenn B 7.28.1953 Whittier, CA BR/TR 6-2/200# d6.3																								
1978	Atl N	7	14	1	3	0	0	0	1	1-0	0	2	.214	.267	.214	32	-1	0-0	.909	-1	90	0	/3-5	-0.2
MADISON, ART Arthur B 1.14.1871 Clarksburg, MA D 1.27.1933 N.Adams, MA BR/TR 5-9/165# d9.9																								
1895	Phi N	11	34	6	12	3	0	0	8	1	0	1	.353	.371	.441	109	0	4	.955	-1	96	0	/S-6,2-3,3-2	0.0
1899	Pit N	42	118	20	32	2	4	0	19	11	1		.271	.338	.356	91	-2	1	.953	-5	89	71	2-19,S-15/3-2	-0.5
Total	2	53	152	26	44	5	4	0	27	12	1	1	.289	.345	.375	95	-2	5	.926	-6	90	82	/2-22,S-21,3-4	-0.5
MADISON, SCOTTI Charles Scott B 9.12.1959 Pensacola, FL BB/TR 5-11/195# d7.6																								
1985	Det A	6	11	0	0	0	0	0	1	2-0	0	0	.000	.143	.000	-54	-2	0-0	1.000	0	0	0	/CD	-0.2

Year	Tm Lg	G	AB	R	H	2B	3B	HR	RBI	BB-IB	HP	SO	AVG	OBP	SLG	AOPS	ABR	SB-CS	FA	FR	Rng	Thr	G at Pos	BFW
1986	Det A	2	7	0	0	0	0	0	1	0-0	0	3	.000	.000	.000	-99	-2	0-0	.667	-0	51	580	/3D	-0.2
1987	KC A	7	15	4	4	3	0	0	0	1-0	0	5	.267	.313	.467	100	0	0-0	1.000	-2	141	234	/1-4,C-3	-0.2
1988	KC A	16	35	4	6	2	0	0	2	4-0	0	5	.171	.256	.229	37	-3	1-0	1.000	1	0	0	/C-4,O-3(2-0-1),1-2,D-4	-0.2
1989	Cin N	40	98	13	17	7	0	1	7	8-2	1	9	.173	.241	.276	46	-7	0-1	1.000	1	99	81	3-26	-0.6
Total	5	71	166	21	27	12	0	1	11	15-2	1	22	.163	.232	.253	37	-14	1-1	.985	-1	97	103	/3-27,D-8,C-8,1-6,O-3(2-0-1)	-1.4
MADJESKI, ED Edward William (born Edward William Majewski) B 7.20.1908 Far Rockaway, NY D 11.11.1994 Montgomery, OH BR/TR 5-11/178# d5.2																								
1932	Phi A	17	35	4	8	0	0	0	3	3	0	6	.229	.289	.229	35	-3	0-0	1.000	1	_99_	_133_	/C-8	-0.2
1933	Phi A	51	142	17	40	4	0	0	17	4	0	21	.282	.301	.310	62	-8	0-0	.958	-4	_86_	_61_	C-41	-0.9
1934	Phi A	8	8	1	3	1	0	0	2	0	0	1	.375	.375	.500	129	0	0-0	.000	-1	_0_	_0_	/C	0.0
	Chi A	85	281	36	62	14	2	5	32	14	1	31	.221	.260	.338	52	-22	2-0	.973	-3	_64_	_123_	C-79	-1.8
	Year	93	289	37	65	15	2	5	34	14	1	32	.225	.263	.343	54	-21	2-0	.971	-4	_64_	_123_	C-80	-1.8
1937	NY N	5	15	0	3	0	0	0	2	0	0	2	.200	.200	.200	9	-2	0	1.000	-1	_104_	_111_	/C-5	-0.3
Total	4	166	481	58	116	19	2	5	56	21	1	61	.241	.274	.320	53	-35	2-0	.970	-7	_73_	_107_	C-134	-3.2
MADLOCK, BILL Bill B 1.2.1951 Memphis, TN BR/TR 5-11/185# d9.7 C2																								
1973	Tex A	21	77	16	27	5	3	1	5	7-0	1	9	.351	.412	.532	171	7	3-2	.918	-4	79	47	3-21	0.3
1974	Chi N	128	453	65	142	21	5	9	54	42-8	5	39	.313	.374	.442	124	15	11-7	.946	-8	96	55	*3-121	0.6
1975	Chi N★	130	514	77	182	29	7	7	64	42-5	3	34	**.354**	.402	.479	139	27	9-7	.943	-3	102	59	*3-128	2.4
1976	Chi N	142	514	68	174	36	1	15	84	56-15	**11**	27	**.339**	.412	.500	146	34	15-11	.961	-9	93	85	*3-136	2.5
1977	SF N	140	533	70	161	28	1	12	46	43-14	6	33	.302	.360	.426	111	9	13-10	.949	-20	86	77	*3-126/2-6	-1.4
1978	SF N	122	447	76	138	26	3	15	44	48-11	3	39	.309	.378	.481	145	27	16-5	.974	-8	102	78	*2-114/1-3	2.8
1979	SF N	69	249	37	65	9	2	7	41	18-3	0	19	.261	.309	.398	99	-2	11-3	.976	-9	88	78	2-63/1-5	-0.7
	†Pit N	85	311	48	102	17	3	7	44	34-8	1	22	.328	.390	.469	129	14	21-8	.969	-9	89	82	3-85	0.6
	Year	154	560	85	167	26	5	14	85	52-11	1	41	.298	.355	.438	117	13	32-11	.969	-18	89	82	3-85,2-63/1-5	-0.1
1980	Pit N	137	494	62	137	22	4	10	53	45-12	4	33	.277	.341	.399	105	3	16-10	.955	-16	85	99	*3-127,1-12	-1.6
1981	Pit N★	82	279	35	95	23	1	6	45	34-7	3	17	**.341**	.412	.495	153	21	18-6	.956	-0	102	139	3-78	2.3
1982	Pit N	154	568	92	181	33	3	19	95	48-16	4	39	.319	.368	.488	136	27	18-6	.952	-7	93	101	*3-146/1-3	2.0
1983	Pit N★	130	473	68	153	21	0	12	68	49-10	2	24	**.323**	.386	.444	127	19	3-4	.958	-16	82	106	*3-126	0.0
1984	Pit N	103	403	38	102	16	0	4	44	26-5	1	29	.253	.297	.323	75	-14	3-1	.942	-11	85	112	3-98/1	-2.8
1985	Pit N	110	399	49	100	23	1	10	41	39-2	5	42	.251	.323	.388	100	0	3-3	.940	-11	92	58	3-98,1-12	-1.4
	†LA N	34	114	20	41	4	0	2	15	10-0	3	11	.360	.422	.447	149	8	7-1	.948	4	107	165	3-32	1.3
	Year	144	513	69	141	27	1	12	56	49-2	8	53	.275	.345	.402	110	8	10-4	.943	-7	95	82	*3-130,1-12	-0.1
1986	LA N	111	379	38	106	17	0	10	60	30-4	5	43	.280	.336	.404	112	6	3-3	.910	-2	97	48	*3-101/1-2	0.2
1987	LA N	21	61	5	11	1	0	3	7	6-0	1	5	.180	.265	.344	61	-4	0-0	.912	-2	84	86	3-16/1	-0.6
	†Det A	87	326	56	91	17	0	14	50	28-1	10	45	.279	.351	.460	119	9	4-3	.989	-2	78	94	D-64,1-22/3	0.4
Total	15	1806	6594	920	2008	348	34	163	860	605-121	68	510	.305	.365	.442	123	206	174-90	.948	-132	92	86	*3-1440,2-183/D-64,1-61	6.9
MADRID, SAL Salvador B 6.9.1920 ElPaso, TX D 2.24.1977 Ft.Wayne, IN BR/TR 5-9/165# d9.17																								
1947	Chi N	8	24	0	3	1	0	0	1	1	0	6	.125	.160	.167	-14	-4	0	.956	2	118	126	/S-8	-0.1
MAGADAN, DAVE David Joseph B 9.30.1962 Tampa, FL BL/TR 6-3/200# d9.7 C1																								
1986	NY N	10	18	3	8	0	0	0	3	3-0	0	1	.444	.524	.444	175	2	0-0	1.000	1	128	130	/1-9	0.2
1987	NY N	85	192	21	61	13	1	3	24	22-2	0	22	.318	.386	.443	126	8	0-0	.981	5	122	86	3-50,1-13	1.2
1988	†NY N	112	314	39	87	15	0	1	35	60-4	2	39	.277	.393	.334	117	12	0-1	.988	2	93	95	1-71,3-48	1.0
1989	NY N	127	374	47	107	22	3	4	41	49-6	1	37	.286	.367	.393	124	14	1-0	.991	3	117	98	1-87,3-28	1.2
1990	NY N	144	451	74	148	28	6	6	72	74-4	2	55	.328	.417	.457	143	31	2-1	**.998**	4	98	79	*1-113,3-19	2.8
1991	NY N	124	418	58	108	23	0	4	51	83-3	2	50	.258	.378	.342	106	9	1-1	.996	4	105	94	*1-122	0.4
1992	NY N	99	321	33	91	9	1	3	28	56-3	0	44	.283	.390	.346	111	8	1-0	.941	-14	81	70	3-93/1-2	-0.6
1993	Fla N	66	227	22	65	12	0	4	29	44-4	1	30	.286	.400	.392	108	5	0-1	.961	5	105	115	3-63/1-2	1.0
	Sea A	71	228	27	59	11	0	1	21	36-3	0	33	.259	.356	.320	83	-4	2-0	.991	2	78	106	1-41,3-27/D-2	-0.5
1994	Fla N	74	211	30	58	7	0	1	17	39-0	1	25	.275	.386	.322	86	-2	0-0	.958	-4	96	73	3-48,1-16	-0.7
1995	Hou N	127	348	44	109	24	0	2	51	71-9	0	56	.313	.428	.399	129	21	2-1	.922	-8	92	64	*3-100,1-11	1.3
1996	Chi N	78	169	23	43	10	0	3	17	29-3	0	23	.254	.360	.367	91	-1	0-2	.963	-4	96	72	3-51,1-10	-0.5
1997	Oak A	128	271	38	82	10	1	4	30	50-1	2	40	.303	.414	.391	114	9	1-0	.940	4	113	134	3-49,1-30,D-25	0.9
1998	Oak A	35	109	12	35	8	0	1	13	13-1	0	12	.321	.390	.422	115	3	0-1	.918	4	126	195	3-30/1-7	0.6
1999	SD N	116	248	20	68	12	1	2	30	45-2	0	36	.274	.377	.355	97	1	1-3	.969	-2	94	79	3-52,1-42	-0.3
2000	SD N	95	132	13	36	7	0	2	21	32-1	0	23	.273	.410	.371	108	4	0-0	.952	2	93	63	3-29/1-8,S-2,D-2	0.5
2001	SD N	91	128	12	32	7	0	1	12	12-0	1	20	.250	.317	.328	74	-5	0-0	.950	-2	83	74	3-22/1-9,2SD	-0.7
Total	16	1582	4159	516	1197	218	13	42	495	718-46	12	546	.288	.390	.377	112	115	11-11	.951	0	98	92	3-709,1-593/D-31,S-3,2	7.8
MAGALLANES, EVER Everado (Espinoza) B 11.6.1965 Chihuahua, Mexico BL/TR 5-10/165# d5.17																								
1991	Cle A	3	2	0	0	0	0	0	0	1-0	0	1	.000	.333	.000	1	0	0-0	1.000	-0	98	0	/S-2	0.0
MAGEE, LEE Leo Christopher (born Leopold Christopher Hoernschemeyer) B 6.4.1889 Cincinnati, OH D 3.14.1966 Columbus, OH BB/TR 5-11/165# d7.4 M1 OF Total (230-LF 285-CF 8-RF)																								
1911	StL N	26	69	9	18	1	1	0	8	8	0	8	.261	.338	.304	82	-2	4	.975	-2	83	91	2-18/S-3	-0.3
1912	StL N	128	458	60	133	13	8	0	40	39	1	29	.290	.347	.354	94	-4	16	.956	6	104	134	O-85(LF),2-23/1-6,S	-0.2
1913	StL N	137	531	54	142	13	7	2	31	34	2	30	.267	.314	.330	85	-11	23-26	.982	11	104	**134**	*O-108(108-3-1),2-22/1-6,S-2	-1.0
1914	StL N	142	529	59	150	23	4	2	40	42	1	24	.284	.337	.353	107	4	36	.970	1	91	115	*O-102(2-100-0),1-39/2-6	-0.3
1915	Bro F	121	452	87	146	19	10	4	49	22	1	19	.323	.356	.436	123	5	34	.937	1	100	99	*2-115/1-2,M	0.9
1916	NY A	131	510	57	131	18	4	3	45	50	1	31	.257	.324	.325	93	-4	29-25	.975	-1	99	91	*O-128(21-107-0)/2-2	-1.8
1917	NY A	51	173	17	38	4	1	0	8	13	1	18	.220	.278	.254	62	-8	3	.938	-4	84	100	O-50(2-48-0)	-1.7
	StL A	36	112	11	19	1	0	0	4	6	0	6	.170	.212	.179	20	-11	3	.971	6	124	137	3-20/2-6,1-5,O(RF)	-0.5
	Year	87	285	28	57	5	1	0	12	19	1	24	.200	.252	.225	46	-19	6	.938	2	84	99	O-51(2-48-1),3-20/2-6,1-5	-2.2
1918	Cin N	119	459	61	133	22	13	0	28	28	0	19	.290	.331	.394	123	11	19	.956	7	101	**139**	*2-114/3-3	2.2
1919	Bro N	45	181	16	43	7	2	0	7	5	1	8	.238	.262	.298	67	-8	5	.938	-3	104	64	2-36/3-9	-1.1
	Chi N	79	267	36	78	12	4	1	17	18	1	16	.292	.339	.378	115	5	14	.978	-5	85	128	O-45(12-27-6),S-13,3-10/2-7	-0.2
	Year	124	448	52	121	19	6	1	24	23	2	24	.270	.309	.346	95	-3	19	.978	-8	85	128	O-45(12-27-6),2-43,3-19,S-13	-1.3
Total	9	1015	3741	467	1031	133	54	12	277	265	9	208	.276	.325	.350	98	-23	186-51	.969	17	97	116	O-519C,2-349/1-58,3-42,S-19	-4.0
MAGEE, SHERRY Sherwood Robert B 8.6.1884 Clarendon, PA D 3.13.1929 Philadelphia, PA BR/TR 5-11/179# d6.29 U1 OF Total (1601-LF 140-CF 125-RF)																								
1904	Phi N	95	364	51	101	15	12	3	57	14	2		.277	.308	.409	125	8	11	.921	5	165	52	O-94(19-1-74)/1	1.0
1905	Phi N	**155**	603	100	180	24	17	5	98	44	8		.299	.354	.420	135	25	48	.963	10	92	122	*O-155(LF)	2.6
1906	Phi N	**154**	563	77	159	36	8	6	67	52	5		.282	.348	.407	135	23	55	.982	12	95	44	*O-154(LF)	2.9
1907	Phi N	140	503	75	165	28	12	4	**85**	53	4		.328	.396	.455	169	41	46	.978	8	68	154	*O-139(LF)	4.5
1908	Phi N	143	508	79	144	30	16	2	57	49	11		.283	.359	.417	143	25	40	.970	3	85	124	*O-142(LF)	2.3
1909	Phi N	143	522	60	141	33	14	2	66	43	11		.270	.339	.398	128	16	38	.970	-7	54	0	*O-143(LF)	0.1
1910	Phi N	154	519	**110**	172	39	17	6	**123**	94	12	36	**.331**	**.445**	**.507**	**172**	**53**	49	.974	-12	92	47	*O-154(126-23-5)	3.4
1911	Phi N	121	445	79	128	32	5	15	94	49	6	33	.288	.366	.483	135	20	22	**.981**	1	103	81	*O-120(120-0-1)	1.6
1912	Phi N	132	464	79	142	25	9	6	66	55	7	54	.306	.388	.438	118	12	30	.963	-11	96	43	*O-124(LF)/1-6	-0.4
1913	Phi N	138	470	92	144	36	6	11	70	38	9	36	.306	.369	.479	136	22	23-8	.968	-11	92	41	*O-123(106-8-9)/1-4	0.8
1914	Phi N	146	544	96	**171**	**39**	11	15	**103**	55	3	42	.314	.380	**.509**	154	35	25	.940	5	115	39	O-67(LF),S-39,1-32/2-8	4.2
1915	Bos N	156	571	72	160	34	12	2	87	54	7	39	.280	.350	.392	130	22	15-12	.981	7	109	95	*O-135(34-102-0),1-21	2.0
1916	Bos N	122	419	44	101	17	5	3	54	44	6	52	.241	.322	.327	104	3	10	.978	-7	95	45	*O-120(102-3-19)/1-2,S	-1.1
1917	Bos N	72	246	24	63	8	4	1	29	13	3	23	.256	.302	.333	100	-1	7	.954	2	109	89	O-65(63-0-2)/1-2	-0.2
	Cin N	45	137	17	44	8	4	0	23	16	2	7	.321	.400	.438	164	11	4	.989	4	110	141	O-41(29-0-12)/1-2	1.5
	Year	117	383	41	107	16	8	1	52	29	5	30	.279	.338	.371	124	11	11	.967	6	109	109	*O-106(92-0-14)/1-4	1.3
1918	Cin N	115	400	46	119	15	13	2	**76**	37	9	18	.298	.370	.415	142	20	14	.981	-2	93	100	1-66,O-38(34-2-1)/2-6	1.7
1919	†Cin N	56	163	11	35	6	1	0	21	26	4	19	.215	.337	.264	84	-1	4	.990	-3	106	17	O-47(44-1-2)/23	-0.7
Total	16	2087	7441	1112	2169	425	166	83	1176	736	109	359	.291	.364	.427	137	334	441-20	.970	5	96	71	*O-1861L,1-136/S-40,2-15,3	26.2
MAGEE, WENDELL Wendell Errol B 8.3.1972 Hattiesburg, MS BR/TR 6/225# d8.16																								
1996	Phi N	38	142	9	29	7	0	2	14	9-0	0	33	.204	.252	.296	43	-12	0-0	.978	3	120	94	O-37(6-18-18)	-1.0
1997	Phi N	38	115	7	23	4	0	1	9	9-1	0	20	.200	.254	.261	36	-11	1-4	.960	4	129	129	O-38(CF)	-0.8
1998	Phi N	20	75	9	22	6	1	1	11	7-0	0	11	.293	.354	.440	106	1	0-0	.941	-1	86	80	O-19(LF)	-0.1

Year	Tm Lg	G	AB	R	H	2B	3B	HR	RBI	BB-IB	HP	SO	AVG	OBP	SLG	AOPS	ABR	SB-CS	FA	FR	Rng	Thr	G at Pos	BFW
1999	Phi N	12	14	4	5	1	0	2	5	1-0	0	4	.357	.400	.857	201	2	0-0	1.000	0	133	0	/O-4(1-2-1)	0.2
2000	Det A	91	186	31	51	4	2	7	31	10-0	0	28	.274	.310	.430	87	-5	1-0	1.000	-2	88	95	O-76(18-5-56)/D-6	-0.8
2001	Det A	90	207	26	44	11	4	5	17	23-1	1	44	.213	.293	.377	79	-7	3-0	.992	2	97	208	O-74(21-36-19),D-11	-0.6
2002	Det A	97	347	34	94	19	1	6	35	10-0	1	64	.271	.289	.383	83	-10	2-4	.982	8	115	125	O-91(5-78-9)/D-4	-0.3
Total	7	386	1086	120	268	52	8	24	122	69-2	2	204	.247	.291	.376	76	-42	7-8	.981	13	107	129	O-339(70-177-103)/D-21	-3.4
MAGGERT, HARL Harl Vestin B 2.13.1883 Cromwell, IN D 1.7.1963 Fresno, CA BL/TR 5-8/155# d9.4 s-Harl																								
1907	Pit N	3	6	1	0	0	0	0	0	2	0		.000	.250	.000	-21	-1	1	1.000	0	0	0	/O-2(LF)	-0.1
1912	Phi A	74	242	39	62	8	6	1	13	36	2		.256	.357	.351	107	3	10	.939	-5	90	65	O-61(39-17-5)	-0.5
Total	2	77	248	40	62	8	6	1	13	38	2		.250	.354	.343	104	2	11	.942	-5	87	63	/O-63(41-17-5)	-0.6
MAGGERT, HARL Harl Warren B 5.4.1914 Los Angeles, CA D 7.10.1986 Citrus Heights, CA BR/TR 6/190# d4.19 f-Harl																								
1938	Bos N	66	89	12	25	3	0	3	19	10	0	20	.281	.354	.416	123	3	0	.944	0	94	153	O-10(8-0-2)/3-8	0.3
MAGNER, STUBBY Edmund Burke B 2.20.1888 Kalamazoo, MI D 9.6.1956 Chillicothe, OH BR/TR 5-3/135# d7.12																								
1911	NY A	13	33	3	7	0	0	0	4	4	0		.212	.297	.212	40	-3	1	.970	0	100	137	/S-6,2-5	-0.2
MAGNER, JOHN John T. B 1855 St.Louis, MO 5-7.5/170# d7.14 U1																								
1879	Cin N	1	4	0	0	0	0	0	1	0		1	.000	.000	.000	-99	-1		.500	-1	0	0	/O(CF)	-0.1
MAGOON, GEORGE George Henry "Maggie" or "Topsy" B 3.27.1875 St.Albans, ME D 12.6.1943 Rochester, NH BR/TR 5-10/160# d6.29																								
1898	Bro N	93	343	35	77	7	0	1	39	30	3		.224	.293	.254	57	-19	7	.925	10	113	94	S-93	-0.4
1899	Bal N	62	207	26	53	8	3	0	31	26	5		.256	.353	.324	82	-4	7	.923	0	101	84	S-62	-0.1
	Chi N	59	189	24	43	5	1	0	21	24	6		.228	.333	.265	67	-7	5	.896	5	107	154	S-59	0.0
	Year	121	396	50	96	13	4	0	52	50	11		.242	.344	.295	75	-11	12	.909	5	104	118	*S-121	-0.1
1901	Cin N	127	460	47	116	16	7	1	53	52	2		.252	.331	.324	97	0	15	.919	-18	90	78	*S-112,2-15	-1.4
1902	Cin N	45	162	29	44	9	2	0	23	13	5		.272	.344	.352	105	1	7	.930	3	116	102	2-41/S-3	0.5
1903	Cin N	42	139	6	30	6	0	0	9	19	1		.216	.314	.259	58	-7	2	.971	2	97	75	2-32/3-9	-0.5
	Chi A	94	334	32	76	11	3	0	25	30	6		.228	.303	.278	79	-7	4	.936	-25	89	81	2-94	-3.3
Total	5	522	1834	199	439	62	16	2	201	194	28		.239	.321	.294	78	-43	47	.916	-23	101	99	S-329,2-182/3-9	-5.2
MAGRANN, TOM Thomas Joseph B 12.9.1963 Hollywood, FL BR/TR 6-3/177# d9.7																								
1989	Cle A	9	10	0	0	0	0	0	0	0-0	0	4	.000	.000	.000	-98	-3	0-0	1.000	1	34	163	/C-9	-0.2
MAGRUDER, CHRIS Christopher James B 4.26.1977 Tacoma, WA BB/TR 5-11/200# d9.4																								
2001	Tex A	17	29	3	5	0	0	0	1	1-0	1	5	.172	.226	.172	7	-4	0-0	1.000	2	150	225	O-12(8-1-3)	-0.2
2002	Cle A	87	258	34	56	15	1	6	29	15-2	1	55	.217	.261	.353	63	-14	2-0	.987	-1	102	51	O-83(45-20-27)	-1.7
2003	Cle A	9	26	3	9	2	1	1	3	3-0	1	6	.346	.433	.615	178	3	0-1	1.000	-1	76	0	/O-8(5-0-3)	0.1
Total	3	113	313	40	70	17	2	7	33	19-2	3	66	.224	.273	.358	67	-15	2-1	.989	-0	104	61	O-103(58-21-33)	-1.8
MAGUIRE, FREDDIE Frederick Edward B 5.10.1899 Roxbury, MA D 11.3.1961 Boston, MA BR/TR 5-11/155# d9.22																								
1922	NY N	5	12	4	4	0	0	0	1	0	0	1	.333	.333	.333	72	-1	1-0	.944	1	140	77	/2-3	0.1
1923	†NY N	41	30	11	6	1	0	0	2	2	0	4	.200	.250	.233	29	-3	1-0	.881	5	149	205	2-16/3	0.2
1928	Chi N	140	574	67	160	24	7	1	41	25	3	38	.279	.312	.350	74	-23	6	.976	**49**	**112**	**140**	*2-138	2.9
1929	Bos N	138	496	54	125	26	8	0	41	19	3	40	.252	.284	.337	55	-37	8	.971	8	102	114	*2-138/S	-2.3
1930	Bos N	146	516	54	138	21	5	0	52	20	2	22	.267	.297	.328	53	-41	4	.969	-2	97	104	*2-146	-3.5
1931	Bos N	148	492	36	112	18	2	0	26	16	5	26	.228	.259	.272	45	-39	3	**.976**	10	**105**	103	*2-148	-2.0
Total	6	618	2120	226	545	90	22	1	163	82	13	131	.257	.289	.322	57	-144	23-0	.971	71	105	116	2-589/S3	-4.6
MAGUIRE, JACK Jack B 2.5.1925 St.Louis, MO D 9.28.2001 Kerrville, TX BR/TR 5-11/165# d4.18																								
1950	NY N	29	40	3	7	2	0	0	3	3	0	13	.175	.233	.225	21	-5	0	1.000	2	114	429	/O-9(4-0-5),1-2	-0.3
1951	NY N	16	20	6	8	1	1	1	4	2	0	2	.400	.455	.700	204	3	0-0	1.000	1	133	233	/O-8(RF)	0.4
	Pit N	8	5	1	0	0	0	0	0	1	0	0	.000	.167	.000	-50	-1	0-0	1.000	1	205	0	/23	-0.1
	Year	24	25	7	8	1	1	1	4	3	0	2	.320	.393	.560	151	2	0-0	1.000	2	98	95	/O-8(RF),23	0.3
	StL A	41	127	15	31	2	1	1	14	12	0	21	.244	.309	.299	63	-7	1-0	.969	-1	98	95	O-26(LF)/3-5,2-2	-1.0
Total	2	94	192	25	46	5	2	2	21	18	0	36	.240	.305	.318	66	-10	1-0	.979	3	105	166	/O-43(30-0-13),3-6,2-3,1-2	-1.0
MAHADY, JIM James Bernard B 4.22.1901 Cortland, NY D 8.9.1936 Cortland, NY BR/TR 5-11/170# d10.2																								
1921	NY N	1	0	0	0	0	0	0	0	0	0	0	—	—	—	—	0	0-0	1.000	0	133	0	/2	0.0
MAHAN, ART Arthur Leo B 6.8.1913 Somerville, MA BL/TL 5-11/178# d4.30																								
1940	Phi N	146	544	55	133	24	5	2	39	40	1	37	.244	.297	.318	73	-21	4	.992	4	109	100	*1-145/P	-3.1
MAHAR, FRANK Frank Edward B 12.4.1878 Natick, MA D 12.5.1961 Somerville, MA TR 5-10.5/?# d8.29																								
1902	Phi N	1	1	0	0	0	0	0	0	0	0		.000	.000	.000	-99	0	0	—	0			H	0.0
MAHARG, BILLY William Joseph B 3.19.1881 Philadelphia, PA D 11.20.1953 Philadelphia, PA BR/TR 5-4.5/155# d5.18																								
1912	Det A	1	1	0	0	0	0	0	0	0	0		.000	.000	.000	-99	0	0	1.000	0	215	0	/3	0.0
1916	Phi N	1	1	0	0	0	0	0	0	0	0	0	.000	.000	.000	-97	0	0	—	-0	0	0	/O(RF)	0.0
Total	2	2	2	0	0	0	0	0	0	0	0	0	.000	.000	.000	-99	0	0	.000	0	0	0	/O(RF)3	0.0
MAHER, TOM Thomas Francis B 7.6.1870 Philadelphia, PA D 8.25.1929 Philadelphia, PA d4.24																								
1902	Phi N	1	0	0	0	0	0	0	0	0	0		—	—	—	—	0	0	—	0			R	0.0
MAHLBERG, GREG Gregory John B 8.8.1952 Milwaukee, WI BR/TR 5-10/180# d9.24																								
1978	Tex A	1	1	0	0	0	0	0	0	0-0	0	0	.000	.000	.000	-99	0	0-0	1.000	-0	0	584	/C	0.0
1979	Tex A	7	17	2	2	0	0	1	1	2-0	0	4	.118	.211	.294	35	-2	0-0	1.000	-2	62	0	/C-7	-0.4
Total	2	8	18	2	2	0	0	1	1	2-0	0	4	.111	.200	.278	28	-2	0-0	1.000	-2	57	44	/C-8	-0.4
MAHONEY, DAN Daniel J. B 3.20.1864 Springfield, MA D 2.1.1904 Springfield, MA BR/TR 5-9.5/165# d8.20																								
1892	Cin N	5	21	1	4	0	1	0	1	1	0	4	.190	.227	.286	56	-1	0	.943	1	*124*	*120*	/C-5	0.0
1895	Was N	6	12	2	2	0	0	0	1	0	0	0	.167	.167	.167	-14	-2	0	1.000	-1	*73*	*117*	/C-2,1	-0.2
Total	2	11	33	3	6	0	1	0	2	1	0	4	.182	.206	.242	28	-3	0	.949	1	*118*	*120*	/C-7,1	-0.2
MAHONEY, DANNY Daniel Joseph B 9.6.1888 Haverhill, MA D 9.28.1960 Utica, NY BR/TR 5-6.5/145# d5.15																								
1911	Cin N	1	0	0	0	0	0	0	0	0	0	0	—	—	—	—	0	0	—	0			R	0.0
MAHONEY, MIKE George W. "Big Mike" B 12.5.1873 Boston, MA D 1.3.1940 Boston, MA BR 6-4/220# d5.18																								
1897	Bos N	2	2	1	1	0	0	0	1	0	0		.500	.500	.500	155	0	0	1.000	0	*0*	*0*	/CP	0.0
1898	StL N	2	7	0	0	0	0	0	0	0	0		.000	.000	.000	-98	-2	0	.920	-0	106	81	/1-2	-0.2
Total	2	4	9	1	1	0	0	0	1	0	0		.111	.111	.111	-36	-2	0	.920	-0	106	81	/1-2,PC	-0.2
MAHONEY, JIM James Thomas "Moe" B 5.26.1934 Englewood, NJ BR/TR 6/175# d7.28 C7																								
1959	Bos A	31	23	10	3	0	0	1	4	3-0	0	7	.130	.231	.261	33	-2	0-0	.940	4	130	76	S-30	0.3
1961	Was A	43	108	10	26	0	1	0	6	5-0	0	23	.241	.274	.259	44	-9	1-2	.968	8	120	148	S-31/2-2	0.1
1962	Cle A	41	74	12	18	4	0	3	5	3-2	0	14	.243	.269	.419	86	-2	0-0	.964	5	113	113	S-23/2-8,3	0.4
1965	Hou N	5	5	0	1	0	0	0	0	0-0	0	3	.200	.200	.200	14	-1	0-0	1.000	0	49	364	/S-5	0.0
Total	4	120	210	32	48	4	1	4	15	11-2	0	47	.229	.266	.314	57	-14	1-2	.962	17	118	130	/S-89,2-10,3	0.8
MAHONEY, MIKE Michael John B 12.5.1972 Des Moines, IA BR/TR 6-1/200# d9.8																								
2000	Chi N	4	7	1	2	1	0	0	1	1-0	1	0	.286	.444	.429	125	0	0-0	1.000	-1	104	0	/C-4	-0.1
2002	Chi N	16	29	2	6	3	0	0	3	1-1	0	10	.207	.233	.310	45	-2	0-0	1.000	2	0	154	C-16	0.0
Total	2	20	36	3	8	4	0	0	4	2-1	1	10	.222	.282	.333	63	-2	0-0	1.000	0	16	130	/C-20	-0.1
MAIER, BOB Robert Phillip B 9.5.1915 Dunellen, NJ D 8.4.1993 S.Plainfield, NJ BR/TR 5-8/180# d4.17																								
1945	†Det A	132	486	58	128	25	7	1	34	38	0	32	.263	.317	.350	88	-8	7-11	.936	-15	85	80	*3-124/O-5(LF)	-2.6
MAILHO, EMIL Emil Pierre "Lefty" B 12.16.1909 Berkeley, CA BL/TL 5-10/165# d4.14																								
1936	Phi A	21	18	5	1	0	0	0	0	5	0	3	.056	.261	.056	-18	-3	0-0	1.000	0	123	0	/O(LF)	-0.3

Year	Tm Lg	G	AB	R	H	2B	3B	HR	RBI	BB-IB	HP	SO	AVG	OBP	SLG	AOPS	ABR	SB-CS	FA	FR	Rng	Thr	G at Pos	BFW
MAISEL, CHARLIE Charles Louis B 4.21.1894 Catonsville, MD D 8.25.1953 Baltimore, MD BR/TR 6/?# d10.2																								
1915	Bal F	1	4	0	0	0	0	0	0	0	0	0	.000	.000	.000	-97	-1	0	1.000	0	*138*	*90*	/C	-0.1
MAISEL, FRITZ Frederick Charles "Flash" B 12.23.1889 Catonsville, MD D 4.22.1967 Baltimore, MD BR/TR 5-7.5/170# d8.11 b-George																								
1913	NY A	51	187	33	48	4	3	0	12	34	0	20	.257	.371	.310	99	1	25	.950	-2	91	44	3-51	0.1
1914	NY A	150	548	78	131	23	9	2	47	76	2	69	.239	.334	.325	98	1	**74**-17	.928	-17	85	91	*3-148	-0.2
1915	NY A	135	530	77	149	16	6	4	46	48	1	35	.281	.342	.357	109	5	51-12	.940	-9	88	96	*3-134	0.7
1916	NY A	53	158	18	36	5	0	0	7	20	1	18	.228	.318	.259	72	-5	4	.980	-4	95	33	O-26(CF),3-11/2-4	-1.0
1917	NY A	113	404	46	80	4	4	0	20	36	2	18	.198	.267	.228	51	-24	29	.967	-3	97	92	*2-100/3-7	-2.8
1918	StL A	90	284	43	66	4	2	0	16	46	1	17	.232	.341	.261	84	-3	11	.949	-3	94	67	3-79/O(RF)	-0.5
Total	6	592	2111	295	510	56	24	6	148	260	7	177	.242	.327	.299	88	-25	194-<u>29</u>	.938	-38	89	83	3-430,2-104/O-27(0-26-1)	-3.7
MAISEL, GEORGE George John B 3.12.1892 Catonsville, MD D 11.20.1968 Baltimore, MD BR/TR 5-10.5/180# d5.1 b-Fritz																								
1913	StL A	11	18	2	3	2	0	0	1	1	0	7	.167	.211	.278	44	-1	0	.833	-1	80	0	/O-5(2-3-0)	-0.2
1916	Det A	8	5	2	0	0	0	0	0	0	0	2	.000	.000	.000	-97	-1	0	.857	1	210	457	/3-3	0.0
1921	Chi N	111	393	54	122	7	2	0	43	11	3	13	.310	.334	.338	78	-12	17-7	.978	-1	102	84	*O-108(0-107-1)	-1.6
1922	Chi N	38	84	9	16	1	1	0	6	8	0	2	.190	.261	.226	26	-9	1-3	1.000	0	103	77	O-26(2-13-11)	-1.1
Total	4	168	500	67	141	10	3	0	50	20	3	24	.282	.314	.314	66	-23	18-<u>10</u>	.979	-0	102	81	O-139(4-123-12)/3-3	-2.9
MAJESKI, HANK Henry "Heeney" B 12.13.1916 Staten Island, NY D 8.9.1991 Staten Island, NY BR/TR 5-9/180# d5.17 Mil 1943-45																								
1939	Bos N	106	367	35	100	16	1	7	54	18	2	30	.272	.310	.379	91	-6	2	.945	10	113	118	3-99	0.7
1940	Bos N	3	3	0	0	0	0	0	0	0	0	0	.000	.000	.000	-99	-1	0	—	0			H	-0.1
1941	Bos N	19	55	5	8	5	0	0	3	1	0	13	.145	.161	.236	11	-7	0	.911	0	104	86	3-11	-0.6
1946	NY A	8	12	1	1	0	1	0	0	0	0	3	.083	.083	.250	-9	-2	0-0	.750	-1	73	0	/3-2	-0.3
	Phi A	78	264	25	66	14	3	1	25	26	1	13	.250	.320	.337	84	-6	3-2	.967	11	114	134	3-72	0.5
	Year	86	276	26	67	14	4	1	25	26	1	16	.243	.310	.333	80	-8	3-2	.964	10	113	131	3-74	0.2
1947	Phi A	141	479	54	134	26	5	8	72	53	5	31	.280	.358	.405	110	7	1-0	**.988**	8	104	**119**	*3-134/S-4,2	1.5
1948	Phi A	148	590	88	183	41	4	12	120	48	6	43	.310	.368	.454	118	14	2-1	**.975**	3	103	72	*3-142/S-8	1.6
1949	Phi A	114	448	62	124	26	5	9	67	29	4	23	.277	.326	.417	99	-4	0-1	.957	-5	96	138	*3-113	-0.9
1950	Chi A	122	414	47	128	18	2	6	46	42	3	34	.309	.377	.406	103	2	1-4	.970	8	106	**132**	*3-112	0.8
1951	Chi A	12	35	4	9	4	0	0	6	1	0	0	.257	.278	.371	76	-1	0-0	.950	0	116	156	/3-9	-0.1
	Phi A	89	323	41	92	19	4	5	42	35	2	24	.285	.358	.415	106	3	1-2	.974	13	123	95	3-88	1.5
	Year	101	358	45	101	23	4	5	48	36	2	24	.282	.351	.411	104	2	1-2	.972	13	122	99	3-97	1.4
1952	Phi A	34	117	14	30	2	2	2	20	19	1	10	.256	.365	.359	96	0	0-1	.976	3	114	109	3-34	0.3
	Cle A	36	54	7	16	2	0	0	9	7	0	7	.296	.377	.333	106	1	0-0	.913	-1	80	182	3-11/2-3	0.0
	Year	70	171	21	46	4	2	2	29	26	1	17	.269	.369	.351	101	1	0-1	.966	3	108	122	3-45/2-3	0.3
1953	Cle A	50	50	6	15	1	0	2	12	3	1	8	.300	.352	.440	116	1	0-0	1.000	-1	85	84	2-10/3-7,O(LF)	0.0
1954	†Cle A	57	121	10	34	4	0	3	17	7	0	14	.281	.320	.388	92	-2	0-0	.990	1	99	98	2-25,3-10	0.0
1955	Cle A	36	48	3	9	2	0	2	6	8-0	2	3	.188	.322	.354	80	-1	0-0	1.000	-1	75	137	/3-9,2-4	-0.2
	Bal A	16	41	2	7	1	0	0	2	2-1	0	4	.171	.209	.195	10	-5	0-0	1.000	-2	93	81	/3-8,2-5	-0.7
	Year	52	89	5	16	3	0	2	8	10-1	2	7	.180	.275	.281	50	-6	0-0	1.000	-3	86	103	3-17/2-9	-0.9
Total	13	1069	3421	404	956	181	27	57	501	299-<u>1</u>	27	260	.279	.342	.398	100	-7	10-<u>11</u>	.968	48	107	113	3-861/2-48,S-12,O(LF)	4.0
MAKSUDIAN, MIKE Michael Bryant B 5.28.1966 Belleville, IL BL/TR 5-11/220# d9.2																								
1992	Tor A	3	3	0	0	0	0	0	0	0-0	0	0	.000	.000	.000	-96	-1	0-0	—	0	0	0	/1	-0.1
1993	Min A	5	12	2	2	1	0	0	2	4-0	0	2	.167	.353	.250	71	0	0-0	1.000	1	233	93	/1-4,3	0.1
1994	Chi N	26	26	6	7	2	0	0	4	10-0	0	4	.269	.472	.346	120	2	0-1	1.000	1	120	170	/1-3,C-2,3-2	0.2
Total	3	34	41	8	9	3	0	0	6	14-0	0	6	.220	.411	.293	92	1	0-1	1.000	2	187	119	/1-8,3-3,C-2	0.2
MALAVE, JOSE Jose Francisco B 5.31.1971 Cumana, Venezuela BR/TR 6-2/212# d5.23																								
1996	Bos A	41	102	12	24	3	0	4	17	2-0	1	25	.235	.257	.382	58	-7	0-0	.978	-3	82	55	O-38(8-0-30)	-1.0
1997	Bos A	4	4	0	0	0	0	0	0	0-0	0	2	.000	.000	.000	-98	-1	0-0	1.000	0	129	0	/O-4(LF)	-0.1
Total	2	45	106	12	24	3	0	4	17	2-0	1	27	.226	.248	.368	52	-8	0-0	.979	-2	84	53	/O-42(12-0-30)	-1.1
MALAY, CHARLIE Charles Francis B 6.13.1879 Brooklyn, NY D 9.18.1949 Brooklyn, NY BB/TR 5-11.5/175# d4.24 s-Joe																								
1905	Bro N	102	349	33	88	7	2	1	31	22	2		.252	.300	.292	83	-8	13	.932	-3	101	66	2-75,O-25(1-23-1)/S	-1.2
MALAY, JOE Joseph Charles B 10.25.1905 Brooklyn, NY D 3.19.1989 Bridgeport, CT BL/TL 6/175# d9.7 f-Charlie																								
1933	NY N	8	24	0	3	0	0	0	2	0	0	0	.125	.125	.125	-29	-4	0	1.000	2	195	49	/1-8	-0.3
1935	NY N	1	1	0	1	0	0	0	0	0	0	0	1.000	1.000	1.000	447	0	0	—	0			H	0.0
Total	2	9	25	0	4	0	0	0	2	0	0	0	.160	.160	.160	-9	-4	0	1.000	2	195	49	/1-8	-0.3
MALDONADO, CANDY Candido (Guadarrama) B 9.5.1960 Humacao, P.R. BR/TR 6/190# d9.7																								
1981	LA N	11	12	0	1	0	0	0	0	0-0	0	5	.083	.083	.083	-55	-2	0-0	1.000	0	140	0	/O-9(4-0-5)	-0.3
1982	LA N	6	4	0	0	0	0	0	0	1-1	0	2	.000	.200	.000	-41	-1	0-0	1.000	1	253	0	/O-3(3-0-1)	0.0
1983	†LA N	42	62	5	12	1	1	1	6	5-0	0	14	.194	.254	.290	51	-4	0-0	1.000	-2	81	0	O-33(12-3-19)	-0.8
1984	LA N	116	254	25	68	14	0	5	28	19-0	1	29	.268	.318	.382	98	-1	0-3	.955	-5	89	96	*O-102(7-31-67)/3-4	-1.0
1985	†LA N	121	213	20	48	7	1	5	19	19-4	0	40	.225	.288	.338	77	-7	1-1	.984	1	92	161	*O-113(44-57-24)	-0.9
1986	SF N	133	405	49	102	31	3	18	85	20-4	3	77	.252	.289	.477	114	5	4-4	.983	1	93	147	*O-101(47-6-62)/3	0.1
1987	†SF N	118	442	69	129	28	4	20	85	34-4	6	78	.292	.346	.509	131	18	8-8	.973	-8	82	89	*O-116(4-0-115)	0.3
1988	SF N	142	499	53	127	23	1	12	68	37-1	7	89	.255	.311	.377	102	1	6-5	.962	-4	96	75	*O-139(RF)	-0.9
1989	†SF N	129	345	39	75	23	0	9	41	37-4	3	69	.217	.296	.362	91	-4	4-1	.974	1	100	118	*O-116(RF)	-0.6
1990	Cle A	155	590	76	161	32	2	22	95	49-4	5	134	.273	.330	.446	117	12	3-5	.993	5	106	101	*O-134(104-0-41),D-20	1.1
1991	Mil A	34	111	11	23	6	0	5	20	13-0	0	23	.207	.288	.396	90	-2	1-0	.976	-2	88	0	O-24(12-0-13)	-0.4
	†Tor A	52	177	26	49	9	0	7	28	23-4	6	53	.277	.375	.446	123	6	3-0	.990	-2	95	71	O-52(52-0-1)/D-9	0.4
	Year	86	288	37	72	15	0	12	48	36-4	6	76	.250	.342	.427	111	5	4-0	.986	-4	93	50	O-76(64-0-14)/D-9	0.0
1992	†Tor A	137	489	64	133	25	4	20	66	59-3	7	112	.272	.357	.462	123	15	2-2	.978	1	96	138	*O-132(129-0-4)/D-4	1.2
1993	Chi N	70	140	8	26	5	0	3	15	13-0	1	40	.186	.260	.286	47	-11	0-0	.914	-1	86	134	O-41(29-0-14)	-1.4
	Cle A	28	81	11	20	2	0	5	20	11-2	0	18	.247	.333	.457	112	1	0-1	.976	-1	90	65	O-26(2-0-25)/D-2	-0.2
1994	Cle A	42	92	14	18	5	1	5	12	19-1	0	31	.196	.333	.435	96	-1	1-1	1.000	-0	87	0	D-25/O-5(LF)	-0.3
1995	Tor A	61	160	22	43	13	0	7	25	25-0	2	45	.269	.368	.481	121	6	1-1	.988	-3	87	66	O-58(26-0-38)/D	0.1
	Tex A	13	30	6	7	3	0	2	5	7-0	0	5	.233	.378	.533	131	2	0-1	1.000	1	111	165	O-11(9-0-4)	0.2
	Year	74	190	28	50	16	0	9	30	32-0	2	50	.263	.370	.489	123	7	1-2	.990	-2	91	82	O-69(35-0-42)/D	0.3
Total	15	1410	4106	498	1042	227	17	146	618	391-32	41	864	.254	.322	.424	107	33	34-33	.977	-20	94	103	*O-1215(489-97-688)/D-61,3-5	-3.4
MALER, JIM James Michael B 8.16.1958 New York, NY BR/TR 6-4/230# d9.3																								
1981	Sea A	12	23	1	8	1	0	0	2	2-0	1	1	.348	.423	.391	131	1	1-0	1.000	-0	71	126	/1-5,D-2	0.1
1982	Sea A	64	221	18	50	8	3	4	26	12-3	3	35	.226	.274	.344	67	-11	0-0	.991	2	108	95	1-57/D-5	-1.3
1983	Sea A	26	66	5	12	1	0	1	3	5-0	2	11	.182	.260	.242	38	-6	0-3	1.000	0	88	58	1-19/D-5	-0.8
Total	3	102	310	24	70	10	3	5	31	19-3	6	47	.226	.283	.326	65	-16	1-3	.994	2	102	90	/1-81,D-12	-2.0
MALINOSKY, TONY Anthony Francis B 10.5.1909 Collinsville, IL BR/TR 5-10.5/165# d4.26																								
1937	Bro N	35	79	7	18	2	0	0	3	9	0	11	.228	.307	.253	53	-5	0	.833	-6	88	132	3-13,S-11	-1.1
MALKMUS, BOBBY Robert Edward B 7.4.1931 Newark, NJ BR/TR 5-9/180# d6.1																								
1957	Mil N	13	22	6	2	0	1	0	0	3-0	0	3	.091	.200	.182	4	-3	0-0	.972	2	127	116	/2-7	-0.1
1958	Was A	41	70	5	13	2	1	0	3	4-0	0	15	.186	.230	.243	31	-7	0-0	.964	2	104	92	2-26/3-2,S	-0.3
1959	Was A	6	0	0	0	0	0	0	0	0-0	0	0	—	—	—	—	0	0-0	—	0			R	0.0
1960	Phi N	79	133	16	28	4	1	1	12	11-0	0	28	.211	.267	.278	51	-9	2-2	1.000	4	109	158	S-29,2-23,3-12	-0.4
1961	Phi N	121	342	39	79	8	2	7	31	20-1	2	43	.231	.276	.327	61	-20	1-3	.988	11	107	121	2-58,S-34,3-25	-0.4
1962	Phi N	8	5	3	1	1	0	0	0	0-0	0	1	.200	.200	.400	58	0	0-0	1.000	1	228	266	/S	0.1
Total	6	268	572	69	123	15	5	8	46	38-1	2	90	.215	.265	.301	53	-39	3-5	.982	20	108	110	2-114/S-65,3-39	-1.1
MALLETT, JERRY Gerald Gordon B 9.18.1935 Bonne Terre, MO BR/TR 6-5/208# d9.19																								
1959	Bos A	4	15	1	4	0	0	0	1	1-0	0	3	.267	.313	.267	58	-1	0-0	1.000	2	108	572	/O-4(CF)	0.1

Year	Tm Lg	G	AB	R	H	2B	3B	HR	RBI	BB-IB	HP	SO	AVG	OBP	SLG	AOPS	ABR	SB-CS	FA	FR	Rng	Thr	G at Pos	BFW
MALLON, LES Leslie Clyde B 11.21.1905 Sweetwater, TX D 4.17.1991 Granbury, TX BR/TR 5-8/160# d4.14																								
1931	Phi N	122	375	41	116	19	2	1	45	29	0	40	.309	.359	.379	91	-4	0	.956	6	103	88	2-97/1-5,S-3,3-3	0.8
1932	Phi N	103	347	44	90	16	0	5	31	28	2	28	.259	.318	.349	71	-14	1	.955	-24	85	77	2-88/3-5	-3.2
1934	Bos N	42	166	23	49	6	1	0	18	15	0	12	.295	.354	.343	95	-1	0	.967	-5	103	69	2-42	-0.3
1935	Bos N	116	412	48	113	24	2	2	25	28	1	37	.274	.322	.357	89	-6	3	.975	-9	97	74	2-73,3-36/O(RF)	-0.9
Total	4	383	1300	156	368	65	5	8	119	100	3	117	.283	.336	.359	85	-25	4	.962	-32	96	79	2-300/3-44,1-5,S-3,O(RF)	-3.6
MALLONEE, BEN Howard Bennett "Lefty" B 3.31.1894 Baltimore, MD D 2.19.1978 Baltimore, MD BL/TL 5-6/150# d9.14																								
1921	Phi A	7	25	2	6	1	0	0	4	1	0	2	.240	.269	.280	40	-2	1-0	1.000	0	96	126	/O-6(CF)	-0.2
MALLONEE, JULE Julius Norris B 4.4.1900 Charlotte, NC D 12.26.1934 Charlotte, NC BL/TR 6-2/180# d8.4																								
1925	Chi A	2	3	1	0	0	0	0	0	1	0	0	.000	.250	.000	-34	-1	0-0	1.000	-0	62	0	/O(CF)	-0.1
MALLORY, JIM James Baugh "Sunny Jim" B 9.1.1918 Lawrenceville, VA D 8.6.2001 Greenville, NC BR/TR 6-1/170# d9.8 Mil 1942-44																								
1940	Was A	4	12	2	2	0	0	0	0	1	0	1	.167	.231	.167	5	-2	0-0	1.000	0	130	0	/O-3(1-1-1)	-0.2
1945	StL N	13	43	3	10	2	0	0	5	0	0	2	.233	.233	.279	41	-4	0	.923	-0	99	126	O-11(8-3-2)	-0.4
	NY N	37	94	10	28	1	0	0	9	6	0	7	.298	.340	.309	80	-3	1	.979	-0	94	127	O-21(8-9-4)	-0.4
	Year	50	137	13	38	3	0	0	14	6	0	9	.277	.308	.299	68	-6	1	.959	-0	96	127	O-32(16-12-6)	-0.8
Total	2	54	149	15	40	3	0	0	14	7	0	10	.268	.301	.289	63	-9	1-0	.964	0	99	114	/O-35(17-13-7)	-1.0
MALLORY, SHELDON Sheldon B 7.16.1953 Argo, IL BL/TL 6-2/175# d4.10																								
1977	Oak A	64	126	19	27	4	1	0	5	11-0	3	18	.214	.291	.262	53	-8	12-5	.977	1	112	127	O-45(9-17-21)/1-4,D-7	-0.7
MALLOY, MARTY Marty Thomas B 4.6.1972 Gainesville, FL BL/TR 5-10/160# d9.6																								
1998	†Atl N	11	28	3	5	1	0	1	1	2-0	0	2	.179	.233	.321	44	-2	0-0	1.000	1	106	93	2-10	-0.1
2002	Fla N	24	25	1	3	0	0	0	1	2-0	0	8	.120	.185	.120	-16	-4	0-0	1.000	-0	72	98	/2-3,3-2	-0.5
Total	2	35	53	4	8	1	0	1	2	4-0	0	10	.151	.211	.226	16	-6	0-0	1.000	1	100	94	/2-13,3-2	-0.6
MALMBERG, HARRY Harry William "Swede" B 7.31.1925 Fairfield, AL D 10.29.1976 San Francisco, CA BR/TR 6-1/170# d4.12 C2																								
1955	Det A	67	208	25	45	5	2	0	19	29-2	0	19	.216	.310	.260	56	-12	0-1	.985	3	109	91	2-65	-0.5
MALONE, EDDIE Edward Russell B 6.16.1920 Chicago, IL BR/TR 5-10/175# d7.17																								
1949	Chi A	55	170	17	46	7	2	1	16	29	0	19	.271	.377	.353	97	0	2-1	.990	-2	*83*	*85*	C-51	0.1
1950	Chi A	31	71	2	16	2	0	0	10	10	0	8	.225	.321	.254	50	-5	0-0	1.000	1	*70*	*119*	C-21	-0.3
Total	2	86	241	19	62	9	2	1	26	39	0	27	.257	.361	.324	83	-5	2-1	.993	-0	*79*	*94*	/C-72	-0.2
MALONE, FERGY Fergus G. B 1842 , Ireland D 1.1.1905 Seattle, WA BR/TL 5-8/156# d6.3 M3 U1																								
1871	Ath NA	27	134	33	46	7	1	1	33	9		4	.343	.385	.433	136	7	9-3	.856	9			*C-27	1.1
1872	Ath NA	41	213	46	60	5	3	0	39	4		5	.282	.295	.333	92	-2	3-0	**.884**	5			C-24,1-17	0.2
1873	Phi NA	**53**	259	59	75	11	2	0	41	14		7	.290	.326	.347	97	-1	6-1	.898	5			*C-53/SM	0.3
1874	Chi NA	47	223	33	56	5	0	0	28	4		0	.251	.264	.274	72	-7	2-1	.820	3			*C-47,M	-0.3
1875	Phi NA	29	123	15	28	2	1	0	10	1		2	.228	.234	.260	69	-4	1-0	.919	-3	25	53	1-22/C-6,O-2(CF)	-0.5
1876	Phi N	22	96	14	22	2	0	0	6	0		1	.229	.229	.250	60	-4		.777	-2			C-20/O-3(RF),S	-0.5
1884	Phi U	1	4	0	1	0	0	0		0			.250	.250	.250	56	0		.818	-1			/CM	-0.1
Total	5 NA	197	952	186	265	30	7	1	151	32		18	.278	.302	.328	93	-7	21-5	.000	19			C-157/1-39,O-2(CF),S	0.8
Total	2	23	100	14	23	2	0	0	6	0		1	.230	.230	.250	60	-4		.780	-3			/C-21,O-3(RF),S	-0.6
MALONE, LEW Lewis Aloysius B 3.13.1897 Baltimore, MD D 2.17.1972 Brooklyn, NY BR/TR 5-11/175# d5.31 Mil 1918																								
1915	Phi A	76	201	17	41	4	4	1	17	21	1	40	.204	.283	.279	70	-8	7-1	.919	-6	87	44	2-43,3-12/O-4(RF),S-2	-1.2
1916	Phi A	5	4	1	0	0	0	0	0	1	0	2	.000	.200	.000	-42	-1	0	1.000	-0	0	0	/S	-0.1
1917	Bro N	1	0	1	0	0	0	0	0	0	0	0	—	—	—	—	0	0	—	0			R	0.0
1919	Bro N	51	162	9	33	7	3	0	11	6	0	18	.204	.232	.284	54	-10	1	.934	-7	83	66	3-47/2-2,S-2	-1.7
Total	4	133	367	28	74	11	7	1	28	28	1	60	.202	.260	.278	62	-19	8-1	.910	-13	84	65	/3-59,2-45,S-5,O-4(RF)	-3.0
MALONE, MARTIN Martin d6.20 ▲																								
1872	Eck NA	5	16	2	6	0	0	0	3	1		3	.375	.412	.375	169	2	0-1	.333	-3	0	0	/O-3(0-1-2),P-2,2-2	-0.1
MALONEY, JOHN John d9.15																								
1876	NY N	2	7	1	2	0	1	0	2	0		1	.286	.286	.571	206	1		.800	-0	0	0	/O-2(CF)	0.0
1877	Har N	1	4	0	1	0	0	0	0	0		0	.250	.250	.250	65	0		.250	-1	0	0	/O(CF)	-0.1
Total	2	3	11	1	3	0	1	0	2	0		1	.273	.273	.455	152	1		.556	-2	0	0	/O-3(CF)	-0.1
MALONEY, PAT Patrick William B 1.19.1888 Grosvenor Dale, CT D 6.27.1979 Pawtucket, RI BR/TR 6/150# d6.19																								
1912	NY A	25	79	9	17	1	0	0	4	6	1		.215	.279	.228	43	-6	3	.926	-1	111	56	O-20(CF)	-0.8
MALONEY, BILLY William Alphonse B 6.5.1878 Lewiston, ME D 9.2.1960 Breckenridge, TX BL/TR 5-10/177# d5.2																								
1901	Mil A	86	290	42	85	3	4	0	22	7	8		.293	.328	.331	87	-5	11	.952	-4	*78*	***124***	C-72/O-8(CF)	-0.2
1902	StL A	30	112	8	23	3	0	0	11	6	2		.205	.258	.232	37	-9	0	.906	-3	112	194	O-23(1-0-22)/C-7	-1.2
	Cin N	27	89	13	22	4	0	1	7	2	1		.247	.272	.326	77	-3	8	.848	-0	199	0	O-18(10-6-2)/C-7	-0.3
1905	Chi N	145	558	78	145	17	14	2	56	43	11		.260	.325	.351	98	-2	**59**	.954	-1	90	96	*O-145(0-12-134)	-1.0
1906	Bro N	151	566	71	125	15	7	0	32	49	3		.221	.286	.272	80	-13	38	.966	9	102	130	*O-151(0-149-2)	-1.3
1907	Bro N	144	502	51	115	7	10	0	32	31	10		.229	.287	.283	86	-10	25	.967	1	89	99	*O-144(CF)	-1.8
1908	Bro N	113	359	31	70	5	7	3	17	24	5		.195	.255	.273	71	-13	14	.947	2	87	130	*O-103(5-95-3)/C-4	-1.8
Total	6	696	2476	294	585	54	42	6	177	162	40		.236	.294	.299	83	-55	155	.954	5	94	111	O-592(16-414-163)/C-90	-7.6
MALZONE, FRANK Frank James B 2.28.1930 Bronx, NY BR/TR 5-10/180# d9.17																								
1955	Bos A	6	20	2	7	1	0	0	1	1-0	0	3	.350	.381	.400	101	0	0-0	1.000	2	152	103	/3-4	0.2
1956	Bos A	27	103	15	17	3	1	2	11	9-0	0	8	.165	.230	.272	29	-11	1-0	.931	2	117	77	3-26	-0.9
1957	Bos A★	153	634	82	185	31	5	15	103	31-1	1	41	.292	.323	.427	98	-3	2-1	**.954**	21	**120**	**101**	*3-153	1.8
1958	Bos A★	**155**	627	76	185	30	2	15	87	33-3	4	53	.295	.333	.421	100	-1	1-3	.950	17	**118**	106	*3-155	1.5
1959	Bos A★	**154**	604	90	169	34	2	19	92	42-6	1	58	.280	.323	.437	103	2	6-0	.953	10	**109**	**131**	*3-154	1.2
1960	Bos A★	152	595	60	161	30	2	14	79	36-4	4	42	.271	.313	.398	89	-10	2-3	.948	14	**109**	104	*3-151	0.2
1961	Bos A	151	590	74	157	21	4	14	87	44-3	1	49	.266	.314	.386	85	-14	1-3	.950	2	102	138	*3-149	-1.3
1962	Bos A	156	619	74	175	20	3	21	95	35-2	0	43	.283	.319	.426	96	-5	0-1	.967	10	105	107	*3-156	0.3
1963	Bos A★	151	580	66	169	25	2	15	71	31-5	3	45	.291	.327	.419	105	3	0-2	.964	3	99	64	*3-148	0.5
1964	Bos A☆	148	537	62	142	19	0	13	56	37-1	2	43	.264	.312	.372	86	-10	0-0	.959	7	98	89	*3-143	-0.4
1965	Bos A	106	364	40	87	20	0	3	34	28-0	1	38	.239	.293	.319	70	-14	1-1	.969	1	100	104	3-96	-1.4
1966	Cal A	82	155	6	32	5	0	2	12	10-1	0	11	.206	.253	.277	54	-9	0-0	.925	-3	91	51	3-35	-1.4
Total	12	1441	5428	647	1486	239	21	133	728	337-26	17	434	.274	.315	.399	91	-72	14-14	.955	84	107	103	*3-1370	0.3
MANCUSO, GUS August Rodney "Blackie" B 12.5.1905 Galveston, TX D 10.26.1984 Houston, TX BR/TR 5-10/185# d4.30 C1 b-Frank																								
1928	StL N	11	38	2	7	0	1	0	3	0	0	5	.184	.184	.237	9	-5	0	.984	2	*138*	*90*	C-11	-0.2
1930	†StL N	76	227	39	83	17	2	7	59	18	1	16	.366	.415	.551	127	10	1	.969	1	*114*	*100*	C-61	1.4
1931	†StL N	67	187	13	49	16	1	1	23	18	0	13	.262	.327	.374	85	-3	2	.972	5	*100*	*140*	C-56	0.5
1932	StL N	103	310	25	88	23	1	5	43	30	0	15	.284	.347	.413	100	1	0	.977	4	*74*	***125***	C-82	1.0
1933	†NY N	144	481	39	127	17	2	6	56	48	0	21	.264	.331	.345	95	-2	0	.972	-1	*105*	*102*	*C-142	0.6
1934	NY N	122	383	32	94	14	0	7	46	27	0	19	.245	.295	.337	70	-17	0	.977	4	*110*	*118*	*C-122	-0.5
1935	NY N★	128	447	33	133	18	2	5	56	30	0	16	.298	.342	.380	95	-3	1	.972	-4	***117***	*99*	*C-126	0.1
1936	†NY N	139	519	55	156	21	3	9	63	39	1	28	.301	.351	.405	104	3	0	.977	7	*134*	*111*	*C-138	1.8
1937	†NY N★	86	287	30	80	17	1	4	39	17	0	20	.279	.319	.387	90	-4	1	.982	11	*159*	***110***	C-81	1.2
1938	NY N	52	158	19	55	8	0	2	15	17	0	13	.348	.411	.437	132	8	0	.977	3	*127*	*77*	C-44	1.3
1939	Chi N	80	251	17	58	10	0	2	17	24	0	19	.231	.298	.295	59	-14	0	.981	2	*127*	*93*	C-76	-0.8
1940	Bro N	60	144	16	33	8	0	0	16	13	0	7	.229	.293	.285	56	-8	0	.982	5	*123*	*92*	C-56	-0.1
1941	StL N	106	328	25	75	13	1	2	37	37	1	19	.229	.309	.293	66	-14	0	.989	8	*125*	*101*	*C-105	0.0
1942	StL N	5	13	0	1	0	0	0	1	0	0	0	.077	.077	.077	-51	-2	0	.917	-1	*0*	*0*	/C-3	-0.3
	NY N	39	109	4	21	1	1	0	8	14	0	7	.193	.285	.220	48	-7	1	.982	2	*129*	*92*	C-38	-0.3
	Year	44	122	4	22	1	1	0	9	14	0	7	.180	.265	.205	38	-10	1	.977	1	*120*	*86*	C-41	-0.6
1943	NY N	94	252	11	50	5	0	2	20	28	2	16	.198	.284	.242	52	-15	0	.974	-4	*80*	*96*	C-77	-1.6

Year	Tm Lg	G	AB	R	H	2B	3B	HR	RBI	BB-IB	HP	SO	AVG	OBP	SLG	AOPS	ABR	SB-CS	FA	FR	Rng	Thr	G at Pos	BFW
1944	NY N	78	195	15	49	4	1	1	25	30	0	20	.251	.351	.297	84	-3	0	.976	2	*107*	*111*	C-72	0.2
1945	Phi N	70	176	11	35	5	0	0	16	28	0	10	.199	.309	.227	52	-10	2	.988	-2	*69*	*123*	C-70	-0.9
Total	17	1460	4505	386	1194	197	16	53	543	418	5	264	.265	.328	.351	85	-85	8	.977	44	*113*	*106*	*C-1360	3.4
MANCUSO, FRANK Frank Octavius B 5.23.1918 Houston, TX BR/TR 6/195# d4.18 b-Gus																								
1944	†StL A	88	244	19	50	11	0	1	24	20	2	32	.205	.271	.262	50	-16	1-0	.953	-6	*91*	*70*	C-87	-1.8
1945	StL A	119	365	39	98	13	3	1	38	46	2	44	.268	.354	.329	94	-1	0-2	.989	-4	*101*	*74*	*C-115	0.1
1946	StL A	87	262	22	63	8	3	3	23	30	2	31	.240	.323	.328	78	-7	1-0	.973	-14	*62*	*74*	C-85	-1.9
1947	Was A	43	131	5	30	5	1	0	13	5	0	11	.229	.257	.282	51	-9	0-0	.958	-4	*96*	*92*	C-35	-1.2
Total	4	337	1002	85	241	37	7	5	98	101	6	118	.241	.314	.306	74	-33	2-2	.972	-28	*88*	*75*	C-322	-4.8
MANDA, CARL Carl Alan B 11.16.1888 Little River, KS D 3.9.1983 Artesia, NM BR/TR 5-10/170# d9.11																								
1914	Chi A	9	15	2	4	0	0	0	1	3	0	3	.267	.389	.267	99	0	1	.971	3	144	60	/2-7	0.3
MANEY, VINCENT S. Vincent B 10.14.1887 Batavia, NY D 3.13.1952 Batavia, NY BR/TR 6/175# d5.18																								
1912	Det A	1	2	0	0	0	0	0	0	1	1		.000	.500	.000	48	0	0	.833	-0	71	315	/S	0.0
MANGAN, JIM James Daniel B 9.24.1929 San Francisco, CA BR/TR 5-10/190# d4.16 Mil 1953																								
1952	Pit N	11	13	1	2	0	0	0	2	1	0	3	.154	.214	.154	4	-2	0-0	.833	-1	*47*	*279*	/C-4	-0.2
1954	Pit N	14	26	2	5	0	0	0	2	4	0	9	.192	.300	.192	32	-3	0-0	1.000	-0	*53*	*88*	/C-7	-0.2
1956	NY N	20	20	2	2	0	0	0	1	4-0	0	6	.100	.250	.100	-1	-3	0-0	1.000	0	*153*	*0*	C-15	-0.2
Total	3	45	59	5	9	0	0	0	5	9-0	0	18	.153	.265	.153	15	-8	0-0	.985	-0	*96*	*72*	/C-26	-0.6
MANGUAL, ANGEL Angel Luis (Guilbe) B 3.19.1947 Juana Diaz, P.R. BR/TR 5-10/180# d9.15 b-Pepe																								
1969	Pit N	6	4	1	1	1	0	0	0	0-0	0	0	.250	.250	.500	108	0	0-0	.000	-0	0	0	/O-3(2-0-1)	0.0
1971	†Oak A	94	287	32	82	8	1	4	30	17-1	0	27	.286	.324	.362	97	-2	1-4	.988	-2	99	66	O-81(17-57-9)	-0.8
1972	†Oak A	91	272	19	67	13	2	5	32	14-1	1	48	.246	.285	.364	97	-2	0-1	.971	3	112	81	O-74(2-22-52)	-0.3
1973	†Oak A	74	192	20	43	4	1	3	13	8-1	1	34	.224	.257	.302	61	-11	1-1	.947	-1	103	72	O-50(14-17-21),D-14/1-2,2	-1.5
1974	†Oak A	115	365	37	85	14	4	9	43	17-2	0	59	.233	.265	.367	87	-9	3-0	.961	0	104	111	O-74(26-28-29),D-37/3	-1.2
1975	Oak A	62	109	13	24	3	0	1	6	3-0	0	18	.220	.241	.275	47	-8	0-1	.978	-1	95	60	O-39(21-6-14),D-15	-1.1
1976	Oak A	8	12	0	2	1	0	0	1	0-0	0	1	.167	.167	.250	22	-1	0-1	1.000	0	61	429	/O-7(RF)	-0.2
Total	7	450	1241	122	304	44	8	22	125	59-5	2	187	.245	.279	.346	83	-33	5-8	.969	-1	103	85	O-328(82-130-133)/D-66,1-2,32	-5.1
MANGUAL, PEPE Jose Manuel (Guilbe) B 5.23.1952 Ponce, P.R. BR/TR 5-10/165# d9.6 b-Angel																								
1972	Mon N	8	11	2	3	0	0	0	0	1-0	0	5	.273	.333	.273	73	0	0-1	1.000	-1	37	0	/O-3(2-0-1)	-0.2
1973	Mon N	33	62	9	11	2	1	3	7	6-0	0	18	.177	.246	.387	71	-3	2-4	.966	-1	85	0	O-22(20-1-1)	-0.6
1974	Mon N	23	61	10	19	3	0	0	4	5-0	0	15	.311	.353	.361	98	0	5-0	1.000	-2	69	0	O-22(18-2-8)	-0.2
1975	Mon N	140	514	84	126	16	2	9	45	74-1	4	115	.245	.340	.337	86	-8	33-11	.972	-11	88	90	*O-138(1-135-2)	-2.0
1976	Mon N	66	215	34	56	9	1	3	16	50-2	2	49	.260	.403	.353	112	7	17-7	.968	1	106	77	O-62(34-36-1)	0.7
	NY N	41	102	15	19	5	2	1	9	10-0	0	32	.186	.259	.304	63	-5	7-3	.985	1	104	116	O-38(12-22-5)	-0.5
	Year	107	317	49	75	14	3	4	25	60-2	2	81	.237	.361	.338	99	2	24-10	.973	2	105	89	*O-100(46-58-6)	0.2
1977	NY N	8	7	1	1	0	0	0	2	1-0	0	4	.143	.250	.143	9	-1	0-0	.833	0	241	0	/O-4(2-2-0)	-0.1
Total	6	319	972	155	235	35	6	16	83	147-3	6	238	.242	.341	.340	89	-10	64-26	.972	-14	92	78	O-289(89-198-18)	-2.9
MANGUS, GEORGE George Graham B 5.22.1890 Red Creek, NY D 8.10.1933 Rutland, MA BL/TR 5-11.5/165# d8.20																								
1912	Phi N	10	25	2	5	3	0	0	3	1	0	6	.200	.231	.320	47	-2	0	.750	-2	80	0	/O-5(LF)	-0.4
MANION, CLYDE Clyde Jennings "Pete" B 10.30.1896 Big River, MO D 9.4.1967 Detroit, MI BR/TR 5-11/175# d5.5																								
1920	Det A	32	80	4	22	4	1	0	8	4	1	7	.275	.318	.350	79	-3	0-0	.940	-3	*92*	*114*	C-30	-0.3
1921	Det A	12	10	0	2	0	0	0	2	2	1	2	.200	.385	.200	53	-1	0-0	1.000	0	*80*	*312*	C-3	0.0
1922	Det A	42	69	9	19	4	1	0	12	4	0	6	.275	.315	.362	79	-2	0-1	.932	-3	*83*	*47*	C-22/1	-0.5
1923	Det A	23	22	0	3	0	0	0	2	2	0	2	.136	.208	.136	-8	-4	0-0	.857	-1	*82*	*147*	/C-3,1	-0.4
1924	Det A	14	13	1	3	0	0	0	2	1	0	1	.231	.286	.231	35	-1	0-0	.750	-1	*61*	*0*	/C-3,1	-0.2
1926	Det A	75	176	15	35	4	0	0	14	24	0	16	.199	.295	.222	36	-16	1-1	.972	-3	*87*	*102*	C-74	-1.6
1927	Det A	1	0	0	0	0	0	0	0	1	0	0	—	1.000	—	174	0	0-0	—	0			H	0.0
1928	StL A	76	243	25	55	5	1	2	31	15	1	18	.226	.274	.280	44	-20	3-0	.980	5	*100*	*83*	C-71	-1.0
1929	StL A	35	111	16	27	2	0	0	11	15	0	3	.243	.333	.261	53	-7	1-0	.976	3	*155*	*80*	C-34	-0.1
1930	StL A	57	148	12	32	1	0	1	11	24	0	17	.216	.326	.243	45	-12	0-1	.985	7	*141*	*144*	C-56	-0.2
1932	Cin N	49	135	7	28	4	0	0	12	14	0	16	.207	.282	.237	43	-11	0	.970	1	*88*	*92*	C-47	-0.8
1933	Cin N	36	84	3	14	1	0	0	3	8	0	7	.167	.239	.179	21	-9	0	.981	2	*93*	*114*	C-34	-0.5
1934	Cin N	25	54	4	10	0	0	0	4	4	0	7	.185	.241	.185	16	-6	0	1.000	2	*93*	*148*	C-24	-0.4
Total	13	477	1145	96	250	25	3	3	112	118	3	102	.218	.293	.253	45	-92	5-3	.973	9	*106*	*103*	C-401/1-3	-6.0
MANKOWSKI, PHIL Philip Anthony B 1.9.1953 Buffalo, NY BL/TR 6/180# d8.30																								
1976	Det A	24	85	9	23	2	1	1	4	4-0	0	8	.271	.300	.353	88	-2	0-0	.971	2	103	211	3-23	0.1
1977	Det A	94	286	21	79	7	3	3	27	16-4	2	41	.276	.318	.353	79	-9	1-2	.964	12	118	103	3-85/2	0.2
1978	Det A	88	222	28	61	8	0	4	20	22-3	2	28	.275	.344	.365	97	0	2-3	.972	2	106	148	3-80/D	0.0
1979	Det A	42	99	11	22	4	0	0	8	10-4	0	16	.222	.286	.263	50	-7	0-0	.963	2	104	121	3-36/D	-0.5
1980	NY N	8	12	1	2	1	0	0	1	2-0	0	4	.167	.286	.250	52	-1	0-0	.571	-1	93	0	/3-3	-0.2
1982	NY N	13	35	2	8	1	0	0	4	1-0	0	6	.229	.237	.257	42	-3	0-1	.957	-0	107	123	3-13	-0.4
Total	6	269	739	72	195	23	4	8	64	55-11	4	103	.264	.315	.338	79	-22	3-6	.962	17	110	131	3-240/D-2,2	-0.8
MANLOVE, CHARLIE Charles Henry Weeks "Chick" B 10.8.1862 Philadelphia, PA D 2.12.1952 Altoona, PA BR/TR 5-9/165# d5.31																								
1884	Alt U	2	7	1	3	0	0	0		0			.429	.429	.429	158	0		1.000	-1			/CO(CF)	0.0
	NY N	3	10	0	0	0	0	0	0	0		4	.000	.000	.000	-98	-2		.833	-0			/C-3,O(RF)	-0.2
Total	1	5	17	1	3	0	0	0	0	0		4	.176	.176	.176	9	-2		.880	-1			/C-4,O-2(0-1-1)	-0.2
MANN, GARTH Ben Garth "Red" B 11.16.1915 Brandon, TX D 9.11.1980 Italy, TX BR/TR 6/155# d5.14																								
1944	Chi N	1	0	1	0	0	0	0	0	0	0	0	—	—	—	—	0	0	—	0			R	0.0
MANN, FRED Fred J. B 4.1.1858 Sutton, VT D 4.6.1916 Springfield, MA BL/TR 5-10.5/178# d5.1 OF Total (39-LF 444-CF 28-RF)																								
1882	Wor N	19	77	12	18	5	0	0	7	2		15	.234	.253	.299	74	-2		.703	-5	81	75	3-18/1	-0.6
	Phi AA	29	121	13	28	7	4	0		4			.231	.256	.355	98	-1		.798	-7	68	109	3-29	-0.7
1883	Col AA	96	394	61	98	18	13	1		18			.249	.282	.368	117	9		.854	-4	104	194	*O-82(2-80-0)/1-9,3-6,S	0.1
1884	Col AA	99	366	70	101	12	18	7		25	11		.276	.341	.464	174	31		.857	-8	65	79	*O-97(CF)/2-2	1.8
1885	Pit AA	99	391	60	99	17	6	0	41	31	6		.253	.318	.327	106	4		.908	-10	59	69	*O-97(CF)/3-3	-0.8
1886	Pit AA	116	440	85	110	16	14	2	60	45	11		.250	.335	.364	119	11	26	.878	-4	71	100	*O-116(0-115-1)	0.3
1887	Cle AA	64	259	45	80	15	7	2	41	23	9		.309	.385	.444	135	13	25	.879	0	102	142	O-64(37-0-27)	1.0
	Phi AA	55	229	42	63	14	6	0	32	15	6		.275	.336	.389	102	0	16	.917	-2	85	114	O-55(CF)	-0.3
	Year	119	488	87	143	29	13	2	73	38	15		.293	.362	.418	119	13	41	.896	-2	95	130	*O-119(37-55-27)	0.7
Total	6	577	2277	388	597	104	68	12	181	163	43	15	.262	.323	.383	122	65	67	.881	-40	78	112	O-511C/3-56,1-10,2-2,S	0.8
MANN, JOHNNY John Leo B 2.4.1898 Fontanet, IN D 3.31.1977 Terre Haute, IN BR/TR 5-11/160# d4.18																								
1928	Chi A	6	6	0	2	0	0	0	1	1	0	0	.333	.429	.333	104	0	0-0	1.000	0	125	0	/3-2	0.0
MANN, KELLY Kelly John B 8.17.1967 Santa Monica, CA BR/TR 6-3/215# d9.4																								
1989	Atl N	7	24	1	5	2	0	0	1	0-0	1	6	.208	.240	.292	50	-2	0-0	1.000	2	88	165	/C-7	0.1
1990	Atl N	11	28	2	4	1	0	1	2	0-0	0	6	.143	.143	.286	14	-3	0-0	1.000	-2	78	108	C-10	-0.6
Total	2	18	52	3	9	3	0	1	3	0-0	1	12	.173	.189	.288	30	-5	0-0	1.000	-1	83	135	/C-17	-0.5
MANN, LES Leslie "Major" B 11.18.1893 Lincoln, NE D 1.14.1962 Pasadena, CA BR/TR 5-9/172# d4.30																								
1913	Bos N	120	407	54	103	24	7	3	51	18	4	73	.253	.291	.369	86	-9	7-16	.960	1	103	95	*O-120(12-103-6)	-2.0
1914	†Bos N	126	389	44	96	16	11	4	40	24	1	50	.247	.292	.375	99	-3	9	.952	10	104	**161**	*O-123(5-104-14)	-0.1
1915	Chi F	135	470	74	144	12	**19**	4	58	36	1	40	.306	.357	.438	131	9	18	.969	5	110	97	*O-130(94-7-33)/S	0.8
1916	Chi N	127	415	46	113	13	9	2	29	19	2	31	.272	.307	.361	95	-3	11-7	.972	-3	99	77	*O-115(74-20-26)	-1.3
1917	Chi N	117	444	63	121	19	10	1	44	27	1	46	.273	.316	.367	101	0	14	.953	-1	88	141	*O-116(106-11-2)	-0.7
1918	†Chi N	129	489	69	141	27	7	2	55	38	2	45	.288	.342	.384	118	11	21	.961	-5	88	107	*O-129(LF)	0.0
1919	Chi N	80	299	31	68	8	8	1	22	11	1	29	.227	.257	.318	72	-12	12	.982	1	101	101	O-78(LF)	-1.6

Year	Tm Lg	G	AB	R	H	2B	3B	HR	RBI	BB-IB	HP	SO	AVG	OBP	SLG	AOPS	ABR	SB-CS	FA	FR	Rng	Thr	G at Pos	BFW
	Bos N	40	145	15	41	6	4	3	20	9	1	14	.283	.329	.441	136	6	7	.929	2	97	165	O-40(LF)	0.6
	Year	120	444	46	109	14	12	4	42	20	2	43	.245	.281	.358	92	-6	19	.962	2	100	123	*O-118(LF)	-1.0
1920	Bos N	115	424	48	117	7	8	3	32	38	4	42	.276	.341	.351	104	2	7-7	.980	0	99	102	*O-110(102-0-8)	-0.4
1921	StL N	97	256	57	84	12	7	7	30	23	3	28	.328	.390	.512	140	14	5-5	.969	3	105	114	O-79(1-66-12)	1.3
1922	StL N	84	147	42	51	14	1	2	20	16	1	12	.347	.415	.497	141	10	0-1	.978	1	109	78	O-57(10-47-0)	0.8
1923	StL N	38	89	20	33	5	2	5	11	9	1	5	.371	.434	.640	184	11	0-0	.979	1	104	135	O-26(5-6-16)	1.0
	Cin N	8	1	1	0	0	0	0	0	0	0	0	.000	.000	.000	-99	0	0-0	—	0			H	0.0
	Year	46	90	21	33	5	2	5	11	9	1	5	.367	.430	.633	181	10	0-0	.979	1	104	135	O-26(5-6-16)	1.0
1924	Bos N	32	102	13	28	7	4	0	10	8	1	10	.275	.333	.422	105	1	1-0	1.000	1	104	121	O-28(7-0-21)	0.0
1925	Bos N	60	184	27	63	11	4	2	20	5	4	11	.342	.373	.478	127	7	6-1	.992	3	107	110	O-57(5-11-41)	0.6
1926	Bos N	50	129	23	39	8	2	1	20	9	0	9	.302	.348	.419	116	3	5	.966	2	108	142	O-46(17-17-16)	0.3
1927	Bos N	29	66	8	17	3	1	0	6	8	0	3	.258	.338	.333	87	-1	2	.955	2	101	202	O-24(5-3-17)	-0.1
	NY N	29	67	13	22	4	1	2	10	8	0	7	.328	.400	.507	142	4	2	1.000	-0	85	142	O-22(15-5-2)	0.3
	Year	58	133	21	39	7	2	2	16	16	0	10	.293	.369	.421	116	3	4	.973	1	94	175	O-46(20-8-19)	0.2
1928	NY N	82	193	29	51	7	1	2	25	18	1	9	.264	.330	.342	76	-7	2	.952	-3	91	64	O-68(3-14-63)	-1.3
Total	16	1498	4716	677	1332	203	106	44	503	324	28	464	.282	.332	.398	109	43	129-37	.966	18	100	113	*O-1368(708-414-277)/S	-1.8

MANNING, JIMMY James H. B 1.31.1862 Fall River, MA D 10.22.1929 Edinburg, TX BB/TR 5-7/157# d5.16 M1

Year	Tm Lg	G	AB	R	H	2B	3B	HR	RBI	BB-IB	HP	SO	AVG	OBP	SLG	AOPS	ABR	SB-CS	FA	FR	Rng	Thr	G at Pos	BFW
1884	Bos N	89	345	52	83	8	6	2	35	19		47	.241	.280	.316	88	-5		.878	-3	95	97	O-73(1-72-0)/S-9,2-9,3-3	-0.9
1885	Bos N	84	306	34	63	8	9	2	27	19		36	.206	.252	.310	84	-6		.898	7	130	131	*O-83(12-63-8)/S	-0.1
	Det N	20	78	15	21	4	0	1	9	4		10	.269	.305	.359	114	1		.802	-6	83	113	S-20	-0.4
	Year	104	384	49	84	12	9	3	36	23		46	.219	.263	.320	90	-4		.898	1	130	131	O-83(12-63-8),S-21	-0.5
1886	Det N	26	97	14	18	2	3	0	7	6		10	.186	.233	.268	50	-6	7	.947	0	85	158	O-26(LF)/S	-0.6
1887	Det N	13	52	5	10	1	0	0	3	5	1	4	.192	.276	.212	36	-4	3	.867	-5	0	0	O-10(LF)/S-3	-0.8
1889	KC AA	132	506	68	103	16	7	3	68	54	13	61	.204	.297	.281	61	-27	58	.927	-8	154	63	O-69(LF),2-63/S3	-2.9
Total	5	364	1384	188	298	39	25	8	149	107	14	168	.215	.278	.297	73	-47	68	.903	-15	118	102	O-261(118-135-8)/2-72,S-35,3-4	-5.7

MANNING, JACK John E. B 12.20.1853 Braintree, MA D 8.15.1929 Boston, MA BR/TR 5-8.5/158# d4.23 M1 ▲ OF NA (2-LF 2-CF 69-RF) OF Total (2-LF 16-CF 605-RF)

Year	Tm Lg	G	AB	R	H	2B	3B	HR	RBI	BB-IB	HP	SO	AVG	OBP	SLG	AOPS	ABR	SB-CS	FA	FR	Rng	Thr	G at Pos	BFW
1873	Bos NA	31	154	28	41	4	1	0	21	1		14	.266	.271	.305	65	-8	5-2	.920	-1	168	132	1-28/O-7(2-0-5)	-0.5
1874	Bal NA	42	174	32	61	8	2	0	18	2		2	.351	.358	.420	149	9	0-0	.839	-5	109	0	P-22,2-22/S-4,13	-0.1
	Har NA	1	5	1	1	0	0	0	0	0		0	.200	.200	.200	27	0	0-0	.167	-2	38	0	/3	-0.2
	Year	43	179	33	62	8	2	0	18	2		2	.346	.354	.413	146	9	0-0	.793	-7	109	0	P-22,2-22/S-4,3-2,1	-0.3
1875	Bos NA	77	348	71	94	11	3	1	46	2		9	.270	.274	.328	104	1	5-5	.802	-1	151	117	*O-65(0-2-64),P-27/1-3,3	0.3
1876	Bos N	**70**	288	52	76	13	0	2	25	7		5	.264	.281	.330	101	1		.777	-4	85	0	*O-56(0-1-55),P-34/S2	-0.3
1877	Cin N	57	252	47	80	16	7	0	36	5		6	.317	.331	.437	157	17		.742	-10	87	30	S-26,1-17,O-12(1-10-1),P-10/2-2,M	0.5
1878	Bos N	**60**	248	41	63	10	1	0	23	10		16	.254	.283	.302	86	-4		.753	-15	57	45	*O-59(0-3-56)/P-3	-1.8
1880	Cin N	48	190	20	41	6	3	2	17	7		15	.216	.244	.311	87	-2		.798	-3	108	45	O-47(0-2-47)/1	-0.6
1881	Buf N	1	1	0	0	0	0	0	0	0		0	.000	.000	.000	-99	0		1.000	1	1112	0	/O(LF)	0.0
1883	Phi N	98	420	60	112	31	5	0	37	20		37	.267	.300	.364	110	8		.853	7	167	108	*O-98(RF)	1.2
1884	Phi N	104	424	71	115	29	4	5	52	40		67	.271	.334	.394	134	20		.847	0	129	194	*O-104(RF)	1.7
1885	Phi N	107	445	61	114	24	4	3	40	37		27	.256	.313	.348	116	10		.896	-6	106	119	*O-107(RF)	0.3
1886	Bal AA	137	556	78	124	18	7	1	45	50	3		.223	.291	.286	83	-10	24	.887	-9	71	72	*O-137(RF)	-1.8
Total	3 NA	151	681	132	197	23	6	1	85	5	0	25	.289	.294	.345	105	2	10-7	.000	-8	139	108	/O-72R,P-49,1-32,2-22,S-4,3-3	-0.5
Total	9	682	2824	430	725	147	31	13	275	176	3	173	.257	.301	.345	108	40	24-0	.844	-39	106	94	O-621R/P-47,S-27,1-18,2-3	-0.8

MANNING, RICK Richard Eugene B 9.2.1954 Niagara Falls, NY BL/TR 6-1/180# d5.23

Year	Tm Lg	G	AB	R	H	2B	3B	HR	RBI	BB-IB	HP	SO	AVG	OBP	SLG	AOPS	ABR	SB-CS	FA	FR	Rng	Thr	G at Pos	BFW
1975	Cle A	120	480	69	137	16	5	3	35	44-2	2	62	.285	.347	.358	100	0	19-11	.974	10	115	133	*O-118(28-69-32)/D	0.6
1976	Cle A	138	552	73	161	24	7	6	43	41-1	0	75	.292	.337	.393	116	10	16-10	.987	-2	99	82	*O-136(CF)	0.4
1977	Cle A	68	252	33	57	7	3	5	18	21-0	0	35	.226	.282	.337	71	-11	9-5	.990	1	111	43	O-68(CF)	-1.0
1978	Cle A	148	566	65	149	27	3	3	50	38-1	1	62	.263	.309	.337	83	-13	12-12	.995	-3	98	78	*O-144(CF)	-2.0
1979	Cle A	144	560	67	145	12	2	3	51	55-3	1	48	.259	.323	.304	71	-22	30-8	.986	7	110	97	*O-141(CF)/D	-1.3
1980	Cle A	140	471	55	110	17	4	3	52	63-11	2	66	.234	.321	.306	74	-15	12-6	.990	1	104	76	*O-139(CF)	-1.5
1981	Cle A	**103**	360	47	88	15	3	4	33	40-2	0	57	.244	.318	.336	90	-4	25-3	.987	8	116	101	*O-103(CF)	0.8
1982	Cle A	152	562	71	152	18	2	8	44	54-5	0	60	.270	.334	.352	89	-8	12-8	.978	-7	93	98	*O-152(CF)	-1.6
1983	Cle A	50	194	20	54	6	0	1	10	12-1	0	22	.278	.319	.325	75	-7	7-3	.987	-1	104	31	O-50(CF)	-0.8
	Mil A	108	375	40	86	14	4	3	33	26-4	1	40	.229	.279	.312	68	-17	11-2	.991	-1	107	14	*O-108(CF)	-1.8
	Year	158	569	60	140	20	4	4	43	38-5	1	62	.246	.292	.316	71	-24	18-5	.990	-2	106	20	*O-158(CF)	-2.6
1984	Mil A	119	341	53	85	10	5	7	31	34-1	1	32	.249	.318	.370	94	-3	5-7	.987	-13	84	31	*O-114(CF)/D	-1.9
1985	Mil A	79	216	19	47	9	1	2	18	14-0	0	19	.218	.265	.296	54	-14	1-0	.976	-2	101	50	O-74(1-57-17)/D-2	-1.7
1986	Mil A	89	205	31	52	7	3	8	27	17-2	1	20	.254	.310	.434	98	-1	5-3	.988	4	115	81	O-83(40-29-18)/D-5	0.0
1987	Mil A	97	114	21	26	7	1	0	13	12-0	0	18	.228	.299	.307	60	-6	4-0	.958	-1	102	45	O-78(21-8-51)/D-2	-0.8
Total	13	1555	5248	664	1349	189	43	56	458	471-33	9	616	.257	.317	.341	84	-111	168-78	.985	-1	104	75	*O-1508(90-1317-118)/D-12	-12.6

MANNING, TIM Timothy Edward B 12.3.1853 Henley-On-Thames, England D 6.11.1934 Oak Park, IL BR/TR 5-10/170# d5.1

Year	Tm Lg	G	AB	R	H	2B	3B	HR	RBI	BB-IB	HP	SO	AVG	OBP	SLG	AOPS	ABR	SB-CS	FA	FR	Rng	Thr	G at Pos	BFW
1882	Pro N	21	76	7	8	0	0	0	8	5		13	.105	.160	.105	-13	-9		.787	-9	79	72	S-17/C-4	-1.7
1883	Bal AA	35	121	23	26	5	0	0		14			.215	.296	.256	77	-2		.913	3	106	53	2-35	0.2
1884	Bal AA	91	341	49	70	14	5	2		26	7		.205	.275	.293	82	-6		.907	-2	96	73	*2-91	-0.5
1885	Bal AA	43	157	17	32	8	1	0	16	10	3		.204	.265	.268	70	-5		.919	2	103	99	2-41/3-3	-0.1
	Pro N	10	35	3	2	1	0	0	0	1		11	.057	.083	.086	-47	-6		.854	-3	74	69	S-10	-0.8
Total	4	200	730	99	138	28	6	2	24	56		24	.189	.256	.252	63	-28		.911	-10	100	75	2-167/S-27,C-4,3-3	-2.9

MANNO, DON Donald D. B 5.4.1915 Williamsport, PA D 3.11.1995 Williamsport, PA BR/TR 6-1/190# d9.22

Year	Tm Lg	G	AB	R	H	2B	3B	HR	RBI	BB-IB	HP	SO	AVG	OBP	SLG	AOPS	ABR	SB-CS	FA	FR	Rng	Thr	G at Pos	BFW
1940	Bos N	3	7	1	2	0	0	1	4	0	0	2	.286	.286	.714	177	1	0	1.000	0	134	0	/O-2(RF)	0.1
1941	Bos N	22	30	2	5	1	0	0	4	3	0	7	.167	.242	.200	27	-3	0	1.000	-1	94	0	/O-5(LF),3-3,1	-0.4
Total	2	25	37	3	7	1	0	1	8	3	0	9	.189	.250	.297	56	-2	0	1.000	-1	109	0	/O-7(5-0-2),3-3,1	-0.3

MANRIQUE, FRED Fred Eloy (Reyes) B 11.5.1961 Edo Bolivar, Venezuela BR/TR 6-1/175# d8.23

Year	Tm Lg	G	AB	R	H	2B	3B	HR	RBI	BB-IB	HP	SO	AVG	OBP	SLG	AOPS	ABR	SB-CS	FA	FR	Rng	Thr	G at Pos	BFW
1981	Tor A	14	28	1	4	0	0	0	1	0-0	1	12	.143	.172	.143	-8	-4	0-1	.949	1	124	144	S-11/3-2,D	-0.3
1984	Tor A	10	9	0	3	0	0	0	1	0-0	0	1	.333	.333	.333	82	0	0-0	.938	1	136	204	/2-9,D	0.1
1985	Mon N	9	13	5	4	1	1	1	1	1-0	0	3	.308	.357	.769	219	2	0-0	1.000	1	115	0	/2-2,S-2,3	0.3
1986	StL N	13	17	2	3	0	0	1	1	1-0	0	1	.176	.222	.353	57	-1	1-0	1.000	-2	60	0	/3-4,2	-0.3
1987	Chi A	115	298	30	77	13	3	4	29	19-1	1	69	.258	.302	.362	74	-11	5-3	.984	-4	105	120	2-92,S-23/D-5	-0.9
1988	Chi A	140	345	43	81	10	6	5	37	21-1	3	54	.235	.283	.342	75	-13	6-5	.985	5	105	108	*2-129,S-12/D	-0.5
1989	Chi A	65	187	23	56	13	1	2	30	8-1	2	30	.299	.333	.412	112	3	0-4	.961	-9	90	91	2-57/S-2,3D	-0.6
	Tex A	54	191	23	55	12	0	2	22	9-0	0	33	.288	.318	.382	96	-1	4-1	.963	-4	87	112	S-37,2-17/3-6	-0.2
	Year	119	378	46	111	25	1	4	52	17-1	2	63	.294	.326	.397	104	1	4-5	.952	-12	89	86	2-74,S-39/3-7,D	-0.8
1990	Min A	69	228	22	54	10	0	5	29	4-0	2	35	.237	.254	.346	63	-12	2-0	.974	-7	96	103	2-67/D	-1.7
1991	Oak A	9	21	2	3	0	0	0	0	2-0	0	1	.143	.217	.143	2	-3	0-0	.955	-0	83	52	/S-7,2-2	-0.3
Total	9	498	1337	151	340	59	11	20	151	65-3	9	239	.254	.292	.360	79	-40	18-14	.976	-17	101	106	2-376/S-94,3-14,D-10	-4.4

MANSELL, JOHN John B 1861 Auburn, NY D 2.20.1925 Romulus, NY BL 5-10/168# d5.9 b-Mike b-Tom

Year	Tm Lg	G	AB	R	H	2B	3B	HR	RBI	BB-IB	HP	SO	AVG	OBP	SLG	AOPS	ABR	SB-CS	FA	FR	Rng	Thr	G at Pos	BFW
1882	Phi AA	31	126	17	30	3	1	0	17	4			.238	.262	.278	77	-3		.791	-5	54	0	O-31(CF)	-0.9

MANSELL, MIKE Michael R. B 1.15.1858 Auburn, NY D 12.4.1902 Auburn, NY BL 5-11/175# d5.1 b-John b-Tom

Year	Tm Lg	G	AB	R	H	2B	3B	HR	RBI	BB-IB	HP	SO	AVG	OBP	SLG	AOPS	ABR	SB-CS	FA	FR	Rng	Thr	G at Pos	BFW
1879	Syr N	67	242	24	52	4	2	1	13	5		45	.215	.231	.260	69	-7		.881	15	71	103	*O-67(LF)	0.3
1880	Cin N	53	187	22	36	6	2	2	12	4		37	.193	.209	.278	64	-7		.865	12	102	196	O-53(LF)	0.2
1882	Pit AA	**79**	347	59	96	**18**	**16**	2		7			.277	.291	.438	150	17		.829	3	86	55	*O-79(LF)	1.6
1883	Pit AA	96	412	90	106	12	13	3		25			.257	.300	.371	120	10		.883	3	59	39	*O-96(LF)	0.9
1884	Pit AA	27	100	15	14	0	3	1		7	1		.140	.204	.230	42	-6		.796	-1	60	110	O-27(24-0-3)	-0.8
	Phi AA	20	70	6	14	1	1	0		5	0		.200	.253	.243	59	-3		.762	-2	48	0	O-20(16-4-0)	-0.5
	Ric AA	29	113	21	34	2	5	0		8	3		.301	.363	.407	153	7		.763	-3	106	125	O-29(0-2-27)	0.3
	Year	76	283	42	62	3	9	1		20	4		.219	.280	.304	90	-3		.775	-6	72	82	O-76(40-6-30)	-1.0
Total	5	371	1471	237	352	43	42	9	25	61	4	82	.239	.271	.344	106	11		.854	26	76	86	O-371(335-6-30)	2.0

MANSELL, TOM Thomas E. "Brick" B 1.1.1855 Auburn, NY D 10.6.1934 Auburn, NY BL/TR 5-8/160# d5.1 b-John b-Mike

Year	Tm Lg	G	AB	R	H	2B	3B	HR	RBI	BB-IB	HP	SO	AVG	OBP	SLG	AOPS	ABR	SB-CS	FA	FR	Rng	Thr	G at Pos	BFW
1879	Tro N	40	177	29	43	6	0	0	11	3		9	.243	.256	.277	81	-3		.742	-7	31	82	O-40(38-2-0)	-1.2

Year	Tm Lg	G	AB	R	H	2B	3B	HR	RBI	BB-IB	HP	SO	AVG	OBP	SLG	AOPS	ABR	SB-CS	FA	FR	Rng	Thr	G at Pos	BFW
	Syr N	1	4	0	1	0	0	0	0	0		0	.250	.250	.250	74	0		1.000	-0	0	0	/O(RF)	0.0
	Year	41	181	29	44	6	0	0	11	3		9	.243	.255	.276	81	-3		.747	-7	30	80	O-41(38-2-1)	-1.2
1883	Det N	34	131	22	29	4	1	0	10	8		13	.221	.266	.267	66	-5		.758	-4	149	73	O-34(RF)/P	-0.8
	StL AA	28	112	23	45	8	1	0	24	7			.402	.437	.491	188	11		.786	-6	18	0	O-28(25-2-1)	0.4
1884	Cin AA	65	266	49	66	4	6	0	23	15	5		.248	.301	.308	94	-2		.752	-10	25	0	O-65(41-25-1)	-1.2
	Col AA	23	77	9	15	1	3	0	6	6	1		.195	.262	.286	85	-1		.667	-3	85	0	O-23(LF)	-0.4
	Year	88	343	58	81	5	9	0	29	21	6		.236	.292	.303	93	-3		.739	-12	39	0	O-88(64-25-1)	-1.6
Total	3	191	767	132	199	23	11	0	74	39	6	22	.259	.300	.318	100	0		.751	-29	54	33	O-191(127-29-37)/P	-3.2
MANTILLA, FELIX Felix (Lamela) B 7.29.1934 Isabela, P.R. BR/TR 6/160# d6.21 OF Total (74-LF 76-CF 10-RF)																								
1956	Mil N	35	53	9	15	1	1	0	3	1-0	1	8	.283	.309	.340	79	-2	0-1	1.000	5	144	138	S-15/3-3	0.4
1957	†Mil N	71	182	28	43	9	1	4	21	14-2	2	34	.236	.296	.363	82	-5	2-0	.931	5	108	116	S-35,2-13/3-7,O(CF)	0.3
1958	†Mil N	85	226	37	50	5	1	7	19	20-2	0	20	.221	.282	.345	72	-10	2-0	.987	-3	90	76	O-43(12-33-0),2-21/S-5,3-2	-1.3
1959	Mil N	103	251	26	54	5	0	3	19	16-1	2	31	.215	.266	.271	48	-19	6-1	.970	0	105	98	2-60,S-23/3-9,O-7(CF)	-1.4
1960	Mil N	63	148	21	38	7	0	3	11	7-1	1	16	.257	.291	.365	86	-3	3-1	.956	-8	71	70	2-26,S-25/O-8(3-5-0)	-0.9
1961	Mil N	45	93	13	20	3	0	1	5	10-0	1	16	.215	.298	.280	58	-6	1-1	.933	-3	94	101	S-19,2-10,O-10(2-6-2)/3-6	-0.8
1962	NY N	141	466	54	128	17	4	11	59	37-0	5	51	.275	.330	.399	94	-4	3-1	.948	-4	106	124	3-95,S-25,2-14	-0.6
1963	Bos A	66	178	27	56	8	0	6	15	20-1	0	14	.315	.384	.461	131	8	2-1	.965	-1	93	117	S-27,O-11(CF)/2-5	0.9
1964	Bos A	133	425	69	123	20	1	30	64	41-1	4	46	.289	.357	.553	142	24	0-1	.984	-1	97	110	O-48(36-5-8),2-45/3-7,S-6	2.6
1965	Bos A★	150	534	60	147	17	2	18	92	79-5	8	84	.275	.374	.416	118	16	7-3	.976	-17	89	81	*2-123,O-27(20-8-0)/1-2	0.9
1966	Hou N	77	151	16	33	5	0	6	22	11-0	2	32	.219	.279	.371	85	-3	1-0	.990	-2	42	90	1-14,3-14/2-9,O(LF)	-0.6
Total	11	969	2707	360	707	97	10	89	330	256-13	26	352	.261	.329	.403	100	-4	27-10	.977	-28	93	83	2-326,S-180,O-156C,3-143/1-16	-0.5
MANTLE, MICKEY Mickey Charles "The Commerce Comet" B10.20.1931 Spavinaw, OK D8.13.1995 Dallas, TX BB/TR 5-11/198# d4.17 C1 HF1974 OF Total (129-LF 1745-CF 146-RF)																								
1951	†NY A	96	341	61	91	11	5	13	65	43	0	74	.267	.349	.443	117	7	8-7	.959	-5	90	74	O-86(0-3-85)	-0.1
1952	†NY A☆	142	549	94	171	37	7	23	87	75	0	111	.311	.394	.530	166	**48**	4-1	.968	-6	90	132	*O-141(0-121-20)/3	3.9
1953	†NY A★	127	461	105	136	24	3	21	92	79	0	90	.295	.398	.497	145	31	8-4	.982	-3	97	95	*O-121(0-116-4)/S	2.3
1954	NY A★	146	543	**129**	163	17	12	27	102	102	0	107	.300	.408	.525	160	47	5-2	.975	-4	88	156	*O-144(0-143-1)/S-4,2	3.8
1955	†NY A★	147	517	121	158	25	**11**	**37**	99	**113**-6	3	97	.306	**.431**	**.611**	**181**	**62**	8-1	.995	-1	97	129	*O-145(CF)/S-2	**5.5**
1956	†NY A★	150	533	**132**	188	22	5	**52**	**130**	112-6	2	99	**.353**	.464	**.705**	**213**	**90**	10-1	.990	0	100	105	*O-144(CF)	**8.1**
1957	†NY A★	144	474	**121**	173	28	6	34	94	**146**-23	0	75	.365	.512	.665	223	**94**	16-3	.979	-8	95	64	*O-139(CF)	**8.2**
1958	†NY A★	150	519	**127**	158	21	1	**42**	97	**129-13**	2	120	.304	.443	.592	**189**	**71**	18-3	.977	-8	94	62	*O-150(CF)	**6.0**
1959	NY A★	144	541	104	154	23	4	31	75	93-6	2	126	.285	.390	.514	**152**	**41**	21-3	**.995**	-1	101	72	*O-143(CF)	**3.6**
1960	†NY A★	153	527	**119**	145	17	6	**40**	94	111-6	1	125	.275	.399	.558	**166**	**51**	14-3	.991	-9	90	100	*O-150(CF)	**3.8**
1961	†NY A★	153	514	**132**	163	16	6	54	128	**126**-9	0	112	.317	.448	**.687**	**210**	**86**	12-1	.983	-7	97	76	*O-150(CF)	7.4
1962	†NY A★	123	377	96	121	15	1	30	89	**122**-9	1	78	.321	**.486**	**.605**	**198**	**63**	9-0	.978	-11	86	73	*O-117(0-94-23)	**5.0**
1963	†NY A✳	65	172	40	54	8	0	15	35	40-4	0	32	.314	.441	.622	197	25	2-1	.990	-2	99	74	O-52(CF)	2.2
1964	†NY A★	143	465	92	141	25	2	35	111	99-**18**	0	102	.303	**.423**	.591	**177**	**53**	6-3	.978	-13	84	38	*O-132(17-102-13)	3.8
1965	NY A✳	122	361	44	92	12	1	19	46	73-7	0	76	.255	.379	.452	136	20	4-1	.966	-3	94	50	*O-108(LF)	1.2
1966	NY A	108	333	40	96	12	1	23	56	57-5	0	76	.288	.389	.538	171	32	1-1	1.000	-5	94	41	O-97(4-93-0)	2.6
1967	NY A★	144	440	63	108	17	0	22	55	107-7	1	113	.245	.391	.434	150	34	1-1	.993	4	115	92	*1-131	3.3
1968	NY A★	144	435	57	103	14	1	18	54	106-7	1	97	.237	.385	.398	143	29	6-2	.988	-2	99	102	*1-131	2.3
Total	18	2401	8102	1677	2415	344	72	536	1509	1733-126	13	1710	.298	.421	.557	173	884	153-38	.982	-83	94	88	*O-2019C,1-262/S-7,23	72.9
MANTO, JEFF Jeffrey Paul B 8.23.1964 Bristol, PA BR/TR 6-3/210# d6.7 OF Total (LF)																								
1990	Cle A	30	76	12	17	5	1	2	14	21-1	0	18	.224	.392	.395	121	3	0-1	.990	1	132	103	1-25/3-5	0.3
1991	Cle A	47	128	15	27	7	0	2	13	14-0	4	22	.211	.306	.313	72	-5	2-0	.929	-1	97	203	3-32,1-14/C-5,O(LF)	-0.6
1993	Phi N	8	18	0	1	0	0	0	0	0-0	1	3	.056	.105	.056	-56	-4	0-0	1.000	-0	84	0	/3-6,S	-0.5
1995	Bal A	89	254	31	65	9	0	17	38	24-0	2	69	.256	.325	.492	107	1	0-3	.959	-2	91	117	3-69,D-13/1-4	-0.2
1996	Bos A	10	30	5	8	3	1	2	4	3-0	1	6	.267	.353	.633	140	2	0-0	.963	4	134	99	/2-4,S-4	0.6
	Sea A	21	54	7	10	3	0	1	4	9-0	0	12	.185	.302	.296	52	-4	0-1	.971	0	104	82	3-16/O(LF)D	-0.4
	Bos A	12	18	3	2	0	0	0	2	5-0	0	6	.111	.304	.111	11	-2	0-0	.960	3	146	77	3-10/1	0.0
	Year	43	102	15	20	6	1	3	10	17-0	1	24	.196	.317	.363	70	-5	0-1	.967	7	118	80	3-26/2-4,S-4,D-2,O(LF)1	0.2
1997	Cle A	16	30	3	8	3	0	2	7	1-0	0	10	.267	.290	.567	113	0	0-0	1.000	-2	72	0	/3-7,1-6,O(LF)	-0.2
1998	Cle A	7	14	3	1	0	0	0	1	1-0	0	5	.071	.133	.071	-43	-3	0-0	1.000	-5	0	23	/1-4,3-2,2	-0.9
	Det A	16	30	6	8	2	0	1	3	3-0	1	11	.267	.353	.433	102	0	1-0	.977	-2	0	68	1-10/O(LF)D	-0.2
	Cle A	8	23	5	7	1	0	2	5	1-0	0	5	.304	.333	.609	134	1	0-1	1.000	-3	12	0	/3-6,1-3	-0.3
	Year	31	67	14	16	3	0	3	9	5-0	1	21	.239	.301	.418	83	-2	1-1	.979	-10	18	54	1-17/3-8,D-6,2O(LF)	-1.4
1999	Cle A	12	25	5	5	0	0	1	2	11-0	0	11	.200	.444	.320	95	1	0-0	1.000	1	110	148	3-10/1	0.2
	NY A	6	8	0	1	0	0	0	0	2-0	0	4	.125	.300	.125	14	-1	0-0	1.000	0	112	80	/1-3,3	-0.1
	Year	18	33	5	6	0	0	1	2	13-0	0	15	.182	.413	.273	78	0	0-0	1.000	1	108	146	3-11/1-4	0.1
2000	Col N	7	5	2	4	2	0	1	4	2-0	0	0	.800	.857	1.800	437	3	0-0	1.000	0	0	1047	/13	0.3
Total	9	289	713	97	164	35	2	31	97	97-1	9	182	.230	.329	.415	94	-8	3-6	.960	-6	92	123	3-165/1-72,D-21,2-5,S-5,C-5,0-4L	-2.0
MANUEL, CHARLIE Charles Fuqua B 1.4.1944 Northfork, WV BL/TR 6-4/200# d4.8 M3 C8																								
1969	†Min A	83	164	14	34	6	0	2	24	28-4	0	33	.207	.320	.280	69	-6	1-0	.967	-3	82	69	O-46(41-1-4)	-1.1
1970	†Min A	59	64	4	12	0	0	1	7	6-2	1	17	.188	.260	.234	39	-5	0-0	1.000	-1	66	0	O-11(9-0-2)	-0.7
1971	Min A	18	16	1	2	1	0	0	1	1-0	0	8	.125	.176	.188	3	-2	0-0	—	-0	0	0	/O(RF)	-0.2
1972	Min A	63	122	6	25	5	0	1	8	4-0	1	16	.205	.233	.270	48	-8	0-0	.977	1	91	233	O-28(20-0-9)	-0.9
1974	LA N	4	3	0	1	0	0	0	1	1-0	0	0	.333	.500	.333	142	0	0-0	—	0			H	0.0
1975	LA N	15	15	0	2	0	0	0	2	0-0	0	3	.133	.133	.133	-27	-3	0-0	—	0			H	-0.3
Total	6	242	384	25	76	12	0	4	43	40-6	2	77	.198	.273	.260	52	-24	1-0	.973	-3	83	120	/O-86(70-1-16)	-3.2
MANUEL, JERRY Jerry B 12.23.1953 Hahira, GA BB/TR (BR 1981-82) 6/165# d9.18 M6 C7																								
1975	Det A	6	18	0	1	0	0	0	0	0-0	0	4	.056	.056	.056	-66	-4	0-0	.944	2	140	99	/2-6	-0.1
1976	Det A	54	43	4	6	1	0	0	2	3-0	1	9	.140	.213	.163	11	-5	1-0	.921	-1	108	64	2-47/S-4,D	-0.4
1980	Mon N	7	6	0	0	0	0	0	0	0-0	0	2	.000	.000	.000	-99	-2	0-0	.941	1	142	0	/S-7	0.0
1981	†Mon N	27	55	10	11	5	0	3	10	6-1	0	11	.200	.270	.455	104	0	0-0	.987	-3	80	115	2-23/S-2	-0.2
1982	SD N	2	5	0	1	0	1	0	1	1-0	0	0	.200	.333	.600	165	0	0-0	1.000	-2	0	172	/2S3	-0.1
Total	5	96	127	14	19	6	1	3	13	10-1	1	26	.150	.214	.283	42	-11	1-0	.949	-2	99	91	/2-77,S-14,3D	-0.8
MANUSH, FRANK Frank Benjamin B 9.18.1883 Tuscumbia, AL D 1.5.1965 Laguna Beach, CA BR/TR 5-10.5/175# d8.31 b-Heinie																								
1908	Phi A	23	77	6	12	2	1	0	0	2	1		.156	.188	.208	27	-6	2	.933	-4	71	89	3-20/2-2	-1.2
MANUSH, HEINIE Henry Emmett B 7.20.1901 Tuscumbia, AL D 5.12.1971 Sarasota, FL BL/TL 6-1/200# d4.20 C2 HF1964 b-Frank																								
1923	Det A	109	308	59	103	20	5	4	54	20	**17**	21	.334	.406	.471	133	15	3-5	.953	-6	93	61	O-79(72-0-7)	0.2
1924	Det A	120	422	83	122	24	8	9	68	27	**16**	30	.289	.355	.448	108	3	14-5	.979	-7	97	35	*O-106(99-1-6)/1	-1.0
1925	Det A	99	278	46	84	14	3	5	47	24	2	21	.302	.362	.428	101	0	8-3	.982	0	98	107	O-73(13-56-5)	-0.2
1926	Det A	136	498	95	188	35	8	14	86	31	6	28	**.378**	.421	.564	153	37	11-5	.967	-10	96	60	*O-120(11-104-5)	2.2
1927	Det A	151	593	102	177	31	18	6	90	47	4	29	.298	.354	.442	104	1	12-8	.971	-9	94	60	*O-149(3-147-0)	-1.4
1928	StL A	**154**	638	104	**241**	**47**	20	13	108	39	0	14	.378	.414	.575	153	46	16-5	.992	-2	104	40	*O-154(LF)	3.3
1929	StL A	142	574	85	204	**45**	10	6	81	43	1	24	.355	.401	.500	126	23	9-9	.987	-5	93	77	*O-141(LF)	0.5
1930	StL A	49	198	26	65	16	4	2	29	5	0	7	.328	.345	.480	103	0	3-1	.990	3	105	147	O-48(LF)	0.0
	Was A	88	356	74	129	33	8	7	65	26	0	17	.362	.406	.559	141	22	4-3	.988	-3	93	78	O-86(LF)	1.2
	Year	137	554	100	194	49	12	9	94	31	0	24	.350	.385	.531	128	22	7-4	.989	-0	97	102	*O-134(LF)	1.2
1931	Was A	146	616	110	189	41	11	6	70	36	6	27	.307	.351	.438	106	4	3-3	.977	-12	86	50	*O-143(LF)	-1.5
1932	Was A	149	625	121	214	41	14	14	116	36	5	29	.342	.383	.520	133	29	7-2	.988	-1	101	54	*O-146(LF)	1.9
1933	†Was A	**153**	658	115	**221**	32	**17**	5	95	36	2	18	.336	.372	.459	120	17	6-4	.982	-3	99	64	*O-150(LF)	0.5
1934	Was A★	137	556	88	194	42	11	11	89	36	3	23	.349	.392	.523	140	31	7-3	.980	-2	105	43	*O-131(130-1-0)	2.0
1935	Was A	119	479	68	131	26	9	4	56	35	4	17	.273	.328	.390	88	-10	2-0	.985	2	102	84	*O-111(LF)	-1.3
1936	Bos A	82	313	43	91	15	5	0	45	17	1	11	.291	.329	.371	69	-16	1-3	.966	-4	90	57	O-72(LF)	-2.2
1937	Bro N	132	466	57	155	25	7	4	73	40	3	24	.333	.389	.442	123	16	6	.970	-6	94	64	*O-123(RF)	0.3
1938	Bro N	17	51	9	12	3	1	0	6	5	0	4	.235	.304	.333	73	-2	1	1.000	1	118	88	O-12(RF)	-0.2
	Pit N	15	13	2	4	1	1	0	4	2	0	0	.308	.400	.538	155	1	0	—	0			H	0.1
	Year	32	64	11	16	4	2	0	10	7	0	4	.250	.324	.375	90	-1	1	1.000	1	118	88	O-12(RF)	-0.1

Year	Tm Lg	G	AB	R	H	2B	3B	HR	RBI	BB-IB	HP	SO	AVG	OBP	SLG	AOPS	ABR	SB-CS	FA	FR	Rng	Thr	G at Pos	BFW
1939	Pit N	10	12	0	0	0	0	0	1	1	0	1	.000	.077	.000	-79	-3	0	1.000	-0	74	0	/O(RF)	-0.3
Total	17	2008	7654	1287	2524	491	160	110	1183	506	70	345	.330	.377	.479	121	214	113-59	.979	-63	97	62	*O-1845(1379-309-159)/1	4.1
MANWARING, KIRT Kirt Dean B 7.15.1965 Elmira, NY BR/TR 5-11/190# d9.15																								
1987	SF N	6	7	0	1	0	0	0	0	0-0	1	1	.143	.250	.143	8	-1	0-0	.909	-1	206	0	/C-6	-0.2
1988	SF N	40	116	12	29	7	0	1	15	2-0	3	21	.250	.279	.336	80	-3	0-1	.979	-3	109	92	C-40	-0.5
1989	†SF N	85	200	14	42	4	2	0	18	11-1	4	28	.210	.264	.250	49	-14	2-1	.982	1	148	86	C-81	-1.0
1990	SF N	8	13	0	2	0	1	0	1	0-0	0	3	.154	.154	.308	25	-2	0-0	1.000	0	92	0	/C-8	-0.1
1991	SF N	67	178	16	40	9	0	0	19	9-0	3	22	.225	.271	.275	57	-10	1-1	.988	1	131	90	C-67	-0.7
1992	SF N	109	349	24	85	10	5	4	26	29-0	5	42	.244	.311	.335	88	-6	2-1	.994	7	**172**	127	*C-108	0.7
1993	SF N	130	432	48	119	15	1	5	49	41-13	6	76	.275	.345	.350	90	-5	1-3	**.998**	7	**154**	122	*C-130	0.9
1994	SF N	97	316	30	79	17	1	1	29	25-3	3	50	.250	.308	.320	68	-15	1-1	.993	2	108	102	C-97	-0.6
1995	SF N	118	379	21	95	15	2	4	36	27-6	10	72	.251	.314	.332	74	-14	1-0	.990	-12	121	77	*C-118	-1.9
1996	SF N	49	145	9	34	6	0	1	14	16-1	3	24	.234	.319	.297	67	-6	0-1	.993	-1	120	161	C-49	-0.5
	Hou N	37	82	5	18	3	0	0	4	3-0	2	16	.220	.264	.256	41	-7	0-0	.995	2	113	194	C-37	-0.4
	Year	86	227	14	52	9	0	1	18	19-1	5	40	.229	.300	.282	59	-13	0-1	**.994**	1	117	**173**	C-86	-0.9
1997	Col N	104	337	22	76	6	4	1	27	30-0	2	78	.226	.291	.276	41	-29	1-5	.994	-15	87	84	*C-100	-4.0
1998	Col N	110	291	30	72	12	3	2	26	38-3	3	49	.247	.339	.330	64	-14	1-5	.988	-2	90	116	*C-108	-1.1
1999	Col N	48	137	17	41	7	1	2	14	12-1	5	23	.299	.374	.409	78	-4	0-0	.981	-6	72	83	C-44/D	-0.7
Total	13	1008	2982	248	733	111	20	21	278	243-28	50	505	.246	.311	.318	68	-130	10-19	.991	-22	123	106	C-993/D	-10.1
MAPES, CLIFF Clifford Franklin B 3.13.1922 Sutherland, NE D 12.5.1996 Pryor, OK BL/TR 6-3/205# d4.20																								
1948	NY A	53	88	19	22	11	1	1	12	6	0	13	.250	.298	.432	94	-1	1-1	.958	3	109	321	O-21(9-6-6)	0.1
1949	†NY A	111	304	56	75	13	3	7	38	58	1	50	.247	.369	.378	98	0	6-0	.976	6	103	**186**	*O-108(4-58-49)	0.5
1950	†NY A	108	356	60	88	14	6	12	61	47	2	61	.247	.338	.421	96	-4	1-6	.950	-4	93	105	*O-102(4-21-80)	-1.1
1951	NY A	45	51	6	11	3	1	2	8	4	0	14	.216	.273	.431	92	-1	0-0	1.000	0	115	0	O-34(2-3-29)	-0.1
	StL A	56	201	32	55	7	2	7	30	26	1	33	.274	.360	.433	110	3	0-1	.983	0	100	100	O-53(15-12-31)	0.0
	Year	101	252	38	66	10	3	9	38	30	1	47	.262	.343	.433	109	2	0-1	.986	0	103	82	O-87(17-15-60)	-0.1
1952	Det A	86	193	26	38	7	0	9	23	27	0	42	.197	.295	.373	84	-5	0-1	.967	-2	94	87	O-63(5-18-43)	-0.9
Total	5	459	1193	199	289	55	13	38	172	168	4	213	.242	.338	.406	97	-8	8-9	.969	4	99	135	O-381(39-118-238)	-1.5
MAPLE, HOWARD Howard Albert "Mape" B 7.20.1903 Adrian, MO D 11.9.1970 Portland, OR BL/TR 5-7/175# d5.19																								
1932	Was A	44	41	6	10	0	1	0	7	7	1	7	.244	.367	.293	74	-1	0-0	1.000	-1	*153*	*86*	C-41	-0.2
MAPPES, GEORGE George Richard "Dick" B 12.25.1865 St.Louis, MO D 2.20.1934 St.Louis, MO d9.23																								
1885	Bal AA	6	19	2	4	0	1	0	0	1	0		.211	.250	.316	79	-1		.875	-2	76	43	/2-6	-0.2
1886	StL N	6	14	1	2	0	0	0	0	1		5	.143	.200	.143	6	-2	0	1.000	-1			/C-3,3-2,2	-0.2
Total	2	12	33	3	6	0	1	0	0	2		5	.182	.229	.242	48	-3	0	.848	-3			/2-7,C-3,3-2	-0.4
MARANVILLE, RABBIT Walter James Vincent B 11.11.1891 Springfield, MA D 1.5.1954 New York, NY BR/TR 5-5/155# d9.10 Mil 1918 M1 HF1954																								
1912	Bos N	26	86	8	18	2	0	0	8	9	1	14	.209	.292	.233	44	-7	1	.929	1	110	90	S-26	-0.4
1913	Bos N	143	571	68	141	13	8	2	48	68	3	62	.247	.330	.308	81	-12	25-19	.949	17	**106**	93	*S-143	1.4
1914	†Bos N	156	586	74	144	23	6	4	78	45	6	56	.246	.306	.326	88	-9	28	.938	**50**	**116**	**168**	*S-156	**5.5**
1915	Bos N	149	509	51	124	23	6	2	43	45	2	65	.244	.308	.324	96	-3	18-12	.941	20	103	107	*S-149	3.0
1916	Bos N	155	604	79	142	16	13	4	38	50	2	69	.235	.296	.325	94	-5	32-15	**.947**	23	101	**133**	*S-155	3.4
1917	Bos N	142	561	69	146	19	13	3	43	40	2	47	.260	.312	.357	111	6	27	.947	14	100	106	*S-142	3.3
1918	Bos N	11	38	3	12	0	1	0	3	4	0	0	.316	.381	.368	134	2	0	.932	-1	89	43	S-11	0.2
1919	Bos N	131	480	44	128	18	10	5	43	36	1	23	.267	.319	.377	113	7	12	.941	**26**	108	**126**	*S-131	4.6
1920	Bos N	134	493	48	131	19	15	1	43	28	0	24	.266	.305	.371	98	-4	14-11	.948	15	105	97	*S-133	2.1
1921	Pit N	153	612	90	180	25	12	1	70	47	3	38	.294	.347	.379	90	-8	25-12	.962	-17	97	94	*S-153	-0.7
1922	Pit N	**155**	672	115	198	26	15	0	63	61	2	43	.295	.355	.378	88	-11	24-13	.961	3	95	104	*S-138,2-18	0.7
1923	Pit N	141	581	78	161	19	9	1	41	42	1	34	.277	.327	.346	76	-21	14-11	**.965**	11	**101**	**111**	*S-141	0.5
1924	Pit N	152	594	62	158	33	20	2	71	35	0	53	.266	.307	.399	86	-14	18-14	**.973**	5	103	**123**	*2-152	-0.5
1925	Chi N	75	266	37	62	10	3	0	23	29	0	20	.233	.308	.293	54	-18	6-5	.955	2	102	106	S-74,M	-0.8
1926	Bro N	78	234	32	55	8	5	0	24	26	0	24	.235	.312	.312	69	-10	7	.948	7	102	79	S-60,2-18	0.4
1927	StL N	9	29	0	7	1	0	0	0	2	0	2	.241	.290	.276	51	-2	0	.962	2	121	125	/S-9	0.1
1928	†StL N	112	366	40	88	14	10	1	34	36	1	27	.240	.310	.342	69	-18	3	.969	-9	98	87	*S-112/2-2	-1.4
1929	Bos N	146	560	87	159	26	10	0	55	47	4	33	.284	.344	.366	79	-18	13	.961	21	**110**	108	*S-145/2	1.7
1930	Bos N	142	558	85	157	26	8	2	43	48	5	23	.281	.344	.367	75	-23	9	**.965**	-14	91	96	*S-138/3-4	-1.9
1931	Bos N	145	562	69	146	22	5	0	33	56	2	34	.260	.329	.317	77	-17	9	.949	-24	93	103	*S-137,2-11	-3.1
1932	Bos N	149	571	67	134	20	4	0	37	46	3	28	.235	.295	.284	59	-33	4	**.975**	4	103	104	*2-149	-1.9
1933	Bos N	143	478	46	104	15	4	0	38	36	1	34	.218	.274	.266	59	-26	2	.971	-28	87	106	*2-142	-4.8
1935	Bos N	23	67	3	10	2	0	0	5	3	0	3	.149	.186	.179	-2	-10	0	.963	-3	94	110	2-20	-1.1
Total	23	2670	10078	1255	2605	380	177	28	884	839	39	756	.258	.318	.340	82	-254	291-112	.952	126	102	109	*S-2153,2-513/3-4	10.3
MARION, RED John Wyeth B 3.14.1914 Richburg, SC D 3.13.1975 San Jose, CA BR/TR 6-2/175# d9.16 b-Marty																								
1935	Was A	4	11	1	2	1	0	1	1	0	0	2	.182	.182	.545	85	0	0-0	.833	0	67	463	/O-3(1-1-1)	0.0
1943	Was A	14	17	2	3	0	0	0	1	3	0	1	.176	.300	.176	42	-1	0-0	1.000	0	119	0	/O-4(LF)	-0.1
Total	2	18	28	3	5	1	0	1	2	3	0	3	.179	.258	.321	63	-1	0-0	.923	0	93	232	/O-7(5-1-1)	-0.1
MARION, MARTY Martin Whiteford "Slats" or "The Octopus" B 12.1.1917 Richburg, SC BR/TR 6-2/170# d4.16 M6 C2 b-Red																								
1940	StL N	125	435	44	121	18	1	3	46	21	0	34	.278	.311	.345	76	-14	9	.949	-8	95	101	*S-125	-1.4
1941	StL N	**155**	547	50	138	22	3	3	58	42	2	48	.252	.308	.320	72	-20	8	.954	2	101	103	*S-155	-0.7
1942	†StL N	147	485	66	134	**38**	5	0	54	48	1	50	.276	.343	.375	102	3	8	.960	6	99	113	*S-147	2.1
1943	†StL N★	129	418	38	117	15	3	1	52	32	2	37	.280	.334	.337	90	-5	1	.970	16	103	**138**	*S-128	2.2
1944	†StL N★	144	506	50	135	26	2	6	63	43	0	50	.267	.324	.362	91	-6	1	**.972**	3	98	**126**	*S-144	0.9
1945	StL N✻	123	430	63	119	27	5	1	59	39	2	39	.277	.340	.370	95	-3	2	.967	-6	97	**114**	*S-122	0.1
1946	†StL N★	146	498	51	116	29	4	3	46	59	3	53	.233	.318	.325	79	-12	1	.973	**18**	**104**	**125**	*S-145	1.5
1947	StL N★	149	540	57	147	19	6	4	74	49	1	58	.272	.334	.352	79	-16	3	**.981**	16	99	**123**	*S-141	0.8
1948	StL N✻	144	567	70	143	26	4	4	43	37	0	54	.252	.298	.333	67	-27	1	**.974**	10	103	106	*S-142	-0.8
1949	StL N☆	134	515	61	140	31	2	5	70	37	2	42	.272	.323	.369	81	-13	0	.976	12	106	99	*S-134	0.7
1950	StL N★	106	372	36	92	10	2	4	40	44	0	55	.247	.327	.317	67	-17	1	.978	2	100	112	*S-101	-0.9
1952	StL A	67	186	16	46	11	0	2	19	19	1	17	.247	.320	.339	81	-4	0-2	.980	-6	89	118	S-63,M	-0.8
1953	StL A	3	7	0	0	0	0	0	0	0	0	0	.000	.000	.000	-98	-2	0-0	1.000	-1	0	0	/3-2,M	-0.3
Total	13	1572	5506	602	1448	272	37	36	624	470	14	537	.263	.323	.345	81	-136	35-2	.969	65	100	115	*S-1547/3-2	3.4
MARIS, ROGER Roger Eugene (born Roger Eugene Maras) B 9.10.1934 Hibbing, MN D 12.14.1985 Houston, TX BL/TR 6/204# d4.16																								
1957	Cle A	116	358	61	84	9	5	14	51	60-5	1	79	.235	.344	.405	106	3	8-4	.975	7	110	147	*O-112(26-87-8)	0.5
1958	Cle A	51	182	26	41	5	1	9	27	17-2	0	33	.225	.287	.412	94	-2	4-2	.967	2	103	173	O-47(0-27-23)	-0.2
	KC A	99	401	61	99	14	3	19	53	28-1	2	52	.247	.298	.439	99	-3	0-0	.975	-3	91	107	O-99(0-21-90)	-1.0
	Year	150	583	87	140	19	4	28	80	45-3	2	85	.240	.294	.431	97	-5	4-2	.972	-1	95	129	*O-146(0-48-113)	-1.2
1959	KC A★	122	433	69	118	21	7	16	72	58-5	3	53	.273	.359	.464	123	14	2-1	.975	3	109	107	*O-117(0-6-113)	1.3
1960	†NY A★	136	499	98	141	18	7	39	**112**	70-4	3	65	.283	.371	**.581**	164	42	2-2	.985	1	105	70	*O-131(0-7-128)	3.6
1961	†NY A★	161	590	**132**	159	16	4	**61**	**142**	94-0	7	67	.269	.372	.620	170	57	0-0	.968	-11	85	78	*O-160(0-11-156)	3.5
1962	†NY A★	157	590	92	151	34	1	33	100	87-11	6	78	.256	.356	.485	128	25	1-0	.991	-7	97	47	*O-154(0-64-103)	1.0
1963	†NY A	90	312	53	84	14	1	23	53	35-3	2	40	.269	.346	.542	146	19	1-0	.988	3	107	114	O-86(0-1-86)	1.7
1964	†NY A	141	513	86	144	12	2	26	71	62-1	6	78	.281	.364	.464	127	19	3-0	.996	-8	90	65	*O-137(0-32-105)	0.3
1965	NY A	46	155	22	37	7	0	8	27	29-1	0	29	.239	.357	.439	126	6	0-0	.971	-3	88	37	O-43(RF)	0.0
1966	NY A	119	348	37	81	9	2	13	43	36-3	3	60	.233	.307	.382	101	0	0-0	.993	-6	84	61	O-95(0-1-94)	-1.3
1967	†StL N	125	410	64	107	18	7	9	55	52-3	4	61	.261	.346	.405	117	10	0-0	.991	2	108	62	*O-118(0-2-118)	0.5
1968	†StL N	100	310	25	79	18	2	5	45	24-3	1	38	.255	.307	.374	106	2	0-0	.983	1	108	57	O-84(RF)	-0.3
Total	12	1463	5101	826	1325	195	42	275	851	652-42	38	733	.260	.345	.476	128	192	21-9	.982	-23	99	83	*O-1383(26-259-1151)	9.6
MARKLAND, GENE Cleneth Eugene "Mousey" B 12.26.1919 Detroit, MI D 6.15.1999 Barefoot Bay, FL BR/TR 5-10/160# d4.25																								
1950	Phi A	5	8	2	1	0	0	0	0	3	0	0	.125	.364	.125	30	-1	0-0	1.000	-0	92	31	/2-5	-0.1

Year	Tm Lg	G	AB	R	H	2B	3B	HR	RBI	BB-IB	HP	SO	AVG	OBP	SLG	AOPS	ABR	SB-CS	FA	FR	Rng	Thr	G at Pos	BFW
MARNIE, HARRY Harry Sylvester B 7.6.1918 Philadelphia, PA D 1.7.2002 Philadelphia, PA BR/TR 6-1/178# d9.15 Mil 1943-45																								
1940	Phi N	11	34	4	6	0	0	0	4	4	0	2	.176	.263	.176	24	-3	0	.984	4	132	123	2-11	0.1
1941	Phi N	61	158	12	38	3	3	0	11	13	0	25	.241	.298	.297	71	-7	0	.990	2	93	91	2-39,S-16/3-3	-0.2
1942	Phi N	24	30	3	5	0	0	0	0	1	0	2	.167	.194	.167	6	-4	1	.971	5	155	175	2-11/S-7,3	0.1
Total	3	96	222	19	49	3	3	0	15	18	0	29	.221	.279	.261	55	-14	1	.987	10	107	105	/2-61,S-23,3-4	0.0
MAROLEWSKI, FRED Fred Daniel "Fritz" B 10.6.1928 Chicago, IL BR/TR 6-2.5/205# d9.19																								
1953	StL N	1	0	0	0	0	0	0	0	0	0	0	—	—	—	—	0	0-0	—	0	0	0	/1	0.0
MARQUARDT, OLLIE Albert Ludwig B 9.22.1902 Toledo, OH D 2.7.1968 Port Clinton, OH BR/TR 5-9/156# d4.14																								
1931	Bos A	17	39	4	7	1	0	0	2	3	0	4	.179	.238	.205	18	-5	0-1	.946	-2	105	66	2-13/S3	-0.6
MARQUEZ, GONZALO Gonzalo Enrique (Moya) B 3.31.1946 Carupano, Venezuela D 12.20.1984 Valencia, Venezuela BL/TL 5-11/180# d8.11																								
1972	†Oak A	23	21	2	8	0	0	0	4	3-0	1	4	.381	.462	.381	167	2	1-1	.929	-0	119	90	/1-2	0.2
1973	Oak A	23	25	1	6	1	0	0	2	0-0	0	4	.240	.240	.280	49	-2	0-0	—	-0	0	0	/2-2,1O(RF)D	-0.2
	Chi N	19	58	5	13	2	0	1	4	3-1	1	4	.224	.270	.310	57	-3	0-0	.994	2	135	103	1-18	-0.3
1974	Chi N	11	11	1	0	0	0	0	0	1-1	0	2	.000	.083	.000	-72	-3	0-0	1.000	0	0	0	/1	-0.3
Total	3	76	115	9	27	3	0	1	10	7-2	2	14	.235	.286	.287	62	-6	1-1	.989	2	132	101	/1-22,2-2,DO(RF)	-0.6
MARQUEZ, LUIS Luis Angel (Sanchez) "Canena" B 10.28.1925 Aguadilla, P.R. D 3.1.1988 Aguadilla, P.R. BR/TR 5-10.5/174# d4.18																								
1951	Bos N	68	122	19	24	5	1	0	11	10	3	20	.197	.274	.254	46	-9	4-4	1.000	3	123	67	O-43(21-23-3)	-0.8
1954	Chi N	17	12	2	1	0	0	0	0	2	0	4	.083	.214	.083	-19	-2	3-0	1.000	1	140	0	O-14(4-10-0)	-0.1
	Pit N	14	9	3	1	0	0	0	0	4	0	0	.111	.385	.111	37	-1	0-0	1.000	0	136	0	/O-4(1-1-2)	0.0
	Year	31	21	5	2	0	0	0	0	6	0	4	.095	.296	.095	7	-3	3-0	1.000	1	139	0	O-18(5-11-2)	-0.1
Total	2	99	143	24	26	5	1	0	11	16	3	24	.182	.278	.231	40	-12	7-4	1.000	4	125	57	/O-61(26-34-5)	-0.9
MARQUIS, BOB Robert Rudolph B 12.23.1924 Oklahoma City, OK BL/TL 6-1/170# d4.17																								
1953	Cin N	40	44	9	12	1	1	2	3	4	0	11	.273	.333	.477	107	0	0-0	.905	-0	116	0	O-10(2-8-0)	0.0
MARQUIS, ROGER Roger Julian "Noonie" B 4.5.1937 Holyoke, MA BL/TL 6/190# d9.25																								
1955	Bal A	1	1	0	0	0	0	0	0	0-0	0	0	.000	.000	.000	-99	0	0-0	—	-0	0	0	/O(RF)	0.0
MARR, LEFTY Charles W. B 9.19.1862 Cincinnati, OH D 1.11.1912 New Britain, CT BL/TL 5-9/180# d10.3																								
1886	Cin AA	8	29	2	8	1	1	0	2	1	1		.276	.323	.379	116	0	1	.696	-2	61	0	/O-8(CF)	-0.2
1889	Col AA	**139**	546	110	167	26	**15**	1	75	87	6	32	.306	.407	.414	141	35	29	.856	7	106	101	3-66,O-47(0-1-47),S-26/1-2,C	3.6
1890	Cin N	130	527	91	157	17	12	1	73	46	6	29	.298	.361	.381	117	11	44	.930	-7	115	152	O-64(RF),3-63/S-3	0.4
1891	Cin N	72	286	32	74	9	7	0	32	25	2	15	.259	.323	.339	92	-3	16	.835	-9	58	0	O-72(RF)	-1.1
	Cin AA	14	57	9	11	1	0	0	4	7	0	4	.193	.281	.211	38	-5	2	.923	-1	42	0	O-14(RF)	-0.5
Total	4	363	1445	244	417	54	35	2	186	166	15	80	.289	.368	.379	118	38	92	.853	-11	80	57	O-205(0-9-197),3-129/S-29,1-2,C	2.2
MARRERO, ELI Elieser B 11.17.1973 Havana, Cuba BR/TR 6-1/180# d9.3																								
1997	StL N	17	45	4	11	2	0	2	7	2-1	0	13	.244	.271	.422	81	-2	4-0	.969	1	122	173	C-17	0.1
1998	StL N	83	254	28	62	18	1	4	20	28-5	0	42	.244	.318	.370	81	-7	6-2	.991	0	133	95	C-73/1-2	-0.1
1999	StL N	114	317	32	61	13	1	6	34	18-4	1	56	.192	.236	.297	34	-34	11-2	.987	0	143	119	C-96,1-20	-2.6
2000	†StL N	53	102	21	23	3	1	5	17	9-0	3	16	.225	.302	.422	81	-4	5-0	1.000	5	277	118	C-38/1-7	0.4
2001	†StL N	86	203	37	54	11	3	6	23	15-2	0	36	.266	.312	.438	93	-3	6-3	.984	4	129	66	C-65,O-15(8-0-7)/1-6	0.5
2002	†StL N	131	397	63	104	19	1	18	66	40-11	0	72	.262	.327	.451	109	2	14-2	.985	6	104	166	*O-106(39-36-46),C-44/1-4	0.9
2003	StL N	41	107	10	24	4	2	2	20	7-0	0	18	.224	.267	.355	64	-6	0-1	.980	3	114	73	O-31(10-6-21)/C-6,1-2	-0.4
Total	7	525	1425	195	339	70	9	43	187	119-23	4	253	.238	.295	.390	78	-54	46-10	.987	19	142	102	C-339,O-152(57-42-74)/1-41	-1.2
MARRERO, ORESTE Oreste Vilato (Vazquez) B 10.31.1969 Bayamon, P.R. BL/TL 6/195# d8.12																								
1993	Mon N	32	81	10	17	5	1	1	4	14-0	0	16	.210	.326	.333	74	-3	1-3	.991	-1	93	121	1-32	-0.6
1996	LA N	10	8	2	3	1	0	0	1	1-0	0	3	.375	.444	.500	161	1	0-0	1.000	0	0	0	/1	0.1
Total	2	42	89	12	20	6	1	1	5	15-0	0	19	.225	.337	.348	81	-2	1-3	.991	-1	93	120	/1-33	-0.5
MARRIOTT, WILLIAM William Earl B 4.18.1893 Pratt, KS D 8.11.1969 Berkeley, CA BL/TR 6/170# d9.6 Mil 1918																								
1917	Chi N	3	6	0	0	0	0	0	0	0	0	1	.000	.000	.000	-93	-1	0	.667	-0	77	0	/O(LF)	-0.2
1920	Chi N	14	43	7	12	4	2	0	5	6	0	5	.279	.367	.465	135	2	1-1	.892	-3	94	31	2-14	-0.1
1921	Chi N	30	38	3	12	1	1	0	7	4	0	1	.316	.381	.395	105	0	0-1	.826	-1	81	53	/2-6,S3O(LF)	-0.1
1925	Bos N	103	370	37	99	9	1	1	40	28	2	26	.268	.322	.305	67	-18	3-8	.928	-3	103	74	3-89/O(LF)	-1.7
1926	Bro N	109	360	39	96	13	9	3	42	17	2	20	.267	.303	.378	84	-10	12	.927	-6	97	37	*3-104	-1.0
1927	Bro N	6	9	0	1	0	1	0	1	2	0	2	.111	.273	.333	61	-1	0	.889	0	105	0	/3-2	0.0
Total	6	265	826	86	220	27	14	4	95	57	4	55	.266	.317	.347	78	-28	16-10	.925	-14	100	57	3-196/2-20,O-3(LF),S	-3.1
MARSANS, ARMANDO Armando B 10.3.1887 Matanzas, Cuba D 9.3.1960 Havana, Cuba BR/TR 5-10/157# d7.4 OF Total (51-LF 459-CF 71-RF)																								
1911	Cin N	58	138	17	36	2	2	0	11	15	3	11	.261	.346	.304	86	-2	11	.968	-3	99	48	O-34(5-16-13)/13	-0.7
1912	Cin N	110	416	59	132	19	7	1	38	20	3	17	.317	.353	.404	110	4	35	.975	-1	106	77	O-98(7-82-13)/1-6	-0.3
1913	Cin N	118	435	49	129	7	6	0	38	17	3	25	.297	.327	.340	91	-6	37-11	.963	-2	98	106	O-94(3-56-37),1-22/3-2,S	-1.0
1914	Cin N	36	124	16	37	3	0	0	22	14	1	6	.298	.374	.323	105	1	13	.916	-1	100	85	O-36(LF)	-0.1
	StL F	9	40	5	14	0	2	0	2	3	0	0	.350	.395	.450	123	1	4	.927	-1	88	244	/2-7,S-2	0.0
1915	StL F	36	124	16	22	3	0	0	6	14	0	5	.177	.261	.202	29	-13	5	.975	2	94	164	O-35(CF)	-1.5
1916	StL A	151	528	51	134	12	1	1	60	57	6	41	.254	.333	.286	91	-5	46-26	.977	-2	95	111	*O-150(CF)	-1.8
1917	StL A	75	257	31	59	12	0	0	20	20	0	6	.230	.285	.276	74	-8	11	.963	-5	100	33	O-67(CF)/3-5,2	-1.9
	NY A	25	88	10	20	4	0	0	15	8	0	3	.227	.292	.273	72	-3	6	.974	2	113	107	O-25(CF)	-0.3
	Year	100	345	41	79	16	0	0	35	28	0	9	.229	.287	.275	73	-11	17	.967	-3	104	55	O-92(CF)/3-5,2	-2.2
1918	NY A	37	123	13	29	5	1	0	9	5	0	3	.236	.266	.293	67	-5	3	.943	-4	91	45	O-36(0-28-8)	-1.3
Total	8	655	2273	267	612	67	19	2	221	173	16	117	.269	.325	.318	88	-36	171-37	.967	-13	99	90	O-575C/1-29,2-8,3-8,S-3	-8.9
MARSH, FRED Fred Francis B 1.5.1924 Valley Falls, KS BR/TR 5-10/180# d4.19																								
1949	Cle A	1	0	0	0	0	0	0	0	0	0	0	—	—	—	—	0	0-0	—	0			R	0.0
1951	StL A	130	445	44	108	21	4	4	43	36	0	56	.243	.299	.335	69	-20	4-4	.928	3	**103**	**113**	*3-117/S-3,2-2	-1.8
1952	StL A	11	24	3	5	1	0	0	1	5	0	4	.208	.345	.250	65	-1	0-1	.963	0	109	86	/2-9,S-3	0.0
	Was A	9	24	1	1	0	0	0	1	1	0	4	.042	.080	.042	-68	-6	0-0	1.000	-2	59	103	/2-5,O-2(LF)	-0.8
	StL A	76	223	25	64	8	1	2	26	22	0	29	.287	.351	.359	95	-1	3-2	.945	-10	97	216	S-57,3-21	-0.9
	Year	96	271	29	70	9	1	2	28	28	0	37	.258	.328	.321	79	-7	3-3	.945	-12	89	109	S-60,3-21,2-14/O-2(LF)	-1.7
1953	Chi A	67	95	22	19	1	0	2	2	13	1	26	.200	.303	.274	55	-6	0-3	.940	3	101	158	3-32,S-17/1-5,2-2	-0.3
1954	Chi A	62	98	21	30	5	2	0	4	9	0	16	.306	.364	.398	105	1	4-2	.975	10	132	158	3-36/S-3,1-2,O(RF)	1.1
1955	Bal A	89	303	30	66	7	1	2	19	35-1	1	33	.218	.300	.267	58	-18	1-2	.983	-17	82	89	2-76,3-18,S-16	-3.0
1956	Bal A	20	24	2	3	0	0	0	0	4-0	0	3	.125	.250	.125	2	-3	1-0	.929	-1	99	115	/S-8,3-8,2-5	-0.4
Total	7	465	1236	148	296	43	8	10	96	125-1	2	171	.239	.310	.311	69	-54	13-14	.928	-13	107	121	3-232,S-107/2-99,1-7,O-3(2-0-1)	-6.1
MARSH, TOM Thomas Owen B 12.27.1965 Toledo, OH BR/TR 6-2/180# d6.5																								
1992	Phi N	42	125	7	25	3	2	2	16	2-0	1	23	.200	.215	.304	47	-10	0-1	.971	-1	105	0	O-35(25-0-12)	-1.3
1994	Phi N	8	18	3	5	1	1	0	3	1-0	0	1	.278	.316	.444	93	0	0-0	.889	-0	95	0	/O-7(3-0-4)	-0.1
1995	Phi N	43	109	13	32	3	1	3	15	4-0	0	25	.294	.316	.422	93	-2	0-1	.939	0	102	141	O-29(24-4-1)	-0.3
Total	3	93	252	23	62	7	4	5	34	7-0	1	49	.246	.266	.365	71	-12	0-2	.952	-1	103	56	/O-71(52-4-17)	-1.7
MARSHALL, CHARLIE Charles Anthony (born Charles Anthony Marchlewicz) B 8.28.1919 Wilmington, DE BR/TR 5-10.5/178# d6.14																								
1941	StL N	1	0	0	0	0	0	0	0	0	0	0	—	—	—	—	0	0	1.000	-0	*0*	*0*	/C	0.0
MARSHALL, DAVE David Lewis B 1.14.1943 Artesia, CA BL/TR 6-1/190# d9.7																								
1967	SF N	1	0	0	0	0	0	0	0	0-0	0	0	—	—	—	—	0	0-0	—	0			R	0.0
1968	SF N	76	174	17	46	5	1	1	16	20-2	1	37	.264	.338	.322	101	1	2-1	.924	-2	83	100	O-50(24-0-28)	-0.5
1969	SF N	110	267	32	62	7	1	2	33	40-3	5	68	.232	.340	.288	80	-5	1-8	.956	-5	85	70	O-87(79-0-17)	-1.7
1970	NY N	92	189	21	46	10	1	6	29	17-0	0	43	.243	.304	.402	88	-4	4-1	.973	-0	102	76	O-43(12-0-33)	-0.5
1971	NY N	100	214	28	51	9	1	3	21	26-3	2	54	.238	.322	.332	88	-3	3-1	.989	-1	100	59	O-64(25-0-39)	-0.7
1972	NY N	72	156	21	39	5	0	4	11	22-1	1	28	.250	.346	.359	103	1	3-3	.972	-2	107	0	O-42(1-4-38)	-0.3
1973	SD N	39	49	4	14	5	0	0	4	8-0	1	9	.286	.390	.388	128	3	0-1	1.000	-1	100	0	/O-8(RF)	0.1

Year	Tm Lg	G	AB	R	H	2B	3B	HR	RBI	BB-IB	HP	SO	AVG	OBP	SLG	AOPS	ABR	SB-CS	FA	FR	Rng	Thr	G at Pos	BFW
Total	7	490	1049	123	258	41	4	16	114	133-9	10	239	.246	.333	.338	92	-7	13-15	.966	-10	94	61	O-294(141-4-163)	-3.6
MARSHALL, DOC Edward Harbert "Eddie" B 6.4.1906 New Albany, MS D 9.1.1999 Lake San Marcos, CA BR/TR 5-11/150# d9.28																								
1929	NY N	5	15	6	6	2	0	0	2	1	0	0	.400	.438	.533	140	1	0	1.000	-1	94	0	/2-5	0.0
1930	NY N	78	223	33	69	5	3	0	21	13	1	9	.309	.350	.359	73	-10	0	.947	-1	96	92	S-45,2-17/3-5	-0.6
1931	NY N	68	194	15	39	6	2	0	10	8	0	8	.201	.233	.253	31	-20	1	.956	2	103	102	2-47,S-11/3-3	-1.4
1932	NY N	68	226	18	56	8	1	0	28	6	1	11	.248	.270	.292	52	-16	1	.922	-3	98	100	S-63	-1.4
Total	4	219	658	72	170	21	6	0	61	28	2	28	.258	.291	.309	56	-45	2	.931	-3	96	98	S-119/2-69,3-8	-3.4
MARSHALL, JOE Joseph Hanley "Home Run Joe" B 2.19.1876 Audubon, MN D 9.11.1931 Santa Monica, CA BR/TR 5-8/170# d9.7																								
1903	Pit N	10	23	2	6	1	2	0	2	0	0		.261	.261	.478	106	0	0	1.000	-2	71	115	/S-3,O-3(2-1-0),2	-0.2
1906	StL N	33	95	2	15	1	2	0	7	6	1		.158	.216	.211	34	-8	0	.903	1	246	0	O-23(RF)/1-4	-0.9
Total	2	43	118	4	21	2	4	0	9	6	1		.178	.224	.263	50	-8	0	.903	-1	242	0	/O-26(2-1-23),1-4,S-3,2	-1.1
MARSHALL, KEITH Keith Alan B 7.2.1951 San Francisco, CA BR/TR 6-2/175# d4.7																								
1973	KC A	8	9	0	2	1	0	0	3	1-0	0	4	.222	.300	.333	73	0	0-0	1.000	-0	94	0	/O-8(5-2-2)	-0.1
MARSHALL, MIKE Michael Allen B 1.12.1960 Libertyville, IL BR/TR 6-5/220# d9.7																								
1981	†LA N	14	25	2	5	3	0	0	1	1-0	1	4	.200	.259	.320	66	-1	0-0	1.000	-1	0	200	/1-3,3-3,O-2(1-0-1)	-0.3
1982	LA N	49	95	10	23	3	0	5	9	13-1	1	23	.242	.336	.432	117	2	2-0	1.000	-2	79	0	O-19(3-0-16),1-13	-0.1
1983	†LA N	140	465	47	132	17	1	17	65	43-4	5	127	.284	.347	.434	117	10	7-3	.976	-6	92	46	*O-109(RF),1-33	-0.2
1984	LA N☆	134	495	68	127	27	0	21	65	40-6	3	93	.257	.315	.438	111	6	4-3	.981	-1	95	102	*O-118(116-0-4),1-15	-0.1
1985	†LA N	135	518	72	152	27	2	28	95	37-6	3	137	.293	.342	.515	141	26	3-10	.991	-5	86	106	*O-125(1-0-124)/1-7	1.2
1986	LA N	103	330	47	77	11	0	19	53	27-3	4	90	.233	.298	.439	109	2	4-4	.963	-3	89	112	O-97(1-0-97)	-0.7
1987	LA N	104	402	45	118	19	0	16	72	18-2	4	79	.294	.327	.460	109	4	0-5	.987	-9	80	60	*O-102(RF)	-1.2
1988	†LA N	144	542	63	150	27	2	20	82	24-7	7	93	.277	.314	.445	120	11	4-1	.966	-2	86	98	O-90(RF),1-53	0.4
1989	LA N	105	377	41	98	21	1	11	42	33-4	5	78	.260	.325	.408	111	5	2-5	.978	-5	95	38	*O-102(RF)	-0.4
1990	NY N	53	163	24	39	8	1	6	27	7-0	3	40	.239	.278	.411	89	-3	0-2	.993	-0	88	77	1-42/O(RF)	-0.7
	†Bos A	30	112	10	32	6	1	4	12	4-0	1	26	.286	.316	.464	111	1	0-0	1.000	0	157	95	D-14/1-8,O-8(RF)	0.0
1991	Bos A	22	62	4	18	4	0	1	7	0-0	0	19	.290	.290	.403	86	-1	0-0	.979	-2	0	114	/1-5,O-4(1-0-3),D-7	-0.4
	Cal A	2	7	0	0	0	0	0	0	0-0	0	1	.000	.000	.000	-99	-2	0-0	1.000	0	157	239	/1D	-0.2
	Year	24	69	4	18	4	0	1	7	0-0	0	20	.261	.261	.362	67	-3	0-0	.984	-2	31	138	/D-8,1-6,O-4(1-0-3)	-0.6
Total	11	1035	3593	433	971	173	8	148	530	247-33	37	810	.270	.321	.446	115	60	26-33	.978	-35	89	78	O-777(123-0-657),1-180/D-22,3-3	-2.7
MARSHALL, MAX Milo May B 9.18.1913 Shenandoah, IA D 9.16.1993 Salem, OR BL/TR 6-1/180# d5.10 Mil 1944-45																								
1942	Cin N	131	530	49	135	17	6	7	43	34	1	38	.255	.301	.349	90	-9	4	.976	-11	91	27	*O-129(43-11-79)	-3.0
1943	Cin N	132	508	55	120	11	8	4	39	34	2	52	.236	.287	.313	74	-19	8	.981	-5	92	89	*O-129(RF)	-3.5
1944	Cin N	66	229	36	56	13	2	4	23	21	0	10	.245	.308	.371	94	-2	3	.965	1	104	89	O-59(1-0-58)	-0.6
Total	3	329	1267	140	311	41	16	15	105	89	3	100	.245	.297	.339	84	-30	15	.975	-16	94	63	O-317(44-11-266)	-7.1
MARSHALL, JIM Rufus James B 5.25.1931 Danville, IL BL/TL 6-1/190# d4.15 M4 C1																								
1958	Bal A	85	191	17	41	4	3	5	19	18-1	0	30	.215	.280	.346	76	-7	3-2	1.000	-2	75	99	1-52/O-8(3-0-5)	-1.2
	Chi N	26	81	12	22	2	0	5	11	12-0	1	13	.272	.372	.481	126	3	1-0	.992	-1	73	81	1-15,O-11(RF)	0.2
1959	Chi N	108	294	39	74	10	1	11	40	33-1	0	39	.252	.324	.405	95	-2	0-1	.997	3	110	102	1-72/O-8(7-0-3)	-0.4
1960	SF N	75	118	19	28	2	2	2	13	17-1	0	24	.237	.331	.339	90	-2	0-1	.968	-3	67	85	1-28/O-6(LF)	-0.6
1961	SF N	44	36	5	8	0	0	1	7	3-0	0	8	.222	.275	.306	58	-2	0-0	1.000	0	200	175	/1-4,O-2(1-0-1)	-0.2
1962	NY N	17	32	6	11	1	0	3	4	3-0	0	6	.344	.400	.656	175	3	0-0	1.000	0	115	127	/1-5,O(RF)	0.3
	Pit N	55	100	13	22	5	1	2	12	15-0	0	19	.220	.319	.350	80	-3	1-0	1.000	1	108	121	1-26	-0.3
	Year	72	132	19	33	6	1	5	16	18-0	0	25	.250	.338	.424	103	1	1-0	1.000	1	109	122	1-31/O(RF)	0.0
Total	5	410	852	111	206	24	7	29	106	101-3	1	139	.242	.320	.388	93	-10	5-4	.994	-1	93	101	1-202/O-36(17-0-21)	-2.2
MARSHALL, WILLARD Willard Warren B 2.8.1921 Richmond, VA D 11.5.2000 Norwood, NJ BL/TR 6-1/205# d4.14 Mil 1943-45																								
1942	NY N★	116	401	41	103	9	2	11	59	26	3	20	.257	.307	.372	98	-3	1	.975	1	94	**157**	*O-107(67-46-1)	-0.7
1946	NY N	131	510	63	144	18	3	13	48	33	1	29	.282	.327	.406	107	2	3	.978	-4	89	125	*O-125(51-59-15)	-0.9
1947	NY N★	**155**	587	102	171	19	6	36	107	67	2	30	.291	.366	.528	134	26	3	.972	9	108	142	*O-155(RF)	3.0
1948	NY N	143	537	72	146	21	8	14	86	64	1	34	.272	.350	.419	107	5	2	.983	1	93	148	*O-142(RF)	0.1
1949	NY N★	141	499	81	153	19	3	12	70	78	1	20	.307	.401	.429	123	19	4	.974	2	105	100	*O-138(2-0-136)	1.7
1950	Bos N	105	298	38	70	10	2	5	40	36	1	5	.235	.319	.332	77	-10	1	.958	4	101	191	O-85(14-9-64)	-0.9
1951	Bos N	136	469	65	132	24	7	11	62	48	2	18	.281	.351	.433	118	11	0-3	**1.000**	-3	93	99	*O-136(RF)	0.4
1952	Bos N	21	66	5	15	4	1	2	11	4	0	4	.227	.271	.409	89	-1	0-0	.938	0	82	186	O-16(RF)	-0.2
	Cin N	107	397	52	106	23	1	8	46	37	2	21	.267	.333	.390	100	0	0-1	.985	2	97	138	*O-105(RF)	-0.2
	Year	128	463	57	121	27	2	10	57	41	2	25	.261	.324	.393	99	-1	0-1	.979	2	95	145	*O-121(RF)	-0.4
1953	Cin N	122	357	51	95	14	6	17	62	41	0	28	.266	.342	.482	111	5	0-0	.995	5	102	157	O-95(RF)	0.6
1954	Chi A	47	71	7	18	2	0	1	7	11	0	9	.254	.349	.324	84	-1	0-0	.960	-1	84	99	O-29(7-0-22)	-0.3
1955	Chi A	22	41	6	7	0	0	0	6	13-1	0	1	.171	.364	.171	48	-2	0-0	.957	-1	105	0	O-12(4-0-8)	-0.3
Total	11	1246	4233	583	1160	163	39	130	604	458-1	13	219	.274	.347	.423	109	51	14-4	.979	15	98	135	*O-1145(145-114-895)	2.3
MARSHALL, BILL William Henry B 2.14.1911 Dorchester, MA D 5.5.1977 Sacramento, CA BR/TR 5-8.5/156# d6.20																								
1931	Bos A	1	0	1	0	0	0	0	0	0	0	0	—	—	—	—	0	0-0	—	0			R	0.0
1934	Cin N	6	8	0	1	0	0	0	0	0	0	2	.125	.125	.125	-34	-2	0	.875	0	133	0	/2-2	-0.1
Total	2	7	8	1	1	0	0	0	0	0	0	2	.125	.125	.125	-34	-2	0-0	.875	0	133	0	/2-2	-0.1
MARSHALL, DOC William Riddle B 9.22.1875 Butler, PA D 12.11.1959 Clinton, IL BR/TR 6/185# d4.15																								
1904	Phi N	8	20	1	2	0	0	0	1	0	0		.100	.100	.100	-40	-3	0	.944	1	*87*	*185*	/C-7	-0.2
	NY N	1	0	0	0	0	0	0	0	0	0		—	—	—	—	0	0	—	-0	*0*	*0*	/C	0.0
	Bos N	13	43	3	9	0	1	0	2	2	0		.209	.244	.256	56	-2	2	.955	0	*87*	*126*	C-10/O(LF)	-0.2
	NY N	10	17	3	6	1	0	0	2	1	0		.353	.389	.412	141	1	0	.955	1	*0*	*0*	/C-2,O-2(1-0-1),2	0.2
	Year	32	80	7	17	1	1	0	5	3	0		.213	.241	.250	52	-5	2	.952	1	*98*	*145*	C-20/O-3(2-0-1),2	-0.2
1906	NY N	38	102	8	17	3	2	0	7	7	2		.167	.234	.235	45	-7	7	1.000	1	169	0	O-16(1-3-13),C-13/1-2	-0.6
	StL N	39	123	6	34	4	1	0	10	6	1		.276	.315	.325	104	0	1	.961	1	*87*	*108*	C-38	0.5
	Year	77	225	14	51	7	3	0	17	13	3		.227	.278	.284	76	-7	8	.969	2	*90*	*108*	C-51,O-16(1-3-13)/1-2	-0.1
1907	StL N	84	268	19	54	8	2	2	18	12	4		.201	.246	.269	64	-12	2	.952	-3	*81*	***123***	C-83	-0.8
1908	StL N	6	14	0	1	0	0	0	1	0	0		.071	.071	.071	-57	-2	0	1.000	1	*74*	*92*	/C-6	-0.2
	Chi N	12	20	4	6	0	1	0	3	0	0		.300	.300	.400	118	0	0	1.000	2	*120*	*197*	/C-4,O-3(0-1-2)	0.2
	Year	18	34	4	7	0	1	0	4	0	0		.206	.206	.265	49	-2	0	1.000	3	*83*	*113*	C-10/O-3(0-1-2)	0.0
1909	Bro N	50	149	7	30	7	1	0	10	6	0		.201	.232	.262	55	-8	3	.968	-4	*88*	*96*	C-49/O(RF)	-0.9
Total	5	261	756	51	159	23	8	2	54	34	7		.210	.251	.270	64	-33	15	.961	-1	*86*	*115*	C-213/O-23(3-4-17),1-2,2	-2.0
MARTEL, DOC Leon Alphonse "Marty" B 1.29.1883 Weymouth, MA D 10.11.1947 Washington, DC BR/TR 6/185# d7.6																								
1909	Phi N	24	41	1	11	3	1	0	7	4	0		.268	.333	.390	123	1	0	.974	3	*109*	*130*	C-12	0.5
1910	Bos N	10	31	0	4	0	0	0	1	2	0	3	.129	.182	.129	-9	-4	0	.980	-0	101	91	1-10	-0.5
Total	2	34	72	1	15	3	1	0	8	6	0	3	.208	.269	.278	64	-3	0	.974	2	*109*	*130*	/C-12,1-10	0.0
MARTIN, AL Albert (a/k/a Albert May In 1872) d5.7																								
1872	Eck NA	4	18	2	5	0	0	0	1	0		0	.278	.278	.278	84	0	0-0	.700	-2	69	59	/2-4	-0.2
1874	Atl NA	7	29	1	4	0	0	0	1	0		1	.138	.138	.138	-13	-3	0-0	.646	-3	102	57	/2-6,O(LF)	-0.5
1875	Atl NA	6	26	1	3	0	0	0	1	0		0	.115	.115	.115	-22	-3	0-0	.909	-0	0	0	/O-6(CF)	-0.3
Total	3 NA	17	73	4	12	0	0	0	3	0		1	.164	.164	.164	9	-6	0-0	.000	-6	89	58	/2-10,O-7(1-6-0)	-1.0
MARTIN, AL Albert Lee B 11.24.1967 West Covina, CA BL/TL 6-2/210# d7.28																								
1992	Pit N	12	12	1	2	0	1	0	2	0-0	0	5	.167	.154	.333	39	-1	0-0	1.000	0	119	0	/O-7(LF)	-0.1
1993	Pit N	143	480	85	135	26	8	18	64	42-5	1	122	.281	.338	.481	117	10	16-9	.975	-6	94	73	*O-136(81-63-6)	0.3
1994	Pit N	82	276	48	79	12	4	9	33	34-3	2	56	.286	.367	.457	112	5	15-6	.979	-1	89	177	O-77(67-13-0)	0.3
1995	Pit N	124	439	70	124	25	3	13	41	44-6	2	92	.282	.351	.442	105	4	20-11	.977	-0	97	124	*O-121(95-42-0)	0.1
1996	Pit N	155	630	101	189	40	1	18	72	54-2	2	116	.300	.354	.452	109	9	38-12	.965	-16	78	58	*O-152(142-26-0)	-0.8
1997	Pit N	113	423	64	123	24	7	13	59	45-7	3	83	.291	.359	.473	115	9	23-7	.957	-13	63	114	*O-110(LF)	-0.5
1998	Pit N	125	440	57	105	15	2	12	47	32-2	5	91	.239	.296	.364	72	-19	20-3	.985	2	99	89	*O-114(LF)/D-2	-1.8

Year	Tm Lg	G	AB	R	H	2B	3B	HR	RBI	BB-IB	HP	SO	AVG	OBP	SLG	AOPS	ABR	SB-CS	FA	FR	Rng	Thr	G at Pos	BFW
1999	Pit N	143	541	97	150	36	8	24	63	49-5	1	119	.277	.337	.506	110	6	20-3	.952	-13	80	38	*O-133(LF)	-0.8
2000	SD N	93	346	62	106	13	6	11	27	28-5	2	54	.306	.360	.474	117	7	6-8	.950	-7	79	77	O-89(LF)	-0.4
	†Sea A	42	134	19	31	2	4	4	9	8-0	2	31	.231	.283	.396	72	-7	4-1	.963	3	117	163	O-35(20-7-9)/D-2	-0.4
2001	†Sea A	100	283	41	68	15	2	7	42	37-4	2	59	.240	.330	.382	93	-2	9-3	.971	2	109	81	O-73(72-1-1),D-16	-0.3
2003	TB A	100	238	19	60	12	2	3	26	17-4	2	51	.252	.306	.357	76	-9	2-2	1.000	0	112	0	D-57,O-13(8-0-5)/1	-1.2
Total	11	1232	4242	664	1172	220	48	132	485	390-43	24	879	.276	.339	.444	103	12	173-65	.969	-49	87	89	*O-1060(938-152-21)/D-77,1	-5.6
MARTIN, BILLY Alfred Manuel B 5.16.1928 Berkeley, CA D 12.25.1989 Johnson City, NY BR/TR 5-11.5/165# d4.18 Mil 1954 M16 C5																								
1950	NY A	34	36	10	9	1	0	1	8	3	0	3	.250	.308	.361	73	-2	0-0	.976	-2	75	82	2-22/3	-0.3
1951	†NY A	51	58	10	15	1	2	0	2	4	2	9	.259	.328	.345	85	-1	0-1	.988	9	137	171	2-23/S-6,3-2,O(CF)	0.8
1952	†NY A	109	363	32	97	13	3	3	33	22	8	31	.267	.323	.344	91	-5	3-6	.984	18	112	**130**	*2-107	1.8
1953	†NY A	149	587	72	151	24	6	15	75	43	6	56	.257	.314	.395	94	-8	6-7	.985	2	100	**117**	*2-146,S-18	0.4
1955	†NY A	20	70	8	21	2	0	1	9	7-1	0	9	.300	.354	.371	100	0	1-2	.977	2	106	161	2-17/S-3	0.3
1956	†NY A★	121	458	76	121	24	5	9	49	30-0	3	56	.264	.310	.397	90	-9	7-3	.980	-6	98	**114**	*2-105,3-16	-0.7
1957	NY A	43	145	12	35	5	2	1	12	3-0	1	14	.241	.257	.324	60	-9	2-1	.947	-2	99	101	2-26,3-13	-0.9
	KC A	73	265	33	68	9	3	9	27	12-0	3	20	.257	.295	.415	91	-5	7-1	.987	-14	82	76	2-52,3-20/S-2	-1.5
	Year	116	410	45	103	14	5	10	39	15-0	4	34	.251	.282	.383	80	-13	9-2	.973	-16	88	84	2-78,3-33/S-2	-2.4
1958	Det A	131	498	56	127	19	1	7	42	16-0	3	62	.255	.279	.339	65	-24	5-3	.958	-13	86	103	S-88,3-41	-3.1
1959	Cle A	73	242	37	63	7	0	9	24	8-2	3	18	.260	.290	.401	92	-4	0-2	.997	-10	87	87	2-67/3-4	-1.0
1960	Cin N	103	317	34	78	17	1	3	16	27-5	0	34	.246	.304	.334	74	-11	0-1	.975	-13	88	97	2-97	-1.8
1961	Mil N	6	6	1	0	0	0	0	0	0-0	0	1	.000	.000	.000	-99	-2	0-0	—	0			H	-0.2
	Min A	108	374	44	92	15	5	6	36	13-0	3	42	.246	.275	.361	65	-20	3-2	.963	-11	92	92	*2-105/S	-2.3
Total	11	1021	3419	425	877	137	28	64	333	188-8	32	355	.257	.300	.369	81	-100	34-29	.980	-39	97	108	2-767,S-118/3-97,O(CF)	-8.5
MARTIN, PHONNEY Alphonse Case B 8.4.1845 New York, NY D 5.24.1933 Hollis, NY 5-7/148# d4.26 M1 ▲																								
1872	Tro NA	**25**	119	27	36	2	1	0	14	0		1	.303	.303	.336	95	-1	0-0	.780	-2	0	0	O-25(RF)/P-8	-0.1
	Eck NA	18	78	13	15	1	1	0	9	2		3	.192	.213	.231	43	-4	3-2	.833	1	98	0	P-10/O-9(RF),M	0.0
	Year	43	197	40	51	3	2	0	23	2		4	.259	.266	.294	76	-4	3-2	.776	-1	59	0	O-34(RF),P-18	-0.1
1873	Mut NA	31	140	12	31	1	0	0	14	0		4	.221	.221	.229	34	-11	1-1	.680	-6	0	0	O-30(RF)/P-6	-1.0
Total	2 NA	74	337	52	82	4	2	0	37	2		8	.243	.248	.267	58	-16	4-3	.000	-7	33	0	/O-64(RF),P-24	-1.1
MARTIN, BABE Boris Michael (born Boris Michael Martinovich) B 3.28.1920 Seattle, WA BR/TR 5-11.5/194# d9.25																								
1944	StL A	2	4	0	3	1	0	0	1	0	0	0	.750	.750	1.000	376	1	0-0	1.000	-0	82	0	/O(LF)	0.1
1945	StL A	54	185	13	37	5	2	2	16	11	0	24	.200	.245	.281	50	-13	0-1	.992	6	117	162	O-48(43-0-6)/1-6	-1.1
1946	StL A	3	9	0	2	0	0	0	1	1	0	2	.222	.300	.222	45	-1	0-0	1.000	0	*107*	*0*	/C-2	0.0
1948	Bos A	4	4	0	2	0	0	0	0	0	0	1	.500	.500	.500	158	0	0-0	—	0	*0*	*0*	/C	0.0
1949	Bos A	2	2	0	0	0	0	0	0	0	0	0	.000	.000	.000	-93	-1	0-0	—	0	*0*	*0*	/C	-0.1
1953	StL A	4	2	0	0	0	0	0	0	1	0	0	.000	.333	.000	-4	0	0-0	—	0	*0*	*0*	/C	0.0
Total	6	69	206	13	44	6	2	2	18	13	0	27	.214	.260	.291	56	-14	0-1	.992	6	117	160	/O-49(44-0-6),1-6,C-5	-1.1
MARTIN, FRANK Frank B 2.28.1879 Chicago, IL D 9.30.1924 Chicago, IL d6.30																								
1897	Lou N	2	8	1	2	0	0	0	0	0	0		.250	.250	.250	33	-1	0	.813	-1	117	0	/2-2	-0.1
1898	Chi N	1	4	0	0	0	0	0	0	0	0		.000	.000	.000	-99	-1	0	1.000	-0	56	0	/2	-0.1
1899	NY N	17	54	5	14	2	0	0	1	2	1		.259	.298	.296	66	-3	0	.824	-0	97	171	3-17	-0.2
Total	3	20	66	6	16	2	0	0	1	2	1		.242	.275	.273	52	-5	0	.824	-1	97	171	/3-17,2-3	-0.4
MARTIN, HERSH Hershel Ray B 9.19.1909 Birmingham, AL D 11.17.1980 Cuba, MO BB/TR 6-2/190# d4.23																								
1937	Phi N	141	579	102	164	35	7	8	49	69	2	66	.283	.362	.409	101	3	11	.978	-3	98	76	*O-139(3-136-0)	-0.4
1938	Phi N☆	120	466	58	139	36	6	3	39	34	1	48	.298	.347	.421	113	9	8	.965	-2	105	73	*O-116(0-115-2)	0.4
1939	Phi N	111	393	59	111	28	5	1	22	42	2	27	.282	.355	.387	102	2	4	.976	3	112	61	O-95(9-73-13)	0.2
1940	Phi N	33	83	10	21	6	1	0	5	9	0	9	.253	.326	.349	90	-1	1	.979	1	92	257	O-23(0-19-4)	0.0
1944	NY A	85	328	49	99	12	4	9	47	34	2	26	.302	.371	.445	128	12	5-2	.964	0	97	114	O-80(78-2-0)	0.8
1945	NY A	117	408	53	109	18	6	7	53	65	0	31	.267	.368	.392	115	10	4-1	.984	1	104	86	*O-102(97-3-2)	0.6
Total	6	607	2257	331	643	135	29	28	215	253	7	207	.285	.359	.408	109	35	33-3	.974	0	103	86	O-555(187-348-21)	1.6
MARTIN, JERRY Jerry Lindsey B 5.11.1949 Columbia, SC BR/TR 6-1/195# d9.7 f-Barney																								
1974	Phi N	13	14	2	3	1	0	0	1	1-0	0	5	.214	.267	.286	52	-1	0-0	1.000	-1	59	0	O-11(6-3-2)	-0.2
1975	Phi N	57	113	15	24	7	1	2	11	11-4	1	16	.212	.288	.345	72	-4	2-2	.979	2	111	143	O-49(8-41-0)	-0.3
1976	†Phi N	130	121	30	30	7	0	2	15	7-0	0	28	.248	.287	.355	80	-3	3-2	.975	-2	100	0	*O-110(73-23-15)/1	-0.8
1977	†Phi N	116	215	34	56	16	3	6	28	18-2	4	42	.260	.328	.447	101	0	6-4	.984	-1	95	91	*O-106(45-18-51)/1	-0.3
1978	†Phi N	128	266	40	72	13	4	9	36	28-3	1	65	.271	.339	.451	119	6	9-5	.987	4	105	147	*O-112(48-22-55)	0.8
1979	Chi N	150	534	74	145	34	3	19	73	38-3	3	85	.272	.321	.453	100	0	2-4	.981	-9	88	113	*O-144(0-140-4)	-1.2
1980	Chi N	141	494	57	112	22	2	23	73	38-6	2	107	.227	.281	.419	88	-10	8-3	.978	-12	83	85	*O-129(5-103-42)	-2.5
1981	SF N	72	241	23	58	5	3	4	25	21-2	3	52	.241	.308	.336	85	-5	6-2	.993	-5	86	88	O-64(10-58-0)	-1.2
1982	KC A	147	519	52	138	22	1	15	65	38-0	2	138	.266	.316	.399	95	-4	1-1	.980	1	110	39	*O-142(11-3-134)/D-3	-1.0
1983	KC A	13	44	4	14	2	0	2	13	1-0	0	7	.318	.313	.500	125	1	1-0	.957	-2	80	0	O-13(RF)	-0.1
1984	NY N	51	91	6	14	1	0	3	5	6-0	0	29	.154	.206	.264	32	-9	0-0	1.000	2	123	169	O-30(9-0-21)/1-3	-0.8
Total	11	1018	2652	337	666	130	17	85	345	207-20	16	574	.251	.307	.409	93	-29	38-23	.982	-22	96	87	O-910(215-411-337)/1-5,D-3	-7.6
MARTIN, JACK John Christopher B 4.19.1887 Plainfield, NJ D 7.4.1980 Plainfield, NJ BR/TR 5-9/159# d4.25																								
1912	NY A	71	231	30	52	6	1	0	17	37	6		.225	.347	.260	70	-7	14	.898	-2	104	77	S-65/3-4,2	-0.4
1914	Bos N	33	85	10	18	2	0	0	5	6	0	7	.212	.264	.235	49	-5	0	.949	0	96	167	3-26/12	-0.5
	Phi N	83	292	26	74	5	3	0	21	27	1	29	.253	.319	.291	77	-8	6	.930	-3	96	73	S-83	-0.6
	Year	116	377	36	92	7	3	0	26	33	1	36	.244	.307	.279	71	-13	6	.930	-3	96	73	S-83,3-26/12	-1.1
Total	2	187	608	66	144	13	4	0	43	70	7	36	.237	.323	.271	71	-20	20	.915	-5	100	75	S-148/3-30,2-2,1	-1.5
MARTIN, PEPPER Johnny Leonard Roosevelt "The Wild Horse Of The Osage" B 2.29.1904 Temple, OK D 3.5.1965 McAlester, OK BR/TR 5-8/170# d4.16 C1																								
1928	†StL N	39	13	11	4	0	0	0	0	1	1	2	.308	.400	.308	86	0	2	1.000	0	157	0	/O-4(RF)	0.0
1930	StL N	6	1	5	0	0	0	0	0	0	0	0	.000	.000	.000	-97	0	0	—	0			H	0.0
1931	†StL N	123	413	68	124	32	8	7	75	30	2	40	.300	.351	.467	114	8	16	.967	0	99	116	*O-110(CF)	0.5
1932	StL N	85	323	47	77	19	6	4	34	30	1	31	.238	.305	.372	79	-10	9	.976	-3	86	178	O-69(5-64-0),3-15	-1.4
1933	StL N★	145	599	**122**	189	36	12	8	57	67	3	46	.316	.387	.456	133	28	**26**	.943	-5	93	68	*3-145	2.9
1934	†StL N★	110	454	76	131	25	11	5	49	32	1	41	.289	.337	.425	96	-3	**23**	.936	-5	96	50	*3-107/P	-0.4
1935	StL N★	135	539	121	161	41	6	9	54	33	2	58	.299	.341	.447	106	5	20	.904	-14	86	108	*3-114,O-16(1-5-10)	-0.6
1936	StL N	143	572	121	177	36	11	11	76	58	0	66	.309	.373	.469	126	21	**23**	.976	-7	93	97	*O-127(0-3-124),3-15/P	0.6
1937	StL N☆	98	339	60	103	27	8	5	38	33	0	50	.304	.366	.475	124	12	9	.973	7	110	154	O-82(0-40-42)/3-5	1.5
1938	StL N	91	269	34	79	18	2	2	38	18	1	34	.294	.340	.398	97	-1	4	.986	-2	107	21	O-62(1-38-23)/3-4	-0.5
1939	StL N	88	281	48	86	17	7	3	37	30	1	35	.306	.375	.448	113	6	6	.975	-4	99	105	O-51(8-37-8),3-22	0.1
1940	StL N	86	228	28	72	15	4	3	39	22	1	24	.316	.378	.456	122	7	6	.974	4	102	211	O-63(16-10-40)/3-2	0.8
1944	StL N	40	86	15	24	4	0	2	4	15	0	11	.279	.386	.395	118	3	2	.980	-1	105	46	O-29(0-7-22)	0.1
Total	13	1189	4117	756	1227	270	75	59	501	369	13	438	.298	.358	.443	112	76	146	.973	-28	99	117	O-613(31-314-273),3-429/P-2	3.6
MARTIN, J. C. Joseph Clifton B 12.13.1936 Axton, VA BL/TR 6-2/200# d9.10 C1																								
1959	Chi A	3	4	0	1	0	0	0	1	0-0	0	1	.250	.250	.250	38	0	0-0	.667	-0	119	0	/3-2	-0.1
1960	Chi A	7	20	0	2	1	0	0	2	0-0	0	6	.100	.100	.150	-34	-4	0-0	1.000	-0	90	0	/3-5,1	-0.4
1961	Chi A	110	274	26	63	8	3	5	32	21-2	2	31	.230	.290	.336	68	-14	1-2	.988	4	122	93	1-60,3-36	-1.2
1962	Chi A	18	26	0	2	0	0	0	2	0-0	0	3	.077	.077	.077	-59	-6	0-0	1.000	-1	*104*	*0*	/C-6,13	-0.6
1963	Chi A	105	259	25	53	11	1	5	28	26-6	1	35	.205	.278	.313	67	-11	0-0	.983	14	129	125	C-98/1-3,3	0.6
1964	Chi A	122	294	23	58	10	1	4	22	16-7	2	30	.197	.241	.279	46	-22	0-0	.986	8	*165*	*94*	*C-120	-1.0
1965	Chi A	119	230	21	60	12	0	2	21	24-10	2	29	.261	.333	.339	98	0	2-1	.982	-2	*92*	*109*	*C-112/1-4,3-2	0.1
1966	Chi A	67	157	13	40	5	3	2	20	14-6	1	24	.255	.316	.363	103	0	0-0	.982	-0	*78*	*98*	C-63	0.2
1967	Chi A	101	252	22	59	12	1	4	22	30-4	1	41	.234	.317	.337	97	0	4-4	.987	6	87	77	C-96/1	1.0
1968	NY N	78	244	20	55	9	2	3	31	21-3	5	31	.225	.298	.316	84	-4	0-0	.994	-3	*99*	*98*	C-53,1-14	-0.6
1969	†NY N	66	177	12	37	5	1	4	21	12-1	0	32	.209	.257	.316	59	-10	0-0	.996	-4	121	33	C-48/1-2	-1.3
1970	Chi N	40	77	11	12	1	0	1	4	20-7	1	11	.156	.333	.208	44	-5	0-0	.983	-0	128	119	C-36/1-3	-0.4
1971	Chi N	47	125	13	33	5	0	2	17	12-6	2	16	.264	.336	.352	84	-2	1-1	.996	2	72	125	C-43/O(LF)	0.2

Year	Tm Lg	G	AB	R	H	2B	3B	HR	RBI	BB-IB	HP	SO	AVG	OBP	SLG	AOPS	ABR	SB-CS	FA	FR	Rng	Thr	G at Pos	BFW
1972	Chi N	25	50	3	12	3	0	0	7	5-1	0	9	.240	.304	.300	67	-2	1-0	.970	-3	41	29	C-17	-0.4
Total	14	908	2189	189	487	82	12	32	230	201-53	17	299	.222	.291	.315	72	-80	9-8	.987	22	*110*	*95*	C-692/1-89,3-47,O(LF)	-3.9
MARTIN, MIKE Joseph Michael B 12.3.1958 Portland, OR BL/TR 6-2/193# d8.15																								
1986	Chi N	8	13	1	1	1	0	0	0	2-1	0	4	.077	.200	.154	-1	-2	0-0	1.000	-3	43	101	/C-8	-0.5
MARTIN, JOE Joseph Samuel "Silent Joe" B 1.1.1876 Hollidaysburg, PA D 5.25.1964 Altoona, PA BL/TR 5-9.5/155# d4.28																								
1903	Was A	35	119	11	27	4	5	0	7	5	0		.227	.258	.345	78	-4	2	.892	-4	106	66	2-15,3-13/O-7(1-0-6)	-0.8
	StL A	44	173	18	37	6	4	0	7	6	2		.214	.249	.295	64	-8	0	.983	-2	138	281	O-38(4-0-34)/2-6,3	-1.2
	Year	79	292	29	64	10	9	0	14	11	2		.219	.252	.315	70	-12	2	.959	-6	119	242	O-45(5-0-40),2-21,3-14	-2.0
MARTIN, NORBERTO Norberto Edonal (McDonald) B 12.10.1966 San Pedro De Macoris, D.R. BR/TR 5-10/164# d9.20 OF Total (12-LF 7-RF)																								
1993	Chi A	8	14	3	5	0	0	0	2	1-0	0	1	.357	.400	.357	108	0	0-0	.957	1	88	181	/2-5,D	0.1
1994	Chi A	45	131	19	36	7	1	1	16	9-0	0	16	.275	.317	.366	78	-4	4-2	.982	-6	79	69	2-28/S-6,3-5,O-2(LF),D	-0.8
1995	Chi A	72	160	17	43	7	4	2	17	3-0	1	25	.269	.281	.400	80	-6	5-0	.950	2	95	112	2-17,O-12(5-0-7),D-10/3-9,S-7	-0.2
1996	Chi A	70	140	30	49	7	0	1	14	6-0	0	17	.350	.374	.421	107	1	10-2	.943	7	94	158	S-24,D-22,2-10/3-3	0.9
1997	Chi A	71	213	24	64	7	1	2	27	6-0	0	31	.300	.320	.371	83	-6	1-4	.960	-12	71	77	S-28,3-17/2-9,D-6	-1.6
1998	Ana A	79	195	20	42	2	0	1	13	6-0	0	29	.215	.236	.241	25	-22	3-1	.982	4	110	108	2-54,D-10/3-5,O-5(LF),S-2	-1.5
1999	Tor A	9	27	3	6	2	0	0	0	4-0	2	4	.222	.364	.296	70	-1	0-0	.974	1	126	148	/2-8,S	0.1
Total	7	354	880	116	245	32	6	7	89	35-0	3	123	.278	.306	.352	72	-38	23-9	.976	-3	103	101	2-131/S-68,D-50,3-39,O-19L	-3.0
MARTIN, STU Stuart McGuire B 11.17.1913 Rich Square, NC D 1.11.1997 Severn, NC BL/TR 6/155# d4.14																								
1936	StL N☆	92	332	63	99	21	4	6	41	29	1	27	.298	.356	.440	114	6	17	.949	-14	92	105	2-83/S-3	-0.2
1937	StL N	90	223	34	58	6	1	1	17	32	0	18	.260	.353	.309	80	-5	3	.946	-6	96	102	2-48/1-9,S	-0.9
1938	StL N	114	417	54	116	26	2	1	27	30	1	28	.278	.328	.357	84	-9	4	.967	-4	99	95	2-99	-0.6
1939	StL N	120	425	60	114	26	7	3	30	33	3	40	.268	.325	.384	85	-9	4	**.977**	-2	97	96	*2-107/1	-0.5
1940	StL N	112	369	45	88	12	6	4	32	33	0	35	.238	.301	.336	71	-15	4	.972	-16	78	22	3-73,2-33	-2.8
1941	Pit N	88	233	37	71	13	2	0	19	10	3	17	.305	.341	.378	103	1	2	.972	-0	105	87	2-53/3-2,1	0.4
1942	Pit N	42	120	16	27	4	2	1	12	8	0	10	.225	.273	.317	71	-5	1	.979	-8	84	81	2-30/1S	-1.2
1943	Chi N	64	118	13	26	4	0	0	5	15	0	10	.220	.308	.254	64	-5	1	.980	3	119	99	2-22/3-8,1-2	-0.2
Total	8	722	2237	322	599	112	24	16	183	190	8	185	.268	.327	.361	86	-41	36	.966	-47	97	95	2-475/3-83,1-14,S-5	-6.0
MARTIN, GENE Thomas Eugene B 1.12.1947 Americus, GA BL/TR 6-0.5/190# d7.28																								
1968	Was A	9	11	1	4	1	0	1	1	0-0	0	1	.364	.364	.727	232	2	0-0	—	-1	0	0	/O-2(LF)	0.1
MARTIN, JOE William Joseph "Smokey Joe" B 8.28.1911 Seymour, MO D 9.28.1960 Buffalo, NY BR/TR 5-11.5/181# d4.27																								
1936	NY N	7	15	0	4	1	0	0	2	0	1	4	.267	.313	.333	75	-1	0	1.000	0	104	193	/3-7	0.0
1938	Chi A	1	0	0	0	0	0	0	0	0	0	0	—	—	—	—	0	0-0	—	0			R	0.0
Total	2	8	15	0	4	1	0	0	2	0	1	4	.267	.313	.333	75	-1	0-0	1.000	0	104	193	/3-7	0.0
MARTIN, BILLY William Lloyd B 2.13.1894 Washington, DC D 9.14.1949 Arlington, VA BR/TR 5-8.5/170# d10.6																								
1914	Bos N	1	3	0	0	0	0	0	0	0	0	0	.000	.000	.000	-99	-1	0	.500	-1	57	0	/S	-0.2
MARTINEZ, SANDY Angel Sandy (Martinez) B 10.3.1970 Villa Mella, D.R. BL/TR 6-2/200# d6.24																								
1995	Tor A	62	191	12	46	12	0	2	25	7-0	1	45	.241	.270	.335	57	-12	0-0	.986	1	178	80	C-61	-0.7
1996	Tor A	76	229	17	52	9	3	3	18	16-0	4	58	.227	.288	.332	57	-16	0-0	.993	4	131	91	C-75	-0.7
1997	Tor A	3	2	1	0	0	0	0	0	1-0	0	1	.000	.333	.000	-3	0	0-0	.933	0	32	209	/C-3	0.0
1998	†Chi N	45	87	7	23	9	1	0	7	13-0	1	21	.264	.363	.391	96	0	1-0	.985	3	116	64	C-33	0.4
1999	Chi N	17	30	1	5	0	0	1	1	0-0	0	11	.167	.167	.267	7	-4	0-0	.959	0	490	0	C-12	-0.4
2000	Fla N	10	18	1	4	2	0	0	0	0-0	0	8	.222	.222	.333	39	-2	0-0	1.000	1	161	0	/C-9	0.0
2001	Mon N	1	1	0	0	0	0	0	0	0-0	0	0	.000	.000	.000	-98	0	0-0	1.000	0	6	0	/C	0.0
Total	7	214	558	39	130	32	4	6	51	37-0	6	144	.233	.286	.337	60	-34	1-0	.987	9	160	78	C-194	-1.4
MARTINEZ, CARLOS Carlos Alberto Escobar (born Alberto Escobar (Martinez)) B 8.11.1964 LaGuaira, Venezuela BR/TR 6-5/175# d9.2																								
1988	Chi A	17	55	5	9	1	0	0	0	0-0	0	12	.164	.164	.182	-3	-8	1-0	.909	0	118	40	3-15/D-2	-0.8
1989	Chi A	109	350	44	105	22	0	5	32	21-2	1	57	.300	.340	.406	112	6	4-1	.912	-5	98	106	3-68,1-34,O-10(LF)/D	-0.1
1990	Chi A	92	272	18	61	6	5	4	24	10-2	0	40	.224	.252	.327	62	-16	0-4	.988	-6	75	84	1-82/O(LF)D	-2.9
1991	Cle A	72	257	22	73	14	0	5	30	10-2	2	43	.284	.310	.397	95	-2	3-2	.968	-4	63	125	D-41,1-31	-1.0
1992	Cle A	69	228	23	60	9	1	5	35	7-0	1	21	.263	.283	.377	87	-5	1-2	.996	-6	95	152	1-37,3-28/D-4	-1.4
1993	Cle A	80	262	26	64	10	0	5	31	20-3	0	29	.244	.295	.340	71	-11	1-1	.934	-7	78	89	3-35,1-22,D-19	-2.1
1995	Cal A	26	61	7	11	1	0	1	9	6-2	1	7	.180	.265	.246	34	-6	0-0	.968	1	112	374	3-16/1-4,D-2	-0.5
Total	7	465	1485	145	383	63	6	25	161	74-11	5	209	.258	.293	.359	81	-42	10-10	.986	-26	74	98	1-210,3-162/D-72,O-11(LF)	-8.8
MARTINEZ, CARMELO Carmelo (Salgado) B 7.28.1960 Dorado, P.R. BR/TR 6-2/220# d8.22																								
1983	Chi N	29	89	8	23	3	0	6	16	4-0	0	19	.258	.287	.494	108	0	0-0	.992	0	94	104	1-26/3O(LF)	-0.1
1984	†SD N	149	488	64	122	28	2	13	66	68-4	4	82	.250	.340	.395	108	7	1-3	.976	11	113	128	*O-142(LF)/1-2	1.2
1985	SD N	150	514	64	130	28	1	21	72	87-4	3	82	.253	.362	.434	124	20	0-4	.978	5	102	115	*O-150(LF)/1-3	1.7
1986	SD N	113	244	28	58	10	0	9	25	35-2	1	46	.238	.333	.389	101	1	1-1	.978	1	90	152	O-60(LF),1-26/3	-0.1
1987	SD N	139	447	59	122	21	2	15	70	70-5	3	82	.273	.372	.430	117	13	5-5	.968	-1	94	137	O-78(LF),1-65	0.5
1988	SD N	121	365	48	86	12	0	18	65	35-3	0	57	.236	.301	.416	106	2	1-1	.993	8	117	164	O-64(55-0-11),1-41	0.6
1989	SD N	111	267	23	59	12	2	6	39	32-3	0	54	.221	.302	.348	86	-5	0-0	.982	3	96	166	O-65(LF),1-32	-0.5
1990	Phi N	71	198	23	48	8	0	8	31	29-0	0	37	.242	.339	.404	104	1	2-1	.994	-1	98	120	1-43,O-20(20-0-1)	-0.2
	†Pit N	12	19	3	4	1	0	2	4	1-0	0	5	.211	.250	.579	126	0	0-0	1.000	1	216	240	/1-5,O-2(LF)	0.1
	Year	83	217	26	52	9	0	10	35	30-0	0	42	.240	.332	.419	106	2	2-1	.995	0	106	128	1-48,O-22(22-0-1)	-0.1
1991	Pit N	11	16	1	4	0	0	0	0	1-0	0	2	.250	.294	.250	55	-1	0-0	.945	-1	31	65	/1-8	-0.3
	KC A	44	121	17	25	6	0	4	17	27-3	0	25	.207	.351	.355	96	0	0-1	.991	3	127	95	1-43/D	0.0
	Cin N	53	138	12	32	5	0	6	19	15-1	0	37	.232	.301	.399	93	-1	0-0	.985	0	72	88	1-25,O-16(LF)	-0.3
Total	9	1003	2906	350	713	134	7	108	424	404-25	11	528	.245	.337	.408	108	37	10-16	.980	30	105	134	O-598(588-0-12),1-319/3-2,D	2.6
MARTINEZ, TINO Constantino B 12.7.1967 Tampa, FL BL/TR 6-2/210# d8.20																								
1990	Sea A	24	68	4	15	4	0	0	5	9-0	0	9	.221	.308	.279	66	-3	0-0	1.000	0	95	157	1-23	-0.4
1991	Sea A	36	112	11	23	2	0	4	9	11-0	0	24	.205	.272	.330	67	-5	0-0	.993	2	119	103	1-29/D-5	-0.6
1992	Sea A	136	460	53	118	19	2	16	66	42-9	2	77	.257	.316	.411	103	1	2-1	.995	4	116	88	1-78,D-47	-0.2
1993	Sea A	109	408	48	108	25	1	17	60	45-9	5	56	.265	.343	.456	112	7	0-3	.997	-2	85	98	*1-103/D-6	-0.6
1994	Sea A	97	329	42	86	21	0	20	61	29-2	1	52	.261	.320	.508	108	3	1-2	.997	1	94	88	1-82/D-8	-0.4
1995	†Sea A★	141	519	92	152	35	3	31	111	62-15	4	91	.293	.369	.551	135	27	0-0	.993	4	104	71	*1-139/D	1.7
1996	†NY A	155	595	82	174	28	0	25	117	68-4	2	85	.292	.364	.466	109	8	2-1	**.996**	-2	88	91	*1-151/D-3	-0.7
1997	†NY A★	158	594	96	176	31	2	44	141	75-14	3	75	.296	.371	.577	146	39	3-1	.994	7	116	102	*1-150/D-9	3.1
1998	†NY A	142	531	92	149	33	1	28	123	61-3	6	83	.281	.355	.505	127	21	2-1	.992	1	103	109	*1-142	0.9
1999	†NY A	159	589	95	155	27	2	28	105	69-7	3	86	.263	.341	.458	103	2	3-4	.995	7	115	85	*1-158	-0.5
2000	†NY A	155	569	69	147	37	4	16	91	52-9	8	74	.258	.328	.422	89	-10	4-1	.994	-1	94	86	*1-154	-2.3
2001	†NY A	154	589	89	165	24	2	34	113	42-2	2	89	.280	.329	.501	113	9	1-2	.996	5	105	91	*1-149/D-3	0.0
2002	†StL N	150	511	63	134	25	1	21	75	58-9	2	71	.262	.337	.438	109	4	3-2	.996	-2	94	106	*1-149	-1.2
2003	StL N	138	476	66	130	25	2	15	69	53-7	9	71	.273	.352	.429	108	6	1-1	**.997**	-0	101	91	*1-126/D-5	-0.5
Total	14	1754	6350	902	1732	336	20	299	1146	676-90	47	943	.273	.344	.473	113	109	22-19	.995	24	102	93	*1-1633/D-87	-1.7
MARTINEZ, DAVE David B 9.26.1964 New York, NY BL/TL 5-10/175# d6.15 OF Total (144-LF 857-CF 731-RF)																								
1986	Chi N	53	108	13	15	1	1	1	7	6-0	1	22	.139	.190	.194	6	-14	4-2	.988	2	114	117	O-46(9-39-1)	-1.3
1987	Chi N	142	459	70	134	18	8	8	36	57-4	2	96	.292	.372	.418	105	4	16-8	.980	2	101	149	*O-139(14-134-3)	0.6
1988	Chi N	75	256	27	65	10	1	4	34	21-5	2	46	.254	.311	.348	86	-4	7-3	.970	-3	96	66	O-72(0-70-2)	-0.8
	Mon N	63	191	24	49	3	5	2	12	17-3	0	48	.257	.316	.356	89	-3	16-6	.992	0	97	86	O-60(1-44-22)	-0.3
	Year	138	447	51	114	13	6	6	46	38-8	2	94	.255	.313	.351	87	-8	23-9	.979	-3	96	75	*O-132(1-114-24)	-1.1
1989	Mon N	126	361	41	99	16	7	3	27	27-2	0	57	.274	.324	.382	100	-1	23-4	.967	-4	86	144	*O-118(0-104-38)	-0.3
1990	Mon N	118	391	60	109	13	5	11	39	24-2	1	48	.279	.321	.422	107	2	13-11	.989	2	105	110	*O-108(0-103-22)/P	0.2
1991	Mon N	124	396	47	117	18	5	7	42	20-3	3	54	.295	.332	.419	112	5	16-7	.982	2	98	152	*O-112(36-34-54)	0.6
1992	Cin N	135	393	47	100	20	5	3	31	42-4	0	54	.254	.323	.354	90	-5	12-8	.991	2	104	145	*O-111(3-105-6),1-21	-0.6
1993	SF N	91	241	28	58	12	1	5	27	27-3	0	39	.241	.317	.361	84	-6	6-3	.993	1	96	163	O-73(3-43-34)	-0.5

Year	Tm Lg	G	AB	R	H	2B	3B	HR	RBI	BB-IB	HP	SO	AVG	OBP	SLG	AOPS	ABR	SB-CS	FA	FR	Rng	Thr	G at Pos	BFW
1994	SF N	97	235	23	58	9	3	4	27	21-1	2	22	.247	.314	.362	79	-8	3-4	1.000	2	110	103	O-58(3-3-53),1-25	-1.0
1995	Chi A	119	303	49	93	16	4	5	37	32-2	1	41	.307	.371	.436	115	7	8-2	.976	-2	102	77	O-59(30-5-32),1-47/PD	0.1
1996	Chi A	146	440	85	140	20	8	10	53	52-1	3	52	.318	.393	.468	123	16	15-7	.988	1	106	65	*O-121(3-73-73),1-23	1.3
1997	Chi A	145	504	78	144	16	6	12	55	55-7	3	69	.286	.356	.413	105	4	12-6	.996	4	105	103	*O-105(4-45-75),1-52/D	0.2
1998	TB A	90	309	31	79	11	0	3	20	35-4	2	52	.256	.334	.320	70	-13	8-7	.994	3	100	153	O-86(0-2-85)/1D	-1.4
1999	TB A	143	514	79	146	25	5	6	66	60-3	5	76	.284	.361	.387	91	-6	13-6	.985	-7	90	91	*O-140(2-52-93)	-1.5
2000	TB A	29	104	12	27	4	2	1	12	10-1	0	17	.260	.319	.365	75	-4	1-4	1.000	2	88	274	O-28(RF)	-0.5
	Chi N	18	54	5	10	1	1	0	1	2-0	0	8	.185	.214	.241	15	-7	1-0	1.000	-0	104	0	O-10(9-1-0)/1-9	-0.8
	Tex A	38	119	14	32	4	1	2	12	14-2	1	20	.269	.351	.370	82	-3	2-1	1.000	4	130	93	O-35(RF)/1-4	-0.1
	Tor A	47	180	29	56	10	1	2	22	24-0	1	28	.311	.393	.411	101	1	4-2	.982	6	108	249	O-47(RF)	0.4
	Year	114	403	55	115	18	4	5	46	48-3	2	65	.285	.362	.387	87	-6	7-7	.992	11	109	209	*O-110(RF)/1-4	-0.1
2001	†Atl N	120	237	33	68	11	3	2	20	21-0	1	44	.287	.347	.384	87	-4	3-3	1.000	-0	91	76	O-52(27-0-28),1-10/D	-0.7
Total	16	1919	5795	795	1599	238	72	91	580	567-47	28	893	.276	.341	.389	95	-39	183-94	.986	15	100	123	*O-1580C,1-192/D-8,P-2	-6.4
MARTINEZ, DOMINGO Domingo Emilio (La Fontaine) B 8.4.1967 Santo Domingo, D.R. BR/TR 6-2/215# d9.11																								
1992	Tor A	7	8	2	5	0	0	1	3	0-0	0	1	.625	.625	1.000	333	2	0-0	1.000	-1	0	113	/1-7	0.2
1993	Tor A	8	14	2	4	0	0	1	3	1-0	0	7	.286	.333	.500	120	0	0-0	1.000	1	172	75	/1-7,3	0.0
Total	2	15	22	4	9	0	0	2	6	1-0	0	8	.409	.435	.682	196	2	0-0	1.000	-0	101	91	/1-14,3	0.2
MARTINEZ, EDGAR Edgar B 1.2.1963 New York, NY BR/TR 5-11/175# d9.12																								
1987	Sea A	13	43	6	16	5	2	0	5	2-0	1	5	.372	.413	.581	152	3	0-0	1.000	0	91	50	3-12/D	0.3
1988	Sea A	14	32	0	9	4	0	0	5	4-0	0	7	.281	.351	.406	110	1	0-0	.929	-4	46	65	3-13	-0.3
1989	Sea A	65	171	20	41	5	0	2	20	17-1	3	26	.240	.314	.304	74	-5	2-1	.949	-6	80	106	3-61	-1.1
1990	Sea A	144	487	71	147	27	2	11	49	74-3	5	62	.302	.397	.433	131	24	1-4	.928	-5	95	65	*3-143/D-2	1.9
1991	Sea A	150	544	98	167	35	1	14	52	84-9	8	72	.307	.405	.452	137	33	0-3	.962	3	103	91	*3-144/D-2	3.4
1992	Sea A★	135	528	100	181	**46**	3	18	73	54-2	4	61	**.343**	.404	.544	164	46	14-4	.943	2	100	129	*3-103,D-28/1-2	4.9
1993	Sea A	42	135	20	32	7	0	4	13	28-1	0	19	.237	.366	.378	100	1	0-0	.889	-7	41	42	D-24,3-16	-0.7
1994	Sea A	89	326	47	93	23	1	13	51	53-3	3	42	.285	.387	.482	121	12	6-2	.950	5	100	119	3-64,D-23	1.5
1995	†Sea A★	**145**	511	**121**	182	**52**	0	29	113	116-19	8	87	**.356**	**.479**	.628	**184**	**74**	4-3	.800	-2	47	0	*D-138/3-4,1-3	**5.7**
1996	Sea A★	139	499	121	163	52	2	26	103	123-12	8	84	.327	.464	.595	166	61	3-3	.967	-1	41	89	*D-134/1-4,3-2	4.5
1997	†Sea A★	155	542	104	179	35	1	28	108	119-11	11	86	.330	.456	.554	164	61	2-4	.986	0	100	86	*D-144/1-7,3	4.6
1998	Sea A	154	556	86	179	46	1	29	102	106-4	3	96	.322	**.429**	.565	157	53	1-1	1.000	2	277	101	*D-147/1-4	4.1
1999	Sea A	142	502	86	169	35	1	24	86	97-6	6	99	.337	**.447**	.554	158	51	7-2	1.000	-0	84	47	*D-134/1-5	3.8
2000	†Sea A★	153	556	100	180	31	0	37	**145**	96-8	5	95	.324	.423	.579	156	52	3-0	1.000	0	99	215	*D-146/1-2	3.9
2001	†Sea A★	132	470	80	144	40	1	23	116	93-9	9	90	.306	.423	.543	163	50	4-1	1.000	-0	0	0	*D-127/1	4.0
2002	Sea A	97	328	42	91	23	0	15	59	67-8	6	69	.277	.403	.485	141	24	1-1	—	0	0	0	D-91	1.7
2003	Sea A★	145	497	72	146	25	0	24	98	92-7	7	95	.294	.406	.489	141	34	0-1	—	0	0	0	*D-140	2.3
Total	17	1914	6727	1174	2119	491	15	297	1198	1225-103	87	1095	.315	.423	.525	151	575	48-30	.946	-13	95	93	*D-1281,3-563/1-28	44.5
MARTINEZ, FELIX Felix (Mata) B 5.18.1974 Nagua, D.R. BB/TR 6/168# d9.3																								
1997	KC A	16	31	3	7	1	1	0	3	6-0	0	8	.226	.351	.323	76	-1	0-0	.975	-3	73	106	S-12/D-2	-0.3
1998	KC A	34	85	7	11	1	1	0	5	5-0	1	21	.129	.187	.165	-7	-14	3-1	.956	-1	96	123	S-32/2-2	-1.2
1999	KC A	6	7	1	1	0	0	0	0	0-0	0	0	.143	.143	.143	-26	-1	0-0	—	-2	0	0	/S-2,2	-0.3
2000	TB A	106	299	42	64	11	4	2	17	32-0	8	68	.214	.305	.298	55	-21	9-3	.976	34	124	116	*S-106	2.0
2001	TB A	77	219	24	54	13	1	1	14	10-0	5	46	.247	.294	.329	65	-11	6-5	.944	-6	92	100	S-67,2-10	-1.2
Total	5	239	641	77	137	26	7	3	39	53-0	14	143	.214	.287	.290	50	-48	18-9	.964	22	107	111	S-219/2-13,D-2	-1.0
MARTINEZ, TONY Gabriel Antonio (Diaz) B 3.18.1940 Perico, Cuba D 8.24.1991 Miami, FL BR/TR 5-10/165# d4.9 Mil 1970																								
1963	Cle A	43	141	10	22	4	0	0	8	5-0	0	18	.156	.184	.184	4	-18	1-1	.961	-12	78	77	S-41	-3.0
1964	Cle A	9	14	1	3	1	0	0	2	0-0	0	2	.214	.214	.286	38	-1	0-1	1.000	2	115	209	/2-4,S	0.1
1965	Cle A	4	3	0	0	0	0	0	0	0-0	0	0	.000	.000	.000	-99	-1	0-0	—	0			H	-0.1
1966	Cle A	17	17	2	5	0	0	0	0	1-0	0	6	.294	.333	.294	82	0	1-1	.833	-0	90	0	/S-5,2-4	0.0
Total	4	73	175	13	30	5	0	0	10	6-0	0	26	.171	.198	.200	13	-20	2-3	.958	-10	79	81	/S-47,2-8	-3.0
MARTINEZ, GREG Gregory Alfred B 1.27.1972 Las Vegas, NV BB/TR 5-10/168# d3.31																								
1998	Mil N	13	3	2	0	0	0	0	0	1-0	0	2	.000	.250	.000	-27	-1	2-0	—	-1	0	0	/O-6(LF)	-0.1
MARTINEZ, BUCK John Albert B 11.7.1948 Redding, CA BR/TR 5-10/190# d6.18 Mil 1970 M2																								
1969	KC A	72	205	14	47	6	1	4	23	8-2	0	25	.229	.258	.327	62	-11	0-0	.972	3	125	83	C-55/O(RF)	-0.6
1970	KC A	6	9	1	1	0	0	0	0	2-0	0	1	.111	.273	.111	10	-1	0-0	.958	-0	72	315	/C-5	-0.1
1971	KC A	22	46	3	7	2	0	0	1	5-0	0	9	.152	.231	.196	23	-5	0-1	.968	-0	106	46	C-21	-0.5
1973	KC A	14	32	2	8	1	0	1	6	4-0	0	5	.250	.333	.375	92	0	0-0	.966	-1	187	57	C-14	0.0
1974	KC A	43	107	10	23	3	1	1	8	14-0	2	19	.215	.317	.290	71	-4	0-1	.977	-0	101	58	C-38	-0.3
1975	KC A	80	226	15	51	9	2	3	23	21-0	1	28	.226	.293	.323	72	-8	1-0	.980	-4	76	107	C-79	-1.0
1976	†KC A	95	267	24	61	13	3	5	34	16-1	0	45	.228	.269	.356	82	-7	0-0	.991	3	89	108	C-94	0.0
1977	KC A	29	80	3	18	4	0	1	9	3-0	0	12	.225	.253	.313	53	-5	0-0	.993	1	116	66	C-28	-0.4
1978	Mil A	89	256	26	56	10	1	1	20	14-1	0	42	.219	.255	.277	51	-17	1-1	.978	-1	120	75	C-89	-1.5
1979	Mil A	69	196	17	53	8	0	4	26	8-0	0	25	.270	.296	.372	80	-6	0-1	.967	-5	133	100	C-68/P	-0.9
1980	Mil A	76	219	16	49	9	0	3	17	12-0	1	33	.224	.266	.306	58	-13	1-0	.985	5	115	101	C-76	-0.4
1981	Tor A	45	128	13	29	8	1	4	21	11-0	1	16	.227	.287	.398	92	-2	1-0	.991	2	105	88	C-45	0.3
1982	Tor A	96	260	26	63	17	0	10	37	24-1	0	34	.242	.301	.423	90	-4	1-1	.988	8	170	90	C-93	0.8
1983	Tor A	88	221	27	56	14	0	10	33	29-0	0	39	.253	.337	.452	109	3	0-1	.989	-2	149	67	C-85	0.4
1984	Tor A	102	232	24	51	13	1	5	37	29-0	2	49	.220	.301	.349	80	-6	0-3	.995	-1	126	68	C-98/D	-0.5
1985	Tor A	42	99	11	16	3	0	4	14	10-0	1	12	.162	.239	.313	50	-7	0-0	.988	3	112	109	C-42	-0.2
1986	Tor A	81	160	13	29	8	0	2	12	20-0	0	25	.181	.271	.269	47	-12	0-0	.994	-2	112	76	C-78/D	-1.1
Total	17	1049	2743	245	618	128	10	58	321	230-5	8	419	.225	.284	.343	73	-105	5-10	.984	9	119	87	*C-1008/D-2,PO(RF)	-6.0
MARTINEZ, JOSE Jose (Azcuiz) B 7.26.1942 Cardenas, Cuba BR/TR 5-10/190# d6.18 C15																								
1969	Pit N	77	168	20	45	6	0	1	16	9-0	1	32	.268	.309	.321	78	-5	1-3	.975	6	113	123	2-42,S-20/3-5,O-2(LF)	0.3
1970	Pit N	19	20	1	1	0	0	0	0	1-0	0	5	.050	.095	.050	-61	-5	0-0	1.000	2	40	0	/3-7,2-4,S	-0.3
Total	2	96	188	21	46	6	0	1	16	10-0	1	37	.245	.286	.293	63	-10	1-3	.966	7	116	126	/2-46,S-21,3-12,O-2(LF)	0.0
MARTINEZ, MANNY Manuel (De Jesus) B 10.3.1970 San Pedro De Macoris, D.R. BR/TR 6-2/169# d6.14																								
1996	Sea A	9	17	3	4	2	1	0	3	3-0	0	5	.235	.350	.471	105	0	2-0	1.000	1	103	563	/O-8(2-4-3)	0.2
	Phi N	13	36	2	8	0	2	0	0	1-0	1	11	.222	.263	.333	55	-3	2-1	.955	1	112	168	O-11(1-1-10)	-0.2
1998	Pit N	73	180	21	45	11	2	6	24	9-0	2	44	.250	.290	.433	87	-4	0-3	.989	-3	95	0	O-62(26-37-3)	-0.9
1999	Mon N	137	331	48	81	12	7	2	26	17-0	0	51	.245	.279	.341	58	-23	19-6	.968	5	108	208	*O-126(0-126-1)	-1.4
Total	3	232	564	74	138	25	12	8	53	30-0	3	111	.245	.284	.374	69	-30	23-10	.974	4	104	154	O-207(29-168-17)	-2.3
MARTINEZ, MARTY Orlando (Oliva) B 8.23.1941 Havana, Cuba BB/TR (BR 1962) 6-1/175# d5.2 M1 C4 OF Total (LF)																								
1962	Min A	37	18	13	3	0	1	0	3	3-0	0	4	.167	.286	.278	51	-1	0-0	.920	4	241	144	S-11/3	0.3
1967	Atl N	44	73	14	21	2	1	0	5	11-1	1	11	.288	.384	.342	112	2	0-1	.920	-0	103	115	S-25/2-9,C-3,3-2,1	0.3
1968	Atl N	113	356	34	82	5	3	0	12	29-4	2	28	.230	.291	.261	67	-14	6-6	.955	-3	95	121	S-54,3-37,2-16,C-14	-1.4
1969	Hou N	78	198	14	61	5	4	0	15	10-1	0	21	.308	.340	.374	102	0	0-0	1.000	-2	79	116	O-21(LF),S-17,3-15/C-7,P2	-0.2
1970	Hou N	75	150	12	33	3	0	0	12	9-0	0	22	.220	.264	.240	38	-14	0-0	.990	-3	97	68	S-29,3-10/C-6,2-4	-1.4
1971	Hou N	32	62	4	16	3	1	0	4	3-0	0	6	.258	.292	.339	80	-2	1-0	.968	-1	103	80	/2-9,S-7,1-4,3-3	-0.1
1972	StL N	9	7	0	3	0	0	0	2	0-0	0	1	.429	.429	.429	146	0	0-0	1.000	-0	57	0	/S-3,2-2,3	0.0
	Oak A	22	40	3	5	0	0	0	1	3-0	0	6	.125	.186	.125	-7	-5	0-0	.944	1	70	68	2-17/S-6,3	-0.4
	Tex A	26	41	3	6	1	1	0	3	2-0	0	8	.146	.182	.220	21	-4	0-1	.944	-2	57	38	/S-5,3-4,2	-0.7
	Year	48	81	6	11	1	1	0	4	5-0	0	14	.136	.184	.173	8	-10	0-1	.946	-1	69	67	2-18,S-11/3-5	-1.1
Total	7	436	945	97	230	19	11	0	57	70-6	3	107	.243	.296	.287	70	-38	7-8	.950	-6	100	102	S-157/3-74,2-59,C-30,O-21L,1-5,P	-3.6
MARTINEZ, PABLO Pablo Made (Valera) B 6.29.1969 Sabana Grande, D.R. BB/TR 5-10/155# d7.20																								
1996	Atl N	4	2	1	1	0	0	0	0	0-0	0	0	.500	.500	.500	156	0	0-1	1.000	-1	63	172	/S	-0.1
MARTINEZ, RAMON Ramon E. B 10.10.1972 Philadelphia, PA BR/TR 6-1/170# d6.20																								
1998	SF N	19	19	4	6	1	0	0	0	4-0	0	2	.316	.435	.368	121	1	0-0	1.000	2	113	176	2-14	0.3

Year	Tm Lg	G	AB	R	H	2B	3B	HR	RBI	BB-IB	HP	SO	AVG	OBP	SLG	AOPS	ABR	SB-CS	FA	FR	Rng	Thr	G at Pos	BFW
1999	SF N	61	144	21	38	6	0	5	19	14-0	0	17	.264	.327	.410	92	-2	1-2	.992	5	124	114	2-27,S-12,3-11/D	0.4
2000	†SF N	88	189	30	57	13	2	6	25	15-1	1	22	.302	.354	.487	119	5	3-2	.991	-6	87	112	S-44,2-32/1-2,3-2	0.2
2001	SF N	128	391	48	99	18	3	5	37	38-6	5	52	.253	.323	.353	82	-11	1-2	.974	2	89	66	3-70,2-42,S-24	-0.6
2002	†SF N	72	181	26	49	10	2	4	25	14-2	4	26	.271	.335	.414	104	0	2-0	.950	-4	93	138	S-40,2-17/1-4,0-3(LF),3-2	-0.1
2003	†Chi N	108	293	30	83	16	1	3	34	24-1	2	50	.283	.333	.375	88	-5	0-1	.979	-1	80	111	2-42,3-37,S-32/1-2	-0.2
Total	6	476	1217	159	332	64	8	23	140	109-10	12	169	.273	.334	.395	94	-12	7-7	.989	-2	99	111	2-174,S-152,3-122/1-8,0-3(LF),D	0.0

MARTINEZ, CHITO Reyenaldo Ignacio B 12.19.1965 Belize City, British Honduras (Belize) BL/TL 5-10/180# d7.5

Year	Tm Lg	G	AB	R	H	2B	3B	HR	RBI	BB-IB	HP	SO	AVG	OBP	SLG	AOPS	ABR	SB-CS	FA	FR	Rng	Thr	G at Pos	BFW
1991	Bal A	67	216	32	58	12	1	13	33	11-0	0	51	.269	.303	.514	127	6	1-1	.982	1	102	106	O-54(1-0-53)/1D	0.5
1992	Bal A	83	198	26	53	10	1	5	25	31-4	2	47	.268	.366	.404	114	5	0-1	.973	0	101	117	O-52(RF)/D-4	0.4
1993	Bal A	8	15	0	0	0	0	0	0	4-2	0	4	.000	.211	.000	-37	-3	0-0	1.000	-1	37	0	/O-5(RF),D-2	-0.4
Total	3	158	429	58	111	22	2	18	58	46-6	2	102	.259	.330	.445	115	8	1-2	.978	1	100	109	O-111(1-0-110)/D-10,1	0.5

MARTINEZ, HECTOR Rodolfo Hector (Santos) B 5.11.1939 Las Villas, Cuba D 12.1999 , Cuba BR/TR 5-10/160# d9.30

Year	Tm Lg	G	AB	R	H	2B	3B	HR	RBI	BB-IB	HP	SO	AVG	OBP	SLG	AOPS	ABR	SB-CS	FA	FR	Rng	Thr	G at Pos	BFW
1962	KC A	1	1	0	0	0	0	0	0	0-0	0	1	.000	.000	.000	-96	0	0-0	—	0			H	0.0
1963	KC A	6	14	2	4	0	0	1	3	1-0	1	3	.286	.375	.500	135	1	0-1	1.000	-0	100	0	/O-3(CF)	0.0
Total	2	7	15	2	4	0	0	1	3	1-0	1	4	.267	.353	.467	120	1	0-1	1.000	-0	100	0	/O-3(CF)	0.0

MARTINEZ, TED Teodoro Noel (Encarnacion) B 12.10.1947 Barahona, D.R. BR/TR (BB 1973 (part)) 6/165# d7.18

Year	Tm Lg	G	AB	R	H	2B	3B	HR	RBI	BB-IB	HP	SO	AVG	OBP	SLG	AOPS	ABR	SB-CS	FA	FR	Rng	Thr	G at Pos	BFW
1970	NY N	4	16	0	1	0	0	0	0	0-0	0	3	.063	.063	.063	-66	-4	0-0	1.000	0	76	153	/2-4,S	-0.3
1971	NY N	38	125	16	36	5	2	1	10	4-2	3	22	.288	.323	.384	102	0	6-0	.976	-7	83	120	S-23,2-13/3-3,O(LF)	-0.3
1972	NY N	103	330	22	74	5	5	1	19	12-2	1	49	.224	.254	.279	52	-22	7-4	.994	-12	72	39	2-47,S-42,O-15(6-4-5)/3-2	-3.1
1973	†NY N	92	263	34	67	11	0	1	14	13-2	2	38	.255	.294	.308	68	-12	3-5	.941	-8	91	58	S-44,0-21(4-18-0),3-14/2-5	-1.8
1974	NY N	116	334	32	73	15	7	2	43	14-4	0	40	.219	.247	.323	61	-20	3-2	.952	-1	96	83	S-75,3-12,2-11,0-10(1-9-0)	-1.3
1975	StL N	16	21	1	4	2	0	0	2	0-0	0	2	.190	.190	.286	30	-2	0-0	1.000	0	118	0	/O-7(3-0-4),2-2,S3	-0.2
	†Oak A	86	87	7	15	0	0	0	3	2-0	1	9	.172	.200	.172	6	-11	1-1	.955	-8	77	74	S-45,2-31,3-14	-1.7
1977	LA N	67	137	21	41	6	1	1	10	2-0	0	20	.299	.309	.380	84	-4	3-4	.992	3	109	192	2-27,S-13,3-12	0.1
1978	LA N	54	55	13	14	1	0	1	5	4-1	1	14	.255	.317	.327	80	-1	3-2	.912	0	88	68	S-17,3-16,2-10	0.0
1979	LA N	81	112	19	30	5	1	0	2	4-1	0	16	.268	.293	.330	71	-5	3-2	.769	-14	42	74	3-23,S-21,2-18	-1.8
Total	9	657	1480	165	355	50	16	7	108	55-12	8	213	.240	.270	.309	62	-81	29-20	.956	-46	88	82	S-282,2-168/3-97,O-54(15-31-9)	-10.4

MARTINEZ, VICTOR Victor Jesus B 12.23.1978 Ciudad Bolivar, Venezuela BB/TR 6-2/170# d9.10

Year	Tm Lg	G	AB	R	H	2B	3B	HR	RBI	BB-IB	HP	SO	AVG	OBP	SLG	AOPS	ABR	SB-CS	FA	FR	Rng	Thr	G at Pos	BFW
2002	Cle A	12	32	2	9	1	0	1	5	3-0	0	2	.281	.333	.406	100	0	0-0	.983	-2	40	100	/C-9,D	-0.2
2003	Cle A	49	159	15	46	4	0	1	16	13-0	1	21	.289	.345	.333	83	-4	1-1	.996	3	108	102	C-40/D-5	0.2
Total	2	61	191	17	55	5	0	2	21	16-0	1	23	.288	.343	.346	86	-4	1-1	.994	1	97	102	/C-49,D-6	0.0

MARTY, JOE Joseph Anton B 9.1.1913 Sacramento, CA D 10.4.1984 Sacramento, CA BR/TR 6/182# d4.22 Mil 1942-45

Year	Tm Lg	G	AB	R	H	2B	3B	HR	RBI	BB-IB	HP	SO	AVG	OBP	SLG	AOPS	ABR	SB-CS	FA	FR	Rng	Thr	G at Pos	BFW
1937	Chi N	88	290	41	84	17	2	5	44	28	2	30	.290	.356	.414	104	2	3	.976	-3	97	60	O-84(1-83-0)	-0.3
1938	†Chi N	76	235	32	57	8	3	7	35	18	3	26	.243	.305	.391	88	-5	0	.987	-2	93	113	O-68(0-64-6)	-0.9
1939	Chi N	23	76	6	10	1	0	2	10	4	0	13	.132	.175	.224	6	-11	2	.933	-0	73	273	O-21(1-1-19)	-1.2
	Phi N	91	299	32	76	12	6	9	44	24	0	27	.254	.310	.425	98	-3	1	.974	3	103	151	O-79(6-56-18)/P	-0.2
	Year	114	375	38	86	13	6	11	54	28	0	40	.229	.283	.384	79	-13	3	.968	3	97	174	*O-100(7-57-37)/P	-1.4
1940	Phi N	123	455	52	123	21	8	13	50	17	1	50	.270	.298	.437	105	-1	2	.974	-1	104	74	*O-118(0-115-3)	-0.5
1941	Phi N	137	477	60	128	19	3	8	39	51	4	41	.268	.344	.371	105	4	6	.964	-8	93	71	*O-132(0-131-1)	-0.8
Total	5	538	1832	223	478	78	22	44	222	142	10	187	.261	.318	.400	97	-14	14	.972	-11	97	95	O-502(8-450-47)/P	-3.9

MARTYN, BOB Robert Gordon B 8.15.1930 Weiser, ID BL/TR 6/176# d6.18

Year	Tm Lg	G	AB	R	H	2B	3B	HR	RBI	BB-IB	HP	SO	AVG	OBP	SLG	AOPS	ABR	SB-CS	FA	FR	Rng	Thr	G at Pos	BFW
1957	KC A	58	131	10	35	2	4	1	12	11-3	0	20	.267	.322	.366	87	-3	1-3	.976	1	103	117	O-49(13-9-28)	-0.5
1958	KC A	95	226	25	59	10	7	2	23	26-5	0	36	.261	.336	.394	99	0	1-4	.967	1	104	95	O-63(27-1-45)	-0.3
1959	KC A	1	1	0	0	0	0	0	0	0-0	0	0	.000	.000	.000	-98	0	0-0	—	0			R	0.0
Total	3	154	358	35	94	12	11	3	35	37-8	0	56	.263	.330	.383	94	-3	2-7	.970	1	104	104	O-112(40-10-73)	-0.8

MARTZ, GARY Gary Arthur B 1.10.1951 Spokane, WA BR/TR 6-4/210# d7.8

Year	Tm Lg	G	AB	R	H	2B	3B	HR	RBI	BB-IB	HP	SO	AVG	OBP	SLG	AOPS	ABR	SB-CS	FA	FR	Rng	Thr	G at Pos	BFW
1975	KC A	1	1	0	0	0	0	0	0	0-0	0	0	.000	.000	.000	-97	0	0-0	1.000	0	411	0	/O(LF)	0.0

MARZANO, JOHN John Robert B 2.14.1963 Philadelphia, PA BR/TR 5-11/197# d7.31

Year	Tm Lg	G	AB	R	H	2B	3B	HR	RBI	BB-IB	HP	SO	AVG	OBP	SLG	AOPS	ABR	SB-CS	FA	FR	Rng	Thr	G at Pos	BFW
1987	Bos A	52	168	20	41	11	0	5	24	7-0	3	41	.244	.283	.399	77	-6	0-1	.986	4	114	97	C-52	0.0
1988	Bos A	10	29	3	4	1	0	0	1	1-0	0	3	.138	.167	.172	-5	-4	0-0	1.000	3	86	111	C-10	0.0
1989	Bos A	7	18	5	8	3	0	1	3	0-0	0	2	.444	.421	.778	224	3	0-0	1.000	-1	98	113	/C-7	0.2
1990	Bos A	32	83	8	20	4	0	0	6	5-0	0	10	.241	.281	.289	58	-5	0-1	1.000	3	84	100	C-32	-0.1
1991	Bos A	49	114	10	30	8	0	0	9	1-0	1	16	.263	.271	.333	64	-6	0-0	.985	-3	130	122	C-48	-0.6
1992	Bos A	19	50	4	4	2	1	0	1	2-0	1	12	.080	.132	.160	-17	-8	0-0	.968	-2	79	87	C-18/D	-0.9
1995	Tex A	2	6	1	2	0	0	0	0	0-0	0	0	.333	.333	.333	72	0	0-0	1.000	-0	27	281	/C-2	0.0
1996	Sea A	41	106	8	26	6	0	0	6	7-0	4	15	.245	.316	.302	57	-7	0-0	.986	-2	123	35	C-39	-0.6
1997	Sea A	39	87	7	25	3	0	1	10	7-0	0	15	.287	.340	.356	83	-2	0-0	.976	-2	85	105	C-37/D	-0.3
1998	Sea A	50	133	13	31	7	1	4	12	9-1	9	24	.233	.325	.391	85	-3	0-0	.997	4	92	95	C-48/D	0.4
Total	10	301	794	79	191	45	2	11	72	39-1	18	138	.241	.289	.344	67	-38	0-2	.988	4	103	94	C-293/D-3	-1.9

MASHORE, CLYDE Clyde Wayne B 5.29.1945 Concord, CA BR/TR 5-11/184# d7.11

Year	Tm Lg	G	AB	R	H	2B	3B	HR	RBI	BB-IB	HP	SO	AVG	OBP	SLG	AOPS	ABR	SB-CS	FA	FR	Rng	Thr	G at Pos	BFW
1969	Cin N	2	1	1	0	0	0	0	0	0-0	0	0	.000	.000	.000	-95	0	0-0	—	0			H	0.0
1970	Mon N	13	25	2	4	0	0	1	3	4-2	0	11	.160	.276	.280	49	-2	0-0	1.000	-1	77	0	O-10(2-8-0)	-0.3
1971	Mon N	66	114	20	22	5	0	1	7	10-1	0	22	.193	.258	.263	48	-8	1-0	.967	-2	91	0	O-47(19-29-5)/3	-1.2
1972	Mon N	93	176	23	40	7	1	3	23	14-1	0	41	.227	.278	.330	73	-7	6-1	.988	-2	87	85	O-74(23-8-46)	-1.1
1973	Mon N	67	103	12	21	3	0	3	14	15-0	0	28	.204	.300	.320	71	-4	4-3	.958	3	102	189	O-44(43-3-1)/2	-0.3
Total	5	241	419	58	87	15	1	8	47	43-4	0	102	.208	.278	.305	64	-21	11-4	.974	-3	91	84	O-175(87-48-52)/23	-2.9

MASHORE, DAMON Damon Wayne B 10.31.1969 Ponce, P.R. BR/TR 5-11/195# d6.5

Year	Tm Lg	G	AB	R	H	2B	3B	HR	RBI	BB-IB	HP	SO	AVG	OBP	SLG	AOPS	ABR	SB-CS	FA	FR	Rng	Thr	G at Pos	BFW
1996	Oak A	50	105	20	28	7	1	3	12	16-0	1	31	.267	.366	.438	105	1	4-0	.985	-1	94	45	O-48(35-7-15)	0.0
1997	Oak A	92	279	55	69	10	2	3	18	50-1	5	82	.247	.370	.330	86	-3	5-4	.991	9	108	246	O-89(28-71-6)	0.5
1998	Ana A	43	98	13	23	6	0	2	11	9-0	3	22	.235	.318	.357	75	-3	1-0	1.000	-1	95	54	O-35(1-7-28)/D-7	-0.5
Total	3	185	482	88	120	23	3	8	41	75-1	9	135	.249	.359	.359	88	-5	10-4	.991	7	102	161	O-172(64-85-49)/D-7	0.0

MASI, PHIL Philip Samuel B 1.6.1916 Chicago, IL D 3.29.1990 Mt.Prospect, IL BR/TR 5-10/180# d4.23

Year	Tm Lg	G	AB	R	H	2B	3B	HR	RBI	BB-IB	HP	SO	AVG	OBP	SLG	AOPS	ABR	SB-CS	FA	FR	Rng	Thr	G at Pos	BFW
1939	Bos N	46	114	14	29	7	2	1	14	9	1	15	.254	.315	.377	92	-2	0	.960	-1	*148*	*93*	C-42	-0.1
1940	Bos N	63	138	11	27	4	1	1	14	14	0	14	.196	.270	.261	50	-10	0	.966	-1	*105*	*126*	C-52	-0.8
1941	Bos N	87	180	17	40	8	2	3	18	16	0	13	.222	.286	.339	79	-6	4	.978	-5	*95*	*95*	C-83	-0.7
1942	Bos N	57	87	14	19	3	1	0	9	12	0	4	.218	.313	.276	74	-3	2	.961	0	*75*	*159*	C-39/O-4(1-0-4)	-0.1
1943	Bos N	80	238	27	65	9	1	2	28	27	0	20	.273	.347	.345	102	1	7	.991	-7	*57*	*128*	C-73	-0.2
1944	Bos N	89	251	33	69	13	5	3	23	31	0	20	.275	.355	.402	108	3	4	.977	-1	*65*	*141*	C-63,1-12/3-2	0.5
1945	Bos N✳	114	371	55	101	25	4	7	46	42	1	32	.272	.348	.418	112	6	9	.980	1	*101*	*114*	C-95/1-7	1.2
1946	Bos N★	133	397	52	106	17	5	3	62	55	1	41	.267	.358	.358	102	2	5	.981	-8	*81*	*87*	*C-124	0.1
1947	Bos N★	126	411	54	125	22	4	9	50	47	1	27	.304	.377	.443	120	12	7	**.989**	-3	*82*	*111*	*C-123	1.5
1948	†Bos N★	113	376	43	95	19	0	5	44	35	1	26	.253	.318	.343	80	-10	2	.988	0	*93*	*76*	*C-109	-0.5
1949	Bos N	37	105	13	22	2	0	0	6	14	0	10	.210	.303	.229	47	-8	1	.993	-1	*100*	*87*	C-37	-0.7
	Pit N	48	135	16	37	6	1	2	13	17	0	16	.274	.355	.378	94	-1	1	.994	1	*118*	*109*	C-44/1-2	0.2
	Year	85	240	29	59	8	1	2	19	31	0	26	.246	.332	.313	74	-8	2	**.994**	0	*110*	*99*	C-81/1-2	-0.5
1950	Chi A	122	377	38	105	17	2	7	55	49	3	36	.279	.366	.390	96	-1	2-1	**.996**	2	*73*	*108*	*C-114	0.6
1951	Chi A	84	225	24	61	11	2	4	28	32	2	27	.271	.367	.391	107	3	1-0	.979	0	*80*	*54*	C-78	0.7
1952	Chi A	30	63	9	16	1	1	0	7	10	0	10	.254	.356	.302	84	-1	0-0	.956	-1	*72*	*66*	C-25	-0.1
Total	14	1229	3468	420	917	164	31	47	417	410	10	311	.264	.344	.370	97	-15	45-1	.983	-24	*87*	*102*	*C-1101/1-21,O-4(1-0-4),3-2	1.6

MASKREY, HARRY Harry H. B 12.21.1861 Mercer, PA D 8.17.1930 Mercer, PA d9.21 b-Leech

Year	Tm Lg	G	AB	R	H	2B	3B	HR	RBI	BB-IB	HP	SO	AVG	OBP	SLG	AOPS	ABR	SB-CS	FA	FR	Rng	Thr	G at Pos	BFW
1882	Lou AA	1	4	0	0	0	0	0		0			.000	.000	.000	-99	-1		.000	-1	0	0	/O(CF)	-0.1

MASKREY, LEECH Samuel Leech B 2.11.1854 Mercer, PA D 4.1.1922 Mercer, PA BR/TR 5-8/150# d5.2 b-Harry

Year	Tm Lg	G	AB	R	H	2B	3B	HR	RBI	BB-IB	HP	SO	AVG	OBP	SLG	AOPS	ABR	SB-CS	FA	FR	Rng	Thr	G at Pos	BFW
1882	Lou AA	76	288	30	65	14	2	0		9			.226	.249	.288	85	-3		.902	-2	60	58	*O-76(75-0-1)/2	-0.6
1883	Lou AA	96	361	50	73	13	8	1		10			.202	.224	.291	70	-11		.914	10	103	46	*O-96(45-41-14)/S	-0.3
1884	Lou AA	105	412	48	103	13	4	0	36	17	1		.250	.281	.301	94	-2		.896	4	88	81	*O-103(97-0-7)/3-3,S	0.0

Year	Tm Lg	G	AB	R	H	2B	3B	HR	RBI	BB-IB	HP	SO	AVG	OBP	SLG	AOPS	ABR	SB-CS	FA	FR	Rng	Thr	G at Pos	BFW
1885	Lou AA	109	423	54	97	8	11	1	46	19	4		.229	.269	.307	82	-10		.899	-4	48	59	*O-108(LF)/3-3	-1.5
1886	Lou AA	5	19	1	3	1	0	0	2	1	0		.158	.200	.211	27	-2	0	.800	-1	0	0	/O-5(3-0-2)	-0.2
	Cin AA	27	98	7	19	3	1	0	10	5	1		.194	.240	.245	51	-6	4	.926	-1	91	116	O-26(0-7-19)/3-2	-0.6
	Year	32	117	8	22	4	1	0	12	6	1		.188	.234	.239	47	-7	4	.915	-2	79	101	O-31(3-7-21)/3-2	-0.8
Total	5	418	1601	190	360	52	26	2	94	61	6		.225	.256	.294	80	-34	4	.904	6	75	64	O-414(328-48-43)/3-8,S-2,2	-3.2
MASON, CHARLIE Charles E. B 6.25.1853 New Orleans, LA D 10.21.1936 Philadelphia, PA BR/TR ?/175# d4.26 M1																								
1875	Cen NA	12	47	5	11	0	0	0	3	0		1	.234	.234	.234	69	-1	0-0	.719	-0	174	0	O-10(3-0-7)/1-2,C	-0.1
	Was NA	8	33	2	3	0	0	0	1	0		3	.091	.091	.091	-38	-4	0-0	.909	2	251	0	/O-8(LF),P	-0.1
	Year	20	80	7	14	0	0	0	4	0		4	.175	.175	.175	23	-6	0-0	.796	2	205	0	O-18(11-0-7)/1-2,CP	-0.2
1883	Phi AA	1	2	0	1	0	0	0	1	0			.500	.500	.500	204	0		—	-0	0	0	/O(RF)	0.0
MASON, DON Donald Stetson B 12.20.1944 Boston, MA BL/TR 5-11/160# d4.14																								
1966	SF N	42	25	8	3	0	0	1	1	0-0	0	2	.120	.120	.240	-3	-4	0-1	.905	2	157	88	/2-9	-0.2
1967	SF N	4	3	0	0	0	0	0	0	0-0	0	0	.000	.000	.000	-99	-1	0-0	1.000	0	239	0	/2-2	0.0
1968	SF N	10	19	3	3	0	0	0	1	1-0	0	4	.158	.200	.158	9	-2	1-1	1.000	-1	79	0	/2-5,S-4,3-2	-0.4
1969	SF N	104	250	43	57	4	2	0	13	36-0	0	29	.228	.324	.260	67	-10	1-5	.956	2	108	127	2-51,3-21/S-7	-0.7
1970	SF N	46	36	4	5	0	0	0	1	5-0	0	7	.139	.244	.139	5	-5	0-0	.950	-3	61	32	2-14	-0.7
1971	SD N	113	344	43	73	12	1	2	11	27-0	0	35	.212	.270	.270	57	-20	6-4	.965	-6	97	80	2-90/3-3	-2.2
1972	SD N	9	11	1	2	0	0	0	0	1-0	0	1	.182	.250	.182	26	-1	0-0	.692	-2	96	0	/2-3	-0.3
1973	SD N	8	8	0	0	0	0	0	0	0-0	0	2	.000	.000	.000	-99	-2	0-0	.750	0	199	420	/2	-0.2
Total	8	336	696	102	143	16	3	3	27	70-0	0	80	.205	.278	.250	52	-45	8-11	.955	-6	101	92	2-175/3-26,S-11	-4.7
MASON, JIM James Percy B 8.14.1950 Mobile, AL BL/TR 6-2/190# d9.26																								
1971	Was A	3	9	0	3	0	0	0	0	1-0	0	3	.333	.400	.333	116	0	0-0	.955	2	144	54	/S-3	0.2
1972	Tex A	46	147	10	29	3	0	0	10	9-0	1	39	.197	.247	.218	41	-11	0-0	.948	-7	94	66	S-32,3-10	-1.7
1973	Tex A	92	238	23	49	7	2	3	19	23-0	0	48	.206	.273	.290	62	-12	0-1	.947	-2	98	91	S-74,2-19/3	-0.6
1974	NY A	152	440	41	110	18	6	5	37	35-1	0	87	.250	.302	.352	90	-6	1-2	.964	0	98	103	*S-152	1.0
1975	NY A	94	223	17	34	3	2	2	16	22-0	0	49	.152	.228	.211	25	-23	0-2	.955	-1	93	110	S-93/2	-1.7
1976	†NY A	93	217	17	39	7	1	1	14	9-0	0	37	.180	.210	.235	31	-19	0-0	.966	5	108	123	S-93	-0.6
1977	Tor A	22	79	10	13	3	0	0	2	7-0	0	10	.165	.233	.203	20	-9	1-1	.971	-3	82	66	S-22	-0.9
	Tex A	36	55	9	12	3	0	1	7	6-0	0	10	.218	.290	.327	69	-2	0-0	.976	2	111	115	S-32/3D	0.1
	Year	58	134	19	25	6	0	1	9	13-0	0	20	.187	.257	.254	40	-11	1-1	.973	-1	95	88	S-54/3D	-0.8
1978	Tex A	55	105	10	20	4	0	0	3	5-0	0	17	.190	.227	.229	28	-10	0-0	.938	-4	103	84	S-42,3-11/2D	-1.2
1979	Mon N	40	71	3	13	5	1	0	6	7-1	0	16	.183	.256	.282	47	-5	0-2	.966	-4	84	84	S-33/3-6	-0.8
Total	9	633	1584	140	322	53	12	12	114	124-2	1	316	.203	.259	.275	54	-97	2-8	.959	-11	98	100	S-576/3-29,2-21,D-2	-6.2
MASSA, GORDON Gordon Richard "Moose" or "Duke" B 9.2.1935 Cincinnati, OH BL/TR 6-3/210# d9.24 Mil 1959																								
1957	Chi N	6	15	2	7	1	0	0	3	4-0	0	3	.467	.579	.533	205	3	0-0	1.000	-2	*68*	*0*	/C-6	0.1
1958	Chi N	2	2	0	0	0	0	0	0	0-0	0	2	.000	.000	.000	-99	-1	0-0	—	0			H	-0.1
Total	2	8	17	2	7	1	0	0	3	4-0	0	5	.412	.524	.471	172	2	0-0	1.000	-2	*68*	*0*	/C-6	0.0
MASSEY, ROY Roy Hardee "Red" B 10.9.1890 Sevierville, TN D 6.23.1954 Atlanta, GA BL/TR 5-11/170# d4.16																								
1918	Bos N	66	203	20	59	6	2	0	18	23	0	20	.291	.363	.340	120	6	1	.954	-2	91	106	O-45(21-29-0)/3-2,1S	0.1
MASSEY, BILL William Harry "Big Bill" B 1.1871 Philadelphia, PA D 10.9.1940 Manila, Philippines BR/TR 5-11/168# d9.18																								
1894	Cin N	13	53	7	15	3	0	0	5	3	0	2	.283	.321	.340	57	-4	0	.991	-2	86	227	1-10/2-2,3	-0.4
MASSEY, MIKE William Herbert B 9.28.1893 Galveston, TX D 10.17.1971 Shreveport, LA BB/TR 6/195# d4.12																								
1917	Bos N	31	91	12	18	0	0	0	2	15	1	15	.198	.318	.198	63	-3	2	.900	-7	91	89	2-25	-1.1
MASTELLER, DAN Dan Patrick B 3.17.1968 Toledo, OH BL/TL 6/185# d6.23																								
1995	Min A	71	198	21	47	12	0	3	21	18-0	1	19	.237	.303	.343	68	-9	1-2	.994	-2	81	112	1-48,O-22(6-0-16)/D-8	-1.5
MATA, VICTOR Victor Jose (Abreu) B 6.17.1961 Santiago, D.R. BR/TR 6-1/165# d7.22																								
1984	NY A	30	70	8	23	5	0	1	6	0-0	1	12	.329	.333	.443	119	2	1-1	.942	-2	92	0	O-28(2-21-8)	-0.1
1985	NY A	6	7	1	1	0	0	0	0	0-0	0	0	.143	.143	.143	-22	-1	0-0	1.000	-1	27	0	/O-3(1-1-2)	-0.2
Total	2	36	77	9	24	5	0	1	6	0-0	1	12	.312	.316	.416	106	1	1-1	.943	-3	87	0	/O-31(3-22-10)	-0.3
MATCHICK, TOM John Thomas B 9.7.1943 Hazleton, PA BL/TR 6/175# d9.2																								
1967	Det A	8	6	1	1	0	0	0	0	0-0	0	2	.167	.167	.167	-1	-1	0-0	1.000	0	0	0	/S	-0.1
1968	†Det A	80	227	18	46	6	2	3	14	10-3	4	46	.203	.248	.286	60	-11	0-2	.950	-2	94	99	S-59,2-13/1-6	-1.2
1969	Det A	94	298	25	72	11	2	0	32	15-3	0	51	.242	.276	.292	57	-18	3-0	.972	-7	101	117	2-47,3-27/S-6,1-2	-2.2
1970	Bos A	10	14	2	1	0	0	0	0	2-0	0	2	.071	.188	.071	-24	-2	0-1	1.000	-0	105	0	/3-2,2S	-0.3
	KC A	55	158	11	31	3	2	0	11	5-2	1	23	.196	.226	.241	29	-16	0-0	.985	11	115	138	S-43,2-10/3	0.0
	Year	65	172	13	32	3	2	0	11	7-2	1	25	.186	.222	.227	24	-18	0-1	.985	11	115	138	S-44,2-11/3-3	-0.3
1971	Mil A	42	114	6	25	1	0	1	7	7-0	0	23	.219	.264	.254	48	-8	3-2	.979	0	98	90	3-41/2	-0.9
1972	Bal A	3	9	0	2	0	0	0	0	0-0	0	1	.222	.222	.222	32	-1	0-1	.857	-1	78	0	/3-3	-0.2
Total	6	292	826	63	178	21	6	4	64	39-8	5	148	.215	.254	.270	49	-57	6-6	.967	1	100	113	S-110/3-74,2-72,1-8	-4.9
MATEO, HENRY Henry Antonio (Valera) B 10.14.1976 Santo Domingo, D.R. BB/TR 5-11/180# d7.28																								
2001	Mon N	5	9	1	3	1	0	0	0	0-0	0	1	.333	.333	.444	97	0	0-0	.818	-1	104	0	/2-2	-0.1
2002	Mon N	22	23	1	4	0	1	0	0	2-1	0	6	.174	.240	.261	32	-3	2-0	1.000	2	204	111	/2-3,S-2	0.0
2003	Mon N	100	154	29	37	3	1	0	7	11-0	3	38	.240	.304	.273	47	-12	11-1	.970	3	106	137	2-43,O-10(2-2-6)/S-2,D-3	-0.6
Total	3	127	186	31	44	4	2	0	7	13-1	3	45	.237	.297	.280	48	-15	13-1	.962	4	111	126	/2-48,O-10(2-2-6),S-4,D-3	-0.7
MATEO, RUBEN Ruben Amaury B 2.10.1978 San Cristobal, D.R. BR/TR 6/170# d6.12																								
1999	Tex A	32	122	16	29	9	1	5	18	4-0	1	28	.238	.268	.451	75	-5	3-0	1.000	-3	80	156	O-31(CF)	-0.6
2000	Tex A	52	206	32	60	11	0	7	19	10-1	5	34	.291	.339	.447	95	-2	6-0	.980	1	102	150	O-52(CF)	0.1
2001	Tex A	40	129	18	32	5	2	1	13	9-0	6	28	.248	.322	.341	74	-5	1-0	.986	-3	92	0	O-39(RF)	-0.9
2002	Cin N	46	86	11	22	6	0	2	7	6-0	2	20	.256	.319	.395	88	-2	0-0	1.000	-1	93	84	O-24(0-2-23)	-0.3
2003	Cin N	74	207	16	50	9	0	3	18	12-1	3	53	.242	.290	.329	63	-12	0-0	.982	-1	101	62	O-54(4-14-39)	-1.4
Total	5	244	750	93	193	40	3	18	75	41-2	17	163	.257	.309	.391	79	-26	10-0	.986	-6	95	91	O-200(4-99-101)	-3.1
MATHENY, MIKE Michael Scott B 9.22.1970 Columbus, OH BR/TR 6-3/205# d4.7																								
1994	Mil A	28	53	3	12	3	0	1	2	3-0	2	13	.226	.293	.340	60	-3	0-1	.989	-1	83	98	C-27	-0.3
1995	Mil A	80	166	13	41	9	1	0	21	12-0	2	28	.247	.306	.313	58	-10	2-1	.986	-2	125	60	C-80	-0.8
1996	Mil A	106	313	31	64	15	2	8	46	14-0	3	80	.204	.243	.342	45	-28	3-2	.985	-5	114	97	*C-104/D	-2.4
1997	Mil A	123	320	29	78	16	1	4	32	17-0	7	68	.244	.294	.338	64	-17	0-1	.993	11	103	109	*C-121/1-2	0.1
1998	Mil N	108	320	24	76	13	0	6	27	11-0	7	63	.237	.278	.334	60	-19	1-0	.987	-12	84	83	*C-107	-2.5
1999	Tor A	57	163	16	35	6	0	3	17	12-0	1	37	.215	.271	.307	47	-14	0-0	.995	8	80	126	C-57	-0.2
2000	StL N	128	417	43	109	22	1	6	47	32-8	4	96	.261	.317	.362	72	-18	0-0	.994	16	163	149	*C-124/1-8	0.5
2001	†StL N	121	381	40	83	12	0	7	42	28-5	4	76	.218	.276	.304	51	-29	0-1	.995	15	**210**	88	*C-121/1-2	-0.7
2002	†StL N	110	315	31	77	12	1	3	35	32-6	2	49	.244	.313	.317	73	-14	1-3	.994	3	127	91	*C-106/1	-0.5
2003	StL N	141	441	43	111	18	2	8	47	44-16	2	81	.252	.320	.356	80	-13	1-1	**1.000**	-3	155	53	*C-138/1-4	-0.8
Total	10	1002	2889	273	686	126	8	46	316	205-35	34	591	.237	.293	.334	63	-165	8-10	.993	29	134	95	C-985/1-17,D	-7.6
MATHES, JOE Joseph John B 7.28.1891 Milwaukee, WI D 12.21.1978 St.Louis, MO BB/TR 6-0.5/180# d9.19																								
1912	Phi A	4	14	0	2	0	0	0	0	0	1		.143	.200	.143	-2	-2	0	.889	-0	115	0	/3-4	-0.2
1914	StL F	26	85	10	25	3	0	0	6	9	0	11	.294	.362	.329	85	-3	1	.938	-4	91	60	2-23	-0.6
1916	Bos N	2	0	0	0	0	0	0	0	0	0	0	—	—	—	—	0	0	.000	-1	0	0	/2-2	-0.1
Total	3	32	99	10	27	3	0	0	6	9	1	11	.273	.339	.303	74	-5	1	.921	-5	90	59	/2-25,3-4	-0.9
MATHEWS, EDDIE Edwin Lee B 10.13.1931 Texarkana, TX D 2.18.2001 LaJolla, CA BL/TR 6-1/200# d4.15 M3 C2 HF1978																								
1952	Bos N	145	528	80	128	23	5	25	58	59	1	115	.242	.320	.447	114	8	6-4	.957	-9	92	85	*3-142	-0.1
1953	Mil N★	**157**	579	110	175	31	8	**47**	135	99	2	83	.302	.406	.627	**175**	65	1-3	.939	1	99	105	*3-157	6.1
1954	Mil N	138	476	96	138	21	4	40	103	113	2	61	.290	.423	.603	**177**	58	10-3	.966	-2	**99**	**128**	*3-127,O-10(LF)	5.4
1955	Mil N★	141	499	108	144	23	5	41	101	**109**-20	1	98	.289	.413	.601	175	58	3-4	.952	-7	98	84	*3-137	4.9

Year	Tm Lg	G	AB	R	H	2B	3B	HR	RBI	BB-IB	HP	SO	AVG	OBP	SLG	AOPS	ABR	SB-CS	FA	FR	Rng	Thr	G at Pos	BFW
1956	Mil N☆	151	552	103	150	21	2	37	95	91-17	1	86	.272	.373	.518	146	37	6-0	.944	-14	97	92	*3-150	2.5
1957	†Mil N★	148	572	109	167	28	9	32	94	90-5	0	79	.292	.387	.540	157	48	3-1	.964	-4	102	98	*3-147	4.3
1958	†Mil N☆	149	546	97	137	18	1	31	77	85-5	2	85	.251	.349	.458	123	19	5-0	.955	5	110	89	*3-149	2.5
1959	Mil N★	148	594	118	182	16	8	**46**	114	80-2	3	71	.306	.390	.593	172	60	2-1	.961	2	103	92	*3-148	6.0
1960	Mil N★	153	548	108	152	19	7	39	124	111-3	2	113	.277	.397	.551	**170**	**57**	7-3	.950	-15	92	85	*3-153	4.3
1961	Mil N★	152	572	103	175	23	6	32	91	**93**-3	2	95	.306	.402	.535	156	49	12-7	.961	-6	97	108	*3-151	4.2
1962	Mil N★	152	536	106	142	25	6	29	90	**101**-7	2	90	.265	.381	.496	138	32	4-2	.964	0	101	92	*3-140/1-7	3.1
1963	Mil N	158	547	82	144	27	4	23	84	**124**-14	1	119	.263	**.399**	.453	147	41	3-4	**.968**	11	111	135	*3-121,O-42(LF)	5.1
1964	Mil N	141	502	83	117	19	1	23	74	85-5	1	100	.233	.344	.412	112	10	2-2	.962	-1	94	94	*3-128/1-7	0.8
1965	Mil N	156	546	77	137	23	0	32	95	73-7	3	110	.251	.341	.469	125	19	1-0	.956	8	108	81	*3-153	2.8
1966	Atl N	134	452	72	113	21	4	16	53	63-6	0	82	.250	.341	.420	109	7	1-1	.946	-1	99	**134**	*3-127	0.6
1967	Hou N	101	328	39	78	13	2	10	38	48-12	1	65	.238	.333	.381	109	5	2-4	.987	-3	97	87	1-79,3-24	-0.4
	Det A	36	108	14	25	3	0	6	19	15-0	2	23	.231	.331	.426	121	3	0-0	.933	-2	76	0	3-21,1-13	0.0
1968	†Det A	31	52	4	11	0	0	3	8	5-1	0	12	.212	.281	.385	97	0	0-0	.974	1	95	151	/1-6,3-6	0.0
Total	17	2391	8537	1509	2315	354	72	512	1453	1444-107	26	1487	.271	.376	.509	145	576	68-39	.956	-36	100	98	*3-2181,1-112/O-52(LF)	52.1
MATHEWS, NELSON Nelson Elmer B 7.21.1941 Columbia, IL BR/TR 6-4/195# d9.9 s-Timothy																								
1960	Chi N	3	8	1	2	0	0	0	0	0-0	0	2	.250	.250	.250	38	-1	0-0	1.000	0	124	0	/O-2(RF)	-0.1
1961	Chi N	3	9	0	1	0	0	0	0	0-0	0	2	.111	.111	.111	-40	-2	0-0	1.000	0	118	0	/O-2(CF)	-0.2
1962	Chi N	15	49	5	15	2	0	2	13	5-0	2	4	.306	.393	.469	126	2	3-3	.962	-1	90	0	O-14(CF)	0.0
1963	Chi N	61	155	12	24	3	2	4	10	16-2	0	48	.155	.234	.277	44	-11	3-4	.979	-3	93	36	O-46(CF)	-1.8
1964	KC A	157	573	58	137	27	5	14	60	43-7	1	143	.239	.293	.377	82	-14	2-3	.968	-3	105	45	*O-154(CF)	-2.4
1965	KC A	67	184	17	39	7	7	2	15	24-4	0	49	.212	.300	.359	89	-3	0-2	.981	0	108	40	O-57(25-26-8)	-0.6
Total	6	306	978	93	218	39	14	22	98	88-13	3	248	.223	.288	.359	78	-29	8-12	.972	-7	103	40	O-275(25-242-10)	-5.1
MATHEWS, BOBBY Robert T. B 11.21.1851 Baltimore, MD D 4.17.1898 Baltimore, MD BR/TR 5-5.5/140# d5.4 U3 ▲																								
1871	Kek NA	**19**	89	15	24	3	1	0	10	2		0	.270	.286	.326	74	-2	2-1	.840	-1	79	145	P-19	0.0
1872	Bal NA	50	222	36	50	2	0	0	22	3		2	.225	.236	.234	43	-16	3-1	.780	-5	75	95	*P-49/O-8(RF),3-3	-0.3
1873	Mut NA	52	223	40	43	3	3	0	14	10		3	.193	.227	.233	37	-17	1-1	.780	-3	80	47	*P-52/O-5(RF)	-0.2
1874	Mut NA	**65**	298	46	72	6	1	0	30	3		4	.242	.249	.268	64	-12	2-0	.774	-2	94	108	*P-65/3O(LF)	-0.1
1875	Mut NA	70	264	23	48	6	2	0	15	2		5	.182	.188	.220	39	-16	1-2	.838	-6	81	72	*P-70/O(LF)	-0.2
1876	NY N	56	218	19	40	4	1	0	9	3		2	.183	.195	.211	40	-12		.810	-3	96	0	*P-56/O(RF)	-0.1
1877	Cin N	15	59	5	10	0	0	0	0	1		2	.169	.183	.169	13	-5		.862	-3	79	0	P-15/O(LF)S	-0.2
1879	Pro N	43	173	25	35	2	0	1	10	7		12	.202	.233	.231	55	-8		.956	-4	99	0	P-27,O-21(RF)/3-5	-0.8
1881	Pro N	16	57	6	11	1	0	0	4	5		6	.193	.258	.211	50	-3		.810	-2	82	264	P-14/O-5(RF)	-0.2
	Bos N	19	71	2	12	2	0	0	4	0		5	.169	.169	.197	15	-7		.818	-2	74	0	O-18(1-9-9)/P-5	-0.8
	Year	35	128	8	23	3	0	0	8	5		11	.180	.211	.203	32	-10		.811	-4	64	0	O-23(1-9-14),P-19	-1.0
1882	Bos N	45	169	17	38	6	0	0	13	8		18	.225	.260	.260	67	-6		.867	-8	63	67	P-34,O-13(RF)/S	-0.7
1883	Phi AA	45	167	15	31	2	0	0	11	5			.186	.209	.198	29	-14		.874	-1	88	101	P-44/O-3(1-1-1)	-0.1
1884	Phi AA	49	184	26	34	5	1	0		7	0		.185	.215	.223	40	-12		.775	-3	90	57	P-49/O(RF)	-0.1
1885	Phi AA	48	179	22	30	3	0	0	12	10	0		.168	.212	.184	24	-15		.881	-0	96	55	P-48/O(RF)	0.0
1886	Phi AA	24	88	16	21	3	0	0	10	3	0		.239	.264	.273	67	-3	1	.843	-0	112	**266**	P-24/O(RF)	0.0
1887	Phi AA	7	25	5	5	0	0	0	0	4	0		.200	.310	.200	44	0	0	.889	0	118	386	/P-7	0.0
Total	5 NA	256	1096	160	237	20	7	0	91	20	0	14	.216	.230	.247	49	-63	9-5	.000	-15	83	86	P-255/O-15(2-0-13),3-4	-0.8
Total	10	367	1390	158	267	28	2	1	73	53	0	45	.192	.222	.217	42	-85	1-0	.845	-25	91	76	P-323/O-65(3-10-53),3-5,S-2	-3.0
MATHISON, JIMMY James Michael Ignatius B 11.11.1878 Baltimore, MD D 7.4.1911 Baltimore, MD TR d8.29																								
1902	Bal A	29	91	12	24	2	1	0	7	9	6		.264	.368	.308	85	-1	2	.889	-4	85	86	3-28/S	-0.4
MATIAS, JOHN John Roy B 8.15.1944 Honolulu, HI BL/TL 5-11/170# d4.7																								
1970	Chi A	58	117	7	22	2	0	2	6	3-1	1	22	.188	.215	.256	28	-12	1-0	.941	-0	55	219	O-22(5-0-17),1-18	-1.4
MATOS, FRANCISCO Francisco Aguirre (Mancebo) B 7.23.1969 Santo Domingo, D.R. BR/TR 6-1/160# d7.17																								
1994	Oak A	14	28	1	7	1	0	0	2	1-0	0	2	.250	.267	.286	49	-2	1-0	.925	-2	90	71	2-12/D-2	-0.3
MATOS, JULIUS Julius B 12.12.1974 New York, NY BR/TR 5-11/175# d5.31																								
2002	SD N	76	185	19	44	3	0	2	19	9-0	2	33	.238	.279	.286	58	-13	1-1	.963	3	107	101	2-49,3-17/S-4,O-3(RF),1-2,D	-0.9
2003	KC A	28	57	7	15	1	0	2	7	1-0	0	12	.263	.276	.386	63	-3	1-0	1.000	-3	55	0	3-13,2-11/S-2,O(RF)D	-0.6
Total	2	104	242	26	59	4	0	4	26	10-0	2	45	.244	.278	.310	59	-16	2-1	.964	-1	110	98	/2-60,3-30,S-6,O-4(RF),D-2,1-2	-1.5
MATOS, LUIS Luis David B 10.30.1978 Bayamon, P.R. BR/TR 6/180# d6.19																								
2000	Bal A	72	182	21	41	6	3	1	17	12-0	3	30	.225	.281	.308	52	-14	13-4	.988	6	121	96	O-69(1-44-25)/D-3	-0.7
2001	Bal A	31	98	16	21	7	0	4	12	11-0	1	30	.214	.300	.408	89	-2	7-0	.985	0	99	119	O-31(1-23-10)	0.0
2002	Bal A	17	31	0	4	1	0	0	1	1-0	0	6	.129	.156	.161	-16	-5	1-0	1.000	-1	84	0	O-14(2-6-7)/D	-0.6
2003	Bal A	109	439	70	133	23	3	13	45	28-0	7	90	.303	.353	.458	117	10	15-7	.987	4	108	101	*O-107(0-106-4)/D-2	1.5
Total	4	229	750	107	199	37	6	18	75	52-0	11	156	.265	.321	.403	92	-11	36-11	.988	9	109	98	O-221(4-179-46)/D-6	0.2
MATOS, PASCUAL Pascual (Cuevas) B 12.23.1974 Barahona, D.R. BR/TR 6-2/180# d5.11																								
1999	Atl N	6	8	0	1	0	0	0	2	0-0	0	1	.125	.125	.125	-37	-2	0-0	1.000	0	59	0	/C-5	-0.1
MATRANGA, DAVE David Michael B 1.8.1977 Orange, CA BR/TR 6/170# d6.27																								
2003	Hou N	6	5	1	1	0	0	1	1	0-0	0	2	.200	.200	.800	138	0	0-0	1.000	-0	0	0	/2-2	0.0
MATSUI, HIDEKI Hideki B 6.12.1974 Ishikawa, Japan BL/TR 6-1/210# d3.31																								
2003	†NY A★	**163**	623	82	179	42	1	16	106	63-5	3	86	.287	.353	.435	109	10	2-2	.977	-1	94	147	*O-159(118-46-0)/D-4	0.4
MATTHEWS, GARY Gary Nathaniel Jr. B 8.25.1974 San Francisco, CA BB/TR 6-3/200# d6.4 f-Gary																								
1999	SD N	23	36	4	8	0	0	0	7	9-0	0	9	.222	.378	.222	62	-2	2-0	1.000	-0	109	0	O-17(6-2-10)	-0.2
2000	Chi N	80	158	24	30	1	2	4	14	15-1	1	28	.190	.264	.297	43	-15	3-0	.978	3	110	136	O-61(46-21-1)	-1.2
2001	Chi N	106	258	41	56	9	1	9	30	38-2	1	55	.217	.320	.364	81	-8	5-3	.976	-2	98	78	*O-100(20-88-1)	-0.9
	Pit N	46	147	22	36	6	1	5	14	22-0	0	45	.245	.341	.401	90	-2	3-2	.971	-3	99	43	O-44(CF)	-0.4
	Year	152	405	63	92	15	2	14	44	60-2	1	100	.227	.328	.378	84	-9	8-5	.974	-5	98	66	*O-144(20-132-1)	-1.3
2002	NY N	2	1	0	0	0	0	0	0	0-0	0	0	.000	.000	.000	-99	0	0-0	—	0			/H	0.0
	Bal A	109	344	54	95	25	3	7	38	43-1	1	69	.276	.355	.427	113	8	15-5	.969	-4	92	106	*O-100(16-16-76)/D-2	0.2
2003	Bal A	41	162	21	33	12	1	2	20	9-0	1	29	.204	.250	.327	53	-11	0-3	1.000	-1	95	110	O-40(CF)/D	-1.3
	SD N	103	306	50	83	19	1	4	22	34-0	1	66	.271	.346	.379	98	0	12-5	.993	-2	98	45	O-92(33-35-35)	-0.4
Total	5	510	1412	216	341	72	9	31	145	170-4	5	301	.242	.324	.371	85	-30	40-18	.981	-9	98	81	O-454(121-246-123)/D-3	-4.2
MATTHEWS, GARY Gary Nathaniel Sr. B 7.5.1950 San Fernando, CA BR/TR 6-3/190# d9.6 C4 s-Gary																								
1972	SF N	20	62	11	18	1	1	4	14	7-2	0	13	.290	.357	.532	149	4	0-1	.971	-1	101	0	O-19(10-0-9)	0.2
1973	SF N	148	540	74	162	22	10	12	58	58-7	1	83	.300	.367	.444	119	14	17-5	.983	1	93	110	*O-145(144-0-1)	0.9
1974	SF N	154	561	87	161	27	6	16	82	70-5	3	69	.287	.368	.442	120	16	11-9	.970	-1	95	85	*O-151(150-0-1)	0.6
1975	SF N	116	425	67	119	22	3	12	58	65-5	2	53	.280	.377	.431	119	13	13-4	.967	3	102	127	*O-113(LF)	1.1
1976	SF N	156	587	79	164	28	4	20	84	75-3	1	94	.279	.359	.443	124	19	12-5	.975	-11	81	71	*O-156(LF)	0.0
1977	Atl N	148	555	89	157	25	5	17	64	67-3	2	90	.283	.362	.438	101	2	22-8	.965	1	93	117	*O-145(LF)	-0.1
1978	Atl N	129	474	75	135	20	5	18	62	61-2	2	92	.285	.366	.462	118	12	8-7	.969	-1	101	99	*O-127(1-0-127)	0.4
1979	Atl N★	156	631	97	192	34	5	27	90	60-5	0	75	.304	.363	.502	125	22	18-6	.974	-5	96	93	*O-156(RF)	1.1
1980	Atl N	155	571	79	159	17	3	19	75	42-2	0	93	.278	.325	.419	104	1	11-3	.960	-8	95	64	*O-143(6-0-137)	-1.4
1981	†Phi N	101	359	62	108	21	3	9	67	59-2	3	42	.301	.398	.451	136	20	15-2	.963	-1	93	132	*O-100(LF)	1.9
1982	Phi N	**162**	616	89	173	31	1	19	83	66-1	2	87	.281	.349	.427	114	13	21-4	.966	-2	91	116	*O-162(LF)	0.8
1983	†Phi N	132	446	66	115	18	2	10	50	69-3	0	81	.258	.352	.374	104	5	13-9	.974	-3	86	136	*O-122(LF)	-0.3
1984	†Chi N	147	491	101	143	21	2	14	82	**103**-2	3	97	.291	**.410**	.428	126	23	17-8	.955	-7	88	68	*O-145(LF)	1.2
1985	Chi N	97	298	45	70	12	0	13	40	59-2	2	64	.235	.362	.406	104	4	2-0	.977	-2	85	130	O-85(LF)	-0.1
1986	Chi N	123	370	49	96	16	1	21	46	60-1	0	59	.259	.361	.478	121	11	3-2	.940	-7	80	82	*O-105(LF)	0.0
1987	Chi N	44	42	3	11	3	0	0	8	4-1	0	11	.262	.326	.333	72	-2	0-0	1.000	-0	92	0	/O-2(LF)	-0.2
	Sea A	45	119	10	28	1	0	3	15	15-0	0	22	.235	.319	.319	67	-6	0-1	—	0	0	0	D-39	-0.7
Total	16	2033	7147	1083	2011	319	51	234	978	940-46	21	1125	.281	.364	.439	116	171	183-74	.968	-44	92	99	*O-1876(1446-0-431)/D-39	5.4

Year	Tm Lg	G	AB	R	H	2B	3B	HR	RBI	BB-IB	HP	SO	AVG	OBP	SLG	AOPS	ABR	SB-CS	FA	FR	Rng	Thr	G at Pos	BFW
MATTHEWS, BOB Robert B Camden, NJ d9.25																								
1891	Phi AA	1	3	1	1	0	0	0	0	0	2	1	.333	.600	.333	167	1	0	—	-0	0	0	/O(RF)	0.0
MATTHEWS, WID Wid Curry "Matty" B 10.20.1896 Raleigh, IL D 10.5.1965 Hollywood, CA BL/TL 5-8.5/155# d4.18																								
1923	Phi A	129	485	52	133	11	6	1	25	50	1	27	.274	.343	.328	76	-17	16-16	.947	-15	95	20	*O-127(2-125-0)	-3.8
1924	Was A	53	169	25	51	10	4	0	13	11	3	4	.302	.355	.408	100	-1	3-8	.985	5	109	177	O-44(1-43-0)	0.0
1925	Was A	10	9	2	4	0	0	0	1	0	0	1	.444	.444	.444	129	0	0-0	1.000	0	106	0	/O(CF)	0.0
Total	3	192	663	79	188	21	10	1	39	61	4	32	.284	.348	.350	83	-18	19-24	.957	-10	98	58	O-172(3-169-0)	-3.8
MATTHIAS, STEVE Stephen J. B 1860 Mitchellville, MD BR/TR 5-8/160# d4.20																								
1884	CP U	37	142	24	39	7	1	0		5			.275	.299	.338	93	-5		.840	1	95	92	S-36/O-2(CF)	-0.3
MATTICK, BOBBY Robert James B 12.5.1915 Sioux City, IA BR/TR 5-11/178# d5.5 M2 f-Wally																								
1938	Chi N	1	1	0	1	0	0	0	1	0	0	0	1.000	1.000	1.000	439	0	0	—	-0	0	0	/S	0.0
1939	Chi N	51	178	16	51	12	1	0	23	6	1	19	.287	.314	.365	80	-5	1	.927	4	110	84	S-48	0.2
1940	Chi N	128	441	30	96	15	0	0	33	19	0	33	.218	.250	.252	39	-37	5	.946	8	108	103	*S-126/3	-2.1
1941	Cin N	20	60	8	11	3	0	0	7	8	0	7	.183	.279	.233	45	-4	1	.982	-1	90	97	S-12/3-5,2	-0.4
1942	Cin N	6	10	0	2	1	0	0	0	0	0	1	.200	.200	.300	45	-1	0	1.000	0	91	85	/S-3	0.0
Total	5	206	690	54	161	31	1	0	64	33	1	60	.233	.269	.281	52	-47	7	.943	11	107	97	S-190/3-6,2	-2.3
MATTICK, WALLY Walter Joseph "Chink" B 3.12.1887 St.Louis, MO D 11.5.1968 Los Altos, CA BR/TR 5-10/180# d4.11 s-Bobby																								
1912	Chi A	90	285	45	74	7	9	1	35	27	5		.260	.334	.358	101	0	16	.982	-5	91	70	O-79(2-66-10)	-1.1
1913	Chi A	71	207	15	39	8	1	0	11	18	0	16	.188	.253	.237	44	-15	3	.977	2	91	152	O-64(7-56-0)	-1.8
1918	StL N	8	14	0	2	0	0	0	1	2	2	3	.143	.333	.143	49	-1	0	1.000	0	84	182	/O-3(RF)	-0.1
Total	3	169	506	60	115	15	10	1	47	47	7	19	.227	.302	.302	77	-16	19	.980	-3	91	107	O-146(9-122-13)	-3.0
MATTIMORE, MIKE Michael Joseph B 1859 Renovo, PA D 4.28.1931 Butte, MT BL/TL 5-8.5/160# d5.3 ▲																								
1887	NY N	8	32	5	8	1	0	0	4	0	0	6	.250	.250	.281	50	-2	1	.889	-1	47	0	/P-7,O-2(CF)	-0.1
1888	Phi AA	41	142	22	38	6	5	0	12	12	2		.268	.333	.380	129	5	16	.915	4	137	338	P-26,O-16(1-1-15)	0.4
1889	Phi AA	23	73	10	17	1	2	1	8	9	2	7	.233	.333	.342	94	-1	6	.944	-2	0	0	O-12(3-5-4)/1-7,P-5	-0.2
	KC AA	19	75	6	12	1	1	0	5	3	0	16	.160	.192	.200	11	-9	0	.844	-1	82	0	O-19(19-1-0)/P	-0.9
	Year	42	148	16	29	2	3	1	13	12	2	23	.196	.265	.270	52	-10	6	.873	-3	56	0	O-31(22-6-4)/1-7,P-6	-1.1
1890	Bro AA	33	129	14	17	1	1	0	7	16	2		.132	.238	.155	17	-13	11	.887	-4	106	0	P-19,O-14(0-1-13)	-0.8
Total	4	124	451	57	92	10	9	1	36	40	6	29	.204	.278	.273	64	-20	34	.853	-5	69	105	/O-63(23-10-32),P-58,1-7	-1.6
MATTINGLY, DON Donald Arthur B 4.20.1961 Evansville, IN BL/TL 6/175# d9.8 OF Total (33-LF 2-CF 47-RF)																								
1982	NY A	7	12	0	2	0	0	0	1	0-0	0	1	.167	.154	.167	-8	-2	0-0	1.000	2	200	603	/O-6(5-0-1),1	0.0
1983	NY A	91	279	34	79	15	4	4	32	21-5	1	31	.283	.333	.409	108	3	0-0	.974	-5	86	97	O-48(13-1-39),1-42/2	-0.7
1984	NY A★	153	603	91	**207**	**44**	2	23	110	41-8	1	33	**.343**	.381	.537	**159**	47	1-1	**.996**	16	**135**	**115**	*1-133,O-19(13-1-6)	5.4
1985	NY A★	159	652	107	211	**48**	3	35	**145**	56-13	2	41	.324	.371	.567	159	52	2-2	**.995**	-10	75	117	*1-159	3.1
1986	NY A★	**162**	677	117	**238**	**53**	2	31	113	53-11	1	35	.352	.394	**.573**	**163**	**59**	0-0	**.996**	-2	88	101	*1-160/3-3,D	4.6
1987	NY A★	141	569	93	186	38	2	30	115	51-13	1	38	.327	.378	.559	147	39	1-4	**.996**	-1	97	108	*1-140/D	2.7
1988	NY A★	144	599	94	186	37	0	18	88	41-14	3	29	.311	.353	.462	129	23	1-0	.993	-2	98	105	*1-143/O(LF)D	1.1
1989	NY A★	158	631	79	191	37	2	23	113	51-18	1	30	.303	.351	.477	134	28	3-0	.995	-4	90	105	*1-145,D-17/O(RF)	1.4
1990	NY A	102	394	40	101	16	0	5	42	28-13	3	20	.256	.308	.335	80	-11	1-0	.997	8	130	102	1-89,D-13/O(LF)	-1.0
1991	NY A	152	587	64	169	35	0	9	68	46-11	4	42	.288	.339	.394	103	3	2-0	.996	-3	88	**124**	*1-127,D-22	-0.9
1992	NY A	157	640	89	184	40	0	14	86	39-7	1	43	.287	.327	.416	108	6	3-0	**.997**	6	113	103	*1-143,D-15	0.2
1993	NY A	134	530	78	154	27	2	17	86	61-9	2	42	.291	.364	.445	121	16	0-0	**.998**	1	100	**116**	*1-130/D-5	0.5
1994	NY A	97	372	62	113	20	1	6	51	60-7	0	24	.304	.397	.411	114	11	0-0	**.998**	5	122	**123**	1-97	0.7
1995	†NY A	128	458	59	132	32	2	7	49	40-7	1	35	.288	.341	.413	98	-1	0-2	.994	0	98	91	*1-125/D	-1.2
Total	14	1785	7003	1007	2153	442	20	222	1099	588-136	21	444	.307	.358	.471	128	273	14-9	.996	13	100	109	*1-1634/D-76,O-76R,3-3,2	15.9
MATTIS, RALPH Ralph "Matty" B 8.24.1890 Philadelphia, PA D 9.13.1960 Williamsport, PA BR/TR 5-11/172# d4.22																								
1914	Pit F	36	85	14	21	4	1	0	8	9	1	11	.247	.326	.318	77	-4	2	.938	2	106	167	O-24(12-0-12)	-0.3
MATTOX, CLOY Cloy Mitchell "Monk" B 11.24.1902 Leesville, VA D 8.3.1985 Danville, VA BL/TR 5-8/168# d9.1 b-Jim																								
1929	Phi A	3	6	0	1	0	0	0	0	1	0	1	.167	.286	.167	19	-1	0-0	.875	-0	*85*	*145*	/C-3	-0.1
MATTOX, JIM James Powell B 12.17.1896 Leesville, VA D 10.12.1973 Myrtle Beach, SC BL/TR 5-9.5/168# d4.30 b-Cloy																								
1922	Pit N	29	51	11	15	1	1	0	3	1	0	3	.294	.308	.353	69	-3	0-0	.984	1	*98*	*78*	C-21	-0.1
1923	Pit N	22	32	4	6	1	1	0	1	0	2	5	.188	.235	.281	35	-3	0-0	.960	0	*111*	*139*	/C-8	-0.2
Total	2	51	83	15	21	2	2	0	4	1	2	8	.253	.279	.325	56	-6	0-0	.978	1	*102*	*97*	/C-29	-0.3
MATUSZEK, LEN Leonard James B 9.27.1954 Toledo, OH BL/TR 6-2/195# d9.3																								
1981	Phi N	13	11	1	3	1	0	0	1	3-1	0	1	.273	.429	.364	121	1	0-1	1.000	1	0	538	/13	0.1
1982	Phi N	25	39	1	3	1	0	0	3	1-0	1	10	.077	.119	.103	-36	-7	0-1	.750	-2	83	0	/3-8,1-3	-1.0
1983	Phi N	28	80	12	22	6	1	4	16	4-1	0	14	.275	.306	.525	129	3	0-1	1.000	-1	72	58	1-21	0.0
1984	Phi N	101	262	40	65	17	1	12	43	39-4	4	54	.248	.350	.458	125	10	4-3	.990	5	136	79	1-81/O(LF)	1.1
1985	Tor A	62	151	23	32	6	2	2	15	11-0	0	24	.212	.259	.318	57	-9	2-1	1.000	0	126	63	D-54/1-5	-1.1
	†LA N	43	63	10	14	2	1	3	13	8-2	1	14	.222	.307	.429	111	1	0-1	1.000	0	120	0	O-17(LF),1-10/3	0.0
1986	LA N	91	199	26	52	7	0	9	28	21-1	1	47	.261	.333	.432	118	4	2-2	1.000	-0	80	116	O-37(35-0-2),1-31	0.1
1987	LA N	16	15	0	1	0	0	0	0	1-0	0	4	.067	.125	.067	-49	-3	0-0	1.000	0	173	0	/1-3	-0.3
Total	7	379	820	113	192	40	5	30	119	88-9	7	168	.234	.309	.405	99	0	8-10	.990	4	119	80	1-155/O-55(53-0-2),D-54,3-10	-1.1
MAUCH, GENE Gene William "Skip" B 11.18.1925 Salina, KS BR/TR 5-10/165# d4.18 Mil 1944-45 M26 C1																								
1944	Bro N	5	15	2	2	1	0	0	2	2	0	3	.133	.235	.200	24	-1	0	1.000	-1	75	120	/S-5	-0.2
1947	Pit N	16	30	8	9	0	0	0	1	7	0	6	.300	.432	.300	95	0	0	.963	-3	88	0	/2-6,S-4	-0.2
1948	Bro N	12	13	1	2	0	0	0	0	1	0	4	.154	.214	.154	1	-2	0	.950	0	82	109	/2-7,S	-0.2
	Chi N	53	138	18	28	3	2	1	7	26	0	10	.203	.329	.275	68	-6	1	.925	-3	90	130	2-26,S-19	-0.6
	Year	65	151	19	30	3	2	1	7	27	0	14	.199	.320	.265	62	-8	1	.929	-3	89	127	2-33,S-20	-0.8
1949	Chi N	72	150	15	37	6	2	1	7	21	0	15	.247	.339	.333	83	-3	3	.971	8	124	108	2-25,S-19/3-7	0.7
1950	Bos N	48	121	17	28	5	0	1	15	14	1	9	.231	.316	.298	67	-6	1	.968	-3	95	82	2-28/3-7,S-5	-0.6
1951	Bos N	19	20	5	2	0	0	0	1	7	0	4	.100	.333	.100	24	-2	0-0	1.000	-1	89	50	S-10/3-3,2-2	-0.2
1952	StL N	7	3	0	0	0	0	0	0	1	0	2	.000	.250	.000	-25	0	0-0	.500	-1	0	0	/S-2	-0.1
1956	Bos A	7	25	4	8	0	0	0	1	3-0	0	3	.320	.393	.320	80	-1	0-0	.935	-1	100	85	/2-6	-0.1
1957	Bos A	65	222	23	60	10	3	2	28	22-0	1	26	.270	.335	.369	88	-3	1-0	.962	-8	95	94	2-58	-0.7
Total	9	304	737	93	176	25	7	5	62	104-0	2	82	.239	.333	.312	75	-24	6-0	.958	-12	98	96	2-158/S-65,3-17	-2.2
MAUL, AL Albert Joseph "Smiling Al" B 10.9.1865 Philadelphia, PA D 5.3.1958 Philadelphia, PA BR/TR 6/175# d6.20 ▲																								
1884	Phi U	1	4	0	0	0	0	0		0			.000	.000	.000	-99	-1		1.000	-0	55	0	/P	0.0
1887	Phi N	16	56	15	17	2	2	1	4	15	0	10	.304	.451	.464	146	4	5	.818	-2	0	0	/O-8(7-1-0),P-7,1-2	0.0
1888	Pit N	74	259	21	54	9	4	0	31	21	3	45	.208	.276	.274	83	-4	9	.975	0	59	115	1-38,O-34(0-3-31)/P-3	-0.7
1889	Pit N	68	257	37	71	6	6	4	44	29	3	41	.276	.356	.393	121	7	18	.946	10	134	179	O-64(39-0-25)/P-6	1.3
1890	Pit P	45	162	31	42	6	2	0	21	22	0	12	.259	.348	.321	86	-2	5	.904	5	123	205	P-30,O-15(11-3-1)/S	0.2
1891	Pit N	47	149	15	28	2	4	0	14	20	0	28	.188	.284	.255	59	-8	4	.878	1	132	223	O-40(20-12-8)/P-8	-0.6
1893	Was N	44	134	10	34	8	4	0	12	33	1	14	.254	.405	.373	110	4	1	.889	-0	105	40	P-37/O-7(5-0-2)	0.0
1894	Was N	41	124	23	30	3	3	2	20	14	7	11	.242	.352	.363	75	-5	1	.877	2	129	0	P-28,O-12(1-0-11)	-0.1
1895	Was N	22	72	9	18	5	2	0	16	6	0	7	.250	.308	.375	76	-3	0	.933	0	104	255	P-16/O-4(2-0-2)	-0.1
1896	Was N	8	28	6	8	1	1	0	5	3	0	2	.286	.355	.393	97	2	0	.923	-1	65	169	/P-8	0.0
1897	Was N	1	1	0	0	0	0	0	0	0	0		.000	.000	.000	-99	0	0	1.000	0	219	0	/P	0.0
	Bal N	2	3	0	1	0	0	0	0	0	0		.333	.333	.333	76	0	0	1.000	-0	55	0	/P-2	0.0
	Year	3	4	0	1	0	0	0	0	0	0		.250	.250	.250	32	0	0	1.000	-0	88	0	/P-3	0.0
1898	Bal N	29	93	21	19	3	2	0	10	16	2		.204	.333	.280	75	-2	1	.978	-6	64	0	P-28/O(CF)	-0.3
1899	Bro N	4	11	2	3	0	0	0	0	1	0		.273	.333	.273	66	0	0	.900	0	137	0	/P-4	0.0
1900	Phi N	5	15	2	3	0	0	0	1	2	0		.200	.294	.200	38	0	0	.917	0	115	0	/P-5	0.0
1901	NY N	3	8	1	3	0	0	0	1	0	0		.375	.375	.375	123	1	0	1.000	0	145	0	/P-3	0.0
Total	15	410	1376	193	331	45	30	7	179	182	16	170	.241	.336	.332	91	-7	44	.910	9	105	94	P-187,O-185(85-20-80)/1-40,S	-0.3

Year	Tm Lg	G	AB	R	H	2B	3B	HR	RBI	BB-IB	HP	SO	AVG	OBP	SLG	AOPS	ABR	SB-CS	FA	FR	Rng	Thr	G at Pos	BFW
MAULDIN, MARK Marshall Reese B 11.5.1914 Atlanta, GA D 9.2.1990 Union City, GA BR/TR 5-11/170# d9.10																								
1934	Chi A	10	38	3	10	2	0	1	3	0	0	3	.263	.263	.395	66	-2	0-0	.906	-0	95	155	3-10	-0.2
MAURER, ROB Robert John B 1.7.1967 Evansville, IN BL/TL 6-3/210# d9.8																								
1991	Tex A	13	16	0	1	1	0	0	2	2-0	1	6	.063	.211	.125	-5	-2	0-0	1.000	1	366	193	/1-4,D-2	-0.1
1992	Tex A	8	9	1	2	0	0	0	1	1-0	0	2	.222	.300	.222	50	-1	0-0	1.000	0	98	0	/1-3,D	-0.1
Total	2	21	25	1	3	1	0	0	3	3-0	1	8	.120	.241	.160	14	-3	0-0	1.000	1	220	88	/1-7,D-3	-0.2
MAURO, CARMEN Carmen Louis B 11.10.1926 St.Paul, MN BL/TR 6/167# d10.1																								
1948	Chi N	3	5	2	1	0	0	1	1	2	0	0	.200	.429	.800	235	1	0	1.000	0	117	0	/O-2(0-1-1)	0.1
1950	Chi N	62	185	19	42	4	3	1	10	13	2	31	.227	.285	.297	54	-13	3	.946	-4	92	56	O-49(18-1-30)	-1.9
1951	Chi N	13	29	3	5	1	0	0	3	2	1	6	.172	.250	.207	24	-3	0-0	.900	-0	97	166	/O-6(0-5-1)	-0.4
1953	Bro N	8	9	1	0	0	0	0	0	0	0	4	.000	.000	.000	-98	-3	0-0	1.000	0	96	0	/O(RF)	-0.3
	Was A	17	23	1	4	0	1	0	2	1	0	3	.174	.208	.261	27	-3	0-0	1.000	1	114	344	/O-6(3-3-0)	-0.2
	Phi A	64	165	14	44	4	4	0	17	19	0	21	.267	.342	.339	81	-4	3-4	.969	2	108	135	O-49(4-38-7)/3	-0.5
	Year	81	188	15	48	4	5	0	19	20	0	24	.255	.327	.330	76	-7	3-4	.971	3	108	151	O-55(7-41-7)/3	-0.7
Total	4	167	416	40	96	9	8	2	33	37	3	65	.231	.298	.305	61	-25	6-4	.958	-1	100	104	O-113(25-48-40)/3	-3.2
MAVIS, BOB Robert Henry B 4.8.1918 Milwaukee, WI BL/TR 5-7/160# d9.17																								
1949	Det A	1	0	0	0	0	0	0	0	0	0	0	—	—	—	—	0	0-0	—	0			R	0.0
MAXVILL, DAL Charles Dallan B 2.18.1939 Granite City, IL BR/TR 5-11/160# d6.10 C7																								
1962	StL N	79	189	20	42	3	1	1	18	17-2	1	39	.222	.287	.265	46	-14	1-2	.962	-0	97	121	S-76/3	-1.0
1963	StL N	53	51	12	12	2	0	0	3	6-0	0	11	.235	.316	.275	66	-2	0-0	.974	3	102	127	S-24/2-9,3-3	0.2
1964	†StL N	37	26	4	6	0	0	0	4	0-0	0	7	.231	.231	.231	28	-3	1-0	.972	2	99	167	2-15,S-13/3O(RF)	0.1
1965	StL N	68	89	10	12	2	2	0	10	7-3	1	15	.135	.206	.202	14	-10	0-0	.993	6	110	149	2-49,S-12	-0.2
1966	StL N	134	394	25	96	14	3	0	24	37-9	2	61	.244	.312	.294	69	-15	3-0	.967	17	**109**	125	*S-128/2-5,O(LF)	1.4
1967	†StL N	152	476	37	108	14	4	1	41	48-12	1	66	.227	.297	.279	67	-20	0-2	.974	-1	101	91	*S-148/2-7	-0.9
1968	†StL N	151	459	51	116	8	5	1	24	52-9	1	71	.253	.329	.298	91	-4	0-2	.969	-9	96	107	*S-151	-0.2
1969	StL N	132	372	27	65	10	2	2	32	44-2	1	52	.175	.263	.228	39	-30	1-1	.969	14	107	113	*S-131	-0.1
1970	StL N	152	399	35	80	5	2	0	28	51-3	0	56	.201	.287	.223	39	-34	0-0	**.982**	28	**118**	110	*S-136,2-22	0.8
1971	StL N	142	356	31	80	10	1	0	24	43-3	1	45	.225	.307	.258	60	-17	1-2	.979	11	**108**	89	*S-140	0.7
1972	StL N	105	276	22	61	6	1	1	23	31-4	0	47	.221	.299	.261	61	-14	0-1	.980	5	99	116	S-95,2-11	0.1
	†Oak A	27	36	2	9	1	0	0	1	1-0	0	11	.250	.270	.278	67	-2	0-1	.983	-1	108	123	2-24/S-4	-0.2
1973	Oak A	29	19	0	4	0	0	0	1	1-0	0	3	.211	.250	.211	33	-2	0-0	.966	-3	76	118	S-18,2-11/3	-0.4
	Pit N	74	217	19	41	4	3	0	17	22-2	0	40	.189	.261	.235	40	-18	0-0	.971	7	109	105	S-74	-0.3
1974	Pit N	8	22	3	4	0	0	0	0	2-0	0	4	.182	.250	.182	23	-2	0-0	.946	1	106	205	/S-8	-0.1
	†Oak A	60	52	3	10	0	0	0	2	8-0	0	10	.192	.300	.192	47	-3	0-0	1.000	-2	95	40	2-30,S-29/3	-0.2
1975	Oak A	20	10	1	2	0	0	0	0	0-0	0	0	.200	.200	.200	14	-1	0-0	.955	-2	80	35	S-20/2-2	-0.3
Total	14	1423	3443	302	748	79	24	6	252	370-49	8	538	.217	.293	.259	57	-191	7-11	.973	76	105	108	*S-1207,2-185/3-7,O-2(1-0-1)	-0.6
MAXWELL, CHARLIE Charles Richard "Smokey" B 4.8.1927 Lawton, MI BL/TL 5-11/185# d9.20																								
1950	Bos A	3	8	1	0	0	0	0	0	1	0	3	.000	.111	.000	-63	-2	0-0	1.000	0	124	0	/O-2(RF)	-0.2
1951	Bos A	49	80	8	15	1	0	3	12	9	0	18	.188	.270	.313	52	-6	0-1	.926	-1	96	0	O-13(5-0-8)	-0.8
1952	Bos A	8	15	0	1	1	0	0	0	3	0	11	.067	.222	.133	0	-2	0-0	.966	1	233	44	/1-3,O-3(0-1-2)	-0.1
1954	Bos A	74	104	9	26	4	1	0	5	12	0	21	.250	.328	.308	67	-4	3-0	1.000	-1	85	104	O-27(21-3-6)	-0.5
1955	Bal A	4	4	0	0	0	0	0	0	0-0	0	1	.000	.000	.000	-99	-1	0-0	—	0			H	-0.1
	Det A	55	109	19	29	7	1	7	18	8-0	2	20	.266	.325	.541	134	4	0-0	.967	1	107	145	O-26(22-0-4)/1-2	0.4
	Year	59	113	19	29	7	1	7	18	8-0	2	21	.257	.315	.522	126	3	0-0	.967	1	107	145	O-26(22-0-4)/1-2	0.3
1956	Det A☆	141	500	96	163	14	3	28	87	79-1	2	74	.326	.414	.534	150	37	1-1	.987	6	107	121	*O-136(134-0-2)	3.4
1957	Det A★	138	492	75	136	23	3	24	82	76-7	5	84	.276	.377	.482	130	22	3-2	**.997**	10	114	80	*O-137(137-0-3)	2.4
1958	Det A	131	397	56	108	14	4	13	65	64-4	0	54	.272	.369	.426	111	8	6-1	.986	-1	102	65	*O-114(113-0-3),1-14	0.1
1959	Det A	145	518	81	130	12	2	31	95	81-5	6	91	.251	.357	.461	117	13	0-2	.986	4	107	70	*O-136(LF)	0.8
1960	Det A	134	482	70	114	16	5	24	81	58-6	6	75	.237	.325	.440	102	0	5-0	**.996**	-1	98	57	*O-120(LF)	-0.7
1961	Det A	79	131	11	30	4	2	5	18	20-2	1	24	.229	.333	.405	94	-1	0-0	.965	1	112	109	O-25(22-0-4)	-0.1
1962	Det A	30	67	5	13	2	0	1	9	8-1	0	10	.194	.273	.269	47	-5	0-0	.966	-0	109	0	O-15(RF)/1	-0.6
	Chi A	69	206	30	61	8	3	9	43	34-3	0	32	.296	.394	.495	139	12	0-0	.990	-1	95	65	O-56(49-0-7)/1-6	0.8
	Year	99	273	35	74	10	3	10	52	42-4	0	42	.271	.365	.440	115	7	0-0	.985	-1	98	51	O-71(49-0-22)/1-7	0.2
1963	Chi A	71	130	17	30	4	2	3	17	31-2	0	27	.231	.370	.362	111	3	0-0	1.000	-1	80	150	O-24(LF),1-17	0.0
1964	Chi A	2	2	0	0	0	0	0	0	0-0	0	0	.000	.000	.000	-99	-1	0-0	—	0			H	-0.1
Total	14	1133	3245	478	856	110	26	148	532	484-31	22	545	.264	.360	.451	116	77	18-7	.988	18	104	82	O-834(783-4-55)/1-43	4.7
MAXWELL, JASON Jason Ramond B 3.26.1972 Lewisburg, TN BR/TR 6/185# d9.1																								
1998	Chi N	7	3	2	1	0	0	1	2	0-0	0	2	.333	.333	1.333	301	1	0-0	1.000	0	296	0	/2	0.1
2000	Min A	64	111	14	27	6	0	1	11	9-0	1	32	.243	.298	.324	57	-7	2-1	.967	4	133	114	2-30,3-19/S-5,O-2(0-1-1),D-7	-0.1
2001	Min A	39	68	4	13	4	0	1	10	9-2	0	23	.191	.286	.294	52	-5	2-0	.893	-4	91	77	S-12,3-11/2-9,D-6	-0.7
Total	3	110	182	20	41	10	0	3	23	18-2	1	57	.225	.294	.330	59	-11	4-1	.974	1	124	82	/2-40,3-30,S-17,D-13,O-2(0-1-1)	-0.7
MAY, CARLOS Carlos B 5.17.1948 Birmingham, AL BL/TR 6/215# d9.6 b-Lee																								
1968	Chi A	17	67	4	12	1	0	0	1	3-1	0	15	.179	.214	.194	24	-6	0-0	.960	-2	80	0	O-17(15-0-2)	-1.1
1969	Chi A★	100	367	62	103	18	2	18	62	58-7	6	66	.281	.385	.488	137	20	1-4	.982	-4	83	126	*O-100(80-0-22)	0.9
1970	Chi A	150	555	83	158	28	4	12	68	79-9	3	96	.285	.373	.414	114	13	12-5	.991	-2	81	135	*O-141(LF)/1-7	0.3
1971	Chi A	141	500	64	147	21	7	7	70	62-5	6	61	.294	.375	.406	119	14	16-7	.986	-2	93	85	*1-130/O-9(LF)	0.2
1972	Chi A☆	148	523	83	161	26	3	12	68	79-14	9	70	.308	.405	.438	149	36	23-14	.983	-6	84	119	*O-145(LF)/1-5	2.5
1973	Chi A	149	553	62	148	20	0	20	96	53-5	5	73	.268	.334	.412	106	5	8-6	.992	0	91	150	D-75,O-70(LF)/1-2	-0.2
1974	Chi A	149	551	66	137	19	2	8	58	46-3	1	76	.249	.306	.334	82	-13	8-9	.988	1	98	122	*O-129(LF),D-13	-2.2
1975	Chi A	128	454	55	123	19	2	8	53	67-13	9	46	.271	.373	.374	111	10	12-7	.989	3	129	98	1-63,O-46(LF),D-19	0.5
1976	Chi A	20	63	7	11	2	0	0	3	9-0	0	5	.175	.278	.206	43	-4	4-0	1.000	-1	92	0	D-10/O-9(LF)	-0.5
	†NY A	87	288	38	80	11	2	3	40	34-2	5	32	.278	.358	.361	114	6	1-1	.950	-1	112	0	D-71/O-7(LF),1	0.4
	Year	107	351	45	91	13	2	3	43	43-2	5	37	.259	.344	.333	101	2	5-1	.933	-1	103	0	D-81,O-16(LF)/1	-0.1
1977	NY A	65	181	21	41	7	1	2	16	17-4	1	24	.227	.292	.309	66	-8	0-0	1.000	-1	60	0	D-53/O-4(2-0-2)	-1.1
	Cal A	11	18	0	6	0	0	0	1	5-0	0	1	.333	.478	.333	131	1	0-0	1.000	0	107	43	/1-3,D	0.1
	Year	76	199	21	47	7	1	2	17	22-4	1	25	.236	.311	.312	73	-7	0-0	1.000	-0	60	0	D-54/O-4(2-0-2),1-3	-1.0
Total	10	1165	4120	545	1127	172	23	90	536	512-63	45	565	.274	.357	.392	111	74	85-53	.984	-13	87	127	O-677(653-0-26),D-242,1-211	-0.2
MAY, DAVE David La France B 12.23.1943 New Castle, DE BL/TR 5-10.5/186# d7.28 s-Derrick																								
1967	Bal A	36	85	12	20	1	1	1	7	6-2	0	13	.235	.286	.306	75	-3	0-0	.969	-0	99	87	O-19(1-0-18)	-0.5
1968	Bal A	84	152	15	29	6	3	0	7	19-3	1	27	.191	.285	.270	69	-5	3-3	.984	-4	83	43	O-61(1-16-47)	-1.4
1969	†Bal A	78	120	8	29	6	0	3	10	9-0	2	23	.242	.305	.367	86	-2	2-1	.940	1	94	204	O-40(RF)	-0.3
1970	Bal A	25	31	6	6	0	1	1	6	4-0	0	4	.194	.286	.355	75	-1	0-0	1.000	-1	47	0	/O-9(RF)	-0.3
	Mil A	100	342	36	82	8	1	7	31	44-6	2	56	.240	.329	.330	82	-8	8-6	.989	4	112	98	O-99(0-99-1)	-0.7
	Year	125	373	42	88	8	2	8	37	48-6	2	60	.236	.325	.332	81	-9	8-6	.989	2	108	93	*O-108(0-99-10)	-1.0
1971	Mil A	144	501	74	139	20	3	16	65	50-4	3	59	.277	.343	.425	119	12	15-9	.975	5	109	113	*O-142(2-94-48)	1.3
1972	Mil A	143	500	49	119	20	2	9	45	47-8	3	56	.238	.306	.340	94	-4	11-13	.985	5	111	100	*O-138(CF)	-0.5
1973	Mil A★	156	624	96	189	23	4	25	93	44-6	5	78	.303	.352	.473	134	26	6-7	.979	-7	97	76	*O-152(CF)/D-2	1.4
1974	Mil A	135	477	56	108	15	1	10	42	28-4	3	73	.226	.273	.325	72	-19	4-3	.989	1	100	109	*O-121(5-17-108)/D-8	-2.5
1975	Atl N	82	203	28	56	8	0	12	40	25-3	2	27	.276	.361	.493	130	8	1-1	.964	-0	101	90	O-53(13-17-24)	0.6
1976	Atl N	105	214	27	46	5	3	3	23	26-3	1	31	.215	.300	.308	69	-9	5-1	.972	2	101	141	O-60(41-0-19)	-0.9
1977	Tex A	120	340	46	82	14	1	7	42	32-1	4	43	.241	.311	.350	80	-9	4-3	.969	1	100	121	*O-111(21-2-92)/D-5	-1.3
1978	Mil A	39	77	9	15	4	0	2	11	9-1	2	10	.195	.295	.325	74	-2	0-0	.944	1	99	212	O-16(4-7-5)/D-8	-0.2
	Pit N	5	4	0	0	0	0	0	0	1-0	0	1	.000	.200	.000	-38	-1	1-0	—	0			H	-0.1
Total	12	1252	3670	462	920	130	20	96	422	344-41	28	501	.251	.318	.375	97	-17	60-47	.978	6	102	104	*O-1021(88-542-411)/D-23	-5.4
MAY, DERRICK Derrick Brant B 7.14.1968 Rochester, NY BL/TR 6-4/225# d9.6 f-Dave																								
1990	Chi N	17	61	8	15	3	0	1	11	2-0	0	7	.246	.270	.344	63	-3	1-0	.972	0	104	89	O-17(LF)	-0.3
1991	Chi N	15	22	4	5	2	0	1	3	2-0	0	1	.227	.280	.455	102	0	0-0	1.000	1	111	365	/O-7(LF)	0.1

Year	Tm Lg	G	AB	R	H	2B	3B	HR	RBI	BB-IB	HP	SO	AVG	OBP	SLG	AOPS	ABR	SB-CS	FA	FR	Rng	Thr	G at Pos	BFW
1992	Chi N	124	351	33	96	11	0	8	45	14-4	3	40	.274	.306	.373	89	-6	5-3	.969	-8	81	65	*O-108(98-0-14)	-1.8
1993	Chi N	128	465	62	137	25	2	10	77	31-6	1	41	.295	.336	.422	104	2	10-3	.970	-3	95	90	*O-122(121-0-2)	-0.4
1994	Chi N	100	345	43	98	19	2	8	51	30-4	0	34	.284	.340	.420	99	-1	3-2	.994	-2	93	75	O-92(LF)	-0.6
1995	Mil A	32	113	15	28	3	1	1	9	5-0	1	18	.248	.286	.319	54	-8	0-1	.971	-0	106	48	O-32(LF)	-0.9
	Hou N	78	206	29	62	15	1	8	41	19-0	1	24	.301	.358	.500	134	10	5-0	.974	-4	91	0	O-55(43-0-12)/1	0.5
1996	Hou N	109	259	24	65	12	3	5	33	30-8	2	33	.251	.330	.378	95	-2	2-2	.970	5	117	145	O-71(70-0-3)	0.0
1997	Phi N	83	149	8	34	5	1	1	13	8-3	0	26	.228	.266	.295	47	-12	4-1	.961	3	113	167	O-56(7-0-49)	-1.0
1998	Mon N	85	180	13	43	8	0	5	15	11-1	0	24	.239	.281	.367	70	-8	0-0	.984	-0	87	131	O-48(LF)/D-2	-1.0
1999	Bal A	26	49	5	13	0	0	4	12	4-0	0	6	.265	.315	.510	112	0	0-0	1.000	1	119	491	/O-5(2-0-3),D-9	0.1
Total	10	797	2200	244	596	103	10	52	310	156-26	8	254	.271	.319	.398	92	-28	30-12	.975	-6	96	92	O-613(537-0-83)/D-11,1	-5.3
MAY, JERRY Jerry Lee B 12.14.1943 Staunton, VA D 6.30.1996 Swoope, VA BR/TR 6-2.5/195# d9.19																								
1964	Pit N	11	31	1	8	0	0	0	3	3-0	0	9	.258	.314	.258	66	-1	0-0	.988	2	*111*	*70*	C-11	0.1
1965	Pit N	4	2	0	1	0	0	0	1	0-0	0	0	.500	.500	.500	182	0	0-0	1.000	-0	*0*	*0*	/C-4	0.0
1966	Pit N	42	52	6	13	4	0	1	2	2-1	1	15	.250	.291	.385	86	-1	0-1	.984	4	*129*	*120*	C-41	0.4
1967	Pit N	110	325	23	88	13	2	3	22	36-19	3	55	.271	.348	.351	100	1	0-0	.993	1	*116*	*94*	*C-110	0.8
1968	Pit N	137	416	26	91	15	2	1	33	41-12	3	80	.219	.293	.272	72	-13	0-0	.988	1	*108*	*110*	*C-135	-0.7
1969	Pit N	62	190	21	44	8	0	7	23	9-0	2	53	.232	.268	.384	84	-5	1-1	.994	-6	142	95	C-52	-0.9
1970	Pit N	51	139	13	29	4	2	1	16	21-6	1	25	.209	.313	.288	65	-7	0-0	.994	11	110	185	C-45	0.7
1971	KC A	71	218	16	55	13	2	1	24	27-8	0	37	.252	.329	.344	93	-1	0-0	.997	0	107	99	C-71	0.2
1972	KC A	53	116	10	22	5	1	1	4	14-2	0	13	.190	.277	.276	65	-5	0-0	.979	-6	78	95	C-41	-1.1
1973	KC A	11	30	4	4	1	1	0	2	3-0	1	5	.133	.235	.233	30	-3	0-0	.940	-3	42	32	C-11	-0.6
	NY N	4	8	0	2	0	0	0	0	1-0	0	1	.250	.333	.250	65	0	0-0	1.000	0	0	0	/C-4	0.0
Total	10	556	1527	120	357	63	10	15	130	157-48	11	293	.234	.307	.318	81	-35	1-2	.990	3	*110*	*106*	C-525	-1.1
MAY, LEE Lee Andrew B 3.23.1943 Birmingham, AL BR/TR 6-3/205# d9.1 C9 b-Carlos																								
1965	Cin N	5	4	1	0	0	0	0	0	0-0	0	1	.000	.000	.000	-94	-1	0-0	—	0			H	-0.1
1966	Cin N	25	75	14	25	5	1	2	10	0-0	0	14	.333	.333	.507	119	2	0-1	.972	-1	88	112	1-16	0.0
1967	Cin N	127	438	54	116	29	2	12	57	19-3	10	80	.265	.308	.422	97	-1	4-8	.994	1	89	86	1-81,O-48(32-0-16)	-1.1
1968	Cin N	146	559	78	162	32	1	22	80	34-11	6	100	.290	.337	.469	132	21	4-7	.996	-1	93	93	*1-122,O-33(11-0-22)	1.2
1969	Cin N★	158	607	85	169	32	3	38	110	45-8	6	142	.278	.331	.529	132	23	5-4	.993	0	104	95	*1-156/O-7(5-0-2)	1.1
1970	†Cin N	153	605	78	153	34	2	34	94	38-5	2	125	.253	.297	.484	106	1	1-1	.993	-1	100	114	*1-153	-1.2
1971	Cin N★	147	553	85	154	17	3	39	98	42-2	4	135	.278	.332	.532	145	29	3-0	.994	-5	88	109	*1-143	1.4
1972	Hou N★	148	592	87	168	31	2	29	98	52-12	2	145	.284	.343	.490	137	27	3-1	.996	-3	86	109	*1-146	1.3
1973	Hou N	148	545	65	147	24	3	28	105	34-10	2	122	.270	.310	.479	117	10	1-1	.993	-2	91	94	*1-144	-0.4
1974	Hou N	152	556	59	149	26	0	24	85	17-2	7	97	.268	.294	.444	110	3	1-0	.994	2	106	103	*1-145	-0.6
1975	Bal A	146	580	67	152	28	3	20	99	36-8	5	91	.262	.308	.424	113	7	1-2	.993	4	**113**	**134**	*1-144/D-2	0.0
1976	Bal A	148	530	61	137	17	4	25	**109**	41-8	3	104	.258	.312	.447	130	16	4-1	.996	3	114	93	1-94,D-52	1.3
1977	Bal A	150	585	75	148	16	2	27	99	38-5	0	119	.253	.296	.426	101	-2	2-2	.995	-3	88	123	*1-110,D-39	-1.3
1978	Bal A	148	556	56	137	16	1	25	80	31-5	1	110	.246	.286	.414	101	-3	5-2	.973	-0	83	105	*D-140/1-4	-0.8
1979	†Bal A	124	456	59	116	15	0	19	69	28-4	1	100	.254	.297	.412	93	-7	3-4	.913	-1	0	125	*D-117/1-2	-1.2
1980	Bal A	78	222	20	54	10	2	7	31	15-1	0	53	.243	.289	.401	88	-4	2-0	1.000	-0	71	70	D-58/1-7	-0.6
1981	†KC A	26	55	3	16	3	0	0	8	3-0	0	14	.291	.328	.345	95	0	0-1	1.000	-1	47	142	/1-8,D-4	-0.2
1982	KC A	42	91	12	28	5	2	3	12	14-1	0	18	.308	.393	.505	147	6	0-0	.989	-1	79	102	1-32/D-2	0.4
Total	18	2071	7609	959	2031	340	31	354	1244	487-85	49	1570	.267	.313	.459	116	127	39-35	.994	-8	97	106	*1-1507,D-414/O-88(48-0-40)	-0.8
MAY, PINKY Merrill Glend B 1.18.1911 Laconia, IN D 9.4.2000 Corydon, IN BR/TR 5-11.5/165# d4.21 Mil 1944-45 s-Milt																								
1939	Phi N	135	464	49	133	27	3	2	62	41	1	20	.287	.346	.371	95	-2	4	**.956**	10	**106**	109	*3-132	1.2
1940	Phi N★	136	501	59	147	24	2	1	48	58	4	33	.293	.371	.355	105	7	2	.954	16	**118**	58	*3-135/S	2.7
1941	Phi N	142	490	46	131	17	4	0	39	55	2	30	.267	.344	.318	91	-5	2	**.972**	**24**	**111**	107	*3-140	2.4
1942	Phi N	115	345	25	82	15	0	0	18	51	1	17	.238	.338	.281	86	-3	3	.963	**19**	**123**	120	*3-107	2.0
1943	Phi N	137	415	31	117	19	2	1	48	56	1	21	.282	.369	.345	111	8	2	**.963**	9	**108**	90	*3-132	1.9
Total	5	665	2215	210	610	102	11	4	215	261	9	121	.275	.354	.337	98	5	13	.962	77	113	95	3-646/S	10.2
MAY, MILT Milton Scott B 8.1.1950 Gary, IN BL/TR 6/190# d9.8 C14 f-Pinky																								
1970	Pit N	5	4	1	2	1	0	0	2	0-0	1	0	.500	.600	.750	265	1	0-0	—	0			H	0.1
1971	†Pit N	49	126	15	35	1	0	6	25	9-3	0	16	.278	.321	.429	113	1	0-0	1.000	4	330	97	C-31	0.8
1972	†Pit N	57	139	12	39	10	0	0	14	10-2	0	13	.281	.325	.353	96	-1	0-0	.985	3	139	121	C-33	0.5
1973	Pit N	101	283	29	76	8	1	7	31	34-12	2	26	.269	.349	.378	105	2	0-1	.973	-6	101	93	C-79	0.0
1974	Hou N	127	405	47	117	17	4	7	54	39-8	1	33	.289	.349	.402	116	8	0-1	**.993**	3	97	**123**	*C-116	1.7
1975	Hou N	111	386	29	93	15	1	4	52	26-3	0	41	.241	.287	.316	73	-16	1-2	.986	8	87	**176**	*C-102	-0.4
1976	Det A	6	25	2	7	1	0	0	1	0-0	0	1	.280	.280	.320	73	-1	0-0	1.000	2	133	147	/C-6	0.1
1977	Det A	115	397	32	99	9	3	12	46	26-2	0	31	.249	.291	.378	78	-13	0-0	.986	6	117	106	*C-111	-0.2
1978	Det A	105	352	24	88	9	0	10	37	27-3	2	26	.250	.305	.361	85	-8	0-0	.979	2	108	95	C-94	-0.2
1979	Det A	6	11	1	3	2	0	0	3	1-1	0	1	.273	.333	.455	107	0	0-0	1.000	0	35	0	/C-5	0.0
	Chi A	65	202	23	51	13	0	7	28	14-1	2	27	.252	.306	.421	94	-2	0-0	.981	2	106	105	C-65	0.2
	Year	71	213	24	54	15	0	7	31	15-2	2	28	.254	.307	.423	95	-2	0-0	.982	2	103	100	C-70	0.2
1980	SF N	111	358	27	93	16	2	6	50	25-4	1	40	.260	.305	.366	90	-5	0-1	.986	2	98	108	*C-103	0.0
1981	SF N	97	316	20	98	17	0	2	33	34-10	0	29	.310	.376	.383	118	9	1-4	.989	-3	82	93	C-93	0.9
1982	SF N	114	395	29	104	19	0	9	39	28-8	0	38	.263	.311	.380	93	-4	0-1	.987	-4	79	144	*C-110	-0.4
1983	SF N	66	186	18	46	6	0	6	20	21-6	0	23	.247	.324	.376	96	-1	2-2	.981	-1	90	102	C-56	0.0
	Pit N	7	12	0	3	0	0	0	0	1-1	0	1	.250	.308	.250	55	-1	0-0	1.000	1	52	242	/C-4	0.0
	Year	73	198	18	49	6	0	6	20	22-7	0	24	.247	.323	.369	94	-2	2-2	.983	-0	88	110	C-60	0.0
1984	Pit N	50	96	4	17	3	0	1	8	10-1	0	15	.177	.255	.240	40	-8	0-1	.993	2	97	83	C-26	-0.5
Total	15	1192	3693	313	971	147	11	77	443	305-65	9	361	.263	.318	.371	93	-39	4-13	.986	21	105	116	*C-1034	2.6
MAYBERRY, JOHN John Claiborn B 2.18.1949 Detroit, MI BL/TL 6-3/220# d9.10 C2																								
1968	Hou N	4	9	0	0	0	0	0	0	0-0	1	2	.000	.100	.000	-69	-2	0-0	1.000	-1	0	55	/1-2	-0.3
1969	Hou N	5	4	0	0	0	0	0	0	1-0	0	1	.000	.200	.000	-41	-1	0-0	—	0			H	-0.1
1970	Hou N	50	148	23	32	3	2	5	14	21-6	2	33	.216	.318	.365	87	-3	1-1	.995	3	125	85	1-45	-0.3
1971	Hou N	46	137	16	25	0	1	7	14	13-2	2	32	.182	.260	.350	74	-6	0-0	.997	-4	57	68	1-37	-1.4
1972	KC A	149	503	65	150	24	3	25	100	78-13	3	74	.298	.394	.507	168	45	0-2	**.995**	-1	96	**120**	*1-146	3.5
1973	KC A★	152	510	87	142	20	2	26	100	**122**-**17**	2	79	.278	**.417**	.478	141	34	3-0	.994	-6	84	110	*1-149/D	1.8
1974	KC A★	126	427	63	100	13	1	22	69	77-11	6	72	.234	.358	.424	118	12	4-2	.990	-3	95	112	*1-106,D-16	0.1
1975	KC A	156	554	95	161	38	1	34	106	**119**-16	4	73	.291	.416	.547	**167**	**55**	5-3	.988	1	104	97	*1-131,D-27	4.5
1976	†KC A	161	594	76	138	22	2	13	95	82-7	2	73	.232	.322	.342	95	-1	3-2	.996	-3	93	105	*1-160/D-2	-1.8
1977	†KC A	153	543	73	125	22	1	23	82	83-9	7	86	.230	.336	.401	100	2	1-3	**.995**	-5	83	103	*1-145/D-8	-1.3
1978	Tor A	152	515	51	129	15	2	22	70	60-2	4	57	.250	.329	.416	107	5	1-2	.993	-13	60	101	*1-139/D-7	-1.8
1979	Tor A	137	464	61	127	22	1	21	74	69-7	5	60	.274	.372	.461	122	17	1-1	.995	-7	80	103	*1-135	0.1
1980	Tor A	149	501	62	124	19	2	30	82	77-9	3	80	.248	.349	.473	118	13	0-0	.994	-5	86	106	*1-136/D-8	-0.1
1981	Tor A	94	290	34	72	6	1	17	43	44-4	8	45	.248	.360	.452	125	10	1-1	.993	-8	67	97	1-80,D-10	-0.2
1982	Tor A	17	33	7	9	0	0	2	3	7-1	1	5	.273	.405	.455	127	2	0-0	1.000	-1	36	94	D-13/1-4	0.0
	NY A	69	215	20	45	7	0	8	27	28-2	5	38	.209	.313	.353	84	-4	0-0	.996	-2	78	104	1-63/D-4	-1.0
	Year	86	248	27	54	7	0	10	30	35-3	6	43	.218	.326	.367	90	-3	0-0	.996	-3	75	103	1-67,D-17	-1.0
Total	15	1620	5447	733	1379	211	19	255	879	881-106	55	810	.253	.360	.439	122	178	20-17	.994	-53	85	104	*1-1478/D-96	1.7
MAYE, LEE Arthur Lee B 12.11.1934 Tuscaloosa, AL D 7.17.2002 Riverside, CA BL/TR 6-2/190# d7.17																								
1959	Mil N	51	140	17	42	5	1	4	16	7-2	1	26	.300	.338	.436	114	2	2-2	.976	2	109	98	O-44(24-0-21)	0.1
1960	Mil N	41	83	14	25	6	0	0	2	7-2	1	21	.301	.359	.373	110	2	5-0	.968	-1	95	72	O-19(15-0-4)	0.1
1961	Mil N	110	373	68	101	11	5	14	41	36-2	3	50	.271	.337	.440	112	5	10-1	.972	-3	99	72	O-96(26-0-72)	-0.1
1962	Mil N	99	349	40	85	10	0	10	41	25-2	1	58	.244	.294	.358	77	-12	9-3	.977	-1	106	32	O-94(38-60-2)	-1.6
1963	Mil N	124	442	67	120	22	7	11	34	36-2	3	52	.271	.329	.428	118	10	14-2	.983	-2	100	53	*O-111(70-73-3)	0.5
1964	Mil N	153	588	96	179	**44**	5	10	74	34-3	4	54	.304	.346	.447	121	17	5-10	.961	-3	100	83	*O-135(54-92-0)/3-5	0.6
1965	Mil N	15	53	8	16	2	0	2	7	2-0	1	6	.302	.339	.453	120	1	0-0	.962	1	92	289	O-13(4-9-0)	0.1
	Hou N	108	415	38	104	17	7	3	36	20-3	1	37	.251	.285	.347	83	-11	1-5	.953	-2	96	104	*O-103(92-11-3)	-2.1

Year	Tm Lg	G	AB	R	H	2B	3B	HR	RBI	BB-IB	HP	SO	AVG	OBP	SLG	AOPS	ABR	SB-CS	FA	FR	Rng	Thr	G at Pos	BFW
	Year	123	468	46	120	19	7	5	43	22-3	2	43	.256	.291	.359	88	-10	1-5	.954	-1	96	124	*O-116(96-20-3)	-2.0
1966	Hou N	115	358	38	103	12	4	9	36	20-5	0	26	.288	.323	.419	113	5	4-3	.949	-1	100	71	O-97(LF)	-0.2
1967	Cle A	115	297	43	77	20	4	9	27	26-4	1	47	.259	.321	.444	123	8	3-3	.981	-4	90	49	O-77(23-10-54)/2	0.0
1968	Cle A	109	299	20	84	13	2	4	26	15-0	1	24	.281	.316	.378	112	3	0-0	.984	3	113	103	O-80(71-0-10)/1	0.3
1969	Cle A	43	108	9	27	5	0	1	15	8-2	1	15	.250	.305	.324	74	-4	1-0	.982	1	125	0	O-28(26-0-2)	-0.4
	Was A	71	238	41	69	9	3	9	26	20-0	0	25	.290	.345	.466	132	9	1-3	.944	-4	99	23	O-65(6-4-56)	0.2
	Year	114	346	50	96	14	3	10	41	28-2	1	40	.277	.332	.422	112	4	2-3	.957	-3	107	16	O-93(32-4-58)	-0.2
1970	Was A	96	255	28	67	12	1	7	30	21-1	1	32	.263	.321	.400	103	0	4-2	1.000	-5	71	104	O-68(6-0-63)/3	-0.8
	Chi A	6	6	0	1	0	0	0	1	0-0	0	1	.167	.167	.167	-8	-1	0-0	—	0			H	-0.1
	Year	102	261	28	68	12	1	7	31	21-1	1	33	.261	.318	.395	100	-1	4-2	1.000	-5	71	104	O-68(6-0-63)/3	-0.9
1971	Chi A	32	44	6	9	2	0	1	7	5-1	0	7	.205	.280	.318	69	-2	0-0	1.000	0	82	217	O-10(2-0-8)	-0.2
Total	13	1288	4048	533	1109	190	39	94	419	282-29	19	481	.274	.323	.410	108	32	59-34	.970	-20	99	73	*O-1040(554-259-298)/3-6,12	-3.6

MAYER, ED Edward H. B 8.16.1866 Marshall, IL D 5.18.1913 Chicago, IL 5-8.5/155# d4.19

Year	Tm Lg	G	AB	R	H	2B	3B	HR	RBI	BB-IB	HP	SO	AVG	OBP	SLG	AOPS	ABR	SB-CS	FA	FR	Rng	Thr	G at Pos	BFW
1890	Phi N	120	484	49	117	25	5	1	70	22	8	36	.242	.286	.320	75	-17	20	.878	-11	90	111	*3-117/O-4(CF)	-2.3
1891	Phi N	68	268	24	50	2	4	0	31	14	4	29	.187	.238	.224	34	-24	7	.895	-3	103	65	3-31,O-29(4-24-1)/S-7,2	-2.4
Total	2	188	752	73	167	27	9	1	101	36	12	65	.222	.269	.286	60	-41	27	.882	-13	93	102	3-148/O-33(4-28-1),S-7,2	-4.7

MAYER, SAM Samuel Frankel (born Samuel Frankel Erskine) B 2.28.1893 Atlanta, GA D 7.1.1962 Atlanta, GA BR/TL 5-10/164# d9.14 b-Erskine

Year	Tm Lg	G	AB	R	H	2B	3B	HR	RBI	BB-IB	HP	SO	AVG	OBP	SLG	AOPS	ABR	SB-CS	FA	FR	Rng	Thr	G at Pos	BFW
1915	Was A	11	29	5	7	0	0	1	4	4	0	2	.241	.333	.345	101	0	1-2	1.000	0	97	96	/O-9(1-0-8),P1	-0.1

MAYER, WALLY Walter A. B 7.8.1890 Cincinnati, OH D 11.18.1951 Minnetonka, MN BR/TR 5-11/168# d9.28 Mil 1918

Year	Tm Lg	G	AB	R	H	2B	3B	HR	RBI	BB-IB	HP	SO	AVG	OBP	SLG	AOPS	ABR	SB-CS	FA	FR	Rng	Thr	G at Pos	BFW
1911	Chi A	1	3	0	0	0	0	0	0	2	0		.000	.400	.000	16	0	0	.900	-0	*190*	*64*	/C	0.0
1912	Chi A	9	9	1	0	0	0	0	0	1	0		.000	.100	.000	-73	-2	0	1.000	-0	*95*	*44*	/C-6	-0.2
1914	Chi A	40	85	7	14	3	1	0	5	14	1	23	.165	.290	.224	55	-4	1-1	.968	5	*133*	*109*	C-33/3	0.3
1915	Chi A	22	54	3	12	3	1	0	5	5	0	8	.222	.288	.315	78	-2	0-2	.990	1	*181*	*61*	C-20	0.0
1917	Bos A	4	12	2	2	0	0	0	0	5	0	2	.167	.412	.167	78	0	0	.964	1	*125*	*125*	/C-4	0.2
1918	Bos A	26	49	7	11	4	0	0	5	7	0	7	.224	.321	.306	91	0	0	.964	-0	*108*	*89*	C-23	0.1
1919	StL A	30	62	2	14	4	1	0	5	8	0	11	.226	.314	.323	77	-2	0	.959	3	*107*	*123*	C-25	0.3
Total	7	132	274	22	53	14	3	0	20	42	1	51	.193	.303	.266	68	-10	1-3	.969	8	*131*	*98*	C-112/3	0.7

MAYES, PADDY Adair Bushyhead B 3.17.1885 Locust Grove, OK D 5.28.1962 Fayetteville, AR BL/TR 5-11/160# d6.11

Year	Tm Lg	G	AB	R	H	2B	3B	HR	RBI	BB-IB	HP	SO	AVG	OBP	SLG	AOPS	ABR	SB-CS	FA	FR	Rng	Thr	G at Pos	BFW
1911	Phi N	5	5	1	0	0	0	0	0	1	1	2	.000	.286	.000	-17	-1	0	1.000	0	0	0	/O-2	0.0

MAYNARD, BUSTER James Walter B 3.25.1913 Henderson, NC D 9.7.1977 Durham, NC BR/TR 5-11/170# d9.17 Mil 1944-45

Year	Tm Lg	G	AB	R	H	2B	3B	HR	RBI	BB-IB	HP	SO	AVG	OBP	SLG	AOPS	ABR	SB-CS	FA	FR	Rng	Thr	G at Pos	BFW
1940	NY N	7	29	6	8	2	2	1	2	2	0	6	.276	.323	.586	145	1	0	.929	-1	87	0	/O-7(0-3-4)	0.0
1942	NY N	89	190	17	47	4	1	4	32	19	1	19	.247	.319	.342	93	-2	3	.982	5	105	160	O-58(7-48-4),3-10/2	0.2
1943	NY N	121	393	43	81	8	2	9	32	24	0	27	.206	.252	.305	60	-22	3	.965	-2	86	145	O-74(25-39-13),3-22	-2.9
1946	NY N	7	4	2	0	0	0	0	0	1	0	1	.000	.200	.000	-41	-1	0	.750	-0	103	0	/O-3(0-1-2)	-0.1
Total	4	224	616	68	136	14	5	14	66	46	1	53	.221	.276	.328	74	-24	6	.967	2	93	140	O-142(32-91-23)/3-32,2	-2.8

MAYNARD, CHICK Le Roy Evans B 11.2.1896 Turners Falls, MA D 1.31.1957 Bangor, ME BL/TR 5-9/150# d6.27

Year	Tm Lg	G	AB	R	H	2B	3B	HR	RBI	BB-IB	HP	SO	AVG	OBP	SLG	AOPS	ABR	SB-CS	FA	FR	Rng	Thr	G at Pos	BFW
1922	Bos A	12	24	1	3	0	0	0	0	3	0	2	.125	.222	.125	-8	-4	0-1	.872	-3	90	26	S-12	-0.6

MAYNE, BRENT Brent Danem B 4.19.1968 Loma Linda, CA BL/TR 6-1/190# d9.18

Year	Tm Lg	G	AB	R	H	2B	3B	HR	RBI	BB-IB	HP	SO	AVG	OBP	SLG	AOPS	ABR	SB-CS	FA	FR	Rng	Thr	G at Pos	BFW
1990	KC A	5	13	2	3	0	0	0	1	3-0	0	3	.231	.375	.231	74	0	0-1	.970	0	52	74	/C-5	0.0
1991	KC A	85	231	22	58	8	0	3	31	23-4	0	42	.251	.315	.325	78	-7	2-4	.987	-0	82	104	C-80/D	-0.4
1992	KC A	82	213	16	48	10	0	0	18	11-0	0	26	.225	.260	.272	49	-15	0-4	.990	3	146	94	C-62/3-8,D	-1.0
1993	KC A	71	205	22	52	9	1	2	22	18-7	1	31	.254	.317	.337	72	-8	3-2	.995	-0	81	84	C-68/D	-0.5
1994	KC A	46	144	19	37	5	1	2	20	14-1	0	27	.257	.323	.347	70	-7	1-0	.996	2	94	96	C-42/D-3	-0.2
1995	KC A	110	307	23	77	18	1	1	27	25-1	3	41	.251	.313	.326	66	-15	0-1	.995	11	108	57	*C-103	0.1
1996	NY N	70	99	9	26	6	0	1	6	12-1	0	22	.263	.342	.354	88	-1	0-1	1.000	-8	54	21	C-21	-0.8
1997	Oak A	85	256	29	74	12	0	6	22	18-1	4	33	.289	.343	.406	97	-1	1-0	.996	-12	88	95	C-83	-0.7
1998	SF N	94	275	26	75	15	0	3	32	37-3	1	47	.273	.359	.360	96	0	2-1	.991	-7	88	70	C-88	-0.2
1999	SF N	117	322	39	97	32	0	2	39	43-5	5	65	.301	.389	.419	114	10	2-2	.995	-2	96	116	*C-105	1.3
2000	Col N	117	335	36	101	21	0	6	64	47-13	1	48	.301	.381	.418	83	-7	1-3	.990	0	101	79	*C-105/P	-0.2
2001	Col N	49	160	15	53	7	0	0	20	16-3	0	24	.331	.385	.375	82	-3	0-0	.997	8	118	114	C-44/1	0.7
	KC A	51	166	13	40	4	1	2	20	10-2	1	17	.241	.283	.313	54	-11	1-2	.993	-3	101	91	C-49	-1.1
2002	KC A	101	326	35	77	8	2	4	30	34-1	2	54	.236	.309	.310	59	-19	4-4	.993	-1	115	100	C-99	-1.4
2003	KC A	113	372	39	91	17	1	6	36	32-5	3	59	.245	.307	.344	64	-19	0-2	.994	-1	104	102	*C-112	-1.3
Total	14	1196	3424	345	909	172	7	38	388	343-47	21	539	.265	.333	.353	77	-103	17-27	.993	-10	100	90	*C-1066/3-8,D-6,1P	-5.7

MAYO, EDDIE Edward Joseph "Hotshot" (born Edward Joseph Mayoski) B 4.15.1910 Holyoke, MA BL/TR 5-11/178# d5.22 C4

Year	Tm Lg	G	AB	R	H	2B	3B	HR	RBI	BB-IB	HP	SO	AVG	OBP	SLG	AOPS	ABR	SB-CS	FA	FR	Rng	Thr	G at Pos	BFW
1936	†NY N	46	141	11	28	4	1	1	8	11	0	12	.199	.257	.262	40	-12	0	.981	3	111	191	3-40	-0.8
1937	Bos N	65	172	19	39	6	1	1	18	15	1	20	.227	.293	.291	65	-8	1	.956	-5	90	37	3-50	-1.2
1938	Bos N	8	14	2	3	0	0	1	4	1	0	0	.214	.267	.429	98	0	0	.923	1	114	332	/3-6,S-2	0.1
1943	Phi A	128	471	49	103	10	1	0	28	34	5	32	.219	.278	.244	54	-28	2-0	**.976**	0	93	74	*3-123	-2.9
1944	Det A	154	607	76	151	18	3	5	63	57	4	23	.249	.317	.313	76	-18	9-13	.978	**34**	**114**	**121**	*2-143,S-11	2.2
1945	†Det A✶	134	501	71	143	24	3	10	54	47	0	29	.285	.347	.405	111	7	7-7	**.980**	20	**112**	115	*2-124	3.5
1946	Det A	51	202	21	51	9	2	0	22	14	0	12	.252	.301	.317	68	-9	6-2	.965	-6	92	93	2-49	-1.2
1947	Det A	142	535	66	149	28	4	6	48	48	0	28	.279	.338	.379	96	-3	3-7	.983	-14	93	83	*2-142	-1.1
1948	Det A	106	370	35	92	20	1	2	42	30	3	19	.249	.310	.324	67	-18	1-9	.975	-7	91	83	2-86,3-10	-2.3
Total	9	834	3013	350	759	119	16	26	287	257	13	175	.252	.313	.328	78	-89	29-38	.978	26	103	102	2-544,3-229/S-13	-3.7

MAYO, JACKIE John Lewis B 7.26.1925 Litchfield, IL BL/TR 6-1/190# d9.19

Year	Tm Lg	G	AB	R	H	2B	3B	HR	RBI	BB-IB	HP	SO	AVG	OBP	SLG	AOPS	ABR	SB-CS	FA	FR	Rng	Thr	G at Pos	BFW
1948	Phi N	12	35	7	8	2	1	0	3	7	2	7	.229	.386	.343	101	1	1	1.000	1	114	114	O-11(LF)	0.1
1949	Phi N	45	39	3	5	0	0	0	2	4	0	5	.128	.209	.128	-8	-6	0	.889	0	123	117	O-25(0-1-24)	-0.6
1950	†Phi N	18	36	1	8	3	0	0	3	2	0	5	.222	.263	.306	50	-3	0	.958	-0	113	0	O-15(LF)	-0.3
1951	Phi N	9	7	1	1	0	0	0	0	0	0	0	.143	.143	.143	-23	-1	0-0	1.000	0	147	0	/O-5(LF)	-0.1
1952	Phi N	50	119	13	29	5	0	1	4	12	0	17	.244	.313	.311	74	-4	1-3	1.000	3	111	48	O-27(24-1-2)/1-6	-0.4
1953	Phi N	5	4	0	0	0	0	0	0	0	0	1	.000	.000	.000	-99	-1	0-0	—	-0	0	0	/O(RF)	-0.1
Total	6	139	240	25	51	10	1	1	12	25	2	35	.213	.292	.275	56	-14	2-3	.972	4	114	62	/O-84(55-2-27),1-6	-1.4

MAYS, WILLIE Willie Howard "Say Hey" B 5.6.1931 Westfield, AL BR/TR 5-11/180# d5.25 Mil 1952 C6 HF1979

Year	Tm Lg	G	AB	R	H	2B	3B	HR	RBI	BB-IB	HP	SO	AVG	OBP	SLG	AOPS	ABR	SB-CS	FA	FR	Rng	Thr	G at Pos	BFW
1951	†NY N	121	464	59	127	22	5	20	68	57	2	60	.274	.356	.472	120	13	7-4	.976	2	105	110	*O-121(CF)	1.2
1952	NY N	34	127	17	30	2	4	4	23	16	1	17	.236	.326	.409	102	0	4-1	.991	4	110	161	O-34(CF)	0.4
1954	†NY N★	151	565	119	195	33	**13**	41	110	66	2	57	**.345**	.411	**.667**	176	61	8-5	.985	10	109	112	*O-151(CF)	**6.2**
1955	NY N★	152	580	123	185	18	**13**	**51**	127	79-13	4	60	.319	.400	**.659**	**176**	**62**	24-4	.982	12	102	**195**	*O-152(CF)	**6.8**
1956	NY N★	152	578	101	171	27	8	36	84	68-20	1	65	.296	.369	.557	146	37	**40**-10	.979	6	104	126	*O-152(CF)	4.1
1957	NY N★	152	585	112	195	26	**20**	35	97	76-15	1	62	.333	.407	**.626**	**174**	**61**	**38**-19	.980	1	100	121	*O-150(CF)	**5.6**
1958	SF N★	152	600	**121**	208	33	11	29	96	78-12	1	56	.347	.419	.583	**167**	**59**	**31**-6	.980	7	106	136	*O-151(CF)	**6.3**
1959	SF N★	151	575	125	180	43	5	34	104	65-9	2	58	.313	.381	.583	157	47	**27**-4	.984	-3	101	72	*O-147(2-146-0)	4.1
1960	SF N★	153	595	107	**190**	29	12	29	103	61-11	4	70	.319	.381	.555	164	51	25-10	.981	4	105	108	*O-152(CF)	5.0
1961	SF N★	154	572	**129**	176	32	3	40	123	81-15	2	77	.308	.393	.584	162	52	18-9	.980	0	107	64	*O-153(CF)	4.7
1962	†SF N★	162	621	130	189	36	5	**49**	141	78-11	4	85	.304	.384	.615	167	58	18-2	.991	7	115	57	*O-161(CF)	**6.2**
1963	SF N★	157	596	115	187	32	7	38	103	66-5	2	83	.314	.380	.582	176	58	8-3	.981	4	**111**	69	*O-157(CF)/S	**6.1**
1964	SF N★	157	578	121	171	21	9	**47**	111	82-13	1	72	.296	.383	**.607**	**171**	**54**	19-5	.984	5	110	103	*O-155(CF)/1S3	5.8
1965	SF N★	157	558	118	177	21	3	**52**	112	76-16	0	71	.317	**.398**	**.645**	**184**	**62**	9-4	.983	6	105	154	*O-151(1-147-5)	**6.6**
1966	SF N★	152	552	99	159	29	4	37	103	70-11	2	81	.288	.368	.556	149	37	5-1	.982	2	106	75	*O-150(1-145-5)	3.6
1967	SF N★	141	486	83	128	22	2	22	70	51-7	2	92	.263	.334	.453	125	16	6-0	.976	-3	101	44	*O-134(CF)	1.1
1968	SF N★	148	498	84	144	20	5	23	79	67-7	2	81	.289	.372	.488	158	36	12-6	.978	2	106	90	*O-142(CF)/1	4.0
1969	SF N★	117	403	64	114	17	3	13	58	49-7	3	71	.283	.362	.437	126	15	6-2	.976	-10	87	63	*O-108(0-106-2)/1	0.3
1970	SF N★	139	478	94	139	15	2	28	83	79-3	3	90	.291	.390	.506	141	30	5-0	.975	-2	101	89	*O-129(CF)/1-5	2.5
1971	†SF N★	136	417	82	113	24	5	18	61	**112**-11	3	123	.271	**.425**	.482	160	41	23-3	.970	-4	104	47	O-84(CF),1-48	3.7
1972	SF N	19	49	8	9	2	0	0	3	17-1	0	5	.184	.394	.224	79	0	3-0	1.000	-1	91	0	O-14(CF)	-0.1
	NY N★	69	195	27	52	9	1	8	19	43-5	1	43	.267	.402	.446	144	14	1-5	.974	0	108	120	O-49(1-48-0),1-11	1.1

Year	Tm Lg	G	AB	R	H	2B	3B	HR	RBI	BB-IB	HP	SO	AVG	OBP	SLG	AOPS	ABR	SB-CS	FA	FR	Rng	Thr	G at Pos	BFW
	Year	88	244	35	61	11	1	8	22	60-6	1	48	.250	.400	.402	131	14	4-5	.979	-1	104	93	O-63(1-62-0),1-11	1.0
1973	†NY N★	66	209	24	44	10	0	6	25	27-0	1	47	.211	.303	.344	81	-5	1-0	.991	1	115	85	O-45(5-43-9),1-17	-0.7
Total	22	2992	10881	2062	3283	523	140	660	1903	1464-192	44	1526	.302	.384	.557	157	859	338-103	.981	50	105	100	*O-2842(10-2827-21)/1-84,S-2,3	84.6
MAZEROSKI, BILL William Stanley "Maz" B 9.5.1936 Wheeling, WV BR/TR 5-11.5/183# d7.7 C3 HF2001																								
1956	Pit N	81	255	30	62	8	1	3	14	18-1	0	24	.243	.293	.318	66	-13	0-0	.981	9	111	110	2-81	0.2
1957	Pit N	148	526	59	149	27	7	8	54	27-2	1	49	.283	.318	.407	96	-4	3-3	.978	3	108	105	*2-144	0.9
1958	Pit N★	152	567	69	156	24	6	19	68	25-3	3	71	.275	.308	.439	98	-4	1-1	.980	18	**113**	110	*2-152	2.4
1959	Pit N★	135	493	50	119	15	6	7	59	29-1	1	54	.241	.283	.339	66	-26	1-3	.981	-6	100	**121**	*2-133	-2.3
1960	†Pit N★	151	538	58	147	21	5	11	64	40-15	1	50	.273	.320	.392	95	-5	4-0	**.989**	**27**	**108**	**143**	*2-151	3.5
1961	Pit N	152	558	71	148	21	2	13	59	26-10	3	55	.265	.298	.380	79	-18	2-1	.975	**36**	**115**	**128**	*2-152	3.0
1962	Pit N★	159	572	55	155	24	9	14	81	37-**16**	2	47	.271	.315	.418	95	-6	0-3	.985	**40**	**111**	**135**	*2-159	4.7
1963	Pit N✳	142	534	43	131	22	3	8	52	32-6	0	46	.245	.286	.343	80	-14	2-0	.984	**51**	**125**	**151**	*2-138	5.3
1964	Pit N☆	**162**	601	66	161	22	8	10	64	29-11	0	52	.268	.300	.381	91	-9	1-1	.975	**35**	**118**	**119**	*2-162	4.1
1965	Pit N	130	494	52	134	17	1	6	54	18-5	2	34	.271	.294	.346	81	-13	2-1	**.988**	**27**	**116**	**143**	*2-127	2.5
1966	Pit N	**162**	621	56	163	22	7	16	82	31-9	1	62	.262	.296	.398	91	-9	4-3	**.992**	**40**	**116**	**149**	*2-162	4.7
1967	Pit N★	**163**	639	62	167	25	3	9	77	30-7	0	55	.261	.292	.352	84	-15	1-2	.981	19	**109**	116	*2-163	1.9
1968	Pit N	143	506	36	127	18	2	3	42	38-10	2	38	.251	.304	.312	87	-8	3-4	.981	20	**114**	**124**	*2-142	2.7
1969	Pit N	67	227	13	52	7	1	3	25	22-3	2	16	.229	.298	.308	73	-8	1-1	.988	14	113	115	2-65	1.0
1970	†Pit N	112	367	29	84	14	0	7	39	27-9	2	40	.229	.283	.324	64	-19	2-0	.987	20	114	128	*2-102	0.8
1971	†Pit N	70	193	17	49	3	1	1	16	15-1	0	8	.254	.303	.295	72	-7	0-0	.986	-4	100	82	2-46/3-7	-1.0
1972	†Pit N	34	64	3	12	4	0	0	3	3-1	0	5	.188	.217	.250	35	-5	0-0	.986	1	106	96	2-15/3-3	-0.4
Total	17	2163	7755	769	2016	294	62	138	853	447-110	20	706	.260	.299	.367	84	-183	27-23	.983	348	113	126	*2-2094/3-10	34.0
MAZZERA, MEL Melvin Leonard "Mike" B 1.31.1914 Stockton, CA D 12.17.1997 Stockton, CA BL/TL 5-11/180# d9.9																								
1935	StL A	12	30	4	7	2	0	1	2	4	0	9	.233	.324	.400	82	-1	0-0	.950	0	105	161	O-10(4-3-3)	-0.1
1937	StL A	7	7	1	2	2	0	0	0	0	0	2	.286	.286	.571	110	0	0-0	—	0			H	0.0
1938	StL A	86	204	33	57	8	2	6	29	12	3	25	.279	.329	.426	88	-5	1-1	.976	2	93	230	O-47(25-8-14)	-0.4
1939	StL A	33	110	21	33	5	2	3	22	10	1	20	.300	.364	.464	108	1	0-0	.983	0	105	57	O-25(18-0-7)	0.0
1940	Phi N	69	156	16	37	5	4	0	13	19	0	15	.237	.320	.321	80	-4	1	.985	1	90	202	O-42(26-2-16),1-11	-0.5
Total	5	207	507	75	136	22	8	10	66	45	4	71	.268	.333	.402	90	-9	2-1	.978	3	96	175	O-124(73-13-40)/1-11	-1.0
MAZZILLI, LEE Lee Louis B 3.25.1955 New York, NY BB/TR 6-1/185# d9.7 C4																								
1976	NY N	24	77	9	15	2	0	2	7	14-0	1	10	.195	.323	.299	83	-1	5-4	.983	2	112	165	O-23(2-21-0)	0.0
1977	NY N	159	537	66	134	24	3	6	46	72-6	3	72	.250	.340	.339	87	-8	22-15	.992	3	108	95	*O-156(CF)	-0.6
1978	NY N	148	542	78	148	28	5	16	61	69-6	1	82	.273	.353	.432	124	18	20-13	.987	-1	101	96	*O-144(CF)	1.6
1979	NY N★	158	597	78	181	34	4	15	79	93-5	0	74	.303	.395	.449	135	33	34-12	.989	-5	94	111	*O-143(CF),1-15	3.0
1980	NY N	152	578	82	162	31	4	16	76	82-11	3	92	.280	.370	.431	127	24	41-15	.983	-4	83	99	1-92,O-66(CF)	1.8
1981	NY N	95	324	36	74	14	5	6	34	46-3	2	53	.228	.324	.358	96	-1	17-7	.970	-1	102	75	O-89(51-40-0)	-0.4
1982	Tex A	58	195	23	47	8	0	4	17	28-0	1	26	.241	.339	.344	93	-1	11-6	.945	-2	88	65	O-26(11-15-2),D-24	-0.4
	NY A	37	128	20	34	2	0	6	17	15-0	1	15	.266	.347	.422	112	2	2-3	.995	-2	54	136	1-23/O-2(LF),D-9	-0.2
	Year	95	323	43	81	10	0	10	34	43-0	2	41	.251	.342	.375	100	1	13-9	.949	-4	89	60	D-33,O-28(13-15-2),1-23	-0.6
1983	Pit N	109	246	37	59	9	0	5	24	49-1	2	43	.240	.365	.337	95	1	15-5	.985	-1	102	122	O-57(5-53-0)/1-7	0.1
1984	Pit N	111	266	37	63	11	1	4	21	40-2	1	42	.237	.338	.331	89	-3	8-1	.989	-6	82	42	O-74(LF)/1-5	-1.1
1985	Pit N	92	117	20	33	8	0	1	9	29-1	0	17	.282	.425	.376	127	7	4-1	.986	-1	63	129	1-19/O-5(3-3-0)	0.6
1986	Pit N	61	93	18	21	2	1	1	8	26-1	0	25	.226	.392	.301	93	1	3-3	1.000	-1	104	0	O-18(16-3-0)/1-7	-0.1
	†NY N	39	58	10	16	3	0	2	7	12-1	2	11	.276	.417	.431	138	4	1-1	1.000	-1	120	0	O-10(8-0-2)/1-8	0.3
	Year	100	151	28	37	5	1	3	15	38-2	2	36	.245	.401	.351	109	4	4-4	1.000	-2	110	0	O-28(24-3-2),1-15	0.2
1987	NY N	88	124	26	38	8	1	3	24	21-3	0	14	.306	.399	.460	136	8	5-3	1.000	-1	87	101	O-25(12-2-13),1-13	0.5
1988	†NY N	68	116	9	17	2	0	0	12	12-0	1	16	.147	.227	.164	16	-13	4-1	1.000	-1	100	147	O-18(13-0-6),1-16	-1.6
1989	NY N	48	60	10	11	2	0	2	7	17-0	0	19	.183	.364	.317	101	1	3-0	.889	-1	93	0	O-10(4-1-5)/1-8	0.0
	†Tor A	28	66	12	15	3	0	4	11	17-1	2	16	.227	.395	.455	143	5	2-0	.944	-1	96	74	D-19/1-2,O-2(RF)	0.4
Total	14	1475	4124	571	1068	191	24	93	460	642-41	20	627	.259	.359	.385	109	77	197-90	.986	-24	100	92	O-868(201-647-30),1-215/D-52	3.9
McALEER, JIMMY James Robert "Loafer" B 7.10.1864 Youngstown, OH D 4.29.1931 Youngstown, OH BR/TR 6/175# d4.24 M11																								
1889	Cle N	110	447	66	105	6	6	0	35	30	4	49	.235	.289	.275	59	-26	37	.955	8	136	237	*O-110(CF)	-2.0
1890	Cle P	86	341	58	91	8	7	1	42	37	1	33	.267	.340	.340	89	-4	21	.940	6	90	109	O-86(CF)	-0.1
1891	Cle N	136	565	97	135	16	11	1	61	49	5	47	.239	.305	.312	77	-18	51	.924	5	88	26	*O-136(124-13-0)	-1.5
1892	†Cle N	149	571	92	136	26	7	4	70	63	4	54	.238	.318	.329	92	-5	40	.948	5	74	133	*O-149(CF)	-0.9
1893	Cle N	91	350	63	83	5	1	2	41	35	4	21	.237	.314	.274	53	-24	32	.928	-1	98	91	*O-91(2-89-0)	-2.6
1894	Cle N	64	253	36	73	15	1	2	40	13	3	17	.289	.331	.379	68	-14	14	.953	3	85	126	O-64(CF)	-1.2
1895	†Cle N	**132**	532	85	144	17	3	0	68	38	6	37	.271	.326	.314	62	-31	32	.934	-2	70	25	*O-132(CF)	-3.4
1896	†Cle N	116	455	70	131	16	4	1	54	47	5	32	.288	.361	.347	82	-11	24	.958	3	107	131	*O-116(CF)	-1.3
1897	Cle N	24	91	6	20	2	0	0	10	7	1		.220	.283	.242	37	-8	4	.947	-0	94	0	O-24(1-23-0)	-0.9
1898	Cle N	106	366	47	87	3	0	0	48	46	5		.238	.331	.246	67	-13	7	.965	1	70	131	*O-104(1-102-1)/2-2	-1.7
1901	Cle A	3	7	0	1	0	0	0	0	0	0		.143	.143	.143	-22	-1	0	1.000	-0	0	0	/O-2(CF),P3M	-0.1
1902	StL A	2	3	0	2	0	0	0	0	0	0		.667	.667	.667	274	1	0	—	-0	0	0	/O-2(0-1-1),M	0.1
1907	StL A	2	0	0	0	0	0	0	0	0	0		—	—	—	—	0	0	—	0			RM	0.0
Total	13	1021	3981	620	1008	114	40	11	469	365	38	290	.253	.322	.310	72	-154	262	.944	28	90	106	*O-1016(128-887-2)/2-2,3P	-15.6
McALEESE, JACK John James B 1877 Sharon, PA D 11.15.1950 New York, NY BR/TR 5-8/?# d8.10																								
1901	Chi A	1	1	0	0	0	0	0	0	0	0		.000	.000	.000	-99	0	0	1.000	0	117	0	/P	0.0
1909	StL A	85	267	33	57	7	0	0	12	32	9		.213	.318	.240	82	-3	18	.910	-1	119	93	O-79(27-32-20)/3-2	-0.8
Total	2	86	268	33	57	7	0	0	12	32	9		.213	.317	.239	82	-3	18	.910	-1	119	93	/O-79(27-32-20),3-2,P	-0.8
McALLESTER, BILL William Lusk B 12.29.1889 Chattanooga, TN D 3.3.1970 Chattanooga, TN BR/TR 6/175# d5.2																								
1913	StL A	49	85	3	13	4	0	0	6	11	0	12	.153	.250	.200	33	-7	2	.908	-2	*110*	*84*	C-39	-0.8
McALLISTER, SPORT Lewis William B 7.23.1874 Austin, MS D 7.17.1962 Wyandotte, MI BB/TR 5-11/180# d8.7 ▲ OF Total (17-LF 10-CF 123-RF)																								
1896	Cle N	8	27	2	6	2	0	0	1	0	1	2	.222	.250	.296	41	-2	1	.500	-1	0	0	/O-4(RF),C-2,P	-0.3
1897	Cle N	43	137	23	30	5	1	0	11	12	1		.219	.287	.270	45	-11	3	.894	-4	59	0	O-28(1-3-24)/S-4,P-4,1-3,C-2,2	-1.3
1898	Cle N	17	57	8	13	3	1	0	9	5	0		.228	.290	.316	75	-2	0	.941	0	87	0	/P-9,O-8(0-4-4)	-0.1
1899	Cle N	113	418	29	99	6	8	1	31	19	2		.237	.273	.297	61	-24	5	.943	-11	94	107	O-79(9-3-70),C-17/3-7,1-6,S-3,P-3,2	-3.4
1901	Det A	90	306	45	92	9	4	3	57	15	5		.301	.344	.386	97	-2	17	.898	-13	*107*	*92*	C-35,1-28,O-11(5-0-6),3-10/S-3	-1.1
1902	Det A	21	67	8	14	1	0	1	8	2	1		.209	.243	.269	41	-6	0	1.000	0	307	93	/1-5,S-5,2-3,C-2,3-2,O(LF)	-0.5
	Bal A	3	11	0	1	0	0	0	1	1	0		.091	.167	.091	-26	-2	0	.923	-0	118	0	/2-2,1	-0.2
	Det A	45	162	11	34	4	2	0	24	3	1		.210	.229	.259	34	-15	1	.991	-1	307	93	1-21,O-11(1-0-10)/C-7,3-4,S	-1.5
	Year	69	240	19	49	5	2	1	33	6	2		.204	.230	.254	33	-22	1	.992	-1	105	96	1-27,O-12(2-0-10)/C-9,S-6,3-6,2-5,D	-2.2
1903	Det A	78	265	31	69	8	2	0	22	10	4		.260	.297	.306	84	-5	5	.888	-6	96	80	S-46,C-18/O-5(RF),3-4,1	-0.8
Total	7	418	1450	157	358	38	18	5	164	67	15	2	.247	.287	.308	67	-69	32	.914	-35	87	89	O-147R/C-83,1-65,S-62,3-27,P-17,2	-9.2
McANANY, JIM James B 9.4.1936 Los Angeles, CA BR/TR 5-10/196# d9.19																								
1958	Chi A	5	13	0	0	0	0	0	0	0-0	0	5	.000	.000	.000	-99	-4	0-0	1.000	0	126	0	/O-3(RF)	-0.4
1959	†Chi A	67	210	22	58	9	3	0	27	19-4	1	26	.276	.339	.348	90	-3	2-1	.966	0	94	171	O-67(4-2-63)	-0.5
1960	Chi A	3	2	0	0	0	0	0	0	0-0	0	2	.000	.000	.000	-99	-1	0-0	—	0			H	-0.1
1961	Chi N	11	10	1	3	1	0	0	0	1-0	0	3	.300	.364	.400	101	0	0-0	—	-0	0	0	/O(RF)	0.0
1962	Chi N	7	6	0	0	0	0	0	0	1-0	0	2	.000	.143	.000	-56	-1	0-0	—	0			H	-0.1
Total	5	93	241	23	61	10	3	0	27	21-4	1	38	.253	.316	.320	75	-9	2-1	.968	0	96	161	/O-71(4-2-67)	-1.1
McATEE, BUB Michael James "Butch" B 3.1845 Troy, NY D 10.18.1876 Troy, NY TR 5-9/160# d5.8																								
1871	Chi NA	26	135	34	37	8	2	0	10	5	2		.274	.300	.363	81	-5	5-3	.943	1	117	130	*1-26	-0.2
1872	Tro NA	**25**	126	30	28	3	1	0	15	3	2		.222	.240	.262	54	-7	0-2	.948	1	67	70	1-25	-0.4
Total	2 NA	51	261	64	65	11	3	0	25	8	4		.249	.271	.314	69	-12	5-5	.000	2	93	101	/1-51	-0.6
McAULEY, IKE James Earl B 8.19.1891 Wichita, KS D 4.6.1928 Des Moines, IA BR/TR 5-9.5/150# d9.10																								
1914	Pit N	15	24	3	3	0	0	0	0	0	0	8	.125	.125	.125	-27	-4	0	.900	0	104	266	/S-5,3-3,2-2	-0.4

Year	Tm Lg	G	AB	R	H	2B	3B	HR	RBI	BB-IB	HP	SO	AVG	OBP	SLG	AOPS	ABR	SB-CS	FA	FR	Rng	Thr	G at Pos	BFW
1915	Pit N	5	15	0	2	1	0	0	0	0	0	6	.133	.133	.200	0	-2	0	.917	-1	90	90	/S-5	-0.3
1916	Pit N	4	8	1	2	0	0	0	1	0	0	1	.250	.250	.250	53	0	0	.938	0	83	178	/S-4	0.0
1917	StL N	3	7	0	2	0	0	0	1	0	0	1	.286	.286	.286	78	0	0	.833	-1	58	0	/S-3	-0.2
1925	Chi N	37	125	10	35	7	2	0	11	11	1	12	.280	.343	.368	80	-3	1-0	.949	-7	79	95	S-37	-0.6
Total	5	64	179	14	44	8	2	0	13	11	1	28	.246	.293	.313	62	-9	1-0	.940	-9	81	109	/S-54,3-3,2-2	-1.5

McAULIFFE, GENE Eugene Leo B 2.28.1872 Randolph, MA D 4.29.1953 Randolph, MA BR/TR 6-1/180# d8.17

Year	Tm Lg	G	AB	R	H	2B	3B	HR	RBI	BB-IB	HP	SO	AVG	OBP	SLG	AOPS	ABR	SB-CS	FA	FR	Rng	Thr	G at Pos	BFW
1904	Bos N	1	2	0	1	0	0	0	0	0	0		.500	.500	.500	217	0	0	.667	-1	*75*	*156*	/C	0.0

McAULIFFE, DICK Richard John B 11.29.1939 Hartford, CT BL/TR 5-11/176# d9.17

Year	Tm Lg	G	AB	R	H	2B	3B	HR	RBI	BB-IB	HP	SO	AVG	OBP	SLG	AOPS	ABR	SB-CS	FA	FR	Rng	Thr	G at Pos	BFW
1960	Det A	8	27	2	7	0	1	0	1	2-0	0	6	.259	.310	.333	72	-1	0-0	.884	0	107	145	/S-7	-0.1
1961	Det A	80	285	36	73	12	4	6	33	24-0	4	39	.256	.322	.389	87	-6	2-3	.933	-20	80	103	S-55,3-22	-2.2
1962	Det A	139	471	50	124	20	5	12	63	64-3	0	76	.263	.349	.403	99	0	4-2	.965	-25	78	71	2-70,3-49,S-16	-1.8
1963	Det A	150	568	77	149	18	6	13	61	64-1	0	75	.262	.334	.384	98	-1	11-5	.963	-21	91	91	*S-133,2-15	-0.9
1964	Det A	162	557	85	134	18	7	24	66	77-8	3	96	.241	.334	.427	109	7	8-5	.958	-7	100	89	*S-160	1.5
1965	Det A★	113	404	61	105	13	6	15	54	49-4	2	62	.260	.342	.433	118	9	6-9	.956	-12	89	95	*S-112	0.6
1966	Det A★	124	430	83	118	16	8	23	56	66-2	3	80	.274	.373	.509	148	28	5-7	.964	-5	98	82	*S-105,3-15	3.2
1967	Det A★	153	557	92	133	16	7	22	65	105-4	7	118	.239	.364	.411	126	22	6-5	.965	-4	97	**115**	*2-145,S-43	3.3
1968	†Det A	151	570	**95**	142	24	10	16	56	82-8	2	99	.249	.344	.411	125	19	8-7	.986	-21	88	105	*2-148/S-5	1.1
1969	Det A	74	271	49	71	10	5	11	33	47-1	0	41	.262	.369	.458	125	10	2-5	.976	5	102	92	2-72	1.9
1970	Det A	146	530	73	124	21	1	12	50	101-7	3	62	.234	.358	.345	95	0	5-6	.975	14	105	91	*2-127,S-15,3-12	2.2
1971	Det A	128	477	67	99	16	6	18	57	53-4	5	67	.208	.293	.379	86	-10	4-1	.987	11	101	106	*2-123/S-7	1.1
1972	†Det A	122	408	47	98	16	3	8	30	59-7	2	59	.240	.339	.353	103	3	0-0	.975	-5	90	94	*2-116/S-3,3	0.7
1973	Det A	106	343	39	94	18	1	12	47	49-5	1	52	.274	.366	.437	118	9	0-4	.986	3	103	96	*2-102/S-2,D	1.8
1974	Bos A	100	272	32	57	13	1	5	24	39-5	1	40	.210	.310	.320	76	-7	2-0	.971	-6	91	99	2-53,3-40/S-3,D-3	-1.0
1975	Bos A	7	15	0	2	0	0	0	1	1-0	0	2	.133	.188	.133	-7	-2	0-0	.769	-2	73	105	/3-7	-0.5
Total	16	1763	6185	888	1530	231	71	197	697	882-59	33	974	.247	.343	.403	108	80	63-59	.977	-94	95	98	2-971,S-666,3-146/D-4	10.9

McAVOY, GEORGE George Robert B 3.12.1884 E.Liverpool, OH d7.17

Year	Tm Lg	G	AB	R	H	2B	3B	HR	RBI	BB-IB	HP	SO	AVG	OBP	SLG	AOPS	ABR	SB-CS	FA	FR	Rng	Thr	G at Pos	BFW
1914	Phi N	1	1	0	0	0	0	0	0	0	0	0	.000	.000	.000	-94	0	0	—	0			H	0.0

McAVOY, WICKEY James Eugene B 10.22.1894 Rochester, NY D 7.6.1973 Rochester, NY BR/TR 5-11/172# d9.29

Year	Tm Lg	G	AB	R	H	2B	3B	HR	RBI	BB-IB	HP	SO	AVG	OBP	SLG	AOPS	ABR	SB-CS	FA	FR	Rng	Thr	G at Pos	BFW
1913	Phi A	4	9	0	1	0	0	0	0	0	1	4	.111	.200	.111	-9	-1	0	1.000	1	*132*	*156*	/C-4	0.0
1914	Phi A	8	16	1	2	0	1	0	0	0	0	4	.125	.125	.250	13	-2	0	.971	0	*94*	*127*	/C-8	-0.1
1915	Phi A	68	184	12	35	7	2	0	6	11	0	32	.190	.236	.250	47	-13	0-2	.931	-7	*64*	*150*	C-64	-1.7
1917	Phi A	10	24	1	6	1	0	1	4	0	0	3	.250	.250	.417	105	0	0	.955	1	*85*	*182*	/C-8	0.1
1918	Phi A	83	271	14	66	5	3	0	32	13	2	23	.244	.283	.284	70	-11	5	.960	4	*87*	***119***	C-74/P1O(RF)	-0.1
1919	Phi A	62	170	10	24	5	2	0	11	14	0	21	.141	.207	.194	13	-20	1	.973	-3	*76*	*130*	C-57	-2.1
Total	6	235	674	38	134	18	8	1	53	38	3	87	.199	.245	.254	47	-47	6-2	.954	-4	*79*	*133*	C-215/O(RF)1P	-3.9

McBRIDE, ALGIE Algernon Griggs B 5.23.1869 Washington, DC D 1.10.1956 Georgetown, OH BL/TL 5-9/152# d5.12

Year	Tm Lg	G	AB	R	H	2B	3B	HR	RBI	BB-IB	HP	SO	AVG	OBP	SLG	AOPS	ABR	SB-CS	FA	FR	Rng	Thr	G at Pos	BFW
1896	Chi N	9	29	2	7	1	1	1	7	7	0	3	.241	.389	.448	116	1	0	.917	-0	73	0	/O-9(LF)	0.0
1898	Cin N	120	486	94	147	14	12	2	43	51	12		.302	.383	.393	114	10	16	.959	3	105	75	*O-120(4-115-1)	0.4
1899	Cin N	64	251	57	87	12	5	1	23	30	7		.347	.431	.446	138	15	5	.950	-1	87	84	O-64(5-45-14)	0.9
1900	Cin N	112	436	59	120	15	8	4	59	25	4		.275	.320	.374	94	-5	12	.915	-5	73	140	*O-110(14-10-86)	-1.5
1901	Cin N	30	123	19	29	7	0	2	18	7	1		.236	.282	.341	86	-2	0	.968	-2	28	0	O-28(11-19-0)	-0.5
	NY N	68	264	27	74	11	0	2	29	12	2		.280	.317	.345	95	-2	3	.948	-3	100	135	O-65(RF)	-0.7
	Year	98	387	46	103	18	0	4	47	19	3		.266	.306	.344	92	-4	3	.956	-5	78	93	O-93(11-19-65)	-1.2
Total	5	403	1589	258	464	60	26	12	179	132	26	3	.292	.356	.385	108	17	36	.946	-9	86	96	O-396(43-189-166)	-1.4

McBRIDE, BAKE Arnold Ray B 2.3.1949 Fulton, MO BL/TR 6-2/190# d7.26

Year	Tm Lg	G	AB	R	H	2B	3B	HR	RBI	BB-IB	HP	SO	AVG	OBP	SLG	AOPS	ABR	SB-CS	FA	FR	Rng	Thr	G at Pos	BFW
1973	StL N	40	63	8	19	3	0	0	5	4-0	2	10	.302	.352	.349	98	0	0-1	.976	2	136	132	O-17(1-16-0)	0.1
1974	StL N	150	559	81	173	19	5	6	56	43-9	13	57	.309	.369	.394	115	12	30-11	.990	1	105	97	*O-144(CF)	1.2
1975	StL N	116	413	70	124	10	9	5	36	34-1	1	52	.300	.354	.404	107	3	26-8	.990	4	113	63	*O-107(CF)	0.7
1976	StL N☆	72	272	40	91	13	4	3	24	18-0	6	28	.335	.386	.445	135	12	10-5	.981	4	116	118	O-66(CF)	1.6
1977	StL N	43	122	21	32	5	1	4	20	7-2	0	19	.262	.298	.418	93	-2	9-3	1.000	-3	75	118	O-33(CF)	-0.5
	†Phi N	85	280	55	95	20	5	11	41	25-2	3	25	.339	.392	.564	149	19	27-4	.986	2	102	125	O-73(0-21-54)	2.3
	Year	128	402	76	127	25	6	15	61	32-4	3	44	.316	.364	.520	133	18	36-7	.990	-2	94	123	*O-106(0-54-54)	1.8
1978	†Phi N	122	472	68	127	20	4	10	49	28-3	5	68	.269	.315	.392	96	-4	28-3	**.996**	4	108	88	*O-119(0-1-118)	-0.1
1979	Phi N	151	582	82	163	16	12	12	60	41-3	4	77	.280	.328	.411	98	-3	25-14	.989	13	122	103	*O-147(RF)	0.3
1980	†Phi N	137	554	68	171	33	10	9	87	26-4	5	58	.309	.342	.453	115	10	13-10	.990	2	112	53	*O-133(0-1-133)	0.5
1981	†Phi N	58	221	26	60	17	1	2	21	11-1	0	25	.271	.303	.385	91	-3	5-0	.987	-4	83	51	O-56(RF)	-0.9
1982	Cle A	27	85	8	31	3	3	0	13	2-1	0	12	.365	.375	.471	132	3	2-2	1.000	-1	103	0	O-22(RF)	0.1
1983	Cle A	70	230	21	67	8	1	1	18	9-2	1	26	.291	.318	.348	81	-6	8-2	.977	1	105	137	O-46(RF),D-15	-0.6
Total	11	1071	3853	548	1153	167	55	63	430	248-28	40	457	.299	.345	.420	109	41	183-63	.989	24	109	88	O-963(1-389-576)/D-15	4.7

McBRIDE, GEORGE George Florian B 11.20.1880 Milwaukee, WI D 7.2.1973 Milwaukee, WI BR/TR 5-11/170# d9.12 M1 C3

Year	Tm Lg	G	AB	R	H	2B	3B	HR	RBI	BB-IB	HP	SO	AVG	OBP	SLG	AOPS	ABR	SB-CS	FA	FR	Rng	Thr	G at Pos	BFW
1901	Mil A	3	12	0	2	0	0	0	0	1	0		.167	.231	.167	12	-1	0	1.000	0	86	201	/S-3	-0.1
1905	Pit N	27	87	9	19	4	0	0	7	6	1		.218	.277	.264	60	-4	2	.902	-2	93	171	3-17/S-8	-0.6
	StL N	81	281	22	61	1	2	2	34	14	4		.217	.264	.256	57	-16	10	.938	-4	106	90	S-80/1	-1.7
	Year	108	368	31	80	5	2	2	41	20	5		.217	.267	.258	58	-20	12	.935	-5	106	90	S-88,3-17/1	-2.3
1906	StL N	90	313	24	53	8	2	0	13	17	1		.169	.215	.208	33	-25	5	.944	2	103	101	S-90	-2.3
1908	Was A	**155**	518	47	120	10	6	0	34	41	3		.232	.292	.274	92	-5	12	.948	33	106	**121**	*S-155	3.7
1909	Was A	**156**	504	38	118	16	0	0	34	36	7		.234	.294	.266	81	-10	17	**.935**	13	100	101	*S-156	0.9
1910	Was A	154	514	54	118	19	4	1	55	61	8		.230	.321	.288	95	0	11	.939	**33**	107	110	*S-154	4.1
1911	Was A	**154**	557	58	131	11	4	0	59	52	10		.235	.312	.269	64	-26	15	.941	27	110	106	*S-154	1.2
1912	Was A	152	521	56	118	13	7	1	52	38	7		.226	.288	.284	63	-26	17	**.941**	**28**	105	116	*S-152	1.2
1913	Was A	150	499	52	107	18	7	1	52	43	7	46	.214	.286	.285	66	-22	12	**.960**	9	100	109	*S-150	-0.3
1914	Was A	156	503	49	102	12	4	0	24	43	6	70	.203	.274	.243	53	-29	12-14	**.958**	10	97	**129**	*S-156	-1.2
1915	Was A	146	476	54	97	8	6	1	30	29	1	60	.204	.251	.252	50	-32	10-5	**.968**	7	96	98	*S-146	-1.5
1916	Was A	139	466	36	106	15	4	1	36	23	5	58	.227	.271	.283	67	-21	8	.957	14	101	104	*S-139	0.3
1917	Was A	50	141	6	27	3	0	0	9	10	4	17	.191	.265	.213	46	-9	1	.943	0	96	91	S-41/3-6,2-2	-0.7
1918	Was A	18	53	2	7	0	0	0	1	0	0	11	.132	.132	.132	-21	-8	1	.986	1	106	84	S-14/2-2	-0.7
1919	Was A	15	40	3	8	1	1	0	4	3	0	6	.200	.256	.275	49	-3	0	.932	-0	100	41	S-15	-0.2
1920	Was A	13	41	6	9	1	0	0	3	2	0	3	.220	.256	.244	34	-4	0-0	.966	-3	84	62	S-13	-0.6
Total	16	1659	5526	516	1203	140	47	7	447	419	64	271	.218	.281	.264	65	-241	133-19	.948	168	102	108	*S-1626/3-23,2-4,1	1.5

McBRIDE, JOHN John F. d10.12

Year	Tm Lg	G	AB	R	H	2B	3B	HR	RBI	BB-IB	HP	SO	AVG	OBP	SLG	AOPS	ABR	SB-CS	FA	FR	Rng	Thr	G at Pos	BFW
1890	Phi AA	1	2	0	0	0	0	0	0	0	0		.000	.000	.000	-99	-1	0	1.000	1	632	0	/O(CF)	0.0

McBRIDE, TOM Thomas Raymond B 11.2.1914 Bonham, TX D 12.26.2001 Wichita Falls, TX BR/TR 6/190# d4.23

Year	Tm Lg	G	AB	R	H	2B	3B	HR	RBI	BB-IB	HP	SO	AVG	OBP	SLG	AOPS	ABR	SB-CS	FA	FR	Rng	Thr	G at Pos	BFW
1943	Bos A	26	96	11	23	3	1	0	7	7	0	3	.240	.291	.292	70	-4	2-0	.984	-0	96	109	O-24(0-21-3)	-0.5
1944	Bos A	71	216	29	53	7	3	0	24	8	1	13	.245	.276	.306	67	-10	4-0	.992	4	103	203	O-57(23-14-22)/1-5	-0.9
1945	Bos A	100	344	38	105	11	7	1	47	26	0	17	.305	.354	.387	112	4	2-2	.984	1	95	142	O-81(15-50-22),1-11	0.2
1946	†Bos A	61	153	21	46	5	2	0	19	9	0	6	.301	.340	.359	90	-2	0-1	1.000	-2	93	37	O-43(10-2-32)	-0.6
1947	Bos A	2	5	0	1	0	0	0	0	0	0	0	.200	.200	.200	11	-1	0-0	1.000	1	80	1087	/O(RF)	0.0
	Was A	56	166	19	45	4	2	0	15	15	0	9	.271	.331	.319	84	-4	3-1	.972	-0	104	66	O-51(43-4-5)/3	-0.7
	Year	58	171	19	46	4	2	0	15	15	0	9	.269	.328	.316	81	-5	3-1	.973	1	103	95	O-52(43-4-6)/3	-0.7
1948	Was A	92	206	22	53	9	1	1	29	28	0	15	.257	.346	.325	81	-5	2-2	.983	5	108	204	O-55(25-0-30)	-0.2
Total	6	408	1186	140	326	39	16	2	141	93	1	63	.275	.328	.340	88	-22	13-6	.985	9	100	141	O-312(116-91-115)/1-16,3	-2.7

McCABE, SWAT James Arthur B 11.20.1881 Towanda, PA D 12.9.1944 Bristol, CT BL/TR 5-10/187# d9.23

Year	Tm Lg	G	AB	R	H	2B	3B	HR	RBI	BB-IB	HP	SO	AVG	OBP	SLG	AOPS	ABR	SB-CS	FA	FR	Rng	Thr	G at Pos	BFW
1909	Cin N	3	11	2	6	1	0	0	0	0	0		.545	.545	.636	269	2	1	.625	-1	0	0	/O-3(CF)	0.1
1910	Cin N	13	35	3	9	1	0	0	5	1	1	2	.257	.297	.286	73	-1	0	1.000	1	102	172	/O-9(RF)	-0.1
Total	2	16	46	5	15	2	0	0	5	1	1	2	.326	.354	.370	118	1	1	.875	-0	74	125	/O-12(0-3-9)	0.0

Year	Tm Lg	G	AB	R	H	2B	3B	HR	RBI	BB-IB	HP	SO	AVG	OBP	SLG	AOPS	ABR	SB-CS	FA	FR	Rng	Thr	G at Pos	BFW
McCABE, JOE Joseph Robert B 8.27.1938 Indianapolis, IN BR/TR 6/190# d4.18																								
1964	Min A	14	19	1	3	0	0	0	2	0-0	0	8	.158	.150	.158	-12	-3	0-0	1.000	0	*162*	*110*	C-12	-0.3
1965	Was A	14	27	1	5	0	0	1	5	4-0	0	13	.185	.281	.296	68	-1	1-0	.972	-1	*99*	*201*	C-11	-0.2
Total	2	28	46	2	8	0	0	1	7	4-0	0	21	.174	.231	.239	36	-4	1-0	.986	-1	*126*	*162*	/C-23	-0.5
McCABE, BILL William Francis B 10.28.1892 Chicago, IL D 9.2.1966 Chicago, IL BB/TR (BL 1918) 5-9.5/180# d4.16																								
1918	†Chi N	29	45	9	8	0	1	0	5	4	0	7	.178	.245	.222	42	-3	2	.939	3	126	24	2-13/O-4(1-0-2)	0.0
1919	Chi N	33	84	8	13	3	1	0	5	9	2	15	.155	.253	.214	41	-6	3	.950	-1	101	72	O-20(0-1-19)/S-4,3	-0.9
1920	Chi N	3	2	1	1	0	0	0	0	0	0	0	.500	.500	.500	184	0	0-0	—	0			H	0.0
	†Bro N	41	68	10	10	0	0	0	3	2	0	6	.147	.171	.147	-8	-9	1-2	.882	0	111	92	S-13/O-6(LF),2-4,3-3	-1.0
	Year	44	70	11	11	0	0	0	3	2	0	6	.157	.181	.157	-2	-9	1-2	.882	0	111	92	S-13/O-6(LF),2-4,3-3	-1.0
Total	3	106	199	28	32	3	2	0	13	15	2	28	.161	.227	.196	26	-18	6-2	.943	2	103	86	/O-30(7-1-21),S-17,2-17,3-4	-1.9
McCAFFERY, HARRY Harry Charles B 11.25.1858 St.Louis, MO D 4.19.1928 St.Louis, MO BR/TR 5-10.5/185# d6.15 U1 ▲																								
1882	Lou AA	1	4	1	1	0	0	0		0			.250	.250	.250	73	0		1.000	-0	44	0	/2	0.0
	StL AA	38	153	23	42	8	6	0		3			.275	.288	.405	127	4		.891	3	196	337	O-23(5-0-18)/2-8,3-7,1	0.6
	Year	39	157	24	43	8	6	0		3			.274	.287	.401	125	3		.891	3	196	337	O-23(5-0-18)/2-9,3-7,1	0.6
1883	StL AA	5	18	0	1	0	0	0	1	1			.056	.105	.056	-44	-3		.900	2	332	2340	/O-5(CF)	-0.1
1885	Cin AA	1	5	0	0	0	0	0	0	0	0		.000	.000	.000	-98	-1		.000	-0	0	0	/P	0.0
Total	3	45	180	24	44	8	6	0	1	4	0		.244	.261	.356	101	0		.893	4	218	665	/O-28(5-5-18),2-9,3-7,P1	0.5
McCAFFREY, SPARROW Charles P. B 1868 Philadelphia, PA D 4.29.1894 Philadelphia, PA ?/120# d8.13																								
1889	Col AA	2	1	1	1	0	0	0	0	1	0	0	1.000	1.000	1.000	495	1	0	—	-0			/C-2	0.0
McCALL, BRIAN Brian Allen "Bam" B 1.25.1943 Kentfield, CA BL/TL 5-10/170# d9.18																								
1962	Chi A	4	8	2	3	0	0	2	3	0-0	0	2	.375	.375	1.125	287	2	0-0	1.000	0	122	0	/O(CF)	0.2
1963	Chi A	3	7	1	0	0	0	0	0	1-0	0	2	.000	.125	.000	-62	-2	0-0	1.000	-0	99	0	/O-2(RF)	-0.2
Total	2	7	15	3	3	0	0	2	3	1-0	0	4	.200	.250	.600	126	0	0-0	1.000	0	110	0	/O-3(0-1-2)	0.0
McCANDLESS, JACK Scott Cook B 5.5.1891 Pittsburgh, PA D 8.17.1961 Pittsburgh, PA BL/TR 6/170# d9.10																								
1914	Bal F	11	31	5	8	0	1	0	1	3	1	0	.258	.343	.323	79	-1	0	1.000	-0	94	91	/O-8(0-1-7)	-0.2
1915	Bal F	117	406	47	87	6	7	5	34	41	6	99	.214	.296	.300	66	-25	9	.945	1	100	111	*O-105(23-58-25)	-3.3
Total	2	128	437	52	95	6	8	5	35	44	7	99	.217	.299	.302	67	-26	9	.948	1	100	110	O-113(23-59-32)	-3.5
McCANN, EMMETT Robert Emmett B 3.4.1902 Philadelphia, PA D 4.15.1937 Philadelphia, PA BR/TR 5-11/150# d4.19																								
1920	Phi A	13	34	4	9	1	1	0	3	3	1	1	.265	.342	.353	83	-1	0-1	.907	-0	99	79	S-11	-0.1
1921	Phi A	52	157	15	35	5	0	0	15	4	0	6	.223	.242	.255	27	-18	2-1	.949	-3	101	81	S-32/3-9,2-2,1	-1.6
1926	Bos A	6	3	0	0	0	0	0	0	1	0	1	.000	.250	.000	-32	-1	0-0	1.000	-0	0	0	/S3	-0.1
Total	3	71	194	19	44	6	1	0	18	8	1	8	.227	.261	.268	36	-20	2-2	.939	-4	100	80	/S-44,3-10,2-2,1	-1.8
McCARDELL, ROGER Roger Morton B 8.29.1932 Gorsuch Mills, MD D 11.13.1996 Perry Point, MD BR/TR 6/200# d5.8																								
1959	SF N	4	4	0	0	0	0	0	0	0-0	0	0	.000	.000	.000	-99	-1	0-0	1.000	0	*0*	*0*	/C-3	-0.1
McCARREN, BILL William Joseph B 11.4.1895 Fortenia, PA D 9.11.1983 Denver, CO BR/TR 5-11.5/170# d5.4																								
1923	Bro N	69	216	28	53	10	1	3	27	22	4	39	.245	.326	.343	79	-6	0-1	.927	-2	92	102	3-66/O(RF)	-0.5
McCARTHY, ALEX Alexander George B 5.12.1888 Chicago, IL D 3.12.1978 Salisbury, MD BR/TR 5-9/150# d10.7																								
1910	Pit N	3	12	1	1	0	1	0	0	0	0	2	.083	.083	.250	-3	-2	0	.875	0	115	187	/S-3	-0.2
1911	Pit N	50	150	18	36	5	1	2	31	14	0	24	.240	.305	.327	74	-6	4	.981	3	91	112	S-33,2-11/3O(LF)	0.0
1912	Pit N	111	401	53	111	12	4	1	41	30	3	26	.277	.332	.334	84	-9	8	.962	-9	95	119	*2-105/3-4	-1.6
1913	Pit N	31	74	7	15	5	0	0	10	7	3	7	.203	.298	.270	66	-3	1-2	.902	-1	93	89	S-12,3-12/2-6	-0.4
1914	Pit N	57	173	14	26	0	1	1	14	6	3	17	.150	.192	.179	11	-20	2	.975	6	118	139	3-36,2-10/S-6	-1.4
1915	Pit N	21	49	3	10	0	1	0	3	5	1	10	.204	.291	.245	64	-2	1-2	.950	1	90	67	/2-9,S-5,3-4,1	-0.2
	Chi N	23	72	4	19	3	0	1	6	5	2	7	.264	.329	.347	105	1	2-3	.972	7	105	165	2-12,3-12/S	0.8
	Year	44	121	7	29	3	1	1	9	10	3	17	.240	.313	.306	88	-2	3-5	.964	8	99	126	2-21,3-16/S-6,1	0.6
1916	Chi N	37	107	10	26	2	3	0	6	11	5	7	.243	.341	.318	93	0	1	.931	-2	106	76	2-34/S-3	-0.2
	Pit N	50	146	11	29	3	0	0	3	15	2	10	.199	.282	.219	54	-7	3	.955	-4	84	95	S-39/2-7,3-5	-1.0
	Year	87	253	21	55	5	3	0	9	26	7	17	.217	.308	.261	72	-7	4	.951	-6	83	92	S-42,2-41/3-5	-1.2
1917	Pit N	49	151	15	33	4	0	0	8	11	1	13	.219	.276	.245	58	-7	1	.964	3	82	229	3-26,2-13/S-9	-0.3
Total	8	432	1335	136	306	34	11	5	122	104	20	123	.229	.295	.282	67	-55	23-7	.957	3	100	111	2-207,S-111,3-100/1O(LF)	-4.5
McCARTHY, JERRY Jerome Francis B 5.23.1923 Brooklyn, NY D 10.3.1965 Oceanside, NY BL/TL 6-1/205# d6.19																								
1948	StL A	2	3	0	1	0	0	0	0	0	0	0	.333	.333	.333	76	0	0-0	.600	-1	0	0	/1-2	-0.1
McCARTHY, JACK John Arthur B 3.26.1869 Gilbertville, MA D 9.11.1931 Chicago, IL BL/TL 5-9/155# d8.3																								
1893	Cin N	49	195	28	55	8	3	0	22	22	0	7	.282	.355	.354	86	-4	6	.887	-1	88	0	O-47(10-1-37)/1-2	-0.6
1894	Cin N	40	167	29	45	9	1	0	21	17	3	6	.269	.348	.335	63	-10	3	.895	2	142	0	O-25(5-0-20),1-15	-0.7
1898	Pit N	137	537	75	155	13	12	4	78	34	4		.289	.336	.380	107	3	7	.935	4	98	93	*O-137(LF)	-0.5
1899	Pit N	139	565	109	173	22	17	4	69	39	4		.306	.355	.427	114	9	28	.962	-5	87	105	*O-139(133-6-0)	-0.8
1900	Chi N	124	503	68	148	16	7	0	48	24	2		.294	.329	.354	92	-7	22	.944	-1	117	90	*O-123(96-1-26)	-1.6
1901	Cle A	86	343	60	110	14	7	0	32	30	4		.321	.382	.402	123	12	9	.949	1	83	183	O-86(85-1-0)	0.7
1902	Cle A	95	359	45	102	31	5	0	41	24	0		.284	.329	.398	105	3	12	.944	-4	50	0	O-95(LF)	-0.6
1903	Cle A	108	415	47	110	20	8	0	43	19	1		.265	.299	.352	96	-2	15	.964	-3	84	173	*O-108(LF)	-1.2
	Chi N	24	101	11	28	5	0	0	14	4	0		.277	.305	.327	82	-3	8	.947	-1	103	154	O-24(LF)	-0.5
1904	Chi N	115	432	36	114	14	2	0	51	23	4		.264	.307	.306	89	-6	14	.961	-7	56	0	*O-115(25-90-0)	-1.9
1905	Chi N	59	170	16	47	4	3	0	14	10	1		.276	.320	.335	92	-2	8	.986	2	191	410	O-37(18-19-0)/1-6	-0.2
1906	Bro N	91	322	23	98	13	1	0	35	20	1		.304	.347	.351	128	10	9	.924	2	122	38	O-86(83-3-0)	0.8
1907	Bro N	25	91	4	20	2	0	0	8	2	0		.220	.237	.242	54	-5	4	1.000	-3	0	0	O-25(LF)	-1.1
Total	12	1092	4200	551	1205	171	66	8	476	268	24	13	.287	.333	.365	101	-2	145	.946	-12	91	91	*O-1047(844-121-83)/1-23	-8.2
McCARTHY, JOHNNY John Joseph B 1.7.1910 Chicago, IL D 9.13.1973 Mundelein, IL BL/TL 6-1.5/185# d9.2 Mil 1943-45																								
1934	Bro N	17	39	7	7	2	0	1	5	2	0	2	.179	.220	.308	42	-3	0	.961	1	157	170	1-13	-0.4
1935	Bro N	22	48	9	12	1	1	0	4	2	0	9	.250	.280	.313	60	-3	1	.982	-3	0	135	1-19	-0.7
1936	NY N	4	16	1	7	0	0	1	2	0	0	1	.438	.438	.625	185	2	1	.981	1	213	157	/1-4	0.2
1937	†NY N	114	420	53	117	19	3	10	65	24	3	37	.279	.322	.410	96	-3	2	.987	3	112	**113**	*1-110	-1.0
1938	NY N	134	470	55	128	13	4	8	59	39	1	28	.272	.329	.368	91	-7	3	.993	-3	92	114	*1-125	-2.1
1939	NY N	50	80	12	21	6	1	1	11	3	1	8	.262	.298	.400	85	-2	0	1.000	-2	28	130	1-12/O-4(0-1-3),P	-0.5
1940	NY N	51	67	6	16	4	0	0	5	2	0	8	.239	.261	.299	53	-4	0	1.000	1	139	131	/1-6	-0.4
1941	NY N	14	40	1	13	3	0	0	12	3	0	0	.325	.372	.400	115	1	0	.987	1	143	60	/1-8,O(LF)	0.1
1943	Bos N	78	313	32	95	24	6	2	33	10	1	19	.304	.327	.438	122	7	1	.996	-1	99	79	1-78	0.2
1946	Bos N	2	7	0	1	0	0	0	1	2	0	0	.143	.333	.143	37	0	0	1.000	-1	0	209	/1-2	-0.1
1948	NY N	56	57	6	15	0	1	2	12	3	0	2	.263	.300	.404	88	-1	0	.966	-1	56	99	/1-6	-0.2
Total	11	542	1557	182	432	72	16	25	209	90	6	114	.277	.319	.392	95	-13	8	.990	-2	99	109	1-383/O-5(1-1-3),P	-4.9
McCARTHY, JOE Joseph N. B 12.25.1881 Syracuse, NY D 1.12.1937 Syracuse, NY BR/TR d9.27																								
1905	NY A	1	2	0	0	0	0	0	0	0	0		.000	.000	.000	-90	0	0	1.000	-0	*59*	*210*	/C	-0.1
1906	StL N	15	37	3	9	2	0	0	2	2	0		.243	.282	.297	84	-1	0	.984	-1	*77*	*99*	C-15	-0.1
Total	2	16	39	3	9	2	0	0	2	2	0		.231	.268	.282	74	-1	0	.985	-1	*76*	*105*	/C-16	-0.2
McCARTHY, TOMMY Thomas Francis Michael B 7.24.1863 Boston, MA D 8.5.1922 Boston, MA BR/TR 5-7/170# d7.10 M1 HF1957 ▲ OF Total (514-LF 32-CF 647-RF)																								
1884	Bos U	53	209	37	45	2	2	0		6			.215	.237	.244	47	-20		.794	0	104	65	O-48(41-2-7)/P-7	-1.7
1885	Bos N	40	148	16	27	2	0	0	11	5		25	.182	.209	.196	33	-11		.865	1	96	0	O-40(39-0-1)	-1.0
1886	Phi N	8	27	6	5	2	1	0	3	2		3	.185	.241	.333	73	-1	1	.818	-1	82	0	/O-8(RF),P	-0.1
1887	Phi N	18	70	7	13	4	0	0	6	2	1	5	.186	.219	.243	27	-7	15	.897	-7	95	0	/O-8(6-2-0),2-5,S-3,3-2	-1.2
1888	†StL AA	131	511	107	140	20	3	1	68	38	3		.274	.328	.331	100	-1	93	.931	26	**189**	**306**	*O-131(0-12-119)/P-2	2.1
1889	StL AA	**140**	604	136	176	24	7	2	63	46	6	26	.291	.348	.364	91	-10	57	.893	12	138	**200**	*O-140(1-3-137)/2-2,P	0.1
1890	StL AA	133	548	137	192	28	9	6	69	66	11		.350	.430	.467	144	30	**83**	.893	6	107	135	*O-102(2-0-100),3-32/2M	3.1
1891	StL AA	134	570	124	176	20	6	8	92	49	10	19	.309	.374	.407	107	2	37	.898	1	124	129	*O-112(7-0-106),2-14,S-12/3-2,P	0.2

Year	Tm Lg	G	AB	R	H	2B	3B	HR	RBI	BB-IB	HP	SO	AVG	OBP	SLG	AOPS	ABR	SB-CS	FA	FR	Rng	Thr	G at Pos	BFW
1892	†Bos N	**152**	603	119	146	19	5	4	63	93	4	29	.242	.347	.310	91	-5	53	.883	0	117	85	*O-152(0-1-151)	-1.1
1893	Bos N	116	462	107	160	28	6	5	111	64	3	10	.346	.429	.465	128	20	46	.902	2	149	109	*O-108(88-3-17)/2-7,S-3	1.1
1894	Bos N	127	539	118	188	21	8	13	126	59	6	17	.349	.419	.490	110	8	43	.904	10	128	199	*O-127(119-9-0)/S-2,2P	0.5
1895	Bos N	117	452	90	131	13	2	2	73	72	3	12	.290	.391	.341	83	-9	18	.885	-10	94	57	*O-109(LF)/2-9	-2.4
1896	Bro N	104	377	62	94	8	4	3	47	34	3	17	.249	.316	.316	71	-16	22	.920	-3	140	168	*O-103(102-0-1)	-2.4
Total	13	1273	5120	1066	1493	191	53	44	732	536	50	163	.292	.364	.375	99	-20	468	.897	37	130	146	*O-1188R/2-39,3-36,S-20,P-13	-2.8
McCARTHY, BILL William John B 2.14.1886 Boston, MA D 2.4.1928 Washington, DC TR d6.5																								
1905	Bos N	1	3	0	0	0	0	0	0	0	0		.000	.000	.000	-99	-1	0	.667	-1	*153*	*80*	/C	-0.2
1907	Cin N	3	8	1	1	0	0	0	0	0	0		.125	.125	.125	-21	-1	0	1.000	-0	*110*	*164*	/C-3	-0.1
Total	2	4	11	1	1	0	0	0	0	0	0		.091	.091	.091	-43	-2	0	.842	-1	*126*	*133*	/C-4	-0.3
McCARTON, FRANK Francis B 10.6.1854 Middletown, CT D 6.17.1907 New York, NY d4.26																								
1872	Man NA	19	82	19	25	5	0	0	12	3		4	.305	.329	.366	120	3	0-0	.743	-3	52	0	O-19(0-18-1)	0.0
McCARTY, DAVID David Andrew B 11.23.1969 Houston, TX BR/TL 6-5/215# d5.17																								
1993	Min A	98	350	36	75	15	2	2	21	19-0	1	80	.214	.257	.286	45	-28	2-6	.959	6	101	187	O-67(38-2-34),1-36/D-2	-2.9
1994	Min A	44	131	21	34	8	2	1	12	7-1	5	32	.260	.322	.374	79	-4	2-1	.981	3	157	80	1-32,O-14(9-0-5)	-0.4
1995	Min A	25	55	10	12	3	1	0	4	4-0	1	18	.218	.279	.309	54	-4	0-1	.993	-1	93	101	1-18/O-5(2-0-4)	-0.6
	SF N	12	20	1	5	1	0	0	2	2-0	0	4	.250	.318	.300	66	-1	1-0	.833	-1	97	0	/O-4(RF),1-2	-0.2
1996	SF N	91	175	16	38	3	0	6	24	18-0	2	43	.217	.294	.337	70	-8	2-1	.990	-1	71	114	1-51,O-20(5-0-15)	-1.2
1998	Sea A	8	18	1	5	0	0	1	2	5-0	0	4	.278	.435	.444	130	1	1-0	1.000	-1	102	0	/O-5(RF),1-2	0.0
2000	KC A	103	270	34	75	14	2	12	53	22-1	0	68	.278	.329	.478	98	-2	0-0	.992	10	160	127	1-63,O-11(7-0-4)/SD	0.2
2001	KC A	98	200	26	50	10	0	7	26	24-1	1	45	.250	.328	.405	86	-4	0-0	.988	2	128	133	1-68/O-9(8-0-1),D-7	-0.7
2002	KC A	13	32	3	3	1	0	1	2	2-0	0	10	.094	.147	.219	-4	-5	0-0	1.000	0	97	73	/1-9,D-2	-0.6
	TB A	12	34	2	6	0	0	1	2	4-0	2	9	.176	.300	.265	53	-2	0-0	1.000	1	102	176	O-11(LF)	-0.2
	Year	25	66	5	9	1	0	2	4	6-0	2	19	.136	.230	.242	24	-7	0-0	1.000	1	102	176	O-11(LF)/1-9,D-2	-0.8
2003	Oak A	8	26	2	7	2	0	0	2	1-0	0	7	.269	.286	.346	68	-1	0-0	1.000	-1	55	0	/O-5(LF),1-3	-0.3
	†Bos A	16	27	4	11	3	0	1	6	2-0	0	7	.407	.448	.630	176	3	0-0	1.000	-1	72	0	/O-8(7-0-1),1-5,D	0.2
	Year	24	53	6	18	5	0	1	8	3-0	0	14	.340	.368	.491	123	2	0-0	1.000	-2	64	0	O-13(12-0-1)/1-8,D	-0.1
Total	9	528	1338	156	321	60	7	32	156	110-3	12	327	.240	.301	.367	73	-55	8-9	.989	16	127	110	1-289,O-159(92-2-73)/D-19,S	-6.7
McCARTY, LEW George Lewis B 11.17.1888 Milton, PA D 6.9.1930 Reading, PA BR/TR 5-11.5/192# d8.30																								
1913	Bro N	9	26	1	6	0	0	0	2	2	0	2	.231	.286	.231	47	-2	0	1.000	0	96	80	/C-9	-0.1
1914	Bro N	90	284	20	72	14	2	1	30	14	2	22	.254	.293	.327	83	-7	1	.970	-2	*88*	*102*	C-84	-0.2
1915	Bro N	84	276	19	66	9	4	0	19	7	1	23	.239	.261	.301	68	-12	7-4	.969	-7	*85*	*107*	C-81	-1.4
1916	Bro N	55	150	17	47	6	1	0	13	14	3	16	.313	.383	.367	127	6	4	.985	-1	94	99	C-27,1-17	0.7
	NY N	25	68	6	27	3	4	0	9	7	0	9	.397	.453	.559	222	10	0	.993	1	114	78	C-24	1.4
	Year	80	218	23	74	9	5	0	22	21	3	25	.339	.405	.427	155	15	4	.989	0	104	89	C-51,1-17	2.1
1917	†NY N	56	162	15	40	3	2	2	19	14	1	6	.247	.311	.327	99	0	1	.979	-2	*107*	*56*	C-54	0.2
1918	NY N	86	257	16	69	7	3	0	24	17	3	13	.268	.321	.319	97	-1	3	.975	-6	*97*	*65*	C-75	0.0
1919	NY N	85	210	17	59	5	4	2	21	18	1	15	.281	.341	.371	115	4	2	.970	-6	*99*	*74*	C-59	0.3
1920	NY N	36	38	2	5	0	0	0	0	4	0	2	.132	.214	.132	1	-5	2-0	1.000	1	*145*	*116*	/C-5	-0.3
	StL N	5	7	0	2	0	0	0	0	5	0	0	.286	.583	.286	160	1	0-0	1.000	-1	*82*	*138*	/C-3	0.1
	Year	41	45	2	7	0	0	0	0	9	0	2	.156	.296	.156	33	-3	2-0	1.000	1	*122*	*124*	/C-8	-0.2
1921	StL N	1	1	0	0	0	0	0	0	0	0	1	.000	.000	.000	-99	0	0-0	—	0			H	0.0
Total	9	532	1479	113	393	47	20	5	137	102	11	109	.266	.318	.335	97	-6	20-4	.975	-22	*96*	*85*	C-421/1-17	0.7
McCARVER, TIM James Timothy B 10.16.1941 Memphis, TN BL/TR 6-1/195# d9.10 OF Total (15-LF 1-RF)																								
1959	StL N	8	24	3	4	1	0	0	0	2-0	0	1	.167	.231	.208	17	-3	0-0	.971	-1	*98*	*87*	/C-6	-0.4
1960	StL N	10	10	3	2	0	0	0	0	0-0	0	2	.200	.200	.200	9	-1	0-0	1.000	0	*0*	*0*	/C-5	-0.1
1961	StL N	22	67	5	16	2	1	1	6	0-0	0	5	.239	.239	.343	47	-5	0-0	.969	-1	*90*	*103*	C-20	-0.5
1963	StL N	127	405	39	117	12	7	4	51	27-5	2	43	.289	.333	.383	97	-1	5-2	.994	-4	*81*	*88*	*C-126	0.1
1964	†StL N	143	465	53	134	19	3	9	52	40-15	1	44	.288	.343	.400	101	1	2-0	.987	-5	*107*	*56*	*C-137	0.4
1965	StL N	113	409	48	113	17	2	11	48	31-11	1	26	.276	.327	.408	97	-1	5-1	**.995**	-6	*90*	*71*	*C-111	-0.1
1966	StL N★	150	543	50	149	19	**13**	12	68	36-10	2	38	.274	.319	.424	105	2	9-6	.992	3	*117*	*86*	*C-148	1.2
1967	†StL N★	138	471	68	139	26	3	14	69	54-19	5	32	.295	.369	.452	137	24	8-8	**.997**	6	***144***	*109*	*C-130	3.8
1968	†StL N	128	434	35	110	15	6	5	48	26-8	1	31	.253	.295	.350	95	-4	4-3	.986	4	*133*	*78*	*C-109	0.6
1969	StL N	138	515	46	134	27	3	7	51	49-9	2	26	.260	.323	.365	93	-4	4-9	.986	6	88	81	*C-136	0.6
1970	Phi N	44	164	16	47	11	1	4	14	14-4	1	10	.287	.346	.439	112	3	2-2	.991	-1	70	73	C-44	0.3
1971	Phi N	134	474	51	132	20	5	8	46	43-7	1	26	.278	.337	.392	107	4	5-3	.985	-9	59	125	*C-125	0.1
1972	Phi N	45	152	14	36	8	0	2	14	17-2	2	15	.237	.318	.329	83	-3	1-2	.989	-0	96	61	C-40	-0.2
	Mon N	77	239	19	60	5	1	5	20	19-3	1	14	.251	.309	.343	84	-6	4-4	.990	7	100	126	C-45,O-14(14-0-1)/3-6	0.2
	Year	122	391	33	96	13	1	7	34	36-5	3	29	.246	.313	.338	83	-8	5-6	.990	7	98	95	C-85,O-14(14-0-1)/3-6	0.0
1973	StL N	130	331	30	88	16	4	3	49	38-6	2	31	.266	.339	.366	97	0	2-0	.986	-7	67	88	1-77,C-11	-1.3
1974	StL N	74	106	13	23	0	1	0	11	22-0	3	6	.217	.353	.236	72	-3	0-1	.969	-3	51	139	C-21/1-6	-0.5
	Bos A	11	28	3	7	1	0	0	1	4-2	0	1	.250	.344	.286	77	-1	1-0	1.000	1	71	76	/C-8,D-2	0.1
1975	Bos A	12	21	1	8	2	1	0	3	1-1	0	3	.381	.409	.571	161	2	0-0	.957	1	61	70	/C-7,1	0.2
	Phi N	47	59	6	15	2	0	1	7	14-3	0	7	.254	.397	.339	102	1	0-0	.984	1	61	129	C-10/1	0.3
1976	†Phi N	90	155	26	43	11	2	3	29	35-2	1	14	.277	.409	.432	136	10	2-1	1.000	6	77	69	C-41/1-2	1.8
1977	†Phi N	93	169	28	54	13	2	6	30	28-1	2	11	.320	.410	.527	146	13	3-5	.988	1	83	107	C-42/1-3	1.4
1978	†Phi N	90	146	18	36	9	1	1	14	28-6	2	24	.247	.367	.342	101	2	2-2	.995	5	158	150	C-34,1-11	0.8
1979	Phi N	79	137	13	33	5	1	1	12	19-5	1	12	.241	.333	.314	76	-4	2-0	.989	6	148	123	C-31/O(LF)	0.4
1980	Phi N	6	5	2	1	1	0	0	2	1-0	0	0	.200	.333	.400	98	0	0-0	1.000	-0	0	0	/1-2	0.0
Total	21	1909	5529	590	1501	242	57	97	645	548-119	30	422	.271	.337	.388	102	26	61-49	.990	9	*101*	*90*	*C-1387,1-103/O-15L,3-6,D-2	9.2
McCAULEY, AL Allen A. B 3.4.1863 Indianapolis, IN D 8.24.1917 Wayne Twnshp., IN BL/TL 6/180# d6.21 ▲																								
1884	Ind AA	17	53	7	10	0	1	0	5	12	2		.189	.358	.226	97	1		1.000	1	144	286	P-10/1-5,O-3(RF)	0.0
1890	Phi N	116	418	63	102	25	7	1	42	57	8	38	.244	.346	.344	99	1	8	.973	-6	63	107	*1-116	-1.4
1891	Was AA	59	206	36	58	5	8	1	31	30	2	13	.282	.378	.398	128	8	9	.969	-1	95	71	1-59	0.2
Total	3	192	677	106	170	30	16	2	78	99	12	51	.251	.357	.352	107	10	17	.971	-6	73	97	1-180/P-10,O-3(RF)	-1.2
McCAULEY, JIM James Adelbert B 3.24.1863 Stanley, NY D 9.14.1930 Canandaigua, NY BL/TR 6/180# d9.17																								
1884	StL AA	1	2	0	0	0	0	0		0	0		.000	.000	.000	-97	0		.818	0			/C	0.0
1885	Buf N	24	84	4	15	2	1	0	7	11		12	.179	.274	.226	61	-3		.936	2			C-21/O-4(CF)	0.1
	Chi N	3	6	1	1	0	0	0	0	2		3	.167	.375	.167	70	0		.800	-2			/C-2,O-2(RF)	-0.1
	Year	27	90	5	16	2	1	0	7	13		15	.178	.282	.222	62	-3		.927	1			C-23/O-6(0-4-2)	0.0
1886	Bro AA	11	30	5	7	1	0	0	3	11	0		.233	.439	.267	122	2	2	.846	-2			C-11	0.1
Total	3	39	122	10	23	3	1	0	10	24	0	15	.189	.322	.230	76	-1	2	.893	-1			/C-35,O-6(0-4-2)	0.1
McCAULEY, PAT Patrick F. B 6.10.1870 Ware, MA D 1.17.1917 Hoboken, NJ TR 5-10.5/156# d9.5																								
1893	StL N	5	16	0	1	0	0	0	0	0	0	1	.063	.063	.063	-67	-4	0	.808	-1	*83*	*136*	/C-5	-0.3
1896	Was N	26	84	14	21	3	0	3	11	7	1	8	.250	.315	.393	86	-2	3	.917	-2	*87*	*124*	C-24/O(RF)	-0.1
1903	NY A	6	19	0	1	0	0	0	1	0	0		.053	.053	.053	-64	-4	0	.920	-2	*99*	*51*	/C-6	-0.5
Total	3	37	119	14	23	3	0	3	12	7	1	9	.193	.244	.294	44	-10	3	.900	-4	*88*	*114*	/C-35,O(RF)	-0.9
McCAULEY, BILL William H. B 12.20.1869 Washington, DC D 1.27.1926 Washington, DC d8.31																								
1895	Was N	1	2	0	0	0	0	0	0	0	0	0	.000	.000	.000	-99	-1	0	.714	0	143	0	/S	0.0
McCHESNEY, HARRY Harry Vincent "Pud" B 6.1.1880 Pittsburgh, PA D 8.11.1960 Pittsburgh, PA BR/TR 5-9/165# d9.17																								
1904	Chi N	22	88	9	23	6	2	0	11	4	0		.261	.293	.375	106	0	2	.967	-2	75	142	O-22(0-1-21)	-0.3
McCLAIN, SCOTT Scott Michael B 5.19.1972 Simi Valley, CA BR/TR 6-3/209# d5.14																								
1998	TB A	9	20	2	2	0	0	0	0	2-0	1	6	.100	.217	.100	-13	-3	0-0	.966	-1	192	38	/1-5,3-3	-0.4
McCLANAHAN, PETE Robert Hugh B 10.24.1906 Coldspring, TX D 10.28.1987 Mont Belvieu, TX BR/TR 5-9/170# d4.24																								
1931	Pit N	7	4	2	2	0	0	0	0	2	0	0	.500	.667	.500	220	1	0	—	0			H	0.1

Year	Tm Lg	G	AB	R	H	2B	3B	HR	RBI	BB-IB	HP	SO	AVG	OBP	SLG	AOPS	ABR	SB-CS	FA	FR	Rng	Thr	G at Pos	BFW
McCLELLAN, HARVEY Harvey McDowell "Little Mac" B 12.22.1894 Cynthiana, KY D 11.6.1925 Cynthiana, KY BR/TR 5-9.5/143# d5.31																								
1919	Chi A	7	12	2	4	0	0	0	1	1	0	1	.333	.385	.333	102	0	0	1.000	-0	141	330	/3-3,S-2	0.0
1920	Chi A	10	18	4	6	1	1	0	5	4	0	1	.333	.455	.500	153	2	2-0	.917	-2	54	0	/S-4,3-2	0.0
1921	Chi A	63	196	20	35	4	1	1	14	14	1	18	.179	.237	.224	18	-25	2-3	.968	14	123	40	2-21,S-15,O-15(RF)/3-5	-1.0
1922	Chi A	91	301	28	68	17	3	2	28	16	3	32	.226	.272	.322	55	-21	3-2	.971	-3	103	111	3-71/S-8,2-2,O(CF)	-1.8
1923	Chi A	141	550	67	129	29	3	1	41	27	0	44	.235	.270	.304	52	-41	14-11	.958	-17	95	92	*S-139/2-2	-4.3
1924	Chi A	32	85	9	15	3	0	0	9	6	1	7	.176	.239	.212	17	-11	2-0	.938	2	120	64	S-21/2-7,3O(RF)	-0.6
Total	6	344	1162	130	257	54	8	4	98	68	5	103	.221	.267	.292	46	-96	23-16	.952	-7	99	90	S-189/3-82,2-32,O-17(0-1-16)	-7.7
McCLELLAN, BILL William Henry B 3.22.1856 Chicago, IL D 7.3.1929 Chicago, IL BL/TL 5-5.5/156# d5.20																								
1878	Chi N	48	205	26	46	6	1	0	29	2		13	.224	.232	.263	59	-9		.866	-8	97	94	*2-42/S-5,O(RF)	-1.5
1881	Pro N	68	259	30	43	3	1	0	16	15		21	.166	.212	.185	26	-21		.855	-7	91	117	S-50,O-17(0-1-16)/2	-2.5
1883	Phi N	80	326	42	75	21	4	1	33	19		18	.230	.272	.328	89	-2		.849	5	105	91	*S-78/O-2(CF),3	0.5
1884	Phi N	111	450	71	116	13	2	3	33	28		43	.258	.301	.316	99	1		.852	-9	95	81	*S-111/O(CF)	-0.4
1885	Bro AA	**112**	464	85	124	22	7	0	46	28	6		.267	.317	.345	108	5		.837	-7	78	117	3-57,2-55	0.1
1886	Bro AA	**141**	595	131	152	33	9	1	68	56	2		.255	.322	.346	108	7	43	.907	-8	98	97	*2-141	0.3
1887	Bro AA	136	548	109	144	24	6	1	53	80	6		.263	.363	.334	94	-1	70	.879	-21	97	87	*2-136	-1.4
1888	Bro AA	74	278	33	57	7	3	0	21	40	1		.205	.307	.252	80	-4	13	.905	-7	89	128	2-56,O-18(0-1-17)	-0.9
	Cle AA	22	72	6	16	0	0	0	5	6	0		.222	.282	.222	64	-3	6	.875	-1	179	0	O-15(RF)/2-5,S-2	-0.4
	Year	96	350	39	73	7	3	0	26	46	1		.209	.302	.246	77	-7	19	.897	-8	90	132	2-61,O-33(0-1-32)/S-2	-1.3
Total	8	792	3197	533	773	129	33	6	304	274	15	95	.242	.305	.308	90	-27	132	.893	-63	97	97	2-436,S-246/3-58,O-54(0-5-49)	-6.2
McCLENDON, LLOYD Lloyd Glenn B 1.11.1959 Gary, IN BR/TR 5-11/195# d4.6 M3 C4																								
1987	Cin N	45	72	8	15	5	0	2	13	4-0	0	15	.208	.247	.361	57	-5	1-0	.981	-1	121	65	C-12/1-5,3O(LF)	-0.5
1988	Cin N	72	137	9	30	4	0	3	14	15-1	2	22	.219	.301	.314	75	-4	4-0	1.000	3	181	65	C-23,O-17(11-0-6),1-12/3-2	-0.1
1989	†Chi N	92	259	47	74	12	1	12	40	37-3	1	31	.286	.368	.479	133	12	6-4	.962	-5	92	90	O-45(LF),1-28/3-6,C-5	0.4
1990	Chi N	49	107	5	17	3	0	1	10	14-2	0	21	.159	.254	.215	29	-10	1-0	.980	3	117	0	O-23(LF)/C-8,1-8	-0.9
	Pit N	4	3	1	1	0	0	1	2	0-0	0	1	.333	.333	1.333	349	1	0-0	—	-0	0	0	/O(LF)	0.1
	Year	53	110	6	18	3	0	2	12	14-2	0	22	.164	.256	.245	37	-9	1-0	.980	3	116	0	O-24(LF)/C-8,1-8	-0.8
1991	†Pit N	85	163	24	47	7	0	7	24	18-0	2	23	.288	.366	.460	133	7	2-1	.966	-2	69	152	O-32(14-0-18),1-22/C-2	0.4
1992	†Pit N	84	190	26	48	8	1	3	20	28-0	2	24	.253	.350	.353	102	2	1-3	.964	-4	84	0	O-60(10-0-50),1-18	-0.5
1993	Pit N	88	181	21	40	11	1	2	19	23-1	0	17	.221	.306	.326	70	-7	0-3	.967	-1	96	90	O-61(21-0-47)/1-6	-1.1
1994	Pit N	51	92	9	22	4	0	4	12	4-0	1	11	.239	.278	.413	76	-4	0-1	.967	-1	88	89	O-20(12-0-9)/1-2	-0.6
Total	8	570	1204	150	294	54	3	35	154	143-7	8	165	.244	.325	.381	94	-8	15-12	.966	-7	91	69	O-260(138-0-130),1-101/C-50,3-9	-2.8
McCLESKEY, JEFF Jefferson Lamar B 11.6.1891 Americus, GA D 5.11.1971 Americus, GA BL/TR 5-11/160# d9.8																								
1913	Bos N	2	3	0	0	0	0	0	0	1	0	0	.000	.250	.000	-25	0	0	.750	-1	47	0	/3-2	-0.1
McCLOSKEY B Brooklyn, NY d5.25																								
1875	Was NA	11	40	1	7	0	0	0	4	1		2	.175	.195	.175	31	-3	0-1	.673	-6			C-11	-0.8
McCLOSKEY, BILL William George B 5.1854 , PA 5-8/155# d8.18																								
1884	Wil U	9	30	0	3	0	0	0		0			.100	.100	.100	-38	-6		.588	-0	262	0	/O-5(3-3-0),C-5	-0.6
McCLURE, HAL Harold Murray "Mac" B 8.8.1859 Lewisburg, PA D 3.1.1919 Lewisburg, PA BR/TR 6/165# d5.10																								
1882	Bos N	2	6	1	2	0	0	0	0	0		1	.333	.333	.333	114	0		.750	-1	0	0	/O-2(RF)	0.0
McCLURE, LARRY Lawrence Ledwith B 10.3.1885 Wayne, WV D 8.31.1949 Huntington, WV BR/TR 5-6.5/130# d7.26																								
1910	NY A	1	1	0	0	0	0	0	0	0	0		.000	.000	.000	-95	0	0	—	-0	0	0	/O(LF)	0.0
McCONNELL, AMBY Ambrose Moses B 4.29.1883 N.Pownal, VT D 5.20.1942 Utica, NY BL/TR 5-7/150# d4.17																								
1908	Bos A	140	502	77	140	10	6	2	43	38	11		.279	.343	.335	117	10	31	.939	-16	95	86	*2-126/S-3	-0.5
1909	Bos A	121	453	61	108	7	8	0	36	34	6		.238	.300	.289	84	-8	26	.954	11	**112**	101	*2-121	0.4
1910	Bos A	11	35	6	6	0	0	0	1	5	2		.171	.310	.171	50	-2	4	.959	-1	108	0	2-10	-0.3
	Chi A	33	120	13	33	2	3	0	5	7	1		.275	.320	.342	112	1	4	.952	-0	97	109	2-32	0.1
	Year	44	155	19	39	2	3	0	6	12	3		.252	.318	.303	97	-1	8	.954	-1	100	81	2-42	-0.2
1911	Chi A	104	396	45	111	11	5	1	34	23	7		.280	.331	.341	90	-6	7	**.973**	0	100	102	*2-103	-0.4
Total	4	409	1506	202	398	30	22	3	119	107	27		.264	.324	.319	98	-5	72	.954	-6	102	94	2-392/S-3	-0.7
McCONNELL, GEORGE George Neely "Slats" B 9.16.1877 Shelbyville, TN D 5.10.1964 Chattanooga, TN BR/TR 6-3/190# d4.13 ▲																								
1909	NY A	13	43	4	9	0	1	0	5	1	0		.209	.227	.256	52	-3	1	.964	2	154	116	1-11/P-2	-0.2
1912	NY A	42	91	11	27	4	2	0	8	4	1		.297	.333	.385	99	0	0	.913	5	**146**	193	P-23/1-2	0.2
1913	NY A	39	67	4	12	2	0	0	2	0	0	11	.179	.179	.209	13	-8	0	.965	4	140	115	P-35/1	0.2
1914	Chi N	1	2	0	0	0	0	0	0	0	0	1	.000	.000	.000	-99	0	0	1.000	0	162	0	/P	0.0
1915	Chi F	53	125	14	31	6	2	1	18	0	1	16	.248	.254	.352	74	4	2	.974	3	113	144	P-44	0.0
1916	Chi N	28	57	2	9	0	0	0	0	2	1	4	.158	.200	.158	10	-2	0	.952	2	111	218	P-28	0.0
Total	6	176	385	35	88	12	5	1	33	7	3	32	.229	.248	.294	57	-9	3	.953	15	126	161	P-133/1-14	0.2
McCONNELL, SAM Samuel Faulkner B 6.8.1895 Philadelphia, PA D 6.27.1981 Phoenixville, PA BL/TR 5-6.5/150# d4.19																								
1915	Phi A	6	11	1	2	1	0	0	0	1	0	3	.182	.250	.273	58	-1	0	.842	1	134	0	/3-5	0.0
McCORMACK, DON Donald Ross B 9.18.1955 Omak, WA BR/TR 6-3/205# d9.30																								
1980	Phi N	2	1	0	1	0	0	0	0	0-0	0	0	1.000	1.000	1.000	436	0	0-0	1.000	1	0	0	/C-2	0.1
1981	Phi N	3	4	0	1	0	0	0	0	0-0	0	1	.250	.250	.250	40	0	0-0	1.000	-0	0	165	/C-3	0.0
Total	2	5	5	0	2	0	0	0	0	0-0	0	1	.400	.400	.400	121	0	0-0	1.000	1	0	126	/C-5	0.1
McCORMICK, FRANK Frank Andrew "Buck" B 6.9.1911 New York, NY D 11.21.1982 Manhasset, NY BR/TR 6-4/205# d9.11 C2																								
1934	Cin N	12	16	1	5	2	1	0	5	0	0	1	.313	.313	.563	132	1	0	.941	-1	0	76	/1-2	0.0
1937	Cin N	24	83	5	27	5	0	0	9	2	0	4	.325	.341	.386	102	0	1	1.000	1	123	123	1-20/2-4,O(RF)	-0.1
1938	Cin N★	**151**	640	89	**209**	40	4	5	106	18	3	17	.327	.348	.425	115	11	1	.995	-4	89	103	*1-151	-0.7
1939	†Cin N★	**156**	630	99	**209**	41	4	18	**128**	40	2	16	.332	.374	.495	131	26	1	**.996**	1	97	**117**	*1-156	1.3
1940	†Cin N★	**155**	618	93	**191**	**44**	3	19	127	52	5	26	.309	.367	.482	131	27	2	**.995**	-1	95	**130**	*1-155	1.1
1941	Cin N★	**154**	603	77	162	31	5	17	97	40	4	13	.269	.318	.421	107	3	2	**.995**	-0	94	108	*1-154	-1.2
1942	Cin N★	145	564	58	156	24	0	13	89	45	2	18	.277	.332	.388	111	7	1	.993	5	111	**124**	*1-144	-0.2
1943	Cin N✳	126	472	56	143	28	0	8	59	29	1	15	.303	.345	.413	120	11	2	.995	4	**111**	116	*1-120	0.9
1944	Cin N☆	153	581	85	177	37	3	20	102	57	4	17	.305	.371	.482	144	34	7	.992	12	**133**	122	*1-153	3.8
1945	Cin N✳	152	580	68	160	33	0	10	81	56	5	22	.276	.345	.384	105	4	6	.994	4	**109**	90	*1-151	0.1
1946	Phi N★	135	504	46	143	20	2	11	66	36	1	21	.284	.333	.397	110	4	2	**.999**	5	**108**	83	*1-134	0.5
1947	Phi N	15	40	7	9	2	0	1	8	3	0	2	.225	.279	.350	69	-2	0	.989	-1	63	115	1-12	-0.3
	Bos N	81	212	24	75	18	2	2	43	11	0	8	.354	.386	.486	133	10	2	.996	-1	90	92	1-46	0.7
	Year	96	252	31	84	20	2	3	51	14	0	10	.333	.368	.464	123	8	2	.995	-2	85	96	1-58	0.4
1948	†Bos N	75	180	14	45	9	2	4	34	10	0	9	.250	.289	.389	84	-5	0	.987	2	126	112	1-50	-0.4
Total	13	1534	5723	722	1711	334	26	128	954	399	27	189	.299	.348	.434	118	131	27	.995	28	105	110	*1-1448/2-4,O(RF)	5.5
McCORMICK, MOOSE Harry Elwood B 2.28.1881 Philadelphia, PA D 7.9.1962 Lewisburg, PA BL/TL 5-11/180# d4.14																								
1904	NY N	59	203	28	54	9	5	1	26	13	4		.266	.323	.374	110	2	13	.916	-4	47	124	O-55(2-52-1)	-0.5
	Pit N	66	238	25	69	10	6	2	23	13	2		.290	.332	.408	124	6	6	.940	-3	94	0	O-66(18-0-48)	0.0
	Year	125	441	53	123	19	11	3	49	26	6		.279	.328	.392	118	8	19	.928	-7	72	58	*O-121(20-52-49)	-0.5
1908	Phi N	11	22	0	2	0	0	0	2	2	0		.091	.167	.091	-17	-3	0	1.000	0	0	0	/O-5(LF)	-0.4
	NY N	73	252	31	76	16	3	0	32	4	1		.302	.315	.389	119	4	6	.901	-8	36	113	O-65(59-0-12)	-0.9
	Year	84	274	31	78	16	3	0	34	6	1		.285	.302	.365	108	1	6	.910	-8	33	105	O-70(64-0-12)	-1.3
1909	NY N	110	413	68	120	21	8	3	27	49	5		.291	.373	.402	138	20	4	.924	-10	90	198	*O-110(87-0-23)	0.5
1912	†NY N	42	39	4	13	4	1	0	8	6	0	9	.333	.422	.487	144	3	1	.667	-1	54	0	/O-6(1-1-4),1	0.2
1913	†NY N	57	80	9	22	2	3	0	15	5	0	13	.275	.318	.375	97	-1	0	.909	-0	103	72	O-15(0-2-13)	-0.2
Total	5	418	1247	165	356	62	26	6	133	92	12	22	.285	.340	.391	122	31	30	.920	-26	70	118	O-322(172-55-101)/1	-1.3
McCORMICK, JIM James Ambrose B 11.2.1868 Spencer, MA D 2.1.1948 Saco, ME BR/TR 6-1/160# d9.10																								
1892	StL N	3	11	0	0	0	0	0	0	1	0	5	.000	.083	.000	-78	-2	0	1.000	-0	102	0	/2-2,3	-0.2

Year	Tm Lg	G	AB	R	H	2B	3B	HR	RBI	BB-IB	HP	SO	AVG	OBP	SLG	AOPS	ABR	SB-CS	FA	FR	Rng	Thr	G at Pos	BFW
McCORMICK, JERRY John B Philadelphia, PA D 9.19.1905 Philadelphia, PA d5.1																								
1883	Bal AA	93	389	40	102	16	6	0		2			.262	.266	.334	89	-6		.799	1	101	87	*3-93	-0.3
1884	Phi U	**67**	295	41	84	12	2	0		4			.285	.294	.339	99	-9		.811	11	118	118	3-54/2-5,O-5(5-0-1),S-3,P	0.3
	Was U	42	157	23	34	8	2	0		1			.217	.222	.293	57	-13		.792	-3	72	149	3-38/S-4	-1.4
	Year	109	452	64	118	20	4	0		5			.261	.269	.323	84	-23		**.806**	9	101	129	3-92/S-7,2-5,O-5(5-0-1),P	-1.1
Total	2	202	841	104	220	36	10	0		7			.262	.268	.328	86	-28		.802	9	101	108	3-185/S-7,O-5(5-0-1),2-5,P	-1.4
McCORMICK, MIKE Michael J. "Kid" or "Dude" B 5.1883 , Scotland D 11.18.1953 Jersey City, NJ BR/TR 5-3/155# d4.14																								
1904	Bro N	105	347	28	64	5	4	0	27	43	2		.184	.278	.222	56	-17	22	**.914**	-2	93	**181**	*3-104/2	-1.7
McCORMICK, MIKE Myron Winthrop B 5.6.1917 Angels Camp, CA D 4.14.1976 Ventura, CA BR/TR 6/200# d4.16 Mil 1943-45																								
1940	†Cin N	110	417	48	125	20	0	1	30	13	3	36	.300	.326	.355	87	-8	8	.986	2	102	102	*O-107(51-50-6)	-1.1
1941	Cin N	110	369	52	106	17	3	4	31	30	0	24	.287	.341	.382	103	1	4	.976	2	101	119	*O-101(82-19-0)	-0.2
1942	Cin N	40	135	18	32	2	3	1	11	13	0	7	.237	.304	.319	82	-3	0	.990	-0	104	61	O-38(13-26-0)	-0.5
1943	Cin N	4	15	0	2	0	0	0	0	2	0	0	.133	.235	.133	8	-2	0	.909	-1	83	0	/O-4(CF)	-0.3
1946	Cin N	23	74	10	16	2	0	0	5	8	0	4	.216	.293	.243	55	-4	0	1.000	-1	96	50	O-21(CF)	-0.7
	Bos N	59	164	23	43	6	2	1	16	11	0	7	.262	.309	.341	83	-4	0	.973	-1	110	27	O-48(10-33-5)	-0.7
	Year	82	238	33	59	8	2	1	21	19	0	11	.248	.304	.311	75	-8	0	.982	-2	105	35	O-69(10-54-5)	-1.4
1947	Bos N	92	284	42	81	13	7	3	36	20	0	21	.285	.332	.412	99	-2	1	.981	-3	94	84	O-79(26-62-1)	-0.7
1948	†Bos N	115	343	45	104	22	7	1	39	32	0	34	.303	.363	.417	112	6	1	.975	-1	96	106	*O-100(56-34-20)	0.1
1949	†Bro N	55	139	17	29	5	1	2	14	14	0	12	.209	.281	.302	54	-9	1	1.000	0	97	106	O-49(38-7-5)	-1.1
1950	NY N	4	4	0	0	0	0	0	0	0	0	2	.000	.000	.000	-99	-1	0	—	0			H	-0.1
	Chi A	55	138	16	32	4	3	0	10	16	0	6	.232	.312	.304	60	-9	0-1	.982	2	107	130	O-44(2-42-0)	-0.7
1951	Was A	81	243	31	70	9	3	1	23	29	0	20	.288	.364	.362	98	0	1-2	.966	3	106	156	O-62(24-12-28)	0.0
Total	10	748	2325	302	640	100	29	14	215	188	3	173	.275	.330	.361	90	-35	16-3	.980	3	101	100	O-653(302-310-65)	-6.0
McCORMICK, BARRY William J. B 12.25.1874 Maysville, KY D 1.28.1956 Cincinnati, OH TR 5-9/?# d9.25 U13																								
1895	Lou N	3	12	2	3	0	1	0	0	0	0	0	.250	.250	.417	75	-1	1	1.000	-1	96	141	/S-2,2	-0.1
1896	Chi N	45	168	22	37	3	1	1	23	14	0	30	.220	.280	.268	43	-14	9	.835	-5	98	93	3-35/S-6,2-3,O(RF)	-1.6
1897	Chi N	101	419	87	112	8	10	2	55	33	2		.267	.324	.348	75	-17	44	.851	2	108	137	3-56,S-46/2	-1.1
1898	Chi N	137	530	76	131	15	9	2	78	47	5		.247	.314	.321	82	-13	15	.888	3	**112**	**171**	*3-136/S2	-0.7
1899	Chi N	102	376	48	97	15	2	2	52	25	4		.258	.311	.324	76	-12	14	.941	1	110	124	2-99/S-3	-0.6
1900	Chi N	110	379	35	83	13	5	3	48	38	1		.219	.292	.303	67	-17	8	.907	-9	98	94	S-84,3-21/2-5	-2.0
1901	Chi N	115	427	45	100	15	6	1	32	31	1		.234	.288	.304	74	-14	12	.911	-4	103	103	*S-112/3-3	-1.4
1902	StL A	**139**	504	55	124	14	4	3	51	37	5		.246	.304	.308	71	-20	10	.905	-15	92	**142**	*3-132/S-7,O(CF)	-3.0
1903	StL A	61	207	13	45	6	1	1	16	18	1		.217	.283	.271	69	-7	5	.969	-1	95	85	2-28,3-28/S-4	-0.7
	Was A	63	219	14	47	10	2	0	23	10	2		.215	.255	.279	59	-11	3	.960	9	112	115	2-63	-0.2
	Year	124	426	27	92	16	3	1	39	28	3		.216	.269	.275	64	-18	8	.962	8	107	106	2-91,3-28/S-4	-0.9
1904	Was A	113	404	36	88	11	1	0	39	27	4		.218	.274	.250	67	-14	9	.938	4	**109**	106	*2-113	-1.1
Total	10	989	3645	433	867	110	42	15	417	280	25	30	.238	.297	.303	71	-140	130	.885	-18	103	145	3-411,2-314,S-265/O-2(0-1-1)	-12.5
McCOSKY, BARNEY William Barney B 4.11.1917 Coal Run, PA D 9.6.1996 Venice, FL BL/TR 6-1/184# d4.18 Mil 1943-45																								
1939	Det A	147	611	120	190	33	14	4	58	70	2	45	.311	.384	.430	100	1	20-4	.986	3	108	57	*O-145(CF)	0.3
1940	†Det A	143	589	123	**200**	39	**19**	4	57	67	1	41	.340	.408	.491	120	19	13-9	.983	-5	96	70	*O-141(CF)	1.0
1941	Det A	127	494	80	160	25	8	3	55	61	3	33	.324	.401	.425	108	8	8-3	.985	-0	104	59	*O-122(21-101-0)	0.4
1942	Det A	154	600	75	176	28	11	7	50	68	0	37	.293	.365	.412	109	8	11-5	.981	0	105	58	*O-154(145-7-2)	0.0
1946	Det A	25	91	11	18	5	0	1	11	17	0	9	.198	.324	.286	67	-3	0-0	.966	-2	90	63	O-24(CF)	-0.6
	Phi A	92	308	33	109	17	4	1	34	43	0	13	.354	.433	.445	146	22	2-2	.981	-1	104	39	O-85(CF)	1.8
	Year	117	399	44	127	22	4	2	45	60	0	22	.318	.407	.409	127	18	2-2	.978	-4	101	45	O-109(CF)	1.2
1947	Phi A	137	546	77	179	22	7	1	52	57	4	29	.328	.395	.399	119	16	1-4	.983	-0	100	80	*O-136(114-23-0)	0.5
1948	Phi A	135	515	95	168	21	5	0	46	68	0	22	.326	.405	.386	111	11	1-3	.990	-2	96	94	*O-134(LF)	-0.2
1950	Phi A	66	179	19	43	10	1	0	11	22	0	12	.240	.323	.307	63	-10	0-0	.987	-2	91	35	O-42(LF)	-1.4
1951	Phi A	12	27	4	8	2	0	1	1	3	0	4	.296	.367	.481	125	1	0-0	1.000	-0	101	0	/O-7(5-0-2)	0.0
	Cin N	25	50	2	16	2	1	1	11	4	0	2	.320	.370	.460	120	1	0-0	1.000	-1	84	0	O-11(4-7-1)	0.0
	Cle A	31	61	8	13	3	0	0	2	8	0	5	.213	.304	.262	57	-3	1-0	1.000	-0	107	0	O-16(1-2-13)	-0.4
1952	Cle A	54	80	14	17	4	1	1	6	8	0	5	.213	.284	.325	74	-3	1-1	.944	-2	80	0	O-19(11-0-9)	-0.6
1953	Cle A	22	21	3	4	3	0	0	3	1	0	4	.190	.227	.333	51	-1	0-0	—	0			H	-0.1
Total	11	1170	4172	664	1301	214	71	24	397	497	10	261	.312	.386	.414	109	67	58-31	.984	-13	101	63	*O-1036(477-535-27)	0.7
McCOVEY, WILLIE Willie Lee "Stretch" B 1.10.1938 Mobile, AL BL/TL 6-4/210# d7.30 HF1986																								
1959	SF N	52	192	32	68	9	5	13	38	22-1	4	35	.354	.429	.656	189	24	2-0	.989	-1	89	77	1-51	2.0
1960	SF N	101	260	37	62	15	3	13	51	45-4	0	53	.238	.349	.469	130	12	1-1	.985	-3	87	82	1-71	0.5
1961	SF N	106	328	59	89	12	3	18	50	37-3	5	60	.271	.350	.491	126	12	1-2	.985	-2	93	81	1-84	0.4
1962	†SF N	91	229	41	67	6	1	20	54	29-1	0	35	.293	.368	.590	156	17	3-3	.976	0	106	63	O-57(45-0-12),1-17	1.3
1963	SF N★	152	564	103	158	19	5	**44**	102	50-5	11	119	.280	.350	.566	161	42	1-1	.942	-2	98	84	*O-135(134-0-2),1-23	3.4
1964	SF N	130	364	55	80	14	1	18	54	61-5	5	73	.220	.336	.412	108	6	2-1	.935	-6	79	110	O-83(78-0-5),1-26	-0.5
1965	SF N	160	540	93	149	17	4	39	92	88-5	6	118	.276	.381	.539	152	40	0-4	.991	-5	84	88	*1-156	2.5
1966	SF N★	150	502	85	148	26	6	36	96	76-10	6	100	.295	.391	.586	163	45	2-1	.984	-6	88	90	*1-145	3.1
1967	SF N	135	456	73	126	17	4	31	91	71-17	6	110	.276	.378	.535	162	38	3-3	.989	1	106	111	*1-127	3.3
1968	SF N★	148	523	81	153	16	4	**36**	**105**	72-20	5	71	.293	.378	**.545**	**176**	**49**	4-2	.985	4	116	92	*1-146	**5.0**
1969	SF N★	149	491	101	157	26	2	**45**	**126**	121-**45**	4	66	.320	**.453**	**.656**	**212**	**81**	0-0	.992	-5	90	107	*1-148	**6.6**
1970	SF N★	152	495	98	143	39	2	39	126	**137-40**	3	75	.289	.444	**.612**	**183**	**67**	0-0	.989	12	**132**	95	*1-146	**6.5**
1971	†SF N★	105	329	45	91	13	0	18	70	64-**21**	4	57	.277	.396	.480	151	25	0-2	.983	-2	100	110	1-95	1.6
1972	SF N	81	263	30	56	8	0	14	35	38-5	2	45	.213	.316	.403	102	1	0-0	.986	-4	79	95	1-74	-1.0
1973	SF N	130	383	52	102	14	3	29	75	105-**25**	1	78	.266	.420	.546	161	37	1-0	.988	2	110	102	*1-117	3.1
1974	SD N	128	344	53	87	19	1	22	63	96-9	1	76	.253	.416	.506	164	35	1-0	.987	-6	76	65	*1-104	2.2
1975	SD N	122	413	43	104	17	0	23	68	57-8	3	80	.252	.345	.460	130	16	1-0	.986	1	113	107	*1-115	1.0
1976	SD N	71	202	20	41	9	0	7	36	21-7	1	39	.203	.281	.351	86	-4	0-0	.991	7	163	108	1-51	-0.2
	Oak A	11	24	0	5	0	0	0	0	3-1	0	4	.208	.296	.208	52	-1	0-0	—	0			/D-9	-0.2
1977	SF N	141	478	54	134	21	0	28	86	67-16	0	106	.280	.367	.500	131	22	3-0	.989	-7	78	95	*1-136	0.7
1978	SF N	108	351	32	80	19	2	12	64	36-8	0	57	.228	.298	.396	97	-3	1-0	.987	-2	92	80	1-97	-1.0
1979	SF N	117	353	34	88	9	0	15	57	36-2	1	70	.249	.318	.402	103	0	0-2	.987	1	104	87	1-89	-0.5
1980	SF N	48	113	8	23	8	0	1	16	13-2	1	23	.204	.285	.301	67	-5	0-0	.992	-2	75	85	1-27	-0.8
Total	22	2588	8197	1229	2211	353	46	521	1555	1345-260	69	1550	.270	.374	.515	148	556	26-22	.987	-27	99	94	*1-2045,O-275(257-0-19)/D-9	39.0
McCOY, ART Arthur Gray B 7.1864 Danville, PA D 3.22.1904 Danville, PA ?/168# d7.8																								
1889	Was N	2	6	0	0	0	0	0	0	2	0	1	.000	.250	.000	-29	-1	0	.889	-1	38	0	/2-2	-0.2
McCOY, BENNY Benjamin Jenison B 11.9.1915 Jenison, MI BL/TR 5-9/170# d9.14 Mil 1942-45																								
1938	Det A	7	15	2	3	1	0	0	0	1	0	2	.200	.250	.267	28	-2	0-0	.963	1	136	144	/2-6,3	-0.1
1939	Det A	55	192	38	58	13	6	1	33	29	0	26	.302	.394	.448	107	3	3-1	.958	-1	101	87	2-34,S-16	0.4
1940	Phi A	134	490	56	126	26	5	7	62	65	1	44	.257	.345	.373	88	-8	2-2	.951	-10	102	90	*2-130/3	-1.0
1941	Phi A	141	517	86	140	12	7	8	61	95	0	50	.271	.384	.368	102	5	3-3	.963	-11	104	96	*2-135	0.2
Total	4	337	1214	182	327	52	18	16	156	190	1	122	.269	.369	.381	97	-2	8-6	.957	-22	103	93	2-305/S-16,3-2	-0.5
McCRACKEN, QUINTON Quinton Antoine B 3.16.1970 Wilmington, NC BB/TR 5-8/170# d9.17																								
1995	Col N	3	1	0	0	0	0	0	0	0-0	0	1	.000	.000	.000	-78	0	0-0	—	-0	0	0	/O(CF)	0.0
1996	Col N	124	283	50	82	13	6	3	40	32-4	1	62	.290	.363	.410	84	-6	17-6	.957	-7	82	84	O-93(8-85-4)	-1.1
1997	Col N	147	325	69	95	11	1	3	36	42-0	1	62	.292	.374	.360	76	-10	28-11	.980	-4	94	114	*O-132(CF)	-1.0
1998	TB A	155	614	77	179	38	7	7	59	41-1	3	107	.292	.335	.410	92	-8	19-10	.992	5	95	193	*O-153(58-103-0)	-0.3
1999	TB A	40	148	20	37	6	1	1	18	14-0	1	23	.250	.317	.324	64	-8	6-5	.988	-2	96	43	O-40(26-20-0)	-1.0
2000	TB A	15	31	5	4	0	0	0	2	6-0	0	4	.129	.270	.129	6	-4	0-1	1.000	-0	104	0	O-11(9-3-0)	-0.5
2001	Min A	24	64	7	14	2	2	0	3	5-0	0	13	.219	.275	.313	53	-5	0-1	1.000	-1	85	0	O-10(6-2-3)/D-9	-0.6
2002	†Ari N	123	349	60	108	27	8	3	40	32-0	2	68	.309	.367	.458	111	4	5-4	.995	4	110	100	O-97(7-31-68)	0.5
2003	Ari N	115	203	17	46	5	2	0	18	15-2	0	34	.227	.276	.271	41	-18	5-1	.983	-5	75	42	O-55(10-16-34)/D	-2.3
Total	9	746	2018	305	565	102	27	17	216	187-7	8	374	.280	.341	.383	81	-55	80-39	.985	-10	94	117	O-592(124-393-109)/D-10	-6.3

Year	Tm Lg	G	AB	R	H	2B	3B	HR	RBI	BB-IB	HP	SO	AVG	OBP	SLG	AOPS	ABR	SB-CS	FA	FR	Rng	Thr	G at Pos	BFW
McCRAW, TOM Tommy Lee B 11.21.1940 Malvern, AR BL/TL 6/183# d6.4 C22																								
1963	Chi A	102	280	38	71	11	3	6	33	21-1	3	46	.254	.309	.379	94	-3	15-4	.993	-2	88	112	1-97	-0.8
1964	Chi A	125	368	47	96	11	5	6	36	32-4	4	65	.261	.325	.367	95	-3	15-7	.992	-1	87	122	1-84,O-36(32-2-3)	-0.9
1965	Chi A	133	273	38	65	12	1	5	21	25-4	3	48	.238	.309	.344	91	-3	12-7	.993	1	130	95	1-72,O-64(37-31-3)	-0.7
1966	Chi A	151	389	49	89	16	4	5	48	29-7	5	40	.229	.288	.329	83	-9	20-11	.990	3	121	94	*1-121,O-41(29-0-16)	-1.3
1967	Chi A	125	453	55	107	18	3	11	45	33-2	1	55	.236	.288	.362	95	-4	24-10	.991	11	**140**	**114**	*1-123/O-6(1-4-1)	0.1
1968	Chi A	136	477	51	112	16	12	9	44	36-9	5	58	.235	.293	.375	101	-1	20-5	.986	3	119	107	*1-135	-0.4
1969	Chi A	93	240	21	62	12	2	2	25	21-6	3	24	.258	.326	.350	85	-5	1-3	.989	-6	91	98	1-44,O-41(11-16-17)	-1.6
1970	Chi A	129	332	39	73	11	2	6	31	21-3	4	50	.220	.273	.319	61	-18	12-3	.987	0	135	99	1-59,O-49(21-12-18)	-2.3
1971	Was A	122	207	33	44	6	4	7	25	19-2	5	38	.213	.291	.382	96	-2	3-3	.958	-3	102	33	O-60(26-1-37),1-30	-0.9
1972	Cle A	129	391	43	101	13	5	7	33	41-5	4	47	.258	.333	.371	106	3	12-10	1.000	1	103	37	O-84(42-22-24),1-38	-0.4
1973	Cal A	99	264	25	70	7	0	3	24	30-1	2	42	.265	.343	.326	97	0	3-2	1.000	4	91	156	O-34(32-1-1),1-25/D-8	-0.1
1974	Cal A	56	119	21	34	8	0	3	17	12-2	0	13	.286	.348	.429	131	5	2-1	1.000	2	94	56	1-29,O-12(7-0-5)/D-3	0.5
	Cle A	45	112	17	34	8	0	3	17	5-0	1	11	.304	.336	.455	128	4	0-1	.990	2	130	115	1-38/O(CF)	0.3
	Year	101	231	38	68	16	0	6	34	17-2	1	24	.294	.343	.442	130	9	2-2	.994	3	115	91	1-67,O-13(7-1-5)/D-3	0.8
1975	Cle A	23	51	7	14	1	1	2	5	7-2	0	7	.275	.362	.451	129	2	4-1	1.000	-1	79	96	1-16/O-3(LF)	0.0
Total	13	1468	3956	484	972	150	42	75	404	332-48	40	544	.246	.309	.362	94	-34	143-68	.991	12	116	106	1-911,O-431(241-90-125)/D-11	-8.5
McCRAY, RODNEY Rodney Duncan B 9.13.1963 Detroit, MI BR/TR 5-10/175# d4.30																								
1990	Chi A	32	6	8	0	0	0	0	0	1-0	0	4	.000	.143	.000	-58	-1	6-0	1.000	0	135	0	O-13(3-7-4)/D-7	0.0
1991	Chi A	17	7	2	2	0	0	0	0	0-0	0	2	.286	.286	.286	60	0	1-1	1.000	1	162	0	/O-8(4-2-2),D-6	0.0
1992	NY N	18	1	3	1	0	0	0	1	0-0	0	0	1.000	1.000	1.000	475	0	2-0	1.000	0	153	0	O-13(1-1-11)	0.1
Total	3	67	14	13	3	0	0	0	1	1-0	0	6	.214	.267	.214	36	-1	9-1	1.000	1	150	0	/O-34(8-10-17),D-13	0.1
McCREA, FRANK Francis William B 9.6.1896 Jersey City, NJ D 2.25.1981 Dover, NJ BR/TR 5-9/155# d9.26																								
1925	Cle A	1	5	1	1	0	0	0	0	0	0	0	.200	.200	.200	2	-1	0-0	1.000	-0	*65*	*0*	/C	-0.1
McCREDIE, WALT Walter Henry B 11.29.1876 Manchester, IA D 7.29.1934 Portland, OR BL/TR 6-2/195# d4.20																								
1903	Bro N	56	213	40	69	5	0	0	20	24	2		.324	.397	.347	116	6	10	.925	-4	79	165	O-56(RF)	0.0
McCREERY, TOM Thomas Livingston B 10.19.1874 Beaver, PA D 7.3.1941 Beaver, PA BB/TR 5-11/180# d6.8 ▲ OF Total (39-LF 203-CF 390-RF)																								
1895	Lou N	31	108	18	35	3	1	0	10	8	1	15	.324	.376	.370	99	0	3	.875	-4	49	0	O-18(RF)/P-8,S-4,31	-0.4
1896	Lou N	115	441	87	155	23	**21**	7	65	42	1	58	.351	.409	.546	156	34	26	.916	0	126	87	*O-111(0-2-109)/2P	2.4
1897	Lou N	91	344	55	96	5	6	4	40	40	0		.279	.354	.363	93	-3	13	.859	-6	100	74	*O-91(1-1-89)	-1.2
	NY N	49	177	36	53	8	5	1	28	22	1		.299	.380	.418	114	4	15	.900	-1	160	85	O-45(RF)/2-3	0.1
	Year	140	521	91	149	13	11	5	68	62	1		.286	.363	.382	100	1	28	.871	-6	120	78	*O-136(1-1-134)/2-3	-1.1
1898	NY N	35	121	15	24	4	3	1	17	19	0		.198	.307	.306	78	-3	3	.820	-5	85	0	O-35(1-0-35)	-0.9
	Pit N	53	190	33	59	5	7	2	20	26	0		.311	.394	.442	142	10	3	.934	-1	88	66	O-51(0-46-5)	0.6
	Year	88	311	48	83	9	10	3	37	45	0		.267	.360	.389	117	7	6	.901	-6	87	39	O-86(1-46-40)	-0.3
1899	Pit N	119	460	77	149	21	9	3	65	47	3		.324	.390	.428	125	17	11	.911	-12	102	48	O-98(15-50-33)/S-9,2-7	0.0
1900	Pit N	43	132	20	29	4	3	1	13	16	0		.220	.304	.318	71	-5	2	.887	1	179	169	O-35(17-1-17)/P	-0.6
1901	Bro N	91	335	47	97	11	14	3	53	32	2		.290	.355	.433	124	9	13	.947	1	83	70	O-82(4-78-0)/1-4,S-2	0.6
1902	Bro N	112	430	49	105	8	4	4	57	29	2		.244	.295	.309	86	-8	16	.979	-1	94	97	*1-108/O-4(1-0-3)	-1.2
1903	Bro N	40	141	13	37	5	2	0	10	20	0		.262	.354	.326	97	0	5	.892	-3	72	149	O-38(0-2-36)	-0.5
	Bos N	23	83	15	18	2	1	1	10	9	0		.217	.293	.301	72	-3	6	.900	-1	59	115	O-23(CF)	-0.5
	Year	63	224	28	55	7	3	1	20	29	0		.246	.332	.317	88	-3	11	.896	-4	67	136	O-61(0-25-36)	-1.0
Total	9	802	2962	465	857	99	76	27	388	310	10	73	.289	.359	.401	113	52	116	.906	-30	106	83	O-631R,1-113/S-15,2-11,P-10,3	-1.6
McCUE, FRANK Frank Aloysius B 10.4.1898 Chicago, IL D 7.5.1953 Chicago, IL BB/TR 5-9/150# d9.15																								
1922	Phi A	2	5	0	0	0	0	0	0	0	0	0	.000	.000	.000	-97	-1	0-0	—	-0	0	0	/3-2	-0.2
McCULLOUGH, CLYDE Clyde Edward B 3.4.1917 Nashville, TN D 9.18.1982 San Francisco, CA BR/TR 5-11.5/180# d4.28 Mil 1944-45 C4																								
1940	Chi N	9	26	4	4	1	0	0	1	5	0	5	.154	.290	.192	36	-2	0	1.000	1	*108*	*76*	/C-7	0.0
1941	Chi N	125	418	41	95	9	2	9	53	34	2	67	.227	.289	.323	75	-16	5	.982	-6	*89*	*93*	*C-119	-1.5
1942	Chi N	109	337	39	95	22	1	5	31	25	0	47	.282	.331	.398	117	7	7	.980	0	*110*	*108*	C-97	1.3
1943	Chi N	87	266	20	63	5	2	2	23	24	1	33	.237	.302	.293	73	-9	6	.977	-10	*126*	*41*	C-81	-1.6
1946	Chi N	95	307	38	88	18	5	4	34	22	2	39	.287	.338	.417	116	5	2	.991	-3	*111*	*74*	C-89	0.7
1947	Chi N	86	234	25	59	12	4	3	30	20	1	20	.252	.314	.376	86	-6	1	.984	4	*110*	*107*	C-64	0.2
1948	Chi N☆	69	172	10	36	4	2	1	7	15	0	25	.209	.273	.273	50	-13	0	.973	1	*93*	*125*	C-51	-0.9
1949	Pit N	91	241	30	57	9	3	4	21	24	4	30	.237	.316	.349	76	-8	1	.985	6	*122*	*100*	C-90	0.2
1950	Pit N	103	279	28	71	16	4	6	34	31	5	35	.254	.340	.405	92	-3	3	.985	-4	*126*	*95*	*C-100	-0.2
1951	Pit N	92	259	26	77	9	2	8	39	27	1	31	.297	.366	.440	113	5	2-0	.988	6	*108*	*109*	C-87	1.6
1952	Pit N	66	172	10	40	5	1	1	15	10	2	18	.233	.283	.291	58	-10	0-1	.981	4	*82*	*143*	C-61/1	-0.4
1953	Chi N☆	77	229	21	59	3	2	6	23	15	0	23	.258	.303	.367	72	-10	0-0	.987	-2	*84*	*112*	C-73	-0.9
1954	Chi N	31	81	9	21	7	0	3	17	5	1	5	.259	.310	.457	96	-1	0-0	.981	-2	*61*	*26*	C-26/3-3	-0.2
1955	Chi N	44	81	7	16	0	0	0	10	8-3	1	15	.198	.272	.198	29	-8	0-0	.989	3	*77*	*79*	C-37	-0.4
1956	Chi N	14	19	0	4	1	0	0	1	0-0	0	5	.211	.200	.263	27	-2	0-0	1.000	0	*60*	*129*	/C-7	-0.1
Total	15	1098	3121	308	785	121	28	52	339	265-3	20	398	.252	.314	.358	85	-71	27-1	.984	-2	*105*	*95*	C-989/3-3,1	-2.2
McCURDY, HARRY Harry Henry "Hank" B 9.15.1899 Stevens Point, WI D 7.21.1972 Houston, TX BL/TR 5-11/187# d7.4																								
1922	StL N	13	27	3	8	2	2	0	5	1	0	1	.296	.321	.519	119	0	0-0	.967	-1	*95*	*94*	/C-9,1-2	0.0
1923	StL N	67	185	17	49	11	2	0	15	11	0	11	.265	.306	.346	73	-7	3-1	.969	-6	*94*	*68*	C-58	-0.9
1926	Chi A	44	86	16	28	7	2	1	11	6	0	10	.326	.370	.488	127	3	0-1	.974	-2	*126*	*73*	C-25/1-8	0.2
1927	Chi A	86	262	34	75	19	3	1	27	32	1	24	.286	.366	.393	99	1	6-4	.972	-1	*115*	*84*	C-82	0.5
1928	Chi A	49	103	12	27	10	0	2	13	8	0	15	.262	.315	.417	92	-1	1-3	.964	-1	*130*	*52*	C-34	-0.2
1930	Phi N	80	148	23	49	6	2	1	25	15	0	12	.331	.393	.419	90	-2	0	.966	-6	*76*	*95*	C-41	-0.5
1931	Phi N	66	150	21	43	9	0	1	25	23	0	16	.287	.382	.367	95	0	2	.968	-3	*75*	*111*	C-45	0.0
1932	Phi N	62	136	13	32	6	1	1	14	17	1	13	.235	.325	.316	65	-6	0	.974	-1	*89*	*76*	C-42	-0.5
1933	Phi N	73	54	9	15	1	0	2	12	16	1	6	.278	.451	.407	130	3	0	—	0	*0*	*0*	/C-2	0.4
1934	Cin N	3	6	0	0	0	0	0	1	0	0	0	.000	.000	.000	-99	-2	0	1.000	1	293	212	/1	-0.1
Total	10	543	1157	148	326	71	12	9	148	129	3	108	.282	.355	.387	92	-11	12-9	.970	-19	*100*	*82*	C-338/1-11	-1.1
McDANIEL, TERRY Terrence Keith B 12.6.1966 Kansas City, MO BR/TR 5-9/205# d8.31																								
1991	NY N	23	29	3	6	1	0	0	2	1-0	0	11	.207	.233	.241	34	-3	2-0	1.000	1	128	0	O-14(7-5-4)	-0.2
McDAVID, RAY Ray Darnell B 7.20.1971 San Diego, CA BL/TR 6-3/190# d7.15																								
1994	SD N	9	28	2	7	1	0	0	2	1-0	0	8	.250	.276	.286	48	-2	1-0	1.000	-1	83	0	/O-7(4-2-1)	-0.3
1995	SD N	11	17	2	3	0	0	0	0	2-0	0	6	.176	.263	.176	19	-2	1-1	1.000	-1	72	0	/O-7(CF)	-0.3
Total	2	20	45	4	10	1	0	0	2	3-0	0	14	.222	.271	.244	37	-4	2-1	1.000	-1	79	0	/O-14(4-9-1)	-0.6
McDERMOTT, RED Frank A. B 11.12.1889 Philadelphia, PA D 9.11.1964 Philadelphia, PA BR/TR 5-6/150# d8.6																								
1912	Det A	5	15	2	4	1	0	0	0	0	1		.267	.313	.333	87	0	1	1.000	0	86	187	/O-5(LF)	0.0
McDERMOTT, MICKEY Maurice Joseph "Maury" B 8.29.1929 Poughkeepsie, NY D 8.7.2003 Phoenix, AZ BL/TL 6-2/170# d4.24 C1 ▲																								
1948	Bos A	7	8	2	3	1	0	0	0	0	0	0	.375	.375	.500	125	1	0-0	1.000	1	197	0	/P-7	0.0
1949	Bos A	12	33	3	7	3	0	0	6	3	0	6	.212	.278	.303	50	1	0-0	.941	-0	94	0	P-12	0.0
1950	Bos A	39	44	11	16	5	0	0	12	9	0	3	.364	.472	.477	131	7	0-0	.938	1	110	52	P-38	0.0
1951	Bos A	43	66	8	18	1	1	1	6	3	1	14	.273	.314	.364	76	2	0-1	.950	2	114	196	P-34	0.0
1952	Bos A	36	62	10	14	1	1	1	7	4	0	11	.226	.273	.323	60	2	0-0	.944	0	86	47	P-30	0.0
1953	Bos A	45	93	9	28	8	0	1	13	2	0	13	.301	.316	.419	92	7	0-1	.957	1	120	124	P-32	0.0
1954	Was A	54	95	7	19	3	0	0	4	7	0	12	.200	.255	.232	36	3	0-0	.955	1	118	72	P-30	0.0
1955	Was A	70	95	10	25	4	0	1	10	6-0	1	16	.263	.311	.337	79	8	1-0	.943	0	115	54	P-31	0.0
1956	†NY A	46	52	4	11	0	0	1	4	8-0	0	13	.212	.317	.269	58	3	0-0	1.000	-0	92	167	P-23	0.0
1957	KC A	58	49	6	12	1	0	4	7	9-2	0	16	.245	.362	.510	133	2	0-0	.960	1	147	0	P-29/1-2	0.0
1958	Det A	4	3	0	1	0	0	0	1	0-0	0	2	.333	.333	.333	78	0	0-0	—	-0	0	0	/P-2	0.0
1961	StL N	22	14	1	1	1	0	0	3	0-0	0	4	.071	.071	.143	-41	-1	0-0	1.000	-0	63	0	P-19	0.0
	KC A	7	5	0	1	1	0	0	1	1-0	0	2	.200	.333	.400	93	1	0-0	.500	-0	0	0	/P-4	0.0

Year	Tm Lg	G	AB	R	H	2B	3B	HR	RBI	BB-IB	HP	SO	AVG	OBP	SLG	AOPS	ABR	SB-CS	FA	FR	Rng	Thr	G at Pos	BFW
Total	12	443	619	71	156	29	2	9	74	52-2	2	112	.252	.312	.349	76	36	1-2	.951	5	111	84	P-291/1-2	0.0
McDERMOTT, TERRY Terrence Michael B 3.20.1951 Rockville Cen., NY BR/TR 6-3/205# d9.12																								
1972	LA N	9	23	2	3	0	0	0	0	2-0	0	8	.130	.200	.130	-5	-3	0-0	1.000	-0	68	97	/1-7	-0.4
McDERMOTT, SANDY Thomas Nathaniel B 3.15.1856 Zanesville, OH D 11.23.1922 Mansfield, OH d6.18																								
1885	Bal AA	1	0	0	0	0	0	0	0	0	0		—	—	—	—	0		—	-0	0	0	/2	0.0
McDONALD d5.18																								
1872	Eck NA	1	4	0	0	0	0	0	0	0		0	.000	.000	.000	-99	-1	0-0	.333	-1	59	0	/S	-0.2
McDONALD, TEX Charles E. (born Charles C. Crabtree) B 1.31.1891 Farmersville, TX D 3.31.1943 Houston, TX BL/TR 5-10/160# d4.11																								
1912	Cin N	61	140	16	36	3	4	1	15	13	2	24	.257	.329	.357	90	-2	5	.915	-8	81	49	S-42	-0.8
1913	Cin N	11	10	1	3	0	0	0	2	0	0	1	.300	.300	.300	72	0	0	—	-0	0	0	/S	-0.1
	Bos N	62	145	24	52	4	4	0	18	15	1	17	.359	.422	.441	144	9	4-6	.869	-2	104	169	3-31/2-6,O(RF)	0.7
	Year	73	155	25	55	4	4	0	20	15	1	18	.355	.415	.432	140	8	4-6	.869	-2	104	169	3-31/2-6,SO(RF)	0.6
1914	Pit F	67	223	27	71	16	7	3	29	13	2	23	.318	.361	.493	132	6	9	.925	3	82	270	O-29(RF),2-27/S-5	0.8
	Buf F	69	250	32	74	13	6	3	32	20	2	26	.296	.353	.432	111	0	11	.953	-2	103	71	O-61(2-1-58),2-10	-0.6
	Year	136	473	59	145	29	13	6	61	33	4	49	.307	.357	.461	121	5	20	.943	1	96	135	O-90(2-1-87),2-37/S-5	0.2
1915	Buf F	87	251	31	68	9	6	6	39	27	2	34	.271	.346	.426	114	1	5	.924	-5	96	53	O-65(12-0-53)	-0.8
Total	4	357	1019	131	304	45	27	13	135	88	9	125	.298	.359	.434	118	14	34-6	.936	-14	96	101	O-156(14-1-141)/S-48,2-43,3-31	-0.8
McDONALD, JACK Daniel B 1847 Brooklyn, NY D 11.23.1880 Brooklyn, NY 5-11/154# d5.2																								
1872	Atl NA	15	62	9	16	3	1	0	4	0		1	.258	.258	.339	70	-3	0-0	.720	-2	0	0	O-15(1-0-14)	-0.3
McDONALD, DAVE David Bruce B 5.20.1943 New Albany, IN BL/TR 6-3/215# d9.15																								
1969	NY A	9	23	0	5	1	0	0	2	2-0	0	5	.217	.280	.261	54	-1	0-1	.960	-1	84	47	/1-7	-0.3
1971	Mon N	24	39	3	4	2	0	1	4	4-0	0	14	.103	.178	.231	17	-4	0-0	.983	-1	81	146	/1-8,O(LF)	-0.6
Total	2	33	62	3	9	3	0	1	6	6-0	0	19	.145	.214	.242	31	-5	0-1	.972	-1	82	101	/1-15,O(LF)	-0.9
McDONALD, DONZELL Donzell B 2.20.1975 Long Beach, CA BB/TR 5-11/180# d4.19																								
2001	NY A	5	3	0	1	0	0	0	0	0-0	0	2	.333	.333	.333	76	0	0-0	1.000	-0	94	0	/O-3(1-2-0)	0.0
2002	KC A	10	22	3	4	2	0	0	1	4-0	0	5	.182	.296	.273	50	-1	1-0	1.000	-2	25	0	/O-7(LF)	-0.3
Total	2	15	25	3	5	2	0	0	1	4-0	0	7	.200	.300	.280	53	-1	1-0	1.000	-2	35	0	/O-10(8-2-0)	-0.3
McDONALD, ED Edward C. B 10.28.1886 Albany, NY D 3.11.1946 Albany, NY BR/TR 6/180# d8.5																								
1911	Bos N	54	175	28	36	7	3	1	21	40	2	39	.206	.359	.297	78	-3	11	.955	-2	95	121	3-53/S	-0.4
1912	Bos N	121	459	70	119	23	6	2	34	70	5	91	.259	.363	.349	94	-1	22	.940	1	99	109	*3-118	0.2
1913	Chi N	1	0	0	0	0	0	0	0	0	0	0	—	—	—	—	0	0	—	0			R	0.0
Total	3	176	634	98	155	30	9	3	55	110	7	130	.244	.362	.334	89	-4	33	.945	-1	98	113	3-171/S	-0.2
McDONALD, JIM James B Philadelphia, PA BR/TR 6/180# d6.2																								
1902	NY N	2	9	0	3	0	0	0	1	0	0		.333	.333	.333	107	0	0	1.000	-0	0	0	/O-2(RF)	0.0
McDONALD, JIM James Augustus B 8.6.1860 San Francisco, CA D 9.14.1914 San Francisco, CA d6.20																								
1884	Was U	2	6	0	1	0	0	0		0			.167	.167	.167	1	-1		.700	-1			/CO(RF)	-0.2
	Pit AA	38	145	11	23	3	0	0		2	0		.159	.170	.179	14	-13		.795	-5	97	74	3-22,O-15(1-12-2)/2	-1.7
1885	Buf N	5	14	0	0	0	0	0	0	0		4	.000	.000	.000	-97	-3		.875	1	135	102	/S-4,O(CF)	-0.2
Total	2	45	165	11	24	3	0	0	0	2		4	.145	.156	.164	4	-17		.795	-5			/3-22,O-17(1-13-3),S-4,2C	-2.1
McDONALD, JASON Jason Adam B 3.20.1972 Modesto, CA BB/TR 5-8/175# d6.5																								
1997	Oak A	78	236	47	62	11	4	4	14	36-0	1	49	.263	.361	.394	99	0	13-8	.961	-2	100	64	O-74(17-66-0)	-0.1
1998	Oak A	70	175	25	44	9	0	1	16	27-0	3	33	.251	.359	.320	81	-4	10-4	.956	4	106	221	O-60(11-33-25)	0.1
1999	Oak A	100	187	26	39	2	1	3	8	25-0	3	48	.209	.310	.278	54	-13	6-3	.993	4	113	85	O-89(31-53-13)/2D	-0.9
2000	Tex A	38	94	15	22	5	0	3	13	17-0	1	25	.234	.357	.383	86	-2	4-4	.988	7	124	314	O-32(11-3-26)	0.3
Total	4	286	692	113	167	27	5	11	51	105-0	8	155	.241	.347	.342	81	-19	33-19	.973	14	109	148	O-255(70-155-64)/D-5,2	-0.6
McDONALD, JOHN John Joseph B 9.24.1974 New London, CT BR/TR 5-11/175# d7.4																								
1999	Cle A	18	21	2	7	0	0	0	0	0-0	0	3	.333	.333	.333	68	-1	0-1	1.000	3	149	244	/2-7,S-6	0.2
2000	Cle A	9	9	0	4	0	0	0	0	0-0	0	1	.444	.444	.444	124	0	0-0	1.000	0	93	66	/S-7,2-2	0.1
2001	Cle A	17	22	1	2	1	0	0	0	1-0	1	7	.091	.167	.136	-18	-4	0-0	.955	-1	83	55	/S-9,2-3,3-3	-0.4
2002	Cle A	93	264	35	66	11	3	1	12	10-0	5	50	.250	.288	.326	65	-14	3-0	.986	12	118	107	2-64,S-21,3-10/D	0.3
2003	Cle A	82	214	21	46	9	1	1	14	11-0	2	31	.215	.258	.280	44	-18	3-3	.980	-7	110	134	2-37,S-27,3-23	-2.1
Total	5	219	530	59	125	21	4	2	26	22-0	8	92	.236	.275	.302	54	-37	6-4	.985	8	116	120	2-113/S-70,3-36,D	-1.9
McDONALD, JOE Malcolm Joseph B 4.9.1888 , TX D 5.30.1963 Baytown, TX BR/TR 5-11/175# d9.6																								
1910	StL A	10	32	4	5	0	0	0	1	1	0		.156	.182	.156	6	-4	0	.821	-2	77	156	3-10	-0.6
McDONALD, KEITH William Keith B 2.8.1973 Yokosuka, Japan BR/TR 6-2/215# d7.4																								
2000	StL N	6	7	3	3	0	0	3	5	2-0	0	1	.429	.556	1.714	441	4	0-0	1.000	1	83	0	/C-4	0.4
2001	StL N	2	2	0	0	0	0	0	0	0-0	0	1	.000	.000	.000	-99	-1	0-0	1.000	0	0	0	/C-2	0.0
Total	2	8	9	3	3	0	0	3	5	2-0	0	2	.333	.455	1.333	329	3	0-0	1.000	1	66	0	/C-6	0.4
McDONNELL, JIM James William "Mack" B 8.15.1922 Gagetown, MI D 4.24.1993 Detroit, MI BL/TR 5-11/165# d9.23																								
1943	Cle A	2	1	1	0	0	0	0	0	2	0	1	.000	.667	.000	108	0	0-0	1.000	-0	*0*	*0*	/C	0.0
1944	Cle A	20	43	5	10	0	0	0	4	4	0	3	.233	.298	.233	55	-3	0-0	.900	-2	*91*	*73*	C-13	-0.4
1945	Cle A	28	51	3	10	2	0	0	8	2	0	4	.196	.226	.235	36	-4	0-0	.980	5	*104*	*123*	C-23	0.1
Total	3	50	95	9	20	2	0	0	12	8	0	8	.211	.272	.232	48	-7	0-0	.953	2	*97*	*101*	/C-37	-0.3
McDONOUGH, ED Edward Sebastian B 9.11.1886 Elgin, IL D 9.2.1926 Elgin, IL BR/TR 6/160# d8.3																								
1909	Phi N	1	1	0	0	0	0	0	0	0	0		.000	.000	.000	-99	0	0	1.000	0	*0*	*294*	/C	0.0
1910	Phi N	5	9	1	1	0	0	0	0	0	0	1	.111	.111	.111	-34	-2	0	1.000	-1	*82*	*51*	/C-4	-0.2
Total	2	6	10	1	1	0	0	0	0	0	0	1	.100	.100	.100	-40	-2	0	1.000	-0	*70*	*87*	/C-5	-0.2
McDOUGALD, GIL Gilbert James B 5.19.1928 San Francisco, CA BR/TR 6-1/180# d4.20																								
1951	†NY A	131	402	72	123	23	4	14	63	56	4	54	.306	.396	.488	143	25	14-5	.949	-8	91	167	3-82,2-55	2.1
1952	†NY A★	152	555	65	146	16	5	11	78	57	4	73	.263	.336	.369	102	1	6-5	.968	16	**113**	**149**	*3-117,2-38	1.9
1953	†NY A	141	541	82	154	27	7	10	83	60	5	65	.285	.361	.416	113	10	3-4	.953	7	105	**124**	*3-136,2-26	1.7
1954	NY A	126	394	66	102	22	2	12	48	62	5	64	.259	.364	.416	118	12	3-4	.989	10	103	138	2-92,3-35	2.8
1955	†NY A	141	533	79	152	10	8	13	53	65-2	2	77	.285	.361	.407	109	6	6-4	**.985**	22	106	**127**	*2-126,3-17	3.7
1956	†NY A☆	120	438	79	136	13	3	13	56	68-1	3	59	.311	.405	.443	128	20	3-8	.970	9	97	129	S-92,2-31/3-5	3.5
1957	†NY A★	141	539	87	156	25	**9**	13	62	59-1	4	71	.289	.362	.442	121	16	2-5	.976	17	101	**131**	*S-121,2-21/3-7	4.4
1958	†NY A★	138	503	69	126	19	1	14	65	59-1	3	75	.250	.329	.376	98	-1	6-2	.977	1	97	**112**	*2-115,S-19	1.1
1959	NY A★	127	434	44	109	16	8	4	34	35-3	3	40	.251	.309	.353	85	-10	0-3	.989	9	104	115	2-53,S-52,3-25	0.5
1960	†NY A	119	337	54	87	16	4	8	34	38-0	3	45	.258	.337	.401	105	2	2-4	.945	2	106	116	3-84,2-42	0.5
Total	10	1336	4676	697	1291	187	51	112	576	559-8	36	623	.276	.356	.410	112	81	45-44	.984	85	101	116	2-599,3-508,S-284	22.2
McDOWELL, ODDIBE Oddibe B 8.25.1962 Hollywood, FL BL/TL 5-9/165# d5.19																								
1985	Tex A	111	406	63	97	14	5	18	42	36-2	3	85	.239	.304	.431	98	-3	25-7	.993	6	109	147	*O-103(CF)/D-4	0.6
1986	Tex A	154	572	105	152	24	7	18	49	65-5	1	112	.266	.341	.427	105	4	33-15	.991	-3	89	177	*O-148(CF)/D	0.1
1987	Tex A	128	407	65	98	26	4	14	52	51-0	0	99	.241	.324	.428	97	-1	24-2	.989	-2	97	107	*O-125(CF)	0.1
1988	Tex A	120	437	55	108	19	5	6	37	41-2	2	89	.247	.311	.355	85	-9	33-10	.989	-6	93	41	*O-113(CF)/D-3	-1.3
1989	Cle A	69	239	33	53	5	2	3	22	25-0	1	36	.222	.296	.297	67	-11	12-5	.992	1	99	136	O-64(63-1-0)/D-2	-1.1
	Atl N	76	280	56	85	18	4	7	24	27-3	0	37	.304	.365	.471	134	12	15-10	.978	0	107	58	O-68(CF)	1.2
1990	Atl N	113	305	47	74	14	0	7	25	21-0	2	53	.243	.295	.357	74	-11	13-2	.971	-8	83	53	O-72(12-60-1)	-1.8
1994	Tex A	59	183	34	48	5	1	1	15	28-0	0	39	.262	.355	.317	77	-5	14-2	.983	-1	103	66	O-53(0-31-27)/D-2	-0.4
Total	7	830	2829	458	715	125	28	74	266	294-12	9	550	.253	.323	.395	94	-24	169-53	.987	-13	97	107	O-746(75-649-28)/D-12	-2.6
McELVEEN, PRYOR Pryor Mynatt "Humpty" B 11.5.1881 Atlanta, GA D 10.27.1951 Pleasant Hill, TN BR/TR 5-10/168# d4.26 OF Total (1-LF 3-CF 7-RF)																								
1909	Bro N	81	258	22	51	8	1	3	25	14	1		.198	.242	.271	61	-13	6	.938	-3	93	111	3-37,O-13(1-3-7),S-10/1-5,2-5	-1.7

Year	Tm Lg	G	AB	R	H	2B	3B	HR	RBI	BB-IB	HP	SO	AVG	OBP	SLG	AOPS	ABR	SB-CS	FA	FR	Rng	Thr	G at Pos	BFW
1910	Bro N	74	213	19	48	8	3	1	26	22	3	47	.225	.307	.305	81	-5	6	.943	-7	79	161	3-54/S-6,2-3,C	-1.1
1911	Bro N	16	31	1	6	0	0	0	5	0	0	3	.194	.194	.194	9	-4	0	.929	-2	66	177	/2-5,S	-0.6
Total	3	171	502	42	105	16	4	4	56	36	4	50	.209	.268	.281	67	-22	12	.941	-12	85	141	/3-91,S-17,2-13,O-13R,1-5,C	-3.4
McELWEE, LEE Leland Stanford B 5.23.1894 LaMesa, CA D 2.8.1957 Union, ME BR/TR 5-10.5/160# d7.3																								
1916	Phi A	54	155	9	41	3	0	0	10	8	0	17	.265	.301	.284	79	-4	0	.883	1	96	114	3-30/O-9(RF),2-3,1S	-0.4
McELYEA, FRANK Frank B 8.4.1918 Hawthorne Twsp., IL D 4.19.1987 Evansville, IN BR/TR 6-6/221# d9.10 Mil 1943-45																								
1942	Bos N	7	4	2	0	0	0	0	0	0	0	0	.000	.000	.000	-99	-1	0	1.000	0	200	0	/O(LF)	-0.1
McEWING, JOE Joseph Earl B 10.19.1972 Bristol, PA BR/TR 5-10/170# d9.2 OF Total (150-LF 39-CF 77-RF)																								
1998	StL N	10	20	5	4	1	0	0	1	1-0	1	3	.200	.273	.250	39	-2	0-1	1.000	-1	83	106	/2-6,O-3(1-1-1)	-0.3
1999	StL N	152	513	65	141	28	4	9	44	41-8	6	87	.275	.333	.398	84	-13	7-4	.980	8	104	88	2-96,O-66(32-23-19)/3-6,1-2,S	-0.2
2000	†NY N	87	153	20	34	14	1	2	19	5-0	1	29	.222	.248	.366	56	-11	3-1	1.000	-3	94	74	O-52(43-11-6),3-19,2-16/S-4	-1.2
2001	NY N	116	283	41	80	17	3	8	30	17-0	10	57	.283	.342	.449	109	3	8-5	1.000	-0	89	71	O-62(48-2-25),3-25,S-12/2-5,1-3,D	0.2
2002	NY N	105	196	22	39	8	1	3	26	9-0	3	50	.199	.242	.296	46	-17	4-4	1.000	1	129	0	O-35(10-1-24),S-21,1-20,2-13,3-10	-1.7
2003	NY N	119	278	31	67	11	0	1	16	25-4	3	57	.241	.309	.291	60	-16	3-0	.995	4	89	88	2-55,S-42,O-18(16-1-2)/1-5,3-2	-0.8
Total	6	589	1443	184	365	79	9	23	136	98-12	24	283	.253	.308	.368	76	-56	25-15	.997	8	107	70	O-236L,2-191/S-80,3-62,1-30,D	-4.0
McFADDEN, GUY Guy G. B 9.3.1872 Topeka, KS D 3.10.1911 Topeka, KS d8.24																								
1895	StL N	4	14	1	3	0	0	0	2	0	0	2	.214	.214	.214	11	-2	0	.968	-1	0	135	/1-4	-0.2
McFADDEN, LEON Leon B 4.26.1944 Little Rock, AR BR/TR 6-2/195# d9.6																								
1968	Hou N	16	47	2	13	1	0	0	1	6-2	0	10	.277	.358	.298	101	0	1-0	.968	-1	102	38	S-16	0.1
1969	Hou N	44	74	3	13	2	0	0	3	4-0	0	9	.176	.218	.203	19	-8	1-2	.944	-2	91	0	O-17(4-0-13)/S-8	-1.1
1970	Hou N	2	0	0	0	0	0	0	0	0-0	0	0	—	—	—	—	0	0-0	—	0			R	0.0
Total	3	62	121	5	26	3	0	0	4	10-2	0	19	.215	.275	.240	50	-8	2-2	.966	-3	98	26	/S-24,O-17(4-0-13)	-1.0
McFARLAN, ALEX Alexander Shepherd B 11.11.1866 , KY D 3.2.1939 Pewee Valley, KY 5-9/165# d6.19 b-Dan																								
1892	Lou N	14	42	2	7	0	0	0	1	8	0	11	.167	.300	.167	46	-2	1	.773	-2	56	0	O-12(RF)/2-2	-0.4
McFARLAND, CHRIS Christopher B 8.17.1861 Fall River, MA D 5.24.1918 New Bedford, MA 5-9/170# d4.19																								
1884	Bal U	3	14	2	3	1	0	0		0			.214	.214	.286	46	-1		.571	-1	0	0	/O-3(CF),P	-0.2
McFARLAND, ED Edward William B 8.3.1874 Cleveland, OH D 11.28.1959 Cleveland, OH BR/TR 5-10/180# d7.7																								
1893	Cle N	8	22	5	9	2	1	0	6	1	1	2	.409	.458	.591	168	2	0	1.000	-1	0	0	/O-5(CF),3-2,C	0.0
1896	StL N	83	290	48	70	13	4	3	36	15	1	17	.241	.281	.345	67	-15	7	.961	1	*85*	***144***	C-80/O-2(RF)	-0.6
1897	StL N	31	107	14	35	5	2	1	17	8	0		.327	.374	.439	117	2	2	.965	-5	*68*	*124*	C-23/1-3,O-3(LF),2	0.0
	Phi N	38	130	18	29	3	5	1	16	14	2		.223	.308	.346	75	-5	2	.951	-2	*104*	*98*	C-37	-0.3
	Year	69	237	32	64	8	7	2	33	22	2		.270	.337	.388	93	-3	4	.957	-7	*89*	*109*	C-60/1-3,O-3(LF),2	-0.3
1898	Phi N	121	429	65	121	21	5	3	71	44	2		.282	.352	.375	113	8	4	.960	2	*110*	*102*	*C-121	2.0
1899	Phi N	96	324	59	108	22	9	2	57	36	2		.333	.403	.475	146	21	9	.968	11	*109*	*103*	C-94	3.6
1900	Phi N	94	344	50	105	14	8	0	38	29	3		.305	.364	.392	110	5	9	**.963**	-12	*78*	*112*	C-93/3	0.1
1901	Phi N	74	295	33	84	14	2	1	32	18	0		.285	.326	.356	96	-2	11	.970	2	*99*	***113***	C-74	0.8
1902	Chi A	75	246	29	56	9	2	1	25	19	3		.228	.291	.293	65	-11	8	.967	7	*128*	*90*	C-69/1	0.2
1903	Chi A	61	201	15	42	7	2	1	19	14	1		.209	.264	.279	66	-8	3	.968	0	*110*	*101*	C-56/1	-0.2
1904	Chi A	50	160	22	44	11	3	0	20	17	1		.275	.348	.381	136	7	2	.975	-4	*117*	*77*	C-49	0.9
1905	Chi A	80	250	24	70	13	4	0	31	23	2		.280	.345	.364	130	9	5	.973	8	*132*	*94*	C-70	2.6
1906	†Chi A	12	23	0	4	1	0	0	3	3	0		.174	.269	.217	54	-1	0	.973	0	*161*	*46*	/C-7	0.0
1907	Chi A	52	138	11	39	9	1	0	8	12	0		.283	.340	.362	128	5	3	.972	-1	*118*	*92*	C-43	0.9
1908	Bos A	19	48	5	10	2	1	0	4	1	0		.208	.224	.292	66	-2	0	.978	3	*100*	*128*	C-13	0.3
Total	14	894	3007	398	826	146	49	13	383	254	18	19	.275	.335	.369	104	15	65	.967	10	*106*	*105*	C-830/O-10(3-5-2),1-5,3-3,2	10.3
McFARLAND, HERM Hermas Walter B 3.11.1870 Des Moines, IA D 9.21.1935 Richmond, VA BL/TR 5-6/150# d4.21																								
1896	Lou N	30	110	11	21	4	1	1	12	9	0	14	.191	.252	.273	40	-10	4	.833	-3	103	264	O-28(3-18-9)/C	-1.3
1898	Cin N	19	64	10	18	1	3	0	11	7	1		.281	.361	.391	108	0	3	.968	-1	47	0	O-17(13-3-1)	-0.2
1901	Chi A	132	473	83	130	21	9	4	59	75	9		.275	.384	.383	116	15	33	.946	5	82	83	*O-132(LF)	1.2
1902	Chi A	7	27	5	5	0	0	0	4	2	0		.185	.241	.185	20	-3	1	1.000	-0	0	0	/O-7(2-0-5)	-0.3
	Bal A	61	242	54	78	19	6	3	36	36	4		.322	.418	.488	144	16	10	.965	4	146	52	O-61(CF)	1.6
	Year	68	269	59	83	19	6	3	40	38	4		.309	.402	.457	133	14	11	.967	4	132	47	O-68(2-61-5)	1.3
1903	NY A	103	362	41	88	16	9	5	45	46	3		.243	.333	.378	106	4	13	.939	-3	79	72	*O-103(39-58-7)	-0.5
Total	5	352	1278	204	340	61	28	13	167	175	17	14	.266	.362	.388	110	22	64	.941	2	91	83	O-348(189-140-22)/C	0.5
McFARLAND, HOWIE Howard Alexander B 3.7.1910 ElReno, OK D 4.7.1993 Wichita, KS BR/TR 6/175# d7.16																								
1945	Was A	6	11	0	1	0	0	0	2	0	0	3	.091	.091	.091	-52	-2	0-0	1.000	0	61	639	/O-3(1-0-2)	-0.2
McFARLANE, ORLANDO Orlando Dejesus (Quesada) B 6.28.1938 Oriente, Cuba BR/TR 6/180# d4.23																								
1962	Pit N	8	23	0	2	0	0	0	1	1-0	0	4	.087	.125	.087	-42	-5	0-0	1.000	1	*117*	*113*	/C-8	-0.3
1964	Pit N	37	78	5	19	5	0	0	1	4-2	0	27	.244	.280	.308	66	-3	0-0	.983	-3	*88*	*117*	C-35/O(RF)	-0.6
1966	Det A	49	138	16	35	7	0	5	13	9-1	1	46	.254	.304	.413	102	0	0-0	.991	-0	*134*	*104*	C-33	0.1
1967	Cal A	12	22	0	5	0	0	0	3	1-0	0	7	.227	.250	.227	47	-2	0-0	.935	-2	68	144	/C-6	-0.3
1968	Cal A	18	31	1	9	0	0	0	2	5-1	0	9	.290	.389	.290	112	1	0-0	.977	-0	46	56	/C-9	0.1
Total	5	124	292	22	70	12	0	5	20	20-4	1	93	.240	.290	.332	78	-9	0-0	.985	-4	*107*	*107*	/C-91,O(RF)	-1.0
McGAFFIGAN, PATSY Mark Andrew B 9.12.1888 Carlyle, IL D 12.22.1940 Carlyle, IL BR/TR 5-8/140# d4.16 Mil 1918																								
1917	Phi N	19	60	5	10	1	0	0	6	0	0	7	.167	.167	.183	7	-7	1	.920	1	103	82	S-17/O(RF)	-0.5
1918	Phi N	54	192	17	39	3	2	1	8	16	1	23	.203	.268	.255	56	-10	3	.948	-8	98	84	2-53/S	-1.9
Total	2	73	252	22	49	4	2	1	14	16	1	30	.194	.245	.238	45	-17	4	.948	-7	98	84	/2-53,S-18,O(RF)	-2.4
McGAH, EDDIE Edward Joseph B 9.30.1921 Oakland, CA D 9.30.2002 Oakland, CA BR/TR 6/183# d4.26																								
1946	Bos A	15	37	2	8	1	1	0	1	7	0	7	.216	.341	.297	75	-1	0-0	.981	-1	*116*	*68*	C-14	-0.2
1947	Bos A	9	14	1	0	0	0	0	2	3	0	0	.000	.176	.000	-45	-3	0-0	.964	1	*151*	*79*	/C-7	-0.1
Total	2	24	51	3	8	1	1	0	3	10	0	7	.157	.295	.216	41	-4	0-0	.975	-0	*127*	*71*	/C-21	-0.3
McGANN, AMBROSE Ambrose B 1875 Baltimore, MD ?/170# d5.2																								
1895	Lou N	20	73	9	21	5	2	0	9	8	0	6	.288	.358	.411	105	1	6	.852	-2	86	25	/S-8,3-6,O-5(RF)	-0.1
McGANN, DAN Dennis Lawrence "Cap" B 7.15.1871 Shelbyville, KY D 12.13.1910 Louisville, KY BB/TR 6/190# d8.8																								
1896	Bos N	43	171	25	55	6	7	2	30	12	5	10	.322	.383	.474	118	4	2	.905	-11	89	64	2-43	-0.5
1898	Bal N	145	535	99	161	18	8	5	106	53	39		.301	.404	.393	126	22	33	.983	2	98	102	*1-145	2.2
1899	Bro N	63	214	49	52	11	4	2	32	21	19		.243	.362	.360	96	0	16	.985	1	102	137	1-61	0.1
	Was N	76	280	65	96	9	8	5	58	14	18		.343	.410	.486	147	18	11	.990	3	101	77	1-76	1.8
	Year	139	494	114	148	20	12	7	90	35	**37**		.300	.389	.431	124	18	27	**.988**	4	101	105	*1-137	1.9
1900	StL N	121	444	79	132	10	9	4	58	32	**24**		.297	.376	.387	112	8	26	**.990**	-1	85	63	*1-121/2	0.6
1901	StL N	103	423	73	115	15	9	6	56	16	**23**		.272	.333	.392	116	8	17	.984	-3	85	**127**	*1-103	0.3
1902	Bal A	68	250	40	79	10	8	0	42	19	6		.316	.378	.420	116	5	17	.987	3	113	117	1-68	0.7
	NY N	61	227	25	68	5	7	0	21	12	8		.300	.356	.383	130	7	12	.981	1	109	112	1-61	0.8
1903	NY N	129	482	75	130	21	6	3	50	32	12		.270	.331	.357	93	-5	36	**.988**	-1	85	97	*1-129	-0.8
1904	NY N	141	517	81	148	22	6	6	71	36	**18**		.286	.354	.387	123	15	42	**.991**	3	98	119	*1-141	1.6
1905	†NY N	136	491	88	147	23	14	5	75	55	**19**		.299	.391	.434	143	28	22	**.991**	5	102	101	*1-136	3.1
1906	NY N	134	451	62	107	14	8	0	37	60	13		.237	.344	.304	100	3	30	**.995**	4	99	102	*1-133	0.4
1907	NY N	81	262	29	78	9	1	2	36	29	7		.298	.383	.363	129	11	9	.994	5	113	95	1-81	1.6
1908	Bos N	135	475	52	114	8	5	2	55	38	**19**		.240	.321	.291	97	0	9	.988	6	125	**124**	*1-121/2-9	0.5
Total	12	1436	5222	842	1482	181	100	42	727	429	230	10	.284	.364	.381	117	124	282	.989	16	100	105	*1-1376/2-53	12.4
McGARR, CHIPPY James B. B 5.10.1863 Worcester, MA D 6.6.1904 Worcester, MA BR/TR 5-7/168# d7.11 U1																								
1884	CP U	19	70	10	11	2	0	0		0			.157	.157	.186	4	-10		.905	-3	74	56	2-13/O-6(5-0-1)	-1.2
1886	Phi AA	71	267	41	71	9	3	2	31	9	2		.266	.295	.345	99	-1	17	.850	-1	100	110	S-71	0.0
1887	Phi AA	**137**	536	93	158	23	6	1	63	23	2		.295	.326	.366	93	-7	84	.875	-1	95	123	*S-137	-0.3

Year	Tm Lg	G	AB	R	H	2B	3B	HR	RBI	BB-IB	HP	SO	AVG	OBP	SLG	AOPS	ABR	SB-CS	FA	FR	Rng	Thr	G at Pos	BFW
1888	StL AA	34	132	17	31	1	0	0	13	6	0		.235	.268	.242	58	-7	25	.895	-6	99	109	2-33/S	-1.1
1889	KC AA	25	108	22	31	3	0	0	16	6	1	11	.287	.330	.315	79	-3	12	.857	-2	78	282	3-11/O-6(2-0-4),2-5,S-3	-0.4
	Bal AA	3	7	1	1	0	0	0	0	1	0	1	.143	.250	.143	13	-1	0	.583	-2	53	0	/S-3	-0.3
	Year	28	115	23	32	3	0	0	16	7	1	12	.278	.325	.304	76	-4	12	.857	-5	78	282	3-11/O-6(2-0-4),S-6,2-5	-0.7
1890	Bos N	121	487	68	115	12	7	1	51	34	4	38	.236	.291	.296	66	-23	39	**.933**	-3	95	78	*3-115/S-5,O(RF)	-2.1
1893	Cle N	63	249	38	77	12	0	0	28	20	1	15	.309	.363	.357	86	-5	24	.886	0	103	66	3-63	-0.3
1894	Cle N	128	523	94	144	24	6	2	74	28	3	29	.275	.316	.356	59	-37	31	.902	-6	95	90	*3-128	-3.1
1895	†Cle N	113	422	86	114	14	2	2	59	35	1	33	.270	.328	.327	65	-23	19	.872	-5	98	93	*3-109/2-4	-2.1
1896	†Cle N	113	455	68	122	16	4	1	53	22	0	30	.268	.302	.327	62	-26	16	.924	-7	96	132	*3-113/C	-2.7
Total	10	827	3256	538	875	116	28	9	388	184	14	157	.269	.311	.330	71	-143	267	.903	-35	96	98	3-539,S-220/2-55,O-13(7-0-6),C	-13.6
McGARR, JIM James Vincent "Reds" B 11.9.1888 Philadelphia, PA D 7.21.1981 Miami, FL BR/TR 5-9.5/170# d5.18																								
1912	Det A	1	4	0	0	0	0	0	0	0	0		.000	.000	.000	-99	-1	0	.800	-0	124	0	/2	-0.1
McGARVEY, DAN Daniel Francis B 12.2.1887 Philadelphia, PA D 3.7.1947 Philadelphia, PA d5.18																								
1912	Det A	1	3	0	0	0	0	0	0	1	1		.000	.400	.000	18	0	0	.667	1	0	0	/O	0.1
McGEACHY, JACK John Charles B 5.23.1864 Clinton, MA D 4.5.1930 Cambridge, MA BR/TR 5-8/165# d6.17 ▲																								
1886	Det N	6	27	3	9	0	1	0	4	0		3	.333	.333	.407	120	0	2	.875	-1	89	0	/O-6(LF)	0.0
	StL N	59	226	31	46	12	3	2	24	1		37	.204	.207	.310	59	-11	8	.880	0	138	173	O-55(CF)/2-2,3-2	-1.1
	Year	65	253	34	55	12	4	2	28	1		40	.217	.220	.320	66	-11	10	.880	-0	133	157	O-61(6-55-0)/2-2,3-2	-1.1
1887	Ind N	99	405	49	109	17	3	1	56	5	1	16	.269	.280	.333	72	-16	27	.894	4	125	85	*O-98(0-97-2)/3P	-1.2
1888	Ind N	118	452	45	99	15	2	0	30	5	2	21	.219	.231	.261	56	-23	49	.932	5	137	117	*O-117(2-6-109)/SP	-1.9
1889	Ind N	131	532	83	142	32	1	2	63	9	2	39	.267	.282	.342	73	-22	37	.918	8	144	170	*O-131(RF)/P-3	-1.4
1890	Bro P	104	443	84	108	24	4	1	65	19	2	12	.244	.278	.323	57	-30	21	.906	-3	81	24	*O-104(22-31-52)	-2.8
1891	Phi AA	50	201	24	46	4	3	2	13	6	1	12	.229	.255	.308	61	-12	9	.920	2	115	0	O-50(4-12-34)	-1.0
	Bos AA	41	178	26	45	2	1	1	21	12	1	8	.253	.304	.292	72	-7	11	.910	-4	57	0	O-41(38-0-3)	-1.0
	Year	91	379	50	91	6	4	3	34	18	2	20	.240	.278	.301	66	-19	20	.916	-2	89	0	O-91(42-12-37)	-2.0
Total	6	608	2464	345	604	106	18	9	276	57	9	148	.245	.265	.314	65	-121	164	.909	11	119	94	O-602(72-201-331)/P-5,3-3,2-2,S	-10.4
McGEARY, MIKE Michael Henry B 1851 Philadelphia, PA BR/TR 5-7/138# d5.9 M3																								
1871	Tro NA	**29**	148	42	39	4	0	0	12	6		0	.264	.292	.291	67	-6	**20**-4	**.897**	-1			*C-26/S-3	-0.3
1872	Ath NA	**47**	225	68	81	9	2	0	35	2		1	.360	.366	.418	140	10	13-8	.867	5			C-23,S-23/O(RF)	1.0
1873	Ath NA	**52**	275	63	83	8	1	0	31	1		1	.302	.304	.338	84	-7	4-6	.804	-5	95	105	*S-43,C-14/3	-1.0
1874	Ath NA	54	271	61	87	10	2	0	22	1		2	.321	.324	.373	113	2	10-2	.837	8			C-28,S-26/O-4(RF)	0.9
1875	Phi NA	68	310	71	90	6	2	0	37	1		1	.290	.293	.323	109	2	19-4	.743	1	84	71	3-27,2-23,S-18/O-3(0-1-2),M	0.2
1876	StL N	61	276	48	72	3	0	0	30	2		1	.261	.266	.272	84	-4		.889	8	112	117	*2-56/C-5,O(CF)3	0.5
1877	StL N	57	258	35	65	3	2	0	20	2		6	.252	.258	.279	73	-8		.883	6	102	82	2-39,3-19	0.1
1879	Pro N	**85**	374	62	103	7	2	0	35	5		13	.275	.285	.305	96	-2		.884	1	97	80	*2-73,3-12	0.3
1880	Pro N	18	59	5	8	0	0	0	1	0		6	.136	.136	.136	-8	-6		.887	4	147	101	3-17/2-2,SM	-0.2
	Cle N	31	111	14	28	2	1	0	6	4		3	.252	.278	.288	94	-1		.887	-5	81	140	3-29/O-2(RF)	-0.5
	Year	49	170	19	36	2	1	0	7	4		9	.212	.230	.235	60	-7		.887	-1	99	129	3-46/2-2,O-2(RF),S	-0.7
1881	Cle N	11	41	1	9	0	0	0	5	0		6	.220	.220	.220	41	-3		.724	-5	64	69	3-11,M	-0.7
1882	Det N	34	133	14	19	4	1	0	2	2		20	.143	.156	.188	10	-13		.928	4	102	51	S-33/2-3	-0.7
Total	5 NA	250	1229	305	380	37	7	0	137	11		5	.309	.315	.351	104	1	66-24	.000	9			S-113/C-91,3-28,2-23,O-8(0-1-7)	0.8
Total	6	297	1252	179	304	19	6	0	99	15		55	.243	.252	.268	72	-37		.885	13			2-173/3-89,S-34,C-5,O-3(0-1-2)	-1.2
McGEE, DAN Daniel Aloysius B 9.29.1911 New York, NY D 12.4.1991 Lakehurst, NJ BR/TR 5-8.5/152# d7.14																								
1934	Bos N	7	22	2	3	0	0	0	1	3	0	6	.136	.240	.136	4	-3	0	.951	1	118	79	/S-7	-0.1
McGEE, FRANK Francis De Sales B 4.28.1899 Columbus, OH D 1.30.1934 Columbus, OH BR/TR 5-11.5/175# d9.19																								
1925	Was A	2	3	0	0	0	0	0	0	0	0	1	.000	.000	.000	-99	-1	0-0	1.000	0	147	125	/1-2	-0.1
McGEE, PAT Patrick B Philadelphia, PA D 6.21.1889 New York, NY d9.24																								
1874	Atl NA	16	65	4	11	1	0	0	6	0		3	.169	.169	.185	15	-5	0-0	.795	-2	46	0	O-15(6-9-0)/S-2,2	-0.6
1875	Mut NA	25	95	4	17	2	0	0	9	0		10	.179	.179	.200	30	-7	0-0	.848	-2	53	0	O-25(CF)	-0.8
	Atl NA	18	65	3	10	3	1	0	5	1		4	.154	.167	.231	42	-3	0-0	.912	5	381	229	O-13(CF)/2-6,3	0.1
	Year	43	160	7	27	5	1	0	14	1		14	.169	.174	.213	34	-10	0-0	.875	3	161	75	O-38(CF)/2-6,3	-0.7
Total	2 NA	59	225	11	38	6	1	0	20	1		17	.169	.173	.204	29	-15	0-0	.000	1	125	52	/O-53(6-47-0),2-7,S-2,3	-1.3
McGEE, WILLIE Willie Dean B 11.2.1958 San Francisco, CA BB/TR 6-1/175# d5.10																								
1982	†StL N	123	422	43	125	12	8	4	56	12-2	2	58	.296	.318	.391	97	-4	24-12	.958	-11	91	46	*O-117(1-116-0)	-1.6
1983	StL N★	147	601	75	172	22	8	5	75	26-2	0	98	.286	.314	.374	90	-10	39-8	.987	-4	97	93	*O-145(CF)	-1.0
1984	StL N	145	571	82	166	19	11	6	50	29-2	1	80	.291	.325	.394	104	0	43-10	.985	3	103	126	*O-141(CF)	0.8
1985	†StL N★	152	612	114	**216**	26	**18**	10	82	34-2	0	86	**.353**	.384	.503	148	36	56-16	.978	0	102	118	*O-149(3-146-0)	4.3
1986	StL N	124	497	65	127	22	7	7	48	37-7	1	82	.256	.306	.370	87	-10	19-16	**.991**	-1	102	114	*O-121(CF)	-1.5
1987	†StL N★	153	620	76	177	37	11	11	105	24-5	2	90	.285	.312	.434	94	-8	16-4	.981	-8	93	100	*O-152(CF)/S	-1.5
1988	StL N★	137	562	73	164	24	6	3	50	32-5	1	84	.292	.329	.372	100	-1	41-6	.975	-3	96	140	*O-135(CF)	0.3
1989	StL N	58	199	23	47	10	2	3	17	10-0	1	34	.236	.275	.352	76	-7	8-6	.976	-2	97	80	O-47(CF)	-1.0
1990	StL N	125	501	76	168	32	5	3	62	38-6	1	86	**.335**	.382	.437	125	18	28-9	.957	4	105	**182**	*O-124(0-118-6)	2.4
	†Oak A	29	113	23	31	3	2	0	15	10-0	0	18	.274	.333	.336	91	-1	3-0	.986	0	103	73	O-28(CF)/D	-0.1
1991	SF N	131	497	67	155	30	3	4	43	34-3	2	74	.312	.357	.408	119	13	17-9	.978	-5	95	80	*O-128(0-89-48)	0.6
1992	SF N	138	474	56	141	20	2	1	36	29-3	1	88	.297	.339	.354	102	1	13-4	.976	1	95	150	*O-119(0-31-90)	0.0
1993	SF N	130	475	53	143	28	1	4	46	38-7	1	67	.301	.353	.389	102	2	10-9	.979	-3	93	98	*O-126(RF)	-0.8
1994	SF N	45	156	19	44	3	0	5	23	15-2	0	24	.282	.337	.397	97	-1	3-0	.988	-1	98	64	O-42(RF)	-0.3
1995	†Bos A	67	200	32	57	11	3	2	15	9-0	0	41	.285	.311	.400	82	-6	5-2	.973	3	94	250	O-64(3-27-47)	-0.4
1996	†StL N	123	309	52	95	15	2	5	41	18-2	2	60	.307	.348	.417	102	1	5-2	.962	1	95	149	O-83(35-11-42)/1-6	-0.1
1997	StL N	122	300	29	90	19	4	3	38	22-2	0	59	.300	.347	.420	101	0	8-2	.981	-1	87	154	O-81(18-18-53)/D-3	-0.2
1998	StL N	120	269	27	68	10	1	3	34	14-5	0	49	.253	.287	.331	63	-15	7-2	.938	1	92	159	O-88(56-6-38)/1D	-1.6
1999	StL N	132	271	25	68	7	0	0	20	17-3	0	60	.251	.293	.277	46	-23	7-4	.972	-4	89	58	O-89(30-19-43)/1-3	-2.7
Total	18	2201	7649	1010	2254	350	94	79	856	448-58	15	1238	.295	.333	.396	100	-15	352-121	.976	-31	97	117	*O-1979(146-1351-535)/1-10,D-7,S	-4.4
McGEEHAN, DAN Daniel De Sales B 6.7.1885 Jeddo, PA D 7.12.1955 Hazleton, PA BR/TR 5-6/135# d4.22 b-Conny																								
1911	StL N	3	9	0	2	0	0	0	1	0	0	1	.222	.222	.222	25	-1	0	.818	-1	80	0	/2-3	-0.2
McGHEE, ED Warren Edward B 9.29.1924 Perry, AR D 2.13.1986 Memphis, TN BR/TR 5-11/170# d9.20																								
1950	Chi A	3	6	0	1	0	1	0	0	0	0	1	.167	.167	.500	67	-1	0-0	1.000	-0	71	0	/O(RF)	-0.1
1953	Phi A	104	358	36	94	11	4	1	29	32	3	43	.263	.328	.324	74	-13	4-3	.982	5	117	47	O-99(1-97-1)	-1.3
1954	Phi A	21	53	5	11	2	0	2	9	4	0	8	.208	.259	.358	69	-3	0-1	.933	-0	115	0	O-13(2-11-0)	-0.4
	Chi A	42	75	12	17	1	0	0	5	12	0	8	.227	.333	.240	57	-4	5-0	.982	2	102	227	O-34(5-18-11)	-0.2
	Year	63	128	17	28	3	0	2	14	16	0	16	.219	.303	.289	62	-7	5-1	.960	2	107	138	O-47(7-29-11)	-0.6
1955	Chi A	26	13	6	1	0	0	0	0	6-0	0	1	.077	.368	.077	24	-1	2-1	.923	0	131	0	O-17(5-12-0)	-0.1
Total	4	196	505	59	124	14	5	3	43	54-0	3	61	.246	.321	.311	70	-22	11-5	.975	7	115	69	O-164(13-138-13)	-2.1
McGHEE, BILL William Mac "Fibber" B 9.5.1905 Shawmut, AL D 3.10.1984 Decatur, GA BL/TL 5-10.5/185# d7.5																								
1944	Phi A	77	287	27	83	12	0	1	19	21	0	20	.289	.338	.341	96	-2	2-1	.989	-1	95	82	1-75	-0.7
1945	Phi A	93	250	24	63	6	1	0	19	24	1	16	.252	.320	.284	76	-7	3-2	.989	-3	86	47	O-48(40-0-9)/1-8	-1.5
Total	2	170	537	51	146	18	1	1	38	45	1	36	.272	.329	.315	87	-9	5-3	.990	-4	98	85	/1-83,O-48(40-0-9)	-2.2
McGILVRAY, BILL William Alexander "Big Bill" B 4.29.1883 Portland, OR D 5.23.1952 Denver, CO BL/TL 6/160# d4.17																								
1908	Cin N	2	2	0	0	0	0	0	0	0	0		.000	.000	.000	-99	0	0	—	0			H	-0.1
McGINLEY, TIM Timothy S. B 1854 Philadelphia, PA D 11.2.1899 Oakland, CA 5-9.5/155# d4.30																								
1875	Cen NA	13	52	5	12	0	1	0	5	0		4	.231	.231	.269	80	-1	0-0	.646	-6			C-12/O-2(RF)	-0.6
	NH NA	32	131	13	36	3	1	0	10	0		7	.275	.275	.313	119	3	1-1	.807	-7			C-32,3-2	-0.3
	Year	45	183	18	48	3	2	0	15	0		11	.262	.262	.301	107	2	1-1	.762	-13			C-44/O-2(RF),3-2	-0.9
1876	Bos N	9	40	5	6	0	0	0	2	0		1	.150	.150	.150	0	-4		.600	-4	0	0	/O-6(CF),C-3	-0.7

Year	Tm Lg	G	AB	R	H	2B	3B	HR	RBI	BB-IB	HP	SO	AVG	OBP	SLG	AOPS	ABR	SB-CS	FA	FR	Rng	Thr	G at Pos	BFW
McGINN, FRANK Frank J. B 1869 Cincinnati, OH D 11.19.1897 Cincinnati, OH d6.9																								
1890	Pit N	1	4	0	0	0	0	0	0	0	0	2	.000	.000	.000	-99	-1	0	1.000	-0	0	0	/O(CF)	-0.1
McGINNIS, RUSS Russell Brent B 6.18.1963 Coffeyville, KS BR/TR 6-3/225# d6.3																								
1992	Tex A	14	33	2	8	4	0	0	4	3-0	0	7	.242	.306	.364	90	0	0-0	1.000	-3	76	75	C-10/1-2,3-2	-0.3
1995	KC A	3	5	1	0	0	0	0	0	1-0	0	1	.000	.167	.000	-51	-1	0-0	1.000	-1	0	0	/13O(LF)	-0.2
Total	2	17	38	3	8	4	0	0	4	4-0	0	8	.211	.286	.316	69	-1	0-0	1.000	-4	76	75	/C-10,3-3,1-3,O(LF)	-0.5
McGLONE, JOHN John T. B 1864 Brooklyn, NY D 11.24.1927 Brooklyn, NY TR 5-10/165# d10.7																								
1886	Was N	4	15	2	1	0	0	0	1	0		3	.067	.067	.067	-64	-3	0	.846	-1	55	0	/3-4	-0.4
1887	Cle AA	21	79	14	20	2	1	0	10	7	3		.253	.337	.304	82	-2	15	.854	1	90	75	3-21	-0.1
1888	Cle AA	55	203	22	37	1	3	1	22	16	2		.182	.249	.232	56	-10	26	.787	-6	89	65	3-48/O-7(CF)	-1.4
Total	3	80	297	38	58	3	4	1	33	23	5	3	.195	.265	.242	58	-15	41	.810	-7	88	65	/3-73,O-7(CF)	-1.9
McGOVERN, ART Arthur John B 2.27.1882 St.John, NB, CAN D 11.14.1915 Thornton, RI BR/TR 5-10/160# d4.21																								
1905	Bos A	15	44	1	5	1	0	0	1	4	1		.114	.204	.136	9	-4	0	.951	-2	*120*	*61*	C-15	-0.6
McGOWAN, BEAUTY Frank Bernard B 11.8.1901 Branford, CT D 5.6.1982 Hamden, CT BL/TR 5-11/190# d4.12																								
1922	Phi A	99	300	36	69	10	5	1	20	40	1	46	.230	.323	.307	63	-16	6-5	.965	6	108	145	O-82(0-56-28)	-1.5
1923	Phi A	95	287	41	73	9	1	1	19	36	1	25	.254	.340	.303	69	-12	4-3	.971	2	99	132	O-79(26-17-36)	-1.5
1928	StL A	47	168	35	61	13	4	2	18	16	2	15	.363	.425	.524	143	11	2-1	.962	-1	105	61	O-47(0-11-37)	0.6
1929	StL A	125	441	62	112	26	6	2	51	61	1	34	.254	.346	.354	78	-13	5-2	.975	2	97	124	*O-117(0-34-84)	-1.9
1937	Bos N	9	12	0	1	0	0	0	0	1	0	2	.083	.154	.083	-37	-2	0	1.000	-0	89	0	/O-2(RF)	-0.3
Total	5	375	1208	174	316	58	16	6	108	154	5	122	.262	.347	.351	80	-32	17-11	.970	9	101	122	O-327(26-118-187)	-4.6
McGRAW, JOHN John Joseph "Mugsy" or "Little Napoleon" B 4.7.1873 Truxton, NY D 2.25.1934 New Rochelle, NY BL/TR 5-7/155# d8.26 M33 HF1937 OF Total (21-LF 9-CF 30-RF)																								
1891	Bal AA	33	115	17	31	3	5	0	14	12	4	17	.270	.359	.383	111	1	4	.811	-12	70	98	S-21/O-9(RF),2-3	-0.8
1892	Bal N	79	286	41	77	13	2	1	26	32	6	21	.269	.355	.339	107	4	15	.897	3	149	85	O-34(8-6-20),2-34/S-8,3-3	0.6
1893	Bal N	127	480	123	154	9	10	5	64	101	16	11	.321	.454	.412	129	28	38	.894	-17	90	82	*S-117,O-11(10-0-1)	1.3
1894	†Bal N	124	512	156	174	18	14	1	92	91	13	12	.340	.451	.436	110	13	78	.892	1	107	98	*3-118/2-6	1.2
1895	†Bal N	96	388	110	143	13	6	2	48	60	5	9	.369	.459	.448	131	22	61	.878	8	119	**148**	*3-95/2	2.5
1896	†Bal N	23	77	20	25	2	2	0	14	11	2	4	.325	.422	.403	116	2	13	.833	-2	97	157	3-18/1	0.0
1897	†Bal N	106	391	90	127	15	3	0	48	99	9		.325	**.471**	.379	126	25	44	.886	-12	91	**134**	*3-105	1.3
1898	Bal N	143	515	**143**	176	8	10	0	53	**112**	19		.342	.475	.396	148	44	43	.900	-8	97	96	*3-137/O-3(CF)	3.5
1899	Bal N	117	399	**140**	156	13	3	1	33	**124**	14		.391	**.547**	.446	165	53	73	.945	1	102	85	*3-117,M	4.9
1900	StL N	99	334	84	115	10	4	2	33	85	23		.344	**.505**	.416	157	38	29	.909	-6	97	58	*3-99	3.1
1901	Bal A	73	232	71	81	14	9	0	28	61	**14**		.349	.508	.487	169	29	24	.890	-14	78	56	3-69,M	1.5
1902	Bal A	20	63	14	18	3	2	1	3	17	2		.286	.451	.444	143	5	5	.864	-5	63	202	3-19,M	0.0
	NY N	35	107	13	25	0	0	0	5	26	4		.234	.401	.234	98	3	7	.926	-2	99	96	S-34,M	0.2
1903	NY N	12	11	2	3	0	0	0	1	1	3		.273	.467	.273	109	1	1	—	-1	0	0	/2-2,O-2(LF),S3M	-0.1
1904	NY N	5	12	0	4	0	0	0	0	3	0		.333	.467	.333	142	1	0	.947	2	129	381	/2-2,S-2,M	0.3
1905	NY N	3	0	0	0	0	0	0	0	0	0		—	—	—	—	0	1	—	-0	0	0	/O(LF)M	0.0
1906	NY N	4	2	0	0	0	0	0	0	1	0		.000	.333	.000	4	0	0	—	-0	0	0	/3M	0.0
Total	16	1099	3924	1024	1309	121	70	13	462	836	134	74	.334	.466	.410	135	269	436	.898	-65	99	102	3-782,S-183/O-60R,2-48,1	19.5
McGRIFF, FRED Frederick Stanley B 10.31.1963 Tampa, FL BL/TL 6-3/215# d5.17																								
1986	Tor A	3	5	1	1	0	0	0	0	0-0	0	2	.200	.200	.200	9	-1	0-0	1.000	-0	0	0	/1D	-0.1
1987	Tor A	107	295	58	73	16	0	20	43	60-4	1	104	.247	.376	.505	128	14	3-2	.983	-1	84	56	D-90,1-14	0.9
1988	Tor A	154	536	100	151	35	4	34	82	79-3	4	149	.282	.376	.552	156	42	6-1	**.997**	-3	90	113	*1-153	2.9
1989	†Tor A	161	551	98	148	27	3	**36**	92	119-12	4	132	.269	.399	.525	**162**	**51**	7-4	.989	2	109	109	*1-159/D-2	4.1
1990	Tor A	153	557	91	167	21	1	35	88	94-12	2	108	.300	.400	.530	156	44	5-3	.996	10	124	99	*1-147/D-6	4.4
1991	SD N	153	528	84	147	19	1	31	106	105-**26**	2	135	.278	.396	.494	146	36	4-1	.990	-10	79	113	*1-153	1.6
1992	SD N★	152	531	79	152	30	4	**35**	104	96-23	1	108	.286	.394	.556	164	48	8-6	.991	-0	100	89	*1-151	3.8
1993	SD N	83	302	52	83	11	1	18	46	42-4	1	55	.275	.361	.497	126	11	4-3	.983	-7	75	77	1-83	-0.4
	†Atl N	68	255	59	79	18	1	19	55	34-2	1	51	.310	.392	.612	163	23	1-0	.992	0	100	114	1-66	1.7
	Year	151	557	111	162	29	2	37	101	76-6	2	106	.291	.375	.549	143	34	5-3	.987	-7	86	94	*1-149	1.3
1994	Atl N★	113	424	81	135	25	1	34	94	50-8	1	76	.318	.389	.623	156	34	7-3	.994	-3	86	86	*1-112	2.1
1995	†Atl N★	**144**	528	85	148	27	1	27	93	65-6	5	99	.280	.361	.489	119	15	3-6	.996	3	101	100	*1-144	0.3
1996	†Atl N★	159	617	81	182	37	1	28	107	68-12	2	116	.295	.365	.494	118	17	7-3	.992	8	115	102	*1-158	0.9
1997	†Atl N	152	564	77	156	25	1	22	97	68-4	4	112	.277	.356	.441	106	5	5-0	.990	-2	95	111	*1-149	-0.9
1998	TB A	151	564	73	160	33	0	19	81	79-9	2	118	.284	.371	.443	109	10	7-2	.995	-4	88	**123**	*1-135,D-14	-0.6
1999	TB A	144	529	75	164	30	1	32	104	86-11	1	107	.310	.405	.552	140	34	1-0	.989	6	121	**109**	*1-125,D-18	2.5
2000	TB A★	158	566	82	157	18	0	27	106	91-10	0	120	.277	.373	.452	110	10	2-0	.993	-7	83	108	*1-144,D-10	-1.0
2001	TB A	97	343	40	109	18	0	19	61	40-9	0	69	.318	.387	.536	143	22	1-1	.986	4	120	85	1-74,D-17	1.6
	Chi N	49	170	27	48	7	2	12	41	26-4	3	37	.282	.383	.559	148	12	0-1	.990	-2	77	85	1-49	0.5
2002	Chi N	146	523	67	143	27	2	30	103	63-6	4	99	.273	.353	.505	129	19	1-2	.993	-9	67	76	*1-137/D-2	-0.3
2003	LA N	86	297	32	74	14	0	13	40	31-4	1	66	.249	.322	.428	99	-1	0-0	.989	-3	85	114	1-79	-1.1
Total	18	2433	8685	1342	2477	438	24	491	1543	1296-169	39	1863	.285	.378	.511	134	445	72-38	.992	-19	96	102	*1-2233,D-161	22.9
McGRIFF, TERRY Terence Roy B 9.23.1963 Fort Pierce, FL BR/TR 6-2/195# d7.11																								
1987	Cin N	34	89	6	20	3	0	2	11	8-0	0	17	.225	.289	.326	60	-5	0-0	.983	2	98	111	C-33	-0.2
1988	Cin N	35	96	9	19	3	0	1	4	12-0	0	31	.198	.284	.260	56	-5	1-0	.990	0	74	141	C-32	-0.3
1989	Cin N	6	11	1	3	0	0	0	2	2-1	0	3	.273	.385	.273	88	0	0-0	.929	0	63	86	/C-6	0.1
1990	Cin N	2	4	0	0	0	0	0	0	0-0	0	1	.000	.000	.000	-96	-1	0-0	1.000	0	23	535	/C	-0.1
	Hou N	4	5	0	0	0	0	0	0	0-0	0	0	.000	.000	.000	-99	-1	0-0	.900	-1	54	0	/C-4	-0.3
	Year	6	9	0	0	0	0	0	0	0-0	0	1	.000	.000	.000	-99	-2	0-0	.938	-1	43	193	/C-5	-0.4
1993	Fla N	3	7	0	0	0	0	0	0	1-0	0	2	.000	.125	.000	-60	-2	0-0	1.000	-0	0	0	/C-3	-0.2
1994	StL N	42	114	10	25	6	0	0	13	13-1	2	11	.219	.308	.272	55	-7	0-0	.991	2	79	131	C-39	-0.3
Total	6	126	326	26	67	12	0	3	30	36-2	2	65	.206	.287	.270	51	-21	1-0	.985	3	79	126	C-118	-1.3
McGRILLIS, MARK Mark A. B 10.22.1872 Philadelphia, PA D 5.16.1935 Philadelphia, PA 6/148# d9.17																								
1892	StL N	1	3	0	0	0	0	0	0	0	0	1	.000	.000	.000	-99	-1	0	1.000	0	131	0	/3	-0.1
McGUCKIN, JOE Joseph W. B 3.13.1862 Paterson, NJ D 12.31.1903 Yonkers, NY 5-8.5/160# d8.27																								
1890	Bal AA	11	37	2	4	0	0	0	2	6	1		.108	.250	.108	6	-4	3	.962	3	200	230	O-11(RF)	-0.1
McGUINNESS, JOHN John James B 1857 , Ireland D 12.19.1916 Binghamton, NY 5-10.5/150# d5.6																								
1876	NY N	1	4	0	0	0	0	0	0	0		0	.000	.000	.000	-99	-1		.500	-2	79	0	/2C	-0.2
1879	Syr N	12	51	7	15	1	1	0	4	0		6	.294	.294	.353	126	1		.928	-1	94	129	1-12	0.0
1884	Phi U	53	220	25	52	8	1	0		5			.236	.253	.282	67	-15		.959	-0	81	88	1-48/2-5,S	-1.8
Total	3	66	275	32	67	9	2	0	4	5		6	.244	.257	.291	75	-15		.954	-2	84	96	/1-60,2-6,SC	-2.0
McGUIRE, JIM James A. B 2.4.1875 Dunkirk, NY D 1.26.1917 Buffalo, NY TR d9.10																								
1901	Cle A	18	69	4	16	2	0	0	3	0	0		.232	.232	.261	38	-6	0	.913	0	93	134	S-18	-0.5
McGUIRE, DEACON James Thomas B 11.18.1863 Youngstown, OH D 10.31.1936 Duck Lake, MI BR/TR 6-1/185# d6.21 M6 C6 OF Total (4-LF 4-CF 25-RF)																								
1884	Tol AA	45	151	12	28	7	0	1		5	1		.185	.217	.252	50	-8		.906	-6			C-41/O-4(1-3-0),S-3	-1.0
1885	Det N	34	121	11	23	4	2	0	9	5		23	.190	.222	.256	54	-6		.920	9			C-31/O-3(LF)	0.5
1886	Phi N	50	167	25	33	7	1	2	18	19		25	.198	.280	.287	72	-5	2	.899	-5			C-49/O(RF)	-0.6
1887	Phi N	41	150	22	46	6	6	2	23	11	2	8	.307	.362	.467	121	4	3	.884	-1			C-41	0.5
1888	Phi N	12	51	7	17	4	2	0	11	4	0	9	.333	.382	.490	167	4	0	.800	-5			C-10/3-2	0.0
	Det N	3	13	0	0	0	0	0	0	0	0	4	.000	.000	.000	-99	-3	0	.810	-2			/C-3	-0.5
	Year	15	64	7	17	4	2	0	11	4	0	13	.266	.309	.391	116	1	0	.802	-7			C-13/3-2	-0.5
	Cle AA	26	94	15	24	1	3	1	13	7	4		.255	.333	.362	126	3	2	.891	-1			C-17/1-6,O-3(RF)	0.2
1890	Roc AA	87	331	46	99	16	4	4	53	21	8		.299	.356	.408	135	14	8	.938	11	*115*	*86*	C-71,1-15/O-3(0-1-2),P	2.6
1891	Was AA	114	413	55	125	22	10	3	66	43	10	34	.303	.382	.426	138	21	10	.911	-13	*87*	*111*	*C-98,O-18(RF)/3-3,1	1.3
1892	Was N	97	315	46	73	14	4	4	43	61	2	49	.232	.360	.340	115	9	7	.936	-15	*67*	*103*	C-89/1-8,O(RF)	0.2

Year	Tm Lg	G	AB	R	H	2B	3B	HR	RBI	BB-IB	HP	SO	AVG	OBP	SLG	AOPS	ABR	SB-CS	FA	FR	Rng	Thr	G at Pos	BFW
1893	Was N	63	237	29	61	14	3	1	26	26	3	12	.257	.338	.354	86	-4	3	.889	-9	78	98	C-50,1-12	-0.7
1894	Was N	104	425	67	130	18	6	6	78	33	7	19	.306	.366	.419	91	-6	11	.918	-17	71	110	*C-104	-1.1
1895	Was N	**133**	538	89	181	30	8	10	97	40	5	18	.336	.388	.478	124	18	17	.937	-1	78	**142**	*C-133/S	2.3
1896	Was N	108	389	60	125	25	3	2	70	30	6	14	.321	.379	.416	109	6	12	.936	-6	87	92	*C-98/1	0.8
1897	Was N	93	327	51	112	17	7	4	53	21	2		.343	.386	.474	127	12	9	.947	-1	80	123	C-73/1-6	1.5
1898	Was N	131	489	59	131	18	3	1	57	24	6		.268	.310	.323	82	-12	10	.967	-8	65	103	C-93,1-37,M	-1.2
1899	Was N	59	199	25	54	3	1	1	12	16	3		.271	.335	.312	79	-6	3	.973	-8	77	110	C-56/1	-0.8
	Bro N	46	157	22	50	12	4	0	23	12	5		.318	.385	.446	125	6	4	.971	2	92	107	C-46	1.0
	Year	105	356	47	104	15	5	1	35	28	8		.292	.357	.371	99	0	7	.972	-6	84	109	*C-102/1	0.2
1900	†Bro N	71	241	20	69	15	2	0	34	19	4		.286	.348	.365	91	-2	2	.952	-5	93	97	C-69	-0.1
1901	Bro N	85	301	28	89	16	4	0	40	18	3		.296	.342	.375	105	2	4	.960	-9	79	96	C-81/1-3	0.1
1902	Det A	73	229	27	52	14	1	2	23	24	0		.227	.300	.323	71	-8	0	.952	-6	82	88	C-70	-0.8
1903	Det A	72	248	15	62	12	1	0	21	19	1		.250	.306	.306	87	-3	3	.960	-8	77	96	C-69/1	-0.5
1904	NY A	101	322	17	67	12	2	0	20	27	3		.208	.276	.258	66	-11	2	.970	6	95	108	C-97/1	0.5
1905	NY A	72	228	9	50	7	2	0	33	18	5		.219	.291	.268	69	-7	3	.975	-3	114	85	C-71	-0.3
1906	NY A	51	144	11	43	5	0	0	14	12	3		.299	.365	.333	108	2	3	.966	0	108	75	C-49/1	0.7
1907	NY A	1	1	0	0	0	0	0	0	0	0		.000	.000	.000	-93	0	0	1.000	0	0	255	/C	0.0
	Bos A	6	4	1	3	0	0	1	1	0	0		.750	.750	1.500	620	2	0	—	0			HM	0.2
	Year	7	5	1	3	0	0	1	1	0	0		.600	.600	1.200	470	2	0	1.000	0	0	255	/C	0.2
1908	Bos A	1	1	0	0	0	0	0	0	0	0		.000	.000	.000	-97	0	0	—	0			HM	0.0
	Cle A	1	4	0	1	1	0	0	2	0	0		.250	.250	.500	142	0	0	1.000	-0	0	0	/1	0.0
	Year	2	5	0	1	1	0	0	2	0	0		.200	.200	.400	93	0	0	1.000	-0	0	0	/1	0.0
1910	Cle A	1	3	0	1	0	0	0	0	0	1		.333	.500	.333	159	0	0	1.000	-1	53	118	/CM	0.0
1912	Det A	1	2	1	1	0	0	0	0	0	0		.500	.500	.500	192	0	0	.714	-0	129	194	/C	0.0
Total	26	1782	6295	770	1750	300	79	45	840	515	84	215	.278	.341	.372	101	22	118	.938	-101	74	91	*C-1612/1-94,O-33R,3-5,S-4,P	4.8

McGUIRE, MICKEY M C Adolphus B 1.18.1941 Dayton, OH BR/TR 5-10/170# d9.7

Year	Tm Lg	G	AB	R	H	2B	3B	HR	RBI	BB-IB	HP	SO	AVG	OBP	SLG	AOPS	ABR	SB-CS	FA	FR	Rng	Thr	G at Pos	BFW
1962	Bal A	6	4	0	0	0	0	0	0	0-0	0	0	.000	.000	.000	-99	-1	0-0	1.000	-0	88	0	/S-5	-0.1
1967	Bal A	10	17	2	4	0	0	0	2	0-0	0	2	.235	.235	.235	40	-1	0-0	1.000	-3	36	0	/2-4	-0.5
Total	2	16	21	2	4	0	0	0	2	0-0	0	2	.190	.190	.190	11	-2	0-0	1.000	-3	88	0	/S-5,2-4	-0.6

McGUIRE, RYAN Ryan Byron B 11.23.1971 Bellflower, CA BL/TL 6-2/210# d6.5

Year	Tm Lg	G	AB	R	H	2B	3B	HR	RBI	BB-IB	HP	SO	AVG	OBP	SLG	AOPS	ABR	SB-CS	FA	FR	Rng	Thr	G at Pos	BFW
1997	Mon N	84	199	22	51	15	2	3	17	19-1	0	34	.256	.320	.397	87	-4	1-4	.960	2	109	126	O-44(21-2-22),1-30/D-3	-0.6
1998	Mon N	130	210	17	39	9	0	1	10	32-0	0	55	.186	.292	.243	44	-17	0-0	.980	-2	101	66	1-78,O-46(33-7-8)	-2.2
1999	Mon N	88	140	17	31	7	2	2	18	27-0	0	33	.221	.347	.343	78	-4	1-1	.997	8	165	71	1-58,O-23(16-1-7)	0.0
2000	NY N	1	2	0	0	0	0	0	0	1-0	0	0	.000	.333	.000	-6	0	0-0	1.000	0	215	0	/O(RF)	0.0
2001	Fla N	48	54	8	10	2	0	1	8	7-0	0	15	.185	.270	.278	46	-4	1-0	1.000	1	139	0	/O-9(RF),1-4	-0.4
2002	Bal A	17	26	0	2	1	0	0	2	2-0	0	7	.077	.143	.115	-32	-5	0-0	1.000	0	99	113	/1-7,D	-0.5
Total	6	368	631	64	133	34	4	7	55	88-1	0	144	.211	.306	.311	62	-34	3-5	.992	10	124	84	1-177,O-123(70-10-47)/D-4	-3.7

McGUIRE, BILL William Patrick B 2.14.1964 Omaha, NE BR/TR 6-3/205# d8.2

Year	Tm Lg	G	AB	R	H	2B	3B	HR	RBI	BB-IB	HP	SO	AVG	OBP	SLG	AOPS	ABR	SB-CS	FA	FR	Rng	Thr	G at Pos	BFW
1988	Sea A	9	16	1	3	0	0	0	2	3-0	0	2	.188	.316	.188	43	-1	0-0	1.000	-3	69	54	/C-9	-0.3
1989	Sea A	14	28	2	5	0	0	1	4	2-0	0	6	.179	.233	.286	44	-2	0-0	1.000	2	119	63	C-14	0.0
Total	2	23	44	3	8	0	0	1	6	5-0	0	8	.182	.265	.250	44	-3	0-0	1.000	-1	100	60	/C-23	-0.3

McGUNNIGLE, BILL William Henry "Gunner" B 1.1.1855 Boston, MA D 3.9.1899 Brockton, MA BR/TR 5-9/155# d5.2 M5 ▲

Year	Tm Lg	G	AB	R	H	2B	3B	HR	RBI	BB-IB	HP	SO	AVG	OBP	SLG	AOPS	ABR	SB-CS	FA	FR	Rng	Thr	G at Pos	BFW
1879	Buf N	47	171	22	30	0	1	0	5	5		24	.175	.199	.187	27	-13		.918	3	87	0	O-34(RF),P-14	-0.7
1880	Buf N	7	22	0	4	0	0	0	1	0		4	.182	.182	.182	23	-2		1.000	-2	54	0	/P-5,O-3(1-1-1)	-0.2
	Wor N	1	4	0	0	0	0	0	0	0		2	.000	.000	.000	-92	-1		1.000	-0	0	0	/O(1-0-1)	-0.1
	Year	8	26	0	4	0	0	0	1	0		6	.154	.154	.154	5	-3		1.000	-2	54	0	/P-5,O-4(2-1-2)	-0.3
1882	Cle N	1	5	2	1	0	0	0	0	0		1	.200	.200	.200	30	0		—	-0	0	0	/O(CF)	0.0
Total	3	56	202	24	35	0	1	0	6	5		31	.173	.193	.183	25	-16		.900	1	77	0	/O-39(2-2-36),P-19	-1.0

McGWIRE, MARK Mark David B 10.1.1963 Pomona, CA BR/TR 6-5/225# d8.22

Year	Tm Lg	G	AB	R	H	2B	3B	HR	RBI	BB-IB	HP	SO	AVG	OBP	SLG	AOPS	ABR	SB-CS	FA	FR	Rng	Thr	G at Pos	BFW
1986	Oak A	18	53	10	10	1	0	3	9	4-0	1	18	.189	.259	.377	76	-2	0-1	.833	-4	78	40	3-16	-0.6
1987	Oak A★	151	557	97	161	28	4	**49**	118	71-8	5	131	.289	.370	**.618**	168	54	1-1	.992	-7	85	80	*1-145/3-8,O-3(RF)	3.5
1988	†Oak A★	155	550	87	143	22	1	32	99	76-4	4	117	.260	.352	.478	135	27	0-0	.993	-10	78	97	*1-154/O(RF)	0.6
1989	†Oak A★	143	490	74	113	17	0	33	95	83-5	3	94	.231	.339	.467	132	22	1-1	.995	5	110	108	*1-141/D-2	1.7
1990	†Oak A★	156	523	87	123	16	0	39	108	**110**-9	7	116	.235	.370	.489	146	36	2-1	.997	-8	83	**108**	*1-154/D-2	1.7
1991	Oak A✳	154	483	62	97	22	0	22	75	93-3	3	116	.201	.330	.383	103	5	2-1	.997	-1	94	93	*1-152	-0.7
1992	†Oak A★	139	467	87	125	22	0	42	104	90-12	5	105	.268	.385	**.585**	**180**	52	0-1	.995	-13	69	101	*1-139	2.9
1993	Oak A	27	84	16	28	6	0	9	24	21-5	1	19	.333	.467	.726	231	17	0-1	1.000	-2	77	90	1-25	1.2
1994	Oak A	47	135	26	34	3	0	9	25	37-3	0	40	.252	.413	.474	140	10	0-0	.988	-3	74	89	1-40/D-5	0.4
1995	Oak A✳	104	317	75	87	13	0	39	90	88-5	11	77	.274	.441	.685	200	52	1-1	.986	-1	98	85	1-91,D-10	3.8
1996	Oak A★	130	423	104	132	21	0	**52**	113	116-16	8	112	.312	**.467**	**.730**	**201**	72	0-0	.990	-5	87	**125**	*1-109,D-18	5.0
1997	Oak A★	105	366	48	104	24	0	34	81	58-8	4	98	.284	.383	.628	162	34	1-0	.994	-3	90	94	*1-101	2.1
	StL N	51	174	38	44	3	0	24	42	43-8	5	61	.253	.411	.684	183	22	2-0	.998	-1	88	101	1-50	1.6
1998	StL N★	155	509	130	152	21	0	**70**	147	**162**-28	6	155	.299	**.470**	**.752**	**218**	**97**	1-0	.992	-9	87	101	*1-151	**7.1**
1999	StL N★	153	521	118	145	21	1	**65**	**147**	133-**21**	2	141	.278	.424	.697	**177**	64	0-0	.990	-6	89	97	*1-151	4.2
2000	†StL N✳	89	236	60	72	8	0	32	73	76-12	7	78	.305	.483	.746	204	43	1-0	.998	-9	49	93	1-70	2.6
2001	†StL N	97	299	48	56	4	0	29	64	56-3	3	118	.187	.316	.492	107	2	0-0	.994	-8	62	95	1-90	-1.4
Total	16	1874	6187	1167	1626	252	6	583	1414	1317-150	75	1596	.263	.394	.588	165	607	12-8	.993	-83	85	98	*1-1763/D-37,3-24,O-4(RF)	35.7

McHALE, JIM James Bernard "J.B." B 12.17.1875 Miners Mills, PA D 6.17.1959 Los Angeles, CA BR/TR 5-11/165# d4.14

Year	Tm Lg	G	AB	R	H	2B	3B	HR	RBI	BB-IB	HP	SO	AVG	OBP	SLG	AOPS	ABR	SB-CS	FA	FR	Rng	Thr	G at Pos	BFW
1908	Bos A	21	67	9	15	2	2	0	7	4	1		.224	.278	.313	90	-1	4	.970	-1	104	0	O-19(1-18-0)	-0.3

McHALE, JOHN John Joseph B 9.21.1921 Detroit, MI BL/TR 6/200# d5.28 Mil 1943

Year	Tm Lg	G	AB	R	H	2B	3B	HR	RBI	BB-IB	HP	SO	AVG	OBP	SLG	AOPS	ABR	SB-CS	FA	FR	Rng	Thr	G at Pos	BFW
1943	Det A	4	3	0	0	0	0	0	0	1	0	1	.000	.250	.000	-23	0	0-0	—	0			H	0.0
1944	Det A	1	1	0	0	0	0	0	0	0	0	0	.000	.000	.000	-95	0	0-0	—	0			H	0.0
1945	†Det A	19	14	0	2	0	0	0	1	1	1	4	.143	.250	.143	14	-1	0-0	1.000	0	302	0	/1-3	-0.1
1947	Det A	39	95	10	20	1	0	3	11	7	0	24	.211	.265	.316	59	-6	1-1	.995	-1	82	64	1-25	-0.8
1948	Det A	1	1	0	0	0	0	0	0	0	0	0	.000	.000	.000	-97	0	0-0	—	0			H	0.0
Total	5	64	114	10	22	1	0	3	12	9	1	29	.193	.258	.281	49	-7	1-1	.995	-0	87	63	/1-28	-0.9

McHALE, BOB Robert Emmet "Rabbit" B 2.25.1872 Michigan Bluff, CA D 6.9.1952 Sacramento, CA d5.9

Year	Tm Lg	G	AB	R	H	2B	3B	HR	RBI	BB-IB	HP	SO	AVG	OBP	SLG	AOPS	ABR	SB-CS	FA	FR	Rng	Thr	G at Pos	BFW
1898	Was N	11	33	5	6	2	0	0	7	1	3		.182	.270	.242	47	-2	1	.900	-1	0	0	/O-9(CF),S1	-0.3

McHENRY, AUSTIN Austin Bush "Mac" B 9.22.1895 Wrightsville, OH D 11.27.1922 Jefferson Twsp., OH BR/TR 5-11/152# d6.22

Year	Tm Lg	G	AB	R	H	2B	3B	HR	RBI	BB-IB	HP	SO	AVG	OBP	SLG	AOPS	ABR	SB-CS	FA	FR	Rng	Thr	G at Pos	BFW
1918	StL N	80	272	32	71	12	6	1	29	21	2	24	.261	.319	.360	111	3	8	.952	1	89	159	O-80(LF)	0.0
1919	StL N	110	371	41	106	19	11	1	47	19	1	57	.286	.322	.404	125	10	7	.985	4	93	**164**	*O-103(73-26-7)	1.0
1920	StL N	137	504	66	142	19	11	10	65	25	0	73	.282	.316	.423	115	7	8-11	.952	4	102	129	*O-133(89-52-0)	0.1
1921	StL N	152	574	92	201	37	8	17	102	38	2	48	.350	.393	.531	145	37	10-20	.965	5	114	70	*O-152(146-0-6)	2.5
1922	StL N	64	238	31	72	18	3	5	43	14	1	27	.303	.344	.466	112	4	2-2	.935	5	104	171	O-61(LF)	0.3
Total	5	543	1959	262	592	105	39	34	286	117	6	229	.302	.343	.448	126	61	35-33	.960	19	102	128	O-529(449-78-13)	3.9

McHENRY, VANCE Vance Loren B 7.10.1956 Chico, CA BR/TR 5-9/165# d8.13

Year	Tm Lg	G	AB	R	H	2B	3B	HR	RBI	BB-IB	HP	SO	AVG	OBP	SLG	AOPS	ABR	SB-CS	FA	FR	Rng	Thr	G at Pos	BFW
1981	Sea A	15	18	3	4	0	0	0	2	1-0	0	1	.222	.263	.222	39	-1	0-0	.893	-2	90	137	S-13/D	-0.3
1982	Sea A	3	1	0	0	0	0	0	0	0-0	0	0	.000	.000	.000	-97	0	0-0	.500	-0	0	0	/SD	0.0
Total	2	18	19	3	4	0	0	0	2	1-0	0	1	.211	.250	.211	32	-1	0-0	.867	-2	88	135	/S-14,D-2	-0.3

McILVEEN, IRISH Henry Cooke B 7.27.1880 Belfast, Ireland D 10.18.1960 Lorain, OH BL/TL 5-11.5/180# d7.10

Year	Tm Lg	G	AB	R	H	2B	3B	HR	RBI	BB-IB	HP	SO	AVG	OBP	SLG	AOPS	ABR	SB-CS	FA	FR	Rng	Thr	G at Pos	BFW
1906	Pit N	5	5	1	2	0	0	0	0	0	0		.400	.400	.400	143	0	0	1.000	0	100	0	/P-2	0.0
1908	NY A	44	169	17	36	3	3	0	8	14	1		.213	.277	.266	76	-5	6	.949	-1	77	0	O-44(13-1-30)	-0.8
1909	NY A	4	3	0	0	0	0	0	0	1	0		.000	.250	.000	-20	0	0	—	0			H	0.0
Total	3	53	177	18	38	3	3	0	8	15	1		.215	.280	.266	76	-5	6	.949	-0	77	0	/O-44(13-1-30),P-2	-0.8

Year	Tm Lg	G	AB	R	H	2B	3B	HR	RBI	BB-IB	HP	SO	AVG	OBP	SLG	AOPS	ABR	SB-CS	FA	FR	Rng	Thr	G at Pos	BFW
McINNIS, STUFFY John Phalen "Jack" B 9.19.1890 Gloucester, MA D 2.16.1960 Ipswich, MA BR/TR 5-9.5/162# d4.12 Mil 1918 M1																								
1909	Phi A	19	46	4	11	0	0	1	4	2	1		.239	.286	.304	85	-1	0	.886	-1	92	111	S-14	-0.2
1910	Phi A	38	73	10	22	2	4	0	12	7	0		.301	.363	.438	152	4	3	.927	-4	83	80	S-17/2-5,3-4,O(LF)	0.1
1911	†Phi A	126	468	76	150	20	10	3	77	25	5		.321	.361	.425	121	11	23	.982	-15	85	122	1-97,S-24	-0.4
1912	Phi A	**153**	568	83	186	25	13	3	101	49	3		.327	.384	.433	138	28	27	.984	3	110	**121**	*1-153	2.7
1913	†Phi A	148	543	79	176	30	4	4	90	45	6	31	.324	.382	.416	137	26	16	**.992**	-1	89	110	*1-148	2.2
1914	†Phi A	149	576	74	181	12	8	1	95	19	4	27	.314	.341	.368	118	8	25-19	**.995**	0	90	109	*1-149	0.4
1915	Phi A	119	456	44	143	14	4	0	49	14	2	17	.314	.337	.362	113	4	8-8	.989	6	**116**	81	*1-119	0.6
1916	Phi A	140	512	42	151	25	3	1	60	25	3	19	.295	.331	.361	114	6	7	.992	7	115	93	*1-140	1.1
1917	Phi A	150	567	50	172	19	4	0	44	33	0	19	.303	.342	.351	113	7	18	.993	2	99	86	*1-150	0.5
1918	†Bos A	117	423	40	115	11	5	0	56	19	2	10	.272	.306	.322	91	-7	10	**.992**	5	114	88	1-94,3-23	-0.4
1919	Bos A	120	440	32	134	12	5	1	58	23	1	11	.305	.341	.361	103	0	8	.995	3	104	**133**	*1-118	0.0
1920	Bos A	148	559	50	166	21	3	2	71	18	2	19	.297	.321	.356	83	-16	6-11	**.996**	-2	92	118	*1-148	-2.3
1921	Bos A	152	584	72	179	31	10	0	76	21	4	9	.307	.335	.394	88	-13	2-4	**.999**	4	103	109	*1-152	-1.8
1922	Cle A	142	537	58	164	28	7	1	78	15	1	5	.305	.325	.389	85	-14	1-5	**.997**	-5	81	94	*1-140	-2.8
1923	Bos N	154	607	70	191	23	9	2	95	26	0	12	.315	.343	.392	97	-4	7-8	.991	4	112	107	*1-154	-1.1
1924	Bos N	146	581	57	169	23	7	1	59	15	2	6	.291	.311	.360	83	-16	9-3	.994	7	**118**	101	*1-146	-1.8
1925	†Pit N	59	155	19	57	10	4	0	24	17	2	1	.368	.437	.484	126	7	1-1	.993	1	111	127	1-46	0.5
1926	Pit N	47	127	12	38	6	1	0	13	7	0	3	.299	.336	.362	83	-3	1	.988	-1	94	126	1-40	-0.6
1927	Phi N	1	0	0	0	0	0	0	0	0	0	0	—	—	—	—	0	0	1.000	-0	0	0	/1M	0.0
Total	19	2128	7822	872	2405	312	101	20	1062	380	38	189	.307	.343	.381	106	27	172-59	.993	15	102	106	*1-1995/S-55,3-27,2-5,O(LF)	-3.3
McINTOSH, TIM Timothy Allen B 3.21.1965 Minneapolis, MN BR/TR 5-11/195# d9.3																								
1990	Mil A	5	5	1	1	0	0	1	1	0-0	0	2	.200	.200	.800	168	0	0-0	.875	-1	107	0	/C-4	-0.1
1991	Mil A	7	11	2	4	1	0	1	1	0-0	0	4	.364	.364	.727	199	1	0-0	—	-0	0	0	/O-4(LF),1D	0.1
1992	Mil A	35	77	7	14	3	0	0	6	3-0	2	9	.182	.229	.221	28	-8	1-3	.983	1	60	65	C-14,O-10(9-0-1)/1-7,D-3	-0.7
1993	Mil A	1	0	0	0	0	0	0	0	0-0	0	0	—	—	—	—	0	0-0	—	-0	0	0	/C	0.0
	Mon N	20	21	2	2	1	0	0	2	0-0	0	7	.095	.095	.143	-36	-4	0-0	1.000	-0	72	0	/O-7(2-0-6),C-5	-0.4
1996	NY A	3	3	0	0	0	0	0	0	0-0	0	0	.000	.000	.000	-99	-1	0-0	—	-0	0	0	/C13	-0.1
Total	5	71	117	12	21	5	0	2	10	3-0	2	22	.179	.211	.274	34	-12	1-3	.973	-1	60	48	/C-25,O-21(15-0-7),1-9,D-5,3	-1.2
McINTYRE, MATTY Matthew W. B 6.12.1880 Stonington, CT D 4.2.1920 Detroit, MI BL/TL 5-11/175# d7.3																								
1901	Phi A	82	308	38	85	12	4	0	46	30	3		.276	.346	.341	87	-5	11	.921	-4	72	0	O-82(LF)	-1.2
1904	Det A	152	578	74	146	11	10	2	46	44	4		.253	.310	.317	101	1	11	.959	12	94	85	*O-152(151-0-1)	0.4
1905	Det A	131	495	59	130	21	5	0	30	48	2		.263	.330	.325	107	5	9	.968	18	126	172	*O-131(LF)	1.7
1906	Det A	133	493	63	128	19	11	0	39	56	2		.260	.338	.343	110	7	29	.982	12	147	198	*O-133(132-1-0)	1.3
1907	Det A	20	81	6	23	1	1	0	9	7	0		.284	.341	.321	107	1	3	1.000	3	119	170	O-20(LF)	0.3
1908	†Det A	151	569	**105**	168	24	13	0	28	83	7		.295	.392	.383	146	33	20	**.977**	16	97	81	*O-151(LF)	4.6
1909	†Det A	125	476	65	116	18	9	1	34	54	3		.244	.325	.326	101	2	13	.975	-1	87	29	*O-122(119-3-0)	-0.7
1910	Det A	83	305	40	72	15	5	0	25	39	0		.236	.323	.318	94	-1	4	.946	2	103	110	O-77(58-17-2)	-0.4
1911	Chi A	146	569	102	184	19	11	1	52	64	5		.323	.397	.401	127	22	17	.948	-3	105	76	*O-146(0-31-115)	1.1
1912	Chi A	49	84	10	14	0	0	0	10	14	2		.167	.300	.167	36	-6	3	1.000	-0	100	71	O-25(14-1-10)	-0.8
Total	10	1072	3958	562	1066	140	69	4	319	439	28		.269	.346	.343	110	59	120	.964	55	105	98	*O-1039(858-53-128)	6.3
McIVOR, OTTO Edward Otto B 7.26.1884 Greenville, TX D 5.4.1954 Dallas, TX BB/TL 5-11.5/175# d4.18																								
1911	StL N	30	62	11	14	2	1	1	9	9	1	14	.226	.333	.339	91	-1	0	.926	-1	93	54	O-17(3-6-8)	-0.3
McKAY, CODY Cody Dean B 1.11.1974 Vancouver, BC, CAN BL/TR 6/212# d9.22 f-Dave																								
2002	Oak A	2	3	0	2	0	0	0	2	0-0	0	1	.667	.500	.667	256	1	0-0	1.000	0	0	0	/C	0.1
McKAY, DAVE David Lawrence B 3.14.1950 Vancouver, BC, CAN BB/TR (BR 1975-76, 77 (part)) 6-1/195# d8.22 C20 s-Cody																								
1975	Min A	33	125	8	32	4	1	2	16	6-0	1	14	.256	.291	.352	81	-4	1-1	.923	1	95	172	3-33	-0.3
1976	Min A	45	138	8	28	2	0	0	8	9-0	4	27	.203	.272	.217	43	-10	1-2	.911	-1	101	186	3-41/S-2,D	-1.2
1977	Tor A	95	274	18	54	4	3	3	22	7-0	2	51	.197	.222	.266	32	-27	2-1	.968	-4	97	81	2-40,3-32,S-20/D-2	-2.8
1978	Tor A	145	504	59	120	20	8	7	45	20-2	1	91	.238	.268	.351	71	-21	4-4	.984	-2	98	96	*2-140/S-3,3-2,D	-1.7
1979	Tor A	47	156	19	34	9	0	0	12	7-0	1	19	.218	.256	.276	43	-12	1-1	.974	7	109	107	2-46/3-2	-0.3
1980	Oak A	123	295	29	72	16	1	1	29	10-0	6	57	.244	.283	.315	68	-13	1-1	.977	-8	91	72	2-62,3-54,S-10	-1.9
1981	†Oak A	79	224	25	59	11	1	4	21	16-0	2	43	.263	.313	.375	104	1	4-1	.926	-4	93	52	3-43,2-38/S-7	-0.1
1982	Oak A	78	212	25	42	4	1	4	17	11-0	0	35	.198	.235	.283	44	-17	6-1	.968	-9	88	68	2-59,3-16/S-3	-2.3
Total	8	645	1928	191	441	70	15	21	170	86-2	17	337	.229	.266	.313	62	-103	20-12	.976	-20	97	89	2-385,3-223/S-45,D-4	-10.6
McKEAN, ED Edwin John "Mack" B 6.6.1864 Grafton, OH D 8.16.1919 Cleveland, OH BR/TR 5-9/160# d4.16 OF Total (47-LF 4-CF 1-RF)																								
1887	Cle AA	132	539	97	154	16	13	2	54	60	1		.286	.358	.375	108	7	76	.847	-5	95	87	*S-123/2-8,O-4(LF)	0.4
1888	Cle AA	131	548	94	164	21	15	6	68	28	6		.299	.340	.425	149	28	52	.909	5	100	65	S-78,O-48(43-4-1)/2-9,3	3.1
1889	Cle N	123	500	88	159	22	8	5	75	42	4	25	.318	.375	.424	126	16	35	.907	9	105	101	*S-122/2	2.5
1890	Cle N	**136**	530	95	157	15	14	7	61	87	6	25	.296	.401	.417	141	31	23	.903	-12	97	91	*S-134/2-3	2.0
1891	Cle N	**141**	603	115	170	13	12	6	69	64	1	19	.282	.352	.373	107	4	14	.887	-12	99	82	*S-141	-0.4
1892	†Cle N	129	531	76	139	14	10	0	93	49	1	29	.262	.325	.326	93	-5	19	.862	-44	85	72	*S-129	-4.0
1893	Cle N	125	545	103	169	29	24	4	133	50	4	14	.310	.372	.473	117	9	16	.902	-3	100	112	*S-125	1.0
1894	Cle N	**130**	554	116	198	30	15	8	128	49	2	12	.357	.412	.509	116	13	33	.905	-20	91	81	*S-130	0.0
1895	†Cle N	**132**	569	131	194	32	17	8	119	46	7	26	.341	.397	.499	123	17	13	.907	-20	93	86	*S-132	0.3
1896	†Cle N	133	571	100	193	29	12	7	112	45	2	9	.338	.388	.468	118	13	13	.915	-34	88	113	*S-133	-1.2
1897	Cle N	125	523	83	143	21	14	2	78	40	4		.273	.330	.379	82	-16	15	.920	-28	90	82	*S-125	-3.2
1898	Cle N	151	604	89	172	23	1	9	94	56	1		.285	.346	.371	107	6	11	.932	-31	86	84	*S-151	-1.6
1899	StL N	67	277	40	72	7	3	3	40	20	0		.260	.310	.339	76	-10	4	.886	-9	94	93	S-42,1-15,2-10	-1.5
Total	13	1655	6894	1227	2084	272	158	67	1124	636	39	159	.302	.365	.417	114	113	324	.900	-205	94	89	*S-1565/O-52L,2-31,1-15,3	-2.6
McKECHNIE, BILL William Boyd "Deacon" B 8.7.1886 Wilkinsburg, PA D 10.29.1965 Bradenton, FL BB/TR 5-10/160# d9.8 M25 C7 HF1962 OF Total (1-CF 1-RF)																								
1907	Pit N	3	8	0	1	0	0	0	0	0	0		.125	.125	.125	-21	-1	0	1.000	-0	97	0	/3-2,2	-0.1
1910	Pit N	71	212	23	46	1	2	0	12	11	0	23	.217	.256	.241	42	-16	4	.971	4	106	98	2-36,S-14/3-8,1-4	-1.2
1911	Pit N	104	321	40	73	8	7	2	37	28	2	18	.227	.293	.315	68	-15	9	.975	-0	98	99	1-57,2-17,S-12/3-6	-1.6
1912	Pit N	24	73	8	18	0	1	0	4	4	0	5	.247	.286	.274	54	-5	2	.978	-0	104	0	3-13/S-4,2-3,1-2	-0.4
1913	Bos N	1	4	1	0	0	0	0	0	0	1	1	.000	.200	.000	-39	-1	0	1.000	-0	94	0	/O(CF)	-0.1
	NY A	45	112	7	15	0	0	0	8	8	1	17	.134	.198	.134	-2	-15	2	.950	4	114	143	2-28/S-7,3-2	-1.1
1914	Ind F	149	570	107	173	24	6	2	38	53	5	36	.304	.368	.377	93	-11	47	.939	23	**117**	122	*3-149	1.6
1915	New F	127	451	49	113	22	5	1	43	41	2	31	.251	.316	.328	86	-16	28	.956	1	96	98	*3-117/O(RF)M	-1.3
1916	NY N	71	260	22	64	9	1	0	17	7	1	20	.246	.269	.288	75	-8	7	.940	-2	98	87	3-71	-1.0
	Cin N	37	130	4	36	3	0	0	10	3	0	12	.277	.293	.300	84	-3	4	.960	-2	90	119	3-35	-0.4
	Year	108	390	26	100	12	1	0	27	10	1	32	.256	.277	.292	78	-11	11	.947	-4	95	97	*3-106	-1.4
1917	Cin N	48	134	11	34	3	1	0	15	7	1	7	.254	.296	.291	84	-3	5	.943	-4	88	119	2-26,S-13/3-4	-0.7
1918	Pit N	**126**	435	34	111	13	9	2	43	24	2	22	.255	.297	.340	91	-6	12	.966	-1	95	131	*3-126	-0.4
1920	Pit N	40	133	13	29	3	1	1	13	4	0	7	.218	.241	.278	47	-9	7-4	.943	-2	90	78	3-20,S-10/2-6,1	-1.1
Total	11	846	2843	319	713	86	33	8	240	190	15	199	.251	.301	.313	76	-109	127-4	.952	19	101	107	3-553,2-117/1-64,S-60,O-2C	-7.8
McKEE, FRANK Frank B Philadelphia, PA d6.11																								
1884	Was U	4	17	2	3	0	0	0		1			.176	.222	.176	23	-2		.200	-2	141	0	/O-3(RF),3-2,C	-0.3
McKEE, RED Raymond Ellis B 7.20.1890 Shawnee, OH D 8.5.1972 Saginaw, MI BL/TR 5-11/180# d4.19																								
1913	Det A	68	187	18	53	3	4	1	20	21	1	21	.283	.359	.358	112	3	7	.950	-10	*83*	*104*	C-62	-0.2
1914	Det A	34	64	7	12	1	1	0	8	14	1	16	.188	.342	.234	71	-1	1-2	.964	-5	*85*	*71*	C-27	-0.5
1915	Det A	55	106	10	29	5	0	1	17	13	0	16	.274	.353	.349	105	1	1	.954	-5	*93*	*83*	C-35	-0.1
1916	Det A	32	76	3	16	1	2	0	4	6	0	11	.211	.268	.276	61	-4	0	.955	-4	84	107	C-26	-0.7
Total	4	189	433	38	110	10	7	2	49	54	2	64	.254	.339	.323	95	-1	9-2	.954	-24	*86*	*95*	C-150	-1.5
McKEEL, WALT Walt Thomas B 1.17.1972 Wilson, NC BR/TR 6-2/200# d9.14																								
1996	Bos A	1	0	0	0	0	0	0	0	0-0	0	0	—	—	—	—	0	0-0	—	-0	0	0	/C	0.0

Year	Tm Lg	G	AB	R	H	2B	3B	HR	RBI	BB-IB	HP	SO	AVG	OBP	SLG	AOPS	ABR	SB-CS	FA	FR	Rng	Thr	G at Pos	BFW
1997	Bos A	5	3	0	0	0	0	0	0	0-0	0	1	.000	.000	.000	-98	-1	0-0	1.000	0	0	0	/C-4,1	-0.1
2002	Col N	5	13	1	4	0	0	0	0	0-0	0	3	.308	.308	.308	57	-1	0-0	1.000	-2	26	0	/C-5	-0.2
Total	3	11	16	1	4	0	0	0	0	0-0	0	4	.250	.250	.250	30	-2	0-0	1.000	-2	21	0	/C-10,1	-0.3
McKEEVER, JIM James B 4.19.1861 St.John, NB, CAN D 8.19.1897 Boston, MA 5-10/170# d4.17																								
1884	Bos U	16	66	13	9	0	0	0		0			.136	.136	.136	-17	-12		.869	-4			C-12/O-4(RF)	-1.4
McKELVEY, JOHN John Wellington B 8.27.1847 Rochester, NY D 5.31.1944 Rochester, NY BR/TR 5-7.5/175# d4.19																								
1875	NH NA	43	188	26	43	3	1	0	10	5		8	.229	.249	.255	86	-1	3-1	.656	-9	88	68	O-39(0-4-35)/3-5	-0.6
McKELVY, RUSS Russell Errett B 9.8.1854 Swissvale, PA D 10.19.1915 Omaha, NE BR/TR d5.1 ▲																								
1878	Ind N	**63**	253	33	57	4	3	2	36	5		38	.225	.240	.289	84	-3		.846	5	113	82	*O-62(CF)/P-4	-0.1
1882	Pit AA	1	4	0	0	0	0	0		0			.000	.000	.000	-99	-1		—	-0	0	0	/O(RF)	-0.1
Total	2	64	257	33	57	4	3	2	36	5		38	.222	.237	.284	81	-4		.846	4	113	82	/O-63(0-62-1),P-4	-0.2
McKENNA, ED Edward J. B St.Louis, MO d7.29																								
1874	Phi NA	1	4	0	0	0	0	0	0	0		1	.000	.000	.000	-97	-1	0-0	1.000	0	0	0	/1	-0.1
1877	StL N	1	5	0	1	0	0	0	0	0		1	.200	.200	.200	28	0		1.000	-0	0	0	/O(CF)	-0.1
1884	Was U	32	117	19	22	1	0	0		4			.188	.215	.197	26	-14		.876	-8			C-23,O-10(0-2-8)/3-7	-1.9
Total	2	33	122	19	23	1	0	0	0	4		1	.189	.214	.197	26	-14		1.000	-8			/C-23,O-11(0-3-8),3-7	-2.0
McKEOUGH, DAVE David J. B 12.1.1863 Utica, NY D 7.11.1901 Utica, NY 5-7/158# d4.22																								
1890	Roc AA	62	218	38	49	5	0	0	20	29	0		.225	.316	.248	72	-6	14	.929	2	*114*	*112*	C-47,S-13/2-2,3	0.0
1891	Phi AA	15	54	4	14	1	1	0	3	8	0	6	.259	.355	.315	92	0	0	.854	-4	*109*	*84*	C-14/S	-0.3
Total	2	77	272	42	63	6	1	0	23	37	0	6	.232	.324	.261	76	-6	14	.912	-2	*113*	*105*	/C-61,S-14,2-2,3	-0.3
McKINNEY, RICH Charles Richard B 11.22.1946 Piqua, OH BR/TR 5-11/185# d6.26 OF Total (6-LF 27-RF)																								
1970	Chi A	43	119	12	20	5	0	4	17	11-0	1	25	.168	.242	.311	50	-8	3-2	.931	1	95	44	3-23,S-11	-0.7
1971	Chi A	114	369	35	100	11	2	8	46	35-1	2	37	.271	.334	.377	99	-1	0-0	.968	-8	93	79	2-67,O-25(RF)/3-5	-0.5
1972	NY A	37	121	10	26	2	0	1	7	7-0	0	13	.215	.258	.256	55	-7	1-0	.917	-1	110	86	3-33	-1.0
1973	Oak A	48	65	9	16	3	0	1	7	7-0	0	4	.246	.319	.338	90	-1	0-0	.900	-1	96	84	3-17/2-7,O-3(LF),D-6	-0.2
1974	Oak A	5	7	0	1	0	0	0	0	0-0	0	0	.143	.143	.143	-19	-1	0-0	1.000	-1	0	0	/2-3	-0.3
1975	Oak A	8	7	0	1	0	0	0	2	1-0	0	2	.143	.200	.143	14	-1	0-0	1.000	-0	0	0	/1D	-0.1
1977	Oak A	86	198	13	35	7	0	6	21	16-0	0	43	.177	.236	.303	47	-15	0-1	.978	-2	101	93	1-32,D-18/3-7,O-5(3-0-2),2-3	-2.0
Total	7	341	886	79	199	28	2	20	100	77-1	3	124	.225	.286	.328	73	-34	4-3	.911	-12	103	77	/3-85,2-80,1-33,O-33R,D-26,S-11	-4.8
McKINNEY, BOB Robert Francis B 10.4.1875 McSherrystown, PA D 8.19.1946 Hanover, PA BR/TR 5-7/165# d7.23																								
1901	Phi A	2	2	0	0	0	0	0	0	0	0		.000	.000	.000	-96	-1	0	—	-1	0	0	/23	-0.1
McKINNON, ALEX Alexander J. B 8.14.1856 Boston, MA D 7.24.1887 Charlestown, MA BR 5-11.5/170# d5.1 M1																								
1884	NY N	**116**	470	66	128	21	13	3	73	8		62	.272	.285	.391	108	2		.955	-2	93	102	*1-116	-0.9
1885	StL N	100	411	42	121	21	6	1	44	8		31	.294	.308	.382	130	13		**.978**	-2	77	96	*1-100,M	0.3
1886	StL N	122	491	75	148	24	7	8	72	21		23	.301	.330	.428	138	22	10	.963	-6	79	105	*1-119/O-3(CF)	0.5
1887	Pit N	48	200	26	68	16	4	1	30	8	0	9	.340	.365	.475	142	12	6	.977	3	139	101	1-48	0.9
Total	4	386	1572	209	465	82	30	13	219	45	0	125	.296	.315	.411	127	49	16	.967	-6	90	101	1-383/O-3(CF)	0.8
McKNIGHT, JIM James Arthur B 6.1.1936 Bee Branch, AR D 2.24.1994 Van Buren County, AR BR/TR 6-1/185# d9.22 s-Jeff																								
1960	Chi N	3	6	0	2	0	0	0	1	0-0	0	1	.333	.333	.333	84	0	0-0	.667	-1	71	152	/2O(RF)	-0.1
1962	Chi N	60	85	6	19	0	1	0	5	2-0	0	13	.224	.241	.247	30	-9	0-0	.955	2	125	168	/3-9,O-5(RF),2-2	-0.7
Total	2	63	91	6	21	0	1	0	6	2-0	0	14	.231	.247	.253	34	-9	0-0	.955	1	125	168	/3-9,O-6(RF),2-3	-0.8
McKNIGHT, JEFF Jefferson Alan B 2.18.1963 Conway, AR BB/TR 6/188# d6.6 f-Jim OF Total (10-LF 6-RF)																								
1989	NY N	6	12	2	3	0	0	0	0	2-0	0	1	.250	.357	.250	80	0	0-0	1.000	-1	97	101	/2-4,13S	-0.2
1990	Bal A	29	75	11	15	2	0	1	4	5-0	1	17	.200	.259	.267	49	-5	0-0	1.000	-1	115	83	1-15/0-8(4-0-4),2-5,SD	-0.7
1991	Bal A	16	41	2	7	1	0	0	2	2-0	0	7	.171	.209	.195	13	-5	1-0	1.000	-0	64	282	/O-7(6-0-1),1-2,D-4	-0.6
1992	NY N	31	85	10	23	3	1	2	13	2-0	0	8	.271	.287	.400	94	-1	0-1	.980	1	113	89	2-14/1-9,3-3,S-3,O(RF)	-0.1
1993	NY N	105	164	19	42	3	1	2	13	13-0	1	31	.256	.311	.323	72	-7	0-0	.943	0	99	109	S-29,2-15,1-10/3-9,C	-0.5
1994	NY N	31	27	1	4	1	0	0	2	4-0	0	12	.148	.250	.185	18	-3	0-0	1.000	-0	0	0	/1-2	-0.3
Total	6	218	404	45	94	10	2	5	34	28-0	2	76	.233	.284	.304	63	-21	1-1	.996	-1	102	81	/1-39,2-38,S-34,O-16L,3-13,D-5,C	-2.4
McLANE, ED Edward Cameron B 8.20.1881 Weston, MA D 8.21.1975 Baltimore, MD BR/TR 5-10/179# d10.6																								
1907	Bro N	1	2	0	0	0	0	0	0	0	1		.000	.333	.000	5	0	0	.333	-1	0	0	/O(RF)	-0.1
McLARNEY, ART Arthur James B 12.20.1908 Ft.Worden, WA D 12.20.1984 Seattle, WA BB/TR 6/168# d8.23																								
1932	NY N	9	23	2	3	1	0	0	3	1	0	3	.130	.167	.174	-8	-4	0	1.000	-1	87	84	/S-7	-0.4
McLARRY, POLLY Howard Zell B 3.25.1891 Leonard, TX D 11.4.1971 Bonham, TX BL/TR 6/185# d9.2																								
1912	Chi A	2	2	0	0	0	0	0	0	0	0		.000	.000	.000	-99	-1	0	—	0			H	-0.1
1915	Chi N	68	127	16	25	3	0	1	12	14	0	20	.197	.277	.244	58	-6	2-2	.957	1	105	45	2-21,1-18	-0.6
Total	2	70	129	16	25	3	0	1	12	14	0	20	.194	.273	.240	56	-7	2-2	.957	1	105	45	/2-21,1-18	-0.7
McLAUGHLIN, BARNEY Bernard B 1857 , Ireland D 2.13.1921 Lowell, MA BR/TR d8.2 b-Frank ▲																								
1884	KC U	42	162	15	37	7	3	0		9			.228	.269	.309	86	-7		.762	-1	184	360	O-24(4-3-17),2-12/P-7,S-2	-0.7
1887	Phi N	50	205	26	45	8	3	1	26	11	1	27	.220	.263	.302	53	-14	2	.879	-14	90	71	2-50	-2.2
1890	Syr AA	86	329	43	87	8	1	2	40	47	2		.264	.360	.313	110	8	13	.902	-6	96	82	S-86	0.3
Total	3	178	696	84	169	23	7	3	66	67	3	27	.243	.312	.309	86	-13	15	.900	-22	97	80	/S-88,2-62,O-24(4-3-17),P-7	-2.6
McLAUGHLIN, FRANK Francis Edward B 6.19.1856 Lowell, MA D 4.5.1917 Lowell, MA BR/TR 5-9/160# d8.9 b-Barney ▲																								
1882	Wor N	15	55	7	12	0	2	1	4	0		11	.218	.218	.345	76	-2		.760	-4	99	44	S-14/O(CF)	-0.5
1883	Pit AA	29	114	15	25	2	0	1		6			.219	.258	.263	71	-3		.802	-0	112	64	S-25/O-4(0-3-1),2-2,P-2	-0.2
1884	Cin U	16	67	10	16	4	1	2		2			.239	.261	.418	95	-3		.740	-6	73	139	S-16	-0.7
	CP U	15	67	11	16	4	1	0		1			.239	.250	.328	74	-4		.888	3	114	179	2-14/SO(RF)	0.0
	KC U	32	123	17	28	11	0	1		9			.228	.280	.341	101	-3		.847	-6	105	58	2-10,0-10(2-6-2)/3-9,S-5,P-2	-0.7
	Year	63	257	38	60	19	2	3		12			.233	.268	.358	92	-10		.873	-9	111	134	2-24,S-22,O-11(2-6-3)/3-9,P-2	-1.4
Total	3	107	426	60	97	21	4	5	4	18		11	.228	.259	.331	85	-15		.769	-13	98	83	/S-61,2-26,O-16(2-10-4),3-9,P-4	-2.1
McLAUGHLIN, JAMES James B San Francisco, CA d5.3																								
1884	Was U	10	37	3	7	3	0	0		0			.189	.189	.270	39	-4		.696	-4	75	0	/S-9,3	-0.7
McLAUGHLIN, KID James Anson "Sunshine" B 4.12.1888 Randolph, NY D 11.13.1934 Allegany, NY BL/TR 5-8.5/158# d6.30																								
1914	Cin N	3	2	1	0	0	0	0	0	0	0	0	.000	.000	.000	-97	0	0	1.000	0	130	0	/O-2(CF)	-0.1
McLAUGHLIN, JIM James Robert B 1.3.1902 St.Louis, MO D 12.18.1968 Mount Vernon, IL BR/TR 5-8.5/168# d4.18																								
1932	StL A	1	1	0	0	0	0	0	1	0	0	0	.000	.000	.000	-95	0	0-0	—	-0	0	0	/3	0.0
McLAUGHLIN, TOM Thomas B 3.28.1860 Louisville, KY D 7.21.1921 Louisville, KY TR d7.17																								
1883	Lou AA	42	146	16	28	1	2	0		5			.192	.219	.226	47	-8		.844	2	118	129	S-19,0-17(8-9-1)/1-5,3-2,2-2	-0.5
1884	Lou AA	98	335	41	67	11	6	0	21	22	6		.200	.262	.269	77	-7		.892	13	109	**171**	*S-94/3-4,2	0.8
1885	Lou AA	**112**	411	49	87	13	9	2	41	15	3		.212	.245	.302	72	-14		.883	-1	92	112	*2-93,S-19	-0.9
1886	NY AA	74	250	27	34	3	1	0	16	26	1		.136	.220	.156	20	-21	13	.886	7	102	62	S-63,2-10/O(LF)	-1.1
1891	Was AA	14	41	9	11	0	1	0	3	7	2	6	.268	.400	.317	111	1	3	.871	1	98	128	S-14	0.2
Total	5	340	1183	142	227	28	19	2	81	75	12	6	.192	.247	.253	62	-49	16	.886	22	106	128	S-209,2-106/O-18(9-9-1),3-6,1-5	-1.5
McLAURIN, RALPH Ralph Edgar B 5.23.1885 Kissimmee, FL D 2.11.1943 McColl, SC d9.5																								
1908	StL N	8	22	2	5	0	0	0	0	0	0		.227	.227	.227	47	-1	0	.875	-1	0	0	/O-6(LF)	-0.3
McLEAN, LARRY John Bannerman B 7.18.1881 Fredericton, NB, CAN D 3.24.1921 Boston, MA BR/TR 6-5/228# d4.26																								
1901	Bos A	9	19	4	4	1	0	0	2	0	0		.211	.211	.263	31	-2	1	1.000	0	107	114	/1-5	-0.1
1903	Chi N	1	4	0	0	0	0	0	1	1	0		.000	.200	.000	-42	-1	0	.889	0	*182*	*67*	/C	-0.1
1904	StL N	27	84	5	14	2	1	0	4	4	0		.167	.205	.214	31	-7	1	.954	-4	*88*	*52*	C-24	-0.9

Year	Tm Lg	G	AB	R	H	2B	3B	HR	RBI	BB-IB	HP	SO	AVG	OBP	SLG	AOPS	ABR	SB-CS	FA	FR	Rng	Thr	G at Pos	BFW
1906	Cin N	12	35	3	7	2	0	0	2	4	0		.200	.282	.257	65	-1	0	.954	-1	101	90	C-12	-0.1
1907	Cin N	113	374	35	108	9	9	0	54	13	0		.289	.313	.361	107	0	4	.975	-0	100	91	C-89,1-13	1.0
1908	Cin N	99	309	24	67	9	4	1	28	15	2		.217	.258	.282	74	-10	2	.963	-3	108	101	C-69,1-19	-0.8
1909	Cin N	95	324	26	83	12	2	2	36	21	3		.256	.307	.324	97	-2	1	.978	-3	89	106	C-95	0.5
1910	Cin N	127	423	27	126	14	7	2	71	26	1	23	.298	.340	.378	114	6	4	.983	7	118	104	*C-119	2.4
1911	Cin N	107	328	24	94	7	2	0	34	20	1	18	.287	.330	.320	85	-7	1	.968	14	132	110	C-98	1.5
1912	Cin N	102	333	17	81	15	1	1	27	18	1	15	.243	.284	.303	63	-18	1	.973	-1	94	109	C-98	-1.1
1913	StL N	48	152	7	41	9	0	0	12	6	0	9	.270	.297	.329	80	-4	0	.981	-7	71	112	C-42	-0.8
	†NY N	30	75	3	24	4	0	0	9	4	0	4	.320	.354	.373	107	1	1	.953	-1	114	65	C-28	0.2
	Year	78	227	10	65	13	0	0	21	10	0	13	.286	.316	.344	89	-3	1	.970	-8	86	96	C-70	-0.6
1914	NY N	79	154	8	40	6	0	0	14	4	1	9	.260	.283	.299	76	-5	4	.973	-0	133	69	C-74	-0.2
1915	NY N	13	33	0	5	0	0	0	4	0	0	1	.152	.152	.152	-9	-4	0	.985	1	89	161	C-12	-0.4
Total	13	862	2647	183	694	90	26	6	298	136	9	79	.262	.301	.323	86	-54	20	.973	2	106	100	C-761/1-37	1.1

McLEMORE, MARK Mark Tremell B 10.4.1964 San Diego, CA BB/TR 5-11/195# d9.13 OF Total (249-LF 21-CF 147-RF)

Year	Tm Lg	G	AB	R	H	2B	3B	HR	RBI	BB-IB	HP	SO	AVG	OBP	SLG	AOPS	ABR	SB-CS	FA	FR	Rng	Thr	G at Pos	BFW
1986	Cal A	5	4	0	0	0	0	0	0	1-0	0	2	.000	.200	.000	-40	-1	0-1	1.000	2	171	86	/2-2	0.0
1987	Cal A	138	433	61	102	13	3	3	41	48-0	0	72	.236	.310	.300	66	-21	25-8	.974	-8	93	**117**	*2-132/S-6,D-3	-1.8
1988	Cal A	77	233	38	56	11	2	2	16	25-0	0	28	.240	.312	.330	83	-5	13-7	.979	4	107	138	2-63/3-5,D	0.1
1989	Cal A	32	103	12	25	3	1	0	14	7-0	1	19	.243	.295	.291	68	-5	6-1	.966	4	111	147	2-27/D	0.2
1990	Cal A	20	48	4	7	2	0	0	2	4-0	0	9	.146	.212	.188	13	-6	1-0	1.000	-5	79	62	/2-8,S-8,D	-1.0
	Cle A	8	12	2	2	0	0	0	0	0-0	0	6	.167	.167	.167	-7	-2	0-0	1.000	1	73	395	/3-4,2-3,D	-0.1
	Year	28	60	6	9	2	0	0	2	4-0	0	15	.150	.203	.183	9	-7	1-0	1.000	-4	85	94	2-11/S-8,3-4,D-2	-1.1
1991	Hou N	21	61	6	9	1	0	0	2	6-0	0	13	.148	.221	.164	11	-7	0-1	.975	-1	103	83	2-19	-0.9
1992	Bal A	101	228	40	56	7	2	0	27	21-1	0	26	.246	.308	.294	68	-10	11-5	.978	2	103	121	2-70,D-17	-0.6
1993	Bal A	148	581	81	165	27	5	4	72	64-4	1	92	.284	.353	.368	91	-6	21-15	.987	12	109	141	*O-124(RF),2-25/3-4,D	0.0
1994	Bal A	104	343	44	88	11	1	3	29	51-3	1	50	.257	.354	.321	72	-13	20-5	.981	2	99	98	2-96/O-7(RF),D	-0.3
1995	Tex A	129	467	73	122	20	5	5	41	59-6	3	71	.261	.346	.358	82	-11	21-11	.986	-2	103	0	O-73(69-0-5),2-66/D-2	-1.1
1996	†Tex A	147	517	84	150	23	4	5	46	87-5	0	69	.290	.389	.379	92	-3	27-10	.985	24	109	113	*2-147/O(RF)	2.7
1997	Tex A	89	349	47	91	17	2	1	25	40-1	2	54	.261	.338	.330	72	-13	7-5	.980	-1	104	106	2-89/O(LF)	-1.0
1998	†Tex A	126	461	79	114	15	1	5	53	89-1	2	64	.247	.369	.317	78	-11	12-4	.975	-5	94	90	*2-122/D-2	-0.8
1999	†Tex A	144	566	105	155	20	7	6	45	83-2	0	79	.274	.363	.366	84	-12	16-8	.983	10	106	102	*2-135,O-11(4-0-7)	0.4
2000	†Sea A	138	481	72	118	23	1	3	46	81-2	1	78	.245	.353	.316	74	-16	30-14	.987	-1	96	103	*2-129,O-14(14-1-0)	-0.9
2001	†Sea A	125	409	78	117	16	9	5	57	69-0	0	84	.286	.384	.406	117	12	39-7	.988	-5	97	121	O-68(63-8-2),3-36,S-35/2-9,D-2	1.4
2002	Sea A	104	337	54	91	17	2	7	41	61-1	1	63	.270	.380	.395	112	8	18-10	.972	-2	109	45	O-88(82-12-1),3-14/2-2,SD	0.4
2003	Sea A	99	309	34	72	15	2	2	37	38-0	2	71	.233	.318	.314	71	-12	5-5	.972	1	98	130	S-38,3-29,O-16(LF),D-11/2-6	-1.0
Total	18	1755	5942	914	1540	241	47	51	594	834-26	14	950	.259	.349	.341	82	-134	272-117	.981	31	101	109	*2-1150,O-403L/3-92,S-88,D-47	-4.3

McLEOD, RALPH Ralph Alton B 10.19.1916 N.Quincy, MA BL/TL 6/170# d9.14

Year	Tm Lg	G	AB	R	H	2B	3B	HR	RBI	BB-IB	HP	SO	AVG	OBP	SLG	AOPS	ABR	SB-CS	FA	FR	Rng	Thr	G at Pos	BFW
1938	Bos N	6	7	1	2	1	0	0	0	0	0	2	.286	.286	.429	105	0	0	1.000	0	98	0	/O(LF)	0.0

McLEOD, JIM Soule James B 9.12.1908 Jones, LA D 8.3.1981 Little Rock, AR BR/TR 6/187# d5.22

Year	Tm Lg	G	AB	R	H	2B	3B	HR	RBI	BB-IB	HP	SO	AVG	OBP	SLG	AOPS	ABR	SB-CS	FA	FR	Rng	Thr	G at Pos	BFW
1930	Was A	18	34	3	9	1	0	0	1	1	1	5	.265	.306	.294	53	-2	1-1	1.000	-1	101	0	3-10/S-7	-0.2
1932	Was A	7	0	1	0	0	0	0	0	1	0	0	—	1.000	—	183	0	0-0	1.000	0	145	0	/S	0.0
1933	Phi N	67	232	20	45	6	1	0	15	12	1	25	.194	.237	.228	30	-21	1	.914	-3	101	85	3-67/S	-2.3
Total	3	92	266	24	54	7	1	0	16	14	2	30	.203	.248	.237	33	-23	2-1	.922	-3	101	76	/3-77,S-9	-2.5

McMAHON, JACK John Henry B 10.15.1869 Waterbury, CT D 12.30.1894 Bridgeport, CT BR/TL 5-10/165# d8.8

Year	Tm Lg	G	AB	R	H	2B	3B	HR	RBI	BB-IB	HP	SO	AVG	OBP	SLG	AOPS	ABR	SB-CS	FA	FR	Rng	Thr	G at Pos	BFW
1892	NY N	40	147	21	33	5	7	1	24	10	1	9	.224	.278	.374	98	-2	3	.973	-3	74	68	1-36/C-5	-0.4
1893	NY N	11	30	5	10	2	1	0	4	2	0	0	.333	.375	.467	122	1	0	.891	-1	101	103	C-11	0.0
Total	2	51	177	26	43	7	8	1	28	12	1	9	.243	.295	.390	103	-1	3	.973	-4	74	68	/1-36,C-16	-0.4

McMANUS, FRANK Francis E. B 9.21.1875 Lawrence, MA D 9.1.1923 Syracuse, NY TR 5-7/150# d9.14

Year	Tm Lg	G	AB	R	H	2B	3B	HR	RBI	BB-IB	HP	SO	AVG	OBP	SLG	AOPS	ABR	SB-CS	FA	FR	Rng	Thr	G at Pos	BFW
1899	Was N	7	21	3	8	1	0	0	2	2	0		.381	.435	.429	139	1	3	.931	-1	78	162	/C-7	0.1
1903	Bro N	2	7	0	0	0	0	0	0	0	0		.000	.000	.000	-99	-2	0	.929	0	90	135	/C-2	-0.1
1904	Det A	1	0	0	0	0	0	0	0	0	0		—	—	—	—	0	0	—	0	0	0	/C	0.0
	NY A	4	7	0	0	0	0	0	0	0	0		.000	.000	.000	-96	-2	0	.900	-1	81	0	/C-4	-0.2
	Year	5	7	0	0	0	0	0	0	0	0		.000	.000	.000	-97	-2	0	.900	-1	76	0	/C-5	-0.2
Total	3	14	35	3	8	1	0	0	2	2	0		.229	.270	.257	50	-3	3	.925	-1	80	125	/C-14	-0.2

McMANUS, JIM James Michael B 7.20.1936 Brookline, MA BL/TL 6-4/215# d9.21

Year	Tm Lg	G	AB	R	H	2B	3B	HR	RBI	BB-IB	HP	SO	AVG	OBP	SLG	AOPS	ABR	SB-CS	FA	FR	Rng	Thr	G at Pos	BFW
1960	KC A	5	13	3	4	0	0	1	2	1-0	0	2	.308	.357	.538	138	1	0-0	1.000	-0	48	34	/1-3	0.0

McMANUS, MARTY Martin Joseph B 3.14.1900 Chicago, IL D 2.18.1966 St.Louis, MO BR/TR 5-10.5/160# d9.26 M2

Year	Tm Lg	G	AB	R	H	2B	3B	HR	RBI	BB-IB	HP	SO	AVG	OBP	SLG	AOPS	ABR	SB-CS	FA	FR	Rng	Thr	G at Pos	BFW
1920	StL A	1	3	0	1	0	1	0	1	0	0	0	.333	.333	1.000	236	0	0-0	.667	-1	95	0	/3	0.0
1921	StL A	121	412	49	107	19	8	3	64	27	2	30	.260	.308	.367	68	-22	5-3	.952	-12	91	87	2-96,3-13/1-9,S-2	-2.9
1922	StL A	**154**	606	88	189	34	11	11	109	38	6	41	.312	.358	.459	108	5	9-6	.964	1	96	130	*2-153/1	1.0
1923	StL A	**154**	582	86	180	35	10	15	94	49	4	50	.309	.367	.481	116	11	14-10	.960	-4	91	112	*2-133,1-20	0.9
1924	StL A	123	442	71	147	23	5	5	80	55	2	40	.333	.409	.441	112	10	13-9	.972	8	102	103	*2-119	2.0
1925	StL A	**154**	587	108	169	**44**	8	13	90	73	5	69	.288	.371	.457	104	4	5-11	.967	2	97	94	*2-154/O(RF)	0.6
1926	StL A	149	549	102	156	30	10	9	68	55	1	62	.284	.350	.424	97	-4	5-7	.958	12	104	113	3-84,2-61/1-4	1.3
1927	Det A	108	369	60	99	19	7	9	69	34	1	38	.268	.332	.431	95	-4	8-7	.960	0	95	93	S-39,2-35,3-22/1-6	0.1
1928	Det A	139	500	78	144	37	5	8	73	51	1	32	.288	.355	.430	104	3	11-13	.955	2	101	69	3-92,1-45/S-2	0.6
1929	Det A	154	599	99	168	32	8	18	90	60	1	52	.280	.347	.451	103	2	16-11	.972	7	101	89	*3-150/S-8	1.7
1930	Det A	132	484	74	155	40	4	9	89	59	2	28	.320	.396	.475	118	15	**23**-8	**.966**	7	100	**100**	*3-130/S-3,1	3.0
1931	Det A	107	362	39	98	17	3	3	53	49	2	22	.271	.361	.359	87	-6	7-3	.950	7	109	120	3-79,2-21/1	0.6
	Bos A	17	62	8	18	4	0	1	9	8	0	1	.290	.371	.403	110	1	1-1	1.000	6	151	299	3-11/2-7	0.7
	Year	124	424	47	116	21	3	4	62	57	2	23	.274	.362	.366	90	-5	8-4	.956	13	114	142	3-90,2-28/1	1.3
1932	Bos A	93	302	39	71	19	4	5	24	36	0	30	.235	.317	.374	80	-9	1-2	.969	1	107	80	2-49,3-30/S-2,1M	-0.4
1933	Bos A	106	366	51	104	30	4	3	36	49	0	21	.284	.369	.413	108	6	3-0	.957	-2	97	73	3-76,2-26/1-4,M	0.8
1934	Bos N	119	435	56	120	18	0	8	47	32	3	42	.276	.330	.372	95	-3	5	.964	-6	103	92	2-73,3-37	-0.3
Total	15	1831	6660	1008	1926	401	88	120	996	675	30	558	.289	.357	.430	101	9	126-91	.965	29	98	104	2-927,3-725/1-92,S-56,O(RF)	9.7

McMATH, JIMMY Jimmy Lee B 8.10.1949 Tuscaloosa, AL BL/TL 6-1.5/195# d9.7

Year	Tm Lg	G	AB	R	H	2B	3B	HR	RBI	BB-IB	HP	SO	AVG	OBP	SLG	AOPS	ABR	SB-CS	FA	FR	Rng	Thr	G at Pos	BFW
1968	Chi N	6	14	0	2	0	0	0	2	0-0	0	6	.143	.143	.143	-13	-2	0-0	1.000	0	116	0	/O-3(LF)	-0.2

McMILLAN, GEORGE George A. "Reddy" B 9.1.1863 Ontario, , CAN D 4.18.1920 Cleveland, OH 5-8/175# d8.11

Year	Tm Lg	G	AB	R	H	2B	3B	HR	RBI	BB-IB	HP	SO	AVG	OBP	SLG	AOPS	ABR	SB-CS	FA	FR	Rng	Thr	G at Pos	BFW
1890	NY N	10	35	4	5	0	0	0	1	7	0	4	.143	.286	.143	26	-3	1	.800	-2	58	0	O-10(1-0-9)	-0.4

McMILLAN, NORM Norman Alexis "Bub" B 10.5.1895 Latta, SC D 9.28.1969 Marion, SC BR/TR 6/175# d4.12 OF Total (15-CF 12-RF)

Year	Tm Lg	G	AB	R	H	2B	3B	HR	RBI	BB-IB	HP	SO	AVG	OBP	SLG	AOPS	ABR	SB-CS	FA	FR	Rng	Thr	G at Pos	BFW
1922	†NY A	33	78	7	20	1	2	0	11	6	0	10	.256	.310	.321	63	-5	4-1	.921	-3	92	0	O-26(0-15-12)/3-5	-0.8
1923	Bos A	131	459	37	116	24	5	0	42	28	2	44	.253	.299	.327	64	-25	13-5	.942	3	88	93	3-67,2-34,S-28	-1.2
1924	StL A	76	201	25	56	12	2	0	27	12	4	17	.279	.332	.358	73	-8	6-4	.966	-3	96	94	2-37,3-19/S-7,1-2	-0.8
1928	Chi N	49	123	11	27	2	2	1	12	13	1	19	.220	.299	.293	56	-8	0	.977	2	116	136	2-19,3-18	-0.5
1929	†Chi N	124	495	77	134	35	5	5	55	36	3	43	.271	.324	.392	76	-19	13	.944	6	101	111	*3-120	-0.5
Total	5	413	1356	157	353	74	16	6	147	95	10	133	.260	.313	.352	69	-65	36-10	.944	5	95	93	3-229/2-90,S-35,O-26C,1-2	-3.8

McMILLAN, ROY Roy David B 7.17.1929 Bonham, TX D 11.2.1997 Bonham, TX BR/TR 5-11/170# d4.17 M2 C7

Year	Tm Lg	G	AB	R	H	2B	3B	HR	RBI	BB-IB	HP	SO	AVG	OBP	SLG	AOPS	ABR	SB-CS	FA	FR	Rng	Thr	G at Pos	BFW
1951	Cin N	85	199	21	42	4	0	1	8	17	0	26	.211	.273	.246	40	-17	0-0	.963	2	101	85	S-54,3-12/2	-1.2
1952	Cin N	**154**	540	60	132	32	2	7	57	45	3	81	.244	.306	.350	82	-13	4-5	.971	10	**107**	97	*S-154	0.6
1953	Cin N	**155**	557	51	130	15	4	5	43	43	1	52	.233	.290	.302	54	-38	2-4	.972	10	**109**	**115**	*S-155	-1.6
1954	Cin N	**154**	588	86	147	21	2	4	42	47	5	54	.250	.308	.313	61	-33	4-2	.959	7	99	**124**	*S-154	-1.3
1955	Cin N	151	470	50	126	21	2	1	37	66-7	7	33	.268	.364	.328	81	-9	4-4	.969	**18**	**110**	**120**	*S-150	2.0
1956	Cin N★	150	479	51	126	16	7	3	62	76-9	5	54	.263	.366	.344	88	-5	4-3	**.975**	**29**	**114**	**108**	*S-150	3.7
1957	Cin N★	151	448	50	122	25	5	1	55	66-8	6	44	.272	.371	.357	91	-2	5-1	**.977**	-7	98	94	*S-151	0.4
1958	Cin N	145	393	48	90	18	3	1	25	47-5	1	33	.229	.312	.298	60	-22	5-2	**.980**	2	100	96	*S-145	-0.9
1959	Cin N	79	246	38	65	14	2	9	24	27-3	4	27	.264	.345	.447	106	3	0-2	.974	-2	93	112	S-73	0.6
1960	Cin N	124	399	42	94	12	2	10	42	35-5	4	40	.236	.301	.351	77	-13	2-0	.964	-10	99	108	*S-116,2-10	-1.4

Year	Tm Lg	G	AB	R	H	2B	3B	HR	RBI	BB-IB	HP	SO	AVG	OBP	SLG	AOPS	ABR	SB-CS	FA	FR	Rng	Thr	G at Pos	BFW
1961	Mil N	154	505	42	111	16	0	7	48	61-2	4	86	.220	.305	.293	65	-25	2-4	**.975**	-2	107	115	*S-154	-1.4
1962	Mil N	137	468	66	115	13	0	12	41	60-0	5	53	.246	.336	.350	87	-7	2-2	.972	2	102	109	*S-135	0.6
1963	Mil N	100	320	35	80	10	1	4	29	17-2	2	25	.250	.291	.325	78	-9	1-5	.979	6	107	123	S-94	0.3
1964	Mil N	8	13	1	4	0	0	0	2	0-0	0	2	.308	.308	.308	73	-1	1-0	.933	-1	73	113	/S-8	-0.1
	NY N	113	379	30	80	8	2	1	25	14-2	4	16	.211	.246	.251	42	-30	3-1	.976	1	105	92	*S-111	-2.1
	Year	121	392	31	84	8	2	1	27	14-2	4	18	.214	.248	.253	43	-31	4-1	.975	0	104	93	*S-119	-2.2
1965	NY N	157	528	44	128	19	2	1	42	24-1	4	60	.242	.280	.292	64	-26	1-0	.964	-0	106	87	*S-153	-1.5
1966	NY N	76	220	24	47	9	1	1	12	20-3	2	25	.214	.284	.277	59	-12	1-1	.975	6	110	91	S-71	-0.1
Total	16	2093	6752	739	1639	253	35	68	594	665-47	57	711	.243	.314	.321	72	-259	41-36	.972	70	105	106	*S-2028/3-12,2-11	-3.4
McMILLAN, TOM Thomas Erwin B 9.13.1951 Richmond, VA BR/TR 5-9/165# d9.17																								
1977	Sea A	2	5	0	0	0	0	0	0	0-0	0	0	.000	.000	.000	-99	-1	0-0	1.000	0	89	141	/S-2	-0.1
McMILLAN, TOMMY Thomas Law "Rebel" B 4.18.1888 Pittston, PA D 7.15.1966 Orlando, FL BR/TR 5-5/130# d8.19																								
1908	Bro N	43	147	9	35	3	0	0	3	9	3		.238	.296	.259	80	-3	5	.873	-7	91	111	S-29,O-14(CF)	-1.1
1909	Bro N	108	373	18	79	15	1	0	24	20	1		.212	.254	.257	61	-18	11	.914	-11	96	81	*S-105/2-2,3	-2.9
1910	Bro N	23	74	2	13	1	0	0	2	6	0	10	.176	.237	.189	26	-7	4	.898	-2	99	79	S-23	-0.9
	Cin N	82	248	20	46	0	3	0	13	31	2	23	.185	.281	.210	46	-17	7	.927	8	111	95	S-82	-0.7
	Year	105	322	22	59	1	3	0	15	37	2	33	.183	.271	.205	41	-24	11	**.921**	6	**108**	92	*S-105	-1.6
1912	NY A	41	149	24	34	2	0	0	12	15	1		.228	.303	.242	53	-9	18	.948	-3	92	91	S-41	-1.0
Total	4	297	991	73	207	21	4	0	54	81	7	33	.209	.273	.238	56	-54	45	.917	-15	100	90	S-280/O-14(CF),2-2,3	-6.6
McMILLON, BILLY William Edward B 11.17.1971 Otero, NM BL/TL 5-11/172# d7.26																								
1996	Fla N	28	51	4	11	0	0	0	4	5-1	0	14	.216	.286	.216	36	-5	0-0	1.000	-1	92	0	O-15(LF)	-0.6
1997	Fla N	13	18	0	2	1	0	0	1	0-0	0	7	.111	.111	.167	-30	-3	0-0	1.000	0	110	0	/O-2(LF)	-0.3
	Phi N	24	72	10	21	4	1	2	13	6-0	0	17	.292	.333	.458	109	1	2-1	.957	2	126	170	O-21(19-0-2)	0.2
	Year	37	90	10	23	5	1	2	14	6-0	0	24	.256	.293	.400	83	-3	2-1	.960	3	125	155	O-23(21-0-2)	-0.1
2000	Det A	46	123	20	37	7	1	4	24	19-0	1	19	.301	.388	.472	123	5	1-0	.964	1	137	0	D-24,O-15(3-0-13)	0.4
2001	Det A	20	34	1	3	1	0	1	4	2-0	1	12	.088	.162	.206	-4	-5	0-0	1.000	0	111	0	/O-7(1-0-6),D-3	-0.5
	Oak A	20	58	6	17	7	1	0	10	5-0	1	13	.293	.354	.448	111	1	1-0	.950	-2	60	106	O-16(15-0-2)/D	-0.2
	Year	40	92	7	20	8	1	1	14	7-0	2	25	.217	.284	.359	70	-4	1-0	.967	-2	72	82	O-23(16-0-8)/D-4	-0.7
2003	†Oak A	66	153	15	41	11	0	6	26	19-1	2	36	.268	.354	.458	111	3	0-0	.979	-2	98	0	O-36(35-0-1)/1-3,D-9	0.0
Total	5	217	509	56	132	31	3	13	82	56-2	5	118	.259	.333	.409	95	-3	4-1	.971	-2	102	56	O-112(90-0-24)/D-37,1-3	-1.0
McMULLEN, HUGH Hugh Raphael B 12.16.1901 LaCygne, KS D 5.23.1986 Whittier, CA BB/TR 6-1/180# d9.19																								
1925	NY N	5	15	1	2	1	0	0	0	0	0	3	.133	.133	.200	-17	-3	0-0	1.000	-1	*91*	*0*	/C-5	-0.3
1926	NY N	57	91	5	17	2	0	0	6	2	0	18	.187	.204	.209	11	-12	1	.942	-2	*86*	*104*	C-56	-1.1
1928	Was A	1	1	0	0	0	0	0	0	0	0	1	.000	.000	.000	-99	0	0-0	—	0			H	0.0
1929	Cin N	1	1	0	0	0	0	0	0	0	0	0	.000	.000	.000	-99	0	0	1.000	0	*0*	*0*	/C	0.0
Total	4	64	108	6	19	3	0	0	6	2	0	22	.176	.191	.204	5	-15	1-0	.947	-3	*85*	*92*	/C-62	-1.4
McMULLEN, KEN Kenneth Lee B 6.1.1942 Oxnard, CA BR/TR 6-3/195# d9.17 OF Total (12-LF 8-RF)																								
1962	LA N	6	11	0	3	0	0	0	0	0-0	0	3	.273	.273	.273	50	-1	0-0	1.000	-0	53	0	/O-2(LF)	-0.1
1963	LA N	79	233	16	55	9	0	5	28	20-2	1	46	.236	.297	.339	89	-3	1-2	.933	1	101	90	3-71/2O(LF)	-0.3
1964	LA N	24	67	3	14	0	0	1	2	3-1	0	7	.209	.243	.254	43	-5	0-1	.991	-2	87	78	1-13/3-4,O-3(1-0-2)	-0.9
1965	Was A	150	555	75	146	18	6	18	54	47-4	4	90	.263	.323	.414	110	6	2-0	.954	5	102	97	*3-142/O-8(3-0-5),1	1.1
1966	Was A	147	524	48	122	19	4	13	54	44-1	0	89	.233	.289	.359	87	-10	3-1	.951	-5	97	112	*3-141/1-8,O(RF)	-1.7
1967	Was A	146	563	73	138	22	2	16	67	46-2	1	84	.245	.301	.377	104	1	5-3	.965	9	108	**153**	*3-145	1.0
1968	Was A	151	557	66	138	11	2	20	62	63-5	3	66	.248	.326	.382	118	12	1-3	.962	8	105	93	*3-145,S-11	2.1
1969	Was A	158	562	83	153	25	2	19	87	70-6	1	103	.272	.349	.425	123	18	4-5	.976	21	**110**	109	*3-154	3.9
1970	Was A	15	59	5	12	2	0	0	3	5-0	0	10	.203	.266	.237	42	-5	0-0	.971	5	119	207	3-15	0.0
	Cal A	124	422	50	98	9	3	14	61	59-10	3	81	.232	.329	.367	96	-2	1-0	.959	8	102	139	*3-122	0.6
	Year	139	481	55	110	11	3	14	64	64-10	3	91	.229	.321	.351	89	-7	1-0	**.960**	13	104	**147**	*3-137	0.6
1971	Cal A	160	593	63	148	19	2	21	68	53-10	3	74	.250	.312	.395	107	3	1-1	.966	-6	98	84	*3-158	-0.4
1972	Cal A	137	472	36	127	18	1	9	34	48-2	0	59	.269	.335	.369	116	9	1-2	.970	1	96	100	*3-137	1.0
1973	LA N	42	85	6	21	5	0	5	18	6-1	0	13	.247	.297	.482	118	1	0-0	.922	5	145	71	3-24	0.6
1974	†LA N	44	60	5	15	1	0	3	12	2-0	0	12	.250	.274	.417	95	-1	0-0	1.000	0	104	0	/3-7,2-3	-0.1
1975	LA N	39	46	4	11	1	1	2	14	7-0	0	12	.239	.340	.435	119	1	0-0	1.000	1	86	0	3-11/1-3	0.2
1976	Oak A	98	186	20	41	6	2	5	23	22-3	1	33	.220	.305	.355	97	-1	1-1	.952	-3	104	44	3-35,1-26,D-23/O-5(LF),2	-0.6
1977	Mil A	63	136	15	31	7	1	5	19	15-0	0	33	.228	.305	.404	91	-2	0-0	.978	1	138	109	D-29,1-11/3-7	-0.2
Total	16	1583	5131	568	1273	172	26	156	606	510-47	17	815	.248	.316	.383	105	21	20-19	.961	49	103	108	*3-1318/1-62,D-52,O-20L,S-11,2-5	6.2
McMULLIN, FRED Frederick Drury B 10.13.1891 Scammon, KS D 11.20.1952 Los Angeles, CA BR/TR 5-11/170# d8.27																								
1914	Det A	1	1	0	0	0	0	0	0	0	0	1	.000	.000	.000	-97	0	0	.667	-0	97	0	/S	0.0
1916	Chi A	68	187	8	48	3	0	0	10	19	2	30	.257	.332	.273	81	-4	9	.950	-3	93	113	3-63/S-2,2	-0.5
1917	†Chi A	59	194	35	46	2	1	0	12	27	3	17	.237	.339	.258	81	-3	9	.932	-10	86	58	3-52/S-2	-1.3
1918	Chi A	70	235	32	65	7	0	1	16	25	4	26	.277	.356	.319	103	2	8	.941	-3	102	69	3-69/2	0.1
1919	†Chi A	60	170	31	50	8	4	0	19	11	5	18	.294	.355	.388	108	2	4	.931	-2	100	157	3-46/2-5	0.1
1920	Chi A	46	127	14	25	1	4	0	13	9	1	13	.197	.255	.268	39	-12	1-1	.962	-3	94	81	3-29/2-3,S	-1.5
Total	6	304	914	120	234	21	9	1	70	91	15	105	.256	.333	.302	85	-15	31-1	.942	-21	95	94	3-259/2-10,S-6	-3.1
McMULLIN, JOHN John F. "Lefty" B 1848 Philadelphia, PA D 4.11.1881 Philadelphia, PA BR/TL 5-9/160# d5.9 ▲																								
1871	Tro NA	**29**	136	38	38	0	5	0	32	8		6	.279	.319	.353	92	-2	11-1	.871	-0	100	44	*P-29/S	0.0
1872	Mut NA	54	236	47	60	6	1	0	24	11		6	.254	.287	.288	83	-2	8-2	.871	3	46	0	*O-53(41-1-11)/P-3	0.3
1873	Ath NA	**52**	227	54	62	7	1	0	28	8		4	.273	.298	.313	76	-8	9-1	.822	-4	41	81	*O-51(LF)/P	-0.6
1874	Ath NA	**55**	260	61	90	10	2	2	32	8		13	.346	.366	.423	140	10	4-3	.771	-6	62	80	*O-55(5-51-1)	0.3
1875	Phi NA	54	222	33	57	9	4	2	19	5		12	.257	.273	.360	114	3	6-10	.835	-1	47	132	*O-54(22-32-0)/P-4	0.0
Total	5 NA	244	1081	233	307	32	13	4	135	40		41	.284	.310	.349	102	1	38-17	.000	-8	49	71	O-213(119-84-12)/P-37,S	0.0
McNABB, CARL Carl Mac "Skinny" B 1.25.1917 Stevenson, AL BR/TR 5-9/155# d4.20																								
1945	Det A	1	1	0	0	0	0	0	0	0	0	1	.000	.000	.000	-94	0	0-0	—	0			H	0.0
McNAIR, ERIC Donald Eric "Boob" B 4.12.1909 Meridian, MS D 3.11.1949 Meridian, MS BR/TR 5-8.5/160# d9.20																								
1929	Phi A	4	8	2	4	1	0	0	3	0	0	0	.500	.500	.625	181	1	1-0	1.000	-0	75	0	/S-4	0.1
1930	†Phi A	78	237	27	63	12	2	0	34	9	1	19	.266	.296	.333	57	-16	5-2	.915	-11	78	68	S-31,3-29/2-5,O(RF)	-2.0
1931	†Phi A	79	280	41	76	10	1	5	33	11	3	19	.271	.306	.368	72	-12	1-4	.915	-4	98	220	3-47,2-16,S-13	-1.3
1932	Phi A	135	554	87	158	**47**	3	18	95	28	3	29	.285	.323	.478	101	-1	8-4	.953	-12	92	111	*S-133	-0.2
1933	Phi A	89	310	57	81	15	4	7	48	15	3	32	.261	.302	.403	84	-9	2-1	.966	-2	95	99	S-46,2-27	-0.5
1934	Phi A	151	599	80	168	20	4	17	82	35	1	42	.280	.321	.412	91	-12	7-8	.951	8	102	108	*S-151	0.6
1935	Phi A	137	526	55	142	22	2	4	57	35	3	33	.270	.319	.342	72	-23	3-7	.955	-17	91	95	*S-121,3-11/1-2	-3.2
1936	Bos A	128	494	68	141	36	2	4	74	27	5	34	.285	.329	.391	73	-22	3-3	.966	-10	91	96	S-84,2-35,3-11	-2.1
1937	Bos A	126	455	60	133	29	4	12	76	30	3	33	.292	.340	.453	94	-5	10-7	.969	-6	99	91	*2-106/S-9,3-4,1	-0.4
1938	Bos A	46	96	9	15	1	1	0	7	3	0	6	.156	.182	.188	-7	-17	0-1	.870	1	119	58	S-15,2-14/3-3	-1.3
1939	Chi A	129	479	62	155	18	5	7	82	38	1	41	.324	.375	.426	102	1	17-9	.937	1	97	134	*3-103,2-19/S-9	0.7
1940	Chi A	66	251	26	57	13	1	7	31	12	1	26	.227	.265	.371	62	-15	1-7	.958	-16	91	71	2-65/3	-2.9
1941	Det A	23	59	5	11	1	0	0	3	4	1	4	.186	.250	.203	19	-7	0-0	.970	-1	91	0	3-11/S-3	-0.7
1942	Det A	26	68	5	11	2	0	1	4	3	0	5	.162	.197	.235	20	-7	0-1	.881	-5	76	67	S-21	-1.3
	Phi A	34	103	8	25	2	0	0	4	11	0	5	.243	.316	.262	64	-5	1-0	.952	-5	92	60	S-29/2	-0.7
	Year	60	171	13	36	4	0	1	8	14	0	10	.211	.270	.251	46	-13	1-1	.927	-10	86	63	S-50/2	-2.0
Total	14	1251	4519	592	1240	229	29	82	633	261	25	328	.274	.318	.392	80	-149	59-54	.949	-79	94	99	S-669,2-288,3-220/1-3,O(RF)	-15.2
McNALLY, MIKE Michael Joseph "Minooka Mike" B 9.9.1892 Minooka, PA D 5.29.1965 Bethlehem, PA BR/TR 5-11/150# d4.21 Mil 1918																								
1915	Bos A	23	53	7	8	0	1	0	0	3	0	7	.151	.196	.189	16	-6	0-2	.891	-1	92	154	3-18/2-5	-0.8
1916	†Bos A	87	135	28	23	0	0	0	9	10	0	19	.170	.228	.170	20	-14	9	.964	2	116	103	2-35,3-14/S-7,O(CF)	-1.2
1917	Bos A	42	50	9	15	1	0	0	2	6	0	3	.300	.375	.320	113	1	3	.935	3	118	60	3-14/S-9,2-6	0.5
1919	Bos A	33	42	10	11	4	0	0	6	1	0	2	.262	.279	.357	83	-1	4	.950	5	125	86	S-11,3-11/2-3	0.5

Year	Tm Lg	G	AB	R	H	2B	3B	HR	RBI	BB-IB	HP	SO	AVG	OBP	SLG	AOPS	ABR	SB-CS	FA	FR	Rng	Thr	G at Pos	BFW
1920	Bos A	93	312	42	80	5	1	0	23	31	1	24	.256	.326	.279	64	-16	13-10	.930	-8	100	115	2-76/S-8,1-6	-2.2
1921	†NY A	71	215	36	56	4	2	1	24	14	0	15	.260	.306	.312	56	-15	5-6	.974	14	132	60	3-49,2-16	0.1
1922	†NY A	52	143	20	36	2	2	0	18	16	1	14	.252	.331	.294	63	-8	3-0	.983	-2	94	95	3-34/2-9,S-4,1	-0.7
1923	NY A	30	38	5	8	0	0	0	1	3	0	4	.211	.268	.211	27	-4	2-0	1.000	-1	116	77	S-13/3-7,2-5	-0.4
1924	NY A	49	69	11	17	0	0	0	2	7	0	5	.246	.316	.246	46	-6	1-1	.985	5	119	125	2-25,3-13/S-6	0.0
1925	Was A	12	21	1	3	0	0	0	0	1	0	4	.143	.182	.143	-17	-4	0-0	1.000	-1	91	97	/3-7,S-2,2	-0.4
Total	10	492	1078	169	257	16	6	1	85	92	2	97	.238	.299	.267	54	-73	40-19	.946	18	108	109	2-181,3-167/S-60,1-7,O(CF)	-4.6
McNAMARA, GEORGE George Francis B 1.11.1901 Chicago, IL D 6.12.1990 Hinsdale, IL BL/TR 6/175# d9.28																								
1922	Was A	3	11	3	3	0	0	0	1	1	0	2	.273	.333	.273	63	-1	0-0	1.000	-0	74	0	/O-3(RF)	-0.1
McNAMARA, JIM James Patrick B 6.10.1965 Nashua, NH BL/TR 6-4/210# d4.9																								
1992	SF N	30	74	6	16	1	0	1	9	6-2	0	25	.216	.275	.270	58	-4	0-0	.993	-1	179	60	C-30	-0.5
1993	SF N	4	7	0	1	0	0	0	1	0-0	0	1	.143	.143	.143	-24	-1	0-0	1.000	-0	144	0	/C-4	-0.2
Total	2	34	81	6	17	1	0	1	10	6-2	0	26	.210	.264	.259	51	-5	0-0	.993	-2	176	55	/C-34	-0.7
McNAMARA, DINNY John Raymond B 9.16.1905 Lexington, MA D 12.20.1963 Arlington, MA BL/TR 5-9/165# d7.2																								
1927	Bos N	11	9	3	0	0	0	0	0	0	0	3	.000	.000	.000	-99	-3	0	1.000	1	180	0	/O-3(CF)	-0.2
1928	Bos N	9	4	2	1	0	0	0	0	0	0	1	.250	.250	.250	33	0	0	1.000	1	198	0	/O-3(0-1-2)	0.0
Total	2	20	13	5	1	0	0	0	0	0	0	4	.077	.077	.077	-63	-3	0	1.000	1	188	0	/O-6(0-4-2)	-0.2
McNAMARA, BOB Robert Maxey B 9.19.1916 Denver, CO BR/TR 5-10/170# d5.27																								
1939	Phi A	9	9	0	2	1	0	0	3	1	0	1	.222	.300	.333	63	0	0-0	1.000	-0	109	0	/3-5,S-2,12	-0.1
McNAMARA, TOM Thomas Henry B 11.5.1895 Roxbury, MA D 5.5.1974 Danvers, MA BR/TR 6-2/200# d6.25																								
1922	Pit N	1	1	0	0	0	0	0	0	0	0	0	.000	.000	.000	-99	0	0-0	—	0			H	0.0
McNEALY, RUSTY Robert Lee B 8.12.1958 Sacramento, CA BL/TL 5-8/160# d9.4																								
1983	Oak A	15	4	5	0	0	0	0	0	0-0	0	0	.000	.000	.000	-99	-1	0-1	1.000	1	216	0	/O-5(1-4-1),D-7	-0.1
McNEELY, EARL George Earl B 5.12.1898 Sacramento, CA D 7.16.1971 Sacramento, CA BR/TR 5-9/155# d8.9 C3																								
1924	†Was A	43	179	31	59	5	6	0	15	5	2	21	.330	.355	.425	104	-1	3-1	.973	-1	101	79	O-42(0-42-2)	-0.2
1925	†Was A	122	385	76	110	14	2	3	37	48	9	54	.286	.378	.356	89	-5	15-16	.975	2	99	123	*O-112(7-103-2)/1	-0.9
1926	Was A	124	442	84	134	20	12	0	48	44	5	28	.303	.373	.403	105	3	18-6	.969	1	108	83	*O-118(65-52-2)	-0.1
1927	Was A	73	185	40	51	10	4	0	16	11	1	13	.276	.320	.373	80	-6	11-4	.977	-1	98	83	O-47(3-32-14)/1-4	-0.8
1928	StL A	127	496	66	117	27	7	0	44	37	**8**	39	.236	.299	.319	61	-29	8-6	.984	5	100	150	*O-120(2-1-118)	-3.3
1929	StL A	69	230	27	56	8	1	1	18	7	2	13	.243	.272	.300	45	-19	2-1	.980	-3	91	74	O-62(18-2-42)	-2.5
1930	StL A	76	235	33	64	19	1	0	20	22	2	14	.272	.340	.362	75	-8	8-3	.939	-2	86	94	O-38(8-26-4),1-27	-1.2
1931	StL A	49	102	12	23	4	0	0	15	9	0	5	.225	.288	.265	45	-8	4-4	.969	-0	93	137	O-37(2-23-12)/1	-0.9
Total	8	683	2254	369	614	107	33	4	213	183	29	187	.272	.335	.354	78	-73	69-41	.974	0	99	109	O-576(105-281-196)/1-33	-9.9
McNEELY, JEFF Jeffrey Lavern B 10.18.1969 Monroe, NC BR/TR 6-2/190# d9.5																								
1993	Bos A	21	37	10	11	1	1	0	1	7-0	0	9	.297	.409	.378	106	1	6-0	.917	-3	73	0	O-13(CF)/D-3	0.0
McNEIL, NORM Norman Francis B 10.22.1892 Chicago, IL D 4.11.1942 Buffalo, NY BR/TR 5-11/180# d6.21																								
1919	Bos A	5	9	0	3	0	0	0	1	1	0	0	.333	.400	.333	113	0	0	.818	-1	*91*	*68*	/C-5	-0.1
McNERTNEY, JERRY Gerald Edward B 8.7.1936 Boone, IA BR/TR 6-1/195# d4.16 C1																								
1964	Chi A	73	186	16	40	5	0	3	23	19-4	3	24	.215	.290	.290	66	-8	0-0	.987	8	*179*	*90*	C-69	0.2
1966	Chi A	44	59	3	13	0	0	0	1	7-0	0	6	.220	.303	.220	57	-3	1-1	.969	3	*87*	*138*	C-37	0.1
1967	Chi A	56	123	8	28	6	0	3	13	6-3	2	14	.228	.275	.350	87	-2	0-0	.996	4	81	214	C-52	0.4
1968	Chi A	74	169	18	37	4	1	3	18	18-3	2	29	.219	.300	.308	84	-3	0-0	.985	6	88	114	C-64/1	0.7
1969	Sea A	128	410	39	99	18	1	8	55	29-3	0	63	.241	.291	.349	80	-12	1-0	.988	-5	82	112	*C-122	-1.3
1970	Mil A	111	296	27	72	11	1	6	22	22-4	4	33	.243	.302	.348	79	-9	1-4	.984	-4	64	121	C-94,1-13	-1.2
1971	StL N	56	128	15	37	4	2	4	22	12-1	0	14	.289	.343	.445	119	3	0-0	.985	-3	147	40	C-36	0.2
1972	StL N	39	48	3	10	3	1	0	9	6-1	0	16	.208	.291	.313	74	-2	0-0	.982	2	159	205	C-10	0.1
1973	Pit N	9	4	0	1	0	0	0	0	0-0	0	0	.250	.250	.250	40	0	0-0	1.000	-0	0	172	/C-9	0.0
Total	9	590	1423	129	337	51	6	27	163	119-19	11	199	.237	.298	.338	81	-36	3-5	.987	10	*100*	*119*	C-493/1-14	-0.8
McNULTY, PAT Patrick Howard B 2.27.1899 Cleveland, OH D 5.4.1963 Hollywood, CA BL/TR 5-11/160# d9.5																								
1922	Cle A	22	59	10	16	2	1	0	5	9	0	5	.271	.368	.339	85	-1	4-1	.956	-1	103	0	O-22(1-19-2)	-0.3
1924	Cle A	101	291	46	78	13	5	0	26	33	2	22	.268	.347	.347	78	-9	10-7	.961	-2	93	106	O-75(11-20-44)	-1.5
1925	Cle A	118	373	70	117	18	2	6	43	47	1	23	.314	.392	.421	105	4	7-7	.965	4	100	**157**	*O-111(3-29-81)	0.1
1926	Cle A	48	56	3	14	2	1	0	6	5	0	9	.250	.311	.321	65	-3	0-1	.909	0	68	387	/O-9(2-5-2)	-0.3
1927	Cle A	19	41	3	13	1	0	0	4	4	0	3	.317	.378	.341	87	-1	1-2	.906	-0	103	92	O-12(1-11-0)	-0.2
Total	5	308	820	132	238	36	9	6	84	98	3	62	.290	.368	.378	91	-10	22-18	.957	1	97	128	O-229(18-84-129)	-2.2
McNULTY, BILL William Francis B 8.29.1946 Sacramento, CA BR/TR 6-4/205# d7.9																								
1969	Oak A	5	17	0	0	0	0	0	0	0-0	0	10	.000	.000	.000	-99	-5	0-0	1.000	2	122	667	/O-5(LF)	-0.3
1972	Oak A	4	10	0	1	0	0	0	0	2-0	0	1	.100	.250	.100	7	-1	0-0	.800	-2	35	0	/3-3	-0.3
Total	2	9	27	0	1	0	0	0	0	2-0	0	11	.037	.103	.037	-61	-6	0-0	1.000	0	122	667	/O-5(LF),3-3	-0.6
McPHEE, BID John Alexander B 11.1.1859 Massena, NY D 1.3.1943 San Diego, CA BR/TR 5-8/152# d5.2 M2 HF2000																								
1882	Cin AA	78	311	43	71	8	7	1	31	11			.228	.255	.309	84	-6		**.920**	-4	90	**130**	*2-78	-0.7
1883	Cin AA	96	367	61	90	10	10	2	42	18			.245	.281	.343	95	-3		**.928**	4	97	**149**	*2-96	0.4
1884	Cin AA	**112**	450	107	125	8	7	5	64	27	6		.278	.327	.360	118	8		.924	15	103	154	*2-112	2.5
1885	Cin AA	110	431	78	114	12	4	0	46	19	7		.265	.306	.311	94	-3		**.936**	4	103	116	*2-110	0.5
1886	Cin AA	140	560	139	150	23	12	**8**	70	59	5		.268	.343	.395	127	17	40	**.939**	27	**104**	**133**	*2-140	**4.2**
1887	Cin AA	129	540	137	156	20	**19**	2	87	55	5		.289	.360	.407	111	7	95	.924	23	**109**	**147**	*2-129	2.8
1888	Cin AA	111	458	88	110	12	10	4	51	43	5		.240	.312	.336	102	0	54	**.940**	26	107	**164**	*2-111	2.8
1889	Cin AA	135	540	109	145	25	7	5	57	60	4	29	.269	.346	.369	100	0	63	**.946**	**37**	112	**133**	*2-135/3	3.6
1890	Cin N	132	528	125	135	16	22	3	39	82	6	26	.256	.362	.386	119	13	55	.942	26	104	**130**	*2-132	3.9
1891	Cin N	**138**	562	107	144	14	16	6	38	74	2	35	.256	.345	.370	107	5	33	**.954**	24	109	123	*2-138	3.0
1892	Cin N	144	573	111	157	19	12	4	60	84	7	48	.274	.373	.370	127	22	44	.948	23	105	146	*2-144	4.7
1893	Cin N	127	491	101	138	17	11	3	68	94	4	20	.281	.401	.379	105	7	25	.954	**31**	**109**	**168**	*2-127	3.6
1894	Cin N	128	483	113	151	21	10	5	93	91	6	23	.313	.428	.429	103	6	33	.945	30	**113**	115	*2-128	3.2
1895	Cin N	115	432	107	129	24	12	1	75	73	8	30	.299	.409	.417	109	9	30	.955	12	101	114	*2-115	2.1
1896	Cin N	117	433	81	132	18	7	1	87	51	10	18	.305	.391	.386	98	0	48	**.978**	8	101	130	*2-117	1.2
1897	Cin N	81	282	45	85	13	7	1	39	35	4		.301	.386	.408	103	1	9	.966	13	106	129	2-81	1.5
1898	Cin N	133	486	72	121	26	9	1	60	66	2		.249	.341	.346	91	-5	21	.956	-13	97	**145**	*2-130/O-3(RF)	-1.1
1899	Cin N	112	377	60	105	17	7	1	65	40	7		.279	.358	.369	98	0	18	.955	-4	98	109	*2-106/O(CF)	0.1
Total	18	2138	8304	1684	2258	303	189	53	1072	982	88	229	.272	.355	.373	106	78	568	.944	283	104	136	*2-2129/O-4(0-1-3),3	38.3
McQUAID, MART Mortimer Martin B 6.28.1861 Chicago, IL D 3.5.1928 Chicago, IL 5-9/160# d8.15																								
1891	StL AA	4	11	1	4	2	0	0	1	0	0	1	.364	.364	.545	139	0	1	1.000	0	88	112	/2-3,O(LF)	0.1
1898	Was N	1	4	0	0	0	0	0	0	0	0		.000	.000	.000	-99	-1	0	.333	-1	0	0	/O(LF)	-0.2
Total	2	5	15	1	4	2	0	0	1	0	0	1	.267	.267	.400	82	-1	1	1.000	-1	88	112	/2-3,O-2(LF)	-0.1
McQUAIG, JERRY Gerald Joseph B 1.31.1912 Douglas, GA BR/TR 5-11/183# d8.25																								
1934	Phi A	7	16	2	1	0	0	0	1	2	0	4	.063	.167	.063	-40	-3	0-0	.889	-1	95	0	/O-6(5-0-1)	-0.4
McQUERY, MOX William Thomas B 6.28.1861 Garrard Co., KY D 6.12.1900 Cincinnati, OH 6-4/?# d8.20																								
1884	Cin U	35	132	31	37	5	0	2		8			.280	.321	.364	99	-4		.978	1	80	88	1-35	-0.5
1885	Det N	70	278	34	76	15	4	3	30	8		29	.273	.294	.388	119	5		.976	3	117	88	1-70	0.2
1886	KC N	122	449	62	111	27	4	4	38	36		44	.247	.303	.352	93	-4	4	.969	1	108	90	*1-122	-1.2
1890	Syr AA	122	461	64	142	17	6	2	55	53	3		.308	.383	.384	141	27	26	.972	-1	94	93	*1-122	1.3
1891	Was AA	68	261	40	63	9	4	2	37	18	6	19	.241	.305	.330	86	-5	3	.977	1	107	85	1-68	-0.9
Total	5	417	1581	231	429	73	18	13	160	123	9	92	.271	.327	.365	110	19	33	.973	5	103	90	1-417	-1.1

Year	Tm Lg	G	AB	R	H	2B	3B	HR	RBI	BB-IB	HP	SO	AVG	OBP	SLG	AOPS	ABR	SB-CS	FA	FR	Rng	Thr	G at Pos	BFW
McQUILLEN, GLENN Glenn Richard "Red" B 4.19.1915 Strasburg, VA D 6.8.1989 Gardenville, MD BR/TR 6/198# d6.16 Mil 1943-45																								
1938	StL A	43	116	14	33	4	0	0	13	4	0	12	.284	.308	.319	57	-8	0-1	.971	1	122	0	O-30(LF)	-0.8
1941	StL A	7	21	4	7	2	1	0	3	1	0	2	.333	.364	.524	128	1	0-1	.933	-0	108	0	/O-6(3-0-3)	0.0
1942	StL A	100	339	40	96	15	12	3	47	10	1	17	.283	.306	.425	103	-2	1-1	.969	-6	93	32	O-77(68-0-9)	-1.3
1946	StL A	59	166	24	40	3	3	1	12	19	0	18	.241	.319	.313	73	-6	0-2	.977	3	94	299	O-48(44-0-5)	-0.6
1947	StL A	1	1	0	0	0	0	0	0	0	0	0	.000	.000	.000	-98	0	0-0	—	0			H	0.0
Total	5	210	643	82	176	24	16	4	75	34	1	49	.274	.311	.379	87	-15	1-5	.970	-2	99	93	O-161(145-0-17)	-2.7
McQUINN, GEORGE George Hartley B 5.29.1910 Arlington, VA D 12.24.1978 Alexandria, VA BL/TL 5-11/165# d4.14																								
1936	Cin N	38	134	5	27	3	4	0	13	10	1	22	.201	.262	.284	50	-10	0	.992	1	111	100	1-38	-1.2
1938	StL A	148	602	100	195	42	7	12	82	58	1	49	.324	.384	.477	115	14	4-5	.992	1	95	92	*1-148	0.0
1939	StL A☆	154	617	101	195	37	13	20	94	65	2	42	.316	.383	.515	125	22	6-5	.993	10	123	80	*1-154	1.5
1940	StL A☆	151	594	78	166	39	10	16	84	57	0	58	.279	.343	.460	104	2	3-3	**.992**	9	**126**	112	*1-150	-0.3
1941	StL A	130	495	93	147	28	4	18	80	74	0	30	.297	.388	.479	124	19	5-4	**.995**	7	117	102	*1-125	1.3
1942	StL A☆	145	554	86	145	32	5	12	78	60	1	77	.262	.335	.403	105	3	1-1	.991	1	103	96	*1-144	-0.9
1943	StL A	125	449	53	109	19	2	12	74	56	0	65	.243	.327	.374	103	1	4-3	.992	2	104	84	*1-122	-0.3
1944	†StL A★	146	516	83	129	26	3	11	72	85	1	74	.250	.357	.376	103	5	4-3	**.994**	-6	80	93	*1-146	-0.9
1945	StL A✳	139	483	69	134	31	3	7	61	65	1	51	.277	.364	.398	115	11	1-1	.991	4	107	82	*1-136	0.9
1946	Phi A	136	484	47	109	23	6	3	35	64	1	62	.225	.317	.316	78	-14	4-2	.988	2	106	88	*1-134	-1.7
1947	†NY A★	144	517	84	157	24	3	13	80	78	0	66	.304	.395	.437	132	25	0-2	.994	-2	89	98	*1-142	1.8
1948	NY A★	94	302	33	75	11	4	11	41	40	0	38	.248	.336	.421	102	-1	0-2	.993	-1	90	106	1-90	-0.5
Total	12	1550	5747	832	1588	315	64	135	794	712	8	634	.276	.357	.424	109	77	32-31	.992	28	104	94	*1-1529	-0.3
McRAE, BRIAN Brian Wesley B 8.27.1967 Bradenton, FL BB/TR 6/185# d8.7 f-Hal																								
1990	KC A	46	168	21	48	8	3	2	23	9-0	0	29	.286	.318	.405	104	0	4-3	1.000	1	110	47	O-45(CF)	0.1
1991	KC A	152	629	86	164	28	9	8	64	24-1	2	99	.261	.288	.372	81	-19	20-11	.993	-2	106	26	*O-150(CF)	-2.1
1992	KC A	149	533	63	119	23	5	4	52	42-1	6	88	.223	.285	.308	65	-25	18-5	.993	1	102	95	*O-148(CF)	-2.4
1993	KC A	153	627	78	177	28	9	12	69	37-1	4	105	.282	.325	.413	92	-9	23-14	.983	-6	98	48	*O-153(CF)	-1.3
1994	KC A	114	436	71	119	22	6	4	40	54-3	6	67	.273	.359	.378	87	-7	28-8	.988	-12	85	34	*O-110(CF)/D-4	-1.4
1995	Chi N	137	580	92	167	38	7	12	48	47-1	7	92	.288	.348	.440	108	7	27-8	.991	-2	104	53	*O-137(CF)	1.0
1996	Chi N	157	624	111	172	32	5	17	66	73-6	12	84	.276	.360	.425	104	5	37-9	.986	-12	92	24	*O-155(CF)	0.0
1997	Chi N	108	417	63	100	27	5	6	28	52-2	4	62	.240	.329	.372	81	-11	14-6	.996	-2	103	60	*O-107(CF)	-1.0
	NY N	45	145	23	36	5	2	5	15	13-0	2	22	.248	.317	.414	93	-2	3-4	.957	-6	77	56	O-41(CF)	-0.8
	Year	153	562	86	136	32	7	11	43	65-2	6	84	.242	.326	.383	84	-13	17-10	.987	-7	96	59	*O-148(CF)	-1.8
1998	NY N	159	552	79	146	36	5	21	79	80-3	5	90	.264	.360	.462	117	15	20-11	.987	-13	86	86	*O-154(CF)	0.4
1999	NY N	96	298	35	66	12	1	8	36	39-1	5	57	.221	.320	.349	72	-13	2-6	.994	-11	80	24	O-87(CF)	-2.4
	Col N	7	23	1	6	2	0	1	1	2-0	2	7	.261	.370	.478	89	0	0-0	1.000	-1	90	0	/O-7(CF)	-0.1
	Year	103	321	36	72	14	1	9	37	41-1	7	64	.224	.323	.358	73	-13	2-6	.994	-12	81	22	O-94(CF)	-2.5
	Tor A	31	82	11	16	3	1	3	11	16-1	2	22	.195	.340	.366	79	-2	0-1	1.000	-0	90	130	D-15,O-13(CF)	-0.4
Total	10	1354	5114	734	1336	264	58	103	532	488-20	57	824	.261	.331	.396	92	-61	196-86	.990	-63	96	52	*O-1307(CF)/D-19	-10.4
McRAE, HAL Harold Abraham B 7.10.1945 Avon Park, FL BR/TR 5-11/180# d7.11 M6 C10 s-Brian OF Total (360-LF 33-CF 94-RF)																								
1968	Cin N	17	51	1	10	1	0	0	2	4-2	0	14	.196	.255	.216	40	-4	1-1	.926	-3	79	95	2-16	-0.7
1970	†Cin N	70	165	18	41	6	1	8	23	15-2	1	23	.248	.313	.442	100	-1	0-2	.981	-3	89	41	O-46(46-0-1)/3-6,2	-0.7
1971	Cin N	99	337	39	89	24	2	9	34	11-0	2	35	.264	.291	.427	103	0	3-2	.966	-0	94	109	O-91(66-28-0)	-0.5
1972	†Cin N	61	97	9	27	4	0	5	26	2-0	2	10	.278	.295	.474	126	3	0-0	.867	-3	101	0	O-12(0-3-9),3-11	-0.1
1973	KC A	106	338	36	79	18	3	9	50	34-2	6	38	.234	.312	.385	89	-5	2-2	.963	-1	96	110	O-64(3-0-63),D-37/3-2	-1.0
1974	KC A	148	539	71	167	36	4	15	88	54-6	5	68	.310	.375	.475	136	26	11-8	.950	2	115	49	D-90,O-56(40-0-19)/3	2.3
1975	KC A★	126	480	58	147	38	6	5	71	47-7	4	47	.306	.366	.442	126	18	11-8	.986	-4	88	86	*O-114(112-2-0),D-12/3	0.7
1976	†KC A★	149	527	75	175	34	5	8	73	64-7	8	43	.332	**.407**	.461	154	**40**	22-12	.970	0	104	95	*D-117,O-31(LF)	3.7
1977	†KC A	**162**	641	104	191	**54**	11	21	92	59-5	**13**	43	.298	.366	.515	137	34	18-14	.958	5	109	275	*D-115,O-47(LF)	3.2
1978	†KC A	156	623	90	170	39	5	16	72	51-6	6	62	.273	.329	.429	110	8	17-8	1.000	0	55	557	*D-153/O-3(LF)	0.5
1979	KC A	101	393	55	113	32	4	10	74	38-0	4	46	.288	.351	.466	117	10	5-4	—	0	0	0	*D-100	0.7
1980	†KC A	124	489	73	145	39	5	14	83	29-4	8	56	.297	.342	.483	123	15	10-2	1.000	-1	99	0	*D-110/O-9(LF)	1.3
1981	†KC A	101	389	38	106	23	2	7	36	34-3	2	33	.272	.330	.396	111	6	3-4	.909	0	128	0	D-97/O-4(2-0-2)	0.2
1982	KC A★	159	613	91	189	**46**	8	27	**133**	55-7	5	61	.308	.369	.542	146	39	4-4	.500	-1	45	0	*D-158/O(LF)	3.3
1983	KC A	157	589	84	183	41	6	12	82	50-7	10	68	.311	.372	.462	128	24	2-3	—	0	0	0	*D-156	1.9
1984	†KC A	106	317	30	96	13	4	3	42	34-3	1	47	.303	.363	.397	112	6	0-3	—	0	0	0	D-94	0.2
1985	†KC A	112	320	41	83	19	0	14	70	44-3	1	45	.259	.349	.450	117	9	0-1	—	0	0	0	*D-106	0.5
1986	KC A	112	278	22	70	14	0	7	37	18-4	1	39	.252	.298	.378	81	-8	0-0	—	0	0	0	D-75	-1.0
1987	KC A	18	32	5	10	3	0	1	9	5-1	0	1	.313	.405	.500	135	2	0-0	—	0			/D-7	0.2
Total	19	2084	7218	940	2091	484	66	191	1097	648-69	79	779	.290	.351	.454	122	222	109-78	.966	-8	97	103	*D-1427,O-478L/3-21,2-17	14.7
McREMER d6.20																								
1884	Was U	1	3	0	0	0	0	0		0			.000	.000	.000	-99	-1		1.000	0	0	0	/O(RF)	-0.1
McREYNOLDS, KEVIN Walter Kevin B 10.16.1959 Little Rock, AR BR/TR 6-1/210# d6.2																								
1983	SD N	39	140	15	31	3	1	4	14	12-1	0	29	.221	.277	.343	75	-5	2-1	.989	0	92	190	O-38(3-32-10)	-0.6
1984	†SD N	147	525	68	146	26	6	20	75	34-8	0	69	.278	.317	.465	119	11	3-6	.991	10	113	122	*O-143(CF)	1.9
1985	SD N	152	564	61	132	24	4	15	75	43-6	3	81	.234	.290	.371	85	-13	4-0	.993	9	111	125	*O-150(CF)	-0.5
1986	SD N	158	560	89	161	31	6	26	96	66-6	1	83	.287	.358	.504	140	30	8-6	.977	2	102	96	*O-154(108-109-3)	2.8
1987	NY N	151	590	86	163	32	5	29	95	39-5	1	70	.276	.318	.495	119	12	14-1	.987	1	101	79	*O-150(LF)	0.9
1988	†NY N	147	552	82	159	30	2	27	99	38-3	4	56	.288	.336	.496	144	29	21-0	.985	6	93	**213**	*O-147(147-1-0)	3.7
1989	NY N	148	545	74	148	25	3	22	85	46-10	1	74	.272	.326	.450	127	17	15-7	.969	8	112	129	*O-145(LF)	2.2
1990	NY N	147	521	75	140	23	1	24	82	71-11	1	61	.269	.353	.455	122	17	9-2	.988	-2	88	147	*O-144(LF)	1.2
1991	NY N	143	522	65	135	32	1	16	74	49-7	2	46	.259	.322	.416	108	5	6-6	.993	1	99	116	*O-141(125-33-2)	0.2
1992	KC A	109	373	45	92	25	0	13	49	67-3	0	48	.247	.357	.418	115	10	7-1	.986	-7	90	55	*O-106(94-0-12)/D	0.1
1993	KC A	110	351	44	86	22	4	11	42	37-6	1	56	.245	.316	.425	92	-4	2-2	.990	0	99	89	*O-104(LF)/D	-0.8
1994	NY N	51	180	23	46	11	2	4	21	20-1	0	34	.256	.328	.406	91	-2	2-0	1.000	-0	100	34	O-47(LF)	-0.4
Total	12	1502	5423	727	1439	284	35	211	807	522-67	14	707	.265	.328	.447	116	107	93-32	.987	27	101	119	*O-1469(1067-468-27)/D-2	10.7
McSHANNIC, PETE Peter Robert B 3.20.1864 Pittsburgh, PA D 11.30.1946 Toledo, OH BB/TR 5-7/190# d9.15																								
1888	Pit N	26	98	5	19	1	0	0	5	1	2	9	.194	.218	.204	38	-7	3	.907	-1	95	29	3-26	-0.7
McSORLEY, TRICK John Bernard B 12.6.1852 St.Louis, MO D 2.9.1936 St.Louis, MO BR/TR 5-4/142# d5.6																								
1875	RS NA	15	52	4	11	0	0	0	2	0		3	.212	.212	.212	53	-2	3-0	.745	0	121	0	/3-9,O-7(6-1-0)	-0.1
1884	Tol AA	21	68	12	17	1	0	0		3	0		.250	.282	.265	77	-2		.974	1	150	207	1-16/O-5(LF),3P	-0.2
1885	StL N	2	6	2	3	1	0	0	1	2		1	.500	.625	.667	340	2		.400	-2	29	0	/3-2	0.0
1886	StL AA	5	20	1	3	3	0	0	0	0	0		.150	.150	.300	38	-1	0	.765	-3	66	0	/S-5	-0.4
Total	3	28	94	15	23	5	0	0	1	5	0	1	.245	.283	.298	85	-1	0-0	.745	-3	150	207	/1-16,S-5,O-5(LF),3-3,P	-0.6
McSWEENEY, PAUL Paul A. B 4.3.1867 St.Louis, MO D 8.12.1951 St.Louis, MO d9.20																								
1891	StL AA	3	12	2	3	1	0	0	2	0	1	0	.250	.308	.333	73	0	1	.643	-3	69	0	/2-3,3	-0.3
McTAMANY, JIM James Edward B 7.1.1863 Philadelphia, PA D 4.16.1916 Lenni, PA BR/TR 5-8/190# d8.15																								
1885	Bro AA	35	131	21	36	7	2	1	13	9	0		.275	.321	.382	121	3		.896	-4	0	0	O-35(LF)	-0.1
1886	Bro AA	111	418	86	106	23	10	2	56	54	10		.254	.353	.371	126	15	18	.893	11	150	145	*O-111(0-107-4)	2.0
1887	Bro AA	134	520	123	134	22	10	1	68	76	12		.258	.365	.344	97	1	66	.918	6	147	162	*O-134(CF)	0.2
1888	KC AA	130	516	94	127	12	10	4	41	67	11		.246	.345	.331	110	7	55	.913	0	121	87	*O-130(0-80-50)	0.4
1889	Col AA	**139**	529	113	146	21	7	4	52	116	1	66	.276	.407	.365	127	28	40	.902	-7	107	128	*O-139(CF)	1.5
1890	Col AA	125	466	**140**	120	27	7	1	48	**112**	4		.258	.405	.352	132	30	43	.940	0	80	**198**	*O-125(CF)	2.3
1891	Col AA	81	304	59	76	17	9	3	35	58	2	48	.250	.374	.395	127	13	20	.929	-3	71	137	O-81(CF)	0.7
	Phi AA	58	218	57	49	6	3	3	21	43	5	44	.225	.365	.321	96	1	13	.901	-1	97	47	O-58(0-57-1)	-0.1
	Year	139	522	116	125	23	12	6	56	101	7	92	.239	.370	.364	114	14	33	.917	-4	82	99	*O-139(0-138-1)	0.6
Total	7	813	3102	693	794	135	58	19	334	535	45	158	.256	.373	.355	117	98	255	.913	3	109	130	O-813(35-723-55)	6.9

Year	Tm Lg	G	AB	R	H	2B	3B	HR	RBI	BB-IB	HP	SO	AVG	OBP	SLG	AOPS	ABR	SB-CS	FA	FR	Rng	Thr	G at Pos	BFW
McVEY, CAL Calvin Alexander B8.30.1850 Montrose, IA D8.20.1926 San Francisco, CA BR/TR 5-9/170# d5.5 M3 ▲ OF NA (4-LF 32-CF 66-RF) OF Total (1-LF 1-CF 6-RF)																								
1871	Bos NA	29	153	43	**66**	9	5	0	43	1		2	.431	.435	.556	177	14	6-0	.873	2			*C-29/O-5(RF),3	1.1
1872	Bos NA	46	237	56	76	10	2	0	41	1		1	.321	.324	.380	110	1	6-1	.869	6			*C-39,O-11(2-0-9)/3	0.6
1873	Bal NA	38	192	49	73	5	5	2	35	3		2	.380	.390	.490	160	13	2-1	**.907**	-1			C-25/O-6(1-4-1),S-5,2-4,1-3,3-2,M	0.8
1874	Bos NA	70	343	**91**	**123**	21	6	3	**71**	1		3	.359	.360	.481	159	20	5-0	.710	-2	91	0	*O-57(0-8-49),C-23	1.7
1875	Bos NA	**82**	389	89	138	**36**	9	3	**87**	1		5	.355	.356	**.517**	193	35	7-0	.949	7	**129**	155	*1-55,O-23(1-20-2),C-16/P-3	3.7
1876	Chi N	63	308	62	107	15	0	1	53	2		4	.347	.352	.406	136	10		.959	4	110	**145**	*1-55,P-11/C-6,O(LF)3	0.9
1877	Chi N	**60**	266	58	98	9	7	0	36	8		11	.368	.387	.455	147	13		.859	-10			*C-40,3-17,P-17/21	0.2
1878	Cin N	**61**	271	43	83	10	4	2	28	5		10	.306	.319	.395	147	14		.814	-10	82	89	*3-61/C-3,M	0.6
1879	Cin N	**81**	354	64	105	18	6	0	55	8		13	.297	.312	.381	134	13		.946	-7	27	101	*1-72/O-7(0-1-6),P-3,3CM	0.2
Total	5 NA	265	1314	328	476	81	27	8	277	7		13	.362	.366	.483	161	83	26-2	.000	12			C-132,O-102R/1-58,S-5,2-4,3-4,P	7.9
Total	4	265	1199	227	393	52	17	3	172	23		38	.328	.340	.407	140	50		.951	-23			1-128/3-80,C-50,P-31,O-8R,2	1.9
McVEY, GEORGE George W. B 9.16.1865 Port Jervis, NY D 5.3.1896 Quincy, IL BR/TR 6-1/185# d9.19																								
1885	Bro AA	6	21	2	3	0	0	0	1	2	0		.143	.217	.143	15	-2		.967	0	0	139	/1-3,C-3	-0.2
McWILLIAMS, BILL William Henry B 11.28.1910 Dubuque, IA D 1.21.1997 Garland, TX BR/TR 6/185# d7.8																								
1931	Bos A	2	2	0	0	0	0	0	0	0	0	1	.000	.000	.000	-99	-1	0-0	—	0			H	-0.1
MEACHAM, BOB Robert Andrew B 8.25.1960 Los Angeles, CA BB/TR (BR 1987-88) 6-1/180# d6.30																								
1983	NY A	22	51	5	12	2	0	0	4	4-0	1	10	.235	.304	.275	63	-2	8-0	.929	4	124	103	S-18/3-4	0.5
1984	NY A	99	360	62	91	13	4	2	25	32-0	3	70	.253	.312	.328	83	-8	9-5	.955	-12	91	87	S-96/2-2	-1.0
1985	NY A	156	481	70	105	16	2	1	47	54-1	5	102	.218	.302	.266	59	-26	25-7	.963	-20	87	112	*S-155	-2.7
1986	NY A	56	161	19	36	7	1	0	10	17-0	3	39	.224	.309	.280	62	-8	3-6	.948	-4	101	100	S-56	-0.8
1987	NY A	77	203	28	55	11	1	5	21	19-0	6	33	.271	.349	.409	102	1	6-5	.961	-5	94	93	S-56,2-25/D	0.1
1988	NY A	47	115	18	25	9	0	0	7	14-0	2	22	.217	.308	.296	72	-4	7-1	.959	-7	81	101	S-24,2-21/3-5	-0.8
Total	6	457	1371	202	324	58	8	8	114	140-1	20	276	.236	.313	.308	73	-47	58-24	.957	-44	92	101	S-405/2-48,3-9,D	-4.7
MEAD, CHARLIE Charles Richard B 4.9.1921 Vermilion, AL, CAN BL/TR 6-1.5/185# d8.28																								
1943	NY N	37	146	9	40	6	1	1	13	10	0	15	.274	.321	.349	93	-2	3	.976	-0	100	77	O-37(0-3-34)	-0.5
1944	NY N	39	78	5	14	1	0	1	8	5	0	7	.179	.229	.231	30	-8	0	.981	4	115	245	O-23(13-3-7)	-0.5
1945	NY N	11	37	4	10	1	0	1	6	5	0	2	.270	.357	.378	103	0	0	.962	1	93	285	O-11(0-1-11)	0.1
Total	3	87	261	18	64	8	1	3	27	20	0	24	.245	.299	.318	75	-10	3	.975	4	103	158	/O-71(13-7-52)	-0.9
MEADOWS, LOUIE Michael Ray B 4.29.1961 Maysville, NC BL/TL 5-11/190# d7.3																								
1986	Hou N	6	6	1	2	0	0	0	0	0-0	0	0	.333	.333	.333	87	0	1-0	—	-0	0	0	/O(RF)	0.0
1988	Hou N	35	42	5	8	0	1	2	3	6-0	0	8	.190	.292	.381	95	0	4-2	1.000	1	128	237	O-10(7-1-3)	0.1
1989	Hou N	31	51	5	9	0	0	3	10	1-0	0	14	.176	.189	.353	55	-4	1-2	1.000	-2	65	0	O-14(12-0-4)/1	-0.6
1990	Hou N	15	14	3	2	0	0	0	0	2-0	0	4	.143	.250	.143	11	-2	0-0	1.000	-0	107	0	/O-9(7-0-2)	-0.2
	Phi N	15	14	1	1	0	0	0	0	1-0	0	2	.071	.133	.071	-42	-3	0-0	1.000	-1	32	0	/O-4(3-2-0)	-0.3
	Year	30	28	4	3	0	0	0	0	3-0	0	6	.107	.194	.107	-15	-4	0-0	1.000	-1	84	0	O-13(10-2-2)	-0.5
Total	4	102	127	15	22	0	1	5	13	10-0	0	28	.173	.232	.307	54	-9	6-4	1.000	-1	91	82	/O-38(29-3-10),1	-1.0
MEARA, CHARLIE Charles Edward "Goggy" B 4.16.1891 New York, NY D 2.8.1962 Bronx, NY BL/TR 5-10/160# d6.1																								
1914	NY A	4	7	2	2	0	0	0	1	2	0	2	.286	.444	.286	120	0	0-1	1.000	-0	105	0	/O-3(0-2-2)	0.0
MEARES, PAT Patrick James B 9.6.1968 Salina, KS BR/TR 6/188# d5.5																								
1993	Min A	111	346	33	87	14	3	0	33	7-0	1	52	.251	.266	.309	55	-23	4-5	.961	-0	101	105	*S-111	-1.6
1994	Min A	80	229	29	61	12	1	2	24	14-0	2	50	.266	.310	.354	72	-10	5-1	.963	-2	98	98	S-79	-0.5
1995	Min A	116	390	57	105	19	4	12	49	15-0	11	68	.269	.311	.431	91	-7	10-4	.965	-3	100	93	*S-114/O-3(0-2-1)	0.0
1996	Min A	152	517	66	138	26	7	8	67	17-1	9	90	.267	.298	.391	72	-24	9-4	.965	-27	83	92	*S-150/O(CF)	-3.6
1997	Min A	134	439	63	121	23	3	10	60	18-0	16	86	.276	.323	.410	90	-7	7-7	.969	15	**112**	**112**	*S-134	1.6
1998	Min A	149	543	56	141	26	3	9	70	24-1	6	86	.260	.296	.368	71	-24	7-4	.966	-9	96	100	*S-149	-2.1
1999	Pit N	21	91	15	28	4	0	0	7	9-0	2	20	.308	.382	.352	88	-1	0-0	.939	1	110	96	S-21	0.1
2000	Pit N	132	462	55	111	22	2	13	47	36-6	8	91	.240	.305	.381	73	-21	1-0	.967	22	**115**	118	*S-126	1.0
2001	Pit N	87	270	27	57	11	1	4	25	10-3	2	45	.211	.244	.304	40	-25	0-2	.973	3	111	110	2-85	-1.9
Total	9	982	3287	401	849	157	24	58	382	150-11	57	588	.258	.299	.374	73	-142	43-27	.965	-1	101	103	S-884/2-85,O-4(0-3-1)	-7.0
MEDEIROS, RAY Ray Antone "Pep" B 5.9.1926 Oakland, CA BR/TR 5-10/163# d4.25																								
1945	Cin N	1	0	0	0	0	0	0	0	0	0	0	—	—	—	—	0	0	—	0			R	0.0
MEDINA, LUIS Luis Main B 3.26.1963 Santa Monica, CA BR/TL 6-4/200# d9.2																								
1988	Cle A	16	51	10	13	0	0	6	8	2-0	2	18	.255	.309	.608	146	3	0-0	1.000	-0	86	111	1-16	0.1
1989	Cle A	30	83	8	17	1	0	4	8	6-0	0	35	.205	.258	.361	72	-4	0-1	.500	-1	48	0	D-25/O-3(1-0-2),1	-0.6
1991	Cle A	5	16	0	1	0	0	0	0	1-0	0	7	.063	.118	.063	-48	-3	0-0	—	0			/D-5	-0.4
Total	3	51	150	18	31	1	0	10	16	9-0	2	60	.207	.261	.413	85	-4	0-1	1.000	-1	85	110	/D-30,1-17,O-3(1-0-2)	-0.9
MEDWICK, JOE Joseph Michael "Ducky" or "Muscles" B 11.24.1911 Carteret, NJ D 3.21.1975 St.Petersburg, FL BR/TR 5-10/187# d9.2 HF1968																								
1932	StL N	26	106	13	37	12	1	2	12	2	1	10	.349	.367	.538	136	5	3	.970	-1	95	96	O-26(7-19-0)	0.4
1933	StL N	148	595	92	182	40	10	18	98	26	2	56	.306	.337	.497	129	20	5	.980	7	103	150	*O-147(LF)	2.0
1934	†StL N★	149	620	110	198	40	**18**	18	106	21	1	83	.319	.343	.529	122	16	3	.960	3	105	97	*O-149(144-0-5)	1.0
1935	StL N★	**154**	634	132	224	46	13	23	126	30	4	59	.353	.386	.576	149	42	4	.965	3	108	74	*O-154(LF)	3.4
1936	StL N★	**155**	636	115	**223**	**64**	13	18	**138**	34	4	33	.351	.387	.577	157	49	3	.985	14	**114**	141	*O-155(LF)	5.2
1937	StL N★	**156**	633	**111**	**237**	**56**	10	**31**	**154**	41	2	50	**.374**	.414	**.641**	**179**	**68**	4	**.988**	4	107	81	*O-156(LF)	6.0
1938	StL N★	146	590	100	190	**47**	8	21	**122**	42	2	41	.322	.369	.536	138	30	0	.974	8	109	105	*O-144(LF)	3.0
1939	StL N★	150	606	98	201	48	8	14	117	45	2	44	.332	.380	.507	128	24	6	.976	5	106	113	*O-149(LF)	2.1
1940	StL N	37	158	21	48	12	0	3	20	6	0	8	.304	.329	.437	104	1	0	.988	-1	101	37	O-37(LF)	-0.2
	Bro N★	106	423	62	127	18	12	14	66	26	3	28	.300	.345	.499	123	11	2	.980	4	107	92	*O-103(LF)	0.9
	Year	143	581	83	175	30	12	17	86	32	3	36	.301	.341	.482	118	12	2	.982	3	105	77	*O-140(LF)	0.7
1941	†Bro N★	133	538	100	171	33	10	18	88	38	1	35	.318	.364	.517	140	26	2	.983	-3	90	116	*O-131(130-0-1)	1.6
1942	Bro N★	142	553	69	166	37	4	4	96	32	0	25	.300	.338	.403	115	9	2	.990	-3	99	55	*O-140(LF)	-0.1
1943	Bro N	48	173	13	47	10	0	0	25	10	1	8	.272	.315	.329	86	-3	1	.971	-3	88	60	O-42(LF)	-0.9
	NY N	78	324	41	91	20	3	5	45	9	0	14	.281	.300	.407	103	-1	0	.988	3	100	138	O-74(LF)/1-3	-0.3
	Year	126	497	54	138	30	3	5	70	19	1	22	.278	.306	.380	97	-4	1	.983	-0	96	113	*O-116(LF)/1-3	-1.2
1944	NY N★	128	490	64	165	24	3	7	85	38	1	24	.337	.386	.441	133	21	2	.993	7	**114**	89	*O-122(LF)	2.1
1945	NY N	26	92	14	28	4	0	3	11	2	0	2	.304	.319	.446	110	1	2	.979	-1	95	63	O-23(LF)	-0.2
	Bos N	66	218	17	62	13	0	0	26	12	1	12	.284	.325	.344	85	-4	3	1.000	2	97	261	O-38(LF),1-15	-0.6
	Year	92	310	31	90	17	0	3	37	14	1	14	.290	.323	.374	93	-4	5	.992	1	96	185	O-61(LF),1-15	-0.8
1946	Bro N	41	77	7	24	4	0	2	18	6	1	5	.312	.369	.442	128	3	0	1.000	-1	106	0	O-18(LF)/1	0.1
1947	StL N	75	150	19	46	12	0	4	28	16	0	12	.307	.373	.467	117	4	0	1.000	0	95	122	O-43(7-0-36)	0.3
1948	StL N	20	19	0	4	0	0	0	2	1	0	2	.211	.250	.211	24	-2	0	—	-0	0	0	/O(RF)	-0.2
Total	17	1984	7635	1198	2471	540	113	205	1383	437	26	551	.324	.362	.505	133	320	42	.980	47	104	103	*O-1852(1790-19-43)/1-19	25.6
MEE, TOMMY Thomas William "Judge" B 3.18.1890 Chicago, IL D 5.16.1981 Chicago, IL BR/TR 5-8/165# d6.14																								
1910	StL A	8	19	1	3	2	0	0	1	0	0		.158	.158	.263	34	-1	0	.828	-1	116	0	/S-6,23	-0.3
MEEK, DAD Frank J. B 3.14.1867 St.Louis, MO D 12.22.1922 St.Louis, MO 6/?# d5.10																								
1889	StL AA	2	2	2	1	0	0	0	1	0	0	0	.500	.500	.500	164	0	1	.667	0			/C-2	0.0
1890	StL AA	4	16	3	5	0	0	0	1	0	0		.313	.313	.313	74	-1	1	.913	1	*96*	*129*	/C-4	0.1
Total	2	6	18	5	6	0	0	0	2	0	0	0	.333	.333	.333	84	-1	2	.898	1	*87*	*118*	/C-6	0.1
MEEKS, SAMMY Samuel Mack B 4.23.1923 Anderson, SC BR/TR 5-9/160# d4.29																								
1948	Was A	24	33	4	4	1	0	0	2	1	0	12	.121	.147	.152	-21	-6	0-0	.939	-1	93	120	S-10/2	-0.6
1949	Cin N	16	36	10	11	2	0	2	6	2	0	6	.306	.342	.528	128	1	1	1.000	4	117	177	/2-8,S-3	0.5
1950	Cin N	39	95	7	27	5	0	1	8	6	0	14	.284	.327	.368	82	-2	1	.951	-2	95	89	S-29/3-2	-0.3
1951	Cin N	23	35	4	8	0	0	0	2	0	0	4	.229	.229	.229	23	-4	1-0	.929	-1	47	215	/3-4,S	-0.5
Total	4	102	199	25	50	8	0	3	18	9	0	36	.251	.284	.337	64	-11	3-0	.953	-1	97	104	/S-43,2-9,3-6	-0.9

Year	Tm Lg	G	AB	R	H	2B	3B	HR	RBI	BB-IB	HP	SO	AVG	OBP	SLG	AOPS	ABR	SB-CS	FA	FR	Rng	Thr	G at Pos	BFW
MEIER, DUTCH Arthur Ernst B 3.30.1879 St.Louis, MO D 3.23.1948 Chicago, IL BR/TR 5-10/175# d5.12																								
1906	Pit N	82	273	32	70	11	4	0	16	13	3		.256	.298	.326	90	-4	4	.975	-6	90	164	O-52(29-6-18),S-17	-1.2
MEIER, DAVE David Keith B 8.8.1959 Helena, MT BR/TR 6/185# d4.3																								
1984	Min A	59	147	18	35	8	1	0	13	6-0	1	9	.238	.271	.306	57	-9	0-1	.978	-1	99	71	O-50(41-0-10)/3D	-1.2
1985	Min A	71	104	15	27	6	0	1	8	18-0	1	12	.260	.374	.346	93	0	0-6	.987	-0	102	44	O-63(55-3-4)/D-3	-0.4
1987	Tex A	13	21	4	6	1	0	0	0	0-0	0	4	.286	.286	.333	63	-1	0-0	.917	-0	100	0	/O-8(6-0-2)	-0.2
1988	Chi N	2	5	0	2	0	0	0	1	0-0	0	1	.400	.400	.400	125	0	0-0	1.000	-1	0	0	/3	-0.1
Total	4	145	277	37	70	15	1	1	22	24-0	2	26	.253	.316	.325	73	-10	0-7	.978	-2	100	54	O-121(102-3-16)/D-7,3-2	-1.9
MEINERT, WALT Walter Henry B 12.11.1890 New York, NY D 11.9.1958 Decatur, IL BL/TL 5-7.5/150# d9.6																								
1913	StL A	4	8	1	3	0	0	0	0	1	0	3	.375	.444	.375	144	1	1	1.000	-0	120	0	/O-2(RF)	0.0
MEINKE, FRANK Frank Louis B 10.18.1863 Chicago, IL D 11.8.1931 Chicago, IL BR 5-10.5/172# d5.1 s-Bob ▲																								
1884	Det N	92	341	28	56	5	7	6	24	6		89	.164	.179	.273	42	-23		.839	-2	100	135	S-51,P-35/O-4(1-0-4),3-3,2-3	-1.3
1885	Det N	1	3	0	0	0	0	0	0	0		1	.000	.000	.000	-99	-1		1.000	0	0	0	/O(LF)P	0.0
Total	2	93	344	28	56	5	7	6	24	6		90	.163	.177	.270	41	-24		.839	-2	100	135	/S-51,P-36,O-5(2-0-4),2-3,3-3	-1.3
MEINKE, BOB Robert Bernard B 6.25.1887 Chicago, IL D 12.29.1952 Chicago, IL BR/TR 5-10/135# d8.22 f-Frank																								
1910	Cin N	2	1	0	0	0	0	0	0	1	0	0	.000	.500	.000	51	0	0	1.000	1	144	0	/S-2	0.1
MEISTER, GEORGE George B. B 6.5.1864 Dorzbach, Germany D 8.24.1908 Pittsburgh, PA ?/160# d8.15																								
1884	Tol AA	34	119	9	23	6	0	0		3	5		.193	.244	.244	58	-5		.817	-7	72	91	3-34	-1.1
MEISTER, JOHN John F. B 5.10.1863 Allentown, PA D 1.17.1923 Philadelphia, PA 5-8/175# d8.24																								
1886	NY AA	45	186	35	44	7	3	2	21	4	0		.237	.253	.339	92	-2	1	.906	-5	88	94	2-45	-0.5
1887	NY AA	39	158	24	35	6	2	1	21	16	2		.222	.301	.304	72	-5	9	.930	-5	91	248	O-22(CF),2-14/3-3,S	-0.9
Total	2	84	344	59	79	13	5	3	42	20	2		.230	.276	.323	82	-7	10	.905	-10	89	96	/2-59,O-22(CF),3-3,S	-1.4
MEISTER, KARL Karl Daniel "Dutch" B 5.15.1891 Marietta, OH D 8.15.1967 Marietta, OH BR/TR 6/178# d8.10																								
1913	Cin N	4	7	1	2	1	0	0	2	0	0	4	.286	.286	.429	103	0	0	.667	-1	59	0	/O-4(1-3-0)	-0.1
MEIXELL, MOXIE Merton Merrill B 10.18.1887 Lake Crystal, MN D 8.17.1982 Los Angeles, CA BL/TR 5-10/168# d7.7																								
1912	Cle A	3	2	0	1	0	0	0	0	0	0		.500	.500	.500	181	0	0	—	-0	0	0	/O(RF)	0.0
MEJIA, MIGUEL Miguel B 3.25.1975 San Pedro De Macoris, D.R. BR/TR 6-1/155# d4.4																								
1996	†StL N	45	23	10	2	0	0	0	0	0-0	0	10	.087	.087	.087	-54	-5	6-3	.933	-0	112	0	O-21(5-11-6)	-0.5
MEJIA, ROBERTO Roberto Antonio (Diaz) B 4.14.1972 Hato Mayor, D.R. BR/TR 5-11/160# d7.15																								
1993	Col N	65	229	31	53	14	5	5	20	13-1	1	63	.231	.275	.402	68	-11	4-1	.963	-1	102	88	2-65	-0.8
1994	Col N	38	116	11	28	8	1	4	14	15-2	0	33	.241	.326	.431	82	-3	3-1	.959	-5	91	79	2-34	-0.5
1995	Col N	23	52	5	8	1	0	1	4	0-0	1	17	.154	.167	.231	3	-7	0-1	.971	-5	73	42	2-16	-1.2
1997	StL N	7	14	0	1	1	0	0	2	0-0	0	5	.071	.067	.143	-46	-3	0-0	.900	-1	94	224	/2-3,O(1-0-1)	-0.4
Total	4	133	411	47	90	24	6	10	40	28-3	2	118	.219	.270	.380	60	-24	7-3	.961	-11	95	82	2-118/O(1-0-1)	-2.9
MEJIAS, ROMAN Roman (Gomez) B 8.9.1930 Abreus, Cuba BR/TR 6/175# d4.13																								
1955	Pit N	71	167	14	36	8	1	3	21	9-0	0	13	.216	.256	.329	55	-11	1-3	.926	2	90	278	O-44(30-1-14)	-1.2
1957	Pit N	58	142	12	39	7	4	2	15	6-1	1	13	.275	.309	.423	97	-1	2-2	1.000	3	98	268	O-42(7-7-29)	0.0
1958	Pit N	76	157	17	42	3	2	5	19	2-1	1	27	.268	.280	.408	82	-5	2-0	.973	3	116	90	O-57(41-10-8)	-0.5
1959	Pit N	96	276	28	65	6	1	7	28	21-7	5	48	.236	.298	.341	71	-12	1-2	.970	2	102	143	O-85(15-21-52)	-1.3
1960	Pit N	3	1	1	0	0	0	0	0	0-0	0	1	.000	.000	.000	-99	0	0-0	—	0			H	0.0
1961	Pit N	4	1	1	0	0	0	0	0	0-0	0	1	.000	.000	.000	-99	0	0-0	1.000	0	162	0	/O-2(LF)	0.0
1962	Hou N	146	566	82	162	12	3	24	76	30-1	6	83	.286	.326	.445	114	8	12-4	.946	-5	96	91	*O-142(1-1-141)	-0.5
1963	Bos A	111	357	43	81	18	0	11	39	14-2	3	36	.227	.260	.370	72	-14	4-1	.973	-2	99	116	O-86(7-65-15)	-1.9
1964	Bos A	62	101	14	24	3	1	2	4	7-1	1	16	.238	.294	.347	74	-4	0-0	.962	2	117	155	O-37(14-13-11)	-0.3
Total	9	627	1768	212	449	57	12	54	202	89-13	17	238	.254	.294	.391	86	-39	22-12	.963	5	100	137	O-495(117-118-270)	-5.7
MEJIAS, SAM Samuel Elias B 5.9.1952 Santiago, D.R. BR/TR 6/170# d9.6 C7																								
1976	StL N	18	21	1	3	1	0	0	0	2-1	0	2	.143	.217	.190	16	-2	2-0	1.000	1	120	156	O-17(3-1-13)	-0.1
1977	Mon N	74	101	14	23	4	1	3	8	2-0	0	17	.228	.243	.376	65	-6	1-0	.966	-0	101	106	O-56(4-21-31)	-0.7
1978	Mon N	67	56	9	13	1	0	0	6	2-1	0	5	.232	.259	.250	43	-4	0-0	.949	0	98	142	O-52(24-4-25)/P	-0.5
1979	Chi N	31	11	4	2	0	0	0	0	2-0	0	5	.182	.308	.182	34	-1	0-0	.875	-1	71	0	O-23(15-5-3)	-0.2
	Cin N	7	2	1	1	0	0	0	0	0-0	0	0	.500	.500	.500	173	0	0-0	1.000	-0	48	0	/O-5(CF)	0.0
	Year	38	13	5	3	0	0	0	0	2-0	0	5	.231	.333	.231	53	-1	0-0	.889	-1	68	0	O-28(15-10-3)	-0.2
1980	Cin N	71	108	16	30	5	1	1	10	6-0	1	13	.278	.322	.370	93	-1	4-2	.989	3	106	160	O-67(8-50-17)	0.1
1981	Cin N	66	49	6	14	2	0	0	7	2-1	0	9	.286	.302	.327	80	-1	1-0	.972	-1	83	73	O-58(0-16-42)	-0.3
Total	6	334	348	51	86	13	2	4	31	16-3	1	51	.247	.281	.330	69	-15	8-2	.973	1	99	121	O-278(54-102-131)/P	-1.7
MELE, DUTCH Albert Ernest B 1.11.1915 New York, NY D 2.12.1975 Hollywood, FL BL/TL 6-0.5/195# d9.14																								
1937	Cin N	6	14	1	2	1	0	0	1	1	0	1	.143	.200	.214	13	-2	0	1.000	-1	28	0	/O-5(2-0-3)	-0.3
MELE, SAM Sabath Anthony B 1.21.1923 Astoria, NY BR/TR 6-1/187# d4.15 M7 C3																								
1947	Bos A	123	453	71	137	14	8	12	73	37	1	35	.302	.356	.448	114	7	0-3	.992	-1	95	126	*O-116(3-29-87)/1	0.1
1948	Bos A	66	180	25	42	12	1	2	25	13	2	21	.233	.292	.344	66	-9	1-1	.971	-1	104	60	O-55(3-0-52)	-1.1
1949	Bos A	18	46	1	9	1	1	0	7	7	0	14	.196	.302	.261	46	-4	2-0	.955	-1	91	95	O-11(RF)	-0.4
	Was A	78	264	21	64	12	2	3	25	17	0	34	.242	.288	.337	67	-14	2-1	.966	0	98	119	O-63(1-24-44),1-11	-1.6
	Year	96	310	22	73	13	3	3	32	24	0	48	.235	.290	.326	63	-18	4-1	.964	-0	97	115	O-74(1-24-55),1-11	-2.0
1950	Was A	126	435	57	119	21	6	12	86	51	1	40	.274	.351	.432	105	2	2-0	.990	-0	94	102	O-99(6-26-72),1-16	-0.2
1951	Was A	143	558	58	153	**36**	7	5	94	32	1	31	.274	.315	.391	92	-9	2-3	.993	2	108	90	*O-124(2-17-107),1-15	-1.2
1952	Was A	9	28	2	12	3	0	2	10	1	0	2	.429	.448	.750	237	5	0-0	.917	-1	94	0	/O-7(0-1-6)	0.4
	Chi A	123	423	46	105	18	2	14	59	48	2	40	.248	.328	.400	101	0	1-2	1.000	-6	86	95	*O-112(RF)/1-3	-1.1
	Year	132	451	48	117	21	2	16	69	49	2	42	.259	.335	.421	109	4	1-2	.994	-7	86	90	*O-119(0-1-118)/1-3	-0.7
1953	Chi A	140	481	64	132	26	8	12	82	58	0	47	.274	.353	.437	109	6	3-1	.996	-8	83	115	*O-138(0-4-138)/1-2	-0.7
1954	Bal A	72	230	17	55	9	4	5	32	18	0	26	.239	.290	.378	90	-5	1-0	.962	-2	88	136	O-62(40-0-24)	-1.0
	Bos A	42	132	22	42	6	0	7	23	12	2	12	.318	.378	.523	132	6	0-1	.994	-2	63	96	1-22,O-13(3-0-13)	0.2
	Year	114	362	39	97	15	4	12	55	30	2	38	.268	.322	.431	107	2	1-1	.961	-4	87	132	O-75(43-0-37),1-22	-0.8
1955	Bos A	14	31	1	4	2	0	0	1	0-0	0	7	.129	.125	.194	-13	-5	1-0	1.000	2	100	534	/O-7(6-0-1)	-0.3
	Cin N	35	62	4	13	1	0	2	7	5-0	1	13	.210	.279	.323	56	-4	0-1	.960	-0	110	0	O-13(12-0-1)/1	-0.5
1956	Cle A	57	114	17	29	7	0	4	20	12-0	0	20	.254	.320	.421	94	-1	0-1	.969	1	96	175	O-20(14-0-6)/1-8	-0.2
Total	10	1046	3437	406	916	168	39	80	544	311-0	10	342	.267	.328	.408	97	-25	15-14	.985	-16	94	109	O-840(90-101-674)/1-79	-7.6
MELENDEZ, FRANCISCO Francisco Javier (Villegas) B 1.25.1964 Rio Piedras, P.R. BL/TL 6/190# d8.26																								
1984	Phi N	21	23	0	3	0	0	0	2	1-0	0	5	.130	.167	.130	-15	-4	0-0	1.000	1	174	35	1-10	-0.3
1986	Phi N	9	8	0	2	0	0	0	0	0-0	0	2	.250	.250	.250	37	-1	0-0	1.000	-0	0	0	/1-2	-0.1
1987	SF N	12	16	2	5	0	0	1	1	0-0	0	3	.313	.313	.500	117	0	0-0	1.000	-1	0	0	/1-5	0.0
1988	SF N	23	26	1	5	0	0	0	3	3-0	0	2	.192	.276	.192	38	-2	0-0	1.000	-1	0	119	/1-6,O(LF)	-0.3
1989	Bal A	9	11	1	3	0	0	0	3	1-0	0	2	.273	.308	.273	75	0	0-0	1.000	0	101	167	/1-5	-0.1
Total	5	74	84	4	18	0	0	1	9	5-0	0	14	.214	.256	.250	43	-7	0-0	1.000	-1	83	79	/1-28,O(LF)	-0.8
MELENDEZ, LUIS Luis Antonio (Santana) B 8.11.1949 Aibonito, P.R. BR/TR 6/165# d9.7																								
1970	StL N	21	70	11	21	1	0	0	8	2-0	0	12	.300	.315	.314	69	-3	3-0	1.000	0	90	179	O-18(0-5-13)	-0.3
1971	StL N	88	173	25	39	3	1	0	11	24-1	0	29	.225	.320	.254	62	-8	2-0	.959	-1	100	97	O-66(4-20-45)	-1.2
1972	StL N	118	332	32	79	11	3	5	28	25-0	1	34	.238	.292	.334	79	-10	5-4	.959	1	107	91	*O-105(4-69-40)	-1.4
1973	StL N	121	341	35	91	18	1	2	35	27-2	0	50	.267	.319	.343	84	-7	2-7	.990	2	103	131	O-95(2-65-30)	-1.0
1974	StL N	83	124	15	27	4	3	0	8	11-0	1	9	.218	.283	.298	64	-6	2-2	.977	1	119	0	O-46(23-22-10)/S	-0.7
1975	StL N	110	291	33	77	8	5	2	27	16-3	0	25	.265	.301	.347	77	-10	3-2	.983	-0	102	62	O-89(36-49-7)	-1.4
1976	StL N	20	24	0	3	0	0	0	0	0-0	0	3	.125	.125	.125	-29	-4	0-0	1.000	1	163	0	/O-8(4-4-0)	-0.3
	SD N	72	119	15	29	5	0	0	5	3-1	0	12	.244	.260	.286	60	-7	1-1	.988	1	112	0	O-60(24-29-10)	-0.8

Year	Tm Lg	G	AB	R	H	2B	3B	HR	RBI	BB-IB	HP	SO	AVG	OBP	SLG	AOPS	ABR	SB-CS	FA	FR	Rng	Thr	G at Pos	BFW
	Year	92	143	15	32	5	0	0	5	3-1	0	15	.224	.238	.259	44	-11	1-1	.990	2	117	0	O-68(28-33-10)	-1.1
1977	SD N	8	3	1	0	0	0	0	0	1-0	0	1	.000	.250	.000	-29	-1	0-0	1.000	0	172	0	/O-2(CF)	0.0
Total	8	641	1477	167	366	50	13	9	122	109-7	2	175	.248	.299	.318	73	-56	18-16	.977	5	105	84	O-489(97-265-155)/S	-7.1
MELHUSE, ADAM Adam Michael B 3.27.1972 Santa Clara, CA BB/TR 6-2/185# d6.16																								
2000	LA N	1	1	0	0	0	0	0	0	0-0	0	1	.000	.000	.000	-99	0	0-0	—	0			/H	0.0
	Col N	23	23	3	4	0	1	0	4	3-0	0	5	.174	.269	.261	28	-3	0-0	1.000	-0	94	75	/1-3,CO(RF)	-0.3
	Year	24	24	3	4	0	1	0	4	3-0	0	6	.167	.259	.250	24	-3	0-0	1.000	-0	94	75	/1-3,CO(RF)	-0.3
2001	Col N	40	71	5	13	2	0	1	8	6-0	0	18	.183	.241	.254	24	-8	1-0	.991	-4	54	23	C-23/1	-1.1
2003	†Oak A	40	77	13	23	7	0	5	14	9-0	0	19	.299	.372	.584	145	5	0-0	.993	0	93	95	C-33/3-2,1	0.7
Total	3	104	172	21	40	9	1	6	26	18-0	0	43	.233	.302	.401	72	-6	1-0	.992	-4	76	64	/C-57,1-5,3-2,O(RF)	-0.7
MELILLO, SKI Oscar Donald "Spinach" B 8.4.1899 Chicago, IL D 11.14.1963 Chicago, IL BR/TR 5-8/150# d4.18 M1 C13																								
1926	StL A	99	385	54	98	18	5	1	30	32	2	31	.255	.315	.335	66	-20	6-7	.965	10	106	120	2-88,3-11	-0.7
1927	StL A	107	356	45	80	18	2	0	26	25	0	28	.225	.276	.287	45	-30	3-6	.935	3	99	122	*2-101	-2.5
1928	StL A	51	132	9	25	2	0	0	9	9	0	11	.189	.241	.205	18	-16	2-1	.961	0	97	101	2-28,3-19	-1.4
1929	StL A	141	494	57	146	17	10	5	67	29	2	30	.296	.337	.401	86	-12	11-6	.973	**20**	110	**118**	*2-141	1.2
1930	StL A	149	574	62	147	30	10	5	59	23	2	44	.256	.287	.369	63	-35	15-9	.979	25	**112**	110	*2-148	-0.5
1931	StL A	151	617	88	189	34	11	2	75	37	0	29	.306	.346	.407	94	-7	7-11	.968	**35**	**113**	**123**	*2-151	3.3
1932	StL A	**154**	612	71	148	19	11	3	66	36	2	42	.242	.286	.324	54	-44	6-6	.981	11	104	104	*2-153	-2.2
1933	StL A	132	496	50	145	23	6	3	79	29	1	18	.292	.333	.381	83	-13	12-10	**.991**	**22**	105	**133**	*2-130	1.6
1934	StL A	144	552	54	133	19	3	2	55	28	1	27	.241	.279	.297	45	-47	4-6	**.981**	17	102	110	*2-141	-2.1
1935	StL A	19	62	8	13	3	0	0	5	8	0	4	.210	.300	.258	43	-5	0-0	.970	-0	108	73	2-18	-0.4
	Bos A	106	400	45	104	13	2	1	39	38	2	22	.260	.327	.310	61	-23	3-2	.973	17	109	120	*2-105	0.1
	Year	125	462	53	117	16	2	1	44	46	2	26	.253	.324	.303	59	-28	3-2	**.973**	17	**109**	114	*2-123	-0.3
1936	Bos A	98	327	39	74	12	4	0	32	28	0	16	.226	.287	.287	40	-32	0-0	.980	-7	87	107	2-93	-3.0
1937	Bos A	26	56	8	14	2	0	0	6	5	0	4	.250	.311	.286	50	-4	0-1	.939	-3	77	80	2-19/S-2,3-2	-0.6
Total	12	1377	5063	590	1316	210	64	22	548	327	12	306	.260	.306	.340	64	-288	69-65	.973	151	105	115	*2-1316/3-32,S-2	-7.2
MELLANA, JOE Joseph Peter B 3.11.1905 Oakland, CA D 11.1.1969 Larkspur, CA BR/TR 5-10/180# d9.21																								
1927	Phi A	4	7	1	2	0	0	0	2	0	0	1	.286	.286	.286	46	-1	0-0	.889	1	201	273	/3-2	0.1
MELLOR, BILL William Harpin B 6.6.1874 Camden, NJ D 11.5.1940 Bridgeton, RI BR/TR 6/190# d7.28																								
1902	Bal A	10	36	4	13	3	0	0	5	3	0		.361	.410	.444	131	2	1	.978	-1	41	17	1-10	0.0
MELO, JUAN Juan Esteban B 11.11.1976 Bani, D.R. BB/TR 6-3/206# d9.2																								
2000	SF N	11	13	0	1	0	0	0	0	0-0	0	5	.077	.077	.077	-66	-3	0-0	1.000	-2	57	0	/2-6	-0.5
MELOAN, PAUL Paul B. "Molly" B 8.23.1888 Paynesville, MO D 2.11.1950 Taft, CA BR/TL 5-10.5/175# d8.2																								
1910	Chi A	65	222	23	54	6	6	0	23	17	6		.243	.314	.324	104	1	4	.948	4	90	192	O-65(RF)	0.2
1911	Chi A	1	3	0	1	0	0	0	1	0	0		.333	.333	.333	89	0	0	.000	-1	0	0	/O(RF)	-0.1
	StL A	64	206	30	54	11	2	3	14	15	2		.262	.318	.379	98	-1	7	.904	-4	96	70	O-54(1-0-53)	-0.7
	Year	65	209	30	55	11	2	3	15	15	2		.263	.319	.378	98	-1	7	.893	-4	94	69	O-55(1-0-54)	-0.8
Total	2	130	431	53	109	17	8	3	38	32	8		.253	.316	.350	101	0	11	.923	-0	92	138	O-120(1-0-119)	-0.6
MELTON, DAVE David Olin B 10.3.1928 Pampa, TX BR/TR 6/185# d4.17																								
1956	KC A	3	3	0	1	0	0	0	0	0-0	0	0	.333	.333	.333	76	0	0-0	1.000	0	139	0	/O-3(LF)	0.0
1958	KC A	9	6	0	0	0	0	0	0	0-0	0	5	.000	.000	.000	-98	-2	0-0	1.000	0	210	0	/O-2(LF)	-0.2
Total	2	12	9	0	1	0	0	0	0	0-0	0	5	.111	.111	.111	-39	-2	0-0	1.000	0	161	0	/O-5(LF)	-0.2
MELTON, BILL William Edwin B 7.7.1945 Gulfport, MS BR/TR 6-2/200# d5.4																								
1968	Chi A	34	109	5	29	8	0	2	16	10-0	0	32	.266	.322	.394	117	2	1-1	.968	-0	114	89	3-33	0.2
1969	Chi A	157	556	67	142	26	2	23	87	56-7	5	106	.255	.326	.433	106	4	1-2	.952	-0	102	117	*3-148,O-11(3-0-8)	0.2
1970	Chi A	141	514	74	135	15	1	33	96	56-2	9	107	.263	.340	.488	123	15	2-4	1.000	7	86	171	O-71(RF),3-70	1.8
1971	Chi A☆	150	543	72	146	18	2	**33**	86	61-5	11	87	.269	.352	.492	133	23	3-3	.968	24	115	90	*3-148	4.8
1972	Chi A	57	208	22	51	5	0	7	30	23-2	0	31	.245	.319	.370	103	1	1-1	.935	3	104	110	3-56	0.4
1973	Chi A	152	560	83	155	29	1	20	87	75-7	2	66	.277	.363	.439	121	18	4-4	.953	10	109	104	*3-151/D	2.7
1974	Chi A	136	495	63	120	17	0	21	63	59-3	5	60	.242	.326	.404	107	5	3-2	.939	-8	93	103	*3-123,D-11	-0.4
1975	Chi A	149	512	62	123	16	0	15	70	78-1	8	106	.240	.346	.359	99	2	5-4	.945	-8	93	78	*3-138,D-11	-0.8
1976	Cal A	118	341	31	71	17	3	6	42	44-2	2	53	.208	.300	.328	90	-4	2-0	.992	-5	88	102	D-51,1-30,3-21	-1.2
1977	Cle A	50	133	17	32	11	0	0	14	17-0	2	21	.241	.331	.323	83	-2	1-3	1.000	-1	89	97	1-15,D-14,3-13	-0.5
Total	10	1144	3971	496	1004	162	9	160	591	479-29	44	669	.253	.337	.419	112	64	23-24	.949	22	104	100	3-901/D-88,O-82(3-0-79),1-45	7.2
MELUSKEY, MITCH Mitchell Wade B 9.18.1973 Yakima, WA BB/TR 6/185# d8.30																								
1998	Hou N	8	8	1	2	1	0	0	0	1-0	0	4	.250	.333	.375	88	0	0-0	1.000	0	0	0	/C-3	0.0
1999	Hou N	10	33	4	7	1	0	1	3	5-1	0	6	.212	.316	.333	65	-2	1-0	1.000	-1	55	151	C-10	-0.1
2000	Hou N	117	337	47	101	21	0	14	69	55-10	4	74	.300	.401	.487	117	11	1-0	.982	-8	83	81	*C-103/3	0.9
2002	Det A	8	27	3	6	0	0	0	1	5-0	1	3	.222	.353	.222	65	-1	0-0	1.000	-2	223	148	/C-8	-0.2
2003	Hou N	12	9	1	1	1	0	0	2	2-0	0	2	.111	.250	.222	30	-1	0-0	—	0			/H	-0.2
Total	5	155	414	56	117	24	0	15	75	68-11	5	89	.283	.386	.449	108	7	2-0	.985	-10	91	91	C-124/3	0.4
MELVIN, BOB Robert Paul B 10.28.1961 Palo Alto, CA BR/TR 6-4/205# d5.25 M1 C4																								
1985	Det A	41	82	10	18	4	1	0	4	3-0	0	21	.220	.247	.293	47	-6	0-0	.989	3	91	72	C-41	-0.2
1986	SF N	89	268	24	60	14	2	5	25	15-1	0	69	.224	.262	.347	71	-12	3-2	.988	6	103	140	C-84/3	-0.3
1987	†SF N	84	246	31	49	8	0	11	31	17-3	0	44	.199	.249	.366	64	-14	0-4	.998	7	127	155	C-78/1	-0.6
1988	SF N	92	273	23	64	13	1	8	27	13-0	0	46	.234	.268	.377	87	-6	0-2	.984	-4	149	68	C-89/1	-0.7
1989	Bal A	85	278	22	67	10	1	1	32	15-3	0	53	.241	.279	.295	64	-14	1-4	.991	-10	99	88	C-75/D-9	-2.2
1990	Bal A	93	301	30	73	14	1	5	37	11-1	0	53	.243	.267	.346	73	-12	0-1	.997	-4	108	77	C-76,D-10/1	-1.3
1991	Bal A	79	228	11	57	10	0	1	23	11-2	0	46	.250	.279	.307	66	-11	0-0	.998	-1	91	85	C-72/D-4	-0.8
1992	KC A	32	70	5	22	5	0	0	6	5-0	0	13	.314	.351	.386	106	1	0-0	1.000	-0	102	106	C-21/1-3	0.1
1993	Bos A	77	176	13	39	7	0	3	23	7-0	1	44	.222	.251	.313	49	-13	0-0	.994	-3	116	39	C-76/1	-1.3
1994	NY A	9	14	2	4	0	0	1	3	0-0	0	3	.286	.286	.500	101	0	0-0	1.000	-1	64	178	/C-4,1-4,D	-0.1
	Chi A	11	19	3	3	0	0	0	1	1-0	0	4	.158	.200	.158	-6	-3	0-0	1.000	-0	53	0	C-11	-0.3
	Year	20	33	5	7	0	0	1	4	1-0	0	7	.212	.235	.303	39	-3	0-0	1.000	-1	56	41	C-15/1-4,D	-0.4
Total	10	692	1955	174	456	85	6	35	212	98-10	1	396	.233	.268	.337	69	-90	4-13	.993	-9	111	93	C-627/D-24,1-11,3	-7.7
MENCH, KEVIN Kevin Ford B 1.7.1978 Wilmington, DE BR/TR 6/215# d4.9																								
2002	Tex A	110	366	52	95	20	2	15	60	31-0	8	83	.260	.327	.448	99	-1	1-1	.990	0	98	117	*O-106(57-1-62)/D-2	-0.5
2003	Tex A	38	125	15	40	12	0	2	11	10-0	3	17	.320	.381	.464	112	3	1-1	.984	-2	87	51	O-35(34-3-2)	-0.1
Total	2	148	491	67	135	32	2	17	71	41-0	11	100	.275	.341	.452	103	2	2-2	.989	-2	95	101	O-141(91-4-64)/D-2	-0.6
MENDEZ, CARLOS Carlos Alberto (Castillo) B 6.18.1974 Caracas, Venezuela BR/TR 6/210# d5.22																								
2003	Bal A	26	45	3	10	2	0	0	5	0-0	0	12	.222	.217	.267	29	-5	0-0	.939	-0	111	29	/1-9,D-8	-0.5
MENDEZ, DONALDO Donaldo Alfonso B 6.7.1978 Barquisimeto, Venezuela BR/TR 6-1/155# d4.5																								
2001	SD N	46	118	11	18	2	1	1	5	5-2	3	37	.153	.206	.212	9	-17	1-2	.920	-6	94	72	S-46	-2.1
2003	SD N	26	84	10	19	6	0	2	9	7-1	2	32	.226	.298	.369	81	-2	1-0	.951	-4	96	60	S-26	-0.5
Total	2	72	202	21	37	8	1	3	14	12-3	5	69	.183	.245	.277	39	-19	2-2	.933	-11	95	67	/S-72	-2.6
MENDOZA, CARLOS Carlos Ramon B 11.4.1974 Bolivar, Venezuela BL/TL 5-11/160# d9.3																								
1997	NY N	15	12	6	3	0	0	0	1	4-0	2	2	.250	.500	.250	108	1	0-0	1.000	0	80	0	/O-3(2-3-0)	0.0
2000	Col N	13	10	0	1	0	0	0	0	1-0	0	4	.100	.182	.100	-21	-2	0-1	.000	-1	0	0	/O-3(LF)	-0.3
Total	2	28	22	6	4	0	0	0	1	5-0	2	6	.182	.379	.182	47	-1	0-1	.833	-1	64	0	/O-6(5-3-0)	-0.3
MENDOZA, MINNIE Cristobal Rigoberto (Carreras) B 11.16.1933 Ceiba Del Agua, Cuba BR/TR 6/180# d4.9 C1																								
1970	Min A	16	16	2	3	0	0	0	2	0-0	0	1	.188	.188	.188	4	-2	0-0	1.000	1	168	0	/3-5,2-4	-0.2
MENDOZA, MARIO Mario (Aizpuru) B 12.26.1950 Chihuahua, Mexico BR/TR 5-11/187# d4.26																								
1974	†Pit N	91	163	10	36	1	2	0	15	8-2	1	35	.221	.259	.252	46	-13	1-1	.964	-4	106	66	S-87	-1.0

Year	Tm Lg	G	AB	R	H	2B	3B	HR	RBI	BB-IB	HP	SO	AVG	OBP	SLG	AOPS	ABR	SB-CS	FA	FR	Rng	Thr	G at Pos	BFW
1975	Pit N	56	50	8	9	1	0	0	2	3-0	0	17	.180	.226	.200	19	-6	0-0	.952	-4	95	78	S-53/3	-0.7
1976	Pit N	50	92	6	17	5	0	0	12	4-1	0	15	.185	.216	.239	30	-9	0-1	.967	1	107	111	S-45/3-2,2	-0.5
1977	Pit N	70	81	-5	16	3	0	0	4	3-0	0	10	.198	.226	.235	23	-9	0-0	.928	-5	99	100	S-45,3-19/P	-1.2
1978	Pit N	57	55	5	12	1	0	1	3	2-1	3	9	.218	.283	.291	58	-3	3-1	.980	-1	114	53	2-21,3-18,S-14	-0.3
1979	Sea A	148	373	26	74	10	3	1	29	9-0	1	62	.198	.216	.249	26	-40	3-0	.968	7	107	102	*S-148	-1.9
1980	Sea A	114	277	27	68	6	3	2	14	16-0	0	42	.245	.286	.310	63	-15	3-4	.959	-1	101	108	*S-114	-0.7
1981	Tex A	88	229	18	53	6	1	0	22	7-0	1	25	.231	.254	.266	54	-14	2-1	.970	6	109	97	S-88	-0.1
1982	Tex A	12	17	1	2	0	0	0	0	0-0	0	4	.118	.118	.118	-37	-3	0-0	.882	-1	84	157	S-12	-0.3
Total	9	686	1337	106	287	33	9	4	101	52-4	6	219	.215	.245	.262	41	-112	12-8	.961	-2	104	96	S-606/3-40,2-22,P	-6.7
MENECHINO, FRANK Frank B 1.7.1971 Staten Island, NY BR/TR 5-9/175# d9.7																								
1999	Oak A	9	9	0	2	0	0	0	0	0-0	0	4	.222	.222	.222	15	-1	0-0	1.000	0	100	139	/S-5,3	-0.1
2000	†Oak A	66	145	31	37	9	1	6	26	20-0	1	45	.255	.345	.455	104	1	1-4	.973	10	121	114	2-51/S-5,3-4,PD	1.1
2001	†Oak A	139	471	82	114	22	2	12	60	79-0	19	97	.242	.369	.374	97	2	2-3	.978	18	111	**119**	*2-136/S-3,3D	2.5
2002	Oak A	38	132	22	27	7	0	3	15	20-0	1	32	.205	.312	.326	70	-5	0-0	.992	-5	103	51	2-32/3-4,S-2,D	-0.9
2003	†Oak A	43	83	10	16	0	0	2	9	19-1	4	16	.193	.364	.265	70	-3	0-0	.986	-0	103	120	2-22,3-19/S-3,D	-0.2
Total	5	295	840	145	196	38	3	23	110	138-1	25	194	.233	.354	.368	91	-6	3-7	.979	22	111	108	2-241/3-29,S-18,D-7,P	2.4
MENEFEE, JOCK John B 1.15.1868 Rowlesburg, WV D 3.11.1953 Belle Vernon, PA BR/TR 6/165# d8.17 ▲																								
1892	Pit N	2	3	0	0	0	0	0	0	0	0	0	.000	.000	.000	-99	-1	0	1.000	0	0	0	/O(RF)P	0.0
1893	Lou N	22	73	10	20	2	1	0	12	13	1	5	.274	.391	.329	100	1	2	.913	2	126	97	P-15/O-7(1-2-4)	0.1
1894	Lou N	29	79	7	13	1	0	0	4	8	1	7	.165	.250	.177	5	-12	2	.940	2	113	0	P-28/2	0.1
	Pit N	13	47	6	12	1	2	0	7	3	0	3	.255	.300	.362	59	0	2	.909	2	142	0	P-13	0.0
	Year	42	126	13	25	2	2	0	11	11	1	10	.198	.268	.246	26	-16	4	.928	4	123	0	P-41/2	0.1
1895	Pit N	2	0	0	0	0	0	0	0	0	0	0	—	—	—	—	0	0	.667	0	220	0	/P-2	0.0
1898	NY N	1	5	0	0	0	0	0	0	0	0		.000	.000	.000	-99	-1	0	.750	0	135	0	/P	0.0
1900	Chi N	17	46	5	5	0	0	0	4	2	2		.109	.180	.109	-20	-3	0	.889	-2	71	126	P-16	0.0
1901	Chi N	48	152	19	39	5	3	0	13	8	8		.257	.327	.329	94	-1	4	.913	-2	103	132	O-24(5-1-18),P-21/1-2,2	-0.3
1902	Chi N	65	216	24	50	4	1	0	15	15	7		.231	.303	.259	76	-5	4	.952	-5	62	130	O-23(1-0-21),P-22,1-18/3-2,2	-1.0
1903	Chi N	22	64	3	13	3	0	0	2	3	0		.203	.239	.250	40	-5	0	.896	3	140	0	P-20/1-2	0.1
Total	9	221	685	74	152	16	7	0	57	52	19	15	.222	.295	.266	60	-27	14	.918	0	110	50	P-139/O-55(7-3-44),1-22,2-3,3-2	-1.0
MENKE, DENIS Denis John B 7.21.1940 Bancroft, IA BR/TR 6/190# d4.14 C20 OF Total (3-LF 2-RF)																								
1962	Mil N	50	146	12	28	3	1	2	16	16-0	2	38	.192	.277	.267	49	-11	0-1	.980	2	97	92	2-20,3-15/S-9,1-2,O(LF)	-0.7
1963	Mil N	146	518	58	121	16	4	11	50	37-4	6	106	.234	.289	.344	83	-12	6-7	.976	6	108	106	S-82,3-51,2-22/1O(LF)	0.1
1964	Mil N	151	505	79	143	29	5	20	65	68-13	4	77	.283	.368	.479	137	27	4-2	.964	7	103	101	*S-141,2-15/3-6	4.8
1965	Mil N	71	181	16	44	13	1	4	18	18-3	1	28	.243	.313	.392	97	0	1-3	.967	-4	100	80	S-54/1-8,3-4	-0.2
1966	Atl N	138	454	55	114	20	4	15	60	71-8	6	87	.251	.355	.412	112	10	0-7	.955	-20	91	83	*S-106,3-39/1-7	-0.4
1967	Atl N	129	418	37	95	14	3	7	39	65-5	3	62	.227	.333	.325	91	-3	5-7	.965	-15	95	96	*S-124/3-3	-0.9
1968	Hou N	150	542	56	135	23	6	6	56	64-6	6	81	.249	.334	.347	107	7	5-8	.982	-9	91	65	*2-119,S-35/1-5,3-4	0.9
1969	Hou N★	154	553	72	149	25	5	10	90	87-12	4	87	.269	.369	.387	115	15	2-7	.956	-11	90	83	*S-131,2-23/1-9,3	1.9
1970	Hou N★	154	562	82	171	26	6	13	92	82-10	5	80	.304	.392	.441	130	27	6-5	.954	-17	95	80	*S-133,2-21/1-5,3-5,O-3(1-0-2)	2.6
1971	Hou N	146	475	57	117	26	3	1	43	59-4	2	68	.246	.328	.320	88	-6	4-5	.997	-4	89	103	*1-101,3-32,S-17/2-5	-1.8
1972	†Cin N	140	447	41	104	19	2	9	50	58-2	5	76	.233	.322	.345	97	-1	0-1	.955	-4	103	105	*3-130,1-11	-0.7
1973	†Cin N	139	241	38	46	10	0	3	26	69-6	2	53	.191	.368	.270	86	0	1-1	.966	-0	104	123	*3-123/S-7,2-5,1	0.0
1974	Hou N	30	29	2	3	1	0	0	1	4-0	0	10	.103	.206	.138	-1	-4	0-0	1.000	1	89	264	1-12/3-7,2-3,S-2	-0.3
Total	13	1598	5071	605	1270	225	40	101	606	698-73	46	853	.250	.343	.370	104	49	34-54	.961	-68	97	91	S-841,3-420,2-233,1-162/O-5L	5.3
MENOSKY, MIKE Michael William "Leaping Mike" B 10.16.1894 Glen Campbell, PA D 4.11.1983 Detroit, MI BL/TR 5-10/163# d4.18 Mil 1918																								
1914	Pit F	68	140	26	37	4	1	2	9	16	3	30	.264	.352	.350	92	-3	5	.942	0	111	91	O-41(6-3-32)	-0.5
1915	Pit F	17	21	3	2	0	0	0	1	2	1	0	.095	.208	.095	-13	-4	2	.917	-0	122	0	/O-9(6-1-2)	-0.4
1916	Was A	11	37	5	6	1	1	0	3	1	0	10	.162	.184	.243	29	-4	1	.952	2	92	265	/O-9(1-8-0)	-0.3
1917	Was A	114	322	46	83	12	10	1	34	45	6	55	.258	.359	.366	123	10	22	.982	11	121	126	O-94(93-0-1)	1.8
1919	Was A	116	342	62	98	15	3	6	39	44	7	46	.287	.379	.401	120	11	13	.979	1	108	65	*O-103(87-15-1)	0.7
1920	Bos A	141	532	80	158	24	9	3	64	65	9	52	.297	.383	.393	110	11	23-19	.961	-5	93	89	*O-141(LF)	-0.2
1921	Bos A	133	477	77	143	18	5	3	45	60	9	45	.300	.388	.377	99	2	12-6	.970	-4	97	72	*O-133(LF)	-1.1
1922	Bos A	126	406	61	115	16	5	3	32	40	5	33	.283	.355	.369	90	-6	9-5	.977	6	108	108	*O-103(74-4-26)	-0.8
1923	Bos A	84	188	22	43	8	4	0	25	22	0	19	.229	.310	.314	64	-10	3-6	.920	3	96	214	O-49(28-18-3)	-1.1
Total	9	810	2465	382	685	98	38	18	252	295	40	290	.278	.364	.370	100	7	90-36	.967	13	103	100	O-682(569-49-65)	-1.9
MENSOR, ED Edward "The Midget" B 11.7.1886 Woodville, OR D 4.20.1970 Salem, OR BB/TR 5-6/145# d7.15																								
1912	Pit N	39	99	19	26	3	2	0	1	23	0	12	.263	.402	.333	104	2	10	.955	-1	104	72	O-32(0-20-12)	-0.1
1913	Pit N	44	56	9	10	1	0	0	1	8	1	13	.179	.292	.196	43	-4	2-4	.971	2	107	236	O-18(1-16-1)/2S	-0.4
1914	Pit N	44	89	15	18	2	1	1	6	22	2	13	.202	.372	.281	99	2	2	.969	0	117	54	O-25(4-10-11)	0.0
Total	3	127	244	43	54	6	3	1	8	53	3	38	.221	.367	.283	89	0	14-4	.964	1	110	95	/O-75(5-46-24),S2	-0.5
MENZE, TED Theodore Charles B 11.4.1897 St.Louis, MO D 12.23.1969 St.Louis, MO BR/TR 5-9/172# d4.23																								
1918	StL N	1	3	0	0	0	0	0	0	0	0	2	.000	.000	.000	-99	-1	0	1.000	-0	73	0	/O(LF)	-0.1
MEOLI, RUDY Rudolph Bartholomew B 5.1.1951 Troy, NY BL/TR 5-9/165# d9.9																								
1971	Cal A	7	3	0	0	0	0	0	0	0-0	0	1	.000	.000	.000	-99	-1	0-0	—	0			H	-0.1
1973	Cal A	120	305	36	68	12	1	2	23	31-1	0	38	.223	.290	.289	70	-12	2-4	.933	-11	90	94	S-95,3-13/2-8	-1.4
1974	Cal A	36	90	9	22	2	0	0	3	8-0	0	10	.244	.306	.267	70	-3	2-4	.946	2	124	0	3-20/S-8,12	-0.2
1975	Cal A	70	126	12	27	2	1	0	6	15-0	0	20	.214	.298	.246	59	-7	3-0	.976	-5	110	73	S-28,3-15,2-11/D-3	-0.9
1978	Chi N	47	29	10	3	0	1	0	2	6-0	0	4	.103	.257	.172	20	-3	1-0	.900	1	94	0	/2-6,3-5	-0.2
1979	Phi N	30	73	2	13	4	1	0	6	9-1	0	15	.178	.268	.260	43	-6	2-0	.984	2	96	74	S-16,2-15/3	-0.2
Total	6	310	626	69	133	20	4	2	40	69-2	0	88	.212	.289	.267	61	-32	10-8	.944	-11	94	91	S-147/3-54,2-41,D-3,1	-3.0
MERCADO, ORLANDO Orlando (Rodriguez) B 11.7.1961 Arecibo, P.R. BR/TR 6/195# d9.13 C2																								
1982	Sea A	9	17	1	2	0	0	1	6	0-0	0	5	.118	.118	.294	8	-2	0-0	1.000	-2	82	54	/C-8,D	-0.4
1983	Sea A	66	178	10	35	11	2	1	16	14-0	1	27	.197	.256	.298	51	-12	2-2	.995	1	81	61	C-65	-0.9
1984	Sea A	30	78	5	17	3	1	0	5	4-0	1	12	.218	.265	.282	52	-5	1-0	.992	-5	82	101	C-29	-1.0
1986	Tex A	46	102	7	24	1	1	1	7	6-0	1	13	.235	.279	.294	56	-6	0-1	.996	7	81	115	C-45	0.2
1987	Det A	10	22	2	3	0	0	0	1	2-0	0	0	.136	.208	.136	-6	-3	0-0	.980	1	115	79	C-10	-0.2
	LA N	7	5	1	3	1	0	0	1	1-0	0	1	.600	.667	.800	294	2	0-0	1.000	-1	206	0	/C-7	0.1
1988	Oak A	16	24	3	3	0	0	1	1	3-0	0	8	.125	.222	.250	33	-2	0-0	.959	-3	97	37	C-16	-0.5
1989	Min A	19	38	1	4	0	0	0	1	4-0	0	4	.105	.190	.105	-14	-6	1-0	1.000	3	146	75	C-19	-0.2
1990	NY N	42	90	10	19	1	0	3	7	8-3	2	11	.211	.290	.322	68	-4	0-0	.991	-4	75	47	C-40	-0.7
	Mon N	8	8	0	2	0	0	0	0	0-0	0	1	.250	.250	.250	39	-1	0-0	1.000	-0	49	84	/C-8	-0.1
	Year	50	98	10	21	1	0	3	7	8-3	2	12	.214	.287	.316	66	-5	0-0	.992	-4	72	51	C-48	-0.8
Total	8	253	562	40	112	17	4	7	45	42-3	5	82	.199	.259	.281	48	-39	4-3	.993	-3	88	74	C-247/D	-3.7
MERCED, ORLANDO Orlando Luis (Villanueva) B 11.2.1966 Hato Rey, P.R. BL/TR (BB 1990-92, 93 (part)) 5-11/170# d6.27 OF Total (93-LF 617-RF)																								
1990	Pit N	25	24	3	5	1	0	0	0	1-0	0	9	.208	.240	.250	36	-2	0-0	—	-0	0	0	/CO(RF)	-0.2
1991	†Pit N	120	411	83	113	17	2	10	50	64-4	1	81	.275	.373	.399	119	13	8-4	.988	-4	90	100	*1-105/O-7(RF)	0.3
1992	†Pit N	134	405	50	100	28	5	6	60	52-8	2	63	.247	.332	.385	105	4	5-4	.995	2	107	111	*1-114,O-17(RF)	-0.3
1993	Pit N	137	447	68	140	26	4	8	70	77-10	1	64	.313	.414	.443	130	24	3-3	.965	8	114	158	*O-109(RF),1-42	2.3
1994	Pit N	108	386	48	105	21	3	9	51	42-5	1	58	.272	.343	.412	95	-2	4-1	.981	-5	87	71	O-68(RF),1-55	-1.4
1995	Pit N	132	487	75	146	29	4	15	83	52-9	1	74	.300	.365	.468	117	12	7-2	.976	2	101	109	*O-107(4-0-104),1-35	0.7
1996	Pit N	120	453	69	130	24	1	17	80	51-5	0	74	.287	.357	.457	110	7	8-4	.988	10	107	179	*O-115(RF)/1	1.2
1997	Tor A	98	368	45	98	23	2	9	40	47-1	3	62	.266	.352	.413	99	0	7-3	.985	5	103	169	O-96(RF)/1D	0.1
1998	Min A	63	204	22	59	12	0	5	33	17-3	1	29	.289	.345	.422	97	-1	1-4	.982	-0	94	115	1-38,O-13(RF)/D-8	-0.5
	Bos A	9	9	0	0	0	0	0	2	2-0	0	3	.000	.167	.000	-46	-2	0-0	1.000	0	297	0	/O(RF)D	-0.2
	Year	72	213	22	59	12	0	5	35	19-3	1	32	.277	.336	.404	91	-3	1-4	.982	0	94	115	1-38,O-14(RF)/D-9	-0.7
	Chi N	12	10	2	3	0	0	1	5	1-0	0	2	.300	.333	.600	143	1	0-0	1.000	0	201	0	/O-4(LF)	0.1
1999	Mon N	93	194	25	52	12	1	8	26	26-0	0	27	.268	.353	.464	108	2	2-1	.962	2	108	141	O-44(LF)/1-7,D-2	0.2

Year	Tm Lg	G	AB	R	H	2B	3B	HR	RBI	BB-IB	HP	SO	AVG	OBP	SLG	AOPS	ABR	SB-CS	FA	FR	Rng	Thr	G at Pos	BFW
2001	†Hou N	94	137	19	36	6	1	6	29	14-1	1	32	.263	.333	.453	96	-1	5-1	.975	-1	98	76	O-31(11-0-21)/3-2,1	-0.2
2002	Hou N	123	251	35	72	13	3	6	30	26-5	0	50	.287	.350	.434	105	1	4-0	.980	5	108	251	O-56(20-0-44)/1-7,3D	0.4
2003	Hou N	123	212	20	49	17	2	3	26	15-2	1	33	.231	.283	.373	67	-11	3-2	.959	2	106	293	O-31(10-0-21),1-12/3-2,D-7	-1.0
Total	13	1391	3998	564	1108	229	28	103	585	487-53	12	661	.277	.355	.426	106	45	57-29	.978	26	104	157	O-700R,1-418/D-20,3-5,C	1.5
MERCEDES, HENRY Henry Felipe (Perez) B 7.23.1969 Santo Domingo, D.R. BR/TR 6-1/210# d4.22																								
1992	Oak A	9	5	1	4	0	1	0	1	0-0	0	1	.800	.800	1.200	479	2	0-0	.875	-1	41	0	/C-9	0.1
1993	Oak A	20	47	5	10	2	0	0	3	2-0	1	15	.213	.260	.255	42	-4	1-1	.987	-1	180	155	C-18/D	-0.4
1995	KC A	23	43	7	11	2	0	0	9	8-0	1	13	.256	.370	.302	81	-1	0-0	.986	-4	92	90	C-22	-0.4
1996	KC A	4	4	1	1	0	0	0	0	0-0	0	1	.250	.250	.250	27	0	0-0	1.000	-1	67	0	/C-4	-0.1
1997	Tex A	23	47	4	10	4	0	0	4	6-0	0	25	.213	.302	.298	54	-3	0-0	.988	-3	92	21	C-23	-0.5
Total	5	79	146	18	36	8	1	0	17	16-0	2	55	.247	.325	.315	71	-6	1-1	.983	-11	115	82	/C-76,D	-1.3
MERCEDES, LUIS Luis Roberto (Santana) B 2.15.1968 San Pedro De Macoris, D.R. BR/TR 6/180# d9.8																								
1991	Bal A	19	54	10	11	2	0	0	2	4-0	0	9	.204	.259	.241	41	-4	0-0	1.000	-2	74	0	O-15(13-0-3)/D	-0.7
1992	Bal A	23	50	7	7	2	0	0	4	8-0	1	9	.140	.267	.180	28	-5	0-1	.956	3	146	219	O-16(1-2-13)/D-7	-0.2
1993	Bal A	10	24	1	7	2	0	0	0	5-0	0	4	.292	.414	.375	109	1	1-1	1.000	-0	68	172	/O-8(RF),D-2	0.0
	SF N	18	25	1	4	0	1	0	3	1-0	2	3	.160	.250	.240	33	-3	0-1	1.000	-1	52	0	/O-5(1-3-1)	-0.4
Total	3	70	153	19	29	6	1	0	9	18-0	3	25	.190	.286	.242	47	-11	1-3	.976	-0	96	112	/O-44(15-5-25),D-10	-1.3
MERCER, WIN George Barclay B 6.20.1874 Chester, WV D 1.12.1903 San Francisco, CA BR/TR 5-7/140# d4.21 ▲ OF Total (21-LF 25-CF 30-RF)																								
1894	Was N	53	165	29	48	5	2	2	29	9	0	20	.291	.328	.382	73	-8	9	.944	1	108	40	P-50/O-4(RF)	0.0
1895	Was N	64	201	26	51	9	1	1	26	12	3	33	.254	.306	.323	63	-11	7	.874	-6	82	74	P-44/S-7,O-6(1-0-5),3-3,2	-0.7
1896	Was N	49	156	23	38	1	1	1	14	9	4	18	.244	.302	.282	54	-11	9	.856	0	98	86	P-46/O(CF)	0.0
1897	Was N	50	139	23	44	2	5	0	19	6	2		.317	.354	.403	100	8	7	.858	-2	88	149	P-47	0.0
1898	Was N	80	249	38	80	3	5	2	25	18	1		.321	.369	.398	120	6	14	.863	-6	85	96	P-33,S-23,O-19(2-17-0)/3-5,2	-0.1
1899	Was N	108	375	73	112	6	7	1	35	32	4		.299	.360	.360	99	-1	16	.846	-10	78	68	3-62,P-23,O-16(15-0-1)/S1	-1.1
1900	NY N	76	248	32	73	4	0	0	27	26	2		.294	.366	.310	92	-1	15	.931	0	110	159	P-33,3-19,O-14(RF)/S-7,2-3	-0.1
1901	Was A	51	140	26	42	7	2	0	16	23	1		.300	.402	.379	119	5	10	.944	-1	97	58	P-24,O-16(3-7-6)/1-7,S3	0.1
1902	Det A	35	100	8	18	2	0	0	6	6	0		.180	.226	.200	19	-2	1	.935	3	125	66	P-35	0.0
Total	9	566	1773	278	506	39	23	7	197	141	17	<u>71</u>	.285	.344	.345	87	-15	88	.903	-19	101	89	P-335/3-90,O-76R,S-39,1-8,2-5	-1.9
MERCER, JOHN John Locke B 6.22.1892 Taylortown, LA D 12.22.1982 Shreveport, LA BL/TL 5-10.5/155# d6.25																								
1912	StL N	1	1	0	0	0	0	0	0	0	0	0	.000	.000	.000	-99	0	0	.500	-0	0	0	/1	-0.1
MERCHANT, ANDY James Anderson B 8.30.1950 Mobile, AL BL/TR 5-11/185# d9.28																								
1975	Bos A	1	4	1	2	0	0	0	0	1-0	0	0	.500	.600	.500	197	1	0-0	1.000	-1	73	232	/C	0.0
1976	Bos A	2	2	0	0	0	0	0	0	0-0	0	2	.000	.000	.000	-89	0	0-0	1.000	0	0	0	/C	0.0
Total	2	3	6	1	2	0	0	0	0	1-0	0	2	.333	.429	.333	109	1	0-0	1.000	-0	66	209	/C-2	0.0
MEREWETHER, ART Arthur Francis "Merry" B 7.7.1902 E.Providence, RI D 2.2.1997 Bayside, NY BR/TR 5-9.5/155# d7.10																								
1922	Pit N	1	1	0	0	0	0	0	0	0	0	0	.000	.000	.000	-99	0	0-0	—	0			H	0.0
MERKLE, FRED Frederick Charles (born Carl Frederick Rudolf Merkle) B 12.20.1888 Watertown, WI D 3.2.1956 Daytona Beach, FL BR/TR 6-1/190# d9.21 C2																								
1907	NY N	15	47	0	12	1	0	0	5	1	0		.255	.271	.277	69	-2	0	.949	-1	88	65	1-15	-0.4
1908	NY N	38	41	6	11	2	1	1	7	4	0		.268	.333	.439	140	2	0	1.000	-1	33	106	1-11/O-5(2-0-3),23	0.1
1909	NY N	79	236	15	45	9	1	0	20	16	1		.191	.245	.237	49	-14	8	.976	-3	82	105	1-70/2	-2.1
1910	NY N	144	506	75	148	35	14	4	70	44	3	59	.292	.353	.441	131	18	23	.981	1	103	111	*1-144	1.7
1911	†NY N	149	541	80	153	24	10	12	84	43	6	60	.283	.342	.431	112	6	49	.985	16	**143**	101	*1-148	1.8
1912	†NY N	129	479	82	148	22	6	11	84	42	8	70	.309	.374	.449	121	13	37	.980	-1	101	122	*1-129	0.9
1913	†NY N	153	563	78	147	30	12	3	69	41	3	60	.261	.315	.373	95	-5	35-18	.986	-4	88	121	*1-153	-1.2
1914	NY N	146	512	71	132	25	7	7	63	52	1	80	.258	.327	.375	112	8	23	.990	4	110	114	*1-146	0.8
1915	NY N	140	505	52	151	25	3	4	62	36	2	39	.299	.348	.384	129	17	20-15	.989	-2	88	101	*1-110,O-30(0-27-5)	1.1
1916	NY N	112	401	45	95	19	3	7	44	33	8	46	.237	.308	.352	108	4	17	.984	0	103	103	*1-112	0.2
	†Bro N	23	69	6	16	1	0	0	2	7	1	4	.232	.312	.246	70	-2	2	.992	-1	60	43	1-15/O-4(3-1-0)	-0.4
	Year	135	470	51	111	20	3	7	46	40	9	50	.236	.308	.336	102	2	19	.985	-0	98	97	*1-127/O-4(3-1-0)	-0.2
1917	Bro N	2	8	1	1	1	0	0	0	0	0	1	.125	.125	.250	13	-1	0	1.000	0	86	76	/1-2	-0.1
	Chi N	146	549	65	146	30	9	3	57	42	4	60	.266	.323	.370	104	3	13	.983	-4	86	96	*1-140/O-6(5-1-0)	-0.5
	Year	148	557	66	147	31	9	3	57	42	4	61	.264	.320	.368	103	2	13	.983	-4	86	96	*1-142/O-6(5-1-0)	-0.6
1918	†Chi N	129	482	55	143	25	5	3	65	35	4	36	.297	.349	.388	122	13	21	.990	1	100	98	*1-129	1.2
1919	Chi N	133	498	52	133	20	6	3	62	33	2	35	.267	.315	.349	99	-1	20	.985	-10	71	98	*1-132/2	-1.6
1920	Chi N	92	330	33	94	20	4	3	38	24	1	32	.285	.335	.397	108	3	3-5	.985	1	105	89	1-85/O(LF)	0.1
1925	NY A	7	13	4	5	1	0	0	1	1	0	1	.385	.429	.462	128	1	1-0	1.000	-0	48	124	/1-5	0.0
1926	NY A	1	2	0	0	0	0	0	0	0	0	0	.000	.000	.000	-99	-1	0-0	1.000	-0	0	0	/1	-0.1
Total	16	1638	5782	720	1580	290	81	61	733	454	44	<u>583</u>	.273	.331	.383	109	62	272-<u>38</u>	.985	-5	98	105	*1-1547/O-46(11-29-8),2-3,3	1.5
MERLONI, LOU Louis William B 4.6.1971 Framingham, MA BR/TR 5-10/188# d5.10 OF Total (5-LF 1-RF)																								
1998	Bos A	39	96	10	27	6	0	1	15	7-1	2	20	.281	.343	.375	85	-2	1-0	.974	-2	94	72	2-32/3-5,S	-0.2
1999	†Bos A	43	126	18	32	7	0	1	13	8-0	2	16	.254	.307	.333	62	-7	0-0	.956	2	94	105	S-24/3-9,2-8,10(LF)D	-0.3
2000	Bos A	40	128	10	41	11	2	0	18	4-1	1	22	.320	.341	.438	94	-1	1-0	.928	0	100	53	3-40	-0.1
2001	Bos A	52	146	21	39	10	0	3	13	6-0	3	31	.267	.306	.397	84	-3	2-1	.987	1	97	81	S-45/2-5,3	0.1
2002	Bos A	84	194	28	48	12	2	4	18	20-0	5	35	.247	.332	.392	90	-2	1-2	.988	4	94	92	2-66/3-8,S-5,1-3,O-2(1-0-1)	0.4
2003	SD N	65	151	20	41	7	2	1	17	22-2	1	33	.272	.362	.364	101	1	2-3	.925	1	104	86	3-25,S-23,2-10/1-2,O-2(LF)	0.3
	Bos A	15	30	4	7	1	0	0	1	4-0	0	8	.233	.324	.267	57	-2	0-0	1.000	1	53	148	/2-7,3-7,O(LF)	0.0
Total	6	338	871	111	235	54	6	10	95	71-4	14	165	.270	.332	.380	86	-16	7-6	.978	8	92	88	2-128/S-98,3-95,O-6L,1-6,D-3	0.2
MERRILL, ED Edward Mason B 5.1860 Maysville, KY D 1.29.1946 Elmwood Park, IL 5-11/176# d5.5																								
1882	Lou AA	1	0	0	0	0	0	0		0			—	—	—	—		0	—	-0	0	0	/O(CF)	0.0
	Wor N	2	8	0	1	0	0	0	0	0		1	.125	.125	.125	-19	-1		.714	-0	112	0	/3-2	-0.1
1884	Ind AA	55	196	14	35	3	1	0		6	1		.179	.207	.204	35	-13		.900	-3	96	60	2-55	-1.4
Total	2	58	204	14	36	3	1	0	<u>0</u>	6	1	<u>1</u>	.176	.204	.201	33	-14		.900	-4	96	60	/2-55,3-2,O(CF)	-1.5
MERRIMAN, LLOYD Lloyd Archer "Citation" B 8.2.1924 Clovis, CA BL/TL 6/195# d4.24 Mil 1952																								
1949	Cin N	103	287	35	66	12	5	4	26	21	1	36	.230	.285	.348	68	-14	2	.969	1	102	128	O-86(CF)	-1.5
1950	Cin N	92	298	44	77	15	3	2	31	30	2	23	.258	.330	.349	79	-9	6	.989	-4	93	65	O-84(2-81-1)	-1.5
1951	Cin N	114	359	34	87	23	2	5	36	31	0	34	.242	.303	.359	76	-12	8-4	.997	6	117	55	*O-102(31-76-0)	-1.0
1954	Cin N	73	112	12	30	8	1	0	16	23	3	10	.268	.397	.357	98	1	3-0	.981	-0	112	0	O-25(9-0-16)	0.1
1955	Chi A	1	1	0	0	0	0	0	0	0-0	0	0	.000	.000	.000	-97	0	0-0	—	0			H	0.0
	Chi N	72	145	15	31	6	1	1	8	21-0	0	21	.214	.311	.290	62	-8	1-0	.977	-1	95	73	O-47(8-36-3)	-1.0
Total	5	455	1202	140	291	64	12	12	117	126-<u>0</u>	6	124	.242	.316	.345	75	-42	20-<u>4</u>	.985	2	105	73	O-344(50-279-20)	-4.9
MERRITT, GEORGE George Washington B 4.14.1880 Paterson, NJ D 2.21.1938 Memphis, TN TR 6/160# d9.6 ▲																								
1901	Pit N	4	11	2	3	0	1	0	0	0	2		.273	.385	.455	139	1	0	1.000	-0	82	0	/P-3	0.0
1902	Pit N	2	9	2	3	1	0	0	2	0	0		.333	.333	.444	135	0	0	1.000	1	297	0	/O-2(LF)	0.1
1903	Pit N	9	27	4	4	0	1	0	3	2	1		.148	.233	.222	29	-3	1	.889	-1	0	0	/O-7(1-0-6),P	-0.4
Total	3	15	47	8	10	1	2	0	5	2	3		.213	.288	.319	74	-2	1	.929	-1	93	0	/O-9(3-0-6),P-4	-0.3
MERRITT, HERM Herman G. B 11.12.1900 Independence, KS D 5.26.1927 Kansas City, MO BR/TR d8.24																								
1921	Det A	20	46	3	17	1	2	0	6	1	1	5	.370	.396	.478	123	1	1-0	.882	-5	64	0	S-17	-0.3
MERRITT, JOHN John Howard B 10.12.1894 Tupelo, MS D 11.3.1955 Tupelo, MS BR/TL 5-11/170# d9.27																								
1913	NY N	1	0	0	0	0	0	0	0	0	0	0	—	—	—	—	0	0	—	-0	0	0	/O(RF)	0.0
MERRITT, BILL William Henry B 7.30.1870 Lowell, MA D 11.17.1937 Lowell, MA BR/TR 5-7/160# d8.8 OF Total (4-LF 1-CF 1-RF)																								
1891	Chi N	11	42	4	9	1	0	0	4	2	0	2	.214	.250	.238	42	-3	0	.955	-1	*131*	*109*	C-11/1	-0.3
1892	Lou N	46	168	22	33	4	2	1	13	11	0	15	.196	.246	.262	58	-9	3	.940	-5	*89*	*105*	C-46	-0.9
1893	Bos N	39	141	30	49	6	3	3	26	13	0	13	.348	.403	.496	128	5	3	.945	0	*131*	*56*	C-37/O-2(LF)	0.7
1894	Bos N	10	26	3	6	1	0	0	6	8	0	0	.231	.412	.269	62	-1	0	.881	1	*118*	*89*	/C-8,O(CF)	0.0

Year	Tm Lg	G	AB	R	H	2B	3B	HR	RBI	BB-IB	HP	SO	AVG	OBP	SLG	AOPS	ABR	SB-CS	FA	FR	Rng	Thr	G at Pos	BFW
	Pit N	36	109	18	30	1	2	1	18	15	0	7	.275	.363	.349	73	-5	2	.952	0	*102*	*130*	C-28/1-4,O-2(LF)	-0.2
	Cin N	30	117	17	38	6	1	1	22	10	2	3	.325	.388	.419	91	-2	4	.956	-1	*99*	*115*	C-25/3-3,1O(RF)	0.0
	Year	76	252	38	74	8	3	2	46	33	2	10	.294	.380	.373	80	-7	6	.942	0	*103*	*118*	C-61/1-5,O-4(2-1-1),3-3	-0.2
1895	Cin N	22	79	9	14	2	0	0	12	6	0	5	.177	.235	.203	13	-11	2	.955	0	*103*	*100*	C-20/2	-0.7
	Pit N	67	239	32	68	5	1	0	27	18	2	16	.285	.340	.314	73	-9	2	.935	-7	*88*	*93*	C-63/1-2	-0.8
	Year	89	318	41	82	7	1	0	39	24	2	21	.258	.314	.286	57	-20	4	.939	-6	*92*	*95*	C-83/1-2,2	-1.5
1896	Pit N	77	282	26	82	8	2	1	42	18	1	10	.291	.336	.344	83	-7	3	.941	-6	*84*	*121*	C-62/3-5,2-3,1-3,S-2	-0.6
1897	Pit N	62	209	21	55	6	1	1	26	9	1		.263	.297	.316	64	-11	2	.946	-8	*83*	*79*	C-53/1-7	-1.3
1899	Bos N	1	2	0	0	0	0	0	0	0	1		.000	.333	.000	-5	0	0	1.000	0	*120*	*211*	/C	0.0
Total	8	401	1414	182	384	40	12	8	196	110	7	71	.272	.327	.334	75	-53	21	.942	-25	*96*	*99*	C-354/1-18,3-8,O-6L,2-4,S-2	-4.1

MERSON, JACK John Warren B 1.17.1922 Elkridge, MD D 4.28.2000 Elkridge, MD BR/TR 5-11/175# d9.14

1951	Pit N	13	50	6	18	2	2	1	14	1	0	7	.360	.373	.540	138	2	0-0	.987	2	122	64	2-13	0.5
1952	Pit N	111	398	41	98	20	2	5	38	22	1	38	.246	.287	.344	72	-15	1-1	.978	-0	99	107	2-81,3-27	-1.2
1953	Bos A	1	4	0	0	0	0	0	0	0	0	0	.000	.000	.000	-95	-1	0-0	.875	0	127	0	/2	-0.1
Total	3	125	452	47	116	22	4	6	52	23	1	45	.257	.294	.363	78	-14	1-1	.978	2	103	99	/2-95,3-27	-0.8

MERTES, SAM Samuel Blair "Sandow" B 8.6.1872 San Francisco, CA D 3.11.1945 San Francisco, CA BR/TR 6/225# d6.30 OF Total (687-LF 182-CF 110-RF)

1896	Phi N	37	143	20	34	4	4	0	14	8	2	10	.238	.288	.322	61	-9	19	.907	-1	63	0	O-35(1-33-1)/S2	-1.0
1898	Chi N	83	269	45	80	4	8	1	47	34	6		.297	.388	.383	121	8	27	.880	0	149	308	O-60(4-5-53),S-14/2-4,1-2	0.6
1899	Chi N	117	426	83	127	13	16	9	81	33	0		.298	.349	.467	126	12	45	.923	-2	121	93	*O-108(16-47-46)/1-3,S	0.3
1900	Chi N	127	481	72	142	25	4	7	60	42	3		.295	.356	.407	114	10	38	.923	-4	112	133	O-88(10-78-0),1-33/S-7	0.0
1901	Chi A	**137**	545	94	151	16	17	5	98	52	6		.277	.347	.396	108	6	46	.940	-10	94	101	*2-132/O-5(LF)	-0.3
1902	Chi A	129	497	60	140	23	7	1	79	37	2		.282	.334	.362	97	-2	46	.922	3	**160**	158	*O-120(111-0-9)/S-5,C-2,P123	-0.5
1903	NY N	138	517	100	145	**32**	14	7	**104**	61	3		.280	.360	.437	122	15	45	**.973**	8	126	117	*O-137(LF)/C1	1.4
1904	NY N	148	532	83	147	28	11	4	78	54	3		.276	.346	.393	123	15	47	.956	-2	90	21	*O-147(130-17-0)/S	0.5
1905	†NY N	150	551	81	154	27	17	5	108	56	5		.279	.351	.417	126	17	52	.960	-9	51	73	*O-150(149-2-0)	-0.1
1906	NY N	71	253	37	60	9	6	1	33	29	3		.237	.323	.332	102	1	21	.970	0	107	0	O-71(71-0-1)	-0.4
	StL N	53	191	20	47	7	4	0	19	16	0		.246	.304	.325	100	0	10	.890	-5	63	0	O-53(LF)	-0.9
	Year	124	444	57	107	16	10	1	52	45	3		.241	.315	.329	101	0	31	.938	-5	89	0	*O-124(124-0-1)	-1.3
Total	10	1190	4405	695	1227	188	108	40	721	422	33	10	.279	.346	.398	114	73	396	.938	-22	105	92	O-974L,2-138/1-40,S-29,C-3,3P	-0.4

MERULLO, LENNIE Leonard Richard B 5.5.1917 Boston, MA BR/TR 5-11/168# d9.12 gs-Matt

1941	Chi N	7	17	3	6	1	0	0	1	2	0	0	.353	.421	.412	140	1	1	.968	1	107	156	/S-7	0.3
1942	Chi N	143	515	53	132	23	3	2	37	35	5	45	.256	.310	.324	89	-8	14	.946	-1	102	93	*S-143	0.2
1943	Chi N	129	453	37	115	18	3	1	25	26	2	42	.254	.297	.313	78	-14	7	.940	-6	100	97	*S-125	-1.1
1944	Chi N	66	193	20	41	8	1	1	16	16	1	18	.212	.276	.280	57	-11	3	.937	1	101	86	S-56/1	-0.6
1945	†Chi N	121	394	40	94	18	0	2	37	31	2	30	.239	.297	.299	68	-17	7	.948	1	99	96	*S-118	-0.8
1946	Chi N	65	126	14	19	8	0	0	7	11	0	13	.151	.219	.214	24	-13	2	.946	8	117	106	S-44	-0.2
1947	Chi N	108	373	24	90	16	1	0	29	15	2	26	.241	.274	.290	52	-27	4	.949	6	101	116	*S-108	-1.4
Total	7	639	2071	191	497	92	8	6	152	136	12	174	.240	.291	.301	69	-89	38	.945	12	102	99	S-601/1	-3.6

MERULLO, MATT Matthew Bates B 8.4.1965 Winchester, MA BL/TR 6-2/200# d4.12 gf-Lennie

1989	Chi A	31	81	5	18	1	0	1	8	6-0	0	14	.222	.273	.272	56	-5	0-1	.973	-4	78	45	C-27/D	-0.8
1991	Chi A	80	140	8	32	1	0	5	21	9-1	0	18	.229	.268	.343	72	-6	0-0	.989	-3	64	163	C-27,1-16/D-6	-0.9
1992	Chi A	24	50	3	9	1	1	0	3	1-0	1	8	.180	.208	.240	27	-5	0-0	.971	-2	88	66	C-16/D	-0.7
1993	Chi A	8	20	1	1	0	0	0	0	0-0	0	1	.050	.050	.050	-75	-5	0-0	—	0			/D-6	-0.5
1994	Cle A	4	10	1	1	0	0	0	0	2-0	0	1	.100	.250	.100	-5	-2	0-0	.957	-2	35	0	/C-4	-0.3
1995	Min A	76	195	19	55	14	1	1	27	14-0	3	27	.282	.335	.379	87	-4	0-1	.987	-10	67	47	C-46,D-13/1-2	-1.1
Total	6	223	496	37	116	17	2	7	59	32-1	4	69	.234	.281	.319	64	-27	0-2	.981	-21	71	67	C-120/D-27,1-18	-4.3

MESNER, STEVE Stephan Mathias B 1.13.1918 Los Angeles, CA D 4.6.1981 San Diego, CA BR/TR 5-9/178# d9.23

1938	Chi N	2	4	2	1	0	0	0	0	1	0	1	.250	.400	.250	80	0	0	.667	-1	80	0	/S	-0.1
1939	Chi N	17	43	7	12	4	0	0	6	3	1	4	.279	.340	.372	90	0	0	.927	1	124	109	S-12/23	0.2
1941	StL N	24	69	8	10	1	0	0	10	5	0	6	.145	.203	.159	3	-9	0	.958	3	108	246	3-22	-0.6
1943	Cin N	137	504	53	137	26	1	0	52	26	1	20	.272	.309	.327	85	-10	6	.944	-1	102	130	*3-130	-1.0
1944	Cin N	121	414	31	100	17	4	1	47	34	1	20	.242	.301	.309	75	-14	1	.951	-8	**99**	**120**	*3-120	-2.2
1945	Cin N	150	540	52	137	19	1	1	52	52	2	18	.254	.322	.298	74	-18	4	.971	15	**113**	127	*3-148/2-3	-0.1
Total	6	451	1574	153	397	67	6	2	167	121	5	69	.252	.308	.306	75	-51	11	.956	10	105	131	3-421/S-13,2-4	-3.8

MESSENGER, BOBBY Charles Walter B 3.19.1884 Bangor, ME D 7.10.1951 Bath, ME BB/TR 5-10.5/165# d8.30

1909	Chi A	31	112	18	19	1	1	0	0	13	2		.170	.268	.196	49	-6	7	.950	-2	102	126	O-31(RF)	-1.0
1910	Chi A	9	26	7	6	0	1	0	4	4	2		.231	.375	.308	119	1	3	.846	-0	66	190	/O-8(LF)	0.0
1911	Chi A	13	17	4	2	0	1	0	0	3	0		.118	.250	.235	37	-2	0	.875	-1	97	0	/O-4(LF)	-0.2
1914	StL A	1	2	0	0	0	0	0	0	0	0	0	.000	.000	.000	-99	-1	0	—	0	0	0	/O(RF)	-0.1
Total	4	54	157	29	27	1	3	0	4	20	4	0	.172	.282	.217	57	-8	10	.918	-3	94	126	/O-44(12-0-32)	-1.3

MESSITT, JACK Thomas John B 7.27.1874 Philadelphia, PA D 9.22.1934 Chicago, IL 5-9/177# d9.14

1899	Lou N	3	11	0	1	0	0	0	0	0	0		.091	.091	.091	-50	-2	0	1.000	1	*134*	*219*	/C-3	-0.1

METCALFE, AL Alfred Tristram B 12.31.1852 Brooklyn, NY D 9.2.1914 Brooklyn, NY d5.27

1875	Mut NA	8	32	2	7	0	0	0	1	0		3	.219	.219	.219	50	-2	2-0	.667	-1	113	0	/3-5,O-2(RF),S	-0.2

METCALFE, MIKE Michael Henry B 1.2.1973 Quantico, VA BR/TR 5-10/175# d9.18

1998	LA N	4	1	0	0	0	0	0	0	0-0	0	1	.000	.000	.000	-99	0	2-0	—	-0	0	0	/2	0.0
2000	LA N	4	12	0	1	0	0	0	0	1-0	0	2	.083	.154	.083	-40	-3	0-0	1.000	-1	115	0	/O-4(3-1-0),2	-0.3
Total	2	8	13	0	1	0	0	0	0	1-0	0	3	.077	.143	.077	-45	-3	2-0	1.000	-1	115	0	/O-4(3-1-0),2-2	-0.3

METHA, SCAT Frank Joseph B 12.13.1913 Los Angeles, CA D 3.2.1975 Fountain Valley, CA BR/TR 5-11/165# d4.22

1940	Det A	26	37	6	9	0	1	0	3	2	0	8	.243	.282	.297	46	-3	0-1	.960	2	113	101	2-10/3-6	-0.1

METHENY, BUD Arthur Beauregard B 6.1.1915 St.Louis, MO D 1.2.2003 Virginia Beach, VA BL/TL 5-11/190# d4.27

1943	†NY A	103	360	51	94	18	2	9	36	39	0	34	.261	.333	.397	113	5	2-3	.963	-9	88	16	O-91(RF)	-1.1
1944	NY A	137	518	72	124	16	1	14	67	56	2	57	.239	.316	.355	89	-8	5-5	.956	-7	90	90	*O-132(11-0-121)	-2.5
1945	NY A	133	509	64	126	18	2	8	53	54	4	31	.248	.325	.338	88	-7	5-2	.984	-6	90	94	*O-128(RF)	-2.2
1946	NY A	3	3	0	0	0	0	0	0	0	0	0	.000	.000	.000	-99	-1	0-0	—	0			H	-0.1
Total	4	376	1390	187	344	52	5	31	156	149	6	122	.247	.323	.359	94	-11	12-10	.968	-22	89	72	O-351(11-0-340)	-5.9

METKOVICH, CATFISH George Michael B 10.8.1920 Angels Camp, CA D 5.17.1995 Costa Mesa, CA BL/TL 6-1/185# d7.16

1943	Bos A	78	321	34	79	14	4	5	27	19	3	38	.246	.294	.361	90	-6	1-3	.955	-3	92	100	O-76(0-54-25)/1-2	-1.4
1944	Bos A	134	549	94	152	28	8	9	59	31	3	57	.277	.319	.406	108	3	13-4	.962	0	102	97	O-82(0-81-3),1-50	-0.1
1945	Bos A	138	539	65	140	26	3	5	62	51	6	70	.260	.331	.347	94	-3	19-6	.985	-3	101	108	1-97,O-42(0-29-14)	-1.2
1946	†Bos A	86	281	42	69	15	2	4	25	36	1	39	.246	.333	.356	88	-4	8-3	.948	-7	88	48	O-81(6-2-73)	-1.3
1947	Cle A	126	473	68	120	22	7	5	40	32	1	51	.254	.302	.362	86	-11	5-3	.989	-3	101	24	*O-119(0-119-2)/1	-1.8
1949	Chi A	93	338	50	80	9	4	5	45	41	1	24	.237	.321	.331	75	-13	5-4	.968	-8	94	17	O-87(9-79-1)	-2.4
1951	Pit N	120	423	51	124	21	3	3	40	28	1	23	.293	.338	.378	90	-6	3-2	.994	-2	95	68	O-69(3-66-0),1-37	-1.1
1952	Pit N	125	373	41	101	18	3	7	41	32	4	29	.271	.335	.391	98	-1	5-2	.988	-6	79	102	1-72,O-33(5-21-8)	-1.0
1953	Pit N	26	41	5	6	0	1	1	7	6	0	3	.146	.255	.268	37	-4	0-0	1.000	-1	0	44	/1-5,O-4(0-3-1)	-0.5
	Chi N	61	124	19	29	9	0	2	12	16	1	10	.234	.326	.355	76	-4	2-1	1.000	-1	111	44	O-38(10-11-18)/1-7	-0.6
	Year	87	165	24	35	9	1	3	19	22	1	13	.212	.309	.333	66	-8	2-1	1.000	-1	110	77	O-42(10-14-19),1-12	-1.1
1954	Mil N	68	123	7	34	5	1	1	15	15	1	15	.276	.352	.358	94	-1	0-0	1.000	2	129	110	1-18,O-13(RF)	0.0
Total	10	1055	3585	476	934	167	36	47	373	307	22	359	.261	.322	.367	91	-50	61-28	.976	-31	97	59	O-644(33-465-158),1-289	-11.4

METRO, CHARLIE Charles (born Charles Moreskonich) B 4.28.1919 Nanty Glo, PA BR/TR 5-11.5/178# d5.4 M2 C3

1943	Det A	44	40	12	8	0	0	0	2	3	0	6	.200	.256	.200	32	-3	1-1	.966	1	139	0	O-14(1-11-2)	-0.3
1944	Det A	38	78	8	15	0	1	0	5	3	0	10	.192	.222	.218	25	-8	1-0	1.000	0	106	66	O-20(9-10-2)	-0.9
	Phi A	24	40	4	4	0	0	0	1	7	0	6	.100	.234	.100	-3	-5	0-0	1.000	1	117	195	O-11(9-0-2)/3-5,2-2	-0.5
	Year	62	118	12	19	0	1	0	6	10	0	16	.161	.227	.178	16	-13	1-0	1.000	1	109	101	O-31(18-10-4)/3-5,2-2	-1.4

Year	Tm Lg	G	AB	R	H	2B	3B	HR	RBI	BB-IB	HP	SO	AVG	OBP	SLG	AOPS	ABR	SB-CS	FA	FR	Rng	Thr	G at Pos	BFW
1945	Phi A	65	200	18	42	10	1	3	15	23	0	33	.210	.291	.315	76	-6	1-1	.972	-2	90	106	O-57(53-1-4)	-1.2
Total 3		171	358	42	69	10	2	3	23	36	0	55	.193	.266	.257	51	-22	3-2	.980	0	100	94	O-102(72-22-10)/3-5,2-2	-2.9
METZ, LENNY Leonard Raymond B 7.6.1899 Louisville, CO D 2.24.1953 Denver, CO BR/TR 5-10.5/170# d9.11																								
1923	Phi N	12	37	4	8	0	0	0	3	4	1	3	.216	.310	.216	37	-3	0-0	.969	0	75	83	/2-6,S-6	-0.2
1924	Phi N	7	7	1	2	0	0	0	1	1	0	0	.286	.375	.286	71	0	0-0	.846	-0	121	71	/S-6	0.0
1925	Phi N	11	14	1	0	0	0	0	0	0	0	2	.000	.000	.000	-92	-4	0-0	1.000	1	113	0	/S-9,2-2	-0.3
Total 3		30	58	6	10	0	0	0	4	5	1	5	.172	.250	.172	11	-7	0-0	.951	1	114	74	/S-21,2-8	-0.5
METZGER, ROGER Roger Henry B 10.10.1947 Fredericksburg, TX BB/TR (BL 1970, 80) 6/165# d6.16																								
1970	Chi N	1	2	0	0	0	0	0	0	0-0	0	0	.000	.000	.000	-89	-1	0-0	.833	1	157	217	/S	0.0
1971	Hou N	150	562	64	132	14	**11**	0	26	44-4	4	50	.235	.294	.299	70	-23	15-6	.977	-4	96	100	*S-148	-0.9
1972	Hou N	**153**	641	84	142	12	3	2	38	60-1	1	71	.222	.288	.259	58	-35	23-9	.971	5	100	105	*S-153	-1.1
1973	Hou N	154	580	67	145	11	**14**	1	35	39-0	3	70	.250	.299	.322	73	-23	10-4	**.982**	-18	90	90	*S-149	-2.4
1974	Hou N	143	572	66	145	18	10	0	30	37-1	0	73	.253	.297	.320	76	-20	9-7	.976	-7	98	99	*S-143	-1.2
1975	Hou N	127	450	54	102	7	9	2	26	41-10	0	39	.227	.289	.296	68	-22	4-5	.977	16	**110**	104	*S-126	0.9
1976	Hou N	152	481	37	101	13	8	0	29	52-10	0	63	.210	.286	.270	65	-23	1-1	**.986**	0	98	97	*S-150/2-2	-0.6
1977	Hou N	97	269	24	50	9	6	0	16	32-3	0	24	.186	.272	.264	49	-20	2-0	.973	-9	96	93	S-96/2	-2.0
1978	Hou N	45	123	11	27	4	1	0	6	12-3	0	9	.220	.287	.268	61	-7	0-0	.964	-4	88	97	S-42/2	-0.7
	SF N	75	235	17	61	6	1	0	17	12-0	0	17	.260	.294	.294	68	-11	8-1	.974	-13	85	82	S-74	-1.6
	Year	120	358	28	88	10	2	0	23	24-3	0	26	.246	.292	.285	66	-17	8-1	.970	-17	86	87	*S-116/2	-2.3
1979	SF N	94	259	24	65	7	8	0	31	23-2	0	31	.251	.311	.340	83	-7	11-3	.956	-1	98	80	S-78,2-10/3	0.0
1980	SF N	28	27	5	2	0	0	0	0	3-0	0	2	.074	.167	.074	-31	-5	0-0	.971	-3	73	84	S-13/2	-0.7
Total 11		1219	4201	453	972	101	71	5	254	355-34	8	449	.231	.291	.293	67	-197	83-36	.976	-38	97	96	*S-1173/2-15,3	-10.3
METZIG, WILLIAM William Andrew B 12.4.1918 Ft.Dodge, IA BR/TR 6-1/180# d9.19 Mil 1945																								
1944	Chi A	5	16	1	2	0	0	0	1	1	0	4	.125	.176	.125	-13	-2	0-0	1.000	1	118	65	/2-5	-0.1
METZLER, ALEX Alexander B 1.4.1903 Fresno, CA D 11.30.1973 Fresno, CA BL/TR 5-9/167# d9.16																								
1925	Chi N	9	38	2	7	2	0	0	2	3	0	7	.184	.244	.237	23	-4	0-0	1.000	2	96	351	/O-9(CF)	-0.3
1926	Phi A	20	67	8	16	3	0	0	12	7	0	5	.239	.311	.284	53	-5	1-0	1.000	1	97	180	O-17(15-1-1)	-0.4
1927	Chi A	134	543	87	173	29	11	3	61	61	9	39	.319	.396	.429	117	15	15-11	.965	7	109	111	*O-134(0-133-4)	1.5
1928	Chi A	139	464	71	141	18	14	3	55	77	6	30	.304	.410	.422	121	17	15-8	.968	-1	102	84	*O-134(50-43-46)	0.8
1929	Chi A	146	568	80	156	23	13	2	49	80	3	45	.275	.367	.371	92	-5	9-5	.960	-5	92	103	*O-142(132-10-0)	-2.0
1930	Chi A	56	79	12	14	4	0	0	5	11	0	6	.177	.278	.228	31	-8	0-2	.969	-0	99	85	O-27(21-1-5)	-0.9
	StL A	56	209	30	54	6	3	1	23	21	0	12	.258	.326	.330	65	-11	5-1	.951	-6	85	46	O-56(1-36-19)	-1.8
	Year	112	288	42	68	10	3	1	28	32	0	18	.236	.313	.302	57	-19	5-3	.955	-7	88	54	O-83(22-37-24)	-2.7
Total 6		560	1968	290	561	85	41	9	207	260	18	144	.285	.374	.384	97	-1	45-27	.965	-2	99	101	O-519(219-233-75)	-3.1
MEULENS, HENSLEY Hensley Filemon Acasio "Bam-Bam" B 6.23.1967 Willemstad, Curacao BR/TR 6-3/212# d8.23																								
1989	NY A	8	28	2	5	0	0	0	1	2-0	0	8	.179	.233	.179	18	-3	0-1	.875	2	141	68	/3-8	-0.2
1990	NY A	23	83	12	20	7	0	3	10	9-0	3	25	.241	.337	.434	113	2	1-0	.963	2	106	205	O-23(LF)	0.3
1991	NY A	96	288	37	64	8	1	6	29	18-1	4	97	.222	.276	.319	64	-15	3-0	.967	2	110	106	O-73(61-0-13),D-13/1-7	-1.5
1992	NY A	2	5	1	3	0	0	1	1	1-0	0	0	.600	.667	1.200	416	2	0-0	1.000	0	113	814	/3-2	0.2
1993	NY A	30	53	8	9	1	1	2	5	8-0	0	19	.170	.279	.340	67	-3	0-1	1.000	-2	93	0	O-24(22-0-1)/1-3,3	-0.5
1997	Mon N	16	24	6	7	1	0	2	6	4-0	0	10	.292	.379	.583	152	2	0-1	1.000	-1	65	0	O-8(LF),1-3	0.0
1998	Ari N	7	15	1	1	0	0	1	1	0-0	0	6	.067	.067	.267	-18	-3	0-0	1.000	1	105	499	/O-4(RF)	-0.2
Total 7		182	496	67	109	17	2	15	53	42-1	7	165	.220	.288	.353	76	-18	4-3	.972	4	105	118	O-132(114-0-18)/1-13,D-13,3-11	-1.9
MEUSEL, IRISH Emil Frederick B 6.9.1893 Oakland, CA D 3.1.1963 Long Beach, CA BR/TR 5-11.5/178# d10.1 C1 b-Bob																								
1914	Was A	1	2	0	0	0	0	0	0	0	0	0	.000	.000	.000	-96	0	0	1.000	-0	97	0	/O(LF)	-0.1
1918	Phi N	124	473	48	132	25	6	4	62	30	1	21	.279	.323	.383	108	4	18	.972	2	106	94	*O-120(71-45-0)/2-4	-0.1
1919	Phi N	135	521	65	159	26	7	5	59	15	2	13	.305	.327	.411	113	7	24	.968	-3	99	79	*O-128(59-15-54)	-0.3
1920	Phi N	138	518	75	160	27	8	14	69	32	0	27	.309	.349	.473	129	18	17-11	.929	-5	94	99	*O-129(99-0-43)/1-3	0.6
1921	Phi N	84	343	59	121	21	7	12	51	18	0	17	.353	.385	.560	136	17	8-4	.929	0	87	160	O-84(38-1-46)	1.0
	†NY N	62	243	37	80	12	6	2	36	15	2	12	.329	.373	.453	117	6	5-9	.971	0	93	133	O-62(62-0-1)	-0.1
	Year	146	586	96	201	33	13	14	87	33	2	29	.343	.380	.515	129	23	13-13	.947	0	89	149	*O-146(100-1-47)	0.9
1922	†NY N	154	617	100	204	28	17	16	132	35	2	33	.331	.369	.509	123	18	12-10	.980	-10	88	79	*O-154(LF)	-0.5
1923	†NY N	146	595	102	177	22	14	19	**125**	38	1	16	.297	.341	.477	115	9	8-8	.949	-9	90	75	*O-145(LF)	-1.2
1924	†NY N	139	549	75	170	26	9	6	102	33	2	18	.310	.351	.423	109	6	11-7	.967	-8	100	28	*O-138(LF)	-1.2
1925	NY N	135	516	82	169	35	8	21	111	26	3	19	.328	.363	.548	135	24	5-4	.959	-6	86	125	*O-126(118-0-8)	0.8
1926	NY N	129	449	51	131	25	10	6	65	16	4	18	.292	.322	.432	103	-1	5	.958	-4	92	100	*O-112(LF)	-1.3
1927	Bro N	42	74	7	18	3	1	1	7	11	0	5	.243	.341	.351	85	-1	0	1.000	0	93	134	O-17(11-0-6)	-0.2
Total 11		1289	4900	701	1521	250	93	106	819	269	17	199	.310	.348	.464	118	107	113-53	.959	-43	94	92	*O-1216(1008-61-158)/2-4,1-3	-2.6
MEUSEL, BOB Robert William "Long Bob" B 7.19.1896 San Jose, CA D 11.28.1977 Downey, CA BR/TR 6-3/190# d4.14 b-Irish																								
1920	NY A	119	460	75	151	40	7	11	83	20	2	72	.328	.359	.517	126	15	4-4	.947	-8	94	112	O-64(16-0-48),3-45/1-2	0.4
1921	†NY A	149	598	104	190	40	16	24	135	34	2	88	.318	.356	.559	128	20	17-6	.934	4	97	143	*O-147(10-0-137)	1.3
1922	†NY A	121	473	61	151	26	11	16	84	40	3	58	.319	.376	.522	129	18	13-8	.950	2	88	**174**	*O-121(47-1-74)	1.1
1923	†NY A	132	460	59	144	29	10	9	91	31	2	52	.313	.359	.478	117	9	13-15	.953	-1	92	126	*O-121(78-0-43)	-0.3
1924	NY A	143	579	93	188	40	11	12	120	32	5	43	.325	.365	.494	120	14	26-14	.951	-4	92	110	*O-143(93-2-49)/3-2	0.1
1925	NY A	**156**	624	101	181	34	12	**33**	**138**	54	1	55	.290	.348	.542	125	18	13-14	.985	-6	95	65	*O-131(86-0-46),3-27	0.1
1926	†NY A	108	413	73	130	22	3	12	81	37	1	32	.315	.373	.470	121	11	16-17	.960	-6	100	37	*O-107(68-1-38)	-0.5
1927	†NY A	135	516	75	174	47	9	8	103	45	2	58	.337	.393	.510	137	28	24-10	.950	-4	92	110	*O-131(83-0-48)	1.5
1928	†NY A	131	518	77	154	45	5	11	113	39	2	56	.297	.349	.467	116	12	6-9	.975	2	96	124	*O-131(87-0-44)	0.1
1929	NY A	100	391	46	102	15	3	10	57	17	0	42	.261	.292	.391	79	-15	2-5	.968	3	109	96	O-96(56-0-40)	-2.0
1930	Cin N	113	443	62	128	30	8	10	62	26	1	63	.289	.330	.460	93	-7	9	.962	-3	95	100	*O-112(70-39-4)	-1.4
Total 11		1407	5475	826	1693	368	95	156	1067	375	21	619	.309	.356	.497	119	123	143-102	.958	-20	95	110	*O-1304(694-43-571)/3-74,1-2	0.4
MEYER, BENNY Bernhard "Earache" B 1.21.1885 Hematite, MO D 2.6.1974 Festus, MO BR/TR 5-9/170# d4.9 C6																								
1913	Bro N	38	87	12	17	0	1	1	10	10	0	14	.195	.278	.253	51	-6	8-3	.943	-1	97	98	O-26(2-17-7)/C	-0.8
1914	Bal F	143	500	76	152	18	10	5	40	71	4	53	.304	.395	.410	116	6	23	.916	-9	94	71	*O-132(12-2-118)/S-4	-0.9
1915	Bal F	35	120	20	29	2	0	0	5	37	1	13	.242	.424	.258	91	0	6	.931	-4	96	22	O-34(RF)	-0.6
	Buf F	93	333	37	77	8	6	1	29	40	1	37	.231	.316	.300	72	-17	9	.947	-5	88	83	O-88(73-0-15)	-2.9
	Year	128	453	57	106	10	6	1	34	77	2	50	.234	.348	.289	78	-17	15	.943	-9	90	65	O-122(73-0-49)	-3.5
1925	Phi N	1	1	1	1	1	0	0	0	0	0	0	1.000	1.000	2.000	594	1	0-0	—	-0	0	0	/2	0.1
Total 4		310	1041	146	276	29	17	7	84	158	6	117	.265	.365	.346	95	-16	46-3	.931	-19	93	71	O-280(87-19-174)/S-4,2C	-5.1
MEYER, DAN Daniel Thomas B 8.3.1952 Hamilton, OH BL/TR 5-11/180# d9.14																								
1974	Det A	13	50	5	10	1	1	3	7	1-1	1	1	.200	.231	.440	86	-1	1-0	.967	0	122	0	O-12(LF)	-0.2
1975	Det A	122	470	56	111	17	3	8	47	26-1	2	25	.236	.277	.336	70	-20	8-3	.950	-2	88	77	O-74(LF),1-46	-3.0
1976	Det A	105	294	37	74	8	4	2	16	17-0	0	22	.252	.292	.327	78	-9	10-0	.988	-4	82	122	O-47(LF),1-19/D	-1.6
1977	Sea A	159	582	75	159	24	4	22	90	43-4	1	51	.273	.320	.442	107	4	11-8	.992	-1	97	98	*1-159	-0.6
1978	Sea A	123	444	38	101	18	1	8	56	24-6	0	39	.227	.264	.327	66	-21	7-3	.989	-2	98	115	*1-121/O-2(LF),D	-3.1
1979	Sea A	144	525	72	146	21	7	20	74	29-10	4	35	.278	.317	.459	106	2	11-7	.936	-9	96	111	*3-101,O-31(LF),1-15	-1.0
1980	Sea A	146	531	56	146	25	6	11	71	31-4	1	42	.275	.314	.407	96	-5	8-4	.961	-11	76	112	*O-123(LF)/3-5,1-4,D-7	-2.1
1981	Sea A	83	252	26	66	10	1	3	22	10-1	0	16	.262	.291	.345	80	-7	4-3	.961	-4	91	137	3-49,O-14(13-1-0)/1-3,D-3	-1.3
1982	Oak A	120	383	28	92	17	3	8	59	18-3	0	33	.240	.271	.363	77	-14	1-1	.990	-1	91	84	1-58,D-38,O-11(4-0-8)	-2.0
1983	Oak A	69	169	15	32	9	0	1	13	19-2	0	11	.189	.268	.260	50	-11	0-0	.987	-3	70	86	1-41,D-12,O-11(9-0-2)/3	-1.7
1984	Oak A	20	22	1	7	3	1	0	4	0-0	0	2	.318	.318	.545	143	1	0-0	.944	0	233	93	/1-3,D	0.1
1985	Oak A	14	12	2	0	0	0	0	0	1-0	0	2	.000	.077	.000	-83	-3	0-0	—	0	0	0	/3O(RF)D	-0.3
Total 12		1118	3734	411	944	153	31	86	459	219-32	10	277	.253	.293	.379	86	-84	61-29	.991	-35	94	100	1-469,O-326(315-1-11),3-157/D-64	-16.8
MEYER, GEORGE George Francis B 8.3.1909 Chicago, IL D 1.3.1992 Hoffman Estates, IL BR/TR 5-9/160# d9.3																								
1938	Chi A	24	81	10	24	2	2	0	9	11	1	17	.296	.387	.370	89	-1	3-1	.967	2	116	69	2-24	0.2

Year	Tm Lg	G	AB	R	H	2B	3B	HR	RBI	BB-IB	HP	SO	AVG	OBP	SLG	AOPS	ABR	SB-CS	FA	FR	Rng	Thr	G at Pos	BFW
MEYER, DUTCH Lambert Dalton B 10.6.1915 Waco, TX D 1.19.2003 Fort Worth, TX BR/TR 5-10.5/181# d6.23 Mil 1943-44																								
1937	Chi N	1	0	0	0	0	0	0	0	0	0	0	—	—	—	—	0	0	—	0			R	0.0
1940	Det A	23	58	12	15	3	0	0	6	4	1	10	.259	.317	.310	58	-3	2-0	.960	-1	98	60	2-21	-0.3
1941	Det A	46	153	12	29	9	1	1	14	8	0	13	.190	.230	.281	31	-15	1-1	.972	2	92	77	2-40	-1.1
1942	Det A	14	52	5	17	3	0	2	9	4	1	4	.327	.386	.500	137	3	0-1	.989	5	124	146	2-14	0.8
1945	Cle A	130	524	71	153	29	8	7	48	40	0	32	.292	.342	.418	125	15	2-4	.978	-28	84	79	*2-130	-0.8
1946	Cle A	72	207	13	48	5	3	0	16	26	1	16	.232	.321	.285	75	-7	0-1	.977	-10	91	67	2-64	-1.5
Total	6	286	994	113	262	49	12	10	93	82	3	75	.264	.322	.367	94	-7	5-7	.977	-32	90	79	2-269	-2.9
MEYER, LEO Leo B 3.29.1888 , IA D 9.2.1968 Smyrna, DE TR d9.27																								
1909	Bro N	7	23	1	3	0	0	0	0	2	0		.130	.200	.130	3	-3	0	.882	-1	89	63	/S-7	-0.4
MEYER, SCOTT Scott William B 8.19.1957 Evergreen Park, IL BR/TR 6-1/195# d9.10																								
1978	Oak A	8	9	1	1	1	0	0	0	0-0	0	4	.111	.111	.222	-9	-1	0-0	1.000	-0	120	0	/C-7	-0.1
MEYER, JOEY Tanner Joe B 5.10.1962 Honolulu, HI BR/TR 6-3/260# d4.4																								
1988	Mil A	103	327	22	86	18	0	11	45	23-2	1	88	.263	.313	.419	102	0	0-1	.986	-0	101	99	D-66,1-33	-0.4
1989	Mil A	53	147	13	33	6	0	7	29	12-1	0	36	.224	.274	.408	93	-2	1-0	.982	-1	87	143	D-31,1-18	-0.4
Total	2	156	474	35	119	24	0	18	74	35-3	1	124	.251	.300	.416	100	-2	1-1	.984	-1	97	113	/D-97,1-51	-0.8
MEYER, BILLY William Adam B 1.14.1892 Knoxville, TN D 3.31.1957 Knoxville, TN BR/TR 5-9.5/170# d9.6 M5																								
1913	Chi A	1	1	0	1	0	0	0	0	0	0	0	1.000	1.000	1.000	490	0	0	.857	0	*0*	*130*	/C	0.1
1916	Phi A	50	138	6	32	2	2	1	12	8	0	11	.232	.274	.297	75	-5	3	.961	-2	63	145	C-48	-0.4
1917	Phi A	62	162	9	38	5	1	0	9	7	1	14	.235	.271	.278	68	-7	0	.962	1	*84*	*110*	C-55	-0.1
Total	3	113	301	15	71	7	3	1	21	15	1	25	.236	.274	.289	73	-12	3	.960	-0	*74*	*126*	C-104	-0.4
MEYERLE, LEVI Levi Samuel "Long Levi" B 7.1845 Philadelphia, PA D 11.4.1921 Philadelphia, PA BR/TR 6-1/177# d5.20 ▲ OF NA (2-LF 29-RF) OF Total (1-CF 4-RF)																								
1871	Ath NA	26	130	45	64	9	3	**4**	40	2		1	**.492**	**.500**	**.700**	**243**	**23**	4-0	.646	-9	67	32	*3-26/P	0.9
1872	Ath NA	27	146	31	48	10	5	1	31	0		1	.329	.329	.486	147	7	0-0	.773	3	165	0	O-26(RF)/3	0.9
1873	Phi NA	48	238	53	83	14	4	3	59	2		0	.349	.354	.479	140	10	5-0	.746	-7	89	106	*3-48/S	0.2
1874	Chi NA	53	254	65	100	19	1	1	45	3		4	**.394**	**.401**	.488	**182**	**23**	3-1	.833	-12	79	113	2-31,3-14/S-5,O-5(2-0-3)	0.7
1875	Phi NA	68	301	55	95	14	8	1	54	0		2	.316	.316	.425	149	13	7-2	.859	-6	98	99	2-36,3-20,1-16	0.5
1876	Phi N	55	256	46	87	12	8	0	34	3		2	.340	.347	.449	165	17		.791	-4	101	75	*3-49/O-3(RF),2-3,P-2	1.3
1877	Cin N	27	107	11	35	7	2	0	15	0		4	.327	.327	.430	154	7		.822	0	99	88	S-18,2-12/O(CF)	0.7
1884	Phi U	3	11	0	1	1	0	0		0			.091	.091	.182	-21	-2		.789	-1	0	127	/1-2,O(RF)	-0.3
Total	5 NA	222	1069	249	390	66	21	10	229	7		8	.365	.369	.494	166	76	19-3	.000	-30	76	99	3-109/2-67,O-31R,1-16,S-6,P	3.2
Total	3	85	374	57	123	20	10	0	49	3		6	.329	.334	.436	156	22		.791	-4	101	75	/3-49,S-18,2-15,O-5R,1-2,P-2	1.7
MEYERS, CHAD Chad William B 8.8.1975 Omaha, NE BR/TR 6/190# d8.6																								
1999	Chi N	43	142	17	33	9	0	0	4	9-1	3	27	.232	.292	.296	50	-11	4-2	.983	-7	89	71	2-32,O-14(4-10-0)	-1.5
2000	Chi N	36	52	8	9	2	0	0	5	3-0	1	11	.173	.228	.212	13	-7	1-0	1.000	-1	94	115	/2-8,3-8	-0.8
2001	Chi N	18	17	1	2	0	0	0	0	2-0	4	5	.118	.348	.118	30	-2	0-1	1.000	2	172	82	/2-4,O-4(2-2-0),3	0.0
2003	Sea A	9	1	1	0	0	0	0	0	0-0	0	0	.000	.000	.000	-99	0	1-0	—	-0	0	0	/O-3(LF),D-6	0.0
Total	4	106	212	27	44	11	0	0	9	14-1	8	43	.208	.281	.259	39	-20	6-3	.987	-6	95	78	/2-44,O-21(9-12-0),3-9,D-6	-2.3
MEYERS, HENRY Henry L. B 1860 Philadelphia, PA D 6.28.1898 Harrisburg, PA d8.30																								
1890	Phi AA	5	19	2	3	0	0	0	1	1	1		.158	.238	.158	17	-2	2	.684	-2	67	0	/3-5	-0.4
MEYERS, CHIEF John Tortes B 7.29.1880 Riverside, CA D 7.25.1971 San Bernardino, CA BR/TR 5-11/194# d4.16																								
1909	NY N	90	220	15	61	10	5	1	30	22	6		.277	.359	.382	128	8	3	.963	2	*117*	*87*	C-64	1.7
1910	NY N	127	365	25	104	18	0	1	62	40	4	18	.285	.362	.342	106	4	5	.969	2	*99*	*101*	*C-117	1.9
1911	†NY N	133	391	48	130	18	9	1	61	25	13	33	.332	.392	.432	126	14	7	.979	10	*130*	*76*	*C-128	3.3
1912	†NY N	126	371	60	133	16	5	6	54	47	8	20	.358	.441	.477	147	26	8	.973	5	*124*	*84*	*C-122	4.0
1913	†NY N	120	378	37	118	18	5	3	47	37	9	22	.312	.387	.410	127	15	7-9	.967	6	**117**	97	*C-116	3.0
1914	NY N	134	381	33	109	13	5	1	55	34	8	25	.286	.357	.354	116	8	4	.970	-2	*130*	*96*	*C-126	1.7
1915	NY N	110	289	24	67	10	5	1	26	26	7	18	.232	.311	.311	94	-2	4-4	**.986**	-6	*89*	*87*	C-96	-0.1
1916	†Bro N	80	239	21	59	10	3	0	21	26	6	15	.247	.336	.314	97	1	2	.984	5	104	104	C-74	1.4
1917	Bro N	47	132	8	28	3	0	0	3	13	0	7	.212	.283	.235	58	-6	4	.974	-4	*97*	*77*	C-44	-0.8
	Bos N	25	68	5	17	4	4	0	4	4	2	4	.250	.311	.426	133	2	0	1.000	5	*124*	*123*	C-24	1.1
	Year	72	200	13	45	7	4	0	7	17	2	11	.225	.292	.300	82	-4	4	.984	1	*107*	*94*	C-68	0.3
Total	9	992	2834	276	826	120	41	14	363	274	63	162	.291	.367	.378	117	70	44-13	.974	24	*114*	*91*	C-911	17.2
MEYERS, LOU Lewis Henry "Crazy Horse" B 12.9.1859 Cincinnati, OH D 11.30.1920 Cincinnati, OH BR/TR 5-11/165# d5.10																								
1884	Cin U	2	3	1	0	0	0	0		1			.000	.250	.000	-17	-1		.667	-1			/C-2,O(RF)	-0.1
MICELOTTA, MICKEY Robert Peter B 10.20.1928 Corona, NY BR/TR 5-11/185# d4.20																								
1954	Phi N	13	3	2	0	0	0	0	0	1	0	1	.000	.250	.000	-28	-1	0-0	1.000	0	145	0	/S	-0.1
1955	Phi N	4	4	0	0	0	0	0	0	0-0	0	0	.000	.000	.000	-99	-1	0-0	1.000	-0	74	184	/S-2	-0.1
Total	2	17	7	2	0	0	0	0	0	1-0	0	1	.000	.125	.000	-64	-2	0-0	1.000	-0	88	147	/S-3	-0.2
MICHAEL, GENE Eugene Richard "Stick" B 6.2.1938 Kent, OH BB/TR 6-2/183# d7.15 M4 C8																								
1966	Pit N	30	33	9	5	2	1	0	2	0-0	0	7	.152	.152	.273	15	-4	0-0	.903	2	132	253	/S-8,2-2,3	-0.1
1967	LA N	98	223	20	45	3	1	0	7	11-0	2	30	.202	.246	.224	39	-18	1-3	.950	-1	100	81	S-83	-1.6
1968	NY A	61	116	8	23	3	0	1	8	2-0	1	23	.198	.218	.250	43	-8	3-2	.939	-5	95	79	S-43/P	-1.2
1969	NY A	119	412	41	112	24	4	2	31	43-1	1	56	.272	.341	.364	101	1	7-4	.968	0	102	103	*S-118	1.6
1970	NY A	134	435	42	93	10	1	2	38	50-5	0	93	.214	.292	.255	56	-26	3-1	.957	-1	102	113	*S-123/3-4,2-3	-1.2
1971	NY A	139	456	36	102	15	0	3	35	48-8	3	64	.224	.299	.276	69	-18	3-3	.973	25	**117**	119	*S-136	2.3
1972	NY A	126	391	29	91	7	4	1	32	32-4	1	45	.233	.290	.279	73	-14	4-2	.969	24	117	126	*S-121	2.7
1973	NY A	129	418	30	94	11	1	3	47	26-0	0	51	.225	.270	.278	56	-25	1-3	.965	11	107	110	*S-129	-0.1
1974	NY A	81	177	19	46	9	0	0	13	14-0	0	24	.260	.313	.311	82	-4	0-0	.970	2	102	106	2-45,S-39/3-2	0.3
1975	Det A	56	145	15	31	2	0	3	13	8-0	0	28	.214	.253	.290	51	-10	0-0	.938	0	98	109	S-44/2-7,3-4	-0.5
Total	10	973	2806	249	642	86	12	15	226	234-18	8	421	.229	.288	.284	66	-126	22-18	.962	58	107	110	S-844/2-57,3-11,P	2.2
MICHAELS, CASS Casimir Eugene (Played In 1943 Under Real Name Of Casimir Eugene Kwietniewski) B3.4.1926 Detroit, MI D11.12.1982 Grosse Pointe, MI BR/TR 5-11/175# d8.19																								
1943	Chi A	2	7	0	0	0	0	0	0	0	0	0	.000	.000	.000	-99	-2	0-0	1.000	-1	37	0	/3-2	-0.3
1944	Chi A	27	68	4	12	4	1	0	5	2	0	5	.176	.200	.265	33	-6	0-0	.930	2	111	97	S-21/3-3	-0.3
1945	Chi A	129	445	47	109	8	5	2	54	37	3	28	.245	.307	.299	78	-13	8-7	.936	8	105	93	*S-126/2	0.4
1946	Chi A	91	291	37	75	8	0	1	22	29	4	36	.258	.333	.296	80	-7	9-3	.957	1	104	112	2-66,3-13/S-6	-0.1
1947	Chi A	110	355	31	97	15	4	3	34	39	3	28	.273	.350	.363	102	1	10-5	.982	9	111	126	2-60,3-44/S-2	1.4
1948	Chi A	145	484	47	120	12	6	5	56	69	2	42	.248	.344	.329	82	-12	8-2	.957	16	111	100	S-85,2-55/O(CF)	1.3
1949	Chi A★	**154**	561	73	173	27	9	6	83	101	3	50	.308	.417	.421	126	25	5-7	.976	15	**111**	109	*2-154	4.5
1950	Chi A	36	138	21	43	6	3	4	19	13	1	8	.312	.375	.486	122	4	0-0	.964	-3	80	122	2-35	0.2
	Was A★	106	388	48	97	8	4	4	47	55	1	39	.250	.345	.322	75	-14	2-3	.975	7	107	100	*2-104	-0.2
	Year	142	526	69	140	14	7	8	66	68	2	47	.266	.352	.365	88	-10	2-3	.972	3	100	105	*2-139	0.0
1951	Was A	138	485	59	125	20	4	4	45	61	1	41	.258	.342	.340	86	-8	1-1	.964	-22	100	84	*2-128	-2.3
1952	Was A	22	86	10	20	4	1	1	7	7	0	15	.233	.290	.337	77	-3	0-0	.977	-2	106	92	2-22	-0.3
	StL A	55	166	21	44	8	2	3	25	23	0	16	.265	.354	.392	104	1	1-0	.916	-0	105	129	3-42/2-8	0.1
	Phi A	55	200	22	50	4	5	1	18	23	1	11	.250	.330	.335	80	-5	3-0	.993	-9	86	74	2-55	-1.2
	Year	132	452	53	114	16	8	5	50	53	1	42	.252	.332	.356	89	-7	4-0	.989	-11	92	81	2-85,3-42	-1.4
1953	Phi A	117	411	53	103	10	0	12	42	51	1	56	.251	.335	.363	85	-9	7-0	.970	-12	96	87	*2-110	-1.1
1954	Chi A	101	282	35	74	13	2	7	44	56	4	31	.262	.392	.397	113	8	10-4	.958	-2	96	66	3-91/2-2	0.6
Total	12	1288	4367	508	1142	147	46	53	501	566	24	406	.262	.349	.353	92	-40	64-32	.973	6	103	101	2-800,S-240,3-195/O(CF)	2.7
MICHAELS, JASON Jason Drew B 5.4.1976 Tampa, FL BR/TR 6/204# d4.6																								
2001	Phi N	6	6	0	1	0	0	0	1	0-0	0	2	.167	.167	.167	-14	-1	0-0	—	-0	0	0	/O(LF)	-0.1
2002	Phi N	81	105	16	28	10	3	2	11	13-1	1	33	.267	.347	.476	125	3	1-1	1.000	-1	76	254	O-26(6-14-7)/3D	0.2
2003	Phi N	76	109	20	36	11	0	5	17	15-1	1	22	.330	.416	.569	164	11	0-0	.976	1	92	237	O-38(23-5-13)	1.1

Year	Tm Lg	G	AB	R	H	2B	3B	HR	RBI	BB-IB	HP	SO	AVG	OBP	SLG	AOPS	ABR	SB-CS	FA	FR	Rng	Thr	G at Pos	BFW
Total	3	163	220	36	65	21	3	7	29	28-2	2	57	.295	.377	.514	141	13	1-1	.985	0	85	242	/O-65(30-19-20),D-2,3	1.2
MICHAELS, RALPH Ralph Joseph B 5.3.1902 Etna, PA D 8.5.1988 Monroeville, PA BR/TR 5-10.5/178# d4.16																								
1924	Chi N	8	11	0	4	0	0	0	2	0	0	1	.364	.364	.364	95	0	0-0	.929	-0	95	73	/S-4	0.0
1925	Chi N	22	50	10	14	1	0	0	6	6	0	9	.280	.357	.300	69	-2	1-0	.975	2	121	190	3-15/12S	0.1
1926	Chi N	2	0	1	0	0	0	0	0	0	0	0	—	—	—	—	0	0	—	0			H	0.0
Total	3	32	61	11	18	1	0	0	8	6	0	10	.295	.358	.311	73	-2	1-0	.975	2	121	190	/3-15,S-5,21	0.1
MICKELSON, ED Edward Allen B 9.9.1926 Ottawa, IL BR/TR 6-3/205# d9.18																								
1950	StL N	5	10	1	1	0	0	0	0	2	0	3	.100	.250	.100	-4	-2	0	1.000	1	182	32	/1-4	-0.1
1953	StL A	7	15	1	2	1	0	0	2	2	0	6	.133	.235	.200	18	-2	0-0	1.000	0	111	71	/1-3	-0.2
1957	Chi N	6	12	0	0	0	0	0	1	0-0	0	4	.000	.000	.000	-99	-3	0-0	1.000	1	169	151	/1-2	-0.3
Total	3	18	37	2	3	1	0	0	3	4-0	0	13	.081	.171	.108	-23	-7	0-0	1.000	2	155	77	/1-9	-0.6
MIDKIFF, EZRA Ezra Millington "Salt Rock" B 11.13.1882 Salt Rock, WV D 3.20.1957 Huntington, WV BL/TR 5-10/180# d10.5																								
1909	Cin N	1	2	0	0	0	0	0	0	0	0		.000	.000	.000	-99	0	0	.000	-1	0	0	/3	-0.1
1912	NY A	21	86	9	21	1	0	0	9	7	0		.244	.301	.256	56	-5	4	.901	2	120	32	3-21	-0.3
1913	NY A	83	284	22	56	9	1	0	14	12	1	33	.197	.232	.236	37	-23	9	.957	14	121	105	3-76/S-4,2-2	-0.8
Total	3	105	372	31	77	10	1	0	23	19	1	33	.207	.247	.239	41	-28	13	.942	15	120	90	/3-98,S-4,2-2	-1.2
MIENTKIEWICZ, DOUG Douglas Andrew B 6.19.1974 Toledo, OH BL/TR 6-2/195# d9.18																								
1998	Min A	8	25	1	5	1	0	0	2	4-0	0	3	.200	.310	.240	45	-2	1-1	1.000	-1	61	50	/1-8	-0.3
1999	Min A	118	327	34	75	21	3	2	32	43-3	4	51	.229	.324	.330	66	-16	1-1	**.997**	-2	89	91	*1-110	-2.6
2000	Min A	3	14	0	6	0	0	0	4	0-0	0	0	.429	.400	.429	114	0	0-0	1.000	-1	0	109	/1-3	-0.1
2001	Min A	151	543	77	166	39	1	15	74	67-6	9	92	.306	.387	.464	121	20	2-6	**.997**	-9	74	83	*1-148/D-2	-0.4
2002	†Min A	143	467	60	122	29	1	10	64	74-8	6	69	.261	.365	.392	102	4	1-2	.996	-6	81	90	*1-143	-1.4
2003	†Min A	142	487	67	146	38	1	11	65	74-4	5	55	.300	.393	.450	122	20	4-1	.997	-8	78	83	*1-139/O-3(RF),23D	0.0
Total	6	565	1863	239	520	128	6	38	241	262-21	24	270	.279	.371	.415	105	26	9-11	.997	-26	79	86	1-551/O-3(RF),D-3,32	-4.8
MIERKOWICZ, ED Edward Frank "Butch" or "Mouse" B 3.6.1924 Wyandotte, MI BR/TR 6-4/205# d8.31																								
1945	†Det A	10	15	0	2	2	0	0	2	1	0	3	.133	.188	.267	29	-1	0-0	1.000	-0	109	0	/O-6(LF)	-0.2
1947	Det A	21	42	6	8	1	0	1	1	1	0	12	.190	.209	.286	36	-4	1-0	.947	-0	104	0	O-10(LF)	-0.5
1948	Det A	3	5	0	1	0	0	0	1	2	0	2	.200	.429	.200	69	0	0-0	1.000	0	128	0	/O(LF)	0.0
1950	StL N	1	1	0	0	0	0	0	0	0	0	1	.000	.000	.000	-95	0	0	—	0			H	0.0
Total	4	35	63	6	11	3	0	1	4	4	0	18	.175	.224	.270	36	-5	1-0	.968	-0	108	0	/O-17(LF)	-0.7
MIESKE, MATT Matthew Todd B 2.13.1968 Midland, MI BR/TR 6/192# d5.3																								
1993	Mil A	23	58	9	14	0	0	3	7	4-0	0	14	.241	.290	.397	84	-2	0-2	.936	-1	96	78	O-22(1-9-12)	-0.4
1994	Mil A	84	259	39	67	13	1	10	38	21-0	3	62	.259	.320	.432	88	-5	3-5	.976	0	99	122	O-80(6-0-80)/D	-0.9
1995	Mil A	117	267	42	67	13	1	12	48	27-0	4	45	.251	.323	.442	93	-3	2-4	.979	5	112	130	*O-108(RF)/D-2	-0.3
1996	Mil A	127	374	46	104	24	3	14	64	26-2	2	76	.278	.324	.471	95	-4	1-5	.996	7	**114**	95	*O-122(9-10-108)	-0.3
1997	Mil A	84	253	39	63	15	3	5	21	19-2	0	50	.249	.300	.391	78	-9	1-0	.962	-1	93	146	O-74(26-0-52)/D-5	-1.2
1998	Chi N	77	97	16	29	7	0	1	12	11-1	1	17	.299	.373	.402	101	1	0-0	.974	-2	83	67	O-62(50-3-12)	-0.2
1999	Sea A	24	41	11	15	0	0	4	7	2-1	0	9	.366	.395	.659	166	4	0-0	1.000	2	133	162	O-20(6-3-13)/D	0.5
	†Hou N	54	109	13	31	5	0	5	22	6-1	0	22	.284	.316	.468	98	-1	0-0	1.000	2	120	69	O-37(30-0-7)	0.0
2000	Hou N	62	81	7	14	1	2	1	5	7-0	1	17	.173	.247	.272	29	-9	0-0	.933	-1	75	0	O-18(14-0-4)	-1.1
	Ari N	11	8	3	2	0	0	1	2	1-0	0	1	.250	.300	.625	131	0	0-0	1.000	0	886	0	/O(RF)	0.1
	Year	73	89	10	16	1	2	2	7	8-0	1	18	.180	.253	.303	38	-9	0-0	.941	-1	85	0	O-19(14-0-5)	-1.0
Total	8	663	1547	225	406	78	10	56	226	124-7	11	313	.262	.318	.434	90	-28	7-16	.979	12	105	110	O-544(142-25-397)/D-9	-3.8
MIGGINS, LARRY Lawrence Edward "Irish" B 8.20.1925 Bronx, NY BR/TR 6-4/198# d10.3																								
1948	StL N	1	1	1	0	0	0	0	0	0	0	0	.000	.000	.000	-95	0	0	—	0			H	0.0
1952	StL N	42	96	7	22	5	1	2	10	3	0	19	.229	.253	.365	69	-5	0-1	.967	-2	87	0	O-25(23-0-2)/1	-0.8
Total	2	43	97	8	22	5	1	2	10	3	0	19	.227	.250	.361	67	-5	0-1	.967	-2	87	0	/O-25(23-0-2),1	-0.8
MIHALIC, JOHN John Michael B 11.13.1911 Cleveland, OH D 4.24.1987 Ft.Oglethorpe, GA BR/TR 5-11/172# d9.18																								
1935	Was A	6	22	4	5	3	0	0	6	2	0	3	.227	.292	.364	71	-1	1-0	.966	-0	96	133	/S-6	0.0
1936	Was A	25	88	15	21	2	1	0	8	14	0	14	.239	.343	.284	60	-5	2-1	.972	1	101	147	2-25	-0.2
1937	Was A	38	107	13	27	5	2	0	8	17	0	9	.252	.355	.336	79	-3	2-1	.981	1	98	126	2-28/S-3	0.0
Total	3	69	217	32	53	10	3	0	22	33	0	26	.244	.344	.318	70	-9	5-2	.977	2	99	136	/2-53,S-9	-0.2
MIKSIS, EDDIE Edward Thomas B 9.11.1926 Burlington, NJ BR/TR 6-0.5/185# d6.17 Mil 1945 OF Total (34-LF 106-CF 88-RF)																								
1944	Bro N	26	91	12	20	2	0	0	11	6	0	11	.220	.268	.242	45	-7	4	.896	-4	78	275	3-15,S-10	-1.1
1946	Bro N	23	48	3	7	0	0	0	5	3	1	3	.146	.212	.146	2	-6	0	.970	-0	96	0	3-13/2	-0.7
1947	†Bro N	45	86	18	23	1	0	4	10	9	0	8	.267	.337	.419	96	-1	0	1.000	2	113	82	2-13,O-11(LF)/3-5,S-2	0.0
1948	Bro N	86	221	28	47	7	1	2	16	19	1	27	.213	.278	.281	50	-16	5	.967	-1	96	66	2-54,3-22/S-5	-1.4
1949	†Bro N	50	113	17	25	5	0	1	6	7	0	8	.221	.267	.292	48	-8	3	.978	4	111	79	3-29/S-4,2-3,1	-0.5
1950	Bro N	51	76	13	19	2	1	2	10	5	0	10	.250	.296	.382	75	-3	3	.964	1	80	61	2-15,S-15/3-7	-0.1
1951	Bro N	19	10	6	2	1	0	0	0	1	1	2	.200	.333	.300	70	0	0-0	1.000	1	150	699	/3-6,2	0.1
	Chi N	102	421	48	112	13	3	4	35	33	0	36	.266	.319	.340	76	-15	11-5	.969	1	106	85	*2-102	-0.7
	Year	121	431	54	114	14	3	4	35	34	1	38	.265	.320	.339	76	-15	11-5	.969	2	106	85	*2-103/3-6	-0.6
1952	Chi N	93	383	44	89	20	1	2	19	20	1	32	.232	.272	.305	59	-22	4-4	.950	-14	91	63	2-54,S-40	-3.2
1953	Chi N	142	577	61	145	17	6	8	39	33	1	59	.251	.293	.343	64	-32	13-4	.954	-15	96	91	2-92,S-53	-3.4
1954	Chi N	38	99	9	20	3	0	2	3	3	0	9	.202	.225	.293	33	-10	1-0	.961	2	104	101	2-21/3-2,O(LF)	-0.6
1955	Chi N	131	481	52	113	14	2	9	41	32-3	0	55	.235	.282	.328	62	-27	3-6	**.989**	-1	100	66	*O-111(0-76-41),3-18	-3.5
1956	Chi N	114	356	54	85	10	3	9	27	32-2	1	40	.239	.303	.360	79	-11	4-2	.975	1	99	55	3-48,O-33(6-25-2),2-19/S-2	-1.0
1957	StL N	49	38	3	8	0	0	1	2	7-1	0	7	.211	.333	.289	68	-2	0-0	1.000	-0	97	0	O-31(11-3-18)	-0.2
	Bal A	1	1	0	0	0	0	0	0	0-0	0	0	.000	.000	.000	-99	0	0-0	—	0			H	0.0
1958	Bal A	3	2	0	0	0	0	0	0	0-0	0	1	.000	.000	.000	-99	-1	0-0	—	-0	0	0	/S	-0.1
	Cin N	69	50	15	7	0	0	0	4	5-0	0	5	.140	.218	.140	-2	-7	1-1	1.000	3	142	0	O-32(5-2-27),3-14/2-7,S-5,1	-0.5
Total	14	1042	3053	383	722	95	17	44	228	215-6	6	313	.236	.288	.322	62	-168	52-22	.962	-22	100	81	2-382,O-219C,3-179,S-137/1-2	-16.9
MILAN, HORACE Horace Robert B 4.7.1894 Linden, TN D 6.29.1955 Texarkana, AR BR/TR 5-9/175# d8.29 Mil 1918 b-Clyde																								
1915	Was A	11	27	6	11	1	1	0	7	8	0	7	.407	.543	.519	214	5	2	1.000	-1	79	0	O-10(2-4-4)	0.4
1917	Was A	31	73	8	21	3	1	0	9	4	2	9	.288	.342	.356	114	1	4	.932	-1	120	0	O-23(LF)	-0.1
Total	2	42	100	14	32	4	2	0	16	12	2	16	.320	.404	.400	144	6	6	.944	-2	108	0	/O-33(25-4-4)	0.3
MILAN, CLYDE Jesse Clyde "Deerfoot" B 3.25.1887 Linden, TN D 3.3.1953 Orlando, FL BL/TR 5-9/168# d8.19 M1 C17 b-Horace																								
1907	Was A	48	183	22	51	3	3	0	9	8	4		.279	.323	.328	117	3	8	.929	4	203	68	O-47(0-30-17)	0.5
1908	Was A	130	485	55	116	10	12	1	32	38	7		.239	.304	.315	110	5	29	.959	5	126	156	*O-122(CF)	0.4
1909	Was A	130	400	36	80	12	4	1	15	31	6		.200	.268	.257	69	-14	10	.972	5	130	86	*O-120(29-89-2)	-1.7
1910	Was A	142	531	89	148	17	6	0	16	71	15		.279	.379	.333	129	23	44	.946	8	99	154	*O-142(CF)	2.6
1911	Was A	**154**	616	109	194	24	8	3	35	74	7		.315	.395	.394	123	22	58	.957	7	102	131	*O-154(CF)	1.8
1912	Was A	**154**	601	105	184	19	11	1	79	63	5		.306	.377	.379	116	13	**88**	.935	7	102	148	*O-154(CF)	1.0
1913	Was A	154	579	92	174	18	9	3	54	58	3	25	.301	.367	.378	116	12	**75**	.932	-12	88	83	*O-154(CF)	-1.2
1914	Was A	115	437	63	129	19	11	1	39	32	2	26	.295	.346	.396	118	8	38-21	.949	-6	96	71	*O-113(1-112-0)	-0.5
1915	Was A	153	573	83	165	13	7	2	66	53	5	32	.288	.353	.346	107	5	40-19	.946	-6	102	61	*O-151(CF)	-1.0
1916	Was A	150	565	58	154	14	3	1	45	56	5	31	.273	.343	.313	98	0	34-21	.961	14	**114**	136	*O-149(CF)	0.4
1917	Was A	155	579	60	170	15	4	0	48	58	6	26	.294	.364	.333	114	11	20	.962	-6	96	86	*O-153(CF)	-0.6
1918	Was A	128	503	56	146	18	5	0	56	36	5	14	.290	.344	.346	110	5	26	.972	-4	95	90	*O-124(CF)	-0.9
1919	Was A	88	321	43	92	12	6	0	37	40	3	16	.287	.371	.361	107	4	11	.953	-1	103	83	O-86(CF)	-0.2
1920	Was A	126	506	70	163	22	5	3	41	28	5	12	.322	.364	.403	106	4	10-12	.971	4	109	88	*O-123(115-0-8)	0.0
1921	Was A	113	406	55	117	19	11	1	40	37	2	13	.288	.351	.397	95	-4	4-5	.931	3	98	147	O-99(34-15-52)	-0.9
1922	Was A	42	74	8	17	5	0	0	5	2	0	2	.230	.250	.297	44	-6	0-0	1.000	1	91	249	O-12(3-0-9),M	-0.6
Total	16	1982	7359	1004	2100	240	105	17	617	685	80	197	.285	.353	.353	109	91	495-78	.953	21	106	109	*O-1903(182-1635-88)	-0.9

Year	Tm Lg	G	AB	R	H	2B	3B	HR	RBI	BB-IB	HP	SO	AVG	OBP	SLG	AOPS	ABR	SB-CS	FA	FR	Rng	Thr	G at Pos	BFW
MILBOURNE, LARRY Lawrence William B 2.14.1951 Port Norris, NJ BB/TR 6/165# d4.6																								
1974	Hou N	112	136	31	38	2	1	0	9	10-0	0	14	.279	.329	.309	83	-3	6-2	.974	2	112	86	2-87/S-8,O-4(LF)	0.2
1975	Hou N	73	151	17	32	1	2	1	9	6-1	1	14	.212	.245	.265	45	-12	1-2	.968	-2	95	130	2-43,S-22	-1.1
1976	Hou N	59	145	22	36	4	0	0	7	14-0	1	10	.248	.319	.276	77	-4	6-1	.965	-3	98	84	2-32	-0.4
1977	Sea A	86	242	24	53	10	0	2	21	6-0	2	20	.219	.239	.285	44	-19	3-1	.982	4	112	108	2-41,S-40/3D	-1.0
1978	Sea A	93	234	31	53	6	2	2	20	9-1	0	6	.226	.254	.295	55	-15	5-7	.989	4	96	65	3-32,S-23,2-15,D-10	-1.1
1979	Sea A	123	356	40	99	13	4	2	26	19-2	0	20	.278	.313	.354	79	-11	5-3	.981	3	113	92	S-65,2-49,3-11	-0.3
1980	Sea A	106	258	31	68	6	6	0	26	19-4	1	13	.264	.313	.333	78	-9	7-6	.976	3	113	114	2-38,S-34/3-6,D-8	-0.2
1981	†NY A	61	163	24	51	7	2	1	12	9-2	1	14	.313	.351	.399	118	3	2-0	.955	-2	89	84	S-39,2-14/3-3,D-3	0.6
1982	NY A	14	27	2	4	1	0	0	0	1-0	0	4	.148	.179	.185	0	-4	0-1	.917	-2	62	0	/S-9,2-3,3-3	-0.5
	Min A	29	98	9	23	1	1	0	1	7-0	0	8	.235	.283	.265	51	-7	1-1	.981	-7	76	82	2-26	-1.3
	Cle A	82	291	29	80	11	4	2	25	12-0	2	20	.275	.301	.361	83	-7	2-5	.981	-3	99	83	2-63,S-21/3-9,D	-0.7
	Year	125	416	40	107	13	5	2	26	20-0	2	32	.257	.289	.327	70	-18	3-7	.979	-12	93	87	2-92,S-30,3-12/D	-2.5
1983	Phi N	41	66	3	16	0	1	0	4	4-0	0	7	.242	.282	.273	56	-4	2-1	.963	-3	83	39	2-27/S-8,3-3	-0.6
	NY A	31	70	5	14	4	0	0	2	5-0	1	10	.200	.263	.257	46	-5	1-1	1.000	2	104	85	2-19/S-6,3-4	-0.2
1984	Sea A	79	211	22	56	5	1	1	22	12-0	0	16	.265	.304	.313	72	-8	0-2	.900	-7	74	87	3-40,2-14/S-5,D-6	-1.6
Total	11	989	2448	290	623	71	24	11	184	133-10	9	176	.254	.293	.317	70	-105	41-33	.974	-10	102	98	2-471,S-280,3-112/D-29,O-4(LF)	-8.2
MILES, AARON Aaron Wade B 12.15.1976 Pittsburg, CA BB/TR 5-8/170# d9.11																								
2003	Chi A	8	12	3	4	3	0	0	2	0-0	0	0	.333	.333	.583	134	1	0-0	1.000	0	130	0	/2-3,D-2	0.1
MILES, DON Donald Ray B 3.13.1936 Indianapolis, IN BL/TR 6-1/210# d9.9																								
1958	LA N	8	22	2	4	0	0	0	0	0-0	1	6	.182	.217	.182	7	-3	0-0	1.000	1	140	0	/O-5(LF)	-0.3
MILES, DEE Wilson Daniel B 2.15.1909 Kellerman, AL D 11.2.1976 Birmingham, AL BL/TR 6/175# d7.7																								
1935	Was A	60	215	28	57	5	2	0	29	7	1	13	.265	.291	.307	57	-15	6-4	.970	1	102	129	O-45(RF)	-1.6
1936	Was A	25	59	8	14	1	2	0	7	1	0	5	.237	.250	.322	43	-6	0-1	.958	0	103	102	O-10(1-0-9)	-0.6
1939	Phi A	106	320	49	96	17	6	1	37	15	0	17	.300	.331	.400	88	-7	3-4	.968	-3	96	72	O-77(1-20-57)	-1.3
1940	Phi A	88	236	26	71	9	6	1	23	8	1	18	.301	.327	.403	90	-5	1-1	.945	0	106	82	O-50(15-18-18)	-0.7
1941	Phi A	80	170	14	53	7	1	0	15	4	1	8	.312	.331	.365	86	-4	0-1	1.000	2	115	73	O-35(25-2-8)	-0.4
1942	Phi A	99	346	41	94	12	5	0	22	12	2	10	.272	.300	.335	79	-11	5-3	.984	0	99	109	O-81(9-46-28)	-1.5
1943	Bos A	45	121	9	26	2	2	0	10	3	0	3	.215	.234	.264	45	-9	0-2	.968	-1	89	159	O-25(1-24-0)	-1.2
Total	7	503	1467	175	411	53	24	2	143	50	5	74	.280	.306	.353	76	-57	15-16	.971	1	101	100	O-323(52-110-165)	-7.3
MILEY, MIKE Michael Wilfred B 3.30.1953 Yazoo City, MS D 1.6.1977 Baton Rouge, LA BB/TR (BR 1975 (part)) 6-1/185# d7.6																								
1975	Cal A	70	224	17	39	3	2	4	26	16-0	1	54	.174	.230	.259	42	-19	0-1	.939	-9	86	123	S-70	-2.0
1976	Cal A	14	38	4	7	2	0	0	4	4-1	0	8	.184	.256	.237	50	-2	1-0	.981	-3	74	122	S-14	-0.3
Total	2	84	262	21	46	5	2	4	30	20-1	1	62	.176	.234	.256	43	-21	1-1	.945	-11	84	123	/S-84	-2.3
MILLAN, FELIX Felix Bernardo (Martinez) B 8.21.1943 Yabucoa, P.R. BR/TR 5-11/172# d6.2																								
1966	Atl N	37	91	20	25	6	0	0	5	2-2	0	6	.275	.290	.341	74	-3	3-1	.973	-4	90	85	2-25/S3	-0.5
1967	Atl N	41	136	13	32	3	3	2	6	4-1	2	10	.235	.266	.346	75	-5	0-3	.972	2	112	97	2-41	-0.1
1968	Atl N	149	570	49	165	22	2	1	33	22-7	6	26	.289	.321	.340	99	-1	6-6	.980	-3	101	109	*2-145	0.9
1969	†Atl N★	**162**	652	98	174	23	5	6	57	34-5	8	35	.267	.310	.345	83	-16	14-3	**.980**	-18	94	76	*2-162	-2.1
1970	Atl N✱	142	590	100	183	25	5	2	37	35-2	5	23	.310	.352	.380	91	-7	16-5	.979	-11	89	95	*2-142	-0.7
1971	Atl N★	143	577	65	167	20	8	2	45	37-7	3	22	.289	.332	.362	92	-6	11-7	.982	6	101	119	*2-141	0.9
1972	Atl N	125	498	46	128	19	3	1	38	23-1	3	28	.257	.292	.313	66	-22	6-4	.987	-11	96	84	*2-120	-2.8
1973	†NY N	153	638	82	185	23	4	3	37	35-3	6	22	.290	.332	.353	91	-8	2-2	.989	4	95	102	*2-153	0.6
1974	NY N	136	518	50	139	15	2	1	33	31-2	8	14	.268	.317	.311	78	-16	5-1	.979	-10	87	96	*2-134	-1.7
1975	NY N	**162**	676	81	191	37	2	1	56	36-2	**12**	28	.283	.329	.348	92	-7	1-6	.972	-23	86	89	*2-162	-2.3
1976	NY N	139	531	55	150	25	2	1	35	41-5	7	19	.282	.341	.343	101	1	2-4	.977	-15	84	90	*2-136	-0.6
1977	NY N	91	314	40	78	11	2	2	21	18-3	3	9	.248	.294	.315	67	-15	1-1	.977	-9	83	92	2-89	-2.0
Total	12	1480	5791	699	1617	229	38	22	403	318-40	63	242	.279	.322	.343	87	-105	67-43	.980	-90	93	95	*2-1450/3S	-10.4
MILLAR, KEVIN Kevin Charles B 9.24.1971 Los Angeles, CA BR/TR 6-1/195# d4.11																								
1998	Fla N	2	2	1	1	0	0	0	0	1-0	0	0	.500	.667	.500	224	1	0-0	.833	1	221	704	/3-2	0.1
1999	Fla N	105	351	48	100	17	4	9	67	40-2	7	64	.285	.362	.433	108	5	1-0	.995	-4	87	105	1-94/3O(LF)	-0.7
2000	Fla N	123	259	36	67	14	3	14	42	36-0	8	47	.259	.364	.498	121	8	0-0	.989	6	159	79	1-34,O-18(17-0-1),3-13/D-6	1.1
2001	Fla N	144	449	62	141	39	5	20	85	39-2	5	70	.314	.374	.557	141	28	0-0	.986	-7	92	38	O-86(27-0-66),1-15,3-10/D-6	1.5
2002	Fla N	126	438	58	134	41	0	16	57	40-0	5	74	.306	.366	.509	138	22	0-2	.985	0	97	92	*O-108(89-0-22)/1-2,3-2,D-6	1.8
2003	†Bos A	148	544	83	150	30	1	25	96	60-5	5	108	.276	.348	.472	112	10	3-2	.996	6	115	98	*1-101,O-31(19-0-12),D-19	0.5
Total	6	648	2043	288	593	141	13	84	347	216-9	30	363	.290	.362	.495	124	74	4-4	.995	3	107	98	1-246,O-244(153-0-101)/D-37,3-28	4.3
MILLARD, FRANK Frank E. B 7.4.1865 E.St.Louis, IL D 7.4.1892 Dallas, TX d5.4																								
1890	StL AA	1	1	0	0	0	0	0	0	1	0		.000	.500	.000	42	0	0	.625	-0	153	0	/2	0.0
MILLER, CORKY Abraham Philip B 3.18.1976 Yucaipa, CA BR/TR 6-1/225# d9.4																								
2001	Cin N	17	49	5	9	2	0	3	7	4-0	2	16	.184	.263	.408	70	-2	1-0	.991	3	108	186	C-17	0.2
2002	Cin N	39	114	9	29	10	0	3	15	9-2	4	20	.254	.328	.421	97	-1	0-0	.992	5	138	78	C-38	0.6
2003	Cin N	14	30	4	8	0	0	0	1	5-0	2	7	.267	.395	.267	82	0	0-0	1.000	-0	45	99	C-11	0.0
Total	3	70	193	18	46	12	0	6	23	18-2	8	43	.238	.323	.394	88	-3	1-0	.993	8	116	110	/C-66	0.8
MILLER, DUSTY Charles Bradley B 9.10.1868 Oil City, PA D 9.3.1945 Memphis, TN BL/TR 5-11.5/170# d9.23																								
1889	Bal AA	11	40	4	6	1	1	0	6	2	1	11	.150	.209	.225	23	-4	3	.636	-8	69	0	/S-8,O-3(2-1-0)	-1.0
1890	StL AA	26	96	17	21	5	3	1	10	8	0		.219	.279	.365	78	-4	4	.872	3	195	351	O-24(9-15-0)/S-3	-0.2
1895	Cin N	**132**	529	103	177	31	16	10	112	33	4	34	.335	.378	.510	123	15	43	.937	10	129	183	*O-132(0-11-121)	1.5
1896	Cin N	125	504	91	162	38	12	4	93	33	4	30	.321	.368	.468	112	7	76	.902	-2	120	173	*O-125(1-0-124)	-0.1
1897	Cin N	119	440	83	139	27	1	4	70	48	8		.316	.393	.409	105	5	29	.929	2	108	64	*O-119(RF)	0.1
1898	Cin N	152	586	99	175	24	12	3	90	38	9		.299	.351	.396	106	3	32	.929	5	106	79	*O-152(RF)	0.0
1899	Cin N	81	327	45	83	12	6	0	37	9	3		.254	.280	.327	65	-17	18	.927	6	144	123	O-81(1-2-79)	-1.4
	StL N	10	39	3	8	1	0	0	3	3	1		.205	.279	.231	40	-3	1	.875	-1	64	249	O-10(CF)	-0.5
	Year	91	366	48	91	13	6	0	40	12	4		.249	.280	.317	62	-20	19	.921	4	135	137	O-91(1-12-79)	-1.9
Total	7	656	2561	445	771	139	51	22	421	174	30	75	.301	.353	.421	103	2	206	.923	15	121	133	O-646(13-39-595)/S-11	-1.6
MILLER, BRUCE Charles Bruce B 3.4.1947 Fort Wayne, IN BR/TR 6-1/185# d8.4																								
1973	SF N	12	21	1	3	0	0	0	2	2-1	0	3	.143	.217	.143	2	-3	0-0	.900	0	124	0	/3-4,2-3,S	-0.3
1974	SF N	73	198	19	55	7	1	0	16	11-2	1	15	.278	.316	.323	76	-6	1-1	.938	8	138	46	3-41,S-13/2-9	0.4
1975	SF N	99	309	22	74	6	3	1	31	15-0	1	26	.239	.275	.288	55	-20	0-1	.949	5	97	101	3-68,2-21/S-6	-1.5
1976	SF N	12	25	1	4	1	0	0	2	2-1	0	5	.160	.222	.200	20	-3	0-0	.920	-3	93	83	/2-8,3-2	-0.5
Total	4	196	553	43	136	14	4	1	51	30-4	2	49	.246	.285	.291	59	-32	1-2	.944	11	111	78	3-115/2-41,S-20	-1.9
MILLER, CHARLIE Charles Elmer B 1.4.1892 Warrensburg, MO D 4.23.1972 Warrensburg, MO TR d9.18																								
1912	StL A	1	2	0	0	0	0	0	0	0	0		.000	.000	.000	-99	-1	0	1.000	0	142	0	/S	0.0
MILLER, CHARLIE Charles Hess B 12.30.1877 Conestoga, PA D 1.13.1951 Millersville, PA BR/TR 6/190# d10.2																								
1915	Bal F	1	1	0	0	0	0	0	0	0	0	0	.000	.000	.000	-97	0	0	—	0			H	0.0
MILLER, CHUCK Charles Marion B 9.18.1889 Woodville, OH D 6.16.1961 Houston, TX BL/TL 5-8.5/155# d9.19																								
1913	StL N	4	12	0	2	0	0	0	1	0	0	2	.167	.167	.167	-5	-2	0	1.000	-0	85	0	/O-3(2-0-1)	-0.2
1914	StL N	36	36	4	7	1	0	0	2	3	0	9	.194	.256	.222	43	-3	2	1.000	1	107	153	O-14(6-5-2)	-0.2
Total	2	40	48	4	9	1	0	0	3	3	0	11	.188	.235	.208	31	-5	2	1.000	0	100	103	/O-17(8-5-3)	-0.4
MILLER, DUSTY Dakin Evans B 9.3.1876 Malvern, IA D 4.19.1950 Stockton, CA BL/TR 5-10/175# d4.17																								
1902	Chi N	51	187	17	46	4	1	0	13	7	7		.246	.299	.278	80	-4	10	.955	2	132	0	O-51(46-1-4)	-0.6
MILLER, DAMIAN Damian Donald B 10.13.1969 LaCrosse, WI BR/TR 6-3/202# d8.10																								
1997	Min A	25	66	5	18	1	0	2	13	2-0	0	12	.273	.282	.379	73	-3	0-0	1.000	-2	249	61	C-20/D-3	-0.3
1998	Ari N	57	168	17	48	14	2	3	14	11-2	2	43	.286	.337	.446	104	1	1-0	.986	1	121	94	C-46/O-2(RF),1D	0.5

Year	Tm Lg	G	AB	R	H	2B	3B	HR	RBI	BB-IB	HP	SO	AVG	OBP	SLG	AOPS	ABR	SB-CS	FA	FR	Rng	Thr	G at Pos	BFW
1999	Ari N	86	296	35	80	19	0	11	47	19-3	2	78	.270	.316	.446	90	-5	0-0	.991	16	90	143	C-86	1.5
2000	Ari N	100	324	43	89	24	0	10	44	36-4	1	74	.275	.347	.441	95	-2	2-2	.992	0	111	127	C-97/1-2,S	0.4
2001	†Ari N	123	380	45	103	19	0	13	47	35-9	4	80	.271	.337	.424	90	-5	0-1	.993	29	92	126	*C-121	2.9
2002	†Ari N★	101	297	40	74	22	0	11	42	38-5	3	88	.249	.340	.434	97	-2	0-0	**.997**	11	122	108	*C-100	1.5
2003	†Chi N	114	352	34	82	19	1	9	36	39-6	1	91	.233	.310	.369	78	-12	1-0	.997	21	126	113	*C-114	1.6
Total	7	606	1883	219	494	118	3	59	243	180-29	13	466	.262	.329	.422	90	-28	4-3	.994	77	113	119	C-584/D-5,1-3,O-2(RF),S	8.1

MILLER, DARRELL Darrell Keith B 2.26.1958 Washington, DC BR/TR 6-2/200# d8.14

1984	Cal A	17	41	5	7	0	0	0	1	4-0	0	9	.171	.244	.171	17	-5	0-0	.990	-1	76	114	1-16/O(LF)	-0.7
1985	Cal A	51	48	8	18	2	1	2	7	1-0	1	10	.375	.400	.583	166	4	0-1	.952	2	126	205	O-45(1-3-41)/C3D	0.5
1986	Cal A	33	57	6	13	2	1	0	4	4-0	0	8	.228	.274	.298	58	-3	0-0	1.000	-5	41	0	O-23(11-3-9),C-10/D-2	-0.9
1987	Cal A	53	108	14	26	5	0	4	16	9-0	2	13	.241	.303	.398	89	-2	1-0	.984	0	171	144	C-33,O-18(14-0-4)/3D	-0.1
1988	Cal A	70	140	21	31	4	1	2	7	9-0	5	29	.221	.292	.307	70	-6	2-1	.987	1	99	113	C-53/O-8(7-2-0),D	-0.3
Total	5	224	394	54	95	13	3	8	35	27-0	8	69	.241	.300	.350	80	-12	3-2	.987	-3	118	120	/C-97,O-95(34-8-54),1-16,D-8,3-2	-1.5

MILLER, BING Edmund John B 8.30.1894 Vinton, IA D 5.7.1966 Philadelphia, PA BR/TR 6/185# d4.16 C17 b-Ralph

1921	Was A	114	420	57	121	28	8	9	71	25	4	50	.288	.334	.457	105	1	3-4	.945	-0	102	89	*O-109(92-3-14)	-0.8
1922	Phi A	143	535	90	179	29	12	21	90	24	7	42	.335	.371	.551	134	23	10-10	.977	5	102	132	*O-139(15-90-36)	1.9
1923	Phi A	123	458	68	137	25	4	12	64	27	4	34	.299	.344	.450	106	2	9-3	.978	-2	103	67	*O-119(104-0-15)	-0.8
1924	Phi A	113	398	62	136	22	4	6	62	12	10	24	.342	.376	.462	114	7	11-5	.973	-3	94	89	O-94(10-9-75)/1-7	-0.2
1925	Phi A	124	474	78	151	29	10	10	81	19	8	14	.319	.355	.485	105	1	11-6	.975	-8	89	60	*O-115(22-0-96),1-12	-1.6
1926	Phi A	38	110	13	32	6	2	2	13	11	0	6	.291	.355	.436	100	0	4-1	1.000	-2	99	34	O-34(10-0-26)/1	-0.3
	StL A	94	353	60	117	27	5	4	50	22	7	12	.331	.382	.470	116	8	7-9	.939	2	108	116	O-94(26-16-54)	0.2
	Year	132	463	73	149	33	7	6	63	33	7	18	.322	.376	.462	112	8	11-10	.950	1	106	97	*O-128(36-16-80)/1	-0.1
1927	StL A	143	492	83	160	32	7	5	75	30	9	26	.325	.375	.449	109	6	8-7	.970	3	111	72	*O-126(37-61-29)	0.1
1928	Phi A	139	510	76	168	34	7	8	85	27	**8**	24	.329	.372	.471	117	12	10-6	.968	-1	107	60	*O-133(28-43-66)	0.2
1929	†Phi A	147	556	84	184	32	16	8	93	40	4	25	.331	.380	.489	118	13	24-10	.970	-1	107	64	*O-145(9-4-133)	0.2
1930	†Phi A	**154**	585	89	177	38	7	9	100	47	3	22	.303	.357	.438	96	-3	13-13	.976	4	**111**	78	*O-154(0-13-142)	-1.2
1931	†Phi A	137	534	75	150	43	5	8	77	36	**10**	16	.281	.338	.425	94	-5	5-3	.987	5	**115**	55	*O-137(RF)	-0.8
1932	Phi A	95	305	40	90	17	4	7	58	20	2	11	.295	.343	.446	99	-1	7-3	.979	4	118	52	O-84(5-0-79)	-0.2
1933	Phi A	67	120	22	33	7	1	2	17	12	1	7	.275	.346	.400	96	-1	4-2	1.000	-1	99	57	O-30(10-3-18)/1-6	-0.2
1934	Phi A	81	177	22	43	10	2	1	22	16	1	14	.243	.309	.339	70	-8	1-0	1.000	0	101	70	O-46(4-0-42)	-1.0
1935	Bos A	78	138	18	42	8	1	3	26	10	1	8	.304	.356	.442	99	-1	0-1	.962	-0	101	99	O-29(1-0-28)	-0.2
1936	Bos A	30	47	9	14	2	1	1	6	5	1	5	.298	.377	.447	97	0	0-0	1.000	0	88	141	O-13(7-0-7)	-0.1
Total	16	1820	6212	946	1934	389	96	116	990	383	80	340	.311	.359	.461	108	54	127-83	.971	5	105	77	*O-1601(380-242-997)/1-26	-4.8

MILLER, EDDIE Edward Lee B 6.29.1957 San Pablo, CA BB/TR 5-9/175# d9.5

1977	Tex A	17	6	7	2	0	0	0	1	1-0	0	1	.333	.429	.333	110	0	3-1	1.000	-0	88	0	/O-2(CF),D-3	0.0
1978	Atl N	6	21	5	3	1	0	0	2	2-0	1	4	.143	.250	.190	22	-2	3-0	1.000	-2	53	0	/O-5(2-3-0)	-0.3
1979	Atl N	27	113	12	35	1	0	0	5	5-1	2	24	.310	.350	.319	78	-3	15-2	.988	1	114	50	O-27(1-27-0)	0.0
1980	Atl N	11	19	3	3	0	0	0	0	0-0	0	5	.158	.158	.158	-11	-3	1-2	1.000	-2	46	0	/O-9(1-8-0)	-0.6
1981	Atl N	50	134	29	31	3	1	0	7	7-1	3	29	.231	.285	.269	56	-8	23-5	.985	-0	101	72	O-36(28-2-7)	-0.7
1982	Det A	14	25	3	1	0	0	0	0	4-0	3	4	.040	.250	.040	-14	-4	0-3	1.000	-0	80	195	/O-8(0-3-5),D	-0.6
1984	SD N	13	14	4	4	0	1	1	2	0-0	0	4	.286	.286	.643	155	1	4-0	1.000	1	62	828	/O-8(0-4-4)	0.2
Total	7	138	332	63	79	5	2	1	17	19-2	9	71	.238	.297	.274	57	-19	49-13	.989	-3	95	98	/O-95(32-49-16),D-4	-2.0

MILLER, EDDIE Edward Robert "Eppie" B 11.26.1916 Pittsburgh, PA D 7.31.1997 Lake Worth, FL BR/TR 5-9/180# d9.9

1936	Cin N	5	10	0	1	0	0	0	0	1	0	1	.100	.182	.100	-24	-2	0	.938	-1	112	54	/S-4,2	-0.2
1937	Cin N	36	60	3	9	3	1	0	5	3	0	8	.150	.190	.233	15	-7	0	.926	3	107	126	S-30/3-4	-0.3
1939	Bos N	77	296	32	79	12	2	4	31	16	5	21	.267	.315	.361	88	-6	4	.970	10	106	141	S-77	1.0
1940	Bos N★	151	569	78	157	33	3	14	79	41	5	43	.276	.330	.418	111	8	8	**.970**	15	99	**118**	*S-151	3.4
1941	Bos N★	154	585	54	140	27	3	6	68	35	5	72	.239	.288	.326	76	-20	8	**.966**	13	104	**120**	*S-154	0.4
1942	Bos N★	142	534	47	130	28	2	6	47	22	4	42	.243	.279	.337	81	-15	11	**.983**	6	**105**	93	*S-142	0.2
1943	Cin N★	154	576	49	129	26	4	2	71	33	4	43	.224	.271	.293	64	-28	8	**.979**	**24**	105	130	*S-154	0.9
1944	Cin N✳	**155**	536	48	112	21	5	4	55	41	3	41	.209	.269	.289	59	-30	9	.971	12	**106**	125	*S-155	-0.6
1945	Cin N	115	421	46	100	27	2	13	49	18	4	38	.238	.275	.404	89	-9	4	**.975**	6	105	95	*S-115	0.7
1946	Cin N✳	91	299	30	58	10	0	6	36	25	1	34	.194	.258	.288	57	-18	5	.970	16	111	161	S-88	0.3
1947	Cin N✳	151	545	69	146	**38**	4	19	87	49	4	40	.268	.333	.457	109	5	5	.972	-6	94	91	*S-151	0.8
1948	Phi N	130	468	45	115	20	1	14	61	19	4	40	.246	.281	.382	79	-16	1	.966	-12	93	89	*S-122	-2.1
1949	Phi N	85	266	21	55	10	1	6	29	29	4	21	.207	.294	.320	66	-13	1	.986	-11	86	104	2-82/S	-2.0
1950	StL N	64	172	17	39	8	0	3	22	19	1	21	.227	.307	.326	64	-9	0	.980	10	120	96	S-51/2	0.3
Total	14	1510	5337	539	1270	263	28	97	640	351	44	465	.238	.290	.352	80	-160	64	.972	85	103	114	*S-1395/2-84,3-4	2.8

MILLER, ED Edwin J. "Big Ed" B 11.24.1888 Annville, PA D 4.17.1980 S.Lebanon Twsp, PA BR/TR 6/180# d6.29

1912	StL A	13	46	4	9	1	0	0	5	2	1		.196	.245	.217	34	-4	1	.951	-4	43	75	/1-8,S-5	-0.8
1914	StL A	41	58	8	8	0	1	0	4	4	2	13	.138	.219	.172	18	-6	1-3	.981	-2	66	162	/1-8,2-5,O-5(RF),3-2	-1.0
1918	Cle A	32	96	9	22	4	3	0	3	12	1	10	.229	.321	.333	89	-1	2	.977	2	126	118	1-22/O-4(1-0-3)	0.0
Total	3	86	200	21	39	5	4	0	12	18	4	23	.195	.275	.260	58	-11	4-3	.972	-4	99	114	/1-38,O-9(1-0-8),2-5,S-5,3-2	-1.8

MILLER, ELMER Elmer B 7.28.1890 Sandusky, OH D 11.28.1944 Beloit, WI BR/TR 6/175# d4.26

1912	StL N	12	37	5	7	1	0	0	3	4	0	9	.189	.268	.216	34	-3	1	1.000	1	118	66	O-11(4-3-4)	-0.3
1915	NY A	26	83	4	12	1	0	0	3	4	1	14	.145	.193	.157	5	-10	0	.955	-2	92	34	O-26(0-20-6)	-1.5
1916	NY A	43	152	12	34	3	2	1	18	11	1	18	.224	.280	.289	70	-6	8	.969	4	101	161	O-42(18-9-15)	-0.5
1917	NY A	114	379	43	95	11	3	3	35	40	**9**	44	.251	.336	.319	99	1	11	.961	-4	91	108	*O-112(33-53-26)	-1.0
1918	NY A	67	202	18	49	9	2	1	22	19	3	17	.243	.317	.322	91	-2	4	.947	2	99	141	O-62(3-53-6)	-0.6
1921	†NY A	56	242	41	72	9	8	4	36	19	3	16	.298	.356	.450	102	0	2-2	.947	-1	91	133	O-56(CF)	-0.4
1922	NY A	51	172	31	46	7	2	3	18	11	0	12	.267	.311	.384	79	-6	2-3	.982	1	95	150	O-51(7-41-3)	-0.8
	Bos A	44	147	16	28	2	3	4	16	5	1	10	.190	.222	.327	42	-14	3-1	.957	-1	97	82	O-35(2-33-0)	-1.6
	Year	95	319	47	74	9	5	7	34	16	1	22	.232	.271	.357	62	-20	5-4	.970	-0	96	120	O-86(9-74-3)	-2.4
Total	7	413	1414	170	343	43	20	16	151	113	18	140	.243	.307	.335	80	-40	31-6	.960	-2	95	121	O-395(67-268-60)	-6.7

MILLER, ELMER Elmer Joseph "Lefty" B 4.17.1903 Detroit, MI D 1.8.1987 Corona, CA BL/TL 5-11/189# d6.21 ▲

1929	Phi N	31	38	3	9	1	0	1	4	1	0	5	.237	.256	.342	44	-4	0	.750	2	82	0	/P-8,O-4(RF)	-0.1

MILLER, KOHLY Frank A. B 1.1874 Cumru Township, PA D 3.29.1951 Reading, PA d9.16

1892	Was N	1	3	0	0	0	0	0	0	0	0	1	.000	.000	.000	-99	-1	0	.400	-1	74	0	/S	-0.2
	StL N	1	4	0	0	0	0	0	0	0	0	0	.000	.000	.000	-99	-1	0	.500	-1	0	0	/3	-0.2
	Year	2	7	0	0	0	0	0	0	0	0	1	.000	.000	.000	-99	-2	0	.400	-2	74	0	/S3	-0.4
1897	Phi N	3	11	2	2	0	0	0	1	2	0		.182	.308	.182	32	-1	0	.857	-2	45	104	/2-3	-0.3
Total	2	5	18	2	2	0	0	0	1	2	0	1	.111	.200	.111	-13	-3	0	.857	-4	45	104	/2-3,3S	-0.7

MILLER, GEORGE George C. B 2.19.1853 Newport, KY D 7.24.1929 Norwood, OH BR/TR 5-5/160# d9.6

1877	Cin N	11	37	4	6	1	0	0	3	5		2	.162	.262	.189	50	-1		.918	-0			C-11	-0.1
1884	Cin AA	6	20	6	5	1	1	0	3	1	1		.250	.318	.400	127	1		.975	2			/C-6	0.3
Total	2	17	57	10	11	2	1	0	6	6	1	2	.193	.281	.263	79	0		.938	2			/C-17	0.2

MILLER, DOGGIE George Frederick "Foghorn" or "Calliope" B 8.15.1864 Brooklyn, NY D 4.6.1909 Brooklyn, NY BR/TR 5-6/145# d5.1 M1 OF Total (146-LF 68-CF 96-RF)

1884	Pit AA	89	347	46	78	10	2	0		13	2		.225	.257	.265	71	-10		.798	-2	131	56	O-49(48-0-1),C-36/3-3,2	-1.0
1885	Pit AA	42	166	19	27	3	1	0	13	4	0		.163	.182	.193	19	-15		.893	-6			C-33/O-6(3-3-0),S-2,3-2	-1.6
1886	Pit AA	83	317	70	80	15	1	2	36	43	1		.252	.343	.325	110	6	35	.918	-14			C-61,O-22(12-10-1)/2	-0.3
1887	Pit N	87	342	58	83	17	4	1	34	35	2	13	.243	.317	.325	85	-5	33	.928	-20			C-73,O-14(2-11-1)/3	-1.7
1888	Pit N	103	404	50	112	17	5	0	36	18	7	16	.277	.319	.344	122	11	27	.908	-12			C-68,O-32(25-5-2)/3-4	0.4
1889	Pit N	104	422	77	113	25	3	6	56	31	2	11	.268	.321	.384	107	3	16	.889	-7			C-76,O-27(6-5-16)/3-3	0.2
1890	Pit N	**138**	549	85	150	24	3	4	66	68	4	11	.273	.357	.350	120	19	32	.850	4	121	100	3-88,O-25(1-2-22),S-13,C-10/2-6	2.3
1891	Pit N	135	548	80	156	19	6	4	57	59	3	26	.285	.357	.363	113	10	35	.938	-9	*105*	*110*	C-41,*S*-37,3-34,O-24(22-0-2)/1	0.5
1892	Pit N	149	623	103	158	15	12	2	59	69	7	14	.254	.335	.326	99	0	28	.906	1	98	91	O-76(24-30-23),C-63,S-19/3-2	0.3

Year	Tm Lg	G	AB	R	H	2B	3B	HR	RBI	BB-IB	HP	SO	AVG	OBP	SLG	AOPS	ABR	SB-CS	FA	FR	Rng	Thr	G at Pos	BFW
1893	Pit N	41	154	23	28	6	1	0	17	17	5	8	.182	.284	.234	39	-13	3	.916	-1	*98*	*100*	C-40	-0.9
1894	StL N	127	481	93	163	9	11	8	86	58	4	9	.339	.414	.453	109	8	17	.832	-11	90	73	3-52,C-41,2-18,1-12/O-4(2-0-2),SM	0.1
1895	StL N	122	494	81	144	15	4	5	74	25	6	12	.291	.333	.368	82	-14	18	.829	-21	81	74	3-46,C-47,O-21(RF)/S-9,1-6	-2.6
1896	Lou N	98	324	54	89	17	4	1	33	27	2	9	.275	.334	.361	86	-6	16	.922	-11	*78*	*118*	C-48,2-25/O-8(1-2-5),3-8,1-3,S-2	-1.1
Total	13	1318	5171	839	1381	192	57	33	567	467	45	129	.267	.333	.345	97	-6	260	.918	-108	*43*	*48*	C-637,O-308L,3-243/S-83,2-51,1	-5.4
MILLER, HUGHIE Hugh Stanley "Cotton" B 12.28.1887 St.Louis, MO D 12.24.1945 Jefferson Barracks, MO BR/TR 6-1.5/175# d6.18																								
1911	Phi N	1	0	0	0	0	0	0	0	0	0	0	—	—	—	—	0	0	—	0			R	0.0
1914	StL F	132	490	51	109	20	5	0	46	27	1	57	.222	.264	.284	47	-44	4	.990	0	95	68	*1-130	-5.1
1915	StL F	7	6	0	3	1	0	0	3	0	0	0	.500	.500	.667	216	1	0	1.000	-0	0	0	/1-6	0.1
Total	3	140	496	51	112	21	5	0	49	27	1	57	.226	.267	.288	49	-43	4	.990	-0	94	67	1-136	-5.0
MILLER, JAKE Jacob George (born Jacob George Muenzing) B 12.1.1895 Baltimore, MD D 8.24.1974 Towson, MD BR/TR 5-10/170# d7.15																								
1922	Pit N	3	11	0	1	0	0	0	0	2	0	0	.091	.231	.091	-14	-2	1-0	.889	-0	114	0	/O-3(RF)	-0.2
MILLER, HACK James Eldridge B 2.13.1913 Celeste, TX D 11.21.1966 Dallas, TX BR/TR 5-11.5/215# d4.18																								
1944	Det A	5	5	1	1	0	0	1	3	1	0	1	.200	.333	.800	207	1	0-0	1.000	0	*0*	*269*	/C-5	0.1
1945	Det A	2	4	0	3	0	0	0	1	0	0	0	.750	.750	.750	315	1	0-0	1.000	0	*0*	*0*	/C-2	0.1
Total	2	7	9	1	4	0	0	1	4	1	0	1	.444	.500	.778	250	2	0-0	1.000	1	*0*	*152*	/C-7	0.2
MILLER, JIM James McCurdy "Rabbit" B 10.2.1880 Pittsburgh, PA D 2.7.1937 Pittsburgh, PA BR/TR 5-8/165# d9.9																								
1901	NY N	18	58	3	8	0	0	0	3	6	0		.138	.219	.138	5	-7	1	.936	-2	99	98	2-18	-0.9
MILLER, JOHN John Allen B 3.14.1944 Alhambra, CA BR/TR 5-11/195# d9.11																								
1966	NY A	6	23	1	2	0	0	1	2	0-0	0	9	.087	.087	.217	-16	-4	0-0	1.000	-1	0	63	/1-3,O-3(LF)	-0.5
1969	LA N	26	38	3	8	1	0	1	1	2-0	0	9	.211	.250	.316	62	-2	0-0	1.000	-2	18	0	/O-6(LF),1-5,3-2,2	-0.5
Total	2	32	61	4	10	1	0	2	3	2-0	0	18	.164	.190	.279	33	-6	0-0	1.000	-3	48	0	/O-9(LF),1-8,3-2,2	-1.0
MILLER, DOTS John Barney B 9.9.1886 Kearny, NJ D 9.5.1923 Saranac Lake, NY BR/TR 5-11.5/170# d4.16 Mil 1918																								
1909	†Pit N	151	560	71	156	31	13	3	87	39	3		.279	.329	.396	115	8	14	**.953**	-12	102	113	*2-150	-0.3
1910	Pit N	120	444	45	101	13	10	1	48	33	2	41	.227	.284	.309	69	-19	11	.946	-15	95	93	*2-119/1S	-3.5
1911	Pit N	137	470	82	126	17	8	6	78	51	7	48	.268	.348	.377	99	-1	17	.943	-3	98	**137**	*2-129	-0.1
1912	Pit N	148	567	74	156	33	12	4	87	37	4	45	.275	.324	.397	98	-4	18	.985	-0	102	**124**	*1-147	-0.8
1913	Pit N	154	580	75	158	24	20	7	90	37	1	52	.272	.317	.419	114	7	20-13	.985	-4	92	86	*1-150/S-3	-0.2
1914	StL N	155	573	67	166	27	10	4	88	34	9	52	.290	.339	.393	119	12	16	.993	-6	107	97	1-91,S-60/2-5	0.9
1915	StL N	150	553	73	146	17	10	2	72	43	6	48	.264	.324	.342	101	0	27-19	.991	3	99	102	1-94,2-55/3-9,S-3	0.2
1916	StL N	143	505	47	120	22	7	1	46	40	5	49	.238	.300	.315	89	-6	18	.993	7	98	110	1-93,2-38,S-21/3	0.0
1917	StL N	148	544	61	135	15	9	2	45	33	3	52	.248	.295	.320	91	-7	14	.960	17	112	135	2-92,1-46,S-11	1.3
1919	StL N	101	346	38	80	10	4	1	24	13	3	23	.231	.265	.292	72	-13	6	.981	3	107	93	1-68,2-28	-1.3
1920	Phi N	98	343	41	87	12	2	1	27	16	1	17	.254	.289	.309	68	-14	13-6	.948	-7	87	115	2-59,3-17,S-12/1-9,O(CF)	-2.0
1921	Phi N	84	320	37	95	11	3	0	23	15	1	27	.297	.330	.350	74	-11	3-5	.940	3	110	132	3-41,1-38/2-6	-0.9
Total	12	1589	5805	711	1526	232	108	32	715	391	45	454	.263	.314	.357	95	-48	177-43	.988	-14	101	104	1-737,2-681,S-111/3-68,O(CF)	-6.7
MILLER, JOE Joseph A. B 2.17.1861 Baltimore, MD D 4.23.1928 Wheeling, WV BR 5-9.5/165# d5.1																								
1884	Tol AA	105	423	46	101	12	8	1		26	1		.239	.284	.312	91	-4		.864	2	98	102	*S-105	0.0
1885	Lou AA	98	339	44	62	9	5	0	24	28	2		.183	.249	.239	55	-17		.891	2	102	104	*S-79,3-11/2-8	-1.1
Total	2	203	762	90	163	21	13	1	24	54	3		.214	.269	.280	75	-21		.876	4	100	103	S-184/3-11,2-8	-1.1
MILLER, JOE Joseph Wick B 7.24.1850 , Germany D 8.30.1891 White Bear Lake, MN 5-10.5/169# d6.26																								
1872	Nat NA	1	4	0	1	0	0	0	0	0		0	.250	.250	.250	46	0	0-0	.923	-0	0	0	/1	0.0
1875	Wes NA	**13**	50	4	6	1	0	0	0	0		3	.120	.120	.140	-9	-5	0-0	.870	5	107	109	2-13	-0.1
	Chi NA	15	54	1	8	0	0	0	1	0		7	.148	.148	.148	3	-5	0-0	.788	-3	100	54	2-14/O(1-0-1)	-0.8
	Year	28	104	5	14	1	0	0	1	0		10	.135	.135	.144	-3	-11	0-0	.832	2	104	82	2-27/O(1-0-1)	-0.9
Total	2 NA	29	108	5	15	1	0	0	1	0		10	.139	.139	.148	-1	-10	0-0	.832	2	104	82	/2-27,O(1-0-1)1	-0.9
MILLER, KEITH Keith Alan B 6.12.1963 Midland, MI BR/TR 5-11/185# d6.16 OF Total (49-LF 65-CF 28-RF)																								
1987	NY N	25	51	14	19	2	2	0	1	2-0	1	6	.373	.407	.490	144	3	8-1	.967	-2	97	74	2-16	0.3
1988	NY N	40	70	9	15	1	1	1	5	6-0	0	10	.214	.276	.300	69	-3	0-5	.946	-9	59	43	2-16/S-8,3-6,O(RF)	-1.4
1989	NY N	57	143	15	33	7	0	1	7	5-0	1	27	.231	.262	.301	63	-7	6-0	.967	-1	81	78	2-23,O-14(0-10-4)/S-8,3-2	-0.7
1990	NY N	88	233	42	60	8	0	1	12	23-1	2	46	.258	.327	.305	76	-7	16-3	.980	8	133	40	O-61(7-53-5),2-11/S-4	0.3
1991	NY N	98	275	41	77	22	1	4	23	23-0	5	44	.280	.345	.411	113	6	14-4	.972	12	106	113	2-60,O-28(14-2-17)/3-2,S-2	2.1
1992	KC A	106	416	57	118	24	4	4	38	31-0	14	46	.284	.352	.389	105	4	16-6	.971	-9	93	99	2-93,O-16(LF)/D	-0.1
1993	KC A	37	108	9	18	3	0	0	3	8-0	1	19	.167	.229	.194	15	-13	3-1	.889	-3	87	64	3-21/O-4(LF),2-3,D-6	-1.6
1994	KC A	5	15	1	2	0	0	0	0	0-0	0	3	.133	.133	.133	-30	-3	0-0	1.000	0	105	440	/O-4(LF),3-2	-0.3
1995	KC A	9	15	2	5	0	0	1	3	2-0	0	4	.333	.412	.533	142	1	0-0	1.000	1	156	938	/O-4(4-0-1),D-4	0.2
Total	9	465	1326	190	347	67	8	12	92	100-1	24	205	.262	.323	.351	88	-19	63-20	.969	-3	94	98	2-222,O-132C/3-33,S-22,D-11	-1.2
MILLER, ED L. Edward B Tecumseh, MI d7.18																								
1884	Tol AA	8	24	2	6	0	0	0	1	1	0		.250	.280	.250	72	-1		.615	-0	210	0	/O-8(6-1-2)	-0.1
MILLER, HACK Laurence H. B 1.1.1894 New York, NY D 9.16.1971 Oakland, CA BR/TR 5-9/195# d9.22																								
1916	Bro N	3	3	0	1	0	1	0	1	1	0	1	.333	.500	1.000	345	1	0	1.000	-0	58	0	/O-3(0-2-1)	0.1
1918	†Bos A	12	29	2	8	2	0	0	4	0	0	4	.276	.276	.345	89	-1	0	1.000	-1	86	0	O-10(9-1-0)	-0.2
1922	Chi N	122	466	61	164	28	5	12	78	26	2	39	.352	.389	.511	128	19	3-3	.959	-3	92	105	*O-116(115-0-2)	0.6
1923	Chi N	135	485	74	146	24	2	20	88	27	4	39	.301	.343	.482	116	9	6-5	.978	3	96	143	*O-129(LF)	0.1
1924	Chi N	53	131	17	44	8	1	4	25	8	1	11	.336	.379	.504	133	6	1-0	.948	-3	92	35	O-32(LF)	0.1
1925	Chi N	24	86	10	24	3	2	2	9	2	1	9	.279	.303	.430	84	-3	0-1	.878	-3	83	55	O-21(LF)	-0.7
Total	6	349	1200	164	387	65	11	38	205	64	8	103	.322	.361	.490	120	31	10-9	.962	-6	93	109	O-311(306-3-3)	0.0
MILLER, LEMMIE Lemmie Earl B 6.2.1960 Dallas, TX BR/TR 6-1/190# d5.22																								
1984	LA N	8	12	1	2	0	0	0	0	1-0	0	2	.167	.231	.167	13	-1	0-0	1.000	-0	75	0	/O-5(4-0-1)	-0.2
MILLER, OTTO Lowell Otto "Moonie" B 6.1.1889 Minden, NE D 3.29.1962 Brooklyn, NY BR/TR 6/196# d7.16 C11																								
1910	Bro N	31	66	5	11	3	0	0	2	2	1	19	.167	.203	.212	22	-7	1	.987	6	*106*	*104*	C-28	0.1
1911	Bro N	25	62	7	13	2	2	0	8	0	0	4	.210	.210	.306	46	-5	2	.927	-4	*79*	*124*	C-22	-0.8
1912	Bro N	98	316	35	88	18	1	1	31	18	4	50	.278	.325	.351	88	-5	11	.975	8	*94*	*112*	C-94	1.1
1913	Bro N	104	320	26	87	11	7	0	26	10	0	31	.272	.294	.350	81	-9	7-12	.971	9	103	103	*C-103/1	0.6
1914	Bro N	54	169	17	39	6	1	0	9	7	0	20	.231	.261	.278	59	-9	0	.964	-2	*89*	*98*	C-50/1	-0.7
1915	Bro N	84	254	20	57	4	6	0	25	6	1	28	.224	.245	.287	60	-14	3	.981	2	*91*	*95*	C-83	-0.4
1916	†Bro N	73	216	16	55	9	2	1	17	7	1	29	.255	.281	.329	85	-4	6	.968	4	103	80	C-69	0.6
1917	Bro N	92	274	19	63	5	4	1	17	14	2	29	.230	.272	.288	70	-10	5	.979	0	*102*	*94*	C-91	-0.3
1918	Bro N	75	228	8	44	6	1	0	8	9	2	20	.193	.230	.228	40	-17	1	.972	2	*90*	*99*	C-62/1	-1.1
1919	Bro N	51	164	18	37	5	0	0	5	7	0	14	.226	.257	.256	53	-9	2	.966	-0	*89*	*94*	C-51	-0.6
1920	†Bro N	90	301	16	87	9	2	0	33	9	1	18	.289	.312	.332	82	-7	0-5	**.986**	-2	*99*	*66*	C-89	-0.4
1921	Bro N	91	286	22	67	8	6	1	27	9	1	26	.234	.260	.315	50	-22	2-1	.972	4	*87*	*104*	C-91	-1.2
1922	Bro N	59	180	20	47	11	1	1	23	6	0	13	.261	.285	.350	63	-10	0-0	.968	-1	*76*	*114*	C-57	-0.7
Total	13	927	2836	229	695	97	33	5	231	104	13	301	.245	.275	.308	67	-128	40-18	.973	25	*94*	*97*	C-890/1-3	-3.8
MILLER, KEITH Neal Keith B 3.7.1963 Dallas, TX BB/TR 5-11/175# d4.23																								
1988	Phi N	47	48	4	8	3	0	0	6	5-0	0	13	.167	.245	.229	36	-4	0-0	1.000	-0	57	0	/O-4(2-1-1),3-3,S	-0.5
1989	Phi N	8	10	0	3	1	0	0	0	0-0	0	3	.300	.300	.400	98	0	0-0	1.000	-0	69	0	/O-2(CF)	0.0
Total	2	55	58	4	11	4	0	0	6	5-0	0	16	.190	.254	.259	47	-4	0-0	1.000	-1	62	0	/O-6(2-3-1),3-3,S	-0.5
MILLER, NORM Norman Calvin B 2.5.1946 Los Angeles, CA BL/TR 5-11/195# d9.11 Mil 1967																								
1965	Hou N	11	15	2	3	0	1	0	1	1-0	0	7	.200	.250	.333	67	-1	0-0	1.000	-0	84	0	/O-2(LF)	-0.1
1966	Hou N	11	34	1	5	0	0	1	3	2-1	0	8	.147	.194	.235	20	-4	0-0	1.000	-0	111	0	/O-8(5-0-3),3-2	-0.5
1967	Hou N	64	190	15	39	9	3	1	14	19-2	0	42	.205	.278	.300	68	-8	2-0	.967	1	107	103	O-53(LF)	-1.0
1968	Hou N	79	257	35	61	18	2	6	28	22-1	5	48	.237	.304	.393	112	4	6-5	.971	-4	100	18	O-74(2-7-65)	-0.6

Year	Tm Lg	G	AB	R	H	2B	3B	HR	RBI	BB-IB	HP	SO	AVG	OBP	SLG	AOPS	ABR	SB-CS	FA	FR	Rng	Thr	G at Pos	BFW
1969	Hou N	119	409	58	108	21	4	4	50	47-3	7	77	.264	.348	.364	102	3	4-4	.984	-1	97	99	*O-114(8-14-97)	-0.4
1970	Hou N	90	226	29	54	9	0	4	29	41-7	1	33	.239	.357	.332	90	-1	3-1	.947	-1	90	147	O-72(4-3-68)/C	-0.5
1971	Hou N	45	74	5	19	5	0	2	10	5-0	1	13	.257	.313	.405	105	0	0-0	1.000	-1	93	0	O-20(0-6-15)/C	-0.2
1972	Hou N	67	107	18	26	4	0	4	13	13-0	1	23	.243	.331	.393	107	1	1-0	1.000	-2	82	72	O-29(6-10-13)	-0.1
1973	Hou N	3	3	0	0	0	0	0	0	0-0	0	2	.000	.000	.000	-99	-1	0-0	—	-0	0	0	/O(RF)	-0.1
	Atl N	9	8	2	3	1	0	1	6	3-0	0	3	.375	.500	.875	267	2	0-0	.667	-0	39	0	/O(LF)	0.2
	Year	12	11	2	3	1	0	1	6	3-0	0	5	.273	.400	.636	181	1	0-0	.667	-0	34	0	/O-2(1-0-1)	0.1
1974	Atl N	42	41	1	7	1	0	1	5	7-1	0	9	.171	.292	.268	55	-2	0-0	1.000	0	55	484	O-4(1-0-4)	-0.3
Total	10	540	1364	166	325	68	10	24	159	160-15	15	265	.238	.323	.356	95	-7	16-10	.972	-8	96	86	O-378(82-40-266)/C-2,3-2	-3.6
MILLER, ORLANDO Orlando (Salmon) B 1.13.1969 Changuinola, Panama BR/TR 6-1/180# d7.8																								
1994	Hou N	16	40	3	13	0	1	2	9	2-2	2	12	.325	.386	.525	142	2	1-0	1.000	-1	99	68	S-11/2-3	0.2
1995	Hou N	92	324	36	85	20	1	5	36	22-8	5	71	.262	.319	.377	89	-6	3-4	.964	4	102	99	S-89	0.4
1996	Hou N	139	468	43	120	26	2	15	58	14-4	10	116	.256	.291	.417	92	-8	3-7	.958	-13	95	85	*S-117,3-29	-1.4
1997	Det A	50	111	13	26	7	1	2	10	5-0	4	24	.234	.289	.369	72	-5	1-0	.979	-0	102	132	S-31,D-11/3-4,1-3	-0.4
Total	4	297	943	95	244	53	5	24	113	43-14	21	223	.259	.305	.402	90	-17	8-11	.964	-11	99	94	S-248/3-33,D-11,1-3,2-3	-1.2
MILLER, OTTO Otis Louis B 2.2.1901 Belleville, IL D 7.26.1959 Belleville, IL BR/TR 5-10.5/168# d4.17																								
1927	StL A	51	76	8	17	5	0	0	8	8	1	5	.224	.306	.289	53	-5	0-1	.938	-1	100	88	S-35,3-11	-0.5
1930	Bos A	112	370	49	106	22	5	0	40	26	0	21	.286	.333	.373	82	-10	2-4	.948	-1	110	95	3-83,2-15	-0.7
1931	Bos A	107	389	38	106	12	1	0	43	15	1	20	.272	.301	.308	64	-21	1-1	.953	2	112	97	3-75,2-25	-1.4
1932	Bos A	2	2	0	0	0	0	0	0	0	0	0	.000	.000	.000	-99	-1	0-0	—	0			H	-0.1
Total	4	272	837	95	229	39	6	0	91	49	2	46	.274	.315	.335	71	-37	3-6	.949	-0	111	98	3-169/2-40,S-35	-2.7
MILLER, RALPH Ralph Joseph B 2.29.1896 Ft.Wayne, IN D 3.18.1939 Ft.Wayne, IN BR/TR 6/190# d4.14																								
1920	Phi N	97	338	28	74	14	1	0	28	11	1	32	.219	.246	.266	45	-24	3-4	.940	5	110	97	3-91/1-3,S-2,O(LF)	-1.9
1921	Phi N	57	204	19	62	10	0	3	26	6	1	10	.304	.327	.397	84	-5	3-5	.910	-1	99	88	S-46,3-10	-0.1
1924	†Was A	9	15	1	2	0	0	0	0	1	0	1	.133	.188	.133	-17	-3	0-0	.941	0	120	67	/2-3	-0.2
Total	3	163	557	48	138	24	1	3	54	18	2	43	.248	.274	.311	59	-32	6-9	.927	4	112	105	3-101/S-48,2-3,1-3,O(LF)	-2.2
MILLER, RAY Raymond Peter B 2.12.1888 Pittsburgh, PA D 4.7.1927 Pittsburgh, PA BL/TL 5-10/168# d4.14 Mil 1918																								
1917	Cle A	19	21	1	4	1	0	0	2	8	0	3	.190	.414	.238	92	1	0	1.000	1	226	0	/1-4	0.2
	Pit N	6	27	1	4	1	0	0	0	2	0	3	.148	.207	.185	20	-3	0	1.000	0	117	124	/1-6	-0.3
Total	1	25	48	2	8	2	0	0	2	10	0	6	.167	.310	.208	56	-2	0	1.000	2	156	80	/1-10	-0.1
MILLER, RICK Richard Alan B 4.19.1948 Grand Rapids, MI BL/TL 6/185# d9.4																								
1971	Bos A	15	33	9	11	5	0	1	7	8-0	0	8	.333	.452	.576	180	4	0-2	.969	2	140	145	O-14(4-4-6)	0.5
1972	Bos A	89	98	13	21	4	1	3	15	11-0	0	27	.214	.291	.367	91	-1	0-2	.967	5	114	312	O-75(24-47-4)	0.2
1973	Bos A	143	441	65	115	17	7	6	43	51-2	3	59	.261	.339	.372	95	-2	12-7	.978	-0	107	46	*O-137(15-71-61)	-0.8
1974	Bos A	114	280	41	73	8	1	5	22	37-2	0	47	.261	.347	.350	94	-1	13-2	.989	9	115	116	*O-105(21-77-7)	0.8
1975	†Bos A	77	108	21	21	2	1	0	15	21-6	0	20	.194	.326	.231	55	-6	3-2	.981	5	136	78	O-65(25-15-26)	-0.2
1976	Bos A	105	269	40	76	15	3	0	27	34-2	0	47	.283	.359	.361	100	1	11-10	.991	9	126	75	O-82(17-37-32)/D-4	0.7
1977	Bos A	86	189	34	48	9	3	0	24	22-1	3	30	.254	.341	.333	76	-6	11-5	.992	-2	87	114	O-79(2-29-48)/D	-0.9
1978	Cal A	132	475	66	125	25	4	1	37	54-1	4	70	.263	.341	.339	96	0	3-13	.989	8	112	108	*O-129(0-93-36)	0.1
1979	†Cal A	120	427	60	125	15	5	2	28	50-1	1	69	.293	.367	.365	102	3	5-4	.989	8	**120**	42	*O-117(CF)/D-2	0.9
1980	Cal A	129	412	52	113	14	3	2	38	48-4	1	71	.274	.349	.337	92	-3	7-3	.984	7	108	147	*O-118(0-98-24)	0.3
1981	Bos A	97	316	38	92	17	2	2	33	28-1	1	36	.291	.349	.377	103	2	3-5	.987	-8	87	88	O-95(CF)	-0.8
1982	Bos A	135	409	50	104	13	2	4	38	40-2	2	41	.254	.323	.325	75	-14	5-6	.983	-10	87	76	*O-127(CF)	-2.6
1983	Bos A	104	262	41	75	10	2	2	21	28-1	1	30	.286	.356	.363	92	-2	3-3	.993	0	102	91	O-66(6-22-40)/1-2,D-2	-0.4
1984	Bos A	95	123	17	32	5	1	0	12	17-0	0	22	.260	.348	.317	82	-2	1-1	.974	-1	82	93	O-31(0-21-10)/1-8	-0.4
1985	Bos A	41	45	5	15	2	0	0	9	5-0	0	6	.333	.392	.378	110	1	1-0	1.000	0	127	0	/O-8(4-1-3),D-4	0.1
Total	15	1482	3887	552	1046	161	35	28	369	454-23	16	583	.269	.346	.350	92	-26	78-65	.986	31	107	95	*O-1248(118-854-297)/D-13,1-10	-2.5
MILLER, ROD Rodney Carter B 1.16.1940 Portland, OR BL/TR 5-10/160# d9.28																								
1957	Bro N	1	1	0	0	0	0	0	0	0-0	0	1	.000	.000	.000	-91	0	0-0	—	0			H	0.0
MILLER, DOC Roy Oscar B 2.4.1883 Chatham, ON, CAN D 7.31.1938 Jersey City, NJ BL/TL 5-10.5/170# d5.4																								
1910	Chi N	1	1	0	0	0	0	0	0	0	0	0	.000	.000	.000	-99	0	0	—	0			H	0.0
	Bos N	130	482	48	138	27	4	3	55	33	1	52	.286	.333	.378	103	1	17	.951	-8	98	52	*O-130(6-0-127)	-1.4
	Year	131	483	48	138	27	4	3	55	33	1	52	.286	.333	.377	102	0	17	.951	-8	98	52	*O-130(6-0-127)	-1.4
1911	Bos N	146	577	69	**192**	36	3	7	91	43	0	43	.333	.379	.442	120	15	32	.961	3	99	129	*O-146(0-3-143)	1.0
1912	Bos N	51	201	26	47	8	1	2	24	14	1	17	.234	.287	.313	63	-11	6	.948	2	91	156	O-50(RF)	-1.1
	Phi N	67	177	24	51	12	5	0	21	9	0	13	.288	.323	.412	94	-2	3	.986	2	96	160	O-40(RF)	-0.2
	Year	118	378	50	98	20	6	2	45	23	1	30	.259	.303	.360	78	-13	9	.964	4	93	158	O-90(RF)	-1.3
1913	Phi N	69	87	9	30	6	0	0	11	6	2	6	.345	.400	.414	127	4	2-1	.800	-2	61	0	O-12(RF)	0.1
1914	Cin N	93	192	8	49	7	2	0	33	16	0	18	.255	.313	.313	83	-4	4	.976	-2	105	34	O-47(23-3-23)	-0.9
Total	5	557	1717	184	507	96	15	12	235	121	4	149	.295	.343	.390	102	3	64-1	.958	-5	97	100	O-425(29-6-395)	-2.5
MILLER, RUDY Rudel Charles B 7.12.1900 Kalamazoo, MI D 1.22.1994 Kalamazoo, MI BR/TR 6-1/180# d9.19																								
1929	Phi A	2	4	1	1	0	0	0	1	3	0	0	.250	.571	.250	115	1	0-0	.750	-1	72	0	/3-2	0.0
MILLER, TOM Thomas P. "Reddy" B 1850 Philadelphia, PA D 5.29.1876 Philadelphia, PA d10.24																								
1874	Ath NA	4	16	1	8	0	0	0	5	0		0	.500	.500	.500	204	2	0-0	.793	0			/C-4,O(0-1-1)	0.1
1875	StL NA	56	214	18	35	2	0	0	12	1		8	.164	.167	.173	20	-15	2-0	.827	-4			*C-53/3-2	-1.7
Total	2 NA	60	230	19	43	2	0	0	17	1		8	.187	.190	.196	37	-13	2-0	.000	-4			/C-57,3-2,O(0-1-1)	-1.6
MILLER, TOM Thomas Royall B 7.5.1897 Powhatan Court House, VA D 8.13.1980 Richmond, VA BL/TR 5-11/180# d7.29																								
1918	Bos N	2	2	0	0	0	0	0	0	0	0	0	.000	.000	.000	-99	0	1	—	0			H	-0.1
1919	Bos N	7	6	2	2	0	0	0	0	0	0	1	.333	.333	.333	105	0	0	—	0			H	0.0
Total	2	9	8	2	2	0	0	0	0	0	0	1	.250	.250	.250	53	0	1	.000	0				-0.1
MILLER, WARD Ward Taylor "Windy" or "Grump" B 7.5.1884 Mt.Carroll, IL D 9.4.1958 Dixon, IL BL/TR 5-11/177# d4.14																								
1909	Pit N	15	56	2	8	0	1	0	4	4	1		.143	.213	.179	20	-5	2	.967	-2	50	0	O-14(CF)	-0.9
	Cin N	43	113	17	35	3	1	0	4	6	0		.310	.345	.354	118	2	9	.981	-0	61	0	O-26(17-16-3)	0.0
	Year	58	169	19	43	3	2	0	8	10	1		.254	.300	.296	84	-4	11	.976	-2	57	0	O-40(17-30-3)	-0.9
1910	Cin N	81	126	21	30	6	0	0	10	22	1	13	.238	.356	.286	92	0	10	.944	2	94	207	O-26(0-11-15)	0.1
1912	Chi N	86	241	45	74	11	4	0	22	26	1	18	.307	.377	.386	109	4	11	.943	-5	90	70	O-64(13-38-14)	-0.4
1913	Chi N	80	203	23	48	5	7	1	16	34	1	33	.236	.349	.345	98	0	13-15	.980	4	107	110	O-63(47-11-5)	-0.1
1914	StL F	121	402	49	118	17	7	4	50	59	10	36	.294	.397	.400	112	4	18	.953	5	**115**	86	*O-111(74-31-6)	0.3
1915	StL F	154	536	80	164	19	9	1	63	79	5	39	.306	.400	.381	114	7	33	.963	4	111	85	*O-154(LF)	0.5
1916	StL A	146	485	72	129	17	5	1	50	72	9	76	.266	.371	.328	116	13	25-21	.943	-9	96	69	*O-136(3-0-133)	-0.5
1917	StL A	43	82	13	17	1	1	1	2	16	2	15	.207	.350	.280	96	1	7	.966	-1	71	166	O-25(12-4-9)	-0.1
Total	8	769	2244	322	623	79	35	8	221	318	30	230	.278	.375	.355	108	26	128-36	.957	-1	101	84	O-619(320-125-185)	-1.1
MILLER, WARREN Warren Lemuel "Gitz" B 7.14.1885 Philadelphia, PA D 8.12.1956 Philadelphia, PA BL/TL 5-10/160# d7.29																								
1909	Was A	26	51	5	11	0	0	0	1	4	0		.216	.273	.216	57	-2	0	1.000	1	152	0	O-15(1-10-4)	-0.3
1911	Was A	21	34	3	5	0	0	0	0	0	0		.147	.147	.147	-18	-6	0	.778	-1	72	104	/O-9(1-0-8)	-0.6
Total	2	47	85	8	16	0	0	0	1	4	0		.188	.225	.188	25	-8	0	.931	-0	123	38	/O-24(2-10-12)	-0.9
MILLER, BILL William Alexander B 5.23.1879 Bad Schwalbach, Germany D 9.8.1957 Ashtabula, OH BL/TL 6-2/170# d8.23																								
1902	Pit N	1	5	0	1	0	0	0	2	0			.200	.200	.200	23	0	0	—	0	0	0	/O(RF)	-0.1
MILLETTE, JOE Joseph Anthony B 8.12.1966 Walnut Creek, CA BR/TR 6-1/180# d7.16																								
1992	Phi N	33	78	5	16	0	0	0	2	5-2	2	10	.205	.271	.205	37	-7	1-0	.974	4	120	106	S-26/3-3,2	-0.1
1993	Phi N	10	10	3	2	0	0	0	2	1-0	0	2	.200	.273	.200	29	-1	0-0	1.000	1	130	47	/S-7,3-3	0.1
Total	2	43	88	8	18	0	0	0	4	6-2	2	12	.205	.271	.205	36	-8	1-0	.978	5	121	98	/S-33,3-6,2	0.0

Year	Tm Lg	G	AB	R	H	2B	3B	HR	RBI	BB-IB	HP	SO	AVG	OBP	SLG	AOPS	ABR	SB-CS	FA	FR	Rng	Thr	G at Pos	BFW
MILLIARD, RALPH Ralph Gregory B 12.30.1973 Willemstad, Curacao BR/TR 5-11/170# d5.12																								
1996	Fla N	24	62	7	10	2	0	0	1	14-1	0	16	.161	.312	.194	40	-5	2-0	.955	5	123	116	2-24	0.1
1997	Fla N	8	30	2	6	0	0	0	2	3-0	2	3	.200	.314	.200	40	-3	1-1	1.000	4	138	176	/2-8	0.2
1998	NY N	10	1	3	0	0	0	0	0	0-0	0	1	.000	.000	.000	-99	-1	0-0	.833	-1	77	0	/2-5,S	-0.1
Total	3	42	93	12	16	2	0	0	3	17-1	2	20	.172	.310	.194	38	-8	3-1	.963	9	126	130	/2-37,S	0.2
MILLIES, WALLY Walter Louis B 10.18.1906 Chicago, IL D 2.28.1995 Oak Lawn, IL BR/TR 5-10.5/170# d9.23																								
1934	Bro N	2	7	0	0	0	0	0	0	0	0	0	.000	.000	.000	-99	-2	0	1.000	0	*55*	*0*	/C-2	-0.2
1936	Was A	74	215	26	67	10	2	0	25	11	0	8	.312	.345	.377	83	-6	1-0	.968	-0	*87*	*141*	C-72	-0.2
1937	Was A	59	179	21	40	7	1	0	28	9	0	15	.223	.261	.274	36	-18	1-0	.971	0	*101*	*126*	C-56	-1.4
1939	Phi N	84	205	12	48	3	0	0	12	9	1	5	.234	.270	.249	41	-17	0	.964	-10	*54*	***127***	C-84	-2.4
1940	Phi N	26	43	1	3	0	0	0	0	4	0	4	.070	.149	.070	-39	-8	0	.958	0	*89*	*93*	C-24	-0.7
1941	Phi N	1	2	0	0	0	0	0	0	0	0	0	.000	.000	.000	-99	-1	0	.800	0	*0*	*469*	/C	-0.1
Total	6	246	651	60	158	20	3	0	65	33	1	32	.243	.280	.283	47	-52	2-0	.966	-10	*79*	*129*	C-239	-5.0
MILLIGAN, JOCKO John B 8.8.1861 Philadelphia, PA D 8.29.1923 Philadelphia, PA BR/TR 6/192# d5.1																								
1884	Phi AA	66	268	39	77	20	3	3		8	0		.287	.308	.418	126	7		**.939**	10			C-65/O(CF)	2.1
1885	Phi AA	67	265	35	71	15	4	2	39	7	1		.268	.289	.377	103	0		.935	9			C-61/1-6,O-2(RF)	1.2
1886	Phi AA	75	301	52	76	17	3	5	45	21	0		.252	.301	.379	111	3	18	.919	1			C-40,1-29/O-5(0-4-1),3-2	0.4
1887	Phi AA	95	377	54	114	27	4	2	50	21	3		.302	.344	.411	110	5	8	.966	1	83	90	1-50,C-47/O(CF)	0.4
1888	†StL AA	63	219	19	55	6	2	5	37	17	2		.251	.311	.365	105	0	3	.941	9			C-58/1-5	1.2
1889	StL AA	72	273	53	100	30	2	12	76	16	3	19	.366	.408	.623	170	22	2	.933	9			C-66/1-9	3.0
1890	Phi P	62	234	38	69	9	3	3	57	19	6	19	.295	.363	.397	101	0	2	.893	2	*98*	*92*	C-59/1-3	0.6
1891	Phi AA	118	455	75	138	**35**	12	11	106	56	15	51	.303	.397	.505	158	34	2	.939	-1	*108*	*77*	C-87,1-32	3.2
1892	Was N	88	323	40	89	20	9	4	43	26	3	24	.276	.335	.430	135	13	2	.947	-4	*67*	*134*	C-59,1-28	1.2
1893	Bal N	24	102	19	25	5	2	1	19	5	2	7	.245	.294	.363	73	-5	2	.981	2	149	74	1-22/C	-0.2
	NY N	42	147	16	34	5	6	1	25	14	1	14	.231	.302	.367	77	-6	2	.934	8	*99*	*152*	C-42	0.5
	Year	66	249	35	59	10	8	2	44	19	3	21	.237	.299	.365	75	-11	4	.932	9	*99*	*148*	C-43,1-22	0.3
Total	10	772	2964	440	848	189	50	49	497	210	36	134	.286	.341	.433	123	73	41	.930	44	*39*	*44*	C-585,1-184/O-9(0-6-3),3-2	13.6
MILLIGAN, RANDY Randy Andre B 11.27.1961 San Diego, CA BR/TR 6-1/228# d9.12																								
1987	NY N	3	1	0	0	0	0	0	0	1-0	0	1	.000	.500	.000	49	0	0-0	—	0			/H	0.0
1988	Pit N	40	82	10	18	5	0	3	8	20-0	1	24	.220	.379	.390	123	4	1-2	.987	-1	98	128	1-25/O-2(LF)	0.1
1989	Bal A	124	365	56	98	23	5	12	45	74-2	3	75	.268	.394	.458	144	25	9-5	.995	1	109	100	*1-117/D	2.0
1990	Bal A	109	362	64	96	20	1	20	60	88-3	2	68	.265	.408	.492	157	33	6-3	.990	5	121	115	1-98/D-9	3.0
1991	Bal A	141	483	57	127	17	2	16	70	84-4	2	108	.263	.373	.406	121	17	0-5	.990	2	111	105	*1-106,D-25/O-9(LF)	0.9
1992	Bal A	137	462	71	111	21	1	11	53	106-0	4	81	.240	.383	.361	108	11	0-1	.994	-6	84	110	*1-129/D-6	-0.5
1993	Cin N	83	234	30	64	11	1	6	29	46-0	1	49	.274	.394	.406	115	7	0-2	.994	6	132	104	1-61/O-9(LF)	0.7
	Cle A	19	47	7	20	7	0	0	7	14-0	0	4	.426	.557	.574	206	9	0-0	1.000	-1	81	145	1-18/D	0.7
1994	Mon N	47	82	10	19	2	0	2	12	14-1	0	21	.232	.337	.329	76	-3	0-0	.978	2	140	116	1-33	-0.3
Total	8	703	2118	305	553	106	10	70	284	447-10	13	431	.261	.391	.420	127	103	16-18	.992	8	108	109	1-587/D-42,O-20(LF)	6.6
MILLS, JACK Abbott Paige B 10.23.1889 S.Williamstown, MA D 6.3.1973 Washington, DC BL/TR 6/165# d7.1																								
1911	Cle A	13	17	5	5	0	0	0	1	1	1		.294	.368	.294	85	0	1	1.000	1	147	185	/3-7	0.1
MILLS, CHARLIE Charles F. B 9.1844 Brooklyn, NY D 4.10.1874 Brooklyn, NY 6/?# d5.18 U2																								
1871	Mut NA	32	146	27	36	4	3	0	22	1		0	.247	.252	.315	68	-5	2-0	.866	-1			*C-29/O-4(RF),3	-0.3
1872	Mut NA	6	31	6	4	0	0	0	2	0		0	.129	.129	.129	-22	-4	0-0	.667	-1	0	0	/O-4(RF),C-3	-0.4
Total	2 NA	38	177	33	40	4	3	0	24	1		0	.226	.230	.282	53	-9	2-0	.000	-2			/C-32,O-8(RF),3	-0.7
MILLS, BUSTER Colonel Buster "Bus" B 9.16.1908 Ranger, TX D 12.1.1991 Arlington, TX BR/TR 5-11.5/195# d4.18 Mil 1943-45 M1 C7																								
1934	StL N	29	72	7	17	4	1	1	8	4	2	11	.236	.295	.361	70	-3	0	1.000	-1	104	0	O-18(0-17-1)	-0.4
1935	Bro N	17	56	12	12	2	1	1	7	5	4	11	.214	.323	.339	80	-1	0	.971	-1	96	0	O-17(11-6-0)	-0.3
1937	Bos A	123	505	85	149	25	8	7	58	46	6	41	.295	.361	.418	92	-6	11-8	.946	-5	94	84	*O-120(107-10-5)	-1.7
1938	StL A	123	466	66	133	24	4	3	46	43	3	46	.285	.350	.373	81	-13	7-8	.964	2	104	113	*O-113(106-6-1)	-1.7
1940	NY A	34	63	10	25	3	3	1	15	7	0	5	.397	.457	.587	176	7	0-0	1.000	-1	93	0	O-14(12-0-2)	0.5
1942	Cle A	80	195	19	54	4	2	1	26	23	0	18	.277	.353	.333	99	0	5-4	.973	4	113	107	O-53(13-37-3)	0.2
1946	Cle A	9	22	1	6	0	0	0	3	3	0	5	.273	.360	.273	84	0	0-1	1.000	-0	96	0	/O-6(LF)	-0.1
Total	7	415	1379	200	396	62	19	14	163	131	15	137	.287	.355	.390	91	-16	23-21	.964	-2	101	85	O-341(255-76-12)	-3.5
MILLS, EVERETT Everett B 1.20.1845 Newark, NJ D 6.22.1908 Newark, NJ 6-1/174# d5.5 M1																								
1871	Oly NA	**32**	157	38	43	6	4	1	24	3		1	.274	.287	.382	95	0	2-3	.967	3	98	120	*1-32	0.2
1872	Bal NA	55	266	55	79	14	2	0	34	3		2	.297	.305	.365	100	-1	0-2	.931	1	91	87	*1-55,M	0.0
1873	Bal NA	54	262	64	87	20	9	0	56	2		1	.332	.337	.477	140	12	1-0	**.949**	2	65	101	*1-53/O(CF)	1.1
1874	Har NA	**53**	244	39	69	6	1	0	19	4		2	.283	.294	.316	91	-3	1-1	.920	-2	88	58	*1-53	-0.3
1875	Har NA	80	342	59	89	8	4	1	48	0		3	.260	.260	.316	94	-3	6-4	.945	2	78	**166**	*1-80	0.0
1876	Har N	63	254	28	66	8	1	0	23	1		3	.260	.263	.299	80	-6		.939	-2	63	78	*1-63	-1.0
Total	5 NA	274	1271	255	367	54	20	2	181	12		9	.289	.295	.367	105	5	10-10	.000	6	82	111	1-273/O(CF)	1.0
MILLS, FRANK Frank Le Moyne B 5.13.1895 Knoxville, OH D 8.31.1983 Youngstown, OH BL/TR 6/180# d9.22																								
1914	Cle A	4	8	0	1	0	0	0	0	1	0	2	.125	.222	.125	4	-1	0	.900	-1	*75*	*162*	/C-2	-0.2
MILLS, BRAD James Bradley B 1.19.1957 Exeter, CA BL/TR 6/195# d6.8 C5																								
1980	Mon N	21	60	1	18	1	0	0	8	5-1	0	6	.300	.348	.317	88	-1	0-1	.977	-1	78	131	3-18	-0.2
1981	†Mon N	17	21	3	5	1	0	0	1	2-1	0	1	.238	.304	.286	67	-1	0-0	1.000	-1	70	0	/3-7,2-2	-0.2
1982	Mon N	54	67	6	15	3	0	1	2	5-0	0	11	.224	.278	.313	64	-3	0-0	.867	-3	60	84	3-13	-0.7
1983	Mon N	14	20	1	5	0	0	0	1	2-0	0	3	.250	.318	.250	60	-1	0-0	1.000	-0	102	0	/3-3,1	-0.2
Total	4	106	168	11	43	5	0	1	12	14-2	0	21	.256	.311	.304	73	-6	0-1	.959	-5	74	92	/3-41,2-2,1	-1.3
MILLS, RUPERT Rupert Frank B 10.12.1892 Newark, NJ D 7.20.1929 Lake Hopatcong, NJ BR/TR 6-2/185# d6.23																								
1915	New F	41	134	12	27	5	1	0	16	6	1	21	.201	.241	.254	42	-13	6	.976	-0	108	110	1-37	-1.6
MILLS, BILL William Henry B 11.2.1920 Boston, MA BR/TR 5-10/175# d5.19																								
1944	Phi A	5	4	0	1	0	0	0	0	1	0	1	.250	.400	.250	89	0	0-0	—	0	*0*	*0*	/C	0.0
MILNE, PETE William James B 4.10.1925 Mobile, AL D 4.11.1999 Mobile, AL BL/TR 6-1/180# d9.15																								
1948	NY N	12	27	0	6	0	1	0	2	1	0	6	.222	.250	.296	47	-2	0	.867	-1	90	0	/O-9(2-5-2)	-0.4
1949	NY N	31	29	5	7	1	0	1	6	3	0	6	.241	.313	.379	85	-1	0	1.000	0	130	0	/O(LF)	-0.1
1950	NY N	4	4	1	1	0	1	0	1	0	0	0	.250	.250	.750	151	0	0	—	0			H	0.0
Total	3	47	60	6	14	1	2	1	9	4	0	13	.233	.281	.367	73	-3	0	.882	-1	94	0	/O-10(3-5-2)	-0.5
MILNER, BRIAN Brian Tate B 11.17.1959 Fort Worth, TX BR/TR 6-2/200# d6.23																								
1978	Tor A	2	9	3	4	0	1	0	2	0-0	0	1	.444	.444	.667	204	1	0-0	.800	-2	58	0	/C-2	-0.1
MILNER, EDDIE Eddie James B 5.21.1955 Columbus, OH BL/TL 5-11/173# d9.2																								
1980	Cin N	6	3	1	0	0	0	0	0	0-0	0	0	.000	.000	.000	-99	-1	0-0	—	0			/H	-0.1
1981	Cin N	8	5	0	1	1	0	0	1	1-0	0	1	.200	.333	.400	106	0	0-0	1.000	-0	105	0	/O-4(2-0-2)	0.0
1982	Cin N	113	407	61	109	23	5	4	31	41-1	2	40	.268	.338	.378	98	0	18-12	.987	4	107	113	*O-107(65-30-37)	0.0
1983	Cin N	146	502	77	131	23	6	9	33	68-2	1	60	.261	.350	.384	100	1	41-12	.990	13	**118**	142	*O-139(0-138-1)	1.9
1984	Cin N	117	336	44	78	8	4	7	29	51-3	2	50	.232	.333	.342	87	-5	21-13	.983	14	**127**	162	*O-108(CF)	0.9
1985	Cin N	145	453	82	115	19	7	3	33	61-3	1	31	.254	.342	.347	89	-5	35-13	.983	14	**122**	**173**	*O-135(CF)	1.2
1986	Cin N	145	424	70	110	22	6	15	47	36-2	0	56	.259	.317	.446	104	1	18-11	.990	3	112	93	*O-127(CF)	0.3
1987	†SF N	101	214	38	54	14	0	4	19	24-3	0	33	.252	.328	.374	90	-3	10-9	.993	-2	107	0	O-84(CF)	-0.6
1988	Cin N	23	51	3	9	1	0	0	2	4-0	0	9	.176	.236	.196	24	-5	2-2	.968	0	101	178	O-15(2-11-2)	-0.6
Total	9	804	2395	376	607	111	28	42	195	286-14	6	280	.253	.333	.376	94	-17	145-72	.987	47	116	125	O-719(69-633-42)	3.0
MILNER, JOHN John David "The Hammer" B 12.28.1949 Atlanta, GA D 1.4.2000 East Point, GA BL/TL 6/185# d9.15																								
1971	NY N	9	18	1	3	1	0	0	1	0-0	0	3	.167	.167	.222	9	-2	0-0	1.000	1	179	624	/O-3(LF)	-0.1

Year	Tm Lg	G	AB	R	H	2B	3B	HR	RBI	BB-IB	HP	SO	AVG	OBP	SLG	AOPS	ABR	SB-CS	FA	FR	Rng	Thr	G at Pos	BFW
1972	NY N	117	362	52	86	12	2	17	38	51-1	5	74	.238	.340	.423	118	9	2-1	.965	3	106	125	O-91(88-0-3),1-10	0.7
1973	†NY N	129	451	69	108	12	3	23	72	62-6	1	84	.239	.329	.432	112	7	1-1	.989	-4	89	89	1-95,O-29(LF)	-0.7
1974	NY N	137	507	70	128	19	0	20	63	66-9	0	77	.252	.337	.408	110	7	10-2	.994	1	100	96	*1-133	-0.2
1975	NY N	91	220	24	42	11	0	7	29	33-4	2	22	.191	.302	.336	81	-6	1-1	.985	6	113	92	O-31(29-2-0),1-29	-0.4
1976	NY N	127	443	56	120	25	4	15	78	65-1	0	53	.271	.362	.447	137	23	0-7	.985	2	103	102	*O-112(LF),1-12	1.6
1977	NY N	131	388	43	99	20	3	12	57	61-7	0	55	.255	.353	.415	111	8	6-2	.994	1	99	107	1-87,O-22(21-0-1)	0.4
1978	Pit N	108	295	39	80	17	0	6	38	34-6	0	25	.271	.342	.390	101	1	5-0	1.000	1	113	22	O-69(68-0-1),1-28	0.0
1979	†Pit N	128	326	52	90	9	4	16	60	53-6	1	37	.276	.373	.475	126	12	3-5	.958	0	111	50	O-64(LF),1-48	0.8
1980	Pit N	114	238	31	58	6	0	8	34	52-2	0	29	.244	.378	.370	108	5	2-2	.991	-4	85	111	1-70,O-11(10-0-1)	-0.3
1981	Pit N	34	59	6	14	1	0	2	9	5-0	0	3	.237	.292	.356	82	-2	0-0	.980	-2	25	44	/1-8,O-8(LF)	-0.5
	†Mon N	31	76	6	18	5	0	3	9	12-2	0	6	.237	.341	.421	114	2	0-1	.978	0	117	102	1-21	0.1
	Year	65	135	12	32	6	0	5	18	17-2	0	9	.237	.320	.393	100	0	0-1	.979	-2	96	89	1-29/O-8(LF)	-0.4
1982	Mon N	26	28	1	3	0	0	0	2	4-0	0	2	.107	.212	.107	-6	-4	0-0	1.000	0	88	193	/1-5	-0.4
	Pit N	33	25	5	6	2	0	2	8	6-1	1	3	.240	.406	.560	163	2	1-0	1.000	0	0	1163	/1	0.3
	Year	59	53	6	9	2	0	2	10	10-1	1	5	.170	.308	.321	76	-1	1-0	1.000	0	85	229	/1-6	-0.1
Total	12	1215	3436	455	855	140	16	131	498	504-45	10	473	.249	.344	.413	112	62	31-22	.991	6	99	102	1-547,O-440(432-2-6)	1.3

MILOSEVICH, MIKE Michael "Mollie" B 1.13.1915 Zeigler, IL D 2.3.1966 E.Chicago, IN BR/TR 5-10.5/172# d4.30

Year	Tm Lg	G	AB	R	H	2B	3B	HR	RBI	BB-IB	HP	SO	AVG	OBP	SLG	AOPS	ABR	SB-CS	FA	FR	Rng	Thr	G at Pos	BFW
1944	NY A	94	312	27	77	11	4	0	32	30	0	37	.247	.313	.308	75	-10	1-2	.954	5	100	121	S-91	0.1
1945	NY A	30	69	5	15	2	0	0	7	6	1	6	.217	.289	.246	54	-4	0-0	.957	0	98	110	S-22/2	-0.3
Total	2	124	381	32	92	13	4	0	39	36	1	43	.241	.309	.297	71	-14	1-2	.954	5	100	119	S-113/2	-0.2

MINCHER, DON Donald Ray B 6.24.1938 Huntsville, AL BL/TR 6-3/213# d4.18

Year	Tm Lg	G	AB	R	H	2B	3B	HR	RBI	BB-IB	HP	SO	AVG	OBP	SLG	AOPS	ABR	SB-CS	FA	FR	Rng	Thr	G at Pos	BFW
1960	Was A	27	79	10	19	4	1	2	5	11-0	0	11	.241	.330	.392	96	0	0-1	.977	-4	36	69	1-20	-0.6
1961	Min A	35	101	18	19	5	1	5	11	22-0	0	11	.188	.333	.406	91	-1	0-1	.969	-1	95	117	1-29	-0.4
1962	Min A	86	121	20	29	1	1	9	29	34-3	0	24	.240	.406	.488	134	7	0-0	.978	-1	86	97	1-25	0.4
1963	Min A	82	225	41	58	8	0	17	42	30-0	3	51	.258	.351	.520	138	12	0-0	.983	-4	75	85	1-60	0.5
1964	Min A	120	287	45	68	12	4	23	56	27-2	0	51	.237	.300	.547	130	10	0-0	.992	1	102	93	1-76	0.6
1965	†Min A	128	346	43	87	17	3	22	65	49-**15**	2	73	.251	.344	.509	134	16	1-3	.992	-4	81	97	1-99/O(LF)	0.5
1966	Min A	139	431	53	108	30	0	14	62	58-9	2	68	.251	.340	.418	110	8	3-2	.992	4	107	73	*1-130	0.4
1967	Cal A★	147	487	81	133	23	3	25	76	69-9	4	69	.273	.367	.487	157	36	0-3	.994	-1	97	96	*1-142/O(RF)	2.8
1968	Cal A	120	399	35	94	12	1	13	48	43-6	4	65	.236	.312	.368	111	5	0-2	.991	-2	92	**116**	*1-113	-0.5
1969	Sea A★	140	427	53	105	14	0	25	78	78-13	5	69	.246	.366	.454	131	20	10-11	.995	6	113	91	*1-122	1.5
1970	Oak A	140	463	62	114	18	0	27	74	56-11	3	71	.246	.327	.460	120	12	5-4	.990	-2	97	106	*1-137	-0.1
1971	Oak A	28	92	9	22	6	1	2	8	20-3	0	14	.239	.375	.391	120	3	1-1	.996	3	134	55	1-27	0.4
	Was A	100	323	35	94	15	1	10	45	53-4	2	52	.291	.389	.437	143	21	2-1	.990	1	108	109	1-88	1.6
	Year	128	415	44	116	21	2	12	53	73-7	2	66	.280	.386	.427	138	24	3-2	**.991**	4	**114**	96	*1-115	2.0
1972	Tex A	61	191	23	45	10	0	6	39	46-1	2	23	.236	.384	.382	136	12	2-1	.994	5	136	91	1-59	1.4
	†Oak A	47	54	2	8	1	0	0	5	10-0	0	16	.148	.281	.167	37	-4	0-2	.988	-1	68	69	1-11	-0.7
	Year	108	245	25	53	11	0	6	44	56-1	2	39	.216	.363	.335	115	8	2-3	.993	4	127	88	1-70	0.7
Total	13	1400	4026	530	1003	176	16	200	643	606-76	27	668	.249	.348	.450	127	157	24-32	.990	-2	99	95	*1-1138/O-2(1-0-1)	7.8

MINCHER, ED Edward M. B 6.17.1850 Baltimore, MD D 12.8.1918 Brooklyn, NY d5.4

Year	Tm Lg	G	AB	R	H	2B	3B	HR	RBI	BB-IB	HP	SO	AVG	OBP	SLG	AOPS	ABR	SB-CS	FA	FR	Rng	Thr	G at Pos	BFW
1871	Kek NA	9	36	4	8	0	0	0	5	0		0	.222	.222	.222	28	-3	1-0	.852	0	0	0	/O-9(LF)	-0.2
1872	Nat NA	**11**	53	5	5	0	0	0	4	0		1	.094	.094	.094	-36	-9	0-0	.837	2	83	0	O-11(LF)	-0.5
Total	2 NA	20	89	9	13	0	0	0	9	0		1	.146	.146	.146	-11	-12	1-0	.000	2	47	0	/O-20(LF)	-0.7

MINNEHAN, DAN Daniel Joseph B 11.28.1865 Troy, NY D 8.8.1929 Troy, NY BR/TR 5-10/145# d9.20

Year	Tm Lg	G	AB	R	H	2B	3B	HR	RBI	BB-IB	HP	SO	AVG	OBP	SLG	AOPS	ABR	SB-CS	FA	FR	Rng	Thr	G at Pos	BFW
1895	Lou N	8	34	6	13	0	0	0	6	1	0	1	.382	.400	.382	109	0	0	.920	0	92	284	/3-7,O-2(CF)	0.1

MINOR, DAMON Damon Reed B 1.5.1974 Canton, OH BL/TL 6-7/230# d9.2 b-Ryan

Year	Tm Lg	G	AB	R	H	2B	3B	HR	RBI	BB-IB	HP	SO	AVG	OBP	SLG	AOPS	ABR	SB-CS	FA	FR	Rng	Thr	G at Pos	BFW
2000	SF N	10	9	3	4	0	0	3	6	2-0	0	1	.444	.545	1.444	409	4	0-0	1.000	-0	0	0	/1-4	0.3
2001	SF N	19	45	3	7	1	0	0	3	3-1	0	8	.156	.208	.178	1	-7	0-0	.989	-1	64	49	1-11	-0.9
2002	SF N	83	173	21	41	6	0	10	24	24-6	2	34	.237	.333	.445	112	2	0-0	.997	-1	89	105	1-44/D-3	-0.2
Total	3	112	227	27	52	7	0	13	33	29-7	2	43	.229	.319	.432	103	-1	0-0	.995	-2	81	90	/1-59,D-3	-0.8

MINOR, RYAN Ryan Dale B 1.5.1974 Canton, OH BR/TR 6-7/225# d9.13 b-Damon

Year	Tm Lg	G	AB	R	H	2B	3B	HR	RBI	BB-IB	HP	SO	AVG	OBP	SLG	AOPS	ABR	SB-CS	FA	FR	Rng	Thr	G at Pos	BFW
1998	Bal A	9	14	3	6	1	0	0	1	0-0	0	3	.429	.429	.500	143	1	0-0	.833	-0	87	0	/3-6,1-3,D	0.0
1999	Bal A	46	124	13	24	7	0	3	10	8-0	0	43	.194	.241	.323	44	-11	1-0	.963	6	120	132	3-45/1	-0.4
2000	Bal A	32	84	4	11	1	0	0	3	3-0	1	20	.131	.170	.143	-20	-16	0-0	.927	-1	84	126	3-26/1-5	-1.6
2001	Mon N	55	95	10	15	2	0	2	13	9-0	1	31	.158	.234	.242	24	-11	0-1	.970	-6	64	0	3-24/O-2(LF),1D	-1.7
Total	4	142	317	30	56	11	0	5	27	20-0	2	97	.177	.228	.259	25	-37	1-1	.951	-1	97	97	3-101/1-10,D-4,O-2(LF)	-3.7

MINOSO, MINNIE Saturnino Orestes Armas (Arrieta) (born Orestes Arrieta (Armas)) B 11.29.1922 Havana, Cuba BR/TR 5-10/175# d4.19 C5 OF Total (1512-LF 83-CF 87-RF)

Year	Tm Lg	G	AB	R	H	2B	3B	HR	RBI	BB-IB	HP	SO	AVG	OBP	SLG	AOPS	ABR	SB-CS	FA	FR	Rng	Thr	G at Pos	BFW
1949	Cle A	9	16	2	3	0	0	1	1	2	2	2	.188	.350	.375	94	0	0-1	1.000	-0	115	0	/O-7(RF)	-0.1
1951	Cle A	8	14	3	6	2	0	0	2	1	2	1	.429	.529	.571	209	3	0-0	.952	-0	97	27	/1-7	0.2
	Chi A★	138	516	109	167	32	14	10	74	71	**14**	41	.324	.419	.498	150	39	31-10	.961	-9	88	69	O-82(44-2-41),3-68/S	2.8
	Year	146	530	112	173	34	**14**	10	76	72	**16**	42	.326	.422	.500	152	42	**31**-10	.961	-9	88	69	O-82(44-2-41),3-68/1-7,S	3.0
1952	Chi A★	147	569	96	160	24	9	13	61	71	**14**	46	.281	.375	.424	121	17	**22**-16	.979	-4	92	107	*O-143(70-63-10)/3-9,S	0.5
1953	Chi A★	151	556	104	174	24	8	15	104	74	**17**	43	.313	.410	.466	132	28	**25**-16	.967	2	96	146	*O-147(145-0-2),3-10	2.1
1954	Chi A★	153	568	119	182	29	**18**	19	116	77	**16**	46	.320	.411	**.535**	154	44	18-11	.978	6	103	133	*O-146(120-16-13)/3-9	4.1
1955	Chi A	139	517	79	149	26	7	10	70	76-3	10	43	.288	.387	.424	115	14	19-8	.971	6	99	162	*O-138(135-2-7)/3-2	1.3
1956	Chi A	151	545	106	172	29	**11**	21	88	86-4	**23**	40	.316	.425	.525	149	42	12-6	.974	-4	96	88	*O-148(147-0-1)/3-8,1	2.9
1957	Chi A★	153	568	96	176	**36**	5	12	103	79-5	**21**	54	.310	.408	.454	136	34	18-15	.984	-2	92	105	*O-152(LF)/3	2.2
1958	Cle A	149	556	94	168	25	2	24	80	59-3	**15**	53	.302	.383	.484	141	32	14-14	.975	6	104	144	*O-147(LF)/3	2.8
1959	Cle A★	148	570	92	172	32	0	21	92	54-2	**17**	46	.302	.377	.468	136	30	8-10	.985	9	105	145	*O-148(LF)	2.8
1960	Chi A★	**154**	591	89	**184**	32	4	20	105	52-2	**13**	63	.311	.374	.481	132	27	17-13	.980	-2	88	126	*O-154(152-0-5)	1.5
1961	Chi A	152	540	91	151	28	3	14	82	67-2	**16**	46	.280	.369	.420	114	14	9-4	.956	-1	99	92	*O-147(LF)	0.5
1962	StL N	39	97	14	19	5	0	1	10	7-0	3	17	.196	.271	.278	44	-8	4-0	.972	-0	89	137	O-27(LF)	-0.8
1963	Was A	109	315	38	72	12	2	4	30	33-1	8	38	.229	.315	.317	79	-8	8-6	.955	-3	76	80	O-74(LF)/3-8	-1.6
1964	Chi A	30	31	4	7	0	0	1	5	5-1	1	3	.226	.351	.323	91	0	0-0	1.000	0	129	0	/O-5(4-0-1)	0.0
1976	Chi A	3	8	0	1	0	0	0	0	0-0	0	2	.125	.125	.125	-27	-1	0-0	—	0			/D-3	-0.1
1980	Chi A	2	2	0	0	0	0	0	0	0-0	0	0	.000	.000	.000	-99	-1	0-0	—	0			/H	-0.1
Total	17	1835	6579	1136	1963	336	83	186	1023	814-23	192	584	.298	.389	.459	130	306	205-130	.974	4	96	120	*O-1665L,3-116/1-8,D-3,S-2	21.0

MIRABELLI, DOUG Douglas Anthony B 10.18.1970 Kingman, AZ BR/TR 6-1/205# d8.27

Year	Tm Lg	G	AB	R	H	2B	3B	HR	RBI	BB-IB	HP	SO	AVG	OBP	SLG	AOPS	ABR	SB-CS	FA	FR	Rng	Thr	G at Pos	BFW
1996	SF N	9	18	2	4	1	0	0	1	3-0	0	4	.222	.333	.278	66	-1	0-0	1.000	-2	104	0	/C-8	-0.2
1997	SF N	6	7	0	1	0	0	0	0	1-0	0	3	.143	.250	.143	6	-1	0-0	1.000	0	158	0	/C-6	-0.1
1998	SF N	10	17	2	4	2	0	1	4	2-0	0	6	.235	.316	.529	124	1	0-0	.974	-0	115	253	C-10	0.1
1999	SF N	33	87	10	22	6	0	1	10	9-1	1	25	.253	.327	.356	79	-3	0-0	1.000	-3	125	132	C-30	-0.4
2000	†SF N	82	230	23	53	10	2	6	28	36-2	2	57	.230	.337	.370	85	-5	1-0	.985	-11	98	107	C-80	-1.0
2001	Tex A	23	49	4	5	2	0	2	3	10-0	0	21	.102	.254	.265	36	-5	0-0	.990	-0	157	246	C-23/D	-0.4
	Bos A	54	141	16	38	8	0	9	26	17-2	4	36	.270	.360	.518	128	6	0-0	.995	-0	65	141	C-52/D	0.8
	Year	77	190	20	43	10	0	11	29	27-2	4	57	.226	.332	.453	103	1	0-0	.994	-1	91	171	C-75/D-2	0.4
2002	Bos A	57	151	17	34	7	0	7	25	17-0	3	33	.225	.312	.411	89	-2	0-0	1.000	-1	63	170	C-50/D-4	0.0
2003	†Bos A	62	163	23	42	13	0	6	18	11-0	1	36	.258	.307	.448	94	-2	0-0	.988	-3	62	114	C-55/1-2,D-4	-0.1
Total	8	336	863	97	203	49	2	32	115	106-5	11	221	.235	.324	.408	91	-12	1-0	.992	-20	88	136	C-314/D-10,1-2	-1.3

MIRANDA, WILLY Guillermo (Perez) B 5.24.1926 Velasco, Cuba D 9.7.1996 Baltimore, MD BB/TR 5-9.5/150# d5.6

Year	Tm Lg	G	AB	R	H	2B	3B	HR	RBI	BB-IB	HP	SO	AVG	OBP	SLG	AOPS	ABR	SB-CS	FA	FR	Rng	Thr	G at Pos	BFW
1951	Was A	7	9	2	4	0	0	0	0	0	0	0	.444	.444	.444	143	0	0-0	.818	-1	40	0	/S-2,1	-0.1
1952	Chi A	12	8	1	2	1	0	0	0	3	0	0	.250	.455	.375	131	1	0-0	1.000	3	144	156	/S-4,3-4,2	0.4
	StL A	7	11	2	1	0	1	0	1	3	0	1	.091	.286	.273	54	-1	0-0	.900	-1	100	37	/S-7	-0.2
	Chi A	58	142	13	31	3	1	0	7	10	1	14	.218	.275	.254	47	-10	1-0	.975	6	144	156	S-50/23	-0.2
	Year	77	161	16	34	4	2	0	8	16	1	15	.211	.287	.261	52	-10	1-0	.970	7	111	105	S-61/3-5,2-2	0.0
1953	StL A	17	6	2	1	0	0	0	0	1	0	1	.167	.286	.167	24	-1	1-1	.933	1	106	77	/S-8,3-6	0.1
	NY A	48	58	12	13	0	0	1	5	5	0	10	.224	.286	.276	54	-4	1-1	.984	9	118	154	S-45	0.6

Year	Tm Lg	G	AB	R	H	2B	3B	HR	RBI	BB-IB	HP	SO	AVG	OBP	SLG	AOPS	ABR	SB-CS	FA	FR	Rng	Thr	G at Pos	BFW
	Year	65	64	14	14	0	0	1	5	6	0	11	.219	.286	.266	51	-5	2-2	.979	10	117	148	S-53/3-6	0.7
1954	NY A	92	116	12	29	4	2	1	12	10	0	10	.250	.300	.345	82	-3	0-3	.948	9	107	146	S-88/2-4,3	0.8
1955	Bal A	153	487	42	124	12	6	1	38	42-4	1	58	.255	.313	.310	74	-19	4-3	.958	20	**110**	105	*S-153/2	1.3
1956	Bal A	148	461	38	100	16	4	2	34	46-3	0	73	.217	.287	.282	55	-31	3-6	.962	4	103	99	*S-147	-1.6
1957	Bal A	115	314	29	61	3	0	0	20	24-2	0	42	.194	.249	.204	28	-32	2-1	.966	-3	101	91	*S-115	-2.8
1958	Bal A	102	214	15	43	6	0	1	8	14-2	0	25	.201	.250	.243	38	-19	1-1	.962	-7	91	112	*S-102	-2.0
1959	Bal A	65	88	8	14	5	0	0	7	7-0	0	16	.159	.221	.216	21	-10	0-0	.974	11	124	150	S-47,3-11/2-5	0.3
Total	9	824	1914	176	423	50	14	6	132	165-11	2	250	.221	.282	.271	54	-129	13-16	.962	51	105	108	S-768/3-23,2-12,1	-3.4
MISSE, JOHN John Beverly B 5.30.1885 Highland, KS D 3.18.1970 St.Joseph, MO BR/TR 5-8/150# d5.26																								
1914	StL F	99	306	28	60	8	1	0	22	36	0	52	.196	.281	.229	38	-31	3	.948	1	105	76	2-50,S-48/3-2	-2.7
MITCHELL, CLARENCE Clarence Elmer B 2.22.1891 Franklin, NE D 11.6.1963 Grand Island, NE BL/TL 5-11.5/190# d6.2 Mil 1918 C2 ▲																								
1911	Det A	5	4	2	2	0	0	0	0	1	0		.500	.600	.500	198	1	0	1.000	-1	52	0	/P-5	0.0
1916	Cin N	56	117	11	28	2	1	0	11	4	0	6	.239	.264	.274	67	-5	1	.985	-0	107	**290**	P-29/1-9,O-3(LF)	-0.2
1917	Cin N	47	90	13	25	3	0	0	5	5	0	5	.278	.316	.311	97	0	0	.982	0	100	128	P-32/1-6,O-5(LF)	0.0
1918	Bro N	10	24	2	6	1	1	0	2	0	0	3	.250	.250	.375	90	-1	0	.750	-1	51	0	/O-6(RF),1-2,P	-0.2
1919	Bro N	34	49	7	18	1	0	1	2	4	0	4	.367	.415	.449	156	6	0	.976	1	115	112	P-23	0.0
1920	†Bro N	55	107	9	25	2	2	0	11	8	0	9	.234	.287	.290	64	-5	1-0	1.000	1	139	0	P-19,1-11/O-4(2-0-2)	-0.4
1921	Bro N	46	91	11	24	5	0	0	12	5	2	7	.264	.316	.319	66	-4	3-1	.945	3	127	**326**	P-37/1-4	0.1
1922	Bro N	56	155	21	45	6	3	3	28	19	1	6	.290	.371	.426	106	2	0-0	.992	4	130	108	1-42/P-5	0.2
1923	Phi N	53	78	10	21	3	2	1	9	4	0	11	.269	.305	.397	75	3	0-0	.880	-3	55	98	P-29	0.0
1924	Phi N	69	102	7	26	3	0	0	13	2	1	7	.255	.276	.284	45	0	1-0	**1.000**	3	126	135	P-30	0.0
1925	Phi N	52	92	7	18	2	0	0	13	5	0	9	.196	.237	.217	16	-12	2-0	**1.000**	4	132	289	P-32/1-2	0.2
1926	Phi N	39	78	8	19	4	0	0	6	5	0	5	.244	.289	.295	55	-5	0	.986	4	140	107	P-28/1-4	0.2
1927	Phi N	18	42	5	10	2	0	1	6	2	0	1	.238	.273	.357	67	2	0	.963	0	120	88	P-13	0.0
1928	Phi N	5	4	0	1	0	0	0	0	0	0	0	.250	.250	.250	30	0	0	1.000	0	215	0	/P-3	0.0
	†StL N	19	56	0	7	1	0	0	1	0	0	3	.125	.125	.143	-30	-4	0	.982	2	137	164	P-19	0.0
	Year	24	60	0	8	1	0	0	1	0	0	3	.133	.133	.150	-26	-4	0	**.983**	3	**140**	158	P-22	0.0
1929	StL N	26	66	9	18	3	1	0	9	4	0	6	.273	.314	.348	63	4	1	.974	-1	96	132	P-25	0.0
1930	StL N	1	2	0	1	0	0	0	0	0	0	0	.500	.500	.500	138	0	0	—	-0	0	0	/P	0.0
	NY N	24	47	9	12	1	0	0	1	1	0	5	.255	.271	.277	33	0	0	1.000	2	134	60	P-24	0.0
	Year	25	49	9	13	1	0	0	1	1	0	5	.265	.280	.286	38	1	0	1.000	2	131	59	P-25	0.0
1931	NY N	27	73	5	16	2	0	1	4	2	0	4	.219	.240	.288	42	2	0	.885	-2	83	83	P-27	0.0
1932	NY N	8	10	2	2	0	0	0	0	1	0	1	.200	.273	.200	30	0	0	.833	-1	48	0	/P-8	0.0
Total	18	650	1287	138	324	41	10	7	133	72	4	92	.252	.293	.315	64	-16	9-1	.972	15	114	155	P-390/1-80,O-18(12-0-8)	-0.1
MITCHELL, FRED Frederick Francis (born Frederick Francis Yapp) B 6.5.1878 Cambridge, MA D 10.13.1970 Newton, MA BR/TR 5-9.5/185# d4.27 M7 C3 ▲ OF Total (1-LF 2-CF)																								
1901	Bos A	20	44	5	7	0	2	0	4	2	0		.159	.196	.250	23	-5	0	.875	-1	106	223	P-17/2-2,S	-0.1
1902	Bos A	1	1	0	0	0	0	0	0	0	0		.000	.000	.000	-97	0	0	.667	0	171	2645	/P	0.0
	Phi A	20	48	7	9	1	1	0	3	1	0		.188	.204	.250	24	-5	1	.942	2	136	267	P-18/O(CF)	0.1
	Year	21	49	7	9	1	1	0	3	1	0		.184	.200	.245	22	-5	1	.927	2	137	352	P-19/O(CF)	0.1
1903	Phi N	29	95	11	19	4	0	0	10	0	0		.200	.200	.242	27	-1	0	.857	-3	81	150	P-28	0.0
1904	Phi N	25	82	9	17	3	1	0	3	5	0		.207	.253	.268	63	-4	1	.981	3	154	0	P-13/1-9,3-2,O(CF)	0.0
	Bro N	8	24	3	7	1	1	0	6	1	1		.292	.346	.417	139	3	0	.906	1	128	341	/P-8	0.0
	Year	33	106	12	24	4	2	0	9	6	1		.226	.274	.302	80	-3	1	.952	4	144	129	P-21/1-9,3-2,O(CF)	0.0
1905	Bro N	27	79	4	15	0	0	0	8	4	1		.190	.238	.190	30	-7	0	.881	-1	123	113	P-12/1-7,3-4,SO(LF)	-0.6
1910	NY A	68	196	16	45	7	2	0	18	9	3		.230	.274	.286	71	-7	6	.968	-9	*96*	*90*	C-62	-1.2
1913	Bos N	4	3	0	1	0	0	0	0	0	0	2	.333	.333	.333	89	0	0	—	0			H	0.0
Total	7	202	572	55	120	16	7	0	52	22	5	2	.210	.245	.262	52	-26	8	.904	-8	115	182	/P-97,C-62,1-16,3-6,O-3C,S-2,2-2	-1.8
MITCHELL, JOHNNY John Franklin B 8.9.1894 Detroit, MI D 11.4.1965 Birmingham, MI BB/TR 5-8/155# d5.21																								
1921	NY A	13	42	4	11	1	0	0	2	4	0	4	.262	.326	.286	56	-3	1-0	.958	-4	110	44	/S-7,2-5	-0.6
1922	NY A	4	4	1	0	0	0	0	0	0	0	1	.000	.000	.000	-98	-1	0-0	1.000	-0	79	0	/S-4	-0.1
	Bos A	59	203	20	51	4	1	1	8	16	4	17	.251	.318	.296	61	-12	1-2	.962	-3	101	103	S-58	-0.8
	Year	63	207	21	51	4	1	1	8	16	4	18	.246	.313	.290	58	-13	1-2	.963	-3	101	102	S-62	-0.9
1923	Bos A	92	347	40	78	15	4	0	19	34	1	18	.225	.296	.291	55	-23	7-11	.961	4	102	87	S-87/2-5	-1.2
1924	Bro N	64	243	42	64	10	0	1	16	37	0	22	.263	.361	.317	86	-3	3-1	.951	0	97	74	S-64	0.5
1925	Bro N	97	336	45	84	8	3	0	18	28	0	19	.250	.308	.292	55	-23	2-0	.947	-2	95	89	S-90	-1.4
Total	5	329	1175	152	288	38	8	2	63	119	5	81	.245	.317	.296	62	-65	14-14	.955	-5	99	87	S-310/2-10	-3.6
MITCHELL, KEITH Keith Alexander B 8.6.1969 San Diego, CA BR/TR 5-10/180# d7.23																								
1991	†Atl N	48	66	11	21	0	0	2	5	8-0	0	12	.318	.392	.409	118	2	3-1	.970	-1	91	89	O-34(24-1-10)	0.1
1994	Sea A	46	128	21	29	2	0	5	15	18-0	1	22	.227	.324	.359	75	-5	0-0	.980	-4	84	0	O-38(27-3-11)/D-6	-0.9
1996	Cin N	11	15	2	4	1	0	1	3	1-0	0	3	.267	.313	.533	117	0	0-0	.875	-0	109	0	O-5(2-1-2)	0.0
1998	Bos A	23	33	4	9	2	0	0	6	7-1	0	5	.273	.400	.333	92	0	1-0	1.000	-1	60	0	D-12,O-10(4-0-6)	-0.2
Total	4	128	242	38	63	5	0	8	29	34-1	1	42	.260	.353	.380	91	-3	4-1	.969	-6	85	27	/O-87(57-5-29),D-18	-1.0
MITCHELL, KEVIN Kevin Darnell B 1.13.1962 San Diego, CA BR/TR 5-11/210# d9.4 OF Total (756-LF 6-CF 53-RF)																								
1984	NY N	7	14	0	3	0	0	0	1	0-0	0	3	.214	.214	.214	21	-2	0-1	.833	-0	81	457	/3-5	-0.2
1986	†NY N	108	328	51	91	22	2	12	43	33-0	1	61	.277	.344	.466	125	11	3-3	.983	4	105	73	O-68(40-6-29),S-24/3-7,1-2	1.4
1987	SD N	62	196	19	48	7	1	7	26	20-3	0	38	.245	.313	.398	91	-3	0-0	.945	3	113	106	3-51/O-3(LF)	-0.1
	†SF N	69	268	49	82	13	1	15	44	28-1	2	50	.306	.376	.530	144	16	9-6	.962	-1	100	93	3-68/O-3(2-0-1),S	1.4
	Year	131	464	68	130	20	2	22	70	48-4	2	88	.280	.350	.474	121	13	9-6	.954	2	106	99	*3-119/O-6(5-0-1),S	1.3
1988	SF N	148	505	60	127	25	7	19	80	48-7	5	85	.251	.319	.442	123	13	5-5	.943	0	106	122	*3-102,O-40(LF)	1.2
1989	†SF N★	154	543	100	158	34	6	**47**	**125**	87-**32**	3	115	.291	.387	**.635**	**194**	**67**	3-4	.978	-2	96	92	*O-147(LF)/3-2	**6.2**
1990	SF N★	140	524	90	152	24	2	35	93	58-9	2	87	.290	.360	.544	151	35	4-7	.971	-0	97	87	*O-138(LF)	3.0
1991	SF N	113	371	52	95	13	1	27	69	43-8	5	57	.256	.338	.515	142	20	2-3	.970	-1	97	108	*O-100(LF)/1	1.6
1992	Sea A	99	360	48	103	24	0	9	67	35-4	3	46	.286	.351	.428	117	9	0-2	1.000	-1	98	91	O-69(LF),D-26	0.4
1993	Cin N	93	323	56	110	21	3	19	64	25-4	1	48	.341	.385	.601	160	27	1-0	.957	2	100	124	O-87(85-0-2)	2.5
1994	Cin N	95	310	57	101	18	1	30	77	59-15	3	62	.326	.429	.681	188	42	2-0	.972	1	89	184	O-89(LF)/1	3.8
1996	Bos A	27	92	9	28	4	0	2	13	11-0	1	14	.304	.385	.413	100	0	0-0	.935	-3	78	0	O-21(1-0-21)/D-4	-0.3
	Cin N	37	114	18	37	11	0	6	26	26-2	0	16	.325	.447	.579	168	13	0-0	.978	-1	102	0	O-31(LF)/1-3	1.0
1997	Cle A	20	59	7	9	1	0	4	11	9-2	1	11	.153	.275	.373	65	-3	1-0	.000	-0	0	0	D-16/O(LF)	-0.4
1998	Oak A	51	127	14	29	7	1	2	21	9-0	0	26	.228	.279	.346	63	-7	0-0	1.000	-1	88	0	D-23,O-10(LF)/1-2	-0.9
Total	13	1223	4134	630	1173	224	25	234	760	491-87	27	719	.284	.360	.520	143	238	30-31	.971	-2	96	99	O-807L,3-235/D-69,S-25,1-9	20.6
MITCHELL, DALE Loren Dale B 8.23.1921 Colony, OK D 1.5.1987 Tulsa, OK BL/TL 6-1/195# d9.15																								
1946	Cle A	11	44	7	19	3	0	0	5	1	0	2	.432	.444	.500	175	4	1-0	1.000	-0	105	0	O-11(CF)	0.4
1947	Cle A	123	493	69	156	16	10	1	34	23	0	14	.316	.347	.396	109	3	2-5	.977	-6	88	101	*O-115(83-42-1)	-1.2
1948	†Cle A	141	608	82	204	30	8	4	56	45	2	17	.336	.383	.431	119	15	13-18	**.991**	0	96	113	*O-140(140-1-0)	0.1
1949	Cle A★	149	640	81	**203**	16	**23**	3	56	43	0	11	.317	.360	.428	110	4	10-3	**.994**	-3	95	87	*O-149(LF)	-0.9
1950	Cle A	130	506	81	156	27	5	3	49	67	1	21	.308	.390	.399	106	7	3-7	.972	-11	87	33	*O-127(LF)	-1.4
1951	Cle A	134	510	83	148	21	7	11	62	53	1	16	.290	.358	.424	117	11	7-7	.992	-9	89	32	*O-124(LF)	-0.9
1952	Cle A★	134	511	61	165	26	3	5	58	52	1	9	.323	.387	.415	132	22	6-6	.992	-7	93	25	*O-128(LF)	0.6
1953	Cle A	134	500	76	150	26	4	13	60	42	0	20	.300	.354	.446	118	11	3-1	.970	-10	90	23	*O-125(LF)	-0.5
1954	†Cle A	53	60	6	17	1	0	1	6	9	0	1	.283	.377	.350	98	0	0-0	.889	-0	69	327	/O-6(LF),1	0.0
1955	Cle A	61	58	4	15	2	1	0	10	4-2	0	3	.259	.302	.328	68	-3	0-0	1.000	0	107	208	/1-8,O-3(LF)	-0.3
1956	Cle A	38	30	2	4	0	0	0	6	7-1	0	2	.133	.297	.133	17	-3	0-0	—	-0	0	0	/O(LF)	-0.3
	†Bro N	19	24	3	7	1	0	0	1	0-0	0	3	.292	.292	.333	63	-1	0-0	1.000	-0	90	0	/O-2(LF)	-0.2
Total	11	1127	3984	555	1244	169	61	41	403	346-3	5	119	.312	.368	.416	114	70	45-47	.985	-47	91	62	O-931(888-54-1)/1-9	-4.6
MITCHELL, MIKE Michael Francis B 12.12.1879 Springfield, OH D 7.16.1961 Phoenix, AZ BR/TR 6-1/185# d4.11																								
1907	Cin N	148	558	64	163	17	12	3	47	37	3		.292	.339	.382	121	12	17	.962	24	**200**	186	*O-146(3-0-144)/1-2	3.3
1908	Cin N	119	406	41	90	9	6	1	37	46	2		.222	.304	.281	89	-4	18	.959	2	110	56	*O-118(3-0-115)/1	-0.9
1909	Cin N	145	523	83	162	17	**17**	4	86	57	0		.310	.378	.430	152	30	37	.962	5	100	64	*O-145(RF)/1	3.2

Year	Tm Lg	G	AB	R	H	2B	3B	HR	RBI	BB-IB	HP	SO	AVG	OBP	SLG	AOPS	ABR	SB-CS	FA	FR	Rng	Thr	G at Pos	BFW
1910	Cin N	**156**	583	79	167	16	**18**	5	88	59	4	56	.286	.356	.401	126	17	35	.958	-2	99	92	*O-149(0-22-127)/1-7	0.9
1911	Cin N	142	529	74	154	22	22	2	84	44	2	34	.291	.348	.427	121	11	35	.971	9	114	113	*O-140(1-0-139)	1.2
1912	Cin N	147	552	60	156	14	13	4	78	41	1	43	.283	.333	.377	97	-5	23	.947	-1	106	85	*O-144(RF)	-1.3
1913	Chi N	82	279	37	73	11	6	4	35	32	1	33	.262	.340	.387	107	3	15-8	.941	1	100	119	O-82(72-0-10)	0.0
	Pit N	54	199	25	54	8	2	1	16	14	0	15	.271	.319	.347	94	-2	8-10	.946	3	110	112	O-54(CF)	-0.5
	Year	136	478	62	127	19	8	5	51	46	1	48	.266	.331	.370	102	1	23-18	.943	4	104	116	*O-136(72-54-10)	-0.5
1914	Pit N	76	273	31	64	11	5	2	23	16	1	16	.234	.279	.333	86	-6	5	.984	6	124	81	O-76(RF)	-0.5
	Was A	55	193	20	55	5	3	1	20	22	1	19	.285	.361	.358	112	3	9-7	.957	2	98	142	O-53(47-0-6)	0.2
Total	8	1124	4095	514	1138	130	104	27	514	368	15	216	.278	.340	.380	114	59	202-25	.959	49	118	103	*O-1107(126-76-905)/1-11	5.6
MITCHELL, BOBBY Robert Van B 4.7.1955 Salt Lake City, UT BL/TL 5-10/170# d9.1																								
1980	LA N	9	3	1	1	0	0	0	0	1-0	0	0	.333	.500	.333	139	0	0-0	1.000	0	139	0	/O-8(0-7-1)	0.0
1981	LA N	10	8	0	1	0	0	0	0	1-0	0	4	.125	.222	.125	1	-1	0-0	1.000	0	122	0	/O-7(1-6-1)	-0.1
1982	Min A	124	454	48	113	11	6	2	28	54-4	2	53	.249	.331	.313	76	-14	8-9	.997	11	116	105	*O-121(5-115-6)	-0.6
1983	Min A	59	152	26	35	4	2	1	15	28-2	1	21	.230	.354	.303	80	-3	1-1	.990	-2	89	84	O-44(1-43-0)	-0.6
Total	4	202	617	75	150	15	8	3	43	84-6	3	78	.243	.336	.308	76	-18	9-10	.996	8	110	98	O-180(7-171-8)	-1.3
MITCHELL, BOBBY Robert Vance B 10.22.1943 Norristown, PA BR/TR 6-4/190# d7.5																								
1970	NY A	10	22	1	5	2	0	0	4	2-0	1	3	.227	.320	.318	81	0	0-2	1.000	2	177	0	/O-7(0-2-5)	0.0
1971	Mil A	35	55	7	10	1	1	2	6	6-1	0	18	.182	.262	.345	72	-2	0-2	.974	2	121	228	O-19(2-7-10)	-0.2
1973	Mil A	47	130	12	29	6	0	5	20	5-1	0	32	.223	.250	.385	79	-4	4-1	.960	-2	77	0	O-20(10-0-10),D-19	-0.8
1974	Mil A	88	173	27	42	6	2	5	20	18-1	1	46	.243	.314	.387	103	0	7-6	.969	-1	96	88	D-53,O-26(10-2-14)	-0.3
1975	Mil A	93	229	39	57	14	3	9	41	25-1	0	69	.249	.320	.454	117	5	3-4	.992	2	108	49	O-72(LF),D-11	0.2
Total	5	273	609	86	143	29	6	21	91	56-4	2	168	.235	.299	.406	100	-1	14-15	.984	3	107	68	O-144(94-11-39)/D-83	-1.1
MITTERLING, RALPH Ralph "Sarge" B 4.19.1890 Freeburg, PA D 1.22.1956 Pittsburgh, PA BR/TR 5-10/165# d7.7																								
1916	Phi A	13	39	1	6	0	0	0	2	3	0	6	.154	.214	.154	11	-4	0	.944	-1	85	86	O-12(1-11-0)	-0.6
MITTERWALD, GEORGE George Eugene B 6.7.1945 Berkeley, CA BR/TR 6-2/206# d9.15 C5																								
1966	Min A	3	5	1	1	0	0	0	0	0-0	0	0	.200	.200	.200	14	-1	0-0	1.000	0	*70*	*0*	/C-3	0.0
1968	Min A	11	34	1	7	1	0	0	1	3-0	0	8	.206	.270	.235	52	-2	0-0	.961	-1	67	36	C-10	-0.2
1969	†Min A	69	187	18	48	8	0	5	13	17-1	3	47	.257	.327	.380	96	-1	0-1	.987	9	135	74	C-63/O(LF)	1.1
1970	†Min A	117	369	36	82	12	2	15	46	34-6	2	84	.222	.291	.388	84	-9	3-5	.996	26	141	128	*C-117	2.2
1971	Min A	125	388	38	97	13	1	13	44	39-9	0	104	.250	.316	.389	97	-2	3-3	.986	-2	102	97	*C-120	0.0
1972	Min A	64	163	12	30	4	1	1	8	9-2	0	37	.184	.225	.239	37	-13	0-1	.984	5	75	152	C-61	-0.7
1973	Min A	125	432	50	112	15	0	16	64	39-0	5	111	.259	.326	.405	101	0	3-1	.992	4	97	99	*C-122/D-3	1.0
1974	Chi N	78	215	17	54	7	0	7	28	18-4	2	42	.251	.310	.381	90	-3	1-3	.974	-6	65	142	C-68	-0.7
1975	Chi N	84	200	19	44	4	3	5	26	19-7	0	42	.220	.285	.345	72	-8	0-0	.976	3	118	188	C-59,1-10	-0.4
1976	Chi N	101	303	19	65	7	0	5	28	16-2	0	63	.215	.249	.287	49	-21	1-2	.981	-2	93	113	C-64,1-25	-2.4
1977	Chi N	110	349	40	83	22	0	9	43	28-7	1	69	.238	.295	.378	72	-14	3-1	.989	10	108	130	*C-109/1	0.1
Total	11	887	2645	251	623	93	7	76	301	222-38	13	607	.236	.296	.362	80	-74	14-17	.987	47	*105*	*118*	C-796/1-36,D-3,O(LF)	-0.0
MIZE, JOHNNY John Robert "The Big Cat" B 1.7.1913 Demorest, GA D 6.2.1993 Demorest, GA BL/TR 6-2/215# d4.16 Mil 1943-45 C1 HF1981																								
1936	StL N	126	414	76	136	30	8	19	93	50	1	32	.329	.402	.577	162	36	1	.994	0	96	78	1-97/O-8(RF)	2.5
1937	StL N★	145	560	103	204	40	7	25	113	56	5	57	.364	.427	.595	171	56	2	.988	-14	67	91	*1-144	2.9
1938	StL N	149	531	85	179	34	**16**	27	102	74	4	47	.337	.422	**.614**	172	53	0	.989	-0	100	96	*1-140	3.9
1939	StL N★	153	564	104	197	44	14	**28**	108	92	4	49	**.349**	.444	**.626**	**174**	**62**	0	.987	-3	91	94	*1-152	**4.3**
1940	StL N★	155	579	111	182	31	13	**43**	**137**	82	5	49	.314	.404	**.636**	**173**	**57**	7	.990	-6	82	83	*1-153	3.6
1941	StL N★	126	473	67	150	**39**	8	16	100	70	1	45	.317	.406	.535	153	35	4	.994	4	107	110	*1-122	2.7
1942	NY N★	142	541	97	165	25	7	26	**110**	60	5	39	.305	.380	**.521**	161	41	3	**.995**	-2	90	98	*1-138	2.7
1946	NY N★	101	377	70	127	18	3	22	70	62	5	26	.337	.437	.576	185	44	3	.989	6	121	97	*1-101	4.8
1947	NY N★	154	586	**137**	177	26	2	**51**	**138**	74	4	42	.302	.384	.614	160	48	2	**.996**	9	119	93	*1-154	5.0
1948	NY N★	152	560	110	162	26	4	**40**	125	94	4	37	.289	.395	.564	156	45	4	.991	3	108	97	*1-152	4.2
1949	NY N★	106	388	59	102	15	0	18	62	50	3	19	.263	.351	.441	111	6	1	.994	2	106	95	*1-101	0.5
	†NY A	13	23	4	6	1	0	1	2	4	1	2	.261	.393	.435	119	1	0-0	.980	-0	77	87	/1-6	0.0
1950	†NY A	90	274	43	76	12	0	25	72	29	2	24	.277	.351	.595	143	14	0-1	.996	-2	78	117	1-72	0.9
1951	†NY A	113	332	37	86	14	1	10	49	36	4	24	.259	.339	.398	102	1	1-0	.994	-3	81	119	1-93	-0.4
1952	†NY A	78	137	9	36	9	0	4	29	11	2	15	.263	.327	.416	112	2	0-0	.987	0	106	155	1-27	0.2
1953	†NY A★	81	104	6	26	3	0	4	27	12	2	17	.250	.339	.394	101	0	0-0	1.000	-0	89	171	1-15	-0.1
Total	15	1884	6443	1118	2011	367	83	359	1337	856	52	524	.312	.397	.562	157	501	28-1	.992	-7	96	97	*1-1667/O-8(RF)	37.7
MIZEROCK, JOHN John Joseph B 12.8.1960 Punxsutawney, PA BL/TR 5-11/190# d4.12 M1 C2																								
1983	Hou N	33	85	8	13	4	1	1	10	12-2	1	15	.153	.263	.259	49	-6	0-0	.967	-2	101	112	C-33	-0.7
1985	Hou N	15	38	6	9	4	0	0	6	2-0	1	8	.237	.293	.342	79	-1	0-0	.966	2	74	121	C-15	0.1
1986	Hou N	44	81	9	15	1	1	1	6	24-2	1	16	.185	.374	.259	81	-1	0-0	.987	-1	106	54	C-42	0.0
1989	Atl N	11	27	1	6	0	0	0	2	0-0	0	3	.222	.222	.222	27	-3	0-0	1.000	1	301	73	C-11	-0.1
Total	4	103	231	24	43	9	2	2	24	38-4	3	42	.186	.307	.268	64	-11	0-0	.979	0	118	87	C-101	-0.7
MIZEUR, BILL William Francis "Bad Bill" B 6.22.1897 Nokomis, IL D 8.27.1976 Decatur, IL BL/TR 6/180# d9.30																								
1923	StL A	1	1	0	0	0	0	0	0	0	0	0	.000	.000	.000	-95	0	0-0	—	0			H	0.0
1924	StL A	1	1	0	0	0	0	0	0	0	0	0	.000	.000	.000	-94	0	0-0	—	0			H	0.0
Total	2	2	2	0	0	0	0	0	0	0	0	0	.000	.000	.000	-94	0	0-0	.979	0				0.0
MOATES, DAVE David Allan B 1.30.1948 Great Lakes, IL BL/TL 5-9/163# d9.21																								
1974	Tex A	1	0	0	0	0	0	0	0	0-0	0	0	—	—	—	—	0	0-0	—	0			R	0.0
1975	Tex A	54	175	21	48	9	0	3	14	13-0	0	15	.274	.321	.377	99	0	9-2	.984	0	93	184	O-51(1-49-1)/D	0.0
1976	Tex A	85	137	21	33	7	1	0	13	11-2	0	18	.241	.293	.307	75	-4	6-3	.991	3	102	137	O-66(8-37-25)/D-7	-0.2
Total	3	140	312	42	81	16	1	3	27	24-2	0	33	.260	.309	.346	88	-4	15-5	.987	4	97	162	O-117(9-86-26)/D-8	-0.2
MOELLER, CHAD Chad Edward B 2.18.1975 Upland, CA BR/TR 6-3/207# d6.20																								
2000	Min A	48	128	13	27	3	1	1	9	9-0	0	33	.211	.261	.273	35	-13	1-0	.979	2	175	51	C-48	-0.8
2001	Ari N	25	56	8	13	0	1	1	2	6-1	0	12	.232	.306	.321	59	-4	0-0	1.000	-4	82	112	C-25	-0.6
2002	†Ari N	37	105	10	30	11	1	2	16	17-3	0	23	.286	.385	.467	116	3	0-1	.997	9	101	95	C-35	1.3
2003	Ari N	78	239	29	64	17	1	7	29	23-11	2	59	.268	.335	.435	90	-3	1-2	.987	-5	84	93	C-76	-0.4
Total	4	188	528	60	134	31	4	11	56	55-15	2	127	.254	.325	.390	79	-17	2-3	.989	1	110	85	C-184	-0.5
MOELLER, DANNY Daniel Edward B 3.23.1885 DeWitt, IA D 4.14.1951 Florence, AL BB/TR 5-11/165# d9.24																								
1907	Pit N	11	42	4	12	1	1	0	3	4	0		.286	.348	.357	119	1	2	.800	-1	76	327	O-11(RF)	-0.1
1908	Pit N	36	109	14	21	3	1	0	9	9	0		.193	.254	.239	57	-5	4	.950	-3	0	0	O-27(3-1-23)	-1.2
1912	Was A	132	519	90	143	26	10	6	46	52	4		.276	.346	.399	112	8	30	.944	3	98	124	*O-132(31-0-101)	0.3
1913	Was A	153	589	88	139	15	10	5	42	72	3	103	.236	.322	.321	86	-10	62	.926	3	104	116	*O-153(16-0-137)	-1.6
1914	Was A	151	571	83	143	19	10	1	45	71	7	89	.250	.341	.324	96	-1	26-25	.930	-1	101	104	*O-150(1-1-149)	-1.4
1915	Was A	118	438	65	99	11	10	2	23	59	1	63	.226	.319	.311	87	-7	32-10	.952	-5	89	90	*O-116(21-0-95)	-1.6
1916	Was A	78	240	30	59	8	1	1	23	30	2	35	.246	.335	.300	92	-2	13	.963	4	101	165	O-63(23-0-40)	-0.1
	Cle A	25	30	5	2	0	0	0	1	5	0	6	.067	.200	.067	-19	-4	2	1.000	-0	108	0	/O-8(3-2-3),2	-0.5
	Year	103	270	35	61	8	1	1	24	35	2	41	.226	.319	.274	78	-6	15	.966	4	101	154	O-71(26-2-43)/2	-0.6
Total	7	704	2538	379	618	83	43	15	192	302	17	296	.243	.328	.328	93	-20	171-35	.938	-2	95	113	O-660(98-4-559)/2	-6.2
MOFFETT, JOE Joseph W. B 6.1859 Wheeling, WV 6/179# d5.6 b-Sam																								
1884	Tol AA	56	204	17	41	5	3	0		2	0		.201	.209	.255	49	-12		.957	-5	46	115	1-38,3-11/2-4,O-3(1-3-0)	-1.8
MOFFETT, SAM Samuel R. B 3.14.1857 Wheeling, WV D 5.5.1907 Butte, MT BR/TR 6/175# d5.15 b-Joe ▲																								
1884	Cle N	67	256	26	47	12	2	0	15	8		56	.184	.208	.246	41	-17		.827	6	186	0	O-42(13-1-28),P-24/1-2,32	-0.7
1887	Ind N	11	41	6	5	1	0	0	1	1	0	6	.122	.143	.146	-20	-7	2	.857	-1	75	0	/P-6,O-5(1-2-3)	-0.2
1888	Ind N	10	35	6	4	0	0	0	0	5	0	4	.114	.225	.114	11	-3	0	.750	-2	41	342	/P-7,O-3(CF)	-0.2
Total	3	88	332	38	56	13	2	0	16	14	0	66	.169	.202	.220	30	-27	2	.821	2	169	0	/O-50(14-6-31),P-37,1-2,23	-1.1

Year	Tm Lg	G	AB	R	H	2B	3B	HR	RBI	BB-IB	HP	SO	AVG	OBP	SLG	AOPS	ABR	SB-CS	FA	FR	Rng	Thr	G at Pos	BFW
MOHARDT, JOHN John Henry B 1.21.1898 Pittsburgh, PA D 11.24.1961 LaJolla, CA BR/TR 5-10/165# d4.15																								
1922	Det A	5	1	2	1	0	0	0	0	1	0	0	1.000	1.000	1.000	436	1	0-1	1.000	0	407	0	/O-3(1-1-1)	0.1
MOHLER, KID Ernest Follette B 12.13.1870 Oneida, IL D 11.4.1961 San Francisco, CA BR/TL 5-4.5/145# d9.29																								
1894	Was N	3	9	0	1	0	0	0	0	2	0	4	.111	.273	.111	-5	-2	0	.952	1	106	65	/2-3	-0.1
MOHR, DUSTAN Dustan Kyle B 6.19.1976 Hattiesburg, MS BR/TR 6/210# d8.29																								
2001	Min A	20	51	6	12	2	0	0	4	5-0	0	17	.235	.298	.275	53	-3	1-1	1.000	2	139	0	O-19(6-0-15)/D	-0.2
2002	†Min A	120	383	55	103	23	2	12	45	31-3	1	86	.269	.325	.433	98	-1	6-3	.992	5	115	62	*O-113(28-1-94)/D-3	-0.1
2003	Min A	121	348	50	87	22	0	10	36	33-0	1	106	.250	.314	.399	87	-7	5-2	.976	3	117	35	*O-110(30-11-77)/D-6	-0.7
Total	3	261	782	111	202	47	2	22	85	69-3	2	209	.258	.319	.408	90	-11	12-6	.985	10	118	45	O-242(64-12-186)/D-10	-1.0
MOKAN, JOHNNIE John Leo B 9.23.1895 Buffalo, NY D 2.10.1985 Buffalo, NY BR/TR 5-7/165# d4.15																								
1921	Pit N	19	52	7	14	3	2	0	9	5	0	3	.269	.333	.404	92	-1	0-0	.946	-0	122	0	O-15(6-0-7)	-0.2
1922	Pit N	31	89	9	23	3	1	0	8	9	0	3	.258	.327	.315	65	-4	0-1	.903	-2	72	134	O-23(3-0-20)	-0.7
	Phi N	47	151	20	38	7	1	3	27	16	1	25	.252	.327	.371	73	-6	1-0	.905	-3	83	113	O-37(36-2-3)/3-2	-1.1
	Year	78	240	29	61	10	2	3	35	25	1	28	.254	.327	.350	70	-10	1-1	.905	-5	79	120	O-60(39-2-23)/3-2	-1.8
1923	Phi N	113	400	76	125	23	3	10	48	53	6	31	.313	.401	.460	113	10	6-11	.969	5	101	**150**	*O-105(84-21-2)/3	0.5
1924	Phi N	96	366	50	95	15	1	7	44	30	3	27	.260	.321	.363	74	-13	7-5	.986	-2	95	90	O-94(93-2-0)	-2.2
1925	Phi N	75	209	30	69	11	2	6	42	27	4	9	.330	.417	.488	120	7	3-5	.984	-4	97	21	O-68(36-32-2)	0.0
1926	Phi N	127	456	68	138	23	5	6	62	41	4	31	.303	.365	.414	104	3	4	.967	-1	92	117	*O-123(67-0-67)	-0.7
1927	Phi N	74	213	22	61	13	2	0	33	25	0	21	.286	.361	.366	94	-1	5	.962	-2	91	95	O-63(27-9-28)	-0.7
Total	7	582	1936	282	563	98	17	32	273	206	18	150	.291	.364	.409	97	-5	26-22	.966	-9	94	104	O-528(352-66-129)/3-3	-5.1
MOLE, FENTON Fenton Le Roy "Muscles" B 6.14.1925 San Leandro, CA BL/TL 6-1.5/200# d9.1																								
1949	NY A	10	27	2	5	2	1	0	2	3	0	5	.185	.267	.333	58	-2	0-0	1.000	1	117	160	/1-8	-0.1
MOLINA, BENGIE Benjamin Jose B 7.20.1974 Rio Piedras, P.R. BR/TR 5-11/200# d9.21 b-Jose																								
1998	Ana A	2	1	0	0	0	0	0	0	0-0	0	0	.000	.000	.000	-99	0	0-0	1.000	-0	0	0	/C-2	0.0
1999	Ana A	31	101	8	26	5	0	1	10	6-0	2	6	.257	.312	.337	66	-5	0-1	.991	8	127	109	C-30	0.4
2000	Ana A	130	473	59	133	20	2	14	71	23-0	6	33	.281	.318	.421	84	-13	1-0	.991	9	105	**129**	*C-127/D-2	0.4
2001	Ana A	96	325	31	85	11	0	6	40	16-3	8	51	.262	.309	.351	73	-13	0-1	.991	0	107	106	C-94/D	-0.7
2002	†Ana A	122	428	34	105	18	0	5	47	15-3	4	34	.245	.274	.322	59	-26	0-0	**.999**	13	142	122	*C-121	-0.5
2003	Ana A	119	409	37	115	24	0	14	71	13-2	2	31	.281	.304	.443	98	-3	1-1	.993	13	128	147	*C-117	1.6
Total	6	500	1737	169	464	78	2	40	239	73-8	22	155	.267	.302	.383	78	-60	2-3	.993	43	121	126	C-491/D-3	1.2
MOLINA, IZZY Islay B 6.3.1971 New York, NY BR/TR 6/200# d8.15																								
1996	Oak A	14	25	0	5	2	0	0	1	1-0	0	3	.200	.231	.280	29	-3	0-0	1.000	-3	46	0	C-12/D	-0.5
1997	Oak A	48	111	6	22	3	1	3	7	3-0	0	17	.198	.219	.324	40	-11	0-0	.992	-4	73	87	C-48	-1.2
1998	Oak A	6	2	1	1	0	0	0	0	0-0	0	0	.500	.500	.500	165	0	0-0	1.000	0	32	0	/C-5	0.1
2002	Bal A	1	3	1	1	0	0	0	0	0-0	0	0	.333	.333	.333	82	0	0-0	1.000	0	54	390	/C	0.0
Total	4	69	141	8	29	5	1	3	8	4-0	0	20	.206	.228	.319	41	-14	0-0	.993	-6	68	80	/C-66,D	-1.6
MOLINA, JOSE Jose Benjamin (Matta) B 6.3.1975 Bayamon, P.R. BR/TR 6-1/195# d9.6 b-Bengie																								
1999	Chi N	10	19	3	5	1	0	0	1	2-1	0	4	.263	.333	.316	67	-1	0-0	1.000	1	100	150	C-10	0.1
2001	Ana A	15	37	8	10	3	0	2	4	3-0	0	8	.270	.325	.514	113	1	0-0	1.000	2	77	230	C-15	0.4
2002	†Ana A	29	70	5	19	3	0	0	5	5-0	0	15	.271	.312	.314	70	-3	0-2	.983	4	84	151	C-29	0.2
2003	Ana A	53	114	12	21	4	0	0	6	1-0	3	26	.184	.210	.219	15	-14	0-0	.996	-2	112	82	C-53	-1.4
Total	4	107	240	28	55	11	0	2	16	11-1	3	53	.229	.268	.300	51	-17	0-2	.993	6	98	130	C-107	-0.7
MOLINARO, BOB Robert Joseph B 5.21.1950 Newark, NJ BL/TR 6/190# d9.18																								
1975	Det A	6	19	2	5	0	1	0	1	1-0	0	0	.263	.300	.368	84	-1	0-0	1.000	0	83	243	/O-6(RF)	-0.1
1977	Det A	4	4	0	1	1	0	0	0	0-0	0	2	.250	.250	.500	94	0	0-0	—	0			H	0.0
	Chi A	1	2	0	1	0	0	0	0	0-0	0	1	.500	.500	.500	174	0	1-0	1.000	-0	90	0	/O(RF)	0.0
	Year	5	6	0	2	1	0	0	0	0-0	0	3	.333	.333	.500	119	0	1-0	1.000	-0	90	0	/O(RF)	0.0
1978	Chi A	105	286	39	75	5	5	6	27	19-2	3	12	.262	.314	.378	93	-4	22-6	1.000	-3	88	58	O-62(12-1-50),D-32	-0.8
1979	Bal A	8	6	0	0	0	0	0	0	1-0	0	3	.000	.143	.000	-60	-1	1-0	1.000	0	164	0	/O-5(LF)	-0.1
1980	Chi A	119	344	48	100	16	4	5	36	26-7	7	29	.291	.348	.404	107	4	18-7	.957	-2	97	93	O-49(LF),D-47	0.0
1981	Chi A	47	42	7	11	1	1	1	9	8-1	1	1	.262	.377	.405	133	2	1-0	1.000	0	114	0	/O-2(1-0-1),D-4	0.2
1982	Chi N	65	66	6	13	1	0	1	12	6-1	0	5	.197	.264	.258	45	-5	1-1	1.000	-1	27	0	/O-4(LF)	-0.7
	Phi N	19	14	0	4	0	0	0	2	3-1	0	1	.286	.412	.286	96	0	1-0	—	0			H	0.0
	Year	84	80	6	17	1	0	1	14	9-2	0	6	.213	.292	.262	55	-5	2-1	1.000	-1	27	0	/O-4(LF)	-0.7
1983	Phi N	19	18	1	2	1	0	1	3	0-0	0	2	.111	.105	.333	19	-2	0-0	—	0			H	-0.3
	Det A	8	2	3	0	0	0	0	0	1-0	0	1	.000	.333	.000	1	0	1-1	—	0			/D	0.0
Total	8	401	803	106	212	25	11	14	90	65-12	11	57	.264	.324	.375	95	-7	46-15	.980	-6	91	77	O-129(71-1-58)/D-84	-1.8
MOLITOR, PAUL Paul Leo B 8.22.1956 St.Paul, MN BR/TR 6/185# d4.7 C3 HF2004																								
1978	Mil A	125	521	73	142	26	4	6	45	19-2	4	54	.273	.301	.372	89	-9	30-12	.976	5	108	100	2-91,S-31/3D	0.7
1979	Mil A	140	584	88	188	27	16	9	62	48-5	2	48	.322	.372	.469	126	20	33-13	.979	6	**113**	97	*2-122,S-10/D-8	3.5
1980	Mil A✳	111	450	81	137	29	2	9	37	48-4	3	48	.304	.372	.438	126	18	34-7	.971	6	104	123	2-91,S-12/3D	3.4
1981	†Mil A	64	251	45	67	11	0	2	19	25-1	3	29	.267	.341	.335	100	1	10-6	.976	-2	90	129	O-46(0-43-4),D-16	-0.2
1982	†Mil A	160	666	**136**	201	26	8	19	71	69-1	1	93	.302	.366	.450	132	29	41-9	.942	-3	99	**150**	*3-150/S-4,D-6	3.0
1983	Mil A	152	608	95	164	28	6	15	47	59-4	2	74	.270	.333	.410	113	10	41-8	.966	2	105	112	*3-146/D-2	1.6
1984	Mil A	13	46	3	10	1	0	0	6	2-0	0	8	.217	.245	.239	38	-4	1-0	.933	3	156	219	/3-7,D-4	0.0
1985	Mil A★	140	576	93	171	28	3	10	48	54-6	1	80	.297	.356	.408	110	9	21-7	.953	3	101	115	*3-135/D-4	1.2
1986	Mil A	105	437	62	123	24	6	9	55	40-0	0	81	.281	.340	.426	104	2	20-5	.944	0	94	155	3-91,D-10/O-4(LF)	0.3
1987	Mil A	118	465	**114**	164	**41**	5	16	75	69-2	2	67	.353	.438	.566	159	44	45-10	.947	-6	85	109	D-58,3-41,2-19	4.0
1988	Mil A★	154	609	115	190	34	6	13	60	71-8	2	54	.312	.384	.452	132	28	41-10	.941	-5	96	96	*3-105,D-49/2	2.8
1989	Mil A	155	615	84	194	35	4	11	56	64-4	4	67	.315	.379	.439	133	28	27-11	.950	11	115	97	*3-112,D-28,2-16	4.2
1990	Mil A	103	418	64	119	27	6	12	45	37-4	1	51	.285	.343	.464	125	13	18-3	.988	7	112	87	2-60,1-37/3-2,D-4	2.2
1991	Mil A★	158	665	**133**	**216**	32	**13**	17	75	77-16	6	62	.325	.399	.489	148	45	19-8	.986	-2	94	130	*D-112,1-46	3.7
1992	Mil A★	158	609	89	195	36	7	12	89	73-12	3	66	.320	.389	.461	142	36	31-6	.996	-5	70	117	*D-108,1-48	3.0
1993	†Tor A★	160	636	121	**211**	37	5	22	111	77-3	3	71	.332	.402	.509	144	41	22-4	.985	-2	79	78	*D-137,1-23	3.0
1994	Tor A★	**115**	454	86	155	30	4	14	75	55-4	1	48	.341	.410	.518	138	27	20-0	1.000	0	88	139	*D-110/1-5	2.2
1995	Tor A	130	525	63	142	31	2	15	60	61-1	5	57	.270	.350	.423	101	2	12-0	—	0	0	0	*D-129	-0.4
1996	Min A	161	660	99	**225**	41	8	9	113	56-10	3	72	.341	.390	.468	115	17	18-6	.993	1	117	91	*D-143,1-17	0.7
1997	Min A	135	538	63	164	32	4	10	89	45-8	0	73	.305	.351	.435	104	4	11-4	.991	-0	97	64	*D-122,1-12	-0.4
1998	Min A	126	502	75	141	29	5	4	69	45-5	1	41	.281	.335	.382	87	-9	9-2	1.000	1	124	57	*D-115/1-9	-1.5
Total	21	2683	10835	1782	3319	605	114	234	1307	1094-100	47	1244	.306	.369	.448	122	352	504-131	.950	20	102	122	*D-1174,3-791,2-400,1-197/SO	37.0
MOLLENKAMP, FRED Frederick Henry B 3.15.1890 Cincinnati, OH D 11.1.1948 Cincinnati, OH 6-2/195# d8.29																								
1914	Phi N	3	8	0	1	0	0	0	0	2	0	0	.125	.300	.125	26	-1	0	1.000	2	328	129	/1-3	0.1
MOLLWITZ, FRITZ Frederick August B 6.16.1890 Coburg, Germany D 10.3.1967 Bradenton, FL BR/TR 6-2/170# d9.26																								
1913	Chi N	2	7	1	3	0	0	0	0	0	0	0	.429	.429	.429	145	0	0	1.000	-0	0	0	/1-2	0.0
1914	Chi N	13	20	0	3	0	0	0	1	0	0	3	.150	.150	.150	-11	-3	1	.962	-0	66	0	/1-4,O(RF)	-0.4
	Cin N	32	111	12	18	2	0	0	5	3	2	9	.162	.198	.180	12	-12	2	.991	1	112	105	1-32	-1.3
	Year	45	131	12	21	2	0	0	6	3	2	12	.160	.191	.176	9	-15	3	.989	1	108	97	1-36/O(RF)	-1.7
1915	Cin N	153	525	36	136	21	3	1	51	15	1	49	.259	.281	.316	79	-15	19-11	**.996**	-0	95	**122**	*1-153	-2.1
1916	Cin N	65	183	12	41	4	4	0	16	5	0	12	.224	.245	.290	65	-9	6	.981	-1	100	104	1-54	-1.2
	Chi N	33	71	1	19	2	0	0	11	7	0	6	.268	.333	.296	85	-1	4	.976	-1	123	95	1-19/O-6(4-0-2)	-0.2
	Year	98	254	13	60	6	4	0	27	12	0	18	.236	.271	.291	71	-9	10	.980	-1	105	102	1-73/O-6(4-0-2)	-1.4
1917	Pit N	36	140	15	36	4	1	0	12	8	0	8	.257	.297	.300	81	-3	4	.994	-1	87	69	1-36/2	-0.6
1918	Pit N	119	432	43	116	12	7	0	45	23	0	24	.269	.305	.329	90	-6	23	.990	-1	95	101	*1-119	-1.1
1919	Pit N	56	168	11	29	2	4	0	12	15	2	18	.173	.249	.232	43	-12	9	.994	-3	69	91	1-53/O(RF)	-1.8
	StL N	25	83	7	19	3	0	0	5	7	0	3	.229	.289	.265	71	-3	2	.994	1	102	139	1-25	-0.3
	Year	81	251	18	48	5	4	0	17	22	2	21	.191	.262	.243	52	-15	11	.994	-2	80	108	1-78/O(RF)	-2.1

Year	Tm Lg	G	AB	R	H	2B	3B	HR	RBI	BB-IB	HP	SO	AVG	OBP	SLG	AOPS	ABR	SB-CS	FA	FR	Rng	Thr	G at Pos	BFW
Total	7	534	1740	138	420	50	19	1	158	83	5	132	.241	.278	.294	72	-64	70-11	.991	-5	94	106	1-497/O-8(4-0-4),2	-9.0
MONACO, BLAS Blas B 11.16.1915 San Antonio, TX D 2.10.2000 San Antonio, TX BB/TR 5-11/170# d8.18																								
1937	Cle A	5	7	0	2	0	1	0	2	0	1	2	.286	.375	.571	134	0	0-0	1.000	0	107	0	/2-3	0.0
1946	Cle A	12	6	2	0	0	0	0	0	1	0	1	.000	.143	.000	-62	-1	0-0	—	0			H	-0.1
Total	2	17	13	2	2	0	1	0	2	1	1	3	.154	.267	.308	53	-1	0-0	1.000	0	107	0	/2-3	-0.1
MONAHAN, SHANE Shane Hartland B 8.12.1974 Syosset, NY BL/TR 6/195# d7.9																								
1998	Sea A	62	211	17	51	8	1	4	28	8-0	0	53	.242	.269	.346	59	-14	1-2	.992	2	111	91	O-62(61-3-2)	-1.4
1999	Sea A	16	15	3	2	0	0	0	0	0-0	0	6	.133	.133	.133	-32	-3	0-0	1.000	-0	105	0	/O-9(7-0-3),D-3	-0.3
Total	2	78	226	20	53	8	1	4	28	8-0	0	59	.235	.261	.332	53	-17	1-2	.992	1	111	86	/O-71(68-3-5),D-3	-1.7
MONCEWICZ, FREDDIE Frederick Alfred B 9.1.1903 Brockton, MA D 4.23.1969 Brockton, MA BR/TR 5-8.5/175# d6.19																								
1928	Bos A	3	1	0	0	0	0	0	0	0	0	1	.000	.000	.000	-99	0	0-0	1.000	0	101	0	/S-2	0.0
MONCHAK, ALEX Alex B 12.22.1919 Bayonne, NJ BR/TR 6/180# d6.22 C17																								
1940	Phi N	19	14	1	2	0	0	0	0	0	0	6	.143	.143	.143	-22	-2	1	.833	-1	91	92	/S-9,2	-0.3
MONDAY, RICK Robert James B 11.20.1945 Batesville, AR BL/TL 6-3/200# d9.3																								
1966	KC A	17	41	4	4	1	1	0	2	6-0	0	16	.098	.213	.171	12	-5	1-1	.964	-0	99	146	O-15(CF)	-0.6
1967	KC A	124	406	52	102	14	6	14	58	42-2	2	107	.251	.322	.419	122	10	3-6	.972	9	109	**221**	*O-113(3-110-0)	1.5
1968	Oak A★	148	482	56	132	24	7	8	49	72-7	4	143	.274	.371	.402	142	27	14-6	.978	-3	94	121	*O-144(CF)	2.4
1969	Oak A	122	399	57	108	17	4	12	54	72-11	5	100	.271	.388	.424	133	21	12-3	.964	-9	96	40	*O-119(CF)	1.0
1970	Oak A	112	376	63	109	19	7	10	37	58-0	2	99	.290	.387	.457	137	21	17-11	.981	-3	103	45	*O-109(CF)	1.5
1971	†Oak A	116	355	53	87	9	3	18	56	49-5	0	93	.245	.335	.439	121	9	6-9	.984	-5	94	93	*O-111(CF)	0.0
1972	Chi N	138	434	68	108	22	5	11	42	78-8	1	102	.249	.362	.399	105	6	12-9	**.996**	-10	87	78	*O-134(0-132-2)	-0.8
1973	Chi N	149	554	93	148	24	5	26	56	92-7	1	124	.267	.372	.469	123	19	5-12	.973	-9	93	101	*O-148(CF)	0.4
1974	Chi N	142	538	84	158	19	7	20	58	70-6	2	94	.294	.375	.467	130	22	7-9	.984	-9	87	118	*O-139(CF)	0.7
1975	Chi N	136	491	89	131	29	4	17	60	83-12	1	95	.267	.373	.446	121	17	8-3	.973	-7	96	74	*O-131(CF)	0.7
1976	Chi N	137	534	107	145	20	5	32	77	60-8	2	125	.272	.346	.507	129	19	5-9	.993	-2	105	61	*O-103(5-99-0),1-32	1.0
1977	†LA N	118	392	47	90	13	1	15	48	60-6	0	109	.230	.330	.383	91	-4	1-4	.991	-16	78	43	*O-115(0-114-1)/1-3	-2.3
1978	†LA N★	119	342	54	87	14	1	19	57	49-11	1	100	.254	.348	.468	127	12	2-4	.995	-6	92	50	*O-103(11-80-30)/1	0.4
1979	LA N	12	33	2	10	0	0	0	2	5-0	0	6	.303	.395	.303	94	0	0-0	.964	0	123	0	O-10(0-8-3)	0.0
1980	LA N	96	194	35	52	7	1	10	25	28-3	1	49	.268	.363	.469	133	9	2-2	.969	-4	93	30	O-50(1-31-25)	0.4
1981	†LA N	66	130	24	41	1	2	11	25	24-3	1	42	.315	.423	.608	198	17	1-2	.962	-3	85	40	O-41(6-0-37)	1.3
1982	LA N	104	210	37	54	6	4	11	42	39-6	1	51	.257	.372	.481	142	12	2-1	.943	-5	70	116	O-57(18-0-40)/1-4	0.5
1983	†LA N	99	178	21	44	7	1	6	20	29-9	0	42	.247	.351	.399	108	3	0-0	.969	-2	97	41	O-44(14-0-31)/1-4	-0.1
1984	LA N	31	47	4	9	2	0	1	7	8-3	0	16	.191	.309	.298	72	-2	0-0	.987	-1	79	48	1-10/O-2(2-0-1)	-0.3
Total	19	1986	6136	950	1619	248	64	241	775	924-107	24	1513	.264	.361	.443	124	213	98-91	.979	-84	94	86	*O-1688(60-1490-170)/1-54	7.7
MONDESI, RAUL Raul Ramon (Avelino) B 3.12.1971 San Cristobal, D.R. BR/TR 5-11/202# d7.19																								
1993	LA N	42	86	13	25	3	1	4	10	4-0	0	16	.291	.322	.488	120	2	4-1	.951	2	110	174	O-40(20-6-17)	0.3
1994	LA N	112	434	63	133	27	8	16	56	16-5	2	78	.306	.333	.516	126	13	11-8	.965	1	94	**194**	*O-112(0-15-109)	0.9
1995	†LA N★	139	536	91	153	23	6	26	88	33-4	4	96	.285	.328	.496	126	16	27-4	.980	9	106	174	*O-138(0-24-114)	2.3
1996	†LA N	157	634	98	188	40	7	24	88	32-9	5	122	.297	.334	.495	125	20	14-7	.967	7	113	103	*O-157(RF)	1.8
1997	LA N	159	616	95	191	42	5	30	87	44-7	6	105	.310	.360	.541	143	36	32-15	.989	9	118	87	*O-159(RF)	3.7
1998	LA N	148	580	85	162	26	5	30	90	30-4	3	112	.279	.316	.497	117	10	16-10	.980	-9	92	67	*O-148(0-94-54)	-0.1
1999	LA N	159	601	98	152	29	5	33	99	71-6	3	134	.253	.332	.483	110	6	36-9	.982	-3	101	66	*O-158(0-1-158)	0.1
2000	Tor A	96	388	78	105	22	2	24	67	32-0	3	73	.271	.329	.523	108	3	22-6	.967	1	105	75	O-96(RF)	0.1
2001	Tor A	149	572	88	144	26	4	27	84	73-3	6	128	.252	.342	.453	105	4	30-11	.972	-1	89	179	*O-149(RF)	-0.2
2002	Tor A	75	299	51	67	16	1	15	45	31-1	3	57	.224	.301	.435	90	-5	9-2	.984	-2	96	76	O-62(RF),D-13	-0.9
	†NY A	71	270	39	65	18	0	11	43	28-2	2	46	.241	.315	.430	96	-1	6-4	.969	-6	81	93	O-70(0-11-59)/D	-1.0
	Year	146	569	90	132	34	1	26	88	59-3	5	103	.232	.308	.432	93	-6	15-6	.976	-8	88	85	*O-132(0-11-121),D-14	-1.9
2003	NY A	98	361	56	93	23	3	16	49	38-6	2	66	.258	.330	.471	110	5	17-7	.986	3	103	129	O-97(RF)/D	0.4
	Ari N	45	162	27	49	8	1	8	22	18-0	1	31	.302	.372	.512	117	4	5-4	.964	-1	103	38	O-43(0-2-42)	0.1
Total	11	1450	5539	882	1527	303	48	264	828	450-47	40	1064	.276	.333	.491	116	113	229-88	.976	9	101	113	*O-1429(20-153-1273)/D-15	7.5
MONEY, DON Donald Wayne "Brooks" B 6.7.1947 Washington, DC BR/TR 6-1/190# d4.10																								
1968	Phi N	4	13	1	3	2	0	0	2	2-1	0	4	.231	.333	.385	115	0	0-1	1.000	-1	74	156	/S-4	0.0
1969	Phi N	127	450	41	103	22	2	6	42	43-5	1	83	.229	.296	.327	77	-14	1-3	.969	18	111	101	*S-126	1.9
1970	Phi N	120	447	66	132	25	4	14	66	43-6	7	68	.295	.361	.463	124	15	4-7	.961	5	96	119	*3-119/S-2	1.8
1971	Phi N	121	439	40	98	22	8	7	38	31-10	3	80	.223	.276	.358	79	-13	4-1	.953	7	110	132	3-68,O-40(LF),2-20	-0.7
1972	Phi N	152	536	54	119	16	2	15	52	41-5	2	92	.222	.278	.343	74	-19	5-7	**.978**	15	102	**128**	*3-151/S-2	-0.8
1973	Mil A	145	556	75	158	28	2	11	61	53-3	3	53	.284	.347	.401	113	11	22-5	**.971**	-11	93	94	*3-124,S-21	0.4
1974	Mil A☆	159	629	85	178	32	3	15	65	62-5	2	80	.283	.346	.415	120	17	19-6	**.989**	-7	98	123	*3-157/2D	1.2
1975	Mil A	109	405	58	112	16	1	15	43	31-1	3	51	.277	.331	.432	114	6	7-9	.951	-6	91	108	3-99/S-7	-0.1
1976	Mil A★	117	439	51	117	18	4	12	62	47-2	0	50	.267	.333	.408	120	11	6-5	.958	-2	95	116	*3-103,D-10/S	0.8
1977	Mil A✳	152	570	86	159	28	3	25	83	57-2	7	70	.279	.348	.470	122	17	8-5	.981	18	**111**	112	*2-116,O-23(LF),3-15/D-7	3.9
1978	Mil A★	137	518	88	152	30	2	14	54	48-2	7	70	.293	.361	.440	124	17	3-0	.994	6	100	105	1-61,2-36,3-25,D-15/S-2	2.2
1979	Mil A	92	350	52	83	20	1	6	38	40-0	2	47	.237	.316	.351	81	-9	1-0	1.000	-3	124	140	D-33,3-26,1-19,2-16	-1.3
1980	Mil A	86	289	39	74	17	1	17	46	40-0	1	36	.256	.348	.498	133	13	0-0	.940	1	104	169	3-55,1-14,D-14/2-2	1.2
1981	†Mil A	60	185	17	40	7	0	2	14	19-0	1	27	.216	.288	.286	71	-7	0-0	.977	-7	92	83	3-56/1D	-1.6
1982	†Mil A	96	275	40	78	14	3	16	55	32-2	1	38	.284	.360	.531	150	19	0-2	.923	3	117	66	D-66,3-16,1-11/2	1.8
1983	Mil A	43	114	5	17	5	0	1	8	11-1	0	17	.149	.220	.219	24	-12	0-0	.980	4	142	0	D-28,3-11/1-2	-0.9
Total	16	1720	6215	798	1623	302	36	176	729	600-45	40	866	.261	.328	.406	106	52	80-51	.968	39	99	118	*3-1025,2-192,D-176,S-165,1/O	9.8
MONROE, CRAIG Craig Keystone B 2.27.1977 Texarkana, TX BR/TR 6-1/195# d7.28																								
2001	Tex A	27	52	8	11	1	0	2	5	6-0	0	18	.212	.293	.346	65	-3	2-0	1.000	4	135	292	O-24(6-0-21)/D	0.1
2002	Det A	13	25	3	3	1	0	1	1	0-0	1	5	.120	.154	.280	13	-3	0-2	.950	1	133	245	/O-9(4-0-5),D-3	-0.3
2003	Det A	128	425	51	102	18	1	23	70	27-2	2	89	.240	.287	.449	98	-4	4-2	.970	1	99	122	*O-108(75-2-38),D-13	-0.8
Total	3	168	502	62	116	20	1	26	76	33-2	3	112	.231	.281	.430	90	-10	6-4	.973	6	105	149	O-141(85-2-64)/D-17	-1.0
MONROE, FRANK Frank W. B Hamilton, OH d7.18																								
1884	Ind AA	2	8	1	0	0	0	0		0	0		.000	.000	.000	-99	-2		1.000	-1	0	0	/O(RF)C	-0.3
MONROE, JOHN John Allen B 8.24.1898 Farmersville, TX D 6.19.1956 Conroe, TX BL/TR 5-10/160# d4.16																								
1921	NY N	19	21	4	3	0	0	1	3	3	1	6	.143	.280	.286	50	-2	0-0	.846	-1	98	44	/2-8,S	-0.2
	Phi N	41	133	13	38	4	2	1	8	11	1	9	.286	.345	.368	82	-3	2-2	.938	4	122	85	2-28/3-9	0.2
	Year	60	154	17	41	4	2	2	11	14	2	15	.266	.335	.357	79	-4	2-2	.920	3	118	78	2-36/3-9,S	0.0
MONTAGUE, ED Edward Francis B 7.24.1905 San Francisco, CA D 6.17.1988 Daly City, CA BR/TR 5-10/165# d5.14																								
1928	Cle A	32	51	12	12	0	1	0	3	6	2	7	.235	.339	.275	62	-3	0-0	.914	2	117	123	S-15/3-9	0.0
1930	Cle A	58	179	37	47	5	2	1	16	37	1	38	.263	.392	.330	82	-3	1-5	.917	-7	91	76	S-46,3-13	-0.6
1931	Cle A	64	193	27	55	8	3	1	26	21	1	22	.285	.358	.373	87	-3	3-4	.924	13	118	86	S-64	1.2
1932	Cle A	66	192	29	47	5	1	0	24	21	2	24	.245	.326	.281	55	-13	3-3	.891	-14	88	75	S-57,3-11	-2.2
Total	4	220	615	105	161	18	7	2	69	85	6	91	.262	.357	.324	74	-22	7-12	.912	-6	102	82	S-182/3-33	-1.6
MONTANEZ, WILLIE Guillermo (Naranjo) B 4.1.1948 Catano, P.R. BL/TL 6-1/193# d4.12																								
1966	Cal A	8	2	2	0	0	0	0	0	0-0	0	2	.000	.000	.000	-99	-1	1-0	1.000	0	0	1093	/1-2	0.0
1970	Phi N	18	25	3	6	0	0	0	3	1-1	0	4	.240	.269	.240	39	-2	0-0	1.000	1	89	306	O-10(1-0-9)/1-5	-0.2
1971	Phi N	158	599	78	153	27	6	30	99	67-14	3	105	.255	.327	.471	126	19	4-7	.972	-6	93	114	*O-158(0-137-24)/1-9	0.7
1972	Phi N	147	531	60	131	**39**	3	13	64	58-13	1	108	.247	.320	.405	103	3	1-3	.985	8	106	**201**	*O-130(CF),1-14	0.6
1973	Phi N	146	552	69	145	16	5	11	65	46-7	6	80	.263	.324	.370	90	-8	2-6	.994	-2	91	103	1-99,O-51(RF)	-2.3
1974	Phi N	143	527	55	160	33	1	7	79	32-6	3	57	.304	.343	.410	107	5	3-6	.992	-2	92	108	*1-137/O(RF)	-1.0
1975	Phi N	21	84	9	24	8	0	2	16	4-0	0	12	.286	.315	.452	108	1	1-0	.990	2	134	122	1-21	0.1
	SF N	135	518	52	158	26	2	8	85	45-8	4	50	.305	.359	.409	110	8	5-3	.994	-1	93	99	*1-134	-0.4
	Year	156	602	61	182	34	2	10	101	49-8	4	62	.302	.353	.415	110	8	6-3	.993	1	99	102	*1-155	-0.3

Year	Tm Lg	G	AB	R	H	2B	3B	HR	RBI	BB-IB	HP	SO	AVG	OBP	SLG	AOPS	ABR	SB-CS	FA	FR	Rng	Thr	G at Pos	BFW
1976	SF N	60	230	22	71	15	2	2	20	15-5	1	15	.309	.351	.417	115	4	2-1	.989	3	125	108	1-58	0.3
	Atl N	103	420	52	135	14	0	9	64	21-6	0	32	.321	.353	.419	112	6	0-4	.986	-8	76	96	*1-103	-1.3
	Year	163	650	74	206	29	2	11	84	36-11	1	47	.317	.352	.418	113	10	2-5	.987	-4	94	100	*1-161	-1.0
1977	Atl N★	136	544	70	156	31	1	20	68	35-3	0	60	.287	.328	.458	97	-2	1-1	.992	-6	80	74	*1-134	-1.7
1978	NY N	159	609	66	156	32	0	17	96	60-19	1	92	.256	.320	.392	103	2	9-4	.995	2	103	108	*1-158	-0.6
1979	NY N	109	410	36	96	19	0	5	47	25-7	1	48	.234	.277	.317	65	-21	0-1	.989	3	115	107	*1-108	-2.6
	Tex A	38	144	19	46	6	0	8	24	8-1	1	14	.319	.357	.528	137	7	0-1	.995	1	112	84	1-19,D-17	0.6
1980	SD N	128	481	39	132	12	4	6	63	36-9	3	52	.274	.325	.353	96	-4	3-4	.994	4	114	107	*1-124	-0.9
	Mon N	14	19	1	4	0	0	0	1	3-1	0	3	.211	.318	.211	50	-1	0-1	1.000	-0	86	0	/1-4	-0.2
	Year	142	500	40	136	12	4	6	64	39-10	3	55	.272	.325	.348	94	-5	3-5	.994	4	113	104	*1-128	-1.1
1981	Mon N	26	62	6	11	0	1	0	5	4-0	0	9	.177	.227	.210	24	-6	0-0	.992	1	128	86	1-16	-0.7
	Pit N	29	38	2	10	0	0	1	1	1-0	0	2	.263	.282	.342	74	-2	0-0	1.000	-1	23	81	1-11	-0.3
	Year	55	100	8	21	0	1	1	6	5-0	0	11	.210	.248	.260	43	-8	0-0	.995	-0	95	84	1-27	-1.0
1982	Pit N	36	32	4	9	1	0	0	1	3-3	0	3	.281	.343	.313	82	-1	0-0	1.000	0	178	166	/1-2,O-2(LF)	-0.1
	Phi N	18	16	0	1	0	0	0	1	1-0	0	3	.063	.118	.063	-47	-3	0-0	1.000	0	190	0	/1-6	-0.3
	Year	54	48	4	10	1	0	0	2	4-3	0	6	.208	.269	.229	40	-4	0-0	1.000	1	186	58	/1-8,O-2(LF)	-0.4
Total	14	1632	5843	645	1604	279	25	139	802	465-103	24	751	.275	.327	.402	101	4	32-42	.992	0	99	101	*1-1164,O-352(2-267-85)/D-17	-10.3

MONTEAGUDO, RENE Rene (Miranda) B 3.12.1916 Havana, Cuba D 9.14.1973 Hialeah, FL BL/TL 5-7/165# d9.6 s-Aurelio ▲

Year	Tm Lg	G	AB	R	H	2B	3B	HR	RBI	BB-IB	HP	SO	AVG	OBP	SLG	AOPS	ABR	SB-CS	FA	FR	Rng	Thr	G at Pos	BFW
1938	Was A	5	6	0	3	0	0	0	1	0	0	0	.500	.500	.500	162	1	0-0	1.000	-1	24	0	/P-5	0.0
1940	Was A	27	33	4	6	1	1	0	1	1	0	4	.182	.206	.273	24	0	0-0	.941	-1	60	83	P-27	0.0
1944	Was A	10	38	2	11	2	0	0	4	0	0	1	.289	.289	.342	84	-1	0-0	.929	-0	82	201	/O-9(RF)	-0.2
1945	Phi N	114	193	26	58	6	0	0	15	28	0	7	.301	.389	.332	104	3	2	.918	-2	82	196	O-35(12-0-23),P-14	-0.1
Total	4	156	270	32	78	9	1	0	21	29	0	12	.289	.358	.330	94	3	2-0	.889	-4	57	98	/P-46,O-44(12-0-32)	-0.3

MONTEMAYOR, FELIPE Felipe Angel "Monty" B 2.7.1930 Monterrey, Mexico BL/TL 6-2/185# d4.14

Year	Tm Lg	G	AB	R	H	2B	3B	HR	RBI	BB-IB	HP	SO	AVG	OBP	SLG	AOPS	ABR	SB-CS	FA	FR	Rng	Thr	G at Pos	BFW
1953	Pit N	28	55	5	6	4	0	0	2	4	3	13	.109	.210	.182	3	-8	0-0	1.000	1	100	205	O-12(1-11-0)	-0.7
1955	Pit N	36	95	10	20	1	3	2	8	18-2	1	24	.211	.342	.347	85	-2	1-0	.957	-3	89	0	O-28(6-14-9)	-0.5
Total	2	64	150	15	26	5	3	2	10	22-2	4	37	.173	.295	.287	55	-10	1-0	.974	-2	93	67	/O-40(7-25-9)	-1.2

MONTGOMERY, AL Alvin Atlas B 7.3.1920 Loving, NM D 4.26.1942 Waverly, VA BR/TR 5-10.5/185# d6.20

Year	Tm Lg	G	AB	R	H	2B	3B	HR	RBI	BB-IB	HP	SO	AVG	OBP	SLG	AOPS	ABR	SB-CS	FA	FR	Rng	Thr	G at Pos	BFW
1941	Bos N	42	52	4	10	1	0	0	4	9	1	8	.192	.323	.212	55	-3	0	.976	-3	95	92	C-30	-0.5

MONTGOMERY, RAY Raymond James B 8.8.1969 Bronxville, NY BR/TR 6-3/195# d7.3

Year	Tm Lg	G	AB	R	H	2B	3B	HR	RBI	BB-IB	HP	SO	AVG	OBP	SLG	AOPS	ABR	SB-CS	FA	FR	Rng	Thr	G at Pos	BFW
1996	Hou N	12	14	4	3	1	0	1	4	1-0	0	5	.214	.267	.500	105	0	0-0	1.000	0	121	0	/O-6(5-1-2)	0.0
1997	Hou N	29	68	8	16	4	1	0	4	5-0	0	18	.235	.276	.324	62	-4	0-0	1.000	1	94	195	O-18(2-2-15)	-0.4
1998	Hou N	6	5	2	2	0	0	0	0	0-0	0	0	.400	.400	.400	114	0	0-0	1.000	0	155	0	O-2(1-0-1)	0.0
Total	3	47	87	14	21	5	1	1	8	6-0	0	23	.241	.281	.356	72	-4	0-0	1.000	1	100	160	/O-26(8-3-18)	-0.4

MONTGOMERY, BOB Robert Edward B 4.16.1944 Nashville, TN BR/TR 6-1/203# d9.6

Year	Tm Lg	G	AB	R	H	2B	3B	HR	RBI	BB-IB	HP	SO	AVG	OBP	SLG	AOPS	ABR	SB-CS	FA	FR	Rng	Thr	G at Pos	BFW
1970	Bos A	22	78	8	14	2	0	1	4	6-0	1	20	.179	.244	.244	33	-7	0-0	.981	0	99	143	C-22	-0.6
1971	Bos A	67	205	19	49	11	2	2	24	16-4	3	43	.239	.300	.341	77	-6	1-0	.989	-6	93	68	C-66	-0.9
1972	Bos A	24	77	7	22	1	0	2	7	3-0	0	17	.286	.309	.377	99	0	0-0	.985	-3	106	49	C-22	-0.2
1973	Bos A	34	128	18	41	6	2	7	25	7-0	0	36	.320	.353	.563	146	7	0-0	.974	-0	80	118	C-33	0.8
1974	Bos A	88	254	26	64	10	0	4	38	13-1	1	50	.252	.287	.339	75	-8	3-0	.977	-3	98	101	C-79/D-5	-0.8
1975	†Bos A	62	195	16	44	10	1	2	26	4-0	1	37	.226	.241	.318	53	-12	1-1	.987	-7	104	86	C-53/1-6,D-3	-1.8
1976	Bos A	31	93	10	23	3	1	3	13	5-1	0	20	.247	.283	.398	88	-2	0-1	.983	-3	102	77	C-30/D	-0.4
1977	Bos A	17	40	6	12	2	0	2	7	4-0	1	9	.300	.370	.500	123	1	0-0	.982	-3	89	78	C-15	-0.1
1978	Bos A	10	29	2	7	1	1	0	5	2-0	0	12	.241	.290	.345	70	-1	0-0	.976	-0	299	83	C-10	-0.1
1979	Bos A	32	86	13	30	4	1	0	7	4-1	0	24	.349	.374	.419	109	1	1-0	.984	-4	71	32	C-31	-0.2
Total	10	387	1185	125	306	50	8	23	156	64-7	7	268	.258	.296	.372	83	-27	6-2	.983	-29	100	85	C-361/D-9,1-6	-4.3

MONTOYO, CHARLIE Jose Carlos (Diaz) B 10.17.1965 Florida, P.R. BR/TR 5-10/170# d9.7

Year	Tm Lg	G	AB	R	H	2B	3B	HR	RBI	BB-IB	HP	SO	AVG	OBP	SLG	AOPS	ABR	SB-CS	FA	FR	Rng	Thr	G at Pos	BFW
1993	Mon N	4	5	1	2	1	0	0	3	0-0	0	0	.400	.400	.600	157	0	0-0	—	-1	0	0	/2-3	-0.1

MONTREUIL, AL Allan Arthur B 8.23.1943 New Orleans, LA BR/TR 5-5/158# d9.1

Year	Tm Lg	G	AB	R	H	2B	3B	HR	RBI	BB-IB	HP	SO	AVG	OBP	SLG	AOPS	ABR	SB-CS	FA	FR	Rng	Thr	G at Pos	BFW
1972	Chi N	5	11	0	1	0	0	0	0	1-0	0	4	.091	.167	.091	-23	-2	0-0	1.000	-1	75	46	/2-5	-0.3

MONZON, DAN Daniel Francisco B 5.17.1946 Bronx, NY D 1.21.1996 Santo Domingo, D.R. BR/TR 5-10/182# d4.25

Year	Tm Lg	G	AB	R	H	2B	3B	HR	RBI	BB-IB	HP	SO	AVG	OBP	SLG	AOPS	ABR	SB-CS	FA	FR	Rng	Thr	G at Pos	BFW
1972	Min A	55	55	13	15	1	0	0	5	8-0	0	12	.273	.365	.291	92	0	1-0	.977	1	102	37	2-13/3-5,S-3,O(LF)	0.2
1973	Min A	39	76	10	17	1	1	0	4	11-0	1	9	.224	.326	.263	66	-3	1-0	.968	1	81	93	2-17,3-14/O(LF)	-0.1
Total	2	94	131	23	32	2	1	0	9	19-0	1	21	.244	.342	.275	77	-3	2-0	.971	2	90	69	/2-30,3-19,S-3,O-2(LF)	0.1

MOOCK, JOE Joseph Geoffrey B 3.12.1944 Plaquemine, LA BL/TR 6-1/180# d9.1

Year	Tm Lg	G	AB	R	H	2B	3B	HR	RBI	BB-IB	HP	SO	AVG	OBP	SLG	AOPS	ABR	SB-CS	FA	FR	Rng	Thr	G at Pos	BFW
1967	NY N	13	40	2	9	2	0	0	5	0-0	0	7	.225	.225	.275	43	-3	0-0	.917	1	113	165	3-12	-0.2

MOOLIC, GEORGE George Henry "Prunes" B 3.12.1865 Lawrence, MA D 2.19.1915 Methuen, MA BR/TR 5-7/145# d5.1

Year	Tm Lg	G	AB	R	H	2B	3B	HR	RBI	BB-IB	HP	SO	AVG	OBP	SLG	AOPS	ABR	SB-CS	FA	FR	Rng	Thr	G at Pos	BFW
1886	Chi N	16	56	9	8	3	0	0	2	2		17	.143	.172	.196	10	-6	0	.945	3			C-15/O-2(RF)	-0.2

MOON, WALLY Wallace Wade B 4.3.1930 Bay, AR BL/TR 6/175# d4.13 C1

Year	Tm Lg	G	AB	R	H	2B	3B	HR	RBI	BB-IB	HP	SO	AVG	OBP	SLG	AOPS	ABR	SB-CS	FA	FR	Rng	Thr	G at Pos	BFW
1954	StL N	151	635	106	193	29	9	12	76	71	1	73	.304	.371	.435	109	10	18-10	.978	-7	93	93	*O-148(10-139-0)	-0.4
1955	StL N	152	593	86	175	24	8	19	76	47-4	3	65	.295	.349	.459	113	10	11-11	.975	-5	93	70	*O-100(34-44-28),1-51	-0.5
1956	StL N	149	540	86	161	22	11	16	68	80-7	1	50	.298	.390	.469	129	25	12-9	.988	-0	92	97	O-97(0-1-96),1-52	1.8
1957	StL N★	142	516	86	152	28	5	24	73	62-12	1	57	.295	.367	.508	131	23	5-6	.966	-10	86	80	*O-133(89-13-48)	0.5
1958	StL N	108	290	36	69	10	3	7	38	47-5	0	30	.238	.342	.366	85	-5	2-3	.984	-3	90	90	O-82(31-8-54)	-1.2
1959	†LA N★	145	543	93	164	26	**11**	19	74	81-1	3	64	.302	.394	.495	126	23	15-6	.983	-6	83	116	*O-143(128-4-29)/1	0.9
1960	LA N	138	469	74	140	21	6	13	69	67-4	1	53	.299	.383	.452	121	16	6-10	.986	2	91	156	*O-127(115-0-18)	0.9
1961	LA N	134	463	79	152	25	3	17	88	89-9	1	79	.328	**.434**	.505	137	30	7-5	.970	-8	88	52	*O-133(126-0-19)	1.4
1962	LA N	95	244	36	59	9	1	4	31	30-3	1	33	.242	.326	.336	84	-5	5-2	.981	-1	104	95	O-36(24-0-12),1-32	-0.9
1963	LA N	122	343	41	90	13	2	8	48	45-5	1	43	.262	.345	.382	119	9	5-5	.962	-6	89	35	O-96(48-3-60)	-0.3
1964	LA N	68	118	8	26	2	1	2	9	12-3	0	22	.220	.292	.305	74	-4	1-1	1.000	-1	99	0	O-23(6-0-17)	-0.7
1965	†LA N	53	89	6	18	3	0	1	11	13-3	0	22	.202	.304	.270	67	-3	2-0	1.000	-1	85	95	O-23(10-0-13)	-0.5
Total	12	1457	4843	737	1399	212	60	142	661	644-56	13	591	.289	.371	.445	117	129	89-68	.978	-47	90	89	*O-1141(621-212-394),1-136	1.0

MOORE, AL Albert James B 8.4.1902 Brooklyn, NY D 11.29.1974 , At Sea N.Y.To P.R BR/TR 5-10/174# d9.27

Year	Tm Lg	G	AB	R	H	2B	3B	HR	RBI	BB-IB	HP	SO	AVG	OBP	SLG	AOPS	ABR	SB-CS	FA	FR	Rng	Thr	G at Pos	BFW
1925	NY N	2	8	0	1	0	0	0	0	1	0	2	.125	.222	.125	-9	-1	0-1	1.000	-0	91	0	/O-2(LF)	-0.2
1926	NY N	28	81	12	18	4	0	0	10	5	0	7	.222	.267	.272	46	-6	2	.966	2	97	199	O-20(5-16-0)	-0.5
Total	2	30	89	12	19	4	0	0	10	6	0	9	.213	.263	.258	41	-7	2-1	.968	2	96	181	/O-22(7-16-0)	-0.7

MOORE, JUNIOR Alvin Earl B 1.25.1953 Waskom, TX BR/TR 5-11/185# d8.2

Year	Tm Lg	G	AB	R	H	2B	3B	HR	RBI	BB-IB	HP	SO	AVG	OBP	SLG	AOPS	ABR	SB-CS	FA	FR	Rng	Thr	G at Pos	BFW
1976	Atl N	20	26	1	7	1	0	0	2	4-0	1	4	.269	.387	.308	93	0	0-0	.929	1	118	146	/3-6,2O(LF)	0.1
1977	Atl N	112	361	41	94	9	3	5	34	33-0	1	29	.260	.323	.343	71	-15	4-5	.942	4	103	58	*3-104/2	-1.4
1978	Chi A	24	65	8	19	0	1	0	4	6-0	0	7	.292	.352	.323	90	-1	1-1	.857	0	87	0	D-12/3-6,O-5(LF)	-0.1
1979	Chi A	88	201	24	53	6	2	1	23	12-0	0	20	.264	.300	.328	71	-9	0-2	.966	-2	95	91	O-61(52-0-12),D-10/2-2	-1.3
1980	Chi A	45	121	9	31	4	1	1	10	7-0	0	11	.256	.295	.331	72	-5	0-2	.929	-1	93	92	3-34/O-3(LF),1D	-0.7
Total	5	289	774	83	204	20	7	7	73	62-0	2	71	.264	.318	.335	73	-30	5-10	.936	3	101	66	3-150/O-70(61-0-12),D-24,2-4,1	-3.4

MOORE, ANSE Anselm Winn B 9.22.1917 Delhi, LA D 10.29.1993 Pearl, MS BL/TR 6-1/190# d4.17

Year	Tm Lg	G	AB	R	H	2B	3B	HR	RBI	BB-IB	HP	SO	AVG	OBP	SLG	AOPS	ABR	SB-CS	FA	FR	Rng	Thr	G at Pos	BFW
1946	Det A	51	134	16	28	4	0	1	8	12	1	9	.209	.279	.261	48	-9	1-1	.971	-0	100	81	O-32(17-0-15)	-1.2

MOORE, ARCHIE Archie Francis B 8.30.1941 Upper Darby, PA BL/TL 6-2/190# d4.20

Year	Tm Lg	G	AB	R	H	2B	3B	HR	RBI	BB-IB	HP	SO	AVG	OBP	SLG	AOPS	ABR	SB-CS	FA	FR	Rng	Thr	G at Pos	BFW
1964	NY A	31	23	4	4	2	0	0	1	2-0	0	9	.174	.240	.261	39	-2	0-0	1.000	1	119	0	/O-8(0-5-3),1-7	-0.2
1965	NY A	9	17	1	7	2	0	1	4	4-1	0	4	.412	.524	.706	248	4	0-0	.889	0	79	319	/O-5(1-0-5)	0.4
Total	2	40	40	5	11	4	0	1	5	6-1	0	13	.275	.370	.450	128	2	0-0	.929	1	90	230	/O-13(1-5-8),1-7	0.2

MOORE, CHARLEY Charles Wesley B 12.1.1884 Jackson Co., IN D 7.29.1970 Portland, OR BR/TR 5-10/160# d4.16

Year	Tm Lg	G	AB	R	H	2B	3B	HR	RBI	BB-IB	HP	SO	AVG	OBP	SLG	AOPS	ABR	SB-CS	FA	FR	Rng	Thr	G at Pos	BFW
1912	Chi N	5	9	2	2	0	1	0	2	0	0	1	.222	.222	.444	80	0	0	.800	0	81	0	/S-2,23	0.0

Year	Tm Lg	G	AB	R	H	2B	3B	HR	RBI	BB-IB	HP	SO	AVG	OBP	SLG	AOPS	ABR	SB-CS	FA	FR	Rng	Thr	G at Pos	BFW
MOORE, CHARLIE Charles William B 6.21.1953 Birmingham, AL BR/TR 5-11/180# d9.8 OF Total (49-LF 8-CF 341-RF)																								
1973	Mil A	8	27	0	5	0	1	0	3	2-1	0	4	.185	.241	.259	42	-2	0-0	.981	2	67	197	/C-8	0.0
1974	Mil A	72	204	17	50	10	4	0	19	21-0	0	34	.245	.316	.333	87	-3	3-4	.985	0	78	62	C-61/D-6	-0.1
1975	Mil A	73	241	26	70	20	1	1	29	17-0	0	31	.290	.336	.394	106	2	1-5	.960	-2	105	87	C-47,O-22(16-0-6)/D	0.0
1976	Mil A	87	241	33	46	7	4	3	16	43-0	1	45	.191	.314	.290	80	-5	1-2	.969	1	89	149	C-49,O-28(LF)/3D	-0.4
1977	Mil A	138	375	42	93	15	6	5	45	31-0	1	39	.248	.306	.360	81	-10	1-7	.980	-1	94	91	*C-137	-0.8
1978	Mil A	96	268	30	72	7	1	5	31	12-0	0	24	.269	.300	.358	84	-7	4-2	.983	4	**140**	68	C-95	0.1
1979	Mil A	111	337	45	101	16	2	5	38	29-1	1	32	.300	.355	.404	105	3	8-5	.979	12	98	101	*C-106	1.8
1980	Mil A	111	320	42	93	13	2	2	30	24-2	0	28	.291	.336	.363	96	-2	10-5	.989	-2	139	68	*C-105	0.1
1981	†Mil A	48	156	16	47	8	3	1	9	12-0	0	13	.301	.351	.410	125	5	1-4	.970	1	106	79	C-34/O-8(3-0-5),D-6	0.6
1982	†Mil A	133	456	53	116	22	4	6	45	29-2	1	49	.254	.299	.360	86	-10	2-10	.988	8	101	163	*O-115(RF),C-20/2	-1.0
1983	Mil A	151	529	65	150	27	6	2	49	55-5	4	42	.284	.354	.369	108	7	11-4	.978	-7	95	76	*O-150(RF)/C-7,D	-0.7
1984	Mil A	70	188	13	44	7	1	2	17	10-0	1	26	.234	.275	.314	66	-9	0-4	.984	-1	108	61	O-61(0-7-56)/C-7	-1.4
1985	Mil A	105	349	35	81	13	4	0	31	27-0	1	53	.232	.288	.292	60	-19	4-0	.977	5	114	123	*C-102/O-3(RF)	-1.0
1986	Mil A	80	235	24	61	12	3	3	39	21-1	0	38	.260	.317	.374	86	-5	5-5	.992	17	133	140	C-72/O-4(0-1-3),2D	1.4
1987	Tor A	51	107	15	23	10	1	1	7	13-0	1	12	.215	.306	.355	73	-4	0-0	.984	2	82	64	C-44/O-5(2-0-3)	-0.1
Total	15	1334	4033	456	1052	187	43	36	408	346-12	11	470	.261	.319	.355	89	-59	51-57	.980	40	110	96	C-894,O-396R/D-18,2-2,3	-1.5
MOORE, DEE D C B 4.6.1914 Hedley, TX D 7.2.1997 Williston, ND BR/TR 5-11/190# d9.12 Mil 1944-45																								
1936	Cin N	6	10	4	4	2	1	0	1	0	0	3	.400	.400	.800	230	2	0	1.000	-0	202	0	/P-2,C	0.1
1937	Cin N	7	13	2	1	0	0	0	0	1	1	2	.077	.200	.077	-23	-2	0	.931	1	*80*	*143*	/C-6	-0.1
1943	Bro N	37	79	8	20	3	0	0	12	11	0	8	.253	.344	.291	84	-1	1	.982	-4	*94*	*100*	C-15/3-9	-0.5
	Phi N	37	113	13	27	4	1	1	8	15	0	8	.239	.328	.319	91	-1	0	.960	-1	*98*	*111*	C-21/O-6(LF),3-5,1	-0.1
	Year	74	192	21	47	7	1	1	20	26	0	16	.245	.335	.307	88	-2	1	.968	-5	*97*	*107*	C-36,3-14/O-6(LF),1	-0.6
1946	Phi N	11	13	2	1	0	0	0	1	7	0	3	.077	.400	.077	41	0	0	1.000	-0	*74*	*88*	/C-6,1-2	0.0
Total	4	98	228	29	53	9	2	1	22	34	1	24	.232	.335	.303	85	-2	1	.962	-4	*90*	*105*	/C-49,3-14,O-6(LF),1-3,P-2	-0.6
MOORE, GENE Eugene Jr. "Rowdy" B 8.26.1909 Lancaster, TX D 3.12.1978 Jackson, MS BL/TL 5-11/175# d9.19 f-Gene																								
1931	Cin N	4	14	2	2	1	0	0	1	0	0	0	.143	.143	.214	-6	-2	0	1.000	0	111	0	/O-3(LF)	-0.2
1933	StL N	11	38	6	15	3	2	0	8	4	0	10	.395	.452	.579	183	4	1	.967	-0	109	0	O-10(CF)	0.4
1934	StL N	9	18	2	5	1	0	0	1	2	0	2	.278	.350	.333	79	0	0	.923	-0	112	0	/O-3(CF)	-0.1
1935	StL N	3	3	0	0	0	0	0	0	0	0	1	.000	.000	.000	-96	-1	0	—	0			H	-0.1
1936	Bos N	151	637	91	185	38	12	13	67	40	3	80	.290	.335	.449	117	12	6	.977	13	102	186	*O-151(RF)	1.6
1937	Bos N☆	148	561	88	159	29	10	16	70	61	4	73	.283	.358	.456	132	24	11	.978	11	**113**	128	*O-148(RF)	2.6
1938	Bos N	54	180	27	49	8	3	3	19	16	2	20	.272	.338	.400	114	3	1	.981	1	107	95	O-47(RF)	0.1
1939	Bro N	107	306	45	69	13	6	3	39	40	0	50	.225	.315	.337	73	-12	4	.961	-4	88	110	O-86(2-1-83)/1	-2.0
1940	Bro N	10	26	3	7	2	0	0	2	1	0	3	.269	.296	.346	72	-1	0	1.000	-1	89	0	O-6(RF)	-0.2
	Bos N	103	363	46	106	24	1	5	39	25	0	32	.292	.338	.405	110	5	2	.986	6	108	147	O-94(0-1-94)	0.5
	Year	113	389	49	113	26	1	5	41	26	0	35	.290	.335	.401	107	3	2	.986	5	107	140	*O-100(0-1-100)	0.3
1941	Bos N	129	397	42	108	17	8	5	43	45	2	37	.272	.349	.393	114	7	5	.968	5	106	147	*O-110(1-28-84)	0.7
1942	Was A	1	2	0	0	0	0	0	0	0	0	1	.000	.000	.000	-99	-1	0-0	—	-0	0	0	/O(CF)	-0.1
1943	Was A	92	254	41	68	14	3	2	39	19	1	29	.268	.321	.370	106	1	0-2	.985	2	105	119	O-57(24-1-32)/1	-0.1
1944	†StL A	110	390	56	93	13	6	6	58	24	1	37	.238	.284	.349	76	-14	0-5	.968	2	110	77	O-98(RF)/1	-2.1
1945	StL A	110	354	48	92	16	2	5	50	40	1	26	.260	.337	.359	97	-1	1-3	.970	0	101	110	*O-100(1-0-99)	-0.8
Total	14	1042	3543	497	958	179	53	58	436	317	14	401	.270	.333	.400	105	24	31-10	.975	36	105	128	O-914(31-45-842)/1-3	0.2
MOORE, FERDIE Ferdinand Depage B 2.21.1896 Camden, NJ D 5.6.1947 Atlantic City, NJ d10.2																								
1914	Phi A	2	4	1	2	0	0	0	1	0	0	2	.500	.500	.500	209	0	0	.895	-1	0	0	/1-2	0.0
MOORE, GARY Gary Douglas B 2.24.1945 Tulsa, OK BR/TL 5-10/175# d5.3																								
1970	LA N	7	16	2	3	0	2	0	0	0-0	0	1	.188	.188	.438	65	-1	1-0	1.000	-1	70	0	/O-5(RF),1	-0.2
MOORE, EDDIE Graham Edward B 1.18.1899 Barlow, KY D 2.10.1976 Ft.Myers, FL BR/TR 5-7/165# d9.25																								
1923	Pit N	6	26	6	7	1	0	0	1	2	0	3	.269	.321	.308	65	-1	1-0	.923	-3	63	63	/S-6	-0.3
1924	Pit N	72	209	47	75	8	4	2	13	27	2	12	.359	.437	.464	139	13	6-7	.988	3	105	134	O-35(1-0-34),3-13/2-4	1.2
1925	†Pit N	142	547	106	163	29	8	6	77	73	2	26	.298	.383	.413	97	0	19-7	.952	-6	95	119	*2-122,O-15(RF)/3-3	-0.2
1926	Pit N	43	132	19	30	8	1	0	19	12	0	6	.227	.292	.303	57	-8	3	.911	-6	84	119	2-24/3-9,S	-1.3
	Bos N	54	184	17	49	3	2	0	15	16	0	12	.266	.325	.304	77	-6	6	.973	-4	93	112	2-39,S-14/3	-0.8
	Year	97	316	36	79	11	3	0	34	28	0	18	.250	.311	.304	68	-14	9	.950	-11	90	115	2-63,S-15,3-10	-2.1
1927	Bos N	112	411	53	124	14	4	1	32	39	1	17	.302	.364	.363	103	3	5	.947	-8	93	65	3-52,2-39,O-16(1-11-4)/S	-0.1
1928	Bos N	68	215	27	51	9	0	2	18	19	0	12	.237	.299	.307	62	-12	7	.958	5	112	161	O-54(LF)/2	-1.2
1929	Bro N	111	402	48	119	18	6	0	48	44	3	16	.296	.370	.371	86	-8	3	.955	-14	93	67	2-74,S-36/O-2(RF),3	-1.4
1930	Bro N	76	196	24	55	13	1	1	20	21	2	7	.281	.356	.372	77	-6	1	.991	2	111	111	2-23,O-23(13-7-3),S-17/3	-0.4
1932	NY N	37	87	9	23	3	0	1	6	9	1	6	.264	.340	.333	84	-2	1	.930	1	96	92	S-21/3-6,2-5	0.1
1934	Cle A	27	65	4	10	2	0	0	8	10	0	4	.154	.267	.185	18	-8	0-0	.932	0	95	107	2-18/3-3,S-2	-0.6
Total	10	748	2474	360	706	108	26	13	257	272	11	121	.285	.359	.366	89	-35	52-14	.956	-31	95	104	2-349,O-145(69-18-58)/S-98,3-89	-5.0
MOORE, HARRY Henry S. d4.17																								
1884	Was U	111	461	77	155	23	5	1		19			.336	.363	.414	139	10		.820	-7	63	98	*O-105(102-2-1)/S-8	0.0
MOORE, JACKIE Jackie Spencer B 2.19.1939 Jay, FL BR/TR 6/180# d4.18 M3 C26																								
1965	Det A	21	53	2	5	0	0	0	2	6-2	0	12	.094	.183	.094	-17	-8	0-0	.985	2	*147*	*83*	C-20	-0.6
MOORE, JIMMY James William B 4.24.1903 Paris, TN D 3.7.1986 Memphis, TN BR/TR 6-0.5/187# d4.17																								
1930	Chi A	16	39	4	8	2	0	0	2	6	1	3	.205	.326	.256	52	-3	0-0	.900	1	94	311	O-11(LF)	-0.2
	†Phi A	15	50	10	19	3	0	2	12	2	0	4	.380	.404	.560	136	3	1-1	.958	-0	98	113	O-13(8-1-4)	0.1
	Year	31	89	14	27	5	0	2	14	8	1	7	.303	.367	.427	100	0	1-1	.932	1	96	197	O-24(19-1-4)	-0.1
1931	†Phi A	49	143	18	32	5	1	2	21	11	1	13	.224	.284	.315	54	-10	0-1	.973	2	105	118	O-36(24-2-10)	-1.0
Total	2	80	232	32	59	10	1	4	35	19	2	20	.254	.316	.358	71	-10	1-2	.958	2	102	148	/O-60(43-3-14)	-1.1
MOORE, JERRIE Jeremiah S. B Detroit, MI D 9.26.1890 Wayne, MI BL 5-11/170# d4.17																								
1884	Alt U	20	80	10	25	3	1	1		0			.313	.313	.412	116	-1		.800	-8			C-12/O-9(1-2-6)	-0.7
	Cle N	9	30	1	6	0	0	0	10	0		5	.200	.200	.200	25	-3		.887	-2			/C-9	-0.3
1885	Det N	6	23	2	4	1	0	0	0	1		3	.174	.208	.217	38	-2		.800	-2			/C-6	-0.3
Total	2	35	133	13	35	4	1	1	10	1		8	.263	.269	.331	83	-6		.830	-12			/C-27,O-9(1-2-6)	-1.3
MOORE, JOHNNY John Francis B 3.23.1902 Waterville, CT D 4.4.1991 Bradenton, FL BL/TR 5-10.5/175# d9.15																								
1928	Chi N	4	4	0	0	0	0	0	0	0	0	0	.000	.000	.000	-99	-1	0	—	0			H	-0.1
1929	Chi N	37	63	13	18	1	0	2	8	4	1	6	.286	.338	.397	81	-2	0	.971	1	110	100	O-15(10-4-1)	-0.2
1931	Chi N	39	104	19	25	3	1	2	16	7	0	5	.240	.288	.346	69	-5	1	.964	0	95	193	O-22(12-9-1)	-0.6
1932	†Chi N	119	443	59	135	24	5	13	64	22	3	38	.305	.342	.470	117	9	4	.983	-4	91	119	*O-109(4-91-14)	0.2
1933	Cin N	135	514	60	135	19	5	1	44	29	3	16	.263	.306	.325	81	-13	4	.974	3	102	118	*O-132(75-57-0)	-1.7
1934	Cin N	16	42	5	8	1	1	0	5	3	0	2	.190	.244	.262	36	-4	0	1.000	-0	109	0	O-10(RF)	-0.5
	Phi N	116	458	68	157	34	6	11	93	40	1	18	.343	.397	.515	125	18	7	.981	8	104	175	*O-115(10-0-108)	1.8
	Year	132	500	73	165	35	7	11	98	43	1	20	.330	.384	.494	120	15	7	.983	8	104	161	*O-125(10-0-118)	1.3
1935	Phi N	153	600	84	194	33	3	19	93	45	5	50	.323	.375	.483	117	15	4	.973	-10	78	117	*O-150(2-0-148)	-0.4
1936	Phi N	124	472	85	155	24	3	16	68	26	1	22	.328	.365	.494	117	11	1	.948	-6	96	54	*O-112(78-0-35)	-0.2
1937	Phi N	96	307	46	98	16	2	9	59	18	0	18	.319	.357	.472	114	6	2	.943	-0	93	147	O-72(30-2-42)	0.1
1945	Chi N	7	6	0	1	0	0	0	2	1	0	1	.167	.286	.167	28	-1	0	—	0			H	-0.1
Total	10	846	3013	439	926	155	26	73	452	195	14	176	.307	.352	.449	109	33	23	.970	-9	94	120	O-737(221-163-359)	-1.7
MOORE, JO-JO Joseph Gregg "The Gause Ghost" B 12.25.1908 Gause, TX D 4.1.2001 Bryan, TX BL/TR 5-11/155# d9.17																								
1930	NY N	3	5	1	1	0	0	0	0	0	0	1	.200	.200	.200	-3	-1	0	1.000	-0	75	0	/O(CF)	-0.1
1931	NY N	4	8	0	2	1	0	0	3	0	0	1	.250	.250	.375	68	0	1	1.000	-0	96	0	/O(LF)	0.0
1932	NY N	86	361	53	110	15	2	2	27	20	0	18	.305	.341	.374	94	-3	4	.982	-3	88	115	O-86(85-1-0)	-1.1
1933	†NY N	132	524	56	153	16	5	0	42	21	3	27	.292	.323	.342	91	-7	4	.966	2	90	**185**	*O-132(111-21-0)	-1.3
1934	NY N✶	139	580	106	192	37	4	15	61	31	5	23	.331	.370	.486	130	24	5	.954	-13	81	83	*O-131(112-20-0)	0.5

Year	Tm Lg	G	AB	R	H	2B	3B	HR	RBI	BB-IB	HP	SO	AVG	OBP	SLG	AOPS	ABR	SB-CS	FA	FR	Rng	Thr	G at Pos	BFW
1935	NY N★	155	681	108	201	28	9	15	71	53	8	24	.295	.353	.429	111	10	5	.972	-1	98	96	*O-155(LF)	0.1
1936	†NY N☆	152	649	110	205	29	9	7	63	37	6	27	.316	.358	.421	110	8	2	.981	8	94	**224**	*O-149(LF)	0.8
1937	†NY N★	142	580	89	180	37	10	6	57	46	3	37	.310	.364	.440	116	13	7	.975	-8	83	120	*O-140(LF)	-0.3
1938	NY N☆	125	506	76	153	23	6	11	56	22	3	27	.302	.335	.437	110	5	2	.978	-5	88	88	*O-114(LF)	-0.7
1939	NY N	138	562	80	151	23	2	10	47	45	1	17	.269	.324	.370	85	-12	5	.986	3	95	159	*O-136(LF)	-1.7
1940	NY N★	138	543	83	150	33	4	6	46	43	7	30	.276	.337	.385	98	-1	7	.982	-2	93	95	*O-133(LF)	-1.1
1941	NY N	121	428	47	117	16	2	7	40	30	1	15	.273	.322	.369	93	-5	4	.972	-2	100	66	*O-116(112-4-0)	-1.3
Total	12	1335	5427	809	1615	258	53	79	513	348	37	247	.298	.344	.408	105	31	46	.975	-21	91	125	*O-1294(1248-47-0)	-6.2
MOORE, KELVIN Kelvin Orlando B 9.26.1957 Leroy, AL BR/TL 6-1/195# d8.28																								
1981	†Oak A	14	47	5	12	0	1	1	3	5-0	0	15	.255	.327	.362	103	0	1-0	1.000	-1	72	81	1-13	-0.2
1982	Oak A	21	67	6	15	1	1	2	6	3-0	0	23	.224	.250	.358	70	-3	0-1	.971	-2	75	57	1-20	-0.7
1983	Oak A	41	124	12	26	4	0	5	16	10-0	1	39	.210	.272	.363	78	-4	2-4	.994	-3	70	115	1-40	-1.0
Total	3	76	238	23	53	5	2	8	25	18-0	1	77	.223	.277	.361	81	-7	3-5	.989	-6	72	93	/1-73	-1.9
MOORE, KERWIN Kerwin Lamar B 10.29.1970 Detroit, MI BB/TR 6-1/190# d8.30																								
1996	Oak A	22	16	4	1	1	0	0	0	2-0	0	6	.063	.167	.125	-25	-3	1-0	1.000	-0	103	0	O-18(CF)/D-2	-0.3
MOORE, MOLLY Maurice d6.30																								
1875	Atl NA	21	86	5	19	4	0	0	5	0		4	.221	.221	.267	79	-1	0-1	.747	-4	111	0	S-14/1-8,O-2(RF),C23	-0.5
MOORE, RANDY Randolph Edward B 6.21.1906 Naples, TX D 6.12.1992 Mt.Pleasant, TX BL/TR 6/185# d4.12 OF Total (66-LF 13-CF 339-RF)																								
1927	Chi A	6	15	0	0	0	0	0	0	0	0	2	.000	.000	.000	-99	-5	0-0	1.000	1	119	257	/O-4(RF)	-0.4
1928	Chi A	24	61	6	13	4	1	0	5	3	0	5	.213	.250	.311	47	-5	0-2	.946	0	117	63	O-16(2-0-14)	-0.7
1930	Bos N	83	191	24	55	9	0	2	34	10	0	13	.288	.323	.366	69	-10	3	.986	1	113	121	O-34(11-12-11),3-13	-0.9
1931	Bos N	83	192	19	50	8	1	3	34	13	1	3	.260	.311	.359	83	-5	1	.952	1	93	180	O-29(17-1-11),3-22/2	-0.5
1932	Bos N	107	351	41	103	21	2	3	43	15	0	11	.293	.322	.390	94	-3	1	.987	-2	94	54	O-41(RF),3-31,1-22/C	-0.9
1933	Bos N	135	497	64	150	23	7	8	70	40	2	16	.302	.356	.425	133	21	3	.979	-1	101	92	*O-122(12-0-110),1-10	1.2
1934	Bos N	123	422	55	120	21	2	7	64	40	0	16	.284	.346	.393	105	4	2	.965	-0	108	114	O-72(16-0-56),1-37	-0.4
1935	Bos N	125	407	42	112	20	4	4	42	26	0	16	.275	.319	.373	93	-5	1	.950	1	104	130	O-78(7-0-71),1-21	-1.0
1936	Bro N	42	88	4	21	3	0	0	14	8	0	1	.239	.302	.273	55	-5	0	.964	-2	91	0	O-21(RF)	-0.8
1937	Bro N	13	22	3	3	1	0	0	2	3	0	2	.136	.240	.182	16	-3	0	.889	-0	*106*	*109*	C-10	-0.3
	StL N	8	7	0	0	0	0	0	0	0	0	0	.000	.000	.000	-98	-2	0	—	-0	0	0	/O(LF)	-0.2
	Year	21	29	3	3	1	0	0	2	3	0	2	.103	.188	.138	-10	-4	0	.889	-1	*106*	*109*	C-10/O(LF)	-0.5
Total	10	749	2253	258	627	110	17	27	308	158	3	85	.278	.326	.378	95	-18	11-2	.969	-2	103	104	O-418R/1-90,3-66,C-11,2	-4.9
MOORE, BOBBY Robert Vincent B 10.27.1965 Cincinnati, OH BR/TR 5-9/165# d9.5																								
1991	KC A	18	14	3	5	1	0	0	0	1-0	0	2	.357	.400	.429	129	1	3-2	1.000	0	102	0	O-13(9-5-0)	0.0
MOORE, TERRY Terry Bluford B 5.27.1912 Vernon, AL D 3.29.1995 Collinsville, IL BR/TR 5-11/195# d4.16 Mil 1943-45 M1 C7																								
1935	StL N	119	456	63	131	34	3	6	53	15	3	40	.287	.314	.414	90	-6	13	.984	7	109	109	*O-117(CF)	-0.3
1936	StL N	143	590	85	156	39	4	5	47	37	1	52	.264	.309	.369	82	-15	9	.977	13	112	139	*O-133(CF)	-0.5
1937	StL N	115	461	76	123	17	3	5	43	32	2	41	.267	.317	.349	79	-14	13	.988	8	112	100	*O-106(CF)	-0.8
1938	StL N	94	312	49	85	21	3	4	21	46	0	19	.272	.366	.397	104	3	9	.987	4	114	77	O-75(CF)/3-6	0.6
1939	StL N★	130	417	65	123	25	2	17	77	43	1	38	.295	.362	.487	119	11	6	**.994**	8	102	**175**	*O-121(CF)/P	1.6
1940	StL N★	136	537	92	163	33	4	17	64	42	2	44	.304	.356	.475	121	15	18	.987	13	**120**	104	*O-133(CF)	2.5
1941	StL N★	122	493	86	145	26	4	6	68	52	2	31	.294	.364	.400	108	6	3	.984	0	95	140	*O-121(0-121-1)	0.3
1942	†StL N★	130	489	80	141	26	3	6	49	56	2	26	.288	.364	.391	112	9	10	.986	-8	92	80	*O-126(CF)/3	-0.2
1946	†StL N	91	278	32	73	14	1	3	28	18	2	26	.263	.312	.353	85	-6	0	.982	-2	97	89	O-66(CF)	-1.0
1947	StL N	127	460	61	130	17	1	7	45	38	1	39	.283	.339	.370	84	-10	1	.983	-7	92	71	*O-120(CF)	-2.1
1948	StL N	91	207	30	48	11	0	4	18	27	0	12	.232	.321	.343	75	-7	0	.993	-3	94	53	O-71(CF)	-1.1
Total	11	1298	4700	719	1318	263	28	80	513	406	16	368	.280	.340	.399	98	-14	82	.985	33	104	108	*O-1189(0-1189-1)/3-7,P	-1.0
MOORE, SCRAPPY William Allen B 12.16.1892 St.Louis, MO D 10.13.1964 Little Rock, AR BR/TR 5-8/153# d6.21																								
1917	StL A	4	8	1	1	0	0	0	0	1	0	0	.125	.222	.125	6	-1	0	.750	-0	100	651	/3-2	-0.1
MOORE, BILL William Henry "Willie" B 12.12.1903 Kansas City, MO D 5.24.1972 Kansas City, MO BL/TR 5-11/170# d9.7																								
1926	Bos A	5	18	2	3	0	0	0	0	0	0	2	.167	.167	.167	-13	-3	0-0	1.000	0	*66*	*155*	/C-5	-0.3
1927	Bos A	44	69	7	15	2	0	0	4	13	0	8	.217	.341	.246	56	-4	0-0	.938	-2	*68*	*112*	C-42	-0.4
Total	2	49	87	9	18	2	0	0	4	13	0	10	.207	.310	.230	43	-7	0-0	.946	-2	*68*	*119*	/C-47	-0.7
MOORE, BILL William Ross B 10.10.1960 Los Angeles, CA BR/TL 6-1/185# d7.19																								
1986	Mon N	6	12	0	2	0	0	0	0	0-0	0	4	.167	.167	.167	-8	-2	0-0	1.000	-0	59	61	/1-3,O(RF)	-0.2
MORA, ANDRES Andres (Ibarra) B 5.25.1955 Rio Bravo, Mexico BR/TR 6/180# d4.13																								
1976	Bal A	73	220	18	48	11	0	6	25	13-0	0	49	.218	.258	.350	83	-6	1-0	.951	0	99	152	D-34,O-31(30-0-2)	-0.8
1977	Bal A	77	233	32	57	8	2	13	44	5-1	1	53	.245	.261	.464	100	-2	0-0	1.000	-7	70	55	O-57(LF)/3D	-1.2
1978	Bal A	76	229	21	49	8	0	8	14	13-1	1	47	.214	.258	.354	75	-9	0-1	.978	1	105	100	O-69(LF)/D	-1.1
1980	Cle A	9	18	0	2	0	0	0	0	0-0	0	0	.111	.111	.111	-39	-3	0-0	1.000	-0	99	0	/O-3(2-0-1)	-0.4
Total	4	235	700	71	156	27	2	27	83	31-2	2	149	.223	.256	.383	83	-20	1-1	.978	-6	91	92	O-160(158-0-3)/D-40,3	-3.5
MORA, MELVIN Melvin B 2.2.1972 Agua Negra, Venezuela BR/TR 5-10/160# d5.30 OF Total (170-LF 158-CF 29-RF)																								
1999	†NY N	66	31	6	5	0	0	0	1	4-0	1	7	.161	.278	.161	15	-4	2-1	1.000	-1	98	0	O-45(28-11-8)/2-4,3-3,S	-0.4
2000	NY N	79	215	35	56	13	2	6	30	18-3	2	48	.260	.317	.423	90	-4	7-3	.958	-6	89	68	S-44,O-28(12-16-3)/2-4,3-4	-0.6
	Bal A	53	199	25	58	9	3	2	17	17-0	4	32	.291	.359	.397	96	-1	5-8	.952	2	107	88	S-52/2	0.3
2001	Bal A	128	436	49	109	28	0	7	48	41-2	14	91	.250	.329	.362	88	-6	11-4	.987	7	105	86	O-88(CF),S-43/2	0.6
2002	Bal A	149	557	86	130	30	4	19	64	70-2	20	108	.233	.338	.404	102	3	16-10	.989	16	109	152	*O-104(74-31-5),S-41,2-12/D-3	1.9
2003	Bal A★	96	344	68	109	17	1	15	48	49-0	12	71	.317	.418	.503	148	27	6-3	.994	5	102	205	O-79(56-12-13),S-11/2-6,1	2.9
Total	5	571	1782	269	467	97	10	49	208	199-7	53	357	.262	.350	.410	104	15	47-29	.989	25	105	135	O-344L,S-192/2-28,3-7,D-3,1	4.7
MORALES, JOSE Jose Manuel (Hernandez) B 12.30.1944 Frederiksted, V.I. BR/TR 6/195# d8.13 C9																								
1973	Oak A	6	14	0	4	1	0	0	1	1-0	0	5	.286	.313	.357	100	0	0-1	—	0			/D-3	0.0
	Mon N	5	5	0	2	0	0	0	0	0-0	0	0	.400	.400	.400	118	0	0-0	—	0			H	0.0
1974	Mon N	25	26	3	7	4	0	1	5	1-0	0	7	.269	.296	.538	123	1	0-0	.800	-1	0	0	/C-2	0.0
1975	Mon N	93	163	18	49	6	1	2	24	14-9	0	21	.301	.354	.387	102	0	0-2	.983	5	191	103	1-27/O-6(LF),C-5	0.3
1976	Mon N	104	158	12	50	11	0	4	37	3-3	2	20	.316	.333	.462	120	4	0-0	.977	-0	208	73	1-21,C-12	0.3
1977	Mon N	65	74	3	15	4	1	1	9	5-3	0	12	.203	.247	.324	55	-5	0-0	1.000	-2	51	104	/C-8,1-8	-0.8
1978	Min A	101	242	22	76	13	1	2	38	20-3	1	35	.314	.363	.401	114	5	0-1	—	0	0	0	D-77/C1O(LF)	0.3
1979	Min A	92	191	21	51	5	1	2	27	14-5	2	27	.267	.319	.335	75	-7	0-0	1.000	-0	0	0	D-77/1	-0.9
1980	Min A	97	241	36	73	17	2	8	36	22-4	1	19	.303	.361	.490	123	8	0-0	1.000	-0	0	0	D-86/C-2,1-2	0.5
1981	Bal A	38	86	6	21	3	0	2	14	3-0	0	13	.244	.270	.349	77	-3	0-0	1.000	-0	0	66	D-22/1-3	-0.4
1982	Bal A	3	3	0	0	0	0	0	0	0-0	0	2	.000	.000	.000	-99	-1	0-0	—	0			/H	-0.1
	LA N	35	30	1	9	1	0	1	8	4-0	0	8	.300	.382	.433	131	1	0-0	—	0			H	0.0
1983	†LA N	47	53	4	15	3	0	3	8	1-0	0	11	.283	.296	.509	120	1	0-0	.951	-1	84	77	/1-4	0.0
1984	LA N	22	19	0	3	0	0	0	0	1-1	0	2	.158	.200	.158	2	-3	0-0	—	0			H	-0.3
Total	12	733	1305	126	375	68	6	26	207	89-28	6	182	.287	.332	.408	102	1	0-4	.981	1	166	96	D-265/1-67,C-30,O-7(LF)	-1.1
MORALES, JERRY Julio Ruben (Torres) B 2.18.1949 Yabucao, P.R. BR/TR 5-10/175# d9.5 C2																								
1969	SD N	19	41	5	8	2	0	1	6	5-0	0	7	.195	.283	.317	71	-2	0-2	1.000	2	105	259	O-19(10-9-1)	-0.1
1970	SD N	28	58	6	9	0	1	1	4	3-0	0	11	.155	.197	.241	17	-7	0-0	.926	-2	86	0	O-26(23-0-4)	-1.0
1971	SD N	12	17	1	2	0	0	0	1	2-0	0	2	.118	.211	.118	-5	-2	1-0	1.000	-0	89	0	/O-7(4-1-2)	-0.3
1972	SD N	115	347	38	83	15	7	4	18	35-3	0	54	.239	.307	.357	96	-3	4-6	.987	5	108	139	O-96(34-56-12)/3-4	-0.3
1973	SD N	122	388	47	109	23	2	9	34	27-3	0	55	.281	.325	.420	115	7	6-5	.991	2	107	77	*O-100(31-50-27)	0.4
1974	Chi N	151	534	70	146	21	7	15	82	46-3	2	63	.273	.330	.423	106	3	2-12	.975	-5	95	54	*O-143(83-32-41)	-1.3
1975	Chi N	153	578	62	156	21	0	12	91	50-9	5	65	.270	.328	.369	91	-7	3-7	.979	-3	95	111	*O-151(0-20-136)	-2.0
1976	Chi N	140	537	66	147	17	0	16	67	41-7	0	49	.274	.323	.395	95	-4	3-8	.983	-0	100	104	*O-136(3-8-131)	-1.4
1977	Chi N★	136	490	56	142	34	5	11	69	43-4	2	75	.290	.348	.447	101	1	0-3	.985	-13	81	98	*O-128(6-125-3)	-1.4
1978	StL N	130	457	44	109	19	8	4	46	33-1	1	44	.239	.288	.341	77	-15	4-4	.977	-4	102	56	*O-126(0-34-94)	-2.6

Year	Tm Lg	G	AB	R	H	2B	3B	HR	RBI	BB-IB	HP	SO	AVG	OBP	SLG	AOPS	ABR	SB-CS	FA	FR	Rng	Thr	G at Pos	BFW
1979	Det A	129	440	50	93	23	1	14	56	30-0	2	56	.211	.260	.364	65	-23	10-4	.986	-7	88	75	*O-119(18-20-88)/D-7	-3.4
1980	NY N	94	193	19	49	7	1	3	30	13-2	1	31	.254	.293	.347	84	-5	2-3	.973	-2	94	97	O-63(3-55-6)	-0.8
1981	Chi N	84	245	27	70	6	2	1	25	22-0	1	29	.286	.343	.339	91	-2	1-1	.986	-3	94	44	O-72(17-49-8)	-0.8
1982	Chi N	65	116	14	33	2	2	4	30	9-1	0	7	.284	.333	.440	112	1	1-2	1.000	5	110	299	O-41(12-36-4)	0.5
1983	Chi N	63	87	11	17	9	0	0	11	7-0	0	19	.195	.253	.299	51	-6	0-0	1.000	-0	89	109	O-29(17-10-3)	-0.7
Total	15	1441	4528	516	1173	199	36	95	570	366-33	14	567	.259	.313	.382	91	-64	37-57	.983	-26	96	92	*O-1256(261-505-560)/D-7,3-4	-15.2

MORALES, RICH Richard Angelo B 9.20.1943 San Francisco, CA BR/TR 5-11/170# d8.8 C2

Year	Tm Lg	G	AB	R	H	2B	3B	HR	RBI	BB-IB	HP	SO	AVG	OBP	SLG	AOPS	ABR	SB-CS	FA	FR	Rng	Thr	G at Pos	BFW
1967	Chi A	8	10	0	0	0	0	0	0	0-0	0	2	.000	.000	.000	-99	-3	0-0	.944	-1	97	51	/S-7	-0.3
1968	Chi A	10	29	2	5	0	0	0	0	2-0	0	5	.172	.226	.172	22	-3	0-0	.966	0	186	260	/S-7,2-5	-0.2
1969	Chi A	55	121	12	26	0	1	0	6	7-0	2	18	.215	.269	.231	39	-10	1-0	.976	5	123	90	2-38,S-13/3	-0.2
1970	Chi A	62	112	6	18	2	0	1	2	9-0	1	16	.161	.228	.205	20	-12	1-0	.967	-1	108	88	S-24,3-20,2-12	-1.2
1971	Chi A	84	185	19	45	8	0	2	14	22-4	4	26	.243	.336	.319	84	-3	2-3	.976	-6	95	52	S-57,3-18/2-3,O(RF)	-0.5
1972	Chi A	110	287	24	59	7	1	2	20	19-2	3	49	.206	.261	.258	54	-17	2-3	.968	-5	94	76	S-86,2-16,3-14	-1.5
1973	Chi A	7	4	1	0	0	0	0	1	1-0	0	1	.000	.200	.000	-38	-1	0-0	1.000	0	123	0	/3-5,2-2	-0.1
	SD N	90	244	9	40	6	1	0	16	27-6	0	36	.164	.245	.197	27	-25	0-1	.988	15	113	90	2-79,S-10	-0.5
1974	SD N	54	61	8	12	3	0	1	5	8-1	0	6	.197	.290	.295	67	-3	1-0	.933	0	99	71	S-29,2-18/3-6,1	-0.1
Total	8	480	1053	81	205	26	3	6	64	95-13	10	159	.195	.267	.242	46	-77	7-7	.970	7	99	74	S-233,2-173/3-64,1O(RF)	-4.6

MORALES, WILLIE William Anthony B 9.7.1972 Tucson, AZ BR/TR 5-10/182# d4.9

Year	Tm Lg	G	AB	R	H	2B	3B	HR	RBI	BB-IB	HP	SO	AVG	OBP	SLG	AOPS	ABR	SB-CS	FA	FR	Rng	Thr	G at Pos	BFW
2000	Bal A	3	11	1	3	1	0	0	0	0-0	0	3	.273	.273	.364	62	-1	0-0	1.000	2	0	278	/C-3	0.1

MORAN, CHARLIE Charles Barthell "Uncle Charlie" B 2.22.1878 Nashville, TN D 6.14.1949 Horse Cave, KY BR/TR 5-8/180# d9.9 U22 ▲

Year	Tm Lg	G	AB	R	H	2B	3B	HR	RBI	BB-IB	HP	SO	AVG	OBP	SLG	AOPS	ABR	SB-CS	FA	FR	Rng	Thr	G at Pos	BFW
1903	StL N	4	14	2	6	0	0	0	1	0	0		.429	.429	.429	149	1	1	1.000	-1	46	0	/P-3,S	0.0
1908	StL N	21	63	2	11	1	2	0	2	0	0		.175	.175	.254	38	-5	0	.903	-5	65	133	C-16	-1.0
Total	2	25	77	4	17	1	2	0	3	0	0		.221	.221	.286	61	-4	1	.903	-6	65	133	/C-16,P-3,S	-1.0

MORAN, CHARLES Charles Vincent B 3.26.1879 Washington, DC D 4.11.1934 Washington, DC TR d4.29

Year	Tm Lg	G	AB	R	H	2B	3B	HR	RBI	BB-IB	HP	SO	AVG	OBP	SLG	AOPS	ABR	SB-CS	FA	FR	Rng	Thr	G at Pos	BFW
1903	Was A	98	373	41	84	14	5	1	24	33	5		.225	.297	.298	77	-9	8	**.943**	6	100	106	S-96/2-2	0.0
1904	Was A	62	243	27	54	10	0	0	7	23	0		.222	.289	.263	77	-5	7	.919	-6	94	85	S-61/3	-1.1
	StL A	82	272	15	47	3	1	0	14	25	0		.173	.242	.191	40	-18	2	.937	-3	109	27	3-81/O(RF)	-2.1
	Year	144	515	42	101	13	1	0	21	48	0		.196	.265	.225	58	-23	9	.938	-9	109	27	3-82,S-61/O(RF)	-3.2
1905	StL A	27	82	6	16	1	0	0	5	10	1		.195	.290	.207	62	-3	3	.954	-3	98	132	2-20/3-5	-0.7
Total	3	269	970	89	201	28	6	1	50	91	6		.207	.279	.252	66	-35	20	.935	-6	98	98	S-157/3-87,2-22,O(RF)	-3.9

MORAN, HERBIE John Herbert B 2.16.1884 Costello, PA D 9.21.1954 Clarkson, NY BL/TR 5-5/150# d4.16

Year	Tm Lg	G	AB	R	H	2B	3B	HR	RBI	BB-IB	HP	SO	AVG	OBP	SLG	AOPS	ABR	SB-CS	FA	FR	Rng	Thr	G at Pos	BFW
1908	Phi A	19	59	4	9	0	0	0	4	6	1		.153	.242	.153	27	-5	1	.952	0	47	0	O-19(0-10-9)	-0.6
	Bos N	8	29	3	8	0	0	0	2	2	2		.276	.364	.276	106	0	1	1.000	2	168	1021	/O-8(LF)	0.2
1909	Bos N	8	31	8	7	1	0	0	0	5	0		.226	.333	.258	80	0	0	1.000	0	98	0	/O-8(LF)	-0.1
1910	Bos N	20	67	11	8	0	0	0	3	13	2	14	.119	.280	.119	17	-6	6	.958	4	98	245	O-20(11-0-9)	-0.4
1912	Bro N	130	508	77	140	18	10	1	40	69	5	38	.276	.368	.356	102	4	28	.961	2	98	118	*O-129(2-73-55)	-0.3
1913	Bro N	132	515	71	137	15	5	0	26	45	7	29	.266	.333	.315	83	-10	21-16	.950	-1	104	88	*O-129(3-6-121)	-1.9
1914	Cin N	107	395	43	93	10	5	1	35	41	3	29	.235	.312	.294	78	-10	26	.954	-7	93	70	*O-107(1-24-82)	-2.5
	†Bos N	41	154	24	41	3	1	0	4	17	2	11	.266	.347	.299	93	-1	4	.940	-5	80	70	O-41(0-17-30)	-0.8
	Year	148	549	67	134	13	6	1	39	58	5	40	.244	.322	.295	82	-11	30	.950	-11	90	70	*O-148(1-41-112)	-3.3
1915	Bos N	130	419	59	84	13	5	0	21	66	8	41	.200	.320	.255	79	-7	16-10	.964	1	92	140	*O-123(15-12-101)	-1.3
Total	7	595	2177	300	527	60	26	2	135	264	30	162	.242	.332	.296	83	-35	103-26	.957	-4	96	118	O-584(48-142-407)	-7.7

MORAN, PAT Patrick Joseph B 2.7.1876 Fitchburg, MA D 3.7.1924 Orlando, FL BR/TR 5-10/180# d5.15 M9

Year	Tm Lg	G	AB	R	H	2B	3B	HR	RBI	BB-IB	HP	SO	AVG	OBP	SLG	AOPS	ABR	SB-CS	FA	FR	Rng	Thr	G at Pos	BFW
1901	Bos N	52	180	12	38	5	1	2	18	3	1		.211	.228	.283	44	-14	3	.973	-2	130	55	C-28,1-13/3-4,S-3,O-3(RF),2	-1.3
1902	Bos N	80	251	22	60	5	5	1	24	17	6		.239	.303	.311	89	-4	6	**.982**	3	107	99	C-71/1-3,O(RF)	0.7
1903	Bos N	109	389	40	102	25	5	7	54	29	11		.262	.331	.406	114	7	8	.967	13	97	**121**	*C-107/1	2.9
1904	Bos N	113	398	26	90	11	3	4	34	18	4		.226	.267	.299	77	-12	10	.957	1	86	107	C-72,3-39/1-2	-0.3
1905	Bos N	85	267	22	64	11	5	2	22	8	3		.240	.270	.341	83	-7	3	**.986**	0	79	99	C-78	0.1
1906	†Chi N	70	226	22	57	13	1	0	35	7	2		.252	.281	.319	82	-5	6	.979	8	161	97	C-61	1.0
1907	†Chi N	65	198	8	45	5	1	1	19	10	2		.227	.271	.278	68	-8	5	.973	2	112	106	C-59	0.0
1908	Chi N	50	150	12	39	5	1	0	12	13	1		.260	.323	.307	97	0	6	.968	-0	110	103	C-45	0.5
1909	Chi N	77	246	18	54	11	1	1	23	16	4		.220	.278	.285	73	-8	2	.984	5	128	96	C-74	0.5
1910	Phi N	68	199	13	47	7	1	0	11	17	3	16	.236	.306	.281	69	-8	6	.989	-0	94	104	C-56	-0.3
1911	Phi N	34	103	2	19	3	0	0	8	3	0	13	.184	.208	.214	18	-12	0	.984	-2	86	104	C-32	-1.1
1912	Phi N	13	26	1	3	1	0	0	1	1	0	7	.115	.148	.154	-16	-4	0	.955	-1	89	71	C-13	-0.5
1913	Phi N	1	1	0	0	0	0	0	0	0	0	0	.000	.000	.000	-96	0	0	—	0			H	0.0
1914	Phi N	1	0	0	0	0	0	0	1	0	0	0	—	—	—	—	0	0	—	-0	0	0	/C	0.0
Total	14	818	2634	198	618	102	24	18	262	142	37	36	.235	.283	.312	78	-75	55	.976	27	107	102	C-697/3-43,1-19,O-4(RF),S-3,2	2.2

MORAN, AL Richard Alan B 12.5.1938 Detroit, MI BR/TR 6-1.5/190# d4.9

Year	Tm Lg	G	AB	R	H	2B	3B	HR	RBI	BB-IB	HP	SO	AVG	OBP	SLG	AOPS	ABR	SB-CS	FA	FR	Rng	Thr	G at Pos	BFW
1963	NY N	119	331	26	64	5	2	1	23	36-1	1	60	.193	.274	.230	46	-23	3-7	.951	6	**109**	86	*S-116/3	-1.1
1964	NY N	16	22	2	5	0	0	0	4	2-0	0	2	.227	.280	.227	50	-1	0-0	.957	2	130	101	S-15/3	0.1
Total	2	135	353	28	69	5	2	1	27	38-1	1	62	.195	.274	.229	46	-24	3-7	.951	8	110	87	S-131/3-2	-1.0

MORAN, ROY Roy Ellis "Deedle" B 9.17.1884 Vincennes, IN D 7.18.1966 Atlanta, GA BR/TR 5-8/155# d9.3

Year	Tm Lg	G	AB	R	H	2B	3B	HR	RBI	BB-IB	HP	SO	AVG	OBP	SLG	AOPS	ABR	SB-CS	FA	FR	Rng	Thr	G at Pos	BFW
1912	Was A	7	13	1	2	0	0	0	0	8	0		.154	.476	.154	82	1	3	.889	-0	73	158	/O-6(5-1-0)	0.0

MORAN, BILL William L. B 10.10.1869 Joliet, IL D 4.8.1916 Joliet, IL 5-10.5/175# d5.7

Year	Tm Lg	G	AB	R	H	2B	3B	HR	RBI	BB-IB	HP	SO	AVG	OBP	SLG	AOPS	ABR	SB-CS	FA	FR	Rng	Thr	G at Pos	BFW
1892	StL N	24	81	2	11	1	0	0	5	2	0	12	.136	.157	.148	-8	-11	0	.898	-5	96	91	C-22/O-2(LF)	-1.3
1895	Chi N	15	55	8	9	2	1	1	9	3	1	2	.164	.220	.291	29	-6	2	.827	-3	94	109	C-15	-0.7
Total	2	39	136	10	20	3	1	1	14	5	1	14	.147	.183	.206	10	-17	2	.871	-8	95	99	/C-37,O-2(LF)	-2.0

MORAN, BILLY William Nelson B 11.27.1933 Montgomery, AL BR/TR 5-11/185# d4.15

Year	Tm Lg	G	AB	R	H	2B	3B	HR	RBI	BB-IB	HP	SO	AVG	OBP	SLG	AOPS	ABR	SB-CS	FA	FR	Rng	Thr	G at Pos	BFW
1958	Cle A	115	257	26	58	11	0	1	18	13-1	0	23	.226	.262	.280	51	-18	3-2	.960	3	110	89	2-74,S-38	-1.0
1959	Cle A	11	17	1	5	0	0	0	2	0-0	0	1	.294	.294	.294	64	-1	0-0	1.000	-1	103	52	/2-6,S-5	-0.2
1961	LA A	54	173	17	45	7	1	2	22	17-1	1	16	.260	.328	.347	73	-6	0-0	.966	-1	95	93	2-51/S-2	-0.3
1962	LA A★	160	659	90	186	25	3	17	74	39-2	4	80	.282	.324	.407	99	-3	5-1	.986	17	108	92	*2-160	2.8
1963	LA A	153	597	67	164	29	5	7	65	31-2	3	57	.275	.310	.375	98	-3	1-1	.973	12	**107**	102	*2-151	2.3
1964	LA A	50	198	26	53	10	1	0	11	13-1	1	20	.268	.315	.328	88	-3	1-3	.929	-4	93	60	3-47/2-3,S	-0.9
	Cle A	69	151	14	31	6	0	1	10	18-3	1	16	.205	.291	.265	57	-8	0-1	.972	0	97	61	3-42,2-15/1-2	-0.9
	Year	119	349	40	84	16	1	1	21	31-4	2	36	.241	.304	.301	73	-12	1-4	.947	-4	95	60	3-89,2-18/1-2,S	-1.8
1965	Cle A	22	24	1	3	0	0	0	0	2-0	1	5	.125	.222	.125	1	-3	0-0	1.000	1	116	176	/2-7,S	-0.2
Total	7	634	2076	242	545	88	10	28	202	133-10	11	218	.263	.308	.355	85	-45	10-8	.976	26	106	95	2-467/3-89,S-47,1-2	1.6

MORANDINI, MICKEY Michael Robert B 4.22.1966 Kittanning, PA BL/TR 5-11/171# d9.1

Year	Tm Lg	G	AB	R	H	2B	3B	HR	RBI	BB-IB	HP	SO	AVG	OBP	SLG	AOPS	ABR	SB-CS	FA	FR	Rng	Thr	G at Pos	BFW
1990	Phi N	25	79	9	19	4	0	1	3	6-0	0	19	.241	.294	.329	71	-3	3-0	.990	-4	98	78	2-25	-0.6
1991	Phi N	98	325	38	81	11	4	1	20	29-0	2	45	.249	.313	.317	79	-9	13-2	.986	-0	101	91	2-97	-0.5
1992	Phi N	127	422	47	112	8	8	3	30	25-2	0	64	.265	.305	.344	84	-11	8-3	.991	9	106	96	*2-124/S-3	0.3
1993	†Phi N	120	425	57	105	19	9	3	33	34-2	5	73	.247	.309	.355	79	-14	13-2	.990	-7	96	74	*2-111	-1.3
1994	Phi N	87	274	40	80	16	5	2	26	34-5	4	33	.292	.378	.409	103	2	10-5	.985	1	100	85	2-79	0.7
1995	Phi N★	127	494	65	140	34	7	6	49	42-3	9	80	.283	.350	.417	101	1	9-6	.989	2	98	98	*2-122	0.9
1996	Phi N	140	539	64	135	24	6	3	32	49-0	9	87	.250	.321	.334	73	-21	26-5	.982	-2	97	105	*2-137	-1.2
1997	Phi N	150	553	83	163	40	2	1	39	62-0	8	91	.295	.371	.380	98	2	16-13	.990	-16	85	96	*2-146/S	-0.8
1998	†Chi N	154	582	93	172	20	4	8	53	72-4	9	84	.296	.380	.385	99	2	13-1	**.993**	-22	92	72	*2-152	-1.0
1999	Chi N	144	456	60	110	18	5	4	37	48-2	6	61	.241	.319	.329	66	-24	6-6	.991	-1	101	97	*2-132	-1.9
2000	Phi N	91	302	31	76	13	3	0	22	29-1	4	54	.252	.324	.315	62	-17	5-2	.987	-8	88	85	2-85	-2.0
	Tor A	35	107	10	29	2	1	0	7	7-0	0	23	.271	.316	.308	57	-7	1-0	.993	-0	99	123	2-35	-0.5
Total	11	1298	4558	597	1222	209	54	32	351	437-19	56	714	.268	.338	.359	84	-99	123-45	.989	-47	96	91	*2-1245/S-4	-7.9

MORBAN, JOSE Jose B 12.2.1979 Santiago, D.R. BR/TR 6-1/170# d4.6

Year	Tm Lg	G	AB	R	H	2B	3B	HR	RBI	BB-IB	HP	SO	AVG	OBP	SLG	AOPS	ABR	SB-CS	FA	FR	Rng	Thr	G at Pos	BFW
2003	Bal A	61	71	14	10	0	0	2	5	3-0	1	21	.141	.187	.225	8	-10	8-0	1.000	-3	51	121	S-14,D-13,2-12/3	-1.0

Year	Tm Lg	G	AB	R	H	2B	3B	HR	RBI	BB-IB	HP	SO	AVG	OBP	SLG	AOPS	ABR	SB-CS	FA	FR	Rng	Thr	G at Pos	BFW
MORDECAI, MIKE Michael Howard B 12.13.1967 Birmingham, AL BR/TR 5-11/175# d5.8 OF Total (1-LF 1-CF 2-RF)																								
1994	Atl N	4	4	1	1	0	0	1	3	1-0	0	0	.250	.400	1.000	244	1	0-0	1.000	-0	105	0	/S-4	0.1
1995	†Atl N	69	75	10	21	6	0	3	11	9-0	0	16	.280	.353	.480	115	2	0-0	1.000	-2	84	165	2-21/1-9,3-6,S-6,O(CF)	0.0
1996	†Atl N	66	108	12	26	5	0	2	8	9-1	0	24	.241	.297	.343	65	-6	1-0	.985	0	113	113	2-20,3-10/S-6,1	-0.4
1997	Atl N	61	81	8	14	2	1	0	3	6-0	0	16	.173	.227	.222	19	-10	0-1	1.000	-2	54	129	3-19/2-4,S-4,1-3,O(RF)D	-1.2
1998	Mon N	73	119	12	24	4	2	3	10	9-0	0	20	.202	.258	.345	58	-8	1-0	.953	-6	108	68	S-30,2-21,3-11/1	-1.2
1999	Mon N	109	226	29	53	10	2	5	25	20-0	1	31	.235	.297	.363	68	-12	2-5	.962	-1	93	136	2-38,S-38,3-32/1	-1.1
2000	Mon N	86	169	20	48	16	0	4	16	12-0	1	34	.284	.335	.450	93	-2	2-2	.937	-1	102	126	3-58,S-10/2-9,1-3	-0.2
2001	Mon N	96	254	28	71	17	2	3	32	19-1	1	53	.280	.330	.398	86	-5	2-2	.974	-8	86	33	3-42,2-32/S-4,C1O(RF)D	-1.1
2002	Mon N	55	74	9	15	4	0	0	4	8-3	1	14	.203	.289	.257	44	-6	1-1	.931	-0	98	133	3-28/2-4,1-3,S-3,O(LF)	-0.6
	Fla N	38	77	10	22	4	0	0	7	5-1	1	13	.286	.337	.338	85	-2	1-1	.988	1	105	93	S-24/3-7,1	0.0
	Year	93	151	19	37	8	0	0	11	13-4	2	27	.245	.313	.298	63	-8	2-2	.947	1	92	171	3-35,S-27/2-4,1-4,O(LF)	-0.6
2003	†Fla N	65	89	11	19	4	0	2	8	8-3	0	21	.213	.276	.326	59	-6	3-0	.976	-7	82	107	S-14,2-12,3-12/1	-1.0
Total	10	722	1276	150	314	72	7	23	127	106-9	5	242	.246	.305	.368	73	-54	13-12	.958	-25	90	86	3-225,2-161,S-143/1-24,O-4R,D-2,C	-6.7
MOREHART, RAY Raymond Anderson B 12.2.1899 Terrell, TX D 1.13.1989 Dallas, TX BL/TR 5-9/157# d8.9																								
1924	Chi A	31	100	10	20	4	2	0	8	17	0	7	.200	.316	.280	56	-6	3-1	.873	-9	92	94	S-27/2-2	-1.2
1926	Chi A	73	192	27	61	10	3	0	21	11	1	15	.318	.358	.401	101	0	3-11	.950	-5	103	61	2-48	-0.7
1927	NY A	73	195	45	50	7	2	1	20	29	0	18	.256	.353	.328	80	-5	4-4	.945	1	109	104	2-53	-0.3
Total	3	177	487	82	131	21	7	1	49	57	1	40	.269	.347	.347	83	-11	10-16	.946	-12	105	83	2-103/S-27	-2.2
MOREJON, DANNY Daniel (Torres) B 7.21.1930 Havana, Cuba BR/TR 6-1/175# d7.11																								
1958	Cin N	12	26	4	5	0	0	0	1	9-1	0	2	.192	.400	.192	60	-1	1-0	1.000	-1	87	0	O-11(2-6-3)	-0.2
MORELAND, KEITH Bobby Keith B 5.2.1954 Dallas, TX BR/TR 6/200# d10.1 OF Total (119-LF 560-RF)																								
1978	Phi N	1	2	0	0	0	0	0	0	0-0	0	0	.000	.000	.000	-99	-1	0-0	1.000	-1	7	0	/C	-0.1
1979	Phi N	14	48	3	18	3	2	0	8	3-0	0	5	.375	.412	.521	148	3	0-0	1.000	-1	78	105	C-13	0.3
1980	†Phi N	62	159	13	50	8	0	4	29	8-2	0	14	.314	.341	.440	112	2	3-1	.967	-1	80	128	C-39/3-4,O-2(RF)	0.4
1981	†Phi N	61	196	16	50	7	0	6	37	15-1	1	13	.255	.307	.383	92	-2	1-2	.982	-3	72	112	C-50/3-7,1-2,O-2(RF)	-0.5
1982	Chi N	138	476	50	124	17	2	15	68	46-8	3	71	.261	.326	.399	100	0	0-6	.989	2	104	140	O-86(54-0-35),C-44/3-2	-0.2
1983	Chi N	154	533	76	161	30	3	16	70	68-8	3	73	.302	.378	.460	127	21	0-3	.976	-10	88	69	*O-151(RF)/C-3	0.3
1984	†Chi N	140	495	59	138	17	3	16	80	34-5	3	71	.279	.326	.422	101	0	1-4	.976	-8	89	97	*O-103(1-0-102),1-29/3-8,C-3	-1.7
1985	Chi N	161	587	74	180	30	3	14	106	68-7	1	58	.307	.374	.440	116	15	12-3	.976	-8	87	103	*O-148(RF),1-12,3-11/C-2	0.0
1986	Chi N	156	586	72	159	30	0	12	79	53-10	0	48	.271	.326	.384	90	-7	3-6	.980	-8	84	139	*O-121(RF),3-24,C-13,1-12	-2.4
1987	Chi N	153	563	63	150	29	1	27	88	39-4	0	66	.266	.309	.465	99	-2	3-3	.934	7	106	102	*3-150/1	0.2
1988	SD N	143	511	40	131	23	0	5	64	40-6	0	51	.256	.305	.331	86	-9	2-3	.994	-2	100	115	1-73,O-64(LF)/3-2	-2.1
1989	Det A	90	318	34	95	16	0	5	35	27-5	2	33	.299	.357	.396	115	7	3-2	1.000	-2	60	76	D-51,1-31,3-12/C	0.1
	Bal A	33	107	11	23	4	0	1	10	4-0	0	12	.215	.243	.280	49	-8	0-0	—	0	0	0	D-29	-0.9
	Year	123	425	45	118	20	0	6	45	31-5	2	45	.278	.330	.367	99	-1	3-2	1.000	-2	60	76	D-80,1-31,3-12/C	-0.8
Total	12	1306	4581	511	1279	214	14	121	674	405-56	13	515	.279	.335	.411	103	19	28-33	.979	-34	89	103	O-677R,3-220,C-169,1-160/D-80	-6.6
MORELOCK, HARRY A. Harry B 11.1869 Philadelphia, PA d8.21																								
1891	Phi N	4	14	1	1	0	0	0	0	3	0	3	.071	.235	.071	-9	-2	0	.824	-2	77	0	/S-4	-0.4
1892	Phi N	1	3	0	0	0	0	0	0	1	0	0	.000	.250	.000	-23	0	0	.600	-1	44	0	/3	-0.1
Total	2	5	17	1	1	0	0	0	0	4	0	3	.059	.238	.059	-11	-2	0	.824	-3	77	0	/S-4,3	-0.5
MORENO, JOSE Jose De Los Santos (born De Los Santos Mauricio (Moreno)) B 11.1.1957 Santo Domingo, D.R. BB/TR 6/175# d5.24																								
1980	NY N	37	46	6	9	2	1	2	9	3-2	0	12	.196	.240	.413	83	-1	1-0	.917	2	120	393	/2-4,3-4	0.1
1981	SD N	34	48	5	11	2	0	0	6	1-1	0	8	.229	.245	.271	50	-3	4-1	1.000	1	101	176	/O-9(4-0-5),2	-0.3
1982	Cal A	11	3	3	0	0	0	0	0	2-0	0	0	.000	.400	.000	21	0	0-2	1.000	-1	65	0	/2-2,D	-0.1
Total	3	82	97	14	20	4	1	2	15	6-3	0	20	.206	.250	.330	66	-4	5-3	1.000	3	101	176	/O-9(4-0-5),2-7,3-4,D	-0.3
MORENO, OMAR Omar Renan (Quintero) B 10.24.1952 Puerto Armuelles, Panama BL/TL 6-2/180# d9.6																								
1975	Pit N	6	6	1	1	0	0	0	0	1-0	0	1	.167	.286	.167	28	-1	1-0	.000	-1	0	0	/O(LF)	-0.1
1976	Pit N	48	122	24	33	4	1	2	12	16-0	1	24	.270	.357	.369	106	1	15-5	.960	1	111	146	O-42(CF)	0.4
1977	Pit N	150	492	69	118	19	9	7	34	38-5	1	102	.240	.295	.358	72	-21	53-16	.977	5	109	113	*O-147(CF)	-1.1
1978	Pit N	155	515	95	121	15	7	2	33	81-4	3	104	.235	.339	.303	78	-13	**71**-22	.984	5	108	110	*O-152(CF)	-0.1
1979	†Pit N	162	695	110	196	21	12	8	69	51-9	3	104	.282	.333	.381	90	-10	**77**-21	.975	5	111	88	*O-162(CF)	0.3
1980	Pit N	**162**	676	87	168	20	**13**	2	36	57-11	2	101	.249	.306	.325	76	-23	96-33	.990	11	110	133	*O-162(CF)	-0.3
1981	Pit N	**103**	434	62	120	18	8	1	35	26-4	3	76	.276	.319	.362	91	-6	39-14	.997	2	107	81	*O-103(CF)	-0.1
1982	Pit N	158	645	82	158	18	9	3	44	44-2	1	121	.245	.292	.315	68	-28	60-26	.983	1	104	108	*O-157(CF)	-2.6
1983	Hou N	97	405	48	98	12	11	0	25	22-3	1	72	.242	.282	.326	73	-18	30-13	.977	3	102	171	O-97(CF)	-1.5
	NY A	48	152	17	38	9	1	1	17	8-0	0	31	.250	.287	.342	75	-5	7-3	.992	-1	100	37	O-48(CF)	-0.7
1984	NY A	117	355	37	92	12	6	4	38	18-1	1	48	.259	.294	.361	84	-9	20-11	.985	-1	96	138	*O-108(CF)/D	-1.1
1985	NY A	34	66	12	13	4	1	1	4	1-0	0	16	.197	.209	.333	47	-5	1-1	1.000	3	132	184	O-26(3-19-4)/D	-0.2
	KC A	24	70	9	17	1	3	2	12	3-0	1	8	.243	.280	.429	91	-1	0-1	1.000	-3	67	83	O-21(0-13-8)	-0.5
	Year	58	136	21	30	5	4	3	16	4-0	1	24	.221	.246	.382	70	-6	1-2	1.000	0	99	132	O-47(3-32-12)/D	-0.7
1986	Atl N	118	359	46	84	18	6	4	27	21-2	0	77	.234	.276	.351	68	-17	17-16	.970	0	95	127	O-97(18-12-71)	-2.4
Total	12	1382	4992	699	1257	171	87	37	386	387-41	17	885	.252	.306	.343	79	-156	487-182	.982	30	105	114	*O-1323(22-1221-83)/D-2	-10.0
MORGAN, CHET Chester Collins "Chick" B 6.6.1910 Cleveland, MS D 9.20.1991 Pasadena, TX BL/TR 5-9/160# d4.19																								
1935	Det A	14	23	2	4	1	0	0	1	5	0	0	.174	.321	.217	43	-2	0-0	.909	-0	110	0	/O-4(LF)	-0.2
1938	Det A	74	306	50	87	6	1	0	27	20	1	12	.284	.330	.310	58	-20	5-6	.980	-2	96	85	O-74(6-68-0)	-2.3
Total	2	88	329	52	91	7	1	0	28	25	1	12	.277	.330	.304	57	-22	5-6	.977	-2	97	80	/O-78(10-68-0)	-2.5
MORGAN, DAN Daniel B 5.1853 , MO D 1.30.1910 St.Louis, MO d5.4 ▲																								
1875	RS NA	**19**	69	11	18	4	0	0	1	5		4	.261	.311	.319	132	3	2-1	.824	-4	79	0	O-10(3-7-0)/P-7,3-7	-0.1
1878	Mil N	14	56	2	11	0	0	0	5	3		9	.196	.237	.196	41	-4		.769	-4	47	0	O-13(0-1-12)/3-3,2	-0.7
MORGAN, ED Edward Carre B 5.22.1904 Cairo, IL D 4.9.1980 New Orleans, LA BR/TR 6-0.5/180# d4.11																								
1928	Cle A	76	265	42	83	24	6	4	54	21	1	17	.313	.366	.494	123	8	5-5	.968	2	124	122	1-36,O-21(0-18-3),3-14	0.8
1929	Cle A	93	318	60	101	19	10	3	37	37	2	24	.318	.392	.469	116	8	4-3	.908	-8	74	108	O-80(RF)	-0.6
1930	Cle A	150	584	122	204	47	11	26	136	62	1	66	.349	.413	.601	148	42	8-4	.987	-1	107	103	*1-129,O-19(RF)	2.9
1931	Cle A	131	462	87	162	33	4	11	86	83	1	46	.351	.451	.511	144	35	4-5	.984	2	112	107	*1-117/3-3	2.3
1932	Cle A	144	532	96	156	32	7	4	68	94	3	44	.293	.402	.402	102	6	7-6	.985	-10	81	88	*1-142/3	-1.6
1933	Cle A	39	121	10	32	3	3	1	13	7	0	9	.264	.305	.364	73	-5	1-1	.997	2	128	65	1-32/O(LF)	-0.6
1934	Bos A	138	528	95	141	28	4	3	79	81	2	46	.267	.367	.352	80	-13	7-1	.988	-6	80	94	*1-137	-2.9
Total	7	771	2810	512	879	186	45	52	473	385	10	252	.313	.398	.467	117	81	36-25	.986	-18	97	97	1-593,O-121(1-18-102)/3-18	0.3
MORGAN, EDDIE Edwin Willis "Pepper" B 11.19.1914 Brady Lake, OH D 6.27.1982 Lakewood, OH BL/TL 5-10/160# d4.14																								
1936	StL N	8	18	4	5	0	0	1	3	2	0	4	.278	.350	.444	113	0	0	.889	-1	102	0	/O-4(RF)	0.0
1937	Bro N	31	48	4	9	3	0	0	5	9	0	7	.188	.316	.250	55	-3	0	.984	-2	24	83	/1-7,O-7(1-1-5)	-0.5
Total	2	39	66	8	14	3	0	1	8	11	0	11	.212	.325	.303	70	-3	0	.842	-2	90	123	/O-11(1-1-9),1-7	-0.5
MORGAN, BILL Henry William B 10.1857 Washington, DC d8.17																								
1882	Pit AA	17	66	10	17	2	1	0		4			.258	.300	.318	114	1		.688	-6	0	418	O-11(RF)/C-7	-0.4
1884	Ric AA	6	20	0	2	0	0	0		1	0		.100	.143	.100	-20	-3		.850	-2			/C-3,O-2(RF),2	-0.4
	Bal U	2	9	1	2	0	0	0		1			.222	.300	.222	55	-1		.909	-1			/C2O(RF)	-0.1
Total	2	25	95	11	21	2	1	0		6			.221	.267	.263	78	-3		.727	-9			/O-14(RF),C-11,2-2	-0.9
MORGAN, RED James Edward B 10.6.1883 Neola, IA D 3.25.1981 New York, NY BR/TR d6.20																								
1906	Bos A	88	307	20	66	6	3	1	21	16	7		.215	.270	.264	67	-12	7	.866	-11	82	98	3-88	-2.3
MORGAN, JOE Joe Leonard B 9.19.1943 Bonham, TX BL/TR 5-7/160# d9.21 HF1990																								
1963	Hou N	8	25	5	6	0	1	0	3	5-0	0	5	.240	.367	.320	106	0	1-0	.909	-3	74	50	/2-7	-0.2
1964	Hou N	10	37	4	7	0	0	0	0	6-0	0	7	.189	.302	.189	44	-3	0-1	.949	-1	80	66	2-10	-0.4
1965	Hou N	157	601	100	163	22	12	14	40	**97**-1	3	77	.271	.373	.418	132	29	20-9	.969	-9	99	81	*2-157	3.7

Year	Tm Lg	G	AB	R	H	2B	3B	HR	RBI	BB-IB	HP	SO	AVG	OBP	SLG	AOPS	ABR	SB-CS	FA	FR	Rng	Thr	G at Pos	BFW
1966	Hou N✶	122	425	60	121	14	8	5	42	89-3	3	43	.285	.410	.391	134	25	11-8	.965	-20	90	79	*2-117	1.6
1967	Hou N	133	494	73	136	27	11	6	42	81-5	2	51	.275	.378	.411	131	23	29-5	.979	-4	95	76	*2-130/O(LF)	3.7
1968	Hou N	10	20	6	5	0	1	0	0	7-0	0	4	.250	.444	.350	144	2	3-0	.882	-2	54	79	/2-5,O(LF)	0.0
1969	Hou N	147	535	94	126	18	5	15	43	110-1	1	74	.236	.365	.372	110	11	49-14	.972	3	90	95	*2-132,O-14(12-2-0)	2.9
1970	Hou N★	144	548	102	147	28	9	8	52	102-3	1	55	.268	.383	.396	114	16	42-13	.979	11	106	101	*2-142	3.9
1971	Hou N	160	583	87	149	27	**11**	13	56	88-2	1	52	.256	.351	.407	118	16	40-8	.986	-7	100	89	*2-157	2.6
1972	†Cin N★	149	552	**122**	161	23	4	16	73	**115**-1	6	44	.292	**.417**	.435	152	45	58-17	**.990**	-6	100	103	*2-149	5.9
1973	†Cin N★	157	576	116	167	35	2	26	82	111-3	4	61	.290	.406	.493	157	50	67-15	.990	5	102	109	*2-154	**7.5**
1974	Cin N★	149	512	107	150	31	3	22	67	120-8	3	69	.293	**.427**	.494	160	49	58-12	.982	2	97	110	*2-142	7.0
1975	†Cin N★	146	498	107	163	27	6	17	94	**132**-3	3	52	.327	**.466**	.508	**169**	**57**	67-10	**.986**	2	103	112	*2-142	**8.0**
1976	†Cin N★	141	472	113	151	30	5	27	111	114-8	1	41	.320	**.444**	**.576**	**186**	**61**	60-9	.981	-14	87	104	*2-133	**6.7**
1977	Cin N★	153	521	113	150	21	6	22	78	117-2	2	58	.288	.417	.478	138	34	49-10	**.993**	-3	89	117	*2-151	4.6
1978	Cin N★	132	441	68	104	27	0	13	75	79-3	2	40	.236	.347	.385	107	7	19-5	.980	-23	85	69	*2-124	-0.7
1979	†Cin N★	127	436	70	109	26	1	9	32	93-11	1	45	.250	.379	.376	107	10	28-6	.980	-12	93	101	*2-121	0.8
1980	†Hou N	141	461	66	112	17	5	11	49	**93**-6	0	47	.243	.367	.373	117	15	24-6	.988	-11	92	96	*2-130	1.4
1981	SF N	90	308	47	74	16	1	8	31	66-7	0	37	.240	.371	.377	116	10	14-5	.991	-4	97	112	2-87	1.3
1982	SF N	134	463	68	134	19	4	14	61	85-4	2	60	.289	.400	.438	135	26	24-4	.989	-3	102	94	*2-120/3-3	3.4
1983	†Phi N	123	404	72	93	20	1	16	59	89-1	4	54	.230	.370	.403	117	14	18-2	.971	17	107	96	*2-117	4.1
1984	Oak A	116	365	50	89	21	0	6	43	66-4	1	39	.244	.356	.351	105	6	8-3	.977	-16	85	98	*2-100/D-5	-0.4
Total	22	2649	9277	1650	2517	449	96	268	1133	1865-76	40	1015	.271	.392	.427	133	503	689-162	.981	-97	96	97	*2-2527/O-16(14-2-0),D-5,3-3	67.4
MORGAN, JOE Joseph Michael B 11.19.1930 Walpole, MA BL/TR 5-10/170# d4.14 M4 C5																								
1959	Mil N	13	23	2	5	1	0	0	1	2-0	0	4	.217	.280	.261	49	-2	0-0	.913	-2	91	34	/2-7	-0.3
	KC A	20	21	2	4	0	1	0	3	3-0	0	7	.190	.292	.286	58	-1	0-0	1.000	-0	82	0	/3-2	-0.2
1960	Phi N	26	83	5	11	2	2	0	2	6-1	0	11	.133	.191	.205	8	-11	0-0	.971	1	105	78	3-24	-1.1
	Cle A	22	47	6	14	2	0	2	4	6-0	0	4	.298	.377	.468	131	2	0-0	.889	-2	95	41	3-12/O-2(RF)	0.1
1961	Cle A	4	10	0	2	0	0	0	0	1-0	0	3	.200	.273	.200	29	-1	0-0	1.000	0	125	0	/O-2(CF)	-0.1
1964	StL N	3	3	0	0	0	0	0	0	0-0	0	2	.000	.000	.000	-92	-1	0-0	—	0			H	-0.1
Total	4	88	187	15	36	5	3	2	10	18-1	0	31	.193	.263	.283	49	-14	0-0	.944	-3	101	63	/3-38,2-7,O-4(0-2-2)	-1.7
MORGAN, KEVIN Kevin Lee B 3.3.1970 Lafayette, LA BR/TR 6-1/170# d6.15																								
1997	NY N	1	1	0	0	0	0	0	0	0-0	0	0	.000	.000	.000	-99	0	0-0	1.000	0	235	0	/3	0.0
MORGAN, RAY Raymond Caryll B 6.14.1889 Baltimore, MD D 2.15.1940 Baltimore, MD BR/TR 5-8.5/155# d8.7																								
1911	Was A	25	89	11	19	2	0	0	5	4	0		.213	.247	.236	36	-8	2	.900	-2	95	31	3-25	-0.9
1912	Was A	81	273	40	65	10	7	1	30	29	3		.238	.318	.337	87	-5	12	.939	-9	87	90	2-76/S-4,3	-1.3
1913	Was A	138	481	58	131	19	8	0	57	68	6	63	.272	.369	.345	107	7	19	.950	-8	93	**141**	*2-134/S-4	0.2
1914	Was A	147	491	50	126	22	8	1	49	62	10	34	.257	.352	.340	104	5	24-17	.948	-13	90	**128**	*2-146	-0.7
1915	Was A	62	193	21	45	5	4	0	21	30	2	15	.233	.342	.301	91	-1	6-5	.965	-3	100	114	2-57/S-2,3-2	-0.4
1916	Was A	99	315	41	84	12	4	1	29	59	10	29	.267	.398	.340	123	14	14	.957	-11	94	104	2-82/S-9,1-3,3	0.4
1917	Was A	101	338	32	90	9	1	1	33	40	1	29	.266	.346	.308	101	2	7	.961	-8	88	113	2-95/3-3	-0.5
1918	Was A	88	300	25	70	11	1	0	30	28	6	14	.233	.311	.277	79	-7	4	.959	-8	98	88	2-80/O-2(RF)	-1.6
Total	8	741	2480	278	630	90	33	4	254	320	38	184	.254	.348	.322	98	7	88-22	.953	-61	92	115	2-670/3-32,S-19,1-3,O-2(RF)	-4.8
MORGAN, BOBBY Robert Morris B 6.29.1926 Oklahoma City, OK BR/TR 5-9/175# d4.18																								
1950	Bro N	67	199	38	45	10	3	7	21	32	3	43	.226	.342	.412	95	-1	0	.969	8	122	154	3-52,S-10	0.7
1952	†Bro N	67	191	36	45	8	0	7	16	46	3	35	.236	.392	.387	115	7	2-2	.968	1	108	121	3-60/2-5,S-4	0.7
1953	†Bro N	69	196	35	51	6	2	7	33	33	1	47	.260	.370	.418	103	2	2-2	.920	-2	98	99	3-36,S-21	0.0
1954	Phi N	135	455	58	119	25	2	14	50	70	0	68	.262	.357	.418	102	3	3-1	.954	-19	93	91	*S-129/3-8,2-5	-0.5
1955	Phi N	136	483	61	112	20	2	10	49	73-0	0	72	.232	.331	.344	81	-11	6-4	.980	-17	87	87	2-88,S-41/3-6,1	-1.9
1956	Phi N	8	25	1	5	0	0	0	1	6-0	0	4	.200	.355	.200	56	-1	0-0	.857	-1	94	101	/3-5,2-3	-0.2
	StL N	61	113	14	22	7	0	3	20	15-0	0	24	.195	.287	.336	67	-5	0-2	.980	-1	101	52	2-13,3-11/S-6	-0.6
	Year	69	138	15	27	7	0	3	21	21-0	0	28	.196	.300	.312	65	-6	0-2	.877	-1	102	70	3-16,2-16/S-6	-0.8
1957	Phi N	2	0	0	0	0	0	0	0	0-0	0	0	—	—	—	—	0	0-0	1.000	-0	0	0	/2	0.0
	Chi N	125	425	43	88	20	2	5	27	52-1	1	87	.207	.294	.299	61	-23	5-0	.976	8	110	80	*2-116,3-12	-0.5
	Year	127	425	43	88	20	2	5	27	52-1	1	87	.207	.294	.299	61	-23	5-0	**.976**	8	**110**	80	*2-117,3-12	-0.5
1958	Chi N	1	1	0	0	0	0	0	0	0-0	0	1	.000	.000	.000	-99	0	0-0	—	0			H	0.0
Total	8	671	2088	286	487	96	11	53	217	327-1	8	381	.233	.338	.366	88	-29	18-11	.978	-24	100	80	2-231,S-211,3-190/1	-2.3
MORGAN, VERN Vernon Thomas B 8.8.1928 Emporia, VA D 11.8.1975 Minneapolis, MN BL/TR 6-1/190# d8.10 C7																								
1954	Chi N	24	64	3	15	2	0	0	2	1	0	10	.234	.242	.266	33	-6	0-0	.895	-3	91	38	3-15	-0.9
1955	Chi N	7	7	1	1	0	0	0	1	3-0	0	4	.143	.400	.143	52	0	0-0	.667	-1	62	0	/3-2	-0.1
Total	2	31	71	4	16	2	0	0	3	4-0	0	14	.225	.263	.254	36	-6	0-0	.864	-4	88	34	/3-17	-1.0
MORGAN, BILL William B 1856 Brooklyn, NY D 9.9.1908 New York, NY d8.6																								
1883	Pit AA	32	114	12	18	2	1	0		7			.158	.207	.193	31	-8		.825	-2	93	58	S-21/O-6(1-4-1),C-5,2-2	-0.8
1884	Was AA	45	162	8	28	1	1	0		8	1		.173	.216	.191	39	-10		.781	-4	70	92	O-31(17-2-13),C-12/2-2,S-2	-1.2
Total	2	77	276	20	46	3	2	0		15	1		.167	.212	.192	35	-18		.771	-6	64	84	/O-37(18-6-14),S-23,C-17,2-4	-2.0
MORHARDT, MOE Meredith Goodwin B 1.16.1937 Manchester, CT BL/TL 6-1/185# d9.7																								
1961	Chi N	7	18	3	5	0	0	0	1	3-0	0	5	.278	.381	.278	78	0	0-0	.962	-1	64	154	/1-7	-0.2
1962	Chi N	18	16	1	2	0	0	0	2	2-0	0	8	.125	.222	.125	-4	-2	0-0	—	0			H	-0.2
Total	2	25	34	4	7	0	0	0	3	5-0	0	13	.206	.308	.206	39	-2	0-0	.962	-1	64	154	/1-7	-0.4
MORIARITY, GENE Eugene John B 1.5.1865 Holyoke, MA BL/TL 5-8/130# d6.18 ▲																								
1884	Bos N	4	16	1	1	0	0	0	0	0		8	.063	.063	.063	-61	-3		.714	-0	131	0	/O-4(1-3-0)	-0.3
	Ind AA	10	37	4	8	0	2	0	4	0	0		.216	.216	.324	76	-1		.769	-1	76	0	/O-7(RF),P-2,3	-0.2
1885	Det N	11	39	1	1	1	0	0	0	0		10	.026	.026	.051	-75	-7		.905	-0	59	0	/O-6(1-0-5),3-4,SP	-0.7
1892	StL N	47	177	20	31	4	1	3	19	4	3	37	.175	.207	.260	43	-13	7	.820	1	112	0	O-47(LF)	-1.6
Total	3	72	269	26	41	5	3	3	23	4	3	55	.152	.174	.227	24	-24	7	.822	-1	103	0	/O-64(49-3-12),3-5,P-3,S	-2.8
MORIARTY, ED Edward Jerome B 10.12.1912 Holyoke, MA D 9.29.1991 Holyoke, MA BR/TR 5-10.5/180# d6.21																								
1935	Bos N	8	34	4	11	2	1	1	1	0	0	6	.324	.324	.529	136	1	0	.923	-3	103	0	/2-8	-0.1
1936	Bos N	6	6	1	1	0	0	0	0	0	0	1	.167	.167	.167	-11	-1	0	—	0			H	-0.1
Total	2	14	40	5	12	2	1	1	1	0	0	7	.300	.300	.475	114	0	0	.923	-3	103	0	/2-8	-0.2
MORIARTY, GEORGE George Joseph B 6.7.1884 Chicago, IL D 4.8.1964 Miami, FL BR/TR 6/185# d9.27 M2 U22 b-Bill																								
1903	Chi N	1	5	1	0	0	0	0	0	0	0		.000	.000	.000	-99	-1	0	1.000	-0	39	0	/3	-0.2
1904	Chi N	4	13	0	0	0	0	0	0	1	0		.000	.071	.000	-77	-3	0	.778	-1	66	0	/3-2,O-2(CF)	-0.4
1906	NY A	65	197	22	46	7	7	0	23	17	1		.234	.298	.340	90	-3	8	.912	0	98	82	3-39,O-15(14-2-0)/1-5,2	-0.3
1907	NY A	126	437	51	121	16	5	0	43	25	3		.277	.320	.336	101	0	28	.899	-9	93	81	3-91,1-22/O-9(1-4-3),2-8,S	-0.7
1908	NY A	101	348	25	82	12	1	0	27	11	5		.236	.269	.276	76	-9	22	.976	7	85	108	1-52,3-28,O-10(8-0-2)/2-4	-0.4
1909	†Det A	133	473	43	129	20	4	1	39	24	1		.273	.309	.338	100	-1	34	**.939**	-1	**111**	84	*3-106,1-24	0.1
1910	Det A	136	490	53	123	24	3	2	60	33	7		.251	.308	.324	92	-4	33	.927	1	**107**	88	*3-134	0.0
1911	Det A	130	478	51	116	20	4	1	60	27	3		.243	.287	.308	63	-25	28	.929	-5	104	57	*3-129/1	-2.6
1912	Det A	105	375	38	93	23	1	0	54	26	11		.248	.316	.315	83	-7	30	.987	-7	65	52	1-71,3-33	-1.5
1913	Det A	104	347	29	83	5	2	0	30	24	7	25	.239	.302	.265	67	-14	33	.938	-1	104	65	3-94/O-7(LF)	-1.4
1914	Det A	132	465	56	118	19	5	1	40	39	5	27	.254	.318	.323	90	-6	34-15	.956	16	**125**	91	*3-126/1-3	1.7
1915	Det A	31	38	2	8	1	0	0	0	5	1	7	.211	.318	.237	63	-1	1-1	.875	-0	115	101	3-12/12O(CF)	-0.2
1916	Chi A	7	5	1	1	0	0	0	0	2	0	0	.200	.429	.200	88	0	0	1.000	0	740	0	/13	0.1
Total	13	1075	3671	372	920	147	32	5	376	234	44	59	.251	.303	.312	84	-74	251-16	.931	0	108	79	3-796,1-180/O-44(30-9-5),2-14,S	-5.8
MORIARTY, MIKE Michael Thomas B 3.8.1974 Camden, NJ BR/TR 6/195# d4.11																								
2002	Bal A	8	16	0	3	1	0	0	3	0-0	0	2	.188	.188	.250	16	-2	0-1	1.000	3	146	0	/S-4,2-2,3	0.1
MORIARTY, BILL William Joseph B 8.1883 Chicago, IL D 12.25.1916 Elgin, IL BR/TR 6-2/180# d4.29 b-George																								
1909	Cin N	6	20	1	4	1	0	0	1	0	0		.200	.200	.250	40	-1	2	.944	-0	84	89	/S-6	-0.2

Year	Tm Lg	G	AB	R	H	2B	3B	HR	RBI	BB-IB	HP	SO	AVG	OBP	SLG	AOPS	ABR	SB-CS	FA	FR	Rng	Thr	G at Pos	BFW
MORLEY, BILL William M. (born William Morley Jennings) B 1.23.1890 Holland, MI D 5.14.1985 Lubbock, TX BR/TR 5-11/170# d9.8																								
1913	Was A	2	3	0	0	0	0	0	0	0	0	0	.000	.000	.000	-98	-1	0	—	-0	0	0	/2	-0.1
MORMAN, RUSS Russell Lee B 4.28.1962 Independence, MO BR/TR 6-4/220# d8.3																								
1986	Chi A	49	159	18	40	5	0	4	17	16-0	2	36	.252	.324	.358	84	-3	1-0	.989	-4	72	85	1-47	-1.0
1988	Chi A	40	75	8	18	2	0	0	3	3-0	0	17	.240	.269	.267	51	-5	0-0	.981	-3	65	83	1-22,O-10(LF)/D-3	-0.9
1989	Chi A	37	58	5	13	2	0	0	8	6-1	0	16	.224	.292	.259	59	-3	1-0	.988	-1	94	116	1-35/D	-0.5
1990	KC A	12	37	5	10	4	2	1	3	3-0	0	3	.270	.317	.568	147	2	0-0	1.000	0	57	238	/O-8(LF),1-3,D	0.2
1991	KC A	12	23	1	6	0	0	0	1	1-1	0	5	.261	.292	.261	54	-1	0-0	1.000	-0	81	47	/1-8,O-2(LF),D	-0.2
1994	Fla N	13	33	2	7	0	1	1	2	2-0	1	9	.212	.278	.364	64	-2	0-0	.987	1	157	153	/1-8	-0.2
1995	Fla N	34	72	9	20	2	1	3	7	3-0	1	12	.278	.316	.458	101	0	0-0	.955	-1	83	0	O-18(6-0-12)/1-3	-0.2
1996	Fla N	6	6	0	1	1	0	0	0	1-0	0	2	.167	.286	.333	65	0	0-0	1.000	-0	0	535	/1-2	0.0
1997	Fla N	4	7	3	2	1	0	1	2	0-0	0	2	.286	.286	.857	194	1	1-0	1.000	0	0	1726	/O-2(RF),1	0.1
Total	9	207	470	51	117	17	4	10	43	35-2	4	102	.249	.304	.366	82	-11	3-0	.989	-8	87	95	1-129/O-40(26-0-14),D-6	-2.7
MORNEAU, JUSTIN Justin Ernest George B C., , CAN BL/TR 6-4/200# d6.10																								
2003	Min A	40	106	14	24	4	0	4	16	9-1	0	30	.226	.287	.377	73	-4	0-0	.971	0	152	32	D-23/1-7	-0.6
MORONKO, JEFF Jeffrey Robert B 8.17.1959 Houston, TX BR/TR 6-2/190# d9.1																								
1984	Cle A	7	19	1	3	1	0	0	3	3-0	0	5	.158	.273	.211	35	-2	0-0	.895	-0	69	190	/3-6,D	-0.2
1987	NY A	7	11	0	1	0	0	0	0	0-0	1	2	.091	.167	.091	-29	-2	0-0	1.000	0	141	0	/3-3,S-2,O-2(1-0-1)	-0.2
Total	2	14	30	1	4	1	0	0	3	3-0	1	7	.133	.235	.167	12	-4	0-0	.926	-0	91	132	/3-9,O-2(1-0-1),S-2,D	-0.4
MORRILL, JOHN John Francis "Honest John" B 2.19.1855 Boston, MA D 4.2.1932 Brookline, MA BR/TR 5-10.5/155# d4.24 M8 ▲ OF Total (2-LF 12-CF 12-RF)																								
1876	Bos N	66	278	38	73	5	2	0	26	3		5	.263	.270	.295	87	-4		.857	5	110	133	2-37,C-23/O-5(1-3-1),1-3	0.3
1877	Bos N	**61**	242	47	73	5	1	0	28	6		15	.302	.319	.331	101	0		.864	-9	76	36	3-30,1-18,O-11(RF)/2-3	-0.8
1878	Bos N	**60**	233	26	56	5	1	0	23	5		16	.240	.256	.270	68	-9		.957	2	130	**139**	*1-59/O(CF)3	-0.8
1879	Bos N	**84**	348	56	98	18	5	0	49	14		32	.282	.309	.362	118	7		.878	1	87	34	3-51,1-33	0.7
1880	Bos N	**86**	342	51	81	16	8	2	44	11		37	.237	.261	.348	108	3		.966	2	220	114	1-46,3-40/P-3	0.4
1881	Bos N	81	311	47	90	19	3	1	39	12		30	.289	.316	.379	123	9		.969	7	138	76	*1-74/2-4,P-3,3-2	1.3
1882	Bos N	83	349	73	101	19	11	2	54	18		29	.289	.324	.424	137	14		.964	-2	76	63	*1-76/S-3,2-2,O(CF)3PM	0.5
1883	Bos N	97	404	83	129	33	16	6	68	15		68	.319	.344	.525	155	26		**.974**	-1	76	93	*1-81/O-7(CF),3-6,S-2,2-2,P-2,M	1.5
1884	Bos N	111	438	80	114	19	7	3	61	30		87	.260	.308	.356	109	5		.971	2	125	96	*1-91,2-17/P-7,3-2,O(LF)M	-0.1
1885	Bos N	111	394	74	89	20	7	4	44	64		78	.226	.334	.343	124	15		.969	0	103	108	*1-92,2-17/3-2,M	0.7
1886	Bos N	117	430	86	106	25	6	7	69	56		81	.247	.333	.381	120	13	9	.895	-8	87	78	S-55,1-42,2-20/PM	0.3
1887	Bos N	**127**	504	79	141	32	6	12	81	37	1	86	.280	.330	.438	110	7	19	.984	4	109	102	*1-127,M	0.0
1888	Bos N	135	486	60	96	18	7	4	39	55	2	68	.198	.282	.288	80	-9	21	.979	9	**147**	104	*1-133/2-2,M	-1.3
1889	Was N	44	146	20	27	5	0	2	16	30	1	23	.185	.328	.260	70	-4	12	.980	-1	104	60	1-40/3-3,2PM	-0.8
1890	Bos P	2	7	1	1	0	0	0	2	2	0	1	.143	.333	.143	28	-1	0	.750	-1	88	0	/S1	-0.1
Total	15	1265	4912	821	1275	239	80	43	643	358	4	656	.260	.310	.367	111	72	61	.971	11	124	101	1-916,3-138,2-105/S-61,O-26C,CP	1.8
MORRIS, DOYT Doyt Theodore B 7.15.1916 Stanley, NC D 7.4.1984 Gastonia, NC BR/TR 6-4/195# d6.6																								
1937	Phi A	6	13	0	2	0	0	0	0	0	0	3	.154	.154	.154	-23	-3	0-0	1.000	0	111	0	/O-3(2-1-0)	-0.2
MORRIS, E. E. B Trenton, NJ d9.11																								
1884	Bal U	1	3	0	0	0	0	0		0			.000	.000	.000	-91	-1		—	-0	0	0	/O(CF)P	-0.1
MORRIS, JOHN John Daniel B 2.23.1961 N.Bellmore, NY BL/TL 6-1/185# d8.5																								
1986	StL N	39	100	8	24	0	1	1	14	7-2	0	15	.240	.287	.290	61	-6	6-2	.986	2	130	0	O-31(5-4-26)	-0.5
1987	†StL N	101	157	22	41	6	4	3	23	11-4	1	22	.261	.314	.408	88	-3	5-2	.989	0	113	0	O-74(2-8-68)	-0.5
1988	StL N	20	38	3	11	2	1	0	3	1-0	0	7	.289	.308	.395	99	0	0-0	.857	-2	65	0	O-16(11-3-2)	-0.3
1989	StL N	96	117	8	28	4	1	2	14	4-0	0	22	.239	.264	.342	70	-5	1-0	1.000	-2	94	0	O-51(10-11-32)	-0.8
1990	StL N	18	18	0	2	0	0	0	0	3-0	0	6	.111	.238	.111	-1	-2	0-0	1.000	-0	87	0	/O-6(0-1-5)	-0.3
1991	Phi N	85	127	15	28	2	1	1	6	12-4	1	25	.220	.293	.276	61	-7	2-0	.974	-0	104	51	O-57(11-27-24)	-0.8
1992	Cal A	43	57	4	11	1	0	1	3	4-1	1	11	.193	.258	.263	46	-4	1-0	1.000	-1	94	0	O-14(5-0-9)/D-6	-0.5
Total	7	402	614	60	145	15	8	8	63	42-11	3	108	.236	.288	.326	69	-27	15-4	.981	-3	106	12	O-249(44-54-166)/D-6	-3.7
MORRIS, WALTER John Walter B 1.31.1880 Rockwall, TX D 8.2.1961 Dallas, TX BR/TR 5-11/?# d8.31																								
1908	StL N	23	73	1	13	1	1	0	2	0	0		.178	.178	.219	28	-6	1	.938	2	103	109	S-23	-0.4
MORRIS, P. P. B Rockford, IL d5.14																								
1884	Was U	1	3	0	0	0	0	0		0			.000	.000	.000	-99	-1		.750	-0	113	0	/S	-0.1
MORRIS, WARREN Warren Randall B 1.11.1974 Alexandria, LA BL/TR 5-11/190# d4.5																								
1999	Pit N	147	511	65	147	20	3	15	73	59-3	2	88	.288	.360	.427	99	0	3-7	.979	3	104	111	*2-144	0.7
2000	Pit N	144	528	68	137	31	2	3	43	65-3	2	78	.259	.341	.343	75	-19	7-10	.979	19	**114**	97	*2-134	0.5
2001	Pit N	48	103	6	21	6	0	2	11	3-0	2	9	.204	.239	.320	42	-9	2-3	.965	2	122	105	2-29/3	-0.6
2002	Min A	4	7	0	0	0	0	0	0	0-0	0	1	.000	.000	.000	-99	-2	0-0	1.000	0	117	91	/2-4	-0.2
2003	Det A	97	346	37	94	13	2	6	37	23-1	1	42	.272	.316	.373	88	-7	4-2	.987	12	111	138	2-89	0.9
Total	5	440	1495	176	399	70	7	26	164	150-7	7	218	.267	.334	.375	83	-37	16-22	.980	36	110	112	2-400/3	1.3
MORRIS, HAL William Harold B 4.9.1965 Fort Rucker, AL BL/TL 6-4/215# d7.29																								
1988	NY A	15	20	1	2	0	0	0	0	0-0	0	9	.100	.100	.100	-44	-4	0-0	1.000	0	125	0	/O-4(3-0-2),D	-0.4
1989	NY A	15	18	2	5	0	0	0	4	1-0	0	4	.278	.316	.278	69	-1	0-0	1.000	-0	109	0	/O-5(2-0-3),1-2,D	-0.1
1990	†Cin N	107	309	50	105	22	3	7	36	21-4	1	32	.340	.381	.498	135	15	9-3	.995	1	104	104	1-80/O-6(LF)	1.2
1991	Cin N	136	478	72	152	33	1	14	59	46-7	1	61	.318	.374	.479	135	23	10-4	.992	6	116	103	*1-128/O(LF)	2.2
1992	Cin N	115	395	41	107	21	3	6	53	45-8	2	53	.271	.347	.385	105	4	6-6	**.999**	7	**116**	91	*1-109	0.2
1993	Cin N	101	379	48	120	18	0	7	49	34-4	2	51	.317	.371	.420	112	8	2-2	.994	3	106	81	1-98	0.1
1994	Cin N	112	436	60	146	30	4	10	78	34-8	5	62	.335	.385	.491	129	19	6-2	.994	2	102	94	*1-112	1.1
1995	†Cin N	101	359	53	100	25	2	11	51	29-7	1	58	.279	.333	.451	105	2	1-1	.994	5	119	**116**	1-99	-0.2
1996	Cin N	142	528	82	165	32	4	16	80	50-5	5	76	.313	.374	.479	123	19	7-5	.993	-2	95	94	*1-140	0.4
1997	Cin N	96	333	42	92	20	1	1	33	23-2	3	43	.276	.328	.351	77	-11	3-1	.990	-3	86	101	1-89	-2.2
1998	KC A	127	472	50	146	27	2	1	40	32-6	1	52	.309	.350	.381	89	-7	1-0	.990	-2	127	98	1-46,O-39(LF),D-39	-1.5
1999	Cin N	80	102	10	29	9	0	0	16	10-0	0	21	.284	.348	.373	80	-3	0-0	.991	-1	78	112	1-25/O-4(LF),D	-0.5
2000	Cin N	59	63	9	14	2	1	2	6	12-3	1	10	.222	.351	.381	84	-1	0-0	1.000	3	239	100	1-16/O(RF)D	0.1
	Det A	40	106	15	33	7	0	1	8	19-1	0	16	.311	.416	.406	112	3	0-0	.990	1	109	101	1-38/O(LF)	0.1
Total	13	1246	3998	535	1216	246	21	76	513	356-55	22	548	.304	.361	.433	110	66	45-24	.994	19	107	98	1-982/O-61(56-0-6),D-43	0.5
MORRISON, JIM James Forrest B 9.23.1952 Pensacola, FL BR/TR 5-11/182# d9.18 OF Total (9-LF 3-RF)																								
1977	Phi N	5	7	3	3	0	0	0	1	1-0	0	1	.429	.500	.429	145	1	0-0	.875	-0	119	0	/3-5	0.0
1978	†Phi N	53	108	12	17	1	1	3	10	10-1	1	21	.157	.235	.269	40	-9	1-1	.968	11	122	144	2-31/3-3,O(LF)	0.3
1979	Chi A	67	240	38	66	14	0	14	35	15-0	4	48	.275	.324	.508	122	7	11-3	.982	5	100	102	2-48,3-29	1.4
1980	Chi A	**162**	604	66	171	40	0	15	57	36-2	8	74	.283	.329	.424	106	5	9-6	.969	9	101	96	*2-161/SD	2.3
1981	Chi A	90	290	27	68	8	1	10	34	10-0	2	29	.234	.261	.372	84	-8	3-2	.956	9	108	92	3-87/2D	-0.1
1982	Chi A	51	166	17	37	7	3	7	19	13-0	0	15	.223	.279	.428	91	-3	0-1	.914	-10	85	101	3-50/D	-1.5
	Pit N	44	86	10	24	4	1	4	15	5-0	0	14	.279	.309	.488	119	2	2-0	.964	1	100	65	3-26/O-2(LF),2S	0.3
1983	Pit N	66	158	16	48	7	2	6	25	9-1	2	25	.304	.347	.487	126	5	2-6	.973	1	104	119	2-28,3-26/S-7	0.6
1984	Pit N	100	304	38	87	14	2	11	45	20-1	1	52	.286	.328	.454	119	7	0-1	.938	-4	98	89	3-61,2-26/S-2,1	0.2
1985	Pit N	92	244	17	62	10	0	4	22	8-1	1	44	.254	.277	.344	75	-9	3-0	.961	1	90	106	3-59,2-15/O(LF)	-0.8
1986	Pit N	154	537	58	147	35	4	23	88	47-5	4	88	.274	.334	.482	120	14	9-8	.946	-12	95	49	*3-151/2S	-0.1
1987	Pit N	96	348	41	92	22	1	9	46	27-3	1	57	.264	.315	.411	91	-5	8-5	.975	4	105	89	3-82,S-17/2-9	-0.1
	†Det A	34	117	15	24	1	1	4	19	2-0	1	26	.205	.221	.333	47	-10	2-1	.962	4	152	37	3-16/2-3,S-3,O-3(1-0-2),1D	-0.5
1988	Det A	24	74	7	16	5	0	0	6	0-0	0	14	.216	.216	.284	40	-6	0-2	1.000	-0	0	130	D-14/1-4,3-4,O-2(1-0-1),S	-0.8
	Atl N	51	92	6	14	2	0	2	13	10-1	0	13	.152	.229	.239	35	-8	0-1	.933	-2	84	34	3-20/O-4(LF),P-3	-1.0
Total	12	1089	3375	371	876	170	16	112	435	213-15	25	521	.260	.305	.419	98	-17	50-37	.949	16	100	79	3-619,2-324/S-33,D-25,O-13L,1-6,P	0.2

Year	Tm Lg	G	AB	R	H	2B	3B	HR	RBI	BB-IB	HP	SO	AVG	OBP	SLG	AOPS	ABR	SB-CS	FA	FR	Rng	Thr	G at Pos	BFW
MORRISON, JON Jonathan W. B 1859 London, ON, CAN 5-9.5/167# d8.1																								
1884	Ind AA	44	182	26	48	6	8	1		7	4		.264	.306	.401	132	6		.784	2	107	282	O-44(CF)	0.6
1887	NY AA	9	34	7	4	0	0	0	3	6	1		.118	.268	.118	10	-4	0	.600	-4	0	0	/O-9(CF)	-0.7
Total	2	53	216	33	52	6	8	1	3	13	5		.241	.299	.356	110	2	0	.756	-2	89	235	/O-53(CF)	-0.1
MORRISON, TOM Thomas J. B 8.1870 St.Louis, MO D 3.27.1902 St.Louis, MO 5-3/145# d9.18																								
1895	Lou N	6	22	3	6	0	2	0	4	1	0	1	.273	.304	.455	100	0	0	1.000	-1	59	108	/S-3,3-3	-0.1
1896	Lou N	8	27	3	4	1	0	0	0	4	0	4	.148	.258	.185	19	-3	0	.864	1	131	0	/3-5,O-2(RF),S	-0.2
Total	2	14	49	6	10	1	2	0	4	5	0	5	.204	.278	.306	55	-3	0	.839	-1	117	0	/3-8,S-4,O-2(RF)	-0.3
MORRISSEY, JACK John Albert "King" B 5.2.1876 Lansing, MI D 10.30.1936 Lansing, MI BB/TR 5-10/160# d9.18																								
1902	Cin N	12	39	5	11	1	1	0	3	4	0		.282	.349	.359	108	0	0	.941	-1	96	87	2-11/O(LF)	0.0
1903	Cin N	29	89	14	22	1	0	0	9	14	0		.247	.350	.258	67	-3	3	.922	-9	82	0	2-17/O-8(6-2-0),S-2	-1.3
Total	2	41	128	19	33	2	1	0	12	18	0		.258	.349	.289	78	-3	3	.930	-10	87	32	/2-28,O-9(7-2-0),S-2	-1.3
MORRISSEY, JOHN John J. B 12.30.1856 Janesville, WI D 4.29.1884 Janesville, WI d5.2 b-Tom																								
1881	Buf N	12	47	3	10	2	0	0	3	0		3	.213	.213	.255	47	-3		.865	-1	103	0	3-12	-0.4
1882	Det N	2	7	1	2	0	0	0	0	0		2	.286	.286	.286	84	0		.714	-1	23	0	/3-2	-0.1
Total	2	14	54	4	12	2	0	0	3	0		5	.222	.222	.259	52	-3		.841	-3	90	0	/3-14	-0.5
MORRISSEY, JO-JO Joseph Anselm B 1.16.1904 Warren, RI D 5.2.1950 Worcester, MA BR/TR 6-1.5/178# d4.12																								
1932	Cin N	89	269	15	65	10	1	0	13	14	1	15	.242	.282	.286	55	-17	2	.967	4	102	78	S-45,2-42,3-12/O(LF)	-0.9
1933	Cin N	148	534	43	123	20	0	0	26	20	2	22	.230	.261	.268	52	-34	5	.964	-6	113	98	2-88,S-63,3-15	-3.3
1936	Chi A	17	38	3	7	1	0	0	6	2	0	3	.184	.225	.211	8	-6	0-0	.895	-1	97	103	/3-9,S-4,2	-0.5
Total	3	254	841	61	195	31	1	0	45	36	3	40	.232	.266	.271	51	-57	7-0	.971	-3	112	102	2-131,S-112/3-36,O(LF)	-4.7
MORRISSEY, TOM Thomas J. B 1861 Janesville, WI D 9.23.1941 Janesville, WI 5-11/180# d9.27 b-John																								
1884	Mil U	**12**	47	3	8	2	0	0		0			.170	.170	.213	28	-5		.710	-1	71	147	3-12	-0.6
MORSE, BUD Newell Obediah B 9.4.1904 Berkeley, CA D 4.6.1987 Sparks, NV BL/TR 5-9/150# d9.14																								
1929	Phi A	8	27	1	2	0	0	0	0	0	0	2	.074	.074	.074	-60	-7	0-0	.975	1	103	78	/2-8	-0.6
MORSE, HAP Peter Raymond "Pete" B 12.6.1886 St.Paul, MN D 6.19.1974 St.Paul, MN BR/TR 5-8/160# d4.18																								
1911	StL N	4	8	0	0	0	0	0	0	1	0	2	.000	.111	.000	-70	-2	0	.750	-1	89	0	/S-2,O(LF)	-0.3
MORTON, CHARLIE Charles Hazen B 10.12.1854 Kingsville, OH D 12.9.1921 Massillon, OH BR/TR ?/150# d5.2 M3 U1 ▲																								
1882	Pit AA	25	103	12	29	0	3	0		5			.282	.315	.340	127	3		.816	1	159	0	O-25(CF)/3-3,S	0.2
	StL AA	9	32	2	2	0	1	0		2			.063	.118	.125	-17	-4		.708	-4	79	48	/2-7,O-3(1-2-0)	-0.7
	Year	34	135	14	31	0	4	0		7			.230	.268	.289	90	-2		.821	-3	155	0	O-28(1-27-0)/2-7,3-3,S	-0.5
1884	Tol AA	32	111	11	18	6	2	0		7	0		.162	.212	.252	49	-6		.861	-0	79	78	3-16,O-15(14-0-1)/P-3,2M	-0.5
1885	Det N	22	79	9	14	1	2	0	3	5		10	.177	.226	.241	51	-4		.750	-1	103	85	3-18/S-4,M	-0.4
Total	3	88	325	34	63	7	8	0	3	19		10	.194	.238	.265	66	-11		.841	-4	144	0	/O-43(15-27-1),3-37,2-8,S-5,P-3	-1.4
MORTON, GUY Guy Jr. "Moose" B 11.4.1930 Tuscaloosa, AL BR/TR 6-2/200# d9.17 f-Guy																								
1954	Bos A	1	1	0	0	0	0	0	0	0	0	1	.000	.000	.000	-90	0	0-0	—	0			H	0.0
MORTON, BUBBA Wycliffe Nathaniel B 12.13.1931 Washington, DC BR/TR 5-10.5/180# d4.19																								
1961	Det A	77	108	26	31	5	1	2	19	9-1	1	25	.287	.342	.407	98	0	3-1	.952	1	111	76	O-30(8-2-20)	-0.1
1962	Det A	90	195	30	51	6	3	4	17	32-0	0	32	.262	.366	.385	99	0	1-1	.991	4	115	166	O-62(1-30-33)/1-3	0.1
1963	Det A	6	11	2	1	0	0	0	2	2-0	0	1	.091	.231	.091	-5	-2	0-0	.875	-0	120	0	/O-3(CF)	-0.2
	Mil N	15	28	1	5	0	0	0	4	2-1	1	3	.179	.258	.179	28	-3	0-0	1.000	0	115	0	/O-9(6-3-0)	-0.3
1966	Cal A	15	50	4	11	1	0	0	4	2-0	0	6	.220	.250	.240	43	-4	1-1	1.000	0	97	124	O-14(RF)	-0.5
1967	Cal A	80	201	23	63	9	3	0	32	22-1	2	29	.313	.387	.388	135	9	0-3	1.000	-2	96	31	O-61(9-0-55)	0.3
1968	Cal A	81	163	13	44	6	0	1	18	14-0	4	18	.270	.341	.325	107	2	2-1	.985	-1	102	48	O-50(3-0-47)/3	-0.2
1969	Cal A	87	172	18	42	10	1	7	32	28-1	3	29	.244	.356	.436	128	7	0-0	1.000	2	101	166	O-49(6-0-43)/1	0.8
Total	7	451	928	117	248	37	8	14	128	111-4	11	143	.267	.351	.370	106	9	7-7	.988	3	104	97	O-278(33-38-212)/1-4,3	-0.1
MORYN, WALT Walter Joseph "Moose" B 4.12.1926 St.Paul, MN D 7.21.1996 Winfield, IL BL/TR 6-2/205# d6.29																								
1954	Bro N	48	91	16	25	4	2	2	14	7	1	11	.275	.330	.429	94	-1	0-0	.881	0	95	199	O-20(6-0-15)	-0.2
1955	Bro N	11	19	3	5	1	0	1	3	5-1	0	4	.263	.417	.474	132	1	0-0	.833	-1	67	0	/O-7(1-0-6)	0.0
1956	Chi N	147	529	69	151	27	3	23	67	50-2	3	67	.285	.348	.478	122	16	4-2	.983	6	104	144	*O-141(1-0-140)	1.8
1957	Chi N	149	568	76	164	33	0	19	88	50-6	3	90	.289	.348	.447	114	12	0-2	.960	7	113	131	*O-147(RF)	1.4
1958	Chi N☆	143	512	77	135	26	7	26	77	62-7	**8**	83	.264	.350	.494	123	17	1-2	.978	-1	105	42	*O-141(LF)	0.8
1959	Chi N	117	381	41	89	14	1	14	48	44-2	3	66	.234	.316	.386	87	-7	0-0	.989	0	94	119	*O-104(97-1-9)	-1.2
1960	Chi N	38	109	12	32	4	0	2	11	13-0	0	19	.294	.366	.385	108	2	2-1	.964	-1	96	83	O-30(25-0-5)	0.0
	StL N	75	200	24	49	4	3	11	35	17-4	0	38	.245	.299	.460	97	-2	0-0	.990	1	107	90	O-62(29-0-39)	-0.3
	Year	113	309	36	81	8	3	13	46	30-4	0	57	.262	.323	.434	101	0	2-1	.981	1	103	88	O-92(54-0-44)	-0.3
1961	StL N	17	32	0	4	2	0	0	2	1-0	0	5	.125	.152	.188	-10	-5	0-0	.889	-1	91	0	/O-7(3-0-4)	-0.6
	Pit N	40	65	6	13	1	0	3	9	2-0	1	10	.200	.235	.354	53	-5	0-0	.950	1	95	236	O-11(6-0-5)	-0.4
	Year	57	97	6	17	3	0	3	11	3-0	1	15	.175	.208	.299	31	-10	0-0	.931	0	94	157	O-18(9-0-9)	-1.0
Total	8	785	2506	324	667	116	16	101	354	251-22	19	393	.266	.335	.446	108	28	7-7	.972	14	104	109	O-670(309-1-370)	1.3
MOSCHITTO, ROSS Rosaire Allen B 2.15.1945 Fresno, CA BR/TR 6-2/175# d4.15 Mil 1966																								
1965	NY A	96	27	12	5	0	0	1	3	0-0	0	12	.185	.179	.296	35	-2	0-0	.941	2	151	0	O-89(10-55-24)	-0.1
1967	NY A	14	9	1	1	0	0	0	0	1-0	0	2	.111	.200	.111	-6	-1	0-0	1.000	0	49	779	/O-8(2-4-2)	-0.1
Total	2	110	36	13	6	0	0	1	3	1-0	0	14	.167	.184	.250	25	-3	0-0	.944	2	140	87	/O-97(12-59-26)	-0.2
MOSEBY, LLOYD Lloyd Anthony B 11.5.1959 Portland, AR BL/TR 6-3/200# d5.24 C1																								
1980	Tor A	114	389	44	89	24	1	9	46	25-4	4	85	.229	.281	.365	73	-15	4-6	.982	2	96	152	*O-104(12-6-86)/D-6	-1.9
1981	Tor A	100	378	36	88	16	2	9	43	24-3	1	86	.233	.278	.357	78	-12	11-8	.989	-3	99	62	*O-100(0-80-21)	-1.8
1982	Tor A	147	487	51	115	20	9	9	52	33-3	8	106	.236	.294	.370	74	-18	11-7	.992	-4	100	45	*O-145(CF)	-2.3
1983	Tor A	151	539	104	170	31	7	18	81	51-4	5	85	.315	.376	.499	132	24	27-8	.983	4	104	116	*O-147(CF)	2.9
1984	Tor A	158	592	97	166	28	**15**	18	92	78-9	8	122	.280	.368	.470	126	23	39-9	.990	4	108	77	*O-156(CF)	3.0
1985	†Tor A	152	584	92	151	30	7	18	70	76-4	4	91	.259	.345	.426	108	8	37-15	.980	-10	93	70	*O-152(CF)	-0.1
1986	Tor A★	152	589	89	149	24	5	21	86	64-3	6	122	.253	.329	.418	100	0	32-11	.984	-8	93	75	*O-147(CF)/D-3	-0.6
1987	Tor A	155	592	106	167	27	4	26	96	70-4	2	124	.282	.358	.473	116	14	39-7	.980	-17	78	107	*O-153(CF)/D-2	0.2
1988	Tor A	128	472	77	113	17	7	10	42	70-6	6	93	.239	.343	.369	99	1	31-8	.984	-9	91	34	*O-125(11-117-6)/D	-0.5
1989	†Tor A	135	502	72	111	25	3	11	43	56-1	6	101	.221	.306	.349	86	-9	24-7	.986	-12	88	45	*O-120(CF),D-14	-2.0
1990	Det A	122	431	64	107	16	5	14	51	48-3	5	77	.248	.329	.406	104	2	17-5	.983	3	101	153	*O-116(14-104-0)/D-4	0.6
1991	Det A	74	260	37	68	15	1	6	35	21-2	3	43	.262	.321	.396	97	-1	8-1	.955	-4	98	28	O-64(LF)/D-7	-0.5
Total	12	1588	5815	869	1494	273	66	169	737	616-46	58	1135	.257	.332	.414	102	17	280-92	.984	-55	96	82	*O-1529(101-1327-113)/D-37	-3.0
MOSER, ARNIE Arnold Robert B 8.9.1915 Houston, TX D 8.15.2002 Houston, TX BR/TR 5-11/165# d6.20																								
1937	Cin N	5	5	0	0	0	0	0	0	0	0	2	.000	.000	.000	-99	-1	0	—	0			H	-0.1
MOSES, JERRY Gerald Braheen B 8.9.1946 Yazoo City, MS BR/TR 6-3/210# d5.9																								
1965	Bos A	4	4	1	1	0	0	1	1	0-0	0	2	.250	.250	1.000	224	1	0-0	—	0			H	0.1
1968	Bos A	6	18	2	6	0	0	2	4	1-0	0	4	.333	.368	.667	196	2	0-1	.963	-2	246	0	/C-6	0.0
1969	Bos A	53	135	13	41	9	1	4	17	5-1	1	23	.304	.326	.474	117	3	0-1	.981	-7	90	94	C-36	-0.3
1970	Bos A☆	92	315	26	83	18	1	6	35	21-9	2	45	.263	.313	.384	85	-6	1-1	.990	6	103	71	C-88/O(LF)	0.3
1971	Cal A	69	181	12	41	8	2	4	15	10-4	0	34	.227	.266	.359	82	-6	0-0	.977	1	78	149	C-63/O(RF)	-0.2
1972	Cle A	52	141	9	31	3	0	4	14	11-3	3	29	.220	.290	.326	81	-3	0-0	.982	-1	130	118	C-39/1-3	-0.3
1973	NY A	21	59	5	15	2	0	0	3	2-0	0	6	.254	.270	.288	62	-3	0-0	1.000	5	112	73	C-17/D	0.2
1974	Det A	74	198	19	47	6	3	4	19	11-2	2	38	.237	.282	.359	81	-6	0-1	.985	-1	109	88	C-74	-0.4
1975	SD N	13	19	1	3	2	0	0	1	2-0	0	3	.158	.238	.263	42	-1	0-0	.900	-1	51	0	/C-5	-0.3
	Chi A	2	2	1	1	0	1	0	0	0-0	0	0	.500	.500	1.500	441	1	0-0	1.000	-0	0	0	/1D	0.1
Total	9	386	1072	89	269	48	8	25	109	63-19	8	184	.251	.295	.381	89	-18	1-4	.984	-0	104	95	C-328/1-4,D-2,O-2(1-0-1)	-0.8

Year	Tm Lg	G	AB	R	H	2B	3B	HR	RBI	BB-IB	HP	SO	AVG	OBP	SLG	AOPS	ABR	SB-CS	FA	FR	Rng	Thr	G at Pos	BFW
MOSES, JOHN John William B 8.9.1957 Los Angeles, CA BB/TL 5-10/170# d8.23 C4																								
1982	Sea A	22	44	7	14	5	1	1	3	4-0	0	5	.318	.375	.545	145	3	5-1	.947	-1	69	279	O-19(8-3-9)	0.3
1983	Sea A	93	130	19	27	4	1	0	6	12-0	1	20	.208	.280	.254	46	-9	11-5	.979	3	87	297	O-71(34-31-7),D-10	-0.8
1984	Sea A	19	35	3	12	1	1	0	2	2-0	1	5	.343	.395	.429	129	1	1-0	1.000	-1	84	131	O-19(7-14-0)/D	0.1
1985	Sea A	33	62	4	12	0	0	0	3	2-0	0	8	.194	.219	.194	14	-8	5-2	1.000	-3	71	85	O-29(1-28-0)	-1.0
1986	Sea A	103	399	56	102	16	3	3	34	34-3	0	65	.256	.311	.333	76	-13	25-18	.987	-4	88	185	O-93(2-91-0)/1-7,D-4	-1.9
1987	Sea A	116	390	58	96	16	4	3	38	29-2	3	49	.246	.301	.331	65	-20	23-15	.987	-3	94	120	*O-100(0-97-4)/1-16,D-5	-2.4
1988	Min A	105	206	33	65	10	3	2	12	15-2	2	21	.316	.366	.422	117	5	11-6	1.000	1	113	35	O-82(29-20-43)/D-2	0.5
1989	Min A	129	242	33	68	12	3	1	31	19-1	1	23	.281	.333	.368	92	-2	14-7	.988	3	**117**	73	*O-108(39-26-63)/1-2,PD	-0.1
1990	Min A	115	172	26	38	3	1	1	14	19-1	2	19	.221	.303	.267	58	-9	2-3	1.000	0	108	68	O-85(16-23-52),D-10/1-6,P-2	-1.1
1991	Det A	13	21	5	1	1	0	0	1	2-0	0	7	.048	.130	.095	-36	-4	4-0	1.000	-1	91	0	O-12(11-0-1)	-0.4
1992	Sea A	21	22	3	3	1	0	0	1	5-0	0	4	.136	.296	.182	37	-2	0-0	1.000	-1	95	0	O-18(17-1-1)/D	-0.3
Total	11	769	1723	247	438	69	17	11	145	143-9	10	226	.254	.313	.333	75	-58	101-57	.990	-5	97	127	O-636(164-334-180)/D-36,1-31,P-3-7.1	
MOSES, WALLY Wallace B 10.8.1910 Uvalda, GA D 10.10.1990 Vidalia, GA BL/TL 5-10/160# d4.17 C16																								
1935	Phi A	85	345	60	112	21	3	5	35	25	3	18	.325	.375	.446	113	6	3-4	.943	-1	101	103	O-80(RF)	0.0
1936	Phi A	146	585	98	202	35	11	7	66	62	2	32	.345	.410	.479	121	20	12-6	.974	0	101	93	*O-144(0-136-9)	1.5
1937	Phi A☆	**154**	649	113	208	48	13	25	86	54	2	38	.320	.374	.550	132	29	9-7	.958	5	108	111	*O-154(RF)	2.2
1938	Phi A	142	589	86	181	29	8	8	49	58	0	31	.307	.369	.424	101	0	15-5	.966	4	**112**	87	*O-139(RF)	-0.2
1939	Phi A	115	437	68	134	28	7	3	33	44	0	23	.307	.370	.423	105	3	7-4	.965	-1	96	119	*O-103(0-5-100)	-0.3
1940	Phi A	142	537	91	166	41	9	9	50	75	2	44	.309	.396	.469	126	23	6-4	.974	5	110	92	*O-133(0-2-131)	1.9
1941	Phi A	116	438	78	132	31	4	4	35	62	0	27	.301	.388	.418	116	13	3-3	.975	8	**114**	109	*O-109(RF)	1.3
1942	Chi A	146	577	73	156	28	4	7	49	74	0	27	.270	.353	.369	106	6	16-10	.980	6	106	129	*O-145(3-14-130)	0.3
1943	Chi A	150	599	82	147	22	**12**	3	48	55	1	47	.245	.310	.337	89	-10	56-14	.979	7	**110**	106	*O-148(0-23-125)	-0.5
1944	Chi A	136	535	82	150	26	9	3	34	52	1	22	.280	.345	.379	108	6	21-7	.975	-2	100	77	*O-134(RF)	-0.3
1945	Chi A∗	140	569	79	168	**35**	15	2	50	69	2	33	.295	.373	.420	134	25	11-5	.977	6	**115**	85	*O-139(RF)	2.4
1946	Chi A	56	168	20	46	9	1	4	16	17	1	20	.274	.344	.411	115	3	2-2	1.000	-2	96	63	O-36(2-14-22)	0.0
	†Bos A	48	175	23	36	11	3	2	17	14	1	15	.206	.268	.337	65	-9	2-4	.979	-1	99	72	O-44(0-2-43)	-1.3
	Year	104	343	43	82	20	4	6	33	31	2	35	.239	.306	.373	88	-6	4-6	.989	-3	98	68	O-80(2-16-65)	-1.3
1947	Bos A	90	255	32	70	18	2	2	27	27	0	16	.275	.344	.384	95	-1	3-0	.974	-4	93	47	O-58(RF)	-0.7
1948	Bos A	78	189	26	49	12	1	2	29	21	2	19	.259	.340	.365	83	-4	5-0	.981	1	108	61	O-45(RF)	-0.4
1949	Phi A	110	308	49	85	19	3	1	25	51	1	19	.276	.381	.367	102	3	1-3	.983	-0	101	88	O-92(1-1-91)	-0.1
1950	Phi A	88	265	47	70	16	5	2	21	40	2	17	.264	.365	.385	94	-2	0-1	.987	3	107	128	O-62(4-7-51)	-0.1
1951	Phi A	70	136	17	26	6	0	0	9	21	1	9	.191	.304	.235	46	-10	2-2	.984	1	112	51	O-27(RF)	-1.0
Total	17	2012	7356	1124	2138	435	110	89	679	821	21	457	.291	.364	.416	109	101	174-81	.973	35	106	96	*O-1792(10-204-1587)	4.7
MOSKIMAN, DOC William Bankhead B 12.20.1879 Oakland, CA D 1.11.1953 San Leandro, CA BR/TR 6/170# d8.23																								
1910	Bos A	5	9	1	1	0	0	0	1	2	0		.111	.273	.111	20	-1	0	1.000	0	143	185	/1-2,O(RF)	-0.1
MOSOLF, JIM James Frederick B 8.21.1905 Puyallup, WA D 12.28.1979 Dallas, OR BL/TR 5-10/186# d9.9																								
1929	Pit N	8	13	3	6	1	1	0	2	1	0	1	.462	.500	.692	188	2	0	1.000	0	128	0	/O-3(LF)	0.2
1930	Pit N	40	51	16	17	2	1	0	9	8	0	7	.333	.424	.412	103	1	0	.765	-1	76	120	O-12(1-1-9)/P	-0.1
1931	Pit N	39	44	7	11	1	0	1	8	8	0	5	.250	.365	.341	92	0	0	1.000	-1	73	0	/O-4(3-0-1)	-0.1
1933	Chi N	31	82	13	22	5	1	1	9	5	2	8	.268	.326	.390	104	0	0	.964	1	107	122	O-22(19-3-0)	0.0
Total	4	118	190	39	56	9	3	2	28	22	2	21	.295	.374	.405	107	3	0	.929	-1	99	101	/O-41(26-4-10),P	0.0
MOSQUERA, JULIO Julio Alberto (Cervantes) B 1.29.1972 Panama City, Panama BR/TR 6/165# d8.17																								
1996	Tor A	8	22	2	5	2	0	0	2	0-0	1	3	.227	.261	.318	46	-2	0-1	1.000	1	203	0	/C-8	-0.1
1997	Tor A	3	8	0	2	1	0	0	0	0-0	0	2	.250	.250	.375	60	0	0-0	1.000	-0	135	151	/C-3	-0.1
Total	2	11	30	2	7	3	0	0	2	0-0	1	5	.233	.258	.333	49	-2	0-1	1.000	0	187	36	/C-11	-0.2
MOSS, CHARLIE Charles Crosby B 3.20.1911 Meridian, MS D 10.9.1991 Meridian, MS BR/TR 5-10/160# d5.19																								
1934	Phi A	10	10	3	2	0	0	0	1	0	0	0	.200	.200	.200	4	-1	0-0	1.000	-1	*56*	*0*	/C-6	-0.2
1935	Phi A	4	3	1	1	0	0	0	1	1	0	0	.333	.500	.333	120	0	0-0	—	0	*0*	*0*	/C	0.0
1936	Phi A	33	44	2	11	1	1	0	10	6	0	5	.250	.340	.318	65	-2	1-0	.929	-2	*73*	*82*	C-19	-0.4
Total	3	47	57	6	14	1	1	0	12	7	0	5	.246	.328	.298	58	-3	1-0	.935	-3	*70*	*72*	/C-26	-0.6
MOSS, HOWIE Howard Glenn B 10.17.1919 Gastonia, NC D 5.7.1989 Baltimore, MD BR/TR 5-11.5/185# d4.14 Mil 1945																								
1942	NY N	7	14	0	0	0	0	0	0	0	0	4	.000	.000	.000	-99	-4	0	1.000	-0	105	0	/O-3(2-1-0)	-0.4
1946	Cin N	7	26	1	5	0	0	0	1	0	1	4	.192	.222	.192	19	-3	0	1.000	0	89	155	/O-6(RF)	-0.3
	Cle A	8	32	2	2	0	0	0	0	3	0	9	.063	.143	.063	-44	-6	0-1	.857	-1	89	0	/3-8	-0.9
Total	2	22	72	3	7	0	0	0	1	3	1	17	.097	.145	.097	-32	-13	0-1	1.000	-1	94	105	/O-9(2-1-6),3-8	-1.6
MOSS, LES John Lester B 5.14.1925 Tulsa, OK BR/TR 5-11/205# d9.10 M2 C13																								
1946	StL A	12	35	4	13	3	0	0	5	3	1	5	.371	.436	.457	142	2	1-0	.968	-0	*66*	*64*	C-12	0.3
1947	StL A	96	274	17	43	5	2	6	27	35	1	48	.157	.255	.255	41	-23	0-0	.983	-7	*73*	*106*	C-96	-2.6
1948	StL A	107	335	35	86	12	1	14	46	39	0	50	.257	.334	.424	98	-2	0-0	.988	-8	*62*	*104*	*C-103	-0.6
1949	StL A	97	278	28	81	11	0	10	39	49	1	32	.291	.399	.439	117	8	0-1	.970	-3	*98*	*103*	C-83	0.8
1950	StL A	84	222	24	59	6	0	8	34	26	0	32	.266	.343	.401	87	-5	0-1	.957	-3	*97*	*119*	C-60	-0.5
1951	StL A	16	47	5	8	2	0	1	7	6	0	8	.170	.264	.277	45	-4	0-0	.967	-1	*101*	*171*	C-12	-0.4
	Bos A	71	202	18	40	6	0	3	26	25	1	34	.198	.289	.272	48	-15	0-0	.984	-1	*119*	*63*	C-69	-1.3
	Year	87	249	23	48	8	0	4	33	31	1	42	.193	.285	.273	47	-18	0-0	**.981**	-2	***116***	*81*	C-81	-1.7
1952	StL A	52	118	11	29	3	0	3	12	15	0	13	.246	.331	.347	86	-2	0-1	.957	-3	*99*	*108*	C-39	-0.4
1953	StL A	78	239	21	66	14	1	2	28	18	1	31	.276	.329	.368	86	-5	0-1	.978	-7	*87*	*86*	C-71	-0.8
1954	Bal A	50	126	7	31	3	0	0	5	14	0	16	.246	.321	.270	68	-5	0-0	.972	-3	*81*	*120*	C-38	-0.7
1955	Bal A	29	56	5	19	1	0	2	6	7-1	0	4	.339	.413	.464	146	4	0-1	1.000	1	*85*	*82*	C-17	0.5
	Chi A	32	59	5	15	2	0	2	7	6-1	1	10	.254	.333	.390	91	-1	0-0	.990	1	*126*	*64*	C-32	0.1
	Year	61	115	10	34	3	0	4	13	13-2	1	14	.296	.372	.426	116	3	0-1	.994	2	*108*	*72*	C-49	0.6
1956	Chi A	56	127	20	31	4	0	10	22	18-0	0	15	.244	.338	.512	120	3	0-0	.994	-3	*130*	*65*	C-49	0.1
1957	Chi A	42	115	10	31	3	0	2	12	20-1	0	18	.270	.375	.348	99	1	0-0	.980	-4	*89*	*43*	C-39	-0.2
1958	Chi A	2	1	0	0	0	0	0	0	1-0	0	0	.000	.500	.000	51	0	0-0	—	0			H	0.0
Total	13	824	2234	210	552	75	4	63	276	282-3	6	316	.247	.333	.369	86	-44	1-5	.978	-41	*90*	*94*	C-720	-5.7
MOSTIL, JOHNNY John Anthony "Bananas" B 6.1.1896 Chicago, IL D 12.10.1970 Midlothian, IL BR/TR 5-8.5/168# d6.20																								
1918	Chi A	10	33	4	9	2	2	0	4	1	0	6	.273	.294	.455	125	1	1	.923	-2	88	123	/2-9	-0.1
1921	Chi A	100	326	43	98	21	7	3	42	28	13	35	.301	.379	.436	109	5	10-12	.946	-3	94	103	O-91(1-90-0)/2	-0.4
1922	Chi A	132	458	74	139	28	14	7	70	38	**14**	39	.303	.375	.472	120	13	14-10	.966	0	107	67	*O-123(18-105-0)	0.6
1923	Chi A	153	546	91	159	37	15	3	64	62	12	51	.291	.376	.430	113	11	41-16	.974	15	**116**	126	*O-143(0-135-8)/3-5,S	2.3
1924	Chi A	118	385	75	125	22	5	4	49	45	4	41	.325	.401	.439	120	13	7-11	.974	7	109	130	*O-102(1-90-12)	1.2
1925	Chi A	153	605	**135**	181	36	16	2	50	**90**	**12**	52	.299	.400	.421	115	17	**43**-20	**.985**	-2	102	64	*O-153(CF)	1.1
1926	Chi A	148	600	120	197	41	15	4	42	79	**10**	55	.328	.415	.467	135	33	**35**-14	.968	**50**	**219**	**194**	*O-147(CF)	7.8
1927	Chi A	13	16	3	2	0	0	0	1	0	1	1	.125	.176	.125	-21	-3	1-0	.857	0	84	427	/O-6(CF)	-0.2
1928	Chi A	133	503	69	136	19	8	0	51	66	4	54	.270	.360	.340	86	-8	23-20	.976	12	**115**	123	*O-131(0-120-11)	-0.4
1929	Chi A	12	35	4	8	3	0	0	3	6	0	2	.229	.341	.314	71	-1	1-1	.963	0	97	99	O-11(0-10-1)	-0.2
Total	10	972	3507	618	1054	209	82	23	376	415	70	336	.301	.386	.427	113	81	176-104	.971	77	118	110	O-907(20-856-32)/2-10,3-5,S	11.7
MOTA, ANDY Andres Alberto (Matos) B 3.4.1966 Santo Domingo, D.R. BR/TR 5-10/180# d8.31 b-Jose f-Manny																								
1991	Hou N	27	90	4	17	2	0	1	6	1-0	0	17	.189	.198	.244	25	-9	2-0	.970	-8	86	78	2-27	-1.8
MOTA, JOSE Jose Manuel (Matos) B 3.16.1965 Santo Domingo, D.R. BB/TR 5-9/155# d5.25 b-Andy f-Manny																								
1991	SD N	17	36	4	8	0	0	0	2	2-0	1	7	.222	.282	.222	42	-3	0-0	.962	-2	91	97	2-13/S-3	-0.4
1995	KC A	2	2	0	0	0	0	0	0	0-0	0	0	.000	.000	.000	-99	-1	0-0	1.000	0	174	0	/2-2	0.0
Total	2	19	38	4	8	0	0	0	2	2-0	1	7	.211	.268	.211	35	-4	0-0	.965	-1	95	92	/2-15,S-3	-0.4
MOTA, MANNY Manuel Rafael (Geronimo) B 2.18.1938 Santo Domingo, D.R. BR/TR 5-11/168# d4.16 C10 s-Andy s-Jose																								
1962	SF N	47	74	9	13	1	0	0	9	7-0	1	8	.176	.253	.189	22	-8	3-2	1.000	2	116	362	O-27(22-2-4)/3-7,2-3	-0.6
1963	Pit N	59	126	20	34	2	3	0	7	7-0	1	18	.270	.313	.333	86	-3	0-2	.953	-3	83	57	O-37(35-2-2)/2	-0.8

Year	Tm Lg	G	AB	R	H	2B	3B	HR	RBI	BB-IB	HP	SO	AVG	OBP	SLG	AOPS	ABR	SB-CS	FA	FR	Rng	Thr	G at Pos	BFW
1964	Pit N	115	271	43	75	8	3	5	32	10-0	3	31	.277	.309	.384	94	-3	4-1	.961	-1	100	99	O-93(57-50-7)/C2	-0.6
1965	Pit N	121	294	47	82	7	6	4	29	22-0	2	32	.279	.330	.384	101	0	2-2	.985	-2	91	123	O-95(35-60-15)	-0.5
1966	Pit N	116	322	54	107	16	7	5	46	25-1	4	28	.332	.383	.472	137	17	7-7	.994	-3	97	56	O-96(45-52-12)/3-4	1.0
1967	Pit N	120	349	53	112	14	8	4	56	14-2	2	46	.321	.343	.441	125	10	3-2	.988	3	96	180	O-99(48-48-13)/3-2	0.9
1968	Pit N	111	331	35	93	10	2	1	33	20-4	1	19	.281	.320	.332	99	-1	4-2	.981	-3	93	86	O-92(50-31-22)/23	-0.8
1969	Mon N	31	89	6	28	1	1	0	0	6-0	0	11	.315	.358	.348	98	0	1-3	.907	-3	94	0	O-22(1-17-5)	-0.5
	LA N	85	294	35	95	6	4	3	30	26-1	1	25	.323	.377	.401	128	11	5-4	.969	1	90	186	O-80(75-4-10)	0.8
	Year	116	383	41	123	7	5	3	30	32-1	1	36	.321	.372	.389	120	10	6-7	.954	-1	91	146	*O-102(76-21-15)	0.3
1970	LA N	124	417	63	127	12	6	3	37	47-4	3	37	.305	.377	.384	110	7	11-6	.973	-0	95	106	*O-111(109-1-4)/3	0.1
1971	LA N	91	269	24	84	13	5	0	34	20-5	1	20	.312	.361	.398	122	8	4-3	.965	-4	88	67	O-80(62-0-24)	-0.1
1972	LA N	118	371	57	120	16	5	5	48	27-6	5	15	.323	.375	.434	133	16	4-4	.993	-7	86	48	O-99(96-3-0)	0.4
1973	LA N★	89	293	33	92	11	2	0	23	25-9	1	12	.314	.368	.365	109	4	1-3	1.000	-7	72	84	O-74(LF)	-0.8
1974	†LA N	66	57	5	16	2	0	0	16	5-4	1	4	.281	.328	.316	91	-1	0-0	1.000	-0	35	0	/O-3(LF)	-0.1
1975	LA N	52	49	3	13	1	0	0	10	5-0	2	1	.265	.357	.286	84	-1	0-0	1.000	1	165	0	/O-5(LF)	0.0
1976	LA N	50	52	1	15	3	0	0	13	7-3	0	5	.288	.367	.346	107	1	0-0	1.000	2	189	485	/O-6(LF)	0.3
1977	†LA N	49	38	5	15	1	0	1	4	10-3	0	0	.395	.521	.500	176	5	1-1	1.000	0	116	0	/O(LF)	0.5
1978	†LA N	37	33	2	10	1	0	0	6	3-1	0	4	.303	.361	.333	95	0	0-0	—	0			H	-0.1
1979	LA N	47	42	1	15	0	0	0	3	3-0	0	4	.357	.400	.357	110	1	0-0	—	-0	0	0	/O(LF)	0.1
1980	LA N	7	7	0	3	0	0	0	2	0-0	0	0	.429	.429	.429	143	0	0-0	—	0			/H	0.0
1982	LA N	1	1	0	0	0	0	0	0	0-0	0	0	.000	.000	.000	-99	0	0-0	—	0			/H	0.0
Total	20	1536	3779	496	1149	125	52	31	438	289-43	28	320	.304	.355	.389	112	63	50-42	.979	-23	92	103	*O-1021(725-270-118)/3-15,2-6,C	-0.8
MOTLEY, DARRYL Darryl De Wayne B 1.21.1960 Muskogee, OK BR/TR 5-9/196# d8.10																								
1981	KC A	42	125	15	29	4	0	2	8	7-0	1	15	.232	.276	.312	70	-5	1-3	.968	3	114	112	O-39(2-0-38)	-0.5
1983	KC A	19	68	9	16	1	2	3	11	2-0	1	8	.235	.264	.441	91	-1	2-1	.978	1	108	148	O-18(3-2-15)/D	-0.1
1984	†KC A	146	522	64	148	25	6	15	70	28-2	1	73	.284	.319	.441	108	4	10-12	.984	2	106	76	*O-138(105-3-45)	-0.3
1985	†KC A	123	383	45	85	20	1	17	49	18-2	2	57	.222	.257	.413	81	-12	6-4	.967	-5	94	59	*O-114(44-0-76)/D-7	-2.2
1986	KC A	72	217	22	44	9	1	7	20	11-1	0	31	.203	.241	.350	57	-14	0-2	.979	-6	79	50	O-66(3-1-62)/D-2	-2.4
	Atl N	5	10	1	2	1	0	0	0	1-1	0	1	.200	.273	.300	55	-1	0-0	1.000	-0	104	0	/O-3(RF)	-0.1
1987	Atl N	6	8	0	0	0	0	0	1	0-0	0	1	.000	.000	.000	-95	-2	0-0	1.000	-0	97	0	/O-2(LF)	-0.2
Total	6	413	1333	156	324	60	10	44	159	67-6	5	186	.243	.280	.402	86	-31	19-22	.976	-6	99	73	O-380(159-6-239)/D-10	-5.8
MOTT, BITSY Elisha Matthew B 6.12.1918 Arcadia, FL D 2.25.2001 Brandon, FL BR/TR 5-8/155# d4.17																								
1945	Phi N	90	289	21	64	8	0	0	22	27	1	25	.221	.290	.249	52	-18	2	.944	12	110	119	S-63,2-27/3-7	-0.1
MOTTOLA, CHAD Charles Edward B 10.15.1971 Augusta, GA BR/TR 6-3/220# d4.23																								
1996	Cin N	35	79	10	17	3	0	3	6	6-1	0	16	.215	.271	.367	66	-4	2-2	1.000	0	98	134	O-31(0-1-30)	-0.5
2000	Tor A	3	9	1	2	0	0	0	2	0-0	1	4	.222	.300	.222	34	-1	0-0	1.000	-0	103	0	/O-3(RF)	-0.1
2001	Fla N	5	7	1	0	0	0	0	1	2-0	0	2	.000	.200	.000	-36	-1	0-0	1.000	1	142	575	/O-5(2-1-4)	0.0
Total	3	43	95	12	19	3	0	3	9	8-1	1	22	.200	.267	.326	55	-6	2-2	1.000	2	103	166	/O-39(2-2-37)	-0.6
MOTTON, CURT Curtell Howard B 9.24.1940 Darnell, LA BR/TR 5-7.5/175# d7.5 C1																								
1967	Bal A	27	65	5	13	2	0	2	9	5-0	2	14	.200	.267	.323	78	-2	0-1	.973	1	125	0	O-18(18-0-1)	-0.3
1968	Bal A	83	217	27	43	7	0	8	25	31-0	1	43	.198	.298	.341	94	-1	1-3	.989	0	101	62	O-54(LF)	-0.5
1969	†Bal A	56	89	15	27	6	0	6	21	13-0	1	10	.303	.398	.573	167	8	3-1	1.000	-2	87	0	O-20(16-0-4)	0.6
1970	Bal A	52	84	16	19	3	1	3	19	18-0	1	20	.226	.369	.393	109	2	1-2	1.000	0	104	90	O-21(20-0-2)	0.1
1971	†Bal A	38	53	13	10	1	0	4	8	10-0	0	12	.189	.317	.434	112	1	0-0	1.000	0	94	138	O-16(12-0-5)	0.0
1972	Mil A	6	6	1	1	0	0	1	2	1-0	0	2	.167	.286	.667	181	1	0-0	—	-0	0	0	/O-3(LF)	0.0
	Cal A	42	39	6	6	1	0	0	1	5-0	0	12	.154	.250	.179	31	-3	0-0	1.000	0	130	0	/O-9(LF)	-0.4
	Year	48	45	7	7	1	0	1	3	6-0	0	14	.156	.255	.244	52	-3	0-0	1.000	0	122	0	O-12(LF)	-0.4
1973	Bal A	5	6	2	2	0	0	1	4	1-0	0	1	.333	.429	.833	250	1	0-0	—	-0	0	0	/O(LF)D	0.1
1974	†Bal A	7	8	0	0	0	0	0	0	2-0	0	2	.000	.200	.000	-40	-1	0-0	1.000	0	162	0	/O-2(RF),D	-0.1
Total	8	316	567	85	121	20	1	25	89	86-0	5	116	.213	.319	.384	105	6	5-7	.991	0	104	52	O-144(133-0-14)/D-2	-0.5
MOTZ, FRANK Frank H. B 10.1.1868 Freeburg, PA D 3.18.1944 Akron, OH 6/160# d8.27																								
1890	Phi N	1	2	1	0	0	0	0	0	1	0	1	.000	.333	.000	-1	0	1	1.000	0	315	411	/1	0.0
1893	Cin N	43	156	16	40	7	1	2	25	19	4	10	.256	.352	.353	85	-3	3	.981	6	162	102	1-43	0.2
1894	Cin N	18	69	8	14	4	0	0	12	9	1	1	.203	.304	.261	36	-7	2	.995	4	174	80	1-18	-0.3
Total	3	62	227	25	54	11	1	2	37	29	5	12	.238	.337	.322	68	-10	6	.985	10	168	100	/1-62	-0.1
MOULTON, ALLIE Albert Theodore B 1.16.1886 Medway, MA D 7.10.1968 Peabody, MA BR/TR 5-6/155# d9.25																								
1911	StL A	4	15	4	1	0	0	0	1	4	0		.067	.263	.067	-6	-2	0	.938	-0	133	0	/2-4	-0.2
MOUNTAIN, FRANK Frank Henry B 5.17.1860 Ft.Edward, NY D 11.19.1939 Schenectady, NY BR/TR 5-11/185# d7.19 ▲																								
1880	Tro N	2	9	1	2	0	0	0	0	0		4	.222	.222	.222	49	0		1.000	0	118	0	/P-2	0.0
1881	Det N	7	25	0	4	1	1	0	4	2		8	.160	.222	.280	55	0		.923	-1	52	0	/P-7	0.0
1882	Wor N	5	16	1	1	0	0	0	1	0		5	.063	.063	.063	-58	-2		.889	-1	75	0	/P-5	0.0
	Phi AA	9	36	5	12	3	0	0		2			.333	.368	.417	154	2		.917	1	136	0	/P-8,O(RF)	0.1
	Wor N	20	70	8	19	2	2	2	5	3		18	.271	.301	.443	132	2		.870	-2	75	0	P-13/O-6(1-5-0),1-2,S	-0.1
1883	Col AA	70	276	36	60	14	5	3		9			.217	.242	.337	92	-1		.848	1	101	99	P-59,O-12(8-4-0)	0.0
1884	Col AA	58	210	26	50	7	3	4		9	4		.238	.283	.357	117	5		.919	3	121	0	P-42,O-17(9-7-1)	0.2
1885	Pit AA	5	20	1	2	0	1	0	1	1	0		.100	.143	.200	8	-1		.846	0	131	0	/P-5	0.0
1886	Pit AA	18	55	6	8	1	1	0	2	13	1		.145	.319	.200	64	-1	3	.959	-0	100	87	1-16/P-2	-0.3
Total	7	194	717	84	158	28	13	9	13	39	5	35	.220	.265	.333	96	4	3	.880	2	106	52	P-143/O-36(18-16-2),1-18,S	-0.1
MOUTON, JAMES James Raleigh B 12.29.1968 Denver, CO BR/TR 5-9/175# d4.4																								
1994	Hou N	99	310	43	76	11	0	2	16	27-0	5	69	.245	.315	.300	65	-16	24-5	.982	0	102	92	O-96(1-19-80)	-1.5
1995	Hou N	104	298	42	78	18	2	4	27	25-1	4	59	.262	.326	.376	91	-4	25-8	1.000	-1	95	88	O-94(38-22-38)	-0.5
1996	Hou N	122	300	40	79	15	1	3	34	38-2	0	55	.263	.343	.350	91	-3	21-9	.971	3	103	157	*O-108(79-29-5)	-0.1
1997	Hou N	86	180	24	38	9	1	3	23	18-0	2	30	.211	.287	.322	62	-10	9-7	1.000	-3	91	40	O-61(9-39-14)	-1.4
1998	SD N	55	63	8	12	2	1	0	7	7-1	0	11	.190	.268	.254	42	-5	4-3	.969	-0	96	97	O-33(16-4-14)/D	-0.6
1999	Mon N	95	122	18	32	5	1	2	13	18-1	2	31	.262	.364	.369	89	-2	6-2	.981	-0	92	127	O-56(32-16-11)/D	-0.2
2000	Mil N	87	159	28	37	7	1	2	17	30-0	3	43	.233	.363	.327	78	-4	13-4	.989	1	99	127	O-45(19-23-7)	-0.3
2001	Mil N	75	138	20	34	8	0	2	10	11-0	6	40	.246	.329	.348	77	-4	7-3	.965	2	111	102	O-53(21-28-7)	-0.3
Total	8	723	1570	223	386	75	7	18	147	174-5	22	338	.246	.328	.337	78	-48	109-41	.983	1	99	106	O-546(215-180-176)/D-2	-4.9
MOUTON, LYLE Lyle Joseph B 5.13.1969 Lafayette, LA BR/TR 6-4/240# d6.7																								
1995	Chi A	58	179	23	54	16	0	5	27	19-0	2	46	.302	.373	.475	125	7	1-0	.990	3	105	166	O-53(29-0-30)/D-2	0.8
1996	Chi A	87	214	25	63	8	1	7	39	22-4	2	50	.294	.361	.439	107	2	3-0	.970	-2	95	43	O-47(21-0-29),D-28	-0.2
1997	Chi A	88	242	26	65	9	0	5	23	14-1	1	66	.269	.308	.368	80	-8	4-4	.969	1	113	28	O-67(16-0-55),D-11	-1.0
1998	Bal A	18	39	5	12	2	0	2	7	4-0	0	8	.308	.372	.513	129	2	0-0	1.000	-0	89	135	O-16(6-0-12)/D-2	0.1
1999	Mil N	14	17	2	3	1	0	1	3	2-0	0	3	.176	.263	.412	68	-1	0-0	1.000	-1	26	0	/O-3(2-0-1)	-0.2
2000	Mil N	42	97	14	27	7	1	2	16	10-0	1	29	.278	.349	.433	99	0	1-0	.978	3	98	301	O-27(22-1-4)	0.2
2001	Fla N	21	17	1	1	0	0	0	1	0-0	0	7	.059	.059	.059	-72	-4	0-0	1.000	-1	54	0	O-11(6-0-5)	-0.5
Total	7	328	805	96	225	43	2	22	116	71-5	6	209	.280	.339	.420	99	-2	9-4	.978	3	102	107	O-224(102-1-136)/D-43	-0.8
MOWE, RAY Raymond Benjamin B 7.12.1889 Rochester, IN D 8.14.1968 Sarasota, FL BL/TR 5-7.5/160# d9.25																								
1913	Bro N	5	9	0	1	0	0	0	0	0	1	1	.111	.200	.111	-10	-1	0	.941	0	102	98	/S-2	-0.1
MOWREY, MIKE Harry Harlan B 4.20.1884 Browns Mill, PA D 3.20.1947 Chambersburg, PA BR/TR 5-10/180# d9.24																								
1905	Cin N	7	30	4	8	1	0	0	6	1	0		.267	.290	.300	69	-1	0	.759	-1	116	110	/3-7	-0.2
1906	Cin N	21	53	3	17	3	0	0	6	5	0		.321	.379	.377	130	2	2	.930	2	114	58	3-15/2S	0.4
1907	Cin N	138	448	43	113	16	6	1	44	35	1		.252	.308	.321	93	-4	10	.929	-16	84	87	*3-127,S-11	-1.8
1908	Cin N	77	227	17	50	9	1	0	23	12	2		.220	.266	.269	73	-7	5	.936	-5	102	90	3-56/S-3,O-3(LF),2	-1.3
1909	Cin N	38	115	10	22	5	0	0	5	20	0		.191	.311	.235	70	-3	2	.947	0	111	137	3-22,S-13	-0.2
	StL N	12	29	3	7	1	0	0	4	4	0		.241	.333	.276	95	0	1	.921	-1	85	0	/2-7,3-2	-0.1
	Year	50	144	13	29	6	0	0	9	24	0		.201	.315	.243	75	-3	3	.948	-1	112	135	3-24,S-13/2-7	-0.3

Year	Tm Lg	G	AB	R	H	2B	3B	HR	RBI	BB-IB	HP	SO	AVG	OBP	SLG	AOPS	ABR	SB-CS	FA	FR	Rng	Thr	G at Pos	BFW
1910	StL N	143	489	69	138	24	6	2	70	67	6	38	.282	.375	.368	121	16	21	.927	14	114	**139**	*3-141	3.6
1911	StL N	137	471	59	126	29	7	0	61	59	5	46	.268	.355	.359	103	4	15	.944	7	107	96	*3-134/S	1.5
1912	StL N	114	408	59	104	13	8	2	50	46	3	29	.255	.335	.341	87	-7	19	.931	2	105	**139**	*3-108	-0.2
1913	StL N	132	450	61	117	18	4	0	33	53	3	40	.260	.342	.318	90	-4	21-15	.953	18	**121**	**129**	*3-131	1.7
1914	Pit N	79	284	24	72	7	5	1	25	22	4	20	.254	.316	.324	94	-2	8	.960	-1	103	82	3-78	-0.1
1915	Pit F	151	521	56	146	26	6	1	49	66	5	39	.280	.367	.359	105	-1	40	**.959**	-17	90	72	*3-151	-1.5
1916	†Bro N	144	495	57	121	22	6	0	60	50	5	60	.244	.320	.313	92	-3	16	**.965**	-2	99	87	*3-144	0.0
1917	Bro N	83	271	20	58	9	5	0	25	29	1	25	.214	.292	.284	75	-7	7	.952	-1	103	102	3-80/2-2	-0.7
Total	13	1276	4291	485	1099	183	54	7	461	469	35	297	.256	.334	.329	96	-17	167-15	.944	-0	103	103	*3-1196/S-29,2-11,O-3(LF)	1.1

MOWRY, JOE Joseph Aloysius B 4.6.1908 St.Louis, MO D 2.9.1994 St.Louis, MO BB/TR 6/198# d5.13

Year	Tm Lg	G	AB	R	H	2B	3B	HR	RBI	BB-IB	HP	SO	AVG	OBP	SLG	AOPS	ABR	SB-CS	FA	FR	Rng	Thr	G at Pos	BFW
1933	Bos N	86	249	25	55	8	5	0	20	15	3	22	.221	.273	.293	67	-11	1	.994	1	108	37	O-64(48-5-11)	-1.5
1934	Bos N	25	79	9	17	3	0	1	4	3	0	13	.215	.244	.291	46	-6	0	.976	1	112	66	O-20(4-0-16)/2	-0.6
1935	Bos N	81	136	17	36	8	1	1	13	11	1	13	.265	.324	.360	91	-2	0	.970	1	107	137	O-45(30-2-13)	-0.2
Total	3	192	464	51	108	19	6	2	37	29	4	48	.233	.284	.313	71	-19	1	.985	3	108	66	O-129(82-7-40)/2	-2.3

MOYNAHAN, MIKE Michael B 1856 Chicago, IL D 4.9.1899 Chicago, IL BL/TR d8.20

Year	Tm Lg	G	AB	R	H	2B	3B	HR	RBI	BB-IB	HP	SO	AVG	OBP	SLG	AOPS	ABR	SB-CS	FA	FR	Rng	Thr	G at Pos	BFW
1880	Buf N	27	100	12	33	5	1	0	14	6		9	.330	.368	.400	157	6		.862	-3	91	99	S-27	0.4
1881	Cle N	33	135	12	31	5	1	0	8	3		14	.230	.246	.281	69	-5		.883	-2	35	166	O-32(LF)/3	-0.9
	Det N	1	4	1	1	0	0	0	0	0		1	.250	.250	.250	55	0		.857	0	111	0	/3	0.0
	Year	34	139	13	32	5	1	0	8	3		15	.230	.246	.281	69	-5		.883	-2	35	166	O-32(LF)/3-2	-0.9
1883	Phi AA	95	400	90	124	18	10	1	67	31			.310	.360	.412	135	15		.833	-0	101	69	*S-95	1.5
1884	Phi AA	1	4	0	0	0	0	0		0	0		.000	.000	.000	-94	-1		.500	-1	0	0	/O(CF)	-0.1
	Cle N	12	45	9	13	2	1	0	6	7		11	.289	.385	.378	136	2		.852	-1	107	0	/2-6,S-3,O-3(1-0-2)	0.2
Total	4	169	688	124	202	30	13	1	95	47		35	.294	.339	.379	125	17		.837	-7	100	77	S-125/O-36(33-1-2),2-6,3-2	1.1

MUELLER, HEINIE Clarence Francis B 9.16.1899 Creve Coeur, MO D 1.23.1975 DeSoto, MO BL/TL 5-8/158# d9.25

Year	Tm Lg	G	AB	R	H	2B	3B	HR	RBI	BB-IB	HP	SO	AVG	OBP	SLG	AOPS	ABR	SB-CS	FA	FR	Rng	Thr	G at Pos	BFW
1920	StL N	4	22	0	7	1	0	0	1	2	0	4	.318	.375	.364	117	1	1-0	1.000	-0	110	0	/O-4(1-0-4)	0.0
1921	StL N	55	176	25	62	10	6	1	34	11	2	22	.352	.397	.494	137	9	2-4	.976	-1	102	76	O-54(0-51-3)	0.5
1922	StL N	61	159	20	43	7	2	3	26	14	0	18	.270	.329	.396	91	-3	2-1	.947	1	96	143	O-44(10-34-0)	-0.3
1923	StL N	78	265	39	91	16	9	5	41	18	3	16	.343	.392	.528	144	16	4-3	.963	3	108	100	O-74(0-71-3)	1.5
1924	StL N	92	296	39	78	12	6	2	37	19	2	16	.264	.312	.365	82	-8	8-7	.962	-0	106	81	O-53(2-42-9),1-27	-1.3
1925	StL N	78	243	33	76	16	4	1	26	17	3	11	.313	.365	.424	99	0	0-3	.955	0	103	95	O-72(2-57-13)	-0.4
1926	StL N	52	191	36	51	7	5	3	28	11	7	6	.267	.330	.403	93	-2	8	.950	0	96	123	O-51(0-21-30)	-0.5
	NY N	85	305	36	76	6	2	4	29	21	1	17	.249	.300	.321	68	-14	7	.950	1	97	135	O-82(10-38-35)	-1.9
	Year	137	496	72	127	13	7	7	57	32	8	23	.256	.312	.353	78	-17	15	.950	1	97	**131**	*O-133(10-59-65)	-2.4
1927	NY N	84	190	33	55	6	1	3	19	25	4	12	.289	.384	.379	105	3	2	.944	-4	100	22	O-56(49-5-2)/1	-0.4
1928	Bos N	42	151	25	34	3	1	0	19	17	3	9	.225	.316	.258	54	-10	1	.985	3	107	152	O-41(4-37-0)	-0.8
1929	Bos N	46	93	10	19	2	1	0	11	12	1	12	.204	.302	.247	39	-9	2	1.000	-0	100	56	O-24(4-11-10)	-1.0
1935	StL A	16	27	0	5	1	0	0	1	1	0	4	.185	.214	.222	12	-4	0-0	.955	0	204	127	/1-3,O-2(1-1-0)	-0.4
Total	11	693	2118	296	597	87	37	22	272	168	26	147	.282	.342	.389	94	-21	37-18	.960	3	102	101	O-557(83-368-109)/1-31	-5.0

MUELLER, DON Donald Frederick "Mandrake The Magician" B 4.14.1927 St.Louis, MO BL/TR 6/185# d8.2 f-Walter

Year	Tm Lg	G	AB	R	H	2B	3B	HR	RBI	BB-IB	HP	SO	AVG	OBP	SLG	AOPS	ABR	SB-CS	FA	FR	Rng	Thr	G at Pos	BFW
1948	NY N	36	81	12	29	4	1	1	9	0	0	3	.358	.358	.469	121	2	0	.973	1	92	229	O-22(18-1-1)	0.2
1949	NY N	51	56	5	13	4	0	0	1	5	0	6	.232	.295	.304	61	-3	0	1.000	-0	108	0	/O-6(2-0-4)	-0.3
1950	NY N	132	525	60	153	15	6	7	84	10	3	26	.291	.309	.383	80	-18	1	.986	-2	99	82	*O-125(3-0-122)	-2.3
1951	NY N	122	469	58	130	10	7	16	69	19	1	13	.277	.307	.431	95	-6	1-1	.983	-2	107	48	*O-115(RF)	-1.2
1952	NY N	122	456	61	128	14	7	12	49	34	2	24	.281	.333	.421	107	3	2-1	.987	-3	99	73	*O-120(RF)	-0.4
1953	NY N	131	480	56	160	12	2	6	60	19	1	13	.333	.360	.404	97	-3	2-0	.972	-4	94	82	*O-122(11-0-111)	-1.0
1954	†NY N★	153	619	90	**212**	35	8	4	71	22	2	17	.342	.363	.444	110	8	2-3	.979	-5	90	102	*O-153(RF)	-0.3
1955	NY N★	147	605	67	185	21	4	8	83	19-4	3	12	.306	.326	.393	91	-9	1-2	.976	-14	86	41	*O-146(RF)	-2.9
1956	NY N	138	453	38	122	12	1	5	41	15-2	0	7	.269	.290	.333	68	-21	0-1	.989	-9	89	41	*O-117(RF)	-3.6
1957	NY N	135	450	45	116	7	1	6	37	13-3	1	16	.258	.280	.318	60	-26	2-0	.989	1	89	**167**	*O-115(RF)	-3.0
1958	Chi A	70	166	7	42	5	0	0	16	11-3	0	9	.253	.298	.283	62	-9	0-0	.968	-2	86	101	O-43(RF)	-1.2
1959	Chi A	4	4	0	2	0	0	0	0	0-0	0	0	.500	.500	.500	178	0	0-0	—	0			H	0.0
Total	12	1245	4364	499	1292	139	37	65	520	167-12	13	146	.296	.322	.390	89	-82	11-8	.982	-38	94	81	*O-1084(34-1-1047)	-16.0

MUELLER, HEINIE Emmett Jerome B 7.20.1912 St.Louis, MO D 10.3.1986 Orlando, FL BB/TR 5-6/167# d4.19 Mil 1942-45

Year	Tm Lg	G	AB	R	H	2B	3B	HR	RBI	BB-IB	HP	SO	AVG	OBP	SLG	AOPS	ABR	SB-CS	FA	FR	Rng	Thr	G at Pos	BFW
1938	Phi N	136	444	53	111	12	4	4	34	64	1	43	.250	.346	.322	87	-6	2	.967	-21	87	64	*2-111,3-21	-2.0
1939	Phi N	115	341	46	95	19	4	9	43	33	0	34	.279	.342	.437	111	5	4	.964	-6	87	101	2-51,3-17,O-17(4-0-13)/S	0.1
1940	Phi N	97	263	24	65	13	2	3	28	37	2	23	.247	.344	.346	95	-1	2	.966	-5	87	68	2-34,O-31(29-0-2),3-13/1-2	-0.5
1941	Phi N	93	233	21	53	11	1	1	22	22	3	24	.227	.302	.296	72	-9	2	.980	2	94	106	2-29,O-21(0-1-20),3-19	-0.5
Total	4	441	1281	144	324	55	11	17	127	156	6	124	.253	.337	.353	93	-11	10	.968	-30	88	79	2-225/3-70,O-69(33-1-35),1-2,S	-2.9

MUELLER, RAY Ray Coleman "Iron Man" B 3.8.1912 Pittsburg, KS D 6.29.1994 Lower Paxton Township, PA BR/TR 5-9/175# d5.11 Mil 1945 C2

Year	Tm Lg	G	AB	R	H	2B	3B	HR	RBI	BB-IB	HP	SO	AVG	OBP	SLG	AOPS	ABR	SB-CS	FA	FR	Rng	Thr	G at Pos	BFW
1935	Bos N	42	97	10	22	5	0	3	11	3	0	11	.227	.250	.371	70	-5	0	.978	-1	87	174	C-40	-0.4
1936	Bos N	24	71	5	14	4	0	0	5	5	0	17	.197	.250	.254	38	-6	0	.986	-2	158	55	C-23	-0.6
1937	Bos N	64	187	21	47	9	2	2	26	18	0	36	.251	.317	.353	90	-3	1	.995	6	198	93	C-57	0.6
1938	Bos N	83	274	23	65	8	6	4	35	16	1	28	.237	.282	.354	82	-9	3	.993	2	165	105	C-75	-0.2
1939	Pit N	86	180	14	42	8	1	2	18	14	0	22	.233	.289	.322	65	-9	0	.971	-1	114	96	C-81	-0.7
1940	Pit N	4	3	1	1	0	0	0	1	2	0	0	.333	.600	.333	165	1	0	1.000	0	59	211	/C-4	0.1
1943	Cin N	141	427	50	111	19	4	8	52	56	1	42	.260	.347	.379	111	7	1	.988	20	118	**129**	*C-140	3.8
1944	Cin N★	**155**	555	54	159	24	4	10	73	53	4	47	.286	.353	.398	115	11	4	.983	1	**154**	55	*C-155	2.3
1946	Cin N	114	378	35	96	18	4	8	48	27	3	37	.254	.309	.386	100	-2	0	**.994**	10	124	**116**	*C-100	1.4
1947	Cin N	71	192	17	48	11	0	6	33	16	1	25	.250	.311	.401	88	-4	1	.984	0	101	124	C-55	-0.1
1948	Cin N	14	34	2	7	1	0	0	2	4	0	3	.206	.289	.235	45	-3	0	.982	-0	73	82	C-10	-0.2
1949	Cin N	32	106	7	29	4	0	1	13	5	2	13	.274	.319	.340	76	-4	1	1.000	-1	121	107	C-31	-0.3
	NY N	56	170	17	38	2	2	5	23	13	0	14	.224	.279	.347	67	-9	1	.982	1	92	85	C-56	-0.6
	Year	88	276	24	67	6	2	6	36	18	2	27	.243	.294	.344	70	-13	2	.988	-1	103	93	C-87	-0.9
1950	NY N	4	11	0	1	1	0	0	0	0	0	2	.091	.091	.182	-30	-2	0	1.000	1	113	0	/C-4	-0.1
	Pit N	67	156	17	42	7	0	6	24	11	1	14	.269	.321	.429	92	-2	2	.996	2	125	110	C-63	0.2
	Year	71	167	17	43	8	0	6	24	11	1	16	.257	.307	.413	85	-4	2	.996	3	124	102	C-67	0.1
1951	Bos N	28	70	8	11	2	0	1	9	7	0	11	.157	.234	.229	27	-7	0-0	1.000	2	78	163	C-23	-0.5
Total	14	985	2911	281	733	123	23	56	373	250	13	322	.252	.314	.368	91	-46	14-0	.988	40	131	101	C-917	4.7

MUELLER, WALTER Walter John B 12.6.1894 Central, MO D 8.16.1971 St.Louis, MO BR/TR 5-8/160# d5.7 s-Don

Year	Tm Lg	G	AB	R	H	2B	3B	HR	RBI	BB-IB	HP	SO	AVG	OBP	SLG	AOPS	ABR	SB-CS	FA	FR	Rng	Thr	G at Pos	BFW
1922	Pit N	32	122	21	33	5	1	2	18	5	1	7	.270	.305	.377	74	-5	1-0	.976	4	108	179	O-31(RF)	-0.3
1923	Pit N	40	111	11	34	4	4	0	20	4	1	6	.306	.336	.414	95	-1	2-2	.941	0	113	76	O-26(19-0-7)	-0.3
1924	Pit N	30	50	6	13	1	1	0	8	4	1	4	.260	.327	.320	73	-2	1-0	1.000	2	96	409	O-15(8-5-2)	0.0
1926	Pit N	19	62	8	15	0	1	0	3	0	0	2	.242	.242	.274	37	-6	0	.969	1	102	145	O-15(14-0-1)	-0.6
Total	4	121	345	46	95	10	7	2	49	13	3	19	.275	.307	.362	74	-14	4-2	.966	8	107	165	/O-87(41-5-41)	-1.2

MUELLER, BILL William Lawrence "Hawk" B 11.9.1920 Bay City, MI D 10.24.2001 Glenview, IL BR/TR 6-1.5/180# d8.29 Mil 1943-45

Year	Tm Lg	G	AB	R	H	2B	3B	HR	RBI	BB-IB	HP	SO	AVG	OBP	SLG	AOPS	ABR	SB-CS	FA	FR	Rng	Thr	G at Pos	BFW
1942	Chi A	26	85	5	14	1	0	0	5	12	1	9	.165	.276	.176	29	-8	2-1	.978	6	114	351	O-26(0-23-3)	-0.2
1945	Chi A	13	9	3	0	0	0	0	0	2	0	1	.000	.182	.000	-47	-2	1-0	.778	-0	124	0	/O-7(0-5-2)	-0.2
Total	2	39	94	8	14	1	0	0	5	14	1	10	.149	.266	.160	22	-10	3-1	.960	6	115	323	/O-33(0-28-5)	-0.4

MUELLER, BILL William Richard B 3.17.1971 Maryland Heights, MO BB/TR 5-11/175# d4.18

Year	Tm Lg	G	AB	R	H	2B	3B	HR	RBI	BB-IB	HP	SO	AVG	OBP	SLG	AOPS	ABR	SB-CS	FA	FR	Rng	Thr	G at Pos	BFW
1996	SF N	55	200	31	66	15	1	0	19	24-0	1	26	.330	.401	.415	121	8	0-0	.966	-2	95	141	3-45/2-8	0.7
1997	†SF N	128	390	51	114	26	3	7	44	48-1	3	71	.292	.369	.428	113	9	4-3	.956	4	103	97	*3-122	1.4
1998	SF N	145	534	93	157	27	0	9	59	79-1	1	83	.294	.383	.395	113	13	3-3	.952	2	106	141	*3-137,2-10	1.6
1999	SF N	116	414	61	120	24	0	2	36	65-1	3	52	.290	.388	.362	99	3	4-2	.958	-4	95	96	*3-108/2-3	0.0
2000	†SF N	153	560	97	150	29	4	10	55	52-0	6	62	.268	.333	.387	89	-10	4-2	**.974**	-3	95	99	*3-145/2-2	-1.1
2001	Chi N	70	210	38	62	12	1	6	23	37-3	3	19	.295	.403	.448	128	11	1-1	.942	0	96	64	3-64/2	1.1
2002	Chi N	103	353	51	94	19	4	7	37	51-2	0	41	.266	.355	.402	106	2	0-0	.973	1	92	103	*3-101	0.4
	SF N	8	13	0	2	0	0	0	1	1-0	0	1	.154	.214	.154	1	-2	0-0	1.000	-0	76	0	/3-3	-0.2

Year	Tm Lg	G	AB	R	H	2B	3B	HR	RBI	BB-IB	HP	SO	AVG	OBP	SLG	AOPS	ABR	SB-CS	FA	FR	Rng	Thr	G at Pos	BFW
	Year	111	366	51	96	19	4	7	38	52-2	0	42	.262	.350	.393	102	0	0-0	.974	0	92	101	*3-104	0.2
2003	†Bos A	146	524	85	171	45	5	19	85	59-2	7	77	**.326**	.398	.540	142	34	1-4	.951	1	105	101	*3-135,2-10/SD	3.4
Total	8	924	3198	507	936	197	18	60	359	416-10	24	432	.293	.375	.422	112	68	17-15	.959	-1	99	105	3-860/2-34,D-3,S	7.3
MULDOON, MIKE Michael D. B 4.9.1858 Westmeath County, Ireland 5-8/165# d5.1																								
1882	Cle N	**84**	341	50	84	17	5	6	45	10		28	.246	.268	.378	108	3		.880	3	103	158	*3-61,O-23(21-2-0)	0.6
1883	Cle N	98	378	54	86	22	3	0	29	10		39	.228	.247	.302	67	-14		.825	-9	88	77	*3-98/O-2(RF)	-1.9
1884	Cle N	110	422	46	101	16	6	2	38	18		67	.239	.270	.320	82	-9		.833	-7	98	106	*3-109/O(RF)2	-1.3
1885	Bal AA	102	410	47	103	20	6	2	52	20	4		.251	.293	.344	102	1		.870	-2	98	106	*3-101/2	0.1
1886	Bal AA	101	381	57	76	13	8	0	23	34	2		.199	.269	.276	72	-12	12	.912	3	101	68	2-57,3-44	-0.5
Total	5	495	1932	254	450	88	28	10	187	92	6	134	.233	.270	.323	86	-31	12	.846	-12	97	103	3-413/2-59,O-26(21-2-3)	-3.0
MULLANE, TONY Anthony John "Count" or "The Apollo Of The Box" B1.20.1859 Cork, Ireland D4.25.1944 Chicago, IL BB/TR (BL 1882, TB 1882 part, 1893 part) 5-10.5/165# d8.27 ▲ OF Total (57-LF 59-CF 39-RF)																								
1881	Det N	5	19	0	5	0	0	0	1	0		0	.263	.263	.263	63	0		.882	0	83	0	/P-5	0.0
1882	Lou AA	77	303	46	78	13	1	0		13			.257	.288	.307	107	3		.959	10	117	**299**	*P-55,1-13,O-12(1-12-1)/2-2	0.5
1883	StL AA	83	307	38	69	11	6	0	33	13			.225	.256	.300	74	-9		.851	2	103	204	P-53,O-30(13-10-7)/2-3,1-2	-0.2
1884	Tol AA	95	352	49	97	19	3	3		33	1		.276	.339	.372	127	12		.889	5	126	296	P-67,O-19(14-0-4)/1-7,3-6,S2	0.4
1886	Cin AA	91	324	59	73	12	5	0	39	25	1		.225	.283	.293	78	-9	20	.899	-1	102	235	P-63,O-27(2-23-2)/1-4,3-2,S2	-0.5
1887	Cin AA	56	199	35	44	6	3	3	23	16	4		.221	.292	.327	71	-8	20	.944	-1	85	**282**	P-48/O-9(7-2-0)	-0.1
1888	Cin AA	51	175	27	44	4	4	1	16	8	3		.251	.296	.337	97	-1	12	.888	-1	97	48	P-44/1-4,O-3(RF),2-2	-0.1
1889	Cin AA	63	196	53	58	16	4	0	29	27	2	21	.296	.387	.418	125	7	24	.920	-3	83	0	P-33,3-18,O-12(4-5-3)/1-4	0.1
1890	Cin N	81	286	41	79	9	8	0	34	39	6	30	.276	.375	.364	116	7	19	.941	-7	78	0	O-28(8-2-18),P-25,3-21,S-10/1	-0.2
1891	Cin N	64	209	16	31	1	2	0	10	18	4	33	.148	.229	.172	17	-22	4	.958	0	106	66	P-51,O-12(6-5-1)/3-4	-0.3
1892	Cin N	39	118	14	20	3	1	0	9	9	3	8	.169	.246	.212	39	-9	4	.926	5	132	183	P-37/1-2	0.2
1893	Cin N	16	52	11	15	0	0	1	6	5	3	3	.288	.383	.346	92	0	1	.939	0	107	113	P-15/3	0.0
	Bal N	38	114	15	26	2	1	0	14	5	0	14	.228	.261	.263	39	-11	5	.943	2	110	107	P-34/O-2(LF),1	0.0
	Year	54	166	26	41	2	1	1	20	10	3	17	.247	.302	.289	56	-11	6	.942	2	109	109	P-49/O-2(LF),31	0.0
1894	Bal N	21	53	3	21	3	0	0	9	6	2	3	.396	.475	.453	119	5	2	.889	-1	73	128	P-21	0.0
	Cle N	4	13	0	1	0	0	0	0	4	0	2	.077	.294	.077	-6	-1	1	.944	2	225	485	/P-4	0.0
	Year	25	66	3	22	3	0	0	9	10	2	5	.333	.436	.379	94	4	3	.911	1	105	204	P-25	0.0
Total	13	784	2720	407	661	99	38	8	223	221	29	114	.243	.307	.316	87	-36	112	.918	13	106	180	P-555,O-154C/3-52,1-38,S-12,2-9	-0.2
MULLEAVY, GREG Gregory Thomas "Moe" B 9.25.1905 Detroit, MI D 2.1.1980 Arcadia, CA BR/TR 5-9/167# d7.4 C7																								
1930	Chi A	77	289	27	76	14	5	0	28	20	0	23	.263	.311	.346	69	-14	5-2	.918	-8	99	91	S-73	-1.2
1932	Chi A	1	3	0	0	0	0	0	0	0	0	0	.000	.000	.000	-99	-1	0-0	1.000	0	87	207	/2	-0.1
1933	Bos A	1	0	1	0	0	0	0	0	0	0	0	—	—	—	—	0	0-0	—	0			R	0.0
Total	3	79	292	28	76	14	5	0	28	20	0	23	.260	.308	.342	67	-15	5-2	.918	-8	99	91	/S-73,2	-1.3
MULLEN d8.17																								
1872	Cle NA	1	4	1	0	0	0	0	0	0		0	.000	.000	.000	-99	-1	0-0	.400	-1	0	0	/O(RF)	-0.1
MULLEN, CHARLIE Charles George B 3.15.1889 Seattle, WA D 6.6.1963 Seattle, WA BR/TR 5-10.5/155# d5.18																								
1910	Chi A	41	123	15	24	2	1	0	13	4	0		.195	.220	.228	42	-9	4	.982	1	115	145	1-37/O-2(RF)	-0.9
1911	Chi A	20	59	7	12	2	1	0	5	5	0		.203	.266	.271	51	-4	1	.969	0	107	27	1-20	-0.4
1914	NY A	93	323	33	84	8	0	0	44	33	2	55	.260	.332	.285	86	-4	11-17	.994	3	106	130	1-93	-0.9
1915	NY A	40	90	11	24	1	0	0	7	10	0	12	.267	.340	.278	85	-1	5-2	.982	1	120	0	1-27	-0.1
1916	NY A	59	146	11	39	9	1	0	18	9	0	13	.267	.310	.342	94	-1	7	.943	-5	73	72	2-20,1-17/O-6(1-2-3)	-0.7
Total	5	253	741	77	183	22	3	0	87	61	2	80	.247	.306	.285	78	-19	28-19	.988	-0	109	100	1-194/2-20,O-8(1-2-5)	-3.0
MULLEN, MOON Ford Parker B 2.9.1917 Olympia, WA BL/TR 5-9/165# d4.18 Mil 1945																								
1944	Phi N	118	464	51	124	9	4	0	31	28	4	32	.267	.315	.304	77	-15	4	.963	-6	98	81	*2-114/3	-1.5
MULLEN, JOHN John B Philadelphia, PA BL/TL d9.9																								
1876	Phi N	1	3	0	0	0	0	0	0	0		0	.000	.000	.000	-99	-1		.714	-0			/C	-0.1
MULLEN, BILLY William John B 1.23.1896 St.Louis, MO D 5.4.1971 St.Louis, MO BR/TR 5-8/160# d10.2																								
1920	StL A	2	4	0	0	0	0	0	0	0	0	0	.000	.000	.000	-97	-1	0-0	1.000	-0	71	0	/2	-0.2
1921	StL A	4	4	0	0	0	0	0	0	2	0	1	.000	.333	.000	-8	-1	0-0	1.000	0	90	0	/3-2	0.0
1923	Bro N	4	11	1	3	0	0	0	0	0	0	0	.273	.273	.273	46	-1	0-0	.875	-0	115	0	/3-4	-0.1
1926	Det A	11	13	2	1	0	0	0	0	5	0	1	.077	.333	.077	11	-1	1-0	.875	-1	87	0	/3-9	-0.2
1928	StL A	15	18	2	7	1	0	0	2	3	0	4	.389	.476	.444	139	1	0-0	.867	0	111	141	/3-6	0.1
Total	5	36	50	5	11	1	0	0	2	10	0	6	.220	.350	.240	56	-3	1-0	.884	-1	102	47	/3-21,2	-0.4
MULLER, FREDDIE Frederick William B 12.21.1907 Newark, CA D 10.20.1976 Davis, CA BR/TR 5-10/170# d7.8																								
1933	Bos A	15	48	6	9	1	1	0	3	5	0	5	.188	.264	.250	37	-5	1-0	.923	-3	94	82	2-14	-0.6
1934	Bos A	2	1	1	0	0	0	0	0	1	0	0	.000	.500	.000	36	0	0-0	.800	-1	47	0	/23	-0.1
Total	2	17	49	7	9	1	1	0	3	6	0	5	.184	.273	.245	38	-5	1-0	.914	-3	91	77	/2-15,3	-0.7
MULLIGAN, EDDIE Edward Joseph B 8.27.1894 St.Louis, MO D 3.15.1982 San Rafael, CA BR/TR 5-9/152# d9.23																								
1915	Chi N	11	22	5	8	1	0	0	2	5	0	1	.364	.481	.409	170	2	2-2	.907	0	91	233	S-10/3	0.3
1916	Chi N	58	189	13	29	3	4	0	9	8	3	30	.153	.200	.212	24	-17	1	.888	-3	103	109	S-58	-1.9
1921	Chi A	151	609	82	153	21	12	1	45	32	4	53	.251	.293	.330	59	-40	13-18	.955	-12	94	95	*3-151/S	-4.4
1922	Chi A	103	372	39	87	14	8	0	31	22	1	32	.234	.278	.315	55	-26	7-7	.971	3	108	84	3-84/S-7	-1.8
1928	Pit N	27	43	4	10	2	0	0	1	3	0	4	.233	.283	.279	45	-3	0	.929	0	92	253	/3-6,2-4	-0.3
Total	5	350	1235	143	287	41	24	1	88	70	8	120	.232	.278	.307	54	-84	23-27	.961	-12	99	94	3-242/S-76,2-4	-8.1
MULLIGAN, JOHN John d6.14																								
1884	Was U	1	4	2	1	0	0	0		0			.250	.250	.250	54	0		1.000	1	113	0	/3	0.0
MULLIGAN, SEAN Sean Patrick B 4.25.1970 Lynwood, CA BR/TR 6-2/205# d9.1																								
1996	SD N	2	1	0	0	0	0	0	0	0-0	0	0	.000	.000	.000	-99	0	0-0	—	0			/H	0.0
MULLIN, HENRY Henry J. B 4.1862 St.John, NB, CAN D 11.8.1927 Beverly, MA BR 5-9/160# d6.4																								
1884	Was AA	34	120	13	17	3	1	0		8	0		.142	.195	.183	27	-9		.869	1	107	0	O-34(4-29-1)/3	-0.8
	Bos U	2	8	1	0	0	0	0		0			.000	.000	.000	-99	-2		1.000	2	505	1160	/O-2(CF)	0.0
Total	1	36	128	14	17	3	1	0		8			.133	.184	.172	18	-11		.882	3	137	88	/O-36(4-31-1),3	-0.8
MULLIN, JIM James Henry B 10.16.1883 New York, NY D 1.24.1925 Philadelphia, PA BR/TR 5-10/173# d6.1																								
1904	Phi A	22	52	5	14	1	0	1	5	3	1		.269	.321	.346	106	0	2	.985	-3	66	68	/1-7,2-5,S-2,O(LF)	-0.3
	Was A	27	102	10	19	2	2	0	4	4	1		.186	.224	.245	49	-6	3	.981	5	111	98	2-27	-0.1
	Phi A	19	58	4	10	0	0	0	4	2	3		.172	.238	.172	29	-5	2	.984	-1	66	68	1-19	-0.6
	Year	68	212	19	43	3	2	1	13	9	5		.203	.252	.250	58	-10	7	.965	1	109	97	2-32,1-26/S-2,O(LF)	-1.0
1905	Was A	50	163	18	31	7	6	0	13	5	0		.190	.214	.307	67	-7	5	.928	-2	100	85	2-40/1-6	-1.0
Total	2	118	375	37	74	10	8	1	26	14	5		.197	.236	.275	62	-18	12	.946	-1	104	91	/2-72,1-32,S-2,O(LF)	-2.0
MULLIN, PAT Patrick Joseph B 11.1.1917 Trotter, PA D 8.14.1999 Brownsville, PA BL/TR 6-2/190# d9.18 Mil 1942-45 C8																								
1940	Det A	4	4	0	0	0	0	0	0	0	0	0	.000	.000	.000	-91	-1	0-0	—	-0	0	0	/O(CF)	-0.1
1941	Det A	54	220	42	76	11	5	5	23	18	2	18	.345	.400	.509	126	8	5-1	.944	-4	93	52	O-51(CF)	0.3
1946	Det A	93	276	34	68	13	4	3	35	25	1	36	.246	.311	.355	81	-7	3-5	.949	-2	91	133	O-75(0-1-75)	-1.3
1947	Det A☆	116	398	62	102	28	6	15	62	63	1	66	.256	.359	.470	126	14	3-8	.988	4	107	128	*O-106(RF)	1.3
1948	Det A★	138	496	91	143	16	11	23	80	77	1	57	.288	.385	.504	132	21	1-2	.972	-2	101	75	*O-131(0-10-123)	1.4
1949	Det A	104	310	55	83	8	6	12	59	42	1	29	.268	.357	.448	112	4	1-2	.989	-2	97	73	O-79(61-18-3)	-0.3
1950	Det A	69	142	16	31	5	0	6	23	20	0	23	.218	.315	.380	75	-6	1-4	1.000	1	94	164	O-32(21-0-13)	-0.7
1951	Det A	110	295	41	83	11	6	12	51	40	0	38	.281	.367	.481	128	10	2-2	.939	-5	91	69	O-83(76-4-6)	0.0
1952	Det A	97	255	29	64	13	5	7	35	31	0	30	.251	.332	.424	108	2	4-2	.979	3	102	151	O-65(60-2-5)	0.1
1953	Det A	79	97	11	26	1	0	4	17	14	0	15	.268	.360	.402	107	1	0-1	.944	-1	83	133	O-14(10-0-4)	0.0
Total	10	864	2493	381	676	106	43	87	385	330	6	312	.271	.358	.453	115	46	20-27	.970	-8	98	101	O-637(228-87-335)	0.7

Year	Tm Lg	G	AB	R	H	2B	3B	HR	RBI	BB-IB	HP	SO	AVG	OBP	SLG	AOPS	ABR	SB-CS	FA	FR	Rng	Thr	G at Pos	BFW
MULLINIKS, RANCE Steven Rance B 1.15.1956 Tulare, CA BL/TR 6/170# d6.18																								
1977	Cal A	78	271	36	73	13	2	3	21	23-2	1	36	.269	.329	.365	93	-3	1-1	.963	3	101	83	S-77	0.8
1978	Cal A	50	119	6	22	3	1	1	6	8-0	1	23	.185	.238	.252	41	-10	2-0	.953	-6	81	97	S-47/D-2	-1.2
1979	Cal A	22	68	7	10	0	0	1	8	4-0	1	14	.147	.192	.191	8	-9	0-0	.957	-5	68	92	S-22	-1.2
1980	KC A	36	54	8	14	3	0	0	6	7-0	0	10	.259	.339	.315	81	-1	0-0	.981	-3	86	61	S-18,2-14	-0.3
1981	KC A	24	44	6	10	3	0	0	5	2-0	0	7	.227	.261	.295	61	-2	0-1	.900	-1	94	129	2-10/S-7,3-5	-0.3
1982	Tor A	112	311	32	76	25	0	4	35	37-1	1	49	.244	.326	.363	82	-6	3-2	.938	-5	91	84	*3-102,S-16	-1.3
1983	Tor A	129	364	54	100	34	3	10	49	57-5	1	43	.275	.373	.467	122	14	0-2	.971	-4	87	59	*3-116,S-15/2-2	0.7
1984	Tor A	125	343	41	111	21	5	3	42	33-3	1	44	.324	.383	.440	123	12	2-3	**.968**	-6	91	77	*3-119/S-3,2	0.4
1985	†Tor A	129	366	55	108	26	1	10	57	55-2	0	54	.295	.383	.454	126	16	2-0	**.971**	-9	88	97	*3-119	0.5
1986	Tor A	117	348	50	90	22	0	11	45	43-1	1	60	.259	.340	.417	103	2	1-1	**.975**	5	108	90	*3-110/2D	0.5
1987	Tor A	124	332	37	103	28	1	11	44	34-1	0	55	.310	.371	.500	127	14	1-1	.927	-5	98	113	3-96,D-22/S	0.7
1988	Tor A	119	337	49	101	21	1	12	48	56-3	0	57	.300	.395	.475	143	22	1-0	1.000	-1	63	0	*D-108/3-7	1.8
1989	†Tor A	103	273	25	65	11	2	3	29	34-6	0	40	.238	.320	.326	85	-5	0-0	.985	2	106	236	D-73,3-29	-0.6
1990	Tor A	57	97	11	28	4	0	2	16	22-2	0	19	.289	.417	.392	126	5	2-1	.949	-3	79	150	3-22,D-10/1-3	0.2
1991	†Tor A	97	240	27	60	12	1	2	24	44-2	0	44	.250	.364	.333	92	-1	0-0	1.000	-2	44	0	D-81/3-5	-0.5
1992	Tor A	3	2	1	1	0	0	0	0	1-0	0	0	.500	.667	.500	221	0	0-0	—	0			/D-2	0.0
Total	16	1325	3569	445	972	226	17	73	435	460-28	7	555	.272	.354	.407	107	48	15-12	.961	-41	93	93	3-730,D-303,S-206/2-28,1-3	0.2
MULLINS, FRAN Francis Joseph B 5.14.1957 Oakland, CA BR/TR 6/180# d9.1																								
1980	Chi A	21	62	9	12	4	0	0	3	9-0	0	8	.194	.292	.258	53	-4	0-1	.981	-1	85	173	3-21	-0.6
1984	SF N	57	110	8	24	8	0	2	10	9-0	0	29	.218	.277	.345	77	-4	3-1	.969	4	119	108	S-28,3-28/2-4	0.2
1986	Cle A	28	40	3	7	4	0	0	5	2-0	0	11	.175	.209	.275	33	-4	0-0	.953	2	129	78	2-13,S-11/1D	0.0
Total	3	106	212	20	43	16	0	2	18	20-0	0	48	.203	.269	.307	61	-12	3-2	.968	5	96	127	/3-49,S-39,2-17,D1	-0.4
MULVEY, JOE Joseph H. B 10.27.1858 Providence, RI D 8.21.1928 Philadelphia, PA BR/TR 5-11.5/178# d5.31																								
1883	Pro N	4	16	1	2	1	0	0	2	0		1	.125	.125	.188	-6	-2		.692	-2	77	0	/S-4	-0.4
	Phi N	3	12	2	6	1	0	0	3	0		1	.500	.500	.583	250	2		.750	-1	44	171	/3-3	0.1
	Year	7	28	3	8	2	0	0	5	0		2	.286	.286	.357	96	0		.692	-3	77	0	/S-4,3-3	-0.3
1884	Phi N	100	401	47	92	11	2	2	32	4		49	.229	.237	.282	66	-16		.834	13	115	151	*3-100	-0.1
1885	Phi N	107	443	74	119	25	6	6	64	3		18	.269	.274	.393	116	6		.848	-5	95	96	*3-107	0.3
1886	Phi N	107	430	71	115	16	10	2	53	15		31	.267	.292	.365	98	-3	27	.879	-19	87	18	*3-107/O(RF)	-1.8
1887	Phi N	111	474	93	136	21	6	2	78	21	3	14	.287	.321	.369	86	-10	43	.865	-17	86	106	*3-111	-2.2
1888	Phi N	100	398	37	86	12	3	0	39	9	1	33	.216	.235	.261	55	-21	18	.891	-13	89	72	*3-100	-3.2
1889	Phi N	129	544	77	157	21	9	6	77	23	1	25	.289	.319	.393	91	-12	23	.893	1	104	83	*3-129	-0.8
1890	Phi P	120	519	96	149	26	16	5	87	27	3	36	.287	.326	.428	98	-6	20	.857	-17	87	72	*3-120	-1.6
1891	Phi AA	113	453	62	115	9	13	5	66	17	4	32	.254	.287	.364	86	-13	11	.894	1	96	98	*3-113	-0.9
1892	Phi N	25	98	9	14	1	1	0	4	6	1	9	.143	.200	.173	13	-11	2	.883	2	105	139	3-25	-0.8
1893	Was N	55	226	21	53	9	4	0	19	7	2	8	.235	.264	.310	54	-16	2	.874	5	112	88	3-55	-0.9
1895	Bro N	13	49	8	15	4	1	0	8	2	0	0	.306	.333	.429	104	0	1	.917	1	99	50	3-13	0.1
Total	12	987	4063	598	1059	157	71	28	532	134	15	257	.261	.287	.355	84	-102	147	.871	-53	96	88	3-983/S-4,O(RF)	-12.2
MUMPHREY, JERRY Jerry Wayne B 9.9.1952 Tyler, TX BB/TR 6-2/185# d9.10																								
1974	StL N	5	2	2	0	0	0	0	0	0-0	0	0	.000	.000	.000	-99	-1	0-0	—	-0	0	0	/O(LF)	-0.1
1975	StL N	11	16	2	6	2	0	0	1	4-0	0	3	.375	.500	.500	172	2	0-0	1.000	1	174	0	/O-3(RF)	0.3
1976	StL N	112	384	51	99	15	5	1	26	37-0	1	53	.258	.322	.331	86	-7	22-6	.993	5	113	98	O-94(15-77-12)	-0.2
1977	StL N	145	463	73	133	20	10	2	38	47-6	1	70	.287	.354	.387	100	0	22-15	.971	6	111	100	*O-133(49-67-34)	0.3
1978	StL N	125	367	41	96	13	4	2	37	30-0	1	40	.262	.317	.335	84	-8	14-10	.995	-1	89	141	*O-116(48-30-48)	-1.4
1979	StL N	124	339	53	100	10	3	3	32	26-2	0	39	.295	.341	.369	94	-3	8-11	.984	-3	96	44	*O-114(83-19-20)	-1.2
1980	SD N	160	564	61	168	24	3	4	59	49-4	0	90	.298	.352	.372	109	7	52-5	.974	-3	100	97	*O-153(CF)	1.4
1981	†NY A	80	319	44	98	11	5	6	32	24-1	0	27	.307	.354	.429	127	10	14-9	.966	3	112	113	O-79(CF)	1.3
1982	NY A	123	477	76	143	24	10	9	68	50-4	0	66	.300	.364	.449	124	16	11-3	.986	0	104	63	*O-123(CF)	1.7
1983	NY A	83	267	41	70	11	4	7	36	28-2	0	33	.262	.327	.412	107	2	2-3	.983	7	113	154	O-83(CF)	0.8
	Hou N	44	143	17	48	10	2	1	17	22-3	1	23	.336	.425	.455	154	12	5-0	.990	-2	97	50	O-43(CF)	1.1
1984	Hou N★	151	524	66	152	20	3	9	83	56-7	0	79	.290	.355	.391	119	14	15-7	.988	-8	93	67	*O-137(CF)	0.6
1985	Hou N	130	444	52	123	25	2	8	61	37-8	0	57	.277	.329	.396	106	3	6-7	.969	-2	100	81	*O-126(0-58-68)	-0.4
1986	Chi N	111	309	37	94	11	2	5	32	26-4	0	45	.304	.355	.401	101	1	2-3	.982	-0	102	64	O-92(39-65-21)	-0.2
1987	Chi N	118	309	41	103	19	2	13	44	35-6	0	47	.333	.400	.534	140	18	1-1	.992	-1	94	105	O-85(78-1-6)	1.4
1988	Chi N	63	66	3	9	2	0	0	9	7-2	0	16	.136	.219	.167	12	-7	0-0	1.000	-1	69	0	/O-4(LF)	-0.9
Total	15	1585	4993	660	1442	217	55	70	575	478-49	4	688	.289	.349	.396	109	59	174-80	.981	2	102	90	*O-1386(317-935-212)	4.5
MUNCE, JOHN John Lewis "Big John" B 11.18.1857 Philadelphia, PA D 3.15.1917 Philadelphia, PA 5-8.5/160# d8.19																								
1884	Wil U	7	21	1	4	0	0	0		1			.190	.227	.190	27	-3		.667	-0	136	0	/O-7(0-2-6)	-0.3
MUNCH, JAKE Jacob Ferdinand B 11.16.1890 Morton, PA D 6.8.1966 Lansdowne, PA BL/TL 6-2.5/170# d5.27																								
1918	Phi A	22	30	3	8	0	1	0	0	0	0	5	.267	.267	.333	80	-1	0	.667	-1	67	0	/O-3(0-1-2),1-2	-0.2
MUNDINGER, GEORGE George B 11.20.1854 New Orleans, LA D 10.12.1910 Covington, LA BR/TR 6-2/200# d5.9																								
1884	Ind AA	3	8	1	2	0	0	0	3	0	0		.250	.250	.250	65	0		.750	-2			/C-3	-0.2
MUNDY, BILL William Edward B 6.28.1889 Salineville, OH D 9.23.1958 Kalamazoo, MI BL/TL 5-10/154# d8.17																								
1913	Bos A	16	47	4	12	0	0	0	4	4	0	12	.255	.314	.255	65	-2	0	.952	-3	47	53	1-14	-0.5
MUNN, HORATIO Horatio Brinsmade B 7.26.1851 Newark, NJ D 2.17.1910 Brooklyn, NY d9.6																								
1875	Atl NA	1	4	0	0	0	0	0	0	0		0	.000	.000	.000	-99	-1	0-0	.833	-0	111	0	/2	-0.1
MUNOZ, JOSE Jose Luis B 11.11.1967 Chicago, IL BB/TR 5-11/165# d4.7																								
1996	Chi A	17	27	7	7	0	0	0	1	4-0	0	1	.259	.355	.259	62	-1	0-0	.923	-3	72	51	/2-7,S-2,3O(LF)D	-0.3
MUNOZ, NOE Noe B 11.11.1967 Escatepec, Mexico BR/TR 6-2/180# d4.30																								
1995	LA N	2	1	0	0	0	0	0	0	0-0	0	0	.000	.000	.000	-99	0	0-0	1.000	1	0	0	/C-2	0.0
MUNOZ, PEDRO Pedro Javier (Gonzalez) B 9.19.1968 Ponce, P.R. BR/TR 5-10/207# d9.1																								
1990	Min A	22	85	13	23	4	1	0	5	2-0	0	16	.271	.281	.341	70	-4	3-0	.972	-2	81	69	O-21(3-0-19)/D	-0.6
1991	Min A	51	138	15	39	7	1	7	26	9-0	1	31	.283	.327	.500	121	3	3-0	.989	3	116	114	O-44(10-0-39)/D-2	0.6
1992	Min A	127	418	44	113	16	3	12	71	17-1	1	90	.270	.298	.409	94	-6	4-5	.987	-0	95	106	*O-122(7-0-117)/D-3	-1.1
1993	Min A	104	326	34	76	11	1	13	38	25-2	3	97	.233	.294	.393	82	-10	1-2	.983	-5	89	80	*O-102(64-0-41)	-1.9
1994	Min A	75	244	35	72	15	2	11	36	19-0	2	67	.295	.348	.508	118	6	0-0	.965	-2	102	26	O-58(42-0-19),D-12	0.0
1995	Min A	104	376	45	113	17	0	18	58	19-0	3	86	.301	.338	.489	112	5	0-3	.926	-3	57	225	D-77,O-25(1-0-24)/1-3	-0.5
1996	Oak A	34	121	17	31	5	0	6	18	9-1	0	31	.256	.308	.446	89	-3	0-0	1.000	-3	56	0	D-18,O-14(RF)	-0.7
Total	7	517	1708	203	467	75	8	67	252	100-4	10	418	.273	.315	.444	100	-9	11-10	.980	-12	92	89	O-386(127-0-273),D-113/1-3	-4.2
MUNSON, RED Clarence Hanford B 7.31.1883 Cincinnati, OH D 2.19.1957 Mishawaka, IN TR d8.28																								
1905	Phi N	9	26	1	3	1	0	0	2	0	0		.115	.115	.154	-21	-4	0	.857	-1	*120*	*89*	/C-8	-0.4
MUNSON, ERIC Eric Walter B 10.3.1977 San Diego, CA BL/TR 6-3/220# d7.18																								
2000	Det A	3	5	0	0	0	0	0	1	0-0	0	1	.000	.000	.000	-99	-2	0-0	.941	-1	0	167	/1-3	-0.2
2001	Det A	17	66	4	10	3	1	1	6	3-0	0	21	.152	.188	.273	20	-8	0-1	.994	1	121	92	1-17	-0.9
2002	Det A	18	59	3	11	0	0	2	5	6-0	1	11	.186	.269	.288	52	-4	0-0	.970	0	121	88	D-14/1-4	-0.5
2003	Det A	99	313	28	75	9	0	18	50	35-1	1	61	.240	.312	.441	105	2	3-0	.920	-13	90	79	3-91/D-3	-1.0
Total	4	137	443	35	96	12	1	21	62	44-1	2	94	.217	.286	.391	83	-12	3-1	.920	-13	90	79	/3-91,1-24,D-17	-2.6
MUNSON, JOE Joseph Martin Napoleon (born Joseph Martin Napoleon Carlson) B 11.6.1899 Renovo, PA D 2.24.1991 Drexel Hill, PA BL/TR 5-9/184# d9.18																								
1925	Chi N	9	35	5	13	3	1	0	3	3	1	1	.371	.436	.514	140	2	1-1	1.000	-0	95	80	/O-9(RF)	0.1
1926	Chi N	33	101	17	26	2	2	3	15	8	1	4	.257	.318	.406	93	-2	0	.898	-2	95	67	O-28(16-0-12)	-0.6
Total	2	42	136	22	39	5	3	3	18	11	2	5	.287	.349	.434	105	0	1-1	.922	-2	95	70	/O-37(16-0-21)	-0.5

Year	Tm Lg	G	AB	R	H	2B	3B	HR	RBI	BB-IB	HP	SO	AVG	OBP	SLG	AOPS	ABR	SB-CS	FA	FR	Rng	Thr	G at Pos	BFW
MUNSON, THURMAN Thurman Lee B 6.7.1947 Akron, OH D 8.2.1979 Canton, OH BR/TR 5-11/191# d8.8																								
1969	NY A	26	86	6	22	1	2	1	9	10-1	0	10	.256	.330	.349	94	-1	0-1	.986	1	207	103	C-25	0.1
1970	NY A	132	453	59	137	25	4	6	53	57-6	7	56	.302	.386	.415	128	20	5-7	.989	13	**167**	96	*C-125	3.9
1971	NY A★	125	451	71	113	15	4	10	42	52-1	7	65	.251	.335	.368	106	4	6-5	**.998**	8	**221**	113	*C-117/O(RF)	1.8
1972	NY A	140	511	54	143	16	3	7	46	47-5	3	58	.280	.343	.364	115	9	6-7	.977	4	**185**	77	*C-132	2.1
1973	NY A★	147	519	80	156	29	4	20	74	48-4	4	64	.301	.362	.487	143	29	4-6	.984	15	158	98	*C-142/D	5.0
1974	NY A★	144	517	64	135	19	2	13	60	44-12	1	66	.261	.316	.381	103	1	2-0	.974	6	123	70	*C-137/D-4	1.4
1975	NY A★	157	597	83	190	24	3	12	102	45-8	6	52	.318	.366	.429	128	22	3-2	.972	18	151	111	*C-130,D-22/1-2,O-2(1-0-1),3	4.5
1976	†NY A★	152	616	79	186	27	1	17	105	29-6	9	38	.302	.337	.432	127	19	14-11	.981	1	111	94	*C-121,D-21,O-11(2-0-9)	2.5
1977	†NY A★	149	595	85	183	28	5	18	100	39-8	2	55	.308	.351	.462	121	16	5-6	.984	3	111	92	*C-136,D-10	2.3
1978	†NY A✳	154	617	73	183	27	1	6	71	35-6	3	70	.297	.332	.373	102	1	2-3	.986	9	128	103	*C-125,D-14,O-13(RF)	1.4
1979	NY A	97	382	42	110	18	3	3	39	32-2	0	37	.288	.340	.374	95	-2	1-2	.978	3	**181**	85	C-88/1-3,D-5	0.4
Total	11	1423	5344	696	1558	229	32	113	701	438-59	42	571	.292	.346	.410	117	118	48-50	.982	81	153	94	*C-1278/D-77,O-27(3-0-24),1-5,3	25.4
MUNYAN, JOHN John Baird B 11.14.1860 Chester, PA D 2.18.1945 Endicott, NY d7.12																								
1887	Cle AA	16	58	9	14	1	1	0	6	3	0		.241	.279	.293	61	-3	4	.762	-1	64	0	O-12(3-3-6)/C-3,3-2	-0.3
1890	Col AA	2	7	1	1	0	0	0	0	0	1		.143	.250	.143	17	-1	0	.667	0	281	0	/O-2(CF)	-0.1
	StL AA	96	342	61	91	15	7	4	42	32	7		.266	.341	.386	100	-2	11	.939	-1	*100*	*99*	C-83/O-7(LF),2-5,3-3,S	0.3
	Year	98	349	62	92	15	7	4	42	32	8		.264	.339	.381	99	-3	11	.939	-1	*100*	*99*	C-83/O-9(7-2-0),2-5,3-3,S	0.2
1891	StL AA	60	176	41	41	4	3	0	19	41	4	39	.233	.389	.290	82	-3	13	.940	-4	*115*	*82*	C-43,O-12(4-0-8)/S-5,3-3	-0.3
Total	3	174	583	112	147	20	11	4	67	76	12	39	.252	.350	.345	90	-9	28	.937	-6	*101*	*91*	C-129/O-33(14-5-14),3-8,S-6,2-5	-0.4
MURCER, BOBBY Bobby Ray B 5.20.1946 Oklahoma City, OK BL/TR 5-11/180# d9.8 Mil 1967 OF Total (56-LF 789-CF 839-RF)																								
1965	NY A	11	37	2	9	0	1	1	4	5-0	0	12	.243	.333	.378	102	0	0-0	.932	4	110	195	S-11	0.5
1966	NY A	21	69	3	12	1	1	0	5	4-0	0	5	.174	.219	.217	27	-7	2-2	.931	-3	94	38	S-18	-1.0
1969	NY A	152	564	82	146	24	4	26	82	50-2	3	103	.259	.319	.454	120	12	7-5	.964	-6	94	45	*O-118(0-27-99),3-31	0.0
1970	NY A	159	581	95	146	23	3	23	78	87-5	2	100	.251	.348	.420	118	15	15-10	.992	-4	93	139	*O-155(CF)	0.7
1971	NY A★	146	529	94	175	25	6	25	94	91-13	0	60	.331	**.427**	.543	**185**	**62**	14-8	.985	-14	83	103	*O-143(CF)	4.7
1972	NY A★	153	585	**102**	171	30	7	33	96	63-7	2	67	.292	.361	.537	171	49	11-9	.992	-4	97	105	*O-151(CF)	4.5
1973	NY A★	160	616	83	187	29	2	22	95	50-6	3	67	.304	.357	.464	135	27	6-7	.985	-7	92	119	*O-160(CF)	1.6
1974	NY A★	156	606	69	166	25	4	10	88	57-10	2	59	.274	.332	.378	108	6	14-5	.978	-5	85	178	*O-156(0-59-101)	-0.4
1975	SF N★	147	526	80	157	29	4	11	91	91-6	2	45	.298	.396	.432	127	23	9-5	.981	-11	77	108	*O-144(0-2-143)	0.6
1976	SF N	147	533	73	138	20	2	23	90	84-10	4	78	.259	.362	.433	122	17	12-7	.961	-6	96	88	*O-146(RF)	0.5
1977	Chi N	154	554	90	147	18	3	27	89	80-13	3	77	.265	.355	.455	106	5	16-7	.980	-12	82	94	*O-150(RF)/2S	-1.4
1978	Chi N	146	499	66	140	22	6	9	64	80-15	0	57	.281	.376	.403	106	7	14-5	.979	-16	79	74	*O-138(0-33-121)	-1.4
1979	Chi N	58	190	22	49	4	1	7	22	36-2	1	20	.258	.374	.400	103	2	2-3	1.000	2	111	95	O-54(RF)	0.0
	NY A	74	264	42	72	12	0	8	33	25-2	2	32	.273	.339	.409	103	1	1-1	.983	-2	98	87	O-70(12-59-7)	-0.1
1980	†NY A	100	297	41	80	9	1	13	57	34-2	2	28	.269	.339	.438	116	6	2-0	.955	-4	90	59	O-59(44-0-18),D-33	0.0
1981	†NY A	50	117	14	31	6	0	6	24	12-1	0	15	.265	.331	.470	131	4	0-0	—	0	0	0	D-33	0.4
1982	NY A	65	141	12	32	6	0	7	30	12-2	1	15	.227	.288	.418	94	-2	2-1	—	0	0	0	D-47	-0.3
1983	NY A	9	22	2	4	2	0	1	1	1-0	0	1	.182	.217	.409	71	-1	0-0	—	0			/D-5	-0.1
Total	17	1908	6730	972	1862	285	45	252	1043	862-96	27	841	.277	.357	.445	124	226	127-75	.981	-88	89	105	*O-1644R,D-118/3-31,S-30,2	8.8
MURCH, SIMMY Simeon Augustus B 11.21.1880 Castine, ME D 6.6.1939 Exeter, NH BR/TR 6-2/220# d9.20																								
1904	StL N	13	51	3	7	1	0	0	1	1	0		.137	.154	.157	-4	-6	0	.905	-1	101	166	/2-6,3-6,S	-0.7
1905	StL N	4	9	0	1	0	0	0	0	0	0		.111	.111	.111	-35	-2	0	.750	-2	0	0	/2-2,S	-0.4
1908	Bro N	6	11	1	2	1	0	0	0	1	0		.182	.250	.273	70	0	0	.964	-1	0	99	/1-2	-0.1
Total	3	23	71	4	10	2	0	0	1	2	0		.141	.164	.169	3	-8	0	.880	-4	83	136	/2-8,3-6,1-2,S-2	-1.2
MURDOCH, WILBUR Wilbur Edwin B 3.14.1875 Avon, NY D 10.29.1941 Los Angeles, CA d8.29																								
1908	StL N	27	62	5	16	3	0	0	5	3	0		.258	.292	.306	96	0	4	.913	-2	0	0	O-16(13-5-0)	-0.3
MURNANE, TIM Timothy Hayes B 6.4.1852 Naugatuck, CT D 2.7.1917 Boston, MA BL/TR 5-9.5/172# d4.26 M1																								
1872	Man NA	23	114	28	41	1	1	0	16	0		0	.360	.360	.386	137	5	1-2	.905	-4	0	62	1-23	0.1
1873	Ath NA	41	176	53	39	2	1	1	10	8		13	.222	.255	.261	50	-12	8-2	.785	-3	55	0	O-30(0-24-6),1-10/2-6	-1.0
1874	Ath NA	21	82	11	17	2	0	0	11	1		3	.207	.217	.232	40	-6	0-1	.857	-3	132	0	O-14(0-1-13)/2-6,1-3	-0.7
1875	Phi NA	69	313	71	85	5	0	1	30	7		7	.272	.287	.297	100	-1	**30**-9	.918	1	86	74	1-31,O-26(1-24-1),2-15	0.3
1876	Bos N	69	308	60	87	4	3	2	34	8		12	.282	.301	.334	109	3		.927	-4	44	130	*1-65/O-3(2-1-0),2	-0.4
1877	Bos N	35	140	23	39	7	1	1	15	6		7	.279	.308	.364	107	1		.815	0	102	280	O-30(0-25-5)/1-5	0.0
1878	Pro N	49	188	35	45	6	1	0	14	8		12	.239	.270	.282	82	-3		.940	1	**168**	111	*1-48/O(CF)	-0.5
1884	Bos U	76	311	55	73	5	2	0		22			.235	.285	.264	68	-21		.950	-4	39	40	1-63,O-16(1-0-15),M	-2.7
Total	4 NA	154	685	163	182	10	2	2	67	16		23	.266	.282	.295	84	-14	39-14	.000	-9	47	0	/O-70(1-49-20),1-67,2-27	-1.3
Total	4	229	947	173	244	22	7	3	63	44		31	.258	.291	.305	90	-20		.938	-8	81	92	1-181/O-50(3-27-20),2	-3.6
MURPHY d8.16																								
1884	Bos U	1	3	0	0	0	0	0		1			.000	.250	.000	-18	0		.333	-2			/CO(LF)	-0.2
MURPHY, CLARENCE Clarence d6.17																								
1886	Lou AA	1	3	0	0	0	0	0	0	0	0		.000	.000	.000	-95	-1	0	1.000	0	0	0	/O(LF)	-0.1
MURPHY, CONNIE Cornelius David "Stone Face" B 11.1.1870 Northfield, MA D 12.14.1945 New Bedford, MA BL/TR 5-8/155# d9.17																								
1893	Cin N	6	17	3	3	1	0	0	2	1	0	2	.176	.222	.235	21	-2	0	.917	-1	*115*	*30*	/C-4	-0.3
1894	Cin N	1	4	0	0	0	0	0	0	1	0	1	.000	.200	.000	-47	-1	0	.500	-1	*81*	*106*	/C	-0.1
Total	2	7	21	3	3	1	0	0	2	2	0	3	.143	.217	.190	6	-3	0	.857	-2	*108*	*45*	/C-5	-0.4
MURPHY, DALE Dale Bryan B 3.12.1956 Portland, OR BR/TR 6-5/215# d9.13 OF Total (101-LF 1044-CF 747-RF)																								
1976	Atl N	19	65	3	17	6	0	0	9	7-0	0	9	.262	.333	.354	89	-1	0-0	.974	-1	59	151	C-19	-0.1
1977	Atl N	18	76	5	24	8	1	2	14	0-0	0	8	.316	.316	.526	108	1	0-1	.954	-3	56	66	C-18	-0.1
1978	Atl N	151	530	66	120	14	3	23	79	42-3	3	145	.226	.284	.394	80	-16	11-7	.984	2	116	81	*1-129,C-21	-2.2
1979	Atl N	104	384	53	106	7	2	21	57	38-5	2	67	.276	.340	.469	111	5	6-1	.980	-12	85	97	1-76,C-27	-1.0
1980	Atl N★	156	569	98	160	27	2	33	89	59-9	1	133	.281	.349	.510	133	24	9-6	.985	-1	96	127	*O-154(4-129-21)/1	2.1
1981	Atl N	104	369	43	91	12	1	13	50	44-8	0	72	.247	.325	.390	100	0	14-5	.981	-2	92	151	*O-103(0-102-1)/1-3	-0.2
1982	†Atl N★	**162**	598	113	168	23	2	36	**109**	93-9	3	134	.281	.378	.507	140	34	23-11	.979	-0	105	54	*O-162(65-118-8)	3.2
1983	Atl N★	**162**	589	131	178	24	4	36	**121**	90-12	2	110	.302	.393	**.540**	146	39	30-4	.985	-3	96	119	*O-160(28-136-2)	4.0
1984	Atl N★	**162**	607	94	176	32	8	**36**	100	79-20	2	134	.290	.372	**.547**	145	36	19-7	.987	-11	88	108	*O-160(CF)	2.6
1985	Atl N★	**162**	616	**118**	185	32	2	**37**	111	**90**-15	1	141	.300	.388	.539	148	42	10-3	.980	-20	81	78	*O-161(CF)	2.2
1986	Atl N★	160	614	89	163	29	7	29	83	75-5	2	141	.265	.347	.477	118	15	7-7	.981	-20	82	64	*O-159(0-155-6)	-0.8
1987	Atl N★	159	566	115	167	27	1	44	105	115-**29**	7	136	.295	.417	.580	154	48	16-6	.977	5	105	123	*O-159(RF)	4.5
1988	Atl N	156	592	77	134	35	4	24	77	74-16	2	125	.226	.313	.421	104	4	3-5	.992	11	105	183	*O-156(RF)	0.9
1989	Atl N	154	574	60	131	16	0	20	84	65-10	2	142	.228	.306	.361	88	-9	3-2	.985	-7	95	61	*O-151(0-82-70)	-2.0
1990	Atl N	97	349	38	81	14	0	17	55	41-11	1	84	.232	.312	.418	94	-3	9-2	.981	1	108	45	O-97(RF)	-0.4
	Phi N	57	214	22	57	9	1	7	28	20-3	0	46	.266	.328	.416	104	1	0-1	.992	-0	95	99	O-55(1-1-53)	-0.2
	Year	154	563	60	138	23	1	24	83	61-14	1	130	.245	.318	.417	98	-2	9-3	.985	1	103	65	*O-152(1-1-150)	-0.6
1991	Phi N	153	544	66	137	33	1	18	81	48-3	0	93	.252	.309	.415	104	2	1-0	.983	-1	103	56	*O-147(RF)	-0.3
1992	Phi N	18	62	5	10	1	0	2	7	1-0	0	13	.161	.175	.274	25	-6	0-0	.950	-3	68	0	O-16(1-0-16)	-1.1
1993	Col N	26	42	1	6	1	0	0	7	5-1	0	15	.143	.224	.167	8	-5	0-0	1.000	0	91	148	O-13(2-0-11)	-0.6
Total	18	2180	7960	1197	2111	350	39	398	1266	986-159	28	1748	.265	.346	.469	119	211	161-68	.983	-66	96	98	*O-1853C,1-209/C-85	10.5
MURPHY, DANNY Daniel Francis B 8.11.1876 Philadelphia, PA D 11.22.1955 Jersey City, NJ BR/TR 5-9/175# d9.17 C6																								
1900	NY N	22	74	11	20	1	0	0	6	8	0		.270	.341	.284	77	-2	4	.888	-4	89	102	2-22	-0.4
1901	NY N	5	20	0	4	0	0	0	0	1	0		.200	.238	.200	29	-2	0	.895	-2	85	0	/2-5	-0.4
1902	Phi A	76	291	48	91	11	8	1	48	13	4		.313	.351	.416	107	2	12	.963	-13	86	69	2-76	-1.0
1903	Phi A	133	513	66	140	31	11	1	60	13	3		.273	.295	.382	97	-3	17	.949	-13	88	73	*2-133	-1.6
1904	Phi A	150	557	78	160	30	17	7	77	22	5		.287	.320	.440	132	18	22	.941	14	103	84	*2-150	3.7
1905	†Phi A	151	537	71	149	34	4	6	71	42	8		.277	.339	.389	129	18	23	.955	-12	92	76	*2-151	0.8
1906	Phi A	119	448	48	135	28	6	2	60	21	6		.301	.341	.404	129	14	17	.955	-11	90	95	*2-119	0.4

Year	Tm Lg	G	AB	R	H	2B	3B	HR	RBI	BB-IB	HP	SO	AVG	OBP	SLG	AOPS	ABR	SB-CS	FA	FR	Rng	Thr	G at Pos	BFW
1907	Phi A	124	469	51	127	23	3	2	57	30	2		.271	.317	.345	109	5	11	.965	7	101	73	*2-122	1.4
1908	Phi A	142	525	51	139	28	7	4	66	32	2		.265	.309	.368	112	6	16	.963	7	110	146	O-84(2-12-70),2-56/1-2	1.1
1909	Phi A	149	541	61	152	28	14	5	69	35	6		.281	.332	.412	132	18	19	**.977**	-4	87	126	*O-149(RF)	0.8
1910	†Phi A	151	560	70	168	28	18	4	64	31	1		.300	.338	.436	143	24	18	.974	-3	102	74	*O-151(RF)	1.6
1911	†Phi A	141	508	104	167	27	11	6	66	50	8		.329	.398	.461	142	29	22	.961	7	87	**153**	*O-136(RF)/2-4	2.8
1912	Phi A	36	130	27	42	6	2	2	20	16	1		.323	.401	.446	147	8	8	.891	-4	81	44	O-36(RF)	0.3
1913	Phi A	40	59	3	19	5	1	0	6	4	0	8	.322	.365	.441	139	3	0	1.000	-1	62	0	/O-9(RF)	0.2
1914	Bro F	52	161	16	49	9	0	4	32	17	1	16	.304	.374	.435	121	3	4	.986	2	102	115	O-46(1-0-45)	0.2
1915	Bro F	5	6	0	1	0	0	0	0	0	0	0	.167	.167	.167	-6	-1	0	1.000	-0	77	0	/2O(RF)	-0.2
Total	16	1496	5399	705	1563	289	102	44	702	335	47	24	.289	.336	.405	124	140	193	.953	-32	94	79	2-839,O-612(3-12-597)/1-2	9.7
MURPHY, DANNY Daniel Francis B 8.23.1942 Beverly, MA BL/TR 5-11/185# d6.18 ▲																								
1960	Chi N	31	75	7	9	2	0	1	6	4-0	1	13	.120	.175	.187	-1	-11	0-0	.976	0	105	77	O-21(0-16-5)	-1.2
1961	Chi N	4	13	3	5	0	0	2	3	1-0	0	5	.385	.429	.846	225	2	0-0	1.000	0	87	345	/O-4(RF)	0.2
1962	Chi N	14	35	5	7	3	1	0	3	2-0	0	9	.200	.243	.343	53	-2	0-0	1.000	-1	59	0	/O-5(2-1-6)	-0.4
1969	Chi A	17	1	0	0	0	0	0	0	2-0	0	0	.000	.667	.000	95	1	0-0	1.000	-0	86	0	P-17	0.0
1970	Chi A	51	6	3	2	0	0	1	1	2-0	0	2	.333	.500	.833	252	2	0-0	.933	-1	84	112	P-51	0.0
Total	5	117	130	18	23	5	1	4	13	11-0	1	29	.177	.246	.323	53	-8	0-0	.947	-1	85	81	/P-68,O-30(2-17-15)	-1.4
MURPHY, DANNY Daniel Joseph "Handsome Dan" B 9.10.1864 Brooklyn, NY D 12.14.1915 Brooklyn, NY ?/156# d4.26																								
1892	NY N	8	26	2	3	0	0	0	0	5	0	4	.115	.258	.115	14	-2	0	.900	-2	*69*	*72*	/C-8	-0.4
MURPHY, DAVE David Francis "Dirty Dave" B 5.4.1876 Adams, MA D 4.8.1940 Adams, MA TR d8.28																								
1905	Bos N	3	11	0	2	0	0	0	1	0	0		.182	.182	.182	9	-1	0	1.000	-1	97	0	/S-2,3	-0.3
MURPHY, DWAYNE Dwayne Keith B 3.18.1955 Merced, CA BL/TR 6-1/185# d4.8 C6																								
1978	Oak A	60	52	15	10	2	0	0	5	7-0	0	14	.192	.279	.231	50	-3	0-1	1.000	2	121	88	O-45(21-12-14)/D-5	-0.2
1979	Oak A	121	388	57	99	10	4	11	40	84-6	1	80	.255	.387	.387	116	13	15-11	.988	4	103	131	*O-118(2-115-3)	1.5
1980	Oak A	159	573	86	157	18	2	13	68	102-7	2	96	.274	.384	.380	119	21	26-15	.990	12	113	115	*O-158(CF)	3.1
1981	†Oak A	107	390	58	98	10	3	15	60	73-6	2	91	.251	.369	.408	131	18	10-4	.985	3	109	89	*O-106(CF)/D	2.2
1982	Oak A	151	543	84	129	15	1	27	94	94-2	3	122	.238	.349	.418	116	14	26-8	.983	10	109	137	*O-147(CF)/SD	2.5
1983	Oak A	130	471	55	107	17	2	17	75	62-4	0	105	.227	.314	.380	97	-2	7-5	.979	3	108	91	*O-124(CF)/D-7	0.0
1984	Oak A	153	559	93	143	18	2	33	88	74-1	3	111	.256	.342	.472	133	25	4-5	.988	11	111	138	*O-153(CF)	3.3
1985	Oak A	152	523	77	122	21	3	20	59	84-3	3	123	.233	.340	.400	111	10	4-5	.989	-2	104	61	*O-150(CF)	0.6
1986	Oak A	98	329	50	83	11	3	9	39	56-4	4	80	.252	.364	.386	114	9	3-1	.993	6	111	119	O-97(CF)/D	1.4
1987	Oak A	82	219	39	51	7	0	8	35	58-2	0	61	.233	.388	.374	113	8	4-4	.984	0	106	33	O-79(CF)/12	0.7
1988	Det A	49	144	14	36	5	0	4	19	24-2	1	26	.250	.361	.368	109	3	1-1	1.000	3	116	51	O-43(4-35-10)/D-3	0.5
1989	Phi N	98	156	20	34	5	0	9	27	29-2	0	44	.218	.341	.423	117	4	0-1	.986	-1	99	52	O-52(30-5-19)	0.2
Total	12	1360	4347	648	1069	139	20	166	609	747-39	19	953	.246	.356	.402	116	120	100-61	.987	53	109	102	*O-1272(57-1181-46)/D-18,21S	15.8
MURPHY, ED Edward Joseph B 8.23.1918 Joliet, IL D 12.10.1991 Joliet, IL BR/TR 5-11/190# d9.10 Mil 1943-45																								
1942	Phi N	13	28	2	7	2	0	0	4	2	0	4	.250	.300	.321	86	0	0	1.000	-0	72	126	/1-8	-0.2
MURPHY, TONY Francis J. B 7.1859 Brooklyn, NY D 12.15.1915 New York, NY 5-6/145# d10.15																								
1884	NY AA	1	3	1	1	0	0	0		0	0		.333	.333	.333	121	0		1.000	-0			/C	0.0
MURPHY, FRANK Francis Patrick B 4.16.1875 N.Tarrytown, NY D 11.4.1912 Central Islip, NY TR d7.2																								
1901	Bos N	45	176	13	46	5	3	1	18	4	1		.261	.282	.341	73	-7	6	.939	3	164	71	O-45(LF)	-0.6
	NY N	35	130	10	21	3	0	0	8	6	0		.162	.199	.185	12	-15	2	.847	-9	90	34	2-23,O-12(LF)	-2.4
	Year	80	306	23	67	8	3	1	26	10	1		.219	.246	.275	49	-21	8	.940	-6	149	59	O-57(LF),2-23	-3.0
MURPHY, DUMMY Herbert Courtland B 12.18.1886 Olney, IL D 8.10.1962 Tallahassee, FL BR/TR 5-10/165# d4.14																								
1914	Phi N	9	26	1	4	1	0	0	3	0	1	4	.154	.185	.192	12	-3	0	.864	0	102	58	/S-9	-0.2
MURPHY, HOWARD Howard B 1.1.1882 Birmingham, AL D 10.5.1926 Fort Worth, TX BL/TR 5-8.5/150# d8.4																								
1909	StL N	25	60	3	12	0	0	0	3	4	0		.200	.250	.200	42	-4	1	.925	-1	86	0	O-19(CF)	-0.7
MURPHY, EDDIE John Edward B 10.2.1891 Hancock, NY D 2.21.1969 Dunmore, PA BL/TR 5-9/155# d8.26																								
1912	Phi A	33	142	24	45	4	1	0	6	11	1		.317	.370	.359	113	3	7	.947	-0	90	118	O-33(RF)	0.0
1913	†Phi A	137	508	105	150	14	7	1	30	70	10	44	.295	.391	.356	122	18	21	.942	-11	85	72	*O-135(RF)	0.0
1914	†Phi A	148	573	101	156	12	9	3	43	87	**12**	46	.272	.379	.340	121	19	36-32	.941	-7	92	80	*O-148(RF)	0.1
1915	Phi A	68	260	37	60	3	4	0	17	29	3	15	.231	.315	.273	79	-7	13-3	.899	-2	78	125	O-58(RF)/3-6	-1.0
	Chi A	70	273	51	86	11	5	0	26	39	5	12	.315	.410	.392	136	14	20-12	.952	-2	104	81	O-70(3-0-67)	1.0
	Year	138	533	88	146	14	9	0	43	68	8	27	.274	.365	.334	109	8	33-15	.933	-4	94	99	*O-128(3-0-125)/3-6	0.0
1916	Chi A	51	105	14	22	5	1	0	4	9	2	5	.210	.284	.276	68	-4	3	1.000	-1	98	91	O-24(RF)/3	-0.7
1917	Chi A	53	51	9	16	2	1	0	16	5	1	1	.314	.386	.392	135	2	4	1.000	-1	48	0	/O-9(1-0-8)	0.2
1918	Chi A	91	286	36	85	9	3	0	23	22	1	18	.297	.350	.350	110	3	6	.958	-7	101	36	O-63(1-0-62)/2-8	-0.7
1919	†Chi A	30	35	8	17	4	0	0	5	7	0	0	.486	.571	.600	228	7	0	.917	0	111	163	/O-6(2-0-4)	0.7
1920	Chi A	58	118	22	40	2	1	0	19	12	1	4	.339	.405	.373	107	2	1-3	.886	2	75	340	O-19(RF)/3-3	0.2
1921	Chi A	6	5	1	1	0	0	0	0	0	0	0	.200	.200	.200	2	-1	0-0	—	0			H	-0.1
1926	Pit N	16	17	3	2	0	0	0	6	3	0	0	.118	.250	.118	2	-2	0	1.000	0	114	0	/O-3(LF)	-0.3
Total	11	761	2373	411	680	66	32	4	195	294	36	145	.287	.374	.346	114	54	111-50	.942	-28	91	88	O-568(10-0-558)/3-10,2-8	-0.6
MURPHY, JOHN John Patrick B 1879 New Haven, CT D 4.20.1949 Andover, MA 5-7.5/160# d9.10																								
1902	StL N	1	3	1	2	1	0	0	1	1	0		.667	.750	1.000	458	1	0	1.000	-1	0	0	/3	0.1
1903	Det A	5	22	1	4	1	0	0	1	0	0		.182	.182	.227	23	-2	0	.852	-1	103	58	/S-5	-0.3
Total	2	6	25	2	6	2	0	0	2	1	0		.240	.269	.320	79	-1	0	.852	-1	103	58	/S-5,3	-0.2
MURPHY, LEO Leo Joseph "Red" B 1.7.1889 Terre Haute, IN D 8.12.1960 Racine, WI BR/TR 6-1/179# d5.2																								
1915	Pit N	31	41	4	4	0	0	0	4	4	0	12	.098	.178	.098	-16	-6	0	.932	-2	*77*	*118*	C-20	-0.8
MURPHY, MIKE Michael Jerome B 8.19.1888 Forestville, PA D 10.26.1952 Johnson City, NY BR/TR 5-9/170# d5.17																								
1912	StL N	1	1	0	0	0	0	0	1	0	0	0	.000	.000	.000	-99	0	0	—	0	*0*	*0*	/C	0.0
1916	Phi A	14	27	0	3	0	0	0	1	1	0	3	.111	.143	.111	-25	-4	0	.973	-3	51	75	C-12	-0.7
Total	2	15	28	0	3	0	0	0	2	1	0	3	.107	.138	.107	-28	-4	0	.973	-3	*50*	*74*	/C-13	-0.7
MURPHY, MORGAN Morgan Edward B 2.14.1867 E.Providence, RI D 10.3.1938 Providence, RI BR/TR 5-8/160# d4.22																								
1890	Bos P	68	246	38	56	10	2	2	32	24	2	31	.228	.301	.309	59	-15	16	.903	14	*154*	*83*	C-67/S-2,O(CF)3	0.3
1891	Bos AA	106	402	60	87	11	4	4	54	36	5	58	.216	.289	.294	68	-18	17	**.954**	**27**	***140***	*99*	*C-104/O-4(1-2-1)	1.5
1892	Cin N	74	234	29	46	8	2	2	24	25	1	57	.197	.277	.274	67	-9	4	.955	2	*118*	*69*	C-74	0.0
1893	Cin N	57	200	25	47	5	1	1	19	14	3	35	.235	.295	.285	53	-14	1	.932	-3	*110*	*77*	C-56/1	-1.0
1894	Cin N	76	261	42	70	9	0	1	37	26	1	36	.268	.337	.314	56	-19	6	.901	-6	*99*	*101*	C-75/S3	-1.5
1895	Cin N	25	82	15	22	2	0	0	16	11	0	8	.268	.355	.293	66	-4	6	.907	-1	*104*	*85*	C-25	-0.3
1896	StL N	49	175	12	45	5	2	0	11	8	0	14	.257	.290	.309	60	-11	1	.926	-6	*85*	*99*	C-48	-1.1
1897	StL N	63	211	13	36	2	0	0	12	6	1		.171	.197	.180	-0	-31	1	.946	-12	*68*	*125*	C-54/1-8	-3.4
1898	Pit N	5	16	0	2	0	0	0	2	1	1		.125	.176	.125	-14	-2	0	.957	1	*110*	*136*	/C-5	-0.1
	Phi N	25	86	6	17	3	0	0	11	6	1		.198	.258	.233	43	-6	0	.964	1	*111*	*118*	C-25	-0.3
	Year	30	102	6	19	3	0	0	13	7	1		.186	.245	.216	34	-9	0	.963	2	*111*	*121*	C-30	-0.4
1900	Phi N	11	36	2	10	0	1	0	3	0	0		.278	.278	.333	69	-2	0	.980	-0	*78*	*116*	C-11	-0.1
1901	Phi A	9	28	5	6	1	0	0	6	0	0		.214	.214	.250	27	-3	0	.929	-0	*107*	*79*	/C-8,1	-0.2
Total	11	568	1977	247	444	56	12	10	227	157	14	239	.225	.286	.280	53	-134	53	.936	16	*114*	*94*	C-552/1-10,O-5(1-3-1),S-3,3-2	-6.2
MURPHY, PAT Patrick J. B 1.2.1857 Auburn, MA D 5.16.1927 Worcester, MA TR 5-10/160# d9.2																								
1887	NY N	17	56	4	12	2	0	0	4	2	0	4	.214	.241	.250	38	-5	1	.847	-1			C-17	-0.3
1888	†NY N	28	106	11	18	1	0	0	4	6	0	11	.170	.214	.179	27	-9	3	.913	2			C-28	-0.4
1889	NY N	9	28	5	10	1	1	1	4	2	0	0	.357	.400	.571	170	2	0	.872	-1			/C-9	0.1
1890	NY N	32	119	14	28	5	1	0	9	14	1	13	.235	.321	.294	79	-3	3	.905	-4	*99*	*100*	C-29/O-3(1-1-1),S	-0.4
Total	4	86	309	34	68	9	2	1	21	24	1	28	.220	.278	.272	64	-15	7	.895	-4	*34*	*34*	/C-83,O-3(1-1-1),S	-1.0

Year	Tm Lg	G	AB	R	H	2B	3B	HR	RBI	BB-IB	HP	SO	AVG	OBP	SLG	AOPS	ABR	SB-CS	FA	FR	Rng	Thr	G at Pos	BFW
MURPHY, LARRY Patrick Lawrence B 3.17.1857 , , CAN D 10.6.1911 Indianapolis, IN BL 5-8/170# d5.30																								
1891	Was AA	101	400	73	106	15	3	1	35	63	5	27	.265	.372	.325	104	7	29	.874	-6	56	67	*O-101(69-3-30)	-0.1
MURPHY, DICK Richard Lee B 10.25.1931 Cincinnati, OH BL/TL 5-11/170# d6.13 Mil 1955																								
1954	Cin N	6	1	1	0	0	0	0	0	0	0	1	.000	.000	.000	-97	0	0-0	—	0			H	0.0
MURPHY, BUZZ Robert R. B 4.26.1895 Denver, CO D 5.11.1938 Denver, CO BL/TL 5-8.5/155# d7.14																								
1918	Bos N	9	32	6	12	2	3	1	9	3	0	5	.375	.429	.719	259	6	0	1.000	-1	89	0	/O-9(LF)	0.5
1919	Was A	79	252	19	66	7	4	0	28	19	5	32	.262	.326	.321	83	-6	5	.959	3	112	91	O-73(19-54-0)	-0.8
Total	2	88	284	25	78	9	7	1	37	22	5	37	.275	.338	.366	101	0	5	.961	2	110	82	/O-82(28-54-0)	-0.3
MURPHY, BILLY William Eugene B 5.7.1944 Pineville, LA BR/TR 6-1/190# d4.15																								
1966	NY N	84	135	15	31	4	1	3	13	7-0	1	34	.230	.271	.341	71	-6	1-2	.955	1	85	285	O-57(8-48-1)	-0.7
MURPHY, WILLIE William H. "Gentle Willie" B 3.23.1864 Springfield, MA BL 5-11/198# d5.1																								
1884	Cle N	42	168	18	38	3	3	1	9	1		23	.226	.231	.298	63	-8		.720	-7	72	0	O-42(34-3-5)	-1.5
	Was AA	5	21	3	10	0	0	0		1	2		.476	.542	.476	266	4		.700	0	0	0	/O-4(LF),3	0.4
Total	1	47	189	21	48	3	3	1	9	2	2	23	.254	.269	.317	83	-4		.718	-7	66	0	/O-46(38-3-5),3	-1.1
MURPHY, YALE William Henry "Tot" or "Midget" B 11.11.1869 Southville, MA D 2.14.1906 Southville, MA BL/TR 5-3/125# d4.19																								
1894	†NY N	75	283	65	77	6	2	0	28	52	0	23	.272	.385	.307	69	-12	28	.898	-10	87	63	S-49,O-21(1-0-20)/3-3,21	-1.5
1895	NY N	51	184	35	37	6	2	0	16	27	0	13	.201	.303	.255	46	-14	7	.944	-4	78	175	O-33(29-2-2)/S-8,3-8,2	-1.7
1897	NY N	5	8	1	0	0	0	0	1	2	0		.000	.200	.000	-46	-2	0	.800	-2	46	0	/S-3,2-2	-0.3
Total	3	131	475	101	114	12	4	0	45	81	0	36	.240	.351	.282	59	-28	35	.890	-15	87	64	/S-60,O-54(30-2-22),3-11,2-4,1	-3.5
MURRAY, TONY Anthony Joseph B 4.30.1904 Chicago, IL D 3.19.1974 Chicago, IL BR/TR 5-10.5/154# d10.6																								
1923	Chi N	2	4	0	1	0	0	0	0	0	1	0	.250	.400	.250	75	0	0-0	1.000	-0	82	0	/O-2(1-2-1)	0.0
MURRAY, CALVIN Calvin Duane B 7.30.1971 Dallas, TX BR/TR 5-11/190# d6.22																								
1999	SF N	15	19	1	5	2	0	0	5	2-0	0	4	.263	.333	.368	83	0	1-0	1.000	-1	66	0	/O-9(3-6-0)	-0.1
2000	†SF N	108	194	35	47	12	1	2	22	29-0	3	33	.242	.348	.345	83	-4	9-3	.980	0	108	61	*O-106(2-104-0)	-0.3
2001	SF N	106	326	54	80	14	2	6	25	32-0	3	57	.245	.319	.356	80	-10	8-8	.979	3	116	87	*O-104(CF)	-0.7
2002	Tex A	37	77	16	13	5	1	0	1	6-0	1	15	.169	.238	.260	31	-8	4-0	1.000	2	105	150	O-34(0-33-1)/D-2	-0.5
	SF N	11	12	0	0	0	0	0	0	1-0	0	2	.000	.077	.000	-81	-3	0-0	.917	1	122	458	O-10(5-4-3)	-0.3
Total	4	277	628	106	145	33	4	8	53	70-0	7	111	.231	.314	.334	72	-25	22-11	.981	5	111	95	O-263(10-251-4)/D-2	-1.9
MURRAY, EDDIE Eddie Clarence B 2.24.1956 Los Angeles, CA BB/TR 6-2/200# d4.7 C6 b-Rich HF2002																								
1977	Bal A	160	611	81	173	29	2	27	88	48-6	1	104	.283	.333	.470	125	19	0-1	.992	-3	70	108	*D-111,1-42/O-3(LF)	1.0
1978	Bal A☆	**161**	610	85	174	32	3	27	95	70-7	1	97	.285	.356	.480	143	35	6-5	.997	3	101	115	*1-157/3-3,D	2.8
1979	†Bal A	**159**	606	90	179	30	2	25	99	72-9	2	78	.295	.369	.475	132	28	10-2	.994	-1	96	109	*1-157/D-2	1.8
1980	Bal A	158	621	100	186	36	2	32	116	54-10	2	71	.300	.354	.519	138	32	7-2	.994	-9	76	115	*1-154/D	1.4
1981	Bal A★	99	378	57	111	21	2	**22**	**78**	40-10	1	43	.294	.360	.534	156	27	2-3	**.999**	11	**136**	110	1-99	3.1
1982	Bal A★	151	550	87	174	30	1	32	110	70-**18**	1	82	.316	.391	.549	157	44	7-2	**.997**	3	106	90	*1-149/D-2	3.8
1983	†Bal A★	156	582	115	178	30	3	33	111	86-13	3	90	.306	.393	.538	**158**	**48**	5-1	.993	4	109	104	*1-153/D-2	4.3
1984	Bal A★	**162**	588	97	180	26	3	29	110	**107-25**	2	87	.306	**.410**	.509	157	**51**	10-2	.992	10	124	114	*1-159/D-3	5.2
1985	Bal A★	156	583	111	173	37	1	31	124	84-12	2	68	.297	.383	.523	151	43	5-2	.987	12	128	110	*1-154/D-2	4.5
1986	Bal A☆	137	495	61	151	25	1	17	84	78-7	0	49	.305	.396	.463	136	28	3-0	.989	-2	96	101	*1-119,D-16	1.9
1987	Bal A	160	618	89	171	28	3	30	91	73-6	0	80	.277	.352	.477	121	18	1-2	.993	12	127	112	*1-156/D-4	1.9
1988	Bal A	**161**	603	75	171	27	2	28	84	75-8	0	78	.284	.361	.474	136	30	5-2	.989	10	137	111	*1-103,D-58	3.1
1989	LA N	**160**	594	66	147	29	1	20	88	87-24	2	85	.247	.342	.401	115	13	7-2	**.996**	10	118	116	*1-159/3-2	1.3
1990	LA N	155	558	96	184	22	3	26	95	82-**21**	1	64	.330	.414	.520	160	49	8-5	.992	1	99	91	*1-150	4.0
1991	LA N★	153	576	69	150	23	1	19	96	55-17	0	74	.260	.321	.403	106	4	10-3	.995	6	110	100	*1-149/3	0.0
1992	NY N	156	551	64	144	37	2	16	93	66-8	0	74	.261	.336	.423	117	13	4-2	.991	-5	87	101	*1-154	-0.2
1993	NY N	154	610	77	174	28	1	27	100	40-4	0	61	.285	.325	.467	112	8	2-2	.988	2	108	101	*1-154	-0.5
1994	Cle A	108	433	57	110	21	1	17	76	31-6	0	53	.254	.302	.425	85	-11	8-4	.988	-2	76	111	D-82,1-26	-2.0
1995	†Cle A	113	436	68	141	21	0	21	82	39-5	0	65	.323	.375	.516	128	18	5-1	.984	3	162	85	D-95,1-18	1.2
1996	Cle A	88	336	33	88	9	1	12	45	34-2	0	45	.262	.326	.402	84	-9	3-0	1.000	0	137	0	D-87/1	-1.3
	†Bal A	64	230	36	59	12	0	10	34	27-4	0	42	.257	.327	.439	94	-2	1-0	—	0	0	0	D-62	-0.6
	Year	152	566	69	147	21	1	22	79	61-6	0	87	.260	.327	.417	88	-11	4-0	1.000	0	137	0	*D-149/1	-1.9
1997	Ana A	46	160	13	35	7	0	3	15	13-0	0	24	.219	.273	.319	55	-11	1-0	—	0	0	0	D-45	-1.3
	LA N	9	7	0	2	0	0	0	3	2-0	0	2	.286	.444	.286	104	0	0-0	—	0			/H	0.0
Total	21	3026	11336	1627	3255	560	35	504	1917	1333-222	18	1516	.287	.359	.476	130	475	110-43	.993	66	108	106	*1-2413,D-573/3-6,O-3(LF)	35.4
MURRAY, ED Edward Francis B 5.8.1895 Mystic, CT D 11.8.1970 Cheyenne, WY BR/TR 5-6/145# d6.24																								
1917	StL A	1	1	0	0	0	0	0	0	0	0	1	.000	.000	.000	-99	0	0	—	-0	0	0	/S	0.0
MURRAY, GLENN Glenn Everett B 11.23.1970 Manning, SC BR/TR 6-2/225# d5.10																								
1996	Phi N	38	97	8	19	3	0	2	6	7-0	0	36	.196	.250	.289	41	-9	1-1	1.000	1	117	66	O-27(1-2-24)	-0.8
MURRAY, JIM James Oscar B 1.16.1878 Galveston, TX D 4.25.1945 Galveston, TX BR/TL 5-10/180# d9.2																								
1902	Chi N	12	47	3	8	0	0	0	1	2	0		.170	.204	.170	16	-5	0	1.000	-1	64	0	O-12(RF)	-0.6
1911	StL A	31	102	8	19	5	0	3	11	5	0		.186	.224	.324	54	-7	0	.935	0	106	93	O-25(0-1-24)	-0.8
1914	Bos N	39	112	10	26	4	2	0	12	6	1	24	.232	.277	.304	73	-4	2	.941	-4	75	32	O-32(18-1-13)	-1.0
Total	3	82	261	21	53	9	2	3	24	13	1	24	.203	.244	.287	56	-16	2	.949	-5	86	51	/O-69(18-2-49)	-2.4
MURRAY, MIAH Jeremiah J. B 1.1.1865 Boston, MA D 1.11.1922 Boston, MA BR/TR 5-11.5/170# d5.17 U1																								
1884	Pro N	8	27	1	5	0	0	0	1	1		8	.185	.214	.185	27	-2		.836	-4			/C-7,O(CF)1	-0.5
1885	Lou AA	12	43	4	8	0	0	0	3	2	1		.186	.239	.186	36	-3		.863	-1			C-12/1-2	-0.2
1888	Was N	12	42	1	4	1	0	0	3	1	0	7	.095	.116	.119	-27	-6	0	.912	0			C-10/1-2	-0.5
1891	Was AA	2	8	0	0	0	0	0	0	0	0	1	.000	.000	.000	-99	-2	0	1.000	1	*87*	*63*	/C-2	-0.1
Total	4	34	120	6	17	1	0	0	7	4	1	16	.142	.176	.150	3	-13	0	.884	-3	*7*	*5*	/C-31,1-5,O(CF)	-1.3
MURRAY, RED John Joseph B 3.4.1884 Arnot, PA D 12.4.1958 Sayre, PA BR/TR 5-10.5/190# d6.16																								
1906	StL N	46	144	18	37	9	7	1	16	9	1		.257	.305	.438	137	5	5	.962	-1	194	0	O-34(4-11-20)/C-7	0.4
1907	StL N	132	485	46	127	10	10	7	46	24	3		.262	.301	.367	113	4	23	.935	3	132	82	*O-131(124-1-6)	-0.2
1908	StL N	**154**	593	64	167	19	15	7	62	37	8		.282	.332	.400	140	24	48	.914	-3	118	84	*O-154(0-89-67)	1.7
1909	NY N	149	570	74	150	15	12	**7**	91	45	2		.263	.319	.368	112	5	48	.947	2	142	22	*O-149(29-0-120)	0.1
1910	NY N	149	553	78	153	27	8	4	87	52	6	51	.277	.345	.376	110	7	57	.948	6	103	135	*O-148(24-0-124)	0.7
1911	†NY N	140	488	70	142	27	15	3	78	43	5	37	.291	.354	.426	114	8	48	.954	-6	95	75	*O-131(50-2-83)	-0.4
1912	†NY N	143	549	83	152	26	20	3	92	27	8	45	.277	.320	.413	97	-6	38	**.968**	5	109	101	*O-143(27-0-117)	-0.8
1913	†NY N	147	520	70	139	21	3	2	59	34	6	28	.267	.320	.331	85	-10	35-25	.965	9	110	127	*O-147(32-1-116)	-1.0
1914	NY N	86	139	19	31	6	3	0	23	9	0	7	.223	.270	.309	75	-5	11	1.000	0	114	48	O-49(16-0-34)	-0.7
1915	NY N	45	127	12	28	1	2	3	11	7	0	15	.220	.261	.331	83	-4	2-3	.959	-0	96	111	O-34(1-30-3)	-0.7
	Chi N	51	144	20	43	6	1	0	11	8	1	8	.299	.340	.354	110	2	6-5	.966	2	116	91	O-40(7-11-25)/2	0.2
	Year	96	271	32	71	7	3	3	22	15	1	23	.262	.303	.343	98	-2	8-8	.963	2	107	100	O-74(8-41-28)/2	-0.5
1917	NY N	22	22	1	1	1	0	0	3	4	0	3	.045	.192	.091	-12	-3	0	1.000	-0	117	0	O-11(4-4-3)/C	-0.3
Total	11	1264	4334	555	1170	168	96	37	579	299	40	194	.270	.323	.379	108	27	321-33	.950	18	118	86	*O-1171(318-149-718)/C-8,2	-1.0
MURRAY, LARRY Larry B 4.1.1953 Chicago, IL BB/TR 5-11/179# d9.7																								
1974	NY A	6	1	1	0	0	0	0	0	0-0	0	0	.000	.000	.000	-99	0	0-1	—	-0	0	0	/O-3(1-1-2)	-0.1
1975	NY A	6	1	1	0	0	0	0	0	0-0	0	0	.000	.000	.000	-99	0	0-0	1.000	-0	66	0	/O-4(2-1-1)	0.0
1976	NY A	8	10	2	1	0	0	0	2	1-0	0	2	.100	.182	.100	-16	-1	2-0	1.000	0	84	340	/O-7(0-6-1)	-0.1
1977	Oak A	90	162	19	29	5	2	1	9	17-2	0	36	.179	.257	.253	40	-14	12-3	.992	0	101	83	O-78(27-36-22)/SD	-1.3
1978	Oak A	11	12	1	1	0	0	0	0	3-0	0	2	.083	.267	.083	3	-1	0-0	1.000	-0	90	0	/O-6(5-0-1)	-0.2
1979	Oak A	105	226	25	42	11	2	2	20	28-1	0	34	.186	.275	.279	53	-15	6-6	.963	7	122	142	O-90(24-12-57)/2-3	-1.2
Total	6	226	412	49	73	16	4	3	31	49-3	0	74	.177	.264	.257	44	-31	20-10	.975	7	111	119	O-188(59-56-84)/2-3,D-3,S	-2.9

Year	Tm Lg	G	AB	R	H	2B	3B	HR	RBI	BB-IB	HP	SO	AVG	OBP	SLG	AOPS	ABR	SB-CS	FA	FR	Rng	Thr	G at Pos	BFW
MURRAY, RAY Raymond Lee "Deacon" B 10.12.1917 Spring Hope, NC D 4.9.2003 Fort Worth, TX BR/TR 6-3/204# d4.25																								
1948	Cle A	4	4	0	0	0	0	0	0	0	0	3	.000	.000	.000	-99	-1	0-0	—	0			H	-0.1
1950	Cle A	55	139	16	38	8	2	1	13	12	0	13	.273	.331	.381	85	-4	1-0	.972	-1	*122*	*116*	C-45	-0.3
1951	Cle A	1	1	0	1	0	0	0	1	0	0	0	1.000	1.000	1.000	468	1	0-0	1.000	1	*0*	*0*	/C	0.1
	Phi A	40	122	10	26	6	0	0	13	14	0	8	.213	.294	.262	50	-8	0-0	.985	1	*136*	*147*	C-39	-0.6
	Year	41	123	10	27	6	0	0	14	14	0	8	.220	.299	.268	53	-8	0-0	.986	1	*134*	*145*	C-40	-0.5
1952	Phi A	44	136	14	28	5	0	1	10	9	0	13	.206	.255	.265	42	-11	0-0	.995	4	*129*	*191*	C-42	-0.4
1953	Phi A	84	268	25	76	14	3	6	41	18	1	25	.284	.331	.425	99	-1	0-0	.989	4	*148*	*127*	C-78	0.7
1954	Bal A	22	61	4	15	4	1	0	2	2	0	5	.246	.270	.344	73	-3	0-0	.989	0	*81*	*132*	C-21	-0.2
Total	6	250	731	69	184	37	6	8	80	55	1	67	.252	.305	.352	75	-27	1-0	.987	8	*132*	*141*	C-226	-0.8
MURRAY, RICH Richard Dale B 7.6.1957 Los Angeles, CA BR/TR 6-4/195# d6.7 b-Eddie																								
1980	SF N	53	194	19	42	8	2	4	24	11-1	0	48	.216	.259	.340	67	-9	2-1	.987	1	113	78	1-53	-1.2
1983	SF N	4	10	0	2	0	0	0	1	0-0	0	3	.200	.200	.200	11	-1	0-0	1.000	-0	63	57	/1-3	-0.2
Total	2	57	204	19	44	8	2	4	25	11-1	0	51	.216	.256	.333	65	-10	2-1	.988	1	111	77	/1-56	-1.4
MURRAY, BOBBY Robert Hayes B 7.4.1894 St.Albans, VT D 1.4.1979 Nashua, NH BL/TR 5-7/155# d9.24																								
1923	Was A	10	37	2	7	1	0	0	2	1	0	4	.189	.211	.216	13	-5	1-0	1.000	2	121	0	3-10	-0.2
MURRAY, TOM Thomas W. B 1866 Paterson, NJ BR 5-7/150# d6.20																								
1894	Phi N	1	2	0	0	0	0	0	0	0	0	2	.000	.000	.000	-99	-1	0	.833	-1	36	0	/S	-0.1
MURRAY, BILL William Allenwood "Dasher" B 9.6.1893 Vinalhaven, ME D 9.14.1943 Boston, MA BB/TR 5-11/165# d6.27																								
1917	Was A	8	21	2	3	0	1	0	4	2	0	2	.143	.217	.238	39	-2	1	.889	-2	79	85	/2-6,S	-0.4
MURRELL, IVAN Ivan Augustus (Peters) B 4.24.1945 Almirante, Panama BR/TR 6-2/196# d9.28																								
1963	Hou N	2	5	1	1	0	0	0	0	0-0	0	2	.200	.200	.200	17	-1	0-0	1.000	0	106	0	/O-2(CF)	-0.1
1964	Hou N	10	14	1	2	1	0	0	1	0-0	0	6	.143	.133	.214	-1	-2	0-0	1.000	-0	60	0	/O-5(4-0-1)	-0.2
1967	Hou N	10	29	2	9	0	0	0	1	1-1	0	9	.310	.333	.310	88	-1	1-0	.846	-1	100	0	/O-6(5-0-1)	-0.2
1968	Hou N	32	59	3	6	1	1	0	3	1-0	0	17	.102	.117	.153	-20	-9	0-0	.931	2	103	312	O-15(4-2-9)	-0.9
1969	SD N	111	247	19	63	10	6	3	25	11-1	2	65	.255	.291	.381	91	-5	3-4	.959	3	114	82	O-72(23-41-14)/1-2	-0.5
1970	SD N	125	347	43	85	9	3	12	35	17-5	4	93	.245	.287	.392	84	-10	9-7	.970	5	109	133	*O-101(61-24-20)/1	-1.1
1971	SD N	103	255	23	60	6	3	7	24	7-1	3	60	.235	.263	.365	82	-8	5-2	.978	2	100	47	O-72(55-16-2)	-1.0
1972	SD N	5	7	0	1	0	0	0	1	0-0	0	3	.143	.143	.143	-20	-1	0-0	1.000	0	106	0	/O(RF)	-0.1
1973	SD N	93	210	23	48	13	1	9	21	2-0	0	52	.229	.236	.429	87	-6	2-0	.959	2	101	95	O-37(10-18-12),1-24	-0.6
1974	Atl N	73	133	11	33	1	1	2	12	5-1	0	35	.248	.273	.316	62	-7	0-0	.983	3	130	149	O-32(13-9-13),1-13	-0.6
Total	10	564	1306	126	308	41	15	33	123	44-9	9	342	.236	.265	.366	77	-50	20-13	.965	16	108	104	O-343(175-112-73)/1-40	-5.3
MURTAUGH, DANNY Daniel Edward B 10.8.1917 Chester, PA D 12.2.1976 Chester, PA BR/TR 5-9/165# d7.6 Mil 1943-45 M15 C2																								
1941	Phi N	85	347	34	76	8	1	0	11	26	1	31	.219	.275	.248	50	-24	**18**	.978	3	98	86	2-85/S	-1.6
1942	Phi N	144	506	48	122	16	4	0	27	49	2	39	.241	.311	.289	80	-13	13	.939	8	101	87	S-60,3-53,2-32	0.3
1943	Phi N	113	451	65	123	17	4	1	35	57	2	23	.273	.357	.335	104	4	4	.974	3	99	104	*2-113	1.5
1946	Phi N	6	19	1	4	1	0	1	3	2	0	2	.211	.286	.421	102	0	0	.958	-2	72	0	/2-6	-0.2
1947	Bos N	3	8	0	1	0	0	0	0	1	0	2	.125	.222	.125	-6	-1	0	1.000	-0	91	71	/2-2,3-2	-0.1
1948	Pit N	146	514	56	149	21	5	1	71	60	1	40	.290	.365	.356	94	-2	10	.979	3	101	111	*2-146	0.9
1949	Pit N	75	236	16	48	7	2	2	24	29	0	17	.203	.291	.275	51	-16	2	.975	2	95	120	2-74	-1.0
1950	Pit N	118	367	34	108	20	5	2	37	47	1	42	.294	.376	.392	99	1	2	.976	3	104	103	*2-108	0.9
1951	Pit N	77	151	9	30	7	0	1	11	16	2	19	.199	.284	.265	47	-11	0-0	.970	-0	98	105	2-65/3-3	-0.9
Total	9	767	2599	263	661	97	21	8	219	287	9	215	.254	.331	.317	81	-62	49-0	.975	19	100	102	2-631/S-61,3-58	-0.2
MUSER, TONY Anthony Joseph B 8.1.1947 Van Nuys, CA BL/TL 6-2/190# d9.14 M6 C11																								
1969	Bos A	2	9	0	1	0	0	0	1	1-0	0	1	.111	.200	.111	-10	-1	0-0	1.000	1	226	174	/1-2	-0.1
1971	Chi A	11	16	2	5	0	1	0	0	1-0	0	1	.313	.353	.438	119	0	0-0	.963	0	182	44	/1-4	0.0
1972	Chi A	44	61	6	17	2	2	1	9	2-0	0	6	.279	.302	.426	113	0	1-1	.986	-1	83	97	1-29/O(RF)	-0.2
1973	Chi A	109	309	38	88	14	3	4	30	33-0	0	36	.285	.352	.388	105	3	8-4	.992	-3	86	106	1-89,D-13/O-2(LF)	-0.6
1974	Chi A	103	206	16	60	5	1	1	18	6-0	1	22	.291	.313	.340	86	-4	1-4	.998	-4	51	108	1-80,D-13	-1.5
1975	Chi A	43	111	11	27	3	0	0	6	7-1	0	8	.243	.286	.270	58	-6	2-1	.993	2	121	125	1-41	-0.7
	Bal A	80	82	11	26	3	0	0	11	8-0	0	9	.317	.374	.354	115	2	0-0	.996	-0	93	129	1-62	0.0
	Year	123	193	22	53	6	0	0	17	15-1	0	17	.275	.324	.306	83	-4	2-1	.994	1	109	127	*1-103	-0.7
1976	Bal A	136	326	25	74	7	1	1	30	21-4	0	34	.227	.270	.264	62	-16	1-1	.991	3	**121**	106	*1-109,O-12(8-4-0),D-10	-2.2
1977	Bal A	120	118	14	27	6	0	0	7	13-5	0	16	.229	.301	.280	65	-5	1-2	.992	1	136	199	1-77,O-11(5-6-0)/D	-0.6
1978	Mil A	15	30	0	4	1	1	0	5	3-0	0	5	.133	.212	.233	25	-3	0-0	.988	-0	95	61	1-12	-0.4
Total	9	663	1268	123	329	41	9	7	117	95-10	1	138	.259	.309	.323	82	-30	14-13	.992	-2	99	115	1-505/D-37,O-26(15-10-1)	-6.3
MUSIAL, STAN Stanley Frank "Stan The Man" B 11.21.1920 Donora, PA BL/TL 6/175# d9.17 Mil 1945 HF1969																								
1941	StL N	12	47	8	20	4	0	1	7	2	0	1	.426	.449	.574	175	5	1	1.000	-0	93	113	O-11(3-0-8)	0.4
1942	†StL N	140	467	87	147	32	10	10	72	62	2	25	.315	.397	.490	148	30	6	.984	7	**117**	74	*O-135(133-2-2)	3.2
1943	†StL N★	**157**	617	108	**220**	**48**	**20**	13	81	72	2	18	**.357**	**.425**	**.562**	**176**	**61**	9	.982	5	108	88	*O-155(34-10-117)	**5.7**
1944	†StL N★	146	568	112	**197**	**51**	14	12	94	90	5	28	.347	**.440**	**.549**	**174**	**61**	7	.987	3	105	99	*O-146(1-38-124)	**5.5**
1946	†StL N★	**156**	624	**124**	**228**	**50**	**20**	16	103	73	3	31	**.365**	.434	**.587**	**180**	**66**	7	.989	-3	83	135	*1-114,O-42(LF)	**5.8**
1947	StL N★	149	587	113	183	30	13	19	95	80	4	24	.312	.398	.504	132	28	4	.994	-6	81	118	*1-149	1.6
1948	StL N★	**155**	611	**135**	**230**	**46**	**18**	39	**131**	79	3	34	**.376**	**.450**	**.702**	**196**	**82**	7	.981	-2	98	85	*O-155(41-64-76)/1-2	**7.2**
1949	StL N★	**157**	612	128	**207**	**41**	**13**	36	123	107	2	38	.338	**.438**	.624	174	67	3	**.991**	-10	89	74	*O-156(3-72-117)/1	5.1
1950	StL N★	146	555	105	192	41	7	28	109	87	3	36	**.346**	.437	**.596**	**161**	**53**	5	.964	-7	91	39	O-77(56-14-10),1-69	3.8
1951	StL N★	152	578	**124**	205	30	**12**	32	108	98	1	40	**.355**	.449	.614	**182**	**70**	4-5	.974	2	102	150	O-91(84-10-1),1-60	6.1
1952	StL N★	**154**	578	**105**	**194**	**42**	6	21	91	96	2	29	**.336**	.432	**.538**	**167**	**58**	7-7	.987	-10	94	49	*O-129(21-106-9),1-25/P	4.2
1953	StL N★	**157**	593	127	200	**53**	9	30	113	**105**	0	32	.337	**.437**	.609	169	**66**	3-4	.984	-9	92	66	*O-157(141-9-26)	4.4
1954	StL N★	**153**	591	**120**	195	**41**	9	35	126	103	4	39	.330	.428	.607	166	61	1-7	**.990**	-5	92	96	*O-152(8-0-147),1-10	4.7
1955	StL N★	**154**	562	97	179	30	5	33	108	80-19	**8**	39	.319	.408	.566	156	48	5-4	.992	7	**127**	99	*1-110,O-51(21-0-33)	4.5
1956	StL N★	**156**	594	87	184	33	6	27	**109**	75-15	3	39	.310	.386	.522	142	37	2-0	.993	6	**124**	**119**	*1-103,O-53(3-0-51)	3.6
1957	StL N★	134	502	82	176	38	3	29	102	66-**19**	2	34	**.351**	**.422**	.612	172	54	1-1	.992	0	101	**125**	*1-130	4.6
1958	StL N★	135	472	64	159	35	2	17	62	72-**26**	1	26	.337	.423	.528	145	35	0-0	.989	7	**122**	111	*1-124	3.5
1959	StL N★	115	341	37	87	13	2	14	44	60-11	0	25	.255	.364	.428	104	4	0-2	.990	4	116	106	1-90/O-3(LF)	0.2
1960	StL N★	116	331	49	91	17	1	17	63	41-7	2	34	.275	.354	.486	118	9	1-1	.990	-2	96	44	O-59(53-0-6),1-29	0.2
1961	StL N★	123	372	46	107	22	4	15	70	52-17	1	35	.288	.371	.489	116	10	0-0	**.994**	4	102	140	*O-103(LF)	0.9
1962	StL N★	135	433	57	143	18	1	19	82	64-4	3	46	.330	.416	.508	135	24	3-0	.977	-5	88	78	*O-119(97-0-23)	1.4
1963	StL N★	124	337	34	86	10	2	12	58	35-9	2	43	.255	.325	.404	100	1	2-0	.968	-2	101	22	O-96(LF)	-0.6
Total	22	3026	10972	1949	3630	725	177	475	1951	1599-127	53	696	.331	.417	.559	157	930	78-31	.984	-16	98	82	*O-1890(943-325-750),*1-1016/P	76.0
MUSSER, DANNY William Daniel B 9.5.1905 Zion, PA D 3.2.2000 Upper Sandusky, OH BL/TR 5-9.5/160# d9.18																								
1932	Was A	1	2	0	1	0	0	0	0	0	0	0	.500	.500	.500	162	0	0-0	—	-0	0	0	/3	0.0
MYATT, GEORGE George Edward "Mercury", "Stud" or "Foghorn" B 6.14.1914 Denver, CO D 9.14.2000 Orlando, FL BL/TR 5-11/167# d8.16 M2 C23																								
1938	NY N	43	170	27	52	2	1	3	10	14	1	13	.306	.362	.382	104	1	10	.919	5	108	130	S-24,3-19	0.9
1939	NY N	22	53	7	10	2	0	0	3	6	0	6	.189	.271	.226	35	-5	2	.907	0	108	124	3-14	-0.4
1943	Was A	42	53	11	13	3	0	0	3	13	0	7	.245	.394	.302	109	2	3-0	.930	-1	113	59	2-11/S-2,3-2	0.2
1944	Was A	140	538	86	153	19	6	0	40	54	7	44	.284	.357	.342	105	5	26-10	.957	-20	87	93	*2-121,S-15/O-3(RF)	-0.6
1945	Was A	133	490	81	145	17	7	1	39	63	2	43	.296	.378	.365	127	19	30-11	.972	-15	88	88	2-94,O-32(1-0-31)/3-6,S	1.0
1946	Was A	15	34	7	8	1	0	0	4	2	1	3	.235	.297	.265	61	-2	1-1	.900	-2	85	68	/3-7,2-2	-0.4
1947	Was A	12	7	1	0	0	0	0	0	4	0	4	.000	.364	.000	6	-1	0-0	1.000	0	152	0	/2	-0.1
Total	7	407	1345	220	381	44	14	4	99	156	11	120	.283	.362	.346	108	19	72-22	.962	-32	89	89	2-229/3-48,S-42,O-35(1-0-34)	0.6
MYATT, GLENN Glenn Calvin B 7.9.1897 Argenta, AR D 8.9.1969 Houston, TX BL/TR 5-11/165# d4.15																								
1920	Phi A	70	196	14	49	8	3	0	18	12	0	22	.250	.293	.321	62	-11	1-3	.900	-3	77	151	O-37(1-0-36),C-22	-1.5
1921	Phi A	44	69	6	14	2	0	0	5	6	0	7	.203	.267	.232	28	-8	1-0	.939	0	*97*	*139*	C-27	-0.6
1923	Cle A	92	220	36	63	7	6	3	40	16	1	18	.286	.338	.414	97	-2	0-2	.934	-5	*122*	*53*	C-69	-0.4
1924	Cle A	105	342	55	117	22	7	8	73	33	1	12	.342	.402	.518	134	17	6-1	.978	-9	*89*	*76*	C-95	1.4

Year	Tm Lg	G	AB	R	H	2B	3B	HR	RBI	BB-IB	HP	SO	AVG	OBP	SLG	AOPS	ABR	SB-CS	FA	FR	Rng	Thr	G at Pos	BFW
1925	Cle A	106	358	51	97	15	9	11	54	29	2	24	.271	.329	.455	97	-5	3-1	.973	-9	*120*	*66*	C-98/O(LF)	-0.7
1926	Cle A	56	117	14	29	5	2	0	13	13	0	13	.248	.323	.325	69	-5	1-0	1.000	1	*162*	*61*	C-35	-0.2
1927	Cle A	55	94	15	23	6	0	2	8	12	1	7	.245	.336	.372	83	-2	1-1	.978	2	*118*	*153*	C-26	0.1
1928	Cle A	58	125	9	36	7	2	1	15	13	0	13	.288	.355	.400	97	0	0-2	.967	-5	*88*	*82*	C-30	-0.4
1929	Cle A	59	129	14	30	4	1	1	17	7	1	5	.233	.277	.302	47	-11	0-1	.976	-1	*87*	*129*	C-41	-0.9
1930	Cle A	86	265	30	78	23	2	2	37	18	1	17	.294	.342	.419	88	-4	2-3	.977	-5	*81*	*97*	C-71	-0.5
1931	Cle A	65	195	21	48	14	2	1	29	21	0	13	.246	.319	.354	73	-8	2-1	.991	-2	*103*	*127*	C-53	-0.6
1932	Cle A	82	252	45	62	12	1	8	46	27	3	21	.246	.326	.397	81	-7	2-2	.988	-3	*116*	*75*	C-65	-0.7
1933	Cle A	40	77	10	18	4	0	0	7	15	2	8	.234	.372	.286	73	-2	0-1	.965	0	*129*	*162*	C-27	-0.1
1934	Cle A	36	107	18	34	6	1	0	12	13	0	5	.318	.392	.393	101	1	1-0	.980	-1	*114*	*64*	C-34	0.2
1935	Cle A	10	36	1	3	1	0	0	2	4	0	3	.083	.175	.111	-24	-7	0-0	1.000	-1	*101*	*75*	C-10	-0.7
	NY N	13	18	2	4	0	1	1	6	0	0	3	.222	.222	.500	90	-1	0	1.000	-1	*66*	*0*	/C-4	-0.1
1936	Det A	27	78	5	17	1	0	0	5	9	0	4	.218	.299	.231	32	-8	0-0	1.000	-1	*114*	*119*	C-27	-0.7
Total	16	1004	2678	346	722	137	37	38	387	248	12	195	.270	.334	.391	85	-63	20-18	.974	-41	*107*	*90*	C-734/O-38(2-0-36)	-6.4

MYER, BUDDY Charles Solomon B 3.16.1904 Ellisville, MS D 10.31.1974 Baton Rouge, LA BL/TR 5-10.5/163# d9.26

Year	Tm Lg	G	AB	R	H	2B	3B	HR	RBI	BB-IB	HP	SO	AVG	OBP	SLG	AOPS	ABR	SB-CS	FA	FR	Rng	Thr	G at Pos	BFW
1925	†Was A	4	8	1	2	0	0	0	0	0	0	1	.250	.250	.250	28	-1	0-0	1.000	-1	66	0	/S-4	-0.2
1926	Was A	132	434	66	132	18	6	1	62	45	0	19	.304	.370	.380	98	-1	10-11	.928	-17	93	76	*S-118/3-8	-0.7
1927	Was A	15	51	7	11	1	0	0	7	8	0	3	.216	.322	.235	47	-4	3-1	.933	-2	90	115	S-15	-0.4
	Bos A	133	469	59	135	22	11	2	47	48	4	15	.288	.359	.394	97	-2	9-5	.940	6	102	105	*S-101,3-14,O-10(LF)/2	1.4
	Year	148	520	66	146	23	11	2	54	56	4	18	.281	.355	.379	92	-6	12-6	.939	4	100	106	*S-116,3-14,O-10(LF)/2	1.0
1928	Bos A	147	536	78	168	26	6	1	44	53	4	28	.313	.379	.390	104	5	**30**-16	.967	6	108	**133**	*3-144	2.0
1929	Was A	141	563	80	169	29	10	3	82	63	2	33	.300	.373	.403	99	0	19-7	.958	-12	93	92	2-88,3-53	-0.4
1930	Was A	138	541	97	164	18	8	2	61	58	2	31	.303	.373	.377	90	-7	14-11	.965	-14	92	**114**	*2-134/O-2(1-0-1)	-1.6
1931	Was A	139	591	114	173	33	11	4	56	58	4	42	.293	.360	.406	100	1	11-14	**.984**	-13	90	109	*2-137	-0.6
1932	Was A	143	577	120	161	38	16	5	52	69	4	33	.279	.360	.426	104	4	12-7	.975	-17	92	**112**	*2-139	-0.4
1933	†Was A	131	530	95	160	29	15	4	61	60	1	29	.302	.374	.436	115	12	6-8	.978	1	99	127	*2-129	1.8
1934	Was A	139	524	103	160	33	8	3	57	102	1	32	.305	.419	.416	121	23	6-6	.975	-8	100	107	*2-135	2.1
1935	Was A☆	151	616	115	215	36	11	5	100	96	4	40	**.349**	.440	.468	139	42	7-6	.979	7	95	**123**	*2-151	5.3
1936	Was A	51	156	31	42	5	2	0	15	42	1	11	.269	.427	.327	94	2	7-2	.985	3	100	108	2-43	0.7
1937	Was A☆	125	430	54	126	16	10	1	65	78	5	41	.293	.407	.384	105	7	2-6	.966	-16	90	107	*2-119/O(LF)	-0.2
1938	Was A	127	437	79	147	22	8	6	71	93	1	32	.336	.454	.465	140	34	9-5	**.982**	-3	100	105	*2-121	3.5
1939	Was A	83	258	33	78	10	3	1	32	40	0	18	.302	.396	.376	106	4	4-1	.968	3	100	113	2-65	1.1
1940	Was A	71	210	28	61	14	4	0	29	34	0	10	.290	.389	.395	111	5	6-3	.967	6	110	86	2-54	1.3
1941	Was A	53	107	14	27	3	1	0	9	18	0	10	.252	.360	.299	80	-2	2-0	.982	-3	87	83	2-24	-0.4
Total	17	1923	7038	1174	2131	353	130	38	850	965	33	428	.303	.389	.406	108	122	157-109	.974	-74	96	110	*2-1340,S-238,3-219/O-13(12-0-1)	14.3

MYERS, GEORGE George D. B 11.13.1860 Buffalo, NY D 12.14.1926 Buffalo, NY BR/TR 5-8/170# d5.2

Year	Tm Lg	G	AB	R	H	2B	3B	HR	RBI	BB-IB	HP	SO	AVG	OBP	SLG	AOPS	ABR	SB-CS	FA	FR	Rng	Thr	G at Pos	BFW
1884	Buf N	78	325	34	59	9	2	2	32	13		33	.182	.213	.240	41	-22		.837	-14			C-49,O-34(16-18-0)	-3.0
1885	Buf N	89	326	40	67	7	2	0	19	23		40	.206	.258	.239	60	-14		.899	-4			C-69,O-23(0-21-1)	-1.3
1886	StL N	79	295	26	56	7	3	0	27	18		42	.190	.236	.234	46	-18	6	.928	-5			C-72/O-6(0-5-1),3	-1.6
1887	Ind N	69	235	25	51	8	1	1	20	22	5	7	.217	.298	.272	61	-11	26	.929	-8			C-50,O-15(3-7-5)/1-6,3	-1.3
1888	Ind N	66	248	36	59	9	0	2	16	16	3	14	.238	.292	.298	87	-3	28	.929	-4			C-47,3-14,O-10(2-1-7)/1	-0.3
1889	Ind N	43	149	22	29	3	0	0	12	17	4	13	.195	.294	.215	42	-11	12	.909	0	158	106	O-23(6-17-0),C-18/1	-0.9
Total	6	424	1578	183	321	43	8	5	126	109	12	149	.203	.260	.250	56	-79	72	.901	-34			C-305,O-111(27-69-14)/3-16,1-8	-8.4

MYERS, GREG Gregory Richard B 4.14.1966 Riverside, CA BL/TR 6-2/205# d9.12

Year	Tm Lg	G	AB	R	H	2B	3B	HR	RBI	BB-IB	HP	SO	AVG	OBP	SLG	AOPS	ABR	SB-CS	FA	FR	Rng	Thr	G at Pos	BFW
1987	Tor A	7	9	1	1	0	0	0	0	0-0	0	3	.111	.111	.111	-40	-2	0-0	1.000	2	0	0	/C-7	0.0
1989	Tor A	17	44	0	5	2	0	0	1	2-0	0	9	.114	.152	.159	-12	-7	0-1	1.000	2	103	84	C-11/D-6	-0.4
1990	Tor A	87	250	33	59	7	1	5	22	22-0	0	33	.236	.293	.332	75	-9	0-1	.993	1	118	105	C-87	-0.4
1991	Tor A	107	309	25	81	22	0	8	36	21-4	0	45	.262	.306	.411	94	-3	0-0	.979	-8	77	89	*C-104	-0.6
1992	Tor A	22	61	4	14	6	0	1	13	5-0	0	5	.230	.279	.377	81	-1	0-0	.991	-1	61	110	C-18/D	-0.2
	Cal A	8	17	0	4	1	0	0	0	0-0	0	6	.235	.235	.294	47	-1	0-0	1.000	0	51	57	/C-8	-0.1
	Year	30	78	4	18	7	0	1	13	5-0	0	11	.231	.271	.359	74	-3	0-0	.993	-1	59	98	C-26/D	-0.3
1993	Cal A	108	290	27	74	10	0	7	40	17-2	2	47	.255	.298	.362	75	-11	3-3	.986	-7	71	102	C-97/D-2	-1.3
1994	Cal A	45	126	10	31	6	0	2	8	10-3	0	27	.246	.299	.341	64	-7	0-2	.991	1	123	161	C-41/D	-0.4
1995	Cal A	85	273	35	71	12	2	9	38	17-3	1	49	.260	.304	.418	87	-7	0-1	.989	3	131	86	C-61,D-16	-0.1
1996	Min A	97	329	37	94	22	3	6	47	19-3	0	52	.286	.320	.426	86	-8	0-0	.985	-2	121	100	C-90	-0.4
1997	Min A	62	165	24	44	11	1	5	28	16-2	0	29	.267	.328	.436	97	-1	0-0	.986	-2	103	111	C-38,D-10	-0.1
	Atl N	9	9	0	1	0	0	0	1	1-0	0	3	.111	.200	.111	-16	-2	0-0	1.000	1	40	273	/C-2	0.0
1998	†SD N	69	171	19	42	10	0	4	20	17-1	0	36	.246	.312	.374	87	-4	0-1	.987	-1	107	110	C-52	-0.2
1999	SD N	50	128	9	37	4	0	3	15	13-2	0	14	.289	.355	.391	96	-1	0-0	.986	-6	89	73	C-41	-0.5
	†Atl N	34	72	10	16	2	0	2	9	13-2	0	16	.222	.337	.333	72	-3	0-0	.994	6	196	110	C-31	0.4
	Year	84	200	19	53	6	0	5	24	26-4	0	30	.265	.348	.370	86	-4	0-0	.990	-1	132	88	C-72	-0.1
2000	Bal A	43	125	9	28	6	0	3	12	8-0	0	29	.224	.271	.344	57	-9	0-0	1.000	-3	59	110	C-28/D-8	-0.9
2001	Bal A	25	74	11	20	2	0	4	18	8-0	0	17	.270	.341	.459	114	1	0-0	1.000	-2	61	175	D-11/C-8	0.0
	†Oak A	33	87	13	16	1	0	7	13	13-1	0	21	.184	.290	.437	88	-2	0-0	1.000	1	114	120	C-28/D-2	0.0
	Year	58	161	24	36	3	0	11	31	21-1	0	38	.224	.313	.447	99	-1	0-0	1.000	-1	101	133	C-36,D-13	0.0
2002	†Oak A	65	144	15	32	5	0	6	21	26-3	0	36	.222	.341	.382	92	-1	0-0	.997	6	95	156	C-53/D	0.7
2003	Tor A	121	329	51	101	19	0	15	52	37-2	0	57	.307	.374	.502	127	13	0-3	.982	-9	77	74	C-81,D-22	0.6
Total	16	1094	3012	333	771	148	7	87	394	265-28	3	534	.256	.314	.396	87	-65	3-12	.988	-18	99	104	C-886/D-80	-3.9

MYERS, HENRY Henry C. B 5.1858 Philadelphia, PA D 4.18.1895 Philadelphia, PA BR/TR 5-9/159# d8.20 M1 ▲

Year	Tm Lg	G	AB	R	H	2B	3B	HR	RBI	BB-IB	HP	SO	AVG	OBP	SLG	AOPS	ABR	SB-CS	FA	FR	Rng	Thr	G at Pos	BFW
1881	Pro N	1	4	0	0	0	0	0	0	0		2	.000	.000	.000	-99	-1		1.000	-0	76	0	/S	-0.1
1882	Bal AA	69	294	43	53	3	0	0		12			.180	.212	.190	40	-17		.822	-6	**107**	76	*S-68/P-6,M	-1.9
1884	Wil U	6	24	3	3	0	0	0		0			.125	.125	.125	-23	-4		.875	4	108	0	/S-5,2	-0.1
Total	3	76	322	46	56	3	0	0	0	12		2	.174	.204	.183	32	-22		.826	-3	107	70	/S-74,P-6,2	-2.1

MYERS, HY Henry Harrison B 4.27.1889 E.Liverpool, OH D 5.1.1965 Minerva, OH BR/TR 5-9.5/175# d8.30 OF Total (5-LF 1150-CF 28-RF)

Year	Tm Lg	G	AB	R	H	2B	3B	HR	RBI	BB-IB	HP	SO	AVG	OBP	SLG	AOPS	ABR	SB-CS	FA	FR	Rng	Thr	G at Pos	BFW
1909	Bro N	6	22	1	5	1	0	0	6	2	0		.227	.292	.273	78	-1	1	1.000	-1	0	0	/O-6(RF)	-0.1
1911	Bro N	13	43	2	7	1	0	0	0	2	0	3	.163	.200	.186	9	-5	1	.889	-1	88	124	O-13(0-12-1)	-0.7
1914	Bro N	70	227	35	65	3	9	0	17	7	3	24	.286	.316	.379	104	-1	2	.964	-5	90	59	O-60(4-45-12)	-1.0
1915	Bro N	153	605	69	150	21	7	2	46	17	6	51	.248	.275	.316	77	-19	19-22	.964	-2	93	119	*O-153(CF)	-3.9
1916	†Bro N	113	412	54	108	12	14	3	36	21	6	35	.262	.308	.381	108	2	17	.969	-5	93	82	*O-106(0-105-1)	-1.2
1917	Bro N	120	471	37	126	15	10	1	41	18	0	25	.268	.294	.348	94	-5	5	.982	-6	104	67	O-66(0-62-4),1-22,2-19,3-15	-1.7
1918	Bro N	107	407	36	104	9	8	4	40	20	1	26	.256	.292	.346	95	-4	17	.975	8	108	119	*O-107(CF)	-0.5
1919	Bro N	133	512	62	157	23	**14**	5	**73**	23	2	34	.307	.339	**.436**	129	16	13	.979	4	109	76	*O-131(CF)	1.1
1920	†Bro N	154	582	83	177	36	**22**	4	80	35	1	54	.304	.345	.462	126	18	9-13	.978	-1	101	78	*O-152(CF)/3-2	0.4
1921	Bro N	144	549	51	158	14	4	4	68	22	2	51	.288	.318	.350	74	-21	8-6	.968	-4	85	136	*O-124(CF),2-21/3	-3.0
1922	Bro N	153	618	82	196	20	9	6	89	13	0	26	.317	.331	.408	90	-12	9-10	.974	-1	101	88	*O-152(CF)/2	-1.9
1923	StL N	96	330	29	99	18	2	2	48	12	3	19	.300	.330	.385	90	-5	5-3	.977	7	108	138	O-87(CF)	-0.2
1924	StL N	43	124	12	26	5	1	1	15	3	0	10	.210	.228	.290	39	-11	1-2	.945	-2	107	100	O-22(1-17-4),3-12/2-3	-1.4
1925	StL N	1	1	0	0	0	0	0	0	0	0	0	.000	.000	.000	-98	0	0-0	—	0			H	0.0
	Cin N	3	6	1	1	1	0	0	0	0	0	0	.167	.167	.333	25	-1	0-0	1.000	0	110	0	/O-3(CF)	-0.1
	StL N	1	1	1	1	0	0	0	0	0	0	0	1.000	1.000	1.000	403	0	0-0	—	0			H	0.0
	Year	5	8	2	2	1	0	0	0	0	0	0	.250	.250	.375	58	-1	0-0	1.000	0	110	0	/O-3(CF)	-0.1
Total	14	1310	4910	555	1380	179	100	32	559	195	24	358	.281	.312	.378	95	-49	107-56	.972	-7	99	98	*O-1182C/2-44,3-30,1-22	-14.2

MYERS, BERT James Albert B 4.8.1874 Frederick, MD D 10.12.1915 Washington, DC BR/TR 5-10/?# d4.25

Year	Tm Lg	G	AB	R	H	2B	3B	HR	RBI	BB-IB	HP	SO	AVG	OBP	SLG	AOPS	ABR	SB-CS	FA	FR	Rng	Thr	G at Pos	BFW
1896	StL N	122	454	47	116	12	8	0	37	40	3	32	.256	.320	.317	71	-19	8	.867	-6	96	82	*3-121/S	-2.0
1898	Was N	31	110	14	29	1	4	0	13	13	0		.264	.341	.345	97	-1	2	.835	-3	94	123	3-31	-0.3
1900	Phi N	7	28	5	5	1	0	0	2	3	0		.179	.258	.214	31	-3	1	.909	1	128	260	/3-7	-0.1
Total	3	160	592	66	150	14	12	0	52	56	3	32	.253	.321	.318	74	-23	11	.863	-8	97	99	3-159/S	-2.4

Year	Tm Lg	G	AB	R	H	2B	3B	HR	RBI	BB-IB	HP	SO	AVG	OBP	SLG	AOPS	ABR	SB-CS	FA	FR	Rng	Thr	G at Pos	BFW
MYERS, AL James Albert "Cod" B 10.22.1863 Danville, IL D 12.24.1927 Marshall, IL BR/TR 5-8.5/165# d9.27																								
1884	Mil U	**12**	46	6	15	6	0	0		0			.326	.326	.457	249	7		.848	3	93	48	2-12	0.9
1885	Phi N	93	357	25	73	13	2	1	28	11		41	.204	.228	.261	59	-16		.884	-16	98	85	*2-93	-2.7
1886	KC N	118	473	69	131	22	9	4	51	22		42	.277	.309	.387	104	0	3	.913	2	**108**	88	*2-118	0.6
1887	Was N	105	362	45	84	9	5	2	36	40	2	26	.232	.312	.301	76	-10	18	.909	-9	95	68	2-78,S-27	-1.3
1888	Was N	132	502	46	104	12	7	2	46	37	6	46	.207	.270	.271	78	-11	20	.918	-22	95	71	*2-132	-2.8
1889	Was N	46	176	24	46	3	0	0	20	22	1	7	.261	.347	.278	81	-3	10	.942	1	94	104	2-46	-0.1
	Phi N	75	305	52	82	14	2	0	28	36	4	9	.269	.354	.328	84	-7	8	.853	-14	101	88	2-75	-1.5
	Year	121	481	76	128	17	2	0	48	58	5	16	.266	.351	.310	83	-10	18	.886	-14	98	94	*2-121	-1.6
1890	Phi N	117	487	95	135	29	7	2	81	57	10	46	.277	.365	.378	114	10	44	.948	6	94	129	*2-117	1.8
1891	Phi N	135	514	67	118	27	2	2	69	69	9	46	.230	.331	.302	83	-9	8	.937	-12	98	111	*2-135	-1.4
Total	8	833	3222	429	788	135	34	13	359	294	32	263	.245	.314	.320	88	-39	111	.914	-61	98	93	2-806/S-27	-6.5
MYERS, LYNN Lynnwood Lincoln B 2.23.1914 Enola, PA D 1.19.2000 Harrisburg, PA BR/TR 5-6.5/145# d7.13 b-Billy																								
1938	StL N	70	227	18	55	10	2	1	19	9	0	25	.242	.271	.317	58	-13	9	.944	-1	101	94	S-69	-1.0
1939	StL N	74	117	24	28	6	1	0	10	12	0	23	.239	.310	.308	63	-6	1	.897	-0	95	133	S-36,3-13/2-5	-0.4
Total	2	144	344	42	83	16	3	1	29	21	0	48	.241	.285	.314	60	-19	10	.930	-2	99	105	S-105/3-13,2-5	-1.4
MYERS, HAP Ralph Edward B 4.8.1888 San Francisco, CA D 6.30.1967 San Francisco, CA BR/TR 6-3/175# d4.16																								
1910	Bos A	3	6	0	2	0	0	0	0	0	0		.333	.333	.333	106	0	0	1.000	1	64	648	/O-2(RF)	0.1
1911	StL A	11	37	4	11	1	0	0	1	1	0		.297	.316	.324	82	-1	0	.976	-2	43	93	1-11	-0.3
	Bos A	13	38	3	14	2	0	0	0	4	0		.368	.429	.421	139	2	4	.947	-1	87	103	1-12	0.1
	Year	24	75	7	25	3	0	0	1	5	0		.333	.375	.373	111	1	4	.963	-3	65	98	1-23	-0.2
1913	Bos N	140	524	74	143	20	1	2	50	38	9	48	.273	.333	.326	87	-8	57-18	.987	5	115	81	*1-135	0.0
1914	Bro F	92	305	61	67	10	5	1	29	44	2	43	.220	.322	.295	69	-17	43	.989	1	102	101	1-88	-1.9
1915	Bro F	118	341	61	98	9	1	1	36	32	2	39	.287	.352	.328	93	-7	28	.990	1	105	93	*1-107	-0.9
Total	5	377	1251	203	335	42	7	4	116	119	13	130	.268	.338	.322	85	-31	132-18	.987	5	106	90	1-353/O-2(RF)	-2.9
MYERS, RICHIE Richard B 4.7.1930 Sacramento, CA BR/TR 5-6/150# d4.21																								
1956	Chi N	4	1	1	0	0	0	0	0	0-0	0	0	.000	.000	.000	-99	0	0-0	—	0			H	0.0
MYERS, ROD Roderick Demond B 1.14.1973 Conroe, TX BL/TL 6/190# d6.21																								
1996	KC A	22	63	9	18	7	0	1	11	7-0	0	16	.286	.357	.444	101	0	3-2	1.000	-2	80	0	O-19(4-15-1)	-0.2
1997	KC A	31	101	14	26	7	0	2	9	17-0	1	22	.257	.370	.386	95	0	4-0	.982	-1	95	61	O-26(12-9-10)	-0.1
Total	2	53	164	23	44	14	0	3	20	24-0	1	38	.268	.365	.409	98	0	7-2	.989	-4	89	38	/O-45(16-24-11)	-0.3
MYERS, BILLY William Harrison B 8.14.1910 Enola, PA D 4.10.1995 Carlisle, PA BR/TR 5-8/168# d4.16 b-Lynn																								
1935	Cin N	117	445	60	119	15	10	5	36	29	2	81	.267	.315	.380	89	-9	10	.939	2	101	125	*S-112	0.1
1936	Cin N	98	323	45	87	9	6	6	27	28	0	56	.269	.328	.390	99	-2	6	.938	4	101	118	S-98	0.9
1937	Cin N	124	335	35	84	13	3	7	43	44	1	57	.251	.339	.370	97	-1	0	.948	7	107	99	*S-121/2-6	1.4
1938	Cin N	134	442	57	112	18	6	12	47	41	0	80	.253	.317	.403	99	-2	2	.939	-2	100	105	*S-123,2-11	0.6
1939	†Cin N	151	509	79	143	18	6	9	56	71	0	90	.281	.369	.393	104	5	4	.951	3	100	**113**	*S-151	1.9
1940	†Cin N	90	282	33	57	14	2	5	30	30	2	56	.202	.283	.319	65	-13	0	.961	-3	99	135	S-88	-1.1
1941	Chi N	24	63	10	14	1	0	1	4	7	1	25	.222	.310	.286	71	-2	1	.939	2	108	113	S-19/2	0.2
Total	7	738	2399	319	616	88	33	45	243	250	6	445	.257	.328	.377	93	-24	23	.946	13	101	115	S-712/2-18	4.0
NADY, XAVIER Xavier Clifford B 11.14.1978 Salinas, CA BR/TR 6-4/220# d9.30																								
2000	SD N	1	1	1	1	0	0	0	0	0-0	0	0	1.000	1.000	1.000	438	1	0-0	—	0			/H	0.0
2003	SD N	110	371	50	99	17	1	9	39	24-0	6	74	.267	.321	.391	93	-5	6-2	.968	1	93	193	*O-105(RF)	-0.8
Total	2	111	372	51	100	17	1	9	39	24-0	6	74	.269	.323	.392	94	-4	6-2	.968	1	93	193	O-105(RF)	-0.8
NAEHRING, TIM Timothy James B 2.1.1967 Cincinnati, OH BR/TR 6-2/205# d7.15																								
1990	Bos A	24	85	10	23	6	0	2	12	8-1	0	15	.271	.333	.412	102	0	0-0	.918	2	105	96	S-19/3-5,2	0.3
1991	Bos A	20	55	1	6	1	0	0	3	6-0	0	15	.109	.197	.127	-8	-8	0-0	.956	-0	107	86	S-17/3-2,2	-0.7
1992	Bos A	72	186	12	43	8	0	3	14	18-0	3	31	.231	.308	.323	72	-7	0-0	.992	11	110	116	S-30,2-23,3-10/O(LF)D	0.7
1993	Bos A	39	127	14	42	10	0	1	17	10-0	0	26	.331	.377	.433	111	2	1-0	.973	-3	91	122	2-15,D-10/3-9,S-4	0.0
1994	Bos A	80	297	41	82	18	1	7	42	30-1	4	56	.276	.349	.414	92	-3	1-3	.981	5	108	106	2-49,3-11/1-8,S-8,D-7	0.3
1995	†Bos A	126	433	61	133	27	2	10	57	77-5	4	66	.307	.415	.448	121	18	0-2	.954	7	108	109	*3-124/D	2.3
1996	Bos A	116	430	77	124	16	0	17	65	49-4	4	63	.288	.363	.444	102	1	2-1	.963	8	106	78	*3-116/2	1.0
1997	Bos A	70	259	38	74	18	1	9	40	38-0	1	40	.286	.375	.467	117	8	1-1	.981	-9	88	87	3-68/D	0.0
Total	8	547	1872	254	527	104	4	49	250	236-11	16	312	.282	.365	.420	102	11	5-7	.962	21	100	92	3-345/2-90,S-78,D-23,1-8,O(LF)	3.9
NAGEL, BILL William Taylor B 8.19.1915 Memphis, TN D 10.8.1981 Freehold, NJ BR/TR 6-1/190# d4.20																								
1939	Phi A	105	341	39	86	19	4	12	39	25	2	86	.252	.307	.437	90	-7	2-1	.944	-12	96	82	2-56,3-43/P	-1.4
1941	Phi N	17	56	2	8	1	1	0	6	3	0	14	.143	.186	.196	8	-7	0	.935	2	123	100	2-12/O-2(LF),3	-0.5
1945	Chi A	67	220	21	46	10	3	3	27	15	1	41	.209	.263	.323	71	-9	3-1	.984	-2	89	90	1-57/3	-1.5
Total	3	189	617	62	140	30	8	15	72	43	3	141	.227	.281	.374	77	-23	5-2	.942	-13	101	85	/2-68,1-57,3-45,O-2(LF),P	-3.4
NAGELSEN, LOU Louis Marcellus (born Louis Marcellus Nageleisen) B 6.29.1887 Piqua, OH D 10.21.1965 Fort Wayne, IN BR/TR 6-2/180# d9.10																								
1912	Cle A	2	3	0	0	0	0	0	0	0	0		.000	.000	.000	-97	-1	0	1.000	-0	*84*	*0*	/C-2	-0.1
NAGELSON, RUSS Russell Charles B 9.19.1944 Cincinnati, OH BL/TR 6/205# d9.11																								
1968	Cle A	5	3	0	1	0	0	0	0	2-0	0	2	.333	.600	.333	192	1	0-0	—	0			H	0.1
1969	Cle A	12	17	1	6	0	0	0	0	3-1	0	3	.353	.450	.353	123	1	0-0	1.000	-0	72	0	/O-3(1-0-2),1	0.1
1970	Cle A	17	24	3	3	1	0	1	2	3-0	0	9	.125	.222	.292	39	-2	0-0	1.000	-0	84	0	/O-4(1-0-3)	-0.3
	Det A	28	32	5	6	0	0	0	2	5-0	0	6	.188	.297	.188	36	-3	0-0	1.000	-0	88	0	/O-4(3-0-2),1	-0.3
	Year	45	56	8	9	1	0	1	4	8-0	0	15	.161	.266	.232	38	-5	0-0	1.000	-1	86	0	/O-8(4-0-5),1	-0.6
Total	3	62	76	9	16	1	0	1	4	13-1	0	20	.211	.326	.263	64	-3	0-0	1.000	-1	83	0	/O-11(5-0-7),1-2	-0.4
NAGLE, TOM Thomas Edward B 10.30.1865 Milwaukee, WI D 3.9.1946 Milwaukee, WI BR/TR 5-10/150# d4.22																								
1890	Chi N	38	144	21	39	5	1	1	11	7	3	24	.271	.318	.340	88	-3	4	.939	-4	*111*	*62*	C-33/O-6(RF)	-0.3
1891	Chi N	8	25	3	3	0	0	0	1	1	0	3	.120	.154	.120	-20	-4	0	.906	-2	*137*	*62*	/C-7,O(LF)	-0.5
Total	2	46	169	24	42	5	1	1	12	8	3	27	.249	.294	.308	73	-7	4	.935	-5	*115*	*62*	/C-40,O-7(1-0-6)	-0.8
NAHORODNY, BILL William Gerard B 8.31.1953 Hamtramck, MI BR/TR 6-2/200# d9.27																								
1976	Phi N	3	5	0	1	1	0	0	0	0-0	0	0	.200	.200	.400	65	0	0-0	1.000	-0	31	0	/C-2	0.0
1977	Chi A	7	23	3	6	1	0	1	4	2-0	0	3	.261	.308	.435	104	0	0-0	1.000	-1	79	67	/C-7	-0.1
1978	Chi A	107	347	29	82	11	2	8	35	23-0	2	52	.236	.285	.349	77	-11	1-0	.980	-4	81	82	*C-104/1-4,D	-1.2
1979	Chi A	65	179	20	46	10	0	6	29	18-1	0	23	.257	.322	.413	98	-1	0-1	.973	-1	63	115	C-60/D-3	0.0
1980	Atl N	59	157	14	38	12	0	5	18	8-1	2	21	.242	.287	.414	91	-2	0-2	.990	-6	83	99	C-54/1	-0.7
1981	Atl N	14	13	0	3	1	0	0	2	1-1	0	3	.231	.286	.308	67	-1	0-0	1.000	0	0	0	/C-3,1	-0.1
1982	Cle A	39	94	6	21	5	1	4	18	2-0	0	9	.223	.237	.426	79	-3	0-0	1.000	-5	92	62	C-35	-0.7
1983	Det A	2	1	0	0	0	0	0	0	1-0	0	0	.000	.500	.000	53	0	0-0	—	0			/H	0.0
1984	Sea A	12	25	2	6	0	0	1	3	1-0	2	7	.240	.310	.360	89	0	0-1	.976	-2	132	44	C-10/1	-0.3
Total	9	308	844	74	203	41	3	25	109	56-3	6	118	.241	.290	.385	85	-18	1-4	.983	-19	80	87	C-275/1-7,D-4	-3.1
NALEWAY, FRANK Frank "Chick" B 7.5.1902 Chicago, IL D 1.28.1949 Chicago, IL BR/TR 5-9.5/165# d9.16																								
1924	Chi A	1	2	0	0	0	0	0	0	1	0	0	.000	.333	.000	-10	0	0-0	.750	-1	73	0	/S	-0.1
NANCE, DOC William G. "Kid" (born Willie G. Cooper) B 8.2.1876 Ft.Worth, TX D 5.28.1958 Fort Worth, TX BR/TR 5-7/165# d8.19																								
1897	Lou N	35	120	25	29	5	3	3	17	20	1		.242	.355	.408	105	1	3	.986	3	161	386	O-35(0-7-28)	0.2
1898	Lou N	22	76	13	24	5	0	1	16	12	1		.316	.416	.421	142	5	2	.946	2	235	274	O-22(RF)	0.6
1901	Det A	132	461	72	129	24	5	3	66	51	3		.280	.355	.373	98	0	9	.932	2	118	155	*O-132(130-0-2)	-0.5
Total	3	189	657	110	182	34	8	7	99	83	5		.277	.362	.385	104	6	14	.943	8	139	211	O-189(130-7-52)	0.3
NAPLES, AL Aloysius Francis B 8.29.1927 St.George, NY BR/TR 5-9/168# d6.25																								
1949	StL A	2	7	0	1	1	0	0	0	0	0	1	.143	.143	.286	12	-1	0-0	.875	-1	116	0	/S-2	-0.1

Year	Tm Lg	G	AB	R	H	2B	3B	HR	RBI	BB-IB	HP	SO	AVG	OBP	SLG	AOPS	ABR	SB-CS	FA	FR	Rng	Thr	G at Pos	BFW
NAPOLEON, DANNY Daniel B 1.11.1942 Claysburg, PA BR/TR 5-11/190# d4.14																								
1965	NY N	68	97	5	14	1	1	0	7	8-1	2	23	.144	.222	.175	15	-11	0-0	.941	0	117	0	O-15(14-0-1)/3-7	-1.3
1966	NY N	12	33	2	7	2	0	0	0	1-0	0	10	.212	.235	.273	42	-3	0-1	.929	0	89	188	O-10(LF)	-0.4
Total	2	80	130	7	21	3	1	0	7	9-1	2	33	.162	.225	.200	22	-14	0-1	.938	0	108	61	/O-25(24-0-1),3-7	-1.7
NARAGON, HAL Harold Richard B 10.1.1928 Zanesville, OH BL/TR 6/175# d9.23 Mil 1952 C7																								
1951	Cle A	3	8	0	2	0	0	0	0	1	1	0	.250	.400	.250	83	0	0-0	.929	-0	*82*	*0*	/C-2	0.0
1954	†Cle A	46	101	10	24	2	2	0	12	9	0	12	.238	.300	.297	63	-5	0-0	1.000	0	*108*	*120*	C-45	-0.4
1955	Cle A	57	127	12	41	9	2	1	14	15-0	0	8	.323	.394	.449	122	4	1-0	.991	-1	*112*	*86*	C-52	0.6
1956	Cle A	53	122	11	35	3	1	3	18	13-2	1	9	.287	.355	.402	99	0	0-0	.988	-6	*78*	*49*	C-48	-0.5
1957	Cle A	57	121	12	31	1	1	0	8	12-1	1	9	.256	.326	.281	69	-5	0-0	.990	-2	*75*	*85*	C-39	-0.6
1958	Cle A	9	9	2	3	0	1	0	0	0-0	0	0	.333	.333	.556	144	0	0-0	—	0			H	0.0
1959	Cle A	14	36	6	10	4	1	0	5	3-0	1	2	.278	.341	.444	121	1	0-0	1.000	-1	*81*	*59*	C-10	0.0
	Was A	71	195	12	47	3	2	0	11	8-0	1	9	.241	.272	.277	52	-13	0-1	.993	-5	*62*	*56*	C-54	-1.6
	Year	85	231	18	57	7	3	0	16	11-0	2	11	.247	.283	.303	63	-12	0-1	.994	-6	*65*	*56*	C-64	-1.6
1960	Was A	33	92	7	19	2	0	0	5	8-2	1	4	.207	.275	.228	39	-8	0-0	.978	-1	*133*	*169*	C-29	-0.8
1961	Min A	57	139	10	42	2	1	2	11	4-0	1	8	.302	.326	.374	82	-4	0-0	.994	-2	*96*	*75*	C-36	-0.5
1962	Min A	24	35	1	8	1	0	0	3	3-1	0	1	.229	.282	.257	47	-3	0-0	1.000	0	*210*	*0*	/C-9	-0.2
Total	10	424	985	83	262	27	11	6	87	76-6	7	62	.266	.321	.334	77	-33	1-1	.991	-17	*94*	*82*	C-324	-4.0
NARLESKI, BILL William Edward "Cap" B 6.9.1899 Perth Amboy, NJ D 6.20.1964 Laurel Springs, NJ BR/TR 5-9/160# d4.18 s-Ray																								
1929	Bos A	96	260	30	72	16	1	0	25	21	1	22	.277	.333	.346	77	-8	4-4	.957	-9	97	98	S-51,2-29/3-7	-1.2
1930	Bos A	39	98	11	23	9	0	0	7	7	3	5	.235	.306	.327	63	-5	0-0	.915	-6	84	121	S-19,3-14/2-5	-0.8
Total	2	135	358	41	95	25	1	0	32	28	4	27	.265	.326	.341	73	-13	4-4	.949	-15	95	102	/S-70,2-34,3-21	-2.0
NARRON, JERRY Jerry Austin B 1.15.1956 Goldsboro, NC BL/TR 6-3/205# d4.13 M2 C10																								
1979	NY A	61	123	17	21	3	1	4	18	9-0	0	26	.171	.226	.309	44	-10	0-0	.973	-4	108	66	C-56/D	-1.2
1980	Sea A	48	107	7	21	3	0	4	18	13-2	0	18	.196	.279	.336	68	-5	0-0	.992	-6	96	82	C-39/D	-1.0
1981	Sea A	76	203	13	45	5	0	3	17	16-3	2	35	.222	.285	.291	64	-10	0-0	.996	-13	70	70	C-65	-2.1
1983	Cal A	10	22	1	3	0	0	1	4	1-0	0	3	.136	.174	.273	21	-3	0-0	.895	-1	90	156	/C-6,D	-0.3
1984	Cal A	69	150	9	37	5	0	3	17	8-1	1	12	.247	.286	.340	74	-6	0-0	.994	-5	95	89	C-46/1-7	-0.9
1985	Cal A	67	132	12	29	4	0	5	14	11-2	0	17	.220	.280	.364	75	-5	0-0	1.000	3	78	130	C-45/1D	-0.1
1986	†Cal A	57	95	5	21	3	1	1	8	9-0	1	14	.221	.292	.305	65	-5	0-0	.988	-0	114	132	C-51/D-2	-0.4
1987	Sea A	4	8	0	0	0	0	0	0	0-0	0	2	.000	.000	.000	-95	-2	0-0	1.000	-1	44	168	/C-3	-0.3
Total	8	392	840	64	177	23	2	21	96	67-8	4	127	.211	.270	.318	62	-46	0-0	.989	-26	91	92	C-311/D-12,1-8	-6.3
NARRON, SAM Samuel B 8.25.1913 Middlesex, NC D 12.31.1996 Middlesex, NC BR/TR 5-10/180# d9.15 C13																								
1935	StL N	4	7	0	3	0	0	0	0	0	0	0	.429	.429	.429	126	0	0	1.000	0	*0*	*0*	/C	0.0
1942	StL N	10	10	0	4	0	0	0	1	0	0	0	.400	.400	.400	125	0	0	1.000	-0	*0*	*0*	/C-2	0.0
1943	†StL N	10	11	0	1	0	0	0	0	1	0	2	.091	.167	.091	-24	-2	0	1.000	1	*0*	*0*	/C-3	-0.1
Total	3	24	28	0	8	0	0	0	1	1	0	2	.286	.310	.286	67	-2	0	1.000	0	*0*	*0*	/C-6	-0.1
NASH, COTTON Charles Francis B 7.24.1942 Jersey City, NJ BR/TR 6-6/220# d9.1																								
1967	Chi A	3	3	1	0	0	0	0	0	1-0	0	0	.000	.250	.000	-21	0	0-0	.833	-1	0	393	/1-3	-0.1
1969	Min A	6	9	0	2	0	0	0	0	1-0	0	2	.222	.300	.222	47	-1	0-0	1.000	1	272	0	/1-6,O(LF)	0.0
1970	Min A	4	4	1	1	0	0	0	2	1-0	0	1	.250	.400	.250	82	0	0-1	1.000	-0	0	251	/1-2	-0.1
Total	3	13	16	2	3	0	0	0	2	3-0	0	3	.188	.316	.188	45	-1	0-1	.965	0	155	141	/1-11,O(LF)	-0.2
NASH, KEN Kenneth Leland (Played One Game In 1912 Under Name Of Costello) B 7.14.1888 Weymouth, MA D 2.16.1977 Epsom, NH BB/TR 5-8/140# d7.4																								
1912	Cle A	11	23	2	4	0	0	0	0	3	0		.174	.269	.174	27	-2	0	.826	-2	86	61	/S-8	-0.4
1914	StL N	24	51	4	14	3	1	0	6	6	0	10	.275	.351	.373	116	1	0	.875	-5	73	0	3-10/2-6,S-3	-0.4
Total	2	35	74	6	18	3	1	0	6	9	0	10	.243	.325	.311	87	-1	0	.760	-7	79	56	/S-11,3-10,2-6	-0.8
NASH, BILLY William Mitchell B 6.24.1865 Richmond, VA D 11.15.1929 E.Orange, NJ BR/TR 5-8.5/167# d8.5 M1 U1 OF Total (6-LF 1-CF 1-RF)																								
1884	Ric AA	**45**	166	31	33	8	8	1		12	7		.199	.281	.361	109	2		.828	9	114	158	3-45	1.1
1885	Bos N	26	94	9	24	4	0	0	11	2		9	.255	.271	.298	87	-1		.864	-2	83	139	3-19/2-8	-0.3
1886	Bos N	109	417	61	117	11	8	1	45	24		28	.281	.320	.353	107	3	16	.863	-6	96	84	*3-90,S-17/O-2(1-1-0)	-0.1
1887	Bos N	121	475	100	140	24	12	6	94	60	2	30	.295	.376	.434	123	16	43	.884	7	103	96	*3-117/O-5(4-0-1)	2.1
1888	Bos N	135	526	71	149	18	15	4	75	50	4	46	.283	.350	.397	134	21	20	**.913**	18	**119**	**141**	*3-105,2-31	4.1
1889	Bos N	128	481	84	132	20	2	3	76	79	2	44	.274	.379	.343	97	0	26	.905	11	102	117	*3-128/P	1.2
1890	Bos P	129	488	103	130	28	6	5	90	88	4	43	.266	.383	.379	97	0	26	.866	19	**111**	**171**	*3-129/P	1.6
1891	Bos N	**140**	537	92	148	24	9	5	95	74	5	50	.276	.369	.382	106	4	28	.900	-12	83	111	*3-140	-0.5
1892	†Bos N	135	526	94	137	25	5	4	95	59	3	42	.260	.338	.350	99	-1	31	**.898**	25	117	**125**	*3-135/O(LF)	2.4
1893	Bos N	128	485	115	141	27	6	10	123	85	2	29	.291	.399	.433	112	9	30	**.923**	2	100	107	*3-128	1.1
1894	Bos N	132	512	132	148	23	6	8	87	91	3	23	.289	.399	.404	87	-9	20	**.933**	4	98	116	*3-132	-0.2
1895	Bos N	**133**	513	97	149	24	6	10	110	74	3	19	.290	.383	.419	99	-1	18	.881	-11	87	145	*3-133	-0.8
1896	Phi N	65	227	29	56	9	1	3	30	34	4	21	.247	.355	.335	83	-4	3	.911	8	112	117	3-65,M	0.4
1897	Phi N	104	337	45	87	20	2	0	39	60	2		.258	.373	.329	89	-1	4	.919	-9	94	101	3-79,S-19/2-4	-0.7
1898	Phi N	20	70	9	17	2	1	0	9	11	0		.243	.346	.300	89	0	0	.958	-1	77	203	3-20	-0.1
Total	15	1550	5854	1072	1608	267	87	60	979	803	41	384	.275	.366	.381	103	38	265	.897	62	101	123	*3-1465/2-43,S-36,O-8L,P-2	11.3
NATAL, BOB Robert Marcel B 11.13.1965 Long Beach, CA BR/TR 5-11/190# d7.18 C2																								
1992	Mon N	5	6	0	0	0	0	0	0	1-0	0	1	.000	.143	.000	-57	-1	0-0	.909	-1	40	0	/C-4	-0.2
1993	Fla N	41	117	3	25	4	1	1	6	6-0	4	22	.214	.273	.291	49	-9	1-0	1.000	2	104	100	C-38	-0.5
1994	Fla N	10	29	2	8	2	0	0	2	5-0	0	5	.276	.382	.345	89	0	1-0	.983	2	74	145	/C-8	0.2
1995	Fla N	16	43	2	10	2	1	2	6	1-0	0	9	.233	.244	.465	83	-1	0-0	.988	0	167	86	C-13	0.0
1996	Fla N	44	90	4	12	1	1	0	2	15-5	0	31	.133	.257	.167	15	-11	0-1	.976	-3	88	111	C-43	-1.2
1997	Fla N	4	4	2	2	1	0	1	3	2-0	0	0	.500	.571	1.500	468	2	0-0	1.000	1	0	0	/C-4	0.3
Total	6	120	289	13	57	10	3	4	19	30-5	4	68	.197	.279	.294	52	-20	2-1	.986	1	100	103	C-110	-1.4
NATON, PETE Peter Alphonsus B 9.9.1931 Flushing, NY BR/TR 6-1/200# d6.16 Mil 1953																								
1953	Pit N	6	12	2	2	0	0	0	1	2	0	1	.167	.286	.167	22	-1	0-0	1.000	-1	*75*	*0*	/C-4	-0.2
NAVA, SANDY Vincent P. (born Irwin Sandy) B 4.12.1850 San Francisco, CA D 6.15.1906 Baltimore, MD 5-6/155# d5.5																								
1882	Pro N	28	97	15	20	2	0	0	7	1		13	.206	.214	.227	42	-6		.867	-6			C-27/O(RF)	-0.9
1883	Pro N	29	100	18	24	4	2	0	16	3		17	.240	.262	.320	74	-3		.813	-3			C-27/O-2(1-0-1)	-0.4
1884	Pro N	34	116	10	11	0	0	0	6	11		35	.095	.173	.095	-13	-15		.887	-0			C-27/S-6,2	-1.1
1885	Bal AA	8	27	2	5	1	0	0	4	1	0		.185	.214	.222	39	-2		.825	-4			/C-8	-0.4
1886	Bal AA	2	5	0	1	0	0	0	0	0	0		.200	.200	.200	26	0	1	.500	-1	54	0	/SC	-0.2
Total	5	101	345	45	61	7	2	0	33	16	0	65	.177	.213	.209	33	-26	1	.857	-14			/C-90,S-7,O-3(1-0-2),2	-3.0
NAVARRO, TITO Norberto (Rodriguez) B 9.12.1970 Rio Piedras, P.R. BB/TR 5-10/165# d9.6																								
1993	NY N	12	17	1	1	0	0	0	1	0-0	0	4	.059	.059	.059	-69	-4	0-0	1.000	1	118	0	/S-2	-0.3
NAYLOR, EARL Earl Eugene B 5.19.1919 Kansas City, MO D 1.16.1990 Winter Haven, FL BR/TR 6/190# d4.15 Mil 1944-45 ▲																								
1942	Phi N	76	168	9	33	4	1	0	14	11	0	18	.196	.246	.232	42	-13	1	.984	-4	87	37	O-34(2-22-11),P-20	-1.6
1943	Phi N	33	120	12	21	2	0	3	14	12	1	16	.175	.256	.267	53	-8	1	.964	3	107	176	O-33(CF)	-0.6
1946	Bro N	3	2	1	0	0	0	0	0	0	0	1	.000	.000	.000	-99	-1	0	—	0			H	-0.1
Total	3	112	290	22	54	6	1	3	28	23	1	35	.186	.248	.245	46	-22	2	.971	-0	98	113	/O-67(2-55-11),P-20	-2.3
NEAGLE, JACK John Henry B 1.2.1858 Syracuse, NY D 9.20.1904 Syracuse, NY BR/TR 5-6/155# d7.8 ▲																								
1879	Cin N	3	12	1	2	0	0	0	2	0		0	.167	.167	.167	11	-1		—	-0	0	0	/O-2(0-1-1),P-2	0.0
1883	Phi N	18	73	6	12	1	0	0	4	1		9	.164	.176	.178	9	-8		.840	-2	39	0	O-12(11-1-0)/P-8	-0.6
	Bal AA	9	35	3	10	4	0	0		2			.286	.324	.400	128	1		.769	-1	97	0	/P-6,O-5(1-0-4)	-0.1
	Pit AA	27	101	14	19	0	1	0		5			.188	.226	.208	43	-6		.839	-2	87	0	P-16,O-15(0-8-7)	-0.4
	Year	36	136	17	29	4	1	0		7			.213	.252	.257	66	-5		.818	-3	90	0	P-22,O-20(1-8-11)	-0.5
1884	Pit AA	43	148	13	22	6	0	0		6	1		.149	.187	.189	23	-12		.760	-5	87	62	P-38/O-6(2-2-2)	-0.4

Year	Tm Lg	G	AB	R	H	2B	3B	HR	RBI	BB-IB	HP	SO	AVG	OBP	SLG	AOPS	ABR	SB-CS	FA	FR	Rng	Thr	G at Pos	BFW
Total	3	100	369	37	65	11	1	0	6	14	1	9	.176	.208	.211	36	-26		.785	-11	85	36	/P-70,O-40(14-12-14)	-1.5
NEAL, CHARLIE Charles Lenard B 1.30.1931 Longview, TX D 11.18.1996 Dallas, TX BR/TR 5-10/165# d4.17																								
1956	†Bro N	62	136	22	39	5	1	2	14	14-1	0	19	.287	.353	.382	91	-1	2-2	.972	2	105	120	2-51/S	0.3
1957	Bro N	128	448	62	121	13	7	12	62	53-0	8	83	.270	.356	.411	96	-1	11-4	.949	-1	100	102	*S-100,3-23/2-3	0.8
1958	LA N	140	473	87	120	9	6	22	65	61-4	5	91	.254	.341	.438	102	1	7-6	.976	13	99	**123**	*2-132/S-9	2.4
1959	†LA N★	151	616	103	177	30	**11**	19	83	43-2	4	86	.287	.337	.464	103	2	17-6	**.989**	18	98	112	*2-151/S	3.3
1960	LA N★	139	477	60	122	23	2	8	40	48-2	1	75	.256	.321	.363	83	-10	5-5	.977	-18	83	104	*2-136/S-3	-2.0
1961	LA N	108	341	40	80	6	1	10	48	30-6	1	49	.235	.297	.346	65	-18	3-2	.976	1	92	93	*2-104	-0.9
1962	NY N	136	508	59	132	14	9	11	58	56-1	0	90	.260	.330	.388	91	-7	2-8	.970	-1	109	95	2-85,S-39,3-12	0.0
1963	NY N	72	253	26	57	12	1	3	18	27-3	1	49	.225	.302	.316	77	-7	1-2	.961	4	110	96	3-66/S-8	-0.3
	Cin N	34	64	2	10	1	0	0	3	5-0	0	15	.156	.217	.172	13	-7	0-1	.927	-3	60	0	3-19/2S	-1.1
	Year	106	317	28	67	13	1	3	21	32-3	1	64	.211	.286	.287	64	-14	1-3	.955	1	101	78	3-85/S-9,2	-1.4
Total	8	970	3316	461	858	113	38	87	391	337-19	20	557	.259	.329	.394	90	-48	48-36	.978	17	96	108	2-663,S-162,3-120	2.5
NEAL, OFFA Theophilus Fountain B 6.5.1876 Benton, IL D 4.11.1950 Mt.Vernon, IL BL/TR 6/185# d9.30																								
1905	NY N	4	13	0	0	0	0	0	0	0	0		.000	.000	.000	-98	-3	0	1.000	0	63	791	/3-3,2	-0.3
NEALE, GREASY Alfred Earle B 11.5.1891 Parkersburg, WV D 11.2.1973 Lake Worth, FL BL/TR (BB 1916-18 (partS)) 6/170# d4.12 C1																								
1916	Cin N	138	530	53	139	13	5	0	20	19	6	79	.262	.295	.306	87	-10	17	.973	7	104	127	*O-133(79-55-2)	-1.2
1917	Cin N	121	385	40	113	14	9	3	33	24	5	36	.294	.343	.400	133	14	25	.979	2	103	100	*O-119(79-27-13)	1.2
1918	Cin N	107	371	57	100	11	11	1	32	24	6	38	.270	.324	.367	112	4	23	**.981**	7	117	90	*O-102(78-12-12)	0.7
1919	†Cin N	139	500	57	121	10	12	1	54	47	7	51	.242	.316	.316	93	-4	28	.959	-1	104	77	*O-138(24-5-109)	-1.5
1920	Cin N	150	530	55	135	10	7	3	46	45	8	48	.255	.322	.317	85	-9	29-12	.987	12	119	97	*O-150(0-3-148)	-0.4
1921	Phi N	22	57	7	12	1	0	0	1	14	0	9	.211	.366	.228	56	-3	3-4	.842	-3	68	0	O-16(RF)	-0.8
	Cin N	63	241	39	58	10	5	0	12	22	1	16	.241	.307	.324	70	-10	9-6	.964	-1	101	81	O-60(1-8-53)	-1.6
	Year	85	298	46	70	11	5	0	13	36	1	25	.235	.319	.305	67	-13	12-10	.950	-4	96	68	O-76(1-8-69)	-2.4
1922	Cin N	25	43	11	10	2	1	0	2	6	2	3	.233	.353	.326	77	-1	5-2	.864	-1	87	76	O-16(5-0-11)	-0.3
1924	Cin N	3	4	0	0	0	0	0	0	0	0	1	.000	.000	.000	-99	-1	0-0	1.000	0	116	0	/O-2(LF)	-0.1
Total	8	768	2661	319	688	71	50	8	200	201	35	281	.259	.319	.332	94	-20	139-24	.972	20	108	95	O-736(268-110-364)	-4.0
NEALON, JIM James Joseph B 12.15.1884 Sacramento, CA D 4.2.1910 San Francisco, CA BR/TR 6-1.5/?# d4.12																								
1906	Pit N	**154**	556	82	142	21	12	3	**83**	53	6		.255	.327	.353	107	4	15	.987	1	102	**132**	*1-154	0.3
1907	Pit N	105	381	29	98	10	8	0	47	23	1		.257	.301	.325	95	-4	11	.978	0	106	69	*1-104	-0.6
Total	2	259	937	111	240	31	20	3	130	76	7		.256	.317	.342	102	0	26	.983	1	104	107	1-258	-0.3
NEEDHAM, TOM Thomas Joseph "Deerfoot" B 5.17.1879 Steubenville, OH D 12.14.1926 Steubenville, OH BR/TR 5-10/180# d5.12																								
1904	Bos N	84	269	18	70	12	3	4	19	11	1		.260	.292	.372	108	1	3	.945	-3	*88*	***124***	C-77/O(CF)	0.6
1905	Bos N	83	271	21	59	6	1	2	17	24	5		.218	.293	.269	70	-10	3	.949	-14	*73*	***121***	C-77/O-3(CF),1-2	-1.7
1906	Bos N	83	285	11	54	8	2	1	12	13	2		.189	.230	.242	49	-18	3	.962	-9	*81*	*115*	C-76/2-5,1-2,30(CF)	-2.3
1907	Bos N	86	260	19	51	6	2	1	19	18	6		.196	.264	.246	60	-12	4	.967	-16	*73*	*107*	C-78/1	-2.4
1908	NY N	54	91	8	19	3	0	0	11	12	6		.209	.339	.242	82	-1	0	.975	4	*147*	*84*	C-47	0.7
1909	Chi N	13	28	3	4	0	0	0	0	0	0		.143	.143	.143	-11	-4	0	.980	1	*137*	*59*	/C-7	-0.3
1910	†Chi N	31	76	9	14	3	1	0	10	10	1	10	.184	.287	.250	57	-4	1	.982	4	*146*	*82*	C-27/1	0.2
1911	Chi N	27	62	4	12	2	0	0	5	9	2	14	.194	.315	.226	52	-4	2	.984	6	*170*	*113*	C-23	0.4
1912	Chi N	33	90	12	16	5	0	0	10	7	3	13	.178	.260	.233	36	-8	3	.994	2	*125*	*104*	C-32	-0.4
1913	Chi N	20	42	5	10	4	1	0	11	4	0	8	.238	.304	.381	95	0	0	.962	3	123	158	C-14/1	0.3
1914	Chi N	9	17	3	2	1	0	0	3	1	0	4	.118	.167	.176	2	-2	1	.943	0	*109*	*160*	/C-7	-0.1
Total	11	523	1491	113	311	50	10	8	117	109	26	49	.209	.274	.272	66	-62	20	.963	-24	*97*	*112*	C-465/1-7,2-5,O-5(CF),3	-5.0
NEEL, TROY Troy Lee B 9.14.1965 Freeport, TX BL/TR 6-4/210# d5.30																								
1992	Oak A	24	53	8	14	3	0	3	9	5-0	1	15	.264	.339	.491	137	2	0-1	.846	-0	97	311	/O-9(LF),1-2,D-9	0.2
1993	Oak A	123	427	59	124	21	0	19	63	49-5	4	101	.290	.367	.473	132	20	3-5	.981	-1	100	92	D-85,1-34	0.9
1994	Oak A	83	278	43	74	13	0	15	48	38-5	2	61	.266	.357	.475	123	10	2-3	.994	-1	85	105	1-45,D-35	0.2
Total	3	230	758	110	212	37	0	37	120	92-10	7	177	.280	.362	.475	129	32	5-9	.986	-2	90	98	D-129/1-81,O-9(LF)	1.3
NEEMAN, CAL Calvin Amandus B 2.18.1929 Valmeyer, IL BR/TR 6-1/192# d4.16																								
1957	Chi N	122	415	37	107	17	1	10	39	22-5	3	87	.258	.298	.376	81	-12	0-0	.990	-0	*85*	***146***	*C-118	-0.6
1958	Chi N	76	201	30	52	7	0	12	29	21-2	3	41	.259	.336	.473	113	4	0-0	.992	-1	*81*	*96*	C-71	0.6
1959	Chi N	44	105	7	17	2	0	3	9	11-2	0	23	.162	.241	.267	36	-10	0-0	.994	-4	*57*	*60*	C-38	-1.3
1960	Chi N	9	13	0	2	1	0	0	0	0-0	0	5	.154	.154	.231	4	-2	0-0	1.000	2	*99*	*163*	/C-9	0.0
	Phi N	59	160	13	29	6	2	4	13	16-2	2	42	.181	.264	.319	59	-9	0-0	.979	1	*64*	*153*	C-52	-0.7
	Year	68	173	13	31	7	2	4	13	16-2	2	47	.179	.257	.312	55	-11	0-0	.982	2	*67*	*154*	C-61	-0.7
1961	Phi N	19	31	0	7	1	0	0	2	4-1	0	8	.226	.306	.258	55	-2	1-0	.986	1	*97*	*122*	C-19	-0.1
1962	Pit N	24	50	5	9	1	1	1	5	3-0	0	10	.180	.226	.300	40	-5	0-0	.983	5	*114*	*124*	C-24	0.1
1963	Cle A	9	9	0	0	0	0	0	0	1-0	0	5	.000	.100	.000	-70	-2	0-0	1.000	1	144	296	/C-9	-0.1
	Was A	14	18	1	1	0	0	0	0	1-0	0	0	.056	.105	.056	-54	-4	0-0	.970	1	167	121	C-12	-0.2
	Year	23	27	1	1	0	0	0	0	2-0	0	5	.037	.103	.037	-59	-6	0-0	.985	2	156	201	C-21	-0.3
Total	7	376	1002	93	224	35	4	30	97	79-12	8	221	.224	.284	.356	72	-42	1-0	.988	5	*83*	*129*	C-352	-2.3
NEFF, DOUG Douglas Williams B 10.8.1891 Harrisonburg, VA D 5.23.1932 Cape Charles, VA BR/TR 5-9/141# d6.26																								
1914	Was A	3	2	0	0	0	0	0	0	0	0	0	.000	.000	.000	-96	0	0	.889	1	146	0	/S-3	0.0
1915	Was A	30	60	1	10	1	0	0	4	4	0	6	.167	.219	.183	20	-6	1-2	.867	-4	91	81	3-12,2-10/S-7	-1.1
Total	2	33	62	1	10	1	0	0	4	4	0	6	.161	.212	.177	16	-6	1-2	.867	-4	91	81	/3-12,2-10,S-10	-1.1
NEIGHBORS, CY Flemon Cecil B 9.23.1880 Fayetteville, MO D 5.20.1964 Tacoma, WA BR 5-10/178# d4.29																								
1908	Pit N	1	0	0	0	0	0	0	0	0	0		—	—	—	—	0	0	—	-0	0	0	/O(LF)	0.0
NEIGHBORS, BOB Robert Otis B 11.9.1917 Talihina, OK D 8.8.1952 , North Korea (MIA) BR/TR 5-11/165# d9.16																								
1939	StL A	7	11	3	2	0	0	1	1	0	0	1	.182	.182	.455	56	-1	0-0	.917	-0	90	64	/S-5	-0.1
NEILL, MIKE Michael Robert B 4.27.1970 Martinsville, VA BL/TL 6-2/190# d7.27																								
1998	Oak A	6	15	2	4	1	0	0	0	2-0	0	4	.267	.353	.333	82	0	0-0	1.000	1	157	0	/O-6(4-2-0)	0.1
NEILL, TOMMY Thomas White B 11.7.1919 Hartselle, AL D 9.22.1980 Houston, TX BL/TR 6-2/200# d9.10																								
1946	Bos N	13	45	8	12	2	0	0	7	2	0	1	.267	.298	.311	72	-2	0	1.000	-0	91	115	O-13(LF)	-0.3
1947	Bos N	7	10	1	2	0	1	0	0	1	1	2	.200	.333	.400	96	0	0	1.000	-0	73	0	/O-2(1-0-1)	0.0
Total	2	20	55	9	14	2	1	0	7	3	1	3	.255	.305	.327	77	-2	0	1.000	-0	89	102	/O-15(14-0-1)	-0.3
NEIS, BERNIE Bernard Edmund B 9.26.1895 Bloomington, IL D 11.29.1972 Inverness, FL BB/TR (BR 1920-21) 5-7/160# d4.14																								
1920	†Bro N	95	249	38	63	11	2	2	22	26	2	35	.253	.329	.337	89	-3	9-9	.957	1	100	118	O-83(11-7-65)	-0.7
1921	Bro N	102	230	34	59	5	4	4	34	25	1	41	.257	.332	.365	81	-6	9-7	.946	1	93	151	O-77(11-24-45)/2	-1.0
1922	Bro N	61	70	15	16	4	1	1	9	13	0	8	.229	.349	.357	83	-1	3-2	.897	1	106	163	O-27(7-3-17)	-0.2
1923	Bro N	126	445	78	122	17	4	5	37	36	1	38	.274	.330	.364	85	-10	8-8	.941	2	96	146	*O-111(13-87-11)	-1.4
1924	Bro N	80	211	43	64	8	3	4	26	27	1	17	.303	.385	.427	121	7	4-2	.937	-2	97	87	O-62(19-22-22)	0.1
1925	Bos N	106	355	47	101	20	2	5	45	38	0	19	.285	.354	.394	100	1	8-10	.970	7	117	93	O-87(9-76-2)	0.2
1926	Bos N	30	93	16	20	5	2	0	8	8	0	10	.215	.277	.312	64	-5	4	.925	0	110	87	O-23(15-8-0)	-0.6
1927	Cle A	32	96	17	29	9	0	4	18	18	0	9	.302	.412	.521	140	6	0-1	.978	2	106	159	O-29(5-24-0)	0.7
	Chi A	45	76	9	22	5	0	0	11	10	0	9	.289	.372	.355	92	0	1-0	.927	1	107	129	O-21(6-9-7)	0.0
	Year	77	172	26	51	14	0	4	29	28	0	18	.297	.395	.448	120	6	1-1	.962	3	106	149	O-50(11-33-7)	0.7
Total	8	677	1825	297	496	84	18	25	210	201	5	186	.272	.346	.379	94	-11	46-39	.950	13	102	124	O-520(96-260-169)/2	-2.9
NEITZKE, ERNIE Ernest Fredrich B 11.13.1894 Toledo, OH D 4.27.1977 Sylvania, OH BR/TR 5-10/180# d6.2																								
1921	Bos A	11	25	3	6	0	0	0	2	4	0	4	.240	.345	.240	53	-2	0-0	.875	-0	89	109	/O-8(4-1-3),P-2	-0.2
NELSON, BRY Bryant Lawrence B 1.27.1974 Crossett, AR BB/TR 5-10/205# d5.14																								
2002	Bos A	25	34	6	9	3	0	0	2	4-0	0	1	.265	.342	.353	84	-1	1-1	.964	0	86	53	2-11,O-11(7-2-2)/D	0.0

Year	Tm Lg	G	AB	R	H	2B	3B	HR	RBI	BB-IB	HP	SO	AVG	OBP	SLG	AOPS	ABR	SB-CS	FA	FR	Rng	Thr	G at Pos	BFW
NELSON, DAVE David Earl B 6.20.1944 Fort Sill, OK BR/TR (BB 1968 (part)) 5-10/160# d4.11 C11 OF Total (6-LF 10-CF 1-RF)																								
1968	Cle A	88	189	26	44	4	5	0	19	17-0	1	35	.233	.295	.307	85	-4	23-7	.987	-5	81	95	2-59,S-14	-0.1
1969	Cle A	52	123	11	25	0	0	0	6	9-1	1	26	.203	.259	.203	31	-11	4-3	.966	7	111	129	2-33/O-2(1-0-1)	-0.2
1970	Was A	47	107	5	17	1	0	0	4	7-0	0	24	.159	.207	.168	6	-14	2-1	.986	4	113	117	2-33	-0.8
1971	Was A	85	329	47	92	11	3	5	33	23-2	1	29	.280	.328	.377	105	1	17-8	.938	-12	89	86	3-84/2	-1.1
1972	Tex A	145	499	68	113	16	3	2	28	67-3	5	81	.226	.324	.283	85	-7	51-17	.945	-5	95	99	*3-119,O-15(5-10-0)	-0.9
1973	Tex A★	142	576	71	165	24	4	7	48	34-3	0	78	.286	.325	.378	102	0	43-16	.984	-5	94	91	*2-140	0.8
1974	Tex A	121	474	71	112	13	1	3	42	34-0	4	72	.236	.291	.287	69	-19	25-13	.969	2	97	86	*2-120/D	-0.9
1975	Tex A	28	80	9	17	1	0	2	10	8-1	1	10	.213	.289	.300	68	-3	6-0	.959	0	97	113	2-23/D	0.0
1976	†KC A	78	153	24	36	4	2	1	17	14-0	0	26	.235	.298	.307	77	-5	15-5	.975	-2	98	74	2-46,D-22/1-3	-0.4
1977	KC A	27	48	8	9	3	1	0	4	7-0	0	11	.188	.291	.292	59	-3	1-3	.926	-2	81	82	2-11/D-7	-0.5
Total	10	813	2578	340	630	77	19	20	211	220-10	13	392	.244	.305	.312	81	-65	187-73	.976	-18	96	94	2-466,3-203/D-31,O-17C,S-14,1-3	-4.1
NELSON, ROCKY Glenn Richard B 11.18.1924 Portsmouth, OH BL/TL 5-11/178# d4.27																								
1949	StL N	82	244	28	54	8	4	4	32	11	1	12	.221	.258	.336	55	-17	1	1.000	-3	70	101	1-70	-2.2
1950	StL N	76	235	27	58	10	4	1	20	26	1	9	.247	.324	.336	71	-10	4	.992	4	123	112	1-70	-0.8
1951	StL N	9	18	3	4	1	0	0	1	1	0	0	.222	.263	.278	45	-1	0-0	1.000	-1	47	167	/1-4,O(LF)	-0.2
	Pit N	71	195	29	52	7	4	1	14	10	0	7	.267	.302	.359	75	-8	1-1	.990	1	115	105	1-32,O-12(LF)	-0.9
	Year	80	213	32	56	8	4	1	15	11	0	7	.263	.299	.352	73	-9	1-1	.991	1	109	111	1-36,O-13(LF)	-1.1
	Chi A	6	5	0	0	0	0	0	0	1	0	0	.000	.167	.000	-53	-1	0-0	—	0			H	-0.1
1952	†Bro N	37	39	6	10	1	0	0	3	7	0	4	.256	.370	.282	82	-1	0-0	1.000	-1	0	89	/1-5	-0.1
1954	Cle A	4	4	0	0	0	0	0	0	0	0	1	.000	.000	.000	-98	-1	0-0	1.000	-0	0	230	/1-2	-0.1
1956	Bro N	31	96	7	20	2	0	4	15	4-1	0	10	.208	.235	.354	53	-7	0-0	.991	1	118	124	1-25	-0.7
	StL N	38	56	6	13	5	0	3	8	6-1	0	6	.232	.306	.482	108	1	0-0	1.000	1	165	127	1-14/O-8(LF)	0.1
	Year	69	152	13	33	7	0	7	23	10-2	0	16	.217	.262	.401	73	-6	0-0	.993	2	128	125	1-39/O-8(LF)	-0.6
1959	Pit N	98	175	31	51	11	0	6	32	23-4	3	19	.291	.379	.457	124	7	0-0	.994	-4	68	150	1-56/O-2(1-0-1)	0.1
1960	†Pit N	93	200	34	60	11	1	7	35	24-5	5	15	.300	.382	.470	133	10	1-2	.996	1	104	127	1-73	0.8
1961	Pit N	75	127	15	25	5	1	5	13	17-2	2	11	.197	.301	.370	77	-4	0-0	.996	-1	86	119	1-35	-0.7
Total	9	620	1394	186	347	61	14	31	173	130-13	12	94	.249	.317	.379	84	-32	7-3	.995	-1	97	119	1-386/O-23(22-0-1)	-4.8
NELSON, JAMIE James Victor B 9.5.1959 Clinton, OK BR/TR 5-11/180# d7.21																								
1983	Sea A	40	96	9	21	3	0	1	5	13-1	0	12	.219	.309	.281	62	-5	4-2	.978	1	71	156	C-39	-0.2
NELSON, CANDY John W B 3.14.1849 Brooklyn, NY D 9.4.1910 Brooklyn, NY BL/TR 5-6/145# d6.11																								
1872	Tro NA	4	20	2	7	0	0	0	4	0		2	.350	.350	.350	114	0	0-0	1.000	-1	0	0	/O-3(CF),S	0.0
	Eck NA	18	76	12	19	5	1	0	9	2		3	.250	.269	.342	102	2	1-0	.837	-0	120	93	/2-8,O-8(CF),3-4	0.1
	Year	22	96	14	26	5	1	0	13	2		5	.271	.286	.344	105	2	1-0	.813	-1	0	0	O-11(CF)/2-8,3-4,S	0.1
1873	Mut NA	36	168	28	55	4	1	0	22	1		2	.327	.331	.363	107	1	2-0	.867	-9	74	41	2-27/3-6,O-6(RF),C1	-0.7
1874	Mut NA	**65**	297	55	73	7	5	0	31	**9**		5	.246	.268	.303	80	-7	6-0	.824	-18	77	57	*2-51,S-14/O(CF)	-2.1
1875	Mut NA	70	276	28	55	7	1	0	23	9		0	.199	.225	.232	56	-12	4-2	.855	-1	97	93	2-49,3-23/S-2,O(LF)	-1.4
1878	Ind N	19	84	12	11	1	0	0	5	5		11	.131	.180	.143	8	-7		.841	-7	81	22	S-19	-1.3
1879	Tro N	28	106	17	28	7	1	0	10	8		4	.264	.316	.349	127	4		.834	2	105	123	S-24/O-4(LF)	0.6
1881	Wor N	24	103	13	29	1	0	1	15	5		6	.282	.315	.320	95	-1		.898	2	115	70	S-24	0.2
1883	NY AA	**97**	417	75	127	19	6	0		31			.305	.353	.379	130	14		.875	-7	85	105	*S-97	0.9
1884	†NY AA	111	432	114	110	15	3	1		**74**	9		.255	.375	.310	129	21		.879	-16	84	71	*S-110/2	0.8
1885	NY AA	107	420	98	107	12	4	1	30	**61**	3		.255	.353	.310	115	13		.892	17	106	103	*S-107/3	2.9
1886	NY AA	109	413	89	93	7	2	0	23	64	2		.225	.332	.252	91	2	14	.855	-5	95	83	S-73,O-36(0-28-8)	-0.1
1887	NY AA	68	257	61	63	5	1	0	24	48	8		.245	.380	.272	88	1	29	.895	10	165	365	O-37(0-1-36),S-32/2	0.9
	NY N	1	2	0	0	0	0	0	0	0	0	1	.000	.000	.000	-99	-1	0	—	-0	0	0	/3	-0.1
1890	Bro AA	60	223	44	56	3	2	0	12	35	5		.251	.365	.283	94	1	12	.866	-6	113	105	S-57/O-4(RF)	-0.3
Total	4 NA	193	837	125	209	23	8	0	89	21	0	12	.250	.268	.296	81	-16	13-2	.000	-28	86	69	2-135/3-33,O-19(1-12-6),S-17,1C	-4.1
Total	9	624	2457	523	624	70	19	3	119	331	27	22	.254	.349	.302	108	47	55-0	.875	-9	96	93	S-543/O-81(4-29-48),3-2,2-2	4.5
NELSON, RAY Raymond "Kell" (born Raymond Nelson Kellogg) B 8.4.1875 Holyoke, MA D 1.8.1961 Mt.Vernon, NY BR/TR 5-9/150# d5.6																								
1901	NY N	39	130	12	26	2	0	0	7	10	1		.200	.262	.215	41	-10	3	.885	-4	113	70	2-39	-1.3
NELSON, RICKY Ricky Lee B 5.8.1959 Eloy, AZ BL/TR 6/200# d5.17																								
1983	Sea A	98	291	32	74	13	3	5	36	17-3	0	50	.254	.294	.371	79	-9	7-4	.971	-3	81	179	O-91(46-1-50)/D	-1.5
1984	Sea A	9	15	2	3	0	0	1	2	2-0	0	4	.200	.294	.400	91	0	0-0	1.000	0	147	0	/O-2(RF),D-3	0.0
1985	Sea A	6	2	2	0	0	0	0	0	0-0	0	1	.000	.000	.000	-99	-1	0-0	1.000	-0	87	0	/O-3(RF)	-0.1
1986	Sea A	10	12	2	2	0	0	0	1	0-0	0	4	.167	.167	.167	-9	-2	1-0	.667	-0	164	0	/O(CF)D	-0.2
Total	4	123	320	38	79	13	3	6	39	19-3	0	59	.247	.288	.363	75	-12	8-4	.965	-3	82	175	/O-97(46-2-55),D-9	-1.8
NELSON, ROB Robert Augustus B 5.17.1964 Pasadena, CA BL/TL 6-4/215# d9.9																								
1986	Oak A	5	9	1	2	1	0	0	0	1-0	0	4	.222	.300	.333	78	0	0-0	.800	-0	135	129	/1-2,D	0.0
1987	Oak A	7	24	1	4	1	0	0	0	0-0	0	12	.167	.167	.208	-2	-4	0-0	.968	2	221	113	/1-7	-0.2
	SD N	10	11	0	1	0	0	0	1	1-0	0	8	.091	.167	.091	-31	-2	0-0	1.000	-0	0	122	/1-2	-0.3
1988	SD N	7	21	4	4	0	0	1	3	2-0	0	9	.190	.261	.333	71	-1	0-0	.981	0	129	141	/1-5	-0.1
1989	SD N	42	82	6	16	0	1	3	7	20-1	0	29	.195	.353	.329	96	0	1-3	.991	3	151	110	1-31	0.1
1990	SD N	5	5	0	0	0	0	0	0	0-0	0	4	.000	.000	.000	-99	-1	0-0	—	0			/H	-0.2
Total	5	76	152	12	27	2	1	4	11	24-1	0	66	.178	.290	.283	62	-8	1-3	.983	5	156	116	/1-47,D	-0.7
NELSON, TEX Robert Sydney "Babe" B 8.7.1936 Dallas, TX BL/TL 6-3/220# d6.22																								
1955	Bal A	25	31	4	6	0	0	0	1	7-0	0	13	.194	.342	.194	50	-2	0-0	.889	1	70	582	/O-6(LF),1-2	-0.2
1956	Bal A	39	68	5	14	2	0	0	5	7-0	0	22	.206	.276	.235	40	-6	0-0	.939	1	98	277	O-24(9-0-16)	-0.5
1957	Bal A	15	23	2	5	0	2	0	5	1-0	1	5	.217	.280	.391	87	-1	0-0	1.000	-1	81	0	/O-8(2-0-6)	-0.1
Total	3	79	122	11	25	2	2	0	11	15-0	1	40	.205	.295	.254	52	-9	0-0	.938	1	90	280	/O-38(17-0-22),1-2	-0.8
NELSON, TOMMY Thomas Cousineau B 5.1.1917 Chicago, IL D 9.24.1973 San Diego, CA BR/TR 5-11.5/180# d4.17																								
1945	Bos N	40	121	6	20	2	0	0	6	4	0	13	.165	.192	.182	4	-16	1	.910	-4	106	185	3-20,2-12	-2.0
NEN, DICK Richard Le Roy B 9.24.1939 South Gate, CA BL/TL 6-2/205# d9.18 s-Robb																								
1963	LA N	7	8	2	1	0	0	1	1	3-1	0	3	.125	.364	.500	157	1	0-0	1.000	-1	0	0	/1-5	0.0
1965	Was A	69	246	18	64	7	1	6	31	19-1	1	47	.260	.312	.370	96	-2	1-2	.993	8	152	90	1-65	0.2
1966	Was A	94	235	20	50	8	0	6	30	28-2	0	46	.213	.294	.323	79	-6	0-2	.990	-1	95	93	1-76	-1.3
1967	Was A	110	238	21	52	7	1	6	29	21-4	0	39	.218	.280	.332	84	-5	0-1	.995	1	109	117	1-65/O(LF)	-0.9
1968	Chi N	81	94	8	17	1	1	2	16	6-2	0	17	.181	.225	.277	48	-6	0-0	.987	-1	84	81	1-52	-1.0
1970	Was A	6	5	1	1	0	0	0	0	0-0	0	0	.200	.200	.200	11	-1	0-0	1.000	0	653	0	/1	0.0
Total	6	367	826	70	185	23	3	21	107	77-10	1	152	.224	.288	.335	82	-19	1-5	.992	7	115	96	1-264/O(LF)	-3.0
NESS, JACK John Charles B 11.11.1884 Chicago, IL D 12.4.1957 DeLand, FL BR/TR 6-2/165# d5.9																								
1911	Det A	12	39	6	6	0	0	0	2	2	0		.154	.195	.154	-2	-5	0	.977	1	122	72	1-12	-0.5
1916	Chi A	75	258	32	69	7	5	1	34	9	7	32	.267	.310	.345	96	-3	4	.979	-5	77	133	1-69	-1.0
Total	2	87	297	38	75	7	5	1	36	11	7	32	.253	.295	.320	82	-8	4	.978	-4	84	124	/1-81	-1.5
NETTLES, GRAIG Graig B 8.20.1944 San Diego, CA BL/TR 6/186# d9.6 C2 b-Jim OF Total (58-LF 2-CF 13-RF)																								
1967	Min A	3	3	0	1	1	0	0	0	0-0	0	0	.333	.333	.667	175	0	0-0	—	0			H	0.0
1968	Min A	22	76	13	17	2	1	5	8	7-1	1	20	.224	.298	.474	125	2	0-0	.968	1	112	245	O-16(2-1-13)/3-5,1-3	0.2
1969	†Min A	96	225	27	50	9	2	7	26	32-1	1	47	.222	.319	.373	92	-2	1-2	.987	1	99	62	O-54(53-1-0),3-21	-0.4
1970	Cle A	157	549	81	129	13	1	26	62	81-3	3	77	.235	.336	.404	99	-1	3-1	**.967**	26	112	126	*3-154/O-3(LF)	2.6
1971	Cle A	158	598	78	156	18	1	28	86	82-6	3	56	.261	.350	.435	112	10	7-4	.973	**46**	**125**	**148**	*3-158	**5.9**
1972	Cle A	150	557	65	141	28	0	17	70	57-5	4	50	.253	.325	.395	110	8	2-3	.956	8	**111**	90	*3-150	1.6
1973	NY A	160	552	65	129	18	0	22	81	78-3	7	76	.234	.334	.386	107	6	0-0	.953	33	**128**	138	*3-157/D-2	3.8
1974	NY A	155	566	74	139	21	1	22	75	59-8	3	75	.246	.316	.403	109	6	1-0	.961	**20**	112	85	*3-154/S	2.6
1975	NY A★	157	581	71	155	24	4	21	91	51-3	2	88	.267	.322	.430	115	10	1-3	.964	13	106	104	*3-157	2.1
1976	†NY A	158	583	88	148	29	2	**32**	93	62-6	4	94	.254	.327	.475	135	24	11-6	.965	17	**115**	**122**	*3-158/S	4.3
1977	†NY A★	158	589	99	150	23	4	37	107	68-8	3	79	.255	.333	.496	124	18	2-5	.974	-4	96	112	*3-156/D	1.0

Year	Tm Lg	G	AB	R	H	2B	3B	HR	RBI	BB-IB	HP	SO	AVG	OBP	SLG	AOPS	ABR	SB-CS	FA	FR	Rng	Thr	G at Pos	BFW
1978	†NY A★	159	587	81	162	23	2	27	93	59-6	6	69	.276	.343	.460	128	22	1-1	.975	-5	96	106	*3-159/S-2	1.4
1979	NY A★	145	521	71	132	15	1	20	73	59-6	0	53	.253	.325	.401	98	-2	1-2	.966	7	105	114	*3-144	0.2
1980	†NY A★	89	324	52	79	14	0	16	45	42-5	1	42	.244	.331	.435	110	5	0-0	.960	-7	91	104	3-88/S	-0.3
1981	†NY A	103	349	46	85	7	1	15	46	47-4	1	49	.244	.333	.398	112	6	0-2	.972	4	98	91	3-97/D-4	0.7
1982	NY A	122	405	47	94	11	2	18	55	51-4	1	49	.232	.317	.402	98	-1	1-5	.934	-2	97	101	*3-113/D-3	-0.6
1983	NY A	129	462	56	123	17	3	20	75	51-2	3	65	.266	.341	.446	120	12	0-1	.956	-9	93	69	*3-126/D	0.1
1984	†SD N	124	395	56	90	11	1	20	65	58-4	5	55	.228	.329	.413	109	5	0-0	.936	-11	90	82	*3-119	-0.8
1985	SD N★	137	440	66	115	23	1	15	61	72-5	0	59	.261	.363	.420	121	15	0-0	.959	-9	90	79	*3-130	0.4
1986	SD N	126	354	36	77	9	0	16	55	41-8	2	62	.218	.300	.379	88	-7	0-1	.941	-3	93	86	*3-114	-1.2
1987	Atl N	112	177	16	37	8	1	5	33	22-4	0	25	.209	.294	.350	67	-8	1-0	.951	-1	92	130	3-40/1-6	-1.0
1988	Mon N	80	93	5	16	4	0	1	14	9-2	0	19	.172	.240	.247	40	-7	0-0	.818	-1	95	177	3-12/1-5	-1.0
Total	22	2700	8986	1193	2225	328	28	390	1314	1088-94	50	1209	.248	.329	.421	110	121	32-36	.961	124	105	106	*3-2412/O-73L,1-14,D-11,S-5	21.6
NETTLES, JIM James William B 3.2.1947 San Diego, CA BL/TL 6/186# d9.7 b-Graig																								
1970	Min A	13	20	3	5	0	0	0	0	1-0	0	5	.250	.286	.250	48	-1	0-1	1.000	-1	83	0	O-11(5-1-5)	-0.3
1971	Min A	70	168	17	42	5	1	6	24	19-2	0	24	.250	.321	.399	101	0	3-2	.986	5	120	101	O-62(2-57-3)	0.3
1972	Min A	102	235	28	48	5	2	4	15	32-3	1	52	.204	.302	.294	74	-7	4-3	.982	-0	99	111	O-78(12-58-8)/1	-1.1
1974	Det A	43	141	20	32	5	1	6	17	15-1	1	26	.227	.306	.404	99	0	3-4	1.000	-2	96	33	O-41(8-4-30)	-0.5
1979	KC A	11	23	0	2	0	0	0	1	3-0	0	2	.087	.192	.087	-21	-4	0-0	1.000	1	139	0	/O-8(7-0-1),1	-0.4
1981	Oak A	1	0	0	0	0	0	0	0	0-0	0	0	—	—	—	—	0	0-0	—	-0	0	0	/O(RF)	0.0
Total	6	240	587	68	129	15	4	16	57	70-6	2	109	.220	.304	.341	83	-12	10-10	.988	3	105	81	O-201(34-120-48)/1-2	-2.0
NETTLES, MORRIS Morris B 1.26.1952 Los Angeles, CA BL/TL 6-1/170# d4.26																								
1974	Cal A	56	175	27	48	4	0	0	8	16-0	0	38	.274	.335	.297	88	-2	20-11	.990	-5	90	0	O-54(3-37-14)	-0.9
1975	Cal A	112	294	50	68	11	0	0	23	26-2	1	57	.231	.295	.269	65	-13	22-15	.974	3	113	76	O-90(39-38-17)/D-9	-1.4
Total	2	168	469	77	116	15	0	0	31	42-2	1	95	.247	.310	.279	74	-15	42-26	.980	-2	104	47	O-144(42-75-31)/D-9	-2.3
NETZEL, MILO Miles A. B 5.12.1886 Eldred, PA D 3.18.1938 Oxnard, CA BL/TL d9.16																								
1909	Cle A	10	37	2	7	1	0	0	3	3	0		.189	.250	.216	46	-2	1	.800	-2	82	156	/3-6,O-2(LF)	-0.5
NEU, OTTO Otto Adam B 9.24.1894 Springfield, OH D 9.19.1932 Kenton, OH BR/TR 5-11/170# d7.10																								
1917	StL A	1	0	0	0	0	0	0	0	0	0	0	—	—	—	—	0	0	—	-0	0	0	/S	0.0
NEUN, JOHNNY John Henry B 10.28.1900 Baltimore, MD D 3.28.1990 Baltimore, MD BB/TL 5-10.5/175# d4.14 M3 C3																								
1925	Det A	60	75	15	20	3	3	0	4	9	0	12	.267	.345	.387	87	-2	2-3	.990	-1	66	67	1-13	-0.4
1926	Det A	97	242	47	72	14	4	0	15	27	1	26	.298	.370	.388	97	-1	4-7	.993	-2	78	95	1-49	-0.7
1927	Det A	79	204	38	66	9	4	0	27	35	2	13	.324	.427	.407	116	7	22-7	.980	-3	85	107	1-53	0.2
1928	Det A	36	108	15	23	3	1	0	5	7	0	10	.213	.261	.259	36	-10	2-2	.975	0	115	90	1-25	-1.1
1930	Bos N	81	212	39	69	12	2	2	23	21	1	18	.325	.389	.429	101	1	9	.991	0	101	101	1-55	-0.2
1931	Bos N	79	104	17	23	1	3	0	11	11	1	14	.221	.302	.288	62	-6	2	.994	0	99	106	1-36	-0.7
Total	6	432	945	171	273	42	17	2	85	110	5	93	.289	.366	.376	91	-11	41-19	.987	-6	91	99	1-231	-2.9
NEVIN, ALEXANDER Alexander Brown B 10.3.1850 Allegheny City, PA D 10.10.1921 Pensacola, FL d5.6																								
1873	Res NA	13	55	7	11	1	2	0	1	1		4	.200	.214	.291	53	-3	0-0	.561	-6	79	0	3-12/2O(RF)	-0.7
NEVIN, PHIL Phillip Joseph B 1.19.1971 Fullerton, CA BR/TR 6-2/180# d6.11 OF Total (81-LF 38-RF)																								
1995	Hou N	18	60	4	7	1	0	0	1	7-1	1	13	.117	.221	.133	-4	-9	1-0	.933	-1	95	146	3-16	-1.0
	Det A	29	96	9	21	3	1	2	12	11-0	3	27	.219	.318	.333	70	-4	0-0	.963	-1	90	108	O-27(LF)/D-2	-0.6
1996	Det A	38	120	15	35	5	0	8	19	8-0	1	39	.292	.338	.533	117	2	1-0	.943	3	121	124	3-24/O-9(LF),C-4,D	0.6
1997	Det A	93	251	32	59	16	1	9	35	25-1	1	68	.235	.306	.414	87	-5	0-1	.986	-2	91	175	O-40(LF),D-30,3-17/1-7,C	-1.1
1998	Ana A	75	237	27	54	8	1	8	27	17-0	5	67	.228	.291	.371	71	-11	0-0	.989	-9	85	100	C-69/1-2,D-3	-1.5
1999	SD N	128	383	52	103	27	0	24	85	51-1	1	82	.269	.352	.527	130	17	1-0	.982	11	116	124	3-67,C-31,O-13(5-0-9),1-11/D	2.7
2000	SD N	143	538	87	163	34	1	31	107	59-9	4	121	.303	.374	.543	138	31	2-0	.929	-8	97	86	*3-142	2.3
2001	SD N★	149	546	97	167	31	0	41	126	71-7	4	147	.306	.388	.588	162	51	4-4	.930	5	108	109	*3-145/D	5.4
2002	SD N	107	407	53	116	16	0	12	57	38-4	1	87	.285	.344	.413	113	5	4-0	.928	2	103	119	3-71,1-36	0.4
2003	SD N	59	226	30	63	8	0	13	46	21-1	0	44	.279	.339	.487	124	7	2-0	.996	-1	104	101	1-31,O-29(RF)	0.2
Total	9	839	2864	406	788	149	4	148	515	308-24	21	695	.275	.348	.485	120	84	15-5	.938	0	104	107	3-482,O-118L,C-105/1-87,D-38	7.4
NEWELL, JOHN John A. B 1.14.1868 Wilmington, DE D 1.28.1919 Wilmington, DE BR/TL 5-9/170# d7.22																								
1891	Pit N	5	18	1	2	0	0	0	2	0	1	0	.111	.158	.111	-22	-3	0	.846	-1	114	0	/3-5	-0.3
NEWELL, T. E. T. E. B St.Louis, MO d8.8																								
1877	StL N	1	3	0	0	0	0	0	0	0		0	.000	.000	.000	-99	-1		.833	0	96	0	/S	-0.1
NEWFIELD, MARC Marc Alexander B 10.19.1972 Sacramento, CA BR/TR 6-4/205# d7.6																								
1993	Sea A	22	66	5	15	3	0	1	7	2-0	1	8	.227	.257	.318	54	-4	0-1	—	-1	0	0	D-15/O-5(LF)	-0.7
1994	Sea A	12	38	3	7	1	0	1	4	2-0	0	4	.184	.225	.289	31	-4	0-0	1.000	-1	53	0	/O-3(LF),D-9	-0.4
1995	Sea A	24	85	7	16	3	0	3	14	3-1	1	16	.188	.225	.329	42	-8	0-0	1.000	-0	110	0	O-24(23-0-1)	-0.8
	SD N	21	55	6	17	5	1	1	7	2-0	0	8	.309	.333	.491	118	1	0-0	1.000	1	110	134	O-19(LF)	0.1
1996	SD N	84	191	27	48	11	0	5	26	16-1	2	44	.251	.311	.387	89	-3	1-1	.970	-4	89	0	O-51(30-0-23)/1-2	-0.8
	Mil A	49	179	21	55	15	0	7	31	11-1	4	26	.307	.354	.508	112	3	0-1	.990	-2	91	83	O-49(LF)	-0.1
1997	Mil A	50	157	14	36	8	0	1	18	14-0	2	27	.229	.295	.299	57	-10	0-0	.977	-2	93	0	O-28(LF),D-18	-1.3
1998	Mil N	93	186	15	44	7	0	3	25	19-1	1	29	.237	.306	.323	67	-9	0-1	.962	-1	94	108	O-55(LF)/D	-1.1
Total	6	355	957	98	238	53	1	22	132	69-4	11	162	.249	.303	.375	77	-34	1-4	.981	-8	93	54	O-234(212-0-24)/D-43,1-2	-5.1
NEWHAN, DAVID David Matthew B 9.7.1973 Fullerton, CA BL/TR 5-10/180# d6.4																								
1999	SD N	32	43	7	6	1	0	2	6	1-0	0	11	.140	.159	.302	14	-6	2-1	.970	4	117	149	2-19/13	-0.2
2000	SD N	14	20	5	3	1	0	1	2	6-1	0	7	.150	.346	.350	82	0	0-0	1.000	-1	132	0	/2-3,O-5(RF),3-2	-0.1
	Phi N	10	17	3	3	0	0	0	0	2-0	0	6	.176	.263	.176	14	-2	0-0	1.000	3	158	221	/2-5	0.1
	Year	24	37	8	6	1	0	1	2	8-1	0	13	.162	.311	.270	51	-3	0-0	1.000	2	153	180	/2-8,O-5(RF),3-2	0.0
2001	Phi N	7	6	2	2	1	0	0	1	1-0	0	0	.333	.375	.500	143	0	0-0	1.000	-1	0	0	/2	0.0
Total	3	63	86	17	14	3	0	3	9	10-1	0	24	.163	.247	.302	41	-8	2-1	.980	5	121	150	/2-28,O-5(RF),3-3,1	-0.2
NEWMAN, AL Albert Dwayne B 6.30.1960 Kansas City, MO BB/TR 5-9/183# d6.14 C1 OF Total (11-LF 1-CF)																								
1985	Mon N	25	29	7	5	1	0	0	1	3-0	0	4	.172	.250	.207	31	-3	2-1	1.000	2	125	108	2-15/S-2	0.0
1986	Mon N	95	185	23	37	3	0	1	8	21-2	0	20	.200	.279	.232	44	-14	11-11	.967	1	105	109	2-59,S-22	-1.2
1987	†Min A	110	307	44	68	15	5	0	29	34-0	0	27	.221	.298	.303	58	-18	15-11	.982	-0	92	103	S-55,2-47,3-12/O-2(LF),D-5	-1.3
1988	Min A	105	260	35	58	7	0	0	19	29-0	0	34	.223	.301	.250	54	-15	12-3	.966	-8	81	149	3-60,S-28,2-23/D-2	-2.0
1989	Min A	141	446	62	113	18	2	0	38	59-0	2	46	.253	.341	.303	78	-11	25-12	.980	-13	91	83	2-84,3-37,S-31/O-4(4-1-0),D-2	-2.0
1990	Min A	144	388	43	94	14	0	0	30	33-0	2	34	.242	.304	.278	60	-20	13-6	.993	1	99	115	2-89,S-48,3-28/O-3(LF)	-1.5
1991	†Min A	118	246	25	47	5	0	0	19	23-0	1	21	.191	.260	.211	31	-23	4-5	.987	-2	88	112	S-55,2-35,3-35/1O(LF)D	-2.3
1992	Tex A	116	246	25	54	5	0	0	12	34-0	1	26	.220	.317	.240	60	-12	9-6	.983	4	105	82	2-72,3-28,S-20/O(LF)D	-0.6
Total	8	854	2107	264	476	68	7	1	156	236-2	6	212	.226	.304	.266	58	-116	91-55	.984	-15	101	96	2-424,S-261,3-200/D-13,O-11L,1	-10.9
NEWMAN, CHARLIE Charles "Decker" B 11.5.1868 Juda, WI D 11.23.1947 San Diego, CA BR/TR d7.11																								
1892	NY N	3	12	1	4	0	0	0	1	2	0	0	.333	.429	.333	133	1	3	.750	-0	216	0	/O-3(LF)	0.0
	Chi N	16	61	4	10	0	0	0	2	1	0	6	.164	.177	.164	3	-7	2	.950	-1	46	228	O-16(LF)	-0.9
	Year	19	73	5	14	0	0	0	3	3	0	6	.192	.224	.192	26	-7	5	.917	-2	76	188	O-19(LF)	-0.9
NEWMAN, JEFF Jeffrey Lynn B 9.11.1948 Fort Worth, TX BR/TR 6-2/218# d6.30 M1 C10																								
1976	Oak A	43	77	5	15	4	0	0	4	4-0	0	12	.195	.235	.247	43	-6	0-0	.981	5	169	135	C-43	0.1
1977	Oak A	94	162	17	36	9	0	4	15	4-1	1	24	.222	.244	.352	61	-9	2-0	.970	-3	118	**138**	C-94/P	-0.9
1978	Oak A	105	268	25	64	7	1	9	32	18-2	1	40	.239	.288	.373	90	-5	0-3	.969	-2	95	84	C-61,1-36/D-2	-0.7
1979	Oak A☆	143	516	53	119	17	2	22	71	27-2	1	88	.231	.267	.399	82	-16	2-1	.977	2	124	**129**	C-81,1-46/3-7,D-7	-1.4
1980	Oak A	127	438	37	102	19	1	15	56	25-8	1	81	.233	.273	.384	85	-11	3-4	.982	-15	86	59	1-60,C-55/3-2,2D	-2.8
1981	†Oak A	68	216	17	50	12	0	3	15	9-1	0	28	.231	.260	.329	73	-8	0-2	.995	0	136	102	C-37,1-30	-0.9
1982	Oak A	72	251	19	50	11	0	6	30	14-1	0	49	.199	.240	.315	54	-17	0-1	.989	-4	73	84	C-67/1-3,3D	-1.9
1983	Bos A	59	132	11	25	4	0	3	7	10-1	2	31	.189	.255	.288	46	-10	0-1	.990	0	88	135	C-51/D-6	-0.9

Year	Tm Lg	G	AB	R	H	2B	3B	HR	RBI	BB-IB	HP	SO	AVG	OBP	SLG	AOPS	ABR	SB-CS	FA	FR	Rng	Thr	G at Pos	BFW
1984	Bos A	24	63	5	14	2	0	1	3	5-0	0	16	.222	.275	.302	58	-4	0-0	.992	0	92	80	C-24	-0.2
Total	9	735	2123	189	475	85	4	63	233	116-16	6	369	.224	.264	.357	73	-86	7-12	.981	-16	108	108	C-513,1-175/D-25,3-10,2P	-9.6
NEWNAM, PATRICK Patrick Henry B 12.10.1880 Hempstead, TX D 6.20.1938 San Antonio, TX BL/TR 6/180# d5.29																								
1910	StL A	103	384	45	83	3	8	2	26	29	2		.216	.275	.281	79	-11	16	.972	-3	97	100	*1-103	-1.8
1911	StL A	20	62	11	12	4	0	0	5	12	3		.194	.351	.258	74	-1	4	.986	1	110	112	1-20	-0.1
Total	2	123	446	56	95	7	8	2	31	41	5		.213	.287	.278	78	-12	20	.974	-3	99	102	1-123	-1.9
NEWSOME, SKEETER Lamar Ashby B 10.18.1910 Phenix City, AL D 8.31.1989 Columbus, GA BR/TR 5-9/170# d4.19																								
1935	Phi A	59	145	18	30	7	1	1	10	5	0	9	.207	.233	.290	35	-15	2-1	.956	2	97	120	S-24,2-13/3-4,O(RF)	-1.0
1936	Phi A	127	471	41	106	15	2	0	46	25	1	27	.225	.266	.265	32	-52	13-4	.957	10	**108**	99	*S-123/2-2,3O(LF)	-2.8
1937	Phi A	122	438	53	111	22	1	1	30	37	0	22	.253	.312	.315	59	-28	11-5	.954	10	106	97	*S-122	-0.8
1938	Phi A	17	48	7	13	4	0	0	7	1	0	4	.271	.286	.354	61	-3	1-1	.971	1	109	75	S-15	-0.1
1939	Phi A	99	248	22	55	9	1	0	17	19	0	12	.222	.277	.266	40	-23	5-7	.950	0	100	91	S-93/2-2	-1.7
1941	Bos A	93	227	28	51	6	0	2	17	22	1	11	.225	.296	.278	51	-16	10-4	.958	9	109	99	S-69,2-23	-0.2
1942	Bos A	29	95	7	26	6	0	0	9	9	0	5	.274	.337	.337	87	-1	2-1	.925	1	118	194	3-12,2-10/S-7	0.1
1943	Bos A	114	449	48	119	21	2	1	22	21	2	21	.265	.301	.327	82	-11	5-6	.962	9	105	103	S-98,3-15	0.5
1944	Bos A	136	472	41	114	26	3	0	41	33	0	21	.242	.291	.309	72	-17	4-3	.963	9	104	90	*S-126/2-8,3	0.2
1945	Bos A	125	438	45	127	30	1	1	48	20	1	15	.290	.322	.370	98	-2	6-3	.963	16	103	100	2-82,S-33,3-11	2.3
1946	Phi N	112	375	35	87	10	2	1	23	30	0	23	.232	.289	.277	63	-19	4	.955	-10	98	81	*S-107/2-3,3-2	-2.4
1947	Phi N	95	310	36	71	8	2	2	22	24	0	24	.229	.284	.287	54	-21	4	.969	3	105	130	S-85/2-6,3-3	-1.3
Total	12	1128	3716	381	910	164	15	9	292	246	5	194	.245	.293	.304	62	-208	67-35	.959	59	105	99	S-902,2-149/3-49,O-2(1-0-1)	-7.2
NEWSON, WARREN Warren Dale B 7.3.1964 Newnan, GA BL/TL 5-7/202# d5.29																								
1991	Chi A	71	132	20	39	5	0	4	25	28-1	0	34	.295	.419	.424	137	8	2-2	.962	-3	74	142	O-50(16-1-34)/D-3	0.4
1992	Chi A	63	136	19	30	3	0	1	11	37-2	0	38	.221	.387	.265	87	0	3-0	1.000	1	87	199	O-50(17-0-33)/D-4	0.1
1993	†Chi A	26	40	9	12	0	0	2	6	9-1	0	12	.300	.429	.450	139	3	0-0	1.000	-0	96	0	D-10/O-5(2-0-3)	0.2
1994	Chi A	63	102	16	26	5	0	2	7	14-1	0	23	.255	.345	.363	84	-2	1-0	.979	1	115	68	O-34(9-0-26)/D-3	-0.2
1995	Chi A	51	85	19	20	0	2	3	9	23-0	1	27	.235	.404	.388	112	3	1-1	.978	2	128	86	O-24(12-0-14)/D-7	0.3
	†Sea A	33	72	15	21	2	0	2	6	16-0	0	18	.292	.420	.403	114	2	1-0	.971	-0	101	93	O-23(18-2-4)	0.2
	Year	84	157	34	41	2	2	5	15	39-0	1	45	.261	.411	.395	114	5	2-1	.975	2	115	89	O-47(30-2-18)/D-7	0.5
1996	†Tex A	91	235	34	60	14	1	10	31	37-1	0	82	.255	.355	.451	97	-1	3-0	.992	4	111	130	O-66(8-0-58)/D-9	0.1
1997	Tex A	81	169	23	36	10	1	10	23	31-2	0	53	.213	.333	.462	100	0	3-0	.949	-0	110	37	O-58(20-0-44)/D-9	-0.1
1998	Tex A	10	21	1	4	1	0	0	2	1-1	0	5	.190	.227	.238	20	-2	0-0	1.000	0	125	0	/O-6(LF),D-3	-0.2
Total	8	489	992	156	248	40	4	34	120	196-9	1	292	.250	.374	.401	103	11	14-3	.978	5	103	111	O-316(108-3-216)/D-48	0.8
NIARHOS, GUS Constantine Gregory B 12.6.1920 Birmingham, AL BR/TR 6/165# d6.9 C3																								
1946	NY A	37	40	11	9	1	1	0	2	11	0	2	.225	.392	.300	94	0	1-0	.989	4	*143*	*137*	C-29	0.5
1948	NY A	83	228	41	61	12	2	0	19	52	0	15	.268	.404	.338	99	3	1-3	.990	6	*105*	*99*	C-82	1.2
1949	†NY A	32	43	7	12	2	1	0	6	13	1	8	.279	.456	.372	120	2	0-0	1.000	3	*83*	*83*	C-30	0.6
1950	NY A	1	0	0	0	0	0	0	0	0	0	0	—	—	—	—	0	0-0	—	0			R	0.0
	Chi A	41	105	17	34	4	0	0	16	14	1	6	.324	.408	.362	101	1	0-0	.978	4	*86*	*97*	C-36	0.7
	Year	42	105	17	34	4	0	0	16	14	1	6	.324	.408	.362	101	1	0-0	.978	4	*86*	*97*	C-36	0.7
1951	Chi A	66	168	27	43	6	0	1	10	47	0	9	.256	.419	.310	101	4	4-3	.985	3	*79*	*82*	C-59	1.0
1952	Bos A	29	58	4	6	0	0	0	4	12	1	9	.103	.268	.103	6	-7	0-0	.992	4	*142*	*102*	C-25	-0.2
1953	Bos A	16	35	6	7	1	1	0	2	4	1	4	.200	.300	.286	56	-2	0-1	.985	2	*100*	*76*	C-16	0.0
1954	Phi N	3	5	0	1	0	0	0	0	0	0	1	.200	.200	.200	5	-1	0-0	1.000	1	*0*	*0*	/C-3	0.0
1955	Phi N	7	9	1	1	0	0	0	0	0-0	0	2	.111	.111	.111	-42	-2	0-0	1.000	1	*72*	*179*	/C-7	-0.1
Total	9	315	691	114	174	26	5	1	59	153-0	4	56	.252	.390	.308	89	-2	6-7	.988	27	*99*	*95*	C-287	3.7
NICHOLAS, DON Donald Leigh B 10.30.1930 Phoenix, AZ BL/TR 5-7/150# d4.16																								
1952	Chi A	3	2	0	0	0	0	0	0	0	0	0	.000	.000	.000	-99	-1	0-0	—	0			H	-0.1
1954	Chi A	7	0	3	0	0	0	0	0	1	0	0	—	1.000	—	185	0	0-1	—	0			H	0.0
Total	2	10	2	3	0	0	0	0	0	1	0	0	.000	.333	.000	-2	-1	0-1	.988	0				-0.1
NICHOLL, SAM Samuel Anderson B 4.20.1869 County Antrim, Ireland D 4.19.1937 Steubenville, OH BR/TR 5-10/178# d10.5																								
1888	Pit N	8	22	3	1	0	0	0	0	2	0	2	.045	.125	.045	-48	-4	0	.952	1	90	0	/O-8(CF)	-0.3
1890	Col AA	14	56	7	9	0	0	0	4	2	0		.161	.190	.161	4	-7	3	.903	2	178	375	O-14(LF)	-0.5
Total	2	22	78	10	10	0	0	0	4	4	0	2	.128	.171	.128	-10	-11	3	.923	2	152	266	/O-22(14-8-0)	-0.8
NICHOLLS, SIMON Simon Burdette B 7.18.1882 Germantown, MD D 3.12.1911 Baltimore, MD BL/TR 5-11.5/165# d9.18																								
1903	Det A	2	8	0	3	0	0	0	0	0	0		.375	.375	.375	129	0	0	.600	-2	49	0	/S-2	-0.2
1906	Phi A	12	44	1	8	1	0	0	1	3	0		.182	.234	.205	36	-3	0	.965	-0	89	112	S-12	-0.4
1907	Phi A	124	460	75	139	12	2	0	23	24	1		.302	.338	.337	113	6	13	.930	-13	93	50	S-82,2-28,3-13	-0.4
1908	Phi A	150	550	58	119	17	3	4	31	35	1		.216	.265	.280	72	-17	14	.913	-20	89	69	*S-120,2-23/3-7	-3.8
1909	Phi A	21	71	10	15	2	1	0	3	3	0		.211	.243	.268	60	-3	0	.889	-2	81	80	S-14/3-5,1	-0.6
1910	Cle A	3	0	0	0	0	0	0	0	0	0		—	—	—	—	0	0	.000	-1	0	0	/S-3	-0.1
Total	6	312	1133	144	284	32	6	4	58	65	2		.251	.292	.300	86	-17	27	.917	-38	90	64	S-233/2-51,3-25,1	-5.5
NICHOLS, AL Albert H. B Brooklyn, NY 5-11/180# d4.24																								
1875	Atl NA	32	131	4	20	2	0	0	9	0		6	.153	.153	.168	13	-10	0-0	.785	8	122	194	3-32	-0.3
1876	NY N	**57**	212	20	38	4	0	0	9	2		3	.179	.187	.198	33	-13		.779	4	114	16	*3-57	-0.7
1877	Lou N	6	19	1	4	0	1	0	0	0		2	.211	.211	.316	54	-1		.706	2	147	0	/2-3,S31	0.1
Total	2	63	231	21	42	4	1	0	9	2		5	.182	.189	.208	35	-14		.785	6	115	16	/3-58,2-3,1S	-0.6
NICHOLS, ART Arthur Francis (born Arthur Francis Meikle) B 7.14.1871 Manchester, NH D 8.9.1945 Willimantic, CT BR/TR 5-10/175# d9.16																								
1898	Chi N	14	42	7	12	1	0	0	6	4	3		.286	.388	.310	101	1	6	.968	2	*146*	*94*	C-14	0.3
1899	Chi N	17	47	5	12	2	0	1	11	0	2		.255	.286	.362	79	-2	3	.931	-1	*106*	*70*	C-15	-0.1
1900	Chi N	8	25	1	5	0	0	0	0	3	0		.200	.286	.200	36	-2	1	.938	-1	*99*	*101*	/C-7	-0.2
1901	StL N	93	308	50	75	11	3	1	33	10	10		.244	.290	.308	77	-9	14	.960	-0	*94*	*93*	C-47,O-40(0-29-11)	-0.7
1902	StL N	73	251	36	67	12	0	1	31	21	4		.267	.333	.327	108	3	18	.984	-6	76	79	1-56,C-11/O-4(0-1-3)	-0.3
1903	StL N	36	120	13	23	2	0	0	9	12	3		.192	.281	.208	42	-9	9	.972	-5	21	82	1-25/O-7(LF),C-2	-1.4
Total	6	241	793	112	194	28	3	3	90	50	22		.245	.308	.299	81	-18	51	.952	-11	*103*	*92*	/C-96,1-81,O-51(7-30-14)	-2.4
NICHOLS, CARL Carl Edward B 10.14.1962 Los Angeles, CA BR/TR 6/208# d9.14																								
1986	Bal A	5	5	0	0	0	0	0	0	1-1	0	4	.000	.167	.000	-51	-1	0-0	1.000	-1	71	0	/C-5	-0.2
1987	Bal A	13	21	4	8	1	0	0	3	1-0	0	4	.381	.409	.429	126	1	0-0	1.000	-1	81	121	C-13	0.0
1988	Bal A	18	47	2	9	1	0	0	1	3-0	0	10	.191	.235	.213	29	-5	0-0	.987	6	98	228	C-13/O-3(RF)	0.2
1989	Hou N	8	13	0	1	0	0	0	2	0-0	0	3	.077	.077	.077	-58	-3	0-0	1.000	0	190	0	/C-6	-0.3
1990	Hou N	32	49	7	10	3	0	0	11	8-1	1	11	.204	.317	.265	67	-2	0-0	.986	3	114	110	C-15/1-3,O(LF)	0.2
1991	Hou N	20	51	3	10	3	0	0	1	5-1	0	17	.196	.268	.255	51	-3	0-0	.971	1	151	154	C-17	-0.1
Total	6	96	186	16	38	8	0	0	18	18-3	1	49	.204	.274	.247	49	-13	0-0	.985	8	118	143	/C-69,O-4(1-0-3),1-3	-0.2
NICHOLS, ROY Roy B 3.3.1921 Little Rock, AR D 4.3.2002 Hot Springs, AR BR/TR 5-11/155# d5.6																								
1944	NY N	11	9	3	2	1	0	0	0	2	0	2	.222	.364	.333	97	0	0	1.000	1	177	0	/23	0.1
NICHOLS, REID Thomas Reid B 8.5.1958 Ocala, FL BR/TR 5-11/165# d9.16 C1 OF Total (124-LF 247-CF 62-RF)																								
1980	Bos A	12	36	5	8	0	1	0	3	3-0	0	8	.222	.282	.278	51	-3	0-1	.962	-1	85	141	/O-9(CF),D	-0.4
1981	Bos A	39	48	13	9	0	1	0	3	2-0	0	6	.188	.216	.229	28	-5	0-1	1.000	-0	84	315	O-27(1-25-1)/3D	-0.6
1982	Bos A	92	245	35	74	16	1	7	33	14-1	1	28	.302	.341	.461	112	4	5-3	.989	3	97	199	O-82(30-57-2)/D-4	0.6
1983	Bos A	100	274	35	78	22	1	6	22	26-2	3	36	.285	.352	.438	108	4	7-5	.994	1	102	84	O-72(11-32-30),D-18/S	0.2
1984	Bos A	74	124	14	28	5	1	1	14	12-1	3	18	.226	.307	.306	68	-5	2-1	.988	0	93	138	O-48(17-26-4)/D	-0.6
1985	Bos A	21	32	3	6	1	0	1	3	2-0	1	4	.188	.250	.313	53	-2	1-0	.933	-1	75	0	O-10(2-7-1)/2-3,D-4	-0.3
	Chi A	51	118	20	35	7	1	1	15	15-1	0	13	.297	.373	.398	108	2	5-5	1.000	-1	97	52	O-48(25-27-8)/D	0.0
	Year	72	150	23	41	8	1	2	18	17-1	1	17	.273	.347	.380	96	0	6-5	.988	-2	93	42	O-58(27-34-9)/D-5,2-3	-0.3
1986	Chi A	74	136	9	31	4	0	2	18	11-0	0	23	.228	.282	.301	58	-8	5-4	.989	2	107	128	O-53(31-14-11)/2-2,D-3	-0.7
1987	Mon N	77	147	22	39	8	2	4	20	14-1	1	13	.265	.329	.429	97	-1	2-1	.990	3	112	188	O-59(7-50-5)/3-3	0.2

Year	Tm Lg	G	AB	R	H	2B	3B	HR	RBI	BB-IB	HP	SO	AVG	OBP	SLG	AOPS	ABR	SB-CS	FA	FR	Rng	Thr	G at Pos	BFW
Total	8	540	1160	156	308	63	8	22	131	99-6	9	149	.266	.326	.391	91	-14	27-21	.990	7	99	142	O-408C/D-39,2-5,3-4,S	-1.6
NICHOLSON, DAVE David Lawrence B 8.29.1939 St.Louis, MO BR/TR 6-2/215# d5.24																								
1960	Bal A	54	113	17	21	1	1	5	11	20-0	0	55	.186	.308	.345	77	-4	0-2	.982	1	93	162	O-44(34-0-11)	-0.5
1962	Bal A	97	173	25	30	4	1	9	15	27-0	1	76	.173	.289	.364	79	-6	3-4	.983	4	112	148	O-80(34-20-27)	-0.6
1963	Chi A	126	449	53	103	11	4	22	70	63-0	0	175	.229	.319	.419	108	5	2-1	.970	0	92	117	*O-123(LF)	-0.2
1964	Chi A	97	294	40	60	6	1	13	39	52-0	3	126	.204	.329	.364	95	-1	0-2	.972	-0	98	99	O-92(91-0-1)	-0.7
1965	Chi A	54	85	11	13	2	1	2	12	9-0	0	40	.153	.234	.271	46	-6	0-0	1.000	-2	82	0	O-36(25-12-1)	-1.0
1966	Hou N	100	280	36	69	8	4	10	31	46-6	3	92	.246	.356	.411	122	9	1-1	.968	5	103	208	O-90(13-5-73)	0.9
1967	Atl N	10	25	2	5	0	0	0	1	2-1	0	9	.200	.250	.200	34	-2	0-0	1.000	0	85	244	/O-7(7-1-0)	-0.3
Total	7	538	1419	184	301	32	12	61	179	219-7	7	573	.212	.318	.381	97	-5	6-10	.974	7	98	136	O-472(327-38-113)	-2.4
NICHOLSON, FRED Fred "Shoemaker" B 9.1.1894 Honey Grove, TX D 1.23.1972 Kilgore, TX BR/TR 5-10.5/173# d4.11 Mil 1918																								
1917	Det A	13	14	4	4	1	0	0	1	1	0	2	.286	.333	.357	111	0	0	1.000	-0	104	0	/O-3(1-0-2)	0.0
1919	Pit N	30	66	8	18	2	2	1	6	6	0	11	.273	.333	.409	118	1	2	.939	1	108	113	O-17(13-1-3)/1	0.1
1920	Pit N	99	247	33	89	16	7	4	30	18	0	31	.360	.404	.530	162	19	9-6	.957	3	104	129	O-58(28-18-13)	2.0
1921	Bos N	83	245	36	80	11	7	5	41	17	0	29	.327	.370	.490	133	11	5-4	.983	-1	105	65	O-59(57-0-3)/1-4,2-2	0.5
1922	Bos N	78	222	31	56	4	5	2	29	23	5	24	.252	.336	.342	79	-7	5-7	.915	-1	109	69	O-63(20-0-44)	-1.4
Total	5	303	794	112	247	34	21	12	107	65	5	97	.311	.367	.452	124	24	21-17	.950	0	106	90	O-200(119-19-65)/1-5,2-2	1.2
NICHOLSON, KEVIN Kevin Ronald B 3.29.1976 Vancouver, BC, CAN BB/TR 5-10/190# d6.23																								
2000	SD N	37	97	7	21	6	1	1	8	4-0	1	31	.216	.255	.330	50	-8	1-0	.983	1	111	69	S-30/2-4	-0.4
NICHOLSON, OVID Ovid Edward B 12.30.1888 Salem, IN D 3.24.1968 Salem, IN BL/TR 5-9.5/155# d9.17																								
1912	Pit N	6	11	2	5	0	0	0	3	1	0	2	.455	.500	.455	164	1	0	1.000	0	125	0	/O-4(LF)	0.1
NICHOLSON, PARSON Thomas Clark "Deacon" B 4.14.1863 Blaine, OH D 2.28.1917 Bellaire, OH 5-9/148# d9.14																								
1888	Det N	24	85	11	22	2	3	1	9	2	1	7	.259	.284	.388	111	1	6	.935	-0	105	68	2-24	0.1
1890	Tol AA	**134**	523	78	140	16	11	4	72	42	9		.268	.333	.363	102	-1	46	.929	-7	102	83	*2-134/C	-0.3
1895	Was N	10	38	7	7	2	1	0	5	7	0	4	.184	.311	.289	56	-2	6	.797	-2	101	88	S-10	-0.3
Total	3	168	646	96	169	20	15	5	86	51	10	11	.262	.325	.362	100	-2	58	.930	-9	102	81	2-158/S-10,C	-0.5
NICHOLSON, BILL William Beck "Swish" B 12.11.1914 Chestertown, MD D 3.8.1996 Chestertown, MD BL/TR 6/205# d6.13																								
1936	Phi A	11	12	2	0	0	0	0	0	0	0	5	.000	.000	.000	-99	-4	0-0	1.000	0	106	0	/O(RF)	-0.4
1939	Chi N	58	220	37	65	12	5	5	38	20	0	29	.295	.354	.464	116	4	0	.955	-1	101	89	O-58(RF)	0.0
1940	Chi N★	135	491	78	146	27	7	25	98	50	3	67	.297	.366	.534	148	31	2	.950	-6	91	101	*O-123(43-0-81)	1.8
1941	Chi N★	147	532	74	135	26	1	26	98	82	3	91	.254	.357	.453	132	23	1	.971	4	111	85	*O-143(3-0-140)	1.8
1942	Chi N	152	588	83	173	22	11	21	78	76	**8**	80	.294	.382	.476	156	42	8	.986	7	107	127	*O-151(RF)	**4.1**
1943	Chi N★	**154**	608	95	188	30	9	**29**	**128**	71	5	86	.309	.386	.531	166	50	4	.978	3	107	96	*O-154(RF)	4.5
1944	Chi N★	156	582	**116**	167	35	8	**33**	**122**	93	6	71	.287	.391	.545	162	49	3	.979	-2	96	105	*O-156(RF)	3.8
1945	†Chi N✳	151	559	82	136	28	4	13	88	92	6	73	.243	.356	.377	106	8	4	.990	-2	99	86	*O-151(RF)	-0.4
1946	Chi N	105	296	36	65	13	2	8	41	44	2	44	.220	.325	.358	95	-1	1	.973	2	120	51	O-80(RF)	-0.2
1947	Chi N	148	487	69	119	28	1	26	75	87	5	83	.244	.364	.466	124	18	1	**.990**	-5	99	57	*O-140(RF)	0.9
1948	Chi N	143	494	68	129	24	5	19	67	81	5	60	.261	.371	.445	125	19	2	.980	-5	95	72	*O-136(RF)	1.0
1949	Phi N	98	299	42	70	8	3	11	40	45	5	53	.234	.344	.391	99	0	1	.995	3	102	118	O-91(RF)	0.0
1950	Phi N	41	58	3	13	2	1	3	10	8	0	16	.224	.318	.448	101	0	0	.952	-1	109	0	O-15(RF)	-0.1
1951	Phi N	85	170	23	41	9	2	8	30	25	1	24	.241	.342	.459	115	4	0-1	.987	-1	105	29	O-41(RF)	0.1
1952	Phi N	55	88	17	24	3	0	6	19	14	3	26	.273	.390	.511	150	6	0-0	1.000	-1	109	0	O-19(RF)	0.5
1953	Phi N	38	62	12	13	5	1	2	16	12	0	20	.210	.338	.419	97	0	0-0	1.000	-1	77	0	O-12(RF)	-0.2
Total	16	1677	5546	837	1484	272	60	235	948	800	52	828	.268	.365	.465	133	249	27-1	.979	-4	102	87	*O-1471(46-0-1427)	17.2
NICOL, GEORGE George Edward B 10.17.1870 Barry, IL D 8.4.1924 Milwaukee, WI TL 5-7/155# d9.23 ▲																								
1890	StL AA	3	7	4	2	1	0	0	1	4	0		.286	.545	.429	164	1	0	1.000	-0	0	0	/P-3	0.0
1891	Chi N	3	6	0	2	0	1	0	3	0	0	1	.333	.333	.667	189	1	0	.000	-1	0	0	/P-3	0.0
1894	Pit N	9	22	8	9	1	0	0	3	0	0	1	.409	.409	.455	109	2	0	.800	-1	48	0	/P-9	0.0
	Lou N	28	112	12	38	6	4	0	19	2	2	4	.339	.362	.464	105	0	4	.791	-4	52	102	O-26(RF)/P-2	-0.4
	Year	37	134	20	47	7	4	0	22	2	2	5	.351	.370	.463	105	1	4	.791	-5	52	102	O-26(RF),P-11	-0.4
Total	3	43	147	24	51	8	5	0	26	6	2	6	.347	.381	.469	112	4	4	.791	-6	52	102	/O-26(RF),P-17	-0.4
NICOL, HUGH Hugh B 1.1.1858 Campsie, Scotland D 6.27.1921 Lafayette, IN BR/TR 5-4/145# d5.3 M1																								
1881	Chi N	26	108	13	22	2	0	0	7	4		12	.204	.232	.222	42	-7		.932	4	168	110	O-26(2-12-12)/S	-0.4
1882	Chi N	47	186	19	37	9	1	1	16	7		29	.199	.228	.274	57	-9		.887	11	275	55	O-47(RF)/S-8	0.1
1883	StL AA	94	368	73	105	13	3	0	39	18			.285	.319	.337	105	2		.916	10	181	247	*O-84(1-1-84),2-11	1.0
1884	StL AA	**110**	442	79	116	14	5	0		22	3		.262	.302	.317	99	-1		.873	17	**264**	113	*O-87(RF),2-23/S3	1.4
1885	†StL AA	**112**	425	59	88	11	1	0	45	34	3		.207	.271	.238	59	-19		.888	12	173	64	*O-111(RF)/3	-0.8
1886	StL AA	67	253	44	52	6	3	0	19	26	0		.206	.280	.253	64	-11	38	.942	-4	116	0	O-57(0-1-56)/S-8,2-4	-1.3
1887	Cin AA	125	475	122	102	18	2	1	34	86	5		.215	.341	.267	69	-16	**138**	.918	-3	98	24	*O-125(0-6-119)	-1.6
1888	Cin AA	135	548	112	131	10	2	1	35	67	7		.239	.330	.270	88	-5	103	.957	-3	71	69	*O-125(RF),2-12/S	-0.8
1889	Cin AA	122	474	82	121	7	8	2	58	54	5	35	.255	.338	.316	84	-10	80	.918	2	101	85	*O-115(RF)/2-7,3-3	-0.7
1890	Cin N	50	186	28	39	1	4	0	19	19	0	12	.210	.283	.258	58	-10	24	.921	-6	95	188	O-46(RF)/S-3,2	-1.5
Total	10	888	3465	631	813	91	29	5	272	337	23	88	.235	.307	.282	78	-86	383	.912	38	144	91	O-823(3-20-802)/2-58,S-22,3-5	-4.6
NICOSIA, STEVE Steven Richard B 8.6.1955 Paterson, NJ BR/TR 5-10/185# d7.8																								
1978	Pit N	3	5	0	0	0	0	0	0	1-0	0	0	.000	.167	.000	-48	-1	0-0	1.000	0	37	278	/C	-0.1
1979	†Pit N	70	191	22	55	16	0	4	13	23-7	0	17	.288	.364	.435	112	4	0-2	.991	1	130	74	C-65	0.7
1980	Pit N	60	176	16	38	8	0	1	22	19-5	1	16	.216	.291	.278	60	-9	0-1	.984	-1	128	61	C-58	-0.8
1981	Pit N	54	169	21	39	10	1	2	18	13-2	0	10	.231	.286	.337	74	-6	3-1	.982	-1	106	70	C-52	-0.5
1982	Pit N	39	100	6	28	3	0	1	7	11-4	0	13	.280	.348	.340	91	-1	0-1	.990	2	104	112	C-35/O-3(LF)	0.2
1983	Pit N	21	46	4	6	2	0	1	1	1-0	0	7	.130	.149	.239	6	-6	0-0	.988	-3	71	59	C-15	-0.9
	SF N	15	33	4	11	0	0	0	6	3-1	0	2	.333	.389	.333	105	0	0-0	.984	2	107	28	/C-9	0.2
	Year	36	79	8	17	2	0	1	7	4-1	0	9	.215	.253	.278	47	-6	0-0	.986	-2	86	46	C-24	-0.7
1984	SF N	48	132	9	40	11	2	2	19	8-0	0	14	.303	.336	.462	129	5	1-1	.985	-11	74	52	C-41	-0.5
1985	Mon N	42	71	4	12	2	0	1	7	7-0	0	11	.169	.244	.197	26	-7	1-0	.988	-3	125	0	C-23/1-2	-1.0
	Tor A	6	15	0	4	0	0	0	1	0-0	0	0	.267	.267	.267	46	-1	0-0	1.000	2	246	168	/C-6	0.0
Total	8	358	938	86	233	52	3	11	88	86-19	1	90	.248	.310	.345	82	-22	5-6	.987	-13	112	68	C-305/O-3(LF),1-2	-2.7
NIEBERGALL, CHARLIE Charles Arthur "Nig" B 5.23.1899 New York, NY D 8.29.1982 Holiday, FL BR/TR 5-10/160# d6.17																								
1921	StL N	5	6	1	1	0	0	0	0	0	0	0	.167	.167	.167	-12	-1	0-0	1.000	-0	*52*	*203*	/C-3	-0.1
1923	StL N	9	28	2	3	1	0	0	1	2	0	2	.107	.167	.143	-18	-5	0-0	1.000	-0	*99*	*75*	/C-7	-0.5
1924	StL N	40	58	6	17	6	0	0	7	3	1	9	.293	.339	.397	98	0	0-0	.951	0	*111*	*117*	C-34	0.1
Total	3	54	92	9	21	7	0	0	8	5	1	11	.228	.276	.304	55	-6	0-0	.966	-1	*105*	*107*	/C-44	-0.5
NIEHAUS, AL Albert Bernard B 6.1.1899 Cincinnati, OH D 10.14.1931 Cincinnati, OH BR/TR 5-11/175# d4.22																								
1925	Pit N	17	64	7	14	8	0	0	7	1	1	5	.219	.242	.344	45	-5	0-0	.962	-2	82	89	1-15	-0.7
	Cin N	51	147	16	44	10	2	0	14	13	1	10	.299	.360	.395	95	-1	1-4	.988	2	123	134	1-45	-0.2
	Year	68	211	23	58	18	2	0	21	14	2	15	.275	.326	.379	80	-6	1-4	.981	0	111	121	1-60	-0.9
NIEHOFF, BERT John Albert B 5.13.1884 Louisville, CO D 12.8.1974 Inglewood, CA BR/TR 5-10.5/170# d10.4 C1																								
1913	Cin N	2	8	0	0	0	0	0	0	0	0	2	.000	.000	.000	-99	-2	0	.917	1	177	0	/3-2	-0.1
1914	Cin N	142	484	46	117	16	9	4	49	38	1	77	.242	.298	.337	86	-10	20	.924	8	106	83	*3-134/2-3	0.2
1915	†Phi N	148	529	61	126	27	2	2	49	30	1	63	.238	.280	.308	77	-15	21-11	.946	-5	97	103	*2-148	-1.9
1916	Phi N	146	548	65	133	**42**	4	4	61	37	1	57	.243	.292	.356	95	-3	20-14	.936	1	102	120	*2-144/3-2	0.0
1917	Phi N	114	361	30	92	17	4	2	42	23	2	29	.255	.303	.341	93	-3	8	.945	13	112	89	2-96/1-7,3-6	1.3
1918	StL N	22	84	5	15	2	0	0	5	3	0	10	.179	.207	.202	26	-8	2	.975	2	102	120	2-22	-0.6
	NY N	7	23	3	6	0	0	0	1	0	0	4	.261	.261	.261	60	-1	0	.871	-3	71	89	/2-7	-0.4
	Year	29	107	8	21	2	0	0	6	3	0	14	.196	.218	.215	33	-9	2	.954	-1	95	113	2-29	-1.0
Total	6	581	2037	210	489	104	19	12	207	131	5	242	.240	.288	.327	84	-42	71-25	.943	16	102	106	2-420,3-144/1-7	-1.5

Year	Tm Lg	G	AB	R	H	2B	3B	HR	RBI	BB-IB	HP	SO	AVG	OBP	SLG	AOPS	ABR	SB-CS	FA	FR	Rng	Thr	G at Pos	BFW
NIEKRO, LANCE Lance Joseph B 1.29.1979 Winter Haven, FL BR/TR 6-3/210# d9.5 f-Joe																								
2003	SF N	5	5	2	1	1	0	0	2	0-0	0	1	.200	.200	.400	53	0	0-0	1.000	-0	0	156	/1-3	-0.1
NIELSEN, MILT Milton Robert B 2.8.1925 Tyler, MN BL/TL 5-11/190# d9.27																								
1949	Cle A	3	9	1	1	0	0	0	0	2	0	4	.111	.273	.111	4	-1	0-0	1.000	-0	87	0	/O-3(CF)	-0.2
1951	Cle A	16	6	1	0	0	0	0	0	1	0	1	.000	.143	.000	-63	-1	0-0	—	0			H	-0.1
Total	2	19	15	2	1	0	0	0	0	3	0	5	.067	.222	.067	-22	-2	0-0	1.000	-0	87	0	/O-3(CF)	-0.3
NIEMAN, BUTCH Elmer Le Roy B 2.8.1918 Herkimer, KS D 11.2.1993 Topeka, KS BL/TL 6-2/195# d5.2																								
1943	Bos N	101	335	39	84	15	8	7	46	39	1	39	.251	.331	.406	114	5	4	.963	1	99	131	O-93(76-1-16)	0.1
1944	Bos N	134	468	65	124	16	6	16	65	47	0	47	.265	.332	.427	108	4	5	.975	-1	96	116	*O-126(86-0-46)	-0.5
1945	Bos N	97	247	43	61	15	0	14	56	43	1	33	.247	.361	.478	131	11	11	.932	-2	100	84	O-57(43-0-14)	0.6
Total	3	332	1050	147	269	46	14	37	167	129	2	119	.256	.339	.432	116	20	20	.961	-1	98	114	O-276(205-1-76)	0.2
NIEMAN, BOB Robert Charles B 1.26.1927 Cincinnati, OH D 3.10.1985 Corona, CA BR/TR 5-11/195# d9.14																								
1951	StL A	12	43	6	16	3	1	2	8	3	0	5	.372	.413	.628	174	4	0-0	.962	-0	94	115	O-11(LF)	0.3
1952	StL A	131	478	66	138	22	2	18	74	46	1	73	.289	.352	.456	120	12	0-4	.976	1	101	107	*O-125(32-0-94)	0.7
1953	Det A	142	508	72	143	32	5	15	69	57	0	57	.281	.354	.453	118	12	0-3	.979	1	103	93	*O-135(74-0-64)	0.6
1954	Det A	91	251	24	66	14	1	8	35	22	0	32	.263	.319	.422	105	1	0-2	.984	-1	100	55	O-62(LF)	-0.4
1955	Chi A	99	272	36	77	11	2	11	53	36-1	2	37	.283	.366	.460	119	7	1-0	.976	-2	94	78	O-78(29-0-52)	0.2
1956	Chi A	14	40	3	12	1	0	2	4	4-2	0	4	.300	.364	.475	118	1	0-1	1.000	0	119	0	O-10(RF)	0.0
	Bal A	114	388	60	125	20	6	12	64	86-3	0	59	.322	.442	.497	161	40	1-5	.980	3	112	49	*O-114(LF)	3.3
	Year	128	428	63	137	21	6	14	68	90-5	0	63	.320	.436	.495	156	40	1-6	.982	3	**113**	45	*O-124(114-0-10)	3.3
1957	Bal A	129	445	61	123	17	6	13	70	63-3	2	86	.276	.363	.429	125	16	4-4	.980	4	105	98	*O-120(116-0-4)	1.3
1958	Bal A	105	366	56	119	20	2	16	60	44-5	0	57	.325	.395	.522	159	30	2-8	.961	-3	96	63	*O-100(LF)	2.1
1959	Bal A	118	360	49	105	18	2	21	60	42-3	2	55	.292	.367	.528	146	23	1-2	.973	3	105	115	O-97(LF)	2.0
1960	StL N	81	188	19	54	13	5	4	31	24-1	2	31	.287	.372	.473	120	6	0-1	.940	-5	86	0	O-55(53-0-2)	-0.2
1961	StL N	6	17	0	8	1	0	0	2	0-0	0	2	.471	.471	.529	150	1	0-0	1.000	-0	54	0	/O-4(LF)	0.1
	Cle A	39	65	2	23	6	0	2	10	7-0	0	4	.354	.417	.538	157	6	1-0	.960	0	106	119	O-12(7-0-5)	0.5
1962	Cle A	2	1	0	0	0	0	0	1	0-0	0	1	.000	.000	.000	-99	0	0-0	—	0			H	0.0
	†SF N	30	30	1	9	2	0	1	3	1-0	0	9	.300	.323	.467	111	0	0-0	1.000	0	113	0	/O-3(LF)	0.0
Total	12	1113	3452	455	1018	180	32	125	544	435-18	9	512	.295	.373	.474	132	159	10-30	.975	1	102	80	O-926(702-0-231)	10.5
NIEMIEC, AL Alfred Joseph B 5.18.1911 Meriden, CT D 10.29.1995 Kirkland, WA BR/TR 5-11/158# d9.19																								
1934	Bos A	9	32	2	7	0	0	0	3	3	0	4	.219	.286	.219	30	-3	0-0	1.000	3	121	131	/2-9	0.0
1936	Phi A	69	203	22	40	3	2	1	20	26	1	16	.197	.291	.246	35	-22	2-2	.972	5	109	89	2-52/S-5	-1.2
Total	2	78	235	24	47	3	2	1	23	29	1	20	.200	.291	.243	34	-25	2-2	.976	8	111	95	/2-61,S-5	-1.2
NIETO, TOM Thomas Andrew B 10.27.1960 Downey, CA BR/TR 6-1/205# d5.10																								
1984	StL N	33	86	7	24	4	0	3	12	5-2	0	18	.279	.312	.430	112	1	0-0	.994	0	120	94	C-32	0.3
1985	†StL N	95	253	15	57	10	2	0	34	26-8	3	37	.225	.305	.281	65	-11	0-2	.990	-6	115	45	C-95	-1.6
1986	Mon N	30	65	5	13	3	1	1	7	6-1	1	21	.200	.278	.323	66	-3	0-1	.978	-9	48	46	C-30	-1.2
1987	Min A	41	105	7	21	7	1	1	12	8-0	3	24	.200	.276	.314	54	-7	0-0	.996	-3	67	79	C-40/D	-0.8
1988	Min A	24	60	1	4	0	0	0	0	1-0	1	17	.067	.097	.067	-52	-12	0-0	.991	0	123	55	C-24	-1.2
1989	Phi N	11	20	1	3	0	0	0	0	6-0	1	7	.150	.370	.150	54	-1	0-0	1.000	1	85	31	C-11	0.1
1990	Phi N	17	30	1	5	0	0	0	4	3-0	1	11	.167	.265	.167	21	-3	0-0	.984	-0	94	78	C-17	-0.3
Total	7	251	619	37	127	24	4	5	69	55-11	10	135	.205	.280	.281	56	-36	0-3	.991	-17	99	60	C-249/D	-4.7
NIEVES, JOSE Jose Miguel (Pinto) B 6.16.1975 Guacara, Venezuela BR/TR 6-1/180# d8.7 OF Total (1-CF 1-RF)																								
1998	Chi N	2	1	0	0	0	0	0	0	0-0	0	0	.000	.000	.000	-97	0	0-0	—	-0	0	0	/S	-0.1
1999	Chi N	54	181	16	45	9	1	2	18	8-0	4	25	.249	.291	.343	62	-11	0-2	.935	1	112	91	S-52	-0.6
2000	Chi N	82	198	17	42	6	3	5	24	11-1	0	43	.212	.251	.348	51	-16	1-1	.949	-2	108	38	3-39,S-24/2-7	-1.6
2001	Ana A	29	53	5	13	3	1	2	3	2-0	2	20	.245	.298	.453	92	-1	0-1	1.000	5	127	184	2-11,S-10/3-2,1D	0.4
2002	Ana A	45	97	17	28	2	0	0	6	2-0	0	14	.289	.303	.309	63	-5	1-1	.938	-7	74	92	2-18,S-13/3-5,1-3,O-2(0-1-1)	-1.1
Total	5	212	530	55	128	20	5	9	51	23-1	6	102	.242	.278	.349	61	-33	2-5	.945	-3	101	91	S-100/3-46,2-36,D-4,1-4,O-2C	-3.0
NIEVES, MELVIN Melvin Ramos B 12.28.1971 San Juan, P.R. BB/TR 6-2/210# d9.1																								
1992	Atl N	12	19	0	4	1	0	0	1	2-0	0	7	.211	.286	.263	53	-1	0-0	.727	-1	99	0	/O-6(3-0-3)	-0.2
1993	SD N	19	47	4	9	0	0	2	3	3-0	1	21	.191	.255	.319	52	-3	0-0	.931	-0	116	0	O-15(RF)	-0.5
1994	SD N	10	19	2	5	1	0	1	4	3-0	0	10	.263	.364	.474	120	1	0-0	1.000	1	145	365	/O-6(2-0-4)	0.2
1995	SD N	98	234	32	48	6	1	14	38	19-0	5	88	.205	.276	.419	84	-7	2-3	.990	0	96	149	O-79(62-6-15)/1-2	-0.9
1996	Det A	120	431	71	106	23	4	24	60	44-2	6	158	.246	.322	.485	101	-1	1-2	.943	-1	98	122	*O-105(21-0-84),D-11	-0.7
1997	Det A	116	359	46	82	18	1	20	64	39-6	5	157	.228	.311	.451	97	-3	1-7	.979	0	103	70	O-99(0-2-99),D-10	-0.9
1998	Cin N	83	119	8	30	4	0	2	17	26-1	0	42	.252	.381	.336	91	0	0-0	1.000	-1	89	82	O-25(3-0-22)/D-3	-0.2
Total	7	458	1228	163	284	53	6	63	187	136-9	17	483	.231	.314	.438	94	-14	4-12	.962	-1	100	106	O-335(91-8-242)/D-24,1-2	-3.2
NIEVES, WILBERT Wilbert B 9.25.1977 San Juan, P.R. BR/TR 5-11/190# d7.21																								
2002	SD N	28	72	2	13	3	1	0	3	4-4	0	15	.181	.224	.250	29	-8	1-0	.971	-0	121	54	C-27	-0.7
NILAND, TOM Thomas James "Honest Tom" B 4.14.1870 Brookfield, MA D 4.30.1950 Lynn, MA BR/TR 5-11/160# d4.19																								
1896	StL N	18	68	3	12	0	1	0	3	5	1	4	.176	.243	.206	20	-8	0	.913	-3	115	207	O-13(6-0-7)/S-5	-1.0
NILES, HARRY Herbert Clyde B 9.10.1880 Buchanan, MI D 4.18.1953 Sturgis, MI BR/TR 5-8/175# d4.24																								
1906	StL A	142	541	71	124	14	4	2	31	46	6		.229	.297	.281	85	-9	30	.967	11	**256**	193	*O-108(0-6-102),3-34	-0.2
1907	StL A	120	492	65	142	9	5	2	35	28	3		.289	.331	.339	114	7	19	.949	-3	102	112	*2-116/O(RF)	0.6
1908	NY A	95	361	43	90	14	6	4	24	25	4		.249	.305	.355	113	5	18	.928	-17	89	52	2-85/O-7(1-1-5)	-1.4
	Bos A	18	33	4	8	0	0	1	3	6	1		.242	.375	.333	127	1	3	1.000	-1	89	88	/2-8,S-2	0.1
	Year	113	394	47	98	14	6	5	27	31	5		.249	.312	.353	114	6	21	.934	-18	89	55	2-93/O-7(1-1-5),S-2	-1.3
1909	Bos A	145	546	65	134	12	5	1	38	39	13		.245	.311	.291	88	-7	27	.952	-2	127	85	*O-117(77-12-28),3-13/S-9,2-5	-1.7
1910	Bos A	18	57	6	12	3	0	1	3	4	0		.211	.262	.316	79	-1	1	.920	0	105	108	O-15(4-0-11)	-0.2
	Cle A	70	240	25	51	6	4	1	18	15	3		.213	.267	.283	72	-9	9	.975	-5	97	105	O-50(13-0-37)/S-7,3-5	-1.7
	Year	88	297	31	63	9	4	2	21	19	3		.212	.266	.290	73	-10	10	.962	-5	99	106	O-65(17-0-48)/S-7,3-5	-1.9
Total	5	608	2270	279	561	58	24	12	152	163	30		.247	.306	.310	95	-13	107	.960	-16	165	125	O-298(95-19-184),2-214/3-52,S-18	-4.5
NILES, BILL William E. B 1.11.1867 Covington, KY D 7.3.1936 Springfield, OH ?/160# d5.13																								
1895	Pit N	11	37	2	8	0	0	0	0	5	0	2	.216	.310	.216	39	-3	2	.930	0	94	68	3-10/2	-0.2
NILL, RABBIT George Charles B 7.14.1881 Ft.Wayne, IN D 5.24.1962 Fort Wayne, IN BR/TR 5-7/160# d9.27																								
1904	Was A	15	48	4	8	0	1	0	3	5	2		.167	.273	.208	54	-2	0	.878	-3	89	66	2-15	-0.6
1905	Was A	103	319	46	58	7	3	3	31	33	5		.182	.269	.251	68	-11	12	.897	-1	98	135	3-52,2-33/S-6	-1.1
1906	Was A	89	315	37	74	8	2	0	15	47	3		.235	.340	.273	97	2	16	.882	2	97	112	S-31,2-25,3-15,O-15(CF)	0.5
1907	Was A	66	215	21	47	7	3	0	25	15	4		.219	.282	.279	86	-3	6	.962	0	99	74	2-39,O-18(17-0-1)/3	-0.4
	Cle A	12	43	5	12	1	0	0	2	3	0		.279	.326	.302	100	0	2	.815	-2	107	134	/3-7,S-4	-0.2
	Year	78	258	26	59	8	3	0	27	18	4		.229	.289	.283	88	-3	8	.962	-2	99	74	2-39,O-18(17-0-1)/3-8,S-4	-0.6
1908	Cle A	11	23	3	5	0	0	0	0	1	0		.217	.217	.217	41	-2	0	.833	-1	109	120	/S-6,O-3(2-0-2),2	-0.2
Total	5	296	963	116	204	23	9	3	77	103	14		.212	.297	.264	82	-16	36	.943	-5	104	83	2-113/3-75,S-47,O-36(19-15-3)	-2.0
NILSSON, DAVE David Wayne B 12.14.1969 Brisbane, Australia BL/TR 6-3/215# d5.18 OF Total (80-LF 105-RF)																								
1992	Mil A	51	164	15	38	8	0	4	25	17-1	0	18	.232	.304	.354	85	-3	2-2	.992	1	142	78	C-46/1-3,D-2	0.0
1993	Mil A	100	296	35	76	10	2	7	40	37-5	0	36	.257	.336	.375	93	-3	3-6	.981	-8	90	74	C-91/1-4,D-4	-0.7
1994	Mil A	109	397	51	109	28	3	12	69	34-9	0	61	.275	.326	.451	95	-4	1-0	.994	-5	72	58	C-60,D-43/1-5	-0.7
1995	Mil A	81	263	41	73	12	1	12	53	24-4	2	41	.278	.337	.468	103	0	2-0	.981	1	97	143	O-58(15-0-47),D-14/1-7,C-2	-0.2
1996	Mil A	123	453	81	150	33	2	17	84	57-6	3	68	.331	.407	.525	129	22	2-3	.965	-1	88	121	O-61(6-0-55),D-40,1-24/C-2	1.2
1997	Mil A	156	554	71	154	33	0	20	81	65-8	2	88	.278	.352	.446	107	6	2-3	.991	-3	84	129	1-74,D-59,O-22(LF)	-0.8
1998	Mil N	102	309	39	83	14	1	12	56	33-1	1	48	.269	.339	.437	103	1	2-2	.984	-6	77	134	1-49,O-37(37-0-3)/C-7	-1.0
1999	Mil N★	115	343	56	106	19	1	21	62	53-6	2	64	.309	.400	.554	141	23	1-2	.991	-16	63	100	*C-101/D	1.1
Total	8	837	2779	389	789	157	10	105	470	320-40	10	424	.284	.356	.461	110	42	15-18	.988	-39	86	78	C-309,O-178R,1-166,D-163	-1.1

Year	Tm Lg	G	AB	R	H	2B	3B	HR	RBI	BB-IB	HP	SO	AVG	OBP	SLG	AOPS	ABR	SB-CS	FA	FR	Rng	Thr	G at Pos	BFW
NIVAR, RAMON Ramon A. B 2.22.1980 San Cristobal, D.R. BR/TR 5-10/170# d7.30																								
2003	Tex A	28	90	9	19	1	2	0	7	4-0	1	10	.211	.253	.267	34	-9	4-2	.961	2	108	267	O-26(CF)/D	-0.6
NIX, LAYNCE Laynce Michael B 10.30.1980 Houston, TX BL/TL 6/190# d7.10																								
2003	Tex A	53	184	25	47	10	0	8	30	9-0	0	53	.255	.289	.440	82	-5	3-0	.963	3	123	39	O-52(5-21-37)	-0.3
NIXON, AL Albert Richard "Humpty Dumpty" B 4.11.1886 Atlantic City, NJ D 11.9.1960 Opelousas, LA BR/TL 5-7.5/164# d9.4																								
1915	Bro N	14	26	3	6	1	0	0	2	2	0	4	.231	.286	.269	67	-1	1-1	1.000	0	85	130	O-14(8-1-1)	-0.1
1916	Bro N	1	2	0	2	0	0	0	0	0	0	0	1.000	1.000	1.000	501	1	0	—	-0	0	0	/O(LF)	0.1
1918	Bro N	6	11	1	5	0	0	0	0	0	0	0	.455	.455	.455	178	1	0	1.000	0	123	0	/O-4(2-0-1)	0.1
1921	Bos N	55	138	25	33	6	3	1	9	7	1	11	.239	.281	.348	69	-7	3-2	.980	2	115	83	O-43(22-10-13)	-0.7
1922	Bos N	86	318	35	84	14	4	2	22	9	0	19	.264	.284	.352	66	-17	6-6	.975	2	115	65	O-79(48-22-11)	-2.0
1923	Bos N	88	321	53	88	12	4	0	19	24	5	14	.274	.334	.336	81	-9	2-3	.987	7	105	141	O-80(14-62-4)	-0.6
1926	Phi N	93	311	38	91	18	2	4	41	13	1	20	.293	.323	.402	90	-5	5	.977	2	104	100	O-88(CF)	-0.6
1927	Phi N	54	154	18	48	7	0	0	18	5	0	5	.312	.333	.357	84	-4	1	.969	2	116	74	O-44(0-43-1)	-0.3
1928	Phi N	25	64	7	15	2	0	0	7	6	0	4	.234	.300	.266	47	-5	1	1.000	1	113	66	O-20(10-0-10)	-0.5
Total	9	422	1345	180	372	60	13	7	118	66	7	77	.277	.314	.356	78	-46	19-12	.980	16	110	95	O-373(105-226-41)	-4.6
NIXON, TROT Christopher Trotman B 4.11.1974 Durham, NC BL/TL 6-1/195# d9.21																								
1996	Bos A	2	4	2	2	1	0	0	0	0-0	0	1	.500	.500	.750	206	1	1-0	1.000	0	134	0	/O-2(RF)	0.1
1998	†Bos A	13	27	3	7	1	0	0	0	1-0	0	3	.259	.286	.296	51	-2	0-0	1.000	1	148	0	/O-7(1-0-6),D-2	-0.1
1999	†Bos A	124	381	67	103	22	5	15	52	53-1	3	75	.270	.357	.472	108	5	3-1	.968	-7	95	38	*O-121(RF)	-0.7
2000	Bos A	123	427	66	118	27	8	12	60	63-2	2	85	.276	.368	.461	106	5	8-1	.991	1	100	109	*O-118(0-6-115)/D	0.2
2001	Bos A	148	535	100	150	31	4	27	88	79-1	7	113	.280	.376	.505	129	25	7-4	.973	-5	95	85	*O-145(0-70-83)/D	1.5
2002	Bos A	152	532	81	136	36	3	24	94	65-2	5	109	.256	.338	.470	111	9	4-2	.984	-1	102	79	*O-152(0-13-145)	0.1
2003	†Bos A	134	441	81	135	24	6	28	87	65-4	3	96	.306	.396	.578	150	33	4-2	.983	-4	97	58	*O-130(0-1-129)	2.1
Total	7	696	2347	400	651	142	26	106	381	326-10	20	482	.277	.366	.496	120	76	27-10	.980	-16	98	73	O-675(1-90-601)/D-4	3.2
NIXON, OTIS Otis Junior B 1.9.1959 Columbus Co., NC BB/TR 6-2/180# d9.9 b-Donell																								
1983	NY A	13	14	2	2	0	0	0	0	1-0	0	5	.143	.200	.143	-4	-2	2-0	.938	1	129	303	/O-9(0-4-5)	-0.1
1984	Cle A	49	91	16	14	0	0	0	1	8-0	0	11	.154	.220	.154	6	-12	12-6	1.000	2	105	124	O-46(43-4-0)	-1.1
1985	Cle A	104	162	34	38	4	0	3	9	8-0	0	27	.235	.271	.315	60	-9	20-11	.971	6	122	170	O-80(53-26-0),D-11	-0.4
1986	Cle A	105	95	33	25	4	1	0	8	13-0	0	12	.263	.352	.326	88	-1	23-6	.969	3	110	132	O-95(84-14-0)/D-5	0.3
1987	Cle A	19	17	2	1	0	0	0	1	3-0	0	4	.059	.200	.059	-26	-3	2-3	1.000	1	121	0	O-17(11-7-0)/D-2	-0.3
1988	Mon N	90	271	47	66	8	2	0	15	28-0	0	42	.244	.312	.288	71	-10	46-13	.994	-1	101	55	O-82(25-61-0)	-0.6
1989	Mon N	126	258	41	56	7	2	0	21	33-1	0	36	.217	.306	.260	62	-12	37-12	.988	-1	102	61	O-98(13-92-1)	-1.0
1990	Mon N	119	231	46	58	6	2	1	20	28-0	0	33	.251	.331	.307	80	-6	50-13	.994	2	102	145	O-88(21-71-0)/S	0.2
1991	Atl N	124	401	81	119	10	1	0	26	47-3	2	40	.297	.371	.327	93	-2	72-21	.987	3	107	92	*O-115(55-17-48)	0.7
1992	†Atl N	120	456	79	134	14	2	2	22	39-0	0	54	.294	.348	.346	92	-4	41-18	.991	10	119	93	*O-111(2-102-16)	0.8
1993	†Atl N	134	461	77	124	12	3	1	24	61-2	0	63	.269	.351	.315	80	-11	47-13	.990	1	105	68	*O-116(0-115-2)	-0.3
1994	Bos A	103	398	60	109	15	1	0	25	55-1	0	65	.274	.360	.317	74	-14	42-10	.989	-2	98	76	*O-103(CF)	-0.9
1995	Tex A	139	589	87	174	21	2	0	45	58-1	0	85	.295	.357	.338	81	-15	50-21	.989	-5	98	56	*O-138(CF)	-1.5
1996	Tor A	125	496	87	142	15	1	1	29	71-1	1	68	.286	.377	.327	80	-12	54-13	.994	1	108	66	*O-125(CF)	-0.2
1997	Tor A	103	401	54	105	12	1	1	26	52-0	0	54	.262	.343	.304	71	-15	47-10	.996	-3	102	20	*O-102(CF)/D	-1.0
	LA N	42	175	30	48	6	2	1	18	13-0	0	24	.274	.323	.349	83	-5	12-2	.990	-1	103	51	O-42(CF)	-0.3
1998	Min A	110	448	71	133	6	6	1	20	44-0	2	56	.297	.361	.344	84	-10	37-7	.989	-3	100	59	*O-108(CF)	-0.6
1999	†Atl N	84	151	31	31	2	1	0	8	23-1	0	15	.205	.309	.232	40	-14	26-7	.981	-5	77	0	O-52(50-5-0)	-1.6
Total	17	1709	5115	878	1379	142	27	11	318	585-10	5	694	.270	.343	.314	77	-157	620-186	.989	8	104	74	*O-1527(357-1136-72)/D-19,S	-7.9
NIXON, DONELL Robert Donell B 12.31.1961 Evergreen, NC BR/TR 6-1/185# d4.7 b-Otis																								
1987	Sea A	46	132	17	33	4	0	3	12	13-0	2	28	.250	.327	.348	75	-5	21-7	1.000	0	101	77	O-32(1-32-0)/D-6	-0.2
1988	SF N	59	78	15	27	3	0	0	6	10-0	0	12	.346	.420	.385	138	5	11-8	.983	1	117	0	O-46(32-15-0)	0.5
1989	†SF N	95	166	23	44	2	0	1	15	11-1	0	30	.265	.311	.295	76	-5	10-3	.967	-3	96	0	O-64(15-29-26)	-0.9
1990	Bal A	8	20	1	5	2	0	0	2	1-0	0	7	.250	.286	.350	79	-1	5-0	1.000	-1	68	0	/O-4(LF),D-3	0.0
Total	4	208	396	56	109	11	0	4	35	35-1	2	77	.275	.337	.333	88	-6	47-18	.983	-3	102	24	O-146(52-76-26)/D-9	-0.6
NIXON, RUSS Russell Eugene B 2.19.1935 Cleves, OH BL/TR 6-1/200# d4.20 M5 C12																								
1957	Cle A	62	185	15	52	7	1	2	18	12-7	0	12	.281	.323	.362	88	-3	0-1	.984	-5	72	124	C-57	-0.6
1958	Cle A	113	376	42	113	17	4	9	46	13-4	0	38	.301	.322	.439	111	3	0-3	.991	-8	84	83	*C-101	-0.1
1959	Cle A	82	258	23	62	10	3	1	29	15-1	0	28	.240	.277	.314	66	-13	0-0	.985	-6	89	88	C-74	-1.6
1960	Cle A	25	82	6	20	5	0	1	6	6-2	2	6	.244	.308	.341	79	-2	0-1	.993	-1	86	89	C-25	-0.2
	Bos A	80	272	24	81	17	3	5	33	13-3	0	23	.298	.329	.438	102	0	0-1	.987	-9	103	87	C-74	-0.6
	Year	105	354	30	101	22	3	6	39	19-5	2	29	.285	.324	.415	97	-2	0-2	.989	-10	99	88	C-99	-0.8
1961	Bos A	87	242	24	70	12	2	1	19	13-1	2	19	.289	.327	.368	84	-5	0-1	.975	-4	86	82	C-66	-0.6
1962	Bos A	65	151	11	42	7	2	1	19	8-3	0	14	.278	.313	.371	81	-4	0-0	1.000	-3	80	36	C-38	-0.5
1963	Bos A	98	287	27	77	18	1	5	30	22-5	4	32	.268	.327	.390	98	0	0-0	.992	-5	137	72	C-76	-0.1
1964	Bos A	81	163	10	38	7	0	1	20	14-3	2	29	.233	.297	.294	64	-8	0-0	.990	-3	77	71	C-45	-1.0
1965	Bos A	59	137	11	37	5	1	0	11	6-2	0	23	.270	.295	.321	72	-5	0-0	.981	-6	68	72	C-38	-1.0
1966	Min A	51	96	5	25	2	1	0	7	7-3	1	13	.260	.314	.302	74	-3	0-0	.986	-2	92	54	C-32	-0.4
1967	Min A	74	170	16	40	6	1	1	22	18-3	0	29	.235	.304	.300	74	-5	0-0	.994	-3	104	80	C-69	-0.6
1968	Bos A	29	85	1	13	2	0	0	6	7-1	0	13	.153	.217	.176	19	-8	0-0	.994	-4	83	108	C-27	-1.3
Total	12	906	2504	215	670	115	19	27	266	154-38	11	279	.268	.310	.361	84	-53	0-7	.988	-58	92	82	C-722	-8.6
NOBLE, RAY Rafael Miguel (Magee) B 3.15.1919 Central Hatillo, Cuba D 5.9.1998 Brooklyn, NY BR/TR 5-11/210# d4.18																								
1951	†NY N	55	141	16	33	6	0	5	26	6	0	26	.234	.265	.383	72	-6	0-0	.974	-2	142	54	C-41	-0.7
1952	NY N	6	5	0	0	0	0	0	0	0	0	1	.000	.000	.000	-99	-1	0-0	1.000	0	0	0	/C-5	-0.1
1953	NY N	46	97	15	20	0	1	4	14	19	3	14	.206	.353	.351	83	-2	1-0	.982	-0	146	90	C-41	-0.1
Total	3	107	243	31	53	6	1	9	40	25	3	41	.218	.299	.362	74	-9	1-0	.979	-2	142	71	/C-87	-0.9
NOBOA, JUNIOR Milciades Arturo (Diaz) B 11.10.1964 Azua, D.R. BR/TR 5-10/160# d8.22 OF Total (3-LF 13-RF)																								
1984	Cle A	23	11	3	4	0	0	0	0	0-0	0	2	.364	.364	.364	100	0	1-0	1.000	-3	74	103	2-19/D	-0.2
1987	Cle A	39	80	7	18	2	1	0	7	3-1	0	6	.225	.253	.275	40	-7	1-0	.983	-3	94	59	2-21/S-8,3-5,D	-0.8
1988	Cal A	21	16	4	1	0	0	0	0	0-0	0	1	.063	.063	.063	-67	-4	0-0	.967	2	139	154	/2-9,S-3,3-2	-0.2
1989	Mon N	21	44	3	10	0	0	0	1	1-0	0	3	.227	.244	.227	35	-4	0-0	1.000	4	143	118	2-13/S-4,3	0.1
1990	Mon N	81	158	15	42	7	2	0	14	7-2	1	14	.266	.294	.335	78	-5	4-1	1.000	-15	63	73	2-31/O-9(2-0-7),3-8,S-7,P	-2.0
1991	Mon N	67	95	5	23	3	0	1	2	1-1	0	8	.242	.250	.305	56	-6	2-3	1.000	-1	71	0	/O-7(1-0-6),2-6,3-2,S-2,1	-0.8
1992	NY N	46	47	7	7	0	0	0	3	3-0	1	8	.149	.212	.149	5	-6	0-0	.977	3	133	139	2-16/3-3,S-2	-0.3
1994	Oak A	17	40	3	13	1	1	0	6	2-0	0	5	.325	.357	.400	104	0	1-0	.943	-1	92	98	2-14/S	0.0
	Pit N	2	2	0	0	0	0	0	0	0-0	0	0	.000	.000	.000	-99	-1	0-0	1.000	0	286	0	/S	0.0
Total	8	317	493	47	118	13	4	1	33	17-4	2	47	.239	.265	.288	54	-33	9-4	.981	-14	95	95	2-129/S-28,3-21,O-16R,D-2,1P	-4.2
NOCE, PAUL Paul David B 12.16.1959 San Francisco, CA BR/TR 5-10/175# d6.1																								
1987	Chi N	70	180	17	41	9	2	3	14	6-1	2	49	.228	.261	.350	58	-12	5-3	.983	11	112	116	2-36,S-35/3-2	0.3
1990	Cin N	1	1	0	1	0	0	0	0	0-0	0	0	1.000	1.000	1.000	434	0	0-0	—	0			/H	0.0
Total	2	71	181	17	42	9	2	3	14	6-1	2	49	.232	.265	.354	60	-12	5-3	.983	11	112	116	/2-36,S-35,3-2	0.3
NOFTSKER, GEORGE George Washington B 8.24.1859 Shippensburg, PA D 5.8.1931 Shippensburg, PA BR/TR 5-8/135# d4.17																								
1884	Alt U	7	25	0	1	0	0	0		0			.040	.040	.040	-75	-6		.818	0	0	0	/O-5(0-1-4),C-3	-0.5
NOKES, MATT Matthew Dodge B 10.31.1963 San Diego, CA BL/TR 6-1/185# d9.3																								
1985	SF N	19	53	3	11	2	0	2	5	1-0	1	9	.208	.236	.358	67	-3	0-0	.977	-2	67	23	C-14	-0.4
1986	Det A	7	24	2	8	1	0	1	2	1-1	0	1	.333	.360	.500	132	1	0-0	1.000	1	147	43	/C-7	0.2
1987	†Det A★	135	461	69	133	14	2	32	87	35-2	6	70	.289	.345	.536	135	21	2-1	.992	-6	103	55	*C-109,D-19/O-3(3-0-1),3-2	1.8
1988	Det A	122	382	53	96	18	0	16	53	34-3	1	58	.251	.313	.424	109	4	0-1	.989	5	135	101	*C-110/D-4	1.4
1989	Det A	87	268	15	67	10	0	9	39	17-1	2	37	.250	.298	.388	95	-3	1-0	.978	-4	81	135	C-51,D-33	-0.5
1990	Det A	44	111	12	30	5	1	3	8	4-3	2	14	.270	.305	.414	99	-1	0-0	.984	-5	90	195	D-24,C-19	-0.5
	NY A	92	240	21	57	4	0	8	32	20-3	4	33	.237	.307	.367	84	-6	2-2	.995	-4	75	177	C-46,D-30/O-2(RF)	-0.9

Year	Tm Lg	G	AB	R	H	2B	3B	HR	RBI	BB-IB	HP	SO	AVG	OBP	SLG	AOPS	ABR	SB-CS	FA	FR	Rng	Thr	G at Pos	BFW
	Year	136	351	33	87	9	1	11	40	24-6	6	47	.248	.306	.373	89	-6	2-2	.993	-9	79	182	C-65,D-54/O-2(RF)	-1.4
1991	NY A	135	456	52	122	20	0	24	77	25-5	5	49	.268	.308	.469	113	6	3-2	.992	-10	73	97	*C-130/D-3	0.3
1992	NY A	121	384	42	86	9	1	22	59	37-11	3	62	.224	.293	.424	101	-2	0-1	.993	-14	72	84	*C-111	-1.0
1993	NY A	76	217	25	54	8	0	10	35	16-2	2	31	.249	.303	.424	97	-2	0-0	.992	-10	70	95	C-56,D-11	-0.9
1994	NY A	28	79	11	23	3	0	7	19	5-0	0	16	.291	.329	.595	138	4	0-0	.975	-2	116	50	C-17/1-4,D-5	0.3
1995	Bal A	26	49	4	6	1	0	2	6	4-0	0	11	.122	.185	.265	16	-6	0-0	.989	1	56	94	C-16/D-2	-0.5
	Col N	10	11	1	2	1	0	0	0	1-1	0	4	.182	.250	.273	29	-1	0-0	.909	0	0	0	/C-3	-0.1
Total	11	902	2735	310	695	96	4	136	422	200-32	26	395	.254	.308	.441	106	12	8-7	.990	-49	90	95	C-689,D-131/O-5(3-0-3),1-4,3-2	-0.8
NOLAN, JOE Joseph William B 5.12.1951 St.Louis, MO BL/TR 6/190# d9.21																								
1972	NY N	4	10	0	0	0	0	0	0	1-0	0	3	.000	.091	.000	-74	-2	0-0	.938	-1	130	133	/C-3	-0.3
1975	Atl N	4	4	0	1	0	0	0	0	1-0	0	0	.250	.400	.250	80	0	0-0	1.000	0	0	0	/C	0.0
1977	Atl N	62	82	13	23	3	0	3	9	13-1	0	12	.280	.375	.427	103	1	1-0	1.000	-3	55	68	C-19	-0.2
1978	Atl N	95	213	22	49	7	3	4	22	34-5	1	28	.230	.339	.347	83	-4	3-2	.979	-9	78	46	C-61	-1.1
1979	Atl N	89	230	28	57	9	3	4	21	27-3	3	28	.248	.333	.365	85	-4	1-3	.983	-9	62	71	C-74	-1.2
1980	Atl N	17	22	2	6	1	0	0	2	2-0	0	4	.273	.333	.318	80	-1	0-0	1.000	1	66	137	/C-6	0.1
	Cin N	53	154	14	48	7	0	3	24	13-0	0	8	.312	.353	.416	117	4	0-0	.982	-4	63	96	C-51	0.2
	Year	70	176	16	54	8	0	3	26	15-0	0	12	.307	.350	.403	112	3	0-0	.983	-3	63	99	C-57	0.3
1981	Cin N	81	236	25	73	18	1	1	26	24-6	1	19	.309	.371	.407	120	7	1-2	**.995**	-7	81	45	C-81	0.3
1982	Bal A	77	219	24	51	7	1	6	35	16-1	0	35	.233	.278	.356	75	-8	1-1	.978	-3	72	116	C-72	-0.9
1983	†Bal A	73	184	25	51	11	1	5	24	16-1	2	31	.277	.342	.429	113	3	0-0	.980	-7	96	56	C-65	-0.1
1984	Bal A	35	62	2	18	1	1	1	9	12-4	0	10	.290	.400	.387	123	3	0-0	.962	-0	95	312	D-11/C-6	0.2
1985	Bal A	31	38	1	5	2	0	0	6	5-1	0	5	.132	.227	.184	16	-4	0-0	1.000	0	59	0	/C-5,D-4	-0.4
Total	11	621	1454	156	382	66	10	27	178	164-22	7	183	.263	.336	.378	95	-5	7-8	.984	-41	75	74	C-444/D-15	-3.4
NONNENKAMP, RED Leo William B 7.7.1910 St.Louis, MO D 12.3.2000 Little Rock, AR BL/TL 5-11/165# d9.6																								
1933	Pit N	1	1	0	0	0	0	0	0	0	0	1	.000	.000	.000	-99	0	0	—	0			H	0.0
1938	Bos A	87	180	37	51	4	1	0	18	21	0	13	.283	.358	.317	67	-9	6-1	.968	3	111	152	O-39(5-5-29)/1-5	-0.7
1939	Bos A	58	75	12	18	2	1	0	5	12	0	6	.240	.345	.293	62	-4	0-1	.962	-1	99	0	O-15(7-4-4)	-0.5
1940	Bos A	9	7	0	0	0	0	0	1	0	1	4	.000	.125	.000	-62	-2	0-0	—	0			H	-0.2
Total	4	155	263	49	69	6	2	0	24	33	1	24	.262	.347	.300	62	-15	6-2	.966	2	108	117	/O-54(12-9-33),1-5	-1.4
NOONAN, PETE Peter John B 11.24.1881 W.Stockbridge, MA D 2.11.1965 Great Barrington, MA BR/TR 6/180# d6.20																								
1904	Phi A	39	114	13	23	3	1	2	13	1	0		.202	.209	.298	56	-6	1	.969	-2	*100*	*110*	C-22,1-10	-0.7
1906	Chi N	5	3	0	1	0	0	0	0	0	0		.333	.333	.333	102	0	0	1.000	0	0	2150	/1	0.0
	StL N	44	125	8	21	1	3	1	9	11	0		.168	.235	.248	53	-7	1	.957	-2	*82*	*111*	C-23,1-16	-0.8
	Year	49	128	8	22	1	3	1	9	11	0		.172	.237	.250	54	-8	1	.957	-2	*82*	*111*	C-23,1-17	-0.8
1907	StL N	74	237	19	53	7	3	1	16	9	0		.224	.252	.291	73	-9	3	.951	-3	*83*	*95*	C-70	-0.6
Total	3	162	479	40	98	11	7	4	38	21	0		.205	.238	.282	64	-22	5	.955	-7	*85*	*101*	C-115/1-27	-2.1
NORDBROOK, TIM Timothy Charles B 7.7.1949 Baltimore, MD BR/TR 6-1/180# d9.13																								
1974	Bal A	6	15	4	4	0	0	0	1	2-0	0	2	.267	.353	.267	83	0	1-0	1.000	0	100	133	/S-5,2	0.1
1975	Bal A	40	34	6	4	1	0	0	0	7-0	0	7	.118	.268	.147	21	-3	0-0	.970	-2	110	90	S-37/2-3	-0.4
1976	Bal A	27	22	4	5	0	0	0	0	3-0	0	5	.227	.320	.227	66	-1	0-0	1.000	-3	52	58	2-14,S-12/D	-0.3
	Cal A	5	8	1	0	0	0	0	0	1-0	0	3	.000	.111	.000	-70	-2	1-0	.941	-1	89	0	/S-4,2	-0.2
	Year	32	30	5	5	0	0	0	0	4-0	0	8	.167	.265	.167	30	-3	1-0	.978	-4	94	90	S-16,2-15/D	-0.5
1977	Chi A	15	20	2	5	0	0	0	1	7-0	0	4	.250	.429	.250	95	1	1-0	.850	-4	70	59	S-11/3D	-0.2
	Tor A	24	63	9	11	0	1	0	1	4-0	0	11	.175	.224	.206	18	-7	1-0	.989	-3	89	71	S-24	-0.8
	Year	39	83	11	16	0	1	0	2	11-0	0	15	.193	.284	.217	39	-7	2-0	.947	-7	84	68	S-35/D-2,3	-1.0
1978	Tor A	7	0	1	0	0	0	0	0	0-0	1	0	—	1.000	—	200	0	0-0	1.000	0	119	112	/S-7	0.1
	Mil A	2	5	0	0	0	0	0	0	1-0	0	1	.000	.167	.000	-49	-1	0-0	.909	0	158	0	/S-2	0.0
	Year	9	5	1	0	0	0	0	0	1-0	1	1	.000	.286	.000	-13	-1	0-0	.941	1	141	48	/S-9	0.1
1979	Mil A	2	2	0	1	0	0	0	0	0-0	0	0	.500	.500	.500	171	0	0-0	1.000	-1	0	0	/S-2	-0.1
Total	6	128	169	27	30	1	1	0	3	25-0	1	33	.178	.286	.195	38	-13	4-0	.961	-13	95	79	S-104/2-19,D-3,3	-1.8
NORDHAGEN, WAYNE Wayne Oren B 7.4.1948 Thief River Falls, MN BR/TR 6-2/205# d7.16																								
1976	Chi A	22	53	6	10	2	0	0	5	4-0	0	12	.189	.233	.226	39	-4	0-0	1.000	1	118	167	O-10(RF)/C-5,D-6	-0.4
1977	Chi A	52	124	16	39	7	3	4	22	2-0	0	12	.315	.323	.516	125	3	1-0	.944	-4	83	45	O-46(12-2-34)/C-3,D-2	-0.2
1978	Chi A	68	206	28	62	16	0	5	35	5-0	0	18	.301	.310	.451	113	3	0-1	.941	-6	79	100	O-36(19-0-18),D-16,C-12	-0.5
1979	Chi A	78	193	20	54	15	0	7	25	13-2	0	22	.280	.324	.466	111	3	0-0	1.000	1	98	562	D-47,O-12(6-0-7)/C-5,P-2	0.1
1980	Chi A	123	415	45	115	22	4	15	59	10-3	1	45	.277	.294	.458	104	0	0-1	.969	-3	88	120	O-74(45-0-33),D-32	-0.8
1981	Chi A	65	208	19	64	8	1	6	33	10-0	1	25	.308	.338	.442	127	6	0-1	.947	-4	81	111	O-60(25-1-36)	-0.1
1982	Tor A	44	115	8	32	3	0	1	14	9-1	0	13	.278	.328	.330	75	-4	0-2	1.000	-0	73	175	D-32,O-10(10-0-1)	-0.6
	Pit N	1	4	0	2	0	0	0	2	0-0	0	1	.500	.500	.500	175	0	0-0	1.000	-0	100	0	/O(LF)	0.0
	Tor A	28	70	4	18	3	0	0	6	1-0	0	9	.257	.264	.300	51	-5	0-0	—	0	0	0	D-28	-0.6
1983	Chi N	21	35	1	5	1	0	1	4	0-0	1	5	.143	.162	.257	15	-4	0-0	1.000	-1	65	0	/O-7(LF)	-0.6
Total	8	502	1423	147	401	77	8	39	205	54-6	3	162	.282	.306	.429	101	-2	1-5	.962	-17	85	124	O-256(125-3-139),D-163/C-25,P-2	-3.7
NORDYKE, LOU Louis Ellis B 8.7.1876 Brighton, IA D 9.27.1945 Los Angeles, CA BL/TR 6/185# d4.18																								
1906	StL A	25	53	4	13	1	0	0	7	10	0		.245	.365	.264	102	1	3	.942	-3	53	261	1-12	-0.2
NOREN, IRV Irving Arnold B 11.29.1924 Jamestown, NY BL/TL 6/190# d4.18 C5																								
1950	Was A	138	542	80	160	27	10	14	98	67	2	77	.295	.375	.459	118	14	5-2	.984	9	102	184	*O-121(CF),1-17	1.8
1951	Was A	129	509	82	142	33	5	8	86	51	0	35	.279	.345	.411	105	3	10-7	.978	12	117	113	*O-126(CF)	1.2
1952	Was A	12	49	4	12	3	1	0	2	6	0	3	.245	.327	.347	91	-1	1-0	1.000	2	115	196	O-12(CF)	0.1
	†NY A	93	272	36	64	13	2	5	21	26	6	34	.235	.316	.353	91	-4	4-2	1.000	-3	91	83	O-60(18-18-25),1-19	-0.9
	Year	105	321	40	76	16	3	5	23	32	6	37	.237	.318	.352	91	-4	5-2	1.000	-1	96	107	O-72(18-30-25),1-19	-0.8
1953	†NY A	109	345	55	92	12	6	6	46	42	2	39	.267	.350	.388	103	1	3-3	.991	3	100	143	O-96(21-44-38)	0.0
1954	NY A★	125	426	70	136	21	6	12	66	43	1	38	.319	.377	.481	140	23	4-6	.980	1	99	107	*O-116(55-23-49)/1	1.7
1955	†NY A	132	371	49	94	19	1	8	59	43-5	3	33	.253	.331	.375	92	-4	5-2	.980	4	108	104	*O-126(117-10-3)	-0.6
1956	NY A	29	37	4	8	1	0	0	6	12-2	0	7	.216	.408	.243	78	0	0-0	.875	-0	58	253	O-10(4-0-6)/1	-0.1
1957	KC A	81	160	8	34	8	0	2	16	11-2	1	19	.213	.267	.300	54	-10	0-0	.990	-1	86	117	1-25/O-6(RF)	-1.3
	StL N	17	30	3	11	4	1	1	10	4-2	0	6	.367	.429	.667	189	4	0-1	1.000	-1	66	0	/O-8(1-0-7)	0.3
1958	StL N	117	178	24	47	9	1	4	22	13-2	4	21	.264	.327	.393	87	-3	0-1	.974	-2	96	34	O-77(59-14-10)	-0.8
1959	StL N	8	8	0	1	1	0	0	0	0-0	0	2	.125	.125	.250	-3	-1	0-0	—	-0	0	0	/O-2(LF),1	-0.1
	Chi N	65	156	27	50	6	2	4	19	13-1	3	24	.321	.384	.462	125	6	2-0	1.000	2	106	137	O-40(16-6-18)/1	0.7
	Year	73	164	27	51	7	2	4	19	13-1	3	26	.311	.372	.451	118	4	2-0	1.000	2	105	136	O-42(18-6-18)/1-2	0.6
1960	Chi N	12	11	0	1	0	0	0	1	3-0	0	4	.091	.286	.091	9	-1	0-0	.833	-0	0	213	/1O(RF)	-0.2
	LA N	26	25	1	5	0	0	1	1	1-0	0	8	.200	.231	.320	46	-2	0-0	—	0			H	-0.2
	Year	38	36	1	6	0	0	1	2	4-0	0	12	.167	.250	.250	36	-3	0-0	1.000	-0	0	213	/1O(RF)	-0.4
Total	11	1093	3119	443	857	157	35	65	453	335-14	22	350	.275	.348	.410	106	25	34-24	.984	27	103	124	O-801(293-374-163)/1-66	1.6
NORMAN, DAN Daniel Edmund B 1.11.1955 Los Angeles, CA BR/TR (BB 1908 (part)) 6-2/195# d9.27																								
1977	NY N	7	16	2	4	1	0	0	0	4-0	0	2	.250	.400	.313	99	0	0-0	1.000	-1	88	0	/O-6(0-1-6)	0.0
1978	NY N	19	64	7	17	0	1	4	10	2-0	0	14	.266	.284	.484	116	1	1-0	1.000	-0	99	70	O-18(1-0-18)	-0.1
1979	NY N	44	110	9	27	3	1	3	11	10-2	1	26	.245	.311	.373	90	-2	2-0	.967	1	95	169	O-33(8-0-25)	-0.2
1980	NY N	69	92	5	17	1	1	2	9	6-0	0	14	.185	.235	.283	45	-7	5-0	1.000	-1	78	99	O-19(9-0-10)	-0.8
1982	Mon N	53	66	6	14	3	0	2	7	7-0	0	20	.212	.288	.348	76	-2	0-1	.969	-1	91	87	O-31(17-6-8)	-0.4
Total	5	192	348	29	79	8	3	11	37	29-2	1	76	.227	.287	.362	81	-10	8-1	.981	-2	92	109	O-107(35-7-67)	-1.5
NORMAN, BILL Henry Willis Patrick B 7.16.1910 St.Louis, MO D 4.21.1962 Milwaukee, WI BR/TR 6-2/190# d8.8 M2 C2																								
1931	Chi A	24	55	7	10	2	0	0	6	4	0	10	.182	.237	.218	22	-6	0-1	.933	1	117	96	O-17(3-14-0)	-0.6
1932	Chi A	13	48	6	11	3	1	0	2	2	0	3	.229	.260	.333	56	-3	0-0	.917	-1	72	233	O-13(1-11-1)	-0.4
Total	2	37	103	13	21	5	1	0	8	6	0	13	.204	.248	.272	38	-9	0-1	.928	-0	97	156	/O-30(4-25-1)	-1.0

Year	Tm Lg	G	AB	R	H	2B	3B	HR	RBI	BB-IB	HP	SO	AVG	OBP	SLG	AOPS	ABR	SB-CS	FA	FR	Rng	Thr	G at Pos	BFW
NORMAN, LES Leslie Eugene B 2.25.1969 Warren, MI BR/TR 6-1/185# d5.29																								
1995	KC A	24	40	6	9	0	1	0	4	6-0	0	6	.225	.326	.275	58	-3	0-1	.958	-1	88	131	O-17(4-5-8)/D-5	-0.4
1996	KC A	54	49	9	6	0	0	0	0	6-0	1	14	.122	.232	.122	-7	-8	1-1	1.000	2	129	89	O-38(15-3-20)/D-7	-0.6
Total	2	78	89	15	15	0	1	0	4	12-0	1	20	.169	.275	.191	22	-11	1-2	.986	1	112	107	/O-55(19-8-28),D-12	-1.0
NORMAN, NELSON Nelson Augusto B 5.23.1958 San Pedro De Macoris, D.R. BB/TR (BR 1978, 1979 (part)) 6-2/160# d5.20 C1																								
1978	Tex A	23	34	1	9	2	0	0	1	0-0	0	5	.265	.265	.324	64	-2	0-0	.984	5	146	118	S-18/3-6	0.4
1979	Tex A	147	343	36	76	9	3	0	21	19-0	0	41	.222	.260	.265	43	-28	4-1	.952	-29	83	86	*S-142/2	-4.4
1980	Tex A	17	32	4	7	0	0	0	1	1-0	0	1	.219	.242	.219	28	-3	0-1	.943	5	124	145	S-17	0.3
1981	Tex A	7	13	1	3	1	0	0	2	1-0	0	2	.231	.267	.308	75	0	0-0	.963	3	153	186	/S-5	0.3
1982	Pit N	3	3	0	0	0	0	0	0	0-0	0	0	.000	.000	.000	-97	-1	0-0	—	-1	0	0	/2-2,S	-0.2
1987	Mon N	1	4	0	0	0	0	0	0	0-0	0	1	.000	.000	.000	-97	-1	0-0	.667	-1	37	0	/S	-0.2
Total	6	198	429	42	95	12	3	0	25	21-0	0	50	.221	.256	.263	42	-35	4-2	.954	-18	93	95	S-184/3-6,2-3	-3.8
NORRIS, JIM James Francis B 12.20.1948 Brooklyn, NY BL/TL 5-10/175# d4.7																								
1977	Cle A	133	440	59	119	23	6	2	37	64-4	0	57	.270	.360	.364	102	4	26-17	.982	8	116	108	*O-124(3-74-49)/1-3	0.9
1978	Cle A	113	315	41	89	14	5	2	27	42-4	0	20	.283	.364	.378	111	6	12-7	.988	4	109	126	O-78(26-5-51),D-15/1-6	0.6
1979	Cle A	124	353	50	87	15	6	3	30	44-1	0	35	.246	.327	.348	83	-8	15-10	.982	3	117	34	O-93(47-23-28),D-13	-0.8
1980	Tex A	119	174	23	43	5	0	0	16	23-2	0	16	.247	.327	.276	72	-6	6-3	1.000	-3	84	101	O-82(7-19-57),1-10/D	-1.1
Total	4	489	1282	173	338	57	17	7	110	173-11	0	128	.264	.348	.351	95	-4	59-37	.985	12	110	91	O-377(83-121-185)/D-29,1-19	-0.4
NORRIS, LEO Leo John B 5.17.1908 Bay St.Louis, MS D 2.13.1987 Zachary, LA BR/TR 5-11/165# d4.14																								
1936	Phi N	**154**	581	64	154	27	4	11	76	39	3	79	.265	.315	.382	79	-18	4	.936	-3	93	84	*S-121,2-38	-1.0
1937	Phi N	116	381	45	98	24	3	9	36	21	0	53	.257	.296	.407	82	-10	3	.949	-8	94	83	2-74,3-24,S-20	-1.2
Total	2	270	962	109	252	51	7	20	112	60	3	132	.262	.307	.392	80	-28	7	.940	-11	94	84	S-141,2-112/3-24	-2.2
NORTH, BILLY William Alex B 5.15.1948 Seattle, WA BB/TR (BR 1971) 5-11/185# d9.3																								
1971	Chi N	8	16	3	6	0	0	0	0	4-1	1	6	.375	.524	.375	138	1	1-1	1.000	-1	42	0	/O-6(1-0-5)	-0.1
1972	Chi N	66	127	22	23	2	3	0	4	13-1	1	33	.181	.262	.244	40	-10	6-0	.955	-1	89	146	O-48(9-26-15)	-1.2
1973	Oak A	146	554	98	158	10	5	5	34	78-5	3	89	.285	.376	.348	111	11	53-20	.980	15	**120**	136	*O-138(0-136-2)/D-6	2.8
1974	†Oak A	149	543	79	141	20	5	4	33	69-1	5	86	.260	.347	.337	105	6	**54**-26	.991	11	119	92	*O-138(CF)/D-8	1.7
1975	†Oak A	140	524	74	143	17	5	1	43	81-3	4	80	.273	.373	.330	103	6	30-12	.975	11	120	106	*O-138(4-134-0)/D	1.6
1976	Oak A	154	590	91	163	20	5	2	31	73-3	2	95	.276	.356	.337	109	9	**75**-29	.978	-4	99	74	*O-144(0-137-7)/D-8	0.8
1977	Oak A	56	184	32	48	3	3	1	9	32-2	2	25	.261	.376	.326	95	0	17-13	.983	-4	93	31	O-52(CF)/D	-0.5
1978	Oak A	24	52	5	11	4	0	0	5	9-2	2	13	.212	.344	.288	86	0	3-2	1.000	-1	88	120	O-17(CF)	-0.1
	†LA N	110	304	54	71	10	0	0	10	65-2	2	48	.234	.371	.266	81	-3	27-8	.975	-3	101	40	*O-103(1-102-0)	-0.5
1979	SF N	142	460	87	119	15	4	5	30	96-3	1	84	.259	.386	.341	108	11	58-24	.987	1	105	98	*O-130(CF)	1.6
1980	SF N	128	415	73	104	12	1	1	19	81-5	1	78	.251	.373	.292	90	-1	45-19	.982	4	111	82	*O-115(1-114-0)	0.6
1981	SF N	46	131	22	29	7	0	1	12	26-0	1	28	.221	.354	.298	88	0	26-8	.966	-3	93	42	O-37(CF)	-0.1
Total	11	1169	3900	640	1016	120	31	20	230	627-28	25	665	.261	.365	.323	99	30	395-162	.981	26	108	90	*O-1066(16-1023-29)/D-24	6.6
NORTHEN, HUB Hubbard Elwin B 8.16.1885 Atlanta, TX D 10.1.1947 Shreveport, LA BL/TL 5-8/175# d9.10																								
1910	StL A	26	96	6	19	1	0	0	16	5	0		.198	.238	.208	42	-7	2	.926	-3	94	54	O-26(CF)	-1.2
1911	Cin N	1	0	0	0	0	0	0	0	0	0	0	—	—	—	—	0	0	—	0			H	0.0
	Bro N	19	76	16	24	2	2	0	1	14	1	9	.316	.429	.395	137	5	4	.911	0	96	164	O-19(CF)	0.4
	Year	20	76	16	24	2	2	0	1	14	1	9	.316	.429	.395	137	5	4	.911	0	96	164	O-19(CF)	0.4
1912	Bro N	118	412	54	116	26	6	3	46	41	4	46	.282	.352	.396	109	5	8	.950	-6	92	76	*O-102(10-43-49)	-0.7
Total	3	164	584	76	159	29	8	3	63	60	5	55	.272	.345	.365	103	3	14	.939	-8	93	85	O-147(10-88-49)	-1.5
NORTHEY, RON Ronald James B 4.26.1920 Mahanoy City, PA D 4.16.1971 Pittsburgh, PA BL/TR 5-10/195# d4.14 Mil 1945 C3 s-Scott																								
1942	Phi N	127	402	31	101	13	2	5	31	28	0	33	.251	.300	.331	89	-7	2	.952	2	104	130	*O-109(RF)	-1.2
1943	Phi N	147	586	72	163	31	5	16	68	51	3	52	.278	.339	.430	127	18	2	.978	1	97	122	*O-145(RF)	1.0
1944	Phi N	152	570	72	164	35	9	22	104	67	4	51	.288	.367	.496	146	34	1	.981	1	90	141	*O-151(RF)	2.5
1946	Phi N	128	438	55	109	24	6	16	62	39	2	59	.249	.313	.441	116	6	1	.971	-4	97	68	*O-111(RF)	-0.1
1947	Phi N	13	47	7	12	3	0	0	3	6	0	3	.255	.340	.319	79	-1	1	1.000	-0	87	106	O-13(RF)	-0.2
	StL N	110	311	52	91	19	3	15	63	48	2	29	.293	.391	.518	133	16	0	.949	-3	87	137	O-94(15-0-79)/3-2	1.0
	Year	123	358	59	103	22	3	15	66	54	2	32	.288	.384	.492	127	15	1	.955	-3	87	133	*O-107(15-0-92)/3-2	0.8
1948	StL N	96	246	40	79	10	1	13	64	38	4	25	.321	.420	.528	147	17	0	.989	-4	86	54	O-67(RF)	1.2
1949	StL N	90	265	28	69	18	2	7	50	31	0	15	.260	.338	.423	98	0	0	.980	-8	73	68	O-73(RF)	-1.1
1950	Cin N	27	77	11	20	5	0	5	9	15	0	6	.260	.380	.519	134	4	0	.955	-2	79	0	O-24(RF)	0.1
	Chi N	53	114	11	32	9	0	4	20	10	0	9	.281	.339	.465	110	2	0	.976	0	88	168	O-27(RF)	0.1
	Year	80	191	22	52	14	0	9	29	25	0	15	.272	.356	.487	120	6	0	.969	-2	84	102	O-51(RF)	0.2
1952	Chi N	1	1	0	0	0	0	0	0	0	0	0	.000	.000	.000	-99	0	0-0	—	0			H	0.0
1955	Chi A	14	14	1	5	2	0	1	4	3-0	0	3	.357	.471	.714	209	2	0-0	1.000	-0	66	0	/O-2(RF)	0.2
1956	Chi A	53	48	4	17	2	0	3	23	8-2	0	1	.354	.417	.583	168	5	0-0	1.000	0	75	490	/O-4(3-0-3)	0.5
1957	Chi A	40	27	0	5	1	0	0	7	11-1	0	5	.185	.410	.222	80	0	0-0	—	0			H	0.0
	Phi N	33	26	1	7	0	0	1	5	6-1	0	6	.269	.406	.385	118	1	0-0	—	0			H	0.1
Total	12	1084	3172	385	874	172	28	108	513	361-4	15	297	.276	.352	.450	124	97	7-0	.972	-17	92	112	O-820(18-0-804)/3-2	4.1
NORTHEY, SCOTT Scott Richard B 10.15.1946 Philadelphia, PA BR/TR 6/175# d9.2 f-Ron																								
1969	KC A	20	61	11	16	2	2	1	7	7-0	0	19	.262	.338	.410	108	0	6-3	.973	-0	99	104	O-18(CF)	0.0
NORTHRUP, JIM James Thomas B 11.24.1939 Breckenridge, MI BL/TR 6-3/190# d9.30																								
1964	Det A	5	12	1	1	1	0	0	0	0-0	0	3	.083	.083	.167	-32	-2	1-0	1.000	-0	98	0	/O-2(0-2-1)	-0.2
1965	Det A	80	219	20	45	12	3	2	16	12-1	2	50	.205	.253	.315	60	-12	1-1	.976	-3	98	0	O-54(10-6-38)	-1.9
1966	Det A	123	419	53	111	24	6	16	58	33-4	4	52	.265	.322	.465	121	11	4-7	.980	8	117	126	*O-113(3-11-106)	1.1
1967	Det A	144	495	63	134	18	6	10	61	43-6	3	83	.271	.332	.392	110	6	7-1	.972	-2	106	37	*O-143(65-94-39)	-0.1
1968	†Det A	154	580	76	153	29	7	21	90	50-4	4	87	.264	.324	.447	129	19	4-5	.979	4	**113**	78	*O-151(12-47-103)	1.5
1969	Det A	148	543	79	160	31	5	25	66	52-1	3	83	.295	.358	.508	135	24	4-2	.985	5	111	83	*O-143(29-89-49)	2.4
1970	Det A	139	504	71	132	21	3	24	80	58-6	7	68	.262	.343	.458	119	13	3-6	.993	2	110	47	*O-136(34-39-78)	0.7
1971	Det A	136	459	72	124	27	2	16	71	60-9	2	43	.270	.355	.442	121	14	7-4	.981	-3	94	64	*O-108(42-68-39),1-32	0.5
1972	†Det A	134	426	40	111	15	2	8	42	38-6	2	47	.261	.324	.362	101	0	4-7	.978	-2	95	103	*O-127(50-42-72)/1-2	-0.9
1973	Det A	119	404	55	124	14	7	12	44	38-6	1	41	.307	.366	.465	125	13	4-4	.982	2	105	90	*O-116(51-10-78)	0.9
1974	Det A	97	376	41	89	12	1	11	42	36-4	0	46	.237	.300	.362	88	-6	0-0	.973	-1	104	66	O-97(0-2-97)	-1.3
	Mon N	21	54	3	13	1	0	2	8	5-1	0	9	.241	.305	.370	84	-1	0-0	1.000	-3	57	0	O-13(7-0-6)	-0.5
	Bal A	8	7	2	4	0	0	1	3	2-1	0	1	.571	.667	1.000	386	3	0-0	1.000	1	95	644	/O-6(4-0-2),D	0.3
1975	Bal A	84	194	27	53	13	0	5	29	22-1	2	22	.273	.348	.418	125	7	0-1	.979	-6	80	65	O-58(3-56-0)/D-3	-0.1
Total	12	1392	4692	603	1254	218	42	153	610	449-50	30	635	.267	.333	.429	115	89	39-38	.981	2	105	73	*O-1267(310-466-708)/1-34,D-4	2.4
NORTON, FRANK Frank Prescott B 6.1845 , NY D 8.1.1920 Greenwich, CT d5.5																								
1871	Oly NA	1	1	0	0	0	0	0	0	0		1	.000	.000	.000	-99	0	0-0	.000	-1	0	0	/3O(RF)	0.0
NORTON, GREG Gregory Blakemoor B 7.6.1972 San Leandro, CA BB/TR 6-1/190# d8.18 OF Total (24-LF 7-RF)																								
1996	Chi A	11	23	4	5	0	0	2	3	4-0	0	6	.217	.333	.478	107	0	0-1	.778	-3	35	0	/S-6,3-2,D-2	-0.3
1997	Chi A	18	34	5	9	2	2	0	1	2-0	0	8	.265	.306	.441	96	0	0-0	.864	-1	105	0	3-11/D-2	-0.1
1998	Chi A	105	299	38	71	17	2	9	36	26-1	2	77	.237	.301	.398	83	-8	3-3	.994	-5	65	92	1-79,3-11/2D	-1.9
1999	Chi A	132	436	62	111	26	0	16	50	69-3	2	93	.255	.358	.424	99	1	4-4	.922	-6	95	88	*3-120,1-26/D	-0.5
2000	Chi A	71	201	25	49	6	1	6	28	26-0	2	47	.244	.333	.373	78	-7	1-0	.926	-10	68	66	3-47,1-17/D-3	-1.6
2001	Col N	117	225	30	60	13	2	13	40	19-2	0	65	.267	.321	.516	92	-3	1-0	1.000	-8	65	109	O-25(22-0-4),3-24,1-13/D	-1.1
2002	Col N	113	168	19	37	8	1	7	37	24-0	0	52	.220	.314	.405	79	-6	2-3	.896	-4	77	108	3-22,1-15/O-2(LF),D	-1.1
2003	Col N	114	179	19	47	15	0	6	31	16-0	1	47	.263	.325	.447	87	-3	2-1	.924	-2	94	56	3-34/1-9,O-3(RF)	-0.5
Total	8	681	1565	202	389	87	8	59	226	186-6	7	395	.249	.329	.427	89	-26	13-12	.918	-39	87	76	3-271,1-159/O-30L,D-12,S-6,2	-7.1
NORWOOD, WILLIE Willie B 11.7.1950 Greene County, AL BR/TR 6/185# d4.21																								
1977	Min A	39	83	15	19	3	0	3	9	6-0	0	17	.229	.281	.373	78	-3	6-1	.952	-0	113	0	O-28(3-20-8)/D-5	-0.2
1978	Min A	125	428	56	109	22	3	8	46	28-0	3	64	.255	.301	.376	89	-7	25-10	.944	-4	94	94	*O-115(101-14-4)/D-6	-1.4
1979	Min A	96	270	32	67	13	3	6	30	20-2	0	51	.248	.299	.385	80	-8	9-5	.974	-3	91	90	O-71(0-44-28),D-14	-1.3

Year	Tm Lg	G	AB	R	H	2B	3B	HR	RBI	BB-IB	HP	SO	AVG	OBP	SLG	AOPS	ABR	SB-CS	FA	FR	Rng	Thr	G at Pos	BFW
1980	Min A	34	73	6	12	2	0	1	8	3-0	0	13	.164	.197	.233	16	-9	1-1	1.000	1	129	0	O-17(0-5-17)/D-9	-0.8
Total	4	294	854	109	207	40	6	18	93	57-2	3	145	.242	.290	.367	79	-27	41-17	.959	-6	97	77	O-231(104-83-57)/D-34	-3.7
NOSSEK, JOE Joseph Rudolph B 11.8.1940 Cleveland, OH BR/TR 6/178# d4.18 C27																								
1964	Min A	7	1	1	0	0	0	0	0	0-0	0	0	.000	.000	.000	-99	0	0-0	—	-0	0	0	/O-2(1-1-0)	0.0
1965	†Min A	87	170	19	37	9	0	2	16	7-1	1	22	.218	.250	.306	55	-10	2-0	.970	-1	99	77	O-48(2-46-2)/3-9	-1.2
1966	Min A	4	0	0	0	0	0	0	0	0-0	0	0	—	—	—	—	0	0-0	—	-0	0	0	/O-2(CF)	0.0
	KC A	87	230	13	60	10	3	1	27	8-1	0	21	.261	.285	.343	83	-6	4-2	.983	5	109	199	O-78(12-65-3)/3	-0.3
	Year	91	230	13	60	10	3	1	27	8-1	0	21	.261	.285	.343	82	-6	4-2	.983	5	109	199	O-80(12-67-3)/3	-0.3
1967	KC A	87	166	12	34	6	1	0	10	4-1	0	26	.205	.221	.253	42	-13	2-0	.982	4	126	76	O-63(35-32-0)	-1.1
1969	Oak A	13	6	0	0	0	0	0	0	0-0	0	0	.000	.000	.000	-99	-2	0-0	1.000	-0	98	0	O-12(9-3-0)	-0.2
	StL N	9	5	2	1	0	0	0	0	0-0	0	3	.200	.200	.200	12	-1	0-0	1.000	0	262	0	/O(CF)	0.0
1970	StL N	1	1	0	0	0	0	0	0	0-0	0	0	.000	.000	.000	-98	0	0-0	—	0			H	0.0
Total	6	295	579	47	132	25	4	3	53	19-3	1	72	.228	.252	.301	60	-32	8-2	.980	8	112	131	O-206(59-150-5)/3-10	-2.8
NOVIKOFF, LOU Louis Alexander "The Mad Russian" B 10.12.1915 Glendale, AZ D 9.30.1970 South Gate, CA BR/TR 5-10/185# d4.15 Mil 1945																								
1941	Chi N	62	203	22	49	8	0	5	24	11	1	15	.241	.284	.355	82	-6	0	1.000	-1	91	91	O-54(51-0-3)	-1.0
1942	Chi N	128	483	48	145	25	5	7	64	24	3	28	.300	.337	.416	125	12	3	.964	-3	90	136	*O-120(LF)	0.4
1943	Chi N	78	233	22	65	7	3	0	28	18	1	15	.279	.333	.335	95	-2	0	.980	-6	85	39	O-61(60-1-0)	-1.1
1944	Chi N	71	139	15	39	4	2	3	19	10	0	11	.281	.329	.403	106	0	1	.976	-3	77	57	O-29(28-1-0)	-0.4
1946	Phi N	17	23	0	7	1	0	0	3	1	0	2	.304	.333	.348	96	0	0	1.000	0	142	0	/O-3(LF)	0.0
Total	5	356	1081	107	305	45	10	15	138	64	5	71	.282	.325	.384	107	4	4	.976	-12	89	97	O-267(262-2-3)	-2.1
NOVOTNEY, RUBE Ralph Joseph B 8.5.1924 Streator, IL D 7.16.1987 Redondo Beach, CA BR/TR 6/187# d4.29																								
1949	Chi N	22	67	4	18	2	1	0	6	3	0	11	.269	.300	.328	70	-3	0	.958	-2	*64*	*101*	C-20	-0.4
NUNAMAKER, LES Leslie Grant B 1.25.1889 Aurora, NE D 11.14.1938 Hastings, NE BR/TR 6-2/190# d4.28																								
1911	Bos A	62	183	18	47	4	3	0	19	12	0		.257	.303	.311	72	-7	1	.972	4	*100*	*101*	C-59	0.1
1912	Bos A	35	103	15	26	5	2	0	6	6	3		.252	.313	.340	82	-3	2	.971	-1	*113*	*74*	C-35	-0.1
1913	Bos A	29	65	9	14	5	2	0	9	8	1	8	.215	.311	.354	92	-1	2	.977	1	*100*	*66*	C-27	0.3
1914	Bos A	5	5	0	1	0	0	0	0	1	0	0	.200	.333	.200	61	0	0	1.000	0	*120*	*306*	/C-3,1	0.0
	NY A	87	257	19	68	10	3	2	29	22	2	34	.265	.327	.350	104	1	11-9	.971	3	*92*	*116*	C-70/1-5	1.0
	Year	92	262	19	69	10	3	2	29	23	2	34	.263	.328	.347	103	1	11-9	.971	3	*92*	*118*	C-73/1-6	1.0
1915	NY A	87	249	24	56	6	3	0	17	23	1	24	.225	.293	.273	70	-10	3-2	.964	-4	*93*	*100*	C-77/1-2	-0.8
1916	NY A	91	260	25	77	14	7	0	28	34	1	21	.296	.380	.404	133	11	4	.983	2	126	**99**	C-79	2.1
1917	NY A	104	310	22	81	9	2	0	33	21	1	25	.261	.310	.303	86	-6	5	.976	3	*125*	*102*	C-91	0.5
1918	StL A	85	274	22	71	9	2	0	22	28	5	16	.259	.339	.307	98	0	6	.979	-3	*81*	*111*	C-81/1O(RF)	0.4
1919	Cle A	26	56	6	14	1	1	0	7	2	0	6	.250	.276	.304	59	-3	0	.927	-3	*132*	*80*	C-16	-0.5
1920	†Cle A	34	54	10	18	3	3	0	14	4	0	5	.333	.379	.500	128	2	1-0	.963	1	*124*	*89*	C-17/1-6	0.4
1921	Cle A	46	131	16	47	7	2	0	25	11	0	8	.359	.408	.443	115	3	1-1	.970	2	*101*	*60*	C-46	0.7
1922	Cle A	25	43	8	13	2	0	0	7	4	0	3	.302	.362	.349	85	-1	0-0	.936	-3	*88*	*48*	C-13	-0.3
Total	12	716	1990	194	533	75	30	2	216	176	14	150	.268	.332	.339	95	-14	36-12	.972	3	*104*	*97*	C-614/1-15,O(RF)	3.8
NUNEZ, ABRAHAM Abraham B 2.5.1977 Haina, D.R. BB/TR 6-3/210# d9.3																								
2002	Fla N	19	17	2	2	0	0	0	1	0-0	0	5	.118	.118	.118	-38	-4	0-1	1.000	-0	101	0	O-15(2-12-1)	-0.4
NUNEZ, ABRAHAM Abraham Orlando (Adames) B 3.16.1976 Santo Domingo, D.R. BB/TR 5-11/160# d8.27																								
1997	Pit N	19	40	3	9	2	2	0	6	3-0	1	10	.225	.289	.375	73	-2	1-0	1.000	1	103	97	S-12/2-9	0.0
1998	Pit N	24	52	6	10	2	0	1	2	12-0	0	14	.192	.344	.288	68	-2	4-2	.930	3	110	108	S-23	0.2
1999	Pit N	90	259	25	57	8	0	0	17	28-0	1	54	.220	.299	.251	41	-23	9-1	.953	11	108	104	S-65,2-14	-0.6
2000	Pit N	40	91	10	20	1	0	1	8	8-1	0	14	.220	.283	.264	40	-9	0-0	.978	4	118	86	S-21/2-6	-0.3
2001	Pit N	115	301	30	79	11	4	1	21	28-1	1	53	.262	.326	.336	71	-13	8-2	.990	17	114	119	2-48,S-48/3O(LF)	0.9
2002	Pit N	112	253	28	59	14	1	2	15	27-1	2	44	.233	.311	.320	69	-12	3-4	.991	15	127	133	2-46,S-24/D	0.5
2003	Pit N	118	311	37	77	8	7	4	35	26-1	3	53	.248	.310	.357	72	-14	9-3	.979	0	109	101	2-71,S-23/3	-0.8
Total	7	518	1307	139	311	46	14	9	104	132-4	8	242	.238	.311	.315	63	-75	34-12	.964	50	112	103	S-216,2-194/3-2,DO(LF)	-0.1
NUNNALLY, JON Jonathan Keith B 11.9.1971 Pelham, NC BL/TR 5-10/190# d4.26																								
1995	KC A	119	303	51	74	15	6	14	42	51-5	2	86	.244	.357	.472	112	5	6-4	.971	1	108	81	*O-107(16-7-92)/D-4	0.2
1996	KC A	35	90	16	19	5	1	5	17	13-2	0	25	.211	.308	.456	91	-2	0-0	.968	-0	112	0	O-29(7-0-24)/D-4	-0.3
1997	KC A	13	29	8	7	0	1	1	4	5-0	0	7	.241	.353	.414	97	0	0-0	1.000	-1	74	0	/O-9(1-0-8)	-0.2
	Cin N	65	201	38	64	12	3	13	35	26-0	2	51	.318	.400	.602	157	17	7-3	.984	2	109	108	O-60(14-46-11)	1.8
1998	Cin N	74	174	29	36	9	0	7	20	34-3	1	38	.207	.335	.379	88	-2	3-4	.956	5	122	151	O-70(6-24-53)	0.0
1999	Bos A	10	14	4	4	1	0	0	1	0-0	0	6	.286	.286	.357	61	-1	0-0	—	-0	0	0	/O-2(1-0-1),D-3	-0.1
2000	NY N	48	74	16	14	5	1	2	6	17-0	0	26	.189	.337	.365	82	-2	3-1	.977	4	115	403	O-34(25-11-4)	0.2
Total	6	364	885	162	218	47	12	42	125	146-10	5	239	.246	.354	.469	111	15	19-12	.971	10	111	112	O-311(70-88-193)/D-11	1.6
NUNNARI, TALMADGE Talmadge Raphael B 4.9.1975 Pensacola, FL BL/TL 6-1/205# d9.7																								
2000	Mon N	18	5	2	1	0	0	0	1	6-1	0	2	.200	.583	.200	122	1	0-0	1.000	-0	89	36	1-14	0.1
NUSZ, EMORY Emory Moberly B 4.2.1866 Frederick, MD D 8.3.1893 Point Of Rocks, MD d4.26																								
1884	Was U	1	4	1	0	0	0	0		0			.000	.000	.000	-99	-1		.500	-1	0	0	/O(LF)	-0.2
NUTTER, DIZZY Everett Clarence B 8.27.1893 Roseville, OH D 7.25.1958 Battle Creek, MI BL/TR 5-9/160# d9.7																								
1919	Bos N	18	52	4	11	0	0	0	3	4	0	5	.212	.268	.212	47	-3	1	1.000	1	97	191	O-12(CF)	-0.3
NYCE, CHARLIE Charles Reiff (born Charles Reiff Nice) B 7.1.1870 Philadelphia, PA D 5.9.1908 Philadelphia, PA 5-8/160# d5.28																								
1895	Bos N	9	35	7	8	5	0	2	9	4	1	2	.229	.325	.543	113	0	0	.889	-1	99	120	/S-9	0.0
NYMAN, CHRIS Christopher Curtis B 6.6.1955 Pomona, CA BR/TR 6-4/200# d7.28 b-Nyls																								
1982	Chi A	28	65	6	16	1	0	0	2	3-0	0	9	.246	.279	.262	50	-5	3-2	.994	1	111	108	1-24/O-2(1-0-1)	-0.5
1983	Chi A	21	28	12	8	0	0	2	4	4-0	1	7	.286	.394	.500	139	2	2-2	1.000	-0	88	113	1-10,D-10	0.0
Total	2	49	93	18	24	1	0	2	6	7-0	1	16	.258	.317	.333	78	-3	5-4	.996	1	103	110	/1-34,D-10,O-2(1-0-1)	-0.5
NYMAN, NYLS Nyls Wallace Rex B 3.7.1954 Detroit, MI BL/TR 6/170# d9.6 b-Chris																								
1974	Chi A	5	14	5	9	2	1	0	4	0-0	1	1	.643	.667	.929	347	4	1-0	1.000	1	128	588	/O-3(LF)	0.6
1975	Chi A	106	327	36	74	6	3	2	28	11-0	2	34	.226	.255	.281	51	-22	10-4	.958	-3	98	97	O-94(62-26-8)/D-4	-2.9
1976	Chi A	8	15	2	2	1	0	0	1	0-0	0	3	.133	.133	.200	-3	-2	1-0	1.000	0	135	0	/O-7(6-1-0)	-0.2
1977	Chi A	1	1	0	0	0	0	0	0	0-0	0	0	.000	.000	.000	-99	0	0-0	—	0			H	0.0
Total	4	120	357	43	85	9	4	2	33	11-0	3	38	.238	.266	.303	60	-20	12-4	.962	-1	101	105	O-104(71-27-8)/D-4	-2.5
OAKES, REBEL Ennis Telfair B 12.17.1883 Arizona, LA D 3.1.1948 Lisbon, LA BL/TR 5-8/170# d4.14 M2																								
1909	Cin N	120	415	55	112	10	5	3	31	40	5		.270	.341	.340	112	6	23	.979	-1	101	87	*O-113(4-99-10)	0.0
1910	StL N	131	468	50	118	14	6	0	43	38	5	38	.252	.315	.308	85	-10	18	.939	-7	97	72	*O-127(3-118-6)	-2.4
1911	StL N	154	551	69	145	13	6	2	59	41	5	35	.263	.320	.319	81	-15	25	.961	6	104	117	*O-151(1-150-0)	-1.9
1912	StL N	136	495	57	139	19	5	3	58	31	4	24	.281	.328	.358	90	-8	26	.947	-5	102	72	*O-136(CF)	-2.2
1913	StL N	147	539	60	158	14	5	0	49	43	4	32	.293	.350	.338	98	-1	22-26	.968	-9	91	77	*O-145(CF)	-2.5
1914	Pit F	145	571	82	178	18	10	7	75	35	7	22	.312	.359	.415	111	-1	28	.960	1	98	108	*O-145(CF),M	-1.1
1915	Pit F	153	580	55	161	24	5	0	82	37	2	19	.278	.323	.336	86	-20	21	.973	-6	104	55	*O-153(0-152-1),M	-3.9
Total	7	986	3619	428	1011	112	42	15	397	265	32	170	.279	.334	.346	95	-49	163-26	.961	-21	100	84	O-970(8-945-17)	-14.0
OANA, PRINCE Henry Kawaihoa B 1.22.1908 Waipahu, HI D 6.19.1976 Austin, TX BR/TR 6-2/193# d4.22 ▲																								
1934	Phi N	6	21	3	5	1	0	0	3	0	0	1	.238	.238	.286	35	-2	0	1.000	0	129	0	/O-4(LF)	-0.2
1943	Det A	20	26	5	10	2	1	1	7	1	0	2	.385	.407	.654	193	4	0-0	.750	-0	87	493	P-10	0.0
1945	Det A	4	5	0	1	0	0	0	0	0	0	0	.200	.200	.200	15	0	0-0	1.000	-0	47	0	/P-3	0.0
Total	3	30	52	8	16	3	1	1	10	1	0	3	.308	.321	.462	108	2	0-0	.778	-0	77	372	/P-13,O-4(LF)	-0.2
OATES, JOHNNY Johnny Lane B 1.21.1946 Sylva, NC BL/TR 5-11/188# d9.17 M11 C7																								
1970	Bal A	5	18	2	5	0	1	0	2	2-0	0	0	.278	.333	.389	102	0	0-0	.939	-1	229	65	/C-4	-0.1
1972	Bal A	85	253	20	66	12	1	4	21	28-8	0	31	.261	.332	.364	105	2	5-7	**.995**	4	133	87	C-82	0.9

Year	Tm Lg	G	AB	R	H	2B	3B	HR	RBI	BB-IB	HP	SO	AVG	OBP	SLG	AOPS	ABR	SB-CS	FA	FR	Rng	Thr	G at Pos	BFW
1973	Atl N	93	322	27	80	6	0	4	27	22-4	1	31	.248	.299	.304	63	-16	1-4	.981	-2	92	128	C-86	-1.6
1974	Atl N	100	291	22	65	10	0	1	21	23-10	0	24	.223	.278	.268	52	-19	2-3	.992	12	107	102	C-91	-0.3
1975	Atl N	8	18	0	4	1	0	0	0	1-0	0	4	.222	.263	.278	48	-1	0-0	1.000	-1	98	73	/C-6	-0.2
	Phi N	90	269	28	77	14	0	1	25	33-10	0	29	.286	.359	.349	95	0	1-0	.990	9	163	109	C-82	1.2
	Year	98	287	28	81	15	0	1	25	34-10	0	33	.282	.354	.345	92	-2	1-0	.990	8	159	107	C-88	1.0
1976	†Phi N	37	99	10	25	2	0	0	8	8-0	0	12	.253	.308	.273	64	-5	0-1	.994	2	122	100	C-33	-0.2
1977	†LA N	60	156	18	42	4	0	3	11	11-4	0	11	.269	.314	.353	80	-5	1-0	.987	3	87	106	C-56	0.0
1978	†LA N	40	75	5	23	1	0	0	6	5-1	0	3	.307	.350	.320	89	-1	0-1	.956	-2	100	96	C-24	-0.3
1979	LA N	26	46	4	6	2	0	0	2	4-1	0	1	.130	.200	.174	3	-6	0-1	.975	1	78	143	C-20	-0.6
1980	NY A	39	64	6	12	3	0	1	3	2-0	1	3	.188	.224	.281	38	-6	1-2	.991	-3	126	160	C-39	-0.8
1981	NY A	10	26	4	5	1	0	0	0	2-0	0	0	.192	.250	.231	40	-2	0-0	.963	-2	53	63	C-10	-0.4
Total	11	593	1637	146	410	56	2	14	126	141-38	2	149	.250	.309	.313	73	-59	11-19	.987	20	117	108	C-533	-2.4
OBANDO, SHERMAN Sherman Omar (Gainor) B 1.23.1970 Bocas Del Toro, Panama BR/TR 6-4/215# d4.10																								
1993	Bal A	31	92	8	25	2	0	3	15	4-0	1	26	.272	.309	.391	83	-3	0-0	.929	0	125	0	D-21/O-8(1-0-7)	-0.4
1995	Bal A	16	38	0	10	1	0	0	3	2-0	0	12	.263	.293	.289	53	-3	1-0	.923	0	143	0	/O-7(RF),D-7	-0.2
1996	Mon N	89	178	30	44	9	0	8	22	22-1	1	48	.247	.332	.433	98	-1	2-0	.962	1	110	85	O-47(RF)	-0.1
1997	Mon N	41	47	3	6	1	0	2	9	6-0	1	14	.128	.241	.277	35	-5	0-0	1.000	-0	98	0	O-15(1-0-14)/D-2	-0.5
Total	4	177	355	41	85	13	0	13	49	34-1	3	100	.239	.310	.386	81	-12	3-0	.957	1	113	60	/O-77(2-0-75),D-30	-1.2
OBERBECK, HENRY Henry A. B 5.17.1858 , MO D 8.26.1921 St.Louis, MO d5.7 ▲																								
1883	Pit AA	2	9	1	2	1	0	0	0				.222	.222	.333	80	0		1.000	0	0	173	/1-2	0.0
	StL AA	4	14	0	0	0	0	0	0				.000	.000	.000	-95	-3		.833	1	259	1371	/O-4(3-1-0)	-0.2
	Year	6	23	1	2	1	0	0	0				.087	.087	.130	-30	-3		.833	1	259	1371	/O-4(3-1-0),1-2	-0.2
1884	Bal U	33	125	19	23	4	0	0	3				.184	.203	.216	25	-15		.878	1	140	86	O-28(1-0-27)/3-8,P-2	-1.2
	KC U	27	90	7	17	3	0	0	7				.189	.247	.222	50	-8		.823	6	149	115	3-15/O-7(3-3-1),P-6,1-3	-0.1
	Year	60	215	26	40	7	0	0	10				.186	.222	.219	34	-24		.908	7	115	70	O-35(4-3-28),3-23/P-8,1-3	-1.3
Total	2	66	238	27	42	8	0	0	10				.176	.210	.210	28	-26		.901	8	129	203	/O-39(7-4-28),3-23,P-8,1-5	-1.5
OBERKFELL, KEN Kenneth Ray B 5.4.1956 Highland, IL BL/TR 6/210# d8.22																								
1977	StL N	9	9	0	1	0	0	0	1	0-0	0	3	.111	.111	.111	-41	-2	0-0	1.000	-0	94	114	/2-6	-0.2
1978	StL N	24	50	7	6	1	0	0	0	3-0	0	1	.120	.170	.140	-13	-8	0-0	.987	2	116	97	2-17/3-4	-0.5
1979	StL N	135	369	53	111	19	5	1	35	57-9	4	35	.301	.396	.388	115	11	4-1	**.985**	0	105	105	*2-117,3-17/S-2	1.8
1980	StL N	116	422	58	128	27	6	3	46	51-8	1	23	.303	.377	.417	118	13	4-4	.989	-2	104	98	*2-101,3-16	1.6
1981	StL N	102	376	43	110	12	6	2	45	37-6	0	28	.293	.353	.372	104	2	13-5	.956	9	116	**146**	*3-102/S	1.1
1982	†StL N	137	470	55	136	22	5	2	34	40-6	1	31	.289	.345	.370	99	0	11-9	**.972**	14	**121**	112	*3-135/2	1.2
1983	StL N	151	488	62	143	26	5	3	38	61-5	1	27	.293	.371	.385	110	9	12-6	**.960**	6	**112**	**152**	*3-127,2-32/S	1.5
1984	StL N	50	152	17	47	11	1	0	11	16-2	1	10	.309	.379	.395	121	5	1-2	.967	4	116	109	3-46/2-2,S	0.8
	Atl N	50	172	21	40	8	1	1	10	15-1	0	17	.233	.289	.308	65	-8	1-3	.964	-4	95	113	3-45/2-4	-1.4
	Year	100	324	38	87	19	2	1	21	31-3	1	27	.269	.331	.349	90	-3	2-5	.966	0	105	111	3-91/2-6,S	-0.6
1985	Atl N	134	412	30	112	19	4	3	35	51-6	6	38	.272	.359	.359	96	0	1-2	.963	1	108	93	*3-117,2-16	0.0
1986	Atl N	151	503	62	136	24	3	5	48	83-6	2	40	.270	.373	.360	98	3	7-4	.976	18	**120**	118	*3-130,2-41	2.1
1987	Atl N	135	508	59	142	29	2	3	48	48-5	2	29	.280	.342	.362	83	-11	3-3	.979	-2	105	92	*3-126,2-11	-1.5
1988	Atl N	120	422	42	117	20	4	3	40	32-6	2	28	.277	.325	.365	95	-2	4-5	.951	-7	94	107	*3-113/2	-1.0
	Pit N	20	54	7	12	2	0	0	2	5-1	0	6	.222	.288	.259	59	-3	0-0	1.000	-3	89	58	2-11/S-3,3-2,1	-0.6
	Year	140	476	49	129	22	4	3	42	37-7	2	34	.271	.321	.353	91	-5	4-5	.952	-10	95	105	*3-115,2-12/S-3,1	-1.6
1989	Pit N	14	40	2	5	1	0	0	2	2-0	0	2	.125	.163	.150	-9	-6	0-0	.988	0	89	69	/1-9,2-3	-0.7
	†SF N	83	116	17	37	5	1	2	15	8-0	2	8	.319	.367	.431	133	5	0-1	.971	-2	102	51	3-38/1-7,2-7	0.3
	Year	97	156	19	42	6	1	2	17	10-0	2	10	.269	.316	.359	97	-1	0-1	.971	-1	102	51	3-38,1-16,2-10	-0.4
1990	Hou N	77	150	10	31	6	1	1	12	15-1	1	17	.207	.281	.280	57	-9	1-1	.935	-3	104	129	3-24,1-11,2-11	-1.3
1991	Hou N	53	70	7	16	4	0	0	14	14-4	0	8	.229	.357	.286	88	0	0-0	1.000	-0	130	107	1-13/3-4	-0.1
1992	Cal A	41	91	6	24	1	0	0	10	8-2	0	5	.264	.317	.275	69	-4	0-1	.986	-7	74	35	2-21/1-2,D-5	-1.1
Total	16	1602	4874	558	1354	237	44	29	446	546-68	23	356	.278	.351	.362	97	-5	62-47	.965	24	110	114	*3-1046,2-402/1-43,S-8,D-5	2.0
O'BERRY, MIKE Preston Michael B 4.20.1954 Birmingham, AL BR/TR 6-2/195# d4.8																								
1979	Bos A	43	59	8	10	1	0	1	4	5-0	1	16	.169	.242	.237	29	-6	0-0	.957	-3	120	58	C-43	-0.8
1980	Chi N	19	48	7	10	1	0	0	5	5-0	0	13	.208	.273	.229	41	-4	0-0	.982	2	98	173	C-19	-0.1
1981	Cin N	55	111	6	20	3	1	1	5	14-0	0	19	.180	.272	.252	49	-7	0-0	.983	-3	113	116	C-55	-0.9
1982	Cin N	21	45	5	10	2	0	0	3	10-0	0	13	.222	.364	.267	77	-1	0-0	.990	-0	127	141	C-21	0.0
1983	Cal A	26	60	7	10	1	0	1	5	3-0	0	11	.167	.206	.233	21	-7	0-0	1.000	-2	154	91	C-26	-0.8
1984	NY A	13	32	3	8	2	0	0	5	2-0	0	2	.250	.294	.313	71	-1	0-0	1.000	-0	548	227	C-12/3	-0.1
1985	Mon N	20	21	2	4	0	0	0	0	4-0	0	3	.190	.320	.190	49	-1	1-0	1.000	-1	57	202	C-20	-0.1
Total	7	197	376	38	72	10	1	3	27	43-0	1	77	.191	.274	.247	46	-27	1-0	.984	-8	147	126	C-196/3	-2.8
OBRADOVICH, JIM James Thomas B 9.13.1949 Fort Campbell, KY BL/TL 6-2/200# d9.12																								
1978	Hou N	10	17	3	3	0	1	0	2	1-1	0	3	.176	.222	.294	47	-1	0-0	1.000	-0	52	43	/1-3	-0.2
O'BRIEN d8.2																								
1887	Was N	1	4	0	0	0	0	0	0	0	0	2	.000	.000	.000	-99	-1	0	.714	-0	131	0	/2	-0.1
O'BRIEN, CHARLIE Charles Hugh B 5.1.1960 Tulsa, OK BR/TR 6-2/190# d6.2																								
1985	Oak A	16	11	3	3	1	0	0	1	3-0	0	3	.273	.429	.364	129	1	0-0	.958	-1	0	71	C-16	0.0
1987	Mil A	10	35	2	7	3	1	0	0	4-0	0	4	.200	.282	.343	63	-2	0-1	1.000	5	151	265	C-10	0.3
1988	Mil A	40	118	12	26	6	0	2	9	5-0	0	16	.220	.252	.322	59	-7	0-1	.991	8	122	101	C-40	0.3
1989	Mil A	62	188	22	44	10	0	6	35	21-1	9	11	.234	.339	.383	104	2	0-0	.986	5	125	96	C-62	1.1
1990	Mil A	46	145	11	27	7	2	0	11	11-1	2	26	.186	.253	.262	45	-11	0-0	.992	2	130	97	C-46	-0.6
	NY N	28	68	6	11	3	0	0	9	10-2	1	8	.162	.272	.206	36	-6	0-0	.986	6	117	174	C-28	0.2
1991	NY N	69	168	16	31	6	0	2	14	17-1	4	25	.185	.272	.256	51	-11	0-2	.991	8	83	115	C-67	0.0
1992	NY N	68	156	15	33	12	0	2	13	16-1	1	18	.212	.289	.327	75	-5	0-1	.979	1	106	164	C-64	-0.1
1993	NY N	67	188	15	48	11	0	4	23	14-1	2	14	.255	.312	.378	85	-4	1-1	.986	6	102	119	C-65	0.6
1994	Atl N	51	152	24	37	11	0	8	28	15-2	3	24	.243	.322	.474	102	0	0-0	.991	1	131	84	C-48	0.4
1995	†Atl N	67	198	18	45	7	0	9	23	29-2	6	40	.227	.343	.399	92	-2	0-1	.992	-3	66	105	C-64	-0.1
1996	Tor A	109	324	33	77	17	0	13	44	29-1	17	68	.238	.331	.410	87	-7	0-1	.995	13	142	95	*C-105	1.1
1997	Tor A	69	225	22	49	15	1	4	27	22-1	11	45	.218	.311	.347	73	-8	0-2	.995	27	177	142	C-69	2.1
1998	Chi A	57	164	12	43	9	0	4	18	9-0	2	31	.262	.303	.390	82	-5	0-0	.988	-5	78	123	C-57	-0.6
	Ana A	5	11	1	2	0	0	0	0	1-0	0	2	.182	.250	.182	15	-1	0-0	1.000	-0	128	172	/C-5	-0.1
	Year	62	175	13	45	9	0	4	18	10-0	2	33	.257	.300	.377	78	-6	0-0	.989	-6	81	126	C-62	-0.7
1999	Ana A	27	62	3	6	0	0	1	4	1-0	2	12	.097	.136	.145	-28	-12	0-0	.993	8	159	114	C-27	-0.3
2000	Mon N	9	19	1	4	1	0	1	2	2-1	0	7	.211	.286	.421	73	-1	0-0	1.000	-3	44	0	/C-9	-0.3
Total	15	800	2232	216	493	119	4	56	261	209-14	60	354	.221	.303	.353	75	-79	1-10	.990	79	117	117	C-782	4.0
O'BRIEN, EDDIE Edward Joseph B 12.11.1930 S.Amboy, NJ BR/TR 5-9/165# d4.25 Mil 1954 C1 twb-Johnny ▲																								
1953	Pit N	89	261	21	62	5	3	0	14	17	2	30	.238	.289	.280	50	-20	6-1	.935	-12	96	78	S-81	-2.4
1955	Pit N	75	236	26	55	3	1	0	8	18-0	1	13	.233	.290	.254	47	-18	4-5	.993	1	99	201	O-56(1-56-0)/3-7,S-4	-2.1
1956	Pit N	63	53	17	14	2	0	0	3	2-0	0	2	.264	.291	.302	61	-3	1-1	.978	7	129	151	S-23/O-6(5-1-0),3-4,2-2,P	0.6
1957	Pit N	3	4	0	0	0	0	0	0	0-0	0	0	.000	.000	.000	-99	-1	0-0	1.000	0	103	695	/P-3	0.0
1958	Pit N	1	0	0	0	0	0	0	0	0-0	0	0	—	—	—	—	0	0-0	—	-0	0	0	/P	0.0
Total	5	231	554	64	131	10	4	0	25	37-0	3	45	.236	.288	.269	48	-42	11-7	.942	-4	101	88	S-108/O-62(6-57-0),3-11,P-5,2-2	-3.9
O'BRIEN, DINK Frank Aloysius B 9.13.1894 San Francisco, CA D 11.4.1971 Monterey Park, CA BR/TR 5-8/160# d4.26																								
1923	Phi N	15	21	3	7	2	0	0	0	2	0	1	.333	.391	.429	104	0	0-0	.909	-1	*80*	*162*	/C-9	0.0
O'BRIEN, GEORGE George Joseph B 11.4.1889 Cleveland, OH D 3.24.1966 Columbus, OH BR/TR 6/185# d8.16																								
1915	StL A	3	9	1	2	0	0	0	0	1	0	2	.222	.300	.222	59	0	0	.933	-1	*98*	*93*	/C-3	-0.1
O'BRIEN, JOHN John E. B 10.22.1851 Columbus, OH D 12.31.1914 Fall River, MA TR 5-11.5/187# d4.19																								
1884	Bal U	18	77	7	19	1	1	0	2				.247	.266	.286	61	-6		.865	-1	63	257	O-18(3-14-1)	-0.7

Year	Tm Lg	G	AB	R	H	2B	3B	HR	RBI	BB-IB	HP	SO	AVG	OBP	SLG	AOPS	ABR	SB-CS	FA	FR	Rng	Thr	G at Pos	BFW
O'BRIEN, JOHN John J. "Chewing Gum" B 7.14.1870 St.John, NB, CAN D 5.13.1913 Lewiston, ME BL/TR 5-9/175# d4.22																								
1891	Bro N	43	167	22	41	4	2	0	26	12	3	17	.246	.308	.293	76	-5	4	.854	-18	80	76	2-43	-2.0
1893	Chi N	4	14	3	5	0	1	0	1	2	1	2	.357	.471	.500	160	1	0	.900	-2	68	55	/2-4	0.0
1895	Lou N	128	539	82	138	10	4	1	50	45	10	20	.256	.325	.295	65	-27	15	.938	7	105	95	*2-125/1-3	-1.2
1896	Lou N	49	186	24	63	9	1	2	24	13	1	7	.339	.385	.430	119	5	4	.919	-3	96	81	2-49	0.4
	Was N	73	270	38	72	6	3	4	33	27	5	12	.267	.344	.356	85	-6	4	.952	6	104	103	2-73	0.2
	Year	122	456	62	135	15	4	6	57	40	6	19	.296	.361	.386	98	-1	8	.938	3	101	94	*2-122	0.6
1897	Was N	86	320	37	78	12	2	3	45	19	11		.244	.309	.322	67	-16	6	.942	4	96	139	2-86	-0.6
1899	Bal N	39	135	14	26	4	0	1	17	15	2		.193	.283	.244	43	-10	4	.966	6	107	145	2-39	-0.3
	Pit N	79	279	26	63	2	4	1	33	21	2		.226	.285	.272	53	-19	8	.946	-2	98	106	2-79	-1.6
	Year	118	414	40	89	6	4	2	50	36	4		.215	.284	.263	50	-29	12	.953	4	101	119	*2-118	-1.9
Total	6	501	1910	246	486	47	17	12	229	154	35	58	.254	.322	.316	72	-77	45	.936	-3	99	106	2-498/1-3	-5.1
O'BRIEN, JACK John Joseph B 2.5.1873 Watervliet, NY D 6.10.1933 Watervliet, NY BL/TR 6-1/165# d4.14																								
1899	Was N	127	468	68	132	11	5	6	51	31	3		.282	.331	.365	92	-6	17	.926	6	115	91	*O-121(LF)/3-4	-1.0
1901	Was A	11	45	5	8	0	0	0	5	3	1		.178	.245	.178	19	-5	2	.929	-0	0	0	O-11(LF)	-0.5
	Cle A	92	375	54	106	14	5	0	39	22	4		.283	.329	.347	91	-4	13	.941	-0	81	143	O-92(31-0-61)/3	-0.8
	Year	103	420	59	114	14	5	0	44	25	5		.271	.320	.329	83	-9	15	.939	-1	71	126	*O-103(42-0-61)/3	-1.3
1903	†Bos A	96	338	44	71	14	4	3	38	21	3		.210	.262	.302	65	-14	10	.958	-7	115	111	O-71(2-68-1),3-11/2-4,S	-2.5
Total	3	326	1226	171	317	39	14	9	133	77	11		.259	.308	.335	82	-29	42	.937	-2	100	108	O-295(165-68-62)/3-16,2-4,S	-4.8
O'BRIEN, JACK John K. (born John K. Bryne) B 6.12.1860 Philadelphia, PA D 11.20.1910 Philadelphia, PA BR/TR 5-10/184# d5.2 OF Total (5-LF 36-CF 31-RF)																								
1882	Phi AA	62	241	44	73	13	3	3	37	13			.303	.339	.419	145	11		**.925**	10			C-45,O-18(0-6-12)/31	2.2
1883	Phi AA	94	390	74	113	14	10	0	70	25			.290	.333	.377	117	6		.876	-1			C-58,O-25(CF),3-19/S	0.7
1884	Phi AA	36	138	25	39	6	1	1		9	3		.283	.340	.362	121	3		.930	1			C-30/O-5(CF),1	0.6
1885	Phi AA	62	225	35	60	9	1	2	30	20	5		.267	.340	.342	109	3		.903	-4			C-43/S-9,1-7,O-3(RF),3-2	0.2
1886	Phi AA	105	423	65	107	25	7	0	56	38	7		.253	.325	.345	109	5	23	.918	-12			C-36,3-27,1-24,S-10/2-7,O-3(RF)	-0.4
1887	Bro AA	30	123	18	28	4	1	1	17	6	0		.228	.264	.301	57	-8	8	.839	-5			C-25/O-4(1-0-3),2	-0.9
1888	Bal AA	57	196	25	44	11	5	0	18	17	4		.224	.300	.332	105	2	14	.925	-11			C-37,O-13(4-0-9)/1-7	-0.6
1890	Phi AA	109	433	80	113	24	14	4	80	52	12		.261	.356	.409	126	14	31	.976	4	122	92	*1-109/O(RF)C	0.8
Total	8	555	2169	366	577	106	42	11	308	180	31		.266	.331	.369	115	36	76	.903	-17			C-275,1-149/O-72C,3-49,S-20,2-8	2.6
O'BRIEN, JOHNNY John Thomas B 12.11.1930 S.Amboy, NJ BR/TR 5-9/170# d4.19 Mil 1951 twb-Eddie ▲																								
1953	Pit N	89	279	28	69	13	2	2	22	21	4	36	.247	.309	.330	67	-13	1-1	.982	0	102	90	2-77/S	-0.8
1955	Pit N	84	278	22	83	15	2	1	25	20-1	1	19	.299	.346	.378	94	-2	1-1	.969	3	105	94	2-78	0.6
1956	Pit N	73	104	13	18	1	0	0	3	5-0	0	7	.173	.209	.183	7	-14	0-0	.959	1	112	84	2-53/P-8,S	-0.9
1957	Pit N	34	35	7	11	2	1	0	1	1-0	2	4	.314	.368	.429	117	1	0-0	.857	-2	62	0	P-16/S-8,2-2	-0.1
1958	Pit N	3	1	1	0	0	0	0	0	0-0	0	1	.000	.000	.000	-99	0	0-0	—	0			H	0.0
	StL N	12	2	3	0	0	0	0	0	1-0	0	0	.000	.333	.000	-2	0	0-0	1.000	-0	97	0	/S-5,P2	0.0
	Year	15	3	4	0	0	0	0	0	1-0	0	1	.000	.250	.000	-26	-1	0-0	1.000	-0	97	0	/S-5,P2	0.0
1959	Mil N	44	116	16	23	4	0	1	8	11-1	1	15	.198	.271	.259	47	-9	0-0	.987	-2	96	126	2-37	-0.8
Total	6	339	815	90	204	35	5	4	59	59-2	8	82	.250	.306	.320	68	-37	2-2	.974	1	103	96	2-248/P-25,S-15	-2.0
O'BRIEN, PETE Peter J. B 6.17.1877 Binghamton, NY D 1.31.1917 Jersey City, NJ BL/TR 5-7/170# d9.21																								
1901	Cin N	16	54	1	11	1	0	1	3	2	0		.204	.232	.278	51	-4	0	.889	-2	89	111	2-15	-0.6
1906	StL A	151	524	44	122	9	4	2	57	42	3		.233	.293	.277	82	-10	25	.933	-36	81	86	*2-120,3-20,S-11	-5.1
1907	Cle A	43	145	9	33	5	2	0	6	7	0		.228	.263	.290	76	-4	1	.949	-4	115	92	2-15,3-12,S-12	-0.8
	Was A	39	134	6	25	3	1	0	12	12	1		.187	.259	.224	59	-6	4	.912	3	115	0	3-26,S-13/2	-0.2
	Year	82	279	15	58	8	3	0	18	19	1		.208	.261	.258	68	-10	5	.911	-1	111	51	3-38,S-25,2-16	-1.0
Total	3	249	857	60	191	18	7	3	78	63	4		.223	.279	.271	76	-24	30	.930	-39	85	89	2-151/3-58,S-36	-6.7
O'BRIEN, PETE Peter James B 6.16.1867 Chicago, IL D 6.30.1937 York Township, IL BR/TR 5-9.5/165# d4.29																								
1890	Chi N	27	106	15	30	7	0	3	16	5	0	10	.283	.315	.434	113	1	4	.929	-2	94	111	2-27	0.0
O'BRIEN, PETE Peter Michael B 2.9.1958 Santa Monica, CA BL/TL 6-1/198# d9.3																								
1982	Tex A	20	67	13	16	4	1	4	13	6-0	0	8	.239	.297	.507	124	2	1-0	1.000	-0	76	155	O-11(LF)/1-3,D-4	0.1
1983	Tex A	154	524	53	124	24	5	8	53	58-2	1	62	.237	.313	.347	83	-11	5-4	.993	13	**141**	100	*1-133,O-27(9-0-18)/D	-0.8
1984	Tex A	142	520	57	149	26	2	18	80	53-8	0	50	.287	.348	.448	116	12	3-5	.992	1	101	86	*1-141/O(RF)	0.3
1985	Tex A	159	573	69	153	34	3	22	92	69-4	1	53	.267	.342	.452	115	13	5-10	.995	-6	83	93	*1-159	-0.5
1986	Tex A	156	551	86	160	23	3	23	90	87-11	0	66	.290	.385	.468	128	24	4-4	.992	1	98	95	*1-155	1.5
1987	Tex A	159	569	84	163	26	1	23	88	59-6	0	61	.286	.348	.457	113	10	0-4	.992	15	**129**	90	*1-158/O-2(RF),D	1.4
1988	Tex A	156	547	57	149	24	1	16	71	72-9	0	73	.272	.352	.408	111	10	1-4	.995	13	129	95	*1-155/D	1.1
1989	Cle A	155	554	75	144	24	1	12	55	83-17	2	48	.260	.356	.372	104	6	3-1	.994	5	113	88	*1-154/D	0.0
1990	Sea A	108	366	32	82	18	0	5	27	44-1	2	33	.224	.308	.314	74	-12	0-0	.995	5	122	87	1-97/O-6(LF),D-6	-1.3
1991	Sea A	152	560	58	139	29	3	17	88	44-7	1	61	.248	.300	.402	93	-6	0-1	**.997**	2	103	118	*1-132,D-18,O-13(LF)	-1.4
1992	Sea A	134	396	40	88	15	1	14	52	40-8	0	27	.222	.289	.371	85	-9	2-1	.996	3	115	109	1-81,D-36	-1.2
1993	Sea A	72	210	30	54	7	0	7	27	26-4	0	21	.257	.335	.390	94	-2	0-0	.988	2	202	197	D-52/1-9,O(LF)	-0.4
Total	12	1567	5437	654	1421	254	21	169	736	641-77	7	563	.261	.336	.409	104	37	24-34	.994	54	113	96	*1-1377,D-120/O-61(40-0-21)	-1.2
O'BRIEN, RAY Raymond Joseph B 10.31.1892 St.Louis, MO D 3.31.1942 St.Louis, MO BL/TL 5-9/175# d6.27																								
1916	Pit N	16	57	5	12	3	2	0	3	1	0	14	.211	.224	.333	69	-2	0	.864	-0	70	204	O-14(7-0-7)	-0.4
O'BRIEN, SYD Sydney Lloyd B 12.18.1944 Compton, CA BR/TR 6-1/185# d4.15																								
1969	Bos A	100	263	47	64	10	5	9	29	15-0	1	37	.243	.287	.422	91	-5	2-3	.939	-0	111	115	3-53,S-15,2-12	-0.5
1970	Chi A	121	441	48	109	13	2	8	44	22-1	2	62	.247	.285	.340	69	-20	3-3	.938	6	102	125	3-68,2-43/S-5	-1.2
1971	Cal A	90	251	25	50	8	1	5	21	15-4	1	33	.199	.247	.299	58	-15	0-2	.961	-10	85	101	S-52/2-7,3-6,1O(RF)	-2.1
1972	Cal A	36	39	10	7	2	0	1	1	6-0	0	10	.179	.289	.308	82	-1	0-0	.889	-2	103	139	/3-8,S-4,2-3,1	-0.3
	Mil A	31	58	5	12	2	0	1	5	2-0	0	13	.207	.230	.293	57	-3	0-1	.852	-2	110	196	/3-9,2-7	-0.7
	Year	67	97	15	19	4	0	2	6	8-0	0	23	.196	.255	.299	68	-4	0-1	.861	-5	108	178	3-17,2-10/S-4,1	-1.0
Total	4	378	1052	135	242	35	8	24	100	60-5	4	155	.230	.273	.347	72	-44	5-9	.934	-8	106	121	3-144/S-76,2-72,1-2,O(RF)	-4.8
O'BRIEN, TOMMY Thomas Edward "Obie" B 12.19.1918 Anniston, AL D 11.5.1978 Anniston, AL BR/TR 5-11/195# d4.24																								
1943	Pit N	89	232	35	72	12	7	2	26	15	0	24	.310	.352	.448	126	7	0	.964	-2	94	99	O-48(17-0-31)/3-9	0.2
1944	Pit N	85	156	27	39	6	2	3	20	21	1	12	.250	.343	.372	97	0	1	.965	-0	84	176	O-48(15-0-33)/3	-0.2
1945	Pit N	58	161	23	54	6	5	0	18	9	1	13	.335	.374	.435	120	4	0	.961	-2	97	63	O-45(12-0-33)	0.0
1949	Bos A	49	125	24	28	5	0	3	10	21	0	12	.224	.336	.336	73	-5	1-0	.984	-2	91	76	O-32(0-8-25)	-0.7
1950	Bos A	9	31	0	4	1	0	0	3	3	0	5	.129	.206	.161	-5	-5	0-0	1.000	-0	84	175	/O-9(3-4-2)	-0.5
	Was A	3	9	1	1	0	0	0	1	1	0	0	.111	.200	.111	-20	-2	0-0	1.000	1	110	425	/O-3(2-0-1)	-0.1
	Year	12	40	1	5	1	0	0	4	4	0	5	.125	.205	.150	-8	-7	0-0	1.000	1	92	248	O-12(5-4-3)	-0.6
Total	5	293	714	110	198	30	14	8	78	70	2	66	.277	.344	.392	100	-1	2-0	.970	-5	92	111	O-185(49-12-125)/3-10	-1.3
O'BRIEN, TOM Thomas H. B 6.22.1860 Salem, MA D 4.21.1921 Worcester, MA BR/TR 6-1/185# d6.14																								
1882	Wor N	22	89	9	18	1	1	0	7	1		10	.202	.211	.236	42	-6		.789	-3	81	0	O-20(16-4-0)/2-2,3	-0.9
1883	Bal AA	33	138	16	37	6	4	0		5			.268	.294	.370	109	1		.825	-4	105	60	2-29/O-4(CF)	-0.2
1884	Bos U	103	449	80	118	31	8	4		12			.263	.282	.394	105	-11		.853	0	100	82	*2-99/O-3(1-1-1),1-2,C	-0.7
1885	Bal AA	8	33	4	7	3	0	0	5	2	0		.212	.257	.303	78	-1		.932	1	235	38	/1-6,2-2	0.0
1887	NY AA	31	129	13	25	3	2	0	18	2	1		.194	.212	.248	29	-13	10	.963	-3	87	90	1-20/O-8(2-4-2),3-2,2-2,P	-1.4
1890	Roc AA	73	273	36	52	6	5	0	31	30	1		.190	.273	.249	58	-14	6	.971	-4	74	113	1-68/2-8	-2.1
Total	6	270	1111	158	257	50	20	4	61	52	2	10	.231	.267	.323	79	-44	16	.846	-13	102	79	2-142/1-96,O-35(19-13-3),3-3,PC	-5.3
O'BRIEN, TOM Thomas J. B 2.20.1873 Verona, PA D 2.4.1901 Phoenix, AZ 5-11/170# d5.10 OF Total (169-LF 61-CF 32-RF)																								
1897	†Bal N	50	147	25	37	6	0	0	32	20	2		.252	.349	.293	70	-5	7	.968	1	81	70	1-25,O-24(13-1-10)	-0.5
1898	Bal N	18	60	9	13	0	0	0	14	10	1		.217	.338	.217	59	-3	0	.833	-0	130	831	O-16(RF)	-0.3
	Pit N	107	413	53	107	10	8	1	45	25	11		.259	.318	.329	87	-7	13	.924	-6	155	186	O-69(10-59-0),1-21/3-8,2-7,S-4	-1.6
	Year	125	473	62	120	10	8	1	59	35	12		.254	.321	.315	84	-10	13	.911	-6	150	310	O-85(10-59-16),1-21/3-8,2-7,S-4	-1.9
1899	NY N	151	577	101	171	22	10	6	77	44	4		.296	.350	.400	109	7	23	.933	-4	104	110	*O-128(125-0-3),3-21/S-2,21	-0.7
1900	†Pit N	102	376	61	109	22	6	3	61	21	13		.290	.349	.404	107	3	12	.961	-10	69	111	1-65,O-25(21-1-3)/2-4,S-2	-0.8

Year	Tm Lg	G	AB	R	H	2B	3B	HR	RBI	BB-IB	HP	SO	AVG	OBP	SLG	AOPS	ABR	SB-CS	FA	FR	Rng	Thr	G at Pos	BFW
Total	4	428	1573	249	437	60	24	10	229	120	31		.278	.341	.366	97	-5	55	.928	-18	120	187	O-262L,1-112/3-29,2-12,S-8	-3.9
O'BRIEN, DARBY William D. B 9.1.1863 Peoria, IL D 6.15.1893 Peoria, IL BR/TR 6-1/186# d4.16																								
1887	NY AA	127	522	97	157	30	13	5	73	40	4		.301	.355	.437	126	18	49	.913	7	102	83	*O-121(121-1-0),1-10/S-2,3P	1.8
1888	Bro AA	136	532	105	149	27	6	2	65	30	7		.280	.327	.365	122	13	55	.932	1	66	23	*O-136(LF)	0.9
1889	†Bro AA	136	567	146	170	30	11	5	80	61	16	76	.300	.384	.418	128	22	91	.906	-8	53	92	*O-136(LF)	0.9
1890	†Bro N	85	350	78	110	28	6	2	63	32	4	43	.314	.378	.446	139	18	38	.960	0	90	67	O-85(44-42-0)	1.3
1891	Bro N	103	395	79	100	18	6	5	57	39	7	53	.253	.331	.367	104	2	31	.951	2	67	35	*O-103(LF)	0.1
1892	Bro N	122	490	72	119	14	5	1	56	29	3	52	.243	.289	.298	81	-12	57	.956	1	77	71	*O-122(115-3-4)	-2.1
Total	6	709	2856	577	805	147	47	20	394	231	41	224	.282	.344	.387	117	61	321	.934	3	75	62	O-703(655-46-4)/1-10,S-2,P3	2.9
O'BRIEN, BILLY William Smith B 3.14.1860 Albany, NY D 5.26.1911 Kansas City, MO BR/TR 6/185# d9.27 ▲																								
1884	StP U	8	30	1	7	3	0	0		0			.233	.233	.333	129	0		.840	2	138	0	/3-8,P-2	0.2
	KC U	4	17	2	4	0	0	0		0			.235	.235	.235	49	-2		.714	1	177	0	/3-3,1	-0.1
	Year	12	47	3	11	3	0	0		0			.234	.234	.298	92	-2		.795	3	151	0	3-11/P-2,1	0.1
1887	Was N	113	453	71	126	16	12	**19**	73	21	5	17	.278	.317	.492	130	16	11	.974	-4	69	91	*1-104/O-4(1-3-0),3-4,2-2	0.2
1888	Was N	133	528	42	119	15	2	9	66	9	0	70	.225	.238	.313	80	-13	10	.975	-4	81	82	*1-132/3	-2.8
1889	Was N	2	8	1	0	0	0	0	0	1	0	1	.000	.111	.000	-72	-2	0	1.000	-0	0	0	/1-2	-0.2
1890	Bro AA	96	388	47	108	25	8	4	67	28	3		.278	.332	.415	124	10	5	.973	-3	90	111	*1-96	-0.1
Total	5	356	1424	164	364	59	22	32	206	59	8	88	.256	.289	.395	109	9	26	.974	-8	80	92	1-335/3-16,O-4(1-3-0),2-2,P-2	-2.8
OCHOA, ALEX Alex B 3.29.1972 Miami Lakes, FL BR/TR 6/185# d9.18																								
1995	NY N	11	37	7	11	1	0	0	0	2-0	0	10	.297	.333	.324	77	-1	1-0	1.000	1	120	160	O-10(RF)	0.0
1996	NY N	82	282	37	83	19	3	4	33	17-0	2	30	.294	.336	.426	105	2	4-3	.966	1	97	160	O-76(RF)	-0.1
1997	NY N	113	238	31	58	14	1	3	22	18-0	2	32	.244	.300	.349	72	-10	3-4	.982	-2	86	149	O-88(0-4-84)/D	-1.5
1998	Min A	94	249	35	64	14	2	2	25	10-0	1	35	.257	.288	.353	65	-13	6-3	.969	-0	91	179	O-74(21-4-52)/D-3	-1.5
1999	Mil N	119	277	47	83	16	3	8	40	45-2	5	43	.300	.404	.466	121	11	6-4	.979	-2	93	110	O-85(50-9-31)/D	0.6
2000	Cin N	118	244	50	77	21	3	13	58	24-3	3	27	.316	.378	.586	137	14	9-4	.977	2	107	107	O-95(74-3-37)	1.3
2001	Cin N	90	349	48	101	20	4	7	35	24-0	2	53	.289	.337	.430	93	-4	12-9	.989	1	100	102	O-85(3-0-85)/D	-0.8
	Col N	58	187	25	47	10	3	1	17	21-0	2	23	.251	.330	.353	64	-10	5-4	.990	2	97	184	O-52(33-2-21)	-0.9
	Year	148	536	73	148	30	7	8	52	45-0	4	76	.276	.334	.403	81	-15	17-13	.989	3	99	132	*O-137(36-2-106)/D	-1.7
2002	Mil N	85	215	32	55	9	0	6	21	32-2	2	30	.256	.357	.381	100	0	8-5	.993	6	119	130	O-72(18-2-61)	0.3
	†Ana A	37	65	8	18	7	0	2	10	10-0	0	5	.277	.373	.477	124	3	2-2	.975	-1	87	152	O-36(7-0-31)	0.1
Total	8	807	2143	320	597	131	19	46	261	203-7	19	288	.279	.344	.422	96	-8	56-38	.981	10	98	139	O-673(206-24-488)/D-6	-2.5
OCK, WHITEY Harold David B 3.17.1912 Brooklyn, NY D 3.18.1975 Mt.Kisco, NY BR/TR 5-11/180# d9.29																								
1935	Bro N	1	3	0	0	0	0	0	0	1	0	2	.000	.250	.000	-27	-1	0	1.000	-0	*0*	*0*	/C	-0.1
O'CONNELL, DANNY Daniel Francis B 1.21.1927 Paterson, NJ D 10.2.1969 Clifton, NJ BR/TR 6/180# d7.14 Mil 1951 C2																								
1950	Pit N	79	315	39	92	16	1	8	32	24	0	33	.292	.342	.425	97	-1	7	.977	7	103	95	S-65,3-12	0.9
1953	Pit N	149	588	88	173	26	8	7	55	57	4	42	.294	.361	.401	99	0	3-4	.958	7	**110**	66	*3-104,2-47	0.9
1954	Mil N	146	541	61	151	28	4	2	37	38	2	46	.279	.326	.357	84	-13	2-2	.979	6	106	114	*2-103,3-35/1-8,S	0.0
1955	Mil N	124	453	47	102	15	4	6	40	28-2	5	43	.225	.276	.316	60	-27	2-2	.981	14	**111**	92	*2-114/3-7,S	-0.5
1956	Mil N	139	498	71	119	17	9	2	42	76-0	4	42	.239	.342	.321	86	-8	3-3	.985	-4	**104**	**119**	*2-138/3-4,S	-0.2
1957	Mil N	48	183	29	43	9	1	1	8	19-0	2	20	.235	.312	.311	74	-6	1-0	.982	6	108	137	2-48	0.4
	NY N	95	364	57	97	18	3	7	28	33-0	2	30	.266	.330	.390	93	-3	8-3	.980	5	105	115	2-68,3-30	0.8
	Year	143	547	86	140	27	4	8	36	52-0	4	50	.256	.324	.364	87	-9	9-3	.981	12	106	124	*2-116,3-30	1.2
1958	SF N	107	306	44	71	12	2	3	23	51-0	0	35	.232	.340	.314	77	-9	2-1	.986	2	104	100	*2-104/3-3	0.0
1959	SF N	34	58	6	11	3	0	0	0	5-0	0	15	.190	.254	.241	34	-5	0-1	.927	3	118	131	3-26/2-8	-0.3
1961	Was A	138	493	61	128	30	1	1	37	77-0	3	62	.260	.361	.331	88	-4	15-5	.939	5	115	90	3-73,2-61	0.7
1962	Was A	84	236	24	62	7	2	2	18	23-1	0	28	.263	.327	.335	80	-7	5-1	.961	1	106	176	3-41,2-22	-0.3
Total	10	1143	4035	527	1049	181	35	39	320	431-3	22	396	.260	.333	.351	84	-83	48-22	.980	53	106	108	2-713,3-335/S-68,1-8	2.4
O'CONNELL, JIMMY James Joseph B 2.11.1901 Sacramento, CA D 11.11.1976 Bakersfield, CA BL/TR 5-10.5/175# d4.17																								
1923	†NY N	87	252	42	63	9	2	6	39	34	5	32	.250	.351	.373	92	-2	7-3	.980	-10	87	25	O-64(CF)/1-8	-1.4
1924	NY N	52	104	24	33	4	2	2	18	11	1	16	.317	.388	.452	128	4	2-1	.952	-2	88	95	O-29(1-15-14)/2	0.2
Total	2	139	356	66	96	13	4	8	57	45	6	48	.270	.361	.396	102	2	9-4	.974	-11	87	41	/O-93(1-79-14),1-8,2	-1.2
O'CONNELL, JOHN John Charles B 6.13.1904 Verona, PA D 10.17.1992 Canton, OH BR/TR 6/170# d8.16																								
1928	Pit N	1	1	0	0	0	0	0	0	0	0	0	.000	.000	.000	-96	0	0	1.000	1	*0*	*594*	/C	0.0
1929	Pit N	2	7	1	1	1	0	0	0	1	0	1	.143	.250	.286	32	-1	0	1.000	-0	*100*	*0*	/C-2	-0.1
Total	2	3	8	1	1	1	0	0	0	1	0	1	.125	.222	.250	17	-1	0	1.000	0	*80*	*119*	/C-3	-0.1
O'CONNELL, JOHN John Joseph D 5.14.1908 Derry, NH 5-9.5/170# d8.22																								
1891	Bal AA	8	29	2	5	1	0	0	7	3	0	6	.172	.250	.207	31	-3	2	.938	-2	99	0	/S-3,2-3,O-2(RF)	-0.4
1902	Det A	8	22	1	4	0	0	0	0	3	0		.182	.280	.182	29	-2	0	.919	0	113	79	/2-6,1-2	-0.2
Total	2	16	51	3	9	1	0	0	7	6	0	6	.176	.263	.196	30	-5	2	.885	-2	99	85	/2-9,S-3,1-2,O-2(RF)	-0.6
O'CONNELL, PAT Patrick H. B 6.10.1861 Bangor, ME D 1.24.1943 Lewiston, ME BL/TR 5-10/175# d7.22																								
1886	Bal AA	42	166	20	30	3	2	0	8	11	1		.181	.236	.223	45	-10	10	.782	-6	58	0	O-41(CF)/1P	-1.6
O'CONNOR, DAN Daniel Cornelius B 8.1868 Guelph, ON, CAN D 3.3.1942 Guelph, ON, CAN BL/TR 6-2/185# d6.3																								
1890	Lou AA	6	26	3	12	1	1	0	5	1	0		.462	.481	.577	217	4	5	1.000	-1	0	117	/1-6	0.2
O'CONNOR, JOHNNY John Charles "Bucky" B 12.1.1891 Cahirciveen, Ireland D 5.30.1982 Bonner Springs, KS BR/TR 5-9/?# d9.16																								
1916	Chi N	1	0	0	0	0	0	0	0	0	0	0	—	—	—	—	0	0	—	0	0	0	/C	0.0
O'CONNOR, JACK John Joseph "Rowdy Jack" or "Peach Pie" B6.2.1869 St.Louis, MO D11.14.1937 St.Louis, MO BR/TR 5-10/170# d4.20 M1 OF Total (42-LF 113-CF 217-RF)																								
1887	Cin AA	12	40	4	4	0	0	0	1	2	0		.100	.143	.100	-31	-7	3	.947	2	166	414	/O-7(LF),C-5	-0.4
1888	Cin AA	36	137	14	28	3	1	1	17	6	1		.204	.243	.263	59	-7	12	.795	-2	141	0	O-34(11-21-2)/C-2	-0.9
1889	Col AA	107	398	69	107	17	7	4	60	33	4	37	.269	.331	.377	107	3	26	**.955**	-1			C-84,O-19(3-0-16)/2-4,1-3	0.7
1890	Col AA	121	457	89	148	14	10	2	66	38	1		.324	.377	.411	142	23	29	**.962**	11	*105*	*99*	*C-106/O-9(3-4-2),S-8,2-2,3	3.7
1891	Col AA	56	229	28	61	12	3	0	37	11	0	14	.266	.300	.345	90	-4	10	.878	0	113	205	O-40(7-0-33),C-21	-0.2
1892	†Cle N	140	572	71	142	22	5	1	58	25	2	48	.248	.282	.309	76	-19	17	.935	12	124	127	*O-106(6-0-100),C-34	-0.9
1893	Cle N	96	384	72	110	23	1	4	75	29	3	12	.286	.341	.383	87	-8	29	.949	5	*112*	*104*	C-56,O-44(2-27-15)	0.0
1894	Cle N	86	330	67	104	23	7	2	51	15	0	7	.315	.345	.445	86	-9	15	.942	10	*160*	*77*	C-45,O-33(1-27-5)/1-7	0.2
1895	Cle N	90	343	52	100	14	10	0	58	31	3	22	.292	.355	.391	87	-8	11	.927	0	*119*	*96*	C-48,1-41/3	-0.3
1896	†Cle N	68	256	41	76	11	1	1	43	15	3	12	.297	.343	.359	81	-7	15	.966	2	*149*	*82*	C-37,1-17,O-12(0-3-9)	-0.2
1897	Cle N	103	397	49	115	21	4	2	69	26	3		.290	.338	.378	84	-10	20	.941	-8	46	0	O-52(0-30-22),1-36,C-13	-1.7
1898	Cle N	131	478	50	119	17	4	1	56	26	2		.249	.291	.308	72	-18	8	.983	9	122	99	1-69,C-48,O-15(2-1-12)	-0.6
1899	StL N	84	289	33	73	5	6	0	43	15	4		.253	.299	.311	66	-15	7	.943	6	*125*	*87*	C-57,1-26	-0.4
1900	StL N	10	32	4	7	0	0	0	6	2	2		.219	.306	.219	46	-2	0	.957	-0	*92*	*87*	C-10	-0.2
	†Pit N	43	147	15	35	4	1	0	19	3	2		.238	.263	.279	49	-11	5	.944	-4	*130*	*96*	C-40/1-2	-1.0
	Year	53	179	19	42	4	1	0	25	5	4		.235	.271	.268	49	-13	5	.947	-4	*122*	*94*	C-50/1-2	-1.2
1901	Pit N	61	202	16	39	7	3	0	22	10	2		.193	.238	.257	42	-15	2	.978	3	*131*	*90*	C-59	-0.7
1902	Pit N	49	170	13	50	1	2	1	28	3	0		.294	.306	.341	96	-2	2	.979	0	*140*	*100*	C-42/1-6,O(RF)	0.2
1903	NY A	64	212	13	43	4	1	0	12	8	1		.203	.235	.231	38	-16	4	.988	2	*110*	*80*	C-63/1	-0.9
1904	StL A	14	47	4	10	1	0	0	2	2	0		.213	.245	.234	55	-2	0	.943	-4	*87*	*72*	C-14	-0.5
1906	StL A	55	174	8	33	0	0	0	11	2	0		.190	.199	.190	23	-16	4	.990	6	*94*	*109*	C-51	-0.6
1907	StL A	25	89	2	14	2	0	0	4	0	2		.157	.176	.180	13	-9	0	.991	-2	*87*	*97*	C-25	-0.9
1910	StL A	1	0	0	0	0	0	0	0	0	0		—	—	—	—	0	0	1.000	-0	*30*	*0*	/CM	0.0
Total	21	1452	5383	714	1418	201	66	19	738	302	35	152	.263	.307	.336	79	-159	219	.962	46	*106*	*84*	C-861,O-372R,1-208/S-8,2-6,3-2	-5.6
O'CONNOR, PADDY Patrick Francis B 8.4.1879 County Kerry, Ireland D 8.17.1950 Springfield, MA BR/TR 5-8/168# d4.17 C4																								
1908	Pit N	12	16	1	3	0	0	0	2	0	0		.188	.188	.188	20	-2	0	.889	-1	*117*	*51*	/C-4	-0.3
1909	†Pit N	9	16	1	5	1	0	0	3	0	0		.313	.313	.375	104	0	0	.700	-1	*116*	*52*	/C-3,3	-0.1
1910	Pit N	6	4	0	1	0	0	0	0	1	0	1	.250	.400	.250	85	0	0	1.000	-0	*0*	*0*	/C	0.0
1914	StL N	10	9	0	0	0	0	0	0	2	1	2	.000	.250	.000	-24	-1	0	1.000	-0	*84*	*99*	/C-7	-0.2

Year	Tm Lg	G	AB	R	H	2B	3B	HR	RBI	BB-IB	HP	SO	AVG	OBP	SLG	AOPS	ABR	SB-CS	FA	FR	Rng	Thr	G at Pos	BFW
1915	Pit F	70	219	15	50	10	1	0	16	14	1	30	.228	.278	.283	58	-16	4	.987	7	118	108	C-66	-0.3
1918	NY A	1	3	0	1	0	0	0	0	0	0	1	.333	.333	.333	99	0	0	1.000	-0	66	191	/C	0.0
Total	6	108	267	17	60	11	1	0	21	17	2	34	.225	.276	.273	57	-19	4	.979	4	116	105	/C-82,3	-0.9

O'DEA, KEN James Kenneth B 3.16.1913 Lima, NY D 12.17.1985 Lima, NY BL/TR 6/180# d4.21

Year	Tm Lg	G	AB	R	H	2B	3B	HR	RBI	BB-IB	HP	SO	AVG	OBP	SLG	AOPS	ABR	SB-CS	FA	FR	Rng	Thr	G at Pos	BFW
1935	†Chi N	76	202	30	52	13	2	6	38	26	1	18	.257	.345	.431	106	2	0	.964	-1	107	101	C-63	0.5
1936	Chi N	80	189	36	58	10	3	2	38	38	0	18	.307	.423	.423	126	9	0	.979	-1	117	90	C-55	1.1
1937	Chi N	83	219	31	66	7	5	4	32	24	0	26	.301	.370	.434	113	4	1	.985	-4	117	80	C-64	0.3
1938	†Chi N	86	247	22	65	12	1	3	33	12	0	18	.263	.297	.356	77	-8	1	.970	1	110	83	C-71	-0.3
1939	NY N	52	97	7	17	1	0	3	11	10	0	16	.175	.252	.278	42	-8	0	.947	-2	86	99	C-30	-0.9
1940	NY N	48	96	9	23	4	1	0	12	16	0	15	.240	.348	.302	80	-2	0	.992	3	143	172	C-31	0.3
1941	NY N	59	89	13	19	5	1	3	17	8	0	20	.213	.278	.393	86	-2	0	1.000	1	110	106	C-14	0.0
1942	†StL N	58	192	22	45	7	1	5	32	17	0	23	.234	.297	.359	85	-4	0	.979	9	159	134	C-49	0.9
1943	†StL N	71	203	15	57	11	2	3	25	19	1	25	.281	.345	.399	110	3	0	.989	6	176	104	C-56	1.2
1944	†StL N	85	265	35	66	11	2	6	37	37	1	29	.249	.343	.374	100	1	1	.994	7	141	89	C-69	1.2
1945	StL N✶	100	307	36	78	18	2	4	43	50	0	31	.254	.359	.365	99	1	0	**.995**	4	99	**128**	C-91	1.1
1946	StL N	22	57	2	7	2	0	1	3	8	0	8	.123	.231	.211	25	-6	0	.991	3	152	120	C-22	-0.1
	Bos N	12	32	4	7	0	0	0	2	8	0	4	.219	.375	.219	70	-1	0	1.000	-1	72	108	C-12	-0.1
	Year	34	89	6	14	2	0	1	5	16	0	12	.157	.286	.213	41	-7	0	.994	3	126	116	C-34	-0.2
Total	12	832	2195	262	560	101	20	40	323	273	3	251	.255	.338	.374	95	-11	3	.983	27	125	106	C-627	5.2

O'DEA, PAUL Paul "Lefty" B 7.3.1920 Cleveland, OH D 12.11.1978 Cleveland, OH BL/TL 6/200# d4.19

Year	Tm Lg	G	AB	R	H	2B	3B	HR	RBI	BB-IB	HP	SO	AVG	OBP	SLG	AOPS	ABR	SB-CS	FA	FR	Rng	Thr	G at Pos	BFW
1944	Cle A	76	173	25	55	9	0	0	13	23	1	21	.318	.401	.370	126	7	2-2	.949	-2	93	68	O-41(36-0-5)/P-3,1-3	0.3
1945	Cle A	87	221	21	52	2	2	1	21	20	0	26	.235	.299	.276	70	-9	3-0	.992	3	115	77	O-53(RF)/P	-1.0
Total	2	163	394	46	107	11	2	1	34	43	1	47	.272	.345	.317	95	-2	5-2	.975	0	106	73	/O-94(36-0-58),P-4,1-3	-0.7

ODOM, HEINIE Herman Boyd B 10.13.1900 Rusk, TX D 8.31.1970 Rusk, TX BB/TR 6/170# d4.22

Year	Tm Lg	G	AB	R	H	2B	3B	HR	RBI	BB-IB	HP	SO	AVG	OBP	SLG	AOPS	ABR	SB-CS	FA	FR	Rng	Thr	G at Pos	BFW
1925	NY A	1	1	0	1	0	0	0	0	0	0	0	1.000	1.000	1.000	416	0	0-0	1.000	0	148	0	/3	0.1

O'DONNELL, HARRY Harry Herman "Butch" B 4.2.1894 Philadelphia, PA D 1.31.1958 Philadelphia, PA BR/TR 5-8/175# d4.30

Year	Tm Lg	G	AB	R	H	2B	3B	HR	RBI	BB-IB	HP	SO	AVG	OBP	SLG	AOPS	ABR	SB-CS	FA	FR	Rng	Thr	G at Pos	BFW
1927	Phi N	16	16	1	1	0	0	0	2	2	0	2	.063	.167	.063	-36	-3	0	1.000	-0	72	72	C-12	-0.3

O'DONNELL, JOHN John B Littlestown, PA d7.16

Year	Tm Lg	G	AB	R	H	2B	3B	HR	RBI	BB-IB	HP	SO	AVG	OBP	SLG	AOPS	ABR	SB-CS	FA	FR	Rng	Thr	G at Pos	BFW
1884	Phi U	1	4	0	1	0	0	0		0			.250	.250	.250	56	0		.545	-2			/C	-0.2

O'DOUL, LEFTY Francis Joseph B 3.4.1897 San Francisco, CA D 12.7.1969 San Francisco, CA BL/TL 6/180# d4.29 ▲

Year	Tm Lg	G	AB	R	H	2B	3B	HR	RBI	BB-IB	HP	SO	AVG	OBP	SLG	AOPS	ABR	SB-CS	FA	FR	Rng	Thr	G at Pos	BFW
1919	NY A	19	16	2	4	0	0	0	1	1	0	2	.250	.294	.250	53	-1	1	.500	-0	75	0	/P-3,O(RF)	-0.1
1920	NY A	13	12	2	2	1	0	0	1	1	0	1	.167	.231	.250	26	-1	0-0	—	-0	0	0	/P-2,O(CF)	-0.1
1922	NY A	8	9	0	3	1	0	0	4	0	0	2	.333	.333	.444	99	1	0-0	1.000	0	102	0	/P-6	0.0
1923	Bos A	36	35	2	5	0	0	0	4	2	0	3	.143	.189	.143	-12	-6	0-0	.958	1	153	0	P-23/O(RF)	0.0
1928	NY N	114	354	67	113	19	4	8	46	30	0	8	.319	.372	.463	117	8	9	.962	-7	86	62	O-94(LF)	-0.5
1929	Phi N	**154**	638	152	**254**	35	6	32	122	76	4	19	**.398**	**.465**	.622	157	59	2	.971	3	100	128	*O-154(139-0-15)	4.5
1930	Phi N	140	528	122	202	37	7	22	97	63	5	21	.383	.453	.604	142	39	3	.953	-5	102	33	*O-131(LF)	2.1
1931	Bro N	134	512	85	172	32	11	7	75	48	3	16	.336	.396	.482	136	27	5	.954	-2	104	58	*O-132(LF)	1.6
1932	Bro N	148	595	120	219	32	8	21	90	50	7	20	**.368**	.423	.555	164	54	11	.979	-5	99	44	*O-148(LF)	4.0
1933	Bro N	43	159	14	40	5	1	5	21	15	1	6	.252	.320	.390	106	1	2	.947	-2	101	32	O-41(LF)	-0.3
	†NY N★	78	229	31	70	9	1	9	35	29	2	17	.306	.388	.472	147	15	1	.974	-3	91	82	O-63(32-0-31)	0.9
	Year	121	388	45	110	14	2	14	56	44	3	23	.284	.361	.438	130	16	3	.962	-5	95	61	*O-104(73-0-31)	0.6
1934	NY N	83	177	27	56	4	3	9	46	18	1	7	.316	.383	.525	144	10	2	.968	-4	84	38	O-38(27-0-11)	0.5
Total	11	970	3264	624	1140	175	41	113	542	333	23	122	.349	.413	.532	142	206	36-0	.964	-24	98	65	O-804(744-1-59)/P-34	12.6

ODWELL, FRED Frederick William "Fritz" B 9.25.1872 Downsville, NY D 8.19.1948 Downsville, NY BL/TR 5-9.5/160# d4.16

Year	Tm Lg	G	AB	R	H	2B	3B	HR	RBI	BB-IB	HP	SO	AVG	OBP	SLG	AOPS	ABR	SB-CS	FA	FR	Rng	Thr	G at Pos	BFW
1904	Cin N	129	468	75	133	22	10	1	58	26	8		.284	.333	.380	110	5	30	.956	12	109	133	*O-126(107-14-5)/2	1.0
1905	Cin N	130	468	79	113	10	9	**9**	65	26	8		.241	.293	.359	85	-11	21	.967	2	106	114	*O-126(56-4-66)	-1.6
1906	Cin N	58	202	20	45	5	4	0	21	15	3		.223	.286	.287	76	-6	11	.963	2	134	0	O-57(RF)	-0.8
1907	Cin N	94	274	24	74	5	7	0	24	22	5		.270	.336	.339	107	2	10	.975	6	77	69	O-84(77-0-8)/2	0.3
Total	4	411	1412	198	365	42	30	10	168	89	24		.258	.313	.352	96	-10	72	.964	22	105	94	O-393(240-18-136)/2-2	-1.1

OERTEL, CHUCK Charles Frank "Ducky" or "Snuffy" B 3.12.1931 Coffeyville, KS D 10.4.2000 Royal Oak, MI BL/TR 5-8/165# d9.1

Year	Tm Lg	G	AB	R	H	2B	3B	HR	RBI	BB-IB	HP	SO	AVG	OBP	SLG	AOPS	ABR	SB-CS	FA	FR	Rng	Thr	G at Pos	BFW
1958	Bal A	14	12	4	2	0	0	1	1	1-1	0	1	.167	.231	.417	78	0	0-0	1.000	0	111	0	/O-2(2-0-1)	-0.1

OESTER, RON Ronald John B 5.5.1956 Cincinnati, OH BB/TR 6-2/190# d9.10 C7

Year	Tm Lg	G	AB	R	H	2B	3B	HR	RBI	BB-IB	HP	SO	AVG	OBP	SLG	AOPS	ABR	SB-CS	FA	FR	Rng	Thr	G at Pos	BFW
1978	Cin N	6	8	1	3	0	0	0	1	0-0	0	2	.375	.375	.375	110	0	0-0	1.000	1	117	138	/S-6	0.1
1979	Cin N	6	3	0	0	0	0	0	0	0-0	0	1	.000	.000	.000	-99	-1	0-0	1.000	0	112	0	/S-2	-0.1
1980	Cin N	100	303	40	84	16	2	2	20	26-7	1	44	.277	.336	.363	95	-2	6-2	.980	-15	89	98	2-79,S-17/3-3	-1.2
1981	Cin N	105	354	45	96	16	7	5	42	42-8	0	49	.271	.342	.398	110	5	2-5	.980	5	99	101	*2-103/S-9	1.6
1982	Cin N	151	549	63	143	19	4	9	47	35-8	0	82	.260	.303	.359	83	-13	5-6	.972	3	97	107	*2-118,S-29,3-13	-0.3
1983	Cin N	157	549	63	145	23	5	11	58	49-14	1	106	.264	.322	.384	93	-6	2-2	.977	-25	87	80	*2-154	-2.4
1984	Cin N	150	553	54	134	26	3	3	38	41-7	1	97	.242	.295	.316	69	-23	7-2	.980	-15	89	80	*2-147/S	-3.0
1985	Cin N	152	526	59	155	26	3	1	34	51-17	0	65	.295	.354	.361	97	-1	5-0	.989	9	100	103	*2-149	1.8
1986	Cin N	153	523	52	135	23	2	8	44	52-16	1	84	.258	.325	.356	84	-11	9-2	.978	15	106	108	*2-151	1.5
1987	Cin N	69	237	28	60	9	6	2	23	22-4	0	51	.253	.317	.367	77	-8	2-3	.974	1	96	88	2-69	-0.4
1988	Cin N	54	150	20	42	7	0	0	10	9-3	0	24	.280	.319	.327	83	-3	0-2	.995	-0	93	105	2-49/S-5	-0.3
1989	Cin N	109	305	23	75	15	0	1	14	32-8	0	47	.246	.318	.305	76	-8	1-0	.985	3	97	82	*2-102/S-2	-0.3
1990	†Cin N	64	154	10	46	10	1	0	13	10-1	0	29	.299	.339	.377	93	-1	1-2	.982	-8	82	70	2-50/3-3	-0.9
Total	13	1276	4214	458	1118	190	33	42	344	369-93	4	681	.265	.323	.356	87	-72	40-26	.980	-27	95	94	*2-1171/S-71,3-19	-3.9

O'FARRELL, BOB Robert Arthur B 10.19.1896 Waukegan, IL D 2.20.1988 Waukegan, IL BR/TR 5-9.5/180# d9.5 M2

Year	Tm Lg	G	AB	R	H	2B	3B	HR	RBI	BB-IB	HP	SO	AVG	OBP	SLG	AOPS	ABR	SB-CS	FA	FR	Rng	Thr	G at Pos	BFW
1915	Chi N	2	3	0	1	0	0	0	0	0	0	0	.333	.333	.333	102	0	0	.667	-1	63	184	/C-2	-0.1
1916	Chi N	1	0	0	0	0	0	0	0	0	0	0	—	—	—	—	0	0	—	0	0	0	/C	0.0
1917	Chi N	3	8	1	3	2	0	0	1	1	0	0	.375	.444	.625	209	1	1	1.000	-1	88	73	/C-3	0.1
1918	†Chi N	52	113	9	32	7	3	1	14	10	1	15	.283	.347	.425	132	4	0	.974	-3	98	108	C-45	0.4
1919	Chi N	49	125	11	27	4	2	0	9	7	0	10	.216	.258	.280	61	-6	2	.965	-1	96	112	C-38	-0.5
1920	Chi N	94	270	29	67	11	4	3	19	34	0	23	.248	.332	.352	95	-1	1-0	.956	-2	100	117	C-86	0.5
1921	Chi N	96	260	32	65	12	7	4	32	18	0	14	.250	.299	.396	82	-8	2-0	.967	-4	95	112	C-90	-0.6
1922	Chi N	128	392	68	127	18	8	4	60	79	1	34	.324	.439	.441	125	20	5-3	.977	15	121	**143**	*C-125	4.1
1923	Chi N	131	452	73	144	25	4	12	84	67	1	38	.319	.408	.471	131	23	10-3	.976	9	111	102	*C-124	3.9
1924	Chi N	71	183	25	44	6	2	3	28	30	0	13	.240	.347	.344	85	-3	2-0	.984	1	115	94	C-57	0.2
1925	Chi N	17	22	2	4	0	1	0	3	2	0	5	.182	.250	.273	33	-2	0-0	1.000	-1	104	0	/C-3	-0.3
	StL N	94	317	37	88	13	2	3	32	46	2	26	.278	.373	.360	86	-5	0-1	.975	1	114	81	C-92	0.2
	Year	111	339	39	92	13	3	3	35	48	2	31	.271	.365	.354	83	-7	0-1	.975	0	114	79	C-95	-0.1
1926	†StL N	147	492	63	144	30	9	7	68	61	0	44	.293	.371	.433	111	9	1	.983	13	127	101	*C-146	**3.2**
1927	StL N	61	178	19	47	10	1	0	18	23	0	22	.264	.348	.331	80	-4	3	.979	1	91	146	C-53,M	0.0
1928	StL N	16	52	6	11	1	0	0	4	13	0	9	.212	.369	.231	59	-2	2	.985	0	135	37	C-14	-0.1
	NY N	75	133	23	26	6	0	2	20	34	0	16	.195	.359	.286	70	-4	2	.988	1	136	72	C-63	-0.1
	Year	91	185	29	37	7	0	2	24	47	0	25	.200	.362	.270	67	-7	4	.987	1	136	63	C-77	-0.2
1929	NY N	91	248	35	76	14	3	4	42	28	3	30	.306	.384	.435	103	2	3	.979	-2	138	28	C-84	0.4
1930	NY N	94	249	37	75	16	4	4	54	31	1	21	.301	.381	.446	101	1	1	.973	-1	101	101	C-69	0.4
1931	NY N	85	174	11	39	8	3	1	19	21	1	23	.224	.311	.322	72	-7	0	.980	2	142	90	C-80	-0.2
1932	NY N	50	67	7	16	3	0	0	8	11	1	10	.239	.354	.284	76	-2	0	.969	0	101	88	C-41	0.0
1933	StL N	55	163	16	39	4	2	2	20	15	0	25	.239	.303	.325	76	-5	0	.970	-4	89	94	C-50	-0.7
1934	Cin N	44	123	10	30	8	3	1	9	11	0	19	.244	.306	.382	85	-3	0	.993	-0	96	131	C-42,M	-0.1
	Chi N	22	67	3	15	3	0	0	5	3	0	11	.224	.257	.269	42	-6	0	1.000	2	128	108	C-22	-0.3
	Year	66	190	13	45	11	3	1	14	14	0	30	.237	.289	.342	70	-8	0	.996	1	107	123	C-64	-0.4
1935	StL N	14	10	0	0	0	0	0	0	2	0	0	.000	.167	.000	-49	-2	0	1.000	0	59	0	/C-8	-0.2
Total	21	1492	4101	517	1120	201	58	51	549	547	11	408	.273	.360	.388	97	0	35-7	.976	26	113	101	*C-1338	10.2

Year	Tm Lg	G	AB	R	H	2B	3B	HR	RBI	BB-IB	HP	SO	AVG	OBP	SLG	AOPS	ABR	SB-CS	FA	FR	Rng	Thr	G at Pos	BFW
OFFERMAN, JOSE Jose Antonio (Dono) B 11.8.1968 San Pedro De Macoris, D.R. BB/TR 6/165# d8.19 OF Total (5-LF 1-CF 3-RF)																								
1990	LA N	29	58	7	9	0	0	1	7	4-1	0	14	.155	.210	.207	15	-7	1-0	.946	-3	85	59	S-27	-0.9
1991	LA N	52	113	10	22	2	0	0	3	25-2	1	32	.195	.345	.212	62	-4	3-2	.945	-1	106	89	S-50	-0.2
1992	LA N	149	534	67	139	20	8	1	30	57-4	0	98	.260	.331	.333	90	-6	23-16	.935	-13	96	87	*S-149	-0.9
1993	LA N	158	590	77	159	21	6	1	62	71-7	2	75	.269	.346	.331	88	-8	30-13	.950	-7	98	99	*S-158	0.0
1994	LA N	72	243	27	51	8	4	1	25	38-4	0	38	.210	.314	.288	63	-13	2-1	.967	4	98	104	S-72	-0.3
1995	†LA N★	119	429	69	123	14	6	4	33	69-0	3	67	.287	.389	.375	113	11	2-7	.932	-4	95	99	*S-115	1.4
1996	KC A	151	561	85	170	33	8	5	47	74-3	1	98	.303	.384	.417	103	5	24-10	.994	4	121	116	1-96,2-38,S-36/O(CF)	0.6
1997	KC A	106	424	59	126	23	6	2	39	41-3	0	64	.297	.359	.394	94	-3	9-10	.981	-12	92	102	*2-101/D	-1.1
1998	KC A	158	607	102	191	28	**13**	7	66	89-1	5	96	.315	.403	.438	117	18	45-12	.974	6	105	114	*2-152/D-6	3.5
1999	†Bos A★	149	586	107	172	37	**11**	8	69	96-5	2	79	.294	.391	.435	108	11	18-12	.975	-22	82	91	*2-128,D-17/1-8	-0.7
2000	Bos A	116	451	73	115	14	3	9	41	70-0	1	70	.255	.354	.359	80	-13	0-8	.981	6	97	96	2-80,1-38/D-9	-0.8
2001	Bos A	128	524	76	140	23	3	9	49	61-2	1	97	.267	.342	.374	89	-8	5-2	.974	3	93	77	2-91,1-43	-0.3
2002	Bos A	72	237	39	55	10	0	4	27	33-0	1	29	.232	.325	.325	73	-8	8-5	.994	1	114	124	1-41,D-24/O-2(RF)	-1.2
	Sea A	29	47	9	11	2	1	1	4	4-0	0	9	.234	.294	.383	81	-1	1-1	1.000	2	174	55	1-11/O-6(5-0-1),2D	0.0
	Year	101	284	48	66	12	1	5	31	37-0	1	38	.232	.320	.335	75	-10	9-6	.995	4	124	113	1-52,D-28/O-8(5-0-3),2	-1.2
Total	13	1488	5404	807	1483	235	69	53	502	732-32	17	866	.274	.361	.373	94	-26	171-99	.943	-35	97	98	S-607,2-591,1-237/D-61,O-9L	-0.9
OFFICE, ROWLAND Rowland Johnie B 10.25.1952 Sacramento, CA BL/TL 6/170# d8.5																								
1972	Atl N	2	5	1	2	0	0	0	0	1-0	0	2	.400	.500	.400	145	0	0-0	1.000	0	106	0	/O(CF)	0.0
1974	Atl N	131	248	20	61	16	1	3	31	16-2	0	30	.246	.288	.355	77	-8	5-3	.994	-7	93	0	*O-119(1-118-0)	-1.8
1975	Atl N	126	355	30	103	14	1	3	30	23-4	3	41	.290	.337	.361	91	-4	2-2	.967	-5	93	98	*O-107(1-106-0)	-1.3
1976	Atl N	99	359	51	101	17	1	4	34	37-3	2	49	.281	.348	.368	98	0	2-8	.986	-8	91	55	O-92(CF)	-1.3
1977	Atl N	124	428	42	103	13	1	5	39	23-1	3	58	.241	.282	.311	53	-28	2-4	.988	2	104	126	*O-104(1-103-0)/1	-2.9
1978	Atl N	146	404	40	101	13	1	9	40	22-2	6	52	.250	.297	.354	73	-15	8-6	.990	2	108	68	*O-136(CF)	-1.5
1979	Atl N	124	277	35	69	14	2	2	37	27-2	2	33	.249	.320	.336	74	-9	5-4	.988	-5	92	79	O-97(CF)	-1.6
1980	Mon N	116	292	36	78	13	4	6	30	36-1	0	39	.267	.343	.401	108	4	3-3	.987	-7	92	31	O-97(3-27-68)	-0.7
1981	Mon N	26	40	4	7	0	0	0	0	4-0	0	6	.175	.250	.175	22	-4	0-0	.938	-1	84	0	O-15(0-3-12)	-0.6
1982	Mon N	3	3	0	1	1	0	0	0	0-0	0	1	.333	.333	.667	170	0	0-0	1.000	0	436	0	/O(LF)	0.1
1983	NY A	2	2	0	0	0	0	0	1	0-0	0	0	.000	.000	.000	-99	-1	0-0	1.000	-0	92	0	/O-2(CF)	-0.1
Total	11	899	2413	259	626	101	11	32	242	189-15	16	311	.259	.315	.350	79	-65	27-30	.985	-29	97	67	O-771(7-687-80)/1	-11.7
OGLESBY, JIM James Dorn B 8.10.1905 Schofield, MO D 9.1.1955 Tulsa, OK BL/TL 6/190# d4.14																								
1936	Phi A	3	11	0	2	0	0	0	2	2	0	0	.182	.308	.182	24	-1	0-0	1.000	0	143	83	/1-3	-0.1
OGLIVIE, BEN Benjamin Ambrosio (Palmer) B 2.11.1949 Colon, Panama BL/TL 6-2/170# d9.4 C1																								
1971	Bos A	14	38	2	10	3	0	0	4	0-0	0	5	.263	.263	.342	66	-2	0-0	.958	2	130	176	O-11(10-0-1)	-0.1
1972	Bos A	94	253	27	61	10	2	8	30	18-2	1	61	.241	.293	.391	97	-1	1-1	.981	-2	87	113	O-65(32-0-33)	-0.8
1973	Bos A	58	147	16	32	9	1	2	9	9-2	2	32	.218	.269	.333	66	-7	1-1	.983	-0	96	101	O-32(4-0-28),D-13	-0.9
1974	Det A	92	252	28	68	11	3	4	29	34-6	0	38	.270	.353	.385	109	4	12-3	.947	-3	85	82	O-63(61-0-2),1-10/D-4	-0.1
1975	Det A	100	332	45	95	14	1	9	36	16-0	2	62	.286	.319	.416	103	0	11-8	.975	4	111	65	O-86(76-0-10)/1-5,D-2	-0.2
1976	Det A	115	305	36	87	12	3	15	47	11-3	3	44	.285	.313	.492	129	9	9-4	.986	1	104	160	O-64(16-12-36)/1-9,D	0.8
1977	Det A	132	450	63	118	24	2	21	61	40-2	3	80	.262	.325	.464	107	4	9-9	.976	2	100	118	*O-118(RF)/D-2	-0.1
1978	Mil A	128	469	71	142	29	4	18	72	52-10	0	69	.303	.370	.497	142	26	11-7	.980	-2	103	82	O-89(65-0-25),D-27,1-11	2.0
1979	Mil A	139	514	88	145	30	4	29	81	48-12	2	56	.282	.343	.525	131	21	12-5	.985	-2	101	76	*O-120(102-0-23),D-13/1-9	1.3
1980	Mil A★	156	592	94	180	26	2	**41**	118	54-**19**	5	71	.304	.362	.563	156	43	11-9	.978	13	112	147	*O-152(150-1-2)/D-4	4.8
1981	†Mil A	107	400	53	97	15	2	14	72	37-10	6	49	.243	.310	.395	109	4	2-2	.982	-8	91	39	*O-101(99-2-0)/D-6	-0.9
1982	†Mil A★	159	602	92	147	22	1	34	102	70-13	4	81	.244	.326	.453	119	15	3-5	.982	6	102	147	*O-159(LF)	1.2
1983	Mil A★	125	411	49	115	19	3	13	66	60-12	4	64	.280	.371	.436	133	21	4-6	.985	2	103	87	*O-113(LF)/D-8	1.7
1984	Mil A	131	461	49	121	16	2	12	60	44-5	1	56	.262	.327	.384	100	0	0-6	.970	-3	96	71	*O-125(113-0-23)/D	-1.1
1985	Mil A	101	341	40	99	17	2	10	61	37-3	2	51	.290	.354	.440	119	10	0-2	.965	-2	101	66	O-91(48-0-54)/D-4	0.3
1986	Mil A	103	346	31	98	20	1	5	53	30-6	0	33	.283	.334	.390	95	-2	1-2	.991	4	118	141	O-50(50-0-2),D-42	-0.1
Total	16	1754	5913	784	1615	277	33	235	901	560-105	35	852	.273	.336	.450	119	145	87-70	.978	12	101	101	*O-1439(1098-15-357),D-127/1-44	7.8
OGRODOWSKI, BRUCE Ambrose Francis "Brusie" B 2.17.1912 Hoytville, PA D 3.5.1956 San Francisco, CA BR/TR 5-11/175# d4.14																								
1936	StL N	94	237	28	54	15	1	1	20	10	0	20	.228	.259	.312	53	-16	0	.989	1	*120*	*78*	C-85	-1.1
1937	StL N	90	279	37	65	10	3	3	31	11	2	17	.233	.267	.323	58	-17	2	.984	0	*90*	*88*	C-87	-1.2
Total	2	184	516	65	119	25	4	4	51	21	2	37	.231	.263	.318	56	-33	2	.986	1	*103*	*84*	C-172	-2.3
O'HAGEN, HAL Harry P. B 9.30.1873 Washington, DC D 1.14.1913 Newark, NJ 6/173# d9.24																								
1892	Was N	1	4	1	1	0	0	0	0	0	0	2	.250	.250	.250	53	0	0	1.000	0	*79*	*323*	/C	0.0
1902	Chi N	33	115	11	22	1	3	0	10	11	0		.191	.262	.252	60	-6	9	.983	3	147	128	1-33	-0.3
	NY N	4	11	0	1	0	0	0	0	0	0		.091	.091	.091	-44	-2	0	1.000	0	0	0	/O-4(0-3-1)	-0.2
	Cle A	3	13	2	5	2	0	0	1	0	0		.385	.385	.538	160	1	2	1.000	1	170	0	/1-3	0.2
	NY N	22	73	5	11	2	1	0	8	2	2		.151	.195	.205	24	-7	3	.973	-0	109	115	1-18/O-4(RF)	-0.8
	Year	59	199	16	34	3	4	0	18	13	2		.171	.229	.226	52	-14	12	.980	3	133	123	1-51/O-8(0-3-5)	-1.3
Total	2	63	216	19	40	5	4	0	19	13	2	2	.185	.238	.245	49	-14	14	.981	4	136	116	/1-54,O-8(0-3-5),C	-1.1
O'HALLORAN, GREG Gregory Joseph B 5.21.1968 Toronto, ON, CAN BL/TR 6-2/205# d5.16																								
1994	Fla N	12	11	1	2	0	0	0	1	0-0	0	1	.182	.167	.182	-5	-2	0-0	1.000	0	0	0	/C	-0.2
O'HARA, KID James Francis B 12.19.1875 Wilkes-Barre, PA D 12.1.1954 Canton, OH BB/TR 5-7.5/152# d9.15																								
1904	Bos N	8	29	3	6	0	0	0	0	4	0		.207	.303	.207	60	-1	1	.923	0	196	0	/O-8(RF)	-0.2
O'HARA, TOM Thomas F. B 7.13.1885 Waverly, NY D 6.8.1954 Denver, CO d9.19																								
1906	StL N	14	53	8	16	1	0	0	0	3	0		.302	.339	.321	110	1	3	.889	-2	0	0	O-14(LF)	-0.2
1907	StL N	48	173	11	41	2	1	0	5	12	0		.237	.286	.260	74	-6	1	.943	-2	73	113	O-47(24-0-23)	-1.2
Total	2	62	226	19	57	3	1	0	5	15	0		.252	.299	.274	82	-5	4	.930	-4	57	88	/O-61(38-0-23)	-1.4
O'HARA, BILL William Alexander B 8.14.1883 Toronto, ON, CAN D 6.13.1931 Jersey City, NJ BL/TR 5-10/165# d4.15																								
1909	NY N	115	360	48	85	9	3	1	30	41	2		.236	.318	.286	86	-5	31	.978	4	132	132	*O-111(11-89-11)	-0.6
1910	StL N	9	20	1	3	0	0	0	2	1	0	3	.150	.190	.150	-0	-3	0	1.000	0	86	208	/O-4(CF),P1	-0.3
Total	2	124	380	49	88	9	3	1	32	42	2	3	.232	.311	.279	82	-8	31	.979	4	130	135	O-115(11-93-11)/1P	-0.9
OJEDA, MIGUEL Miguel Arturo B 1.29.1975 Sonora, Mexico BR/TR 6-2/190# d5.17																								
2003	SD N	61	141	13	33	6	0	4	22	18-2	3	26	.234	.331	.362	89	-2	1-1	.981	-1	91	59	C-48/1-2	0.0
OJEDA, AUGIE Octavio Augie B 12.20.1974 Los Angeles, CA BB/TR 5-9/165# d6.4																								
2000	Chi N	28	77	10	17	3	1	2	8	10-1	0	9	.221	.307	.364	71	-4	0-1	.989	-1	106	83	S-25/2-4	-0.3
2001	Chi N	78	144	16	29	5	1	1	12	12-1	2	20	.201	.269	.271	43	-13	1-0	.913	3	125	157	3-35,S-31,2-10	-0.7
2002	Chi N	30	70	4	13	4	0	0	4	5-0	1	5	.186	.247	.243	34	-7	1-0	.966	0	106	45	S-16,2-10/3-5	-0.5
2003	Chi N	12	25	2	3	0	0	0	0	1-1	1	5	.120	.185	.120	-18	-4	0-0	1.000	-1	91	95	/S-7,2-5,3	-0.4
Total	4	148	316	32	62	12	2	3	24	28-3	4	39	.196	.267	.275	43	-28	2-1	.981	1	97	71	/S-79,3-41,2-29	-1.9
OKRIE, LEN Leonard Joseph B 7.16.1923 Detroit, MI BR/TR 6/185# d6.16 C5 f-Frank																								
1948	Was A	19	42	1	10	0	1	0	1	1	0	7	.238	.256	.286	45	-4	0-0	.981	1	*154*	*235*	C-17	-0.2
1950	Was A	17	27	1	6	0	0	0	2	6	1	7	.222	.382	.222	61	-1	0-0	1.000	1	*66*	*176*	C-17	0.0
1951	Was A	5	8	1	1	1	0	0	0	2	0	1	.125	.300	.250	51	0	0-0	.850	-0	*125*	*216*	/C-5	0.0
1952	Bos A	1	1	0	0	0	0	0	0	0	0	1	.000	.000	.000	-93	0	0-0	1.000	-0	*0*	*0*	/C	0.0
Total	4	42	78	3	17	1	1	0	3	9	1	16	.218	.307	.256	51	-5	0-0	.965	1	*116*	*208*	/C-40	-0.2
OLANDER, JIM James Bentley B 2.21.1963 Tucson, AZ BR/TR 6-1/185# d9.20																								
1991	Mil A	12	9	2	0	0	0	0	0	2-0	0	5	.000	.182	.000	-46	-2	0-0	1.000	0	115	0	/O-9(2-5-1),D-2	-0.2
OLDFIELD, DAVE David B 12.18.1864 Philadelphia, PA D 8.28.1939 Philadelphia, PA BB/TL 5-7/175# d6.28																								
1883	Bal AA	1	4	0	0	0	0	0		0			.000	.000	.000	-97	-1		.667	-1			/C	-0.2
1885	Bro AA	10	25	2	8	1	0	0	2	3	1		.320	.414	.360	145	2		.873	-1			/C-9,O-2(0-1-1)	0.1
1886	Bro AA	14	55	7	13	1	0	0	5	2	0		.236	.263	.255	62	-3	1	.833	-3			C-13/SO(RF)	-0.4

Year	Tm Lg	G	AB	R	H	2B	3B	HR	RBI	BB-IB	HP	SO	AVG	OBP	SLG	AOPS	ABR	SB-CS	FA	FR	Rng	Thr	G at Pos	BFW
	Was N	21	71	2	10	2	0	0	2	5		15	.141	.197	.169	13	-7	0	.899	-3			C-12/O-9(0-3-6)	-0.8
Total	3	46	155	11	31	4	0	0	9	10		15	.200	.253	.226	50	-9	1	.857	-7			/C-35,O-12(0-4-8),S	-1.3
OLDHAM, JOHN John Hardin B 11.6.1932 Salinas, CA BR/TL 6-3/198# d9.2																								
1956	Cin N	1	0	0	0	0	0	0	0	0-0	0	0	—	—	—	—	0	0-0	—	0			R	0.0
OLDIS, BOB Robert Carl B 1.5.1928 Preston, IA BR/TR 6-1/185# d4.28 C5																								
1953	Was A	7	16	0	4	0	0	0	3	1	0	2	.250	.294	.250	49	-1	0-0	1.000	1	*119*	*82*	/C-7	0.0
1954	Was A	11	24	1	8	1	0	0	0	1	0	3	.333	.360	.375	107	0	0-0	.941	-1	*99*	*61*	/C-8,3-2	-0.1
1955	Was A	6	6	1	0	0	0	0	0	1-0	0	0	.000	.143	.000	-62	-1	0-0	1.000	-0	*60*	*222*	/C-6	-0.1
1960	†Pit N	22	20	1	4	1	0	0	1	1-0	0	2	.200	.238	.250	34	-2	0-0	1.000	1	*264*	*61*	C-22	0.0
1961	Pit N	4	5	0	0	0	0	0	0	0-0	0	0	.000	.000	.000	-99	-1	0-0	1.000	2	*0*	*219*	/C-4	0.0
1962	Phi N	38	80	9	21	1	0	1	10	13-0	0	10	.262	.366	.313	87	-1	0-1	.987	1	*121*	*123*	C-30	0.1
1963	Phi N	47	85	8	19	3	0	0	8	3-1	0	5	.224	.250	.259	47	-6	0-0	.979	2	*90*	*112*	C-43	-0.3
Total	7	135	236	20	56	6	0	1	22	20-<u>1</u>	0	22	.237	.297	.275	60	-12	0-1	.983	6	*116*	*110*	C-120/3-2	-0.4
OLDRING, RUBE Reuben Henry B 5.30.1884 New York, NY D 9.9.1961 Bridgeton, NJ BR/TR 5-10/186# d10.2 OF Total (455-LF 627-CF 48-RF)																								
1905	NY A	8	30	2	9	0	1	1	6	2	0		.300	.344	.467	140	1	4	.967	4	120	136	/S-8	0.5
1906	Phi A	59	174	15	42	10	1	0	19	2	3		.241	.263	.310	77	-5	7	.897	1	99	119	3-49/S-3,2-2,1	-0.3
1907	Phi A	117	441	48	126	27	8	1	40	7	5		.286	.305	.390	118	7	29	.974	-10	69	0	*O-117(0-116-1)	-0.9
1908	Phi A	116	434	38	96	14	2	1	39	18	9		.221	.267	.270	70	-14	13	.941	-2	65	79	*O-116(21-95-0)	-2.6
1909	Phi A	90	326	39	75	13	8	1	28	20	6		.230	.287	.328	92	-4	17	.963	-0	65	46	O-89(32-56-1)/1	-0.9
1910	Phi A	134	546	79	168	27	14	4	57	23	4		.308	.340	.430	143	23	17	**.978**	-5	96	74	*O-134(1-130-3)	1.3
1911	†Phi A	121	495	84	147	11	14	3	59	21	5		.297	.332	.394	104	-1	21	**.979**	-8	92	71	*O-119(CF)	-1.6
1912	Phi A	99	395	61	119	14	5	1	24	10	3		.301	.324	.370	102	-1	17	.974	-3	103	58	O-98(11-87-0)	-1.1
1913	†Phi A	137	538	101	152	27	9	5	71	34	2	37	.283	.328	.394	113	7	40	.968	-3	109	57	*O-131(LF)/S-5	-0.1
1914	†Phi A	119	466	68	129	21	7	3	49	18	3	35	.277	.308	.371	108	1	14-16	.965	-3	104	46	*O-117(105-11-1)	-1.1
1915	Phi A	107	408	49	101	23	3	6	42	22	4	21	.248	.293	.363	100	-3	11-6	.982	4	114	74	O-96(88-8-0)/3-8	-0.3
1916	Phi A	40	146	10	36	8	3	0	14	9	0	9	.247	.290	.342	95	-2	1	.897	-3	80	118	O-40(LF)	-0.7
	NY A	43	158	17	37	8	0	1	12	12	0	13	.234	.288	.304	76	-5	6	.957	-3	102	20	O-43(0-2-41)	-1.1
	Year	83	304	27	73	16	3	1	26	21	0	22	.240	.289	.322	85	-7	7	.926	-6	91	70	O-83(40-2-41)	-1.8
1918	Phi A	49	133	5	31	2	1	0	11	8	1	10	.233	.282	.263	64	-6	0	.949	-4	75	66	O-30(26-3-1)/2-2,3-2	-1.2
Total	13	1239	4690	616	1268	205	76	27	471	206	45	<u>125</u>	.270	.307	.364	103	-2	197-<u>22</u>	.966	-35	91	58	*O-1130C/3-59,S-16,2-4,1-2	-10.1
O'LEARY, CHARLEY Charles Timothy B 10.15.1882 Chicago, IL D 1.6.1941 Chicago, IL BR/TR 5-7/165# d4.14 C19																								
1904	Det A	135	456	39	97	10	3	1	16	21	4		.213	.254	.254	63	-20	9	.933	4	102	110	*S-135	-1.3
1905	Det A	148	512	47	109	13	1	0	33	29	3		.213	.259	.242	59	-24	13	.933	-4	94	83	*S-148	-2.6
1906	Det A	128	443	34	97	13	2	2	34	17	3		.219	.253	.271	62	-20	8	.926	-7	95	83	*S-127	-2.5
1907	†Det A	139	465	61	112	19	1	0	34	32	6		.241	.298	.286	83	-8	11	.943	-6	95	78	*S-138	-1.1
1908	†Det A	65	211	21	53	9	3	0	17	9	4		.251	.295	.322	96	-1	4	.920	-9	90	80	S-64/2	-1.0
1909	†Det A	76	261	29	53	10	0	0	13	6	1		.203	.224	.241	45	-17	9	.922	-4	106	63	3-54,2-15/S-4,O-2(1-0-1)	-2.3
1910	Det A	65	211	23	51	7	1	0	9	9	1		.242	.276	.284	71	-8	7	.935	-0	94	78	2-38,S-18/3-6	-0.7
1911	Det A	74	256	29	68	8	2	0	25	21	6		.266	.336	.313	77	-7	10	.966	3	105	78	2-67/3-6	-0.3
1912	Det A	3	10	1	2	0	0	0	1	0	0		.200	.200	.200	15	-1	0	1.000	1	158	0	/2-3	0.0
1913	StL N	121	406	32	88	15	5	0	31	20	4	34	.217	.260	.278	55	-25	3-12	.951	-6	99	58	*S-103,2-15	-2.9
1934	StL A	1	1	1	1	0	0	0	0	0	0	0	1.000	1.000	1.000	385	0	0-0	—	0			H	0.0
Total	11	955	3232	317	731	104	18	3	213	164	32	<u>34</u>	.226	.270	.272	67	-131	74-<u>12</u>	.935	-29	97	83	S-737,2-139/3-66,O-2(1-0-1)	-14.7
O'LEARY, DAN Daniel "Hustling Dan" B 10.22.1856 Detroit, MI D 6.24.1922 Chicago, IL BL 5-10/165# d9.3 M1																								
1879	Pro N	2	7	1	3	0	0	0	2	0		0	.429	.429	.429	187	1		—	-0	0	0	/O-2(RF)	0.1
1880	Bos N	3	12	1	3	2	0	0	1	0		3	.250	.250	.417	126	0		1.000	-1	0	0	/O-3(RF)	0.0
1881	Det N	2	8	0	0	0	0	0	0	0		2	.000	.000	.000	-96	-2		.714	-1	0	0	/O-2(CF)	-0.3
1882	Wor N	6	22	2	4	1	0	0	2	5		5	.182	.333	.227	82	0		.800	-2	0	0	/O-6(CF)	-0.2
1884	Cin U	32	132	14	34	0	2	1		5			.258	.285	.311	74	-8		.862	1	99	0	O-32(22-10-0),M	-0.8
Total	5	45	181	18	44	3	2	1	<u>5</u>	10		<u>10</u>	.243	.283	.298	75	-9		.843	-2	76	0	/O-45(22-18-5)	-1.2
O'LEARY, TROY Troy Franklin B 8.4.1969 Compton, CA BL/TL 6/196# d5.9																								
1993	Mil A	19	41	3	12	3	0	0	3	5-0	0	9	.293	.370	.366	100	0	0-0	1.000	1	111	112	O-19(15-0-5)	0.1
1994	Mil A	27	66	9	18	1	1	2	7	5-0	1	12	.273	.329	.409	86	-2	1-1	1.000	1	101	153	O-21(13-0-10)/D	-0.1
1995	Bos A	112	399	60	123	31	6	10	49	29-4	1	64	.308	.355	.491	114	8	5-3	.976	-1	98	94	*O-105(16-13-91)/D-3	0.2
1996	Bos A	149	497	68	129	28	5	15	81	47-3	4	80	.260	.327	.427	87	-11	3-2	.971	-8	87	91	*O-146(66-17-110)	-2.2
1997	Bos A	146	499	65	154	32	4	15	80	39-7	2	70	.309	.358	.479	115	10	0-5	.979	-2	97	92	*O-142(24-0-119)/D	0.0
1998	†Bos A	156	611	95	165	36	8	23	83	36-2	5	108	.270	.314	.468	98	-4	2-2	.990	1	99	99	*O-155(LF)	-0.9
1999	†Bos A	157	596	84	167	36	4	28	103	56-5	4	91	.280	.343	.495	108	6	1-2	.993	1	98	94	*O-157(157-0-2)	0.0
2000	Bos A	138	513	68	134	30	4	13	70	44-2	2	76	.261	.320	.411	81	-15	0-2	.988	-5	88	112	*O-137(LF)	-2.4
2001	Bos A	104	341	50	82	16	6	13	50	25-2	5	73	.240	.298	.437	91	-6	1-3	.994	-1	100	58	O-89(52-0-41)/D-4	-1.1
2002	Mon N	97	273	27	78	12	2	3	37	34-5	3	47	.286	.371	.377	93	-3	1-2	.977	-1	104	25	O-70(69-0-1)/D-3	-0.6
2003	†Chi N	93	174	18	38	9	0	5	28	14-1	1	31	.218	.275	.356	66	-9	3-0	1.000	-0	90	.139	O-51(28-0-24)	-1.0
Total	11	1198	4010	547	1100	234	40	127	591	334-31	28	661	.274	.332	.448	97	-26	17-22	.985	-14	96	92	*O-1092(732-30-403)/D-12	-8.0
OLERUD, JOHN John Garrett B 8.5.1968 Seattle, WA BL/TL 6-5/220# d9.3																								
1989	Tor A	6	8	2	3	0	0	0	0	0-0	0	1	.375	.375	.375	114	0	0-0	1.000	0	168	0	/1-5,D	0.0
1990	Tor A	111	358	43	95	15	1	14	48	57-6	1	75	.265	.364	.430	120	11	0-2	.986	-1	89	75	D-90,1-18	0.6
1991	†Tor A	139	454	64	116	30	1	17	68	68-9	6	84	.256	.353	.438	115	12	0-2	.996	-3	88	76	*1-135/D	-0.1
1992	†Tor A	138	458	68	130	28	0	16	66	70-11	1	61	.284	.375	.450	126	18	1-0	.994	-2	91	70	*1-133/D	0.8
1993	†Tor A★	158	551	109	200	**54**	2	24	107	114-**33**	7	65	**.363**	**.473**	.599	**186**	**77**	0-2	.992	-2	94	90	*1-137,D-20	**5.8**
1994	Tor A	108	384	47	114	29	2	12	67	61-12	3	53	.297	.393	.477	124	16	1-2	.993	1	98	94	*1-104/D-3	0.7
1995	Tor A	135	492	72	143	32	0	8	54	84-10	4	54	.291	.398	.404	110	12	0-0	.997	-3	90	82	*1-133	-0.3
1996	Tor A	125	398	59	109	25	0	18	61	60-6	10	37	.274	.382	.472	115	11	1-0	.998	-3	85	134	*1-101,D-15	-0.1
1997	NY N	154	524	90	154	34	1	22	102	85-5	13	67	.294	.400	.489	138	33	0-0	.995	4	112	117	*1-146	2.3
1998	NY N	160	557	91	197	36	4	22	93	96-11	4	73	.354	.447	.551	165	59	2-2	.996	3	104	101	*1-157	4.5
1999	†NY N	162	581	107	173	39	0	19	96	125-5	11	66	.298	.427	.463	130	36	3-0	.994	3	105	107	*1-160	2.3
2000	†Sea A	159	565	84	161	45	0	14	103	102-11	4	96	.285	.392	.439	115	19	0-2	**.996**	15	**134**	114	*1-158	1.7
2001	†Sea A★	159	572	91	173	32	1	21	95	94-19	5	70	.302	.401	.472	138	37	3-1	.993	8	**119**	106	*1-158	2.9
2002	Sea A	154	553	85	166	39	0	22	102	98-6	5	66	.300	.403	.490	143	40	0-0	.996	4	105	**107**	*1-152/D-2	2.8
2003	Sea A	152	539	64	145	35	0	10	83	84-7	6	67	.269	.372	.390	105	9	0-1	.998	10	**121**	115	*1-152	0.4
Total	15	2020	6994	1076	2079	473	12	239	1145	1198-151	80	935	.297	.402	.471	132	390	11-14	.995	35	105	101	*1-1849,D-133	24.3
OLIN, FRANK Franklin Walter B 1.9.1860 Woodford, VT D 5.21.1951 St.Louis, MO BL d7.4																								
1884	Was AA	21	83	12	32	4	1	0		7	0		.386	.433	.458	216	11		.775	-6	77	37	2-12,O-11(1-7-3)	0.5
	Was U	1	4	0	0	0	0	0		0			.000	.000	.000	-99	-1		—	0	0	0	/O(LF)	-0.1
	Tol AA	26	86	16	22	0	1	1		5	1		.256	.304	.314	99	0		.875	2	141	0	O-26(LF)	0.1
1885	Det N	1	4	1	2	0	0	0	0	0		0	.500	.500	.500	224	1		.667	-0	80	0	/3	0.0
Total	2	49	177	29	56	4	2	1	<u>0</u>	12		<u>0</u>	.316	.363	.379	148	11		.849	-5	126	83	/O-38(28-7-3),2-12,3	0.5
OLIVA, JOSE Jose (Galvez) B 3.3.1971 San Pedro De Macoris, D.R. D 12.22.1997 San Cristobal, D.R. BR/TR 6-3/215# d7.1																								
1994	Atl N	19	59	9	17	5	0	6	11	7-0	0	10	.288	.364	.678	160	5	0-1	.932	0	99	84	3-16	0.5
1995	Atl N	48	109	7	17	4	0	5	12	7-0	0	22	.156	.207	.330	38	-11	0-0	.902	-3	84	88	3-25/1	-1.3
	StL N	22	74	8	9	1	0	2	8	5-0	2	24	.122	.195	.216	9	-10	0-0	.977	-2	86	142	3-18/1-2	-1.2
	Year	70	183	15	26	5	0	7	20	12-0	2	46	.142	.202	.284	26	-21	0-0	.933	-5	85	111	3-43/1-3	-2.5
Total	2	89	242	24	43	10	0	13	31	19-0	2	56	.178	.242	.380	60	-16	0-1	.932	-5	89	103	/3-59,1-3	-2.0
OLIVA, TONY Pedro (Lopez) B 7.20.1940 Pinar Del Rio, Cuba BL/TR 6-2/190# d9.9 C10																								
1962	Min A	9	9	3	4	1	0	0	3	3-0	0	2	.444	.583	.556	201	2	0-0	1.000	0	119	0	/O-2(RF)	0.2
1963	Min A	7	7	0	3	0	0	0	1	0-0	0	2	.429	.429	.429	138	0	0-0	—	0			H	0.0
1964	Min A★	161	672	**109**	**217**	**43**	9	32	94	34-8	6	68	**.323**	.359	.557	150	43	12-6	.981	-1	107	51	*O-159(2-9-154)	3.2

Year	Tm Lg	G	AB	R	H	2B	3B	HR	RBI	BB-IB	HP	SO	AVG	OBP	SLG	AOPS	ABR	SB-CS	FA	FR	Rng	Thr	G at Pos	BFW
1965	†Min A★	149	576	107	**185**	40	5	16	98	55-12	4	64	**.321**	.378	.491	141	32	19-9	.964	3	106	108	*O-147(0-8-143)	2.7
1966	Min A★	159	622	99	**191**	32	7	25	87	42-10	5	72	.307	.353	.502	135	27	13-7	.972	7	114	100	*O-159(0-19-140)	2.6
1967	Min A★	146	557	76	161	**34**	6	17	83	44-12	8	61	.289	.347	.463	128	20	11-3	.987	8	**119**	89	*O-146(RF)	2.1
1968	Min A★	128	470	54	136	24	5	18	68	45-**16**	7	61	.289	.357	.477	145	26	10-9	.983	2	108	102	*O-126(RF)	2.1
1969	†Min A✱	153	637	97	**197**	**39**	4	24	101	45-12	3	66	.309	.355	.496	134	27	10-13	.982	6	107	112	*O-152(RF)	2.3
1970	†Min A★	157	628	96	**204**	**36**	7	23	107	38-12	3	67	.325	.364	.514	138	31	5-4	.968	13	**122**	116	*O-157(0-3-154)	3.6
1971	Min A✱	126	487	73	164	30	3	22	81	25-8	2	44	**.337**	.369	**.546**	152	31	4-1	.969	-2	98	78	*O-121(RF)	2.5
1972	Min A	10	28	1	9	1	0	0	1	2-0	0	5	.321	.367	.357	111	0	0-0	.857	-2	50	0	/O-9(8-0-1)	-0.2
1973	Min A	146	571	63	166	20	0	16	92	45-14	4	44	.291	.345	.410	108	6	2-1	—	0	0	0	*D-142	0.2
1974	Min A	127	459	43	131	16	2	13	57	27-11	2	31	.285	.325	.414	109	4	0-1	—	0	0	0	*D-112	0.1
1975	Min A	131	455	46	123	10	0	13	58	41-15	**13**	45	.270	.344	.378	104	3	0-1	—	0	0	0	*D-120	-0.1
1976	Min A	67	123	3	26	3	0	1	16	2-1	2	13	.211	.234	.260	44	-9	0-0	—	0	0	0	D-32	-1.0
Total	15	1676	6301	870	1917	329	48	220	947	448-131	59	645	.304	.353	.476	130	243	86-55	.975	34	110	94	*O-1178(10-39-1139),D-406	20.3

OLIVARES, ED Edward (Balzac) B 11.5.1938 Mayaguez, P.R. BR/TR 5-11/180# d9.16 s-Omar

1960	StL N	3	5	0	0	0	0	0	0	0-0	0	3	.000	.000	.000	-92	-1	0-0	.500	-0	76	0	/3	-0.2
1961	StL N	21	30	2	5	0	0	0	1	0-0	0	4	.167	.161	.167	-10	-5	1-0	1.000	-0	106	0	O-10(5-0-5)	-0.5
Total	2	24	35	2	5	0	0	0	1	0-0	0	7	.143	.139	.143	-21	-6	1-0	1.000	-1	106	0	/O-10(5-0-5),3	-0.7

OLIVER, AL Albert B 10.14.1946 Portsmouth, OH BL/TL 6/195# d9.23

1968	Pit N	4	8	1	1	0	0	0	0	0-0	0	4	.125	.125	.125	-25	-1	0-0	1.000	0	117	0	/O(RF)	-0.2
1969	Pit N	129	463	55	132	19	2	17	70	21-11	13	38	.285	.333	.445	119	10	8-5	.991	-1	82	110	*1-106,O-21(13-0-8)	0.0
1970	†Pit N	151	551	63	149	33	5	12	83	35-8	14	35	.270	.326	.414	100	-1	1-1	.986	-1	96	74	O-80(28-0-54),1-77	-1.1
1971	†Pit N	143	529	69	149	31	7	14	64	27-2	5	72	.282	.317	.446	116	9	4-3	.981	-1	107	61	*O-116(CF),1-25	0.4
1972	†Pit N★	140	565	88	176	27	4	12	89	34-4	5	44	.312	.352	.437	127	19	2-4	.985	-9	96	47	*O-138(CF)/1-3	0.5
1973	Pit N	158	654	90	191	38	7	20	99	22-1	5	52	.292	.316	.463	118	12	6-0	.964	-11	90	72	*O-109(CF),1-50	-0.5
1974	†Pit N	147	617	96	198	38	12	11	85	33-1	5	58	.321	.358	.475	137	27	10-1	.986	-3	107	46	O-98(CF),1-49	2.1
1975	†Pit N★	155	628	90	176	39	8	18	84	25-3	5	73	.280	.309	.454	112	6	4-2	.987	-6	98	52	*O-153(CF)/1-4	-0.4
1976	Pit N★	121	443	62	143	22	5	12	61	26-7	5	29	.323	.363	.476	137	20	6-2	.984	-3	106	58	*O-106(CF)/1-3	1.6
1977	Pit N	154	568	75	175	29	6	19	82	40-9	4	38	.308	.353	.481	119	15	13-16	.981	-1	105	62	*O-148(128-36-0)	0.6
1978	Tex A	133	525	65	170	35	5	14	89	31-6	2	41	.324	.358	.490	138	25	8-9	.987	0	96	112	*O-107(100-8-0),D-26	1.9
1979	Tex A	136	492	69	159	28	4	12	76	34-8	4	34	.323	.367	.470	127	18	4-5	.975	-3	93	114	*O-119(49-71-0),D-10	1.1
1980	Tex A★	**163**	656	96	209	43	3	19	117	39-9	5	47	.319	.357	.480	132	28	5-7	.973	-2	99	80	*O-157(141-0-16)/1D	1.8
1981	Tex A★	102	421	53	130	29	1	4	55	24-10	2	28	.309	.348	.411	125	13	3-0	1.000	-0	0	0	*D-101/1	1.1
1982	Mon N★	160	617	90	**204**	**43**	2	22	**109**	61-15	4	59	**.331**	.392	.514	149	42	5-2	.986	-12	76	87	*1-159	2.2
1983	Mon N★	157	614	70	184	**38**	3	8	84	44-17	2	44	.300	.347	.410	110	9	1-3	.990	-0	101	83	*1-153/O(RF)	-0.2
1984	SF N	91	339	27	101	19	2	0	34	20-4	1	27	.298	.339	.366	101	0	2-2	.985	1	110	75	1-82	-0.4
	Phi N	28	93	9	29	7	0	0	14	7-2	0	9	.312	.360	.387	108	1	1-2	.987	-2	50	65	1-19/O-5(LF)	-0.3
	Year	119	432	36	130	26	2	0	48	27-6	1	36	.301	.343	.370	103	2	3-4	.985	-2	99	73	*1-101/O-5(LF)	-0.7
1985	LA N	35	79	1	20	5	0	0	8	5-0	0	11	.253	.294	.316	74	-3	1-0	.882	-2	52	200	O-17(LF)	-0.5
	†Tor A	61	187	20	47	6	1	5	23	7-2	1	13	.251	.282	.374	76	-7	0-0	1.000	-0	0	0	D-59/1	-0.9
Total	18	2368	9049	1189	2743	529	77	219	1326	535-119	82	756	.303	.344	.451	122	242	84-64	.980	-55	99	72	*O-1376(481-835-80),1-733,D-200	8.8

OLIVER, DAVE David Jacob B 4.7.1951 Stockton, CA BL/TR 5-11/175# d9.25 C10

1977	Cle A	7	22	2	7	0	1	0	3	4-0	1	0	.318	.444	.409	139	1	0-0	.949	0	84	165	/2-7	0.2

OLIVER, GENE Eugene George B 3.22.1935 Moline, IL BR/TR 6-2/225# d6.6

1959	StL N	68	172	14	42	9	0	6	28	7-0	0	41	.244	.271	.401	72	-7	3-2	.955	-1	110	43	O-42(41-0-3)/C-9,1-5	-1.0
1961	StL N	22	52	8	14	2	0	4	9	6-1	2	10	.269	.367	.538	124	2	0-0	1.000	1	*83*	*97*	C-15/O(LF)	0.3
1962	StL N	122	345	42	89	19	1	14	45	50-4	1	59	.258	.352	.441	102	2	5-2	.991	-0	*106*	*106*	C-98/O-8(6-0-2),1-3	0.6
1963	StL N	39	102	10	23	4	0	6	18	13-3	0	19	.225	.308	.441	105	1	0-0	.981	-1	*81*	*88*	C-35	0.1
	Mil N	95	296	34	74	12	2	11	47	27-1	5	59	.250	.320	.416	112	5	4-4	.985	-8	60	106	1-55,O-35(LF)/C-2	-0.8
	Year	134	398	44	97	16	2	17	65	40-4	5	78	.244	.317	.422	110	5	4-4	.985	-9	60	106	1-55,C-37,O-35(LF)	-0.7
1964	Mil N	93	279	45	77	15	1	13	49	17-0	1	41	.276	.319	.477	120	7	3-7	.982	-5	79	97	1-76/C	-0.4
1965	Mil N	122	392	56	106	20	0	21	58	36-5	3	61	.270	.336	.482	127	14	5-4	.976	1	*88*	*147*	C-64,1-52/O(LF)	1.5
1966	Atl N	76	191	19	37	9	1	8	24	16-3	0	43	.194	.255	.377	72	-8	2-0	.990	7	*117*	*107*	C-48/1-5,O-2(LF)	0.2
1967	Atl N	17	51	8	10	2	0	3	6	6-0	0	8	.196	.281	.412	97	0	0-0	.962	-1	*78*	*136*	C-13/1	-0.1
	Phi N	85	263	29	59	16	0	7	34	29-3	1	56	.224	.300	.365	90	-3	2-2	.987	-4	*102*	*68*	C-79/1-2	-0.4
	Year	102	314	37	69	18	0	10	40	35-3	1	64	.220	.297	.373	91	-3	2-2	.983	-5	98	79	C-92/1-3	-0.5
1968	Bos A	16	35	2	5	0	0	0	1	4-1	1	12	.143	.250	.143	20	-3	0-0	.984	-1	51	88	C-10/O(RF)	-0.4
	Chi N	8	11	1	4	0	0	0	1	3-0	0	2	.364	.500	.364	152	1	0-0	1.000	0	0	0	/1-2,CO(LF)	0.1
1969	Chi N	23	27	0	6	3	0	0	0	1-1	1	9	.222	.276	.333	62	-1	0-0	1.000	2	153	0	/C-6	0.1
Total	10	786	2216	268	546	111	5	93	320	215-22	15	420	.246	.315	.427	103	10	24-21	.985	-10	*97*	*104*	C-381,1-201/O-91(87-0-6)	-0.2

OLIVER, JOE Joseph Melton B 7.24.1965 Memphis, TN BR/TR 6-3/210# d7.15

1989	Cin N	49	151	13	41	8	0	3	23	6-1	1	28	.272	.300	.384	92	-2	0-0	.986	4	121	79	C-47	0.4
1990	†Cin N	121	364	34	84	23	0	8	52	37-15	2	75	.231	.304	.360	79	-10	1-1	**.992**	12	150	110	*C-118	0.9
1991	Cin N	94	269	21	58	11	0	11	41	18-5	0	53	.216	.265	.379	76	-10	0-0	.980	-1	92	88	C-90	-0.6
1992	Cin N	143	485	42	131	25	1	10	57	35-19	1	75	.270	.316	.388	97	-2	2-3	.992	7	122	93	*C-141/1	1.3
1993	Cin N	139	482	40	115	28	0	14	75	27-2	1	91	.239	.276	.384	76	-18	0-0	.992	-6	92	117	*C-133,1-12/O(RF)	-1.6
1994	Cin N	6	19	1	4	0	0	1	5	2-1	0	3	.211	.286	.368	70	-1	0-0	.980	1	75	171	/C-6	0.1
1995	Mil A	97	337	43	92	20	0	12	51	27-1	3	66	.273	.332	.439	93	-4	2-4	.982	-6	74	113	C-91/1-2,D-6	-0.4
1996	Cin N	106	289	31	70	12	1	11	46	28-6	2	54	.242	.311	.405	87	-6	2-0	.992	5	107	93	C-97/1-3,O-3(2-0-1)	0.4
1997	Cin N	111	349	28	90	13	0	14	43	25-1	5	58	.258	.313	.415	89	-7	1-3	.990	-3	108	92	*C-106/1-4	-0.4
1998	Det A	50	155	8	35	8	0	4	22	7-0	0	33	.226	.253	.355	57	-10	0-1	.982	-2	128	101	C-48/1-2	-0.9
	Sea A	29	85	12	19	3	0	2	10	10-0	0	15	.224	.305	.329	65	-4	1-0	.984	-5	85	84	C-29	-0.7
	Year	79	240	20	54	11	0	6	32	17-0	0	48	.225	.272	.346	60	-15	1-1	.983	-6	112	95	C-77/1-2	-1.6
1999	Pit N	45	134	10	27	8	0	1	13	10-0	0	33	.201	.253	.284	37	-13	2-0	.993	-0	113	48	C-44	-1.0
2000	†Sea A	69	200	33	53	13	1	10	35	14-1	0	38	.265	.313	.490	102	0	2-1	.995	-3	98	71	C-66/1D	0.1
2001	NY A	12	36	3	9	1	0	1	2	1-0	0	12	.250	.263	.361	64	-2	0-0	.991	1	65	61	C-12	0.0
	Bos A	5	12	1	3	1	0	0	1	1-0	0	3	.250	.308	.333	68	-1	0-0	.971	-2	60	69	/C-5	-0.2
	Year	17	48	4	12	2	0	1	3	2-0	0	15	.250	.275	.354	65	-3	0-0	.986	-1	64	63	C-17	-0.2
Total	13	1076	3367	320	831	174	3	102	476	248-52	15	637	.247	.299	.391	83	-90	13-13	.989	2	108	96	*C-1033/1-25,D-7,O-4(2-0-2)	-2.6

OLIVER, NATE Nathaniel "Peewee" B 12.13.1940 St.Petersburg, FL BR/TR 5-10/160# d4.9

1963	LA N	65	163	23	39	2	3	1	9	13-0	1	25	.239	.298	.307	80	-5	3-4	.961	2	98	106	2-57/S-2	0.0
1964	LA N	99	321	28	78	9	0	0	21	31-6	0	57	.243	.309	.271	70	-12	7-4	.967	-12	93	82	2-98/S	-1.6
1965	LA N	8	1	3	1	0	0	0	0	0-0	0	0	1.000	1.000	1.000	498	1	1-0	1.000	0	109	0	/2-2	0.1
1966	†LA N	80	119	17	23	2	0	0	3	13-2	1	17	.193	.276	.210	41	-9	3-3	.977	6	109	100	2-68/S-2,3	0.0
1967	LA N	77	232	18	55	6	2	0	7	13-0	2	50	.237	.283	.280	67	-10	3-2	.973	-6	93	74	2-39,S-32/O(LF)	-1.3
1968	SF N	36	73	3	13	2	0	0	1	1-0	0	13	.178	.189	.205	18	-7	0-1	.950	-1	126	162	2-14,S-13/3	-0.8
1969	NY A	1	1	0	0	0	0	0	0	0-0	0	0	.000	.000	.000	-99	0	0-0	—	0			H	0.0
	Chi N	44	44	15	7	3	0	1	4	1-0	1	10	.159	.196	.295	32	-4	0-1	1.000	1	105	140	2-13	-0.3
Total	7	410	954	107	216	24	5	2	45	72-8	5	172	.226	.283	.268	62	-46	17-15	.969	-9	99	95	2-291/S-50,3-2,O(LF)	-3.9

OLIVER, BOB Robert Lee B 2.8.1943 Shreveport, LA BR/TR 6-2/215# d9.10 s-Darren OF Total (15-LF 48-CF 165-RF)

1965	Pit N	3	2	1	0	0	0	0	0	0-0	0	0	.000	.000	.000	-99	-1	0-0	1.000	0	152	0	/O-3(LF)	0.0
1969	KC A	118	394	43	100	8	4	13	43	21-2	2	74	.254	.294	.393	91	-8	5-5	.977	4	107	170	O-98(9-48-45),1-12/3-8	-0.9
1970	KC A	160	612	83	159	24	6	27	99	42-4	3	126	.260	.309	.451	108	3	3-3	.993	-8	85	105	*1-115,3-46	-1.5
1971	KC A	128	373	35	91	12	2	8	52	14-3	5	88	.244	.277	.351	79	-12	0-0	.988	1	96	129	1-68,O-48(1-0-47)/3-2	-1.9
1972	KC A	16	63	7	17	2	1	1	6	2-0	0	12	.270	.292	.381	100	0	1-0	.979	2	141	83	O-16(RF)	0.1
	Cal A	134	509	47	137	20	4	19	70	27-8	3	97	.269	.307	.436	127	13	4-3	.994	-6	74	88	*1-127/O-8(1-0-7)	-0.4
	Year	150	572	54	154	22	5	20	76	29-8	3	109	.269	.305	.430	124	13	5-3	.994	-4	74	88	*1-127,O-24(1-0-23)	-0.3
1973	Cal A	151	544	51	144	24	1	18	89	33-7	5	100	.265	.311	.412	111	6	1-1	.952	0	99	53	3-49,O-47(RF),1-32,D-12	0.0
1974	Cal A	110	359	22	89	9	1	8	55	16-2	1	51	.248	.277	.345	84	-9	2-1	.985	-12	66	96	1-57,3-46/O-4(1-0-3),D	-2.6

Year	Tm Lg	G	AB	R	H	2B	3B	HR	RBI	BB-IB	HP	SO	AVG	OBP	SLG	AOPS	ABR	SB-CS	FA	FR	Rng	Thr	G at Pos	BFW
	Bal A	9	20	1	3	2	0	0	4	0-0	0	5	.150	.150	.250	14	-2	1-1	.974	1	258	33	/1-4,D	-0.2
	Year	119	379	23	92	11	1	8	59	16-2	1	56	.243	.271	.340	81	-11	3-2	.984	-11	80	91	1-61,3-46/O-4(1-0-3),D-2	-2.8
1975	NY A	18	38	3	5	1	0	0	1	1-0	0	9	.132	.154	.158	-12	-6	0-0	1.000	-1	59	228	/1-8,3D	-0.7
Total	8	847	2914	293	745	102	19	94	419	156-26	19	562	.256	.295	.400	100	-16	17-14	.991	-19	81	99	1-423,O-224R,3-152/D-17	-8.1
OLIVER, TOM Thomas Noble "Rebel" B 1.15.1903 Montgomery, AL D 2.26.1988 Montgomery, AL BR/TR 6/168# d4.14 C4																								
1930	Bos A	**154**	646	86	189	34	2	0	46	42	3	25	.293	.339	.351	78	-20	6-6	.982	6	107	75	*O-154(CF)	-2.0
1931	Bos A	148	586	52	162	35	5	0	70	25	1	17	.276	.307	.353	77	-21	4-6	**.993**	6	102	122	*O-148(CF)	-1.9
1932	Bos A	122	455	39	120	23	3	0	37	25	2	12	.264	.305	.327	66	-24	1-6	.983	3	101	121	*O-116(CF)	-2.4
1933	Bos A	90	244	25	63	9	1	0	23	13	0	7	.258	.296	.303	60	-15	1-1	.985	8	113	196	O-86(CF)	-0.8
Total	4	514	1931	202	534	101	11	0	176	105	6	61	.277	.316	.340	73	-80	12-19	.986	22	105	117	O-504(CF)	-7.1
OLIVO, MIGUEL Miguel Eduardo (Pena) B 7.15.1978 Villa Vasquez, D.R. BR/TR 6-1/215# d9.15																								
2002	Chi A	6	19	2	4	1	0	1	5	2-0	0	5	.211	.286	.421	83	-1	0-0	1.000	-1	299	71	/C-6	-0.1
2003	Chi A	114	317	37	75	19	1	6	27	19-0	4	80	.237	.287	.360	69	-15	6-4	.988	15	158	82	*C-113	0.6
Total	2	120	336	39	79	20	1	7	32	21-0	4	85	.235	.287	.363	70	-16	6-4	.988	14	166	81	C-119	0.5
OLMEDO, REY Rainer Gustavo B 5.31.1981 Maracay, Venezuela BB/TR 5-11/150# d5.25																								
2003	Cin N	79	230	24	55	6	1	0	17	13-0	0	46	.239	.280	.274	46	-19	1-1	.929	-10	97	71	S-51,2-18	-2.5
OLMO, LUIS Luis Francisco (Rodriguez) (born Luis Francisco Rodriquez (Olmo)) B 8.11.1919 Arecibo, P.R. BR/TR 5-11.5/190# d7.23																								
1943	Bro N	57	238	39	72	6	4	4	37	8	0	20	.303	.325	.412	112	2	3	.957	-1	96	122	O-57(1-54-2)	-0.1
1944	Bro N	136	520	65	134	20	5	9	85	17	2	37	.258	.284	.367	84	-14	10	.971	-13	119	91	O-64(3-61-1),2-42,3-31	-2.8
1945	Bro N	141	556	62	174	27	**13**	10	110	36	1	33	.313	.356	.462	127	17	15	.971	-8	98	105	*O-106(100-6-0),3-31/2	0.4
1949	†Bro N	38	105	15	32	4	1	1	14	5	0	11	.305	.336	.390	91	-2	2	.950	-1	91	157	O-34(17-16-1)	-0.3
1950	Bos N	69	154	23	35	7	1	5	22	18	0	23	.227	.308	.383	86	-4	3	.974	-2	99	37	O-55(18-11-24)/3	-0.7
1951	Bos N	21	56	4	11	1	1	0	4	4	0	4	.196	.250	.250	38	-5	0-1	1.000	-0	83	187	O-16(10-6-2)	-0.6
Total	6	462	1629	208	458	65	25	29	272	88	3	128	.281	.319	.405	102	-6	33-1	.968	-25	101	105	O-332(149-154-30)/3-63,2-43	-4.1
OLSEN, BARNEY Bernard Charles B 9.11.1919 Everett, MA D 3.30.1977 Everett, MA BR/TR 5-11/179# d8.23																								
1941	Chi N	24	73	13	21	6	1	1	4	4	0	11	.288	.325	.438	118	1	0	.947	1	103	188	O-23(CF)	0.2
OLSON, GREG Gregory William B 9.6.1960 Marshall, MN BR/TR 6/200# d6.27																								
1989	Min A	3	2	0	1	0	0	0	0	0-0	0	0	.500	.500	.500	171	0	0-0	1.000	-0	39	0	/C-3	0.0
1990	Atl N★	100	298	36	78	12	1	7	36	30-4	2	51	.262	.332	.379	90	-4	1-1	.987	-4	102	76	C-97/3	-0.3
1991	†Atl N	133	411	46	99	25	0	6	44	44-3	3	48	.241	.316	.345	82	-9	1-1	.995	1	99	80	*C-127	-0.1
1992	Atl N	95	302	27	72	14	2	3	27	34-4	1	31	.238	.316	.328	78	-8	2-1	.998	5	96	**140**	C-94	0.2
1993	†Atl N	83	262	23	59	10	0	4	24	29-0	1	27	.225	.304	.309	64	-13	1-0	.988	-3	97	91	C-81	-1.1
Total	5	414	1275	132	309	61	3	20	131	137-11	7	157	.242	.317	.342	79	-34	5-3	.992	-2	98	96	C-402/3	-1.3
OLSON, IVY Ivan Massie B 10.14.1885 Kansas City, MO D 9.1.1965 Inglewood, CA BR/TR 5-10.5/175# d4.12 C4 OF Total (8-LF 2-RF)																								
1911	Cle A	140	545	89	142	20	8	1	50	34	6		.261	.311	.332	79	-17	20	.909	-16	95	98	*S-139/3	-2.3
1912	Cle A	125	467	68	118	13	1	0	33	21	4		.253	.291	.285	63	-23	16	.917	2	101	52	S-56,3-36,2-21/O-3(LF)	-1.6
1913	Cle A	104	370	47	92	13	3	0	32	22	3	28	.249	.296	.300	72	-14	7	.953	2	102	69	3-73,1-21/2	-1.1
1914	Cle A	89	310	22	75	6	2	1	20	13	1	24	.242	.275	.284	65	-14	15-9	.942	7	104	114	S-31,2-23,3-19/O-6(5-0-1),1-3	-0.5
1915	Cin N	63	207	18	48	5	4	0	14	12	0	13	.232	.274	.295	71	-8	10-6	.938	7	112	106	2-39,3-15/1-7	0.0
	Bro N	18	26	2	2	0	1	0	3	1	0	0	.077	.111	.154	-20	-4	0	.909	-2	80	85	/S-7,23O(RF)	-0.6
	Year	81	233	20	50	5	5	0	17	13	0	13	.215	.256	.279	61	-12	10-6	.938	5	111	105	2-40,3-16/1-7,S-7,O(RF)	-0.6
1916	†Bro N	108	351	29	89	13	4	1	38	21	1	27	.254	.298	.322	88	-5	14	.920	-14	91	70	*S-103/2-3,1	-1.4
1917	Bro N	139	580	64	156	18	5	2	38	14	4	34	.269	.291	.328	87	-10	6	.941	-6	97	89	*S-133/3-6	-0.8
1918	Bro N	**126**	506	63	121	16	4	1	17	27	6	18	.239	.286	.292	77	-14	21	.918	-23	88	81	*S-126	-3.2
1919	Bro N	140	590	73	**164**	14	9	1	38	30	3	12	.278	.316	.337	94	-5	26	.947	-4	92	95	*S-140	0.2
1920	†Bro N	143	637	71	162	13	11	1	46	20	1	19	.254	.278	.314	68	-29	4-7	.935	-9	93	87	*S-125,2-21	-3.3
1921	Bro N	151	652	88	174	22	10	3	35	28	4	26	.267	.301	.345	68	-31	4-9	.943	7	100	97	*S-133,2-20	-1.1
1922	Bro N	136	551	63	150	26	6	1	47	25	2	10	.272	.306	.347	69	-27	8-5	.960	-4	101	88	2-85,S-51	-2.1
1923	Bro N	82	292	33	76	11	1	1	35	14	1	10	.260	.296	.315	63	-16	5-0	.974	6	104	85	2-72/3-4,1-2,S-2	-0.7
1924	Bro N	10	27	0	6	1	0	0	0	3	0	1	.222	.300	.259	53	-2	0-0	.941	-1	76	148	/S-8,2-2	-0.2
Total	14	1574	6111	730	1575	191	69	13	446	285	36	222	.258	.295	.318	74	-219	156-36	.932	-48	94	90	*S-1054,2-288,3-155/1-34,O-10L	-18.7
OLSON, KARL Karl Arthur "Ole" B 7.6.1930 Kentfield, CA BR/TR 6-3/205# d6.30 Mil 1952																								
1951	Bos A	5	10	0	1	0	0	0	0	0	0	3	.100	.100	.100	-42	-2	0-0	1.000	0	122	0	/O-5(2-0-3)	-0.2
1953	Bos A	25	57	5	7	2	0	1	6	1	0	9	.123	.138	.211	-7	-9	0-0	.970	0	103	93	O-24(23-2-0)	-1.0
1954	Bos A	101	227	25	59	12	2	1	20	12	0	23	.260	.293	.344	68	-10	2-1	.957	2	93	225	O-78(29-36-16)	-1.1
1955	Bos A	26	48	7	12	1	2	0	1	1-0	0	10	.250	.265	.354	60	-3	0-0	1.000	0	101	113	O-21(11-8-5)	-0.3
1956	Was A	106	313	34	77	10	2	4	22	28-1	1	41	.246	.305	.329	69	-15	1-1	.990	-4	94	71	*O-101(16-84-3)	-2.3
1957	Was A	8	12	2	2	0	0	0	0	1-0	0	2	.167	.231	.167	10	-2	0-0	1.000	0	124	0	/O-6(2-4-0)	-0.2
	Det A	8	14	1	2	0	0	0	1	0-0	0	6	.143	.143	.143	-21	-2	0-0	1.000	-0	98	0	/O-5(4-1-0)	-0.3
	Year	16	26	3	4	0	0	0	1	1-0	0	8	.154	.185	.154	-6	-4	0-0	1.000	0	112	0	O-11(6-5-0)	-0.5
Total	6	279	681	74	160	25	6	6	50	43-1	1	94	.235	.278	.316	57	-43	3-2	.979	-1	96	121	O-240(87-135-27)	-5.4
OLSON, MARV Marvin Clement "Sparky" B 5.28.1907 Gayville, SD D 2.5.1998 Tyndall, SD BR/TR 5-7/160# d9.13																								
1931	Bos A	15	53	8	10	1	0	0	5	9	0	3	.189	.306	.208	40	-4	0-0	.963	1	103	87	2-15	-0.3
1932	Bos A	115	403	58	100	14	6	0	25	61	0	26	.248	.347	.313	74	-14	1-5	.955	-10	96	94	*2-106/3	-1.8
1933	Bos A	3	1	1	0	0	0	0	0	0	0	1	.000	.000	.000	-99	0	0-0	—	-0	0	0	/2	0.0
Total	3	133	457	67	110	15	6	0	30	70	0	30	.241	.342	.300	70	-18	1-5	.956	-10	97	93	2-122/3	-2.1
O'MALLEY, TOM Thomas Patrick B 12.25.1960 Orange, NJ BL/TR 6/190# d5.8																								
1982	SF N	92	291	26	80	12	4	2	27	33-9	1	39	.275	.350	.364	100	1	0-3	.965	-1	100	70	3-83/2S	-0.2
1983	SF N	135	410	40	106	16	1	5	45	52-4	4	47	.259	.345	.339	94	-2	2-4	.940	-2	101	67	*3-117	-0.7
1984	SF N	13	25	2	3	0	0	0	0	2-0	0	2	.120	.185	.120	-13	-4	0-0	1.000	-1	77	105	/3-7	-0.5
	Chi A	12	16	0	2	0	0	0	3	0-0	0	5	.125	.125	.125	-29	-3	0-0	1.000	-1	22	0	/3-6	-0.4
1985	Bal A	8	14	1	1	0	0	1	2	0-0	0	2	.071	.071	.286	-8	-2	0-0	.833	-1	56	0	/3-3	-0.4
1986	Bal A	56	181	19	46	9	0	1	18	17-1	0	21	.254	.317	.320	76	-6	0-1	.938	2	105	95	3-55	-0.5
1987	Tex A	45	117	10	32	8	0	1	12	15-1	0	9	.274	.351	.368	92	-1	0-0	.962	-1	97	47	3-40/2	-0.2
1988	Mon N	14	27	3	7	0	0	0	2	3-1	0	4	.259	.323	.259	69	-1	0-0	.905	1	130	0	/3-7	0.0
1989	NY N	9	11	2	6	2	0	0	8	0-0	0	2	.545	.545	.727	274	2	0-0	1.000	-0	40	0	/3-3	0.2
1990	NY N	82	121	14	27	7	0	3	14	11-1	0	20	.223	.286	.355	76	-4	0-0	.983	-0	76	134	3-38/1-3	-0.4
Total	9	466	1213	117	310	54	5	13	131	133-17	5	151	.256	.329	.340	87	-20	2-8	.951	-5	98	73	3-359/1-3,2-2,S	-3.1
O'MARA, OLLIE Oliver Edward B 3.8.1891 St.Louis, MO D 10.24.1989 Reno, NV BR/TR 5-9/155# d9.8																								
1912	Det A	1	4	0	0	0	0	0	0	0	0		.000	.000	.000	-99	-1	0	.857	0	127	0	/S	-0.1
1914	Bro N	67	247	41	65	10	2	1	7	16	3	26	.263	.316	.332	91	-3	14	.918	-10	94	76	S-63	-0.9
1915	Bro N	149	577	77	141	26	3	0	31	51	2	40	.244	.308	.300	83	-11	11-12	.906	-36	91	69	*S-149	-4.3
1916	†Bro N	72	193	18	39	5	2	0	15	12	0	20	.202	.249	.249	52	-11	10	.898	-7	89	149	S-51	-1.6
1918	Bro N	121	450	29	96	8	1	1	24	7	10	18	.213	.242	.242	48	-29	11	.951	-1	100	76	*3-121	-2.9
1919	Bro N	2	7	1	0	0	0	0	0	0	0	0	.000	.000	.000	-98	-2	0	.875	-1	62	0	/3-2	-0.3
Total	6	412	1478	166	341	49	8	2	77	86	15	104	.231	.280	.279	69	-57	46-12	.907	-53	91	86	S-264,3-123	-10.1
O'MEARA, ED Thomas Edward B 12.12.1872 Chicago, IL D 2.16.1902 Fort Wayne, IN BR d9.29																								
1895	Cle N	1	1	1	0	0	0	0	0	1	0	0	.000	.500	.000	34	0	0	.500	-0	*86*	*200*	/C	0.0
1896	Cle N	12	33	5	5	0	0	0	0	5	0	7	.152	.263	.152	10	-4	0	.914	-0	*144*	*75*	/C-9,1	-0.3
Total	2	13	34	6	5	0	0	0	0	6	0	7	.147	.275	.147	12	-4	0	.892	-0	*141*	*82*	/C-10,1	-0.3
O'NEAL d10.23																								
1874	Har NA	1	3	0	0	0	0	0	0	0		1	.000	.000	.000	-95	-1	0-0	.667	1	1254	0	/O(RF)	0.0
O'NEIL, DENNY Dennis B 11.22.1866 Holyoke, MA D 11.15.1922 Rushville, IN BL/TL 6-2.5/200# d6.18																								
1893	StL N	7	25	3	3	0	0	0	2	4	0	0	.120	.241	.120	-3	-4	3	.986	-1	0	75	/1-7	-0.4

Year	Tm Lg	G	AB	R	H	2B	3B	HR	RBI	BB-IB	HP	SO	AVG	OBP	SLG	AOPS	ABR	SB-CS	FA	FR	Rng	Thr	G at Pos	BFW
O'NEIL, MICKEY George Michael B 4.12.1900 St.Louis, MO D 4.8.1964 St.Louis, MO BR/TR 5-10/185# d9.12 C1																								
1919	Bos N	11	28	3	6	0	0	0	1	1	0	7	.214	.241	.214	39	-2	0	.981	2	107	144	C-11	0.1
1920	Bos N	112	304	19	86	5	4	0	28	21	5	20	.283	.339	.326	96	-2	4-4	.962	7	112	**135**	*C-105/2	1.4
1921	Bos N	98	277	26	69	9	4	2	29	23	0	21	.249	.307	.332	73	-11	2-2	.968	4	114	**138**	C-95	-0.1
1922	Bos N	83	251	18	56	5	2	0	26	14	1	11	.223	.267	.259	38	-24	1-0	.978	-0	101	126	C-79	-1.8
1923	Bos N	96	306	29	65	7	4	0	20	17	2	14	.212	.258	.261	39	-28	3-2	.973	6	92	**137**	C-95	-1.5
1924	Bos N	106	362	32	89	4	1	0	22	14	1	27	.246	.276	.262	47	-28	4-3	.985	-2	81	110	*C-106	-2.3
1925	Bos N	70	222	29	57	6	5	2	30	21	2	16	.257	.327	.356	81	-7	1-2	.972	-6	109	59	C-69	-0.8
1926	Bro N	75	201	19	42	5	3	0	20	23	1	8	.209	.293	.264	52	-14	3	.965	-3	76	113	C-74	-1.2
1927	Was A	5	6	0	0	0	0	0	0	0	0	1	.000	.000	.000	-99	-2	0-0	1.000	-0	75	0	/C-4	-0.2
	NY N	16	38	2	5	0	0	0	3	5	0	2	.132	.233	.132	-0	-5	0	.969	2	114	138	C-16	-0.3
Total	9	672	1995	177	475	41	23	4	179	139	12	127	.238	.292	.288	58	-123	18-13	.972	11	98	120	C-654/2	-6.7
O'NEIL, JOHN John Francis B 4.19.1920 Shelbiana, KY BR/TR 5-9/155# d4.16																								
1946	Phi N	46	94	12	25	3	0	0	9	5	0	12	.266	.303	.298	73	-4	0	.940	0	100	97	S-32	-0.2
O'NEILL, FRED Frederick James "Tip" B 1865 London, ON, CAN D 3.7.1892 London, ON, CAN 5-7/142# d5.3																								
1887	NY AA	6	26	4	8	1	1	0	3	1	1		.308	.357	.423	123	1	3	.800	-1	142	0	/O-6(0-1-5)	0.0
O'NEILL, HARRY Harry Mink B 5.8.1917 Philadelphia, PA D 3.6.1945 Iwo Jima, Marianas Islands BR/TR 6-3/205# d7.23																								
1939	Phi A	1	0	0	0	0	0	0	0	0	0	0	—	—	—	—	0	0-0	—	0	0	0	/C	0.0
O'NEILL, TIP James Edward B 5.25.1858 Woodstock, ON, CAN D 12.31.1915 Montreal, PQ, CAN BR/TR 6-1.5/167# d5.5 ▲																								
1883	NY N	23	76	8	15	3	0	0	5	3		15	.197	.228	.237	42	-5		.917	-2	79	0	P-19/O-7(0-1-6)	-0.2
1884	StL AA	78	297	49	82	13	11	3	54	12	2		.276	.309	.424	132	9		.811	-5	51	59	O-64(59-5-0),P-17/1	0.0
1885	†StL AA	52	206	44	72	7	4	3	38	13	4		.350	.399	.466	165	15		.881	-2	66	67	O-52(LF)	1.1
1886	†StL AA	138	579	106	190	28	14	3	**107**	47	7		.328	.385	.440	151	33	9	.927	8	61	107	*O-138(LF)	3.2
1887	†StL AA	124	517	**167**	**225**	**52**	**19**	**14**	**123**	50	5		**.435**	**.490**	**.691**	**205**	**71**	30	.895	-7	39	49	*O-124(LF)	**4.8**
1888	†StL AA	130	529	96	**177**	24	10	5	98	44	4		**.335**	.390	.446	151	28	26	.937	-1	37	26	*O-130(LF)	2.2
1889	StL AA	134	534	123	179	33	8	9	110	72	5	37	.335	.419	.478	137	25	28	.936	-4	46	57	*O-134(LF)	1.5
1890	Chi P	137	577	112	174	20	16	3	75	65	5	36	.302	.377	.407	105	3	29	.926	-13	31	21	*O-137(LF)	-1.0
1891	StL AA	127	514	111	166	28	4	10	95	61	9	33	.323	.404	.451	126	16	25	.935	-12	23	0	*O-127(LF)	0.1
1892	Cin N	109	419	63	105	14	6	2	52	53	3	25	.251	.339	.327	103	3	14	.922	-4	72	81	*O-109(LF)	-1.0
Total	10	1052	4248	879	1385	222	92	52	757	420	44	146	.326	.392	.458	140	198	161	.917	-41	46	50	*O-1022(1010-6-6)/P-36,1	10.7
O'NEILL, JIM James Leo B 2.23.1893 Minooka, PA D 9.5.1976 Chambersburg, PA BR/TR 5-10.5/165# d4.15 b-Jack b-Mike b-Steve																								
1920	Was A	86	294	27	85	17	7	1	40	13	2	30	.289	.324	.405	95	-4	7-3	.943	-9	100	68	S-80/2-2	-0.6
1923	Was A	23	33	6	9	1	0	0	3	1	0	3	.273	.294	.303	60	-2	0-0	.946	2	110	115	/2-8,3-4,SO(RF)	0.0
Total	2	109	327	33	94	18	7	1	43	14	2	33	.287	.321	.394	91	-6	7-3	.943	-7	100	68	/S-81,2-10,3-4,O(RF)	-0.6
O'NEILL, JOHN John J. B New York, NY TR d9.6																								
1899	NY N	2	7	0	0	0	0	0	0	0	0		.000	.000	.000	-99	-2	0	.929	0	79	159	/C-2	-0.1
1902	NY N	2	8	0	0	0	0	0	0	0	0		.000	.000	.000	-99	-2	0	.933	0	128	145	/C-2	-0.2
Total	2	4	15	0	0	0	0	0	0	0	0		.000	.000	.000	-99	-4	0	.931	0	104	152	/C-4	-0.3
O'NEILL, JACK John Joseph B 1.10.1873 Maam, Ireland D 6.29.1935 Minooka, PA BR/TR 5-10/165# d4.21 b-Jim b-Mike b-Steve																								
1902	StL N	63	192	13	27	1	1	0	12	13	5		.141	.214	.156	15	-19	2	.973	-2	93	104	C-59	-1.6
1903	StL N	75	246	23	58	9	1	0	27	13	5		.236	.288	.280	64	-11	11	.972	9	95	110	C-74	0.4
1904	Chi N	51	168	8	36	5	0	1	19	6	4		.214	.258	.262	61	-8	1	.981	5	127	96	C-49	0.2
1905	Chi N	53	172	16	34	4	2	0	12	8	11		.198	.277	.244	54	-10	6	.974	7	120	90	C-50	0.3
1906	Bos N	61	167	14	30	5	1	0	4	12	2		.180	.243	.222	46	-11	0	.971	4	92	108	C-48/1-2,O(RF)	-0.2
Total	5	303	945	74	185	24	5	1	74	52	27		.196	.258	.235	49	-59	20	.974	23	104	102	C-280/1-2,O(RF)	-0.9
O'NEILL, PAUL Paul Andrew B 2.25.1963 Columbus, OH BL/TL 6-4/215# d9.3																								
1985	Cin N	5	12	1	4	1	0	0	1	0-0	0	2	.333	.333	.417	103	0	0-0	1.000	1	89	767	/O-2(LF)	0.1
1986	Cin N	3	2	0	0	0	0	0	0	1-0	0	1	.000	.333	.000	-0	0	0-0	—	0			/H	0.0
1987	Cin N	84	160	24	41	14	1	7	28	18-1	0	29	.256	.331	.488	109	2	2-1	.949	0	112	93	O-42(14-10-22)/1-2,P	0.1
1988	Cin N	145	485	58	122	25	3	16	73	38-5	2	65	.252	.306	.414	102	0	8-6	.984	1	103	90	*O-118(0-8-114),1-21	-0.4
1989	Cin N	117	428	49	118	24	2	15	74	46-8	2	64	.276	.346	.446	122	12	20-5	.983	-0	97	111	*O-115(0-4-115)	1.2
1990	†Cin N	145	503	59	136	28	0	16	78	53-13	2	103	.270	.339	.421	104	4	13-11	.993	3	99	128	*O-141(0-1-141)	0.2
1991	Cin N★	152	532	71	136	36	0	28	91	73-14	1	107	.256	.346	.481	126	19	12-7	.994	9	108	123	*O-150(RF)	2.4
1992	Cin N	148	496	59	122	19	1	14	66	77-15	2	85	.246	.346	.373	102	4	6-3	**.997**	9	108	131	*O-143(RF)	0.9
1993	NY A	141	498	71	155	34	1	20	75	44-5	2	69	.311	.367	.504	137	25	2-4	.992	-8	86	78	*O-138(46-0-103)/D-2	1.0
1994	NY A★	103	368	68	132	25	1	21	83	72-13	0	56	**.359**	.460	.603	179	48	5-4	.995	1	100	96	O-99(12-0-90)/D-4	4.0
1995	†NY A★	127	460	82	138	30	4	22	96	71-8	1	76	.300	.387	.526	138	28	1-2	.987	-5	96	38	*O-121(25-0-107)/D-4	1.5
1996	†NY A	150	546	89	165	35	1	19	91	102-8	4	76	.302	.411	.474	124	26	0-1	**1.000**	3	104	72	*O-146(RF)/1D	1.9
1997	†NY A★	149	553	89	179	42	0	21	117	75-8	0	92	.324	.399	.514	139	35	10-7	.984	-1	98	76	*O-146(RF)/1-2,D-2	2.4
1998	†NY A★	152	602	95	191	40	2	24	116	57-2	2	103	.317	.372	.510	133	30	15-1	.987	1	99	102	*O-150(RF)/D	2.4
1999	†NY A	153	597	70	170	39	4	19	110	66-1	2	89	.285	.353	.459	108	7	11-9	.974	1	102	99	*O-151(RF)	0.0
2000	†NY A	142	566	79	160	26	0	18	100	51-2	0	90	.283	.336	.424	93	-6	14-9	.993	4	112	56	*O-140(RF)/D-2	-0.8
2001	†NY A	137	510	77	136	33	1	21	70	48-4	2	59	.267	.330	.459	104	3	22-3	.981	-10	91	13	*O-130(RF)/D-6	-0.9
Total	17	2053	7318	1041	2105	451	21	281	1269	892-107	22	1166	.288	.363	.470	121	237	141-73	.988	9	101	88	*O-1932(99-23-1848)/1-26,D-24,P	16.0
O'NEILL, PEACHES Philip Bernard B 8.30.1879 Anderson, IN D 8.2.1955 Anderson, IN BR/TR 5-11/165# d4.16																								
1904	Cin N	8	15	0	4	0	0	0	1	1	0		.267	.313	.267	73	0	0	.900	-2	73	64	/C-5,1	-0.3
O'NEILL, STEVE Stephen Francis B 7.6.1891 Minooka, PA D 1.26.1962 Cleveland, OH BR/TR 5-10/165# d9.18 M14 C4 b-Jim b-Jack b-Mike																								
1911	Cle A	9	27	1	4	1	0	0	1	4	1		.148	.281	.185	31	-2	2	.986	2	100	123	/C-9	0.0
1912	Cle A	69	215	17	49	4	0	0	14	12	1		.228	.272	.247	47	-15	2	.961	7	97	108	C-68	-0.3
1913	Cle A	80	234	19	69	13	3	0	29	10	2	24	.295	.329	.376	103	0	5	.973	9	119	100	C-80	1.6
1914	Cle A	87	269	28	68	12	2	0	20	15	0	35	.253	.292	.312	79	-8	1-3	.956	-2	88	**113**	C-82/1	-0.4
1915	Cle A	121	386	32	91	14	2	2	34	26	5	41	.236	.293	.298	75	-13	2-3	.968	9	107	103	*C-115	0.6
1916	Cle A	130	378	30	89	23	0	0	29	24	4	33	.235	.288	.296	71	-13	2	.971	6	110	88	*C-128	0.4
1917	Cle A	129	370	21	68	10	2	0	29	41	4	55	.184	.272	.222	47	-22	2	.980	5	105	103	*C-127	-0.8
1918	Cle A	114	359	34	87	8	7	1	35	48	7	22	.242	.343	.312	89	-3	5	**.983**	9	123	104	*C-113	1.7
1919	Cle A	125	398	46	115	35	7	2	47	48	5	21	.289	.373	.427	117	11	4	.977	0	**139**	84	*C-123	2.2
1920	†Cle A	149	489	63	157	39	5	3	55	69	3	39	.321	.408	.440	121	19	3-5	.976	2	114	79	*C-148	3.1
1921	Cle A	106	335	39	108	22	1	1	50	57	2	22	.322	.424	.403	110	9	0-1	.982	4	93	68	*C-105	1.9
1922	Cle A	133	392	33	122	27	4	2	65	73	3	25	.311	.423	.416	118	16	2-2	.974	-15	81	75	*C-130	0.8
1923	Cle A	113	330	31	82	12	0	0	50	64	2	34	.248	.374	.285	75	-8	0-4	.968	-6	118	56	*C-111	-0.9
1924	Bos A	106	307	29	73	15	1	0	38	63	2	23	.238	.371	.293	73	-9	0-2	.970	-1	99	98	C-92	-0.4
1925	NY A	35	91	7	26	5	0	1	13	10	1	3	.286	.363	.374	89	-1	0-0	.946	1	101	108	C-31	0.2
1927	StL A	74	191	14	44	7	0	1	22	20	0	6	.230	.303	.283	51	-14	0-3	.983	1	106	149	C-60	-1.0
1928	StL A	10	24	4	7	1	0	0	6	8	1	0	.292	.485	.333	115	1	0-0	.958	-3	67	67	C-10	-0.1
Total	17	1590	4795	448	1259	248	34	13	537	592	43	383	.263	.349	.337	88	-52	30-23	.972	28	108	92	*C-1532/1	8.6
O'NEILL, BILL William John B 1.22.1880 St.John, NB, CAN D 7.20.1920 Woodhaven, NY BB/TR 5-11/175# d5.7																								
1904	Bos A	17	51	7	10	1	0	0	5	2	0		.196	.226	.216	38	-4	0	.933	-3	0	0	/O-9(8-1-0),S-2	-0.7
	Was A	95	365	33	89	10	1	1	16	22	4		.244	.294	.285	85	-6	22	.893	-9	98	36	O-93(14-79-0)/2-3	-2.2
	Year	112	416	40	99	11	1	1	21	24	4		.238	.286	.276	79	-10	22	.896	-12	90	33	*O-102(22-80-0)/2-3,S-2	-2.9
1906	†Chi A	94	330	37	82	4	1	1	21	22	3		.248	.301	.276	83	-6	19	.949	-2	112	49	O-93(0-7-87)	-1.4
Total	2	206	746	77	181	15	2	2	42	46	7		.243	.293	.276	81	-16	41	.919	-14	100	41	O-195(22-87-87)/2-3,S-2	-4.3
ONIS, RALPH Manuel Dominguez "Curly" B 10.24.1908 Tampa, FL D 1.4.1995 Tampa, FL BR/TR 5-9/180# d4.27																								
1935	Bro N	1	1	0	1	0	0	0	0	0	0	0	1.000	1.000	1.000	449	0	0	.500	-0	0	0	/C	0.0

Year	Tm Lg	G	AB	R	H	2B	3B	HR	RBI	BB-IB	HP	SO	AVG	OBP	SLG	AOPS	ABR	SB-CS	FA	FR	Rng	Thr	G at Pos	BFW
ONSLOW, EDDIE Edward Joseph B 2.17.1893 Meadville, PA D 5.8.1981 Dennison, OH BL/TL 6/170# d8.7 b-Jack																								
1912	Det A	36	128	11	29	1	2	1	13	3	1		.227	.250	.289	56	-8	3	.972	-4	75	108	1-35	-1.3
1913	Det A	17	55	7	14	1	0	0	8	5	1	9	.255	.328	.273	77	-1	1	.990	-1	70	95	1-17	-0.3
1918	Cle A	2	6	0	1	0	0	0	0	0	0	1	.167	.167	.167	1	-1	0	.000	-1	0	0	/O(LF)	-0.2
1927	Was A	9	18	1	4	1	0	0	1	1	0	0	.222	.263	.278	41	-2	0-0	1.000	0	90	125	/1-5	-0.2
Total	4	64	207	19	48	3	2	1	22	9	2	10	.232	.271	.280	59	-12	4-0	.979	-5	74	105	/1-57,O(LF)	-2.0
ONSLOW, JACK John James B 10.13.1888 Scottdale, PA D 12.22.1960 Concord, MA BR/TR 5-11/180# d5.2 M2 C7 b-Eddie																								
1912	Det A	36	69	7	11	1	0	0	4	10	2		.159	.284	.174	33	-6	1	.948	-4	*84*	*110*	C-35/O(CF)	-0.7
1917	NY N	9	8	1	2	1	0	0	0	0	1	1	.250	.333	.375	121	0	0	.929	-1	*110*	*59*	/C-9	0.0
Total	2	45	77	8	13	2	0	0	4	10	3	1	.169	.289	.195	41	-6	1	.947	-4	*86*	*105*	/C-44,O(CF)	-0.7
ONTIVEROS, STEVE Steven Robert B 10.26.1951 Bakersfield, CA BB/TR 6/185# d8.5																								
1973	SF N	24	33	3	8	0	0	1	5	4-0	0	7	.242	.324	.333	79	-1	0-0	1.000	1	200	53	/1-5,O(RF)	0.0
1974	SF N	120	343	45	91	15	1	4	33	57-4	3	41	.265	.375	.350	99	2	0-0	.929	-4	93	111	3-75,1-19/O-2(1-0-1)	-0.3
1975	SF N	108	325	21	94	16	0	3	31	55-4	2	44	.289	.391	.366	108	7	2-0	.923	3	106	90	3-89/O-8(2-0-7),1-4	0.9
1976	SF N	59	74	8	13	3	0	0	5	6-0	1	11	.176	.244	.216	31	-7	0-0	1.000	-1	113	192	/3-7,O-7(4-3-2),1-4	-0.8
1977	Chi N	156	546	54	163	32	3	10	68	81-4	3	69	.299	.390	.423	107	9	3-3	.955	3	106	97	*3-155	1.0
1978	Chi N	82	276	34	67	14	4	1	22	34-3	0	33	.243	.321	.333	75	-8	0-2	.965	12	123	118	3-77/1	0.2
1979	Chi N	152	519	58	148	28	2	4	57	58-7	7	68	.285	.362	.370	92	-3	0-1	.941	2	101	104	*3-142/1	-0.3
1980	Chi N	31	77	7	16	3	0	1	3	14-1	0	17	.208	.330	.286	68	-3	0-0	.929	-0	104	32	3-24	-0.3
Total	8	732	2193	230	600	111	10	24	224	309-23	16	290	.274	.365	.366	94	-4	5-6	.944	17	105	101	3-569/1-34,O-18(7-3-11)	0.4
OQUENDO, JOSE Jose Manuel (Contreras) B 7.4.1963 Rio Piedras, P.R. BB/TR (BR 1983 (part)) 5-10/160# d5.2 C5 OF Total (11-LF 7-CF 47-RF)																								
1983	NY N	120	328	29	70	7	0	1	17	19-2	2	60	.213	.260	.244	41	-27	8-9	.960	0	106	103	*S-116	-1.8
1984	NY N	81	189	23	42	5	0	0	10	15-2	2	26	.222	.284	.249	52	-12	10-1	.972	0	92	102	S-67	-0.4
1986	StL N	76	138	20	41	4	1	0	13	15-4	0	20	.297	.359	.341	97	0	2-3	.956	-9	90	109	S-29,2-21/3O(LF)	-0.7
1987	†StL N	116	248	43	71	9	0	1	24	54-6	0	29	.286	.408	.335	99	3	4-4	1.000	9	118	210	O-46(8-3-37),2-32,S-23/3-8,1-3,P	1.3
1988	StL N	148	451	36	125	10	1	7	46	52-7	0	40	.277	.350	.350	101	2	4-6	.997	8	106	116	2-69,3-47,S-17,1-16,O-15(2-4-9)/PC	1.2
1989	StL N	163	556	59	162	28	7	1	48	79-7	0	59	.291	.375	.372	112	12	3-5	**.994**	25	**110**	**124**	*2-156/S-7,1	4.3
1990	StL N	156	469	38	118	17	5	1	37	74-8	0	46	.252	.350	.316	85	-7	1-1	**.996**	-2	102	88	*2-150/S-4	-0.5
1991	StL N	127	366	37	88	11	4	1	26	67-13	1	48	.240	.357	.301	87	-3	1-2	.988	9	109	112	*2-118,S-22/1-3,P	0.9
1992	StL N	14	35	3	9	3	1	0	3	5-1	0	3	.257	.350	.400	115	1	0-0	1.000	1	121	147	/2-9,S-5	0.2
1993	StL N	46	73	7	15	0	0	0	4	12-1	0	8	.205	.314	.205	44	-5	0-0	.988	5	122	100	S-22,2-16	0.1
1994	StL N	55	129	13	34	2	2	0	9	21-4	0	16	.264	.364	.310	80	-3	1-1	.945	-8	77	56	S-28,2-16	-0.8
1995	StL N	88	220	31	46	8	3	2	17	35-3	0	21	.209	.316	.300	64	-11	1-1	.981	7	110	122	2-62,S-24/3-2,O(RF)	0.0
Total	12	1190	3202	339	821	104	24	14	254	448-58	5	376	.256	.346	.317	85	-50	35-33	.992	46	107	114	2-649,S-364/O-63R,3-58,1-23,P-3,C	3.8
ORAN, TOM Thomas B 1847 , CA D 9.22.1886 St.Louis, MO d5.4																								
1875	RS NA	**19**	81	7	15	3	1	0	10	1		1	.185	.195	.247	58	-3	3-2	.633	-4	102	0	O-19(0-2-17)/S	-0.5
ORAVETZ, ERNIE Ernest Eugene B 1.24.1932 Johnstown, PA BB/TL 5-4/145# d4.11																								
1955	Was A	100	263	24	71	5	1	0	25	26-0	1	19	.270	.336	.297	76	-9	1-2	.967	-5	94	24	O-57(0-17-42)	-1.6
1956	Was A	88	137	20	34	3	2	0	11	27-0	0	20	.248	.370	.299	79	-3	1-0	.946	-1	97	103	O-31(20-3-9)	-0.5
Total	2	188	400	44	105	8	3	0	36	53-0	1	39	.262	.348	.298	77	-12	2-2	.961	-5	95	48	/O-88(20-20-51)	-2.1
ORDAZ, LUIS Luis Javier B 8.12.1975 Maracaibo, Venezuela BR/TR 5-11/170# d9.3																								
1997	StL N	12	22	3	6	1	0	0	1	1-0	0	2	.273	.304	.318	64	-1	3-0	.964	-1	93	102	S-11	-0.1
1998	StL N	57	153	9	31	5	0	0	8	12-1	0	18	.203	.261	.235	32	-15	2-0	.945	6	118	121	S-54/3-2,2	-0.5
1999	StL N	10	9	3	1	0	0	0	2	1-0	0	2	.111	.200	.111	-18	-2	1-0	.786	-1	77	192	/S-8,23	-0.2
2000	KC A	65	104	17	23	2	0	0	11	5-0	1	10	.221	.257	.240	28	-12	4-2	.986	-10	72	117	S-38,2-22	-1.8
2001	KC A	28	56	8	14	3	0	0	4	3-0	1	8	.250	.295	.304	55	-4	0-0	.987	5	129	177	2-19/S-8,3D	0.2
2002	KC A	33	94	11	21	2	0	0	4	12-0	0	13	.223	.308	.245	45	-7	2-3	.982	-6	90	78	2-28/3-6,S-2	-1.2
Total	6	205	438	51	96	13	0	0	30	34-1	2	53	.219	.276	.249	38	-41	12-5	.947	-7	104	118	S-121/2-71,3-10,D	-3.6
ORDENANA, TONY Antonio (Rodriguez) "Mosquito" B 10.30.1918 Guanabacoa, Cuba D 9.29.1988 Miami, FL BR/TR 5-9/158# d10.3																								
1943	Pit N	1	4	0	2	0	0	0	3	0	0	0	.500	.500	.500	183	0	0	1.000	1	136	150	/S	0.1
ORDONEZ, MAGGLIO Magglio (Delgado) B 1.28.1974 Caracas, Venezuela BR/TR 5-11/170# d8.29																								
1997	Chi A	21	69	12	22	6	0	4	11	2-0	0	8	.319	.338	.580	139	4	1-2	1.000	1	118	87	O-19(RF)	0.3
1998	Chi A	145	535	70	151	25	2	14	65	28-1	9	53	.282	.326	.415	94	-6	9-7	.985	5	108	97	*O-145(0-22-136)	-0.7
1999	Chi A★	157	624	100	188	34	3	30	117	47-4	1	64	.301	.349	.510	116	13	13-6	.991	7	107	111	*O-153(RF)/D-2	1.2
2000	†Chi A★	153	588	102	185	34	3	32	126	60-3	2	64	.315	.371	.546	129	25	18-4	.983	-3	91	114	*O-152(RF)	1.5
2001	Chi A★	160	593	97	181	40	1	31	113	70-7	5	70	.305	.382	.533	133	30	25-7	.983	-3	94	108	*O-155(0-1-155)/D-3	2.1
2002	Chi A	153	590	116	189	47	1	38	135	53-2	7	77	.320	.381	.597	153	45	7-5	.986	-4	96	87	*O-150(RF)/D	3.2
2003	Chi A★	160	606	95	192	46	3	29	99	57-1	7	73	.317	.380	.546	140	36	9-5	.994	4	106	82	*O-157(0-4-154)/D-2	3.0
Total	7	949	3605	592	1108	232	13	178	666	317-18	31	409	.307	.365	.527	128	147	82-36	.988	7	101	100	O-931(0-27-919)/D-8	10.6
ORDONEZ, REY Reynaldo B 1.11.1971 Havana, Cuba BR/TR 5-9/160# d4.1																								
1996	NY N	151	502	51	129	12	4	1	30	22-12	1	53	.257	.289	.303	59	-31	1-3	.962	10	**106**	109	*S-150	-1.1
1997	NY N	120	356	35	77	5	3	1	33	18-3	1	36	.216	.255	.256	36	-35	11-5	**.983**	10	112	113	*S-118	-1.6
1998	NY N	153	505	46	124	20	2	1	42	23-7	1	60	.246	.278	.299	53	-35	3-6	.975	-1	93	96	*S-151	-2.7
1999	†NY N	154	520	49	134	24	2	1	60	49-12	1	59	.258	.319	.317	65	-28	8-4	**.994**	6	98	106	*S-154	-0.9
2000	NY N	45	133	10	25	5	0	0	9	17-2	0	16	.188	.278	.226	31	-14	0-0	.965	-5	90	83	S-44	-1.5
2001	NY N	149	461	31	114	24	4	3	44	34-17	1	43	.247	.299	.336	68	-23	3-2	.980	-3	93	100	*S-148	-1.5
2002	NY N	144	460	53	117	25	2	1	42	24-11	2	46	.254	.292	.324	68	-24	2-2	.969	1	99	96	*S-142	-1.3
2003	TB A	34	117	14	37	11	0	3	22	2-0	1	12	.316	.328	.487	115	2	0-2	.970	5	110	134	S-34	0.9
Total	8	950	3054	289	757	126	17	11	282	189-64	8	325	.248	.291	.311	60	-188	28-24	.976	22	100	103	S-941	-9.7
ORENGO, JOE Joseph Charles B 11.29.1914 San Francisco, CA D 7.24.1988 San Francisco, CA BR/TR 6/185# d4.18																								
1939	StL N	7	3	0	0	0	0	0	0	0	0	1	.000	.000	.000	-94	-1	0	.667	-1	72	0	/S-7	-0.2
1940	StL N	129	415	58	119	23	4	7	56	65	0	90	.287	.383	.412	113	10	9	.952	-5	95	96	2-77,3-34,S-19	1.2
1941	NY N	77	252	23	54	11	2	4	25	28	2	49	.214	.298	.321	73	-9	1	.958	10	105	108	3-59/S-9,2-6	0.4
1943	NY N	83	266	28	58	8	2	6	29	36	0	46	.218	.311	.331	85	-5	1	.992	5	121	67	1-82	-0.5
	Bro N	7	15	1	3	2	0	0	1	4	0	2	.200	.368	.333	103	0	0	1.000	-0	100	0	/3-6	0.0
	Year	90	281	29	61	10	2	6	30	40	0	48	.217	.315	.331	86	-5	1	.992	5	121	67	1-82/3-6	-0.5
1944	Det A	46	154	14	31	10	0	0	10	20	1	29	.201	.297	.266	58	-8	1-1	.903	3	104	123	S-29,3-11/1-5,2-2	-0.3
1945	Chi A	17	15	5	1	0	0	0	1	3	0	2	.067	.222	.067	-15	-2	0-0	.923	-0	100	0	/3-7,2	-0.3
Total	6	366	1120	129	266	54	8	17	122	156	3	219	.237	.332	.346	88	-15	12-1	.957	11	97	93	3-117/1-87,2-86,S-64	0.3
ORIE, KEVIN Kevin Leonard B 9.1.1972 West Chester, PA BR/TR 6-4/210# d4.1																								
1997	Chi N	114	364	40	100	23	5	8	44	39-3	5	57	.275	.350	.431	102	1	2-2	.971	13	110	84	*3-112/S-3	1.4
1998	Chi N	64	204	24	37	14	0	2	21	18-0	3	35	.181	.253	.279	40	-18	1-1	.966	1	100	72	3-57	-1.7
	Fla N	48	175	23	46	8	1	6	17	14-2	5	24	.263	.335	.423	103	0	1-0	.939	5	113	51	3-48	0.6
	Year	112	379	47	83	22	1	8	38	32-2	8	59	.219	.291	.346	67	-18	2-1	.952	6	106	62	*3-105	-1.1
1999	Fla N	77	240	26	61	16	0	6	29	22-1	3	43	.254	.322	.396	86	-5	1-0	.961	4	111	74	3-64/1	-0.1
2002	Chi N	13	32	4	9	3	0	0	5	1-0	1	4	.281	.306	.375	88	-1	0-0	.895	-2	77	55	3-12	-0.2
Total	4	316	1015	117	253	64	6	22	116	94-6	17	163	.249	.320	.389	85	-23	5-3	.960	21	108	73	3-293/S-3,1	-0.0
ORME, GEORGE George William B 9.16.1891 Lebanon, IN D 3.16.1962 Indianapolis, IN BR/TR 5-10/160# d9.14																								
1920	Bos A	4	6	4	2	0	0	0	1	3	0	0	.333	.556	.333	146	1	0-0	1.000	0	146	0	/O-3(0-1-2)	0.1
ORNDORFF, JESS Jesse Walworth Thayer B 1.15.1881 Chicago, IL D 9.28.1960 Cardiff-By-The- Sea, CA BB/TR 6/168# d4.18																								
1907	Bos N	5	17	0	2	0	0	0	0	0	0		.118	.118	.118	-26	-3	0	.900	-2	*69*	*125*	/C-5	-0.5
O'ROURKE, FRANK James Francis "Blackie" B 11.28.1894 Hamilton, ON, CAN D 5.14.1986 Chatham, NJ BR/TR 5-10.5/165# d6.12																								
1912	Bos N	61	196	11	24	3	1	0	16	11	2	50	.122	.177	.148	-10	-31	1	.915	-10	97	67	S-59/3	-3.7
1917	Bro N	64	198	18	47	7	1	0	15	14	2	25	.237	.294	.283	75	-5	11	.954	3	106	59	3-58	-0.1

Year	Tm Lg	G	AB	R	H	2B	3B	HR	RBI	BB-IB	HP	SO	AVG	OBP	SLG	AOPS	ABR	SB-CS	FA	FR	Rng	Thr	G at Pos	BFW
1918	Bro N	4	12	0	2	0	0	0	2	1	0	3	.167	.231	.167	22	-1	0	.857	1	138	103	/2-2,O	0.0
1920	Was A	14	54	8	16	1	0	0	5	2	0	5	.296	.321	.315	71	-2	2-1	.952	1	94	195	S-13/3	0.0
1921	Was A	123	444	51	104	17	8	3	54	26	7	56	.234	.287	.329	60	-29	6-7	.922	-11	96	90	*S-122	-2.6
1922	Bos A	67	216	28	57	14	3	1	17	20	3	28	.264	.335	.370	84	-5	6-6	.909	-11	90	70	S-49,3-20	-1.0
1924	Det A	47	181	28	50	11	2	0	19	12	3	19	.276	.332	.359	79	-6	7-4	.970	6	109	116	2-40/S-7	0.2
1925	Det A	124	482	88	141	40	7	5	57	32	11	37	.293	.350	.436	100	-1	5-8	**.971**	15	107	98	*2-118/3-6	1.4
1926	Det A	111	363	43	88	16	1	1	41	35	7	33	.242	.321	.300	62	-20	8-6	.936	4	95	176	3-60,2-41,S-10	-1.1
1927	StL A	140	538	85	144	25	3	1	39	64	**12**	43	.268	.358	.331	77	-16	18-8	.955	11	99	101	*3-121,2-16/1-3	0.4
1928	StL A	99	391	54	103	24	3	1	62	21	1	19	.263	.303	.348	68	-18	10-2	.954	-11	81	74	3-96/S-2	-2.1
1929	StL A	**154**	585	81	147	23	9	2	62	41	5	28	.251	.306	.332	62	-35	14-7	.943	-17	87	113	*3-151/2-3,S-2	-3.9
1930	StL A	115	400	52	107	15	4	1	41	35	0	30	.268	.326	.333	65	-21	11-9	.950	6	97	111	3-84,S-23/1-3	-0.8
1931	StL A	8	9	0	2	0	0	0	0	0	0	1	.222	.222	.222	17	-1	1-1	1.000	0	144	0	/S-2,1	-0.1
Total	14	1131	4069	547	1032	196	42	15	430	314	53	377	.254	.315	.333	68	-191	100-59	.949	-11	93	101	3-598,S-289,2-220/1-7,O	-13.4
O'ROURKE, JIM James Henry "Orator Jim" B9.1.1850 Bridgeport, CT D1.8.1919 Bridgeport, CT BR/TR 5-8/185# d4.26 M5 U1 HF1945 b-John s-Queenie z OF NA (44-CF 22-RF) OF Total (770-LF 419-CF 195-RF)																								
1872	Man NA	23	99	25	27	5	0	0	16	4		0	.273	.301	.323	98	1	1-0	.735	-2	118	27	S-15/C-9,3-2,1	-0.1
1873	Bos NA	57	280	79	98	21	2	1	49	15		3	.350	.383	.450	135	11	9-5	.912	1	139	**157**	1-34,O-21(RF),C-12	1.0
1874	Bos NA	70	331	82	104	15	8	**5**	61	4		5	.314	.322	.453	138	12	11-2	.943	1	90	**177**	*1-70	1.2
1875	Bos NA	75	358	97	106	13	7	**6**	72	9		6	.296	.313	.422	148	16	17-5	.800	-5	109	79	O-45(0-44-1),3-27/1-6,C	1.0
1876	Bos N	**70**	312	61	102	17	3	2	43	15		17	.327	.358	.420	156	19		.856	-3	61	38	*O-68(9-60-0)/1-2,C	1.1
1877	Bos N	**61**	265	**68**	96	14	4	0	23	**20**		9	.362	**.407**	.445	162	20		.846	-2	74	0	*O-60(23-35-3)/1	1.2
1878	Bos N	**60**	255	44	71	17	7	1	29	5		21	.278	.292	.412	120	5		.860	1	100	189	*O-57(CF)/1-2,C-2	0.3
1879	Pro N	81	362	69	126	19	9	1	46	13		10	.348	**.371**	.459	174	29		.785	-10	85	149	*O-56(2-0-56),1-20/C-5,3-3	1.7
1880	Bos N	**86**	363	71	100	20	11	**6**	45	21		8	.275	.315	.441	158	22		.907	-3	127	58	O-37(15-4-19),1-19,S-17,3-10/C-9	1.9
1881	Buf N	**83**	348	71	105	21	7	0	30	27		18	.302	.352	.402	139	17		.821	-19	72	86	*3-56,O-18(LF)/C-8,S-3,1M	-0.1
1882	Buf N	**84**	370	62	104	15	6	2	37	13		13	.281	.305	.370	114	5		.866	-1	87	83	*O-81(5-77-0)/S-2,C-2,3M	0.1
1883	Buf N	94	436	102	143	29	8	1	38	15		13	.328	.350	.438	135	18		.866	-9	60	0	O-61(60-1-0),C-33/3-8,S-3,P-2,M	0.8
1884	Buf N	108	467	119	**162**	33	7	5	63	35		17	**.347**	.392	.480	167	36		.894	-7	36	77	*O-86(LF),1-18,C-10/P-4,3M	2.3
1885	NY N	**112**	477	119	143	21	**16**	5	42	40		21	.300	.354	.442	158	31		.940	-16	49	0	*O-112(CF)/C-8	1.0
1886	NY N	105	440	106	136	26	6	1	34	39		21	.309	.365	.402	132	18	14	.926	5	91	58	O-63(1-62-0),C-47/1-2	2.3
1887	NY N	103	397	73	113	15	13	3	88	36	5	11	.285	.352	.411	116	10	46	.890	-7			C-40,3-38,O-28(19-6-3)/2-2	0.5
1888	†NY N	107	409	50	112	16	6	4	50	24	3	30	.274	.319	.372	121	10	25	.960	1	89	39	O-87(75-3-9),C-15/1-4,3-2	0.9
1889	†NY N	128	502	89	161	36	7	3	81	40	1	34	.321	.372	.438	126	16	33	.893	-7	75	47	*O-128(LF)/C	0.6
1890	NY P	111	478	112	172	37	5	9	115	33	8	20	.360	.410	.515	135	22	23	.930	2	117	72	*O-111(10-1-100)	1.7
1891	NY N	**136**	555	92	164	28	7	5	95	26	6	29	.295	.334	.398	118	11	19	.906	-1	92	30	*O-126(126-1-0),C-14	0.7
1892	NY N	115	448	62	136	28	5	0	56	30	5	30	.304	.354	.388	126	14	16	.913	-8	64	27	*O-111(106-0-5)/C-4,1	-0.3
1893	Was N	129	547	75	157	22	5	2	95	49	8	26	.287	.354	.356	92	-6	15	.927	5	110	56	O-87(LF),1-33/C-9,M	-0.6
1904	NY N	1	4	1	1	0	0	0	0	0	0		.250	.250	.250	52	0	0	.800	-1	*109*	*0*	/C	-0.1
Total	4 NA	225	1068	283	335	54	17	12	198	32	0	14	.314	.334	.430	137	40	38-12	.000	-6	100	167	1-111/O-66C,3-29,C-22,S-15	3.1
Total	19	1774	7435	1446	2304	414	132	50	1010	481	36	348	.310	.355	.421	133	297	191-0	.898	-79	82	53	*O-1377L,C-209,3-119,1-103/SP2	16.0
O'ROURKE, CHARLIE James Patrick B 6.22.1937 Walla Walla, WA BR/TR 6-2/195# d6.16																								
1959	StL N	2	2	0	0	0	0	0	0	0-0	0	0	.000	.000	.000	-94	-1	0-0	—	0			H	-0.1
O'ROURKE, QUEENIE James Stephen B 12.26.1883 Bridgeport, CT D 12.22.1955 Sparrows Point, MD BR/TR 5-7/150# d8.15 f-Jim																								
1908	NY A	34	108	5	25	1	0	0	3	4	0		.231	.259	.241	62	-5	4	1.000	-2	71	0	O-14(LF),S-11/2-4,3-3	-0.9
O'ROURKE, JOHN John B 8.23.1849 Bridgeport, CT D 6.23.1911 Boston, MA BL/TL 6/190# d5.1 b-Jim																								
1879	Bos N	72	317	69	108	17	11	6	**62**	8		32	.341	.357	**.521**	181	26		.882	0	62	122	*O-71(0-70-1)	2.1
1880	Bos N	81	313	30	86	22	8	3	36	18		32	.275	.314	.425	153	18		.871	4	103	0	*O-81(3-78-1)	1.8
1883	NY AA	77	315	49	85	19	5	2		21			.270	.315	.381	118	7		.856	-7	79	139	*O-76(CF)/1	-0.3
Total	3	230	945	148	279	58	24	11	98	47		64	.295	.329	.442	150	51		.871	-3	82	86	O-228(3-224-2)/1	3.6
O'ROURKE, JOE Joseph Leo Jr. B 10.28.1904 Philadelphia, PA D 6.27.1990 Philadelphia, PA BL/TR 5-7/145# d4.19 f-Patsy																								
1929	Phi N	3	3	0	0	0	0	0	0	0	0	1	.000	.000	.000	-94	-1	0	—	0			H	-0.1
O'ROURKE, PATSY Joseph Leo Sr. B 4.13.1881 Philadelphia, PA D 4.18.1956 Philadelphia, PA BR/TR 5-7/160# d4.16 s-Joe																								
1908	StL N	53	164	8	32	4	2	0	16	14	1		.195	.263	.244	65	-6	2	.860	-8	101	59	S-53	-1.5
O'ROURKE, TOM Thomas Joseph B 10.1865 New York, NY D 7.19.1929 New York, NY TR 5-9/158# d5.11																								
1887	Bos N	22	78	12	12	3	0	0	10	7	1	6	.154	.233	.192	19	-8	4	.777	-7			C-21/O(RF)3	-1.2
1888	Bos N	20	74	3	13	0	0	0	4	1	0	9	.176	.187	.176	16	-7	2	.881	1			C-20/O(RF)	-0.5
1890	NY N	2	7	1	0	0	0	0	0	1	0	0	.000	.125	.000	-63	-1	0	.864	0	*95*	*180*	/C-2	-0.1
	Syr AA	41	153	16	33	8	0	0	12	12	1		.216	.277	.268	68	-6	2	.907	-15	*79*	*77*	C-40/1	-1.6
Total	3	85	312	32	58	11	0	0	26	21	2	15	.186	.242	.221	39	-22	8	.867	-21	*41*	*42*	/C-83,O-2(RF),13	-3.4
O'ROURKE, TIM Timothy Patrick "Voiceless Tim" B 5.18.1864 Chicago, IL D 4.20.1938 Seattle, WA BL/TR 5-10/170# d5.27 OF Total (32-LF 1-CF 40-RF)																								
1890	Syr AA	87	332	48	94	13	6	1	46	36	4		.283	.360	.367	128	13	22	.866	-8	92	65	3-87	0.6
1891	Col AA	34	136	22	38	1	3	0	12	15	2	7	.279	.359	.331	104	1	9	.879	0	101	129	3-34	0.2
1892	Bal N	63	239	40	74	8	4	0	35	24	0	19	.310	.373	.377	123	7	12	.869	-8	95	72	S-58/O-4(2-1-1),3	0.1
1893	Bal N	31	135	22	49	4	1	0	19	12	2	4	.363	.423	.407	119	4	5	.980	-2	26	0	O-25(LF)/3-5,S	0.0
	Lou N	92	352	80	99	8	4	0	53	77	8	15	.281	.421	.327	108	13	22	.865	-11	90	101	S-60,O-26(4-0-22)/3-6	0.3
	Year	123	487	102	148	12	5	0	72	89	10	19	.304	.422	.349	112	17	27	.861	-13	89	99	S-61,O-51(29-0-22),3-11	0.3
1894	Lou N	55	220	46	61	3	3	0	27	23	2	9	.277	.351	.318	67	-11	9	.977	-1	145	144	1-30,O-18(1-0-17)/S-3,3-3,2	-1.0
	StL N	18	71	10	20	4	1	0	10	8	0	3	.282	.354	.366	74	-3	2	.861	-2	85	99	3-18	-0.4
	Was N	7	25	4	5	2	1	0	2	2	0	1	.200	.259	.360	49	-2	0	.909	0	105	0	/2-4,S-3	-0.2
	Year	80	316	60	86	9	5	0	39	33	2	13	.272	.345	.332	67	-16	11	.977	-3	145	144	1-30,3-21,O-18(1-0-17)/S-6,2-5	-1.6
Total	5	387	1510	272	440	43	23	1	204	197	18	58	.291	.380	.352	105	22	81	.861	-31	93	85	3-154,S-125/O-73R,1-30,2-5	-0.4
ORR, DAVE David L. B 9.29.1859 New York, NY D 6.2.1915 Richmond Hill, NY BR/TR 5-11/250# d5.17 M1 ▲																								
1883	NY AA	1	4	1	1	1	0	0		0			.250	.250	.500	130	0		1.000	0	0	0	/1	0.0
	NY N	1	3	0	0	0	0	0	0	0		1	.000	.000	.000	-99	-1		1.000	0	0	0	/O(LF)	-0.1
	NY AA	12	46	5	15	3	3	2	11	0			.326	.326	.652	198	5		.938	-2	0	0	1-12	0.2
1884	†NY AA	110	458	82	**162**	32	13	9	112	5	1		**.354**	.362	.539	**195**	**46**		.960	-5	64	69	*1-110/O-3(RF)	2.8
1885	NY AA	107	444	76	152	29	**21**	6	77	8	3		.342	.358	**.543**	189	42		.966	-3	73	86	*1-107/P-3	2.6
1886	NY AA	136	571	93	**193**	25	**31**	7	91	17	5		.338	.363	**.527**	**193**	**56**	16	**.981**	0	79	95	*1-136	3.8
1887	NY AA	84	345	63	127	25	10	2	66	22	1		.368	.408	.516	164	29	17	.969	-1	107	90	1-81/O-3(CF),M	1.7
1888	Bro AA	99	394	57	120	20	5	1	59	7	8		.305	.330	.388	130	12	11	.979	4	121	106	*1-99	0.6
1889	Col AA	134	560	70	183	31	12	4	87	9	2	38	.327	.340	.446	129	18	12	.983	9	**130**	81	*1-134	1.3
1890	Bro P	107	464	89	172	32	13	6	124	30	4	11	.371	.414	.534	144	26	10	.972	-5	78	100	*1-107	0.9
Total	8	791	3289	536	1125	198	108	37	627	98	24	50	.342	.366	.502	163	233	66	.973	-1	92	89	1-787/O-7(1-3-3),P-3	13.8
ORR, BILLY William John B 4.22.1891 San Francisco, CA D 3.10.1967 St.Helena, CA BR/TR 5-11/168# d5.3																								
1913	Phi A	30	67	6	13	1	1	0	7	4	0	10	.194	.239	.239	41	-5	1	.967	-2	98	22	S-16/1-3,3-3,2-2	-0.7
1914	Phi A	10	24	3	4	1	1	0	1	2	0	5	.167	.231	.292	59	-1	1-1	.810	-3	93	0	/S-6,3	-0.5
Total	2	40	91	9	17	2	2	0	8	6	0	15	.187	.237	.253	46	-6	2-1	.927	-5	97	16	/S-22,3-4,1-3,2-2	-1.2
ORSATTI, ERNIE Ernest Ralph B 9.8.1902 Los Angeles, CA D 9.4.1968 Canoga Park, CA BL/TL 5-7.5/154# d9.4																								
1927	StL N	27	92	15	29	7	3	0	12	11	0	12	.315	.388	.457	122	3	2	.922	-1	97	98	O-26(0-6-20)	0.1
1928	†StL N	27	69	10	21	6	0	3	15	10	1	11	.304	.400	.522	137	4	0	1.000	-1	92	136	O-17(2-0-15)/1-5	0.2
1929	StL N	113	346	64	115	21	7	3	39	33	2	43	.332	.394	.460	110	6	7	.974	6	108	159	O-77(9-2-67),1-10	0.4
1930	†StL N	48	131	24	42	8	4	1	15	12	1	18	.321	.382	.466	100	0	1	.985	3	120	93	1-22,O-11(RF)	0.1
1931	†StL N	70	158	27	46	16	6	0	19	14	0	16	.291	.349	.468	113	3	1	.988	-1	104	0	O-45(30-6-9)/1	-0.1
1932	StL N	101	375	44	126	27	6	2	44	18	1	29	.336	.368	.456	117	9	5	.976	-7	92	45	O-96(40-55-1)/1	-0.2
1933	StL N	120	436	55	130	21	6	0	38	33	0	33	.298	.348	.374	101	1	14	.986	-2	103	68	*O-107(6-96-5)/1-3	-0.4
1934	†StL N	105	337	39	101	14	4	0	31	27	1	31	.300	.353	.365	87	-5	6	.986	-3	96	84	O-90(CF)	-1.0
1935	StL N	90	221	28	53	9	3	1	24	18	0	25	.240	.297	.321	64	-11	10	.975	-1	100	66	O-60(6-26-28)	-1.4

Year	Tm Lg	G	AB	R	H	2B	3B	HR	RBI	BB-IB	HP	SO	AVG	OBP	SLG	AOPS	ABR	SB-CS	FA	FR	Rng	Thr	G at Pos	BFW
Total	9	701	2165	306	663	129	39	10	237	176	6	218	.306	.360	.416	102	10	46	.979	-7	99	84	O-529(93-281-156)/1-42	-2.3

ORSINO, JOHN John Joseph "Horse" B 4.22.1938 Teaneck, NJ BR/TR 6-3/215# d7.14

Year	Tm Lg	G	AB	R	H	2B	3B	HR	RBI	BB-IB	HP	SO	AVG	OBP	SLG	AOPS	ABR	SB-CS	FA	FR	Rng	Thr	G at Pos	BFW
1961	SF N	25	83	5	23	3	2	4	12	3-0	1	13	.277	.310	.506	116	1	0-0	.959	-2	*84*	*87*	C-25	0.0
1962	†SF N	18	48	4	13	2	0	0	4	5-0	0	11	.271	.333	.313	78	-1	0-0	.963	-1	*124*	*64*	C-16	-0.2
1963	Bal A	116	379	53	103	18	1	19	56	38-6	9	53	.272	.349	.475	134	18	2-3	.990	-2	101	96	*C-109/1-3	2.1
1964	Bal A	81	248	21	55	10	0	8	23	23-3	2	55	.222	.290	.359	81	-7	0-0	.976	-1	*82*	*99*	C-66/1-5	-0.4
1965	Bal A	77	232	30	54	10	2	9	28	23-2	5	51	.233	.313	.409	102	1	1-0	.987	-6	*99*	*99*	C-62/1-5	-0.2
1966	Was A	14	23	1	4	1	0	0	0	0-0	0	7	.174	.174	.217	12	-3	0-0	1.000	-0	99	126	/1-5,C-2	-0.3
1967	Was A	1	1	0	0	0	0	0	0	0-0	0	1	.000	.000	.000	-99	0	0-0	—	0			H	0.0
Total	7	332	1014	114	252	44	5	40	123	92-11	17	191	.249	.319	.420	106	9	3-3	.982	-12	*95*	*95*	C-280/1-18	1.0

ORSULAK, JOE Joseph Michael B 5.31.1962 Glen Ridge, NJ BL/TL 6-1/196# d9.1

Year	Tm Lg	G	AB	R	H	2B	3B	HR	RBI	BB-IB	HP	SO	AVG	OBP	SLG	AOPS	ABR	SB-CS	FA	FR	Rng	Thr	G at Pos	BFW
1983	Pit N	7	11	0	2	0	0	0	1	0-0	0	2	.182	.167	.182	1	-2	0-1	1.000	1	37	1952	/O-4(CF)	-0.1
1984	Pit N	32	67	12	17	1	2	0	3	1-0	1	7	.254	.271	.328	69	-3	3-1	1.000	1	112	98	O-25(7-12-5)	-0.2
1985	Pit N	121	397	54	119	14	6	0	21	26-3	1	27	.300	.342	.365	100	-1	24-11	.976	4	103	157	*O-115(41-72-16)	0.2
1986	Pit N	138	401	60	100	19	6	2	19	28-2	1	38	.249	.299	.342	75	-14	24-11	.981	2	97	**159**	*O-120(9-46-73)	-1.5
1988	Bal A	125	379	48	109	21	3	8	27	23-2	3	30	.288	.331	.422	113	6	9-8	.979	4	108	105	*O-117(36-14-76)	0.6
1989	Bal A	123	390	59	111	22	5	7	55	41-6	2	35	.285	.351	.421	122	12	5-3	.985	6	109	124	*O-109(20-0-91)/D-5	1.5
1990	Bal A	124	413	49	111	14	3	11	57	46-9	1	48	.269	.343	.397	110	5	6-8	.989	9	**124**	68	*O-109(30-0-80)/D-5	1.0
1991	Bal A	143	486	57	135	22	1	5	43	28-1	4	45	.278	.321	.358	92	-6	6-2	.997	17	108	**286**	*O-132(85-1-68)/D-2	0.8
1992	Bal A	117	391	45	113	18	3	4	39	28-5	4	34	.289	.342	.381	100	0	5-4	.983	2	102	122	*O-110(14-0-98)/D	-0.2
1993	NY N	134	409	59	116	15	4	8	35	28-1	2	25	.284	.331	.399	96	-3	5-4	.978	1	99	132	*O-114(66-40-23)/1-4	-0.5
1994	NY N	96	292	39	76	3	0	8	42	16-2	3	21	.260	.299	.353	72	-13	4-2	.979	-4	81	146	O-90(18-13-63)/1-6	-2.0
1995	NY N	108	290	41	82	19	2	1	37	19-2	1	35	.283	.323	.372	87	-5	1-3	.965	-4	88	69	O-86(56-0-31)/1	-1.3
1996	Fla N	120	217	23	48	6	1	2	19	16-1	0	38	.221	.274	.286	50	-16	1-1	.956	3	99	255	O-59(30-14-19)/1-2	-1.5
1997	Mon N	106	150	13	34	12	1	1	7	18-0	0	17	.227	.310	.340	70	-6	0-1	1.000	-1	80	156	O-63(37-0-26),1-15/D	-1.0
Total	14	1494	4293	559	1173	186	37	57	405	318-34	23	402	.273	.324	.374	93	-46	93-60	.982	41	102	150	*O-1253(449-216-669)/1-28,D-14	-4.2

ORTA, JORGE Jorge (Nunez) B 11.26.1950 Mazatlan, Mexico BL/TR 5-10/175# d4.15 OF Total (96-LF 3-CF 246-RF)

Year	Tm Lg	G	AB	R	H	2B	3B	HR	RBI	BB-IB	HP	SO	AVG	OBP	SLG	AOPS	ABR	SB-CS	FA	FR	Rng	Thr	G at Pos	BFW
1972	Chi A	51	124	20	25	3	1	3	11	6-0	1	37	.202	.244	.315	64	-6	3-3	.958	0	86	147	S-18,2-14/3-9	-0.4
1973	Chi A	128	425	46	113	9	10	6	40	37-3	1	87	.266	.323	.376	94	-5	8-8	.969	-23	91	85	*2-122/S	-2.1
1974	Chi A	139	525	73	166	31	2	10	67	40-1	3	88	.316	.365	.440	128	20	9-5	.971	-4	100	99	*2-123,D-10/S-3	2.4
1975	Chi A✳	140	542	64	165	26	10	11	83	48-7	4	67	.304	.363	.450	128	19	16-9	.978	-3	99	94	*2-135/D-2	2.5
1976	Chi A	158	636	74	174	29	8	14	72	38-2	5	77	.274	.316	.410	112	7	24-8	.971	0	100	164	O-77(76-0-2),3-49,D-31	0.5
1977	Chi A	144	564	71	159	27	8	11	84	46-3	2	49	.282	.334	.417	105	3	4-4	.970	-40	80	67	*2-139	-3.0
1978	Chi A	117	420	45	115	19	2	13	53	42-3	4	39	.274	.340	.421	114	8	1-2	.984	-12	87	81	*2-114/D-2	0.2
1979	Chi A	113	325	49	85	18	3	11	46	44-2	1	33	.262	.348	.437	111	6	1-5	.978	-11	85	72	D-62,2-41	-0.7
1980	Cle A☆	129	481	78	140	18	3	10	64	71-2	2	44	.291	.379	.403	116	13	6-5	.982	9	118	116	*O-120(0-2-118)/D-7	1.6
1981	Cle A	88	338	50	92	14	3	5	34	21-3	1	43	.272	.312	.376	100	-1	4-3	.994	1	88	181	O-86(0-1-86)	-0.5
1982	LA N	86	115	13	25	5	0	2	8	12-3	1	13	.217	.295	.313	73	-4	0-1	.947	2	135	102	O-17(1-0-16)	-0.4
1983	Tor A	103	245	30	58	6	3	10	38	19-0	0	29	.237	.287	.408	85	-6	1-2	1.000	0	88	148	D-70,O-17(5-0-12)	-0.9
1984	†KC A	122	403	50	120	23	7	9	50	28-8	2	39	.298	.343	.457	119	10	0-1	.980	-3	91	0	D-83,O-26(14-0-12)/2	0.3
1985	†KC A	110	300	32	80	21	1	4	45	22-5	2	28	.267	.317	.383	92	-3	2-1	—	0	0	0	D-85	-0.5
1986	KC A	106	336	35	93	14	2	9	46	23-3	0	34	.277	.321	.411	96	-2	0-3	—	0	0	0	D-87	-0.6
1987	KC A	21	50	3	9	4	0	2	4	3-1	0	8	.180	.226	.380	55	-3	0-0	—	0	0	0	D-12	-0.4
Total	16	1755	5829	733	1619	267	63	130	745	500-46	29	715	.278	.334	.412	108	56	79-60	.974	-84	91	85	2-689,D-451,O-343R/3-58,S-22	-2.0

ORTEGA, BILL William (Bobadilla) B 7.24.1975 Havana, Cuba BR/TR 6-4/205# d9.7

Year	Tm Lg	G	AB	R	H	2B	3B	HR	RBI	BB-IB	HP	SO	AVG	OBP	SLG	AOPS	ABR	SB-CS	FA	FR	Rng	Thr	G at Pos	BFW
2001	StL N	5	5	0	1	0	0	0	0	0-0	0	1	.200	.200	.200	4	-1	0-0	—	0			/H	-0.1

ORTENZIO, FRANK Frank Joseph B 2.24.1951 Fresno, CA BR/TR 6-2/215# d9.9

Year	Tm Lg	G	AB	R	H	2B	3B	HR	RBI	BB-IB	HP	SO	AVG	OBP	SLG	AOPS	ABR	SB-CS	FA	FR	Rng	Thr	G at Pos	BFW
1973	KC A	9	25	1	7	2	0	1	6	2-0	0	6	.280	.333	.480	118	1	0-0	.983	1	161	73	/1-7,D	0.1

ORTH, AL Albert Lewis "Smiling Al" or "The Curveless Wonder" B 9.5.1872 Tipton, IN D 10.8.1948 Lynchburg, VA BL/TR 6/200# d8.15 U6 ▲ OF Total (20-LF 21-CF 14-RF)

Year	Tm Lg	G	AB	R	H	2B	3B	HR	RBI	BB-IB	HP	SO	AVG	OBP	SLG	AOPS	ABR	SB-CS	FA	FR	Rng	Thr	G at Pos	BFW
1895	Phi N	11	45	8	16	4	0	1	13	1	0	6	.356	.370	.511	125	4	0	.842	-2	70	0	P-11	0.0
1896	Phi N	25	82	12	21	3	3	1	13	3	0	11	.256	.282	.402	80	3	2	.901	1	111	109	P-25	0.0
1897	Phi N	53	152	26	50	7	4	1	17	3	0		.329	.342	.447	110	1	5	.929	0	107	46	P-36/O-6(3-3-0)	0.0
1898	Phi N	39	123	17	36	6	4	1	14	3	0		.293	.310	.431	117	1	1	.959	0	100	49	P-32/O(RF)	0.0
1899	Phi N	22	62	5	13	3	1	1	5	1	0		.210	.222	.339	55	-4	2	.793	-4	52	0	P-21/O(LF)	-0.2
1900	Phi N	39	129	6	40	4	1	1	21	2	1		.310	.326	.380	95	-1	2	.943	1	103	156	P-33/O-3(CF)	0.0
1901	Phi N	41	128	14	36	6	0	1	15	3	1		.281	.303	.352	88	-2	3	.945	2	116	102	P-35/O-4(CF)	0.1
1902	Was A	56	175	20	38	3	2	2	10	9	0		.217	.255	.291	51	-12	2	.923	0	100	86	P-38,O-13(1-4-8)/1S	-0.3
1903	Was A	55	162	19	49	9	7	0	11	4	1		.302	.323	.444	126	4	3	.920	-2	102	0	P-36/S-7,O-4(2-0-2),1-2	-0.1
1904	Was A	31	102	7	22	3	1	0	11	1	2		.216	.238	.265	60	-5	2	.816	-2	50	0	O-18(12-6-0),P-10	-0.8
	NY A	24	64	6	19	1	1	0	7	0	1		.297	.308	.344	101	0	2	.968	0	107	82	P-20/O-2(0-1-1)	0.0
	Year	55	166	13	41	4	2	0	18	1	3		.247	.265	.295	76	-5	4	.969	-2	106	53	P-30,O-20(12-7-1)	-0.8
1905	NY A	55	131	13	24	3	1	1	8	4	1		.183	.213	.244	40	-9	2	.940	-1	103	38	P-40/1O(RF)	-0.1
1906	NY A	47	135	12	37	2	2	1	17	6	0		.274	.305	.341	93	-2	2	.934	-1	99	38	P-45/O(RF)	0.0
1907	NY A	44	105	11	34	6	0	1	13	4	1		.324	.355	.410	133	4	1	.920	2	122	41	P-36/O(LF)	0.1
1908	NY A	38	69	4	20	1	2	0	4	2	0		.290	.310	.362	117	5	0	.980	-1	99	154	P-21	0.0
1909	NY A	22	34	3	9	0	1	0	5	5	0		.265	.359	.324	115	1	1	1.000	-1	92	0	/2-6,P	-0.1
Total	15	602	1698	183	464	61	30	12	184	51	8	17	.273	.298	.366	91	-12	30	.932	-8	102	63	P-440/O-55C,S-8,2-6,1-4	-1.4

ORTIZ, JUNIOR Adalberto Colon B 10.24.1959 Humacao, P.R. BR/TR 5-11/176# d9.20

Year	Tm Lg	G	AB	R	H	2B	3B	HR	RBI	BB-IB	HP	SO	AVG	OBP	SLG	AOPS	ABR	SB-CS	FA	FR	Rng	Thr	G at Pos	BFW
1982	Pit N	7	15	1	3	1	0	0	0	1-0	0	3	.200	.250	.267	43	-1	0-0	1.000	-0	227	48	/C-7	-0.1
1983	Pit N	5	8	1	1	0	0	0	0	1-0	0	0	.125	.222	.125	-1	-1	0-0	1.000	1	0	0	/C-4	0.0
	NY N	68	185	10	47	5	0	0	12	3-0	1	34	.254	.270	.281	53	-12	1-0	.965	-6	70	95	C-67	-1.6
	Year	73	193	11	48	5	0	0	12	4-0	1	34	.249	.268	.275	51	-13	1-0	.967	-5	67	91	C-71	-1.6
1984	NY N	40	91	6	18	3	0	0	11	5-0	0	15	.198	.235	.231	33	-8	1-0	.980	-5	97	93	C-32	-1.3
1985	Pit N	23	72	4	21	2	0	1	5	3-1	0	17	.292	.320	.361	91	-1	1-0	.985	-1	94	137	C-23	-0.1
1986	Pit N	49	110	11	37	6	0	0	14	9-0	0	13	.336	.380	.391	112	2	0-1	.983	-3	99	81	C-36	0.0
1987	Pit N	75	192	16	52	8	1	1	22	15-1	0	23	.271	.322	.339	75	-7	0-2	.975	-2	93	121	C-72	-0.6
1988	Pit N	49	118	8	33	6	0	2	18	9-0	2	9	.280	.336	.381	109	1	1-4	.983	-3	92	41	C-40	-0.1
1989	Pit N	91	230	16	50	6	1	1	22	20-4	2	20	.217	.282	.265	61	-12	2-2	.995	-12	69	96	C-84	-2.2
1990	Min A	71	170	18	57	7	1	0	18	12-0	2	16	.335	.384	.388	110	3	0-4	1.000	-1	154	89	C-68/D-3	0.3
1991	†Min A	61	134	9	28	5	1	0	11	15-0	1	12	.209	.293	.261	52	-8	0-1	.995	-2	177	96	C-60	-0.8
1992	Cle A	86	244	20	61	7	0	0	24	12-0	4	23	.250	.296	.279	63	-12	1-3	.989	-7	92	98	C-86	-1.6
1993	Cle A	95	249	19	55	13	0	0	20	11-1	5	26	.221	.267	.273	46	-19	1-0	.990	3	112	127	C-95	-1.0
1994	Tex A	29	76	3	21	2	0	0	9	5-0	1	11	.276	.329	.303	65	-4	0-1	.992	-2	145	153	C-28	-0.4
Total	13	749	1894	142	484	71	4	5	186	121-7	18	222	.256	.305	.305	69	-79	8-18	.986	-40	105	101	C-702/D-3	-9.5

ORTIZ, DAVID David Americo (Arias) B 11.18.1975 Santo Domingo, D.R. BL/TL 6-4/230# d9.2

Year	Tm Lg	G	AB	R	H	2B	3B	HR	RBI	BB-IB	HP	SO	AVG	OBP	SLG	AOPS	ABR	SB-CS	FA	FR	Rng	Thr	G at Pos	BFW
1997	Min A	15	49	10	16	3	0	1	6	2-0	0	19	.327	.353	.449	106	0	0-0	.989	1	155	119	1-11/D	0.1
1998	Min A	86	278	47	77	20	0	9	46	39-3	5	72	.277	.371	.446	111	6	1-0	.989	-0	102	92	1-70,D-10	-0.1
1999	Min A	10	20	1	0	0	0	0	0	5-0	0	12	.000	.200	.000	-41	-4	0-0	1.000	-0	0	204	/1D	-0.4
2000	Min A	130	415	59	117	36	1	10	63	57-2	0	81	.282	.364	.446	101	2	1-0	.996	-1	82	78	D-88,1-27	-0.6
2001	Min A	89	303	46	71	17	1	18	48	40-8	1	68	.234	.324	.475	105	2	1-0	1.000	-1	49	40	D-80/1-8	-0.4
2002	†Min A	125	412	52	112	32	1	20	75	43-0	3	87	.272	.339	.500	120	12	1-2	.990	-1	80	89	D-95,1-15	0.3
2003	†Bos A	128	448	79	129	39	2	31	101	58-8	1	83	.288	.369	.592	145	30	0-0	.992	-0	96	55	D-74,1-45	1.9
Total	7	583	1925	294	522	147	5	89	339	244-21	10	422	.271	.353	.491	116	48	4-2	.992	-2	97	80	D-353,1-177	0.8

ORTIZ, HECTOR Hector (Montanez) B 10.14.1969 Rio Piedras, P.R. BR/TR 6/205# d9.14

Year	Tm Lg	G	AB	R	H	2B	3B	HR	RBI	BB-IB	HP	SO	AVG	OBP	SLG	AOPS	ABR	SB-CS	FA	FR	Rng	Thr	G at Pos	BFW
1998	KC A	4	4	1	0	0	0	0	0	0-0	0	0	.000	.000	.000	-97	-1	0-0	1.000	-1	0	0	/C-3,1	-0.2
2000	KC A	26	88	15	34	6	0	0	5	8-1	1	8	.386	.443	.455	124	4	0-0	.993	-2	85	107	C-26	0.3
2001	KC A	56	154	12	38	6	1	0	11	9-0	1	24	.247	.293	.299	52	-11	1-3	.990	6	126	121	C-55/D	-0.2

Year	Tm Lg	G	AB	R	H	2B	3B	HR	RBI	BB-IB	HP	SO	AVG	OBP	SLG	AOPS	ABR	SB-CS	FA	FR	Rng	Thr	G at Pos	BFW
2002	Tex A	7	14	1	3	1	0	1	2	1-0	0	1	.214	.267	.500	93	0	0-0	.957	-2	0	0	/C-7	-0.2
Total	4	93	260	29	75	13	1	1	18	18-1	2	33	.288	.339	.358	77	-8	1-3	.990	1	103	108	/C-91,D1	-0.3
ORTIZ, JAVIER Javier Victor B 1.22.1963 Boston, MA BR/TR 6-4/220# d6.15																								
1990	Hou N	30	77	7	21	5	1	1	10	12-0	0	11	.273	.367	.403	116	2	1-1	.978	-1	98	65	O-25(20-1-9)	0.1
1991	Hou N	47	83	7	23	4	1	1	5	14-0	0	14	.277	.381	.386	123	3	0-0	1.000	-0	77	177	O-24(15-0-11)	0.2
Total	2	77	160	14	44	9	2	2	15	26-0	0	25	.275	.374	.394	120	5	1-1	.987	-1	88	116	/O-49(35-1-20)	0.3
ORTIZ, JOSE Jose Daniel (Santos) B 6.13.1977 Santo Domingo, D.R. BR/TR 5-9/160# d9.15																								
2000	Oak A	7	11	4	2	0	0	0	1	2-0	0	3	.182	.308	.182	29	-1	0-0	.857	-1	70	71	/2-3,D-4	-0.2
2001	Oak A	11	42	4	7	0	0	0	3	3-0	0	5	.167	.217	.167	5	-6	1-0	.951	-2	84	124	2-10/D	-0.7
	Col N	53	204	38	52	8	1	13	35	14-0	4	36	.255	.314	.495	86	-5	3-1	.965	1	111	97	2-51	-0.1
2002	Col N	65	192	22	48	7	1	1	12	16-0	3	30	.250	.315	.313	60	-11	2-0	.987	-5	100	70	2-53/3	-1.3
Total	3	136	449	68	109	15	2	14	51	35-0	7	74	.243	.305	.379	68	-23	6-1	.973	-7	103	87	2-117/D-5,3	-2.3
ORTIZ, JOSE Jose Luis (Irizarry) B 6.25.1947 Ponce, P.R. BR/TR 5-9.5/155# d9.4																								
1969	Chi A	16	11	0	3	1	0	0	2	1-1	0	0	.273	.333	.364	90	0	0-0	1.000	0	58	420	/O-8(2-5-2)	0.0
1970	Chi A	15	24	4	8	1	0	0	1	2-0	1	2	.333	.407	.375	113	1	1-0	1.000	1	66	706	/O-8(1-5-2)	0.2
1971	Chi N	36	88	10	26	7	1	0	3	4-0	3	10	.295	.347	.398	96	0	2-2	1.000	-2	88	72	O-30(0-29-1)	-0.3
Total	3	67	123	14	37	9	1	0	6	7-1	4	12	.301	.358	.390	99	1	3-2	1.000	-0	81	222	/O-46(3-39-5)	-0.1
ORTIZ, LUIS Luis Alberto (Galarza) B 5.25.1970 Santo Domingo, D.R. BR/TR 6/190# d8.31																								
1993	Bos A	9	12	0	3	0	0	0	1	0-0	0	2	.250	.250	.250	33	-1	0-0	1.000	-1	50	272	/3-5,D-3	-0.2
1994	Bos A	7	18	3	3	2	0	0	6	1-0	0	5	.167	.182	.278	23	-2	0-0	—	0			/D-6	-0.2
1995	Tex A	41	108	10	25	5	2	1	18	6-0	0	18	.231	.270	.343	57	-7	0-1	.867	-8	83	40	3-35/D-3	-1.4
1996	Tex A	3	7	1	2	0	1	1	1	0-0	0	1	.286	.286	1.000	196	1	0-0	—	0			/D	0.1
Total	4	60	145	14	33	7	3	2	26	7-0	0	26	.228	.256	.359	58	-9	0-1	.875	-8	81	57	/3-40,D-13	-1.7
ORTIZ, ROBERTO Roberto Gonzalo (Nunez) B 6.30.1915 Camaguey, Cuba D 9.15.1971 Miami, FL BR/TR 6-4/200# d9.6 b-Baby																								
1941	Was A	22	79	10	26	1	2	1	17	3	0	10	.329	.354	.430	112	1	0-1	.860	-0	97	178	O-21(RF)	-0.1
1942	Was A	20	42	4	7	1	3	1	4	5	1	11	.167	.271	.405	89	-1	0-0	.941	0	97	174	/O-9(1-0-8)	-0.2
1943	Was A	1	4	0	1	0	0	0	0	0	0	0	.250	.250	.250	48	0	0-1	1.000	0	126	0	/O(RF)	-0.1
1944	Was A	85	316	36	80	11	4	5	35	19	**8**	47	.253	.312	.361	96	-3	4-1	.949	-2	106	37	O-80(10-0-71)	-1.0
1949	Was A	40	129	12	36	3	0	1	11	9	0	12	.279	.326	.326	74	-5	0-0	.946	1	90	204	O-32(4-0-28)	-0.5
1950	Was A	39	75	4	17	2	1	0	8	7	1	12	.227	.301	.280	52	-6	0-0	1.000	-0	86	170	O-19(RF)	-0.6
	Phi A	6	14	1	1	0	0	0	3	0	0	3	.071	.071	.071	-65	-4	0-0	1.000	-0	98	0	/O-3(1-0-3)	-0.4
	Year	45	89	5	18	2	1	0	11	7	1	15	.202	.268	.247	34	-9	0-0	1.000	-0	88	144	O-22(1-0-22)	-1.0
Total	6	213	659	67	168	18	10	8	78	43	10	95	.255	.310	.349	84	-18	4-3	.942	-2	100	103	O-165(16-0-151)	-2.9
ORTON, JOHN John Andrew B 12.8.1965 Santa Cruz, CA BR/TR 6-1/192# d8.20																								
1989	Cal A	16	39	4	7	1	0	0	4	2-0	0	17	.179	.220	.205	21	-4	0-0	.988	2	135	116	C-16	-0.2
1990	Cal A	31	84	8	16	5	0	1	6	5-0	1	31	.190	.244	.286	49	-6	0-1	.987	-1	113	91	C-31	-0.6
1991	Cal A	29	69	7	14	4	0	0	3	10-0	1	17	.203	.313	.261	60	-3	0-1	.994	6	93	144	C-28/D	0.3
1992	Cal A	43	114	11	25	3	0	2	12	7-0	2	32	.219	.276	.298	61	-6	1-1	.981	7	128	130	C-43	0.3
1993	Cal A	37	95	5	18	5	0	1	4	7-0	1	24	.189	.252	.274	40	-8	1-2	.980	6	116	82	C-35/O(LF)	-0.1
Total	5	156	401	35	80	18	0	4	29	31-0	5	121	.200	.265	.274	49	-27	2-5	.985	19	117	112	C-153/O(LF)D	-0.3
ORWOLL, OSSIE Oswald Christian B 11.17.1900 Portland, OR D 5.8.1967 Decorah, IA BL/TL 6/174# d4.13 ▲																								
1928	Phi A	64	170	28	52	13	2	0	22	16	0	24	.306	.366	.406	100	0	3-1	.983	-1	96	131	1-34,P-27	-0.2
1929	Phi A	30	51	6	13	2	1	0	6	2	0	11	.255	.283	.333	56	-4	0-0	1.000	-1	93	328	P-12/O-9(1-8-0)	-0.3
Total	2	94	221	34	65	15	3	0	28	18	0	35	.294	.347	.389	90	-4	3-1	.970	-2	85	72	/P-39,1-34,O-9(1-8-0)	-0.5
OSBORN, FRED Wilferd Pearl "Ossie" B 11.28.1883 Nevada, OH D 9.2.1954 Upper Sandusky, OH BL/TR 5-9/178# d6.8																								
1907	Phi N	56	163	22	45	2	3	0	9	3	2		.276	.298	.325	97	-2	4	1.000	-2	48	0	O-36(8-26-1)/1	-0.6
1908	Phi N	152	555	62	148	19	12	2	44	30	1		.267	.305	.355	107	2	16	.969	-5	71	67	*O-152(0-146-6)	-1.1
1909	Phi N	58	189	14	35	4	1	0	19	12	1		.185	.238	.217	41	-13	6	.979	7	175	172	O-54(CF)	-1.0
Total	3	266	907	98	228	25	16	2	72	45	4		.251	.290	.321	91	-13	26	.975	1	93	84	O-242(8-226-7)/1	-2.7
OSBORNE, FRED Frederick W. B Hampton, IA TL d7.14 ▲																								
1890	Pit N	41	168	24	40	8	3	1	14	6	1	18	.238	.269	.339	87	-4	0	.828	-1	125	0	O-35(28-1-6)/P-8	-0.4
OSBORNE, BOBO Lawrence Sidney B 10.12.1935 Chattahoochee, GA BL/TR 6-1/205# d6.27 f-Tiny																								
1957	Det A	11	27	4	4	1	0	0	1	3-0	0	7	.148	.233	.185	15	-3	0-0	1.000	-0	110	0	/O-5(RF),1-4	-0.4
1958	Det A	2	2	0	0	0	0	0	0	0-0	0	0	.000	.000	.000	-93	-1	0-0	—	0			H	-0.1
1959	Det A	86	209	27	40	7	1	3	21	16-0	2	41	.191	.254	.278	44	-16	1-0	.983	-1	96	101	1-56/O(RF)	-2.0
1961	Det A	71	93	8	20	7	0	2	13	20-0	0	15	.215	.354	.355	88	-1	1-0	.957	-2	70	129	/3-8,1-11	-0.3
1962	Det A	64	74	12	17	1	0	0	7	16-0	1	25	.230	.374	.243	68	-2	0-0	.857	-2	85	0	3-13/1-7,C	-0.5
1963	Was A	125	358	42	76	14	1	12	44	49-7	3	83	.212	.308	.358	87	-5	0-0	.988	-5	103	101	1-81,3-16	-1.6
Total	6	359	763	93	157	30	2	17	86	104-7	6	171	.206	.304	.317	71	-28	2-0	.987	-11	99	98	1-159/3-37,O-6(RF),C	-4.9
OSIK, KEITH Keith Richard B 10.22.1968 Port Jefferson, NY BR/TR 6/185# d4.5 OF Total (3-LF 1-RF)																								
1996	Pit N	48	140	18	41	14	1	1	14	14-1	1	22	.293	.361	.429	105	2	1-0	.977	-5	69	127	C-41/3-2,O-2(LF)	0.0
1997	Pit N	49	105	10	27	9	1	0	7	9-1	1	21	.257	.322	.362	77	-3	0-1	.989	-1	133	112	C-32/2-4,13	-0.3
1998	Pit N	39	98	8	21	4	0	0	7	13-2	2	16	.214	.316	.255	53	-6	1-2	1.000	3	109	113	C-26/3-7	-0.2
1999	Pit N	66	167	12	31	3	1	2	13	11-0	1	30	.186	.239	.251	25	-20	0-0	.997	2	121	89	C-50/P	-1.5
2000	Pit N	46	123	11	36	6	1	4	22	14-0	5	11	.293	.387	.455	113	3	3-0	.992	-5	83	73	C-26,3-12/1-5,PD	0.0
2001	Pit N	56	120	9	25	4	0	2	13	13-0	3	24	.208	.299	.292	53	-8	1-0	.995	-0	83	101	C-39/1-5,3-3,2-2,O(RF)	-0.6
2002	Pit N	55	100	6	16	3	0	2	11	6-0	1	25	.160	.211	.250	24	-12	0-0	.993	5	75	77	C-27/3-4,1-3,2O(LF)	-0.5
2003	Mil N	80	241	22	60	12	0	2	21	31-0	3	44	.249	.342	.324	76	-7	0-1	.991	1	90	113	C-78	-0.2
Total	8	439	1094	96	257	55	4	13	108	111-4	17	193	.235	.314	.328	67	-51	6-4	.991	-1	95	104	C-319/3-29,1-14,2-7,O-4L,P-2,D	-3.3
OSTDIEK, HARRY Henry Girard B 4.12.1881 Ottumwa, IA D 5.6.1956 Minneapolis, MN BR/TR 5-11/185# d9.10																								
1904	Cle A	7	18	1	3	0	1	0	3	3	1		.167	.318	.278	90	0	1	.946	-0	*110*	*91*	/C-7	0.0
1908	Bos A	1	3	0	0	0	0	0	0	0	0		.000	.000	.000	-97	-1	0	.889	-0	*123*	*98*	/C	-0.1
Total	2	8	21	1	3	0	1	0	3	3	1		.143	.280	.238	65	-1	1	.935	-0	*112*	*92*	/C-8	-0.1
OSTEEN, CHAMP James Champlin B 2.24.1877 Hendersonville, NC D 12.14.1962 Greenville, SC BL/TR 5-8/150# d9.18																								
1903	Was A	10	40	4	8	0	2	0	4	2	1		.200	.256	.300	65	-2	0	.938	1	96	102	S-10	-0.1
1904	NY A	28	107	15	21	1	4	2	9	1	2		.196	.218	.336	71	-4	0	.930	-0	114	71	3-17/S-8,1-4	-0.5
1908	StL N	29	112	2	22	4	0	0	11	0	1		.196	.204	.232	41	-8	0	.847	-4	80	114	S-17,3-12	-1.4
1909	StL N	16	45	6	9	1	0	0	7	7	0		.200	.308	.222	69	-1	1	.879	-4	101	0	S-16	-0.6
Total	4	83	304	27	60	6	6	2	31	10	4		.197	.233	.276	60	-15	1	.890	-8	91	72	/S-51,3-29,1-4	-2.6
OSTERGARD, RED Roy Lund B 5.16.1896 Denmark, WI D 1.13.1977 Hemet, CA BR/TR 5-10.5/175# d6.14																								
1921	Chi A	12	11	2	4	0	0	0	0	0	0	2	.364	.364	.364	87	0	0-0	—	0			H	0.0
OSTERHOUT, CHARLIE Charles H. B 1856 Syracuse, NY D 5.21.1933 Syracuse, NY TR d6.23																								
1879	Syr N	2	8	0	0	0	0	0	0	0		0	.000	.000	.000	-99	-2		1.000	-0	0	0	/O(CF)C	-0.2
OSTROSSER, BRIAN Brian Leonard B 6.17.1949 Hamilton, ON, CAN BL/TR 6/175# d8.5																								
1973	NY N	4	5	0	0	0	0	0	0	0-0	0	2	.000	.000	.000	-99	-1	0-0	1.000	-1	71	0	/S-4	-0.2
OSTROWSKI, JOHNNY John Thaddeus B 10.17.1917 Chicago, IL D 11.13.1992 Chicago, IL BR/TR 5-10.5/170# d9.24																								
1943	Chi N	10	29	2	6	0	1	0	3	3	1	8	.207	.303	.276	69	-1	0	1.000	-1	89	0	/O-5(LF),3-4	-0.3
1944	Chi N	8	13	2	2	1	0	0	2	1	0	4	.154	.214	.231	25	-1	0	.500	-1	31	0	/O-2(LF)	-0.2
1945	Chi N	7	10	4	3	2	0	0	1	0	0	0	.300	.300	.500	123	0	0	.750	-1	63	0	/3-4	0.0
1946	Chi N	64	160	20	34	4	2	3	12	20	0	31	.213	.300	.319	77	-5	1	.934	0	111	89	3-50/2	-0.5
1948	Bos A	1	1	0	0	0	0	0	0	0	0	1	.000	.000	.000	-95	0	0-0	—	0			H	0.0
1949	Chi A	49	158	19	42	9	4	5	31	15	1	41	.266	.333	.468	115	2	4-3	.944	-1	100	106	O-41(40-0-3)/3-8	-0.2

Year	Tm Lg	G	AB	R	H	2B	3B	HR	RBI	BB-IB	HP	SO	AVG	OBP	SLG	AOPS	ABR	SB-CS	FA	FR	Rng	Thr	G at Pos	BFW
1950	Chi A	21	45	9	10	1	1	2	2	9	1	8	.222	.364	.422	104	0	0-0	1.000	0	106	106	O-14(6-1-8)	0.0
	Was A	55	141	16	32	2	1	4	23	20	1	31	.227	.327	.340	75	-6	2-0	.947	1	111	92	O-45(34-7-4)	-0.6
	Chi A	1	4	1	2	1	0	0	0	0	0	1	.500	.500	.750	223	1	0-0	1.000	-0	106	106	/O(CF)	0.0
	Year	77	190	26	44	4	2	6	25	29	2	40	.232	.339	.368	85	-5	2-0	.958	2	109	94	O-60(40-9-12)	-0.6
Total	7	216	561	73	131	20	9	14	74	68	4	125	.234	.321	.376	89	-10	7-3	.950	-2	103	93	O-108(87-9-15)/3-66,2	-1.8
OTANEZ, WILLIS Willis Alexander B 4.19.1973 Las Vega Baja, D.R. BR/TR 6-1/200# d8.25																								
1998	Bal A	3	5	0	1	0	0	0	0	0-0	0	2	.200	.200	.200	5	-1	0-0	1.000	-0	56	0	/O-2(RF)	-0.1
1999	Bal A	29	80	7	17	3	0	2	11	6-0	1	16	.213	.273	.325	55	-6	0-0	.917	-3	80	62	3-22/1-5,D-3	-0.8
	Tor A	42	127	21	32	8	0	5	13	9-0	1	30	.252	.307	.433	85	-3	0-0	.953	-3	71	191	3-24,1-13/D-2	-0.6
	Year	71	207	28	49	11	0	7	24	15-0	2	46	.237	.293	.391	73	-9	0-0	.934	-6	76	125	3-46,1-18/D-5	-1.4
Total	2	74	212	28	50	11	0	7	24	15-0	2	48	.236	.291	.387	72	-10	0-0	.934	-6	76	125	/3-46,1-18,D-5,O-2(RF)	-1.5
OTERO, REGGIE Regino Jose (Gomez) B 9.7.1915 Havana, Cuba D 10.21.1988 Hialeah, FL BL/TR 6/165# d9.2 C8																								
1945	Chi N	14	23	1	9	0	0	0	5	2	0	2	.391	.440	.391	135	1	0	.967	-0	110	116	/1-8	0.1
OTERO, RICKY Ricardo (Figueroa) B 4.15.1972 Vega Baja, P.R. BB/TR 5-7/150# d4.26																								
1995	NY N	35	51	5	7	2	0	0	1	3-0	0	10	.137	.185	.176	-4	-8	2-1	1.000	2	130	145	O-23(15-9-0)	-0.6
1996	Phi N	104	411	54	112	11	7	2	32	34-0	2	30	.273	.330	.348	79	-13	16-10	.985	7	111	165	*O-100(CF)	-0.5
1997	Phi N	50	151	20	38	6	2	0	3	19-0	1	15	.252	.339	.318	73	-6	0-3	1.000	6	124	247	O-42(1-40-1)	-0.1
Total	3	189	613	79	157	19	9	2	36	56-0	3	55	.256	.320	.326	71	-27	18-14	.990	14	116	184	O-165(16-149-1)	-1.2
OTIS, AMOS Amos Joseph B 4.26.1947 Mobile, AL BR/TR 5-11/166# d9.6 C4																								
1967	NY N	19	59	6	13	2	0	0	1	5-0	1	13	.220	.292	.254	59	-3	0-4	1.000	-0	77	250	O-16(2-14-3)/3	-0.6
1969	NY N	48	93	6	14	3	1	0	4	6-1	0	27	.151	.202	.204	14	-11	1-0	1.000	1	104	233	O-35(16-18-1)/3-3	-1.1
1970	KC A★	159	620	91	176	**36**	9	11	58	68-3	1	67	.284	.353	.424	114	13	33-2	.990	0	98	141	*O-159(CF)	1.6
1971	KC A★	147	555	80	167	26	4	15	79	40-2	2	74	.301	.345	.443	125	16	**52**-8	.990	8	112	109	*O-144(CF)	3.1
1972	KC A✱	143	540	75	158	28	2	11	54	50-3	3	59	.293	.352	.413	129	20	28-12	.992	-2	103	66	*O-137(CF)	1.8
1973	KC A★	148	583	89	175	21	4	26	93	63-5	1	47	.300	.368	.484	129	22	13-9	.986	-4	96	102	*O-135(CF),D-14	1.4
1974	KC A	146	552	87	157	31	9	12	73	58-4	2	67	.284	.348	.438	120	15	18-5	.986	-2	104	73	*O-143(CF)/D-2	1.2
1975	KC A	132	470	87	116	26	6	9	46	66-1	4	48	.247	.342	.385	103	4	39-11	.988	-5	94	102	*O-130(CF)	0.0
1976	†KC A★	153	592	93	165	**40**	2	18	86	55-7	5	100	.279	.341	.444	129	22	26-7	.992	-17	87	43	*O-152(CF)	0.5
1977	†KC A	142	478	85	120	20	8	17	78	71-5	0	88	.251	.342	.433	110	8	23-7	.991	-7	91	103	*O-140(CF)	0.2
1978	†KC A	141	486	74	145	30	7	22	96	66-7	4	54	.298	.380	.525	150	34	32-8	**.995**	2	103	103	*O-136(CF)/D	3.9
1979	KC A	151	577	100	170	28	2	18	90	68-8	3	92	.295	.369	.444	117	15	30-5	**.992**	-4	93	110	*O-146(CF)/D-4	1.5
1980	†KC A	107	394	56	99	16	3	10	53	39-0	3	70	.251	.316	.383	92	-4	16-1	.988	-0	103	79	*O-105(CF)	-0.2
1981	†KC A	99	372	49	100	22	3	9	57	31-1	2	59	.269	.321	.417	114	7	16-7	.993	4	109	94	O-97(13-86-1)/D	1.1
1982	KC A	125	475	73	136	25	3	11	88	37-3	2	65	.286	.335	.421	108	5	9-5	.997	-8	92	61	*O-125(CF)	-0.3
1983	KC A	98	356	35	93	16	3	4	41	27-3	0	63	.261	.313	.357	84	-8	5-2	.996	-1	97	90	O-96(0-55-41)/D	-1.2
1984	Pit N	40	97	6	16	4	0	0	10	7-0	0	15	.165	.213	.206	21	-10	0-0	.964	3	103	248	O-32(LF)	-0.9
Total	17	1998	7299	1092	2020	374	66	193	1007	757-53	33	1008	.277	.343	.425	114	145	341-93	.991	-31	98	97	*O-1928(63-1825-46)/D-23,3-4	12.0
OTIS, BILL Paul Franklin B 12.24.1889 Scituate, MA D 12.15.1990 Duluth, MN BL/TR 5-10.5/150# d7.4																								
1912	NY A	4	17	1	1	0	0	0	2	3	0		.059	.200	.059	-24	-3	0	.917	0	97	148	/O-4(CF)	-0.3
OTT, MEL Melvin Thomas "Master Melvin" B 3.2.1909 Gretna, LA D 11.21.1958 New Orleans, LA BL/TR 5-9/170# d4.27 M7 HF1951																								
1926	NY N	35	60	7	23	2	0	0	4	1	0	9	.383	.393	.417	120	2	1	.913	1	92	329	O-10(LF)	0.2
1927	NY N	82	163	23	46	7	3	1	19	13	0	9	.282	.335	.380	91	-2	2	.982	-3	79	75	O-32(13-21-0)	-0.7
1928	NY N	124	435	69	140	26	4	18	77	52	2	36	.322	.397	.524	138	25	3	.970	-1	92	127	*O-115(5-1-108)/2-5,3	1.5
1929	NY N	150	545	138	179	37	2	42	151	**113**	6	38	.328	.449	.635	166	61	6	.973	7	97	156	*O-149(RF)/2	5.0
1930	NY N	148	521	122	182	34	5	25	119	103	2	35	.349	**.458**	.578	152	50	9	.969	4	99	126	*O-146(RF)	3.7
1931	NY N	138	497	104	145	23	8	29	115	**80**	2	44	.292	.392	.545	**153**	38	10	.981	3	96	140	*O-137(0-71-66)	3.4
1932	NY N	**154**	566	119	180	30	8	**38**	123	**100**	4	39	.318	**.424**	.601	**175**	**64**	6	.984	-1	103	70	*O-154(RF)	**5.2**
1933	†NY N	152	580	98	164	36	1	23	103	**75**	2	48	.283	.367	.467	139	32	1	.983	-8	89	89	*O-152(0-19-143)	1.6
1934	NY N★	**153**	582	119	190	29	10	**35**	**135**	85	3	43	.326	.415	.591	**170**	**59**	0	.974	-13	84	84	*O-153(0-16-137)	3.6
1935	NY N★	152	593	113	191	33	6	31	114	82	3	58	.322	.407	.555	159	51	7	**.990**	1	98	113	*O-137(RF),3-15	4.2
1936	†NY N★	150	534	120	175	28	6	**33**	135	111	5	41	.328	.448	**.588**	**179**	**65**	6	.985	-5	85	122	*O-148(RF)	4.8
1937	†NY N★	151	545	99	160	28	2	**31**	95	**102**	3	69	.294	.408	.523	149	41	7	.939	-2	105	75	3-60,O-91(RF)	3.5
1938	NY N★	150	527	**116**	164	23	6	**36**	116	118	5	47	.311	**.442**	.583	**178**	**62**	2	.957	2	106	78	*3-113,O-37(RF)	**6.4**
1939	NY N★	125	396	85	122	23	2	27	80	100	1	50	.308	**.449**	.581	173	47	2	.973	-7	91	68	O-96(RF),3-20	3.4
1940	NY N★	151	536	89	155	27	3	19	79	100	6	50	.289	.407	.457	137	32	6	.982	-0	99	104	*O-111(RF),3-42	2.6
1941	NY N★	148	525	89	150	29	0	27	90	100	3	68	.286	.403	.495	149	38	5	.968	0	93	153	*O-145(1-0-144)	3.0
1942	NY N★	152	549	**118**	162	21	0	**30**	93	**109**	3	61	.295	.415	.497	**165**	**50**	6	.990	-4	91	110	*O-152(RF),M	3.9
1943	NY N★	125	380	65	89	12	2	18	47	95	3	48	.234	.391	.418	133	21	7	.975	-2	98	103	*O-111(RF)/3M	1.3
1944	NY N★	120	399	91	115	16	4	26	82	90	3	47	.288	.423	.544	171	42	2	.986	-3	102	57	*O-103(RF)/3-4,M	3.3
1945	NY N✱	135	451	73	139	23	0	21	79	71	**8**	41	.308	.411	.499	150	33	1	.983	-4	92	100	*O-118(RF),M	2.1
1946	NY N	31	68	2	5	1	0	1	4	8	0	15	.074	.171	.132	-13	-10	0	1.000	0	88	149	O-16(RF),M	-1.2
1947	NY N	4	4	0	0	0	0	0	0	0	0	0	.000	.000	.000	-99	-1	0	—	0			HM	-0.1
Total	22	2730	9456	1859	2876	488	72	511	1860	1708	64	896	.304	.414	.533	155	800	89	.980	-34	94	111	*O-2313(29-128-2167),3-256/2-6	60.7
OTT, ED Nathan Edward B 7.11.1951 Muncy, PA BL/TR 5-10/198# d6.10 C7																								
1974	Pit N	7	5	1	0	0	0	0	0	0-0	0	1	.000	.000	.000	-99	-1	0-0	1.000	0	216	0	/O-2(RF)	-0.1
1975	Pit N	5	5	0	1	0	0	0	0	0-0	0	0	.200	.200	.200	11	-1	0-0	1.000	-0	0	0	/C-2	-0.1
1976	Pit N	27	39	2	12	2	0	0	5	3-1	0	5	.308	.349	.359	103	0	0-0	1.000	-0	139	187	/C-8	0.0
1977	Pit N	104	311	40	82	14	3	7	38	32-6	2	41	.264	.334	.395	93	-3	7-7	.982	4	144	90	C-90	0.3
1978	Pit N	112	379	49	102	18	4	9	38	27-6	0	56	.269	.315	.409	97	-2	4-1	.975	-4	104	78	C-97/O-4(LF)	-0.2
1979	†Pit N	117	403	49	110	20	2	7	51	26-8	0	62	.273	.314	.385	86	-8	0-1	.994	-1	109	78	*C-116	-0.4
1980	Pit N	120	392	35	102	14	0	8	41	33-8	0	47	.260	.317	.357	87	-7	1-6	.983	6	117	114	*C-117/O-3(LF)	0.2
1981	Cal A	75	258	20	56	8	1	2	22	17-1	1	42	.217	.266	.279	58	-14	2-1	.979	-2	93	123	C-72	-1.4
Total	8	567	1792	196	465	76	10	33	195	138-30	3	254	.259	.311	.368	86	-36	14-16	.983	3	114	96	C-502/O-9(7-0-2)	-1.7
OTT, BILLY William Joseph B 11.23.1940 New York, NY BB/TR 6-1/180# d9.4																								
1962	Chi N	12	28	3	4	0	0	1	2	2-0	0	10	.143	.200	.250	19	-3	0-0	1.000	0	89	204	/O-7(RF)	-0.4
1964	Chi N	20	39	4	7	3	0	0	1	3-0	0	10	.179	.238	.256	38	-3	0-1	1.000	-1	91	0	O-10(RF)	-0.5
Total	2	32	67	7	11	3	0	1	3	5-0	0	20	.164	.222	.254	30	-6	0-1	1.000	-0	90	90	/O-17(RF)	-0.9
OTTEN, JOHN John G. B 8.1870 , Netherlands D 10.17.1905 Chicago, IL TR ?/175# d7.5																								
1895	StL N	26	87	8	21	0	0	0	8	5	0	8	.241	.283	.241	36	-8	2	.947	-5	*77*	*75*	C-24/O-2(1-1-0)	-0.9
OTTERSON, BILLY William John B 5.4.1862 Pittsburgh, PA D 9.21.1940 Pittsburgh, PA BR/TR 5-7/124# d9.4																								
1887	Bro AA	30	100	16	20	4	1	2	15	8	0		.200	.259	.320	60	-6	8	.859	3	108	147	S-30	-0.1
OUELLETTE, PHIL Philip Roland B 11.10.1961 Salem, OR BB/TR 6/190# d9.10																								
1986	SF N	10	23	1	4	0	0	0	0	3-0	0	3	.174	.269	.174	26	-2	0-0	1.000	-0	85	75	/C-9	-0.2
OULLIBER, JOHNNY John Andrew B 2.24.1911 New Orleans, LA D 12.26.1980 New Orleans, LA BR/TR 5-11/165# d7.25																								
1933	Cle A	22	75	9	20	1	0	0	3	4	1	5	.267	.313	.280	55	-5	0-0	1.000	-2	80	0	O-18(12-0-6)	-0.8
OUTEN, CHINK William Austin B 6.17.1905 Mt.Holly, NC D 9.11.1961 Durham, NC BL/TR 6/200# d4.16																								
1933	Bro N	93	153	20	38	10	0	4	17	20	0	15	.248	.335	.392	112	3	1	.982	-6	*92*	*64*	C-56	-0.1
OUTLAW, JIMMY James Paulus B 1.20.1913 Orme, TN BR/TR 5-8/168# d4.20																								
1937	Cin N	49	165	18	45	7	3	0	11	3	1	31	.273	.290	.352	77	-6	2	.914	4	117	74	3-41	-0.1
1938	Cin N	4	0	1	0	0	0	0	0	0	0	0	—	—	—	—	0	0	—	0			R	0.0
1939	Bos N	65	133	15	35	2	0	0	5	10	0	14	.263	.315	.278	65	-7	1	.964	0	111	43	O-39(15-22-2)/3-2	-0.8
1943	Det A	20	67	8	18	1	0	1	6	8	0	4	.269	.347	.328	91	-1	0-0	1.000	-0	87	162	O-16(4-3-9)	-0.2
1944	Det A	139	535	69	146	20	6	3	57	41	2	40	.273	.327	.350	88	-8	7-8	.964	-4	89	133	*O-137(71-6-60)	-2.3
1945	†Det A	132	446	56	121	16	5	0	34	45	0	33	.271	.338	.330	88	-6	6-7	.967	-2	87	143	*O-105(82-17-8),3-21	-1.6

Year	Tm Lg	G	AB	R	H	2B	3B	HR	RBI	BB-IB	HP	SO	AVG	OBP	SLG	AOPS	ABR	SB-CS	FA	FR	Rng	Thr	G at Pos	BFW
1946	Det A	92	299	36	78	14	2	2	31	29	1	24	.261	.328	.341	82	-7	5-4	1.000	-5	87	189	O-43(26-10-9),3-38	-1.5
1947	Det A	70	127	20	29	7	1	0	15	21	0	14	.228	.338	.299	76	-3	3-1	.983	-2	107	0	O-37(21-3-13)/3-9	-0.6
1948	Det A	74	198	33	56	12	0	0	25	31	1	15	.283	.383	.343	91	-1	0-1	.920	-0	101	101	3-47,O-13(10-0-3)	-0.2
1949	Det A	5	4	1	1	0	0	0	0	0	0	1	.250	.250	.250	32	0	0-0	—	0			H	0.0
Total	10	650	1974	257	529	79	17	6	184	188	5	176	.268	.333	.334	85	-39	24-21	.972	-9	92	127	O-390(229-61-104),3-158	-7.3

OVERBAY, LYLE Lyle Stefan B 1.28.1977 Centralia, WA BL/TL 6-2/215# d9.19

Year	Tm Lg	G	AB	R	H	2B	3B	HR	RBI	BB-IB	HP	SO	AVG	OBP	SLG	AOPS	ABR	SB-CS	FA	FR	Rng	Thr	G at Pos	BFW
2001	Ari N	2	2	0	1	0	0	0	0	0-0	0	1	.500	.500	.500	151	0	0-0	—	0			/H	0.0
2002	Ari N	10	10	0	1	0	0	0	1	0-0	0	5	.100	.100	.100	-42	-2	0-0	—	0			/H	-0.3
2003	Ari N	86	254	23	70	20	0	4	28	35-7	2	67	.276	.365	.402	91	-2	1-0	.997	6	125	86	1-75	-0.2
Total	3	98	266	23	72	20	0	4	29	35-7	2	73	.271	.357	.391	87	-4	1-0	.997	6	125	86	/1-75	-0.5

OWEN, MICKEY Arnold Malcolm B 4.4.1916 Nixa, MO BR/TR 5-10/190# d5.2 Mil 1945 C2

Year	Tm Lg	G	AB	R	H	2B	3B	HR	RBI	BB-IB	HP	SO	AVG	OBP	SLG	AOPS	ABR	SB-CS	FA	FR	Rng	Thr	G at Pos	BFW
1937	StL N	80	234	17	54	4	2	0	20	15	0	13	.231	.277	.265	47	-18	1	.974	-2	89	109	C-78	-1.5
1938	StL N	122	397	45	106	25	2	4	36	32	2	14	.267	.325	.370	86	-7	2	.980	1	91	113	*C-116	0.1
1939	StL N	131	344	32	89	18	2	3	35	43	2	28	.259	.344	.349	82	-8	6	.982	6	120	91	*C-126	0.4
1940	StL N	117	307	27	81	16	2	0	27	34	2	13	.264	.341	.329	81	-7	4	.980	1	86	118	*C-113	0.0
1941	†Bro N★	128	386	32	89	15	2	1	44	34	2	14	.231	.296	.288	62	-19	1	.995	9	**160**	87	*C-128	-0.3
1942	Bro N★	133	421	53	109	16	3	0	44	44	1	17	.259	.330	.311	87	-6	10	.987	8	144	94	*C-133	1.1
1943	Bro N☆	106	365	31	95	11	2	0	54	25	1	15	.260	.309	.301	77	-11	4	.987	-5	97	96	*C-100/3-3,S	-1.1
1944	Bro N☆	130	461	43	126	20	3	1	42	36	0	17	.273	.326	.336	88	-7	4	.979	-8	87	98	*C-125/2	-0.8
1945	Bro N	24	84	5	24	9	0	0	11	10	1	2	.286	.368	.393	113	2	0	.963	-2	105	96	C-24	0.2
1949	Chi N	62	198	15	54	9	3	2	18	12	1	13	.273	.318	.379	88	-4	1	.969	-3	65	148	C-59	-0.4
1950	Chi N	86	259	22	63	11	0	2	21	13	1	16	.243	.282	.309	56	-17	2	.978	-1	66	**119**	C-86	-1.4
1951	Chi N	58	125	10	23	6	0	0	15	19	0	13	.184	.292	.232	42	-10	1-0	.969	2	66	133	C-57	-0.6
1954	Bos A	32	68	6	16	3	0	1	11	9	0	6	.235	.309	.324	70	-3	0-1	.989	-1	70	73	C-30	-0.3
Total	13	1209	3649	338	929	163	21	14	378	326	13	181	.255	.318	.322	76	-115	36-1	.982	4	103	105	*C-1175/3-3,2S	-4.6

OWEN, DAVE Dave B 4.25.1958 Cleburne, TX BB/TR 6-2/170# d9.6 b-Spike

Year	Tm Lg	G	AB	R	H	2B	3B	HR	RBI	BB-IB	HP	SO	AVG	OBP	SLG	AOPS	ABR	SB-CS	FA	FR	Rng	Thr	G at Pos	BFW
1983	Chi N	16	22	1	2	0	1	0	2	2-0	0	7	.091	.160	.182	-3	-3	1-0	1.000	1	119	105	S-14/3-3	-0.1
1984	Chi N	47	93	8	18	2	2	1	10	8-1	2	15	.194	.269	.290	53	-6	1-2	.969	1	111	127	S-35/3-6,2-4	-0.3
1985	Chi N	22	19	6	7	0	0	0	4	1-0	0	5	.368	.400	.368	105	0	1-1	.917	-1	132	166	/S-7,3-7,2-4	-0.1
1988	KC A	7	5	0	0	0	0	0	0	0-0	0	3	.000	.000	.000	-99	-1	0-0	.941	2	110	343	/S-7	0.0
Total	4	92	139	15	27	2	3	1	16	11-1	2	30	.194	.260	.273	47	-10	3-3	.969	3	114	140	/S-63,3-16,2-8	-0.5

OWEN, LARRY Lawrence Thomas B 5.31.1955 Cleveland, OH BR/TR 5-11/185# d8.14

Year	Tm Lg	G	AB	R	H	2B	3B	HR	RBI	BB-IB	HP	SO	AVG	OBP	SLG	AOPS	ABR	SB-CS	FA	FR	Rng	Thr	G at Pos	BFW
1981	Atl N	13	16	0	0	0	0	0	0	1-0	0	4	.000	.059	.000	-80	-4	0-0	.964	0	57	50	C-10	-0.4
1982	Atl N	2	3	1	1	1	0	0	0	0-0	0	1	.333	.333	.667	167	0	0-0	1.000	-0	61	360	/C-2	0.0
1983	Atl N	17	17	0	2	0	0	0	1	0-0	0	2	.118	.118	.118	-32	-3	0-1	.970	-1	120	0	C-16	-0.4
1985	Atl N	26	71	7	17	3	0	2	12	8-3	0	17	.239	.313	.366	85	-1	0-0	.966	1	78	75	C-25	0.0
1987	KC A	76	164	17	31	6	0	5	14	16-0	0	51	.189	.260	.317	51	-12	0-0	.983	17	122	136	C-75	0.7
1988	KC A	37	81	5	17	1	0	1	3	9-0	2	23	.210	.304	.259	59	-4	0-0	.989	2	127	91	C-37	0.0
Total	6	171	352	30	68	11	0	8	30	34-3	2	98	.193	.267	.293	51	-24	0-1	.980	19	112	106	C-165	-0.1

OWEN, MARV Marvin James “Freck” B 3.22.1906 Agnew, CA D 6.22.1991 Mountain View, CA BR/TR 6-1/175# d4.16

Year	Tm Lg	G	AB	R	H	2B	3B	HR	RBI	BB-IB	HP	SO	AVG	OBP	SLG	AOPS	ABR	SB-CS	FA	FR	Rng	Thr	G at Pos	BFW
1931	Det A	105	377	35	84	11	6	3	39	29	2	38	.223	.282	.308	53	-27	2-2	.937	-1	95	94	S-37,3-37,1-27/2-4	-2.4
1933	Det A	138	550	77	144	24	9	2	65	44	4	56	.262	.321	.349	76	-20	2-2	.944	-10	90	83	*3-136	-2.4
1934	†Det A	**154**	565	79	179	34	9	8	96	59	4	37	.317	.385	.451	115	13	3-3	.956	-6	84	**118**	*3-154	1.1
1935	†Det A	134	483	52	127	24	5	2	71	43	2	37	.263	.326	.346	76	-17	1-4	.958	-9	87	112	*3-131	-2.1
1936	Det A	**154**	583	72	172	20	4	9	105	53	7	41	.295	.361	.389	85	-14	9-6	.952	-2	93	**112**	*3-153/1-2	-1.0
1937	Det A	107	396	48	114	22	5	1	45	41	2	24	.288	.358	.376	83	-10	3-4	**.970**	-2	102	78	*3-106	-0.8
1938	Chi A	141	577	84	162	23	6	6	55	45	4	31	.281	.337	.373	76	-23	6-4	.948	-1	**106**	**112**	*3-140	-1.7
1939	Chi A	58	194	22	46	9	0	0	15	16	2	15	.237	.302	.284	49	-15	4-5	.953	-3	90	116	3-55	-1.6
1940	Bos A	20	57	4	12	0	0	0	6	8	0	4	.211	.308	.211	36	-5	0-0	.962	2	99	191	/3-9,1-8	-0.4
Total	9	1011	3782	473	1040	167	44	31	497	338	27	283	.275	.339	.367	80	-118	30-30	.953	-32	94	106	3-921/1-37,S-37,2-4	-11.3

OWEN, SPIKE Spike Dee B 4.19.1961 Cleburne, TX BB/TR 5-10/170# d6.25 b-Dave

Year	Tm Lg	G	AB	R	H	2B	3B	HR	RBI	BB-IB	HP	SO	AVG	OBP	SLG	AOPS	ABR	SB-CS	FA	FR	Rng	Thr	G at Pos	BFW
1983	Sea A	80	306	36	60	11	3	2	21	24-0	2	44	.196	.257	.271	44	-24	10-6	.970	6	99	92	S-80	-1.0
1984	Sea A	152	530	67	130	18	8	3	43	46-0	3	63	.245	.308	.326	77	-17	16-8	.977	16	102	86	*S-151	1.5
1985	Sea A	118	352	41	91	10	6	6	37	34-0	0	27	.259	.322	.372	89	-6	11-5	.975	25	113	102	*S-117	3.0
1986	Sea A	112	402	46	99	22	6	0	35	34-1	1	42	.246	.305	.331	73	-15	1-3	.972	36	121	128	*S-112	3.1
	†Bos A	42	126	21	23	2	1	1	10	17-0	1	9	.183	.283	.238	44	-10	3-1	.976	-0	87	139	S-42	-0.6
	Year	154	528	67	122	24	7	1	45	51-1	2	51	.231	.300	.309	66	-25	4-4	**.973**	**36**	**112**	131	*S-154	2.5
1987	Bos A	132	437	50	113	17	7	2	48	53-2	1	43	.259	.337	.343	80	-12	11-8	.975	-12	92	88	*S-130	-1.1
1988	†Bos A	89	257	40	64	14	1	5	18	27-0	2	27	.249	.324	.370	90	-3	0-1	.967	-2	94	76	S-76/D-7	0.1
1989	Mon N	142	437	52	102	17	4	6	41	76-25	3	44	.233	.349	.332	95	0	3-2	**.979**	10	101	96	*S-142	2.2
1990	Mon N	149	453	55	106	24	5	5	35	70-12	0	60	.234	.333	.342	91	-4	8-6	**.989**	-19	89	77	*S-148	-1.3
1991	Mon N	139	424	39	108	22	8	3	26	42-11	1	61	.255	.321	.366	95	-3	2-6	.986	7	105	105	*S-133	1.2
1992	Mon N	122	386	52	104	16	3	7	40	50-3	0	30	.269	.348	.381	109	6	9-4	.982	-4	95	76	*S-116	1.1
1993	NY A	103	334	41	78	16	2	2	20	29-2	0	30	.234	.294	.311	65	-17	3-2	.968	6	113	78	S-96/D-2	-0.4
1994	Cal A	82	268	30	83	17	2	3	37	49-0	1	17	.310	.418	.422	116	9	2-8	.956	-6	93	140	3-70/S-5,1-4,2D	0.2
1995	Cal A	82	218	17	50	9	3	1	28	18-1	0	22	.229	.288	.312	57	-14	3-2	.945	-7	75	75	3-29,S-25,2-16	-1.9
Total	13	1544	4930	587	1211	215	59	46	439	569-57	15	519	.246	.324	.341	83	-110	82-62	.977	55	101	93	*S-1373/3-99,2-17,D-11,1-4	6.1

OWENS, JAYHAWK Claude Jayhawk B 2.10.1969 Cincinnati, OH BR/TR 6-1/200# d6.6

Year	Tm Lg	G	AB	R	H	2B	3B	HR	RBI	BB-IB	HP	SO	AVG	OBP	SLG	AOPS	ABR	SB-CS	FA	FR	Rng	Thr	G at Pos	BFW
1993	Col N	33	86	12	18	5	0	3	6	6-1	2	30	.209	.277	.372	62	-5	1-0	.957	-2	103	134	C-32	-0.5
1994	Col N	6	12	4	3	0	1	0	1	3-0	0	3	.250	.400	.417	97	0	0-0	1.000	0	150	221	/C-6	0.0
1995	†Col N	18	45	7	11	2	0	4	12	2-0	1	16	.244	.286	.556	91	-1	0-0	.988	3	302	133	C-16	0.3
1996	Col N	73	180	31	43	9	1	4	17	27-0	1	56	.239	.338	.367	70	-7	4-1	.974	-2	97	134	C-68	-0.5
Total	4	130	323	54	75	16	2	11	36	38-1	4	104	.232	.318	.396	72	-13	5-1	.973	-1	127	138	C-122	-0.7

OWENS, ERIC Eric Blake B 2.3.1971 Danville, VA BR/TR 6-1/185# d6.6 OF Total (291-LF 201-CF 251-RF)

Year	Tm Lg	G	AB	R	H	2B	3B	HR	RBI	BB-IB	HP	SO	AVG	OBP	SLG	AOPS	ABR	SB-CS	FA	FR	Rng	Thr	G at Pos	BFW
1995	Cin N	2	2	0	2	0	0	0	1	0-0	0	0	1.000	1.000	1.000	432	1	0-0	—	-1	0	0	/3-2	0.0
1996	Cin N	88	205	26	41	6	0	0	9	23-1	1	38	.200	.281	.229	37	-18	16-2	.986	-1	95	137	O-52(LF)/2-6,3-5	-1.8
1997	Cin N	27	57	8	15	0	0	0	3	4-0	0	11	.263	.311	.263	52	-4	3-2	.938	-5	69	0	O-18(9-8-1)/2-2	-0.9
1998	Mil N	34	40	5	5	2	0	1	4	2-0	0	6	.125	.167	.250	8	-6	0-0	1.000	-1	73	369	O-16(10-5-2)/2-4	-0.7
1999	SD N	149	440	55	117	22	3	9	61	38-2	3	50	.266	.327	.391	88	-9	33-7	.990	-1	104	74	*O-116(69-47-27),1-12/3-4,2	-0.8
2000	SD N	145	583	87	171	19	7	6	51	45-4	4	63	.293	.346	.381	90	-10	29-14	**1.000**	3	105	67	*O-144(65-34-68)/2	-1.0
2001	Fla N	119	400	51	101	16	1	5	28	29-2	0	59	.253	.302	.335	67	-20	8-6	.984	-5	89	100	*O-106(1-37-72)/D	-2.8
2002	Fla N	131	385	44	104	15	5	4	37	31-1	0	33	.270	.324	.366	88	-9	26-9	.975	9	114	163	*O-121(75-22-39)	-0.2
2003	Ana A	111	241	29	65	6	0	1	20	10-0	1	24	.270	.300	.307	64	-13	11-8	.971	2	108	89	O-97(10-48-42)/D-3	-1.3
Total	9	806	2353	305	621	86	16	26	214	182-10	9	284	.264	.318	.347	76	-88	126-48	.985	-1	102	102	O-670L/2-14,1-12,3-11,D-4	-9.5

OWENS, FRANK Frank Walter “Yip” B 1.26.1886 Toronto, ON, CAN D 7.2.1958 Minneapolis, MN BR/TR 6/170# d9.11

Year	Tm Lg	G	AB	R	H	2B	3B	HR	RBI	BB-IB	HP	SO	AVG	OBP	SLG	AOPS	ABR	SB-CS	FA	FR	Rng	Thr	G at Pos	BFW
1905	Bos A	1	2	0	0	0	0	0	0	0	0		.000	.000	.000	-99	0	0	1.000	-0	0	198	/C	-0.1
1909	Chi A	64	174	12	35	4	1	0	17	8	2		.201	.245	.236	54	-9	3	.959	-6	94	85	C-57	-1.2
1914	Bro F	58	184	15	51	7	3	2	20	9	1	16	.277	.314	.380	89	-6	2	.967	-11	78	96	C-58	-1.4
1915	Bal F	99	334	32	84	14	7	3	28	17	1	34	.251	.290	.362	80	-15	4	.976	-2	107	105	C-99	-0.9
Total	4	222	694	59	170	25	11	5	65	34	4	50	.245	.284	.334	77	-30	9	.969	-20	96	98	C-215	-3.6

OWENS, JACK Furman Lee B 5.6.1908 Converse, SC D 11.14.1958 Greenville, SC BR/TR 6-1/186# d9.21

Year	Tm Lg	G	AB	R	H	2B	3B	HR	RBI	BB-IB	HP	SO	AVG	OBP	SLG	AOPS	ABR	SB-CS	FA	FR	Rng	Thr	G at Pos	BFW
1935	Phi A	2	8	0	2	0	0	0	1	0	0	1	.250	.250	.250	30	-1	0-0	.900	-0	82	180	/C-2	-0.1

OWENS, RED Thomas Llewellyn B 11.1.1874 Pottsville, PA D 8.20.1952 Harrisburg, PA BR/TR d7.28

Year	Tm Lg	G	AB	R	H	2B	3B	HR	RBI	BB-IB	HP	SO	AVG	OBP	SLG	AOPS	ABR	SB-CS	FA	FR	Rng	Thr	G at Pos	BFW
1899	Phi N	8	21	0	1	0	0	0	1	2	0		.048	.130	.048	-52	-4	0	.914	-0	104	91	/2-8	-0.4
1905	Bro N	43	168	14	36	6	2	1	20	6	0		.214	.241	.292	63	-8	1	.929	2	98	118	2-43	-0.6
Total	2	51	189	14	37	6	2	1	21	8	0		.196	.228	.265	49	-12	1	.927	2	99	115	/2-51	-1.0

Year	Tm Lg	G	AB	R	H	2B	3B	HR	RBI	BB-IB	HP	SO	AVG	OBP	SLG	AOPS	ABR	SB-CS	FA	FR	Rng	Thr	G at Pos	BFW
OXLEY, HENRY Henry Havelock B 1.4.1858 Covehead, PE, CAN D 10.12.1945 Somerville, MA 5-11/163# d7.30																								
1884	NY N	2	4	0	0	0	0	0	0	1		2	.000	.200	.000	-31	-1		.900	0			/C-2	0.0
	NY AA	1	3	0	0	0	0	0		0	0		.000	.000	.000	-99	-1		.889	-0			/C	-0.1
Total	1	3	7	0	0	0	0	0	0	1	0	2	.000	.125	.000	-56	-2		.895	0			/C-3	-0.1
OYLER, ANDY Andrew Paul "Pepper" B 5.5.1880 Newville, PA D 10.24.1970 E.Pennsboro Twsp., PA BR/TR 5-6.5/138# d5.8																								
1902	Bal A	27	77	9	17	1	0	1	6	8	3		.221	.318	.273	62	-4	3	.947	-4	67	36	3-20/O-3(0-2-1),S-2,2	-0.7
OYLER, RAY Raymond Francis B 8.4.1938 Indianapolis, IN D 1.26.1981 Seattle, WA BR/TR 5-11/165# d4.18																								
1965	Det A	82	194	22	36	6	0	5	13	21-3	0	61	.186	.265	.294	58	-11	1-0	.955	1	105	61	S-57,2-11/13	-0.5
1966	Det A	71	210	16	36	8	3	1	9	23-4	3	62	.171	.263	.252	48	-14	0-0	.965	9	107	116	S-69	0.0
1967	Det A	148	367	33	76	14	2	1	29	37-3	2	91	.207	.281	.264	61	-17	0-2	.964	13	107	99	*S-146	0.7
1968	†Det A	111	215	13	29	6	1	1	12	20-0	2	59	.135	.213	.186	22	-20	0-2	.977	-6	89	82	*S-111	-2.4
1969	Sea A	106	255	24	42	5	0	7	22	31-0	2	80	.165	.260	.267	48	-18	1-2	.965	3	104	87	*S-106	-0.6
1970	Cal A	24	24	2	2	0	0	0	1	3-0	0	6	.083	.185	.083	-24	-4	0-0	1.000	-4	60	33	S-13/3-2	-0.8
Total	6	542	1265	110	221	39	6	15	86	135-10	9	359	.175	.258	.251	48	-84	2-6	.966	16	102	90	S-502/2-11,3-3,1	-3.6
OZUNA, PABLO Pablo Jose B 8.25.1974 Santo Domingo, D.R. BR/TR 6/160# d4.23																								
2000	Fla N	14	24	2	8	1	0	0	0	0-0	0	2	.333	.333	.375	82	-1	1-0	.967	-1	96	70	/2-7	-0.1
2002	Fla N	34	47	4	13	2	2	0	3	1-0	1	3	.277	.300	.404	92	-1	1-1	.967	-2	85	65	2-10/O(CF)	-0.3
2003	Col N	17	40	5	8	1	0	0	2	2-0	2	6	.200	.273	.225	28	-4	3-0	.981	4	140	155	/2-8,O-5(CF),S-3	0.1
Total	3	65	111	11	29	4	2	0	5	3-0	3	11	.261	.297	.333	64	-6	5-1	.974	2	109	100	/2-25,O-6(CF),S-3	-0.3
PABOR, CHARLIE Charles Henry B 9.24.1846 New York, NY D 4.23.1913 New Haven, CT BL/TL 5-8/155# d5.4 M2 ▲																								
1871	Cle NA	**29**	142	24	42	2	4	0	18	1		3	.296	.301	.366	96	0	1-0	.773	-4	103	0	*O-28(LF)/P-7,M	-0.2
1872	Cle NA	21	92	12	19	0	0	0	7	0		0	.207	.207	.207	29	-7	0-0	.863	-0	47	209	O-19(LF)/P-2	-0.4
1873	Atl NA	**55**	228	36	82	9	3	0	41	6		3	.360	.376	.425	154	17	2-0	.811	-3	51	62	*O-55(LF)	1.2
1874	Phi NA	17	77	11	17	0	1	0	1	0		0	.221	.221	.247	48	-5	0-1	.553	-2	196	210	O-17(2-3-13)	-0.5
1875	Atl NA	42	153	14	36	2	2	0	11	1		1	.235	.240	.275	90	0	0-0	.803	1	71	60	O-42(LF)/PM	0.1
	NH NA	6	23	4	8	0	2	0	2	0		1	.348	.348	.522	227	3	0-0	.818	-1	0	0	/O-6(LF),M	0.2
	Year	48	176	18	44	2	4	0	13	1		2	.250	.254	.307	108	2	0-0	.804	-0	63	53	O-48(LF)/P	0.3
Total	5 NA	170	715	101	204	13	12	0	80	8		8	.285	.293	.337	103	8	3-1	.000	-10	77	83	O-167(152-3-13)/P-10	0.4
PABST, ED Edward D. A. B 1868 St.Louis, MO D 6.19.1940 St.Louis, MO 5-11/170# d9.26																								
1890	Phi AA	8	25	7	10	2	0	0	3	5	0		.400	.500	.480	190	3	3	.963	3	232	0	/O-8(LF)	0.5
	StL AA	4	14	1	2	0	1	0	0	0	0		.143	.143	.286	23	-2	0	1.000	1	259	0	/O-4(LF)	0.0
	Year	12	39	8	12	2	1	0	3	5	0		.308	.386	.410	129	1	3	.972	4	240	0	O-12(LF)	0.5
PACIOREK, JIM James Joseph B 6.7.1960 Detroit, MI BR/TR 6-3/203# d4.9 b-John b-Tom																								
1987	Mil A	48	101	16	23	5	0	2	10	12-0	0	20	.228	.302	.337	69	-4	1-0	.980	-3	75	84	1-21,3-15/O-5(4-0-1),D-2	-0.7
PACIOREK, JOHN John Francis B 2.11.1945 Detroit, MI BR/TR 6-2/200# d9.29 b-Jim b-Tom																								
1963	Hou N	1	3	4	3	0	0	0	3	2-0	0	0	1.000	1.000	1.000	509	2	0-0	1.000	-0	95	0	/O(RF)	0.2
PACIOREK, TOM Thomas Marian B 11.2.1946 Detroit, MI BR/TR 6-4/215# d9.12 b-Jim b-John OF Total (476-LF 73-CF 281-RF)																								
1970	LA N	8	9	2	2	1	0	0	0	0-0	1	3	.222	.300	.333	73	0	0-0	1.000	-0	45	0	/O-3(1-0-2)	-0.1
1971	LA N	2	2	0	1	0	0	0	1	0-0	0	0	.500	.500	.500	196	0	0-0	1.000	0	243	0	/O(LF)	0.0
1972	LA N	11	47	4	12	4	0	1	6	1-0	0	7	.255	.271	.404	92	-1	1-0	.979	1	97	92	/1-6,O-6(1-0-5)	0.0
1973	LA N	96	195	26	51	8	0	5	18	11-2	1	35	.262	.304	.379	92	-3	3-3	.979	-3	90	54	O-77(36-22-25)/1-4	-0.9
1974	†LA N	85	175	23	42	8	6	1	24	10-1	1	32	.240	.282	.371	86	-5	1-3	.944	-4	92	33	O-77(44-23-15)/1	-1.2
1975	LA N	62	145	14	28	8	0	1	5	11-1	0	29	.193	.250	.269	46	-11	4-3	.972	-3	93	0	O-54(30-2-25)	-1.7
1976	Atl N	111	324	39	94	10	4	4	36	19-2	3	57	.290	.333	.383	97	-2	2-3	.983	-7	82	56	O-84(38-7-44),1-12/3	-1.5
1977	Atl N	72	155	20	37	8	0	3	15	6-2	0	46	.239	.262	.348	57	-9	1-0	.984	-1	88	82	1-32/O-9(4-2-3),3	-1.2
1978	Atl N	5	9	2	3	0	0	0	0	0-0	0	1	.333	.333	.333	78	0	0-0	1.000	-0	0	82	/1-2	-0.1
	Sea A	70	251	32	75	20	3	4	30	15-0	0	39	.299	.336	.450	121	6	2-2	.980	-2	88	88	O-54(53-4-0),D-12/1-3	0.1
1979	Sea A	103	310	38	89	23	4	6	42	28-1	5	62	.287	.353	.445	113	6	6-4	1.000	-1	101	40	O-75(47-0-29),1-15	0.1
1980	Sea A	126	418	44	114	19	1	15	59	17-1	1	67	.273	.301	.431	98	-3	3-2	1.000	-2	95	73	O-60(19-1-41),1-36,D-23	-1.0
1981	Sea A★	104	405	50	132	28	2	14	66	35-3	4	50	.326	.379	.509	150	26	13-10	.974	3	104	128	*O-103(84-12-14)	2.5
1982	Chi A	104	382	49	119	27	4	11	55	24-3	9	53	.312	.361	.490	133	17	3-3	.993	3	116	109	*1-102/O-6(LF)	1.4
1983	†Chi A	115	420	65	129	32	3	9	63	25-4	3	58	.307	.347	.462	117	10	6-1	1.000	-3	97	91	1-67,O-55(30-0-27)/D-2	0.2
1984	Chi A	111	363	35	93	21	2	4	29	25-4	4	69	.256	.308	.358	81	-9	6-0	.993	-9	57	115	1-67,O-41(25-0-17)	-2.2
1985	Chi A	46	122	14	30	2	0	0	9	8-0	1	22	.246	.293	.262	53	-8	2-0	.970	0	94	97	O-23(21-0-2),D-12/1-6	-0.9
	NY N	46	116	14	33	3	1	1	11	6-1	1	14	.284	.325	.353	92	-2	1-0	1.000	-2	89	0	O-29(6-0-24)/1-8	-0.5
1986	Tex A	88	213	17	61	7	0	4	22	3-0	3	41	.286	.305	.376	82	-6	1-3	.967	3	74	271	O-25(22-0-3),1-23,3-21/SD	-0.5
1987	Tex A	27	60	6	17	3	0	3	12	1-0	1	19	.283	.302	.483	105	0	0-1	1.000	1	139	155	1-12,O-12(8-0-5)/D-3	0.0
Total	18	1392	4121	494	1162	232	30	86	503	245-25	38	704	.282	.325	.415	102	6	55-38	.979	-26	93	75	O-794L,1-396/D-61,3-23,S	-7.5
PACK, FRANKIE Frank B 4.10.1928 Morristown, TN D 1.26.2000 Hendersonville, NC BL/TR 6/190# d6.5																								
1949	StL A	1	1	0	0	0	0	0	0	0	0	1	.000	.000	.000	-96	0	0-0	—	0			H	0.0
PADDEN, DICK Richard Joseph "Brains" B 9.17.1870 Martins Ferry, OH D 10.31.1922 Martins Ferry, OH BR/TR 5-10/165# d7.15																								
1896	Pit N	61	219	33	53	4	8	2	24	14	2	9	.242	.294	.361	75	-10	8	.931	-14	78	56	2-61	-1.8
1897	Pit N	**134**	517	84	146	16	10	2	58	38	16		.282	.350	.364	92	-5	18	.941	4	95	78	*2-134	0.4
1898	Pit N	128	463	61	119	7	6	2	43	35	19		.257	.335	.311	87	-7	11	.947	-1	103	97	*2-128	-0.2
1899	Was N	134	451	66	125	20	7	2	61	24	17		.277	.337	.366	94	-4	27	.913	5	103	96	S-85,2-48	0.7
1901	StL N	123	489	71	125	17	7	2	62	31	11		.256	.315	.331	92	-5	26	.950	-1	**101**	121	*2-115/S-8	-0.4
1902	StL A	117	413	54	109	26	3	1	40	30	9		.264	.327	.349	89	-5	11	**.967**	12	105	**141**	*2-117	0.8
1903	StL A	29	94	7	19	3	0	0	6	9	5		.202	.306	.234	65	-3	5	.955	2	104	164	2-29	-0.1
1904	StL A	132	453	42	108	19	4	0	36	40	**18**		.238	.325	.298	104	5	23	.959	-16	95	80	*2-132	-1.1
1905	StL A	16	58	5	10	1	1	0	4	3	0		.172	.213	.224	41	-4	3	.950	-0	104	50	2-16	-0.5
Total	9	874	3157	423	814	113	46	11	334	224	97	9	.258	.326	.333	90	-38	132	.950	-8	97	97	2-780/S-93	-2.2
PADDEN, TOM Thomas Francis B 10.6.1908 Manchester, NH D 6.10.1973 Manchester, NH BR/TR 5-11.5/170# d5.29																								
1932	Pit N	47	118	13	31	6	1	0	10	9	0	7	.263	.315	.331	75	-4	0	.985	-1	*81*	*88*	C-43	-0.3
1933	Pit N	30	90	5	19	2	0	0	8	2	1	6	.211	.237	.233	35	-8	0	.984	3	*76*	*129*	C-27	-0.3
1934	Pit N	82	237	27	76	12	2	0	22	30	1	23	.321	.399	.388	109	5	3	.978	-6	*69*	***13***	C-76	0.3
1935	Pit N	97	302	35	82	9	1	1	30	48	0	26	.272	.371	.318	84	-4	1	.966	8	*83*	*124*	C-94	0.9
1936	Pit N	88	281	22	70	9	2	1	31	22	0	41	.249	.304	.306	63	-15	0	.976	1	*77*	***127***	C-87	-0.9
1937	Pit N	35	98	14	28	2	0	0	8	13	0	11	.286	.369	.306	85	-1	1	.983	2	*62*	*145*	C-34	0.2
1943	Phi N	17	41	5	12	0	0	0	1	2	1	6	.293	.341	.293	87	-1	0	1.000	2	*84*	*60*	C-16	0.2
	Was A	3	3	1	0	0	0	0	0	1	0	1	.000	.250	.000	-25	0	0-0	1.000	0	*0*	*0*	/C-2	0.0
Total	7	399	1170	122	318	40	6	2	110	127	3	121	.272	.345	.321	80	-28	5-0	.977	9	*76*	*93*	C-379	0.1
PADDOCK, DEL Delmar Harold B 6.8.1887 Volga, SD D 2.6.1952 Remer, MN BL/TR 5-9/165# d4.14																								
1912	Chi A	1	1	0	0	0	0	0	0	0	0		.000	.000	.000	-99	0	0	—	0			H	0.0
	NY A	46	156	26	45	5	3	1	14	23	4		.288	.393	.378	114	4	9	.894	-5	90	71	3-41/2-2,O(RF)	0.0
	Year	47	157	26	45	5	3	1	14	23	4		.287	.391	.376	113	4	9	.894	-5	90	71	3-41/2-2,O(RF)	0.0
PADGETT, DON Don Wilson B 12.5.1911 Caroleen, NC D 12.9.1980 High Point, NC BL/TR 6/190# d4.23 Mil 1942-45																								
1937	StL N	123	446	62	140	22	6	10	74	30	0	43	.314	.357	.457	117	10	4	.955	1	108	81	*O-109(0-6-102)	0.4
1938	StL N	110	388	59	105	26	5	8	65	18	0	28	.271	.303	.425	93	-5	0	.962	6	102	231	O-71(3-5-63),1-16/C-6	-0.4
1939	StL N	92	233	38	93	15	3	5	53	18	1	11	.399	.444	.554	157	19	1	.978	-1	*120*	*61*	C-61/1-6	2.1
1940	StL N	93	240	24	58	15	1	6	41	26	2	14	.242	.321	.387	89	-3	1	.962	-6	*86*	*107*	C-72/1-2	-0.5
1941	StL N	107	324	39	80	18	0	5	44	21	0	16	.247	.293	.349	75	-11	0	.959	-6	96	25	O-62(59-0-3),C-18/1-2	-2.0
1946	Bro N	19	30	2	5	1	0	1	9	4		0	4	.167	.265	.300	59	-2	0	1.000	0	*195*	*67*	C-10	-0.1
	Bos N	44	98	6	25	3	0	2	21	5	0	7	.255	.291	.347	80	-3	0	.939	-5	*80*	*109*	C-26	-0.7
	Year	63	128	8	30	4	0	3	30	9	0	11	.234	.285	.336	75	-5	0	.954	-5	*106*	*99*	C-36	-0.8

Year	Tm Lg	G	AB	R	H	2B	3B	HR	RBI	BB-IB	HP	SO	AVG	OBP	SLG	AOPS	ABR	SB-CS	FA	FR	Rng	Thr	G at Pos	BFW
1947	Phi N	75	158	14	50	8	1	0	24	16	1	5	.316	.383	.380	107	2	0	.962	-5	*71*	*117*	C-39	-0.1
1948	Phi N	36	74	3	17	3	0	0	7	3	0	2	.230	.260	.270	44	-6	0	.957	-3	*63*	*30*	C-19	-0.8
Total	8	699	1991	247	573	111	16	37	338	141	4	130	.288	.336	.415	101	1	6	.962	-18	*96*	*86*	C-251,O-242(62-11-168)/1-26	-2.1
PADGETT, ERNIE Ernest Kitchen "Red" B 3.1.1899 Philadelphia, PA D 4.15.1957 E.Orange, NJ BR/TR 5-8/155# d10.3																								
1923	Bos N	4	11	3	2	0	0	0	0	2	0	0	.182	.308	.182	33	-1	0-0	.947	1	92	190	/S-2,2	0.0
1924	Bos N	138	502	42	128	25	9	1	46	37	3	56	.255	.310	.347	79	-15	4-9	.967	-9	102	108	*3-113,2-29	-1.9
1925	Bos N	86	256	31	78	9	7	0	29	14	0	14	.305	.341	.395	96	-3	3-5	.964	-15	85	76	2-47,S-18/3-7	-1.6
1926	Cle A	36	62	7	13	0	1	0	6	8	0	3	.210	.300	.242	42	-5	1-0	.930	1	116	158	3-29/S-2	-0.3
1927	Cle A	7	7	1	2	0	0	0	0	0	0	2	.286	.286	.286	48	-1	0-0	1.000	-0	60	0	/2-4	-0.1
Total	5	271	838	84	223	34	17	1	81	61	3	75	.266	.318	.351	80	-25	8-14	.957	-23	102	113	3-149/2-81,S-22	-3.9
PAEPKE, DENNIS Dennis Ray B 4.17.1945 Long Beach, CA BR/TR 6/202# d6.2																								
1969	KC A	12	27	2	3	1	0	0	0	2-0	0	3	.111	.172	.148	-10	-4	0-0	1.000	2	72	99	/C-8	-0.2
1971	KC A	60	152	11	31	6	0	2	14	8-1	0	29	.204	.242	.283	49	-11	0-0	.994	0	83	82	C-32,O-17(1-0-16)	-1.1
1972	KC A	2	6	0	0	0	0	0	0	1-1	0	2	.000	.143	.000	-55	-1	0-0	.842	-0	30	172	/C-2	-0.1
1974	KC A	6	12	0	2	0	0	0	0	1-0	0	2	.167	.231	.167	15	-1	0-1	1.000	-1	45	352	/C-4,O(RF)	-0.2
Total	4	80	197	13	36	7	0	2	14	12-2	0	36	.183	.229	.249	36	-17	0-1	.984	1	76	106	/C-46,O-18(1-0-17)	-1.6
PAFKO, ANDY Andrew "Handy Andy" or "Pruschka" B 2.25.1921 Boyceville, WI BR/TR 6/190# d9.24 C3																								
1943	Chi N	13	58	7	22	3	0	0	10	2	0	5	.379	.400	.431	142	3	1	1.000	-2	87	0	O-13(CF)	0.1
1944	Chi N	128	469	47	126	16	2	6	62	28	4	23	.269	.315	.350	87	-9	2	.983	10	100	**215**	*O-123(0-123-1)	-0.2
1945	†Chi N✳	144	534	64	159	24	12	12	110	45	**8**	36	.298	.361	.455	129	19	5	**.995**	-0	100	98	*O-140(CF)	1.4
1946	Chi N	65	234	18	66	6	4	3	39	27	4	15	.282	.366	.380	114	5	4	.978	3	93	211	O-64(CF)	0.6
1947	Chi N★	129	513	68	155	25	7	13	66	31	3	39	.302	.346	.454	115	9	4	.985	-1	99	102	*O-127(CF)	0.5
1948	Chi N★	142	548	82	171	30	2	26	101	50	5	50	.312	.375	.516	145	33	3	.938	10	109	**121**	*3-139	4.2
1949	Chi N★	144	519	79	146	29	2	18	69	63	**9**	33	.281	.369	.449	121	17	4	.987	-6	90	120	O-98(1-89-9),3-49	0.8
1950	Chi N★	146	514	95	156	24	8	36	92	69	11	32	.304	.397	.591	158	43	4	.978	-4	94	104	*O-144(0-138-6)	3.4
1951	Chi N	49	178	26	47	5	3	12	35	17	4	10	.264	.342	.528	128	6	1-1	.992	-1	91	142	O-48(CF)	0.4
	Bro N	84	277	42	69	11	0	18	58	35	8	27	.249	.350	.484	120	8	1-4	.993	-0	92	128	O-76(70-9-0)	0.1
	Year	133	455	68	116	16	3	30	93	52	**12**	37	.255	.347	.501	123	14	2-5	.993	-1	92	134	*O-124(70-57-0)	0.5
1952	†Bro N	150	551	76	158	17	5	19	85	64	5	48	.287	.366	.439	121	16	4-3	.988	0	90	**175**	*O-139(105-12-38),3-13	0.9
1953	Mil N	140	516	70	153	23	4	17	72	37	3	33	.297	.347	.455	114	10	2-1	.976	-8	92	49	*O-139(RF)	-0.4
1954	Mil N	138	510	61	146	22	4	14	69	37	4	36	.286	.335	.427	105	2	1-2	.969	-6	93	75	*O-138(0-7-131)	-0.9
1955	Mil N	86	252	29	67	3	5	5	34	7-1	4	23	.266	.293	.377	81	-9	1-2	.980	-3	101	25	O-58(1-7-52),3-12	-1.4
1956	Mil N	45	93	15	24	5	0	2	9	10-0	0	13	.258	.330	.376	95	0	0-0	.978	-1	94	125	O-37(33-0-5)	-0.3
1957	†Mil N	83	220	31	61	6	1	8	27	10-2	1	22	.277	.308	.423	102	-1	1-0	.982	-2	101	25	O-69(32-1-36)	-0.5
1958	†Mil N	95	164	17	39	7	1	3	23	15-3	2	17	.238	.306	.348	80	-5	0-0	1.000	2	115	55	O-93(80-3-17)	-0.5
1959	Mil N	71	142	17	31	8	2	1	15	14-1	1	15	.218	.293	.324	70	-6	0-0	.978	-0	108	35	O-64(40-22-9)	-0.9
Total	17	1852	6292	844	1796	264	62	213	976	561-7	76	477	.285	.350	.449	118	141	38-13	.984	-7	96	110	*O-1570(362-803-443),3-213	7.3
PAGAN, JOSE Jose Antonio (Rodriguez) B 5.5.1935 Barceloneta, P.R. BR/TR 5-9/165# d8.4 C5 OF Total (83-LF 10-RF)																								
1959	SF N	31	46	7	8	1	0	0	1	2-0	0	8	.174	.208	.196	9	-6	1-0	.900	1	103	118	3-18/S-5,2-3	-0.5
1960	SF N	18	49	8	14	2	2	0	2	1-0	0	6	.286	.300	.408	97	-1	2-2	.917	-5	61	37	S-11/3	-0.6
1961	SF N	134	434	38	110	15	2	5	46	31-7	2	45	.253	.306	.332	72	-18	8-5	.964	-19	87	70	*S-132/O-4(3-0-2)	-2.6
1962	†SF N	164	580	73	150	25	6	7	57	47-4	1	77	.259	.312	.359	82	-15	13-9	**.973**	-23	90	86	*S-164	-2.5
1963	SF N	148	483	46	113	12	1	6	39	26-5	4	67	.234	.277	.300	67	-21	10-7	.970	-18	91	84	*S-143/2O(LF)	-3.0
1964	SF N	134	367	33	82	10	1	1	28	35-10	1	66	.223	.289	.264	57	-20	5-4	.958	-23	86	80	*S-132/O-8(6-0-2)	-3.6
1965	SF N	26	83	10	17	4	0	0	5	8-2	0	9	.205	.272	.253	48	-5	1-0	.941	-5	94	53	S-26	-0.9
	Pit N	42	38	6	9	1	0	0	1	1-0	1	7	.237	.275	.263	52	-2	1-0	.923	2	143	192	3-15/S-7	0.1
	Year	68	121	16	26	5	0	0	6	9-2	1	16	.215	.273	.256	50	-8	2-0	.923	-2	99	66	S-33,3-15	-0.8
1966	Pit N	109	368	44	97	15	6	4	54	13-3	4	38	.264	.292	.370	84	-9	0-2	.949	-1	103	118	3-83,S-18/2-3,O-3(LF)	-1.1
1967	Pit N	81	211	17	61	6	2	1	19	10-3	3	28	.289	.323	.351	95	-2	1-1	.938	8	133	94	3-25,O-23(LF),S-16/2-2,C	0.6
1968	Pit N	80	163	24	36	7	1	4	21	11-3	3	32	.221	.278	.350	90	-2	2-3	.924	-1	102	72	3-30,O-19(LF)/S-8,2-2,1	-0.5
1969	Pit N	108	274	29	78	11	4	9	42	17-2	1	46	.285	.325	.453	119	6	1-0	.954	-2	92	99	3-44,O-23(21-0-2)/2	0.3
1970	†Pit N	95	230	21	61	14	1	7	29	20-1	0	24	.265	.321	.426	101	0	1-1	.957	1	98	154	3-53/O-4(1-0-3),12	0.0
1971	†Pit N	57	158	16	38	1	0	5	15	16-2	1	25	.241	.311	.342	86	-3	0-0	.980	-1	94	135	3-41/O-3(LF),1-2	-0.5
1972	Pit N	53	127	11	32	9	0	3	8	5-0	1	17	.252	.284	.394	93	-1	0-0	.899	-8	69	67	3-32/O-2(LF)	-1.0
1973	Phi N	46	78	4	16	5	0	0	5	1-1	0	15	.205	.213	.269	33	-7	0-1	.958	-1	76	48	3-16/1-5,O-2(1-0-1),2	-0.9
Total	15	1326	3689	387	922	138	26	52	372	244-43	22	510	.250	.298	.344	79	-106	46-35	.963	-96	90	80	S-662,3-358/O-92L,2-14,1-9,C	-16.7
PAGE, MIKE Michael Randy B 7.12.1940 Woodruff, SC BL/TR 6-2.5/210# d6.30																								
1968	Atl N	20	28	1	5	0	0	0	1	1-0	0	9	.179	.207	.179	16	-3	0-0	1.000	-0	92	0	/O-6(1-0-5)	-0.4
PAGE, MITCHELL Mitchell Otis B 10.15.1951 Los Angeles, CA BL/TR 6-2/205# d4.9 C5																								
1977	Oak A	145	501	85	154	28	8	21	75	78-6	6	95	.307	.405	.521	153	40	42-5	.954	5	111	116	*O-133(131-0-5)/D-8	4.5
1978	Oak A	147	516	62	147	25	7	17	70	53-6	4	95	.285	.355	.459	135	23	23-19	.973	-0	102	61	*O-114(112-0-2),D-33	1.6
1979	Oak A	133	478	51	118	11	2	9	42	52-5	3	93	.247	.323	.335	83	-11	17-16	1.000	-1	59	0	*D-126/O-4(LF)	-1.8
1980	Oak A	110	348	58	85	10	4	17	51	35-3	1	87	.244	.311	.443	113	5	14-7	—	0	0	0	*D-101	0.2
1981	Oak A	34	92	9	13	1	0	4	13	7-0	0	29	.141	.200	.283	40	-8	2-1	—	0	0	0	D-29	-0.9
1982	Oak A	31	78	14	20	5	0	4	7	7-1	2	24	.256	.333	.474	124	3	3-4	—	0	0	0	D-24	0.1
1983	Oak A	57	79	16	19	3	0	0	1	10-0	2	22	.241	.341	.278	77	-2	3-3	1.000	0	128	0	D-34,O-10(7-0-3)	-0.3
1984	Pit N	16	12	2	4	1	0	0	0	3-0	0	4	.333	.467	.417	150	1	0-0	—	0			H	0.1
Total	8	673	2104	297	560	84	21	72	259	245-21	18	449	.266	.346	.429	118	51	104-55	.963	4	106	89	D-355,O-261(254-0-10)	3.5
PAGEL, KARL Karl Douglas B 3.29.1955 Madison, WI BL/TL 6-2/190# d9.21																								
1978	Chi N	2	2	0	0	0	0	0	0	0-0	0	2	.000	.000	.000	-89	-1	0-0	—	0			H	-0.1
1979	Chi N	1	1	0	0	0	0	0	0	0-0	0	1	.000	.000	.000	-91	0	0-0	—	0			/H	0.0
1981	Cle A	14	15	3	4	0	2	1	4	4-1	0	1	.267	.421	.733	230	2	0-0	1.000	1	225	142	/1-6,D	0.4
1982	Cle A	23	18	3	3	0	0	0	2	7-1	0	11	.167	.400	.167	63	0	0-0	.970	-0	81	66	1-10/D	-0.1
1983	Cle A	8	20	1	6	0	0	0	1	0-0	0	5	.300	.300	.300	63	-1	0-0	.000	-0	0	0	/O(LF)D	-0.1
Total	5	48	56	7	13	0	2	1	7	11-2	0	20	.232	.358	.357	99	0	0-0	.985	1	155	105	/1-16,D-7,O(LF)	0.1
PAGLIARONI, JIM James Vincent "Pag" B 12.8.1937 Dearborn, MI BR/TR 6-4/210# d8.13 Mil 1956-57																								
1955	Bos A	1	0	0	0	0	0	0	1	0-0	0	0	—	.000	—	—	0	0-0	—	0	*0*	*0*	/C	0.0
1960	Bos A	28	62	7	19	5	2	2	9	13-0	1	11	.306	.434	.548	158	6	0-0	.990	-2	*116*	*65*	C-18	0.5
1961	Bos A	120	376	50	91	17	0	16	58	55-0	4	74	.242	.342	.415	100	1	1-1	.984	-4	*85*	*78*	*C-108	0.1
1962	Bos A	90	260	39	67	14	0	11	37	36-0	5	55	.258	.359	.438	110	5	2-1	.987	-4	*80*	*92*	C-73	0.4
1963	Pit N	92	252	27	58	5	0	11	26	36-8	2	57	.230	.330	.381	104	2	0-0	.988	2	*85*	*119*	C-85	0.8
1964	Pit N	97	302	33	89	12	3	10	36	41-4	2	56	.295	.383	.454	135	15	1-0	.992	-2	*100*	*83*	C-96	1.9
1965	Pit N	134	403	42	108	15	0	17	65	41-11	3	84	.268	.337	.432	115	8	0-0	.994	1	***144***	*69*	*C-131	1.6
1966	Pit N	123	374	37	88	20	0	11	49	50-9	4	71	.235	.329	.377	96	0	0-5	**.997**	-9	*102*	*55*	*C-118	-0.5
1967	Pit N	44	100	4	20	1	1	0	9	16-5	1	26	.200	.314	.230	59	-5	0-0	.984	0	*114*	*79*	C-38	-0.4
1968	Oak A	66	199	19	49	4	0	6	20	24-1	2	42	.246	.330	.357	115	4	0-0	.997	-7	82	76	C-63	0.0
1969	Oak A	14	27	1	4	1	0	1	2	5-0	1	2	.148	.303	.296	71	-1	0-0	.981	3	64	217	/C-7	0.2
	Sea A	40	110	10	29	4	1	5	14	13-1	0	16	.264	.333	.455	123	3	0-0	.988	-7	45	96	C-29/1-2,O(RF)	-0.3
	Year	54	137	11	33	5	1	6	16	18-1	1	18	.241	.327	.423	113	2	0-0	.987	-5	49	120	C-36/1-2,O(RF)	-0.1
Total	11	849	2465	269	622	98	7	90	326	330-39	25	494	.252	.344	.407	109	38	4-7	.991	-30	*99*	*81*	C-767/1-2,O(RF)	4.3
PAGLIARULO, MIKE Michael Timothy B 3.15.1960 Medford, MA BL/TR (BB 1985 (1 game)) 6-2/195# d7.7																								
1984	NY A	67	201	24	48	15	3	7	34	15-0	0	46	.239	.288	.448	105	1	0-0	.955	-2	90	147	3-67	-0.2
1985	NY A	138	380	55	91	16	2	19	62	45-4	4	86	.239	.324	.442	111	5	0-0	.951	-17	84	76	*3-134	-1.3
1986	NY A	149	504	71	120	24	3	28	71	54-10	4	120	.238	.316	.464	111	6	4-1	.953	-3	99	106	*3-143/S-2	0.2
1987	NY A	150	522	76	122	26	3	32	87	53-9	2	111	.234	.305	.479	105	2	1-3	.959	-2	101	**130**	*3-147/1	-0.3
1988	NY A	125	444	46	96	20	1	15	67	37-9	2	104	.216	.276	.367	80	-13	1-0	.943	-5	100	79	*3-124	-1.7
1989	NY A	74	223	19	44	10	0	4	16	19-0	2	43	.197	.266	.296	59	-12	1-1	.936	-2	106	58	3-69/D	-1.4

Year	Tm Lg	G	AB	R	H	2B	3B	HR	RBI	BB-IB	HP	SO	AVG	OBP	SLG	AOPS	ABR	SB-CS	FA	FR	Rng	Thr	G at Pos	BFW
	SD N	50	148	12	29	7	0	3	14	18-4	1	39	.196	.287	.304	69	-6	2-0	.936	-5	96	44	3-49	-1.0
1990	SD N	128	398	29	101	23	2	7	38	39-3	3	66	.254	.322	.374	91	-4	1-3	.955	-5	95	103	*3-116	-1.1
1991	†Min A	121	365	38	102	20	0	6	36	21-3	3	55	.279	.322	.384	91	-5	1-2	.965	15	**120**	**158**	*3-118/2	1.0
1992	Min A	42	105	10	21	4	0	0	9	1-0	1	17	.200	.213	.238	26	-11	1-0	.962	2	116	70	3-37/D	-0.8
1993	Min A	83	253	31	74	16	4	3	23	18-2	5	34	.292	.350	.423	107	2	6-6	.984	-0	102	85	3-79	0.2
	Bal A	33	117	24	38	9	0	6	21	8-0	1	15	.325	.373	.556	140	6	0-0	.937	-1	88	126	3-28/1-4	0.5
	Year	116	370	55	112	25	4	9	44	26-2	6	49	.303	.357	.465	118	9	6-6	.969	-1	98	96	*3-107/1-4	0.7
1995	Tex A	86	241	27	56	16	0	4	27	15-2	1	49	.232	.277	.349	61	-14	0-0	.963	6	111	124	3-68,1-11	-0.8
Total	11	1246	3901	462	942	206	18	134	505	343-46	29	785	.241	.306	.407	93	-43	18-16	.955	-18	100	104	*3-1179/1-16,D-2,S-2,2	-6.7
PAGNOZZI, TOM Thomas Alan B 7.30.1962 Tucson, AZ BR/TR 6-1/190# d4.12																								
1987	†StL N	27	48	8	9	1	0	2	9	4-2	0	13	.188	.250	.333	52	-4	1-0	1.000	-2	353	66	C-25/1	-0.5
1988	StL N	81	195	17	55	9	0	0	15	11-1	0	32	.282	.319	.328	86	-4	0-0	.971	-1	85	157	C-28,1-28/3-5	-0.6
1989	StL N	52	80	3	12	2	0	0	3	6-2	1	19	.150	.216	.175	13	-9	0-0	.982	-6	61	91	C-38/1-2,3	-1.5
1990	StL N	69	220	20	61	15	0	2	23	14-1	1	37	.277	.321	.373	91	-3	1-1	.989	11	128	155	C-63/1-2	1.2
1991	StL N	140	459	38	121	24	5	2	57	36-6	4	63	.264	.319	.351	89	-7	9-13	.991	9	122	**138**	*C-139/1-3	0.7
1992	StL N★	139	485	33	121	26	3	7	44	28-9	1	64	.249	.290	.359	86	-10	2-5	**.999**	-10	115	78	*C-138	-1.4
1993	StL N	92	330	31	85	15	1	7	41	19-6	1	30	.258	.296	.373	80	-10	1-0	.991	-6	112	100	C-92	-0.9
1994	StL N	70	243	21	66	12	1	7	40	21-5	0	39	.272	.327	.416	94	-2	0-0	**.998**	1	**189**	116	C-70/1	0.3
1995	StL N	62	219	17	47	14	1	2	15	11-0	1	31	.215	.254	.315	50	-16	0-1	.995	2	98	145	C-61	-1.1
1996	†StL N	119	407	48	110	23	0	13	55	24-2	2	78	.270	.311	.423	93	-5	4-1	.990	-1	126	104	*C-116/1	0.2
1997	StL N	25	50	4	11	3	0	1	8	1-0	0	7	.220	.235	.340	49	-4	0-0	1.000	-3	142	59	C-13/1-2,3	-0.6
1998	StL N	51	160	7	35	9	0	1	10	14-0	0	37	.219	.280	.294	52	-11	0-0	.982	-3	86	98	C-44	-1.1
Total	12	927	2896	247	733	153	11	44	320	189-34	11	450	.253	.299	.359	80	-85	18-21	.992	-7	124	113	C-827/1-40,3-7	-5.3
PALACIOS, REY Robert Rey B 11.8.1962 Brooklyn, NY BR/TR 5-10/190# d9.8																								
1988	KC A	5	11	2	1	0	0	0	0	0-0	0	4	.091	.091	.091	-48	-2	0-0	1.000	1	77	0	/C-3,3D	-0.2
1989	KC A	55	47	12	8	2	0	1	8	2-0	1	14	.170	.216	.277	39	-4	0-1	.958	-1	68	0	3-21,1-18,C-13/O(RF)D	-0.5
1990	KC A	41	56	8	13	3	0	2	9	5-0	0	24	.232	.295	.393	92	-1	2-2	.992	1	104	56	C-27/1-7,3-3,O(RF)	0.1
Total	3	101	114	22	22	5	0	3	17	7-0	1	42	.193	.244	.316	57	-7	2-3	.994	1	103	55	/C-43,1-25,3-25,D-3,O-2(RF)	-0.6
PALMEIRO, ORLANDO Orlando B 1.19.1969 Hoboken, NJ BL/TL 5-11/155# d7.1																								
1995	Cal A	15	20	3	7	0	0	0	1	1-0	0	1	.350	.381	.350	93	0	0-0	1.000	-0	93	0	/O-7(3-4-0),D	0.0
1996	Cal A	50	87	6	25	6	1	0	6	8-1	2	13	.287	.361	.379	87	-1	0-1	1.000	-3	80	0	O-31(7-17-8)/D-4	-0.4
1997	Ana A	74	134	19	29	2	2	0	8	17-1	1	11	.216	.307	.261	51	-10	2-2	.975	-1	101	60	O-52(4-45-4),D-11	-1.1
1998	Ana A	75	165	28	53	7	2	0	21	20-1	0	11	.321	.395	.388	104	2	5-4	1.000	1	118	0	O-54(46-6-4)/D-3	0.1
1999	Ana A	109	317	46	88	12	1	1	23	39-1	6	30	.278	.364	.331	81	-8	5-5	.994	1	101	118	O-92(60-1-35),D-10	-1.0
2000	Ana A	108	243	38	73	20	2	0	25	38-0	2	20	.300	.395	.399	101	2	4-1	.984	3	103	167	O-72(40-2-31),D-19	0.2
2001	Ana A	104	230	29	56	10	1	2	23	25-2	3	24	.243	.319	.322	70	-10	6-6	.989	-0	102	74	O-59(26-7-28),D-30	-1.4
2002	†Ana A	110	263	35	79	12	1	0	31	30-1	0	22	.300	.368	.354	95	-1	7-2	.993	1	104	74	O-86(33-11-47)/D-6	-0.2
2003	StL N	141	317	37	86	13	1	3	33	32-3	2	31	.271	.336	.347	84	-7	3-3	**1.000**	5	112	129	*O-112(42-17-62)	-0.5
Total	9	786	1776	241	496	82	11	6	171	210-10	16	163	.279	.357	.348	85	-33	32-24	.992	7	105	92	O-565(261-110-219)/D-84	-4.3
PALMEIRO, RAFAEL Rafael (Corrales) B 9.24.1964 Havana, Cuba BL/TL 6/188# d9.8																								
1986	Chi N	22	73	9	18	4	0	3	12	4-0	1	6	.247	.295	.425	89	-1	1-1	.900	1	102	166	O-20(19-0-3)	-0.2
1987	Chi N	84	221	32	61	15	1	14	30	20-1	1	26	.276	.336	.543	124	7	2-2	1.000	-2	95	41	O-45(44-0-2),1-18	0.3
1988	Chi N★	152	580	75	178	41	5	8	53	38-6	3	34	.307	.349	.436	120	15	12-2	.983	-0	100	67	*O-147(145-2-3)/1-5	1.3
1989	Tex A	156	559	76	154	23	4	8	64	63-3	6	48	.275	.354	.374	104	5	4-3	.991	9	117	85	*1-147/D-6	0.4
1990	Tex A	154	598	72	**191**	35	6	14	89	40-6	3	59	.319	.361	.468	131	24	3-3	.995	-3	89	98	*1-146/D-6	1.0
1991	Tex A★	159	631	115	203	**49**	3	26	88	68-10	6	72	.322	.389	.532	156	50	4-3	.992	-6	86	84	*1-157/D-2	3.2
1992	Tex A	159	608	84	163	27	4	22	85	72-8	10	83	.268	.352	.434	124	20	2-3	.995	13	122	92	*1-156/D-2	2.1
1993	Tex A	160	597	**124**	176	40	2	37	105	73-22	5	85	.295	.371	.554	153	44	22-3	.997	18	138	96	*1-160	4.9
1994	Bal A	111	436	82	139	32	0	23	76	54-1	2	63	.319	.392	.550	134	23	7-3	.996	-1	93	102	*1-111	1.1
1995	Bal A	143	554	89	172	30	2	39	104	62-5	3	65	.310	.380	.583	145	35	3-1	.997	10	118	108	*1-142	3.0
1996	†Bal A	162	626	110	181	40	2	39	142	95-12	3	96	.289	.381	.546	133	33	8-0	.995	6	113	111	*1-159/D-3	2.3
1997	†Bal A	158	614	95	156	24	2	38	110	67-7	5	109	.254	.329	.485	113	10	5-2	.993	6	111	102	*1-155/D-3	0.1
1998	Bal A★	**162**	619	98	183	36	1	43	121	79-8	7	91	.296	.379	.565	144	41	11-7	.994	8	114	98	*1-159/D-3	3.1
1999	†Tex A★	158	565	96	183	30	1	47	148	97-14	3	69	.324	.420	.630	157	51	2-4	.996	-2	74	91	*D-128,1-28	3.4
2000	Tex A	158	565	102	163	29	3	39	120	103-17	3	77	.288	.397	.558	137	34	2-1	.995	-3	88	82	*1-108,D-46	1.7
2001	Tex A	160	600	98	164	33	0	47	123	101-8	7	90	.273	.381	.563	140	37	1-1	.992	4	116	107	*1-113,D-46	2.6
2002	Tex A	155	546	99	149	34	0	43	105	104-16	6	94	.273	.391	.571	145	39	2-0	.994	10	138	96	1-97,D-55	3.4
2003	Tex A	154	561	92	146	21	2	38	112	84-9	5	77	.260	.359	.508	116	13	2-0	.996	5	133	108	D-97,1-55	0.7
Total	18	2567	9553	1548	2780	543	38	528	1687	1224-153	79	1244	.291	.373	.522	134	480	93-39	.994	72	111	97	*1-1916,D-397,O-212(208-2-8)	34.4
PALMER, DEAN Dean William B 12.27.1968 Tallahassee, FL BR/TR 6-2/195# d9.1																								
1989	Tex A	16	19	0	2	2	0	0	1	0-0	0	12	.105	.100	.211	-13	-3	0-0	.667	-0	82	0	/3-6,SO(LF)D	-0.3
1991	Tex A	81	268	38	50	9	2	15	37	32-0	3	98	.187	.281	.403	88	-5	0-2	.944	-9	82	53	3-50,O-29(LF)/D-5	-1.5
1992	Tex A	152	541	74	124	25	0	26	72	62-2	4	154	.229	.311	.420	107	4	10-4	.945	-1	92	90	*3-150	0.4
1993	Tex A	148	519	88	127	31	2	33	96	53-4	8	154	.245	.321	.503	123	15	11-10	.922	-14	91	82	*3-148/S	0.1
1994	Tex A	93	342	50	84	14	2	19	59	26-0	2	89	.246	.302	.465	94	-5	3-4	.912	-3	105	54	3-91	-0.7
1995	Tex A	36	119	30	40	6	0	9	24	21-1	4	21	.336	.448	.613	170	13	1-1	.948	2	113	148	3-36	1.5
1996	†Tex A	154	582	98	163	26	2	38	107	59-4	5	145	.280	.348	.527	112	9	2-0	.953	-19	84	63	*3-154/D	-0.8
1997	Tex A	94	355	47	87	21	0	14	55	26-2	1	84	.245	.296	.423	81	-11	1-0	.959	-4	97	61	3-93	-1.3
	KC A	49	187	23	52	10	1	9	31	15-0	2	50	.278	.335	.487	109	2	1-2	.924	-8	87	97	3-48/D	-0.6
	Year	143	542	70	139	31	1	23	86	41-2	3	134	.256	.310	.445	91	-9	2-2	.948	-12	94	74	*3-141/D	-1.9
1998	KC A★	152	572	84	159	27	2	34	119	48-3	6	134	.278	.333	.510	114	10	8-2	.921	-24	81	80	*3-129,D-22	-1.2
1999	Det A	150	560	92	147	25	2	38	100	57-3	10	153	.262	.339	.518	114	10	3-3	.945	-5	96	**105**	*3-141/D-9	0.6
2000	Det A	145	524	73	134	22	2	29	102	66-2	4	146	.256	.338	.471	106	4	4-2	.914	-15	92	72	*3-115,1-20,D-14	-1.1
2001	Det A	57	216	34	48	11	0	11	40	27-0	3	59	.222	.317	.426	98	-1	4-1	—	0	0	0	D-57	-0.4
2002	Det A	4	12	0	0	0	0	0	0	1-0	0	5	.000	.077	.000	-82	-3	0-0	—	0			/D-4	-0.4
2003	Det A	26	86	3	12	2	0	0	6	9-0	2	28	.140	.235	.163	9	-11	0-0	1.000	1	162	0	D-22/13	-1.2
Total	14	1357	4902	734	1229	231	15	275	849	502-21	54	1332	.251	.324	.472	106	28	48-31	.935	-98	92	80	*3-1162,D-141/O-30(LF),1-21,S-2	-6.9
PALMER, EDDIE Edwin Henry "Baldy" B 6.1.1893 Petty, TX D 1.9.1983 Marlow, OK BR/TR 5-9.5/175# d9.6																								
1917	Phi A	16	52	7	11	1	0	0	5	7	0	7	.212	.305	.231	65	-2	1	.898	0	106	49	3-13/S	-0.1
PALMISANO, JOE Joseph B 11.19.1902 West Point, GA D 11.5.1971 Albuquerque, NM BR/TR 5-8/160# d5.31																								
1931	Phi A	19	44	5	10	2	0	0	4	6	0	3	.227	.320	.273	54	-3	0-0	.960	-1	*109*	77	C-16/2	-0.3
PALYS, STAN Stanley Francis B 5.1.1930 Blakely, PA BR/TR 6-2/190# d9.20																								
1953	Phi N	2	2	0	0	0	0	0	0	1	0	0	.000	.333	.000	-4	0	0-0	—	-0	0	0	/O(RF)	0.0
1954	Phi N	2	4	0	1	0	0	0	0	1	0	1	.250	.400	.250	74	0	0-0	1.000	0	113	0	/O(RF)	0.0
1955	Phi N	15	52	8	15	3	0	1	8	6-0	0	5	.288	.362	.404	105	1	1-0	1.000	0	103	93	O-15(3-4-8)	0.0
	Cin N	79	222	29	51	14	0	7	30	12-0	1	35	.230	.271	.387	69	-10	1-1	.992	2	113	78	O-55(LF)/1	-1.1
	Year	94	274	37	66	17	0	8	38	18-0	1	40	.241	.289	.391	75	-10	2-1	.993	3	111	81	O-70(58-4-8)/1	-1.1
1956	Cin N	40	53	5	12	0	0	2	5	6-0	0	13	.226	.300	.340	69	-2	0-0	.929	-1	97	0	O-10(7-0-4)	-0.4
Total	4	138	333	42	79	17	0	10	43	26-0	1	54	.237	.293	.378	74	-11	2-1	.988	2	109	72	/O-82(65-4-14),1	-1.5
PANKOVITS, JIM James Franklin B 8.6.1955 Pennington Gap, VA BR/TR 5-10/195# d5.27 OF Total (28-LF 20-RF)																								
1984	Hou N	53	81	6	23	7	0	1	14	2-0	0	20	.284	.298	.407	105	0	2-1	.925	-3	80	138	2-15/S-4/O-3(LF)	-0.2
1985	Hou N	75	172	24	42	3	0	4	14	17-1	1	29	.244	.316	.331	84	-4	1-0	.983	2	112	108	O-33(14-0-20),2-21/S3	-0.2
1986	†Hou N	70	113	12	32	6	1	1	7	11-1	0	25	.283	.347	.381	103	1	1-1	.969	2	102	99	2-26/O-5(LF),C	0.4
1987	Hou N	50	61	7	14	2	0	1	8	6-1	0	13	.230	.299	.311	64	-3	2-0	1.000	3	95	140	/2-9,O-6(LF),3-4	0.0
1988	Hou N	68	140	13	31	7	1	2	12	8-0	2	28	.221	.272	.329	75	-5	2-1	.939	-5	93	128	2-31,3-11/1-2	-1.0
1990	Bos A	2	0	0	0	0	0	0	0	0-0	0	0	—	—	—	—	0	0-0	—	-1	0	0	/2-2	-0.1
Total	6	318	567	62	142	25	2	9	55	44-3	3	115	.250	.307	.349	86	-11	8-3	.961	-1	96	116	2-104/O-47L,3-16,S-5,1-2,C	-1.1

Year	Tm Lg	G	AB	R	H	2B	3B	HR	RBI	BB-IB	HP	SO	AVG	OBP	SLG	AOPS	ABR	SB-CS	FA	FR	Rng	Thr	G at Pos	BFW
PAPE, KEN Kenneth Wayne B 10.1.1951 San Antonio, TX BR/TR 5-11/195# d5.17																								
1976	Tex A	21	23	7	5	1	0	1	4	3-1	2	2	.217	.357	.391	117	1	0-1	.968	3	167	161	/S-6,3-4,2D	0.4
PAPI, STAN Stanley Gerard B 2.4.1951 Fresno, CA BR/TR 6/178# d4.11																								
1974	StL N	8	4	0	1	0	0	0	1	0-0	0	0	.250	.250	.250	40	0	0-0	1.000	1	83	443	/S-7,2	0.0
1977	Mon N	13	43	5	10	2	1	0	4	1-0	0	9	.233	.250	.326	55	-3	1-0	.952	-4	66	0	3-10/S-2,2	-0.7
1978	Mon N	67	152	15	35	11	0	0	11	10-1	2	28	.230	.285	.303	65	-7	0-0	.976	-2	93	84	S-22,3-15/2-5	-0.8
1979	Bos A	50	117	9	22	8	0	1	6	5-0	0	20	.188	.221	.282	33	-11	0-0	.982	7	118	119	2-26,S-21/D	-0.2
1980	Bos A	1	0	0	0	0	0	0	0	0-0	0	0	—	—	—	—	0	0-0	—	-0	0	0	/3	0.0
	Det A	46	114	12	27	3	4	3	17	5-0	0	24	.237	.267	.412	82	-4	0-0	.973	-6	80	88	2-31,3-11/S-5/1	-0.8
	Year	47	114	12	27	3	4	3	17	5-0	0	24	.237	.267	.412	82	-4	0-0	.973	-6	80	88	2-31,3-12/S-5,1	-0.8
1981	Det A	40	93	8	19	2	1	3	12	3-0	0	18	.204	.224	.344	61	-5	1-0	.941	-0	106	74	3-32/120(LF)D	-0.6
Total	6	225	523	49	114	26	6	7	51	24-1	2	99	.218	.253	.331	60	-30	2-0	.931	-4	93	74	/3-69,2-65,S-57,D-4,1-2,O(LF)	-3.1
PAPPAS, ERIK Erik Daniel B 4.25.1966 Chicago, IL BR/TR 6/190# d4.19																								
1991	Chi N	7	17	1	3	0	0	0	2	1-0	0	5	.176	.222	.176	13	-2	0-0	1.000	1	89	116	/C-6	-0.1
1993	StL N	82	228	25	63	12	0	1	28	35-2	0	35	.276	.368	.342	95	0	1-3	.982	6	110	102	C-63,O-16(1-0-15)/1-2	0.9
1994	StL N	15	44	8	4	1	0	0	5	10-0	1	13	.091	.259	.114	6	-6	0-0	.955	-5	69	21	C-15	-1.0
Total	3	104	289	34	70	13	0	1	35	46-2	1	53	.242	.342	.298	76	-8	1-3	.978	3	101	87	/C-84,O-16(1-0-15),1-2	-0.2
PAQUETTE, CRAIG Craig Harold B 3.28.1969 Long Beach, CA BR/TR 6/190# d6.1 OF Total (131-LF 75-RF)																								
1993	Oak A	105	393	35	86	20	4	12	46	14-2	0	108	.219	.245	.382	70	-20	4-2	.950	-8	91	87	*3-104/O(LF)D	-2.6
1994	Oak A	14	49	0	7	2	0	0	0	0-0	0	14	.143	.143	.184	-18	-9	1-0	1.000	1	95	139	3-14	-0.7
1995	Oak A	105	283	42	64	13	1	13	49	12-0	1	88	.226	.256	.417	77	-12	5-2	.935	-11	73	103	3-75,O-20(18-0-2)/S-8,1-3	-2.1
1996	KC A	118	429	61	111	15	1	22	67	23-2	2	101	.259	.296	.452	87	-11	5-3	.891	-8	99	60	3-51,O-47(LF),1-19,S-11/D-6	-2.0
1997	KC A	77	252	26	58	15	1	8	33	10-0	2	57	.230	.263	.393	67	-13	2-2	.935	-0	100	133	3-72/O-4(LF)	-1.2
1998	NY N	7	19	3	5	2	0	0	0	0-0	0	6	.263	.263	.368	65	-1	1-0	1.000	-2	34	198	/3-4,1-2,O(LF)	-0.3
1999	StL N	48	157	21	45	6	0	10	37	6-0	0	38	.287	.309	.516	104	0	1-0	.955	3	90	0	O-27(3-0-25),3-10/2-7,1-6	0.2
2000	†StL N	134	384	47	94	24	2	15	61	27-1	2	83	.245	.294	.435	82	-12	4-3	.942	-7	84	88	3-86,O-31(18-0-16),1-28,2-13	-2.0
2001	†StL N	123	340	47	96	17	0	15	64	18-1	5	67	.282	.326	.465	103	0	3-1	1.000	-5	80	66	O-56(32-0-26),3-33,1-23/2-4	-0.7
2002	Det A	72	252	20	49	14	1	4	20	10-0	0	53	.194	.223	.306	42	-22	1-0	.936	-2	99	63	3-49,1-14/O-8(4-0-4),D-5	-2.4
2003	Det A	11	33	2	5	0	0	0	0	0-0	0	5	.152	.152	.152	-21	-6	0-0	1.000	-1	38	113	/1-5,O-5(3-0-2)	-0.7
Total	11	814	2591	304	620	128	10	99	377	120-6	12	620	.239	.274	.411	76	-106	27-13	.941	-39	91	95	3-498,O-200L,1-100/2-24,S-19,D	-14.5
PARDO, AL Alberto Judas B 9.8.1962 Oviedo, Spain BB/TR 6-2/187# d7.3																								
1985	Bal A	34	75	3	10	1	0	0	1	3-0	0	15	.133	.167	.147	-14	-12	0-0	.979	-3	50	43	C-29	-1.4
1986	Bal A	16	51	3	7	1	0	1	3	0-0	0	14	.137	.137	.216	-6	-8	0-0	.987	-2	103	94	C-14/D	-0.9
1988	Phi N	2	2	0	0	0	0	0	0	0-0	0	2	.000	.000	.000	-98	-1	0-0	1.000	-0	0	0	/C-2	-0.1
1989	Phi N	1	1	0	0	0	0	0	0	0-0	0	0	.000	.000	.000	-99	0	0-0	1.000	0	0	0	/C	0.0
Total	4	53	129	6	17	2	0	1	4	3-0	0	31	.132	.152	.171	-12	-21	0-0	.982	-5	68	60	/C-46,D	-2.4
PAREDES, JOHNNY Johnny Alfonso (Isambert) B 9.2.1962 Maracaibo, Venezuela BR/TR 5-11/165# d4.29																								
1988	Mon N	35	91	6	17	2	0	1	10	9-0	3	17	.187	.282	.242	49	-6	5-2	.976	-1	100	131	2-28/O(RF)	-0.6
1990	Det A	6	8	2	1	0	0	0	0	1-0	0	0	.125	.222	.125	-0	-1	0-0	.917	-0	98	115	/2-4	-0.1
	Mon N	3	6	0	2	1	0	0	1	1-1	0	0	.333	.429	.500	161	1	0-0	.889	-0	116	192	/2-2	0.0
1991	Det A	16	18	4	6	0	0	0	0	0-0	0	1	.333	.333	.333	84	0	1-1	.958	-1	91	150	/2-7,3SD	-0.1
Total	3	60	123	12	26	3	0	1	11	11-1	3	18	.211	.292	.260	56	-6	6-3	.965	-2	100	136	/2-41,D-2,S30(RF)	-0.8
PARENT, FREDDY Frederick Alfred B 11.25.1875 Biddeford, ME D 11.2.1972 Sanford, ME BR/TR 5-7/154# d7.14 OF Total (34-LF 102-CF 12-RF)																								
1899	StL N	2	8	0	1	0	0	0	1	0	0		.125	.125	.125	-31	-1	0	.889	-0	93	157	/2-2	-0.2
1901	Bos A	**138**	517	87	158	23	9	4	59	41	9		.306	.367	.408	117	13	16	.918	-2	100	115	*S-138	1.4
1902	Bos A	**138**	567	91	156	31	8	3	62	24	4		.275	.309	.374	86	-12	16	.932	0	102	108	*S-138	-0.7
1903	†Bos A	139	560	83	170	31	17	4	80	13	6		.304	.326	.441	122	13	24	.930	8	103	82	*S-139	2.6
1904	Bos A	155	591	85	172	22	9	6	77	28	6		.291	.330	.389	120	12	20	.929	-10	98	107	*S-155	0.9
1905	Bos A	**153**	602	55	141	16	5	0	33	47	6		.234	.296	.277	81	-12	25	.920	-11	99	109	*S-153	-2.0
1906	Bos A	149	600	67	141	14	10	1	49	31	4		.235	.277	.297	80	-16	16	.933	-4	99	104	*S-143/2-6	-1.7
1907	Bos A	114	409	51	113	19	5	1	26	22	5		.276	.321	.355	116	7	12	.978	-1	186	73	O-47(26-13-9),S-43/3-7,2-5	0.6
1908	Chi A	119	391	28	81	7	5	0	35	50	2		.207	.300	.251	81	-6	9	.930	2	107	100	*S-118	-0.1
1909	Chi A	136	472	61	123	10	5	0	30	46	7		.261	.335	.303	106	5	32	.929	14	114	115	S-98,O-38(7-30-1)/2	2.3
1910	Chi A	81	258	23	46	6	1	1	16	29	2		.178	.266	.221	55	-13	14	.970	-3	87	65	O-62(1-59-2),2-11/S-4,3	-2.0
1911	Chi A	3	9	2	4	1	0	0	3	2	0		.444	.545	.556	214	2	0	1.000	1	123	0	/2-3	0.2
Total	12	1327	4984	633	1306	180	74	20	471	333	51		.262	.315	.340	99	-8	184	.927	-7	102	106	*S-1129,O-147C/2-28,3-8	1.3
PARENT, MARK Mark Alan B 9.16.1961 Ashland, OR BR/TR 6-5/225# d9.20																								
1986	SD N	8	14	1	2	0	0	0	0	1-0	0	3	.143	.200	.143	-4	-2	0-0	.889	-2	38	0	/C-3	-0.4
1987	SD N	12	25	0	2	0	0	0	2	0-0	0	9	.080	.080	.080	-60	-6	0-0	1.000	-0	190	0	C-10	-0.6
1988	SD N	41	118	9	23	3	0	6	15	6-0	0	23	.195	.232	.373	73	-5	0-0	.986	6	172	84	C-36	0.3
1989	SD N	52	141	12	27	4	0	7	21	8-2	0	34	.191	.229	.369	70	-6	1-0	1.000	6	143	90	C-41/1	0.2
1990	SD N	65	189	13	42	11	0	3	16	16-3	0	29	.222	.283	.328	67	-9	1-0	.992	2	94	90	C-60	-0.3
1991	Tex A	3	1	0	0	0	0	0	0	0-0	0	1	.000	.000	.000	-99	0	0-0	1.000	0	0	0	/C-3	0.0
1992	Bal A	17	34	4	8	1	0	2	4	3-0	1	7	.235	.316	.441	107	0	0-0	.988	3	122	93	C-16	0.4
1993	Bal A	22	54	7	14	2	0	4	12	3-0	0	14	.259	.293	.519	110	0	0-0	.989	-3	161	16	C-21/D	-0.1
1994	Chi N	44	99	8	26	4	0	3	16	13-1	1	24	.263	.348	.394	96	0	0-1	.976	-1	88	170	C-37	0.0
1995	Pit N	69	233	25	54	9	0	15	33	23-2	0	62	.232	.301	.464	96	-2	0-0	.990	-4	101	151	C-67	-0.2
	Chi N	12	32	5	8	2	0	3	5	3-0	0	7	.250	.314	.594	135	1	0-0	1.000	3	165	143	C-10	0.5
	Year	81	265	30	62	11	0	18	38	26-2	0	69	.234	.302	.479	101	-1	0-0	**.992**	-1	108	**150**	C-77	0.3
1996	Det A	38	104	13	25	6	0	7	17	3-0	0	27	.240	.259	.500	87	-3	0-0	.994	-4	121	142	C-33/1	-0.5
	†Bal A	18	33	4	6	1	0	2	6	2-0	0	10	.182	.229	.394	54	-3	0-0	.987	0	172	67	C-18	-0.2
	Year	56	137	17	31	7	0	9	23	5-0	0	37	.226	.252	.474	79	-6	0-0	.992	-4	135	122	C-51/1	-0.7
1997	Phi N	39	113	4	17	3	0	0	8	7-0	0	39	.150	.198	.177	-0	-17	0-1	.996	-5	89	136	C-38	-2.0
1998	Phi N	34	113	7	25	4	0	1	13	10-0	0	30	.221	.278	.283	49	-8	1-1	.987	-6	119	86	C-34	-1.2
Total	13	474	1303	112	279	50	0	53	168	98-8	2	319	.214	.268	.375	71	-60	3-3	.990	-4	119	110	C-427/1-2,D	-4.1
PARIS, KELLY Kelly Jay B 10.17.1957 Encino, CA BR/TR 6/180# d9.1																								
1982	StL N	12	29	1	3	0	0	0	1	0-0	0	7	.103	.100	.103	-42	-6	0-0	.867	2	125	382	/3-5,S-4	-0.4
1983	Cin N	56	120	13	30	6	0	0	7	15-1	1	22	.250	.336	.300	75	-3	8-2	1.000	-4	116	0	3-16,2-10/S-7,1-3	-0.6
1985	Bal A	5	9	0	0	0	0	0	0	0-0	0	1	.000	.000	.000	-99	-3	0-0	.857	-1	61	0	/2-2,D-2	-0.4
1986	Bal A	5	10	0	2	0	0	0	0	0-0	0	3	.200	.200	.200	9	-1	0-1	.857	0	130	240	/3-3,D-2	-0.1
1988	Chi A	14	44	6	11	0	0	3	6	0-0	0	6	.250	.250	.455	93	-1	0-0	1.000	-0	75	136	/1-9,3-4,D	-0.2
Total	5	92	212	20	46	6	0	3	14	15-1	1	39	.217	.270	.288	54	-14	8-3	.944	-4	121	85	/3-28,1-12,2-12,S-11,D-5	-1.7
PARISSE, TONY Louis Peter B 6.25.1911 Philadelphia, PA D 6.2.1956 Philadelphia, PA BR/TR 5-10/165# d9.22																								
1943	Phi A	6	17	0	3	0	0	0	1	2	0	2	.176	.263	.176	30	-1	0-0	1.000	0	*81*	*173*	/C-5	-0.1
1944	Phi A	4	4	0	0	0	0	0	0	0	0	1	.000	.000	.000	-99	-1	0-0	.500	-1	*0*	*0*	/C-2	-0.2
Total	2	10	21	0	3	0	0	0	1	2	0	3	.143	.217	.143	6	-2	0-0	.960	-0	*74*	*158*	/C-7	-0.3
PARKER, ACE Clarence McKay B 5.17.1912 Portsmouth, VA BR/TR 6/180# d4.24																								
1937	Phi A	38	94	8	11	0	1	2	13	4	0	17	.117	.153	.202	-11	-17	0-0	.905	-3	93	91	S-19/2-9,O-5(2-3-0)	-1.8
1938	Phi A	56	113	12	26	5	0	0	12	10	0	16	.230	.293	.274	44	-10	1-2	.972	-3	91	57	S-26/2-9,3-9	-1.1
Total	2	94	207	20	37	5	1	2	25	14	0	33	.179	.231	.242	19	-27	1-2	.934	-6	92	75	/S-45,2-18,3-9,O-5(2-3-0)	-2.9
PARKER, PAT Clarence Perkins B 5.22.1893 Somerville, MA D 3.21.1967 Claremont, NH BR/TR 5-7/160# d8.10																								
1915	StL A	3	6	0	1	0	0	0	1	0	0	3	.167	.167	.167	-0	-1	0-1	1.000	0	133	0	/O-2(RF)	-0.1
PARKER, DAVE David Gene B 6.9.1951 Grenada, MS BL/TR 6-5/230# d7.12 C2																								
1973	Pit N	54	139	17	40	9	1	4	14	2-1	2	27	.288	.308	.453	111	1	1-1	.964	3	122	130	O-39(4-16-19)	0.3
1974	†Pit N	73	220	27	62	10	3	4	29	10-1	3	53	.282	.322	.409	107	1	3-3	.964	2	104	158	O-49(11-14-27)/1-6	0.0

Year	Tm Lg	G	AB	R	H	2B	3B	HR	RBI	BB-IB	HP	SO	AVG	OBP	SLG	AOPS	ABR	SB-CS	FA	FR	Rng	Thr	G at Pos	BFW
1975	†Pit N	148	558	75	172	35	10	25	101	38-4	5	89	.308	.357	**.541**	148	33	8-6	.972	5	110	71	*O-141(RF)	3.0
1976	Pit N	138	537	82	168	28	10	13	90	30-6	2	80	.313	.349	.475	132	20	19-7	.956	1	104	102	*O-134(RF)	1.7
1977	Pit N★	159	637	107	**215**	**44**	8	21	88	58-13	7	107	**.338**	.397	.531	143	40	17-19	.965	23	**118**	**203**	*O-158(RF)/2	5.1
1978	Pit N	148	581	102	194	32	12	30	117	57-**23**	2	92	**.334**	.394	**.585**	163	**48**	20-7	.960	1	105	98	*O-147(RF)	**4.5**
1979	†Pit N★	158	622	109	193	45	7	25	94	67-14	9	101	.310	.380	.526	140	35	20-4	.960	0	104	108	*O-158(RF)	3.1
1980	Pit N★	139	518	71	153	31	1	17	79	25-5	2	69	.295	.327	.458	116	10	10-7	.965	1	100	130	*O-130(RF)	0.4
1981	Pit N★	67	240	29	62	14	3	9	48	9-3	2	25	.258	.287	.454	106	0	6-2	.941	-4	99	21	O-60(RF)	-0.7
1982	Pit N	73	244	41	66	19	3	6	29	22-2	1	45	.270	.330	.447	113	4	7-5	.957	-3	97	47	O-63(RF)	-0.2
1983	Pit N	144	552	68	154	29	4	12	69	28-6	0	89	.279	.311	.411	97	-4	12-9	.973	0	111	32	*O-142(RF)	-1.3
1984	Cin N	156	607	73	173	28	0	16	94	41-10	1	89	.285	.328	.410	103	2	11-10	.974	-2	104	60	*O-151(RF)	-1.0
1985	Cin N★	160	635	88	198	**42**	4	34	**125**	52-**24**	3	80	.312	.365	.551	146	38	5-13	.972	6	109	110	*O-159(RF)	3.3
1986	Cin N★	**162**	637	89	174	31	3	31	116	56-16	1	126	.273	.330	.477	116	12	1-6	.970	-9	91	68	*O-159(RF)	-0.7
1987	Cin N	153	589	77	149	28	0	26	97	44-13	8	104	.253	.311	.433	91	-9	7-3	.967	4	103	134	*O-142(RF)/1-9	-1.2
1988	†Oak A	101	377	43	97	18	1	12	55	32-2	0	70	.257	.314	.406	104	1	0-1	.953	-0	88	164	D-61,O-34(LF)/1	-0.2
1989	†Oak A	144	553	56	146	27	0	22	97	38-13	1	91	.264	.308	.432	112	7	0-0	1.000	0	104	0	*D-140/O(RF)	0.2
1990	Mil A☆	157	610	71	176	30	3	21	92	41-11	4	102	.289	.330	.451	119	14	4-7	.960	-1	0	168	*D-153/1-3	0.7
1991	Cal A	119	466	45	108	22	2	11	56	29-3	3	91	.232	.279	.358	76	-17	3-2	—	0	0	0	*D-119	-2.1
	Tor A	13	36	2	12	4	0	0	3	4-0	0	7	.333	.400	.444	128	2	0-1	—	0	0	0	D-11	0.1
	Year	132	502	47	120	26	2	11	59	33-3	3	98	.239	.288	.365	80	-15	3-3	—	0	0	0	*D-130	-2.0
Total	19	2466	9358	1272	2712	526	75	339	1493	683-170	56	1537	.290	.339	.471	121	238	154-113	.965	27	105	101	*O-1867(49-30-1791),D-484/1-19,2	15.0
PARKER, DIXIE Douglas Woolley B 4.24.1895 Forest Home, AL D 5.15.1972 Tuscaloosa, AL BL/TR 5-11/160# d7.28																								
1923	Phi N	4	5	0	1	0	0	0	1	0	0	1	.200	.200	.200	5	-1	0-0	.500	-1	*47*	*0*	/C-2	-0.2
PARKER, SALTY Francis James B 7.8.1913 E.St.Louis, IL D 7.27.1992 Houston, TX BR/TR 6/173# d8.13 M2 C16																								
1936	Det A	11	25	6	7	2	0	0	4	2	0	3	.280	.333	.360	71	-1	0-2	.906	2	111	151	/S-7,1-2	0.0
PARKER, WES Maurice Wesley B 11.13.1939 Evanston, IL BB/TL 6-1/180# d4.19																								
1964	LA N	124	214	29	55	7	1	3	10	14-3	1	45	.257	.303	.341	88	-4	5-4	.971	3	108	86	O-69(9-15-49),1-31	-0.5
1965	†LA N	154	542	80	129	24	7	8	51	75-1	5	95	.238	.334	.352	101	3	13-7	**.997**	4	104	105	*1-154/O(CF)	-0.3
1966	†LA N	156	475	67	120	17	5	12	51	69-9	5	83	.253	.351	.385	114	11	7-3	.992	0	95	83	*1-140,O-14(2-7-5)	0.4
1967	LA N	139	413	56	102	16	5	5	31	65-10	7	83	.247	.358	.346	112	9	10-5	**.996**	5	116	95	*1-112,O-18(CF)	0.8
1968	LA N	135	468	42	112	22	2	3	27	49-6	2	87	.239	.312	.314	96	-1	4-6	**.999**	3	103	93	*1-114,O-28(22-6-1)	-0.8
1969	LA N	132	471	76	131	23	4	13	68	56-6	2	46	.278	.353	.427	128	18	4-1	.995	1	100	95	*1-128/O-2(0-1-1)	0.9
1970	LA N	**161**	614	84	196	**47**	4	10	111	79-18	0	70	.319	.392	.458	134	33	8-2	**.996**	4	109	92	*1-161	2.5
1971	LA N	157	533	69	146	24	1	6	62	63-5	1	63	.274	.347	.356	107	7	6-1	.996	5	116	**111**	*1-148,O-18(1-0-18)	0.1
1972	LA N	130	427	45	119	14	3	4	59	62-5	1	43	.279	.367	.354	110	8	3-5	**.997**	4	**113**	108	*1-120/O-5(0-3-2)	0.1
Total	9	1288	4157	548	1110	194	32	64	470	532-63	24	615	.267	.351	.375	112	84	60-34	.996	28	108	98	*1-1108,O-155(34-51-76)	3.2
PARKER, RICK Richard Alan B 3.20.1963 Kansas City, MO BR/TR 6/185# d5.4																								
1990	SF N	54	107	19	26	5	0	2	14	10-0	1	15	.243	.314	.346	84	-2	6-1	.978	-2	90	63	O-35(13-5-23)/2-2,3S	-0.4
1991	SF N	13	14	0	1	0	0	0	1	1-0	0	5	.071	.133	.071	-42	-3	0-0	1.000	0	140	0	/O-4(4-1-0)	-0.3
1993	Hou N	45	45	11	15	3	0	0	4	3-0	0	8	.333	.375	.400	112	1	1-2	1.000	-1	89	0	O-16(3-13-1)/2S	-0.1
1994	NY N	8	16	1	1	0	0	0	0	0-0	0	2	.063	.063	.063	-68	-4	0-0	1.000	1	139	282	/O-6(4-1-3)	-0.3
1995	LA N	27	29	3	8	0	0	0	4	2-0	0	4	.276	.323	.276	66	-1	1-1	1.000	1	130	201	O-21(19-1-1)/3-2,S-2	-0.1
1996	LA N	16	14	2	4	1	0	0	1	0-0	1	2	.286	.333	.357	89	0	1-0	1.000	-1	30	0	/O-4(1-3-0)	-0.1
Total	6	163	225	36	55	9	0	2	24	16-0	2	36	.244	.300	.311	69	-9	9-4	.990	-0	102	96	/O-86(44-24-28),S-4,3-3,2-3	-1.3
PARKER, BILLY William David B 1.14.1947 Hayneville, AL D 2.9.2003 Sun City West, AZ BR/TR 5-8/168# d9.9																								
1971	Cal A	20	70	4	16	0	1	1	6	2-0	0	20	.229	.250	.300	59	-4	1-1	.958	-4	97	100	2-20	-0.8
1972	Cal A	36	80	11	17	2	0	2	8	9-0	0	17	.213	.286	.313	85	-2	0-2	.951	-0	77	108	3-21/2-9,O-5(LF),S	-0.3
1973	Cal A	38	102	14	23	2	1	0	7	8-1	1	23	.225	.286	.265	61	-5	0-1	.959	-8	71	72	2-32/S-3,D	-1.2
Total	3	94	252	29	56	4	2	3	21	19-1	1	60	.222	.276	.290	68	-11	1-4	.963	-12	85	89	/2-61,3-21,O-5(LF),S-4,D	-2.3
PARKINSON, FRANK Frank Joseph "Parky" B 3.23.1895 Dickson City, PA D 7.4.1960 Trenton, NJ BR/TR 5-11/175# d4.13																								
1921	Phi N	108	391	36	99	20	2	5	32	13	0	81	.253	.277	.353	61	-22	3-4	.931	9	**111**	89	*S-105/3	-0.2
1922	Phi N	141	545	86	150	18	6	15	70	55	2	93	.275	.344	.413	86	-12	3-4	.963	**28**	**117**	98	*2-139	1.8
1923	Phi N	67	219	21	53	12	0	3	28	13	1	31	.242	.288	.338	58	-13	0-4	.950	2	105	99	2-37,S-15,3-11	-1.0
1924	Phi N	62	156	14	33	7	0	1	19	14	1	28	.212	.281	.276	44	-12	3-1	.952	6	109	128	3-28,S-21,2-10	-0.3
Total	4	378	1311	157	335	57	8	24	149	95	4	233	.256	.308	.366	69	-59	9-13	.962	44	115	99	2-186,S-141/3-40	0.3
PARKS, ART Artie William B 11.1.1911 Paris, AR D 12.6.1989 Little Rock, AR BL/TR 5-9/170# d9.25																								
1937	Bro N	7	16	2	5	2	0	0	0	2	0	2	.313	.389	.438	122	1	0	1.000	1	67	469	/O-4(LF)	0.1
1939	Bro N	71	239	27	65	13	2	1	19	28	0	14	.272	.348	.356	86	-4	2	.977	-3	97	41	O-65(32-0-34)	-1.1
Total	2	78	255	29	70	15	2	1	19	30	0	16	.275	.351	.361	89	-3	2	.978	-3	96	61	/O-69(36-0-34)	-1.0
PARKS, DEREK Derek Gavin B 9.29.1968 Covina, CA BR/TR 6/205# d9.11																								
1992	Min A	7	6	1	2	0	0	0	0	1-0	1	1	.333	.500	.333	133	0	0-0	1.000	-0	40	100	/C-7	0.0
1993	Min A	7	20	3	4	0	0	0	1	1-0	0	2	.200	.238	.200	19	-2	0-0	.970	-1	98	0	/C-7	-0.3
1994	Min A	31	89	6	17	6	0	1	9	4-0	2	20	.191	.242	.292	37	-9	0-1	.993	-4	84	141	C-31	-1.0
Total	3	45	115	10	23	6	0	1	10	6-0	3	23	.200	.258	.278	40	-11	0-1	.989	-5	83	113	/C-45	-1.3
PARKS, BILL William Robert B 6.4.1849 Easton, PA D 10.10.1911 Easton, PA BR/TR 5-8/150# d4.26 M1 ▲																								
1875	Was NA	27	111	13	20	0	0	0	6	1		1	.180	.188	.180	29	-7	1-1	.836	3	137	0	O-17(16-1-0),P-14,M	-0.1
	Phi NA	2	6	0	1	0	0	0	0	0		1	.167	.167	.167	16	-1	0-0	.500	-0	0	0	/P-2,O-2(LF)	0.0
	Year	29	117	13	21	0	0	0	6	1		2	.179	.186	.179	29	-8	1-1	.833	2	125	0	O-19(18-1-0),P-16	-0.1
1876	Bos N	1	4	0	0	0	0	0	0	0		0	.000	.000	.000	-98	-1		.750	-0	0	0	/O(LF)	-0.1
PARRILLA, SAM Samuel (Monge) B 6.12.1943 Santurce, P.R. D 2.9.1994 Brooklyn, NY BR/TR 5-11/185# d4.11																								
1970	Phi N	11	16	0	2	1	0	0	0	1-0	0	4	.125	.176	.188	-3	-2	0-0	1.000	0	125	0	/O-3(LF)	-0.2
PARRISH, LANCE Lance Michael B 6.15.1956 Clairton, PA BR/TR 6-3/220# d9.5 C4																								
1977	Det A	12	46	10	9	2	0	3	7	5-0	0	12	.196	.275	.435	85	-1	0-0	1.000	4	388	101	C-12	0.3
1978	Det A	85	288	37	63	11	3	14	41	11-0	3	71	.219	.254	.424	85	-8	0-0	.987	7	161	81	C-79	0.3
1979	Det A	143	493	65	136	26	3	19	65	49-2	2	105	.276	.343	.456	110	7	6-7	.989	7	121	121	*C-142	1.8
1980	Det A★	144	553	79	158	34	6	24	82	31-3	3	109	.286	.325	.499	120	13	6-4	.990	5	128	95	*C-121,D-16/1-5,O-5(1-0-4)	2.2
1981	Det A	96	348	39	85	18	2	10	46	34-6	0	52	.244	.311	.394	98	-1	2-3	.993	4	124	104	C-90/D-5	0.6
1982	Det A★	133	486	75	138	19	2	32	87	40-5	1	99	.284	.338	.529	134	20	3-4	.989	17	142	107	*C-132/O(LF)	4.2
1983	Det A★	155	605	80	163	42	3	27	114	44-7	1	106	.269	.314	.483	120	15	1-3	.995	11	**150**	131	*C-131,D-27	3.0
1984	†Det A★	147	578	75	137	16	2	33	98	41-6	2	120	.237	.287	.443	100	-3	2-3	.991	16	**156**	99	*C-127,D-22	1.7
1985	Det A✳	140	549	64	150	27	1	28	98	41-5	2	90	.273	.323	.479	118	12	2-6	.993	2	128	99	*C-120,D-22	1.7
1986	Det A★	91	327	53	84	6	1	22	62	38-3	5	83	.257	.340	.483	122	9	0-0	.989	11	131	115	C-85/D-6	2.3
1987	Phi N	130	466	42	114	21	0	17	67	47-2	1	104	.245	.313	.399	85	-10	0-1	.989	-2	85	110	*C-127	-0.8
1988	Phi N★	123	424	44	91	17	2	15	60	47-7	2	93	.215	.293	.370	88	-7	0-0	.988	0	83	119	*C-117/1	0.0
1989	Cal A	124	433	48	103	12	1	17	50	42-6	2	104	.238	.306	.388	97	-3	1-1	.993	-0	114	75	*C-122/D-2	0.4
1990	Cal A★	133	470	54	126	14	0	24	70	46-4	5	107	.268	.338	.451	122	13	2-2	.993	19	**136**	127	*C-131/1-4,D	3.8
1991	Cal A	119	402	38	87	12	0	19	51	35-2	5	117	.216	.285	.388	85	-10	0-1	.997	12	125	115	*C-111/1-3,D-5	0.8
1992	Cal A	24	83	7	19	2	0	4	11	5-1	0	22	.229	.270	.398	85	-2	0-0	.975	-4	66	141	C-22/D-2	-0.5
	Sea A	69	192	19	45	11	1	8	21	19-2	1	48	.234	.304	.427	103	0	1-1	.995	-1	55	128	C-34,1-16,D-14	-0.1
	Year	93	275	26	64	13	1	12	32	24-3	1	70	.233	.294	.418	98	-2	1-1	.987	-5	60	134	C-56,D-16,1-16	-0.6
1993	Cle A	10	20	2	4	1	0	1	2	4-0	0	5	.200	.333	.400	97	0	1-0	.950	1	38	222	C-10	0.2
1994	Pit N	40	126	10	34	5	0	3	16	18-1	1	28	.270	.363	.381	94	-1	1-1	.988	1	118	92	C-38/1	0.2
1995	Tor A	70	178	15	36	9	0	4	22	15-0	1	52	.202	.265	.320	53	-13	0-0	1.000	10	93	169	C-67/D	0.1
Total	19	1988	7067	856	1782	305	27	324	1070	612-62	37	1527	.252	.313	.440	105	30	28-37	.991	118	125	110	*C-1818,D-123/1-30,O-6(2-0-4)	22.2
PARRISH, LARRY Larry Alton B 11.10.1953 Winter Haven, FL BR/TR 6-3/215# d9.6 M2 C2 OF Total (3-LF 405-RF)																								
1974	Mon N	25	69	9	14	5	0	0	4	6-2	2	19	.203	.286	.275	54	-4	0-0	.986	5	125	74	3-24	0.1

Year	Tm Lg	G	AB	R	H	2B	3B	HR	RBI	BB-IB	HP	SO	AVG	OBP	SLG	AOPS	ABR	SB-CS	FA	FR	Rng	Thr	G at Pos	BFW
1975	Mon N	145	532	50	146	32	5	10	65	28-5	4	74	.274	.314	.410	96	-4	4-5	.919	-8	98	126	*3-143/2S	-1.4
1976	Mon N	154	543	65	126	28	5	11	61	41-2	2	91	.232	.285	.363	81	-15	2-6	.945	7	105	116	*3-153	-1.1
1977	Mon N	123	402	50	99	19	2	11	46	37-9	4	71	.246	.314	.386	90	-6	2-4	.936	-5	103	63	*3-115	-1.4
1978	Mon N	144	520	68	144	39	4	15	70	32-9	2	103	.277	.321	.454	116	9	2-3	.947	-12	92	86	*3-139	-0.6
1979	Mon N★	153	544	83	167	39	2	30	82	41-11	2	101	.307	.357	.551	146	33	5-1	.947	-16	89	98	*3-153	1.5
1980	Mon N	126	452	55	115	27	3	15	72	36-6	4	80	.254	.310	.427	105	2	2-6	.949	-6	92	80	*3-124	-0.7
1981	†Mon N	97	349	41	85	19	3	8	44	28-2	0	73	.244	.297	.384	92	-5	0-0	.935	-17	75	51	3-95	-2.5
1982	Tex A	128	440	59	116	15	0	17	62	30-0	4	84	.264	.314	.414	104	1	5-2	.962	-9	78	142	*O-124(RF)/3-3,D-2	-1.4
1983	Tex A	145	555	76	151	26	4	26	88	46-8	3	91	.272	.326	.474	121	14	0-0	.962	-13	79	107	*O-132(RF),D-13	-0.6
1984	Tex A	156	613	72	175	42	1	22	101	42-7	6	116	.285	.336	.465	116	13	2-4	.982	-0	90	156	O-81(2-0-80),D-63,3-12	0.6
1985	Tex A	94	346	44	86	11	1	17	51	33-2	1	77	.249	.314	.434	101	0	0-2	.991	-4	84	90	O-69(RF),D-22/3-2	-1.0
1986	Tex A	129	464	67	128	22	1	28	94	52-7	2	114	.276	.347	.509	127	17	3-1	.935	-6	69	39	D-98,3-30	0.8
1987	Tex A★	152	557	79	149	22	1	32	100	49-7	3	154	.268	.328	.483	112	8	3-1	.918	-7	57	119	*D-122,3-28/O(LF)	-0.3
1988	Tex A	68	248	22	47	9	1	7	26	20-2	2	79	.190	.253	.319	58	-14	0-0	—	0	0	0	D-67	-1.7
	†Bos A	52	158	10	41	5	0	7	26	8-0	1	32	.259	.298	.424	96	-1	0-1	.988	3	129	86	1-36,D-14	-0.2
	Year	120	406	32	88	14	1	14	52	28-2	3	111	.217	.270	.360	73	-16	0-1	.988	3	129	86	D-81,1-36	-1.9
Total	15	1891	6792	850	1789	360	33	256	992	529-79	42	1359	.263	.318	.439	106	48	30-36	.941	-88	93	91	*3-1021,O-407R,D-401/1-36,S2	-9.9

PARROTT, TOM Thomas William "Tacky Tom" B 4.10.1868 Portland, OR D 1.1.1932 Dundee, OR BR/TR 5-10.5/170# d6.18 b-Jiggs ▲ OF Total (15-LF 88-CF 28-RF)

Year	Tm Lg	G	AB	R	H	2B	3B	HR	RBI	BB-IB	HP	SO	AVG	OBP	SLG	AOPS	ABR	SB-CS	FA	FR	Rng	Thr	G at Pos	BFW
1893	Chi N	7	27	4	7	1	0	0	3	1	0	2	.259	.286	.296	56	-2	0	.800	-1	17	0	/P-4,3-2,2	-0.1
	Cin N	24	68	5	13	1	1	1	9	1	0	9	.191	.203	.279	27	-8	0	.915	1	117	90	P-22/O(LF)	0.0
	Year	31	95	9	20	2	1	1	12	2	0	11	.211	.227	.284	35	-10	0	.906	0	102	77	P-26/3-2,2O(LF)	-0.1
1894	Cin N	68	229	51	74	12	6	4	40	17	1	10	.323	.372	.480	101	-1	4	.929	2	113	92	P-41,O-13(9-2-2),1-12/S32	0.0
1895	Cin N	64	201	35	69	13	7	3	41	11	0	8	.343	.377	.522	126	6	10	.922	1	107	100	P-41,1-14/O-9(1-8-0)	0.1
1896	StL N	118	474	62	138	13	12	7	70	11	0	24	.291	.307	.414	93	-9	12	.951	7	98	154	*O-108(4-78-26)/P-7,1-6	-0.7
Total	4	281	999	157	301	40	26	15	163	41	1	53	.301	.329	.438	96	-14	26	.940	11	108	145	O-131C,P-115/1-32,3-3,2-2,S	-0.7

PARROTT, JIGGS Walter Edward B 7.14.1871 Portland, OR D 4.16.1898 Phoenix, AZ 5-11/160# d7.11 b-Tom

Year	Tm Lg	G	AB	R	H	2B	3B	HR	RBI	BB-IB	HP	SO	AVG	OBP	SLG	AOPS	ABR	SB-CS	FA	FR	Rng	Thr	G at Pos	BFW
1892	Chi N	78	333	38	67	8	5	2	22	8	1	30	.201	.222	.273	49	-23	7	.891	-1	96	63	3-78	-2.1
1893	Chi N	110	455	54	111	10	9	1	65	13	1	25	.244	.267	.312	54	-33	25	.904	10	**108**	109	*3-99/2-7,O-4(RF)	-1.8
1894	Chi N	126	525	82	130	17	9	3	65	16	3	35	.248	.274	.331	43	-53	30	.932	-3	100	91	*2-125/3	-3.9
1895	Chi N	3	4	0	1	0	0	0	0	0	0	0	.250	.250	.250	27	0	0	—	-1	0	0	/O(LF)S1	-0.1
Total	4	317	1317	174	309	35	23	6	152	37	5	90	.235	.258	.310	48	-109	62	.899	6	103	89	3-178,2-132/O-5(1-0-4),1S	-7.9

PARSONS, CASEY Casey Robert B 4.14.1954 Wenatchee, WA BL/TR 6-1/180# d5.31

Year	Tm Lg	G	AB	R	H	2B	3B	HR	RBI	BB-IB	HP	SO	AVG	OBP	SLG	AOPS	ABR	SB-CS	FA	FR	Rng	Thr	G at Pos	BFW
1981	Sea A	36	22	6	5	1	0	1	5	1-0	2	4	.227	.308	.409	105	0	0-0	1.000	2	134	387	O-24(3-2-19)/1	0.2
1983	Chi A	8	5	1	1	0	0	0	0	2-1	0	1	.200	.429	.200	77	0	0-0	1.000	0	194	0	/O-3(0-1-2),D-2	0.0
1984	Chi A	1	1	0	0	0	0	0	0	0-0	0	1	.000	.000	.000	-96	0	0-0	—	0			/H	0.0
1987	Cle A	18	25	2	4	0	0	1	5	0-0	0	5	.160	.160	.280	13	-3	0-0	1.000	0	189	0	/O-2(0-1-1),1D	-0.3
Total	4	63	53	9	10	1	0	2	10	3-1	2	11	.189	.254	.321	57	-3	0-0	1.000	3	141	341	/O-29(3-4-22),D-7,1-2	-0.1

PARSONS, DIXIE Edward Dixon B 5.12.1916 Talladega, AL D 10.31.1991 Longview, TX BR/TR 6-2/180# d8.16

Year	Tm Lg	G	AB	R	H	2B	3B	HR	RBI	BB-IB	HP	SO	AVG	OBP	SLG	AOPS	ABR	SB-CS	FA	FR	Rng	Thr	G at Pos	BFW
1939	Det A	5	1	0	0	0	0	0	0	1	0	1	.000	.500	.000	36	0	0-0	1.000	0	*0*	*0*	/C-4	0.0
1942	Det A	63	188	8	37	4	0	2	11	13	0	22	.197	.249	.250	37	-16	1-0	.981	8	*106*	*112*	C-62	-0.5
1943	Det A	40	106	2	15	3	0	0	4	6	0	16	.142	.188	.170	4	-13	0-0	.975	4	*99*	*154*	C-40	-0.8
Total	3	108	295	10	52	7	0	2	15	20	0	39	.176	.229	.220	26	-29	1-0	.979	11	*103*	*127*	C-106	-1.3

PARSONS, JOHN John S. B Napoleon, OH 5-6/138# d10.15

Year	Tm Lg	G	AB	R	H	2B	3B	HR	RBI	BB-IB	HP	SO	AVG	OBP	SLG	AOPS	ABR	SB-CS	FA	FR	Rng	Thr	G at Pos	BFW
1884	Cin AA	1	3	0	0	0	0	0		0	0		.000	.000	.000	-95	-1		1.000	-0	0	0	/O(RF)	-0.1

PARTEE, ROY Roy Robert B 9.7.1917 Los Angeles, CA D 12.26.2000 Eureka, CA BR/TR 5-10/180# d4.23 Mil 1945

Year	Tm Lg	G	AB	R	H	2B	3B	HR	RBI	BB-IB	HP	SO	AVG	OBP	SLG	AOPS	ABR	SB-CS	FA	FR	Rng	Thr	G at Pos	BFW
1943	Bos A	96	299	30	84	14	2	0	31	39	2	33	.281	.368	.341	106	4	0-0	.983	-5	*95*	*100*	C-91	0.5
1944	Bos A	89	280	18	68	12	0	2	41	37	1	29	.243	.333	.307	85	-4	0-1	.989	-3	*95*	*93*	C-85	-0.3
1946	†Bos A	40	111	13	35	5	2	0	9	13	0	14	.315	.387	.396	113	2	0-0	.974	-4	*126*	*71*	C-38	0.0
1947	Bos A	60	169	14	39	2	0	0	16	18	0	23	.231	.305	.243	50	-11	0-0	.975	-0	*90*	*62*	C-54	-0.9
1948	StL A	82	231	14	47	8	1	0	17	25	1	21	.203	.284	.247	41	-20	2-2	.982	-4	*67*	*62*	C-76	-2.0
Total	5	367	1090	89	273	41	5	2	114	132	4	120	.250	.334	.303	78	-29	2-3	.982	-17	*91*	*82*	C-344	-2.7

PARTENHEIMER, STEVE Harold Philip B 8.30.1891 Greenfield, MA D 6.16.1971 Mansfield, OH BR/TR 5-8.5/145# d6.28 s-Stan

Year	Tm Lg	G	AB	R	H	2B	3B	HR	RBI	BB-IB	HP	SO	AVG	OBP	SLG	AOPS	ABR	SB-CS	FA	FR	Rng	Thr	G at Pos	BFW
1913	Det A	1	2	0	0	0	0	0	0	1	0	1	.000	.333	.000	-1	0	0	.750	-0	156	0	/3	0.0

PARTRIDGE, JAY James Bugg B 11.15.1902 Mountville, GA D 1.14.1974 Nashville, TN BL/TR 5-11/160# d4.12

Year	Tm Lg	G	AB	R	H	2B	3B	HR	RBI	BB-IB	HP	SO	AVG	OBP	SLG	AOPS	ABR	SB-CS	FA	FR	Rng	Thr	G at Pos	BFW
1927	Bro N	146	572	72	149	17	6	7	40	20	3	36	.260	.289	.348	70	-27	9	.938	-13	93	80	*2-140	-3.6
1928	Bro N	37	73	18	18	0	1	0	12	13	1	6	.247	.368	.274	71	-3	2	.908	-4	86	76	2-18/3-2	-0.6
Total	2	183	645	90	167	17	7	7	52	33	4	42	.259	.299	.340	70	-30	11	.935	-17	92	80	2-158/3-2	-4.2

PASCHAL, BEN Benjamin Edwin B 10.13.1895 Enterprise, AL D 11.10.1974 Charlotte, NC BR/TR 5-11/185# d8.16

Year	Tm Lg	G	AB	R	H	2B	3B	HR	RBI	BB-IB	HP	SO	AVG	OBP	SLG	AOPS	ABR	SB-CS	FA	FR	Rng	Thr	G at Pos	BFW
1915	Cle A	9	9	0	1	0	0	0	0	0	0	3	.111	.111	.111	-33	-2	0	—	0			H	-0.2
1920	Bos A	9	28	5	10	0	0	0	5	5	0	2	.357	.455	.357	122	1	1-0	1.000	0	94	123	/O-7(RF)	0.1
1924	NY A	4	12	2	3	1	0	0	3	1	0	0	.250	.308	.333	65	-1	0-0	1.000	0	66	470	/O-4(CF)	0.0
1925	NY A	89	247	49	89	16	5	12	56	22	2	29	.360	.417	.611	161	22	14-9	.953	-1	98	100	O-66(16-14-36)	1.5
1926	†NY A	96	258	46	74	12	3	7	32	26	1	35	.287	.354	.438	108	2	7-6	.935	1	101	147	O-74(12-17-47)	-0.2
1927	NY A	50	82	16	26	9	2	2	16	4	0	10	.317	.349	.549	134	4	0-2	.976	0	113	59	O-27(11-4-12)	0.2
1928	†NY A	65	79	12	25	6	1	1	15	8	0	11	.316	.379	.456	122	3	1-0	1.000	0	103	84	O-25(16-1-8)	0.2
1929	NY A	42	72	13	15	3	0	2	11	6	0	3	.208	.269	.333	58	-5	1-2	.951	1	113	134	O-20(12-4-4)	-0.5
Total	8	364	787	143	243	47	11	24	138	72	3	93	.309	.369	.488	123	24	24-19	.953	2	102	121	O-223(67-44-114)	1.1

PASEK, JOHNNY John Paul B 6.25.1905 Niagara Falls, NY D 3.13.1976 Niagara Falls, NY BR/TR 5-10/175# d7.28

Year	Tm Lg	G	AB	R	H	2B	3B	HR	RBI	BB-IB	HP	SO	AVG	OBP	SLG	AOPS	ABR	SB-CS	FA	FR	Rng	Thr	G at Pos	BFW
1933	Det A	28	61	6	15	4	0	0	4	7	0	7	.246	.324	.311	68	-3	2-0	.989	-1	*58*	*129*	C-28	-0.2
1934	Chi A	4	9	1	3	0	0	0	0	1	0	1	.333	.400	.333	88	0	0-0	1.000	-0	*61*	*144*	/C-4	0.0
Total	2	32	70	7	18	4	0	0	4	8	0	8	.257	.333	.314	70	-3	2-0	.990	-2	*58*	*131*	/C-32	-0.2

PASKERT, DODE George Henry B 8.28.1881 Cleveland, OH D 2.12.1959 Cleveland, OH BR/TR 5-11/165# d9.21 OF Total (146-LF 1461-CF 35-RF)

Year	Tm Lg	G	AB	R	H	2B	3B	HR	RBI	BB-IB	HP	SO	AVG	OBP	SLG	AOPS	ABR	SB-CS	FA	FR	Rng	Thr	G at Pos	BFW
1907	Cin N	16	50	10	14	4	0	1	8	2	2		.280	.333	.420	130	2	2	.973	1	149	0	O-16(CF)	0.2
1908	Cin N	118	395	40	96	14	4	1	36	27	4		.243	.298	.306	96	-2	25	.953	5	103	84	*O-116(77-34-5)	-0.4
1909	Cin N	104	322	49	81	7	4	0	33	34	2		.252	.327	.298	95	-1	23	.968	1	98	115	O-82(36-46-1)/1-6	-0.5
1910	Cin N	144	506	63	152	21	5	2	46	70	3	60	.300	.389	.374	128	21	51	.957	9	110	128	*O-139(6-126-8)/1-2	2.4
1911	Phi N	**153**	560	96	153	18	5	4	47	70	4	70	.273	.358	.345	96	-1	28	.979	1	102	88	*O-153(2-146-7)	-1.1
1912	Phi N	145	540	102	170	37	5	2	43	91	7	67	.315	.420	.413	120	21	36	.967	-0	103	89	*O-141(CF)/2-2,3	1.1
1913	Phi N	124	454	83	119	21	9	4	29	65	3	69	.262	.358	.374	105	5	12-17	.972	11	114	111	*O-120(1-119-0)	0.5
1914	Phi N	132	451	59	119	25	6	3	44	56	3	68	.264	.349	.366	106	5	23	.958	8	112	133	*O-128(CF)/S-4	0.5
1915	†Phi N	109	328	51	80	17	4	3	39	35	1	38	.244	.319	.348	100	1	9-6	.970	-3	91	95	O-92(19-74-1)/1-5	-0.9
1916	Phi N	149	555	82	155	30	7	8	46	54	3	76	.279	.346	.402	125	18	22-21	.983	-5	96	78	*O-146(2-145-0)/S	0.0
1917	Phi N	141	546	78	137	27	11	4	43	62	3	63	.251	.331	.363	108	7	19	**.984**	-11	83	98	*O-138(CF)	-1.7
1918	†Chi N	127	461	69	132	24	3	3	59	53	2	49	.286	.362	.371	121	14	20	.980	-8	92	74	*O-121(CF)/3-6	-0.3
1919	Chi N	88	270	21	53	11	3	2	29	28	1	33	.196	.274	.281	67	-10	7	.969	-5	82	126	O-80(3-76-3)	-2.3
1920	Chi N	139	487	57	136	22	10	5	71	64	3	58	.279	.366	.396	117	13	16-14	.956	-2	92	122	*O-137(0-136-1)	0.1
1921	Cin N	27	92	8	16	1	1	0	4	4	0	8	.174	.208	.207	11	-12	0-2	.984	1	112	61	O-24(0-15-9)	-1.4
Total	15	1716	6017	868	1613	279	77	42	577	715	41	659	.268	.350	.361	108	81	293-60	.969	2	100	100	*O-1633C/1-13,3-7,S-5,2-2	-3.8

PASLEY, KEVIN Kevin Patrick B 7.22.1953 Bronx, NY BR/TR 6/185# d10.2

Year	Tm Lg	G	AB	R	H	2B	3B	HR	RBI	BB-IB	HP	SO	AVG	OBP	SLG	AOPS	ABR	SB-CS	FA	FR	Rng	Thr	G at Pos	BFW
1974	LA N	1	0	0	0	0	0	0	0	0-0	0	0	—	—	—	—	0	0-0	1.000	0	0	0	/C	0.0
1976	LA N	23	52	4	12	2	0	0	2	3-1	0	7	.231	.273	.269	55	-3	0-0	.971	1	81	112	C-23	-0.2
1977	LA N	2	3	0	1	0	0	0	0	0-0	0	0	.333	.333	.333	80	0	0-0	1.000	-1	30	0	/C-2	-0.1
	Sea A	4	13	1	5	0	0	0	2	1-0	0	2	.385	.429	.385	125	0	0-0	1.000	-1	252	0	/C-4	-0.1
1978	Sea A	25	54	3	13	5	0	1	5	2-0	0	4	.241	.268	.389	83	-1	0-0	1.000	-1	108	0	C-25	-0.1
Total	4	55	122	8	31	7	0	1	9	6-1	0	13	.254	.289	.336	76	-4	0-0	.986	-2	107	50	/C-55	-0.5

Year	Tm Lg	G	AB	R	H	2B	3B	HR	RBI	BB-IB	HP	SO	AVG	OBP	SLG	AOPS	ABR	SB-CS	FA	FR	Rng	Thr	G at Pos	BFW
PASQUA, DAN Daniel Anthony B 10.17.1961 Yonkers, NY BL/TL 6/203# d5.30																								
1985	NY A	60	148	17	31	3	1	9	25	16-4	1	38	.209	.289	.426	96	-2	0-0	1.000	4	129	114	O-37(31-0-6),D-14	0.0
1986	NY A	102	280	44	82	17	0	16	45	47-3	3	78	.293	.399	.525	151	22	2-0	.987	-1	102	84	O-81(71-0-12)/1-5,D-3	1.7
1987	NY A	113	318	42	74	7	1	17	42	40-3	1	99	.233	.319	.421	96	-3	0-2	.985	0	107	46	O-74(61-0-14),D-20,1-12	-0.7
1988	Chi A	129	422	48	96	16	2	20	50	46-5	3	100	.227	.307	.417	101	0	1-0	**.996**	6	110	90	*O-112(65-0-52)/1-7,D-2	0.3
1989	Chi A	73	246	26	61	9	1	11	47	25-1	1	58	.248	.315	.427	111	3	1-2	.993	3	110	72	O-66(52-0-20)/D-5	0.3
1990	Chi A	112	325	43	89	27	3	13	58	37-7	2	66	.274	.347	.495	137	16	1-1	.962	3	108	228	D-57,O-43(21-0-22)	1.7
1991	Chi A	134	417	71	108	22	5	18	66	62-4	3	86	.259	.358	.465	129	17	0-2	.991	-3	99	92	1-83,O-59(9-0-51)/D-8	0.7
1992	Chi A	93	265	26	56	16	1	6	33	36-1	1	57	.211	.305	.347	84	-5	0-1	.963	-2	100	79	O-81(RF)/1-5,D	-1.0
1993	†Chi A	78	176	22	36	10	1	5	20	26-1	0	51	.205	.302	.358	80	-5	2-2	.984	-2	89	137	O-37(11-0-26),1-32/D-6	-1.0
1994	Chi A	11	23	2	5	2	0	2	4	0-0	0	9	.217	.217	.565	95	0	0-0	.867	-0	148	0	/O-5(1-0-5),1-3	-0.1
Total	10	905	2620	341	638	129	15	117	390	335-29	15	642	.244	.330	.438	112	43	7-10	.984	8	105	92	O-595(322-0-289),1-147,D-116	1.9
PASQUELLA, MIKE Michael John "Toney" (born Michael John Pasquariello) B 11.7.1898 Philadelphia, PA D 4.5.1965 Bridgeport, CT BR/TR 5-11/167# d7.9																								
1919	Phi N	1	1	1	1	0	0	0	0	0	0	0	1.000	1.000	1.000	469	0	0	—	0	0	0	/1	0.0
	StL N	1	1	0	0	0	0	0	0	0	0	1	.000	.000	.000	-99	0	0	—	0			H	0.0
	Year	2	2	1	1	0	0	0	0	0	0	1	.500	.500	.500	200	0	0	—	0	0	0	/1	0.0
PASTORNICKY, CLIFF Clifford Scott B 11.18.1958 Seattle, WA BR/TR 5-10/170# d6.14																								
1983	KC A	10	32	4	4	0	0	2	5	0-0	0	3	.125	.125	.313	16	-4	0-0	.929	-0	111	0	3-10	-0.4
PATE, BOB Robert Wayne B 12.3.1953 Los Angeles, CA BR/TR 6-3.5/200# d6.2																								
1980	Mon N	23	39	3	10	2	0	0	5	3-0	0	6	.256	.295	.308	73	-1	0-1	1.000	-1	86	0	O-18(2-0-16)	-0.4
1981	Mon N	8	6	0	2	0	0	0	0	1-0	0	0	.333	.429	.333	117	0	0-0	1.000	-0	97	0	/O-5(1-2-2)	0.0
Total	2	31	45	3	12	2	0	0	5	4-0	0	6	.267	.314	.311	79	-1	0-1	1.000	-1	87	0	/O-23(3-2-18)	-0.4
PATEK, FREDDIE Frederick Joseph "The Flea" B 10.9.1944 Seguin, TX BR/TR 5-5/148# d6.3																								
1968	Pit N	61	208	31	53	4	2	2	18	12-0	2	37	.255	.298	.322	89	-3	18-7	.976	0	105	84	S-52/O-5(2-0-3),3	0.2
1969	Pit N	147	460	48	110	9	1	5	32	53-15	1	86	.239	.318	.296	75	-15	15-8	.954	-10	90	96	*S-146	-0.8
1970	†Pit N	84	237	42	58	10	5	1	19	29-1	0	46	.245	.322	.342	81	-6	8-2	.971	13	109	111	S-65	1.4
1971	KC A	147	591	86	158	21	**11**	6	36	44-3	5	80	.267	.323	.371	97	-4	49-14	.968	22	105	**126**	*S-147	4.3
1972	KC A✳	136	518	59	110	25	4	0	32	47-4	3	64	.212	.280	.276	67	-21	33-7	.971	**38**	**120**	**140**	*S-136	4.2
1973	KC A	135	501	82	117	19	5	5	45	54-0	3	63	.234	.311	.321	73	-17	36-14	.966	**40**	**119**	**125**	*S-135	4.1
1974	KC A	149	537	72	121	18	6	3	38	77-1	3	69	.225	.324	.298	76	-14	33-15	.967	8	**106**	**119**	*S-149	1.4
1975	KC A	136	483	58	110	14	5	5	45	42-0	2	65	.228	.291	.308	68	-21	32-7	.959	4	102	101	*S-136/D	0.3
1976	†KC A★	144	432	58	104	19	3	1	43	50-5	2	63	.241	.318	.306	84	-7	51-15	.962	-7	98	111	*S-143/D	0.8
1977	†KC A	154	497	72	130	26	6	5	60	41-2	5	84	.262	.320	.368	88	-8	**53**-13	.958	-17	92	84	*S-154	-0.3
1978	†KC A★	138	440	54	109	23	1	2	46	42-1	1	56	.248	.312	.318	76	-13	38-11	.949	-21	87	113	*S-137	-1.6
1979	KC A	106	306	30	77	17	0	1	37	16-0	3	42	.252	.293	.317	64	-15	11-12	.955	-24	85	88	*S-104	-3.1
1980	Cal A	86	273	41	72	10	5	5	34	15-1	1	26	.264	.302	.392	92	-4	7-6	.953	-18	84	78	S-81	-1.5
1981	Cal A	27	47	3	11	1	1	0	5	1-0	0	6	.234	.250	.298	57	-3	1-0	.983	-2	84	96	2-16/3-7,S-3	-0.4
Total	14	1650	5530	736	1340	216	55	41	490	523-33	31	787	.242	.309	.324	79	-151	385-131	.962	24	100	108	*S-1588/2-16,3-8,O-5(2-0-3),D-2	9.0
PATRICK, BOB Robert Lee B 10.27.1917 Ft.Smith, AR D 10.6.1999 Ft.Smith, AR BR/TR 6-2/190# d9.20 Mil 1943-45																								
1941	Det A	5	7	2	2	0	0	0	0	0	0	1	.286	.286	.286	47	-1	0-0	.750	-0	90	0	/O-3(LF)	-0.1
1942	Det A	4	8	1	2	1	0	1	3	1	0	0	.250	.333	.750	185	1	0-0	1.000	0	116	0	/O-3(RF)	0.1
Total	2	9	15	3	4	1	0	1	3	1	0	1	.267	.313	.533	118	0	0-0	.889	-0	105	0	/O-6(3-0-3)	0.0
PATTEE, HARRY Harry Ernest B 1.17.1882 Charlestown, MA D 7.17.1971 Lynchburg, VA BL/TR 5-8/149# d4.14																								
1908	Bro N	80	264	19	57	5	2	0	9	25	1		.216	.286	.250	74	-7	24	.964	11	111	70	2-74	0.5
PATTERSON, DAN Daniel Thomas B 1846 New York, NY TL 5-9/143# d5.18																								
1871	Mut NA	32	151	31	31	2	0	0	13	1		0	.205	.211	.219	26	-13	2-1	.824	-2	58	0	*O-31(9-0-22)/2-2	-0.8
1872	Eck NA	12	47	6	10	1	0	0	3	0		2	.213	.213	.234	44	-2	0-3	.861	3	272	321	O-11(2-9-0)/1	0.0
1874	Mut NA	1	5	1	2	0	0	0	2	0		0	.400	.400	.400	153	0	0-0	1.000	0	0	0	/1O(LF)	0.0
1875	Atl NA	12	45	4	9	0	0	0	4	0		0	.200	.200	.200	45	-2	1-0	.636	-5	67	0	/2-7,O-7(RF)	-0.6
Total	4 NA	57	248	42	52	3	0	0	22	1		2	.210	.213	.222	35	-17	3-4	.000	-4	99	72	/O-50(12-9-29),2-9,1-2	-1.4
PATTERSON, COREY Donald Corey B 8.13.1979 Atlanta, GA BL/TR 5-10/175# d9.19																								
2000	Chi N	11	42	9	7	1	0	2	2	3-0	1	14	.167	.239	.333	43	-4	1-1	.963	-0	109	0	O-11(CF)	-0.4
2001	Chi N	59	131	26	29	3	0	4	14	6-0	3	33	.221	.266	.336	59	-9	4-0	.976	1	117	0	O-54(13-45-1)	-0.7
2002	Chi N	153	592	71	150	30	5	14	54	19-1	8	142	.253	.284	.392	81	-22	18-3	.990	-4	99	71	*O-147(CF)	-2.2
2003	Chi N	83	329	49	98	17	7	13	55	15-2	1	77	.298	.329	.511	117	6	16-5	.975	-6	87	74	O-82(CF)	0.2
Total	4	306	1094	155	284	51	12	33	125	43-3	13	266	.260	.293	.419	88	-29	39-9	.983	-10	98	60	O-294(13-285-1)	-3.1
PATTERSON, GEORGE George d4.24																								
1884	Phi U	2	7	0	1	0	0	0		0			.143	.143	.143	-14	-1		.500	-0	221	0	/O-2(1-0-1)	-0.1
PATTERSON, HAM Hamilton B 10.13.1877 Belleville, IL D 11.25.1945 E.St.Louis, IL BR/TR 6-2/185# d5.18 b-Pat																								
1909	StL A	17	49	2	10	1	0	0	5	0	0		.204	.204	.224	38	-4	1	1.000	-1	54	66	/1-6,O-6(LF)	-0.6
	Chi A	1	3	2	0	0	0	0	0	1	0		.000	.250	.000	-21	0	0	1.000	1	416	0	/1	0.0
	Year	18	52	4	10	1	0	0	5	1	0		.192	.208	.212	35	-4	1	1.000	0	96	58	/1-7,O-6(LF)	-0.6
PATTERSON, HANK Henry Joseph Colquit B 7.17.1907 San Francisco, CA D 9.30.1970 Panorama City, CA BR/TR 5-11.5/170# d9.5 C1																								
1932	Bos A	1	1	0	0	0	0	0	0	0	0	0	.000	.000	.000	-99	0	0-0	—	0	*0*	*0*	/C	0.0
PATTERSON, JARROD Jarrod Lane B 9.7.1973 Montgomery, AL BL/TR 6-1/195# d6.16																								
2001	Det A	13	41	6	11	1	1	2	4	0-0	2	4	.268	.302	.488	108	0	0-1	.923	-4	69	0	3-13	-0.4
2003	KC A	13	22	3	4	0	0	0	0	3-1	0	6	.182	.280	.182	23	-2	0-0	.000	-1	0	0	/3-4,1-2,D-4	-0.3
Total	2	26	63	9	15	1	1	2	4	3-1	2	10	.238	.294	.381	75	-2	0-1	.889	-5	63	0	/3-17,D-4,1-2	-0.7
PATTERSON, JOHN John Allen B 2.11.1967 Key West, FL BB/TR 5-9/160# d4.6																								
1992	SF N	32	103	10	19	1	1	0	4	5-0	1	24	.184	.229	.214	28	-10	5-1	.960	2	98	144	2-22/O-5(CF)	-0.8
1993	SF N	16	16	1	3	0	0	1	2	0-0	0	5	.188	.188	.375	48	-1	0-1	—	0			H	-0.3
1994	SF N	85	240	36	57	10	1	3	32	16-0	11	43	.237	.315	.325	70	-10	13-3	.979	-6	94	93	2-63	-1.2
1995	SF N	95	205	27	42	5	3	1	14	14-1	12	41	.205	.294	.273	52	-14	4-2	.983	-5	89	117	2-53	-1.7
Total	4	228	564	74	121	16	5	5	52	35-1	24	113	.215	.289	.287	56	-35	22-7	.977	-10	93	110	2-138/O-5(CF)	-4.0
PATTERSON, CLAIRE Lorenzo Claire B 10.5.1887 Arkansas City, KS D 3.28.1913 Mojave, CA BL/TR 6- /180# d9.5																								
1909	Cin N	4	8	0	1	0	0	0	1	0	0		.125	.125	.125	-23	-1	0	1.000	0	0	0	/O-2(LF)	-0.1
PATTERSON, MIKE Michael Lee B 1.26.1958 Santa Monica, CA BL/TR 5-10/170# d4.15																								
1981	Oak A	12	23	4	8	1	1	0	1	2-1	0	5	.348	.400	.478	160	2	0-1	1.000	-0	94	0	/O-5(2-0-3),D-2	0.1
	NY A	4	9	2	2	0	2	0	0	0-0	0	0	.222	.222	.667	150	0	0-0	1.000	0	120	0	/O-4(3-0-1)	0.0
	Year	16	32	6	10	1	3	0	1	2-1	0	5	.313	.353	.531	158	2	0-1	1.000	-0	105	0	/O-9(5-0-4),D-2	0.1
1982	NY A	11	16	3	3	1	0	1	1	2-0	0	6	.188	.278	.438	94	0	1-0	1.000	-2	42	0	/O-9(2-7-0),D	-0.2
Total	2	27	48	9	13	2	3	1	2	4-1	0	11	.271	.327	.500	135	2	1-1	1.000	-2	77	0	/O-18(7-7-4),D-3	-0.1
PATTERSON, PAT William Jennings Bryan B 1.29.1901 Belleville, IL D 10.1.1977 St.Louis, MO BR/TR 6/175# d4.14 b-Ham																								
1921	NY N	23	35	5	14	0	0	1	5	2	0	5	.400	.432	.486	142	2	0-1	.970	2	156	0	3-14/S-7	0.5
PATTON, GENE Gene Tunney B 7.8.1926 Coatesville, PA BL/TR 5-10/165# d6.17 Mil 1945																								
1944	Bos N	1	0	0	0	0	0	0	0	0	0	0	—	—	—	—	0	0	—	0			R	0.0
PATTON, BILL George William B 10.12.1912 Cornwall, PA D 3.15.1986 Philadelphia, PA BR/TR 6-2/180# d6.29																								
1935	Phi A	9	10	1	3	1	0	0	2	2	0	3	.300	.417	.400	113	0	0-0	1.000	0	*59*	*499*	/C-3	0.1
PATTON, TOM Thomas Allen B 9.5.1935 Honey Brook, PA BR/TR 5-9.5/185# d4.30																								
1957	Bal A	1	2	0	0	0	0	0	0	0-0	0	0	.000	.000	.000	-99	-1	0-0	1.000	1	*0*	*520*	/C	0.0

Year	Tm Lg	G	AB	R	H	2B	3B	HR	RBI	BB-IB	HP	SO	AVG	OBP	SLG	AOPS	ABR	SB-CS	FA	FR	Rng	Thr	G at Pos	BFW
PAUL, JOSH Joshua William B 5.19.1975 Evanston, IL BR/TR 6-1/185# d9.7																								
1999	Chi A	6	18	2	4	1	0	0	1	0-0	0	4	.222	.222	.278	26	-2	0-0	1.000	1	67	0	/C-6	-0.1
2000	†Chi A	36	71	15	20	3	2	1	8	5-0	1	17	.282	.338	.423	90	-1	1-0	.974	2	114	179	C-34/O(LF)	0.2
2001	Chi A	57	139	20	37	11	0	3	18	13-0	0	25	.266	.327	.410	90	-2	6-2	.980	-2	73	69	C-56	0.0
2002	Chi A	33	104	11	25	4	0	0	11	9-0	1	22	.240	.302	.279	57	-6	2-0	.990	0	82	39	C-32/O(LF)	-0.4
2003	Chi A	13	17	6	6	0	0	0	4	3-0	0	3	.353	.450	.353	115	1	0-0	1.000	-2	171	270	C-11/D	-0.1
	Chi N	3	6	0	0	0	0	0	0	0-0	0	3	.000	.000	.000	-99	-2	0-0	1.000	1	108	410	/C-3	0.0
Total	5	148	355	54	92	19	2	4	42	30-0	2	74	.259	.318	.358	76	-12	9-2	.984	1	90	97	C-142/O-2(LF),D	-0.4
PAUL, LOU Louis BR/TR d9.5																								
1876	Phi N	3	12	2	2	1	0	0	0	0		0	.167	.167	.250	37	-1		.643	-2			/C-3	-0.2
PAULA, CARLOS Carlos (Conill) B 11.28.1927 Havana, Cuba D 4.25.1983 Miami, FL BR/TR 6-3/195# d9.6																								
1954	Was A	9	24	2	4	1	0	0	2	2	0	4	.167	.231	.208	22	-3	0-0	1.000	1	118	266	/O-6(LF)	-0.2
1955	Was A	115	351	34	105	20	7	6	45	17-3	2	43	.299	.332	.447	115	5	2-3	.941	-4	96	77	O-85(6-0-80)	-0.2
1956	Was A	33	82	8	15	2	1	3	13	8-0	0	15	.183	.250	.341	56	-6	0-2	.974	-1	104	0	O-20(9-0-11)	-0.8
Total	3	157	457	44	124	23	8	9	60	27-3	2	62	.271	.311	.416	99	-4	2-5	.950	-4	99	74	O-111(21-0-91)	-1.2
PAULETTE, GENE Eugene Edward B 5.26.1891 Centralia, IL D 2.8.1966 Little Rock, AR BR/TR 6/150# d6.16 OF Total (1-LF 3-CF 10-RF)																								
1911	NY N	10	12	1	2	0	0	0	1	0	0	1	.167	.167	.167	-6	-2	0	.938	-1	63	0	/1-7,S3	-0.3
1916	StL A	5	4	1	2	0	0	0	0	1	0	1	.500	.600	.500	242	1	0	—	0			H	0.1
1917	StL A	12	22	3	4	0	0	0	0	3	0	3	.182	.280	.182	43	-1	0	.982	-0	108	36	/1-5,2-3,3	-0.2
	StL N	95	332	32	88	21	7	0	34	16	2	16	.265	.303	.370	109	3	9	.993	-2	88	142	1-93	-0.2
1918	StL N	125	461	33	126	15	3	0	52	27	2	16	.273	.316	.319	97	-2	11	.983	1	97	**108**	1-97,S-12/2-7,O-6(1-1-3),3-2,P	-0.4
1919	StL N	43	144	11	31	6	0	0	11	9	0	6	.215	.261	.257	60	-7	4	.990	2	116	114	1-35/S-3	-0.6
	Phi N	67	243	20	63	8	3	1	31	19	1	10	.259	.316	.329	88	-3	10	.957	-2	95	100	2-58,O-10(0-2-7)/1	-0.5
	Year	110	387	31	94	14	3	1	42	28	1	16	.243	.296	.302	78	-10	14	.957	0	95	100	2-58,1-36,O-10(0-2-7)/S-3	-1.1
1920	Phi N	143	562	59	162	16	6	1	36	33	4	16	.288	.332	.343	90	-7	9-8	.988	6	**120**	95	*1-139/S-2	-0.5
Total	6	500	1780	160	478	66	19	2	165	108	9	69	.269	.314	.330	92	-18	43-8	.988	4	105	111	1-377/2-68,S-18,O-16R,3-4,P	-2.6
PAUXTIS, SI Simon Francis B 7.20.1885 Pittston, PA D 3.13.1961 Philadelphia, PA BR/TR 6- /175# d9.18																								
1909	Cin N	4	8	2	1	0	0	0	0	0	1		.125	.222	.125	8	-1	0	1.000	-1	*85*	*47*	/C-4	-0.1
PAVLETICH, DON Donald Stephen B 7.13.1938 Milwaukee, WI BR/TR 5-11/209# d4.20 Mil 1957-58																								
1957	Cin N	1	1	0	0	0	0	0	0	0-0	0	0	.000	.000	.000	-93	0	0-0	—	0			H	0.0
1959	Cin N	1	0	1	0	0	0	0	0	0-0	0	0	—	—	—	—	0	0-0	—	0			R	0.0
1962	Cin N	34	63	7	14	3	0	1	7	8-1	0	18	.222	.310	.317	67	-3	0-0	1.000	0	92	83	1-25/C-2	-0.4
1963	Cin N	71	183	18	38	11	0	5	18	17-3	0	12	.208	.274	.350	76	-5	0-0	.991	-3	63	71	1-57,C-13	-1.1
1964	Cin N	34	91	12	22	4	0	5	11	10-1	0	17	.242	.314	.451	109	1	0-0	.983	-2	*83*	*51*	C-27/1	0.1
1965	Cin N	68	191	25	61	11	1	8	32	23-5	1	27	.319	.394	.513	144	12	1-1	.986	-3	*79*	*79*	C-54/1-9	1.2
1966	Cin N	83	235	29	69	13	2	12	38	18-3	1	37	.294	.344	.519	126	8	1-0	.975	-8	*68*	*121*	C-55,1-10	0.3
1967	Cin N	74	231	25	55	14	3	6	34	21-7	4	38	.238	.310	.403	93	-2	2-1	.986	-2	*78*	*93*	C-66/1-6,3	-0.1
1968	Cin N	46	98	11	28	3	1	2	11	8-2	2	23	.286	.352	.398	117	2	0-0	1.000	-0	84	89	1-22/C-5	0.1
1969	Chi A	78	188	26	46	12	0	6	33	28-4	0	45	.245	.338	.404	103	2	0-0	.974	-4	49	124	C-51,1-13	-0.2
1970	Bos A	32	65	4	9	1	1	0	6	10-0	0	15	.138	.250	.185	21	-7	1-0	1.000	-3	125	123	1-16,C-10	-1.1
1971	Bos A	14	27	5	7	1	0	1	3	5-0	0	5	.259	.375	.407	113	1	0-0	.973	-1	43	62	/C-8	0.0
Total	12	536	1373	163	349	73	8	46	193	148-26	8	237	.254	.328	.420	103	9	5-2	.983	-25	*74*	*90*	C-291,1-159/3	-1.2
PAWELEK, TED Theodore John "Porky" B 8.15.1919 Chicago Heights, IL D 2.12.1964 Chicago Heights, IL BL/TR 5-10.5/202# d9.13																								
1946	Chi N	4	4	0	1	1	0	0	0	0	0	0	.250	.250	.500	112	0	0	—	-0	*0*	*0*	/C	0.0
PAWLOSKI, STAN Stanley Walter B 9.6.1931 Wanamie, PA BR/TR 6-1/175# d9.24																								
1955	Cle A	2	8	0	1	0	0	0	0	0-0	0	2	.125	.125	.125	-31	-2	0-0	1.000	1	154	0	/2-2	-0.1
PAYNE, FRED Frederick Thomas B 9.2.1880 Camden, NY D 1.16.1954 Camden, NY BR/TR 5-10/162# d4.21																								
1906	Det A	72	222	23	60	5	5	0	20	13	2		.270	.316	.338	102	0	4	.966	2	*106*	*81*	C-47,O-17(1-12-4)	0.6
1907	†Det A	53	169	17	28	2	2	0	14	7	5		.166	.221	.201	34	-13	4	.981	5	*106*	*98*	C-46/O-5(3-1-1)	-0.4
1908	Det A	20	45	3	3	0	0	0	2	3	3		.067	.176	.067	-20	-6	1	.954	-2	*86*	*70*	C-17/O(RF)	-0.8
1909	Chi A	32	82	8	20	2	0	0	12	5	1		.244	.295	.268	82	-2	0	.987	-1	*90*	*113*	C-27/O-3(RF)	0.0
1910	Chi A	91	252	17	56	5	4	0	19	11	2		.222	.260	.274	70	-10	6	.974	2	***118***	*87*	C-78/O-2(RF)	-0.1
1911	Chi A	66	133	14	27	2	1	1	19	8	2		.203	.259	.256	45	-10	6	.963	0	*144*	*81*	C-56	-0.7
Total	6	334	903	82	194	16	12	1	86	47	15		.215	.265	.262	64	-41	21	.972	7	*113*	*89*	C-271/O-28(4-13-11)	-1.4
PAYNTER, GEORGE George Washington (born George Washington Paner) B 7.6.1871 Cincinnati, OH D 10.1.1950 Cincinnati, OH BR/TR 5-9/125# d8.12																								
1894	StL N	1	4	0	0	0	0	0	0	1	0	0	.000	.200	.000	-48	-1	1	1.000	1	854	0	/O(CF)	0.0
PAYTON, JAY Jason Lee B 11.22.1972 Zanesville, OH BR/TR 5-10/185# d9.1																								
1998	NY N	15	22	2	7	1	0	0	0	1-0	0	4	.318	.348	.364	89	0	0-0	1.000	0	75	354	O-10(8-0-1)	0.0
1999	NY N	13	8	1	2	1	0	0	1	0-0	1	2	.250	.333	.375	81	0	1-2	1.000	0	106	0	/O-6(5-2-0)	-0.1
2000	†NY N	149	488	63	142	23	1	17	62	30-0	3	60	.291	.331	.447	100	-2	5-11	.981	-1	103	93	*O-146(4-143-0)	-0.5
2001	NY N	104	361	44	92	16	1	8	34	18-1	5	52	.255	.298	.371	76	-14	4-3	.984	1	107	118	*O-103(CF)	-1.2
2002	NY N	87	275	33	78	6	3	8	31	21-0	1	34	.284	.336	.415	104	-1	4-1	.994	-1	96	152	O-82(1-81-0)	0.0
	Col N	47	170	36	57	14	4	8	28	8-0	3	20	.335	.376	.606	135	8	3-3	1.000	2	106	122	O-44(32-16-2)	0.8
	Year	134	445	69	135	20	7	16	59	29-0	4	54	.303	.351	.488	118	8	7-4	.996	1	100	141	*O-126(33-97-2)	0.8
2003	Col N	157	600	93	181	32	5	28	89	43-3	7	77	.302	.354	.512	108	6	6-4	.987	3	109	64	*O-151(149-8-3)	0.4
Total	6	572	1924	272	559	93	14	69	245	121-4	20	249	.291	.337	.461	102	-3	23-24	.987	5	105	102	O-542(199-353-6)	-0.6
PEACOCK, JOHNNY John Gaston B 1.10.1910 Fremont, NC D 10.17.1981 Wilson, NC BL/TR 5-11/165# d9.23																								
1937	Bos A	9	32	3	10	2	1	0	6	1	0	0	.313	.333	.438	89	-1	0-0	.980	1	*126*	*138*	/C-9	0.1
1938	Bos A	72	195	29	59	7	1	1	39	17	0	4	.303	.358	.364	78	-7	4-1	.984	-5	*101*	*52*	C-57/1O(LF)	-0.8
1939	Bos A	92	274	33	76	11	4	0	36	29	0	11	.277	.347	.347	75	-10	1-1	.972	-6	*87*	*77*	C-84	-1.0
1940	Bos A	63	131	20	37	4	1	0	13	23	0	10	.282	.390	.328	85	-2	1-1	.994	-6	*90*	*77*	C-48	-0.6
1941	Bos A	79	261	28	74	20	1	0	27	21	1	3	.284	.339	.368	85	-5	2-1	.988	-2	*102*	*90*	C-70	-0.2
1942	Bos A	88	286	17	76	7	3	0	25	21	0	11	.266	.316	.311	74	-10	1-1	.988	-2	*103*	*112*	C-82	-0.8
1943	Bos A	48	114	7	23	3	1	0	7	10	0	9	.202	.266	.246	49	-7	1-1	.972	-1	*102*	*97*	C-32	-0.8
1944	Bos A	4	4	0	0	0	0	0	0	0	0	0	.000	.000	.000	-99	-1	0-0	1.000	0	*0*	*0*	/C-2	-0.1
	Phi N	83	253	21	57	9	3	0	21	31	0	15	.225	.310	.285	70	-10	1	.990	1	*103*	*106*	C-73/2	-0.5
1945	Phi N	33	74	6	15	6	0	0	6	6	0	0	.203	.262	.284	53	-5	1	.969	-4	*70*	*87*	C-23	-0.7
	Bro N	48	110	11	28	5	1	0	14	24	0	10	.255	.388	.318	98	1	2	.975	0	*107*	*71*	C-38	0.3
	Year	81	184	17	43	11	1	0	20	30	0	10	.234	.341	.304	82	-3	3	.973	-3	*94*	*76*	C-61	-0.4
Total	9	619	1734	175	455	74	16	1	194	183	1	73	.262	.333	.325	76	-57	14-6	.983	-24	*98*	*89*	C-518/2O(LF)1	-5.1
PEAK, ELIAS Elias B 5.23.1859 Philadelphia, PA D 12.17.1916 Philadelphia, PA d4.19																								
1884	Bos U	1	3	2	2	0	0	0		1			.667	.750	.667	338	1		1.000	-0	0	0	/O(RF)	0.1
	Phi U	54	215	35	42	6	4	0		7			.195	.221	.260	49	-20		.825	-8	106	78	2-47/O-5(4-0-1),S-2	-2.4
	Year	55	218	37	44	6	4	0		8			.202	.230	.266	54	-19		.825	-8	106	78	2-47/O-6(4-0-2),S-2	-2.3
PEARCE, HARRY Harry James B 7.12.1889 Philadelphia, PA D 1.8.1942 Philadelphia, PA BR/TR 5-9/158# d10.2																								
1917	Phi N	7	16	2	4	3	0	0	2	0	1	4	.250	.294	.438	118	0	0	.967	3	166	59	/S-4	0.4
1918	Phi N	60	164	16	40	3	2	0	18	9	3	31	.244	.295	.287	73	-5	5	.944	-0	110	89	2-46/S-2,13	-0.5
1919	Phi N	68	244	24	44	3	3	0	9	8	1	27	.180	.209	.217	26	-22	6	.948	-0	101	107	2-43,S-23/3-2	-2.3
Total	3	135	424	42	88	9	5	0	29	17	5	62	.208	.247	.252	48	-27	11	.946	3	106	97	/2-89,S-29,3-3,1	-2.4
PEARCE, DICKEY Richard J. B 2.29.1836 Brooklyn, NY D 9.18.1908 Wareham, MA BR/TR 5-3.5/161# d5.18 M2 U2																								
1871	Mut NA	**33**	163	31	44	5	0	0	20	4		1	.270	.287	.301	76	-3	0-0	.793	-7	92	114	*S-33	-0.7
1872	Mut NA	44	206	32	39	2	1	1	22	4		1	.189	.205	.223	34	-14	1-1	**.844**	2	103	162	*S-42/O-2(1-0-1),M	-1.0
1873	Atl NA	**55**	262	42	72	6	0	1	23	8		2	.275	.296	.309	90	0	3-0	.777	2	116	96	*S-55/12	0.1
1874	Atl NA	**56**	255	48	75	1	0	0	26	6		1	.294	.310	.298	109	5	1-0	**.845**	8	**109**	69	*S-56/3-2,2	0.9

Year	Tm Lg	G	AB	R	H	2B	3B	HR	RBI	BB-IB	HP	SO	AVG	OBP	SLG	AOPS	ABR	SB-CS	FA	FR	Rng	Thr	G at Pos	BFW
1875	StL NA	**70**	311	51	77	6	3	0	29	7		7	.248	.264	.286	100	2	8-3	.830	11	**113**	150	*S-70/P-2,M	1.0
1876	StL N	25	102	12	21	1	0	0	10	3		5	.206	.229	.216	51	-5		.902	3	109	170	S-23/O(LF)2	-0.1
1877	StL N	8	29	1	5	0	0	0	4	1		4	.172	.200	.172	19	-3		.950	3	126	169	/S-8	0.0
Total	5 NA	258	1197	204	307	20	4	2	120	29		12	.256	.274	.285	84	-10	13-4	.000	17	108	118	S-256/P-2,3-2,2-2,O-2(1-0-1),1	0.3
Total	2	33	131	13	26	1	0	0	14	4		9	.198	.222	.206	44	-8		.914	6	113	170	S-31,2O(LF)	-0.1
PEARCE, DUCKY William C. B 3.17.1885 Corning, OH D 5.22.1933 Brownstown, IN BR/TR 6-1/185# d7.1																								
1908	Cin N	2	2	0	0	0	0	0	0	0	0		.000	.000	.000	-99	0	0	1.000	1	*121*	*195*	/C-2	0.0
1909	Cin N	2	2	0	0	0	0	0	0	0	0		.000	.000	.000	-99	0	0	1.000	-0	*63*	*0*	/C-2	-0.1
Total	2	4	4	0	0	0	0	0	0	0	0		.000	.000	.000	-99	0	0	1.000	1	*102*	*130*	/C-4	-0.1
PEARSON, ALBIE Albert Gregory B 9.12.1934 Alhambra, CA BL/TL 5-5/141# d4.14																								
1958	Was A	146	530	63	146	25	5	3	33	64-1	2	31	.275	.354	.358	99	1	7-8	.980	-3	101	75	*O-141(0-136-6)	-0.9
1959	Was A	25	80	9	15	1	0	0	2	14-0	0	3	.188	.309	.200	43	-6	1-1	.974	-3	84	0	O-21(0-11-10)	-1.0
	Bal A	80	138	22	32	4	2	0	6	13-0	0	5	.232	.296	.290	64	-7	4-0	.987	1	109	97	O-50(22-16-16)	-0.7
	Year	105	218	31	47	5	2	0	8	27-0	0	8	.216	.301	.257	56	-13	5-1	.983	-2	99	60	O-71(22-27-26)	-1.7
1960	Bal A	48	82	17	20	2	0	1	6	17-0	0	3	.244	.370	.305	87	-1	4-0	.975	-1	95	78	O-32(11-7-15)	-0.1
1961	LA A	144	427	92	123	21	3	7	41	96-1	3	40	.288	.420	.400	109	11	11-3	.956	-4	96	91	*O-113(1-46-76)	0.2
1962	LA A	160	614	**115**	160	29	6	5	42	95-3	1	36	.261	.360	.352	96	0	15-6	.989	-5	98	100	*O-160(0-143-17)	-0.9
1963	LA A★	154	578	92	176	26	5	6	47	92-5	3	37	.304	.402	.398	133	31	17-10	.983	-4	99	105	*O-148(2-135-15)	2.4
1964	LA A	107	265	34	59	5	1	2	16	35-2	1	22	.223	.316	.272	72	-9	6-4	.978	-5	93	23	O-66(10-52-7)	-1.8
1965	Cal A	122	360	41	100	17	2	4	21	51-0	2	17	.278	.370	.369	114	9	12-1	.988	-2	95	86	*O-101(7-12-87)	0.3
1966	Cal A	2	3	0	0	0	0	0	0	0-0	0	1	.000	.000	.000	-99	-1	0-0	—	-0	0	0	/O(LF)	-0.1
Total	9	988	3077	485	831	130	24	28	214	477-12	12	195	.270	.369	.355	102	28	77-33	.980	-24	98	84	O-833(54-558-249)	-2.6
PECHOUS, CHARLIE Charles Edward B 10.5.1896 Chicago, IL D 9.13.1980 Kenosha, WI BR/TR 6/170# d9.14																								
1915	Chi F	18	51	4	9	3	0	0	4	4	0	15	.176	.236	.235	35	-5	1	.938	-0	113	0	3-18	-0.6
1916	Chi N	22	69	5	10	1	1	0	4	3	0	21	.145	.181	.188	12	-7	1	.940	6	137	70	3-22	-0.1
1917	Chi N	13	41	2	10	0	0	0	1	2	1	9	.244	.295	.244	61	-2	1	1.000	-2	67	0	/3-7,S-5	-0.4
Total	3	53	161	11	29	4	1	0	9	9	1	45	.180	.228	.217	32	-14	3	.947	3	118	35	/3-47,S-5	-1.1
PECK, HAL Harold Arthur B 4.20.1917 Big Bend, WI D 4.13.1995 Milwaukee, WI BL/TL 5-11/175# d5.13																								
1943	Bro N	1	1	0	0	0	0	0	0	0	0	0	.000	.000	.000	-99	0	0	—	0			H	0.0
1944	Phi A	2	8	0	2	0	0	0	1	0	0	2	.250	.250	.250	44	-1	0-2	1.000	-0	89	0	/O-2(RF)	-0.2
1945	Phi A	112	449	51	124	22	9	5	39	37	0	28	.276	.331	.399	112	5	5-3	.943	-10	85	80	*O-110(RF)	-1.3
1946	Phi A	48	150	14	37	8	2	2	11	16	0	14	.247	.319	.367	92	-2	1-2	.981	-0	85	158	O-35(RF)	-0.4
1947	Cle A	114	392	58	115	18	2	8	44	27	2	31	.293	.342	.411	112	5	3-3	.983	-2	97	80	O-97(3-0-95)	-0.1
1948	†Cle A	45	63	12	18	3	0	0	8	4	0	8	.286	.328	.333	78	-2	1-0	1.000	-1	93	0	/O-9(1-0-9)	-0.3
1949	Cle A	33	29	1	9	1	0	0	9	3	0	3	.310	.375	.345	93	0	0-0	1.000	0	147	0	/O-2(RF)	0.0
Total	7	355	1092	136	305	52	13	15	112	87	2	86	.279	.334	.392	106	5	10-10	.965	-13	90	87	O-255(4-0-253)	-2.3
PECKINPAUGH, ROGER Roger Thorpe B 2.5.1891 Wooster, OH D 11.17.1977 Cleveland, OH BR/TR 5-10.5/165# d9.15 M8																								
1910	Cle A	15	45	1	9	0	0	0	6	1	1		.200	.234	.200	36	-3	3	.906	-5	89	60	S-14	-0.9
1912	Cle A	70	236	18	50	4	1	1	22	16	0		.212	.262	.250	45	-17	11	.924	-1	98	77	S-68	-1.5
1913	Cle A	1	0	1	0	0	0	0	0	0	0	0	—	—	—	—	0	0	—	0			H	0.0
	NY A	95	340	35	91	10	7	1	32	24	0	47	.268	.316	.347	94	-4	19	.931	-3	103	79	S-93	-0.1
	Year	96	340	36	91	10	7	1	32	24	0	47	.268	.316	.347	94	-4	19	.931	-3	103	79	S-93	-0.1
1914	NY A	**157**	570	55	127	14	6	3	51	51	1	73	.223	.288	.284	72	-20	38-17	.956	5	105	82	*S-157,M	-0.2
1915	NY A	142	540	67	119	18	7	5	44	49	3	72	.220	.289	.307	79	-16	19-12	.942	5	**106**	114	*S-142	0.0
1916	NY A	145	552	65	141	22	8	4	58	62	1	50	.255	.332	.346	101	1	18	.946	-0	102	96	*S-145	1.2
1917	NY A	148	543	63	141	24	7	0	41	64	2	46	.260	.340	.330	103	4	17	.934	7	102	133	*S-148	2.3
1918	NY A	122	446	59	103	15	3	0	43	43	3	41	.231	.303	.278	74	-14	12	.961	**22**	**113**	**148**	*S-122	1.9
1919	NY A	122	453	89	138	20	2	7	33	59	4	37	.305	.390	.404	122	16	10	.943	**26**	**116**	**139**	*S-121	5.1
1920	NY A	139	534	109	144	26	6	8	54	72	0	47	.270	.356	.386	93	-4	8-12	.962	8	102	113	*S-137	1.1
1921	†NY A	149	577	128	166	25	7	8	71	84	2	44	.288	.380	.397	96	-1	2-2	.948	-3	96	111	*S-149	1.1
1922	Was A	147	520	62	132	14	4	2	48	55	3	36	.254	.329	.308	70	-22	11-6	.951	18	**109**	120	*S-147	1.2
1923	Was A	154	568	73	150	18	4	2	62	64	1	30	.264	.340	.320	78	-17	10-8	.948	**22**	**107**	**127**	*S-154	2.0
1924	†Was A	155	523	72	142	20	5	2	73	72	0	45	.272	.360	.340	84	-11	9-6	.963	11	105	**119**	*S-155	1.5
1925	†Was A	126	422	67	124	16	4	4	64	49	0	23	.294	.367	.379	91	-5	13-4	.952	-14	92	102	*S-124/1	-0.4
1926	Was A	57	147	19	35	4	1	1	14	28	0	12	.238	.360	.299	75	-4	3-0	.960	-1	96	96	S-46/1	-0.1
1927	Chi A	68	217	23	64	6	3	0	23	21	1	6	.295	.360	.350	87	-4	2-3	.964	0	104	106	S-60	0.1
Total	17	2012	7233	1006	1876	256	75	48	739	814	22	609	.259	.336	.335	87	-121	205-70	.949	97	104	112	*S-1982/1-2	14.3
PECOTA, BILL William Joseph B 2.16.1960 Redwood City, CA BR/TR 6-2/190# d9.19 OF Total (13-LF 2-CF 19-RF)																								
1986	KC A	12	29	3	6	2	0	0	2	3-0	1	3	.207	.294	.276	58	-2	0-2	.974	4	163	62	3-12/S-2,D-4	0.2
1987	KC A	66	156	22	43	5	1	3	14	15-0	1	25	.276	.343	.378	89	-2	5-0	.977	9	113	129	S-36,3-17,2-15/D	1.0
1988	KC A	90	178	25	37	3	3	1	15	18-0	2	34	.208	.286	.275	58	-10	7-2	.976	7	110	96	S-41,3-21,1-11/O-9(3-0-6),D-4,2-3,C	0.0
1989	KC A	65	83	21	17	4	2	3	5	7-1	1	9	.205	.275	.410	91	-1	5-0	.988	1	104	75	S-29,O-15(4-2-9),2-12/3-7,1-4,D	0.2
1990	KC A	87	240	43	58	15	2	5	20	33-0	1	39	.242	.336	.383	102	1	8-5	.986	10	97	73	2-50,S-21,3-11/O-6(4-0-3),1-4,D-2	1.4
1991	KC A	125	398	53	114	23	2	6	45	41-6	2	45	.286	.356	.399	108	5	16-7	.983	-3	97	82	*3-102,2-34/S-9,1-8,D-2,O(LF)P	0.4
1992	NY N	117	269	28	61	13	0	2	26	25-3	1	40	.227	.293	.297	69	-11	9-3	.926	8	102	140	3-48,S-39,2-38/P1	0.1
1993	†Atl N	72	62	17	20	2	1	0	5	2-0	0	5	.323	.344	.387	94	-1	1-1	1.000	-1	86	0	3-23/2-4,O(RF)	-0.2
1994	Atl N	64	112	11	24	5	0	2	16	16-1	0	16	.214	.310	.313	62	-6	1-0	.974	6	122	112	3-31/2O(LF)	0.1
Total	9	698	1527	223	380	72	11	22	148	160-11	9	216	.249	.323	.354	87	-27	52-20	.968	43	109	99	3-272,S-177,2-157/O-33R,1-28,DPC	3.2
PEDEN, LES Leslie Earl "Gooch" B 9.17.1923 Azle, TX D 2.11.2002 Jacksonville, FL BR/TR 6-1.5/212# d4.17 C1																								
1953	Was A	9	28	4	7	1	0	1	1	4	0	3	.250	.344	.393	101	0	0-0	1.000	0	*89*	*110*	/C-8	0.0
PEDERSON, STU Stuart Russell B 1.28.1960 Palo Alto, CA BL/TL 6/185# d9.8																								
1985	LA N	8	4	1	0	0	0	0	1	0-0	0	2	.000	.000	.000	-99	-1	0-0	1.000	0	120	0	/O-5(3-0-2)	-0.1
PEDRE, JORGE Jorge Enrique B 10.12.1966 Culver City, CA BR/TR 5-11/210# d9.7																								
1991	KC A	10	19	2	5	1	1	0	3	3-0	0	5	.263	.364	.421	116	0	0-0	.971	-2	51	110	/C-9,1	-0.1
1992	Chi N	4	4	0	0	0	0	0	0	0-0	0	1	.000	.000	.000	-98	-1	0-0	1.000	-1	0	0	/C-4	-0.2
Total	2	14	23	2	5	1	1	0	3	3-0	0	6	.217	.308	.348	81	-1	0-0	.973	-2	44	95	/C-13,1	-0.3
PEDRIQUE, AL Alfredo Jose (Garcia) B 8.11.1960 Aragua, Venezuela BR/TR 6- /155# d4.14																								
1987	NY N	5	6	1	0	0	0	0	0	1-0	0	2	.000	.143	.000	-61	-1	0-0	1.000	1	147	0	/S-4,2	0.0
	Pit N	88	246	23	74	10	1	1	27	18-4	3	27	.301	.354	.362	90	-3	5-4	.968	-5	93	114	S-76/3-3,2-2	-0.1
	Year	93	252	24	74	10	1	1	27	19-4	3	29	.294	.349	.353	87	-4	5-4	.969	-3	94	111	S-80/2-3,3-3	-0.1
1988	Pit N	50	128	7	23	5	0	0	4	8-2	1	17	.180	.234	.219	31	-11	0-0	.974	5	112	115	S-46/3-5	-0.4
1989	Det A	31	69	1	14	3	0	0	5	2-0	0	15	.203	.225	.246	34	-6	0-0	.960	4	104	63	3-12,S-12/2-8	-0.1
Total	3	174	449	32	111	18	1	1	36	29-6	4	61	.247	.298	.298	64	-21	5-4	.971	6	100	112	S-138/3-20,2-11	-0.6
PEDROES, CHICK Charles P. B 10.27.1869 Chicago, IL D 8.6.1927 Chicago, IL d8.21																								
1902	Chi N	2	6	0	0	0	0	0	0	0	0		.000	.000	.000	-99	-1	0	1.000	-0	0	0	/O-2(RF)	-0.2
PEEL, HOMER Homer Hefner B 10.10.1902 Port Sullivan, TX D 4.8.1997 Shreveport, LA BR/TR 5-9.5/170# d9.13																								
1927	StL N	2	2	0	0	0	0	0	0	0	0	1	.000	.000	.000	-97	-1	0	—	-0	0	0	/O(RF)	-0.1
1929	Phi N	53	156	16	42	12	1	0	19	12	2	7	.269	.329	.359	66	-8	1	.990	0	103	61	O-39(1-36-2)/1	-0.8
1930	StL N	26	73	9	12	2	0	0	10	3	0	4	.164	.197	.192	-5	-13	0	.968	-2	92	0	O-21(6-0-15)	-1.4
1933	†NY N	84	148	16	38	1	1	1	12	14	1	10	.257	.325	.297	80	-4	0	.962	-3	81	48	O-45(35-9-1)	-0.9
1934	NY N	21	41	7	8	0	0	1	3	1	0	2	.195	.214	.268	29	-4	0	.929	-1	76	0	O-10(0-8-2)	-0.6
Total	5	186	420	48	100	15	2	2	44	30	3	24	.238	.294	.298	53	-30	1	.974	-6	91	40	O-116(42-53-21)/1	-3.8
PEERSON, JACK Jack Chiles B 8.28.1910 Brunswick, GA D 10.23.1966 Ft.Walton Beach, FL BR/TR 5-11/175# d9.7																								
1935	Phi A	10	19	3	6	1	0	0	1	1	0	1	.316	.350	.368	87	0	0-0	.952	-1	105	0	/S-4	-0.1
1936	Phi A	8	34	7	11	1	1	0	5	0	0	3	.324	.324	.412	82	-1	0-1	.942	2	127	87	/S-7,2	0.1

Year	Tm Lg	G	AB	R	H	2B	3B	HR	RBI	BB-IB	HP	SO	AVG	OBP	SLG	AOPS	ABR	SB-CS	FA	FR	Rng	Thr	G at Pos	BFW
Total	2	18	53	10	17	2	1	0	6	1	0	4	.321	.333	.396	84	-1	0-1	.945	2	120	59	/S-11,2	0.0
PEETE, CHARLIE Charles "Mule" B 2.22.1929 Franklin, VA D 11.27.1956 Caracas, Venezuela BL/TR 5-9.5/190# d7.17																								
1956	StL N	23	52	3	10	2	2	0	6	6-0	1	10	.192	.288	.308	60	-3	0-2	1.000	1	88	256	O-21(CF)	-0.4
PEFFER, MONTE Monte (born Montague Pfeiffer) B 10.8.1891 New York, NY D 9.27.1941 New York, NY BR/TR 5-4.5/147# d9.29																								
1913	Phi A	1	3	0	0	0	0	0	0	0	1	1	.000	.250	.000	-26	0	0	.800	-0	123	0	/S	-0.1
PEGUERO, JULIO Julio Cesar B 9.7.1968 San Isidro, D.R. BB/TR 6/160# d4.8																								
1992	Phi N	14	9	3	2	0	0	0	0	3-0	0	3	.222	.417	.222	86	0	0-0	1.000	0	104	0	O-14(0-9-5)	0.0
PEGUES, STEVE Steven Antone B 5.21.1968 Pontotoc, MS BR/TR 6-2/190# d7.6																								
1994	Cin N	11	10	1	3	0	0	0	0	1-0	0	3	.300	.364	.300	76	0	0-0	.833	0	195	0	/O-4(3-0-1)	0.0
	Pit N	7	26	1	10	2	0	0	2	1-0	0	2	.385	.407	.462	124	1	1-0	1.000	-2	57	0	/O-7(5-2-0)	0.0
	Year	18	36	2	13	2	0	0	2	2-0	0	5	.361	.395	.417	112	1	1-0	.929	-1	80	0	O-11(8-2-1)	0.0
1995	Pit N	82	171	17	42	8	0	6	16	4-0	1	36	.246	.263	.398	71	-8	1-2	.954	1	113	80	O-53(31-4-25)	-0.9
Total	2	100	207	19	55	10	0	6	18	6-0	1	41	.266	.286	.401	78	-7	2-2	.950	-0	107	66	/O-64(39-6-26)	-0.9
PEITZ, HEINIE Henry Clement B 11.28.1870 St.Louis, MO D 10.23.1943 Cincinnati, OH BR/TR 5-11/165# d10.15 C1 b-Joe ▲ OF Total (4-LF 7-RF)																								
1892	StL N	1	3	0	0	0	0	0	0	0	0	0	.000	.000	.000	-99	-1	0	1.000	-0	*101*	*0*	/C	-0.1
1893	StL N	96	362	53	92	12	9	1	45	54	1	20	.254	.353	.345	86	-7	12	.948	3	*87*	*110*	C-74,S-11,O-10(4-0-6)/1-5	0.2
1894	StL N	99	338	52	89	19	9	3	49	43	1	21	.263	.348	.399	80	-12	14	.897	3	86	61	3-47,C-39,1-14/P	-0.3
1895	StL N	90	334	44	95	14	12	2	65	29	2	20	.284	.345	.416	97	-3	9	.937	-10	*77*	*111*	C-71,1-11,3-10	-0.5
1896	Cin N	68	211	33	63	12	5	2	34	30	0	15	.299	.386	.431	108	3	7	.968	11	*142*	*68*	C-67	1.6
1897	Cin N	77	266	35	78	11	7	1	44	18	1		.293	.340	.398	89	-6	3	**.979**	16	*156*	*85*	C-71/P-2	1.4
1898	Cin N	105	330	49	90	15	5	1	43	35	3		.273	.348	.358	96	-2	9	.945	10	***166***	*78*	*C-101	1.6
1899	Cin N	94	293	45	79	13	2	1	43	46	2		.270	.372	.338	94	0	11	.977	7	***130***	*84*	C-92/P	1.3
1900	Cin N	91	294	34	75	14	1	2	34	20	7		.255	.318	.330	81	-7	5	.958	7	*116*	*99*	C-80/1-8	0.7
1901	Cin N	82	269	24	82	13	5	1	24	23	2		.305	.364	.401	130	11	3	.982	3	*112*	*90*	C-49,2-21/3-6,1-2	1.9
1902	Cin N	112	387	54	122	22	5	1	60	24	9		.315	.369	.406	127	13	7	.919	3	90	129	2-48,C-47/1-6,3-6	2.1
1903	Cin N	105	358	45	93	15	3	0	42	37	1		.260	.331	.318	77	-10	7	.970	3	*122*	*82*	C-78,1-11/3-9,2-4	0.0
1904	Cin N	84	272	32	66	13	2	1	30	14	1		.243	.282	.316	78	-7	1	.975	5	*104*	*104*	C-64,1-18/3	0.4
1905	Pit N	88	278	18	62	10	0	0	27	24	2		.223	.289	.259	62	-12	2	.965	-2	*118*	*93*	C-87/2	-0.6
1906	Pit N	40	125	13	30	8	0	0	20	13	2		.240	.321	.304	91	-1	1	.979	1	*122*	*87*	C-38	0.5
1913	StL N	3	4	1	1	0	1	0	0	0	0	0	.250	.250	.750	182	0	0	.625	-1	86	77	/C-2,O(RF)	-0.1
Total	16	1235	4124	532	1117	191	66	16	560	410	34	76	.271	.342	.361	92	-41	91	.963	58	*122*	*93*	C-961/3-79,1-75,2-74,O-11R,S-11,P	10.1
PEITZ, JOE Joseph B 11.8.1869 St.Louis, MO D 12.4.1919 St.Louis, MO d6.28 b-Heinie																								
1894	StL N	7	26	10	11	2	3	0	3	6	0	1	.423	.531	.731	202	5	2	.818	-1	67	283	/O-7(RF)	0.3
PELAEZ, ALEX Alejandro B 4.6.1976 San Diego, CA BR/TR 5-9/190# d5.16																								
2002	SD N	3	8	0	2	0	0	0	0	0-0	0	0	.250	.250	.250	38	-1	0-0	1.000	-0	148	325	/123	-0.1
PELLAGRINI, EDDIE Edward Charles B 3.13.1918 Boston, MA BR/TR 5-9/165# d4.22																								
1946	Bos A	22	71	7	15	3	1	2	4	3	1	18	.211	.253	.366	68	-3	1-0	.891	-2	88	140	3-14/S-9	-0.6
1947	Bos A	74	231	29	47	8	1	4	19	23	2	35	.203	.281	.299	57	-14	2-2	.926	-7	93	107	3-42,S-26	-2.0
1948	StL A	105	290	31	69	8	3	2	27	34	1	40	.238	.320	.307	65	-15	1-2	.964	18	110	123	S-98	0.8
1949	StL A	79	235	26	56	8	1	2	15	14	1	24	.238	.284	.306	54	-17	2-1	.961	3	104	84	S-76	-0.9
1951	Phi N	86	197	31	46	4	5	5	30	23	4	25	.234	.326	.381	91	-3	5-1	.990	-12	95	64	2-53/S-8,3-6	-1.2
1952	Cin N	46	100	15	17	2	0	1	3	8	0	18	.170	.231	.220	26	-10	1-0	.983	4	116	106	2-22/1-8,S3	-0.5
1953	Pit N	78	174	16	44	3	2	4	19	14	0	20	.253	.309	.362	75	-7	1-1	.972	-2	93	60	2-31,3-12/S-3	-0.7
1954	Pit N	73	125	12	27	6	0	0	16	9	4	21	.216	.288	.264	46	-10	0-0	.968	2	113	129	3-31/2-7,S	-0.8
Total	8	563	1423	167	321	42	13	20	133	128	13	201	.226	.295	.316	62	-79	13-7	.956	4	104	99	S-222,2-113,3-106/1-8	-5.9
PELLOW, KIT Kit Donovan B 8.28.1973 Kansas City, MO BR/TR 6-1/205# d8.14																								
2002	KC A	29	63	6	15	1	0	1	5	9-0	1	21	.238	.342	.302	66	-3	1-1	.844	1	135	185	3-12,1-10/D-5	-0.2
2003	Col N	11	18	6	8	3	1	1	4	0-0	2	4	.444	.476	.889	222	3	0-0	1.000	-1	69	0	/C-7,1O(LF)	0.2
Total	2	40	81	12	23	4	1	2	9	9-0	3	25	.284	.372	.432	101	0	1-1	.844	-0	135	185	/3-12,1-11,C-7,D-5,O(LF)	0.0
PELOUZE, LOUIS Louis Henri B 9.10.1863 Fort Monroe, VA D 1.9.1939 New York, NY BL/TL 6/175# d7.24																								
1886	StL N	1	3	0	0	0	0	0	0	0		2	.000	.000	.000	-99	-1	0	1.000	0	0	0	/O(CF)	-0.1
PELTIER, DAN Daniel Edward B 6.30.1968 Clifton Park, NY BL/TL 6-1/200# d6.26																								
1992	Tex A	12	24	1	4	0	0	0	2	0-0	0	3	.167	.167	.167	-7	-4	0-0	.857	-2	53	0	O-10(1-0-9)	-0.5
1993	Tex A	65	160	23	43	7	1	1	17	20-0	1	27	.269	.352	.344	92	-1	0-4	.950	-2	83	130	O-55(2-0-54)/1-5	-0.7
1996	SF N	31	59	3	15	2	0	0	9	7-1	0	9	.254	.328	.288	68	-3	0-0	1.000	-1	72	113	1-13/O(LF)	-0.5
Total	3	108	243	27	62	9	1	1	28	27-1	1	39	.255	.330	.313	77	-8	0-4	.943	-5	79	113	/O-66(4-0-63),1-18	-1.7
PELTZ, JOHN John B 4.23.1861 New Orleans, LA D 2.27.1906 New Orleans, LA BR/TR 5-8/175# d5.1																								
1884	Ind AA	106	393	40	86	13	17	3		7	2		.219	.236	.361	95	-4		.818	5	81	30	*O-106(LF)	-0.1
1888	Bal AA	1	4	1	1	0	0	0	0	0	0		.250	.250	.250	62	0	1	.500	-0	0	0	/O(LF)	-0.1
1890	Bro AA	98	384	55	87	9	6	1	33	32	2		.227	.289	.289	73	-14	10	.904	1	107	137	*O-98(CF)	-1.4
	Syr AA	5	17	2	3	1	1	0	2	3	0		.176	.300	.353	103	0	0	.857	1	316	665	/O-5(CF)	0.1
	Tol AA	20	73	8	18	2	2	0	13	3	1		.247	.286	.329	79	-3	7	.886	-0	108	171	O-20(CF)	-0.3
	Year	123	474	65	108	12	9	1	48	38	3		.228	.289	.297	75	-16	17	.900	1	114	158	*O-123(CF)	-1.6
Total	3	230	871	106	195	25	26	4	48	45	5		.224	.266	.326	84	-21	18	.865	6	98	98	O-230(107-123-0)	-1.8
PEMBERTON, BROCK Brock B 11.5.1953 Tulsa, OK BB/TL 6-3/190# d9.10																								
1974	NY N	11	22	0	4	0	0	0	1	0-0	0	3	.182	.182	.182	2	-3	0-1	1.000	1	193	138	/1-4	-0.3
1975	NY N	2	2	0	0	0	0	0	0	0-0	0	1	.000	.000	.000	-99	-1	0-0	—	0			H	-0.1
Total	2	13	24	0	4	0	0	0	1	0-0	0	4	.167	.167	.167	-7	-4	0-1	1.000	1	193	138	/1-4	-0.4
PEMBERTON, RUDY Rudy Hector (Perez) B 12.17.1969 San Pedro De Macoris, D.R. BR/TR 6-1/185# d4.26																								
1995	Det A	12	30	3	9	3	1	0	3	1-0	1	5	.300	.344	.467	109	0	0-0	1.000	-1	95	0	/O-8(6-0-2),D-3	0.0
1996	Bos A	13	41	11	21	8	0	1	10	2-0	2	4	.512	.556	.780	228	9	3-1	1.000	-3	42	0	O-13(1-0-12)	0.5
1997	Bos A	27	63	8	15	2	0	2	10	4-0	3	13	.238	.314	.365	75	-2	0-0	.949	0	94	170	O-23(RF)	-0.3
Total	3	52	134	22	45	13	1	3	23	7-0	6	22	.336	.395	.515	131	7	3-1	.968	-3	79	84	/O-44(7-0-37),D-3	0.2
PENA, BERT Adalberto (Rivera) B 7.11.1959 Santurce, P.R. BR/TR 5-11/165# d9.14																								
1981	Hou N	4	2	0	1	0	0	0	0	0-0	0	0	.500	.500	.500	194	0	0-0	1.000	-0	55	325	/S-3	0.0
1983	Hou N	4	8	0	1	0	0	0	0	2-0	0	2	.125	.300	.125	23	-1	0-0	1.000	-2	72	110	/S-4	-0.2
1984	Hou N	24	39	3	8	1	0	1	4	3-1	0	8	.205	.262	.308	64	-2	0-0	.956	1	101	71	S-21	0.0
1985	Hou N	20	29	7	8	2	0	0	4	1-0	0	6	.276	.290	.345	82	-1	0-0	1.000	-2	98	0	/3-7,S-6,2-2	-0.3
1986	Hou N	15	29	3	6	1	0	0	2	5-2	0	5	.207	.324	.241	60	-1	1-0	.907	1	96	51	S-10/3-2,2	0.0
1987	Hou N	21	46	5	7	0	0	0	0	2-0	1	7	.152	.204	.152	-4	-7	0-0	.982	-4	81	37	S-19/3	-0.9
Total	6	88	153	18	31	4	0	1	10	13-3	1	28	.203	.268	.248	45	-12	1-0	.953	-6	88	64	/S-63,3-10,2-3	-1.4
PENA, ANGEL Angel Maria B 2.16.1975 San Pedro De Macoris, D.R. BR/TR 5-10/225# d9.8																								
1998	LA N	6	13	1	3	0	0	0	0	0-0	0	6	.231	.231	.231	23	-2	0-0	1.000	1	200	107	/C-4	-0.1
1999	LA N	43	120	14	25	6	0	4	21	12-0	0	24	.208	.276	.358	64	-7	0-1	.989	-1	92	128	C-43	-0.5
2001	LA N	22	54	3	11	1	0	1	2	1-0	0	17	.204	.214	.278	29	-6	0-0	1.000	6	107	107	C-15	0.1
Total	3	71	187	18	39	7	0	5	23	13-0	0	47	.209	.256	.326	52	-15	0-1	.993	6	102	121	/C-62	-0.5
PENA, TONY Antonio Francisco (Padilla) B 6.4.1957 Monte Cristi, D.R. BR/TR 6/181# d9.1 M2 C1 b-Ramon																								
1980	Pit N	8	21	1	9	1	1	0	1	0-0	0	4	.429	.429	.571	174	2	0-1	.952	1	78	95	/C-6	0.3
1981	Pit N	66	210	16	63	9	1	2	17	8-2	1	23	.300	.326	.381	98	-1	1-2	.985	8	**173**	86	C-64	0.9
1982	Pit N★	138	497	53	147	28	4	11	63	17-3	4	57	.296	.323	.435	107	3	2-5	.982	7	**145**	106	*C-137	1.5
1983	Pit N	151	542	51	163	22	3	15	70	31-8	0	73	.301	.338	.435	110	6	6-7	.992	6	128	90	*C-149	1.7
1984	Pit N★	147	546	77	156	27	2	15	78	36-5	4	79	.286	.333	.425	112	8	12-8	.991	22	**137**	111	*C-146	3.8

Year	Tm Lg	G	AB	R	H	2B	3B	HR	RBI	BB-IB	HP	SO	AVG	OBP	SLG	AOPS	ABR	SB-CS	FA	FR	Rng	Thr	G at Pos	BFW
1985	Pit N★	147	546	53	136	27	2	10	59	29-4	0	67	.249	.284	.361	81	-16	12-8	.988	22	**139**	120	*C-146/1	1.3
1986	Pit N★	144	510	56	147	26	2	10	52	53-6	1	69	.288	.356	.406	107	6	9-10	.981	16	115	122	*C-139/1-4	2.7
1987	†StL N	116	384	40	82	13	4	5	44	36-9	1	54	.214	.281	.307	55	-25	6-1	.988	7	131	68	*C-112/1-4,O-2(RF)	-1.3
1988	StL N	149	505	55	133	23	1	10	51	33-11	1	60	.263	.308	.372	94	-5	6-2	**.994**	10	130	91	*C-142/1-3	1.5
1989	StL N★	141	424	36	110	17	2	4	37	35-19	2	33	.259	.318	.337	85	-8	5-3	**.997**	13	103	103	*C-134/O(RF)	1.3
1990	†Bos A	143	491	62	129	19	1	7	56	43-3	1	71	.263	.322	.348	84	-10	8-6	.995	10	93	100	*C-142/1	0.8
1991	Bos A	141	464	45	107	23	2	5	48	37-1	4	53	.231	.291	.321	66	-21	8-3	.995	12	107	91	*C-140	-0.1
1992	Bos A	133	410	39	99	21	1	1	38	24-0	1	61	.241	.284	.305	61	-21	3-2	.993	19	121	84	*C-132	0.5
1993	Bos A	126	304	20	55	11	0	4	19	25-0	2	46	.181	.246	.257	34	-29	1-3	.995	20	138	76	*C-125/D	-0.2
1994	Cle A	40	112	18	33	8	1	2	10	9-0	0	11	.295	.341	.438	100	0	0-1	.996	2	90	106	C-40	0.3
1995	†Cle A	91	263	25	69	15	0	5	28	14-1	1	44	.262	.302	.376	74	-10	1-0	.987	-1	74	80	C-91	-0.5
1996	†Cle A	67	174	14	34	4	0	1	27	15-0	0	25	.195	.255	.236	26	-20	0-1	.992	6	112	120	C-67	-1.0
1997	Chi A	31	67	4	11	1	0	0	8	8-0	0	13	.164	.250	.179	16	-8	0-0	1.000	-2	58	43	C-30/3	-0.9
	†Hou N	9	19	2	4	3	0	0	2	2-0	0	3	.211	.273	.368	72	-1	0-0	1.000	2	55	48	/C-8	0.2
Total	18	1988	6489	667	1687	298	27	107	708	455-72	23	846	.260	.309	.364	84	-150	80-63	.991	178	121	97	*C-1950/1-13,O-3(RF),3D	12.8
PENA, CARLOS Carlos Felipe B 5.17.1978 Santo Domingo, D.R. BL/TL 6-2/210# d9.5																								
2001	Tex A	22	62	6	16	4	1	3	12	10-0	0	17	.258	.361	.500	119	2	0-0	.987	2	147	87	1-16/D	0.2
2002	Oak A	40	124	12	27	4	0	7	16	15-0	1	38	.218	.305	.419	90	-2	0-0	.997	8	177	83	1-40	0.2
	Det A	75	273	31	69	13	4	12	36	26-0	2	73	.253	.321	.462	111	4	2-2	.996	-7	62	110	1-73/D-2	-1.1
	Year	115	397	43	96	17	4	19	52	41-0	3	111	.242	.316	.448	104	1	2-2	.996	0	102	101	*1-113/D-2	-0.9
2003	Det A	131	452	51	112	21	6	18	50	53-1	6	123	.248	.332	.440	111	7	4-5	.990	-0	108	114	*1-128/D	-0.6
Total	3	268	911	100	224	42	11	40	114	104-1	9	251	.246	.327	.448	109	11	6-7	.992	1	108	106	1-257/D-4	-1.3
PENA, ELVIS Elvis (Mendez) B 9.15.1976 San Pedro De Macoris, D.R. BB/TR 5-11/164# d9.2																								
2000	Col N	10	9	1	3	1	0	0	1	1-0	0	1	.333	.400	.444	90	0	1-0	1.000	-0	103	228	/S-3,2	0.0
2001	Mil N	15	40	5	9	2	0	0	6	6-0	1	6	.225	.333	.275	64	-2	2-0	.980	3	136	116	2-11	0.2
Total	2	25	49	6	12	3	0	0	7	7-0	1	7	.245	.345	.306	70	-2	3-0	.980	3	134	115	/2-12,S-3	0.2
PENA, GERONIMO Geronimo (Martinez) B 3.29.1967 Distrito Nacional, D.R. BB/TR 6-1/195# d9.5																								
1990	StL N	18	45	5	11	2	0	0	2	4-0	1	14	.244	.314	.289	69	-2	1-1	.982	2	111	135	2-11	0.0
1991	StL N	104	185	38	45	8	3	5	17	18-1	5	45	.243	.322	.400	103	1	15-5	.976	-7	94	107	2-83/O-4(LF)	-0.4
1992	StL N	62	203	31	62	12	1	7	31	24-0	5	37	.305	.386	.478	150	14	13-8	.984	11	116	136	2-57	2.8
1993	StL N	74	254	34	65	19	2	5	30	25-0	4	71	.256	.330	.406	98	0	13-5	.966	3	112	121	2-64	0.7
1994	StL N	83	213	33	54	13	1	11	34	24-1	6	54	.254	.344	.479	114	5	9-1	.990	3	105	124	2-59/3	1.2
1995	StL N	32	101	20	27	6	1	1	8	16-1	1	30	.267	.367	.376	98	0	3-2	.976	-1	102	112	2-25	0.0
1996	Cle A	5	9	1	1	0	0	1	2	1-0	0	4	.111	.200	.444	57	-1	0-0	—	-1	0	0	/3-3,2	-0.1
Total	7	378	1010	162	265	60	8	30	124	112-3	22	255	.262	.345	.427	111	17	54-22	.978	9	107	122	2-300/3-4,O-4(LF)	4.2
PENA, ROBERTO Roberto Cesar "Baby" (born Roberto Cesar Zapata (Pena)) B 4.17.1937 Santo Domingo, D.R. D 7.23.1982 Santiago, D.R. BR/TR 5-8/175# d4.12																								
1965	Chi N	51	170	17	37	5	1	2	12	16-4	2	19	.218	.291	.294	64	-8	1-2	.930	-5	102	97	S-50	-1.0
1966	Chi N	6	17	0	3	2	0	0	1	0-0	0	4	.176	.176	.294	28	-2	0-0	.957	-1	84	73	/S-5	-0.2
1968	Phi N	138	500	56	130	13	2	1	38	34-2	2	63	.260	.307	.300	84	-10	3-5	.954	5	99	119	*S-133	0.6
1969	SD N	139	472	44	118	16	3	4	30	21-0	3	63	.250	.286	.322	73	-19	0-3	.977	-2	104	89	S-65,2-33,3-27,1-12	-1.6
1970	Oak A	19	58	4	15	1	0	0	3	3-0	0	4	.259	.295	.276	61	-3	1-1	.961	-3	89	48	S-12/3-5	-0.5
	Mil A	121	416	36	99	19	1	3	42	25-4	2	45	.238	.282	.310	63	-21	3-5	.981	-13	94	95	S-99,2-15/1-7	-2.4
	Year	140	474	40	114	20	1	3	45	28-4	2	49	.241	.283	.306	63	-24	4-6	**.979**	-16	93	90	*S-111,2-15/1-7,3-5	-2.9
1971	Mil A	113	274	17	65	9	3	3	28	15-3	1	37	.237	.279	.325	71	-11	2-1	.996	1	88	87	1-50,3-37,S-23/2	-1.2
Total	6	587	1907	174	467	65	10	13	154	114-13	10	235	.245	.290	.310	72	-74	10-17	.962	-18	99	102	S-387/1-69,3-69,2-49	-6.3
PENA, WILY MO Wily Mo B 1.23.1982 Laguna Salada, D.R. BR/TR 6-3/215# d9.10																								
2002	Cin N	13	18	1	4	0	0	1	1	0-0	0	11	.222	.222	.389	58	-1	0-0	1.000	-1	68	0	/O-4(3-0-1)	-0.2
2003	Cin N	80	165	20	36	6	1	5	16	12-2	3	53	.218	.283	.358	67	-9	3-2	.977	-2	95	41	O-47(8-26-14)/3	-1.2
Total	2	93	183	21	40	6	1	6	17	12-2	3	64	.219	.278	.361	66	-10	3-2	.978	-3	93	38	/O-51(11-26-15),3	-1.4
PENCE, ELMER Elmer Clair B 8.17.1900 Valley Springs, CA D 9.17.1968 San Francisco, CA BR/TR 6/185# d8.23																								
1922	Chi A	1	0	0	0	0	0	0	0	0	0	0	—	—	—	—	0	0-0	1.000	0	164	0	/O(RF)	0.0
PENDLETON, JIM James Edward B 1.7.1924 St.Charles, MO D 3.20.1996 Houston, TX BR/TR 6/185# d4.17 OF Total (189-LF 42-CF 63-RF)																								
1953	Mil N	120	251	48	75	12	4	7	27	7	2	36	.299	.323	.462	108	2	6-5	.961	7	114	138	*O-105(75-15-25)/S-7	0.5
1954	Mil N	71	173	20	38	3	1	1	16	4	0	21	.220	.236	.266	33	-18	2-1	.950	1	98	167	O-50(23-18-11)	-1.9
1955	Mil N	8	10	0	0	0	0	0	0	0-0	0	2	.000	.000	.000	-99	-3	0-0	1.000	-1	0	0	/S3O(CF)	-0.4
1956	Mil N	14	11	0	0	0	0	0	0	1-0	0	3	.000	.083	.000	-80	-3	0-0	1.000	-0	99	0	/S-3,3-2,12	-0.3
1957	Pit N	46	59	9	18	1	1	0	9	9-1	1	14	.305	.394	.356	110	1	0-0	.917	-2	80	217	/O-9(2-1-6),3-2,S	0.0
1958	Pit N	3	3	0	1	0	0	0	0	0-0	0	0	.333	.333	.333	79	0	0-0	—	0			H	0.0
1959	Cin N	65	113	13	29	2	0	3	9	8-2	1	18	.257	.309	.354	75	-4	3-0	.971	3	115	181	O-24(LF),3-16/S-3	-0.2
1962	Hou N	117	321	30	79	12	2	8	36	14-2	2	57	.246	.279	.371	79	-11	0-0	.963	-3	100	79	O-90(65-7-21)/1-8,3-3,S-2	-1.9
Total	8	444	941	120	240	30	8	19	97	43-5	6	151	.255	.290	.365	76	-36	11-6	.959	5	104	127	O-279L/3-24,S-17,1-9,2	-4.2
PENDLETON, TERRY Terry Lee B 7.16.1960 Los Angeles, CA BB/TR 5-9/180# d7.18 C2																								
1984	StL N	67	262	37	85	16	3	1	33	16-3	0	32	.324	.357	.420	123	8	20-5	.943	9	117	91	3-66	1.9
1985	†StL N	149	559	56	134	16	3	5	69	37-4	0	75	.240	.285	.306	66	-26	17-12	.965	26	121	111	*3-149	-0.3
1986	StL N	159	578	56	138	26	5	1	59	34-10	1	59	.239	.279	.306	63	-31	24-6	.962	19	118	**150**	*3-156/O(RF)	-1.1
1987	†StL N	159	583	82	167	29	4	12	96	70-6	2	74	.286	.360	.412	103	4	19-12	.949	5	108	100	*3-158	0.7
1988	StL N	110	391	44	99	20	2	6	53	21-4	2	51	.253	.293	.361	86	-8	3-3	.963	14	118	81	*3-101	0.6
1989	StL N	162	613	83	162	28	5	13	74	44-3	0	81	.264	.313	.390	97	-4	9-5	**.971**	**35**	**129**	101	*3-161	3.4
1990	StL N	121	447	46	103	20	2	6	58	30-8	1	58	.230	.277	.324	66	-22	7-5	.947	8	111	106	*3-117	-1.4
1991	†Atl N	153	586	94	**187**	34	8	22	86	43-8	1	70	**.319**	.363	.517	138	28	10-2	.950	20	**114**	**139**	*3-148	5.1
1992	†Atl N★	160	640	98	**199**	39	1	21	105	37-8	0	67	.311	.345	.473	123	19	5-2	.960	7	101	109	*3-158	2.8
1993	†Atl N	161	633	81	172	33	1	17	84	36-5	3	97	.272	.311	.408	91	-10	5-1	.959	11	102	138	*3-161	0.3
1994	Atl N	77	309	25	78	18	3	7	30	12-3	0	57	.252	.280	.398	73	-13	2-0	.950	3	96	113	3-77	-0.9
1995	Fla N	133	513	70	149	32	1	14	78	38-7	2	84	.290	.339	.439	104	2	1-2	.952	3	97	107	*3-129	0.6
1996	Fla N	111	406	30	102	20	1	7	58	26-5	3	75	.251	.298	.357	75	-15	0-2	.961	6	103	126	*3-108	-0.9
	†Atl N	42	162	21	33	6	0	4	17	15-1	0	36	.204	.271	.315	51	-12	2-1	.939	1	99	88	3-41	-1.0
	Year	153	568	51	135	26	1	11	75	41-6	3	111	.238	.290	.345	68	-27	2-3	.955	6	102	116	*3-149	-1.9
1997	Cin N	50	113	11	28	9	0	1	17	12-1	0	14	.248	.320	.354	75	-4	2-1	.942	-7	70	24	3-32	-1.0
1998	KC A	79	237	17	61	10	0	3	29	15-1	0	49	.257	.299	.338	64	-13	1-0	.957	1	105	74	D-40,3-23	-1.4
Total	15	1893	7032	851	1897	356	39	140	946	486-77	15	979	.270	.316	.391	92	-97	127-59	.957	159	110	113	*3-1785/D-40,O(RF)	7.4
PENN, SHANNON Shannon Dion B 9.11.1969 Cincinnati, OH BB/TR 5-10/160# d4.28																								
1995	Det A	3	9	0	3	0	0	0	0	1-0	0	2	.333	.400	.333	94	0	0-0	.864	2	138	248	/2-3	0.2
1996	Det A	6	14	0	1	0	0	0	1	0-0	0	3	.071	.071	.071	-64	-4	0-0	—	-0	0	0	/O(LF)D	-0.3
Total	2	9	23	0	4	0	0	0	1	1-0	0	5	.174	.208	.174	-1	-4	0-0	.864	2	138	248	/D-4,2-3,O(LF)	-0.1
PENNYFEATHER, WILL William Nathaniel B 5.25.1968 Perth Amboy, NJ BR/TR 6-2/195# d6.27																								
1992	Pit N	15	9	2	2	0	0	0	0	0-0	0	0	.222	.222	.222	26	-1	0-0	1.000	0	113	0	O-10(1-6-5)	-0.1
1993	Pit N	21	34	4	7	1	0	0	2	0-0	0	6	.206	.206	.235	18	-4	0-1	1.000	-1	94	0	O-17(1-15-2)	-0.5
1994	Pit N	4	3	0	0	0	0	0	0	0-0	0	0	.000	.000	.000	-99	-1	0-0	—	-0	0	0	/O(LF)	-0.1
Total	3	40	46	6	9	1	0	0	2	0-0	0	6	.196	.196	.217	11	-6	0-1	1.000	-1	98	0	/O-28(3-21-7)	-0.7
PEOPLES, JIMMY James Elsworth B 10.8.1863 Big Beaver, MI D 8.29.1920 Detroit, MI TR 5-8/200# d5.29 U1 ▲ OF Total (5-LF 6-CF 24-RF)																								
1884	Cin AA	69	267	28	45	2	2	1	16	6	0		.169	.187	.202	26	-22		.829	-2	93	160	S-47,C-14,O-10(0-4-6)/31	-2.1
1885	Cin AA	7	22	1	4	0	0	0	1	1	0		.182	.217	.182	27	-2		.826	-1			/C-5,P-2,O(RF)	-0.2
	Bro AA	41	151	21	30	4	1	1	15	5	1		.199	.229	.258	53	-8		.902	-0			C-37/S-2,13O(CF)	-0.5
	Year	48	173	22	34	4	1	1	16	6	1		.197	.228	.249	50	-10		.896	-1			C-42/P-2,O-2(0-1-1),S-2,13	-0.7
1886	Bro AA	93	340	43	74	7	3	3	38	20	0		.218	.261	.282	70	-13	20	.879	14			C-76,S-14/O-8(4-1-3),3	0.6
1887	Bro AA	73	268	36	68	14	2	1	38	16	4		.254	.306	.332	77	-9	22	.853	-4			C-57/O-8(1-0-7),S-4,1-4,2	-0.6

Year	Tm Lg	G	AB	R	H	2B	3B	HR	RBI	BB-IB	HP	SO	AVG	OBP	SLG	AOPS	ABR	SB-CS	FA	FR	Rng	Thr	G at Pos	BFW
1888	Bro AA	32	103	15	20	5	3	0	17	8	1		.194	.259	.301	79	-2	10	.904	4			C-25/S-5,O-2(RF)	0.4
1889	Col AA	29	100	13	23	6	2	1	16	6	0	8	.230	.274	.360	84	-2	3	.922	-4			C-22/O-5(RF),2-2,S	-0.4
Total	6	344	1251	157	264	38	13	7	141	62	6	8	.211	.252	.279	62	-58	55	.887	7			C-236/S-73,O-35R,1-6,2-3,3-3,P-2	-2.8
PEPITONE, JOE Joseph Anthony "Pepi" B 10.9.1940 Brooklyn, NY BL/TL 6-2/200# d4.10 C1																								
1962	NY A	63	138	14	33	3	2	7	17	3-0	0	21	.239	.255	.442	86	-4	1-1	1.000	-1	92	0	O-32(14-7-13),1-16	-0.7
1963	†NY A★	157	580	79	157	16	3	27	89	23-2	7	63	.271	.304	.448	109	4	3-5	.995	5	113	**114**	*1-143,O-16(0-7-9)	-0.1
1964	†NY A★	160	613	71	154	12	3	28	100	24-7	3	63	.251	.281	.418	90	-11	2-1	.988	7	**124**	112	*1-155,O-30(0-28-3)	-1.5
1965	NY A★	143	531	51	131	18	3	18	62	43-11	2	59	.247	.305	.394	98	-3	4-2	**.997**	1	99	117	*1-115,O-41(2-3-36)	-1.1
1966	NY A	152	585	85	149	21	4	31	83	29-6	2	58	.255	.290	.463	118	10	4-3	**.995**	9	**125**	**104**	*1-119,O-55(0-49-9)	1.1
1967	NY A	133	501	45	126	18	3	13	64	34-4	3	62	.251	.301	.377	104	1	1-3	.976	-7	94	90	*O-123(CF)/1-6	-1.2
1968	NY A	108	380	41	93	9	3	15	56	37-9	1	45	.245	.311	.403	119	8	8-2	.980	-10	85	62	O-92(4-88-0),1-12	-0.6
1969	NY A	135	513	49	124	16	3	27	70	30-11	1	42	.242	.284	.442	105	-1	8-6	**.995**	-4	88	118	*1-132	-1.7
1970	Hou N	75	279	44	70	9	5	14	35	18-9	1	28	.251	.298	.470	107	0	5-2	.995	-1	90	116	1-50,O-28(15-3-13)	-0.5
	Chi N	56	213	38	57	9	2	12	44	15-2	0	15	.268	.313	.498	102	0	0-2	.992	-1	107	35	O-56(CF),1-13	-0.3
	Year	131	492	82	127	18	7	26	79	33-11	1	43	.258	.304	.482	105	0	5-4	.989	-1	109	42	O-84(15-59-13),1-63	-0.8
1971	Chi N	115	427	50	131	19	4	16	61	24-8	4	41	.307	.347	.482	117	9	1-2	.990	-4	104	102	1-95,O-23(1-22-0)	-0.3
1972	Chi N	66	214	23	56	5	0	8	21	13-4	3	22	.262	.309	.397	91	-3	1-2	.997	-1	89	120	1-66	-1.0
1973	Chi N	31	112	16	30	3	0	3	18	8-0	1	6	.268	.320	.375	86	-2	3-1	.985	-0	100	122	1-28	-0.4
	Atl N	3	11	0	4	0	0	0	1	1-0	0	1	.364	.417	.364	110	0	0-0	.963	-1	0	192	/1-3	-0.1
	Year	34	123	16	34	3	0	3	19	9-0	1	7	.276	.328	.374	88	-2	3-1	.983	-1	90	129	1-31	-0.5
Total	12	1397	5097	606	1315	158	35	219	721	302-73	28	526	.258	.301	.432	105	8	41-32	.993	-7	106	112	1-953,O-496(36-386-83)	-8.4
PEPLOSKI, HENRY Henry Stephen "Pep" B 9.15.1905 Garlin, Poland D 1.28.1982 Dover, NJ BL/TR 5-9/155# d9.19 b-Pepper																								
1929	Bos N	6	10	1	2	0	0	0	1	1	0	3	.200	.273	.200	20	-1	0	1.000	-0	82	0	/3-2	-0.1
PEPLOSKI, PEPPER Joseph Aloysius B 9.12.1891 Brooklyn, NY D 7.13.1972 New York, NY BR/TR 5-8/155# d6.24 b-Henry																								
1913	Det A	2	4	1	2	0	0	0	0	0	0	0	.500	.500	.500	196	0	0	1.000	-0	78	0	/3-2	0.0
PEPPER, DON Donald Hoyte B 10.8.1943 Saratoga Sprgs., NY BL/TR 6-4.5/215# d9.10																								
1966	Det A	4	3	0	0	0	0	0	0	0-0	0	1	.000	.000	.000	-98	-1	0-0	1.000	-0	0	0	/1	-0.1
PEPPER, RAY Raymond Watson B 8.5.1905 Decatur, AL D 3.24.1996 Belle Mina, AL BR/TR 6-2/195# d4.15																								
1932	StL N	21	57	3	14	2	1	0	7	5	0	13	.246	.306	.316	66	-3	1	.971	0	104	108	O-17(16-0-1)	-0.3
1933	StL N	3	9	2	2	0	0	1	2	0	0	1	.222	.222	.556	110	0	0	1.000	-0	86	0	/O-2(LF)	0.0
1934	StL A	148	564	71	168	24	6	7	101	29	1	67	.298	.333	.399	81	-17	1-4	.963	3	100	133	*O-136(101-37-1)	-2.1
1935	StL A	92	261	20	66	15	3	4	37	20	0	32	.253	.306	.379	73	-11	0-2	.982	-1	92	113	O-57(27-4-26)	-1.5
1936	StL A	75	124	13	35	5	0	2	23	5	0	23	.282	.310	.371	66	-7	0-2	.941	-1	93	73	O-18(2-5-11)	-0.9
Total	5	339	1015	109	285	46	10	14	170	59	1	136	.281	.321	.387	77	-38	2-8	.967	1	98	121	O-230(148-46-39)	-4.8
PERALTA, JHONNY Jhonny Antonio B 5.28.1982 Santiago, D.R. BR/TR 6-1/180# d6.12																								
2003	Cle A	77	242	24	55	10	1	4	21	20-0	4	65	.227	.295	.326	67	-12	1-3	.976	1	108	94	S-72/3-6	-0.6
PERCONTE, JACK John Patrick B 8.31.1954 Joliet, IL BL/TR 5-10/160# d9.13																								
1980	LA N	14	17	2	4	0	0	0	2	2-0	0	1	.235	.316	.235	57	-1	3-0	1.000	2	122	107	/2-9	0.2
1981	LA N	8	9	2	2	0	1	0	1	2-0	0	2	.222	.364	.444	133	0	1-1	1.000	4	291	355	/2-2	0.5
1982	Cle A	93	219	27	52	4	4	0	15	22-1	0	25	.237	.303	.292	66	-10	9-3	.976	-6	100	51	2-82/D-2	-1.2
1983	Cle A	14	26	1	7	1	0	0	0	5-0	0	2	.269	.387	.308	91	0	3-1	.950	7	161	215	2-13	0.8
1984	Sea A	155	612	93	180	24	4	0	31	57-1	5	47	.294	.357	.346	97	0	29-6	.981	5	100	85	*2-150	1.8
1985	Sea A	125	485	60	128	17	7	2	23	50-0	3	36	.264	.335	.340	85	-9	31-2	.986	16	108	105	*2-125	1.9
1986	Chi A	24	73	6	16	1	0	0	4	11-1	0	10	.219	.321	.233	52	-5	2-0	.990	-8	76	79	2-24	-1.1
Total	7	433	1441	191	389	47	16	2	76	149-3	8	123	.270	.340	.329	86	-25	78-13	.982	21	103	89	2-405/D-2	2.9
PEREZ, ANTONIO Antonio Miguel B 1.26.1980 Bani, D.R. BR/TR 5-11/170# d5.14																								
2003	TB A	48	125	19	31	6	1	2	12	18-0	1	34	.248	.345	.360	89	-2	4-1	.990	-13	77	56	2-31/3-6,S-6,D-3	-1.2
PEREZ, TONY Atanasio (Rigal) B 5.14.1942 Ciego De Avila, Cuba BR/TR 6-2/205# d7.26 M2 C6 HF2000 s-Eduardo																								
1964	Cin N	12	25	1	2	1	0	0	1	3-0	0	9	.080	.179	.120	-14	-4	0-0	.981	-2	0	51	/1-6	-0.6
1965	Cin N	104	281	40	73	14	4	12	47	21-5	2	67	.260	.315	.466	110	3	0-2	.989	-1	87	96	1-93	-0.4
1966	Cin N	99	257	25	68	10	4	4	39	14-2	2	44	.265	.304	.381	83	-6	1-0	.989	-6	59	89	1-75	-1.6
1967	Cin N★	156	600	78	174	28	7	26	102	33-10	4	102	.290	.328	.490	119	13	0-3	.963	-19	82	56	*3-139,1-18/2	-0.9
1968	Cin N★	160	625	93	176	25	7	18	92	51-13	6	92	.282	.338	.430	123	17	3-2	.952	6	106	100	*3-160	2.6
1969	Cin N★	160	629	103	185	31	2	37	122	63-7	2	131	.294	.357	.526	138	31	4-2	.937	-3	105	114	*3-160	2.9
1970	†Cin N★	158	587	107	186	28	6	40	129	83-13	4	134	.317	.401	.589	162	52	8-3	.923	-5	99	122	*3-153/1-8	4.6
1971	Cin N	158	609	72	164	22	3	25	91	51-5	1	120	.269	.325	.438	117	12	4-1	.959	5	108	117	*3-148,1-44	1.7
1972	†Cin N	136	515	64	146	33	7	21	90	55-15	0	121	.283	.349	.497	148	31	4-2	.993	-5	86	**110**	*1-136	1.6
1973	†Cin N	151	564	73	177	33	3	27	101	74-10	3	117	.314	.393	.527	162	49	3-1	.991	-2	99	**110**	*1-151	3.6
1974	Cin N★	158	596	81	158	28	2	28	101	61-7	2	112	.265	.331	.460	123	16	1-3	**.996**	-5	83	99	*1-157	-0.1
1975	†Cin N★	137	511	74	144	28	3	20	109	54-6	3	101	.282	.350	.466	124	16	1-2	.993	-6	86	113	*1-132	-0.1
1976	†Cin N★	139	527	77	137	32	6	19	91	50-9	5	88	.260	.328	.452	117	11	10-5	.996	-6	82	104	*1-136	-0.5
1977	Mon N	154	559	71	158	32	6	19	91	63-15	2	111	.283	.352	.463	122	17	4-3	.992	5	115	79	*1-148	1.3
1978	Mon N	148	544	63	158	38	3	14	78	38-9	2	104	.290	.336	.449	120	13	2-0	.991	2	108	114	*1-145	0.7
1979	Mon N	132	489	58	132	29	4	13	73	38-4	3	82	.270	.322	.425	104	2	2-1	.991	-4	88	87	*1-129	-1.0
1980	Bos A	151	585	73	161	31	3	25	105	41-11	1	93	.275	.320	.467	108	5	1-0	.993	-4	90	115	*1-137,D-13	-0.8
1981	Bos A	84	306	35	77	11	3	9	39	27-0	0	66	.252	.310	.395	97	-2	0-0	.993	-1	94	119	1-56,D-23	-0.8
1982	Bos A	69	196	18	51	14	2	6	31	19-3	0	48	.260	.326	.444	103	1	0-1	.857	0	169	0	D-46/1-2	-0.1
1983	†Phi N	91	253	18	61	11	2	6	43	28-1	1	57	.241	.316	.372	92	-3	1-0	.998	1	98	81	1-69	-0.5
1984	Cin N	71	137	9	33	6	1	2	15	11-2	0	21	.241	.295	.343	76	-4	0-0	.990	-2	73	85	1-31	-0.8
1985	Cin N	72	183	25	60	8	0	6	33	22-1	0	22	.328	.396	.470	136	9	0-2	.995	-3	76	102	1-50	0.4
1986	Cin N	77	200	14	51	12	1	2	29	25-2	0	25	.255	.333	.355	87	-3	0-0	.984	-3	87	127	1-55	-0.9
Total	23	2777	9778	1272	2732	505	79	379	1652	925-150	43	1867	.279	.341	.463	122	276	49-33	.992	-54	90	103	*1-1778,3-760/D-82,2	10.3
PEREZ, DANNY Daniel B 2.26.1971 ElPaso, TX BR/TR 5-10/188# d6.30																								
1996	Mil A	4	4	0	0	0	0	0	0	0-0	0	0	.000	.000	.000	-96	-1	0-0	1.000	0	155	0	/O-3(2-1-0)	-0.1
PEREZ, EDUARDO Eduardo Atanasio B 9.11.1969 Cincinnati, OH BR/TR 6-4/215# d7.27 f-Tony																								
1993	Cal A	52	180	16	45	6	2	4	30	9-0	2	39	.250	.292	.372	75	-7	5-4	.962	2	110	88	3-45/D-3	-0.5
1994	Cal A	38	129	10	27	7	0	5	16	12-1	0	29	.209	.275	.380	66	-7	3-0	.997	-2	74	97	1-38	-1.1
1995	Cal A	29	71	9	12	4	1	1	7	12-0	2	9	.169	.302	.296	58	-4	0-2	.883	-2	88	85	3-23/D	-0.7
1996	Cin N	18	36	8	8	0	0	3	5	5-1	0	9	.222	.317	.472	104	0	0-0	1.000	1	147	111	/1-8,3-3	0.0
1997	Cin N	106	297	44	75	18	0	16	52	29-1	2	76	.253	.321	.475	104	1	5-1	.996	-2	83	80	1-67,O-12(11-0-1)/3-8,D	-0.6
1998	Cin N	84	172	20	41	4	0	4	30	21-2	2	45	.238	.325	.331	73	-7	0-1	.985	7	157	113	1-51/3O(LF)	-0.4
1999	StL N	21	32	6	11	2	0	1	9	7-0	0	6	.344	.462	.500	143	3	0-0	1.000	1	125	350	/O-6(LF),1-5	0.3
2000	StL N	35	91	9	27	4	0	3	10	5-0	3	19	.297	.350	.440	98	0	1-0	1.000	1	100	122	1-24/O-4(LF),3-2	-0.1
2002	†StL N	96	154	22	31	9	0	10	26	17-0	3	36	.201	.290	.455	99	-2	0-0	.982	2	125	294	O-35(7-0-29),1-10/3-6,D	-0.1
2003	StL N	105	253	47	72	16	0	11	41	29-1	4	53	.285	.365	.478	123	9	5-2	.966	-2	114	30	O-71(10-0-64),3-12/1-5,D	0.5
Total	10	584	1415	191	349	70	3	58	226	146-6	18	321	.247	.322	.423	94	-14	19-10	.994	6	103	99	1-208,O-129(39-0-94),3-100/D-7	-2.7
PEREZ, EDDIE Eduardo Rafael B 5.4.1968 Ciudad Ojeda, Venezuela BR/TR 6-1/175# d9.10																								
1995	Atl N	7	13	1	4	1	0	1	4	0-0	0	2	.308	.308	.615	132	0	0-0	1.000	3	0	0	/C-5,1	0.3
1996	†Atl N	68	156	19	40	9	1	4	17	8-0	1	19	.256	.293	.404	78	-5	0-0	.993	-4	160	67	C-54/1-7	-0.7
1997	†Atl N	73	191	20	41	5	0	6	18	10-0	2	35	.215	.259	.335	54	-14	0-1	.988	-2	87	84	C-64/1-6	-1.3
1998	†Atl N	61	149	18	50	12	0	6	32	15-0	2	28	.336	.404	.537	145	10	1-1	.997	0	76	115	C-45/1-8,D	1.2
1999	†Atl N	104	309	30	77	17	0	7	30	17-4	6	40	.249	.299	.372	69	-15	0-1	.993	6	122	89	C-98/1-2	-0.4
2000	Atl N	7	22	0	4	1	0	0	3	0-0	0	2	.182	.182	.227	2	-3	0-0	.976	-1	71	60	/C-7	-0.4
2001	Atl N	5	10	0	3	0	0	0	0	0-0	0	2	.300	.300	.300	55	-1	0-0	1.000	-1	66	0	/C-5	-0.2
2002	Cle A	42	117	6	25	9	0	0	4	5-0	1	25	.214	.252	.291	45	-9	0-0	.988	-1	83	154	C-42	-0.8

Year	Tm Lg	G	AB	R	H	2B	3B	HR	RBI	BB-IB	HP	SO	AVG	OBP	SLG	AOPS	ABR	SB-CS	FA	FR	Rng	Thr	G at Pos	BFW
2003	Mil N	107	350	26	95	17	1	11	45	17-3	0	47	.271	.304	.420	88	-7	0-1	.991	-14	75	91	*C-102	-1.6
Total	9	474	1317	120	339	71	2	35	153	72-7	12	200	.257	.300	.394	79	-44	1-4	.991	-15	97	94	C-422/1-24,D	-3.9
PEREZ, MARTY Martin Roman B 2.28.1946 Visalia, CA BR/TR 5-11/160# d9.9																								
1969	Cal A	13	13	3	3	0	0	0	0	2-0	0	1	.231	.333	.231	63	-1	0-0	1.000	4	145	278	/S-7,2-2,3-2	0.4
1970	Cal A	3	3	0	0	0	0	0	1	0-0	0	0	.000	.000	.000	-99	-1	0-0	.833	-1	57	155	/S-2	-0.1
1971	Atl N	130	410	28	93	15	3	4	32	25-5	1	44	.227	.272	.307	60	-22	1-2	.955	-13	97	**115**	*S-126/2	-2.3
1972	Atl N	141	479	33	109	13	1	1	28	30-1	3	55	.228	.276	.265	50	-31	0-3	.957	-34	87	84	*S-141	-5.4
1973	Atl N	141	501	66	125	15	5	8	57	49-1	2	66	.250	.316	.347	79	-14	2-3	.962	-6	102	91	*S-139	-0.6
1974	Atl N	127	447	51	116	20	5	2	34	35-1	1	51	.260	.314	.340	80	-12	2-0	.985	-4	100	108	*2-102,S-14/3-6	-0.9
1975	Atl N	120	461	50	127	14	2	2	34	37-2	0	44	.275	.327	.328	80	-13	2-2	.985	-4	100	94	*2-116/S-7	-0.9
1976	Atl N	31	96	12	24	4	0	1	6	8-0	0	9	.250	.305	.323	74	-3	0-0	.976	0	98	99	2-18,S-17/3-2	-0.1
	SF N	93	332	37	86	13	1	2	26	30-0	0	28	.259	.318	.322	80	-8	3-4	.979	1	107	89	2-89/S-5	-0.2
	Year	124	428	49	110	17	1	3	32	38-0	0	37	.257	.315	.322	79	-11	3-4	.978	1	106	90	*2-107,S-22/3-2	-0.3
1977	NY A	1	4	0	2	0	0	0	0	0-0	0	1	.500	.500	.500	175	0	0-0	1.000	1	207	621	/3	0.1
	Oak A	115	373	32	86	14	5	2	23	29-0	3	65	.231	.290	.311	65	-18	1-3	.974	4	109	80	*2-105,3-12/S-4	-1.0
	Year	116	377	32	88	14	5	2	23	29-0	3	66	.233	.292	.313	66	-18	1-3	.974	5	109	80	*2-105,3-13/S-4	-0.9
1978	Oak A	16	12	1	0	0	0	0	0	0-0	0	5	.000	.000	.000	-99	-3	0-0	1.000	0	99	112	3-11/S-3,2	-0.3
Total	10	931	3131	313	771	108	22	22	241	245-10	10	369	.246	.301	.316	70	-126	11-17	.958	-51	96	98	S-465,2-434/3-34	-11.3
PEREZ, NEIFI Neifi Neftali (Diaz) B 6.2.1973 Villa Mella, D.R. BB/TR 6/175# d8.31																								
1996	Col N	17	45	4	7	2	0	0	3	0-0	0	8	.156	.156	.200	-6	-7	2-2	.972	-1	86	146	S-14/2-4	-0.7
1997	Col N	83	313	46	91	13	10	5	31	21-4	1	43	.291	.333	.444	83	-8	4-3	.975	26	131	123	S-45,2-41/3-2	2.2
1998	Col N	**162**	647	80	177	25	9	9	59	38-0	1	70	.274	.313	.382	67	-31	5-6	.975	**29**	**113**	**123**	*S-162/C	1.0
1999	Col N	157	690	108	193	27	**11**	12	70	28-0	1	54	.280	.307	.403	62	-41	13-5	.981	27	**109**	**112**	*S-157	-0.1
2000	Col N	**162**	651	92	187	39	11	10	71	30-6	0	63	.287	.314	.427	69	-31	3-6	.978	**37**	**115**	117	*S-162	1.5
2001	Col N	87	382	65	114	19	8	7	47	16-1	0	49	.298	.326	.445	79	-12	6-2	.976	7	102	114	S-87	0.3
	KC A	49	199	18	48	7	1	1	12	10-0	1	19	.241	.277	.302	49	-15	3-4	.978	8	107	130	S-46/2-4	-0.3
2002	KC A	145	554	65	131	20	4	3	37	20-2	0	53	.236	.260	.303	45	-45	8-9	.972	6	102	113	*S-139/2-5	-2.8
2003	†SF N	120	328	27	84	19	4	1	31	14-3	0	23	.256	.285	.348	66	-17	3-2	.987	22	109	130	2-57,S-45/3-2	1.0
Total	8	982	3809	505	1032	171	58	48	361	177-16	4	382	.271	.301	.384	64	-207	47-39	.977	162	110	119	S-857,2-111/3-4,C	2.1
PEREZ, ROBERT Robert Alexander (Jimenez) B 6.4.1969 Bolivar, Venezuela BR/TR 6-3/205# d7.20																								
1994	Tor A	4	8	0	1	0	0	0	0	0-0	0	1	.125	.125	.125	-35	-2	0-0	1.000	0	60	555	/O-4(2-0-2)	-0.1
1995	Tor A	17	48	2	9	2	0	1	3	0-0	0	5	.188	.188	.292	22	-6	0-0	1.000	0	119	0	O-15(5-0-11)	-0.6
1996	Tor A	86	202	30	66	10	0	2	21	8-0	1	17	.327	.354	.406	92	-2	3-0	.983	1	102	80	O-79(59-0-25)/D-2	-0.3
1997	Tor A	37	78	4	15	4	1	2	6	0-0	0	16	.192	.192	.346	36	-8	0-0	1.000	-1	102	0	O-25(17-0-9)/D-7	-0.9
1998	Sea A	17	35	3	6	1	0	2	6	0-0	0	5	.171	.171	.371	36	-4	0-0	1.000	1	112	158	O-17(2-0-15)	-0.3
	Mon N	52	106	9	25	1	0	1	8	2-0	1	23	.236	.255	.274	40	-10	0-0	.852	-2	56	239	O-29(LF)	-1.2
2001	NY A	6	15	1	4	1	0	0	0	1-0	0	7	.267	.313	.333	69	-1	0-1	1.000	-0	94	0	/O-5(0-3-2),D	-0.1
	Mil N	2	5	0	0	0	0	0	0	0-0	0	0	.000	.000	.000	-99	-2	0-0	1.000	0	146	0	/O(RF)	-0.1
Total	6	221	497	49	126	19	1	8	44	11-0	2	74	.254	.271	.344	58	-35	3-1	.976	-1	96	99	O-175(114-3-65)/D-10	-3.6
PEREZ, SANTIAGO Santiago Alberto B 12.30.1975 Santo Domingo, D.R. BB/TR 6-2/185# d6.3																								
2000	Mil N	24	52	8	9	2	0	0	2	8-2	1	9	.173	.290	.212	32	-5	4-0	.917	-2	105	108	S-20	-0.5
2001	SD N	43	81	13	16	1	0	0	4	15-0	0	29	.198	.320	.210	46	-6	5-1	.947	-3	110	108	O-26(9-10-8)/S-8,2-2	-0.8
Total	2	67	133	21	25	3	0	0	6	23-2	1	38	.188	.308	.211	40	-11	9-1	.913	-5	93	87	/S-28,O-26(9-10-8),2-2	-1.3
PEREZ, TIMO Timoniel B 4.8.1975 Bani, D.R. BL/TL 5-9/167# d9.1																								
2000	†NY N	24	49	11	14	4	1	1	3	3-0	1	5	.286	.333	.469	106	0	1-1	.970	2	120	272	O-19(8-7-8)	0.2
2001	NY N	85	239	26	59	9	1	5	22	12-0	2	25	.247	.287	.356	69	-12	1-6	1.000	4	108	133	O-73(6-8-62)	-1.2
2002	NY N	136	444	52	131	27	6	8	47	23-2	2	36	.295	.331	.437	108	1	10-6	.979	7	111	148	*O-122(24-93-17)	0.8
2003	NY N	127	346	32	93	21	0	4	42	18-1	2	29	.269	.301	.364	77	-12	5-6	.989	1	100	117	*O-104(58-49-14)	-1.4
Total	4	372	1078	121	297	61	8	18	114	56-3	7	95	.276	.312	.397	89	-23	17-19	.986	14	107	140	O-318(96-157-101)	-1.6
PEREZ, TOMAS Tomas Orlando B 12.29.1973 Barquisimeto, Venezuela BB/TR 5-11/165# d5.3																								
1995	Tor A	41	98	12	24	3	1	1	8	7-0	0	18	.245	.292	.327	62	-6	0-1	.954	-2	99	88	S-31/2-7,3	-0.6
1996	Tor A	91	295	24	74	13	4	1	19	25-0	1	29	.251	.311	.332	63	-17	1-2	.970	6	105	133	2-75,3-11/S-5	-0.7
1997	Tor A	40	123	9	24	3	2	0	9	11-0	1	28	.195	.267	.252	36	-12	1-1	.993	8	105	119	S-32/2-8	-0.1
1998	Tor A	6	9	1	1	0	0	0	0	1-0	0	3	.111	.200	.111	-16	-2	0-0	1.000	-1	56	52	/S-4,2	-0.2
2000	Phi N	45	140	17	31	7	1	1	13	11-2	0	30	.221	.278	.307	47	-12	1-1	.976	-6	79	83	S-44	-1.4
2001	Phi N	62	135	11	41	7	1	3	19	7-1	2	22	.304	.347	.437	104	1	0-1	1.000	7	110	108	2-29/3-9,S-8,O(RF)	0.8
2002	Phi N	92	212	22	53	13	1	5	20	21-6	1	40	.250	.319	.392	94	-3	1-0	.994	9	113	119	2-50,3-14,S-13/1-3,P	0.8
2003	Phi N	125	298	39	79	18	1	5	33	23-11	0	54	.265	.316	.383	87	-6	0-1	.953	1	99	150	3-58,2-26/1-9,S-4	-0.4
Total	8	502	1310	135	327	64	11	16	121	106-20	5	224	.250	.307	.352	72	-57	4-7	.980	22	108	117	2-196,S-141/3-93,1-12,PO(RF)	-1.8
PEREZCHICA, TONY Antonio Llamas (Gonzales) B 4.20.1966 Mexicali, Mexico BR/TR 5-11/165# d9.7																								
1988	SF N	7	8	1	1	0	0	0	1	2-0	0	1	.125	.273	.125	27	-1	0-0	1.000	-2	59	0	/2-6	-0.3
1990	SF N	4	3	1	1	0	0	0	0	1-0	0	2	.333	.500	.333	139	0	0-0	1.000	-1	0	0	/2-2,S-2	-0.1
1991	SF N	23	48	2	11	4	1	0	3	2-0	0	12	.229	.260	.354	73	-2	0-1	.947	-3	90	72	S-13/2-6	-0.4
	Cle A	17	22	4	8	2	0	0	0	3-0	0	5	.364	.440	.455	147	2	0-0	1.000	-3	43	50	/S-6,3-3,2-2,D	-0.1
1992	Cle A	18	20	2	2	1	0	0	1	2-0	0	6	.100	.182	.150	-6	-3	0-0	.875	-3	131	0	/3-9,2-4,S-4,D	-0.6
Total	4	69	101	10	23	7	1	0	5	10-0	0	26	.228	.295	.317	74	-4	0-1	.944	-11	73	53	/S-25,2-20,3-12,D-2	-1.5
PERKINS, BRODERICK Broderick Phillip B 11.23.1954 Pittsburg, CA BL/TL 5-10/180# d7.7																								
1978	SD N	62	217	14	52	14	1	2	33	5-2	0	29	.240	.253	.341	71	-10	4-0	.993	4	135	138	1-59	-0.8
1979	SD N	57	87	8	23	0	0	0	8	8-2	0	12	.264	.323	.264	67	-4	0-0	.982	-0	105	124	1-28	-0.5
1980	SD N	43	100	18	37	9	0	2	14	11-1	0	10	.370	.432	.520	175	11	2-1	.988	-2	94	110	1-20,O-10(RF)	0.8
1981	SD N	92	254	27	71	18	3	2	40	14-4	0	16	.280	.314	.398	110	2	0-4	.997	-1	94	104	1-80/O-3(1-0-2)	-0.5
1982	SD N	125	347	32	94	10	4	2	34	26-10	3	20	.271	.325	.340	92	-4	2-1	.994	2	110	99	1-98,O-11(4-0-7)	-0.9
1983	Cle A	79	184	23	50	10	0	0	24	9-3	0	19	.272	.299	.326	71	-7	1-5	.991	-1	33	101	1-19,O-17(5-0-12),D-16	-1.2
1984	Cle A	58	66	5	13	1	0	0	4	7-1	1	10	.197	.276	.212	39	-5	0-0	1.000	-0	0	220	D-10/1-2	-0.6
Total	7	516	1255	127	340	62	8	8	157	80-23	4	116	.271	.313	.352	90	-17	9-11	.993	1	106	111	1-306/O-41(10-0-31),D-26	-3.7
PERKINS, CY Ralph Foster B 2.27.1896 Gloucester, MA D 10.2.1963 Philadelphia, PA BR/TR 5-10.5/158# d9.25 M1 C17																								
1915	Phi A	7	20	2	4	1	0	0	0	3	0	3	.200	.304	.250	68	-1	0	.920	-1	*69*	***89***	/C-6	-0.1
1917	Phi A	6	18	1	3	0	0	0	2	2	0	1	.167	.250	.167	28	-2	0	.978	2	*97*	*164*	/C-6	0.1
1918	Phi A	68	218	9	41	4	1	1	14	8	0	15	.188	.217	.229	34	-18	1	.990	9	*89*	*126*	C-60	-0.5
1919	Phi A	101	305	22	77	12	7	2	29	27	0	22	.252	.313	.357	87	-6	2	.971	0	*79*	***135***	C-87/S-8	0.2
1920	Phi A	148	492	40	128	24	6	5	52	28	2	35	.260	.303	.364	75	-19	5-6	.979	15	*98*	***145***	*C-146/2	0.6
1921	Phi A	141	538	58	155	31	4	12	73	32	1	32	.288	.329	.428	91	-9	5-9	.971	0	*88*	*118*	*C-141	-0.1
1922	Phi A	148	505	58	135	20	6	6	69	40	1	30	.267	.322	.366	77	-18	1-7	.984	0	*107*	*115*	*C-141	-1.1
1923	Phi A	143	500	53	135	34	5	2	65	65	2	30	.270	.356	.370	90	-5	1-3	.971	-5	*104*	*93*	*C-137	-0.2
1924	Phi A	128	392	31	95	19	4	0	32	31	4	20	.242	.304	.311	58	-25	3-4	.983	0	*105*	*85*	*C-128	-1.7
1925	Phi A	65	140	21	43	10	0	1	18	26	3	6	.307	.426	.400	104	3	0-0	.980	6	*115*	*84*	C-58/3	1.1
1926	Phi A	63	148	14	43	6	0	0	19	18	1	7	.291	.371	.331	80	-4	0-2	.984	8	*113*	*102*	C-55	0.6
1927	Phi A	59	137	11	35	7	2	1	15	12	0	8	.255	.315	.358	70	-6	0-2	.979	1	*118*	*83*	C-54/1	-0.3
1928	Phi A	19	29	1	5	0	0	0	1	1	0	1	.172	.200	.172	-1	-4	0-1	.982	2	*122*	*88*	C-19	-0.2
1929	Phi A	38	76	4	16	4	0	0	9	5	0	4	.211	.259	.263	34	-8	0-0	.990	1	*89*	*88*	C-38	-0.5
1930	Phi A	20	38	1	6	2	0	0	4	2	0	3	.158	.200	.211	4	-6	0-0	.964	-0	*114*	*31*	C-19/1	-0.5
1931	NY A	16	47	3	12	1	0	0	7	1	1	4	.255	.286	.277	51	-3	0-0	1.000	-3	*90*	*0*	C-16	-0.5
1934	Det A	1	1	0	0	0	0	0	0	0	0	0	.000	.000	.000	-99	0	0-0	—	0			H	0.0
Total	17	1171	3604	329	933	175	35	30	409	301	15	221	.259	.319	.352	75	-131	18-34	.978	35	*99*	*110*	*C-1111/S-8,1-2,32	-3.1
PERLOZZO, SAM Samuel Benedict B 3.4.1951 Cumberland, MD BR/TR 5-9/170# d9.13 C17																								
1977	Min A	10	24	6	7	0	2	0	0	2-0	0	3	.292	.346	.458	119	0	0-0	1.000	-3	76	43	2-10/3	-0.2

Year	Tm Lg	G	AB	R	H	2B	3B	HR	RBI	BB-IB	HP	SO	AVG	OBP	SLG	AOPS	ABR	SB-CS	FA	FR	Rng	Thr	G at Pos	BFW
1979	SD N	2	2	0	0	0	0	0	0	1-0	0	0	.000	.333	.000	-1	0	0-0	.500	-1	0	0	/2-2	-0.1
Total	2	12	26	6	7	0	2	0	0	3-0	0	3	.269	.345	.423	110	0	0-0	.967	-4	70	40	/2-12,3	-0.3
PERRIN, JOHN John Stephenson B 2.4.1898 Escanaba, MI D 6.24.1969 Detroit, MI BL/TR 5-9/160# d7.11																								
1921	Bos A	4	13	3	3	0	0	0	1	0	0	3	.231	.231	.231	19	-2	0-0	1.000	-1	33	0	/O-4(RF)	-0.2
PERRINE, NIG John Grover B 1.14.1885 Clinton, WI D 8.13.1948 Kansas City, MO BR/TR 5-9/160# d4.11																								
1907	Was A	44	146	13	25	4	1	0	15	13	3		.171	.253	.212	53	-7	10	.946	-4	86	152	2-24,S-18/3-2	-1.1
PERRING, GEORGE George Wilson B 8.13.1884 Sharon, WI D 8.20.1960 Beloit, WI BR/TR (BB 1909 (1 game)) 6/190# d4.25																								
1908	Cle A	89	310	23	67	8	5	0	19	16	0		.216	.255	.274	72	-11	8	.928	-11	100	114	S-48,3-41	-2.2
1909	Cle A	88	283	26	63	10	9	0	20	19	5		.223	.283	.322	87	-5	6	.932	2	105	71	3-67,S-11/2-4	-0.1
1910	Cle A	39	122	14	27	6	3	0	8	3	0		.221	.240	.320	74	-4	3	.931	1	106	96	3-33/1-4	-0.4
1914	KC F	144	496	68	138	28	10	2	69	59	0	39	.278	.355	.387	106	-3	7	.934	9	118	127	*3-101,1-41/PS	0.8
1915	KC F	**153**	553	67	143	23	7	7	67	55	1	30	.259	.327	.363	98	-11	10	.958	11	108	98	*3-102,1-31,2-31/S	0.3
Total	5	513	1764	198	438	75	34	9	183	152	6	69	.248	.310	.345	93	-34	34	.939	11	108	92	3-344/1-76,S-61,2-35,P	-1.6
PERRY, BOYD Boyd Glenn B 3.21.1914 Snow Camp, NC D 6.29.1990 Burlington, NC BR/TR 5-10/158# d5.23																								
1941	Det A	36	83	9	15	5	0	0	11	10	0	9	.181	.269	.241	32	-8	1-0	.974	0	103	95	S-25,2-11	-0.6
PERRY, CHAN Chan Everett B 9.13.1972 Live Oak, FL BR/TR 6-2/200# d8.3																								
2000	Cle A	13	14	1	1	0	0	0	0	0-0	0	5	.071	.071	.071	-62	-4	0-0	1.000	0	110	0	/O-7(1-0-6),1D	-0.3
2002	KC A	5	11	0	1	0	0	0	3	0-0	0	1	.091	.091	.091	-46	-2	0-0	1.000	0	98	74	/1-5	-0.3
Total	2	18	25	1	2	0	0	0	3	0-0	0	6	.080	.080	.080	-55	-6	0-0	1.000	0	110	0	/O-7(1-0-6),1-6,D-4	-0.6
PERRY, CLAY Clayton Shields B 12.18.1881 Clayton, WI D 1.13.1954 Rice Lake, WI BR/TR 5-10.5/175# d9.2																								
1908	Det A	7	17	0	2	0	0	0	0	0	1		.118	.167	.118	-7	-2	0	.850	-1	91	160	/3-7	-0.3
PERRY, GERALD Gerald June B 10.30.1960 Savannah, GA BL/TR 6/190# d8.11 C4																								
1983	Atl N	27	39	5	14	2	0	1	6	5-0	0	4	.359	.422	.487	144	3	0-1	.982	-2	0	102	/1-7,O(LF)	0.0
1984	Atl N	122	347	52	92	12	2	7	47	61-5	2	38	.265	.372	.372	104	5	15-12	.988	-8	78	112	1-64,O-53(LF)	-1.0
1985	Atl N	110	238	22	51	5	0	3	13	23-1	0	28	.214	.282	.273	53	-15	9-5	.985	-2	101	104	1-55/O(LF)	-2.1
1986	Atl N	29	70	6	19	2	0	2	11	8-1	0	4	.271	.342	.386	96	0	0-1	.889	-3	53	0	O-21(21-0-1)/1	-0.5
1987	Atl N	142	533	77	144	35	2	12	74	48-1	1	63	.270	.329	.411	91	-6	42-16	.990	-11	77	110	*1-136/O-7(LF)	-2.2
1988	Atl N★	141	547	61	164	29	1	8	74	36-9	1	49	.300	.338	.400	108	6	29-14	.988	1	106	91	*1-141	-0.3
1989	Atl N	72	266	24	67	11	0	4	21	32-5	3	28	.252	.337	.338	92	-2	10-6	.987	1	108	103	1-72	-0.6
1990	KC A	133	465	57	118	22	2	8	57	39-4	3	56	.254	.313	.361	90	-6	17-4	.986	1	109	94	D-68,1-51	-0.8
1991	StL N	109	242	29	58	8	4	6	36	22-1	0	34	.240	.300	.380	90	-4	15-8	.989	-5	72	93	1-61/O-5(4-0-1)	-1.2
1992	StL N	87	143	13	34	8	0	1	18	15-4	1	23	.238	.311	.315	81	-3	3-6	.987	-4	60	142	1-29	-1.1
1993	StL N	96	98	21	33	5	0	4	16	18-2	0	23	.337	.440	.510	157	9	1-1	.976	-1	56	82	1-15/O(RF)	0.7
1994	StL N	60	77	12	25	7	0	3	18	15-1	0	12	.325	.435	.532	153	7	1-1	.990	-2	54	99	1-13	0.4
1995	StL N	65	79	4	13	4	0	0	5	6-0	0	12	.165	.224	.215	16	-10	0-0	1.000	-1	54	63	1-11	-1.1
Total	13	1193	3144	383	832	150	11	59	396	328-34	11	374	.265	.333	.376	95	-16	142-75	.988	-35	90	102	1-656/O-89(87-0-3),D-68	-9.8
PERRY, HERBERT Herbert Edward B 9.15.1969 Live Oak, FL BR/TR 6-2/210# d5.3																								
1994	Cle A	4	9	1	1	0	0	0	1	3-1	1	1	.111	.357	.111	36	-1	0-0	1.000	1	176	48	/1-2,3-2	0.0
1995	†Cle A	52	162	23	51	13	1	3	23	13-0	4	28	.315	.376	.463	116	4	1-3	1.000	-1	91	87	1-45/3D	-0.1
1996	Cle A	7	12	1	1	1	0	0	0	1-0	0	2	.083	.154	.167	-19	-2	1-0	1.000	-0	85	109	/1-5,3	-0.2
1999	TB A	66	209	29	53	10	1	6	32	16-1	10	42	.254	.331	.397	85	-5	0-0	.955	5	111	162	3-42,1-14,D-10/O-6(LF)	-0.1
2000	TB A	7	28	2	6	1	0	0	1	2-0	0	7	.214	.267	.250	32	-3	0-0	.938	-1	86	85	/3-7,1	-0.3
	†Chi A	109	383	69	118	29	1	12	61	22-1	9	68	.308	.356	.483	109	5	4-1	.969	6	103	95	*3-104/1-3,D-3	1.1
	Year	116	411	71	124	30	1	12	62	24-1	9	75	.302	.350	.467	104	3	4-1	.967	5	102	94	*3-111/1-4,D-3	0.8
2001	Chi A	92	285	38	73	21	1	7	32	23-1	7	55	.256	.326	.411	90	-4	2-2	.940	-6	93	48	3-68,1-12,D-10	-1.1
2002	Tex A	132	450	64	124	24	1	22	77	34-1	6	66	.276	.333	.480	108	4	4-2	.951	-1	96	87	*3-112,1-12/O(LF)D	0.4
2003	Tex A	11	24	1	4	1	0	0	2	0-0	0	3	.167	.167	.208	-2	-4	0-0	1.000	0	145	73	/1-5,3-2	-0.3
Total	8	480	1562	228	431	100	5	50	229	114-5	37	272	.276	.337	.442	98	-6	12-8	.955	3	99	91	3-339/1-99,D-35,O-7(LF)	-0.6
PERRY, BOB Melvin Gray B 9.14.1934 New Bern, NC BR/TR 6-2/180# d5.17																								
1963	LA A	61	166	16	42	9	0	3	14	9-2	3	31	.253	.300	.361	91	-2	1-1	.946	-5	90	33	O-55(7-23-26)	-1.0
1964	LA A	70	221	19	61	8	1	3	16	14-0	0	52	.276	.318	.362	99	-1	1-1	.975	-5	90	52	O-62(0-62-1)	-0.8
Total	2	131	387	35	103	17	1	6	30	23-2	3	83	.266	.310	.362	95	-3	2-2	.962	-9	90	43	O-117(7-85-27)	-1.8
PERRY, HANK William Henry "Socks" B 7.28.1886 Howell, MI D 7.18.1956 Pontiac, MI BL/TR 5-11/190# d4.12																								
1912	Det A	13	36	3	6	1	0	0	0	3	0		.167	.231	.194	23	-4	0	1.000	1	108	164	/O-7(CF)	-0.3
PESKY, JOHNNY John Michael (born John Michael Paveskovich) B 9.27.1919 Portland, OR BL/TR 5-9/168# d4.14 Mil 1943-45 M3 C13																								
1942	Bos A	147	620	105	**205**	29	9	2	51	42	2	36	.331	.375	.416	118	14	12-7	.955	20	**110**	109	*S-147	4.5
1946	†Bos A★	153	621	115	**208**	43	4	2	55	65	3	29	.335	.401	.427	124	23	9-8	.969	12	106	104	*S-153	4.6
1947	Bos A	155	638	106	**207**	27	8	0	39	72	0	22	.324	.393	.392	110	11	12-9	.976	-10	95	95	*S-133,3-22	0.9
1948	Bos A	143	565	124	159	26	6	3	55	99	6	32	.281	.394	.365	98	3	3-5	.951	7	**113**	**136**	*3-141	0.8
1949	Bos A	148	604	111	185	27	7	2	69	100	4	19	.306	.408	.384	103	7	8-4	.970	19	108	**139**	*3-148	2.5
1950	Bos A	127	490	112	153	22	6	1	49	104	5	31	.312	.437	.388	103	9	2-1	.974	16	105	112	*3-116/S-8	2.3
1951	Bos A	131	480	93	150	20	6	3	41	84	2	15	.313	.417	.398	110	11	2-2	.961	2	105	95	*S-106,3-11/2-5	2.0
1952	Bos A	25	67	10	10	2	0	0	2	15	1	5	.149	.313	.179	36	-5	0-3	.917	-4	82	0	3-19/S-2	-1.1
	Det A	69	177	26	45	4	0	1	9	41	0	11	.254	.394	.294	93	1	1-2	.952	-2	89	100	S-41,2-22/3-3	0.1
	Year	94	244	36	55	6	0	1	11	56	1	16	.225	.372	.262	77	-4	1-5	.953	-6	88	101	S-43,3-22,2-22	-1.0
1953	Det A	103	308	43	90	22	1	2	24	27	2	10	.292	.353	.390	102	1	3-7	.991	-7	96	83	2-73	-0.2
1954	Det A	20	17	5	3	0	0	1	1	3	0	1	.176	.300	.353	80	-1	0-0	—	0			H	-0.1
	Was A	49	158	17	40	4	3	0	9	10	0	7	.253	.296	.316	72	-7	1-1	.979	-4	101	81	2-37/S	-0.8
	Year	69	175	22	43	4	3	1	10	13	0	8	.246	.296	.320	72	-8	1-1	.979	-4	101	81	2-37/S	-0.9
Total	10	1270	4745	867	1455	226	50	17	404	662	25	218	.307	.394	.386	106	67	53-49	.964	50	103	101	S-591,3-460,2-137	15.5
PETAGINE, ROBERTO Roberto Antonio (Guerra) B 6.7.1971 Nueva Esparta, Venezuela BL/TL 6-1/170# d4.4																								
1994	Hou N	8	7	0	0	0	0	0	0	1-0	0	3	.000	.125	.000	-67	-2	0-0	1.000	-0	0	0	/1-2	-0.2
1995	SD N	89	124	15	29	8	0	3	17	26-2	0	41	.234	.367	.371	99	1	0-0	.996	-0	98	89	1-51/O-2(1-0-1)	-0.2
1996	NY N	50	99	10	23	3	0	4	17	9-1	3	27	.232	.313	.384	87	-2	0-2	.996	1	113	91	1-40	-0.4
1997	NY N	12	15	2	1	0	0	0	2	3-0	0	6	.067	.222	.067	-21	-3	0-0	1.000	1	193	0	/1-6,O(LF)	-0.2
1998	Cin N	34	62	14	16	2	1	3	7	16-0	0	11	.258	.405	.468	129	3	1-0	1.000	2	110	102	1-15,O-15(1-0-15)	0.4
Total	5	193	307	41	69	13	1	10	43	55-3	3	88	.225	.346	.371	92	-3	1-2	.997	3	108	87	1-114/O-18(3-0-16)	-0.6
PETERMAN, BILL William David B 3.20.1921 Philadelphia, PA D 3.13.1999 Philadelphia, PA BR/TR 6-2/185# d4.26 Mil 1943-45																								
1942	Phi N	1	1	0	1	0	0	0	0	0	0	0	1.000	1.000	1.000	512	1	0	—	0	*0*	*0*	/C	0.0
PETERS, JOHN John Paul B 4.8.1850 Louisiana, MO D 1.4.1924 St.Louis, MO BR/TR 5-7/180# d5.23																								
1874	Chi NA	55	239	39	69	10	0	1	25	2		11	.289	.295	.343	103	1	2-2	.799	2	104	75	S-36,2-19	0.0
1875	Chi NA	**69**	297	40	85	16	2	0	34	0		3	.286	.286	.354	120	6	12-6	.871	9	109	158	*S-65/2-6	1.1
1876	Chi N	**66**	316	70	111	14	2	1	47	3		2	.351	.357	.418	141	12		**.932**	1	91	**146**	*S-66/P	1.3
1877	Chi N	**60**	265	45	84	10	3	0	41	1		7	.317	.320	.377	106	1		.883	**20**	**116**	**164**	*S-60	2.0
1878	Mil N	55	246	33	76	6	1	0	22	5		8	.309	.323	.341	111	2		.853	2	114	96	2-34,S-22	0.6
1879	Chi N	**83**	379	45	93	13	2	1	31	1		19	.245	.247	.298	74	-11		.837	-7	99	79	*S-83	-1.4
1880	Pro N	86	359	30	82	5	0	0	24	5		15	.228	.239	.242	66	-13		**.900**	-4	94	**139**	*S-86	-1.2
1881	Buf N	54	229	21	49	8	1	0	25	3		12	.214	.224	.258	52	-13		.869	2	100	88	S-53/O(RF)	-0.7
1882	Pit AA	78	333	46	96	10	1	0		4			.288	.297	.324	115	5		.883	6	103	**114**	*S-77/2	1.2
1883	Pit AA	8	28	3	3	0	0	0		0			.107	.107	.107	-32	-4		.818	2	121	150	/S-8	-0.2
1884	Pit AA	1	4	0	0	0	0	0		0	0		.000	.000	.000	-99	-1		.667	-1	40	0	/S	-0.2
Total	2 NA	124	536	79	154	26	2	1	59	2	0	14	.287	.290	.349	112	7	14-8	.000	11	107	129	S-101/2-25	1.1
Total	9	491	2159	293	594	66	10	2	190	22	0	63	.275	.282	.318	94	-22		.881	20	100	119	S-456/2-35,O(RF)P	1.4

Year	Tm Lg	G	AB	R	H	2B	3B	HR	RBI	BB-IB	HP	SO	AVG	OBP	SLG	AOPS	ABR	SB-CS	FA	FR	Rng	Thr	G at Pos	BFW
PETERS, JOHN John William "Big Pete" or "Shotgun" B 7.14.1893 Kansas City, KS D 2.21.1932 Kansas City, MO BR/TR 6/192# d5.1																								
1915	Det A	1	3	0	0	0	0	0	0	0	0	1	.000	.000	.000	-95	-1	0	1.000	1	*136*	*191*	/C	0.0
1918	Cle A	1	1	0	0	0	0	0	0	1	0	1	.000	.500	.000	46	0	0	.500	-1	*0*	*140*	/C	-0.1
1921	Phi N	55	155	7	45	4	0	3	23	6	3	13	.290	.329	.374	79	-5	1-0	.933	-11	*65*	*69*	C-44	-1.3
1922	Phi N	55	143	15	35	9	1	4	24	9	4	18	.245	.308	.406	75	-5	0-1	.953	-5	*81*	*73*	C-39	-0.8
Total	4	112	302	22	80	13	1	7	47	16	7	33	.265	.317	.384	76	-11	1-1	.934	-16	*73*	*74*	/C-85	-2.2
PETERS, RICK Richard Devin B 11.21.1955 Lynwood, CA BB/TR 5-9/170# d9.8																								
1979	Det A	12	19	3	5	0	0	0	2	5-0	0	3	.263	.417	.263	85	0	0-0	.000	-2	0	0	/3-3,2-2,O(LF)D	-0.2
1980	Det A	133	477	79	139	19	7	2	42	54-2	6	48	.291	.369	.373	102	3	13-7	.977	-4	103	13	*O-109(8-97-5),D-11	-0.2
1981	Det A	63	207	26	53	7	3	0	15	29-2	2	28	.256	.351	.319	91	-1	1-6	.991	3	114	141	O-38(5-33-0),D-19	-0.1
1983	Oak A	55	178	20	51	7	0	0	20	12-0	1	21	.287	.327	.326	88	-3	4-9	.986	7	131	100	O-47(6-30-16)/D-8	0.1
1986	Oak A	44	38	7	7	1	0	0	1	7-1	0	7	.184	.311	.211	49	-2	2-2	1.000	1	120	0	O-27(19-7-1)/2	-0.2
Total	5	307	919	135	255	34	10	2	80	107-5	9	107	.277	.356	.343	95	-3	20-24	.983	4	112	54	O-222(39-167-22)/D-41,2-3,3-3	-0.6
PETERS, RUSTY Russell Dixon B 12.14.1914 Roanoke, VA D 2.21.2003 Harrisonburg, VA BR/TR 5-11/170# d4.14 Mil 1945-46																								
1936	Phi A	45	119	12	26	3	2	3	16	4	0	28	.218	.244	.353	47	-11	1-1	.898	-1	96	95	S-25,3-10/O-2(LF),2	-1.0
1937	Phi A	116	339	39	88	17	6	3	43	41	0	59	.260	.339	.372	80	-10	4-4	.966	-9	96	84	2-70,3-31,S-13	-1.3
1938	Phi A	2	7	0	0	0	0	0	0	0	0	1	.000	.000	.000	-99	-2	0-0	.714	-2	41	0	/S-2	-0.4
1940	Cle A	30	71	5	17	3	2	0	7	4	0	14	.239	.280	.338	61	-4	1-0	.922	-2	82	119	/2-9,S-6,3-6,1	-0.5
1941	Cle A	29	63	6	13	2	0	0	2	7	0	10	.206	.286	.238	42	-5	0-1	.891	0	115	92	S-11/3-9,2-3	-0.5
1942	Cle A	34	58	6	13	5	1	0	2	2	0	14	.224	.250	.345	70	-3	0-0	.944	0	119	101	S-24/23	-0.1
1943	Cle A	79	215	22	47	6	2	1	19	18	1	29	.219	.282	.279	69	-9	1-1	.913	-5	92	119	3-46,S-14/2-6,O-2(LF)	-1.4
1944	Cle A	88	282	23	63	13	3	1	24	15	2	35	.223	.268	.301	65	-14	2-1	.976	-2	103	97	2-63,S-13/3-8	-1.2
1946	Cle A	9	21	0	6	0	0	0	2	1	0	1	.286	.318	.286	74	-1	0-1	1.000	1	94	99	/S-7	0.0
1947	StL A	39	47	10	16	4	0	0	2	6	0	8	.340	.415	.426	131	2	0-0	.955	3	108	118	2-13/S-2	0.6
Total	10	471	1222	123	289	53	16	8	117	98	3	199	.236	.295	.326	69	-57	9-9	.966	-15	98	95	2-166,S-117,3-111/O-4(LF),1	-5.8
PETERSEN, CHRIS Christopher Ronald B 11.6.1970 Boston, MA BR/TR 5-11/180# d5.25																								
1999	Col N	7	13	1	2	0	0	0	2	2-0	0	3	.154	.267	.154	8	-2	0-0	.955	3	136	208	/2-6,S	0.1
PETERSON, BUDDY Carl Francis B 4.23.1925 Portland, OR BR/TR 5-9.5/170# d9.14																								
1955	Chi A	6	21	7	6	1	0	0	2	3-0	1	2	.286	.400	.333	96	0	0-0	.962	-1	88	124	/S-6	0.0
1957	Bal A	7	17	1	3	2	0	0	0	2-0	0	2	.176	.263	.294	55	-1	0-0	.963	-1	82	87	/S-7	-0.2
Total	2	13	38	8	9	3	0	0	2	5-0	1	4	.237	.341	.316	80	-1	0-0	.962	-1	85	106	/S-13	-0.2
PETERSON, CAP Charles Andrew B 8.15.1942 Tacoma, WA D 5.16.1980 Tacoma, WA BR/TR 6-2/195# d9.12 OF Total (142-LF 139-RF)																								
1962	SF N	4	6	1	1	0	0	0	0	1-0	0	4	.167	.286	.167	25	-1	0-0	1.000	-1	62	164	/S-2	-0.1
1963	SF N	22	54	7	14	2	0	1	2	2-0	0	13	.259	.286	.352	83	-1	0-0	.917	-5	86	0	/2-8,3-5,O-3(2-0-1),S	-0.6
1964	SF N	66	74	8	15	1	1	1	8	3-1	0	20	.203	.234	.284	44	-6	0-0	1.000	-1	95	0	O-10(10-0-1)/1-2,23	-0.7
1965	SF N	63	105	14	26	7	0	3	15	10-2	0	16	.248	.310	.400	97	0	0-0	1.000	-1	80	110	O-27(23-0-4)	-0.2
1966	SF N	89	190	13	45	6	1	2	19	11-1	1	32	.237	.279	.311	63	-10	2-0	1.000	0	96	80	O-51(50-0-1)/1-2	-1.2
1967	Was A	122	405	35	97	17	2	8	46	32-1	3	61	.240	.299	.351	95	-3	0-3	.970	-1	103	72	*O-101(18-0-88)	-1.3
1968	Was A	94	226	20	46	8	1	3	18	18-3	1	31	.204	.262	.288	70	-9	2-1	1.000	-2	95	68	O-53(14-0-39)	-1.5
1969	Cle A	76	110	8	25	3	0	1	14	24-3	1	18	.227	.365	.282	82	-1	0-0	.977	-0	106	125	O-30(25-0-5)/3-4	-0.3
Total	8	536	1170	106	269	44	5	19	122	101-11	6	195	.230	.292	.325	80	-31	4-4	.983	-9	99	78	O-275L/3-10,2-9,1-4,S-3	-5.9
PETERSON, HARDY Harding William B 10.17.1929 Perth Amboy, NJ BR/TR 6/205# d5.5																								
1955	Pit N	32	81	7	20	6	0	1	10	7-1	1	7	.247	.311	.358	79	-2	0-0	.965	3	*87*	*220*	C-31	0.1
1957	Pit N	30	73	10	22	2	1	2	11	9-2	0	10	.301	.378	.438	122	2	0-1	.985	1	*110*	*126*	C-30	0.5
1958	Pit N	2	6	0	2	0	0	0	0	1-0	0	0	.333	.429	.333	108	0	0-0	1.000	-0	*56*	*0*	/C-2	0.0
1959	Pit N	2	1	0	0	0	0	0	0	0-0	0	0	.000	.000	.000	-99	0	0-0	1.000	0	*0*	*0*	/C-2	0.0
Total	4	66	161	17	44	8	1	3	21	17-3	1	17	.273	.344	.391	99	0	0-1	.976	4	*96*	*166*	/C-65	0.6
PETERSON, BOB Robert A. B 7.16.1884 Philadelphia, PA D 11.27.1962 Evesham Township, NJ BR/TR 6-1/160# d4.18																								
1906	Bos A	39	118	10	24	1	1	1	9	11	1		.203	.277	.254	67	-4	1	.899	-9	*81*	*101*	C-30/2-3,1-2,O(LF)	-1.2
1907	Bos A	4	13	1	1	0	0	0	0	0	0		.077	.077	.077	-51	-2	0	1.000	0	*113*	*84*	/C-4	-0.2
Total	2	43	131	11	25	1	1	1	9	11	1		.191	.259	.237	56	-6	1	.910	-9	*85*	*99*	/C-34,2-3,1-2,O(LF)	-1.4
PETOSKEY, TED Frederick Lee B 1.5.1911 St.Charles, MI D 11.30.1996 Elgin, SC BR/TR 5-11.5/183# d9.9																								
1934	Cin N	6	7	0	0	0	0	0	1	0	0	5	.000	.000	.000	-99	-2	0	1.000	1	164	992	/O-2(CF)	-0.1
1935	Cin N	4	5	0	2	0	0	0	0	0	0	1	.400	.400	.400	119	0	1	1.000	-0	52	0	/O-2(1-1-0)	0.0
Total	2	10	12	0	2	0	0	0	1	0	0	6	.167	.167	.167	-11	-2	1	1.000	1	123	627	/O-4(1-3-0)	-0.1
PETRALLI, GENO Eugene James B 9.25.1959 Sacramento, CA BL/TR (BB 1982-86, 87 (part)) 6-2/185# d9.4 OF Total (1-LF 2-RF)																								
1982	Tor A	16	44	3	16	2	0	0	1	4-0	0	6	.364	.417	.409	117	1	0-0	.981	-1	77	66	C-12/3-3	0.0
1983	Tor A	6	4	0	0	0	0	0	0	1-0	0	1	.000	.200	.000	-37	-1	0-0	1.000	-0	0	0	/C-5,D	-0.1
1984	Tor A	3	3	0	0	0	0	0	0	0-0	0	0	.000	.000	.000	-97	-1	0-0	1.000	0	0	0	/CD	0.0
1985	Tex A	42	100	7	27	2	0	0	11	8-0	1	12	.270	.319	.290	71	-4	1-0	.990	-2	64	105	C-41	-0.4
1986	Tex A	69	137	17	35	9	3	2	18	5-0	0	14	.255	.282	.409	83	-4	3-0	.988	-7	87	39	C-41,3-15/2-2,D-2	-0.9
1987	Tex A	101	202	28	61	11	2	7	31	27-2	2	29	.302	.388	.480	129	9	0-2	.995	-4	59	144	C-63,3-17/1-5,2-4,O-3(1-0-2),D-2	0.6
1988	Tex A	129	351	35	99	14	2	7	36	41-5	2	52	.282	.356	.393	108	5	0-1	.981	1	79	142	C-85,D-23/3-9,1-2,2-2	0.9
1989	Tex A	70	184	18	56	7	0	4	23	17-1	2	24	.304	.368	.408	117	4	0-0	.989	-1	74	116	C-49,D-16	0.6
1990	Tex A	133	325	28	83	13	1	0	21	50-3	3	49	.255	.357	.302	87	-3	0-2	.991	-2	106	108	*C-118/3-7,2-3	0.0
1991	Tex A	87	199	21	54	8	1	2	20	21-1	0	25	.271	.339	.352	94	-1	2-1	.972	-7	81	113	C-66/3-7,D-5	-0.6
1992	Tex A	94	192	11	38	12	0	1	18	20-2	0	34	.198	.274	.276	56	-11	0-0	.990	-1	143	126	C-54,D-14/3-4,2-2	-1.0
1993	Tex A	59	133	16	32	5	0	1	13	22-3	0	17	.241	.348	.301	79	-3	2-0	.990	-9	73	122	C-39/23D	-0.9
Total	12	809	1874	184	501	83	9	24	192	216-17	10	263	.267	.344	.360	95	-9	8-6	.987	-33	87	116	C-574/D-66,3-63,2-14,1-7,O-3R	-1.8
PETRICK, BEN Benjamin Wayne B 4.7.1977 Salem, OR BR/TR 6/195# d9.1																								
1999	Col N	19	62	13	20	3	0	4	12	10-0	0	13	.323	.417	.565	114	2	1-0	.982	-7	65	36	C-19	-0.4
2000	Col N	52	146	32	47	10	1	3	20	20-2	2	33	.322	.401	.466	97	0	1-2	.985	-3	96	60	C-48	-0.1
2001	Col N	85	244	41	58	15	3	11	39	31-3	3	67	.238	.327	.459	83	-6	3-3	.984	-6	81	74	C-77/1-2	-0.8
2002	Col N	38	95	10	20	3	1	5	11	9-0	1	33	.211	.283	.421	74	-4	0-1	.952	-1	88	0	O-16(15-2-0),C-14	-0.5
2003	Col N	3	2	0	0	0	0	0	0	0-0	0	1	.000	.000	.000	-88	-1	0-0	1.000	1	201	3625	/O-2(1-1-0),C	0.0
	Det A	43	120	18	27	6	0	4	12	8-0	0	30	.225	.273	.375	74	-5	0-0	.969	-1	91	126	O-32(18-14-3)/C-6,1-2	-0.6
Total	5	240	669	114	172	37	5	27	94	78-5	6	177	.257	.336	.448	87	-14	5-6	.984	-18	85	62	C-165/O-50(34-17-3),1-4	-2.4
PETROCELLI, RICO Americo Peter B 6.27.1943 Brooklyn, NY BR/TR 6/185# d9.21																								
1963	Bos A	1	4	0	1	1	0	0	1	0-0	0	1	.250	.250	.500	101	0	0-0	.833	-0	69	0	/S	0.0
1965	Bos A	103	323	38	75	15	2	13	33	36-4	1	71	.232	.309	.412	98	-1	0-2	.958	9	110	83	S-93	1.6
1966	Bos A	139	522	58	124	20	1	18	59	41-2	3	99	.238	.295	.383	85	-10	1-1	.954	5	106	88	*S-127/3-5	0.6
1967	†Bos A★	142	491	53	127	24	2	17	66	49-9	5	93	.259	.330	.420	112	8	2-4	.970	5	103	98	*S-141	2.6
1968	Bos A	123	406	41	95	17	2	12	46	31-2	4	73	.234	.292	.374	95	-2	0-1	**.978**	11	109	106	*S-117/1	2.1
1969	Bos A★	154	535	92	159	32	2	40	97	98-13	1	68	.297	.403	.589	167	50	3-5	**.981**	6	102	107	*S-153/3	**7.5**
1970	Bos A	157	583	82	152	31	3	29	103	67-6	2	82	.261	.334	.473	114	11	1-1	.970	-0	94	89	*S-141,3-18	2.7
1971	Bos A	158	553	82	139	24	4	28	89	91-5	2	108	.251	.354	.461	122	18	2-0	**.976**	-1	99	111	*3-156	1.7
1972	Bos A	147	521	62	125	15	2	15	75	78-9	2	91	.240	.339	.363	104	5	0-1	.970	5	94	**126**	*3-146	1.0
1973	Bos A	100	356	44	87	13	1	13	45	47-3	1	64	.244	.333	.396	99	0	0-0	.980	6	105	125	3-99	0.6
1974	Bos A	129	454	53	121	23	1	15	76	48-4	2	74	.267	.336	.421	110	6	1-0	.962	-13	90	96	*3-116/D-9	-0.7
1975	†Bos A	115	402	31	96	15	1	7	59	41-1	3	66	.239	.310	.333	76	-12	0-2	.960	-13	92	60	*3-113/D	-2.8
1976	Bos A	85	240	17	51	7	1	3	24	34-3	0	36	.213	.307	.287	67	-9	0-5	.967	-3	95	104	3-73/2-5,1SD	-1.5
Total	13	1553	5390	653	1352	237	22	210	773	661-61	26	926	.251	.332	.420	108	64	10-22	.969	17	103	96	S-774,3-727/D-14,2-5,1-2	15.4
PETTEE, PAT Patrick E. B 1.10.1863 Natick, MA D 10.9.1934 Natick, MA BR/TR 5-10/170# d4.8																								
1891	Lou AA	2	5	1	0	0	0	0	0	3	0	1	.000	.375	.000	9	0	1	.818	-1	98	116	/2-2	-0.1

Year	Tm Lg	G	AB	R	H	2B	3B	HR	RBI	BB-IB	HP	SO	AVG	OBP	SLG	AOPS	ABR	SB-CS	FA	FR	Rng	Thr	G at Pos	BFW
PETTIGREW, NED Jim Ned B 8.25.1881 Honey Grove, TX D 8.20.1952 Duncan, OK BR/TR 5-11/175# d4.23																								
1914	Buf F	2	2	0	0	0	0	0	0	0	0	0	.000	.000	.000	-98	-1	0	—	0			H	-0.1
PETTINI, JOE Joseph Paul B 1.26.1955 Wheeling, WV BR/TR 5-9/165# d7.10 C2																								
1980	SF N	63	190	19	44	3	1	1	9	17-1	0	33	.232	.295	.274	61	-10	5-2	.955	-13	81	72	S-42,3-18/2-8	-2.0
1981	SF N	35	29	3	2	1	0	0	2	4-0	0	5	.069	.182	.103	-18	-5	1-0	.920	-2	102	31	2-12,S-12/3-9	-0.6
1982	SF N	29	39	5	8	1	0	0	2	3-0	0	4	.205	.262	.231	39	-3	0-1	.934	-3	87	72	S-26/3	-0.5
1983	SF N	61	86	11	16	0	1	0	7	9-1	0	11	.186	.260	.209	33	-8	4-1	.949	1	89	119	S-26,2-14,3-12	-0.4
Total 4		188	344	38	70	5	2	1	20	33-2	0	53	.203	.272	.238	45	-26	10-4	.943	-16	84	85	S-106/3-40,2-34	-3.5
PETTIS, GARY Gary George B 4.3.1958 Oakland, CA BB/TR 6-1/165# d9.13 C3																								
1982	Cal A	10	5	5	1	0	0	1	1	0-0	0	2	.200	.200	.800	159	0	0-0	1.000	1	99	798	/O-8(1-6-1)	0.1
1983	Cal A	22	85	19	25	2	3	3	6	7-0	0	15	.294	.348	.494	130	3	8-3	.982	1	82	362	O-21(0-20-1)	0.4
1984	Cal A	140	397	63	90	11	6	2	29	60-1	3	115	.227	.332	.300	77	-11	48-17	.983	6	106	145	*O-134(CF)	-0.2
1985	Cal A	125	443	67	114	10	8	1	32	62-0	0	125	.257	.347	.323	86	-7	56-9	.990	9	108	162	*O-122(CF)	0.9
1986	†Cal A	154	539	93	139	23	4	5	58	69-2	0	132	.258	.339	.343	88	-7	50-13	.985	11	**113**	109	*O-153(CF)/D	0.8
1987	Cal A	133	394	49	82	13	2	1	17	52-0	1	124	.208	.302	.259	53	-26	24-5	.980	6	115	39	*O-131(CF)	-1.7
1988	Det A	129	458	65	96	14	4	3	36	47-0	1	85	.210	.285	.277	60	-24	44-10	.987	6	110	90	*O-126(CF)/D-2	-1.4
1989	Det A	119	444	77	114	8	6	1	18	84-0	0	106	.257	.375	.309	97	2	43-15	.988	-2	105	16	*O-119(CF)	0.3
1990	Tex A	136	423	66	101	16	8	3	31	57-0	4	118	.239	.333	.336	88	-6	38-15	.993	1	95	170	*O-128(CF)/D-2	-0.3
1991	Tex A	137	282	37	61	7	5	0	19	54-0	0	91	.216	.341	.277	75	-8	29-13	.977	1	107	87	*O-126(CF)/D-3	-0.6
1992	SD N	30	30	0	6	1	0	0	0	2-0	0	11	.200	.250	.233	37	-2	1-0	.952	0	134	0	O-14(0-13-1)	-0.2
	Det A	48	129	27	26	4	3	1	12	27-0	0	34	.202	.338	.302	81	-3	13-4	.993	3	113	76	O-46(CF)	0.1
Total 11		1183	3629	568	855	109	49	21	259	521-3	9	958	.236	.332	.310	80	-89	354-104	.986	41	107	108	*O-1128(1-1125-3)/D-8	-1.8
PETTIT, BOB Robert Henry B 7.19.1861 Williamstown, MA D 11.1.1910 Derby, CT BL/TR 5-9/160# d9.3																								
1887	Chi N	32	138	29	36	3	3	2	12	8	0	15	.261	.301	.370	76	-6	16	.894	-1	145	0	O-32(RF)/CP	-0.6
1888	Chi N	43	169	23	43	1	4	4	23	7	1	9	.254	.288	.379	104	0	7	.931	-0	133	246	O-43(0-2-42)	-0.1
1891	Mil AA	21	80	10	14	4	0	1	5	7	3	7	.175	.267	.262	43	-6	2	.932	-3	116	32	/2-9,O-7(3-2-2),3-6	-0.8
Total 3		96	387	62	93	8	7	7	40	22	4	31	.240	.288	.351	79	-12	25	.919	-4	131	126	/O-82(3-4-76),2-9,3-6,PC	-1.5
PEVEY, MARTY Marty Ashley B 12.25.1962 Savannah, GA BL/TR 6-1/185# d5.16 C1																								
1989	Mon N	13	41	2	9	1	1	0	3	0-0	0	8	.220	.220	.293	45	-3	0-0	.985	-4	50	107	C-11/O(RF)	-0.7
PEZOLD, LARRY Lorenz Johannes B 6.22.1893 New Orleans, LA D 10.22.1957 Baton Rouge, LA BR/TR 5-9.5/175# d7.27																								
1914	Cle A	23	71	4	16	0	1	0	5	9	0	6	.225	.313	.254	68	-3	2-3	.827	-1	105	63	3-20/O(RF)	-0.5
PFEFFER, FRED Nathaniel Frederick "Fritz" or "Dandelion" B 3.17.1860 Louisville, KY D 4.10.1932 Chicago, IL BR/TR 5-10.5/184# d5.1 M1 ▲ OF Total (2-CF 1-RF)																								
1882	Tro N	**85**	330	26	72	7	4	1	43	1		24	.218	.221	.273	60	-15		.857	10	105	133	*S-83/2-2	-0.2
1883	Chi N	96	371	41	87	22	7	1	45	8		50	.235	.251	.340	71	-14		.887	16	108	**141**	*2-79,S-18/31	0.5
1884	Chi N	**112**	467	105	135	10	10	25	101	25		47	.289	.325	.514	148	22		.903	**43**	**117**	**185**	*2-112/P	**6.0**
1885	†Chi N	112	469	90	113	12	7	5	73	26		47	.241	.281	.328	85	-10		.893	22	112	**159**	*2-109/P-5,O(RF)	1.5
1886	†Chi N	118	474	88	125	17	8	7	95	36		46	.264	.316	.378	96	-5	30	.903	8	94	**148**	*2-118/1	0.7
1887	Chi N	123	479	95	133	21	6	16	89	34	1	20	.278	.327	.447	100	-3	57	.917	23	98	**133**	*2-123/O-2(CF)	2.0
1888	Chi N	**135**	517	90	129	22	10	8	57	32	3	38	.250	.297	.377	106	2	64	.931	**38**	**104**	**151**	*2-135	**4.4**
1889	Chi N	134	531	85	128	15	7	7	77	53	3	51	.241	.313	.335	77	-19	45	.943	10	104	113	*2-134	-0.3
1890	Chi P	124	499	86	128	21	8	5	80	44	2	23	.257	.319	.361	78	-18	27	.916	20	98	**129**	*2-124	0.5
1891	Chi N	**137**	498	93	123	12	9	7	77	79	3	60	.247	.353	.349	105	5	40	.921	24	105	**137**	*2-137	3.0
1892	Lou N	124	470	78	121	14	9	2	76	67	2	36	.257	.353	.338	119	14	27	.932	8	104	**149**	*2-116,1-10/PM	2.5
1893	Lou N	125	508	85	129	29	12	3	75	51	0	18	.254	.322	.376	93	-6	32	.939	12	101	118	*2-125	0.9
1894	Lou N	105	414	70	128	12	15	5	61	30	1	14	.309	.357	.447	100	-2	32	.939	15	103	134	*2-91,S-15/P	1.4
1895	Lou N	11	45	8	13	1	0	0	5	5	0	3	.289	.360	.311	79	-1	2	.742	-3	67	122	/S-5,2-3,1-3	-0.3
1896	NY N	4	14	1	2	0	0	0	4	1	1	1	.143	.250	.143	5	-2	0	.760	-2	82	0	/2-4	-0.3
	Chi N	94	360	45	88	16	7	2	52	23	2	20	.244	.294	.344	65	-20	22	.947	7	105	107	*2-94	-0.7
	Year	98	374	46	90	16	7	2	56	24	3	21	.241	.292	.337	63	-22	22	.939	5	104	103	2-98	-1.0
1897	Chi N	32	114	10	26	0	1	0	11	12	3		.228	.318	.246	48	-8	5	.883	-4	94	104	2-32	-1.0
Total 16		1671	6560	1096	1680	231	120	94	1021	527	21	<u>498</u>	.256	.313	.371	93	-80	383	.920	246	104	137	*2-1538,S-121/1-15,P-8,O-3C,3	20.6
PFEIL, BOBBY Robert Raymond B 11.13.1943 Passaic, NJ BR/TR 6-1/180# d6.26																								
1969	NY N	62	211	20	49	9	0	0	10	7-0	1	27	.232	.260	.275	49	-15	0-1	.976	-3	101	120	3-49,2-11/O-2(LF)	-1.8
1971	Phi N	44	70	5	19	3	0	2	9	6-1	0	9	.271	.329	.400	106	0	1-1	1.000	-2	101	292	3-15/C-4,O-3(2-0-1),12S	-0.1
Total 2		106	281	25	68	12	0	2	19	13-1	1	36	.242	.278	.306	63	-15	1-2	.980	-4	101	158	/3-64,2-12,O-5(4-0-1),C-4,S1	-1.9
PFISTER, GEORGE George Edward B 9.4.1918 Bound Brook, NJ D 8.14.1997 Somerset, NJ BR/TR 6/200# d9.27 C1																								
1941	Bro N	1	2	0	0	0	0	0	0	0	0	0	.000	.000	.000	-96	-1	0	—	0	*0*	*0*	/C	-0.1
PFYL, MONTE Meinhard Charles B 5.11.1884 St.Louis, MO D 10.18.1945 San Francisco, CA BL/TL 6-3/190# d7.30																								
1907	NY N	1	0	0	0	0	0	0	0	0	0	0	—	—	—		0	0	—	0	0	0	/1	0.0
PHELAN, ART Arthur Thomas "Dugan" B 8.14.1887 Niantic, IL D 12.27.1964 Ft.Worth, TX BR/TR 5-8/160# d6.25																								
1910	Cin N	23	42	7	9	0	0	0	4	7	0	6	.214	.327	.214	61	-2	5	1.000	-0	112	0	/3-8,2-5,O-3(LF),S	-0.2
1912	Cin N	130	461	56	112	9	11	3	54	46	2	37	.243	.314	.330	79	-15	25	.924	-1	102	103	*3-127/2-3	-1.2
1913	Chi N	91	261	41	65	11	6	2	35	29	3	26	.249	.331	.360	97	-1	8-8	.931	-2	100	82	2-46,3-38/S	-0.3
1914	Chi N	25	46	5	13	2	1	0	3	4	0	3	.283	.340	.370	111	1	0	.905	-1	110	0	/3-7,2-3,S-2	0.0
1915	Chi N	133	448	41	98	16	7	3	35	55	2	42	.219	.307	.306	86	-7	12-9	.939	-2	94	92	*3-110,2-24	-0.6
Total 5		402	1258	150	297	38	25	8	131	141	7	114	.236	.317	.325	86	-24	50-<u>17</u>	.931	-6	99	89	3-290/2-81,S-4,O-3(LF)	-2.3
PHELAN, DAN Daniel T. B 7.23.1864 Thomaston, CT D 12.7.1945 West Haven, CT BL 5-10/175# d4.18																								
1890	Lou AA	8	32	4	8	1	1	0	4	0	0		.250	.250	.344	77	-1	1	.975	0	99	0	/1-8	-0.2
PHELAN, DICK James Dickson B 12.10.1854 Towanda, PA D 2.13.1931 San Antonio, TX BR d4.17																								
1884	Bal U	101	402	63	99	13	3	3		12			.246	.268	.316	69	-28		.872	-12	94	104	*2-100/3-5,O(CF)	-3.2
1885	Buf N	4	16	2	2	0	0	1	3	0		3	.125	.125	.313	37	-1		.808	-1	120	102	/2-4	-0.1
	StL N	2	4	1	1	1	0	0	1	0		2	.250	.250	.500	147	0		1.000	-0	0	0	/3-2	0.0
	Year	6	20	3	3	1	0	1	4	0		5	.150	.150	.350	58	-1		.808	-1	120	102	/2-4,3-2	-0.1
Total 2		107	422	66	102	14	3	4	<u>4</u>	12		<u>5</u>	.242	.263	.318	69	-29		.869	-13	95	104	2-104/3-7,O(CF)	-3.3
PHELPS, NEALY Cornelius Carman B 11.19.1840 New York, NY D 2.12.1885 New York, NY d7.1																								
1871	Kek NA	1	3	0	0	0	0	0	0	1		0	.000	.250	.000	-20	0	0-0	.889	-0	0	205	/1	0.0
1873	Mut NA	1	6	0	0	0	0	0	0	0		0	.000	.000	.000	-99	-1	0-0	1.000	0	0	0	/1O(RF)	-0.1
1874	Mut NA	6	24	5	3	0	0	0	2	0		0	.125	.125	.125	-19	-3	0-0	.818	1	196	610	/O-6(RF)	-0.1
1875	Mut NA	2	6	1	2	1	0	0	0	0		1	.333	.333	.500	176	0	0-0	1.000	1	389	0	/O-2(RF)	0.1
1876	NY N	1	3	0	0	0	0	0	0	0		1	.000	.000	.000	-99	-1		.667	-0	0	0	/O(CF)	-0.1
	Phi N	1	4	0	0	0	0	0	0	0		0	.000	.000	.000	-99	-1		.571	-1			/C	-0.2
	Year	2	7	0	0	0	0	0	0	0		1	.000	.000	.000	-99	-1		.667	-2	0	0	/O(CF)C	-0.3
Total 4 NA		10	39	6	5	1	0	0	2	1		1	.128	.150	.154	-3	-4	0-0	.000	1			/O-9(RF),1-2	-0.1
PHELPS, ED Edward Jaykill "Yaller" B 3.3.1879 Albany, NY D 1.31.1942 E.Greenbush, NY BR/TR 5-11/185# d9.3																								
1902	Pit N	18	61	5	13	1	0	0	6	4	2		.213	.284	.230	57	-3	2	.968	-3	*120*	*66*	C-13/1-5	-0.5
1903	†Pit N	81	273	32	77	7	3	2	31	17	6		.282	.338	.352	94	-3	2	.980	0	***133***	*81*	C-76/1-3	0.4
1904	Pit N	94	302	29	73	5	5	0	28	15	5		.242	.289	.278	73	-10	2	.964	-6	*106*	*84*	C-91/1	-0.7
1905	Cin N	44	156	18	36	5	3	0	18	12	5		.231	.306	.301	73	-5	4	.949	-3	*94*	*85*	C-44	-0.4
1906	Cin N	12	40	3	11	0	2	1	5	3	0		.275	.326	.450	136	1	2	.987	-0	*95*	*85*	C-12	0.3
	Pit N	43	118	9	28	3	1	0	12	9	2		.237	.302	.280	78	-3	1	.971	-1	*121*	*66*	C-40	0.0
	Year	55	158	12	39	3	3	1	17	12	2		.247	.308	.323	93	-2	3	.975	-1	*114*	*71*	C-52	0.3
1907	Pit N	43	113	11	24	1	0	0	12	9	2		.212	.282	.221	57	-5	1	.979	1	*126*	*92*	C-35/1	-0.1
1908	Pit N	34	64	3	15	2	2	0	11	2	1		.234	.269	.328	90	-1	0	.977	0	*127*	*71*	C-20	0.1
1909	StL N	104	306	43	76	13	1	0	22	39	9		.248	.350	.297	108	6	7	.954	-14	*75*	*92*	C-83	-0.1

Year	Tm Lg	G	AB	R	H	2B	3B	HR	RBI	BB-IB	HP	SO	AVG	OBP	SLG	AOPS	ABR	SB-CS	FA	FR	Rng	Thr	G at Pos	BFW
1910	StL N	93	270	25	71	4	2	0	37	36	3	29	.263	.356	.293	93	-1	9	.976	-18	73	81	C-80	-1.2
1912	Bro N	52	111	8	32	4	3	0	23	16	2	15	.288	.388	.378	114	3	1	.976	-2	86	93	C-32	0.3
1913	Bro N	15	18	0	4	0	0	0	0	1	0	2	.222	.263	.222	38	-1	0	.875	-1	71	60	/C-4	-0.3
Total	11	633	1832	186	460	45	20	3	205	163	37	46	.251	.325	.302	88	-22	31	.968	-46	101	83	C-530/1-10	-2.2
PHELPS, BABE Ernest Gordon "Blimp" B 4.19.1908 Odenton, MD D 12.10.1992 Odenton, MD BL/TR 6-2/225# d9.17																								
1931	Was A	3	3	0	1	0	0	0	0	0	0	0	.333	.333	.333	75	0	0-0	—	0			H	0.0
1933	Chi N	3	7	0	2	0	0	0	2	0	0	1	.286	.286	.286	64	0	0	1.000	1	0	228	/C-2	0.0
1934	Chi N	44	70	7	20	5	2	2	12	1	0	8	.286	.296	.500	111	1	0	.981	-1	145	143	C-18	0.0
1935	Bro N	47	121	17	44	7	2	5	22	9	0	10	.364	.408	.579	165	11	0	.957	-0	114	97	C-34	1.2
1936	Bro N	115	319	36	117	23	2	5	57	27	3	18	.367	.421	.498	145	22	1	.977	-10	65	112	C-98/O(RF)	1.6
1937	Bro N	121	409	42	128	37	3	7	58	25	3	28	.313	.357	.469	121	12	2	.971	-3	85	104	*C-111	1.5
1938	Bro N✳	66	208	33	64	12	2	5	46	23	1	15	.308	.379	.457	126	8	2	.980	-2	82	87	C-55	0.9
1939	Bro N★	98	323	33	92	21	2	6	42	24	1	24	.285	.336	.418	98	-1	0	.980	3	110	93	C-92	0.7
1940	Bro N★	118	370	47	109	24	5	13	61	30	1	27	.295	.349	.492	122	11	2	.977	-4	121	55	C-99/1	1.2
1941	Bro N	16	30	3	7	3	0	2	4	1	0	2	.233	.258	.533	114	0	0	.971	-0	227	0	C-11	0.1
1942	Pit N	95	257	21	73	11	1	9	41	20	4	24	.284	.345	.440	126	8	2	.959	-3	87	99	C-72	1.0
Total	11	726	2117	239	657	143	19	54	345	160	13	157	.310	.362	.472	124	72	9-0	.974	-19	97	92	C-592/1O(RF)	8.2
PHELPS, JOSH Joshua Lee B 5.12.1978 Anchorage, AK BR/TR 6-3/215# d6.13																								
2000	Tor A	1	1	0	0	0	0	0	0	0-0	0	1	.000	.000	.000	-97	0	0-0	1.000	-0	0	0	/C	0.0
2001	Tor A	8	12	3	0	0	0	0	1	2-0	0	5	.000	.143	.000	-56	-3	1-0	1.000	0	74	161	/C-7	-0.2
2002	Tor A	74	265	41	82	20	1	15	58	19-0	3	82	.309	.362	.562	136	13	0-0	1.000	-0	0	112	D-71/1-2	0.8
2003	Tor A	119	396	57	106	18	1	20	66	39-3	17	115	.268	.358	.470	114	9	1-2	.967	-1	83	33	*D-106/1-8	0.0
Total	4	202	674	101	188	38	2	35	125	60-3	20	203	.279	.355	.497	119	19	2-2	.971	-1	72	43	D-177/1-10,C-8	0.6
PHELPS, KEN Kenneth Allen B 8.6.1954 Seattle, WA BL/TL 6-1/209# d9.20																								
1980	KC A	3	4	0	0	0	0	0	0	0-0	0	2	.000	.000	.000	-99	-1	0-0	1.000	-0	0	243	/1-2	-0.1
1981	KC A	21	22	1	3	0	1	0	1	1-0	0	13	.136	.174	.227	15	-3	0-0	1.000	0	451	0	/1-2,D-4	-0.2
1982	Mon N	10	8	0	2	0	0	0	0	0-0	1	3	.250	.333	.250	64	0	0-0	—	0			H	-0.1
1983	Sea A	50	127	10	30	4	1	7	16	13-0	0	25	.236	.301	.449	101	0	0-0	1.000	2	116	60	1-22,D-19	-0.1
1984	Sea A	101	290	52	70	9	0	24	51	61-5	5	73	.241	.378	.521	149	21	3-3	.987	-1	62	84	D-84/1-9	1.7
1985	Sea A	61	116	18	24	3	0	9	24	24-2	0	33	.207	.343	.466	118	3	2-0	1.000	-1	58	116	D-25/1-8	0.2
1986	Sea A	125	344	69	85	16	4	24	64	88-6	6	96	.247	.406	.526	151	29	2-3	.983	-4	82	118	1-55,D-52	1.9
1987	Sea A	120	332	68	86	13	1	27	68	80-5	8	75	.259	.410	.548	145	25	1-1	1.000	-0	0	0	*D-114/1	2.0
1988	Sea A	72	190	37	54	8	0	14	32	51-2	1	35	.284	.434	.547	167	20	1-0	.952	-0	105	89	D-68/1-3	1.8
	NY A	45	107	17	24	5	0	10	22	19-3	0	26	.224	.339	.551	147	7	0-0	—	0	0	0	D-24/1	0.6
	Year	117	297	54	78	13	0	24	54	70-5	1	61	.263	.402	.549	160	27	1-0	.952	-0	101	85	D-92/1-4	2.4
1989	NY A	86	185	26	46	3	0	7	29	27-2	0	47	.249	.340	.378	105	2	0-0	.980	-1	35	99	D-55/1-8	-0.1
	†Oak A	11	9	0	1	1	0	0	0	4-0	0	0	.111	.385	.222	78	0	0-0	—	-0	0	0	/1D	0.0
	Year	97	194	26	47	4	0	7	29	31-2	0	47	.242	.342	.371	104	2	0-0	.980	-1	28	80	D-56/1-9	-0.1
1990	Oak A	32	59	6	11	2	0	1	6	12-1	0	10	.186	.319	.271	71	-2	0-0	.964	0	176	171	D-15/1-5	-0.2
	Cle A	24	61	4	7	0	0	0	0	10-2	0	11	.115	.239	.115	2	-8	1-0	1.000	-0	92	41	1-14/D-6	-0.9
	Year	56	120	10	18	2	0	1	6	22-3	0	21	.150	.280	.192	36	-10	1-0	.992	0	106	63	D-21,1-19	-1.1
Total	11	761	1854	308	443	64	7	123	313	390-28	21	449	.239	.374	.480	132	93	10-7	.987	-5	86	95	D-467,1-131	6.5
PHILLEY, DAVE David Earl B 5.16.1920 Paris, TX BB/TR 6/188# d9.6 Mil 1943-45																								
1941	Chi A	7	9	4	2	1	0	0	0	3	0	3	.222	.417	.333	102	0	0-0	—	-0	0	0	/O-2(LF)	0.0
1946	Chi A	17	68	10	24	2	3	0	17	4	0	4	.353	.389	.471	145	4	5-0	.983	3	113	197	O-17(16-1-0)	0.6
1947	Chi A	143	551	55	142	25	11	2	45	35	1	39	.258	.303	.354	85	-14	21-16	.986	-1	97	97	*O-133(39-95-0)/3-4	-2.2
1948	Chi A	137	488	51	140	28	3	5	42	50	0	33	.287	.353	.387	100	0	8-10	.978	10	100	**200**	*O-128(6-123-0)	0.4
1949	Chi A	146	598	84	171	20	8	0	44	54	2	51	.286	.347	.346	86	-13	13-4	.977	-2	95	115	*O-145(0-3-143)	-1.7
1950	Chi A	**156**	619	69	150	21	5	14	80	52	1	57	.242	.302	.360	71	-31	6-3	.980	5	100	141	*O-154(0-70-103)	-2.9
1951	Chi A	7	25	0	6	2	0	0	2	2	0	3	.240	.296	.320	68	-1	0-0	.938	-1	100	0	/O-6(LF)	-0.2
	Phi A	125	468	71	123	18	7	7	59	63	3	38	.263	.354	.376	95	-2	9-6	.978	-3	92	125	*O-120(2-116-2)/3-2	-0.9
	Year	132	493	71	129	20	7	7	61	65	3	41	.262	.351	.373	94	-4	9-6	.976	-4	92	118	*O-126(8-116-2)/3-2	-1.1
1952	Phi A	151	586	80	154	25	4	7	71	59	4	35	.263	.334	.355	86	-10	11-4	.991	7	106	112	*O-149(CF)/3-2	-0.7
1953	Phi A	**157**	620	80	188	30	9	9	59	51	2	35	.303	.358	.424	106	5	13-5	.981	-4	92	128	*O-157(0-31-129)/3	-0.4
1954	†Cle A	133	452	48	102	13	3	12	60	57	0	48	.226	.308	.347	79	-14	2-4	.984	-4	99	64	*O-129(1-0-129)	-2.4
1955	Cle A	43	104	15	31	4	2	2	9	12-2	0	10	.298	.368	.433	111	2	0-2	1.000	0	98	108	O-34(2-0-32)	0.0
	Bal A	83	311	50	93	13	3	6	41	34-2	0	38	.299	.367	.418	119	8	1-2	.970	-3	95	92	O-82(46-2-48)/3-2	0.1
	Year	126	415	65	124	17	5	8	50	46-4	0	48	.299	.367	.422	116	9	1-4	.976	-2	96	96	*O-116(48-2-80)/3-2	0.1
1956	Bal A	32	117	13	24	4	2	1	17	18-3	0	13	.205	.309	.299	67	-6	3-1	.935	-1	101	95	O-31(23-0-16)/3-5	-0.7
	Chi A	86	279	44	74	14	2	4	47	28-0	1	27	.265	.328	.373	85	-6	1-3	.978	-4	69	88	1-51,O-30(17-0-19)	-1.4
	Year	118	396	57	98	18	4	5	64	46-3	1	40	.247	.322	.351	80	-12	4-4	.965	-5	99	98	O-61(40-0-35),1-51/3-5	-2.1
1957	Chi A	22	71	9	23	4	0	0	9	4-0	0	10	.324	.360	.380	102	0	1-1	.975	-0	121	0	O-17(RF)/1-2	-0.1
	Det A	65	173	15	49	8	1	2	16	7-0	0	16	.283	.309	.376	85	-4	3-1	.996	3	147	80	1-27,O-12(4-0-8)/3	-0.3
	Year	87	244	24	72	12	1	2	25	11-0	0	26	.295	.324	.377	90	-4	4-2	.965	2	115	0	O-29(4-0-25),1-29/3	-0.4
1958	Phi N	91	207	30	64	11	4	3	31	15-3	1	20	.309	.357	.444	113	4	1-1	1.000	-2	98	0	O-24(RF),1-18	0.0
1959	Phi N	99	254	32	74	18	2	7	37	18-3	1	27	.291	.339	.461	109	3	0-0	1.000	0	106	156	O-34(RF),1-24	0.1
1960	Phi N	14	15	2	5	2	0	0	4	3-1	0	2	.333	.444	.467	149	1	0-0	—	-1	0	0	/O-3(2-0-1),1-2	0.1
	SF N	39	61	5	10	0	0	1	7	6-0	0	14	.164	.239	.213	26	-6	0-0	.941	-1	97	0	O-10(LF)/3-3	-0.8
	Year	53	76	7	15	2	0	1	11	9-1	0	16	.197	.282	.263	53	-5	0-0	.941	-2	93	0	O-13(12-0-1)/3-3,1-2	-0.7
	Bal A	14	34	6	9	2	1	1	5	4-0	0	5	.265	.342	.471	119	1	1-0	1.000	-1	99	0	/O-8(6-0-2),3	0.0
1961	Bal A	99	144	13	36	9	2	1	23	10-0	0	20	.250	.293	.361	78	-5	2-0	1.000	-3	68	0	O-25(22-0-3)/1	-0.8
1962	Bos A	38	42	3	6	2	0	0	4	5-0	1	3	.143	.250	.190	20	-5	0-0	1.000	-0	101	0	/O-4(RF)	-0.5
Total	18	1904	6296	789	1700	276	72	84	729	594-14	17	551	.270	.334	.377	91	-89	101-63	.981	-2	98	115	*O-1454(204-590-714),1-125/3-21	-14.7
PHILLIPS, ADOLFO Adolfo Emilio (Lopez) B 12.16.1941 Bethania, Panama BR/TR 6/177# d9.2																								
1964	Phi N	13	13	4	3	0	0	0	0	3-0	0	3	.231	.375	.231	76	0	0-0	1.000	1	114	654	/O-4(3-2-1)	0.1
1965	Phi N	41	87	14	20	4	0	3	5	5-0	0	34	.230	.272	.379	83	-2	3-3	1.000	-1	102	0	O-32(2-30-0)	-0.4
1966	Phi N	2	3	1	0	0	0	0	0	0-0	0	0	.000	.000	.000	-99	-1	0-0	1.000	-0	87	0	/O(CF)	-0.1
	Chi N	116	416	68	109	29	1	16	36	43-3	12	135	.262	.348	.452	119	12	32-15	.978	5	101	180	*O-111(CF)	1.7
	Year	118	419	69	109	29	1	16	36	43-3	12	135	.260	.346	.449	118	12	32-15	.979	5	101	**178**	*O-112(CF)	1.6
1967	Chi N	144	448	66	120	20	7	17	70	80-**29**	6	93	.268	.384	.458	134	23	24-10	.981	8	106	**164**	*O-141(CF)	3.1
1968	Chi N	143	439	49	106	20	5	13	33	47-20	5	90	.241	.320	.399	108	5	9-7	.979	2	100	130	*O-141(CF)	0.3
1969	Chi N	28	49	5	11	3	1	0	1	16-3	1	15	.224	.424	.327	100	1	1-3	.956	-0	112	0	O-25(1-24-0)	-0.1
	Mon N	58	199	25	43	4	4	4	7	19-1	1	62	.216	.286	.337	74	-8	6-5	.981	-1	97	106	O-53(CF)	-1.1
	Year	86	248	30	54	7	5	4	8	35-4	2	77	.218	.318	.335	80	-6	7-8	.973	-2	101	77	O-78(1-77-0)	-1.2
1970	Mon N	92	214	36	51	6	3	6	21	36-1	2	51	.238	.352	.379	96	0	7-1	.985	-1	106	32	O-75(6-71-0)	-0.1
1972	Cle A	12	7	2	0	0	0	0	0	2-0	0	2	.000	.222	.000	-29	-1	0-0	1.000	0	129	0	O-10(6-2-2)	-0.1
Total	8	649	1875	270	463	86	21	59	173	251-57	27	485	.247	.343	.410	110	29	82-44	.980	13	103	129	O-593(18-576-3)	3.3
PHILLIPS, BRANDON Brandon Emil B 6.28.1981 Raleigh, NC BR/TR 5-11/185# d9.13																								
2002	Cle A	11	31	5	8	3	1	0	4	3-0	1	6	.258	.343	.419	103	0	0-0	.957	0	108	61	2-11	0.1
2003	Cle A	112	370	36	77	18	1	6	33	14-0	3	77	.208	.242	.311	46	-30	4-5	.981	16	112	112	*2-109	-0.9
Total	2	123	401	41	85	21	2	6	37	17-0	4	83	.212	.251	.319	51	-30	4-5	.979	16	112	108	2-120	-0.8
PHILLIPS, J. R. Charles Gene B 4.29.1970 West Covina, CA BL/TL 6-1/185# d9.3																								
1993	SF N	11	16	1	5	1	1	1	4	0-0	0	5	.313	.313	.688	164	1	0-0	.971	-0	88	45	/1-5	0.1
1994	SF N	15	38	1	5	0	0	1	3	1-0	0	13	.132	.150	.211	-7	-6	1-0	.989	1	154	103	1-10	-0.6
1995	SF N	92	231	27	45	9	0	9	28	19-2	0	69	.195	.256	.351	60	-15	1-1	.993	-3	85	95	1-79/O(LF)	-2.4
1996	SF N	15	25	3	5	0	0	2	5	1-0	0	13	.200	.231	.440	75	-1	0-0	.981	-1	51	87	1-10	-0.3
	Phi N	35	79	9	12	5	0	5	10	10-1	1	38	.152	.256	.405	70	-4	0-0	.957	3	178	119	O-15(RF),1-11	-0.2
	Year	50	104	12	17	5	0	7	15	11-1	1	51	.163	.250	.413	71	-5	0-0	.992	2	54	102	1-21,O-15(RF)	-0.5

Year	Tm Lg	G	AB	R	H	2B	3B	HR	RBI	BB-IB	HP	SO	AVG	OBP	SLG	AOPS	ABR	SB-CS	FA	FR	Rng	Thr	G at Pos	BFW
1997	Hou N	13	15	2	2	0	0	1	4	0-0	0	7	.133	.125	.333	18	-2	0-0	1.000	-0	0	106	/1-3,O-3(RF)	-0.2
1998	Hou N	36	58	4	11	0	0	2	9	7-1	0	22	.190	.277	.293	51	-4	0-0	.962	-1	101	107	1-12/O-6(LF)	-0.6
1999	Col N	25	39	5	9	4	0	2	4	0-0	1	13	.231	.250	.487	63	-2	0-0	.933	2	103	848	/O-7(1-0-6),1-4	0.0
Total	7	242	501	52	94	19	1	23	67	38-4	2	180	.188	.247	.367	59	-33	2-1	.989	1	87	97	1-134/O-32(8-0-24)	-4.2
PHILLIPS, DAMON Damon Roswell "Dee" B 6.8.1919 Corsicana, TX BR/TR 6/176# d7.19 Mil 1945																								
1942	Cin N	28	84	4	17	2	0	0	6	7	0	5	.202	.264	.226	44	-6	0	.964	3	110	124	S-27	-0.1
1944	Bos N	140	489	35	126	30	1	1	53	28	2	34	.258	.301	.329	74	-17	1	.932	2	109	155	3-90,S-60	-1.0
1946	Bos N	2	2	0	1	0	0	0	0	0	0	0	.500	.500	.500	182	0	0	—	0			H	0.0
Total	3	170	575	39	144	32	1	1	59	35	2	39	.250	.296	.315	70	-23	1	.932	5	109	155	/3-90,S-87	-1.1
PHILLIPS, EDDIE Edward David B 2.17.1901 Worcester, MA D 1.26.1968 Buffalo, NY BR/TR 6/178# d5.4																								
1924	Bos N	3	3	0	0	0	0	0	0	0	0	2	.000	.000	.000	-99	-1	0-0	1.000	-0	*0*	*817*	/C	-0.1
1929	Det A	68	221	24	52	13	1	2	21	20	1	16	.235	.302	.330	62	-13	0-1	.967	-8	*74*	*87*	C-63	-1.6
1931	Pit N	106	353	30	82	18	3	7	44	41	3	49	.232	.317	.360	82	-8	1	.986	-5	*99*	*74*	*C-103	-0.7
1932	NY A	9	31	4	9	1	0	2	4	2	0	3	.290	.333	.516	123	1	1-0	1.000	1	*113*	*122*	/C-9	0.2
1934	Was A	56	169	6	33	6	1	2	16	26	1	24	.195	.306	.278	54	-12	1-0	.984	-5	*148*	*98*	C-53	-1.2
1935	Cle A	70	220	18	60	16	1	1	41	15	0	21	.273	.319	.368	76	-8	0-0	.980	-7	*111*	*71*	C-69	-1.0
Total	6	312	997	82	236	54	6	14	126	104	5	115	.237	.312	.345	72	-41	3-1	.980	-24	*105*	*82*	C-298	-4.4
PHILLIPS, EDDIE Howard Edward B 7.8.1931 St.Louis, MO BB/TR 6-1/180# d9.10																								
1953	StL N	9	0	4	0	0	0	0	0	0	0	0	—	—	—	—	0	0-0	—	0			R	0.0
PHILLIPS, JACK Jack Dorn "Stretch" B 9.6.1921 Clarence, NY BR/TR 6-4/193# d8.22																								
1947	†NY A	16	36	5	10	0	1	1	2	3	0	5	.278	.333	.417	109	0	0-0	.986	-2	17	118	1-10	-0.2
1948	NY A	1	2	0	0	0	0	0	0	0	0	1	.000	.000	.000	-99	-1	0-0	.889	-0	0	0	/1	-0.1
1949	NY A	45	91	16	28	4	1	1	10	12	0	9	.308	.388	.407	110	2	1-0	.977	-2	73	110	1-38	-0.2
	Pit N	18	56	6	13	3	1	0	3	4	0	6	.232	.283	.321	60	-3	1	1.000	-0	94	91	1-16/3	-0.4
1950	Pit N	69	208	25	61	7	6	5	34	20	0	17	.293	.355	.457	108	2	1	.986	1	119	96	1-54/3-3,P	0.1
1951	Pit N	70	156	12	37	7	3	0	12	15	0	17	.237	.304	.321	66	-7	1-2	.991	-1	88	107	1-53/3-4	-1.0
1952	Pit N	1	1	0	0	0	0	0	0	0	0	0	.000	.000	.000	-97	0	0-0	1.000	-0	0	451	/1	0.0
1955	Det A	55	117	15	37	8	2	1	20	10-0	0	12	.316	.364	.444	121	3	0-0	.992	-2	77	71	1-35/3-3	0.0
1956	Det A	67	224	31	66	13	2	1	20	21-0	0	19	.295	.354	.384	95	-1	1-1	.981	-2	97	99	1-56/2O(LF)	-0.6
1957	Det A	1	1	1	0	0	0	0	0	0-0	0	0	.000	.000	.000	-97	0	0-0	—	0			H	0.0
Total	9	343	892	111	252	42	16	9	101	85-0	0	86	.283	.344	.396	95	-5	5-3	.986	-8	92	98	1-264/3-11,O(LF)2P	-2.4
PHILLIPS, JASON Jason Lloyd B 9.27.1976 LaMesa, CA BR/TR 6-1/177# d9.19																								
2001	NY N	6	7	2	1	1	0	0	0	0-0	0	1	.143	.143	.286	7	-1	0-0	1.000	0	96	0	/C-5	-0.1
2002	NY N	11	19	4	7	0	0	1	3	1-0	1	1	.368	.409	.526	160	2	0-0	1.000	-0	0	89	/C-7	0.2
2003	NY N	119	403	45	120	25	0	11	58	39-3	10	50	.298	.373	.442	116	10	0-1	.990	-6	91	104	1-84,C-29	-0.1
Total	3	136	429	51	128	26	0	12	61	40-3	11	52	.298	.371	.443	116	11	0-1	.990	-6	91	104	/1-84,C-41	0.0
PHILLIPS, BUBBA John Melvin B 2.24.1928 West Point, MS D 6.22.1993 Hattiesburg, MS BR/TR 5-9/180# d4.30																								
1955	Det A	95	184	18	43	4	0	3	23	14-1	2	20	.234	.289	.304	63	-10	2-1	.992	3	120	47	O-65(61-2-4)/3-4	-1.0
1956	Chi A	67	99	16	27	6	0	2	11	6-0	1	12	.273	.321	.394	87	-2	1-2	1.000	3	128	124	O-35(6-7-22)/3-2	0.0
1957	Chi A	121	393	38	106	13	3	7	42	28-3	3	32	.270	.322	.372	89	-7	5-3	.958	11	115	111	3-97,O-20(1-13-8)	0.3
1958	Chi A	84	260	26	71	10	0	5	30	15-3	1	14	.273	.310	.369	89	-4	3-0	.954	1	103	149	3-47,O-37(19-15-4)	-0.4
1959	†Chi A	117	379	43	100	27	1	5	40	27-7	4	28	.264	.319	.380	92	-4	1-1	.951	3	109	85	*3-100,O-23(8-14-1)	-0.2
1960	Cle A	113	304	34	63	14	1	4	33	14-3	4	37	.207	.249	.299	50	-22	1-0	.953	-4	90	113	3-85,O-25(15-3-7)/S	-2.8
1961	Cle A	143	546	64	144	23	1	18	72	29-4	5	61	.264	.305	.408	92	-9	1-0	.958	-16	83	77	*3-143	-2.5
1962	Cle A	148	562	53	145	26	0	10	54	20-0	7	55	.258	.289	.358	76	-20	4-0	.977	-11	88	60	*3-145/O-3(CF),2	-3.1
1963	Det A	128	464	42	114	11	2	5	45	19-1	4	42	.246	.276	.310	63	-23	6-2	.961	1	97	125	*3-117/O-5(CF)	-2.4
1964	Det A	46	87	14	22	1	0	3	6	10-2	0	13	.253	.327	.368	92	-1	1-2	.983	1	105	149	3-22/O(LF)	0.0
Total	10	1062	3278	348	835	135	8	62	356	182-24	31	314	.255	.297	.358	79	-102	25-11	.960	-6	96	97	3-762,O-214(111-62-46)/2S	-12.1
PHILLIPS, TONY Keith Anthony B 4.25.1959 Atlanta, GA BB/TR 5-10/175# d5.10 OF Total (566-LF 97-CF 169-RF)																								
1982	Oak A	40	81	11	17	2	2	0	8	12-0	2	26	.210	.326	.284	73	-3	2-3	.953	-0	107	90	S-39	0.0
1983	Oak A	148	412	54	102	12	3	4	35	48-1	2	70	.248	.327	.320	85	-8	16-5	.941	-20	101	110	*S-101,2-63/3-4,D	-1.5
1984	Oak A	154	451	62	120	24	3	4	37	42-1	0	86	.266	.325	.359	97	-1	10-6	.941	-8	106	107	S-91,2-90/O(LF)	0.1
1985	Oak A	42	161	23	45	12	2	4	17	13-0	0	34	.280	.331	.453	122	5	3-2	.980	3	108	108	3-31,2-24	0.7
1986	Oak A	118	441	76	113	14	5	5	52	76-0	3	82	.256	.367	.345	103	6	15-10	.976	7	115	71	2-88,3-30/O-4(CF),SD	1.6
1987	Oak A	111	379	48	91	20	0	10	46	57-1	0	76	.240	.337	.372	95	-1	7-6	.974	1	103	73	2-87,3-11/S-9,O-2(1-0-1),D	0.4
1988	†Oak A	79	212	32	43	8	4	2	17	36-0	1	50	.203	.320	.307	80	-5	0-2	.913	-13	78	99	3-32,O-31(24-6-3),2-27,S-10/1-3,D-2	-1.9
1989	†Oak A	143	451	48	118	15	6	4	47	58-2	3	66	.262	.345	.348	101	2	3-8	.985	-8	104	96	2-84,3-49,S-17,O-16(13-0-4)/1	-0.6
1990	Det A	152	573	97	144	23	5	8	55	99-0	4	85	.251	.364	.351	100	5	19-9	.931	15	112	92	*3-104,2-47,S-11/O-8(4-1-4),D-4	2.3
1991	Det A	146	564	87	160	28	4	17	72	79-5	3	95	.284	.371	.438	122	19	10-5	.992	23	123	111	O-56(25-9-23),3-46,2-36,D-18,S-13	4.2
1992	Det A	159	606	**114**	167	32	3	10	64	114-2	1	93	.276	.387	.388	118	21	12-10	.968	11	122	72	O-69(14-24-35),2-57,D-34,3-20/S	3.0
1993	Det A	151	566	113	177	27	0	7	57	**132**-5	4	102	.313	.443	.398	130	35	16-11	.969	10	106	80	*O-108(70-9-34),2-51/3D	4.2
1994	Det A	114	438	91	123	19	3	19	61	95-3	2	105	.281	.409	.468	126	21	13-5	.980	8	112	83	*O-104(LF),2-12/D-6	2.5
1995	Cal A	139	525	119	137	21	1	27	61	113-6	3	135	.261	.394	.459	122	22	13-10	.924	7	107	122	3-88,O-48(47-8-0)/D-2	2.5
1996	Chi A	153	581	119	161	29	3	12	63	**125**-9	4	132	.277	.404	.399	111	17	13-8	.981	10	110	122	*O-150(150-2-0)/2-2,1	1.9
1997	Chi A	36	129	23	40	6	0	2	9	29-0	1	29	.310	.440	.403	127	8	4-1	.972	3	129	183	O-28(RF)/3-9	0.9
	Ana A	105	405	73	107	28	2	6	48	73-5	2	89	.264	.376	.388	101	4	9-9	.968	-12	88	78	2-43,O-35(31-2-3),D-26/3	-0.9
	Year	141	534	96	147	34	2	8	57	102-5	3	118	.275	.392	.391	107	12	13-10	.970	-9	108	107	O-63(31-2-31),2-43,D-26,3-10	0.0
1998	Tor A	13	48	9	17	5	0	1	7	9-1	2	6	.354	.467	.521	158	5	0-0	.960	-1	98	0	O-13(11-0-4)	0.4
	NY N	52	188	25	42	11	0	3	14	38-0	0	44	.223	.351	.330	83	-3	1-1	.967	-2	95	62	O-51(43-0-15)	-0.7
1999	Oak A	106	406	76	99	24	4	15	49	71-3	5	94	.244	.362	.433	107	6	11-3	.974	-7	97	107	2-66,O-62(28-32-15)/3-2,SD	0.2
Total	18	2161	7617	1300	2023	360	50	160	819	1319-44	42	1499	.266	.374	.389	109	155	177-114	.973	25	108	92	O-786L,2-777,3-428,S-294,D-101/1	19.3
PHILLIPS, MARR Marr B. B 6.16.1857 Pittsburgh, PA D 4.1.1928 Pittsburgh, PA BR 5-6.5/164# d5.1																								
1884	Ind AA	97	413	41	111	18	8	0		5	1		.269	.279	.351	107	3		.862	16	**112**	62	*S-97	1.9
1885	Det N	33	139	13	29	5	0	0	17	0		13	.209	.209	.245	46	-8		.881	0	105	54	S-33	-0.7
	Pit AA	4	15	1	4	0	0	0	2	2	0		.267	.353	.267	99	0		.875	-1	94	193	/S-4	0.0
1890	Roc AA	64	257	18	53	8	0	0	34	16	3		.206	.261	.237	51	-16	10	.918	5	106	123	S-64	-0.8
Total	3	198	824	73	197	31	8	0	53	23	4	13	.239	.263	.296	79	-21	10	.884	20	108	83	S-198	0.4
PHILLIPS, MIKE Michael Dwaine B 8.19.1950 Beaumont, TX BL/TR 6-1/185# d4.15																								
1973	SF N	63	104	18	25	3	4	1	9	6-0	1	17	.240	.288	.375	79	-4	0-3	.931	-7	83	50	3-28,S-20/2-7	-1.0
1974	SF N	100	283	19	62	6	1	2	20	14-0	1	37	.219	.258	.269	45	-21	4-5	.909	3	116	95	3-34,2-30,S-23	-1.7
1975	SF N	10	31	3	6	0	0	0	1	6-0	0	4	.194	.324	.194	44	-2	1-0	.969	3	106	108	/2-6,3-6	0.1
	NY N	116	383	31	98	10	7	1	28	25-5	1	47	.256	.300	.326	78	-13	3-0	.944	-4	95	82	*S-115/2	-0.3
	Year	126	414	34	104	10	7	1	29	31-5	1	51	.251	.302	.316	76	-15	4-0	.944	-1	95	82	*S-115/2-7,3-6	-0.2
1976	NY N	87	262	30	67	4	6	4	29	25-8	0	29	.256	.315	.363	99	-1	2-2	.955	-1	88	71	S-53,2-19,3-10	0.4
1977	NY N	38	86	5	18	2	1	1	3	2-0	2	15	.209	.244	.291	45	-7	0-1	1.000	-2	84	64	S-24/3-9,2-4	-0.8
	StL N	48	87	17	21	3	2	0	9	9-1	1	13	.241	.320	.322	74	-3	1-0	.971	3	105	134	2-31/S-5,3-5	0.1
	Year	86	173	22	39	5	3	1	12	11-1	3	28	.225	.283	.306	60	-10	1-1	.973	1	98	116	2-35,S-29,3-14	-0.7
1978	StL N	76	164	14	44	8	1	1	28	13-2	2	25	.268	.317	.348	91	-2	0-0	.971	3	98	107	2-55,S-10/3	0.4
1979	StL N	44	97	10	22	3	1	1	6	10-0	1	9	.227	.306	.309	68	-4	0-0	.973	4	126	101	S-25,2-16/3	0.2
1980	StL N	63	128	13	30	5	0	0	7	9-3	0	17	.234	.283	.273	55	-8	0-0	.971	7	126	153	S-37/2-9,3-8	0.2
1981	SD N	14	29	1	6	0	1	0	0	0-0	0	3	.207	.207	.276	39	-3	1-0	.979	2	105	122	/2-9,S	0.0
	†Mon N	34	55	5	12	2	0	0	4	5-0	0	15	.218	.279	.255	53	-3	0-1	.974	-3	88	92	S-26/2-6	-0.5
	Year	48	84	6	18	2	1	0	4	5-0	0	18	.214	.256	.262	49	-6	1-1	.974	-1	89	101	S-27,2-15	-0.5
1982	Mon N	14	8	0	1	0	0	0	1	0-0	0	3	.125	.111	.125	-29	-1	0-0	1.000	-0	88	55	2-10/S-2	-0.2
1983	Mon N	5	2	0	0	0	0	0	0	0-0	0	0	.000	.000	.000	-99	-1	0-0	.000	-2	0	0	/S-3,3-2	-0.2
Total	11	712	1719	166	412	46	24	11	145	124-19	9	234	.240	.291	.314	70	-73	12-12	.956	5	100	94	S-344,2-203,3-104	-3.3

PHILLIPS, DICK Richard Eugene B 11.24.1931 Racine, WI D 3.29.1998 Burnaby, BC, CAN BL/TR 6/180# d4.15 C1

Year	Tm Lg	G	AB	R	H	2B	3B	HR	RBI	BB-IB	HP	SO	AVG	OBP	SLG	AOPS	ABR	SB-CS	FA	FR	Rng	Thr	G at Pos	BFW
1962	SF N	5	3	1	0	0	0	0	1	1-0	0	1	.000	.250	.000	-27	-1	0-0	1.000	-0	0	0	/1	-0.1
1963	Was A	124	321	33	76	8	0	10	32	29-0	2	35	.237	.300	.355	84	-7	1-0	.994	3	129	128	1-68/2-5,3-4	-0.8
1964	Was A	109	234	17	54	6	1	2	23	27-0	1	22	.231	.307	.291	70	-9	1-2	.994	2	112	117	1-61/3-4	-1.2
1966	Was A	25	37	3	6	0	0	0	4	2-1	1	5	.162	.225	.162	13	-4	0-0	1.000	-0	63	53	/1-5	-0.5
Total	4	263	595	54	136	14	1	12	60	59-1	4	63	.229	.298	.316	74	-21	2-2	.995	4	119	120	1-135/3-8,2-5	-2.6

PHILLIPS, BILL William B. B 1857 St.John, NB, CAN D 10.7.1900 Chicago, IL BR/TR 6/202# d5.1

Year	Tm Lg	G	AB	R	H	2B	3B	HR	RBI	BB-IB	HP	SO	AVG	OBP	SLG	AOPS	ABR	SB-CS	FA	FR	Rng	Thr	G at Pos	BFW
1879	Cle N	81	365	58	99	15	4	0	29	2		20	.271	.275	.334	101	0		.954	-4	120	66	*1-75,C-11/O-2(0-1-1)	-0.6
1880	Cle N	**85**	334	41	85	14	10	1	36	6		29	.254	.268	.365	115	4		.963	2	**110**	**101**	*1-85	0.3
1881	Cle N	**85**	357	51	97	18	10	1	44	5		19	.272	.282	.387	114	5		.966	-1	78	**113**	*1-85	0.0
1882	Cle N	78	335	40	87	17	7	4	47	7		18	.260	.275	.388	114	5		.971	3	112	142	*1-78/C	0.1
1883	Cle N	97	382	42	94	29	8	2	40	8		49	.246	.262	.380	93	-3		.967	-2	68	116	*1-97	-1.2
1884	Cle N	111	464	58	128	25	12	3	46	18		80	.276	.303	.401	115	7		.959	-2	93	110	*1-111	-0.4
1885	Bro AA	99	391	65	118	16	11	3	63	27	11		.302	.364	.422	147	21		**.973**	0	91	82	*1-99	1.1
1886	Bro AA	**141**	585	68	160	26	15	0	72	33	1		.274	.313	.369	113	6	13	.978	-2	73	90	*1-141	-0.7
1887	Bro AA	132	533	82	142	34	11	2	101	45	6		.266	.330	.383	97	-2	16	**.982**	4	107	91	*1-132	-0.8
1888	KC AA	129	509	57	120	20	10	1	56	27	7		.236	.284	.320	88	-9	10	.980	3	117	97	*1-129	-1.6
Total	10	1038	4255	562	1130	214	98	17	534	178	25	215	.266	.299	.374	109	34	39	.971	2	96	100	*1-1032/C-12,O-2(0-1-1)	-3.8

PHYLE, BILL William Joseph B 6.25.1875 Duluth, MN D 8.6.1953 Los Angeles, CA TR d9.17 ▲

Year	Tm Lg	G	AB	R	H	2B	3B	HR	RBI	BB-IB	HP	SO	AVG	OBP	SLG	AOPS	ABR	SB-CS	FA	FR	Rng	Thr	G at Pos	BFW
1898	Chi N	4	9	1	1	0	0	0	0	2	0		.111	.273	.111	11	0	0	.800	-1	70	0	/P-3	0.0
1899	Chi N	10	34	2	6	0	0	0	1	0	0		.176	.176	.176	-3	-2	0	.935	0	108	167	P-10	0.0
1901	NY N	25	66	8	12	2	0	0	3	2	0		.182	.206	.212	22	-7	0	.903	1	112	0	P-24/S	0.0
1906	StL N	22	73	6	13	3	1	0	4	5	0		.178	.231	.247	51	-4	2	.935	1	102	84	3-21	-0.3
Total	4	61	182	17	32	5	1	0	8	9	0		.176	.215	.214	28	-13	2	.907	2	107	51	/P-37,3-21,S	-0.3

PIATT, ADAM Adam David B 2.8.1976 Chicago, IL BR/TR 6-2/195# d4.24

Year	Tm Lg	G	AB	R	H	2B	3B	HR	RBI	BB-IB	HP	SO	AVG	OBP	SLG	AOPS	ABR	SB-CS	FA	FR	Rng	Thr	G at Pos	BFW
2000	†Oak A	60	157	24	47	5	5	5	23	23-0	1	44	.299	.392	.490	125	6	0-1	.950	-6	79	65	O-29(8-0-22),3-13,D-13/1-3	-0.2
2001	Oak A	36	95	9	20	5	1	0	6	13-0	0	26	.211	.300	.284	57	-6	0-0	.962	0	92	172	O-32(RF)/D	-0.7
2002	†Oak A	55	137	18	32	8	0	5	18	12-0	2	33	.234	.303	.401	85	-3	2-1	1.000	-4	84	43	O-50(40-0-12)/1	-0.8
2003	Oak A	47	100	6	24	10	0	4	15	6-0	0	30	.240	.280	.460	91	-1	1-2	.978	-2	79	119	O-38(32-0-7)/1D	-0.5
	TB A	14	32	5	6	3	0	2	3	3-0	0	16	.188	.250	.469	87	-1	0-0	1.000	-1	55	0	/O-7(1-0-6),D-4	-0.2
	Year	61	132	11	30	13	0	6	18	9-0	0	46	.227	.273	.462	90	-2	1-2	.981	-4	75	98	O-45(33-0-13)/D-6,1	-0.7
Total	4	212	521	62	129	31	6	16	65	57-0	3	149	.248	.323	.422	94	-5	3-4	.977	-13	82	91	O-156(81-0-79)/D-20,3-13,1-5	-2.4

PIAZZA, MIKE Michael Joseph B 9.4.1968 Norristown, PA BR/TR 6-3/197# d9.1

Year	Tm Lg	G	AB	R	H	2B	3B	HR	RBI	BB-IB	HP	SO	AVG	OBP	SLG	AOPS	ABR	SB-CS	FA	FR	Rng	Thr	G at Pos	BFW
1992	LA N	21	69	5	16	3	0	1	7	4-0	1	12	.232	.284	.319	71	-3	0-0	.990	-1	123	70	C-16	-0.3
1993	LA N★	149	547	81	174	24	2	35	112	46-6	3	86	.318	.370	.561	155	41	3-4	.989	5	97	123	*C-146/1	5.3
1994	LA N★	107	405	64	129	18	0	24	92	33-10	1	65	.319	.370	.541	143	24	1-3	.985	-10	91	82	*C-104	1.9
1995	†LA N★	112	434	82	150	17	0	32	93	39-10	1	80	.346	.400	.606	**177**	46	1-0	.990	-2	94	83	*C-112	5.0
1996	†LA N★	148	547	87	184	16	0	36	105	81-21	1	93	.336	.422	.563	171	58	0-3	.992	-13	72	76	*C-146	5.1
1997	LA N★	152	556	104	201	32	1	40	124	69-11	3	77	.362	.431	.638	**191**	**75**	5-1	.986	-3	93	89	*C-139/D-7	7.8
1998	LA N	37	149	20	42	5	0	9	30	11-4	0	27	.282	.329	.497	121	4	0-0	.993	4	56	120	C-37	0.9
	Fla N	5	18	1	5	0	1	0	5	0-0	0	0	.278	.263	.389	77	-1	0-0	.968	0	82	89	/C-4	0.0
	NY N★	109	394	67	137	33	0	23	76	47-10	2	53	.348	.417	.607	168	41	1-0	.989	4	83	102	C-99/D-4	5.0
	Year	151	561	88	184	38	1	32	111	58-14	2	80	.328	.390	.570	154	44	1-0	.990	8	76	106	*C-140/D-4	5.9
1999	†NY N★	141	534	100	162	25	0	40	124	51-11	1	70	.303	.361	.575	137	28	2-2	.989	-13	84	93	*C-137/D	2.2
2000	†NY N✶	136	482	90	156	26	0	38	113	58-10	3	69	.324	.398	.614	158	42	4-2	**.997**	-10	66	97	*C-124/D-5	3.8
2001	NY N★	141	503	81	151	29	0	36	94	67-19	2	87	.300	.384	.573	150	38	0-2	.991	-12	61	97	*C-131/D-5	3.2
2002	NY N★	135	478	69	134	23	2	33	98	57-9	3	82	.280	.359	.544	143	26	0-3	.986	-18	53	88	*C-121/D-6	1.4
2003	NY N	68	234	37	67	13	0	11	34	35-3	1	40	.286	.377	.483	128	10	0-0	.982	-7	51	169	C-64/1	0.7
Total	12	1461	5350	888	1708	264	6	358	1107	598-124	22	841	.319	.388	.572	156	429	17-20	.989	-76	78	97	*C-1380/D-28,1-2	42.0

PICCIOLO, ROB Robert Michael B 2.4.1953 Santa Monica, CA BR/TR 6-2/185# d4.9 C14 OF Total (2-LF 1-RF)

Year	Tm Lg	G	AB	R	H	2B	3B	HR	RBI	BB-IB	HP	SO	AVG	OBP	SLG	AOPS	ABR	SB-CS	FA	FR	Rng	Thr	G at Pos	BFW
1977	Oak A	148	419	35	84	12	3	2	22	9-0	1	55	.200	.218	.258	30	-42	1-4	.966	-8	97	88	*S-148	-3.8
1978	Oak A	78	93	16	21	1	0	2	7	2-0	0	13	.226	.242	.301	55	-6	1-1	.958	-5	83	108	S-41,2-19,3-13	-0.9
1979	Oak A	115	348	37	88	16	2	2	27	3-1	1	45	.253	.261	.328	61	-20	2-1	.964	-14	88	68	*S-105/2-6,3-4,O(LF)	-2.3
1980	Oak A	95	271	32	65	9	2	5	18	2-0	0	63	.240	.245	.343	64	-15	1-1	.977	-25	75	79	S-49,2-47/O(LF)	-3.4
1981	†Oak A	82	179	23	48	5	3	4	13	5-0	1	22	.268	.290	.397	102	-1	0-1	.981	-16	84	78	S-82	-1.1
1982	Oak A	18	49	3	11	1	0	0	3	1-0	0	10	.224	.240	.245	35	-4	1-0	.979	4	117	104	S-18	0.2
	Mil A	22	21	7	6	1	0	0	1	1-0	0	4	.286	.318	.333	84	0	0-0	1.000	-2	44	60	2-11/S-6,D	-0.2
	Year	40	70	10	17	2	0	0	4	2-0	0	14	.243	.264	.271	50	-5	1-0	.973	2	113	102	S-24,2-11/D	0.0
1983	Mil A	14	27	2	6	3	0	0	1	0-0	0	4	.222	.214	.333	55	-2	0-0	1.000	1	106	227	/S-7,2-2,3-2,1D	0.0
1984	Cal A	87	119	18	24	6	0	1	9	0-0	0	21	.202	.200	.277	31	-11	0-1	.974	0	101	83	S-66,3-13/2-9,O(RF)	-0.8
1985	Oak A	71	102	19	28	2	0	1	8	2-0	0	17	.275	.288	.324	73	-4	3-2	.889	-3	100	111	3-19,2-17,1-13,D-10/S-9	-0.7
Total	9	730	1628	192	381	56	10	17	109	25-1	3	254	.234	.246	.312	55	-105	9-11	.970	-66	91	84	S-531,2-111/3-51,1-14,D-12,0-3L	-13.0

PICCIUTO, NICK Nicholas Thomas B 8.27.1921 Newark, NJ D 1.10.1997 Winchester, VA BR/TR 5-8.5/165# d5.11

Year	Tm Lg	G	AB	R	H	2B	3B	HR	RBI	BB-IB	HP	SO	AVG	OBP	SLG	AOPS	ABR	SB-CS	FA	FR	Rng	Thr	G at Pos	BFW
1945	Phi N	36	89	7	12	6	0	0	6	6	0	17	.135	.189	.202	9	-11	0	.839	-5	89	55	3-30/2-4	-1.6

PICINICH, VAL Valentine John B 9.8.1896 New York, NY D 12.5.1942 Nobleboro, ME BR/TR 5-9/165# d7.25 Mil 1918 C1

Year	Tm Lg	G	AB	R	H	2B	3B	HR	RBI	BB-IB	HP	SO	AVG	OBP	SLG	AOPS	ABR	SB-CS	FA	FR	Rng	Thr	G at Pos	BFW
1916	Phi A	40	118	8	23	3	1	0	5	6	0	33	.195	.234	.237	44	-9	1	.967	-5	60	102	C-37	-1.2
1917	Phi A	2	6	0	2	0	0	0	0	1	0	2	.333	.429	.333	135	0	0	.786	-1	*78*	*53*	/C-2	-0.1
1918	Was A	47	148	13	34	3	3	0	12	9	0	25	.230	.274	.291	72	-6	0	.960	-3	*103*	*79*	C-46	-0.5
1919	Was A	80	212	18	58	12	3	3	22	17	1	43	.274	.330	.401	106	1	6	.978	10	*96*	*123*	C-69	1.7
1920	Was A	48	133	14	27	6	2	3	14	9	1	33	.203	.259	.346	61	-8	0-0	.978	6	*103*	*96*	C-45	0.1
1921	Was A	45	141	10	39	9	0	0	12	16	1	21	.277	.354	.340	82	-3	0-3	.966	2	*154*	*70*	C-45	0.1
1922	Was A	76	210	16	48	12	2	0	19	23	2	33	.229	.311	.305	64	-11	1-0	.976	5	*102*	*92*	C-76	-0.1
1923	Bos A	87	268	33	74	21	1	2	31	46	2	32	.276	.386	.384	103	4	3-5	.957	-2	*80*	*128*	C-81	0.5
1924	Bos A	69	161	25	44	6	3	1	24	29	3	19	.273	.394	.366	97	0	5-1	.951	-3	*94*	*96*	C-52	0.1
1925	Bos A	90	251	31	64	21	0	1	25	33	1	21	.255	.344	.351	77	-8	2-0	.968	-9	*70*	*75*	C-74/1-2	-1.1
1926	Cin N	89	240	33	63	16	1	2	31	29	0	22	.262	.342	.363	92	-2	4	.967	-3	*108*	*78*	C-86	0.0
1927	Cin N	65	173	16	44	8	3	0	12	24	0	15	.254	.345	.335	85	-3	3	.980	0	*83*	*51*	C-61	0.1
1928	Cin N	96	324	29	98	15	1	7	35	20	0	25	.302	.343	.420	100	-1	1	.983	-1	*103*	*108*	C-93	0.5
1929	Bro N	93	273	28	71	16	6	4	31	34	0	24	.260	.342	.407	86	-6	3	.979	-8	*59*	***137***	C-85	-0.9
1930	Bro N	23	46	4	10	3	0	0	3	5	0	6	.217	.294	.283	41	-4	1	.944	-1	*94*	*109*	C-22	-0.4
1931	Bro N	24	45	5	12	4	0	1	4	4	0	9	.267	.327	.422	100	0	1	.967	-0	*107*	*55*	C-15	0.1
1932	Bro N	41	70	8	18	6	0	1	11	4	0	8	.257	.297	.386	84	-2	0	.985	-1	*99*	*75*	C-24	-0.2
1933	Bro N	6	6	1	1	1	0	0	0	0	0	1	.167	.167	.333	42	0	0	.889	-0	*54*	*217*	/C-6	-0.1
	Pit N	16	52	6	13	4	0	1	7	5	0	10	.250	.316	.385	99	0	0	.982	-2	*81*	*72*	C-16	-0.1
	Year	22	58	7	14	5	0	1	7	5	0	11	.241	.302	.379	95	0	0	.969	-2	*78*	*88*	C-22	-0.2
Total	18	1037	2877	298	743	166	26	26	298	314	11	382	.258	.334	.361	86	-58	31-9	.970	-15	*92*	*96*	C-935/1-2	-1.5

PICK, CHARLIE Charles Thomas B 4.10.1888 Brookneal, VA D 6.26.1954 Lynchburg, VA BL/TR 5-10/160# d9.20

Year	Tm Lg	G	AB	R	H	2B	3B	HR	RBI	BB-IB	HP	SO	AVG	OBP	SLG	AOPS	ABR	SB-CS	FA	FR	Rng	Thr	G at Pos	BFW
1914	Was A	10	23	0	9	0	0	0	1	4	0	4	.391	.481	.391	157	2	1-2	.833	0	73	237	/O-7(6-0-1)	0.1
1915	Was A	3	2	0	0	0	0	0	0	0	0	0	.000	.000	.000	-98	0	0	—	0			H	-0.1
1916	Phi A	121	398	29	96	10	3	0	20	40	3	24	.241	.315	.281	83	-8	25-16	.899	5	102	103	*3-108/O-8(5-3-0)	-0.1
1918	†Chi N	29	89	13	29	4	1	0	12	14	0	4	.326	.417	.393	144	6	7	.964	-0	104	74	2-20/3-8	0.7
1919	Chi N	75	269	27	65	8	6	0	18	14	5	12	.242	.292	.316	82	-6	17	.946	5	109	109	2-71/3-3	0.0
	Bos N	34	114	12	29	1	1	1	7	7	5	5	.254	.325	.307	94	-1	4	.924	-5	86	130	2-21/3-5,O-3(2-1-0),1-2	-0.6
	Year	109	383	39	94	9	7	1	25	21	10	17	.245	.302	.313	86	-7	21	.942	-0	104	113	2-92/3-8,O-3(2-1-0),1-2	-0.6
1920	Bos N	95	383	34	105	16	6	2	28	23	3	11	.274	.320	.363	100	0	10-16	.952	0	105	92	2-94	-0.2
Total	6	367	1278	115	333	39	17	3	86	102	16	60	.261	.323	.325	95	-7	64-34	.949	5	105	100	2-206,3-124/O-18(13-4-1),1-2	-0.2

Year	Tm Lg	G	AB	R	H	2B	3B	HR	RBI	BB-IB	HP	SO	AVG	OBP	SLG	AOPS	ABR	SB-CS	FA	FR	Rng	Thr	G at Pos	BFW
PICK, EDDIE Edgar Everett B 5.7.1899 Attleboro, MA D 5.13.1967 Santa Monica, CA BB/TR 6/185# d9.13																								
1923	Cin N	9	8	2	3	0	0	0	2	3	0	3	.375	.545	.375	150	1	0-0	1.000	-0	71	0	/O-4(LF)	0.1
1924	Cin N	3	2	0	0	0	0	0	0	0	0	1	.000	.000	.000	-99	-1	0-0	1.000	0	142	0	/O(LF)	-0.1
1927	Chi N	54	181	23	31	5	2	2	15	20	0	26	.171	.254	.254	36	-17	0	.910	-5	83	124	3-49/2O(RF)	-1.9
Total	3	66	191	25	34	5	2	2	17	23	0	30	.178	.266	.257	40	-17	0-0	.910	-5	83	124	/3-49,O-6(5-0-1),2	-1.9
PICKERING, CALVIN Calvin Elroy B 9.29.1976 St.Thomas, V.I. BL/TL 6-5/283# d9.12																								
1998	Bal A	9	21	4	5	0	0	2	3	3-0	0	4	.238	.333	.524	120	0	1-0	.969	-1	0	114	/1-5,D-3	-0.1
1999	Bal A	23	40	4	5	1	0	1	5	11-0	0	16	.125	.314	.225	42	-3	0-0	.960	-1	59	166	/1-8,D-7	-0.4
2001	Cin N	4	4	0	1	0	0	0	1	0-0	0	2	.250	.250	.250	29	0	0-0	—	0			/H	-0.1
	Bos A	17	50	4	14	1	0	3	7	8-0	0	13	.280	.379	.480	123	2	0-0	1.000	-1	71	82	1-12/D-2	0.0
Total	3	53	115	12	25	2	0	6	16	22-0	0	35	.217	.343	.391	91	-1	1-0	.983	-3	57	110	/1-25,D-12	-0.6
PICKERING, OLLIE Oliver Daniel B 4.9.1870 Olney, IL D 1.20.1952 Vincennes, IN BL/TR 5-10/175# d8.9																								
1896	Lou N	45	165	28	50	6	4	1	22	12	0	11	.303	.350	.406	103	0	13	.901	3	187	214	O-45(3-44-0)	0.0
1897	Lou N	64	249	34	62	5	2	1	21	26	2		.249	.325	.297	67	-11	20	.938	4	170	109	O-63(0-62-1)	-1.0
	Cle N	46	182	33	64	5	2	1	22	11	1		.352	.392	.418	108	2	18	.950	-1	76	86	O-46(1-45-1)/2	-0.1
	Year	110	431	67	126	10	4	2	43	37	3		.292	.352	.348	85	-9	38	.943	3	130	99	*O-109(1-107-2)/2	-1.1
1901	Cle A	137	547	102	169	25	6	0	40	58	8		.309	.383	.377	116	16	36	.949	13	125	**204**	*O-137(2-110-25)	2.0
1902	Cle A	69	293	46	75	5	2	3	26	19	2		.256	.306	.317	76	-10	22	.979	-3	62	61	O-64(3-57-4)/1-2	-1.5
1903	Phi A	**137**	512	93	144	18	6	1	36	53	4		.281	.353	.346	105	5	40	.970	3	114	135	*O-135(0-134-1)	0.2
1904	Phi A	124	455	56	103	10	3	0	30	45	2		.226	.299	.262	74	-12	17	.939	-1	99	61	*O-121(10-111-0)	-2.1
1907	StL A	151	576	63	159	15	10	0	60	35	3		.276	.321	.337	110	5	15	.949	-9	75	120	*O-151(0-22-128)	-1.1
1908	Was A	113	373	45	84	7	4	2	30	28	3		.225	.285	.282	92	-4	13	.940	-6	57	35	O-98(0-27-71)	-1.6
Total	8	886	3352	500	910	96	39	9	287	287	25	11	.271	.334	.331	97	-9	194	.949	3	103	116	O-860(19-612-231)/1-2,2	-5.2
PICKERING, URBANE Urbane Henry "Pick" B 6.3.1899 Hoxie, KS D 5.13.1970 Modesto, CA BR/TR 5-10/180# d4.18																								
1931	Bos A	103	341	48	86	13	4	9	52	33	0	53	.252	.318	.393	91	-6	3-4	.967	-1	108	64	3-74,2-16	-0.4
1932	Bos A	132	457	47	119	28	5	2	40	39	1	71	.260	.320	.357	77	-16	3-4	.941	-5	101	103	*3-126/C	-1.6
Total	2	235	798	95	205	41	9	11	92	72	1	124	.257	.319	.372	83	-22	6-8	.951	-6	104	88	3-200/2-16,C	-2.0
PICKETT, DAVE David T. B 5.26.1874 Brookline, MA D 4.22.1950 Easton, MA TR 5-7.5/170# d7.21																								
1898	Bos N	14	43	3	12	1	0	0	3	6	1		.279	.380	.302	91	0	2	.955	-1	67	0	O-14(LF)	-0.1
PICKETT, JOHN John Thomas B 2.20.1866 Chicago, IL D 7.4.1922 Chicago, IL BR/TR 5-10.5/186# d6.6																								
1889	KC AA	53	201	20	45	7	0	0	12	11	2	21	.224	.271	.259	48	-14	7	.900	-11	43	89	O-28(23-4-1),3-14,2-11	-2.2
1890	Phi P	100	407	82	114	7	9	4	64	40	2	17	.280	.347	.371	90	-7	12	.893	-23	91	94	*2-100	-2.1
1892	Bal N	36	141	13	30	2	3	1	12	7	2	10	.213	.260	.291	65	-7	2	.915	-1	103	53	2-36	-0.5
Total	3	189	749	115	189	16	12	5	88	58	6	48	.252	.311	.326	75	-28	21	.900	-34	93	81	2-147/O-28(23-4-1),3-14	-4.8
PICKUP, TY Clarence William B 10.29.1897 Philadelphia, PA D 8.2.1974 Philadelphia, PA BR/TR 6/180# d4.30																								
1918	Phi N	1	1	0	1	0	0	0	0	0	0	0	1.000	1.000	1.000	478	0	0	1.000	0	125	0	/O(RF)	0.0
PIERCE, GRACIE Grayson S. B New York, NY D 8.28.1894 New York, NY BR/TR d5.2 U3																								
1882	Lou AA	9	33	3	10	1	0	0		1			.303	.324	.333	129	1		.864	1	113	131	/2-9	0.2
	Bal AA	41	151	8	30	2	1	0		3			.199	.214	.225	52	-7		.796	-10	92	95	2-38/O-3(RF),S	-1.4
	Year	50	184	11	40	3	1	0		4			.217	.234	.245	66	-6		.808	-8	96	101	2-47/O-3(RF),S	-1.2
1883	Col AA	11	41	5	7	0	0	0		0			.171	.171	.171	11	-4		.744	-2	71	141	/2-6,O-5(0-4-1)	-0.5
	NY N	18	62	3	5	0	1	0	2	1		9	.081	.095	.113	-37	-10		.850	-1	30	183	O-18(0-17-1)/2	-1.1
1884	NY AA	5	20	2	5	1	0	0		0	0		.250	.250	.300	81	0		1.000	-4	0	0	/O-3(0-2-1),2-3	-0.4
Total	3	84	307	21	57	4	2	0	2	5	0	9	.186	.199	.212	36	-20		.795	-15	88	98	/2-57,O-29(0-23-6),S	-3.2
PIERCE, JACK Lavern Jack B 6.2.1948 Laurel, MS BL/TR 6/210# d4.27																								
1973	Atl N	11	20	0	1	0	0	0	0	1-0	0	8	.050	.095	.050	-55	-4	0-0	1.000	0	133	26	/1-6	-0.4
1974	Atl N	6	9	1	1	0	0	0	0	1-0	0	0	.111	.200	.111	-11	-1	0-0	.958	0	160	74	/1-2	-0.1
1975	Det A	53	170	19	40	6	1	8	22	20-1	2	40	.235	.320	.424	105	1	0-0	.971	-4	80	92	1-49	-0.7
Total	3	70	199	20	42	6	1	8	22	22-1	2	48	.211	.293	.372	83	-4	0-0	.973	-4	87	86	/1-57	-1.2
PIERCE, MAURY Maurice B Baltimore, MD d4.23																								
1884	Was U	2	7	0	1	0	0	0		0			.143	.143	.143	-14	-1		.778	-0	52	0	/3-2	-0.1
PIERCY, ANDY Andrew J. B 8.1856 San Jose, CA D 12.27.1932 San Jose, CA TR d5.12																								
1881	Chi N	2	8	1	2	0	0	0	0	0		1	.250	.250	.250	55	0		.750	-1	0	0	/32	-0.2
PIERRE, JUAN Juan D'Vaughn B 8.14.1977 Mobile, AL BL/TL 6/170# d8.7																								
2000	Col N	51	200	26	62	2	0	0	20	13-0	1	15	.310	.353	.320	58	-12	7-6	.975	-2	100	70	O-50(CF)	-1.4
2001	Col N	156	617	108	202	26	11	2	55	41-1	10	29	.327	.378	.415	86	-11	**46**-17	.979	-5	104	38	*O-154(CF)	-1.1
2002	Col N	152	592	90	170	20	5	1	35	31-0	9	52	.287	.332	.343	70	-27	47-12	.995	-2	108	26	*O-149(CF)	-2.1
2003	†Fla N	**162**	668	100	204	28	7	1	41	55-1	5	35	.305	.361	.373	96	-3	**65**-20	.993	2	106	68	*O-161(CF)	0.8
Total	4	521	2077	324	638	76	23	4	151	140-2	25	131	.307	.357	.372	81	-53	165-55	.987	-7	105	48	O-514(CF)	-3.8
PIERSALL, JIM James Anthony B 11.14.1929 Waterbury, CT BR/TR 6/175# d9.7 C1																								
1950	Bos A	6	7	4	2	0	0	0	0	4	0	0	.286	.545	.286	107	1	0-0	1.000	1	152	0	/O-2(CF)	0.1
1952	Bos A	56	161	28	43	8	0	1	16	28	1	26	.267	.379	.335	93	0	3-3	.928	-2	100	77	S-30,O-22(0-1-21)/3	-0.2
1953	Bos A	151	585	76	159	21	9	3	52	41	9	52	.272	.329	.354	80	-17	11-10	.987	11	**117**	106	*O-151(1-2-150)	-1.3
1954	Bos A★	133	474	77	135	24	2	8	38	36	3	42	.285	.338	.395	90	-6	5-1	.985	-2	96	102	*O-126(0-30-96)	-1.3
1955	Bos A	149	515	68	146	25	5	13	62	67-7	2	52	.283	.364	.427	104	4	6-1	.993	1	103	76	*O-147(CF)	-0.2
1956	Bos A★	**155**	601	91	176	**40**	6	14	87	58-2	1	48	.293	.350	.449	99	-1	7-7	**.991**	7	111	94	*O-155(CF)	-0.2
1957	Bos A	151	609	103	159	27	5	19	63	62-1	4	54	.261	.331	.415	98	-2	14-6	.990	1	102	112	*O-151(CF)	-0.7
1958	Bos A	130	417	55	99	13	5	8	48	42-2	0	43	.237	.303	.350	75	-14	12-2	.985	-1	99	110	*O-125(CF)	-2.0
1959	Cle A	100	317	42	78	13	2	4	30	25-1	2	31	.246	.303	.338	79	-9	6-3	.982	-1	104	54	O-91(CF)/3	-1.4
1960	Cle A	138	486	70	137	12	4	18	66	24-3	0	38	.282	.313	.434	104	-1	18-5	.992	6	**115**	64	*O-134(8-127-2)	0.1
1961	Cle A	121	484	81	156	26	7	6	40	43-1	2	46	.322	.378	.442	122	16	8-2	**.991**	6	110	138	*O-120(CF)	1.9
1962	Was A	135	471	38	115	20	4	4	31	39-3	0	53	.244	.301	.329	70	-20	12-7	**.997**	0	105	84	*O-132(CF)	-2.4
1963	Was A	29	94	9	23	1	0	1	5	6-0	0	11	.245	.284	.287	63	-5	4-0	1.000	0	118	0	O-25(CF)	-0.5
	NY N	40	124	13	24	4	1	1	10	10-1	0	14	.194	.250	.266	49	-8	1-2	1.000	-1	87	141	O-38(CF)	-1.2
	LA A	20	52	4	16	1	0	0	4	5-0	0	5	.308	.368	.327	103	0	0-1	1.000	-2	81	0	O-18(1-12-5)	-0.3
1964	LA A	87	255	28	80	11	0	2	13	16-1	0	32	.314	.353	.380	116	5	5-3	1.000	-2	93	55	O-72(48-32-0)	0.0
1965	Cal A	53	112	10	30	5	2	2	12	5-1	1	15	.268	.305	.402	101	0	2-2	.984	0	113	0	O-41(29-10-4)	-0.2
1966	Cal A	75	123	14	26	5	0	0	14	13-0	0	19	.211	.283	.252	58	-6	1-2	.973	1	101	139	O-63(25-14-27)	-0.9
1967	Cal A	5	3	0	0	0	0	0	0	0-0	0	2	.000	.000	.000	-99	-1	0-0	1.000	0	474	0	/O(LF)	-0.1
Total	17	1734	5890	811	1604	256	52	104	591	524-23	25	583	.272	.332	.386	92	-64	115-57	.990	23	106	93	*O-1614(113-1214-305)/S-30,3-2	-10.8
PIERSON, DAVE David P. B 8.20.1855 Wilkes-Barre, PA D 11.11.1922 Newark, NJ BR/TR 5-7/142# d4.25 b-Dick																								
1876	Cin N	57	233	33	55	4	1	0	13	1		9	.236	.239	.262	78	-4		.760	-1			C-31,O-30(1-0-29)/S32P	-0.3
PIERSON, DICK Edmund Dana B 10.24.1857 Wilkes-Barre, PA D 7.20.1922 Newark, NJ TR d6.23 b-Dave																								
1885	NY AA	3	9	1	1	0	0	0	0	2	0		.111	.273	.111	26	-1		.682	-3	61	70	/2-3	-0.3
PIERZYNSKI, A.J. Anthony John B 12.30.1976 Bridgehampton, NY BL/TR 6-3/218# d9.9																								
1998	Min A	7	10	1	3	0	0	0	1	1-0	1	2	.300	.385	.300	89	0	0-0	1.000	2	76	73	/C-6	0.2
1999	Min A	9	22	3	6	2	0	0	3	1-0	1	4	.273	.333	.364	75	-1	0-0	1.000	-1	417	49	/C-9	-0.1
2000	Min A	33	88	12	27	5	1	2	11	5-0	2	14	.307	.354	.455	100	0	1-0	1.000	-2	157	88	C-32	0.0
2001	Min A	114	381	51	110	33	2	7	55	16-4	4	57	.289	.322	.441	97	-2	1-7	.985	2	165	71	*C-110/D	0.5
2002	†Min A★	130	440	54	132	31	6	6	49	13-1	11	61	.300	.334	.439	103	1	1-2	.996	3	143	66	*C-124	1.1
2003	†Min A	137	487	63	152	35	3	11	74	24-12	15	55	.312	.360	.464	115	11	3-1	.993	4	159	64	*C-135	2.3
Total	6	430	1428	184	430	106	12	26	193	60-17	34	193	.301	.341	.447	105	9	6-10	.993	8	159	68	C-416/D	4.0

Year	Tm Lg	G	AB	R	H	2B	3B	HR	RBI	BB-IB	HP	SO	AVG	OBP	SLG	AOPS	ABR	SB-CS	FA	FR	Rng	Thr	G at Pos	BFW
PIET, TONY Anthony Francis (born Anthony Francis Pietruszka) B 12.7.1906 Berwick, PA D 12.1.1981 Hinsdale, IL BR/TR 6/175# d8.15																								
1931	Pit N	44	167	22	50	12	4	0	24	13	1	24	.299	.354	.419	108	2	10	.987	-5	99	62	2-44/S	0.0
1932	Pit N	**154**	574	66	162	25	8	7	85	46	7	56	.282	.343	.390	98	-1	19	.970	-26	92	90	*2-154	-1.7
1933	Pit N	107	362	45	117	21	5	1	42	19	6	28	.323	.367	.417	124	11	12	.955	-8	98	109	2-97	1.0
1934	Cin N	106	421	58	109	20	5	1	38	23	6	44	.259	.307	.337	74	-16	6	.934	-9	98	92	3-51,2-49	-2.0
1935	Cin N	6	5	2	1	1	0	0	2	0	0	0	.200	.200	.400	59	0	0	1.000	0	145	0	/O(RF)	0.0
	Chi A	77	292	47	87	17	5	3	27	33	3	27	.298	.375	.421	103	2	2-1	.975	2	111	85	2-59,3-17	0.8
1936	Chi A	109	352	69	96	15	2	7	42	66	9	48	.273	.400	.386	92	-2	15-5	.966	5	120	108	2-68,3-32	0.9
1937	Chi A	100	332	34	78	15	1	4	38	32	6	36	.235	.314	.322	61	-20	14-6	.939	1	98	77	3-86,2-13	-1.4
1938	Det A	41	80	9	17	6	0	0	14	15	2	11	.213	.351	.287	58	-5	2-4	.919	1	125	90	3-18/2	-0.4
Total	8	744	2585	352	717	132	30	23	312	247	40	274	.277	.350	.378	91	-29	80-16	.967	-39	101	95	2-485,3-204/O(RF)S	-2.8
PIEZ, SANDY Charles William B 10.13.1892 New York, NY D 12.29.1930 Atlantic City, NJ BR/TR 5-10/170# d4.17																								
1914	NY N	37	8	9	3	0	1	0	3	0	0	1	.375	.375	.625	202	1	4	1.000	1	217	0	/O-5(2-2-1)	0.2
PIGNATANO, JOE Joseph Benjamin B 8.4.1929 Brooklyn, NY BR/TR 5-10/180# d4.28 C21																								
1957	Bro N	8	14	0	3	1	0	0	1	0-0	0	5	.214	.214	.286	30	-1	0-0	1.000	2	*135*	*0*	/C-6	0.1
1958	LA N	63	142	18	31	4	0	9	17	16-1	2	26	.218	.306	.437	91	-2	4-1	1.000	6	*154*	*120*	C-57	0.6
1959	†LA N	52	139	17	33	4	1	1	11	21-2	2	15	.237	.346	.302	69	-5	1-0	.997	6	*230*	*93*	C-49	0.3
1960	LA N	58	90	11	21	4	0	2	9	15-2	0	17	.233	.343	.344	83	-1	1-1	.984	9	*169*	*124*	C-40	0.9
1961	KC A	92	243	31	59	10	3	4	22	36-2	4	42	.243	.347	.358	88	-3	2-2	.979	1	*113*	*90*	C-83/3-2	0.1
1962	SF N	7	5	2	1	0	0	0	0	4-0	0	0	.200	.556	.200	114	1	0-0	1.000	0	*93*	*211*	/C-7	0.1
	NY N	27	56	2	13	2	0	0	2	2-0	0	11	.232	.259	.268	41	-5	0-0	.991	2	*101*	*123*	C-25	-0.2
	Year	34	61	4	14	2	0	0	2	6-0	0	11	.230	.299	.262	51	-4	0-0	.992	2	*100*	*132*	C-32	-0.1
Total	6	307	689	81	161	25	4	16	62	94-7	8	116	.234	.332	.351	80	-16	8-4	.990	26	*152*	*103*	C-267/3-2	1.9
PIKE, JAY Jacob Emanuel B Brooklyn, NY d8.27 b-Lip																								
1877	Har N	1	4	0	1	0	0	0	0	0		0	.250	.250	.250	65	0		.000	-1	0	0	/O(RF)	-0.1
PIKE, JESS Jess Willard B 7.31.1915 Dustin, OK D 3.28.1984 San Diego, CA BL/TL 6-3/175# d4.18																								
1946	NY N	16	41	4	7	1	1	1	6	6	0	9	.171	.277	.317	68	-2	0	.929	-2	71	0	O-10(0-6-4)	-0.4
PIKE, LIP Lipman Emanuel B 5.25.1845 New York, NY D 10.10.1893 Brooklyn, NY BL/TL 5-8/158# d5.9 M3 b-Jay OF NA (7-LF 98-CF 88-RF)																								
1871	Tro NA	28	130	43	49	10	7	**4**	39	5		7	.377	.400	.654	194	15	3-2	.850	2	161	0	O-18(RF)/2-7,1-4,M	1.1
1872	Bal NA	56	285	68	85	15	5	**7**	**60**	4		6	.298	.308	.460	127	7	10-1	.875	-10	0	0	O-25(6-5-16),2-24/3-9	-0.1
1873	Bal NA	56	285	71	90	15	8	**4**	51	8		4	.316	.334	.467	136	12	8-1	.747	-3	114	291	*O-56(0-2-54)/2-2	1.0
1874	Har NA	52	234	58	83	**22**	5	1	50	5		1	.355	.368	**.504**	168	17	4-1	.856	7	166	118	O-27(CF),S-20/2-7,3M	1.8
1875	StL NA	**70**	312	61	108	22	12	0	44	3		8	.346	.352	.494	**210**	**35**	25-10	.885	-3	51	120	*O-64(1-64-0),2-10/3-2,S	2.8
1876	StL N	63	282	55	91	19	10	1	50	8		9	.323	.341	.472	178	24		.896	-5	125	**312**	*O-62(CF)/2-2	1.4
1877	Cin N	**58**	262	45	78	12	4	**4**	23	9		7	.298	.321	.420	148	16		.802	-4	141	67	O-38(CF),2-22/S-2,M	0.9
1878	Cin N	31	145	28	47	5	1	0	11	4		9	.324	.342	.372	149	8		.824	-3	56	100	O-31(CF)	0.3
	Pro N	5	22	4	5	0	1	0	4	1		1	.227	.261	.318	90	0		.788	-3	78	0	/2-5	-0.3
	Year	36	167	32	52	5	2	0	15	5		10	.311	.331	.365	140	8		.824	-6	56	100	O-31(CF)/2-5	0.0
1881	Wor N	5	18	1	2	0	0	0	0	4		3	.111	.273	.111	24	-1		.647	-2	65	394	/O-5(CF)	-0.3
1887	NY AA	1	4	0	0	0	0	0	0	0	0		.000	.000	.000	-99	-1	0	1.000	-0	0	0	/O(CF)	-0.1
Total	5 NA	262	1246	301	415	84	37	16	244	25	0	26	.333	.346	.498	162	86	50-15	.000	-7	91	146	O-190C/2-50,S-21,3-12,1-4	6.6
Total	5	163	733	133	223	36	16	5	88	26	0	29	.304	.328	.417	152	46	0-0	.833	-17	112	201	O-137(CF)/2-29,S-2	1.9
PILARCIK, AL Alfred James B 7.3.1930 Whiting, IN BL/TL 5-10/180# d7.13																								
1956	KC A	69	239	28	60	10	1	4	22	30-1	0	32	.251	.333	.351	81	-6	9-2	.976	-4	83	185	O-67(0-64-3)	-1.2
1957	Bal A	142	407	52	113	16	3	9	49	53-6	4	28	.278	.359	.398	116	10	14-7	.996	3	96	**177**	*O-126(2-54-79)	0.9
1958	Bal A	141	379	40	92	21	0	1	24	42-1	2	37	.243	.320	.306	78	-10	7-3	.986	-2	103	63	*O-119(4-32-104)	-1.6
1959	Bal A	130	273	37	77	12	1	3	16	30-1	1	25	.282	.355	.366	101	1	9-3	.978	-4	92	68	*O-106(3-8-102)	-0.5
1960	Bal A	104	194	30	48	5	1	4	17	15-2	4	16	.247	.313	.345	79	-6	0-2	1.000	-1	91	140	O-75(0-2-74)	-0.9
1961	KC A	35	60	9	12	1	1	0	9	6-0	0	7	.200	.269	.250	40	-5	1-0	1.000	1	103	180	O-21(0-2-19)	-0.5
	Chi A	47	62	9	11	1	0	1	6	9-0	0	5	.177	.282	.242	42	-5	1-1	.944	1	106	273	O-17(2-14-1)	-0.5
	Year	82	122	18	23	2	1	1	15	15-0	0	12	.189	.275	.246	41	-10	2-1	.971	2	104	223	O-38(2-16-20)	-1.0
Total	6	668	1614	205	413	66	7	22	143	185-11	11	150	.256	.334	.346	89	-21	41-18	.986	-5	95	132	O-531(11-176-382)	-4.3
PILNEY, ANDY Antone James B 1.19.1913 Frontenac, KS D 9.15.1996 Kenner, LA BR/TR 5-11/174# d6.12																								
1936	Bos N	3	2	0	0	0	0	0	0	0	0	1	.000	.000	.000	-99	-1	0	—	0			H	-0.1
PINELLI, BABE Ralph Arthur (born Rinaldo Angelo Paolinelli) B 10.18.1895 San Francisco, CA D 10.22.1984 Daly City, CA BR/TR 5-9/165# d8.3 U22																								
1918	Chi A	24	78	7	18	1	1	1	7	7	1	8	.231	.302	.308	83	-2	3	.847	-7	72	99	3-24	-0.9
1920	Det A	102	284	33	65	9	3	0	21	25	2	16	.229	.296	.282	55	-19	6-8	.954	12	112	167	3-74,S-18/2	-0.5
1922	Cin N	**156**	547	77	167	19	7	1	72	48	6	37	.305	.368	.371	93	-4	17-22	.945	22	**117**	83	*3-156	2.2
1923	Cin N	117	423	44	117	14	5	0	51	27	0	29	.277	.320	.333	74	-16	10-14	.938	7	**109**	88	*3-116	-0.5
1924	Cin N	144	510	61	156	16	7	0	70	32	5	32	.306	.353	.365	94	-4	23-17	.956	24	**119**	94	*3-143	2.8
1925	Cin N	130	492	68	139	33	6	2	49	22	2	28	.283	.316	.386	80	-15	8-19	.945	17	**124**	113	*3-109,S-17	0.5
1926	Cin N	71	207	26	46	7	4	0	24	15	3	5	.222	.284	.295	58	-13	2	.978	2	127	82	3-40,S-27/2-3	-0.7
1927	Cin N	30	76	11	15	2	0	1	4	6	1	7	.197	.265	.263	43	-6	2	.968	-1	107	73	3-15/S-9,2-5	-0.5
Total	8	774	2617	327	723	101	33	5	298	182	20	162	.276	.328	.346	79	-79	71-80	.947	77	116	100	3-677/S-71,2-9	2.4
PINIELLA, LOU Louis Victor B 8.28.1943 Tampa, FL BR/TR 6-2/198# d9.4 M17 C2																								
1964	Bal A	4	1	0	0	0	0	0	0	0-0	0	0	.000	.000	.000	-99	0	0-0	—	0			H	0.0
1968	Cle A	6	5	1	0	0	0	0	1	0-0	0	0	.000	.000	.000	-99	-1	0-0	1.000	-0	85	0	/O-2(LF)	-0.2
1969	KC A	135	493	43	139	21	6	11	68	33-2	3	56	.282	.325	.416	107	3	2-4	.977	10	112	128	*O-129(126-3-0)	0.5
1970	KC A	144	542	54	163	24	5	11	88	35-6	2	42	.301	.342	.424	111	7	3-6	.984	-1	98	68	*O-139(LF)/1	-0.3
1971	KC A	126	448	43	125	21	5	3	51	21-4	2	43	.279	.311	.368	94	-5	5-3	.986	-2	93	85	*O-115(LF)	-1.5
1972	KC A★	151	574	65	179	**33**	4	11	72	34-9	8	59	.312	.356	.441	138	26	7-2	.976	-2	99	69	*O-150(LF)	1.8
1973	KC A	144	513	53	128	28	1	9	69	30-7	2	65	.250	.291	.361	77	-16	5-7	.986	-7	80	104	*O-128(LF)/D-9	-3.2
1974	NY A	140	518	71	158	26	0	9	70	32-7	2	58	.305	.341	.407	119	12	1-8	.989	9	104	176	*O-130(99-0-34)/1D	1.2
1975	NY A	74	199	7	39	4	1	0	22	16-3	3	22	.196	.262	.226	41	-16	0-0	.986	-1	84	162	O-46(15-0-31),D-12	-2.0
1976	†NY A	100	327	36	92	16	6	3	38	18-8	2	34	.281	.322	.394	110	3	0-1	.982	2	106	113	O-49(10-0-39),D-38	0.1
1977	†NY A	103	339	47	112	19	3	12	45	20-3	1	31	.330	.365	.510	138	17	2-2	.975	-4	82	58	O-51(24-0-27),D-43/1	0.9
1978	†NY A	130	472	67	148	34	5	6	69	34-8	2	36	.314	.361	.445	129	18	3-1	.969	-2	103	58	*O-103(78-2-25),D-23	1.2
1979	NY A	130	461	49	137	22	2	11	69	17-6	2	31	.297	.320	.425	103	0	3-2	.982	1	93	161	*O-112(84-0-29),D-16	-0.4
1980	†NY A	116	321	39	92	18	0	2	27	29-5	0	20	.287	.343	.361	96	-1	0-2	.971	-1	97	134	*O-104(102-1-1)/D-7	-0.6
1981	†NY A	60	159	16	44	9	0	5	18	13-4	0	9	.277	.331	.428	119	4	0-1	.986	2	118	99	O-36(11-0-25),D-19	0.4
1982	NY A	102	261	33	80	17	1	6	37	18-6	1	18	.307	.352	.448	120	7	0-1	1.000	-0	98	87	D-55,O-40(13-0-27)	0.4
1983	NY A	53	148	19	43	9	1	2	16	11-3	1	12	.291	.344	.405	109	2	1-1	.959	-1	87	139	O-43(15-0-28)/D	-0.1
1984	NY A	29	86	8	26	4	1	1	6	7-1	0	5	.302	.355	.407	115	2	0-0	1.000	1	90	210	O-24(15-0-9)/D-2	0.1
Total	18	1747	5867	651	1705	305	41	102	766	368-82	31	541	.291	.333	.409	109	62	32-41	.981	4	97	109	*O-1401(1126-6-275),D-231/1-3	-1.7
PINKHAM, ED Edward B 1849 Brooklyn, NY BL/TL 5-7/142# d5.8 ▲																								
1871	Chi NA	24	95	27	25	5	5	1	17	**18**		3	.263	.381	.453	125	2	5-2	.754	9	159	57	3-18/O-8(RF),P-3	0.7
PINKNEY, GEORGE George Burton B 1.11.1862 Orange Prairie, IL D 11.10.1926 Peoria, IL BR/TR 5-7/160# d8.16																								
1884	Cle N	36	144	18	45	9	0	0	16	10		7	.313	.357	.375	126	5		.848	-6	83	93	2-25,S-11	0.0
1885	Bro AA	110	447	77	124	16	5	0	42	27	7		.277	.328	.336	109	6		.904	-6	101	66	2-57,3-51/S-3	0.2
1886	Bro AA	**141**	597	119	156	22	7	0	37	**70**	0		.261	.339	.322	106	7	32	.858	-16	84	83	*3-141/P	-0.6
1887	Bro AA	**138**	580	133	155	26	6	3	69	61	6		.267	.343	.348	92	-5	59	**.890**	15	107	122	*3-136/S-2	1.0
1888	Bro AA	**143**	575	**134**	156	18	8	4	52	66	12		.271	.358	.351	128	21	51	.898	-27	76	78	*3-143	-0.3
1889	†Bro AA	**138**	545	103	134	25	7	4	82	59	7	43	.246	.327	.339	90	-7	47	**.897**	-9	95	83	*3-138	-1.1
1890	†Bro N	126	485	115	150	20	9	7	83	80	4	19	.309	.411	.431	145	31	47	.933	-16	84	78	*3-126	1.5
1891	Bro N	135	501	80	137	19	6	2	71	67	7	32	.273	.367	.347	109	9	44	.904	-18	89	52	*3-130/S-5	-0.6
1892	StL N	78	290	31	50	3	2	0	25	36	2	26	.172	.268	.197	43	-19	4	.888	-8	92	93	3-78	-2.4

Year	Tm Lg	G	AB	R	H	2B	3B	HR	RBI	BB-IB	HP	SO	AVG	OBP	SLG	AOPS	ABR	SB-CS	FA	FR	Rng	Thr	G at Pos	BFW
1893	Lou N	118	446	64	105	12	6	1	62	50	8	8	.235	.323	.296	71	-17	12	.923	2	105	**114**	*3-118	-1.1
Total	10	1163	4610	874	1212	170	56	21	539	526	53	135	.263	.345	.338	103	31	296	.897	-90	91	86	*3-1061/2-82,S-21,P	-3.4
PINSON, VADA Vada Edward B 8.11.1938 Memphis, TN D 10.21.1995 Oakland, CA BL/TL 5-11/181# d4.15 C16																								
1958	Cin N	27	96	20	26	7	0	1	8	11-0	1	18	.271	.352	.375	88	-1	2-1	1.000	2	98	194	O-27(4-5-18)	0.0
1959	Cin N★	**154**	648	**131**	205	**47**	9	20	84	55-3	1	98	.316	.371	.509	128	26	21-6	.984	9	112	122	*O-154(CF)	3.0
1960	Cin N★	**154**	652	107	187	**37**	12	20	61	47-3	5	96	.287	.339	.472	117	14	32-12	.981	-2	100	92	*O-154(CF)	0.8
1961	†Cin N	**154**	607	101	**208**	34	8	16	87	39-1	1	63	.343	.379	.504	131	27	23-10	.976	9	106	169	*O-153(CF)	3.2
1962	Cin N	155	619	107	181	31	7	23	100	45-7	4	68	.292	.341	.477	114	11	26-8	.989	-2	94	127	*O-152(CF)	0.7
1963	Cin N	**162**	652	96	**204**	37	**14**	22	106	36-3	1	80	.313	.347	.514	141	32	27-8	.979	2	106	90	*O-162(0-147-17)	3.4
1964	Cin N	156	625	99	166	23	11	23	84	42-2	5	99	.266	.316	.448	109	6	8-2	.972	-4	93	150	*O-156(CF)	-0.3
1965	Cin N	159	669	97	204	34	10	22	94	43-3	7	81	.305	.352	.484	125	21	21-8	**.992**	4	106	104	*O-159(CF)	2.3
1966	Cin N	156	618	70	178	35	6	16	76	33-6	5	83	.288	.326	.442	103	3	18-10	.964	-4	100	83	*O-154(0-139-24)	-0.7
1967	Cin N	158	650	90	187	28	**13**	18	66	26-1	3	86	.288	.318	.454	106	4	26-8	.986	-4	99	47	*O-157(CF)	-0.3
1968	Cin N	130	499	60	135	29	6	5	48	32-8	0	59	.271	.311	.383	102	1	17-11	.978	-7	89	88	*O-123(1-120-3)	-1.2
1969	StL N	132	495	58	126	22	6	10	70	35-2	3	63	.255	.303	.384	92	-6	4-4	**.996**	-3	99	64	*O-124(0-1-124)	-1.7
1970	Cle A	148	574	74	164	28	6	24	82	28-7	3	69	.286	.319	.481	113	7	7-6	.982	4	109	94	*O-141(15-14-120)/1-7	0.4
1971	Cle A	146	566	60	149	23	4	11	35	21-0	6	58	.263	.295	.376	82	-14	25-6	.978	1	99	130	*O-141(9-100-39)/1-3	-1.7
1972	Cal A	136	484	56	133	24	2	7	49	30-12	5	54	.275	.321	.376	114	7	17-6	.991	-2	90	123	*O-134(104-15-29)/1	0.0
1973	Cal A	124	466	56	121	14	6	8	57	20-3	0	55	.260	.286	.367	91	-9	5-5	.965	-1	92	144	*O-120(75-32-25)	-1.7
1974	KC A	115	406	46	112	18	2	6	41	21-4	2	45	.276	.312	.374	92	-5	21-5	.980	-3	91	115	*O-110(14-6-91)/1D	-1.1
1975	KC A	103	319	38	71	14	5	4	22	10-4	2	21	.223	.248	.335	63	-17	5-6	.993	-1	96	104	O-82(12-12-59)/1-4,D-5	-2.4
Total	18	2469	9645	1366	2757	485	127	256	1170	574-69	54	1196	.286	.327	.442	110	107	305-122	.981	-4	99	109	*O-2403(234-1676-549)/1-16,D-7	2.7
PIPP, WALLY Walter Clement B 2.17.1893 Chicago, IL D 1.11.1965 Grand Rapids, MI BL/TL 6-1/180# d6.29 Mil 1918																								
1913	Det A	12	31	3	5	0	3	0	5	2	1	6	.161	.235	.355	73	-2	0	.977	-1	85	136	1-10	-0.2
1915	NY A	136	479	59	118	20	13	4	60	66	1	81	.246	.339	.367	112	7	18-7	**.992**	2	104	**125**	*1-134	0.8
1916	NY A	151	545	70	143	20	14	**12**	93	54	2	82	.262	.331	.417	122	12	16	.992	5	111	**112**	*1-148	1.4
1917	NY A	**155**	587	82	143	29	12	**9**	70	60	6	66	.244	.320	.380	112	7	11	.990	4	109	110	*1-155	0.8
1918	NY A	91	349	48	106	15	9	2	44	22	0	34	.304	.345	.415	127	9	11	.988	1	101	130	1-91	0.8
1919	NY A	138	523	74	144	23	10	7	50	39	4	42	.275	.330	.398	103	0	9	.991	0	99	112	*1-138	-0.3
1920	NY A	153	610	109	171	30	14	11	76	48	6	54	.280	.339	.430	99	-3	4-10	.991	0	99	**121**	*1-153	-0.9
1921	†NY A	**153**	588	96	174	35	9	8	97	45	1	28	.296	.347	.427	94	-6	17-10	.991	-5	88	**114**	*1-153	-2.0
1922	†NY A	152	577	96	190	32	10	9	90	56	4	32	.329	.392	.466	120	18	7-12	.993	-6	85	107	*1-152	-0.1
1923	†NY A	144	569	79	173	19	8	6	108	36	6	28	.304	.352	.397	95	-6	6-13	.992	-4	87	99	*1-144	-2.2
1924	NY A	**153**	589	88	174	30	**19**	9	114	51	0	36	.295	.352	.457	108	3	12-5	**.994**	1	98	96	*1-153	-0.5
1925	NY A	62	178	19	41	6	3	3	24	13	1	12	.230	.286	.348	61	-12	3-3	.991	4	131	119	1-47	-1.0
1926	Cin N	155	574	72	167	22	15	6	99	49	5	26	.291	.352	.413	108	5	8	.992	2	104	**123**	*1-155	-0.3
1927	Cin N	122	443	49	115	19	6	2	41	32	0	11	.260	.309	.343	77	-15	2	**.996**	1	97	104	*1-114	-2.2
1928	Cin N	95	272	30	77	11	3	2	26	23	1	13	.283	.341	.368	87	-5	1	.989	1	109	124	1-72	-0.8
Total	15	1872	6914	974	1941	311	148	90	997	596	38	551	.281	.341	.408	104	12	125-60	.992	6	100	113	*1-1819	-6.7
PIRIE, JIM James Moir B 3.31.1853 Ontario, , CAN D 6.2.1934 Dundas, ON, CAN 5-8/169# d9.25																								
1883	Phi N	5	19	1	3	0	0	0	0	0		2	.158	.158	.158	-4	-2		.577	-4	66	65	/S-5	-0.5
PIRKL, GREG Gregory Daniel B 8.7.1970 Long Beach, CA BR/TR 6-5/225# d8.13																								
1993	Sea A	7	23	1	4	0	0	1	4	0-0	0	4	.174	.174	.304	25	-3	0-0	1.000	1	149	186	/1-5,D-2	-0.2
1994	Sea A	19	53	7	14	3	0	6	11	1-1	1	12	.264	.286	.660	133	2	0-0	.983	-1	24	48	D-10/1-7	-0.1
1995	Sea A	10	17	2	4	0	0	0	0	1-0	0	7	.235	.278	.235	35	-2	0-0	1.000	0	109	28	/1-6,D	-0.2
1996	Sea A	7	21	2	4	1	0	1	1	0-0	0	3	.190	.190	.381	40	-2	0-0	1.000	0	160	115	/1-2,D-3	-0.2
	Bos A	2	2	0	0	0	0	0	0	0-0	0	1	.000	.000	.000	-98	-1	0-0	—	0			/H	-0.1
	Year	9	23	2	4	1	0	1	1	0-0	0	4	.174	.174	.348	27	-3	0-0	1.000	0	160	115	/D-3,1-2	-0.3
Total	4	45	116	12	26	4	0	8	16	2-1	1	27	.224	.242	.466	77	-6	0-0	.994	0	93	90	/1-20,D-16	-0.8
PISONI, JIM James Pete B 8.14.1929 St.Louis, MO BR/TR 5-10/169# d9.25																								
1953	StL A	3	12	1	1	0	0	1	1	0	0	5	.083	.083	.333	8	-2	0-0	1.000	-0	106	0	/O-3(0-2-1)	-0.2
1956	KC A	10	30	4	8	0	0	2	5	2-0	0	8	.267	.303	.467	103	0	0-0	.966	3	117	517	/O-9(LF)	0.3
1957	KC A	44	97	14	23	2	2	3	12	10-1	2	17	.237	.318	.392	92	-1	0-0	.989	3	113	138	O-44(0-44-1)	0.0
1959	Mil N	9	24	4	4	1	0	0	0	2-0	0	6	.167	.231	.208	20	-3	0-0	.941	0	95	236	/O-9(2-8-0)	-0.3
	NY A	17	17	2	3	0	1	0	1	1-0	0	9	.176	.222	.294	42	-2	0-0	1.000	1	130	0	O-15(9-3-3)	-0.1
1960	NY A	20	9	1	1	0	0	0	1	1-0	0	2	.111	.200	.111	-14	-1	0-0	.938	1	150	0	O-18(12-6-0)	-0.1
Total	5	103	189	26	40	3	3	6	20	16-1	2	47	.212	.278	.354	71	-9	0-0	.978	7	116	180	/O-98(32-63-5)	-0.4
PITKO, ALEX Alexander "Spunk" B 11.22.1914 Burlington, NJ BR/TR 5-10/180# d9.11																								
1938	Phi N	7	19	2	6	1	0	0	2	3	0	3	.316	.409	.368	118	1	1	.889	-1	86	0	/O-7(RF)	0.0
1939	Was A	4	8	0	1	0	0	0	1	1	0	3	.125	.222	.125	-10	-1	0-0	1.000	-0	87	0	/O-3(2-0-1)	-0.2
Total	2	11	27	2	7	1	0	0	3	4	0	6	.259	.355	.296	80	0	1-0	.917	-1	86	0	/O-10(2-0-8)	-0.2
PITLER, JAKE Jacob Albert B 4.22.1894 New York, NY D 2.3.1968 Binghamton, NY BR/TR 5-8/150# d5.30 C11																								
1917	Pit N	109	382	39	89	8	5	0	23	30	5	24	.233	.297	.280	75	-11	6	**.966**	-15	85	90	*2-106/O-3(1-0-1)	-2.8
1918	Pit N	2	1	1	0	0	0	0	0	1	0	0	.000	.500	.000	55	0	2	.667	-0	97	0	/2	0.0
Total	2	111	383	40	89	8	5	0	23	31	5	24	.232	.298	.279	75	-11	8	.962	-16	85	89	2-107/O-3(1-0-1)	-2.8
PITTARO, CHRIS Christopher Francis B 9.16.1961 Trenton, NJ BB/TR 5-11/170# d4.8																								
1985	Det A	28	62	10	15	3	1	0	7	5-0	0	13	.242	.299	.323	71	-3	1-1	.881	-2	92	37	3-22/2-4,D	-0.5
1986	Min A	11	21	0	2	0	0	0	0	0-0	0	8	.095	.095	.095	-47	-4	0-0	.969	0	92	180	/2-8,S-4	-0.4
1987	Min A	14	12	6	4	0	0	0	0	1-0	0	0	.333	.385	.333	90	0	1-0	1.000	-2	48	108	/2-8,D-2	-0.2
Total	3	53	95	16	21	3	1	0	7	6-0	0	21	.221	.267	.274	48	-7	2-1	.881	-4	92	37	/3-22,2-20,S-4,D-3	-1.1
PITTINGER, PINKY Clarke Alonzo B 2.24.1899 Hudson, MI D 11.4.1977 Ft.Lauderdale, FL BR/TR 5-10/160# d4.15																								
1921	Bos A	40	91	6	18	1	0	0	5	4	0	13	.198	.232	.209	13	-12	3-2	.985	3	117	132	O-27(19-4-4)/3-3,S-2,2	-1.0
1922	Bos A	66	186	16	48	3	0	0	7	9	2	10	.258	.299	.274	51	-14	2-5	.920	-2	97	136	3-33,S-29	-1.2
1923	Bos A	60	177	15	38	5	0	0	15	5	0	10	.215	.236	.243	26	-20	3-1	.959	-8	87	61	2-42,S-10/3-3	-2.5
1925	Chi N	59	173	21	54	7	2	0	15	12	2	7	.312	.364	.376	88	-3	5-4	.940	2	100	69	S-24,3-24	0.2
1927	Cin N	31	84	17	23	5	0	1	10	2	0	5	.274	.291	.369	78	-3	4	.963	1	111	158	2-20/S-9,3-2	-0.1
1928	Cin N	40	38	12	9	0	1	0	4	0	0	1	.237	.237	.289	37	-4	2	.892	4	145	221	S-12/2-4,3-4	0.1
1929	Cin N	77	210	31	62	11	0	0	27	5	2	4	.295	.318	.348	68	-11	8	.956	2	99	130	S-50/3-8,2-4	-0.3
Total	7	373	959	118	252	32	3	1	83	37	6	50	.263	.294	.306	55	-67	27-12	.938	1	102	103	S-136/3-77,2-71,O-27(19-4-4)	-4.8
PITTMAN, JOE Joseph Wayne B 1.1.1954 Houston, TX BR/TR 6-1/180# d4.25																								
1981	†Hou N	52	135	11	38	4	2	0	7	11-3	0	16	.281	.333	.341	97	-1	4-4	.980	-6	90	82	2-35/3-4	-0.6
1982	Hou N	15	10	0	2	1	0	0	0	0-0	0	2	.200	.200	.300	41	-1	0-0	1.000	0	76	0	/3-3,O(RF)	-0.1
	SD N	55	118	16	30	2	0	0	7	9-2	0	13	.254	.307	.271	66	-5	8-3	.964	-6	101	106	2-30,S-13	-0.9
	Year	70	128	16	32	3	0	0	7	9-2	0	15	.250	.299	.273	65	-6	8-3	.964	-6	101	106	2-30,S-13/3-3,O(RF)	-1.0
1984	SF N	17	22	2	5	0	0	0	2	0-0	0	6	.227	.217	.227	29	-2	1-1	.900	-4	89	0	/S-6,2-5,3-2	-0.6
Total	3	139	285	29	75	7	2	0	16	20-5	0	37	.263	.309	.302	77	-9	13-8	.974	-16	94	91	/2-70,S-19,3-9,O(RF)	-2.2
PITTS, GAYLEN Gaylen Richard B 6.6.1946 Wichita, KS BR/TR 6-1/175# d5.12 C5																								
1974	Oak A	18	41	4	10	3	0	0	3	5-0	0	4	.244	.326	.317	92	0	0-0	.909	-1	96	57	3-11/2-6,1	-0.1
1975	Oak A	10	3	1	1	1	0	0	1	0-0	0	0	.333	.333	.667	181	0	0-0	.800	1	124	0	/3-6,S-2,2	0.1
Total	2	28	44	5	11	4	0	0	4	5-0	0	4	.250	.327	.341	98	0	0-0	.895	-0	99	51	/3-17,2-7,S-2,1	0.0
PITZ, HERMAN Herman B 7.18.1865 Brooklyn, NY D 9.3.1924 Far Rockaway, NY 5-6/140# d4.18																								
1890	Bro AA	61	189	26	26	0	0	0	6	45	3		.138	.312	.138	34	-12	25	.885	-11	*82*	*96*	C-34,3-16/O-9(5-0-4),S-2,2	-1.8
	Syr AA	29	95	17	21	0	0	0	3	13	1		.221	.321	.221	67	-3	14	.929	-7	*79*	*108*	C-27/SO(CF)	-0.6
	Year	90	284	43	47	0	0	0	9	58	4		.165	.315	.165	44	-15	39	.906	-17	*81*	*101*	C-61,3-16,O-10(5-1-4)/S-3,2	-2.4

Year	Tm Lg	G	AB	R	H	2B	3B	HR	RBI	BB-IB	HP	SO	AVG	OBP	SLG	AOPS	ABR	SB-CS	FA	FR	Rng	Thr	G at Pos	BFW
PLANTIER, PHIL Phillip Alan B 1.27.1969 Manchester, NH BL/TR 5-11/195# d8.21																								
1990	Bos A	14	15	1	2	1	0	0	3	4-0	1	6	.133	.333	.200	55	-1	0-0	—	-0	0	0	/O(LF)D	-0.1
1991	Bos A	53	148	27	49	7	1	11	35	23-2	1	38	.331	.420	.615	175	16	1-0	.976	2	120	46	O-40(16-0-27)/D-5	1.6
1992	Bos A	108	349	46	86	19	0	7	30	44-8	2	83	.246	.332	.361	89	-4	2-3	.975	1	100	125	O-76(13-0-63),D-23	-0.7
1993	SD N	138	462	67	111	20	1	34	100	61-7	7	124	.240	.335	.509	121	13	4-5	.990	10	106	147	*O-134(LF)	1.7
1994	SD N	96	341	44	75	21	0	18	41	36-6	5	91	.220	.302	.440	93	-4	3-1	.988	1	97	97	O-91(LF)	-0.6
1995	Hou N	22	68	12	17	2	0	4	15	11-1	1	19	.250	.349	.456	123	2	0-0	.962	-2	80	0	O-20(8-0-12)	-0.1
	SD N	54	148	21	38	4	0	5	19	17-2	0	29	.257	.333	.385	92	-2	1-1	.958	3	104	238	O-39(LF)	-0.1
	Year	76	216	33	55	6	0	9	34	28-3	1	48	.255	.339	.407	101	0	1-1	.959	1	96	162	O-59(47-0-12)	-0.2
1996	Oak A	73	231	29	49	8	1	7	31	28-0	3	56	.212	.304	.346	66	-13	2-2	.973	4	102	175	O-68(67-1-1)/D	-1.1
1997	SD N	10	8	0	1	0	0	0	0	2-0	0	3	.125	.300	.125	18	-1	0-0	1.000	0	125	0	/O-3(LF)	-0.1
	StL N	42	113	13	29	8	0	5	18	11-1	3	27	.257	.333	.460	108	1	0-3	.981	-1	96	48	O-32(10-0-23)	-0.2
	Year	52	121	13	30	8	0	5	18	13-1	3	30	.248	.331	.438	103	1	0-3	.982	-1	97	46	O-35(13-0-23)	-0.3
Total	8	610	1883	260	457	90	3	91	292	237-27	23	476	.243	.332	.439	103	7	13-15	.980	17	102	126	O-504(382-1-126)/D-33	0.3
PLARSKI, DON Donald Joseph B 11.9.1929 Chicago, IL D 12.29.1981 St.Louis, MO BR/TR 5-6/160# d7.20																								
1955	KC A	8	11	0	1	0	0	0	0	0-0	0	2	.091	.091	.091	-50	-2	1-0	1.000	-0	105	0	/O-6(CF)	-0.2
PLASKETT, ELMO Elmo Alexander B 6.27.1938 Frederiksted, V.I. D 11.2.1998 Christiansted, V.I. BR/TR 5-10/195# d9.8																								
1962	Pit N	7	14	2	4	0	0	1	3	1-0	0	3	.286	.333	.500	120	0	0-0	1.000	-1	*65*	*0*	/C-4	0.0
1963	Pit N	10	21	1	3	0	0	0	2	0-0	0	5	.143	.143	.143	-17	-3	0-0	1.000	-1	*67*	*0*	/C-5,3	-0.4
Total	2	17	35	3	7	0	0	1	5	1-0	0	8	.200	.222	.286	41	-3	0-0	1.000	-2	*66*	*0*	/C-9,3	-0.4
PLATT, WHITEY Mizell George B 8.21.1920 W.Palm Beach, FL D 7.27.1970 W.Palm Beach, FL BR/TR 6-2/195# d9.16 Mil 1944-45																								
1942	Chi N	4	16	1	1	0	0	0	2	0	0	3	.063	.063	.063	-66	-3	0	1.000	0	87	352	/O-4(2-2-0)	-0.4
1943	Chi N	20	41	2	7	3	0	0	2	1	0	7	.171	.190	.244	25	-4	0	.952	-1	98	0	O-14(7-7-0)	-0.6
1946	Chi A	84	247	28	62	8	5	3	32	17	3	34	.251	.307	.360	89	-5	1-7	.971	-1	96	93	O-61(25-23-14)	-1.2
1948	StL A	123	454	57	123	22	10	7	82	39	2	51	.271	.331	.410	94	-6	1-4	.948	-7	92	60	*O-114(LF)	-2.3
1949	StL A	102	244	29	63	8	2	3	29	24	0	27	.258	.325	.344	74	-10	0-1	.986	1	108	73	O-59(LF)/1-2	-1.3
Total	5	333	1002	117	256	41	17	13	147	81	5	122	.255	.314	.369	83	-28	2-12	.964	-8	97	73	O-252(207-32-14)/1-2	-5.8
PLATTE, AL Alfred Frederick Joseph B 4.13.1890 Grand Rapids, MI D 8.29.1976 Grand Rapids, MI BL/TL 5-7/160# d9.1																								
1913	Det A	9	18	1	2	1	0	0	0	1	0	1	.111	.158	.167	-5	-2	0	.800	-1	96	0	/O-5(LF)	-0.4
PLESS, RANCE Rance B 12.6.1925 Greeneville, TN BR/TR 6/145# d4.21																								
1956	KC A	48	85	4	23	3	1	0	9	10-0	1	13	.271	.354	.329	81	-2	0-1	1.000	2	83	141	1-15/3-5	-0.2
PLEWS, HERB Herbert Eugene B 6.14.1928 Helena, MT BL/TR 5-11/160# d4.18																								
1956	Was A	91	256	24	69	10	7	1	25	26-3	1	40	.270	.337	.375	88	-5	1-2	.947	-2	110	77	2-66/S-5,3-2	-0.3
1957	Was A	104	329	51	89	19	4	1	26	28-1	2	39	.271	.326	.362	90	-4	0-3	.979	-9	90	73	2-79,3-11/S-4	-1.0
1958	Was A	111	380	46	98	12	6	2	29	17-1	1	45	.258	.291	.337	74	-15	2-3	.976	-13	93	83	2-64,3-36	-2.6
1959	Was A	27	40	4	9	0	0	0	2	3-0	0	5	.225	.279	.225	40	-3	0-1	.971	0	96	49	/2-6	-0.3
	Bos A	13	12	0	1	1	0	0	0	0-0	0	4	.083	.083	.167	-32	-2	0-0	.833	0	106	200	/2-2	-0.2
	Year	40	52	4	10	1	0	0	2	3-0	0	9	.192	.236	.212	24	-6	0-1	.951	0	97	65	/2-8	-0.5
Total	4	346	1017	125	266	42	17	4	82	74-5	4	133	.262	.312	.348	80	-29	3-9	.967	-24	97	77	2-217/3-49,S-9	-4.4
PLOCK, WALTER Walter S. B 7.2.1869 Philadelphia, PA D 4.28.1900 Richmond, VA 6-3/180# d8.21																								
1891	Phi N	2	5	2	2	0	0	0	0	0	1	1	.400	.500	.400	159	0	0	.000	-1	0	0	/O-2(CF)	0.0
PLUMMER, BILL William Francis B 3.21.1947 Oakland, CA BR/TR 6-1/200# d4.19 M1 C7																								
1968	Chi N	2	2	0	0	0	0	0	0	0-0	0	1	.000	.000	.000	-94	0	0-0	1.000	-0	*0*	*0*	/C	-0.1
1970	Cin N	4	8	0	1	0	0	0	0	0-0	1	2	.125	.222	.125	-4	-1	0-0	.857	-2	35	0	/C-4	-0.3
1971	Cin N	10	19	0	0	0	0	0	0	0-0	0	4	.000	.000	.000	-99	-5	0-0	1.000	-1	0	172	/C-4,3-2	-0.6
1972	Cin N	38	102	8	19	4	0	2	9	4-2	0	20	.186	.211	.284	44	-8	0-0	.994	-4	224	84	C-36/13	-1.1
1973	Cin N	50	119	8	18	3	0	2	11	18-5	1	26	.151	.268	.227	41	-9	1-0	.994	-5	119	65	C-42/3-5	-1.3
1974	Cin N	50	120	7	27	7	0	2	10	6-0	0	21	.225	.258	.333	67	-6	1-0	.974	-2	116	44	C-49/3	-0.6
1975	Cin N	65	159	17	29	7	0	1	19	24-2	2	28	.182	.291	.245	51	-10	1-0	.990	-8	117	14	C-63	-1.6
1976	Cin N	56	153	16	38	6	1	4	19	14-0	0	36	.248	.311	.379	93	-2	0-2	.977	-2	79	60	C-54	-0.2
1977	Cin N	51	117	10	16	5	0	1	7	17-1	0	34	.137	.244	.205	22	-13	1-1	.986	-3	158	66	C-50	-1.5
1978	Sea A	41	93	6	20	5	0	2	7	12-0	0	19	.215	.305	.333	80	-2	0-0	.978	-11	68	24	C-40	-1.2
Total	10	367	892	72	168	37	1	14	82	95-10	4	191	.188	.267	.279	53	-56	4-3	.984	-36	*120*	*50*	C-343/3-9,1	-8.5
POCOROBA, BIFF Biff B 7.25.1953 Burbank, CA BB/TR (BL 1975 part, 1977 part, 1980 part, 1981-84) 5-10/180# d4.25																								
1975	Atl N	67	188	15	48	7	1	1	22	20-2	0	11	.255	.325	.319	77	-6	0-0	.970	-11	55	79	C-62	-1.4
1976	Atl N	54	174	16	42	7	0	0	14	19-2	0	12	.241	.313	.282	66	-7	1-0	.978	5	114	95	C-54	0.1
1977	Atl N	113	321	46	93	24	1	8	44	57-15	1	27	.290	.394	.445	113	9	3-4	.989	-3	71	**133**	*C-100	0.9
1978	Atl N★	92	289	21	70	8	0	6	34	29-6	2	14	.242	.312	.332	73	-10	0-3	.990	-3	76	88	C-79	-1.1
1979	Atl N	28	38	6	12	4	0	0	4	7-1	0	0	.316	.422	.421	122	2	1-1	.933	0	55	132	/C-7	0.2
1980	Atl N	70	83	7	22	4	0	2	8	11-0	0	11	.265	.347	.386	102	1	1-0	.934	-1	51	27	C-10	0.0
1981	Atl N	57	122	4	22	4	0	0	8	12-1	2	15	.180	.265	.213	36	-10	0-0	.938	-2	80	130	3-21/C-9	-1.3
1982	†Atl N	56	120	5	33	7	0	2	22	13-2	1	12	.275	.351	.383	101	1	0-0	.988	-7	58	112	C-36/3-2	-0.5
1983	Atl N	55	120	11	32	6	0	2	16	12-4	0	7	.267	.331	.367	87	-2	0-0	.983	-5	65	74	C-34	-0.5
1984	Atl N	4	2	1	0	0	0	0	0	2-0	0	0	.000	.500	.000	48	0	0-0	—	0			/H	0.0
Total	10	596	1457	132	374	71	2	21	172	182-33	6	109	.257	.339	.351	86	-22	6-8	.982	-26	74	100	C-391/3-23	-3.6
PODSEDNIK, SCOTT Scott Eric B 3.18.1976 West, TX BL/TL 6/170# d7.6																								
2001	Sea A	5	6	1	1	0	1	0	3	0-0	0	1	.167	.167	.500	70	0	0-0	1.000	-0	63	0	/O-5(3-1-1)	-0.1
2002	Sea A	14	20	2	4	0	0	1	5	4-0	0	6	.200	.320	.350	85	0	0-0	.938	0	127	0	O-11(9-1-2)/D-2	0.0
2003	Mil N	154	558	100	175	29	8	9	58	56-2	4	91	.314	.379	.443	116	14	43-10	.992	2	107	65	*O-139(3-123-13)	2.2
Total	3	173	584	103	180	29	9	10	66	60-2	4	98	.308	.375	.440	115	14	43-10	.989	2	107	61	O-155(15-125-16)/D-2	2.1
POEPPING, MIKE Michael Harold B 8.7.1950 Little Falls, MN BR/TR 6-6/230# d9.6																								
1975	Min A	14	37	0	5	1	0	0	1	5-0	0	7	.135	.238	.162	15	-4	0-0	.950	-1	82	107	O-13(RF)	-0.6
POFAHL, JIMMY James Willard B 6.18.1917 Faribault, MN D 9.14.1984 Owatonna, MN BR/TR 5-11/185# d4.16																								
1940	Was A	119	406	34	95	23	5	2	36	37	0	55	.234	.298	.330	67	-21	2-0	.952	-3	96	98	*S-112/2-4	-1.4
1941	Was A	22	75	9	14	3	2	0	6	10	0	11	.187	.282	.280	52	-5	1-0	.934	-3	101	61	S-21	-0.6
1942	Was A	84	283	22	59	7	2	0	28	29	0	30	.208	.282	.247	50	-19	4-3	.956	-1	96	108	S-49,2-15,3-14	-1.6
Total	3	225	764	65	168	33	9	2	70	76	0	96	.220	.290	.295	59	-45	7-3	.951	-7	97	97	S-182/2-19,3-14	-3.6
POFF, JOHN John William B 10.23.1952 Chillicothe, OH BL/TL 6-2/190# d9.8																								
1979	Phi N	12	19	2	2	1	0	0	1	1-0	0	4	.105	.150	.158	-15	-3	0-0	.875	-0	107	0	/O-4(LF),1	-0.4
1980	Mil A	19	68	7	17	1	2	1	7	3-2	0	7	.250	.282	.368	79	-2	0-0	1.000	-1	104	0	/O-7(RF),1-3,D-7	-0.4
Total	2	31	87	9	19	2	2	1	8	4-2	0	11	.218	.253	.322	57	-5	0-0	.957	-2	105	0	/O-11(4-0-7),D-7,1-4	-0.8
POINTER, AARON Aaron Elton "Hawk" B 4.19.1942 Little Rock, AR BR/TR 6-2/185# d9.22																								
1963	Hou N	2	5	0	1	0	0	0	0	0-0	0	1	.200	.200	.200	17	-1	0-0	1.000	-0	75	0	/O(RF)	-0.1
1966	Hou N	11	26	5	9	1	0	1	5	5-0	1	6	.346	.469	.500	182	3	1-1	1.000	2	95	564	O-11(LF)	0.5
1967	Hou N	27	70	6	11	4	0	1	10	13-1	1	26	.157	.291	.257	62	-3	1-0	.951	1	109	158	O-22(LF)	-0.3
Total	3	40	101	11	21	5	0	2	15	18-1	2	33	.208	.333	.317	91	-1	2-1	.966	3	104	260	/O-34(33-0-1)	0.1
POLANCO, PLACIDO Placido Enrique B 10.10.1975 Santo Domingo, D.R. BR/TR 5-10/168# d7.3																								
1998	StL N	45	114	10	29	3	2	1	11	5-0	1	9	.254	.292	.342	67	-6	2-0	.952	5	124	129	S-28,2-14	0.2
1999	StL N	88	220	24	61	9	3	1	19	15-1	0	24	.277	.321	.359	72	-10	1-3	.979	0	99	102	2-66/3-9,S-9	-0.7
2000	†StL N	118	323	50	102	12	3	5	39	16-0	1	26	.316	.347	.418	93	-5	4-4	.984	4	95	72	2-51,3-35,S-29/1	0.3
2001	†StL N	144	564	87	173	26	4	3	38	25-0	6	43	.307	.342	.383	88	-10	12-3	.985	24	117	104	*3-103,S-42,2-15/D	1.9
2002	StL N	94	342	47	97	19	1	5	27	12-1	4	27	.284	.316	.389	90	-8	3-1	.974	6	110	141	3-78,S-13/2-6	0.0
	Phi N	53	206	28	61	13	1	4	22	14-0	4	14	.296	.353	.427	113	3	2-2	.983	12	126	141	3-53	1.5

Year	Tm Lg	G	AB	R	H	2B	3B	HR	RBI	BB-IB	HP	SO	AVG	OBP	SLG	AOPS	ABR	SB-CS	FA	FR	Rng	Thr	G at Pos	BFW
	Year	147	548	75	158	32	2	9	49	26-1	8	41	.288	.330	.403	98	-5	5-3	.978	18	117	141	*3-131,S-13/2-6	1.5
2003	Phi N	122	492	87	142	30	3	14	63	42-1	8	38	.289	.352	.447	114	10	14-2	.992	5	103	103	2-99,3-21	2.2
Total	6	664	2261	333	665	112	17	33	219	129-3	24	181	.294	.337	.402	94	-26	38-15	.980	56	114	131	3-299,2-251,S-121/D1	5.4
POLAND, HUGH Hugh Reid B 1.19.1913 Tompkinsville, KY D 3.30.1984 Guthrie, KY BL/TR 5-11.5/185# d4.22 Mil 1945																								
1943	NY N	4	12	1	1	0	1	0	2	1	0	0	.083	.154	.250	16	-1	0	.889	-1	*78*	*162*	/C-4	-0.3
	Bos N	44	141	5	27	7	0	0	13	4	0	11	.191	.214	.241	32	-13	0	.973	-5	*58*	*46*	C-38	-1.7
	Year	48	153	6	28	7	1	0	15	5	0	11	.183	.209	.242	30	-14	0	.969	-6	*59*	*53*	C-42	-2.0
1944	Bos N	8	23	1	3	1	0	0	2	0	0	1	.130	.130	.174	-14	-4	0	.939	-0	*67*	*0*	/C-6	-0.4
1946	Bos N	4	6	0	1	1	0	0	0	0	0	0	.167	.167	.333	40	0	0	1.000	-0	*43*	*0*	/C-2	-0.1
1947	Phi N	4	8	0	0	0	0	0	0	0	0	0	.000	.000	.000	-99	-2	0	1.000	0	*47*	*267*	/C-2	-0.2
	Cin N	16	18	1	6	1	0	0	2	1	0	4	.333	.368	.389	102	0	0	.667	-1	*0*	*0*	/C-3	-0.1
	Year	20	26	1	6	1	0	0	2	1	0	4	.231	.259	.269	41	-2	0	.867	-1	*27*	*154*	/C-5	-0.3
1948	Cin N	3	3	0	1	0	0	0	0	0	0	0	.333	.333	.333	84	0	0	—	0			H	0.0
Total	5	83	211	8	39	10	1	0	19	6	0	16	.185	.207	.242	28	-20	0	.958	-7	*58*	*51*	/C-55	-2.8
POLCOVICH, KEVIN Kevin Michael B 6.28.1970 Auburn, NY BR/TR 5-9/170# d5.17																								
1997	Pit N	84	245	37	67	16	1	4	21	21-4	9	45	.273	.350	.396	94	-1	2-2	.969	13	116	83	S-80/2-2,3	1.7
1998	Pit N	81	212	18	40	12	0	0	14	15-2	5	33	.189	.255	.245	33	-21	4-3	.916	14	115	113	S-54,2-15/3-8	-0.3
Total	2	165	457	55	107	28	1	4	35	36-6	14	78	.234	.307	.326	66	-22	6-5	.948	27	116	95	S-134/2-17,3-9	1.4
POLHEMUS, MARK Mark S. "Humpty Dumpty" B 10.4.1862 Brooklyn, NY D 11.12.1923 Lynn, MA 5-6.5/185# d7.13																								
1887	Ind N	20	75	6	18	1	0	0	8	2	0	9	.240	.260	.253	45	-6	4	.744	0	236	0	O-20(RF)	-0.5
POLIDOR, GUS Gustavo Adolfo (Gonzalez) B 10.26.1961 Caracas, Venezuela D 4.28.1995 Caracas, Venezuela BR/TR 6/170# d9.7																								
1985	Cal A	2	1	1	1	0	0	0	0	0-0	0	0	1.000	1.000	1.000	452	0	0-0	1.000	0	207	0	/SO(RF)	0.1
1986	Cal A	6	19	1	5	1	0	0	1	1-0	0	0	.263	.300	.316	69	-1	0-0	1.000	-2	71	89	/2-4,S3	-0.2
1987	Cal A	63	137	12	36	3	0	2	15	2-0	1	15	.263	.277	.328	62	-8	0-0	.983	-12	83	60	S-46,3-11/2-3	-1.6
1988	Cal A	54	81	4	12	3	0	0	4	3-0	0	11	.148	.179	.185	2	-11	0-0	.984	-2	109	64	S-25,3-22/2-3,D	-1.2
1989	Mil A	79	175	15	34	7	0	0	14	6-0	2	18	.194	.230	.234	31	-16	3-0	.923	-5	105	105	3-30,2-29,S-21/D-2	-2.0
1990	Mil A	18	15	0	1	0	0	0	1	0-0	0	1	.067	.067	.067	-63	-3	0-0	1.000	-1	105	0	3-14/2-2,S-2	-0.5
1993	Fla N	7	6	0	1	1	0	0	0	0-0	0	2	.167	.167	.333	28	-1	0-0	—	-0	0	0	/23	-0.1
Total	7	229	434	33	90	15	0	2	35	12-0	3	47	.207	.233	.256	35	-40	3-0	.970	-22	93	75	/S-96,3-79,2-42,D-3,O(RF)	-5.5
POLLY, NICK Nicholas (born Nicholas Joseph Polachanin) B 4.18.1917 Chicago, IL D 1.17.1993 Chicago, IL BR/TR 5-11/190# d9.11																								
1937	Bro N	10	18	2	4	0	0	0	2	0	0	1	.222	.222	.222	21	-2	0	.850	1	142	0	/3-7	-0.1
1945	Bos A	4	7	0	1	0	0	0	1	0	0	1	.143	.143	.143	-17	-1	0-0	1.000	0	99	0	/3-2	-0.1
Total	2	14	25	2	5	0	0	0	3	0	0	2	.200	.200	.200	11	-3	0-0	.870	1	135	0	/3-9	-0.2
POLONIA, LUIS Luis Andrew (Almonte) B 10.12.1964 Santiago, D.R. BL/TL 5-8/152# d4.24																								
1987	Oak A	125	435	78	125	16	10	4	49	32-1	0	64	.287	.335	.398	100	-1	29-7	.979	0	105	40	*O-104(35-69-8),D-18	0.0
1988	†Oak A	84	288	51	84	11	4	2	27	21-0	0	40	.292	.338	.378	104	1	24-9	.988	1	104	73	O-76(76-0-1)/D-2	0.2
1989	Oak A	59	206	31	59	6	4	1	17	9-0	0	15	.286	.315	.369	96	-2	13-4	.985	6	123	104	O-55(LF)	0.3
	NY A	66	227	39	71	11	2	2	29	16-1	2	29	.313	.359	.405	118	5	9-4	.982	3	105	203	O-53(LF)/D-9	0.8
	Year	125	433	70	130	17	6	3	46	25-1	2	44	.300	.338	.388	108	3	22-8	.984	9	114	154	*O-108(LF)/D-9	1.1
1990	NY A	11	22	2	7	0	0	0	3	0-0	0	1	.318	.304	.318	78	-1	1-0	—	0			/D-4	-0.1
	Cal A	109	381	50	128	7	9	2	32	25-1	1	42	.336	.376	.417	125	11	20-14	.980	-6	86	61	O-85(73-13-0),D-11	0.2
	Year	120	403	52	135	7	9	2	35	25-1	1	43	.335	.372	.412	122	10	21-14	.980	-6	86	61	O-85(73-13-0),D-15	0.1
1991	Cal A	150	604	92	179	28	8	2	50	52-4	1	74	.296	.352	.379	103	3	48-23	.981	-6	91	116	*O-143(143-1-0)/D-4	-0.6
1992	Cal A	149	577	83	165	17	4	0	35	45-6	1	64	.286	.337	.329	87	-10	51-21	.980	-1	100	123	O-99(LF),D-47	-1.1
1993	Cal A	152	576	75	156	17	6	1	32	48-7	2	53	.271	.328	.326	74	-21	55-24	.983	4	105	143	*O-141(LF)/D-4	-1.8
1994	NY A	95	350	62	109	21	6	1	36	37-1	4	36	.311	.383	.414	110	6	20-12	.976	-1	94	149	O-84(LF)/D-2	0.2
1995	NY A	67	238	37	62	9	3	2	15	25-1	0	29	.261	.326	.349	78	-8	10-4	1.000	6	118	132	O-64(LF)/D	-0.4
	†Atl N	28	53	6	14	7	0	0	2	3-0	0	9	.264	.304	.396	80	-1	3-0	1.000	-2	51	0	O-15(11-4-1)	-0.3
1996	Bal A	58	175	25	42	4	1	2	14	10-0	1	20	.240	.285	.309	50	-14	8-6	.983	-2	94	49	O-34(32-0-2),D-18	-1.7
	†Atl N	22	31	3	13	0	0	0	2	1-0	0	3	.419	.424	.419	121	1	1-1	.800	-1	53	0	/O-7(LF)	0.0
1999	Det A	87	333	46	108	21	8	10	32	16-0	2	32	.324	.357	.526	121	9	17-9	.986	2	101	181	D-43,O-40(31-0-10)	0.7
2000	Det A	80	267	37	73	10	5	6	25	22-1	1	25	.273	.325	.416	90	-5	8-5	1.000	2	119	156	D-44,O-27(1-0-26)	-0.6
	†NY A	37	77	11	22	4	0	1	5	7-0	0	7	.286	.341	.377	83	-2	4-2	.970	-2	91	0	O-28(22-0-6)/D-7	-0.4
	Year	117	344	48	95	14	5	7	30	29-1	1	32	.276	.329	.407	88	-7	12-7	.987	0	105	80	O-55(23-0-32),D-51	-1.0
Total	12	1379	4840	728	1417	189	70	36	405	369-23	15	543	.293	.342	.383	97	-29	321-145	.983	3	100	110	*O-1055(927-87-54),D-214	-4.6
PONCE, CARLOS Carlos Antonio (Diaz) B 2.7.1959 Rio Piedras, P.R. BR/TR 5-10/170# d8.14																								
1985	Mil A	21	62	4	10	2	0	1	5	1-0	0	9	.161	.169	.242	13	-8	0-0	1.000	-1	60	121	1-10/O-6(5-0-1),D-3	-0.9
POND, RALPH Ralph Benjamin B 5.4.1888 Eau Claire, WI D 9.8.1947 Cleveland, OH TR d6.8																								
1910	Bos A	1	4	0	1	0	0	0	0	0	0		.250	.250	.250	55	0	1	.000	-1	0	0	/O(CF)	-0.1
POOL, HARLIN Harlin Welty "Samson" B 3.13.1908 Lakeport, CA D 2.15.1963 Rodeo, CA BL/TR 5-10/195# d5.30																								
1934	Cin N	99	358	38	117	22	5	2	50	17	7	18	.327	.369	.433	117	9	3	.953	0	99	115	O-94(76-0-18)	0.3
1935	Cin N	28	68	8	12	6	2	0	11	2	0	2	.176	.200	.324	39	-6	0	.962	-1	89	103	O-18(15-0-3)	-0.7
Total	2	127	426	46	129	28	7	2	61	19	7	20	.303	.343	.415	105	3	3	.954	-1	98	114	O-112(91-0-21)	-0.4
POOLE, JIM James Robert "Easy" B 5.12.1895 Taylorsville, NC D 1.2.1975 Hickory, NC BL/TR 6/175# d4.14																								
1925	Phi A	133	480	65	143	29	8	5	67	27	2	37	.298	.338	.423	86	-12	5-4	.982	-8	80	106	*1-123	-2.6
1926	Phi A	112	361	49	106	23	5	8	63	23	2	25	.294	.339	.452	99	-2	4-3	.992	1	99	113	*1-101/O(RF)	-0.7
1927	Phi A	38	99	4	22	2	0	0	10	9	0	6	.222	.287	.242	36	-9	0-0	.993	0	99	75	1-31	-1.0
Total	3	283	940	118	271	54	13	13	140	59	4	68	.288	.333	.415	86	-23	9-7	.987	-7	89	105	1-255/O(RF)	-4.3
POOLE, RAY Raymond Herman B 1.16.1920 Salisbury, NC BL/TR 6/180# d9.9 Mil 1942-45																								
1941	Phi A	2	2	0	0	0	0	0	0	0	0	1	.000	.000	.000	-99	-1	0-0	—	0			H	-0.1
1947	Phi A	13	13	1	3	0	0	0	1	1	0	4	.231	.286	.231	44	-1	0-0	—	0			H	-0.1
Total	2	15	15	1	3	0	0	0	1	1	0	5	.200	.250	.200	25	-2	0-0	.987	0				-0.2
POORMAN, TOM Thomas Iverson B 10.14.1857 Lock Haven, PA D 2.18.1905 Lock Haven, PA BL/TR 5-7/135# d5.5 ▲																								
1880	Buf N	19	70	5	11	1	0	0	1	0		13	.157	.157	.171	11	-6		.879	-0	141	0	P-11,O-10(CF)	-0.3
	Chi N	7	25	3	5	1	2	0	0	0		2	.200	.200	.400	92	0		.778	-2	77	0	/O-7(RF),P-2	-0.1
	Year	26	95	8	16	2	2	0	1	0		15	.168	.168	.232	33	-7		.750	-2	40	0	O-17(0-10-7),P-13	-0.4
1884	Tol AA	94	382	56	89	8	7	0		10	1		.233	.254	.291	75	-12		.845	3	162	183	*O-93(RF)/P	-0.8
1885	Bos N	56	227	44	54	5	3	3	25	7		32	.238	.261	.326	92	-2		.867	-3	83	65	O-56(RF)	-0.6
1886	Bos N	88	371	72	97	16	6	3	41	19		52	.261	.297	.361	102	1	31	.902	3	115	211	*O-88(RF)	0.3
1887	Phi AA	135	585	140	155	18	**19**	4	61	35	10		.265	.317	.381	94	-7	88	.911	2	82	130	*O-135(RF)/2-2,P	-0.5
1888	Phi AA	97	383	76	87	16	6	2	44	31	5		.227	.294	.316	96	-1	46	.898	-10	52	32	*O-97(RF)	-1.1
Total	6	496	2043	396	498	65	43	12	172	102	16	99	.244	.285	.335	90	-27	165	.885	-6	97	125	O-486(0-10-476)/P-15,2-2	-3.1
POPE, DAVE David B 6.17.1921 Talladega, AL D 8.28.1999 Cleveland, OH BL/TR 5-10.5/170# d7.1																								
1952	Cle A	12	34	9	10	1	1	1	4	1	0	7	.294	.314	.471	124	1	0-0	1.000	-1	100	0	O-10(RF)	0.0
1954	†Cle A	60	102	21	30	2	1	4	13	10	0	22	.294	.354	.451	118	2	2-1	1.000	-0	101	69	O-29(18-6-5)	0.1
1955	Cle A	35	104	17	31	5	0	6	22	12-0	1	31	.298	.373	.519	134	5	0-0	.954	-2	100	0	O-31(12-14-7)	0.1
	Bal A	86	222	21	55	8	4	1	30	16-3	2	34	.248	.302	.333	77	-8	5-2	1.000	2	110	70	O-73(19-37-31)	-0.9
	Year	121	326	38	86	13	4	7	52	28-3	3	65	.264	.325	.393	97	-3	5-2	.986	0	107	47	*O-104(31-51-38)	-0.8
1956	Bal A	12	19	1	3	0	0	0	1	0-0	1	7	.158	.200	.158	-5	-3	0-0	1.000	-0	69	0	/O-4(2-0-3)	-0.3
	Cle A	25	70	6	17	3	1	0	3	1-0	0	12	.243	.250	.314	48	-6	0-0	1.000	0	103	104	O-18(4-12-2)	-0.6
	Year	37	89	7	20	3	1	0	4	1-0	1	19	.225	.239	.281	38	-8	0-0	1.000	-0	99	90	O-22(6-12-5)	-0.9
Total	4	230	551	75	146	19	7	12	73	40-3	4	113	.265	.317	.390	92	-9	7-3	.990	-0	104	53	O-165(55-69-58)	-1.6
POPOVICH, PAUL Paul Edward B 8.18.1940 Flemington, WV BB/TR (BR 1964, 66-67) 6/175# d4.19																								
1964	Chi N	1	1	0	1	0	0	0	0	0-0	0	0	1.000	1.000	1.000	447	0	0-0	—	0			H	0.0

Year	Tm Lg	G	AB	R	H	2B	3B	HR	RBI	BB-IB	HP	SO	AVG	OBP	SLG	AOPS	ABR	SB-CS	FA	FR	Rng	Thr	G at Pos	BFW
1966	Chi N	2	6	0	0	0	0	0	0	0-0	0	2	.000	.000	.000	-99	-2	0-0	.889	-1	61	83	/2-2	-0.3
1967	Chi N	49	159	18	34	4	0	0	2	9-0	2	12	.214	.265	.239	43	-12	0-1	.967	-2	95	84	S-31,2-17/3-2	-1.1
1968	LA N	134	418	35	97	8	1	2	25	29-2	1	37	.232	.280	.270	72	-15	1-3	.983	7	103	102	2-89,S-45/3-7	0.1
1969	LA N	28	50	5	10	0	0	0	4	1-0	0	4	.200	.212	.200	18	-6	0-0	.985	-4	93	107	2-23/S-3	-0.9
	Chi N	60	154	26	48	6	0	1	14	18-0	1	14	.312	.387	.370	100	1	0-1	.974	1	97	91	2-25/S-7,3-6,O(CF)	0.4
	Year	88	204	31	58	6	0	1	18	19-0	1	18	.284	.347	.328	85	-3	0-1	.978	-2	95	97	2-48,S-10/3-6,O(CF)	-0.5
1970	Chi N	78	186	22	47	5	1	4	20	18-4	2	18	.253	.324	.355	73	-7	0-1	.990	-2	105	151	2-22,S-17,3-16	-0.7
1971	Chi N	89	226	24	49	7	1	4	28	14-0	0	17	.217	.260	.310	54	-14	0-1	.985	3	111	108	2-40,3-16/S	-0.9
1972	Chi N	58	129	8	25	3	2	1	11	12-2	0	8	.194	.261	.271	47	-9	0-1	.981	12	126	141	2-36/S-8,3	0.6
1973	Chi N	99	280	24	66	6	3	2	24	18-5	1	27	.236	.280	.300	58	-16	3-2	.981	16	113	115	2-84/S-9,3	0.5
1974	†Pit N	59	83	9	18	2	1	0	5	5-1	0	10	.217	.256	.265	49	-6	0-0	.962	-0	109	76	2-12,S-10	-0.6
1975	Pit N	25	40	5	8	1	0	0	1	3-0	1	2	.200	.273	.225	40	-3	0-0	1.000	-2	76	48	/2-8,S-8	-0.4
Total	11	682	1732	176	403	42	9	14	134	127-14	8	151	.233	.286	.292	62	-89	4-10	.982	30	107	111	2-358,S-139/3-49,O(CF)	-3.3
POPPLEIN, GEORGE George J. B 8.1840 Baltimore, MD D 3.31.1901 Baltimore, MD d7.11																								
1873	Mar NA	1	4	0	0	0	0	0	0	0		0	.000	.000	.000	-99	-1	0-0	.500	-0	118	0	/3O(CF)	-0.1
POQUETTE, TOM Thomas Arthur B 10.30.1951 Eau Claire, WI BL/TR 5-10/175# d9.1 C2																								
1973	KC A	21	28	4	6	1	0	0	3	1-0	1	4	.214	.258	.250	43	-2	1-1	.870	-0	100	155	O-20(0-2-18)	-0.3
1976	†KC A	104	344	43	104	18	10	2	34	29-3	4	31	.302	.361	.430	131	13	6-5	.979	-5	100	15	O-98(84-0-17)/D-2	0.3
1977	†KC A	106	342	43	100	23	6	2	33	19-2	5	21	.292	.337	.412	103	1	1-4	1.000	1	106	65	O-96(72-1-28)	-0.3
1978	†KC A	80	204	16	44	9	2	4	30	14-1	0	9	.216	.259	.338	67	-10	2-0	.955	9	142	147	O-63(48-1-17)/D	-0.3
1979	KC A	21	26	1	5	0	0	0	3	1-0	0	4	.192	.214	.192	13	-3	0-0	1.000	-0	60	237	O-10(2-0-8)	-0.4
	Bos A	63	154	14	51	9	0	2	23	8-1	3	7	.331	.365	.429	110	3	2-2	.949	-4	83	81	O-43(3-30-11)/D-4	-0.3
	Year	84	180	15	56	9	0	2	26	9-1	3	11	.311	.343	.394	97	-1	2-2	.954	-4	80	102	O-53(5-30-19)/D-4	-0.7
1981	Bos A	3	2	0	0	0	0	0	0	0-0	0	0	.000	.000	.000	-94	0	0-0	—	-0	0	0	/O-2(LF)	-0.1
	Tex A	30	64	2	10	1	0	0	7	5-0	1	1	.156	.225	.172	18	-7	0-1	.963	-3	73	0	O-18(10-5-3)	-1.1
	Year	33	66	2	10	1	0	0	7	5-0	1	1	.152	.219	.167	14	-7	0-1	.963	-3	71	0	O-20(12-5-3)	-1.2
1982	KC A	24	62	4	9	1	0	0	3	4-0	1	5	.145	.206	.161	3	-8	1-0	.957	1	125	95	O-23(20-0-3)	-0.8
Total	7	452	1226	127	329	62	18	10	136	81-7	15	82	.268	.317	.373	92	-13	13-13	.971	-1	106	70	O-373(241-39-105)/D-7	-3.3
PORTER, COLIN Colin F. B 11.23.1975 Tucson, AZ BL/TL 6-2/200# d5.30																								
2003	Hou N	24	32	5	6	0	0	0	0	1-0	0	17	.188	.212	.188	5	-5	1-0	1.000	-0	100	0	O-14(1-7-6)	-0.5
PORTER, DAN Daniel Edward B 10.17.1931 Decatur, IL BL/TL 6/164# d8.16 Mil 1952																								
1951	Was A	13	19	2	4	0	0	0	0	2	0	4	.211	.286	.211	36	-2	0-0	1.000	-0	94	0	/O-3(RF)	-0.2
PORTER, DARRELL Darrell Ray B 1.17.1952 Joplin, MO D 2.27.2002 Sugar Creek, MO BL/TR 6/193# d9.2																								
1971	Mil A	22	70	4	15	2	0	2	9	9-0	0	20	.214	.300	.329	80	-2	2-2	.977	2	81	229	C-22	0.1
1972	Mil A	18	56	2	7	1	0	1	2	5-0	1	21	.125	.210	.196	22	-6	0-0	.976	3	167	78	C-18	-0.2
1973	Mil A	117	350	50	89	19	2	16	67	57-6	4	85	.254	.363	.457	133	17	5-2	.977	0	101	125	C-90,D-19	2.1
1974	Mil A☆	131	432	59	104	15	4	12	56	50-7	5	88	.241	.326	.377	103	2	8-7	.978	1	114	103	*C-117/D-9	0.7
1975	Mil A	130	409	66	95	12	5	18	60	89-10	5	77	.232	.371	.418	123	16	2-5	.979	-3	96	114	*C-124/D-2	1.7
1976	Mil A	119	389	43	81	14	1	5	32	51-3	1	61	.208	.298	.288	75	-11	2-0	.975	-5	106	74	*C-111/D-2	-1.2
1977	†KC A	130	425	61	117	21	3	16	60	53-6	1	70	.275	.353	.452	118	11	1-0	.982	6	127	88	*C-125/D	2.3
1978	†KC A★	150	520	77	138	27	6	18	78	75-14	2	75	.265	.358	.444	122	17	0-5	.988	2	111	83	*C-145/D-4	2.3
1979	KC A★	157	533	101	155	23	10	20	112	**121**-8	8	65	.291	.421	.484	143	39	3-4	.982	9	133	114	*C-141,D-15	5.1
1980	†KC A★	118	418	51	104	14	2	7	51	69-5	2	50	.249	.354	.342	92	-2	1-1	.978	1	125	106	C-81,D-34	0.2
1981	StL N	61	174	22	39	10	2	6	31	39-7	1	32	.224	.364	.408	117	6	1-2	.979	1	108	107	C-52	0.9
1982	†StL N	120	373	46	86	18	5	12	48	66-6	2	66	.231	.347	.402	109	6	1-1	.983	2	98	106	*C-111	1.3
1983	StL N	145	443	57	116	24	3	15	66	68-12	4	94	.262	.363	.431	120	14	1-3	.989	8	**167**	92	*C-133	2.7
1984	StL N	127	422	56	98	16	3	11	68	60-12	5	79	.232	.331	.363	98	0	5-3	.984	-0	105	102	*C-122	0.6
1985	†StL N	84	240	30	53	12	2	10	36	41-6	1	48	.221	.335	.412	109	4	6-1	.990	5	111	96	C-82	1.4
1986	Tex A	68	155	21	41	6	0	12	29	22-0	1	51	.265	.360	.535	136	8	1-1	.994	-2	46	111	C-25,D-19	0.6
1987	Tex A	85	130	19	31	3	0	7	21	30-4	2	43	.238	.387	.423	115	4	0-0	1.000	-1	69	167	D-35/C-7,1-5	0.3
Total	17	1782	5539	765	1369	237	48	188	826	905-106	45	1025	.247	.354	.409	113	123	39-37	.982	30	116	102	*C-1506,D-140/1-5	20.9
PORTER, IRV Irving Marble B 5.17.1888 Lynn, MA D 2.20.1971 Lynn, MA BB/TR 5-9/155# d8.20																								
1914	Chi A	1	4	1	1	0	0	0	0	0	0	1	.250	.250	.250	51	0	0	1.000	-0	88	0	/O(RF)	0.0
PORTER, JAY J W "J W" B 1.17.1933 Shawnee, OK BR/TR 6-2/180# d7.30 Mil 1953																								
1952	StL A	33	104	12	26	4	1	0	7	10	0	10	.250	.316	.308	72	-4	4-0	.973	0	105	160	O-29(3-26-0)/3-2	-0.4
1955	Det A	24	55	6	13	2	0	0	3	8-0	0	15	.236	.333	.273	66	-2	0-0	1.000	-2	25	94	/1-6,C-4,O-4(LF)	-0.5
1956	Det A	14	21	0	2	0	0	0	3	0-0	0	8	.095	.091	.095	-49	-5	0-0	1.000	-1	*0*	*0*	/C-2,O-2(LF)	-0.5
1957	Det A	58	140	14	35	8	0	2	18	14-1	1	20	.250	.323	.350	82	-3	0-0	.953	0	107	69	O-27(5-0-22),C-12/1-3	-0.4
1958	Cle A	40	85	13	17	1	0	4	19	9-0	1	23	.200	.284	.353	76	-3	0-0	1.000	-2	*89*	*119*	C-20/1-4,3	-0.4
1959	Was A	37	106	8	24	4	0	1	10	11-1	1	16	.226	.300	.292	65	-5	0-0	.993	-2	*57*	*119*	C-34/1-2	-0.5
	StL N	23	33	5	7	3	0	1	2	1-0	1	4	.212	.257	.394	66	-2	0-0	1.000	0	*96*	*119*	C-19/1	-0.1
Total	6	229	544	58	124	22	1	8	62	53-2	4	96	.228	.300	.316	68	-24	4-0	.990	-5	*85*	*112*	/C-91,O-62(14-26-22),1-16,3-3	-2.8
PORTER, BO Marquis Donnell B 7.5.1972 Newark, NJ BR/TR 6-2/195# d5.9																								
1999	Chi N	24	26	2	5	1	0	0	0	2-0	0	13	.192	.250	.231	23	-3	0-0	.941	-0	96	0	O-21(16-5-3)	-0.4
2000	†Oak A	17	13	3	2	0	0	1	2	2-0	0	5	.154	.267	.385	64	-1	0-0	1.000	0	115	0	O-16(1-2-14)	-0.1
2001	Tex A	48	87	18	20	4	2	1	6	9-0	0	34	.230	.296	.356	70	-4	3-2	.969	0	109	63	O-40(18-10-12)/D-2	-0.4
Total	3	89	126	23	27	5	2	2	8	13-0	0	52	.214	.284	.333	60	-8	3-2	.968	0	107	42	/O-77(35-17-29),D-2	-0.9
PORTER, MATTHEW Matthew Sheldon B Kansas City, MO d6.27 M1																								
1884	KC U	3	12	1	1	1	0	0		0			.083	.083	.167	-30	-2		.750	1	272	730	/O-3(CF),M	-0.1
PORTER, DICK Richard Twilley "Wiggles" or "Twitches" B 12.30.1901 Princess Anne, MD D 9.24.1974 Philadelphia, PA BL/TR 5-10/170# d4.16																								
1929	Cle A	71	192	26	63	16	5	1	24	17	1	14	.328	.386	.479	117	5	3-5	.941	-2	86	146	O-28(4-0-24),2-20	0.1
1930	Cle A	119	480	100	168	43	8	4	57	55	3	31	.350	.420	.498	127	22	3-3	.962	-6	85	110	*O-118(RF)	0.6
1931	Cle A	114	414	82	129	24	3	1	38	56	1	36	.312	.395	.391	102	4	6-9	.970	-5	93	72	*O-109(RF)/2	-0.8
1932	Cle A	146	621	106	191	42	8	4	60	64	1	43	.308	.373	.420	99	0	2-4	.982	-13	90	17	*O-145(RF)	-2.2
1933	Cle A	132	499	73	133	19	6	0	41	51	0	42	.267	.335	.329	73	-19	4-4	**.996**	-2	96	78	*O-124(7-0-119)	-2.8
1934	Cle A	13	44	9	10	2	1	1	6	4	0	5	.227	.292	.386	73	-2	0-0	1.000	-1	84	0	O-10(RF)	-0.3
	Bos A	80	265	30	80	13	6	0	56	21	1	15	.302	.355	.396	87	-5	5-2	.940	-5	92	21	O-65(1-0-64)	-1.3
	Year	93	309	39	90	15	7	1	62	25	1	20	.291	.346	.395	85	-7	5-2	.947	-6	91	18	O-75(1-0-74)	-1.6
Total	6	675	2515	426	774	159	37	11	282	268	7	186	.308	.376	.414	99	5	23-27	.973	-34	91	64	O-599(12-0-589)/2-21	-6.7
PORTER, BOB Robert Lee B 7.22.1959 Yuma, AZ BL/TL 5-10/180# d5.13																								
1981	Atl N	17	14	2	4	1	0	0	4	2-0	0	1	.286	.375	.357	106	0	0-0	—	0			/H	0.0
1982	Atl N	24	27	1	3	0	0	0	0	1-0	0	9	.111	.143	.111	-27	-5	0-0	1.000	-1	62	0	/O-4(LF),1	-0.6
Total	2	41	41	3	7	1	0	0	4	3-0	0	10	.171	.227	.195	19	-5	0-0	1.000	-1	62	0	/O-4(LF),1	-0.6
POSADA, JORGE Jorge Rafael (Villeta) B 8.17.1971 Santurce, P.R. BB/TR 6-2/190# d9.4																								
1995	†NY A	1	0	0	0	0	0	0	0	0-0	0	0	—	—	—	—	0	0-0	1.000	0	0	0	/C	0.0
1996	NY A	8	14	1	1	0	0	0	0	1-0	0	6	.071	.133	.071	-46	-3	0-0	1.000	0	0	0	/C-4,D-3	-0.3
1997	†NY A	60	188	29	47	12	0	6	25	30-2	3	33	.250	.359	.410	102	2	1-2	.992	-6	92	57	C-60	-0.1
1998	†NY A	111	358	56	96	23	0	17	63	47-7	0	92	.268	.350	.475	117	10	0-1	.994	5	131	110	C-99/1D	1.8
1999	†NY A	112	379	50	93	19	2	12	57	53-2	3	91	.245	.341	.401	90	-5	1-0	.993	1	86	93	*C-109/1D	0.2
2000	†NY A★	151	505	92	145	35	1	28	86	107-10	8	151	.287	.417	.527	139	35	2-2	.993	4	111	101	*C-142,1-12/D-4	4.3
2001	†NY A★	138	484	59	134	28	1	22	95	62-10	6	132	.277	.363	.475	118	14	2-6	.990	-2	94	99	*C-131/1-2,D-6	1.8
2002	†NY A★	143	511	79	137	40	1	20	99	81-9	3	143	.268	.370	.468	122	19	1-0	.988	5	96	90	*C-138/D-5	3.2
2003	†NY A★	142	481	83	135	24	0	30	101	93-6	10	110	.281	.405	.518	144	35	2-4	.994	11	101	88	*C-137/D-2	5.1
Total	9	866	2920	449	788	181	5	135	526	474-46	33	758	.270	.375	.474	121	107	9-15	.992	18	101	93	C-821/D-27,1-16	16.0

Year	Tm Lg	G	AB	R	H	2B	3B	HR	RBI	BB-IB	HP	SO	AVG	OBP	SLG	AOPS	ABR	SB-CS	FA	FR	Rng	Thr	G at Pos	BFW
POSADA, LEO Leopoldo Jesus (Hernandez) B 4.15.1936 Havana, Cuba BR/TR 5-11/175# d9.21																								
1960	KC A	10	36	8	13	0	2	1	2	3-0	0	7	.361	.410	.556	158	3	1-0	1.000	-0	73	194	/O-9(4-0-8)	0.2
1961	KC A	116	344	37	87	10	4	7	53	36-1	4	84	.253	.321	.366	85	-8	0-0	.973	2	103	114	*O-102(69-20-29)	-1.1
1962	KC A	29	46	6	9	1	1	0	3	7-1	0	14	.196	.302	.261	51	-3	0-0	1.000	0	88	204	O-11(10-0-1)	-0.3
Total	3	155	426	51	109	11	7	8	58	46-2	4	105	.256	.326	.371	87	-8	1-0	.976	2	100	126	O-122(83-20-38)	-1.2
POSE, SCOTT Scott Vernon B 2.11.1967 Davenport, IA BL/TR 5-11/165# d4.5																								
1993	Fla N	15	41	0	8	2	0	0	3	2-0	0	4	.195	.233	.244	26	-4	0-2	1.000	-2	66	0	O-10(6-8-0)	-0.7
1997	†NY A	54	87	19	19	2	1	0	5	9-0	0	11	.218	.292	.264	47	-7	3-1	1.000	-1	88	126	O-45(28-3-17)/D-5	-0.8
1999	KC A	86	137	27	39	3	0	0	12	21-1	0	22	.285	.377	.307	76	-4	6-2	.970	2	96	307	O-25(18-1-6),D-18	-0.3
2000	KC A	47	48	6	9	0	0	0	1	6-0	0	13	.188	.278	.188	20	-6	0-1	1.000	-1	55	0	O-11(3-2-7)/D-4	-0.7
Total	4	202	313	52	75	7	1	0	21	38-1	0	50	.240	.321	.268	53	-21	9-6	.990	-2	84	143	/O-91(55-14-30),D-27	-2.5
POST, LEW Lewis G. B 4.12.1875 Woodland, MI D 8.21.1944 Chicago, IL d9.21																								
1902	Det A	3	12	2	1	0	0	0	2	0	0		.083	.083	.083	-53	-2	0	.800	-1	0	0	/O-3(RF)	-0.3
POST, SAM Samuel Gilbert B 11.17.1896 Richmond, VA D 3.31.1971 Portsmouth, VA BL/TL 6-1.5/170# d4.22																								
1922	Bro N	9	25	3	7	0	0	0	4	1	0	4	.280	.308	.280	53	-2	1-0	.982	-1	32	22	/1-8	-0.3
POST, WALLY Walter Charles B 7.9.1929 St.Wendelin, OH D 1.6.1982 St.Henry, OH BR/TR 6-1/203# d9.18																								
1949	Cin N	6	8	1	2	0	0	0	1	0	0	3	.250	.250	.250	34	-1	0	.750	-0	91	0	/O-3(1-1-1)	-0.1
1951	Cin N	15	41	6	9	3	0	1	7	3	0	4	.220	.273	.366	69	-2	0-0	.963	0	102	126	/O-9(CF)	-0.2
1952	Cin N	19	58	5	9	1	0	2	7	4	1	20	.155	.222	.276	37	-5	0-0	1.000	2	126	86	O-16(15-1-0)	-0.5
1953	Cin N	11	33	3	8	1	0	1	4	4	0	6	.242	.324	.364	78	-1	1-0	.960	1	98	249	O-11(0-4-7)	0.0
1954	Cin N	130	451	46	115	21	3	18	83	26	3	70	.255	.297	.435	86	-11	2-2	.957	2	102	123	*O-116(0-1-115)	-1.4
1955	Cin N	**154**	601	116	186	33	3	40	109	60-5	2	102	.309	.372	.574	139	33	7-4	.978	-1	100	98	*O-154(RF)	2.6
1956	Cin N	143	539	94	134	25	3	36	83	37-2	4	124	.249	.301	.506	105	2	6-0	.969	6	109	124	*O-136(RF)	0.5
1957	Cin N	134	467	68	114	26	2	20	74	33-5	0	84	.244	.291	.437	87	-9	2-2	.985	9	114	137	*O-124(1-0-123)	-0.4
1958	Phi N	110	379	51	107	21	3	12	62	32-5	3	74	.282	.340	.449	109	5	0-2	.952	1	100	145	O-91(2-0-90)	0.1
1959	Phi N	132	468	62	119	17	6	22	94	36-4	3	101	.254	.310	.457	100	-2	0-0	.992	7	107	134	*O-120(2-0-118)	0.0
1960	Phi N	34	84	11	24	6	1	2	12	9-1	0	24	.286	.351	.452	119	2	0-0	1.000	0	110	57	O-22(18-0-5)	0.2
	Cin N	77	249	36	70	14	0	17	38	28-3	0	51	.281	.350	.542	139	13	0-2	.985	3	103	142	O-67(44-0-23)	1.2
	Year	111	333	47	94	20	1	19	50	37-4	0	75	.282	.350	.520	134	16	0-2	.989	3	105	122	O-89(62-0-28)	1.4
1961	†Cin N	99	282	44	83	16	3	20	57	22-1	1	61	.294	.346	.585	140	15	0-1	.959	2	103	115	O-81(41-0-40)	1.2
1962	Cin N	109	285	43	75	10	3	17	62	32-2	2	67	.263	.341	.498	118	7	1-0	.935	-2	91	104	O-90(88-0-2)	0.1
1963	Cin N	5	7	1	0	0	0	0	0	0-0	1	1	.000	.125	.000	-59	-1	0-0	1.000	0	134	0	/O(LF)	-0.2
	Min A	21	47	6	9	0	1	2	6	2-0	0	17	.191	.224	.362	60	-3	0-0	1.000	-1	86	0	O-12(2-0-10)	-0.5
1964	Cle A	5	8	1	0	0	0	0	0	3-0	0	4	.000	.273	.000	-16	-1	0-0	.667	-1	65	0	/O-2(RF)	-0.2
Total	15	1204	4007	594	1064	194	28	210	699	331-28	20	813	.266	.323	.485	109	41	19-13	.970	28	104	121	*O-1055(215-16-826)	2.4
POTTER, MIKE Michael Gary B 5.16.1951 Montebello, CA BR/TR 6-1/195# d9.6																								
1976	StL N	9	16	0	0	0	0	0	0	1-0	0	6	.000	.059	.000	-82	-4	0-0	1.000	1	150	0	/O-4(LF)	-0.4
1977	StL N	5	7	0	0	0	0	0	0	0-0	0	2	.000	.000	.000	-99	-2	0-0	—	-0	0	0	/O(RF)	-0.2
Total	2	14	23	0	0	0	0	0	0	1-0	0	8	.000	.042	.000	-87	-6	0-0	1.000	0	130	0	/O-5(4-0-1)	-0.6
POTTS, JOHN John Frederick "Fred" B 2.6.1887 Tipp City, OH D 9.5.1962 Cleveland, OH BL/TR 5-7/165# d4.18																								
1914	KC F	41	102	14	27	4	0	1	9	25	1	13	.265	.414	.333	110	2	7	.933	-3	91	45	O-31(1-5-25)	-0.2
POTTS, DAN Vivian B 1.1869 Bristol, PA D 8.17.1934 Bristol, PA d10.3																								
1892	Was N	1	4	0	1	0	0	0	0	0	0	1	.250	.250	.250	53	0	0	1.000	0	*59*	*287*	/C	0.0
POULSEN, KEN Ken Sterling B 8.4.1947 Van Nuys, CA BL/TR 6-1/190# d7.3																								
1967	Bos A	5	5	0	1	1	0	0	0	0-0	0	2	.200	.200	.400	68	0	0-0	.667	-0	175	0	/3-2,S	0.0
POWELL, ALONZO Alonzo Sidney B 12.12.1964 San Francisco, CA BR/TR 6-2/190# d4.6																								
1987	Mon N	14	41	3	8	3	0	0	4	5-0	0	17	.195	.283	.268	46	-3	0-0	1.000	-1	70	0	O-11(10-0-1)	-0.5
1991	Sea A	57	111	16	24	6	1	3	12	11-0	1	24	.216	.288	.369	82	-3	0-2	.960	-4	82	0	O-40(24-6-15)/1-7,D-7	-0.8
Total	2	71	152	19	32	9	1	3	16	16-0	1	41	.211	.287	.342	71	-6	0-2	.968	-5	79	0	/O-51(34-6-16),D-7,1-7	-1.3
POWELL, JAKE Alvin Jacob B 7.15.1908 Silver Spring, MD D 11.4.1948 Washington, DC BR/TR 5-11.5/180# d8.3																								
1930	Was A	3	4	1	0	0	0	0	0	0	0	1	.000	.000	.000	-99	-1	0-0	1.000	0	113	0	/O-2(1-0-1)	-0.1
1934	Was A	9	35	6	10	2	0	0	1	4	0	2	.286	.359	.343	85	-1	1-1	.955	1	81	434	/O-9(CF)	0.0
1935	Was A	139	551	88	172	26	10	6	98	37	4	37	.312	.360	.428	107	4	15-7	.976	-2	97	94	*O-136(0-136-1)/2-2	-0.1
1936	Was A	53	210	40	62	11	5	1	30	18	2	21	.295	.357	.410	94	-3	10-4	.951	-5	89	48	O-53(CF)	-0.7
	†NY A	87	328	62	99	13	3	7	48	33	0	30	.302	.366	.424	98	-2	16-7	.976	1	104	87	O-84(42-42-0)	-0.3
	Year	140	538	102	161	24	8	8	78	51	2	51	.299	.362	.418	96	-4	26-11	.967	-4	99	73	*O-137(42-95-0)	-1.0
1937	†NY A	97	365	54	96	22	3	3	45	25	2	36	.263	.314	.364	70	-18	7-5	.981	-1	99	67	O-94(LF)	-2.3
1938	†NY A	45	164	27	42	12	1	2	20	15	2	20	.256	.326	.378	76	-6	3-1	.978	-2	97	31	O-43(37-1-6)	-1.0
1939	NY A	31	86	12	21	4	1	1	9	3	0	8	.244	.270	.349	58	-6	1-2	.983	1	112	64	O-23(19-2-3)	-0.6
1940	NY A	12	27	3	5	0	0	0	2	1	0	4	.185	.214	.185	5	-4	0-0	1.000	1	109	219	/O-7(3-2-2)	-0.3
1943	Was A	37	132	14	35	10	2	0	20	5	1	13	.265	.297	.371	99	-1	3-5	.978	2	105	150	O-33(25-8-0)	-0.2
1944	Was A	96	367	29	88	9	1	1	37	16	0	26	.240	.272	.278	60	-21	7-2	.980	0	105	72	O-90(58-0-32)/3	-2.7
1945	Was A	31	98	4	19	2	0	0	3	8	0	8	.194	.255	.214	40	-8	1-1	.950	-0	108	44	O-27(21-0-6)	-1.1
	Phi N	48	173	13	40	5	0	1	14	8	0	13	.231	.265	.277	52	-12	1	.986	-0	87	152	O-44(4-5-35)	-1.4
Total	11	688	2540	353	689	116	26	22	327	173	11	219	.271	.320	.363	81	-79	65-35	.975	-5	100	87	O-645(304-258-86)/2-2,3	-10.8
POWELL, ABNER Charles Abner "Ab" B 12.15.1860 Shenandoah, PA D 8.7.1953 New Orleans, LA BL/TR 5-7/160# d8.4 ▲																								
1884	Was U	48	191	36	54	10	5	0		3			.283	.294	.387	108	-4		.875	-0	51	0	O-30(0-12-18),P-18/3-2,S2	-0.3
1886	Bal AA	11	39	4	7	2	1	0	7	1	0		.179	.200	.282	52	-2	4	.917	1	175	628	/P-7,O-4(3-0-1)	-0.1
	Cin AA	19	74	13	17	1	1	0	8	4	0		.230	.269	.270	67	-3	0	.760	-0	144	0	O-13(5-6-2)/S-6,P-4	-0.3
	Year	30	113	17	24	3	2	0	15	5	0		.212	.246	.274	62	-5	4	.735	0	106	0	O-17(8-6-3),P-11/S-6	-0.4
Total	2	78	304	53	78	13	7	0	15	8	0		.257	.276	.345	91	-9	4	.817	0	74	0	/O-47(8-18-21),P-29,S-7,3-2,2	-0.7
POWELL, HOSKEN Hosken B 5.14.1955 Selma, AL BL/TL 6-1/185# d4.5																								
1978	Min A	121	381	55	94	20	2	3	31	45-1	0	31	.247	.323	.333	84	-7	11-5	.983	0	99	113	*O-117(RF)	-1.2
1979	Min A	104	338	49	99	17	3	2	36	33-1	3	25	.293	.360	.379	96	-1	5-1	.977	-2	95	95	O-93(8-0-85)/D-5	-0.6
1980	Min A	137	485	58	127	17	5	6	35	32-2	3	46	.262	.312	.355	76	-16	14-3	.968	3	104	115	*O-129(RF)	-1.8
1981	Min A	80	264	30	63	11	3	2	25	17-0	1	31	.239	.286	.326	71	-10	7-4	.970	2	102	143	O-64(12-0-52)/D-8	-1.2
1982	Tor A	112	265	43	73	13	4	3	26	12-2	0	23	.275	.304	.389	82	-7	4-4	.974	-3	99	51	O-75(8-0-68),D-19	-1.4
1983	Tor A	40	83	6	14	0	0	1	7	5-0	0	8	.169	.213	.205	16	-10	2-0	.981	1	127	0	O-33(5-0-29)/1D	-1.0
Total	6	594	1816	241	470	78	17	17	160	144-6	7	164	.259	.314	.349	79	-51	43-17	.975	1	101	101	O-511(33-0-480)/D-33,1	-7.2
POWELL, JIM James Edwin B 8.30.1859 Richmond, VA D 11.20.1929 Butte, MT 5-10/170# d8.5																								
1884	Ric AA	41	151	23	37	8	4	0		7	4		.245	.296	.351	112	2		.943	1	136	76	1-41	0.0
1885	Phi AA	19	75	5	12	0	3	0	5	1	2		.160	.192	.240	34	-6		.973	-0	64	63	1-19	-0.7
Total	2	60	226	28	49	8	7	0	5	8	6		.217	.262	.314	84	-4		.952	1	113	72	/1-60	-0.7
POWELL, BOOG John Wesley B 8.17.1941 Lakeland, FL BL/TR 6-4/240# d9.26																								
1961	Bal A	4	13	0	1	0	0	0	1	0-0	0	2	.077	.077	.077	-61	-3	0-0	1.000	-0	65	0	/O-3(LF)	-0.4
1962	Bal A	124	400	44	97	13	2	15	53	38-5	2	79	.243	.311	.398	95	-4	1-1	.969	-2	102	19	*O-112(LF)/1	-1.1
1963	Bal A	140	491	67	130	22	2	25	82	49-8	0	87	.265	.328	.470	126	16	1-2	.969	-4	87	77	*O-121(121-0-1),1-23	0.5
1964	Bal A	134	424	74	123	17	0	39	99	76-6	2	91	.290	.399	**.606**	176	45	0-0	.974	7	97	246	*O-124(LF)/1-5	4.7
1965	Bal A	144	472	54	117	20	2	17	72	71-13	4	93	.248	.347	.407	112	10	1-1	.992	4	127	106	1-78,O-71(LF)	0.6
1966	†Bal A	140	491	78	141	18	0	34	109	67-9	1	125	.287	.372	.532	159	39	0-4	.989	-8	78	97	*1-136	2.3
1967	Bal A	125	415	53	97	14	1	13	55	55-5	2	94	.234	.324	.366	105	4	1-3	.986	-6	83	104	*1-114	-1.1
1968	Bal A★	154	550	60	137	21	1	22	85	73-12	3	97	.249	.338	.411	127	19	7-1	.990	-5	83	100	*1-149	0.7
1969	†Bal A★	152	533	83	162	25	0	37	121	72-10	1	76	.304	.383	.559	161	43	1-1	.995	-1	97	107	*1-144	3.2
1970	†Bal A★	154	526	82	156	28	0	35	114	104-18	5	80	.297	.412	.549	163	50	1-1	.992	-1	98	100	*1-145	3.8

Year	Tm Lg	G	AB	R	H	2B	3B	HR	RBI	BB-IB	HP	SO	AVG	OBP	SLG	AOPS	ABR	SB-CS	FA	FR	Rng	Thr	G at Pos	BFW
1971	†Bal A✶	128	418	59	107	19	0	22	92	82-11	4	64	.256	.379	.459	139	25	1-0	.995	-2	94	110	*1-124	1.5
1972	Bal A	140	465	53	117	20	1	21	81	65-14	4	92	.252	.346	.434	129	18	4-0	.988	-2	97	**120**	*1-133	0.7
1973	†Bal A	114	370	52	98	13	1	11	54	85-10	0	64	.265	.398	.395	126	18	0-2	.989	4	**121**	**118**	*1-111	1.3
1974	†Bal A	110	344	37	91	13	1	12	45	52-10	0	58	.265	.358	.413	126	13	0-1	.996	4	121	129	*1-102/D	1.0
1975	Cle A	134	435	64	129	18	0	27	86	59-5	1	72	.297	.377	.524	154	31	1-3	**.997**	-2	89	96	*1-121/D-5	2.0
1976	Cle A	95	293	29	63	9	0	9	33	41-3	0	43	.215	.305	.338	91	-3	1-1	.987	1	102	111	1-89	-0.9
1977	LA N	50	41	0	10	0	0	0	5	12-1	0	9	.244	.415	.244	82	0	0-0	.938	-1	0	84	/1-4	-0.1
Total	17	2042	6681	889	1776	270	11	339	1187	1001-140	29	1226	.266	.361	.462	134	321	20-21	.991	-13	97	107	*1-1479,O-431(431-0-1)/D-6	18.7
POWELL, DANTE Le Jon Dante B 8.25.1973 Long Beach, CA BR/TR 6-2/185# d4.15																								
1997	†SF N	27	39	8	12	1	0	1	3	4-0	0	11	.308	.372	.410	108	0	1-1	1.000	-0	107	0	O-22(0-20-2)	0.0
1998	SF N	8	4	2	2	0	0	1	1	3-0	0	0	.500	.714	1.250	429	2	0-0	1.000	-1	49	0	/O-8(CF)	0.2
1999	Ari N	22	25	4	4	3	0	0	1	2-0	0	6	.160	.222	.280	26	-3	2-1	.929	-1	80	0	O-15(0-8-7)	-0.4
2001	SF N	13	6	5	2	0	0	0	0	0-0	0	0	.333	.333	.333	79	0	0-0	1.000	1	172	0	/O-9(5-1-3)	0.0
Total	4	70	74	19	20	4	0	2	5	9-0	0	17	.270	.349	.405	97	-1	3-2	.980	-1	100	0	/O-54(5-37-12)	-0.2
POWELL, MARTIN Martin J. B 3.25.1856 Fitchburg, MA D 2.5.1888 Fitchburg, MA BL/TL 6/170# d6.18																								
1881	Det N	55	219	47	74	9	4	1	38	15		9	.338	.380	.429	148	12		.947	-3	85	150	1-55/C	0.6
1882	Det N	80	338	44	81	13	0	0	29	19		27	.240	.280	.278	80	-7		.940	-5	62	64	*1-80	-1.7
1883	Det N	**101**	421	76	115	17	5	1	48	28		23	.273	.318	.344	106	5		.950	-3	97	115	*1-101	-0.6
1884	Cin U	43	185	46	59	4	2	1		13			.319	.364	.378	116	-2		.940	-2	81	136	1-43	-0.7
Total	4	279	1163	213	329	43	11	3	115	75		59	.283	.326	.347	109	8		.945	-12	82	110	1-279/C	-2.4
POWELL, PAUL Paul Ray B 3.19.1948 San Angelo, TX BR/TR 5-11/185# d4.7																								
1971	Min A	20	31	7	5	0	0	1	2	3-0	0	12	.161	.235	.258	38	-3	0-0	1.000	0	117	0	O-15(CF)	-0.3
1973	LA N	2	1	0	0	0	0	0	0	0-0	0	1	.000	.000	.000	-99	0	0-0	—	-0	0	0	/O(LF)	0.0
1975	LA N	8	10	2	2	1	0	0	0	1-0	0	2	.200	.273	.300	61	-1	0-0	.955	0	39	395	/C-7,O(LF)	0.0
Total	3	30	42	9	7	1	0	1	2	4-0	0	15	.167	.239	.262	41	-4	0-0	1.000	0	107	0	/O-17(2-15-0),C-7	-0.3
POWELL, RAY Raymond Reath "Rabbit" B 11.20.1888 Siloam Springs, AR D 10.16.1962 Chillicothe, MO BL/TR 5-9/160# d4.16 Mil 1918																								
1913	Det A	2	0	0	0	0	0	0	0	0	0	0	—	—	—	—	0	0	—	-0	0	0	/O(CF)	0.0
1917	Bos N	88	357	42	97	10	4	4	30	24	0	54	.272	.318	.356	113	4	12	.976	3	104	112	O-88(CF)	0.1
1918	Bos N	53	188	31	40	7	5	0	20	29	1	30	.213	.321	.303	95	0	2	.949	-1	94	118	O-53(CF)	-0.5
1919	Bos N	123	470	51	111	12	12	2	33	41	4	79	.236	.303	.326	93	-5	16	.951	-1	92	114	*O-122(0-1-120)	-1.4
1920	Bos N	147	609	69	137	12	12	6	29	44	4	83	.225	.282	.314	74	-22	10-18	.956	3	100	118	*O-147(0-147-1)	-3.6
1921	Bos N	149	624	114	191	25	**18**	12	74	58	4	85	.306	.369	.462	125	22	6-17	.954	-9	93	91	*O-149(CF)	0.2
1922	Bos N	142	550	82	163	22	11	6	37	59	4	66	.296	.369	.409	105	5	3-12	.980	6	106	110	*O-136(CF)	0.1
1923	Bos N	97	338	57	102	20	4	4	38	45	1	36	.302	.385	.420	117	10	1-6	.941	-5	97	74	O-84(1-83-0)	0.0
1924	Bos N	74	188	21	49	9	1	1	15	21	1	28	.261	.338	.335	85	-3	1-3	.947	4	104	191	O-46(7-36-3)	-0.2
Total	9	875	3324	467	890	117	67	35	276	321	19	461	.268	.336	.375	102	11	51-56	.959	0	98	110	O-826(8-694-124)	-5.3
POWELL, LEROY Robert Leroy B 10.17.1933 Flint, MI BR/TR 6-1/190# d9.16 Mil 1956																								
1955	Chi A	1	0	0	0	0	0	0	0	0-0	0	0	—	—	—	—	0	0-0	—	0			R	0.0
1957	Chi A	1	0	1	0	0	0	0	0	0-0	0	0	—	—	—	—	0	0-0	—	0			R	0.0
Total	2	2	0	1	0	0	0	0	0	0-0	0	0	—	—	—	—	0	0-0	.959	0				0.0
POWER, TOM Thomas E. B San Francisco, CA D 2.25.1898 San Francisco, CA 5-11/164# d8.27																								
1890	Bal AA	**38**	125	11	26	3	1	0	6	13	2		.208	.293	.248	57	-7	6	.960	-3	68	60	1-26,2-12	-1.0
POWER, VIC Victor Pellot (born Felipe Pellot (Pove)) B 11.1.1927 Arecibo, P.R. BR/TR 5-11/195# d4.13 OF Total (41-LF 56-CF 18-RF)																								
1954	Phi A	127	462	36	118	17	5	8	38	19	2	19	.255	.287	.366	78	-17	2-1	.985	8	107	161	*O-101(33-56-12),1-21/S3	-1.5
1955	KC A★	147	596	91	190	34	10	19	76	35-6	0	27	.319	.354	.505	128	20	0-2	.993	14	**140**	97	*1-144	2.5
1956	KC A★	127	530	77	164	21	5	14	63	24-2	1	16	.309	.340	.447	106	2	2-2	.993	8	130	101	1-76,2-47/O-7(LF)	0.8
1957	KC A	129	467	48	121	15	1	14	42	19-3	3	21	.259	.291	.385	82	-13	3-2	**.998**	11	**148**	96	*1-113/O-6(RF),2-4	-0.9
1958	KC A	52	205	35	62	13	4	4	27	7-0	0	3	.302	.325	.463	112	3	1-1	.992	6	147	120	1-50/2	0.5
	Cle A	93	385	63	122	24	6	12	53	13-2	1	11	.317	.336	.504	133	15	2-1	.977	5	93	139	3-42,1-41,2-27/S-2,O(LF)	2.0
	Year	145	590	98	184	37	**10**	16	80	20-2	1	14	.312	.332	.490	125	17	3-2	.992	11	149	120	1-91,3-42,2-28/S-2,O(LF)	2.5
1959	Cle A★	147	595	102	172	31	6	10	60	40-2	2	22	.289	.334	.412	108	5	9-13	**.995**	10	**147**	98	*1-121,2-21/3-7	0.7
1960	Cle A★	147	580	69	167	26	3	10	84	24-5	0	20	.288	.313	.395	94	-7	9-5	**.996**	20	**147**	107	*1-147/S-5,3-4	0.5
1961	Cle A	147	563	64	151	34	4	5	63	38-5	1	16	.268	.309	.369	85	-13	4-3	.994	14	**132**	82	*1-141/2-7	-0.7
1962	Min A	144	611	80	177	28	2	16	63	22-0	3	35	.290	.316	.421	93	-7	7-1	.993	15	**142**	**121**	*1-142/2-2	0.0
1963	Min A	138	541	65	146	28	2	10	52	22-0	0	24	.270	.297	.384	88	-10	3-1	.992	5	110	111	*1-124,2-18/3-5	-1.0
1964	Min A	19	45	6	10	2	0	0	1	1-0	0	3	.222	.239	.267	40	-4	0-0	.990	1	141	98	1-12/2	-0.3
	LA A	68	221	17	55	6	0	3	13	8-0	1	14	.249	.275	.317	72	-9	1-1	1.000	3	137	87	1-48,3-28/2-5	-0.8
	Year	87	266	23	65	8	0	3	14	9-0	1	17	.244	.269	.308	66	-13	1-1	.998	5	138	90	1-60,3-28/2-6	-1.1
	Phi N	18	48	1	10	4	0	0	3	2-0	0	3	.208	.240	.292	50	-3	0-0	.993	1	126	90	1-17	-0.3
1965	Cal A	124	197	11	51	7	1	1	20	5-1	1	13	.259	.281	.320	72	-8	2-2	.996	6	146	100	*1-107/2-6,3-2	-0.5
Total	12	1627	6046	765	1716	290	49	126	658	279-26	15	247	.284	.315	.411	97	-46	45-35	.994	126	138	102	*1-1304,2-139,O-115C/3-89,S-8	1.0
POWERS, MIKE Ellis Foree B 3.2.1906 Toddspoint, KY D 12.2.1983 Louisville, KY BL/TL 6-1/185# d8.19																								
1932	Cle A	14	33	4	6	4	0	0	5	2	0	2	.182	.229	.303	34	-3	0-0	.917	-1	81	0	/O-8(RF)	-0.4
1933	Cle A	24	47	6	13	2	1	0	2	6	0	6	.277	.358	.362	87	-1	2-1	.952	-1	102	0	O-11(4-0-8)	-0.2
Total	2	38	80	10	19	6	1	0	7	8	0	8	.237	.307	.338	65	-4	2-1	.939	-2	93	0	/O-19(4-0-16)	-0.6
POWERS, JOHN John Calvin B 7.8.1929 Birmingham, AL D 9.25.2001 Birmingham, AL BL/TR 6/190# d9.24																								
1955	Pit N	2	4	0	1	0	0	0	0	0-0	0	0	.250	.250	.250	34	0	0-0	1.000	0	155	0	/O-2(RF)	0.0
1956	Pit N	11	21	0	1	0	0	0	0	1-0	0	4	.048	.091	.048	-63	-5	0-0	1.000	0	115	0	/O-5(4-0-1)	-0.5
1957	Pit N	20	35	7	10	3	0	2	8	5-0	3	9	.286	.409	.543	161	4	0-0	1.000	0	96	185	/O-9(4-0-4)	0.4
1958	Pit N	57	82	6	15	1	0	2	2	8-0	0	19	.183	.256	.268	40	-7	0-0	1.000	1	116	98	O-14(3-0-12)	-0.7
1959	Cin N	43	43	8	11	2	1	2	4	3-0	1	13	.256	.319	.488	108	0	0-0	1.000	-0	103	0	/O-5(4-0-1)	0.0
1960	Bal A	10	18	3	2	0	0	0	0	3-0	0	1	.111	.238	.111	-2	-3	0-0	.833	-1	77	0	/O-4(RF)	-0.4
	Cle A	8	12	2	2	1	1	0	0	2-0	0	2	.167	.286	.417	90	0	0-0	1.000	0	129	0	/O-5(3-0-3)	0.0
	Year	18	30	5	4	1	1	0	0	5-0	0	3	.133	.257	.233	34	-3	0-0	.929	-1	101	0	/O-9(3-0-7)	-0.4
Total	6	151	215	26	42	7	2	6	14	22-0	4	48	.195	.281	.330	64	-11	0-0	.986	1	109	76	/O-44(18-0-27)	-1.2
POWERS, LES Leslie Edwin B 11.5.1909 Seattle, WA D 11.13.1978 Santa Monica, CA BL/TL 6/175# d9.17																								
1938	NY N	2	3	0	0	0	0	0	0	0	0	1	.000	.000	.000	-99	-1	0	—	0			H	-0.1
1939	Phi N	19	52	7	18	1	1	0	2	4	0	6	.346	.393	.404	118	1	0	.983	-2	48	82	1-13	-0.2
Total	2	21	55	7	18	1	1	0	2	4	0	7	.327	.373	.382	106	0	0	.983	-2	48	82	/1-13	-0.3
POWERS, DOC Michael Riley B 9.22.1870 Pittsfield, MA D 4.26.1909 Philadelphia, PA BR/TR d6.12																								
1898	Lou N	34	99	13	27	4	3	1	19	5	0		.273	.308	.404	105	0	1	.962	-3	*81*	*93*	C-22/1-6,O(LF)	-0.1
1899	Lou N	49	169	15	35	8	2	0	22	6	1		.207	.239	.278	42	-14	1	.942	-2	*115*	*59*	C-38/1-7	-1.2
	Was N	14	38	3	10	2	0	0	3	1	0		.263	.282	.316	65	-2	0	.942	-2	*76*	*97*	C-12/1	-0.3
	Year	63	207	18	45	10	2	0	25	7	1		.217	.247	.285	46	-16	1	.942	-4	*107*	*67*	C-50/1-8	-1.5
1901	Phi A	116	431	53	108	26	5	1	47	18	7		.251	.292	.341	72	-17	10	.952	-6	*98*	*98*	*C-111/1-3	-1.1
1902	Phi A	71	246	35	65	7	1	2	39	14	3		.264	.312	.325	74	-9	3	.950	7	*95*	*132*	C-68/1-3	0.3
1903	Phi A	75	247	19	56	11	1	0	23	5	0		.227	.242	.279	54	-14	1	.982	1	*97*	*111*	C-66/1-7	-0.7
1904	Phi A	57	184	11	35	3	0	0	11	6	1		.190	.220	.207	33	-14	3	.965	-3	*104*	*89*	C-56/O(RF)	-1.3
1905	†Phi A	21	60	6	10	0	0	0	5	0	1		.167	.180	.167	10	-6	2	.928	1	*126*	*126*	C-21	-0.4
	NY A	11	33	3	6	1	0	0	2	1	0		.182	.206	.212	29	-3	0	.975	-0	110	68	/1-7,C-4	-0.3
	†Phi A	19	61	2	8	0	0	0	5	3	0		.131	.172	.131	-3	-7	2	.991	-2	*126*	*126*	C-19	-0.9
	Year	51	154	11	24	1	0	0	12	4	1		.156	.182	.162	9	-16	4	.957	-2	*114*	*111*	C-44/1-7	-1.6
1906	Phi A	58	185	5	29	1	0	0	7	1	2		.157	.170	.162	4	-21	2	.974	7	*99*	*112*	C-57/1	-1.0
1907	Phi A	59	159	9	29	3	0	0	9	7	0		.182	.217	.201	33	-12	1	.983	9	*99*	*116*	C-59	0.2
1908	Phi A	62	172	8	31	6	1	0	7	5	3		.180	.217	.227	41	-11	1	.967	0	*75*	*106*	C-60/1-2	-0.7
1909	Phi A	1	4	1	1	0	0	0	0	0	0		.250	.250	.250	57	0	0	1.000	0	*153*	*79*	/C	0.0

Year	Tm Lg	G	AB	R	H	2B	3B	HR	RBI	BB-IB	HP	SO	AVG	OBP	SLG	AOPS	ABR	SB-CS	FA	FR	Rng	Thr	G at Pos	BFW
Total	11	647	2088	183	450	72	13	4	199	72	18		.216	.248	.268	51	-130	27	.965	7	97	104	C-594/1-37,O-2(1-0-1)	-7.5
POWERS, PHIL Phillip B. "Grandmother" B 7.26.1854 New York, NY D 12.22.1914 New York, NY BR/TR 5-7/166# d8.31 U8																								
1878	Chi N	8	31	2	5	1	1	0	2	1		5	.161	.188	.258	42	-2		.930	3			/C-8	0.1
1880	Bos N	37	126	11	18	5	0	0	10	5		15	.143	.176	.183	22	-10		.851	-2			C-37/O-2(1-1-1)	-1.1
1881	Cle N	5	15	1	1	0	0	0	0	1		2	.067	.125	.067	-40	-2		.955	-0			/C-4,3	-0.2
1882	Cin AA	16	60	4	13	1	1	0	5	3			.217	.254	.267	72	-2		.921	3			C-10/1-5,O(RF)	0.1
1883	Cin AA	30	114	16	28	1	4	0	8	3			.246	.265	.325	84	-3		.893	1			C-17,O-13(0-2-11)	-0.1
1884	Cin AA	34	130	10	18	1	0	0	8	5	0		.138	.170	.146	4	-14		.891	6			C-31/O-2(RF),1-2	-0.5
1885	Cin AA	15	60	6	16	2	0	0	7	0	0		.267	.267	.300	77	-2		.833	-3			C-15	-0.3
	Bal AA	9	34	6	4	1	0	0	2	1	0		.118	.143	.147	-8	-4		.844	-3			/C-8,O(RF)	-0.6
	Year	24	94	12	20	3	0	0	9	1	0		.213	.221	.245	47	-6		.837	-6			C-23/O(RF)	-0.9
Total	7	154	570	56	103	12	6	0	42	19	0	22	.181	.207	.223	40	-39		.877	4			C-130/O-19(1-3-16),1-7,3	-2.6
POWIS, CARL Carl Edgar "Jug" B 1.11.1928 Philadelphia, PA D 5.10.1999 Houston, TX BR/TR 6/185# d4.15																								
1957	Bal A	15	41	4	8	3	1	0	2	7-0	1	9	.195	.314	.317	82	-1	2-0	.909	-1	89	112	O-13(RF)	-0.2
POZO, ARQUIMEDEZ Arquimedez (Ortiz) B 8.24.1973 Santo Domingo, D.R. BR/TR 5-10/160# d9.12																								
1995	Sea A	1	1	0	0	0	0	0	0	0-0	0	0	.000	.000	.000	-99	0	0-0	1.000	0	148	0	/2	0.0
1996	Bos A	21	58	4	10	3	1	1	11	2-0	1	10	.172	.210	.310	30	-7	1-0	.930	0	95	51	2-10,3-10	-0.5
1997	Bos A	4	15	0	4	1	0	0	3	0-0	0	5	.267	.250	.333	54	-1	0-0	.947	3	191	136	/3-4	0.2
Total	3	26	74	4	14	4	1	1	14	2-0	1	15	.189	.215	.311	33	-8	1-0	.952	3	139	84	/3-14,2-11	-0.3
PRAMESA, JOHNNY John Steven B 8.28.1925 Barton, OH D 9.9.1996 Los Angeles, CA BR/TR 6-2/210# d4.24																								
1949	Cin N	17	25	2	6	1	0	1	2	3	0	5	.240	.321	.400	91	0	0	.966	-1	92	0	C-13	-0.1
1950	Cin N	74	228	14	70	10	1	5	30	19	1	15	.307	.363	.425	106	2	0	.981	-3	72	116	C-73	0.2
1951	Cin N	72	227	12	52	5	2	6	22	5	0	17	.229	.246	.348	57	-15	0-0	.968	-6	74	83	C-63	-1.9
1952	Chi N	22	46	1	13	1	0	1	5	4	0	4	.283	.340	.370	96	0	0-0	.958	0	63	68	C-17	0.1
Total	4	185	526	29	141	17	3	13	59	31	1	41	.268	.310	.386	84	-13	0-0	.973	-10	73	93	C-166	-1.7
PRATT, DEL Derrill Burnham B 1.10.1888 Walhalla, SC D 9.30.1977 Texas City, TX BR/TR 5-11/175# d4.11 OF Total (3-LF 3-CF 8-RF)																								
1912	StL A	152	570	76	172	26	15	5	69	36	4		.302	.348	.426	125	16	24	.943	13	106	122	*2-122,S-21/O-8(0-3-5),3	3.1
1913	StL A	**155**	592	60	175	31	13	2	87	40	1	57	.296	.341	.402	121	13	37	.951	3	101	104	*2-146/1-9	1.9
1914	StL A	158	584	85	165	34	13	5	65	50	2	45	.283	.341	.411	131	20	37-28	.944	-1	100	95	*2-152/O-5(2-0-3),S	2.2
1915	StL A	**159**	602	61	175	31	11	3	78	26	3	43	.291	.323	.394	119	10	32-23	.965	16	96	130	*2-158	2.9
1916	StL A	**158**	596	64	159	35	12	5	**103**	54	3	56	.267	.331	.391	123	14	26-17	.966	20	105	114	*2-158	4.0
1917	StL A	123	450	40	111	22	8	1	53	33	2	36	.247	.301	.338	98	-2	18	.959	18	103	119	*2-119/1-2	1.9
1918	NY A	**126**	477	65	131	19	7	2	55	35	2	26	.275	.327	.356	104	1	12	.969	10	100	**143**	*2-126	1.5
1919	NY A	140	527	69	154	27	7	4	56	36	4	24	.292	.342	.393	105	3	22	.969	25	**115**	122	*2-140	3.1
1920	NY A	**154**	574	84	180	37	8	4	97	50	3	24	.314	.372	.427	107	7	12-10	.971	13	107	**118**	*2-154	2.1
1921	Bos A	135	521	80	169	36	10	5	102	44	1	10	.324	.378	.461	116	12	8-10	.961	0	101	**137**	*2-134	1.4
1922	Bos A	**154**	607	73	183	44	7	6	86	53	4	20	.301	.361	.427	106	6	7-10	.966	-14	100	91	*2-154	-0.6
1923	Det A	101	297	43	92	18	3	0	40	25	6	9	.310	.375	.391	104	2	6-1	.947	-7	96	77	2-60,1-17,3-12	-0.2
1924	Det A	121	429	56	130	32	3	1	77	31	2	10	.303	.353	.399	95	-3	6-9	.948	-2	108	118	2-65,1-51/3-4,O(LF)	-0.8
Total	13	1836	6826	856	1996	392	117	43	968	513	37	360	.292	.345	.403	112	99	247-108	.960	94	103	116	*2-1688/1-79,S-22,3-17,O-14R	22.5
PRATT, FRANK Francis Bruce "Truckhorse" B 8.24.1897 Blocton, AL D 3.8.1974 Centreville, AL BL/TR 5-9.5/155# d5.13																								
1921	Chi A	1	1	0	0	0	0	0	0	0	0	0	.000	.000	.000	-99	0	0-0	—	0			H	0.0
PRATT, LARRY Lester John B 10.8.1886 Gibson City, IL D 1.8.1969 Peoria, IL BR/TR 6- /183# d9.19																								
1914	Bos A	5	4	0	0	0	0	0	0	0	0	4	.000	.000	.000	-99	-1	0	.923	1	210	233	/C-5	0.0
1915	Bro F	20	49	5	9	1	0	1	2	2	0	18	.184	.216	.265	35	-5	2	.949	-2	82	117	C-17	-0.6
	New F	5	4	2	2	2	0	0	0	3	0	1	.500	.714	1.000	403	2	2	1.000	-0	133	93	/C-3	0.2
	Year	25	53	7	11	3	0	1	2	5	0	19	.208	.276	.321	69	-3	4	.953	-2	86	115	C-20	-0.4
Total	2	30	57	7	11	3	0	1	2	5	0	23	.193	.258	.298	58	-4	4	.949	-1	98	127	/C-25	-0.4
PRATT, TOM Thomas J. B 1.26.1844 Chelsea, MA D 9.28.1908 Philadelphia, PA TL 5-7.5/150# d10.18 U1																								
1871	Ath NA	1	6	2	2	0	0	0	1	0		0	.333	.333	.333	93	0	0-0	.786	-1	0	0	/1	0.0
PRATT, TODD Todd Alan B 2.9.1967 Bellevue, NE BR/TR 6-3/225# d7.29																								
1992	Phi N	16	46	6	13	1	0	2	10	4-0	0	12	.283	.340	.435	118	1	0-0	.972	-1	97	0	C-11	0.1
1993	†Phi N	33	87	8	25	6	0	5	13	5-0	1	19	.287	.330	.529	128	3	0-0	.989	2	138	52	C-26	0.7
1994	Phi N	28	102	10	20	6	1	2	9	12-0	0	29	.196	.281	.333	58	-6	0-1	1.000	0	168	63	C-28	-0.5
1995	Chi N	25	60	3	8	2	0	0	4	6-1	0	21	.133	.209	.167	2	-9	0-0	.981	0	81	73	C-25	-0.7
1997	NY N	39	106	12	30	6	0	2	19	13-0	2	32	.283	.372	.396	105	1	0-1	.990	3	142	148	C-36/D	0.6
1998	NY N	41	69	9	19	9	1	2	18	2-0	0	20	.275	.296	.522	111	1	0-0	.973	-2	132	135	C-16/1-3	0.0
1999	†NY N	71	140	18	41	4	0	3	21	15-0	3	32	.293	.369	.386	96	-1	2-0	.996	2	131	69	C-52/1O(LF)	0.4
2000	†NY N	80	160	33	44	6	0	8	25	22-1	5	31	.275	.378	.463	116	4	0-0	.997	-2	131	106	C-71/D	0.5
2001	NY N	45	80	6	13	5	0	2	4	15-1	2	36	.162	.306	.300	62	-4	1-0	.994	-7	116	16	C-31	-0.9
	Phi N	35	93	12	19	3	0	2	7	19-2	1	25	.204	.345	.301	71	-3	0-0	.985	-3	190	50	C-34/1	-0.4
	Year	80	173	18	32	8	0	4	11	34-3	3	61	.185	.327	.301	67	-8	1-0	.989	-10	157	35	C-65/1	-1.3
2002	Phi N	39	106	14	33	11	0	3	16	24-6	4	28	.311	.449	.500	163	12	2-0	1.000	1	102	70	C-34/1-2	1.5
2003	Phi N	43	125	16	34	10	1	4	20	22-0	6	38	.272	.400	.464	134	8	0-0	.996	-4	60	66	C-35/1-6	0.6
Total	11	495	1174	147	299	69	3	35	166	159-11	24	323	.255	.353	.408	101	7	5-2	.992	-9	125	75	C-399/1-13,D-2,O(LF)	1.9
PREIBISCH, MEL Melvin Adolphus "Primo" B 11.23.1914 Sealy, TX D 4.12.1980 Sealy, TX BR/TR 5-11/185# d9.17																								
1940	Bos N	11	40	3	9	2	0	0	5	2	0	4	.225	.262	.275	51	-3	0	1.000	0	107	111	O-11(CF)	-0.3
1941	Bos N	5	4	0	0	0	0	0	0	1	0	2	.000	.200	.000	-42	-1	0	1.000	0	392	0	/O-2(1-1-1)	-0.1
Total	2	16	44	3	9	2	0	0	5	3	0	6	.205	.255	.250	42	-4	0	1.000	1	110	110	/O-13(1-12-1)	-0.4
PRESCOTT, BOBBY George Bertrand B 3.27.1931 Colon, Panama BR/TR 5-11/180# d6.17																								
1961	KC A	10	12	0	1	0	0	0	0	2-0	0	5	.083	.214	.083	-17	-2	0-0	—	-0	0	0	/O-2(LF)	-0.2
PRESLEY, JIM James Arthur B 10.23.1961 Pensacola, FL BR/TR 6-1/200# d6.24 C3																								
1984	Sea A	70	251	27	57	12	1	10	36	6-1	1	63	.227	.247	.402	78	-9	1-1	.958	-5	85	88	3-69/D	-1.6
1985	Sea A	155	570	71	157	33	1	28	84	44-9	1	100	.275	.324	.484	118	13	2-2	.961	5	109	76	*3-154	1.6
1986	Sea A☆	155	616	83	163	33	4	27	107	32-3	4	172	.265	.303	.463	105	1	0-4	.965	6	105	103	*3-155	0.4
1987	Sea A	152	575	78	142	23	6	24	88	38-1	4	157	.247	.296	.433	86	-14	2-0	.953	11	110	103	*3-148/S-4,D	-0.4
1988	Sea A	150	544	50	125	26	0	14	62	36-1	4	114	.230	.280	.355	74	-20	3-5	.940	-12	85	102	*3-146/D-4	-3.3
1989	Sea A	117	390	42	92	20	1	12	41	21-2	1	107	.236	.275	.385	82	-11	0-0	.924	-3	99	89	3-90,1-30/D	-1.5
1990	Atl N	140	541	59	131	34	1	19	72	29-0	3	130	.242	.282	.414	85	-12	1-1	.930	-2	93	94	*3-133,1-17	-1.6
1991	SD N	20	59	3	8	0	0	1	5	4-1	1	16	.136	.200	.186	10	-7	0-1	.923	-4	73	0	3-16	-1.2
Total	8	959	3546	413	875	181	14	135	495	210-18	19	859	.247	.290	.420	90	-59	9-14	.949	-3	99	93	3-911/1-47,D-7,S-4	-7.6
PRESTON, WALT Walter B. B 4.6.1868 Richmond, VA D 12.23.1937 New Orleans, LA BL/TR 6/175# d4.18																								
1895	Lou N	50	197	42	55	6	4	1	24	17	10	17	.279	.366	.365	95	0	11	.893	-5	142	221	O-26(0-19-7),3-25	-0.5
PRICE, JIM Jimmie William B 10.13.1941 Harrisburg, PA BR/TR 6/195# d4.11																								
1967	Det A	44	92	9	24	4	0	0	8	4-1	0	10	.261	.292	.304	74	-3	0-0	.974	-2	67	82	C-24	-0.5
1968	†Det A	64	132	12	23	4	0	3	13	13-1	1	14	.174	.253	.273	58	-7	0-0	.996	-5	132	19	C-42	-1.2
1969	Det A	72	192	21	45	8	0	9	28	18-1	0	20	.234	.294	.417	95	-2	0-0	.989	-2	67	82	C-51	-0.2
1970	Det A	52	132	12	24	4	0	5	15	21-0	0	23	.182	.290	.326	70	-5	0-0	.979	-4	89	65	C-38	-0.8
1971	Det A	29	54	4	13	2	0	1	7	6-1	1	3	.241	.323	.333	84	-1	0-0	.981	-2	60	113	C-25	-0.2
Total	5	261	602	58	129	22	0	18	71	62-4	2	70	.214	.287	.341	78	-18	0-0	.985	-15	86	67	C-180	-2.9
PRICE, JACKIE John Thomas Reid "Johnny" B 11.13.1912 Winborn, MS D 10.2.1967 San Francisco, CA BL/TR 5-10.5/150# d8.18																								
1946	Cle A	7	13	1	3	0	0	0	0	0	0	0	.231	.231	.231	31	-1	0-0	.947	1	119	50	/S-4	0.0

Year	Tm Lg	G	AB	R	H	2B	3B	HR	RBI	BB-IB	HP	SO	AVG	OBP	SLG	AOPS	ABR	SB-CS	FA	FR	Rng	Thr	G at Pos	BFW
PRICE, JOE Joseph Preston "Lumber" B 4.10.1897 Milligan College, TN D 1.15.1961 Washington, DC BR/TR 6-1.5/187# d9.5																								
1928	NY N	1	1	0	0	0	0	0	0	0	0	1	.000	.000	.000	-99	0	0	—	-0	0	0	/O(CF)	0.0
PRICHARD, BOB Robert Alexander B 10.21.1917 Paris, TX D 9.25.1991 Abilene, TX BL/TL 6-1/195# d6.14																								
1939	Was A	26	85	8	20	5	0	0	8	19	0	16	.235	.375	.294	79	-1	0-2	.992	-1	84	135	1-26	-0.5
PRIDDY, JERRY Gerald Edward B 11.9.1919 Los Angeles, CA D 3.3.1980 N.Hollywood, CA BR/TR 5-11.5/180# d4.17 Mil 1944-45																								
1941	NY A	56	174	18	37	7	0	1	26	18	1	16	.213	.290	.270	50	-13	4-2	.968	6	102	160	2-31,3-14,1-10	-0.5
1942	†NY A	59	189	23	53	9	2	2	28	31	1	27	.280	.385	.381	118	6	0-1	.944	3	101	37	3-35,1-11/2-8,S-3	0.9
1943	Was A	149	560	68	152	31	3	4	62	67	1	76	.271	.350	.359	112	10	5-5	.971	5	103	111	*2-134,S-15/3	2.4
1946	Was A	138	511	54	130	22	8	6	58	57	2	73	.254	.332	.364	100	-1	9-3	.962	-1	104	101	*2-138	0.7
1947	Was A	147	505	42	108	20	3	3	49	62	1	79	.214	.301	.283	65	-24	7-6	.980	-1	98	84	*2-146	-1.8
1948	StL A	151	560	96	166	40	9	8	79	86	1	71	.296	.391	.443	118	17	6-5	.968	**23**	**108**	111	*2-146	4.5
1949	StL A	145	544	83	158	26	4	11	63	80	1	81	.290	.382	.414	106	6	5-3	.968	-2	99	75	*2-145	1.2
1950	Det A	**157**	618	104	171	26	6	13	75	95	3	95	.277	.376	.401	96	-2	2-7	.981	**28**	**114**	**120**	*2-157	3.0
1951	Det A	**154**	584	73	152	22	6	8	57	69	0	73	.260	.338	.360	88	-10	4-3	.980	11	102	99	*2-154/S	1.0
1952	Det A	75	279	37	79	23	3	4	20	42	1	29	.283	.379	.430	124	11	1-8	.968	-2	96	80	2-75	1.1
1953	Det A	65	196	14	46	6	2	1	24	17	1	19	.235	.299	.301	63	-10	1-1	.977	1	97	83	2-45,1-11/3-2	-0.8
Total	11	1296	4720	612	1252	232	46	61	541	624	13	639	.265	.353	.373	97	-10	44-44	.973	70	104	100	*2-1179/3-52,1-32,S-19	11.7
PRIDE, CURTIS Curtis John B 12.17.1968 Washington, DC BL/TR 6/205# d9.14																								
1993	Mon N	10	9	3	4	1	1	1	5	0-0	0	3	.444	.444	1.111	288	2	1-0	1.000	0	439	0	/O-2(LF)	0.3
1995	Mon N	48	63	10	11	1	0	0	2	5-0	0	16	.175	.235	.190	13	-8	3-2	.920	-1	100	0	O-24(24-1-0)	-1.0
1996	Det A	95	267	52	80	17	5	10	31	31-1	0	63	.300	.372	.513	121	8	11-6	.967	1	116	0	O-48(45-0-5),D-31	0.5
1997	Det A	79	162	21	34	4	4	2	19	24-1	1	45	.210	.314	.321	67	-8	6-4	.980	-2	96	0	O-35(34-0-3),D-23	-1.2
	Bos A	2	2	1	1	0	0	1	1	0-0	0	1	.500	.500	2.000	502	1	0-0	—	0			/H	0.1
	Year	81	164	22	35	4	4	3	20	24-1	1	46	.213	.316	.341	73	-7	6-4	.980	-2	96	0	O-35(34-0-3),D-23	-1.1
1998	Atl N	70	107	19	27	6	1	3	9	9-0	3	29	.252	.325	.411	93	-1	4-0	1.000	2	140	0	O-22(8-0-14)/D-2	0.1
2000	Bos A	9	20	4	5	1	0	0	0	1-0	0	7	.250	.286	.300	47	-2	0-0	1.000	0	121	0	/O-9(7-2-0),D	-0.1
2001	Mon N	36	76	8	19	3	1	1	9	9-0	2	22	.250	.345	.355	80	-2	3-2	1.000	1	107	94	O-23(19-1-3)/D-2	-0.2
2003	NY A	4	12	1	1	0	0	1	1	0-0	0	2	.083	.083	.333	3	-2	0-0	1.000	-0	86	0	/O-3(1-0-2)	-0.2
Total	8	353	718	119	182	33	12	19	77	79-2	6	188	.253	.332	.412	90	-12	28-14	.977	0	112	13	O-166(140-4-27)/D-59	-1.7
PRIEST, JOHNNY John Gooding B 6.23.1886 St.Joseph, MO D 11.4.1979 Washington, DC BR/TR 5-11/170# d5.30																								
1911	NY A	8	21	2	3	0	0	0	2	2	1		.143	.250	.143	10	-3	3	.824	-2	65	0	/2-5,3-2	-0.5
1912	NY A	2	2	1	1	0	0	0	1	0	0		.500	.500	.500	176	0	0	—	0			H	0.0
Total	2	10	23	3	4	0	0	0	3	2	1		.174	.269	.174	23	-3	3	.824	-2	65	0	/2-5,3-2	-0.5
PRIETO, ALEX Alejandro Antonio B 6.19.1976 Caracas, Venezuela BR/TR 5-10/200# d7.26																								
2003	Min A	8	11	1	1	0	0	0	0	0-0	0	4	.091	.091	.091	-51	-2	0-0	1.000	-0	97	75	/2-5,S	-0.2
PRINCE, TOM Thomas Albert B 8.13.1964 Kankakee, IL BR/TR 5-11/185# d9.22																								
1987	Pit N	4	9	1	2	1	0	1	2	0-0	0	2	.222	.222	.667	123	0	0-0	1.000	-0	70	88	/C-4	0.0
1988	Pit N	29	74	3	13	2	0	0	6	4-0	0	15	.176	.218	.203	22	-8	0-0	.983	-4	98	61	C-28	-1.1
1989	Pit N	21	52	1	7	4	0	0	5	6-1	0	12	.135	.220	.212	26	-5	1-1	.960	-2	49	122	C-21	-0.7
1990	Pit N	4	10	1	1	0	0	0	0	1-0	0	2	.100	.182	.100	-21	-2	0-1	1.000	0	79	0	/C-3	-0.2
1991	Pit N	26	34	4	9	3	0	1	2	7-0	1	3	.265	.405	.441	140	2	0-0	.984	0	105	190	C-19/1	0.3
1992	Pit N	27	44	1	4	2	0	0	5	6-0	0	9	.091	.192	.136	-3	-6	1-1	.977	2	128	82	C-19/3	-0.4
1993	Pit N	66	179	14	35	14	0	2	24	13-2	7	38	.196	.272	.307	56	-11	1-1	.984	-7	73	96	C-59	-1.4
1994	LA N	3	6	2	2	0	0	0	1	1-0	0	3	.333	.429	.333	109	0	0-0	1.000	1	0	0	/C-3	0.1
1995	LA N	18	40	3	8	2	1	1	4	4-0	0	10	.200	.273	.375	75	-2	0-0	.988	-3	119	99	C-17	-0.4
1996	LA N	40	64	6	19	6	0	1	11	6-2	2	15	.297	.365	.438	123	3	0-0	.994	2	105	63	C-35	0.6
1997	LA N	47	100	17	22	5	0	3	14	5-0	3	15	.220	.275	.360	71	-5	0-0	.996	8	377	143	C-45	0.5
1998	LA N	37	81	7	15	5	1	0	5	7-1	2	24	.185	.267	.272	45	-7	0-0	1.000	2	113	174	C-32	-0.3
1999	Phi N	4	6	1	1	0	0	0	0	1-0	0	1	.167	.286	.167	18	-1	0-0	1.000	0	135	0	/C-4	0.0
2000	Phi N	46	122	14	29	9	0	2	16	13-0	2	31	.238	.321	.361	71	-5	1-0	.996	-0	124	84	C-46	-0.3
2001	Min A	64	196	19	43	4	1	7	23	12-0	6	39	.219	.284	.357	66	-10	3-1	1.000	14	152	120	C-64	0.7
2002	†Min A	51	125	14	28	7	1	4	16	14-0	4	26	.224	.317	.392	88	-2	1-3	.997	2	192	78	C-50	0.2
2003	Min A	24	40	5	8	2	0	2	5	5-0	2	7	.200	.319	.400	87	-1	1-0	1.000	1	360	98	C-22/D-2	0.2
	KC A	8	8	0	2	0	0	0	1	0-0	0	0	.250	.250	.250	29	-1	0-0	1.000	-1	64	0	/C-7,D	-0.2
	Year	32	48	5	10	2	0	2	6	5-0	2	7	.208	.309	.375	76	-2	1-0	1.000	-0	314	83	C-29/D-3	0.0
Total	17	519	1190	113	248	66	4	24	140	105-6	29	252	.208	.286	.331	66	-61	9-8	.992	14	149	103	C-478/D-3,31	-2.4
PRINCE, WALTER Walter Farr B 5.9.1861 Amherst, NH D 3.2.1938 Bristol, NH BL/TR 5-9/150# d8.7																								
1883	Lou AA	4	11	1	2	0	0	0		0			.182	.182	.182	19	-1		.500	-2	0	0	/O-2(RF),1-2,S	-0.3
1884	Det N	7	21	0	3	0	0	0	1	3		4	.143	.250	.143	29	-2		.375	-3	0	0	/O-7(RF)	-0.4
	Was AA	43	166	22	36	3	2	1		13	3		.217	.286	.277	95	1		.940	-5	28	78	1-43	-0.8
	Was U	1	4	0	1	0	0	0		0			.250	.250	.250	54	0		.818	-0	0	0	/1	-0.1
Total	2	55	202	23	42	3	2	1	1	16		4	.208	.276	.257	83	-2		.935	-11	34	74	/1-46,O-9(RF),S	-1.6
PRITCHARD, BUDDY Harold William B 1.25.1936 South Gate, CA BR/TR 6-1/195# d4.21																								
1957	Pit N	23	11	1	1	0	0	0	0	0-0	0	4	.091	.091	.091	-53	-2	0-0	.947	2	112	219	S-10/2-3	0.0
PRITCHETT, CHRIS Christopher Davis B 1.31.1970 Merced, CA BL/TR 6-4/185# d9.6																								
1996	Cal A	5	13	1	2	0	0	0	1	0-0	0	3	.154	.154	.154	-22	-2	0-0	1.000	-0	53	110	/1-5	-0.3
1998	Ana A	31	80	12	23	2	1	2	8	4-0	0	16	.287	.321	.412	89	-2	2-0	.995	2	139	65	1-29/D	-0.1
1999	Ana A	20	45	3	7	1	0	1	2	2-0	0	9	.156	.188	.244	10	-6	1-1	.990	1	129	85	1-15/D-5	-0.7
2000	Phi N	5	11	0	1	0	0	0	0	1-0	0	3	.091	.167	.091	-32	-2	0-0	1.000	1	217	43	/1-3	-0.2
Total	4	61	149	16	33	3	1	3	11	7-0	0	31	.221	.255	.315	46	-12	3-1	.995	4	135	72	/1-52,D-6	-1.3
PROESER, GEORGE George "Yatz" B 5.30.1864 Cincinnati, OH D 10.13.1941 New Burlington, OH BL/TL 5-10/190# d9.15 ▲																								
1888	Cle AA	7	23	5	7	2	0	0	1	1	0		.304	.333	.391	136	2	0	.846	-1	84	0	/P-7	0.0
1890	Syr AA	13	53	11	13	1	1	1	6	10	0		.245	.365	.358	126	2	1	.895	-2	47	0	O-13(RF)	0.1
Total	2	20	76	16	20	3	1	1	7	11	0		.263	.356	.368	129	4	1	.895	-2	47	0	/O-13(RF),P-7	0.1
PROPST, JAKE William Jacob B 3.10.1895 Kennedy, AL D 2.24.1967 Columbus, MS BL/TR 5-10/165# d8.7																								
1923	Was A	1	1	0	0	0	0	0	0	0	0	0	.000	.000	.000	-99	0	0-0	—	0			H	0.0
PROTHRO, DOC James Thompson B 7.16.1893 Memphis, TN D 10.14.1971 Memphis, TN BR/TR 5-10.5/170# d9.26 M3																								
1920	Was A	6	13	2	5	0	0	0	2	0	0	4	.385	.385	.385	107	0	0-0	1.000	0	56	290	/S-2,3-2	0.0
1923	Was A	6	8	2	2	0	1	0	3	1	0	3	.250	.333	.500	124	0	0-0	1.000	2	148	0	/3-6	0.2
1924	Was A	46	159	17	53	11	5	0	24	15	1	11	.333	.394	.465	125	6	4-4	.915	-9	80	96	3-45	-0.1
1925	Bos A	119	415	44	130	23	3	0	51	52	0	21	.313	.390	.383	97	0	9-11	.945	-2	**103**	73	*3-108/S-3	0.3
1926	Cin N	3	5	1	1	0	1	0	1	1	0	1	.200	.333	.600	151	0	0	1.000	-0	114	0	/3-2	0.0
Total	5	180	600	66	191	34	10	0	81	69	1	40	.318	.390	.408	105	6	13-15	.940	-9	98	85	3-163/S-5	0.4
PRUESS, EARL Earl Henry "Gibby" B 4.2.1895 Chicago, IL D 8.28.1979 Branson, MO BR/TR 5-10.5/170# d9.15																								
1920	StL A	1	0	1	0	0	0	0	0	1	0	0	—	1.000	—	176	0	1-0	1.000	0	197	0	/O(RF)	0.1
PRUETT, JIM James Calvin B 12.16.1917 Nashville, TN D 7.29.2003 Waukesha, WI BR/TR 5-10/178# d9.26																								
1944	Phi A	3	4	1	1	0	0	0	0	1	1	0	.250	.500	.250	119	0	0-0	1.000	0	*61*	*269*	/C-2	0.1
1945	Phi A	6	9	1	2	0	0	0	0	1	0	2	.222	.300	.222	53	-1	0-1	1.000	0	*94*	*0*	/C-4	-0.1
Total	2	9	13	2	3	0	0	0	0	2	1	2	.231	.375	.231	77	-1	0-1	1.000	1	*82*	*98*	/C-6	0.0
PRUITT, RON Ronald Ralph B 10.21.1951 Flint, MI BR/TR 6/185# d6.25 OF Total (83-LF 6-CF 77-RF)																								
1975	Tex A	14	17	2	3	0	0	0	0	1-0	0	3	.176	.222	.176	14	-2	0-0	1.000	-1	71	93	C-13/O(LF)	-0.3
1976	Cle A	47	86	7	23	1	1	0	5	16-1	0	8	.267	.375	.302	103	1	2-3	1.000	3	119	251	O-26(12-1-13)/C-6,3-6,1D	0.3
1977	Cle A	78	219	29	63	10	2	2	32	28-0	2	22	.288	.369	.379	109	4	2-3	.972	-4	88	47	O-69(27-3-42)/C-4,3D	-0.3

Year	Tm Lg	G	AB	R	H	2B	3B	HR	RBI	BB-IB	HP	SO	AVG	OBP	SLG	AOPS	ABR	SB-CS	FA	FR	Rng	Thr	G at Pos	BFW
1978	Cle A	71	187	17	44	6	1	6	17	16-3	0	20	.235	.296	.374	88	-4	2-1	.984	-11	55	69	C-48,O-16(12-0-4)/3-2,D-5	-1.4
1979	Cle A	64	166	23	47	7	0	2	21	19-1	0	21	.283	.355	.361	94	-1	2-0	.957	-4	80	51	O-29(19-0-11),D-14,C-11/3-3	-0.6
1980	Cle A	23	36	1	11	1	0	0	4	4-0	0	6	.306	.366	.333	95	0	0-0	1.000	0	87	267	/O-6(0-1-5),3-2,D-2	0.0
	Chi A	33	70	8	21	2	0	2	11	8-1	0	7	.300	.372	.414	116	2	0-0	1.000	-2	111	0	O-11(10-1-0)/C-5,3-3,1D	0.0
	Year	56	106	9	32	3	0	2	15	12-1	0	13	.302	.370	.387	109	2	0-0	1.000	-2	102	102	O-17(10-2-5)/D-9,3-5,C-5,1	0.0
1981	Cle A	5	9	0	0	0	0	0	0	1-0	0	2	.000	.100	.000	-70	-2	0-0	1.000	-1	69	0	/O-3(2-0-1),CD	-0.3
1982	SF N	5	4	1	2	1	0	0	2	1-1	0	1	.500	.600	.750	276	1	0-0	1.000	1	0	0	/CO(RF)	0.2
1983	SF N	1	1	0	0	0	0	0	0	0-0	0	0	.000	.000	.000	-99	0	0-0	—	0			/H	0.0
Total	9	341	795	88	214	28	4	12	92	94-7	2	90	.269	.345	.360	97	-1	8-7	.977	-19	94	75	O-162L/C-89,D-37,3-17,1-2	-2.4
PRYOR, GREG Gregory Russell B 10.2.1949 Marietta, OH BR/TR 6/186# d6.4																								
1976	Tex A	5	8	2	3	0	0	0	1	0-0	0	1	.375	.375	.375	118	0	0-0	1.000	0	92	72	/2-3,S3	0.0
1978	Chi A	82	222	27	58	11	0	2	15	11-0	1	18	.261	.298	.338	78	-7	3-1	.966	2	95	74	2-35,S-28,3-20	-0.1
1979	Chi A	143	476	60	131	23	3	3	34	35-1	2	41	.275	.324	.355	84	-10	3-4	.961	-2	103	72	*S-119,2-25,3-22	-0.1
1980	Chi A	122	338	32	81	18	4	1	29	12-0	2	35	.240	.265	.325	63	-18	2-2	.975	15	115	99	S-76,3-41/2-5,D	0.3
1981	Chi A	47	76	4	17	1	0	0	6	6-0	2	8	.224	.298	.237	57	-4	0-0	.931	-0	101	29	3-27,S-13/2-5	-0.4
1982	KC A	73	152	23	41	10	1	2	12	10-0	0	20	.270	.315	.388	92	-2	2-0	.951	-3	97	109	3-40,2-15,1-14/S-7	-0.4
1983	KC A	68	115	9	25	4	0	1	14	7-0	0	8	.217	.260	.278	49	-8	0-0	.958	1	109	96	3-60/1-6,2-3	-0.8
1984	†KC A	123	270	32	71	11	1	4	25	12-0	3	28	.263	.301	.356	80	-8	0-3	.970	2	100	110	*3-105,2-22/S-2,1D	-0.7
1985	†KC A	63	114	8	25	3	0	1	3	8-0	0	12	.219	.270	.272	49	-8	0-1	.946	-3	111	84	3-26,2-20,S-13/1D	-1.0
1986	KC A	63	112	7	19	4	0	0	7	3-0	0	14	.170	.191	.205	8	-14	1-1	.935	1	118	188	3-35,S-17,2-12/1	-1.3
Total	10	789	1883	204	471	85	9	14	146	104-1	10	185	.250	.291	.327	70	-79	11-12	.952	12	107	108	3-377,S-276,2-145/1-23,D-3	-4.5
PUCCINELLI, GEORGE George Lawrence "Pooch" or "Count" B 6.22.1907 San Francisco, CA D 4.16.1956 San Francisco, CA BR/TR 6-0.5/190# d7.17																								
1930	†StL N	11	16	5	9	1	0	3	8	0	0	1	.563	.563	1.188	298	5	0	1.000	-0	59	0	/O-3(3-0-1)	0.4
1932	StL N	31	108	17	30	8	0	3	11	12	0	13	.278	.350	.435	107	1	1	.942	2	94	298	O-30(24-0-6)	0.2
1934	StL A	10	26	4	6	1	0	2	5	1	1	8	.231	.286	.500	92	-1	0-0	.941	0	108	176	/O-6(LF)	0.0
1936	Phi A	135	457	83	127	30	3	11	78	65	1	70	.278	.369	.429	98	0	2-3	.948	0	104	101	*O-117(1-0-116)	-0.7
Total	4	187	607	109	172	40	3	19	102	78	2	92	.283	.367	.453	105	5	3-3	.947	2	102	143	O-156(34-0-123)	-0.1
PUCKETT, KIRBY Kirby B 3.14.1961 Chicago, IL BR/TR 5-8/210# d5.8 HF2001 OF Total (10-LF 1432-CF 276-RF)																								
1984	Min A	128	557	63	165	12	5	0	31	16-1	4	69	.296	.320	.336	78	-17	14-7	.993	18	117	**179**	*O-128(CF)	0.0
1985	Min A	161	691	80	199	29	13	4	74	41-0	4	87	.288	.330	.385	90	-10	21-12	.984	10	105	182	*O-161(CF)	-0.1
1986	Min A★	161	680	119	223	37	6	31	96	34-4	7	99	.328	.366	.537	138	34	20-12	.986	1	102	94	*O-160(CF)	3.3
1987	†Min A★	157	624	96	**207**	32	5	28	99	32-7	6	91	.332	.367	.534	131	26	12-7	.986	-4	93	126	*O-147(CF)/D-8	2.0
1988	Min A★	158	657	109	**234**	42	5	24	121	23-4	2	83	.356	.375	.545	151	42	6-7	.994	9	106	166	*O-158(CF)	4.9
1989	Min A★	159	635	75	**215**	45	4	9	85	41-9	3	59	**.339**	.379	.465	129	25	11-4	.991	11	109	159	*O-157(CF)/D-2	3.5
1990	Min A★	146	551	82	164	40	3	12	80	57-11	3	73	.298	.365	.446	119	15	5-4	.989	2	102	123	*O-141(9-125-9)/23SD	1.6
1991	†Min A★	152	611	92	195	29	6	15	89	31-4	4	78	.319	.352	.460	118	14	11-5	.985	1	96	161	*O-152(0-144-19)	1.3
1992	Min A★	160	639	104	**210**	38	4	19	110	44-13	6	97	.329	.374	.490	137	31	17-7	.993	-1	99	110	*O-149(CF)/2-2,3-2,SD	3.0
1993	Min A★	156	622	89	184	39	3	22	89	47-7	7	93	.296	.349	.474	119	16	8-6	.994	-3	90	149	*O-139(1-95-47),D-17	1.0
1994	Min A★	108	439	79	139	32	3	20	**112**	28-7	7	47	.317	.362	.540	130	19	6-3	.986	6	103	181	O-95(0-3-95),D-13	1.8
1995	Min A★	137	538	83	169	39	0	23	99	56-18	3	89	.314	.379	.515	130	25	3-2	.981	-2	92	125	*O-109(0-5-106),D-28/23S	1.4
Total	12	1783	7244	1071	2304	414	57	207	1085	450-85	56	965	.318	.360	.477	123	220	134-76	.989	46	101	146	*O-1696C/D-81,3-4,2-4,S-3	23.7
PUHL, JOHN John G. B 1.10.1876 Brooklyn, NY D 8.24.1900 Bayonne, NJ d10.13																								
1898	NY N	2	9	1	2	0	0	0	1	0	0		.222	.222	.222	28	-1	0	.667	-1	102	288	/3-2	-0.1
1899	NY N	1	2	0	0	0	0	0	0	0	1		.000	.333	.000	-6	0	0	.667	-0	110	0	/3	0.0
Total	2	3	11	1	2	0	0	0	1	0	1		.182	.250	.182	24	-1	0	.667	-1	104	213	/3-3	-0.1
PUHL, TERRY Terry Stephen B 7.8.1956 Melville, SK, CAN BL/TR 6-2/200# d7.12																								
1977	Hou N	60	229	40	69	13	5	0	10	30-0	1	31	.301	.385	.402	122	8	10-1	.992	0	98	77	O-59(48-11-1)	0.8
1978	Hou N☆	149	585	87	169	25	6	3	35	48-5	4	46	.289	.343	.368	108	6	32-14	.992	7	112	66	*O-148(43-109-4)	1.2
1979	Hou N	157	600	87	172	22	4	8	49	58-8	4	46	.287	.352	.377	105	5	30-22	**1.000**	-6	97	61	*O-152(6-109-40)	-0.6
1980	†Hou N	141	535	75	151	24	5	13	55	60-3	4	52	.282	.357	.419	126	19	27-11	.991	10	114	126	*O-135(4-30-107)	2.6
1981	†Hou N	96	350	43	88	19	4	3	28	31-5	4	49	.251	.315	.354	96	-2	22-4	**1.000**	0	103	72	O-88(0-20-71)	-0.3
1982	Hou N	145	507	64	133	17	9	8	50	51-2	2	49	.262	.331	.379	106	3	17-9	.989	-4	101	45	*O-138(0-32-122)	-0.6
1983	Hou N	137	465	66	136	25	7	8	44	36-2	2	48	.292	.343	.428	121	12	24-11	.991	-4	100	51	*O-124(0-13-118)	0.4
1984	Hou N	132	449	66	135	19	7	9	55	59-12	1	45	.301	.380	.434	139	25	13-8	.986	-6	91	73	*O-126(8-0-123)	1.3
1985	Hou N	57	194	34	55	14	3	2	23	18-4	1	23	.284	.343	.418	116	4	6-2	1.000	0	100	90	O-53(1-0-53)	0.3
1986	†Hou N	81	172	17	42	10	0	3	14	15-1	0	24	.244	.302	.355	84	-4	3-2	1.000	-2	97	0	O-47(5-0-42)	-0.9
1987	Hou N	90	122	9	28	5	0	2	15	11-0	0	16	.230	.293	.320	65	-6	1-1	.980	1	128	0	O-40(28-5-9)	-0.6
1988	Hou N	113	234	42	71	7	2	3	19	35-3	1	30	.303	.395	.389	131	11	22-4	.983	-0	103	61	O-78(48-1-33)	1.3
1989	Hou N	121	354	41	96	25	4	0	27	45-3	1	39	.271	.353	.364	110	6	9-8	1.000	-1	100	55	*O-103(37-11-64)/1-3	0.1
1990	Hou N	37	41	5	12	1	0	0	8	5-0	1	7	.293	.375	.317	98	0	1-2	1.000	-1	62	0	/O-8(6-2-0),1	-0.2
1991	KC A	15	18	0	4	0	0	0	3	3-1	0	2	.222	.333	.222	57	-1	0-0	—	-0	0	0	/O(LF)D	-0.1
Total	15	1531	4855	676	1361	226	56	62	435	505-49	26	507	.280	.349	.388	113	86	217-99	.993	-7	102	66	*O-1300(235-343-787)/1-4,D-2	4.7
PUIG, RICH Richard Gerald B 3.16.1953 Tampa, FL BL/TR 5-10/165# d9.13																								
1974	NY N	4	10	0	0	0	0	0	0	1-0	0	2	.000	.091	.000	-74	-2	0-0	.923	-0	97	139	/2-3,3	-0.2
PUJOLS, ALBERT Jose Alberto B 1.16.1980 Santo Domingo, D.R. BR/TR 6-3/210# d4.2 OF Total (269-LF 40-RF)																								
2001	†StL N★	161	590	112	194	47	4	37	130	69-6	9	93	.329	.403	.610	159	54	1-3	.964	9	95	128	O-78(39-0-39),3-55,1-42/D-2	5.4
2002	†StL N	157	590	118	185	40	2	34	127	72-13	9	69	.314	.394	.561	156	46	2-4	.978	-4	91	63	*O-118(117-0-1),3-41,1-21/SD	3.6
2003	StL N★	157	591	**137**	**212**	**51**	1	43	124	79-12	10	65	**.359**	.439	.667	192	83	5-1	.986	2	98	106	*O-113(LF),1-62/D	7.5
Total	3	475	1771	367	591	138	7	114	381	220-31	28	227	.334	.412	.613	169	183	8-8	.977	7	95	96	O-309L,1-125/3-96,D-5,S	16.5
PUJOLS, LUIS Luis Bienvenido (Toribio) B 11.18.1955 Santiago Rodriguez, D.R. BR/TR 6-1/195# d9.22 M1 C10																								
1977	Hou N	6	15	0	1	0	0	0	0	0-0	0	5	.067	.067	.067	-70	-4	0-0	1.000	-1	79	225	/C-6	-0.5
1978	Hou N	56	153	11	20	8	1	1	11	12-1	1	45	.131	.198	.216	17	-18	0-0	.981	-6	67	76	C-55/1	-2.4
1979	Hou N	26	75	7	17	2	1	0	8	2-0	0	14	.227	.247	.280	46	-6	0-0	.993	-0	77	13	C-26	-0.5
1980	†Hou N	78	221	15	44	6	1	0	20	13-3	1	29	.199	.245	.235	38	-19	0-0	.990	-5	89	78	C-75/3	-2.3
1981	†Hou N	40	117	5	28	3	1	1	14	10-3	0	17	.239	.297	.308	76	-4	1-0	.995	-1	122	77	C-39	-0.3
1982	Hou N	65	176	8	35	6	2	4	15	10-2	0	40	.199	.242	.324	62	-10	0-3	.991	-5	91	104	C-64	-1.5
1983	Hou N	40	87	4	17	2	0	0	12	5-2	0	14	.195	.234	.218	29	-9	0-0	.971	-4	61	24	C-39	-1.2
1984	KC A	4	5	0	1	0	0	0	1	0-0	0	0	.200	.200	.200	11	-1	0-0	1.000	0	0	0	/C-4	0.0
1985	Tex A	1	1	0	1	0	0	0	0	0-0	0	0	1.000	1.000	1.000	444	0	0-0	1.000	-1	7	0	/C	0.0
Total	9	316	850	50	164	27	6	6	81	52-11	2	164	.193	.240	.260	43	-71	1-3	.987	-23	85	73	C-309/31	-8.7
PULLIAM, HARVEY Harvey Jerome B 10.20.1967 San Francisco, CA BR/TR 6/205# d8.10																								
1991	KC A	18	33	4	9	1	0	3	4	3-1	0	9	.273	.333	.576	146	2	0-0	.917	0	100	155	O-15(11-0-5)	0.2
1992	KC A	4	5	2	1	1	0	0	0	1-0	0	3	.200	.333	.400	102	0	0-0	1.000	0	305	0	/O(LF)D	0.0
1993	KC A	27	62	7	16	5	0	1	6	2-0	1	14	.258	.292	.387	76	-2	0-0	.971	-1	100	0	O-26(12-0-16)	-0.4
1995	Col N	5	5	1	2	1	0	1	3	0-0	0	2	.400	.400	1.200	234	1	0-0	—	-0	0	0	/O(LF)	0.1
1996	Col N	10	15	2	2	0	0	0	0	2-0	0	6	.133	.235	.133	0	-2	0-0	1.000	-0	100	0	/O-3(LF)	-0.2
1997	Col N	59	67	15	19	3	0	3	9	5-0	0	15	.284	.333	.463	86	-1	0-1	.962	0	87	208	O-33(24-1-10)	-0.2
Total	6	123	187	31	49	11	0	8	22	13-1	1	49	.262	.313	.449	89	-2	0-1	.956	-1	98	103	/O-79(52-1-31),D-2	-0.5
PUNTO, NICK Nicholas Paul B 11.8.1977 San Diego, CA BB/TR 5-9/170# d9.9																								
2001	Phi N	4	5	0	2	0	0	0	0	0-0	0	0	.400	.400	.400	111	0	0-0	1.000	-1	67	0	/S	0.0
2002	Phi N	9	6	0	1	0	0	0	0	0-0	0	3	.167	.167	.167	-11	-1	0-0	1.000	0	314	1350	/2S	-0.1
2003	Phi N	64	92	14	20	2	0	1	4	7-1	0	22	.217	.273	.272	45	-8	2-1	.985	2	101	95	2-16/3-9,S-7	-0.4
Total	3	77	103	14	23	2	0	1	4	7-1	0	25	.223	.273	.272	46	-9	2-1	.985	2	104	110	/2-17,3-9,S-9-0.5	
PURCELL, BLONDIE William Aloysius B Paterson, NJ BR/TR 5-9.5/159# d5.1 M1 ▲ OF Total (480-LF 92-CF 430-RF)																								
1879	Syr N	63	277	32	72	6	3	0	25	3		13	.260	.268	.303	99	0		.773	-11	44	0	O-47(0-10-37),P-22/C	-0.9
	Cin N	12	50	10	11	0	0	0	4	0		3	.220	.220	.220	48	-3		.750	0	128	0	O-10(0-7-3)/P-2	-0.2

Year	Tm Lg	G	AB	R	H	2B	3B	HR	RBI	BB-IB	HP	SO	AVG	OBP	SLG	AOPS	ABR	SB-CS	FA	FR	Rng	Thr	G at Pos	BFW
	Year	75	327	42	83	6	3	0	29	3		16	.254	.261	.291	91	-3		.767	-10	61	0	O-57(0-17-40),P-24/C	-1.1
1880	Cin N	77	325	48	95	13	6	1	24	5		13	.292	.303	.378	131	10		.814	-2	117	42	O-55(0-54-2),P-25/S	0.3
1881	Cle N	20	80	3	14	2	1	0	4	5		8	.175	.224	.225	44	-5		.786	-3	73	0	O-20(7-13-0)	-0.8
	Buf N	30	113	15	33	7	2	0	17	8		8	.292	.339	.389	130	4		.706	-5	65	0	O-25(LF)/P-9	-0.3
	Year	50	193	18	47	9	3	0	21	13		16	.244	.291	.321	95	0		.748	-7	69	0	O-45(32-13-0)/P-9	-1.1
1882	Buf N	**84**	380	79	105	18	6	2	40	14		27	.276	.302	.371	113	5		.820	-4	60	0	*O-82(78-5-0)/P-6	-0.2
1883	Phi N	97	425	70	114	20	5	1	32	13		26	.268	.290	.346	101	2		.777	3	114	83	3-46,O-44(LF),P-11,M	0.4
1884	Phi N	103	428	67	108	11	7	1	31	29		30	.252	.300	.318	99	1		.874	1	58	27	*O-103(LF)/P	-0.1
1885	Phi AA	66	304	71	90	15	5	0	22	16	3		.296	.337	.378	119	6		.858	0	122	48	O-66(66-1-0)/P	0.4
	Bos N	21	87	9	19	1	1	0	3	3		15	.218	.244	.253	63	-4		.840	-2	61	0	O-21(LF)	-0.6
1886	Bal AA	26	85	17	19	0	1	0	8	17	2		.224	.365	.247	96	1	13	.867	-0	96	0	O-26(25-1-0)/SP	0.0
1887	Bal AA	140	567	101	142	25	8	4	96	46	10		.250	.318	.344	90	-6	88	.932	-5	74	103	*O-140(RF)/P	-1.0
1888	Bal AA	101	406	53	96	9	4	2	39	27	3		.236	.289	.293	89	-5	16	.906	-6	54	78	*O-100(7-1-95)/S-2,1	-1.1
	Phi AA	18	66	10	11	3	1	0	6	5	1		.167	.236	.242	54	-3	10	.903	-1	96	160	O-17(RF)/3	-0.4
	Year	119	472	63	107	12	5	2	45	32	4		.227	.281	.286	84	-8	26	.905	-7	61	91	*O-117(7-1-112)/S-2,13	-1.5
1889	Phi AA	129	507	72	160	19	7	0	85	50	5	27	.316	.383	.381	119	14	22	.903	-11	60	54	*O-129(RF)	0.2
1890	Phi AA	110	463	110	128	28	3	2	59	43	4		.276	.343	.363	109	5	48	.949	0	93	42	*O-110(104-0-7)	0.3
Total	12	1097	4563	767	1217	177	60	13	495	284	28	<u>170</u>	.267	.314	.340	103	22	197	.870	-45	78	50	0-995L/P-79,3-47,S-4,1C	-4.0

PURDY, PID Everett Virgil B 6.15.1904 Beatrice, NE D 1.16.1951 Beatrice, NE BL/TR 5-6/150# d9.7

Year	Tm Lg	G	AB	R	H	2B	3B	HR	RBI	BB-IB	HP	SO	AVG	OBP	SLG	AOPS	ABR	SB-CS	FA	FR	Rng	Thr	G at Pos	BFW
1926	Chi A	11	33	5	6	2	1	0	6	2	0	1	.182	.229	.303	39	-3	0-1	1.000	0	105	104	/O-9(RF)	-0.4
1927	Cin N	18	62	15	22	2	4	1	12	4	2	3	.355	.412	.565	164	5	0	.946	-3	81	0	O-16(CF)	0.1
1928	Cin N	70	223	32	69	11	1	0	25	23	1	13	.309	.377	.368	97	0	1	.966	-0	106	62	O-61(56-1-4)	-0.5
1929	Cin N	82	181	22	49	7	5	1	16	19	3	8	.271	.350	.381	85	-4	2	.978	1	103	103	O-42(34-0-8)	-0.6
Total	4	181	499	74	146	22	11	2	59	48	6	25	.293	.362	.393	97	-2	3-1	.969	-3	102	70	O-128(90-17-21)	-1.4

PURNELL, JESSE Jesse Rhoades B 5.11.1881 Glenside, PA D 7.4.1966 Philadelphia, PA BL/TR 5-5.5/140# d10.1

Year	Tm Lg	G	AB	R	H	2B	3B	HR	RBI	BB-IB	HP	SO	AVG	OBP	SLG	AOPS	ABR	SB-CS	FA	FR	Rng	Thr	G at Pos	BFW
1904	Phi N	7	19	2	2	0	0	0	1	4	1		.105	.292	.105	25	-1	1	.864	-1	93	0	/3-7	-0.2

PURTELL, BILLY William Patrick B 1.6.1886 Columbus, OH D 3.17.1962 Bradenton, FL BR/TR 5-9/170# d4.16

Year	Tm Lg	G	AB	R	H	2B	3B	HR	RBI	BB-IB	HP	SO	AVG	OBP	SLG	AOPS	ABR	SB-CS	FA	FR	Rng	Thr	G at Pos	BFW
1908	Chi A	26	69	3	9	2	0	0	3	2	0		.130	.155	.159	2	-7	2	.940	5	138	241	3-25	-0.2
1909	Chi A	103	361	34	93	9	3	0	40	19	4		.258	.302	.299	94	-3	14	.929	-1	100	130	3-71,2-32	-0.2
1910	Chi A	102	368	21	82	5	3	1	36	21	4		.223	.272	.261	70	-14	5	.907	-1	102	117	*3-102	-1.3
	Bos A	49	168	15	35	1	2	1	15	18	1		.208	.289	.256	69	-6	2	.908	-4	102	37	3-41/S-8	-1.0
	Year	151	536	36	117	6	5	2	51	39	5		.218	.278	.259	70	-19	7	.907	-4	102	95	*3-143/S-8	-2.3
1911	Bos A	27	82	5	23	5	3	0	7	1	1		.280	.298	.415	99	-1	1	.867	-1	96	47	3-15/2-3,S-3,O(CF)	-0.1
1914	Det A	28	76	4	13	4	0	0	3	2	1	7	.171	.203	.224	27	-7	0-2	.946	-1	107	89	3-16/S-2,2	-0.9
Total	5	335	1124	82	255	26	11	2	104	63	11	<u>7</u>	.227	.275	.275	73	-38	24-<u>2</u>	.915	-2	104	113	3-270/2-36,S-13,O(CF)	-3.7

PUTMAN, ED Eddy William B 9.25.1953 Los Angeles, CA BR/TR 6-1/190# d9.7

Year	Tm Lg	G	AB	R	H	2B	3B	HR	RBI	BB-IB	HP	SO	AVG	OBP	SLG	AOPS	ABR	SB-CS	FA	FR	Rng	Thr	G at Pos	BFW
1976	Chi N	5	7	0	3	0	0	0	0	0-0	0	0	.429	.429	.429	132	0	0-0	1.000	0	0	0	/C-3,1	0.0
1978	Chi N	17	25	2	5	0	0	0	3	4-0	0	6	.200	.310	.200	40	-2	0-0	.950	0	124	111	/3-8,1-3,C-2	-0.2
1979	Det A	21	39	4	9	3	0	2	4	4-0	0	12	.231	.302	.462	99	0	0-1	1.000	-1	102	69	C-16/1-5	-0.1
Total	3	43	71	6	17	3	0	2	7	8-0	0	18	.239	.316	.366	81	-2	0-1	1.000	-0	92	62	/C-21,1-9,3-8	-0.3

PUTNAM, PAT Patrick Edward B 12.3.1953 Bethel, VT BL/TR 6-1/214# d9.2

Year	Tm Lg	G	AB	R	H	2B	3B	HR	RBI	BB-IB	HP	SO	AVG	OBP	SLG	AOPS	ABR	SB-CS	FA	FR	Rng	Thr	G at Pos	BFW
1977	Tex A	11	26	3	8	4	0	0	3	1-1	0	4	.308	.333	.462	113	1	0-1	1.000	-1	33	94	/1-7,D-3	-0.1
1978	Tex A	20	46	4	7	1	0	1	2	2-1	0	5	.152	.188	.239	19	-5	0-0	1.000	0	107	94	D-12/1-4	-0.6
1979	Tex A	139	426	57	118	19	2	18	64	23-6	6	50	.277	.319	.458	109	4	1-6	.994	-0	96	86	1-96,D-32	-0.5
1980	Tex A	147	410	42	108	16	2	13	55	36-6	0	49	.263	.319	.407	102	0	0-2	.992	4	108	101	*1-137/3D	-0.4
1981	Tex A	95	297	33	79	17	2	8	35	17-3	0	38	.266	.304	.418	113	4	4-2	.993	3	116	99	1-94/O-3(3-0-1)	0.2
1982	Tex A	43	122	14	28	8	0	2	9	10-1	1	18	.230	.293	.344	78	-4	0-2	.990	2	119	91	1-39/3O(LF)	-0.5
1983	Sea A	144	469	58	126	23	2	19	67	39-8	3	57	.269	.326	.448	107	4	2-1	.994	4	107	99	*1-125,D-11	0.1
1984	Sea A	64	155	11	31	6	0	2	16	12-1	0	27	.200	.254	.277	49	-11	3-0	1.000	1	97	0	D-30,O-13(LF)/1-6	-1.1
	Min A	14	38	1	3	1	0	0	4	4-0	0	12	.079	.163	.105	-22	-6	0-0	—	0	0	0	D-11	-0.7
	Year	78	193	12	34	7	0	2	20	16-1	0	39	.176	.236	.244	34	-17	3-0	1.000	1	97	0	D-41,O-13(LF)/1-6	-1.8
Total	8	677	1989	223	508	95	8	63	255	144-27	10	260	.255	.306	.406	96	-13	10-14	.993	12	108	97	1-508,D-100/O-17(17-0-1),3-2	-3.6

PYBURN, JIM James Edward B 11.1.1932 Fairfield, AL BR/TR 6/190# d4.17

Year	Tm Lg	G	AB	R	H	2B	3B	HR	RBI	BB-IB	HP	SO	AVG	OBP	SLG	AOPS	ABR	SB-CS	FA	FR	Rng	Thr	G at Pos	BFW
1955	Bal A	39	98	5	20	2	2	0	7	8-0	1	24	.204	.271	.265	48	-8	1-1	1.000	-3	83	22	3-33/O(RF)	-1.1
1956	Bal A	84	156	23	27	3	3	2	11	17-0	0	26	.173	.251	.269	41	-14	4-1	.975	3	106	169	O-77(11-64-3)	-1.3
1957	Bal A	35	40	8	9	0	0	1	2	9-0	0	6	.225	.367	.300	90	0	1-0	1.000	3	125	296	O-28(7-13-9)/C	0.2
Total	3	158	294	36	56	5	5	3	20	34-0	1	56	.190	.275	.272	51	-22	6-2	.982	4	111	200	O-106(18-77-13)/3-33,C	-2.2

PYE, EDDIE Robert Edward B 2.13.1967 Columbia, TN BR/TR 5-10/175# d6.3

Year	Tm Lg	G	AB	R	H	2B	3B	HR	RBI	BB-IB	HP	SO	AVG	OBP	SLG	AOPS	ABR	SB-CS	FA	FR	Rng	Thr	G at Pos	BFW
1994	LA N	7	10	2	1	0	0	0	0	1-0	0	4	.100	.182	.100	-26	-2	0-0	1.000	2	181	227	/2-3,S-3	0.0
1995	LA N	7	8	0	0	0	0	0	0	0-0	0	4	.000	.000	.000	-99	-2	0-0	—	-1	0	0	/3-2	-0.3
Total	2	14	18	2	1	0	0	0	0	1-0	0	8	.056	.105	.056	-61	-4	0-0	1.000	1	131	201	/S-3,2-3,3-2	-0.3

PYTLAK, FRANKIE Frank Anthony B 7.30.1908 Buffalo, NY D 5.8.1977 Buffalo, NY BR/TR 5-7.5/160# d4.22 Mil 1942-45

Year	Tm Lg	G	AB	R	H	2B	3B	HR	RBI	BB-IB	HP	SO	AVG	OBP	SLG	AOPS	ABR	SB-CS	FA	FR	Rng	Thr	G at Pos	BFW
1932	Cle A	12	29	5	7	1	1	0	4	3	1	2	.241	.333	.345	71	-1	0-0	1.000	2	*149*	*94*	C-12	0.1
1933	Cle A	80	248	36	77	10	6	2	33	17	0	10	.310	.355	.423	101	-1	3-4	1.000	10	*136*	*155*	C-69	1.2
1934	Cle A	91	289	46	75	12	4	0	35	36	**5**	11	.260	.352	.329	75	-10	11-2	.989	-6	*105*	*73*	C-88	-0.8
1935	Cle A	55	149	14	44	6	1	1	12	11	1	4	.295	.348	.369	84	-4	3-2	.984	-1	*117*	*110*	C-48	-0.2
1936	Cle A	75	224	35	72	15	4	0	31	24	3	11	.321	.394	.424	101	1	5-2	.996	-2	*88*	*133*	C-58	0.3
1937	Cle A	125	397	60	125	15	6	1	44	52	7	15	.315	.404	.390	100	3	16-5	.986	6	*87*	***132***	*C-115	1.7
1938	Cle A	113	364	46	112	14	7	1	43	36	4	15	.308	.376	.393	95	-3	9-5	.987	-6	*76*	*112*	C-99	-0.2
1939	Cle A	63	183	20	49	2	5	0	14	20	1	5	.268	.343	.333	76	-7	4-1	1.000	4	*111*	*93*	C-51	0.0
1940	Cle A	62	149	16	21	2	1	0	16	17	1	5	.141	.234	.168	6	-21	0-1	.996	7	*143*	*124*	C-58/O(RF)	-1.1
1941	Bos A	106	336	36	91	23	1	2	39	28	1	19	.271	.329	.363	81	-9	5-7	.991	1	*109*	*86*	C-91	-0.4
1945	Bos A	9	17	1	2	0	0	0	0	3	0	0	.118	.250	.118	8	-2	0-0	1.000	0	*86*	*208*	/C-6	-0.1
1946	Bos A	4	14	1	2	0	0	0	1	0	0	0	.143	.143	.143	-19	-2	0-0	1.000	1	*150*	*0*	/C-4	-0.1
Total	12	795	2399	316	677	100	36	7	272	247	24	97	.282	.355	.363	84	-56	56-29	.991	17	*105*	*112*	C-699/O(RF)	0.4

PYZNARSKI, TIM Timothy Matthew B 2.4.1960 Chicago, IL BR/TR 6-2/195# d9.14

Year	Tm Lg	G	AB	R	H	2B	3B	HR	RBI	BB-IB	HP	SO	AVG	OBP	SLG	AOPS	ABR	SB-CS	FA	FR	Rng	Thr	G at Pos	BFW
1986	SD N	15	42	3	10	1	0	0	0	4-0	1	11	.238	.319	.262	63	-2	2-0	.977	-1	93	117	1-13	-0.3

QUALLS, JIM James Robert B 10.9.1946 Exeter, CA BB/TR 5-10/158# d4.10

Year	Tm Lg	G	AB	R	H	2B	3B	HR	RBI	BB-IB	HP	SO	AVG	OBP	SLG	AOPS	ABR	SB-CS	FA	FR	Rng	Thr	G at Pos	BFW
1969	Chi N	43	120	12	30	5	3	0	9	2-0	1	14	.250	.266	.342	62	-6	2-1	1.000	-3	87	57	O-35(CF)/2-4	-1.1
1970	Mon N	9	9	1	1	0	0	0	1	0-0	0	0	.111	.111	.111	-40	-2	0-0	1.000	-0	120	0	/2-2,O-2(LF)	-0.2
1972	Chi A	11	10	0	0	0	0	0	0	0-0	0	2	.000	.000	.000	-98	-2	0-0	1.000	0	121	0	/O(CF)	-0.3
Total	3	63	139	13	31	5	3	0	10	2-0	1	16	.223	.238	.302	46	-10	2-1	1.000	-3	86	54	/O-38(2-36-0),2-6	-1.6

QUEEN, MEL Melvin Douglas B 3.26.1942 Johnson City, NY BL/TR 6-1/197# d4.13 M1 C5 s-Mel ▲

Year	Tm Lg	G	AB	R	H	2B	3B	HR	RBI	BB-IB	HP	SO	AVG	OBP	SLG	AOPS	ABR	SB-CS	FA	FR	Rng	Thr	G at Pos	BFW
1964	Cin N	48	95	7	19	2	0	2	12	4-0	0	19	.200	.232	.284	43	-7	0-1	.977	0	121	0	O-20(RF)	-1.0
1965	Cin N	5	3	0	0	0	0	0	0	0-0	0	1	.000	.000	.000	-94	-1	0-0	1.000	0	169	0	/O(RF)	-0.1
1966	Cin N	56	55	4	7	1	0	0	5	10-1	0	12	.127	.250	.145	16	-6	0-0	1.000	2	128	92	O-32(2-0-31)/P-7	-0.6
1967	Cin N	49	81	6	17	4	0	0	5	4-0	0	10	.210	.244	.259	40	3	2-0	.941	-3	52	106	P-31	0.0
1968	Cin N	10	8	2	1	0	0	0	0	1-0	0	3	.125	.222	.125	6	0	0-0	1.000	0	136	0	/P-5	0.0
1969	Cin N	2	6	0	1	0	0	0	1	0-0	0	2	.167	.167	.167	-6	0	0-0	1.000	-0	52	0	/P-2	0.0
1970	Cal A	37	16	1	4	0	0	0	1	0-0	0	2	.250	.250	.250	40	1	0-0	1.000	-1	57	0	P-34	0.0
1971	Cal A	45	8	0	0	0	0	0	1	1-0	0	0	.000	.100	.000	-71	-1	0-0	.900	-1	76	0	P-44	0.0
1972	Cal A	17	2	0	0	0	0	0	0	1-0	0	1	.000	.333	.000	5	0	0-0	1.000	-0	83	0	P-17	0.0
Total	9	269	274	20	49	7	0	2	25	21-1	0	50	.179	.233	.226	30	-11	2-1	.951	-3	64	53	P-140/O-53(2-0-52)	-1.7

QUEEN, BILLY William Eddleman "Doc" B 11.28.1928 Gastonia, NC BR/TR 6-1/185# d4.13

Year	Tm Lg	G	AB	R	H	2B	3B	HR	RBI	BB-IB	HP	SO	AVG	OBP	SLG	AOPS	ABR	SB-CS	FA	FR	Rng	Thr	G at Pos	BFW
1954	Mil N	3	2	0	0	0	0	0	0	0	0	2	.000	.000	.000	-99	-1	0-0	1.000	0	115	0	/O(RF)	-0.1

Year	Tm Lg	G	AB	R	H	2B	3B	HR	RBI	BB-IB	HP	SO	AVG	OBP	SLG	AOPS	ABR	SB-CS	FA	FR	Rng	Thr	G at Pos	BFW
QUELLICH, GEORGE George William B 2.10.1906 Johnsville, CA D 8.31.1958 Johnsville, CA BR/TR 6-1/180# d8.1																								
1931	Det A	13	54	6	12	5	0	1	11	3	0	4	.222	.263	.370	63	-3	1-0	1.000	1	107	227	O-13(LF)	-0.2
QUEST, JOE Joseph L. B 11.16.1852 New Castle, PA D 11.14.1924 San Diego, CA BR/TR 5-6/150# d8.30 U2																								
1871	Cle NA	3	13	1	3	1	0	0	2	1		0	.231	.286	.308	75	0	0-0	.571	-2	114	0	/2-2,S	-0.2
1878	Ind N	62	278	45	57	3	2	0	13	12		24	.205	.238	.230	63	-9		.876	-0	92	106	*2-62	-0.6
1879	Chi N	**83**	334	38	69	16	1	0	22	9		33	.207	.227	.260	57	-15		**.925**	16	112	97	*2-83	0.4
1880	Chi N	82	300	37	71	12	1	0	27	8		16	.237	.256	.283	78	-7		.895	0	101	89	*2-80/S-2,3	-0.3
1881	Chi N	78	293	35	72	6	0	1	26	2		29	.246	.251	.276	63	-13		**.929**	8	**103**	80	*2-77/S	-0.2
1882	Chi N	42	159	24	32	5	2	0	15	8		16	.201	.240	.258	57	-8		.879	-5	96	106	2-41/S	-1.1
1883	Det N	37	137	22	32	8	2	0	15	10		18	.234	.286	.321	88	-1		.897	-3	92	140	2-37	-0.2
	StL AA	19	78	12	20	3	1	0	10	1			.256	.266	.321	83	-2		.890	-3	92	71	2-19	-0.4
1884	StL AA	81	310	46	64	9	5	0		19	2		.206	.257	.268	69	-11		.893	-11	93	117	*2-81	-1.7
	Pit AA	12	43	2	9	3	0	0		0	1		.209	.227	.279	65	-1		.938	1	110	111	/2-7,S-5	0.0
	Year	93	353	48	73	12	5	0		19	3		.207	.253	.269	69	-12		.897	-10	94	117	2-88/S-5	-1.7
1885	Det N	55	200	24	39	8	2	0	21	14		25	.195	.248	.255	63	-8		.898	-4	96	57	2-39,S-15/O(LF)	-0.9
1886	Phi AA	42	150	14	31	4	1	0	10	20	0		.207	.300	.247	71	-4	5	.847	0	104	115	S-41/2-2	-0.2
Total	9	593	2282	299	496	77	17	1	159	103	3	161	.217	.252	.267	67	-79	5-0	.901	-1	99	97	2-528/S-65,O(LF)3	-5.2
QUICK, HAL James Harold "Blondie" B 10.4.1917 Rome, GA D 3.9.1974 Swansea, IL BR/TR 5-10.5/163# d9.7																								
1939	Was A	12	41	3	10	1	0	0	2	1	1	1	.244	.279	.268	44	-4	1-0	.927	-0	106	98	S-10	-0.3
QUILICI, FRANK Francis Ralph "Guido" B 5.11.1939 Chicago, IL BR/TR 6/175# d7.18 M4 C2																								
1965	†Min A	56	149	16	31	5	1	0	7	15-0	0	33	.208	.280	.255	51	-9	1-1	.990	4	107	136	2-52/S-4	-0.2
1967	Min A	23	19	2	2	1	0	0	0	3-0	0	4	.105	.227	.158	14	-2	0-0	1.000	-2	63	129	2-13/3-8,S	-0.4
1968	Min A	97	229	22	56	11	4	1	22	21-0	1	45	.245	.305	.341	93	-2	0-0	1.000	11	106	104	2-48,3-40/S-6,1	1.4
1969	Min A	118	144	19	25	3	1	2	12	12-0	0	22	.174	.236	.250	36	-13	2-0	.935	7	104	39	3-84,2-36/S	-0.4
1970	†Min A	111	141	19	32	3	0	2	12	15-3	0	16	.227	.297	.291	63	-7	0-2	.987	-4	93	88	2-73,3-27/S	-0.9
Total	5	405	682	78	146	23	6	5	53	66-3	1	120	.214	.281	.287	63	-33	3-3	.993	16	103	108	2-222,3-159/S-13,1	-0.5
QUILLEN, LEE Leon Abner B 5.5.1882 North Branch, MN D 5.14.1965 St.Paul, MN BR/TR 5-10/165# d9.30																								
1906	Chi A	4	9	1	3	0	0	0	0	0	0		.333	.333	.333	112	0	1	.600	-2	66	155	/S-3	-0.2
1907	Chi A	49	151	17	29	5	0	0	14	10	3		.192	.256	.225	56	-7	8	.871	-1	105	87	3-48	-0.8
Total	2	53	160	18	32	5	0	0	14	10	3		.200	.260	.231	59	-7	9	.871	-4	105	87	/3-48,S-3	-1.0
QUINLAN d9.7																								
1874	Phi NA	1	4	0	1	0	0	0	1	0		0	.250	.250	.250	59	0	0-0	1.000	0	132	0	/S	0.0
QUINLAN, FRANK Francis Patrick B 3.9.1869 Marlborough, MA D 5.4.1904 Brockton, MA 5-9/180# d10.5																								
1891	Bos AA	2	5	0	0	0	0	0	0	0	0	2	.000	.000	.000	-99	-1	0	1.000	0	*181*	*91*	/CO(LF)	-0.1
QUINLAN, ROBB Robb William B 3.17.1977 St.Paul, MN BR/TR 6-1/200# d7.28																								
2003	Ana A	38	94	13	27	4	2	0	4	6-0	0	16	.287	.330	.372	88	-2	1-2	.988	-0	87	87	1-33/O(LF)D	-0.5
QUINLAN, FINNERS Thomas Finners B 10.21.1887 Scranton, PA D 2.17.1966 Scranton, PA BL/TL 5-8/154# d9.6																								
1913	StL N	13	50	1	8	0	0	0	1	1	0	9	.160	.176	.160	-4	-7	0	.897	1	99	169	O-12(1-0-11)	-0.7
1915	Chi A	42	114	11	22	3	0	0	7	4	8	11	.193	.270	.219	45	-8	3-4	1.000	1	90	151	O-32(9-10-13)	-0.9
Total	2	55	164	12	30	3	0	0	8	5	8	20	.183	.243	.201	31	-15	3-4	.961	2	93	157	/O-44(10-10-24)	-1.6
QUINLAN, TOM Thomas Raymond B 3.27.1968 St.Paul, MN BR/TR 6-3/200# d9.4																								
1990	Tor A	1	2	0	1	0	0	0	0	0-0	1	1	.500	.667	.500	227	1	0-0	1.000	-1	55	0	/3	0.0
1992	Tor A	13	15	2	1	1	0	0	2	2-0	0	9	.067	.176	.133	-12	-2	0-0	.909	-1	64	0	3-13	-0.4
1994	Phi N	24	35	6	7	2	0	1	3	3-1	0	13	.200	.263	.343	55	-2	0-0	.966	-1	89	57	3-20	-0.3
1996	Min A	4	6	0	0	0	0	0	0	0-0	0	3	.000	.000	.000	-99	-2	0-0	.667	-1	51	0	/3-4	-0.3
Total	4	42	58	8	9	3	0	1	5	5-1	1	26	.155	.234	.259	30	-5	0-0	.932	-4	77	34	/3-38	-1.0
QUINN d5.4																								
1875	Atl NA	2	8	2	1	0	0	0	0	0		0	.125	.125	.125	-15	-1	0-0	.800	-2	0	0	/O-2(0-1-1),S	-0.3
QUINN, FRANK Frank J. B 1876 Grand Rapids, MI D 2.17.1920 Camden, IN 5-8/?# d8.9																								
1899	Chi N	12	34	6	6	0	1	0	1	6	0		.176	.300	.235	49	-2	1	.909	-2	0	0	O-10(4-6-0)/2	-0.5
QUINN, JOHN John Edward "Pick" B 9.12.1885 Framingham, MA D 4.9.1956 Marlboro, MA BR/TR 5-11/150# d10.9																								
1911	Phi N	1	2	0	0	0	0	0	0	0	0	0	.000	.000	.000	-99	-1	0	1.000	-0	*79*	*158*	/C	-0.1
QUINN, JOE Joseph C. B Boston, MA D 3.1893 5-8/162# d9.7																								
1881	Bos N	1	4	0	0	0	0	0	0	0		0	.000	.000	.000	-99	-1		1.000	-0	0	0	/1	-0.1
	Wor N	2	7	0	1	0	0	0	1	1		2	.143	.250	.143	25	-1		.714	-2			/C-2	-0.3
	Year	3	11	0	1	0	0	0	1	1		2	.091	.167	.091	-16	-1		.714	-2			/C-2,1	-0.4
QUINN, JOE Joseph J. B 12.25.1864 Sydney, Australia D 11.12.1940 St.Louis, MO BR/TR 5-7/158# d4.26 M2 OF Total (31-LF 66-CF 27-RF)																								
1884	StL U	103	429	74	116	21	1	0		9			.270	.285	.324	81	-22		.945	-1	**109**	**186**	*1-100/O-3(1-0-2),S	-2.8
1885	StL N	97	343	27	73	8	2	0	15	9		38	.213	.233	.248	59	-15		.875	-3	86	0	O-57(27-13-17),3-31,1-11	-1.9
1886	StL N	75	271	33	63	11	3	1	21	8		31	.232	.254	.306	75	-8	12	.895	-3	131	64	0-48(0-47-1),2-15/1-7,3-4,S-2	-1.2
1888	Bos N	38	156	19	47	8	3	4	29	2	0	5	.301	.310	.468	142	6	12	.914	-5	93	78	2-38	0.3
1889	Bos N	112	444	57	116	13	5	2	69	25	5	21	.261	.308	.327	73	-19	24	.860	-17	89	97	S-63,2-47/3-2	-2.8
1890	Bos P	**130**	509	87	153	19	8	7	82	44	2	24	.301	.359	.411	99	-4	29	**.942**	16	98	113	*2-130	1.3
1891	Bos N	124	508	70	122	8	10	3	63	28	6	28	.240	.288	.313	67	-25	24	.938	-24	89	93	*2-124	-4.0
1892	†Bos N	143	532	63	116	14	1	1	59	35	7	40	.218	.275	.254	55	-30	17	**.951**	5	98	143	*2-143	-1.8
1893	StL N	**135**	547	68	126	18	6	0	71	33	4	7	.230	.279	.285	50	-41	24	.942	-33	83	101	*2-135	-5.7
1894	StL N	106	405	59	116	18	1	4	61	24	1	8	.286	.328	.365	67	-23	25	.952	18	99	**148**	*2-106	0.0
1895	StL N	135	547	86	172	19	9	3	76	37	2	7	.314	.360	.399	97	-3	22	.945	1	96	104	*2-135,M	0.3
1896	StL N	48	191	19	40	6	1	1	17	9	2	5	.209	.252	.267	39	-17	8	.956	2	114	33	2-48	-1.2
	†Bal N	24	82	22	27	1	1	0	5	6	0	1	.329	.375	.366	94	-1	6	.951	-2	84	99	/2-8,O-8(1-1-6),3-5,S	-0.2
	Year	72	273	41	67	7	2	1	22	15	2	6	.245	.290	.297	56	-18	14	.955	-0	110	43	2-56/O-8(1-1-6),3-5,S	-1.4
1897	Bal N	75	285	33	74	11	4	1	45	13	3		.260	.299	.337	68	-14	12	.946	8	114	142	3-37,S-21,2-11/O-6(1-5-0),1-2	-0.4
1898	Bal N	12	32	5	8	1	0	0	5	1	0		.250	.273	.281	58	-2	0	.893	-0	88	114	/3-8,2O(LF)	-0.2
	StL N	103	375	35	94	10	5	0	36	24	3		.251	.301	.304	72	-15	13	.962	-1	105	78	2-62,S-41/O(RF)	-1.0
	Year	115	407	40	102	11	5	0	41	25	3		.251	.299	.302	71	-16	13	.960	-1	105	77	2-63,S-41/3-8,O-2(1-0-1)	-1.2
1899	Cle N	147	615	73	176	24	6	0	72	21	2		.286	.312	.345	86	-13	22	**.962**	11	101	86	*2-147,M	0.3
1900	StL N	22	80	12	21	2	0	1	11	10	0		.262	.344	.325	86	-1	4	.933	-6	81	60	2-14/S-6,3	-0.6
	Cin N	74	266	18	73	5	2	0	25	16	0		.274	.316	.308	74	-10	7	.950	-10	89	90	2-74	-1.5
	Year	96	346	30	94	7	2	1	36	26	0		.272	.323	.312	77	-11	11	.947	-15	88	85	2-88/S-6,3	-2.1
1901	Was A	66	266	33	67	11	2	2	34	11	2		.252	.287	.331	72	-11	7	.954	-6	92	64	2-66	-1.5
Total	17	1769	6883	893	1800	228	70	30	796	365	39	215	.262	.302	.328	74	-268	268	.946	-52	95	101	*2-1304,S-135,O-124C,1-120/3-88	-24.6
QUINN, MARK Mark David B 5.21.1974 LaMirada, CA BR/TR 6-1/175# d9.14																								
1999	KC A	17	60	11	20	4	1	6	18	4-0	1	11	.333	.385	.733	173	6	1-0	.964	-1	81	200	O-15(15-0-1)/D	0.5
2000	KC A	135	500	76	147	33	2	20	78	35-1	3	91	.294	.342	.488	104	2	5-2	.988	1	90	180	O-81(78-1-4),D-48	-0.3
2001	KC A	118	453	57	122	31	2	17	60	12-1	7	69	.269	.298	.459	88	-9	9-5	.976	1	97	124	O-99(49-0-50),D-18	-1.3
2002	KC A	23	76	9	18	4	0	2	11	5-0	2	15	.237	.301	.368	69	-3	2-1	1.000	-1	88	0	O-15(RF)/D-7	-0.5
Total	4	293	1089	153	307	72	5	45	167	56-2	13	186	.282	.324	.481	98	-4	17-8	.981	0	93	143	O-210(142-1-70)/D-74	-1.6
QUINN, PADDY Patrick J. B 8.1849 Chicago, IL D 1.2.1909 Chicago, IL 5-8.5/148# d7.26																								
1871	Kek NA	5	17	8	4	0	0	0	2	4		0	.235	.381	.235	81	0	3-1	.964	2			/C-5	0.1
1875	Wes NA	11	43	4	14	1	0	0	5	0		1	.326	.326	.349	127	1	0-1	.861	1			C-10/O(CF)	0.1
	Har NA	5	13	1	3	0	0	0	1	1		3	.231	.286	.231	78	0	0-1	.833	-1			/C-3,O-3(0-1-2)	-0.1
	Chi NA	17	61	12	14	0	0	0	1	0		2	.230	.230	.230	59	-3	1-1	.778	-4			C-11,O-10(0-9-1)	-0.6

Year	Tm Lg	G	AB	R	H	2B	3B	HR	RBI	BB-IB	HP	SO	AVG	OBP	SLG	AOPS	ABR	SB-CS	FA	FR	Rng	Thr	G at Pos	BFW
	Year	33	117	17	31	1	0	0	7	1		6	.265	.271	.274	87	-2	1-3	.826	-4			C-24,O-14(0-11-3)	-0.6
1877	Chi N	4	14	1	1	0	0	0	0	1		0	.071	.133	.071	-30	-2		.667	-0	114	0	/O-4(RF)	-0.2
Total	2 NA	38	134	25	35	1	0	0	9	5		6	.261	.288	.269	87	-2	4-4	.000	-2			/C-29,O-14(0-11-3)	-0.5
QUINN, TOM Thomas Oscar B 4.25.1864 Annapolis, MD D 7.24.1932 Pittsburgh, PA BR/TR 5-8/180# d9.2																								
1886	Pit AA	3	11	1	0	0	0	0	0	0	0		.000	.000	.000	-99	-3	1	.929	-1			/C-3	-0.3
1889	Bal AA	55	194	18	34	2	1	1	15	19	1	22	.175	.252	.211	32	-18	6	.925	7			C-55	-0.5
1890	Pit P	55	207	23	44	4	3	1	15	17	3	8	.213	.282	.275	54	-14	1	.888	-3	*103*	*84*	C-55	-1.0
Total	3	113	412	42	78	6	4	2	30	36	4	<u>30</u>	.189	.261	.238	40	-35	8	.910	2	*49*	*40*	C-113	-1.8
QUINONES, LUIS Luis Raul B 4.28.1962 Ponce, P.R. BB/TR 5-11/175# d5.27																								
1983	Oak A	19	42	5	8	2	1	0	4	1-0	0	4	.190	.205	.286	37	-4	1-1	1.000	2	129	99	/2-6,3-4,O-4(RF),S-3,D-4	-0.2
1986	SF N	71	106	13	19	1	3	0	11	3-1	1	17	.179	.207	.245	26	-12	3-1	.922	-6	100	101	S-33,3-31/2-8	-1.7
1987	Chi N	49	101	12	22	6	0	0	8	10-0	0	16	.218	.288	.277	49	-7	0-0	.965	-1	89	74	S-28/2-4,3	-0.6
1988	Cin N	23	52	4	12	3	0	1	11	2-1	0	11	.231	.255	.346	70	-2	1-1	.974	1	121	103	S-10/2-4,3-4	-0.1
1989	Cin N	97	340	43	83	13	4	12	34	25-0	3	46	.244	.300	.412	99	-2	2-4	.979	-2	94	85	2-53,3-50/S-5	-0.4
1990	†Cin N	83	145	10	35	7	0	2	17	13-3	1	29	.241	.301	.331	73	-5	1-0	.981	6	122	0	3-22,2-13/S-9,1	0.2
1991	Cin N	97	212	15	47	4	3	4	20	21-3	2	31	.222	.297	.325	72	-8	1-2	.975	-7	101	115	2-33,3-19/S-5	-1.6
1992	Min A	3	5	0	1	0	0	0	1	0-0	0	0	.200	.167	.200	12	-1	0-0	.714	0	120	0	/3SD	-0.1
Total	8	442	1003	102	227	36	11	19	106	75-8	7	154	.226	.282	.341	72	-41	9-9	.937	-8	94	55	3-132,2-121/S-94,D-5,O-4(RF),1	-4.5
QUINONES, REY Rey Francisco (Santiago) B 11.11.1963 Rio Piedras, P.R. BR/TR 5-11/160# d5.17																								
1986	Bos A	62	190	26	45	12	1	2	15	19-0	3	26	.237	.315	.342	79	-5	3-2	.940	-8	92	71	S-62	-0.7
	Sea A	36	122	6	23	4	0	0	7	5-0	0	31	.189	.219	.221	21	-14	1-1	.945	0	99	115	S-36	-1.0
	Year	98	312	32	68	16	1	2	22	24-0	3	57	.218	.279	.295	56	-19	4-3	.942	-8	95	87	S-98	-1.7
1987	Sea A	135	478	55	132	18	2	12	56	26-0	4	71	.276	.317	.397	84	-12	1-3	.959	-4	100	98	*S-135	-0.2
1988	Sea A	140	499	63	124	30	3	12	52	23-1	3	71	.248	.284	.393	84	-12	0-3	.963	8	100	119	*S-135/D-4	0.5
1989	Sea A	7	19	2	2	0	0	0	0	1-0	0	1	.105	.150	.105	-26	-3	0-0	.889	-2	98	70	/S-7	-0.5
	Pit N	71	225	21	47	11	0	3	29	15-2	1	40	.209	.253	.298	62	-12	0-2	.934	-14	95	73	S-69	-2.3
Total	4	451	1533	173	373	75	6	29	159	89-3	11	240	.243	.287	.357	74	-58	5-11	.952	-19	98	98	S-444/D-4	-4.2
QUINTANA, CARLOS Carlos Narcis (Hernandez) B 8.26.1965 Estado Miranda, Venezuela BR/TR 6-2/195# d9.16																								
1988	Bos A	5	6	1	2	0	0	0	2	2-0	0	3	.333	.500	.333	133	0	0-0	1.000	0	106	0	/O-3(RF),D	0.0
1989	Bos A	34	77	6	16	5	0	0	6	7-0	0	12	.208	.274	.273	51	-5	0-0	.926	-2	90	0	O-21(4-1-17)/1D	-0.7
1990	†Bos A	149	512	56	147	28	0	7	67	52-0	2	74	.287	.354	.383	102	3	1-2	.987	13	**133**	96	*1-148/O-3(RF)	0.5
1991	Bos A	149	478	69	141	21	1	11	71	61-2	2	66	.295	.375	.412	113	10	1-0	.993	9	**124**	102	*1-138,O-13(1-0-12)/D	1.0
1993	Bos A	101	303	31	74	5	0	1	19	31-2	2	52	.244	.317	.271	57	-18	1-0	.991	-1	80	102	1-53,O-51(1-0-50)	-2.4
Total	5	438	1376	163	380	59	1	19	165	153-4	6	207	.276	.350	.362	93	-10	3-2	.990	19	123	99	1-340/O-91(6-1-85),D-9	-1.6
QUINTERO, HUMBERTO Humberto B 8.2.1979 Maracaibo, Venezuela BR/TR 6-1/190# d9.3																								
2003	SD N	12	23	1	5	0	0	0	2	1-1	0	6	.217	.250	.217	26	-3	0-0	.982	0	164	68	C-11	-0.2
QUINTON, MARSHALL Marshall J. B Philadelphia, PA 5-11/190# d8.7																								
1884	Ric AA	26	94	12	22	5	0	0		0		1	.234	.242	.287	73	-3		.878	-4			C-14,O-10(RF)/S-2	-0.5
1885	Phi AA	7	29	6	6	1	0	0	4	1		1	.207	.258	.241	55	-1		.869	-2			/C-7	-0.3
Total	2	33	123	18	28	6	0	0	<u>4</u>	1		2	.228	.246	.276	68	-4		.874	-6			/C-21,O-10(RF),S-2	-0.8
QUIRK, JAMIE James Patrick B 10.22.1954 Whittier, CA BL/TR 6-4/200# d9.4 C11 OF Total (24-LF 8-RF)																								
1975	KC A	14	39	2	10	0	0	1	5	2-1	0	7	.256	.293	.333	75	-1	0-0	.909	0	106	161	O-10(LF)/3-2,D	-0.2
1976	†KC A	64	114	11	28	6	0	1	15	2-0	0	22	.246	.252	.325	70	-5	0-0	1.000	-2	56	77	D-19,S-12,3-11/1-2	-0.7
1977	Mil A	93	221	16	48	14	1	3	13	8-2	2	47	.217	.251	.330	57	-13	0-1	.950	1	147	218	D-53,O-10(LF)/3-8	-1.4
1978	KC A	17	29	3	6	2	0	0	2	5-0	0	4	.207	.324	.276	68	-1	0-0	.926	0	96	77	3-10/S-2,D	-0.1
1979	KC A	51	79	8	24	6	1	1	11	5-0	1	13	.304	.353	.443	111	1	0-0	.944	-1	277	0	/C-9,S-5,3-3,D-9	0.1
1980	KC A	62	163	13	45	5	0	5	21	7-2	1	24	.276	.305	.399	92	-2	3-2	.929	-1	111	41	3-28,C-15/O-7(2-0-5),1D	-0.3
1981	KC A	46	100	8	25	7	0	0	10	6-1	1	17	.250	.299	.320	79	-3	0-2	.985	-3	67	74	C-22/3-8,2O(RF)	-0.6
1982	KC A	36	78	8	18	3	0	1	5	3-0	0	15	.231	.256	.308	55	-5	0-0	1.000	1	91	84	C-29/1-6,3O(LF)	-0.3
1983	StL N	48	86	3	18	2	1	2	11	6-0	1	27	.209	.269	.326	64	-5	0-0	.929	-7	66	106	C-22/3-7,S	-1.1
1984	Chi A	3	2	0	0	0	0	0	1	0-0	0	2	.000	.000	.000	-96	-1	0-0	1.000	0	0	0	/3	0.0
	Cle A	1	1	1	1	0	0	1	1	0-0	0	0	1.000	1.000	4.000	1189	1	0-0	—	-0	6	0	/C	0.1
	Year	4	3	1	1	0	0	1	2	0-0	0	2	.333	.250	1.333	324	1	0-0	1.000	-0	0	0	/3C	0.1
1985	†KC A	19	57	3	16	3	1	0	4	2-0	0	9	.281	.305	.368	83	-1	0-0	.986	-2	83	196	C-17/1	-0.3
1986	KC A	80	219	24	47	10	0	8	26	17-3	1	41	.215	.273	.370	72	-9	0-1	.989	18	148	186	C-41,3-24/1-6,O(LF)	0.9
1987	KC A	109	296	24	70	17	0	5	33	28-1	4	56	.236	.307	.345	72	-11	1-0	.986	4	89	107	*C-108/S	-0.3
1988	KC A	84	196	22	47	7	1	8	25	28-2	1	41	.240	.333	.408	107	2	1-5	.982	14	75	109	C-79/13	1.8
1989	NY A	13	24	0	2	0	0	0	0	3-0	0	5	.083	.185	.083	-22	-4	0-1	1.000	0	51	123	/C-6,SD	-0.4
	Oak A	9	10	1	2	0	0	1	1	0-0	0	4	.200	.200	.500	95	0	0-0	.500	0	119	0	/3-3,C-2,1O(RF)	0.0
	Bal A	25	51	5	11	2	0	0	9	9-0	0	11	.216	.328	.255	70	-2	0-1	1.000	4	154	160	C-24	0.3
	Year	47	85	6	15	2	0	1	10	12-0	0	20	.176	.276	.235	47	-6	0-2	1.000	5	129	150	C-32/3-3,SD10(RF)	-0.1
1990	†Oak A	56	121	12	34	5	1	3	26	14-1	1	34	.281	.353	.413	121	4	0-0	.977	2	183	112	C-37/1-8,3-8,O(RF)D	0.7
1991	Oak A	76	203	16	53	4	0	1	17	16-1	2	28	.261	.321	.296	76	-7	0-3	.982	0	80	150	C-54/1-8,3D	-0.5
1992	†Oak A	78	177	13	39	7	1	2	11	16-3	3	28	.220	.294	.305	72	-7	0-0	.973	3	78	122	C-59/1-9,3-2,D	-0.2
Total	18	984	2266	193	544	100	7	43	247	177-17	18	435	.240	.298	.347	78	-69	5-16	.982	32	98	125	C-525,3-118/D-88,1-43,O-32L,S2	-2.5
RAABE, BRIAN Brian Charles B 11.5.1967 New Ulm, MN BR/TR 5-9/177# d9.17																								
1995	Min A	6	14	4	3	0	0	0	1	1-0	0	0	.214	.267	.214	27	-2	0-0	1.000	-0	114	187	/2-4,3-2	-0.2
1996	Min A	7	9	0	2	0	0	0	1	0-0	0	1	.222	.200	.222	13	-1	0-0	.857	-0	97	253	/3-6,2	-0.1
1997	Sea A	2	3	0	0	0	0	0	0	1-0	0	2	.000	.250	.000	-28	-1	0-0	1.000	-1	72	0	/3-2,2	-0.1
	Col N	2	3	0	1	0	0	0	0	0-0	0	1	.333	.333	.333	61	0	0-0	1.000	-0	144	0	/2	0.0
Total	3	17	29	4	6	0	0	0	2	2-0	0	4	.207	.250	.207	21	-4	0-0	.889	-1	66	141	/3-10,2-7	-0.4
RABB, JOHN John Andrew B 6.23.1960 Los Angeles, CA BR/TR 6-1/180# d9.4																								
1982	SF N	2	2	0	1	0	1	0	0	0-0	0	1	.500	.500	1.500	441	1	0-0	1.000	0	217	0	/O(LF)	0.1
1983	SF N	40	104	10	24	9	0	1	14	9-1	0	17	.231	.292	.346	79	-3	1-0	.973	-2	73	58	C-31/O-2(RF)	-0.4
1984	SF N	54	82	10	16	1	0	3	9	10-0	0	33	.195	.283	.317	71	-3	1-1	.988	-2	98	37	1-13/O-8(3-0-6),C-6	-0.6
1985	Atl N	3	2	0	0	0	0	0	0	0-0	0	1	.000	.000	.000	-94	-1	0-0	—	-0	0	0	/O(LF)	-0.1
1988	Sea A	9	14	2	5	2	0	0	4	0-0	0	1	.357	.357	.500	131	1	0-0	1.000	0	194	0	/O-2(RF),1D	0.1
Total	5	108	204	22	46	12	1	4	27	19-1	0	53	.225	.291	.353	81	-5	2-1	.966	-4	72	59	/C-37,1-14,O-14(5-0-10),D-5	-0.9
RABBITT, JOE Joseph Patrick B 1.16.1900 Frontenac, KS D 12.5.1969 Norwalk, CT BL/TR 5-10/165# d9.15																								
1922	Cle A	2	3	1	1	0	0	0	0	0	0	0	.333	.333	.333	74	0	0-0	—	-0	0	0	/O(LF)	0.0
RACKLEY, MARV Marvin Eugene B 7.25.1921 Seneca, SC BL/TL 5-10/170# d4.15																								
1947	Bro N	18	9	2	2	0	0	0	2	1	0	0	.222	.300	.222	39	-1	0	1.000	0	153	0	/O-2(0-1-1)	0.0
1948	Bro N	88	281	55	92	13	5	0	15	19	0	25	.327	.370	.409	107	3	8	.949	-2	91	137	O-74(43-33-1)	-0.3
1949	†Bro N	9	9	2	4	1	0	0	1	1	0	0	.444	.500	.556	175	1	0	1.000	-0	90	0	/O-3(LF)	0.1
	Pit N	11	35	5	11	2	0	0	2	2	0	3	.314	.351	.371	92	0	1	1.000	-0	101	0	/O-8(CF)	-0.1
	†Bro N	54	141	23	41	4	1	1	14	13	0	8	.291	.351	.355	86	-3	1	.986	-2	90	0	O-44(41-3-0)	-0.7
	Year	74	185	30	56	7	1	1	17	16	0	11	.303	.358	.368	91	-2	2	.990	-3	99	0	O-55(44-11-0)	-0.7
1950	Cin N	5	2	0	1	0	0	0	1	0	0	0	.500	.500	.500	163	0	0	—	0			H	0.0
Total	4	185	477	87	151	20	6	1	35	36	0	36	.317	.365	.390	100	0	10	.966	-4	95	82	O-131(87-45-2)	-1.0
RADCLIFF, JOHN John Y. B 6.29.1848 Philadelphia, PA D 7.26.1911 Ocean City, NJ 5-6/140# d5.20																								
1871	Ath NA	**28**	145	47	44	7	5	0	22	6		1	.303	.331	.421	116	3	5-1	.804	3	110	79	*S-28	0.4
1872	Bal NA	56	297	70	86	13	4	1	44	0		2	.290	.290	.370	97	-3	3-3	.771	-5	92	96	*S-50/3-6,2	-0.6
1873	Bal NA	45	244	59	70	5	0	0	33	4		2	.287	.298	.307	81	-6	0-0	.772	-1	125	60	3-24,S-23/2	-0.5
1874	Phi NA	23	103	20	25	7	0	1	14	2		0	.243	.257	.340	87	-1	1-1	.800	-1	57	0	O-15(0-1-14)/2-4,S-3,3-3,1-2	-0.2
1875	Cen NA	5	23	2	4	0	0	0	0	1		0	.174	.208	.174	37	-1	0-0	.651	-1	121	0	/S-5	-0.2

Year	Tm Lg	G	AB	R	H	2B	3B	HR	RBI	BB-IB	HP	SO	AVG	OBP	SLG	AOPS	ABR	SB-CS	FA	FR	Rng	Thr	G at Pos	BFW
Total	5 NA	157	812	198	229	32	9	2	113	13		5	.282	.293	.351	93	-8	9-5	.000	-4	97	85	S-109/3-33,O-15(0-1-14),2-6,1-2	-1.1
RADCLIFF, RIP Raymond Allen B 1.19.1906 Kiowa, OK D 5.23.1962 Enid, OK BL/TL 5-10/170# d9.17 Mil 1944-46																								
1934	Chi A	14	56	7	15	2	1	0	5	0	0	2	.268	.268	.339	54	-4	1-0	.946	-0	118	0	O-14(RF)	-0.5
1935	Chi A	146	623	95	178	28	8	10	68	53	4	21	.286	.346	.404	91	-9	4-4	.968	-17	75	68	*O-142(LF)	-3.3
1936	Chi A★	138	618	120	207	31	7	8	82	44	2	12	.335	.381	.447	100	-1	6-3	.936	-17	79	52	*O-132(LF)	-2.2
1937	Chi A	144	584	105	190	38	10	4	79	53	2	25	.325	.383	.445	108	8	6-1	.966	-3	96	87	*O-139(LF)	-0.1
1938	Chi A	129	503	64	166	23	6	5	81	36	1	17	.330	.376	.429	99	-1	5-7	.979	-3	104	65	O-99(LF),1-23	-1.3
1939	Chi A	113	397	49	105	25	2	2	53	26	2	21	.264	.313	.353	68	-19	6-4	.970	-8	88	18	O-78(10-0-69),1-20	-3.1
1940	StL A	150	584	83	**200**	33	9	7	81	47	1	20	.342	.392	.466	119	17	6-4	.973	-5	93	77	*O-139(116-0-23)/1-4	0.3
1941	StL A	19	71	12	20	2	2	2	14	10	0	1	.282	.370	.451	112	1	1-1	1.000	-2	87	0	O-14(LF)/1-3	-0.2
	Det A	96	379	47	120	14	5	3	40	19	1	13	.317	.351	.404	90	-6	4-4	.970	-5	88	87	O-87(85-0-2)	-1.6
	Year	115	450	59	140	16	7	5	54	29	1	14	.311	.354	.411	94	-5	5-5	.974	-7	88	75	*O-101(99-0-2)/1-3	-1.8
1942	Det A	62	144	13	36	5	0	1	20	9	0	6	.250	.294	.306	64	-7	0-1	.978	0	95	60	O-24(6-0-18)/1-4	-1.0
1943	Det A	70	115	3	30	4	0	0	10	13	1	3	.261	.341	.296	81	-2	1-1	1.000	1	97	75	O-19(2-0-17)/1	-0.3
Total	10	1081	4074	598	1267	205	50	42	533	310	14	141	.311	.362	.417	96	-23	40-30	.967	-59	89	65	O-887(745-0-143)/1-55	-13.3
RADER, DAVE David Martin B 12.26.1948 Claremore, OK BL/TR 5-11/165# d9.5																								
1971	SF N	3	4	0	0	0	0	0	0	0-0	0	0	.000	.000	.000	-99	-1	0-0	1.000	0	0	0	/C	-0.1
1972	SF N	133	459	44	119	14	1	6	41	29-4	3	31	.259	.306	.333	81	-12	1-2	.985	-8	85	99	*C-127	-1.6
1973	SF N	148	462	59	106	15	4	9	41	63-23	6	22	.229	.326	.338	82	-10	0-0	.991	-13	75	77	*C-148	-1.8
1974	SF N	113	323	26	94	16	2	1	26	31-9	0	21	.291	.351	.362	96	-1	1-0	.984	-5	97	76	*C-109	-0.2
1975	SF N	98	292	39	85	15	0	5	31	32-12	1	30	.291	.360	.394	106	3	1-0	.984	-3	85	96	C-94	0.4
1976	SF N	88	255	25	67	15	0	1	22	27-8	0	21	.263	.332	.333	87	-3	2-0	.984	-4	89	74	C-81	-0.4
1977	StL N	66	114	15	30	7	1	1	16	9-0	0	10	.263	.310	.368	85	-2	1-0	.976	3	96	81	C-38	0.2
1978	Chi N	116	305	29	62	13	3	3	36	34-7	1	26	.203	.281	.295	56	-18	1-1	.977	-6	116	126	*C-114	-2.1
1979	Phi N	31	54	3	11	1	1	1	5	6-0	0	7	.204	.283	.315	61	-3	0-0	.932	-5	70	151	C-25	-0.7
1980	Bos A	50	137	14	45	11	0	3	17	14-1	0	12	.328	.388	.474	129	6	1-1	.981	1	93	112	C-34/D-9	0.8
Total	10	846	2405	254	619	107	12	30	235	245-64	11	180	.257	.326	.349	86	-41	8-4	.983	-41	90	93	C-771/D-9	-5.5
RADER, DON Donald Russell B 9.5.1893 Wolcott, IN D 6.26.1983 Walla Walla, WA BL/TR 5-10/164# d7.25																								
1913	Chi A	4	3	1	1	1	0	0	0	0	0	0	.333	.333	.667	193	0	0	.000	-1	0	0	/3O(LF)	0.0
1921	Phi N	9	32	4	9	2	0	0	3	3	0	5	.281	.343	.344	76	-1	0-0	1.000	-2	84	67	/S-9	-0.2
Total	2	13	35	5	10	3	0	0	3	3	0	5	.286	.342	.371	84	-1	0-0	1.000	-3	84	67	/S-9,O(LF)3	-0.2
RADER, DOUG Douglas Lee "Rojo" or "The Red Rooster" B 7.30.1944 Chicago, IL BR/TR 6-3/215# d7.31 M7 C8																								
1967	Hou N	47	162	24	54	10	4	2	26	7-2	2	31	.333	.360	.481	146	9	0-3	.972	-1	93	97	1-36/3-7	0.6
1968	Hou N	98	333	42	89	16	4	6	43	31-3	1	51	.267	.328	.393	119	8	2-2	.930	-2	94	82	3-86/1-5	0.6
1969	Hou N	155	569	62	140	25	3	11	83	62-7	6	103	.246	.325	.359	94	-4	1-5	.945	13	100	126	*3-154/1-4	0.7
1970	Hou N	156	576	90	145	25	3	25	87	57-7	4	102	.252	.322	.436	106	3	3-2	**.966**	25	**118**	128	*3-154/1	2.7
1971	Hou N	135	484	51	118	21	4	12	56	40-2	3	112	.244	.303	.378	95	-4	5-1	.946	7	**110**	**129**	*3-135	0.3
1972	Hou N	152	553	70	131	24	7	22	90	57-8	5	120	.237	.309	.425	110	6	5-5	.958	18	110	119	*3-152	2.4
1973	Hou N	154	574	79	146	26	0	21	89	46-6	3	97	.254	.310	.409	99	-2	4-3	.945	-9	91	80	*3-152	-1.3
1974	Hou N	152	533	61	137	27	3	17	78	60-7	4	131	.257	.334	.415	114	10	7-2	.965	3	104	91	*3-152	1.3
1975	Hou N	129	448	41	100	23	2	12	48	42-3	5	101	.223	.296	.364	89	-8	5-4	**.971**	7	102	106	*3-124/S-2	-0.2
1976	SD N	139	471	45	121	22	4	9	55	55-3	3	102	.257	.335	.378	112	8	3-4	.955	6	108	88	*3-137	1.3
1977	SD N	52	170	19	46	8	3	5	27	33-1	1	40	.271	.392	.441	137	10	0-1	.961	-1	97	104	3-51	0.9
	Tor A	96	313	47	75	18	2	13	40	38-2	3	65	.240	.323	.435	104	2	2-1	.966	4	114	22	3-45,D-34/1-7,O(RF)	0.4
Total	11	1465	5186	631	1302	245	39	155	722	528-51	40	1055	.251	.322	.403	106	38	37-33	.956	71	105	104	*3-1349/1-53,D-34,S-2,O(RF)	9.7
RADFORD, PAUL Paul Revere "Shorty" B 10.14.1861 Roxbury, MA D 2.21.1945 Boston, MA BR/TR 5-6/148# d5.1 ▲ OF Total (33-LF 153-CF 724-RF)																								
1883	Bos N	72	258	46	53	6	3	0	14	9		26	.205	.232	.252	46	-17		.836	-3	105	93	*O-72(1-24-50)	-1.9
1884	†Pro N	97	355	56	70	11	2	1	29	25		43	.197	.250	.248	58	-16		.882	2	125	155	*O-96(RF)/P-2	-1.4
1885	Pro N	105	371	55	90	12	5	0	32	33		43	.243	.304	.302	99	1		.852	3	**155**	**306**	*O-88(2-8-80),S-16/P-3,2	0.3
1886	KC N	122	493	78	113	17	5	0	20	58		48	.229	.310	.284	77	-13	39	.890	6	**155**	151	*O-92(RF),S-30/2	-0.6
1887	NY AA	128	486	127	129	15	5	4	45	**106**	6		.265	.403	.342	114	19	73	.833	0	98	127	S-76,O-37(1-1-36),2-18/P-2	1.7
1888	Bro AA	90	308	48	67	9	3	2	29	35	4		.218	.305	.286	90	-2	33	.944	6	151	72	O-88(0-83-5)/2-2	0.1
1889	Cle N	**136**	487	94	116	21	5	1	46	91	6	37	.238	.365	.308	91	-1	30	.942	-1	92	129	*O-136(0-2-136)/3	-0.3
1890	Cle P	122	466	98	136	24	12	2	62	82	8	28	.292	.406	.408	128	26	25	.895	10	113	160	O-80(6-35-39),S-36/3-7,2-4,P	2.7
1891	Bos AA	133	456	102	118	11	5	0	65	96	5	36	.259	.393	.305	102	8	55	.906	19	**111**	128	*S-131/O-4(LF),P	2.6
1892	Was N	137	510	93	130	19	4	1	37	86	3	47	.255	.366	.314	109	11	35	.933	-2	134	347	O-62(2-0-60),3-54,S-20/2-2	0.8
1893	Was N	124	464	87	106	18	3	2	34	104	8	42	.228	.378	.293	82	-5	32	.901	7	142	79	*O-123(7-0-116)/2P	-0.3
1894	Was N	95	325	61	78	13	5	0	49	65	7	23	.240	.378	.311	70	-13	24	.852	1	109	65	S-47,2-25,O-24(10-0-14)	-0.8
Total	12	1361	4979	945	1206	176	57	13	462	790	47	373	.242	.351	.308	92	-2	346	.901	46	132	150	O-902R,S-356/3-62,2-54,P-10	2.9
RADMANOVICH, RYAN Ryan Ashley B 8.9.1971 Calgary, AL, CAN BL/TR 6-2/200# d4.13																								
1998	Sea A	25	69	5	15	4	0	2	10	4-1	0	25	.217	.260	.362	60	-4	1-1	1.000	-0	87	148	O-24(RF)/1	-0.5
RADTKE, JACK Jack William B 4.14.1913 Denver, CO BB/TR 5-7/160# d8.1																								
1936	Bro N	33	31	8	3	0	0	0	2	4	0	9	.097	.200	.097	-18	-5	3	1.000	2	150	0	2-14/3-5,S-4	-0.3
RAFTER, JACK John Cornelius B 2.20.1875 Troy, NY D 1.5.1943 Troy, NY BR/TR 5-8/165# d9.24																								
1904	Pit N	1	3	0	0	0	0	0	0	0	0		.000	.000	.000	-97	-1	0	1.000	0	*103*	*114*	/C	-0.1
RAFTERY, TOM Thomas Francis B 10.5.1881 Boston, MA D 12.31.1954 Boston, MA BR/TR 5-10.5/175# d4.18																								
1909	Cle A	8	32	6	7	2	1	0	0	4	0		.219	.306	.344	101	0	1	1.000	-1	0	0	/O-8(1-1-6)	-0.1
RAGLAND, TOM Thomas B 6.16.1946 Talladega, AL BR/TR 5-10/155# d4.5																								
1971	Was A	10	23	1	4	0	0	0	0	0-0	1	5	.174	.208	.174	10	-3	0-0	1.000	-2	80	64	2-10	-0.4
1972	Tex A	25	58	3	10	2	0	0	2	5-0	0	11	.172	.238	.207	35	-5	0-1	.982	-3	104	68	2-13/3-5,S-3	-0.8
1973	Cle A	67	183	16	47	7	1	0	12	8-0	1	31	.257	.292	.306	67	-8	2-3	.984	3	101	104	2-65/S-2	-0.3
Total	3	102	264	20	61	9	1	0	14	13-0	2	47	.231	.272	.273	56	-16	2-4	.985	-2	99	95	/2-88,S-5,3-5	-1.5
RAINES, LARRY Lawrence Glenn Hope B 3.9.1930 St.Albans, WV D 1.28.1978 Lansing, MI BR/TR 5-10/165# d4.16																								
1957	Cle A	96	244	39	64	14	0	2	16	19-1	1	40	.262	.318	.344	82	-6	5-2	.922	-5	96	112	3-27,S-25,2-10/O-8(LF)	-1.0
1958	Cle A	7	9	1	0	0	0	0	0	0-0	0	5	.000	.000	.000	-99	-3	0-1	.933	2	157	257	/2-2	-0.1
Total	2	103	253	40	64	14	0	2	16	19-1	1	45	.253	.308	.332	76	-9	5-3	.922	-3	96	112	/3-27,S-25,2-12,O-8(LF)	-1.1
RAINES, TIM Timothy Jr. B 8.31.1979 Memphis, TN BR/TR 5-10/183# d10.1 f-Tim																								
2001	Bal A	7	23	6	4	2	0	0	0	3-0	0	8	.174	.269	.261	43	-2	3-0	1.000	-1	73	0	/O-7(CF)	-0.2
2003	Bal A	20	43	4	6	1	1	0	2	2-0	1	12	.140	.196	.209	7	-6	0-0	.974	2	125	185	O-18(1-17-0)/D	-0.4
Total	2	27	66	10	10	3	1	0	2	5-0	1	20	.152	.222	.227	20	-8	3-0	.980	1	106	119	/O-25(1-24-0),D	-0.6
RAINES, TIM Timothy Sr. "Rock" B 9.16.1959 Sanford, FL BB/TR 5-8/178# d9.11 s-Tim																								
1979	Mon N	6	0	3	0	0	0	0	0	0-0	0	0	—	—	—	—	0	2-0	—	0			/R	0.0
1980	Mon N	15	20	5	1	0	0	0	0	6-0	0	3	.050	.269	.050	-6	-3	5-0	1.000	-1	87	54	/2-7,O(LF)	-0.3
1981	†Mon N★	88	313	61	95	13	7	5	37	45-5	2	31	.304	.391	.438	134	15	**71**-11	.976	-1	98	83	O-81(LF)/2	2.4
1982	Mon N★	156	647	90	179	32	8	4	43	75-9	2	83	.277	.353	.369	101	3	**78**-16	.992	-6	95	72	*O-120(LF),2-36	0.5
1983	Mon N★	156	615	**133**	183	32	8	11	71	97-9	2	70	.298	.393	.429	129	28	**90**-14	.988	9	97	174	*O-154(153-2-0)/2-7	4.6
1984	Mon N★	160	622	106	192	**38**	9	8	60	87-7	2	69	.309	.393	.437	140	37	**75**-10	.988	-1	102	88	*O-160(CF)/2-2	4.9
1985	Mon N★	150	575	115	184	30	13	11	41	81-13	3	60	.320	.405	.475	155	45	70-9	.993	2	101	74	*O-146(LF)	5.4
1986	Mon N★	151	580	91	194	35	10	9	62	78-9	2	60	**.334**	**.413**	.476	146	40	70-9	.979	2	93	129	*O-147(LF)	4.8
1987	Mon N★	139	530	**123**	175	34	8	18	68	90-26	4	52	.330	.429	.526	148	41	50-5	.987	7	108	93	*O-139(LF)	5.0
1988	Mon N	109	429	66	116	19	7	12	48	53-14	2	44	.270	.350	.431	119	11	33-7	.988	2	102	72	*O-108(LF)	1.5
1989	Mon N	145	517	76	148	29	6	9	60	93-18	3	48	.286	.395	.418	132	26	41-9	.996	-5	89	90	*O-139(LF)	2.5
1990	Mon N	130	457	65	131	11	5	9	62	70-8	3	43	.287	.379	.392	119	14	49-16	.976	-8	91	33	*O-123(LF)	0.8
1991	Chi A	155	609	102	163	20	6	5	50	83-9	5	68	.268	.359	.345	98	1	51-15	.990	3	97	157	*O-133(134-1-0),D-19	0.6
1992	Chi A	144	551	102	162	22	9	7	54	81-4	0	48	.294	.380	.405	123	19	45-6	.994	10	112	134	*O-129(129-1-0),D-14	3.2

Year	Tm Lg	G	AB	R	H	2B	3B	HR	RBI	BB-IB	HP	SO	AVG	OBP	SLG	AOPS	ABR	SB-CS	FA	FR	Rng	Thr	G at Pos	BFW
1993	†Chi A	115	415	75	127	16	4	16	54	64-4	3	35	.306	.401	.480	139	25	21-7	**1.000**	-3	91	78	*O-112(LF)	1.9
1994	Chi A	101	384	80	102	15	5	10	52	61-3	1	43	.266	.365	.409	102	2	13-0	.981	1	107	45	O-96(LF)	0.2
1995	Chi A	133	502	81	143	25	4	12	67	70-3	3	52	.285	.374	.422	112	11	13-2	.980	-2	96	102	*O-107(107-0-1),D-22	0.6
1996	†NY A	59	201	45	57	10	0	9	33	34-1	1	29	.284	.383	.468	116	6	10-1	.988	-2	87	96	O-50(LF)/D-2	0.3
1997	†NY A	74	271	56	87	20	2	4	38	41-0	0	34	.321	.403	.454	126	13	8-5	.988	-6	82	31	O-57(LF),D-13	0.4
1998	†NY A	109	321	53	93	13	1	5	47	55-1	3	49	.290	.395	.383	109	7	8-3	.985	-3	78	125	D-56,O-47(LF)	0.0
1999	Oak A	58	135	20	29	5	0	4	17	26-1	0	17	.215	.337	.341	78	-4	4-1	1.000	-1	101	0	O-38(38-1-0)/D-3	-0.5
2001	Mon N	47	78	13	24	8	1	0	4	18-0	0	6	.308	.433	.436	125	4	1-0	1.000	-2	79	0	O-20(LF)	0.2
	Bal A	4	11	1	3	0	0	1	5	0-0	0	3	.273	.250	.545	114	0	0-0	1.000	0	151	0	/O-2(LF),D	0.0
2002	Fla N	98	89	9	17	3	0	1	7	22-4	1	19	.191	.351	.258	72	-3	0-0	.917	1	107	319	O-14(LF)/D	-0.3
Total	23	2502	8872	1571	2605	430	113	170	980	1330-148	42	966	.294	.385	.425	124	338	808-146	.988	-4	98	95	*O-2123(1965-165-1),D-131/2-53	38.7
RAINEY, JOHN John Paul B 7.26.1864 Birmingham, MI D 11.11.1912 Detroit, MI BL/TR 5-10/164# d8.25																								
1887	NY N	17	58	6	17	3	0	0	12	5	0	6	.293	.349	.345	98	0	0	.818	-2	84	128	3-17	-0.2
1890	Buf P	42	166	29	39	5	1	1	20	24	5	15	.235	.349	.295	79	-3	12	.870	0	123	87	O-28(RF)/S-7,3-6,2-2	-0.2
Total	2	59	224	35	56	8	1	1	32	29	5	21	.250	.349	.308	84	-3	12	.870	-2	123	87	/O-28(RF),3-23,S-7,2-2	-0.4
RAJSICH, GARY Gary Louis B 10.28.1954 Youngstown, OH BL/TL 6-2/210# d4.9 b-Dave																								
1982	NY N	80	162	17	42	8	3	2	12	17-3	1	40	.259	.333	.383	100	0	1-3	1.000	-2	95	0	O-35(10-0-26)/1-2	-0.5
1983	NY N	11	36	5	12	3	0	1	3	3-1	1	1	.333	.400	.500	149	3	0-0	1.000	-1	79	111	1-10	0.1
1984	StL N	7	7	1	1	0	0	0	2	2-0	0	1	.143	.300	.143	39	0	0-0	1.000	-0	0	171	/1-3	-0.1
1985	SF N	51	91	5	15	6	0	0	10	17-4	0	22	.165	.296	.231	52	-5	0-1	.990	-1	86	105	1-23	-0.8
Total	4	149	296	28	70	17	3	3	27	39-8	2	64	.236	.328	.345	90	-2	1-4	.994	-4	82	111	/1-38,O-35(10-0-26)	-1.3
RALSTON, DOC Samuel Beryl B 8.3.1885 Pierpont, OH D 8.29.1950 Lancaster, PA BR/TR 6/185# d9.8																								
1910	Was A	21	73	4	15	1	0	0	3	3	2		.205	.256	.219	52	-4	2	.976	2	119	122	O-21(LF)	-0.4
RAMAZZOTTI, BOB Robert Louis B 1.16.1917 Elanora, PA D 2.15.2000 Altoona, PA BR/TR 5-8.5/175# d4.20																								
1946	Bro N	62	120	10	25	4	0	0	7	9	0	13	.208	.264	.242	43	-9	0	.939	2	97	99	3-30,2-16	-0.7
1948	Bro N	4	3	0	0	0	0	0	0	0	0	1	.000	.000	.000	-97	-1	0	1.000	-0	0	0	/3-2,2	-0.1
1949	Bro N	5	13	1	2	0	0	1	3	0	0	3	.154	.154	.385	38	-1	0	.833	-1	63	0	/3-3	-0.2
	Chi N	65	190	14	34	3	1	0	6	5	0	33	.179	.200	.205	9	-25	9	.972	6	111	106	3-36,S-12/2-4	-1.8
	Year	70	203	15	36	3	1	1	9	5	0	36	.177	.197	.217	11	-27	9	.965	5	108	99	3-39,S-12/2-4	-2.0
1950	Chi N	61	145	19	38	3	3	1	6	4	1	16	.262	.287	.345	66	-8	3	.961	-3	108	79	2-31,3-10/S-3	-0.9
1951	Chi N	73	158	13	39	5	2	1	15	10	0	23	.247	.292	.323	64	-8	0-0	.950	6	111	115	S-51/2-6,3	0.1
1952	Chi N	50	183	26	52	5	3	1	12	14	1	14	.284	.338	.361	93	-2	3-1	.979	-1	108	93	2-50	0.0
1953	Chi N	26	39	3	6	2	0	0	4	3	0	4	.154	.214	.205	10	-5	0-0	.911	-2	81	81	2-18	-0.7
Total	7	346	851	86	196	22	9	4	53	45	2	107	.230	.271	.291	52	-59	15-1	.966	8	107	91	2-126/3-82,S-66	-4.3
RAMIREZ, ALEX Alexander Ramon B 10.3.1974 Caracas, Venezuela BR/TR 5-11/180# d9.19																								
1998	Cle A	3	8	1	1	0	0	0	0	0-0	0	3	.125	.125	.125	-34	-2	0-0	.833	-0	127	0	/O-3(2-0-1)	-0.2
1999	Cle A	48	97	11	29	6	1	3	18	3-0	1	26	.299	.327	.474	97	-1	1-1	.920	-1	92	122	O-29(5-1-23),D-14	-0.3
2000	Cle A	41	112	13	32	5	1	5	12	5-0	0	17	.286	.316	.482	96	-1	1-0	.978	-1	95	69	O-31(15-1-16)/D-6	-0.3
	Pit N	43	115	13	24	6	1	4	18	7-2	0	32	.209	.254	.383	58	-8	1-0	.949	-1	101	58	O-31(RF)/1	-1.0
Total	3	135	332	38	86	17	3	12	48	15-2	1	78	.259	.293	.437	80	-12	3-1	.949	-2	98	73	/O-94(22-2-71),D-20,1	-1.8
RAMIREZ, ARAMIS Aramis (Nin) B 6.25.1978 Santo Domingo, D.R. BR/TR 6-1/190# d5.26																								
1998	Pit N	72	251	23	59	9	1	6	24	18-0	4	72	.235	.296	.351	69	-12	0-1	.941	-11	85	107	3-71	-2.3
1999	Pit N	18	56	2	10	2	1	0	7	6-0	0	9	.179	.254	.250	29	-6	0-0	.930	0	103	79	3-17	-0.6
2000	Pit N	73	254	19	65	15	2	6	35	10-0	5	36	.256	.293	.402	75	-11	0-0	.917	-6	101	52	3-72	-1.5
2001	Pit N	158	603	83	181	40	0	34	112	40-4	8	100	.300	.350	.536	122	19	5-4	.945	7	112	117	*3-157	2.6
2002	Pit N	142	522	51	122	26	0	18	71	29-3	8	95	.234	.279	.387	77	-21	2-0	.946	2	106	128	*3-131/D-3	-1.8
2003	Pit N	96	375	44	105	25	1	12	67	25-3	7	68	.280	.330	.448	100	0	1-1	.924	5	119	55	3-96	0.6
	†Chi N	63	232	31	60	7	1	15	39	17-0	3	31	.259	.314	.491	109	1	1-1	.939	3	98	124	3-63	0.5
	Year	159	607	75	165	32	2	27	106	42-3	10	99	.272	.324	.465	103	1	2-2	**.929**	8	**111**	82	*3-159	1.1
Total	6	622	2293	253	602	124	6	91	355	145-10	35	411	.263	.312	.441	94	-30	9-7	.937	-0	106	100	3-607/D-3	-2.5
RAMIREZ, JULIO Julio Cesar (Figueroa) B 8.10.1977 San Juan De La Maguana, D.R. BR/TR 5-11/170# d9.10																								
1999	Fla N	15	21	3	3	1	0	0	2	1-0	0	6	.143	.182	.190	-6	-4	0-1	.950	0	131	0	O-11(CF)	-0.3
2001	Chi A	22	37	2	3	0	0	0	1	2-0	0	15	.081	.128	.081	-42	-8	2-0	.978	3	123	255	O-21(1-21-0)	-0.5
2002	Ana A	29	32	6	9	0	1	1	7	2-0	1	14	.281	.343	.438	106	0	0-2	1.000	0	105	161	O-23(0-15-9)	0.0
2003	Ana A	6	2	1	0	0	0	0	0	0-0	0	0	.000	.000	.000	-99	-1	0-0	.750	0	161	0	/O-5(0-3-2),D	-0.1
Total	4	72	92	12	15	1	1	1	10	5-0	1	35	.163	.214	.228	16	-13	2-3	.969	3	119	168	/O-60(1-50-11),D	-0.9
RAMIREZ, MANNY Manuel Aristides (Onelcida) B 5.30.1972 Santo Domingo, D.R. BR/TR 6/190# d9.2																								
1993	Cle A	22	53	5	9	1	0	2	5	2-0	0	8	.170	.200	.302	33	-5	0-0	1.000	0	155	0	D-20/O(RF)	-0.7
1994	Cle A	91	290	51	78	22	0	17	60	42-4	0	72	.269	.357	.521	124	11	4-2	.994	-1	96	119	O-84(RF)/D-5	0.6
1995	†Cle A★	137	484	85	149	26	1	31	107	75-6	5	112	.308	.402	.558	146	34	6-6	.978	-11	88	35	*O-131(RF)/D-5	1.5
1996	†Cle A	152	550	94	170	45	3	33	112	85-8	3	104	.309	.399	.582	146	41	8-5	.970	1	90	178	*O-149(RF)/D-3	3.1
1997	†Cle A	150	561	99	184	40	0	26	88	79-5	7	115	.328	.415	.538	142	38	2-3	.975	-5	90	109	*O-146(RF)/D-4	2.4
1998	†Cle A★	150	571	108	168	35	2	45	145	76-6	6	121	.294	.377	.599	145	38	5-3	.977	-4	97	90	*O-148(RF)/D-2	2.5
1999	†Cle A★	147	522	131	174	34	3	44	**165**	96-9	13	131	.333	.442	**.663**	**171**	**60**	2-4	.975	-2	100	74	*O-146(RF)/D-2	4.5
2000	Cle A✳	118	439	92	154	34	2	38	122	86-9	3	117	.351	.457	**.697**	184	60	1-1	.986	-7	78	118	O-93(RF),D-25	4.2
2001	Bos A★	142	529	93	162	33	2	41	125	81-**25**	8	147	.306	.405	.609	161	49	0-1	1.000	-3	90	31	D-87,O-55(LF)	3.6
2002	Bos A★	120	436	84	152	31	0	33	107	73-14	8	85	**.349**	**.450**	.647	183	56	0-0	.959	-3	83	157	O-68(64-0-7),D-51	4.5
2003	†Bos A✳	154	569	117	185	36	1	37	104	97-**28**	8	94	.325	**.427**	.587	161	55	3-1	.982	-4	83	150	*O-128(LF),D-26	4.3
Total	11	1383	5004	959	1585	337	14	347	1140	792-114	61	1106	.317	.413	.598	156	437	31-26	.978	-37	90	108	*O-1149(247-0-904),D-230	30.5
RAMIREZ, MARIO Mario (Torres) B 9.12.1957 Yauco, P.R. BR/TR 5-9/159# d4.25																								
1980	NY N	18	24	2	5	0	0	0	0	1-0	0	7	.208	.240	.208	27	-2	0-0	1.000	-1	82	128	/S-7/2-4,3-3	-0.3
1981	SD N	13	13	1	1	0	0	0	1	2-1	0	5	.077	.200	.077	-21	-2	0-0	1.000	1	146	0	/S-2,3-2	-0.1
1982	SD N	13	23	1	4	1	0	0	1	2-0	0	4	.174	.240	.217	30	-2	0-0	.963	1	106	115	/S-8,23	-0.1
1983	SD N	55	107	11	21	6	3	0	12	20-1	1	23	.196	.326	.308	80	-2	0-0	.985	-10	81	74	S-38/3	-0.9
1984	†SD N	48	59	12	7	1	0	2	9	13-1	0	14	.119	.278	.237	46	-4	0-0	.971	-9	69	111	S-33/3-6,2-2	-1.2
1985	SD N	37	60	6	17	0	0	2	5	3-0	0	11	.283	.317	.383	97	-1	0-0	.918	-9	72	105	S-27/2-7	-0.8
Total	6	184	286	33	55	8	3	4	28	41-3	1	64	.192	.295	.283	64	-13	0-0	.970	-27	79	94	S-115/2-14,3-13	-3.4
RAMIREZ, MILT Milton (Barboza) B 4.2.1950 Mayaguez, P.R. BR/TR 5-9/150# d4.11																								
1970	StL N	62	79	8	15	2	1	0	3	8-1	0	9	.190	.264	.241	36	-7	0-1	.923	3	104	141	S-59/3	-0.1
1971	StL N	4	11	2	3	0	0	0	0	2-0	0	1	.273	.385	.273	86	0	0-0	.947	-0	68	47	/S-4	0.0
1979	Oak A	28	62	4	10	1	1	0	3	3-0	0	8	.161	.200	.210	11	-8	0-0	.923	-8	72	0	3-12,2-11/S-8	-1.5
Total	3	94	152	14	28	3	2	0	6	13-1	0	18	.184	.248	.230	30	-15	0-1	.920	-5	102	114	/S-71,3-13,2-11	-1.6
RAMIREZ, ORLANDO Orlando (Leal) B 12.18.1951 Cartagena, Colombia BR/TR 5-10/175# d7.6																								
1974	Cal A	31	86	4	14	0	0	0	7	6-0	0	23	.163	.215	.163	11	-10	2-1	.956	2	98	109	S-31	-0.5
1975	Cal A	44	100	10	24	4	1	0	4	11-0	0	22	.240	.315	.300	80	-2	9-6	.905	-2	88	134	S-40	0.0
1976	Cal A	30	70	3	14	1	0	0	5	6-0	0	11	.200	.263	.214	44	-5	3-2	.966	-3	97	72	S-30	-0.5
1977	Cal A	25	13	6	1	0	0	0	0	0-0	0	3	.077	.077	.077	-60	-3	1-0	1.000	0	98	49	/2-5,S-3,D	-0.2
1979	Cal A	13	12	1	0	0	0	0	0	1-0	1	6	.000	.143	.000	-60	-3	1-0	.844	-2	99	66	S-10/D	-0.3
Total	5	143	281	24	53	5	1	0	16	24-0	1	65	.189	.254	.214	37	-23	16-9	.931	-4	95	104	S-114/2-5,D-2	-1.5
RAMIREZ, RAFAEL Rafael Emilio (Peguero) B 2.18.1958 San Pedro De Macoris, D.R. BR/TR 6/185# d8.4																								
1980	Atl N	50	165	17	44	6	1	2	11	2-0	4	33	.267	.292	.352	76	-6	2-1	.949	1	107	106	S-46	0.0
1981	Atl N	95	307	30	67	16	2	2	20	24-3	1	47	.218	.276	.303	63	-15	7-3	.942	2	105	98	S-95	-0.3
1982	†Atl N	157	609	74	169	24	4	10	52	36-7	3	49	.278	.319	.379	91	-8	27-14	.956	18	106	**140**	*S-157	2.9
1983	Atl N	152	622	82	185	13	5	7	58	36-4	2	48	.297	.337	.368	89	-10	16-12	.949	12	106	**128**	*S-152	1.8
1984	Atl N☆	145	591	51	157	22	4	2	48	26-1	1	70	.266	.295	.327	70	-24	14-17	.959	5	102	113	*S-145	-0.8

Year	Tm Lg	G	AB	R	H	2B	3B	HR	RBI	BB-IB	HP	SO	AVG	OBP	SLG	AOPS	ABR	SB-CS	FA	FR	Rng	Thr	G at Pos	BFW
1985	Atl N	138	568	54	141	25	4	5	58	20-1	0	63	.248	.272	.333	65	-28	2-6	.954	15	**112**	**130**	*S-133	-0.1
1986	Atl N	134	496	57	119	21	1	8	33	21-1	3	60	.240	.273	.335	64	-26	19-8	.952	23	118	125	S-86,3-57/O-3(2-0-1)	0.7
1987	Atl N	56	179	22	47	12	0	1	21	8-0	2	16	.263	.300	.346	68	-8	6-3	.946	1	106	153	S-38,3-12	-0.4
1988	Hou N	155	566	51	156	30	5	6	59	18-6	3	61	.276	.298	.378	98	-4	3-2	.965	-17	90	85	*S-154	-1.0
1989	Hou N	151	537	46	132	20	2	6	54	29-3	0	64	.246	.283	.324	76	-18	3-1	.945	-41	82	84	*S-149	-5.2
1990	Hou N	132	445	44	116	19	3	2	37	24-9	1	46	.261	.299	.330	75	-16	10-5	.953	-15	95	91	*S-129	-2.2
1991	Hou N	101	233	17	55	10	0	1	20	13-1	0	40	.236	.274	.292	64	-12	3-3	.953	-8	81	81	S-45,2-27/3-2	-1.8
1992	Hou N	73	176	17	44	6	0	1	13	7-1	1	24	.250	.283	.301	68	-8	0-0	.961	-3	98	77	S-57/3	-0.8
Total	13	1539	5494	562	1432	224	31	53	484	264-37	21	621	.261	.295	.342	77	-183	112-75	.953	-7	101	110	*S-1386/3-72,2-27,O-3(2-0-1)	-7.2
RAMOS, DOMINGO Domingo Antonio (De Ramos) B 3.29.1958 Santiago, D.R. BR/TR 5-10/155# d9.8																								
1978	NY A	1	0	0	0	0	0	0	0	0-0	0	0	—	—	—	—	0	0-0	—	-0	0	0	/S	0.0
1980	Tor A	5	16	0	2	0	0	0	0	2-0	0	5	.125	.222	.125	-2	-2	0-0	1.000	-0	124	86	/2-2,S-2,D	-0.2
1982	Sea A	8	26	3	4	2	0	0	1	3-0	0	2	.154	.241	.231	30	-2	0-0	.920	-5	57	0	/S-8	-0.7
1983	Sea A	53	127	14	36	4	0	2	10	7-0	1	12	.283	.326	.362	86	-3	3-1	.948	7	112	137	S-28/2-8,3-8,D-2	0.8
1984	Sea A	59	81	6	15	2	0	0	2	5-0	0	12	.185	.233	.210	24	-8	2-2	.911	-2	74	126	3-38,S-13/1-5,2-3	-1.0
1985	Sea A	75	168	19	33	6	0	1	15	17-0	0	23	.196	.267	.250	43	-13	0-1	.951	-5	86	75	S-36,2-20,1-14/3-7	-1.5
1986	Sea A	49	99	8	18	2	0	0	5	8-0	1	13	.182	.250	.202	25	-10	0-1	.966	8	125	75	S-21,2-16/3-8,D-2	-0.1
1987	Sea A	42	103	9	32	6	0	2	11	3-0	1	12	.311	.336	.427	96	-1	0-1	.953	4	109	131	S-25/3-7,2-6,D-2	0.5
1988	Cle A	22	46	7	12	1	0	0	5	3-0	1	7	.261	.308	.283	68	-2	0-0	1.000	1	120	139	2-11/1-5,S-4,3-2	0.0
	Cal A	10	15	3	2	0	0	0	0	0-0	0	0	.133	.133	.133	-26	-3	0-0	1.000	0	117	0	/3-8,O(LF)	-0.3
	Year	32	61	10	14	1	0	0	5	3-0	1	7	.230	.269	.246	47	-4	0-0	1.000	1	120	139	2-11,3-10/1-5,S-4,O(LF)	-0.3
1989	†Chi N	85	179	18	47	6	2	1	19	17-4	2	23	.263	.333	.335	85	-3	1-1	.959	3	129	120	S-42,3-30	0.3
1990	Chi N	98	226	22	60	5	0	2	17	27-1	1	29	.265	.342	.314	77	-6	0-2	.932	-12	55	27	3-66,S-21/2	-1.8
Total	11	507	1086	109	261	34	2	8	85	92-5	7	138	.240	.302	.297	64	-53	6-9	.955	-1	108	109	S-201,3-174/2-67,1-24,D-7,O(LF)	-4.0
RAMOS, CHUCHO Jesus Manuel (Garcia) B 4.12.1918 Maturin, Venezuela D 9.2.1977 Caracas, Venezuela BR/TL 5-10.5/167# d5.7																								
1944	Cin N	4	10	1	5	1	0	0	0	0	0	0	.500	.500	.600	217	1	0	1.000	-0	106	0	/O-3(1-0-3)	0.1
RAMOS, JOHN John Joseph B 8.6.1965 Tampa, FL BR/TR 6/190# d9.18																								
1991	NY A	10	26	4	8	1	0	0	3	1-0	0	3	.308	.310	.346	88	0	0-0	1.000	-2	98	0	/C-5,D-4	-0.2
RAMOS, KEN Kenneth Cecil B 6.6.1967 Sidney, NE BL/TL 6-1/185# d5.16																								
1997	Hou N	14	12	0	0	0	0	0	1	2-0	0	0	.000	.133	.000	-61	-3	0-0	—	-0	0	0	/O-2(1-0-1)	-0.3
RAMOS, BOBBY Roberto B 11.5.1955 Havana, Cuba BR/TR 5-11/208# d9.26 C2																								
1978	Mon N	2	4	0	0	0	0	0	0	0-0	0	1	.000	.000	.000	-99	-1	0-0	1.000	-0	73	0	/C	-0.1
1980	Mon N	13	32	5	5	2	0	0	2	5-0	0	5	.156	.270	.219	38	-3	0-0	.964	-1	113	141	C-12	-0.3
1981	Mon N	26	41	4	8	1	0	1	3	3-0	0	5	.195	.250	.293	53	-3	0-0	.974	0	84	76	C-23	-0.2
1982	NY A	4	11	1	1	0	0	1	2	0-0	0	3	.091	.091	.364	18	-1	0-0	1.000	1	190	93	/C-4	-0.1
1983	Mon N	27	61	2	14	3	1	0	5	8-1	1	11	.230	.329	.311	79	-2	0-0	.984	0	93	125	C-25	-0.1
1984	Mon N	31	83	8	16	1	0	2	5	6-1	0	13	.193	.244	.277	49	-6	0-0	.982	2	74	167	C-31	-0.3
Total	6	103	232	20	44	7	1	4	17	22-2	1	38	.190	.262	.280	53	-16	0-0	.980	2	92	131	/C-96	-1.1
RAMSEY, FERNANDO Fernando David (Ramsey) B 12.20.1965 Rainbow, Panama BR/TR 6-1/175# d9.7																								
1992	Chi N	18	25	0	3	0	0	0	2	0-0	0	6	.120	.120	.120	-31	-4	0-0	1.000	-1	91	0	O-15(CF)	-0.6
RAMSEY, MIKE Michael James B 7.8.1960 Thomson, GA BB/TL 6- /170# d4.6																								
1987	LA N	48	125	18	29	4	2	0	12	10-0	0	32	.232	.287	.296	57	-8	2-4	.973	-4	85	51	O-43(4-38-1)	-1.3
RAMSEY, MIKE Michael Jeffrey B 3.29.1954 Roanoke, VA BB/TR 6-1/170# d9.4																								
1978	StL N	12	5	4	1	0	0	0	0	0-0	0	1	.200	.200	.200	12	-1	0-0	.909	1	108	291	/S-4	0.0
1980	StL N	59	126	11	33	8	1	0	8	3-2	0	17	.262	.279	.341	70	-5	0-0	.960	-3	114	118	2-24,S-20/3-8	-0.6
1981	StL N	47	124	19	32	3	0	0	9	8-1	0	16	.258	.303	.282	65	-6	4-0	.966	5	119	111	S-35/3-5,2O(LF)	0.3
1982	†StL N	112	256	18	59	8	2	1	21	22-3	1	34	.230	.294	.289	63	-13	6-5	.963	-1	96	109	2-43,3-28,S-22/O-2(LF)	-1.1
1983	StL N	97	175	25	46	4	3	1	16	12-2	1	23	.263	.309	.337	80	-5	4-2	.968	-10	88	110	2-66,S-20/3-8,O(LF)	-1.3
1984	StL N	21	15	1	1	1	0	0	0	1-0	0	3	.067	.125	.133	-28	-3	0-0	1.000	1	119	47	/2-7,S-7,3	-0.2
	Mon N	37	70	2	15	1	0	0	3	0-0	0	13	.214	.214	.229	26	-7	0-0	.975	-4	102	132	S-26,2-12	-0.9
	Year	58	85	3	16	2	0	0	3	1-0	0	16	.188	.198	.212	16	-10	0-0	.978	-3	103	148	S-33,2-19/3	-1.1
1985	LA N	9	15	1	2	1	0	0	0	2-0	0	4	.133	.235	.200	24	-2	0-0	.923	-1	121	89	/S-4,2-2	-0.2
Total	7	394	786	81	189	26	6	2	57	48-8	2	111	.240	.285	.296	63	-42	14-7	.964	-12	94	106	2-155,S-138/3-50,O-4(LF)	-4.0
RAMSEY, BILL William Thrace "Square Jaw" B 10.20.1920 Osceola, AR BR/TR 6/175# d4.19																								
1945	Bos N	78	137	16	40	8	0	1	12	4	3	22	.292	.326	.372	93	-1	1	.963	1	116	46	O-43(30-13-0)	-0.2
RAND, DICK Richard Hilton B 3.7.1931 South Gate, CA D 1.22.1996 Moreno Valley, CA BR/TR 6-2/185# d9.16																								
1953	StL N	9	31	3	9	1	0	0	1	2	0	6	.290	.333	.323	72	-1	0-0	.984	1	*99*	*111*	/C-9	0.0
1955	StL N	3	10	1	3	0	0	1	3	1-0	0	1	.300	.364	.600	150	1	0-1	1.000	-1	*65*	*209*	/C-3	-0.1
1957	Pit N	60	105	7	23	2	1	1	9	11-1	0	24	.219	.288	.286	58	-6	0-0	.973	0	*120*	*74*	C-57	-0.4
Total	3	72	146	11	35	3	1	2	13	14-1	0	31	.240	.302	.315	68	-6	0-1	.977	1	*113*	*89*	/C-69	-0.5
RANDA, JOE Joseph Gregory B 12.18.1969 Milwaukee, WI BR/TR 5-11/190# d4.30																								
1995	KC A	34	70	6	12	2	0	1	5	6-0	0	17	.171	.237	.243	25	-8	0-1	.949	-4	104	38	3-22/2-9,D-2	-1.1
1996	KC A	110	337	36	102	24	1	6	47	26-4	1	47	.303	.351	.433	98	-1	13-4	.951	-9	91	81	3-92,2-15/1-7,D	-0.7
1997	Pit N	126	443	58	134	27	9	7	60	41-1	6	64	.302	.366	.451	112	8	4-2	.937	19	117	119	*3-120,2-13	2.8
1998	Det A	138	460	56	117	21	2	9	50	41-1	7	70	.254	.323	.367	79	-14	8-7	.976	8	**112**	107	*3-118,2-20/1D	-0.5
1999	KC A	156	628	92	197	36	8	16	84	50-4	3	80	.314	.363	.473	110	9	5-4	.952	9	**110**	102	*3-156	1.7
2000	KC A	158	612	88	186	29	4	15	106	36-3	6	66	.304	.343	.438	94	-6	6-3	.957	9	108	102	*3-156/D	0.4
2001	KC A	151	581	59	147	34	2	13	83	42-2	6	80	.253	.307	.386	75	-21	3-2	.966	4	104	**129**	*3-137,D-14/2	-1.5
2002	KC A	151	549	63	155	36	5	11	80	46-1	9	69	.282	.341	.426	93	-4	2-1	.972	0	102	53	*3-129,D-19	-0.4
2003	KC A	131	502	80	146	31	1	16	72	41-0	7	61	.291	.348	.452	97	-1	1-0	**.980**	-0	101	54	*3-129/D-2	0.0
Total	9	1155	4182	538	1196	240	32	94	587	329-16	45	554	.286	.341	.426	93	-38	42-24	.961	36	106	93	*3-1059/2-58,D-40,1-8	0.7
RANDALL, SAP James Odell B 8.19.1960 Mobile, AL BB/TR 5-11/195# d8.2																								
1988	Chi A	4	12	1	0	0	0	0	1	2-0	0	3	.000	.133	.000	-57	-3	0-0	1.000	0	155	124	/1-2,O(RF)D	-0.3
RANDALL, NEWT Newton J. B 2.3.1880 New Lowell, ON, CAN D 5.3.1955 Duluth, MN BR/TR 5-10/?# d4.18																								
1907	Chi N	22	78	6	16	4	2	0	4	8	0		.205	.279	.308	79	-2	2	.904	-0	85	134	O-21(1-1-21)	-0.4
	Bos N	75	258	16	55	6	3	0	15	19	7		.213	.285	.260	71	-8	4	.920	-6	92	38	O-73(59-3-12)	-2.1
	Year	97	336	22	71	10	5	0	19	27	7		.211	.284	.271	73	-10	6	.915	-6	90	63	O-94(60-4-33)	-2.5
RANDALL, BOB Robert Lee B 6.10.1948 Norton, KS BR/TR 6-3/180# d4.13 C1																								
1976	Min A	153	475	55	127	18	4	1	34	28-0	8	38	.267	.317	.328	88	-7	3-5	.969	-4	96	**123**	*2-153	-0.2
1977	Min A	103	306	36	73	13	2	0	22	15-0	7	25	.239	.289	.294	60	-17	1-4	.985	12	107	120	*2-101/13D	-0.1
1978	Min A	119	330	36	89	11	3	0	21	24-0	6	22	.270	.329	.321	82	-7	5-3	.983	17	**113**	122	*2-116/3-2,D	1.6
1979	Min A	80	199	25	49	7	0	0	14	15-0	0	17	.246	.299	.281	55	-12	2-2	.983	10	110	131	2-71/3-7,SO(LF)	0.1
1980	Min A	5	15	2	3	1	0	0	0	1-0	0	0	.200	.250	.267	39	-1	0-0	.909	-0	116	138	/3-4,2	-0.1
Total	5	460	1325	154	341	50	9	1	91	83-0	21	102	.257	.310	.311	74	-44	11-14	.979	36	105	123	2-442/3-14,D-2,O(LF)S1	1.3
RANDLE, LEN Leonard Shenoff B 2.12.1949 Long Beach, CA BB/TR (BR 1971) 5-10/169# d6.16 OF Total (62-LF 85-CF 6-RF)																								
1971	Was A	75	215	27	47	11	0	2	13	24-2	1	56	.219	.298	.298	74	-7	1-1	.967	8	106	118	2-66	0.6
1972	Tex A	74	249	23	48	13	0	2	21	13-2	1	51	.193	.235	.269	52	-15	4-5	.952	-0	99	86	2-65/S-4,O-2(CF)	-1.4
1973	Tex A	10	29	3	6	1	1	1	1	0-0	0	2	.207	.207	.414	74	-1	0-2	.964	-3	58	69	/2-5,O-2(CF)	-0.5
1974	Tex A	151	520	65	157	17	4	1	49	29-2	2	43	.302	.338	.356	103	1	26-17	.935	11	96	125	3-89,2-40,O-21(13-5-3)/SD	1.4
1975	Tex A	156	601	85	166	24	7	4	57	57-3	4	80	.276	.341	.359	99	0	16-19	.973	11	104	120	2-79,O-66(7-61-0),3-17/CSD	1.2
1976	Tex A	142	539	53	121	11	6	1	51	46-2	2	63	.224	.286	.273	63	-25	30-15	.971	0	95	89	*2-113,O-30(28-1-1)/3-2,D	-1.9
1977	NY N	136	513	78	156	22	7	5	27	65-3	2	70	.304	.383	.404	117	14	33-21	.961	2	96	**152**	*3-110,2-20/O-6(4-4-0),S	1.5
1978	NY N	132	437	53	102	16	8	2	35	64-7	1	57	.233	.330	.320	86	-7	14-11	.967	-7	91	108	*3-124/2-5	-1.7

Year	Tm Lg	G	AB	R	H	2B	3B	HR	RBI	BB-IB	HP	SO	AVG	OBP	SLG	AOPS	ABR	SB-CS	FA	FR	Rng	Thr	G at Pos	BFW
1979	NY A	20	39	2	7	0	0	0	3	3-0	0	2	.179	.238	.179	15	-5	0-0	1.000	1	94	377	O-11(4-7-0)/D-2	-0.4
1980	Chi N	130	489	67	135	19	6	5	39	50-2	1	55	.276	.343	.370	93	-4	19-13	.929	6	109	40	*3-111,2-17/O-6(4-2-0)	0.1
1981	Sea A	82	273	22	63	9	1	4	25	17-4	1	22	.231	.276	.315	68	-12	11-6	.986	7	111	92	3-59,2-21/O-5(2-1-2),S-3	-0.4
1982	Sea A	30	46	10	8	2	0	0	1	4-0	0	4	.174	.240	.217	26	-5	2-2	.964	0	112	59	D-13/3-9,2-6	-0.5
Total	12	1138	3950	488	1016	145	40	27	322	372-27	15	505	.257	.321	.335	87	-66	156-112	.953	36	99	103	3-521,2-437,O-149C/D-21,S-10,C	-2.0
RANDOLPH, WILLIE Willie Larry B 7.6.1954 Holly Hill, SC BR/TR 5-11/166# d7.29 C10																								
1975	†Pit N	30	61	9	10	1	0	0	3	7-1	0	6	.164	.246	.180	21	-7	1-0	.962	2	115	97	2-14/3	-0.4
1976	†NY A✱	125	430	59	115	15	4	1	40	58-5	3	39	.267	.356	.328	103	4	37-12	.974	11	110	117	*2-124	2.9
1977	†NY A★	147	551	91	151	28	11	4	40	64-1	1	53	.274	.347	.387	102	3	13-6	.980	14	106	**121**	*2-147	2.5
1978	NY A	134	499	87	139	18	6	3	42	82-1	4	51	.279	.381	.357	112	13	36-7	.978	3	99	102	*2-134	2.9
1979	NY A	153	574	98	155	15	13	5	61	95-5	3	39	.270	.374	.368	104	6	33-12	.985	17	108	123	*2-153	3.3
1980	†NY A★	138	513	99	151	23	7	7	46	**119**-4	2	45	.294	.427	.407	133	32	30-5	.976	7	99	100	*2-138	5.0
1981	†NY A★	93	357	59	83	14	3	2	24	57-0	0	24	.232	.336	.305	88	-3	14-5	.977	9	100	**127**	2-93	1.3
1982	NY A	144	553	85	155	21	4	3	36	75-3	3	35	.280	.368	.349	100	3	16-9	.981	11	100	103	*2-142/D	2.2
1983	NY A	104	420	73	117	21	1	2	38	53-0	1	32	.279	.361	.348	100	2	12-4	.979	15	106	109	*2-104	2.4
1984	NY A	142	564	86	162	24	2	2	31	86-4	0	42	.287	.377	.348	108	11	10-6	.983	22	103	119	*2-142	4.0
1985	NY A	143	497	75	137	21	2	5	40	85-3	4	39	.276	.382	.356	107	10	16-9	.985	5	100	110	*2-143	2.3
1986	NY A	141	492	76	136	15	2	5	50	94-0	3	49	.276	.393	.346	105	9	15-2	.972	3	103	107	*2-139/D	2.2
1987	NY A★	120	449	96	137	24	2	7	67	82-1	2	25	.305	.411	.414	122	20	11-1	.981	9	104	115	*2-119/D	3.5
1988	NY A	110	404	43	93	20	1	2	34	55-2	2	39	.230	.322	.300	77	-11	8-4	.988	14	109	**111**	*2-110	0.7
1989	LA N★	145	549	62	155	18	0	2	36	71-2	4	51	.282	.366	.326	102	5	7-6	.987	-5	96	112	*2-140	0.4
1990	LA N	26	96	15	26	4	0	1	9	13-0	1	9	.271	.364	.344	98	0	1-0	.969	-1	96	77	2-26	0.1
	†Oak A	93	292	37	75	9	3	1	21	32-1	1	25	.257	.331	.318	86	-5	6-1	.982	-8	97	128	2-84/D-6	-1.0
1991	Mil A	124	431	60	141	14	3	0	54	75-3	0	38	.327	.424	.374	127	21	4-2	.969	9	**108**	**123**	*2-121/D-2	3.3
1992	NY N	90	286	29	72	11	1	2	15	40-1	4	34	.252	.352	.318	92	-1	1-3	.977	-5	90	118	2-79	-0.5
Total	18	2202	8018	1239	2210	316	65	54	687	1243-37	38	675	.276	.373	.351	105	112	271-94	.980	132	103	113	*2-2152/D-11,3	37.1
RANEW, MERRITT Merritt Thomas B 5.10.1938 Albany, GA BL/TR 5-10/180# d4.13																								
1962	Hou N	71	218	26	51	6	8	4	24	14-5	3	43	.234	.287	.390	87	-6	2-2	.980	-7	*69*	*92*	C-58	-1.0
1963	Chi N	78	154	18	52	8	1	3	15	9-1	2	32	.338	.380	.461	134	7	1-0	.980	-1	*135*	*92*	C-37/1-9	0.7
1964	Chi N	16	33	0	3	0	0	0	1	2-0	1	6	.091	.167	.091	-24	-5	0-0	1.000	1	*160*	*191*	/C-9	-0.4
	Mil N	9	17	1	2	0	0	0	0	0-0	0	3	.118	.118	.118	-33	-3	0-1	1.000	-1	*93*	*165*	/C-3	-0.4
	Year	25	50	1	5	0	0	0	1	2-0	1	9	.100	.151	.100	-27	-8	0-1	1.000	1	*145*	*185*	C-12	-0.8
1965	Cal A	41	91	12	19	4	0	1	10	7-0	0	22	.209	.260	.286	58	-5	0-0	.988	-5	*89*	*84*	C-24	-1.0
1969	Sea A	54	81	11	20	2	0	0	4	10-3	0	14	.247	.330	.272	71	-3	0-0	.969	-4	78	0	C-13/O-3(LF),3	-0.6
Total	5	269	594	68	147	20	9	8	54	42-9	6	120	.247	.301	.352	83	-15	3-3	.982	-16	*94*	*92*	C-144/1-9,O-3(LF),3	-2.7
RANSOM, CODY Bryan Cody B 2.17.1976 Mesa, AZ BR/TR 6-2/190# d9.5																								
2001	SF N	9	7	1	0	0	0	0	0	0-0	0	5	.000	.000	.000	-99	-2	0-0	1.000	-0	134	0	/S-6	-0.2
2002	SF N	7	3	2	2	0	0	0	1	1-1	0	1	.667	.750	.667	298	1	0-0	1.000	-0	76	0	/S-3	0.1
2003	SF N	20	27	7	6	1	0	1	1	1-0	0	11	.222	.250	.370	61	-2	0-0	.963	-2	82	164	S-12	-0.3
Total	3	36	37	10	8	1	0	1	2	2-1	0	17	.216	.256	.324	52	-3	0-0	.973	-2	87	123	/S-21	-0.4
RANSOM, JEFF Jeffrey Dean B 11.11.1960 Fresno, CA BR/TR 5-11/185# d9.5																								
1981	SF N	5	15	2	4	1	0	0	0	1-1	0	1	.267	.313	.333	85	0	0-0	1.000	2	65	63	/C-5	0.2
1982	SF N	15	44	5	7	0	0	0	3	6-0	0	7	.159	.255	.159	20	-5	0-0	.988	-0	79	72	C-14	-0.5
1983	SF N	6	20	3	4	0	0	1	3	4-0	0	7	.200	.333	.350	92	0	0-0	.946	-4	33	39	/C-6	-0.4
Total	3	26	79	10	15	1	0	1	6	11-1	0	15	.190	.286	.241	50	-5	0-0	.980	-2	65	62	/C-25	-0.7
RAPP, EARL Earl Wellington B 5.20.1921 Corunna, MI D 2.13.1992 Swedesboro, NJ BL/TR 6-2/185# d4.28																								
1949	Det A	1	0	0	0	0	0	0	0	1	0	0	—	1.000	—	175	0	0-0	—	0			H	0.0
	Chi A	19	54	3	14	1	1	0	11	5	0	6	.259	.322	.315	71	-2	1-1	.974	2	114	178	O-13(11-0-2)	-0.2
	Year	20	54	3	14	1	1	0	11	6	0	6	.259	.333	.315	74	-2	1-1	.974	2	114	178	O-13(11-0-2)	-0.2
1951	NY N	13	11	0	1	0	0	0	1	2	0	3	.091	.231	.091	-10	-2	0-0	—	0			H	-0.2
	StL A	26	98	14	32	5	3	2	14	11	0	11	.327	.394	.500	137	5	1-0	.979	-0	97	119	O-25(RF)	0.4
1952	StL A	30	49	3	7	4	0	0	4	0	0	8	.143	.143	.224	1	-7	0-0	1.000	-0	112	0	/O-7(RF)	-0.7
	Was A	46	67	7	19	6	0	0	9	6	1	13	.284	.351	.373	105	1	0-0	.917	-1	82	0	O-10(RF)	-0.1
	Year	76	116	10	26	10	0	0	13	6	1	21	.224	.268	.310	61	-6	0-0	.958	-1	95	0	O-17(RF)	-0.8
Total	3	135	279	27	73	16	4	2	39	25	1	41	.262	.325	.369	89	-5	2-1	.973	-0	101	105	/O-55(11-0-44)	-0.8
RAPP, GOLDIE Joseph Aloysius B 2.6.1894 Cincinnati, OH D 7.1.1966 LaMesa, CA BB/TR 5-10/165# d4.13																								
1921	NY N	58	181	21	39	9	1	0	15	15	0	13	.215	.276	.276	46	-14	3-11	.941	9	124	130	3-56	-0.4
	Phi N	52	202	28	56	7	1	1	10	14	0	8	.277	.324	.337	70	-8	6-7	.950	1	97	73	3-50/2	-0.5
	Year	110	383	49	95	16	2	1	25	29	0	21	.248	.301	.308	59	-22	9-18	**.945**	10	**112**	104	*3-106/2	-0.9
1922	Phi N	119	502	58	127	26	3	0	38	32	1	29	.253	.299	.317	54	-34	6-12	.948	3	110	97	*3-117/S-2	-2.5
1923	Phi N	47	179	27	47	5	0	1	10	14	1	14	.263	.320	.307	59	-10	1-1	.947	-0	96	95	3-45	-0.8
Total	3	276	1064	134	269	47	5	2	73	75	2	64	.253	.303	.312	57	-66	16-31	.947	13	108	99	3-268/S-2,2	-4.2
RARIDEN, BILL William Angel "Bedford Bill" B 2.4.1888 Bedford, IN D 8.28.1942 Bedford, IN BR/TR 5-10/168# d8.12																								
1909	Bos N	13	42	1	6	1	0	0	1	4	0		.143	.217	.167	18	-4	1	.912	-3	*80*	*95*	C-13	-0.6
1910	Bos N	49	137	15	31	5	1	1	14	12	1	22	.226	.293	.299	70	-5	1	.962	-2	*87*	*119*	C-49	-0.3
1911	Bos N	70	246	22	56	9	0	0	21	21	0	18	.228	.288	.264	51	-16	3	.952	-8	*77*	*124*	C-65/3-3,2	-1.8
1912	Bos N	79	247	27	55	3	1	1	14	18	2	35	.223	.281	.255	46	-19	3	.964	-6	*91*	*105*	C-73	-1.9
1913	Bos N	95	246	31	58	9	2	3	30	30	2	21	.236	.324	.325	84	-4	5-1	.976	-0	102	99	C-87	0.3
1914	Ind F	131	396	44	93	15	5	0	47	61	0	43	.235	.337	.298	67	-22	12	.981	15	*89*	***112***	*C-130	0.4
1915	New F	142	444	49	120	30	7	0	40	60	3	29	.270	.361	.369	112	3	8	.978	25	***123***	*103*	*C-142	4.3
1916	NY N	120	351	23	78	9	3	1	29	55	3	32	.222	.333	.274	92	0	4	.972	-4	113	85	*C-119	0.7
1917	†NY N	101	266	20	72	10	1	0	25	42	1	17	.271	.372	.316	116	8	3	.971	-10	*102*	*57*	*C-100	0.6
1918	NY N	69	183	15	41	5	1	0	17	15	0	15	.224	.283	.262	68	-7	1	**.984**	-6	*93*	*63*	C-63	-0.9
1919	†Cin N	74	218	16	47	6	3	1	24	17	1	19	.216	.275	.284	70	-8	4	.983	6	*113*	*80*	C-70	0.4
1920	Cin N	39	101	9	25	3	0	0	10	5	0	0	.248	.283	.277	62	-5	2-0	.972	0	*104*	*106*	C-37	-0.2
Total	12	982	2877	272	682	105	24	7	272	340	13	251	.237	.320	.298	78	-79	47-1	.973	7	*102*	*96*	C-948/3-3,2	1.0
RATH, MORRIE Morris Charles B 12.25.1886 Mobeetie, TX D 11.18.1945 Upper Darby, PA BL/TR 5-8.5/160# d9.28 Mil 1918																								
1909	Phi A	7	26	4	7	1	0	0	3	2	3		.269	.387	.308	117	1	1	.846	-1	77	108	/S-4,3-2	0.0
1910	Phi A	18	26	3	4	0	0	0	1	5	0		.154	.290	.154	40	-2	0	.950	-1	87	0	3-11/2-3	-0.3
	Cle A	24	67	5	13	3	0	0	0	10	0		.194	.299	.239	68	-2	2	.950	1	104	127	3-22/S	-0.1
	Year	42	93	8	17	3	0	0	1	15	0		.183	.296	.215	60	-3	2	.950	-0	100	97	3-33/2-3,S	-0.4
1912	Chi A	157	591	104	161	10	2	1	19	95	7		.272	.380	.301	98	5	31	**.963**	16	**108**	91	*2-157	2.4
1913	Chi A	92	295	37	59	2	0	0	12	46	1	22	.200	.310	.207	52	-16	22	.962	-0	102	114	2-86	-1.6
1919	†Cin N	138	537	77	142	13	1	1	29	64	0	24	.264	.343	.298	96	1	17	.974	13	103	114	*2-138	1.7
1920	Cin N	129	506	61	135	7	4	2	28	36	3	24	.267	.319	.308	82	-12	10-11	**.977**	-2	95	101	*2-126/3O(RF)	-1.4
Total	6	565	2048	291	521	36	7	4	92	258	14	70	.254	.342	.285	86	-25	83-11	.970	25	102	104	2-510/3-36,S-5,O(RF)	0.7
RATLIFF, GENE Kelly Eugene B 9.28.1945 Macon, GA BR/TR 6-5/185# d5.15																								
1965	Hou N	4	4	0	0	0	0	0	0	0-0	0	4	.000	.000	.000	-99	-1	0-0	—	0			H	-0.1
RATLIFF, PAUL Paul Hawthorne B 1.23.1944 San Diego, CA BL/TR 6-2/190# d4.14																								
1963	Min A	10	21	2	4	1	0	1	3	2-0	1	7	.190	.292	.381	85	0	0-0	.976	2	88	234	/C-7	0.2
1970	†Min A	69	149	19	40	7	2	5	22	15-2	7	51	.268	.363	.443	119	4	0-0	.980	-10	129	28	C-53	-0.4
1971	Min A	21	44	3	7	1	0	2	6	4-1	0	17	.159	.224	.318	52	-3	0-0	1.000	1	126	63	C-15	-0.1
	Mil A	23	41	3	7	1	0	3	7	5-1	1	21	.171	.277	.415	95	-1	0-0	.966	-0	48	123	C-13	0.0
	Year	44	85	6	14	2	0	5	13	9-2	1	38	.165	.250	.365	72	-4	0-0	.985	1	92	89	C-28	-0.1
1972	Mil A	22	42	1	3	0	0	1	4	2-1	0	23	.071	.114	.143	-25	-7	0-0	1.000	-4	66	106	C-13	-1.2
Total	4	145	297	28	61	10	2	12	42	28-5	9	119	.205	.293	.374	86	-7	0-0	.983	-11	107	70	C-101	-1.5

Year	Tm Lg	G	AB	R	H	2B	3B	HR	RBI	BB-IB	HP	SO	AVG	OBP	SLG	AOPS	ABR	SB-CS	FA	FR	Rng	Thr	G at Pos	BFW
RAUB, TOMMY Thomas Jefferson B 12.1.1870 Raubsville, PA D 2.15.1949 Phillipsburg, NJ BR/TR 5-10/155# d5.3																								
1903	Chi N	36	84	6	19	3	2	0	7	5	1		.226	.278	.310	69	-4	3	.900	-3	*122*	*67*	C-12/1-6,O-5(RF),3-4	-0.6
1906	StL N	24	78	9	22	2	4	0	2	4	1		.282	.325	.410	135	2	2	.957	-4	*73*	*111*	C-22	0.0
Total	2	60	162	15	41	5	6	0	9	9	2		.253	.301	.358	99	-2	5	.940	-7	*88*	*98*	/C-34,1-6,O-5(RF),3-4	-0.6
RAUDMAN, BOB Robert Joyce "Shorty" B 3.14.1942 Erie, PA BL/TL 5-9.5/185# d9.13																								
1966	Chi N	8	29	1	7	2	0	0	2	1-0	0	4	.241	.267	.310	59	-2	0-0	.909	1	70	429	/O-8(LF)	-0.2
1967	Chi N	8	26	0	4	0	0	0	1	1-1	0	4	.154	.185	.154	-2	-3	0-0	.875	-0	88	170	/O-8(RF)	-0.5
Total	2	16	55	1	11	2	0	0	3	2-1	0	8	.200	.228	.236	30	-5	0-0	.889	0	80	289	/O-16(8-0-8)	-0.7
RAWLINGS, JOHNNY John William "Red" B 8.17.1892 Bloomfield, IA D 10.16.1972 Inglewood, CA BR/TR 5-8/158# d4.14																								
1914	Cin N	33	60	9	13	1	0	0	8	6	0	8	.217	.288	.233	54	-3	1	.885	0	115	96	3-10/2-7,S-5	-0.3
	KC F	61	193	19	41	3	0	0	15	22	1	25	.212	.296	.228	46	-17	6	.937	10	118	106	S-61	-0.3
1915	KC F	120	399	40	86	9	2	2	24	27	2	40	.216	.269	.263	52	-33	17	.926	-5	104	86	*S-120	-3.2
1917	Bos N	122	371	37	95	9	4	2	31	38	7	32	.256	.337	.318	107	5	12	.977	3	104	95	2-96,S-17/3O(LF)	1.2
1918	Bos N	111	410	32	85	7	3	0	21	30	2	31	.207	.265	.239	56	-21	10	.956	8	106	91	S-71,2-20,O-18(RF)	-1.1
1919	Bos N	77	275	30	70	8	2	1	16	16	1	20	.255	.298	.309	86	-5	10	.961	-9	95	82	2-58,O-10(7-1-5)/S-5	-1.5
1920	Bos N	5	3	0	0	0	0	0	2	0	0	1	.000	.000	.000	-99	-1	0-0	1.000	-0	67	0	/2	-0.1
	Phi N	98	384	39	90	19	2	3	30	22	1	25	.234	.278	.318	67	-16	9-6	.970	-2	98	101	2-97	-1.8
	Year	103	387	39	90	19	2	3	32	22	1	26	.233	.276	.315	67	-17	9-6	.970	-3	98	101	2-98	-1.9
1921	Phi N	60	254	20	74	14	2	1	16	8	2	12	.291	.318	.374	76	-8	4-5	.954	7	109	103	2-60	0.0
	†NY N	86	307	40	82	8	1	1	30	18	4	19	.267	.316	.309	66	-15	4-4	.970	3	99	163	2-86/S	-1.0
	Year	146	561	60	156	22	3	2	46	26	6	31	.278	.317	.339	71	-23	8-9	**.963**	10	103	**138**	*2-146/S	-1.0
1922	NY N	88	308	46	87	13	8	1	30	23	5	15	.282	.342	.386	87	-6	7-6	.984	-1	99	126	2-77/3-5	-0.5
1923	Pit N	119	461	53	131	18	4	1	45	25	1	29	.284	.322	.347	75	-17	9-0	.958	-8	95	97	*2-119	-1.9
1924	Pit N	3	3	0	1	0	0	0	2	0	0	0	.333	.333	.333	78	0	0-0	—	0			H	0.0
1925	Pit N	36	110	17	31	7	0	2	13	8	1	8	.282	.336	.400	82	-3	0-1	.981	2	106	86	2-29	-0.1
1926	Pit N	61	181	27	42	6	0	0	20	14	0	10	.232	.287	.265	47	-13	3	.970	-1	96	87	2-59	-1.3
Total	12	1080	3719	409	928	122	28	14	303	257	27	275	.250	.303	.309	71	-153	92-22	.968	7	100	106	2-709,S-280/O-29(8-1-23),3-16	-11.9
RAY, IRV Irving Burton "Stubby" B 1.22.1864 Harrington, ME D 2.21.1948 Harrington, ME BL/TR 5-6/165# d7.7																								
1888	Bos N	50	206	26	51	2	3	2	26	6	1	11	.248	.272	.316	85	-4	7	.879	-7	99	49	S-48/2-3	-1.0
1889	Bos N	9	33	8	10	1	0	0	2	4	0	0	.303	.378	.333	94	0	1	.875	-3	83	72	/S-5,3-4	-0.2
	Bal AA	26	106	20	36	4	1	0	17	7	3	6	.340	.397	.396	124	3	12	.784	-8	79	110	S-20/O-6(RF)	-0.4
1890	Bal AA	**38**	139	28	50	6	2	1	20	15	3		.360	.433	.453	154	10	11	.894	-7	88	65	S-38	0.3
1891	Bal AA	103	418	72	116	17	5	0	58	54	4	18	.278	.366	.342	102	2	28	.885	-14	99	43	O-64(RF),S-40	-0.9
Total	4	226	902	154	263	30	11	3	123	86	11	35	.292	.360	.359	109	11	59	.863	-39	89	68	S-151/O-70(RF),3-4,2-3	-2.2
RAY, JOHNNY John Cornelius B 3.1.1957 Chouteau, OK BB/TR 5-11/185# d9.2																								
1981	Pit N	31	102	10	25	11	0	0	6	6-2	0	9	.245	.284	.353	78	-3	0-0	.987	2	109	126	2-31	0.1
1982	Pit N	**162**	647	79	182	30	7	7	63	36-1	1	34	.281	.318	.382	93	-7	16-7	.977	9	102	88	*2-162	1.2
1983	Pit N	151	576	68	163	**38**	7	5	53	35-3	0	26	.283	.323	.399	97	-3	18-9	.983	21	105	111	*2-151	2.8
1984	Pit N	155	555	75	173	**38**	6	6	67	37-2	3	31	.312	.354	.434	122	16	11-6	.984	-3	96	105	*2-149	2.2
1985	Pit N	154	594	67	163	33	3	7	70	46-10	1	24	.274	.325	.375	97	-2	13-9	.976	-19	92	85	*2-151	-1.4
1986	Pit N	155	579	67	174	33	0	7	78	58-10	3	47	.301	.363	.394	107	8	6-9	.993	8	107	98	*2-151	2.3
1987	Pit N	123	472	48	129	19	3	5	54	41-4	0	36	.273	.328	.358	82	-12	4-2	.981	2	100	117	*2-119	-0.4
	Cal A	30	127	16	44	11	0	0	15	3-0	0	10	.346	.359	.433	113	3	0-0	.986	0	106	106	2-29/D	0.4
1988	Cal A★	153	602	75	184	42	7	6	83	36-2	4	38	.306	.345	.429	120	15	4-1	.972	-5	107	89	*2-104,O-40(LF)/D-6	1.3
1989	Cal A	134	530	52	153	16	3	5	62	36-3	0	30	.289	.327	.358	97	-3	6-3	.984	5	101	120	*2-130	0.6
1990	Cal A	105	404	47	112	23	0	5	43	19-2	0	44	.277	.308	.371	91	-5	2-3	.987	15	106	117	*2-100/D	1.2
Total	10	1353	5188	604	1502	294	36	53	594	353-39	12	329	.290	.333	.391	101	7	80-49	.982	36	102	103	*2-1277/O-40(LF),D-8	10.3
RAY, LARRY Larry Dale B 3.11.1958 Madison, IN BL/TR 6-1/195# d9.10																								
1982	Hou N	5	6	0	1	0	0	0	1	0-0	0	4	.167	.143	.167	-7	-1	0-0	1.000	-0	81	0	/O(LF)	-0.1
RAYFORD, FLOYD Floyd Kinnard B 7.27.1957 Memphis, TN BR/TR 5-10/195# d4.17																								
1980	Bal A	8	18	1	4	0	0	0	1	0-0	0	5	.222	.222	.222	22	-2	0-0	.900	-0	106	0	/3-4,2D	-0.2
1982	Bal A	34	53	7	7	0	0	3	5	6-0	0	14	.132	.220	.302	42	-5	0-1	.898	1	114	61	3-27/C-2,D-2	-0.5
1983	StL N	56	104	5	22	4	0	3	14	10-1	0	27	.212	.278	.337	70	-4	1-0	.883	-3	96	83	3-33	-0.8
1984	Bal A	86	250	24	64	14	0	4	27	12-0	3	51	.256	.296	.360	83	-6	0-3	.991	12	87	108	C-66,3-22/1	0.7
1985	Bal A	105	359	55	110	21	1	18	48	10-0	0	69	.306	.324	.521	131	13	3-1	.972	2	107	93	3-78,C-29/D	1.5
1986	Bal A	81	210	15	37	4	0	8	19	15-0	0	50	.176	.231	.310	46	-17	0-0	.912	-1	101	146	3-72,C-10/D	-1.8
1987	Bal A	20	50	5	11	0	0	2	3	2-0	0	9	.220	.250	.340	56	-3	0-0	.980	2	67	107	C-17/3D	-0.1
Total	7	390	1044	112	255	43	1	38	117	55-1	3	225	.244	.283	.397	86	-24	4-5	.931	12	105	105	3-237,C-124/D-6,12	-1.2
RAYMER, FRED Frederick Charles B 11.12.1875 Leavenworth, KS D 6.11.1957 Los Angeles, CA BR/TR 5-11/185# d4.24																								
1901	Chi N	120	463	41	108	14	2	0	43	11	4		.233	.257	.272	56	-27	18	.881	-11	94	59	3-82,S-29/1-5,2-3	-3.5
1904	Bos N	114	419	28	88	12	3	1	27	13	1		.210	.236	.260	55	-23	17	**.958**	5	98	94	*2-114	-1.9
1905	Bos N	137	498	26	105	14	2	0	31	8	6		.211	.232	.247	44	-36	15	.949	-16	94	80	*2-134/1O(LF)	-5.4
Total	3	371	1380	95	301	40	7	1	101	32	11		.218	.242	.259	51	-86	50	.954	-22	96	85	2-251/3-82,S-29,1-6,O(LF)	-10.8
RAYMOND, HARRY Harry H. "Jack" B 2.20.1862 Utica, NY D 3.21.1925 San Diego, CA 5-9/179# d9.9 ▲																								
1888	Lou AA	32	123	8	26	2	0	0	13	1	0		.211	.218	.228	44	-8	7	.884	-2	81	21	3-31/O(RF)	-0.9
1889	Lou AA	130	515	58	123	12	9	0	47	19	3	45	.239	.270	.297	63	-28	19	.886	-3	96	87	*3-129/O(LF)P	-2.4
1890	†Lou AA	123	521	91	135	7	4	2	51	22	3		.259	.293	.299	76	-18	18	.874	-9	88	113	*3-119/S-4	-2.2
1891	Lou AA	14	59	4	12	2	0	0	2	5	2	6	.203	.288	.237	51	-4	3	.898	4	110	179	S-14	0.1
1892	Pit N	12	49	4	4	0	1	0	2	4	0	8	.082	.151	.122	-17	-7	1	.867	-1	95	55	3-12	-0.8
	Was N	4	15	2	1	0	0	0	0	3	0	2	.067	.222	.067	-12	-2	1	.783	0	125	0	/3-4	-0.2
	Year	16	64	6	5	0	1	0	2	7	0	10	.078	.169	.109	-16	-9	2	.838	-1	104	39	3-16	-1.0
Total	5	315	1282	167	301	23	14	2	115	54	8	61	.235	.270	.279	62	-67	49	.878	-11	92	88	3-295/S-18,O-2(1-0-1),P	-6.4
RAYMOND, LOU Louis Anthony (born Louis Anthony Raymondjack) B 12.11.1894 Buffalo, NY D 5.2.1979 Rochester, NY BR/TR 5-10.5/187# d5.2																								
1919	Phi N	1	2	0	1	0	0	0	0	0	0	0	.500	.500	.500	188	0	0	—	-0	0	0	/2	0.0
REACH, AL Alfred James B 5.25.1840 London, England D 1.14.1928 Atlantic City, NJ BL/TL 5-6/155# d5.20 M1 b-Bob																								
1871	Ath NA	26	133	43	47	7	6	0	34	5		6	.353	.377	.496	150	8	2-0	.844	-1	93	119	*2-26	0.4
1872	Ath NA	24	118	21	23	0	0	0	10	4		0	.195	.221	.195	29	-10	1-1	.943	4	207	567	O-20(RF)/1-4	-0.3
1873	Ath NA	16	73	13	16	5	1	0	9	0		0	.219	.219	.315	53	-5	2-0	.875	4	140	85	/2-8,O-8(0-5-3)	0.0
1874	Ath NA	14	55	8	7	2	0	0	2	0		4	.127	.127	.164	-7	-7	0-0	.732	4	277	296	O-14(RF)	-0.2
1875	Ath NA	3	14	4	4	1	0	0	1	0		0	.286	.286	.357	110	0	2-1	1.000	-1	0	0	/O-2(RF),2	-0.1
Total	5 NA	83	393	89	97	15	7	0	56	9		10	.247	.264	.321	73	-14	7-2	.000	10	235	342	/O-44(0-5-39),2-35,1-4	-0.2
REACH, BOB Robert B 8.28.1843 Williamsburg, NY D 5.19.1922 Springfield, MA 5-5/155# d4.23 b-Al																								
1872	Oly NA	2	8	1	2	0	0	0	0	0		0	.250	.250	.250	57	0	0-0	.727	-1	93	0	/S-2	-0.1
1873	Was NA	1	5	1	1	0	0	0	0	0		0	.200	.200	.200	20	0	0-0	.500	-1	67	0	/S	-0.1
Total	2 NA	3	13	2	3	0	0	0	0	0		0	.231	.231	.231	42	0	0-0	.000	-2	83	0	/S-3	-0.2
READY, RANDY Randy Max B 1.8.1960 Fremont, CA BR/TR 5-11/180# d9.4 OF Total (167-LF 6-RF)																								
1983	Mil A	12	37	8	15	3	2	1	6	6-1	0	3	.405	.488	.676	234	7	0-1	1.000	0	91	112	/3-4,D-6	0.7
1984	Mil A	37	123	13	23	6	1	3	13	14-0	0	18	.187	.270	.325	66	-6	0-0	.946	5	121	63	3-36	-0.1
1985	Mil A	48	181	29	48	9	5	1	21	14-0	1	23	.265	.318	.387	93	-2	0-0	.989	-1	107	205	O-37(36-0-3)/3-7,2-3,D-2	-0.5
1986	Mil A	23	79	8	15	4	0	1	4	9-0	0	9	.190	.273	.278	49	-6	2-0	.950	-1	92	0	O-11(LF)/2-7,3-3,D	-0.6
	SD N	1	3	0	0	0	0	0	0	0-0	0	1	.000	.000	.000	-99	-1	0-0	.667	-0	129	0	/3	-0.1
1987	SD N	124	350	69	108	26	6	12	54	67-2	3	44	.309	.423	.520	154	31	7-3	.912	9	117	153	3-52,2-51,O-16(LF)	4.0
1988	SD N	114	331	43	88	16	2	7	39	39-1	3	38	.266	.346	.390	114	7	6-2	.952	-2	99	150	3-57,2-26,O-16(15-0-1)	0.6
1989	SD N	28	67	4	17	2	1	0	5	11-0	0	6	.254	.354	.313	94	0	0-0	.963	3	121	172	3-18/2-2,O(LF)	0.4
	Phi N	72	187	33	50	11	1	8	21	31-0	2	31	.267	.372	.465	140	11	4-3	.962	-3	81	244	O-36(LF),3-14/2-7	0.8

Year	Tm Lg	G	AB	R	H	2B	3B	HR	RBI	BB-IB	HP	SO	AVG	OBP	SLG	AOPS	ABR	SB-CS	FA	FR	Rng	Thr	G at Pos	BFW
	Year	100	254	37	67	13	2	8	26	42-0	2	37	.264	.368	.425	127	11	4-3	.962	1	81	243	O-37(LF),3-32/2-9	1.2
1990	Phi N	101	217	26	53	9	1	1	26	29-0	1	35	.244	.332	.309	79	-5	3-2	1.000	4	67	117	O-30(LF),2-28	-0.1
1991	Phi N	76	205	32	51	10	1	1	20	47-3	1	25	.249	.385	.322	104	4	2-1	.989	-3	93	72	2-66	0.3
1992	†Oak A	61	125	17	25	2	0	3	17	25-1	0	23	.200	.329	.288	80	-3	1-0	1.000	2	102	96	O-24(22-0-2),D-24/3-7,1-4,2-4	-0.2
1993	Mon N	40	134	22	34	8	1	1	10	23-0	1	8	.254	.367	.351	89	-1	2-1	.968	-0	103	113	2-28,1-13/3-3	-0.1
1994	Phi N	17	42	5	16	1	0	1	3	8-0	0	6	.381	.480	.476	147	4	0-1	1.000	-4	83	43	2-11/3	0.0
1995	Phi N	23	29	3	4	0	0	0	0	3-0	0	6	.138	.219	.138	-3	-4	0-1	.967	-2	52	143	/1-3,2	-0.7
Total	13	777	2110	312	547	107	21	40	239	326-8	12	276	.259	.359	.387	108	36	27-15	.979	8	100	92	2-234,3-203,O-171L/D-33,1-20	4.4
REAMS, LEROY Leroy B 8.11.1943 Pine Bluff, AR BL/TR 6-2/175# d5.7																								
1969	Phi N	1	1	0	0	0	0	0	0	0-0	0	1	.000	.000	.000	-99	0	0-0	—	0			H	0.0
REARDON, PHIL Philip Michael B 10.3.1883 Brooklyn, NY D 9.28.1920 Brooklyn, NY BR/TR d9.19																								
1906	Bro N	5	14	0	1	0	0	0	0	0	1		.071	.133	.071	-39	-2	0	.917	1	176	713	/O-4(0-1-3)	-0.2
REBEL, ART Arthur Anthony B 3.4.1915 Cincinnati, OH BL/TL 5-8/180# d4.19																								
1938	Phi N	7	9	2	2	0	0	0	1	1	0	1	.222	.300	.222	47	-1	0	1.000	-0	103	0	/O-3(0-1-2)	-0.1
1945	StL N	26	72	12	25	4	0	0	5	6	0	4	.347	.397	.403	120	2	1	.976	3	110	259	O-18(RF)	0.4
Total	2	33	81	14	27	4	0	0	6	7	0	5	.333	.386	.383	112	1	1	.978	2	109	239	/O-21(0-1-20)	0.3
REBOULET, JEFF Jeffrey Allen B 4.30.1964 Dayton, OH BR/TR 6/169# d5.12 OF Total (7-LF 3-CF 15-RF)																								
1992	Min A	73	137	15	26	7	1	1	16	23-0	1	26	.190	.311	.277	64	-6	3-2	.971	16	126	131	S-36,3-22,2-13/O-7(1-1-5),D	1.2
1993	Min A	109	240	33	62	8	0	1	15	35-0	2	37	.258	.356	.304	79	-5	5-5	.982	10	99	91	S-62,3-35,2-11/O-3(1-2-0),D	0.7
1994	Min A	74	189	28	49	11	1	3	23	18-0	1	23	.259	.327	.376	81	-5	0-0	.963	-4	101	53	S-42,2-14,1-10/3-6,O-4(1-0-3),D	-0.7
1995	Min A	87	216	39	63	11	0	4	23	27-0	1	34	.292	.373	.398	101	1	1-2	.993	9	101	113	S-39,3-22,1-17,2-15/C	1.1
1996	Min A	107	234	20	52	9	0	0	23	25-1	1	34	.222	.298	.261	43	-20	4-2	.987	-11	72	102	S-37,3-36,2-22,1-13/O-7(2-0-6),D-3	-2.7
1997	†Bal A	99	228	26	54	9	0	4	27	23-0	1	44	.237	.307	.329	69	-10	3-0	.977	-7	98	99	2-63,S-22,3-12/O(RF)D	-1.3
1998	Bal A	79	126	20	31	6	0	1	8	19-0	2	34	.246	.351	.317	78	-3	0-1	.974	0	95	117	2-28,S-28,3-23	-0.1
1999	Bal A	99	154	25	25	4	0	0	4	33-0	2	29	.162	.317	.188	35	-14	1-0	.987	11	136	106	3-56,2-36,S-10	-0.1
2000	KC A	66	182	29	44	7	0	0	14	23-0	0	32	.242	.325	.280	54	-12	3-1	.982	5	114	122	2-50,3-11/S-5,D	-0.4
2001	LA N	94	214	35	57	15	2	3	22	33-1	1	48	.266	.367	.397	105	3	0-1	.961	-6	83	135	S-56,2-22/3-7,O-2(LF)	0.1
2002	LA N	38	48	3	10	3	0	0	2	6-0	0	13	.208	.291	.271	57	-3	0-0	.933	-1	148	59	2-11/S-5,3-3,D	-0.4
2003	Pit N	93	261	37	63	10	2	3	25	27-3	4	47	.241	.321	.330	69	-12	2-1	.989	6	110	114	2-76/3-7	-0.2
Total	12	1018	2229	310	536	100	6	20	202	292-5	16	401	.240	.332	.318	71	-86	22-15	.984	29	105	110	2-361,S-342,3-240/1-40,O-24R,DC	-2.8
RECCIUS, JOHN John B 10.29.1859 Louisville, KY D 9.1.1930 Louisville, KY 5-6.5/?# d5.2 b-Phil ▲																								
1882	Lou AA	74	266	46	63	12	3	1		23			.237	.298	.316	113	6		.857	-3	104	**222**	*O-65(0-55-11),P-13	0.1
1883	Lou AA	18	63	10	9	2	0	0	3	7			.143	.229	.175	34	-4		.833	-1	31	264	O-18(0-15-4)/P	-0.4
Total	2	92	329	56	72	14	3	1	<u>3</u>	30			.219	.284	.289	98	2		.851	-3	88	231	/O-83(0-70-15),P-14	-0.3
RECCIUS, PHIL Phillip B 6.7.1862 Louisville, KY D 2.15.1903 Louisville, KY 5-9/163# d9.25 b-John ▲																								
1882	Lou AA	4	15	0	2	0	0	0		0			.133	.133	.133	-10	-2		.778	-0	104	0	/O-4(CF)	-0.2
1883	Lou AA	1	3	1	1	1	0	0		0			.333	.333	.667	231	0		1.000	-0	0	0	/O(RF)	0.0
1884	Lou AA	73	263	23	63	9	2	3	21	5	5		.240	.267	.323	96	-1		.845	-3	102	91	3-51,P-18,S-10	-0.2
1885	Lou AA	102	402	57	97	8	10	1	38	13	1		.241	.267	.318	84	-8		.829	-1	99	**130**	*3-97/P-7	-0.7
1886	Lou AA	5	13	4	4	1	1	0	2	3	1		.308	.471	.538	204	2	0	.889	1	278	0	/O-5(2-0-3),P	0.2
1887	Lou AA	11	37	9	9	2	0	0	4	8	1		.243	.391	.297	92	0	3	.926	1	102	0	O-10(2-0-8)/S	0.1
	Cle AA	62	229	23	47	6	3	0	29	24	5		.205	.295	.258	56	-13	9	.877	10	113	165	3-62/P	-0.1
	Year	73	266	32	56	8	3	0	33	32	6		.211	.309	.263	62	-12	12	.877	11	113	165	3-62,O-10(2-0-8)/SP	0.0
1888	Lou AA	2	9	0	2	1	0	0	4	1	0		.222	.300	.333	105	0	0	.750	-1	78	0	/3-2	-0.1
1890	Roc AA	1	4	0	0	0	0	0	1	0	0		.000	.000	.000	-99	-1	0	—	-0	0	0	/O(RF)	-0.1
Total	8	261	975	117	225	28	16	4	<u>99</u>	54	13		.231	.280	.305	81	-23	12	.848	6	104	130	3-212/P-27,O-21(4-4-13),S-11	-1.1
REDER, JOHNNY John Anthony B 9.24.1909 Lublin, Poland D 4.12.1990 Fall River, MA BR/TR 6/184# d4.16																								
1932	Bos A	17	37	4	5	1	0	0	3	6	0	6	.135	.256	.162	11	-5	0-0	.990	0	152	141	1-10/3	-0.5
REDFERN, BUCK George Howard B 4.7.1902 Asheville, NC D 9.8.1964 Asheville, NC BR/TR 5-11/165# d4.11																								
1928	Chi A	86	261	22	61	6	3	0	35	12	0	19	.234	.267	.280	44	-22	8-4	.953	-2	108	83	2-45,S-33/3	-1.8
1929	Chi A	21	46	0	6	0	0	0	3	3	0	3	.130	.184	.130	-18	-8	1-1	.967	-3	82	29	2-11/3-5,S-4	-1.1
Total	2	107	307	22	67	6	3	0	38	15	0	22	.218	.255	.257	35	-30	9-5	.955	-5	105	77	/2-56,S-37,3-6	-2.9
REDFIELD, JOE Joseph Randall B 1.14.1961 Doylestown, PA BR/TR 6-2/190# d6.4																								
1988	Cal A	1	2	0	0	0	0	0	0	0-0	0	0	.000	.000	.000	-99	-1	0-0	1.000	-0	61	614	/3	-0.1
1991	Pit N	11	18	1	2	0	0	0	0	4-0	0	1	.111	.273	.111	12	-2	0-1	.917	-1	64	373	/3-9	-0.4
Total	2	12	20	1	2	0	0	0	0	4-0	0	1	.100	.250	.100	2	-3	0-1	.923	-1	64	409	/3-10	-0.5
REDMAN, TIKE Julian Jawonn B 3.10.1977 Tuscaloosa, AL BL/TL 5-11/166# d6.30																								
2000	Pit N	9	18	2	6	1	0	1	1	1-0	0	7	.333	.368	.556	130	1	1-0	1.000	2	169	442	/O-6(2-0-4)	0.2
2001	Pit N	37	125	8	28	4	1	1	4	4-0	0	25	.224	.246	.296	39	-12	3-5	.980	6	126	285	O-35(0-28-7)	-0.7
2003	Pit N	56	230	36	76	16	5	3	19	14-0	2	18	.330	.374	.483	119	6	7-3	.985	-2	100	34	O-54(CF)	0.5
Total	3	102	373	46	110	21	6	5	24	19-0	2	50	.295	.332	.424	93	-5	11-8	.983	6	112	139	/O-95(2-82-11)	0.0
REDMAN, PRENTICE Prentice Montezz B 8.23.1979 Tuscaloosa, AL BR/TR 6-3/180# d8.24																								
2003	NY N	15	24	3	3	1	0	1	2	1-0	1	9	.125	.192	.292	25	-3	2-0	1.000	-0	97	0	O-10(0-9-2)	-0.3
REDMON, GLENN Glenn Vincent B 1.11.1948 Detroit, MI BR/TR 5-11/180# d9.8																								
1974	SF N	7	17	0	4	3	0	0	4	1-0	0	3	.235	.278	.412	87	0	0-0	.955	-1	79	79	/2-4	-0.1
REDMON, BILLY William T. B Brooklyn, NY BL/TL d5.4																								
1875	RS NA	**19**	82	12	16	2	0	0	1	2		7	.195	.214	.220	56	-3	3-0	.837	5	130	0	S-19/C-2	0.2
1877	Cin N	3	12	1	3	1	0	0	3	1		1	.250	.308	.333	115	0		.833	1	122	0	/S-3	0.1
1878	Mil N	48	187	16	43	8	0	0	21	8		13	.230	.262	.273	71	-6		.785	-16	83	57	S-39/O-7(0-4-3),3-3,C	-1.9
Total	2	51	199	17	46	9	0	0	24	9		14	.231	.264	.276	73	-6		.791	-16	87	52	/S-42,O-7(0-4-3),3-3,C	-1.8
REDMOND, HARRY Harry John B 9.13.1887 Cleveland, OH D 7.10.1960 Cleveland, OH BR/TR 5-8/170# d9.7																								
1909	Bro N	6	19	3	0	0	0	0	1	0	0		.000	.000	.000	-99	-5	0	.892	2	134	99	/2-5	-0.3
REDMOND, WAYNE Howard Wayne B 11.25.1945 Athens, AL BR/TR 5-10/165# d9.7																								
1965	Det A	4	4	1	0	0	0	0	0	1-0	0	1	.000	.200	.000	-38	-1	0-0	1.000	0	112	0	/O-2(1-1-0)	-0.1
1969	Det A	5	3	0	0	0	0	0	0	0-0	0	2	.000	.000	.000	-96	-1	0-0	—	0			H	-0.1
Total	2	9	7	1	0	0	0	0	0	1-0	0	3	.000	.125	.000	-60	-2	0-0	1.000	0	112	0	/O-2(1-1-0)	-0.2
REDMOND, JACK John McKittrick "Red" (born Jackson Mc Kittrick Redmond) B 9.3.1910 Florence, AZ D 7.27.1968 Garland, TX BL/TR 5-11/185# d4.22																								
1935	Was A	22	34	8	6	1	0	1	7	3	0	1	.176	.243	.294	40	-3	0-0	.978	0	*88*	*82*	C-15	-0.2
REDMOND, MIKE Michael Patrick B 5.5.1971 Seattle, WA BR/TR 6-1/185# d5.31																								
1998	Fla N	37	118	10	39	9	0	2	12	5-2	2	16	.331	.368	.458	122	4	0-0	.992	-3	95	171	C-37	0.3
1999	Fla N	84	242	22	73	9	0	1	27	26-2	5	34	.302	.381	.351	92	-2	0-0	.992	2	122	123	C-82	0.5
2000	Fla N	87	210	17	53	8	1	0	15	13-3	8	19	.252	.316	.300	61	-13	0-0	.996	2	88	124	C-85	-0.5
2001	Fla N	48	141	19	44	4	0	4	14	13-4	2	13	.312	.376	.426	111	3	0-0	.994	1	104	123	C-47	0.6
2002	Fla N	89	256	19	78	15	0	2	28	21-8	8	34	.305	.372	.387	109	3	0-2	.993	5	95	162	C-80/1-2	1.2
2003	†Fla N	59	125	12	30	7	1	0	11	7-0	5	16	.240	.302	.312	65	-7	0-0	.995	-5	47	85	C-37/13	-0.9
Total	6	404	1092	99	317	52	2	9	107	85-19	30	132	.290	.355	.366	92	-12	0-2	.993	4	97	134	C-368/1-3,3	1.2
REDUS, GARY Gary Eugene B 11.1.1956 Athens, AL BR/TR 6-1/185# d9.7																								
1982	Cin N	20	83	12	18	3	2	1	7	5-0	0	21	.217	.258	.337	65	-4	11-2	.970	-1	75	190	O-20(LF)	-0.4
1983	Cin N	125	453	90	112	20	9	17	51	71-4	3	111	.247	.352	.444	115	10	39-14	.972	4	102	123	*O-120(LF)	1.3
1984	Cin N	123	394	69	100	21	3	7	22	52-3	1	71	.254	.338	.376	97	0	48-11	.967	-1	97	80	*O-114(93-24-1)	0.2
1985	Cin N	101	246	51	62	14	4	6	28	44-2	1	52	.252	.366	.415	113	6	48-12	.986	1	106	71	O-85(63-37-0)	1.2

Year	Tm Lg	G	AB	R	H	2B	3B	HR	RBI	BB-IB	HP	SO	AVG	OBP	SLG	AOPS	ABR	SB-CS	FA	FR	Rng	Thr	G at Pos	BFW
1986	Phi N	90	340	62	84	22	4	11	33	47-4	3	78	.247	.343	.432	109	5	25-7	.980	6	110	132	O-89(LF)	1.0
1987	Chi A	130	475	78	112	26	6	12	48	69-0	0	90	.236	.328	.392	89	-7	52-11	.979	3	98	152	*O-123(97-19-20)/D-4	-0.1
1988	Chi A	77	262	42	69	10	4	6	34	33-1	2	52	.263	.342	.401	110	4	26-2	.987	0	92	182	O-68(54-16-2)/D-2	0.8
	Pit N	30	71	12	14	2	0	2	4	15-0	1	19	.197	.341	.310	90	0	5-2	.957	2	124	206	O-19(11-1-7)	0.2
1989	Pit N	98	279	42	79	18	7	6	33	40-3	1	51	.283	.372	.462	143	16	25-6	.987	2	123	93	1-72,O-16(2-1-12)	1.8
1990	†Pit N	96	227	32	56	15	3	6	23	33-0	2	38	.247	.341	.419	114	5	11-5	.988	0	102	94	1-72/O-7(4-1-2)	0.2
1991	†Pit N	98	252	45	62	12	2	7	24	28-2	3	39	.246	.324	.393	104	1	17-3	.990	-3	89	130	1-47,O-33(11-12-11)	-0.2
1992	†Pit N	76	176	26	45	7	3	3	12	17-0	0	25	.256	.321	.381	99	-1	11-4	1.000	-3	79	72	1-36,O-15(2-1-12)	-0.5
1993	Tex A	77	222	28	64	12	4	6	31	23-1	0	35	.288	.351	.459	122	6	4-4	.981	-2	96	87	O-61(5-17-46)/1-5,2D	0.2
1994	Tex A	18	33	2	9	1	0	0	2	4-1	0	6	.273	.351	.303	71	-1	0-0	1.000	0	108	0	/O-7(0-3-4),1-5	-0.2
Total	13	1159	3513	591	886	183	51	90	352	481-21	17	688	.252	.342	.410	107	40	322-83	.974	9	100	124	0-777(571-132-117),1-237/D-7,2	5.5
REECE, BOB Robert Scott B 1.5.1951 Sacramento, CA BR/TR 6-1/190# d4.22																								
1978	Mon N	9	11	2	2	1	0	0	3	0-0	0	4	.182	.182	.273	26	-1	0-0	.947	-1	94	0	/C-9	-0.2
REED, DARREN Darren A. Douglas B 10.16.1965 Ojai, CA BR/TR 6-1/190# d5.1																								
1990	NY N	26	39	5	8	4	1	1	2	3-0	0	11	.205	.262	.436	89	-1	1-0	.955	0	100	188	O-14(2-7-6)	-0.1
1992	Mon N	42	81	10	14	2	0	5	10	6-2	1	23	.173	.239	.383	74	-3	0-0	1.000	-0	95	81	O-29(8-0-21)	-0.5
	Min A	14	33	2	6	2	0	0	4	2-0	0	11	.182	.216	.242	31	-3	0-0	1.000	-0	81	175	O-13(10-0-4)/D	-0.4
Total	2	82	153	17	28	8	1	6	16	11-2	1	45	.183	.240	.366	68	-7	1-0	.987	-0	93	129	/O-56(20-7-31),D	-1.0
REED, HUGH Hugh B 1837 Chicago, IL D 11.3.1883 Chicago, IL d8.26																								
1874	Bal NA	1	4	0	0	0	0	0	0	0		0	.000	.000	.000	-99	-1	0-0	1.000	-0	0	0	/O(RF)	-0.1
REED, JEFF Jeffrey Scott B 11.12.1962 Joliet, IL BL/TR 6-2/190# d4.5																								
1984	Min A	18	21	3	3	3	0	0	1	2-0	0	6	.143	.217	.286	36	-2	0-0	.977	-1	61	73	C-18	-0.2
1985	Min A	7	10	2	2	0	0	0	0	0-0	0	3	.200	.200	.200	9	-1	0-0	1.000	-0	89	116	/C-7	-0.1
1986	Min A	68	165	13	39	6	1	2	9	16-0	1	19	.236	.308	.321	70	-7	1-0	.994	2	83	67	C-64	-0.3
1987	Mon N	75	207	15	44	11	0	1	21	12-1	1	20	.213	.254	.280	42	-17	0-1	.970	-10	85	85	C-74	-2.5
1988	Mon N	43	123	10	27	3	2	0	9	13-1	0	22	.220	.292	.276	62	-6	1-0	.995	-1	72	106	C-39	-0.5
	Cin N	49	142	10	33	6	0	1	7	15-0	0	19	.232	.306	.296	71	-5	0-0	.993	4	112	101	C-49	0.1
	Year	92	265	20	60	9	2	1	16	28-1	0	41	.226	.299	.287	66	-11	1-0	.994	3	94	103	C-88	-0.4
1989	Cin N	102	287	16	64	11	0	3	23	34-5	2	46	.223	.306	.293	71	-10	0-0	.988	-9	81	**149**	C-99	-1.5
1990	†Cin N	72	175	12	44	8	1	3	16	24-5	0	26	.251	.340	.360	89	-2	0-0	.987	-4	74	74	C-70	-0.3
1991	Cin N	91	270	20	72	15	2	3	31	23-3	1	38	.267	.321	.370	92	-3	0-1	.991	3	116	86	C-89	0.5
1992	Cin N	15	25	2	4	0	0	0	2	1-1	0	4	.160	.192	.160	1	-3	0-0	1.000	-0	85	62	/C-6	-0.4
1993	SF N	66	119	10	31	3	0	6	12	16-4	0	22	.261	.346	.437	112	2	0-1	1.000	4	127	130	C-37	0.7
1994	SF N	50	103	11	18	3	0	1	7	11-4	0	21	.175	.254	.233	30	-11	0-0	.993	0	89	56	C-33	-0.9
1995	SF N	66	113	12	30	2	0	0	9	20-3	0	17	.265	.376	.283	79	-2	0-0	.995	5	134	142	C-42	0.4
1996	Col N	116	341	34	97	20	1	8	37	43-8	2	65	.284	.365	.419	87	-5	2-2	.982	-10	95	107	*C-111	-0.9
1997	Col N	90	256	43	76	10	0	17	47	35-1	2	55	.297	.386	.535	112	5	2-1	.987	10	111	107	C-78	1.9
1998	Col N	113	259	43	75	17	1	9	39	37-4	1	57	.290	.377	.467	100	1	0-0	.986	3	105	108	C-99	0.9
1999	Col N	46	106	11	27	5	0	2	11	17-1	1	24	.255	.360	.358	66	-5	0-1	.983	-7	50	146	C-36	-1.0
	Chi N	57	150	18	39	11	2	1	17	28-0	2	34	.260	.381	.380	96	0	1-1	.987	-2	86	92	C-49/3D	0.1
	Year	103	256	29	66	16	2	3	28	45-1	3	58	.258	.373	.371	81	-6	1-2	.985	-9	72	113	C-85/3D	-0.9
2000	Chi N	90	229	26	49	10	0	4	25	44-2	1	68	.214	.342	.310	68	-10	0-1	.990	-6	131	87	C-71	-1.2
Total	17	1234	3101	311	774	144	10	61	323	391-43	14	566	.250	.334	.361	81	-81	7-9	.988	-20	97	102	*C-1071/D3	-5.2
REED, JODY Jody Eric B 7.26.1962 Tampa, FL BR/TR 5-9/165# d9.12																								
1987	Bos A	9	30	4	9	1	1	0	8	4-0	0	0	.300	.382	.400	105	0	1-1	1.000	3	97	195	/S-4,2-2,3	0.3
1988	†Bos A	109	338	60	99	23	1	1	28	45-1	4	21	.293	.380	.376	109	7	1-3	.971	8	98	92	S-94,2-11/3-4,D	2.0
1989	Bos A	146	524	76	151	42	2	3	40	73-0	4	44	.288	.376	.393	111	12	4-5	.967	3	94	85	S-77,2-70/3-4,O(RF)D	2.2
1990	†Bos A	155	598	70	173	**45**	0	5	51	75-4	4	65	.289	.371	.390	108	11	4-4	.990	7	**106**	103	*2-119,S-50/D	2.4
1991	Bos A	153	618	87	175	42	2	5	60	60-2	4	53	.283	.349	.382	98	0	6-5	.982	11	100	110	*2-152/S-6	1.5
1992	Bos A	143	550	64	136	27	1	3	40	62-2	0	44	.247	.321	.316	75	-17	7-8	.982	**30**	**115**	116	*2-142/D	1.6
1993	LA N	132	445	48	123	21	2	2	31	38-10	1	40	.276	.333	.346	88	-7	1-3	**.993**	10	102	96	*2-132	0.8
1994	Mil A	108	399	48	108	22	0	2	37	57-1	2	34	.271	.362	.341	80	-10	5-4	**.995**	7	109	106	*2-106	0.2
1995	SD N	131	445	58	114	18	1	4	40	59-1	5	38	.256	.348	.328	83	-9	6-4	.994	18	100	102	*2-130/S-5	1.4
1996	†SD N	146	495	45	121	20	0	2	49	59-8	3	53	.244	.325	.297	71	-19	2-5	.987	-5	99	103	*2-145	-1.8
1997	Det A	52	112	6	22	2	0	0	8	10-0	3	15	.196	.278	.214	32	-11	3-2	.987	8	131	102	2-41/D-5	-0.2
Total	11	1284	4554	566	1231	263	10	27	392	542-29	30	407	.270	.349	.350	90	-43	40-44	.988	100	105	105	*2-1050,S-236/D-9,3-9,O(RF)	10.4
REED, JACK John Burwell B 2.2.1933 Silver City, MS BR/TR 6/185# d4.23																								
1961	†NY A	28	13	4	2	0	0	0	1	1-0	0	1	.154	.214	.154	0	-2	0-0	.933	0	129	0	O-27(12-14-1)	-0.2
1962	NY A	88	43	17	13	2	1	1	4	4-1	0	7	.302	.362	.465	125	1	2-1	.941	1	136	0	O-75(20-39-16)	0.2
1963	NY A	106	73	18	15	3	1	0	1	9-0	0	14	.205	.293	.274	60	-4	5-1	1.000	2	119	101	O-89(14-30-46)	-0.3
Total	3	222	129	39	30	5	2	1	6	14-1	0	22	.233	.308	.326	76	-5	7-2	.972	4	125	60	O-191(46-83-63)	-0.3
REED, MILT Milton D. B 7.4.1890 Atlanta, GA D 7.27.1938 Atlanta, GA BL/TR 5-9.5/150# d9.9																								
1911	StL N	1	1	0	0	0	0	0	0	0	0	0	.000	.000	.000	-99	0	0	—	0			H	0.0
1913	Phi N	13	24	4	6	1	0	0	0	1	0	5	.250	.280	.292	61	-1	1	.900	-3	85	0	/S-9,2-3	-0.3
1914	Phi N	44	107	10	22	2	1	0	2	10	1	13	.206	.280	.243	52	-6	4	.887	-10	76	32	S-22,2-11/3	-1.7
1915	Bro F	10	31	2	9	1	1	0	8	2	1	0	.290	.353	.387	109	0	2	.864	-4	76	56	S-10	-0.4
Total	4	68	163	16	37	4	2	0	10	13	2	18	.227	.292	.276	63	-7	7	.880	-17	77	37	/S-41,2-14,3	-2.4
REED, TED Ralph Edwin B 10.18.1890 Beaver, PA D 2.16.1959 Beaver, PA BR/TR 5-11/190# d9.10																								
1915	New F	20	77	5	20	1	2	0	4	2	1	7	.260	.287	.325	76	-4	1	.863	-4	77	127	3-20	-0.8
REED, BILLY William Joseph B 11.12.1922 Shawano, WI BL/TR 5-10.5/175# d4.15																								
1952	Bos N	15	52	4	13	0	0	0	0	0	1	5	.250	.264	.250	45	-4	0-0	.931	-4	90	70	2-14	-0.8
REEDER, ICICLE Julius Edward B 1858 Cincinnati, OH D 1.15.1913 Cincinnati, OH BR 6/?# d6.24																								
1884	Cin AA	3	14	0	2	0	0	0		0	0		.143	.143	.143	-6	-2		1.000	-0	0	0	/O-3(LF)	-0.2
	Was U	3	12	0	2	0	0	0		0			.167	.167	.167	1	-2		.500	-1	0	0	/O-3(0-1-2)	-0.3
Total	1	6	26	0	4	0	0	0		0			.154	.154	.154	-3	-4		.714	-1	0	0	/O-6(3-1-2)	-0.5
REEDER, NICK Nicholas (born Nicholas Herchenroeder) B 3.22.1867 Louisville, KY D 9.26.1894 Louisville, KY BR/TR 5-9/189# d4.11																								
1891	Lou AA	1	2	0	0	0	0	0	0	0	0	1	.000	.000	.000	-99	-1	0	1.000	0	131	0	/3	0.0
REESE, RANDY Andrew Jackson B 2.7.1904 Tupelo, MS D 1.10.1966 Tupelo, MS BR/TR 5-11/180# d4.15 OF Total (81-LF 26-CF 15-RF)																								
1927	NY N	97	355	43	94	14	2	4	21	13	4	52	.265	.298	.349	73	-14	5	.912	-1	107	141	3-64,O-16(7-0-9)/1	-1.3
1928	NY N	109	406	61	125	18	4	6	44	13	1	24	.308	.331	.416	94	-5	7	.941	-4	89	65	O-64(59-2-4),2-26/1-6,S-6,3-6	-1.2
1929	NY N	58	209	36	55	11	3	0	21	15	1	19	.263	.316	.344	64	-12	8	.960	2	110	96	2-44/O-8(7-1-0),3-4	-0.8
1930	NY N	67	172	26	47	4	2	4	25	10	0	12	.273	.313	.390	70	-9	1	.957	-4	86	39	O-32(8-23-2),3-10/1	-1.3
Total	4	331	1142	166	321	47	11	14	111	51	6	107	.281	.315	.378	78	-40	21	.954	-7	88	60	0-120L/3-84,2-70,1-8,S-6	-4.6
REESE, POKEY Calvin B 6.10.1973 Columbia, SC BR/TR 5-11/180# d4.1																								
1997	Cin N	128	397	48	87	15	0	4	26	31-2	5	82	.219	.284	.287	49	-30	25-7	.966	-6	90	99	*S-110/2-8,3-8	-2.4
1998	Cin N	59	133	20	34	2	2	1	16	14-1	0	28	.256	.322	.323	71	-6	3-2	.985	-3	96	165	3-32,S-18/2-3	-0.7
1999	Cin N	149	585	85	167	37	5	10	52	35-3	6	81	.285	.330	.417	86	-14	38-7	.991	17	**107**	111	*2-146,S-16	1.6
2000	Cin N	135	518	76	132	20	6	12	46	45-5	6	86	.255	.319	.386	76	-20	29-3	.980	14	110	107	*2-133	0.5
2001	Cin N	133	428	50	96	20	2	9	40	34-4	3	82	.224	.284	.343	59	-27	25-4	.972	5	111	75	S-78,2-51	-1.0
2002	Pit N	119	421	46	111	25	0	4	50	41-4	3	81	.264	.330	.352	83	-11	12-1	.988	**28**	**117**	108	*2-117	2.4
2003	Pit N	37	107	9	23	2	0	1	12	9-1	0	31	.215	.271	.262	40	-10	6-0	.969	11	133	117	2-33	0.4
Total	7	760	2589	334	650	121	15	41	242	209-20	23	471	.251	.310	.357	71	-118	138-24	.984	66	113	108	2-491,S-222/3-40	0.8
REESE, PEE WEE Harold Henry B 7.23.1918 Ekron, KY D 8.14.1999 Louisville, KY BR/TR 5-9/175# d4.23 Mil 1943-45 C1 HF1984																								
1940	Bro N	84	312	58	85	8	4	5	28	45	1	42	.272	.366	.372	98	0	15	.960	-13	87	87	S-83	-0.6

Year	Tm Lg	G	AB	R	H	2B	3B	HR	RBI	BB-IB	HP	SO	AVG	OBP	SLG	AOPS	ABR	SB-CS	FA	FR	Rng	Thr	G at Pos	BFW
1941	†Bro N	152	595	76	136	23	5	2	46	68	3	56	.229	.311	.294	68	-24	10	.946	8	102	97	*S-151	-0.5
1942	Bro N★	151	564	87	144	24	5	3	53	82	0	55	.255	.350	.332	98	2	15	.959	18	103	**122**	*S-151	3.3
1946	Bro N✳	152	542	79	154	16	10	5	60	87	1	71	.284	.384	.378	116	14	10	.966	-4	97	109	*S-152	2.0
1947	†Bro N★	142	476	81	135	24	4	12	73	**104**	2	67	.284	.414	.426	119	19	7	.966	-0	99	115	*S-142	2.7
1948	Bro N★	151	566	96	155	31	4	9	75	79	0	63	.274	.363	.390	100	3	25	.962	6	97	108	*S-149	1.8
1949	†Bro N★	155	617	**132**	172	27	3	16	73	116	4	59	.279	.396	.410	112	16	26	**.977**	1	92	105	*S-155	2.6
1950	Bro N★	141	531	97	138	21	5	11	52	91	1	62	.260	.369	.380	96	-1	17	.963	2	94	105	*S-134/3-7	0.9
1951	Bro N★	154	616	94	176	20	8	10	84	81	2	57	.286	.371	.393	103	5	20-14	.953	-7	92	113	*S-154	0.7
1952	†Bro N★	149	559	94	152	18	8	6	58	86	0	59	.272	.369	.365	103	5	**30**-5	.969	-12	90	99	*S-145	0.7
1953	†Bro N★	140	524	108	142	25	7	13	61	82	4	61	.271	.374	.420	104	6	22-6	.966	1	94	105	*S-135	2.0
1954	Bro N☆	141	554	98	171	35	8	10	69	90	3	62	.309	.404	.455	121	21	8-5	.965	-3	98	81	*S-140	2.9
1955	†Bro N	145	553	99	156	29	4	10	61	78-1	3	60	.282	.371	.403	103	6	8-7	.965	-11	94	101	*S-142	0.6
1956	†Bro N	147	572	85	147	19	2	9	46	56-1	1	69	.257	.322	.344	74	-20	13-4	.965	-2	94	103	*S-136,3-12	-0.9
1957	Bro N	103	330	33	74	3	1	1	29	39-1	1	32	.224	.306	.248	47	-24	5-2	.943	7	120	42	3-75,S-23	-1.5
1958	LA N	59	147	21	33	7	2	4	17	26-0	0	15	.224	.337	.381	88	-2	1-2	.929	-3	95	109	S-22,3-21	-0.4
Total	16	2166	8058	1338	2170	330	80	126	885	1210-3	26	890	.269	.366	.377	98	26	232-45	.962	-12	95	104	*S-2014,3-115	16.3

REESE, JIMMIE James Herman (born James Herman Soloman) B 10.1.1901 New York, NY D 7.13.1994 Santa Ana, CA BL/TR 5-11.5/165# d4.19 C22

Year	Tm Lg	G	AB	R	H	2B	3B	HR	RBI	BB-IB	HP	SO	AVG	OBP	SLG	AOPS	ABR	SB-CS	FA	FR	Rng	Thr	G at Pos	BFW
1930	NY A	77	188	44	65	14	2	3	18	11	0	8	.346	.382	.489	125	7	1-1	.974	-5	86	115	2-48/3-5	0.3
1931	NY A	65	245	41	59	10	2	3	26	17	1	10	.241	.293	.335	68	-12	2-3	.972	2	90	125	2-61	-0.7
1932	StL N	90	309	38	82	15	0	2	26	20	2	19	.265	.314	.333	72	-12	4	.979	11	96	107	2-77	0.4
Total	3	232	742	123	206	39	4	8	70	48	3	37	.278	.324	.373	84	-17	7-4	.975	8	92	115	2-186/3-5	0.0

REESE, RICH Richard Benjamin B 9.29.1941 Leipsic, OH BL/TL 6-3/200# d9.4

Year	Tm Lg	G	AB	R	H	2B	3B	HR	RBI	BB-IB	HP	SO	AVG	OBP	SLG	AOPS	ABR	SB-CS	FA	FR	Rng	Thr	G at Pos	BFW
1964	Min A	10	7	0	0	0	0	0	0	0-0	0	1	.000	.000	.000	-99	-2	0-0	1.000	-0	0	0	/1	-0.2
1965	Min A	14	7	0	2	1	0	0	0	2-1	0	2	.286	.444	.429	143	1	0-0	1.000	0	157	0	/1-6,O(LF)	0.1
1966	Min A	3	2	0	0	0	0	0	0	1-0	0	2	.000	.333	.000	5	0	0-0	—	0			H	0.0
1967	Min A	95	101	13	25	5	0	4	20	8-2	0	17	.248	.300	.416	102	0	0-0	.990	-1	44	69	1-36,O-10(LF)	-0.2
1968	Min A	126	332	40	86	15	2	4	28	18-4	3	36	.259	.301	.352	93	-3	3-1	.991	-0	97	76	1-87,O-15(LF)	-0.9
1969	†Min A	132	419	52	135	24	4	16	69	23-3	5	57	.322	.362	.513	140	21	1-5	.993	-4	87	**122**	*1-117/O-5(LF)	0.8
1970	†Min A	153	501	63	131	15	5	10	56	48-5	7	70	.261	.332	.371	93	-5	5-4	.992	-2	92	90	*1-146	-1.9
1971	Min A	120	329	40	72	8	3	10	39	20-2	5	35	.219	.270	.353	74	-13	7-4	.994	-3	85	103	1-95/O-9(8-0-1)	-2.4
1972	Min A	132	197	23	43	3	2	5	26	25-4	0	27	.218	.305	.330	85	-4	0-1	.988	1	109	100	1-98,O-13(LF)	-0.8
1973	Det A	59	102	10	14	1	0	2	4	7-1	0	17	.137	.193	.206	11	-12	0-0	1.000	-1	93	66	1-37,O-21(21-0-1)	-1.6
	Min A	22	23	7	4	1	1	1	3	6-0	0	6	.174	.345	.435	114	1	0-0	1.000	1	133	136	1-17	0.1
	Year	81	125	17	18	2	1	3	7	13-1	0	23	.144	.225	.248	31	-12	0-0	1.000	-1	107	90	1-54,O-21(21-0-1)	-1.5
Total	10	866	2020	248	512	73	17	52	245	158-22	20	270	.253	.312	.384	95	-16	16-15	.992	-10	92	97	1-640/O-74(73-0-2)	-7.0

REEVES, BOBBY Robert Edwin "Gunner" B 6.24.1904 Hill City, TN D 6.4.1993 Chattanooga, TN BR/TR 5-11/170# d6.9

Year	Tm Lg	G	AB	R	H	2B	3B	HR	RBI	BB-IB	HP	SO	AVG	OBP	SLG	AOPS	ABR	SB-CS	FA	FR	Rng	Thr	G at Pos	BFW
1926	Was A	20	49	4	11	0	1	0	7	6	1	9	.224	.321	.265	56	-3	1-1	.940	-1	87	122	3-16/2S	-0.3
1927	Was A	112	380	37	97	11	5	1	39	21	1	53	.255	.296	.318	60	-24	3-1	.923	-10	98	69	S-96,3-12/2-2	-2.2
1928	Was A	102	353	44	107	16	8	3	42	24	2	47	.303	.351	.419	102	0	4-8	.908	-6	98	85	S-66,2-22/3-8,O(RF)	0.0
1929	Bos A	140	460	66	114	19	2	2	28	60	**7**	57	.248	.343	.311	71	-18	7-8	.912	5	108	**115**	*3-131/2-2,S-2,1	-0.6
1930	Bos A	92	272	41	59	7	4	2	18	50	3	36	.217	.345	.294	66	-13	6-2	.895	0	111	198	3-62,S-15,2-11	-0.6
1931	Bos A	36	84	11	14	2	2	0	1	14	1	16	.167	.293	.238	43	-7	0-1	.912	-7	84	77	2-29/P	-1.2
Total	6	502	1598	203	402	55	22	8	135	175	15	218	.252	.331	.329	73	-65	21-21	.906	-20	107	136	3-229,S-180/2-67,P10(RF)	-4.9

REGALADO, RUDY Rudolph Valentino B 5.21.1930 Los Angeles, CA BR/TR 6-1/185# d4.13

Year	Tm Lg	G	AB	R	H	2B	3B	HR	RBI	BB-IB	HP	SO	AVG	OBP	SLG	AOPS	ABR	SB-CS	FA	FR	Rng	Thr	G at Pos	BFW
1954	†Cle A	65	180	21	45	5	0	2	24	19	4	16	.250	.333	.311	76	-5	0-2	.967	-6	83	86	3-50/2-2	-1.3
1955	Cle A	10	26	2	7	2	0	0	5	2-0	0	4	.269	.321	.346	77	-1	0-0	.955	1	101	158	/3-8,2	0.0
1956	Cle A	16	47	4	11	1	0	0	2	4-0	1	1	.234	.308	.255	49	-3	0-0	.783	-5	44	161	3-14/1	-0.8
Total	3	91	253	27	63	8	0	2	31	25-0	5	21	.249	.327	.304	71	-9	0-2	.944	-10	79	105	/3-72,2-3,1	-2.1

REGAN, JOE Joseph Charles B 7.12.1872 Seymour, CT D 11.18.1948 Hartford, CT BR/TR 6-1/?# d9.21

Year	Tm Lg	G	AB	R	H	2B	3B	HR	RBI	BB-IB	HP	SO	AVG	OBP	SLG	AOPS	ABR	SB-CS	FA	FR	Rng	Thr	G at Pos	BFW
1898	NY N	2	5	1	1	0	0	0	2	0	0		.200	.200	.200	15	-1	0	1.000	-0	0	0	/O-2(RF)	-0.1

REGAN, BILL William Wright B 1.23.1899 Pittsburgh, PA D 6.11.1968 Pittsburgh, PA BR/TR 5-10/155# d6.2

Year	Tm Lg	G	AB	R	H	2B	3B	HR	RBI	BB-IB	HP	SO	AVG	OBP	SLG	AOPS	ABR	SB-CS	FA	FR	Rng	Thr	G at Pos	BFW
1926	Bos A	108	403	40	106	21	3	4	34	23	4	37	.263	.309	.360	77	-15	6-3	.965	16	**112**	105	*2-106	0.3
1927	Bos A	129	468	43	128	37	10	2	66	26	2	51	.274	.315	.408	88	-10	10-10	.960	0	101	99	*2-121	-0.8
1928	Bos A	138	511	53	135	30	6	7	75	21	2	40	.264	.296	.387	80	-17	9-6	.963	15	**109**	110	*2-137/O(RF)	0.1
1929	Bos A	104	371	38	107	27	7	1	54	22	0	38	.288	.328	.407	90	-6	7-5	.962	-13	92	112	2-91,3-10/1	-1.6
1930	Bos A	134	507	54	135	35	10	3	53	25	2	60	.266	.303	.393	78	-19	4-2	.963	-10	100	113	*2-127/3-2	-2.2
1931	Pit N	28	104	8	21	8	0	1	10	5	0	19	.202	.239	.308	46	-8	2	.944	-3	103	79	2-28	-1.0
Total	6	641	2364	236	632	158	36	18	292	122	10	245	.267	.306	.387	81	-75	38-26	.962	5	103	106	2-610/3-12,1O(RF)	-5.2

REGO, TONY Antone (born Antone De Rego) B 10.31.1897 Wailuku, HI D 1.6.1978 Tulsa, OK BR/TR 5-4/165# d6.21

Year	Tm Lg	G	AB	R	H	2B	3B	HR	RBI	BB-IB	HP	SO	AVG	OBP	SLG	AOPS	ABR	SB-CS	FA	FR	Rng	Thr	G at Pos	BFW
1924	StL A	24	59	5	13	1	0	0	5	1	0	3	.220	.233	.237	20	-7	0-0	.972	-1	*95*	*110*	C-23	-0.6
1925	StL A	20	32	5	13	2	1	0	3	3	1	2	.406	.472	.531	147	2	0-0	.979	1	*90*	*183*	C-19	0.4
Total	2	44	91	10	26	3	1	0	8	4	1	5	.286	.323	.341	66	-5	0-0	.975	0	*93*	*137*	/C-42	-0.2

REHG, WALLY Walter Phillip B 8.31.1888 Summerfield, IL D 4.5.1946 Burbank, CA BR/TR 5-8/160# d4.14 Mil 1918

Year	Tm Lg	G	AB	R	H	2B	3B	HR	RBI	BB-IB	HP	SO	AVG	OBP	SLG	AOPS	ABR	SB-CS	FA	FR	Rng	Thr	G at Pos	BFW
1912	Pit N	8	9	1	0	0	0	0	0	0	0	1	.000	.000	.000	-99	-3	0	1.000	0	125	0	/O-2(0-1-1)	-0.3
1913	Bos A	30	101	13	28	3	2	0	9	2	0	7	.277	.291	.347	84	-3	4	.943	-1	91	105	O-26(8-3-15)	-0.5
1914	Bos A	88	151	14	33	4	2	0	11	18	1	11	.219	.306	.272	74	-5	5-8	.980	1	99	106	O-43(16-0-28)	-0.8
1915	Bos A	5	5	2	1	0	0	0	0	0	0	1	.200	.200	.200	20	-1	1	1.000	0	144	0	/O(RF)	0.0
1917	Bos N	87	341	48	92	12	6	1	31	24	1	32	.270	.320	.349	111	4	13	.956	-5	87	84	O-86(RF)	-0.6
1918	Bos N	40	133	6	32	5	1	1	12	5	0	14	.241	.268	.316	81	-4	3	.988	3	108	143	O-38(30-1-7)	-0.2
1919	Cin N	5	12	1	2	0	0	0	3	1	0	0	.167	.231	.167	21	-1	0	.875	1	69	384	/O-5(0-1-3)	-0.1
Total	7	263	752	85	188	24	11	2	66	50	2	66	.250	.299	.319	90	-13	26-8	.965	-1	94	108	O-201(54-6-141)	-2.5

REIBER, FRANK Frank Bernard "Tubby" B 9.19.1909 Huntington, WV D 12.26.2002 Bradenton, FL BR/TR 5-8.5/169# d4.13

Year	Tm Lg	G	AB	R	H	2B	3B	HR	RBI	BB-IB	HP	SO	AVG	OBP	SLG	AOPS	ABR	SB-CS	FA	FR	Rng	Thr	G at Pos	BFW
1933	Det A	13	18	3	5	0	1	1	3	2	0	3	.278	.350	.556	134	1	0-0	.929	-1	*57*	*0*	/C-6	0.0
1934	Det A	3	1	0	0	0	0	0	0	2	0	0	.000	.667	.000	84	0	0-0	—	0			H	0.0
1935	Det A	8	11	3	3	0	0	0	1	3	0	3	.273	.429	.273	88	0	0-0	1.000	-0	*82*	*0*	/C-5	0.0
1936	Det A	20	55	7	15	2	0	1	5	5	0	7	.273	.333	.364	72	-3	0-1	.982	-2	*116*	*93*	C-17/O(RF)	-0.4
Total	4	44	85	13	23	2	1	2	9	12	0	13	.271	.361	.388	89	-2	0-1	.975	-4	*102*	*66*	/C-28,O(RF)	-0.4

REICH, HERMAN Herman Charles B 11.23.1917 Bell, CA BR/TL 6-2/200# d5.3

Year	Tm Lg	G	AB	R	H	2B	3B	HR	RBI	BB-IB	HP	SO	AVG	OBP	SLG	AOPS	ABR	SB-CS	FA	FR	Rng	Thr	G at Pos	BFW
1949	Was A	2	2	0	0	0	0	0	0	0	0	1	.000	.000	.000	-99	-1	0-0	—	0			H	-0.1
	Cle A	1	2	0	1	0	0	0	0	1	0	0	.500	.667	.500	215	1	0-0	—	-0	0	0	/O(RF)	0.0
	Year	3	4	0	1	0	0	0	0	1	0	1	.250	.400	.250	75	0	0-0	—	-0	83	262	/O(RF)	-0.1
	Chi N	108	386	43	108	18	2	3	34	13	1	32	.280	.305	.360	80	-12	4	.989	13	160	75	1-85,O-16(RF)	-0.2
Total	1	111	390	43	109	18	2	3	34	14	1	33	.279	.306	.359	80	-12	4-0	.989	13	160	75	/1-85,O-17(RF)	-0.3

REICHARDT, RICK Frederic Carl B 3.16.1943 Madison, WI BR/TR 6-3/215# d9.1

Year	Tm Lg	G	AB	R	H	2B	3B	HR	RBI	BB-IB	HP	SO	AVG	OBP	SLG	AOPS	ABR	SB-CS	FA	FR	Rng	Thr	G at Pos	BFW
1964	LA A	11	37	0	6	0	0	0	0	1-1	0	12	.162	.184	.162	-3	-5	1-0	1.000	-0	104	0	O-11(CF)	-0.6
1965	Cal A	20	75	8	20	4	0	1	6	5-0	1	12	.267	.321	.360	95	0	4-1	.975	0	102	88	O-20(17-4-0)	-0.1
1966	Cal A	89	319	48	92	5	4	16	44	27-3	**13**	61	.288	.367	.480	145	18	8-4	.976	-0	92	146	O-87(77-20-0)	1.5
1967	Cal A	146	498	56	132	14	2	17	69	35-4	7	90	.265	.320	.404	118	9	5-3	.974	7	105	108	*O-138(LF)	1.0
1968	Cal A	151	534	62	136	20	3	21	73	42-2	18	118	.255	.328	.421	131	20	8-7	.989	4	103	95	*O-148(LF)	1.6
1969	Cal A	137	493	60	125	11	4	13	68	43-5	8	100	.254	.319	.371	99	-2	3-6	.981	6	99	128	*O-136(LF)/1-3	-0.6
1970	Cal A	9	6	1	1	0	0	0	1	3-1	0	0	.167	.400	.167	78	0	0-0	1.000	0	117	0	/O(RF)	0.0
	Was A	107	277	42	70	14	2	15	46	23-2	9	69	.253	.328	.480	127	9	2-4	.985	-2	103	0	O-79(38-18-31)/3	0.3
	Year	116	283	43	71	14	2	15	47	26-3	9	69	.251	.330	.473	126	9	2-4	.985	-2	103	0	O-80(38-18-32)/3	0.3
1971	Chi A	138	496	53	138	14	2	19	62	37-0	6	90	.278	.335	.429	112	7	5-10	.981	-8	91	55	*O-128(117-15-0)/1-9	-1.2
1972	Chi A	101	291	31	73	14	4	8	43	28-1	3	63	.251	.321	.409	114	5	2-2	.981	-7	90	41	O-90(11-84-0)	-0.5
1973	Chi A	46	153	15	42	8	1	3	16	8-0	1	29	.275	.315	.399	96	-1	2-3	1.000	-2	90	42	O-37(30-6-1)/D-6	-0.6

Year	Tm Lg	G	AB	R	H	2B	3B	HR	RBI	BB-IB	HP	SO	AVG	OBP	SLG	AOPS	ABR	SB-CS	FA	FR	Rng	Thr	G at Pos	BFW
	KC A	41	127	15	28	5	2	3	17	11-1	0	28	.220	.279	.362	75	-5	0-1	1.000	0	79	326	D-31/O-7(1-0-6)	-0.6
	Year	87	280	30	70	13	3	6	33	19-1	1	57	.250	.298	.382	86	-6	2-4	1.000	-2	89	76	O-44(31-6-7),D-37	-1.2
1974	KC A	1	1	0	1	0	0	0	0	0-0	0	0	1.000	1.000	1.000	451	0	0-0	—	0			H	0.0
Total	11	997	3307	391	864	109	24	116	445	263-20	66	672	.261	.326	.414	115	55	40-41	.982	-3	98	87	O-882(713-158-39)/D-37,1-12,3	0.2
REICHLE, DICK Richard Wendell B 11.23.1896 Lincoln, IL D 6.13.1967 Richmond Heights, MO BL/TR 6/185# d9.19																								
1922	Bos A	6	24	3	6	1	0	0	0	0	1	2	.250	.280	.292	50	-2	0-0	1.000	-0	100	0	/O-6(CF)	-0.2
1923	Bos A	122	361	40	93	17	3	1	39	22	8	34	.258	.315	.330	69	-17	3-6	.976	-2	94	108	O-93(3-87-4)/1-2	-2.3
Total	2	128	385	43	99	18	3	1	39	22	9	36	.257	.313	.327	68	-19	3-6	.977	-2	94	101	/O-99(3-93-4),1-2	-2.5
REID, JESSIE Jessie Thomas B 6.1.1962 Honolulu, HI BL/TL 6-1/200# d9.9																								
1987	SF N	6	8	1	1	0	0	1	1	1-0	0	5	.125	.222	.500	89	0	0-0	1.000	0	116	0	/O-3(1-0-2)	0.0
1988	SF N	2	2	0	0	0	0	0	0	0-0	0	1	.000	.000	.000	-99	-1	0-0	—	0			H	-0.1
Total	2	8	10	1	1	0	0	1	1	1-0	0	6	.100	.182	.400	54	-1	0-0	1.000	0	116	0	/O-3(1-0-2)	-0.1
REID, SCOTT Scott Donald B 1.7.1947 Chicago, IL BL/TR 6-1/195# d9.10																								
1969	Phi N	13	19	5	4	0	0	0	0	7-1	0	5	.211	.423	.211	85	0	0-1	1.000	-0	83	0	/O-5(2-4-0)	-0.1
1970	Phi N	25	49	5	6	1	0	0	1	11-0	0	22	.122	.283	.143	18	-5	0-0	1.000	5	98	759	O-18(3-12-5)	-0.1
Total	2	38	68	10	10	1	0	0	1	18-1	0	27	.147	.326	.162	37	-5	0-1	1.000	4	95	588	/O-23(5-16-5)	-0.2
REID, BILLY William Alexander B 5.17.1857 London, ON, CAN D 6.26.1940 London, ON, CAN BL/TR 6/170# d5.1																								
1883	Bal AA	24	97	14	27	3	0	0		4			.278	.307	.309	96	0		.842	-5	92	69	2-23/S	-0.4
1884	Pit AA	19	70	11	17	2	0	0		4	1		.243	.293	.271	86	-1		.724	-4	0	0	O-17(LF)/32	-0.5
Total	2	43	167	25	44	5	0	0		8	1		.263	.301	.293	92	-1		.839	-9	91	67	/2-24,O-17(LF),3S	-0.9
REILLEY, DUKE Alexander Aloysius "Midget" B 8.25.1884 Chicago, IL D 3.4.1968 Indianapolis, IN BB/TR 5-4.5/148# d8.28																								
1909	Cle A	20	62	10	13	0	0	0	0	4	0		.210	.258	.210	46	-4	5	.979	1	39	178	O-18(13-5-0)	-0.4
REILLEY, CHARLIE Charles E. B 1856 Hartford, CT BR/TR 5-10/165# d5.1																								
1879	Tro N	62	236	17	54	5	1	0	19	1		20	.229	.232	.258	66	-8		.867	-16			C-49,1-11/O-2(1-0-1)	-2.2
1880	Cin N	30	103	8	21	1	0	0	9	0		5	.204	.204	.214	42	-6		.759	-2	132	0	O-16(1-14-1),C-13/3-4	-0.8
1881	Det N	19	70	8	12	2	0	0	3	0		10	.171	.171	.200	16	-7		.889	-3			C-10/O-4(1-1-2),S-3,3-3,1	-0.9
	Wor N	2	8	2	3	0	0	0	1	0		1	.375	.375	.375	129	0		1.000	-1			/C-2	-0.1
	Year	21	78	10	15	2	0	0	4	0		11	.192	.192	.218	28	-6		.897	-4			C-12/O-4(1-1-2),S-3,3-3,1	-1.0
1882	Pro N	3	11	0	2	0	0	0	2	1		2	.182	.250	.182	41	-1		.714	-2			/C-3	-0.3
1884	Bos U	3	11	1	0	0	0	0		1			.000	.083	.000	-74	-3		1.000	-1	0	0	/O-2(RF),3	-0.3
Total	5	119	439	36	92	8	1	0	34	3		38	.210	.215	.232	48	-25		.867	-25			/C-77,O-24(3-15-6),1-12,3-8,S-3	-4.6
REILLY, ARCH Archer Edwin B 8.17.1891 Alton, IL D 11.29.1963 Columbus, OH BR/TR 5-10/163# d6.1																								
1917	Pit N	1	0	0	0	0	0	0	0	0	0	0	—	—	—	—	0	0	1.000	-0	0	0	/3	0.0
REILLY, BARNEY Bernard Eugene B 2.7.1885 Brockton, MA D 11.15.1934 St.Joseph, MO BR/TR 6- /175# d7.2																								
1909	Chi A	12	25	3	5	0	0	0	3	3	0		.200	.286	.200	56	-1	2	.962	2	124	0	2-11/O(RF)	0.0
REILLY, JOSH William Henry B 5.9.1868 San Francisco, CA D 6.12.1938 San Francisco, CA 5-8/160# d5.2																								
1896	Chi N	9	42	6	9	1	0	0	2	1	0	1	.214	.233	.238	23	-5	2	.857	-2	103	27	/2-8,S	-0.6
REILLY, CHARLIE Charles Thomas "Princeton Charlie" (born Charles Thomas O'Reilly) B 2.15.1867 Princeton, NJ D 12.16.1937 Los Angeles, CA BB/TR 5-11/190# d10.9																								
1889	Col AA	6	23	5	11	1	0	3	6	2	1	2	.478	.538	.913	326	7	9	.923	2	135	0	/3-6	0.7
1890	Col AA	137	530	75	141	23	3	4	77	35	6		.266	.319	.343	102	1	43	**.893**	29	**117**	**143**	*3-137	2.8
1891	Pit N	114	415	43	91	8	5	3	44	29	4	58	.219	.277	.284	65	-19	20	.857	0	104	57	*3-99,S-11/O-4(1-3-0)	-1.6
1892	Phi N	91	331	42	65	7	3	1	24	18	2	43	.196	.242	.245	47	-22	13	.905	9	111	132	3-70,O-15(5-8-2)/2-4	-1.2
1893	Phi N	104	416	64	102	16	7	4	56	33	9	36	.245	.314	.346	76	-16	13	.895	1	99	**114**	*3-104	-1.1
1894	Phi N	40	136	21	40	1	2	0	19	16	3	10	.294	.381	.331	74	-5	9	.874	3	121	81	3-28/O-6(5-0-1),2-4,S1	-0.1
1895	Phi N	49	179	28	48	6	1	0	25	13	5	12	.268	.335	.313	67	-8	7	.900	-2	100	92	S-34,3-11/2-3,O(RF)	-0.7
1897	Was N	101	351	64	97	18	3	2	60	34	11		.276	.359	.362	91	-3	18	.905	16	114	129	*3-101	1.3
Total	8	642	2381	342	595	80	24	17	311	180	41	161	.250	.314	.325	80	-65	132	.890	58	110	113	3-556/S-46,O-26(11-11-4),2-11,1	0.1
REILLY, HAL Harold John B 4.1.1894 Oshkosh, WI D 12.24.1957 Chicago, IL BR/TR 6/180# d6.19																								
1919	Chi N	1	3	0	0	0	0	0	0	0	0	1	.000	.000	.000	-99	-1	0	—	-0	0	0	/O(LF)	-0.1
REILLY, JOHN John Good "Long Jong" B 10.5.1858 Cincinnati, OH D 5.31.1937 Cincinnati, OH BR/TR 6-3/178# d5.18																								
1880	Cin N	73	272	21	56	8	4	0	16	3		36	.206	.215	.265	62	-11		.947	-3	70	100	*1-72/O-3(RF)	-1.7
1883	Cin AA	**98**	437	103	136	21	14	9	79	9			.311	.325	.485	149	21		.961	-1	67	131	*1-98/O(RF)	1.0
1884	Cin AA	105	448	114	152	24	19	**11**	91	5	14		.339	.366	**.551**	186	39		.971	-1	74	125	*1-103/O-3(RF),S	2.7
1885	Cin AA	111	482	92	143	18	11	5	60	11	7		.297	.322	.411	128	13		.963	-3	78	105	*1-107/O-7(0-2-5)	0.0
1886	Cin AA	115	441	92	117	12	11	6	79	31	5		.265	.321	.383	116	6	19	.967	-0	104	**136**	*1-110/O-6(0-5-1)	-0.4
1887	Cin AA	134	551	106	170	35	14	10	96	22	15		.309	.352	.477	127	17	50	.980	-1	79	**142**	*1-127/O-9(1-6-2)	0.4
1888	Cin AA	127	527	112	169	28	14	**13**	**103**	17	18		.321	.363	**.501**	**167**	36	82	.977	0	95	**144**	*1-117,O-10(0-2-8)	2.3
1889	Cin AA	111	427	84	111	24	13	5	66	34	18	37	.260	.340	.412	110	5	43	**.984**	-1	75	**124**	*1-109/O-2(1-1-0)	-0.6
1890	Cin N	133	553	114	166	25	**26**	6	86	16	7	41	.300	.328	.472	133	16	29	.977	-3	82	**122**	*1-132/O(CF)	0.1
1891	Cin N	135	546	60	132	20	13	4	64	9	10	42	.242	.267	.348	78	-19	22	.982	-7	59	116	*1-100,O-36(25-10-1)	-3.3
Total	10	1142	4684	898	1352	215	139	69	740	157	94	156	.289	.325	.438	128	123	245	.972	-22	79	126	*1-1075/O-78(27-27-24),S	0.5
REILLY, JOE Joseph J. B 1861 New York, NY 5-10/140# d6.8																								
1885	NY AA	10	40	6	7	3	0	0	3	2	0		.175	.214	.250	48	-2		.848	-1	85	73	/2-8,3-2	-0.2
REILLY, TOM Thomas Henry B 8.3.1884 St.Louis, MO D 10.18.1918 New Orleans, LA BR/TR 5-10/?# d7.27																								
1908	StL N	29	81	5	14	1	0	1	3	2	0		.173	.193	.222	34	-6	4	.866	-4	94	136	S-29	-1.1
1909	StL N	5	7	0	2	0	1	0	2	0	0		.286	.286	.571	176	0	0	1.000	0	125	0	/S-5	0.1
1914	Cle A	1	1	0	0	0	0	0	0	0	0	0	.000	.000	.000	-96	0	0	—	0			H	0.0
Total	3	35	89	5	16	1	1	1	5	2	0	0	.180	.198	.247	44	-6	4	.875	-4	96	126	/S-34	-1.0
REIMER, KEVIN Kevin Michael B 6.28.1964 Macon, GA BL/TR 6-2/225# d9.13																								
1988	Tex A	12	25	2	3	0	0	1	2	0-0	0	6	.120	.115	.240	-2	-4	0-0	—	-0	0	0	/O(LF)D	-0.4
1989	Tex A	3	5	0	0	0	0	0	0	0-0	0	1	.000	.000	.000	-98	-1	0-0	—	0			/D	-0.1
1990	Tex A	64	100	5	26	9	1	2	15	10-0	1	22	.260	.333	.430	112	2	0-1	.857	-1	97	0	D-21/O-9(5-0-5)	0.0
1991	Tex A	136	394	46	106	22	0	20	69	33-6	7	93	.269	.332	.477	125	12	0-3	.948	-3	101	0	O-66(61-0-6),D-56	0.5
1992	Tex A	148	494	56	132	32	2	16	58	42-5	10	103	.267	.336	.437	120	13	2-4	.949	-0	99	111	*O-110(LF),D-32	0.7
1993	Mil A	125	437	53	109	22	1	13	60	30-4	5	72	.249	.303	.394	88	-9	5-4	.962	1	115	50	D-83,O-37(28-0-10)	-1.5
Total	6	488	1455	162	376	85	4	52	204	115-15	23	297	.258	.320	.430	108	13	7-12	.948	-3	102	66	O-223(205-0-21),D-200	-0.8
REINBACH, MIKE Michael Wayne B 8.6.1949 San Diego, CA D 5.20.1989 Palm Desert, CA BL/TR 6-2/195# d4.7																								
1974	Bal A	12	20	2	5	1	0	0	2	2-1	0	5	.250	.304	.300	81	0	0-0	1.000	0	123	0	/O-3(1-0-2),D-3	0.0
REINECKER, WALLY Walter (born Walter Joseph Smith) B 4.21.1890 Pittsburgh, PA D 4.18.1957 Pittsburgh, PA BR/TR 5-6/150# d9.17																								
1915	Bal F	3	8	0	1	0	0	0	0	0	1	0	.125	.222	.125	-1	-1	0	.571	-2	24	0	/3-3	-0.3
REINHOLZ, ART Arthur August B 1.27.1903 Detroit, MI D 12.29.1980 New Port Richey, FL BR/TR 5-10.5/175# d9.27																								
1928	Cle A	2	3	0	1	0	0	0	0	1	0	0	.333	.500	.333	122	0	0-0	.833	0	153	0	/3-2	0.0
REIPSCHLAGER, CHARLIE Charles W. B 2.1854 D 3.16.1910 Atlantic City, NJ BR/TR 5-6.5/160# d5.2																								
1883	NY AA	37	145	8	27	4	2	0		4			.186	.208	.241	42	-9		.936	7			C-29/O-8(0-7-1)	-0.1
1884	†NY AA	59	233	21	56	13	2	0		1	2		.240	.250	.313	85	-4		.925	16			C-51/O-8(5-2-1)	1.5
1885	NY AA	72	268	29	65	11	1	0	21	9	1		.243	.270	.291	80	-5		.879	1			C-59/O-6(2-3-1),3-6,S2	0.0
1886	NY AA	65	232	21	49	4	6	0	25	9	1		.211	.244	.280	70	-9	2	.884	-2			C-57/O-9(1-6-2)	-0.5
1887	Cle AA	63	231	20	49	8	3	0	17	11	1		.212	.251	.273	47	-17	7	.888	5			C-48,1-16	-0.7
Total	5	296	1109	99	246	40	14	0	63	34	5		.222	.248	.283	66	-44	9	.901	26			C-244/O-31(8-18-5),1-16,3-6,2S	0.2

Year	Tm Lg	G	AB	R	H	2B	3B	HR	RBI	BB-IB	HP	SO	AVG	OBP	SLG	AOPS	ABR	SB-CS	FA	FR	Rng	Thr	G at Pos	BFW
REIS, BOBBY Robert Joseph Thomas B 1.2.1909 Woodside, NY D 5.1.1973 St.Paul, MN BR/TR 6-1/175# d9.19 ▲ OF Total (19-LF 17-CF 15-RF)																								
1931	Bro N	6	17	3	5	0	0	0	2	2	0	0	.294	.368	.294	81	0	0	.933	-1	74	0	/3-6	-0.1
1932	Bro N	1	4	0	1	0	0	0	0	0	0	1	.250	.250	.250	36	0	0	.500	-1	67	0	/3	-0.1
1935	Bro N	52	85	10	21	3	2	0	4	6	0	13	.247	.297	.329	70	-4	2	.950	5	103	274	O-21(4-3-14),P-14/2-4,13	0.0
1936	Bos N	37	60	3	13	2	0	0	5	3	0	6	.217	.254	.250	39	-5	0	1.000	4	160	103	P-35/O-2(CF)	0.1
1937	Bos N	45	86	10	21	5	0	0	6	13	0	12	.244	.343	.302	84	-1	2	1.000	-2	101	0	O-18(6-12-0)/P-4,1-4	-0.4
1938	Bos N	34	49	6	9	0	0	0	4	1	0	3	.184	.200	.184	7	-6	1	1.000	-1	128	0	P-16,O-10(9-0-1)/S-3,C2	-0.5
Total	6	175	301	32	70	10	2	0	21	25	0	35	.233	.291	.279	59	-16	5	1.000	4	147	95	/P-69,O-51L,3-8,1-5,2-5,S-3,C	-1.0
REISER, PETE Harold Patrick B 3.17.1919 St.Louis, MO D 10.25.1981 Palm Springs, CA BL/TR (BB 1940 part,1948-52 part) 5-10.5/185# d7.23 Mil 1943-45 C14																								
1940	Bro N	58	225	34	66	11	4	3	20	15	0	33	.293	.338	.418	101	0	2	.960	-3	95	160	3-30,O-17(5-1-9)/S-5	-0.2
1941	†Bro N★	137	536	**117**	184	**39**	**17**	14	76	46	**11**	71	**.343**	.406	**.558**	**163**	44	4	.981	4	104	127	*O-133(0-133-2)	**4.5**
1942	Bro N★	125	480	89	149	33	5	10	64	48	2	45	.310	.375	.463	142	26	**20**	.969	-8	92	78	*O-125(CF)	1.5
1946	Bro N☆	122	423	75	117	21	5	11	73	55	1	58	.277	.361	.428	122	13	**34**	.978	5	98	168	O-97(69-28-0),3-15	1.2
1947	†Bro N	110	388	68	120	23	2	5	46	68	2	41	.309	.415	.418	117	14	14	.988	-5	97	41	*O-108(51-62-0)	0.4
1948	Bro N	64	127	17	30	8	2	1	19	29	1	21	.236	.382	.354	97	1	4	.981	-2	94	54	O-30(17-10-5)/3-4	-0.2
1949	Bos N	84	221	32	60	8	3	8	40	33	1	42	.271	.369	.443	123	8	3	.980	0	98	115	O-63(27-36-0)/3-4	0.5
1950	Bos N	53	78	12	16	2	0	1	10	18	2	22	.205	.367	.269	75	-2	1	.979	0	116	0	O-24(16-6-0)/3	-0.3
1951	Pit N	74	140	22	38	9	3	2	13	27	0	20	.271	.389	.421	115	4	4-2	.982	-2	91	44	O-27(20-6-1)/3-5	0.1
1952	Cle A	34	44	7	6	1	0	3	7	4	0	16	.136	.208	.364	61	-3	1-1	1.000	0	110	0	O-10(4-6-0)	-0.3
Total	10	861	2662	473	786	155	41	58	368	343	20	369	.295	.380	.450	127	105	87-3	.979	-10	98	93	O-634(209-413-17)/3-59,S-5	7.2
REISING, CHARLIE Charles "Pop" B 8.28.1861 Lanesville, IN D 7.26.1915 Louisville, KY d7.19																								
1884	Ind AA	2	8	0	0	0	0	0		1	0		.000	.111	.000	-62	-1		.400	-1	0	0	/O-2(1-1-1)	-0.3
REISS, AL Albert Allen B 1.8.1909 Elizabeth, NJ D 5.13.1989 Red Bank, NJ BB/TR 5-10.5/165# d6.22																								
1932	Phi A	9	5	0	1	0	0	0	1	1	0	1	.200	.333	.200	40	0	0-0	1.000	0	107	0	/S-6	0.0
REITZ, HEINIE Henry P. B 6.29.1867 Chicago, IL D 11.10.1914 Sacramento, CA BL/TR 5-7/158# d4.27																								
1893	Bal N	**130**	490	90	140	17	13	1	76	65	7	32	.286	.377	.380	100	1	24	.939	4	102	99	*2-130	0.8
1894	†Bal N	108	446	86	135	22	**31**	2	105	42	7	24	.303	.372	.504	105	-1	18	**.968**	21	109	114	*2-97,3-12	1.8
1895	Bal N	71	245	45	72	15	5	0	29	18	3	11	.294	.350	.396	89	-4	15	.938	-3	95	140	2-48,3-18/S	-0.4
1896	†Bal N	120	464	76	133	15	6	4	106	49	2	32	.287	.357	.371	91	-6	28	.952	-22	90	120	*2-118/S-3	-1.9
1897	†Bal N	128	477	76	138	15	6	2	84	50	11		.289	.370	.358	93	-3	23	**.962**	19	**111**	**151**	*2-128	1.8
1898	Was N	132	489	62	148	20	2	2	47	32	9		.303	.357	.364	107	5	11	**.959**	11	101	99	*2-132	2.0
1899	Pit N	35	133	12	35	4	2	0	16	10	0		.263	.315	.323	75	-5	3	.976	0	104	59	2-35	-0.3
Total	7	724	2744	447	801	108	65	11	463	266	39	99	.292	.363	.391	97	-13	122	.955	30	102	115	2-688/3-30,S-4	3.8
REITZ, KEN Kenneth John B 6.24.1951 San Francisco, CA BR/TR 6/185# d9.5																								
1972	StL N	21	78	5	28	4	0	0	10	2-0	0	4	.359	.370	.410	125	2	0-1	.956	-4	71	90	3-20	-0.2
1973	StL N	147	426	40	100	20	2	6	42	9-2	4	25	.235	.256	.333	63	-23	0-1	**.974**	-1	99	90	*3-135/S	-2.7
1974	StL N	154	579	48	157	28	2	7	54	23-7	2	63	.271	.299	.363	86	-13	0-0	**.974**	-20	86	96	*3-151/S-2,2	-3.5
1975	StL N	161	592	43	159	25	1	5	63	22-9	5	54	.269	.298	.340	75	-21	1-1	.946	-15	89	75	*3-160	-3.9
1976	SF N	155	577	40	154	21	1	5	66	24-5	1	48	.267	.293	.333	76	-19	5-4	.959	2	101	109	*3-155/S	-1.9
1977	StL N	157	587	58	153	36	1	17	79	19-4	7	74	.261	.291	.412	88	-12	2-6	**.980**	-0	99	143	*3-157	-1.7
1978	StL N	150	540	41	133	26	2	10	75	23-5	5	61	.246	.280	.357	79	-17	1-0	**.973**	10	**108**	72	*3-150	-1.0
1979	StL N	159	605	42	162	41	2	8	73	25-7	4	85	.268	.299	.382	84	-14	1-0	.972	-11	95	95	*3-158	-2.8
1980	StL N★	151	523	39	141	33	0	8	58	22-5	3	44	.270	.300	.379	86	-10	0-1	**.979**	-7	99	113	*3-150	-2.0
1981	Chi N	82	260	10	56	9	1	2	28	15-3	3	56	.215	.261	.281	53	-16	0-0	**.977**	4	105	83	3-81	-1.4
1982	Pit N	7	10	0	0	0	0	0	0	0-0	1	4	.000	.091	.000	-70	-2	0-0	1.000	0	130	0	/3-4	-0.2
Total	11	1344	4777	366	1243	243	12	68	548	184-47	35	518	.260	.290	.359	79	-145	10-14	.970	-41	97	98	*3-1321/S-4,2	-21.3
RELAFORD, DESI Desmond Lamont B 9.16.1973 Valdosta, GA BB/TR (BL 2003 (part)) 5-8/155# d8.1 OF Total (26-LF 5-CF 25-RF)																								
1996	Phi N	15	40	2	7	2	0	0	1	3-0	0	9	.175	.233	.225	21	-5	1-0	.933	1	80	52	/S-9,2-4	-0.3
1997	Phi N	15	38	3	7	1	2	0	6	5-0	0	6	.184	.279	.316	55	-3	3-0	.977	-1	100	46	S-12	-0.2
1998	Phi N	142	494	45	121	25	3	5	41	33-4	3	87	.245	.293	.338	65	-25	9-5	.960	-7	98	89	*S-137	-2.1
1999	Phi N	65	211	31	51	11	2	1	26	19-2	6	34	.242	.322	.327	63	-12	4-3	.952	8	111	119	S-63	0.1
2000	Phi N	83	253	29	56	12	3	3	30	48-7	9	45	.221	.363	.328	76	-7	5-0	.930	-12	89	94	S-81	-1.2
	SD N	45	157	26	32	2	0	2	16	27-0	3	26	.204	.330	.255	55	-10	8-0	.965	-1	98	120	S-45	-0.6
	Year	128	410	55	88	14	3	5	46	75-7	12	71	.215	.351	.300	68	-18	13-0	.943	-13	92	103	*S-126	-1.8
2001	NY N	120	301	43	91	27	0	8	36	27-1	5	65	.302	.364	.472	122	11	13-5	.969	-9	87	94	2-54,S-25,3-20/P	0.7
2002	Sea A	112	329	55	88	13	2	6	43	33-2	6	51	.267	.339	.374	95	-2	10-3	.964	-5	88	118	S-40,3-38,O-35(25-0-10),2-11/D-4	-0.3
2003	KC A	141	500	70	127	27	5	8	59	40-1	6	70	.254	.315	.376	72	-20	20-4	.981	1	98	89	2-89,3-33,O-20(1-5-15)/S-6,D-5	-1.1
Total	8	738	2323	304	580	120	17	33	258	235-17	38	393	.250	.326	.359	77	-73	73-20	.954	-23	97	98	S-418,2-158/3-91,O-55L,D-9,P	-5.0
REMENTER, BUTCH Willis J. H. B 3.14.1878 Philadelphia, PA D 9.23.1922 Philadelphia, PA BR/TR 5-6.5/180# d10.8																								
1904	Phi N	1	2	0	0	0	0	0	0	0	0		.000	.000	.000	-99	0	0	1.000	-0	*74*	*0*	/C	-0.1
REMSEN, JACK John Jay B 4.1850 Brooklyn, NY BR/TR 5-11/189# d5.2																								
1872	Atl NA	**37**	165	25	39	3	5	1	14	2		6	.236	.246	.333	65	-10	1-2	.797	2	123	**192**	*O-37(CF)	-0.6
1873	Atl NA	50	207	29	61	5	6	1	29	2		2	.295	.301	.391	117	5	1-2	.793	-2	70	136	*O-50(CF)	0.2
1874	Mut NA	64	284	52	65	9	3	2	38	0		5	.229	.229	.303	67	-11	6-0	.864	4	134	139	*O-63(8-57-0)/1-3	-0.4
1875	Har NA	**86**	358	70	96	10	4	0	34	5		4	.268	.278	.318	102	-1	6-3	.887	2	71	48	*O-86(0-81-5)	0.1
1876	Har N	**69**	324	62	89	12	5	1	30	1		15	.275	.277	.352	100	-2		.887	7	102	250	*O-69(3-66-0)	0.2
1877	StL N	33	123	14	32	3	4	0	13	4		3	.260	.283	.350	104	1		.906	0	61	0	O-33(CF)	0.0
1878	Chi N	56	224	32	52	11	1	1	19	**17**		33	.232	.286	.304	88	-2		**.944**	4	95	237	*O-56(CF)	-0.1
1879	Chi N	42	152	14	33	4	2	0	8	2		23	.217	.227	.270	60	-7		.862	-1	64	149	O-31(5-26-0),1-11	-0.9
1881	Cle N	48	172	14	30	4	3	0	13	9		31	.174	.215	.233	43	-11		.873	-2	54	55	O-48(CF)	-1.4
1884	Phi N	12	43	9	9	2	0	0	3	6		9	.209	.306	.256	83	0		.952	1	160	0	O-12(CF)	0.0
	Bro AA	81	301	45	67	6	6	3		23	0		.223	.278	.312	91	-3		.914	3	45	79	*O-81(32-49-0)	-0.2
Total	4 NA	237	1014	176	261	27	18	4	115	9	0	17	.257	.264	.331	88	-17	14-7	.000	5	96	114	O-236(8-225-5)/1-3	-0.7
Total	6	341	1339	190	312	42	21	5	86	62	0	114	.233	.267	.307	84	-24		.900	12	74	135	O-330(40-290-0)/1-11	-2.4
REMY, JERRY Gerald Peter B 11.8.1952 Fall River, MA BL/TR 5-9/165# d4.7																								
1975	Cal A	147	569	82	147	17	5	1	46	45-1	0	55	.258	.311	.311	82	-14	34-21	.982	16	103	109	*2-147	1.2
1976	Cal A	143	502	64	132	14	3	0	28	38-1	0	43	.263	.313	.303	87	-9	35-16	.977	19	109	96	*2-133/D-5	2.2
1977	Cal A	154	575	74	145	19	10	4	44	59-2	2	59	.252	.322	.341	85	-12	41-17	.975	-3	95	92	*2-152/3	-0.4
1978	Bos A☆	148	583	87	162	24	6	2	44	40-0	0	55	.278	.321	.350	81	-15	30-13	.983	1	99	**123**	*2-140/SD	-0.4
1979	Bos A	80	306	49	91	11	2	0	29	26-1	0	25	.297	.350	.346	85	-6	14-9	.970	-18	87	83	2-76	-1.9
1980	Bos A	63	230	24	72	7	2	0	9	10-0	0	14	.313	.339	.361	88	-4	14-6	.977	-2	106	73	2-60/O(RF)	-0.2
1981	Bos A	88	358	55	110	9	1	0	31	36-2	0	30	.307	.368	.338	99	1	9-2	.984	-11	99	91	2-87	-0.4
1982	Bos A	155	636	89	178	22	3	0	47	55-1	2	77	.280	.337	.324	79	-17	16-9	.982	-16	97	96	*2-154	-2.5
1983	Bos A	146	592	73	163	16	5	0	43	40-2	0	35	.275	.320	.319	72	-23	11-3	.990	-17	93	100	*2-144	-3.1
1984	Bos A	30	104	8	26	1	1	0	8	7-0	0	11	.250	.297	.279	58	-6	4-3	.973	-1	101	82	2-24	-0.6
Total	10	1154	4455	605	1226	140	38	7	329	356-10	4	404	.275	.327	.328	82	-105	208-99	.981	-31	99	98	*2-1117/D-9,O(RF)S3	-6.1
RENICK, RICK Warren Richard B 3.16.1944 London, OH BR/TR 6/190# d7.11 C14																								
1968	Min A	42	97	16	21	5	2	3	13	9-1	0	42	.216	.283	.402	101	0	0-0	.946	0	100	84	S-40	0.3
1969	†Min A	71	139	21	34	3	0	5	17	12-1	1	32	.245	.307	.374	88	-3	0-1	.913	-6	82	104	3-30,O-10(8-0-2)/S-6	-0.9
1970	†Min A	81	179	20	41	8	0	7	25	22-0	1	29	.229	.317	.391	93	-2	0-2	.987	1	95	99	3-30,O-25(25-1-0)/S	-0.2
1971	Min A	27	45	4	10	2	0	1	8	5-2	1	14	.222	.308	.333	81	-1	0-0	.846	-2	75	0	/3-7,O-7(LF)	-0.3
1972	Min A	55	93	10	16	2	0	4	8	15-0	0	25	.172	.282	.323	77	-2	0-1	1.000	-2	87	0	O-21(19-0-2)/1-6,3-4,S	-0.6
Total	5	276	553	71	122	20	2	20	71	63-4	3	142	.221	.302	.373	89	-8	0-4	.940	-8	90	86	/3-71,O-63(59-1-4),S-48,1-6	-1.7
RENNA, BILL William Beneditto "Big Bill" B 10.14.1924 Hanford, CA BR/TR 6-3/218# d4.14																								
1953	NY A	61	121	19	38	6	3	2	13	13	1	31	.314	.385	.463	133	5	0-1	.983	-1	101	0	O-40(32-5-3)	0.2
1954	Phi A	123	422	52	98	15	4	13	53	41	3	60	.232	.302	.379	86	-10	1-3	.972	6	106	156	*O-115(1-1-114)	-0.9

Year	Tm Lg	G	AB	R	H	2B	3B	HR	RBI	BB-IB	HP	SO	AVG	OBP	SLG	AOPS	ABR	SB-CS	FA	FR	Rng	Thr	G at Pos	BFW
1955	KC A	100	249	33	53	7	3	7	28	31-0	2	42	.213	.305	.349	75	-10	0-3	.992	0	99	102	O-79(8-0-72)	-1.3
1956	KC A	33	48	12	13	3	0	2	5	3-0	0	10	.271	.314	.458	101	0	1-0	.950	-0	93	138	O-25(22-0-3)	-0.1
1958	Bos A	39	56	5	15	5	0	4	18	6-1	0	14	.268	.339	.571	136	3	0-0	1.000	-0	103	0	O-11(LF)	0.2
1959	Bos A	14	22	2	2	0	0	0	2	5-0	0	9	.091	.259	.091	0	-3	0-0	1.000	-1	68	0	/O-7(LF)	-0.4
Total	6	370	918	123	219	36	10	28	119	99-1	6	166	.239	.315	.391	91	-15	2-7	.979	4	102	113	O-277(81-6-192)	-2.3
RENSA, TONY George Anthony "Pug" B 9.29.1901 Parsons, PA D 1.4.1987 Wilkes-Barre, PA BR/TR 5-10/180# d5.5																								
1930	Det A	20	37	6	10	2	1	1	3	6	1	7	.270	.386	.459	111	1	1-0	.964	-1	*63*	*141*	C-18	0.0
	Phi N	54	172	31	49	11	2	3	31	10	1	18	.285	.328	.424	75	-7	0	.932	-11	*74*	*91*	C-49	-1.3
1931	Phi N	19	29	2	3	1	0	0	2	6	0	2	.103	.257	.138	8	-4	0	.958	1	*69*	*206*	C-17	-0.2
1933	NY A	8	29	4	9	2	1	0	3	1	0	3	.310	.333	.448	112	0	0-1	.977	-1	*125*	*96*	/C-8	0.0
1937	Chi A	26	57	10	17	5	1	0	5	8	0	6	.298	.385	.421	103	1	3-0	.975	1	*119*	*90*	C-23	0.3
1938	Chi A	59	165	15	41	5	0	3	19	25	1	16	.248	.351	.333	71	-7	1-1	.982	6	*125*	*105*	C-57	0.1
1939	Chi A	14	25	3	5	0	0	0	2	1	0	2	.200	.231	.200	11	-3	0-0	.972	0	*105*	*158*	C-13	-0.2
Total	6	200	514	71	134	26	5	7	65	57	3	54	.261	.338	.372	74	-19	5-2	.965	-5	*100*	*111*	C-185	-1.3
RENTERIA, EDGAR Edgar Enrique B 8.7.1976 Barranquilla, Colombia BR/TR 6-1/172# d5.10																								
1996	Fla N	106	431	68	133	18	3	5	31	33-0	2	68	.309	.358	.399	103	2	16-2	.979	14	108	115	*S-106	2.6
1997	†Fla N	154	617	90	171	21	3	4	52	45-1	4	108	.277	.327	.340	80	-19	32-15	.975	-4	92	104	*S-153	-0.9
1998	Fla N★	133	517	79	146	18	2	3	31	48-1	4	78	.282	.347	.342	87	-9	41-22	.966	-7	98	102	*S-129	-0.4
1999	StL N	154	585	92	161	36	2	11	63	53-0	2	82	.275	.334	.400	85	-13	37-8	.959	-11	96	94	*S-151	-0.7
2000	†StL N★	150	562	94	156	32	1	16	76	63-3	1	77	.278	.346	.423	94	-5	21-13	.958	-8	94	92	*S-149	-0.1
2001	†StL N	141	493	54	128	19	3	10	57	39-4	3	73	.260	.314	.371	78	-17	17-4	.961	7	104	109	*S-137/1D	0.2
2002	†StL N	152	544	77	166	36	2	11	83	49-7	4	57	.305	.364	.439	118	12	22-7	.970	-18	97	79	*S-149	0.8
2003	StL N★	157	587	96	194	47	1	13	100	65-12	1	54	.330	.394	.480	133	31	34-7	.975	-26	98	85	*S-156	2.2
Total	8	1147	4336	650	1255	227	17	73	493	395-28	21	597	.289	.348	.400	97	-18	220-78	.968	-52	98	97	*S-1130/D1	3.7
RENTERIA, RICH Richard Avina B 12.25.1961 Harbor City, CA BR/TR 5-9/172# d9.14																								
1986	Pit N	10	12	2	3	1	0	0	1	0-0	0	4	.250	.250	.333	58	-1	0-0	.600	-0	134	0	/3	-0.1
1987	Sea A	12	10	2	1	1	0	0	0	1-0	0	2	.100	.182	.200	1	-1	1-0	.833	0	91	0	/2-4,SD	-0.1
1988	Sea A	31	88	6	18	9	0	0	6	2-0	0	8	.205	.222	.307	45	-6	1-3	.958	1	90	103	D-12,S-11/3-5,2-4	-0.6
1993	Fla N	103	263	27	67	9	2	2	30	21-1	2	31	.255	.314	.327	68	-12	0-2	.989	-3	99	65	2-45,3-25/O(LF)	-1.3
1994	Fla N	28	49	5	11	0	0	2	4	1-0	2	4	.224	.269	.347	57	-3	0-1	.929	2	115	285	3-14/2-6,O-2(LF)	-0.2
Total	5	184	422	42	100	20	2	4	41	25-1	4	49	.237	.285	.322	61	-23	2-6	.986	0	99	73	/2-59,3-45,D-16,S-12,O-3(LF)	-2.3
REPASS, BOB Robert Willis B 11.6.1917 W.Pittston, PA BR/TR 6-1/185# d9.18																								
1939	StL N	3	6	0	2	1	0	0	1	0	0	2	.333	.333	.500	114	0	0	1.000	0	142	137	/2-2	0.1
1942	Was A	81	259	30	62	11	1	2	23	33	1	30	.239	.328	.313	81	-6	6-1	.973	-4	89	70	2-33,3-29,S-11	-0.5
Total	2	84	265	30	64	12	1	2	24	33	1	32	.242	.328	.317	82	-6	6-1	.973	-4	91	72	/2-35,3-29,S-11	-0.4
REPOZ, ROGER Roger Allen B 8.3.1940 Bellingham, WA BL/TL 6-3/195# d9.11																								
1964	NY A	11	1	1	0	0	0	0	0	1-0	0	1	.000	.500	.000	52	0	0-0	1.000	0	121	0	/O-9(RF)	0.0
1965	NY A	79	218	34	48	7	4	12	28	25-4	0	57	.220	.298	.454	112	2	1-1	.993	-2	101	37	O-69(0-65-7)	-0.2
1966	NY A	37	43	4	15	4	1	0	9	4-0	0	8	.349	.396	.488	161	4	0-0	1.000	-1	96	0	O-30(0-28-5)	0.3
	KC A	101	319	40	69	10	3	11	34	44-4	2	80	.216	.314	.370	99	0	3-3	.991	-5	100	34	O-52(8-41-3),1-45	-1.1
	Year	138	362	44	84	14	4	11	43	48-4	2	88	.232	.324	.384	106	4	3-3	.992	-6	99	28	O-82(8-69-8),1-45	-0.8
1967	KC A	40	87	9	21	6	1	2	8	12-1	1	20	.241	.340	.402	122	3	4-2	1.000	3	116	197	O-31(16-9-6)	0.5
	Cal A	74	176	25	44	9	1	5	20	19-1	0	37	.250	.318	.398	116	4	2-2	.959	0	109	102	O-63(6-54-4)	0.2
	Year	114	263	34	65	15	2	7	28	31-2	1	57	.247	.326	.399	118	6	6-4	.972	3	111	133	O-94(22-63-10)	0.7
1968	Cal A	133	375	30	90	8	1	13	54	38-3	3	83	.240	.309	.371	111	5	8-7	.987	1	107	63	*O-114(0-71-52)	0.0
1969	Cal A	103	219	25	36	1	1	8	19	32-2	0	52	.164	.270	.288	59	-13	1-3	.985	2	98	144	O-48(13-22-16),1-31	-1.6
1970	Cal A	137	407	50	97	17	6	18	47	45-6	3	90	.238	.317	.442	112	5	4-2	.995	-1	103	95	*O-110(6-42-68),1-18	-0.1
1971	Cal A	113	297	39	59	11	1	13	41	60-6	1	69	.199	.333	.374	108	5	3-5	1.000	-1	96	104	O-97(5-25-72),1-13	-0.2
1972	Cal A	3	3	0	1	0	0	0	0	0-0	0	2	.333	.333	.333	105	0	0-0	—	0			H	0.0
Total	9	831	2145	257	480	73	19	82	260	280-27	10	499	.224	.314	.390	106	15	26-25	.989	-4	103	84	O-623(54-357-242),1-107	-2.2
REPULSKI, RIP Eldon John B 10.4.1927 Sauk Rapids, MN D 2.10.1993 Waite Park, MN BR/TR 6/195# d4.14																								
1953	StL N	153	567	75	156	25	4	15	66	33	9	71	.275	.325	.413	91	-9	3-6	.987	-10	92	54	*O-153(CF)	-2.6
1954	StL N	152	619	99	175	39	5	19	79	43	4	75	.283	.329	.454	102	1	8-10	.975	-9	94	40	*O-152(137-12-3)	-1.9
1955	StL N	147	512	64	138	28	2	23	73	49-3	4	66	.270	.333	.467	111	8	5-7	.974	-4	100	50	*O-141(110-1-32)	-0.5
1956	StL N★	112	376	44	104	18	3	11	55	24-3	7	46	.277	.330	.428	102	1	2-2	.974	-5	99	48	*O-100(99-1-1)	-1.1
1957	Phi N	134	516	65	134	23	4	20	68	19-0	5	74	.260	.290	.436	95	-6	7-1	.968	0	107	64	*O-130(54-0-84)	-1.1
1958	Phi N	85	238	33	58	9	4	13	40	15-1	4	47	.244	.296	.479	103	0	0-0	.949	-3	89	73	O-56(35-0-21)	-0.7
1959	†LA N	53	94	11	24	4	0	2	14	13-2	0	23	.255	.343	.362	83	-2	0-1	1.000	-2	86	0	O-31(16-2-13)	-0.5
1960	LA N	4	5	0	1	0	0	0	0	0-0	0	1	.200	.200	.200	9	-1	0-0	1.000	-0	85	0	/O-2(RF)	-0.1
	Bos A	73	136	14	33	6	1	3	20	10-0	0	25	.243	.289	.368	75	-5	0-0	1.000	0	107	0	O-33(LF)	-0.7
1961	Bos A	15	25	2	7	1	0	0	1	1-0	0	5	.280	.308	.320	66	-1	0-2	1.000	-0	74	0	/O-4(LF)	-0.2
Total	9	928	3088	407	830	153	23	106	416	207-9	33	433	.269	.319	.436	98	-14	25-29	.976	-34	97	49	O-802(488-169-156)	-9.4
RESSLER, LARRY Lawrence P. B 8.10.1848 , France D 6.12.1918 Reading, PA d4.26																								
1875	Was NA	27	108	17	21	1	0	0	5	0		4	.194	.194	.204	40	-6	4-0	.831	3	281	210	O-20(0-3-17)/2-7	-0.2
RESTELLI, DINO Dino Paul "Dingo" B 9.23.1924 St.Louis, MO BR/TR 6-1.5/191# d6.14																								
1949	Pit N	72	232	41	58	11	0	12	40	35	4	26	.250	.358	.453	113	5	3	.961	-0	103	83	O-61(0-47-14)/1	0.3
1951	Pit N	21	38	1	7	1	0	1	3	2	0	4	.184	.225	.289	36	-4	0-0	.920	0	104	124	O-11(8-4-0)	-0.4
Total	2	93	270	42	65	12	0	13	43	37	4	30	.241	.341	.430	103	1	3-0	.956	-0	103	88	/O-72(8-51-14),1	-0.1
RESTOVICH, MICHAEL Michael Jerome B 1.3.1979 Rochester, MN BR/TR 6-4/233# d9.18																								
2002	Min A	8	13	3	4	0	0	1	1	1-0	0	4	.308	.357	.538	132	1	1-0	1.000	0	111	0	/O-5(4-0-1),D-2	0.1
2003	Min A	24	53	10	15	3	2	0	4	10-0	1	12	.283	.406	.415	116	2	0-0	1.000	-0	95	113	O-17(3-0-14)/D-7	0.1
Total	2	32	66	13	19	3	2	1	5	11-0	1	16	.288	.397	.439	120	3	1-0	1.000	-0	98	94	/O-22(7-0-15),D-9	0.2
RETTENMUND, MERV Mervin Weldon B 6.6.1943 Flint, MI BR/TR 5-10/195# d4.14 C20																								
1968	Bal A	31	64	10	19	5	0	2	7	18-0	1	20	.297	.452	.469	181	8	1-1	1.000	-2	78	87	O-23(4-13-13)	0.6
1969	†Bal A	95	190	27	47	10	3	4	25	28-1	0	28	.247	.338	.395	105	2	6-1	.991	-0	100	74	O-78(45-18-21)	0.0
1970	†Bal A	106	338	60	109	17	2	18	58	38-1	3	59	.322	.394	.544	155	25	13-7	.976	5	111	107	O-93(30-44-36)	2.7
1971	†Bal A	141	491	81	156	23	4	11	75	87-2	4	60	.318	.422	.448	149	37	15-6	.977	1	104	79	*O-134(46-40-72)	3.4
1972	Bal A	102	301	40	70	10	2	6	21	41-0	0	37	.233	.325	.339	95	-1	6-4	.989	2	104	102	O-98(6-23-79)	-0.4
1973	†Bal A	95	321	59	84	17	2	9	44	57-4	4	38	.262	.378	.411	124	13	11-2	.985	5	116	70	O-90(11-2-81)	1.5
1974	Cin N	80	208	30	45	6	0	6	28	37-1	2	39	.216	.337	.332	90	-2	5-1	1.000	-3	92	77	O-69(0-9-60)	-0.7
1975	†Cin N	93	188	24	45	6	1	2	19	35-3	0	22	.239	.356	.314	86	-2	5-0	1.000	-1	101	28	O-61(20-4-38)/3	-0.5
1976	SD N	86	140	16	32	7	0	2	11	29-0	0	23	.229	.361	.321	103	2	4-1	.977	6	127	261	O-43(34-1-11)	0.8
1977	SD N	107	126	23	36	6	1	4	17	33-2	1	28	.286	.432	.444	153	12	1-2	1.000	-2	81	0	O-27(23-1-3)/3	0.9
1978	Cal A	50	108	16	29	5	1	1	14	30-0	2	13	.269	.433	.361	131	7	0-3	.968	-2	89	0	O-22(5-0-17),D-18	0.3
1979	†Cal A	35	76	7	20	2	0	1	10	11-1	1	14	.263	.360	.329	91	0	1-0	1.000	-2	46	0	D-17/O-9(4-0-5)	-0.3
1980	Cal A	2	4	0	1	0	0	0	0	1-0	0	1	.250	.400	.250	84	0	0-0	—	0			/D	0.0
Total	13	1023	2555	393	693	114	16	66	329	445-15	18	382	.271	.381	.406	124	101	68-28	.985	6	104	84	O-747(228-155-436)/D-36,3-2	8.3
RETZER, KEN Kenneth Leo B 4.30.1934 Wood River, IL BL/TR 6/185# d9.9																								
1961	Was A	16	53	7	18	4	0	1	3	4-0	0	5	.340	.386	.472	130	2	1-0	.988	-0	*64*	*147*	C-16	0.3
1962	Was A	109	340	36	97	11	2	8	37	26-4	0	21	.285	.334	.400	98	-2	2-0	.985	1	*113*	*112*	C-99	0.4
1963	Was A	95	265	21	64	10	0	5	31	17-2	2	20	.242	.290	.336	76	-9	2-0	.981	-15	61	130	C-81	-2.1
1964	Was A	17	32	1	3	0	0	0	1	5-1	1	4	.094	.237	.094	-4	-4	0-0	.971	2	*112*	*271*	C-13	-0.2
Total	4	237	690	65	182	25	2	14	72	52-7	3	50	.264	.316	.367	87	-13	5-0	.983	-12	*90*	*130*	C-209	-1.6
REVERING, DAVE David Alvin B 2.12.1953 Roseville, CA BL/TR 6-4/210# d4.8																								
1978	Oak A	152	521	49	141	21	3	16	46	26-5	0	55	.271	.303	.415	106	1	0-1	.989	7	120	88	*1-138/D-3	0.0

Year	Tm Lg	G	AB	R	H	2B	3B	HR	RBI	BB-IB	HP	SO	AVG	OBP	SLG	AOPS	ABR	SB-CS	FA	FR	Rng	Thr	G at Pos	BFW
1979	Oak A	125	472	63	136	25	5	19	77	34-5	1	65	.288	.334	.483	125	15	1-4	.986	1	106	72	*1-104,D-18	0.7
1980	Oak A	106	376	48	109	21	5	15	62	32-6	0	37	.290	.344	.492	136	17	1-0	.989	0	102	74	1-95/D-5	1.2
1981	Oak A	31	87	12	20	1	1	2	10	11-2	1	12	.230	.320	.333	94	-1	0-1	.995	-2	74	60	1-29/D-2	-0.5
	†NY A	45	119	8	28	4	1	2	7	11-5	0	20	.235	.300	.336	84	-3	0-1	.994	5	153	94	1-44	0.0
	Year	76	206	20	48	5	2	4	17	22-7	1	32	.233	.309	.335	88	-3	0-2	.994	3	120	80	1-73/D-2	-0.5
1982	NY A	14	40	2	6	2	0	0	2	3-2	0	4	.150	.205	.200	13	-5	0-0	1.000	-2	30	72	1-13/D	-0.7
	Tor A	55	135	15	29	6	0	5	18	22-1	0	30	.215	.321	.370	83	-3	0-3	1.000	-0	67	118	D-49/1-4	-0.6
	Sea A	29	82	8	17	3	1	3	12	9-0	0	17	.207	.283	.378	78	-3	0-0	.986	-2	71	114	1-27	-0.6
	Year	98	257	25	52	11	1	8	32	34-3	0	51	.202	.292	.346	71	-10	0-3	.992	-4	59	102	D-50,1-44	-1.9
Total	5	557	1832	205	486	83	16	62	234	148-26	2	240	.265	.318	.430	110	18	2-10	.989	8	107	81	1-454/D-78	-0.5
REVILLE, HENRY Henry B Baltimore, MD d10.14																								
1874	Bal NA	1	4	0	0	0	0	0	0	0		0	.000	.000	.000	-99	-1	0-0	1.000	1	627	0	/O(RF)	0.0
REXTER, WILLIAM William H. B Brooklyn, NY d9.25																								
1875	Atl NA	1	4	0	0	0	0	0	0	0		0	.000	.000	.000	-99	-1	0-0	1.000	0	0	0	/O(RF)	-0.1
REYES, GIL Gilberto Rolando (Polanco) B 12.10.1963 Santo Domingo, D.R. BR/TR 6-2/203# d6.11																								
1983	LA N	19	31	1	5	2	0	0	0	0-0	1	5	.161	.188	.226	14	-4	0-0	.944	0	111	137	C-19	-0.3
1984	LA N	4	5	0	0	0	0	0	0	0-0	0	3	.000	.000	.000	-99	-1	0-0	1.000	-0	0	0	/C-2	-0.2
1985	LA N	6	1	0	0	0	0	0	0	1-0	1	1	.000	.667	.000	105	0	0-0	1.000	1	0	203	/C-6	0.2
1987	LA N	1	0	0	0	0	0	0	0	0-0	0	0	—	—	—	—	0	0-0	1.000	0	0	0	/C	0.0
1988	LA N	5	9	1	1	0	0	0	0	0-0	0	3	.111	.111	.111	-37	-2	0-0	1.000	0	207	0	/C-5	-0.1
1989	Mon N	4	5	0	1	0	0	0	1	0-0	0	1	.200	.200	.200	14	-1	0-0	1.000	0	102	0	/C-4	0.0
1991	Mon N	83	207	11	45	9	0	0	13	19-2	1	51	.217	.285	.261	56	-12	2-4	.975	13	134	171	C-80	0.4
Total	7	122	258	13	52	11	0	0	14	20-2	3	64	.202	.266	.244	45	-20	2-4	.973	15	129	157	C-117	0.0
REYES, JOSE Jose Bernabe B 6.11.1983 Villa Gonzalez, D.R. BB/TR 6/160# d6.10																								
2003	NY N	69	274	47	84	12	4	5	32	13-0	0	36	.307	.334	.434	103	0	13-3	.973	3	106	92	S-69	1.0
REYES, NAP Napoleon Aguilera B 11.24.1919 Santiago De Cuba, Cuba D 9.15.1995 Miami, FL BR/TR 6-1/205# d5.19																								
1943	NY N	40	125	13	32	4	2	0	13	4	2	12	.256	.290	.320	76	-4	2	.994	-5	41	78	1-38/3	-1.2
1944	NY N	116	374	38	108	16	5	8	53	15	5	24	.289	.325	.422	109	3	2	.990	2	67	93	1-63,3-37/O-3(LF)	0.3
1945	NY N	122	431	39	124	15	4	5	44	25	**8**	26	.288	.338	.376	97	-3	1	.961	1	105	59	*3-115/1-5	-0.1
1950	NY N	1	1	0	0	0	0	0	0	0	0	0	.000	.000	.000	-99	0	0	.667	-0	0	0	/1	-0.1
Total	4	279	931	90	264	35	11	13	110	44	15	62	.284	.326	.387	99	-4	5	.960	-2	110	67	3-153,1-107/O-3(LF)	-1.1
REYES, RENE Rene B 2.21.1978 Margarita, Venezuela BB/TR 5-11/210# d7.22																								
2003	Col N	53	116	13	30	7	1	2	7	5-0	0	19	.259	.287	.388	65	-6	2-1	.964	0	95	176	O-36(11-5-24)	-0.7
REYNOLDS, CARL Carl Nettles B 2.1.1903 Larue, TX D 5.29.1978 Houston, TX BR/TR 6/194# d9.1																								
1927	Chi A	14	42	5	9	3	0	1	7	5	1	7	.214	.313	.357	75	-2	1-2	1.000	2	134	75	O-13(11-0-2)	-0.1
1928	Chi A	84	291	51	94	21	11	2	36	17	5	13	.323	.371	.491	126	10	15-3	.979	-0	102	85	O-74(15-1-58)	0.6
1929	Chi A	131	517	81	164	24	12	11	67	20	4	37	.317	.348	.474	111	5	19-9	.949	-2	100	96	*O-130(13-21-98)	-0.5
1930	Chi A	138	563	103	202	25	18	22	104	20	7	39	.359	.388	.584	148	36	16-4	.975	4	105	97	*O-132(35-54-47)	2.9
1931	Chi A	118	462	71	134	24	14	6	77	24	6	26	.290	.333	.442	108	3	17-6	.949	-4	95	93	*O-109(11-18-90)	-0.5
1932	Was A	102	406	53	124	28	7	9	63	13	3	19	.305	.332	.475	108	2	8-4	.983	2	114	38	O-95(RF)	-0.1
1933	StL A	135	475	81	136	26	14	8	71	49	3	25	.286	.357	.451	106	3	5-4	.965	-2	101	64	*O-124(123-2-0)	-0.6
1934	Bos A	113	413	61	125	26	9	4	86	27	3	28	.303	.350	.438	95	-4	5-3	.977	-1	101	74	*O-100(2-66-33)	-0.8
1935	Bos A	78	244	33	66	13	4	6	35	24	0	20	.270	.336	.430	91	-4	4-1	.975	4	113	127	O-64(3-1-60)	-0.3
1936	Was A	89	293	41	81	18	2	4	41	21	2	22	.276	.329	.392	82	-9	8-4	.968	1	100	124	O-72(0-4-69)	-1.1
1937	Chi N	7	11	0	3	1	0	0	1	2	0	2	.273	.385	.364	100	0	0	.800	-0	99	0	/O-2(LF)	0.0
1938	†Chi N	125	497	59	150	28	10	3	67	22	3	32	.302	.335	.416	103	1	9	.983	2	104	90	*O-125(63-83-4)	-0.3
1939	Chi N	88	281	33	69	10	6	4	44	16	5	38	.246	.298	.367	76	-11	5	.972	-1	100	85	O-72(3-51-18)	-1.4
Total	13	1222	4495	672	1357	247	107	80	699	260	42	308	.302	.346	.458	107	30	112-40	.970	5	103	86	*O-1112(281-301-574)	-2.2
REYNOLDS, CHARLIE Charles Lawrence B 5.1.1865 Williamsburg, IN D 7.3.1944 Denver, CO BR 5-9/175# d5.8																								
1889	KC AA	1	4	1	1	0	0	0	1	0	0	1	.250	.250	.250	40	0	0	1.000	-1			/C	-0.1
	Bro AA	12	42	5	9	1	1	0	3	1	0	6	.214	.233	.286	47	-3	2	.892	0			C-12	-0.2
	Year	13	46	6	10	1	1	0	4	1	0	7	.217	.234	.283	46	-4	2	.893	-1			C-13	-0.3
REYNOLDS, DANNY Daniel Vance "Squirrel" B 11.27.1919 Stony Point, NC BR/TR 5-11/158# d5.26																								
1945	Chi A	29	72	6	12	2	1	0	4	3	0	8	.167	.200	.222	23	-7	1-2	.947	2	109	94	S-14,2-11	-0.5
REYNOLDS, DON Donald Edward B 4.16.1953 Arkadelphia, AR BR/TR 5-8/178# d4.7 b-Harold																								
1978	SD N	57	87	8	22	2	0	0	10	15-2	0	14	.253	.363	.276	87	-1	1-0	.923	-1	77	159	O-25(22-0-3)	-0.2
1979	SD N	30	45	6	10	1	2	0	6	7-1	0	6	.222	.321	.333	86	-1	0-1	.950	1	86	283	O-14(7-5-2)	-0.1
Total	2	87	132	14	32	3	2	0	16	22-3	0	20	.242	.348	.295	87	-2	1-1	.935	-0	80	206	/O-39(29-5-5)	-0.3
REYNOLDS, CRAIG Gordon Craig B 12.27.1952 Houston, TX BL/TR 6-1/175# d8.1 OF Total (3-LF 1-RF)																								
1975	†Pit N	31	76	8	17	3	0	0	4	3-1	0	5	.224	.253	.263	44	-6	0-1	.969	3	107	90	S-30	-0.1
1976	Pit N	7	4	1	1	0	0	1	1	0-0	0	0	.250	.250	1.000	241	1	0-0	.889	-0	106	100	/S-4,2	0.0
1977	Sea A	135	420	41	104	12	3	4	28	15-1	3	23	.248	.277	.319	63	-23	6-6	.955	8	107	110	*S-134	-0.2
1978	Sea A☆	148	548	57	160	16	7	5	44	36-1	3	41	.292	.336	.374	101	0	9-6	.960	8	108	110	*S-146	2.3
1979	Hou N★	146	555	63	147	20	9	0	39	21-0	2	49	.265	.292	.333	75	-21	12-6	.965	-5	98	115	*S-143	-1.1
1980	†Hou N	137	381	34	86	9	6	3	28	20-1	0	39	.226	.262	.304	63	-21	2-1	.969	5	104	96	*S-135	-0.5
1981	†Hou N	87	323	43	84	10	**12**	4	31	12-2	0	31	.260	.286	.402	99	-4	3-3	.973	1	98	80	S-85	0.5
1982	Hou N	54	118	16	30	2	3	1	7	11-3	1	9	.254	.321	.347	95	-1	3-1	.958	-4	95	86	S-35/3-7	-0.2
1983	Hou N	65	98	10	21	3	0	1	6	6-1	0	10	.214	.260	.276	52	-7	0-1	.956	-7	91	79	2-26,3-15/S-8,O(LF)	-1.4
1984	Hou N	146	527	61	137	15	11	6	60	22-2	0	53	.260	.286	.364	89	-12	7-1	.965	24	112	118	*S-143/3	2.9
1985	Hou N	107	379	43	103	18	8	4	32	12-2	0	30	.272	.293	.393	93	-6	4-4	.977	16	109	115	*S-102/2	2.0
1986	†Hou N	114	313	32	78	7	3	6	41	12-5	0	31	.249	.274	.348	73	-13	3-1	.978	-8	88	87	S-98/1-5,3-4,O-2(1-0-1),P	-1.3
1987	Hou N	135	374	35	95	17	3	4	28	30-8	0	44	.254	.303	.348	77	-13	5-1	.970	-9	90	71	*S-129/3-2	-1.0
1988	Hou N	78	161	20	41	7	0	1	14	8-2	0	23	.255	.290	.317	77	-5	3-0	.970	-3	100	122	S-22,3-19,2-11,1-10	-0.7
1989	Hou N	101	189	16	38	4	0	2	14	19-5	0	18	.201	.274	.254	54	-12	1-0	.979	7	119	110	2-29,S-26,3-10/1-5,P0(LF)	-0.2
Total	15	1491	4466	480	1142	143	65	42	377	227-34	9	406	.256	.291	.345	80	-143	58-32	.966	36	102	102	*S-1240/2-68,3-58,1-20,O-4L,P-2	1.0
REYNOLDS, HAROLD Harold Craig B 11.26.1960 Eugene, OR BB/TR 5-11/165# d9.2 b-Don																								
1983	Sea A	20	59	8	12	4	1	0	1	2-0	0	9	.203	.226	.305	44	-5	0-2	.975	-1	94	112	2-18	-0.5
1984	Sea A	10	10	3	3	0	0	0	0	0-0	1	1	.300	.364	.300	87	0	1-1	1.000	2	127	132	/2-6	0.2
1985	Sea A	67	104	15	15	3	1	0	6	17-0	0	14	.144	.264	.192	27	-10	3-2	.960	5	116	84	2-61	-0.3
1986	Sea A	126	445	46	99	19	4	1	24	29-0	3	42	.222	.275	.290	53	-29	30-12	.977	30	**115**	**122**	*2-126	1.0
1987	Sea A★	160	530	73	146	31	8	1	35	39-0	2	34	.275	.325	.370	80	-15	**60**-20	.977	24	111	108	*2-160	2.3
1988	Sea A★	158	598	61	169	26	**11**	4	41	51-1	2	51	.283	.340	.383	98	-2	35-29	.977	8	102	104	*2-158	0.9
1989	Sea A	153	613	87	184	24	9	0	43	55-1	3	45	.300	.359	.369	103	3	25-18	.980	**25**	**111**	107	*2-151/D	3.1
1990	Sea A	160	642	100	162	36	5	5	55	81-3	3	52	.252	.336	.347	91	-5	31-16	.978	20	**106**	100	*2-160	2.1
1991	Sea A	161	631	95	160	34	6	3	57	72-2	5	63	.254	.332	.341	87	-9	28-8	.978	8	98	121	*2-159/D	0.7
1992	Sea A	140	458	55	113	23	3	3	33	45-1	3	41	.247	.316	.330	81	-11	15-12	.982	8	102	94	*2-134/O(LF)D	0.0
1993	Bal A	145	485	64	122	20	4	4	47	66-3	4	47	.252	.343	.334	80	-12	12-11	.986	3	99	**121**	*2-141/D	-0.3
1994	Cal A	74	207	33	48	10	1	0	11	23-0	1	18	.232	.310	.290	56	-13	10-7	.996	-11	85	69	2-65/D-3	-2.1
Total	12	1374	4782	640	1233	230	53	21	353	480-11	27	417	.258	.327	.341	83	-108	250-138	.979	122	105	107	*2-1339/D-7,O(LF)	7.1
REYNOLDS, R. J. Robert James B 4.19.1959 Sacramento, CA BB/TR 6/190# d9.1																								
1983	LA N	24	55	5	13	0	0	2	11	3-1	0	11	.236	.267	.345	72	-2	5-0	.931	0	87	222	O-18(9-5-7)	-0.2
1984	LA N	73	240	24	62	12	2	2	24	14-0	1	38	.258	.300	.350	84	-6	7-5	.973	-2	90	104	O-63(25-19-34)	-1.1
1985	LA N	73	207	22	55	10	4	0	25	13-0	1	31	.266	.308	.353	88	-4	6-3	.970	-1	99	87	O-54(31-5-24)	-0.7
	Pit N	31	130	22	40	5	3	3	17	9-1	1	18	.308	.357	.462	129	4	12-2	.958	1	105	137	O-31(29-8-0)	0.6
	Year	104	337	44	95	15	7	3	42	22-1	2	49	.282	.327	.395	104	1	18-5	.965	0	101	106	O-85(60-13-24)	-0.1

Year	Tm Lg	G	AB	R	H	2B	3B	HR	RBI	BB-IB	HP	SO	AVG	OBP	SLG	AOPS	ABR	SB-CS	FA	FR	Rng	Thr	G at Pos	BFW
1986	Pit N	118	402	63	108	30	2	9	48	40-4	1	78	.269	.335	.420	105	3	16-9	.955	-7	94	27	*O-112(84-12-44)	-0.8
1987	Pit N	117	335	47	87	24	1	7	51	34-8	0	80	.260	.323	.400	91	-4	14-1	.993	-4	83	118	O-99(29-0-72)	-0.9
1988	Pit N	130	323	35	80	14	2	6	51	20-3	0	62	.248	.288	.359	87	-6	15-2	.974	1	94	177	O-95(19-1-79)	-0.6
1989	Pit N	125	363	45	98	16	2	6	48	34-8	1	66	.270	.331	.375	106	3	22-5	.990	2	100	119	O-98(5-30-72)	0.6
1990	†Pit N	95	215	25	62	10	1	0	19	23-1	0	35	.288	.354	.344	98	0	12-2	.972	-3	88	93	O-59(13-24-26)	-0.2
Total	8	786	2270	288	605	121	17	35	294	190-26	5	419	.267	.321	.381	97	-12	109-29	.973	-13	93	106	O-629(244-104-358)	-3.3

REYNOLDS, RONN Ronn Dwayne B 9.28.1958 Wichita, KS BR/TR 6/200# d9.29

Year	Tm Lg	G	AB	R	H	2B	3B	HR	RBI	BB-IB	HP	SO	AVG	OBP	SLG	AOPS	ABR	SB-CS	FA	FR	Rng	Thr	G at Pos	BFW
1982	NY N	2	4	0	0	0	0	0	0	1-0	0	1	.000	.200	.000	-40	-1	0-0	1.000	-2	153	0	/C-2	-0.2
1983	NY N	24	66	4	13	1	0	0	2	8-1	0	12	.197	.280	.212	40	-5	0-0	.942	-5	76	109	C-24	-0.9
1985	NY N	28	43	4	9	2	0	0	1	0-0	1	18	.209	.227	.256	36	-4	0-0	.990	1	116	178	C-25	-0.3
1986	Phi N	43	126	8	27	4	0	3	10	5-0	0	30	.214	.242	.317	52	-9	0-0	.991	-5	71	84	C-42	-1.3
1987	Hou N	38	102	5	17	4	0	1	7	3-0	0	29	.167	.189	.235	12	-13	0-1	.975	-2	77	103	C-38	-1.4
1990	SD N	8	15	1	1	1	0	0	1	1-0	0	6	.067	.125	.133	-29	-3	0-0	1.000	-1	73	113	/C-8	-0.4
Total	6	143	356	22	67	12	0	4	21	18-1	1	96	.188	.228	.256	32	-35	0-1	.977	-13	81	106	C-139	-4.5

REYNOLDS, TOMMIE Tommie D B 8.15.1941 Arizona, LA BR/TR (BB 1967 (part)) 6-2/190# d9.5 C8

Year	Tm Lg	G	AB	R	H	2B	3B	HR	RBI	BB-IB	HP	SO	AVG	OBP	SLG	AOPS	ABR	SB-CS	FA	FR	Rng	Thr	G at Pos	BFW
1963	KC A	8	19	1	1	1	0	0	0	1-0	1	7	.053	.143	.105	-28	-3	0-0	.800	-1	83	0	/O-5(LF)	-0.5
1964	KC A	31	94	11	19	1	0	2	9	10-0	2	22	.202	.292	.277	58	-5	0-0	.976	-0	98	177	O-25(LF)/3-3	-0.7
1965	KC A	90	270	34	64	11	3	1	22	36-1	0	41	.237	.327	.311	83	-5	9-2	.982	7	109	171	O-83(77-0-6)/3	-0.1
1967	NY N	101	136	16	28	1	0	2	9	11-3	3	26	.206	.278	.257	56	-8	1-1	.971	2	111	147	O-72(42-13-21)/3-5,C	-0.8
1969	Oak A	107	315	51	81	10	0	2	20	34-1	8	29	.257	.343	.308	87	-4	1-3	.979	5	112	75	O-89(81-0-8)	-0.5
1970	Cal A	59	120	11	30	3	1	1	6	6-0	1	10	.250	.291	.317	70	-5	1-1	.969	1	123	56	O-32(4-1-28)/3	-0.6
1971	Cal A	45	86	4	16	3	0	2	8	9-1	3	6	.186	.286	.291	68	-4	0-1	.978	2	106	143	O-26(6-0-23)/3	-0.4
1972	Mil A	72	130	13	26	5	1	2	13	10-0	1	25	.200	.262	.300	68	-5	0-0	.961	3	134	91	O-41(36-0-6)/13	-0.4
Total	8	513	1170	141	265	35	5	12	87	117-6	19	166	.226	.306	.296	73	-39	12-8	.973	19	112	119	O-373(276-14-92)/3-12,1C	-4.0

REYNOLDS, BILL William Dee B 8.14.1884 Eastland, TX D 6.5.1924 Carnegie, OK BR/TR 6/185# d9.15

Year	Tm Lg	G	AB	R	H	2B	3B	HR	RBI	BB-IB	HP	SO	AVG	OBP	SLG	AOPS	ABR	SB-CS	FA	FR	Rng	Thr	G at Pos	BFW
1913	NY A	5	5	0	0	0	0	0	0	0	0	1	.000	.000	.000	-99	-1	0	.917	-0	*72*	*57*	/C-5	-0.1
1914	NY A	4	5	0	2	0	0	0	0	0	0	3	.400	.400	.400	141	0	0	1.000	0	*85*	*138*	/C	0.1
Total	2	9	10	0	2	0	0	0	0	0	0	4	.200	.200	.200	19	-1	0	.941	0	*76*	*81*	/C-6	0.0

RHAWN, BOBBY Robert John "Rocky" B 2.13.1919 Catawissa, PA D 6.9.1984 Danville, PA BR/TR 5-8/180# d9.17

Year	Tm Lg	G	AB	R	H	2B	3B	HR	RBI	BB-IB	HP	SO	AVG	OBP	SLG	AOPS	ABR	SB-CS	FA	FR	Rng	Thr	G at Pos	BFW
1947	NY N	13	45	7	14	3	0	1	3	8	0	1	.311	.415	.444	128	2	0	.913	1	119	76	/2-8,3-5	0.3
1948	NY N	36	44	11	12	2	1	1	8	8	0	6	.273	.385	.432	120	1	3	.872	-1	104	75	S-14/3-7	0.1
1949	NY N	14	29	8	5	0	0	0	2	7	0	2	.172	.333	.172	40	-2	1	.959	2	127	134	/2-8	0.0
	Pit N	3	7	0	1	0	0	0	0	0	0	0	.143	.143	.143	-23	-1	0	.889	0	108	0	/3-2	-0.1
	Year	17	36	8	6	0	0	0	2	7	0	2	.167	.302	.167	29	-3	1	.959	2	127	134	/2-8,3-2	-0.1
	Chi A	24	73	12	15	4	1	0	5	12	0	8	.205	.318	.288	63	-4	0-1	.959	1	101	84	3-19/S-3	-0.3
Total	3	90	198	38	47	9	2	2	18	35	0	17	.237	.352	.333	84	-4	4-1	.963	3	103	111	/3-33,S-17,2-16	0.0

RHEAM, CY Kenneth Johnston B 9.28.1893 Pittsburgh, PA D 10.23.1947 Pittsburgh, PA BR/TR 6- /175# d5.20

Year	Tm Lg	G	AB	R	H	2B	3B	HR	RBI	BB-IB	HP	SO	AVG	OBP	SLG	AOPS	ABR	SB-CS	FA	FR	Rng	Thr	G at Pos	BFW
1914	Pit F	73	214	15	45	5	3	0	20	9	0	33	.210	.242	.262	38	-23	6	.976	-6	59	53	1-43,3-13,2-11/O(LF)	-3.1
1915	Pit F	34	69	10	12	0	0	1	5	1	0	7	.174	.186	.217	13	-9	4	.959	1	129	81	O-22(12-4-6)/1	-1.0
Total	2	107	283	25	57	5	3	1	25	10	0	40	.201	.229	.251	32	-32	10	.976	-4	58	52	/1-44,O-23(13-4-6),3-13,2-11	-4.1

RHIEL, BILLY William Joseph B 8.16.1900 Youngstown, OH D 8.16.1946 Youngstown, OH BR/TR 5-11/175# d4.20

Year	Tm Lg	G	AB	R	H	2B	3B	HR	RBI	BB-IB	HP	SO	AVG	OBP	SLG	AOPS	ABR	SB-CS	FA	FR	Rng	Thr	G at Pos	BFW
1929	Bro N	76	205	27	57	9	4	4	25	19	0	25	.278	.339	.420	89	-4	0	.979	-2	95	59	2-47/3-7,S-2	-0.4
1930	Bos N	20	47	3	8	4	0	0	4	2	0	5	.170	.204	.255	11	-7	0	.947	-2	70	67	3-13/2-2	-0.8
1932	Det A	85	250	30	70	13	3	3	38	17	1	23	.280	.328	.392	82	-7	2-0	.956	-2	85	147	3-37,1-12/O-8(LF),2	-0.8
1933	Det A	19	17	1	3	0	1	0	1	5	0	4	.176	.364	.294	75	-1	0-0	1.000	0	137	0	/O(LF)	0.0
Total	4	200	519	61	138	26	8	7	68	43	1	57	.266	.323	.387	78	-19	2-0	.949	-6	88	136	/3-57,2-50,1-12,O-9(LF),S-2	-2.0

RHODES, DUSTY James Lamar B 5.13.1927 Mathews, AL BL/TR 6/180# d7.15

Year	Tm Lg	G	AB	R	H	2B	3B	HR	RBI	BB-IB	HP	SO	AVG	OBP	SLG	AOPS	ABR	SB-CS	FA	FR	Rng	Thr	G at Pos	BFW
1952	NY N	67	176	34	44	8	1	10	36	23	1	33	.250	.340	.477	123	5	1-0	.917	-2	98	79	O-56(55-2-0)	0.0
1953	NY N	76	163	18	38	7	0	11	30	10	0	28	.233	.277	.479	91	-3	0-1	.965	2	95	182	O-47(25-0-22)	-0.4
1954	†NY N	82	164	31	56	7	3	15	50	18	1	25	.341	.410	.695	181	19	1-0	.984	-1	96	49	O-37(33-2-1)	1.5
1955	NY N	94	187	22	57	5	2	6	32	27-2	0	26	.305	.389	.449	122	7	1-1	.986	-1	94	74	O-45(LF)	0.3
1956	NY N	111	244	20	53	10	3	8	33	30-2	0	41	.217	.301	.381	83	-6	0-0	.958	-2	87	178	O-68(64-0-5)	-1.1
1957	NY N	92	190	20	39	5	1	4	19	18-3	1	34	.205	.276	.305	57	-12	0-0	1.000	-3	90	0	O-44(22-0-23)	-1.7
1959	SF N	54	48	1	9	2	0	0	7	5-3	0	9	.188	.259	.229	34	-5	0-0	—	0			H	-0.5
Total	7	576	1172	146	296	44	10	54	207	131-10	3	196	.253	.328	.445	104	5	3-2	.963	-8	93	101	O-297(244-4-51)	-1.9

RHODES, KARL Karl Derrick "Tuffy" B 8.21.1968 Cincinnati, OH BL/TL 5-11/170# d8.7

Year	Tm Lg	G	AB	R	H	2B	3B	HR	RBI	BB-IB	HP	SO	AVG	OBP	SLG	AOPS	ABR	SB-CS	FA	FR	Rng	Thr	G at Pos	BFW
1990	Hou N	38	86	12	21	6	1	1	3	13-3	0	12	.244	.340	.372	100	0	4-1	.955	1	107	119	O-30(19-9-5)	0.1
1991	Hou N	44	136	7	29	3	1	1	12	14-3	1	26	.213	.289	.272	63	-7	2-2	.958	3	115	135	O-44(RF)	-0.6
1992	Hou N	5	4	0	0	0	0	0	0	0-0	0	2	.000	.000	.000	-99	-1	0-0	—	-0	0	0	/O(1-0-1)	-0.1
1993	Hou N	5	2	0	0	0	0	0	0	0-0	0	0	.000	.000	.000	-99	-1	0-0	1.000	0	110	0	/O-4(1-2-1)	-0.1
	Chi N	15	52	12	15	2	1	3	7	11-0	0	9	.288	.413	.538	155	4	2-0	.970	-0	93	140	O-14(6-14-1)	0.5
	Year	20	54	12	15	2	1	3	7	11-0	0	9	.278	.400	.519	147	4	2-0	.971	-0	94	132	O-18(7-16-2)	0.4
1994	Chi N	95	269	39	63	17	0	8	19	33-1	1	64	.234	.318	.387	84	-6	6-4	.967	-3	90	113	O-76(15-67-1)	-0.8
1995	Chi N	13	16	2	2	0	0	0	2	0-0	0	4	.125	.118	.125	-34	-3	0-0	.889	-0	118	0	O-11(LF)	-0.3
	Bos A	10	25	2	2	1	0	0	1	3-0	0	4	.080	.179	.120	-20	-5	0-0	.947	-1	101	0	/O-9(CF)	-0.5
Total	6	225	590	74	132	29	3	13	44	74-7	2	121	.224	.310	.349	79	-19	14-7	.960	0	101	114	O-189(53-101-53)	-1.8

RHOMBERG, KEVIN Kevin Jay B 11.22.1955 Dubuque, IA BR/TR 6/175# d9.1

Year	Tm Lg	G	AB	R	H	2B	3B	HR	RBI	BB-IB	HP	SO	AVG	OBP	SLG	AOPS	ABR	SB-CS	FA	FR	Rng	Thr	G at Pos	BFW
1982	Cle A	16	18	3	6	0	0	1	1	2-0	0	4	.333	.400	.500	146	1	0-2	.900	1	113	508	/O-7(LF),3D	0.1
1983	Cle A	12	21	2	10	0	0	0	2	2-0	0	4	.476	.500	.476	170	2	1-1	1.000	-1	82	0	/O-9(8-1-0),D	0.1
1984	Cle A	13	8	0	2	0	0	0	0	0-0	0	3	.250	.250	.250	38	-1	0-0	1.000	0	129	0	/O-7(LF),12D	0.0
Total	3	41	47	5	18	0	0	1	3	4-0	0	11	.383	.423	.447	140	2	1-3	.963	1	101	148	/O-23(22-1-0),D-6,213	0.2

RHYNE, HAL Harold J. B 3.30.1899 Paso Robles, CA D 1.7.1971 Orangevale, CA BR/TR 5-8.5/163# d4.18

Year	Tm Lg	G	AB	R	H	2B	3B	HR	RBI	BB-IB	HP	SO	AVG	OBP	SLG	AOPS	ABR	SB-CS	FA	FR	Rng	Thr	G at Pos	BFW
1926	Pit N	109	366	46	92	14	3	2	39	35	6	21	.251	.327	.322	71	-14	1	.967	5	99	123	2-66,S-44/3	-0.3
1927	†Pit N	62	168	21	46	5	0	0	17	14	0	9	.274	.330	.304	66	-8	0	.963	-8	79	95	2-45,3-10/S-7	-1.3
1929	Bos A	120	346	41	87	24	5	0	38	25	4	14	.251	.309	.350	71	-15	4-1	.935	-2	97	112	*S-113/3O(RF)	-0.5
1930	Bos A	107	296	34	60	8	5	0	23	25	2	19	.203	.269	.264	37	-29	1-4	.944	3	107	**117**	*S-107	-1.6
1931	Bos A	147	565	75	154	34	3	0	51	57	2	41	.273	.341	.343	85	-11	3-3	**.963**	18	**115**	88	*S-147	1.6
1932	Bos A	71	207	26	47	12	5	0	14	23	2	14	.227	.310	.333	69	-10	3-2	.966	5	113	96	S-55/3-4,2	-0.1
1933	Chi A	39	83	9	22	1	1	0	10	5	1	9	.265	.315	.301	67	-4	1-1	.955	2	108	125	2-19,3-13/S-2	-0.2
Total	7	655	2031	252	508	98	22	2	192	184	17	127	.250	.318	.323	69	-91	13-11	.950	23	107	104	S-475,2-131/3-29,O(RF)	-2.4

RICE, DEL Delbert B 10.27.1922 Portsmouth, OH D 1.26.1983 Buena Park, CA BR/TR 6-2/190# d5.2 M1 C7

Year	Tm Lg	G	AB	R	H	2B	3B	HR	RBI	BB-IB	HP	SO	AVG	OBP	SLG	AOPS	ABR	SB-CS	FA	FR	Rng	Thr	G at Pos	BFW
1945	StL N	83	253	27	66	17	3	1	28	16	3	33	.261	.313	.364	86	-5	0	.994	5	*97*	*120*	C-77	0.4
1946	†StL N	55	139	10	38	8	1	1	12	8	0	16	.273	.313	.367	89	-2	0	.977	1	*152*	*51*	C-53	0.1
1947	StL N	97	261	28	57	7	3	12	44	36	1	40	.218	.315	.406	87	-6	1	.981	3	*126*	*74*	C-94	0.2
1948	StL N	100	290	24	57	10	1	4	34	37	5	46	.197	.298	.279	54	-18	1	**.996**	11	***292***	*73*	C-99	-0.2
1949	StL N	92	284	25	67	16	1	4	29	30	5	40	.236	.320	.342	74	-10	0	.992	1	*127*	*66*	C-92	-0.5
1950	StL N	130	414	39	101	20	3	9	54	43	5	65	.244	.323	.372	78	-13	0	.984	7	*134*	*91*	*C-130	0.1
1951	StL N	122	374	34	94	13	1	9	47	34	3	26	.251	.319	.364	83	-9	0-0	.985	4	*124*	*90*	*C-120	0.1
1952	StL N	147	495	43	128	27	2	11	65	33	6	38	.259	.313	.388	93	-5	0-1	.992	2	*139*	*95*	*C-147	0.4
1953	StL N✱	135	419	32	99	22	1	6	37	48	6	49	.236	.323	.337	72	-16	0-0	.988	-5	*87*	*91*	*C-135	-1.4
1954	StL N	56	147	13	37	10	1	2	16	16	0	21	.252	.321	.374	81	-4	0-1	.985	1	*165*	*87*	C-52	-0.1
1955	StL N	20	59	6	12	3	0	1	7	7-0	0	6	.203	.284	.305	58	-4	0-0	.964	-4	*89*	*92*	C-18	-0.7
	Mil N	27	71	5	14	0	1	2	7	6-2	0	12	.197	.260	.310	53	-5	0-0	.981	0	*117*	*152*	C-22	-0.4
	Year	47	130	11	26	3	1	3	14	13-2	0	18	.200	.271	.308	55	-9	0-0	.973	-4	*104*	*125*	C-40	-1.1
1956	Mil N	71	188	15	40	9	1	3	17	18-7	0	34	.213	.282	.319	65	-9	0-0	.983	2	*156*	*81*	C-65	-0.5
1957	†Mil N	54	144	15	33	1	1	9	20	17-7	0	37	.229	.309	.438	106	0	0-0	.992	3	*101*	*65*	C-48	0.5

Year	Tm Lg	G	AB	R	H	2B	3B	HR	RBI	BB-IB	HP	SO	AVG	OBP	SLG	AOPS	ABR	SB-CS	FA	FR	Rng	Thr	G at Pos	BFW
1958	Mil N	43	121	10	27	7	0	1	8	8-1	0	30	.223	.271	.306	57	-8	0-0	.995	1	*117*	*89*	C-38	-0.6
1959	Mil N	13	29	3	6	0	0	0	1	2-0	0	3	.207	.250	.207	28	-3	0-0	.956	-1	*132*	*0*	/C-9	-0.3
1960	Chi N	18	52	2	12	3	0	0	4	2-1	0	7	.231	.255	.288	50	-4	0-0	.968	-2	*68*	*105*	C-18	-0.5
	StL N	1	2	0	0	0	0	0	0	1-0	0	0	.000	.333	.000	1	0	0-0	1.000	-0	*0*	*0*	/C	0.0
	Year	19	54	2	12	3	0	0	4	3-1	0	7	.222	.259	.278	49	-4	0-0	.970	-2	*65*	*100*	C-19	-0.5
	Bal A	1	1	0	0	0	0	0	0	0-0	0	0	.000	.000	.000	-99	0	0-0	1.000	0	*0*	*0*	/C	0.0
1961	LA A	44	83	11	20	4	0	4	11	20-5	0	19	.241	.385	.434	107	2	0-1	.994	1	*75*	*138*	C-30	0.3
Total	17	1309	3826	342	908	177	20	79	441	382-23	34	522	.237	.312	.356	78	-119	2-3	.987	30	*136*	*87*	*C-1249	-3.1
RICE, SAM Edgar Charles B 2.20.1890 Morocco, IN D 10.13.1974 Rossmoor, MD BL/TR 5-9/150# d8.7 Mil 1918 HF1963 ▲																								
1915	Was A	4	8	0	3	0	0	0	0	0	0	1	.375	.375	.375	122	1	0	.889	0	131	592	/P-4	0.0
1916	Was A	58	197	26	59	8	3	1	17	15	1	13	.299	.352	.386	123	5	4	.957	2	117	94	O-46(4-0-42)/P-5	0.4
1917	Was A	155	586	77	177	25	7	0	69	50	3	41	.302	.360	.369	124	17	35	.960	5	103	124	*O-155(RF)	1.5
1918	Was A	7	23	3	8	1	0	0	3	2	0	0	.348	.400	.391	141	1	1	1.000	3	94	446	/O-6(RF)	0.4
1919	Was A	141	557	80	179	23	9	3	71	42	7	26	.321	.376	.411	122	16	26	.962	5	113	92	*O-141(RF)	1.4
1920	Was A	**153**	624	83	211	29	9	3	80	39	4	23	.338	.381	.428	117	15	**63**-30	.960	**17**	**121**	124	*O-153(CF)	2.3
1921	Was A	143	561	83	185	39	13	4	79	38	9	10	.330	.382	.467	121	17	26-12	.964	6	109	101	*O-141(0-137-4)	1.7
1922	Was A	**154**	633	91	187	37	13	6	69	48	2	13	.295	.347	.423	105	3	20-9	.951	2	98	143	*O-154(CF)	0.0
1923	Was A	148	595	117	188	35	**18**	3	75	57	6	12	.316	.381	.450	125	20	20-8	.970	7	107	108	*O-147(RF)	1.6
1924	†Was A	154	646	106	**216**	39	14	1	76	46	4	24	.334	.382	.443	116	14	24-13	.967	1	106	89	*O-154(0-34-123)	0.4
1925	†Was A	**152**	649	111	227	31	13	1	87	37	4	10	.350	.388	.442	113	11	26-11	.968	7	106	122	*O-152(0-29-133)	0.7
1926	Was A	**152**	641	98	**216**	32	14	3	76	42	2	20	.337	.380	.445	117	14	24-23	.961	8	106	148	*O-152(0-44-120)	0.8
1927	Was A	142	603	98	179	33	14	2	65	36	0	11	.297	.336	.408	93	-8	19-6	.975	-2	100	81	*O-139(1-0-138)	-1.8
1928	Was A	148	616	95	202	32	15	2	55	49	2	15	.328	.379	.438	115	13	16-3	.973	-10	88	73	*O-147(1-0-147)	-0.6
1929	Was A	150	616	119	199	39	10	1	62	55	4	9	.323	.382	.424	106	7	16-8	.970	3	99	132	*O-147(RF)	-0.1
1930	Was A	147	593	121	207	35	13	1	73	55	3	14	.349	.407	.457	118	18	13-8	.963	3	106	101	*O-145(0-15-133)	0.9
1931	Was A	120	413	81	128	21	8	0	42	35	1	11	.310	.365	.400	100	0	6-5	.970	2	107	76	*O-105(10-11-85)	-0.4
1932	Was A	106	288	58	93	16	7	1	34	32	0	6	.323	.391	.438	116	7	7-4	.972	2	98	143	O-69(10-14-48)	0.5
1933	†Was A	73	85	19	25	4	3	1	12	2	2	7	.294	.326	.447	104	0	0-2	1.000	4	120	285	O-39(8-10-23)	0.2
1934	Cle A	97	335	48	98	19	1	1	33	28	2	9	.293	.351	.364	83	-8	5-1	.963	-6	90	35	O-78(13-0-65)	-1.7
Total	20	2404	9269	1514	2987	498	184	34	1078	708	56	275	.322	.374	.427	113	163	351-143	.965	57	105	110	*O-2270(47-601-1657)/P-9	8.2
RICE, HAL Harold Housten "Hoot" B 2.11.1924 Morganette, WV D 12.22.1997 Bloomington, IN BL/TR 6-1/195# d9.25																								
1948	StL N	8	31	3	10	1	2	0	3	2	0	4	.323	.364	.484	121	1	0	1.000	-0	105	0	/O-8(LF)	0.0
1949	StL N	40	46	3	9	2	1	1	9	3	0	7	.196	.245	.348	55	-3	0	1.000	0	89	286	O-10(LF)	-0.3
1950	StL N	44	128	12	27	3	1	2	11	10	0	10	.211	.268	.297	46	-10	0	.972	1	100	124	O-37(33-0-4)	-1.2
1951	StL N	69	236	20	60	12	1	4	38	24	0	22	.254	.323	.364	84	-5	0-1	.953	-0	98	118	O-63(48-0-16)	-1.0
1952	StL N	98	295	37	85	14	5	7	45	16	0	26	.288	.325	.441	110	3	1-3	.972	-2	96	92	O-81(77-4-5)	-0.5
1953	StL N	8	8	0	2	0	0	0	0	0	0	3	.250	.250	.250	31	-1	0-0	—	0			H	-0.1
	Pit N	78	286	39	89	16	1	4	42	17	0	22	.311	.350	.416	99	0	0-1	.973	8	109	213	O-70(68-0-2)	0.3
	Year	86	294	39	91	16	1	4	42	17	0	25	.310	.347	.412	97	-1	0-1	.973	8	109	213	O-70(68-0-2)	0.2
1954	Pit N	28	81	10	14	4	1	1	9	14	0	24	.173	.295	.284	52	-6	0-2	1.000	3	112	190	O-24(24-0-2)	-0.5
	Chi N	51	72	5	11	0	0	0	5	8	0	15	.153	.235	.153	4	-10	0-0	.897	-0	94	176	O-24(3-0-21)	-1.1
	Year	79	153	15	25	4	1	1	14	22	0	39	.163	.267	.222	29	-16	0-2	.966	3	106	185	O-48(27-0-23)	-1.6
Total	7	424	1183	129	307	52	12	19	162	94	0	133	.260	.314	.372	82	-31	1-7	.969	10	102	145	O-317(271-4-50)	-4.4
RICE, HARRY Harry Francis B 11.22.1901 Ware Station, IL D 1.1.1971 Portland, OR BL/TR 5-9/185# d4.18 OF Total (28-LF 465-CF 421-RF)																								
1923	StL A	4	3	0	0	0	0	0	0	0	0	0	.000	.000	.000	-95	-1	0-0	—	0			H	-0.1
1924	StL A	54	93	19	26	7	0	0	15	7	3	5	.280	.350	.355	77	-3	1-3	.917	-1	94	125	3-15/2-4,1-2,S-2,O-2(1-0-1)	-0.3
1925	StL A	103	354	87	127	25	8	11	47	54	5	15	.359	.450	.568	149	28	8-7	.984	3	102	142	O-85(3-6-76)/1-3,C23	2.2
1926	StL A	148	578	86	181	27	10	9	59	63	4	40	.313	.384	.441	110	9	10-11	.970	3	102	149	*O-133(0-47-87)/3-8,2-4,S-2	0.1
1927	StL A	137	520	90	149	26	9	7	68	50	2	21	.287	.351	.412	94	-5	5-4	.938	11	104	**196**	*O-130(0-44-87)/3-7	-0.3
1928	Det A	131	510	87	154	21	12	6	81	44	2	27	.302	.360	.425	104	2	20-12	.962	-5	101	70	*O-129(CF)/3-2	-0.8
1929	Det A	130	536	97	163	33	7	6	69	61	4	23	.304	.379	.425	106	7	6-11	.960	1	98	119	*O-127(CF)/3-3	0.0
1930	Det A	37	128	16	39	6	0	2	24	19	2	8	.305	.403	.398	102	1	0-3	.944	-1	101	72	O-35(19-0-16)	-0.3
	NY A	100	346	62	103	17	5	7	74	31	3	21	.298	.361	.436	106	3	3-3	.969	2	103	109	O-87(4-83-0)/1-6,3	0.1
	Year	137	474	78	142	23	5	9	98	50	5	29	.300	.372	.426	105	4	3-6	.964	1	102	99	*O-122(23-83-16)/1-6,3	-0.2
1931	Was A	47	162	32	43	5	6	0	15	12	1	10	.265	.320	.370	81	-5	2-1	.968	0	102	90	O-42(1-19-23)	-0.7
1933	Cin N	143	510	44	133	19	6	0	54	35	6	24	.261	.316	.322	84	-11	4	**.991**	4	104	106	*O-141(0-10-131)/3	-1.6
Total	10	1034	3740	620	1118	186	63	48	506	376	32	194	.299	.368	.421	104	25	59-55	.966	17	102	124	O-911C/3-38,1-11,2-9,S-4,C	-1.7
RICE, JIM James Edward B 3.8.1953 Anderson, SC BR/TR 6-2/205# d8.19 C7																								
1974	Bos A	24	67	6	18	2	1	1	13	4-0	1	12	.269	.307	.373	92	-1	0-0	.800	-0	85	0	D-16/O-3(LF)	-0.2
1975	Bos A	144	564	92	174	29	4	22	102	36-7	4	122	.309	.350	.491	126	18	10-5	1.000	-4	87	91	O-90(LF),D-54	0.8
1976	Bos A	153	581	75	164	25	8	25	85	28-2	4	123	.282	.315	.482	118	10	8-5	.967	-2	93	109	O-98(LF),D-54	0.1
1977	Bos A★	160	644	104	206	29	15	**39**	114	53-10	8	120	.320	.376	**.593**	143	37	5-4	.956	-1	94	124	*D-116,O-44(19-0-27)	3.0
1978	Bos A★	**163**	677	121	**213**	25	**15**	**46**	**139**	58-7	5	126	.315	.370	**.600**	153	**44**	7-5	.989	4	95	158	*O-114(101-1-15),D-49	4.1
1979	Bos A★	158	619	117	201	39	6	39	130	57-4	4	97	.325	.381	.596	152	44	9-4	.984	-6	87	83	*O-125(124-0-1),D-33	3.1
1980	Bos A✳	124	504	81	148	22	6	24	86	30-5	4	87	.294	.336	.504	121	13	8-3	.988	-1	92	115	*O-109(LF),D-15	0.7
1981	Bos A	**108**	451	51	128	18	1	17	62	34-3	3	76	.284	.333	.441	116	9	2-2	.988	-2	95	110	*O-108(LF)	0.2
1982	Bos A	145	573	86	177	24	5	24	97	55-6	7	98	.309	.375	.494	129	23	0-1	.969	-6	88	112	*O-145(LF)	1.0
1983	Bos A★	155	626	90	191	34	1	**39**	**126**	52-10	6	102	.305	.361	.550	137	31	0-2	.984	10	103	170	*O-151(LF)/D-4	3.3
1984	Bos A★	159	657	98	184	25	7	28	122	44-8	1	102	.280	.323	.467	111	8	4-0	.989	4	101	110	*O-157(LF)/D-2	0.6
1985	Bos A★	140	546	85	159	20	3	27	103	51-5	2	75	.291	.349	.487	122	16	2-0	.964	-8	86	95	*O-130(LF)/D-7	0.3
1986	†Bos A★	157	618	98	200	39	2	20	110	62-5	4	78	.324	.384	.490	137	33	0-1	.977	8	103	162	*O-156(LF)/D	3.4
1987	Bos A	108	404	66	112	14	0	13	62	45-3	7	77	.277	.357	.408	100	1	1-1	.977	1	85	197	O-94(LF),D-12	-0.3
1988	†Bos A	135	485	57	128	18	3	15	72	48-2	3	89	.264	.330	.406	102	1	1-1	.968	-2	88	0	*D-112,O-19(LF)	-0.5
1989	Bos A	56	209	22	49	10	2	3	28	13-0	1	39	.234	.276	.344	71	-8	1-0	—	0	0	0	D-55	-1.0
Total	16	2089	8225	1249	2452	373	79	382	1451	670-77	64	1423	.298	.352	.502	127	279	58-34	.980	-4	94	125	*O-1543(1504-1-43),D-530	18.6
RICE, LEN Leonard Oliver B 9.2.1918 Lead, SD D 6.13.1992 Sonora, CA BR/TR 6/175# d4.26																								
1944	Cin N	10	4	1	0	0	0	0	0	0	0	0	.000	.000	.000	-99	-1	0	1.000	0	*0*	*0*	/C-5	-0.1
1945	Chi N	32	99	10	23	3	0	0	7	5	0	8	.232	.269	.263	49	-7	2	.976	1	*157*	*55*	C-29	-0.5
Total	2	42	103	11	23	3	0	0	7	5	0	8	.223	.259	.252	44	-8	2	.977	1	*153*	*54*	/C-34	-0.6
RICE, BOB Robert Turnbull B 5.28.1899 Philadelphia, PA D 2.20.1986 Elizabethtown, PA BR/TR 5-10/170# d9.1																								
1926	Phi N	19	54	3	8	0	1	0	10	3	0	4	.148	.193	.185	2	-8	0	.864	0	100	242	3-15/2-2,S-2	-0.7
RICHARD, CHRIS Christopher Robert B 6.7.1974 San Diego, CA BL/TL 6-2/185# d7.17																								
2000	StL N	6	16	1	2	0	0	1	1	2-0	0	2	.125	.222	.313	33	-2	0-0	1.000	0	121	0	/O-3(1-0-2),1-2	-0.2
	Bal A	56	199	38	55	14	2	13	36	15-3	4	38	.276	.335	.563	129	8	7-5	.989	-7	50	106	1-53/O(RF)D	-0.4
2001	Bal A	136	483	74	128	31	3	15	61	45-4	8	100	.265	.335	.435	107	5	11-9	1.000	5	115	102	O-96(0-36-69),D-20,1-18	0.4
2002	Bal A	50	155	15	36	11	0	4	21	12-0	2	30	.232	.292	.381	82	-4	0-3	1.000	-1	63	0	D-36/1-9	-0.9
2003	Col N	19	27	3	6	1	1	1	3	3-0	0	6	.222	.300	.444	80	-1	0-1	1.000	0	110	0	/O-3(LF),1	-0.1
Total	4	267	880	131	227	57	6	34	122	77-7	14	176	.258	.324	.452	105	6	18-18	1.000	-2	115	95	O-103(4-36-72)/1-83,D-57	-1.2
RICHARD, LEE Lee Edward "Bee Bee" B 9.18.1948 Lafayette, LA BR/TR (BB 1975) 5-11/165# d4.7 OF Total (22-CF 1-RF)																								
1971	Chi A	87	260	38	60	7	3	2	17	20-0	1	46	.231	.286	.304	66	-12	8-9	.920	13	119	92	S-68,O-16(CF)	0.6
1972	Chi A	11	29	5	7	0	0	0	1	0-0	0	7	.241	.241	.241	43	-2	1-0	1.000	-0	57	268	/O-6(CF),S	-0.3
1974	Chi A	32	67	5	11	1	0	0	1	5-1	0	8	.164	.222	.179	16	-7	0-0	.821	-2	95	104	3-12/S-6,2-3,O(RF)D	-0.9
1975	Chi A	43	45	11	9	0	1	0	5	4-0	0	7	.200	.265	.244	44	-3	2-3	1.000	-1	97	0	3-12/S-9,2-5,D-5	-0.4
1976	StL N	66	91	12	16	4	2	0	5	4-1	0	9	.176	.211	.264	34	-8	1-0	.975	-3	100	101	2-26,S-12/3	-1.0
Total	5	239	492	71	103	12	6	2	29	33-2	1	77	.209	.259	.270	50	-32	12-12	.923	6	113	102	/S-96,2-34,3-25,O-23C,D-10	-2.0
RICHARDS, GENE Eugene B 9.29.1953 Monticello, SC BL/TL 6/175# d4.6																								
1977	SD N	146	525	79	152	16	11	5	32	60-12	2	80	.290	.363	.390	114	11	56-12	.963	3	93	200	*O-109(72-41-1),1-32	1.7

Year	Tm Lg	G	AB	R	H	2B	3B	HR	RBI	BB-IB	HP	SO	AVG	OBP	SLG	AOPS	ABR	SB-CS	FA	FR	Rng	Thr	G at Pos	BFW
1978	SD N	154	555	90	171	26	12	4	45	64-7	4	80	.308	.381	.420	135	27	37-17	.965	-8	91	88	*O-124(113-26-0),1-26	1.6
1979	SD N	150	545	77	152	17	9	4	41	47-6	8	62	.279	.343	.365	100	-1	24-8	.973	-4	97	73	*O-132(20-102-10)	-0.5
1980	SD N	158	642	91	193	26	8	4	41	61-7	2	73	.301	.363	.385	116	14	61-16	.979	7	100	174	*O-156(156-0-1)	2.3
1981	SD N	104	393	47	113	14	**12**	3	42	53-3	1	44	.288	.373	.407	131	16	20-8	.975	-2	88	148	*O-102(LF)	1.2
1982	SD N	132	521	63	149	13	8	3	28	36-1	2	52	.286	.333	.359	99	-2	30-20	.977	-1	104	98	*O-103(LF)/1-25	-0.9
1983	SD N	95	233	37	64	11	3	3	22	17-1	1	17	.275	.325	.386	100	0	14-5	.980	1	110	57	O-54(LF)	-0.1
1984	SF N	87	135	18	34	4	0	0	4	18-2	0	28	.252	.340	.281	79	-3	5-3	.940	-1	103	59	O-26(15-1-11)	-0.5
Total	8	1026	3549	502	1028	127	63	26	255	356-39	20	436	.290	.357	.383	113	62	247-89	.972	-5	97	124	O-806(634-170-23)/1-83	4.8
RICHARDS, FRED Fred Charles "Fuzzy" B 11.3.1927 Warren, OH BL/TL 6-1.5/185# d9.15																								
1951	Chi N	10	27	1	8	2	0	0	4	2	0	3	.296	.345	.370	91	0	0-0	1.000	1	162	44	/1-9	0.1
RICHARDS, PAUL Paul Rapier B 11.21.1908 Waxahachie, TX D 5.4.1986 Waxahachie, TX BR/TR 6-1.5/180# d4.17 M12																								
1932	Bro N	3	8	0	0	0	0	0	0	0	0	2	.000	.000	.000	-99	-2	0	1.000	2	*122*	*102*	/C-3	0.0
1933	NY N	51	87	4	17	3	0	0	10	3	0	12	.195	.222	.230	30	-8	0	.989	1	*112*	*157*	C-36	-0.6
1934	NY N	42	75	10	12	1	0	0	3	13	0	8	.160	.284	.173	26	-8	0	1.000	2	*118*	*137*	C-37	-0.4
1935	NY N	7	4	0	1	0	0	0	0	2	0	1	.250	.500	.250	110	0	0	1.000	1	*0*	*272*	/C-4	0.1
	Phi A	85	257	31	63	10	1	4	29	24	0	12	.245	.310	.339	68	-13	0-0	.977	-6	*72*	*105*	C-79	-1.3
1943	Det A	100	313	32	69	7	1	5	33	38	1	35	.220	.307	.297	71	-11	1-0	**.986**	16	*102*	***139***	*C-100	1.3
1944	Det A	95	300	24	71	13	0	3	37	35	1	30	.237	.318	.310	76	-9	8-3	.979	17	***191***	***147***	C-90	1.5
1945	†Det A	83	234	26	60	12	1	3	32	19	1	31	.256	.315	.355	88	-4	4-0	**.995**	9	*122*	*102*	C-83	1.2
1946	Det A	57	139	13	28	5	2	0	11	23	0	18	.201	.315	.266	60	-7	2-0	.997	10	*112*	*102*	C-54	0.6
Total	8	523	1417	140	321	51	5	15	155	157	3	149	.227	.305	.301	68	-62	15-3	.987	52	*121*	*125*	C-486	2.4
RICHARDSON B Boston, MA 5-4/136# d7.10																								
1884	CP U	1	4	0	0	0	0	0		0			.000	.000	.000	-99	-1		.667	-1	46	0	/2	-0.2
RICHARDSON, HARDY Abram Harding "Old True Blue" B 4.21.1855 Clarksboro, NJ D 1.14.1931 Utica, NY BR/TR 5-9.5/170# d5.1 ▲ OF Total (375-LF 158-CF 11-RF)																								
1879	Buf N	**79**	336	54	95	18	10	0	37	16		30	.283	.315	.396	130	11		.843	-7	93	150	*3-78/C	0.6
1880	Buf N	83	343	48	89	18	8	0	17	14		37	.259	.289	.359	116	5		.848	-5	98	64	*3-81/C-5	0.3
1881	Buf N	**83**	344	62	100	18	9	2	53	12		27	.291	.315	.413	129	11		.914	23	**217**	88	*O-79(CF)/2-5,S3	2.8
1882	Buf N	83	354	61	96	20	8	2	57	11		33	.271	.293	.390	115	5		.898	19	109	75	*2-83	2.5
1883	Buf N	92	399	73	124	34	7	1	56	22		20	.311	.347	.439	134	17		.903	16	113	80	*2-92	3.1
1884	Buf N	102	439	85	132	27	9	6	60	22		41	.301	.334	.444	138	18		.897	6	106	65	2-71,O-24(CF)/3-5,1-3	2.3
1885	Buf N	96	426	90	136	19	11	6	44	20		22	.319	.350	.458	154	24		.905	9	107	69	2-50,O-48(1-47-0)/SP	3.0
1886	Det N	125	538	125	**189**	27	11	**11**	61	46		27	.351	.402	.504	168	43	42	.899	8	123	43	O-80(LF),2-42/P-4,S-3,3-2	4.5
1887	†Det N	120	543	131	178	25	18	8	94	31	2	40	.328	.366	.484	129	19	29	.941	20	104	105	2-64,O-59(58-1-0)	3.3
1888	Det N	58	266	60	77	18	2	6	32	17	1	23	.289	.335	.440	144	13	13	.925	-0	94	99	2-58	1.5
1889	Bos N	132	536	122	163	33	10	6	79	48	5	44	.304	.367	.437	117	10	47	.924	10	105	115	2-86,O-46(LF)	1.9
1890	Bos P	**130**	555	126	181	26	14	13	**146**	52	0	46	.326	.384	.494	125	16	42	.950	2	56	66	*O-124(LF)/S-6,1	1.2
1891	Bos AA	74	278	45	71	9	4	7	52	40	1	26	.255	.351	.392	114	5	16	.955	-1	48	98	O-60(57-1-2)/3-9,S-4,1-3	0.3
1892	Was N	10	37	2	4	0	0	0	0	5	0	3	.108	.214	.108	-2	-4	2	.941	0	0	0	/O-7(LF),3-2,2	-0.5
	NY N	64	248	36	53	11	5	2	34	21	1	26	.214	.278	.323	83	-6	14	.931	3	105	77	2-33,O-17(2-6-9)/1-9,S-6	-0.2
	Year	74	285	38	57	11	5	2	34	26	1	29	.200	.269	.295	72	-10	16	.933	3	104	75	2-34,O-24(9-6-9)/1-9,S-6,3-2	-0.7
Total	14	1331	5642	1120	1688	303	126	70	822	377	10	445	.299	.344	.435	129	187	205	.915	102	106	86	2-585,O-544L,3-178/S-21,1-16,CP	26.6
RICHARDSON, NOLEN Clifford Nolen B 1.18.1903 Chattanooga, TN D 9.25.1951 Athens, GA BR/TR 6-1.5/170# d4.16																								
1929	Det A	13	21	2	4	0	0	0	2	2	0	1	.190	.261	.190	18	-3	1-1	.839	-4	58	46	S-13	-0.6
1931	Det A	38	148	13	40	9	2	0	16	6	0	3	.270	.299	.358	70	-7	2-1	.946	-1	109	30	3-38	-0.6
1932	Det A	69	155	13	34	5	2	0	12	9	0	13	.219	.262	.277	38	-15	5-2	.986	7	111	110	3-65/S-4	-0.5
1935	NY A	12	46	3	10	1	1	0	5	3	0	1	.217	.265	.283	44	-4	0-0	.922	-5	67	65	S-12	-0.8
1938	Cin N	35	100	8	29	4	0	0	10	3	0	4	.290	.311	.330	78	-3	0	.966	0	101	81	S-35	-0.1
1939	Cin N	1	3	0	0	0	0	0	0	0	0	0	.000	.000	.000	-99	-1	0	1.000	0	89	155	/S	0.0
Total	6	168	473	39	117	19	5	0	45	23	0	22	.247	.282	.309	55	-33	8-4	.969	-2	110	74	3-103/S-65	-2.6
RICHARDSON, DANNY Daniel B 1.25.1863 Elmira, NY D 9.12.1926 New York, NY BR/TR 5-8/165# d5.22 M1 ▲ OF Total (41-LF 51-CF 51-RF)																								
1884	NY N	74	277	36	70	8	1	1	27	16		17	.253	.294	.300	85	-5		.907	2	176	153	O-55(11-7-37),S-19	-0.3
1885	NY N	49	198	26	52	9	3	0	25	10		14	.263	.298	.338	107	2		.950	0	69	0	O-22(10-2-12),3-21/P-9	0.2
1886	NY N	68	237	43	55	9	1	1	27	17		21	.232	.283	.291	74	-7	12	.953	1	64	0	O-64(20-42-2)/P-5,S32	-0.7
1887	NY N	122	450	79	125	19	10	3	62	36	4	25	.278	.337	.384	105	4	41	.928	18	109	106	*2-108,3-14/P	2.1
1888	†NY N	135	561	82	127	16	7	8	61	15	1	35	.226	.248	.323	82	-13	35	**.942**	9	96	97	*2-135	0.1
1889	†NY N	125	497	88	139	22	8	7	100	46	1	37	.280	.342	.398	106	2	32	.934	15	102	108	*2-125	1.9
1890	NY P	123	528	102	135	12	9	4	80	37	2	19	.256	.307	.335	66	-30	37	.900	14	107	112	S-68,2-56	-1.0
1891	NY N	123	516	85	139	18	5	4	51	33	0	27	.269	.313	.347	96	-4	28	.952	**45**	**114**	122	*2-114/S-9	4.0
1892	Was N	142	551	48	132	13	4	3	58	25	1	45	.240	.274	.294	74	-19	25	.931	**45**	111	126	S-93,2-49/3M	3.0
1893	Bro N	54	206	36	46	6	2	0	27	13	3	18	.223	.279	.272	49	-15	7	.949	-12	77	90	2-46/3-5,S-3	-2.1
1894	Lou N	116	430	51	109	17	2	1	40	35	5	31	.253	.317	.309	55	-31	8	.916	5	98	121	*S-107,2-10	-1.5
Total	11	1131	4451	676	1129	149	52	32	558	283	17	289	.254	.301	.332	82	-116	225	.940	142	103	104	2-644,S-300,O-141C/3-42,P-15	5.7
RICHARDSON, JEFF Jeffrey Scott B 8.26.1965 Grand Island, NE BR/TR 6-2/175# d7.14																								
1989	Cin N	53	125	10	21	4	0	2	11	10-0	1	23	.168	.234	.248	37	-10	1-0	.969	-11	76	83	S-39/3-8	-2.0
1991	Pit N	6	4	0	1	0	0	0	0	0-0	0	3	.250	.250	.250	42	0	0-0	—	-1	0	0	/3-3,S-2	-0.1
1993	Bos A	15	24	3	5	2	0	0	2	1-0	0	3	.208	.240	.292	40	-2	0-0	1.000	4	164	96	/2-8,S-5,3D	0.2
Total	3	74	153	13	27	6	0	2	13	11-0	1	29	.176	.235	.255	38	-12	1-0	.971	-8	77	86	/S-46,3-12,2-8,D-2	-1.9
RICHARDSON, KEN Kenneth Franklin B 5.2.1915 Orleans, IN D 12.7.1987 Woodland Hills, CA BR/TR 5-10.5/187# d4.14																								
1942	Phi A	6	15	1	1	0	0	0	0	2	0	0	.067	.176	.067	-30	-3	0-0	1.000	0	88	596	/O-3(1-0-2),13	-0.3
1946	Phi N	6	20	1	3	1	0	0	2	0	0	2	.150	.150	.200	-1	-3	0	.939	-1	95	29	/2-6	-0.4
Total	2	12	35	2	4	1	0	0	2	2	0	2	.114	.162	.143	-14	-6	0-0	.939	-1	95	29	/2-6,O-3(1-0-2),31	-0.7
RICHARDSON, BOBBY Robert Clinton B 8.19.1935 Sumter, SC BR/TR 5-9/170# d8.5																								
1955	NY A	11	26	2	4	0	0	0	3	2-0	0	0	.154	.214	.154	0	-4	1-1	.864	-3	59	30	/2-6,S-4	-0.7
1956	NY A	5	7	1	1	0	0	0	0	0-0	0	1	.143	.143	.143	-25	-1	0-0	1.000	1	57	102	/2-5	-0.1
1957	†NY A☆	97	305	36	78	11	1	0	19	9-3	0	26	.256	.274	.298	58	-18	1-3	.979	4	103	105	2-93	-0.9
1958	†NY A	73	182	18	45	6	2	0	14	8-0	0	5	.247	.276	.302	62	-10	1-3	.973	4	99	112	2-51,3-13/S-2	-0.4
1959	NY A☆	134	469	53	141	18	6	2	33	26-3	0	20	.301	.335	.377	99	-2	5-5	.970	1	98	116	*2-109,S-14,3-12	0.8
1960	†NY A	150	460	45	116	12	3	1	26	35-6	0	19	.252	.303	.298	68	-22	6-6	.973	-5	97	**114**	*2-141,3-11	-1.9
1961	†NY A	162	662	80	173	17	5	3	49	30-1	2	23	.261	.295	.316	67	-34	9-7	.978	-4	91	**135**	*2-161	-2.4
1962	†NY A★	161	692	99	**209**	38	5	8	59	37-1	1	24	.302	.337	.406	103	1	11-9	.982	-3	102	116	*2-161	1.2
1963	†NY A★	151	630	72	167	20	6	3	48	25-0	2	22	.265	.294	.330	76	-22	15-1	.984	13	104	**122**	*2-150	0.7
1964	†NY A★	159	679	90	181	25	4	4	50	28-1	0	36	.267	.294	.333	73	-25	11-2	.982	-16	93	109	*2-157/S	-2.7
1965	NY A★	160	664	76	164	28	2	6	47	37-4	1	39	.247	.287	.322	74	-24	7-5	.981	-2	96	120	*2-158	-1.3
1966	NY A★	149	610	71	153	21	3	7	42	25-1	1	28	.251	.280	.330	78	-19	6-6	.980	10	109	102	*2-147/3-2	0.2
Total	12	1412	5386	643	1432	196	37	34	390	262-20	7	243	.266	.299	.335	77	-180	73-48	.979	0	99	116	*2-1339/3-38,S-21	-7.5
RICHARDSON, TOM Thomas Mitchell B 8.7.1883 Louisville, IL D 11.15.1939 Onawa, IA BR/TR 6/190# d8.2																								
1917	StL A	1	1	0	0	0	0	0	0	0	0	0	.000	.000	.000	-99	0	0	—	0			H	0.0
RICHARDSON, BILL William Henry B 9.24.1878 Salem, IN D 11.6.1949 Sullivan, IN BR/TR 5-11/200# d9.20																								
1901	StL N	15	52	7	11	2	0	2	7	6	0		.212	.293	.365	95	0	1	.981	-1	58	95	1-15	-0.2
RICHARDT, MIKE Michael Anthony B 5.24.1958 Los Angeles, CA BR/TR 6/170# d8.30																								
1980	Tex A	22	71	2	16	2	0	0	8	1-0	0	7	.225	.236	.254	35	-7	0-0	.978	-3	92	75	2-20/D	-0.9
1982	Tex A	119	402	34	97	10	0	3	43	23-1	1	42	.241	.281	.289	61	-22	9-1	.988	11	105	101	2-98,D-15/O-6(LF)	-0.5
1983	Tex A	22	83	9	13	2	1	1	7	2-0	0	11	.157	.174	.241	14	-10	2-1	.992	3	99	116	2-20	-0.6
1984	Tex A	6	9	0	1	0	0	0	0	1-0	0	1	.111	.200	.111	-11	-1	0-1	1.000	0	87	267	/2-4	-0.1
	Hou N	16	15	1	4	1	0	0	2	0-0	0	1	.267	.267	.333	73	-1	0-0	—	0			H	-0.1

Year	Tm Lg	G	AB	R	H	2B	3B	HR	RBI	BB-IB	HP	SO	AVG	OBP	SLG	AOPS	ABR	SB-CS	FA	FR	Rng	Thr	G at Pos	BFW
Total	4	185	580	46	131	15	1	4	60	27-1	1	62	.226	.259	.276	50	-41	11-3	.988	11	102	102	2-142/D-16,O-6(LF)	-2.2
RICHBOURG, LANCE Lance Clayton B 12.18.1897 DeFuniak Springs, FL D 9.10.1975 Crestview, FL BL/TR 5-10.5/160# d7.4																								
1921	Phi N	10	5	2	1	1	0	0	0	0	0	3	.200	.200	.400	51	0	1-1	1.000	1	175	0	/2-4	0.0
1924	Was A	15	32	3	9	2	1	0	1	2	0	6	.281	.324	.406	90	-1	0-0	1.000	1	100	240	/O-7(RF)	0.0
1927	Bos N	115	450	57	139	12	9	2	34	22	1	30	.309	.342	.389	104	0	24	.953	-4	100	74	*O-110(0-3-107)	-1.3
1928	Bos N	148	612	105	206	26	12	2	52	62	2	39	.337	.399	.428	123	22	11	.972	4	114	52	*O-148(RF)	1.3
1929	Bos N	139	557	76	170	24	13	3	56	42	1	26	.305	.355	.411	93	-7	7	.971	5	**108**	97	*O-134(2-0-132)	-1.3
1930	Bos N	130	529	81	161	23	8	3	54	19	2	31	.304	.331	.395	77	-21	13	.971	-2	105	56	*O-128(RF)	-3.0
1931	Bos N	97	286	32	82	11	6	2	29	19	0	14	.287	.331	.388	96	-3	9	.981	-2	102	40	O-71(15-0-56)	-0.9
1932	Chi N	44	148	22	38	2	2	1	21	8	0	4	.257	.295	.318	65	-8	0	.986	-2	91	58	O-33(1-3-29)	-1.2
Total	8	698	2619	378	806	101	51	13	247	174	6	153	.308	.352	.400	97	-18	65-1	.970	-1	106	67	O-631(18-6-607)/2-4	-6.4
RICHIE, ROB Robert Eugene B 9.5.1965 Reno, NV BL/TR 6-2/190# d8.19																								
1989	Det A	19	49	6	13	4	2	1	10	5-1	0	10	.265	.333	.490	132	2	0-1	.917	-1	88	139	O-13(11-0-2)/D-4	0.1
RICHMOND, DON Donald Lester B 10.27.1919 Gillett, PA D 5.24.1981 Elmira, NY BL/TR 6-1/175# d9.16 Mil 1942-45																								
1941	Phi A	9	35	3	7	1	1	0	5	0	0	1	.200	.200	.286	28	-4	0-2	.957	-1	98	195	/3-9	-0.5
1946	Phi A	16	62	3	18	3	0	1	9	0	0	10	.290	.290	.387	89	-1	1-0	.940	-1	90	27	3-16	-0.2
1947	Phi A	19	21	2	4	1	1	0	4	3	0	3	.190	.292	.333	72	-1	0-0	.500	-2	53	0	/3-4,2	-0.3
1951	StL N	12	34	3	3	1	0	1	4	3	0	3	.088	.162	.206	-2	-5	0-1	1.000	3	119	116	3-11	-0.3
Total	4	56	152	11	32	6	2	2	22	6	0	17	.211	.241	.316	51	-11	1-3	.957	-2	99	91	/3-40,2	-1.3
RICHMOND, LEE J Lee B 5.5.1857 Sheffield, OH D 10.1.1929 Toledo, OH TL 5-10/155# d9.27 ▲																								
1879	Bos N	1	6	0	2	0	0	0	1	0		1	.333	.333	.333	118	0		1.000	0	106	0	/P	0.0
1880	Wor N	77	309	44	70	8	4	0	34	9		32	.227	.248	.278	72	-10		.827	-8	82	49	*P-74,O-20(1-1-18)	-0.5
1881	Wor N	61	252	31	63	5	1	0	28	10		10	.250	.279	.278	71	-9		.937	1	113	79	P-53,O-11(0-2-9)	-0.2
1882	Wor N	55	228	50	64	8	9	2	28	9		11	.281	.308	.421	128	6		.889	3	124	66	P-48,O-11(1-1-9)	0.2
1883	Pro N	49	194	41	55	8	6	1	19	15		19	.284	.335	.402	120	4		.714	-8	37	0	O-41(33-3-5),P-12	-0.5
1886	Cin AA	8	29	3	8	0	0	0	3	3	0		.276	.344	.276	92	0	0	.400	-3	0	0	/O-7(CF),P-3	-0.3
Total	6	251	1018	169	262	29	20	3	113	46	0	73	.257	.289	.334	94	-9	0	.886	-15	103	58	P-191/O-90(35-14-41)	-1.3
RICHMOND, JOHN John H. B 3.5.1854 , PA TR 5-9/170# d4.22																								
1875	Ath NA	29	125	29	25	2	0	0	12	1		4	.200	.206	.216	42	-8	1-0	.814	-3	79	136	2-17,O-11(2-3-6)/C-3	-1.0
1879	Syr N	62	254	31	54	8	4	1	23	4		24	.213	.225	.287	76	-5		.875	-7	90	102	O-35(4-29-2),S-28/C-2	-1.1
1880	Bos N	32	129	12	32	3	1	0	9	2		18	.248	.260	.287	88	-2		.844	-7	81	178	S-31/O(CF)	-0.7
1881	Bos N	27	98	13	27	2	2	1	12	6		7	.276	.317	.367	120	2		.969	-0	61	100	O-25(0-24-1)/S-2	0.1
1882	Cle N	41	140	12	24	6	2	0	11	11		27	.171	.232	.243	54	-6		.917	3	143	0	O-41(CF)	-0.4
	Phi AA	18	65	8	12	2	2	0	4	11			.185	.303	.277	91	0		.892	-0	94	0	O-18(0-17-1)	-0.1
1883	Col AA	92	385	63	109	7	8	0		25			.283	.327	.343	126	13		**.877**	28	**123**	88	*S-91/O-2(CF)	**3.8**
1884	Col AA	105	398	57	100	13	7	3		35	3		.251	.317	.342	125	14		.866	-8	93	114	*S-105	0.8
1885	Pit AA	34	131	14	27	2	2	0	12	8	2		.206	.262	.252	64	-5		.849	-9	89	102	S-23,O-11(0-8-3)	-1.2
Total	7	411	1600	210	385	43	28	5	71	102	5	76	.241	.288	.312	101	11		.866	0	99	104	S-280,O-133(4-122-7)/C-2	1.2
RICHTER, AL Allen Gordon B 2.7.1927 Norfolk, VA BR/TR 5-11/165# d9.23																								
1951	Bos A	5	11	1	1	0	0	0	0	3	0	0	.091	.286	.091	5	-1	0-0	1.000	2	112	232	/S-3	0.0
1953	Bos A	1	0	0	0	0	0	0	0	0	0	0	—	—	—	—	0	0-0	1.000	0	93	443	/S	0.0
Total	2	6	11	1	1	0	0	0	0	3	0	0	.091	.286	.091	5	-1	0-0	1.000	2	110	254	/S-4	0.0
RICHTER, JOHN John M. B 2.8.1873 Louisville, KY D 10.4.1927 Louisville, KY 6/178# d10.6																								
1898	Lou N	3	13	1	2	0	0	0	0	0	0		.154	.154	.154	-12	-2	0	.929	0	108	195	/3-3	-0.1
RICKERT, JOE Joseph Francis "Diamond Joe" B 12.12.1876 London, OH D 10.15.1943 Springfield, OH BR/TR 5-10.5/165# d10.12																								
1898	Pit N	2	6	0	1	0	0	0	0	0	0		.167	.167	.167	-5	-1	0	1.000	1	0	0	/O-2(LF)	-0.1
1901	Bos N	13	60	6	10	1	2	0	1	3	0		.167	.206	.250	29	-6	1	.974	2	107	231	O-13(LF)	-0.5
Total	2	15	66	6	11	1	2	0	1	3	0		.167	.203	.242	27	-7	1	.979	2	89	193	/O-15(LF)	-0.6
RICKERT, MARV Marvin August "Twitch" B 1.8.1921 Longbranch, WA D 6.3.1978 Oakville, WA BL/TR 6-2/195# d9.10 Mil 1943-45																								
1942	Chi N	8	26	5	7	0	0	0	1	1	0	5	.269	.296	.269	69	-1	0	1.000	1	106	154	/O-6(CF)	-0.1
1946	Chi N	111	392	44	103	18	3	7	47	28	1	54	.263	.314	.378	98	-3	3	.972	-4	97	59	*O-104(75-19-10)	-1.4
1947	Chi N	71	137	7	20	0	0	2	15	15	0	17	.146	.230	.190	13	-18	0	.982	1	99	106	O-30(18-3-9)/1-7	-1.8
1948	Cin N	8	6	0	1	0	0	0	0	0	0	0	.167	.167	.167	-10	-1	0	—	0			H	-0.1
	†Bos N	3	13	1	3	0	1	0	2	0	1	1	.231	.286	.385	81	-1	0	1.000	1	109	324	/O-3(LF)	0.0
	Year	11	19	1	4	0	1	0	2	0	1	1	.211	.250	.316	54	-1	0	1.000	1	109	324	/O-3(LF)	-0.1
1949	Bos N	100	277	44	81	18	3	6	49	23	0	38	.292	.347	.444	117	6	1	.981	5	107	162	O-75(50-3-25),1-12	0.7
1950	Pit N	17	20	0	3	0	0	0	4	0	0	4	.150	.150	.150	-20	-4	0	—	-0	0	0	/O-3(RF)	-0.4
	Chi A	84	278	38	66	9	2	4	27	21	0	42	.237	.291	.327	60	-18	0-1	.968	-2	105	52	O-78(18-0-63)/1	-2.2
Total	6	402	1149	139	284	45	9	19	145	88	2	161	.247	.302	.352	79	-40	4-1	.976	1	102	93	O-299(164-31-110)/1-20	-5.3
RICKETTS, DAVE David William B 7.12.1935 Pottstown, PA BB/TR 6-2/195# d9.25 C19 b-Dick																								
1963	StL N	3	8	0	2	0	0	0	0	0-0	0	2	.250	.250	.250	41	-1	0-0	1.000	-0	*83*	*0*	/C-3	-0.1
1965	StL N	11	29	1	7	0	0	0	0	1-0	0	3	.241	.267	.241	40	-2	0-0	.977	-2	*79*	*54*	C-11	-0.4
1967	†StL N	52	99	11	27	8	0	1	14	4-0	0	7	.273	.295	.384	96	-1	0-0	1.000	0	*143*	*119*	C-21	0.1
1968	†StL N	20	22	1	3	0	0	0	1	0-0	0	3	.136	.136	.136	-18	-3	0-0	1.000	-0	*0*	*0*	/C	-0.4
1969	StL N	30	44	2	12	1	0	0	5	4-0	0	5	.273	.320	.295	77	-1	0-0	.983	0	36	104	/C-8	-0.1
1970	Pit N	14	11	0	2	0	0	0	0	1-0	0	3	.182	.250	.182	18	-1	0-0	.909	-0	92	221	/C-7	-0.1
Total	6	130	213	15	53	9	0	1	20	10-0	0	23	.249	.278	.305	67	-9	0-0	.988	-2	*101*	*99*	/C-51	-1.0
RICKEY, BRANCH Wesley Branch "The Mahatma" B 12.20.1881 Flat, OH D 12.9.1965 Columbia, MO BL/TR 5-9/175# d6.16 M10 HF1967																								
1905	StL A	1	3	0	0	0	0	0	0	0	0		.000	.000	.000	-99	-1	0	1.000	-0	*75*	*166*	/C	-0.1
1906	StL A	65	201	22	57	7	3	3	24	16	3		.284	.345	.393	137	8	4	.954	-6	*86*	*93*	C-55/O(RF)	0.8
1907	NY A	52	137	16	25	1	3	0	15	11	2		.182	.253	.234	51	-8	4	.846	-4	40	0	O-22(20-1-1),C-11/1-9	-1.4
1914	StL A	2	2	0	0	0	0	0	0	0	0	1	.000	.000	.000	-99	-1	0	—	0			HM	-0.1
Total	4	120	343	38	82	8	6	3	39	27	5	1	.239	.304	.324	97	-2	8	.940	-11	*88*	*90*	/C-67,O-23(20-1-2),1-9	-0.8
RICKLEY, CHRIS Christian B 10.7.1859 Philadelphia, PA D 10.25.1911 Philadelphia, PA 5-8/160# d6.9																								
1884	Phi U	6	25	5	5	2	0	0		2			.200	.259	.280	68	-2		.757	-0	111	156	/S-6	-0.1
RICKS, JOHN John d9.21																								
1891	StL AA	5	18	3	3	0	0	0	0	0	0	2	.167	.167	.167	-4	-3	0	.810	-1	55	0	/3-5	-0.3
1894	StL N	1	1	0	0	0	0	0	0	0	0	0	.000	.000	.000	-99	0	0	.250	-1	0	0	/3	-0.1
Total	2	6	19	3	3	0	0	0	0	0	0	2	.158	.158	.158	-9	-3	0	.720	-3	48	0	/3-6	-0.4
RICO, FRED Alfredo (Cruz) B 7.4.1944 Jerome, AZ BR/TR 5-10/180# d9.1																								
1969	KC A	12	26	2	6	2	0	0	2	9-1	0	10	.231	.429	.308	108	1	0-1	1.000	4	167	319	/O-9(0-2-7),3	0.4
RICO, ART Arthur Raymond B 7.23.1896 Roxbury, MA D 1.3.1919 Boston, MA BR/TR 5-9.5/185# d7.31 Mil 1918																								
1916	Bos N	4	4	0	0	0	0	0	0	0	0	0	.000	.000	.000	-99	-1	0	1.000	-0	109	118	/C-4	-0.1
1917	Bos N	13	14	1	4	1	0	0	2	0	0	2	.286	.286	.357	102	0	0	.950	-1	*104*	*82*	C-11/O-2(LF)	0.0
Total	2	17	18	1	4	1	0	0	2	0	0	2	.222	.222	.278	56	-1	0	.962	-1	*105*	*90*	/C-15,O-2(LF)	-0.1
RICONDA, HARRY Henry Paul B 3.17.1897 New York, NY D 11.15.1958 Mahopac, NY BR/TR 5-10/175# d4.19																								
1923	Phi A	55	175	23	46	11	4	0	12	12	2	18	.263	.317	.371	80	-6	4-2	.911	-1	108	98	3-47/S-2	-0.3
1924	Phi A	83	281	34	71	16	3	1	21	27	2	43	.253	.323	.342	71	-13	3-4	.927	-3	97	108	3-73/S-2	-1.1
1926	Bos N	4	12	1	2	0	0	0	0	2	0	2	.167	.286	.167	27	-1	0	.818	-1	46	0	/3-4	-0.2
1928	Bro N	92	281	22	63	15	4	3	35	20	4	28	.224	.285	.338	63	-16	6	.957	0	94	64	2-53,3-21,S-16	-1.3
1929	Pit N	8	15	3	7	2	0	0	2	0	0	0	.467	.467	.600	158	1	0	.840	-2	67	124	/S-4	0.0
1930	Cin N	1	1	0	0	0	0	0	0	0	0	0	.000	.000	.000	-99	0	0	—	0			H	0.0
Total	6	243	765	83	189	44	11	4	70	61	8	91	.247	.309	.349	71	-35	13-6	.922	-7	101	95	3-145/2-53,S-24	-2.9

Year	Tm Lg	G	AB	R	H	2B	3B	HR	RBI	BB-IB	HP	SO	AVG	OBP	SLG	AOPS	ABR	SB-CS	FA	FR	Rng	Thr	G at Pos	BFW
RIDDLE, JOHN John H. B 2.1864 , PA D 5.5.1931 Camden, NJ BR/TR d9.18																								
1889	Was N	11	37	3	8	3	0	0	3	2	0	8	.216	.256	.297	58	-2	0	.841	1			/C-9,O-2(RF)	-0.1
1890	Phi AA	27	85	7	7	0	1	0	2	17	1		.082	.243	.106	3	-10	4	.914	-3	*84*	*88*	C-13,O-12(9-3-0)/2-2,3	-1.1
Total	2	38	122	10	15	3	1	0	5	19	1	8	.123	.246	.164	20	-12	4	.880	-3	*46*	*48*	/C-22,O-14(9-3-2),2-2,3	-1.2
RIDDLE, JOHNNY John Ludy "Mutt" B 10.3.1905 Clinton, SC D 12.15.1998 Indianapolis, IN BR/TR 5-11/190# d4.17 C11 b-Elmer																								
1930	Chi A	25	58	7	14	3	1	0	4	3	1	6	.241	.290	.328	58	-4	0-0	1.000	-1	*91*	*132*	C-25	-0.4
1937	Was A	8	26	2	7	0	0	0	3	0	1	2	.269	.296	.269	46	-2	0-0	.971	0	*110*	*150*	/C-8	-0.2
	Bos N	2	3	0	0	0	0	0	0	1	0	0	.000	.250	.000	-29	-1	0	1.000	1	*0*	*243*	/C-2	0.0
1938	Bos N	19	57	6	16	1	0	0	2	4	0	2	.281	.328	.298	81	-2	0	.951	3	*162*	*125*	C-19	0.2
1941	Cin N	10	10	2	3	0	0	0	0	0	0	1	.300	.300	.300	69	0	0	1.000	1	*95*	*0*	C-10	0.0
1944	Cin N	1	0	0	0	0	0	0	0	0	0	0	—	—	—	—	0	0	—	0	*0*	*0*	/C	0.0
1945	Cin N	23	45	0	8	0	0	0	2	4	0	6	.178	.245	.178	19	-5	0	1.000	2	*85*	*127*	C-23	-0.2
1948	Pit N	10	15	1	3	0	0	0	0	1	0	2	.200	.250	.200	23	-2	0	1.000	1	*151*	*99*	C-10	-0.1
Total	7	98	214	18	51	4	1	0	11	13	2	19	.238	.288	.266	51	-16	0-0	.983	5	*114*	*124*	/C-98	-0.7
RIEBE, HANK Harvey Donald B 10.10.1921 Cleveland, OH D 4.16.2001 Cleveland, OH BR/TR 5-9.5/175# d8.26 Mil 1943-45																								
1942	Det A	11	35	1	11	2	0	0	2	0	0	6	.314	.314	.371	85	-1	0-0	1.000	0	*101*	*71*	C-11	0.0
1947	Det A	8	7	0	0	0	0	0	2	0	0	2	.000	.000	.000	-97	-2	0-0	1.000	-0	*0*	*0*	/C-3	-0.2
1948	Det A	25	62	0	12	0	0	0	5	3	0	5	.194	.231	.194	13	-8	0-1	1.000	0	*108*	*50*	C-24	-0.7
1949	Det A	17	33	1	6	2	0	0	2	0	0	5	.182	.182	.242	12	-4	1-0	.960	-1	*88*	*152*	C-11	-0.5
Total	4	61	137	2	29	4	0	0	11	3	0	18	.212	.229	.241	26	-15	1-1	.994	-1	*101*	*73*	/C-49	-1.4
RIESGO, NIKCO Damon Nikco B 1.11.1967 Long Beach, CA BR/TR 6-2/185# d4.20																								
1991	Mon N	4	7	1	1	0	0	0	0	3-0	0	1	.143	.400	.143	60	0	0-0	.500	-0	0	638	/O-2(RF)	-0.1
RIGGERT, JOE Joseph Aloysius B 12.11.1886 Janesville, WI D 12.10.1973 Kansas City, MO BR/TR 5-9.5/170# d5.12																								
1911	Bos A	50	146	19	31	4	4	2	13	12	4		.212	.290	.336	75	-6	5	.929	-3	99	37	O-39(21-11-6)	-1.0
1914	Bro N	27	83	6	16	1	3	2	6	4	0	20	.193	.230	.349	70	-4	2	.972	-1	93	92	O-20(1-0-20)	-0.6
	StL N	34	89	9	19	5	2	0	8	5	0	14	.213	.255	.315	70	-4	4	.961	-1	92	103	O-30(9-19-2)	-0.6
	Year	61	172	15	35	6	5	2	14	9	0	34	.203	.243	.331	70	-8	6	.966	-1	92	98	O-50(10-19-22)	-1.2
1919	Bos N	63	240	34	68	8	5	4	17	25	2	30	.283	.356	.408	135	10	9	.950	-2	103	72	O-61(CF)	0.5
Total	3	174	558	68	134	18	14	8	44	46	6	64	.240	.305	.366	98	-4	20	.950	-6	99	71	O-150(31-91-28)	-1.7
RIGGS, ADAM Adam David B 10.4.1972 Steubenville, OH BR/TR 6/195# d8.7																								
1997	LA N	9	20	3	4	1	0	0	1	4-1	0	3	.200	.333	.250	60	-1	1-0	1.000	-1	98	81	/2-8	-0.2
2001	SD N	12	36	2	7	1	0	0	1	2-0	0	8	.194	.237	.222	22	-4	1-1	1.000	-1	86	100	2-11/3	-0.5
2003	Ana A	24	61	11	15	4	1	3	5	9-0	0	9	.246	.343	.492	121	2	3-1	.976	2	170	74	1-10/O-8(LF),2-3,D-3	0.3
Total	3	45	117	16	26	6	1	3	7	15-1	0	20	.222	.311	.368	81	-3	5-2	1.000	-0	91	85	/2-22,1-10,O-8(LF),D-3,3	-0.4
RIGGS, LEW Lewis Sidney B 4.22.1910 Mebane, NC D 8.12.1975 Durham, NC BL/TR 6/175# d4.28 Mil 1943-45																								
1934	StL N	2	1	0	0	0	0	0	0	0	0	1	.000	.000	.000	-94	0	0	—	0			H	0.0
1935	Cin N	142	532	73	148	26	8	5	46	43	2	32	.278	.334	.385	96	-3	8	.928	8	110	99	*3-135	0.9
1936	Cin N★	141	538	69	138	20	12	6	57	38	7	33	.257	.314	.372	90	-10	5	.968	13	116	**108**	*3-140	0.7
1937	Cin N	122	384	43	93	17	5	6	45	24	1	17	.242	.289	.359	79	-13	4	.941	18	121	119	*3-100/2-4,S	0.9
1938	Cin N	142	531	53	134	21	13	2	55	40	5	28	.252	.311	.352	84	-13	3	.947	-1	100	78	*3-140	-0.9
1939	Cin N	22	38	5	6	1	0	0	1	5	0	4	.158	.256	.184	20	-4	1	.957	-0	102	75	3-11	-0.4
1940	†Cin N	41	72	8	21	7	1	1	9	2	0	4	.292	.311	.458	109	1	0	.943	1	118	145	3-11	0.2
1941	†Bro N	77	197	27	60	13	4	5	36	16	0	12	.305	.357	.487	131	7	1	.932	-8	83	56	3-43/12	0.1
1942	Bro N	70	180	20	50	5	0	3	22	13	2	9	.278	.333	.356	100	0	0	.944	-5	86	107	3-46/1	-0.4
1946	Bro N	1	4	0	0	0	0	0	0	0	0	0	.000	.000	.000	-99	-1	0	1.000	0	93	0	/3	-0.1
Total	10	760	2477	298	650	110	43	28	271	181	17	140	.262	.317	.375	91	-36	22	.945	26	107	97	3-627/2-5,1-2,S	1.0
RIGNEY, TOPPER Emory Elmo B 1.7.1897 Groveton, TX D 6.6.1972 San Antonio, TX BR/TR 5-9/150# d4.12																								
1922	Det A	**155**	536	68	161	17	7	2	63	68	1	44	.300	.380	.369	99	2	17-8	.938	-15	98	89	*S-155	0.5
1923	Det A	129	470	63	148	24	11	1	74	55	2	35	.315	.389	.419	115	11	7-5	.944	-10	99	73	*S-129	1.4
1924	Det A	147	499	81	144	29	9	4	94	102	1	39	.289	.410	.407	113	15	11-11	**.967**	8	106	103	*S-146	3.5
1925	Det A	62	146	21	36	5	2	2	18	21	0	15	.247	.341	.349	77	-5	2-2	.934	-9	91	36	S-51/3-4	-1.0
1926	Bos A	148	525	71	142	32	6	4	53	108	0	31	.270	.395	.377	105	10	6-8	**.969**	21	**114**	97	*S-146	4.3
1927	Bos A	8	18	0	2	1	0	0	0	1	0	2	.111	.158	.167	-16	-3	0-0	1.000	-1	62	190	/3-4,S	-0.4
	Was A	45	132	20	36	5	4	0	13	22	1	10	.273	.381	.371	97	0	1-2	.929	-2	93	123	S-32/3-6	0.1
	Year	53	150	20	38	6	4	0	13	23	1	12	.253	.356	.347	84	-3	1-2	.932	-3	91	123	S-33,3-10	-0.3
Total	6	694	2326	324	669	113	39	13	315	377	5	176	.288	.388	.387	104	30	44-36	.953	-8	103	90	S-660/3-14	8.4
RIGNEY, BILL William Joseph "Specs" or "The Cricket" B 1.29.1918 Alameda, CA D 2.20.2001 Walnut Creek, CA BR/TR 6-1/178# d4.16 M18 C1																								
1946	NY N	110	360	38	85	9	1	3	31	36	1	29	.236	.307	.292	70	-14	9	.965	3	107	76	3-73,S-33	-1.1
1947	NY N	130	531	84	142	24	3	17	59	51	5	54	.267	.337	.420	99	-1	7	.974	4	112	84	2-72,3-41,S-24	0.7
1948	NY N★	113	424	72	112	17	3	10	43	47	3	54	.264	.342	.389	97	-2	4	.967	-7	99	80	*2-105/S-7	-0.3
1949	NY N	122	389	53	108	19	6	6	47	47	0	38	.278	.356	.404	103	2	3	.928	-11	95	80	S-81,2-26,3-14	-0.3
1950	NY N	56	83	8	15	2	0	0	8	8	0	13	.181	.253	.205	22	-9	0	.966	3	107	130	2-23,3-11	-0.6
1951	†NY N	44	69	9	16	2	0	4	9	8	1	7	.232	.321	.435	100	0	0-1	.953	3	115	193	3-12/2-9	0.2
1952	NY N	60	90	15	27	5	1	1	14	11	2	6	.300	.388	.411	121	3	2-3	.889	-2	83	220	3-10/2-9,S-4,1	0.2
1953	NY N	19	20	2	5	0	0	0	1	0	0	5	.250	.250	.250	30	-2	0-0	1.000	-0	52	0	/3-2,2	-0.2
Total	8	654	1966	281	510	78	14	41	212	208	12	206	.259	.334	.376	91	-23	25-4	.971	-7	106	84	2-245,3-163,S-149/1	-1.4
RIKARD, CULLEY Culley B 5.9.1914 Oxford, MS D 2.25.2000 Memphis, TN BL/TR 5-11/183# d9.20 Mil 1943-45																								
1941	Pit N	6	20	1	4	1	0	0	0	1	0	1	.200	.238	.250	38	-2	0	1.000	1	129	0	/O-5(3-3-0)	-0.1
1942	Pit N	38	52	6	10	2	1	0	5	7	0	8	.192	.288	.269	62	-2	0	.958	-1	107	0	O-16(2-14-0)	-0.3
1947	Pit N	109	324	57	93	16	4	4	32	50	1	39	.287	.384	.398	105	4	1	.978	-3	103	33	O-79(5-28-45)	-0.1
Total	3	153	396	64	107	19	5	4	37	58	1	48	.270	.365	.374	97	0	1	.978	-3	105	28	O-100(10-45-45)	-0.5
RILES, ERNEST Ernest B 10.2.1960 Cairo, GA BL/TR 6-1/180# d5.14 OF Total (2-LF 3-RF)																								
1985	Mil A	116	448	54	128	12	7	5	45	36-0	2	54	.286	.339	.377	97	-2	2-2	.957	-16	94	83	*S-115/D	-0.7
1986	Mil A	145	524	69	132	24	2	9	47	54-0	1	80	.252	.321	.357	82	-12	7-7	.964	-32	82	86	*S-142	-3.0
1987	Mil A	83	276	38	72	11	1	4	38	30-1	1	47	.261	.329	.351	80	-7	3-4	.935	-8	88	96	3-65,S-21	-1.4
1988	Mil A	41	127	7	32	6	1	1	9	7-0	0	26	.252	.291	.339	75	-4	2-2	.958	-1	96	51	3-28/S-9,D-5	-0.6
	SF N	79	187	26	55	7	2	3	28	10-2	0	33	.294	.323	.401	114	3	1-2	.975	10	142	116	3-30,2-17,S-16	1.3
1989	†SF N	122	302	43	84	13	2	7	40	28-3	2	50	.278	.339	.404	116	6	0-6	.962	-2	91	136	3-83,2-18/S-7,O-5(2-0-3)	0.2
1990	SF N	92	155	22	31	2	1	8	21	26-3	0	26	.200	.313	.381	94	-2	0-0	.986	2	129	106	S-26,2-24,3-10	0.1
1991	Oak A	108	281	30	60	8	4	5	32	31-3	1	42	.214	.290	.324	75	-10	3-2	.939	0	97	126	3-69,S-20/2-7,1-5	-0.9
1992	Hou N	39	61	5	16	1	0	1	4	2-0	0	11	.262	.281	.328	77	-2	1-0	1.000	-1	77	134	/S-6,3-5,1-4,2-2	-0.3
1993	Bos A	94	143	15	27	8	0	5	20	20-3	2	40	.189	.292	.350	69	-6	1-3	1.000	1	119	99	2-20,D-15,3-11/1	-0.7
Total	9	919	2504	309	637	92	20	48	284	244-15	9	409	.254	.319	.365	89	-36	20-28	.964	-49	90	91	S-362,3-301/2-88,D-21,1-10,O-5R	-6.0
RILEY, JIM James Joseph B 11.10.1886 Buffalo, NY D 3.25.1949 Buffalo, NY BR/TR 6/165# d8.2																								
1910	Bos N	1	1	0	0	0	0	0	0	1	0	1	.000	.500	.000	46	0	0	.600	-0	116	0	/O(LF)	0.0
RILEY, JIM James Norman B 5.25.1895 Bayfield, NB, CAN D 5.25.1969 Seguin, TX BL/TR 5-10.5/185# d7.3																								
1921	StL A	4	11	0	0	0	0	0	0	1	0	3	.000	.083	.000	-73	-3	0-0	.818	-2	63	0	/2-4	-0.5
1923	Was A	2	3	1	0	0	0	0	0	2	0	0	.000	.400	.000	12	0	0-0	.882	-1	0	191	/1-2	-0.1
Total	2	6	14	1	0	0	0	0	0	3	0	3	.000	.176	.000	-50	-3	0-0	.818	-3	63	0	/2-4,1-2	-0.6
RILEY, LEE Leon Francis B 8.20.1906 Princeton, NE D 9.13.1970 Schenectady, NY BL/TR 6-1/185# d4.19																								
1944	Phi N	4	12	1	1	1	0	0	1	0	0	0	.083	.083	.167	-32	-2	0	1.000	-1	50	0	/O-3(LF)	-0.3
RILEY, BILLY William James "Pigtail Billy" B 1855 Cincinnati, OH D 11.9.1887 Cincinnati, OH BR/TR 5-10/160# d5.5																								
1875	Wes NA	8	33	4	5	1	0	0	1	1		1	.152	.176	.182	23	-2	0-0	.667	-0	151	0	/O-8(RF)	-0.2
1879	Cle N	43	161	14	23	2	0	0	9	2		26	.143	.153	.155	2	-17		.850	5	120	82	O-43(LF)	-1.4

Year	Tm Lg	G	AB	R	H	2B	3B	HR	RBI	BB-IB	HP	SO	AVG	OBP	SLG	AOPS	ABR	SB-CS	FA	FR	Rng	Thr	G at Pos	BFW
RINGO, FRANK Frank C. B 10.12.1860 Parkville, MO D 4.12.1889 Kansas City, MO BR 5-11/175# d5.1 OF Total (3-LF 11-CF)																								
1883	Phi N	60	221	24	42	10	1	0	12	6		34	.190	.211	.244	42	-14		.847	-8			C-39,O-11(3-8-0)/S-6,3-5,2-2	-1.6
1884	Phi N	26	91	4	12	2	0	0	6	3		19	.132	.160	.154	-1	-10		.783	-14			C-26	-2.1
	Phi AA	2	6	0	0	0	0	0		0	0		.000	.000	.000	-94	-1		.762	-1			/C-2	-0.2
1885	Det N	17	65	12	16	3	0	0	2	0		7	.246	.246	.292	73	-2		.852	0			/C-8,3-8,O(CF)	-0.1
	Pit AA	3	11	0	2	0	0	0	0	0	0		.182	.182	.182	15	-1		.941	1			/C-3	0.1
1886	Pit AA	15	56	3	12	2	2	0	5	1	0		.214	.228	.321	72	-2	0	.934	0	87	190	/1-9,C-6	-0.2
	KC N	16	56	6	13	7	0	0	7	5		10	.232	.295	.357	92	0	0	.904	-4			C-13/O-2(CF),3	-0.3
Total	4	139	506	49	97	24	3	0	32	15		70	.192	.215	.251	46	-30	0	.844	-25			/C-97,3-14,O-14C,1-9,S-6,2-2	-4.4
RINKER, BOB Robert John B 4.21.1921 Audenried, PA D 12.19.2002 Hazleton, PA BR/TR 6/190# d9.6																								
1950	Phi A	3	3	0	1	0	0	0	0	0	0	0	.333	.333	.333	72	0	0-0	—	0	*0*	*0*	/C	0.0
RIOS, ARMANDO Armando B 9.13.1971 Santurce, P.R. BL/TL 5-9/180# d9.1																								
1998	SF N	12	7	3	4	0	0	2	3	3-0	0	2	.571	.700	1.429	469	4	0-0	1.000	0	167	0	/O-5(2-1-2)	0.4
1999	SF N	72	150	32	49	9	0	7	29	24-1	1	35	.327	.420	.527	149	12	7-4	.978	4	114	210	O-53(14-2-39)	1.4
2000	†SF N	115	233	38	62	15	5	10	50	31-4	0	43	.266	.347	.502	121	7	3-2	.959	5	113	161	O-93(19-0-76)/1	0.8
2001	SF N	93	316	38	82	17	3	14	49	34-6	0	73	.259	.330	.465	111	4	3-2	.971	7	114	125	O-87(13-3-76)	0.7
	Pit N	2	3	0	1	0	0	0	1	2-0	0	1	.333	.500	.333	148	1	0-0	—	-1	0	0	/O-2(RF)	0.0
	Year	95	319	38	83	17	3	14	50	36-6	0	74	.260	.332	.464	112	5	3-2	.971	6	112	123	O-89(13-3-78)	0.7
2002	Pit N	76	208	20	55	11	0	1	24	16-1	1	39	.264	.319	.332	75	-8	1-1	1.000	1	92	153	O-56(11-0-47)	-1.0
2003	Chi A	49	104	4	22	3	0	2	11	5-0	0	13	.212	.245	.298	43	-9	0-1	.981	-1	92	91	O-32(9-23-6)/D-4	-1.0
Total	6	419	1021	135	275	55	8	36	167	115-12	2	206	.269	.341	.445	107	11	14-10	.975	15	107	146	O-328(68-29-248)/D-4,1	1.3
RIOS, JUAN Juan Onofre Velez (born Juan Onofre Velez (Rios)) B 6.14.1942 Mayaguez, P.R. D 8.28.1995 Mayaguez, P.R. BR/TR 6-3/185# d4.9																								
1969	KC A	87	196	20	44	5	1	1	5	7-2	3	19	.224	.262	.276	50	-14	1-3	.967	-19	76	77	2-46,S-32/3-4	-3.1
RIPKEN, CAL Calvin Edwin Jr. B 8.24.1960 Havre De Grace, MD BR/TR 6-4/225# d8.10 b-Billy																								
1981	Bal A	23	39	1	5	0	0	0	0	1-0	0	8	.128	.150	.128	-19	-6	0-0	.946	-0	95	96	S-12/3-6	-0.6
1982	Bal A	160	598	90	158	32	5	28	93	46-3	3	95	.264	.317	.475	115	11	3-3	.972	-3	99	89	S-94,3-71	1.6
1983	†Bal A★	**162**	663	**121**	**211**	**47**	2	27	102	58-0	0	97	.318	.371	.517	145	41	0-4	.970	16	**105**	**118**	*S-162	**7.1**
1984	Bal A★	**162**	641	103	195	37	7	27	86	71-1	2	89	.304	.374	.510	146	40	2-1	.971	**39**	**117**	**125**	*S-162	**9.4**
1985	Bal A★	**161**	642	116	181	32	5	26	110	67-1	1	68	.282	.347	.469	125	22	2-3	.967	9	102	115	*S-161	4.6
1986	Bal A★	**162**	627	98	177	35	1	25	81	70-5	4	60	.282	.355	.461	123	21	4-2	.982	10	105	103	*S-162	4.7
1987	Bal A★	**162**	624	97	157	28	3	27	98	81-0	1	77	.252	.333	.436	106	6	3-5	.973	-5	102	104	*S-162	1.6
1988	Bal A★	**161**	575	87	152	25	1	23	81	102-7	2	69	.264	.372	.431	129	27	2-2	.973	4	103	109	*S-161	4.2
1989	Bal A★	**162**	646	80	166	30	0	21	93	57-5	3	72	.257	.317	.401	105	4	3-2	.990	5	107	112	*S-162	2.1
1990	Bal A★	**161**	600	78	150	28	4	21	84	82-18	5	66	.250	.341	.415	115	13	3-1	**.996**	-26	93	91	*S-161	0.0
1991	Bal A★	**162**	650	99	210	46	5	34	114	53-15	5	46	.323	.374	.566	164	55	6-1	**.986**	20	**109**	111	*S-162	**8.6**
1992	Bal A★	**162**	637	73	160	29	1	14	72	64-14	7	50	.251	.323	.366	91	-7	4-3	.984	-10	91	**117**	*S-162	-0.5
1993	Bal A★	**162**	641	87	165	26	3	24	90	65-19	6	58	.257	.329	.420	96	-4	1-4	.977	-5	101	100	*S-162	0.3
1994	Bal A★	**112**	444	71	140	19	3	13	75	32-3	4	41	.315	.364	.459	106	3	1-0	**.985**	-12	95	111	*S-112	0.1
1995	Bal A★	**144**	550	71	144	33	2	17	88	52-6	2	59	.262	.324	.422	92	-7	0-1	**.989**	3	97	118	*S-144	0.6
1996	†Bal A★	**163**	640	94	178	40	1	26	102	59-3	4	78	.278	.341	.466	102	2	1-2	.980	2	101	104	*S-158/3-6	1.4
1997	†Bal A★	**162**	615	79	166	30	0	17	84	56-3	5	73	.270	.331	.402	94	-5	1-0	.949	2	103	98	*3-162/S-3	-0.1
1998	Bal A★	161	601	65	163	27	1	14	61	51-0	4	68	.271	.331	.389	88	-11	0-2	**.979**	-0	97	95	*3-161	-1.0
1999	Bal A★	86	332	51	113	27	0	18	57	13-3	3	31	.340	.368	.584	144	21	0-1	.932	-5	100	85	3-85	1.5
2000	Bal A✳	83	309	43	79	16	0	15	56	23-0	3	37	.256	.310	.453	95	-3	0-0	.974	7	107	131	3-73,D-10	0.3
2001	Bal A	128	477	43	114	16	0	14	68	26-1	2	63	.239	.276	.361	71	-22	0-2	.956	4	102	119	*3-111,D-14	-1.8
Total	21	3001	11551	1647	3184	603	44	431	1695	1129-107	66	1305	.276	.340	.447	113	201	36-39	.979	54	102	109	*S-2302,3-675/D-24	44.1
RIPKEN, BILLY William Oliver B 12.16.1964 Havre De Grace, MD BR/TR 6-1/186# d7.11 b-Cal																								
1987	Bal A	58	234	27	72	9	0	2	20	21-0	0	23	.308	.363	.372	99	0	4-1	.990	2	97	138	2-58	0.6
1988	Bal A	150	512	52	106	18	1	2	34	33-0	5	63	.207	.260	.258	47	-36	8-2	.984	-0	101	108	*2-149/3-2,D	-3.2
1989	Bal A	115	318	31	76	11	2	2	26	22-0	0	53	.239	.284	.305	69	-13	1-2	.985	7	106	118	*2-114/D	-0.4
1990	Bal A	129	406	48	118	28	1	3	38	28-2	4	43	.291	.342	.387	107	4	5-2	.987	-8	98	104	*2-127	-0.1
1991	Bal A	104	287	24	62	11	1	0	14	15-0	0	31	.216	.253	.261	45	-22	0-1	.986	1	100	117	*2-103	-1.9
1992	Bal A	111	330	35	76	15	0	4	36	18-1	3	26	.230	.275	.312	63	-17	2-3	**.993**	0	102	99	*2-108/D-2	-1.5
1993	Tex A	50	132	12	25	4	0	0	11	11-0	4	19	.189	.270	.220	35	-12	0-2	.992	0	92	84	2-34,S-18/3	-1.0
1994	Tex A	32	81	9	25	5	0	0	6	3-0	0	11	.309	.333	.370	81	-2	2-0	.970	1	95	182	3-18,2-12/S-2,1	-0.1
1995	Cle A	8	17	4	7	0	0	2	3	0-0	0	3	.412	.412	.765	195	2	0-0	1.000	-3	50	42	/2-7,3	-0.1
1996	Bal A	57	135	19	31	8	0	2	12	9-0	1	18	.230	.281	.333	55	-9	0-0	.968	1	105	113	2-30,3-25/1	-0.7
1997	Tex A	71	203	18	56	9	1	3	24	9-0	0	32	.276	.300	.374	73	-9	0-1	.971	1	93	92	S-31,2-25,3-13/1-9	-0.5
1998	Det A	27	74	8	20	3	0	0	5	5-0	1	10	.270	.321	.311	66	-4	3-2	.926	-4	100	95	S-21/1-2,2-2,3-2,D	-0.5
Total	12	912	2729	287	674	121	6	20	229	174-3	18	332	.247	.294	.318	69	-118	25-16	.987	-1	101	110	2-769/S-72,3-62,1-13,D-5	-9.4
RIPPLE, JIMMY James Albert B 10.14.1909 Export, PA D 7.16.1959 Greensburg, PA BL/TR 5-10/170# d4.20																								
1936	†NY N	96	311	42	95	17	2	7	47	28	1	15	.305	.365	.441	117	8	1	.980	-5	89	86	O-76(0-75-1)	0.0
1937	†NY N	121	426	70	135	23	3	5	66	29	1	20	.317	.362	.420	110	6	3	.980	-9	86	63	*O-111(0-54-57)	-0.7
1938	NY N	134	501	68	131	21	3	10	60	49	5	21	.261	.333	.375	94	-4	2	.976	-4	90	112	*O-131(0-17-115)	-1.6
1939	NY N	66	123	10	28	4	0	1	12	8	2	7	.228	.286	.285	53	-8	0	1.000	-1	86	130	O-23(9-4-10)	-1.0
	Bro N	28	106	18	35	8	4	0	22	11	1	8	.330	.398	.481	131	5	0	1.000	-2	95	0	O-28(12-1-15)	0.1
	Year	94	229	28	63	12	4	1	34	19	3	15	.275	.339	.376	90	-3	0	1.000	-3	91	54	O-51(21-5-25)	-0.9
1940	Bro N	7	13	0	3	0	0	0	0	2	0	2	.231	.333	.231	55	-1	0	1.000	0	135	0	/O-3(1-0-2)	-0.1
	†Cin N	32	101	15	31	10	0	4	20	13	2	5	.307	.397	.525	151	8	1	1.000	-3	85	0	O-30(27-0-3)	0.4
	Year	39	114	15	34	10	0	4	20	15	2	7	.298	.389	.491	139	7	1	1.000	-2	92	0	O-33(28-0-5)	0.3
1941	Cin N	38	102	10	22	6	1	1	9	9	0	4	.216	.279	.324	69	-4	0	1.000	-1	88	60	O-25(7-0-18)	-0.7
1943	Phi A	32	126	8	30	3	1	0	15	7	1	7	.238	.284	.278	65	-6	0-0	1.000	-2	92	0	O-31(10-0-21)	-1.1
Total	7	554	1809	241	510	92	14	28	251	156	13	89	.282	.343	.395	101	4	7-0	.984	-27	89	72	O-458(66-151-242)	-4.7
RISBERG, SWEDE Charles August B 10.13.1894 San Francisco, CA D 10.13.1975 Red Bluff, CA BR/TR 6/175# d4.11 Mil 1918																								
1917	†Chi A	149	474	59	96	20	8	1	45	59	5	65	.203	.297	.285	76	-13	16	.913	-40	80	97	*S-146	-4.8
1918	Chi A	82	273	36	70	12	3	1	27	23	3	32	.256	.321	.333	96	-1	5	.944	-7	93	122	S-30,3-24,2-12/1-7,O-3(RF)	-0.7
1919	†Chi A	119	414	48	106	19	6	2	38	35	2	38	.256	.317	.345	86	-8	19	.934	-12	95	119	S-97,1-22	-1.5
1920	Chi A	126	458	53	122	21	10	2	65	31	2	45	.266	.316	.369	81	-14	12-10	.934	-7	99	**127**	*S-124	-1.3
Total	4	476	1619	196	394	72	27	6	175	148	12	180	.243	.311	.332	83	-36	52-10	.928	-66	91	114	S-397/1-29,3-24,2-12,O-3(RF)	-8.3
RISING, POP Percival Sumner B 1.2.1872 Industry, PA D 1.28.1938 Rochester, PA TR d8.10																								
1905	Bos A	11	29	2	3	1	1	0	2	2	0		.103	.161	.207	16	-3	0	1.000	0	152	0	/O-6(RF),3	-0.3
RITCHEY, CLAUDE Claude Cassius "Little All Right" B 10.5.1873 Emlenton, PA D 11.8.1951 Emlenton, PA BB/TR 5-6.5/167# d4.22																								
1897	Cin N	101	337	58	95	12	4	0	41	42	5		.282	.370	.341	83	-7	11	.897	-11	92	87	S-70,O-22(10-1-11)/2-8	-1.4
1898	Lou N	151	551	65	140	10	4	5	51	46	9		.254	.322	.314	84	-12	19	.919	-16	87	95	S-80,2-71	-1.9
1899	Lou N	148	540	66	162	16	7	4	73	49	10		.300	.369	.378	105	5	21	.938	-8	97	108	*2-138,S-11	0.3
1900	†Pit N	123	476	62	139	17	8	1	67	29	5		.292	.339	.368	94	-4	18	.952	6	100	113	*2-123	0.7
1901	Pit N	**140**	540	66	160	20	4	1	74	47	5		.296	.358	.354	104	4	15	.941	4	99	**127**	*2-139/S	0.9
1902	Pit N	115	405	54	112	13	1	2	55	53	7		.277	.370	.328	112	9	10	**.966**	6	100	128	*2-114/O(RF)	1.7
1903	†Pit N	138	506	66	145	28	10	0	59	55	3		.287	.360	.381	108	6	15	**.961**	17	**115**	106	*2-137	2.3
1904	Pit N	**156**	544	79	143	22	12	0	51	59	3		.263	.338	.347	109	7	12	.958	1	101	103	*2-156/S-2	1.0
1905	Pit N	153	533	54	136	29	6	0	52	51	3		.255	.324	.332	93	-3	12	**.961**	-6	101	125	*2-153/S-2	-0.8
1906	Pit N	152	484	46	130	21	5	1	62	68	9		.269	.369	.339	116	13	6	**.966**	-1	98	**130**	*2-151	1.4
1907	Bos N	144	499	45	127	17	4	2	51	50	5		.255	.329	.317	103	3	8	**.971**	13	109	100	*2-144	1.9
1908	Bos N	121	421	44	115	10	3	2	36	50	8		.273	.361	.325	121	13	7	.967	13	101	**129**	*2-120	3.1
1909	Bos N	30	87	4	15	1	0	0	3	8	0		.172	.242	.184	31	-7	1	.959	-0	84	118	2-25	-0.8
Total	13	1672	5923	709	1619	216	68	18	675	607	72		.273	.348	.342	101	27	155	.957	18	101	116	*2-1479,S-166/O-23(10-1-12)	8.4

Year	Tm Lg	G	AB	R	H	2B	3B	HR	RBI	BB-IB	HP	SO	AVG	OBP	SLG	AOPS	ABR	SB-CS	FA	FR	Rng	Thr	G at Pos	BFW
RITTER, CHARLIE Charles J. d9.21																								
1885	Buf N	2	6	0	1	0	0	0	0	0		2	.167	.167	.167	8	-1		.813	-0	82	105	/2-2	-0.1
RITTER, FLOYD Floyd Alexander B 6.1.1870 Dorset, OH D 2.7.1943 Stevenson, WA BR/TR 5-8/155# d6.4																								
1890	Tol AA	1	3	0	0	0	0	0	0	0	0		.000	.000	.000	-97	-1	0	.778	-0	*120*	*207*	/C	-0.1
RITTER, LEW Lewis Elmer "Old Dog" B 9.7.1875 Liverpool, PA D 5.27.1952 Harrisburg, PA BR/TR 5-9/150# d9.10																								
1902	Bro N	16	57	5	12	1	0	0	2	1	1		.211	.237	.228	43	-4	2	.973	0	*87*	*87*	C-16	-0.2
1903	Bro N	78	259	26	61	9	6	0	37	19	1		.236	.290	.317	75	-9	9	.940	-22	*67*	*88*	C-74/O-2(1-1-0)	-2.3
1904	Bro N	72	214	23	53	4	1	0	19	20	2		.248	.318	.276	86	-3	17	.966	7	*99*	*107*	C-57/2-5,3	1.0
1905	Bro N	92	311	32	68	10	5	1	28	15	0		.219	.255	.293	68	-14	16	.951	-15	*75*	*98*	C-84/O-4(0-1-3),3-2	-2.1
1906	Bro N	73	226	22	47	1	3	0	15	16	1		.208	.263	.239	61	-11	6	.978	-5	*91*	*93*	C-53/O-9(5-0-5),1-3,3-2	-1.3
1907	Bro N	93	271	15	55	6	1	0	17	18	1		.203	.255	.232	57	-14	5	.969	-6	*88*	*91*	C-89	-1.2
1908	Bro N	38	99	6	19	2	1	0	2	7	0		.192	.245	.232	55	-5	0	.961	-3	*81*	*100*	C-37	-0.6
Total	7	462	1437	129	315	33	17	1	120	96	6		.219	.271	.268	67	-60	55	.960	-43	*83*	*95*	C-410/O-15(6-2-8),3-5,2-5,1-3	-6.7
RITTERSON, WHITEY Edward West B 4.26.1855 Philadelphia, PA D 7.28.1917 Sellersville, PA BR/TR 5-8/?# d5.3																								
1876	Phi N	16	52	8	13	3	0	0	4	0		2	.250	.250	.308	86	-1		.671	-6			C-14/O-4(0-2-2),3	-0.6
RITZ, JIM James L. B 1874 Pittsburgh, PA D 11.10.1896 Pittsburgh, PA 5-8/160# d7.20																								
1894	Pit N	1	4	1	0	0	0	0	0	0	1	0	.000	.200	.000	-49	-1	1	.750	-0	85	537	/3	-0.1
RIVAS, LUIS Luis Wilfredo B 8.30.1979 LaGuaira, Venezuela BR/TR 5-10/175# d9.16																								
2000	Min A	16	58	8	18	4	1	0	6	2-0	0	4	.310	.323	.414	84	-1	2-0	.983	-3	75	86	2-14/S-2	-0.3
2001	Min A	153	563	70	150	21	6	7	47	40-0	6	99	.266	.319	.362	78	-18	31-11	.974	-52	81	72	*2-150	-5.9
2002	†Min A	93	316	46	81	23	4	4	35	19-2	3	51	.256	.305	.392	83	-8	9-4	.986	-29	79	92	2-93	-3.1
2003	†Min A	135	475	69	123	16	9	8	43	30-0	5	65	.259	.308	.381	80	-15	17-7	.982	-31	87	80	*2-134/D	-3.8
Total	4	397	1412	193	372	64	20	19	131	91-2	14	219	.263	.312	.377	80	-42	59-22	.980	-115	82	80	2-391/S-2,D	-13.1
RIVERA, CARLOS Carlos Alberto B 6.10.1978 Fajardo, P.R. BL/TL 5-11/230# d6.22																								
2003	Pit N	78	95	12	21	5	0	3	10	8-2	1	28	.221	.283	.368	68	-5	0-0	.984	-1	91	109	1-60	-0.8
RIVERA, GERMAN German (Diaz) B 7.6.1960 Santurce, P.R. BR/TR 6-2/195# d9.2																								
1983	LA N	13	17	1	6	1	0	0	0	2-0	0	2	.353	.421	.412	132	1	0-1	.929	1	130	0	/3-8	0.1
1984	LA N	94	227	20	59	12	2	2	17	21-5	1	30	.260	.321	.357	92	-2	1-0	.937	10	113	102	3-90	0.7
1985	Hou N	13	36	3	7	2	1	0	2	4-1	0	8	.194	.275	.306	64	-2	0-0	.941	3	140	195	3-11	0.1
Total	3	120	280	24	72	15	3	2	19	27-6	1	40	.257	.322	.354	91	-3	1-1	.937	13	117	107	3-109	0.9
RIVERA, BOMBO Jesus Manuel (Torres) B 8.2.1952 Ponce, P.R. BR/TR 5-10/187# d4.17																								
1975	Mon N	5	9	1	1	0	0	0	0	2-0	0	3	.111	.273	.111	9	-1	0-0	.889	-0	121	0	/O-5(4-0-2)	-0.1
1976	Mon N	68	185	22	51	11	4	2	19	13-1	0	32	.276	.323	.411	103	0	1-0	.950	3	99	215	O-56(44-0-15)	0.1
1978	Min A	101	251	35	68	8	2	3	23	35-1	2	47	.271	.362	.355	101	2	5-3	.982	2	108	95	O-94(32-0-72)/D	0.1
1979	Min A	112	263	37	74	13	5	2	31	17-0	0	40	.281	.324	.392	89	-5	5-5	.989	9	114	222	*O-105(61-1-50)/D-2	0.1
1980	Min A	44	113	13	25	7	0	3	10	4-0	0	20	.221	.248	.363	61	-6	0-0	.922	-2	98	45	O-37(10-0-28)/D	-1.0
1982	KC A	5	10	1	1	0	0	0	0	0-0	0	2	.100	.100	.100	-45	-2	0-0	1.000	-0	78	0	/O-3(2-0-1)	-0.3
Total	6	335	831	109	220	39	11	10	83	71-2	2	144	.265	.323	.374	90	-12	11-8	.970	13	107	151	O-300(153-1-168)/D-4	-1.1
RIVERA, JUAN Juan Luis B 7.3.1978 Guarenas, Venezuela BR/TR 6-2/170# d9.4																								
2001	NY A	3	4	0	0	0	0	0	0	0-0	0	0	.000	.000	.000	-99	-1	0-0	1.000	-0	37	0	/O-3(0-1-2)	-0.2
2002	†NY A	28	83	9	22	5	0	1	6	6-0	0	10	.265	.311	.361	80	-2	1-1	.966	1	102	125	O-28(15-0-15)	-0.3
2003	†NY A	57	173	22	46	14	0	7	26	10-1	0	27	.266	.304	.468	102	0	0-0	.979	-1	97	108	O-56(34-0-22)	-0.2
Total	3	88	260	31	68	19	0	8	32	16-1	0	37	.262	.302	.427	92	-3	1-1	.974	-0	98	112	O-87(49-1-39)	-0.7
RIVERA, LUIS Luis Antonio (Pedraza) B 1.3.1964 Cidra, P.R. BR/TR 5-9/170# d8.3																								
1986	Mon N	55	166	20	34	11	1	0	13	17-0	2	33	.205	.285	.283	58	-9	1-1	.953	-10	87	90	S-55	-1.5
1987	Mon N	18	32	0	5	2	0	0	1	1-0	0	8	.156	.182	.219	5	-4	0-0	.923	-0	109	86	S-15	-0.4
1988	Mon N	123	371	35	83	17	3	4	30	24-4	1	69	.224	.271	.318	66	-17	3-4	.962	-2	99	**128**	*S-116	-1.2
1989	Bos A	93	323	35	83	17	1	5	29	20-1	1	60	.257	.301	.362	81	-8	2-3	.958	-8	92	104	*S-90/2D	-1.0
1990	†Bos A	118	346	38	78	20	0	7	45	25-0	1	58	.225	.279	.344	70	-14	4-3	.965	5	101	97	*S-112/2-3,3	-0.1
1991	Bos A	129	414	64	107	22	3	8	40	35-0	3	86	.258	.318	.384	90	-6	4-4	.959	7	102	113	*S-129	1.0
1992	Bos A	102	288	17	62	11	1	0	29	26-0	3	56	.215	.287	.260	51	-19	4-3	.966	13	112	105	S-93/230(LF)D	0.1
1993	Bos A	62	130	13	27	8	1	1	7	11-0	1	36	.208	.273	.308	53	-9	1-2	.969	-4	102	108	2-27,S-27/3-2,D-7	-1.0
1994	NY N	32	43	11	12	2	1	3	5	4-0	2	14	.279	.367	.581	144	3	0-1	.971	4	124	192	S-11/2-5	0.6
1997	Hou N	7	13	2	3	0	1	0	3	1-0	0	6	.231	.286	.385	76	-1	0-0	.875	-1	70	182	/S-6,2	-0.2
1998	KC A	42	89	14	22	4	0	0	7	7-0	0	17	.247	.302	.292	54	-6	1-1	.961	4	115	126	S-30/2-6,3-6	0.0
Total	11	781	2215	249	516	114	12	28	209	171-5	14	443	.233	.291	.333	70	-90	20-22	.961	7	100	110	S-684/2-44,3-10,D-10,O(LF)	-3.7
RIVERA, JIM Manuel Joseph "Jungle Jim" B 7.22.1922 New York, NY BL/TL 6/196# d4.15																								
1952	StL A	97	336	45	86	13	6	4	30	29	2	59	.256	.319	.366	88	-6	8-7	.976	6	112	103	O-88(8-81-0)	-0.4
	Chi A	53	201	27	50	7	3	3	18	21	0	27	.249	.320	.358	88	-4	13-2	.988	-1	102	47	O-53(CF)	-0.4
	Year	150	537	72	136	20	9	7	48	50	2	86	.253	.319	.363	88	-10	21-9	.980	5	108	81	*O-141(8-134-0)	-0.8
1953	Chi A	**156**	567	79	147	26	**16**	11	78	53	6	70	.259	.329	.420	98	-4	22-15	.976	-8	90	110	*O-156(0-153-3)	-2.0
1954	Chi A	145	490	62	140	16	8	13	61	49	6	68	.286	.356	.431	111	7	18-10	.959	-9	94	49	*O-143(3-28-128)	-0.7
1955	Chi A	147	454	71	120	24	4	10	52	62-6	1	59	.264	.352	.401	100	1	**25**-16	.981	11	102	**230**	*O-143(2-50-115)	0.7
1956	Chi A	139	491	76	125	23	5	12	66	49-2	3	75	.255	.322	.395	88	-9	20-9	.976	2	104	96	*O-134(0-14-122)	-1.0
1957	Chi A	125	402	51	103	21	6	14	52	40-6	3	80	.256	.326	.443	108	4	18-2	.974	-4	100	105	O-86(1-4-83),1-31	-0.2
1958	Chi A	116	276	37	62	8	4	9	35	24-5	1	49	.225	.282	.380	84	-7	21-3	.994	2	100	124	O-99(54-1-45)	-0.5
1959	†Chi A	80	177	18	39	9	4	4	19	11-3	1	19	.220	.266	.384	78	-6	5-3	.976	0	88	186	O-69(21-0-48)	-0.8
1960	Chi A	48	17	17	5	0	0	1	1	3-0	0	3	.294	.400	.471	136	1	4-0	1.000	1	187	0	O-24(9-1-14)	0.3
1961	Chi A	1	0	0	0	0	0	0	0	0-0	0	0	—	—	—	—	0	0-1	—	0			H	0.0
	KC A	64	141	20	34	8	0	2	10	24-0	0	14	.241	.352	.340	84	-2	6-2	.981	-4	81	0	O-43(0-7-36)	-0.7
	Year	65	141	20	34	8	0	2	10	24-0	0	14	.241	.352	.340	84	-2	6-3	.981	-4	81	0	O-43(0-7-36)	-0.7
Total	10	1171	3552	503	911	155	56	83	422	365-22	23	523	.256	.328	.402	96	-25	160-70	.977	-4	99	112	*O-1038(98-392-594)/1-31	-5.7
RIVERA, MIKE Michael R. B 9.8.1976 Rio Piedras, P.R. BR/TR 6/190# d9.18																								
2001	Det A	4	12	2	4	2	0	0	1	0-0	0	2	.333	.333	.500	121	0	0-0	.929	1	70	347	/C-4	0.2
2002	Det A	39	132	11	30	8	1	1	11	4-0	1	35	.227	.254	.326	56	-9	0-0	.990	1	95	138	C-37/D	-0.5
2003	SD N	19	53	2	9	1	0	1	2	5-0	0	11	.170	.241	.245	30	-6	0-0	.986	2	79	85	C-19/1	-0.2
Total	3	62	197	15	43	11	1	2	14	9-0	1	48	.218	.255	.315	53	-15	0-0	.984	5	89	134	/C-60,1D	-0.5
RIVERA, RUBEN Ruben (Moreno) B 11.14.1973 Chorrera, Panama BR/TR 6-3/200# d9.3																								
1995	NY A	5	1	0	0	0	0	0	0	0-0	0	1	.000	.000	.000	-99	0	0-0	1.000	0	174	0	/O-4(LF)	0.0
1996	†NY A	46	88	17	25	6	1	2	16	13-0	2	26	.284	.381	.443	110	2	6-2	1.000	4	125	112	O-45(13-14-19)	0.5
1997	SD N	17	20	2	5	1	0	0	1	2-0	0	9	.250	.318	.300	68	-1	2-1	1.000	1	140	0	/O-7(2-4-4)	0.0
1998	†SD N	95	172	31	36	7	2	6	29	28-0	2	52	.209	.325	.378	92	-2	5-1	.973	-0	100	86	O-91(13-13-73)	-0.4
1999	SD N	147	411	65	80	16	1	23	48	55-1	5	143	.195	.295	.406	82	-14	18-7	.976	5	111	128	*O-143(CF)	-0.6
2000	SD N	135	423	62	88	18	6	17	57	44-1	10	137	.208	.296	.400	79	-16	8-4	.984	1	102	136	*O-132(1-131-0)	-1.2
2001	Cin N	117	263	37	67	13	1	10	34	21-1	5	83	.255	.321	.426	87	-5	6-3	.983	1	107	97	O-99(10-70-21)	-0.4
2002	Tex A	69	158	17	33	4	0	4	14	17-0	5	45	.209	.302	.310	61	-9	4-2	.983	4	120	71	O-67(CF)/D-2	-0.4
2003	SF N	31	50	6	9	2	0	2	4	5-1	0	14	.180	.255	.340	55	-4	1-0	1.000	2	151	0	O-27(9-13-6)	-0.1
Total	9	662	1586	237	343	67	11	64	203	185-4	29	510	.216	.307	.393	82	-49	50-20	.982	18	110	108	O-615(52-455-123)/D-2	-2.6
RIVERS, MICKEY John Milton B 10.31.1948 Miami, FL BL/TL 5-10/165# d8.4 Mil 1971																								
1970	Cal A	17	25	6	8	2	0	0	3	3-0	1	5	.320	.414	.400	130	1	1-0	1.000	0	107	0	/O-5(RF)	0.1
1971	Cal A	79	268	31	71	12	2	1	12	19-1	1	38	.265	.316	.336	91	-4	13-1	.976	-2	94	110	O-76(4-61-18)	-0.5
1972	Cal A	58	159	18	34	6	2	0	7	8-1	1	26	.214	.256	.277	62	-8	4-3	.981	1	116	0	O-48(6-38-7)	-1.0
1973	Cal A	30	129	26	45	6	4	0	16	8-0	1	11	.349	.391	.457	150	8	8-3	.909	-6	81	0	O-29(CF)	0.2
1974	Cal A	118	466	69	133	19	**11**	3	31	39-0	1	47	.285	.341	.393	118	10	30-13	.994	3	106	115	*O-116(CF)	1.2

Year	Tm Lg	G	AB	R	H	2B	3B	HR	RBI	BB-IB	HP	SO	AVG	OBP	SLG	AOPS	ABR	SB-CS	FA	FR	Rng	Thr	G at Pos	BFW
1975	Cal A	155	616	70	175	17	**13**	1	53	43-5	2	42	.284	.331	.359	103	0	**70**-14	.977	1	100	125	*O-152(27-125-0)/D	0.6
1976	†NY A★	137	590	95	184	31	8	8	67	13-0	3	51	.312	.327	.432	123	14	43-7	.986	-1	104	57	*O-136(CF)	1.7
1977	†NY A	138	565	79	184	18	5	12	69	18-4	4	45	.326	.350	.439	115	10	22-14	.982	7	110	118	*O-136(CF)/D	1.5
1978	†NY A	141	559	78	148	25	8	11	48	29-3	3	51	.265	.302	.397	98	-4	25-5	.980	4	108	96	*O-138(CF)	0.3
1979	NY A	74	286	37	82	18	5	3	25	13-2	1	21	.287	.315	.416	99	-1	3-7	.974	-7	82	92	O-69(CF)/D	-1.1
	Tex A	58	247	35	74	9	3	6	25	9-0	1	18	.300	.323	.433	104	0	7-2	.981	1	102	109	O-57(CF)	0.1
	Year	132	533	72	156	27	8	9	50	22-2	2	39	.293	.319	.424	101	-1	10-9	.978	-7	91	100	*O-126(CF)/D	-1.0
1980	Tex A	147	630	96	210	32	6	7	60	20-1	1	34	.333	.353	.437	119	14	18-7	.978	3	94	**208**	*O-141(CF)/D-4	1.8
1981	Tex A	99	399	62	114	21	2	3	26	24-2	1	31	.286	.327	.371	107	3	9-5	.996	-1	88	**207**	O-97(CF)	0.1
1982	Tex A	19	68	6	16	1	1	1	4	0-0	0	7	.235	.232	.324	54	-5	0-0	—	0	0	0	D-16	-0.5
1983	Tex A	96	309	37	88	17	0	1	20	11-0	1	21	.285	.309	.350	83	-7	9-4	.980	0	110	62	D-53,O-23(15-0-8)	-0.9
1984	Tex A	102	313	40	94	13	1	4	33	9-1	0	23	.300	.320	.387	91	-4	5-5	1.000	1	92	177	D-48,O-30(26-2-2)	-0.6
Total	15	1468	5629	785	1660	247	71	61	499	266-20	22	471	.295	.327	.397	106	27	267-90	.982	3	100	117	*O-1253(78-1145-40),D-124	3.0
RIZZO, JOHNNY John Costa B 7.30.1912 Houston, TX D 12.4.1977 Houston, TX BR/TR 6/190# d4.19 Mil 1943-46																								
1938	Pit N	143	555	97	167	31	9	23	111	54	5	61	.301	.368	.514	139	29	1	.951	-11	90	43	*O-140(LF)	0.9
1939	Pit N	94	330	49	86	23	3	6	55	42	3	27	.261	.349	.403	103	3	0	.974	-3	99	36	O-86(LF)	-0.6
1940	Pit N	9	28	1	5	1	0	0	2	5	1	5	.179	.324	.214	51	-2	0	.818	-2	65	0	/O-7(LF)	-0.4
	Cin N	31	110	17	31	6	0	4	17	14	0	14	.282	.363	.445	121	3	1	.974	4	99	260	O-30(LF)	0.5
	Phi N	103	367	53	107	12	2	20	53	37	1	31	.292	.358	.499	139	18	2	.968	5	104	88	O-91(56-23-15)/3-7	1.9
	Year	143	505	71	143	19	2	24	72	56	2	50	.283	.357	.471	130	20	3	.964	7	101	126	*O-128(93-23-15)/3-7	2.0
1941	Phi N	99	235	20	51	9	2	4	24	24	2	34	.217	.295	.323	77	-8	1	.968	2	103	170	O-62(3-8-53)/3-2	-0.9
1942	Bro N	78	217	31	50	8	0	4	27	24	0	25	.230	.307	.323	83	-5	2	.977	2	108	118	O-70(9-0-62)	-0.6
Total	5	557	1842	268	497	90	16	61	289	200	12	197	.270	.345	.435	116	38	7	.964	-3	98	89	O-486(331-31-130)/3-9	0.8
RIZZUTO, PHIL Philip Francis "Scooter" (born Fiero Francis Rizzuto) B 9.25.1917 Brooklyn, NY BR/TR 5-6/160# d4.14 Mil 1943-45 HF1994																								
1941	†NY A	133	515	65	158	20	9	3	46	27	1	36	.307	.343	.398	97	-5	14-5	.957	19	**108**	**141**	*S-128	2.4
1942	†NY A☆	144	553	79	157	24	7	4	68	44	6	40	.284	.343	.374	104	2	22-6	.962	**30**	108	**149**	*S-144	4.6
1946	NY A	126	471	53	121	17	1	2	38	34	6	39	.257	.315	.310	74	-16	14-7	.961	17	104	**129**	*S-125	0.9
1947	†NY A	153	549	78	150	26	9	2	60	57	**8**	31	.273	.350	.364	100	0	11-6	.969	18	99	111	*S-151	2.8
1948	NY A	128	464	65	117	13	2	6	50	60	2	24	.252	.340	.328	79	-14	6-5	.973	-13	87	95	*S-128	-1.8
1949	†NY A	153	614	110	169	22	7	5	65	72	1	34	.275	.352	.358	88	-11	18-6	**.971**	3	94	101	*S-152	0.3
1950	†NY A★	**155**	617	125	200	36	7	7	66	92	7	39	.324	.418	.439	123	26	12-8	**.982**	8	95	108	*S-155	**4.0**
1951	†NY A★	144	540	87	148	21	6	2	43	58	5	27	.274	.350	.346	92	-5	18-3	.968	11	97	**116**	*S-144	1.7
1952	†NY A★	152	578	89	147	24	10	2	43	67	5	42	.254	.337	.341	95	-4	17-6	.976	21	**105**	**127**	*S-152	2.9
1953	†NY A★	134	413	54	112	21	3	2	54	71	4	39	.271	.383	.351	103	6	4-3	.963	3	103	127	*S-133	1.9
1954	NY A	127	307	47	60	11	0	2	15	41	1	23	.195	.291	.251	51	-20	3-2	.968	6	98	**137**	*S-126/2	-0.6
1955	†NY A	81	143	19	37	4	1	1	9	22-1	3	18	.259	.369	.322	88	-1	7-1	.957	-8	84	97	S-79/2	-0.4
1956	NY A	31	52	6	12	0	0	0	6	6-0	0	6	.231	.310	.231	46	-4	3-0	.934	2	106	156	S-30	0.0
Total	13	1661	5816	877	1588	239	62	38	563	651-1	49	398	.273	.351	.355	93	-46	149-58	.968	117	99	121	*S-1647/2-2	18.7
ROACH, MEL Melvin Earl B 1.25.1933 Richmond, VA BR/TR 6-1/190# d7.31 Mil 1955																								
1953	Mil N	5	2	1	0	0	0	0	0	0	0	1	.000	.000	.000	-99	-1	0-0	—	-0	0	0	/2	-0.1
1954	Mil N	3	4	0	0	0	0	0	0	0	0	1	.000	.000	.000	-99	-1	0-0	1.000	-0	0	511	/1	-0.1
1957	Mil N	7	6	1	1	0	0	0	0	0-0	0	3	.167	.167	.167	-11	-1	0-0	1.000	-0	86	0	/2-5	-0.1
1958	Mil N	44	136	14	42	7	0	3	10	6-0	0	15	.309	.336	.426	110	2	0-0	.993	1	109	76	2-27/O-7(4-0-3),1	0.4
1959	Mil N	19	31	1	3	0	0	0	0	2-0	0	4	.097	.152	.097	-35	-6	0-0	.880	-0	117	76	/2-8,O-4(LF),3	-0.6
1960	Mil N	48	140	12	42	12	0	3	18	6-1	1	19	.300	.329	.450	121	4	0-0	.975	-6	98	0	O-21(LF),2-20/13	-0.2
1961	Mil N	13	36	3	6	0	0	1	6	2-0	2	4	.167	.244	.250	35	-3	0-0	1.000	-1	94	0	/O-9(LF),1-2	-0.5
	Chi N	23	39	1	5	2	0	0	1	3-0	0	9	.128	.190	.179	-1	-6	1-0	.981	-1	70	150	/1-7,2-7	-0.7
	Year	36	75	4	11	2	0	1	7	5-0	2	13	.147	.217	.213	16	-9	1-0	1.000	-2	94	0	/O-9(LF),1-9,2-7	-1.2
1962	Phi N	65	105	9	20	4	0	0	8	5-0	0	19	.190	.225	.229	23	-11	0-0	.951	-1	95	76	3-26/2-9,1-4,O-3(LF)	-1.2
Total	8	227	499	42	119	25	0	7	43	24-1	3	75	.238	.275	.331	66	-23	1-0	.969	-9	102	72	/2-77,O-44(41-0-3),3-28,1-16	-3.1
ROACH, MIKE Michael Stephen B 12.23.1869 Driftwood, PA D 11.12.1916 New York, NY 5-7/145# d8.10 b-John																								
1899	Was N	24	78	7	17	1	0	0	7	3	2		.218	.265	.231	37	-7	3	.964	-4	*76*	*73*	C-20/1-3	-0.9
ROACH, ROXEY Wilbur Charles B 11.28.1882 Anita, PA D 12.26.1947 Bay City, MI BR/TR 5-11/160# d5.2																								
1910	NY A	70	220	27	47	9	2	0	20	29	3		.214	.313	.273	79	-4	15	.913	-4	96	139	S-58/O-9(LF)	-0.7
1911	NY A	13	40	4	10	2	1	0	2	6	0		.250	.348	.350	89	0	0	.891	-2	86	179	/S-8,2-5	-0.1
1912	Was A	2	2	1	1	0	0	1	1	0	0		.500	.500	2.000	600	1	0	.500	-1	71	0	/S-2	0.1
1915	Buf F	92	346	35	93	20	3	2	31	17	0	34	.269	.303	.361	85	-13	11	.959	17	108	104	S-92	1.1
Total	4	177	608	67	151	31	6	3	54	52	3	34	.248	.311	.334	85	-16	26	.938	11	102	120	S-160/O-9(LF),2-5	0.4
ROARKE, MIKE Michael Thomas B 11.8.1930 West Warwick, RI BR/TR 6-2/195# d4.19 C20																								
1961	Det A	86	229	21	51	6	1	2	22	20-3	0	31	.223	.283	.284	51	-16	0-0	.988	3	*122*	*96*	C-85	-1.0
1962	Det A	56	136	11	29	4	1	4	14	13-2	1	17	.213	.287	.346	67	-7	0-0	.982	4	*124*	*120*	C-53	0.0
1963	Det A	23	44	5	14	0	0	0	1	2-1	1	3	.318	.362	.318	89	-1	0-0	.986	0	116	116	C-16	0.0
1964	Det A	29	82	4	19	1	0	0	7	10-0	0	10	.232	.315	.244	57	-4	0-0	.994	3	*255*	*115*	C-27	-0.1
Total	4	194	491	41	113	11	2	6	44	45-6	2	61	.230	.296	.297	60	-28	0-0	.987	10	*144*	*108*	C-181	-1.1
ROAT, FRED Frederick R. B 11.10.1867 Oregon, IL D 9.24.1913 Oregon, IL TR d5.10																								
1890	Pit N	57	215	18	48	2	0	2	17	16	3	22	.223	.286	.260	67	-8	7	.847	4	119	103	3-44/1-9,O-4(RF)	-0.4
1892	Chi N	8	31	4	6	0	1	0	2	2	0	3	.194	.242	.258	51	-2	2	.897	-3	97	32	/2-8	-0.4
Total	2	65	246	22	54	2	1	2	19	18	3	25	.220	.281	.260	65	-10	9	.847	1	119	103	/3-44,1-9,2-8,O-4(RF)	-0.8
ROBELLO, TONY Thomas Vardasco B 2.9.1913 San Leandro, CA D 12.25.1994 Fort Worth, TX BR/TR 5-10.5/175# d8.13																								
1933	Cin N	14	30	1	7	3	0	0	3	1	0	5	.233	.258	.333	69	-1	0	1.000	1	121	88	2-11/3-2	0.0
1934	Cin N	2	2	0	0	0	0	0	0	0	0	1	.000	.000	.000	-99	-1	0	—	0			H	-0.1
Total	2	16	32	1	7	3	0	0	3	1	0	6	.219	.242	.313	58	-2	0	1.000	1	121	88	/2-11,3-2	-0.1
ROBERGE, SKIPPY Joseph Albert Armand B 5.19.1917 Lowell, MA D 6.7.1993 Lowell, MA BR/TR 5-11/185# d7.18 Mil 1943-45																								
1941	Bos N	55	167	12	36	6	0	0	15	9	0	18	.216	.256	.251	45	-13	0	.978	4	111	123	2-46/3-5,S-2	-0.6
1942	Bos N	74	172	10	37	7	0	1	12	9	1	19	.215	.258	.273	57	-10	1	.977	5	103	96	2-29,3-27/S-6	-0.2
1946	Bos N	48	169	13	39	6	2	2	20	7	2	12	.231	.270	.325	68	-8	1	.973	2	95	174	3-48	-0.7
Total	3	177	508	35	112	19	2	3	47	25	3	49	.220	.261	.283	57	-31	2	.967	12	105	154	/3-80,2-75,S-8	-1.5
ROBERSON, KEVIN Kevin Lynn B 1.29.1968 Decatur, IL BB/TR 6-4/210# d7.15																								
1993	Chi N	62	180	23	34	4	1	9	27	12-0	3	48	.189	.251	.372	65	-10	0-1	.963	-5	83	56	O-51(14-0-42)	-1.8
1994	Chi N	44	55	8	12	4	0	4	9	2-0	2	14	.218	.271	.509	99	0	0-0	.800	-1	65	242	/O-9(RF)	-0.1
1995	Chi N	32	38	5	7	1	0	4	6	6-0	1	14	.184	.311	.526	118	1	0-1	1.000	-1	78	0	O-11(10-0-1)	0.0
1996	NY N	27	36	8	8	1	0	3	9	7-0	1	17	.222	.348	.500	131	2	0-0	1.000	-1	93	0	O-10(1-0-9)	0.1
Total	4	165	309	44	61	10	1	20	51	27-0	7	93	.197	.275	.430	86	-7	0-2	.955	-6	82	61	/O-81(25-0-61)	-1.8
ROBERTS, BRIAN Brian Michael B 10.9.1977 Durham, NC BB/TR 5-9/170# d6.14																								
2001	Bal A	75	273	42	69	12	3	2	17	13-0	0	36	.253	.284	.341	68	-14	12-3	.939	-4	102	84	S-51,2-12/D-7	-1.1
2002	Bal A	38	128	18	29	6	0	1	11	15-0	1	21	.227	.308	.297	67	-6	9-2	.976	1	105	117	2-25/D-8	-0.3
2003	Bal A	112	460	65	124	22	4	5	41	46-1	1	58	.270	.337	.367	89	-7	23-6	.987	4	103	94	*2-107/S-2,D-4	0.6
Total	3	225	861	125	222	40	7	8	69	74-1	2	115	.258	.316	.348	79	-27	44-11	.983	1	103	99	2-144/S-53,D-19	-0.8
ROBERTS, RED Charles Emory B 8.8.1918 Carrollton, GA D 12.2.1998 Atlanta, GA BR/TR 6/170# d9.3 Mil 1944-45																								
1943	Was A	9	23	1	6	1	0	1	3	4	0	2	.261	.370	.435	140	1	0-0	.778	-4	59	39	/S-6,3	-0.2
ROBERTS, SKIPPER Clarence Ashley B 1.11.1888 Wardner, ID D 12.24.1963 Long Beach, CA BL/TR 5-10.5/175# d6.12																								
1913	StL N	26	41	4	6	2	0	0	3	3	0	13	.146	.205	.195	15	-5	1-2	.859	-3	84	53	C-16	-0.8
1914	Pit F	33	55	7	12	2	1	0	4	1	1	11	.218	.246	.291	46	-5	2	.941	-1	*107*	*77*	C-14	-0.6
	Chi F	4	3	0	1	0	0	0	1	1	0	1	.333	.500	.333	138	0	0	—	0			H	0.0
	Pit F	19	39	5	10	2	1	1	4	1	1	8	.256	.293	.436	98	-1	1	.923	-2	*107*	*77*	/C-9,O(RF)	-0.3

Year	Tm Lg	G	AB	R	H	2B	3B	HR	RBI	BB-IB	HP	SO	AVG	OBP	SLG	AOPS	ABR	SB-CS	FA	FR	Rng	Thr	G at Pos	BFW
	Year	56	97	12	23	4	2	1	9	3	2	20	.237	.275	.351	70	-6	3	.935	-4	*102*	*87*	C-23/O(RF)	-0.9
Total	2	82	138	16	29	6	2	1	12	6	2	33	.210	.253	.304	54	-11	4-2	.906	-7	*95*	*75*	/C-39,O(RF)	-1.7
ROBERTS, CURT Curtis Benjamin B 8.16.1929 Pineland, TX D 11.14.1969 Oakland, CA BR/TR 5-8/165# d4.13																								
1954	Pit N	134	496	47	115	18	7	1	36	55	2	49	.232	.309	.302	62	-28	6-3	.969	5	105	77	*2-131	-1.3
1955	Pit N	6	17	1	2	1	0	0	0	2-0	0	1	.118	.211	.176	4	-2	0-0	.913	-0	112	120	/2-6	-0.2
1956	Pit N	31	62	6	11	5	2	0	4	5-0	0	12	.177	.239	.323	50	-5	1-0	.988	-0	95	108	2-27	-0.4
Total	3	171	575	54	128	24	9	1	40	62-0	2	62	.223	.299	.301	59	-35	7-3	.969	4	104	82	2-164	-1.9
ROBERTS, DAVE David Leonard B 6.30.1933 Panama City, Panama BL/TL 6/172# d9.5																								
1962	Hou N	16	53	3	13	3	0	1	10	8-0	1	8	.245	.349	.358	99	0	0-0	1.000	-1	102	0	O-12(6-0-6)/1-6	-0.1
1964	Hou N	61	125	9	23	4	1	1	7	14-1	1	28	.184	.270	.256	52	-8	0-1	.983	2	136	87	1-34/O-4(LF)	-0.8
1966	Pit N	14	16	3	2	1	0	0	0	0-0	0	7	.125	.125	.188	-15	-2	0-0	.950	0	220	165	/1-2	-0.2
Total	3	91	194	15	38	8	1	2	17	22-1	2	43	.196	.282	.278	60	-10	0-1	.983	2	130	85	/1-42,O-16(10-0-6)	-1.1
ROBERTS, DAVE David Ray B 5.31.1972 Okinawa, Japan BL/TL 5-10/172# d8.7																								
1999	†Cle A	41	143	26	34	4	0	2	12	9-0	0	16	.238	.281	.308	48	-11	11-3	1.000	-1	105	0	O-39(1-38-0)	-1.0
2000	Cle A	19	10	1	2	0	0	0	0	2-0	0	2	.200	.333	.200	39	-1	1-1	1.000	-0	86	0	O-17(12-5-1)	-0.1
2001	Cle A	15	12	3	4	1	0	0	2	1-0	0	2	.333	.385	.417	110	0	0-1	1.000	-0	102	0	O-13(9-2-2)/D-2	0.0
2002	LA N	127	422	63	117	14	7	3	34	48-0	2	51	.277	.353	.365	100	-2	45-10	**1.000**	-3	99	68	*O-117(3-115-0)	0.2
2003	LA N	107	388	56	97	6	5	2	16	43-1	4	39	.250	.331	.307	72	-16	40-14	.976	-6	91	78	*O-105(CF)	-1.7
Total	5	309	975	149	254	25	12	7	64	103-1	6	110	.261	.334	.332	80	-30	97-29	.991	-11	96	60	O-291(25-265-3)/D-2	-2.6
ROBERTS, DAVE David Wayne B 2.17.1951 Lebanon, OR BR/TR 6-3/215# d6.7 C1 OF Total (3-LF 6-CF 10-RF)																								
1972	SD N	100	418	38	102	17	0	5	33	18-1	0	64	.244	.275	.321	74	-16	7-2	.931	-13	97	130	3-84,2-20/S-3,C	-3.0
1973	SD N	127	479	56	137	20	3	21	64	17-3	1	83	.286	.310	.472	124	11	11-2	.942	7	106	111	*3-111,2-12	2.0
1974	SD N	113	318	26	53	10	1	5	18	32-6	2	69	.167	.246	.252	41	-26	2-0	.955	-8	88	72	*3-103/S-3,O(LF)	-3.5
1975	SD N	33	113	7	32	2	0	2	12	13-3	2	19	.283	.367	.354	107	1	3-1	.925	-4	102	98	3-30/2-5	-0.2
1977	SD N	82	186	15	41	14	1	1	23	11-1	1	32	.220	.268	.323	64	-10	2-1	.982	-8	104	104	C-63/2-2,3-2,S	-1.6
1978	SD N	54	97	7	21	4	1	1	7	12-6	1	25	.216	.309	.309	79	-3	0-0	.980	-3	122	87	C-41/1-8,O-2(1-1-0)	-0.5
1979	Tex A	44	84	12	22	2	1	3	14	7-0	0	17	.262	.319	.417	98	-1	1-0	.980	1	169	107	C-14,O-11(1-5-5)/2-8,1-6,3D	0.1
1980	Tex A	101	235	27	56	4	0	10	30	13-2	1	38	.238	.280	.383	83	-7	0-1	.930	-8	76	31	3-37,S-33,C-22/O-5(RF),1-4,2-4	-1.3
1981	†Hou N	27	54	4	13	3	0	1	5	3-0	0	6	.241	.271	.352	83	-1	1-0	.958	-0	135	101	1-10/3-7,2-3,C	-0.2
1982	Phi N	28	33	2	6	1	0	0	2	2-0	0	8	.182	.229	.212	23	-3	0-1	.818	-2	102	0	3-11,C-10/2-7	-0.6
Total	10	709	2017	194	483	77	7	49	208	128-22	8	361	.239	.286	.357	83	-55	27-8	.939	-36	96	97	3-386,C-152/2-61,S-40,1-28,OR,D	-8.8
ROBERTS, BIP Leon Joseph B 10.27.1963 Berkeley, CA BB/TR 5-7/165# d4.7 OF Total (382-LF 72-CF 25-RF)																								
1986	SD N	101	241	34	61	5	2	1	12	14-1	0	29	.253	.293	.303	66	-12	14-12	.971	-3	90	82	2-87	-1.3
1988	SD N	5	9	1	3	0	0	0	0	1-0	0	2	.333	.400	.333	115	0	0-2	.500	-1	33	0	/3-2,2	-0.1
1989	SD N	117	329	81	99	15	8	3	25	49-0	1	45	.301	.391	.422	133	16	21-11	.976	5	104	147	O-54(34-1-21),3-37,S-14/2-9	2.3
1990	SD N	149	556	104	172	36	3	9	44	55-1	6	65	.309	.375	.433	122	18	46-12	.982	5	108	153	O-75(LF),3-56,S-18/2-8	2.9
1991	SD N	117	424	66	119	13	3	3	32	37-0	4	71	.281	.342	.347	92	-4	26-11	.978	-1	100	109	2-68,O-46(19-29-0)	-0.2
1992	Cin N★	147	532	92	172	34	6	4	45	62-4	2	54	.323	.393	.432	131	24	44-16	.993	-3	106	33	O-79(69-16-0),2-42,3-36	2.6
1993	Cin N	83	292	46	70	13	0	1	18	38-1	3	46	.240	.330	.295	70	-11	26-6	.984	1	96	83	2-64,O-11(11-1-0)/3-3,S	-0.4
1994	SD N	105	403	52	129	15	5	2	31	39-1	3	57	.320	.383	.397	107	5	21-7	.976	-12	86	82	2-90,O-20(16-5-0)	-0.1
1995	SD N	73	296	40	90	14	0	2	25	17-1	2	36	.304	.346	.372	92	-3	20-2	.989	6	128	85	O-50(48-4-0),2-25/S-7	0.6
1996	KC A	90	339	39	96	21	2	0	52	25-8	2	38	.283	.331	.357	76	-12	12-9	.986	6	117	114	2-63,D-16,O-11(8-2-1)	-0.4
1997	KC A	97	346	44	107	17	2	1	36	21-2	1	53	.309	.348	.379	88	-6	15-3	.981	-2	101	108	O-84(82-2-0),3-10	-0.7
	†Cle A	23	85	19	23	3	0	3	8	7-0	2	14	.271	.333	.412	92	-1	3-0	.932	1	100	129	2-13,O-10(LF)	0.1
	Year	120	431	63	130	20	2	4	44	28-2	3	67	.302	.345	.385	89	-7	18-3	.982	-0	98	136	O-94(92-2-0),2-13,3-10	-0.6
1998	Det A	34	113	17	28	6	0	0	9	16-0	2	14	.248	.351	.301	72	-4	6-1	1.000	0	33	0	D-29/O-2(LF),2	-0.4
	Oak A	61	182	28	51	11	0	1	15	15-0	2	24	.280	.340	.357	84	-4	10-3	.970	-4	89	123	2-30,O-22(8-12-3)/3-3	-0.6
	Year	95	295	45	79	17	0	1	24	31-0	4	38	.268	.344	.336	79	-8	16-4	.971	-4	90	139	2-31,D-29,O-24(10-12-3)/3-3	-1.0
Total	12	1202	4147	663	1220	203	31	30	352	396-19	30	548	.294	.358	.380	100	6	264-95	.977	-1	98	95	2-501,O-464L,3-147/D-45,S-40	4.3
ROBERTS, LEON Leon Kauffman B 1.22.1951 Vicksburg, MI BR/TR 6-3/200# d9.3 C2																								
1974	Det A	17	63	5	17	3	2	0	7	3-1	0	10	.270	.303	.381	92	-1	0-2	.926	-3	76	0	O-17(0-1-16)	-0.6
1975	Det A	129	447	51	115	17	5	10	38	36-1	4	94	.257	.316	.385	94	-5	3-7	.982	5	112	97	*O-127(RF)/D	-0.9
1976	Hou N	87	235	31	68	11	2	7	33	19-1	3	43	.289	.347	.443	136	10	1-0	.980	-4	89	25	O-60(49-0-12)	0.4
1977	Hou N	19	27	1	2	0	0	0	2	1-0	0	8	.074	.107	.074	-55	-6	0-0	1.000	-0	28	491	/O-9(4-0-6)	-0.7
1978	Sea A	134	472	78	142	21	7	22	92	41-2	8	52	.301	.364	.515	146	28	6-3	.975	6	112	105	*O-128(RF)/D-2	2.8
1979	Sea A	140	450	61	122	24	6	15	54	56-6	2	64	.271	.352	.451	114	9	3-3	.983	5	114	65	*O-136(67-0-69)/D	0.7
1980	Sea A	119	374	48	94	18	3	10	33	43-1	1	59	.251	.325	.396	97	-1	8-4	.984	3	111	81	*O-104(20-20-70)/D-4	-0.2
1981	Tex A	72	233	26	65	17	2	4	31	25-2	1	38	.279	.345	.421	128	9	3-4	.992	-5	91	41	O-71(25-3-46)	0.1
1982	Tex A	31	73	7	17	3	0	1	6	4-1	1	14	.233	.278	.315	67	-3	0-0	1.000	-2	95	0	O-28(11-2-17)/D	-0.6
	Tor A	40	105	6	24	4	0	1	5	7-0	0	16	.229	.274	.295	52	-7	1-1	1.000	-2	74	0	D-21,O-16(LF)	-1.0
	Year	71	178	13	41	7	0	2	11	11-1	1	30	.230	.276	.303	58	-10	1-1	1.000	-4	86	0	O-44(27-2-17),D-22	-1.6
1983	KC A	84	213	24	55	7	0	8	24	17-1	1	27	.258	.313	.404	96	-1	1-1	.979	0	107	63	O-76(41-3-35)/D	-0.4
1984	KC A	29	45	4	10	1	1	0	3	4-0	1	3	.222	.300	.289	63	-2	0-0	1.000	-0	107	0	O-16(10-0-7)/PD	-0.3
Total	11	901	2737	342	731	126	28	78	328	256-16	22	428	.267	.332	.419	108	30	26-25	.982	4	105	72	O-788(243-29-533)/D-34,P	-0.7
ROBERTSON, JIM Alfred James B 1.29.1928 Chicago, IL BR/TR 5-9/183# d4.15																								
1954	Phi A	63	147	9	27	8	0	0	8	23	1	25	.184	.298	.238	48	-10	0-0	.974	-3	*94*	*68*	C-50	-1.1
1955	KC A	6	8	1	2	0	0	0	0	1-0	0	2	.250	.333	.250	58	0	0-0	1.000	0	*0*	*251*	/C-4	0.0
Total	2	69	155	10	29	8	0	0	8	24-0	1	27	.187	.300	.239	49	-10	0-0	.975	-3	*90*	*76*	/C-54	-1.1
ROBERTSON, ANDRE Andre Levett B 10.2.1957 Orange, TX BR/TR 5-10/160# d9.3																								
1981	†NY A	10	19	1	5	1	0	0	0	0-0	0	3	.263	.263	.316	67	-1	1-1	1.000	0	98	65	/S-8,2-3	0.0
1982	NY A	44	118	16	26	5	0	2	9	8-0	0	19	.220	.270	.314	61	-7	0-0	.966	4	98	153	S-27,2-15/3-2	0.0
1983	NY A	98	322	37	80	16	3	1	22	8-0	3	54	.248	.271	.326	67	-16	2-4	.960	11	115	126	S-78,2-29	0.2
1984	NY A	52	140	10	30	5	1	0	6	4-0	0	20	.214	.236	.264	40	-12	0-1	.930	3	105	130	S-49/2-6	-0.4
1985	NY A	50	125	16	41	5	0	2	17	6-0	1	24	.328	.358	.416	116	3	1-2	.867	-6	82	136	3-33,S-14/2-2	-0.4
Total	5	254	724	80	182	32	4	5	54	26-0	4	120	.251	.279	.327	69	-33	4-8	.953	11	107	131	S-176/2-55,3-35	-0.6
ROBERTSON, DARYL Daryl Berdene B 1.5.1936 Cripple Creek, CO BR/TR 6/184# d5.4																								
1962	Chi N	9	19	0	2	0	0	0	2	2-0	0	10	.105	.182	.105	-18	-3	0-0	1.000	-0	112	36	/S-6,3	-0.3
ROBERTSON, DAVE Davis Aydelotte B 9.25.1889 Portsmouth, VA D 11.5.1970 Virginia Beach, VA BL/TL 6/186# d6.5 Def 1918																								
1912	NY N	3	2	0	1	0	0	0	1	0	0	1	.500	.500	.500	169	0	1	1.000	-0	0	0	/1O(LF)	0.0
1914	NY N	82	256	25	68	12	3	2	32	10	2	26	.266	.299	.359	99	-2	9	.950	2	97	141	O-71(15-0-56)	-0.3
1915	NY N	141	544	72	160	17	10	3	58	22	4	52	.294	.326	.379	120	10	22-10	.956	-1	102	86	*O-138(16-0-123)	0.4
1916	NY N	150	587	88	180	18	8	**12**	69	14	3	56	.307	.326	.426	137	21	21-17	.960	-0	101	92	*O-144(RF)	1.3
1917	†NY N	142	532	64	138	16	9	**12**	54	10	2	47	.259	.276	.391	107	0	17	.942	-1	112	66	*O-140(0-1-140)	-0.9
1919	NY N	1	0	0	0	0	0	0	0	0	0	0	—	—	—	—	0	0	—	0			R	0.0
	Chi N	27	96	8	20	2	0	1	10	1	1	10	.208	.224	.260	45	-7	3	.932	-3	86	61	O-25(1-24-0)	-1.3
	Year	28	96	8	20	2	0	1	10	1	1	10	.208	.224	.260	45	-7	3	.932	-3	86	61	O-25(1-24-0)	-1.3
1920	Chi N	134	500	68	150	29	11	10	75	40	1	44	.300	.353	.462	130	19	17-23	.968	-11	87	69	*O-134(LF)	-0.2
1921	Chi N	22	36	7	8	3	0	0	14	1	0	3	.222	.243	.306	44	-3	0-2	1.000	-1	81	0	/O-7(1-6-0)	-0.5
	Pit N	60	230	29	74	18	3	6	48	12	2	16	.322	.361	.504	123	8	4-5	.960	-4	107	26	O-58(2-1-55)	-0.1
	Year	82	266	36	82	21	3	6	62	13	2	19	.308	.345	.477	113	5	4-7	.962	-5	105	24	O-65(3-7-55)	-0.6
1922	NY N	42	47	5	13	2	0	1	3	3	0	7	.277	.320	.383	80	-1	0-0	.909	0	86	193	/O-8(1-6-1)	-0.1
Total	9	804	2830	366	812	117	44	47	364	113	15	262	.287	.318	.409	117	45	94-57	.955	-18	100	79	O-726(171-38-519)/1	-1.7
ROBERTSON, DON Donald Alexander B 10.15.1930 Harvey, IL BL/TL 5-10/180# d4.13																								
1954	Chi N	14	6	2	0	0	0	0	0	0	0	2	.000	.000	.000	-99	-2	0-0	1.000	0	152	0	/O-6(RF)	-0.2

ROBERTSON, GENE Eugene Edward B 12.25.1898 St.Louis, MO D 10.21.1981 Fallon, NV BL/TR 5-7/152# d7.4

Year	Tm Lg	G	AB	R	H	2B	3B	HR	RBI	BB-IB	HP	SO	AVG	OBP	SLG	AOPS	ABR	SB-CS	FA	FR	Rng	Thr	G at Pos	BFW
1919	StL A	5	7	1	1	0	0	0	0	1	0	2	.143	.250	.143	11	-1	0	.750	-1	33	0	/S-2	-0.2
1922	StL A	18	27	2	8	2	1	0	1	1	0	1	.296	.321	.444	95	0	1-0	.875	0	126	0	/3-7,S-6,2	0.1
1923	StL A	78	251	36	62	10	1	0	17	21	2	7	.247	.310	.295	57	-16	4-2	.935	-12	79	50	3-74/2	-2.3
1924	StL A	121	439	70	140	25	4	4	52	36	2	14	.319	.373	.421	99	-1	3-5	.958	-9	91	122	*3-111/2-2	-0.4
1925	StL A	**154**	582	97	158	26	5	14	76	81	4	30	.271	.364	.405	90	-8	10-7	.939	-4	94	**127**	*3-154/S	-0.2
1926	StL A	78	247	23	62	12	6	1	19	17	1	10	.251	.302	.360	69	-12	5-1	.924	-3	102	98	3-55,S-10/2-3	-1.0
1928	†NY A	83	251	29	73	9	0	1	36	14	0	6	.291	.328	.339	78	-8	2-4	.926	-11	83	42	3-70/2-3	-1.6
1929	NY A	90	309	45	92	15	6	0	35	28	1	6	.298	.358	.385	98	-1	3-3	.966	-10	83	45	3-77	-0.7
	Bos N	8	28	1	8	0	0	0	6	1	0	0	.286	.310	.286	51	-2	1	.875	-2	67	0	/3-6,S	-0.3
1930	Bos N	21	59	7	11	1	0	0	7	5	0	3	.186	.250	.203	12	-9	0	.949	-2	83	119	3-17	-0.8
Total	9	656	2200	311	615	100	23	20	249	205	10	79	.280	.344	.373	83	-58	29-22	.941	-52	89	90	3-571/S-20,2-10	-7.4

ROBERTSON, MIKE Michael Francis B 10.9.1970 Norwich, CT BL/TL 6/180# d9.6

Year	Tm Lg	G	AB	R	H	2B	3B	HR	RBI	BB-IB	HP	SO	AVG	OBP	SLG	AOPS	ABR	SB-CS	FA	FR	Rng	Thr	G at Pos	BFW
1996	Chi A	6	7	0	1	1	0	0	0	0-0	0	1	.143	.143	.286	5	-1	0-0	1.000	0	118	182	/1-2,D-2	-0.1
1997	Phi N	22	38	3	8	2	1	0	4	0-0	3	6	.211	.268	.316	52	-3	1-0	1.000	-1	61	56	/1-5,O-5(4-0-1),D	-0.4
1998	Ari N	11	13	0	2	0	0	0	0	0-0	0	2	.154	.154	.154	-19	-2	0-0	—	0			/D-2	-0.2
Total	3	39	58	3	11	3	1	0	4	0-0	3	9	.190	.230	.276	31	-6	1-0	1.000	-1	82	102	/1-7,O-5(4-0-1),D-5	-0.7

ROBERTSON, BOB Robert Eugene B 10.2.1946 Frostburg, MD BR/TR 6-1/210# d9.18

Year	Tm Lg	G	AB	R	H	2B	3B	HR	RBI	BB-IB	HP	SO	AVG	OBP	SLG	AOPS	ABR	SB-CS	FA	FR	Rng	Thr	G at Pos	BFW
1967	Pit N	9	35	4	6	0	0	2	4	3-0	0	12	.171	.237	.343	64	-2	0-0	.990	-0	92	116	/1-9	-0.3
1969	Pit N	32	96	7	20	4	1	1	9	8-0	0	30	.208	.267	.302	61	-5	1-0	.996	1	108	97	1-26	-0.6
1970	†Pit N	117	390	69	112	19	4	27	82	51-2	2	98	.287	.367	.564	150	27	4-1	.995	2	115	131	1-99/3-5,O-3(LF)	2.2
1971	†Pit N	131	469	65	127	18	2	26	72	60-8	4	101	.271	.356	.484	137	23	1-2	.993	14	**139**	100	*1-126	2.8
1972	†Pit N	115	306	25	59	11	0	12	41	41-2	3	84	.193	.291	.346	83	-7	1-1	.993	8	157	124	1-89,O-23(LF),3-11	-0.5
1973	Pit N	119	397	43	95	16	0	14	40	55-4	1	77	.239	.332	.385	101	1	0-4	.995	4	113	96	*1-107	-0.5
1974	†Pit N	91	236	25	54	11	0	16	48	33-1	0	48	.229	.320	.479	127	8	0-0	.991	1	113	93	1-63	0.4
1975	†Pit N	75	124	17	34	4	0	6	18	23-0	2	25	.274	.388	.452	136	7	0-0	.996	2	129	54	1-27	0.7
1976	Pit N	61	129	10	28	5	1	2	25	16-0	0	23	.217	.299	.318	76	-4	0-1	.996	-0	96	126	1-29	-0.7
1978	Sea A	64	174	17	40	5	2	8	28	24-1	1	39	.230	.325	.420	109	2	0-0	1.000	-1	74	115	D-29,1-18	-0.1
1979	Tor A	15	29	1	3	0	0	1	1	3-0	0	9	.103	.188	.207	6	-4	0-0	1.000	1	168	106	/1-9,D-4	-0.3
Total	11	829	2385	283	578	93	10	115	368	317-18	13	546	.242	.331	.434	115	46	7-9	.994	32	123	106	1-602/D-33,O-26(LF),3-16	3.1

ROBERTSON, SHERRY Sherrard Alexander B 1.1.1919 Montreal, PQ, CAN D 10.23.1970 Houghton, SD BL/TR 6/180# d9.8 Mil 1944-45 C1

Year	Tm Lg	G	AB	R	H	2B	3B	HR	RBI	BB-IB	HP	SO	AVG	OBP	SLG	AOPS	ABR	SB-CS	FA	FR	Rng	Thr	G at Pos	BFW
1940	Was A	10	33	4	7	0	1	0	0	5	0	6	.212	.316	.273	58	-2	0-0	.940	1	103	137	S-10	-0.1
1941	Was A	1	3	0	0	0	0	0	0	0	0	3	.000	.000	.000	-99	-1	0-0	.750	-0	95	0	/3	-0.1
1943	Was A	59	120	22	26	4	1	3	14	17	1	19	.217	.319	.342	97	0	0-2	.897	-3	92	23	3-27/S	-0.5
1946	Was A	74	230	30	46	6	3	6	19	30	0	42	.200	.292	.330	78	-8	6-2	.902	-7	97	108	3-38,2-14,S-12/O(RF)	-1.3
1947	Was A	95	266	25	62	9	3	1	23	32	1	52	.233	.318	.301	74	-9	4-5	.949	0	101	131	O-55(LF),3-10/2-4	-1.4
1948	Was A	71	187	19	46	11	3	2	22	24	1	26	.246	.335	.369	90	-3	8-0	.939	-0	106	86	O-51(1-1-49)	-0.3
1949	Was A	110	374	59	94	17	3	11	42	42	1	35	.251	.329	.401	95	-5	10-3	.947	-6	106	68	2-71,3-19,O-13(RF)	-0.6
1950	Was A	71	123	19	32	3	3	2	16	22	0	18	.260	.372	.382	98	0	1-1	.952	-4	85	106	O-14(RF),2-12/3	-0.4
1951	Was A	62	111	14	21	2	1	1	10	9	1	22	.189	.256	.252	38	-10	2-1	.949	2	122	125	O-22(1-0-21)	-0.9
1952	Was A	1	0	0	0	0	0	0	0	0	0	0	—	—	—	—	0	0-0	—	0			R	0.0
	Phi A	43	60	8	12	3	0	0	5	21	0	15	.200	.407	.250	81	0	1-2	.958	-2	89	56	/2-8,O-7(RF),3-2	-0.3
	Year	44	60	8	12	3	0	0	5	21	0	15	.200	.407	.250	81	0	1-2	.958	-2	89	56	/2-8,O-7(RF),3-2	-0.3
Total	10	597	1507	200	346	55	18	26	151	202	5	238	.230	.323	.342	83	-38	32-16	.946	-20	105	107	O-163(57-1-105),2-109/3-98,S-23	-5.9

ROBIDOUX, BILLY JO William Joseph B 1.13.1964 Ware, MA BL/TR 6-1/200# d9.11

Year	Tm Lg	G	AB	R	H	2B	3B	HR	RBI	BB-IB	HP	SO	AVG	OBP	SLG	AOPS	ABR	SB-CS	FA	FR	Rng	Thr	G at Pos	BFW
1985	Mil A	18	51	5	9	2	0	3	8	12-0	0	16	.176	.333	.392	98	0	0-0	1.000	1	83	182	O-11(LF)/1-6,D	0.0
1986	Mil A	56	181	15	41	8	0	1	21	33-1	0	36	.227	.344	.287	72	-6	0-0	.986	-1	96	102	1-43,D-10	-0.9
1987	Mil A	23	62	9	12	0	0	0	4	8-1	0	17	.194	.286	.194	30	-6	0-1	.983	-0	91	171	1-10,D-10	-0.7
1988	Mil A	33	91	9	23	5	0	0	5	8-3	0	14	.253	.307	.308	74	-3	1-1	.983	2	130	102	1-30/D	-0.3
1989	Chi A	16	39	2	5	2	0	0	1	4-0	0	9	.128	.209	.179	11	-5	0-0	.990	-1	88	164	1-15/O(LF)	-0.6
1990	Bos A	27	44	3	8	4	0	1	4	6-1	1	14	.182	.288	.341	74	-1	0-0	.981	-1	74	63	1-11/D-4	-0.3
Total	6	173	468	43	98	21	0	5	43	71-6	1	106	.209	.313	.286	65	-21	1-2	.986	0	104	113	1-115/D-26,O-12(LF)	-2.8

ROBINSON, AARON Aaron Andrew B 6.23.1915 Lancaster, SC D 3.9.1966 Lancaster, SC BL/TR 6-2/205# d5.6 Mil 1943-45

Year	Tm Lg	G	AB	R	H	2B	3B	HR	RBI	BB-IB	HP	SO	AVG	OBP	SLG	AOPS	ABR	SB-CS	FA	FR	Rng	Thr	G at Pos	BFW
1943	NY A	1	1	0	0	0	0	0	0	0	0	1	.000	.000	.000	-99	0	0-0	—	0			H	0.0
1945	NY A	50	160	19	45	6	1	8	24	21	1	23	.281	.368	.481	139	8	0-0	1.000	-4	*74*	*73*	C-45	0.7
1946	NY A	100	330	32	98	17	2	16	64	48	1	39	.297	.388	.506	146	21	0-1	.983	-3	*112*	*101*	C-95	2.4
1947	†NY A☆	82	252	23	68	11	5	5	36	40	0	26	.270	.370	.413	119	7	0-1	.997	-1	*86*	*87*	C-74	1.0
1948	Chi A	98	326	47	82	14	2	8	39	46	0	30	.252	.344	.380	96	-2	0-1	.989	-5	*83*	*112*	C-92	-0.3
1949	Det A	110	331	38	89	12	0	13	56	73	1	21	.269	.402	.423	118	11	0-2	.986	-3	*105*	*96*	*C-108	1.3
1950	Det A	107	283	37	64	7	0	9	37	75	0	35	.226	.388	.346	86	-3	0-1	.993	-0	*140*	*96*	*C-103	0.2
1951	Det A	36	82	3	17	6	0	0	9	17	0	9	.207	.343	.280	70	-3	0-0	1.000	-2	*75*	*116*	C-35	-0.3
	Bos A	26	74	9	15	1	1	2	7	17	0	10	.203	.352	.324	76	-2	0-0	.983	-0	*116*	*84*	C-25	-0.1
	Year	62	156	12	32	7	1	2	16	34	0	19	.205	.347	.301	73	-5	0-0	.991	-2	*95*	*100*	C-60	-0.4
Total	8	610	1839	208	478	74	11	61	272	337	3	194	.260	.375	.412	112	37	0-6	.990	-17	*102*	*97*	C-577	4.9

ROBINSON, VAL Alfred Valentine d5.1

Year	Tm Lg	G	AB	R	H	2B	3B	HR	RBI	BB-IB	HP	SO	AVG	OBP	SLG	AOPS	ABR	SB-CS	FA	FR	Rng	Thr	G at Pos	BFW
1872	Oly NA	7	30	6	6	0	0	0	4	1		1	.200	.226	.200	34	-2	0-0	.750	-0	135	0	/O-7(RF)	-0.1

ROBINSON, BROOKS Brooks Calbert B 5.18.1937 Little Rock, AR BR/TR 6-1/190# d9.17 C1 HF1983

Year	Tm Lg	G	AB	R	H	2B	3B	HR	RBI	BB-IB	HP	SO	AVG	OBP	SLG	AOPS	ABR	SB-CS	FA	FR	Rng	Thr	G at Pos	BFW
1955	Bal A	6	22	0	2	0	0	0	1	0-0	0	10	.091	.091	.091	-55	-5	0-0	.833	-1	89	106	/3-6	-0.7
1956	Bal A	15	44	5	10	4	0	1	1	1-0	0	5	.227	.244	.386	70	-2	0-0	.944	0	109	131	3-14/2	-0.2
1957	Bal A	50	117	13	28	6	1	2	14	7-0	1	10	.239	.286	.359	81	-4	1-0	.971	1	101	91	3-47	-0.3
1958	Bal A	145	463	31	110	16	3	3	32	31-1	5	51	.238	.292	.305	68	-21	1-2	.953	5	99	**122**	*3-140,2-16	-1.7
1959	Bal A	88	313	29	89	15	2	4	24	17-5	2	37	.284	.325	.383	96	-2	2-2	.955	5	105	170	3-87/2	0.2
1960	Bal A★	152	595	74	175	27	9	14	88	35-0	0	49	.294	.329	.440	109	5	2-2	**.977**	15	107	110	*3-152/2-3	1.9
1961	Bal A★	**163**	668	89	192	38	7	7	61	47-2	4	57	.287	.334	.397	99	-2	1-3	**.972**	-8	94	107	*3-163/2-2,S	-1.1
1962	Bal A★	**162**	634	77	192	29	9	23	86	42-3	1	70	.303	.342	.486	129	23	3-1	**.979**	7	103	110	*3-162/S-3,2-2	3.0
1963	Bal A★	161	589	67	148	26	4	11	67	46-4	3	84	.251	.305	.365	91	-8	2-3	**.976**	7	101	**148**	*3-160/S	-0.2
1964	Bal A★	**163**	612	82	194	35	3	28	**118**	51-10	4	64	.317	.368	.521	146	38	1-0	**.972**	-1	98	**147**	*3-163	3.8
1965	Bal A★	144	559	81	166	25	2	18	80	47-9	2	47	.297	.351	.445	123	17	3-0	.967	-9	94	129	*3-143	0.9
1966	†Bal A★	157	620	91	167	35	2	23	100	56-11	5	36	.269	.333	.444	123	19	2-3	**.976**	1	94	93	*3-157	2.0
1967	Bal A★	158	610	88	164	25	5	22	77	54-9	4	54	.269	.328	.434	126	19	1-3	**.980**	**32**	**120**	142	*3-158	5.3
1968	Bal A★	**162**	608	65	154	36	6	17	75	44-11	4	55	.253	.304	.416	118	12	1-1	**.970**	19	**107**	115	*3-162	3.3
1969	†Bal A★	156	598	73	140	21	3	23	84	56-10	3	55	.234	.298	.395	93	-8	2-1	**.976**	11	104	131	*3-156	0.2
1970	†Bal A★	158	608	84	168	31	4	18	94	53-5	4	53	.276	.335	.429	109	7	1-1	.966	-7	93	104	*3-156	-0.1
1971	†Bal A★	156	589	67	160	21	1	20	92	63-8	3	50	.272	.341	.413	115	11	0-0	.968	4	103	123	*3-156	1.5
1972	Bal A★	153	556	48	139	23	2	8	64	43-4	2	45	.250	.303	.342	90	-7	1-0	**.977**	6	103	104	*3-152	-0.1
1973	†Bal A★	155	549	53	141	17	2	9	72	55-5	3	50	.257	.326	.344	90	-7	2-0	.970	5	107	98	*3-154	-0.2
1974	†Bal A★	153	553	46	159	27	0	7	59	56-13	3	47	.288	.353	.374	114	12	2-0	.967	8	109	**137**	*3-153	2.0
1975	Bal A	144	482	50	97	15	1	6	53	44-10	1	33	.201	.267	.274	57	-28	0-0	**.979**	-3	104	122	*3-143	-3.2
1976	Bal A	71	218	16	46	8	2	3	11	8-0	1	24	.211	.240	.307	64	-11	0-0	.969	-3	94	108	3-71	-1.5
1977	Bal A	24	47	3	7	2	0	1	4	4-0	0	4	.149	.212	.255	30	-5	0-0	1.000	0	109	98	3-15	-0.5
Total	23	2896	10654	1232	2848	482	68	268	1357	860-120	53	990	.267	.322	.401	105	53	28-22	.971	95	102	121	*3-2870/2-25,S-5	14.3

ROBINSON, BRUCE Bruce Philip B 4.16.1954 LaJolla, CA BL/TR 6-1/185# d8.19 b-Dave

Year	Tm Lg	G	AB	R	H	2B	3B	HR	RBI	BB-IB	HP	SO	AVG	OBP	SLG	AOPS	ABR	SB-CS	FA	FR	Rng	Thr	G at Pos	BFW
1978	Oak A	28	84	5	21	3	1	0	8	3-0	0	8	.250	.276	.310	68	-4	0-0	.965	8	94	158	C-28	0.5
1979	NY A	6	12	0	2	0	0	0	2	1-0	0	0	.167	.231	.167	9	-2	0-0	.943	1	75	61	/C-6	0.0
1980	NY A	4	5	0	0	0	0	0	0	0-0	0	4	.000	.000	.000	-99	-1	0-0	1.000	-0	0	0	/C-3	-0.1
Total	3	38	101	5	23	3	1	0	10	4-0	0	12	.228	.257	.277	52	-7	0-0	.962	9	88	137	/C-37	0.4

Year	Tm Lg	G	AB	R	H	2B	3B	HR	RBI	BB-IB	HP	SO	AVG	OBP	SLG	AOPS	ABR	SB-CS	FA	FR	Rng	Thr	G at Pos	BFW
ROBINSON, CHARLIE Charles Henry B 7.27.1856 Westerly, RI D 5.18.1913 BL/TR d8.2																								
1884	Ind AA	20	80	11	23	2	0	0		3	0		.287	.313	.313	108	1		.967	1			C-17/S-3,O(RF)	0.3
1885	Bro AA	11	40	5	6	2	1	0	4	3	0		.150	.209	.250	44	-2		.840	-3			C-11	-0.4
Total	2	31	120	16	29	4	1	0	<u>4</u>	6	0		.242	.278	.292	85	-1		.919	-2			/C-28,S-3,O(RF)	-0.1
ROBINSON, RABBIT Clyde B 3.5.1882 Wellsburg, WV D 4.9.1915 Waterbury, CT BR/TR 5-6/148# d4.22																								
1903	Was A	103	373	41	79	10	8	1	20	33	2		.212	.279	.290	69	-14	16	.917	4	113	112	2-45,O-30(0-14-16),S-24/3-5	-1.0
1904	Det A	101	320	30	77	13	6	0	37	29	5		.241	.314	.319	103	2	14	.925	2	106	78	S-30,3-26,O-20(7-0-13),2-19	0.6
1910	Cin N	2	7	0	0	0	0	0	1	1	0	0	.000	.125	.000	-66	-1	0	1.000	-0	78	0	/3-2	-0.2
Total	3	206	700	71	156	23	14	1	58	63	7	<u>0</u>	.223	.294	.300	83	-13	30	.940	6	114	108	/2-64,S-54,O-50(7-14-29),3-33	-0.6
ROBINSON, CRAIG Craig George B 8.21.1948 Abington, PA BR/TR 5-10/165# d9.9																								
1972	Phi N	5	15	0	3	1	0	0	0	1-0	0	2	.200	.250	.267	46	-1	0-0	1.000	2	147	199	/S-4	0.2
1973	Phi N	46	146	11	33	7	0	0	7	0-0	0	25	.226	.226	.274	37	-13	1-1	.945	-5	89	100	S-42/2-4	-1.4
1974	Atl N	145	452	52	104	4	6	0	29	30-4	3	57	.230	.280	.265	52	-30	11-2	.956	-11	95	101	*S-142	-2.5
1975	Atl N	10	17	1	1	0	0	0	0	0-0	0	5	.059	.059	.059	-65	-4	0-0	1.000	-1	75	61	/S-7	-0.4
	SF N	29	29	4	2	1	0	0	0	2-0	0	6	.069	.129	.103	-34	-5	0-0	.941	-1	91	122	S-12/2-9	-0.6
	Year	39	46	5	3	1	0	0	0	2-0	0	11	.065	.104	.087	-45	-9	0-0	.967	-2	84	95	S-19/2-9	-1.0
1976	SF N	15	13	4	4	1	0	0	2	3-0	0	4	.308	.438	.385	131	1	0-1	.952	-0	132	98	/2-7,3-2,S	0.0
	Atl N	15	17	4	4	0	0	0	3	5-0	0	2	.235	.391	.235	81	0	0-0	.952	0	107	43	/2-5,S-2,3	0.0
	Year	30	30	8	8	1	0	0	5	8-0	0	6	.267	.410	.300	102	1	0-1	.952	-0	121	75	2-12/3-3,S-3	0.0
1977	Atl N	27	29	4	6	1	0	0	1	1-0	0	6	.207	.233	.241	25	-3	0-0	1.000	0	83	87	S-23	-0.2
Total	6	292	718	80	157	15	6	0	42	42-4	3	107	.219	.263	.256	44	-55	12-4	.956	-16	93	101	S-233/2-25,3-3	-4.9
ROBINSON, DAVE David Tanner B 5.22.1946 Minneapolis, MN BB/TL 6-1/186# d9.10 b-Bruce																								
1970	SD N	15	38	5	12	2	0	2	6	5-1	0	4	.316	.395	.526	151	3	2-0	1.000	1	123	140	O-13(12-1-0)	0.4
1971	SD N	7	6	0	0	0	0	0	0	1-0	0	3	.000	.143	.000	-61	-1	0-0	—	0			H	-0.1
Total	2	22	44	5	12	2	0	2	6	6-1	0	7	.273	.360	.455	124	2	2-0	1.000	1	123	140	/O-13(12-1-0)	0.3
ROBINSON, EARL Earl John B 11.3.1936 New Orleans, LA BR/TR 6-1/190# d9.10																								
1958	LA N	8	15	3	3	0	0	0	0	1-0	0	4	.200	.250	.200	20	-2	0-0	1.000	1	130	0	/3-6	-0.1
1961	Bal A	96	222	37	59	12	3	8	30	31-1	0	54	.266	.354	.455	119	6	4-3	.973	3	104	120	O-82(6-1-78)	0.4
1962	Bal A	29	63	12	18	3	1	1	4	8-0	0	10	.286	.361	.413	116	2	2-0	1.000	0	117	0	O-17(1-0-16)	0.1
1964	Bal A	37	121	11	33	5	1	3	10	7-0	0	24	.273	.310	.405	98	-1	1-2	.986	2	105	158	O-34(16-20-0)	-0.1
Total	4	170	421	63	113	20	5	12	44	47-1	0	92	.268	.340	.425	109	5	7-5	.980	6	106	113	O-133(23-21-94)/3-6	0.3
ROBINSON, FLOYD Floyd Andrew B 5.9.1936 Prescott, AR BL/TR 5-9/175# d8.10																								
1960	Chi A	22	46	7	13	0	0	0	1	11-0	1	8	.283	.431	.283	98	1	2-3	.960	-1	91	0	O-17(1-4-12)	-0.2
1961	Chi A	132	432	69	134	20	7	11	59	52-3	4	32	.310	.389	.465	129	19	7-4	.991	-1	99	83	*O-106(RF)	1.1
1962	Chi A	156	600	89	187	**45**	10	11	109	72-7	2	47	.312	.384	.475	131	29	4-2	.973	-4	87	136	*O-155(114-0-75)	1.5
1963	Chi A	146	527	71	149	21	6	13	71	62-4	4	43	.283	.361	.419	120	16	4-3	.984	-2	96	88	*O-137(36-0-119)	0.5
1964	Chi A	141	525	83	158	17	3	11	59	70-7	5	41	.301	.388	.408	125	21	9-5	.987	-5	94	64	*O-138(54-0-112)	0.7
1965	Chi A	156	577	70	153	15	6	14	66	76-6	5	51	.265	.352	.385	117	15	4-1	.985	-12	87	57	*O-153(6-1-148)	-0.8
1966	Chi A	127	342	44	81	11	2	5	35	44-4	5	32	.237	.330	.325	96	0	8-2	.962	-8	86	37	*O-113(4-0-111)	-1.5
1967	Cin N	55	130	19	31	6	2	1	10	14-1	0	14	.238	.310	.338	77	-3	3-1	.981	-1	103	0	O-39(4-0-35)	-0.7
1968	Oak A	53	81	5	20	5	0	1	14	4-1	0	10	.247	.276	.346	94	-1	0-0	1.000	-1	81	117	O-18(LF)	-0.2
	Bos A	23	24	1	3	0	0	0	2	3-0	1	4	.125	.250	.125	15	-2	1-0	.833	-1	72	0	O-10(5-0-5)	-0.4
	Year	76	105	6	23	5	0	1	16	7-1	1	14	.219	.270	.295	74	-3	1-0	.963	-1	79	90	O-28(23-0-5)	-0.6
Total	9	1011	3284	458	929	140	36	67	426	408-33	27	282	.283	.365	.409	118	95	42-21	.981	-35	91	77	O-886(242-5-723)	0.0
ROBINSON, FRANK Frank B 8.31.1935 Beaumont, TX BR/TR 6-1/195# d4.17 M13 C7 HF1982 OF Total (820-LF 99-CF 1281-RF)																								
1956	Cin N★	152	572	**122**	166	27	6	38	83	64-7	**20**	95	.290	.379	.558	139	33	8-4	.976	-8	100	48	*O-152(143-10-0)	1.6
1957	Cin N★	150	611	97	197	29	5	29	75	44-5	12	92	.322	.376	.529	131	27	10-2	.989	15	115	116	*O-136(106-32-1),1-24	3.5
1958	Cin N	148	554	90	149	25	6	31	83	62-5	7	80	.269	.350	.504	116	13	10-1	.991	-1	99	109	*O-138(83-53-0),3-11	0.6
1959	Cin N★	146	540	106	168	31	4	36	125	69-9	**8**	93	.311	.391	.583	152	42	18-8	.984	-4	88	**111**	*1-125,O-40(LF)	3.0
1960	Cin N	139	464	86	138	33	6	31	83	82-6	**9**	67	.297	.407	**.595**	169	48	13-6	.993	3	99	97	1-78,O-51(LF)/3	4.4
1961	†Cin N★	153	545	117	176	32	7	37	124	71-**23**	10	64	.323	.404	**.611**	164	52	22-3	.990	4	103	114	*O-150(52-3-99)/3	**4.9**
1962	Cin N★	**162**	609	**134**	208	**51**	2	39	136	76-**16**	**11**	62	.342	**.421**	**.624**	**172**	**65**	18-9	.994	3	109	73	*O-161(9-0-155)	5.6
1963	Cin N	140	482	79	125	19	3	21	91	81-**20**	**14**	69	.259	.379	.442	132	24	26-10	.984	6	104	147	*O-139(116-1-31)/1	2.6
1964	Cin N	156	568	103	174	38	6	29	96	79-**20**	9	67	.306	.396	.548	158	47	23-5	.986	2	106	66	*O-156(77-0-102)	4.4
1965	Cin N★	156	582	109	172	33	5	33	113	70-18	**18**	100	.296	.386	.540	148	40	13-9	.990	-1	104	49	*O-155(7-0-152)	2.9
1966	†Bal A★	155	576	**122**	182	34	2	**49**	**122**	87-11	10	90	**.316**	**.410**	**.637**	**200**	**78**	8-5	.985	-6	96	47	*O-151(20-0-135)/1-3	**6.5**
1967	Bal A✳	129	479	83	149	23	7	30	94	71-14	7	84	.311	.403	.576	189	55	2-3	.990	-6	87	84	*O-126(31-0-95)/1-2	4.3
1968	Bal A	130	421	69	113	27	1	15	52	73-4	12	84	.268	.390	.444	153	32	11-2	.962	-6	90	76	*O-117(55-0-78)/1-3	2.2
1969	†Bal A★	148	539	111	166	19	5	32	100	88-11	**13**	62	.308	.415	.540	164	50	9-3	.987	-2	97	90	*O-134(1-0-134),1-19	4.2
1970	†Bal A★	132	471	88	144	24	1	25	78	69-9	7	70	.306	.398	.520	151	35	2-1	.987	1	99	113	*O-120(RF)/1-7	3.0
1971	†Bal A★	133	455	82	128	16	2	28	99	72-11	9	62	.281	.384	.510	154	34	3-0	.973	-4	103	51	O-92(1-0-91),1-37	2.6
1972	LA N	103	342	41	86	6	1	19	59	55-0	2	76	.251	.353	.442	129	14	2-3	.967	-2	95	88	O-95(9-0-88)	0.6
1973	Cal A	147	534	85	142	29	0	30	97	82-12	10	93	.266	.372	.489	153	40	1-1	.976	3	121	265	*D-127,O-17(LF)	3.9
1974	Cal A★	129	427	75	107	26	2	20	63	75-14	10	85	.251	.371	.461	148	30	5-1	—	-0	0	0	*D-123/O(LF)	2.9
	Cle A	15	50	6	10	1	1	2	5	10-0	0	10	.200	.328	.380	106	1	0-1	.958	-1	0	39	D-11/1-4	-0.1
	Year	144	477	81	117	27	3	22	68	85-14	10	95	.245	.367	.453	143	31	5-2	.808	-1	0	39	*D-134/1-4,O(LF)	2.8
1975	Cle A	49	118	19	28	5	0	9	24	29-3	0	15	.237	.385	.508	152	9	0-0	—	0	0	0	D-42,M	0.8
1976	Cle A	36	67	5	15	0	0	3	10	11-0	0	12	.224	.329	.358	104	0	0-0	1.000	-0	0	119	D-18/1-2,O(LF)M	-0.1
Total	21	2808	10006	1829	2943	528	72	586	1812	1420-218	198	1532	.294	.389	.537	154	769	204-77	.984	-2	101	89	*O-2132R,D-321,1-305/3-13	64.3
ROBINSON, FRED Frederic Henry B 7.6.1856 South Acton, MA D 12.18.1933 Hudson, MA BR/TR d4.17 b-Wilbert																								
1884	Cin U	3	13	1	3	0	0	0		0			.231	.231	.231	37	-1		.727	-2	84	0	/2-3	-0.3
ROBINSON, JACKIE Jack Roosevelt B 1.31.1919 Cairo, GA D 10.24.1972 Stamford, CT BR/TR 5-11/204# d4.15 HF1962 OF Total (161-LF 1-RF)																								
1947	†Bro N	151	590	125	175	31	5	12	48	74	9	36	.297	.383	.427	111	11	**29**	.989	-3	94	**119**	*1-151	0.3
1948	Bro N	147	574	108	170	38	8	12	85	57	**7**	37	.296	.367	.453	117	14	22	**.980**	0	97	**115**	*2-116,1-30/3-6	2.0
1949	†Bro N★	**156**	593	122	203	38	12	16	124	86	8	27	**.342**	.432	.528	150	46	**37**	.981	-4	95	**117**	*2-156	5.0
1950	Bro N★	144	518	99	170	39	4	14	81	80	5	24	.328	.423	.500	139	34	12	**.986**	11	98	**128**	*2-144	**5.0**
1951	Bro N★	153	548	106	185	33	7	19	88	79	9	27	.338	.429	.527	153	45	25-8	**.992**	19	104	**130**	*2-150	**7.3**
1952	†Bro N★	149	510	104	157	17	3	19	75	106	14	40	.308	**.440**	.465	149	42	24-7	.974	4	97	**122**	*2-146	**5.7**
1953	†Bro N★	136	484	109	159	34	7	12	95	74	7	30	.329	.425	.502	137	31	17-4	.981	5	99	144	O-76(LF),3-44/2-9,1-6,S	3.2
1954	Bro N★	124	386	62	120	22	4	15	59	63	7	20	.311	.413	.505	135	23	7-3	1.000	-1	93	109	O-74(73-0-1),3-50/2-4	1.9
1955	†Bro N	105	317	51	81	6	2	8	36	61-5	3	18	.256	.378	.363	96	1	12-3	.966	11	116	132	3-84,O-10(LF)/12	1.3
1956	†Bro N	117	357	61	98	15	2	10	43	60-2	3	32	.275	.382	.412	106	6	12-5	.967	19	132	141	3-72,2-22/1-9,O-2(LF)	2.6
Total	10	1382	4877	947	1518	273	54	137	734	740-<u>7</u>	72	291	.311	.409	.474	131	253	197-<u>30</u>	.983	62	98	123	2-748,3-256,1-197,O-162L/S	34.3
ROBINSON, JACK John W. "Bridgeport" B 7.15.1880 Portland, ME D 7.22.1921 Macon, GA TR d9.6																								
1902	NY N	4	9	0	0	0	0	0	0	0	0		.000	.000	.000	-99	-2	0	1.000	0	*135*	*92*	/C-3	-0.2
ROBINSON, KERRY Kerry Keith B 10.3.1973 St.Louis, MO BL/TL 6/175# d9.22																								
1998	TB A	2	3	0	0	0	0	0	0	0-0	0	1	.000	.000	.000	-98	-1	0-0	1.000	1	294	0	/O-2(LF)	0.0
1999	Cin N	9	1	4	0	0	0	0	0	0-0	0	1	.000	.000	.000	-97	0	0-1	—	-0	0	0	/O-2(LF)	-0.1
2001	†StL N	114	186	34	53	6	1	1	15	12-0	2	20	.285	.330	.344	77	-6	11-2	.981	3	121	77	O-74(42-22-17)	-0.3
2002	†StL N	124	181	27	47	7	4	1	15	11-3	0	29	.260	.301	.359	78	-7	7-4	.977	1	121	0	O-76(52-10-17)/D	-0.7
2003	StL N	116	208	19	52	6	3	1	16	8-3	1	27	.250	.281	.322	59	-14	6-1	1.000	-2	102	0	O-88(36-20-39)	-1.5
Total	5	365	579	84	152	19	8	3	46	31-6	3	78	.263	.301	.339	70	-28	24-8	.986	3	115	26	O-242(134-52-73)/D	-2.6
ROBINSON, WILBERT Wilbert "Uncle Robby" B 6.29.1863 Bolton, MA D 8.8.1934 Atlanta, GA BR/TR 5-8.5/215# d4.19 M19 C3 HF1945 b-Fred																								
1886	Phi AA	87	342	57	69	11	3	1	30	21	3		.202	.254	.260	61	-16	33	.893	-7			C-61,1-22/O-5(0-4-1)	-1.8
1887	Phi AA	68	264	28	60	6	2	1	24	14	1		.227	.269	.277	52	-18	15	.901	2			C-67/1-3,O(CF)	-0.8
1888	Phi AA	66	254	32	62	7	2	1	31	9	0		.244	.270	.299	83	-6	11	.938	21			C-65/1	1.9

Year	Tm Lg	G	AB	R	H	2B	3B	HR	RBI	BB-IB	HP	SO	AVG	OBP	SLG	AOPS	ABR	SB-CS	FA	FR	Rng	Thr	G at Pos	BFW
1889	Phi AA	69	264	31	61	13	2	0	28	6	1	34	.231	.251	.295	56	-16	9	.943	7			C-69	-0.3
1890	Phi AA	82	329	32	78	13	4	4	42	16	3		.237	.279	.337	82	-10	20	.930	-15	*84*	*80*	C-82	-1.6
	Bal AA	14	48	7	13	1	0	0	4	3	0		.271	.314	.292	75	-2	1	.989	6	*119*	*64*	C-11/1-3	0.4
	Year	96	377	39	91	14	4	4	46	19	3		.241	.283	.332	81	-11	21	.938	-9	*88*	*78*	C-93/1-3	-1.2
1891	Bal AA	93	334	25	72	8	5	2	46	16	0	37	.216	.251	.287	54	-23	18	.954	14	***140***	*67*	C-92/O(RF)	-0.1
1892	Bal N	90	330	36	88	14	4	2	57	15	2	35	.267	.303	.352	95	-4	5	.921	-14	*95*	*84*	C-87/1-2,O(RF)	-1.0
1893	Bal N	95	359	49	120	21	3	3	57	26	2	22	.334	.382	.435	115	7	17	.942	-9	*90*	*68*	*C-93/1	0.6
1894	†Bal N	109	414	69	146	21	4	1	98	46	3	18	.353	.421	.430	101	2	12	.944	6	*123*	*77*	*C-109	1.3
1895	†Bal N	77	282	38	74	19	1	0	48	12	1	19	.262	.295	.337	61	-17	11	**.979**	24	***148***	*107*	C-75	1.1
1896	†Bal N	67	245	43	85	9	6	2	38	14	1	13	.347	.385	.457	120	6	9	.948	4	*111*	*73*	C-67	1.3
1897	Bal N	48	181	25	57	9	0	0	23	8	1		.315	.347	.365	88	-3	0	.965	-1	*102*	*72*	C-48	0.0
1898	Bal N	79	289	29	80	12	2	0	38	16	1		.277	.317	.332	84	-6	3	.965	1	*112*	*93*	C-77	0.1
1899	Bal N	108	356	40	101	15	2	0	47	31	2		.284	.344	.337	83	-8	5	.949	-7	*117*	*79*	*C-105	-0.5
1900	StL N	60	210	26	52	5	1	0	28	11	2		.248	.291	.281	59	-12	7	.974	1	*94*	*103*	C-54	-0.6
1901	Bal A	68	239	32	72	12	3	0	26	10	2		.301	.335	.377	93	-3	9	.949	-0	*107*	*81*	C-67	0.3
1902	Bal A	91	335	38	98	16	7	1	57	12	2		.293	.321	.391	93	-5	11	.949	-15	*80*	*86*	C-87,M	-1.1
Total	17	1371	5075	637	1388	212	51	18	722	286	27	178	.273	.316	.346	83	-134	196	.941	16	*87*	*65*	*C-1316/1-32,O-8(0-5-3)	-0.8

ROBINSON, EDDIE William Edward B 12.15.1920 Paris, TX BL/TR 6-2.5/210# d9.9 Mil 1943-45 C3

Year	Tm Lg	G	AB	R	H	2B	3B	HR	RBI	BB-IB	HP	SO	AVG	OBP	SLG	AOPS	ABR	SB-CS	FA	FR	Rng	Thr	G at Pos	BFW
1942	Cle A	8	8	1	1	0	0	0	2	1	0	0	.125	.222	.125	-1	-1	0-0	1.000	-0	0	0	/1	-0.1
1946	Cle A	8	30	6	12	1	0	3	4	2	0	4	.400	.438	.733	238	5	0-0	.988	-2	17	53	/1-8	0.3
1947	Cle A	95	318	52	78	10	1	14	52	30	2	18	.245	.314	.415	105	0	1-0	.994	-3	88	109	1-87	-0.5
1948	†Cle A	134	493	53	125	18	5	16	83	36	2	42	.254	.307	.408	91	-10	1-0	**.995**	-1	94	**114**	*1-131	-1.5
1949	Was A★	143	527	66	155	27	3	18	78	67	**7**	30	.294	.381	.459	125	18	3-4	.987	-2	97	82	*1-143	1.0
1950	Was A	36	129	21	30	4	2	1	13	25	2	4	.233	.365	.318	80	-3	0-0	1.000	0	96	96	1-36	-0.4
	Chi A	119	424	62	133	11	2	20	73	60	5	28	.314	.405	.491	132	21	0-0	.987	-5	84	88	*1-119	1.1
	Year	155	553	83	163	15	4	21	86	85	7	32	.295	.395	.450	120	18	0-0	.990	-5	87	90	*1-155	0.7
1951	Chi A★	151	564	85	159	23	5	29	117	77	3	54	.282	.371	.495	135	27	2-5	.988	-8	85	107	*1-147	1.2
1952	Chi A★	155	594	79	176	33	1	22	104	70	12	49	.296	.382	.466	134	29	2-0	.990	-8	78	106	*1-155	1.6
1953	Phi A★	156	615	64	152	28	4	22	102	63	5	56	.247	.322	.413	94	-7	1-2	.988	-13	70	86	*1-155	-3.0
1954	NY A	85	142	11	37	9	0	3	27	19	0	21	.261	.344	.387	105	1	0-0	.980	1	118	97	1-29	0.1
1955	†NY A	88	173	25	36	1	0	16	42	36-7	5	26	.208	.358	.491	129	7	0-0	.995	-2	74	94	1-46	0.2
1956	NY A	26	54	7	12	1	0	5	11	5-1	3	3	.222	.323	.519	123	1	0-1	1.000	-1	76	112	1-14	0.0
	KC A	75	172	13	34	5	1	2	12	26-1	2	20	.198	.308	.273	55	-11	0-0	.977	-4	75	113	1-47	-1.7
	Year	101	226	20	46	6	1	7	23	31-2	5	23	.204	.312	.332	71	-10	0-1	.983	-4	75	113	1-61	-1.7
1957	Det A	13	9	0	0	0	0	0	0	3-1	1	0	.000	.308	.000	-9	-1	0-0	1.000	0	348	0	/1	-0.1
	Cle A	19	27	1	6	1	0	1	3	0-0	1	3	.222	.241	.370	68	-1	0-0	1.000	0	106	66	/1-7	-0.2
	Bal A	4	3	0	0	0	0	0	0	1-0	0	1	.000	.250	.000	-28	-1	0-0	—	0			H	-0.1
	Year	36	39	1	6	1	0	1	3	4-1	2	4	.154	.261	.256	44	-3	0-0	1.000	1	128	60	/1-8	-0.4
Total	13	1315	4282	546	1146	172	24	172	723	521-10	50	359	.268	.353	.440	113	74	10-12	.990	-48	84	98	*1-1126	-2.1

ROBINSON, YANK William H. B 9.19.1859 Philadelphia, PA D 8.25.1894 St.Louis, MO BR/TR 5-6.5/170# d8.24 ▲ OF Total (52-LF 2-CF 2-RF)

Year	Tm Lg	G	AB	R	H	2B	3B	HR	RBI	BB-IB	HP	SO	AVG	OBP	SLG	AOPS	ABR	SB-CS	FA	FR	Rng	Thr	G at Pos	BFW
1882	Det N	11	39	1	7	1	0	0	2	1		13	.179	.200	.205	30	-3		.800	-3	78	79	S-10/O(CF)P	-0.5
1884	Bal U	102	415	101	111	24	4	3		**37**			.267	.327	.366	100	-12		.831	10	122	128	3-71,S-14,C-11,P-11/2-3	0.3
1885	†StL AA	78	287	63	75	8	8	0	35	29	7		.261	.344	.345	113	5		.862	-2	121	74	O-52(LF),2-19/C-5,3-2,1	0.2
1886	†StL AA	133	481	89	132	26	9	3	71	64	15		.274	.377	.385	132	21	51	.888	-6	102	**133**	*2-125/3-6,O(CF)SP	1.7
1887	†StL AA	125	430	102	131	32	4	1	74	92	17		.305	.445	.405	125	20	75	.899	-12	101	117	*2-117/3-6,O-2(RF),S-2,CP	1.0
1888	†StL AA	134	455	111	105	17	6	3	53	**116**	12		.231	**.400**	.314	117	16	56	.895	-37	87	61	*2-102,S-34	-1.5
1889	StL AA	132	452	97	94	17	3	5	70	**118**	6	55	.208	.378	.292	81	-7	39	.887	-37	85	92	*2-132	-3.4
1890	Pit P	98	306	59	70	10	3	0	38	101	10	33	.229	.434	.281	101	14	17	.887	-19	95	104	*2-98	-0.1
1891	Cin AA	97	342	48	61	9	4	1	37	68	8	51	.178	.328	.237	57	-18	23	.867	-14	101	79	*2-97	-2.5
	StL AA	1	3	0	0	0	0	0	0	0	0	0	.000	.000	.000	-87	-1	0	.750	-1	0	0	/2	-0.1
	Year	98	345	48	61	9	4	1	37	68	8	51	.177	.325	.235	56	-18	23	.866	-15	100	78	2-98	-2.6
1892	Was N	67	218	26	39	4	3	0	19	38	0	29	.179	.301	.225	61	-9	11	.852	-3	100	121	3-58/S-5,2-4	-0.9
Total	10	978	3428	697	825	148	44	16	399	664	75	181	.241	.375	.324	101	26	272	.887	-124	95	99	2-698,3-143/S-66,O-56L,C-17,P1	-5.8

ROBINSON, BILL William Henry B 6.26.1943 McKeesport, PA BR/TR 6-3/205# d9.20 C8

Year	Tm Lg	G	AB	R	H	2B	3B	HR	RBI	BB-IB	HP	SO	AVG	OBP	SLG	AOPS	ABR	SB-CS	FA	FR	Rng	Thr	G at Pos	BFW
1966	Atl N	6	11	1	3	0	1	0	3	0-0	0	1	.273	.273	.455	96	0	0-0	.800	-0	94	0	/O-5(2-0-3)	-0.1
1967	NY A	116	342	31	67	6	1	7	29	28-4	2	56	.196	.259	.281	62	-17	2-2	.968	-2	90	159	*O-102(20-33-53)	-2.7
1968	NY A	107	342	34	82	16	7	6	40	26-3	2	54	.240	.294	.380	107	2	7-6	.985	-4	97	49	O-98(6-51-44)	-0.9
1969	NY A	87	222	23	38	11	2	3	21	16-3	0	39	.171	.226	.279	42	-18	3-1	.963	-1	94	126	O-62(17-19-29)/1	-2.3
1972	Phi N	82	188	19	45	9	1	8	21	5-0	0	30	.239	.258	.426	89	-4	2-3	.982	1	104	63	O-72(13-30-32)	-0.6
1973	Phi N	124	452	62	130	32	1	25	65	27-1	1	91	.288	.326	.529	131	17	5-4	.979	-0	110	104	*O-113(13-44-75),3-14	1.2
1974	Phi N	100	280	32	66	14	1	5	29	17-4	1	61	.236	.280	.346	72	-11	5-3	.971	4	105	174	O-87(40-40-19)	-1.0
1975	†Pit N	92	200	26	56	12	2	6	33	11-4	0	36	.280	.313	.450	112	2	3-1	.991	2	112	93	O-57(31-15-13)	0.3
1976	Pit N	122	393	55	119	22	3	21	64	16-1	1	73	.303	.329	.534	142	18	2-4	.993	-12	95	141	O-78(24-27-29),3-37/1-3	0.2
1977	Pit N	137	507	74	154	32	1	26	104	25-3	3	92	.304	.337	.525	125	16	12-6	.992	-9	78	110	1-86,O-43(41-2-1),3-17	0.1
1978	Pit N	136	499	70	123	36	2	14	80	35-8	5	105	.246	.296	.411	93	-5	14-11	.988	4	105	90	*O-127(111-19-10),3-29/1-3	-0.7
1979	†Pit N	148	421	59	111	17	6	24	75	24-11	1	81	.264	.302	.504	111	4	13-2	.982	-2	97	91	*O-125(119-0-6),1-28/3-3	-0.1
1980	Pit N	100	272	28	78	10	1	12	36	15-2	0	45	.287	.320	.463	116	4	1-4	.985	-4	67	92	1-49,O-41(28-0-14)	-0.6
1981	Pit N	39	88	8	19	3	0	2	8	5-1	0	18	.216	.258	.318	61	-5	1-0	1.000	0	98	77	1-23/O-7(1-0-6),3	-0.6
1982	Pit N	31	71	8	17	3	0	4	12	5-3	0	19	.239	.286	.451	101	0	0-1	1.000	0	117	0	O-22(12-0-11)	-0.1
	Phi N	35	69	6	18	6	0	3	19	7-1	0	15	.261	.321	.478	121	2	1-1	.960	1	85	316	O-19(RF)/1-5	0.2
	Year	66	140	14	35	9	0	7	31	12-4	0	34	.250	.303	.464	111	2	1-2	.984	1	103	140	O-41(12-0-30)/1-5	0.1
1983	Phi N	10	7	0	1	0	0	0	2	1-0	0	4	.143	.250	.143	12	-1	0-0	1.000	-1	0	0	/1-3,3-2,O(LF)	-0.2
Total	16	1472	4364	536	1127	229	29	166	641	263-49	16	820	.258	.300	.438	104	4	71-49	.979	-22	100	106	*O-1059(479-280-364),1-201,3-103	-7.9

ROBLES, RAFAEL Rafael Orlando (Natera) B 10.20.1947 San Pedro De Macoris, D.R. D 8.13.1998 New York, NY BR/TR 6/170# d4.8

Year	Tm Lg	G	AB	R	H	2B	3B	HR	RBI	BB-IB	HP	SO	AVG	OBP	SLG	AOPS	ABR	SB-CS	FA	FR	Rng	Thr	G at Pos	BFW
1969	SD N	6	20	1	2	0	0	0	0	1-0	0	3	.100	.143	.100	-32	-4	1-1	.895	-4	59	28	/S-6	-0.8
1970	SD N	23	89	5	19	1	0	0	3	5-0	1	11	.213	.263	.225	33	-9	3-0	.968	6	122	101	S-23	0.0
1972	SD N	18	24	1	4	0	0	0	0	0-0	0	3	.167	.167	.167	-5	-3	0-0	.952	-3	89	0	S-15/3	-0.6
Total	3	47	133	7	25	1	0	0	3	6-0	1	17	.188	.229	.195	17	-16	4-1	.958	-1	106	71	/S-44,3	-1.4

ROBLES, SERGIO Sergio (Valenzuela) B 4.16.1946 Magdalena, Mexico BR/TR 6-2/190# d8.27

Year	Tm Lg	G	AB	R	H	2B	3B	HR	RBI	BB-IB	HP	SO	AVG	OBP	SLG	AOPS	ABR	SB-CS	FA	FR	Rng	Thr	G at Pos	BFW
1972	Bal A	2	5	0	1	0	0	0	0	0-0	0	0	.200	.200	.200	19	-1	0-0	1.000	-1	0	0	/C	-0.1
1973	Bal A	8	13	0	1	0	0	0	0	3-0	0	1	.077	.250	.077	-4	-2	0-0	1.000	2	0	0	/C-8	0.1
1976	LA N	6	3	0	0	0	0	0	0	0-0	0	2	.000	.000	.000	-99	-1	0-0	1.000	-0	122	0	/C-6	-0.1
Total	3	16	21	0	2	0	0	0	0	3-0	0	3	.095	.208	.095	-11	-4	0-0	1.000	1	28	0	/C-15	-0.1

ROBSON, TOM Thomas James B 1.15.1946 Rochester, NY BR/TR 6-3/215# d9.14 C13

Year	Tm Lg	G	AB	R	H	2B	3B	HR	RBI	BB-IB	HP	SO	AVG	OBP	SLG	AOPS	ABR	SB-CS	FA	FR	Rng	Thr	G at Pos	BFW
1974	Tex A	6	13	2	3	1	0	0	2	4-0	0	3	.231	.412	.308	112	1	0-0	1.000	0	0	1016	/1D	0.1
1975	Tex A	17	35	3	7	0	0	0	2	1-0	0	3	.200	.216	.200	20	-4	0-0	1.000	-0	79	202	/1-5,D-4	-0.4
Total	2	23	48	5	10	1	0	0	4	5-0	0	6	.208	.278	.229	48	-3	0-0	1.000	-0	77	227	/D-9,1-6	-0.3

ROCAP, ADAM Adam B 1854 Philadelphia, PA D 3.29.1892 Philadelphia, PA 5-9/170# d5.5

Year	Tm Lg	G	AB	R	H	2B	3B	HR	RBI	BB-IB	HP	SO	AVG	OBP	SLG	AOPS	ABR	SB-CS	FA	FR	Rng	Thr	G at Pos	BFW
1875	Ath NA	16	69	13	12	1	0	0	4	1		7	.174	.186	.188	27	-5	3-2	.839	-2	154	0	O-12(0-5-7)/2-4	-0.6

ROCCO, MICKEY Michael Dominick B 3.2.1916 St.Paul, MN D 6.1.1997 St.Paul, MN BL/TL 5-11/188# d6.5

Year	Tm Lg	G	AB	R	H	2B	3B	HR	RBI	BB-IB	HP	SO	AVG	OBP	SLG	AOPS	ABR	SB-CS	FA	FR	Rng	Thr	G at Pos	BFW
1943	Cle A	108	405	43	97	14	4	5	46	51	2	40	.240	.328	.331	99	0	1-2	**.995**	-5	81	118	*1-108	-1.2
1944	Cle A	**155**	653	87	174	29	7	13	70	56	1	51	.266	.325	.392	108	5	4-8	.993	17	**142**	105	*1-155	1.2
1945	Cle A	143	565	81	149	28	6	10	56	52	0	40	.264	.326	.388	111	6	0-4	**.992**	4	105	93	*1-141	0.1
1946	Cle A	34	98	8	24	2	0	2	14	15	0	15	.245	.345	.327	94	0	1-1	.996	5	155	79	1-27	0.3
Total	4	440	1721	219	444	73	17	30	186	174	3	146	.258	.327	.372	106	11	6-15	.994	20	115	103	1-431	0.4

ROCHE, JACK John Joseph "Red" B 11.22.1890 Los Angeles, CA D 3.30.1983 Peoria, AZ BR/TR 6-1/178# d5.24

Year	Tm Lg	G	AB	R	H	2B	3B	HR	RBI	BB-IB	HP	SO	AVG	OBP	SLG	AOPS	ABR	SB-CS	FA	FR	Rng	Thr	G at Pos	BFW
1914	StL N	12	9	1	6	2	1	0	3	0	1	1	.667	.700	1.111	441	4	1	.667	-1	*63*	*0*	/C-9	0.3

Year	Tm Lg	G	AB	R	H	2B	3B	HR	RBI	BB-IB	HP	SO	AVG	OBP	SLG	AOPS	ABR	SB-CS	FA	FR	Rng	Thr	G at Pos	BFW
1915	StL N	46	39	2	8	0	1	0	6	4	1	8	.205	.295	.256	68	-2	1	1.000	0	*74*	*323*	/C-4	-0.1
1917	StL N	1	1	0	0	0	0	0	0	0	0	0	.000	.000	.000	-99	0	0	.000	-1	*0*	*0*	/C	-0.1
Total	3	59	49	3	14	2	2	0	9	4	2	9	.286	.364	.408	133	2	2	.750	-2	*60*	*119*	/C-14	0.1
ROCHEFORT, BEN Bennett Harold (born Bennett Harold Rochefort Gilbert) B 8.15.1896 Camden, NJ D 4.2.1981 Red Bank, NJ BL/TR 6-2/185# d10.3																								
1914	Phi A	1	2	0	1	0	0	0	0	0	0	1	.500	.500	.500	209	0	0	1.000	0	352	0	/1	0.1
ROCHELLI, LOU Louis Joseph B 1.11.1919 Staunton, IL D 10.23.1992 Victoria, TX BR/TR 6-1/175# d8.25 Mil 1944-46																								
1944	Bro N	5	17	0	3	0	1	0	2	2	0	6	.176	.263	.294	58	-1	0	.964	-1	100	30	/2-5	-0.1
ROCK, LES Lester Henry (born Lester Henry Schwarzrock) B 8.19.1912 Springfield, MN D 9.9.1991 Davis, CA BL/TR 6-2/184# d9.11																								
1936	Chi A	2	1	0	0	0	0	0	1	0	0	0	.000	.000	.000	-97	0	0-0	—	0	0	0	/1-2	0.0
ROCKENFIELD, IKE Isaac Broc B 11.3.1876 Omaha, NE D 2.21.1927 San Diego, CA BR/TR 5-7/150# d5.5																								
1905	StL A	95	322	40	70	12	0	0	16	46	14		.217	.340	.255	95	3	11	.926	-9	96	76	2-95	-0.6
1906	StL A	27	89	3	21	4	0	0	8	1	4		.236	.277	.281	78	-2	0	.956	-6	81	60	2-26	-0.9
Total	2	122	411	43	91	16	0	0	24	47	18		.221	.328	.260	91	1	11	.933	-15	93	72	2-121	-1.5
ROCKETT, PAT Patrick Edward B 1.9.1955 San Antonio, TX BR/TR 5-11/170# d9.17																								
1976	Atl N	4	5	0	1	0	0	0	0	0-0	0	1	.200	.200	.200	13	-1	0-0	1.000	-1	55	0	/S-2	-0.1
1977	Atl N	93	264	27	67	10	0	1	24	27-2	3	32	.254	.330	.303	64	-13	1-2	.940	-14	85	72	S-84	-1.9
1978	Atl N	55	142	6	20	2	0	0	4	13-3	0	12	.141	.212	.155	4	-18	1-2	.970	-18	71	61	S-51	-3.5
Total	3	152	411	33	88	12	0	1	28	40-5	3	45	.214	.288	.251	43	-32	2-4	.949	-32	80	68	S-137	-5.5
RODGERS, ANDRE Kenneth Andre Ian "Andy" B 12.2.1934 Nassau, Bahamas BR/TR 6-3/200# d4.16																								
1957	NY N	32	86	8	21	2	1	3	9	9-0	1	21	.244	.320	.395	92	-1	0-0	.950	3	104	118	S-20/3-8	0.3
1958	SF N	22	63	7	13	3	1	2	11	4-0	0	14	.206	.243	.381	67	-3	0-0	.972	-2	95	78	S-18	-0.4
1959	SF N	71	228	32	57	12	1	6	24	32-1	1	50	.250	.342	.390	98	0	2-1	.933	-10	93	89	S-66	-0.5
1960	SF N	81	217	22	53	8	5	2	22	24-4	3	44	.244	.325	.355	92	-2	1-1	.953	-3	94	108	S-41,3-21/1-6,O-2(LF)	-0.3
1961	Chi N	73	214	27	57	17	0	6	23	25-1	1	54	.266	.343	.430	103	2	1-1	.983	0	91	95	1-42,S-24/O-2(RF),2	0.1
1962	Chi N	138	461	40	128	20	8	5	44	44-4	3	93	.278	.343	.388	93	-4	5-6	.960	7	**109**	103	*S-133/1	1.3
1963	Chi N	150	516	51	118	17	4	5	33	65-6	9	90	.229	.324	.306	79	-12	5-7	.954	-4	102	118	*S-150	-0.4
1964	Chi N	129	448	50	107	17	3	12	46	53-5	0	88	.239	.317	.371	90	-5	5-1	.965	15	**117**	94	*S-126	2.2
1965	Pit N	75	178	17	51	12	0	2	25	18-3	0	28	.287	.350	.388	108	3	2-1	.950	-3	95	129	S-33,3-15/1-6,2	0.2
1966	Pit N	36	49	6	9	1	0	0	4	8-0	0	7	.184	.293	.204	43	-4	0-1	.913	-1	93	186	/S-5,3-3,O-3(LF),1-2	-0.4
1967	Pit N	47	61	8	14	3	0	2	4	8-2	0	18	.230	.314	.377	98	0	1-1	1.000	1	178	94	/1-9,3-5,S-3,2-2	0.1
Total	11	854	2521	268	628	112	23	45	245	290-26	18	507	.249	.328	.365	90	-26	22-20	.956	3	105	105	S-619/1-66,3-52,O-7(5-0-2),2-4	2.2
RODGERS, BUCK Robert Leroy B 8.16.1938 Delaware, OH BB/TR 6-2/195# d9.8 M13 C9																								
1961	LA A	16	56	8	18	2	0	2	13	1-0	0	6	.321	.333	.464	99	0	0-0	.965	-0	*78*	*163*	C-14	0.0
1962	LA A	155	565	65	146	34	6	6	61	45-6	0	68	.258	.309	.372	86	-12	1-8	.989	2	*109*	*117*	*C-150	-0.5
1963	LA A	100	300	24	70	6	0	4	23	29-2	2	35	.233	.303	.293	73	-11	2-2	.979	-6	118	126	C-85	-1.3
1964	LA A	148	514	38	125	18	3	4	54	40-11	4	71	.243	.299	.313	80	-15	4-3	.987	14	*104*	***137***	*C-146	0.6
1965	Cal A	132	411	33	86	14	3	1	32	35-9	3	61	.209	.271	.265	56	-24	4-5	.991	7	*118*	*89*	*C-128	-1.3
1966	Cal A	133	454	45	107	20	3	7	48	29-8	2	57	.236	.281	.339	81	-12	3-4	.992	-4	*99*	*113*	*C-133	-1.2
1967	Cal A	139	429	29	94	13	3	6	41	34-5	2	55	.219	.277	.305	76	-14	1-4	.991	2	133	122	*C-134/O(LF)	-0.8
1968	Cal A	91	258	13	49	6	0	1	14	16-3	3	48	.190	.244	.225	45	-17	2-1	.985	-2	117	113	C-87	-1.9
1969	Cal A	18	46	4	9	1	0	0	2	5-1	1	8	.196	.288	.217	46	-3	0-0	1.000	-4	47	91	C-18	-0.7
Total	9	932	3033	259	704	114	18	31	288	234-45	17	409	.232	.288	.312	74	-108	17-27	.988	8	*111*	*117*	C-895/O(LF)	-7.1
RODGERS, BILL Wilbur Kincaid "Rawmeat Bill" B 4.18.1887 Pleasant Ridge, OH D 12.24.1978 Goliad, TX BL/TR 5-9.5/170# d4.15																								
1915	Cle A	16	45	8	14	2	0	0	7	8	0	7	.311	.415	.356	128	2	3-3	.945	-3	93	22	2-13	-0.1
	Bos A	11	6	2	0	0	0	0	0	3	0	2	.000	.333	.000	-0	0	0	.900	1	162	0	/2-6	0.0
	Year	27	51	10	14	2	0	0	7	11	0	9	.275	.403	.314	115	2	3-3	.938	-2	101	20	2-19	-0.1
	Cin N	72	213	20	51	13	4	0	12	11	7	29	.239	.299	.338	91	-2	8-5	.947	6	114	141	2-56/S-6,3O(RF)	0.5
1916	Cin N	3	4	0	0	0	0	0	0	0	0	2	.000	.000	.000	-99	-1	0	1.000	-0	68	0	/S	-0.1
Total	2	102	268	30	65	15	4	0	19	22	7	40	.243	.316	.328	93	-1	11-8	.945	3	111	116	/2-75,S-7,O(RF)3	0.3
RODGERS, BILL William Sherman B 12.5.1922 Harrisburg, PA BL/TL 6/162# d9.27 Mil 1945																								
1944	Pit N	2	4	1	1	0	0	0	0	0	0	1	.250	.250	.250	39	0	0	—	-0	0	0	/O(RF)	0.0
1945	Pit N	1	1	0	1	0	0	0	0	0	0	0	1.000	1.000	1.000	440	0	0	—	0			H	0.0
Total	2	3	5	1	2	0	0	0	0	0	0	1	.400	.400	.400	120	0	0	.000	-0	0	0	/O(RF)	0.0
RODIN, ERIC Eric Chapman B 2.5.1930 Orange, NJ D 1.4.1991 Somerville, NJ BR/TR 6-2/215# d9.7																								
1954	NY N	5	6	0	0	0	0	0	0	0	0	2	.000	.000	.000	-99	-2	0-0	1.000	0	109	0	/O-3(0-2-1)	-0.2
RODRIGUEZ, ALEX Alexander Emmanuel "A-Rod" B 7.27.1975 New York, NY BR/TR 6-3/190# d7.8																								
1994	Sea A	17	54	4	11	0	0	0	2	3-0	0	20	.204	.241	.204	17	-7	3-0	.915	-2	91	81	S-17	-0.7
1995	†Sea A	48	142	15	33	6	2	5	19	6-0	0	42	.232	.264	.408	71	-7	4-2	.953	-4	92	52	S-46/D	-0.8
1996	Sea A★	146	601	**141**	215	**54**	1	36	123	59-1	4	104	**.358**	.414	.631	160	57	15-4	.977	-6	95	94	*S-146	5.7
1997	†Sea A★	141	587	100	176	40	3	23	84	41-1	5	99	.300	.350	.496	119	15	29-6	.962	-3	94	90	*S-140/D	2.6
1998	Sea A★	**161**	686	123	**213**	35	5	42	124	45-0	10	121	.310	.360	.560	135	33	46-13	.975	-1	92	88	*S-160/D	4.6
1999	Sea A	129	502	110	143	25	0	42	111	56-2	5	109	.285	.357	.586	140	28	21-7	.977	1	99	107	*S-129	3.8
2000	†Sea A✷	148	554	134	175	34	2	41	132	100-5	7	121	.316	.420	.606	163	57	15-4	.986	6	99	**125**	*S-148	**6.8**
2001	Tex A	**162**	632	**133**	201	34	1	**52**	135	75-6	16	131	.318	.399	.622	159	55	18-3	.976	3	100	107	*S-161/D	**6.9**
2002	Tex A★	**162**	624	125	187	27	2	**57**	**142**	87-12	10	122	.300	.392	.623	156	51	9-4	.987	12	104	96	*S-162	**7.1**
2003	Tex A★	161	607	**124**	181	30	6	**47**	118	87-10	15	126	.298	.396	**.600**	146	42	17-3	**.989**	13	**106**	98	*S-158/D	**6.5**
Total	10	1275	4989	1009	1535	285	22	345	990	559-37	72	995	.308	.382	.581	144	324	177-46	.977	18	98	99	*S-1267/D-5	42.5
RODRIGUEZ, AURELIO Aurelio (Ituarte) B 12.28.1947 Cananea, Mexico D 9.23.2000 Detroit, MI BR/TR 5-10/180# d9.1																								
1967	Cal A	29	130	14	31	3	1	1	8	2-0	0	21	.238	.250	.300	64	-7	1-0	.989	4	117	224	3-29	-0.2
1968	Cal A	76	223	14	54	10	1	1	16	17-2	1	36	.242	.299	.309	88	-3	0-2	.921	-8	87	162	3-70/2-2	-1.4
1969	Cal A	159	561	47	130	17	2	7	49	32-11	2	88	.232	.272	.307	66	-28	5-3	.954	15	109	**135**	*3-159	-1.5
1970	Cal A	17	63	6	17	2	2	0	7	3-0	1	6	.270	.313	.365	90	-1	0-1	1.000	3	109	209	3-17	0.1
	Was A	142	547	64	135	31	5	19	76	37-5	7	81	.247	.300	.426	104	0	15-5	.961	13	117	118	*3-136/S-7	1.6
	Year	159	610	70	152	33	7	19	83	40-5	8	87	.249	.302	.420	102	-1	15-6	.965	16	116	128	*3-153/S-7	1.7
1971	Det A	154	604	68	153	30	7	15	39	27-6	3	93	.253	.288	.401	90	-10	4-6	.953	6	100	105	*3-153/S	-0.7
1972	†Det A	153	601	65	142	23	5	13	56	28-4	2	104	.236	.272	.356	83	-15	2-3	.969	20	105	114	*3-153/S-2	0.5
1973	Det A	160	555	46	123	27	3	9	58	31-0	3	85	.222	.266	.330	63	-28	3-1	.971	5	97	102	*3-160/S	-2.5
1974	Det A	159	571	54	127	23	5	5	49	26-2	1	70	.222	.255	.306	60	-31	2-0	.961	15	107	110	*3-159	-1.7
1975	Det A	151	507	47	124	20	6	13	60	30-1	0	63	.245	.286	.385	85	-13	1-1	.953	27	**116**	105	*3-151	1.3
1976	Det A	128	480	40	115	13	2	8	50	19-3	1	61	.240	.267	.325	71	-19	0-4	**.978**	8	102	92	*3-128	-1.4
1977	Det A	96	306	30	67	14	1	10	32	16-1	0	36	.219	.257	.369	65	-16	1-1	.972	15	124	120	3-95/S	-0.2
1978	Det A	134	385	40	102	25	2	7	43	19-1	3	37	.265	.303	.395	93	-4	0-1	**.987**	6	109	101	*3-131	-0.1
1979	Det A	106	343	27	87	18	0	5	36	11-0	1	40	.254	.277	.350	66	-17	0-2	.956	6	105	124	*3-106/1	-1.3
1980	SD N	89	175	7	35	7	2	2	13	6-0	0	26	.200	.227	.297	48	-13	1-1	.965	2	106	139	3-88/S-2	-1.3
	†NY A	52	164	14	36	6	1	3	14	7-1	0	35	.220	.251	.323	57	-10	0-0	.954	-11	75	57	3-49/2-6	-2.2
1981	†NY A	27	52	4	18	2	0	2	8	2-0	0	10	.346	.370	.500	151	3	0-0	.951	2	104	53	3-20/2-3,1D	0.5
1982	Chi A	118	257	24	62	15	1	3	31	11-0	1	35	.241	.275	.342	68	-11	0-0	.969	9	107	103	*3-112/2-3,S-2	-0.3
1983	Bal A	45	67	0	8	0	0	0	2	0-0	1	13	.119	.130	.119	-31	-12	0-0	.969	-3	86	41	3-45	-1.6
	†Chi A	22	20	1	4	1	0	1	1	0-0	0	3	.200	.200	.400	58	-1	0-0	1.000	2	117	299	3-22	0.1
	Year	67	87	1	12	1	0	1	3	0-0	1	16	.138	.146	.184	-9	-13	0-0	.978	-1	94	108	3-67	-1.5
Total	17	2017	6611	612	1570	287	46	124	648	324-37	27	943	.237	.275	.351	75	-236	35-31	.964	134	106	114	*3-1983/S-16,2-14,D-2,1-2	-12.3
RODRIGUEZ, CARLOS Carlos (Marquez) B 11.1.1967 Mexico City, Mexico BB/TR 5-9/160# d6.16																								
1991	NY A	15	37	1	7	0	0	0	2	1-0	0	2	.189	.211	.189	11	-5	0-0	.957	1	117	148	S-11/2-3	-0.3
1994	Bos A	57	174	15	50	14	1	1	13	11-0	0	13	.287	.330	.397	82	-4	1-0	.973	0	80	94	S-32,2-20/3-4	-0.1
1995	Bos A	13	30	5	10	2	0	0	5	2-0	1	2	.333	.394	.400	104	0	0-0	.960	0	94	84	/2-7,S-6,3	0.1

Year	Tm Lg	G	AB	R	H	2B	3B	HR	RBI	BB-IB	HP	SO	AVG	OBP	SLG	AOPS	ABR	SB-CS	FA	FR	Rng	Thr	G at Pos	BFW
Total	3	85	241	21	67	16	1	1	20	14-0	1	17	.278	.320	.365	75	-9	1-0	.972	1	91	110	/S-49,2-30,3-5	-0.3
RODRIGUEZ, EDWIN Edwin (Morales) B 8.14.1960 Ponce, P.R. BR/TR 5-11/175# d9.28																								
1982	NY A	3	9	2	3	0	0	0	1	1-0	0	1	.333	.400	.333	106	0	0-0	.875	2	205	67	/2-3	0.2
1983	SD N	7	12	1	2	1	0	0	0	1-0	0	3	.167	.231	.250	34	-1	0-0	1.000	-2	79	92	/2-5,S-2,3	-0.3
1985	SD N	1	1	0	0	0	0	0	0	0-0	0	0	.000	.000	.000	-99	0	0-0	—	0			/H	0.0
Total	3	11	22	3	5	1	0	0	1	2-0	0	4	.227	.292	.273	58	-1	0-0	.935	-0	127	83	/2-8,S-2,3	-0.1
RODRIGUEZ, ELLIE Eliseo (Delgado) B 5.24.1946 Fajardo, P.R. BR/TR 5-11/185# d5.26																								
1968	NY A	9	24	1	5	0	0	0	1	3-0	0	3	.208	.296	.208	57	-1	0-0	1.000	-1	128	133	/C-9	-0.2
1969	KC A☆	95	267	27	63	10	0	2	20	31-6	8	26	.236	.333	.296	77	-7	3-2	.990	-7	136	108	C-90	-1.1
1970	KC A	80	231	25	52	8	2	1	15	27-2	4	35	.225	.312	.290	68	-9	2-1	.988	3	73	83	C-75	-0.3
1971	Mil A	115	319	28	67	10	1	1	30	41-5	8	51	.210	.311	.257	64	-13	1-1	.992	10	144	**150**	*C-114	0.1
1972	Mil A☆	116	355	31	101	14	2	2	35	52-5	7	43	.285	.382	.352	123	13	1-4	.983	-4	107	105	*C-114	1.5
1973	Mil A	94	290	30	78	8	1	0	30	41-3	10	28	.269	.376	.303	96	2	4-3	.986	3	123	143	C-75,D-14	0.7
1974	Cal A	140	395	48	100	20	0	7	36	69-6	9	56	.253	.373	.357	119	14	4-5	.992	2	**127**	**119**	*C-137/D	2.3
1975	Cal A	90	226	20	53	6	0	3	27	49-0	6	37	.235	.380	.301	103	5	2-2	.991	-8	71	81	C-90	0.0
1976	LA N	36	66	10	14	0	0	0	9	19-2	3	12	.212	.400	.212	82	0	0-0	.986	2	54	87	C-33	0.3
Total	9	775	2173	220	533	76	6	16	203	332-29	55	291	.245	.356	.308	94	4	17-18	.989	-0	112	114	C-737/D-15	3.3
RODRIGUEZ, HECTOR Hector Antonio (Ordenana) B 6.13.1920 Alquizar, Cuba BR/TR 5-8/165# d4.15																								
1952	Chi A	124	407	55	108	14	0	1	40	47	3	22	.265	.346	.307	82	-8	7-6	.959	5	98	106	*3-113	-0.4
RODRIGUEZ, HENRY Henry Anderson (Lorenzo) B 11.8.1967 Santo Domingo, D.R. BL/TL 6-1/200# d7.5																								
1992	LA N	53	146	11	32	7	0	3	14	8-0	0	30	.219	.258	.329	67	-7	0-0	.960	2	84	290	O-48(17-0-31)/1	-0.7
1993	LA N	76	176	20	39	10	0	8	23	11-2	0	39	.222	.266	.415	84	-5	1-0	.984	-2	78	108	O-48(26-0-23),1-13	-0.9
1994	LA N	104	306	33	82	14	2	8	49	17-2	2	58	.268	.307	.405	91	-6	0-1	.986	3	105	95	O-86(85-0-6),1-17	-0.6
1995	LA N	21	80	6	21	4	1	1	10	5-2	0	17	.262	.306	.375	86	-2	0-1	1.000	-1	103	0	O-20(RF)/1	-0.4
	Mon N	24	58	7	12	0	0	1	5	6-0	0	11	.207	.277	.259	42	-5	0-0	1.000	-1	117	116	1-10/O-8(4-0-4)	-0.7
	Year	45	138	13	33	4	1	2	15	11-2	0	28	.239	.293	.326	65	-7	0-1	.977	-1	94	0	O-28(4-0-24),1-11	-1.1
1996	Mon N★	145	532	81	147	42	1	36	103	37-7	3	160	.276	.325	.562	126	18	2-0	.947	-9	76	113	O-89(88-0-2),1-51	0.2
1997	Mon N	132	476	55	116	28	3	26	83	42-5	2	149	.244	.306	.479	103	-1	3-3	.985	-4	92	53	*O-126(126-0-1)/1-3	-1.0
1998	†Chi N	128	415	56	104	21	1	31	85	54-7	0	113	.251	.334	.530	119	11	1-3	.996	9	115	109	*O-114(LF)/D-5	1.5
1999	Chi N	130	447	72	136	29	0	26	87	56-6	0	113	.304	.381	.544	133	22	2-4	.974	1	100	98	*O-122(LF)/D-2	1.7
2000	Chi N	76	259	37	65	15	1	18	51	22-2	3	76	.251	.314	.525	110	2	1-2	.983	-0	90	126	O-70(70-0-1)	-0.1
	Fla N	36	108	10	29	6	0	2	10	14-0	1	23	.269	.358	.380	91	-1	0-0	1.000	-2	82	63	O-29(24-0-6)	-0.4
	Year	112	367	47	94	21	1	20	61	36-2	4	99	.256	.327	.482	105	1	1-2	.987	-2	88	108	O-99(94-0-7)	-0.5
2001	NY A	5	8	0	0	0	0	0	0	0-0	0	6	.000	.000	.000	-99	-2	0-0	—	0			/D	-0.2
2002	Mon N	20	20	1	1	0	0	0	3	4-0	0	8	.050	.200	.050	-23	-4	0-0	—	-1	0	0	/O-5(4-0-1)	-0.5
Total	11	950	3031	389	784	176	9	160	523	276-33	11	803	.259	.321	.481	107	20	10-14	.980	-4	94	103	O-765(680-0-95)/1-96,D-8	-2.1
RODRIGUEZ, IVAN Ivan (Torres) "Pudge" B 11.27.1971 Manati, P.R. BR/TR 5-9/205# d6.20																								
1991	Tex A	88	280	24	74	16	0	3	27	5-0	0	42	.264	.276	.354	75	-11	0-1	.983	11	138	**132**	C-88	0.5
1992	Tex A★	123	420	39	109	16	1	8	37	24-2	1	73	.260	.300	.360	87	-9	0-0	.983	20	**160**	**134**	*C-116/D-2	1.8
1993	Tex A★	137	473	56	129	28	4	10	66	29-3	4	70	.273	.315	.412	99	-2	8-7	.991	11	133	107	*C-134/D	1.6
1994	Tex A★	99	363	56	108	19	1	16	57	31-5	7	42	.298	.360	.488	117	9	6-3	.992	2	**177**	77	C-99	1.6
1995	Tex A★	130	492	56	149	32	2	12	67	16-2	4	48	.303	.327	.449	98	-3	0-2	.990	13	**198**	108	*C-127/D	1.6
1996	†Tex A★	153	639	116	192	47	3	19	86	38-7	4	55	.300	.342	.473	98	-2	5-0	.989	26	**194**	**122**	*C-146/D-6	3.1
1997	Tex A★	150	597	98	187	34	4	20	77	38-7	8	89	.313	.360	.484	112	10	7-3	.992	23	**253**	109	*C-143/D-5	4.0
1998	†Tex A★	145	579	88	186	40	4	21	91	32-4	3	88	.321	.358	.513	119	15	9-0	.994	16	**262**	109	*C-139/D-6	3.9
1999	†Tex A★	144	600	116	199	29	1	35	113	24-2	1	64	.332	.356	.558	124	18	25-12	.993	18	**257**	96	*C-141/D	4.3
2000	Tex A★	91	363	66	126	27	4	27	83	19-5	1	48	.347	.375	.667	156	29	5-5	**.996**	7	**248**	90	C-87/D	3.7
2001	Tex A	111	442	70	136	24	2	25	65	23-3	4	73	.308	.347	.541	125	14	10-3	.990	13	**308**	118	*C-106/D-5	3.3
2002	Tex A	108	408	67	128	32	2	19	60	25-2	2	71	.314	.353	.542	127	16	5-4	.990	4	**203**	61	*C-100/D-6	2.5
2003	†Fla N	144	511	90	152	36	3	16	85	55-6	6	92	.297	.369	.474	124	19	10-6	.992	1	151	75	*C-138/D	2.8
Total	13	1623	6167	942	1875	380	31	231	914	359-48	45	855	.304	.344	.488	113	103	90-46	.990	164	207	103	*C-1564/D-35	34.7
RODRIGUEZ, JOSE Jose "El Hombre Goma" B 2.23.1894 Havana, Cuba D 1.21.1953 Havana, Cuba BR/TR 5-8/150# d10.5																								
1916	NY N	1	0	0	0	0	0	0	0	0	0	0	—	—	—	—	0	0	—	0			R	0.0
1917	NY N	7	20	2	4	0	1	0	2	2	0	1	.200	.273	.300	78	-1	2	1.000	-1	36	71	/1-7	-0.2
1918	NY N	50	125	15	20	0	2	0	15	12	1	3	.160	.239	.192	33	-10	6	.978	0	91	104	2-40/1-8,3-2	-1.1
Total	3	58	145	17	24	0	3	0	17	14	1	4	.166	.244	.207	39	-11	8	.978	-0	91	104	/2-40,1-15,3-2	-1.3
RODRIGUEZ, LIU Liubiemithz B 11.5.1976 Caracas, Venezuela BB/TR 5-9/170# d6.9																								
1999	Chi A	39	93	8	22	2	2	1	12	12-0	3	11	.237	.343	.333	73	-4	0-0	.985	-8	84	50	2-22,S-14/3	-0.9
RODRIGUEZ, TONY Luis Antonio B 8.15.1970 Rio Piedras, P.R. BR/TR 5-11/165# d7.6																								
1996	Bos A	27	67	7	16	1	0	1	9	4-0	1	8	.239	.292	.299	49	-5	0-0	.979	2	112	78	S-21/3-5	-0.2
RODRIGUEZ, RUBEN Ruben Dario (Martinez) B 8.4.1964 Cabrera, D.R. BR/TR 6-3/190# d9.17																								
1986	Pit N	2	3	0	0	0	0	0	0	0-0	0	1	.000	.000	.000	-98	-1	0-0	1.000	0	95	0	/C-2	-0.1
1988	Pit N	2	5	1	1	0	1	0	1	0-0	0	2	.200	.200	.600	123	0	0-0	1.000	1	0	0	/C-2	0.1
Total	2	4	8	1	1	0	1	0	1	0-0	0	3	.125	.125	.375	36	-1	0-0	1.000	1	45	0	/C-4	0.0
RODRIGUEZ, STEVE Steven James B 11.29.1970 Las Vegas, NV BR/TR 5-8/170# d4.30																								
1995	Bos A	6	8	1	1	0	0	0	0	1-0	0	1	.125	.222	.125	-6	-1	1-0	.667	-1	85	0	/S-4,2D	-0.2
	Det A	12	31	4	6	1	0	0	0	5-0	0	9	.194	.306	.226	41	-3	1-2	.982	-2	100	71	2-12/S	-0.4
	Year	18	39	5	7	1	0	0	0	6-0	0	10	.179	.289	.205	31	-4	2-2	.983	-3	98	66	2-13/S-5,D	-0.6
RODRIGUEZ, VIC Victor Manuel (Rivera) B 7.14.1961 New York, NY BR/TR 5-11/173# d9.5																								
1984	Bal A	11	17	4	7	3	0	0	2	0-0	0	2	.412	.412	.588	177	2	0-0	.958	-0	112	35	/2-7,D	0.2
1989	Min A	6	11	2	5	2	0	0	0	0-0	0	1	.455	.455	.636	191	1	0-0	.900	0	103	202	/3-5,D	0.2
Total	2	17	28	6	12	5	0	0	2	0-0	0	3	.429	.429	.607	183	3	0-0	.958	-0	112	35	/2-7,3-5,D-2	0.4
ROENICKE, GARY Gary Steven B 12.5.1954 Covina, CA BR/TR 6-3/205# d6.8 b-Ron																								
1976	Mon N	29	90	9	20	3	1	2	5	4-0	1	18	.222	.260	.344	69	-4	0-0	.955	0	92	170	O-25(3-0-22)	-0.6
1978	Bal A	27	58	5	15	3	0	3	15	8-0	1	3	.259	.348	.466	138	3	0-1	1.000	-1	74	104	O-20(LF)	0.1
1979	†Bal A	133	376	60	98	16	1	25	64	61-4	12	74	.261	.378	.508	143	25	1-3	.981	0	98	118	*O-130(114-26-8)/D-2	1.9
1980	Bal A	118	297	40	71	13	0	10	28	41-5	6	49	.239	.340	.384	100	1	2-0	**1.000**	3	103	119	*O-113(86-13-38)	0.1
1981	Bal A	85	219	31	59	16	0	3	20	23-1	2	29	.269	.340	.384	110	4	1-2	.983	5	123	43	O-83(45-13-54)	0.5
1982	Bal A	137	393	58	106	25	1	21	74	70-2	9	73	.270	.392	.499	143	27	6-7	.990	9	118	98	*O-125(80-34-42),1-10	3.0
1983	†Bal A	115	323	45	84	13	0	19	64	30-2	4	35	.260	.326	.477	121	9	2-2	.982	-3	93	115	*O-100(79-8-23)/1-7,3-2,D-2	0.2
1984	Bal A	121	326	36	73	19	1	10	44	58-1	4	43	.224	.346	.380	104	4	1-2	.995	-3	93	89	*O-117(85-6-32)	-0.3
1985	Bal A	114	225	36	49	9	0	15	43	44-1	0	36	.218	.342	.458	121	7	2-2	.993	3	104	155	O-89(76-9-9),D-17	0.7
1986	NY A	69	136	11	36	5	0	3	18	27-0	1	30	.265	.388	.368	109	3	1-1	1.000	-2	72	172	O-37(33-3-2),D-15/3-3,1-2	0.0
1987	Atl N	67	151	25	33	8	0	9	28	32-0	1	23	.219	.353	.450	107	2	0-0	.968	-2	88	0	O-44(40-0-4)/1-9	-0.2
1988	Atl N	49	114	11	26	5	0	1	7	8-0	0	15	.228	.279	.298	63	-5	0-0	1.000	-2	92	0	O-35(32-1-2)/1	-0.9
Total	12	1064	2708	367	670	135	4	121	410	406-16	41	428	.247	.351	.434	117	76	16-20	.988	7	101	101	O-918(693-113-236)/D-36,1-29,3-5	4.5
ROENICKE, RON Ronald Jon B 8.19.1956 Covina, CA BB/TL 6/180# d9.2 C4 b-Gary																								
1981	LA N	22	47	6	11	0	0	0	0	6-0	0	8	.234	.321	.234	62	-2	1-1	1.000	2	133	98	O-20(5-6-10)	-0.1
1982	LA N	109	143	18	37	8	0	1	12	21-3	2	32	.259	.359	.336	99	1	5-0	.984	-3	84	43	O-72(21-18-39)	-0.2
1983	LA N	81	145	12	32	4	0	2	12	14-1	0	26	.221	.287	.290	61	-8	3-2	.987	-1	98	43	O-62(9-17-44)	-1.1
	Sea A	59	198	23	50	12	0	4	23	33-1	2	22	.253	.362	.374	100	2	6-2	.993	7	98	362	O-54(16-38-4)/1-8,D	0.7
1984	†SD N	12	20	4	6	1	0	1	2	2-1	0	5	.300	.364	.500	141	1	0-0	1.000	-1	86	0	O-10(7-2-2)	0.0
1985	SF N	65	133	23	34	9	1	3	13	35-3	0	27	.256	.408	.406	136	9	6-2	.984	-1	106	0	O-35(9-6-20)	0.8
1986	Phi N	102	275	42	68	13	1	5	42	61-4	0	52	.247	.381	.356	102	4	2-2	.989	-0	105	63	O-83(24-63-8)	0.2
1987	Phi N	63	78	9	13	3	1	1	4	14-1	0	15	.167	.293	.269	49	-6	1-0	.964	0	102	138	O-26(9-15-4)	-0.6

Year	Tm Lg	G	AB	R	H	2B	3B	HR	RBI	BB-IB	HP	SO	AVG	OBP	SLG	AOPS	ABR	SB-CS	FA	FR	Rng	Thr	G at Pos	BFW
1988	Cin N	14	37	4	5	1	0	0	5	4-0	1	8	.135	.238	.162	16	-4	0-0	1.000	-1	82	0	O-14(0-4-10)	-0.6
Total	8	527	1076	141	256	51	3	17	113	190-14	5	195	.238	.353	.338	92	-3	24-9	.989	2	100	109	O-376(100-169-141)/1-8,D	-0.9
ROETTGER, OSCAR Oscar Frederick Louis "Okkie" B 2.19.1900 St.Louis, MO D 7.4.1986 St.Louis, MO BR/TR 6/170# d7.7 b-Wally ▲																								
1923	NY A	5	2	0	0	0	0	0	0	0	0	0	.000	.000	.000	-98	0	0-0	1.000	0	64	0	/P-5	0.0
1924	NY A	1	0	0	0	0	0	0	0	0	0	0	—	—	—	—	0	0-0	—	0	0	0	/P	0.0
1927	Bro N	5	4	0	0	0	0	0	0	1	1	1	.000	.333	.000	-4	0	0	—	-0	0	0	/O(RF)	-0.1
1932	Phi A	26	60	7	14	1	0	0	6	5	0	4	.233	.292	.250	40	-5	0-0	.978	-1	63	57	1-15	-0.8
Total	4	37	66	7	14	1	0	0	6	6	1	5	.212	.288	.227	34	-5	0-0	.978	-1	63	57	/1-15,P-6,O(RF)	-0.9
ROETTGER, WALLY Walter Henry B 8.28.1902 St.Louis, MO D 9.14.1951 Champaign, IL BR/TR 6-1.5/190# d5.1 b-Oscar																								
1927	StL N	5	1	0	0	0	0	0	0	1	0	0	.000	.500	.000	42	0	0	.500	-1	83	0	/O-3(LF)	-0.1
1928	StL N	68	261	27	89	17	4	6	44	10	3	22	.341	.372	.506	125	9	2	.981	-3	101	31	O-66(33-0-34)	0.1
1929	StL N	79	269	27	68	11	3	3	42	13	0	27	.253	.287	.349	56	-20	0	.993	0	105	66	O-69(7-0-62)	-2.2
1930	NY N	121	420	51	119	15	5	5	51	25	4	29	.283	.330	.379	72	-20	1	**.992**	-3	91	109	*O-114(28-85-4)	-2.5
1931	Cin N	44	185	25	65	11	4	1	20	7	1	9	.351	.378	.470	135	8	1	.990	-0	101	75	O-44(18-2-24)	0.6
	†StL N	45	151	16	43	12	2	0	17	9	3	14	.285	.337	.391	92	-2	0	.974	-3	92	28	O-42(8-7-27)	-0.7
	Year	89	336	41	108	23	6	1	37	16	4	23	.321	.360	.435	114	6	1	.983	-4	97	53	O-86(26-9-51)	-0.1
1932	Cin N	106	347	26	96	18	3	3	43	23	1	24	.277	.323	.372	89	-5	0	.991	2	108	53	O-94(89-5-0)	-0.8
1933	Cin N	84	209	13	50	7	1	1	17	8	0	10	.239	.267	.297	62	-11	0	.977	2	111	88	O-55(26-1-28)	-1.2
1934	Pit N	47	106	7	26	5	1	0	11	3	0	8	.245	.266	.311	53	-7	0	1.000	1	115	64	O-23(19-0-4)	-0.7
Total	8	599	1949	192	556	96	23	19	245	99	12	143	.285	.324	.387	85	-48	4	.986	-4	102	68	O-510(231-100-183)	-7.5
ROETZ, ED Edward Bernard B 8.6.1905 Philadelphia, PA D 3.16.1965 Philadelphia, PA BR/TR 5-10/160# d5.26																								
1929	StL A	16	45	7	11	4	1	0	5	4	0	6	.244	.306	.378	72	-2	0-0	.909	-2	84	140	/S-8,1-5,2-2,3	-0.3
ROGELL, BILLY William George B 11.24.1904 Springfield, IL D 8.9.2003 Sterling Heights, MI BB/TR 5-10.5/163# d4.14																								
1925	Bos A	58	169	12	33	5	1	0	17	11	0	17	.195	.244	.237	22	-21	0-3	.935	6	113	114	2-49/S-6	-1.3
1927	Bos A	82	207	35	55	14	6	2	28	24	0	28	.266	.342	.420	99	-1	3-1	.966	6	123	73	3-53/2-2,O-2(1-0-1)	0.8
1928	Bos A	102	296	33	69	10	4	0	29	22	4	47	.233	.295	.294	56	-19	2-6	.935	-2	104	84	S-67,2-22/O-6(1-2-3),3-3	-1.6
1930	Det A	54	144	20	24	4	2	0	9	15	1	23	.167	.250	.222	20	-18	1-2	.938	3	105	85	S-33,3-13/O(LF)	-1.1
1931	Det A	48	185	21	56	12	3	2	24	24	0	17	.303	.383	.432	110	3	8-8	.958	7	116	84	S-48	1.2
1932	Det A	144	554	88	150	29	6	9	61	50	1	38	.271	.332	.394	84	-14	14-6	.944	11	105	104	*S-139/3-4	0.8
1933	Det A	**155**	587	67	173	42	11	0	57	79	3	33	.295	.381	.404	106	8	6-9	.944	19	104	**133**	*S-155	3.4
1934	†Det A	**154**	592	114	175	32	8	3	100	74	0	36	.296	.374	.392	97	-1	13-3	.962	10	104	108	*S-154	2.1
1935	†Det A	150	560	88	154	23	11	6	71	80	1	29	.275	.367	.387	99	0	3-6	**.971**	11	104	**114**	*S-150	1.9
1936	Det A	146	585	85	160	27	5	6	68	73	3	41	.274	.357	.368	79	-19	14-10	**.965**	2	101	104	*S-146/3	-0.5
1937	Det A	146	536	85	148	30	7	8	64	83	3	48	.276	.376	.403	94	-3	5-5	**.967**	1	99	112	*S-146	0.7
1938	Det A	136	501	76	130	22	8	3	55	86	5	37	.259	.373	.353	78	-14	9-2	.959	10	**106**	109	*S-134	0.6
1939	Det A	74	174	24	40	6	3	2	23	26	0	14	.230	.330	.333	65	-9	3-1	.931	0	95	115	S-43,3-21/2-2	-0.5
1940	Chi N	33	59	7	8	0	0	1	3	2	0	8	.136	.164	.186	-4	-9	1	.900	-4	84	83	S-14/3-9,2-3	-1.2
Total	14	1482	5149	755	1375	256	75	42	609	649	21	416	.267	.351	.370	84	-117	82-62	.956	80	104	109	*S-1235,3-104/2-78,O-9(3-2-4)	5.3
ROGERS, EDDIE Edward Antonio B 8.10.1978 San Pedro De Macoris, D.R. BR/TR 6-1/165# d9.5																								
2002	Bal A	5	3	0	0	0	0	0	0	0-0	0	0	.000	.000	.000	-99	-1	0-0	1.000	1	226	196	/S-4	0.0
ROGERS, EMMETT Emmett E. B 10.11.1870 Hot Springs, AR D 10.24.1941 Fprt Smith, AR BB 5-10/165# d4.19																								
1890	Tol AA	35	110	18	19	3	3	0	7	14	0		.173	.266	.255	52	-7	2	.924	5	*115*	*96*	C-34/O(LF)	0.1
ROGERS, FRALEY Fraley W. B 1850 Brooklyn, NY D 5.10.1881 New York, NY 5-8/184# d4.30																								
1872	Bos NA	45	204	39	56	7	1	1	28	1		4	.275	.278	.333	83	-5	2-0	.790	-3	89	138	*O-41(4-0-38)/1-6	-0.3
1873	Bos NA	2	11	2	4	1	0	0	3	0		2	.364	.364	.455	131	0	0-0	.893	-0	0	96	/1-2	0.0
Total	2 NA	47	215	41	60	8	1	1	31	1		6	.279	.282	.340	85	-5	2-0	.790	-3	89	138	/O-41(4-0-38),1-8	-0.3
ROGERS, JIM James F. B 4.9.1872 Hartford, CT 5-7.5/180# d4.17 M1																								
1896	Was N	38	154	21	43	6	4	1	30	10	0	9	.279	.323	.390	87	-4	3	.882	-2	111	40	3-32/2-6,O(CF)	-0.4
	Lou N	72	290	39	75	8	6	0	38	15	1	14	.259	.297	.328	67	-15	13	.971	-1	115	100	1-60,S-12	-1.3
	Year	110	444	60	118	14	10	1	68	25	1	23	.266	.306	.349	74	-18	16	.971	-3	115	100	1-60,3-32,S-12/2-6,O(CF)	-1.7
1897	Lou N	42	153	22	22	3	2	2	22	23	1		.144	.260	.229	31	-16	4	.929	-3	98	89	2-40/1-3,M	-1.5
Total	2	152	597	82	140	17	12	3	90	48	2	23	.235	.294	.318	63	-35	20	.970	-6	114	97	/1-63,2-46,3-32,S-12,O(CF)	-3.2
ROGERS, JAY Jay Lewis B 8.3.1888 Sandusky, NY D 7.1.1964 Carlisle, NY BR/TR 5-11.5/178# d5.22																								
1914	NY A	5	8	0	0	0	0	0	0	0	0	4	.000	.000	.000	-99	-2	0	.923	-0	*121*	*49*	/C-4	-0.2
ROGERS, PACKY Stanley Frank (born Stanley Frank Hazinski) B 4.26.1913 Swoyersville, PA D 5.15.1998 Elmira, NY BR/TR 5-8/175# d7.12																								
1938	Bro N	23	37	3	7	1	1	0	5	6	0	6	.189	.302	.270	57	-2	0	1.000	-1	94	42	/S-9,3-8,2-3,O(LF)	-0.3
ROGODZINSKI, MIKE Michael George B 2.22.1948 Evanston, IL BL/TR 6/185# d5.4																								
1973	Phi N	66	80	13	19	3	0	2	7	12-1	0	19	.237	.333	.350	88	-1	0-0	.947	0	89	244	O-16(5-0-13)	-0.1
1974	Phi N	17	15	1	1	0	0	0	1	2-0	0	3	.067	.176	.067	-29	-3	0-0	—	-0	0	0	/O(RF)	-0.3
1975	Phi N	16	19	3	5	1	0	0	4	3-0	0	2	.263	.364	.316	86	0	0-1	.667	-1	51	0	/O-2(LF)	-0.1
Total	3	99	114	17	25	4	0	2	12	17-1	0	24	.219	.318	.307	73	-4	0-1	.909	-0	82	199	/O-19(7-0-14)	-0.5
ROHDE, DAVE David Grant B 5.8.1964 Los Altos, CA BB/TR 6-2/180# d4.9																								
1990	Hou N	59	98	8	18	4	0	0	5	9-2	5	20	.184	.283	.224	44	-7	0-0	1.000	-1	108	105	2-32/3-4,S-2	-0.8
1991	Hou N	29	41	3	5	0	0	0	0	5-0	0	8	.122	.217	.122	-2	-6	0-0	1.000	2	123	56	/2-4,3-3,S-3,1	-0.4
1992	Cle A	5	7	0	0	0	0	0	0	2-1	0	3	.000	.222	.000	-34	-1	0-0	.900	1	131	248	/3-5	0.0
Total	3	93	146	11	23	4	0	0	5	16-3	5	31	.158	.262	.185	27	-14	0-0	1.000	1	110	98	/2-36,3-12,S-5,1	-1.2
ROHE, GEORGE George Anthony "Whitey" B 9.15.1875 Cincinnati, OH D 6.10.1957 Cincinnati, OH BR/TR 5-9/165# d5.7																								
1901	Bal A	14	36	7	10	2	0	0	4	5	1		.278	.381	.333	95	0	1	.912	-2	27	94	/1-8,3-6	-0.2
1905	Chi A	34	113	14	24	1	0	1	12	12	4		.212	.310	.248	81	-2	2	.934	-1	89	191	2-17,3-17	-0.3
1906	†Chi A	77	225	14	58	5	1	0	25	16	3		.258	.316	.289	92	-2	8	.926	5	114	133	3-57/2-5,O(LF)	0.5
1907	Chi A	144	494	46	105	11	2	2	51	39	3		.213	.274	.255	71	-15	16	.898	-2	108	199	3-76,2-39,S-30	-1.6
Total	4	269	868	81	197	19	3	3	92	72	11		.227	.294	.266	79	-19	27	.917	-1	110	189	3-156/2-61,S-30,1-8,O(LF)	-1.6
ROHN, DAN Daniel Jay B 1.10.1956 Alpena, MI BL/TR 5-7/165# d9.2																								
1983	Chi N	23	31	3	12	3	2	0	6	2-0	0	2	.387	.424	.613	176	3	1-0	.923	-0	95	73	/2-6,S	0.3
1984	Chi N	25	31	1	4	0	0	1	3	1-0	0	6	.129	.152	.226	6	-4	0-0	1.000	-1	121	173	/3-7,2-5,S-5	-0.5
1986	Cle A	6	10	1	2	0	0	0	2	1-0	0	1	.200	.273	.200	32	-1	0-0	.900	0	178	121	/2-2,3-2,S	0.0
Total	3	54	72	5	18	3	2	1	11	4-0	0	9	.250	.286	.389	82	-2	1-0	.930	-1	103	63	/2-13,3-9,S-7	-0.2
ROHRMEIER, DAN Daniel B 9.27.1965 Cincinnati, OH BR/TR 6/185# d9.3																								
1997	Sea A	7	9	4	3	0	0	0	2	2-0	0	4	.333	.455	.333	111	0	0-0	1.000	0	295	0	/1-3,D-4	0.1
ROHWER, RAY Ray B 6.5.1895 Dixon, CA D 1.24.1988 Davis, CA BL/TL 5-10/155# d4.13																								
1921	Pit N	30	40	6	10	3	2	0	6	4	0	8	.250	.318	.425	93	-1	0-1	.842	0	100	218	O-10(0-3-7)	-0.1
1922	Pit N	53	129	19	38	6	3	3	22	10	1	17	.295	.350	.457	105	1	1-0	.938	1	97	137	O-30(0-2-28)	-0.1
Total	2	83	169	25	48	9	5	3	28	14	1	25	.284	.342	.450	102	0	1-1	.917	1	98	152	/O-40(0-5-35)	-0.2
ROIG, TONY Anton Ambrose B 12.23.1927 New Orleans, LA BR/TR 6-1/180# d9.13																								
1953	Was A	3	8	0	1	1	0	0	0	0	0	1	.125	.125	.250	-1	-1	0-0	1.000	1	114	126	/2-2	0.0
1955	Was A	29	57	3	13	1	1	0	4	2-0	0	15	.228	.254	.281	46	-5	0-0	.932	0	114	126	S-21/3-8,2	-0.4
1956	Was A	44	119	11	25	5	2	0	7	20-0	0	29	.210	.321	.286	62	-6	2-0	.973	5	119	114	2-27,S-19	0.1
Total	3	76	184	14	39	7	3	0	11	22-0	0	45	.212	.295	.283	55	-12	2-0	.927	5	108	99	/S-40,2-30,3-8	-0.3
ROJAS, COOKIE Octavio Victor (Rivas) B 3.6.1939 Havana, Cuba BR/TR 5-10/170# d4.10 M2 C14 OF Total (79-LF 124-CF 10-RF)																								
1962	Cin N	39	86	9	19	2	0	0	6	9-1	1	4	.221	.302	.244	47	-6	1-1	.949	-3	84	92	2-30/3	-0.8
1963	Phi N	64	77	18	17	0	1	1	2	3-0	1	8	.221	.259	.286	57	-5	4-1	.991	9	136	124	2-25/O(LF)	0.7

Year	Tm Lg	G	AB	R	H	2B	3B	HR	RBI	BB-IB	HP	SO	AVG	OBP	SLG	AOPS	ABR	SB-CS	FA	FR	Rng	Thr	G at Pos	BFW
1964	Phi N	109	340	58	99	19	5	2	31	22-0	2	17	.291	.334	.394	107	3	1-3	.967	-5	96	196	O-70(23-54-1),2-20,S-18/C3	-0.3
1965	Phi N★	142	521	78	158	25	3	3	42	42-3	3	33	.303	.356	.380	110	8	5-5	.986	-1	93	105	2-84,O-55(11-41-5),S-11/C-2,1	1.3
1966	Phi N	156	626	77	168	18	1	6	55	35-3	4	46	.268	.310	.329	78	-18	4-6	.983	-9	98	105	*2-106,O-56(30-28-3)/S-2	-2.3
1967	Phi N	147	528	60	137	21	2	4	45	30-3	0	58	.259	.297	.330	79	-15	8-4	.977	-5	97	112	*2-137/O-9(8-1-1),C-3,S-2,P3	-0.9
1968	Phi N	152	621	53	144	19	0	9	48	16-2	0	55	.232	.248	.306	67	-27	4-8	**.987**	15	103	118	*2-150/C	-0.2
1969	Phi N	110	391	35	89	11	1	4	30	23-1	1	28	.228	.269	.292	60	-22	1-6	.980	1	91	107	2-95/O-2(LF)	-1.8
1970	StL N	23	47	2	5	0	0	0	2	3-0	1	4	.106	.176	.106	-22	-8	0-0	1.000	2	125	150	2-10/O-3(LF),S-2	-0.6
	KC A	98	384	36	100	13	3	2	28	20-0	0	29	.260	.296	.326	72	-16	3-7	.982	4	105	109	2-97	-0.8
1971	KC A★	115	414	56	124	22	2	6	59	39-3	2	35	.300	.357	.406	118	11	8-3	**.991**	-4	98	107	*2-111/S-2,O(LF)	1.5
1972	KC A★	137	487	49	127	25	0	3	53	41-5	1	35	.261	.315	.331	94	-3	2-8	.986	-1	105	102	*2-131/3-6,S-2	0.3
1973	KC A★	139	551	78	152	29	3	6	69	37-1	1	38	.276	.320	.372	88	-8	18-4	.982	13	111	110	*2-137	1.6
1974	KC A☆	144	542	52	147	17	1	6	60	30-4	3	43	.271	.309	.339	83	-12	8-4	**.987**	-18	97	94	*2-141	-2.2
1975	KC A	120	406	34	103	18	2	2	37	30-2	0	24	.254	.304	.323	75	-13	4-5	.980	-10	95	92	*2-117/D	-1.7
1976	†KC A	63	132	11	32	6	0	0	16	8-0	0	15	.242	.280	.288	68	-5	2-0	1.000	-6	76	88	2-40/3-6,1D	-1.1
1977	†KC A	64	156	8	39	9	1	0	10	8-2	0	17	.250	.285	.321	65	-8	1-3	.944	3	106	121	3-31,2-16/D-6	-0.5
Total	16	1822	6309	714	1660	254	25	54	593	396-30	20	489	.263	.306	.337	83	-144	74-68	.984	-14	100	106	*2-1447,O-197C/3-46,S-39,DC1P	-7.8
ROJEK, STAN Stanley Andrew B 4.21.1919 N.Tonawanda, NY D 7.9.1997 N.Tonawanda, NY BR/TR 5-10/170# d9.22 Mil 1943-45																								
1942	Bro N	1	0	1	0	0	0	0	0	0	0	0	—	—	—	—	0	0	—	0			R	0.0
1946	Bro N	45	47	11	13	2	1	0	2	4	0	1	.277	.333	.362	96	0	1	.974	2	114	100	S-15/2-6,3-4	0.3
1947	Bro N	32	80	7	21	0	1	0	7	7	0	3	.262	.322	.287	61	-5	1	.971	5	111	131	S-17/3-9,2-7	0.1
1948	Pit N	**156**	641	85	186	27	5	4	51	61	3	41	.290	.355	.367	94	-5	24	.962	-4	102	105	*S-156	0.1
1949	Pit N	144	557	72	136	19	2	0	31	50	2	31	.244	.309	.285	59	-32	4	.966	1	101	103	*S-144	-2.2
1950	Pit N	76	230	28	59	12	1	0	17	18	1	13	.257	.313	.317	64	-12	2	.967	-10	91	99	S-68/2-3	-1.8
1951	Pit N	8	16	0	3	0	0	0	0	0	0	1	.188	.188	.188	1	-2	0-0	.900	-1	107	0	/S-8	-0.3
	StL N	51	186	21	51	7	3	0	14	10	2	10	.274	.318	.344	78	-6	0-3	.974	2	96	123	S-51	-0.3
	Year	59	202	21	54	7	3	0	14	10	2	11	.267	.308	.332	72	-8	0-3	.968	1	97	113	S-59	-0.6
1952	StL A	9	7	0	1	0	0	0	0	2	0	0	.143	.333	.143	35	-1	0-0	1.000	1	141	79	/S-4,2	0.0
Total	8	522	1764	225	470	67	13	4	122	152	8	100	.266	.327	.326	74	-63	32-3	.965	-4	100	105	S-463/2-17,3-13	-4.1
ROLEN, SCOTT Scott Bruce B 4.4.1975 Evansville, IN BR/TR 6-4/210# d8.1																								
1996	Phi N	37	130	10	33	7	0	4	18	13-0	1	27	.254	.322	.400	89	-2	0-2	.954	-7	72	68	3-37	-0.9
1997	Phi N	156	561	93	159	35	3	21	92	76-4	13	138	.283	.377	.469	121	20	16-6	.948	19	103	110	*3-155	4.0
1998	Phi N	160	601	120	174	45	4	31	110	93-6	11	141	.290	.391	.532	139	37	14-7	.970	13	105	98	*3-159	5.1
1999	Phi N	112	421	74	113	28	1	26	77	67-2	3	114	.268	.368	.525	120	14	12-2	.960	16	**112**	114	*3-112	3.0
2000	Phi N	128	483	88	144	32	6	26	89	51-9	5	99	.298	.370	.551	128	20	8-1	.971	5	102	63	*3-128	2.6
2001	Phi N	151	554	96	160	39	1	25	107	74-6	13	127	.289	.378	.498	129	27	16-5	.973	13	111	86	*3-151	4.2
2002	Phi N★	100	375	52	97	21	4	17	66	52-2	8	68	.259	.358	.472	127	13	5-2	.973	8	107	119	*3-100	2.2
	†StL N	55	205	37	57	8	4	14	44	20-2	4	34	.278	.354	.561	143	11	3-2	.958	12	123	170	3-55	2.3
	Year	155	580	89	154	29	8	31	110	72-4	12	102	.266	.357	.503	133	24	8-4	.967	20	113	137	*3-155	4.5
2003	StL N★	154	559	98	160	49	1	28	104	82-5	9	104	.286	.382	.528	141	37	13-3	.969	-3	102	83	*3-153	3.6
Total	8	1053	3889	668	1097	264	24	192	707	528-36	67	852	.282	.374	.510	129	177	87-30	.965	75	106	98	*3-1050	26.1
ROLFE, RED Robert Abial B 10.17.1908 Penacook, NH D 7.8.1969 Gilford, NH BL/TR 5-11.5/170# d6.29 M4 C1																								
1931	NY A	1	0	0	0	0	0	0	0	0	0	0	—	—	—	—	0	0-0	1.000	-0	0	0	/S	0.0
1934	NY A	89	279	54	80	13	2	0	18	26	0	16	.287	.348	.348	86	-6	2-3	.944	-3	87	124	S-46,3-26	-0.5
1935	NY A	**149**	639	108	192	33	9	5	67	57	3	39	.300	.361	.404	103	2	7-3	**.964**	-7	91	96	*3-136,S-17	0.2
1936	†NY A	135	568	116	181	39	**15**	10	70	68	0	38	.319	.392	.493	121	19	3-0	**.957**	1	98	91	*3-133	2.2
1937	†NY A★	154	648	143	179	34	10	4	62	90	1	53	.276	.365	.378	87	-11	4-2	.962	3	96	95	*3-154	-0.2
1938	†NY A☆	151	631	132	196	36	8	10	80	74	3	44	.311	.386	.441	107	8	13-1	.959	-6	96	99	*3-151	0.9
1939	†NY A★	**152**	648	**139**	**213**	**46**	10	14	80	81	1	41	.329	.404	.495	131	32	7-6	.958	-15	89	86	*3-152	2.0
1940	NY A✳	139	588	102	147	26	6	10	53	50	2	48	.250	.311	.366	78	-21	4-2	.949	0	99	96	*3-138	-1.5
1941	†NY A	136	561	106	148	22	5	8	42	57	0	38	.264	.332	.364	85	-13	3-2	.946	-8	94	121	*3-134	-1.5
1942	†NY A	69	265	42	58	8	2	8	25	23	0	18	.219	.281	.355	80	-9	1-1	.959	5	109	159	3-60	-0.2
Total	10	1175	4827	942	1394	257	67	69	497	526	10	335	.289	.360	.413	100	1	44-20	.956	-28	95	101	*3-1084/S-64	1.4
ROLISON, NATE Nathan Mardis B 3.27.1977 Hattiesburg, MS BL/TR 6-6/240# d9.5																								
2000	Fla N	8	13	0	1	0	0	0	2	1-0	0	4	.077	.125	.077	-45	-3	0-0	1.000	0	113	45	/1-4	-0.3
ROLLING, RAY Raymond Copeland B 9.8.1886 Martinsburg, MO D 8.25.1966 St.Paul, MN BR/TR 5-10.5/160# d9.6																								
1912	StL N	5	15	0	3	0	0	0	0	0	0	5	.200	.200	.200	10	-2	0	.947	-1	92	0	/2-4	-0.2
ROLLINGS, RED William Russell B 3.21.1904 Mobile, AL D 12.31.1964 Mobile, AL BL/TR 5-11/167# d4.17																								
1927	Bos A	82	184	19	49	4	1	0	9	12	4	10	.266	.325	.299	64	-10	3-1	.938	-3	98	27	3-44,1-10/2-2	-1.0
1928	Bos A	50	48	7	11	3	1	0	9	6	0	8	.229	.315	.333	72	-2	0-0	1.000	-2	0	222	/1-5,2-4,O-4(2-0-2),3	-0.4
1930	Bos N	52	123	10	29	6	0	0	10	9	0	5	.236	.288	.285	40	-12	2	.973	1	113	119	3-28,2-10	-0.9
Total	3	184	355	36	89	13	2	0	28	27	4	23	.251	.311	.299	57	-24	5-1	.947	-5	103	64	/3-73,2-16,1-15,0-4(2-0-2)	-2.3
ROLLINS, JIMMY James Calvin B 11.27.1978 Oakland, CA BB/TR 5-8/160# d9.17																								
2000	Phi N	14	53	5	17	1	1	0	5	2-0	0	7	.321	.345	.377	82	-2	3-0	.978	-3	66	125	S-13	-0.3
2001	Phi N★	158	656	97	180	29	**12**	14	54	48-2	2	108	.274	.323	.419	93	-9	**46**-8	.979	-19	92	104	*S-157	-0.8
2002	Phi N★	154	637	82	156	33	**10**	11	60	54-3	4	103	.245	.306	.380	87	-17	31-13	.980	1	103	93	*S-152/2	-0.2
2003	Phi N	156	628	85	165	42	6	8	62	54-4	0	113	.263	.320	.387	89	-11	20-12	.979	-1	103	95	*S-154	0.1
Total	4	482	1974	269	518	105	29	33	181	158-9	6	331	.262	.317	.395	90	-39	100-33	.979	-22	98	98	S-476/2	-1.2
ROLLINS, RICH Richard John "Red" B 4.16.1938 Mount Pleasant, PA BR/TR 5-10/185# d6.16																								
1961	Min A	13	17	3	5	1	0	0	3	2-0	1	2	.294	.400	.353	98	0	0-0	1.000	0	105	97	/2-5,3-4	0.1
1962	Min A★	159	624	96	186	23	5	16	96	75-2	6	61	.298	.374	.428	112	13	3-1	.943	-11	94	118	*3-159/S	0.2
1963	Min A	136	531	75	163	23	1	16	61	36-4	8	59	.307	.359	.444	122	16	2-0	.935	-8	94	96	*3-132/2	0.8
1964	Min A	148	596	87	161	25	**10**	12	68	53-3	5	80	.270	.334	.406	104	3	2-5	.947	-8	94	65	*3-146	-0.7
1965	†Min A	140	469	59	117	22	1	5	32	37-7	4	54	.249	.309	.333	79	-12	4-0	.958	-5	98	103	*3-112,2-16	-1.6
1966	Min A	90	269	30	66	7	1	10	40	13-1	4	34	.245	.286	.390	88	-5	0-2	.953	-4	86	134	3-65/2-2,O(LF)	-1.1
1967	Min A	109	339	31	83	11	2	6	39	27-4	3	58	.245	.305	.342	84	-6	1-1	.963	-6	84	99	3-97	-1.4
1968	Min A	93	203	14	49	5	0	6	30	10-2	3	34	.241	.287	.355	89	-3	3-1	.931	-0	105	56	3-56	-0.4
1969	Sea A	58	187	15	42	7	0	4	21	7-0	5	19	.225	.270	.326	68	-9	2-0	.948	5	115	60	3-47/S	-0.3
1970	Mil A	14	25	3	5	1	0	0	5	3-0	0	4	.200	.276	.240	46	-2	0-0	1.000	2	150	213	/3-7	0.0
	Cle A	42	43	6	10	0	0	2	4	3-0	0	5	.233	.283	.372	75	-2	0-0	.600	-2	41	207	/3-5	-0.3
	Year	56	68	9	15	1	0	2	9	6-0	0	9	.221	.280	.324	65	-3	0-0	.900	0	113	211	3-12	-0.3
Total	10	1002	3303	419	887	125	20	77	399	266-23	39	410	.269	.328	.388	98	-7	17-10	.947	-35	95	96	3-830/2-24,S-2,O(LF)	-4.7
ROLLINSON, BILL William (born William Henry Winslow) B 6.10.1856 Fairfield, ME D 9.28.1938 Bristow, VA d6.17																								
1884	Was U	1	3	0	0	0	0	0		0			.000	.000	.000	-99	-1		.714	-0			/C	-0.1
ROLLS, DAMIAN Damian Michael B 9.15.1977 Manhattan, KS BR/TR 6-2/205# d9.3																								
2000	TB A	4	3	0	1	0	0	0	0	0-0	0	1	.333	.333	.333	70	0	0-0	—	-0	0	0	/3D	0.0
2001	TB A	81	237	33	62	11	1	2	12	10-0	0	47	.262	.291	.342	67	-12	12-4	.968	-2	99	79	2-42,O-25(7-18-0)/3D	-1.0
2002	TB A	21	89	15	26	6	1	0	6	3-0	2	16	.292	.330	.382	90	-1	2-5	.947	1	115	76	O-21(4-4-13)	-0.2
2003	TB A	107	373	43	95	20	0	7	46	19-1	7	84	.255	.301	.365	76	-13	11-3	.972	7	109	128	3-73,O-37(6-0-33)/2-2	-0.5
Total	4	213	702	91	184	37	2	9	64	32-1	9	148	.262	.302	.359	75	-26	25-12	.975	6	103	74	/O-83(17-22-46),3-75,2-44,D-7	-1.7
ROMAN, BILL William Anthony B 10.11.1938 Detroit, MI BL/TL 6-4/190# d9.30																								
1964	Det A	3	8	2	3	0	0	1	1	0-0	0	2	.375	.375	.750	201	1	0-0	1.000	0	96	157	/1-2	0.1
1965	Det A	21	27	0	2	0	0	0	0	2-0	0	7	.074	.138	.074	-38	-5	0-0	1.000	-1	41	69	/1-6	-0.6
Total	2	24	35	2	5	0	0	1	1	2-0	0	9	.143	.189	.229	17	-4	0-0	1.000	-1	57	95	/1-8	-0.5
ROMANO, JASON Jason Anthony B 6.24.1979 Tampa, FL BR/TR 6/185# d4.17																								
2002	Tex A	29	54	8	11	4	0	0	4	4-0	0	13	.204	.254	.278	41	-5	2-0	1.000	1	131	0	O-18(11-8-0)/2-8,3D	-0.3

Year	Tm Lg	G	AB	R	H	2B	3B	HR	RBI	BB-IB	HP	SO	AVG	OBP	SLG	AOPS	ABR	SB-CS	FA	FR	Rng	Thr	G at Pos	BFW
	Col N	18	37	9	12	0	1	0	1	3-0	0	11	.324	.375	.378	89	-1	4-1	.952	-2	119	66	2-12/S-5,O-3(CF),3	-0.2
2003	LA N	37	36	3	3	0	0	0	0	1-0	0	8	.083	.108	.083	-52	-8	2-0	1.000	-1	93	0	O-28(9-17-2)/2	-0.9
Total	2	84	127	20	26	4	1	0	5	8-0	0	32	.205	.250	.252	32	-14	8-1	1.000	-2	115	79	/O-49(20-28-2),2-21,S-5,D-4,3-2	-1.4

ROMANO, JOHNNY John Anthony "Honey" B 8.23.1934 Hoboken, NJ BR/TR 5-11/205# d9.12

Year	Tm Lg	G	AB	R	H	2B	3B	HR	RBI	BB-IB	HP	SO	AVG	OBP	SLG	AOPS	ABR	SB-CS	FA	FR	Rng	Thr	G at Pos	BFW
1958	Chi A	4	7	1	2	0	0	0	1	1-0	0	0	.286	.375	.286	86	0	0-0	1.000	0	*0*	*0*	/C-2	0.0
1959	†Chi A	53	126	20	37	5	1	5	25	23-0	1	18	.294	.407	.468	141	8	0-1	.979	0	*80*	*113*	C-38	1.0
1960	Cle A	108	316	40	86	12	2	16	52	37-4	3	50	.272	.349	.475	126	11	0-0	.988	-8	*84*	*85*	C-99	0.7
1961	Cle A★	142	509	76	152	29	1	21	80	61-3	5	60	.299	.377	.483	132	25	0-0	.989	-6	*111*	*103*	*C-141	2.5
1962	Cle A★	135	459	71	120	19	3	25	81	73-0	5	64	.261	.363	.479	130	21	0-1	.990	-3	*104*	*128*	*C-130	2.4
1963	Cle A	89	255	28	55	5	2	10	34	38-4	2	49	.216	.317	.369	94	-2	4-3	.993	-8	112	114	C-71/O-4(LF)	-0.7
1964	Cle A	106	352	46	85	18	1	19	47	51-6	7	83	.241	.346	.460	124	13	2-2	.991	-7	*86*	*98*	C-96/1	1.1
1965	Chi A	122	356	39	86	11	0	18	48	59-3	5	74	.242	.355	.424	129	15	0-2	.992	3	*92*	*101*	*C-111/O-4(LF),1-2	2.3
1966	Chi A	122	329	33	76	12	0	15	47	58-7	1	72	.231	.344	.404	124	12	0-0	.993	4	*79*	*93*	*C-102	2.2
1967	StL N	24	58	1	7	1	0	0	2	13-0	0	15	.121	.282	.138	24	-5	1-0	.983	-1	*167*	*42*	C-20	-0.5
Total	10	905	2767	355	706	112	10	129	417	414-27	29	485	.255	.354	.443	123	98	7-9	.990	-25	*97*	*103*	C-810/O-8(LF),1-3	11.0

ROMANO, TOM Thomas Michael B 10.25.1958 Syracuse, NY BR/TR 5-10/170# d9.1

Year	Tm Lg	G	AB	R	H	2B	3B	HR	RBI	BB-IB	HP	SO	AVG	OBP	SLG	AOPS	ABR	SB-CS	FA	FR	Rng	Thr	G at Pos	BFW
1987	Mon N	7	3	1	0	0	0	0	0	0-0	0	1	.000	.000	.000	-97	-1	0-0	—	-0	0	0	/O-3(LF)	-0.1

ROMERO, MANDY Armando B 10.29.1967 Miami, FL BB/TR 5-11/200# d7.15

Year	Tm Lg	G	AB	R	H	2B	3B	HR	RBI	BB-IB	HP	SO	AVG	OBP	SLG	AOPS	ABR	SB-CS	FA	FR	Rng	Thr	G at Pos	BFW
1997	SD N	21	48	7	10	0	0	2	4	2-0	0	18	.208	.240	.333	52	-4	1-0	1.000	2	67	49	C-19	-0.1
1998	SD N	6	9	1	0	0	0	0	0	1-0	0	3	.000	.100	.000	-77	-2	0-0	.963	1	86	127	/C-6	-0.2
	Bos A	12	13	2	3	1	0	0	1	3-0	0	3	.231	.375	.308	79	0	0-0	1.000	1	0	0	/C-4,D-3	0.1
2003	Col N	3	7	2	3	1	0	0	0	0-0	2	1	.429	.556	.571	171	1	0-0	.938	1	49	232	/C-2	0.2
Total	3	42	77	12	16	2	0	2	5	6-0	2	25	.208	.282	.312	57	-5	1-0	.987	4	64	80	/C-31,D-3	-0.0

ROMERO, ED Edgardo Ralph (Rivera) B 12.9.1957 Santurce, P.R. BR/TR 5-11/175# d7.16 OF Total (17-LF 1-CF 14-RF)

Year	Tm Lg	G	AB	R	H	2B	3B	HR	RBI	BB-IB	HP	SO	AVG	OBP	SLG	AOPS	ABR	SB-CS	FA	FR	Rng	Thr	G at Pos	BFW
1977	Mil A	10	25	4	7	1	0	0	2	4-0	0	3	.280	.379	.320	93	0	0-0	.971	-3	91	56	S-10	-0.2
1980	Mil A	42	104	20	27	7	0	1	10	9-0	0	11	.260	.319	.356	87	-2	2-0	.894	-2	102	115	S-22,2-15/3-3	-0.1
1981	†Mil A	44	91	6	18	3	0	1	10	4-0	0	9	.198	.227	.264	45	-7	0-2	.949	5	92	122	S-22,2-18/3-3	0.0
1982	Mil A	52	144	18	36	8	0	1	7	8-0	0	16	.250	.289	.326	73	-5	0-0	.975	-2	96	123	2-39,S-10/3-2,O(LF)	-0.5
1983	Mil A	59	145	17	46	7	0	1	18	8-0	0	8	.317	.348	.386	112	2	1-0	.962	-11	73	103	S-22,O-15(14-0-1)/3-5,2-3,D-5	-0.7
1984	Mil A	116	357	36	90	12	0	1	31	29-2	1	25	.252	.307	.294	71	-14	3-3	.943	5	131	151	3-59,S-39,2-11/1-4,O(RF)D	-0.5
1985	Mil A	88	251	24	63	11	1	0	21	26-0	0	20	.251	.321	.303	72	-9	1-1	.977	6	108	113	S-43,2-31,O-14(2-0-12)/3	0.2
1986	†Bos A	100	233	41	49	11	0	2	23	18-0	2	16	.210	.270	.283	51	-16	2-0	.959	-8	85	84	S-75,3-18/2-4,O(CF)	-1.8
1987	Bos A	88	235	23	64	5	0	0	14	18-0	0	22	.272	.322	.294	64	-12	0-2	.973	-0	106	108	2-29,S-24,3-24/1-8	-1.0
1988	†Bos A	31	75	3	18	3	0	0	5	3-0	1	8	.240	.272	.280	55	-5	0-0	1.000	-2	66	66	3-15/S-8/2-5,1D	-0.6
1989	Bos A	46	113	14	24	4	0	0	6	7-1	1	7	.212	.260	.248	42	-9	0-2	.983	7	105	126	2-22,3-14,S-10/D-2	-0.2
	Atl N	7	19	1	5	1	0	1	1	0-0	0	0	.263	.263	.474	104	0	0-0	.947	4	141	121	/2-4,S-2,3	0.4
	Mil A	15	50	3	10	3	0	0	3	0-0	0	10	.200	.200	.260	29	-5	0-0	1.000	-3	86	75	2-11/3-4,S	-0.8
1990	Det A	32	70	8	16	3	0	0	4	6-1	0	4	.229	.286	.271	57	-4	0-0	.982	0	95	216	3-27/D-3	-0.4
Total	12	730	1912	218	473	79	1	8	155	140-4	5	159	.247	.298	.302	67	-86	9-10	.958	-4	94	92	S-288,2-192,3-176/O-32L,1-13,D	-6.2

ROMINE, KEVIN Kevin Andrew B 5.23.1961 Exeter, NH BR/TR 5-11/185# d9.5

Year	Tm Lg	G	AB	R	H	2B	3B	HR	RBI	BB-IB	HP	SO	AVG	OBP	SLG	AOPS	ABR	SB-CS	FA	FR	Rng	Thr	G at Pos	BFW
1985	Bos A	24	28	3	6	2	0	0	1	1-0	0	4	.214	.241	.286	42	-2	1-0	1.000	1	114	179	O-23(12-1-12)/D	-0.2
1986	Bos A	35	35	6	9	2	0	0	2	3-0	0	9	.257	.316	.314	72	-1	2-0	1.000	2	123	130	O-33(0-28-5)	0.1
1987	Bos A	9	24	5	7	2	0	0	2	2-0	0	6	.292	.346	.375	89	0	0-0	1.000	0	74	294	/O-7(1-4-3),D-2	0.0
1988	†Bos A	57	78	17	15	2	1	1	6	7-0	0	15	.192	.259	.282	49	-5	2-0	.957	-3	84	0	O-45(5-9-38)/D-5	-0.9
1989	Bos A	92	274	30	75	13	0	1	23	21-1	2	53	.274	.327	.332	82	-6	1-1	.982	1	89	204	O-89(9-48-32)/D-2	-0.7
1990	Bos A	70	136	21	37	7	0	2	14	12-0	1	27	.272	.331	.368	92	-1	4-0	.976	-3	92	0	O-64(16-18-30)/D	-0.5
1991	Bos A	44	55	7	9	2	0	1	7	3-0	0	10	.164	.207	.255	26	-6	1-1	.964	-1	95	0	O-23(10-4-10),D-14	-0.8
Total	7	331	630	89	158	30	1	5	55	49-1	3	124	.251	.306	.325	73	-21	11-2	.980	-3	93	112	O-284(53-112-130)/D-25	-3.0

RONAN, MARC Edward Marcus B 9.19.1969 Ozark, AL BL/TR 6-2/190# d9.21

Year	Tm Lg	G	AB	R	H	2B	3B	HR	RBI	BB-IB	HP	SO	AVG	OBP	SLG	AOPS	ABR	SB-CS	FA	FR	Rng	Thr	G at Pos	BFW
1993	StL N	6	12	0	1	0	0	0	0	0-0	0	5	.083	.083	.083	-56	-3	0-0	1.000	2	0	0	/C-6	-0.1

RONDEAU, HENRI Henri Joseph B 5.7.1887 Danielson, CT D 5.28.1943 Woonsocket, RI BL/TR 5-11/175# d4.11

Year	Tm Lg	G	AB	R	H	2B	3B	HR	RBI	BB-IB	HP	SO	AVG	OBP	SLG	AOPS	ABR	SB-CS	FA	FR	Rng	Thr	G at Pos	BFW
1913	Det A	36	70	5	13	2	0	0	5	14	0	16	.186	.321	.214	58	-3	1	1.000	-2	*77*	*124*	C-16/1-6	-0.4
1915	Was A	14	40	3	7	0	0	0	4	4	0	3	.175	.250	.175	27	-4	1-2	1.000	2	131	136	O-11(LF)	-0.3
1916	Was A	50	162	20	36	5	3	1	28	18	3	18	.222	.311	.309	87	-3	7	.958	3	126	68	O-48(31-0-17)	-0.2
Total	3	100	272	28	56	7	3	1	37	36	3	37	.206	.305	.265	71	-10	9-2	.967	3	127	82	/O-59(42-0-17),C-16,1-6	-0.9

ROOF, GENE Eugene Lawrence B 1.13.1958 Paducah, KY BB/TR 6-2/180# d9.3 C4 b-Phil

Year	Tm Lg	G	AB	R	H	2B	3B	HR	RBI	BB-IB	HP	SO	AVG	OBP	SLG	AOPS	ABR	SB-CS	FA	FR	Rng	Thr	G at Pos	BFW
1981	StL N	23	60	11	18	6	0	0	3	12-2	0	16	.300	.411	.400	129	3	5-1	.950	-1	109	0	O-20(LF)	0.3
1982	StL N	11	15	3	4	0	0	0	2	1-0	0	4	.267	.313	.267	63	-1	2-0	1.000	-0	102	0	/O-5(4-0-2)	-0.1
1983	StL N	6	3	1	0	0	0	0	0	0-0	0	0	.000	.000	.000	-99	-1	0-0	—	-0	0	0	/O(LF)	-0.1
	Mon N	8	12	2	2	2	0	0	1	1-0	0	3	.167	.231	.333	55	-1	0-0	1.000	-0	81	0	/O-5(0-1-4)	-0.1
	Year	14	15	3	2	2	0	0	1	1-0	0	3	.133	.188	.267	25	-2	0-0	1.000	-0	77	0	/O-6(1-1-4)	-0.2
Total	3	48	90	17	24	8	0	0	6	14-2	0	23	.267	.362	.356	102	0	7-1	.958	-1	105	0	/O-31(25-1-6)	0.0

ROOF, PHIL Phillip Anthony B 3.5.1941 Paducah, KY BR/TR 6-3/210# d4.29 C9 b-Gene

Year	Tm Lg	G	AB	R	H	2B	3B	HR	RBI	BB-IB	HP	SO	AVG	OBP	SLG	AOPS	ABR	SB-CS	FA	FR	Rng	Thr	G at Pos	BFW
1961	Mil N	1	0	0	0	0	0	0	0	0-0	0	0	—	—	—	—	0	0-0	1.000	0	*0*	*0*	/C	0.0
1964	Mil N	1	2	0	0	0	0	0	0	0-0	0	1	.000	.000	.000	-99	-1	0-0	1.000	0	*0*	*0*	/C	0.0
1965	Cal A	9	22	1	3	0	0	0	0	0-0	0	6	.136	.136	.136	-23	-4	0-0	.983	3	*153*	*130*	/C-9	0.0
	Cle A	43	52	3	9	1	0	0	3	5-1	1	13	.173	.259	.192	30	-5	0-0	.994	8	*153*	*175*	C-41	0.5
	Year	52	74	4	12	1	0	0	3	5-1	1	19	.162	.225	.176	15	-8	0-0	.992	12	*153*	*162*	C-50	0.5
1966	KC A	127	369	33	77	14	3	7	44	37-6	3	95	.209	.285	.320	76	-11	2-5	.985	-1	*78*	*89*	*C-123/1-2	-0.9
1967	KC A	114	327	23	67	14	5	6	24	23-5	5	85	.205	.266	.333	79	-9	4-1	.991	-4	94	67	*C-113	-0.8
1968	Oak A	34	64	5	12	0	0	1	2	2-0	0	15	.188	.212	.234	37	-5	1-0	.968	-5	71	57	C-32	-1.0
1969	Oak A	106	247	19	58	6	1	2	19	33-3	5	55	.235	.337	.291	81	-5	1-0	.983	-1	127	83	*C-106	-0.2
1970	Mil A	110	321	39	73	7	1	13	37	32-1	5	72	.227	.306	.377	87	-6	3-2	.988	-2	69	108	*C-107/1	-0.4
1971	Mil A	41	114	6	22	2	1	1	10	8-1	1	28	.193	.252	.254	44	-9	0-0	.975	5	196	161	C-39	-0.2
	Min A	31	87	6	21	4	0	0	6	8-0	0	18	.241	.305	.287	67	-4	0-1	.985	6	118	81	C-29	0.4
	Year	72	201	12	43	6	1	1	16	16-1	1	46	.214	.275	.269	54	-12	0-1	.980	11	160	125	C-68	0.2
1972	Min A	61	146	16	30	11	1	3	12	6-0	0	27	.205	.235	.356	71	-6	0-1	.978	-5	133	75	C-61	-1.0
1973	Min A	47	117	10	23	4	1	1	15	13-0	0	27	.197	.277	.274	53	-7	0-0	.992	1	91	95	C-47	-0.5
1974	Min A	44	97	10	19	1	0	2	13	6-0	2	24	.196	.257	.268	50	-7	0-0	1.000	3	96	162	C-44	-0.2
1975	Min A	63	126	18	38	2	0	7	21	9-1	1	28	.302	.353	.484	133	5	0-0	.989	2	95	106	C-63	0.9
1976	Min A	18	46	1	10	3	0	0	4	2-0	0	6	.217	.250	.283	55	-3	0-0	.962	3	50	184	C-12/D	0.1
	Chi A	4	9	0	1	0	0	0	0	0-0	0	3	.111	.111	.111	-35	-2	0-0	1.000	-0	0	164	/C-4	-0.2
	Year	22	55	1	11	3	0	0	4	2-0	0	9	.200	.228	.255	40	-4	0-0	.967	3	39	180	C-16/D	-0.1
1977	Tor A	3	5	0	0	0	0	0	0	0-0	0	0	.000	.000	.000	-99	-1	0-0	1.000	-1	33	237	/C-3	-0.2
Total	15	857	2151	190	463	69	13	43	210	184-18	23	504	.215	.283	.319	73	-80	11-10	.986	15	*100*	*99*	C-835/1-3,D	-3.7

ROOKS, GEORGE George Brinton McClellan (born George Brinton Mc Clellan Ruckser) B 10.21.1863 Chicago, IL D 3.11.1935 Chicago, IL BR/TR 5-11/170# d5.12 gs-Lou Possehl

Year	Tm Lg	G	AB	R	H	2B	3B	HR	RBI	BB-IB	HP	SO	AVG	OBP	SLG	AOPS	ABR	SB-CS	FA	FR	Rng	Thr	G at Pos	BFW
1891	Bos N	5	16	1	2	0	0	0	0	4	0	1	.125	.300	.125	23	-1	0	1.000	1	121	0	/O-5(LF)	-0.1

ROOMES, ROLANDO Rolando Audley B 2.15.1962 Kingston, Jamaica BR/TR 6-3/180# d4.12

Year	Tm Lg	G	AB	R	H	2B	3B	HR	RBI	BB-IB	HP	SO	AVG	OBP	SLG	AOPS	ABR	SB-CS	FA	FR	Rng	Thr	G at Pos	BFW
1988	Chi N	17	16	3	3	0	0	0	0	0-0	0	4	.188	.188	.188	8	-2	0-1	.833	-1	67	0	/O-5(4-0-1)	-0.4
1989	Cin N	107	315	36	83	18	5	7	34	13-0	3	100	.263	.296	.419	100	-1	12-8	.981	5	117	90	*O-100(45-29-37)	0.1
1990	Cin N	30	61	5	13	0	0	2	7	0-0	0	20	.213	.213	.311	41	-5	0-0	1.000	1	115	99	O-19(12-0-7)	-0.5
	Mon N	16	14	1	4	0	1	0	1	1-1	0	6	.286	.333	.429	112	0	0-2	1.000	-0	85	0	/O-6(3-2-1)	-0.1
	Year	46	75	6	17	0	1	2	8	1-1	0	26	.227	.237	.333	54	-5	0-2	1.000	1	110	81	O-25(15-2-8)	-0.6
Total	3	170	406	45	103	18	6	9	42	14-1	3	130	.254	.282	.394	88	-8	12-11	.980	5	114	85	O-130(64-31-46)	-0.9

Year	Tm Lg	G	AB	R	H	2B	3B	HR	RBI	BB-IB	HP	SO	AVG	OBP	SLG	AOPS	ABR	SB-CS	FA	FR	Rng	Thr	G at Pos	BFW
ROONEY, FRANK Frank (born Frank Rovny) B 10.12.1884 Podebrady, Bohemia (Austria-Hungary) D 4.6.1977 Bessemer, MI d4.18																								
1914	Ind F	12	35	1	7	0	1	1	8	1	0	0	.200	.222	.343	47	-3	2	.980	-1	41	122	/1-9	-0.5
ROONEY, PAT Patrick Eugene B 11.28.1957 Chicago, IL BR/TR 6-1/190# d9.9																								
1981	Mon N	4	5	0	0	0	0	0	0	0-0	0	3	.000	.000	.000	-99	-1	0-0	1.000	-0	57	0	/O-2(RF)	-0.2
ROQUE, JORGE Jorge (Vargas) B 4.28.1950 Ponce, P.R. BR/TR 5-10/158# d9.4																								
1970	StL N	5	1	2	0	0	0	0	0	0-0	1	1	.000	.500	.000	45	0	0-0	—	-0	0	0	/O(LF)	0.0
1971	StL N	3	10	2	3	0	0	0	1	0-0	0	3	.300	.300	.300	68	0	1-0	1.000	-0	86	0	/O-3(CF)	-0.1
1972	StL N	32	67	3	7	2	1	1	5	6-0	0	19	.104	.176	.209	10	-8	1-1	.980	-0	112	0	O-24(0-21-3)	-1.0
1973	Mon N	25	61	7	9	2	0	1	6	4-0	1	17	.148	.212	.230	22	-7	2-2	.878	-1	96	180	O-24(1-23-0)	-0.9
Total	4	65	139	14	19	4	1	2	12	10-0	2	40	.137	.204	.223	20	-15	4-3	.934	-2	103	80	/O-52(2-47-3)	-2.0
ROSADO, LUIS Luis (Robles) B 12.6.1955 Santurce, P.R. BR/TR 6/180# d9.8																								
1977	NY N	9	24	1	5	1	0	0	3	1-0	1	3	.208	.250	.250	42	-2	0-0	.980	-2	109	88	/1-7,C	-0.4
1980	NY N	2	4	0	0	0	0	0	0	0-0	0	1	.000	.000	.000	-99	-1	0-0	1.000	-0	0	141	/1	-0.2
Total	2	11	28	1	5	1	0	0	3	1-0	1	4	.179	.219	.214	23	-3	0-0	.983	-2	95	95	/1-8,C	-0.6
ROSAR, BUDDY Warren Vincent B 7.3.1914 Buffalo, NY D 3.13.1994 Rochester, NY BR/TR 5-9/190# d4.29 Def 1944-45																								
1939	NY A	43	105	18	29	5	1	0	12	13	0	10	.276	.356	.343	81	-3	4-0	.980	4	*165*	*63*	C-35	0.3
1940	NY A	73	228	34	68	11	3	4	37	19	2	11	.298	.357	.425	106	2	7-1	.983	2	*140*	*94*	C-63	0.8
1941	†NY A	67	209	25	60	17	2	1	36	22	0	10	.287	.355	.402	101	1	0-0	.996	1	*138*	*83*	C-60	0.5
1942	†NY A☆	69	209	18	48	10	0	2	34	17	0	20	.230	.288	.306	68	-9	1-2	.996	6	*177*	*86*	C-58	0.0
1943	Cle A☆	115	382	53	108	17	1	1	41	33	0	12	.283	.340	.340	106	3	0-4	.983	9	***146***	*123*	*C-114	1.8
1944	Cle A	99	331	29	87	9	3	0	30	34	4	17	.263	.339	.308	89	-4	1-2	**.989**	-0	*93*	*113*	C-98	0.1
1945	Phi A	92	300	23	63	12	1	1	25	20	1	16	.210	.262	.267	54	-18	2-1	.987	-3	*88*	*108*	C-85	-1.7
1946	Phi A★	121	424	34	120	22	2	2	47	36	0	17	.283	.339	.358	96	-2	1-3	**1.000**	10	*123*	*115*	*C-117	1.4
1947	Phi A★	102	359	40	93	20	2	1	33	40	1	13	.259	.335	.334	85	-7	1-3	**.996**	13	*139*	***129***	*C-102	1.2
1948	Phi A★	90	302	30	77	13	0	4	41	39	2	12	.255	.344	.338	82	-7	0-2	**.997**	0	*115*	*85*	C-90	-0.3
1949	Phi A	32	95	7	19	2	0	0	6	16	0	5	.200	.315	.221	45	-7	0-0	.992	-1	*107*	*57*	C-31	-0.7
1950	Bos A	27	84	13	25	2	0	1	12	7	0	4	.298	.352	.357	75	-3	0-0	.991	-1	*125*	*46*	C-25	-0.3
1951	Bos A	58	170	11	39	7	0	1	13	19	0	14	.229	.307	.288	56	-10	0-0	.996	0	*124*	*55*	C-56	-0.7
Total	13	988	3198	335	836	147	15	18	367	315	10	161	.261	.330	.334	84	-64	17-18	.992	41	*127*	*100*	C-934	2.4
ROSARIO, JIMMY Angel Ramon (Ferrer) B 5.5.1945 Bayamon, P.R. BB/TR 5-10/155# d4.8																								
1971	†SF N	92	192	26	43	6	1	0	13	33-4	1	35	.224	.338	.266	75	-5	7-4	1.000	1	110	30	O-67(9-60-1)	-0.5
1972	SF N	7	2	1	0	0	0	0	0	0-0	0	0	.000	.000	.000	-99	-1	0-1	—	-0	0	0	/O(CF)	-0.1
1976	Mil A	15	37	4	7	0	0	1	5	3-0	0	8	.189	.250	.270	53	-2	1-3	1.000	-1	96	0	O-12(11-2-0)/D-2	-0.5
Total	3	114	231	31	50	6	1	1	18	36-4	1	43	.216	.322	.264	70	-8	8-8	1.000	0	108	25	/O-80(20-63-1),D-2	-1.1
ROSARIO, MEL Melvin Gregorio B 5.25.1973 Santo Domingo, D.R. BB/TR 6/191# d9.11																								
1997	Bal A	4	3	0	0	0	0	0	0	0-0	0	1	.000	.000	.000	-99	-1	0-0	.875	-1	87	0	/C-4	-0.2
ROSARIO, SANTIAGO Santiago B 7.25.1939 Guayanilla, P.R. BL/TL 5-11/165# d6.23																								
1965	KC A	81	85	8	20	3	0	2	8	6-0	1	16	.235	.287	.341	81	-2	0-0	.991	-0	91	53	1-31/O-3(2-0-1)	-0.4
ROSARIO, VICTOR Victor Manuel (Rivera) B 8.26.1966 Hato Mayor Del Rey, D.R. BR/TR 5-11/155# d9.6																								
1990	Atl N	9	7	3	1	0	0	0	0	1-0	0	1	.143	.250	.143	10	-1	0-0	1.000	-1	71	0	/S-3,2	-0.2
ROSE, PETE Peter Edward Jr. B 11.16.1969 Cincinnati, OH BL/TR 6-1/180# d9.1 f-Pete																								
1997	Cin N	11	14	2	2	0	0	0	0	2-0	0	9	.143	.250	.143	6	-2	0-0	.600	-1	102	0	/3-2,1	-0.3
ROSE, PETE Peter Edward Sr. "Charlie Hustle" B 4.14.1941 Cincinnati, OH BB/TR 5-11/200# d4.8 M6 s-Pete OF Total (671-LF 70-CF 594-RF)																								
1963	Cin N	157	623	101	170	25	9	6	41	55-0	5	72	.273	.334	.371	101	1	13-15	.971	-18	85	88	*2-157/O(LF)	-0.6
1964	Cin N	136	516	64	139	13	2	4	34	36-0	2	51	.269	.319	.326	79	-14	4-10	.979	-11	88	93	*2-128	-1.7
1965	Cin N★	**162**	670	117	**209**	35	11	11	81	69-2	8	76	.312	.382	.446	124	24	8-3	.975	-18	84	86	*2-162	2.2
1966	Cin N	156	654	97	205	38	5	16	70	37-3	1	61	.313	.351	.460	113	12	4-9	.981	-11	84	84	*2-140,3-16	1.2
1967	Cin N★	148	585	86	176	32	8	12	76	56-9	3	66	.301	.364	.444	117	15	11-6	.982	-5	107	71	*O-123(123-1-0),2-35	0.7
1968	Cin N✳	149	626	94	**210**	42	6	10	49	56-15	4	76	**.335**	**.391**	.470	149	39	3-7	.990	4	94	157	*O-148(0-7-144)/2-3,1	3.5
1969	Cin N★	156	627	**120**	218	33	11	16	82	88-18	5	65	**.348**	.428	.512	155	50	7-10	.988	-3	97	85	*O-156(0-56-101)/2-2	4.0
1970	†Cin N★	159	649	120	**205**	37	9	15	52	73-10	2	64	.316	.385	.470	128	27	12-7	**.997**	-1	100	72	*O-159(1-5-155)	1.8
1971	Cin N★	160	632	86	192	27	4	13	44	68-15	3	50	.304	.373	.421	127	24	13-9	.994	-0	94	108	*O-158(0-1-158)	1.7
1972	†Cin N	**154**	645	107	**198**	31	11	6	57	73-4	7	46	.307	.382	.417	135	32	10-3	.994	10	103	129	*O-154(LF)	3.5
1973	†Cin N★	160	680	115	**230**	36	8	5	64	65-6	6	42	**.338**	.401	.437	139	38	10-7	.992	8	102	127	*O-159(LF)	3.6
1974	Cin N★	**163**	652	**110**	185	**45**	7	3	51	106-14	5	54	.284	.385	.388	119	23	2-4	**.997**	9	109	94	*O-163(LF)	2.2
1975	†Cin N★	**162**	662	**112**	210	**47**	4	7	74	89-8	11	50	.317	.406	.432	130	33	0-1	.963	-22	86	99	*3-137,O-35(LF)	0.8
1976	†Cin N★	**162**	665	**130**	**215**	**42**	6	10	63	86-7	6	54	.323	.404	.450	139	38	9-5	**.969**	-11	94	91	*3-159/O(RF)	2.8
1977	Cin N★	**162**	655	95	204	38	7	9	64	66-7	5	42	.311	.377	.432	115	16	16-4	.958	-19	86	76	*3-161	-0.3
1978	Cin N★	159	655	103	198	**51**	3	7	52	62-6	3	30	.302	.362	.421	119	19	13-9	.961	-14	88	91	*3-156/O-7(LF),1-2	0.2
1979	Phi N★	**163**	628	90	208	40	5	4	59	95-10	2	32	.331	**.418**	.430	128	31	20-11	.995	-2	94	104	*1-159/3-5,2	2.0
1980	†Phi N★	**162**	655	95	185	**42**	1	1	64	66-5	**6**	33	.282	.352	.354	93	-3	12-8	**.997**	12	**127**	92	*1-162	-0.1
1981	†Phi N★	**107**	431	73	**140**	18	5	0	33	46-5	3	26	.325	.391	.390	118	12	4-4	.996	11	132	82	*1-107	1.7
1982	Phi N★	**162**	634	80	172	25	4	3	54	66-9	7	32	.271	.345	.338	90	-6	8-8	.995	6	107	97	*1-162	-1.2
1983	†Phi N	151	493	52	121	14	3	0	45	52-5	2	28	.245	.316	.286	70	-19	7-7	.990	2	115	81	*1-112,O-35(RF)	-2.7
1984	Mon N	95	278	34	72	6	2	0	23	31-3	1	20	.259	.334	.295	82	-6	1-1	.988	8	171	84	1-40,O-28(LF)	-0.1
	Cin N	26	96	9	35	9	0	0	11	9-1	2	7	.365	.430	.458	143	6	0-0	.990	-2	62	79	1-23/,M	0.3
	Year	121	374	43	107	15	2	0	34	40-4	3	27	.286	.359	.337	99	1	1-1	.989	6	129	82	1-63,O-28(LF)	0.2
1985	Cin N★	119	405	60	107	12	2	2	46	86-5	4	35	.264	.395	.319	98	4	8-1	.995	1	99	94	*1-110/,M	0.0
1986	Cin N	72	237	15	52	8	2	0	25	30-0	4	31	.219	.316	.270	61	-12	3-0	.990	-1	101	117	1-61/,M	-1.6
Total	24	3562	14053	2165	4256	746	135	160	1314	1566-167	107	1143	.303	.375	.409	117	384	198-149	.991	-67	100	102	*O-1327L,1-939,3-634,2-628	23.9
ROSE, BOBBY Robert Richard B 3.15.1967 Covina, CA BR/TR 5-11/170# d8.12																								
1989	Cal A	14	38	4	8	1	2	1	3	2-0	1	10	.211	.268	.421	93	-1	0-0	.920	-2	91	69	3-10/2-3	-0.2
1990	Cal A	7	13	5	5	0	0	1	2	2-0	0	1	.385	.467	.615	204	2	0-0	1.000	-1	77	0	/2-4,3-3	0.1
1991	Cal A	22	65	5	18	5	1	1	8	3-0	0	13	.277	.304	.431	102	0	0-0	1.000	1	118	116	/2-8,O-7(6-0-1),3-4,1-3	0.1
1992	Cal A	30	84	10	18	5	0	2	10	8-1	2	9	.214	.295	.345	79	-2	1-1	.953	9	142	115	2-28/1-2	0.7
Total	4	73	200	24	49	11	3	5	23	15-1	3	33	.245	.305	.405	98	-1	1-1	.965	8	132	106	/2-43,3-17,O-7(6-0-1),1-5	0.7
ROSEBORO, JOHNNY John Junior B 5.13.1933 Ashland, OH D 8.16.2002 Los Angeles, CA BL/TR 5-11.5/190# d6.14 C5																								
1957	Bro N	35	69	6	10	2	0	2	6	10-2	0	20	.145	.253	.261	35	-6	0-0	.972	2	*151*	*68*	C-19/1-5	-0.4
1958	LA N☆	114	384	52	104	11	9	14	43	36-2	2	56	.271	.333	.456	104	1	11-8	.987	-7	***132***	*108*	*C-104/O-5(4-1-0)	-0.2
1959	†LA N	118	397	39	92	14	7	10	38	52-11	3	69	.232	.322	.378	81	-11	7-5	.991	9	***211***	*102*	*C-117	0.4
1960	LA N	103	287	22	61	15	3	8	42	44-6	4	53	.213	.323	.369	84	-5	7-6	.993	6	*138*	*94*	C-87/13	0.5
1961	LA N★	128	394	59	99	16	6	18	59	56-8	4	62	.251	.346	.459	104	2	6-4	.986	7	*103*	*89*	*C-125	1.5
1962	LA N★	128	389	45	97	16	7	7	55	50-11	7	60	.249	.341	.380	101	1	12-3	.985	-1	*112*	*85*	*C-128	0.8
1963	†LA N	135	470	50	111	13	7	9	49	36-3	3	50	.236	.291	.351	91	-7	7-6	.992	-2	*129*	*67*	*C-134	-0.3
1964	LA N	134	414	42	119	24	1	3	45	44-9	4	61	.287	.357	.372	115	11	3-3	.993	4	***143***	*110*	*C-128	2.1
1965	†LA N	136	437	42	102	10	0	8	57	34-7	2	51	.233	.289	.311	75	-15	1-6	.994	0	*120*	*85*	*C-131/3	-1.1
1966	†LA N	142	445	47	123	23	2	9	53	44-13	3	51	.276	.343	.398	115	10	3-2	.993	12	***130***	*89*	*C-138	2.9
1967	LA N	116	334	37	91	18	2	4	24	38-12	2	33	.272	.348	.374	117	8	2-4	.984	-5	*117*	*113*	*C-107	0.8
1968	Min A	135	380	31	82	12	0	8	39	46-9	2	57	.216	.300	.311	82	-7	2-3	.991	4	108	75	*C-117	0.2
1969	†Min A★	115	361	33	95	12	0	3	32	39-12	0	44	.263	.333	.321	83	-8	5-5	.980	3	112	76	*C-111	0.0
1970	Was A	46	86	7	20	4	0	1	6	18-5	0	10	.233	.365	.314	94	0	1-1	1.000	-2	71	33	C-30	-0.1
Total	14	1585	4847	512	1206	190	44	104	548	547-110	36	677	.249	.326	.371	95	-26	67-56	.989	31	*129*	*89*	*C-1476/1-6,O-5(4-1-0),3-2	7.1
ROSELLI, BOB Robert Edward B 12.10.1931 San Francisco, CA BR/TR 5-11/185# d8.16																								
1955	Mil N	6	9	1	2	1	0	0	0	1-0	1	4	.222	.364	.333	91	0	0-0	.917	-0	*0*	*204*	/C-2	0.0

Year	Tm Lg	G	AB	R	H	2B	3B	HR	RBI	BB-IB	HP	SO	AVG	OBP	SLG	AOPS	ABR	SB-CS	FA	FR	Rng	Thr	G at Pos	BFW
1956	Mil N	4	2	1	1	0	0	1	1	0-0	0	1	.500	.500	2.000	564	1	0-0	1.000	1	*0*	*0*	/C-3	0.2
1958	Mil N	1	1	0	0	0	0	0	0	0-0	0	0	.000	.000	.000	-99	0	0-0	—	0			H	0.0
1961	Chi A	22	38	2	10	3	0	0	4	0-0	0	11	.263	.263	.342	61	-2	0-0	1.000	-1	*103*	*85*	C-10	-0.2
1962	Chi A	35	64	4	12	3	1	1	5	11-1	1	15	.188	.316	.313	70	-2	1-0	.988	-1	*70*	*79*	C-20	-0.3
Total	5	68	114	8	25	7	1	2	10	12-1	2	31	.219	.305	.351	76	-3	1-0	.986	-1	*70*	*88*	/C-35	-0.3

ROSELLO, DAVE David (Rodriguez) B 6.26.1950 Mayaguez, P.R. BR/TR 5-11/160# d9.10

Year	Tm Lg	G	AB	R	H	2B	3B	HR	RBI	BB-IB	HP	SO	AVG	OBP	SLG	AOPS	ABR	SB-CS	FA	FR	Rng	Thr	G at Pos	BFW
1972	Chi N	5	12	2	3	0	0	1	3	3-0	0	2	.250	.400	.500	139	1	0-0	.846	-0	88	173	/S-5	0.1
1973	Chi N	16	38	4	10	2	0	0	2	2-0	0	4	.263	.300	.316	66	-2	2-2	.964	-1	85	78	2-13/S	-0.2
1974	Chi N	62	148	9	30	7	0	0	10	10-1	0	28	.203	.252	.250	39	-12	1-1	.972	-5	91	130	2-49,S-12	-1.5
1975	Chi N	19	58	7	15	2	0	1	8	9-2	0	8	.259	.348	.345	92	0	0-1	.952	-3	92	58	S-19	-0.2
1976	Chi N	91	227	27	55	5	1	1	11	41-8	1	33	.242	.359	.286	78	-4	1-2	.966	-5	95	100	S-86/2	-0.1
1977	Chi N	56	82	18	18	2	1	1	9	12-1	0	12	.220	.319	.305	62	-4	0-0	.938	-3	108	103	3-21,S-10/2-3	-0.7
1979	Cle A	59	107	20	26	6	1	3	14	15-0	0	27	.243	.328	.402	98	0	1-0	.976	-8	105	61	2-33,3-14,S-11	-0.7
1980	Cle A	71	117	16	29	3	0	2	12	9-0	0	19	.248	.295	.325	71	-5	0-0	.980	-8	80	74	2-43,3-22/S-3,D	-1.1
1981	Cle A	43	84	11	20	4	0	1	7	7-0	0	12	.238	.297	.321	79	-2	0-1	.979	-2	81	92	2-26/3-8,S-4,D-4	-0.3
Total	9	422	873	114	206	31	3	10	76	108-12	1	145	.236	.318	.313	73	-28	5-7	.975	-35	89	90	2-168,S-151/3-65,D-5	-4.7

ROSEMAN, CHIEF James John B 1856 New York, NY D 7.4.1938 Brooklyn, NY BR/TR 5-7/167# d5.1 M1 ▲

Year	Tm Lg	G	AB	R	H	2B	3B	HR	RBI	BB-IB	HP	SO	AVG	OBP	SLG	AOPS	ABR	SB-CS	FA	FR	Rng	Thr	G at Pos	BFW
1882	Tro N	82	331	41	78	21	6	1	29	3		41	.236	.243	.344	90	-3		.853	-5	114	139	*O-82(1-0-81)	-0.8
1883	NY AA	93	398	48	100	13	6	0		11			.251	.271	.314	84	-8		.855	-6	102	169	*O-91(3-8-80)/1-2	-1.3
1884	†NY AA	107	436	97	130	16	11	4		21	6		.298	.339	.413	148	23		.885	-4	58	0	*O-107(4-103-0)	1.4
1885	NY AA	101	410	72	114	13	14	4	46	25	10		.278	.335	.407	139	19		.865	-7	53	30	*O-101(1-99-1)/P	0.7
1886	NY AA	134	559	90	127	19	10	5	53	24	8		.227	.269	.324	93	-4	6	.891	-4	80	148	*O-134(88-44-3)/P	-1.1
1887	Phi AA	21	73	16	16	2	1	0	8	10	5		.219	.352	.274	76	-2	3	.821	-1	147	140	O-21(CF)	-0.2
	NY AA	60	241	30	55	10	1	1	27	9	3		.228	.265	.290	57	-14	3	.868	-5	69	93	O-59(9-36-14)/1-3,P-2	-1.7
	Bro AA	1	3	2	1	0	0	0	1	0	1		.333	.500	.333	133	0	0	1.000	0	0	0	/O(RF)	0.0
	Year	82	317	48	72	12	2	1	36	19	9		.227	.290	.287	63	-15	6	.856	-6	89	104	O-81(9-57-15)/1-3,P-2	-1.9
1890	StL AA	80	302	47	103	26	0	2	58	30	29		.341	.449	.447	144	19	7	.819	-6	82	112	O-58(17-40-1),1-22,M	0.9
	Lou AA	2	8	0	2	0	0	0	0	0	0		.250	.250	.250	48	-1	0	.864	-1	0	351	/1-2	-0.1
	Year	82	310	47	105	26	0	2	58	30	29		.339	.444	.442	142	19	7	.819	-7	82	112	O-58(17-40-1),1-24	0.8
Total	7	681	2761	443	726	120	49	17	222	133	62	41	.263	.312	.360	110	29	19	.866	-38	81	99	O-654(123-351-181)/1-29,P-4	-2.2

ROSEN, AL Albert Leonard "Flip" B 2.29.1924 Spartanburg, SC BR/TR 5-10.5/180# d9.10

Year	Tm Lg	G	AB	R	H	2B	3B	HR	RBI	BB-IB	HP	SO	AVG	OBP	SLG	AOPS	ABR	SB-CS	FA	FR	Rng	Thr	G at Pos	BFW
1947	Cle A	7	9	1	1	0	0	0	0	0	0	3	.111	.111	.111	-39	-2	0-0	—	1	0	0	/3-2,O(LF)	-0.1
1948	†Cle A	5	5	0	1	0	0	0	0	0	0	2	.200	.200	.200	7	-1	0-0	1.000	0	93	0	/3-2	-0.1
1949	Cle A	23	44	3	7	2	0	0	5	7	0	4	.159	.275	.205	28	-5	0-1	1.000	-1	89	51	3-10	-0.6
1950	Cle A	**155**	554	100	159	23	4	**37**	116	100	**10**	72	.287	.405	.543	146	39	5-7	.969	6	**107**	79	*3-154	4.0
1951	Cle A	154	573	82	152	30	1	24	102	85	2	71	.265	.362	.447	125	20	7-5	.958	-10	95	66	*3-154	1.0
1952	Cle A★	148	567	101	171	32	5	28	**105**	75	4	54	.302	.387	.524	162	47	8-6	.958	-15	88	78	*3-147/1-4,S-3	3.3
1953	Cle A★	**155**	599	**115**	201	27	5	**43**	**145**	85	4	48	.336	.422	**.613**	**181**	**68**	8-7	.964	9	**108**	107	*3-154/1S	**7.4**
1954	†Cle A★	137	466	76	140	20	2	24	102	85	3	43	.300	.404	.506	148	34	6-2	.959	-13	81	94	3-87,1-46/2S	1.9
1955	Cle A★	139	492	61	120	13	1	21	81	92-5	4	44	.244	.362	.402	103	4	4-2	.963	-1	89	84	*3-106,1-41	0.1
1956	Cle A	121	416	64	111	18	2	15	61	58-4	0	44	.267	.351	.428	104	3	1-3	.945	-9	93	94	*3-116	-0.7
Total	10	1044	3725	603	1063	165	20	192	717	587-9	27	385	.285	.384	.495	138	207	39-33	.961	-32	96	85	3-932/1-92,S-5,2O(LF)	16.2

ROSEN, GOODY Goodwin George B 8.28.1912 Toronto, ON, CAN D 4.6.1994 Toronto, ON, CAN BL/TL 5-10/155# d9.14

Year	Tm Lg	G	AB	R	H	2B	3B	HR	RBI	BB-IB	HP	SO	AVG	OBP	SLG	AOPS	ABR	SB-CS	FA	FR	Rng	Thr	G at Pos	BFW
1937	Bro N	22	77	10	24	5	1	0	6	6	0	6	.312	.361	.403	106	1	2	.981	1	111	66	O-21(8-13-0)	0.1
1938	Bro N	138	473	75	133	17	11	4	51	65	0	43	.281	.368	.389	106	5	0	**.989**	9	103	**187**	*O-113(13-43-59)	0.9
1939	Bro N	54	183	22	46	6	4	1	12	23	0	21	.251	.335	.344	80	-5	4	1.000	-3	97	0	O-47(1-40-7)	-1.0
1944	Bro N	89	264	38	69	8	3	0	23	26	1	27	.261	.330	.314	83	-6	0	.991	11	119	210	O-65(1-62-3)	0.4
1945	Bro N✻	145	606	126	197	24	11	12	75	50	3	36	.325	.379	.460	134	26	6	.993	-4	101	59	*O-141(CF)	1.8
1946	Bro N	3	3	0	1	0	0	0	0	0	0	1	.333	.333	.333	89	0	0	—	-0	0	0	/O(CF)	0.0
	NY N	100	310	39	87	11	4	5	30	48	0	32	.281	.377	.390	117	8	2	.976	-3	106	36	O-84(0-30-52)	0.3
	Year	103	313	39	88	11	4	5	30	48	0	33	.281	.377	.390	117	8	2	.976	-3	106	36	O-85(0-31-52)	0.3
Total	6	551	1916	310	557	71	34	22	197	218	4	166	.291	.364	.398	111	29	14	.989	11	105	101	O-472(23-330-121)	2.5

ROSENBERG, HARRY Harry B 6.22.1908 San Francisco, CA D 4.13.1997 San Mateo, CA BR/TR 5-9.5/160# d7.15 b-Lou

Year	Tm Lg	G	AB	R	H	2B	3B	HR	RBI	BB-IB	HP	SO	AVG	OBP	SLG	AOPS	ABR	SB-CS	FA	FR	Rng	Thr	G at Pos	BFW
1930	NY N	9	5	1	0	0	0	0	0	1	0	4	.000	.167	.000	-56	-1	0	1.000	0	118	0	/O-3(0-2-1)	-0.1

ROSENBERG, LOU Louis B 3.5.1904 San Francisco, CA D 9.8.1991 Daly City, CA BR/TR 5-7/155# d5.22 b-Harry

Year	Tm Lg	G	AB	R	H	2B	3B	HR	RBI	BB-IB	HP	SO	AVG	OBP	SLG	AOPS	ABR	SB-CS	FA	FR	Rng	Thr	G at Pos	BFW
1923	Chi A	3	4	0	1	0	0	0	0	0	0	1	.250	.250	.250	32	0	0-1	1.000	-1	0	0	/2-2	-0.1

ROSENFELD, MAX Max B 12.23.1902 New York, NY D 3.10.1969 Miami, FL BR/TR 5-8/175# d4.21

Year	Tm Lg	G	AB	R	H	2B	3B	HR	RBI	BB-IB	HP	SO	AVG	OBP	SLG	AOPS	ABR	SB-CS	FA	FR	Rng	Thr	G at Pos	BFW
1931	Bro N	3	9	0	2	1	0	0	0	1	0	1	.222	.300	.333	70	0	0	1.000	-0	100	0	/O-3(CF)	-0.1
1932	Bro N	34	39	8	14	3	0	2	7	0	0	10	.359	.359	.590	153	3	2	.970	1	119	95	O-30(1-10-19)	0.3
1933	Bro N	5	9	0	1	0	0	0	0	1	0	1	.111	.200	.111	-10	-1	0	1.000	0	110	0	/O-2(1-1-0)	-0.2
Total	3	42	57	8	17	4	0	2	7	2	0	12	.298	.322	.474	115	2	2	.978	1	115	66	/O-35(2-14-19)	0.0

ROSENTHAL, LARRY Lawrence John B 5.21.1910 St.Paul, MN D 3.4.1992 Woodbury, MN BL/TL 6-0.5/190# d6.20

Year	Tm Lg	G	AB	R	H	2B	3B	HR	RBI	BB-IB	HP	SO	AVG	OBP	SLG	AOPS	ABR	SB-CS	FA	FR	Rng	Thr	G at Pos	BFW
1936	Chi A	85	317	71	89	15	8	3	46	59	0	37	.281	.394	.407	95	-1	2-0	.977	2	103	92	O-80(CF)	-0.1
1937	Chi A	58	97	20	28	5	3	0	9	9	1	20	.289	.355	.402	90	-2	1-0	.980	1	100	188	O-25(CF)	0.0
1938	Chi A	61	105	14	30	5	1	1	12	12	0	13	.286	.359	.381	83	-3	0-1	.959	0	93	176	O-22(0-22-2)	-0.3
1939	Chi A	107	324	50	86	21	5	10	51	53	0	46	.265	.369	.454	106	4	6-4	.990	-2	97	68	O-93(0-20-75)	-0.3
1940	Chi A	107	276	46	83	14	5	6	42	64	0	32	.301	.432	.453	128	15	2-3	.977	4	116	67	O-92(68-15-11)	1.4
1941	Chi A	20	59	9	14	4	0	0	1	12	0	5	.237	.366	.305	80	-1	0-0	.938	-0	82	203	O-18(0-2-16)	-0.2
	Cle A	45	75	10	14	3	1	1	8	9	0	10	.187	.274	.293	53	-5	1-0	1.000	0	106	87	O-14(5-8-1)/1	-0.5
	Year	65	134	19	28	7	1	1	9	21	0	15	.209	.316	.299	66	-6	1-0	.971	0	93	148	O-32(5-10-17)/1	-0.7
1944	NY A	36	101	9	20	3	0	0	9	19	0	15	.198	.325	.228	57	-5	1-0	.986	2	111	91	O-26(10-5-11)	-0.5
	Phi A	32	54	5	11	2	0	1	6	5	0	9	.204	.271	.296	63	-3	0-0	.960	-1	106	0	O-19(5-0-15)	-0.4
	Year	68	155	14	31	5	0	1	15	24	0	24	.200	.307	.252	60	-7	1-0	.979	1	110	65	O-45(15-5-26)	-0.9
1945	Phi A	28	75	6	15	3	2	0	5	9	0	8	.200	.286	.293	68	-3	0-1	1.000	-1	90	61	O-21(LF)	-0.6
Total	8	579	1483	240	390	75	25	22	189	251	1	195	.263	.370	.392	96	-4	13-9	.979	5	103	89	O-410(109-177-131)/1	-1.5

ROSENTHAL, SI Simon B 11.13.1903 Boston, MA D 4.7.1969 Boston, MA BL/TL 5-9/165# d9.8

Year	Tm Lg	G	AB	R	H	2B	3B	HR	RBI	BB-IB	HP	SO	AVG	OBP	SLG	AOPS	ABR	SB-CS	FA	FR	Rng	Thr	G at Pos	BFW
1925	Bos A	19	72	6	19	5	2	0	8	7	0	3	.264	.329	.389	82	-2	1-0	.919	-1	86	155	O-17(7-0-10)	-0.4
1926	Bos A	104	285	34	76	12	3	4	34	19	2	18	.267	.317	.372	82	-9	4-1	.962	-10	81	0	O-67(48-0-19)	-2.3
Total	2	123	357	40	95	17	5	4	42	26	2	21	.266	.319	.375	82	-11	5-1	.950	-10	82	35	/O-84(55-0-29)	-2.7

ROSER, BUNNY John William Joseph "Jack" B 11.15.1901 St.Louis, MO D 5.6.1979 Rocky Hill, CT BL/TL 5-11/175# d8.24

Year	Tm Lg	G	AB	R	H	2B	3B	HR	RBI	BB-IB	HP	SO	AVG	OBP	SLG	AOPS	ABR	SB-CS	FA	FR	Rng	Thr	G at Pos	BFW
1922	Bos N	32	113	13	27	3	4	0	16	10	1	19	.239	.306	.336	69	-6	2-1	.915	-2	105	55	O-32(LF)	-0.9

ROSKOS, JOHN John Edward B 11.19.1974 Victorville, CA BR/TR 5-11/198# d4.20

Year	Tm Lg	G	AB	R	H	2B	3B	HR	RBI	BB-IB	HP	SO	AVG	OBP	SLG	AOPS	ABR	SB-CS	FA	FR	Rng	Thr	G at Pos	BFW
1998	Fla N	10	10	1	1	0	0	0	0	0-0	0	5	.100	.100	.100	-50	-2	0-0	1.000	0	0	0	/1	-0.2
1999	Fla N	13	12	0	2	2	0	0	1	1-0	0	7	.167	.231	.333	43	-1	0-0	1.000	0	0	0	/C	-0.1
2000	SD N	14	27	0	1	1	0	0	1	3-0	0	7	.037	.133	.074	-49	-6	0-0	.875	-1	72	0	/O-6(4-0-2),1-2	-0.7
Total	3	37	49	1	4	3	0	0	2	4-0	0	19	.082	.151	.143	-26	-9	0-0	.875	-0	72	0	/O-6(4-0-2),1-3,C	-1.0

ROSS, CHET Chester James B 4.1.1917 Buffalo, NY D 2.21.1989 Buffalo, NY BR/TR 6-1/195# d9.15 Mil 1945

Year	Tm Lg	G	AB	R	H	2B	3B	HR	RBI	BB-IB	HP	SO	AVG	OBP	SLG	AOPS	ABR	SB-CS	FA	FR	Rng	Thr	G at Pos	BFW
1939	Bos N	11	31	4	10	1	1	0	0	2	0	10	.323	.364	.419	118	1	0	1.000	1	111	137	/O-8(1-1-7)	0.1
1940	Bos N	149	569	84	160	23	14	17	89	59	3	127	.281	.352	.460	130	21	4	.962	5	106	108	*O-149(LF)	1.8
1941	Bos N	29	50	1	6	1	0	0	4	9	0	17	.120	.254	.140	14	-6	0	1.000	0	97	145	O-12(LF)	-0.6
1942	Bos N	76	220	20	43	7	2	5	19	16	0	37	.195	.250	.314	66	-11	0	.992	0	105	52	O-57(52-0-6)	-1.5
1943	Bos N	94	285	27	62	12	2	7	32	26	1	67	.218	.285	.347	84	-7	1	.977	2	104	111	O-73(LF)	-1.0
1944	Bos N	54	154	20	35	9	2	5	26	12	1	23	.227	.287	.409	91	-3	1	1.000	3	93	238	O-38(25-0-15)	-0.2
Total	6	413	1309	156	316	53	21	34	170	124	5	281	.241	.309	.392	100	-5	6	.976	12	104	116	O-337(312-1-28)	-1.4

ROSS, CODY Cody Joseph B 12.23.1980 Portales, NM BR/TL 5-11/180# d7.4

Year	Tm Lg	G	AB	R	H	2B	3B	HR	RBI	BB-IB	HP	SO	AVG	OBP	SLG	AOPS	ABR	SB-CS	FA	FR	Rng	Thr	G at Pos	BFW
2003	Det A	6	19	1	4	1	0	1	5	1-0	1	3	.211	.286	.421	90	0	0-0	.882	0	126	0	/O-6(RF)	-0.1

ROSS, DAVID David Wade B 3.19.1977 Bainbridge, GA BR/TR 6-2/205# d6.29

Year	Tm Lg	G	AB	R	H	2B	3B	HR	RBI	BB-IB	HP	SO	AVG	OBP	SLG	AOPS	ABR	SB-CS	FA	FR	Rng	Thr	G at Pos	BFW
2002	LA N	8	10	2	2	1	0	1	2	2-0	1	4	.200	.385	.600	169	1	0-0	1.000	0	0	125	/C-6	0.2
2003	LA N	40	124	19	32	7	0	10	18	13-0	2	42	.258	.336	.556	136	6	0-0	.986	-1	61	200	C-38	0.7
Total	2	48	134	21	34	8	0	11	20	15-0	3	46	.254	.340	.560	138	7	0-0	.987	-1	56	194	/C-44	0.9

ROSS, DON Donald Raymond B 7.16.1914 Pasadena, CA D 3.28.1996 Arcadia, CA BR/TR 6-2/200# d4.19 OF Total (11-LF 104-RF)

Year	Tm Lg	G	AB	R	H	2B	3B	HR	RBI	BB-IB	HP	SO	AVG	OBP	SLG	AOPS	ABR	SB-CS	FA	FR	Rng	Thr	G at Pos	BFW
1938	Det A	77	265	22	69	7	1	1	30	29	0	11	.260	.333	.306	58	-17	1-0	.946	5	107	111	3-75	-0.8
1940	Bro N	10	38	4	11	2	0	1	8	3	0	3	.289	.341	.421	103	0	1	.879	-1	97	0	3-10	-0.1
1942	Det A	87	226	29	62	10	2	3	30	36	2	16	.274	.379	.376	104	3	2-1	.964	-4	96	135	O-38(5-0-33),3-20	-0.3
1943	Det A	89	247	19	66	13	0	0	18	20	1	3	.267	.325	.320	82	-5	2-0	.985	-3	92	126	O-38(6-0-32),S-18/2-7,3	-0.9
1944	Det A	66	167	14	35	5	0	2	15	14	1	9	.210	.275	.275	54	-10	2-1	.958	-1	94	83	O-37(RF)/S-2,1	-1.4
1945	Det A	8	29	3	11	4	0	0	4	5	0	1	.379	.471	.517	175	3	2-0	.960	-0	104	0	/3-8	0.4
	Cle A	106	363	26	95	15	1	2	43	42	1	15	.262	.340	.325	97	0	0-4	.958	-11	84	71	*3-106	-1.2
	Year	114	392	29	106	19	1	2	47	47	1	16	.270	.350	.339	104	3	2-4	.958	-11	85	66	*3-114	-0.8
1946	Cle A	55	153	12	41	7	0	3	14	17	0	12	.268	.341	.373	106	1	0-0	.944	-7	73	66	3-41/O-2(RF)	-0.6
Total	7	498	1488	129	390	63	4	12	162	166	5	70	.262	.338	.334	86	-25	10-6	.946	-22	90	75	3-261,O-115R/S-20,2-7,1	-4.9

ROSSI, JOE Joseph Anthony B 3.13.1921 Oakland, CA D 2.20.1999 Oakland, CA BR/TR 6-1/205# d4.20

Year	Tm Lg	G	AB	R	H	2B	3B	HR	RBI	BB-IB	HP	SO	AVG	OBP	SLG	AOPS	ABR	SB-CS	FA	FR	Rng	Thr	G at Pos	BFW
1952	Cin N	55	145	14	32	0	1	1	6	20	1	20	.221	.319	.255	61	-7	1-0	.982	1	*96*	*101*	C-46	-0.4

ROSSMAN, CLAUDE Claude R. B 6.17.1881 Philmont, NY D 1.16.1928 Poughkeepsie, NY BL/TL 6/188# d9.16

Year	Tm Lg	G	AB	R	H	2B	3B	HR	RBI	BB-IB	HP	SO	AVG	OBP	SLG	AOPS	ABR	SB-CS	FA	FR	Rng	Thr	G at Pos	BFW
1904	Cle A	18	62	5	13	5	0	0	6	0	0		.210	.210	.290	58	-3	0	.933	-2	0	0	O-17(0-1-16)	-0.6
1906	Cle A	118	396	49	122	13	2	1	53	17	1		.308	.338	.359	120	8	11	.984	-9	69	**120**	*1-105/O(CF)	-0.3
1907	†Det A	**153**	571	60	158	21	8	0	69	33	2		.277	.318	.342	107	3	20	.981	-14	64	81	*1-153	-1.5
1908	†Det A	138	524	45	154	33	13	2	71	27	1		.294	.330	.418	137	19	8	.981	6	**120**	110	*1-138	2.5
1909	Det A	82	287	16	75	8	3	0	39	13	0		.261	.293	.310	87	-5	10	.981	-6	77	84	1-75	-1.5
	StL A	2	8	0	1	0	0	0	0	0	0		.125	.125	.125	-23	-1	0	1.000	-0	0	0	/O-2(RF)	-0.2
	Year	84	295	16	76	8	3	0	39	13	0		.258	.289	.305	84	-6	10	.981	-6	77	84	1-75/O-2(RF)	-1.7
Total	5	511	1848	175	523	80	26	3	238	90	4		.283	.318	.359	113	21	49	.982	-26	84	99	1-471/O-20(0-2-18)	-1.6

ROSSY, RICO Elam Jose (Ramos) B 2.16.1964 San Juan, P.R. BR/TR 5-10/175# d9.11

Year	Tm Lg	G	AB	R	H	2B	3B	HR	RBI	BB-IB	HP	SO	AVG	OBP	SLG	AOPS	ABR	SB-CS	FA	FR	Rng	Thr	G at Pos	BFW
1991	Atl N	5	1	0	0	0	0	0	0	0-0	0	1	.000	.000	.000	-94	0	0-0	—	-0	0	0	/S	0.0
1992	KC A	59	149	21	32	8	1	1	12	20-1	1	20	.215	.310	.302	71	-5	0-3	.961	1	104	137	S-51/3-9,2-3	-0.2
1993	KC A	46	86	10	19	4	0	2	12	9-0	1	11	.221	.302	.337	68	-4	0-0	.987	-2	103	109	2-24,3-16,S-11	-0.4
1998	Sea A	37	81	12	16	6	0	1	4	6-0	0	13	.198	.253	.309	45	-7	0-0	1.000	5	110	159	3-25/2-6,S-4,D	-0.1
Total	4	147	317	43	67	18	1	4	28	35-1	2	45	.211	.293	.312	63	-16	0-3	.967	4	100	132	/S-67,3-50,2-33,D	-0.7

ROTH, FRANK Francis Charles B 10.11.1878 Chicago, IL D 3.27.1955 Burlington, WI BR/TR 5-10/160# d4.18 C7 b-Braggo

Year	Tm Lg	G	AB	R	H	2B	3B	HR	RBI	BB-IB	HP	SO	AVG	OBP	SLG	AOPS	ABR	SB-CS	FA	FR	Rng	Thr	G at Pos	BFW
1903	Phi N	68	220	27	60	11	4	0	22	9	1		.273	.304	.359	92	-3	3	.935	-8	*85*	*96*	C-60/3	-0.6
1904	Phi N	81	229	28	59	8	1	1	20	12	1		.258	.298	.314	92	-2	8	.958	-10	*77*	*94*	C-67/12	-0.7
1905	StL A	35	107	9	25	3	0	0	7	6	0		.234	.274	.262	74	-3	1	.962	-6	*69*	*110*	C-29	-0.7
1906	Chi A	16	51	4	10	1	1	0	7	3	0		.196	.241	.255	57	-3	1	.990	3	*152*	*95*	C-15	0.2
1909	Cin N	56	147	12	35	7	2	0	16	6	4		.238	.287	.313	87	-3	5	.967	-2	*92*	*90*	C-54	0.0
1910	Cin N	26	29	3	7	2	0	0	3	0	1	2	.241	.267	.310	71	-1	1	.938	-0	*146*	*129*	/C-4,O(LF)	-0.1
Total	6	282	783	83	196	32	8	1	75	36	7	2	.250	.289	.315	86	-15	19	.956	-23	*88*	*96*	C-229/O(LF)213	-1.9

ROTH, BRAGGO Robert Frank B 8.28.1892 Burlington, WI D 9.11.1936 Chicago, IL BR/TR 5-7.5/170# d9.1 b-Frank

Year	Tm Lg	G	AB	R	H	2B	3B	HR	RBI	BB-IB	HP	SO	AVG	OBP	SLG	AOPS	ABR	SB-CS	FA	FR	Rng	Thr	G at Pos	BFW
1914	Chi A	34	126	14	37	4	6	1	10	8	4	25	.294	.355	.444	142	6	3-3	.924	1	92	159	O-34(0-12-22)	0.4
1915	Chi A	70	240	44	60	6	10	3	35	29	3	50	.250	.338	.396	116	4	12-6	.837	-12	68	22	3-35,O-30(29-1-0)	-0.9
	Cle A	39	144	23	43	4	7	4	20	22	2	22	.299	.399	.507	168	12	14-4	.878	-4	78	105	O-39(CF)	0.7
	Year	109	384	67	103	10	17	**7**	55	51	5	72	.268	.361	.438	135	15	26-10	.906	-17	81	122	O-69(29-40-0),3-35	-0.2
1916	Cle A	125	409	50	117	19	7	4	72	38	2	48	.286	.350	.396	117	8	29-14	.954	2	92	**148**	*O-112(0-9-103)	0.6
1917	Cle A	145	495	69	141	30	9	1	72	52	2	73	.285	.355	.388	118	11	51	.957	2	105	101	*O-135(RF)	0.7
1918	Cle A	106	375	53	106	21	12	1	59	53	**8**	41	.283	.383	.411	127	14	36	.936	-4	91	109	*O-106(2-0-104)	0.6
1919	Phi A	48	195	33	63	13	8	5	29	15	2	21	.323	.377	.549	156	13	11	.975	-5	95	15	O-48(RF)	0.6
	Bos A	63	227	32	58	9	4	0	23	24	4	32	.256	.337	.330	93	-2	9	.943	-5	87	85	O-58(1-57-0)	-1.1
	Year	111	422	65	121	22	12	5	52	39	6	53	.287	.355	.431	124	12	20	.955	-10	91	54	*O-106(1-57-48)	-0.5
1920	Was A	138	468	80	136	23	8	9	92	75	6	57	.291	.395	.432	122	18	24-12	.952	-8	85	92	*O-128(7-0-121)	0.5
1921	NY A	43	152	29	43	9	2	2	10	19	2	20	.283	.370	.408	96	0	1-2	.923	-4	88	63	O-37(3-17-17)	-0.7
Total	8	811	2831	427	804	138	73	30	422	335	35	389	.284	.367	.416	122	84	190-41	.944	-37	92	104	O-727(42-135-550)/3-35	1.4

ROTHEL, BOB Robert Burton B 9.17.1923 Columbia Station, OH D 3.21.1984 Huron, OH BR/TR 5-10.5/170# d4.22

Year	Tm Lg	G	AB	R	H	2B	3B	HR	RBI	BB-IB	HP	SO	AVG	OBP	SLG	AOPS	ABR	SB-CS	FA	FR	Rng	Thr	G at Pos	BFW
1945	Cle A	4	10	0	2	0	0	0	0	3	0	1	.200	.385	.200	75	0	0-0	.875	-1	81	0	/3-4	-0.1

ROTHERMEL, BOBBY Edward Hill B 12.18.1870 Fleetwood, PA D 2.11.1927 Detroit, MI BR 5-6.5/148# d6.18

Year	Tm Lg	G	AB	R	H	2B	3B	HR	RBI	BB-IB	HP	SO	AVG	OBP	SLG	AOPS	ABR	SB-CS	FA	FR	Rng	Thr	G at Pos	BFW
1899	Bal N	10	21	1	2	0	0	0	3	1	0		.095	.136	.095	-34	-4	0	.867	-2	93	0	/2-5,3-2,S	-0.6

ROTHFUSS, JACK John Albert B 4.18.1872 Newark, NJ D 4.20.1947 Basking Ridge, NJ BR/TR 5-11.5/195# d8.2

Year	Tm Lg	G	AB	R	H	2B	3B	HR	RBI	BB-IB	HP	SO	AVG	OBP	SLG	AOPS	ABR	SB-CS	FA	FR	Rng	Thr	G at Pos	BFW
1897	Pit N	35	115	20	36	3	1	2	18	5	2		.313	.352	.409	105	0	3	.984	-1	82	56	1-32	0.0

ROTHGEB, CLAUDE Claude James B 1.1.1880 Milford, IL D 7.6.1944 Manitowoc, WI BB 6-0.5/200# d6.17

Year	Tm Lg	G	AB	R	H	2B	3B	HR	RBI	BB-IB	HP	SO	AVG	OBP	SLG	AOPS	ABR	SB-CS	FA	FR	Rng	Thr	G at Pos	BFW
1905	Was A	7	16	2	2	0	0	0	0	0	0		.125	.125	.125	-22	-2	1	.833	0	259	0	/O-4(RF)	-0.3

ROTHROCK, JACK John Huston B 3.14.1905 Long Beach, CA D 2.2.1980 San Bernardino, CA BB/TR 5-11.5/165# d7.28 OF Total (138-LF 194-CF 311-RF)

Year	Tm Lg	G	AB	R	H	2B	3B	HR	RBI	BB-IB	HP	SO	AVG	OBP	SLG	AOPS	ABR	SB-CS	FA	FR	Rng	Thr	G at Pos	BFW
1925	Bos A	22	55	6	19	3	3	0	7	3	0	7	.345	.379	.509	124	2	0-0	.893	-3	86	64	S-22	0.0
1926	Bos A	15	17	3	5	1	0	0	2	3	0	1	.294	.400	.353	101	0	0-0	.692	-2	86	0	/S-2	-0.1
1927	Bos A	117	428	61	111	24	8	1	36	24	2	46	.259	.302	.360	73	-19	5-5	.953	4	100	115	S-40,2-36,3-20,1-13	-1.0
1928	Bos A	117	344	52	92	9	4	3	22	33	1	40	.267	.333	.343	79	-11	12-6	.979	-8	93	22	O-53(26-12-19),3-17,1-16,S-13/2-2,PC	-2.0
1929	Bos A	143	473	70	142	19	7	6	59	43	2	47	.300	.361	.408	100	0	24-13	.970	3	104	95	*O-128(0-126-2)	-0.2
1930	Bos A	45	65	4	18	3	1	0	4	2	0	9	.277	.299	.354	67	-3	0-2	.947	1	105	129	/O-9(1-0-8),3	-0.4
1931	Bos A	133	475	81	132	32	3	4	42	47	0	48	.278	.343	.383	96	-2	13-7	.982	-3	87	149	O-79(75-2-2),2-23/1-8,3-2,S	-0.8
1932	Bos A	12	48	3	10	1	0	0	0	5	0	5	.208	.283	.229	35	-5	3-0	.973	1	112	91	O-12(LF)	-0.4
	Chi A	39	64	8	12	2	1	0	6	5	0	9	.188	.246	.250	31	-7	1-0	.929	-3	100	0	O-19(12-1-6)/3-8,1	-0.9
	Year	51	112	11	22	3	1	0	6	10	0	14	.196	.262	.241	33	-11	4-0	.961	-2	108	64	O-31(24-1-6)/3-8,1	-1.3
1934	†StL N	**154**	647	106	184	35	3	11	72	49	1	56	.284	.336	.399	90	-9	10	.975	3	109	72	*O-154(5-0-149)/2	-1.5
1935	StL N	129	502	76	137	18	5	3	56	57	0	29	.273	.347	.347	84	-10	7	.980	-2	109	38	*O-127(1-1-125)	-2.0
1937	Phi A	88	232	28	62	15	0	0	21	28	0	15	.267	.346	.332	73	-9	1-0	.992	-2	99	44	O-58(6-52-0)/2	-1.1
Total	11	1014	3350	498	924	162	35	28	327	299	6	312	.276	.336	.370	85	-73	76-33	.976	-13	103	74	O-639R/S-78,2-63,3-48,1-38,CP	-10.4

ROUSH, EDD Edd J B 5.8.1893 Oakland City, IN D 3.21.1988 Bradenton, FL BL/TL 5-11/170# d8.20 C1 HF1962

Year	Tm Lg	G	AB	R	H	2B	3B	HR	RBI	BB-IB	HP	SO	AVG	OBP	SLG	AOPS	ABR	SB-CS	FA	FR	Rng	Thr	G at Pos	BFW
1913	Chi A	9	10	2	1	0	0	0	0	0	0	2	.100	.100	.100	-42	-2	0	1.000	-0	109	0	/O-2(CF)	-0.2
1914	Ind F	74	166	26	54	8	4	1	30	6	1	20	.325	.353	.440	104	-2	12	.989	3	124	86	O-43(38-4-1)/1-2	-0.1
1915	New F	145	551	73	164	20	11	3	60	38	6	25	.298	.350	.390	115	1	28	.972	-3	99	92	*O-144(0-143-1)	-1.3
1916	NY N	39	69	4	13	0	1	0	5	1	0	4	.188	.200	.217	30	-6	4	.952	0	86	145	O-15(0-5-10)	-0.8
	Cin N	69	272	34	78	7	14	0	15	13	7	19	.287	.336	.415	133	9	15	.971	2	112	79	O-69(CF)	0.7
	Year	108	341	38	91	7	15	0	20	14	7	23	.267	.309	.375	114	3	19	.969	2	108	88	O-84(0-74-10)	-0.1
1917	Cin N	136	522	82	178	19	14	4	67	27	5	24	**.341**	.379	.454	162	36	21	.962	-2	104	83	*O-134(CF)	2.8
1918	Cin N	113	435	61	145	18	10	5	62	22	2	10	.333	.368	**.455**	**153**	25	24	.960	5	113	87	*O-113(CF)	2.5
1919	†Cin N	133	504	73	162	19	12	4	71	42	6	19	**.321**	.380	.431	147	29	20	.989	5	100	126	*O-133(CF)	2.8
1920	Cin N	149	579	81	196	22	16	4	90	42	3	22	.339	.386	.453	142	31	36-24	.975	10	114	88	*O-139(CF),1-11/2	3.1
1921	Cin N	112	418	68	147	27	12	4	71	31	5	8	.352	.403	.502	145	27	19-17	.980	-2	105	59	*O-108(CF)	1.8
1922	Cin N	49	165	29	58	7	4	1	24	19	3	5	.352	.428	.461	132	9	5-3	.990	1	89	162	O-43(CF)	0.7
1923	Cin N	138	527	88	185	**41**	18	6	88	46	3	16	.351	.406	.531	149	37	10-15	.970	-10	91	77	*O-137(CF)	1.8
1924	Cin N	121	483	67	168	23	**21**	3	72	22	0	11	.348	.376	.501	135	21	17-13	.959	-10	84	102	*O-119(CF)	0.5

Year	Tm Lg	G	AB	R	H	2B	3B	HR	RBI	BB-IB	HP	SO	AVG	OBP	SLG	AOPS	ABR	SB-CS	FA	FR	Rng	Thr	G at Pos	BFW
1925	Cin N	134	540	91	183	28	16	8	83	35	4	14	.339	.383	.494	125	19	22-20	.978	-5	90	115	*O-134(CF)	0.6
1926	Cin N	144	563	95	182	37	10	7	79	38	0	17	.323	.366	.462	125	19	8	.955	-18	79	89	*O-143(CF)/1	-0.5
1927	NY N	140	570	83	173	27	4	7	58	26	1	15	.304	.335	.402	97	-4	18	.975	-6	87	130	*O-138(0-137-1)	-1.6
1928	NY N	46	163	20	41	5	3	2	13	14	1	8	.252	.315	.356	75	-7	1	.955	0	93	198	O-39(CF)	-0.8
1929	NY N	115	450	76	146	19	7	8	52	45	3	16	.324	.390	.451	108	6	6	.982	-6	80	**165**	*O-107(CF)	-0.4
1931	Cin N	101	376	46	102	12	5	1	41	17	3	5	.271	.308	.338	78	-13	2	.981	-3	95	86	O-88(43-45-0)	-1.9
Total	18	1967	7363	1099	2376	339	182	68	981	484	53	260	.323	.369	.446	126	235	268-92	.972	-38	97	102	*O-1848(81-1754-13)/1-14,2	9.7
ROUTCLIFFE, PHIL Philip John "Chicken" B 10.24.1870 Oswego, NY D 10.4.1918 Oswego, NY BR/TR 6/175# d4.21																								
1890	Pit N	1	4	1	1	0	0	0	1	0	1	0	.250	.400	.250	102	0	1	1.000	0	0	0	/O(LF)	0.0
ROWAN, DAVE David (born David Drohan) B 12.6.1882 Elora, ON, CAN D 7.30.1955 Toronto, ON, CAN BL/TL 5-11/175# d5.27																								
1911	StL A	18	65	7	25	1	1	0	11	4	0		.385	.420	.431	143	4	0	.945	-1	99	59	1-18	0.2
ROWAND, AARON Aaron Ryan B 8.29.1977 Portland, OR BR/TR 6-1/200# d6.16																								
2001	Chi A	63	123	21	36	5	0	4	20	15-0	4	28	.293	.385	.431	112	3	5-1	.991	3	109	127	O-61(34-32-11)	0.6
2002	Chi A	126	302	41	78	16	2	7	29	12-1	6	54	.258	.298	.394	81	-9	0-1	.983	6	108	112	*O-120(40-76-7)	-0.4
2003	Chi A	93	157	22	45	8	0	6	24	7-0	3	21	.287	.327	.452	102	0	0-0	1.000	3	94	268	O-87(24-65-12)	0.3
Total	3	282	582	84	159	29	2	17	73	34-1	13	103	.273	.325	.418	94	-6	5-2	.989	12	104	160	O-268(98-173-30)	0.5
ROWDON, WADE Wade Lee B 9.7.1960 Riverhead, NY BR/TR 6-2/180# d9.8																								
1984	Cin N	4	7	0	2	0	0	0	0	0-0	0	1	.286	.286	.286	58	0	0-0	1.000	0	125	161	/S3	0.0
1985	Cin N	5	9	2	2	0	0	0	2	2-0	0	1	.222	.364	.222	64	0	0-0	.667	-1	64	0	/3-4	-0.2
1986	Cin N	38	80	9	20	5	1	0	10	9-0	1	17	.250	.330	.338	82	-2	2-0	.889	-4	117	107	/3-7,S-6,O-5(LF),2-3	-0.5
1987	Chi N	11	31	2	7	1	1	1	4	3-0	0	10	.226	.294	.419	83	-1	0-2	.818	-1	97	0	/3-9	-0.3
1988	Bal A	20	30	1	3	0	0	0	0	0-0	0	6	.100	.100	.100	-45	-6	1-1	.947	3	179	141	/3-8,O-5(LF),D-5	-0.3
Total	5	78	157	14	34	6	2	1	16	14-0	1	35	.217	.283	.299	59	-9	3-3	.866	-4	112	57	/3-29,O-10(LF),S-7,D-5,2-3	-1.3
ROWE, DAVE David Elwood B 10.9.1854 Harrisburg, PA D 12.9.1930 Glendale, CA BR/TR 5-9/180# d5.30 M2 b-Jack ▲ OF Total (9-LF 246-CF 51-RF)																								
1877	Chi N	2	7	0	2	0	0	0	0	0		3	.286	.286	.286	72	0		.667	-0	0	0	/O-2(RF),P	-0.1
1882	Cle N	24	97	13	25	4	3	1	17	4		9	.258	.287	.392	119	2		.837	-3	63	103	O-23(3-20-1)/P	-0.1
1883	Bal AA	59	256	40	80	11	6	0		2			.313	.318	.402	127	6		.798	-6	54	0	O-50(2-0-48)/S-7,1-3,P	0.0
1884	StL U	109	485	95	142	32	11	4		10			.293	.307	.429	117	-5		**.947**	-4	68	**175**	*O-92(CF),S-14/2-2,1-2,P	-1.1
1885	StL N	16	62	8	10	3	0	0	3	5		8	.161	.224	.210	44	-3		.906	-2	35	251	O-16(CF)	-0.5
1886	KC N	105	429	53	103	24	8	3	57	15		43	.240	.266	.354	82	-11	2	.851	-9	61	63	*O-90(4-86-0),S-11/2-4,M	-2.1
1888	KC AA	32	122	14	21	3	4	0	13	6	1		.172	.217	.262	50	-8	2	.914	2	209	81	O-32(CF),M	-0.6
Total	7	347	1458	223	383	77	32	8	90	42	1	63	.263	.284	.376	99	-19	4	.878	-23	75	101	0-305C/S-32,2-6,1-5,P-4	-4.5
ROWE, HARLAND Harland Stimson "Hypie" B 4.20.1896 Springvale, ME D 5.26.1969 Springvale, ME BL/TR 6-1/170# d6.23																								
1916	Phi A	17	36	2	5	1	0	0	3	2	0	8	.139	.184	.167	6	-4	0	.842	-1	96	0	/3-8,O(RF)	-0.6
ROWE, JACK John Charles B 12.8.1856 Hamburg, PA D 4.25.1911 St.Louis, MO BL/TR 5-8/170# d9.6 M1 b-Dave																								
1879	Buf N	8	34	8	12	1	0	0	8	0		1	.353	.353	.382	139	1		.905	0			/C-6,O-2(RF)	0.2
1880	Buf N	79	326	43	82	10	6	1	36	6		17	.252	.265	.328	98	-1		.897	-14			*C-60,O-25(2-6-19)/3-3	-1.4
1881	Buf N	64	246	30	82	11	**11**	1	43	1		12	.333	.336	.480	156	14		.900	-9			C-46/S-7,3-7,O-5(0-1-4)	0.6
1882	Buf N	75	308	43	82	14	5	1	42	12		0	.266	.294	.354	105	1		.950	-6			C-46,S-22/3-7,O(CF)	0.0
1883	Buf N	87	374	65	104	18	7	1	38	15		14	.278	.306	.372	102	1		.899	-16			C-49,O-28(LF),S-18/3-3	-1.0
1884	Buf N	93	400	85	126	14	14	4	61	23		14	.315	.352	.450	146	19		**.943**	-5			C-65,O-30(17-12-1)/S-6	1.7
1885	Buf N	98	421	62	122	28	8	2	51	13		19	.290	.311	.409	127	11		.834	-12	91	115	S-65,C-23,O-12(CF)	0.3
1886	Det N	111	468	97	142	21	9	6	87	26		27	.303	.340	.425	127	14	12	.880	-21	91	95	*S-110/C-3	-0.4
1887	†Det N	124	537	135	171	30	10	6	96	39	3	11	.318	.368	.445	120	14	22	.907	-24	92	95	*S-124	-0.5
1888	Det N	105	451	62	125	19	8	2	74	19	3	28	.277	.311	.368	114	7	10	.861	-9	100	87	*S-105	0.1
1889	Pit N	75	317	57	82	14	3	2	32	22	3	16	.259	.313	.341	91	-4	5	.896	-6	100	105	S-75	-0.6
1890	Buf P	125	504	77	126	22	7	2	76	48	7	18	.250	.324	.333	83	-11	10	**.901**	4	95	96	*S-125,M	-0.3
Total	12	1044	4386	764	1256	202	88	28	644	224	16	177	.286	.323	.392	114	66	59	.882	-117			S-657,C-298,O-103(47-32-26)/3-20	-1.3
ROWELL, BAMA Carvel William B 1.13.1916 Citronelle, AL D 8.16.1993 Citronelle, AL BL/TR 5-11/185# d9.4 Mil 1942-45																								
1939	Bos N	21	59	5	11	2	2	0	6	1	0	4	.186	.200	.288	32	-6	0	.853	-1	82	177	O-16(0-13-3)	-0.8
1940	Bos N	130	486	46	148	19	8	3	58	18	1	22	.305	.331	.395	105	1	12	.953	-2	105	108	*2-115/O-7(0-1-6)	0.6
1941	Bos N	138	483	49	129	23	6	7	60	39	0	36	.267	.322	.383	102	0	11	.935	-8	98	**120**	*2-112,O-14(7-2-6)/3-2	-0.2
1946	Bos N	95	293	37	82	12	6	3	31	29	0	15	.280	.345	.392	108	2	5	.978	3	104	123	O-85(71-14-0)	0.0
1947	Bos N	113	384	48	106	23	2	5	40	18	1	14	.276	.310	.385	86	-9	7	.945	-5	100	58	*O-100(99-2-0)/2-7,3-4	-2.1
1948	Phi N	77	196	15	47	16	2	1	22	8	0	14	.240	.270	.357	70	-9	2	.821	-8	72	149	3-18,O-17(14-0-3),2-12	-1.8
Total	6	574	1901	200	523	95	26	19	217	113	2	105	.275	.316	.382	95	-21	37	.945	-22	101	110	2-246,0-239(191-32-18)/3-24	-4.3
ROWEN, ED W. Edward B 10.22.1857 Bridgeport, CT D 2.22.1892 Bridgeport, CT 5-6/155# d5.1																								
1882	Bos N	83	327	36	81	7	4	1	43	19		18	.248	.289	.303	90	-4		.885	-9	71	108	O-48(RF),C-34/S-6,3	-0.9
1883	Phi AA	49	196	28	43	10	1	0	21	11			.219	.261	.281	68	-7		.855	-2			C-44/O-8(0-5-3),32	-0.5
1884	Phi AA	4	15	4	6	1	0	0	1	1	1		.400	.471	.467	194	2		.806	-2			/C-4	0.0
Total	3	136	538	68	130	18	5	1	65	31	1	18	.242	.284	.299	85	-9		.866	-14			/C-82,O-56(0-5-51),S-6,3-2,2	-1.4
ROWLAND, CHUCK Charlie Leland B 7.23.1899 Warrenton, NC D 1.21.1992 Raleigh, NC BR/TR 6-1/185# d5.11																								
1923	Phi A	5	6	0	0	0	0	0	0	0	0	2	.000	.000	.000	-99	-2	0-0	1.000	0	*77*	*160*	/C-4	-0.2
ROWLAND, RICH Richard Garnet B 2.25.1964 Cloverdale, CA BR/TR 6-1/215# d9.7																								
1990	Det A	7	19	3	3	1	0	0	0	2-1	0	4	.158	.238	.211	26	-2	0-0	.967	-1	47	70	/C-5,D-2	-0.2
1991	Det A	4	4	0	1	0	0	0	1	1-0	0	2	.250	.333	.250	83	0	0-0	1.000	-1	0	0	/C-2,D	0.1
1992	Det A	6	14	2	3	0	0	0	0	3-0	0	3	.214	.353	.214	62	-1	0-0	1.000	-1	74	0	/C-3,13D	-0.2
1993	Det A	21	46	2	10	3	0	0	4	5-0	0	16	.217	.294	.283	56	-3	0-0	.988	1	94	63	C-17/D-3	-0.1
1994	Bos A	46	118	14	27	3	0	9	20	11-0	0	35	.229	.295	.483	92	-2	0-0	.972	-5	105	121	C-39/1D	-0.4
1995	Bos A	14	29	1	5	1	0	0	1	0-0	0	11	.172	.172	.207	-2	-4	0-0	.977	1	140	54	C-11/D-3	-0.3
Total	6	98	230	22	49	8	0	9	26	22-1	0	71	.213	.281	.365	67	-12	0-0	.976	-4	101	92	/C-77,D-15,1-2,3	-1.1
ROXBURGH, JIM James A. B 1.17.1858 San Francisco, CA D 2.21.1934 San Francisco, CA BR/TR 5-10/170# d5.30																								
1884	Bal AA	2	4	1	2	0	0	0		1	1		.500	.667	.500	275	1		.824	-1			/C-2	0.0
1887	Phi AA	2	8	0	1	0	0	0	0	0	0		.125	.125	.125	-30	-1	0	.875	-2			/C-2,2	-0.2
Total	2	4	12	1	3	0	0	0	0	1	1		.250	.357	.250	81	0	0	.840	-2			/C-4,2	-0.2
ROYER, STAN Stanley Dean B 8.31.1967 Olney, IL BR/TR 6-3/195# d9.11																								
1991	StL N	9	21	1	6	1	0	0	1	1-0	0	2	.286	.318	.333	83	0	0-0	1.000	-1	51	0	/3-5	-0.2
1992	StL N	13	31	6	10	2	0	2	9	1-0	0	4	.323	.333	.581	162	2	0-0	.900	0	127	400	/3-5,1-4	0.3
1993	StL N	24	46	4	14	2	0	1	8	2-0	0	14	.304	.333	.413	100	0	0-1	.857	-1	99	85	3-10/1-2	-0.2
1994	StL N	39	57	3	10	5	0	1	2	0-0	0	18	.175	.175	.316	25	-6	0-0	.972	-1	105	57	1-11/3-5	-0.7
	Bos A	4	9	0	1	0	0	0	1	0-0	0	3	.111	.111	.111	-41	-2	0-0	.833	-1	74	0	/3-3,1	-0.2
Total	4	89	164	14	41	10	0	4	21	4-0	0	41	.250	.266	.384	74	-6	0-1	.895	-3	92	92	/3-28,1-18	-1.0
ROYSTER, JERRY Jeron Kennis B 10.18.1952 Sacramento, CA BR/TR 6/165# d8.14 M1 C4 OF Total (123-LF 21-CF 9-RF)																								
1973	LA N	10	19	1	4	0	0	0	2	0-0	0	5	.211	.211	.211	18	-2	1-0	.842	0	121	115	/3-6,2	-0.2
1974	LA N	6	0	2	0	0	0	0	0	0-0	0	0	—	—	—	—	0	0-0	1.000	1	618	0	/23O(RF)	0.1
1975	LA N	13	36	2	9	2	1	0	1	1-0	0	3	.250	.270	.361	77	-1	1-0	1.000	0	81	0	/O-7(1-0-6),2-4,3-3,S	-0.1
1976	Atl N	149	533	65	132	13	1	5	45	52-4	1	53	.248	.313	.304	72	-19	24-13	.962	**25**	**113**	**127**	*3-148/S-2	0.7
1977	Atl N	140	445	64	96	10	2	6	28	38-3	1	67	.216	.278	.288	47	-34	28-10	.953	-12	94	79	3-56,S-51,2-38/O(CF)	-3.9
1978	Atl N	140	529	67	137	17	8	2	35	56-2	3	49	.259	.331	.333	78	-15	27-17	.974	-4	91	84	2-75,S-60/3	-0.9
1979	Atl N	154	601	103	164	25	6	3	51	62-0	0	59	.273	.337	.349	83	-13	35-8	.948	**29**	124	83	3-80,2-77	2.4
1980	Atl N	123	392	42	95	17	5	1	20	37-1	1	48	.242	.309	.319	73	-14	22-13	.948	-7	90	107	2-49,3-48,O-41(LF)	-2.1
1981	Atl N	64	93	13	19	4	1	0	9	7-0	0	14	.204	.257	.269	49	-6	7-5	.950	1	99	105	3-24,2-13	-0.5
1982	†Atl N	108	261	43	77	13	2	2	25	22-1	2	36	.295	.351	.383	102	1	14-6	.943	0	89	61	3-62,O-25(LF),2-16,S-10	0.2
1983	Atl N	91	268	32	63	10	3	3	30	28-2	0	35	.235	.305	.328	71	-10	11-7	.940	8	123	104	3-47,2-26,O-18(LF),S-13	-0.1

Year	Tm Lg	G	AB	R	H	2B	3B	HR	RBI	BB-IB	HP	SO	AVG	OBP	SLG	AOPS	ABR	SB-CS	FA	FR	Rng	Thr	G at Pos	BFW
1984	Atl N	81	227	22	47	13	2	1	21	15-1	1	41	.207	.257	.295	52	-15	6-4	.973	10	128	101	2-29,3-17,S-16,O-11(LF)	-0.3
1985	SD N	90	249	31	70	13	2	5	31	32-1	1	31	.281	.363	.410	118	7	6-5	.975	9	116	111	2-58,3-29/S-7,O-2(0-1-1)	1.9
1986	SD N	118	257	31	66	12	0	5	26	32-3	0	45	.257	.336	.362	95	-1	3-5	.931	4	113	140	3-59,S-24,2-21/O-7(LF)	0.4
1987	Chi A	55	154	25	37	11	0	7	23	19-1	1	28	.240	.324	.448	101	0	2-1	.969	-4	87	88	3-30,O-13(LF)/2-5,D-4	-0.4
	NY A	18	42	1	15	2	0	0	4	4-0	0	4	.357	.413	.405	120	1	2-1	.909	1	88	121	3-13/2SO(LF)	0.2
	Year	73	196	26	52	13	0	7	27	23-1	1	32	.265	.342	.439	104	2	4-2	.954	-3	87	97	3-43,O-14(LF)/2-6,D-4,S	-0.2
1988	Atl N	68	102	8	18	3	0	0	1	6-1	0	16	.176	.222	.206	22	-10	0-0	1.000	0	111	249	O-26(7-19-1),3-10/2-2,S-2	-1.1
Total	16	1428	4208	552	1049	165	33	40	352	411-20	11	534	.249	.315	.333	76	-131	189-95	.951	63	108	100	3-634,2-416,S-187,O-153L/D-4	-3.7

ROYSTER, WILLIE Willie Arthur B 4.11.1954 Clarksville, VA BR/TR 5-11/180# d9.3

Year	Tm Lg	G	AB	R	H	2B	3B	HR	RBI	BB-IB	HP	SO	AVG	OBP	SLG	AOPS	ABR	SB-CS	FA	FR	Rng	Thr	G at Pos	BFW
1981	Bal A	4	4	0	0	0	0	0	0	0-0	0	2	.000	.000	.000	-99	-1	0-0	1.000	-0	0	0	/C-4	-0.1

ROZNOVSKY, VIC Victor Joseph B 10.19.1938 Shiner, TX BL/TR 6-1/180# d6.28

Year	Tm Lg	G	AB	R	H	2B	3B	HR	RBI	BB-IB	HP	SO	AVG	OBP	SLG	AOPS	ABR	SB-CS	FA	FR	Rng	Thr	G at Pos	BFW
1964	Chi N	35	76	2	15	1	0	0	2	5-0	0	18	.197	.244	.211	29	-7	0-1	.976	-3	*111*	*183*	C-26	-1.0
1965	Chi N	71	172	9	38	4	1	3	15	16-1	3	30	.221	.295	.308	70	-7	1-0	.984	1	*92*	*106*	C-63	-0.4
1966	Bal A	41	97	4	23	5	0	1	10	9-4	1	11	.237	.308	.320	82	-2	0-0	.995	-3	*86*	*114*	C-34	-0.4
1967	Bal A	45	97	7	20	5	0	0	10	1-0	0	20	.206	.212	.258	39	-8	0-0	.993	-0	100	144	C-23	-0.8
1969	Phi N	13	13	0	3	0	0	0	1	1-0	0	4	.231	.286	.231	47	-1	0-0	1.000	1	0	0	/C-2	0.0
Total	5	205	455	22	99	15	1	4	38	32-5	4	83	.218	.273	.281	59	-25	1-1	.988	-5	*95*	*126*	C-148	-2.6

RUAN, WILKIN Wilkin B 11.18.1978 Guaymate, D.R. BR/TR 6/170# d9.1

Year	Tm Lg	G	AB	R	H	2B	3B	HR	RBI	BB-IB	HP	SO	AVG	OBP	SLG	AOPS	ABR	SB-CS	FA	FR	Rng	Thr	G at Pos	BFW
2002	LA N	12	11	2	3	1	0	0	3	0-0	0	2	.273	.273	.364	73	-1	0-0	1.000	-0	92	0	/O-5(CF)	-0.1
2003	LA N	21	41	2	9	2	1	0	2	0-0	0	7	.220	.220	.317	40	-4	1-0	1.000	-0	91	178	O-20(CF)	-0.4
Total	2	33	52	4	12	3	1	0	5	0-0	0	9	.231	.231	.327	47	-5	1-0	1.000	-0	91	147	/O-25(CF)	-0.5

RUBELING, AL Albert William B 5.10.1913 Baltimore, MD D 1.28.1988 Baltimore, MD BR/TR 6/185# d4.16

Year	Tm Lg	G	AB	R	H	2B	3B	HR	RBI	BB-IB	HP	SO	AVG	OBP	SLG	AOPS	ABR	SB-CS	FA	FR	Rng	Thr	G at Pos	BFW
1940	Phi A	108	376	49	92	16	6	4	38	48	0	58	.245	.330	.351	78	-12	4-5	.933	-7	96	71	3-98,2-10	-1.5
1941	Phi A	6	19	0	5	0	0	0	2	2	0	1	.263	.333	.263	61	-1	0-0	.833	-2	74	98	/3-6	-0.2
1943	Pit N	47	168	23	44	8	4	0	9	8	0	17	.262	.295	.357	85	-4	0	.974	0	109	106	2-44/3	-0.2
1944	Pit N	92	184	22	45	7	2	4	30	19	2	19	.245	.322	.370	90	-2	4	1.000	1	106	72	O-18(9-0-9),2-17,3-16	-0.2
Total	4	253	747	94	186	31	12	8	79	77	2	95	.249	.321	.355	82	-19	8-5	.939	-7	97	88	3-121/2-71,O-18(9-0-9)	-2.1

RUBERTO, SONNY John Edward B 1.2.1946 Staten Island, NY BR/TR 5-11/175# d5.25 C2

Year	Tm Lg	G	AB	R	H	2B	3B	HR	RBI	BB-IB	HP	SO	AVG	OBP	SLG	AOPS	ABR	SB-CS	FA	FR	Rng	Thr	G at Pos	BFW
1969	SD N	19	21	3	3	0	0	0	0	1-0	0	7	.143	.182	.143	-8	-3	0-0	1.000	1	105	98	C-15	-0.2
1972	Cin N	2	3	0	0	0	0	0	0	0-0	1	1	.000	.250	.000	-25	0	0-0	1.000	-0	47	0	/C-2	-0.1
Total	2	21	24	3	3	0	0	0	0	1-0	1	8	.125	.192	.125	-10	-3	0-0	1.000	1	98	86	/C-17	-0.3

RUBLE, ART William Arthur "Speedy" B 3.11.1903 Knoxville, TN D 11.1.1983 Maryville, TN BL/TR 5-10.5/168# d4.18

Year	Tm Lg	G	AB	R	H	2B	3B	HR	RBI	BB-IB	HP	SO	AVG	OBP	SLG	AOPS	ABR	SB-CS	FA	FR	Rng	Thr	G at Pos	BFW
1927	Det A	56	91	16	15	4	2	0	11	14	1	15	.165	.283	.253	39	-8	2-2	.970	1	104	110	O-43(24-13-7)	-0.9
1934	Phi N	19	54	7	15	4	0	0	8	7	0	3	.278	.361	.352	81	-1	0	.839	-1	86	179	O-14(4-1-10)	-0.3
Total	2	75	145	23	30	8	2	0	19	21	1	18	.207	.311	.290	55	-9	2-2	.929	0	98	133	/O-57(28-14-17)	-1.2

RUCKER, JOHNNY John Joel B 1.15.1917 Crabapple, GA D 8.7.1985 Moultrie, GA BL/TR 6-2/175# d4.16

Year	Tm Lg	G	AB	R	H	2B	3B	HR	RBI	BB-IB	HP	SO	AVG	OBP	SLG	AOPS	ABR	SB-CS	FA	FR	Rng	Thr	G at Pos	BFW
1940	NY N	86	277	38	82	7	5	4	23	7	0	32	.296	.313	.401	95	-4	4	.954	-7	85	64	O-57(CF)	-1.2
1941	NY N	143	622	95	179	38	9	1	42	29	0	61	.288	.320	.383	95	-6	8	.967	-2	97	113	*O-142(CF)	-1.2
1943	NY N	132	505	56	138	19	4	2	46	22	0	44	.273	.304	.339	85	-12	4	.969	-4	98	81	*O-117(CF)	-2.1
1944	NY N	144	587	79	143	14	8	6	39	24	1	48	.244	.275	.325	69	-28	8	.985	-12	82	111	*O-139(CF)	-4.6
1945	NY N	105	429	58	117	19	11	7	51	20	0	36	.273	.305	.417	98	-4	7	.978	-5	95	73	O-98(CF)	-1.3
1946	NY N	95	197	28	52	8	2	1	13	7	3	27	.264	.300	.340	81	-6	4	.948	-5	90	28	O-54(0-50-6)	-1.3
Total	6	705	2617	354	711	105	39	21	214	109	4	248	.272	.302	.366	87	-60	35	.971	-35	92	89	O-607(0-603-6)	-11.7

RUDDERHAM, JOHN John Edmund B 8.30.1863 Quincy, MA D 4.3.1942 Randolph, MA BR/TR 5-8/170# d9.18

Year	Tm Lg	G	AB	R	H	2B	3B	HR	RBI	BB-IB	HP	SO	AVG	OBP	SLG	AOPS	ABR	SB-CS	FA	FR	Rng	Thr	G at Pos	BFW
1884	Bos U	1	4	0	1	0	0	0		0			.250	.250	.250	53	0		.000	-1	0	0	/O(LF)	-0.1

RUDI, JOE Joseph Oden B 9.7.1946 Modesto, CA BR/TR 6-2/200# d4.11 C2

Year	Tm Lg	G	AB	R	H	2B	3B	HR	RBI	BB-IB	HP	SO	AVG	OBP	SLG	AOPS	ABR	SB-CS	FA	FR	Rng	Thr	G at Pos	BFW
1967	KC A	19	43	4	8	2	0	0	1	3-0	0	7	.186	.239	.233	41	-3	0-0	.984	-1	0	18	/1-9,O-6(LF)	-0.6
1968	Oak A	68	181	10	32	5	1	1	12	12-3	2	32	.177	.236	.232	44	-13	1-1	.987	-2	91	34	O-56(55-1-1)	-2.1
1969	Oak A	35	122	10	23	3	1	2	6	5-1	0	16	.189	.220	.279	41	-11	1-1	1.000	1	112	139	O-18(LF),1-11	-1.2
1970	Oak A	106	350	40	108	23	2	11	42	16-1	2	61	.309	.341	.480	129	12	3-1	.982	1	100	138	O-63(58-1-12),1-28	0.9
1971	†Oak A	127	513	62	137	23	4	10	52	28-2	1	62	.267	.304	.386	97	-4	3-2	.996	4	111	68	*O-121(115-0-9)/1-5	-0.8
1972	†Oak A★	147	593	94	**181**	32	**9**	19	75	37-6	2	62	.305	.345	.486	154	36	3-4	.992	-8	88	75	*O-147(LF)/3	2.1
1973	†Oak A★	120	437	53	118	25	1	12	66	30-4	2	72	.270	.315	.414	111	5	0-0	.992	2	106	75	*O-117(LF)/1D	0.0
1974	†Oak A★	158	593	73	174	**39**	4	22	99	34-6	5	92	.293	.334	.484	143	30	2-3	.984	-6	92	76	*O-140(LF),1-27/D-2	1.5
1975	†Oak A★	126	468	66	130	26	6	21	75	40-12	3	56	.278	.338	.494	136	20	2-1	.991	-7	69	102	1-91,O-44(LF)/D-2	0.4
1976	Oak A	130	500	54	135	32	3	13	94	41-10	3	71	.270	.323	.424	124	15	6-1	.989	-4	95	64	*O-126(126-0-1)/1-2,D-2	0.4
1977	Cal A	64	242	48	64	13	2	13	53	22-4	4	48	.264	.333	.496	128	9	1-0	1.000	3	114	70	O-61(LF)/D-3	0.9
1978	Cal A	133	497	58	127	27	1	17	79	28-4	2	82	.256	.295	.416	103	0	2-1	.992	2	105	57	*O-111(LF),D-11,1-10	-0.4
1979	Cal A	90	330	35	80	11	3	11	61	24-3	1	61	.242	.294	.394	87	-7	0-0	.989	2	106	85	O-80(69-0-12)/1-5,D-3	-0.9
1980	Cal A	104	372	42	88	17	1	16	53	17-2	5	84	.237	.277	.417	90	-7	1-0	.991	5	115	74	O-90(89-0-1)/1-6,D-3	-0.6
1981	Bos A	49	122	14	22	3	0	6	24	8-1	2	29	.180	.239	.352	66	-6	0-0	1.000	-1	30	44	D-21/1-5,O(RF)	-0.8
1982	Oak A	71	193	21	41	6	1	5	18	24-0	1	35	.212	.301	.332	77	-6	0-0	.991	-5	65	90	1-49,O-14(4-0-10)/D-3	-1.4
Total	16	1547	5556	684	1468	287	39	179	810	369-59	35	870	.264	.311	.427	112	70	25-15	.991	-15	101	74	*O-1195(1160-2-47),1-249/D-51,3	-2.6

RUDOLPH, DUTCH John Herman B 7.10.1882 Natrona, PA D 4.17.1967 Natrona, PA BL/TL 5-10/160# d7.3

Year	Tm Lg	G	AB	R	H	2B	3B	HR	RBI	BB-IB	HP	SO	AVG	OBP	SLG	AOPS	ABR	SB-CS	FA	FR	Rng	Thr	G at Pos	BFW
1903	Phi N	1	1	0	0	0	0	0	0	0	0		.000	.000	.000	-99	0	0	—	0			H	0.0
1904	Chi N	2	3	0	1	0	0	0	0	0	0		.333	.333	.333	106	0	0	1.000	-0	0	0	/O-2(RF)	0.0
Total	2	3	4	0	1	0	0	0	0	0	0		.250	.250	.250	52	0	0	1.000	-0	0	0	/O-2(RF)	0.0

RUDOLPH, KEN Kenneth Victor B 12.29.1946 Rockford, IL BR/TR 6-1/185# d4.20

Year	Tm Lg	G	AB	R	H	2B	3B	HR	RBI	BB-IB	HP	SO	AVG	OBP	SLG	AOPS	ABR	SB-CS	FA	FR	Rng	Thr	G at Pos	BFW
1969	Chi N	27	34	7	7	1	0	1	6	6-0	0	11	.206	.325	.324	73	-1	0-0	.977	-1	99	0	C-11/O-3(LF)	-0.2
1970	Chi N	20	40	1	4	1	0	0	2	1-1	0	12	.100	.122	.125	-30	-7	0-0	1.000	2	294	172	C-16	-0.5
1971	Chi N	25	76	5	15	3	0	0	7	6-0	1	20	.197	.265	.237	38	-6	0-0	1.000	7	371	219	C-25	0.2
1972	Chi N	42	106	10	25	1	1	2	9	6-0	1	14	.236	.283	.321	64	-5	1-2	.966	3	125	157	C-41	-0.1
1973	Chi N	64	170	12	35	8	1	2	17	7-0	1	25	.206	.239	.300	46	-13	1-4	.970	-5	89	148	C-64	-1.8
1974	SF N	57	158	11	41	3	0	0	10	21-5	1	15	.259	.350	.278	74	-5	0-0	.996	-1	91	69	C-56	-0.3
1975	StL N	44	80	5	16	2	0	1	6	3-0	0	10	.200	.229	.262	35	-7	0-0	.972	-1	77	116	C-31	-0.8
1976	StL N	27	50	1	8	3	0	0	5	1-0	0	7	.160	.176	.220	12	-6	0-0	.940	-0	103	111	C-14	-0.6
1977	SF N	11	15	1	3	0	0	0	0	1-1	0	3	.200	.250	.200	22	-2	0-0	.946	2	214	131	C-11	0.0
	Bal A	11	14	2	4	1	0	0	2	0-0	0	4	.286	.286	.357	79	0	0-0	1.000	3	67	138	C-11	0.2
Total	9	328	743	55	158	23	2	6	64	52-7	4	121	.213	.267	.273	48	-52	2-6	.980	9	140	130	C-280/O-3(LF)	-3.9

RUEL, MUDDY Herold Dominic B 2.20.1896 St.Louis, MO D 11.13.1963 Palo Alto, CA BR/TR 5-9/150# d5.29 Mil 1918 M1 C14

Year	Tm Lg	G	AB	R	H	2B	3B	HR	RBI	BB-IB	HP	SO	AVG	OBP	SLG	AOPS	ABR	SB-CS	FA	FR	Rng	Thr	G at Pos	BFW
1915	StL A	10	14	0	0	0	0	0	1	5	0	5	.000	.263	.000	-22	-2	0	.958	-1	*89*	*61*	/C-6	-0.3
1917	NY A	6	17	1	2	0	0	0	1	2	0	2	.118	.211	.118	0	-2	1	1.000	0	*130*	*96*	/C-6	-0.2
1918	NY A	3	6	0	2	0	0	0	0	2	0	1	.333	.500	.333	148	1	1	1.000	0	*176*	*71*	/C-2	0.1
1919	NY A	79	233	18	56	6	0	0	31	34	1	26	.240	.340	.266	71	-7	4	.975	-1	*110*	*98*	C-79	-0.2
1920	NY A	82	261	30	70	14	1	1	15	15	1	18	.268	.310	.341	70	-11	4-2	.984	3	*114*	*66*	C-80	-0.2
1921	Bos A	113	358	41	99	21	1	1	45	41	1	15	.277	.352	.349	82	-8	2-7	.977	-2	*111*	*95*	*C-109	-0.5
1922	Bos A	116	361	34	92	15	1	0	28	41	1	26	.255	.333	.302	67	-16	4-2	.978	-1	*86*	*84*	*C-112	-1.0
1923	Was A	136	449	63	142	24	3	0	54	55	3	21	.316	.394	.383	111	10	4-6	.980	15	*102*	*123*	*C-133	3.1
1924	†Was A	149	501	50	142	20	2	0	57	62	7	20	.283	.370	.331	84	-9	7-11	.980	21	***147***	*77*	*C-147	1.9
1925	†Was A	127	393	55	122	9	2	0	54	63	4	16	.310	.411	.344	95	1	4-5	.982	15	*109*	*97*	*C-126/1	2.1
1926	Was A	117	368	42	110	22	4	1	53	61	2	14	.299	.401	.389	109	8	7-6	**.989**	1	*98*	*93*	*C-117	1.6
1927	Was A	131	428	61	132	16	5	1	52	63	5	18	.308	.403	.376	104	6	9-6	.988	1	*109*	*87*	*C-128	1.4
1928	Was A	108	350	31	90	18	2	0	55	44	1	14	.257	.342	.320	75	-11	12-10	**.989**	8	***120***	*94*	*C-101/1-2	0.3
1929	Was A	69	188	16	46	4	2	0	20	31	0	7	.245	.352	.287	66	-9	0-5	.990	7	*123*	*140*	C-62	0.1
1930	Was A	66	198	18	50	3	4	0	26	24	3	13	.253	.342	.308	66	-10	1-0	.986	5	*128*	*115*	C-60	-0.1

Year	Tm Lg	G	AB	R	H	2B	3B	HR	RBI	BB-IB	HP	SO	AVG	OBP	SLG	AOPS	ABR	SB-CS	FA	FR	Rng	Thr	G at Pos	BFW
1931	Bos A	33	83	6	25	5	0	0	6	9	0	6	.301	.370	.361	98	0	0-0	.945	0	*122*	*106*	C-30	0.2
	Det A	14	50	1	6	1	0	0	3	5	0	1	.120	.200	.140	-9	-8	0-0	.975	1	*78*	*173*	C-14	-0.5
	Year	47	133	7	31	6	0	0	9	14	0	7	.233	.306	.278	56	-8	0-0	.958	1	*106*	*131*	C-44	-0.3
1932	Det A	51	136	10	32	4	2	0	18	17	0	6	.235	.320	.294	58	-8	1-0	.989	-1	*88*	*107*	C-49	-0.6
1933	StL A	36	63	13	12	2	0	0	8	24	0	4	.190	.414	.222	68	-1	0-0	1.000	3	*118*	*154*	C-28	0.3
1934	Chi A	22	57	4	12	3	0	0	7	8	0	5	.211	.308	.263	47	-4	0-0	.976	-2	*60*	*90*	C-21	-0.5
Total	19	1468	4514	494	1242	187	29	4	534	606	29	238	.275	.365	.332	84	-80	61-60	.982	72	*111*	*97*	*C-1410/1-3	7.0
RUETHER, DUTCH Walter Henry B 9.13.1893 Alameda, CA D 5.16.1970 Phoenix, AZ BL/TL 6-1.5/180# d4.13 Mil 1918 ▲																								
1917	Chi N	31	44	3	12	1	3	0	11	8	0	11	.273	.385	.432	139	2	0	1.000	1	108	297	P-10/1-5	0.1
	Cin N	19	24	1	5	2	0	0	1	3	0	6	.208	.296	.292	84	2	1	.833	-0	98	0	/P-7	0.0
	Year	50	68	4	17	3	3	0	12	11	0	17	.250	.354	.382	122	2	1	.920	0	103	149	P-17/1-5	0.1
1918	Cin N	2	3	0	0	0	0	0	0	0	0	2	.000	.000	.000	-99	0	0	1.000	-0	69	0	/P-2	0.0
1919	†Cin N	42	92	8	24	2	3	0	6	4	0	18	.261	.292	.348	94	5	1	.971	-3	82	57	P-33	0.0
1920	Cin N	45	104	3	20	4	0	0	10	5	0	24	.192	.229	.231	33	-9	0-0	.952	0	102	227	P-37/1	0.0
1921	Bro N	49	97	12	34	5	2	2	13	4	0	9	.351	.376	.505	127	11	1-0	.966	-1	93	126	P-36	0.0
1922	Bro N	67	125	12	26	6	1	2	20	12	1	11	.208	.283	.320	56	6	0-0	**1.000**	-0	90	227	P-35	0.0
1923	Bro N	49	117	6	32	1	0	0	10	12	0	12	.274	.341	.282	68	-5	0-0	.968	-2	82	143	P-34/1	-0.1
1924	Bro N	34	62	5	15	1	1	0	4	5	0	2	.242	.299	.290	60	2	0-0	.981	1	112	154	P-30	0.0
1925	†Was A	55	108	18	36	3	2	1	15	10	0	8	.333	.390	.426	109	1	0-1	.962	-3	83	40	P-30/1	-0.1
1926	Was A	47	92	6	23	2	0	1	11	6	0	10	.250	.296	.304	58	4	0-0	.974	-2	84	86	P-23	0.0
	†NY A	13	21	2	2	0	0	0	0	0	1	1	.095	.136	.095	-39	-2	0-0	.875	-1	55	0	/P-5	0.0
	Year	60	113	8	25	2	0	1	11	6	1	11	.221	.267	.265	40	2	0-0	.957	-3	79	71	P-28	0.0
1927	NY A	35	80	7	21	3	0	1	10	8	0	15	.262	.330	.338	76	5	0-0	**1.000**	0	104	103	P-27	0.0
Total	11	488	969	83	250	30	12	7	111	77	2	129	.258	.314	.335	76	22	3-1	.970	-9	91	132	P-309/1-8	-0.1
RUFER, RUDY Rudolph Joseph B 10.28.1926 Ridgewood, NY BR/TR 6-0.5/165# d9.22																								
1949	NY N	7	15	1	1	0	0	0	2	2	0	0	.067	.176	.067	-32	-3	0	.957	-0	94	79	/S-7	-0.3
1950	NY N	15	11	1	1	0	0	0	0	0	0	1	.091	.091	.091	-52	-2	1	.889	1	165	120	/S-8	-0.2
Total	2	22	26	2	2	0	0	0	2	2	0	1	.077	.143	.077	-40	-5	1	.938	0	111	89	/S-15	-0.5
RUFFING, RED Charles Herbert B 5.3.1904 Granville, IL D 2.17.1986 Mayfield Hts., OH BR/TR 6-1.5/205# d5.31 Mil 1943-44 C1 HF1967 ▲																								
1924	Bos A	8	7	0	1	0	1	0	0	0	0	1	.143	.143	.429	44	0	0-0	1.000	-1	56	0	/P-8	0.0
1925	Bos A	37	79	6	17	4	2	0	11	1	1	22	.215	.235	.316	39	0	0-0	.983	-1	92	111	P-37	0.0
1926	Bos A	37	51	8	10	1	0	1	5	2	0	12	.196	.226	.275	31	1	0-1	.978	-1	81	88	P-37	0.0
1927	Bos A	29	55	5	14	3	1	0	4	0	1	6	.255	.268	.345	59	2	0-0	.978	0	93	49	P-26	0.0
1928	Bos A	60	121	12	38	13	1	2	19	3	0	12	.314	.331	.488	115	13	0-0	.951	-3	78	102	P-42	0.0
1929	Bos A	60	114	9	35	9	0	2	17	2	1	13	.307	.325	.439	97	-1	0-0	.946	-1	88	36	P-35/O-2(LF)	-0.1
1930	Bos A	6	11	2	3	2	0	0	1	0	0	1	.273	.273	.455	84	1	0-0	.667	-1	41	0	/P-4	0.0
	NY A	52	99	15	37	6	2	4	21	7	0	7	.374	.415	.596	160	17	0-0	.938	-3	67	0	P-34	0.0
	Year	58	110	17	40	8	2	4	22	7	0	8	.364	.402	.582	153	17	0-0	.914	-3	64	0	P-38	0.0
1931	NY A	48	109	14	36	8	1	3	12	1	0	13	.330	.336	.505	125	3	0-0	**1.000**	-3	66	42	P-37/O(RF)	-0.1
1932	†NY A	55	124	20	38	6	1	3	19	6	0	10	.306	.338	.444	106	13	0-0	.955	-2	72	133	P-35	0.0
1933	NY A	55	115	10	29	3	1	2	13	7	0	15	.252	.295	.348	74	8	0-0	.964	-0	89	178	P-35	0.0
1934	NY A★	45	113	11	28	3	0	2	13	3	1	17	.248	.274	.327	58	6	0-0	.933	-3	63	83	P-36	0.0
1935	NY A	50	109	13	37	10	0	2	18	3	1	9	.339	.363	.486	125	13	0-0	**1.000**	-2	59	144	P-30	0.0
1936	†NY A	53	127	14	37	5	0	5	22	11	0	12	.291	.348	.449	99	15	0-0	.986	2	113	222	P-33	0.0
1937	†NY A	54	129	11	26	3	0	1	10	13	0	24	.202	.275	.248	32	2	0-0	.974	-4	58	91	P-31	0.0
1938	†NY A☆	45	107	12	24	4	1	3	17	17	0	21	.224	.331	.364	74	9	0-0	**1.000**	-2	73	72	P-31	0.0
1939	†NY A★	44	114	12	35	1	0	1	20	7	0	18	.307	.347	.342	78	8	1-0	.952	-2	81	83	P-28	0.0
1940	NY A★	33	89	8	11	4	0	1	7	3	0	9	.124	.152	.202	-9	-3	0-0	.947	-3	73	86	P-30	0.0
1941	†NY A☆	38	89	10	27	8	1	2	22	4	0	12	.303	.333	.483	115	11	0-0	**1.000**	-3	62	130	P-23	0.0
1942	†NY A☆	30	80	8	20	4	0	1	13	5	1	13	.250	.302	.338	81	6	0-0	.974	-2	77	191	P-24	0.0
1945	NY A	21	46	4	10	0	1	1	5	0	0	8	.217	.217	.326	54	0	0-0	.929	-2	65	94	P-11	0.0
1946	NY A	8	25	1	3	1	0	0	1	1	0	8	.120	.154	.160	-12	-1	0-0	1.000	-1	57	157	/P-8	0.0
1947	Chi A	14	24	2	5	0	0	0	3	1	0	3	.208	.240	.208	26	0	0-0	1.000	-1	82	174	/P-9	0.0
Total	22	882	1937	207	521	98	13	36	273	97	6	266	.269	.306	.389	81	123	1-1	.968	-37	76	104	P-624/O-3(2-0-1)	-0.2
RUIZ, CHICO Hiraldo (Sablon) (born (Hiraldo Sablon (Ruiz)) B 12.5.1938 Santo Domingo, Cuba D 2.9.1972 San Diego, CA BB/TR 6/173# d4.13 OF Total (11-LF 3-RF)																								
1964	Cin N	77	311	33	76	13	2	2	16	7-1	4	41	.244	.269	.318	63	-16	11-3	.942	-7	76	141	3-49,2-30	-2.0
1965	Cin N	29	18	7	2	1	0	0	1	0-0	0	5	.111	.111	.167	-21	-3	1-2	.875	1	130	0	/3-4,S-3	-0.3
1966	Cin N	82	110	13	28	2	1	0	5	5-0	0	14	.255	.287	.291	56	-6	1-2	.927	-1	91	58	3-27/O-8(7-0-1),S-6	-0.8
1967	Cin N	105	250	32	55	12	4	0	13	11-0	2	35	.220	.258	.300	53	-15	9-4	.969	-2	98	87	2-56,3-13,S-11/O-5(3-0-2)	-1.3
1968	Cin N	85	139	15	36	2	1	0	9	12-0	0	18	.259	.316	.288	78	-4	4-3	.979	5	125	108	2-34,1-16/3-5,S-3	0.3
1969	Cin N	88	196	19	48	4	1	0	13	14-3	0	28	.245	.292	.276	58	-11	4-2	.949	-6	99	115	2-39,S-29/3-7,1-2,O(LF)	-1.3
1970	Cal A	68	107	10	26	3	1	0	12	7-1	1	16	.243	.293	.290	64	-5	3-0	.985	-2	100	105	3-27/2-3,S-3,1-2,C	-0.7
1971	Cal A	31	19	4	5	0	0	0	0	2-0	0	7	.263	.333	.263	76	-1	1-0	1.000	-2	45	0	/3-3,2-2	-0.2
Total	8	565	1150	133	276	37	10	2	69	58-5	7	164	.240	.279	.295	60	-61	34-16	.966	-14	102	101	2-164,3-135/S-55,1-20,O-14L,C	-6.3
RUIZ, CHICO Manuel (Cruz) B 11.1.1951 Santurce, P.R. BR/TR 5-11.5/170# d7.29																								
1978	Atl N	18	46	3	13	3	0	0	2	2-1	0	4	.283	.313	.348	76	-1	0-0	.984	1	99	73	2-14/3	0.0
1980	Atl N	25	26	3	8	2	1	0	2	3-0	0	7	.308	.379	.462	129	1	0-1	.875	-0	146	0	3-16/S-4,2-2	0.1
Total	2	43	72	6	21	5	1	0	4	5-1	0	11	.292	.338	.389	95	0	0-1	.880	0	133	0	/3-17,2-16,S-4	0.1
RULLO, JOE Joseph Vincent B 6.16.1916 New York, NY D 10.28.1969 Philadelphia, PA BR/TR 5-11/168# d9.22																								
1943	Phi A	16	55	2	16	3	0	0	6	8	0	7	.291	.381	.345	114	1	0-0	.963	-1	111	89	2-16	0.2
1944	Phi A	35	96	5	16	0	0	0	5	6	1	19	.167	.223	.167	12	-11	1-0	.954	0	101	113	2-33/1O(CF)	-1.0
Total	2	51	151	7	32	3	0	0	11	14	1	26	.212	.283	.232	50	-10	1-0	.957	-0	104	105	/2-49,O(CF)1	-0.8
RUMLER, WILLIAM William George B 3.27.1891 Milford, NE D 5.26.1966 Lincoln, NE BR/TR 6-1/190# d5.4 Mil 1918																								
1914	StL A	34	46	2	8	1	0	0	6	3	1	12	.174	.240	.196	32	-4	2-2	1.000	-1	*81*	*118*	C-10/O-6(RF)	-0.5
1916	StL A	27	37	6	12	3	0	0	10	3	0	7	.324	.375	.405	141	2	0	.971	0	83	61	/C-9	0.3
1917	StL A	78	88	7	23	3	4	1	16	8	0	9	.261	.323	.420	132	3	2	.938	1	97	194	/O-9(3-0-6)	0.3
Total	3	139	171	15	43	7	4	1	32	14	1	28	.251	.312	.357	107	1	4-2	.986	-0	*82*	*90*	/C-19,O-15(3-0-12)	0.1
RUNGE, PAUL Paul William B 5.21.1958 Kingston, NY BR/TR 6/175# d9.25																								
1981	Atl N	10	27	2	7	1	0	0	2	4-0	0	4	.259	.355	.296	84	0	0-0	.911	-2	95	91	S-10	-0.2
1982	Atl N	4	2	0	0	0	0	0	0	0-0	0	0	.000	.000	.000	-96	-1	0-0	—	0			/H	-0.1
1983	Atl N	5	8	0	2	0	0	0	1	1-0	0	4	.250	.333	.250	59	0	0-0	1.000	-1	48	76	/2-2	-0.2
1984	Atl N	28	90	5	24	3	1	0	3	10-0	0	14	.267	.340	.322	81	-2	5-3	.970	7	125	115	2-22/S-7,3-3	0.7
1985	Atl N	50	87	15	19	3	0	1	5	18-0	0	18	.218	.349	.287	76	-2	0-1	.929	2	133	72	3-28/S-5,2-2	0.0
1986	Atl N	7	8	1	2	0	0	0	0	2-0	0	4	.250	.400	.250	79	0	0-0	1.000	-0	114	0	/2-5	0.0
1987	Atl N	27	47	9	10	1	0	3	8	5-0	0	10	.213	.288	.426	82	-1	0-1	.923	-1	94	205	3-10/S-9,2-2	-0.2
1988	Atl N	52	76	11	16	5	0	0	7	14-0	0	21	.211	.330	.276	73	-2	0-0	1.000	-6	84	89	3-19/2-7,S-6	-0.8
Total	8	183	345	43	80	13	1	4	26	54-0	0	75	.232	.334	.310	77	-8	5-5	.941	-2	111	101	/3-60,2-40,S-37	-0.8
RUNNELLS, TOM Thomas William B 4.17.1955 Greeley, CO BB/TR 6/175# d8.9 M2 C2																								
1985	Cin N	28	35	3	7	1	0	0	0	3-0	0	4	.200	.263	.229	37	-3	0-0	1.000	-1	95	103	S-11/2	-0.3
1986	Cin N	12	11	1	1	1	0	0	0	0-0	0	2	.091	.091	.182	-26	-2	0-0	1.000	0	165	160	/2-4,3-3	-0.2
Total	2	40	46	4	8	2	0	0	0	3-0	0	6	.174	.224	.217	23	-5	0-0	1.000	-1	95	103	/S-11,2-5,3-3	-0.5
RUNNELS, PETE James Edward (born James Edward Runnells) B 1.28.1928 Lufkin, TX D 5.20.1991 Pasadena, TX BL/TR 6/170# d7.1 M1 C2																								
1951	Was A	78	273	31	76	12	2	0	25	31	1	24	.278	.354	.337	89	-3	0-3	.949	-15	86	77	S-73	-1.5
1952	Was A	152	555	70	158	18	3	1	64	72	1	55	.285	.368	.333	99	2	0-10	.966	-13	95	100	*S-147/2	-0.5
1953	Was A	137	486	64	125	15	5	2	50	64	3	36	.257	.347	.321	83	-10	3-4	.958	-20	90	122	*S-121,2-11	-2.1
1954	Was A	139	488	75	131	17	15	3	56	78	0	60	.268	.368	.383	112	9	2-3	.953	-17	95	97	*S-107,2-27/O(LF)	0.3

Year	Tm Lg	G	AB	R	H	2B	3B	HR	RBI	BB-IB	HP	SO	AVG	OBP	SLG	AOPS	ABR	SB-CS	FA	FR	Rng	Thr	G at Pos	BFW
1955	Was A	134	503	66	143	16	4	2	49	55-2	1	51	.284	.353	.344	94	-4	3-9	.976	4	103	97	*2-132/S-2	0.7
1956	Was A	147	578	72	179	29	9	8	76	58-2	2	64	.310	.372	.433	113	11	5-5	.995	3	103	88	1-81,2-69/S-3	1.3
1957	Was A	134	473	53	109	18	4	2	35	55-5	2	51	.230	.310	.298	69	-20	2-3	.995	1	97	82	1-72,3-32,2-23	-2.3
1958	Bos A	147	568	103	183	32	5	8	59	87-0	6	49	.322	.416	.438	127	27	1-2	.985	5	**109**	100	*2-106,1-42	3.7
1959	Bos A★	147	560	95	176	33	6	6	57	95-1	1	48	.314	.415	.427	126	25	6-5	.982	6	97	111	*2-101,1-44/S-9	3.6
1960	Bos A★	143	528	80	169	29	2	2	35	71-2	2	51	**.320**	.401	.394	112	13	5-2	**.986**	9	105	101	*2-129,1-57/3-3	3.1
1961	Bos A	143	360	49	114	20	3	3	38	46-2	3	32	.317	.396	.414	115	10	5-1	**.995**	-2	83	**127**	*1-113,3-11/2-7,S	0.4
1962	Bos A★	152	562	80	183	33	5	10	60	79-11	3	57	**.326**	.408	.456	129	27	3-4	.993	-4	89	95	*1-151	1.3
1963	Hou N	124	388	35	98	9	1	2	23	45-2	3	42	.253	.332	.296	89	-4	2-0	.993	-9	86	65	1-70,2-36/3-3	-1.6
1964	Hou N	22	51	3	10	1	0	0	3	8-1	0	7	.196	.305	.216	53	-3	0-0	.986	-2	49	76	1-14	-0.6
Total	14	1799	6373	876	1854	282	64	49	630	844-28	28	627	.291	.375	.378	106	80	37-51	.994	-53	89	96	1-644,2-642,S-463/3-49,O(LF)	5.8
RUSHFORD, JIM James Thomas B 3.24.1974 Chicago, IL BL/TL 6-1/225# d9.3																								
2002	Mil N	23	77	8	11	2	0	1	6	6-0	1	9	.143	.214	.208	14	-10	0-0	.956	-1	105	0	O-22(1-0-21)	-1.2
RUSS, JOHN John B 4.1.1858 Cannelton, IN D 1.18.1912 Louisville, KY d7.4																								
1882	Bal AA	1	3	0	1	0	0	0		0			.333	.333	.333	136	0		—	-0	0	0	/O(CF)P	0.0
RUSSELL, REB Ewell Albert B 4.12.1889 Jackson, MS D 9.30.1973 Indianapolis, IN BL/TL 5-11/185# d4.18 ▲																								
1913	Chi A	54	106	9	20	5	3	1	7	1	1	29	.189	.204	.321	54	3	0	.953	-5	76	108	P-52	0.0
1914	Chi A	46	64	6	17	1	1	0	7	1	0	14	.266	.277	.313	78	3	0	.946	0	104	0	P-38	0.0
1915	Chi A	45	86	11	21	2	3	0	7	4	2	14	.244	.293	.337	86	4	1	.971	-2	83	48	P-41	0.0
1916	Chi A	56	91	9	13	2	0	0	6	0	1	18	.143	.152	.165	-5	-4	1	.974	-2	95	75	P-56	0.0
1917	†Chi A	39	68	4	19	3	3	0	9	2	0	10	.279	.300	.412	115	0	0	.984	-1	93	110	P-35/O(LF)	0.0
1918	Chi A	27	50	2	7	3	0	0	3	0	1	6	.140	.157	.200	8	-6	0	1.000	-1	83	75	P-19/O(RF)	-0.1
1919	Chi A	1	0	0	0	0	0	0	0	0	0	0	—	—	—	—	0	0	—	0	0	0	/P	0.0
1922	Pit N	60	220	51	81	14	8	12	75	14	7	18	.368	.423	.668	175	23	4-2	.968	-1	101	68	O-60(RF)	1.6
1923	Pit N	94	291	49	84	18	7	9	58	20	3	21	.289	.341	.491	115	5	3-1	.970	-0	110	50	O-76(4-0-72)	-0.1
Total	9	422	976	141	262	48	25	22	172	42	15	130	.268	.309	.436	104	28	9-3	.968	-12	88	74	P-242,O-138(5-0-133)	1.4
RUSSELL, RIP Glen David B 1.26.1915 Los Angeles, CA D 9.26.1976 Los Alamitos, CA BR/TR 6-1/180# d5.5																								
1939	Chi N	143	542	55	148	24	5	9	79	36	0	56	.273	.318	.386	87	-11	2	.988	-5	87	85	*1-143	-3.0
1940	Chi N	68	215	15	53	7	2	5	33	8	1	23	.247	.277	.367	78	-8	1	.982	-6	59	55	1-51/3-3	-1.9
1941	Chi N	6	17	1	5	1	0	0	1	1	0	5	.294	.333	.353	97	0	0	.975	0	119	118	/1-5	0.0
1942	Chi N	102	302	32	73	9	0	8	41	17	0	21	.242	.282	.351	88	-6	0	.974	-9	60	107	1-35,2-24,3-10/O-3(LF)	-1.8
1946	†Bos A	80	274	22	57	10	1	6	35	13	1	30	.208	.247	.318	54	-18	1-1	.942	-0	99	172	3-70/2-3	-2.0
1947	Bos A	26	52	8	8	1	0	1	3	8	0	7	.154	.267	.231	36	-4	0-0	.923	1	121	90	3-13	-0.4
Total	6	425	1402	133	344	52	8	29	192	83	2	142	.245	.289	.356	77	-47	4-1	.984	-19	78	82	1-234/3-96,2-27,O-3(LF)	-9.1
RUSSELL, HARVEY Harvey Holmes B 1.10.1887 Marshall, VA D 1.8.1980 Alexandria, VA BL/TR 5-9.5/163# d4.17																								
1914	Bal F	81	168	18	39	3	2	0	13	18	1	17	.232	.310	.274	58	-12	2	.956	-10	*99*	*76*	C-47/SO(1-1-0)	-2.0
1915	Bal F	53	73	5	19	1	2	0	11	14	4	5	.260	.407	.329	105	1	1	.989	-2	*101*	*85*	C-21	0.0
Total	2	134	241	23	58	4	4	0	24	32	5	22	.241	.342	.290	73	-11	3	.965	-12	*100*	*79*	/C-68,O(1-1-0)S	-2.0
RUSSELL, JIM James William B 10.1.1918 Fayette City, PA D 11.24.1987 Pittsburgh, PA BB/TR 6-1/181# d9.12																								
1942	Pit N	5	14	2	1	0	0	0	0	1	0	4	.071	.133	.071	-38	-2	0	1.000	0	129	0	/O-3(CF)	-0.3
1943	Pit N	146	533	79	138	19	11	4	44	77	1	67	.259	.354	.358	102	3	12	.990	4	101	124	*O-134(133-2-2)/1-6	-0.1
1944	Pit N	152	580	109	181	34	14	8	66	79	5	63	.312	.399	.460	136	30	6	.986	9	102	164	*O-149(139-6-4)	3.1
1945	Pit N	146	510	88	145	24	8	12	77	71	5	40	.284	.377	.433	120	15	15	.973	5	109	93	*O-140(139-1-0)	1.2
1946	Pit N	146	516	68	143	29	6	8	50	67	2	54	.277	.362	.403	114	11	11	.966	-7	98	58	*O-134(67-68-0)/1-5	-0.3
1947	Pit N	128	478	68	121	21	8	8	51	63	2	58	.253	.343	.381	89	-7	7	.980	3	109	67	*O-119(1-102-19)	-0.7
1948	Bos N	89	322	44	85	18	1	9	54	46	3	31	.264	.361	.410	110	6	4	.992	-2	103	46	O-84(2-82-0)	0.2
1949	Bos N	130	415	57	96	22	1	8	54	64	2	68	.231	.337	.347	88	-5	3	.975	-8	93	36	*O-120(30-93-0)	-1.8
1950	Bro N	77	214	37	49	8	2	10	32	31	1	36	.229	.329	.425	95	-2	1	.993	4	119	80	O-55(53-3-0)	-0.1
1951	Bro N	16	13	2	0	0	0	0	0	4	1	6	.000	.278	.000	-18	-2	0-0	1.000	-0	96	0	/O-4(LF)	-0.2
Total	10	1035	3595	554	959	175	51	67	428	503	22	427	.267	.360	.400	108	47	59-0	.981	8	103	88	O-942(568-360-25)/1-11	1.0
RUSSELL, JOHN John William B 1.5.1961 Oklahoma City, OK BR/TR 6/200# d6.22 C1 OF Total (88-LF 36-RF)																								
1984	Phi N	39	99	11	28	8	1	2	11	12-2	0	33	.283	.351	.444	123	3	0-1	1.000	-1	100	53	O-29(14-0-18)/C-2	0.1
1985	Phi N	81	216	22	47	12	0	9	23	18-0	0	72	.218	.278	.398	85	-5	2-0	1.000	-5	72	131	O-49(LF),1-18	-1.3
1986	Phi N	93	315	35	76	21	2	13	60	25-2	3	103	.241	.300	.444	100	-1	0-1	.976	-11	67	98	C-89	-0.9
1987	Phi N	24	62	5	9	1	0	3	8	3-0	0	17	.145	.185	.306	26	-7	0-1	.955	-3	114	153	O-10(LF)/C-7	-1.0
1988	Phi N	22	49	5	12	1	0	2	4	3-0	1	15	.245	.302	.388	95	0	0-0	.945	0	49	161	C-15	0.1
1989	Atl N	74	159	14	29	2	0	2	9	8-1	1	53	.182	.225	.233	31	-15	0-0	.990	-1	122	153	C-45,O-14(1-0-15)/1-2,3-2,P	-1.6
1990	Tex A	68	128	16	35	4	0	2	8	11-2	0	41	.273	.331	.352	91	-2	1-0	.980	-1	49	30	C-31,D-19/O-6(LF),1-3,3	-0.2
1991	Tex A	22	27	3	3	0	0	0	1	1-0	0	7	.111	.138	.111	-29	-5	0-0	1.000	-1	68	0	/O-8(6-0-2),C-5,D-5	-0.6
1992	Tex A	7	10	1	1	0	0	0	2	1-0	1	4	.100	.231	.100	2	-1	0-0	1.000	-1	54	243	/C-4,O-2(1-0-1),D	-0.2
1993	Tex A	18	22	1	5	1	0	1	3	2-0	0	10	.227	.292	.409	90	0	0-0	1.000	-2	252	71	C-11/13O(LF)	-0.2
Total	10	448	1087	113	245	50	3	34	129	84-7	6	355	.225	.282	.371	79	-33	3-3	.979	-24	80	101	C-209,O-119L/D-25,1-24,3-4,P	-5.8
RUSSELL, LLOYD Lloyd Opal B 4.10.1913 Atoka, OK D 5.24.1968 Waco, TX BR/TR 5-11/166# d4.26																								
1938	Cle A	2	0	0	0	0	0	0	0	0	0	0	—	—	—	—	0	0-0	—	0			R	0.0
RUSSELL, PAUL Paul A. B 1870 Reading, PA D Pottstown, PA d7.29																								
1894	StL N	3	10	1	1	0	0	0	0	0	0	2	.100	.100	.100	-52	-3	0	1.000	-0	513	0	/O(CF)32	-0.2
RUSSELL, BILL William Ellis B 10.21.1948 Pittsburg, KS BR/TR (BB 1971) 6/175# d4.7 M3 C9 OF Total (62-LF 75-CF 179-RF)																								
1969	LA N	98	212	35	48	6	2	5	15	22-1	1	45	.226	.301	.344	87	-4	4-1	.978	5	121	101	O-86(7-24-62)	-0.2
1970	LA N	81	278	30	72	11	9	0	28	16-1	3	28	.259	.303	.363	82	-8	9-1	.983	7	115	169	O-79(2-23-57)/S	-0.3
1971	LA N	91	211	29	48	7	4	2	15	11-2	0	39	.227	.265	.327	71	-9	6-3	.964	-0	108	94	2-41,O-40(3-8-35)/S-6	-0.8
1972	LA N	129	434	47	118	19	5	4	34	34-9	2	64	.272	.326	.366	99	-1	14-7	.949	10	109	104	*S-121/O-6(1-1-4)	2.6
1973	LA N★	**162**	615	55	163	26	3	4	56	34-20	1	63	.265	.301	.337	81	-17	15-7	.963	-1	101	**118**	*S-162	0.3
1974	†LA N	160	553	61	149	18	6	5	65	53-**25**	4	53	.269	.336	.351	97	-3	14-5	.946	-17	97	84	*S-160/O(RF)	0.1
1975	LA N	84	252	24	52	9	2	0	14	23-6	2	28	.206	.277	.258	52	-17	5-0	.967	-14	93	70	S-83	-2.1
1976	LA N★	149	554	53	152	17	3	5	65	21-9	3	46	.274	.301	.343	85	-13	15-5	.963	-9	98	108	*S-149	-0.3
1977	†LA N	153	634	84	176	28	6	4	51	24-1	2	43	.278	.304	.360	78	-21	16-7	.963	17	108	**130**	*S-153	1.3
1978	†LA N	155	625	72	179	32	4	3	46	30-8	2	34	.286	.320	.365	92	-8	10-6	.962	21	111	113	*S-155	3.1
1979	LA N	153	627	72	170	26	4	7	56	24-2	1	43	.271	.297	.359	80	-19	6-9	.957	-15	98	79	*S-150	-2.2
1980	LA N★	130	466	38	123	23	2	3	34	18-0	3	44	.264	.295	.341	79	-14	13-2	.968	-11	97	84	*S-129	-1.1
1981	†LA N	82	262	20	61	9	2	0	22	19-3	1	20	.233	.284	.282	64	-13	2-1	.965	8	105	115	S-80	0.4
1982	LA N	153	497	64	136	20	2	3	46	63-11	4	30	.274	.357	.340	99	2	10-2	.961	-2	104	82	*S-150	1.8
1983	†LA N	131	451	47	111	13	1	1	30	33-4	4	31	.246	.302	.286	64	-22	13-9	.964	9	104	90	*S-127	0.0
1984	LA N	89	262	25	70	12	1	0	19	25-1	0	24	.267	.329	.321	85	-5	4-4	.965	-3	96	91	S-65,O-18(CF)/2-5	-0.3
1985	LA N	76	169	19	44	6	1	0	13	18-1	1	9	.260	.333	.308	83	-3	4-0	.919	-3	103	104	S-23,O-21(LF)/2-8,3-5	-0.4
1986	LA N	105	216	21	54	11	0	0	18	15-2	2	23	.250	.302	.301	73	-8	7-0	1.000	2	101	111	O-48(28-1-20),S-32/2-8,3	-0.3
Total	18	2181	7318	796	1926	293	57	46	627	483-106	36	667	.263	.310	.338	83	-183	167-69	.960	4	102	99	*S-1746,O-299R/2-62,3-6	1.6
RUSZKOWSKI, HANK Henry Alexander B 11.10.1925 Cleveland, OH D 5.31.2000 Cleveland, OH BR/TR 6/190# d9.26 Mil 1945-46																								
1944	Cle A	3	8	1	3	0	0	0	1	0	0	1	.375	.375	.375	119	0	0-0	1.000	-0	*75*	*222*	/C-2	0.0
1945	Cle A	14	49	2	10	0	0	0	5	4	0	9	.204	.264	.204	38	-4	0-0	.975	2	*95*	*158*	C-14	-0.1
1947	Cle A	23	27	5	7	2	0	3	4	2	0	6	.259	.310	.667	172	2	0-0	1.000	-1	*167*	*213*	C-16	0.2
Total	3	40	84	8	20	2	0	3	10	6	0	16	.238	.289	.369	91	-2	0-0	.981	1	*111*	*176*	/C-32	0.1
RUTH, BABE George Herman "The Bambino," "The Sultan Of Swat" B2.6.1895 Baltimore, MD D8.16.1948 New York, NY BL/TL (BB 1923 (part)) 6-2/215# d7.11 C1 HF1936 ▲ OF Total (1057-LF 64-CF 1131-RF)																								
1914	Bos A	5	10	1	2	1	0	0	2	0	0	4	.200	.200	.300	50	0	0	1.000	-0	106	0	/P-4	0.0
1915	†Bos A	42	92	16	29	10	1	4	21	9	0	23	.315	.376	.576	191	16	0	.976	1	98	148	P-32	0.0
1916	†Bos A	67	136	18	37	5	3	3	15	10	0	23	.272	.322	.419	122	13	0	.973	1	90	172	P-44	0.0

Year	Tm Lg	G	AB	R	H	2B	3B	HR	RBI	BB-IB	HP	SO	AVG	OBP	SLG	AOPS	ABR	SB-CS	FA	FR	Rng	Thr	G at Pos	BFW
1917	Bos A	52	123	14	40	6	3	2	12	12	0	18	.325	.385	.472	163	17	0	.984	2	107	131	P-41	0.0
1918	†Bos A	95	317	50	95	26	11	**11**	66	58	2	58	.300	.411	**.555**	195	37	6	.949	0	92	95	O-59(47-12-0),P-20,1-13	2.7
1919	Bos A	130	432	**103**	139	34	12	**29**	**114**	101	6	58	.322	**.456**	**.657**	**224**	**76**	7	**.996**	10	111	137	*O-111(LF),P-17/1-5	**7.3**
1920	NY A	142	458	**158**	172	36	9	**54**	**137**	**150**	3	80	.376	**.532**	**.847**	**252**	**110**	14-14	.936	-2	96	114	*O-141(36-20-85)/1-2,P	**9.3**
1921	†NY A	152	540	**177**	204	44	16	**59**	**171**	**145**	4	81	.378	**.512**	**.846**	**236**	**118**	17-13	.966	-0	100	87	*O-152(134-18-0)/P-2,1-2	**9.4**
1922	†NY A	110	406	94	128	24	8	35	99	84	1	80	.315	.434	**.672**	**181**	49	2-5	.964	-2	96	99	*O-110(71-0-40)/1	3.5
1923	†NY A	**152**	522	**151**	205	45	13	**41**	**131**	**170**	4	93	.393	**.545**	**.764**	**238**	**119**	17-21	.973	6	110	95	*O-148(68-7-73)/1-4	**10.1**
1924	NY A	**153**	529	**143**	200	39	7	**46**	121	**142**	4	81	**.378**	**.513**	**.739**	**221**	**104**	9-13	.962	3	109	90	*O-152(50-7-99)	**8.4**
1925	NY A	98	359	61	104	12	2	25	66	59	2	68	.290	.393	.543	138	20	2-4	.974	6	105	140	O-98(33-0-66)	1.5
1926	†NY A	152	495	**139**	184	30	5	**47**	**146**	**144**	3	76	.372	**.516**	**.737**	**228**	**103**	11-9	.979	0	105	72	*O-149(82-0-68)/1-2	**8.5**
1927	†NY A	151	540	**158**	192	29	8	**60**	164	**137**	0	89	.356	**.486**	**.772**	**229**	108	7-6	.963	1	104	83	*O-151(56-0-95)	**8.8**
1928	†NY A	**154**	536	**163**	173	29	8	**54**	**142**	**137**	3	87	.323	.463	**.709**	**211**	**92**	4-5	.975	-4	102	59	*O-154(55-0-99)	**7.1**
1929	NY A	135	499	121	172	26	6	**46**	154	72	3	60	.345	.430	**.697**	**199**	**72**	5-3	.984	-5	101	41	*O-133(55-0-78)	**5.4**
1930	NY A	145	518	150	186	28	9	**49**	153	**136**	1	61	.359	**.493**	**.732**	**216**	**100**	10-10	.965	-1	102	86	*O-144(53-0-91)/P	7.6
1931	NY A	145	534	149	199	31	3	**46**	163	**128**	1	51	.373	**.495**	**.700**	**223**	**104**	5-4	.972	-7	95	46	*O-142(51-0-91)/1	**8.1**
1932	†NY A	133	457	120	156	13	5	41	137	**130**	2	62	.341	**.489**	.661	**206**	81	2-2	.961	-1	95	121	*O-128(44-0-87)/1	6.5
1933	NY A★	137	459	97	138	21	3	34	103	**114**	2	90	.301	.442	.582	180	59	4-5	.970	0	101	91	*O-132(55-0-78)/P1	4.7
1934	NY A★	125	365	78	105	17	4	22	84	104	2	63	.288	.448	.537	164	42	1-3	.962	-3	104	40	*O-111(34-0-77)	3.0
1935	Bos N	28	72	13	13	0	0	6	12	20	0	24	.181	.359	.431	121	3	0	.952	-1	96	69	O-26(22-0-4)	0.1
Total	22	2503	8399	2174	2873	506	136	714	2213	2062	43	1330	.342	.474	.690	209	1443	123-117	.968	5	102	87	*O-2241R,P-163/1-32	112.0

RUTHERFORD, JIM James Hollis B 9.26.1886 Stillwater, MN D 9.18.1956 Cleveland, OH BL/TR 6-1/180# d7.12

Year	Tm Lg	G	AB	R	H	2B	3B	HR	RBI	BB-IB	HP	SO	AVG	OBP	SLG	AOPS	ABR	SB-CS	FA	FR	Rng	Thr	G at Pos	BFW
1910	Cle A	1	2	0	1	0	0	0	0	0	0		.500	.500	.500	210	0	0	1.000	0	109	0	/O(CF)	0.0

RUTNER, MICKEY Milton B 3.18.1920 Hempstead, NY BR/TR 5-11/190# d9.11

Year	Tm Lg	G	AB	R	H	2B	3B	HR	RBI	BB-IB	HP	SO	AVG	OBP	SLG	AOPS	ABR	SB-CS	FA	FR	Rng	Thr	G at Pos	BFW
1947	Phi A	12	48	4	12	1	0	1	4	3	0	2	.250	.294	.333	73	-2	0-0	.885	-2	99	118	3-11	-0.4

RYAL, MARK Mark Dwayne B 4.28.1960 Henryetta, OK BL/TL 6-1/185# d9.7

Year	Tm Lg	G	AB	R	H	2B	3B	HR	RBI	BB-IB	HP	SO	AVG	OBP	SLG	AOPS	ABR	SB-CS	FA	FR	Rng	Thr	G at Pos	BFW
1982	KC A	6	13	0	1	0	0	0	0	1-0	0	3	.077	.143	.077	-38	-2	0-0	.900	-0	100	0	/O-5(4-1-0)	-0.3
1985	Chi A	12	33	4	5	3	0	0	3	3-0	0	3	.152	.222	.242	26	-3	0-0	1.000	-0	105	0	O-12(12-1-0)	-0.4
1986	Cal A	13	32	6	12	0	0	2	5	2-1	0	4	.375	.412	.563	164	3	1-0	.900	-0	117	0	/O-6(RF),1-4,D-2	0.2
1987	Cal A	58	100	7	20	6	0	5	18	3-1	0	15	.200	.223	.410	65	-6	0-0	.955	-2	94	0	O-21(6-0-15)/1-4,D-5	-0.8
1989	Phi N	29	33	2	8	2	0	0	5	1-0	0	6	.242	.265	.303	62	-2	0-0	1.000	-0	0	0	/1-4,O-4(2-0-2)	-0.2
1990	Pit N	9	12	0	1	0	0	0	0	0-0	0	3	.083	.083	.083	-56	-3	0-0	1.000	0	109	0	/O-4(3-0-2)	-0.3
Total	6	127	223	19	47	11	0	7	31	10-2	0	34	.211	.245	.354	61	-13	1-0	.957	-3	104	0	/O-52(27-2-25),1-12,D-7	-1.8

RYAN, CONNIE Cornelius Joseph B 2.27.1920 New Orleans, LA D 1.3.1996 Metairie, LA BR/TR 5-11/175# d4.14 Mil 1944-45 M2 C8

Year	Tm Lg	G	AB	R	H	2B	3B	HR	RBI	BB-IB	HP	SO	AVG	OBP	SLG	AOPS	ABR	SB-CS	FA	FR	Rng	Thr	G at Pos	BFW
1942	NY N	11	27	4	5	0	0	0	2	4	0	3	.185	.290	.185	40	-2	1	.944	3	122	102	2-11	0.2
1943	Bos N	132	457	52	97	10	2	1	24	58	0	56	.212	.301	.249	61	-22	7	.962	-20	95	67	*2-100,3-30	-3.9
1944	Bos N★	88	332	56	98	18	5	4	25	36	0	40	.295	.364	.416	114	7	13	.974	12	110	117	2-80,3-14	2.3
1946	Bos N	143	502	55	121	28	8	1	48	55	1	63	.241	.317	.335	84	-10	7	.968	-6	95	85	*2-120,3-24	-1.1
1947	Bos N	150	544	60	144	33	5	5	69	71	1	60	.265	.351	.371	94	-3	5	.973	-6	101	95	*2-150/S	0.0
1948	†Bos N	51	122	14	26	3	0	0	10	21	1	16	.213	.333	.238	58	-6	0	.966	1	111	97	2-40/3-4	-0.3
1949	Bos N	85	208	28	52	13	1	6	20	21	0	30	.250	.319	.409	99	-1	1	.973	3	113	161	3-25,S-18,2-16/1-3	0.3
1950	Bos N	20	72	12	14	2	0	3	6	12	2	9	.194	.326	.347	82	-2	0	1.000	1	101	99	2-20	0.0
	Cin N	106	367	45	95	18	5	3	43	52	1	46	.259	.352	.360	87	-5	4	.973	5	95	97	*2-103	0.5
	Year	126	439	57	109	20	5	6	49	64	3	55	.248	.348	.358	87	-7	4	.978	6	96	97	*2-123	0.5
1951	Cin N	136	473	75	112	17	4	16	53	79	3	72	.237	.350	.391	97	0	11-6	.970	-4	99	82	*2-121/3-3,1-2,O(RF)	0.3
1952	Phi N	**154**	577	81	139	24	6	12	49	69	5	72	.241	.327	.366	93	-5	13-5	.972	-7	103	101	*2-154	-0.2
1953	Phi N	90	247	47	73	14	6	5	26	30	0	35	.296	.372	.462	116	6	5-1	.958	-3	97	101	2-65/1-2	0.8
	Chi A	17	54	6	12	1	0	0	6	9	0	12	.222	.333	.241	55	-3	2-0	.927	-2	91	27	3-16	-0.4
1954	Cin N	1	0	0	0	0	0	0	0	1	0	0	—	1.000	—	182	0	0-0	—	0			H	0.0
Total	12	1184	3982	535	988	181	42	56	381	518	14	514	.248	.337	.357	90	-46	69-12	.970	-22	100	93	2-980,3-116/S-19,1-7,O(RF)	-1.5

RYAN, CYCLONE Daniel R. B 1866 Cappagh White, Ireland D 1.30.1917 Medfield, MA TR 6/200# d8.8

Year	Tm Lg	G	AB	R	H	2B	3B	HR	RBI	BB-IB	HP	SO	AVG	OBP	SLG	AOPS	ABR	SB-CS	FA	FR	Rng	Thr	G at Pos	BFW
1887	NY AA	8	32	4	7	1	0	0	3	3	0		.219	.286	.250	52	-2	1	.938	0	161	162	/1-8,P-2	-0.2
1891	Bos N	1	1	0	0	0	0	0	0	0	0	0	.000	.000	.000	-89	0	0	1.000	0	162	0	/P	0.0
Total	2	9	33	4	7	1	0	0	3	3	0	0	.212	.278	.242	48	-2	1	.938	0	161	162	/1-8,P-3	-0.2

RYAN, MIKE J. B St.Louis, MO d7.25

Year	Tm Lg	G	AB	R	H	2B	3B	HR	RBI	BB-IB	HP	SO	AVG	OBP	SLG	AOPS	ABR	SB-CS	FA	FR	Rng	Thr	G at Pos	BFW
1895	StL N	2	2	0	0	0	0	0	0	0	0	0	.000	.000	.000	-99	-1	0	.000	-1	0	0	/3-2	-0.1

RYAN, JIMMY James Edward "Pony" B 2.11.1863 Clinton, MA D 10.26.1923 Chicago, IL BR/TL 5-9/162# d10.8 ▲ OF Total (393-LF 956-CF 609-RF)

Year	Tm Lg	G	AB	R	H	2B	3B	HR	RBI	BB-IB	HP	SO	AVG	OBP	SLG	AOPS	ABR	SB-CS	FA	FR	Rng	Thr	G at Pos	BFW
1885	Chi N	3	13	2	6	1	0	0	2	1		1	.462	.500	.538	207	2		.737	-1	129	0	/S-2,O(CF)	0.0
1886	†Chi N	84	327	58	100	17	6	4	53	12		28	.306	.330	.431	113	3	10	.828	-1	123	149	O-70(38-8-24)/S-6,3-6,2-5,P-5	0.0
1887	Chi N	126	508	117	145	23	10	11	74	53	6	19	.285	.360	.435	106	2	50	.857	-3	156	190	*O-122(1-97-24)/P-8,2-3	-0.4
1888	Chi N	129	549	115	**182**	**33**	10	**16**	64	35	5	50	.332	.377	**.515**	170	42	60	.878	3	**162**	117	*O-128(0-127-1)/P-8	3.9
1889	Chi N	135	576	140	187	31	14	17	72	70	6	62	.325	.403	.516	149	36	45	.926	-4	168	**243**	*O-106(0-105-1),S-29	2.5
1890	Chi P	118	486	99	165	32	5	6	89	60	4	36	.340	.416	.463	129	22	30	.919	-1	114	123	*O-118(CF)	1.3
1891	Chi N	118	505	110	140	22	15	9	66	53	8	38	.277	.355	.434	129	18	27	.905	1	134	99	*O-117(43-74-0)/S-2,P-2	1.3
1892	Chi N	128	505	105	148	21	11	10	65	61	5	41	.293	.375	.438	144	27	27	.921	-3	129	122	*O-120(CF)/S-9	1.5
1893	Chi N	83	341	82	102	21	7	3	30	59	3	25	.299	.407	.428	124	15	8	.908	-1	130	72	O-73(1-73-1),S-10/P	0.7
1894	Chi N	110	482	133	172	37	7	3	62	51	3	24	.357	.422	.481	111	10	12	.908	6	116	60	*O-110(0-5-106)	0.8
1895	Chi N	108	438	83	139	22	8	6	49	48	6	22	.317	.392	.445	109	5	18	.937	2	113	163	*O-108(RF)	0.1
1896	Chi N	128	489	83	149	24	10	3	86	46	4	16	.305	.369	.413	102	1	29	.912	-1	115	84	*O-128(RF)	-0.6
1897	Chi N	136	520	103	156	33	17	5	85	50	7		.300	.369	.458	113	9	27	.945	7	146	177	*O-136(RF)	0.8
1898	Chi N	144	572	122	185	32	13	4	79	73	5		.323	.405	.446	144	35	29	.914	-8	96	43	*O-144(134-0-10)	1.4
1899	Chi N	125	525	91	158	20	10	3	68	43	3		.301	.357	.394	109	6	9	.956	-2	90	116	*O-125(LF)	-0.7
1900	Chi N	105	415	66	115	25	4	5	59	29	3		.277	.329	.393	102	1	19	.913	-5	87	83	*O-105(49-9-57)	-1.0
1902	Was A	120	484	92	155	32	6	6	44	43	7		.320	.384	.448	129	20	10	.949	1	102	0	*O-120(2-105-13)	1.5
1903	Was A	114	437	42	109	25	4	7	46	17	8		.249	.290	.373	96	-2	9	.970	3	56	30	*O-114(CF)	-0.5
Total	18	2014	8172	1643	2513	451	157	118	1093	804	83	362	.308	.375	.444	123	252	419	.918	-9	120	109	*O-1945C/S-58,P-24,2-8,3-6	12.6

RYAN, JACK John Bernard B 11.12.1868 Haverhill, MA D 8.21.1952 Boston, MA BR/TR 5-10.5/165# d9.2 C7 OF Total (4-LF 4-CF 7-RF)

Year	Tm Lg	G	AB	R	H	2B	3B	HR	RBI	BB-IB	HP	SO	AVG	OBP	SLG	AOPS	ABR	SB-CS	FA	FR	Rng	Thr	G at Pos	BFW
1889	Lou AA	21	79	8	14	1	0	0	2	3	0	17	.177	.207	.190	14	-9	2	.864	-5			C-15/O-4(0-3-1),3-2	-1.1
1890	†Lou AA	93	337	43	73	16	4	0	35	12	0		.217	.244	.288	58	-20	6	.932	15	***136***	*110*	C-89/O-3(1-0-2),S1	0.2
1891	Lou AA	75	253	24	57	5	4	2	25	15	1	40	.225	.271	.300	64	-13	3	.930	-9	*82*	*131*	C-56,1-11/3-6,O-4(3-1-0),2-3	-1.6
1894	Bos N	53	201	39	54	12	7	1	29	13	1	16	.269	.316	.413	69	-12	3	.911	4	*121*	*91*	C-51/1-2	-0.3
1895	Bos N	49	189	22	55	7	0	0	18	6	0	6	.291	.313	.328	61	-12	3	.951	5	*129*	*106*	C-43/2-5,O(RF)	-0.3
1896	Bos N	8	32	2	3	1	0	0	0	0	0	1	.094	.094	.125	-40	-7	0	.911	2	*112*	*108*	/C-8	-0.3
1898	Bro N	87	301	39	57	11	4	0	24	15	2		.189	.233	.252	39	-25	5	.960	-1	*94*	*100*	C-84/3-4,1	-1.7
1899	Bal N	2	4	0	2	1	0	0	1	0	0		.500	.500	.750	229	1	1	1.000	1	*103*	*245*	/C-2	0.1
1901	StL N	83	300	27	59	6	5	0	31	7	1		.197	.218	.250	37	-25	5	.982	3	*97*	*102*	C-65/2-9,1-5,O-3(RF)	-1.6
1902	StL N	76	267	23	48	4	4	0	14	4	1		.180	.195	.225	31	-23	2	.966	-6	*88*	*100*	C-66/1-4,3-4,2-2,S	-2.4
1903	StL N	67	227	18	54	5	1	1	10	10	1		.238	.273	.282	60	-12	2	.971	-5	*82*	*96*	C-47,1-18/S-2	-1.3
1912	Was A	1	1	0	0	0	0	0	0	0	0		.000	.000	.000	-99	0	0	1.000	0	107	0	/3	0.0
1913	Was A	1	1	0	0	0	0	0	0	0	0	0	.000	.000	.000	-98	0	0	1.000	0	*0*	*424*	/C	0.0
Total	13	616	2192	245	476	69	29	4	189	85	7	80	.217	.249	.281	50	-157	32	.947	3	*102*	*102*	C-527/1-42,2-19,3-17,O-15R,S-4	-10.3

RYAN, BUDDY John Budd B 10.6.1885 Denver, CO D 7.9.1956 Sacramento, CA BL/TR 5-9.5/172# d4.11

Year	Tm Lg	G	AB	R	H	2B	3B	HR	RBI	BB-IB	HP	SO	AVG	OBP	SLG	AOPS	ABR	SB-CS	FA	FR	Rng	Thr	G at Pos	BFW
1912	Cle A	93	328	53	89	12	9	1	31	30	6		.271	.343	.372	101	0	12	.963	6	112	125	O-90(56-0-34)	0.2
1913	Cle A	73	243	26	72	6	1	0	32	11	2	13	.296	.332	.329	91	-3	9	.986	-1	101	71	O-68(3-65-0)/1	-0.9
Total	2	166	571	79	161	18	10	1	63	41	8	13	.282	.339	.354	97	-3	21	.973	6	107	102	O-158(59-65-34)/1	-0.7

RYAN, BLONDY John Collins B 1.4.1906 Lynn, MA D 11.28.1959 Swampscott, MA BR/TR 6-1/178# d7.13

Year	Tm Lg	G	AB	R	H	2B	3B	HR	RBI	BB-IB	HP	SO	AVG	OBP	SLG	AOPS	ABR	SB-CS	FA	FR	Rng	Thr	G at Pos	BFW
1930	Chi A	28	87	9	18	0	4	1	10	6	0	13	.207	.258	.333	50	-8	2-0	.875	-1	105	140	3-23/S-2,2	-0.6

Year	Tm Lg	G	AB	R	H	2B	3B	HR	RBI	BB-IB	HP	SO	AVG	OBP	SLG	AOPS	ABR	SB-CS	FA	FR	Rng	Thr	G at Pos	BFW
1933	†NY N	146	525	47	125	10	5	3	48	15	0	62	.238	.259	.293	58	-30	0	.950	17	107	**117**	*S-146	-0.4
1934	NY N	110	385	35	93	19	0	2	41	19	0	68	.242	.277	.306	57	-23	3	.953	10	120	91	3-65,S-30,2-25	-0.8
1935	Phi N	39	129	13	34	3	0	1	10	7	2	20	.264	.312	.310	61	-7	1	.912	0	101	108	S-35/23	-0.4
	NY A	30	105	12	25	1	3	0	11	3	0	10	.238	.259	.305	48	-9	0-0	.908	-6	90	79	S-30	-1.2
1937	†NY N	21	75	10	18	3	1	1	13	6	0	8	.240	.296	.347	73	-3	0	.941	2	100	138	S-19/23	0.0
1938	NY N	12	24	1	5	0	0	0	0	1	0	3	.208	.240	.208	24	-3	0	1.000	-1	118	72	/2-5,3-3,S-2	-0.3
Total	6	386	1330	127	318	36	13	8	133	57	2	184	.239	.271	.304	57	-83	6-0	.936	21	103	114	S-264/3-93,2-33	-3.7

RYAN, JACK John Francis B 5.5.1905 West Mineral, KS D 9.2.1967 Rochester, MN BR/TR 6/185# d6.18

Year	Tm Lg	G	AB	R	H	2B	3B	HR	RBI	BB-IB	HP	SO	AVG	OBP	SLG	AOPS	ABR	SB-CS	FA	FR	Rng	Thr	G at Pos	BFW
1929	Bos A	2	3	0	0	0	0	0	0	0	0	0	.000	.000	.000	-99	-1	0-0	1.000	-0	61	0	/O-2(1-0-1)	-0.1

RYAN, JOHNNY John Joseph B 10.1853 Philadelphia, PA D 3.22.1902 Philadelphia, PA 5-7.5/150# d8.19 ▲

Year	Tm Lg	G	AB	R	H	2B	3B	HR	RBI	BB-IB	HP	SO	AVG	OBP	SLG	AOPS	ABR	SB-CS	FA	FR	Rng	Thr	G at Pos	BFW
1873	Phi NA	2	8	1	2	0	0	0	1	0		0	.250	.250	.250	47	-1	0-0	.727	-0	488	247	/1O(CF)	0.0
1874	Bal NA	**47**	181	29	35	8	1	0	19	5		13	.193	.215	.249	49	-10	3-0	.862	13	105	69	*O-47(LF)/P	0.5
1875	NH NA	37	146	17	23	2	2	0	8	3		12	.158	.174	.199	34	-8	10-4	.796	-8	21	97	O-30(LF),P-10/C-4,S	-1.1
1876	Lou N	64	241	32	61	5	1	1	18	6		23	.253	.271	.295	75	-8		.886	-8	9	50	*O-64(63-1-0)/P	-1.7
1877	Cin N	6	26	2	4	0	1	0	2	1		5	.154	.185	.231	34	-2		.769	-1	0	0	/O-6(1-5-0)	-0.3
Total	3 NA	86	335	47	60	10	3	0	28	8		25	.179	.198	.227	43	-19	13-4	.000	5	72	79	/O-78(77-1-0),P-11,C-4,S1	-0.6
Total	2	70	267	34	65	5	2	1	20	7		28	.243	.263	.288	72	-10		.877	-9	8	46	/O-70(64-6-0),P	-2.0

RYAN, JOHN John M. (Played 1 Game For Washington Under Real Name Of Daniel Sheehan) B Washington, DC d6.11

Year	Tm Lg	G	AB	R	H	2B	3B	HR	RBI	BB-IB	HP	SO	AVG	OBP	SLG	AOPS	ABR	SB-CS	FA	FR	Rng	Thr	G at Pos	BFW
1884	Was U	7	28	2	4	0	1	0		1			.143	.172	.214	17	-4		.667	-1	64	0	/O-7(2-3-2),3	-0.5
	Wil U	2	6	0	1	0	0	0		1			.167	.286	.167	39	-1		.800	-0	0	0	/O-2(1-1-0)	-0.1
	Year	9	34	2	5	0	1	0		2			.147	.194	.206	22	-4		.706	-1	47	0	/O-9(3-4-2),3	-0.6

RYAN, MIKE Michael James B 11.25.1941 Haverhill, MA BR/TR 6-2/205# d10.3 C16

Year	Tm Lg	G	AB	R	H	2B	3B	HR	RBI	BB-IB	HP	SO	AVG	OBP	SLG	AOPS	ABR	SB-CS	FA	FR	Rng	Thr	G at Pos	BFW
1964	Bos A	1	3	0	1	0	0	0	2	1-1	0	0	.333	.500	.333	131	0	0-0	1.000	-0	*0*	*0*	/C	0.0
1965	Bos A	33	107	7	17	0	1	3	9	5-1	0	19	.159	.193	.262	27	-11	0-0	.981	-2	*73*	*136*	C-33	-1.2
1966	Bos A	116	369	27	79	15	3	2	32	29-3	0	68	.214	.271	.287	55	-21	1-0	.992	-7	*68*	*112*	*C-114	-2.4
1967	†Bos A	79	226	21	45	4	2	2	27	26-5	1	42	.199	.282	.261	58	-12	2-0	.988	3	131	87	C-79	-0.5
1968	Phi N	96	296	12	53	6	1	1	15	15-3	0	59	.179	.218	.216	31	-25	0-3	.991	-0	*123*	***150***	C-96	-2.6
1969	Phi N	133	446	41	91	17	2	12	44	30-4	2	66	.204	.256	.332	66	-22	1-1	.991	3	106	103	*C-132	-1.4
1970	Phi N	46	134	14	24	8	0	2	11	16-3	0	24	.179	.265	.284	49	-10	0-0	.992	-10	118	97	C-46	-1.9
1971	Phi N	43	134	9	22	5	1	3	6	10-1	0	32	.164	.222	.284	42	-11	0-0	1.000	7	138	218	C-43	-0.2
1972	Phi N	46	106	6	19	4	0	2	10	10-2	1	25	.179	.254	.274	49	-7	0-0	.992	3	111	110	C-46	-0.2
1973	Phi N	28	69	7	16	1	2	1	5	6-0	0	19	.232	.289	.348	75	-3	0-0	.992	-0	213	103	C-27	-0.2
1974	Pit N	15	30	2	3	0	0	0	0	4-0	0	16	.100	.206	.100	-13	-5	0-0	1.000	1	348	87	C-15	-0.3
Total	11	636	1920	146	370	60	12	28	161	152-23	4	370	.193	.252	.280	51	-127	4-4	.991	-1	*115*	*119*	C-632	-10.9

RYAN, MIKE Michael Sean B 7.6.1977 Indiana, PA BL/TR 5-10/182# d9.20

Year	Tm Lg	G	AB	R	H	2B	3B	HR	RBI	BB-IB	HP	SO	AVG	OBP	SLG	AOPS	ABR	SB-CS	FA	FR	Rng	Thr	G at Pos	BFW
2002	Min A	7	11	3	1	0	0	0	0	0-0	0	2	.091	.091	.091	-51	-2	0-0	1.000	-1	51	0	/O-5(4-3-0)	-0.3
2003	†Min A	27	61	13	24	7	0	5	13	6-0	0	12	.393	.441	.754	207	10	2-1	1.000	3	132	277	O-16(4-0-12)/D-4	1.1
Total	2	34	72	16	25	7	0	5	13	6-0	0	14	.347	.392	.653	169	8	2-1	1.000	2	118	228	/O-21(8-3-12),D-4	0.8

RYAN, ROB Robert James B 6.24.1973 Havre, MT BL/TL 5-11/190# d8.20

Year	Tm Lg	G	AB	R	H	2B	3B	HR	RBI	BB-IB	HP	SO	AVG	OBP	SLG	AOPS	ABR	SB-CS	FA	FR	Rng	Thr	G at Pos	BFW
1999	Ari N	20	29	4	7	1	0	2	5	1-0	0	8	.241	.267	.483	84	-1	0-0	1.000	-0	103	0	/O-5(1-0-4)	-0.1
2000	Ari N	27	27	4	8	1	1	0	2	4-0	1	7	.296	.406	.407	103	0	0-0	1.000	-0	44	0	/O-2(RF),D	0.0
2001	Ari N	1	1	0	0	0	0	0	0	0-0	0	1	.000	.000	.000	-94	0	0-0	—	0			/H	0.0
	Oak A	7	7	0	0	0	0	0	0	0-0	0	5	.000	.000	.000	-99	-2	0-0	1.000	-0	71	0	/O-5(0-4-1),D	-0.2
Total	3	55	64	8	15	2	1	2	7	5-0	1	21	.234	.300	.391	72	-3	0-0	1.000	-1	85	0	/O-12(1-4-7),D-2	-0.3

RYDER, TOM Thomas B 5.9.1863 Dubuque, IA D 7.18.1935 Dubuque, IA BL d7.22

Year	Tm Lg	G	AB	R	H	2B	3B	HR	RBI	BB-IB	HP	SO	AVG	OBP	SLG	AOPS	ABR	SB-CS	FA	FR	Rng	Thr	G at Pos	BFW
1884	StL U	8	28	4	7	1	0	0		2			.250	.300	.286	76	-2		.650	-1	139	0	/O-8(5-3-0)	-0.2

RYE, GENE Eugene Rudolph "Half-Pint" (born Eugene Rudolph Mercantelli) B 11.15.1906 Chicago, IL D 1.21.1980 Park Ridge, IL BL/TR 5-6/165# d4.22

Year	Tm Lg	G	AB	R	H	2B	3B	HR	RBI	BB-IB	HP	SO	AVG	OBP	SLG	AOPS	ABR	SB-CS	FA	FR	Rng	Thr	G at Pos	BFW
1931	Bos A	17	39	3	7	0	0	0	1	2	0	5	.179	.220	.179	6	-5	0-0	.944	-1	94	0	O-10(LF)	-0.6

SABO, ALEX Alexander "Giz" (born Alexsander Szabo) B 2.14.1910 New Brunswick, NJ D 1.3.2001 Tuckerton, NJ BR/TR 6/192# d8.1

Year	Tm Lg	G	AB	R	H	2B	3B	HR	RBI	BB-IB	HP	SO	AVG	OBP	SLG	AOPS	ABR	SB-CS	FA	FR	Rng	Thr	G at Pos	BFW
1936	Was A	4	8	1	3	0	0	0	1	0	0	2	.375	.375	.375	91	0	0-0	.923	0	*100*	*164*	/C-4	0.0
1937	Was A	1	0	0	0	0	0	0	0	0	0	0	—	—	—	—	0	0-0	1.000	-0	*0*	*0*	/C	0.0
Total	2	5	8	1	3	0	0	0	1	0	0	2	.375	.375	.375	91	0	0-0	.929	0	*91*	*150*	/C-5	0.0

SABO, CHRIS Christopher Andrew B 1.19.1962 Detroit, MI BR/TR 6/185# d4.4

Year	Tm Lg	G	AB	R	H	2B	3B	HR	RBI	BB-IB	HP	SO	AVG	OBP	SLG	AOPS	ABR	SB-CS	FA	FR	Rng	Thr	G at Pos	BFW
1988	Cin N★	137	538	74	146	40	2	11	44	29-1	6	52	.271	.314	.414	104	3	46-14	**.966**	10	108	**149**	*3-135/S-2	2.0
1989	Cin N	82	304	40	79	21	1	6	29	25-2	1	33	.260	.316	.395	99	0	14-9	.943	-5	97	96	3-76	-0.5
1990	†Cin N★	148	567	95	153	38	2	25	71	61-7	4	58	.270	.343	.476	118	15	25-10	**.966**	-8	96	83	*3-146	1.0
1991	Cin N★	153	582	91	175	35	3	26	88	44-3	6	79	.301	.354	.505	134	26	19-6	.966	-16	86	98	*3-151	1.2
1992	Cin N	96	344	42	84	19	3	12	43	30-1	1	54	.244	.302	.422	102	0	4-5	.961	-4	90	92	3-93	-0.5
1993	Cin N	148	552	86	143	33	2	21	82	43-5	6	105	.259	.315	.440	101	0	6-4	.967	-12	91	67	*3-148	-1.1
1994	Bal A	68	258	41	66	15	3	11	42	20-2	5	38	.256	.320	.465	95	-3	1-1	.958	-8	74	82	3-37,O-22(9-0-13),D-10	-1.1
1995	Chi A	20	71	10	18	5	0	1	8	3-1	2	12	.254	.295	.366	76	-3	2-0	.909	-1	0	118	D-15/13	-0.4
	StL N	5	13	0	2	1	0	0	3	1-0	0	2	.154	.214	.231	17	-2	1-0	.929	-1	148	65	/1-2,3	-0.2
1996	Cin N	54	125	15	32	7	1	3	16	18-0	1	27	.256	.354	.400	98	0	2-0	.961	5	112	112	3-43	0.5
Total	9	911	3354	494	898	214	17	116	426	274-22	32	460	.268	.326	.445	109	36	120-49	.963	-38	94	97	3-831/D-25,O-22(9-0-13),1-3,S-2	0.9

SACKA, FRANK Frank B 8.30.1924 Romulus, MI D 12.7.1994 Dearborn, MI BR/TR 6/195# d4.29

Year	Tm Lg	G	AB	R	H	2B	3B	HR	RBI	BB-IB	HP	SO	AVG	OBP	SLG	AOPS	ABR	SB-CS	FA	FR	Rng	Thr	G at Pos	BFW
1951	Was A	7	16	1	4	0	0	0	3	0	0	5	.250	.250	.250	36	-2	0-0	.962	1	*163*	*166*	/C-6	-0.1
1953	Was A	7	18	2	5	0	0	0	3	3	0	1	.278	.381	.278	82	0	0-0	1.000	-0	*141*	*138*	/C-6	0.1
Total	2	14	34	3	9	0	0	0	6	3	0	6	.265	.324	.265	62	-2	0-0	.982	2	*151*	*151*	/C-12	0.0

SADEK, MIKE Michael George B 5.30.1946 Minneapolis, MN BR/TR (BB 1979 (part)) 5-9/165# d4.13

Year	Tm Lg	G	AB	R	H	2B	3B	HR	RBI	BB-IB	HP	SO	AVG	OBP	SLG	AOPS	ABR	SB-CS	FA	FR	Rng	Thr	G at Pos	BFW
1973	SF N	39	66	6	11	1	1	0	4	11-0	0	8	.167	.282	.212	38	-5	1-0	.981	3	89	80	C-35	-0.1
1975	SF N	42	106	14	25	5	2	0	9	14-1	0	14	.236	.322	.321	76	-3	1-0	.995	5	92	69	C-38	0.3
1976	SF N	55	93	8	19	2	0	0	7	11-2	1	10	.204	.295	.226	48	-6	0-0	.985	3	95	108	C-51	-0.2
1977	SF N	61	126	12	29	7	0	1	15	12-0	0	5	.230	.297	.310	63	-6	2-1	.992	6	96	151	C-57	0.2
1978	SF N	40	109	15	26	3	0	2	9	10-2	0	11	.239	.303	.321	77	-3	1-0	.975	-3	67	68	C-37	-0.5
1979	SF N	63	126	14	30	5	0	1	11	15-2	1	24	.238	.322	.302	77	-4	1-0	.993	-0	94	80	C-60/O(RF)	-0.2
1980	SF N	64	151	14	38	4	1	1	16	27-6	0	18	.252	.363	.311	93	0	0-0	.974	-1	108	103	C-59	0.1
1981	SF N	19	36	5	6	3	0	0	3	8-0	0	7	.167	.318	.250	64	-1	0-0	.979	3	79	123	C-19	0.3
Total	8	383	813	88	184	30	4	5	74	108-13	2	97	.226	.317	.292	70	-28	6-1	.985	16	92	98	C-356/O(RF)	-0.1

SADLER, DONNIE Donnie Lamont B 6.17.1975 Clifton, TX BR/TR 5-6/165# d4.1 OF Total (47-LF 61-CF 25-RF)

Year	Tm Lg	G	AB	R	H	2B	3B	HR	RBI	BB-IB	HP	SO	AVG	OBP	SLG	AOPS	ABR	SB-CS	FA	FR	Rng	Thr	G at Pos	BFW
1998	†Bos A	58	124	21	28	4	4	3	15	6-0	3	28	.226	.276	.395	71	-6	4-0	.972	-5	85	72	2-50/S-4,D-4	-0.8
1999	†Bos A	49	107	18	30	5	1	0	4	5-0	0	20	.280	.313	.346	66	-6	2-1	.930	-5	76	80	S-14,2-10/3-9,O-8(1-6-1),D-3	-0.9
2000	Bos A	49	99	14	22	5	0	1	10	5-0	1	18	.222	.262	.303	43	-9	3-1	.958	1	116	78	S-19,O-17(3-13-1),2-12/3-3,D-2	-0.6
2001	Cin N	39	84	9	17	3	0	1	3	9-0	0	20	.202	.280	.274	42	-7	3-3	.947	-1	105	109	2-15,S-12/O-8(6-2-2),D	-0.7
	KC A	54	101	19	13	3	0	0	2	9-0	2	17	.129	.212	.158	0	-15	4-1	1.000	15	128	311	O-16(5-4-7),3-15,2-13/S-6	0.1
2002	KC A	35	68	10	13	1	1	0	5	4-0	0	12	.191	.233	.235	23	-8	3-1	.957	-3	108	0	O-15(11-0-4),3-11/2-4,S-4,D-3	-1.0
	Tex A	38	30	6	3	1	0	0	2	3-0	2	7	.100	.229	.133	-0	-4	2-2	1.000	1	126	327	O-18(2-14-3),S-12/3-4,2-2,D	-0.3
	Year	73	98	16	16	2	1	0	7	7-0	2	19	.163	.231	.204	17	-12	5-3	.976	-2	115	122	O-33(13-14-7),S-16,3-15/2-6,D-4	-1.3
2003	Tex A	77	131	27	26	5	2	1	5	13-0	2	34	.198	.277	.290	47	-10	4-3	1.000	-1	95	215	O-41(19-22-7),3-23,S-19/2	-1.0
Total	6	399	744	124	152	27	8	6	46	54-0	10	156	.204	.265	.286	42	-65	25-12	.981	1	102	214	0-123C,2-107/S-90,3-65,D-14	-5.2

SADOWSKI, ED Edward Roman B 1.19.1931 Pittsburgh, PA D 11.6.1993 Garden Grove, CA BR/TR 5-11/175# d4.20 b-Bob b-Ted

Year	Tm Lg	G	AB	R	H	2B	3B	HR	RBI	BB-IB	HP	SO	AVG	OBP	SLG	AOPS	ABR	SB-CS	FA	FR	Rng	Thr	G at Pos	BFW
1960	Bos A	38	93	10	20	2	0	3	8	8-2	1	13	.215	.284	.333	64	-5	0-0	.995	3	*124*	*94*	C-36	-0.1
1961	LA A	69	164	16	38	13	0	4	12	11-1	0	33	.232	.278	.384	68	-7	2-3	.987	3	*82*	*85*	C-56	-0.3
1962	LA A	27	55	4	11	4	0	1	3	2-0	0	14	.200	.228	.327	49	-4	1-0	.968	1	*116*	*84*	C-18	-0.3
1963	LA A	80	174	24	30	1	1	4	15	17-5	0	33	.172	.245	.259	44	-14	2-1	.997	15	139	190	C-68	0.4

Year	Tm Lg	G	AB	R	H	2B	3B	HR	RBI	BB-IB	HP	SO	AVG	OBP	SLG	AOPS	ABR	SB-CS	FA	FR	Rng	Thr	G at Pos	BFW
1966	Atl N	3	9	1	1	0	0	0	1	1-0	0	1	.111	.200	.111	-10	-1	0-0	1.000	0	*109*	*140*	/C-3	-0.1
Total	5	217	495	55	100	20	1	12	39	39-8	1	94	.202	.261	.319	56	-31	5-4	.991	21	*116*	*127*	C-181	-0.4
SADOWSKI, BOB Robert Frank "Sid" B 1.15.1937 St.Louis, MO BL/TR 6/175# d9.16																								
1960	StL N	1	1	0	0	0	0	0	0	1-0	0	0	.000	.500	.000	47	0	0-0	.000	-1	0	0	/2	-0.1
1961	Phi N	16	54	4	7	0	0	0	0	4-0	1	7	.130	.203	.130	-9	-9	1-0	.971	-0	101	124	3-14	-0.9
1962	Chi A	79	130	22	30	3	3	6	24	13-2	0	22	.231	.299	.438	97	-1	0-0	.955	3	111	0	3-16,2-12	0.2
1963	LA A	88	144	12	36	6	0	1	22	15-2	0	34	.250	.317	.313	83	-3	2-1	1.000	-2	111	0	O-25(1-0-24)/3-6,2-4	-0.6
Total	4	184	329	38	73	9	3	7	46	33-4	1	63	.222	.292	.331	73	-13	3-1	.953	-0	96	48	/3-36,O-25(1-0-24),2-17	-1.4
SAENZ, OLMEDO Olmedo (Sanchez) B 10.8.1970 Chitre Herrera, Panama BR/TR 6-2/185# d5.28																								
1994	Chi A	5	14	2	2	0	1	0	0	0-0	0	5	.143	.143	.286	7	-2	0-0	1.000	-1	66	0	/3-5	-0.3
1999	Oak A	97	255	41	70	18	0	11	41	22-1	15	47	.275	.363	.475	117	7	1-1	.938	1	102	165	3-56,1-28/D-8	0.7
2000	†Oak A	76	214	40	67	12	2	9	33	25-2	7	40	.313	.401	.514	133	12	1-0	.923	-2	90	72	D-27,3-18,1-17	0.6
2001	†Oak A	106	305	33	67	21	1	9	32	19-1	13	64	.220	.291	.384	76	-11	0-1	.986	-0	131	91	D-58,1-28,3-14	-1.6
2002	†Oak A	68	156	15	43	10	1	6	18	13-1	7	31	.276	.354	.468	117	4	1-1	1.000	2	84	94	1-34,3-15/D-7	0.4
Total	5	352	944	131	249	61	5	35	124	79-5	42	187	.264	.345	.450	106	10	3-3	.927	0	100	128	3-108,1-107,D-100	-0.2
SAFFELL, TOM Thomas Judson B 7.26.1921 Etowah, TN BL/TR 5-11/170# d7.2																								
1949	Pit N	73	205	36	66	7	1	2	25	21	0	27	.322	.385	.395	107	3	5	.992	-2	96	59	O-53(0-52-2)	-0.1
1950	Pit N	67	182	18	37	7	0	2	6	14	1	34	.203	.264	.275	41	-16	1	.993	4	110	135	O-43(0-42-2)	-1.3
1951	Pit N	49	65	11	13	0	0	1	5	5	0	18	.200	.257	.246	35	-6	1-1	.929	-1	97	112	O-17(1-13-3)	-0.7
1955	Pit N	73	113	21	19	1	0	1	3	15-3	0	22	.168	.266	.204	27	-12	1-0	.964	1	111	91	O-47(6-37-4)	-1.2
	KC A	9	37	5	8	0	0	0	1	4-0	0	7	.216	.293	.216	38	-3	1-0	.962	-1	98	0	/O-9(CF)	-0.4
Total	4	271	602	91	143	15	1	6	40	59-3	1	108	.238	.307	.296	60	-34	9-1	.980	2	104	90	O-169(7-153-11)	-3.7
SAGE, HARRY Harry "Doc" B 3.16.1864 Rock Island, IL D 5.27.1947 Rock Island, IL BR/TR 5-10/185# d4.17																								
1890	Tol AA	81	275	40	41	8	4	2	25	29	2		.149	.235	.229	36	-23	10	.948	18	*115*	***129***	C-80/O(CF)	0.1
SAGER, PONY Samuel B. B 1847 Marshalltown, IA ?/140# d5.6																								
1871	Rok NA	8	39	9	11	0	0	0	5	2		2	.282	.317	.282	78	-1	5-1	.643	-3	90	0	/S-4,O-4(LF)	-0.2
SAGMOEN, MARC Marc Richard B 4.16.1971 Seattle, WA BL/TL 5-11/185# d4.15																								
1997	Tex A	21	43	2	6	2	0	1	4	2-0	0	13	.140	.174	.256	11	-6	0-0	1.000	-1	99	0	O-17(2-0-16)/1D	-0.7
SAIER, VIC Victor Sylvester B 5.4.1891 Lansing, MI D 5.14.1967 E.Lansing, MI BL/TR 5-11/185# d5.3																								
1911	Chi N	86	259	42	67	15	1	1	37	25	7	37	.259	.340	.336	89	-3	11	.980	-4	81	115	1-73	-0.9
1912	Chi N	122	451	74	130	25	14	2	61	34	1	65	.288	.340	.419	107	3	11	.992	-5	77	105	*1-120	-0.6
1913	Chi N	149	519	94	150	15	**21**	14	92	62	5	62	.289	.370	.480	141	27	26-20	.983	-5	87	101	*1-149	1.7
1914	Chi N	153	537	87	129	24	8	18	72	94	4	61	.240	.357	.415	130	22	19	.986	-11	69	78	*1-153	0.9
1915	Chi N	144	497	74	131	35	11	11	64	64	2	62	.264	.350	.445	140	25	29-9	.985	-5	87	88	*1-139	2.1
1916	Chi N	147	498	60	126	25	3	7	50	79	1	68	.253	.356	.357	108	9	20-17	.984	-1	103	97	*1-147	0.4
1917	Chi N	6	21	5	5	1	0	0	2	2	0	1	.238	.304	.286	75	-1	0	1.000	2	224	85	/1-6	0.1
1919	Pit N	58	166	19	37	3	3	2	17	18	2	13	.223	.306	.313	83	-3	5	.985	-5	61	77	1-51	-1.0
Total	8	865	2948	455	775	143	61	55	395	378	22	369	.263	.351	.409	119	79	121-46	.986	-33	84	94	1-838	2.7
ST.CLAIRE, EBBA Edward Joseph B 8.5.1921 Whitehall, NY D 8.22.1982 Whitehall, NY BB/TR 6-1/219# d4.17 s-Randy																								
1951	Bos N	72	220	22	62	17	2	1	25	12	1	24	.282	.322	.391	98	-1	2-0	.977	-0	*82*	*100*	C-62	0.2
1952	Bos N	39	108	5	23	2	0	2	4	8	0	12	.213	.267	.287	56	-7	0-1	.972	1	*101*	*135*	C-34	-0.5
1953	Mil N	33	80	7	16	3	0	2	5	3	0	9	.200	.229	.313	42	-7	0-0	.992	2	*90*	*144*	C-27	-0.4
1954	NY N	20	42	5	11	1	0	2	6	12	1	7	.262	.436	.429	126	2	0-0	.975	1	*134*	*107*	C-16	0.4
Total	4	164	450	39	112	23	2	7	40	35	2	52	.249	.306	.356	81	-13	2-1	.978	4	*94*	*117*	C-139	-0.3
SAKATA, LENN Lenn Haruki B 6.8.1954 Honolulu, HI BR/TR 5-9/160# d7.21																								
1977	Mil A	53	154	13	25	2	0	2	12	9-0	0	22	.162	.209	.214	16	-18	1-3	.985	6	110	132	2-53	-1.0
1978	Mil A	30	78	8	15	4	0	0	3	8-1	0	11	.192	.267	.244	44	-6	1-0	.975	-5	94	79	2-29	-0.9
1979	Mil A	4	14	1	7	2	0	0	1	0-0	0	1	.500	.500	.643	206	2	0-0	1.000	1	110	184	/2-4	0.3
1980	Bal A	43	83	12	16	3	2	1	9	6-0	0	10	.193	.244	.313	53	-6	2-1	.984	1	101	112	2-34/S-4,D	-0.4
1981	Bal A	61	150	19	34	4	0	5	15	11-0	1	18	.227	.282	.353	83	-4	4-0	.963	5	102	107	S-42,2-20	0.6
1982	Bal A	136	343	40	89	18	1	6	31	30-2	4	39	.259	.323	.370	91	-4	7-4	.977	-13	93	95	2-83,S-56	-0.8
1983	†Bal A	66	134	23	34	7	0	3	12	16-0	1	17	.254	.338	.373	97	0	8-4	.990	-3	95	128	2-60/CD	0.0
1984	Bal A	81	157	23	30	1	0	3	11	6-2	0	15	.191	.221	.255	32	-15	4-1	.988	5	117	112	2-76/O(LF)	-0.8
1985	Bal A	55	97	15	22	3	0	3	6	6-0	1	15	.227	.279	.351	73	-4	3-2	.960	-5	94	83	2-50/D	-0.7
1986	Oak A	17	34	4	12	2	0	0	5	3-0	0	6	.353	.395	.412	133	2	0-1	.984	2	119	55	2-16/D	0.4
1987	NY A	19	45	5	12	0	1	2	4	2-0	1	4	.267	.313	.444	99	0	0-1	.929	-0	113	54	3-12/2-6	-0.1
Total	11	565	1289	163	296	46	4	25	109	97-5	8	158	.230	.286	.330	71	-53	30-17	.982	-8	103	109	2-431,S-102/3-12,D-4,O(LF)C	-3.4
SALAS, MARK Mark Bruce B 3.8.1961 Montebello, CA BL/TR 6/205# d6.19																								
1984	StL N	14	20	1	2	1	0	0	1	0-0	0	3	.100	.100	.150	-31	-4	0-0	1.000	-1	50	108	/C-4,O-3(2-0-1)	-0.4
1985	Min A	120	360	51	108	20	5	9	41	18-5	1	37	.300	.332	.458	108	3	0-1	.991	8	100	121	*C-115/D-3	1.5
1986	Min A	91	258	28	60	7	4	8	33	18-2	1	32	.233	.282	.384	78	-9	3-1	.980	0	92	110	C-69/D-8	-0.6
1987	Min A	22	45	8	17	2	0	3	9	5-1	0	6	.378	.431	.622	171	5	0-1	.989	-0	41	28	C-14	0.4
	NY A	50	115	13	23	4	0	3	12	10-0	3	17	.200	.279	.313	58	-7	0-0	1.000	0	102	120	C-41/O(LF)D	-0.6
	Year	72	160	21	40	6	0	6	21	15-1	3	23	.250	.322	.400	91	-2	0-1	.996	-0	85	95	C-55/D-4,O(LF)	-0.2
1988	Chi A	75	196	17	49	7	0	3	9	12-2	3	17	.250	.303	.332	78	-6	0-0	.979	-1	98	121	C-69/D	-0.3
1989	Cle A	30	77	4	17	4	1	2	7	5-1	1	13	.221	.277	.377	81	-2	0-0	1.000	0	57	396	D-20/C-5	-0.3
1990	Det A	74	164	18	38	3	0	9	24	21-2	1	28	.232	.323	.415	104	1	0-0	.988	-6	81	107	C-57/3D	-0.2
1991	Det A	33	57	2	5	1	0	1	7	0-0	2	10	.088	.117	.158	-24	-10	0-0	1.000	-0	68	140	C-11/1-5,D-8	-1.0
Total	8	509	1292	142	319	49	10	38	143	89-13	12	163	.247	.300	.389	86	-29	3-3	.987	1	92	114	C-385/D-47,1-5,O-4(3-0-1),3	-1.5
SALAZAR, ANGEL Argenis Antonio (Yepez) B 11.4.1961 Anaco, Venezuela BR/TR 6/173# d8.10																								
1983	Mon N	36	37	5	8	1	1	0	1	1-0	0	8	.216	.231	.297	47	-3	0-0	.966	-4	69	117	S-34	-0.6
1984	Mon N	80	174	12	27	4	2	0	12	4-0	1	38	.155	.178	.201	7	-22	1-1	.960	-7	91	113	S-80	-2.5
1986	KC A	117	298	24	73	20	2	0	24	7-0	2	47	.245	.266	.326	59	-17	1-1	.978	-2	107	87	*S-115/2	-0.9
1987	KC A	116	317	24	65	7	0	2	21	6-0	0	46	.205	.219	.246	23	-36	4-4	.981	20	**120**	98	*S-116	-0.6
1988	Chi N	34	60	4	15	1	1	0	1	1-1	0	11	.250	.262	.300	58	-3	0-0	.966	1	95	106	S-29/2-2,3	-0.1
Total	5	383	886	69	188	33	6	2	59	19-1	3	150	.212	.230	.270	36	-81	6-6	.974	9	106	99	S-374/2-3,3	-4.7
SALAZAR, LUIS Luis Ernesto (Garcia) B 5.19.1956 Barcelona, Venezuela BR/TR 5-9/180# d8.15 C1 OF Total (161-LF 114-CF 36-RF)																								
1980	SD N	44	169	28	57	4	7	1	25	9-1	1	25	.337	.372	.462	140	8	11-2	.944	-1	99	111	3-42/O-4(0-3-1)	0.8
1981	SD N	109	400	37	121	19	6	3	38	16-2	1	72	.303	.329	.403	116	6	11-8	.955	-1	101	106	3-94,O-23(1-10-14)	0.3
1982	SD N	145	524	55	127	15	5	8	62	23-10	2	80	.242	.274	.336	75	-21	32-9	.938	-2	107	**147**	*3-129,S-18/O(CF)	-2.0
1983	SD N	134	481	52	124	16	2	14	45	17-8	2	80	.258	.285	.387	88	-11	24-9	.949	4	110	98	*3-118,S-19	-0.6
1984	†SD N	93	228	20	55	7	2	3	17	6-1	0	38	.241	.261	.329	65	-12	11-7	.970	4	105	77	3-58,O-24(4-19-2)/S-4	-0.9
1985	Chi A	122	327	39	80	18	2	10	45	12-2	0	60	.245	.267	.404	79	-11	14-4	.968	-6	83	87	O-84(26-68-1),3-39/1-6,D-8	-1.7
1986	Chi A	4	7	1	1	0	0	0	0	1-0	0	3	.143	.250	.143	10	-1	0-0	—	0			/D-2	-0.1
1987	SD N	84	189	13	48	5	0	3	17	14-2	0	30	.254	.302	.328	70	-8	3-3	.957	-6	101	93	3-38,S-22,O-10(4-6-2)/P-2,1	-1.3
1988	Det A	130	452	61	122	14	1	12	62	21-2	3	70	.270	.305	.385	96	-4	6-0	.992	-1	107	127	O-68(60-5-5),S-37,3-31/2-5,1-4	-0.3
1989	SD N	95	246	27	66	7	2	8	22	11-3	1	44	.268	.302	.411	102	-1	1-3	.968	4	112	123	3-72,O-14(2-2-10)/S-9,1-2	0.2
	†Chi N	26	80	7	26	5	0	1	12	4-0	0	13	.325	.357	.425	114	2	0-1	.921	-4	81	35	3-25/O-2(LF)	-0.3
	Year	121	326	34	92	12	2	9	34	15-3	1	57	.282	.316	.414	105	1	1-4	.959	0	104	101	3-97,O-16(4-2-10)/S-9,1-2	-0.1
1990	Chi N	115	410	44	104	13	3	12	47	19-3	4	59	.254	.293	.388	80	-13	3-1	.950	-9	90	91	3-91,O-28(LF)	-2.3
1991	Chi N	103	333	34	86	14	1	14	38	15-1	1	45	.258	.292	.432	97	-3	0-3	.956	-3	106	39	3-86/1-7,O(LF)	-0.7
1992	Chi N	98	255	20	53	7	2	5	25	11-2	0	34	.208	.237	.310	53	-17	1-1	.935	5	126	144	3-40,O-34(33-0-1),S-12/1-5	-1.3
Total	13	1302	4101	438	1070	144	33	94	455	179-37	15	653	.261	.293	.381	88	-86	117-51	.950	-14	104	100	3-863,O-293L,S-121/1-25,D-10,2P	-10.2
SALAZAR, OSCAR Oscar Enrique B 6.27.1978 Maracay, Venezuela BR/TR 5-11/175# d4.10																								
2002	Det A	8	21	2	4	1	0	1	3	1-0	0	2	.190	.227	.381	61	-1	0-0	.938	-2	69	105	/2-6,3S	-0.3

Year	Tm Lg	G	AB	R	H	2B	3B	HR	RBI	BB-IB	HP	SO	AVG	OBP	SLG	AOPS	ABR	SB-CS	FA	FR	Rng	Thr	G at Pos	BFW
SALES, ED Edward A. B 1861 Harrisburg, PA D 8.10.1912 New Haven, CT BL/TR d7.15																								
1890	Pit N	51	189	19	43	7	3	1	23	16	3	15	.228	.298	.312	88	-2	3	.871	-12	91	44	S-51	-1.1
SALKELD, BILL William Franklin B 3.8.1917 Pocatello, ID D 4.22.1967 Los Angeles, CA BL/TR 5-10/190# d4.18 gs-Roger																								
1945	Pit N	95	267	45	83	16	1	15	52	50	0	16	.311	.420	.547	161	24	2	.973	-6	*84*	*100*	C-86	2.2
1946	Pit N	69	160	18	47	8	0	3	19	39	0	16	.294	.432	.400	133	10	2	.972	-3	*68*	*128*	C-51	1.0
1947	Pit N	47	61	5	13	2	0	0	8	6	0	8	.213	.284	.246	41	-5	0	.971	-2	*82*	*101*	C-15	-0.7
1948	†Bos N	78	198	26	48	8	1	8	28	42	1	37	.242	.378	.414	116	6	1	.990	3	*91*	*114*	C-59	1.2
1949	Bos N	66	161	17	41	5	0	5	25	44	1	24	.255	.417	.379	121	8	1	.980	-2	*97*	*75*	C-63	0.8
1950	Chi A	1	3	0	0	0	0	0	0	1	0	0	.000	.250	.000	-33	-1	0-0	1.000	0	*0*	*0*	/C	-0.1
Total	6	356	850	111	232	39	2	31	132	182	2	101	.273	.402	.433	129	42	6-0	.979	-10	*85*	*103*	C-275	4.4
SALMON, CHICO Ruthford Eduardo B 12.3.1940 Colon, Panama D 9.17.2000 Bocas Del Toro, Panama BR/TR 5-10/170# d6.28 OF Total (56-LF 5-CF 64-RF)																								
1964	Cle A	86	283	43	87	17	2	4	25	13-0	2	37	.307	.340	.424	113	5	10-6	1.000	-2	97	40	O-53(1-0-52),2-32,1-13	0.1
1965	Cle A	79	120	20	29	8	0	3	12	5-0	2	19	.242	.281	.383	87	-2	7-4	.985	-2	72	93	1-28,O-17(10-1-6)/2-5,3-5	-0.6
1966	Cle A	126	422	46	108	13	2	7	40	21-2	0	41	.256	.289	.346	82	-11	10-1	.958	-15	83	95	S-61,2-28,1-24,O-10(9-0-1)/3-6	-1.9
1967	Cle A	90	203	19	46	13	1	2	19	17-1	1	29	.227	.288	.330	82	-4	10-4	1.000	9	140	124	O-28(24-4-3),1-24,2-24,S-14/3-4	0.7
1968	Cle A	103	276	24	59	8	1	3	12	12-0	3	30	.214	.253	.283	63	-13	7-7	.971	-8	87	87	2-45,3-18,S-15,O-13(11-0-2),1-11	-2.1
1969	†Bal A	52	91	18	27	5	0	3	12	10-1	2	22	.297	.375	.451	130	4	0-0	1.000	-6	60	106	1-17/2-9,S-9,3-3,O(LF)	-0.1
1970	†Bal A	63	172	19	43	4	0	7	22	8-0	1	30	.250	.287	.395	85	-4	2-2	.946	-14	79	79	S-33,2-12,3-11/1-2	-1.6
1971	Bal A	42	84	11	15	1	0	2	7	3-0	0	21	.179	.205	.262	32	-8	0-0	1.000	-1	57	93	/1-9,2-9,3-6,S-5	-1.0
1972	Bal A	17	16	2	1	1	0	0	0	0-0	0	4	.063	.063	.125	-44	-3	0-0	1.000	-0	0	601	/1-2,3	-0.3
Total	9	658	1667	202	415	70	6	31	149	89-4	11	233	.249	.290	.354	84	-36	46-24	.959	-39	95	79	2-164,S-137,1-130,O-122R/3-54	-6.8
SALMON, TIM Timothy James B 8.24.1968 Long Beach, CA BR/TR 6-3/220# d8.21																								
1992	Cal A	23	79	8	14	1	0	2	6	11-1	1	23	.177	.283	.266	55	-5	1-1	.953	-2	86	67	O-21(RF)	-0.7
1993	Cal A	142	515	93	146	35	1	31	95	82-5	5	135	.283	.382	.536	141	31	5-6	.980	9	110	113	*O-140(0-1-140)/D	3.1
1994	Cal A	100	373	67	107	18	2	23	70	54-2	5	102	.287	.382	.531	131	18	1-3	.966	4	105	121	O-99(RF)	1.4
1995	Cal A	143	537	111	177	34	3	34	105	91-2	6	111	.330	.429	.594	165	55	5-5	.988	7	113	74	*O-142(RF)/D	5.0
1996	Cal A	156	581	90	166	27	4	30	98	93-7	4	125	.286	.386	.501	122	21	4-2	.975	0	96	121	*O-153(RF)/D-3	1.2
1997	Ana A	157	582	95	172	28	1	33	129	95-5	7	142	.296	.394	.517	138	35	9-12	.971	10	107	147	*O-153(RF)/D-4	3.3
1998	Ana A	136	463	84	139	28	1	26	88	90-5	3	100	.300	.410	.533	144	34	0-1	.959	1	126	75	*D-111,O-19(RF)	2.5
1999	Ana A	98	353	60	94	24	2	17	69	63-2	0	82	.266	.372	.490	120	12	4-1	.981	5	110	108	O-89(RF)/D-7	1.2
2000	Ana A	158	568	108	165	36	2	34	97	104-5	6	139	.290	.404	.540	133	32	0-2	.979	6	105	134	*O-124(RF),D-33	2.6
2001	Ana A	137	475	63	108	21	1	17	49	96-4	8	121	.227	.365	.383	96	1	9-3	.989	6	102	156	*O-125(RF),D-12	0.0
2002	†Ana A	138	483	84	138	37	1	22	88	71-3	7	102	.286	.380	.503	134	26	6-3	.986	-4	95	60	*O-111(RF),D-25	1.4
2003	Ana A	148	528	78	145	35	4	19	72	77-3	10	93	.275	.374	.464	125	22	3-1	.958	-1	98	102	O-78(RF),D-68	1.3
Total	12	1536	5537	941	1571	324	22	288	966	927-44	62	1275	.284	.389	.506	131	282	47-40	.977	41	104	114	*O-1254(0-1-1254),D-265	22.3
SALTZGAVER, JACK Otto Hamlin B 1.23.1903 Croton, IA D 2.1.1978 Keokuk, IA BL/TR 5-11/165# d4.12																								
1932	NY A	20	47	10	6	2	1	0	5	10	0	10	.128	.281	.213	31	-5	1-1	.958	-3	72	64	2-16	-0.6
1934	NY A	94	350	64	95	8	1	6	36	48	0	28	.271	.359	.351	90	-4	8-1	.953	-11	84	74	3-84/1-4	-1.1
1935	NY A	61	149	17	39	6	0	3	18	23	2	12	.262	.368	.362	95	0	0-2	.937	-9	86	60	2-25,3-18/1-6	-0.8
1936	NY A	34	90	14	19	5	0	1	13	13	0	18	.211	.311	.300	53	-7	0-0	.972	-4	90	53	3-16/2-6,1-4	-0.8
1937	NY A	17	11	6	2	0	0	0	0	3	0	4	.182	.357	.182	40	-1	0-0	1.000	0	98	281	/1-4	-0.1
1945	Pit N	52	117	20	38	5	3	0	10	8	0	8	.325	.368	.419	114	2	0	.963	-2	95	83	2-31/3	0.2
Total	6	278	764	131	199	26	5	10	82	105	2	80	.260	.351	.347	85	-15	9-4	.957	-28	83	79	3-119/2-78,1-18	-3.2
SAMCOFF, ED Edward William B 9.1.1924 Sacramento, CA BR/TR 5-10/165# d4.21																								
1951	Phi A	4	11	0	0	0	0	0	0	1	0	2	.000	.083	.000	-75	-3	0-0	1.000	-0	80	178	/2-3	-0.3
SAMFORD, RON Ronald Edward B 2.28.1930 Dallas, TX BR/TR 5-11/156# d4.15																								
1954	NY N	12	5	2	0	0	0	0	0	0	0	1	.000	.000	.000	-99	-1	0-1	1.000	0	124	0	/2-3	-0.1
1955	Det A	1	1	0	0	0	0	0	0	0-0	0	1	.000	.000	.000	-99	0	0-0	1.000	0	193	0	/S	0.0
1957	Det A	54	91	6	20	1	2	0	5	6-0	1	15	.220	.276	.275	49	-7	1-0	.964	4	109	133	S-35,2-11/3-4	-0.1
1959	Was A	91	237	23	53	13	0	5	22	11-0	2	29	.224	.262	.342	65	-12	1-0	.947	2	107	96	S-64,2-23	-0.4
Total	4	158	334	31	73	14	2	5	27	17-0	3	46	.219	.261	.317	58	-20	2-1	.952	6	108	106	S-100/2-37,3-4	-0.6
SAMPLE, BILL William Amos B 4.2.1955 Roanoke, VA BR/TR 5-9/175# d9.2																								
1978	Tex A	8	15	2	7	2	0	0	3	0-0	0	3	.467	.467	.600	197	2	0-0	—	-0	0	0	/O-2(LF),D-3	0.2
1979	Tex A	128	325	60	95	21	2	5	35	37-1	2	28	.292	.365	.415	112	7	8-6	1.000	1	96	113	*O-103(91-10-5)/D-9	0.4
1980	Tex A	99	204	29	53	10	0	4	19	18-2	6	15	.260	.335	.368	96	-1	8-5	.973	-4	91	53	O-72(15-18-40)/D-4	-0.6
1981	Tex A	66	230	36	65	16	0	3	25	17-1	7	21	.283	.346	.391	120	7	4-1	.993	-2	92	87	O-64(62-5-0)	0.2
1982	Tex A	97	360	56	94	14	2	10	29	27-0	3	35	.261	.318	.394	99	-1	10-2	.981	-1	98	105	O-91(85-9-0)/D	-0.4
1983	Tex A	147	554	80	152	28	3	12	57	44-2	5	46	.274	.331	.401	103	2	44-8	.988	2	103	70	*O-146(144-2-1)	0.4
1984	Tex A	130	489	67	121	20	2	5	33	29-1	0	46	.247	.286	.327	68	-22	18-6	.986	-4	99	37	*O-122(72-51-3)/D-2	-2.7
1985	NY A	59	139	18	40	5	0	1	15	9-0	2	10	.288	.336	.345	90	-2	2-1	.989	-1	104	39	O-55(51-4-0)	-0.4
1986	Atl N	92	200	23	57	11	0	6	14	14-1	3	26	.285	.338	.430	105	1	4-2	.986	-4	88	30	O-56(10-0-48)/2	-0.4
Total	9	826	2516	371	684	127	9	46	230	195-8	28	230	.272	.329	.384	98	-7	98-31	.987	-12	97	70	O-711(532-99-97)/D-19,2	-3.3
SAMUEL, AMADO Amado Ruperto B 12.6.1938 San Pedro De Macoris, D.R. BR/TR 6-1/170# d4.10																								
1962	Mil N	76	209	16	43	10	0	3	20	12-1	0	54	.206	.248	.297	47	-16	0-2	.958	-2	107	103	S-36,2-28/3-3	-1.5
1963	Mil N	15	17	0	3	1	0	0	0	0-0	0	4	.176	.176	.235	18	-2	0-1	.786	-0	97	151	/S-7,2-4	-0.2
1964	NY N	53	142	7	33	7	0	0	5	4-0	2	24	.232	.264	.282	55	-8	0-1	.945	5	110	151	S-34,3-17/2-3	-0.2
Total	3	144	368	23	79	18	0	3	25	16-1	2	82	.215	.251	.288	49	-26	0-4	.942	3	108	127	/S-77,2-35,3-20	-1.9
SAMUEL, JUAN Juan Milton B 12.9.1960 San Pedro De Macoris, D.R. BR/TR 5-11/170# d8.24 C5 OF Total (34-LF 197-CF 40-RF)																								
1983	†Phi N	18	65	14	18	1	2	2	5	4-1	1	16	.277	.324	.446	114	1	3-2	.916	3	110	87	2-18	0.5
1984	Phi N☆	160	701	105	191	36	**19**	15	69	28-2	7	168	.272	.307	.442	107	2	72-15	.962	-15	95	78	*2-160	0.7
1985	Phi N	161	663	101	175	31	13	19	74	33-2	6	141	.264	.303	.436	102	-2	53-19	.983	1	99	79	*2-159	1.4
1986	Phi N	145	591	90	157	36	12	16	78	26-3	8	142	.266	.302	.448	102	-1	42-14	.967	-5	105	92	*2-143	0.6
1987	Phi N★	160	655	113	178	37	**15**	28	100	60-5	5	162	.272	.335	.502	115	12	35-15	.978	-12	97	94	*2-160	1.1
1988	Phi N	157	629	68	153	32	9	12	67	39-6	12	151	.243	.298	.380	92	-8	33-10	.978	-21	87	90	*2-152/O-3(0-2-1),3	-2.2
1989	Phi N	51	199	32	49	3	1	8	20	18-1	1	45	.246	.311	.392	100	-1	11-3	.993	1	109	80	O-50(CF)	0.2
	NY N	86	333	37	76	13	1	3	28	24-1	10	75	.228	.299	.300	76	-11	31-9	.986	1	103	98	O-84(CF)	-0.7
	Year	137	532	69	125	16	2	11	48	42-2	11	120	.235	.303	.335	85	-11	42-12	.989	2	105	91	*O-134(CF)	-0.5
1990	LA N	143	492	62	119	24	3	13	52	51-5	5	126	.242	.316	.382	95	-4	38-20	.972	-12	86	92	*2-108,O-31(CF)	-1.2
1991	LA N★	153	594	74	161	22	6	12	58	49-4	3	133	.271	.328	.389	104	2	23-8	.978	-5	96	95	*2-152	0.4
1992	LA N	47	122	7	32	3	1	0	15	7-3	1	22	.262	.303	.303	75	-4	2-2	.974	-2	86	70	2-38/O(RF)	-0.6
	KC A	29	102	15	29	5	3	0	8	7-1	1	27	.284	.336	.392	101	0	6-1	.903	-1	78	183	O-18(RF),2-10	-0.1
1993	Cin N	103	261	31	60	10	4	4	26	23-3	3	53	.230	.298	.345	72	-11	9-7	.971	-2	91	87	2-70/1-6,3-4,O-3(2-0-1)	-1.0
1994	Det A	59	136	32	42	9	5	5	21	10-0	3	26	.309	.364	.559	134	6	5-2	1.000	1	92	76	O-27(2-25-0),D-10/2-8,1-2	0.7
1995	Det A	76	171	28	48	10	1	10	34	24-0	2	38	.281	.376	.526	132	8	5-4	.983	-1	109	93	1-37,D-16/O-9(LF),2-6	0.3
	KC A	15	34	3	6	0	0	2	5	5-1	0	11	.176	.282	.353	63	-2	1-0	1.000	-1	39	0	/O-5(LF),1D	-0.3
	Year	91	205	31	54	10	1	12	39	29-1	2	49	.263	.360	.498	121	6	6-4	.984	-2	105	90	1-38,D-23,O-14(LF)/2-6	0.0
1996	Tor A	69	188	34	48	8	3	8	26	15-0	3	65	.255	.319	.457	94	-3	9-1	1.000	-5	77	0	O-24(8-5-15),D-24,1-17	-0.8
1997	Tor A	45	95	13	27	5	4	3	15	10-0	2	28	.284	.364	.516	126	3	5-3	1.000	-3	49	155	D-15/3-9,1-7,2-4,O-2(RF)	0.0
1998	Tor A	43	50	14	9	2	0	1	2	7-0	1	13	.180	.293	.280	50	-4	13-8	.882	-1	98	0	D-11,O-10(8-0-2)/1-3,2-2	-0.5
Total	16	1720	6081	873	1578	287	102	161	703	440-38	74	1442	.259	.315	.420	101	-17	396-143	.973	-76	95	88	*2-1190,O-267C/D-83,1-73,3-14	-1.5
SAMUELS, IKE Samuel Earl B 2.20.1874 Quincy, IL D 2.22.1964 New York, NY BR/TR d8.3																								
1895	StL N	24	74	5	17	2	0	0	5	5	0	7	.230	.278	.257	39	-7	5	.750	-6	92	32	3-21/S-3	-1.0
SANCHEZ, ALEJANDRO Alejandro (Pimentel) B 2.14.1959 San Pedro De Macoris, D.R. BR/TR 6/185# d9.6																								
1982	Phi N	7	14	3	4	1	0	2	4	0-0	0	4	.286	.286	.786	186	1	0-0	1.000	-0	107	0	/O-4(RF)	0.1
1983	Phi N	8	7	2	2	0	0	0	2	0-0	0	2	.286	.286	.286	59	0	0-0	.500	-0	62	0	/O-2(RF)	-0.1
1984	SF N	13	41	3	8	0	1	0	2	0-0	0	12	.195	.195	.244	23	-5	2-3	.952	1	91	280	O-11(3-0-9)	-0.5

Year	Tm Lg	G	AB	R	H	2B	3B	HR	RBI	BB-IB	HP	SO	AVG	OBP	SLG	AOPS	ABR	SB-CS	FA	FR	Rng	Thr	G at Pos	BFW
1985	Det A	71	133	19	33	6	2	6	12	0-0	0	39	.248	.248	.459	89	-3	2-2	.923	-1	93	82	O-31(5-2-24),D-28	-0.6
1986	Min A	8	16	1	2	0	0	0	1	1-0	0	8	.125	.176	.125	-16	-3	0-0	—	-0	0	0	/O(LF)D	-0.3
1987	Oak A	2	3	0	0	0	0	0	0	0-0	0	1	.000	.000	.000	-99	-1	0-0	1.000	-0	91	0	/O(RF)D	-0.1
Total 6		109	214	28	49	7	3	8	21	1-0	0	66	.229	.233	.402	71	-11	4-5	.929	-2	92	128	/O-50(9-2-40),D-32	-1.5
SANCHEZ, ALEX Alexis B 8.26.1976 Havana, Cuba BL/TL 5-10/180# d6.15																								
2001	Mil N	30	68	7	14	3	2	0	4	5-0	0	13	.206	.260	.309	47	-6	6-2	.963	-1	72	237	O-19(3-14-3)	-0.6
2002	Mil N	112	394	55	114	10	7	1	33	31-0	2	62	.289	.343	.358	90	-8	37-14	.982	6	126	19	*O-100(16-86-0)	0.1
2003	Mil N	43	163	15	46	10	3	0	10	7-0	2	28	.282	.316	.380	83	-4	8-6	.990	3	116	152	O-36(CF)	-0.1
	Det A	101	394	43	114	13	5	1	22	18-0	1	46	.289	.320	.355	85	-10	44-18	.979	-1	107	22	O-99(CF)	-0.6
Total 3		286	1019	120	288	36	17	2	69	61-0	5	149	.283	.324	.357	84	-28	95-40	.981	7	114	54	O-254(19-235-3)	-1.2
SANCHEZ, CELERINO Celerino (Perez) B 2.3.1944 Veracruz, Mexico D 5.1.1992 Leon, Mexico BR/TR 5-11/160# d6.13																								
1972	NY A	71	250	18	62	8	3	0	22	12-1	4	30	.248	.292	.304	81	-7	0-0	.939	2	114	98	3-68	-0.5
1973	NY A	34	64	12	14	3	0	1	9	2-0	0	12	.219	.239	.313	57	-4	1-1	1.000	-0	99	0	3-11,D-11/S-2,O-2(RF)	-0.5
Total 2		105	314	30	76	11	3	1	31	14-1	4	42	.242	.281	.306	76	-11	1-1	.943	2	113	89	/3-79,D-11,O-2(RF),S-2	-1.0
SANCHEZ, FREDDY Frederick P. B 12.21.1977 Hollywood, CA BR/TR 5-11/185# d9.10																								
2002	Bos A	12	16	3	3	0	0	0	2	2-0	0	3	.188	.278	.188	27	-2	0-0	1.000	-1	93	51	/2-5,S-5	-0.2
2003	Bos A	20	34	6	8	2	0	0	2	0-0	0	8	.235	.235	.294	38	-3	0-0	1.000	2	158	0	/3-7,S-6,2-3	0.0
Total 2		32	50	9	11	2	0	0	4	2-0	0	11	.220	.250	.260	34	-5	0-0	1.000	1	112	84	/S-11,2-8,3-7	-0.2
SANCHEZ, ORLANDO Orlando (Marquez) B 9.7.1956 Canovanas, P.R. BL/TR 6-1/195# d5.6																								
1981	StL N	27	49	5	14	2	1	0	6	2-1	0	6	.286	.308	.367	90	-1	1-0	.926	-3	71	44	C-18	-0.4
1982	StL N	26	37	6	7	0	1	0	3	5-0	0	5	.189	.286	.243	49	-3	0-0	1.000	-3	49	0	C-15	-0.5
1983	StL N	6	6	0	0	0	0	0	0	0-0	0	4	.000	.000	.000	-99	-2	0-0	1.000	0	0	0	/C	-0.2
1984	KC A	10	10	0	1	1	0	0	2	0-0	0	2	.100	.100	.200	-19	-2	0-0	1.000	0	0	0	/C	-0.1
	Bal A	4	8	0	2	0	0	0	1	0-0	0	2	.250	.250	.250	40	-1	0-0	1.000	0	113	158	/C-4	0.0
	Year	14	18	0	3	1	0	0	3	0-0	0	4	.167	.167	.222	7	-2	0-0	1.000	0	107	149	/C-5	-0.1
Total 4		73	110	11	24	3	2	0	12	7-1	0	19	.218	.263	.282	53	-9	1-0	.962	-6	65	36	/C-39	-1.2
SANCHEZ, REY Rey Francisco (Guadalupe) B 10.5.1967 Rio Piedras, P.R. BR/TR 5-9/170# d9.8																								
1991	Chi N	13	23	1	6	0	0	0	2	4-0	0	3	.261	.370	.261	77	-1	0-0	1.000	-1	80	27	S-10/2-2	-0.1
1992	Chi N	74	255	24	64	14	3	1	19	10-1	3	17	.251	.285	.341	75	-9	2-1	.974	10	104	142	S-68/2-4	0.7
1993	Chi N	105	344	35	97	11	2	0	28	15-7	3	22	.282	.316	.326	74	-13	1-1	.969	27	122	116	S-98	2.0
1994	Chi N	96	291	26	83	13	1	0	24	20-4	7	29	.285	.345	.337	80	-8	2-5	.993	**20**	108	84	2-50,S-30,3-17	1.5
1995	Chi N	114	428	57	119	22	2	3	27	14-2	1	48	.278	.301	.360	75	-16	6-4	.987	2	**109**	87	*2-111/S-4	-0.9
1996	Chi N	95	289	28	61	9	0	1	12	22-6	3	42	.211	.272	.253	39	-26	7-1	.977	21	119	103	S-92	0.3
1997	Chi N	97	205	14	51	9	0	1	12	11-2	0	26	.249	.287	.307	54	-14	4-2	.964	-7	91	63	S-63,2-32/3	-1.6
	†NY A	38	138	21	43	12	0	1	15	5-0	1	21	.312	.338	.420	98	0	0-4	.976	2	108	98	2-37/S-6	0.2
1998	SF N	109	316	44	90	14	2	2	30	16-0	4	47	.285	.325	.361	86	-7	0-0	.977	12	109	97	S-76,2-36	1.0
1999	KC A	134	479	66	141	18	6	2	56	22-2	4	48	.294	.329	.370	77	-18	11-5	.982	29	**119**	115	*S-134	2.0
2000	KC A	143	509	68	139	18	2	1	38	28-0	4	55	.273	.314	.322	60	-31	7-3	.994	19	**112**	108	*S-143	-0.1
2001	KC A	100	390	46	118	14	5	0	28	11-0	2	34	.303	.322	.364	75	-15	9-1	.994	32	126	158	*S-100	2.5
	†Atl N	49	154	10	35	4	1	0	9	4-1	0	15	.227	.245	.266	32	-16	2-0	.986	8	113	122	S-48	-0.4
2002	Bos A	107	357	46	102	12	3	1	38	17-1	2	31	.286	.318	.345	76	-13	2-2	.991	4	100	111	*2-100,S-10	-0.3
2003	NY N	56	174	11	36	3	1	0	12	8-2	0	18	.207	.240	.236	26	-20	1-1	.989	-1	99	87	S-42,2-12	-1.7
	Sea A	46	170	22	50	5	1	0	11	8-1	2	21	.294	.330	.335	80	-5	1-0	.979	-3	88	128	S-46	-0.4
Total 13		1376	4522	519	1235	178	29	13	361	215-29	36	477	.273	.309	.334	69	-212	55-30	.981	175	113	117	S-970,2-384/3-18	4.7
SAND, HEINIE John Henry B 7.3.1897 San Francisco, CA D 11.3.1958 San Francisco, CA BR/TR 5-8/160# d4.17																								
1923	Phi N	132	470	85	107	16	5	4	32	82	4	56	.228	.347	.309	67	-20	7-3	.934	-3	98	106	*S-120,3-11	-0.9
1924	Phi N	137	539	79	132	21	6	6	40	52	4	57	.245	.316	.340	67	-24	5-4	**.959**	2	100	97	*S-137	-0.7
1925	Phi N	148	496	69	138	30	7	3	55	64	3	65	.278	.364	.385	84	-10	1-1	.928	-6	94	100	*S-143	-0.2
1926	Phi N	149	567	99	154	30	5	4	37	66	2	56	.272	.350	.363	88	-8	2	.939	-0	102	85	*S-149	0.7
1927	Phi N	141	535	87	160	22	8	1	49	58	1	59	.299	.369	.376	98	0	5	.949	-4	92	65	S-86,3-58	0.8
1928	Phi N	141	426	38	90	26	1	0	38	60	1	47	.211	.310	.277	53	-28	1	.951	-0	98	95	*S-137	-1.4
Total 6		848	3033	457	781	145	32	18	251	382	15	340	.258	.343	.344	77	-90	21-8	.943	-12	98	93	S-772/3-69	-1.7
SANDBERG, GUS Gustave E. B 2.23.1896 Long Island City, NY D 2.3.1930 Los Angeles, CA BR/TR 6-1/189# d5.11																								
1923	Cin N	7	17	1	3	1	0	0	1	1	0	1	.176	.222	.235	21	-2	0-0	1.000	-0	*117*	*113*	/C-5	-0.2
1924	Cin N	24	52	1	9	0	0	0	3	2	0	7	.173	.204	.173	2	-7	0-0	1.000	0	*94*	*83*	C-24	-0.6
Total 2		31	69	2	12	1	0	0	4	3	0	8	.174	.208	.188	7	-9	0-0	1.000	-0	*99*	*89*	/C-29	-0.8
SANDBERG, JARED Jared Lawrence B 3.2.1978 Olympia, WA BR/TR 6-3/185# d8.7																								
2001	TB A	39	136	13	28	7	0	1	15	10-0	1	45	.206	.265	.279	45	-11	1-0	.944	-1	93	101	3-38/1	-1.1
2002	TB A	102	358	55	82	21	1	18	54	39-3	1	139	.229	.305	.444	98	-2	3-2	.948	-2	98	107	3-97/1-3,D-2	-0.3
2003	TB A	55	136	15	29	10	1	6	23	16-1	2	52	.213	.305	.434	93	-1	0-0	.956	1	106	56	3-50/1S	0.0
Total 3		196	630	83	139	38	2	25	92	65-4	4	236	.221	.297	.406	85	-14	4-2	.949	-2	99	94	3-185/1-5,D-2,S	-1.4
SANDBERG, RYNE Ryne Dee B 9.18.1959 Spokane, WA BR/TR 6-2/180# d9.2																								
1981	Phi N	13	6	2	1	0	0	0	0	0-0	0	1	.167	.167	.167	-5	-1	0-0	1.000	1	85	0	/S-5,2	0.0
1982	Chi N	156	635	103	172	33	5	7	54	36-3	4	90	.271	.312	.372	89	-10	32-12	.970	15	112	88	*3-133,2-24	0.7
1983	Chi N	158	633	94	165	25	4	8	48	51-3	3	79	.261	.316	.351	81	-16	37-11	**.986**	**44**	**121**	**123**	*2-157/S	4.2
1984	†Chi N★	156	636	**114**	200	36	**19**	19	84	52-3	3	101	.314	.367	.520	135	28	32-7	**.993**	22	**112**	103	*2-156	**6.5**
1985	Chi N★	153	609	113	186	31	6	26	83	57-5	1	97	.305	.364	.504	127	22	54-11	.986	13	108	95	*2-153/S	5.3
1986	Chi N★	154	627	68	178	28	5	14	76	46-6	0	79	.284	.330	.411	97	-4	34-11	**.994**	4	104	84	*2-153	1.3
1987	Chi N★	132	523	81	154	25	2	16	59	59-4	2	79	.294	.367	.442	109	8	21-2	.985	5	98	93	*2-131	2.4
1988	Chi N★	155	618	77	163	23	8	19	69	54-3	1	91	.264	.322	.419	107	4	25-10	.987	12	**111**	82	*2-153	2.4
1989	†Chi N★	157	606	**104**	176	25	5	30	76	59-8	4	85	.290	.356	.497	132	24	15-5	.992	-1	103	92	*2-155	3.1
1990	Chi N★	155	615	**116**	188	30	3	**40**	100	50-8	1	84	.306	.354	.559	138	30	25-7	.989	4	106	93	*2-154	4.2
1991	Chi N★	158	585	104	170	32	2	26	100	87-4	2	89	.291	.379	.485	137	31	22-8	**.995**	-3	108	77	*2-157	3.5
1992	Chi N★	158	612	100	186	32	8	26	87	68-4	1	73	.304	.371	.510	145	36	17-6	.990	12	**112**	100	*2-157	5.6
1993	Chi N★	117	456	67	141	20	0	9	45	37-1	2	62	.309	.359	.412	109	6	9-2	.988	1	105	111	*2-115	1.4
1994	Chi N	57	223	36	53	9	5	5	24	23-0	1	40	.238	.312	.390	83	-6	2-3	.987	6	115	98	2-57	0.1
1996	Chi N	150	554	85	135	28	4	25	92	54-4	7	116	.244	.316	.444	96	-4	12-8	.991	-16	101	94	*2-146	-1.4
1997	Chi N	135	447	54	118	26	0	12	64	28-3	2	94	.264	.308	.403	83	-12	7-4	.984	-20	90	81	*2-126/D	-2.6
Total 16		2164	8385	1318	2386	403	76	282	1061	761-59	34	1260	.285	.344	.452	113	136	344-107	.989	99	107	94	*2-1995,3-133/S-7,D	36.7
SANDERS, BEN Alexander Bennett B 2.16.1865 Catharpin, VA D 8.29.1930 Memphis, TN BR/TR 6/210# d6.6 ▲																								
1888	Phi N	57	236	26	58	11	2	1	25	8	2	12	.246	.276	.322	86	-4	13	.929	3	125	81	P-31,O-25(13-6-7)/3	-0.1
1889	Phi N	44	169	21	47	8	2	0	21	6	1	11	.278	.307	.349	76	-6	4	.879	-2	84	36	P-44/O-3(1-2-0)	-0.1
1890	Phi P	52	189	31	59	6	6	0	30	10	0	10	.312	.347	.407	99	-2	2	.924	1	103	171	P-43,O-10(0-3-7)	0.0
1891	Phi AA	40	156	24	39	6	4	1	19	7	2	12	.250	.291	.359	86	-4	2	.839	-4	0	0	O-22(10-0-13),P-19	-0.6
1892	Lou N	54	198	30	54	12	2	3	18	16	1	17	.273	.330	.399	131	7	6	.930	-3	90	150	P-31,1-15/O-9(RF)	0.1
Total 5		247	948	132	257	43	16	5	113	47	6	62	.271	.310	.366	95	-9	27	.916	-5	99	107	P-168/O-69(24-11-36),1-15,3	-0.7
SANDERS, ANTHONY Anthony Marcus B 3.2.1974 Tucson, AZ BR/TR 6-2/200# d4.26																								
1999	Tor A	3	7	1	2	1	0	0	2	0-0	0	2	.286	.286	.429	78	0	0-0	1.000	-0	49	0	/O(LF)D	0.0
2000	Sea A	1	1	1	1	0	0	0	0	0-0	0	0	1.000	1.000	1.000	422	0	0-0	1.000	0	431	0	/O(RF)	0.1
2001	Sea A	9	17	1	3	2	0	0	2	2-0	0	3	.176	.263	.294	49	-1	0-0	1.000	0	121	0	/O-9(8-0-1)	-0.1
Total 3		13	25	3	6	3	0	0	4	2-0	0	5	.240	.296	.360	73	-1	0-0	1.000	0	115	0	/O-11(9-0-2),D-2	0.0
SANDERS, DEION Deion Luwynn B 8.9.1967 Ft.Myers, FL BL/TL 6-1/195# d5.31																								
1989	NY A	14	47	7	11	2	0	2	7	3-1	0	8	.234	.280	.404	92	-1	1-0	.969	-0	95	144	O-14(3-11-0)	-0.1
1990	NY A	57	133	24	21	2	2	3	9	13-0	1	27	.158	.236	.271	42	-11	8-2	.973	-3	83	92	O-42(29-15-0)/D-4	-1.4
1991	Atl N	54	110	16	21	1	2	4	13	12-0	0	23	.191	.270	.345	68	-5	11-3	.952	-1	93	169	O-44(41-5-1)	-0.6

Year	Tm Lg	G	AB	R	H	2B	3B	HR	RBI	BB-IB	HP	SO	AVG	OBP	SLG	AOPS	ABR	SB-CS	FA	FR	Rng	Thr	G at Pos	BFW
1992	†Atl N	97	303	54	92	6	**14**	8	28	18-0	2	52	.304	.346	.495	128	9	26-9	.983	-1	99	100	O-75(12-60-9)	1.0
1993	†Atl N	95	272	42	75	18	6	6	28	16-3	3	42	.276	.321	.452	104	1	19-7	.986	-3	95	33	O-60(5-55-0)	0.0
1994	Atl N	46	191	32	55	10	0	4	21	16-1	1	28	.288	.343	.403	93	-2	19-7	.980	-4	91	0	O-46(CF)	-0.4
	Cin N	46	184	26	51	7	4	0	7	16-0	2	35	.277	.342	.359	84	-4	19-9	1.000	1	104	86	O-45(CF)	-0.2
	Year	92	375	58	106	17	4	4	28	32-1	3	63	.283	.342	.381	88	-6	38-16	.991	-4	97	42	O-91(CF)	-0.6
1995	Cin N	33	129	19	31	2	3	1	10	9-0	2	18	.240	.296	.326	65	-7	16-3	.968	2	117	117	O-33(CF)	-0.2
	SF N	52	214	29	61	9	5	5	18	18-0	2	42	.285	.346	.444	110	2	8-6	.984	-3	101	0	O-52(CF)	0.0
	Year	85	343	48	92	11	8	6	28	27-0	4	60	.268	.327	.399	93	-5	24-9	.977	-0	107	45	O-85(CF)	-0.2
1997	Cin N	115	465	53	127	13	7	5	23	34-2	6	67	.273	.329	.363	81	-14	56-13	.984	-2	102	52	*O-113(37-77-0)	-0.9
2001	Cin N	32	75	6	13	2	0	1	4	4-0	2	10	.173	.235	.240	22	-9	3-4	1.000	3	109	404	O-16(12-4-1)/D-2	-0.7
Total	9	641	2123	308	558	72	43	39	168	159-7	21	352	.263	.319	.392	88	-41	186-63	.982	-11	99	76	O-540(139-403-11)/D-6	-3.5
SANDERS, JOHN John Frank B 11.20.1945 Grand Island, NE BR/TR 6-2/200# d4.13																								
1965	KC A	1	0	0	0	0	0	0	0	0-0	0	0	—	—	—	—	0	0-0	—	0			R	0.0
SANDERS, RAY Raymond Floyd B 12.4.1916 Bonne Terre, MO D 10.28.1983 Washington, MO BL/TR 6-2/185# d4.14																								
1942	†StL N	95	282	37	71	17	2	5	39	42	1	31	.252	.351	.379	106	3	2	.991	-3	79	107	1-77	-0.7
1943	†StL N	144	478	69	134	21	5	11	73	77	1	33	.280	.381	.414	124	17	1	.995	-5	80	**130**	*1-141	0.5
1944	†StL N	154	601	87	177	34	9	12	102	71	2	50	.295	.371	.441	126	21	2	**.994**	-12	64	**136**	*1-152	0.1
1945	StL N	143	537	85	148	29	3	8	78	83	2	55	.276	.375	.385	109	10	3	.986	-5	92	**113**	*1-142	-0.2
1946	Bos N	80	259	43	63	12	0	6	35	50	1	38	.243	.368	.359	105	4	0	.988	3	116	106	1-77	0.5
1948	†Bos N	5	4	0	1	0	0	0	2	1	0	0	.250	.400	.250	81	0	0	—	0			H	0.0
1949	Bos N	9	21	0	3	1	0	0	0	4	0	9	.143	.280	.190	30	-2	0	.984	2	250	40	/1-7	0.0
Total	7	630	2182	321	597	114	19	42	329	328	7	216	.274	.370	.401	115	53	8	.991	-20	85	121	1-596	0.2
SANDERS, REGGIE Reginald Jerome B 9.9.1949 Birmingham, AL BR/TR 6-2/205# d9.1																								
1974	Det A	26	99	12	27	7	0	3	10	5-2	0	20	.273	.308	.434	108	1	1-0	.987	1	119	82	1-25/D	0.0
SANDERS, REGGIE Reginald Laverne B 12.1.1967 Florence, SC BR/TR 6-1/186# d8.22																								
1991	Cin N	9	40	6	8	0	0	1	3	0-0	0	9	.200	.200	.275	31	-4	1-1	1.000	-0	105	0	/O-9(CF)	-0.5
1992	Cin N	116	385	62	104	26	6	12	36	48-2	4	98	.270	.356	.462	127	15	16-7	.978	11	112	**212**	*O-110(53-77-0)	2.6
1993	Cin N	138	496	90	136	16	4	20	83	51-7	5	118	.274	.343	.444	110	6	27-10	.975	2	117	29	*O-137(0-4-135)	0.4
1994	Cin N	107	400	66	105	20	8	17	62	41-1	2	114	.262	.332	.480	110	4	21-9	.975	6	107	155	*O-104(RF)	0.7
1995	†Cin N★	133	484	91	148	36	6	28	99	69-4	8	122	.306	.397	.579	155	40	36-12	.983	4	101	128	*O-130(0-16-125)	4.1
1996	Cin N	81	287	49	72	17	1	14	33	44-4	2	86	.251	.353	.463	113	6	24-8	.988	4	106	131	O-80(RF)	0.8
1997	Cin N	86	312	52	79	19	2	19	56	42-3	3	93	.253	.347	.510	119	9	13-7	.974	3	113	63	O-85(RF)	0.7
1998	Cin N	135	481	83	129	18	6	14	59	51-2	7	137	.268	.346	.418	99	-1	20-9	.978	-4	102	53	*O-131(0-88-57)	-0.5
1999	SD N	133	478	92	136	24	7	26	72	65-1	6	108	.285	.376	.527	136	26	36-13	.975	-3	98	54	*O-129(97-15-41)/D	2.0
2000	†Atl N	103	340	43	79	23	1	11	37	32-2	2	78	.232	.302	.403	76	-13	21-4	.964	-1	92	127	O-96(69-1-27)	-1.5
2001	†Ari N	126	441	84	116	21	3	33	90	46-7	5	126	.263	.337	.549	117	10	14-10	.996	1	102	67	*O-119(RF)	0.4
2002	†SF N	140	505	75	126	23	6	23	85	47-3	12	121	.250	.324	.455	112	4	18-6	.984	9	112	136	*O-137(RF)	0.8
2003	Pit N	130	453	74	129	27	4	31	87	38-4	5	110	.285	.345	.567	130	18	15-5	.983	-1	100	80	*O-120(39-0-91)/D-2	1.3
Total	13	1437	5102	867	1367	270	54	249	802	574-40	61	1320	.268	.347	.488	117	120	262-101	.980	30	105	99	*O-1387(258-210-1001)/D-3	11.3
SANDLOCK, MIKE Michael Joseph B 10.17.1915 Old Greenwich, CT BB/TR (BL 1944) 6-1/185# d9.19																								
1942	Bos N	2	1	1	1	0	0	0	0	0	0	0	1.000	1.000	1.000	496	0	0	—	-0	0	0	/S-2	0.0
1944	Bos N	30	30	1	3	0	0	0	2	5	1	3	.100	.250	.100	1	-4	0	.956	4	143	55	3-22/S-7	0.0
1945	Bro N	80	195	21	55	14	2	2	17	18	1	19	.282	.346	.405	109	2	2	.991	-1	*108*	*79*	C-47,S-22/2-4,3-2	0.5
1946	Bro N	19	34	1	5	0	0	0	0	3	0	4	.147	.216	.147	4	-4	0	.973	4	*130*	*167*	C-17/3	0.0
1953	Pit N	64	186	10	43	5	0	0	12	12	1	19	.231	.281	.258	42	-16	0-0	.991	7	*76*	*170*	C-64	-0.5
Total	5	195	446	34	107	19	2	2	31	38	3	45	.240	.304	.305	66	-22	2-0	.989	14	*94*	*135*	C-128/S-31,3-25,2-4	0.0
SANDS, CHARLIE Charles Duane B 12.17.1947 Newport News, VA BL/TR 6-2/215# d6.21																								
1967	NY A	1	1	0	0	0	0	0	0	0-0	0	1	.000	.000	.000	-99	0	0-0	—	0			H	0.0
1971	†Pit N	28	25	4	5	2	0	1	5	7-1	0	6	.200	.375	.400	120	1	0-0	1.000	-0	41	225	/C-3	0.1
1972	Pit N	1	1	0	0	0	0	0	0	0-0	0	0	.000	.000	.000	-99	0	0-0	—	0			H	0.0
1973	Cal A	17	33	5	9	2	1	1	5	5-1	0	10	.273	.368	.485	150	2	0-0	.917	-5	83	0	C-10	-0.2
1974	Cal A	43	83	6	16	2	0	4	13	23-2	1	17	.193	.370	.361	119	3	0-0	1.000	-0	174	0	D-21/C-5	0.3
1975	Oak A	3	2	0	1	0	0	0	0	1-0	0	1	.500	.667	.500	239	1	0-0	—	0			/D	0.1
Total	6	93	145	15	31	6	1	6	23	36-4	1	35	.214	.372	.393	125	7	0-0	.955	-5	98	34	/D-22,C-18	0.3
SANDT, TOMMY Thomas James B 12.22.1950 Brooklyn, NY BR/TR 5-11/175# d6.29 C16																								
1975	Oak A	1	0	0	0	0	0	0	0	0-0	0	0	—	—	—	—	0	0-0	—	-0	0	0	/2	0.0
1976	Oak A	41	67	6	14	1	0	0	3	7-0	0	9	.209	.284	.224	52	-4	0-0	.966	-4	88	100	S-29/2-9,3-2	-0.6
Total	2	42	67	6	14	1	0	0	3	7-0	0	9	.209	.284	.224	52	-4	0-0	.966	-4	88	100	/S-29,2-10,3-2	-0.6
SANFORD, CHANCE Chance Steven B 6.2.1972 Houston, TX BL/TR 5-10/165# d4.30																								
1998	Pit N	14	28	3	4	1	1	0	3	1-0	0	6	.143	.172	.250	9	-4	0-0	.900	-3	49	217	/3-5,2S	-0.7
1999	LA N	5	8	1	2	0	0	0	2	0-0	0	1	.250	.250	.250	29	-1	0-0	1.000	-1	34	0	/2-2	-0.2
Total	2	19	36	4	6	1	1	0	5	1-0	0	7	.167	.189	.250	13	-5	0-0	.900	-4	49	217	/3-5,2-3,S	-0.9
SANFORD, JACK John Doward B 6.23.1917 Chatham, VA BR/TR 6-3/195# d8.24 Mil 1942-45																								
1940	Was A	34	122	5	24	4	2	0	10	6	0	17	.197	.234	.262	30	-13	0-0	.993	-2	76	132	1-34	-1.7
1941	Was A	3	5	1	2	0	1	0	0	1	0	1	.400	.500	.800	251	1	0-0	1.000	-0	0	97	/1	0.1
1946	Was A	10	26	7	6	0	1	0	1	2	0	6	.231	.286	.308	70	-1	0-0	.971	-2	23	116	/1-6	-0.3
Total	3	47	153	13	32	4	4	0	11	9	0	24	.209	.253	.288	44	-13	0-0	.989	-4	65	128	/1-41	-1.9
SANGUILLEN, MANNY Manuel De Jesus (Magan) B 3.21.1944 Colon, Panama BR/TR 6/193# d7.23																								
1967	Pit N	30	96	6	26	4	0	0	8	4-3	0	12	.271	.300	.313	75	-3	0-1	.986	-3	*104*	*81*	C-28	-0.5
1969	Pit N	129	459	62	139	21	6	5	57	12-4	3	48	.303	.324	.407	106	2	8-4	.981	6	99	115	*C-113	1.3
1970	†Pit N	128	486	63	158	19	9	7	61	17-9	0	45	.325	.344	.444	113	6	2-3	.988	10	155	101	*C-125	2.1
1971	†Pit N☆	138	533	60	170	26	5	7	81	19-13	3	32	.319	.345	.426	118	11	6-4	.994	12	**172**	112	*C-135	3.0
1972	†Pit N★	136	520	55	155	18	8	7	71	21-11	0	38	.298	.322	.404	108	3	1-2	.988	4	157	74	*C-127/O-2(LF)	1.3
1973	Pit N	149	589	64	166	26	7	12	65	17-8	3	29	.282	.301	.411	99	-4	2-5	.983	4	100	73	C-89,O-59(RF)	0.0
1974	†Pit N	151	596	77	171	21	4	7	68	21-9	5	27	.287	.313	.371	95	-7	2-2	.985	1	128	105	*C-151	0.1
1975	†Pit N☆	133	481	60	158	24	4	9	58	48-15	3	31	.328	.391	.451	135	23	5-4	.987	1	114	67	*C-132	3.1
1976	Pit N	114	389	52	113	16	6	2	36	28-14	2	18	.290	.338	.378	103	1	2-4	.978	-2	119	103	*C-111	0.3
1977	Oak A	152	571	42	157	17	5	6	58	22-4	2	35	.275	.302	.354	80	-18	2-5	.985	-3	68	139	C-77,D-58/O-9(RF),1-7	-2.1
1978	Pit N	85	220	15	58	5	1	3	16	9-2	2	10	.264	.296	.336	74	-8	2-2	1.000	-4	68	93	1-40,C-18	-1.5
1979	†Pit N	56	74	8	17	5	2	0	4	2-2	0	5	.230	.247	.351	59	-4	0-0	.947	0	72	155	/C-8,1-5	-0.4
1980	Pit N	47	48	2	12	3	0	0	2	3-2	0	1	.250	.294	.313	68	-2	3-2	.956	-0	127	111	/1-5	-0.2
Total	13	1448	5062	566	1500	205	57	65	585	223-96	23	331	.296	.326	.398	103	0	35-38	.986	26	*127*	*96*	*C-1114/O-70(2-0-68),D-58,1-57	6.5
SANICKI, ED Edward Robert "Butch" B 7.7.1923 Wallington, NJ D 7.6.1998 Old Bridge, NJ BR/TR 5-9/175# d9.14																								
1949	Phi N	7	13	4	3	0	0	3	7	1	0	4	.231	.286	.923	217	2	0	1.000	0	121	0	/O-6(0-1-5)	0.2
1951	Phi N	13	4	1	2	1	0	0	1	1	0	1	.500	.600	.750	265	1	1-0	1.000	0	101	0	O-10(LF)	0.1
Total	2	20	17	5	5	1	0	3	8	2	0	5	.294	.368	.882	231	3	1-0	1.000	0	119	0	/O-16(10-1-5)	0.3
SANKEY, BEN Benjamin Turner B 9.2.1907 Nauvoo, AL D 10.14.2001 Washington, GA BR/TR 5-10/155# d10.5																								
1929	Pit N	2	7	1	1	0	0	0	0	0	0	1	.143	.143	.143	-28	-1	0	.909	-0	101	81	/S-2	-0.2
1930	Pit N	13	30	6	5	0	0	0	0	2	0	3	.167	.219	.167	-5	-5	0	.871	-1	104	56	/S-6,2-4	-0.5
1931	Pit N	57	132	14	30	2	5	0	14	14	0	10	.227	.301	.318	67	-7	0	.920	-8	100	95	S-49/2-2,3-2	-1.1
Total	3	72	169	21	36	2	5	0	14	16	0	14	.213	.281	.284	49	-13	0	.914	-9	100	90	/S-57,2-6,3-2	-1.8
SANTANA, ANDRES Andres Confesor (Belonis) B 2.5.1968 San Pedro De Macoris, D.R. BB/TR 5-11/160# d9.16																								
1990	SF N	6	2	0	0	0	0	0	1	0-0	0	0	.000	.000	.000	-99	-1	0-0	1.000	-1	35	177	/S-3	-0.1

Year	Tm Lg	G	AB	R	H	2B	3B	HR	RBI	BB-IB	HP	SO	AVG	OBP	SLG	AOPS	ABR	SB-CS	FA	FR	Rng	Thr	G at Pos	BFW
SANTANA, PEDRO Pedro B 9.21.1976 San Pedro De Macoris, D.R. BR/TR 5-11/160# d7.16																								
2001	Det A	1	0	0	0	0	0	0	0	0-0	0	0	—	—	—	—	0	0-0	1.000	0	0	0	/2	0.0
SANTANA, RAFAEL Rafael Francisco (De La Cruz) B 1.31.1958 LaRomana, D.R. BR/TR 6-1/165# d4.5 C1																								
1983	StL N	30	14	1	3	0	0	0	2	2-0	1	2	.214	.353	.214	61	-1	0-1	.857	-3	61	70	/2-9,S-6,3-4	-0.4
1984	NY N	51	152	14	42	11	1	1	12	9-0	0	17	.276	.317	.382	97	-1	0-3	.970	-2	79	132	S-50	0.1
1985	NY N	154	529	41	136	19	1	1	29	29-12	0	54	.257	.295	.302	69	-23	1-0	.965	-16	84	96	*S-153	-2.4
1986	†NY N	139	394	38	86	11	0	1	28	36-12	2	43	.218	.285	.254	52	-26	0-0	.973	10	103	107	*S-137/2	-0.4
1987	NY N	139	439	41	112	21	2	5	44	29-10	1	57	.255	.302	.346	75	-17	1-1	.973	13	104	113	*S-138	0.9
1988	NY A	148	480	50	115	12	1	4	38	33-0	1	61	.240	.289	.294	64	-23	1-2	.966	-14	98	102	*S-148	-2.8
1990	Cle A	7	13	3	3	0	0	1	3	0-0	0	0	.231	.231	.462	89	0	0-0	1.000	-2	78	77	/S-7	-0.2
Total	7	668	2021	188	497	74	5	13	156	138-34	5	234	.246	.295	.307	68	-91	3-7	.969	-14	95	106	S-639/2-10,3-4	-5.2
SANTANGELO, F. P. Frank-Paul B 10.24.1967 Livonia, MI BB/TR 5-10/165# d8.2 OF Total (217-LF 195-CF 88-RF)																								
1995	Mon N	35	98	11	29	5	1	1	9	12-0	2	9	.296	.384	.398	103	1	1-1	.979	-2	115	0	O-25(20-2-7)/2-5	-0.2
1996	Mon N	152	393	54	109	20	5	7	56	49-4	11	61	.277	.369	.407	103	4	5-2	.983	10	119	83	*O-124(33-76-18),3-23/2-5,S	1.3
1997	Mon N	130	350	56	87	19	5	5	31	50-1	25	73	.249	.379	.374	99	3	8-5	1.000	1	111	83	O-99(40-13-51),3-32/2-7,S	0.1
1998	Mon N	122	383	53	82	18	0	4	23	44-1	23	72	.214	.330	.292	67	-16	7-3	.983	-2	110	124	O-92(72-23-1),2-35/3	-1.9
1999	SF N	113	254	49	66	17	3	3	26	53-0	11	54	.260	.406	.386	111	8	12-4	.993	-2	99	123	O-81(26-49-9),2-11/3-3,S	0.7
2000	LA N	81	142	19	28	4	0	1	9	21-0	6	33	.197	.322	.246	50	-10	3-2	.983	-3	90	0	O-50(26-27-1)/2-7	-1.3
2001	†Oak A	32	71	16	14	4	0	0	8	11-0	5	17	.197	.341	.254	61	-3	1-1	1.000	-2	96	81	2-20/O-6(0-5-1),3-3,D-2	-0.4
Total	7	665	1691	258	415	87	14	21	162	240-6	83	319	.245	.364	.351	89	-13	37-18	.988	1	109	85	O-477L/2-90,3-62,S-3,D-2	-1.7
SANTIAGO, BENITO Benito (Rivera) B 3.9.1965 Ponce, P.R. BR/TR 6-1/182# d9.14																								
1986	SD N	17	62	10	18	2	0	3	6	2-0	0	12	.290	.308	.468	115	1	0-1	.946	-5	107	44	C-17	-0.4
1987	SD N	146	546	64	164	33	2	18	79	16-2	5	112	.300	.324	.467	111	6	21-12	.976	1	122	98	*C-146	1.4
1988	SD N	139	492	49	122	22	2	10	46	24-2	1	82	.248	.282	.362	86	-11	15-7	.985	10	**213**	93	*C-136	0.8
1989	SD N★	129	462	50	109	16	3	16	62	26-6	1	89	.236	.277	.387	88	-9	11-6	.975	5	**205**	73	*C-127	0.4
1990	SD N✶	100	344	42	93	8	5	11	53	27-2	3	55	.270	.323	.419	103	0	5-5	.980	4	138	92	C-98	1.0
1991	SD N★	152	580	60	155	22	3	17	87	23-5	4	114	.267	.296	.403	93	-8	8-10	.985	8	137	95	*C-151/O(LF)	0.8
1992	SD N★	106	386	37	97	21	0	10	42	21-1	0	52	.251	.287	.383	88	-7	2-5	.982	-7	113	110	*C-103	-1.0
1993	Fla N	139	469	49	108	19	6	13	50	37-2	5	88	.230	.291	.380	74	-18	10-7	.987	-4	103	92	*C-136/O(LF)	-1.4
1994	Fla N	101	337	35	92	14	2	11	41	25-1	1	57	.273	.322	.424	91	-5	1-2	.991	10	141	**135**	C-97	1.0
1995	†Cin N	81	266	40	76	20	0	11	44	24-1	4	48	.286	.351	.485	119	8	2-2	**.996**	7	**150**	60	C-75/1-8	1.8
1996	Phi N	136	481	71	127	21	2	30	85	49-7	1	104	.264	.332	.503	116	9	2-0	.987	2	136	81	*C-114,1-14	1.7
1997	Tor A	97	341	31	83	10	0	13	42	17-1	2	80	.243	.279	.387	72	-15	1-0	.997	0	128	103	C-95/D	-0.8
1998	Tor A	15	29	3	9	5	0	0	4	1-0	0	6	.310	.333	.483	108	0	0-0	1.000	-4	53	0	C-15	-0.3
1999	Chi N	109	350	28	87	18	3	7	36	32-6	2	71	.249	.313	.377	75	-14	1-1	.990	-10	**175**	85	*C-107/1	-1.6
2000	Cin N	89	252	22	66	11	1	8	45	19-8	1	45	.262	.310	.409	80	-9	2-2	.994	6	**221**	71	C-84	0.2
2001	SF N	133	477	39	125	25	4	6	45	23-0	2	78	.262	.295	.369	77	-18	5-4	.994	-3	105	103	*C-130/1-2	-1.3
2002	†SF N★	126	478	56	133	24	5	16	74	27-8	2	73	.278	.315	.450	108	1	4-2	.995	-2	122	75	*C-125	0.7
2003	†SF N	108	401	53	112	21	2	11	56	29-0	2	69	.279	.329	.424	98	-2	0-1	.993	-7	118	44	*C-106	-0.2
Total	18	1923	6753	739	1776	312	40	211	897	422-52	36	1235	.263	.307	.415	93	-91	90-67	.987	13	143	88	*C-1862/1-25,O-2(LF),D	2.8
SANTIAGO, RAMON Ramon D. B 8.31.1979 Las Matas De Farfan, D.R. BB/TR 5-11/150# d5.17																								
2002	Det A	65	222	33	54	5	5	4	20	13-0	8	48	.243	.306	.365	83	-6	8-5	.977	5	114	95	S-63/D	0.4
2003	Det A	141	444	41	100	18	1	2	29	33-0	10	66	.225	.292	.284	58	-27	10-4	.975	-2	106	116	S-85,2-53	-1.8
Total	2	206	666	74	154	23	6	6	49	46-0	18	114	.231	.297	.311	66	-33	18-9	.976	3	109	107	S-148/2-53,D	-1.4
SANTO, RON Ronald Edward B 2.25.1940 Seattle, WA BR/TR 6/190# d6.26 OF Total (7-LF 1-RF)																								
1960	Chi N	95	347	44	87	24	2	9	44	31-5	0	44	.251	.311	.409	97	-2	0-3	.945	-17	83	37	3-94	-2.1
1961	Chi N	154	578	84	164	32	6	23	83	73-7	0	77	.284	.362	.479	120	18	2-3	.937	5	103	**134**	*3-153	2.1
1962	Chi N	**162**	604	44	137	20	4	17	83	65-5	2	94	.227	.302	.358	74	-22	4-1	.955	16	**116**	108	*3-157/S-8	-0.6
1963	Chi N★	**162**	630	79	187	29	6	25	99	42-7	4	92	.297	.339	.481	128	22	6-4	.951	14	**116**	106	*3-162	3.8
1964	Chi N☆	161	592	94	185	33	**13**	30	114	**86**-5	2	96	.313	**.398**	.564	162	51	3-4	.963	19	**119**	117	*3-161	**7.1**
1965	Chi N★	**164**	608	88	173	30	4	33	101	88-7	5	109	.285	.378	.510	144	38	3-1	.957	22	**120**	97	*3-164	6.2
1966	Chi N★	155	561	93	175	21	8	30	94	**95**-7	6	78	.312	**.412**	.538	161	51	4-5	.956	22	114	115	*3-152/S-8	**7.3**
1967	Chi N	161	586	107	176	23	4	31	98	**96**-9	3	103	.300	.395	.512	153	44	1-5	.957	**31**	**117**	**126**	*3-161	**7.6**
1968	Chi N★	162	577	86	142	17	3	26	98	**96**-7	3	106	.246	.354	.421	124	20	3-4	**.971**	20	**115**	**112**	*3-162	4.4
1969	Chi N★	160	575	97	166	18	4	29	123	96-7	2	97	.289	.384	.485	128	24	1-3	.947	7	103	85	*3-160	3.0
1970	Chi N	154	555	83	148	30	4	26	114	92-6	1	108	.267	.369	.476	112	11	2-0	.945	18	109	**135**	*3-152/O(RF)	2.9
1971	Chi N★	154	555	77	148	22	1	21	88	79-8	0	95	.267	.354	.423	105	6	4-0	.958	1	97	120	*3-149/O-6(LF)	0.7
1972	Chi N★	133	464	68	140	25	5	17	74	69-5	4	75	.302	.391	.487	135	24	1-4	.948	14	**116**	94	*3-129/2-3,SO(LF)	3.9
1973	Chi N★	149	536	65	143	29	2	20	77	63-8	4	97	.267	.348	.440	109	8	1-2	.950	-3	99	61	*3-146	0.4
1974	Chi A	117	375	29	83	12	1	5	41	37-1	2	72	.221	.293	.299	69	-14	0-2	.970	1	101	136	D-47,2-39,3-28/1-3,S	-1.4
Total	15	2243	8143	1138	2254	365	67	342	1331	1108-94	38	1343	.277	.362	.464	123	279	35-41	.954	169	110	106	*3-2130/D-47,2-42,S-18,O-8L,1-3	45.3
SANTO DOMINGO, RAFAEL Rafael (Molina) B 11.24.1955 Orocovis, P.R. BB/TR 6/160# d9.7																								
1979	Cin N	7	6	0	1	0	0	0	0	1-0	0	3	.167	.286	.167	26	-1	0-0	—	0			/H	-0.1
SANTOS, ANGEL Angel Ramon B 8.14.1979 Rio Piedras, P.R. BB/TR 5-11/178# d9.8																								
2001	Bos A	9	16	2	2	1	0	0	1	2-0	0	7	.125	.211	.188	10	-2	0-0	.905	-1	90	0	/2-6	-0.3
2003	Cle A	32	76	9	17	3	1	3	6	3-0	0	18	.224	.253	.408	73	-4	1-1	.981	1	108	123	2-28/3-4	-0.2
Total	2	41	92	11	19	4	1	3	7	5-0	0	25	.207	.245	.370	61	-6	1-1	.968	-1	105	102	/2-34,3-4	-0.5
SANTOS, FRANCISCO Francisco B 3.9.1974 Santo Domingo, D.R. BL/TL 6-1/175# d6.18																								
2003	SF N	8	15	2	3	2	0	1	1	0-0	0	3	.200	.200	.533	85	0	0-0	1.000	-0	102	0	/O-3(RF),1	-0.1
SANTOVENIA, NELSON Nelson Gil (Mayol) B 7.27.1961 Pinar Del Rio, Cuba BR/TR 6-3/215# d9.16																								
1987	Mon N	2	1	0	0	0	0	0	0	0-0	0	0	.000	.000	.000	-97	0	0-0	1.000	0	0	0	/C	0.0
1988	Mon N	92	309	26	73	20	2	8	41	24-3	3	77	.236	.294	.392	92	-3	2-3	.983	1	93	108	C-86/1	0.3
1989	Mon N	97	304	30	76	14	1	5	31	24-2	3	37	.250	.307	.352	88	-5	2-1	.981	8	84	135	C-89/1	0.9
1990	Mon N	59	163	13	31	3	1	6	28	8-0	0	31	.190	.222	.331	54	-12	0-3	.980	-3	73	74	C-51	-1.4
1991	Mon N	41	96	7	24	5	0	2	14	2-2	0	18	.250	.255	.365	76	-3	0-0	.976	-1	93	102	C-30/1-7	-0.4
1992	Chi A	2	3	1	1	0	0	1	2	0-0	0	0	.333	.333	1.333	352	1	0-0	1.000	-1	0	261	/C-2	0.0
1993	KC A	4	8	0	1	0	0	0	0	1-0	0	2	.125	.222	.125	-4	-1	0-0	1.000	-1	177	0	/C-4	-0.2
Total	7	297	884	77	206	42	4	22	116	59-7	6	165	.233	.281	.364	82	-23	4-7	.981	4	87	110	C-263/1-9	-0.8
SANTRY, EDWARD Edward B Chicago, IL D 3.6.1899 Chicago, IL d8.7																								
1884	Det N	6	22	1	4	0	0	0	0	1		2	.182	.217	.182	29	-2		.821	-1	82	77	/S-5,2	-0.2
SARDINHA, DANE Dane K. B 4.8.1969 Honolulu, HI BR/TR 6/210# d9.6																								
2003	Cin N	1	2	0	0	0	0	0	0	0-0	0	1	.000	.000	.000	-99	-1	0-0	1.000	-0	0	0	/C	-0.1
SARGENT, JOE Joseph Alexander "Horse Belly" B 9.24.1893 Rochester, NY D 7.5.1950 Rochester, NY BR/TR 5-10/165# d4.27																								
1921	Det A	66	178	21	45	8	5	2	22	24	0	26	.253	.342	.388	86	-4	2-3	.927	-2	91	102	2-24,3-23,S-19	-0.3
SARNI, BILL William Florine B 9.19.1927 Los Angeles, CA D 4.15.1983 Creve Coeur, MO BR/TR 5-11/187# d5.9 C1																								
1951	StL N	36	86	7	15	1	0	0	2	9	0	13	.174	.253	.186	20	-10	1-0	.984	1	*119*	*68*	C-35	-0.7
1952	StL N	3	5	0	1	0	0	0	0	0	0	1	.200	.200	.200	11	-1	0-0	1.000	1	*0*	*0*	/C-3	0.1
1954	StL N	123	380	40	114	18	4	9	70	25	0	42	.300	.337	.439	101	0	3-3	**.996**	-8	*141*	*79*	*C-118	-0.3
1955	StL N	107	325	32	83	15	2	3	34	27-0	1	33	.255	.313	.342	74	-12	1-1	.987	-6	*107*	*105*	C-99	-1.3
1956	StL N	43	148	12	43	7	2	5	22	8-2	1	15	.291	.329	.466	111	2	1-0	.992	1	*97*	*102*	C-41	0.6
	NY N	78	238	16	55	9	3	5	23	20-2	1	31	.231	.290	.357	74	-9	0-1	.993	-0	*118*	*101*	C-78	-0.6
	Year	121	386	28	98	16	5	10	45	28-4	2	46	.254	.305	.399	88	-7	1-1	.992	1	*110*	*101*	*C-119	0.0
Total	5	390	1182	107	311	50	11	22	151	89-4	3	135	.263	.313	.380	84	-30	6-5	.991	-10	*119*	*92*	C-374	-2.2

SASSER, MACKEY Mack Daniel B 8.3.1962 Fort Gaines, GA BL/TR 6-1/210# d7.17 OF Total (41-LF 28-RF)

Year	Tm Lg	G	AB	R	H	2B	3B	HR	RBI	BB-IB	HP	SO	AVG	OBP	SLG	AOPS	ABR	SB-CS	FA	FR	Rng	Thr	G at Pos	BFW
1987	SF N	2	4	0	0	0	0	0	0	0-0	0	0	.000	.000	.000	-99	-1	0-0	1.000	0	0	0	/C	-0.1
	Pit N	12	23	2	5	0	0	0	2	0-0	0	2	.217	.217	.217	16	-3	0-0	1.000	-0	104	0	/C-5	-0.3
	Year	14	27	2	5	0	0	0	2	0-0	0	2	.185	.185	.185	-2	-4	0-0	1.000	-0	79	0	/C-6	-0.4
1988	†NY N	60	123	9	35	10	1	1	17	6-4	0	9	.285	.313	.407	112	2	0-0	.977	1	61	116	C-42/3O(RF)	0.5
1989	NY N	72	182	17	53	14	2	1	22	7-4	0	15	.291	.316	.407	111	2	0-1	.992	-3	89	93	C-62/3	0.2
1990	NY N	100	270	31	83	14	0	6	41	15-9	1	19	.307	.344	.426	111	4	0-0	.975	-5	67	**150**	C-87/1	0.3
1991	NY N	96	228	18	62	14	2	5	35	9-2	1	19	.272	.298	.417	101	-1	0-2	.994	-2	88	95	C-43,O-21(7-0-14),1-10	-0.3
1992	NY N	92	141	7	34	6	0	2	18	3-0	0	10	.241	.248	.326	65	-7	0-0	.989	-8	49	73	C-27,1-12/O-9(7-0-2)	-1.6
1993	Sea A	83	188	18	41	10	2	1	21	15-6	1	30	.218	.274	.309	57	-12	1-0	.946	-2	83	156	O-37(26-0-11),D-19/C-4,1	-1.5
1994	Sea A	3	4	0	0	0	0	0	0	0-0	0	0	.000	.000	.000	-98	-1	0-0	—	-1	0	0	/CO(LF)	-0.2
1995	Pit N	14	26	1	4	1	0	0	0	0-0	0	0	.154	.154	.192	-9	-4	0-0	1.000	-0	118	157	C-11	-0.4
Total	9	534	1189	103	317	69	7	16	156	55-25	3	104	.267	.296	.377	89	-21	1-3	.983	-19	74	115	C-283/O-69L,1-24,D-19,3-2	-3.4

SASSER, ROB Robert Doffell B 3.9.1975 Philadelphia, PA BR/TR 6-3/205# d7.31

Year	Tm Lg	G	AB	R	H	2B	3B	HR	RBI	BB-IB	HP	SO	AVG	OBP	SLG	AOPS	ABR	SB-CS	FA	FR	Rng	Thr	G at Pos	BFW
1998	Tex A	1	1	0	0	0	0	0	0	0-0	0	0	.000	.000	.000	-96	0	0-0	—	0			/H	0.0

SATRIANO, TOM Thomas Victor Nicholas B 8.28.1940 Pittsburgh, PA BL/TR 6-1/190# d7.23

Year	Tm Lg	G	AB	R	H	2B	3B	HR	RBI	BB-IB	HP	SO	AVG	OBP	SLG	AOPS	ABR	SB-CS	FA	FR	Rng	Thr	G at Pos	BFW
1961	LA A	35	96	15	19	5	1	1	8	12-0	1	16	.198	.294	.302	53	-6	2-0	.915	-0	106	127	3-23,2-10/S	-0.6
1962	LA A	10	19	4	8	2	0	2	6	0-0	0	1	.421	.421	.842	238	3	0-0	.833	-0	109	142	/3-5	0.3
1963	LA A	23	50	1	9	1	0	0	2	9-2	0	10	.180	.305	.200	48	-3	0-0	.952	4	159	98	3-13/C-2,1	0.0
1964	LA A	108	255	18	51	9	0	1	17	30-3	0	37	.200	.282	.247	55	-15	0-2	.917	-1	113	86	3-38,1-32,C-25/S-2,2	-1.8
1965	Cal A	47	79	8	13	2	0	1	4	10-1	0	10	.165	.258	.228	40	-6	1-1	1.000	1	94	91	3-15,C-12,2-12/1-3	-0.5
1966	Cal A	103	226	16	54	5	3	0	24	27-2	0	32	.239	.320	.288	78	-6	3-3	.991	-6	*94*	*84*	C-43,1-36,3-25/2-4	-1.2
1967	Cal A	90	201	13	45	7	0	4	21	28-3	0	25	.224	.319	.318	92	-1	1-0	.962	-2	95	89	3-38,C-23,2-15/1-5	-0.2
1968	Cal A	111	297	20	75	9	0	8	35	37-5	1	44	.253	.337	.364	117	7	0-0	.989	-4	109	**142**	C-85,2-14,3-11/1	0.8
1969	Cal A	41	108	5	28	2	0	1	16	18-1	1	15	.259	.364	.306	95	0	0-2	1.000	2	107	97	C-36/1-5,2-2	0.3
	Bos A	47	127	9	24	2	0	0	11	22-7	2	12	.189	.310	.205	46	-8	0-0	.978	0	104	81	C-44	-0.7
	Year	88	235	14	52	4	0	1	27	40-8	3	27	.221	.335	.251	68	-8	0-2	.987	2	105	88	C-80/1-5,2-2	-0.4
1970	Bos A	59	165	21	39	9	1	3	13	21-3	1	23	.236	.326	.358	83	-3	0-0	.985	1	105	68	C-51	0.0
Total	10	674	1623	130	365	53	5	21	157	214-27	6	225	.225	.316	.303	79	-38	7-8	.987	-5	*110*	*106*	C-321,3-168/1-83,2-58,S-3	-3.6

SATURRIA, LUIS Luis Arturo B 7.21.1976 San Pedro De Macoris, D.R. BR/TR 6-2/165# d9.11

Year	Tm Lg	G	AB	R	H	2B	3B	HR	RBI	BB-IB	HP	SO	AVG	OBP	SLG	AOPS	ABR	SB-CS	FA	FR	Rng	Thr	G at Pos	BFW
2000	StL N	12	5	1	0	0	0	0	0	1-0	0	3	.000	.167	.000	-53	-1	0-0	1.000	-1	59	0	/O-9(0-5-4)	-0.2
2001	StL N	13	5	0	1	1	0	0	1	0-0	0	1	.200	.200	.400	50	0	1-0	1.000	-0	75	0	/O-9(3-3-3)	0.0
Total	2	25	10	1	1	1	0	0	1	1-0	0	4	.100	.182	.200	-3	-1	1-0	1.000	-1	65	0	/O-18(3-8-7)	-0.2

SAUCIER, FRANK Francis Field B 5.28.1926 Leslie, MO BL/TR 6-1/180# d7.21 Mil 1952

Year	Tm Lg	G	AB	R	H	2B	3B	HR	RBI	BB-IB	HP	SO	AVG	OBP	SLG	AOPS	ABR	SB-CS	FA	FR	Rng	Thr	G at Pos	BFW
1951	StL A	18	14	4	1	1	0	0	1	3	1	4	.071	.278	.143	16	-2	0-0	.714	-0	126	0	/O-3(1-0-2)	-0.2

SAUER, ED Edward "Horn" B 1.3.1919 Pittsburgh, PA D 7.1.1988 Thousand Oaks, CA BR/TR 6-1/188# d9.17 b-Hank

Year	Tm Lg	G	AB	R	H	2B	3B	HR	RBI	BB-IB	HP	SO	AVG	OBP	SLG	AOPS	ABR	SB-CS	FA	FR	Rng	Thr	G at Pos	BFW
1943	Chi N	14	55	3	15	3	0	0	9	3	1	6	.273	.322	.327	89	-1	1	1.000	0	108	64	O-13(LF)	-0.2
1944	Chi N	23	50	3	11	4	0	0	5	2	0	6	.220	.250	.300	55	-3	0	.960	-0	96	119	O-12(LF)	-0.4
1945	†Chi N	49	93	8	24	4	1	2	11	8	0	23	.258	.317	.387	97	-1	2	1.000	1	106	70	O-26(21-2-3)	-0.1
1949	StL N	24	45	5	10	2	1	0	1	3	0	8	.222	.271	.311	53	-3	0	1.000	-0	76	146	O-10(4-0-7)	-0.4
	Bos N	79	214	26	57	12	0	3	31	17	1	34	.266	.323	.364	89	-3	0	.972	0	106	64	O-71(29-20-25)	-0.6
	Year	103	259	31	67	14	1	3	32	20	1	42	.259	.314	.355	82	-7	0	.974	-0	102	74	O-81(33-20-32)	-1.0
Total	4	189	457	45	117	25	2	5	57	33	2	77	.256	.309	.352	83	-11	3	.981	0	103	76	O-132(79-22-35)	-1.7

SAUER, HANK Henry John B 3.17.1917 Pittsburgh, PA D 8.24.2001 Burlingame, CA BR/TR 6-4/199# d9.9 Mil 1944-45 C1 b-Ed

Year	Tm Lg	G	AB	R	H	2B	3B	HR	RBI	BB-IB	HP	SO	AVG	OBP	SLG	AOPS	ABR	SB-CS	FA	FR	Rng	Thr	G at Pos	BFW
1941	Cin N	9	33	4	10	4	0	0	5	1	0	4	.303	.324	.424	109	0	0	.957	1	102	152	/O-8(LF)	0.0
1942	Cin N	7	20	4	5	0	0	2	4	2	0	2	.250	.318	.550	152	1	0	.976	0	149	254	/1-4	0.1
1945	Cin N	31	116	18	34	1	0	5	20	6	0	16	.293	.328	.431	112	1	2	.972	0	109	0	O-28(LF)/1-3	-0.1
1948	Cin N	145	530	78	138	22	1	35	97	60	4	85	.260	.340	.504	130	20	2	.973	5	100	137	*O-132(LF),1-12	1.5
1949	Cin N	42	152	22	36	6	0	4	16	18	0	19	.237	.318	.355	79	-4	0	.956	4	110	169	O-39(LF)/1	-0.4
	Chi N	96	357	59	104	17	1	27	83	37	3	47	.291	.363	.571	151	24	0	.981	1	95	127	O-96(LF)	1.7
	Year	138	509	81	140	23	1	31	99	55	3	66	.275	.349	.507	129	19	0	.972	4	100	**140**	*O-135(LF)/1	1.3
1950	Chi N★	145	540	85	148	32	2	32	103	60	3	67	.274	.350	.519	127	20	1	.965	-4	85	125	*O-125(LF),1-18	0.6
1951	Chi N	141	525	77	138	19	4	30	89	45	3	77	.263	.325	.486	113	7	2-1	.981	8	102	**165**	*O-132(131-0-1)	0.6
1952	Chi N★	151	567	89	153	31	3	**37**	**121**	77	4	92	.270	.361	.531	143	33	1-2	.983	10	107	147	*O-151(LF)	3.1
1953	Chi N	108	395	61	104	16	5	19	60	50	2	56	.263	.349	.473	109	5	0-0	.970	-1	106	59	*O-105(42-0-64)	0.0
1954	Chi N	142	520	98	150	18	1	41	103	70	6	68	.288	.375	.563	140	30	2-1	.963	-3	103	64	*O-141(9-0-140)	2.2
1955	Chi N	79	261	29	55	8	1	12	28	26-0	2	47	.211	.286	.387	77	-9	0-0	.984	0	100	88	O-68(67-0-1)	-1.3
1956	StL N	75	151	11	45	4	0	5	24	25-3	3	31	.298	.403	.424	124	7	0-0	1.000	-2	90	97	O-37(35-0-2)	0.3
1957	NY N	127	378	46	98	14	1	26	76	49-2	0	59	.259	.343	.508	126	13	1-0	.992	-8	76	70	O-98(LF)	0.0
1958	SF N	88	236	27	59	8	0	12	46	35-2	4	37	.250	.354	.436	111	4	0-0	.950	-4	86	72	O-67(LF)	-0.3
1959	SF N	13	15	1	1	0	0	1	1	0-0	0	7	.067	.067	.267	-17	-3	0-0	—	-0	0	0	/O(LF)	-0.3
Total	15	1399	4796	709	1278	200	19	288	876	561-7	34	714	.266	.347	.496	123	149	11-4	.974	9	98	110	*O-1228(1029-0-208)/1-38	7.7

SAUNDERS, DOUG Douglas Long B 12.13.1969 Yorba Linda, CA BR/TR 6/172# d6.13

Year	Tm Lg	G	AB	R	H	2B	3B	HR	RBI	BB-IB	HP	SO	AVG	OBP	SLG	AOPS	ABR	SB-CS	FA	FR	Rng	Thr	G at Pos	BFW
1993	NY N	28	67	8	14	2	0	0	0	3-0	0	4	.209	.243	.239	30	-7	0-0	.956	2	107	178	2-22/3-4,S	-0.4

SAUNDERS, RUSTY Russell Collier B 3.12.1906 Trenton, NJ D 11.24.1967 Trenton, NJ BR/TR 6-2/205# d9.24

Year	Tm Lg	G	AB	R	H	2B	3B	HR	RBI	BB-IB	HP	SO	AVG	OBP	SLG	AOPS	ABR	SB-CS	FA	FR	Rng	Thr	G at Pos	BFW
1927	Phi A	5	15	2	2	1	0	0	2	3	0	2	.133	.278	.200	24	-2	0-0	.818	-0	78	205	/O-4(LF)	-0.2

SAUTER, AL Albert C. B 9.2.1868 Philadelphia, PA D 7.15.1928 Ocean City, NJ d9.8

Year	Tm Lg	G	AB	R	H	2B	3B	HR	RBI	BB-IB	HP	SO	AVG	OBP	SLG	AOPS	ABR	SB-CS	FA	FR	Rng	Thr	G at Pos	BFW
1890	Phi AA	14	41	1	4	0	0	0	0	11	0		.098	.288	.098	14	-4	0	.850	-3	87	0	3-11/O-2(CF),2-2	-0.6

SAVAGE, DON Donald Anthony B 3.5.1919 Bloomfield, NJ D 12.25.1961 Montclair, NJ BR/TR 6/180# d4.18

Year	Tm Lg	G	AB	R	H	2B	3B	HR	RBI	BB-IB	HP	SO	AVG	OBP	SLG	AOPS	ABR	SB-CS	FA	FR	Rng	Thr	G at Pos	BFW
1944	NY A	71	239	31	63	7	5	4	24	20	1	41	.264	.323	.385	98	-1	1-1	.946	-8	84	100	3-60	-1.0
1945	NY A	34	58	5	13	1	0	0	3	3	0	14	.224	.262	.241	44	-4	1-0	.891	0	103	135	3-14/O-2(LF)	-0.4
Total	2	105	297	36	76	8	5	4	27	23	1	55	.256	.312	.357	88	-5	2-1	.935	-8	87	106	/3-74,O-2(LF)	-1.4

SAVAGE, JIMMIE James Harold B 8.29.1883 Southington, CT D 6.26.1940 New Castle, PA BB/TR 5-5/150# d9.3

Year	Tm Lg	G	AB	R	H	2B	3B	HR	RBI	BB-IB	HP	SO	AVG	OBP	SLG	AOPS	ABR	SB-CS	FA	FR	Rng	Thr	G at Pos	BFW
1912	Phi N	2	3	1	0	0	0	0	0	1	0	0	.000	.250	.000	-27	-1	0	.750	-0	99	0	/2	-0.1
1914	Pit F	132	479	81	136	9	9	1	26	67	0	32	.284	.372	.347	97	-7	17	.963	-4	103	108	O-93(22-5-66),3-29,S-11/2-3	-1.4
1915	Pit F	14	21	0	3	0	0	0	0	1	0	0	.143	.182	.143	-8	-3	0	1.000	-1	113	0	/O-3(RF),3	-0.5
Total	3	148	503	82	139	9	9	1	26	69	0	32	.276	.364	.336	92	-11	17	.964	-5	103	105	/O-96(22-5-69),3-30,S-11,2-4	-2.0

SAVAGE, TED Theodore Edmund (born B 2.21.1936 Venice, IL BR/TR 6-1/185# d4.9

Year	Tm Lg	G	AB	R	H	2B	3B	HR	RBI	BB-IB	HP	SO	AVG	OBP	SLG	AOPS	ABR	SB-CS	FA	FR	Rng	Thr	G at Pos	BFW
1962	Phi N	127	335	54	89	11	2	7	39	40-0	2	66	.266	.345	.373	96	-1	16-5	.974	3	113	63	*O-109(92-12-10)	-0.1
1963	Pit N	85	149	22	29	2	1	5	14	14-1	1	31	.195	.268	.322	69	-6	4-3	.943	-1	82	150	O-47(36-9-2)	-1.0
1965	StL N	30	63	7	10	3	0	1	4	6-1	0	9	.159	.232	.254	34	-5	1-1	.938	-0	102	93	O-20(RF)	-0.7
1966	StL N	16	29	4	5	2	1	0	3	4-0	0	7	.172	.273	.310	61	-1	4-0	1.000	-0	93	0	/O-7(0-2-5)	-0.1
1967	StL N	9	8	1	1	0	0	0	0	0	0	3	.125	.222	.125	2	-1	0-0	—	0			H	-0.1
	Chi N	96	225	40	49	10	1	5	33	40-6	5	54	.218	.346	.338	93	0	7-6	.979	0	97	103	O-86(0-23-66)/3	-0.5
	Year	105	233	41	50	10	1	5	33	41-6	5	57	.215	.342	.330	90	-1	7-6	.979	0	97	103	O-86(0-23-66)/3	-0.6
1968	Chi N	3	8	0	2	0	0	0	0	0-0	0	1	.250	.250	.250	47	-1	0-1	1.000	-0	89	0	/O-2(0-1-2)	-0.1
	LA N	61	126	7	26	6	1	2	7	10-0	1	20	.206	.270	.317	82	-3	1-2	.985	3	112	170	O-39(18-0-24)	-0.3
	Year	64	134	7	28	6	1	2	7	10-0	1	21	.209	.269	.313	80	-4	1-3	.986	3	111	161	O-41(18-1-26)	-0.4
1969	Cin N	68	110	20	25	7	0	2	11	20-0	0	27	.227	.344	.345	90	-1	3-0	.983	1	116	0	O-42(28-12-4)/2	0.0
1970	Mil A	114	276	43	77	10	5	12	50	57-1	2	44	.279	.402	.482	143	18	10-6	.953	-6	87	66	O-82(34-22-33)/1	1.0
1971	Mil A	14	17	2	3	0	0	0	1	5-0	0	4	.176	.364	.176	58	-1	1-0	1.000	-0	87	0	/O-6(6-0-1)	-0.1
	KC A	19	29	2	5	0	0	0	1	3-0	0	6	.172	.250	.172	22	-3	2-0	1.000	0	36	539	/O-9(5-0-5)	-0.3
	Year	33	46	4	8	0	0	0	2	8-0	0	10	.174	.296	.174	36	-4	3-0	1.000	-0	51	380	O-15(11-0-6)	-0.4
Total	9	642	1375	202	321	51	11	34	163	200-9	11	272	.233	.334	.361	94	-5	49-24	.970	-1	100	92	O-449(219-81-172)/123	-2.3

Year	Tm Lg	G	AB	R	H	2B	3B	HR	RBI	BB-IB	HP	SO	AVG	OBP	SLG	AOPS	ABR	SB-CS	FA	FR	Rng	Thr	G at Pos	BFW
SAVERINE, BOB Robert Paul "Rabbit" B 6.2.1941 Norwalk, CT BB/TR 5-9/165# d9.12																								
1959	Bal A	1	0	1	0	0	0	0	0	0-0	0	0	—	—	—	—	0	0-0	—	0			R	0.0
1962	Bal A	8	21	2	5	2	0	0	3	1-0	0	3	.238	.273	.333	66	-1	0-2	1.000	1	123	86	/2-7	0.0
1963	Bal A	115	167	21	39	1	2	1	12	25-0	0	44	.234	.332	.281	77	-5	8-3	.976	1	91	86	O-59(1-58-0),2-19,S-13	-0.1
1964	Bal A	46	34	14	5	1	0	0	0	3-0	0	6	.147	.216	.176	11	-4	3-1	1.000	3	146	49	S-15/O-2(CF)	-0.1
1966	Was A	120	406	54	102	10	4	5	24	27-1	2	62	.251	.300	.333	83	-10	4-3	.972	-8	96	86	2-70,3-26,S-11/O-9(5-0-4)	-1.3
1967	Was A	89	233	22	55	13	0	0	8	17-1	0	34	.236	.287	.292	75	-7	8-7	.957	-12	94	95	2-48,S-10/3-8,O-2(LF)	-1.5
Total	6	379	861	114	206	27	6	6	47	73-2	2	149	.239	.299	.305	76	-27	23-9	.971	-16	96	88	2-144/O-72(8-60-4),S-49,3-34	-3.0
SAWATSKI, CARL Carl Ernest "Swats" B 11.4.1927 Shickshinny, PA D 11.24.1991 Little Rock, AR BL/TR 5-10/210# d9.29 Mil 1951																								
1948	Chi N	2	2	0	0	0	0	0	0	0	0	0	.000	.000	.000	-99	-1	0	—	0			H	-0.1
1950	Chi N	38	103	4	18	1	0	1	7	11	0	19	.175	.254	.214	25	-11	0	.983	-1	*64*	*165*	C-32	-1.1
1953	Chi N	43	59	5	13	3	0	1	5	7	0	7	.220	.303	.322	62	-3	0-0	.943	-1	*88*	*114*	C-15	-0.4
1954	Chi A	43	109	6	20	3	3	1	12	15	0	20	.183	.276	.294	56	-7	0-0	.987	1	*108*	*123*	C-33	-0.5
1957	†Mil N	58	105	13	25	4	0	6	17	10-2	2	15	.238	.316	.448	110	1	0-0	.986	4	*100*	*153*	C-28	0.6
1958	Mil N	10	10	1	1	0	0	0	1	2-0	0	5	.100	.231	.100	-3	-1	0-0	1.000	1	*0*	*280*	/C-3	-0.1
	Phi N	60	183	12	42	4	1	5	12	16-4	3	42	.230	.300	.344	72	-8	0-0	.986	-4	*89*	*65*	C-53	-1.0
	Year	70	193	13	43	4	1	5	13	18-4	3	47	.223	.296	.332	68	-9	0-0	.987	-3	*86*	*72*	C-56	-1.1
1959	Phi N	74	198	15	58	10	0	9	43	32-11	1	36	.293	.392	.480	129	10	0-0	.979	-8	*72*	*116*	C-69	0.5
1960	StL N	78	179	16	41	4	0	6	27	22-2	0	24	.229	.310	.352	75	-6	0-0	.993	-0	*115*	*84*	C-67	-0.4
1961	StL N	86	174	23	52	8	0	10	33	25-7	0	17	.299	.385	.517	125	7	0-0	.996	-2	*80*	*91*	C-60/O(CF)	0.6
1962	StL N	85	222	26	56	9	1	13	42	36-5	0	38	.252	.351	.477	111	4	0-0	.997	-0	*109*	*80*	C-70	0.6
1963	StL N	56	105	12	25	0	0	6	14	15-7	0	28	.238	.333	.410	103	1	2-0	.986	-4	*73*	*92*	C-27	-0.2
Total	11	633	1449	133	351	46	5	58	213	191-38	6	251	.242	.330	.401	92	-14	2-0	.988	-15	*91*	*102*	C-457/O(CF)	-1.5
SAWYER, CARL Carl Everett "Huck" B 10.19.1890 Seattle, WA D 1.17.1957 Los Angeles, CA BR/TR 5-11/160# d9.11																								
1915	Was A	10	32	8	8	1	0	0	3	4	1	5	.250	.351	.281	88	0	2	.964	-2	96	0	/2-6,S-4	-0.2
1916	Was A	16	31	3	6	1	0	0	2	4	1	4	.194	.306	.226	60	-1	3	.963	0	91	151	/2-6,S-5,3	-0.1
Total	2	26	63	11	14	2	0	0	5	8	2	9	.222	.329	.254	74	-1	5	.964	-2	94	71	/2-12,S-9,3	-0.3
SAX, DAVE David John B 9.22.1958 Sacramento, CA BR/TR 6/185# d9.1 b-Steve																								
1982	LA N	2	2	0	0	0	0	0	0	0-0	0	0	.000	.000	.000	-99	-1	0-0	1.000	0	454	0	/O(LF)	0.0
1983	LA N	7	8	0	0	0	0	0	1	0-0	0	0	.000	.000	.000	-99	-2	0-0	.917	-1	30	0	/C-4	-0.3
1985	Bos A	22	36	2	11	3	0	0	6	3-0	0	3	.306	.350	.389	101	0	0-1	.985	-4	52	28	C-16/O-4(2-0-2)	-0.3
1986	Bos A	4	11	1	5	1	0	1	1	0-0	0	1	.455	.455	.818	237	2	0-0	1.000	-0	114	172	/C-2,1	0.2
1987	Bos A	2	3	0	0	0	0	0	0	0-0	0	1	.000	.000	.000	-97	-1	0-0	1.000	1	0	0	/C-2	0.0
Total	5	37	60	3	16	4	0	1	8	3-0	0	5	.267	.297	.383	84	-2	0-1	.980	-4	55	41	/C-24,O-5(3-0-2),1	-0.4
SAX, OLLIE Erik Oliver B 11.5.1904 Branford, CT D 3.21.1982 Newark, NJ BR/TR 5-8/164# d4.13																								
1928	StL A	16	17	4	3	0	0	0	0	5	0	3	.176	.364	.176	45	-1	0-0	.955	2	138	210	/3-9	0.1
SAX, STEVE Stephen Louis B 1.29.1960 Sacramento, CA BR/TR 5-11/185# d8.18 b-Dave																								
1981	†LA N	31	119	15	33	2	0	2	9	7-1	0	14	.277	.317	.345	91	-2	5-7	.975	4	108	135	2-29	0.3
1982	LA N★	150	638	88	180	23	7	4	47	49-1	2	53	.282	.335	.359	97	-3	49-19	.977	3	103	96	*2-149	1.3
1983	†LA N★	155	623	94	175	18	5	5	41	58-3	1	73	.281	.342	.350	93	-6	56-30	.961	-19	90	80	*2-152	-1.5
1984	LA N	145	569	70	138	24	4	1	35	47-3	1	53	.243	.300	.304	71	-22	34-19	.973	23	109	112	*2-141	1.0
1985	†LA N	136	488	62	136	8	4	1	42	54-12	3	43	.279	.352	.318	92	-4	27-11	.969	-5	94	103	*2-135/3	0.1
1986	LA N★	157	633	91	210	43	4	6	56	59-5	3	58	.332	.390	.441	139	35	40-17	.980	2	96	74	*2-154	**4.9**
1987	LA N	157	610	84	171	22	7	6	46	44-5	3	61	.280	.331	.369	88	-12	37-11	.982	4	95	96	*2-152/3O(LF)	0.5
1988	†LA N	160	632	70	175	19	4	5	57	45-6	1	51	.277	.325	.343	95	-5	42-12	.981	-19	92	81	*2-158	-1.5
1989	NY A★	158	651	88	205	26	3	5	63	52-2	1	44	.315	.364	.387	114	13	43-17	**.987**	1	103	107	*2-158	2.2
1990	NY A★	155	615	70	160	24	2	4	42	49-3	4	46	.260	.316	.325	80	-16	43-9	.987	-7	101	93	*2-154	-1.3
1991	NY A	158	652	85	198	38	2	10	56	41-2	3	38	.304	.345	.414	110	8	31-11	.990	-2	100	104	*2-149/3-5,D-4	1.4
1992	Chi A	143	567	74	134	26	4	4	47	43-4	2	42	.236	.290	.317	72	-22	30-12	.972	-26	92	78	*2-141/D	-4.4
1993	Chi A	57	119	20	28	5	0	1	8	8-0	0	6	.235	.283	.303	59	-7	7-3	1.000	-2	78	0	O-32(26-0-6),D-21/2	-1.1
1994	Oak A	7	24	2	6	0	1	0	1	0-0	0	2	.250	.250	.333	53	-2	0-0	1.000	2	111	79	/2-6	0.0
Total	14	1769	6940	913	1949	278	47	54	550	556-47	24	584	.281	.335	.358	95	-45	444-178	.978	-39	98	94	*2-1679/O-33(27-0-6),D-26,3-7	1.9
SAY, JIMMY James I. B 1862 Baltimore, MD D 6.23.1894 Baltimore, MD d7.22 b-Lou																								
1882	Lou AA	1	4	1	1	0	0	0		0			.250	.250	.250	73	0		.333	-1	0	0	/3	-0.1
	Phi AA	22	82	12	17	2	0	1		1			.207	.217	.268	59	-4		.884	4	105	200	S-22	0.1
	Year	23	86	13	18	2	0	1		1			.209	.218	.267	59	-4		.884	3	105	200	S-22/3	0.0
1884	Wil U	16	59	3	13	1	2	0		1			.220	.233	.305	60	-5		.733	-3	75	116	3-16	-0.6
	KC U	2	8	0	2	0	0	0		0			.250	.250	.250	60	-1		.200	-2	38	0	/3-2	-0.2
	Year	18	67	3	15	1	2	0		1			.224	.235	.299	60	-6		.680	-4	72	106	3-18	-0.8
1887	Cle AA	16	64	9	24	5	3	0	12	1	0		.375	.385	.547	163	5	0	.714	-4	85	109	3-16	0.1
Total	3	57	217	25	57	8	5	1	12	3	0		.263	.273	.359	91	-5	0	.690	-6	76	104	/3-35,S-22	-0.7
SAY, LOU Louis I. B 2.4.1854 Baltimore, MD D 6.5.1930 Fallston, MD BR/TR 5-7/145# d4.14 b-Jimmy																								
1873	Mar NA	3	12	1	2	0	0	0	2	0		0	.167	.167	.167	-1	-1	0-0	.667	0	107	0	/S-2,O(RF)	-0.1
1874	Bal NA	18	66	4	14	3	0	0	5	0		1	.212	.212	.258	50	-3	0-0	.786	6	140	0	S-18	0.2
1875	Was NA	11	38	4	10	0	0	0	2	0		7	.263	.263	.263	87	0	0-0	.698	-3	104	0	/S-8,2-2,O(CF)	-0.3
1880	Cin N	48	191	14	38	8	1	0	15	4		31	.199	.215	.251	58	-8		.832	-4	101	76	S-48	-0.9
1882	Phi AA	49	199	35	45	4	3	1	28	8			.226	.256	.291	79	-5		.867	4	107	56	S-49	0.0
1883	Bal AA	74	324	52	83	13	2	1		10			.256	.278	.318	89	-4		.794	3	113	70	*S-74	0.1
1884	Bal U	78	339	65	81	14	2	2		11			.239	.263	.310	66	-24		.795	-2	100	119	*S-78	-2.1
	KC U	17	70	6	14	2	0	1		2			.200	.222	.271	56	-6		.860	7	134	91	S-16/2	0.1
	Year	95	409	71	95	16	2	3		13			.232	.256	.303	65	-30		**.808**	5	**106**	114	S-94/2	-2.0
Total	3 NA	32	116	9	26	3	0	0	9	0		8	.224	.224	.250	57	-4	0-0	.000	3	127	0	/S-28,2-2,O-2(0-1-1)	-0.2
Total	4	266	1123	172	261	41	8	5	43	35		31	.232	.256	.297	73	-47		.820	8	107	84	S-265/2	-2.8
SCALA, JERRY Gerard Michael B 9.27.1924 Bayonne, NJ D 12.14.1993 Fallston, MD BL/TR 5-11/178# d4.22																								
1948	Chi A	3	6	1	0	0	0	0	0	0	0	3	.000	.000	.000	-99	-2	0-0	1.000	0	135	0	/O-2(CF)	-0.2
1949	Chi A	37	120	17	30	7	1	1	13	17	1	19	.250	.348	.350	88	-2	3-3	.988	-2	96	45	O-37(2-35-0)	-0.5
1950	Chi A	40	67	8	13	2	1	0	6	10	0	10	.194	.299	.254	44	-6	0-0	1.000	1	109	81	O-23(1-22-0)	-0.5
Total	3	80	193	26	43	9	2	1	19	27	1	32	.223	.321	.306	67	-10	3-3	.993	-1	101	55	/O-62(3-59-0)	-1.2
SCALZI, SKEETER Frank John B 6.16.1913 Lafferty, OH D 8.25.1984 Pittsburgh, PA BR/TR 5-6/160# d7.21																								
1939	NY N	11	18	3	6	0	0	0	0	3	0	2	.333	.429	.333	106	0	1	.875	1	119	96	/S-5,3	0.1
SCALZI, JOHNNY John Anthony B 3.22.1907 Stamford, CT D 9.27.1962 Port Chester, NY BR/TR 5-7/170# d6.19																								
1931	Bos N	2	1	0	0	0	0	0	0	0	0	1	.000	.000	.000	-99	0	0	—	0			H	0.0
SCANLAN, MORT Mortimer J. B 3.18.1861 Chicago, IL D 12.29.1928 Chicago, IL 6-1/186# d4.21																								
1890	NY N	3	10	0	0	0	0	0	0	2	0	5	.000	.167	.000	-50	-2	1	1.000	-0	0	135	/1-3	-0.2
SCANLAN, PATRICK Patrick J. B 3.25.1861 Nova Scotia, , CAN D 7.17.1913 Springfield, MA d7.4																								
1884	Bos U	6	24	2	7	1	0	0		0			.292	.292	.333	90	-1		.800	0	128	0	/O-6(LF)	-0.1
SCANLON, PAT James Patrick B 9.23.1952 Minneapolis, MN BL/TR 6/180# d9.27																								
1974	Mon N	2	4	1	1	0	0	0	0	0-0	0	1	.250	.250	.250	38	0	0-0	1.000	0	195	0	/3	0.0
1975	Mon N	60	109	5	20	3	1	2	15	17-3	0	25	.183	.294	.284	58	-6	0-1	.957	1	118	94	3-28/1	-0.5
1976	Mon N	11	27	2	5	1	0	1	2	2-0	0	5	.185	.241	.333	59	-2	0-0	.842	-0	112	0	/3-7,1	-0.2
1977	SD N	47	79	9	15	3	0	1	11	12-3	0	20	.190	.297	.266	58	-5	0-0	.957	-2	99	62	2-15,3-11/O(LF)	-0.6
Total	4	120	219	17	41	7	1	4	28	31-6	0	51	.187	.288	.283	58	-13	0-1	.938	-0	118	77	/3-47,2-15,1-2,O(LF)	-1.3
SCARRITT, RUSS Stephen Russell Mallory B 1.14.1903 Pensacola, FL D 12.4.1994 Pensacola, FL BL/TR 5-10.5/165# d4.18																								
1929	Bos A	151	540	69	159	26	17	1	71	34	1	38	.294	.337	.411	94	-7	13-11	.944	-2	96	111	*O-145(134-1-10)	-2.0

Year	Tm Lg	G	AB	R	H	2B	3B	HR	RBI	BB-IB	HP	SO	AVG	OBP	SLG	AOPS	ABR	SB-CS	FA	FR	Rng	Thr	G at Pos	BFW
1930	Bos A	113	447	48	129	17	8	2	48	12	3	49	.289	.312	.376	76	-18	4-7	.967	-0	107	56	*O-110(LF)	-2.6
1931	Bos A	10	39	2	6	1	0	0	1	2	0	2	.154	.195	.179	-1	-6	0-0	1.000	0	98	135	/O-9(LF)	-0.6
1932	Phi N	11	11	0	2	0	0	0	0	1	0	2	.182	.250	.182	16	-1	0	1.000	0	135	0	/O(LF)	-0.1
Total	4	285	1037	119	296	44	25	3	120	49	4	91	.285	.320	.385	82	-32	17-18	.956	-2	101	88	O-265(254-1-10)	-5.3

SCARSELLA, LES Leslie George B 11.23.1913 Santa Cruz, CA D 12.16.1958 San Francisco, CA BL/TL 5-11/185# d9.15

Year	Tm Lg	G	AB	R	H	2B	3B	HR	RBI	BB-IB	HP	SO	AVG	OBP	SLG	AOPS	ABR	SB-CS	FA	FR	Rng	Thr	G at Pos	BFW
1935	Cin N	6	10	4	2	1	0	0	0	3	0	1	.200	.385	.300	89	0	0	1.000	1	238	130	/1-2	0.1
1936	Cin N	115	485	63	152	21	9	3	65	14	2	36	.313	.335	.412	107	2	6	.989	2	108	94	*1-115	-0.7
1937	Cin N	110	329	35	81	11	4	3	34	17	1	26	.246	.285	.331	70	-15	5	.984	-3	89	106	1-65,O-14(12-0-2)	-2.4
1939	Cin N	16	14	0	2	0	0	0	2	0	0	2	.143	.143	.143	-23	-2	0	—	0			H	-0.2
1940	Bos N	18	60	7	18	1	3	0	8	3	1	5	.300	.344	.417	115	1	2	.986	-1	78	137	1-15	-0.2
Total	5	265	898	109	255	34	16	6	109	37	4	70	.284	.315	.378	92	-14	13	.988	-1	101	101	1-197/O-14(12-0-2)	-3.4

SCARSONE, STEVE Steven Wayne B 4.11.1966 Anaheim, CA BR/TR 6-2/195# d5.15 OF Total (1-LF 1-CF)

Year	Tm Lg	G	AB	R	H	2B	3B	HR	RBI	BB-IB	HP	SO	AVG	OBP	SLG	AOPS	ABR	SB-CS	FA	FR	Rng	Thr	G at Pos	BFW
1992	Phi N	7	13	1	2	0	0	0	0	1-0	0	6	.154	.214	.154	6	-2	0-0	1.000	-2	48	74	/2-3	-0.4
	Bal A	11	17	2	3	0	0	0	0	1-0	0	6	.176	.222	.176	13	-2	0-0	.889	-1	54	251	/2-5,3-2,S	-0.3
1993	SF N	44	103	16	26	9	0	2	15	4-0	0	32	.252	.278	.398	82	-3	0-1	1.000	-4	73	110	2-20/3-8,1-6	-0.7
1994	SF N	52	103	21	28	8	0	2	13	10-1	0	20	.272	.330	.408	97	0	0-2	.990	8	118	176	2-22/3-8,1-6,S	0.7
1995	SF N	80	233	33	62	10	3	11	29	18-0	6	82	.266	.333	.476	114	4	3-2	.927	-6	84	113	3-50,2-13,1-11	-0.2
1996	SF N	105	283	28	62	12	1	5	23	25-0	2	91	.219	.286	.322	63	-16	2-3	.973	-4	91	106	2-74,3-14/1S	-1.7
1997	StL N	5	10	0	1	0	0	0	0	2-0	0	5	.100	.250	.100	-4	-2	1-0	1.000	-3	33	0	/2-2,O-2(1-1-0),3	-0.4
1999	KC A	46	68	2	14	5	0	0	6	9-0	0	24	.206	.295	.279	48	-5	1-0	.977	2	123	126	S-16,1-12/2-9,3-3,D-2	-0.2
Total	7	350	830	103	198	44	4	20	86	70-1	8	266	.239	.302	.373	80	-26	7-8	.975	-10	91	120	2-148/3-86,1-36,S-19,D-2,O-2L	-3.2

SCHAAL, PAUL Paul B 3.3.1943 Pittsburgh, PA BR/TR 5-11/180# d9.3

Year	Tm Lg	G	AB	R	H	2B	3B	HR	RBI	BB-IB	HP	SO	AVG	OBP	SLG	AOPS	ABR	SB-CS	FA	FR	Rng	Thr	G at Pos	BFW
1964	LA A	17	32	3	4	0	0	0	0	2-0	0	5	.125	.176	.125	-16	-5	0-1	1.000	0	132	129	/2-9,3-9	-0.6
1965	Cal A	155	483	48	108	12	2	9	45	61-8	1	88	.224	.310	.313	80	-12	6-3	.970	-11	101	68	*3-153/2	-2.5
1966	Cal A	138	386	59	94	15	7	6	24	68-0	5	56	.244	.362	.365	113	10	6-4	.948	-2	104	99	*3-131	0.7
1967	Cal A	99	272	31	51	9	1	6	20	38-3	1	39	.188	.286	.294	76	-8	2-2	.970	-1	98	74	3-88/S-2,2	-1.0
1968	Cal A	60	219	22	46	7	1	2	16	29-0	2	25	.210	.307	.279	82	-4	5-7	.958	12	123	132	3-58	0.7
1969	KC A	61	205	22	54	6	0	1	13	25-2	2	27	.263	.346	.307	84	-3	2-1	.897	-16	81	33	3-49/2-6,S-6	-2.0
1970	KC A	124	380	50	102	12	3	5	35	43-1	1	39	.268	.343	.355	93	-3	7-4	.938	-17	87	64	3-97,S-10/2-6	-2.0
1971	KC A	**161**	548	80	150	31	6	11	63	103-5	2	51	.274	.387	.412	129	26	7-5	.940	-8	101	95	*3-161	1.8
1972	KC A	127	435	47	99	19	3	6	41	61-1	2	59	.228	.323	.326	95	-1	1-3	.947	-11	97	67	*3-123/S	-1.6
1973	KC A	121	396	61	114	14	3	8	42	63-0	5	45	.288	.389	.399	114	10	5-6	.913	-10	100	57	*3-121	-0.2
1974	KC A	12	34	3	6	2	0	1	4	5-0	1	5	.176	.286	.324	75	-1	0-0	.949	1	109	161	3-12	0.0
	Cal A	53	165	10	41	5	0	2	20	18-1	0	27	.248	.322	.315	89	-2	2-2	.903	-9	79	87	3-51	-1.2
	Year	65	199	13	47	7	0	3	24	23-1	1	32	.236	.316	.317	86	-3	2-2	.914	-8	85	102	3-63	-1.2
Total	11	1128	3555	436	869	132	26	57	323	516-21	22	466	.244	.341	.344	98	7	43-38	.943	-72	99	78	*3-1053/2-23,S-19	-7.9

SCHAEFER, GERMANY Herman A. B 2.4.1877 Chicago, IL D 5.16.1919 Saranac Lake, NY BR/TR 5-9/175# d10.5 OF Total (18-LF 13-CF 46-RF)

Year	Tm Lg	G	AB	R	H	2B	3B	HR	RBI	BB-IB	HP	SO	AVG	OBP	SLG	AOPS	ABR	SB-CS	FA	FR	Rng	Thr	G at Pos	BFW
1901	Chi N	2	5	0	3	1	0	0	0	2	0		.600	.714	.800	352	2	0	1.000	0	77	318	/23	0.2
1902	Chi N	81	291	32	57	2	3	0	14	19	2		.196	.250	.223	48	-18	12	.864	-12	93	116	3-75/1-3,O-2(RF),S	-3.0
1905	Det A	153	554	64	135	17	9	2	47	45	1		.244	.302	.318	96	-3	19	.955	9	96	87	*2-151/S-3	0.8
1906	Det A	124	446	48	106	14	3	2	42	32	1		.238	.290	.296	81	-10	31	.948	7	101	100	*2-114/S-7	-0.1
1907	†Det A	109	372	44	96	12	3	1	32	30	0		.258	.313	.315	97	-1	21	.961	-10	90	92	2-74,S-18,3-14/O(RF)	-1.1
1908	†Det A	153	584	96	151	20	10	3	52	37	1		.259	.304	.342	106	2	40	.918	-2	103	150	S-68,2-58,3-29	0.5
1909	Det A	87	280	26	70	12	0	0	22	14	0		.250	.286	.293	79	-7	12	.966	8	114	92	2-86/O(RF)	0.2
	Was A	37	128	13	31	5	1	1	4	6	1		.242	.281	.320	94	-1	2	.941	1	107	144	2-32/3	0.0
	Year	124	408	39	101	17	1	1	26	20	1		.248	.284	.301	84	-8	14	**.960**	9	**112**	106	*2-118/O(RF)3	0.2
1910	Was A	74	229	27	63	6	5	0	14	25	2		.275	.352	.345	124	7	17	.953	3	108	130	2-35,O-26(8-13-5)/3-2	1.0
1911	Was A	125	440	73	147	14	7	0	45	57	1		.334	.412	.398	129	20	22	.980	2	105	**116**	*1-108/O-7(LF)	1.8
1912	Was A	60	166	21	41	7	3	0	19	23	1		.247	.342	.325	90	-1	11	.900	-7	74	221	O-19(RF),1-15,2-15/P	-0.9
1913	Was A	54	100	17	32	1	1	0	7	15	2	12	.320	.419	.350	123	4	6	.926	-3	91	110	2-16/1-6,3-2,PO(RF)	0.1
1914	Was A	30	29	6	7	1	0	0	2	3	0	5	.241	.313	.276	74	-1	4-1	1.000	0	45	0	/2-3,O-3(RF)	0.0
1915	New F	59	154	26	33	5	3	0	8	25	1	11	.214	.328	.286	78	-6	3	.952	-0	76	172	O-17(3-0-14),1-13/3-9,2-2	-0.8
1916	NY A	1	1	0	0	0	0	0	0	0	0	0	.000	.000	.000	-98	0	0	—	0	0	0	/O	0.0
1918	Cle A	1	5	2	0	0	0	0	0	0	0	0	.000	.000	.000	-91	-1	1	1.000	-0	87	0	/2	-0.2
Total	15	1150	3784	495	972	117	48	9	308	333	13	28	.257	.319	.320	96	-14	201-1	.954	-3	99	100	2-588,1-145,3-133/S-97,O-78R,P-2	-1.5

SCHAEFER, JEFF Jeffrey Scott B 5.31.1960 Patchogue, NY BR/TR 5-10/170# d4.7

Year	Tm Lg	G	AB	R	H	2B	3B	HR	RBI	BB-IB	HP	SO	AVG	OBP	SLG	AOPS	ABR	SB-CS	FA	FR	Rng	Thr	G at Pos	BFW
1989	Chi A	15	10	2	1	0	0	0	0	0-0	0	2	.100	.100	.100	-45	-2	1-1	.900	0	130	353	/S-5,2-4,3-4,D	-0.2
1990	Sea A	55	107	11	22	3	0	0	6	3-0	2	11	.206	.239	.234	33	-10	4-1	.933	6	127	218	3-26,S-24/2-3	-0.2
1991	Sea A	84	164	19	41	7	1	1	11	5-0	0	25	.250	.272	.323	64	-9	3-1	.968	-7	81	102	S-46,3-30,2-11/D	-1.2
1992	Sea A	65	70	5	8	2	0	1	3	2-0	0	10	.114	.139	.186	-10	-11	0-1	.922	1	107	50	S-33,3-21/2-7,D-2	-0.9
1994	Oak A	6	8	0	1	0	0	0	0	0-0	0	1	.125	.125	.125	-39	-2	0-0	.800	-1	56	0	/3-3,S-2,1	-0.3
Total	5	225	359	37	73	12	1	2	20	10-0	2	49	.203	.228	.259	35	-34	8-4	.957	-1	91	95	S-110/3-84,2-25,D-4,1	-2.8

SCHAFER, HARRY Harry C. "Silk Stocking" B 8.14.1846 Philadelphia, PA D 2.28.1935 Philadelphia, PA BR/TR 5-9.5/143# d5.5

Year	Tm Lg	G	AB	R	H	2B	3B	HR	RBI	BB-IB	HP	SO	AVG	OBP	SLG	AOPS	ABR	SB-CS	FA	FR	Rng	Thr	G at Pos	BFW
1871	Bos NA	**31**	149	38	42	7	5	0	28	3		1	.282	.296	.396	94	-2	13-4	.684	3	116	190	*3-31	0.1
1872	Bos NA	**48**	226	51	65	10	4	1	35	0		8	.288	.288	.381	98	-2	3-0	.792	4	111	**145**	*3-43/O-5(LF),C-2	0.1
1873	Bos NA	**60**	296	65	79	12	2	2	42	3		4	.267	.274	.341	75	-11	14-7	.703	-15	67	**169**	*3-47,O-13(LF)	-1.9
1874	Bos NA	**71**	327	69	87	10	2	1	45	1		5	.266	.268	.318	83	-7	2-4	.785	6	105	**188**	*3-71/S	-0.4
1875	Bos NA	52	222	49	64	9	0	0	17	1		8	.288	.291	.329	111	2	3-2	.795	3	105	87	*3-51/O(CF)	0.3
1876	Bos N	**70**	286	47	72	11	0	0	35	4		11	.252	.262	.290	82	-5		.810	4	104	122	*3-70	0.1
1877	Bos N	33	141	20	39	5	2	0	13	0		7	.277	.277	.340	90	-2		.621	-11	26	0	O-23(1-0-22)/3-9,S	-1.1
1878	Bos N	2	8	0	1	0	0	0	0	0		1	.125	.125	.125	-16	-1		1.000	-0	0	0	/O-2(RF)	-0.1
Total	5 NA	262	1220	272	337	48	13	4	167	8		26	.276	.281	.347	90	-20	35-17	.000	0	100	156	3-243/O-19(18-1-0),C-2,S	-1.8
Total	3	105	435	67	112	16	2	0	48	4		19	.257	.264	.303	83	-8		.810	-8	95	120	/3-79,O-25(1-0-24),S	-1.1

SCHAFFER, JIMMIE Jimmie Ronald B 4.5.1936 Limeport, PA BR/TR 5-9/185# d5.20 C10

Year	Tm Lg	G	AB	R	H	2B	3B	HR	RBI	BB-IB	HP	SO	AVG	OBP	SLG	AOPS	ABR	SB-CS	FA	FR	Rng	Thr	G at Pos	BFW
1961	StL N	68	153	15	39	7	0	1	16	9-1	1	29	.255	.301	.320	59	-9	0-0	.996	4	*86*	*108*	C-68	-0.3
1962	StL N	70	66	7	16	2	1	0	6	6-0	0	16	.242	.301	.303	58	-4	1-0	.993	4	*120*	*98*	C-69	0.1
1963	Chi N	57	142	17	34	7	0	7	19	11-2	0	35	.239	.294	.437	102	0	0-0	.996	3	*141*	*109*	C-54	0.5
1964	Chi N	54	122	9	25	6	1	2	9	17-4	1	17	.205	.307	.320	74	-4	2-4	.970	-5	*112*	*124*	C-43	-0.9
1965	Chi A	17	31	2	6	3	1	0	1	3-0	0	4	.194	.265	.355	79	-1	0-0	1.000	2	*89*	*114*	C-14	0.1
	NY N	24	37	0	5	2	0	0	0	1-0	0	15	.135	.158	.189	-3	-5	0-0	.968	-1	*97*	*0*	C-21	-0.6
1966	Phi N	8	15	2	2	1	0	1	4	1-0	0	7	.133	.188	.400	58	-1	0-0	.952	-0	*156*	*194*	/C-6	-0.1
1967	Phi N	2	2	1	0	0	0	0	0	1-1	0	1	.000	.333	.000	3	0	0-0	1.000	0	*0*	*0*	/C	0.0
1968	Cin N	4	6	0	1	0	0	0	1	0-0	0	3	.167	.167	.167	0	-1	0-0	1.000	-0	*0*	*0*	/C-2	-0.1
Total	8	304	574	53	128	28	3	11	56	49-8	2	127	.223	.286	.340	69	-25	3-4	.989	5	*111*	*105*	C-278	-1.3

SCHAIVE, JOHNNY John Edward B 2.25.1934 Springfield, IL BR/TR 5-8/175# d9.19

Year	Tm Lg	G	AB	R	H	2B	3B	HR	RBI	BB-IB	HP	SO	AVG	OBP	SLG	AOPS	ABR	SB-CS	FA	FR	Rng	Thr	G at Pos	BFW
1958	Was A	7	24	1	6	0	0	0	1	1-0	0	4	.250	.280	.250	48	-2	0-0	1.000	-1	78	80	/2-6	-0.2
1959	Was A	16	59	3	9	2	0	0	2	0-0	1	7	.153	.167	.186	-3	-8	0-0	.977	2	120	94	2-16	-0.5
1960	Was A	6	12	1	3	1	0	0	0	0-0	0	3	.250	.250	.333	57	-1	0-0	.917	-0	96	114	/2-4	-0.1
1962	Was A	82	225	20	57	15	1	6	29	6-1	0	25	.253	.270	.409	81	-7	0-1	.967	3	110	83	3-49/2-6	-0.4
1963	Was A	3	3	0	0	0	0	0	0	0-0	0	1	.000	.000	.000	-99	-1	0-0	—	0			H	-0.1
Total	5	114	323	25	75	18	1	6	32	7-1	1	40	.232	.249	.350	61	-19	0-1	.967	4	110	83	/3-49,2-32	-1.3

SCHALK, ROY Le Roy John B 11.9.1908 Chicago, IL D 3.11.1990 Gainesville, TX BR/TR 5-10/168# d9.17 Mil 1943

Year	Tm Lg	G	AB	R	H	2B	3B	HR	RBI	BB-IB	HP	SO	AVG	OBP	SLG	AOPS	ABR	SB-CS	FA	FR	Rng	Thr	G at Pos	BFW
1932	NY A	3	12	3	3	1	0	0	0	2	0	2	.250	.357	.333	84	0	0-0	.867	-1	92	55	/2-3	-0.1
1944	Chi A	146	587	47	129	14	4	1	44	45	1	52	.220	.276	.262	55	-35	5-4	.964	-10	97	111	*2-142/S-5	-3.9
1945	Chi A	133	513	50	127	23	1	1	65	32	1	41	.248	.293	.302	75	-17	3-6	.977	10	105	100	*2-133	-0.1
Total	3	282	1112	100	259	38	5	2	109	79	2	95	.233	.285	.281	64	-52	8-10	.970	-0	101	105	2-278/S-5	-4.1

SCHALK, RAY Raymond William "Cracker" B 8.12.1892 Harvel, IL D 5.19.1970 Chicago, IL BR/TR 5-9/165# d8.11 M2 C2 HF1955

Year	Tm Lg	G	AB	R	H	2B	3B	HR	RBI	BB-IB	HP	SO	AVG	OBP	SLG	AOPS	ABR	SB-CS	FA	FR	Rng	Thr	G at Pos	BFW
1912	Chi A	23	63	7	18	2	0	0	8	3	4		.286	.357	.317	96	0	2	.917	1	107	109	C-23	0.3
1913	Chi A	129	401	38	98	15	5	1	38	27	3	36	.244	.297	.314	80	-11	14	.980	10	**129**	82	*C-125	1.0
1914	Chi A	136	392	30	106	13	2	0	36	38	8	24	.270	.347	.314	100	1	24-11	.974	14	**128**	94	*C-125	3.0
1915	Chi A	135	413	46	110	14	4	1	54	62	3	21	.266	.366	.327	104	5	15-18	**.984**	13	**173**	85	*C-134	2.8
1916	Chi A	129	410	36	95	12	9	0	41	41	6	31	.232	.311	.305	84	-8	30-13	**.988**	23	**154**	73	*C-124	3.0
1917	†Chi A	140	424	48	96	12	5	2	51	59	7	27	.226	.331	.292	88	-4	19	.981	16	**140**	95	*C-139	2.7
1918	Chi A	108	333	35	73	6	3	0	22	36	3	22	.219	.301	.255	67	-13	12	.978	1	**124**	77	*C-106	-0.3
1919	†Chi A	131	394	57	111	9	3	0	34	51	2	25	.282	.367	.320	93	-1	11	.981	4	118	95	*C-129	1.4
1920	Chi A	151	485	64	131	25	5	1	61	68	2	19	.270	.362	.348	89	-5	10-4	**.986**	6	**150**	93	*C-151	1.4
1921	Chi A	128	416	32	105	24	4	0	47	40	7	36	.252	.328	.329	69	-19	3-4	**.985**	4	87	**121**	*C-126	-0.7
1922	Chi A	142	442	57	124	22	3	4	60	67	3	36	.281	.379	.371	97	1	12-4	**.989**	19	114	121	*C-142	2.9
1923	Chi A	123	382	42	87	12	2	1	44	39	4	28	.228	.306	.277	55	-25	7-4	.983	1	78	91	*C-121	-1.5
1924	Chi A	57	153	15	30	4	2	1	11	21	2	10	.196	.301	.268	49	-12	1-5	.959	3	83	128	C-56	-0.7
1925	Chi A	125	343	44	94	18	1	0	52	57	3	27	.274	.382	.332	87	-3	11-5	.983	7	**186**	**119**	*C-125	1.1
1926	Chi A	82	226	26	60	9	1	0	32	27	2	11	.265	.349	.314	77	-7	5-1	.977	-2	133	85	C-80	-0.4
1927	Chi A	16	26	2	6	2	0	0	2	2	0	1	.231	.286	.308	55	-2	0-0	1.000	1	117	139	C-15,M	0.0
1928	Chi A	2	1	0	1	0	0	0	1	0	0	0	1.000	1.000	1.000	433	0	1-0	1.000	0	0	0	/CM	0.1
1929	NY N	5	2	0	0	0	0	0	0	0	0	1	.000	.000	.000	-99	-1	0	1.000	1	0	0	/C-5	0.0
Total	18	1762	5306	579	1345	199	49	11	594	638	59	355	.253	.340	.316	83	-104	177-69	.981	121	130	96	*C-1727	16.1

SCHALL, GENE Eugene David B 6.5.1970 Abington, PA BR/TR 6-3/190# d6.16

Year	Tm Lg	G	AB	R	H	2B	3B	HR	RBI	BB-IB	HP	SO	AVG	OBP	SLG	AOPS	ABR	SB-CS	FA	FR	Rng	Thr	G at Pos	BFW
1995	Phi N	24	65	2	15	2	0	0	5	6-1	1	16	.231	.306	.262	51	-5	0-0	.984	-1	105	87	1-14/O-4(LF)	-0.7
1996	Phi N	28	66	7	18	5	1	2	10	12-0	1	15	.273	.392	.470	125	3	0-0	.986	-2	68	118	1-19	0.0
Total	2	52	131	9	33	7	1	2	15	18-1	2	31	.252	.351	.366	89	-2	0-0	.985	-2	84	105	/1-33,O-4(LF)	-0.7

SCHALLER, BIFF Walter B 9.23.1889 Chicago, IL D 10.9.1939 Emeryville, CA BL/TR 5-11/168# d4.30

Year	Tm Lg	G	AB	R	H	2B	3B	HR	RBI	BB-IB	HP	SO	AVG	OBP	SLG	AOPS	ABR	SB-CS	FA	FR	Rng	Thr	G at Pos	BFW
1911	Det A	40	60	8	8	0	1	1	7	4	1		.133	.200	.217	15	-7	1	1.000	2	126	114	O-16(7-9-0)/1	-0.6
1913	Chi A	36	96	12	21	3	0	0	4	20	0	16	.219	.353	.250	78	-1	5	.918	-5	88	0	O-32(LF)	-0.8
Total	2	76	156	20	29	3	1	1	11	24	1	16	.186	.298	.237	54	-8	6	.949	-2	98	31	/O-48(39-9-0),1	-1.4

SCHANG, BOBBY Robert Martin B 12.7.1886 Wales Center, NY D 8.29.1966 Sacramento, CA BR/TR 5-7/165# d9.23 b-Wally

Year	Tm Lg	G	AB	R	H	2B	3B	HR	RBI	BB-IB	HP	SO	AVG	OBP	SLG	AOPS	ABR	SB-CS	FA	FR	Rng	Thr	G at Pos	BFW
1914	Pit N	11	35	0	8	1	1	0	1	0	0	10	.229	.229	.314	64	-2	0	.964	-1	107	74	C-10	-0.2
1915	Pit N	56	125	13	23	6	3	0	4	14	1	32	.184	.271	.280	68	-5	2-2	.974	-4	81	104	C-45	-0.7
	NY N	12	21	1	3	0	0	0	1	4	0	5	.143	.280	.143	31	-2	1	.875	-3	82	73	/C-6	-0.4
	Year	68	146	14	26	6	3	0	5	18	1	37	.178	.273	.260	63	-6	3-2	.960	-7	81	100	C-51	-1.1
1927	StL N	3	5	0	1	0	0	0	0	0	0	0	.200	.200	.200	7	-1	0	1.000	-0	56	0	/C-3	-0.1
Total	3	82	186	14	35	7	4	0	6	18	1	47	.188	.263	.269	62	-10	3-2	.962	-8	86	93	/C-64	-1.4

SCHANG, WALLY Walter Henry B 8.22.1889 S.Wales, NY D 3.6.1965 St.Louis, MO BB/TR 5-10/180# d5.9 C3 b-Bobby

Year	Tm Lg	G	AB	R	H	2B	3B	HR	RBI	BB-IB	HP	SO	AVG	OBP	SLG	AOPS	ABR	SB-CS	FA	FR	Rng	Thr	G at Pos	BFW
1913	†Phi A	79	207	32	55	16	3	3	30	34	9	44	.266	.392	.415	139	13	4	.967	-3	111	95	C-72	1.6
1914	†Phi A	107	307	44	88	11	8	3	45	32	9	33	.287	.371	.404	138	14	7-7	.956	-6	90	110	*C-100	1.7
1915	Phi A	116	359	64	89	9	11	1	44	66	14	47	.248	.385	.343	122	14	18-3	.890	-2	99	104	3-43,O-41(20-21-0),C-26	1.6
1916	Phi A	110	338	41	90	15	8	7	38	38	10	44	.266	.358	.420	140	16	14	.966	-3	100	121	O-61(58-3-0),C-36	1.4
1917	Phi A	118	316	41	90	14	9	3	36	29	**9**	24	.285	.362	.415	139	14	6	.956	-10	72	**120**	C-80,3-12/O-6(2-0-4)	1.1
1918	†Bos A	88	225	36	55	7	1	0	20	46	2	35	.244	.377	.284	101	4	4	.962	-7	101	73	C-57,O-16(14-2-0)/3-5,S	0.0
1919	Bos A	113	330	43	101	16	3	0	55	71	5	42	.306	.436	.373	136	23	15	.972	-1	98	108	*C-103	3.1
1920	Bos A	122	387	58	118	30	7	4	51	64	7	37	.305	.413	.450	134	23	7-7	.958	-7	76	92	C-73,O-40(0-39-1)	1.8
1921	†NY A	134	424	77	134	30	5	6	55	78	5	35	.316	.428	.453	122	19	7-4	.969	-4	101	88	*C-132	2.3
1922	†NY A	124	408	46	130	21	7	1	53	53	6	36	.319	.405	.412	111	9	12-6	.976	2	**135**	112	*C-119	1.9
1923	†NY A	84	272	39	75	8	2	2	29	27	9	17	.276	.360	.342	84	-6	5-2	.970	-5	**120**	86	C-81	-0.5
1924	NY A	114	356	46	104	19	7	5	52	48	4	43	.292	.382	.427	109	5	2-6	.972	-1	108	96	*C-108	1.0
1925	NY A	73	167	17	40	8	1	2	24	17	0	9	.240	.310	.335	65	-9	2-1	.974	2	96	135	C-58	-0.4
1926	StL A	103	285	36	94	19	5	8	50	32	4	20	.330	.405	.516	133	14	5-5	.968	1	126	**144**	C-82/O-3(LF)	1.8
1927	StL A	97	264	40	84	15	2	5	42	41	2	33	.318	.414	.447	119	9	3-2	.976	-5	98	147	C-75	0.9
1928	StL A	91	245	41	70	10	5	3	39	68	4	26	.286	.448	.404	121	13	8-2	.984	-9	84	74	C-82	1.0
1929	StL A	94	249	43	59	10	5	5	36	74	**7**	22	.237	.424	.378	104	6	1-4	**.988**	-0	**134**	89	C-85	1.0
1930	Phi A	45	92	16	16	4	1	1	9	17	1	15	.174	.309	.272	47	-7	0-0	.973	1	103	103	C-36	-0.4
1931	Det A	30	76	9	14	2	0	0	2	14	0	11	.184	.311	.211	38	-6	1-0	.965	-1	72	137	C-30	-0.5
Total	19	1842	5307	769	1506	264	90	59	710	849	107	573	.284	.393	.401	117	168	121-49	.967	-57	102	107	*C-1435,O-167(97-65-5)/3-60,S	20.4

SCHAREIN, ART Arthur Otto "Scoop" B 6.30.1905 Decatur, IL D 7.2.1969 San Antonio, TX BR/TR 5-11/155# d7.6 b-George

Year	Tm Lg	G	AB	R	H	2B	3B	HR	RBI	BB-IB	HP	SO	AVG	OBP	SLG	AOPS	ABR	SB-CS	FA	FR	Rng	Thr	G at Pos	BFW
1932	StL A	81	303	43	92	19	2	0	42	25	3	10	.304	.363	.380	87	-5	4-8	.965	15	114	160	3-77/S-3,2-2	1.0
1933	StL A	123	471	49	96	13	3	0	26	41	1	21	.204	.269	.244	35	-45	7-9	.949	16	117	181	3-95,S-24/2-7	-2.4
1934	StL A	1	2	0	1	0	0	0	2	0	0	0	.500	.500	.500	146	0	0-0	—	0			H	0.0
Total	3	205	776	92	189	32	5	0	70	66	4	31	.244	.306	.298	56	-50	11-17	.956	31	116	171	3-172/S-27,2-9	-1.4

SCHAREIN, GEORGE George Albert "Tom" B 11.21.1914 Decatur, IL D 12.23.1981 Decatur, IL BR/TR 6-1/174# d4.19 b-Art

Year	Tm Lg	G	AB	R	H	2B	3B	HR	RBI	BB-IB	HP	SO	AVG	OBP	SLG	AOPS	ABR	SB-CS	FA	FR	Rng	Thr	G at Pos	BFW
1937	Phi N	146	511	44	123	20	1	0	57	36	2	47	.241	.293	.284	53	-33	13	.947	8	102	104	*S-146	-1.4
1938	Phi N	117	390	47	93	16	4	1	29	16	0	33	.238	.268	.308	60	-23	11	.921	-5	96	80	S-77,2-39/3	-2.1
1939	Phi N	118	399	35	95	17	1	1	33	13	0	40	.238	.262	.293	50	-29	4	.958	-11	91	83	*S-117	-3.3
1940	Phi N	7	17	0	5	0	0	0	0	0	0	3	.294	.294	.294	65	-1	0	.839	-2	82	64	/S-7	-0.2
Total	4	388	1317	126	316	53	6	2	119	65	2	123	.240	.277	.294	54	-86	28	.943	-10	97	91	S-347/2-39,3	-7.0

SCHARF, NICK Edward T. B 7.1858 Baltimore, MD D 5.12.1937 Baltimore, MD TR d5.18

Year	Tm Lg	G	AB	R	H	2B	3B	HR	RBI	BB-IB	HP	SO	AVG	OBP	SLG	AOPS	ABR	SB-CS	FA	FR	Rng	Thr	G at Pos	BFW
1882	Bal AA	10	39	4	8	1	1	1		0			.205	.205	.359	94	0		.727	-2	44	0	/O-9(1-7-1),3	-0.2
1883	Bal AA	3	13	1	2	1	0	0		1			.154	.214	.231	42	-1		.643	-2	62	118	/S-3	-0.3
Total	2	13	52	5	10	2	1	1		1			.192	.208	.327	79	-1		.727	-4	44	0	/O-9(1-7-1),S-3,3	-0.5

SCHEER, AL Allan G. B 10.21.1888 Dayton, OH D 5.6.1959 Logansport, IN BL/TR 5-9/165# d8.2

Year	Tm Lg	G	AB	R	H	2B	3B	HR	RBI	BB-IB	HP	SO	AVG	OBP	SLG	AOPS	ABR	SB-CS	FA	FR	Rng	Thr	G at Pos	BFW
1913	Bro N	6	22	3	5	0	0	0	0	2	0	4	.227	.292	.227	48	-1	1	.800	-1	45	192	/O-6(RF)	-0.2
1914	Ind F	120	363	63	111	23	6	3	45	49	5	39	.306	.396	.427	112	4	9	.926	-1	103	91	*O-102(46-2-54)/2-4,S	-0.2
1915	New F	**155**	546	75	146	25	14	2	60	65	7	38	.267	.353	.375	111	0	31	.971	-4	97	77	*O-155(LF)	-1.1
Total	3	281	931	141	262	48	20	5	105	116	12	81	.281	.368	.392	110	3	41	.953	-5	98	84	O-263(201-2-60)/2-4,S	-1.5

SCHEER, HEINIE Henry B 7.31.1900 New York, NY D 3.21.1976 New Haven, CT BR/TR 5-8/146# d4.20

Year	Tm Lg	G	AB	R	H	2B	3B	HR	RBI	BB-IB	HP	SO	AVG	OBP	SLG	AOPS	ABR	SB-CS	FA	FR	Rng	Thr	G at Pos	BFW
1922	Phi A	51	135	10	23	3	0	4	12	3	0	25	.170	.188	.281	21	-17	1-0	.976	6	126	55	2-30,3-10	-0.9
1923	Phi A	69	210	26	50	8	1	2	21	17	2	41	.238	.301	.314	61	-12	3-4	.971	-5	93	92	2-61	-1.6
Total	2	120	345	36	73	11	1	6	33	20	2	66	.212	.259	.301	46	-29	4-4	.973	1	103	80	/2-91,3-10	-2.5

SCHEEREN, FRITZ Frederick "Dutch" B 9.8.1891 Kokomo, IN D 6.17.1973 Oil City, PA BR/TR 6/180# d9.14

Year	Tm Lg	G	AB	R	H	2B	3B	HR	RBI	BB-IB	HP	SO	AVG	OBP	SLG	AOPS	ABR	SB-CS	FA	FR	Rng	Thr	G at Pos	BFW
1914	Pit N	11	31	4	9	0	1	1	2	1	0	6	.290	.313	.452	132	1	1	.824	-2	95	0	O-10(0-4-7)	-0.1
1915	Pit N	4	3	0	0	0	0	0	0	0	0	0	.000	.000	.000	-99	-1	0	—	-0	0	0	/O(CF)	-0.1
Total	2	15	34	4	9	0	1	1	2	1	0	6	.265	.286	.412	111	0	1	.824	-2	94	0	/O-11(0-5-7)	-0.2

SCHEFFING, BOB Robert Boden B 8.11.1913 Overland, MO D 10.26.1985 Phoenix, AZ BR/TR 6-2/189# d4.27 Mil 1943-45 M6 C5

Year	Tm Lg	G	AB	R	H	2B	3B	HR	RBI	BB-IB	HP	SO	AVG	OBP	SLG	AOPS	ABR	SB-CS	FA	FR	Rng	Thr	G at Pos	BFW
1941	Chi N	51	132	9	32	8	0	1	20	5	0	19	.242	.270	.326	70	-6	2	.966	-3	91	93	C-34	-0.7
1942	Chi N	44	102	7	20	3	0	2	12	7	0	11	.196	.248	.284	58	-6	2	.986	2	111	94	C-32	-0.2
1946	Chi N	63	115	8	32	4	1	0	18	12	0	18	.278	.346	.330	94	-1	0	1.000	-3	117	69	C-40	-0.3
1947	Chi N	110	363	33	96	11	5	5	50	25	0	25	.264	.312	.364	82	-11	2	.984	-2	111	104	C-97	-0.8
1948	Chi N	102	293	23	88	18	2	5	45	22	1	27	.300	.351	.427	114	5	0	.989	-3	94	113	C-78	0.7
1949	Chi N	55	149	12	40	6	1	3	19	9	1	9	.268	.314	.383	88	-3	0	.977	-3	63	115	C-40	-0.4
1950	Chi N	12	16	0	3	1	0	0	1	0	0	2	.188	.188	.250	14	-2	0	.917	-0	64	0	/C-3	-0.2
	Cin N	21	47	4	13	0	0	2	6	4	0	2	.277	.333	.404	93	-1	0	1.000	-2	70	45	C-11	-0.2
	Year	33	63	4	16	1	0	2	7	4	0	4	.254	.299	.365	74	-3	0	.982	-3	69	36	C-14	-0.4
1951	Cin N	47	122	9	31	2	0	2	14	16	1	9	.254	.345	.320	79	-3	0-0	.976	-4	76	63	C-41	-0.5
	StL N	12	18	0	2	0	0	0	2	3	0	5	.111	.238	.111	-3	-3	0-0	1.000	1	119	68	C-11	-0.2

Year	Tm Lg	G	AB	R	H	2B	3B	HR	RBI	BB-IB	HP	SO	AVG	OBP	SLG	AOPS	ABR	SB-CS	FA	FR	Rng	Thr	G at Pos	BFW
	Year	59	140	9	33	2	0	2	16	19	1	14	.236	.331	.293	68	-6	0-0	.980	-3	*83*	*64*	C-52	-0.7
Total	8	517	1357	105	357	53	9	20	187	103	3	127	.263	.316	.360	86	-31	6-0	.984	-18	*96*	*95*	C-387	-2.8
SCHEFFLER, TED Theodore J. B 4.5.1864 New York, NY D 2.24.1949 Jamaica, NY BR/TR 5-10/160# d8.7																								
1888	Det N	27	94	17	19	3	1	0	4	9	2	9	.202	.286	.255	73	-2	4	.847	-4	22	120	O-27(4-23-0)	-0.8
1890	Roc AA	119	445	111	109	12	6	3	34	78	14		.245	.374	.319	113	14	77	.911	8	**140**	131	*O-119(2-0-117)/C	1.9
Total	2	146	539	128	128	15	7	3	38	87	16	9	.237	.360	.308	106	12	81	.899	4	118	129	O-146(6-23-117)/C	1.1
SCHEIBECK, FRANK Frank S. B 6.28.1865 Detroit, MI D 10.22.1956 Detroit, MI BR/TR 5-7/145# d5.9 ▲																								
1887	Cle AA	3	9	2	2	0	0	0	0	2	0		.222	.364	.222	67	0	0	.500	-2	84	0	/S3P	-0.1
1888	Det N	1	4	0	0	0	0	0	0	0	0	0	.000	.000	.000	-99	-1	0	.500	-1	0	0	/S	-0.2
1890	Tol AA	**134**	485	72	117	13	5	1	49	76	5		.241	.350	.295	88	-5	57	.883	2	95	91	*S-134	0.1
1894	Pit N	28	102	20	36	2	3	1	10	11	0	9	.353	.416	.461	112	2	7	.891	-6	71	87	S-11/O-9(8-1-0),3-3,2-2	-0.3
	Was N	52	196	49	45	2	4	0	17	45	4	24	.230	.384	.281	64	-9	11	.876	9	119	63	S-52	0.2
	Year	80	298	69	81	4	7	1	27	56	4	33	.272	.394	.342	81	-7	18	.878	3	111	67	S-63/O-9(8-1-0),3-3,2-2	-0.1
1895	Was N	49	172	18	31	5	2	0	25	17	1	23	.180	.258	.233	27	-19	5	.889	1	101	92	S-45/3-2,2-2	-1.3
1899	Was N	27	94	19	27	4	1	0	9	11	1		.287	.368	.351	99	0	5	.877	-6	91	29	S-27	-0.4
1901	Cle A	93	329	33	70	11	3	0	38	18	2		.213	.258	.264	47	-24	3	.897	-11	92	70	S-92	-2.9
1906	Det A	3	10	1	1	0	0	0	0	2	0		.100	.250	.100	11	-1	0	.889	-0	92	178	/2-3	-0.1
Total	8	390	1401	214	329	37	18	2	148	182	13	56	.235	.328	.291	69	-57	88	.884	-14	97	77	S-363/O-9(8-1-0),2-7,3-6,P	-5.0
SCHEINBLUM, RICHIE Richard Alan B 11.5.1942 New York, NY BB/TR 6-1/180# d9.1																								
1965	Cle A	4	1	1	0	0	0	0	0	0-0	0	0	.000	.000	.000	-99	0	0-0	—	0			H	0.0
1967	Cle A	18	66	8	21	4	2	0	6	5-1	0	10	.318	.361	.439	136	3	0-2	.943	-1	109	0	O-18(RF)	0.0
1968	Cle A	19	55	3	12	5	0	0	5	5-0	1	8	.218	.281	.309	84	-1	0-0	1.000	1	140	0	O-16(6-0-11)	0.0
1969	Cle A	102	199	13	37	5	1	1	13	19-0	0	30	.186	.253	.236	37	-17	0-2	.974	1	98	132	O-50(32-3-15)	-2.0
1971	Was A	27	49	5	7	3	0	0	4	8-0	0	5	.143	.263	.204	36	-4	0-0	.933	4	112	720	O-13(7-0-6)	-0.1
1972	KC A★	134	450	60	135	21	4	8	66	58-3	4	40	.300	.383	.418	139	24	0-1	.965	-5	96	71	*O-119(2-0-119)	1.5
1973	Cin N	29	54	5	12	2	0	1	8	10-1	0	4	.222	.338	.315	88	0	0-0	.960	0	90	178	O-19(1-0-18)	-0.1
	Cal A	77	229	28	75	10	2	3	21	35-6	1	27	.328	.417	.428	150	17	0-0	.969	-1	97	93	O-54(6-0-49)/D-7	1.4
1974	Cal A	10	26	1	4	0	0	0	2	1-0	0	2	.154	.185	.154	-2	-4	0-0	.929	0	132	0	/O-8(4-0-5),D	-0.4
	KC A	36	83	7	15	2	0	0	2	8-0	0	8	.181	.253	.205	31	-7	0-1	—	-0	0	0	D-17/O-2(LF)	-0.9
	Year	46	109	8	19	2	0	0	4	9-0	0	10	.174	.237	.193	24	-11	0-1	.929	0	127	0	D-18,O-10(6-0-5)	-1.3
	StL N	6	6	0	2	0	0	0	0	0-0	0	1	.333	.333	.333	88	0	0-0	—	0			H	0.0
Total	8	462	1218	131	320	52	9	13	127	149-11	6	135	.263	.343	.352	104	11	0-6	.965	0	101	104	O-299(60-3-241)/D-25	-0.6
SCHELL, DANNY Clyde Daniel B 12.26.1927 Fostoria, MI D 5.11.1972 Mayville, MI BR/TR 6-1/195# d4.13																								
1954	Phi N	92	272	25	77	14	3	7	33	17	2	31	.283	.327	.434	97	-2	0-3	.974	0	103	89	O-69(60-3-6)	-0.6
1955	Phi N	2	2	0	0	0	0	0	0	0-0	0	1	.000	.000	.000	-99	-1	0-0	—	0			H	-0.1
Total	2	94	274	25	77	14	3	7	33	17-0	2	32	.281	.324	.431	96	-3	0-3	.974	0	103	89	/O-69(60-3-6)	-0.7
SCHELLHASE, AL Albert Herman "Schelley" B 9.13.1864 Evansville, IN D 1.3.1919 Evansville, IN BR/TR 5-8/148# d5.7																								
1890	Bos N	9	29	1	4	0	0	0	1	1	0	10	.138	.167	.138	-10	-4	0	.778	-1	253	0	/O-5(RF),C-2,S3	-0.4
1891	Lou AA	6	16	3	2	0	0	0	0	1	0	1	.125	.176	.125	-14	-2	2	.929	-1	*83*	*127*	/C-6	-0.3
Total	2	15	45	4	6	0	0	0	1	2	0	11	.133	.170	.133	-11	-6	2	.909	-2	*95*	*121*	/C-8,O-5(RF),3S	-0.7
SCHEMER, MIKE Michael "Lefty" B 11.20.1917 Baltimore, MD D 4.22.1983 Miami, FL BL/TL 6/180# d8.8																								
1945	NY N	31	108	10	36	3	1	1	10	6	0	1	.333	.368	.407	114	2	2	.993	4	145	104	1-27	0.4
1946	NY N	1	1	0	0	0	0	0	0	0	0	0	.000	.000	.000	-99	0	0	—	0			H	0.0
Total	2	32	109	10	36	3	1	1	10	6	0	1	.330	.365	.404	112	2	2	.993	4	145	104	/1-27	0.4
SCHENCK, BILL William G. B 7.1854 Brooklyn, NY D 1.29.1934 Brooklyn, NY 5-7/171# d5.29 ▲																								
1882	Lou AA	60	231	37	60	11	3	0		8			.260	.285	.333	114	4		.814	-5	91	73	*3-58/S-2,P-2	0.0
1884	Ric AA	42	151	14	31	4	0	3		1	1		.205	.216	.291	65	-6		.836	-2	104	79	S-40/2-2	-0.6
1885	Bro AA	1	4	0	0	0	0	0	0	0	0		.000	.000	.000	-99	-1		1.000	0	59	0	/3	-0.1
Total	3	103	386	51	91	15	3	3	0	9	1		.236	.255	.313	92	-3		.817	-7	90	72	/3-59,S-42,2-2,P-2	-0.7
SCHENZ, HANK Henry Leonard B 4.11.1919 New Richmond, OH D 5.12.1988 Cincinnati, OH BR/TR 5-9.5/175# d9.18																								
1946	Chi N	6	11	0	2	0	0	0	1	0	0	0	.182	.182	.182	3	-1	1	1.000	0	98	317	/3-5	-0.1
1947	Chi N	7	14	2	1	0	0	0	0	2	1	1	.071	.235	.071	-16	-2	0	.917	0	130	0	/3-5	-0.2
1948	Chi N	96	337	43	88	17	1	1	14	18	4	15	.261	.306	.326	74	-13	3	.974	-1	96	100	2-78/3-5	-1.0
1949	Chi N	7	14	2	6	0	0	0	1	1	0	0	.429	.467	.429	146	1	2	1.000	1	132	405	/3-5	0.2
1950	Pit N	58	101	17	23	4	2	1	5	6	0	7	.228	.271	.337	57	-7	0	.987	3	107	150	2-21,3-12/S-4	-0.3
1951	Pit N	25	61	5	13	1	0	0	3	0	1	2	.213	.226	.230	22	-7	0-2	.961	-1	87	146	2-19/3-2	-0.8
	†NY N	8	0	1	0	0	0	0	0	0	0	0	—	—	—	—	0	0-0	—	0			R	0.0
	Year	33	61	6	13	1	0	0	3	0	1	2	.213	.226	.230	22	-7	0-2	.961	-1	87	146	2-19/3-2	-0.8
Total	6	207	538	70	133	22	3	2	24	27	6	25	.247	.291	.310	63	-29	6-2	.974	2	96	113	2-118/3-34,S-4	-2.2
SCHEPNER, JOE Joseph Maurice "Gentleman Joe" B 8.10.1895 Aliquippa, PA D 7.25.1959 Mobile, AL BR/TR 5-10/160# d9.11																								
1919	StL A	14	48	2	10	4	0	0	6	1	0	5	.208	.224	.292	43	-4	0	.947	-0	84	121	3-13	-0.4
SCHERBARTH, BOB Robert Elmer B 1.18.1926 Milwaukee, WI BR/TR 6/180# d4.23																								
1950	Bos A	1	0	0	0	0	0	0	0	0	0	0	—	—	—	—	0	0-0	—	0	*0*	*0*	/C	0.0
SCHERER, HARRY Harry d7.24																								
1889	Lou AA	1	3	0	1	0	0	0	0	0	0	0	.333	.333	.333	92	0	0	.500	-1	0	0	/O(CF)	-0.1
SCHIAPPACASSE, LOU Louis Joseph B 3.29.1881 Ann Arbor, MI D 9.20.1910 Ann Arbor, MI BR/TR d9.7																								
1902	Det A	2	5	0	0	0	0	0	1	1	0		.000	.167	.000	-50	-1	0	.000	-1	0	0	/O-2(RF)	-0.2
SCHICK, MORRIE Maurice Francis B 4.17.1892 Chicago, IL D 10.25.1979 Hazel Crest, IL BR/TR 5-11/170# d4.15 Mil 1918																								
1917	Chi N	14	34	3	5	0	0	0	3	3	0	10	.147	.216	.147	11	-4	0	.960	2	103	257	O-12(2-10-0)	-0.3
SCHILLING, CHUCK Charles Thomas B 10.25.1937 Brooklyn, NY BR/TR 5-11/170# d4.11																								
1961	Bos A	158	646	87	167	25	2	5	62	78-0	2	77	.259	.340	.327	77	-19	7-6	**.991**	12	102	104	*2-158	0.6
1962	Bos A	119	413	48	95	17	1	7	35	29-5	4	48	.230	.286	.327	63	-22	1-0	.985	2	98	105	*2-118	-1.0
1963	Bos A	146	576	63	135	25	0	8	33	41-0	5	72	.234	.291	.319	69	-24	3-2	.985	-13	93	84	*2-143	-2.5
1964	Bos A	47	163	18	32	6	0	0	7	15-0	0	22	.196	.263	.233	38	-13	0-1	.974	-1	91	73	2-42	-1.2
1965	Bos A	71	171	14	41	3	2	3	9	13-0	0	17	.240	.292	.333	73	-6	0-1	.976	3	106	81	2-41	0.0
Total	5	541	1969	230	470	76	5	23	146	176-5	11	236	.239	.304	.317	68	-84	11-10	.985	3	98	94	2-502	-4.1
SCHINDLER, BILL William Gibbons B 7.10.1896 Perryville, MO D 2.6.1979 Perryville, MO BR/TR 5-11/160# d9.3																								
1920	StL N	1	2	0	0	0	0	0	0	0	0	1	.000	.000	.000	-99	-1	0-0	1.000	-0	*0*	*0*	/C	-0.1
SCHIRICK, DUTCH Harry Ernest B 6.15.1890 Ruby, NY D 11.12.1968 Kingston, NY BR/TR 5-8/160# d9.17																								
1914	StL A	1	0	0	0	0	0	0	0	1	0	0	—	1.000	—	212	0	2	—	0			H	0.1
SCHLAFLY, LARRY Harry Linton B 9.20.1878 Port Washington, OH D 6.27.1919 Canton, OH BR/TR 5-11/182# d9.18 M2																								
1902	Chi N	10	31	5	10	0	3	0	5	6	0		.323	.432	.516	198	4	2	1.000	-2	0	0	/O-5(RF),2-4,3-2	0.2
1906	Was A	123	426	60	105	13	8	2	30	50	**14**		.246	.345	.329	117	11	29	.961	16	103	93	*2-123	3.1
1907	Was A	24	74	10	10	0	0	1	4	22	3		.135	.354	.176	75	0	7	.928	-8	68	60	2-24	-0.8
1914	Buf F	51	127	16	33	7	1	2	19	12	3	22	.260	.338	.378	93	-3	3	.951	1	106	89	2-23/1-7,C30(LF)M	-0.2
Total	4	208	658	91	158	20	12	5	58	90	20	22	.240	.349	.330	111	12	41	.954	8	98	86	2-174/1-7,O-6(1-0-5),3-3,C	2.3
SCHLEI, ADMIRAL George Henry B 1.12.1878 Cincinnati, OH D 1.24.1958 Huntington, WV BR/TR 5-8.5/179# d4.24																								
1904	Cin N	97	291	25	69	8	3	0	32	17	8		.237	.297	.285	74	-9	7	.977	9	*107*	*101*	C-88	0.9
1905	Cin N	99	314	32	71	8	3	1	36	22	4		.226	.285	.280	62	-15	9	.962	11	*101*	*113*	C-89/1-6	0.5
1906	Cin N	116	388	44	95	13	8	4	54	29	4		.245	.304	.351	100	-1	7	.961	7	*102*	*108*	C-91,1-21	1.6
1907	Cin N	84	246	28	67	3	2	0	27	28	0		.272	.347	.301	99	1	5	.980	6	*103*	*117*	C-67/1-3,O-2(1-0-1)	1.4

Year	Tm Lg	G	AB	R	H	2B	3B	HR	RBI	BB-IB	HP	SO	AVG	OBP	SLG	AOPS	ABR	SB-CS	FA	FR	Rng	Thr	G at Pos	BFW
1908	Cin N	92	300	31	66	6	4	1	22	22	2		.220	.278	.277	79	-7	2	.962	-3	106	94	C-88	-0.2
1909	NY N	92	279	25	68	12	0	0	30	40	2		.244	.343	.287	94	0	4	.963	3	113	109	C-89	1.3
1910	NY N	55	99	10	19	2	1	0	8	14	2	10	.192	.304	.232	57	-5	4	.986	0	96	106	C-49	-0.2
1911	NY N	1	1	0	0	0	0	0	0	0	0	1	.000	.000	.000	-97	0	0	—	0			H	0.0
Total	8	636	1918	195	455	52	21	6	209	172	22	11	.237	.307	.296	83	-36	38	.968	33	105	107	C-561/1-30,O-2(1-0-1)	5.3
SCHLESINGER, RUDY William Cordes B 11.5.1941 Cincinnati, OH BR/TR 6-2/175# d5.4																								
1965	Bos A	1	1	0	0	0	0	0	0	0-0	0	0	.000	.000	.000	-94	0	0-0	—	0			H	0.0
SCHLIEBNER, DUTCH Frederick Paul B 5.19.1891 Charlottenburg, Germany D 4.15.1975 Toledo, OH BR/TR 5-10/180# d4.17																								
1923	Bro N	19	76	11	19	4	0	0	4	5	0	7	.250	.296	.303	60	-4	1-0	.981	2	165	118	1-19	-0.3
	StL A	127	444	50	122	19	6	4	52	39	4	60	.275	.339	.372	82	-12	3-2	.989	-0	98	110	*1-127	-2.0
Total	1	146	520	61	141	23	6	4	56	44	4	67	.271	.333	.362	79	-16	4-2	.988	2	107	111	1-146	-2.3
SCHLUETER, JAY Jay D B 7.31.1949 Phoenix, AZ BR/TR 6/182# d6.18																								
1971	Hou N	7	3	1	1	0	0	0	0	0-0	0	1	.333	.333	.333	92	0	0-0	1.000	0	278	0	/O-2(LF)	0.0
SCHLUETER, NORM Norman John "Duke" B 9.25.1916 Belleville, IL BR/TR 5-10/175# d5.28																								
1938	Chi A	35	118	11	27	5	1	0	7	4	0	15	.229	.254	.288	35	-12	1-0	.952	-2	112	62	C-34	-1.1
1939	Chi A	34	56	5	13	2	1	0	8	1	0	11	.232	.246	.304	39	-5	2-0	.988	0	103	23	C-32	-0.4
1944	Cle A	49	122	2	15	4	0	0	11	12	0	22	.123	.201	.156	3	-16	0-2	.985	-6	84	50	C-43	-2.1
Total	3	118	296	18	55	11	2	0	26	17	0	48	.186	.230	.236	24	-33	3-2	.974	-7	99	49	C-109	-3.6
SCHMANDT, RAY Raymond Henry B 1.25.1896 St.Louis, MO D 2.2.1969 St.Louis, MO BR/TR 6-1/175# d6.24 Mil 1918																								
1915	StL A	3	4	0	0	0	0	0	0	0	0	1	.000	.000	.000	-99	-1	0	1.000	-0	0	0	/1	-0.1
1918	Bro N	34	114	11	35	5	4	0	18	7	0	7	.307	.347	.421	134	4	1	.934	-3	92	61	2-34	0.2
1919	Bro N	47	127	8	21	4	0	0	10	4	0	13	.165	.191	.197	16	-13	0	.911	-1	102	93	2-18,1-12/3-6	-1.6
1920	†Bro N	28	63	7	15	2	1	0	7	3	0	4	.238	.273	.302	63	-3	1-1	.995	3	175	159	1-20	-0.1
1921	Bro N	95	350	42	107	8	5	1	43	11	1	22	.306	.329	.366	81	-10	3-4	.989	0	103	112	1-92	-1.7
1922	Bro N	110	396	54	106	17	3	2	44	21	1	28	.268	.306	.341	67	-20	6-6	.989	4	119	106	*1-110	-2.2
Total	6	317	1054	122	284	36	13	3	122	46	2	75	.269	.301	.337	72	-43	11-11	.990	4	116	113	1-235/2-52,3-6	-5.5
SCHMEES, GEORGE George Edward "Rocky" B 9.6.1924 Cincinnati, OH D 10.30.1998 San Jose, CA BL/TL 6/190# d4.15																								
1952	StL A	34	61	9	8	1	1	0	3	2	0	18	.131	.159	.180	-6	-9	0-0	.932	1	127	90	O-19(9-2-8)/1-2	-0.9
	Bos A	42	64	8	13	3	0	0	3	10	0	11	.203	.311	.250	53	-4	0-1	1.000	0	97	98	O-29(0-18-11)/P-2,1-2	-0.5
	Year	76	125	17	21	4	1	0	6	12	0	29	.168	.241	.216	26	-13	0-1	.960	1	113	94	O-48(9-20-19)/1-4,P-2	-1.4
SCHMIDT, BOSS Charles B 9.12.1880 Coal Hill, AR D 11.14.1932 Clarksville, AR BB/TR 5-11/200# d4.30 b-Walter																								
1906	Det A	68	216	13	47	4	3	0	10	6	1		.218	.242	.264	57	-11	1	.958	8	111	116	C-67	0.3
1907	†Det A	104	349	32	85	6	6	0	23	5	7		.244	.269	.295	77	-11	8	.944	5	107	103	*C-103	0.4
1908	†Det A	122	419	45	111	14	3	1	38	16	3		.265	.297	.320	96	-3	5	.951	2	97	119	*C-121	1.3
1909	†Det A	84	253	21	53	8	2	1	28	7	3		.209	.240	.269	58	-13	7	.955	-6	99	111	C-81/O(RF)	-1.2
1910	Det A	71	197	22	51	7	7	1	23	2	3		.259	.277	.381	99	-2	2	.973	-3	99	94	C-66	0.0
1911	Det A	28	46	4	13	2	1	0	2	0	1		.283	.298	.370	82	-1	0	1.000	-1	90	95	/C-9,O(RF)	-0.2
Total	6	477	1480	137	360	41	22	3	124	36	18		.243	.270	.307	79	-41	23	.955	4	102	110	C-447/O-2(RF)	0.6
SCHMIDT, BUTCH Charles John "Butcher Boy" B 7.19.1886 Baltimore, MD D 9.4.1952 Baltimore, MD BL/TL 6-1.5/200# d5.11																								
1909	NY A	1	2	0	0	0	0	0	0	0	0		.000	.000	.000	-99	0	0	.500	-0	65	0	/P	0.0
1913	Bos N	22	78	6	24	2	2	1	14	2	1	5	.308	.333	.423	113	1	1	.983	1	123	54	1-22	0.1
1914	†Bos N	147	537	67	153	17	9	1	71	43	11	55	.285	.350	.356	111	7	14	.990	2	106	144	*1-147	0.6
1915	Bos N	127	458	46	115	26	7	2	60	36	9	59	.251	.318	.352	107	4	3-10	.987	-4	87	119	*1-127	-0.6
Total	4	297	1075	119	292	45	18	4	145	81	21	119	.272	.335	.358	109	12	18-10	.988	-1	99	128	1-296/P	0.1
SCHMIDT, DAVE David Frederick B 12.22.1956 Mesa, AZ BR/TR 6-1/190# d4.28																								
1981	Bos A	15	42	6	10	1	0	2	3	7-0	0	17	.238	.347	.405	109	1	0-0	1.000	-3	109	66	C-15	-0.2
SCHMIDT, MIKE Michael Jack B 9.27.1949 Dayton, OH BR/TR 6-2/203# d9.12 HF1995																								
1972	Phi N	13	34	2	7	0	0	1	3	5-0	1	15	.206	.325	.294	75	-1	0-0	.964	2	114	208	3-11/2	0.1
1973	Phi N	132	367	43	72	11	0	18	52	62-3	9	136	.196	.324	.373	91	-3	8-2	.954	18	112	136	*3-125/2-4,1-2,S-2	1.6
1974	Phi N★	162	568	108	160	28	7	36	116	106-14	4	138	.282	.395	.546	156	45	23-12	.954	28	117	118	*3-162	7.4
1975	Phi N	158	562	93	140	34	3	38	95	101-10	4	180	.249	.367	.523	139	31	29-12	.954	19	110	119	*3-151,S-10	5.3
1976	†Phi N★	160	584	112	153	31	4	38	107	100-8	11	149	.262	.376	.524	150	41	14-9	.961	18	107	109	*3-160	6.0
1977	†Phi N★	154	544	114	149	27	11	38	101	104-4	9	122	.274	.393	.574	151	41	15-8	.964	27	119	144	*3-149/S-2,2	6.5
1978	†Phi N	145	513	93	129	27	2	21	78	91-12	4	103	.251	.364	.435	122	19	19-6	.963	9	106	162	*3-139/S	2.9
1979	Phi N★	160	541	109	137	25	4	45	114	120-12	3	115	.253	.386	.564	153	42	9-5	.954	17	113	134	*3-157/S-2	5.8
1980	†Phi N✳	150	548	104	157	25	8	48	121	89-10	2	119	.286	.380	.624	169	51	12-5	.946	19	115	135	*3-149	6.9
1981	†Phi N★	102	354	78	112	19	2	31	91	73-18	4	71	.316	.435	.644	195	47	12-4	.956	23	123	127	*3-101	7.2
1982	Phi N★	148	514	108	144	26	3	35	87	107-17	3	131	.280	.403	.547	161	46	14-7	.950	19	109	122	*3-148	6.5
1983	†Phi N★	154	534	104	136	16	4	40	109	128-17	3	148	.255	.399	.524	156	46	7-8	.959	22	110	122	*3-153/S-2	6.5
1984	Phi N★	151	528	93	146	23	3	36	106	92-14	4	116	.277	.383	.536	155	40	5-7	.941	9	112	85	*3-145/1-2,S	4.7
1985	Phi N	158	549	89	152	31	5	33	93	87-8	3	117	.277	.375	.532	148	37	1-3	.993	7	122	100	*1-106,3-54/S	3.7
1986	Phi N★	160	552	97	160	29	1	37	119	89-25	7	84	.290	.390	.547	152	41	1-2	.980	-8	95	134	*3-124,1-35	3.0
1987	Phi N★	147	522	88	153	28	0	35	113	83-15	2	80	.293	.388	.548	141	33	2-1	.971	8	110	122	*3-138/1-9,S-3	3.8
1988	Phi N	108	390	52	97	21	2	12	62	49-10	6	42	.249	.337	.405	111	7	3-0	.939	5	106	89	*3-104/1-3	1.3
1989	Phi N✳	42	148	19	30	7	0	6	28	21-4	0	17	.203	.297	.372	91	-2	0-1	.918	-4	91	118	3-42	-0.6
Total	18	2404	8352	1506	2234	408	59	548	1595	1507-201	79	1883	.267	.380	.527	147	561	174-92	.955	237	111	123	*3-2212,1-157/S-24,2-6	78.6
SCHMIDT, BOB Robert Benjamin B 4.22.1933 St.Louis, MO BR/TR 6-2/205# d4.16																								
1958	SF N☆	127	393	46	96	20	2	14	54	33-5	3	59	.244	.306	.412	90	-6	0-1	.982	-2	113	128	*C-123	-0.3
1959	SF N	71	181	17	44	7	1	5	20	13-4	1	24	.243	.296	.376	80	-6	0-2	1.000	2	100	116	C-70	-0.2
1960	SF N	110	344	31	92	12	1	8	37	26-4	0	51	.267	.317	.378	96	-3	0-3	.981	-5	77	46	*C-108	-0.4
1961	SF N	2	6	0	1	0	0	0	1	0-0	0	1	.167	.143	.167	-12	-1	0-0	1.000	1	80	0	/C-2	0.0
	Cin N	27	70	4	9	0	0	1	4	8-1	0	14	.129	.218	.171	5	-10	0-0	.993	1	89	58	C-27	-0.8
	Year	29	76	4	10	0	0	1	5	8-1	0	15	.132	.212	.171	4	-11	0-0	.994	1	88	53	C-29	-0.8
1962	Was A	88	256	28	62	14	0	10	31	14-2	1	37	.242	.281	.414	86	-6	0-0	.997	1	113	135	C-88	-0.2
1963	Was A	9	15	3	3	1	0	0	0	3-0	0	5	.200	.333	.267	71	0	0-0	1.000	-1	119	0	/C-6	-0.1
1965	NY A	20	40	4	10	1	0	1	3	3-1	0	8	.250	.302	.350	85	-1	0-0	.990	1	117	68	C-20	0.1
Total	7	454	1305	133	317	55	4	39	150	100-17	5	199	.243	.297	.381	84	-33	0-6	.988	-3	100	98	C-444	-1.9
SCHMIDT, WALTER Walter Joseph B 3.20.1887 Coal Hill, AR D 7.4.1973 Modesto, CA BR/TR 5-9/159# d4.13 b-Boss																								
1916	Pit N	64	184	16	35	1	2	2	15	10	1	13	.190	.236	.250	49	-12	3	.976	-0	84	115	C-57	-0.8
1917	Pit N	72	183	9	45	7	0	0	17	11	2	11	.246	.296	.284	76	-5	4	.978	1	77	132	C-61	0.1
1918	Pit N	105	323	31	77	6	3	0	27	17	2	19	.238	.281	.276	68	-13	7	.981	24	160	116	*C-104	2.2
1919	Pit N	85	267	23	67	9	2	0	29	23	0	9	.251	.310	.300	81	-6	5	.982	5	129	102	C-85	0.8
1920	Pit N	94	310	22	86	8	4	0	20	24	4	15	.277	.337	.329	89	-4	9-3	.971	-4	94	94	C-92	0.2
1921	Pit N	114	393	30	111	9	3	0	38	12	2	13	.282	.307	.321	65	-20	10-6	.986	8	138	88	*C-111	-0.4
1922	Pit N	40	152	21	50	11	1	0	22	1	0	5	.329	.333	.414	91	-2	2-1	.995	-3	92	50	C-40	-0.3
1923	Pit N	97	335	39	83	7	2	0	37	22	3	12	.248	.300	.281	53	-23	10-5	.981	-2	117	86	C-96	-1.7
1924	Pit N	58	177	16	43	3	2	1	20	13	0	5	.243	.295	.299	59	-11	6-1	.986	4	145	92	C-57	-0.2
1925	StL N	37	87	9	22	2	1	0	9	4	1	3	.253	.293	.299	51	-7	1-0	.967	5	122	144	C-31	0.0
Total	10	766	2411	216	619	63	20	3	234	137	15	105	.257	.301	.303	68	-103	57-16	.980	38	120	100	C-734	-0.1
SCHMULBACH, HANK Henry Alrives B 1.17.1925 E.St.Louis, IL D 5.3.2001 Belleville, IL BL/TR 5-11/165# d9.27 Mil 1944-46																								
1943	StL A	1	0	1	0	0	0	0	0	0	0	0	—	—	—	—	0	0-0	—	0			R	0.0
SCHNECK, DAVE David Lee B 6.18.1949 Allentown, PA BL/TL 5-10/200# d7.14																								
1972	NY N	37	123	7	23	3	2	3	10	10-2	1	26	.187	.254	.317	63	-7	0-1	.985	-2	97	49	O-33(1-17-16)	-1.1
1973	NY N	13	36	2	7	0	1	0	0	1-1	0	4	.194	.216	.250	29	-4	0-0	1.000	1	137	0	O-12(CF)	-0.3

Year	Tm Lg	G	AB	R	H	2B	3B	HR	RBI	BB-IB	HP	SO	AVG	OBP	SLG	AOPS	ABR	SB-CS	FA	FR	Rng	Thr	G at Pos	BFW
1974	NY N	93	254	23	52	11	1	5	25	16-2	1	43	.205	.254	.315	60	-15	4-1	.974	5	109	161	O-84(23-59-9)	-1.2
Total	3	143	413	32	82	14	4	8	35	27-5	2	73	.199	.251	.310	58	-26	4-2	.979	5	108	115	O-129(24-88-25)	-2.6

SCHNEIDER, BRIAN Brian Duncan B 11.26.1976 Jacksonville, FL BL/TR 6-1/200# d5.26

2000	Mon N	45	115	6	27	6	0	0	11	7-2	0	24	.235	.276	.287	42	-10	0-1	.974	-2	71	111	C-43	-1.0
2001	Mon N	27	41	4	13	3	0	1	6	6-1	0	3	.317	.396	.463	121	2	0-0	1.000	3	136	148	C-14	0.5
2002	Mon N	73	207	21	57	19	2	5	29	21-8	0	41	.275	.339	.459	103	0	1-2	.993	3	129	130	C-65/O-2(1-0-1)	0.7
2003	Mon N	108	335	34	77	26	1	9	46	37-8	2	75	.230	.309	.394	75	-12	0-2	.996	24	**195**	127	C-98/D-2	1.8
Total	4	253	698	65	174	54	3	15	92	71-19	2	143	.249	.318	.400	81	-20	1-5	.992	28	152	126	C-220/D-2,O-2(1-0-1)	2.0

SCHOENDIENST, RED Albert Fred B 2.2.1923 Germantown, IL BB/TR 6/170# d4.17 M14 C17 HF1989

1945	StL N	137	565	89	157	22	6	1	47	21	1	17	.278	.305	.343	78	-19	**26**	.983	1	105	110	*O-118(LF),S-10/2	-2.5
1946	†StL N★	142	606	94	170	28	5	0	34	37	0	27	.281	.322	.343	85	-13	12	**.984**	2	98	**121**	*2-128,3-12/S-4	-0.3
1947	StL N	151	659	91	167	25	9	3	48	48	0	27	.253	.304	.332	66	-33	6	.976	-2	99	118	*2-142/3-5,O(LF)	-2.7
1948	StL N★	119	408	64	111	21	4	4	36	28	0	16	.272	.319	.373	82	-11	1	.980	7	106	108	2-96	0.1
1949	StL N★	151	640	102	190	25	2	3	54	51	2	18	.297	.351	.356	86	-12	8	**.987**	**27**	**114**	116	*2-138,S-14/3-6,O-2(CF)	2.4
1950	StL N★	**153**	642	81	177	**43**	9	7	63	33	2	32	.276	.313	.403	83	-17	3	.985	12	104	114	*2-143,S-10/3	0.3
1951	StL N★	135	553	88	160	32	7	6	54	35	3	23	.289	.335	.405	98	-3	0-1	.990	17	**110**	116	*2-124/S-8	2.1
1952	StL N☆	152	620	91	188	40	7	7	67	42	0	30	.303	.347	.424	113	10	9-6	.977	**36**	**109**	119	*2-142,3-11/S-3	5.4
1953	StL N★	146	564	107	193	35	5	15	79	60	0	23	.342	.405	.502	135	31	3-3	**.983**	**29**	**111**	112	*2-140	**6.5**
1954	StL N★	148	610	98	192	38	8	5	79	54	1	22	.315	.366	.428	107	7	4-2	.980	**28**	**113**	**123**	*2-144	4.5
1955	StL N★	145	553	68	148	21	3	11	51	54-5	4	28	.268	.335	.376	89	-8	7-7	**.985**	-14	97	95	*2-142	-1.2
1956	StL N	40	153	22	48	9	0	0	15	13-0	0	5	.314	.365	.373	100	1	0-1	.995	1	93	114	2-36	0.4
	NY N	92	334	39	99	12	3	2	14	28-1	2	10	.296	.352	.368	95	-2	1-2	.993	-6	94	93	2-85	-0.2
	Year	132	487	61	147	21	3	2	29	41-1	2	15	.302	.356	.370	97	-1	1-3	**.993**	-5	94	99	*2-121	0.2
1957	NY N	57	254	35	78	8	4	9	33	10-0	2	8	.307	.337	.476	116	5	2-1	.984	-0	102	107	2-57	0.9
	†Mil N★	93	394	56	122	23	4	6	32	23-1	1	7	.310	.348	.434	117	9	2-3	.987	9	108	119	2-92/O-2(CF)	2.4
	Year	150	648	91	**200**	31	8	15	65	33-1	3	15	.309	.344	.451	117	14	4-4	.986	9	106	114	*2-149/O-2(CF)	3.3
1958	†Mil N	106	427	47	112	23	1	1	24	31-0	1	21	.262	.313	.328	77	-14	3-1	**.987**	4	104	114	*2-105	-0.2
1959	Mil N	5	3	0	0	0	0	0	0	0-0	0	0	.000	.000	.000	-99	-1	0-0	.667	-1	63	0	/2-4	-0.1
1960	Mil N	68	226	21	58	9	1	1	19	17-4	1	13	.257	.311	.319	79	-7	1-0	.964	-10	93	94	2-62	-1.3
1961	StL N	72	120	9	36	9	0	1	12	12-2	0	6	.300	.364	.400	93	0	1-0	.955	-6	77	72	2-32	-0.5
1962	StL N	98	143	21	43	4	0	2	12	9-2	1	12	.301	.346	.371	84	-3	0-0	.986	0	104	114	2-21/3-4	-0.1
1963	StL N	6	5	0	0	0	0	0	0	0-0	0	1	.000	.000	.000	-91	-1	0-0	—	0			H	-0.1
Total	19	2216	8479	1223	2449	427	78	84	773	606-15	21	346	.289	.337	.387	93	-81	89-27	.983	133	104	112	*2-1834,O-123(119-4-0)/S-49,3-39	15.8

SCHOENECK, JUMBO Louis N. B 3.3.1862 Chicago, IL D 1.20.1930 Chicago, IL BR/TR 6-3/223# d4.20

1884	CP U	90	366	56	116	22	2	2		8			.317	.332	.404	123	0		.956	0	90	93	*1-90	-0.7
	Bal U	16	60	5	15	2	0	0		0			.250	.250	.283	56	-5		.962	2	152	53	1-16	-0.4
	Year	106	426	61	131	24	2	2		8			.308	.320	.387	112	-6		**.957**	2	99	87	*1-106	-1.1
1888	Ind N	48	169	15	40	4	0	0	20	9	2	24	.237	.283	.260	73	-5	11	.974	-1	93	75	1-48/P-2	-1.0
1889	Ind N	16	62	3	15	2	2	0	8	3	2	3	.242	.299	.339	76	-2	1	.978	2	174	79	1-16	-0.1
Total	3	170	657	79	186	30	4	2	28	20	4	27	.283	.308	.350	99	-12	12	.964	3	104	83	1-170/P-2	-2.2

SCHOFIELD, DICK John Richard "Ducky" B 1.7.1935 Springfield, IL BB/TR 5-9/165# d7.3 s-Dick gs-Jayson

1953	StL N	33	39	9	7	0	0	2	4	2	0	11	.179	.220	.333	42	-4	0-0	.917	5	137	147	S-15	0.2
1954	StL N	43	7	17	1	0	1	0	1	0	0	3	.143	.143	.429	42	-1	1-1	1.000	1	144	217	S-11	0.0
1955	StL N	12	4	3	0	0	0	0	0	0-0	0	1	.000	.000	.000	-99	-1	0-0	1.000	0	145	0	/S-3	-0.1
1956	StL N	16	30	3	3	2	0	0	1	0-0	0	6	.100	.100	.167	-30	-5	0-0	.923	-1	85	120	/S-9	-0.6
1957	StL N	65	56	10	9	0	0	0	1	7-0	0	13	.161	.254	.161	14	-7	1-3	.948	5	137	148	S-23	-0.2
1958	StL N	39	108	16	23	4	0	1	8	23-0	0	15	.213	.348	.278	67	-4	0-2	.932	-6	95	65	S-27	-0.8
	Pit N	26	27	4	4	0	1	0	2	3-0	0	6	.148	.226	.222	22	-3	0-1	1.000	0	100	149	/S-5,3-2	-0.3
	Year	65	135	20	27	4	1	1	10	26-0	0	21	.200	.325	.267	59	-7	0-3	.943	-5	96	78	S-32/3-2	-1.1
1959	Pit N	81	145	21	34	10	1	1	9	16-0	0	22	.234	.311	.338	73	-5	1-1	.980	4	113	134	2-28/S-8,O-3(RF)	0.1
1960	†Pit N	65	102	9	34	4	1	0	10	16-4	1	20	.333	.429	.392	126	5	0-1	.947	5	108	147	S-23,2-10/3	1.1
1961	Pit N	60	78	16	15	2	1	0	2	10-0	0	19	.192	.284	.244	42	-7	0-1	.923	6	142	73	3-11/S-9,2-5,O-3(2-0-2)	0.0
1962	Pit N	54	104	19	30	3	0	2	10	17-0	0	22	.288	.382	.375	106	2	0-1	.933	-3	81	61	3-20/2-2,S	-0.2
1963	Pit N	138	541	54	133	18	2	3	32	69-1	3	83	.246	.333	.303	84	-8	2-4	.966	16	107	**135**	*S-117,2-20/3	2.1
1964	Pit N	121	398	50	98	22	5	3	36	54-3	7	60	.246	.345	.349	97	1	1-2	.950	7	105	**118**	*S-111	1.7
1965	Pit N	31	109	13	25	5	0	0	6	15-1	0	19	.229	.317	.275	70	-4	1-0	.974	4	112	153	S-28	0.4
	SF N	101	379	39	77	10	1	2	19	33-0	3	50	.203	.272	.251	47	-26	2-4	.984	-7	93	96	S-93	-2.8
	Year	132	488	52	102	15	1	2	25	48-1	3	69	.209	.282	.256	52	-30	3-4	**.981**	-3	97	109	*S-121	-2.4
1966	SF N	11	16	4	1	0	0	0	0	2-0	0	2	.063	.167	.063	-32	-3	0-0	1.000	1	101	131	/S-8	-0.2
	NY A	25	58	5	9	2	0	0	2	9-0	0	8	.155	.265	.190	36	-5	0-0	.909	1	117	103	S-19	-0.2
	LA N	20	70	10	18	0	0	0	4	8-0	2	8	.257	.350	.257	78	-2	1-1	.923	-3	97	0	3-19/S-3	-0.5
1967	LA N	84	232	23	50	10	1	2	15	31-4	0	40	.216	.307	.293	79	-5	1-2	.976	1	102	97	S-69/2-4,3-2	0.1
1968	†StL N	69	127	14	28	7	1	1	8	13-2	2	31	.220	.303	.315	87	-2	1-2	.973	0	95	63	S-43,2-23	0.2
1969	Bos A	94	226	30	58	9	3	2	20	29-1	4	44	.257	.349	.350	92	-2	0-2	.981	5	120	97	2-37,S-11/3-9,O-5(3-0-2)	0.6
1970	Bos A	76	139	16	26	1	2	1	14	21-2	1	26	.187	.294	.245	48	-10	0-1	.969	-2	97	70	2-15,3-15/S-3	-1.1
1971	Mil A	23	28	2	3	2	0	0	1	2-0	1	8	.107	.194	.179	6	-3	0-0	1.000	-1	96	203	3-12/S-4,2-2	-0.5
	StL N	34	60	7	13	2	0	1	6	10-0	2	9	.217	.347	.300	82	-1	0-0	.935	4	110	103	S-17,2-13/3-3	0.4
Total	19	1321	3083	394	699	113	20	21	211	390-18	26	526	.227	.317	.297	73	-100	12-29	.961	42	103	113	S-660,2-159/3-95,O-11(5-0-7)	-0.6

SCHOFIELD, DICK Richard Craig B 11.21.1962 Springfield, IL BR/TR 5-10/178# d9.8 f-Dick

1983	Cal A	21	54	4	11	2	0	3	4	6-0	1	8	.204	.295	.407	92	-1	0-0	.929	-2	111	78	S-21	0.0
1984	Cal A	140	400	39	77	10	3	4	21	33-0	6	79	.192	.264	.262	47	-29	5-2	**.982**	10	107	117	*S-140	-0.5
1985	Cal A	147	438	50	96	19	3	8	41	35-0	8	70	.219	.287	.331	70	-19	11-4	.963	11	104	**130**	*S-147	0.7
1986	†Cal A	139	458	67	114	17	6	13	57	48-2	5	55	.249	.321	.397	97	-2	23-5	.972	17	105	**134**	*S-137	3.1
1987	Cal A	134	479	52	120	17	3	9	46	37-0	2	63	.251	.305	.355	78	-16	19-3	**.984**	-18	92	101	*S-131/2-2,D	-1.6
1988	Cal A	155	527	61	126	11	6	6	34	40-0	9	57	.239	.303	.317	76	-18	20-5	**.983**	22	110	118	*S-155	1.8
1989	Cal A	91	302	42	69	11	2	4	26	28-0	3	47	.228	.299	.318	76	-10	9-3	.983	-2	102	105	S-90	-0.4
1990	Cal A	99	310	41	79	8	1	1	18	52-3	2	61	.255	.363	.297	89	-2	3-4	.966	10	106	114	S-99	1.5
1991	Cal A	134	427	44	96	9	3	0	31	50-2	3	69	.225	.310	.260	60	-23	8-4	.975	4	99	107	*S-133	-0.9
1992	Cal A	1	3	0	1	0	0	0	0	1-0	0	0	.333	.500	.333	137	0	0-0	1.000	-1	31	0	/S	0.0
	NY N	142	420	52	86	18	2	4	36	60-4	5	82	.205	.309	.286	71	-14	11-4	**.988**	15	104	110	*S-141	1.3
1993	Tor A	36	110	11	21	1	2	0	5	16-0	0	25	.191	.294	.236	44	-9	3-0	.977	5	104	102	S-36	-0.1
1994	Tor A	95	325	38	83	14	1	4	32	34-0	4	62	.255	.332	.342	74	-12	7-7	.972	-8	84	97	S-95	-1.3
1995	LA N	9	10	0	1	0	0	0	0	1-0	0	3	.100	.182	.100	-25	-2	0-0	1.000	3	227	401	/S-3,3	0.1
	Cal A	12	20	1	5	0	0	0	2	4-0	0	2	.250	.375	.250	67	-1	0-0	1.000	-4	83	35	S-12	-0.3
1996	Cal A	13	16	3	4	0	0	0	0	1-0	0	1	.250	.294	.250	39	-2	1-0	.889	-2	36	50	/S-7,2-2,3D	-0.3
Total	14	1368	4299	505	989	137	32	56	353	446-11	48	684	.230	.308	.316	73	-160	120-41	.976	59	102	113	*S-1348/2-4,3-2,D-2	3.1

SCHOMBERG, OTTO Otto H. (born Otto H. Shambrick) B 11.14.1864 Milwaukee, WI D 5.3.1927 Ottawa, KS BL/TL d7.7

1886	Pit AA	72	246	53	67	6	6	1	29	57	4		.272	.417	.358	144	17	7	.966	-7	26	109	1-72	0.4
1887	Ind N	112	419	91	129	18	16	5	83	56	6	32	.308	.397	.463	143	27	21	.958	-10	70	111	*1-112/O(RF)	0.6
1888	Ind N	30	112	11	24	5	1	1	10	10	2	12	.214	.290	.304	88	-1	6	.857	-3	144	0	O-15(RF),1-15	-0.6
Total	3	214	777	155	220	29	23	7	122	123	12	44	.283	.389	.407	136	43	34	.961	-20	49	110	1-199/O-16(RF)	0.4

SCHOONMAKER, JERRY Jerald Lee B 12.14.1933 Seymour, MO BR/TR 5-11/190# d6.11 Mil 1956

1955	Was A	20	46	5	7	0	1	1	4	5-0	0	11	.152	.235	.261	35	-5	1-0	.960	0	92	231	O-15(5-3-7)	-0.5
1957	Was A	30	23	5	2	1	0	0	0	2-0	0	11	.087	.160	.130	-20	-4	0-0	1.000	1	156	0	O-13(5-8-0)	-0.3
Total	2	50	69	10	9	1	1	1	4	7-0	0	22	.130	.211	.217	16	-9	1-0	.975	1	109	168	/O-28(10-11-7)	-0.8

SCHRAMKA, PAUL Paul Edward B 3.22.1928 Milwaukee, WI BL/TL 6/185# d4.14

1953	Chi N	2	0	0	0	0	0	0	0	0	0	0	—	—	—	—	0	0-0	—	-0	0	0	/O(LF)	0.0

SCHRECKENGOST, OSSEE Ossee Freeman (a/k/a Ossee Schreck) B 4.11.1875 New Bethlehem, PA D 7.9.1914 Philadelphia, PA BR/TR 5-10/180# d9.8

Year	Tm Lg	G	AB	R	H	2B	3B	HR	RBI	BB-IB	HP	SO	AVG	OBP	SLG	AOPS	ABR	SB-CS	FA	FR	Rng	Thr	G at Pos	BFW
1897	Lou N	1	3	0	0	0	0	0	0	0	0		.000	.000	.000	-99	-1	0	1.000	0	*117*	*147*	/C	-0.1
1898	Cle N	10	35	5	11	2	3	0	10	0	0		.314	.314	.543	146	1	1	.860	0	*116*	*84*	/C-9	0.2
1899	StL N	6	8	0	0	0	0	0	0	1	0		.000	.111	.000	-67	-2	0	1.000	-0	0	0	/1O(RF)	-0.2
	Cle N	43	150	15	47	8	3	0	10	6	2		.313	.348	.407	115	3	4	.911	-14	*59*	*124*	C-39/1SO(RF)	-0.7
	StL N	66	269	42	77	12	2	2	37	14	1		.286	.324	.368	88	-5	14	.963	-3	0	0	1-41,C-25/2	-0.5
	Year	115	427	57	124	20	5	2	47	21	3		.290	.328	.375	94	-5	18	.927	-17	*87*	*122*	C-64,1-43/O-2(RF),S2	-1.4
1901	Bos A	86	280	37	85	13	5	0	38	19	4		.304	.356	.386	108	3	6	.926	4	*105*	*100*	C-72/1-4	1.3
1902	Cle A	18	74	5	25	0	0	0	9	0	0		.338	.338	.338	91	-1	2	.975	-1	86	62	1-17	-0.2
	Phi A	79	284	45	92	17	2	2	43	9	1		.324	.347	.419	107	2	3	.960	17	*108*	*105*	C-71/1-7,O(CF)	2.4
	Year	97	358	50	117	17	2	2	52	9	1		.327	.345	.402	104	1	5	.960	16	*108*	*105*	C-71,1-24/O(CF)	2.2
1903	Phi A	92	306	26	78	13	4	3	30	11	2		.255	.285	.353	87	-6	0	.975	12	*107*	*105*	C-77,1-10	1.4
1904	Phi A	95	311	23	58	9	1	1	21	5	0		.186	.199	.232	34	-24	3	.979	3	*109*	*81*	C-84/1-9	-1.3
1905	†Phi A	123	420	30	114	19	6	0	45	3	1		.271	.278	.345	96	-4	9	**.984**	9	*117*	*84*	*C-114/1-2	1.7
1906	Phi A	98	338	29	96	20	1	1	41	10	0		.284	.305	.358	104	1	5	.971	8	*97*	*90*	C-89/1-4	1.9
1907	Phi A	101	356	30	97	16	3	0	38	17	0		.272	.306	.334	102	0	4	**.985**	10	*97*	***103***	C-99/1-2	2.2
1908	Phi A	71	207	16	46	7	1	0	16	6	1		.222	.248	.266	63	-9	1	.978	1	*74*	*112*	C-65/1	-0.2
	Chi A	6	16	1	3	0	0	0	0	1	0		.188	.235	.188	38	-1	0	.982	2	*155*	*46*	/C-6	0.2
	Year	77	223	17	49	7	1	0	16	7	1		.220	.247	.260	61	-10	1	.978	3	*83*	*105*	C-71/1	0.0
Total	11	895	3057	304	829	136	31	9	338	102	12		.271	.297	.345	90	-43	52	.970	49	*102*	*98*	C-751/1-99,O-3(0-1-2),2S	8.1

SCHREIBER, HANK Henry Walter B 7.12.1891 Cleveland, OH D 2.23.1968 Indianapolis, IN BR/TR 5-11/165# d4.14 Mil 1918

Year	Tm Lg	G	AB	R	H	2B	3B	HR	RBI	BB-IB	HP	SO	AVG	OBP	SLG	AOPS	ABR	SB-CS	FA	FR	Rng	Thr	G at Pos	BFW
1914	Chi A	1	2	0	0	0	0	0	0	0	0	0	.000	.000	.000	-99	0	0	—	-0	0	0	/O(LF)	-0.1
1917	Bos N	2	7	1	2	0	0	0	0	0	0	1	.286	.286	.286	80	0	0	1.000	-1	39	0	/S3	-0.1
1919	Cin N	19	58	5	13	4	0	0	4	0	0	12	.224	.224	.293	56	-3	0	.984	5	134	281	3-17/S-2	0.2
1921	NY N	4	6	2	2	0	0	0	2	1	0	1	.333	.429	.333	104	0	0-0	.500	-1	0	0	/2-2,S-2,3	-0.1
1926	Chi N	10	18	2	1	1	0	0	0	0	0	1	.056	.056	.111	-55	-4	0	1.000	0	148	0	/S-3,3-3,2	-0.3
Total	5	36	91	10	18	5	0	0	6	1	0	16	.198	.207	.253	34	-7	0-0	.986	4	126	233	/3-22,S-8,2-3,O(LF)	-0.4

SCHREIBER, TED Theodore Henry B 7.11.1938 Brooklyn, NY BR/TR 5-11/175# d4.14

Year	Tm Lg	G	AB	R	H	2B	3B	HR	RBI	BB-IB	HP	SO	AVG	OBP	SLG	AOPS	ABR	SB-CS	FA	FR	Rng	Thr	G at Pos	BFW
1963	NY N	39	50	1	8	0	0	0	2	4-0	1	14	.160	.236	.160	16	-5	0-1	.977	5	140	160	3-17/S-9,2-3	0.0

SCHRIVER, POP William Frederick B 7.11.1865 Brooklyn, NY D 12.27.1932 Brooklyn, NY BR/TR 5-9.5/172# d4.29 OF Total (8-LF 10-CF 5-RF)

Year	Tm Lg	G	AB	R	H	2B	3B	HR	RBI	BB-IB	HP	SO	AVG	OBP	SLG	AOPS	ABR	SB-CS	FA	FR	Rng	Thr	G at Pos	BFW
1886	Bro AA	8	21	2	1	0	0	0	0	2	0		.048	.130	.048	-43	-3	0	.667	1	264	0	/O-5(2-0-3),C-3	-0.2
1888	Phi N	40	134	15	26	5	2	1	23	7	3	21	.194	.250	.284	66	-5	2	.870	-7			C-27/S-6,3-6,O(RF)	-1.0
1889	Phi N	55	211	24	56	10	0	1	19	16	2	8	.265	.323	.327	75	-8	5	.920	1			C-48/2-6,3	-0.2
1890	Phi N	57	223	37	61	9	6	0	35	22	0	15	.274	.339	.368	103	0	9	.916	-2	*105*	*98*	C-34,1-10/3-8,2-3,O-2(LF)	0.0
1891	Chi N	27	90	15	30	1	4	1	21	10	2	9	.333	.412	.467	156	6	1	.964	3	*132*	*84*	C-27/1-2	1.0
1892	Chi N	92	326	40	73	10	6	1	34	27	7	25	.224	.297	.301	80	-8	4	.929	-3	*105*	*100*	C-82,O-10(CF)	-0.4
1893	Chi N	64	229	49	65	8	3	4	34	14	4	9	.284	.336	.397	96	-2	4	.926	1	*90*	*108*	C-56/O-5(4-0-1)	0.3
1894	Chi N	98	354	56	97	12	3	3	49	32	6	21	.274	.344	.350	64	-22	9	.920	-5	*80*	*109*	*C-90/S-3,3-3,1-2	-1.5
1895	NY N	24	92	16	29	2	1	1	16	9	1	10	.315	.382	.391	102	1	3	.898	-3	*94*	*126*	C-18/1-6	-0.1
1897	Cin N	61	178	29	54	12	4	1	30	19	1		.303	.374	.433	106	1	3	.959	5	*155*	*84*	C-53	0.9
1898	Pit N	95	315	25	72	15	3	0	32	23	3		.229	.287	.295	68	-13	0	.957	-2	*105*	*90*	C-92/1	-0.6
1899	Pit N	92	302	31	85	19	5	1	49	24	5		.281	.344	.387	101	1	4	.958	9	*121*	*88*	C-78/1-9	1.5
1900	†Pit N	37	92	12	27	7	0	1	12	10	3		.293	.381	.402	115	3	0	.959	-1	*127*	*67*	C-24/1	0.3
1901	StL N	53	166	17	45	7	3	1	23	12	4		.271	.335	.367	109	2	2	.971	2	*95*	*139*	C-24,1-19	0.6
Total	14	803	2733	368	721	117	40	16	377	227	41	118	.264	.330	.353	88	-47	46	.934	-2	*94*	*86*	C-656/1-50,O-23C,3-18,2-9,S-9	0.6

SCHRODER, BOB Robert James B 12.30.1944 Ridgefield, NJ BL/TR 6/175# d4.20

Year	Tm Lg	G	AB	R	H	2B	3B	HR	RBI	BB-IB	HP	SO	AVG	OBP	SLG	AOPS	ABR	SB-CS	FA	FR	Rng	Thr	G at Pos	BFW
1965	SF N	31	9	4	2	0	0	0	1	1-0	0	1	.222	.300	.222	48	-1	0-0	1.000	2	191	168	/2-4,3	0.1
1966	SF N	10	33	0	8	0	0	0	2	0-0	0	2	.242	.242	.242	34	-3	0-0	.963	-3	80	53	/S-9	-0.6
1967	SF N	62	135	20	31	4	0	0	7	15-3	0	15	.230	.307	.259	64	-6	1-0	.993	-3	101	68	2-45/3-4	-0.7
1968	SF N	35	44	5	7	1	1	0	2	7-0	1	3	.159	.283	.227	56	-2	0-0	.960	-2	103	65	2-12/S-4,3-2	-0.5
Total	4	138	221	29	48	5	1	0	12	23-3	1	21	.217	.293	.249	58	-12	1-0	.989	-7	104	70	/2-61,S-13,3-7	-1.7

SCHROEDER, BILL Alfred William B 9.7.1958 Baltimore, MD BR/TR 6-2/200# d7.13

Year	Tm Lg	G	AB	R	H	2B	3B	HR	RBI	BB-IB	HP	SO	AVG	OBP	SLG	AOPS	ABR	SB-CS	FA	FR	Rng	Thr	G at Pos	BFW
1983	Mil A	23	73	7	13	2	1	3	7	3-0	1	23	.178	.221	.356	60	-5	0-1	.980	-4	97	71	C-23	-0.8
1984	Mil A	61	210	29	54	6	0	14	25	8-2	2	54	.257	.288	.486	115	3	0-1	.987	-9	67	90	C-58/1D	-0.4
1985	Mil A	53	194	18	47	8	0	8	25	12-1	2	61	.242	.290	.407	90	-3	0-1	.987	-7	78	88	C-48/1D	-0.9
1986	Mil A	64	217	32	46	14	0	7	19	9-0	6	59	.212	.262	.373	69	-10	1-0	.995	-3	84	74	C-35,1-19,D-10	-1.2
1987	Mil A	75	250	35	83	12	0	14	42	16-0	3	56	.332	.379	.548	138	13	5-2	.995	-11	94	64	C-67/1-4,D-2	0.5
1988	Mil A	41	122	9	19	2	0	5	10	6-0	2	36	.156	.208	.295	39	-11	0-0	1.000	3	89	89	C-30,1-10/D	-0.6
1989	Cal A	41	138	16	28	2	0	6	15	3-0	0	44	.203	.220	.348	59	-9	0-0	.991	9	80	81	C-33/1-8	0.2
1990	Cal A	18	58	7	13	3	0	4	9	1-0	0	10	.224	.237	.483	98	-1	0-0	1.000	-1	64	130	C-15/1-3	-0.1
Total	8	376	1262	153	303	49	1	61	152	58-3	16	343	.240	.281	.426	91	-23	6-5	.992	-22	82	82	C-309/1-46,D-20	-3.3

SCHU, RICK Richard Spencer B 1.26.1962 Philadelphia, PA BR/TR 6/170# d9.1

Year	Tm Lg	G	AB	R	H	2B	3B	HR	RBI	BB-IB	HP	SO	AVG	OBP	SLG	AOPS	ABR	SB-CS	FA	FR	Rng	Thr	G at Pos	BFW
1984	Phi N	17	29	12	8	2	1	2	5	6-0	0	6	.276	.389	.621	180	3	0-0	.952	-2	68	209	3-15	0.1
1985	Phi N	112	416	54	105	21	4	7	24	38-3	2	78	.252	.318	.373	90	-6	8-6	.933	-15	82	94	*3-111	-2.5
1986	Phi N	92	208	32	57	10	1	8	25	18-1	2	44	.274	.335	.447	111	3	2-2	.913	-1	101	75	3-58	0.1
1987	Phi N	92	196	24	46	6	3	7	23	20-1	2	36	.235	.311	.403	85	-5	0-2	.905	-6	93	37	3-45,1-28	-1.3
1988	Bal A	89	270	22	69	9	4	4	20	21-0	3	49	.256	.316	.363	92	-3	6-4	.937	-8	89	59	3-72/1-4,D-9	-1.1
1989	Bal A	1	0	0	0	0	0	0	0	0-0	0	0	—	—	—	—	0	0-0	1.000	-0	0	0	/2	0.0
	Det A	98	266	25	57	11	0	7	21	24-0	0	37	.214	.278	.335	74	-10	1-2	.934	-3	94	89	3-83/2-5,1-3,S-3,D-9	-1.3
	Year	99	266	25	57	11	0	7	21	24-0	0	37	.214	.278	.335	74	-10	1-2	.934	-3	94	89	3-83/D-9,2-6,1-3,S-3	-1.3
1990	Cal A	61	157	19	42	8	0	6	14	11-0	0	25	.268	.314	.433	110	1	0-0	.918	1	115	154	3-38,1-15/O-4(LF),2	0.2
1991	Phi N	17	22	1	2	0	0	0	2	1-0	0	7	.091	.125	.091	-37	-4	0-0	.667	-1	0	0	/3-3,1	-0.6
1996	Mon N	1	4	0	0	0	0	0	0	0-0	0	0	.000	.000	.000	-98	-1	0-0	.667	-0	94	0	/3	-0.2
Total	9	580	1568	189	386	67	13	41	134	139-5	9	282	.246	.310	.384	91	-22	17-16	.926	-35	91	87	3-426/1-51,D-18,2-7,O-4(LF),S-3	-6.6

SCHUBLE, HEINIE Henry George B 11.1.1906 Houston, TX D 10.2.1990 Baytown, TX BR/TR 5-9/152# d7.8

Year	Tm Lg	G	AB	R	H	2B	3B	HR	RBI	BB-IB	HP	SO	AVG	OBP	SLG	AOPS	ABR	SB-CS	FA	FR	Rng	Thr	G at Pos	BFW
1927	StL N	65	218	29	56	6	2	4	28	7	1	27	.257	.283	.358	69	-11	0	.915	-5	100	110	S-65	-1.0
1929	Det A	92	258	35	60	11	7	2	28	19	1	23	.233	.288	.353	64	-15	3-2	.886	-16	94	82	S-86/3-2	-2.2
1932	Det A	102	340	58	92	20	6	5	52	24	0	37	.271	.319	.409	84	-9	14-5	.941	5	106	80	3-76,S-16	0.1
1933	Det A	49	96	12	21	4	1	0	6	5	0	17	.219	.257	.281	42	-8	2-0	.951	0	113	29	3-23/S-2,2	-0.7
1934	Det A	11	15	2	4	2	0	0	2	1	0	4	.267	.313	.400	83	0	0-0	1.000	0	98	0	/S-3,3-2,2	0.0
1935	Det A	11	8	3	2	0	0	0	0	1	0	0	.250	.333	.250	55	-1	0-0	.714	0	158	1142	/3-2,2	0.0
1936	StL N	2	0	0	0	0	0	0	0	0	0	0	—	—	—	—	0	0	—	-0	0	0	/3	0.0
Total	7	332	935	139	235	43	16	11	116	57	2	108	.251	.296	.367	70	-44	19-7	.906	-16	97	97	S-172,3-106/2-3	-3.8

SCHULMERICH, WES Edward Wesley B 8.21.1901 Hillsboro, OR D 6.26.1985 Corvallis, OR BR/TR 5-11/210# d5.1

Year	Tm Lg	G	AB	R	H	2B	3B	HR	RBI	BB-IB	HP	SO	AVG	OBP	SLG	AOPS	ABR	SB-CS	FA	FR	Rng	Thr	G at Pos	BFW
1931	Bos N	95	327	36	101	17	7	2	43	28	0	30	.309	.363	.422	115	6	0	.966	-4	101	56	O-87(RF)	-0.2
1932	Bos N	119	404	47	105	22	5	11	57	27	5	61	.260	.314	.421	99	-1	5	.968	1	100	101	*O-101(RF)	-0.7
1933	Bos N	29	85	10	21	6	1	1	13	5	0	10	.247	.289	.376	97	-1	0	.980	1	102	148	O-21(RF)	-0.1
	Phi N	97	365	53	122	19	4	8	59	32	4	45	.334	.394	.474	130	16	1	.977	-1	100	78	O-97(LF)	1.0
	Year	126	450	63	143	25	5	9	72	37	4	55	.318	.375	.456	126	16	1	.978	0	100	90	*O-118(97-0-21)	0.9
1934	Phi N	15	52	2	13	1	0	0	1	4	1	8	.250	.316	.269	51	-3	0	.963	-0	100	96	O-13(3-0-10)	-0.4
	Cin N	74	209	21	55	8	3	5	19	22	0	43	.263	.333	.402	98	-1	1	.976	-2	105	21	O-56(13-0-43)	-0.6
	Year	89	261	23	68	9	3	5	20	26	1	51	.261	.330	.375	88	-4	1	.974	-2	104	35	O-69(16-0-53)	-1.0
Total	4	429	1442	169	417	73	20	27	192	118	10	197	.289	.347	.424	109	16	7	.971	-5	101	75	O-375(113-0-262)	-1.0

SCHULT, ART Arthur William "Dutch" B 6.20.1928 Brooklyn, NY BR/TR 6-4/220# d5.17

Year	Tm Lg	G	AB	R	H	2B	3B	HR	RBI	BB-IB	HP	SO	AVG	OBP	SLG	AOPS	ABR	SB-CS	FA	FR	Rng	Thr	G at Pos	BFW
1953	NY A	7	0	3	0	0	0	0	0	0	0	0	—	—	—	—	0	0-0	—	0			R	0.0
1956	Cin N	5	7	3	3	0	0	0	2	1-0	0	1	.429	.500	.429	144	1	0-0	—	-0	0	0	/O(LF)	0.0
1957	Cin N	21	34	4	9	2	0	0	4	0-0	1	2	.265	.286	.324	59	-2	0-0	1.000	1	134	0	/O-5(LF)	-0.2

Year	Tm Lg	G	AB	R	H	2B	3B	HR	RBI	BB-IB	HP	SO	AVG	OBP	SLG	AOPS	ABR	SB-CS	FA	FR	Rng	Thr	G at Pos	BFW
	Was A	77	247	30	65	14	0	4	35	14-0	1	30	.263	.303	.368	84	-6	0-1	.987	-3	60	111	1-35,O-31(14-1-17)	-1.3
1959	Chi N	42	118	17	32	7	0	2	14	7-0	2	14	.271	.320	.381	88	-2	0-0	.985	-3	57	130	1-23,O-15(12-0-6)	-0.6
1960	Chi N	12	15	1	2	1	0	0	1	1-1	0	3	.133	.188	.200	6	-2	0-0	1.000	-0	85	0	/O-4(LF),1	-0.2
Total	5	164	421	58	111	24	0	6	56	23-1	4	50	.264	.306	.363	81	-11	0-1	.987	-6	59	116	/1-59,O-56(36-1-23)	-2.3

SCHULTE, FRANK Frank M. "Wildfire" B 9.17.1882 Cohocton, NY D 10.2.1949 Oakland, CA BL/TR 5-11/170# d9.21

Year	Tm Lg	G	AB	R	H	2B	3B	HR	RBI	BB-IB	HP	SO	AVG	OBP	SLG	AOPS	ABR	SB-CS	FA	FR	Rng	Thr	G at Pos	BFW
1904	Chi N	20	84	16	24	4	3	2	13	2	1		.286	.310	.476	141	3	1	.949	-0	111	0	O-20(LF)	0.2
1905	Chi N	123	493	67	135	15	14	1	47	32	6		.274	.326	.367	102	0	16	.981	-6	86	0	*O-123(107-0-16)	-1.4
1906	†Chi N	146	563	77	158	18	**13**	7	60	31	5		.281	.324	.396	118	8	25	.975	-2	96	**183**	*O-146(RF)	-0.1
1907	†Chi N	97	342	44	98	14	7	2	32	22	5		.287	.339	.386	120	7	7	.973	-3	89	38	O-92(1-0-91)	0.1
1908	†Chi N	102	386	42	91	20	2	1	43	29	3		.236	.294	.306	88	-5	15	.994	-6	63	71	*O-102(12-1-89)	-1.8
1909	Chi N	140	538	57	142	16	11	4	60	24	2		.264	.298	.357	101	-3	23	.968	-12	73	27	*O-140(RF)	-2.4
1910	†Chi N	151	559	93	168	29	15	**10**	68	39	3	57	.301	.349	.460	137	22	22	.968	-6	91	87	*O-150(RF)	1.0
1911	Chi N	154	577	105	173	30	21	**21**	**107**	76	3	71	.300	.384	**.534**	**156**	**40**	23	.971	-7	92	86	*O-154(RF)	2.5
1912	Chi N	139	553	90	146	27	11	12	64	53	7	70	.264	.336	.418	106	3	17	.952	-5	94	92	*O-139(RF)	-0.9
1913	Chi N	132	497	85	138	28	6	9	68	39	5	68	.278	.336	.412	113	8	21-19	.956	-6	92	84	*O-130(1-0-129)	-0.7
1914	Chi N	137	465	54	112	22	7	5	61	39	5	55	.241	.306	.351	95	-3	16	.954	-9	92	58	*O-134(134-0-2)	-1.9
1915	Chi N	151	550	66	137	20	6	12	62	49	2	68	.249	.313	.373	107	4	19-17	.962	5	97	139	*O-147(146-0-4)	0.0
1916	Chi N	72	230	31	68	11	1	5	27	20	0	35	.296	.352	.417	123	7	9	.951	-1	94	127	O-67(66-0-1)	0.4
	Pit N	55	177	12	45	5	3	0	14	17	1	19	.254	.323	.316	96	-1	5	.968	-2	109	37	O-48(20-0-28)	-0.5
	Year	127	407	43	113	16	4	5	41	37	1	54	.278	.339	.373	111	6	14	.958	-2	101	88	*O-115(86-0-29)	-0.1
1917	Pit N	30	103	11	22	5	1	0	7	10	0	14	.214	.283	.282	71	-3	5	.963	0	105	87	O-28(3-0-25)	-0.5
	Phi N	64	149	21	32	10	0	1	15	16	2	22	.215	.299	.302	81	-2	4	.923	-6	74	24	O-42(20-7-15)	-1.2
	Year	94	252	32	54	15	1	1	22	26	2	36	.214	.293	.294	77	-6	9	.943	-6	88	52	O-70(23-7-40)	-1.7
1918	Was A	93	267	35	77	14	3	0	44	47	6	36	.288	.406	.363	135	15	5	.969	2	105	98	O-75(14-1-60)	1.4
Total	15	1806	6533	906	1766	288	124	92	792	545	56	515	.270	.332	.395	114	100	233-36	.966	-64	90	82	*O-1737(544-9-1189)	-5.8

SCHULTE, FRED Fred William "Fritz" (born Fred William Schult) B 1.13.1901 Belvidere, IL D 5.20.1983 Belvidere, IL BR/TR 6-1/183# d4.15

Year	Tm Lg	G	AB	R	H	2B	3B	HR	RBI	BB-IB	HP	SO	AVG	OBP	SLG	AOPS	ABR	SB-CS	FA	FR	Rng	Thr	G at Pos	BFW
1927	StL A	60	189	32	60	16	5	3	34	20	0	14	.317	.383	.503	124	7	5-3	.916	-3	102	67	O-49(CF)	0.2
1928	StL A	146	556	90	159	44	6	7	85	51	1	60	.286	.347	.424	99	-1	6-5	.973	10	108	130	*O-143(CF)	0.2
1929	StL A	121	446	63	137	24	5	3	71	59	1	44	.307	.389	.404	101	3	8-3	**.989**	6	107	93	*O-116(CF)	0.4
1930	StL A	113	392	59	109	23	5	5	62	41	1	44	.278	.348	.401	86	-8	12-8	.966	-5	94	70	O-98(CF)/1-5	-1.6
1931	StL A	134	553	100	168	32	7	9	65	56	1	49	.304	.369	.436	107	6	6-8	.971	-1	96	119	*O-134(CF)	0.0
1932	StL A	146	565	106	166	35	6	9	73	71	0	44	.294	.373	.425	100	2	5-9	.986	-4	96	85	*O-129(3-126-0)/1-5	-0.8
1933	†Was A	144	550	98	162	30	7	5	87	61	1	27	.295	.366	.402	104	4	10-12	.980	8	**112**	94	*O-142(CF)	0.6
1934	Was A	136	524	72	156	32	6	3	73	53	1	34	.298	.363	.399	100	1	3-7	.986	-4	101	46	*O-134(CF)	-0.8
1935	Was A	76	226	33	60	6	4	2	23	26	1	22	.265	.344	.354	83	-6	0-3	.980	-2	97	55	O-56(12-19-26)	-1.0
1936	Pit N	74	238	28	62	7	3	1	17	20	1	20	.261	.320	.328	73	-9	1	.977	-3	96	28	O-55(1-54-0)	-1.3
1937	Pit N	29	20	5	2	0	0	0	3	4	1	3	.100	.280	.100	7	-2	0	.800	-0	116	0	/O-4(1-1-2)	-0.3
Total	11	1179	4259	686	1241	249	54	47	593	462	9	361	.291	.362	.408	98	-3	56-58	.976	2	102	87	*O-1060(17-1016-28)/1-10	-4.4

SCHULTE, HAM Herman Joseph (born Herman Joseph Schultehenrich) B 9.1.1912 St.Louis, MO D 12.21.1993 St.Charles, MO BR/TR 5-8.5/158# d4.16 b-Len

Year	Tm Lg	G	AB	R	H	2B	3B	HR	RBI	BB-IB	HP	SO	AVG	OBP	SLG	AOPS	ABR	SB-CS	FA	FR	Rng	Thr	G at Pos	BFW
1940	Phi N	120	436	44	103	18	2	1	21	32	0	30	.236	.288	.294	63	-22	3	**.980**	-9	91	98	*2-119/S	-2.4

SCHULTE, JOHNNY John Clement B 9.8.1896 Fredericktown, MO D 6.28.1978 St.Louis, MO BL/TR 5-11/190# d4.18 C18

Year	Tm Lg	G	AB	R	H	2B	3B	HR	RBI	BB-IB	HP	SO	AVG	OBP	SLG	AOPS	ABR	SB-CS	FA	FR	Rng	Thr	G at Pos	BFW
1923	StL A	7	3	1	0	0	0	0	1	4	0	0	.000	.571	.000	56	0	0-0	1.000	1	0	289	/C1	0.1
1927	StL N	64	156	35	45	8	2	9	32	47	1	19	.288	.456	.538	160	17	1	.956	0	91	131	C-59	2.0
1928	Phi N	65	113	14	28	2	2	4	17	15	0	12	.248	.336	.407	90	-2	0	.949	-4	77	137	C-34	-0.4
1929	Chi N	31	69	6	18	3	0	0	9	7	0	11	.261	.329	.304	58	-4	0	.978	1	129	133	C-30	-0.2
1932	StL A	15	24	2	5	2	0	0	3	1	0	6	.208	.240	.292	35	-2	0-0	.864	-1	176	0	/C-6	-0.2
	Bos N	10	9	1	2	0	0	1	2	2	0	1	.222	.364	.556	149	1	0	1.000	1	135	0	C-10	0.1
Total	5	192	374	59	98	15	4	14	64	76	1	49	.262	.388	.436	112	10	1-0	.957	-3	99	124	C-140/1	1.4

SCHULTE, JACK John Herman Frank B 11.15.1881 Cincinnati, OH D 8.17.1975 Roseville, MI BR/TR 5-9/180# d8.19

Year	Tm Lg	G	AB	R	H	2B	3B	HR	RBI	BB-IB	HP	SO	AVG	OBP	SLG	AOPS	ABR	SB-CS	FA	FR	Rng	Thr	G at Pos	BFW
1906	Bos N	2	7	0	0	0	0	0	0	0	0		.000	.000	.000	-99	-2	0	1.000	-1	69	0	/S-2	-0.3

SCHULTE, LEN Leonard Bernard (born Leonard Bernard Schultehenrich) B 12.5.1916 St.Charles, MO D 5.6.1986 Orlando, FL BR/TR 5-10/160# d9.27 b-Herman

Year	Tm Lg	G	AB	R	H	2B	3B	HR	RBI	BB-IB	HP	SO	AVG	OBP	SLG	AOPS	ABR	SB-CS	FA	FR	Rng	Thr	G at Pos	BFW
1944	StL A	1	0	0	0	0	0	0	0	1	0	0	—	1.000	—	188	0	0-0	—	0			H	0.0
1945	StL A	119	430	37	106	16	1	0	36	24	0	35	.247	.286	.288	64	-20	0-3	.961	-10	101	69	3-71,2-37,S-14	-3.0
1946	StL A	4	5	1	2	0	0	0	2	0	0	0	.400	.400	.400	118	0	0-0	1.000	0	75	0	/23	0.0
Total	3	124	435	38	108	16	1	0	38	25	0	35	.248	.289	.290	65	-20	0-3	.962	-9	102	68	/3-72,2-38,S-14	-3.0

SCHULTZ, HOWIE Howard Henry "Stretch" or "Steeple" B 7.3.1922 St.Paul, MN BR/TR 6-6/200# d8.16

Year	Tm Lg	G	AB	R	H	2B	3B	HR	RBI	BB-IB	HP	SO	AVG	OBP	SLG	AOPS	ABR	SB-CS	FA	FR	Rng	Thr	G at Pos	BFW
1943	Bro N	45	182	20	49	12	0	1	34	6	2	24	.269	.300	.352	88	-3	3	.986	1	113	69	1-45	-0.4
1944	Bro N	138	526	59	134	32	3	11	83	24	2	67	.255	.290	.390	92	-8	6	.988	-0	98	77	*1-136	-1.6
1945	Bro N	39	142	18	34	8	2	1	19	10	1	14	.239	.294	.345	78	-5	2	.984	2	126	123	1-38	-0.4
1946	Bro N	90	249	27	63	14	1	3	27	16	0	34	.253	.298	.353	84	-6	2	.989	5	124	122	1-87	-0.4
1947	Bro N	2	1	0	0	0	0	0	0	0	0	0	.000	.000	.000	-96	0	0	1.000	-0	0	0	/1	0.0
	Phi N	114	403	30	90	19	1	6	35	21	1	70	.223	.264	.320	56	-27	0	.993	-1	95	105	*1-114	-3.2
	Year	116	404	30	90	19	1	6	35	21	1	70	.223	.263	.319	56	-27	0	.993	-1	95	105	*1-115	-3.2
1948	Phi N	6	13	0	1	0	0	0	1	1	0	2	.077	.143	.077	-40	-3	0	1.000	0	118	153	/1-3	-0.3
	Cin N	36	72	9	12	0	0	2	9	4	0	7	.167	.211	.250	25	-8	2	.982	-3	45	103	1-26	-1.1
	Year	42	85	9	13	0	0	2	10	5	0	9	.153	.200	.224	15	-11	2	.984	-3	54	109	1-29	-1.4
Total	6	470	1588	163	383	85	7	24	208	82	6	218	.241	.281	.349	75	-60	15	.989	4	103	97	1-450	-7.4

SCHULTZ, JOE Joseph Charles Jr. "Dode" B 8.29.1918 Chicago, IL D 1.10.1996 St.Louis, MO BL/TR 5-11/184# d9.27 M2 C14 f-Joe

Year	Tm Lg	G	AB	R	H	2B	3B	HR	RBI	BB-IB	HP	SO	AVG	OBP	SLG	AOPS	ABR	SB-CS	FA	FR	Rng	Thr	G at Pos	BFW
1939	Pit N	4	14	3	4	2	0	0	2	2	0	0	.286	.375	.429	117	0	0	1.000	0	148	0	/C-4	0.1
1940	Pit N	16	36	2	7	0	1	0	4	2	0	1	.194	.237	.250	35	-3	0	.917	-2	75	82	C-13	-0.5
1941	Pit N	2	2	1	1	0	0	0	0	0	0	0	.500	.500	.500	183	0	0	—	0	0	0	/C-2	0.0
1943	StL A	46	92	6	22	5	0	0	8	9	0	8	.239	.307	.293	74	-3	0-1	.979	-4	61	70	C-26	-0.7
1944	StL A	3	8	1	2	0	0	0	0	0	0	1	.250	.250	.250	41	-1	0-0	.818	-1	101	0	/C-3	-0.1
1945	StL A	41	44	1	13	2	0	0	8	3	0	1	.295	.340	.341	93	0	0-0	.941	0	121	0	/C-4	0.0
1946	StL A	42	57	1	22	4	0	0	14	11	0	2	.386	.485	.456	156	5	0-0	1.000	-3	59	0	C-17	0.3
1947	StL A	43	38	3	7	0	0	1	1	4	0	5	.184	.262	.263	45	-3	0-0	—	0			H	-0.3
1948	StL A	43	37	0	7	0	0	0	9	6	0	3	.189	.302	.189	32	-4	0-0	—	0			H	-0.3
Total	9	240	328	18	85	13	1	1	46	37	0	21	.259	.334	.314	81	-9	0-1	.964	-10	77	42	/C-69	-1.5

SCHULTZ, JOE Joseph Charles Sr. "Germany" B 7.24.1893 Pittsburgh, PA D 4.13.1941 Columbia, SC BR/TR 5-11.5/172# d9.28 s-Joe OF Total (104-LF 9-CF 307-RF)

Year	Tm Lg	G	AB	R	H	2B	3B	HR	RBI	BB-IB	HP	SO	AVG	OBP	SLG	AOPS	ABR	SB-CS	FA	FR	Rng	Thr	G at Pos	BFW
1912	Bos N	4	12	1	3	1	0	0	4	0	0	2	.250	.250	.333	58	-1	0	.824	-1	99	80	/2-4	-0.1
1913	Bos N	9	18	2	4	0	0	0	1	2	1	7	.222	.333	.222	59	-1	0	1.000	-0	121	0	/O-5(0-2-3),2	-0.1
1915	Bro N	56	120	13	35	3	2	0	4	10	0	18	.292	.346	.350	109	1	3-4	.894	-4	77	80	3-27/S	-0.3
	Chi N	7	8	1	2	0	0	0	3	0	0	2	.250	.250	.250	51	-1	0	.857	-0	93	0	/2-2	-0.1
	Year	63	128	14	37	3	2	0	7	10	0	20	.289	.341	.344	106	1	3-4	.894	-5	77	80	3-27/2-2,S	-0.4
1916	Pit N	77	204	18	53	8	2	0	22	7	4	14	.260	.298	.319	88	-3	6	.840	-15	89	24	2-24,3-24/O-6(4-0-3),S	-2.0
1919	StL N	88	229	24	58	9	1	2	21	11	0	7	.253	.287	.328	90	-3	4	1.000	-3	95	97	O-49(2-2-46)/2-6,3	-0.9
1920	StL N	99	320	38	84	5	5	0	32	21	0	11	.262	.308	.309	81	-9	5-4	.945	-3	101	72	O-80(2-0-79)	-1.7
1921	StL N	92	275	37	85	20	3	6	45	15	1	11	.309	.347	.469	116	6	4-3	.977	1	109	90	O-67(RF)/3-3,1-2	0.2
1922	StL N	112	344	50	108	13	4	2	64	19	0	10	.314	.350	.392	96	-3	3-1	.976	2	113	65	O-89(33-3-53)	-0.7
1923	StL N	2	7	0	2	0	0	0	1	1	0	0	.286	.375	.286	78	0	0-0	1.000	0	117	0	/O-2(RF)	0.0
1924	StL N	12	12	0	2	0	0	0	2	3	0	0	.167	.333	.167	39	-1	0-0	1.000	-0	41	0	/O-2(1-1-0)	-0.1
	Phi N	88	284	35	80	15	1	5	29	20	0	18	.282	.329	.394	83	-7	6-2	.960	-3	94	92	O-76(54-1-25)	-1.4
	Year	100	296	35	82	15	1	5	31	23	0	18	.277	.329	.385	82	-7	6-2	.960	-3	93	91	O-78(55-2-25)	-1.5
1925	Phi N	24	64	10	22	6	0	0	8	4	0	1	.344	.382	.438	100	0	1-1	.923	0	106	95	O-20(3-0-17)	-0.1
	Cin N	33	62	6	20	3	1	0	13	3	0	1	.323	.354	.403	95	-1	3-1	.950	-1	79	150	O-15(5-0-12)/2	-0.2
	Year	57	126	16	42	9	1	0	21	7	0	2	.333	.368	.421	99	0	4-2	.932	-1	95	117	O-35(8-0-29)/2	-0.3
Total	11	703	1959	235	558	83	19	15	249	116	6	102	.285	.327	.370	93	-23	35-16	.966	-26	103	83	O-411R/3-55,2-38,1-2,S-2	-7.5

Year	Tm Lg	G	AB	R	H	2B	3B	HR	RBI	BB-IB	HP	SO	AVG	OBP	SLG	AOPS	ABR	SB-CS	FA	FR	Rng	Thr	G at Pos	BFW
SCHULZ, JEFF Jeffrey Alan B 6.2.1961 Evansville, IN BL/TR 6-1/190# d9.2																								
1989	KC A	7	9	0	2	0	0	0	1	0-0	0	2	.222	.222	.222	26	-1	0-0	1.000	0	150	0	/O-5(LF)	-0.1
1990	KC A	30	66	5	17	5	1	0	6	6-2	0	13	.258	.319	.364	92	-1	0-0	.943	-1	98	0	O-22(8-0-16)/D	-0.3
1991	Pit N	3	3	0	0	0	0	0	0	0-0	0	2	.000	.000	.000	-99	-1	0-0	—	0			/H	-0.1
Total	3	40	78	5	19	5	1	0	7	6-2	0	17	.244	.298	.333	77	-3	0-0	.951	-1	103	0	/O-27(12-0-16),D	-0.5
SCHULZE, JOHN John H. B 4.1866 St.Louis, MO D 5.19.1941 St.Louis, MO d8.7																								
1891	StL AA	1	2	0	0	0	0	0	0	0	0	0	.000	.000	.000	-87	0	0	1.000	-0	*88*	*186*	/C	0.0
SCHUSTER, BILL William Charles "Broadway Bill" B 8.4.1912 Buffalo, NY D 6.28.1987 ElMonte, CA BR/TR 5-9/164# d9.29																								
1937	Pit N	3	6	2	3	0	0	0	1	1	0	0	.500	.571	.500	193	1	0	1.000	1	120	216	/S-2	0.2
1939	Bos N	2	3	0	0	0	0	0	0	0	0	1	.000	.000	.000	-99	-1	0	.833	-1	100	0	/S3	-0.1
1943	Chi N	13	51	3	15	2	1	0	0	3	0	2	.294	.333	.373	105	0	0	.977	4	109	165	S-13	0.6
1944	Chi N	60	154	14	34	7	1	1	14	12	0	16	.221	.277	.299	62	-8	4	.946	-1	101	100	S-38/2-6	-0.6
1945	†Chi N	45	47	8	9	2	1	0	2	7	0	4	.191	.296	.277	61	-2	2	.949	4	99	142	S-22/2-3,3	0.2
Total	5	123	261	27	61	11	3	1	17	23	0	23	.234	.296	.310	72	-10	6	.954	7	103	126	/S-76,2-9,3-2	0.3
SCHWARTZ, RANDY Douglas Randall B 2.9.1944 Los Angeles, CA BL/TL 6-3/230# d9.8																								
1965	KC A	6	7	0	2	0	0	0	1	0-0	0	4	.286	.286	.286	64	0	0-0	1.000	1	326	0	/1-2	0.0
1966	KC A	10	11	0	1	0	0	0	1	1-0	0	3	.091	.167	.091	-24	-2	0-0	1.000	-0	0	130	/1-2	-0.2
Total	2	16	18	0	3	0	0	0	2	1-0	0	7	.167	.211	.167	10	-2	0-0	1.000	0	163	65	/1-4	-0.2
SCHWARTZ, BILL William August "Pop" or "Scooper Bill" B 4.3.1864 Jamestown, KY D 12.22.1940 Newport, KY BR/TR 6-1/195# d5.3																								
1883	Col AA	2	4	0	1	0	0	0		0			.250	.250	.250	67	0		.600	-2	0	0	/1C	-0.1
1884	Cin U	29	106	14	25	4	0	1		3			.236	.257	.302	64	-8		.837	-6			C-25/O-3(2-1-1),3	-1.0
Total	2	31	110	14	26	4	0	1		3			.236	.257	.300	64	-8		.828	-7			/C-26,O-3(2-1-1),31	-1.1
SCHWARTZ, BILL William Charles "Blab" B 4.22.1884 Cleveland, OH D 8.29.1961 Nashville, TN BR/TR 6-2/185# d5.2																								
1904	Cle A	24	86	5	13	2	0	0	0	0	0		.151	.151	.174	3	-10	4	.980	-4	36	43	1-22/3	-1.7
SCHWEITZER, AL Albert Caspar "Cheese" B 12.23.1882 Cleveland, OH D 1.27.1969 Newark, OH BR/TR 5-6/170# d4.30																								
1908	StL A	64	182	22	53	4	2	1	14	20	4		.291	.374	.352	135	8	6	.952	6	247	202	O-55(0-28-27)	1.4
1909	StL A	27	76	7	17	2	0	0	2	5	3		.224	.298	.250	79	-2	3	.933	-1	88	0	O-22(6-7-9)	-0.4
1910	StL A	113	379	37	87	11	2	2	37	36	4		.230	.303	.285	90	-4	26	.937	-2	93	106	*O-109(1-32-76)	-1.2
1911	StL A	76	237	31	51	11	4	0	34	43	1		.215	.338	.295	80	-4	12	.934	1	97	118	O-68(9-8-51)	-0.7
Total	4	280	874	97	208	28	8	3	87	104	12		.238	.327	.299	95	-2	47	.940	4	127	122	O-254(16-75-163)	-0.9
SCHWERT, PI Pius Louis B 11.22.1892 Angola, NY D 3.11.1941 Washington, DC BR/TR 5-10.5/160# d8.20																								
1914	NY A	3	6	0	0	0	0	0	0	2	0	3	.000	.250	.000	-24	-1	0	.923	0	*85*	*231*	/C-3	0.0
1915	NY A	9	18	6	5	3	0	0	6	1	0	6	.278	.316	.444	128	1	0	.972	0	*102*	*108*	/C-9	0.1
Total	2	12	24	6	5	3	0	0	6	3	0	9	.208	.296	.333	89	0	0	.959	0	*97*	*142*	/C-12	0.1
SCHWIND, ART Arthur Edwin B 11.4.1889 Ft.Wayne, IN D 1.13.1968 Sullivan, IL BB/TR 5-8/150# d10.3																								
1912	Bos N	1	2	0	1	0	0	0	0	0	0	0	.500	.500	.500	171	0	0	—	-0	0	0	/3	0.0
SCHYPINSKI, JERRY Gerald Albert B 9.16.1931 Detroit, MI BL/TR 5-10/170# d8.31																								
1955	KC A	22	69	7	15	2	0	0	5	1-0	0	6	.217	.229	.246	27	-7	0-0	.932	-2	99	95	S-21/2-2	-0.8
SCIOSCIA, MIKE Michael Lorri B 11.27.1958 Upper Darby, PA BL/TR 6-2/220# d4.20 M4 C2																								
1980	LA N	54	134	8	34	5	1	1	8	12-2	0	9	.254	.313	.328	81	-3	1-0	.992	-1	84	112	C-54	-0.3
1981	†LA N	93	290	27	80	10	0	2	29	36-8	1	18	.276	.353	.331	100	1	0-2	.987	1	114	101	C-91	0.6
1982	LA N	129	365	31	80	11	1	5	38	44-11	1	31	.219	.302	.296	70	-14	2-0	.986	-3	112	88	*C-123	-1.2
1983	LA N	12	35	3	11	3	0	1	7	5-1	0	2	.314	.400	.486	145	2	0-0	1.000	0	277	123	C-11	0.3
1984	LA N	114	341	29	93	18	0	5	38	52-10	1	26	.273	.367	.370	110	7	2-1	.985	15	118	127	*C-112	2.8
1985	†LA N	141	429	47	127	26	3	7	53	77-9	5	21	.296	.407	.420	136	26	3-3	.986	10	138	91	*C-139	4.3
1986	LA N	122	374	36	94	18	1	5	26	62-4	3	23	.251	.359	.345	103	5	3-3	.982	4	125	84	*C-119	1.3
1987	LA N	142	461	44	122	26	1	6	38	55-9	1	23	.265	.343	.364	90	-5	7-4	.989	16	132	104	*C-138	1.6
1988	†LA N	130	408	29	105	18	0	3	35	38-12	0	31	.257	.318	.324	88	-6	0-3	.991	15	132	130	*C-123	1.6
1989	LA N★	133	408	40	102	16	0	10	44	52-14	3	29	.250	.338	.363	102	2	0-2	.988	20	131	107	*C-130	3.0
1990	LA N★	135	435	46	115	25	0	12	66	55-14	3	31	.264	.348	.405	110	8	4-1	.989	8	112	86	*C-132	2.4
1991	LA N	119	345	39	91	16	2	8	40	47-3	3	32	.264	.353	.391	113	7	4-3	.990	5	106	71	*C-115	1.9
1992	LA N	117	348	19	77	6	3	3	24	32-4	1	31	.221	.286	.282	63	-17	3-2	.988	11	88	120	*C-108	0.0
Total	13	1441	4373	398	1131	198	12	68	446	567-101	22	307	.259	.344	.356	99	13	29-24	.988	100	120	101	*C-1395	18.3
SCOFFIC, LOU Louis "Weaser" B 5.20.1913 Herrin, IL D 8.28.1997 Herrin, IL BR/TR 5-10/182# d4.16																								
1936	StL N	4	7	2	3	0	0	0	2	1	0	2	.429	.500	.429	153	1	0	.875	-0	129	0	/O-3(RF)	0.0
SCONIERS, DARYL Daryl Anthony B 10.3.1958 San Bernardino, CA BL/TL 6-2/195# d9.13																								
1981	Cal A	15	52	6	14	1	1	1	7	1-0	0	10	.269	.283	.385	91	-1	0-0	1.000	1	116	124	1-12/D-3	-0.1
1982	Cal A	12	13	0	2	0	0	0	2	2-0	0	1	.154	.267	.154	19	-1	0-0	1.000	-0	82	332	/1-3,D	-0.2
1983	Cal A	106	314	49	86	19	3	8	46	17-2	0	41	.274	.310	.430	102	0	4-2	.986	-6	72	99	1-57,D-27/O(LF)	-0.9
1984	Cal A	57	160	14	39	4	0	4	17	13-2	0	17	.244	.301	.344	78	-5	1-2	.990	-2	90	82	1-41/D	-1.0
1985	Cal A	44	98	14	28	6	1	2	12	15-0	0	18	.286	.371	.429	122	4	2-1	.973	-1	30	57	D-20/1-6	0.2
Total	5	234	637	83	169	30	5	15	84	48-4	0	87	.265	.315	.399	97	-3	7-5	.989	-8	81	98	1-119/D-52,O(LF)	-2.0
SCOTT d7.16																								
1884	Bal U	13	53	10	12	1	1	1		2			.226	.255	.340	71	-4		.909	-1	42	257	O-13(RF)/3	-0.4
SCOTT, TONY Anthony B 9.18.1951 Cincinnati, OH BB/TR 6/175# d9.1 C3																								
1973	Mon N	11	1	2	0	0	0	0	0	0-0	0	1	.000	.000	.000	-97	0	0-0	.000	-1	0	0	/O-3(1-1-1)	-0.1
1974	Mon N	19	7	2	2	0	0	0	0	1-0	0	3	.286	.375	.286	82	0	1-1	1.000	-0	101	0	O-16(2-1-14)	-0.1
1975	Mon N	92	143	19	26	4	2	0	11	12-2	3	38	.182	.258	.238	37	-12	5-6	.962	4	110	194	O-71(45-4-28)	-1.2
1977	StL N	95	292	38	85	16	3	3	41	33-4	3	48	.291	.368	.397	107	4	13-10	.996	5	115	95	O-89(3-82-6)	0.7
1978	StL N	96	219	28	50	5	2	1	14	14-1	2	41	.228	.278	.283	59	-13	5-6	.946	-0	93	166	O-77(38-31-10)	-1.7
1979	StL N	153	587	69	152	22	10	6	68	34-4	5	92	.259	.301	.361	80	-18	37-17	.984	6	107	120	*O-151(0-140-14)	-1.2
1980	StL N	143	415	51	104	19	3	0	28	35-9	1	68	.251	.308	.311	72	-15	22-10	**.997**	1	105	63	*O-134(CF)	-1.5
1981	StL N	45	176	21	40	5	2	2	17	5-0	1	22	.227	.253	.313	58	-10	10-7	1.000	-1	100	63	O-44(CF)	-1.3
	†Hou N	55	225	28	66	13	2	2	22	15-1	0	32	.293	.338	.396	113	3	8-3	.985	-2	92	138	O-55(CF)	0.2
	Year	100	401	49	106	18	4	4	39	20-1	1	54	.264	.301	.359	88	-8	18-10	.992	-3	96	105	O-99(CF)	-1.1
1982	Hou N	132	460	43	110	16	3	1	29	15-4	1	56	.239	.262	.293	61	-26	18-4	.982	-5	95	103	*O-129(2-125-3)	-3.2
1983	Hou N	80	186	20	42	6	1	2	17	11-0	0	39	.226	.264	.301	62	-10	5-4	1.000	-1	99	79	O-61(7-30-28)	-1.3
1984	Hou N	25	21	2	4	1	0	0	0	4-1	0	3	.190	.320	.238	63	-1	0-0	1.000	-0	98	0	/O-6(1-5-0)	-0.1
	Mon N	45	71	8	18	4	0	0	5	7-1	0	21	.254	.316	.310	81	-2	1-1	1.000	-0	91	106	O-17(16-1-2)	-0.2
	Year	70	92	10	22	5	0	0	5	11-2	0	24	.239	.317	.293	78	-2	1-1	1.000	-0	93	83	O-23(17-6-2)	-0.3
Total	11	991	2803	331	699	111	28	17	253	186-27	16	464	.249	.297	.327	75	-100	125-69	.986	6	102	107	O-853(115-653-106)	-11.0
SCOTT, DONNIE Donald Malcolm B 8.16.1961 Dunedin, FL BB/TR 5-11/185# d9.30																								
1983	Tex A	2	4	0	0	0	0	0	0	0-0	0	0	.000	.000	.000	-99	-1	0-0	1.000	1	0	273	/C-2	0.0
1984	Tex A	81	235	16	52	9	0	3	20	20-1	0	44	.221	.280	.298	59	-13	0-1	.974	4	117	100	C-80	-0.7
1985	Sea A	80	185	18	41	13	0	4	23	15-0	0	41	.222	.275	.357	72	-7	1-1	.981	-2	82	125	C-74	-0.7
1991	Cin N	10	19	0	3	0	0	0	0	0-0	0	2	.158	.158	.158	-11	-3	0-0	1.000	-4	49	0	/C-8	-0.7
Total	4	173	443	34	96	22	0	7	43	35-1	0	87	.217	.271	.314	60	-24	1-2	.977	-2	100	108	C-164	-2.1
SCOTT, PETE Floyd John B 12.21.1898 Woodland, CA D 5.3.1953 Daly City, CA BR/TR 5-11.5/175# d4.13																								
1926	Chi N	77	189	34	54	13	1	3	34	22	1	31	.286	.363	.413	107	3	3	.968	2	108	118	O-59(34-0-29)/3	0.1
1927	Chi N	71	156	28	49	18	1	0	21	19	1	18	.314	.392	.442	123	6	1	.986	-1	98	73	O-36(1-1-35)	0.3
1928	Pit N	60	177	33	55	10	4	5	33	18	1	14	.311	.378	.497	122	5	1	.979	3	112	155	O-42(29-0-13)/1-8	0.5
Total	3	208	522	95	158	41	6	8	88	59	3	63	.303	.377	.450	117	14	5	.976	5	107	117	O-137(64-1-77)/1-8,3	0.9

Year	Tm Lg	G	AB	R	H	2B	3B	HR	RBI	BB-IB	HP	SO	AVG	OBP	SLG	AOPS	ABR	SB-CS	FA	FR	Rng	Thr	G at Pos	BFW
SCOTT, GARY Gary Thomas B 8.22.1968 New Rochelle, NY BR/TR 6/175# d4.9																								
1991	Chi N	31	79	8	13	3	0	1	5	13-4	3	14	.165	.305	.241	53	-4	0-1	.969	-1	101	136	3-31	-0.6
1992	Chi N	36	96	8	15	2	0	2	11	5-1	0	14	.156	.198	.240	23	-10	0-1	.922	-4	85	68	3-29/S-2	-1.6
Total	2	67	175	16	28	5	0	3	16	18-5	3	28	.160	.250	.240	38	-14	0-2	.946	-5	93	102	/3-60,S-2	-2.2
SCOTT, GEORGE George Charles "Boomer" B 3.23.1944 Greenville, MS BR/TR 6-2/215# d4.12																								
1966	Bos A★	**162**	601	73	147	18	7	27	90	65-13	8	152	.245	.324	.433	105	4	4-0	.991	-1	98	98	*1-158/3-5	-0.6
1967	†Bos A	159	565	74	171	21	7	19	82	63-10	4	119	.303	.373	.465	136	27	10-8	.987	-8	86	107	*1-152/3-2	1.0
1968	Bos A	124	350	23	60	14	0	3	25	26-3	5	88	.171	.236	.237	42	-24	3-5	.987	-1	95	95	*1-112/3-6	-3.7
1969	Bos A	152	549	63	139	14	5	16	52	61-12	4	74	.253	.331	.384	95	-4	4-3	.954	-8	93	121	*3-109,1-53	-1.7
1970	Bos A	127	480	50	142	24	5	16	63	44-5	2	95	.296	.355	.467	117	11	4-11	.934	-9	80	90	3-68,1-59	-0.6
1971	Bos A	146	537	72	141	16	4	24	78	41-5	5	102	.263	.317	.441	106	3	0-3	.992	-6	82	96	*1-143	-1.8
1972	Mil A	152	578	71	154	24	4	20	88	43-4	4	130	.266	.321	.426	123	14	16-4	.992	-3	92	96	*1-139,3-23	0.3
1973	Mil A	158	604	98	185	30	4	24	107	61-6	2	94	.306	.370	.488	144	35	9-5	.994	3	110	100	*1-157/D	2.6
1974	Mil A	158	604	74	170	36	2	17	82	59-5	3	90	.281	.345	.432	124	19	9-9	**.992**	7	**125**	105	*1-148/D-9	1.4
1975	Mil A★	158	617	86	176	26	4	**36**	**109**	51-7	3	97	.285	.341	.515	139	29	6-5	.989	2	109	92	*1-144,D-12/3-5	1.9
1976	Mil A	156	606	73	166	21	5	18	77	53-6	5	118	.274	.334	.414	122	15	0-1	.991	-1	99	100	*1-155	0.1
1977	Bos A★	157	584	103	157	26	5	33	95	57-4	6	112	.269	.337	.500	112	9	1-1	.985	-3	97	118	*1-157	-0.4
1978	Bos A	120	412	51	96	16	4	12	54	44-3	0	86	.233	.305	.379	83	-10	1-1	.991	-11	68	107	*1-113/D-7	-2.9
1979	Bos A	45	156	18	35	9	1	4	23	17-1	0	22	.224	.299	.372	76	-5	0-0	.986	-4	77	107	1-41	-1.1
	KC A	44	146	19	39	8	2	1	20	12-1	2	32	.267	.329	.370	87	-3	1-1	.989	-3	82	81	1-41/3D	-0.7
	NY A	16	44	9	14	3	1	1	6	2-0	0	7	.318	.340	.500	128	2	1-0	1.000	0	0	0	D-15/1	0.1
	Year	105	346	46	88	20	4	6	49	31-2	2	61	.254	.317	.387	87	-6	2-1	.987	-6	79	95	1-83,D-17/3	-1.7
Total	14	2034	7433	957	1992	306	60	271	1051	699-85	53	1418	.268	.333	.435	113	122	69-57	.990	-45	96	101	*1-1773,3-219/D-46	-6.1
SCOTT, JIM James Walter B 9.22.1888 Shenandoah, PA D 5.12.1972 S.Pasadena, FL BR/TR 5-9.5/165# d4.22																								
1914	Pit F	8	24	2	6	1	0	0	1	5	0	0	.250	.379	.292	85	-1	1	.800	-3	88	150	/S-8	-0.3
SCOTT, JOHN John Henry B 1.24.1952 Jackson, MS BR/TR 6-2/165# d9.7																								
1974	SD N	14	15	3	1	0	0	0	0	0-0	0	4	.067	.067	.067	-65	-3	1-0	1.000	1	86	361	/O-8(5-2-1)	-0.3
1975	SD N	25	9	6	0	0	0	0	0	0-0	0	2	.000	.000	.000	-99	-3	2-0	—	-0	0	0	/O(CF)	-0.2
1977	Tor A	79	233	26	56	9	0	2	15	8-0	0	39	.240	.266	.305	54	-15	10-8	.963	-4	90	72	O-67(27-41-0)/D-2	-2.1
Total	3	118	257	35	57	9	0	2	15	8-0	0	45	.222	.245	.280	43	-21	13-8	.965	-3	89	91	/O-76(32-44-1),D-2	-2.6
SCOTT, LE GRANT Le Grant Edward B 7.25.1910 Cleveland, OH D 11.12.1993 Birmingham, AL BL/TL 5-8.5/170# d4.19																								
1939	Phi N	76	232	31	65	15	1	1	26	22	0	14	.280	.343	.366	93	-2	5	.959	1	99	139	O-55(1-1-54)	-0.4
SCOTT, EVERETT Lewis Everett "Deacon" B 11.19.1892 Bluffton, IN D 11.2.1960 Fort Wayne, IN BR/TR 5-8/148# d4.14																								
1914	Bos A	144	539	66	129	15	6	2	37	32	3	43	.239	.286	.301	76	-18	9-14	.949	-11	95	106	*S-143	-2.4
1915	†Bos A	100	359	25	72	11	0	0	28	17	0	21	.201	.237	.231	41	-27	4-7	.961	0	99	96	*S-100	-2.3
1916	†Bos A	123	366	37	85	19	2	0	27	23	3	24	.232	.283	.295	73	-13	8	**.967**	5	102	96	*S-121/23	0.0
1917	Bos A	**157**	528	40	127	24	7	0	50	20	0	46	.241	.268	.313	78	-17	12	**.953**	8	103	105	*S-157	0.3
1918	†Bos A	**126**	443	40	98	11	5	0	43	12	0	16	.221	.242	.269	55	-27	11	**.976**	21	108	79	*S-126	0.2
1919	Bos A	**138**	507	41	141	19	0	0	38	19	1	26	.278	.306	.316	79	-16	8	**.976**	11	104	128	*S-138	0.4
1920	Bos A	**154**	569	41	153	21	12	4	61	21	4	15	.269	.300	.369	80	-20	4-11	**.973**	14	102	112	*S-154	0.1
1921	Bos A	**154**	576	65	151	21	9	1	62	27	0	21	.262	.295	.335	62	-36	5-9	**.972**	**41**	110	**135**	*S-154	1.9
1922	†NY A	**154**	557	64	150	23	5	3	45	23	5	22	.269	.304	.345	67	-28	2-3	**.966**	17	107	104	*S-154	0.5
1923	†NY A	**152**	533	48	131	16	4	6	60	13	2	19	.246	.266	.325	54	-39	1-3	**.961**	-13	95	99	*S-152	-3.6
1924	NY A	**153**	548	56	137	12	6	4	64	21	0	15	.250	.278	.316	53	-42	3-7	.966	10	99	110	*S-153	-1.6
1925	NY A	22	60	3	13	0	0	0	4	2	0	2	.217	.242	.217	17	-8	0-1	.988	2	92	173	S-18	-0.4
	Was A	33	103	10	28	6	1	0	18	4	0	4	.272	.299	.350	65	-6	1-2	.932	-1	95	112	S-30/3-2	-0.4
	Year	55	163	13	41	6	1	0	22	6	0	6	.252	.278	.301	48	-14	1-3	.952	1	94	134	S-48/3-2	-0.8
1926	Chi A	40	143	15	36	10	1	0	13	9	0	8	.252	.296	.336	67	-7	1-3	.955	5	111	105	S-39	0.0
	Cin N	4	6	1	4	0	0	0	1	0	0	0	.667	.667	.667	267	1	0	.875	-1	77	0	/S-4	0.1
Total	13	1654	5837	552	1455	208	58	20	551	243	18	282	.249	.281	.315	65	-303	69-60	.965	108	102	108	*S-1643/3-3,2	-7.2
SCOTT, MILT Milton Parker "Mikado Milt" B 1.17.1866 Chicago, IL D 11.3.1938 Baltimore, MD BR 5-9/160# d9.30																								
1882	Chi N	1	5	1	2	0	0	0	0	0		0	.400	.400	.400	150	0		1.000	0	0	0	/1	0.0
1884	Det N	110	438	29	108	17	5	3	50	9		62	.247	.262	.329	90	-5		.968	-1	82	68	*1-110	-1.4
1885	Det N	38	148	14	39	7	0	0	12	4		16	.264	.283	.311	92	-1		.967	2	136	82	1-38	-0.3
	Pit AA	55	210	15	52	7	1	0	18	5	2		.248	.272	.290	79	-5		.986	3	108	106	1-55	-0.7
1886	Bal AA	137	484	48	92	11	4	2	52	22	9		.190	.239	.242	52	-27	11	.974	8	**137**	57	*1-137/P	-2.7
Total	4	341	1285	107	293	42	10	5	132	40	11	78	.228	.257	.288	74	-38	11	.973	12	114	71	1-341/P	-5.1
SCOTT, DICKIE Richard Edward B 7.19.1962 Ellsworth, ME BR/TR 6-1/170# d5.19																								
1989	Oak A	3	2	0	0	0	0	0	1	0-0	0	0	.000	.000	.000	-99	-1	0-0	—	-0	0	0	/S-3	-0.1
SCOTT, RODNEY Rodney Darrell B 10.16.1953 Indianapolis, IN BB/TR (BR 1975) 6/160# d4.11 OF Total (10-CF 1-RF)																								
1975	KC A	48	15	13	1	0	0	0	0	1-0	0	3	.067	.125	.067	-43	-3	4-2	1.000	-2	39	88	D-22/2-9,S-8,R	-0.5
1976	Mon N	7	10	3	4	0	0	0	0	1-0	0	1	.400	.455	.400	138	1	2-0	1.000	-1	63	86	/2-6,S-3	0.0
1977	Oak A	133	364	56	95	4	4	0	20	43-0	3	50	.261	.342	.294	77	-11	33-18	.963	-10	96	75	2-71,S-70/3-5,O(RF)D	-1.2
1978	Chi N	78	227	41	64	5	1	0	15	43-0	3	41	.282	.403	.313	91	0	27-10	.929	-3	102	176	3-59,O-10(CF)/2-6,S-6	-0.1
1979	Mon N	151	562	69	134	12	5	3	42	66-2	2	82	.238	.319	.294	69	-23	39-12	.980	-5	102	105	*2-113,S-39	-1.4
1980	Mon N	154	567	84	127	13	**13**	0	46	70-0	1	75	.224	.307	.293	69	-23	63-13	.982	-8	96	92	*2-129,S-21	-1.4
1981	†Mon N	95	336	43	69	9	3	0	26	50-0	1	35	.205	.308	.250	60	-16	30-7	.983	-12	94	79	2-93	-2.1
1982	Mon N	14	25	2	5	0	0	0	1	3-0	0	2	.200	.286	.200	37	-2	5-0	.971	-2	74	74	2-12	-0.3
	NY A	10	26	5	5	0	0	0	0	4-0	0	2	.192	.300	.192	39	-2	2-0	.963	-0	100	159	/S-6,2-4	-0.1
Total	8	690	2132	316	504	43	26	3	150	281-2	10	291	.236	.326	.285	71	-79	205-62	.979	-42	96	88	2-443,S-153/3-64,D-23,O-11C	-7.1
SCRANTON, JIM James Dean B 4.5.1960 Torrance, CA BR/TR 6/175# d9.5																								
1984	KC A	2	2	0	0	0	0	0	0	0-0	0	0	.000	.000	.000	-99	-1	0-0	1.000	0	142	753	/S3	0.0
1985	KC A	6	4	1	0	0	0	0	0	0-0	0	0	.000	.000	.000	-99	-1	0-0	1.000	1	148	89	/S-5	0.0
Total	2	8	6	1	0	0	0	0	0	0-0	0	0	.000	.000	.000	-99	-2	0-0	1.000	1	147	163	/S-6,3	0.0
SCRIVENER, CHUCK Wayne Allison B 10.3.1947 Alexandria, VA BR/TR 5-9/170# d9.18																								
1975	Det A	4	16	0	4	1	0	0	0	0-0	0	1	.250	.250	.313	56	-1	1-0	1.000	-1	81	0	/3-3,S-2	-0.2
1976	Det A	80	222	28	49	7	1	2	16	19-0	0	34	.221	.282	.288	65	-10	1-0	.976	13	116	89	2-43,S-37/3-5	1.0
1977	Det A	61	72	10	6	0	0	0	2	5-0	0	9	.083	.143	.083	-35	-14	0-0	.981	0	98	102	S-50/2-8,3-3	-1.1
Total	3	145	310	38	59	8	1	2	18	24-0	0	44	.190	.249	.242	40	-25	2-0	.970	12	103	116	/S-89,2-51,3-11	-0.3
SCRUGGS, TONY Anthony Raymond B 3.19.1966 Riverside, CA BR/TR 6-1/210# d4.8																								
1991	Tex A	5	6	1	0	0	0	0	0	0-0	0	1	.000	.000	.000	-99	-2	0-0	1.000	0	111	0	/O-5(5-1-0)	-0.2
SCUTARO, MARCOS Marcos B 10.30.1975 San Felipe, Venezuela BR/TR 5-10/170# d7.21																								
2002	NY N	27	36	2	8	0	1	1	6	0-0	0	11	.222	.216	.361	55	-3	0-1	1.000	-2	84	0	2-12/S-6,3-3,O(LF)	-0.5
2003	NY N	48	75	10	16	4	0	2	6	13-2	1	14	.213	.333	.347	82	-2	2-0	.981	-5	83	81	2-39/S	-0.5
Total	2	75	111	12	24	4	1	3	12	13-2	1	25	.216	.299	.351	74	-5	2-1	.983	-7	83	71	/2-51,S-7,3-3,O(LF)	-1.0
SEABOL, SCOTT Scott Anthony B 5.17.1975 McKeesport, PA BR/TR 6-4/200# d4.8																								
2001	NY A	1	1	0	0	0	0	0	0	0-0	0	0	.000	.000	.000	-99	0	0-0	—	0			/D	0.0
SEARS, KEN Kenneth Eugene "Ziggy" B 7.6.1917 Streator, IL D 7.17.1968 Bridgeport, TX BL/TR 6-1/200# d5.2 Mil 1944-45																								
1943	NY A	60	187	22	52	7	0	2	22	11	3	18	.278	.328	.348	97	-1	1-3	.974	2	*177*	*96*	C-50	0.4
1946	StL A	7	15	1	5	0	0	0	1	3	0	0	.333	.444	.333	114	1	0-0	1.000	-2	*54*	*0*	/C-4	-0.1
Total	2	67	202	23	57	7	0	2	23	14	3	18	.282	.338	.347	99	0	1-3	.975	1	*170*	*90*	/C-54	0.3
SEARS, TODD Todd Andrew B 10.23.1975 Des Moines, IA BL/TR 6-5/215# d9.17																								
2002	Min A	7	12	2	4	2	0	0	0	0-0	0	1	.333	.333	.500	116	0	0-0	1.000	0	102	128	/1-6	0.0

Year	Tm Lg	G	AB	R	H	2B	3B	HR	RBI	BB-IB	HP	SO	AVG	OBP	SLG	AOPS	ABR	SB-CS	FA	FR	Rng	Thr	G at Pos	BFW
2003	Min A	24	65	7	16	2	0	2	11	7-0	1	15	.246	.324	.369	83	-2	0-0	.990	-0	96	81	1-14/D-6	-0.3
	SD N	9	8	2	2	1	0	0	0	0-0	0	3	.250	.250	.375	66	0	0-0	1.000	0	0	1013	/1	0.0
Total	2	40	85	11	22	5	0	2	11	7-0	1	19	.259	.319	.388	86	-2	0-0	.992	-0	97	99	/1-21,D-6	-0.3
SEBRING, JIMMY James Dennison B 3.22.1882 Liberty, PA D 12.22.1909 Williamsport, PA BL/TR 6/180# d9.8																								
1902	Pit N	19	80	15	26	4	4	0	15	5	0		.325	.365	.475	154	4	2	.974	2	173	312	O-19(RF)	0.6
1903	†Pit N	124	506	71	140	16	13	4	64	32	4		.277	.325	.383	98	-4	20	.927	5	114	**279**	*O-124(RF)	-0.4
1904	Pit N	80	305	28	82	11	7	0	32	17	0		.269	.307	.351	100	-1	8	.959	6	150	162	O-80(RF)	0.2
	Cin N	56	222	22	50	9	2	0	24	14	0		.225	.271	.284	65	-9	8	1.000	4	159	158	O-56(RF)	-0.8
	Year	136	527	50	132	20	9	0	56	31	0		.250	.292	.323	85	-10	16	.974	10	**154**	160	*O-136(RF)	-0.6
1905	Cin N	58	217	31	62	10	5	2	28	14	0		.286	.329	.406	107	1	11	.885	-4	90	116	O-56(RF)	-0.6
1909	Bro N	25	81	11	8	1	1	0	5	11	0		.099	.207	.136	7	-9	3	.951	0	144	150	O-25(0-21-4)	-1.1
	Was A	1	0	0	0	0	0	0	0	0	0		—	—	—	—	0	0	—	-0	0	0	/O(CF)	0.0
Total	5	363	1411	178	368	51	32	6	168	93	4		.261	.308	.355	93	-18	52	.945	13	131	204	O-361(0-22-339)	-2.1
SECORY, FRANK Frank Edward B 8.24.1912 Mason City, IA D 4.7.1995 Port Huron, MI BR/TR 6-1/200# d4.28 U19																								
1940	Det A	1	1	0	0	0	0	0	0	0	0	1	.000	.000	.000	-91	0	0-0	—	0			H	0.0
1942	Cin N	2	5	1	0	0	0	0	1	3	0	2	.000	.375	.000	14	0	0	.857	-0	106	0	/O-2(LF)	-0.1
1944	Chi N	22	56	10	18	1	0	4	17	6	0	8	.321	.387	.554	163	4	1	1.000	-0	112	0	O-17(17-1-0)	0.3
1945	†Chi N	35	57	4	9	1	0	0	6	2	0	7	.158	.186	.175	1	-8	0	1.000	-0	104	0	O-12(10-0-2)	-0.9
1946	Chi N	33	43	6	10	3	0	3	12	6	0	6	.233	.327	.512	139	2	0	.833	-1	84	0	/O-9(LF)	0.0
Total	5	93	162	21	37	5	0	7	36	17	0	24	.228	.302	.389	95	-2	1-0	.964	-2	105	0	/O-40(38-1-2)	-0.7
SEE, CHARLIE Charles Henry "Chad" B 10.13.1896 Pleasantville, NY D 7.19.1948 Bridgeport, CT BL/TR 5-10.5/175# d8.6																								
1919	Cin N	8	14	1	4	0	0	0	1	1	0	0	.286	.333	.286	89	0	0	.833	-1	90	0	/O-4(2-2-0)	-0.1
1920	Cin N	47	82	9	25	4	0	0	15	1	2	7	.305	.329	.354	97	0	2-4	1.000	3	125	130	O-17(0-14-4)/P	0.1
1921	Cin N	37	106	11	26	5	1	1	7	7	1	5	.245	.298	.340	72	-4	3-2	.954	0	101	108	O-30(0-11-18)	-0.6
Total	3	92	202	21	55	9	1	1	23	9	3	12	.272	.313	.342	83	-4	5-6	.967	3	109	110	/O-51(2-27-22),P	-0.6
SEE, LARRY Ralph Laurence B 6.20.1960 Norwalk, CA BR/TR 6-1/195# d9.3																								
1986	LA N	13	20	1	5	2	0	0	2	2-0	0	7	.250	.318	.350	90	0	0-0	.979	1	171	76	/1-9	0.0
1988	Tex A	13	23	0	3	0	0	0	0	1-0	0	8	.130	.167	.130	-15	-4	0-0	1.000	-1	0	0	/C-2,1-2/3D	-0.4
Total	2	26	43	1	8	2	0	0	2	3-0	0	15	.186	.239	.233	32	-4	0-0	.967	0	178	109	/1-11,D-7,C-2,3	-0.4
SEEDS, BOB Ira Robert "Suitcase Bob" B 2.24.1907 Ringgold, TX D 10.28.1993 Erick, OK BR/TR 6/180# d4.19																								
1930	Cle A	85	277	37	79	11	3	3	32	12	0	22	.285	.315	.379	72	-12	1-3	.953	1	102	117	O-70(48-21-1)	-1.6
1931	Cle A	48	134	26	41	4	1	1	10	11	0	11	.306	.359	.373	88	-2	1-0	.966	-1	98	37	O-33(3-1-29)/1-2	-0.4
1932	Cle A	2	4	0	0	0	0	0	0	0	0	0	.000	.000	.000	-94	-1	0-0	—	-0	0	0	/O(RF)	-0.1
	Chi A	116	434	53	126	18	6	2	45	31	3	37	.290	.342	.373	91	-6	5-7	.964	-4	96	82	*O-112(34-34-53)	-1.5
	Year	118	438	53	126	18	6	2	45	31	3	37	.288	.339	.370	89	-8	5-7	.964	-4	96	82	*O-113(34-34-54)	-1.6
1933	Bos A	82	230	26	56	13	4	0	23	21	1	20	.243	.310	.335	71	-10	1-3	.985	0	89	107	1-41,O-32(17-0-16)	-1.4
1934	Bos A	8	6	0	1	0	0	0	1	0	0	1	.167	.167	.167	-13	-1	0-0	—	-0	0	0	/O(RF)	-0.1
	Cle A	61	186	28	46	8	1	0	18	21	1	13	.247	.327	.301	62	-10	2-1	.977	-2	93	56	O-48(26-2-21)	-1.4
	Year	69	192	28	47	8	1	0	19	21	1	14	.245	.322	.297	59	-11	2-1	.977	-3	93	56	O-49(26-2-22)	-1.5
1936	†NY A	13	42	12	11	1	0	4	10	5	0	3	.262	.340	.571	126	1	3-1	1.000	1	115	125	/O-9(1-0-8),3-3	0.1
1938	NY N	81	296	35	86	12	3	9	52	20	1	33	.291	.338	.443	112	4	0	.987	-4	87	100	O-76(37-40-1)	-0.3
1939	NY N	63	173	33	46	5	1	5	26	22	1	31	.266	.352	.393	99	0	1	.975	-4	81	66	O-50(12-38-0)	-0.6
1940	NY N	56	155	18	45	5	2	4	16	17	3	19	.290	.371	.426	118	4	0	.985	-2	82	116	O-40(16-24-0)	0.1
Total	9	615	1937	268	537	77	21	28	233	160	10	190	.277	.336	.382	89	-33	14-15	.970	-16	93	93	O-472(194-160-131)/1-43,3-3	-7.2
SEEREY, PAT James Patrick B 3.17.1923 Wilburton, OK D 4.28.1986 Jennings, MO BR/TR 5-10/200# d6.9																								
1943	Cle A	26	72	8	16	3	0	1	5	4	0	19	.222	.263	.306	70	-3	0-0	.974	1	99	235	O-16(LF)	-0.3
1944	Cle A	101	342	39	80	16	0	15	39	19	1	99	.234	.276	.412	99	-3	0-2	.986	1	100	109	O-86(63-19-4)	-0.7
1945	Cle A	126	414	56	98	22	2	14	56	66	0	97	.237	.342	.401	120	12	1-2	.975	-4	97	69	*O-117(38-28-68)	0.1
1946	Cle A	117	404	57	91	17	2	26	62	65	1	101	.225	.334	.470	131	16	2-3	.981	-2	103	50	*O-115(39-40-43)	0.9
1947	Cle A	82	216	24	37	4	1	11	29	34	0	66	.171	.284	.352	78	-7	0-1	.957	-1	85	181	O-68(53-1-16)	-1.3
1948	Cle A	10	23	7	6	0	0	1	6	7	0	8	.261	.433	.391	123	1	0-0	1.000	-1	62	0	/O-7(RF)	0.0
	Chi A	95	340	44	78	11	0	18	64	61	0	94	.229	.347	.421	107	3	0-0	.981	0	93	130	O-93(82-12-0)	-0.3
	Year	105	363	51	84	11	0	19	70	68	0	102	.231	.353	.419	108	4	0-0	.982	-1	92	124	*O-100(82-12-7)	-0.3
1949	Chi A	4	4	1	0	0	0	0	0	3	0	1	.000	.429	.000	19	0	0-0	1.000	-0	61	0	/O-2(RF)	0.0
Total	7	561	1815	236	406	73	5	86	261	259	2	485	.224	.321	.412	109	19	3-8	.978	-5	96	101	O-504(291-100-140)	-1.6
SEERY, EMMETT John Emmett B 2.13.1861 Princeville, IL D 8.7.1930 Saranac Lake, NY BL/TR 5-7/145# d4.17 OF Total (778-LF 2-CF 138-RF)																								
1884	Bal U	**105**	463	113	144	25	7	2		20			.311	.340	.408	114	-6		.828	3	96	68	*O-103(99-0-5)/C-3,3-2	-0.4
	KC U	1	4	2	2	1	0	0		1			.500	.600	.750	353	1		—	-0	0	0	/O(LF)	0.1
	Year	106	467	115	146	26	7	2		21			.313	.342	.411	116	-5		.828	3	96	68	*O-104(100-0-5)/C-3,3-2	-0.3
1885	StL N	59	216	20	35	7	0	1	14	16		37	.162	.220	.208	42	-13		.874	4	139	63	O-59(49-0-10)/3	-1.0
1886	StL N	**126**	453	73	108	22	6	2	48	57		82	.238	.324	.327	105	7	24	.883	-4	82	51	*O-126(LF)/P-2	0.0
1887	Ind N	122	465	104	104	18	15	4	28	71	4	68	.224	.331	.353	93	-2	48	.891	7	114	45	*O-122(122-1-1)/S	0.1
1888	Ind N	133	500	87	110	20	10	5	50	64	6	73	.220	.316	.330	104	5	80	.939	9	87	126	*O-133(LF)/S	1.1
1889	Ind N	127	526	123	165	26	12	8	59	67	10	59	.314	.401	.454	136	26	19	.909	2	83	88	*O-127(LF)	2.2
1890	Bro P	104	394	78	88	12	7	1	50	70	5	36	.223	.348	.297	69	-17	44	.894	6	105	71	*O-104(LF)	-1.1
1891	Cin AA	97	372	77	106	15	10	4	36	81	8	52	.285	.423	.411	128	17	19	.898	1	98	77	*O-97(17-1-80)	1.4
1892	Lou N	42	154	18	31	6	1	0	15	24	0	19	.201	.309	.253	76	-3	6	.962	4	147	71	O-42(RF)	-0.1
Total	9	916	3547	695	893	152	68	27	300	471	33	426	.252	.345	.356	104	15	240	.896	31	100	75	O-914L/3-3,C-3,S-2,P-2	2.3
SEFCIK, KEVIN Kevin John B 2.10.1971 Tinley Park, IL BR/TR 5-11/175# d9.8 OF Total (91-LF 47-CF 46-RF)																								
1995	Phi N	5	4	1	0	0	0	0	0	0-0	0	2	.000	.000	.000	-99	-1	0-0	1.000	0	86	1057	/3-2	-0.1
1996	Phi N	44	116	10	33	5	3	0	9	9-3	2	16	.284	.341	.379	90	-2	3-0	.986	-2	109	101	S-21,3-20/2	-0.2
1997	Phi N	61	119	11	32	3	0	2	6	4-0	1	9	.269	.298	.345	68	-6	1-2	.961	-4	97	59	2-22,S-10/3-4	-0.9
1998	Phi N	104	169	27	53	7	2	3	20	25-0	7	32	.314	.421	.432	124	8	4-2	.989	1	114	39	O-60(35-8-20)/3-2,2	0.7
1999	Phi N	111	209	28	58	15	3	1	11	29-0	1	24	.278	.368	.392	90	-2	9-4	.986	-4	90	46	O-64(31-19-17),2-15	-0.6
2000	Phi N	99	153	15	36	6	2	0	10	13-0	2	19	.235	.300	.301	53	-11	4-2	1.000	1	116	0	O-50(25-20-9)/D	-1.0
2001	Col N	1	1	0	0	0	0	0	0	0-0	0	0	.000	.000	.000	-82	0	0-0	—	0			/H	0.0
Total	7	425	771	92	212	36	10	6	56	80-3	13	102	.275	.351	.371	86	-14	21-10	.991	-7	106	30	O-174L/2-39,S-31,3-28,D	-2.1
SEGRIST, KAL Kal Hill B 4.14.1931 Greenville, TX BR/TR 6/180# d7.16																								
1952	NY A	13	23	3	1	0	0	0	1	3	0	1	.043	.154	.043	-46	-5	0-0	.971	0	107	115	2-11/3	-0.4
1955	Bal A	7	9	1	3	0	0	0	0	2-0	0	0	.333	.455	.333	123	0	0-0	1.000	0	162	0	/3-3,12	0.1
Total	2	20	32	4	4	0	0	0	1	5-0	0	1	.125	.243	.125	4	-5	0-0	.971	1	109	111	/2-12,3-4,1	-0.3
SEGUI, DAVID David Vincent B 7.19.1966 Kansas City, KS BB/TL 6-1/202# d5.8 f-Diego																								
1990	Bal A	40	123	14	30	7	0	2	15	11-2	1	15	.244	.311	.350	87	-2	0-0	.990	0	105	85	1-36/D-4	-0.5
1991	Bal A	86	212	15	59	7	0	2	22	12-2	0	19	.278	.316	.340	85	-5	1-1	.996	1	125	104	1-42,O-33(28-0-5)/D-4	-0.6
1992	Bal A	115	189	21	44	9	0	1	17	20-3	0	23	.233	.306	.296	68	-8	1-0	.998	1	104	117	1-95,O-18(3-0-15)	-1.0
1993	Bal A	146	450	54	123	27	0	10	60	58-4	0	53	.273	.351	.400	99	1	2-1	.996	4	109	111	*1-144/D	-0.8
1994	NY N	92	336	46	81	17	1	10	43	33-6	1	43	.241	.308	.387	81	-10	0-0	**.996**	-4	95	**115**	1-78,O-21(19-0-2)	-2.1
1995	NY N	33	73	9	24	3	1	2	11	12-1	1	9	.329	.420	.479	144	5	1-3	1.000	-2	57	224	O-18(LF)/1-7	0.2
	Mon N	97	383	59	117	22	3	10	57	28-4	2	38	.305	.355	.457	109	5	1-4	.997	3	109	92	1-97/O-2(LF)	-0.2
	Year	130	456	68	141	25	4	12	68	40-5	3	47	.309	.367	.461	115	10	2-7	.997	2	107	93	*1-104,O-20(LF)	0.0
1996	Mon N	115	416	69	119	30	1	11	58	60-4	0	54	.286	.375	.442	112	10	4-4	.993	7	**119**	94	*1-113	0.5
1997	Mon N	125	459	75	141	22	3	21	68	57-12	1	66	.307	.380	.505	131	21	1-0	.995	-1	96	111	*1-125	0.9
1998	Sea A	143	522	79	159	36	1	19	84	49-4	0	80	.305	.359	.487	119	15	3-1	**.999**	17	**145**	98	*1-134/O(LF)	1.9
1999	Sea A	90	345	43	101	22	3	9	39	32-4	1	43	.293	.352	.452	106	3	1-2	.996	6	130	102	1-90	0.1
	Tor A	31	95	14	30	5	0	5	13	8-0	0	17	.316	.365	.526	123	3	0-0	.955	-0	111	108	D-25/1-4	0.1
	Year	121	440	57	131	27	3	14	52	40-4	1	60	.298	.355	.468	110	6	1-2	.995	6	129	102	1-94,D-25	0.2

Year	Tm Lg	G	AB	R	H	2B	3B	HR	RBI	BB-IB	HP	SO	AVG	OBP	SLG	AOPS	ABR	SB-CS	FA	FR	Rng	Thr	G at Pos	BFW
2000	Tex A	93	351	52	118	29	1	11	57	34-1	0	51	.336	.391	.519	127	15	0-1	1.000	2	121	99	D-52,1-38	0.9
	Cle A	57	223	41	74	13	0	8	46	19-1	1	33	.332	.384	.498	119	7	0-0	1.000	4	148	68	1-35,D-16/O-7(RF)	0.5
	Year	150	574	93	192	42	1	19	103	53-2	1	84	.334	.388	.510	124	22	0-1	1.000	6	134	84	1-73,D-68/O-7(RF)	1.4
2001	Bal A	82	292	48	88	18	1	10	46	49-5	4	61	.301	.406	.473	139	19	1-1	.983	-6	74	93	1-65,D-16	0.6
2002	Bal A	26	95	10	25	4	0	2	16	11-0	0	22	.263	.336	.368	93	-1	0-0	1.000	0	110	225	D-19/1-7	-0.2
2003	Bal A	67	224	26	59	10	1	5	25	26-2	1	47	.263	.341	.384	95	-1	1-0	1.000	1	130	121	D-53/1-8	-0.4
Total	14	1438	4788	675	1392	281	16	138	677	519-55	13	674	.291	.359	.443	110	77	17-18	.995	35	114	102	*1-1118,D-190,O-100(71-0-29)	-0.1
SEGUIGNOL, FERNANDO Fernando Alfredo B 1.19.1975 Bocas Del Toro, Panama BB/TR 6-5/190# d9.5																								
1998	Mon N	16	42	6	11	4	0	2	3	3-0	0	15	.262	.304	.500	111	1	0-0	1.000	3	189	0	/O-9(8-0-1),1-7	0.2
1999	Mon N	35	105	14	27	9	0	5	10	5-1	7	33	.257	.328	.486	107	1	0-0	.989	-2	79	121	1-23/O-8(6-0-3)	-0.3
2000	Mon N	76	162	22	45	8	0	10	22	9-0	3	46	.278	.326	.512	105	0	0-1	.987	-3	87	103	1-30,O-30(17-0-14)/D	-0.5
2001	Mon N	46	50	0	7	2	0	0	5	2-1	1	17	.140	.185	.180	-4	-8	0-0	1.000	1	100	356	O-13(7-0-7)/1-7	-0.7
2003	NY A	5	7	0	1	0	0	0	0	1-0	0	3	.143	.250	.143	8	-1	0-0	1.000	1	290	0	/1-3,D	0.0
Total	5	178	366	42	91	23	0	17	40	20-2	11	114	.249	.303	.451	89	-7	0-1	.986	-1	101	106	/1-70,O-60(38-0-25),D-2	-1.3
SEIBERT, KURT Kurt Elliott B 10.16.1955 Cheverly, MD BB/TR 6/165# d9.3																								
1979	Chi N	7	2	2	0	0	0	0	0	0-0	0	1	.000	.000	.000	-91	-1	0-0	1.000	0	0	0	/2	-0.1
SEIBOLD, SOCKS Harry B 4.3.1896 Philadelphia, PA D 9.21.1965 Philadelphia, PA BR/TR 5-8.5/162# d9.18 Mil 1918 ▲																								
1915	Phi A	10	26	3	3	1	0	0	2	4	0	4	.115	.233	.154	16	-3	0	.714	-4	94	33	/S-7	-0.6
1916	Phi A	5	12	0	2	1	0	0	1	0	0	4	.167	.167	.250	26	-1	0	1.000	1	160	0	/P-3,O(CF)	0.1
1917	Phi A	36	59	6	13	1	1	0	5	4	1	8	.220	.281	.271	70	-2	1	.978	-1	89	111	P-33/O-2(LF)	-0.1
1919	Phi A	15	13	1	2	0	0	0	1	0	0	4	.154	.154	.154	-13	-1	0	.941	0	90	159	P-14	0.0
1929	Bos N	33	70	6	20	2	0	0	9	6	0	6	.286	.342	.314	67	5	0	**1.000**	-1	87	107	P-33	0.0
1930	Bos N	36	90	6	19	2	0	1	5	6	0	6	.211	.260	.267	29	0	0	.941	-3	75	88	P-36	0.0
1931	Bos N	33	70	3	9	0	0	0	2	1	0	9	.129	.141	.129	-28	-4	0	**1.000**	-0	102	183	P-33	0.0
1932	Bos N	28	46	2	7	0	0	0	2	2	0	0	.152	.188	.152	-8	-2	0	1.000	2	123	235	P-28	0.0
1933	Bos N	11	9	0	1	0	0	0	0	2	0	2	.111	.273	.111	14	0	0	1.000	0	123	0	P-11	0.0
Total	9	207	395	27	76	7	1	1	27	25	1	43	.192	.242	.223	25	-8	1	.982	-5	95	131	P-191/S-7,O-3(2-1-0)	-0.6
SEILHEIMER, RICKY Ricky Allen B 8.30.1960 Brenham, TX BL/TR 5-11/185# d7.5																								
1980	Chi A	21	52	4	11	3	1	1	3	4-1	0	15	.212	.268	.365	72	-2	1-0	.946	-8	40	71	C-21	-0.9
SEITZER, KEVIN Kevin Lee B 3.26.1962 Springfield, IL BR/TR 5-11/190# d9.3 OF Total (14-LF 1-CF 1-RF)																								
1986	KC A	28	96	16	31	4	1	2	11	19-0	1	14	.323	.440	.448	140	7	0-0	.987	1	102	94	1-22/O-5(LF),3-3	0.5
1987	KC A★	161	641	105	**207**	33	8	15	83	80-0	2	85	.323	.399	.470	126	27	12-7	.947	10	105	120	*3-141,1-25/O-3(LF),D	3.2
1988	KC A	149	559	90	170	32	5	5	60	72-4	6	64	.304	.387	.406	122	20	10-8	.938	4	104	135	*3-147/O(LF)D	2.3
1989	KC A	160	597	78	168	17	2	4	48	102-7	5	76	.281	.387	.337	107	12	17-8	.950	-3	95	111	*3-159/S-6,O-3(2-1-0),1-2	1.0
1990	KC A	158	622	91	171	31	5	6	38	67-2	2	66	.275	.346	.370	102	3	7-5	.953	7	101	113	*3-152,2-10	1.0
1991	KC A	85	234	28	62	11	3	1	25	29-3	2	21	.265	.350	.350	94	-1	4-1	.940	6	115	69	3-68/D-3	0.6
1992	Mil A	148	540	74	146	35	1	5	71	57-4	2	44	.270	.337	.367	101	2	13-11	**.969**	-5	100	81	*3-146/2-2,1	-0.3
1993	Oak A	73	255	24	65	10	2	4	27	27-1	1	33	.255	.324	.357	90	-4	4-7	.933	-6	85	71	3-46,1-24/O-3(LF),2-2,PDS	-1.3
	Mil A	47	162	21	47	6	0	7	30	17-0	1	15	.290	.359	.457	120	4	3-0	.942	-1	100	124	3-33/1-7,2O(RF)D	0.4
	Year	120	417	45	112	16	2	11	57	44-1	2	48	.269	.338	.396	102	1	7-7	.937	-7	91	93	3-79,1-31/D-6,O-4(3-0-1),2-3,PS	-0.9
1994	Mil A	80	309	44	97	24	2	5	49	30-1	2	38	.314	.375	.453	108	5	2-1	.924	-1	99	95	3-43,1-35/D-4	0.1
1995	Mil A★	132	492	56	153	33	3	5	69	64-2	6	57	.311	.395	.421	107	8	2-0	.968	4	114	128	3-88,1-36,D-14	0.9
1996	Mil A	132	490	74	155	25	3	12	62	73-6	4	68	.316	.406	.453	113	13	6-1	.996	2	118	102	1-65,D-56,3-12	0.6
	†Cle A	22	83	11	32	10	0	1	16	14-1	1	11	.386	.480	.542	159	9	0-0	1.000	2	252	24	D-17/1-5	0.9
	Year	154	573	85	187	35	3	13	78	87-7	5	79	.326	.416	.466	120	22	6-1	.995	4	128	96	D-73,1-70,3-12	1.5
1997	†Cle A	64	198	27	53	14	0	2	24	18-0	0	25	.268	.326	.369	79	-6	0-0	1.000	1	112	118	D-24,1-19,3-13	-0.7
Total	12	1439	5278	739	1557	285	35	74	613	669-31	35	617	.295	.375	.404	110	99	80-49	.949	21	102	107	*3-1051,1-241,D-126/O-16L,2SP	9.2
SELBACH, KIP Albert Karl B 3.24.1872 Columbus, OH D 2.17.1956 Columbus, OH BR/TR 5-7/190# d4.24																								
1894	Was N	97	372	69	114	21	17	7	71	51	0	20	.306	.390	.511	119	11	21	.915	-6	62	59	O-80(45-2-33),S-19	0.0
1895	Was N	130	519	116	168	22	**22**	6	55	71	1	28	.324	.406	.486	131	24	31	.913	16	119	88	*O-119(118-0-1)/S-6,2-5	2.4
1896	Was N	127	487	100	148	17	13	5	100	76	7	28	.304	.405	.423	118	16	49	.946	5	73	60	*O-126(124-0-2)	0.8
1897	Was N	124	486	113	152	25	16	5	59	80	4		.313	.414	.461	131	25	46	.955	12	79	55	*O-124(LF)	2.2
1898	Was N	132	515	88	156	28	11	3	60	64	3		.303	.383	.417	130	22	25	.948	20	130	123	*O-131(127-4-0)/S	2.8
1899	Cin N	141	525	105	156	28	11	3	87	70	6		.297	.386	.410	116	14	38	.953	11	116	166	*O-141(101-40-0)	1.2
1900	NY N	**141**	523	98	176	29	12	4	68	72	8		.337	.425	.461	151	41	36	.951	12	132	**141**	*O-141(LF)	3.7
1901	NY N	125	502	89	145	29	6	1	56	45	2		.289	.350	.376	115	11	8	.942	-9	70	46	*O-125(LF)	-0.4
1902	Bal A	128	503	86	161	27	9	3	60	58	2		.320	.393	.427	122	17	22	.941	10	105	79	*O-127(LF)	1.9
1903	Was A	**140**	533	68	134	23	12	3	49	41	0		.251	.305	.356	96	-3	20	.956	-1	66	49	*O-140(120-0-20)/3	-1.2
1904	Was A	48	178	15	49	8	4	0	14	24	0		.275	.361	.365	132	8	9	.931	1	86	57	O-48(LF)	0.6
	Bos A	98	376	50	97	19	8	0	30	48	3		.258	.347	.351	114	8	10	.961	1	72	81	O-98(LF)	0.4
	Year	146	554	65	146	27	12	0	44	72	3		.264	.351	.356	120	16	19	.950	2	77	73	*O-146(LF)	1.0
1905	Bos A	121	418	54	103	16	6	4	47	67	3		.246	.355	.342	120	13	12	.928	-6	60	35	*O-112(0-20-92)	0.2
1906	Bos A	60	228	15	48	9	2	0	23	18	3		.211	.277	.268	71	-7	7	.966	0	79	122	O-58(LF)	-1.1
Total	13	1612	6165	1066	1807	301	149	44	779	785	42	76	.293	.377	.412	121	200	334	.944	68	91	85	*O-1570(1356-66-148)/S-26,2-5,3	13.5
SELBY, BILL William Frank B 6.11.1970 Monroeville, AL BL/TR 5-9/190# d4.19																								
1996	Bos A	40	95	12	26	4	0	3	6	9-1	0	11	.274	.337	.411	86	-2	1-1	.980	-6	80	56	2-14,3-14/O-6(LF)	-0.7
2000	Cle A	30	46	8	11	1	0	0	4	1-0	1	9	.239	.271	.261	35	-5	0-0	1.000	-1	119	0	O-10(4-0-6)/2-6,3-4,D-6	-0.5
2001	Cin N	36	92	7	21	7	1	2	12	5-1	1	13	.228	.273	.391	67	-5	0-0	1.000	-2	99	114	2-21/3-8,1-2	-0.6
2002	Cle A	65	159	15	34	7	2	6	21	15-2	0	27	.214	.278	.396	79	-5	0-1	.933	-2	95	59	3-33,O-18(13-0-5)/2-6	-0.7
2003	Cle A	27	39	3	4	1	0	0	5	3-0	0	11	.103	.163	.128	-21	-7	0-0	.926	3	159	197	3-10/12O(LF)D	-0.4
Total	5	198	431	45	96	20	3	11	48	33-4	2	71	.223	.279	.360	64	-24	1-2	.917	-7	96	87	/3-69,2-48,O-35(24-0-11),D-8,1-3	-2.9
SELKIRK, GEORGE George Alexander "Twinkletoes" B 1.4.1908 Huntsville, ON, CAN D 1.19.1987 Ft.Lauderdale, FL BL/TR 6-1/182# d8.12 Mil 1943-45																								
1934	NY A	46	176	23	55	7	1	5	38	15	1	17	.313	.370	.449	118	4	1-1	.989	1	105	86	O-46(43-0-7)	0.3
1935	NY A	128	491	64	153	29	12	11	94	44	3	36	.312	.372	.487	128	18	2-7	.975	5	114	88	*O-127(RF)	1.3
1936	†NY A★	137	493	93	152	28	9	18	107	94	1	60	.308	.420	.511	133	29	13-7	.974	2	106	80	*O-135(18-0-118)	2.0
1937	†NY A	78	256	49	84	13	5	18	68	34	2	24	.328	.411	.629	157	22	8-2	.987	4	104	138	O-69(RF)	2.0
1938	†NY A	99	335	58	85	12	5	10	62	68	3	52	.254	.384	.409	99	1	9-4	.973	-3	91	104	O-95(LF)	-0.6
1939	†NY A★	128	418	103	128	17	4	21	101	103	8	49	.306	.452	.517	149	38	12-5	**.989**	-4	98	47	*O-124(86-0-38)	2.6
1940	NY A	118	379	68	102	17	5	19	71	84	3	43	.269	.406	.491	137	24	3-6	.962	-0	95	111	*O-111(79-2-31)	1.5
1941	†NY A	70	164	30	36	5	0	6	25	28	2	30	.220	.340	.360	86	-3	1-0	.967	0	99	107	O-47(19-0-28)	-0.5
1942	†NY A	42	78	15	15	3	0	0	10	16	0	8	.192	.330	.231	60	-3	0-0	1.000	-0	109	0	O-19(RF)	-0.5
Total	9	846	2790	503	810	131	41	108	576	486	23	319	.290	.400	.483	128	130	49-32	.977	4	102	89	O-773(340-2-437)	8.1
SELLERS, RUBE Oliver B 3.7.1881 Duquesne, PA D 1.14.1952 Pittsburgh, PA BR/TR 5-10/180# d8.12																								
1910	Bos N	12	32	3	5	0	0	0	2	6	0	5	.156	.289	.156	29	-3	1	1.000	-1	86	0	/O-9(8-0-1)	-0.4
SELLMAN, FRANK Charles Francis (a/k/a Frank C. Williams 1871-75) B 1852 Baltimore, MD D 5.6.1907 Baltimore, MD d5.4 ▲																								
1871	Kek NA	14	65	14	15	3	0	1	10	4		0	.231	.275	.323	70	-2	1-0	.711	-2	38	157	3-14/C-5,S-2	-0.3
1872	Oly NA	**9**	42	3	10	2	0	0	1	0		1	.238	.238	.286	64	-1	0-2	.788	-3			/C-7,3-2	-0.3
1873	Mar NA	1	3	1	1	0	0	0	0	0		0	.333	.333	.333	129	0	0-0	.000	-0	0	0	/P	0.0
1874	Bal NA	12	54	9	16	3	2	0	7	0		2	.296	.296	.426	130	2	2-0	.304	-15			/C-6,S-6,2-2,3-2,O-2(0-1-1)	-1.0
1875	Was NA	1	3	0	1	0	0	0	0	0		0	.333	.333	.333	137	0	0-0	1.000	0	0	0	/1	0.0
Total	5 NA	37	167	27	43	8	2	1	18	4		3	.257	.275	.347	88	-1	3-2	.000	-20			/C-18,3-18,S-8,O-2(0-1-1),2-2,1P	-1.6
SELPH, CAREY Carey Isom B 12.5.1901 Donaldson, AR D 2.24.1976 Houston, TX BR/TR 5-9.5/175# d5.25																								
1929	StL N	25	51	8	12	1	1	0	7	6	0	4	.235	.316	.294	52	-4	1	.981	-3	85	47	2-16	-0.6
1932	Chi A	116	396	50	112	19	8	0	51	31	4	9	.283	.341	.371	90	-6	7-6	.910	-4	91	109	3-71,2-26	-0.7
Total	2	141	447	58	124	20	9	0	58	37	4	13	.277	.338	.362	85	-10	8-6	.910	-7	91	109	/3-71,2-42	-1.3

Year	Tm Lg	G	AB	R	H	2B	3B	HR	RBI	BB-IB	HP	SO	AVG	OBP	SLG	AOPS	ABR	SB-CS	FA	FR	Rng	Thr	G at Pos	BFW
SEMBER, MIKE Michael David B 2.24.1953 Hammond, IN BR/TR 6/185# d8.18																								
1977	Chi N	3	4	0	1	0	0	0	0	0-0	0	2	.250	.250	.250	31	0	0-0	1.000	0	84	209	/2	0.0
1978	Chi N	9	3	2	1	0	0	0	0	1-0	0	1	.333	.500	.333	122	0	0-0	.667	-0	86	0	/3-7,S	0.0
Total	2	12	7	2	2	0	0	0	0	1-0	0	3	.286	.375	.286	74	0	0-0	.667	-0	86	0	/3-7,S2	0.0
SEMINICK, ANDY Andrew Wasil B 9.12.1920 Pierce, WV BR/TR 5-11/187# d9.14 C5																								
1943	Phi N	22	72	9	13	2	0	2	5	7	0	22	.181	.253	.292	60	-4	0	.930	-0	96	113	C-22/O(LF)	-0.3
1944	Phi N	22	63	9	14	2	1	0	4	6	1	17	.222	.300	.286	68	-3	2	.963	1	118	114	C-11/O-7(LF)	-0.2
1945	Phi N	80	188	18	45	7	2	6	26	18	2	38	.239	.313	.394	98	-1	3	.979	-4	69	121	C-70/3-4,O(LF)	-0.2
1946	Phi N	124	406	55	107	15	5	12	52	39	4	86	.264	.334	.414	115	6	2	.974	-3	93	93	*C-118	1.0
1947	Phi N	111	337	48	85	16	2	13	50	58	5	69	.252	.370	.427	115	9	4	.978	1	72	**120**	*C-107	1.6
1948	Phi N	125	391	49	88	11	3	13	44	58	2	68	.225	.328	.368	90	-6	4	.965	-2	63	153	*C-124	0.0
1949	Phi N★	109	334	52	81	11	2	24	68	69	5	74	.243	.380	.503	138	20	0	.975	3	86	**120**	C-98	2.7
1950	†Phi N	130	393	55	113	15	3	24	68	68	6	50	.288	.400	.524	143	27	0	.976	4	104	80	*C-124	3.6
1951	Phi N	101	291	42	66	8	1	11	37	63	3	67	.227	.370	.375	102	3	1-0	.979	-1	109	92	C-91	0.8
1952	Cin N	108	336	38	86	16	1	14	50	35	2	65	.256	.330	.435	111	4	1-3	.973	-3	92	103	C-99	0.6
1953	Cin N	119	387	46	91	12	0	19	64	49	1	82	.235	.323	.413	90	-6	2-2	.982	-3	130	67	*C-112	-0.4
1954	Cin N	86	247	25	58	9	4	7	30	48	2	39	.235	.362	.389	93	-1	0-0	.989	4	**172**	115	C-82	0.7
1955	Cin N	6	15	1	2	0	0	1	1	0-0	0	3	.133	.133	.333	18	-2	0-0	1.000	1	128	0	/C-5	-0.1
	Phi N	93	289	32	71	12	1	11	34	32-2	6	59	.246	.333	.408	97	-1	1-2	.994	11	112	79	C-88	1.4
	Year	99	304	33	73	12	1	12	35	32-2	6	62	.240	.325	.405	93	-3	1-2	**.994**	12	113	75	C-93	1.3
1956	Phi N	60	161	16	32	3	1	7	23	31-7	1	38	.199	.332	.360	88	-2	3-0	.976	-8	72	109	C-54	-0.7
1957	Phi N	8	11	0	1	0	0	0	0	1-0	0	3	.091	.167	.091	-29	-2	0-0	1.000	0	101	0	/C-8	-0.2
Total	15	1304	3921	495	953	139	26	164	556	582-9	40	780	.243	.347	.417	107	41	23-7	.977	3	98	104	*C-1213/O-9(LF),3-4	10.3
SENERCHIA, SONNY Emanuel Robert B 4.6.1931 Newark, NJ D 11.1.2003 Freehold, NJ BR/TR 6-1/195# d8.22																								
1952	Pit N	29	100	5	22	5	0	3	11	4	0	21	.220	.250	.360	66	-5	0-3	.953	-5	70	72	3-28	-1.1
SENSENDERFER, COUNT John Phillips Jenkins B 12.28.1847 Philadelphia, PA D 5.3.1903 Philadelphia, PA 5-9/170# d5.20																								
1871	Ath NA	25	127	38	41	5	2	0	23	0		1	.323	.323	.394	106	1	5-3	.814	-2	68	196	*O-25(CF)	-0.1
1872	Ath NA	1	5	2	2	0	0	0	1	0		0	.400	.400	.400	146	0	0-1	—	0	0	0	/O(RF)	0.0
1873	Ath NA	20	86	12	24	1	0	0	8	0		2	.279	.279	.291	65	-4	0-2	.827	-0	38	0	O-19(CF)/1	-0.4
1874	Ath NA	5	16	3	3	0	0	0	2	0		0	.188	.188	.188	19	-2	0-0	.625	-1	0	0	/O-5(0-1-4)	-0.2
Total	4 NA	51	234	55	70	6	2	0	34	0		3	.299	.299	.342	85	-5	5-6	.000	-3	51	103	/O-50(0-45-5),1	-0.7
SENTELL, PAUL Leopold Theodore B 8.27.1879 New Orleans, LA D 4.27.1923 Cincinnati, OH BR/TR 5-9/176# d4.12 U2																								
1906	Phi N	63	192	19	44	5	1	1	14	14	3		.229	.292	.281	79	-5	15	.887	-9	99	26	3-33,2-19/O-2(RF),S	-1.5
1907	Phi N	3	3	0	0	0	0	0	0	1	0		.000	.250	.000	-22	0	0	1.000	-1	57	0	/S-2,O(RF)	-0.1
Total	2	66	195	19	44	5	1	1	14	15	3		.226	.291	.277	77	-5	15	.887	-10	99	26	/3-33,2-19,S-3,O-3(RF)	-1.6
SEPKOWSKI, TED Theodore Walter (born Theodore Walter Sczepkowski) B 11.9.1923 Baltimore, MD D 3.8.2002 Severna Park, MD BL/TR 5-11/190# d9.9 Mil 1944-45																								
1942	Cle A	5	10	0	1	0	0	0	0	0	0	3	.100	.100	.100	-46	-2	0-0	.824	-1	113	0	/2-2	-0.3
1946	Cle A	2	8	2	4	1	0	0	1	0	0	0	.500	.500	.625	228	1	0-0	.833	-1	49	225	/3-2	0.1
1947	Cle A	10	8	0	1	1	0	0	0	1	0	1	.125	.222	.250	32	-1	0-0	—	-0	0	0	/O(RF)	-0.1
	NY A	2	0	1	0	0	0	0	0	0	0	0	—	—	—	—	0	0-1	—	0			R	0.0
	Year	12	8	1	1	1	0	0	0	1	0	1	.125	.222	.250	32	-1	0-1	—	-0	0	0	/O(RF)	-0.1
Total	3	19	26	3	6	2	0	0	1	1	0	4	.231	.259	.308	61	-2	0-1	.833	-1	49	225	/3-2,2-2,O(RF)	-0.3
SERENA, BILL William Robert B 10.2.1924 Alameda, CA D 4.17.1996 Hayward, CA BR/TR 5-9.5/175# d9.16																								
1949	Chi N	12	37	3	8	3	0	1	7	7	0	9	.216	.341	.378	95	0	0	.923	-3	76	0	3-11	-0.3
1950	Chi N	127	435	56	104	20	4	17	61	65	1	75	.239	.339	.421	100	0	1	.945	-3	102	86	*3-125	-0.4
1951	Chi N	13	39	8	13	3	1	1	4	11	1	4	.333	.490	.538	173	5	0-2	.941	-2	75	37	3-12	0.2
1952	Chi N	122	390	49	107	21	5	15	61	39	3	83	.274	.345	.469	122	11	1-0	.971	-5	90	53	3-58,2-49	1.0
1953	Chi N	93	275	30	69	10	5	10	52	41	1	46	.251	.350	.433	100	0	0-0	.983	-11	88	68	2-49,3-28	-0.7
1954	Chi N	41	63	8	10	0	1	4	13	14	1	18	.159	.316	.381	81	-2	0-0	.933	-2	107	0	3-12/2-2	-0.4
Total	6	408	1239	154	311	57	16	48	198	177	7	235	.251	.348	.439	108	14	2-2	.951	-25	96	73	3-246,2-100	-0.6
SERNA, PAUL Paul David B 11.16.1958 ElCentro, CA BR/TR 5-8/170# d9.1																								
1981	Sea A	30	94	11	24	2	0	4	9	3-0	2	11	.255	.293	.404	95	-1	2-3	.954	-3	105	45	S-23/2-7	-0.2
1982	Sea A	65	169	15	38	3	0	3	8	4-0	1	13	.225	.246	.296	47	-13	0-5	.936	-3	101	100	S-31,2-18,3-15/D-2	-1.5
Total	2	95	263	26	62	5	0	7	17	7-0	3	24	.236	.263	.335	64	-14	2-8	.945	-6	103	73	/S-54,2-25,3-15,D-2	-1.7
SERVAIS, SCOTT Scott Daniel B 6.4.1967 LaCrosse, WI BR/TR 6-2/195# d7.12																								
1991	Hou N	16	37	0	6	3	0	0	6	4-0	0	8	.162	.244	.243	40	-3	0-0	.988	1	180	91	C-14	-0.1
1992	Hou N	77	205	12	49	9	0	0	15	11-2	5	25	.239	.294	.283	67	-9	0-0	.995	-1	97	67	C-73	-0.6
1993	Hou N	85	258	24	63	11	0	11	32	22-2	5	45	.244	.313	.415	97	-2	0-0	.996	4	100	71	C-82	0.7
1994	Hou N	78	251	27	49	15	1	9	41	10-0	4	44	.195	.235	.371	58	-17	0-0	.996	-2	92	61	C-78	-1.4
1995	Hou N	28	89	7	20	10	0	1	12	9-2	1	15	.225	.300	.371	82	-2	0-1	.977	-1	73	71	C-28	-0.1
	Chi N	52	175	31	50	12	0	12	35	23-6	2	37	.286	.371	.560	145	12	2-1	.981	-1	85	120	C-52	1.4
	Year	80	264	38	70	22	0	13	47	32-8	3	52	.265	.348	.496	125	10	2-2	.980	-1	81	103	C-80	1.3
1996	Chi N	129	445	42	118	20	0	11	63	30-1	14	75	.265	.327	.384	86	-9	0-2	.988	1	99	102	*C-128/1	-0.1
1997	Chi N	122	385	36	100	21	0	6	45	24-7	6	56	.260	.311	.361	74	-15	0-1	.990	0	92	117	*C-118/1D	-0.7
1998	†Chi N	113	325	35	72	15	1	7	36	26-6	5	51	.222	.289	.338	62	-18	1-0	.994	-8	92	94	*C-110/1	-2.0
1999	SF N	69	198	21	54	10	0	5	21	13-2	3	31	.273	.327	.399	89	-4	0-0	.992	-5	88	75	C-62/1	-0.5
2000	Col N	33	101	6	22	4	0	1	13	7-2	1	16	.218	.273	.287	34	-10	0-1	.987	6	80	102	C-32	-0.2
	SF N	7	8	1	2	0	0	0	0	2-1	0	1	.250	.400	.250	75	0	0-0	1.000	0	0	0	/C-6	0.0
	Year	40	109	7	24	4	0	1	13	9-3	1	17	.220	.283	.284	37	-10	0-1	.988	7	74	94	C-38	-0.2
2001	Hou N	11	16	1	6	0	0	0	0	2-0	0	3	.375	.444	.375	109	0	0-0	1.000	2	212	0	/C-9	0.2
Total	11	820	2493	243	611	130	2	63	319	183-31	46	407	.245	.306	.375	79	-77	3-6	.991	-2	94	90	C-792/1-4,D-2	-3.4
SESSI, WALTER Walter Anthony "Watsie" B 7.23.1918 Finleyville, PA D 4.18.1998 Mobile, AL BL/TL 6-3/225# d9.18 Mil 1942-45																								
1941	StL N	5	13	2	0	0	0	0	0	1	0	2	.000	.071	.000	-74	-3	0	.750	-1	65	0	/O-3(RF)	-0.4
1946	StL N	15	14	2	2	0	0	1	2	1	0	4	.143	.200	.357	54	-1	0	—	0			H	-0.1
Total	2	20	27	4	2	0	0	1	2	2	0	6	.074	.138	.185	-9	-4	0	.750	-1	65	0	/O-3(RF)	-0.5
SEVCIK, JOHN John Joseph B 7.11.1942 Oak Park, IL BR/TR 6-2/205# d4.24																								
1965	Min A	12	16	1	1	1	0	0	0	1-0	0	5	.063	.118	.125	-30	-3	0-0	1.000	2	206	184	C-11	0.0
SEVEREID, HANK Henry Levai B 6.1.1891 Story City, IA D 12.17.1968 San Antonio, TX BR/TR 6/175# d5.15 Mil 1918																								
1911	Cin N	37	56	5	17	6	1	0	10	3	1	6	.304	.350	.446	127	2	0	.913	-1	129	79	C-22	0.2
1912	Cin N	50	114	10	27	0	3	0	13	8	0	11	.237	.287	.289	60	-7	0	.943	-6	88	63	C-20/1-7,O-6(5-1-0)	-1.1
1913	Cin N	8	6	0	0	0	0	0	0	1	0	1	.000	.143	.000	-58	-1	0	1.000	-0	56	0	/C-2,O(LF)	-0.2
1915	StL A	80	203	12	45	6	1	1	22	16	0	25	.222	.279	.276	69	-8	2-1	.966	-7	87	91	C-64	-1.1
1916	StL A	100	293	23	80	8	2	0	34	26	4	17	.273	.341	.314	102	1	3	.976	-15	80	85	C-89/13	-0.8
1917	StL A	143	501	45	133	23	4	1	57	28	1	20	.265	.306	.333	99	-3	6	.966	-20	81	100	*C-139/1	-1.2
1918	StL A	51	133	8	34	4	0	0	11	18	3	4	.256	.357	.286	97	1	4	.946	-6	80	95	C-42	-0.2
1919	StL A	112	351	16	87	12	2	0	36	21	4	13	.248	.298	.293	65	-17	2	.983	-2	96	85	*C-103	-1.0
1920	StL A	123	422	46	117	14	5	2	49	33	4	11	.277	.336	.348	79	-13	5-3	.983	-1	95	98	*C-117	-0.3
1921	StL A	143	472	66	153	23	7	2	78	42	0	9	.324	.379	.415	97	-2	7-2	.972	-1	106	97	*C-126	0.6
1922	StL A	137	517	49	166	32	7	3	78	28	0	12	.321	.356	.427	100	-1	1-4	.984	9	119	120	*C-133	1.6
1923	StL A	122	432	50	133	27	6	3	51	31	1	11	.308	.356	.419	98	-2	3-0	**.993**	8	99	98	*C-116	1.4
1924	StL A	137	432	37	133	23	2	4	48	36	1	15	.308	.362	.398	90	-6	1-6	**.989**	-3	93	118	*C-130	-0.2
1925	StL A	34	109	15	40	9	0	1	21	11	0	2	.367	.425	.477	122	4	0-2	.993	-1	85	109	C-31	0.4
	†Was A	50	110	11	39	8	1	0	14	13	0	6	.355	.423	.445	123	5	0-0	.986	3	114	63	C-35	0.8
	Year	84	219	26	79	17	1	1	35	24	0	8	.361	.424	.461	123	9	0-2	.990	2	99	87	C-66	1.2
1926	Was A	22	34	2	7	1	0	0	4	3	0	2	.206	.270	.235	34	-3	0-0	.977	-0	104	96	C-16	-0.3
	†NY A	41	127	13	34	8	1	0	13	13	0	4	.268	.336	.346	79	-4	1-1	.988	-2	82	96	C-40	-0.3

Year	Tm Lg	G	AB	R	H	2B	3B	HR	RBI	BB-IB	HP	SO	AVG	OBP	SLG	AOPS	ABR	SB-CS	FA	FR	Rng	Thr	G at Pos	BFW
	Year	63	161	15	41	9	1	0	17	16	0	6	.255	.322	.323	70	-7	1-1	.985	-2	*86*	*96*	C-56	-0.6
Total	15	1390	4312	408	1245	204	42	17	539	331	19	169	.289	.342	.367	91	-54	35-19	.978	-43	*96*	*99*	*C-1225/1-9,O-7(6-1-0),3	-1.7
SEVERSON, RICH Richard Allen B 1.18.1945 Artesia, CA BR/TR 6/174# d4.10																								
1970	KC A	77	240	22	60	11	1	1	22	16-2	1	33	.250	.300	.317	70	-10	0-0	.962	0	107	120	S-50,2-25	-0.3
1971	KC A	16	30	4	9	0	2	0	1	3-0	0	5	.300	.364	.433	126	1	0-0	1.000	4	154	225	/2-6,S-6,3	0.5
Total	2	93	270	26	69	11	3	1	23	19-2	1	38	.256	.307	.330	76	-9	0-0	.958	4	108	124	/S-56,2-31,3	0.2
SEWARD, GEORGE George T. B St.Louis, MO D 3.28.1904 St.Louis, MO 5-7.5/145# d5.19																								
1875	StL NA	25	96	12	24	2	0	0	8	1		1	.250	.258	.271	92	0	1-0	.817	-2			C-18/O-7(3-1-3),2-2	-0.2
1876	NY N	1	3	0	0	0	0	0	0	0		0	.000	.000	.000	-99	-1		1.000	0	118	0	/2	0.0
1882	StL AA	38	144	23	31	1	1	0		12			.215	.276	.236	71	-4		.776	0	150	118	O-35(6-2-27)/C-5	-0.4
Total	2	39	147	23	31	1	1	0	0	12		0	.211	.270	.231	68	-5		.817	0			/O-35(6-2-27),C-5,2	-0.4
SEWELL, LUKE James Luther B 1.5.1901 Titus, AL D 5.14.1987 Akron, OH BR/TR 5-9/160# d6.30 M10 C4 b-Joe b-Tommy																								
1921	Cle A	3	6	0	0	0	0	0	1	0	0	3	.000	.000	.000	-99	-2	0-0	1.000	1	*112*	*109*	/C-3	-0.1
1922	Cle A	41	87	14	23	5	0	0	10	5	1	8	.264	.312	.322	65	-4	1-1	.963	-2	*88*	*63*	C-39	-0.5
1923	Cle A	10	10	2	2	0	1	0	1	1	0	0	.200	.273	.400	76	-1	0-0	.833	0	*145*	*173*	/C-7	0.0
1924	Cle A	63	165	27	48	9	1	0	17	22	4	13	.291	.387	.358	92	-1	1-0	.959	1	*103*	*87*	C-57	0.4
1925	Cle A	74	220	30	51	10	2	0	18	33	2	18	.232	.337	.295	61	-12	6-2	.971	4	*135*	*90*	C-66/O-2(LF)	-0.3
1926	Cle A	126	433	41	103	16	4	0	46	36	4	27	.238	.302	.293	55	-29	9-3	.983	9	***173***	*63*	*C-125	-1.0
1927	Cle A	128	470	52	138	27	6	0	53	20	4	23	.294	.328	.377	82	-14	4-8	.963	3	***117***	***146***	*C-126	-0.4
1928	Cle A	122	411	52	111	16	9	3	52	26	3	27	.270	.318	.375	81	-13	4-4	.972	8	*106*	***124***	*C-118	0.3
1929	Cle A	124	406	41	96	16	3	1	39	29	0	26	.236	.287	.298	49	-31	6-6	.966	2	*92*	***111***	*C-124	-2.1
1930	Cle A	76	292	40	75	21	2	1	43	14	1	9	.257	.293	.353	61	-18	5-2	.974	-4	*86*	*91*	C-76	-1.4
1931	Cle A	108	375	45	103	30	4	1	53	36	2	17	.275	.341	.384	86	-7	1-1	.980	-6	*103*	*108*	*C-104	-0.7
1932	Cle A	87	300	36	76	20	2	2	52	38	0	24	.253	.337	.353	74	-11	4-5	.978	3	*125*	*85*	C-84	-0.3
1933	†Was A	141	474	65	125	30	4	2	61	48	3	24	.264	.335	.357	84	-10	7-2	.990	1	***181***	*61*	*C-141	0.0
1934	Was A	72	207	21	49	7	3	2	21	22	1	10	.237	.313	.329	68	-10	0-1	.994	0	*150*	*121*	C-50/O-7(2-0-5),1-6,23	-0.8
1935	Chi A	118	421	52	120	19	3	2	67	32	0	18	.285	.336	.359	78	-14	3-2	.988	7	*85*	*99*	*C-112	0.0
1936	Chi A	128	451	59	113	20	5	5	73	54	1	16	.251	.332	.350	66	-25	11-2	.984	13	*122*	*113*	*C-126	-0.2
1937	Chi A☆	122	412	51	111	21	6	1	61	46	0	18	.269	.343	.357	77	-15	4-5	.985	9	*118*	*93*	*C-118	0.1
1938	Chi A	65	211	23	45	4	1	0	27	20	1	20	.213	.284	.242	32	-23	0-0	.985	8	*118*	*130*	C-65	-1.0
1939	Cle A	16	20	1	3	1	0	0	1	3	0	1	.150	.261	.200	20	-2	0-0	.966	-1	*90*	*126*	C-15/1	-0.2
1942	StL A	6	12	1	1	0	0	0	0	1	0	5	.083	.154	.083	-32	-2	0-0	.944	0	*84*	*170*	/C-6,M	-0.2
Total	20	1630	5383	653	1393	272	56	20	696	486	27	307	.259	.323	.341	70	-244	66-44	.978	56	*121*	*100*	*C-1562/O-9(4-0-5),1-7,32	-8.4
SEWELL, JOE Joseph Wheeler B 10.9.1898 Titus, AL D 3.6.1990 Mobile, AL BL/TR 5-6.5/155# d9.10 C2 HF1977 b-Luke b-Tommy																								
1920	†Cle A	22	70	14	23	4	1	0	12	9	1	4	.329	.412	.414	116	2	1-0	.884	1	106	144	S-22	0.4
1921	Cle A	**154**	572	101	182	36	12	4	93	80	11	17	.318	.412	.444	116	18	7-6	.944	-2	99	107	*S-154	3.0
1922	Cle A	153	558	80	167	28	7	2	83	73	6	20	.299	.386	.385	101	4	10-12	.939	9	102	96	*S-139,2-12	2.6
1923	Cle A	**153**	553	98	195	41	10	3	109	98	7	12	.353	.456	.479	147	45	9-6	.930	5	106	104	*S-151	6.2
1924	Cle A	**153**	594	99	188	**45**	5	4	106	67	2	13	.316	.388	.429	109	10	3-3	.960	**22**	**110**	95	*S-153	4.5
1925	Cle A	**155**	608	78	204	37	7	1	98	64	4	4	.336	.402	.424	109	11	7-6	**.967**	**16**	**111**	85	*S-153/2-3	3.9
1926	Cle A	**154**	578	91	187	41	5	4	85	65	8	6	.324	.399	.433	116	16	17-7	.955	1	101	110	*S-154	3.4
1927	Cle A	**153**	569	83	180	48	5	1	92	51	9	7	.316	.382	.424	108	9	3-16	**.962**	5	100	88	*S-153	2.4
1928	Cle A	**155**	588	79	190	40	2	4	70	58	7	9	.323	.391	.418	111	13	7-1	**.963**	26	109	**119**	*S-137,3-19	5.3
1929	Cle A	**152**	578	90	182	38	3	7	73	48	5	4	.315	.372	.427	102	3	6-6	.975	14	**115**	92	*3-152	2.4
1930	Cle A	109	353	44	102	17	6	0	48	41	7	3	.289	.374	.371	86	-6	1-4	.950	0	109	92	3-97	-0.1
1931	NY A	130	484	102	146	22	1	6	64	61	9	8	.302	.390	.388	111	12	1-1	.952	-6	92	66	*3-121/2	0.9
1932	†NY A	125	503	95	137	21	3	11	68	56	3	3	.272	.349	.392	96	-2	0-2	.974	1	93	76	*3-123	0.2
1933	NY A	135	524	87	143	18	1	2	54	71	1	4	.273	.361	.323	87	-6	2-2	.964	4	95	**120**	*3-131	0.1
Total	14	1903	7132	1141	2226	436	68	49	1055	842	80	114	.312	.391	.413	109	129	74-72	.951	94	105	101	*S-1216,3-643/2-16	35.2
SEWELL, TOMMY Thomas Wesley B 4.16.1906 Titus, AL D 7.30.1956 Montgomery, AL BL/TR 5-7.5/155# d6.21 b-Luke b-Joe																								
1927	Chi N	1	1	0	0	0	0	0	0	0	0	0	.000	.000	.000	-99	0	0	—	0			H	0.0
SEXSON, RICHIE Richmond Lockwood B 12.29.1974 Portland, OR BR/TR 6-6/205# d9.14																								
1997	Cle A	5	11	1	3	0	0	0	0	0-0	0	2	.273	.273	.273	41	-1	0-0	1.000	-0	74	0	/1-2,D	-0.1
1998	†Cle A	49	174	28	54	14	1	11	35	6-0	3	42	.310	.344	.592	133	8	1-1	.984	2	126	102	1-45/O-3(LF),D-2	0.5
1999	†Cle A	134	479	72	122	17	7	31	116	34-0	4	117	.255	.305	.514	100	-3	3-3	.988	3	146	96	1-61,O-49(48-0-3),D-24	-0.9
2000	Cle A	91	324	45	83	16	1	16	44	25-0	4	96	.256	.315	.460	92	-5	1-0	1.000	-0	76	99	O-58(LF),1-27,D-10	-1.0
	Mil N	57	213	44	63	14	0	14	47	34-2	3	63	.296	.398	.559	142	14	1-0	.991	9	164	102	1-57	1.7
2001	Mil N	158	598	94	162	24	3	45	125	60-5	6	178	.271	.342	.547	128	22	2-4	.995	9	121	95	*1-158	1.5
2002	Mil N★	157	570	86	159	37	2	29	102	70-7	8	136	.279	.363	.504	131	24	0-0	.995	10	125	99	*1-154/D	1.9
2003	Mil N★	**162**	606	97	165	28	2	45	124	98-7	9	151	.272	.379	.548	142	38	2-3	.993	9	124	89	*1-162	3.0
Total	7	813	2975	467	811	150	16	191	593	327-21	37	785	.273	.349	.526	124	97	10-11	.993	42	130	94	1-666,O-110(109-0-3)/D-38	6.6
SEXTON, CHRIS Christopher Philip B 8.3.1971 Cincinnati, OH BR/TR 5-11/180# d5.3																								
1999	Col N	35	59	9	14	0	1	1	7	11-1	0	10	.237	.357	.322	58	-4	4-2	1.000	0	72	264	O-13(3-9-1),2-10/S-6	-0.3
2000	Cin N	35	100	9	21	4	0	0	10	13-1	2	12	.210	.310	.250	44	-8	4-2	.954	-5	97	72	S-14,2-12/3-3	-1.1
Total	2	70	159	18	35	4	1	1	17	24-2	2	22	.220	.328	.277	50	-12	8-4	.976	-4	93	78	/2-22,S-20,O-13(3-9-1),3-3	-1.4
SEXTON, JIMMY Jimmy Dale B 12.15.1951 Mobile, AL BR/TR 5-10/175# d9.2																								
1977	Sea A	14	37	5	8	1	1	1	3	2-0	0	6	.216	.256	.378	71	-2	1-1	.929	2	124	147	S-12	0.1
1978	Hou N	88	141	17	29	3	2	2	6	13-1	0	28	.206	.273	.298	64	-8	16-2	.981	-10	80	82	S-58/3-8,2-3	-1.1
1979	Hou N	52	43	8	9	0	0	0	1	7-0	0	7	.209	.320	.209	50	-3	1-3	.943	0	107	159	S-11/3-4,2-2	-0.3
1981	Oak A	7	3	3	0	0	0	0	0	0-0	0	2	.000	.000	.000	-99	-1	2-0	1.000	1	344	0	/3D	0.0
1982	Oak A	69	139	19	34	4	0	2	14	9-0	1	24	.245	.289	.317	71	-6	16-0	.957	-10	86	68	S-47/3-8,D-5	-0.9
1983	StL N	6	9	1	1	1	0	0	0	1-1	0	4	.111	.200	.222	17	-1	0-0	1.000	1	143	205	/S-4,3-2	0.1
Total	6	236	372	53	81	9	3	5	24	32-2	1	71	.218	.279	.298	64	-21	36-6	.962	-16	90	91	S-132/3-23,D-6,2-5	-2.1
SEXTON, TOM Thomas William B 3.14.1865 Rock Island, IL D 2.8.1934 Rock Island, IL BL d9.27																								
1884	Mil U	**12**	47	9	11	2	0	0		4			.234	.294	.277	136	2		.853	-1	61	91	S-12	0.1
SEYBOLD, SOCKS Ralph Orlando B 11.23.1870 Washingtonville, OH D 12.22.1921 Greensburg, PA BR/TR 5-11/175# d8.20																								
1899	Cin N	22	85	13	19	5	1	0	8	6	1		.224	.283	.306	60	-5	2	.917	0	119	0	O-22(3-0-19)	-0.5
1901	Phi A	114	449	74	150	24	14	8	90	40	7		.334	.397	.503	142	25	15	.954	-5	79	68	*O-100(2-25-74),1-14	1.4
1902	Phi A	**137**	522	91	165	27	12	**16**	97	43	6		.316	.375	.506	137	24	6	.963	-1	61	81	*O-136(0-16-120)	1.6
1903	Phi A	**137**	522	76	156	**45**	8	8	84	38	6		.299	.353	.462	137	24	5	.964	-1	70	126	*O-120(0-1-119),1-18	1.8
1904	Phi A	143	510	56	149	26	9	3	64	42	4		.292	.351	.396	129	18	12	.975	2	87	145	*O-129(RF),1-13	1.6
1905	†Phi A	133	492	64	135	37	4	6	59	42	8		.274	.341	.402	133	20	5	.983	8	87	153	*O-133(RF)	2.4
1906	Phi A	116	411	41	130	23	2	5	59	30	3		.316	.367	.418	141	20	9	.925	-3	73	102	*O-114(RF)	1.3
1907	Phi A	147	564	58	153	29	4	5	92	40	4		.271	.324	.363	116	10	10	.973	0	100	171	*O-147(RF)	0.5
1908	Phi A	48	130	5	28	2	0	0	3	12	1		.215	.287	.231	64	-5	2	.921	-1	96	0	O-34(RF)	-0.8
Total	9	997	3685	478	1085	218	54	51	556	293	40		.294	.353	.424	129	131	66	.961	-1	82	117	O-935(5-42-889)/1-45	9.3
SEYMOUR, CY James Bentley B 12.9.1872 Albany, NY D 9.20.1919 New York, NY BL/TL 6/200# d4.22 ▲ OF Total (20-LF 1094-CF 224-RF)																								
1896	NY N	12	32	2	7	0	0	0	0	0	0	7	.219	.219	.219	16	-4	0	.857	1	109	164	P-11/O(CF)	0.0
1897	NY N	45	141	13	34	5	1	2	14	4	0		.241	.262	.333	58	-9	3	.853	7	**158**	241	P-39/O-6(2-4-0)	0.2
1898	NY N	80	297	41	82	5	2	4	23	9	1		.276	.300	.347	88	-6	8	.887	6	127	233	P-45,O-35(10-12-15)/2	-0.3
1899	NY N	50	159	25	52	3	2	2	27	4	0		.327	.344	.409	110	1	2	.839	2	130	43	P-32/O-8(2-1-5),1-3,3	0.0
1900	NY N	23	40	9	12	0	0	0	2	3	0		.300	.349	.300	84	-1	0	.828	-0	150	0	P-13/O-3(1-1-2),1	-0.1
1901	Bal A	**134**	547	84	166	19	8	1	77	28	0		.303	.337	.373	93	-7	38	.945	14	135	99	*O-133(4-0-131)/1	0.1
1902	Bal A	72	280	38	75	8	8	3	41	18	2		.268	.317	.386	90	-5	12	.956	2	99	94	O-72(0-3-70)	-0.6
	Cin N	62	244	27	83	8	2	2	37	12	3		.340	.378	.414	132	9	8	.920	2	118	137	O-61(CF)/P3	0.8
1903	Cin N	135	558	85	191	25	15	7	72	33	3		.342	.382	.478	130	19	25	.902	3	76	46	*O-135(CF)	1.5

Year	Tm Lg	G	AB	R	H	2B	3B	HR	RBI	BB-IB	HP	SO	AVG	OBP	SLG	AOPS	ABR	SB-CS	FA	FR	Rng	Thr	G at Pos	BFW
1904	Cin N	131	531	71	166	26	13	5	58	29	3		.313	.352	.439	132	18	11	.951	9	121	88	*O-130(CF)	2.1
1905	Cin N	149	581	95	**219**	**40**	**21**	8	**121**	51	2		**.377**	.429	**.559**	**175**	**52**	21	.947	10	128	**237**	*O-149(CF)	5.6
1906	Cin N	79	307	35	79	7	2	4	38	24	3		.257	.317	.332	98	-1	9	.968	7	97	118	O-79(CF)	0.2
	NY N	72	269	35	86	12	3	4	42	18	1		.320	.365	.431	145	13	20	.978	-2	81	150	O-72(CF)	0.9
	Year	151	576	70	165	19	5	8	80	42	4		.286	.339	.378	120	12	29	.972	5	90	133	*O-151(CF)	1.1
1907	NY N	131	473	46	139	25	8	3	75	36	5		.294	.350	.400	131	16	21	.975	-0	4	59	*O-126(CF)	1.1
1908	NY N	156	587	60	157	23	2	5	92	30	3		.267	.306	.339	101	0	18	.949	5	145	**208**	*O-155(CF)	-0.3
1909	NY N	80	280	37	87	12	5	1	30	25	1		.311	.369	.400	137	12	14	.968	-1	107	138	O-74(1-71-1)	0.8
1910	NY N	79	287	32	76	9	4	1	40	23	2	18	.265	.324	.334	92	-4	10	.936	-7	84	93	O-76(CF)	-1.5
1913	Bos N	39	73	2	13	2	0	0	10	7	1	7	.178	.259	.205	33	-6	2-1	.950	1	95	189	O-18(CF)	-0.6
Total	16	1529	5686	737	1724	229	96	52	799	354	30	32	.303	.347	.405	117	97	222-1	.945	58	102	126	*O-1333C,P-141/1-5,3-2,2	9.9
SHAFER, TILLIE Arthur Joseph B 3.22.1889 Los Angeles, CA D 1.10.1962 Los Angeles, CA BB/TR 5-10/165# d4.24																								
1909	NY N	38	84	11	15	2	1	0	7	14	0		.179	.296	.226	61	-3	6	.750	-3	91	82	3-16,2-13/O-2(0-1-1)	-0.6
1910	NY N	29	21	5	4	1	0	0	1	0	0	6	.190	.190	.238	25	-2	0	.889	2	183	478	/3-8,2-2,S-2	0.0
1912	†NY N	78	163	48	47	4	1	0	23	30	3	19	.288	.408	.325	99	2	22	.879	-5	81	81	S-31,3-16,2-15	0.0
1913	†NY N	138	508	74	146	17	12	5	52	61	5	55	.287	.369	.398	118	13	32-29	.923	-10	89	118	3-79,2-25,S-16,O-15(4-12-0)	0.4
Total	4	283	776	138	212	24	14	5	83	105	8	80	.273	.366	.360	106	10	60-29	.903	-14	95	110	3-119/2-55,S-49,O-17(4-13-1)	-0.2
SHAFER, ORATOR George B 10.1851 Philadelphia, PA D 1.21.1922 Philadelphia, PA BL/TR 5-9/165# d5.23 b-Taylor																								
1874	Har NA	9	35	6	8	0	0	1	3	0		4	.229	.229	.314	69	-1	0-0	.710	-2	0	0	/O-9(8-0-1)	-0.2
	Mut NA	1	5	1	1	0	0	0	0	0		0	.200	.200	.200	28	0	0-0	—	0	0	0	/O(RF)	0.0
	Year	10	40	7	9	0	0	1	3	0		4	.225	.225	.300	64	-2	0-0	.710	-2	0	0	O-10(8-0-2)	-0.2
1875	Phi NA	19	70	10	17	2	1	0	6	0		4	.243	.243	.300	84	-1	2-0	.769	-2	55	307	O-12(3-8-1)/3-5,1-2	-0.2
1877	Lou N	**61**	260	38	74	9	5	3	34	9		17	.285	.309	.392	101	-1		.835	13	179	56	*O-60(0-1-60)/1	1.0
1878	Ind N	**63**	266	48	90	19	6	0	30	13		20	.338	.369	.455	**196**	**29**		.842	8	172	80	*O-63(1-0-63)	**3.3**
1879	Chi N	73	316	53	96	13	0	0	35	6		28	.304	.317	.345	111	3		.801	19	**304**	169	*O-72(RF)/3	2.0
1880	Cle N	83	338	62	90	14	9	0	21	17		36	.266	.301	.361	126	9		.901	15	180	156	*O-83(RF)	2.3
1881	Cle N	**85**	343	48	88	13	6	1	34	23		20	.257	.303	.338	107	4		.880	-0	105	124	*O-85(RF)	0.3
1882	Cle N	**84**	313	37	67	14	2	3	28	27		27	.214	.276	.300	88	-2		.805	-10	90	52	*O-84(2-1-83)	-1.2
1883	Buf N	95	401	67	117	11	3	0	41	27		39	.292	.336	.334	103	1		.861	16	186	87	*O-95(RF)	1.5
1884	StL U	106	467	130	168	**40**	10	2		30			.360	.398	.501	165	25		.870	-3	98	95	*O-100(6-0-96)/2-7,1	1.9
1885	StL N	69	257	30	50	11	2	0	18	19		31	.195	.250	.253	67	-8		.918	10	213	0	O-69(0-1-68)	0.2
	Phi AA	2	9	1	2	0	1	0	1	1	0		.222	.300	.444	125	0		1.000	-0	0	0	/O-2(CF)	0.0
1886	Phi AA	21	82	15	22	3	3	0	8	8	0		.268	.333	.378	121	2	3	.815	0	114	286	O-21(0-18-4)	0.1
1890	Phi AA	100	390	55	110	15	5	1	58	47	5		.282	.367	.354	113	8	29	**.958**	2	102	137	*O-98(RF)/1-3	0.7
Total	2 NA	29	110	17	26	2	1	1	9	0	0	8	.236	.236	.300	76	-2	2-0	.000	-4	29	161	/O-22(11-8-3),3-5,1-2	-0.4
Total	11	842	3442	584	974	162	52	10	308	227	5	218	.283	.328	.369	119	70	32-0	.865	69	156	103	O-832(9-23-807)/2-7,1-5,3	12.1
SHAFER, RALPH Ralph Newton B 3.17.1894 Cincinnati, OH D 2.5.1950 Akron, OH 5-11/?# d7.25																								
1914	Pit N	1	0	0	0	0	0	0	0	0	0	0	—	—	—	—	0	0	—	0			H	0.0
SHAFER, TAYLOR Zachary Taylor B 7.13.1866 Philadelphia, PA D 10.27.1945 Glendale, CA 5-7/155# d4.24 b-Orator																								
1884	Alt U	19	74	11	21	2	0	0		3			.284	.312	.311	88	-3		.889	-2	54	0	O-17(9-7-1)/C-2,3	-0.5
	KC U	44	164	18	28	3	2	0		15			.171	.240	.213	44	-16		.768	-3	115	0	O-41(RF)/C-2,2S3	-1.7
	Bal U	3	13	1	1	0	0	0		0			.077	.077	.077	-48	-3		.750	-0	147	0	/O-3(1-0-3)	-0.3
	Year	66	251	30	50	5	2	0		18			.199	.253	.235	53	-22		.796	-6	101	0	O-61(10-7-45)/C-4,3-2,2S	-2.5
1890	Phi AA	69	261	28	45	3	4	0	21	28	2		.172	.258	.215	40	-20	19	.921	-3	93	103	2-69	-1.8
Total	2	135	512	58	95	8	6	0	21	46	2		.186	.255	.225	46	-42	19	.920	-8	92	102	/2-70,O-61(10-7-45),C-4,3-2,S	-4.3
SHAFFER d9.15																								
1875	Atl NA	1	4	0	0	0	0	0	0	0		0	.000	.000	.000	-99	-1	0-0	.500	-0	0	0	/O(RF)	-0.1
SHAMSKY, ART Arthur Louis B 10.14.1941 St.Louis, MO BL/TL 6-1/175# d4.17																								
1965	Cin N	64	96	13	25	4	3	2	10	10-0	0	29	.260	.330	.427	104	0	1-0	.966	1	104	216	O-18(3-0-15)/1	0.1
1966	Cin N	96	234	41	54	5	0	21	47	32-1	0	45	.231	.321	.521	120	6	0-2	.973	0	104	75	O-74(42-0-33)	0.2
1967	Cin N	76	147	6	29	3	1	3	13	15-5	1	34	.197	.274	.293	56	-8	0-1	.984	1	109	96	O-40(18-0-25)	-1.0
1968	NY N	116	345	30	82	14	4	12	48	21-6	7	58	.238	.292	.406	108	2	1-0	.993	1	103	119	O-82(71-0-12),1-17	-0.2
1969	†NY N	100	303	42	91	9	3	14	47	36-2	3	32	.300	.375	.488	139	16	1-2	.992	-4	96	41	O-78(16-0-63)/1-9	0.7
1970	NY N	122	403	48	118	19	2	11	49	49-13	3	33	.293	.371	.432	115	10	1-1	1.000	3	115	60	O-58(4-0-54),1-56	0.6
1971	NY N	68	135	13	25	6	2	5	18	21-2	1	18	.185	.299	.370	90	-2	1-1	.984	5	112	320	O-38(12-0-27)/1	0.1
1972	Chi N	15	16	1	2	0	0	0	1	3-0	0	3	.125	.263	.125	12	-2	0-0	1.000	-0	66	54	/1-4	-0.2
	Oak A	8	7	0	0	0	0	0	0	1-0	0	2	.000	.125	.000	-64	-1	0-0	—	0			H	-0.2
Total	8	665	1686	194	426	60	15	68	233	188-29	15	254	.253	.330	.427	109	21	5-7	.987	7	105	106	O-388(166-0-229)/1-88	0.1
SHANDLEY, JIM James H. B , NY D 11.4.1904 Brooklyn, NY d5.3																								
1876	NY N	2	8	0	1	0	0	0	0	0		0	.125	.125	.125	-19	-1		.600	-1	0	0	/O-2(0-1-1)	-0.2
SHANER, WALLY Walter Dedaker "Skinny" B 5.24.1900 Lynchburg, VA D 11.13.1992 Las Vegas, NV BR/TR 6-2/195# d5.4																								
1923	Cle A	3	4	1	1	0	0	0	0	1	0	1	.250	.400	.250	74	0	0-0	1.000	-0	102	0	/O-2(LF),3	0.0
1926	Bos A	69	191	20	54	12	2	0	21	17	2	13	.283	.348	.366	89	-3	1-0	.965	-2	97	58	O-48(LF)	-0.9
1927	Bos A	122	406	54	111	33	6	3	49	21	1	35	.273	.311	.406	87	-10	11-4	.955	-1	94	121	*O-108(85-25-10)/1	-1.6
1929	Cin N	13	28	5	9	0	0	1	4	4	0	5	.321	.406	.429	112	1	1	1.000	-1	26	187	/1-8,O-2(LF)	-0.1
Total	4	207	629	80	175	45	8	4	74	43	3	54	.278	.327	.394	89	-12	13-4	.959	-4	95	98	O-160(137-25-10)/1-9,3	-2.6
SHANKS, HOWIE Howard Samuel "Hank" B 7.21.1890 Chicago, IL D 7.30.1941 Monaca, PA BR/TR 5-11/170# d5.9 C5 OF Total (603-LF 55-CF 44-RF)																								
1912	Was A	116	399	52	92	14	7	1	48	40	3		.231	.305	.308	75	-13	21	.962	-2	91	102	*O-114(112-0-2)	-2.0
1913	Was A	109	390	38	99	11	5	1	37	15	3	40	.254	.287	.315	75	-14	24	.978	2	104	89	*O-109(LF)	-1.9
1914	Was A	143	500	44	112	22	10	4	64	29	2	51	.224	.269	.332	78	-16	18-16	.954	-2	102	74	*O-139(94-43-2)	-3.1
1915	Was A	141	492	52	123	19	8	0	47	30	3	42	.250	.297	.321	83	-12	12-14	.982	7	110	141	O-80(75-1-4),3-49,2-10	-0.9
1916	Was A	140	471	51	119	15	7	1	48	41	3	34	.253	.317	.321	92	-5	23-12	.987	7	117	167	O-88(72-3-13),3-31/S-8,1-7	0.0
1917	Was A	126	430	45	87	15	5	0	28	33	6	37	.202	.269	.260	62	-20	15	.929	7	92	110	S-90,O-26(21-5-0)/1-2	-0.9
1918	Was A	120	436	42	112	19	4	1	56	31	4	21	.257	.312	.326	94	-4	23	.957	-6	114	80	O-64(54-2-8),2-48/3-3	-1.3
1919	Was A	135	491	33	122	8	7	1	54	25	3	48	.248	.289	.299	66	-24	13	.922	-16	88	70	S-94,2-34/O-6(LF)	-3.6
1920	Was A	128	444	56	119	16	7	4	37	29	2	43	.268	.316	.363	82	-13	11-6	.951	-4	90	37	3-63,O-35(32-0-3),1-14/2-5,S	-1.6
1921	Was A	**154**	562	81	170	24	**18**	7	69	57	3	38	.302	.370	.447	113	9	11-10	**.960**	3	96	**124**	*3-154/2	1.9
1922	Was A	84	272	35	77	10	9	1	32	25	4	25	.283	.352	.397	100	-1	6-0	.920	5	106	151	3-54,O-27(21-0-6)	0.6
1923	Bos A	131	464	38	118	19	5	3	57	19	1	37	.254	.285	.336	63	-27	6-6	.939	-11	99	103	3-83,2-38/O-6(4-1-1),S	-3.3
1924	Bos A	72	193	22	50	16	3	0	25	21	0	12	.259	.332	.373	81	-5	1-0	.972	6	96	114	S-41,3-22/O-4(RF),1-2,2-2	0.5
1925	NY A	66	155	15	40	3	1	1	18	20	0	15	.258	.343	.310	68	-7	1-0	.938	-4	70	51	3-26,2-21/O-4(3-0-1)	-0.9
Total	14	1665	5699	604	1440	211	96	25	620	415	37	443	.253	.308	.337	82	-152	185-64	.971	-8	115	109	O-702L,3-485,S-235,2-159/1-25	-16.5
SHANLEY, DOC Harry Root B 1890 Granbury, TX D 12.13.1934 St.Petersburg, FL BR/TR 6/174# d9.15																								
1912	StL A	5	8	1	0	0	0	0	1	2	0		.000	.200	.000	-43	-1	0	.833	-1	43	130	/S-4	-0.3
SHANNABROOK, WARREN Warren H. B 11.30.1880 Massillon, OH D 3.10.1964 N.Canton, OH BR/TR 6/170# d8.13																								
1906	Was A	1	2	0	0	0	0	0	0	0	0		.000	.000	.000	-99	0	0	1.000	-0	88	0	/3	-0.1
SHANNON, DAN Daniel Webster B 3.23.1865 Bridgeport, CT D 10.24.1913 Bridgeport, CT 5-9/175# d4.17 M2																								
1889	Lou AA	121	498	90	128	22	12	4	48	42	0	52	.257	.315	.373	97	-3	26	.910	5	**113**	90	*2-121,M	0.5
1890	Phi P	19	75	15	18	5	1	1	16	4	0	12	.240	.278	.373	72	-4	4	.926	-3	96	48	2-19	-0.5
	NY P	83	324	59	70	7	8	3	44	25	1	34	.216	.274	.315	53	-25	21	.908	0	111	98	2-77/S-6	-1.8
	Year	102	399	74	88	12	9	4	60	29	1	46	.221	.275	.326	56	-29	25	.911	-3	108	89	2-96/S-6	-2.3
1891	Was AA	19	67	7	9	2	0	0	3	6	0	9	.134	.205	.164	6	-8	3	.878	1	101	114	S-14/2-5,M	-0.6
Total	3	242	964	171	225	36	21	8	111	77	1	107	.233	.291	.339	73	-40	54	.911	2	110	88	2-222/S-20	-2.4
SHANNON, FRANK John Francis B 12.3.1873 San Francisco, CA D 2.27.1934 Boston, MA 5-3/155# d10.1																								
1892	Was N	1	4	0	1	0	0	0	2	0	0	2	.250	.250	.250	53	0	0	.625	-1	52	0	/S	-0.1

Year	Tm Lg	G	AB	R	H	2B	3B	HR	RBI	BB-IB	HP	SO	AVG	OBP	SLG	AOPS	ABR	SB-CS	FA	FR	Rng	Thr	G at Pos	BFW
1896	Lou N	31	115	14	18	1	1	1	15	13	1	15	.157	.248	.209	22	-13	3	.830	-12	79	52	S-28/3-3	-2.1
Total	2	32	119	14	19	1	1	1	17	13	1	17	.160	.248	.210	23	-13	3	.820	-13	78	50	/S-29,3-3	-2.2
SHANNON, JOE Joseph Aloysius B 2.11.1897 Jersey City, NJ D 7.28.1955 Jersey City, NJ BR/TR 5-11/170# d7.7 twb-Red																								
1915	Bos N	5	10	3	2	0	0	0	1	0	0	3	.200	.200	.200	22	-1	0	.750	-1	68	0	/O-4(1-1-0),2	-0.2
SHANNON, RED Maurice Joseph B 2.11.1897 Jersey City, NJ D 4.12.1970 Jersey City, NJ BB/TR 5-11/170# d10.7 twb-Joe																								
1915	Bos N	1	3	0	0	0	0	0	0	0	0	0	.000	.000	.000	-99	-1	0	.857	0	104	260	/2	-0.1
1917	Phi A	11	35	8	10	0	0	0	7	6	0	9	.286	.390	.286	108	1	2	.875	-1	103	43	S-10	0.1
1918	Phi A	72	225	23	54	6	5	0	16	42	3	52	.240	.367	.311	103	3	5	.898	1	97	139	S-45,2-26	0.8
1919	Phi A	39	155	14	42	7	2	0	14	12	2	28	.271	.331	.342	88	-2	4	.948	-2	106	60	2-37	-0.4
	Bos A	80	290	36	75	11	7	0	17	17	6	42	.259	.313	.345	90	-5	7	.973	-1	98	126	2-79	-0.5
	Year	119	445	50	117	18	9	0	31	29	8	70	.263	.320	.344	89	-7	11	.965	-3	101	105	*2-116	-0.9
1920	Was A	62	222	30	64	8	7	0	30	22	0	32	.288	.352	.387	98	-1	2-5	.919	-13	83	118	S-31,2-16,3-15	-1.3
	Phi A	25	88	4	15	1	1	0	3	4	0	12	.170	.207	.205	9	-12	1-1	.945	1	106	95	S-24	-0.9
	Year	87	310	34	79	9	8	0	33	26	0	44	.255	.313	.335	73	-13	3-6	.931	-12	93	108	S-55,2-16,3-15	-2.2
1921	Phi A	1	1	0	0	0	0	0	0	0	0	0	.000	.000	.000	-99	0	0-0	—	0			H	0.0
1926	Chi N	19	51	9	17	5	0	0	4	6	1	3	.333	.414	.431	126	2	0	.957	-1	100	77	S-13	0.3
Total	7	310	1070	124	277	38	22	0	91	109	12	178	.259	.334	.336	89	-15	21-6	.957	-16	103	99	2-159,S-123/3-15	-2.0
SHANNON, OWEN Owen Dennis Ignatius B 12.22.1879 Omaha, NE D 4.10.1918 Omaha, NE BR/TR d9.6																								
1903	StL A	9	28	1	6	2	0	0	3	1	0		.214	.241	.286	59	-1	0	.957	-0	*133*	*63*	/C-8,1	-0.1
1907	Was A	4	7	0	1	0	0	0	0	0	0		.143	.143	.143	-10	-1	0	1.000	2	*134*	*235*	/C-4	0.1
Total	2	13	35	1	7	2	0	0	3	1	0		.200	.222	.257	47	-2	0	.970	1	*133*	*107*	/C-12,1	0.0
SHANNON, MIKE Thomas Michael "Moonman" B 7.5.1939 St.Louis, MO BR/TR 6-3/195# d9.11																								
1962	StL N	10	15	3	2	0	0	0	0	1-0	0	3	.133	.188	.133	-11	-2	0-0	1.000	1	106	359	/O-7(5-0-2)	-0.2
1963	StL N	32	26	3	8	0	0	1	2	0-0	1	6	.308	.333	.423	106	0	0-1	.944	2	119	396	O-26(13-1-12)	0.1
1964	†StL N	88	253	30	66	8	2	9	43	19-1	0	54	.261	.310	.415	95	-2	4-0	.983	-0	90	142	O-88(9-6-76)	-0.6
1965	StL N	124	244	32	54	17	3	3	25	28-1	2	46	.221	.305	.352	78	-6	2-1	.994	8	122	101	*O-101(1-14-87)/C-4	-0.3
1966	StL N	137	459	61	132	20	6	16	64	37-0	0	106	.288	.339	.462	120	12	8-4	.985	6	110	114	*O-129(14-7-112)/C	1.0
1967	†StL N	130	482	53	118	18	3	12	77	37-6	4	89	.245	.302	.369	93	-5	2-4	.919	-13	92	92	*3-122/O-6(2-2-5)	-2.2
1968	†StL N	156	576	62	153	29	2	15	79	37-5	2	114	.266	.309	.401	114	9	1-2	.952	-11	96	93	*3-156	-0.4
1969	StL N	150	551	51	140	15	5	12	55	49-7	1	87	.254	.315	.365	90	-8	1-4	.945	-18	86	88	*3-149	-3.0
1970	StL N	55	174	18	37	9	2	0	22	16-4	0	20	.213	.275	.287	51	-12	1-1	.919	-19	61	42	3-51	-3.2
Total	9	882	2780	313	710	116	23	68	367	224-24	10	525	.255	.311	.387	96	-14	19-17	.938	-46	88	86	3-478,O-357(44-30-294)/C-5	-8.8
SHANNON, WALLY Walter Charles B 1.23.1933 Cleveland, OH D 2.8.1992 Creve Coeur, MO BL/TR 6/178# d7.9																								
1959	StL N	47	95	5	27	5	0	0	5	0-0	1	12	.284	.292	.337	63	-5	0-0	1.000	-6	50	98	S-21,2-10	-1.0
1960	StL N	18	23	2	4	0	0	0	1	3-1	1	6	.174	.296	.174	30	-2	0-0	1.000	2	142	111	2-15/S	0.1
Total	2	65	118	7	31	5	0	0	6	3-1	2	18	.263	.293	.305	56	-7	0-0	.955	-4	118	76	/2-25,S-22	-0.9
SHANNON, SPIKE William Porter B 2.7.1878 Pittsburgh, PA D 5.16.1940 Minneapolis, MN BB/TR 5-11/180# d4.15 U2																								
1904	StL N	134	500	84	140	10	3	1	26	50	3		.280	.349	.318	111	9	34	**.978**	5	101	**203**	*O-133(13-3-117)	0.7
1905	StL N	140	544	73	146	16	3	0	41	47	0		.268	.327	.309	92	-4	27	**.984**	1	38	65	*O-140(LF)	-1.2
1906	StL N	80	302	36	78	4	0	0	25	36	0		.258	.337	.272	94	-1	15	.972	4	84	113	O-80(LF)	-0.2
	NY N	76	287	42	73	5	1	0	25	34	4		.254	.342	.279	91	-1	18	.958	-5	44	96	O-76(LF)	-1.2
	Year	156	589	78	151	9	1	0	50	70	4		.256	.339	.275	93	-2	33	.966	-2	66	105	*O-156(LF)	-1.4
1907	NY N	**155**	585	**104**	155	12	5	1	33	82	8		.265	.363	.308	107	9	33	.977	2	84	60	*O-155(LF)	0.3
1908	NY N	77	268	34	60	2	1	1	21	28	7		.224	.314	.250	77	-6	13	.976	-3	84	146	O-74(60-0-15)	-1.5
	Pit N	32	127	10	25	0	2	0	12	9	0		.197	.250	.228	53	-7	5	.947	-1	43	0	O-32(8-20-7)	-1.1
	Year	109	395	44	85	2	3	1	33	37	7		.215	.294	.243	69	-13	18	.964	-4	71	98	*O-106(68-20-22)	-2.6
Total	5	694	2613	383	677	49	15	3	183	286	22		.259	.337	.293	96	-1	145	.974	2	72	106	O-690(532-23-139)	-4.2
SHANTZ, BILLY Wilmer Ebert B 7.31.1927 Pottstown, PA D 12.13.1993 Lauderhill, FL BR/TR 6-1/160# d4.13 b-Bobby																								
1954	Phi A	51	164	13	42	9	3	1	17	17	0	23	.256	.326	.366	89	-3	0-0	.975	-9	*83*	*106*	C-51	-1.0
1955	KC A	79	217	18	56	4	1	1	12	11-1	0	14	.258	.293	.300	59	-13	0-0	.990	-7	*117*	*67*	C-78	-1.7
1960	NY A	1	0	0	0	0	0	0	0	0-0	0	0	—	—	—	—	0	0-0	1.000	-0	*0*	*0*	/C	0.0
Total	3	131	381	31	98	13	4	2	29	28-1	0	37	.257	.307	.328	72	-16	0-0	.984	-16	*102*	*83*	C-130	-2.7
SHARMAN, RALPH Ralph Edward "Bally" B 4.11.1895 Cleveland, OH D 5.24.1918 Camp Sheridan, AL BR/TR 5-11/176# d9.10																								
1917	Phi A	13	37	2	11	2	1	0	2	3	1	2	.297	.366	.405	137	2	1	.941	-2	72	68	O-10(2-3-5)	-0.1
SHARON, DICK Richard Louis B 4.15.1950 San Mateo, CA BR/TR 6-2/195# d5.13																								
1973	Det A	91	178	20	43	9	0	7	16	10-0	0	31	.242	.280	.410	87	-4	2-0	.970	4	115	137	O-91(19-7-71)	-0.2
1974	Det A	60	129	12	28	4	0	2	10	14-0	0	29	.217	.292	.295	67	-5	4-4	.989	1	103	109	O-56(23-14-19)	-0.7
1975	SD N	91	160	14	31	7	0	4	20	26-0	0	35	.194	.306	.313	77	-5	0-2	.948	-2	102	32	O-57(39-12-7)	-1.0
Total	3	242	467	46	102	20	0	13	46	50-0	0	95	.218	.293	.345	79	-14	6-6	.969	3	108	97	O-204(81-33-97)	-1.9
SHARP, BILL William Howard B 1.18.1950 Lima, OH BL/TL 5-10/178# d5.26																								
1973	Chi A	77	196	23	54	8	3	4	22	19-2	3	28	.276	.345	.408	109	2	2-3	.981	5	101	238	O-70(11-59-0)/D	0.5
1974	Chi A	100	320	45	81	13	2	4	24	25-2	2	37	.253	.309	.344	86	-6	0-3	.986	1	110	43	O-99(13-7-85)	-1.1
1975	Chi A	18	35	1	7	0	0	0	4	2-0	0	3	.200	.243	.200	26	-3	0-0	.941	-2	76	0	O-14(2-1-11)	-0.6
	Mil A	125	373	37	95	27	3	1	34	19-2	1	26	.255	.289	.351	81	-10	0-3	.994	13	113	157	*O-124(43-82-23)	-0.2
	Year	143	408	38	102	27	3	1	38	21-2	1	29	.250	.285	.338	76	-13	0-3	.991	11	110	143	*O-138(45-83-34)	-0.8
1976	Mil A	78	180	16	44	4	0	0	11	10-0	1	15	.244	.288	.267	64	-8	1-3	.975	6	117	224	O-56(11-10-37)/D-7	-0.5
Total	4	398	1104	122	281	52	8	9	95	75-6	7	109	.255	.304	.341	83	-25	3-12	.985	23	109	142	O-363(80-159-156)/D-8	-1.9
SHARPE, BUD Bayard Heston B 8.6.1881 West Chester, PA D 5.31.1916 Haddock, GA BR/TR 6-1/170# d4.14																								
1905	Bos N	46	170	8	31	3	2	0	11	7	0		.182	.215	.224	31	-15	0	.904	2	205	223	O-42(RF)/C-3,1	-1.6
1910	Pit N	4	16	2	3	0	1	0	1	0	0	2	.188	.188	.313	43	-1	0	1.000	0	131	0	/1-4	-0.1
	Bos N	115	439	30	105	14	3	0	29	14	1	31	.239	.264	.285	58	-25	4	.987	8	128	103	*1-113	-2.1
	Year	119	455	32	108	14	4	0	30	14	1	33	.237	.262	.286	57	-27	4	**.987**	8	**128**	99	*1-117	-2.2
Total	2	165	625	40	139	17	6	0	41	21	1	33	.222	.249	.269	50	-41	4	.987	10	127	99	1-118/O-42(RF),C-3	-3.8
SHARPERSON, MIKE Michael Tyrone B 10.4.1961 Orangeburg, SC D 5.26.1996 Las Vegas, NV BR/TR 6-3/191# d4.6																								
1987	Tor A	32	96	4	20	4	1	0	9	7-0	1	15	.208	.269	.271	43	-8	2-1	.971	-4	85	91	2-32	-1.0
	LA N	10	33	7	9	2	0	0	1	4-1	0	5	.273	.351	.333	85	-1	0-0	1.000	1	131	0	/3-7,2-6	0.0
1988	†LA N	46	59	8	16	1	0	0	4	1-0	1	12	.271	.290	.288	70	-2	0-1	.949	-2	102	128	2-20/3-6,S-4	-0.5
1989	LA N	27	28	2	7	3	0	0	5	4-1	0	7	.250	.333	.357	102	0	0-1	1.000	-1	50	142	/2-4,1-2,3-2,S	-0.1
1990	LA N	129	357	42	106	14	2	3	36	46-6	1	39	.297	.376	.373	111	7	15-6	.949	11	107	91	*3-106,S-15/2-9,1-6	2.0
1991	LA N	105	216	24	60	11	2	2	20	25-0	1	24	.278	.355	.375	108	3	1-3	.981	-2	85	70	3-68,S-16,1-10/2-5	0.1
1992	LA N★	128	317	48	95	21	0	3	36	47-1	0	33	.300	.387	.394	125	13	2-2	.979	18	114	107	2-63,3-60/S-2	3.4
1993	LA N	73	90	13	23	4	0	2	10	5-0	1	17	.256	.299	.367	83	-2	2-0	.945	-0	87	127	2-17/3-6,S-3,10(RF)	-0.2
1995	Atl N	7	7	1	1	1	0	0	2	0-0	0	2	.143	.143	.286	9	-1	0-0	—	-0			/3	-0.1
Total	8	557	1203	149	337	61	5	10	123	139-9	5	154	.280	.355	.364	103	9	22-14	.952	21	104	77	3-256,2-156/S-41,1-19,O(RF)	3.6
SHARROTT, JACK John Henry B 8.13.1869 Bangor, ME D 12.31.1927 Los Angeles, CA BR/TR 5-9/165# d4.22 ▲																								
1890	NY N	32	109	16	22	3	2	0	14	0	0	14	.202	.202	.266	36	-10	6	.932	-1	129	0	P-25/O-9(5-0-4)	-0.3
1891	NY N	10	30	5	10	2	0	1	7	1	0	2	.333	.355	.500	154	4	3	.950	1	105	0	P-10	0.0
1892	NY N	4	8	1	1	0	0	0	0	0	0	1	.125	.125	.125	-25	-1	0	.333	-1	0	0	/O-3(RF),P	-0.2
1893	Phi N	50	152	25	38	4	3	1	22	8	0	14	.250	.287	.336	65	-9	6	.824	-1	114	0	O-33(24-9-5),P-12	-0.9
Total	4	96	299	47	71	9	5	2	43	9	0	31	.237	.260	.321	61	-16	15	.927	-2	120	0	/P-48,O-45(29-9-12)	-1.4
SHAUGHNESSY, SHAG Francis Joseph B 4.8.1883 Amboy, IL D 5.15.1969 Montreal, PQ, CAN BR/TR 6-1.5/185# d4.17 C1																								
1905	Was A	1	3	0	0	0	0	0	0	0	1		.000	.250	.000	-19	0	0	.667	-0	0	0	/O(RF)	-0.1
1908	Phi A	8	29	2	9	0	0	0	1	2	0		.310	.355	.310	109	0	3	1.000	-1	0	0	/O-8(CF)	-0.1
Total	2	9	32	2	9	0	0	0	1	2	1		.281	.343	.281	97	0	3	.938	-1	0	0	/O-9(0-8-1)	-0.2

Year	Tm Lg	G	AB	R	H	2B	3B	HR	RBI	BB-IB	HP	SO	AVG	OBP	SLG	AOPS	ABR	SB-CS	FA	FR	Rng	Thr	G at Pos	BFW
SHAVE, JON Jonathan Taylor B 11.4.1967 Waycross, GA BR/TR 6/185# d5.15																								
1993	Tex A	17	47	3	15	2	0	0	7	0-0	0	8	.319	.306	.362	86	-1	1-3	.917	-2	93	131	/S-9,2-8	-0.3
1998	Min A	19	40	7	10	3	0	1	5	3-0	0	10	.250	.302	.400	79	-1	1-2	1.000	-0	103	124	3-15/1SD	-0.2
1999	Tex A	43	73	10	21	4	0	0	9	5-0	2	17	.288	.350	.342	74	-3	1-0	.953	2	112	118	S-24/1-9,3-6,2D	0.1
Total	3	79	160	20	46	9	0	1	21	8-0	2	35	.287	.326	.363	79	-5	3-5	.942	-0	106	121	/S-34,3-21,1-10,2-9,D-4	-0.4
SHAW, AL Albert Simpson B 3.1.1881 Toledo, IL D 12.30.1974 Danville, IL BL/TR 5-8.5/165# d9.28																								
1907	StL N	9	25	2	7	0	0	0	1	3	1		.280	.379	.280	110	1	1	.947	-1	84	0	/O-9(CF)	0.0
1908	StL N	107	367	40	97	13	4	1	19	25	0		.264	.311	.330	110	3	9	.931	5	200	237	O-91(2-67-22)/S-4,3	0.4
1909	StL N	114	331	45	82	12	7	2	34	55	0		.248	.355	.344	125	12	15	.940	-4	106	30	O-92(0-90-2)	0.3
1914	Bro F	112	376	81	122	27	7	5	49	44	0	59	.324	.395	.473	137	15	24	.955	2	102	109	*O-102(CF)	1.1
1915	KC F	132	448	67	126	22	10	6	67	46	0	45	.281	.348	.415	119	4	15	.942	-12	83	71	*O-124(120-4-0)	-1.4
Total	5	474	1547	235	434	74	28	14	170	173	1	104	.281	.353	.392	123	35	64	.942	-9	119	106	O-418(122-272-24)/S-4,3	0.4
SHAW, AL Alfred "Shoddy" B 10.3.1874 Burslem, England D 3.25.1958 Uhrichsville, OH BR/TR 5-8/170# d6.8																								
1901	Det A	55	171	20	46	7	0	1	23	10	3		.269	.321	.327	76	-5	2	.938	1	119	96	C-42/1-9,3-2,S	-0.1
1907	Bos A	76	198	10	38	1	3	0	7	18	3		.192	.269	.227	59	-9	4	.971	11	124	105	C-73/1	1.0
1908	Chi A	32	49	0	4	1	0	0	2	2	0		.082	.118	.102	-29	-7	0	.953	0	129	72	C-29	-0.6
1909	Bos N	18	41	1	4	0	0	0	0	5	1		.098	.213	.098	-3	-5	0	.975	2	92	123	C-14	-0.2
Total	4	181	459	31	92	9	3	1	32	35	7		.200	.267	.240	53	-26	6	.961	14	120	100	C-158/1-10,3-2,S	0.1
SHAW, BEN Benjamin Nathaniel B 6.18.1893 LaCenter, KY D 3.16.1959 Cleveland, OH BR/TR 5-11.5/190# d4.11 Mil 1918																								
1917	Pit N	2	2	0	0	0	0	0	0	0	0	0	.000	.000	.000	-97	0	0	—	0			H	-0.1
1918	Pit N	21	36	5	7	1	0	0	2	2	2	2	.194	.275	.222	51	-2	0	.981	-1	31	108	/1-9,C-5	-0.3
Total	2	23	38	5	7	1	0	0	2	2	2	2	.184	.262	.211	43	-2	0	.981	-1	31	108	/1-9,C-5	-0.4
SHAW, HUNKY Royal N B 9.29.1884 Yakima, WA D 7.3.1969 Yakima, WA BB/TR 5-8/165# d5.16																								
1908	Pit N	1	1	0	0	0	0	0	0	0	0		.000	.000	.000	-99	0	0	—	0			H	0.0
SHAY, MARTY Arthur Joseph B 4.25.1896 Boston, MA D 2.20.1951 Worcester, MA BR/TR 5-7.5/148# d9.16																								
1916	Chi N	2	7	0	2	0	0	0	0	0	0	1	.286	.286	.286	68	0	0	.917	-0	76	237	/S-2	0.0
1924	Bos N	19	68	4	16	3	1	0	2	5	1	5	.235	.297	.309	65	-3	2-1	.950	-8	69	96	2-19/S	-1.1
Total	2	21	75	4	18	3	1	0	2	5	1	6	.240	.296	.307	66	-3	2-1	.950	-8	69	96	/2-19,S-3	-1.1
SHAY, DANNY Daniel C. B 11.8.1876 Springfield, OH D 12.1.1927 Kansas City, MO TR 5-10/?# d4.30																								
1901	Cle A	19	75	4	17	2	2	0	10	2	2		.227	.266	.307	61	-4	0	.901	-3	89	39	S-19	-0.6
1904	StL N	99	340	45	87	11	1	1	18	39	3		.256	.338	.303	103	3	36	.911	-8	105	93	S-97/2-2	-0.2
1905	StL N	78	281	30	67	12	1	0	28	35	4		.238	.331	.288	88	-2	11	.953	-15	99	106	2-39,S-39	-1.6
1907	NY N	35	79	10	15	1	1	1	6	12	1		.190	.304	.266	76	-2	5	.931	-6	70	24	2-13/S-9,O-2(CF)	-0.9
Total	4	231	775	89	186	26	5	2	62	88	10		.240	.325	.294	90	-5	52	.902	-33	98	75	S-164/2-54,O-2(CF)	-3.3
SHEA, GERRY Gerald J. B 7.26.1881 St.Louis, MO D 5.3.1964 Berkeley, MO TR 5-7/160# d10.1																								
1905	StL N	2	6	0	2	0	0	0	0	0	0		.333	.333	.333	102	0	0	.917	0	85	144	/C-2	0.0
SHEA, NAP John Edward "Napoleon" B 5.23.1874 Ware, MA D 7.8.1968 Bloomfield Hills, MI BR/TR 5-5/155# d9.11																								
1902	Phi N	3	8	1	1	0	0	0	0	1	1		.125	.300	.125	32	-1	0	1.000	-1	75	82	/C-3	-0.1
SHEA, MERV Mervyn David John B 9.5.1900 San Francisco, CA D 1.27.1953 Sacramento, CA BR/TR 5-11/175# d4.23 C8																								
1927	Det A	34	85	5	15	6	3	0	9	7	0	15	.176	.239	.318	43	-8	0-0	.949	-2	97	72	C-31	-0.7
1928	Det A	39	85	8	20	2	3	0	9	9	1	11	.235	.316	.329	69	-4	2-1	.951	1	107	183	C-30	-0.1
1929	Det A	50	162	23	47	6	0	3	24	19	0	18	.290	.365	.383	92	-1	2-1	.964	-7	70	120	C-46	-0.5
1933	Bos A	16	56	1	8	3	0	0	8	4	0	7	.143	.200	.196	5	-8	0-0	1.000	-1	69	145	C-16	-0.7
	StL A	94	279	26	73	11	1	1	27	43	0	26	.262	.360	.319	76	-8	2-0	.995	9	121	113	C-85	0.7
	Year	110	335	27	81	14	1	1	35	47	0	33	.242	.335	.299	65	-15	2-0	**.996**	9	114	117	*C-101	0.0
1934	Chi A	62	176	8	28	3	0	0	5	24	0	19	.159	.260	.176	14	-23	0-1	.972	-3	64	128	C-60	-2.1
1935	Chi A	46	122	8	28	2	0	0	13	30	0	9	.230	.382	.246	64	-5	0-0	.990	6	93	100	C-43	0.3
1936	Chi A	14	24	3	3	0	0	0	2	6	0	5	.125	.300	.125	8	-3	0-0	1.000	1	116	49	C-14	-0.2
1937	Chi A	25	71	7	15	1	0	0	5	15	0	10	.211	.349	.225	48	-5	1-0	.966	3	126	144	C-25	-0.1
1938	Bro N	48	120	14	22	5	0	0	12	28	0	20	.183	.338	.225	56	-6	1	.977	-0	86	90	C-47	-0.4
1939	Det A	4	2	0	0	0	0	0	0	0	0	1	.000	.000	.000	-93	-1	0-0	.500	-1	0	0	/C-4	-0.1
1944	Phi N	7	15	2	4	0	0	1	1	4	0	4	.267	.421	.467	155	1	0	.952	-0	143	94	/C-6	0.1
Total	11	439	1197	105	263	39	7	5	115	189	1	145	.220	.327	.277	58	-71	8-3	.976	7	95	116	C-407	-3.8
SHEAFFER, DANNY Danny Todd B 8.2.1961 Jacksonville, FL BR/TR 6/202# d4.9 OF Total (20-LF 2-CF 9-RF)																								
1987	Bos A	25	66	5	8	1	0	1	5	0-0	0	14	.121	.119	.182	-21	-12	0-0	.977	-5	104	88	C-25	-1.5
1989	Cle A	7	16	1	1	0	0	0	0	2-0	0	2	.063	.167	.063	-32	-3	0-0	—	-0	0	0	/3-2,O(LF)D	-0.3
1993	Col N	82	216	26	60	9	1	4	32	8-0	1	15	.278	.299	.384	72	-9	2-3	.994	-1	114	82	C-65/1-7,O-2(LF),3	-0.7
1994	Col N	44	110	11	24	4	0	1	12	10-0	0	11	.218	.283	.282	41	-9	0-2	.995	2	77	107	C-30/1-2,O(LF)	-0.6
1995	StL N	76	208	24	48	10	1	5	30	23-2	0	38	.231	.306	.361	76	-8	0-0	.993	9	74	99	C-67/1-3,3	0.4
1996	†StL N	79	198	10	45	9	3	2	20	9-0	3	25	.227	.271	.333	59	-12	3-3	.983	4	100	107	C-47,3-17/1-6,O-3(LF)	-0.6
1997	StL N	76	132	10	33	5	0	0	11	8-0	1	17	.250	.296	.288	55	-9	1-0	.957	-2	102	62	3-30,O-22(13-2-9)/C-9,2-3	-1.0
Total	7	389	946	87	219	38	5	13	110	60-2	5	122	.232	.278	.323	56	-62	6-8	.990	7	93	94	C-243/3-51,O-29L,1-18,2-3,D-3	-4.3
SHEAN, DAVE David William B 7.9.1883 Arlington, MA D 5.22.1963 Boston, MA BR/TR 5-11/175# d9.10																								
1906	Phi A	22	75	7	16	3	2	0	3	5	2		.213	.280	.307	81	-2	6	.980	-1	94	70	2-22	-0.3
1908	Phi N	14	48	4	7	2	0	0	2	1	1		.146	.180	.188	17	-4	1	.871	-5	80	52	S-14	-1.1
1909	Phi N	36	112	14	26	2	2	0	4	14	1		.232	.323	.286	88	-1	3	.982	-2	95	78	2-14,1-11/O-3(CF),S	-0.3
	Bos N	75	267	32	66	11	4	1	29	17	2		.247	.297	.330	90	-4	14	.956	7	106	125	2-72	0.5
	Year	111	379	46	92	13	6	1	33	31	3		.243	.305	.317	90	-5	17	.960	6	104	118	2-86,1-11/O-3(CF),S	0.2
1910	Bos N	150	543	52	130	12	7	3	36	42	0	45	.239	.294	.304	71	-22	16	.953	**43**	**116**	**132**	*2-148	2.4
1911	Chi N	54	145	17	28	4	0	0	15	8	1	15	.193	.240	.221	29	-14	4	.947	1	106	59	2-23,S-19/3	-1.2
1912	Bos N	4	10	1	3	0	0	0	0	1	1	2	.300	.417	.300	96	0	0	.917	-0	106	170	/S-4	0.0
1917	Cin N	131	442	36	93	9	5	2	35	22	1	39	.210	.249	.267	61	-22	10	.961	17	**106**	112	*2-131	-0.3
1918	†Bos A	115	425	58	112	16	3	0	34	40	3	25	.264	.331	.315	97	-1	11	.967	-4	97	85	*2-115	-0.4
1919	Bos A	29	100	4	14	0	0	0	8	5	1	7	.140	.189	.140	-7	-15	1	.981	3	100	155	2-29	-1.2
Total	9	630	2167	225	495	59	23	6	166	155	13	133	.228	.284	.285	70	-85	66	.961	59	106	111	2-554/S-38,1-11,O-3(CF),3	-1.9
SHEARER, RAY Ray Solomon B 9.19.1929 Jacobus, PA D 2.21.1982 York, PA BR/TR 6/200# d9.18																								
1957	Mil N	2	2	1	1	0	0	0	0	1-0	0	1	.500	.667	.500	237	1	0-0	—	-0	0	0	/O(LF)	0.1
SHEARON, JOHN John M. B 1870 Pittsburgh, PA D 2.1.1923 Bradford, PA d7.28 ▲																								
1891	Cle N	30	124	10	30	1	1	0	13	1	0	15	.242	.248	.266	48	-9	6	.814	-1	160	0	O-25(4-14-10)/P-6	-0.8
1896	Cle N	16	64	6	11	0	1	0	3	4	0	6	.172	.221	.203	11	-9	3	.818	-4	0	0	O-16(RF)	-1.1
Total	2	46	188	16	41	1	2	0	16	5	0	21	.218	.238	.245	34	-18	9	.815	-5	94	0	/O-41(4-14-26),P-6	-1.9
SHECKARD, JIMMY Samuel James Tilden B 11.23.1878 Upper Chanceford, PA D 1.15.1947 Lancaster, PA BL/TR 5-9/175# d9.14 OF Total (1843-LF 22-CF 214-RF)																								
1897	Bro N	13	49	12	14	3	2	3	14	6	0		.286	.364	.612	164	4	5	.753	-6	100	108	S-11/O-2(RF)	-0.1
1898	Bro N	105	408	51	113	17	9	4	64	37	8		.277	.349	.392	113	6	8	.926	-7	76	52	*O-105(101-4-0)/3	-0.9
1899	Bal N	147	536	104	158	18	10	3	75	56	18		.295	.380	.382	104	5	**77**	.943	19	146	244	*O-146(0-1-146)/1	1.5
1900	Bro N	85	273	74	82	19	10	1	39	42	12		.300	.416	.454	132	14	30	.925	3	125	108	O-78(67-6-5)	1.0
1901	Bro N	133	554	116	196	29	**19**	11	104	47	5		.354	.409	**.534**	168	47	35	.944	5	96	121	*O-121(120-1-0),3-12	4.3
1902	Bal A	4	15	3	4	1	0	0	0	1	0		.267	.313	.333	76	0	2	1.000	-1	0	0	/O-4(CF)	-0.1
	Bro N	123	486	86	129	20	10	4	37	57	5		.265	.349	.372	122	14	23	.964	9	71	128	*O-123(122-1-0)	1.6
1903	Bro N	**139**	515	99	171	29	9	**9**	75	75	6		.332	.423	.476	161	**45**	**67**	.951	**25**	**190**	154	*O-139(LF)	**5.8**
1904	Bro N	143	507	70	121	23	6	1	46	56	2		.239	.317	.314	97	0	21	.956	9	92	95	*O-141(LF)/2-2	0.1
1905	Bro N	130	480	58	140	20	11	3	41	61	7		.292	.380	.398	142	28	23	.967	17	144	130	*O-129(LF)	3.8
1906	†Chi N	149	549	90	144	27	10	1	45	67	6		.262	.349	.353	112	10	30	.986	-2	68	26	*O-149(LF)	0.0
1907	†Chi N	143	484	76	129	23	1	1	36	76	6		.267	.373	.324	112	12	31	.975	-8	68	49	*O-142(LF)	-0.5

Year	Tm Lg	G	AB	R	H	2B	3B	HR	RBI	BB-IB	HP	SO	AVG	OBP	SLG	AOPS	ABR	SB-CS	FA	FR	Rng	Thr	G at Pos	BFW
1908	†Chi N	115	403	54	93	18	3	2	22	62	2		.231	.336	.305	101	4	18	.955	-4	85	89	*O-115(LF)	-0.9
1909	Chi N	148	525	81	134	29	5	1	43	72	1		.255	.346	.335	109	8	15	.967	-5	84	122	*O-148(LF)	-0.5
1910	†Chi N	144	507	82	130	27	6	5	51	83	5	53	.256	.366	.363	114	12	22	.976	8	107	117	*O-143(LF)	1.3
1911	Chi N	156	539	**121**	149	26	11	4	50	**147**	3	58	.276	**.434**	.388	130	34	32	.963	15	107	144	*O-156(LF)	**4.1**
1912	Chi N	146	523	85	128	22	10	3	47	**122**	5	81	.245	.392	.342	102	9	15	.962	9	107	119	*O-146(LF)	1.2
1913	StL N	52	136	18	27	2	1	0	17	41	1	25	.199	.388	.228	79	0	5-7	.953	0	98	105	O-46(16-0-36)	-0.4
	Cin N	47	116	16	22	1	3	0	7	27	0	16	.190	.343	.250	71	-3	6-5	.969	-0	99	96	O-38(9-5-25)	-0.6
	Year	99	252	34	49	3	4	0	24	68	1	41	.194	.368	.238	76	-4	11-12	.960	-0	98	101	O-84(25-5-61)	-1.0
Total	17	2122	7605	1296	2084	354	136	56	813	1135	92	233	.274	.375	.378	120	249	465-12	.958	87	104	113	*O-2071L/3-13,S-11,2-2,1	20.7
SHEEHAN, JIM James Thomas "Big Jim" B 6.3.1913 New Haven, CT D 12.2.2003 BR/TR 6-2/196# d9.26																								
1936	NY N	1	4	0	0	0	0	0	0	0	0	2	.000	.000	.000	-99	-1	0	.833	-0	*0*	*0*	/C	-0.1
SHEEHAN, JACK John Thomas B 4.15.1893 Chicago, IL D 5.29.1987 W.Palm Beach, FL BB/TR 5-8.5/165# d9.11																								
1920	†Bro N	3	5	0	2	1	0	0	0	1	0	0	.400	.500	.600	208	1	0-0	.875	-0	120	0	/S-2,3	0.1
1921	Bro N	5	12	2	0	0	0	0	0	0	0	1	.000	.000	.000	-97	-3	0-0	.900	-0	84	112	/2-2,S3	-0.4
Total	2	8	17	2	2	1	0	0	0	1	0	1	.118	.167	.176	-7	-2	0-0	.909	-1	105	0	/S-3,2-2,3-2	-0.3
SHEEHAN, TOMMY Thomas H. B 11.6.1877 Sacramento, CA D 5.22.1959 Panama City, Panama BR/TR 5-8/160# d8.2																								
1900	NY N	1	2	0	0	0	0	0	0	0	0		.000	.000	.000	-99	-1	0	—	-0	0	0	/S	-0.1
1906	Pit N	95	315	28	76	6	3	1	34	18	1		.241	.284	.289	75	-10	13	.947	-4	97	122	3-90	-1.2
1907	Pit N	75	226	23	62	2	3	0	25	23	0		.274	.341	.310	103	1	10	.941	1	115	42	3-57,S-10	0.4
1908	Bro N	146	468	45	100	18	2	0	29	53	6		.214	.302	.261	83	-6	9	.930	-4	97	73	*3-145	-0.8
Total	4	317	1011	96	238	26	8	1	88	94	7		.235	.305	.280	85	-16	32	.938	-7	101	82	3-292/S-11	-1.7
SHEEHAN, BIFF Timothy James B 2.13.1868 Hartford, CT D 10.21.1923 Hartford, CT BL/TR 5-9/165# d7.22																								
1895	StL N	52	180	24	57	3	6	1	18	20	3	6	.317	.394	.417	111	3	7	.940	-0	135	80	O-41(0-2-39),1-11	0.1
1896	StL N	6	19	0	3	0	0	0	1	4	0	0	.158	.304	.158	25	-2	0	1.000	-0	0	0	/O-6(1-0-5)	-0.2
Total	2	58	199	24	60	3	6	1	19	24	3	6	.302	.385	.392	103	1	7	.948	-1	117	69	/O-47(1-2-44),1-11	-0.1
SHEELY, EARL Earl Homer "Whitey" B 2.12.1893 Bushnell, IL D 9.16.1952 Seattle, WA BR/TR 6-3.5/195# d4.14 s-Bud																								
1921	Chi A	**154**	563	68	171	25	6	11	95	57	7	34	.304	.375	.428	106	5	4-9	.988	6	**119**	108	*1-154	-0.1
1922	Chi A	149	526	72	167	37	4	6	80	60	5	27	.317	.393	.437	117	15	4-6	.993	2	102	96	*1-149	0.6
1923	Chi A	**156**	570	74	169	25	3	4	88	79	5	30	.296	.387	.372	102	5	5-5	.992	-1	95	97	*1-156	-0.7
1924	Chi A	146	535	84	171	34	3	3	103	95	4	28	.320	.426	.411	120	23	7-4	.991	-11	75	85	*1-146	0.3
1925	Chi A	153	600	93	189	43	3	9	111	68	5	23	.315	.389	.442	117	17	3-3	.988	-6	88	109	*1-153	0.1
1926	Chi A	145	525	77	157	40	2	6	89	75	7	13	.299	.394	.417	116	16	3-1	**.995**	-1	93	86	*1-144	0.6
1927	Chi A	45	129	11	27	3	0	2	16	20	1	5	.209	.320	.279	58	-8	1-3	.982	-4	65	101	1-36	-1.4
1929	Pit N	139	485	63	142	22	4	6	88	75	4	24	.293	.392	.392	93	-3	6	**.996**	-1	93	94	*1-139	-1.2
1931	Bos N	147	538	30	147	15	2	1	77	34	2	21	.273	.319	.314	73	-21	0	.992	-2	93	93	*1-143	-3.6
Total	9	1234	4471	572	1340	244	27	48	747	563	40	205	.300	.383	.399	104	49	33-31	.991	-18	94	96	*1-1220	-5.4
SHEELY, BUD Hollis Kimball B 11.26.1920 Spokane, WA D 10.17.1985 Sacramento, CA BL/TR 6-1/200# d7.26 f-Earl																								
1951	Chi A	34	89	2	16	2	0	0	7	6	1	7	.180	.240	.202	21	-10	0-0	.986	2	*86*	*68*	C-33	-0.6
1952	Chi A	36	75	1	18	2	0	0	3	12	1	7	.240	.352	.267	73	-2	0-1	.992	-1	*72*	*97*	C-31	-0.3
1953	Chi A	31	46	4	10	1	0	0	2	9	0	8	.217	.345	.239	58	-2	0-0	1.000	0	*84*	*41*	C-17	-0.1
Total	3	101	210	7	44	5	0	0	12	27	2	22	.210	.305	.233	49	-14	0-1	.991	2	*81*	*73*	/C-81	-1.0
SHEERIN, CHUCK Charles Joseph B 4.17.1909 Brooklyn, NY D 9.27.1986 Valley Stream, NY BR/TR 5-11.5/198# d4.21																								
1936	Phi N	39	72	4	19	4	0	0	4	7	0	18	.264	.329	.319	68	-3	0	.942	-1	103	33	2-17,3-13/S-5	-0.3
SHEETS, ANDY Andrew Mark B 11.19.1971 Baton Rouge, LA BR/TR 6-2/180# d4.22																								
1996	Sea A	47	110	18	21	8	0	0	9	10-0	1	41	.191	.262	.264	34	-11	2-0	.947	3	99	186	3-25,2-18/S-7	-0.7
1997	†Sea A	32	89	18	22	3	0	4	9	7-0	0	34	.247	.299	.416	86	-2	2-0	.872	-5	84	120	3-21/S-9,2-2	-0.5
1998	†SD N	88	194	31	47	5	3	7	29	21-3	1	62	.242	.318	.407	97	-2	7-2	.964	1	109	106	S-39,3-23,2-22/1-2	0.3
1999	Ana A	87	244	22	48	10	0	3	29	14-0	0	59	.197	.236	.275	31	-26	1-2	.966	-22	85	77	S-76/2-7,3	-4.1
2000	Bos A	12	21	1	2	0	0	0	1	0-0	0	3	.095	.095	.095	-50	-5	0-0	1.000	1	108	122	S-10/1D	-0.3
2001	TB A	49	153	10	30	8	0	1	14	12-0	0	35	.196	.251	.268	39	-14	2-0	.990	0	94	96	S-49	-0.9
2002	TB A	41	149	18	37	4	0	4	22	12-0	0	41	.248	.301	.356	76	-5	2-3	.992	3	96	137	2-26,S-11/3-4	-0.1
Total	7	356	960	118	207	38	3	19	113	76-3	2	275	.216	.271	.321	55	-65	16-7	.975	-19	95	88	S-201/2-75,3-74,1-3,D-2	-6.3
SHEETS, LARRY Larry Kent B 12.6.1959 Staunton, VA BL/TR 6-3/225# d9.18 OF Total (192-LF 144-RF)																								
1984	Bal A	8	16	3	7	1	0	1	2	1-0	0	3	.438	.471	.688	221	3	0-0	1.000	1	126	350	/O-7(RF)	0.3
1985	Bal A	113	328	43	86	8	0	17	50	28-2	2	52	.262	.323	.442	110	4	0-1	.875	-1	63	0	D-93/O-9(1-0-8),1	-0.1
1986	Bal A	112	338	42	92	17	1	18	60	21-3	2	56	.272	.317	.488	117	7	2-0	.984	-1	111	57	D-58,O-32(21-0-11)/C-6,1-4,3-2	0.4
1987	Bal A	135	469	74	148	23	0	31	94	31-1	3	67	.316	.358	.563	144	28	1-1	.975	-5	95	60	*O-124(72-0-58)/1-3,D-7	1.7
1988	Bal A	136	452	38	104	19	1	10	47	42-4	6	72	.230	.302	.343	83	-10	1-6	.974	3	94	215	O-76(42-0-36),D-50/1-3	-1.4
1989	Bal A	102	304	33	74	12	1	7	33	26-10	3	58	.243	.305	.359	90	-4	1-1	—	0	0	0	D-88	-0.7
1990	Det A	131	360	40	94	17	2	10	52	24-2	2	42	.261	.308	.403	97	-2	1-3	.981	-2	80	178	O-79(56-0-23),D-44	-0.8
1993	Sea A	11	17	0	2	1	0	0	1	2-0	1	1	.118	.250	.176	17	-2	0-0	1.000	-0	86	0	/O(RF)D	-0.2
Total	8	748	2284	273	607	98	5	94	339	175-22	19	351	.266	.321	.437	109	24	6-12	.976	-5	93	125	D-345,O-328L/1-11,C-6,3-2	-0.8
SHEFFIELD, GARY Gary Antonian B 11.18.1968 Tampa, FL BR/TR 5-11/190# d9.3 OF Total (428-LF 847-RF)																								
1988	Mil A	24	80	12	19	1	0	4	12	7-0	0	7	.237	.295	.400	93	-1	3-1	.967	-11	67	64	S-24	-1.0
1989	Mil A	95	368	34	91	18	0	5	32	27-0	4	33	.247	.303	.337	82	-9	10-6	.959	-11	93	91	S-70,3-21/D-4	-1.5
1990	Mil A	125	487	67	143	30	1	10	67	44-1	3	41	.294	.350	.421	117	12	25-10	.934	-1	105	69	*3-125	1.3
1991	Mil A	50	175	25	34	12	2	2	22	19-1	3	15	.194	.277	.320	69	-7	5-5	.922	-9	80	85	3-43/D-5	-1.7
1992	SD N★	146	557	87	184	34	3	33	100	48-5	6	40	**.330**	.385	.580	168	49	5-6	.961	9	106	109	*3-144	6.0
1993	SD N	68	258	34	76	12	2	10	36	18-0	3	30	.295	.344	.473	115	5	5-1	.905	-7	89	102	3-67	-0.1
	Fla N★	72	236	33	69	8	3	10	37	29-6	6	34	.292	.378	.479	122	8	12-4	.894	-3	103	37	3-66	0.7
	Year	140	494	67	145	20	5	20	73	47-6	9	64	.294	.361	.476	119	13	17-5	.899	-10	96	70	*3-133	0.6
1994	Fla N	87	322	61	89	16	1	27	78	51-11	6	50	.276	.380	.584	144	21	12-6	.970	-3	91	107	O-87(RF)	1.4
1995	Fla N	63	213	46	69	8	0	16	46	55-8	4	45	.324	.467	.587	176	28	19-4	.942	-1	95	116	O-61(3-0-59)	2.5
1996	Fla N★	161	519	118	163	33	1	42	120	142-19	10	66	.314	**.465**	.624	**192**	**80**	16-9	.976	-14	80	77	*O-161(RF)	5.7
1997	†Fla N	135	444	86	111	22	1	21	71	121-11	15	79	.250	.424	.446	135	32	11-7	.980	2	96	152	*O-132(RF)/D	2.7
1998	Fla N	40	136	21	37	11	1	6	28	26-1	2	16	.272	.392	.500	141	9	4-2	.986	0	94	118	O-37(RF)	0.8
	LA N★	90	301	52	95	16	1	16	57	69-11	6	30	.316	.444	.535	168	35	18-5	.994	-2	91	103	O-89(RF)	3.0
	Year	130	437	73	132	27	2	22	85	95-12	8	46	.302	.428	.524	160	45	22-7	.991	-2	92	107	*O-126(RF)	3.8
1999	LA N★	152	549	103	165	20	0	34	101	101-4	4	64	.301	.407	.523	143	40	11-5	.972	-8	84	79	*O-145(LF)/D-3	2.5
2000	LA N★	141	501	105	163	24	3	43	109	101-7	4	71	.325	.438	.643	180	66	4-6	.954	-8	83	64	*O-139(LF)/D-2	4.7
2001	LA N	143	515	98	160	28	2	36	100	94-13	4	67	.311	.417	.583	168	56	10-4	.972	-3	77	189	*O-141(141-0-2)/D-2	4.6
2002	†Atl N	135	492	82	151	26	0	25	84	72-2	11	53	.307	.404	.512	143	31	12-2	.984	-6	90	81	*O-127(RF)/D-4	2.0
2003	†Atl N★	155	576	126	190	37	2	39	132	86-6	8	55	.330	.419	.604	164	57	18-4	.986	-5	95	70	*O-153(RF)	4.6
Total	16	1882	6729	1190	2009	356	23	379	1232	1110-106	99	796	.299	.401	.527	148	512	200-87	.975	-79	88	103	*O-1272R,3-466/S-94,D-21	38.2
SHELBY, JOHN John T. B 2.23.1958 Lexington, KY BB/TR 6-1/175# d9.15 C6																								
1981	Bal A	7	2	2	0	0	0	0	0	0-0	0	1	.000	.000	.000	-99	-1	2-0	1.000	-0	46	0	/O-4(CF)	0.0
1982	Bal A	26	35	8	11	3	0	1	2	0-0	0	5	.314	.314	.486	116	1	0-1	1.000	-1	75	152	O-24(CF)	-0.1
1983	†Bal A	126	325	52	84	15	2	5	27	18-2	0	64	.258	.297	.363	82	-9	15-2	.981	0	93	185	*O-115(CF)/D	-0.6
1984	Bal A	128	383	44	80	12	5	6	30	20-0	0	71	.209	.248	.313	55	-25	12-4	.993	-1	96	136	*O-124(0-118-9)	-2.6
1985	Bal A	69	205	28	58	6	2	7	27	7-0	0	44	.283	.307	.434	103	0	5-1	.981	4	117	95	O-59(9-43-10)/2D	0.4
1986	Bal A	135	404	54	92	14	4	11	49	18-0	2	75	.228	.263	.364	70	-19	18-6	.978	-2	97	84	*O-121(49-56-31)/D-2	-2.2
1987	Bal A	21	32	4	6	0	0	1	3	1-0	0	13	.188	.212	.281	30	-3	0-1	1.000	0	113	0	O-19(0-4-15)/D	-0.4
	LA N	120	476	61	132	26	0	21	69	31-2	1	97	.277	.317	.464	108	4	16-6	.972	-1	98	138	*O-117(CF)	0.3
1988	†LA N	140	494	65	130	23	6	10	64	44-5	0	128	.263	.320	.395	109	5	16-5	.982	-3	96	116	*O-140(CF)	0.2
1989	LA N	108	345	28	63	11	1	1	12	25-5	0	92	.183	.237	.229	35	-30	10-7	.991	-6	92	61	O-98(CF)	-4.0
1990	LA N	25	24	2	6	1	0	0	2	0-0	0	7	.250	.250	.292	50	-2	1-0	1.000	0	121	0	O-12(7-1-4)	-0.2

Year	Tm Lg	G	AB	R	H	2B	3B	HR	RBI	BB-IB	HP	SO	AVG	OBP	SLG	AOPS	ABR	SB-CS	FA	FR	Rng	Thr	G at Pos	BFW
	Det A	78	222	22	55	9	3	4	20	10-0	0	51	.248	.280	.369	80	-7	3-5	.973	2	100	146	O-68(24-35-13)/D-5	-0.8
1991	Det A	53	143	19	22	8	1	3	8	8-1	1	23	.154	.204	.287	34	-13	0-2	.982	4	120	183	O-47(25-26-3)/D-4	-1.1
Total	11	1036	3090	389	739	128	24	70	313	182-15	4	671	.239	.281	.364	79	-99	98-40	.982	-3	98	120	O-948(114-781-85)/D-16,2	-11.1
SHELDON, BOB Bob Mitchell B 11.27.1950 Montebello, CA BL/TR 6/170# d4.10																								
1974	Mil A	10	17	4	2	1	1	0	0	4-0	0	2	.118	.286	.294	67	-1	0-1	1.000	-1	97	0	/2-3,D-4	-0.2
1975	Mil A	53	181	17	52	3	3	0	14	13-0	2	14	.287	.338	.337	92	-2	0-3	.977	1	105	113	2-44/D-6	0.0
1977	Mil A	31	64	9	13	4	1	0	3	6-0	0	9	.203	.268	.297	55	-4	0-0	1.000	-1	80	78	D-17/2-5	-0.6
Total	3	94	262	30	67	8	5	0	17	23-0	2	25	.256	.317	.324	81	-7	0-4	.979	-2	103	106	/2-52,D-27	-0.8
SHELDON, SCOTT Scott Patrick B 11.28.1968 Hammond, IN BR/TR 6-3/185# d5.18 OF Total (4-LF 1-CF 2-RF)																								
1997	Oak A	13	24	2	6	0	0	1	2	1-0	1	6	.250	.308	.375	78	-1	0-0	.939	-3	71	68	S-12/23	-0.3
1998	Tex A	7	16	0	2	0	0	0	1	1-0	0	6	.125	.176	.125	-19	-3	0-0	1.000	2	157	849	/3-3,S-2,1D	0.0
1999	Tex A	2	1	0	0	0	0	0	0	0-0	0	0	.000	.000	.000	-96	0	0-0	1.000	1	497	0	/3-2	0.1
2000	Tex A	58	124	21	35	11	0	4	19	10-0	1	37	.282	.336	.468	101	0	0-0	.970	-0	94	56	S-22,3-15,2-12,1-10/C-3,O-2(2-1-1),P	0.1
2001	Tex A	61	120	11	24	5	0	3	11	3-0	0	35	.200	.216	.317	38	-11	1-1	.951	4	102	18	3-38,S-16/O-3(2-0-1),C	-0.7
Total	5	141	285	34	67	16	0	8	33	15-0	2	84	.235	.275	.375	65	-15	1-1	.961	4	114	112	/3-59,S-52,2-13,1-11,O-5L,C-4,PD	-0.8
SHELLEY, HUGH Hubert Leneirre B 10.26.1910 Rogers, TX D 6.16.1978 Beaumont, TX BR/TR 6/170# d6.25																								
1935	Det A	7	8	1	2	0	0	0	1	2	0	1	.250	.400	.250	74	0	0-0	1.000	0	119	0	/O-5(3-1-1)	0.0
SHELTON, SKEETER Andrew Kemper B 6.29.1888 Huntington, WV D 1.9.1954 Huntington, WV BR/TR 5-11/175# d8.25																								
1915	NY A	10	40	1	1	0	0	0	0	2	0	10	.025	.071	.025	-71	-9	0	1.000	0	87	141	O-10(CF)	-1.0
SHELTON, BEN Benjamin Davis B 9.21.1969 Chicago, IL BR/TL 6-3/210# d6.16																								
1993	Pit N	15	24	3	6	1	0	2	7	3-0	0	3	.250	.333	.542	130	1	0-0	.889	0	90	326	/O-6(LF),1-2	0.1
SHEMO, STEVE Stephen Michael B 4.9.1915 Swoyersville, PA D 4.13.1992 Eden, NC BR/TR 5-11/175# d4.18																								
1944	Bos N	18	31	3	9	2	0	0	1	1	0	3	.290	.313	.355	84	-1	0	.966	2	124	74	2-16/3-2	0.2
1945	Bos N	17	46	4	11	1	0	0	7	1	0	3	.239	.255	.261	43	-4	0	.921	-5	67	23	2-12/3-3,S	-0.8
Total	2	35	77	7	20	3	0	0	8	2	0	6	.260	.278	.299	60	-5	0	.948	-3	98	51	/2-28,3-5,S	-0.6
SHEPARD, JACK Jack Leroy B 5.13.1932 Clovis, CA D 12.31.1994 Atherton, CA BR/TR 6-2/195# d6.19																								
1953	Pit N	2	4	0	1	0	0	0	0	0	0	2	.250	.250	.250	31	0	0-0	.750	-1	*0*	*0*	/C-2	-0.1
1954	Pit N	82	227	24	69	8	2	3	22	26	0	33	.304	.370	.396	103	2	0-0	.977	-2	*56*	*166*	C-67	0.3
1955	Pit N	94	264	24	63	10	2	2	23	33-3	0	25	.239	.321	.314	71	-10	1-0	.982	-7	*72*	*127*	C-77	-1.4
1956	Pit N	100	256	24	62	11	2	7	30	25-5	0	37	.242	.309	.383	87	-5	1-1	.990	3	*102*	*118*	C-86/1-2	0.1
Total	4	278	751	72	195	29	6	12	75	84-8	0	97	.260	.331	.362	86	-13	2-1	.982	-7	*77*	*135*	C-232/1-2	-1.1
SHEPARDSON, RAY Raymond Francis B 5.3.1897 Little Falls, NY D 11.8.1975 Little Falls, NY BR/TR 5-11.5/170# d9.19																								
1924	StL N	3	6	1	0	0	0	0	0	0	0	3	.000	.000	.000	-99	-2	0-0	1.000	0	*97*	*121*	/C-3	-0.2
SHEPHERD, RON Ronald Wayne B 10.27.1960 Longview, TX BR/TR 6-4/175# d9.5																								
1984	Tor A	12	4	0	0	0	0	0	0	0-0	0	3	.000	.000	.000	-97	-1	0-1	1.000	1	86	1367	/O-5(LF),D-4	-0.1
1985	Tor A	38	35	7	4	2	0	0	1	2-0	0	12	.114	.162	.171	-8	-5	3-0	1.000	-0	107	0	O-16(3-13-1),D-15	-0.5
1986	Tor A	65	69	16	14	4	0	2	4	3-0	0	22	.203	.236	.348	55	-4	0-0	1.000	-3	71	0	O-32(12-10-11),D-16	-0.9
Total	3	115	108	23	18	6	0	2	5	5-0	0	37	.167	.204	.278	29	-10	3-1	1.000	-3	83	50	/O-53(20-23-12),D-35	-1.5
SHEPPARD, JOHN John B Baltimore, MD d6.27																								
1873	Mar NA	3	11	1	0	0	0	0	0	0		1	.000	.000	.000	-99	-3	0-0	.500	-2	0	0	/O-2(1-0-1),C	-0.3
SHERIDAN d10.9																								
1875	Atl NA	1	4	0	0	0	0	0	0	0		1	.000	.000	.000	-99	-1	0-0	—	-0	0	0	/O(LF)	-0.1
SHERIDAN, RED Eugene Anthony B 11.14.1896 Brooklyn, NY D 11.25.1975 Queens Village, NY BR/TR 5-10.5/160# d7.3 Mil 1918																								
1918	Bro N	2	4	0	1	0	0	0	0	1	0	0	.250	.400	.250	100	0	1	1.000	-1	58	0	/2-2	0.0
1920	Bro N	3	2	0	0	0	0	0	0	0	0	1	.000	.000	.000	-97	-1	0-0	1.000	1	113	591	/S-3	0.0
Total	2	5	6	0	1	0	0	0	0	1	0	1	.167	.286	.167	37	-1	1-0	1.000	0	113	591	/S-3,2-2	0.0
SHERIDAN, NEILL Neill Rawlins "Wild Horse" B 11.20.1921 Sacramento, CA BR/TR 6-1.5/195# d9.19																								
1948	Bos A	2	1	0	0	0	0	0	0	0	0	1	.000	.000	.000	-95	0	0-0	—	0			H	0.0
SHERIDAN, PAT Patrick Arthur B 12.4.1957 Ann Arbor, MI BL/TR 6-3/175# d9.16																								
1981	KC A	3	1	0	0	0	0	0	0	0-0	0	1	.000	.000	.000	-99	0	0-0	1.000	0	158	0	/O-3(1-0-2)	0.0
1983	KC A	109	333	43	90	12	2	7	36	20-0	0	64	.270	.312	.381	89	-6	12-3	.988	6	115	93	*O-100(28-36-48)	-0.1
1984	†KC A	138	481	64	136	24	4	8	53	41-3	1	91	.283	.338	.399	103	2	19-6	.986	-4	93	98	*O-134(0-35-101)	-0.5
1985	†KC A	78	206	18	47	9	2	3	17	23-2	1	38	.228	.307	.335	76	-7	11-3	.983	-1	97	76	O-69(RF)/D	-0.9
1986	Det A	98	236	41	56	9	1	6	19	21-4	1	57	.237	.300	.360	80	-7	9-2	.977	-3	99	23	O-90(11-51-32)/D-5	-1.0
1987	†Det A	141	421	57	109	19	3	6	49	44-4	1	90	.259	.327	.361	87	-7	18-13	.976	-2	102	78	*O-137(0-26-124)	-1.4
1988	Det A	127	347	47	88	9	5	11	47	44-4	2	64	.254	.339	.403	112	5	8-6	.981	-2	103	38	*O-111(92-9-12)/D-3	0.1
1989	Det A	50	120	16	29	3	0	3	15	17-0	0	21	.242	.333	.342	93	-1	4-0	.982	-1	88	119	O-35(19-7-9)/D-8	-0.1
	†SF N	70	161	20	33	3	4	3	14	13-1	0	45	.205	.264	.329	71	-7	4-1	.983	3	118	77	O-66(8-3-58)	-0.6
1991	NY A	62	113	13	23	3	0	4	7	13-1	0	30	.204	.286	.336	71	-5	1-1	1.000	0	90	183	O-34(3-6-26)/D-2	-0.5
Total	9	876	2419	319	611	91	21	51	257	236-19	6	501	.253	.319	.371	91	-33	86-35	.983	-3	101	77	O-779(162-173-481)/D-19	-5.0
SHERLING, ED Edward Creech "Shine" B 7.17.1897 Coalburg, AL D 11.16.1965 Enterprise, CA BR/TR 6-1/185# d8.13																								
1924	Phi A	4	2	2	1	1	0	0	0	0	0	0	.500	.500	1.000	278	1	0-0	—	0			H	0.1
SHERLOCK, MONK John Clinton B 10.26.1904 Buffalo, NY D 11.26.1985 Buffalo, NY BR/TR 5-10/175# d4.20 b-Vince																								
1930	Phi N	92	299	51	97	18	2	0	38	27	0	28	.324	.380	.398	83	-7	0	.990	3	123	77	1-70/2-5,O(CF)	-0.7
SHERLOCK, VINCE Vincent Thomas "Baldy" B 3.27.1910 Buffalo, NY D 5.11.1997 Cheektowaga, NY BR/TR 6/180# d9.18 b-Monk																								
1935	Bro N	9	26	4	12	1	0	0	6	1	0	2	.462	.481	.500	168	3	1	.907	-2	76	27	/2-8	0.1
SHERMAN, DARRELL Darrell Edward B 12.4.1967 Los Angeles, CA BL/TL 5-9/160# d4.8																								
1993	SD N	37	63	8	14	1	0	0	2	6-0	3	8	.222	.315	.238	51	-4	2-1	1.000	2	143	0	O-26(24-6-1)	-0.2
SHERRILL, DENNIS Dennis Lee B 3.3.1956 Miami, FL BR/TR 6/165# d9.4																								
1978	NY A	2	1	1	0	0	0	0	0	0-0	0	1	.000	.000	.000	-99	0	0-0	—	-0	0	0	/3D	-0.1
1980	NY A	3	4	0	1	0	0	0	0	0-0	0	1	.250	.250	.250	38	0	0-0	1.000	-1	0	0	/S-2,2	-0.1
Total	2	5	5	1	1	0	0	0	0	0-0	0	2	.200	.200	.200	11	0	0-0	1.000	-1	0	0	/S-2,2D3	-0.2
SHERRY, NORM Norman Burt B 7.16.1931 New York, NY BR/TR 5-11/181# d4.12 M2 C16 b-Larry																								
1959	LA N	2	3	0	1	0	0	0	2	0-0	1	0	.333	.500	.333	119	0	0-0	1.000	-0	*0*	*0*	/C-2	0.0
1960	LA N	47	138	22	39	4	1	8	19	12-3	3	29	.283	.353	.500	122	4	0-0	.993	-1	*129*	*66*	C-44	0.5
1961	LA N	47	121	10	31	2	0	5	21	9-2	0	30	.256	.308	.397	78	-4	0-0	.993	3	*103*	*96*	C-45	0.1
1962	LA N	35	88	7	16	2	0	3	16	6-0	1	17	.182	.240	.307	49	-7	0-0	.992	4	*123*	*86*	C-34	-0.1
1963	NY N	63	147	6	20	1	0	2	11	10-1	3	26	.136	.205	.184	13	-17	1-0	.980	2	*120*	*113*	C-61	-1.3
Total	5	194	497	45	107	9	1	18	69	37-6	8	102	.215	.279	.346	69	-24	1-0	.989	9	*118*	*91*	C-186	-0.8
SHETRONE, BARRY Barry Stevan B 7.6.1938 Baltimore, MD D 7.18.2001 Bowie, MD BL/TR 6-2/190# d7.27																								
1959	Bal A	33	79	8	16	1	1	0	5	5-1	0	9	.203	.247	.241	36	-7	3-0	.947	-2	86	0	O-23(5-17-1)	-1.0
1960	Bal A	1	0	1	0	0	0	0	0	0-0	0	0	—	—	—	—	0	0-0	—	0			R	0.0
1961	Bal A	3	7	0	1	0	0	0	1	0-0	0	2	.143	.143	.143	-24	-1	0-0	1.000	-0	91	0	/O-2(CF)	-0.1
1962	Bal A	21	24	3	6	1	0	1	1	0-0	0	5	.250	.250	.417	81	-1	0-0	1.000	1	148	0	/O-6(3-2-1)	0.0
1963	Was A	2	2	0	0	0	0	0	0	0-0	0	0	.000	.000	.000	-99	-1	0-0	—	0			H	-0.1
Total	5	60	112	12	23	2	1	1	7	5-1	0	16	.205	.237	.268	39	-10	3-0	.962	-2	96	0	/O-31(8-21-2)	-1.2
SHETZLINE, JOHN John Henry B 1850 Philadelphia, PA D 12.15.1892 Philadelphia, PA 5-11.5/190# d5.2																								
1882	Bal AA	73	282	23	62	8	3	0		5			.220	.233	.270	75	-7		.800	4	106	138	3-52,2-20/O(RF)S	-0.1

Year	Tm Lg	G	AB	R	H	2B	3B	HR	RBI	BB-IB	HP	SO	AVG	OBP	SLG	AOPS	ABR	SB-CS	FA	FR	Rng	Thr	G at Pos	BFW
SHEVLIN, JIMMY James Cornelius B 7.9.1909 Cincinnati, OH D 10.30.1974 Ft.Lauderdale, FL BL/TL 5-10.5/155# d6.29																								
1930	Det A	28	14	4	2	0	0	0	2	2	0	3	.143	.250	.143	2	-2	0-0	1.000	0	115	0	1-25	-0.2
1932	Cin N	7	24	3	5	2	0	0	4	4	1	0	.208	.345	.292	76	-1	4	.985	-0	85	58	/1-7	-0.2
1934	Cin N	18	39	6	12	2	0	0	6	6	0	5	.308	.400	.359	107	1	0	1.000	1	124	119	1-10	0.1
Total	3	53	77	13	19	4	0	0	12	12	1	8	.247	.356	.299	77	-2	4-0	.995	1	108	70	/1-42	-0.3
SHIELDS, PETE Francis Leroy B 9.21.1891 Swiftwater, MS D 2.11.1961 Jackson, MS BR/TR 6/175# d4.14																								
1915	Cle A	23	72	4	15	6	0	0	6	4	0	14	.208	.250	.292	61	-4	3-3	.974	-0	107	47	1-23	-0.5
SHIELDS, TOMMY Thomas Charles B 8.14.1964 Fairfax, VA BL/TR 6/180# d7.25																								
1992	Bal A	2	0	0	0	0	0	0	0	0-0	0	0	—	—	—	—	0	0-0	—	0			/R	0.0
1993	Chi N	20	34	4	6	1	0	0	1	2-0	0	10	.176	.222	.206	16	-4	0-0	1.000	2	143	173	/2-7,3-7,1O(LF)	-0.2
Total	2	22	34	4	6	1	0	0	1	2-0	0	10	.176	.222	.206	16	-4	0-0	1.000	2	104	136	/3-7,2-7,O(LF)1	-0.2
SHILLING, JIM James Robert B 5.14.1914 Tulsa, OK D 9.12.1986 Tulsa, OK BR/TR 5-11/175# d4.21																								
1939	Cle A	31	98	8	27	7	2	0	12	7	0	9	.276	.324	.388	84	-3	1-0	.935	0	105	105	2-27/S-3	0.0
	Phi N	11	33	3	10	1	3	0	4	1	0	4	.303	.324	.515	126	1	0	.944	-2	79	85	/2-5,S-3,3-3,O(LF)	-0.1
Total	1	42	131	11	37	8	5	0	16	8	0	13	.282	.324	.420	94	-2	1-0	.936	-2	102	103	/2-32,S-6,3-3,O(LF)	-0.1
SHINAULT, GINGER Enoch Erskine B 9.7.1892 Benton, AR D 12.29.1930 Denver, CO BR/TR 5-11/170# d7.4																								
1921	Cle A	22	29	5	11	1	0	0	4	6	0	5	.379	.486	.414	129	2	1-0	.917	1	*103*	*142*	C-20	0.3
1922	Cle A	13	15	1	2	1	0	0	0	0	0	2	.133	.133	.200	-14	-3	0-0	.400	-3	*60*	*0*	C-11	-0.5
Total	2	35	44	6	13	2	0	0	4	6	0	7	.295	.380	.341	85	-1	1-0	.868	-2	*95*	*114*	/C-31	-0.2
SHINDLE, BILLY William B 12.5.1860 Gloucester, NJ D 6.3.1936 Lakeland, NJ BR/TR 5-8.5/155# d10.5																								
1886	Det N	7	26	4	7	0	0	0	4	0		5	.269	.269	.269	62	-1	2	.900	0	118	61	/S-7	-0.1
1887	Det N	22	84	17	24	3	2	0	12	7	0	10	.286	.341	.369	93	-1	13	.818	-3	83	180	3-21/O(LF)	-0.3
1888	Bal AA	135	514	61	107	14	8	1	53	20	8		.208	.249	.272	69	-19	52	**.922**	**38**	120	128	*3-135	2.0
1889	Bal AA	138	567	122	178	24	7	3	64	42	7	37	.314	.369	.397	116	11	56	.862	23	**113**	105	*3-138	3.0
1890	Phi P	**132**	584	127	189	21	21	10	90	40	4	30	.324	.371	.483	124	15	51	.856	8	103	**125**	*S-130/3-2	2.2
1891	Phi N	103	415	68	87	13	1	0	38	33	6	39	.210	.278	.246	51	-26	17	.874	4	106	**156**	*3-100/S-3	-1.7
1892	Bal N	143	619	100	156	20	18	3	50	35	8	34	.252	.301	.357	96	-7	24	.882	37	**130**	114	*3-134/S-9	3.0
1893	Bal N	125	521	100	136	22	11	1	75	66	8	17	.261	.353	.351	86	-10	17	.885	10	**108**	103	*3-125	0.1
1894	Bro N	117	480	94	142	22	9	4	96	29	6	21	.296	.344	.404	86	-12	19	.896	1	96	62	*3-117	-0.7
1895	Bro N	117	481	92	135	21	2	3	70	47	11	28	.281	.358	.351	91	-3	17	.895	-0	106	98	*3-117	-0.1
1896	Bro N	131	516	75	144	24	9	1	61	24	4	20	.279	.316	.366	84	-13	24	.912	-11	93	105	*3-131	-1.8
1897	Bro N	134	542	83	154	32	6	4	105	35	7		.284	.336	.387	96	-3	23	.904	-14	90	76	*3-134	-1.3
1898	Bro N	120	466	50	105	10	3	1	41	10	5		.225	.249	.266	48	-33	3	.911	4	107	128	*3-120	-2.6
Total	13	1424	5815	993	1564	226	97	31	759	388	74	241	.269	.323	.357	88	-102	318	.892	96	107	108	*3-1274,S-149/O(LF)	1.7
SHINES, RAZOR Anthony Raymond "Ray" B 7.18.1956 Durham, NC BB/TR 6-1/210# d9.9																								
1983	Mon N	3	2	0	1	0	0	0	0	0-0	0	0	.500	.500	.500	179	0	0-0	—	-0	0	0	/O(LF)	0.0
1984	Mon N	12	20	0	6	1	0	0	2	0-0	0	3	.300	.286	.350	86	0	0-0	1.000	-1	0	91	/1-3,3	-0.2
1985	Mon N	47	50	0	6	0	0	0	3	4-0	0	9	.120	.185	.120	-14	-8	0-1	.950	0	167	37	/1-5,P	-0.8
1987	Mon N	6	9	0	2	0	0	0	0	1-0	1	0	.222	.364	.222	58	0	1-0	1.000	-0	82	169	/1-2	0.0
Total	4	68	81	0	15	1	0	0	5	5-0	1	12	.185	.239	.198	24	-8	1-1	.975	-1	88	83	/1-10,P3O(LF)	-1.0
SHINJO, TSUYOSHI Tsuyoshi B 1.28.1972 Fukuoka, Japan BR/TR 6-1/185# d4.3																								
2001	NY N	123	400	46	107	23	1	10	56	25-3	7	70	.268	.320	.405	91	-6	4-5	.989	13	**117**	**190**	*O-119(46-53-39)	0.3
2002	†SF N	118	362	42	86	15	3	9	37	24-2	6	46	.238	.294	.370	81	-13	5-0	.980	12	**121**	179	*O-117(1-108-10)	0.0
2003	NY N	62	114	10	22	3	0	1	7	6-1	1	12	.193	.238	.246	28	-13	0-1	.972	7	129	275	O-54(7-50-1)	-0.6
Total	3	303	876	98	215	41	4	20	100	55-6	14	128	.245	.299	.370	78	-32	9-6	.982	31	120	197	O-290(54-211-50)	-0.3
SHINNERS, RALPH Ralph Peter B 10.4.1895 Monches, WI D 7.23.1962 Milwaukee, WI BR/TR 6/180# d4.12																								
1922	NY N	56	135	16	34	4	2	0	15	5	6	22	.252	.308	.311	60	-8	3-5	.915	-4	94	46	O-37(1-30-6)	-1.4
1923	NY N	33	13	5	2	1	0	0	0	2	0	1	.154	.267	.231	33	-1	0-0	1.000	1	171	0	/O-6(2-1-3)	-0.1
1925	StL N	74	251	39	74	9	2	7	36	12	1	19	.295	.330	.430	90	-5	8-5	.982	-2	103	34	O-66(3-56-7)	-0.9
Total	3	163	399	60	110	14	4	7	51	19	7	42	.276	.320	.383	78	-14	11-10	.959	-5	101	38	O-109(6-87-16)	-2.4
SHINNICK, TIM Timothy James "Dandy" or "Good Eye" B 11.6.1867 Exeter, NH D 5.18.1944 Exeter, NH BB/TR 5-9/150# d4.19																								
1890	†Lou AA	133	493	87	126	16	11	1	82	62	8		.256	.348	.339	105	4	62	.925	-31	92	87	*2-130/3-3	-1.9
1891	Lou AA	126	436	77	96	9	11	1	52	54	5	46	.220	.313	.298	76	-14	36	.913	-21	95	94	*2-118/3-7,S	-2.7
Total	2	259	929	164	222	25	22	2	134	116	13	46	.239	.332	.320	91	-10	98	.919	-52	93	90	2-248/3-10,S	-4.6
SHIPKE, BILL William Martin "Skipper Bill" or "Muskrat Bill" (born William Martin Shipkrethaver) B 11.18.1882 St.Louis, MO D 9.10.1940 Omaha, NE BR/TR 5-7/145# d4.23																								
1906	Cle A	2	6	0	0	0	0	0	0	0	0		.000	.000	.000	-99	-1	0	.933	1	124	294	/2-2	-0.1
1907	Was A	64	189	17	37	3	2	1	9	15	2		.196	.262	.249	68	-7	6	.944	8	117	33	3-63	0.3
1908	Was A	111	341	40	71	7	8	0	20	38	5		.208	.297	.276	94	-1	15	.932	-4	96	103	*3-110/2	-0.3
1909	Was A	9	16	2	2	1	0	0	0	2	0		.125	.222	.188	31	-1	0	.905	1	137	154	/3-6,S-2	0.0
Total	4	186	552	59	110	11	10	1	29	55	7		.199	.280	.261	81	-10	21	.935	6	105	80	3-179/2-3,S-2	-0.1
SHIPLEY, CRAIG Craig Barry B 1.7.1963 Parramatta, Australia BR/TR 6-1/185# d6.22 OF Total (4-LF 4-CF 4-RF)																								
1986	LA N	12	27	3	3	1	0	0	4	2-1	1	5	.111	.200	.148	-3	-4	0-0	.914	-3	61	80	S-10/23	-0.7
1987	LA N	26	35	3	9	1	0	0	2	0-0	0	6	.257	.257	.286	45	-3	0-0	.949	-2	95	39	S-18/3-6	-0.4
1989	NY N	4	7	3	1	0	0	0	0	0-0	0	1	.143	.143	.143	-19	-1	0-0	1.000	-1	47	0	/S-3,3-2	-0.2
1991	SD N	37	91	6	25	3	0	1	6	2-0	1	14	.275	.298	.341	77	-3	0-1	.902	-4	75	83	S-19,2-14	-0.6
1992	SD N	52	105	7	26	6	0	0	7	2-1	0	21	.248	.262	.305	59	-6	1-1	.986	5	113	183	S-23,2-11/3-8	0.1
1993	SD N	105	230	25	54	9	0	4	22	10-0	3	31	.235	.275	.326	59	-14	12-3	.964	-6	89	51	S-38,3-37,2-12/O-5(2-3-0)	-1.5
1994	SD N	81	240	32	80	14	4	4	30	9-1	3	28	.333	.362	.475	120	6	6-6	.936	-3	96	88	3-53,S-14,2-13/O-2(1-1-0),1	0.4
1995	Hou N	92	232	23	61	8	1	3	24	8-3	2	28	.263	.291	.345	73	-10	6-1	.982	-3	90	67	3-65,S-11/2-4,1	-1.1
1996	SD N	33	92	13	29	5	0	1	7	2-1	2	15	.315	.337	.402	102	0	7-0	.985	3	114	87	2-17/S-7,3-4,O-3(RF)	0.5
1997	SD N	63	139	22	38	9	0	5	19	7-0	0	20	.273	.306	.446	102	0	1-1	.947	-4	96	59	S-21,2-16/1-4,3-2	-0.3
1998	Ana A	77	147	18	38	7	1	2	17	5-0	5	22	.259	.304	.361	72	-6	0-4	.963	2	80	26	3-48,2-11/1-8,S-5,O-2(1-0-1)	-0.5
Total	11	582	1345	155	364	63	6	20	138	47-7	17	191	.271	.302	.371	80	-41	33-17	.963	-14	90	76	3-226,S-169/2-99,1-14,O-12L	-4.3
SHIRES, ART Charles Arthur "Art The Great" B 8.13.1907 Italy, TX D 7.13.1967 Italy, TX BL/TR 6-1/195# d8.20																								
1928	Chi A	33	123	20	42	6	1	1	11	13	1	10	.341	.409	.431	122	5	0-3	.990	3	138	90	1-32	0.4
1929	Chi A	100	353	41	110	20	7	3	41	32	1	20	.312	.370	.433	108	4	4-5	.991	-0	107	110	1-90/2-3	-0.3
1930	Chi A	37	128	14	33	5	1	1	18	6	0	6	.258	.291	.336	61	-8	2-0	.979	-2	81	67	1-33	-1.1
	Was A	38	84	11	31	5	0	1	19	5	0	5	.369	.404	.464	119	3	1-3	.982	0	113	151	1-21	0.1
	Year	75	212	25	64	10	1	2	37	11	0	11	.302	.336	.387	84	-5	3-3	.980	-2	92	96	1-54	-1.0
1932	Bos N	82	298	32	71	9	3	5	30	25	1	21	.238	.299	.339	74	-11	1	.988	-2	95	100	1-80	-2.1
Total	4	290	986	118	287	45	12	11	119	81	3	62	.291	.347	.395	95	-7	8-11	.988	-1	104	101	1-256/2-3	-3.0
SHIRLEY, BART Barton Arvin B 1.4.1940 Corpus Christi, TX BR/TR 5-10/183# d9.14																								
1964	LA N	18	62	6	17	1	1	0	7	4-2	0	8	.274	.318	.323	87	-1	0-0	.900	0	82	0	3-10/S-8	-0.1
1966	LA N	12	5	2	1	0	0	0	0	0-0	0	2	.200	.200	.200	13	-1	0-0	1.000	1	110	0	/S-5	0.0
1967	NY N	6	12	1	0	0	0	0	0	0-0	0	5	.000	.000	.000	-99	-3	0-0	.917	0	136	66	/2-3	-0.3
1968	LA N	39	83	6	15	3	0	0	4	10-1	0	13	.181	.269	.217	51	-5	0-1	.903	2	103	197	S-21,2-18	-0.1
Total	4	75	162	15	33	4	1	0	11	14-3	0	28	.204	.267	.241	53	-10	0-1	.936	3	107	157	/S-34,2-21,3-10	-0.5
SHIRLEY, MULE Ernest Raeford B 5.21.1901 Snow Hill, NC D 8.3.1955 Goldsboro, NC BL/TL 5-11/180# d5.6																								
1924	†Was A	30	77	12	18	2	2	0	16	3	0	7	.234	.262	.312	49	-6	0-0	.984	0	103	133	1-25	-0.7
1925	Was A	14	23	2	3	1	0	0	2	1	0	7	.130	.167	.174	-14	-4	0-0	1.000	0	92	104	/1-9	-0.4
Total	2	44	100	14	21	3	2	0	18	4	0	14	.210	.240	.280	34	-10	0-0	.988	0	101	127	/1-34	-1.1
SHIVER, IVEY Ivey Merwin "Chick" B 1.22.1906 Sylvester, GA D 8.31.1972 Savannah, GA BR/TR 6-1.5/190# d4.14																								
1931	Det A	2	9	2	1	0	0	0	0	0	0	3	.111	.111	.111	-40	-2	0-0	1.000	-0	64	0	/O-2(CF)	-0.2

Year	Tm Lg	G	AB	R	H	2B	3B	HR	RBI	BB-IB	HP	SO	AVG	OBP	SLG	AOPS	ABR	SB-CS	FA	FR	Rng	Thr	G at Pos	BFW
1934	Cin N	19	59	6	12	1	0	2	6	3	0	15	.203	.242	.322	51	-4	1	1.000	-1	94	0	O-15(RF)	-0.6
Total	2	21	68	8	13	1	0	2	6	3	0	18	.191	.225	.294	38	-6	1-0	1.000	-2	91	0	/O-17(0-2-15)	-0.8
SHOCH, GEORGE George Quintus B 1.6.1859 Philadelphia, PA D 9.30.1937 Philadelphia, PA BR/TR 5-6/158# d9.10 OF Total (99-LF 41-CF 159-RF)																								
1886	Was N	26	95	11	28	2	1	1	18	2		13	.295	.309	.368	114	1	2	.882	-3	47	0	O-25(1-0-24)/S	-0.2
1887	Was N	70	264	47	63	9	1	1	18	21	4	16	.239	.304	.292	71	-9	29	.897	4	124	137	O-63(11-3-49)/S-6,2	-0.5
1888	Was N	90	317	46	58	6	3	2	24	25	9	22	.183	.262	.240	65	-11	23	.900	6	111	39	S-52,O-35(9-0-26)/2P	-0.4
1889	Was N	30	109	12	26	2	0	0	11	20	6	5	.239	.385	.257	86	0	9	.905	3	145	86	O-29(16-0-13)/S	0.2
1891	Mil AA	34	127	29	40	7	1	1	16	18	9	5	.315	.435	.409	118	4	12	.932	3	107	52	S-25/3-9	0.6
1892	Bal N	76	308	42	85	15	3	1	50	24	6	19	.276	.340	.354	107	3	14	.872	-1	105	73	S-57,O-12(8-4-0)/3-7	0.3
1893	Bro N	94	327	53	86	17	1	2	54	48	5	13	.263	.366	.339	92	-1	9	.892	-3	87	0	O-46(32-0-15),3-37,S-11/2-3	-0.5
1894	Bro N	65	243	47	77	6	5	1	37	26	5	6	.317	.394	.395	97	1	16	.926	0	86	70	O-35(1-28-6),3-14/2-9,S-7	0.0
1895	Bro N	61	216	49	56	9	7	0	29	32	5	6	.259	.368	.366	97	1	7	.952	-4	81	77	O-39(16-2-21),2-13/S-6,3-3	-0.4
1896	Bro N	76	250	36	73	7	4	1	28	33	3	10	.292	.381	.364	103	3	11	.941	-6	105	69	2-62,O-10(2-3-5)/3-3,S	0.0
1897	Bro N	85	284	42	79	9	2	0	38	49	5		.278	.393	.324	96	3	6	.941	-3	104	98	2-68,S-13/O-4(3-1-0)	0.3
Total	11	707	2540	414	671	89	28	10	323	298	57	115	.264	.354	.333	93	-5	138	.912	-4	96	67	O-298R,S-180,2-157/3-73,P	-0.6
SHOCKLEY, COSTEN John Costen B 2.8.1942 Georgetown, DE BL/TL 6-2/200# d7.17																								
1964	Phi N	11	35	4	8	0	0	1	2	2-0	0	8	.229	.263	.314	65	-2	0-0	.968	-1	78	119	/1-9	-0.3
1965	Cal A	40	107	5	20	2	0	2	17	9-0	1	16	.187	.252	.262	49	-7	0-0	.996	0	105	123	1-31/O(RF)	-0.9
Total	2	51	142	9	28	2	0	3	19	11-0	1	24	.197	.255	.275	53	-9	0-0	.991	-0	99	122	/1-40,O(RF)	-1.2
SHOEMAKER, CHARLIE Charles Landis B 8.10.1939 Los Angeles, CA D 5.31.1990 Mount Penn, PA BL/TR 5-10/155# d9.9																								
1961	KC A	7	26	5	10	2	0	0	1	2-0	0	2	.385	.429	.462	135	1	0-0	1.000	1	110	63	/2-6	0.3
1962	KC A	5	11	1	2	0	0	0	0	0-0	0	2	.182	.182	.182	-2	-2	0-0	1.000	1	125	58	/2-4	-0.1
1964	KC A	16	52	6	11	2	2	0	3	0-0	0	9	.212	.212	.327	46	-4	0-0	.964	-3	79	49	2-14	-0.7
Total	3	28	89	12	23	4	2	0	4	2-0	0	13	.258	.275	.348	67	-5	0-0	.981	-2	94	54	/2-24	-0.5
SHOFNER, STRICK Frank Strickland B 7.23.1919 Crawford, TX D 10.10.1998 Crawford, TX BL/TR 5-10.5/187# d4.19																								
1947	Bos A	5	13	1	2	0	1	0	0	0	0	3	.154	.154	.308	25	-2	0-0	1.000	1	118	182	/3-4	-0.1
SHOKES, EDDIE Edward Christopher B 1.27.1920 Charleston, SC D 9.14.2002 Winchester, VA BL/TL 6/170# d6.9 Mil 1943-45																								
1941	Cin N	1	1	0	0	0	0	0	0	0	0	1	.000	.000	.000	-99	0	0	—	0			H	0.0
1946	Cin N	31	83	3	10	1	0	0	5	18	0	21	.120	.277	.133	19	-8	1	.996	-2	76	138	1-29	-1.2
Total	2	32	84	3	10	1	0	0	5	18	0	22	.119	.275	.131	18	-8	1	.996	-2	76	138	/1-29	-1.2
SHOOK, RAY Raymond Curtis B 11.18.1889 Perry, OH D 9.16.1970 South Bend, IN BR/TR 5-7.5/155# d4.16																								
1916	Chi A	1	0	0	0	0	0	0	0	0	0	0	—	—	—	—	0	0	—	0			R	0.0
SHOOP, RON Ronald Lee B 9.19.1931 Rural Valley, PA BR/TR 5-11/180# d8.22																								
1959	Det A	3	7	1	1	0	0	0	1	0-0	0	1	.143	.143	.143	-20	-1	0-0	1.000	-0	*0*	*0*	/C-3	-0.2
SHOPAY, TOM Thomas Michael B 2.21.1945 Bristol, CT BL/TR 5-9.5/160# d9.17																								
1967	NY A	8	27	2	8	1	0	2	6	1-1	0	5	.296	.310	.556	161	2	2-0	.917	0	69	393	/O-7(LF)	0.2
1969	NY A	28	48	2	4	0	1	0	0	2-1	0	10	.083	.120	.125	-33	-9	0-1	1.000	1	137	0	O-11(7-0-5)	-1.0
1971	†Bal A	47	74	10	19	2	0	0	5	3-1	0	7	.257	.286	.284	62	-4	2-1	1.000	-0	90	146	O-13(4-0-9)	-0.5
1972	Bal A	49	40	3	9	0	0	0	2	5-0	0	12	.225	.311	.225	60	-2	0-0	1.000	-0	100	0	/O-3(LF)	-0.2
1975	Bal A	40	31	4	5	1	0	0	2	4-0	0	7	.161	.257	.194	31	-3	3-0	1.000	1	109	0	O-13(1-6-6)/CD	-0.1
1976	Bal A	14	20	4	4	0	0	0	1	3-0	0	3	.200	.304	.200	53	-1	1-0	1.000	-1	75	0	O-11(6-2-3)/C	-0.2
1977	Bal A	67	69	15	13	3	0	1	4	8-0	0	7	.188	.273	.275	53	-4	3-3	1.000	2	111	134	O-52(25-28-14)/D-2	-0.3
Total	7	253	309	40	62	7	1	3	20	26-3	0	51	.201	.262	.259	50	-21	11-5	.993	4	104	121	O-110(53-36-37)/D-5,C-2	-2.1
SHORT, DAVE David Orvis B 5.11.1917 Magnolia, AR D 11.22.1983 Shreveport, LA BL/TR 5-11.5/162# d9.16 Mil 1941-45																								
1940	Chi A	4	3	1	1	0	0	0	0	1	0	2	.333	.500	.333	119	0	0-0	—	0			H	0.0
1941	Chi A	3	8	0	0	0	0	0	0	2	0	1	.000	.200	.000	-44	-2	0-0	.800	-1	80	0	/O-2(LF)	-0.2
Total	2	7	11	1	1	0	0	0	0	3	0	3	.091	.286	.091	3	-2	0-0	.800	-1	80	0	/O-2(LF)	-0.2
SHORTEN, CHICK Charles Henry B 4.19.1892 Scranton, PA D 10.23.1965 Scranton, PA BL/TL 6/175# d9.22 Mil 1918																								
1915	Bos A	6	14	1	3	1	0	0	0	0	0	2	.214	.214	.286	51	-1	0	1.000	1	98	254	/O-5(0-4-1)	-0.1
1916	†Bos A	53	112	14	33	2	1	0	11	10	0	8	.295	.352	.330	105	1	1	1.000	-3	95	0	O-33(13-19-1)	-0.4
1917	Bos A	69	168	12	30	4	2	0	16	10	1	10	.179	.229	.226	39	-13	2	.977	-3	100	37	O-43(16-20-7)	-2.0
1919	Det A	95	270	37	85	9	3	0	22	22	0	13	.315	.366	.370	110	4	5	.973	-6	100	19	O-75(0-18-57)	-0.7
1920	Det A	116	364	35	105	9	6	1	40	28	0	14	.288	.339	.354	86	-8	2-4	.989	-0	92	115	O-99(0-31-68)	-1.4
1921	Det A	92	217	33	59	11	3	0	23	20	0	11	.272	.333	.350	75	-8	2-3	.981	-2	98	52	O-51(3-36-12)	-1.2
1922	StL A	55	131	22	36	12	5	2	16	16	0	8	.275	.354	.489	114	2	0-1	1.000	-0	98	69	O-31(4-16-12)	0.0
1924	Cin N	41	69	7	19	3	0	0	6	4	0	2	.275	.315	.319	71	-3	0-0	1.000	-1	71	104	O-15(11-0-4)	-0.4
Total	8	527	1345	161	370	51	20	3	134	110	1	68	.275	.330	.349	87	-26	12-8	.985	-14	96	62	O-352(47-144-162)	-6.2
SHOTTON, BURT Burton Edwin "Barney" B 10.18.1884 Brownhelm, OH D 7.29.1962 Lake Wales, FL BL/TR 5-11/175# d9.13 M11 C8																								
1909	StL A	17	61	5	16	0	1	0	0	5	1		.262	.328	.295	104	0	3	.915	0	85	0	O-17(2-15-0)	-0.1
1911	StL A	139	572	84	146	11	8	0	36	51	1		.255	.317	.302	76	-19	26	.950	3	111	87	*O-139(18-121-0)	-2.5
1912	StL A	154	580	87	168	15	8	2	40	86	9		.290	.390	.353	117	18	35	.941	4	112	90	*O-154(CF)	1.2
1913	StL A	147	549	105	163	23	8	1	28	**99**	1	63	.297	.405	.373	132	28	43	.951	7	104	118	*O-146(CF)	2.7
1914	StL A	154	579	82	156	19	9	0	38	64	2	66	.269	.344	.333	108	6	40-29	.940	-4	103	74	*O-152(CF)	-1.1
1915	StL A	156	559	93	158	18	11	1	30	118	2	62	.283	.409	.360	135	32	43-32	.931	-3	103	78	*O-154(138-5-11)	2.2
1916	StL A	156	614	97	174	23	6	1	36	**110**	0	65	.283	.392	.345	128	27	41-28	.950	8	107	117	*O-156(LF)	3.0
1917	StL A	118	398	48	89	9	1	1	20	62	1	47	.224	.330	.259	83	-5	16	.923	-12	28	36	*O-107(LF)	-2.5
1918	Was A	126	505	68	132	16	7	0	21	67	1	28	.261	.349	.321	104	4	25	.942	-1	105	81	*O-122(67-1-54)	-0.4
1919	StL N	85	270	35	77	13	5	1	20	22	1	25	.285	.341	.381	125	8	16	.927	-4	83	124	O-67(LF)	0.2
1920	StL N	62	180	28	41	5	0	1	12	18	2	14	.228	.305	.272	69	-7	5-1	.959	2	93	175	O-51(41-2-6)	-0.6
1921	StL N	38	48	9	12	1	1	1	7	7	1	4	.250	.357	.375	96	0	0-2	.958	1	107	181	O-11(1-10-0)	0.0
1922	StL N	34	30	5	6	1	0	0	2	4	0	6	.200	.294	.233	39	-3	0-1	1.000	0	398	0	/O-3(1-1-1)	-0.3
1923	StL N	1	0	1	0	0	0	0	0	0	0	0	—	—	—	—	0	0-0	—	0			R	0.0
Total	14	1387	4945	747	1338	154	65	9	290	713	22	380	.271	.365	.333	110	89	293-93	.942	2	98	92	*O-1279(598-607-72)	1.8
SHOUPE, JOHN John F. B 9.30.1851 Cincinnati, OH D 2.13.1920 Cincinnati, OH BL/TL 5-7/140# d5.3																								
1879	Tro N	11	44	5	4	0	0	0	1	0		3	.091	.091	.091	-43	-6		.820	-3	101	0	S-10/2	-0.8
1882	StL AA	2	7	1	0	0	0	0		0			.000	.000	.000	-96	-1		1.000	1	130	0	/2-2	-0.1
1884	Was U	1	4	1	3	0	0	0		0			.750	.750	.750	368	1		.857	2	353	1090	/O(CF)	0.2
Total	3	14	55	7	7	0	0	0	1	0		3	.127	.127	.127	-17	-6		.820	-0	101	0	/S-10,2-3,O(CF)	-0.7
SHOVLIN, JOHN John Joseph "Brode" B 1.14.1891 Drifton, PA D 2.16.1976 Bethesda, MD BR/TR 5-7/163# d6.21																								
1911	Pit N	2	1	1	0	0	0	0	0	0	0	1	.000	.000	.000	-96	0	0	—	0			H	0.0
1919	StL A	9	35	4	7	0	0	0	1	5	0	2	.200	.300	.200	41	-3	0	.936	-1	92	134	/2-9	-0.4
1920	StL A	7	7	2	2	0	0	0	2	0	0	0	.286	.286	.286	50	-1	0-0	1.000	0	117	0	/S-5	0.0
Total	3	18	43	7	9	0	0	0	3	5	0	3	.209	.292	.209	39	-4	0-0	.936	-1	92	134	/2-9,S-5	-0.4
SHUBA, GEORGE George Thomas "Shotgun" B 12.13.1924 Youngstown, OH BL/TR 5-11/180# d7.2																								
1948	Bro N	63	161	21	43	6	0	4	32	34	0	31	.267	.395	.379	107	3	1	.936	-4	91	28	O-56(55-2-1)	-0.4
1949	Bro N	1	1	0	0	0	0	0	0	0	0	0	.000	.000	.000	-96	0	0	—	0			H	0.0
1950	Bro N	34	111	15	23	8	2	3	12	13	2	22	.207	.302	.396	80	-3	2	.984	3	105	219	O-27(LF)	-0.2
1952	†Bro N	94	256	40	78	12	1	9	40	38	0	29	.305	.395	.465	136	14	1-3	.992	-2	98	44	O-67(66-0-1)	0.7
1953	†Bro N	74	169	19	43	12	1	5	23	17	1	20	.254	.326	.426	92	-2	1-2	.984	-3	92	36	O-44(43-0-1)	-0.7
1954	Bro N	45	65	3	10	5	0	2	10	7	1	10	.154	.240	.323	46	-5	0-0	.913	-1	100	0	O-13(7-0-5)	-0.7
1955	†Bro N	44	51	8	14	2	0	1	8	11-1	2	10	.275	.422	.373	110	2	0-0	.909	-1	80	0	/O-9(7-1-2)	0.0
Total	7	355	814	106	211	45	4	24	125	120-1	6	122	.259	.358	.413	104	9	5-5	.967	-8	96	59	O-216(205-3-10)	-1.3

Year	Tm Lg	G	AB	R	H	2B	3B	HR	RBI	BB-IB	HP	SO	AVG	OBP	SLG	AOPS	ABR	SB-CS	FA	FR	Rng	Thr	G at Pos	BFW
SHUGART, FRANK Frank Harry (born Frank Harry Shugarts) B 12.10.1866 Luthersburg, PA D 9.9.1944 Clearfield, PA BL/TR (BB 1897) 5-8/170# d8.23																								
1890	Chi P	29	106	8	20	5	5	0	15	5	1	13	.189	.232	.330	47	-9	5	.881	-3	87	110	S-25/O-5(0-1-4)	-0.9
1891	Pit N	75	320	57	88	19	8	3	33	20	3	26	.275	.324	.412	117	5	21	.902	2	92	131	S-75	0.8
1892	Pit N	137	554	94	148	19	14	0	62	47	4	48	.267	.329	.352	105	2	28	.886	6	104	89	*S-134/C-2,O(RF)	1.4
1893	Pit N	52	210	37	55	7	3	1	32	19	3	15	.262	.332	.338	80	-6	12	.882	-3	103	77	S-51/O(2-1-0)	-0.5
	StL N	59	246	41	69	10	4	0	28	22	6	10	.280	.354	.354	88	-4	13	.907	-6	183	99	O-28(0-19-9),S-23/3-9	-0.8
	Year	111	456	78	124	17	7	1	60	41	9	25	.272	.344	.346	84	-10	25	.868	-8	100	80	S-74,O-29(2-20-9)/3-9	-1.3
1894	StL N	**133**	527	103	154	19	18	7	72	38	9	37	.292	.350	.436	89	-13	21	.912	-9	125	41	*O-122(CF)/S-7,3-7	-2.3
1895	Lou N	113	473	61	125	14	13	4	70	31	4	25	.264	.315	.374	83	-14	14	.874	-18	88	97	*S-88,O-27(0-22-5)	-2.4
1897	Phi N	40	163	20	41	8	2	5	25	8	0		.252	.287	.417	87	-4	5	.872	-10	88	92	S-40	-1.0
1901	Chi A	107	415	62	104	9	12	2	47	28	2		.251	.301	.345	81	-12	12	.885	-11	96	85	*S-107	-1.8
Total	8	745	3014	483	804	110	79	22	384	218	32	174	.267	.323	.378	90	-55	131	.883	-51	95	95	S-550,O-184(2-165-19)/3-16,C-2	-7.5
SHUMPERT, TERRY Terrance Darnell B 8.16.1966 Paducah, KY BR/TR 5-11/185# d5.1 OF Total (84-LF 9-CF 15-RF)																								
1990	KC A	32	91	7	25	6	1	0	8	2-0	1	17	.275	.292	.363	85	-2	3-3	.977	-2	89	79	2-27/D-3	-0.4
1991	KC A	144	369	45	80	16	4	5	34	30-0	5	75	.217	.283	.322	67	-17	17-11	.975	-8	93	94	*2-144	-2.2
1992	KC A	36	94	6	14	5	1	1	11	3-0	0	17	.149	.175	.255	19	-11	2-2	.969	-9	87	85	2-33/SD	-2.0
1993	KC A	8	10	0	1	0	0	0	0	2-0	0	2	.100	.250	.100	-2	-1	1-0	1.000	1	95	119	/2-8	0.0
1994	KC A	64	183	28	44	6	2	8	24	13-0	0	39	.240	.289	.426	79	-7	18-3	.964	-5	102	71	2-38,3-24/SD	-0.7
1995	Bos A	21	47	6	11	3	0	0	3	4-0	0	13	.234	.294	.298	53	-3	3-1	1.000	2	82	97	/2-8,3-5,S-3,D	0.0
1996	Chi N	27	31	5	7	1	0	2	6	2-0	1	11	.226	.286	.452	91	-1	0-1	.923	-1	48	0	3-10/2-4,S	-0.2
1997	SD N	13	33	4	9	3	0	1	6	3-0	0	4	.273	.324	.455	112	1	0-0	.973	-1	78	89	/2-7,O-3(2-0-1),3-2	0.0
1998	Col N	23	26	3	6	1	0	1	2	2-0	0	8	.231	.286	.385	61	-1	0-0	1.000	3	211	188	/2-6	0.1
1999	Col N	92	262	58	91	26	3	10	37	31-2	2	41	.347	.413	.584	119	9	14-0	.988	8	116	99	2-54,O-19(6-9-4),3-14/S-2	2.0
2000	Col N	115	263	52	68	11	7	9	40	28-1	6	40	.259	.340	.456	80	-9	8-4	.967	-2	104	114	O-40(LF),2-23,3-15/S-7,1-6,D	-1.0
2001	Col N	114	242	37	70	14	5	4	24	15-2	3	44	.289	.337	.438	81	-7	14-3	.968	2	108	122	2-41,O-24(LF),3-12/S-4	-0.2
2002	Col N	106	234	30	55	12	1	6	21	21-0	4	41	.235	.304	.372	70	-11	4-1	.974	-1	104	93	2-60/O-8(7-0-1),S-3,3	-0.9
2003	TB A	59	84	14	16	5	2	2	7	10-0	2	17	.190	.289	.369	74	-3	1-0	.978	-3	89	48	D-17,2-14,O-14(5-0-9),3-11/S	-0.7
Total	14	854	1969	295	497	109	26	49	223	166-5	24	369	.252	.315	.409	80	-63	85-29	.977	-17	98	93	2-467,O-108L/3-94,D-25,S-23,1-6	-6.2
SHUPE, VINCE Vincent William B 9.5.1921 E.Canton, OH D 4.5.1962 Canton, OH BL/TL 5-11/180# d7.7																								
1945	Bos N	78	283	22	76	8	0	0	15	17	1	16	.269	.312	.297	69	-12	3	.989	1	107	147	1-77	-1.5
SICKING, ED Edward Joseph B 3.30.1897 St.Bernard, OH D 8.30.1978 Madeira, OH BR/TR 5-9.5/165# d8.26 Mil 1918																								
1916	Chi N	1	1	0	0	0	0	0	0	0	0	0	.000	.000	.000	-90	0	0	—	0			H	0.0
1918	NY N	46	132	9	33	4	0	0	12	6	0	11	.250	.283	.280	73	-4	2	.917	-7	83	0	3-24,2-18/S-3	-1.2
1919	NY N	6	15	2	5	0	0	0	3	1	1	0	.333	.412	.333	127	1	0	.971	2	133	147	/S-6	0.3
	Phi N	61	185	16	40	2	1	0	15	8	1	17	.216	.253	.238	45	-12	4	.925	3	101	167	S-35,2-22	-0.8
	Year	67	200	18	45	2	1	0	18	9	2	17	.225	.265	.245	51	-12	4	.933	5	106	164	S-41,2-22	-0.5
1920	NY N	46	134	11	23	3	1	0	9	10	1	10	.172	.234	.209	28	-12	6-2	.915	-1	101	25	3-28,2-15/S-3	-1.2
	Cin N	37	123	12	33	3	0	0	17	13	0	5	.268	.338	.293	83	-2	2-3	.955	-2	105	77	2-25/S-9,3-2	-0.4
	Year	83	257	23	56	6	1	0	26	23	1	15	.218	.285	.249	55	-14	8-5	.952	-2	103	122	2-40,3-30,S-12	-1.6
1927	Pit N	6	7	1	1	1	0	0	3	1	0	0	.143	.250	.286	40	-1	0	1.000	1	112	89	/2-5	0.0
Total	5	203	597	51	135	13	2	0	59	39	3	43	.226	.277	.255	57	-30	14-5	.965	-3	97	113	/2-85,S-56,3-54	-3.3
SIDDALL, JOE Joseph Todd B 10.25.1967 Windsor, ON, CAN BL/TR 6-1/197# d7.28																								
1993	Mon N	19	20	0	2	1	0	0	1	1-1	0	5	.100	.143	.150	-21	-3	0-0	1.000	-1	75	135	C-15/1O(LF)	-0.4
1995	Mon N	7	10	4	3	0	0	0	1	3-0	1	3	.300	.500	.300	113	1	0-0	.882	-4	35	0	/C-7	-0.3
1996	Fla N	18	47	0	7	1	0	0	3	2-0	0	8	.149	.184	.170	-6	-7	0-0	.977	-2	86	147	C-18	-0.8
1998	Det A	29	65	3	12	3	0	1	6	7-0	0	25	.185	.264	.277	41	-6	0-0	.994	6	116	162	C-27/O(RF)	0.2
Total	4	73	142	7	24	5	0	1	11	13-1	1	41	.169	.244	.225	24	-15	0-0	.983	1	95	142	/C-67,O-2(1-0-1),1	-1.3
SIEBERN, NORM Norman Leroy B 7.26.1933 St.Louis, MO BL/TR 6-3/205# d6.15																								
1956	†NY A	54	162	27	33	1	4	4	21	19-0	0	38	.204	.286	.333	66	-9	1-1	.971	-1	104	27	O-51(LF)	-1.4
1958	†NY A	134	460	79	138	19	5	14	55	66-3	1	87	.300	.388	.454	136	25	5-8	.982	-0	98	100	*O-133(127-11-0)	1.5
1959	NY A	120	380	52	103	17	0	11	53	41-2	2	71	.271	.341	.403	108	5	3-1	.989	-4	94	17	O-93(82-5-9)/1-2	-0.5
1960	KC A	144	520	69	145	31	6	19	69	72-6	2	68	.279	.366	.471	125	19	0-0	.987	-1	107	84	O-75(LF),1-69	1.0
1961	KC A	153	560	68	166	36	5	18	98	82-3	1	91	.296	.384	.475	127	24	2-4	.989	1	101	86	*1-109,O-47(LF)	1.4
1962	KC A★	**162**	600	114	185	25	6	25	117	110-9	1	88	.308	.412	.495	138	36	3-1	.994	2	101	87	*1-162	2.9
1963	KC A☆	152	556	80	151	25	2	16	83	79-6	0	82	.272	.358	.410	110	10	1-4	.991	2	105	90	*1-131,O-16(16-0-1)	0.1
1964	Bal A★	150	478	92	117	24	2	12	56	**106**-3	2	87	.245	.379	.379	114	15	2-3	.995	4	109	**116**	*1-149	1.0
1965	Bal A	106	297	44	76	13	4	8	32	50-7	1	49	.256	.362	.407	117	8	1-2	.991	0	104	121	1-76	0.4
1966	Cal A	125	336	29	83	14	1	5	41	63-7	0	61	.247	.361	.339	107	6	0-1	.992	2	111	134	1-99	0.3
1967	SF N	46	58	6	9	1	1	0	4	14-0	0	13	.155	.319	.207	54	-3	0-0	1.000	-0	96	110	1-15/O-2(LF)	-0.4
	†Bos A	33	44	2	9	0	2	0	7	6-1	0	8	.205	.300	.295	71	-2	0-0	.981	1	105	43	1-13/O(LF)	-0.2
1968	Bos A	27	30	0	2	0	0	0	0	0-0	0	5	.067	.067	.067	-56	-6	0-0	1.000	0	141	114	/1-2,O-2(1-0-1)	-0.7
Total	12	1406	4481	662	1217	206	38	132	636	708-47	10	748	.272	.369	.423	117	128	18-25	.992	4	103	101	1-827,O-420(402-16-11)	5.4
SIEBERT, DICK Richard Walther B 2.19.1912 Fall River, MA D 12.9.1978 Minneapolis, MN BL/TL 6/170# d9.7 s-Paul																								
1932	Bro N	6	7	1	2	0	0	0	0	2	0	2	.286	.444	.286	104	0	0	1.000	-0	0	0	/1-2	0.0
1936	Bro N	2	2	0	0	0	0	0	0	0	0	0	.000	.000	.000	-99	-1	0	1.000	1	0	2806	/O(RF)	0.0
1937	StL N	22	38	3	7	2	0	0	2	4	1	8	.184	.279	.237	41	-3	1	.979	-1	75	44	/1-7	-0.4
1938	StL N	1	1	0	1	0	0	0	0	0	0	0	1.000	1.000	1.000	427	0	0	—	0			H	0.0
	Phi A	48	194	24	55	8	3	0	28	10	3	9	.284	.329	.356	73	-9	2-3	1.000	5	136	81	1-46	-0.7
1939	Phi A	101	402	58	118	28	3	6	47	21	0	22	.294	.329	.423	93	-6	4-1	.991	5	123	81	1-99	-0.9
1940	Phi A	**154**	595	69	170	31	6	5	77	33	2	34	.286	.325	.383	85	-15	8-6	.985	8	125	84	*1-154	-2.0
1941	Phi A	123	467	63	156	28	8	5	79	37	2	22	.334	.385	.460	126	17	1-3	.990	5	119	91	*1-123	1.0
1942	Phi A	153	612	57	159	25	7	2	74	24	3	17	.260	.291	.333	76	-23	4-5	.989	-2	94	80	*1-152	-4.1
1943	Phi A★	146	558	50	140	26	7	1	72	33	2	21	.251	.295	.328	83	-14	6-7	.990	3	108	89	*1-145	-2.2
1944	Phi A	132	468	52	143	27	5	6	52	62	0	17	.306	.387	.423	133	22	2-0	.993	2	102	99	1-74,O-58(42-0-17)	1.9
1945	Phi A	147	573	62	153	29	1	7	51	50	2	33	.267	.328	.358	99	-1	2-7	.991	8	**117**	98	*1-147	-0.3
Total	11	1035	3917	439	1104	204	40	32	482	276	15	185	.282	.332	.379	96	-33	30-32	.990	33	113	88	1-949/O-59(42-0-18)	-7.7
SIEFKE, ED Frederick Edwin B 3.27.1870 New York, NY D 4.18.1893 New York, NY 5-11/168# d5.2																								
1890	Bro AA	16	58	1	8	2	0	0	3	5	0		.138	.206	.172	12	-6	2	.811	-1	124	69	3-16	-0.6
SIEGEL, JOHN John B York, PA d6.9																								
1884	Phi U	8	31	4	7	2	0	0		1			.226	.250	.290	68	-2		.533	-4	61	0	/3-8	-0.6
SIEGLE, JOHNNY John Herbert B 7.8.1874 Urbana, OH D 2.12.1968 Urbana, OH BR/TR 5-10/165# d9.15																								
1905	Cin N	17	56	9	17	1	2	1	8	7	1		.304	.391	.446	135	2	0	.960	-1	51	0	O-16(RF)	0.1
1906	Cin N	22	68	4	8	2	2	0	7	3	2		.118	.178	.206	19	-7	0	.959	0	39	157	O-21(7-14-0)	-0.9
Total	2	39	124	13	25	3	4	1	15	10	3		.202	.277	.315	75	-5	0	.959	-1	44	91	/O-37(7-14-16)	-0.8
SIEMER, OSCAR Oscar Sylvester "Cotton" B 8.14.1901 St.Louis, MO D 12.5.1959 St.Louis, MO BR/TR 5-9/162# d5.20																								
1925	Bos N	16	46	5	14	0	1	1	6	1	0	0	.304	.319	.413	94	-1	0-0	.900	-2	*112*	*99*	C-16	-0.2
1926	Bos N	31	73	3	15	1	0	0	5	2	0	7	.205	.227	.219	22	-8	0	.920	-3	*83*	*65*	C-30	-1.0
Total	2	47	119	8	29	1	1	1	11	3	0	7	.244	.262	.294	51	-9	0-0	.913	-5	*94*	*78*	/C-46	-1.2
SIERRA, RUBEN Ruben Angel (Garcia) B 10.6.1965 Rio Piedras, P.R. BB/TR 6-1/200# d6.1																								
1986	Tex A	113	382	50	101	13	10	16	55	22-3	1	65	.264	.302	.476	106	1	7-8	.972	-2	95	109	*O-107(44-21-68)/D-3	-0.6
1987	Tex A	158	643	97	169	35	4	30	109	39-4	2	114	.263	.302	.470	102	-1	16-11	.963	-1	92	159	*O-157(0-4-156)	-1.0
1988	Tex A	156	615	77	156	32	2	23	91	44-10	1	91	.254	.301	.424	99	-2	18-4	.979	-0	96	118	*O-153(RF)/D	-0.5
1989	Tex A★	**162**	634	101	194	35	**14**	29	**119**	43-2	2	82	.306	.347	**.543**	146	35	8-2	.973	-1	98	112	*O-162(0-2-161)	3.1
1990	Tex A	159	608	70	170	37	2	16	96	49-13	1	86	.280	.330	.426	111	8	9-0	.967	-8	94	65	*O-151(RF)/D-7	-0.3
1991	Tex A★	161	661	110	203	44	5	25	116	56-7	0	91	.307	.357	.502	139	34	16-4	.979	-3	92	126	*O-161(0-3-161)	2.7
1992	Tex A★	124	500	66	139	30	6	14	70	31-6	0	59	.278	.315	.446	117	9	12-4	.970	-6	93	75	*O-119(RF)/D-4	0.0

Year	Tm Lg	G	AB	R	H	2B	3B	HR	RBI	BB-IB	HP	SO	AVG	OBP	SLG	AOPS	ABR	SB-CS	FA	FR	Rng	Thr	G at Pos	BFW
	†Oak A	27	101	17	28	4	1	3	17	14-6	0	9	.277	.359	.426	128	4	2-0	1.000	0	116	0	O-25(RF)/D-2	0.4
	Year	151	601	83	167	34	7	17	87	45-12	0	68	.278	.323	.443	119	13	14-4	.976	-6	97	62	*O-144(RF)/D-6	0.4
1993	Oak A	158	630	77	147	23	5	22	101	52-16	0	97	.233	.288	.390	87	-15	25-5	.977	1	105	89	*O-133(RF),D-25	-1.9
1994	Oak A★	110	426	71	114	21	1	23	92	23-4	0	64	.268	.298	.484	108	2	8-5	.948	-6	85	119	O-98(0-1-97),D-10	-0.9
1995	Oak A	70	264	40	70	17	0	12	42	24-2	0	42	.265	.323	.466	109	3	4-4	.957	-7	82	27	O-62(RF)/D-7	-0.7
	†NY A	56	215	33	56	15	0	7	44	22-2	0	34	.260	.322	.428	96	-1	1-0	.950	0	104	170	D-46,O-10(RF)	-0.4
	Year	126	479	73	126	32	0	19	86	46-4	0	76	.263	.323	.449	103	1	5-4	.956	-6	85	46	O-72(RF),D-53	-1.1
1996	NY A	96	360	39	93	17	1	11	52	40-11	0	58	.258	.327	.403	85	-9	1-3	.984	2	95	243	D-61,O-33(32-0-1)	-1.2
	Det A	46	158	22	35	9	1	1	20	20-1	0	25	.222	.306	.310	57	-10	3-1	.914	-0	109	60	O-23(4-0-19),D-20	-1.2
	Year	142	518	61	128	26	2	12	72	60-12	0	83	.247	.320	.375	76	-19	4-4	.950	2	101	164	D-81,O-56(36-0-20)	-2.4
1997	Cin N	25	90	6	22	5	1	2	7	6-1	0	21	.244	.292	.389	75	-4	0-0	1.000	0	87	203	O-24(12-0-12)	-0.4
	Tor A	14	48	4	10	0	2	1	5	3-1	0	13	.208	.250	.354	56	-4	0-0	.929	-1	90	0	/O-7(6-0-2),D-6	-0.4
1998	Chi A	27	74	7	16	4	1	4	11	3-0	0	11	.216	.247	.459	80	-3	2-0	1.000	-1	82	122	O-14(2-0-12)/D-5	-0.3
2000	Tex A	20	60	5	14	0	0	1	7	4-0	0	9	.233	.281	.283	43	-5	1-0	—	0	0	0	D-14	-0.6
2001	Tex A	94	344	55	100	22	1	23	67	19-0	0	52	.291	.322	.561	124	10	2-0	.937	-3	92	0	D-50,O-36(1-0-35)	0.2
2002	Sea A	122	419	47	113	23	0	13	60	31-5	0	66	.270	.319	.418	97	-2	4-0	.979	-3	94	35	O-60(59-0-1),D-52	-0.9
2003	Tex A	43	133	14	35	9	0	3	12	14-1	0	27	.263	.333	.398	85	-3	1-1	.962	-3	66	92	O-23(20-0-4),D-15	-0.7
	†NY A	63	174	19	48	8	1	6	31	13-2	0	20	.276	.323	.437	100	0	1-0	1.000	-1	84	0	D-32,O-17(6-0-11)	-0.4
	Year	106	307	33	83	17	1	9	43	27-3	0	47	.270	.327	.420	93	-3	2-1	.978	-4	73	55	D-47,O-40(26-0-15)	-1.1
Total	17	2004	7539	1027	2033	403	58	285	1224	572-97	7	1136	.270	.317	.452	107	47	141-52	.970	-41	94	102	*O-1575(186-31-1393),D-360	-6.0

SIEVERS, ROY Roy Edward "Squirrel" B 11.18.1926 St.Louis, MO BR/TR 6-1/195# d4.21 C1

Year	Tm Lg	G	AB	R	H	2B	3B	HR	RBI	BB-IB	HP	SO	AVG	OBP	SLG	AOPS	ABR	SB-CS	FA	FR	Rng	Thr	G at Pos	BFW
1949	StL A	140	471	84	144	28	1	16	91	70	2	75	.306	.398	.471	124	18	1-5	.973	5	101	162	*O-125(51-76-0)/3-7	1.4
1950	StL A	113	370	46	88	20	4	10	57	34	2	42	.238	.305	.395	75	-16	1-3	.983	4	106	183	O-78(10-68-0),3-21	-1.4
1951	StL A	31	89	10	20	2	1	1	11	9	1	21	.225	.303	.303	62	-5	0-0	.985	0	111	48	O-25(9-19-0)	-0.5
1952	StL A	11	30	3	6	3	0	0	5	1	0	4	.200	.226	.300	44	-2	0-0	.968	-1	63	123	/1-7	-0.4
1953	StL A	92	285	37	77	15	0	8	35	32	0	47	.270	.344	.407	100	0	0-1	.992	-6	66	87	1-76	-1.0
1954	Was A	145	514	75	119	26	6	24	102	80	2	77	.232	.331	.446	120	13	2-1	.971	8	110	117	*O-133(LF)/1-8	1.3
1955	Was A	144	509	74	138	20	8	25	106	73-3	4	66	.271	.364	.489	136	25	1-2	.988	-3	101	49	*O-129(LF),1-17/3-2	1.3
1956	Was A★	152	550	92	139	27	2	29	95	100-10	5	88	.253	.370	.467	121	18	0-0	.987	1	98	52	O-78(LF),1-76	0.9
1957	Was A☆	152	572	99	172	23	5	**42**	**114**	76-11	7	55	.301	.388	.579	163	49	1-1	.985	-2	96	86	*O-130(LF),1-21	3.9
1958	Was A	148	550	85	162	18	1	39	108	53-2	4	63	.295	.357	.544	148	34	3-1	.991	-4	92	70	*O-114(LF),1-33	2.2
1959	Was A★	115	385	55	93	19	0	21	49	53-6	2	62	.242	.333	.455	116	8	1-1	.989	5	124	95	1-93,O-13(LF)	0.7
1960	Chi A	127	444	87	131	22	0	28	93	74-**8**	3	69	.295	.396	.534	152	34	1-1	.993	-4	86	**112**	*1-114/O-6(LF)	2.3
1961	Chi A★	141	492	76	145	26	6	27	92	61-4	6	62	.295	.377	.537	144	31	1-0	.993	3	106	85	*1-132	2.5
1962	Phi N	144	477	61	125	19	5	21	80	56-3	7	80	.262	.346	.455	117	11	2-1	.991	4	111	96	*1-130/O-7(3-0-4)	0.8
1963	Phi N	138	450	46	108	19	2	19	82	43-5	5	72	.240	.308	.418	110	6	0-2	.989	-1	96	105	*1-126	-0.3
1964	Phi N	49	120	7	22	3	1	4	16	13-1	1	20	.183	.265	.325	67	-5	0-0	.992	-1	80	102	1-33	-0.9
	Was A	33	58	5	10	1	0	4	11	9-2	0	14	.172	.284	.397	87	-1	0-0	1.000	2	153	168	1-15	0.0
1965	Was A	12	21	3	4	1	0	0	0	4-0	0	3	.190	.320	.238	62	-1	0-0	1.000	-1	30	135	/1-7	-0.2
Total	17	1887	6387	945	1703	292	42	318	1147	841-55	51	920	.267	.354	.475	124	217	14-19	.991	8	100	100	1-888,O-838(676-163-4)/3-30	12.6

SIFFELL, FRANK Frank B 1860 , Germany D 10.26.1909 Philadelphia, PA d6.14

Year	Tm Lg	G	AB	R	H	2B	3B	HR	RBI	BB-IB	HP	SO	AVG	OBP	SLG	AOPS	ABR	SB-CS	FA	FR	Rng	Thr	G at Pos	BFW
1884	Phi AA	7	17	3	3	1	0	0	3	0	1		.176	.222	.235	46	-1		.875	-2			/C-7	-0.2
1885	Phi AA	3	10	0	1	0	0	0	0	0	0		.100	.100	.100	-35	-2		.750	-2			/C-2,O(RF)	-0.3
Total	2	10	27	3	4	1	0	0	3	0	1		.148	.179	.185	16	-3		.841	-4			/C-9,O(RF)	-0.5

SIGAFOOS, FRANK Francis Leonard B 3.21.1904 Easton, PA D 4.12.1968 Indianapolis, IN BR/TR 5-9/170# d9.3

Year	Tm Lg	G	AB	R	H	2B	3B	HR	RBI	BB-IB	HP	SO	AVG	OBP	SLG	AOPS	ABR	SB-CS	FA	FR	Rng	Thr	G at Pos	BFW
1926	Phi A	13	43	4	11	0	0	0	2	0	0	3	.256	.256	.256	32	-4	0-0	.915	-2	99	95	S-12	-0.5
1929	Det A	14	23	3	4	1	0	0	2	5	0	4	.174	.321	.217	41	-2	0-2	.909	-2	66	0	/3-6,S-5	-0.4
	Chi A	7	3	1	1	0	0	0	1	2	0	1	.333	.600	.333	148	1	0-0	1.000	1	172	114	/2-6	0.1
	Year	21	26	4	5	1	0	0	3	7	0	5	.192	.364	.231	56	-1	0-2	.909	-1	66	0	/3-6,2-6,S-5	-0.3
1931	Cin N	21	65	6	11	2	0	0	8	0	1	6	.169	.182	.200	3	-9	0	.881	-2	89	79	3-15/S-2	-1.1
Total	3	55	134	14	27	3	0	0	13	7	1	14	.201	.246	.224	25	-14	0-2	.887	-5	85	64	/3-21,S-19,2-6	-1.9

SIGLIN, PADDY Wesley Peter B 9.24.1891 Aurelia, IA D 8.5.1956 Oakland, CA BR/TR 5-10/160# d9.12

Year	Tm Lg	G	AB	R	H	2B	3B	HR	RBI	BB-IB	HP	SO	AVG	OBP	SLG	AOPS	ABR	SB-CS	FA	FR	Rng	Thr	G at Pos	BFW
1914	Pit N	14	39	4	6	0	0	0	2	4	0	6	.154	.233	.154	16	-4	1	.911	-5	61	30	2-11	-1.0
1915	Pit N	6	7	1	2	0	0	0	0	1	0	2	.286	.375	.286	103	0	1	.800	-0	117	0	/2	0.0
1916	Pit N	3	4	0	1	0	0	0	0	0	0	2	.250	.250	.250	53	0	0	.857	0	55	596	/2-3	0.0
Total	3	23	50	5	9	0	0	0	2	5	0	10	.180	.255	.180	32	-4	2	.895	-5	65	89	/2-15	-1.0

SIGMAN, TRIPP Wesley Triplett B 1.17.1899 Mooresville, NC D 3.8.1971 Augusta, GA BL/TR 6/180# d9.18

Year	Tm Lg	G	AB	R	H	2B	3B	HR	RBI	BB-IB	HP	SO	AVG	OBP	SLG	AOPS	ABR	SB-CS	FA	FR	Rng	Thr	G at Pos	BFW
1929	Phi N	10	29	8	15	1	0	2	9	3	0	1	.517	.563	.759	210	5	0	.944	-1	102	0	O-10(5-5-0)	0.4
1930	Phi N	52	100	15	27	4	1	4	6	6	2	9	.270	.324	.450	79	-4	1	.932	-0	95	156	O-19(3-16-0)	-0.4
Total	2	62	129	23	42	5	1	6	15	9	2	10	.326	.379	.519	108	1	1	.935	-1	97	109	/O-29(8-21-0)	0.0

SILBER, EDDIE Edward James B 6.6.1914 Philadelphia, PA D 10.26.1976 Dunedin, FL BR/TR 5-11/170# d9.3

Year	Tm Lg	G	AB	R	H	2B	3B	HR	RBI	BB-IB	HP	SO	AVG	OBP	SLG	AOPS	ABR	SB-CS	FA	FR	Rng	Thr	G at Pos	BFW
1937	StL A	22	83	10	26	2	0	0	4	5	0	13	.313	.352	.337	74	-3	0-2	.871	-4	73	0	O-21(2-6-15)	-0.8
1939	StL A	1	1	0	0	0	0	0	0	0	0	1	.000	.000	.000	-98	0	0-0	—	0			H	0.0
Total	2	23	84	10	26	2	0	0	4	5	0	14	.310	.348	.333	72	-3	0-2	.871	-4	73	0	/O-21(2-6-15)	-0.8

SILCH, ED Edward "Baldy" B 2.22.1865 St.Louis, MO D 1.15.1895 St.Louis, MO TR 6-2/180# d4.29

Year	Tm Lg	G	AB	R	H	2B	3B	HR	RBI	BB-IB	HP	SO	AVG	OBP	SLG	AOPS	ABR	SB-CS	FA	FR	Rng	Thr	G at Pos	BFW
1888	Bro AA	14	48	5	13	4	0	0	3	4	0		.271	.327	.354	118	1	4	.870	-1	51	0	O-14(0-6-8)	0.0

SILVA, DANNY Daniel James B 10.5.1896 Everett, MA D 4.4.1974 Hyannis, MA BR/TR 6/170# d8.11

Year	Tm Lg	G	AB	R	H	2B	3B	HR	RBI	BB-IB	HP	SO	AVG	OBP	SLG	AOPS	ABR	SB-CS	FA	FR	Rng	Thr	G at Pos	BFW
1919	Was A	1	4	0	1	0	0	0	0	0	0	0	.250	.250	.250	41	0	0	1.000	1	155	0	/3	0.0

SILVERA, AL Aaron Albert B 8.26.1935 San Diego, CA D 7.24.2002 Los Angeles, CA BR/TR 6/180# d6.12

Year	Tm Lg	G	AB	R	H	2B	3B	HR	RBI	BB-IB	HP	SO	AVG	OBP	SLG	AOPS	ABR	SB-CS	FA	FR	Rng	Thr	G at Pos	BFW
1955	Cin N	13	7	3	1	0	0	0	2	0-0	0	1	.143	.143	.143	-23	-1	0-0	—	-0	0	0	/O(LF)	-0.1
1956	Cin N	1	0	0	0	0	0	0	0	0-0	0	0	—	—	—	—	0	0-0	—	0			R	0.0
Total	2	14	7	3	1	0	0	0	2	0-0	0	1	.143	.143	.143	-23	-1	0-0	.000	-0	0	0	/O(LF)	-0.1

SILVERA, CHARLIE Charles Anthony Ryan "Swede" B 10.13.1924 San Francisco, CA BR/TR 5-10/175# d9.29 C6

Year	Tm Lg	G	AB	R	H	2B	3B	HR	RBI	BB-IB	HP	SO	AVG	OBP	SLG	AOPS	ABR	SB-CS	FA	FR	Rng	Thr	G at Pos	BFW
1948	NY A	4	14	1	8	0	1	0	1	0	0	1	.571	.571	.714	243	3	0-0	1.000	-0	*102*	*126*	/C-4	0.3
1949	†NY A	58	130	8	41	2	0	0	13	18	1	5	.315	.403	.331	95	0	2-1	.985	4	*82*	*117*	C-51	0.5
1950	NY A	18	25	2	4	0	0	0	1	1	0	2	.160	.192	.160	-9	-4	0-0	.959	2	*148*	*0*	C-15	-0.2
1951	NY A	18	51	5	14	3	0	1	7	5	0	3	.275	.339	.392	101	0	0-0	1.000	1	*132*	*93*	C-18	0.2
1952	NY A	20	55	4	18	3	0	0	11	5	0	2	.327	.383	.382	121	2	0-3	1.000	-1	*92*	*126*	C-20	0.0
1953	NY A	42	82	11	23	3	1	0	12	9	0	5	.280	.352	.341	91	-1	0-1	.992	4	*121*	*112*	C-39/3	0.4
1954	NY A	20	37	1	10	1	0	0	4	3	1	2	.270	.341	.297	79	-1	0-1	.962	3	*172*	*77*	C-18	0.2
1955	NY A	14	26	1	5	0	0	0	1	6-0	0	4	.192	.344	.192	48	-2	0-0	1.000	2	*184*	*126*	C-11	0.1
1956	NY A	7	9	0	2	0	0	0	0	2-0	0	3	.222	.364	.222	60	0	0-0	.909	-1	*58*	*0*	/C-7	-0.1
1957	Chi N	26	53	1	11	3	0	0	2	4-0	0	5	.208	.263	.264	43	-4	0-0	.982	1	*88*	*214*	C-26	-0.2
Total	10	227	482	34	136	15	2	1	52	53-0	2	32	.282	.356	.328	86	-7	2-6	.985	14	*113*	*116*	C-209/3	1.2

SILVERIO, LUIS Luis Pascual (Delmonte) B 10.23.1956 Villa Gonzalez, D.R. BR/TR 5-11/165# d9.9 C1

Year	Tm Lg	G	AB	R	H	2B	3B	HR	RBI	BB-IB	HP	SO	AVG	OBP	SLG	AOPS	ABR	SB-CS	FA	FR	Rng	Thr	G at Pos	BFW
1978	KC A	8	11	7	6	2	1	0	3	2-0	0	3	.545	.615	.909	315	3	1-1	.833	-1	71	0	/O-6(4-0-2),D-2	0.2

SILVERIO, TOM Tomas Roberto (Veloz) B 10.14.1945 Santiago, D.R. BL/TL 5-10/170# d4.30

Year	Tm Lg	G	AB	R	H	2B	3B	HR	RBI	BB-IB	HP	SO	AVG	OBP	SLG	AOPS	ABR	SB-CS	FA	FR	Rng	Thr	G at Pos	BFW
1970	Cal A	15	15	1	0	0	0	0	0	2-1	0	4	.000	.118	.000	-67	-4	0-1	1.000	-1	30	0	/O-5(1-4-0),1	-0.5
1971	Cal A	3	3	0	1	0	0	0	0	0-0	0	0	.333	.333	.333	96	0	0-0	—	-0	0	0	/O(CF)	0.0
1972	Cal A	13	12	1	2	0	0	0	0	0-0	0	5	.167	.167	.167	-1	-2	0-0	1.000	-0	36	0	/O-4(2-1-1)	-0.2
Total	3	31	30	2	3	0	0	0	0	2-1	0	9	.100	.156	.100	-27	-6	0-1	1.000	-1	32	0	/O-10(3-6-1),1	-0.7

SILVESTRI, DAVE David Joseph B 9.29.1967 St.Louis, MO BR/TR 6/196# d4.27 OF Total (5-LF 1-CF)

Year	Tm Lg	G	AB	R	H	2B	3B	HR	RBI	BB-IB	HP	SO	AVG	OBP	SLG	AOPS	ABR	SB-CS	FA	FR	Rng	Thr	G at Pos	BFW
1992	NY A	7	13	3	4	0	2	0	1	0-0	0	3	.308	.308	.615	154	1	0-0	.889	0	113	127	/S-6	0.1
1993	NY A	7	21	4	6	1	0	1	4	5-0	0	3	.286	.423	.476	146	2	0-0	.955	0	93	153	/S-4,3-3	0.2
1994	NY A	12	18	3	2	0	1	1	2	4-0	0	9	.111	.261	.389	71	-1	0-1	1.000	-0	84	74	/2-9,3-2,S	-0.1

Year	Tm Lg	G	AB	R	H	2B	3B	HR	RBI	BB-IB	HP	SO	AVG	OBP	SLG	AOPS	ABR	SB-CS	FA	FR	Rng	Thr	G at Pos	BFW
1995	NY A	17	21	4	2	0	0	1	4	4-0	1	9	.095	.259	.238	34	-2	0-0	1.000	1	150	61	/2-7,1-4,SD	-0.1
	Mon N	39	72	12	19	6	0	2	7	9-0	0	27	.264	.341	.431	100	0	2-0	1.000	-3	81	22	/S-9,3-8,1-4,2-3,O-3(LF)	-0.1
1996	Mon N	86	162	16	33	4	0	1	17	34-6	0	41	.204	.340	.247	57	-9	2-1	.913	-2	102	83	3-47,S-10/O-2(1-1-0),12	-1.0
1997	Tex A	2	4	0	0	0	0	0	0	0-0	0	1	.000	.000	.000	-95	-1	0-0	—	-1	0	0	/3S	-0.2
1998	TB A	8	14	0	1	0	0	0	0	0-0	0	2	.071	.071	.071	-61	-3	0-0	1.000	-0	61	0	/3-3,2-2,SD	-0.3
1999	Ana A	3	11	0	1	1	0	0	1	0-0	0	1	.091	.091	.182	-33	-2	0-0	1.000	-1	127	0	/2SO(LF)	-0.3
Total	8	181	336	42	68	12	3	6	36	56-6	1	96	.202	.315	.310	65	-15	4-2	.912	-5	106	67	/3-64,S-34,2-23,1-9,O-6L,D-6	-1.8
SILVESTRI, KEN Kenneth Joseph "Hawk" B 5.3.1916 Chicago, IL D 3.31.1992 Tallahassee, FL BB/TR 6-1/200# d4.18 Mil 1942-45 M1 C17																								
1939	Chi A	22	75	6	13	3	0	2	5	6	1	13	.173	.244	.293	36	-8	0-1	.947	0	96	152	C-20	-0.6
1940	Chi A	28	24	5	6	2	0	2	10	4	0	7	.250	.357	.583	138	1	0-0	1.000	-0	0	0	/C	0.1
1941	NY A	17	40	6	10	5	0	1	4	7	0	6	.250	.362	.450	115	1	0-0	1.000	0	129	112	C-13	0.2
1946	NY A	13	21	4	6	1	0	0	1	3	0	7	.286	.375	.333	98	0	0-0	.977	1	111	53	C-12	0.2
1947	NY A	3	10	0	2	0	0	0	0	2	0	2	.200	.333	.200	51	-1	0-0	1.000	-1	76	0	/C-3	-0.1
1949	Phi N	4	4	1	0	0	0	0	0	2	0	1	.000	.333	.000	-3	0	0	1.000	-0	48	268	/C2S	-0.1
1950	†Phi N	11	20	2	5	0	1	0	4	4	1	3	.250	.400	.350	101	0	0	1.000	-1	86	0	/C-9	0.0
1951	Phi N	4	9	2	2	0	0	0	1	3	0	2	.222	.417	.222	78	0	0-0	1.000	-2	68	0	/C-3,2	-0.2
Total	8	102	203	26	44	11	1	5	25	31	2	41	.217	.326	.355	78	-7	0-1	.974	-2	100	102	/C-62,2-2,S	-0.5
SIMMONS, AL Aloysius Harry "Bucketfoot Al" (born Aloys Szymanski) B 5.22.1902 Milwaukee, WI D 5.26.1956 Milwaukee, WI BR/TR 5-11/190# d4.15 C11 HF1953																								
1924	Phi A	**152**	594	69	183	31	9	8	102	30	2	60	.308	.343	.431	98	-5	16-15	.976	-2	95	106	*O-152(51-101-0)	-1.7
1925	Phi A	**153**	654	122	**253**	43	12	24	129	35	1	41	.387	.419	.599	146	43	7-14	.966	-6	103	47	*O-153(CF)	2.5
1926	Phi A	147	583	90	199	53	10	19	109	48	1	49	.341	.392	.564	139	32	11-3	.975	-16	88	76	*O-147(CF)	1.1
1927	Phi A	106	406	86	159	36	11	15	108	31	1	30	.392	.436	.645	168	39	10-2	.985	-1	98	99	*O-105(10-94-1)	3.3
1928	Phi A	119	464	78	163	33	9	15	107	31	3	30	.351	.396	.558	144	28	1-4	.988	-0	97	94	*O-114(LF)	1.7
1929	†Phi A	143	581	114	212	41	9	34	**157**	31	1	38	.365	.398	.642	158	46	4-3	.989	20	**124**	145	*O-142(LF)	5.1
1930	†Phi A	138	554	**152**	211	41	16	36	165	39	1	34	**.381**	.423	.708	173	58	9-2	**.990**	2	101	100	*O-136(129-7-0)	4.5
1931	†Phi A	128	513	105	200	37	13	22	128	47	3	45	**.390**	.444	.641	172	52	3-3	.987	6	108	108	*O-128(125-3-0)	4.6
1932	Phi A	**154**	670	144	**216**	28	9	35	151	47	1	76	.322	.368	.548	129	25	4-2	.980	-6	91	79	*O-154(154-1-0)	1.0
1933	Chi A★	146	605	85	200	29	10	14	119	39	2	49	.331	.373	.481	130	24	5-1	.990	9	111	97	*O-145(144-1-0)	2.4
1934	Chi A★	138	558	102	192	36	7	18	104	53	2	58	.344	.403	.530	135	28	3-2	.987	4	100	122	*O-138(136-2-0)	2.3
1935	Chi A★	128	525	68	140	22	7	16	79	33	2	43	.267	.313	.427	87	-13	4-6	.981	-4	100	49	*O-126(11-115-0)	-2.1
1936	Det A	143	568	96	186	38	6	13	112	49	2	35	.327	.383	.484	112	10	6-4	**.986**	-5	97	68	*O-138(7-134-0)/1	0.2
1937	Was A	103	419	60	117	21	10	8	84	27	4	35	.279	.329	.434	95	-6	3-2	.984	4	109	86	*O-102(98-4-0)	-0.7
1938	Was A	125	470	79	142	23	6	21	95	38	2	40	.302	.357	.511	123	14	2-1	.983	-5	96	47	*O-117(112-8-0)	0.3
1939	Bos N	93	330	39	93	17	5	7	43	22	2	40	.282	.331	.427	110	3	0	.982	1	95	141	O-82(81-1-0)	-0.1
	†Cin N	9	21	0	3	0	0	0	1	2	0	3	.143	.217	.143	-1	-3	0	.938	0	97	233	/O-5(LF)	-0.3
	Year	102	351	39	96	17	5	7	44	24	2	43	.274	.324	.410	103	0	0	.978	1	95	149	O-87(86-1-0)	-0.4
1940	Phi A	37	81	7	25	4	0	1	19	4	0	8	.309	.341	.395	92	-1	0-0	.963	2	125	73	O-18(LF)	0.0
1941	Phi A	9	24	1	3	1	0	0	1	1	0	2	.125	.160	.167	-14	-4	0-0	1.000	0	128	0	/O-5(LF)	-0.4
1943	Bos A	40	133	9	27	5	0	1	12	8	0	21	.203	.248	.263	49	-9	0-1	.986	-1	91	117	O-33(LF)	-1.3
1944	Phi A	4	6	1	3	0	0	0	2	0	0	0	.500	.500	.500	189	1	0-0	1.000	0	120	0	/O-2(LF)	0.1
Total	20	2215	8759	1507	2927	539	149	307	1827	615	30	737	.334	.380	.535	132	362	88-65	.982	4	101	91	*O-2142(1377-771-1)/1	22.5
SIMMONS, BRIAN Brian Lee B 9.4.1973 Lebanon, PA BB/TR 6-2/185# d9.21																								
1998	Chi A	5	19	4	7	0	0	2	6	0-0	0	2	.368	.368	.684	170	2	0-1	1.000	0	111	0	/O-5(2-4-0)	0.1
1999	Chi A	54	126	14	29	3	3	4	17	9-0	0	30	.230	.281	.397	70	-7	4-0	.976	2	113	93	O-46(28-11-9)/D-3	-0.5
2001	Tor A	60	107	8	19	5	0	2	8	8-0	1	26	.178	.239	.280	36	-10	1-0	1.000	1	110	69	O-37(19-12-7)/D-2	-0.9
Total	3	119	252	26	55	8	3	8	31	17-0	1	58	.218	.269	.369	63	-15	5-1	.987	3	112	77	/O-88(49-27-16),D-5	-1.3
SIMMONS, HACK George Washington B 1.29.1885 Brooklyn, NY D 4.26.1942 Arverne, NY BR/TR 5-8/179# d4.15 OF Total (74-LF 1-CF 13-RF)																								
1910	Det A	42	110	12	25	3	1	0	9	10	2		.227	.303	.273	75	-3	1	.984	-0	104	97	1-22/3-7,O-2(0-1-1)	-0.4
1912	NY A	110	401	45	96	17	2	0	41	33	7		.239	.308	.292	68	-16	19	.946	-17	90	75	2-88,1-13/S-4	-3.2
1914	Bal F	114	352	50	95	16	5	1	38	32	6	26	.270	.341	.352	86	-11	7	.894	-3	84	103	O-73(61-0-12),2-26/1-4,S-2,3	-1.7
1915	Bal F	39	88	8	18	7	1	1	14	10	1	9	.205	.293	.341	76	-4	1	1.000	-2	103	0	2-13,O-13(LF)	-0.7
Total	4	305	951	115	234	43	9	2	102	85	16	35	.246	.318	.317	76	-34	28	.953	-21	93	68	2-127/O-88L,1-39,3-8,S-6	-6.0
SIMMONS, JOHN John Earl B 7.7.1924 Birmingham, AL BR/TR 6-1.5/192# d4.22																								
1949	Was A	62	93	12	20	0	0	0	5	11	0	6	.215	.298	.215	38	-8	0-0	1.000	-1	95	75	O-26(18-0-8)	-1.0
SIMMONS, JOE Joseph S. (born Joseph S. Chabriel) B 6.13.1845 New York, NY D 7.24.1901 Jersey City, NJ 5-9/166# d5.8 M2																								
1871	Chi NA	27	129	29	28	6	1	0	17	1		0	.217	.223	.279	39	-11	4-1	.894	-1	34	0	*O-25(0-9-17)/1-2	-0.7
1872	Cle NA	18	90	11	23	5	1	0	9	1		2	.256	.264	.333	87	-1	1-0	.938	1	164	168	1-15/O-3(1-0-2)	0.1
1875	Wes NA	**13**	53	5	9	1	0	0	4	0		2	.170	.170	.189	23	-4	1-2	.733	-0	75	0	O-10(0-9-1)/1-3,M	-0.4
Total	3 NA	58	272	45	60	12	2	0	30	2		4	.221	.226	.279	51	-16	6-3	.000	-0	44	0	/O-38(1-18-20),1-20	-1.0
SIMMONS, NELSON Nelson Bernard B 6.27.1963 Washington, DC BB/TR 6-1/185# d9.4																								
1984	Det A	9	30	4	13	2	0	0	3	2-1	0	5	.433	.469	.500	169	3	1-0	1.000	-0	92	0	/O-5(2-0-4),D-4	0.3
1985	Det A	75	251	31	60	11	0	10	33	26-5	0	41	.239	.306	.402	94	-2	1-0	.945	-2	92	88	O-38(25-0-13),D-31	-0.6
1987	Bal A	16	49	3	13	1	1	1	4	3-0	0	8	.265	.296	.388	85	-1	0-1	1.000	1	104	239	O-13(RF)/D	-0.1
Total	3	100	330	38	86	14	1	11	40	31-6	0	54	.261	.319	.409	99	0	2-1	.963	-1	95	115	/O-56(27-0-30),D-36	-0.4
SIMMONS, TED Ted Lyle B 8.9.1949 Highland Park, MI BB/TR 6/200# d9.21 Mil 1970 OF Total (37-LF 3-RF)																								
1968	StL N	2	3	0	1	0	0	0	0	1-0	0	1	.333	.500	.333	156	0	0-0	1.000	-0	0	0	/C-2	0.0
1969	StL N	5	14	0	3	0	1	0	3	1-0	0	1	.214	.250	.357	73	-1	0-0	.957	-0	64	0	/C-4	-0.1
1970	StL N	82	284	29	69	8	2	3	24	37-5	2	37	.243	.333	.317	74	-10	2-2	.990	-5	109	118	C-79	-1.1
1971	StL N	133	510	64	155	32	4	7	77	36-3	3	50	.304	.347	.424	115	10	1-3	.989	-7	135	96	*C-130	0.9
1972	StL N☆	152	594	70	180	36	6	16	96	29-8	2	57	.303	.336	.465	127	19	1-3	.991	3	79	97	*C-135,1-15	2.7
1973	StL N★	161	619	62	192	36	2	13	91	61-15	2	47	.310	.370	.438	124	22	2-2	.987	10	115	118	*C-153/1-6,O-2(RF)	4.0
1974	StL N☆	152	599	66	163	33	6	20	103	47-8	6	35	.272	.327	.447	117	12	0-0	.986	-6	85	112	*C-141,1-12	1.2
1975	StL N	157	581	80	193	32	3	18	100	63-16	1	35	.332	.396	.491	141	33	1-3	.983	-4	90	80	*C-154/1-2,O-2(LF)	3.6
1976	StL N	150	546	60	159	35	3	5	75	73-**19**	0	35	.291	.371	.394	117	16	0-7	.993	-2	122	**129**	*C-113,1-30/O-7(LF),3-2	1.5
1977	StL N★	150	516	82	164	25	3	21	95	79-**25**	2	37	.318	.408	.500	145	36	2-6	.987	-6	112	97	*C-143/O(RF)	3.5
1978	StL N★	152	516	71	148	40	5	22	80	77-17	3	39	.287	.377	.512	150	37	1-1	.988	-2	77	**142**	*C-134,O-23(LF)	4.1
1979	StL N✳	123	448	68	127	22	0	26	87	61-22	4	34	.283	.369	.507	137	24	0-1	.985	-3	92	87	*C-122	2.6
1980	StL N	145	495	84	150	33	2	21	98	59-13	2	45	.303	.375	.505	140	28	1-0	.985	-6	98	102	*C-129/O-5(LF)	2.8
1981	†Mil A★	100	380	45	82	13	3	14	61	23-2	3	32	.216	.262	.376	88	-8	0-1	.980	-8	95	102	C-75,D-22/1-4	-1.5
1982	†Mil A	137	539	73	145	29	0	23	97	32-5	2	40	.269	.309	.451	114	8	0-0	**.995**	-4	77	129	*C-121,D-15	0.9
1983	Mil A★	153	600	76	185	39	3	13	108	41-6	2	51	.308	.351	.448	129	23	4-2	.975	-6	69	123	C-86,D-66	1.9
1984	Mil A	132	497	44	110	23	2	4	52	30-3	3	40	.221	.269	.300	60	-28	3-0	.995	-3	93	104	D-77,1-37,3-14	-3.6
1985	Mil A	143	528	60	144	28	2	12	76	57-9	1	32	.273	.342	.402	104	4	1-1	.992	-2	82	92	D-99,1-28,C-15/3-2	-0.2
1986	Atl N	76	127	14	32	5	0	4	25	12-5	1	14	.252	.313	.386	89	-2	1-0	.964	-3	112	135	1-14,C-10/3-9	-0.6
1987	Atl N	73	177	20	49	8	0	4	30	21-5	0	23	.277	.350	.390	92	-1	1-1	.984	-1	138	125	1-28,C-15/3-2	-0.4
1988	Atl N	78	107	6	21	6	0	2	11	15-2	0	9	.196	.293	.308	70	-4	0-0	.993	-0	130	71	1-19,C-10	-0.5
Total	21	2456	8680	1074	2472	483	47	248	1389	855-188	39	694	.285	.348	.437	118	218	21-33	.987	-56	97	108	*C-1771,D-279,1-195/O-40L,3-29	21.7
SIMMS, MIKE Michael Howard B 1.12.1967 Orange, CA BR/TR 6-4/185# d9.5																								
1990	Hou N	12	13	3	4	1	0	1	2	0-0	0	4	.308	.308	.615	152	1	0-0	1.000	-0	55	123	/1-6	0.0
1991	Hou N	49	123	18	25	5	0	3	16	18-0	0	38	.203	.301	.317	80	-3	1-0	.889	-2	75	176	O-41(1-0-41)	-0.7
1992	Hou N	15	24	1	6	1	0	1	3	2-0	1	9	.250	.333	.417	116	1	0-0	1.000	0	58	556	/O-9(RF),1	0.1
1994	Hou N	6	12	1	1	1	0	0	0	0-0	0	5	.083	.083	.167	-39	-2	1-0	.857	-0	111	0	/O-3(RF)	-0.3
1995	Hou N	50	121	14	31	4	0	9	24	13-0	3	28	.256	.341	.512	131	5	1-2	.995	-1	105	93	1-25,O-12(RF)	0.1
1996	Hou N	49	68	6	12	2	1	1	8	4-0	1	16	.176	.233	.279	37	-7	1-0	1.000	0	115	0	O-12(9-0-3)/1-5	-0.7
1997	Tex A	59	111	13	28	8	0	5	22	8-1	0	27	.252	.298	.459	90	-2	0-1	.958	-0	115	0	D-28,O-19(2-0-17)/1-2	-0.5
1998	†Tex A	86	186	36	55	11	0	16	46	24-0	3	47	.296	.381	.613	148	13	0-1	1.000	-2	86	52	O-43(3-0-40),D-26,1-16	0.6
1999	Tex A	4	2	0	1	0	0	0	0	0-0	0	1	.500	.500	.500	150	0	0-0	1.000	0	1401	0	/1O(RF)D	0.0

Year	Tm Lg	G	AB	R	H	2B	3B	HR	RBI	BB-IB	HP	SO	AVG	OBP	SLG	AOPS	ABR	SB-CS	FA	FR	Rng	Thr	G at Pos	BFW
Total	9	330	660	92	163	33	1	36	121	69-1	8	175	.247	.323	.464	109	6	4-4	.954	-5	87	104	O-140(15-0-126)/D-56,1-56	-1.4
SIMON, HANK Henry Joseph B 8.25.1862 Hawkinsville, NY D 1.1.1925 Albany, NY BR/TR 5-6/155# d10.7																								
1887	Cle AA	3	10	1	1	0	0	0	0	0	0		.100	.100	.100	-45	-2	0	1.000	-0	0	0	/O-3(LF)	-0.2
1890	Bro AA	89	373	66	96	17	11	0	38	34	2		.257	.323	.362	105	1	23	.951	5	108	99	O-89(LF)	0.4
	Syr AA	38	156	33	47	5	3	2	23	17	0		.301	.370	.410	145	9	12	.941	-2	33	70	O-38(36-2-0)	0.6
	Year	127	529	99	143	22	14	2	61	51	2		.270	.337	.376	116	10	35	.948	3	87	91	*O-127(125-2-0)	1.0
Total	2	130	539	100	144	22	14	2	61	51	2		.267	.333	.371	113	8	35	.949	3	86	90	O-130(128-2-0)	0.8
SIMON, MIKE Michael Edward B 4.13.1883 Hayden, IN D 6.10.1963 Los Angeles, CA BR/TR 5-11/188# d6.27																								
1909	Pit N	12	18	2	3	0	0	0	2	1	0		.167	.211	.167	16	-2	0	.917	0	*171*	*71*	/C-9	-0.1
1910	Pit N	22	50	3	10	0	1	0	5	1	0	2	.200	.216	.240	31	-5	1	1.000	-1	*104*	*74*	C-14	-0.5
1911	Pit N	71	215	19	49	4	3	0	22	10	4	14	.228	.275	.274	52	-15	1	.968	3	*118*	*86*	C-68	-0.6
1912	Pit N	42	113	10	34	2	1	0	11	5	0	9	.301	.331	.336	84	-3	1	.991	3	*135*	*102*	C-40	0.3
1913	Pit N	92	255	23	63	6	2	1	17	10	2	15	.247	.281	.298	68	-11	3-2	.975	9	94	**117**	C-92	0.5
1914	StL F	93	276	21	57	11	2	0	21	18	3	21	.207	.263	.261	41	-27	2	.984	2	*88*	*102*	C-78	-1.9
1915	Bro F	47	142	7	25	5	1	0	12	9	0	12	.176	.225	.225	27	-16	1	.992	-2	*82*	*110*	C-45	-1.6
Total	7	379	1069	85	241	28	10	1	90	54	9	73	.225	.269	.273	51	-79	9-2	.979	14	*102*	*102*	C-346	-3.9
SIMON, RANDALL Randall Carlito B 5.26.1975 Willemstad, Curacao BL/TL 6/180# d9.1																								
1997	Atl N	13	14	2	6	1	0	0	1	1-0	0	2	.429	.467	.500	150	1	0-0	1.000	0	109	110	/1-6	0.1
1998	Atl N	7	16	2	3	0	0	0	4	0-0	0	1	.188	.176	.188	-1	-2	0-0	1.000	-1	42	122	/1-4	-0.3
1999	Atl N	90	218	26	69	16	0	5	25	17-6	1	25	.317	.367	.459	108	3	2-2	.994	-2	80	96	1-70	-0.5
2001	Det A	81	256	28	78	14	2	6	37	15-2	0	28	.305	.341	.445	111	3	0-1	.992	-1	96	109	1-43,D-29	-0.3
2002	Det A	130	482	51	145	17	1	19	82	13-5	4	30	.301	.320	.459	111	5	0-1	.988	-5	76	97	D-65,1-59	-0.9
2003	Pit N	91	307	34	84	14	0	10	51	12-1	2	30	.274	.305	.417	84	-8	0-0	.994	1	109	94	1-80	-1.3
	†Chi N	33	103	13	29	3	0	6	21	4-1	2	7	.282	.318	.485	108	1	0-0	.991	2	120	80	1-29	0.0
	Year	124	410	47	113	17	0	16	72	16-2	4	37	.276	.309	.434	90	-8	0-0	.994	3	112	90	*1-109	-1.3
Total	6	445	1396	156	414	65	3	46	221	62-15	9	123	.297	.328	.446	103	3	2-4	.992	-5	93	97	1-291/D-94	-3.2
SIMON, SYL Sylvester Adam "Sammy" B 12.14.1897 Evansville, IN D 2.28.1973 Chandler, IN BR/TR 5-10.5/170# d10.1																								
1923	StL A	1	1	0	0	0	0	0	0	0	0	0	.000	.000	.000	-95	0	0-0	—	0			H	0.0
1924	StL A	23	32	5	8	1	1	0	6	3	0	5	.250	.314	.344	66	-2	0-0	.889	-1	55	228	/3-6,S-5	-0.2
Total	2	24	33	5	8	1	1	0	6	3	0	5	.242	.306	.333	61	-2	0-0	.889	-1	55	228	/3-6,S-5	-0.2
SIMONS, MEL Melbern Ellis "Butch" B 7.1.1900 Carlyle, IL D 11.10.1974 Paducah, KY BL/TR 5-10/175# d4.14																								
1931	Chi A	68	189	24	52	9	0	0	12	12	0	17	.275	.318	.323	73	-7	1-1	.950	-1	101	89	O-59(15-45-0)	-0.9
1932	Chi A	7	5	0	0	0	0	0	0	0	0	1	.000	.000	.000	-99	-2	0-0	1.000	-0	91	0	/O-6(4-2-0)	-0.2
Total	2	75	194	24	52	9	0	0	12	12	0	18	.268	.311	.314	69	-9	1-1	.951	-1	101	87	/O-65(19-47-0)	-1.1
SIMPSON, HARRY Harry Leon "Suitcase" or "Goody" B 12.3.1925 Atlanta, GA D 4.3.1979 Akron, OH BL/TR 6-1/180# d4.21																								
1951	Cle A	122	332	51	76	7	0	7	24	45	2	48	.229	.325	.313	77	-10	6-4	.971	-4	105	65	O-68(5-8-58),1-50	-1.7
1952	Cle A	146	545	66	145	21	10	10	65	56	2	82	.266	.337	.396	111	6	5-3	.988	-4	101	112	*O-127(0-11-117),1-28	-0.3
1953	Cle A	82	242	25	55	3	1	7	22	18	1	27	.227	.284	.335	68	-12	0-0	.968	-2	100	74	O-69(1-7-62)/1-2	-1.7
1955	Cle A	3	1	1	0	0	0	0	0	2-0	0	0	.000	.667	.000	88	0	0-0	—	0			H	0.0
	KC A	112	396	42	119	16	7	5	52	34-4	2	61	.301	.356	.414	106	3	3-5	.978	-5	94	75	*O-100(4-91-10)/1-3	-0.8
	Year	115	397	43	119	16	7	5	52	36-4	2	61	.300	.358	.413	106	3	3-5	.978	-5	94	75	*O-100(4-91-10)/1-3	-0.8
1956	KC A★	141	543	76	159	22	**11**	21	105	47-8	1	82	.293	.347	.490	119	12	2-3	.965	-13	85	38	*O-111(0-19-96),1-32	-0.7
1957	KC A	50	179	24	53	9	6	6	24	12-2	0	28	.296	.339	.514	128	6	0-1	.996	1	135	83	1-27,O-21(RF)	0.4
	†NY A	75	224	27	56	7	3	7	39	19-0	0	36	.250	.307	.402	94	-3	1-0	.952	-2	77	197	O-42(16-0-26),1-21	-0.8
	Year	125	403	51	109	16	**9**	13	63	31-2	0	64	.270	.321	.452	110	3	1-1	.957	-1	79	155	O-63(16-0-47),1-48	-0.4
1958	NY A	24	51	1	11	2	1	0	6	6-0	1	12	.216	.310	.294	70	-2	0-0	1.000	-1	98	0	O-15(8-0-9)	-0.3
	KC A	78	212	21	56	7	1	7	27	26-3	0	33	.264	.345	.406	104	1	0-2	.990	-3	67	113	1-43,O-11(9-0-2)	-0.6
	Year	102	263	22	67	9	2	7	33	32-3	1	45	.255	.338	.384	98	-1	0-2	.990	-4	67	113	1-43,O-26(17-0-11)	-0.9
1959	KC A	8	14	1	4	0	0	1	2	2-0	1	4	.286	.389	.500	146	1	0-0	1.000	0	94	65	/1-4	0.1
	Chi A	38	75	5	14	5	1	2	13	4-0	0	14	.187	.228	.360	59	-5	0-0	.947	-2	86	0	O-12(RF)/1	-0.7
	Year	46	89	6	18	5	1	3	15	6-0	1	18	.202	.258	.382	75	-4	0-0	.947	-2	111	0	O-12(RF)/1-5	-0.6
	Pit N	9	15	3	4	2	0	0	2	0-0	0	2	.267	.267	.400	75	-1	0-0	1.000	0	111	0	/O-3(1-0-2)	-0.1
Total	8	888	2829	343	752	101	41	73	381	271-17	10	429	.266	.331	.408	102	-4	17-18	.974	-34	95	81	O-579(44-136-415),1-211	-7.2
SIMPSON, JOE Joe Allen B 12.31.1951 Purcell, OK BL/TL 6-3/175# d9.2																								
1975	LA N	9	6	3	2	0	0	0	0	0-0	0	2	.333	.333	.333	89	0	0-0	1.000	-0	89	0	/O-6(CF)	0.0
1976	LA N	23	30	2	4	1	0	0	0	1-0	0	6	.133	.161	.167	-7	-4	0-1	1.000	-0	102	0	O-20(5-6-9)	-0.6
1977	LA N	29	23	2	4	0	0	0	1	2-0	0	6	.174	.240	.174	13	-3	1-1	.957	0	92	131	O-28(5-7-16)/1	-0.3
1978	LA N	10	5	1	2	0	0	0	1	0-0	0	2	.400	.400	.400	125	0	0-0	1.000	0	133	0	O-10(3-2-6)	0.0
1979	Sea A	120	265	29	75	11	0	2	27	11-1	1	21	.283	.312	.347	77	-9	6-3	.966	5	106	183	*O-105(27-5-73)/D-3	-0.7
1980	Sea A	129	365	42	91	15	3	3	34	28-3	1	43	.249	.302	.332	74	-13	17-4	.977	-1	92	139	*O-119(24-36-63)/1-3	-1.6
1981	Sea A	91	288	32	64	11	3	2	30	15-0	1	41	.222	.261	.302	60	-15	12-3	.978	2	105	106	O-88(0-86-2)	-1.4
1982	Sea A	105	296	39	76	14	4	2	23	22-4	2	48	.257	.312	.351	80	-8	8-14	.984	-2	90	136	O-97(32-59-10)	-1.5
1983	KC A	91	119	16	20	2	2	0	8	11-2	2	21	.168	.248	.218	30	-12	1-1	.995	6	128	115	1-54,O-38(4-19-19)/P-2,D	-0.8
Total	9	607	1397	166	338	54	12	9	124	90-10	7	190	.242	.289	.317	67	-64	45-27	.978	10	100	140	O-511(100-226-198)/1-58,D-4,P-2	-6.9
SIMPSON, MARTY Martin B Baltimore, MD d5.14																								
1873	Mar NA	4	15	4	2	0	0	0	2	0		0	.133	.133	.133	-27	-2	0-0	.792	1	181	0	/2-3,C	-0.1
SIMPSON, DICK Richard Charles B 7.28.1943 Washington, DC BR/TR 6-4/176# d9.21																								
1962	LA A	6	8	1	2	1	0	0	1	2-0	0	3	.250	.400	.375	114	0	0-0	1.000	0	128	0	/O-4(4-0-1)	0.0
1964	LA A	21	50	11	7	1	0	2	4	8-0	0	15	.140	.259	.280	55	-3	2-2	1.000	-1	92	0	O-16(CF)	-0.5
1965	Cal A	8	27	2	6	1	0	0	3	2-0	0	8	.222	.267	.259	54	-2	1-0	.875	-1	88	0	/O-8(CF)	-0.3
1966	Cin N	92	84	26	20	2	0	4	14	10-0	2	32	.238	.333	.405	96	0	0-1	.921	-1	106	0	O-64(9-10-46)	-0.3
1967	Cin N	44	54	8	14	3	0	1	6	7-1	0	11	.259	.339	.370	94	0	0-1	.973	2	130	204	O-26(1-4-21)	0.1
1968	StL N	26	56	11	13	0	0	3	8	8-2	0	21	.232	.323	.393	117	1	0-1	1.000	-0	98	83	O-22(RF)	0.0
	Hou N	59	177	25	33	7	2	3	11	20-2	4	61	.186	.282	.299	77	-5	4-4	.970	-3	84	70	O-49(13-16-23)	-1.2
	Year	85	233	36	46	7	2	6	19	28-4	4	82	.197	.292	.322	86	-3	4-5	.979	-3	88	73	O-71(13-16-45)	-1.2
1969	NY A	6	11	2	3	2	0	0	4	3-0	0	6	.273	.429	.455	153	1	0-0	1.000	-0	53	386	/O-5(3-2-0)	0.1
	Sea A	26	51	8	9	2	0	2	5	4-0	0	17	.176	.236	.333	59	-3	3-1	1.000	-1	86	0	O-17(1-16-0)	-0.5
	Year	32	62	10	12	4	0	2	9	7-0	0	23	.194	.275	.355	77	-2	3-1	1.000	-1	78	92	O-22(4-18-0)	-0.4
Total	7	288	518	94	107	19	2	15	56	64-5	6	174	.207	.299	.338	84	-11	10-10	.967	-6	95	66	O-211(31-72-113)	-2.6
SIMS, DUKE Duane B B 6.5.1941 Salt Lake City, UT BL/TR 6-2/205# d9.22																								
1964	Cle A	2	6	0	0	0	0	0	0	0-0	0	2	.000	.000	.000	-99	-2	0-0	1.000	0	*0*	*0*	/C	-0.1
1965	Cle A	48	118	9	21	0	0	6	15	15-2	0	33	.178	.271	.331	69	-5	0-0	.980	1	*131*	*132*	C-40	-0.3
1966	Cle A	52	133	12	35	2	2	6	19	11-1	4	31	.263	.338	.444	122	4	0-1	.975	-3	*155*	*90*	C-48	0.3
1967	Cle A	88	272	25	55	8	2	12	37	30-2	6	64	.202	.294	.379	97	-1	3-3	.989	-6	77	102	C-85	-0.4
1968	Cle A	122	361	48	90	21	0	11	44	62-11	5	68	.249	.366	.399	134	18	1-3	.983	-1	92	105	C-84,1-31/O-4(2-0-2)	2.0
1969	Cle A	114	326	40	77	8	0	18	45	66-5	6	80	.236	.374	.426	120	11	1-2	.991	8	123	96	*C-102/O-3(2-0-1),1	2.3
1970	Cle A	110	345	46	91	12	0	23	56	46-1	6	59	.264	.360	.499	128	13	0-4	.993	1	120	62	C-39,O-36(26-0-10),1-29	1.1
1971	LA N	90	230	23	63	7	2	6	25	30-7	1	39	.274	.357	.400	122	7	0-1	.992	2	105	94	C-74	1.3
1972	LA N	51	151	7	29	7	0	2	11	17-3	1	23	.192	.278	.278	60	-8	0-0	.989	1	100	71	C-48	-0.6
	†Det A	38	98	11	31	4	0	4	19	19-0	1	18	.316	.432	.480	166	9	0-0	.994	-5	70	41	C-25/O-4(RF)	0.6
1973	Det A	80	252	31	61	10	0	8	30	30-1	2	36	.242	.324	.377	92	-2	1-2	.979	-1	79	121	C-68/O-6(5-0-1)	-0.1
	NY A	4	9	3	3	0	0	1	1	3-0	0	1	.333	.500	.667	234	2	0-0	1.000	1	0	288	/CD	0.3
	Year	84	261	34	64	10	0	9	31	33-1	2	37	.245	.331	.387	97	-1	1-2	.979	0	78	124	C-69/O-6(5-0-1),D-2	0.2
1974	NY A	5	15	1	2	1	0	0	2	1-0	0	5	.133	.188	.200	12	-2	0-0	1.000	0	52	0	/CD	-0.2
	Tex A	39	106	7	22	0	0	3	6	8-1	3	24	.208	.280	.292	67	-5	0-0	.970	-1	55	139	C-30/O(RF)D	-0.4
	Year	44	121	8	24	1	0	3	8	9-1	3	29	.198	.269	.281	60	-6	0-0	.971	-0	55	135	C-31/D-5,O(RF)	-0.6

Year	Tm Lg	G	AB	R	H	2B	3B	HR	RBI	BB-IB	HP	SO	AVG	OBP	SLG	AOPS	ABR	SB-CS	FA	FR	Rng	Thr	G at Pos	BFW
Total	11	843	2422	263	580	80	6	100	310	338-34	35	483	.239	.340	.401	111	39	6-16	.986	-3	*101*	*97*	C-646/1-61,O-54(35-0-19),D-7	5.8
SIMS, GREG Gregory Emmett B 6.28.1946 San Francisco, CA BB/TR 6/190# d4.15																								
1966	Hou N	7	6	1	1	0	0	0	0	1-0	0	3	.167	.286	.167	32	-1	0-0	.500	-0	84	0	/O(LF)	-0.1
SINATRO, MATT Matthew Stephen B 3.22.1960 Hartford, CT BR/TR 5-9/175# d9.22 C9																								
1981	Atl N	12	32	4	9	1	1	0	4	5-1	0	4	.281	.378	.375	111	1	1-0	1.000	4	215	140	C-12	0.6
1982	Atl N	37	81	10	11	2	0	1	4	4-0	0	9	.136	.176	.198	4	-11	0-1	1.000	-1	72	101	C-35	-1.2
1983	Atl N	7	12	0	2	0	0	0	2	2-0	0	1	.167	.286	.167	26	-1	0-0	.967	0	67	210	/C-7	-0.1
1984	Atl N	2	4	0	0	0	0	0	0	0-0	0	0	.000	.000	.000	-93	-1	0-0	1.000	-1	33	0	/C-2	-0.2
1987	Oak A	6	3	0	0	0	0	0	0	0-0	0	1	.000	.000	.000	-99	-1	0-0	1.000	-1	60	0	/C-6	-0.1
1988	Oak A	10	9	1	3	2	0	0	5	0-0	0	1	.333	.300	.556	149	1	0-0	1.000	1	0	0	/C-9	0.2
1989	Det A	13	25	2	3	0	0	0	1	1-0	1	3	.120	.185	.120	-13	-4	0-0	1.000	-4	63	104	C-13	-0.7
1990	Sea A	30	50	2	15	1	0	0	4	4-0	0	10	.300	.352	.320	88	-1	1-0	.992	3	94	186	C-28	0.4
1991	Sea A	5	8	1	2	0	0	0	1	1-0	0	1	.250	.333	.250	64	0	0-0	1.000	1	181	0	/C-5	0.1
1992	Sea A	18	28	0	3	0	0	0	0	0-0	0	5	.107	.107	.107	-40	-5	0-0	1.000	-2	183	82	C-18	-0.7
Total	10	140	252	20	48	6	1	1	21	17-1	1	35	.190	.244	.234	34	-22	2-1	.996	1	106	117	C-135	-1.7
SINER, HOSEA Hosea John B 3.20.1885 Shelburn, IN D 6.10.1948 Sullivan, IN BR/TR 5-10.5/185# d7.28																								
1909	Bos N	10	23	1	3	0	0	0	1	2	0		.130	.200	.130	3	-3	0	.909	-1	83	238	/3-5,2S	-0.4
SINGLETON, CHRIS Christopher Verdell B 8.15.1972 Martinez, CA BL/TL 6-2/195# d4.10																								
1999	Chi A	133	496	72	149	31	6	17	72	22-1	1	45	.300	.328	.490	106	2	20-5	.990	12	**118**	113	*O-127(11-121-1)/D-2	1.6
2000	†Chi A	147	511	83	130	22	5	11	62	35-2	1	85	.254	.301	.382	71	-24	22-7	.992	5	106	129	*O-145(19-143-0)	-1.5
2001	Chi A	140	392	57	117	21	5	7	45	20-2	1	61	.298	.331	.431	96	-3	12-11	.991	7	111	124	*O-133(19-121-3)/D-2	0.3
2002	Bal A	136	466	67	122	30	6	9	50	21-0	4	83	.262	.296	.410	91	-8	20-2	.986	-11	88	48	*O-126(CF)/D	-1.3
2003	†Oak A	120	306	38	75	24	1	1	36	26-4	1	55	.245	.301	.340	70	-13	7-2	.969	-12	81	24	*O-113(4-102-8)	-2.3
Total	5	676	2171	317	593	128	23	45	265	124-9	8	329	.273	.311	.415	87	-46	81-27	.987	1	102	92	O-644(53-613-12)/D-5	-3.2
SINGLETON, DUANE Duane Earl B 8.6.1972 Staten Island, NY BL/TR 6-1/170# d8.4																								
1994	Mil A	2	0	0	0	0	0	0	0	0-0	0	0	—	—	—	—	0	0-0	1.000	0	155	0	/O-2(CF)	0.0
1995	Mil A	13	31	0	2	0	0	0	0	1-0	0	10	.065	.094	.065	-55	-7	1-0	1.000	-0	86	193	O-11(3-9-0)	-0.7
1996	Det A	18	56	5	9	1	0	0	3	4-0	1	15	.161	.230	.179	5	-8	0-2	1.000	1	85	354	O-15(3-15-0)	-0.7
Total	3	33	87	5	11	1	0	0	3	5-0	1	25	.126	.183	.138	-16	-15	1-2	1.000	1	87	281	/O-28(6-26-0)	-1.4
SINGLETON, KEN Kenneth Wayne B 6.10.1947 New York, NY BB/TR 6-4/213# d6.24																								
1970	NY N	69	198	22	52	8	0	5	26	30-1	1	48	.263	.361	.379	99	1	1-1	.968	-1	107	30	O-51(26-0-26)	-0.3
1971	NY N	115	298	34	73	5	0	13	46	61-9	2	64	.245	.374	.393	120	10	0-1	.974	-3	93	89	O-96(10-3-85)	0.3
1972	Mon N	142	507	77	139	23	2	14	50	70-5	2	99	.274	.363	.410	118	14	5-10	.972	-4	86	91	*O-137(111-0-29)	0.0
1973	Mon N	**162**	560	100	169	26	2	23	103	123-13	2	91	.302	**.425**	.479	146	42	2-8	.983	-0	89	133	*O-161(2-0-161)	3.2
1974	Mon N	148	511	68	141	20	2	9	74	93-12	0	84	.276	.385	.376	108	10	5-2	.955	-13	86	71	*O-143(RF)	-1.1
1975	Bal A	155	586	88	176	37	4	15	55	118-12	1	82	.300	.415	.454	156	52	3-5	.990	-12	87	65	*O-155(RF)	3.1
1976	Bal A	154	544	62	151	25	2	13	70	79-6	0	76	.278	.366	.403	134	26	2-2	.983	-1	99	91	*O-134(80-0-63),D-19	1.8
1977	Bal A★	152	536	90	176	24	0	24	99	107-13	2	101	.328	.438	.507	168	59	0-1	.986	-3	93	76	*O-150(RF)/D	4.7
1978	Bal A	149	502	67	147	21	2	20	81	98-5	2	94	.293	.409	.462	**154**	42	0-0	.976	-11	93	11	*O-140(4-0-139)/D-5	2.5
1979	†Bal A★	**159**	570	93	168	29	1	35	111	109-**16**	1	118	.295	.405	.533	158	51	3-1	.981	-9	88	78	*O-143(7-0-136),D-16	3.4
1980	Bal A	156	583	85	177	28	3	24	104	92-1	1	94	.304	.397	.485	143	38	0-2	.984	-12	88	28	*O-151(RF)/D-5	1.7
1981	Bal A★	103	363	48	101	16	1	13	49	61-6	0	59	.278	.380	.435	135	19	0-0	**1.000**	-3	95	43	O-72(0-1-72),D-30	1.3
1982	Bal A	156	561	71	141	27	2	14	77	86-2	2	93	.251	.349	.381	102	5	0-1	1.000	1	149	0	*D-148/O-5(2-0-3)	0.0
1983	†Bal A	151	507	52	140	21	3	18	84	99-**19**	1	83	.276	.393	.436	131	26	0-2	—	0	0	0	*D-150	2.1
1984	Bal A	111	363	28	78	7	1	6	36	37-5	0	60	.215	.286	.289	61	-19	0-0	—	0	0	0	*D-103	-2.3
Total	15	2082	7189	985	2029	317	25	246	1065	1263-125	17	1246	.282	.388	.436	132	376	21-36	.980	-71	91	71	*O-1538(242-4-1313),D-477	20.4
SINGTON, FRED Frederic William B 2.24.1910 Birmingham, AL D 8.20.1998 Birmingham, AL BR/TR 6-2/215# d9.23																								
1934	Was A	9	35	2	10	2	0	0	6	4	0	3	.286	.359	.343	85	-1	0-1	.933	-0	81	155	/O-9(3-0-6)	-0.2
1935	Was A	20	22	1	4	0	0	0	3	5	0	1	.182	.333	.182	38	-2	0-0	.889	0	96	335	/O-4(2-0-2)	-0.2
1936	Was A	25	94	13	30	8	0	1	28	15	0	9	.319	.413	.436	116	3	0-0	.946	-1	102	43	O-25(RF)	0.1
1937	Was A	78	228	27	54	15	4	3	36	37	2	33	.237	.348	.377	87	-4	1-1	.961	-0	106	77	O-64(14-0-50)	-0.7
1938	Bro N	17	53	10	19	6	1	2	5	13	1	5	.358	.493	.623	200	9	1	1.000	-1	104	0	O-17(RF)	0.7
1939	Bro N	32	84	13	23	5	0	1	7	15	0	15	.274	.384	.369	100	1	0	.978	-1	98	55	O-22(7-0-15)	-0.1
Total	6	181	516	66	140	36	5	7	85	89	3	66	.271	.382	.401	104	6	2-2	.961	-3	102	70	O-141(26-0-115)	-0.4
SIPEK, DICK Richard Francis B 1.16.1923 Chicago, IL BL/TR 5-9/170# d4.28																								
1945	Cin N	82	156	14	38	6	2	0	13	9	4	15	.244	.302	.308	71	-6	0	.972	0	105	78	O-31(14-0-17)	-0.8
SIPIN, JOHN John White B 8.29.1946 Watsonville, CA BR/TR 6-1.5/175# d5.24																								
1969	SD N	68	229	22	51	12	2	2	9	8-1	1	44	.223	.251	.319	61	-13	2-0	.976	2	113	108	2-60	-0.7
SISCO, STEVE Steven Michael B 12.2.1969 Thousand Oaks, CA BR/TR 5-10/190# d5.6																								
2000	Atl N	25	27	4	5	0	0	1	2	3-0	0	4	.185	.267	.296	42	-3	0-0	1.000	0	140	1423	/O-6(5-0-1),2-5,3-2,D	-0.2
SISLER, GEORGE George Harold "Georgeous George" B3.24.1893 Manchester, OH D3.26.1973 Richmond Heights, MO BL/TL 5-11/170# d6.28 M3 C1 HF1939 s-Dave s-Dick OF Total (12-LF 10-CF 15-RF)																								
1915	StL A	81	274	28	78	10	2	3	29	7	2	27	.285	.307	.369	106	0	10-9	.989	-2	84	102	1-36,O-29(6-8-15),P-15	-0.6
1916	StL A	151	580	83	177	21	11	4	76	40	5	37	.305	.355	.400	133	20	34-26	.985	-2	97	107	*1-141/P-3,O-3(1-2-0),3-2	1.4
1917	StL A	135	539	60	190	30	9	2	52	30	3	19	.353	.390	.453	163	38	37	.985	5	**121**	**117**	*1-133/2-2	4.3
1918	StL A	114	452	69	154	21	9	2	41	40	5	17	.341	.400	.440	159	32	**45**	.990	8	**124**	94	*1-114/P-2	4.0
1919	StL A	132	511	96	180	31	15	10	83	27	5	20	.352	.390	.530	153	33	28	.991	13	**135**	88	*1-131	4.4
1920	StL A	**154**	631	137	**257**	49	18	19	122	46	2	19	**.407**	.449	.632	179	69	42-17	.990	15	**137**	91	*1-154/P	7.9
1921	StL A	138	582	125	216	38	**18**	12	104	34	5	27	.371	.411	.560	137	31	**35**-11	.993	8	**119**	89	*1-138	3.1
1922	StL A	142	586	**134**	**246**	42	**18**	8	105	49	3	14	**.420**	.467	.594	169	**60**	**51**-19	.988	12	**131**	**122**	*1-141	**6.3**
1924	StL A	151	636	94	194	27	10	9	74	31	3	29	.305	.340	.421	90	-12	19-17	.984	1	106	103	*1-151,M	-2.2
1925	StL A	150	649	100	224	21	15	12	105	27	0	24	.345	.371	.479	109	5	11-12	.983	11	**129**	91	*1-150/PM	0.3
1926	StL A	150	613	78	178	21	12	7	71	30	3	30	.290	.327	.398	84	-17	12-8	.987	-3	97	**116**	*1-149/PM	-2.9
1927	StL A	149	614	87	201	32	8	5	97	24	4	15	.327	.357	.430	100	-2	**27**-7	.984	12	**132**	110	*1-149	0.4
1928	Was A	20	49	1	12	1	0	0	2	1	0	2	.245	.260	.265	39	-5	0-1	1.000	-1	0	80	/1-5,O-5(LF)	-0.7
	Bos N	118	491	71	167	26	4	4	68	30	2	15	.340	.380	.434	119	13	11	.988	7	**129**	90	*1-118/P	1.2
1929	Bos N	**154**	629	67	205	40	8	2	79	33	4	17	.326	.363	.424	98	-2	6	.982	4	116	100	*1-154	-0.8
1930	Bos N	116	431	54	133	15	7	3	67	23	2	15	.309	.346	.397	82	-13	7	.987	5	123	105	*1-107	-1.3
Total	15	2055	8267	1284	2812	425	164	102	1175	472	48	327	.340	.379	.468	124	250	375-127	.987	93	120	102	*1-1971/O-37R,P-24,2-2,3-2	24.8
SISLER, DICK Richard Allan B 11.2.1920 St.Louis, MO D 11.20.1998 Nashville, TN BL/TR 6-2/205# d4.16 M2 C13 b-Dave f-George																								
1946	†StL N	83	235	17	61	11	2	3	42	14	2	28	.260	.307	.362	86	-5	0	.988	2	119	117	1-37,O-29(LF)	-0.7
1947	StL N	46	74	4	15	2	1	0	9	3	0	8	.203	.234	.257	29	-8	0	.976	0	119	49	1-10/O-5(LF)	-0.8
1948	Phi N	121	446	60	122	21	3	11	56	47	1	46	.274	.344	.408	105	3	1	.983	-4	93	96	*1-120	-0.5
1949	Phi N	121	412	42	119	19	6	7	50	25	2	38	.289	.333	.415	102	0	0	.987	-9	67	92	1-96	-1.3
1950	†Phi N★	141	523	79	155	29	4	13	83	64	0	50	.296	.373	.442	115	13	1	.987	1	100	89	*O-137(LF)	0.3
1951	Phi N	125	428	46	123	20	5	8	52	40	2	39	.287	.351	.414	107	4	1-0	.968	-1	99	83	*O-111(LF)	-0.5
1952	Cin N	11	27	3	5	1	1	0	4	3	0	5	.185	.267	.296	56	-2	0-0	1.000	-0	103	0	/O-7(3-0-4)	-0.2
	StL N	119	418	48	109	14	5	13	60	29	2	35	.261	.312	.411	99	-3	3-3	.985	4	**115**	**122**	*1-114	-0.3
	Year	130	445	51	114	15	6	13	64	32	2	40	.256	.309	.404	96	-4	3-3	.985	3	**115**	**122**	*1-114/O-7(3-0-4)	-0.5
1953	StL N	32	43	3	11	1	1	0	4	1	0	4	.256	.273	.326	55	-3	0-0	1.000	1	179	112	1-10	-0.2
Total	8	799	2606	302	720	118	28	55	360	226	9	253	.276	.336	.406	101	-1	6-3	.985	-7	97	104	1-387,O-289(285-0-4)	-4.2
SISTI, SIBBY Sebastian Daniel B 7.26.1920 Buffalo, NY BR/TR 5-11/175# d7.21 Mil 1943-45 C2 OF Total (29-LF 14-CF 35-RF)																								
1939	Bos N	63	215	19	49	7	1	1	11	12	0	38	.228	.269	.284	52	-15	4	.994	-1	88	118	2-34,3-17,S-10	-1.3
1940	Bos N	123	459	73	115	19	5	6	34	36	4	64	.251	.311	.353	87	-9	4	.936	-1	99	124	*3-102,2-16	-0.5
1941	Bos N	140	541	72	140	24	3	1	45	38	1	76	.259	.309	.320	81	-15	7	.916	-6	101	105	*3-137/2-2,S-2	-1.6
1942	Bos N	129	407	50	86	11	4	4	35	45	4	55	.211	.296	.287	73	-14	5	.970	-2	101	90	*2-124/O(CF)	-1.0

Year	Tm Lg	G	AB	R	H	2B	3B	HR	RBI	BB-IB	HP	SO	AVG	OBP	SLG	AOPS	ABR	SB-CS	FA	FR	Rng	Thr	G at Pos	BFW
1946	Bos N	1	0	0	0	0	0	0	0	0	0	0	—	—	—	—	0	0	—	-0	0	0	/3	0.0
1947	Bos N	56	153	22	43	8	0	2	15	20	2	17	.281	.371	.373	100	1	2	.947	-8	88	96	S-51/2	-0.4
1948	†Bos N	83	221	30	54	6	2	0	21	31	1	34	.244	.340	.290	73	-7	0	.972	-6	96	88	2-44,S-26	-1.0
1949	Bos N	101	268	39	69	12	0	5	22	34	1	42	.257	.343	.358	93	-2	1	.989	-6	101	64	O-48(21-13-17),2-21,S-18/3	-0.8
1950	Bos N	69	105	21	18	3	1	2	11	16	1	19	.171	.287	.276	52	-7	1	.931	-3	79	85	S-23,2-19,3-13/1O(RF)	-1.0
1951	Bos N	114	362	46	101	20	2	2	38	32	2	50	.279	.341	.362	96	-2	4-5	.944	-16	81	77	S-55,2-52/3-6,1O(RF)	-1.3
1952	Bos N	90	245	19	52	10	1	4	24	14	0	43	.212	.255	.310	58	-15	2-0	.966	-9	90	75	2-33,O-23(8-0-16),S-18/3-9	-2.3
1953	Mil N	38	23	8	5	1	0	0	4	5	0	2	.217	.357	.261	69	-1	0-0	1.000	2	107	51	2-13/S-6,3-4	0.1
1954	Mil N	9	0	2	0	0	0	0	0	0	0	0	—	—	—	—	0	0-0	—	0			R	0.0
Total	13	1016	2999	401	732	121	19	27	260	283	16	440	.244	.313	.324	79	-86	30-5	.973	-56	96	86	2-359,3-290,S-209/O-74R,1-2	-11.1
SIXSMITH, ED Edward B 2.26.1863 Philadelphia, PA D 12.12.1926 Philadelphia, PA BR/TR d9.11																								
1884	Phi N	1	2	0	0	0	0	0	0	0		0	.000	.000	.000	-99	0		1.000	-1			/C	-0.1
SIZEMORE, TED Theodore Crawford B 4.15.1945 Gadsden, AL BR/TR 5-10/165# d4.7 OF Total (16-LF 10-RF)																								
1969	LA N	159	590	69	160	20	5	4	46	45-7	5	40	.271	.328	.342	95	-5	5-5	.979	1	101	112	*2-118,S-46/O(LF)	0.8
1970	LA N	96	340	40	104	10	1	1	34	34-6	0	19	.306	.367	.350	98	0	5-1	.984	-3	101	95	2-86/O-9(8-0-1),S-2	0.3
1971	StL N	135	478	53	126	14	5	3	42	42-5	1	26	.264	.322	.333	83	-10	4-6	.976	17	102	92	2-93,S-39,O-15(7-0-8)/3	1.5
1972	StL N	120	439	53	116	17	4	2	38	37-1	4	36	.264	.324	.335	90	-6	8-3	.976	5	104	99	*2-111	0.8
1973	StL N	142	521	69	147	22	1	1	54	68-0	2	34	.282	.365	.334	96	0	6-4	.981	7	**106**	93	*2-139/3-3	1.7
1974	StL N	129	504	68	126	17	0	2	47	70-2	0	37	.250	.339	.296	80	-11	8-4	.980	15	108	**129**	*2-128/SO(RF)	1.4
1975	StL N	153	562	56	135	23	1	3	49	45-2	2	37	.240	.296	.301	64	-27	1-5	.972	-21	90	83	*2-153	-4.2
1976	LA N	84	266	18	64	8	1	0	18	15-1	0	22	.241	.280	.278	60	-14	2-3	.986	5	103	133	2-71/3-3,C-2	-0.6
1977	†Phi N	152	519	64	146	20	3	4	47	52-21	1	40	.281	.345	.355	85	-10	8-11	.986	15	107	121	*2-152	1.1
1978	†Phi N	108	351	38	77	12	0	0	25	25-8	1	29	.219	.270	.254	48	-25	8-1	.978	10	108	113	*2-107	-0.8
1979	Chi N	98	330	36	82	17	0	2	24	32-7	3	25	.248	.319	.318	68	-13	3-3	.973	23	111	109	2-96	1.4
	Bos A	26	88	12	23	7	0	1	6	4-0	1	5	.261	.301	.375	77	-3	1-0	.993	8	117	150	2-26/C-2	0.6
1980	Bos A	9	23	1	5	1	0	0	0	0-0	0	0	.217	.217	.261	29	-2	0-0	.927	-1	96	132	/2-8	-0.2
Total	12	1411	5011	577	1311	188	21	23	430	469-60	20	350	.262	.325	.321	80	-126	59-46	.979	81	104	108	*2-1288/S-88,O-26L,3-7,C-4	3.8
SKAFF, FRANK Francis Michael B 9.30.1910 LaCrosse, WI D 4.12.1988 Towson, MD BR/TR 5-10/185# d9.11 M1 C4																								
1935	Bro N	6	11	4	6	1	1	0	3	0	0	2	.545	.545	.818	267	2	0	.857	-1	54	0	/3-3	0.2
1943	Phi A	32	64	8	18	2	1	1	8	6	0	11	.281	.343	.391	115	1	0-0	.976	1	142	111	1-18/3-3,S	0.1
Total	2	38	75	12	24	3	2	1	11	6	0	13	.320	.370	.453	138	3	0-0	.976	0	142	111	/1-18,3-6,S	0.3
SKAGGS, DAVE David Lindsey B 6.12.1951 Santa Monica, CA BR/TR 6-2/200# d4.17																								
1977	Bal A	80	216	22	62	9	1	1	24	20-0	0	34	.287	.345	.352	97	0	0-0	.995	-3	116	93	C-80	0.0
1978	Bal A	36	86	6	13	1	1	0	2	9-1	0	14	.151	.232	.186	20	-9	0-1	.988	2	112	106	C-35	-0.7
1979	†Bal A	63	137	9	34	8	0	1	14	13-0	0	14	.248	.313	.328	76	-4	0-0	.984	-4	82	74	C-63	-0.6
1980	Bal A	2	5	0	1	0	0	0	0	0-0	0	1	.200	.200	.200	10	-1	0-0	1.000	0	53	0	/C-2	-0.1
	Cal A	24	66	7	13	0	0	1	9	9-0	0	13	.197	.289	.242	50	-5	0-0	.968	-8	87	28	C-24	-1.2
	Year	26	71	7	14	0	0	1	9	9-0	0	14	.197	.284	.239	47	-5	0-0	.971	-8	85	26	C-26	-1.3
Total	4	205	510	44	123	18	2	3	49	51-1	0	76	.241	.309	.302	72	-19	0-1	.988	-14	102	81	C-204	-2.6
SKETCHLEY, BUD Harry Clement B 3.30.1919 Virden, MB, CAN D 12.19.1979 Los Angeles, CA BL/TL 5-10/180# d4.14																								
1942	Chi A	13	36	1	7	1	0	0	3	7	0	4	.194	.326	.222	57	-2	0-1	.952	0	98	141	O-12(RF)	-0.3
SKIDMORE, ROE Robert Roe B 10.30.1945 Decatur, IL BR/TR 6-3/188# d9.17																								
1970	Chi N	1	1	0	1	0	0	0	0	0-0	0	0	1.000	1.000	1.000	390	0	0-0	—	0			H	0.0
SKIFF, BILL William Franklin B 10.16.1895 New Rochelle, NY D 12.25.1976 Bronxville, NY BR/TR 5-10/170# d5.17																								
1921	Pit N	16	45	7	13	2	0	0	11	0	0	4	.289	.289	.333	63	-2	1-1	.982	-0	*140*	*56*	C-13	-0.2
1926	NY A	6	11	0	1	0	0	0	0	0	0	1	.091	.091	.091	-53	-3	0-0	1.000	-0	*61*	*0*	/C-6	-0.3
Total	2	22	56	7	14	2	0	0	11	0	0	5	.250	.250	.286	40	-5	1-1	.984	-1	*127*	*47*	/C-19	-0.5
SKINNER, ALEXANDER Alexander B 8.14.1856 Chicago, IL D 3.5.1901 Washington, MA d7.12																								
1884	Bal U	1	3	0	1	0	0	0		0			.333	.333	.333	93	0		1.000	0	0	0	/O(RF)	0.0
	CP U	1	3	1	1	0	0	0		0			.333	.333	.333	103	0		—	-0	0	0	/O(CF)	0.0
	Year	2	6	1	2	0	0	0		0			.333	.333	.333	98	0		1.000	-0	0	0	/O-2(0-1-1)	0.0
SKINNER, CAMP Elisha Harrison B 6.25.1897 Douglasville, GA D 8.4.1944 Douglasville, GA BL/TR 5-11/165# d5.2																								
1922	NY A	27	33	1	6	0	0	0	2	0	1	4	.182	.206	.182	2	-5	1-0	1.000	0	118	0	/O-4(1-3-0)	-0.5
1923	Bos A	7	13	1	3	2	0	0	1	0	0	0	.231	.231	.385	60	-1	0-0	—	-0	0	0	/O-2(CF)	-0.1
Total	2	34	46	2	9	2	0	0	3	0	1	4	.196	.213	.239	18	-6	1-0	1.000	-0	114	0	/O-6(1-5-0)	-0.6
SKINNER, JOEL Joel Patrick B 2.21.1961 LaJolla, CA BR/TR 6-4/204# d6.12 M1 C3 f-Bob																								
1983	Chi A	6	11	2	3	0	0	0	1	0-0	0	1	.273	.273	.273	49	-1	0-0	.960	1	113	174	/C-6	0.1
1984	Chi A	43	80	4	17	2	0	0	3	7-0	0	19	.213	.273	.237	42	-6	1-0	.989	4	78	70	C-43	-0.1
1985	Chi A	22	44	9	15	4	1	1	5	5-0	0	13	.341	.408	.545	153	3	0-0	.971	-0	95	130	C-21	0.4
1986	Chi A	60	149	17	30	5	1	4	20	9-0	1	43	.201	.250	.329	55	-10	1-0	.988	-11	115	68	C-60	-1.9
	NY A	54	166	6	43	4	0	1	17	7-0	0	40	.259	.287	.301	62	-9	0-4	.981	1	147	97	C-54	-0.7
	Year	114	315	23	73	9	1	5	37	16-0	1	83	.232	.269	.314	58	-19	1-4	.984	-10	131	83	*C-114	-2.6
1987	NY A	64	139	9	19	4	0	3	14	8-0	1	46	.137	.187	.230	11	-18	0-0	.984	-8	97	108	C-64	-2.4
1988	NY A	88	251	23	57	15	0	4	23	14-0	0	72	.227	.267	.335	68	-11	0-0	.990	-8	**217**	53	C-85/O-2(1-0-1),1	-1.5
1989	Cle A	79	178	10	41	10	0	1	13	9-0	1	42	.230	.271	.303	61	-9	1-1	.990	-8	100	92	C-79	-1.4
1990	Cle A	49	139	16	35	4	1	2	16	7-0	0	44	.252	.288	.338	75	-5	0-0	.996	-4	140	89	C-49	-0.7
1991	Cle A	99	284	23	69	14	0	1	24	14-1	1	67	.243	.279	.303	61	-15	0-2	.991	-0	107	96	C-99	-1.1
Total	9	564	1441	119	329	62	3	17	136	80-1	4	387	.228	.269	.311	60	-81	3-7	.988	-33	129	86	C-560/O-2(1-0-1),1	-9.3
SKINNER, BOB Robert Ralph B 10.3.1931 LaJolla, CA BL/TR 6-4/190# d4.13 M3 C19 s-Joel																								
1954	Pit N	132	470	67	117	15	9	8	46	47	0	59	.249	.316	.370	80	-15	4-0	.986	-2	98	76	*1-118/O-2(RF)	-2.4
1956	Pit N	113	233	29	47	8	3	5	29	26-1	1	50	.202	.282	.326	65	-12	1-1	.977	-5	91	125	O-36(26-0-10),1-23/3	-2.0
1957	Pit N	126	387	58	118	12	6	13	45	38-6	2	50	.305	.370	.468	127	14	10-4	.963	3	100	154	O-93(LF)/1-9,3	1.3
1958	Pit N★	144	529	93	170	33	9	13	70	58-7	2	55	.321	.387	.491	135	28	12-4	.977	7	94	**206**	*O-141(LF)	2.8
1959	Pit N	143	547	78	153	18	4	13	61	67-8	0	65	.280	.357	.399	102	3	10-7	.964	-3	97	75	*O-142(LF)/1	-1.0
1960	†Pit N★	145	571	83	156	33	6	15	86	59-11	1	86	.273	.340	.431	109	8	11-8	.981	-4	90	105	*O-141(LF)	-0.5
1961	Pit N	119	381	61	102	20	3	3	42	51-9	4	49	.268	.358	.360	91	-2	3-5	.973	-2	100	64	O-97(LF)	-1.1
1962	Pit N	144	510	87	154	29	7	20	75	76-5	4	89	.302	.395	.504	140	31	10-4	.960	-5	93	68	*O-139(LF)	2.0
1963	Pit N	34	122	18	33	5	5	0	8	13-1	0	22	.270	.341	.393	110	2	4-1	.983	-2	93	44	O-32(LF)	-0.2
	Cin N	72	194	25	49	10	2	3	17	21-1	2	42	.253	.332	.371	99	0	1-2	1.000	2	102	111	O-51(LF)	-0.1
	Year	106	316	43	82	15	7	3	25	34-2	2	64	.259	.335	.380	103	2	5-3	.993	0	98	81	O-83(LF)	-0.3
1964	Cin N	25	59	6	13	3	0	3	5	4-0	0	12	.220	.270	.424	89	-1	0-0	.913	0	102	136	O-12(LF)	-0.2
	†StL N	55	118	10	32	5	0	1	16	11-2	0	20	.271	.333	.339	83	-2	0-0	.938	-1	90	155	O-31(4-0-27)	-0.5
	Year	80	177	16	45	8	0	4	21	15-2	0	32	.254	.313	.367	85	-3	0-0	.930	-0	94	149	O-43(16-0-27)	-0.7
1965	StL N	80	152	25	47	5	4	5	26	12-2	0	30	.309	.360	.493	126	5	1-0	.935	-2	94	0	O-33(15-0-19)	0.1
1966	StL N	49	45	2	7	1	0	1	5	2-0	1	17	.156	.208	.244	25	-5	0-0	—	0			H	-0.5
Total	12	1381	4318	642	1198	197	58	103	531	485-53	17	646	.277	.351	.421	108	54	67-36	.969	-13	95	106	O-950(893-0-58),1-151/3-2	-2.3
SKIZAS, LOU Louis Peter "The Nervous Greek" B 6.2.1932 Chicago, IL BR/TR 5-11/175# d4.19																								
1956	NY A	6	6	0	1	0	0	0	1	0-0	0	2	.167	.167	.167	-12	-1	0-0	—	0			H	-0.1
	KC A	83	297	39	94	11	3	11	39	15-1	0	17	.316	.346	.485	118	6	3-1	.975	3	100	161	O-74(57-0-18)	0.5
	Year	89	303	39	95	11	3	11	40	15-1	0	19	.314	.343	.479	116	5	3-1	.975	3	100	161	O-74(57-0-18)	0.4
1957	KC A	119	376	34	92	14	1	18	44	27-1	2	15	.245	.297	.431	95	-4	5-2	.976	-2	88	95	O-76(14-0-69),3-32	-1.0
1958	Det A	23	33	4	8	2	0	1	2	5-1	0	1	.242	.342	.394	95	0	0-0	.750	-1	78	0	/O-5(4-0-1),3-4	-0.1
1959	Chi A	8	13	3	1	0	0	0	0	3-0	0	2	.077	.250	.077	-6	-2	0-0	1.000	0	84	438	/O-6(5-0-1)	-0.2
Total	4	239	725	80	196	27	4	30	86	50-3	2	37	.270	.317	.443	102	-1	8-3	.973	-0	93	133	O-161(80-0-89)/3-36	-0.9

Year	Tm Lg	G	AB	R	H	2B	3B	HR	RBI	BB-IB	HP	SO	AVG	OBP	SLG	AOPS	ABR	SB-CS	FA	FR	Rng	Thr	G at Pos	BFW
SKOWRON, BILL William Joseph "Moose" B 12.18.1930 Chicago, IL BR/TR 5-11/195# d4.13																								
1954	NY A	87	215	37	73	12	9	7	41	19	1	18	.340	.392	.577	170	19	2-1	.986	-0	98	126	1-61/3-5,2-2	1.7
1955	†NY A	108	288	46	92	17	3	12	61	21-4	3	32	.319	.369	.524	141	15	1-1	.989	-2	94	115	1-74/3-3	1.0
1956	†NY A	134	464	78	143	21	6	23	90	50-3	6	60	.308	.382	.528	143	27	4-4	.993	4	**112**	**131**	*1-120/3-2	2.3
1957	†NY A★	122	457	54	139	15	5	17	88	31-6	3	60	.304	.347	.470	125	14	3-2	.992	6	119	**113**	*1-115	1.3
1958	†NY A★	126	465	61	127	22	3	14	73	28-1	4	69	.273	.317	.424	107	3	1-1	**.993**	-2	99	**106**	*1-118/3-2	-0.7
1959	NY A★	74	282	39	84	13	5	15	59	20-0	3	47	.298	.349	.539	145	16	1-0	.991	-0	97	115	1-72	1.2
1960	†NY A★	146	538	63	166	34	3	26	91	38-2	2	95	.309	.353	.528	144	31	2-3	.991	9	126	106	*1-142	3.1
1961	†NY A☆	150	561	76	150	23	4	28	89	35-9	8	108	.267	.318	.472	115	8	0-0	.993	1	99	126	*1-149	0.0
1962	†NY A	140	478	63	129	16	6	23	80	36-4	5	99	.270	.325	.473	116	8	0-1	.991	-5	88	106	*1-135	-0.4
1963	†LA N	89	237	19	48	8	0	4	19	13-4	3	49	.203	.252	.287	59	-13	0-1	.991	-1	94	104	1-66/3	-1.9
1964	Was A	73	262	28	71	10	0	13	41	11-2	3	56	.271	.306	.458	110	3	0-0	.994	-2	93	77	1-66	-0.3
	Chi A	73	273	19	80	11	3	4	38	19-4	1	36	.293	.337	.399	108	3	0-0	.998	-0	94	114	1-70	-0.2
	Year	146	535	47	151	21	3	17	79	30-6	4	92	.282	.322	.428	109	5	0-0	.996	-2	94	96	*1-136	-0.5
1965	Chi A✱	146	559	63	153	24	3	18	78	32-4	5	77	.274	.316	.424	116	9	1-3	.994	-6	84	**119**	*1-145	-0.6
1966	Chi A	120	337	27	84	15	2	6	29	26-4	3	45	.249	.308	.359	98	-1	1-1	.991	2	114	132	1-98	-0.4
1967	Chi A	8	8	0	0	0	0	0	1	0-0	0	1	.000	.000	.000	-99	-2	0-0	—	0			H	-0.2
	Cal A	62	123	8	27	2	1	1	10	4-1	4	18	.220	.267	.276	63	-6	0-0	.988	-1	93	82	1-32	-0.9
	Year	70	131	8	27	2	1	1	11	4-1	4	19	.206	.252	.260	53	-8	0-0	.988	-1	93	82	1-32	-1.1
Total	14	1658	5547	681	1566	243	53	211	888	383-48	54	870	.282	.332	.459	121	134	16-18	.992	5	102	114	*1-1463/3-13,2-2	5.0
SKUBE, BOB Robert Jacob B 10.8.1957 Northridge, CA BL/TL 6/180# d9.17																								
1982	Mil A	4	3	0	2	0	0	0	0	0-0	0	0	.667	.667	.667	285	1	0-0	—	-0	0	0	/O(CF)D	0.1
1983	Mil A	12	25	2	5	1	1	0	9	4-0	0	7	.200	.310	.320	80	-1	0-0	1.000	-0	111	0	/O-8(0-4-4),1D	-0.1
Total	2	16	28	2	7	1	1	0	9	4-0	0	7	.250	.344	.357	101	0	0-0	1.000	-0	109	0	/O-9(0-5-4),D-3,1	0.0
SLADE, GORDON Gordon Leigh "Oskie" B 10.9.1904 Salt Lake City, UT D 1.2.1974 Long Beach, CA BR/TR 5-10.5/160# d4.21																								
1930	Bro N	25	37	8	8	2	0	1	2	3	0	5	.216	.275	.351	51	-3	0	.938	6	137	183	S-21	0.4
1931	Bro N	85	272	27	65	13	2	1	29	23	5	28	.239	.310	.313	68	-12	2	.947	10	107	105	S-82/3-2	0.4
1932	Bro N	79	250	23	60	15	1	1	23	11	3	26	.240	.280	.320	62	-13	3	.943	8	100	108	S-55,3-23	-0.1
1933	StL N	39	62	6	7	1	0	0	3	6	0	7	.113	.191	.129	-7	-9	1	.941	0	102	95	S-31/2	-0.8
1934	Cin N	138	555	61	158	19	8	4	52	25	4	34	.285	.320	.369	86	-12	6	.952	5	105	103	S-97,2-39	0.2
1935	Cin N	71	196	22	55	10	0	1	14	16	2	16	.281	.341	.347	88	-3	0	.927	-5	91	94	S-30,2-19/O-8(LF),3-7	-0.5
Total	6	437	1372	147	353	60	11	8	123	84	14	116	.257	.307	.335	73	-52	12	.945	25	104	106	S-316/2-59,3-32,O-8(LF)	-0.4
SLADEN, ART Arthur B 10.28.1860 Dracut, MA D 2.28.1914 Dracut, MA d4.22																								
1884	Bos U	2	7	0	0	0	0	0		0			.000	.000	.000	-99	-2		1.000	-0	0	0	/O-2(RF)	-0.2
SLAGLE, JIMMY James Franklin "Rabbit" or "Shorty" B 7.11.1873 Worthville, PA D 5.10.1956 Chicago, IL BL/TR 5-10.5/144# d4.17																								
1899	Was N	147	599	92	163	15	8	0	41	55	5		.272	.338	.324	83	-13	22	.953	18	91	120	*O-146(CF)	-0.4
1900	Phi N	**141**	574	115	165	16	9	0	45	60	3		.287	.358	.347	96	-2	34	.922	0	112	90	*O-141(LF)	-1.3
1901	Phi N	48	183	20	37	6	2	1	20	16	3		.202	.277	.273	59	-9	5	.930	5	187	206	O-48(LF)	-0.7
	Bos N	66	255	35	69	7	0	0	7	34	1		.271	.359	.298	84	-4	14	.935	-2	133	157	O-66(0-5-61)	-0.8
	Year	114	438	55	106	13	2	1	27	50	4		.242	.325	.288	74	-13	19	.932	3	**157**	178	*O-114(48-5-61)	-1.5
1902	Chi N	117	463	66	146	11	4	0	28	53	0		.315	.386	.356	133	20	41	.965	4	90	125	*O-115(94-22-0)	1.8
1903	Chi N	**139**	543	104	162	20	6	0	44	81	4		.298	.393	.357	117	18	33	.936	-3	78	176	*O-139(115-24-0)	0.7
1904	Chi N	120	481	73	125	12	10	1	31	41	3		.260	.322	.333	102	1	28	.921	-5	94	166	*O-120(102-18-0)	-1.2
1905	Chi N	**155**	568	96	153	19	4	0	37	97	3		.269	.379	.317	104	9	27	.962	-1	129	137	*O-155(33-123-0)	0.1
1906	Chi N	127	498	71	119	8	6	0	33	63	0		.239	.324	.279	83	-8	25	.976	-3	54	147	*O-127(4-123-0)	-1.9
1907	†Chi N	136	489	71	126	6	6	0	32	76	1		.258	.359	.294	99	3	28	.962	-10	83	131	*O-136(4-132-0)	-1.5
1908	Chi N	104	352	38	78	4	1	0	26	43	0		.222	.306	.239	71	-10	17	.976	-6	48	73	*O-101(26-75-0)	-2.5
Total	10	1300	5005	781	1343	124	56	2	344	619	23		.268	.352	.317	97	5	274	.950	-2	95	135	*O-1294(567-668-61)	-7.7
SLATTERY, JACK John Terrence B 1.6.1878 S.Boston, MA D 7.17.1949 Boston, MA BR/TR 6-2/191# d9.28 M1 C2																								
1901	Bos A	1	3	1	1	0	0	0	1	1	0		.333	.500	.333	137	0	0	1.000	0	*124*	*102*	/C	0.1
1903	Cle A	4	11	1	0	0	0	0	0	0	0		.000	.000	.000	-99	-3	0	.885	-1	71	280	/1-2	-0.4
	Chi A	63	211	8	46	3	2	0	20	2	2		.218	.233	.251	47	-14	2	.974	-4	*109*	*80*	C-56/1-5	-1.4
	Year	67	222	9	46	3	2	0	20	2	2		.207	.221	.239	40	-17	2	.974	-5	*109*	*80*	C-56/1-7	-1.8
1906	StL N	3	7	0	2	0	0	0	0	1	0		.286	.375	.286	111	0	0	1.000	-1	*68*	*45*	/C-2	0.0
1909	Was A	32	56	4	12	2	0	0	6	2	1		.214	.254	.250	62	-2	1	.953	-1	128	51	1-11/C-6	-0.4
Total	4	103	288	14	61	5	2	0	27	6	3		.212	.236	.243	47	-19	3	.974	-6	*106*	*79*	/C-65,1-18	-2.1
SLATTERY, MIKE Michael J. B 11.26.1866 Boston, MA D 10.16.1904 Boston, MA BL/TL 6-2/210# d4.17																								
1884	Bos U	106	413	60	86	6	2	0		4			.208	.216	.232	36	-45		.802	4	111	89	*O-96(1-96-0),1-11	-4.0
1888	†NY N	103	391	50	96	12	6	1	35	13	1	28	.246	.272	.315	87	-6	26	.919	-0	93	101	*O-103(4-90-9)	-0.9
1889	†NY N	12	48	7	14	2	0	1	12	4	0	3	.292	.346	.396	107	0	2	.852	-1	86	241	O-12(4-7-1)	-0.1
1890	NY P	97	411	80	126	20	11	5	67	27	2	25	.307	.352	.445	103	-2	18	.905	-12	28	29	*O-97(53-39-9)	-1.3
1891	Cin N	41	158	24	33	3	2	1	16	10	0	10	.209	.256	.272	53	-10	1	.941	-2	62	92	O-41(4-37-0)	-1.2
	Was AA	15	60	8	17	1	0	0	5	4	3	5	.283	.358	.300	93	0	6	.862	-2	41	163	O-15(3-12-0)	-0.2
Total	5	374	1481	229	372	44	21	8	135	62	6	71	.251	.284	.325	77	-63	53	.883	-13	75	85	O-364(69-281-19)/1-11	-7.7
SLAUGHT, DON Donald Martin B 9.11.1958 Long Beach, CA BR/TR 6-1/190# d7.6																								
1982	KC A	43	115	14	32	6	0	3	8	9-0	0	12	.278	.331	.409	102	0	0-0	.994	2	147	70	C-43	0.3
1983	KC A	83	276	21	86	13	4	0	28	11-0	0	27	.312	.336	.388	99	-1	3-1	.964	-7	90	95	C-79/D	-0.4
1984	†KC A	124	409	48	108	27	4	4	42	20-4	2	55	.264	.297	.379	86	-8	0-0	.982	-1	99	105	*C-123/D	-0.4
1985	Tex A	102	343	34	96	17	4	8	35	20-1	6	41	.280	.331	.423	103	1	5-4	.990	-4	97	95	*C-102	0.1
1986	Tex A	95	314	39	83	17	1	13	46	16-0	5	59	.264	.308	.449	101	0	3-2	.993	-11	60	104	C-91/D-2	-0.7
1987	Tex A	95	237	25	53	15	2	8	16	24-3	1	51	.224	.298	.405	84	-6	0-3	.985	-5	71	111	C-85/D-5	-0.9
1988	NY A	97	322	33	91	25	1	9	43	24-3	3	54	.283	.334	.450	120	9	1-0	.979	-9	92	64	C-94/D	0.5
1989	NY A	117	350	34	88	21	3	5	38	30-3	5	57	.251	.315	.371	95	-2	1-1	.991	0	123	112	*C-105/D-3	0.4
1990	†Pit N	84	230	27	69	18	3	4	29	27-2	3	27	.300	.375	.457	134	12	0-1	.979	2	100	109	C-78	1.7
1991	†Pit N	77	220	19	65	17	1	1	29	21-1	3	32	.295	.363	.395	116	6	1-0	.987	2	116	107	C-69/3	1.2
1992	†Pit N	87	255	26	88	17	3	4	37	17-5	2	23	.345	.384	.482	147	16	2-2	.988	1	120	97	C-79	2.2
1993	Pit N	116	377	34	113	19	2	10	55	29-2	6	56	.300	.356	.440	113	7	2-1	.993	-8	88	88	*C-105	0.6
1994	Pit N	76	240	21	69	7	0	2	21	34-2	3	31	.287	.381	.342	90	-2	0-0	.994	0	98	76	C-74	0.3
1995	Pit N	35	112	13	34	6	0	0	13	9-2	1	8	.304	.361	.357	88	-1	0-0	.996	1	72	62	C-33	0.2
1996	Cal A	62	207	23	67	9	0	6	32	13-0	2	20	.324	.366	.454	106	2	0-0	.992	-5	62	126	C-59/D	0.1
	Chi A	14	36	2	9	1	0	0	4	2-0	0	2	.250	.289	.278	47	-3	0-0	.986	-3	56	34	C-12/D	-0.5
	Year	76	243	25	76	10	0	6	36	15-0	2	22	.313	.355	.428	98	-1	0-0	.991	-8	61	110	C-71/D-2	-0.4
1997	SD N	20	20	2	0	0	0	0	0	5-0	0	4	.000	.200	.000	-45	-4	0-0	1.000	-1	104	0	/C-6	-0.5
Total	16	1327	4063	415	1151	235	28	77	476	311-28	42	559	.283	.338	.412	104	26	18-15	.987	-45	95	95	*C-1237/D-15,3	4.2
SLAUGHTER, ENOS Enos Bradsher "Country" B 4.27.1916 Roxboro, NC D 8.12.2002 Durham, NC BL/TR 5-9/192# d4.19 Mil 1943-45 HF1985																								
1938	StL N	112	395	59	109	20	10	8	58	32	0	38	.276	.330	.438	104	1	1	.970	-0	103	90	O-92(1-20-75)	-0.4
1939	StL N	149	604	95	193	**52**	5	12	86	44	5	53	.320	.371	.482	120	18	2	.968	13	118	132	*O-149(RF)	2.2
1940	StL N	140	516	96	158	25	13	17	73	50	2	35	.306	.370	.504	131	21	8	.989	5	111	81	*O-132(RF)	1.8
1941	StL N★	113	425	71	132	22	9	13	76	53	2	28	.311	.390	.496	139	22	4	.947	-11	86	55	*O-108(RF)	0.5
1942	†StL N★	152	591	100	**188**	31	**17**	13	98	88	6	30	.318	.412	.494	153	42	9	.987	0	98	112	*O-151(RF)	3.5
1946	†StL N★	**156**	609	100	183	30	8	18	**130**	69	2	41	.300	.374	.465	131	25	9	.981	2	92	**146**	*O-156(RF)	2.2
1947	StL N★	147	551	100	162	31	13	10	86	59	4	27	.294	.366	.452	111	9	4	.982	2	96	129	*O-142(110-0-32)	0.1
1948	StL N★	146	549	91	176	27	11	11	90	81	1	29	.321	.409	.470	130	25	4	.971	2	107	77	*O-146(107-0-39)	1.8
1949	StL N★	151	568	92	191	34	**13**	13	96	79	1	37	.336	.418	.511	141	36	3	.983	-1	100	78	*O-150(LF)	2.3
1950	StL N★	148	556	82	161	26	7	10	101	66	2	33	.290	.367	.415	100	2	3	.978	-6	94	81	*O-145(20-0-125)	-1.0
1951	StL N★	123	409	48	115	17	8	4	64	67	3	25	.281	.386	.391	109	8	7-2	.995	1	101	109	*O-106(RF)	0.7
1952	StL N★	140	510	73	153	17	12	11	101	70	1	25	.300	.386	.445	130	21	6-1	.989	-2	98	89	*O-137(RF)	1.7
1953	StL N★	143	492	64	143	34	9	6	89	80	5	28	.291	.395	.433	116	16	4-4	**.996**	-8	95	21	*O-137(RF)	0.3

Year	Tm Lg	G	AB	R	H	2B	3B	HR	RBI	BB-IB	HP	SO	AVG	OBP	SLG	AOPS	ABR	SB-CS	FA	FR	Rng	Thr	G at Pos	BFW
1954	NY A	69	125	19	31	4	2	1	19	28	0	8	.248	.386	.336	102	2	0-2	.974	-3	84	0	O-30(3-0-29)	-0.3
1955	NY A	10	9	1	1	0	0	0	1	1-0	0	1	.111	.200	.111	-15	-1	0-0	—	0			H	-0.2
	KC A	108	267	49	86	12	4	5	34	40-4	2	17	.322	.408	.453	132	13	2-3	.985	-1	98	95	O-77(RF)	1.0
	Year	118	276	50	87	12	4	5	35	41-4	2	18	.315	.401	.442	127	12	2-3	.985	-1	98	95	O-77(RF)	0.8
1956	KC A	91	223	37	62	14	3	2	23	29-1	1	20	.278	.362	.395	100	1	1-0	.981	-3	98	25	O-56(19-1-37)	-0.4
	†NY A	24	83	15	24	4	2	0	4	5-0	0	6	.289	.330	.386	91	-1	1-1	1.000	-1	80	75	O-20(17-0-4)	-0.4
	Year	115	306	52	86	18	5	2	27	34-1	1	26	.281	.354	.392	97	-1	2-1	.985	-4	93	38	O-76(36-1-41)	-0.8
1957	†NY A	96	209	24	53	7	1	5	34	40-5	0	19	.254	.369	.368	105	3	0-2	1.000	-3	85	61	O-64(56-0-9)	-0.5
1958	†NY A	77	138	21	42	4	1	4	19	21-0	0	16	.304	.396	.435	133	7	2-0	.957	-2	88	53	O-35(16-0-20)	0.4
1959	NY A	74	99	10	17	2	0	6	21	13-1	0	19	.172	.265	.374	77	-4	1-0	.964	-1	91	0	O-26(9-0-18)	-0.6
	Mil N	11	18	0	3	0	0	0	1	3-0	0	3	.167	.286	.167	27	-2	0-0	1.000	-0	85	0	/O-5(LF)	-0.2
Total	19	2380	7946	1247	2383	413	148	169	1304	1018-11	37	538	.300	.382	.453	122	264	71-15	.980	-17	99	89	*O-2064(513-21-1541)	14.5
SLAYBACK, SCOTTIE Elbert B 10.5.1901 Paducah, KY D 11.30.1979 Cincinnati, OH BR/TR 5-8/165# d9.26																								
1926	NY N	2	8	0	0	0	0	0	0	0	0	0	.000	.000	.000	-99	-2	0	.889	-1	68	0	/2-2	-0.4
SLOAN, BRUCE Bruce Adams "Fatso" B 10.4.1914 McAlester, OK D 9.24.1973 Oklahoma City, OK BL/TL 5-9/195# d4.29																								
1944	NY N	59	104	7	28	4	1	1	9	13	0	8	.269	.350	.356	99	0	0	.935	-2	91	0	O-21(3-0-18)	-0.3
SLOAN, TOD Yale Yeastman B 12.24.1890 Madisonville, TN D 9.12.1956 Akron, OH BL/TR 6/175# d9.22 Mil 1918																								
1913	StL A	7	26	2	7	1	0	0	2	1	1	9	.269	.321	.308	87	0	1	.950	1	125	147	/O-7(RF)	0.0
1917	StL A	109	313	32	72	6	2	2	25	28	7	34	.230	.307	.281	83	-6	8	.963	-1	93	99	O-77(16-1-60)	-1.3
1919	StL A	27	63	9	15	1	3	0	6	12	1	3	.238	.368	.349	99	0	0	.933	1	79	221	O-20(RF)	0.0
Total	3	143	402	43	94	8	5	2	33	41	9	46	.234	.319	.294	86	-6	9	.957	1	94	123	O-104(16-1-87)	-1.3
SLOCUM, RON Ronald Reece B 7.2.1945 Modesto, CA BR/TR 6-2/185# d9.8																								
1969	SD N	13	24	6	7	1	0	1	5	0-0	0	5	.292	.280	.458	112	0	0-0	.938	-1	133	0	/2-4,3-4,S	0.0
1970	SD N	60	71	8	10	2	2	1	11	8-1	1	24	.141	.237	.268	37	-7	0-1	.978	6	75	111	C-19,S-17,3-11/2-9	0.0
1971	SD N	7	18	1	0	0	0	0	0	0-0	1	8	.000	.053	.000	-90	-5	0-0	.905	0	103	0	/3-6	-0.5
Total	3	80	113	15	17	3	2	2	16	8-1	2	37	.150	.218	.265	33	-12	0-1	.887	6	119	123	/3-21,C-19,S-18,2-13	-0.5
SMAJSTRLA, CRAIG Craig Lee B 6.19.1962 Houston, TX BB/TR 5-9/165# d9.6																								
1988	Hou N	8	3	2	0	0	0	0	0	0-0	0	1	.000	.000	.000	-99	-1	0-0	1.000	-0	0	0	/2-2	-0.1
SMALL, CHARLIE Charles Albert B 10.24.1905 Auburn, ME D 1.14.1953 Auburn, ME BL/TR 5-11/180# d7.7																								
1930	Bos A	25	18	1	3	1	0	0	0	2	0	5	.167	.250	.222	22	-2	1-0	1.000	0	153	0	/O(CF)	-0.2
SMALL, HANK George Henry B 7.31.1953 Atlanta, GA BR/TR 6-3/205# d9.27																								
1978	Atl N	1	4	0	0	0	0	0	0	0-0	0	0	.000	.000	.000	-90	-1	0-0	1.000	0	156	119	/1	-0.1
SMALL, JIM James Arthur Patrick B 3.8.1937 Portland, OR BL/TL 6-1.5/180# d6.22																								
1955	Det A	12	4	2	0	0	0	0	0	1-0	0	1	.000	.200	.000	-44	-1	0-0	1.000	1	117	1449	/O-4(3-0-1)	0.0
1956	Det A	58	91	13	29	4	2	0	10	6-0	0	10	.319	.361	.407	102	0	0-0	.940	0	121	0	O-26(4-12-10)	-0.1
1957	Det A	36	42	7	9	2	0	0	0	2-0	0	11	.214	.250	.262	39	-4	0-2	1.000	0	126	0	O-14(8-1-5)	-0.4
1958	KC A	2	4	0	0	0	0	0	0	1-0	0	0	.000	.200	.000	-39	-1	0-0	1.000	-0	99	0	/O(RF)	-0.1
Total	4	108	141	22	38	6	2	0	10	10-0	0	22	.270	.318	.340	75	-6	0-2	.957	1	121	46	/O-45(15-13-17)	-0.6
SMALLEY, ROY Roy Frederick III B 10.25.1952 Los Angeles, CA BB/TR 6-1/185# d4.30 f-Roy																								
1975	Tex A	78	250	22	57	8	0	3	33	30-1	0	42	.228	.309	.296	73	-8	4-0	.941	1	112	96	S-59,2-19/C	0.1
1976	Tex A	41	129	15	29	2	0	1	8	29-3	0	27	.225	.363	.264	85	-1	2-0	.963	-11	86	77	2-38/S-5	-0.9
	Min A	103	384	46	104	16	3	2	36	47-1	2	79	.271	.353	.344	103	3	0-4	.967	10	105	106	*S-103	2.5
	Year	144	513	61	133	18	3	3	44	76-4	2	106	.259	.356	.324	98	2	2-4	.966	-1	104	104	*S-108,2-38	1.6
1977	Min A	150	584	93	135	21	5	6	56	74-1	1	89	.231	.316	.315	75	-19	5-5	.958	20	112	**125**	*S-150	1.5
1978	Min A	158	586	80	160	31	3	19	77	85-3	1	70	.273	.362	.433	122	19	2-8	.970	18	108	**123**	*S-157	**5.2**
1979	Min A★	**162**	621	94	168	28	3	24	95	80-8	4	80	.271	.353	.441	110	10	2-3	.968	**33**	111	**130**	*S-161/1	**5.6**
1980	Min A	133	486	64	135	24	1	12	63	65-4	2	63	.278	.359	.405	103	4	3-3	.975	26	**113**	122	*S-125/1-3,D-3	4.2
1981	Min A	56	167	24	44	7	1	7	22	31-5	0	24	.263	.375	.443	128	7	0-0	.946	-13	81	56	S-37,D-15/1	-0.2
1982	Min A	4	13	2	2	1	0	0	0	3-1	0	4	.154	.313	.231	51	-1	0-0	1.000	1	124	78	/S-4	0.1
	NY A	142	486	55	125	14	2	20	67	68-7	0	100	.257	.346	.418	111	8	0-1	.977	-15	89	85	S-89,3-53/2D	0.1
	Year	146	499	57	127	15	2	20	67	71-8	0	104	.255	.345	.413	109	7	0-1	.979	-14	91	85	S-93,3-53/D-4,2	0.2
1983	NY A	130	451	70	124	24	1	18	62	58-2	2	68	.275	.357	.452	127	18	3-3	.959	-14	87	82	S-91,3-26,1-22	1.0
1984	NY A	67	209	17	50	8	1	7	26	15-2	0	35	.239	.286	.388	89	-4	2-1	.905	-2	108	120	3-35,S-13/1-5,D-5	-0.5
	Chi A	47	135	15	23	4	0	4	13	22-1	0	30	.170	.285	.289	57	-8	1-1	.947	-4	93	105	3-38/S-3,1D	-1.2
	Year	114	344	32	73	12	1	11	39	37-3	0	65	.212	.286	.349	76	-12	3-2	.923	-5	101	113	3-73,S-16/D-7,1-6	-1.7
1985	Min A	129	388	57	100	20	0	12	45	60-3	1	65	.258	.357	.402	102	3	0-2	.987	-3	82	67	D-56,S-49,3-14/1	0.1
1986	Min A	143	459	59	113	20	4	20	57	68-4	0	80	.246	.342	.438	108	6	1-3	.963	-1	73	84	*D-114,S-19/3-8	0.2
1987	†Min A	110	309	32	85	16	1	8	34	36-1	1	52	.275	.352	.411	98	0	2-0	.850	-5	52	0	D-73,3-14/S-4	-0.6
Total	13	1653	5657	745	1454	244	25	163	694	771-47	14	908	.257	.345	.395	103	37	27-34	.966	43	104	109	*S-1069,D-272,3-188/2-58,1-34,C	17.2
SMALLEY, ROY Roy Frederick Jr. B 6.9.1926 Springfield, MO BR/TR 6-3/190# d4.20 s-Roy																								
1948	Chi N	124	361	25	78	11	4	4	36	23	1	76	.216	.265	.302	55	-24	0	.941	11	**107**	**112**	*S-124	-0.7
1949	Chi N	135	477	57	117	21	10	8	35	36	4	77	.245	.304	.382	85	-12	2	.947	18	**108**	107	*S-132	1.3
1950	Chi N	**154**	557	58	128	21	9	21	85	49	4	114	.230	.297	.413	85	-15	2	.945	**20**	**111**	104	*S-154	1.4
1951	Chi N	79	238	24	55	7	4	8	31	25	0	53	.231	.304	.395	85	-6	0-0	.953	-8	94	92	S-74	-1.0
1952	Chi N	87	261	36	58	14	1	5	30	29	2	58	.222	.305	.341	78	-8	0-0	.952	-13	91	69	S-82	-1.7
1953	Chi N	82	253	20	63	9	0	6	25	28	2	57	.249	.329	.356	77	-8	0-0	.932	-8	92	81	S-77	-1.0
1954	Mil N	25	36	5	8	0	0	1	7	4	1	9	.222	.310	.306	67	-2	0-0	.950	2	99	242	/S-9,2-7,1-2	0.1
1955	Phi N	92	260	33	51	11	1	7	39	39-2	2	58	.196	.304	.327	69	-11	0-0	.974	-12	91	70	S-87/23	-1.7
1956	Phi N	65	168	14	38	9	3	0	16	23-4	1	29	.226	.323	.315	74	-6	0-0	.949	-3	99	104	S-60	-0.4
1957	Phi N	28	31	5	5	0	1	1	1	1-0	1	9	.161	.212	.323	42	-3	0-0	.941	-0	97	114	S-20	-0.3
1958	Phi N	1	2	0	0	0	0	0	0	0-0	0	1	.000	.000	.000	-99	-1	0-0	.714	-0	73	160	/S	-0.1
Total	11	872	2644	277	601	103	33	61	305	257-6	18	541	.227	.300	.360	77	-96	4-0	.947	7	101	96	S-820/2-8,1-2,3	-4.1
SMALLEY, WILL William Darwin "Deacon" B 6.27.1871 Oakland, CA D 10.11.1891 Bay City, MI BR/TR d4.19																								
1890	Cle N	**136**	502	62	107	11	1	0	42	60	5	44	.213	.303	.239	60	-23	10	.895	20	**118**	116	*3-136	-0.1
1891	Was AA	11	38	5	6	0	1	0	3	5	0	2	.158	.256	.211	35	-3	0	.762	-1	102	58	/3-9,2-2	-0.4
Total	2	147	540	67	113	11	2	0	45	65	5	46	.209	.300	.237	58	-26	10	.887	19	117	112	3-145/2-2	-0.5
SMAZA, JOE Joseph Paul B 7.7.1923 Detroit, MI D 5.30.1979 Royal Oak, MI BL/TL 5-11/175# d9.18																								
1946	Chi A	2	5	2	1	0	0	0	0	0	0	0	.200	.200	.200	12	-1	0-0	—	-0	0	0	/O(RF)	-0.1
SMILEY, BILL William B. B 1856 Baltimore, MD D 7.11.1884 Baltimore, MD d10.13																								
1874	Bal NA	2	7	0	0	0	0	0	0	0		0	.000	.000	.000	-99	-2	0-0	.786	0	75	0	/3-2	-0.1
1882	StL AA	59	240	30	51	4	2	0		6			.213	.232	.246	59	-11		.885	-8	94	81	*2-57/O-2(1-0-1)	-1.6
	Bal AA	16	61	3	9	0	0	0		0			.148	.148	.148	-0	-6		.843	1	123	96	2-16/S-2	-0.4
	Year	75	301	33	60	4	2	0		6			.199	.215	.226	48	-16		.874	-7	100	84	2-73/O-2(1-0-1),S-2	-2.0
SMITH, EDGAR Albert Edgar B 10.15.1860 North Haven, CT TR 6/200# d6.20																								
1883	Bos N	30	115	10	25	5	3	0	16	5		11	.217	.250	.313	68	-5		.905	-0	46	325	O-30(CF)/C	-0.5
SMITH, ALECK Alexander Benjamin "Broadway Aleck" B 1871 New York, NY D 7.9.1919 New York, NY TR d4.23 OF Total (35-LF 13-CF 10-RF)																								
1897	Bro N	66	237	36	71	13	1	1	39	4	2		.300	.317	.376	87	-5	12	.903	-6	*89*	*118*	C-43,O-18(14-2-2)/1-6	-0.7
1898	Bro N	52	199	25	52	6	5	0	23	3	1		.261	.276	.342	77	-7	7	.909	-8	0	135	O-26(17-5-5),C-20/3-2,2-2,1	-1.4
1899	Bro N	17	61	6	11	0	1	0	6	2	0		.180	.206	.213	15	-7	0	.917	-2	*92*	*69*	C-17	-0.7
	Bal N	41	120	17	46	6	4	0	25	4	3		.383	.417	.500	144	7	7	.951	-1	*118*	*71*	C-36/O-2(RF),1	0.8
	Year	58	181	23	57	6	5	0	31	6	3		.315	.347	.403	101	-1	7	.939	-3	*110*	*70*	C-53/O-2(RF),1	0.1
1900	Bro N	7	25	2	6	0	0	0	3	1	0		.240	.269	.240	39	-2	2	.875	-2	74	0	/3-6,C	-0.4
1901	NY N	26	78	5	11	0	0	0	6	0	0		.141	.141	.141	-19	-12	2	.962	-2	*86*	*85*	C-24	-1.2

Year	Tm Lg	G	AB	R	H	2B	3B	HR	RBI	BB-IB	HP	SO	AVG	OBP	SLG	AOPS	ABR	SB-CS	FA	FR	Rng	Thr	G at Pos	BFW
1902	Bal A	41	145	10	34	3	0	0	21	8	0		.234	.275	.255	45	-11	5	.947	-6	*78*	*100*	C-27/1-7,O-4(LF),2-3,3	-1.4
1903	Bos A	11	33	4	10	1	0	0	4	0	0		.303	.303	.333	86	-1	0	.932	0	*131*	*96*	C-10	0.1
1904	Chi N	10	29	2	6	1	0	0	1	3	0		.207	.281	.241	62	-1	1	.778	-2	0	0	/O-6(CF),C3	-0.3
1906	NY N	16	28	0	5	0	0	0	2	1	0		.179	.207	.179	20	-3	1	1.000	1	*104*	*70*	/C-8,1-3,O(RF)	-0.2
Total	9	287	955	107	252	30	11	1	130	26	6		.264	.288	.321	69	-42	37	.933	-27	*96*	*94*	C-187/O-57L,1-18,3-10,2-5	-5.4
SMITH, AL Alphonse Eugene "Fuzzy" B 2.7.1928 Kirkwood, MO D 1.3.2002 Hammond, IN BR/TR 6/191# d7.10 OF Total (399-LF 87-CF 679-RF)																								
1953	Cle A	47	150	28	36	9	0	3	14	20	3	25	.240	.341	.360	92	-1	2-0	.920	-4	92	59	O-39(4-0-35)/3-2	-0.6
1954	†Cle A	131	481	101	135	29	6	11	50	88	7	65	.281	.398	.435	126	22	2-9	.984	-8	94	100	*O-109(98-0-17),3-21/S-4	0.5
1955	Cle A★	**154**	607	**123**	186	27	4	22	77	93-1	15	77	.306	.407	.473	132	32	11-6	.977	-13	92	57	*O-120(7-9-111),3-45/S-5,2	1.4
1956	Cle A	141	526	87	144	26	5	16	71	84-7	8	72	.274	.378	.433	112	12	6-3	.981	-7	101	69	*O-122(50-23-58),3-28/2	0.0
1957	Cle A	135	507	78	125	23	5	11	49	79-3	4	70	.247	.348	.377	100	2	12-6	.913	-9	87	91	3-84,O-58(18-41-6)	-0.9
1958	Chi A	139	480	61	121	23	5	12	58	48-2	5	77	.252	.323	.396	100	0	3-3	.970	-4	93	92	*O-138(77-2-63)/3	-1.2
1959	†Chi A	129	472	65	112	16	4	17	55	46-3	5	74	.237	.311	.396	94	-5	7-5	.980	-0	99	89	*O-128(84-3-45)/3	-1.3
1960	Chi A★	142	536	80	169	31	3	12	72	50-3	3	65	.315	.374	.451	124	19	8-3	.966	-10	91	53	*O-141(3-5-139)	0.4
1961	Chi A	147	532	88	148	29	4	28	93	56-2	5	67	.278	.348	.506	128	20	4-4	.948	-7	98	80	3-80,O-71(10-3-59)	0.8
1962	Chi A	142	511	62	149	23	8	16	82	57-7	3	60	.292	.363	.462	122	16	3-3	.935	-15	91	44	*3-105,O-39(38-0-2)	-0.2
1963	Bal A	120	368	45	100	17	1	10	39	32-1	3	74	.272	.335	.405	110	5	9-0	.971	-2	97	104	O-97(7-0-92)	0.0
1964	Cle A	61	136	15	22	1	1	4	9	8-1	1	32	.162	.214	.272	34	-13	0-1	1.000	0	104	95	O-48(1-1-46)/3	-1.6
	Bos A	29	51	10	11	4	0	2	7	13-0	1	10	.216	.385	.412	116	2	0-0	.917	-0	96	68	3-10/O-8(2-0-6)	0.1
	Year	90	187	25	33	5	1	6	16	21-1	2	42	.176	.267	.310	59	-11	0-1	.987	0	104	82	O-56(3-1-52),3-11	-1.5
Total	12	1517	5357	843	1458	258	46	164	676	674-30	63	768	.272	.358	.429	113	111	67-43	.974	-79	95	86	*O-1118R,3-378/S-9,2-2	-2.6
SMITH, TONY Anthony B 5.14.1884 Chicago, IL D 2.27.1964 Galveston, TX BR/TR 5-9/150# d8.12																								
1907	Was A	51	139	12	26	1	1	0	8	18	1		.187	.285	.209	63	-5	3	.920	-5	92	71	S-51	-0.9
1910	Bro N	106	321	31	58	10	1	1	16	69	2	53	.181	.329	.227	65	-10	9	.941	9	101	136	*S-101/3-6	0.2
1911	Bro N	13	40	3	6	1	0	0	2	8	0	7	.150	.292	.175	33	-3	1	.870	-1	114	133	S-10/2-3	-0.3
Total	3	170	500	46	90	12	2	1	26	95	3	60	.180	.314	.218	62	-18	13	.931	3	99	117	S-162/3-6,2-3	-1.0
SMITH, KLONDIKE Armstrong Frederick B 1.4.1887 London, England D 11.15.1959 Springfield, MA BL/TL 5-9/160# d9.28																								
1912	NY A	7	27	0	5	1	0	0	0	0	0		.185	.185	.222	15	-3	1	1.000	-1	93	0	/O-7(0-5-2)	-0.4
SMITH, BILLY Billy Edward B 7.14.1953 Jonesboro, LA BB/TR 6-2.5/185# d4.13																								
1975	Cal A	59	143	10	29	5	1	0	14	12-0	0	27	.203	.263	.252	50	-10	1-3	.932	-12	75	73	S-50/1-6,3-2,D-4	-1.8
1976	Cal A	13	8	0	3	0	0	0	0	0-0	0	2	.375	.375	.375	128	0	0-0	.625	-2	81	90	S-10/D	-0.1
1977	Bal A	109	367	44	79	12	2	5	29	33-2	1	71	.215	.281	.300	62	-19	3-2	.991	9	102	130	*2-104/S-5,1-2,3	-0.5
1978	Bal A	85	250	29	65	12	2	5	30	27-3	1	40	.260	.333	.384	108	3	3-0	.986	-1	99	99	2-83/S-2	0.7
1979	†Bal A	68	189	18	47	9	4	6	33	15-1	2	33	.249	.309	.434	102	0	1-0	.980	-5	95	106	2-63/S-5	-0.2
1981	SF N	36	61	6	11	0	0	1	5	9-0	0	16	.180	.282	.230	48	-4	0-0	.971	1	101	118	S-21/2-5,3-3	-0.1
Total	6	370	1018	107	234	38	9	17	111	96-6	4	189	.230	.297	.335	79	-30	8-5	.987	-8	100	114	2-255/S-93,1-8,3-6,D-5	-2.0
SMITH, BOBBY GENE Bobby Gene B 5.28.1934 Hood River, OR BR/TR 5-11/185# d4.16																								
1957	StL N	93	185	24	39	7	1	3	18	13-3	0	35	.211	.260	.308	52	-13	1-1	.973	3	106	156	O-79(0-61-18)	-1.2
1958	StL N	28	88	8	25	3	0	2	5	2-0	1	18	.284	.304	.386	79	-3	1-0	1.000	1	106	118	O-27(0-25-2)	-0.3
1959	StL N	43	60	11	13	1	1	1	7	1-0	0	9	.217	.230	.317	41	-5	0-0	.971	2	112	289	O-32(11-6-15)	-0.4
1960	Phi N	98	217	24	62	5	2	4	27	10-1	0	28	.286	.317	.382	90	-4	2-3	1.000	4	115	89	O-70(65-6-0)/3	-0.4
1961	Phi N	79	174	16	44	7	0	2	18	15-2	1	32	.253	.313	.328	72	-7	0-1	.971	6	111	221	O-47(33-3-12)	-0.4
1962	NY N	8	22	1	3	0	1	0	2	3-0	0	2	.136	.240	.227	26	-2	0-1	1.000	-0	104	0	/O-6(0-3-4)	-0.3
	Chi N	13	29	3	5	0	0	1	2	2-0	0	6	.172	.219	.276	33	-3	0-1	1.000	0	77	283	/O-7(0-6-1)	-0.3
	StL N	91	130	13	30	9	0	0	12	7-0	0	14	.231	.270	.300	48	-9	1-1	1.000	2	100	162	O-80(66-13-7)	-0.9
	Year	112	181	17	38	9	1	1	16	12-0	0	22	.210	.258	.287	43	-15	1-3	1.000	2	98	155	O-93(66-22-12)	-1.5
1965	Cal A	23	57	1	13	3	0	0	5	2-0	1	10	.228	.262	.281	57	-3	0-1	1.000	0	97	130	O-15(14-0-1)	-0.4
Total	7	476	962	101	234	35	5	13	96	55-6	3	154	.243	.284	.331	64	-49	5-9	.986	18	107	156	O-363(189-123-60)/3	-4.6
SMITH, BRICK Brick Dudley B 5.2.1959 Charlotte, NC BR/TR 6-4/225# d9.13																								
1987	Sea A	5	8	1	1	0	0	0	0	2-0	0	4	.125	.300	.125	18	-1	0-0	.963	-0	117	52	/1-3,D	-0.1
1988	Sea A	4	10	1	1	0	0	0	1	0-0	0	1	.100	.100	.100	-42	-2	0-0	1.000	1	172	110	/1-4	-0.1
Total	2	9	18	2	2	0	0	0	1	2-0	0	5	.111	.200	.111	-12	-3	0-0	.983	1	148	85	/1-7,D	-0.2
SMITH, BERNIE Calvin Bernard B 9.4.1941 Ponchatoula, LA BR/TR 5-9/164# d7.31																								
1970	Mil A	44	76	8	21	3	1	1	6	11-1	2	12	.276	.382	.382	110	2	1-3	.979	0	119	0	O-39(2-11-27)	0.0
1971	Mil A	15	36	1	5	1	0	1	3	0-0	1	5	.139	.162	.250	15	-4	0-0	.923	-1	68	178	O-12(3-1-9)	-0.6
Total	2	59	112	9	26	4	1	2	9	11-1	3	17	.232	.317	.339	83	-2	1-3	.967	-1	104	54	/O-51(5-12-36)	-0.6
SMITH, REGGIE Carl Reginald B 4.2.1945 Shreveport, LA BB/TR 6/195# d9.18 Mil 1963 C5 OF Total (3-LF 808-CF 874-RF)																								
1966	Bos A	6	26	1	4	1	0	0	0	0-0	0	5	.154	.154	.192	-1	-3	0-0	.944	-1	100	0	/O-6(CF)	-0.5
1967	†Bos A	158	565	78	139	24	6	15	61	57-11	1	95	.246	.315	.389	99	0	16-6	.983	3	103	117	*O-144(CF)/2-6	0.1
1968	Bos A	155	558	78	148	**37**	5	15	69	64-13	4	77	.265	.342	.430	125	19	22-18	.985	2	107	77	*O-155(CF)	1.7
1969	Bos A★	143	543	87	168	29	7	25	93	54-7	1	67	.309	.368	.527	142	29	7-13	.959	-4	100	91	*O-139(3-136-0)	1.9
1970	Bos A	147	580	109	176	32	7	22	74	51-1	4	60	.303	.361	.497	126	20	10-7	.977	7	108	**167**	*O-145(CF)	2.4
1971	Bos A	159	618	85	175	**33**	2	30	96	63-4	5	82	.283	.352	.489	128	22	11-3	.966	7	108	144	*O-159(0-87-74)	2.6
1972	Bos A★	131	467	75	126	25	4	21	74	68-12	4	63	.270	.365	.475	142	26	15-4	.981	0	103	89	*O-129(0-4-125)	2.4
1973	Bos A	115	423	79	128	23	2	21	69	68-7	1	49	.303	.398	.515	148	29	3-2	.983	4	110	112	*O-104(CF)/1D	3.0
1974	StL N★	143	517	79	160	26	9	23	100	71-10	1	70	.309	.389	.528	158	40	4-3	.976	2	107	95	*O-132(RF)/1	3.5
1975	StL N★	135	477	67	144	26	3	19	76	63-9	3	59	.302	.382	.488	137	25	9-7	.963	-5	103	69	O-69(0-1-68),1-66/3	1.2
1976	StL N	47	170	20	37	7	1	8	23	14-2	1	28	.218	.281	.412	94	-2	1-2	.986	7	104	127	1-17,O-16(0-3-13),3-13	0.2
	LA N	65	225	35	63	8	4	10	26	18-4	1	42	.280	.335	.484	133	8	2-0	.985	1	112	62	O-58(0-1-57)/3	0.7
	Year	112	395	55	100	15	5	18	49	32-6	2	70	.253	.312	.453	116	6	3-2	.989	8	113	131	O-74(0-4-70),1-17,3-14	0.9
1977	†LA N★	148	488	104	150	27	4	32	87	104-11	3	76	.307	**.427**	.576	**168**	52	7-5	.980	-7	93	69	*O-140(0-9-138)	3.9
1978	†LA N★	128	447	82	132	27	2	29	93	70-8	1	90	.295	.382	.559	**164**	39	12-5	.950	-5	95	82	*O-126(0-1-126)	3.0
1979	LA N	68	234	41	64	13	1	10	32	31-3	2	50	.274	.359	.466	126	9	6-5	.988	8	137	104	O-62(0-5-59)	1.4
1980	LA N★	92	311	47	100	13	0	15	55	41-1	1	63	.322	.392	.508	155	24	5-6	.994	6	98	216	O-84(0-7-82)	2.7
1981	†LA N	41	35	5	7	1	0	1	8	7-3	0	8	.200	.318	.314	88	0	0-0	1.000	0	104	92	/1-2	0.0
1982	SF N	106	349	51	99	11	0	18	56	46-9	0	46	.284	.364	.470	133	16	7-0	.982	5	128	92	1-99	1.7
Total	17	1987	7033	1123	2020	363	57	314	1092	890-115	33	1030	.287	.366	.489	136	353	137-86	.976	31	105	110	*O-1668R,1-186/3-15,D-8,2-6	31.9
SMITH, CHARLIE Charles J. B 12.11.1840 Brooklyn, NY D 11.15.1897 Great Neck, NY 5-10.5/150# d5.18																								
1871	Mut NA	14	72	15	19	2	1	0	5	1		1	.264	.274	.319	77	-1	6-0	.688	-1	96	73	3-12/2-3	-0.1
SMITH, POP Charles Marvin B 10.12.1856 Digby, NS, CAN D 4.18.1927 Boston, MA BR/TR 5-11/170# d5.1 U1 OF Total (2-LF 6-CF 6-RF)																								
1880	Cin N	**83**	334	35	69	10	9	0	27	6		36	.207	.221	.290	72	-10		.855	-9	92	85	*2-83	-1.4
1881	Cle N	10	34	1	4	0	0	0	3	0		8	.118	.118	.118	-27	-5		.838	-3	73	0	3-10	-0.7
	Buf N	3	11	3	0	0	0	0	1	3		5	.000	.214	.000	-27	-1		.840	-1	64	215	/2-3	-0.2
	Wor N	11	41	1	3	0	0	0	2	3		5	.073	.136	.073	-31	-6		.955	2	176	265	/O-8(1-4-3),2-3	-0.4
	Year	24	86	5	7	0	0	0	6	6		18	.081	.141	.081	-28	-12		.838	-2	73	0	3-10/O-8(1-4-3),2-6	-1.3
1882	Phi AA	20	65	10	6	0	0	0	2	12			.092	.234	.092	13	-6		.732	-0	93	0	3-11/S-4,O-3(0-2-1),2-2	-0.5
	Lou AA	3	11	1	2	0	0	0		0			.182	.182	.182	24	-1		.778	-1	91	0	/S-3	-0.1
	Year	23	76	11	8	0	0	0	2	12			.105	.227	.105	15	-6		.732	-1	93	0	3-11/S-7,O-3(0-2-1),2-2	-0.6
1883	Col AA	**97**	405	82	106	14	**17**	4		22			.262	.300	.410	137	17		.889	19	**117**	119	*2-73,3-24/P-3	3.4
1884	Col AA	108	445	78	106	18	10	6		20	12		.238	.289	.364	122	12		.905	30	**115**	135	*2-108	4.1
1885	Pit AA	106	453	85	113	11	13	0	35	25	3		.249	.293	.331	98	-1		.922	29	**114**	**123**	*2-106	2.8
1886	Pit AA	126	483	75	105	20	9	2	57	42	6		.217	.288	.308	87	-7	38	**.895**	18	112	108	*S-98,2-28/C	1.3
1887	Pit N	122	456	69	98	12	7	2	54	30	**13**	48	.215	.283	.285	63	-22	30	.914	-12	100	85	*2-89,S-33	-2.5
1888	Pit N	131	481	61	99	15	2	4	52	22	5	78	.206	.248	.270	71	-14	37	.901	1	110	85	S-75,2-56	-0.9
1889	Pit N	72	258	26	54	10	2	5	27	24	6	38	.209	.292	.322	79	-7	12	.897	-1	103	107	S-58/2-9,3-3,O-3(1-0-2)	-0.5
	Bos N	59	208	21	54	13	4	0	32	23	4	30	.260	.345	.361	92	-2	11	.890	-6	86	112	S-59	-0.6

Year	Tm Lg	G	AB	R	H	2B	3B	HR	RBI	BB-IB	HP	SO	AVG	OBP	SLG	AOPS	ABR	SB-CS	FA	FR	Rng	Thr	G at Pos	BFW
	Year	131	466	47	108	23	6	5	59	47	10	68	.232	.315	.339	85	-9	23	.894	-7	94	110	*S-117/2-9,3-3,O-3(1-0-2)	-1.1
1890	Bos N	**134**	463	82	106	16	12	1	53	80	9	81	.229	.353	.322	90	-5	39	.918	-21	97	88	*2-134/S	-1.8
1891	Was AA	27	90	13	16	2	2	0	13	13	2	16	.178	.295	.244	57	-5	2	.919	4	103	112	2-19/S-5,3-4	0.0
Total	12	1112	4238	643	941	141	87	24	358	325	60	345	.222	.287	.313	86	-63	169	.903	50	105	106	2-713,S-336/3-52,O-14C,P-3,C	2.0
SMITH, CHARLEY Charles William B 9.15.1937 Charleston, SC D 11.29.1994 Reno, NV BR/TR 6/177# d9.8																								
1960	LA N	18	60	2	10	1	1	0	5	1-0	0	15	.167	.172	.217	8	-8	0-0	.953	1	96	86	3-18	-0.8
1961	LA N	9	24	4	6	1	0	2	3	1-0	0	6	.250	.280	.542	103	0	0-0	1.000	-1	61	207	/3-4,S-3	0.0
	Phi N	112	411	43	102	13	4	9	47	23-3	5	76	.248	.294	.365	75	-16	3-4	.924	-1	110	102	3-94,S-14	-1.7
	Year	121	435	47	108	14	4	11	50	24-3	5	82	.248	.293	.375	77	-16	3-4	.926	-2	109	105	3-98,S-17	-1.7
1962	Chi A	65	145	11	30	4	0	2	17	9-0	1	32	.207	.256	.276	44	-12	0-1	.944	-0	104	185	3-54	-1.3
1963	Chi A	4	7	0	2	0	1	0	1	0-0	0	2	.286	.286	.571	136	0	0-0	1.000	2	168	722	/S	0.2
1964	Chi A	2	7	1	1	0	1	0	0	1-0	0	1	.143	.250	.429	87	0	0-0	1.000	2	176	481	/3-2	0.2
	NY N	127	443	44	106	12	0	20	58	19-1	3	101	.239	.275	.402	90	-8	2-2	.917	-5	107	64	3-85,S-36,O-13(LF)	-1.3
1965	NY N	135	499	49	122	20	3	16	62	17-3	4	123	.244	.273	.393	89	-10	2-1	.957	10	111	**121**	*3-131/S-6,2	0.0
1966	StL N	116	391	34	104	13	4	10	43	22-4	0	81	.266	.301	.396	93	-5	0-2	.964	-6	94	133	*3-107/S	-1.3
1967	NY A	135	425	38	95	15	3	9	38	32-6	1	110	.224	.278	.336	84	-9	0-2	.947	8	115	116	*3-115	-0.3
1968	NY A	46	70	2	16	4	1	1	7	5-2	0	18	.229	.280	.357	95	-1	0-0	.961	3	120	141	3-13	0.3
1969	Chi N	2	2	0	0	0	0	0	0	0-0	0	0	.000	.000	.000	-89	0	0-0	—	0			H	-0.1
Total	10	771	2484	228	594	83	18	69	281	130-19	14	565	.239	.279	.370	82	-69	7-12	.945	12	108	117	3-623/S-61,O-13(LF),2	-6.1
SMITH, CHRIS Christopher William B 7.18.1957 Torrance, CA BB/TR 6/185# d5.14																								
1981	Mon N	7	7	0	0	0	0	0	0	0-0	0	2	.000	.000	.000	-99	-2	0-0	1.000	0	270	0	/2	-0.2
1982	Mon N	2	2	0	0	0	0	0	0	0-0	0	1	.000	.000	.000	-98	-1	0-0	—	0			/H	-0.1
1983	SF N	22	67	13	22	6	1	1	11	7-1	2	12	.328	.403	.493	153	5	0-0	.976	-2	81	56	1-15/O-4(LF),3	0.3
Total	3	31	76	13	22	6	1	1	11	7-1	2	15	.289	.360	.434	124	2	0-0	.976	-1	81	56	/1-15,O-4(LF),32	0.0
SMITH, EARL Earl Calvin B 3.14.1928 Sunnyside, WA BR/TR 6/185# d4.14																								
1955	Pit N	5	16	1	1	0	0	0	0	4-0	1	2	.063	.286	.063	-1	-2	0-0	1.000	-0	99	0	/O-5(CF)	-0.3
SMITH, EARL Earl Leonard "Sheriff" B 1.20.1891 Oak Hill, OH D 3.14.1943 Portsmouth, OH BB/TR 5-11/170# d9.12																								
1916	Chi N	14	27	2	7	1	1	0	4	2	0	5	.259	.310	.370	98	0	1	.800	-1	52	0	/O-7(6-0-1)	-0.2
1917	StL A	52	199	31	56	7	7	0	10	15	0	21	.281	.332	.387	124	4	5	.977	3	93	155	O-51(22-29-0)	0.4
1918	StL A	89	286	28	77	10	5	0	32	13	1	16	.269	.303	.339	97	-3	13	.952	1	95	127	O-81(54-25-2)	-0.8
1919	StL A	88	252	21	63	12	5	1	36	18	0	27	.250	.300	.349	80	-7	1	.971	7	116	127	O-68(0-4-64)	-0.4
1920	StL A	103	353	45	108	21	8	3	55	13	3	18	.306	.336	.436	100	-1	11-4	.916	-4	98	18	3-70,O-15(4-2-9)	-0.4
1921	StL A	25	78	7	26	4	2	2	14	3	1	4	.333	.366	.513	115	1	0-0	.878	-3	80	0	3-13/O-4(CF)	-0.1
	Was A	59	180	20	39	5	2	2	12	10	2	19	.217	.266	.300	46	-16	1-0	.949	4	108	180	O-43(3-4-36)/3	-1.4
	Year	84	258	27	65	9	4	4	26	13	3	23	.252	.296	.364	69	-14	1-0	.944	1	107	166	O-47(3-8-36),3-14	-1.5
1922	Was A	65	205	22	53	12	2	1	23	8	2	17	.259	.293	.351	71	-10	4-4	.917	3	91	208	O-49(47-0-2)/3-2	-1.0
Total	7	495	1580	176	429	72	32	9	186	82	9	127	.272	.311	.375	90	-32	36-8	.952	8	100	150	O-318(136-68-114)/3-86	-3.9
SMITH, EARL Earl Sutton "Oil" B 2.14.1897 Hot Springs, AR D 6.8.1963 Little Rock, AR BL/TR 5-10.5/180# d4.24																								
1919	NY N	21	36	5	9	2	1	0	8	3	0	3	.250	.308	.361	102	0	1	.973	-2	*88*	*86*	C-14/2	-0.1
1920	NY N	91	262	20	77	7	1	1	30	18	2	16	.294	.344	.340	98	0	5-2	.976	1	*124*	*76*	C-82	0.8
1921	†NY N	89	229	35	77	8	4	10	51	27	1	8	.336	.409	.537	148	16	4-3	.965	-5	*114*	*92*	C-78	1.5
1922	†NY N	90	234	29	65	11	4	9	39	37	3	12	.278	.383	.474	119	7	1-1	.978	1	*133*	*72*	C-75	1.2
1923	NY N	24	34	2	7	1	1	1	4	4	0	1	.206	.289	.382	77	-1	0-0	.975	1	*164*	*100*	C-12	0.0
	Bos N	72	191	22	55	15	1	3	19	22	1	10	.288	.364	.424	112	4	0-1	.975	-2	*82*	*125*	C-54	0.5
	Year	96	225	24	62	16	2	4	23	26	1	11	.276	.353	.418	106	3	0-1	.975	-1	*93*	*122*	C-66	0.5
1924	Bos N	33	59	1	16	3	0	0	8	6	0	3	.271	.338	.322	81	-1	0-1	.946	-2	*83*	*109*	C-13	-0.2
	Pit N	39	111	12	41	10	1	4	21	13	0	4	.369	.435	.586	168	11	2-0	.974	2	*154*	*60*	C-35	1.5
	Year	72	170	13	57	13	1	4	29	19	0	7	.335	.402	.494	140	11	2-1	.967	0	*136*	*72*	C-48	1.3
1925	†Pit N	109	329	34	103	22	3	8	64	31	1	13	.313	.374	.471	107	4	4-1	.968	11	*142*	*87*	C-96	2.0
1926	Pit N	105	292	29	101	17	2	2	46	28	2	7	.346	.407	.438	121	10	1	.964	5	*119*	*84*	C-98	2.0
1927	†Pit N	66	189	16	51	3	1	5	25	21	1	11	.270	.346	.376	87	-3	0	.986	-0	*135*	*61*	C-61	0.0
1928	Pit N	32	85	8	21	6	0	2	11	11	0	7	.247	.333	.388	85	-2	0	.967	-3	*80*	*71*	C-28	-0.3
	†StL N	24	58	3	13	2	0	0	7	5	0	4	.224	.286	.259	42	-5	0	1.000	-0	*127*	*58*	C-18	-0.4
	Year	56	143	11	34	8	0	2	18	16	0	11	.238	.314	.336	68	-6	0	.980	-3	*98*	*66*	C-46	-0.7
1929	StL N	57	145	9	50	8	0	1	22	18	0	6	.345	.417	.421	107	3	0	.962	-3	*115*	*80*	C-50	0.2
1930	StL N	8	10	0	0	0	0	0	0	3	0	1	.000	.231	.000	-36	-2	0	.913	0	*128*	*200*	/C-6	-0.1
Total	12	860	2264	225	686	115	19	46	355	247	11	106	.303	.374	.432	111	41	18-9	.971	5	*123*	*83*	C-720/2	8.6
SMITH, EDGAR Edgar Eugene B 6.12.1862 Providence, RI D 11.3.1892 Providence, RI BR/TR 5-10/160# d5.25 ▲																								
1883	Pro N	2	9	2	2	1	0	0	1	0		2	.222	.222	.333	64	0		1.000	-0	0	0	/1-2,O-2(LF)	-0.1
	Phi N	1	4	1	3	0	0	0	1	0		0	.750	.750	.750	393	1		.000	-1	0	0	/PO(LF)	0.0
	Year	3	13	3	5	1	0	0	2	0		2	.385	.385	.462	158	1		1.000	-1	0	0	/O-3(LF),1-2,P	-0.1
1884	Was AA	14	57	5	5	0	1	0		1	0		.088	.103	.123	-30	-8		.794	4	350	814	O-12(RF)/P-3	-0.2
1885	Pro N	1	4	0	1	0	0	0	0	0		0	.250	.250	.250	64	0		.750	0	148	0	/P	0.0
1890	Cle N	8	24	2	7	0	1	0	4	4	0	1	.292	.393	.375	126	1	0	.900	2	202	0	/P-6,O-2(RF)	0.1
Total	4	26	98	10	18	1	2	0	6	5	0	3	.184	.223	.235	47	-6	0	.816	5	286	828	/O-17(3-0-14),P-11,1-2	-0.2
SMITH, MAYO Edward Mayo B 1.17.1915 New London, MO D 11.24.1977 Boynton Beach, FL BL/TR 6/183# d6.24 M9																								
1945	Phi A	73	203	18	43	5	0	0	11	36	1	13	.212	.333	.236	67	-7	0-1	.976	-3	91	80	O-65(33-27-7)	-1.4
SMITH, ELMER Elmer Ellsworth B 3.23.1868 Pittsburgh, PA D 11.3.1945 Pittsburgh, PA BL/TL 5-11/178# d9.10 ▲																								
1886	Cin AA	9	28	6	8	1	1	0	2	9	0		.286	.459	.393	163	3	0	.600	-2	24	0	P-9/O(LF)	-0.1
1887	Cin AA	52	186	26	47	10	6	0	23	11	1		.253	.298	.371	84	-5	5	.851	-6	74	105	P-52/O-2(CF)	-0.2
1888	Cin AA	40	129	15	29	4	1	0	9	20	0		.225	.329	.271	88	-1	2	.838	-6	76	0	P-40/O-2(CF)	-0.3
1889	Cin AA	29	83	12	23	3	1	2	17	7	2	18	.277	.348	.410	112	5	1	.821	-4	52	0	P-29	0.0
1892	Pit N	138	511	86	140	16	14	4	63	82	1	43	.274	.375	.384	129	20	22	.885	-8	72	0	*O-124(115-2-7),P-17	0.0
1893	Pit N	128	518	121	179	26	23	7	103	77	5	23	.346	.435	.525	158	44	26	.921	4	92	160	*O-128(LF)	2.9
1894	Pit N	126	490	128	175	33	19	6	74	68	5	12	.357	.440	.539	136	31	34	.933	2	83	154	*O-126(121-5-0)/P	1.7
1895	Pit N	125	484	89	146	15	12	1	81	55	6	25	.302	.380	.388	104	5	34	.897	-3	85	48	*O-124(LF)	-0.7
1896	Pit N	122	484	121	175	21	14	6	94	74	8	18	.362	.454	.500	158	46	33	.946	5	79	135	*O-122(LF)	3.3
1897	Pit N	123	467	99	145	19	17	6	54	70	7		.310	.408	.463	135	26	25	.904	3	110	30	*O-123(LF)	1.6
1898	Cin N	123	486	79	166	21	10	1	66	69	2		.342	.425	.432	136	26	20	.949	2	84	120	*O-123(LF)/P	1.6
1899	Cin N	88	343	65	101	13	6	1	24	47	1		.294	.381	.376	106	4	10	.923	-2	88	85	O-88(38-28-22)	-0.3
1900	Cin N	29	111	14	31	4	4	1	18	18	2		.279	.389	.414	125	4	5	.930	-1	74	95	O-27(LF)	0.1
	NY N	85	312	47	81	9	7	2	34	24	2		.260	.317	.353	89	-6	14	.953	-6	95	63	O-83(RF)	-1.4
	Year	114	423	61	112	13	11	3	52	42	4		.265	.337	.369	99	-1	19	.944	-7	89	72	*O-110(27-0-83)	-1.3
1901	Pit N	4	4	0	0	0	0	0	0	2	0		.000	.333	.000	1	0	0	1.000	0	0	0	/O(LF)	0.0
	Bos N	16	57	5	10	2	1	0	3	6	0		.175	.254	.246	41	-4	2	.833	-2	55	0	O-15(4-0-11)	-0.7
	Year	20	61	5	10	2	1	0	3	8	0		.164	.261	.230	40	-5	2	.846	-2	52	0	O-16(5-0-11)	-0.7
Total	14	1237	4693	913	1456	197	136	37	665	639	42	139	.310	.398	.434	126	198	233	.922	-24	86	89	*O-1089(927-39-123),P-149	7.5
SMITH, ELMER Elmer John B 9.21.1892 Sandusky, OH D 8.3.1984 Columbia, KY BL/TR 5-10/165# d9.20 Mil 1918																								
1914	Cle A	13	53	5	17	3	0	0	8	2	0	11	.321	.345	.377	113	1	1-1	1.000	1	103	122	O-13(CF)	0.0
1915	Cle A	144	476	37	118	23	12	3	67	36	0	75	.248	.301	.366	97	-4	10-11	.923	-0	105	101	*O-123(21-0-102)	-1.3
1916	Cle A	79	213	25	59	15	3	3	40	18	1	35	.277	.336	.418	119	5	3	.966	-0	94	111	O-57(1-0-56)	0.2
	Was A	45	168	12	36	10	3	2	27	18	2	28	.214	.298	.345	94	-2	4	.988	2	111	101	O-45(10-0-35)	-0.2
	Year	124	381	37	95	25	6	5	67	36	3	63	.249	.319	.386	108	3	7	.976	2	102	107	*O-102(11-0-91)	0.0
1917	Was A	35	117	8	26	4	3	0	17	5	1	14	.222	.260	.308	74	-4	1	.901	-0	107	103	O-29(27-0-2)	-0.7
	Cle A	64	161	21	42	5	1	3	22	13	0	18	.261	.316	.360	99	-1	6	.986	0	100	99	O-40(8-0-32)	-0.2
	Year	99	278	29	68	9	4	3	39	18	1	32	.245	.293	.338	89	-5	7	.943	0	103	101	O-69(35-0-34)	-0.9
1919	Cle A	114	395	60	110	24	6	9	54	41	5	30	.278	.354	.438	115	8	15	.957	-4	90	83	*O-111(RF)	-0.2

Year	Tm Lg	G	AB	R	H	2B	3B	HR	RBI	BB-IB	HP	SO	AVG	OBP	SLG	AOPS	ABR	SB-CS	FA	FR	Rng	Thr	G at Pos	BFW
1920	†Cle A	129	456	82	144	37	10	12	103	53	3	35	.316	.391	.520	135	23	5-4	.970	-6	101	48	*O-129(RF)	1.0
1921	Cle A	129	431	98	125	28	9	16	85	56	2	46	.290	.374	.508	121	13	0-2	.971	-3	90	104	*O-127(1-0-126)	0.0
1922	Bos A	73	231	43	66	13	6	6	32	25	1	21	.286	.358	.472	116	5	0-3	.947	3	112	109	O-58(0-1-57)	0.2
	†NY A	21	27	1	5	0	0	1	5	3	0	5	.185	.267	.296	46	-2	0-0	.933	1	116	145	O-11(2-0-9)	-0.2
	Year	94	258	44	71	13	6	7	37	28	1	26	.275	.348	.453	108	2	0-3	.945	3	112	112	O-69(2-1-66)	0.0
1923	NY A	70	183	30	56	6	2	7	35	21	0	21	.306	.377	.475	121	5	3-1	.948	1	107	91	O-47(RF)	0.3
1925	Cin N	96	284	47	77	13	7	8	46	28	1	20	.271	.339	.451	102	0	6-5	.967	-1	94	105	O-80(53-2-26)	-0.6
Total	10	1012	3195	469	881	181	62	70	541	319	16	359	.276	.344	.437	112	47	54-27	.957	-9	100	93	O-870(123-16-732)	-1.7
SMITH, MIKE Elwood Hope B 11.16.1904 Norfolk, VA D 5.31.1981 Chesapeake, VA BL/TR 5-11.5/170# d9.4																								
1926	NY N	4	7	0	1	0	0	0	0	0	0	2	.143	.143	.143	-23	-1	0	1.000	0	129	0	/O(LF)	-0.1
SMITH, CARR Emanuel Carr B 4.8.1901 Kernersville, NC D 4.14.1989 Miami, FL BR/TR 6-1/175# d9.23																								
1923	Was A	5	9	0	1	1	0	0	1	0	0	0	.111	.111	.222	-14	-2	0-0	1.000	-0	86	0	/O-4(CF)	-0.2
1924	Was A	5	10	1	2	0	0	0	0	0	0	3	.200	.200	.200	3	-1	0-0	1.000	-0	97	0	/O-4(RF)	-0.2
Total	2	10	19	1	3	1	0	0	1	0	0	3	.158	.158	.211	-5	-3	0-0	1.000	-1	91	0	/O-8(0-4-4)	-0.4
SMITH, ERNIE Ernest Henry "Kansas City Kid" B 10.11.1899 Totowa, NJ D 4.6.1973 Brooklyn, NY BR/TR 5-8/155# d4.17																								
1930	Chi A	24	79	5	19	3	0	0	3	5	0	6	.241	.286	.278	45	-7	2-0	.920	-2	95	64	S-21	-0.6
SMITH, FRANK Frank L. B 11.24.1857 , , CAN D 10.11.1928 Canandaigua, NY d8.6																								
1884	Pit AA	10	36	3	9	0	1	0		0	0		.250	.250	.306	81	-1		.930	-1			/C-7,O-3(1-1-1)	-0.2
SMITH, FRED Fred Vincent B 7.29.1886 Cleveland, OH D 5.28.1961 Cleveland, OH BR/TR 5-11.5/185# d4.17 b-Charlie																								
1913	Bos N	92	285	35	65	9	3	0	27	29	1	55	.228	.302	.281	65	-12	7-11	.920	-10	82	55	3-59,2-14,S-11/O-4(2-1-1)	-2.3
1914	Buf F	145	473	48	104	12	10	2	45	49	3	78	.220	.297	.300	62	-34	24	.930	-3	95	75	*3-127,S-19/1	-3.4
1915	Buf F	35	114	8	27	2	4	0	11	13	1	15	.237	.320	.325	80	-5	2	.920	3	101	111	S-32/3	0.0
	Bro F	110	385	41	95	16	6	5	58	25	3	49	.247	.298	.358	85	-15	21	.920	-2	101	63	S-94,3-15	-1.1
	Year	145	499	49	122	18	10	5	69	38	4	64	.244	.303	.351	84	-20	23	.920	1	101	75	*S-126,3-16	-1.1
1917	StL N	56	165	11	30	0	2	1	17	17	1	22	.182	.262	.224	51	-9	4	.950	6	112	63	3-51/2-2,S	-0.3
Total	4	438	1422	143	321	39	25	8	158	133	9	219	.226	.296	.305	69	-75	58-11	.932	-7	98	76	3-253,S-157/2-16,O-4(2-1-1),1	-7.1
SMITH, GEORGE George Cornelius B 7.7.1937 St.Petersburg, FL D 6.15.1987 St.Petersburg, FL BR/TR 5-10/170# d8.4																								
1963	Det A	52	171	16	37	8	2	0	17	18-1	2	34	.216	.298	.287	63	-8	4-0	.982	7	112	89	2-52	0.4
1964	Det A	5	7	1	2	0	0	0	2	1-0	0	4	.286	.375	.286	86	0	1-0	1.000	0	123	209	/2-3	0.1
1965	Det A	32	53	6	5	0	0	1	1	3-0	0	18	.094	.143	.151	-16	-8	0-0	.984	1	96	134	2-22/S-3,3-3	-0.7
1966	Bos A	128	403	41	86	19	4	8	37	37-6	3	86	.213	.283	.340	71	-15	4-0	.969	5	100	111	*2-109,S-19	0.1
Total	4	217	634	64	130	27	6	9	57	59-7	5	142	.205	.277	.309	62	-31	9-0	.974	12	104	107	2-186/S-22,3-3	-0.1
SMITH, HEINIE George Henry B 10.24.1871 Pittsburgh, PA D 6.25.1939 Buffalo, NY BR/TR 5-9.5/160# d9.8 M1 ▲																								
1897	Lou N	21	76	7	20	3	0	1	7	3	1		.263	.300	.342	72	-3	1	.928	-2	93	111	2-21	-0.4
1898	Lou N	35	121	14	23	4	0	0	13	6	3		.190	.246	.223	35	-10	6	.910	-7	92	64	2-33	-1.5
1899	Pit N	15	53	9	15	3	1	0	12	5	0		.283	.345	.377	98	0	2	.851	-5	96	51	2-15/S	-0.4
1901	NY N	9	29	5	6	2	1	1	4	1	0		.207	.233	.448	99	0	1	.969	-1	93	0	/2-7,P-2	-0.1
1902	NY N	140	517	48	129	19	2	0	34	17	3		.250	.277	.294	77	-15	32	.954	5	98	113	*2-140,M	-0.9
1903	Det A	93	336	36	75	11	3	1	22	19	3		.223	.271	.283	68	-13	12	.928	-1	98	89	2-93	-1.3
Total	6	313	1132	119	268	42	7	3	92	51	10		.237	.276	.294	71	-41	54	.935	-11	97	95	2-309/P-2,S	-4.6
SMITH, GERMANY George J. B 4.21.1863 Pittsburgh, PA D 12.1.1927 Altoona, PA BR/TR 6/175# d4.17																								
1884	Alt U	**25**	108	9	34	8	1	0		1			.315	.321	.407	118	-1		.871	5	122	20	S-25/P	0.5
	Cle N	72	291	31	74	14	4	4	26	2		45	.254	.259	.371	93	-3		.879	6	96	123	2-42,S-30	0.5
1885	Bro AA	108	419	63	108	17	11	4	62	10	0		.258	.275	.379	105	0		.884	**40**	**127**	77	*S-108	3.9
1886	Bro AA	105	426	66	105	17	6	2	45	19	0		.246	.279	.329	89	-7	22	.860	12	112	94	*S-105/O(LF)C	0.8
1887	Bro AA	103	435	79	128	19	16	4	72	13	1		.294	.316	.439	108	1	26	**.886**	**30**	**123**	84	*S-101/3-2	2.7
1888	Bro AA	103	402	47	86	10	7	3	61	22	0		.214	.255	.296	76	-12	27	.844	1	103	130	*S-103/2	-0.7
1889	†Bro AA	121	446	89	103	22	3	3	53	40	1	42	.231	.296	.314	73	-16	35	.899	-6	99	92	*S-120/O(RF)	-1.6
1890	†Bro N	**129**	481	76	92	6	5	1	47	42	3	23	.191	.260	.231	43	-36	24	.904	1	106	114	*S-129	-2.7
1891	Cin N	**138**	512	50	103	11	5	3	53	38	1	32	.201	.258	.260	50	-34	16	.909	12	110	85	*S-138	-1.6
1892	Cin N	139	506	58	123	13	6	8	63	42	0	52	.243	.301	.340	95	-5	19	.920	23	**119**	113	*S-139	2.4
1893	Cin N	130	500	63	118	18	6	4	56	38	2	20	.236	.293	.320	61	-30	14	**.934**	16	110	124	*S-130	-0.6
1894	Cin N	129	492	73	130	34	6	3	79	41	2	28	.264	.323	.376	66	-29	15	.910	19	**116**	**130**	*S-129	-0.3
1895	Cin N	127	503	75	151	23	6	4	74	34	0	24	.300	.345	.394	87	-12	13	.923	1	104	110	*S-127	-0.3
1896	Cin N	120	456	65	131	21	9	3	71	28	1	22	.287	.330	.393	84	-13	22	.926	-10	100	102	*S-120	-1.4
1897	Bro N	112	428	47	86	17	3	0	29	14	4		.201	.233	.255	30	-44	1	.908	-11	106	84	*S-112	-4.3
1898	StL N	51	157	16	25	2	1	1	9	24	1		.159	.275	.204	37	-12	1	.904	-6	105	67	S-51	-1.5
Total	15	1712	6562	907	1597	252	95	47	800	408	16	288	.243	.289	.332	74	-253	235	.902	135	111	100	*S-1667/2-43,3-2,O-2(1-0-1),CP	-4.2
SMITH, JUD Grant Judson B 1.13.1869 Green Oak, MI D 12.7.1947 Los Angeles, CA BR/TR 6/185# d5.21																								
1893	Cin N	17	43	7	10	1	0	1	5	9	0	5	.233	.365	.326	82	-1	1	.750	-1	82	0	/O-9(1-0-8),3-6,S	-0.2
	StL N	4	13	1	1	0	0	0	0	1	1	2	.077	.200	.077	-25	-2	0	.889	1	100	296	/3-4	-0.2
	Year	21	56	8	11	1	0	1	5	10	1	7	.196	.328	.268	58	-3	1	.844	-1	117	381	3-10/O-9(1-0-8),S	-0.4
1896	Pit N	10	35	6	12	2	1	0	4	2	1	2	.343	.395	.457	129	2	3	.909	0	88	178	3-10	0.1
1898	Was N	66	234	33	71	7	5	3	28	22	6		.303	.378	.415	127	8	11	.903	-6	79	85	3-47,S-10/1-7,2	0.3
1901	Pit N	6	21	1	3	1	0	0	0	3	0		.143	.250	.190	28	-2	0	.947	0	106	0	/3-6	-0.1
Total	4	103	346	48	97	11	6	4	37	37	8	9	.280	.363	.382	109	5	15	.900	-7	87	126	/3-73,S-11,O-9(1-0-8),1-7,2	-0.1
SMITH, GREG Gregory Alan B 4.5.1967 Baltimore, MD BB/TR 5-11/170# d9.2																								
1989	Chi N	4	5	1	2	0	0	0	2	0-0	1	0	.400	.500	.400	149	0	0-0	.778	-1	68	118	/2-2	0.0
1990	Chi N	18	44	4	9	2	1	0	5	2-0	0	5	.205	.234	.295	43	-4	1-0	1.000	3	118	105	/2-7,S-7	0.0
1991	LA N	5	3	1	0	0	0	0	0	0-0	0	2	.000	.000	.000	-99	-1	0-0	—	-0	0	0	/2	-0.1
Total	3	27	52	6	11	2	1	0	7	2-0	1	7	.212	.250	.288	47	-5	1-0	.944	2	105	106	/2-10,S-7	-0.1
SMITH, HAL Harold Raymond "Cura" B 6.1.1931 Barling, AR BR/TR 5-11/189# d5.2 C8																								
1956	StL N	75	227	27	64	12	0	5	23	15-4	0	22	.282	.326	.401	94	-2	1-0	.982	-2	90	98	C-66	-0.1
1957	StL N☆	100	333	25	93	12	3	2	37	18-2	0	18	.279	.314	.351	78	-11	2-2	.990	0	107	97	C-97	-0.6
1958	StL N	77	220	13	50	4	1	1	24	14-4	0	14	.227	.272	.268	42	-18	0-0	.989	-3	67	75	C-71	-1.9
1959	StL N★	142	452	35	122	15	3	13	50	15-6	1	28	.270	.295	.403	78	-15	2-6	.989	5	101	**126**	*C-141	-0.5
1960	StL N	127	337	20	77	16	0	2	28	29-13	1	33	.228	.291	.294	56	-20	1-0	.990	17	130	98	*C-124	0.3
1961	StL N	45	125	6	31	4	1	0	10	11-4	1	12	.248	.309	.296	57	-7	0-0	.993	12	99	142	C-45	0.6
1965	Pit N	4	3	0	0	0	0	0	0	0-0	0	1	.000	.000	.000	-99	-1	0-0	1.000	1	0	0	/C-4	0.0
Total	7	570	1697	126	437	63	8	23	172	102-33	3	128	.258	.300	.345	69	-74	6-8	.989	30	102	106	C-548	-2.2
SMITH, HAL Harold Wayne B 12.7.1930 W.Frankfort, IL BR/TR 6/195# d4.11																								
1955	Bal A	135	424	41	115	23	4	4	52	30-2	2	21	.271	.318	.373	93	-6	1-3	.986	-4	77	**141**	*C-125	-0.5
1956	Bal A	77	229	16	60	14	0	3	18	17-3	1	22	.262	.315	.362	85	-5	1-0	.994	3	74	108	C-71	0.1
	KC A	37	142	15	39	9	2	2	24	3-0	0	12	.275	.284	.408	82	-4	1-1	.986	1	86	121	C-37	-0.2
	Year	114	371	31	99	23	2	5	42	20-3	1	34	.267	.303	.380	85	-10	2-1	.991	4	79	113	*C-108	-0.1
1957	KC A	107	360	41	109	26	0	13	41	14-0	1	44	.303	.328	.483	118	8	2-2	.983	-1	89	74	*C-103	1.2
1958	KC A	99	315	32	86	19	2	5	46	25-2	2	47	.273	.323	.394	97	-1	0-0	.949	-2	97	99	3-43,C-31,1-14	-0.3
1959	KC A	108	292	36	84	12	0	5	31	34-0	3	39	.288	.367	.380	104	3	0-3	.953	2	95	87	3-77,C-22	0.5
1960	†Pit N	77	258	37	76	18	2	11	45	22-0	2	48	.295	.351	.508	132	11	1-1	.985	-3	147	81	C-71	1.2
1961	Pit N	67	193	12	43	10	0	3	26	11-1	1	38	.223	.267	.321	55	-12	0-0	.990	-1	142	63	C-65	-1.1
1962	Hou N	109	345	32	81	14	0	12	35	24-1	2	55	.235	.286	.380	84	-9	0-0	.986	-3	69	103	C-92/3-6,1-2	-0.7
1963	Hou N	31	58	1	14	2	0	0	2	4-1	0	15	.241	.290	.276	68	-2	0-0	.985	-2	90	31	C-11	-0.4
1964	Cin N	32	66	6	8	1	0	0	3	12-2	0	20	.121	.256	.136	14	-7	1-0	.983	-2	83	73	C-20	-0.8
Total	10	879	2682	269	715	148	10	58	323	196-12	14	361	.267	.317	.394	94	-24	7-10	.986	-11	96	98	C-648,3-126/1-16	-1.0

Year	Tm Lg	G	AB	R	H	2B	3B	HR	RBI	BB-IB	HP	SO	AVG	OBP	SLG	AOPS	ABR	SB-CS	FA	FR	Rng	Thr	G at Pos	BFW
SMITH, HARRY Harry Thomas B 10.31.1874 Yorkshire, England D 2.17.1933 Salem, NJ BR/TR 5-8.5/165# d7.11 M1																								
1901	Phi A	11	34	3	11	1	0	0	3	2	1		.324	.378	.353	99	0	1	.969	-2	*83*	*110*	/C-9,O(RF)	-0.1
1902	Pit N	50	185	14	35	4	1	0	12	4	1		.189	.211	.222	32	-15	4	.972	2	*146*	*77*	C-50	-0.9
1903	†Pit N	61	212	15	37	3	2	0	19	12	1		.175	.222	.208	22	-22	2	.974	1	*136*	*90*	C-60/O(RF)	-1.5
1904	Pit N	47	141	17	35	3	1	0	18	16	5		.248	.346	.284	92	0	5	.964	-1	*104*	*111*	C-44/O-3(2-0-1)	0.3
1905	Pit N	1	3	0	0	0	0	0	1	0	0		.000	.000	.000	-98	-1	1	1.000	0	*117*	*105*	/C	-0.1
1906	Pit N	1	1	0	0	0	0	0	0	0	0		.000	.000	.000	-96	0	0	.800	0	*0*	*0*	/C	0.0
1907	Pit N	18	38	4	10	1	0	0	1	4	2		.263	.364	.289	103	1	0	.939	-1	*124*	*106*	C-18	0.1
1908	Bos N	41	130	13	32	2	2	1	16	7	2		.246	.295	.315	96	-1	2	.975	-2	*89*	*112*	C-38	0.1
1909	Bos N	43	113	9	19	4	1	0	4	5	0		.168	.203	.221	30	-10	3	.972	1	*87*	*98*	C-31,M	-0.6
1910	Bos N	70	147	8	35	4	0	1	15	5	0	14	.238	.263	.286	57	-8	5	.949	-2	*87*	*127*	C-38	-0.8
Total	10	343	1004	83	214	22	7	2	89	55	12	14	.213	.262	.255	54	-56	23	.967	-4	*113*	*100*	C-290/O-5(2-0-3)	-3.5
SMITH, HARRY Harry W. B 2.5.1856 N.Vernon, IN D 6.4.1898 Queensville, IN BR/TR 6/175# d5.8																								
1877	Chi N	24	94	7	19	1	0	0	3	4		6	.202	.235	.213	37	-7		.853	-7	80	45	2-14,O-10(0-7-3)	-1.2
	Cin N	10	36	4	9	2	1	0	3	1		5	.250	.270	.361	109	1		.879	-1			/C-8,2-3,O-3(CF)	0.0
	Year	34	130	11	28	3	1	0	6	5		11	.215	.244	.254	54	-7		.837	-8	78	40	2-17,O-13(0-10-3)/C-8	-1.2
1889	Lou AA	1	2	0	1	0	0	0	1	0	0	1	.500	.500	.500	189	0	0	—	-1	0	0	/O(CF)C	-0.1
Total	2	35	132	11	29	3	1	0	7	5	0	12	.220	.248	.258	56	-6	0	.837	-9			/2-17,O-14(0-11-3),C-9	-1.3
SMITH, HARVEY Harvey Fetterhoff B 7.24.1871 Union Deposit, PA D 11.12.1962 Harrisburg, PA BL/TR 5-8/160# d8.19																								
1896	Was N	36	131	21	36	7	2	0	17	12	2	7	.275	.345	.359	86	-3	9	.861	1	117	85	3-36	-0.1
SMITH, HAPPY Henry Joseph B 7.14.1883 Coquille, OR D 2.26.1961 San Jose, CA BL/TR 6/185# d4.15																								
1910	Bro N	35	76	6	18	2	0	0	5	4	0	14	.237	.275	.263	59	-4	4	.974	2	106	172	O-16(0-5-11)	-0.3
SMITH, JACK Jack B 6.23.1895 Chicago, IL D 5.2.1972 Westchester, IL BL/TL 5-8/165# d9.30 Mil 1918																								
1915	StL N	4	16	2	3	0	1	0	0	1	0	5	.188	.235	.313	65	-1	0	1.000	-1	70	0	/O-4(3-1-0)	-0.2
1916	StL N	130	357	43	87	6	5	6	34	20	4	50	.244	.291	.339	94	-4	24-16	.949	-4	92	98	*O-120(1-109-11)	-1.8
1917	StL N	137	462	64	137	16	11	3	34	38	1	65	.297	.351	.398	133	18	25	.961	-11	86	72	*O-128(27-65-37)	-0.1
1918	StL N	42	166	24	35	2	1	0	4	7	4	21	.211	.260	.235	53	-9	5	.941	0	85	167	O-42(CF)	-1.4
1919	StL N	119	408	47	91	16	3	0	15	26	1	29	.223	.271	.277	69	-15	30	.960	2	95	132	*O-111(1-36-76)	-2.2
1920	StL N	91	313	53	104	22	5	1	28	25	2	23	.332	.385	.444	143	18	14-9	.963	-2	89	128	O-83(18-57-14)	1.3
1921	StL N	116	411	86	135	22	9	7	33	21	0	24	.328	.361	.477	122	12	11-6	.955	-2	98	89	*O-103(0-19-84)	0.3
1922	StL N	143	510	117	158	23	12	8	46	50	3	30	.310	.375	.449	117	13	18-7	.951	-5	98	73	*O-136(17-79-40)	0.2
1923	StL N	124	407	98	126	16	6	5	41	27	2	20	.310	.356	.415	105	2	32-11	.974	7	**113**	106	*O-109(77-10-23)	0.4
1924	StL N	124	459	91	130	18	6	2	33	33	1	27	.283	.333	.362	88	-8	24-16	.968	9	108	140	*O-114(25-14-77)	-0.8
1925	StL N	80	243	53	61	11	4	4	31	19	1	13	.251	.308	.379	73	-11	20-2	.958	1	105	104	O-64(5-38-28)	-0.9
1926	StL N	1	1	0	0	0	0	0	0	0	0	1	.000	.000	.000	-96	0	0	—	0			H	0.0
	Bos N	96	322	46	100	15	2	2	25	28	2	12	.311	.369	.388	114	7	11	.973	2	105	99	O-83(10-59-15)	0.5
	Year	97	323	46	100	15	2	2	25	28	2	13	.310	.368	.387	113	7	11	.973	2	105	99	O-83(10-59-15)	0.5
1927	Bos N	84	183	27	58	6	4	1	24	16	1	12	.317	.375	.410	119	5	8	.950	2	106	137	O-48(3-14-32)	0.4
1928	Bos N	96	254	30	71	9	2	1	32	21	0	14	.280	.335	.343	82	-7	6	.988	2	109	75	O-65(18-40-7)	-0.9
1929	Bos N	19	20	2	5	0	0	0	2	2	0	2	.250	.318	.250	45	-2	0	.833	-1	108	0	/O-9(2-4-3)	-0.2
Total	15	1406	4532	783	1301	182	71	40	382	334	22	348	.287	.339	.385	103	18	228-67	.961	-1	99	104	*O-1219(207-587-447)	-5.4
SMITH, STUB James A. B 11.26.1876 Elmwood, IL BL/TR 5-6/145# d9.10																								
1898	Bos N	3	10	1	1	0	0	0	0	0	0		.100	.100	.100	-41	-2	0	.933	0	111	0	/S-3	-0.2
SMITH, RED James Carlisle B 4.6.1890 Greenville, SC D 10.11.1966 Atlanta, GA BR/TR 5-11/165# d9.5																								
1911	Bro N	28	111	10	29	6	1	0	19	5	1	13	.261	.299	.333	80	-3	5	.900	-2	99	178	3-28	-0.4
1912	Bro N	128	486	75	139	28	6	4	57	54	4	51	.286	.362	.393	111	8	22	.938	7	106	95	*3-125	1.8
1913	Bro N	151	540	70	160	**40**	10	6	76	45	7	67	.296	.358	.441	124	17	22-19	.933	-2	103	65	*3-151	1.8
1914	Bro N	90	330	39	81	10	8	4	48	30	1	26	.245	.310	.361	97	-2	11	.937	13	108	129	3-90	1.4
	Bos N	60	207	30	65	17	1	3	37	28	2	24	.314	.401	.449	153	15	4	.937	6	108	139	3-60	2.4
	Year	150	537	69	146	27	9	7	85	58	3	50	.272	.346	.395	119	13	15	.937	18	108	133	*3-150	3.8
1915	Bos N	**157**	549	66	145	34	4	2	65	67	1	49	.264	.345	.352	116	14	10-5	.947	-6	94	129	*3-157	1.4
1916	Bos N	150	509	48	132	16	10	3	60	53	3	55	.259	.333	.348	114	9	13	.928	-5	97	75	*3-150	1.0
1917	Bos N	147	505	60	149	31	6	2	62	53	6	61	.295	.369	.392	142	27	16	.925	-23	85	111	*3-147	1.0
1918	Bos N	119	429	55	128	20	3	2	65	45	6	47	.298	.373	.373	133	19	8	.922	3	**110**	78	*3-119	2.9
1919	Bos N	87	241	24	59	6	0	1	25	40	3	22	.245	.359	.282	98	2	6	.981	2	104	55	O-48(17-30-3),3-23	0.2
Total	9	1117	3907	477	1087	208	49	27	514	420	34	415	.278	.353	.377	120	106	117-24	.932	-6	100	101	*3-1050/O-48(17-30-3)	13.5
SMITH, HARRY James Harry B 5.15.1890 Brooklyn, NY D 4.1.1922 Charlotte, NC BR/TR 5-10/180# d9.21																								
1914	NY N	5	7	0	3	0	0	0	2	3	0	1	.429	.600	.429	215	1	1	1.000	1	*166*	*76*	/C-4	0.3
1915	NY N	21	32	1	4	0	1	0	3	6	0	12	.125	.263	.188	40	-2	0-1	.967	-2	*87*	*69*	C-18	-0.4
	Bro F	28	65	5	13	0	0	1	4	7	0	16	.200	.278	.246	48	-6	2	.967	-4	*77*	*95*	C-19/O(RF)	-0.9
1917	Cin N	8	17	0	2	0	0	0	1	2	0	7	.118	.211	.118	2	-2	0	.978	2	*119*	*130*	/C-7	0.1
1918	Cin N	13	27	4	5	1	2	0	4	3	0	6	.185	.267	.370	95	0	1	1.000	-1	*105*	*49*	/C-6,O(CF)	-0.1
Total	4	75	148	10	27	1	3	1	14	21	0	42	.182	.284	.250	59	-9	4-1	.975	-4	*96*	*87*	/C-54,O-2(0-1-1)	-1.0
SMITH, JIMMY James Lawrence "Greenfield Jimmy" B 5.15.1895 Pittsburgh, PA D 1.1.1974 Pittsburgh, PA BB/TR (BR 1914) 5-9/152# d9.26																								
1914	Chi F	3	6	1	3	1	0	0	1	0	0	0	.500	.500	.667	229	1	0	1.000	1	113	434	/S-3	0.2
1915	Chi F	95	318	32	69	11	4	4	30	14	0	65	.217	.250	.314	62	-24	4	.904	-15	91	89	S-92/2	-3.6
	Bal F	33	108	9	19	1	1	1	11	11	1	23	.176	.258	.231	37	-11	3	.883	-3	90	66	S-33	-1.3
	Year	128	426	41	88	12	5	5	41	25	1	88	.207	.252	.293	55	-35	7	.898	-18	91	83	*S-125/2	-4.9
1916	Pit N	36	96	4	18	1	1	0	5	6	3	22	.188	.257	.219	46	-6	0	.929	-2	96	66	S-27/3-6	-0.7
1917	NY N	36	96	12	22	5	1	0	9	9	0	18	.229	.295	.302	86	-1	6	.971	-1	105	60	2-29/S-7	-0.2
1918	Bos N	34	102	8	23	3	4	1	14	3	1	13	.225	.255	.363	91	-2	1	1.000	-3	73	47	2-10/S-9,O-6(2-3-1),3-5	-0.5
1919	†Cin N	28	40	9	11	1	3	1	10	4	0	8	.275	.341	.525	163	3	1	1.000	-1	114	0	/3-6,S-5,2-4,O-4(1-0-3)	0.2
1921	Phi N	67	247	31	57	8	1	4	22	11	1	28	.231	.266	.320	50	-18	2-8	.971	11	119	60	2-66	-0.8
1922	Phi N	38	114	13	25	1	0	1	6	5	1	9	.219	.258	.254	30	-12	1-3	.952	-1	93	120	S-23,2-13/3	-1.2
Total	8	370	1127	119	247	32	15	12	108	63	7	186	.219	.265	.306	60	-70	18-11	.910	-15	92	89	S-199,2-123/3-18,O-10(3-3-4)	-7.9
SMITH, JIM James Lorne B 9.8.1954 Santa Monica, CA BR/TR 6-3/185# d4.12																								
1982	Pit N	42	42	5	10	2	1	0	4	5-0	0	7	.238	.313	.333	80	-1	0-1	.929	0	94	101	S-29/2-3,3	0.0
SMITH, JASON Jason William B 7.24.1977 Meridian, MS BL/TR 6-3/195# d6.17																								
2001	Chi N	2	1	0	0	0	0	0	0	0-0	0	1	.000	.000	.000	-99	0	0-0	1.000	0	0	0	/S	0.0
2002	TB A	26	65	9	13	1	2	1	6	2-0	0	24	.200	.224	.323	44	-6	3-0	.962	-3	102	169	3-12/S-9,2	-0.7
2003	TB A	1	4	0	1	0	0	0	0	0-0	0	0	.250	.250	.250	33	0	0-0	.500	-0	123	607	/3	-0.1
Total	3	29	70	9	14	1	2	1	6	2-0	0	25	.200	.222	.314	41	-6	3-0	.900	-3	104	207	/3-13,S-10,2	-0.8
SMITH, JOHN John B Baltimore, MD d4.14																								
1873	Mar NA	5	19	2	2	0	0	0	1	0		1	.105	.105	.105	-49	-3	0-0	.773	-1	91	0	/S-3,O-2(LF)	-0.3
1874	Bal NA	6	21	2	4	1	0	0	1	0		1	.190	.190	.238	37	-1	0-0	.731	-2	64	0	/S-6	-0.3
1875	NH NA	1	3	0	0	0	0	0	0	1		0	.000	.250	.000	-6	0	0-0	.500	-1	58	0	/S	-0.1
Total	3 NA	12	43	4	6	1	0	0	2	1		2	.140	.159	.163	1	-4	0-0	.000	-4	73	0	/S-10,O-2(LF)	-0.7
SMITH, DWIGHT John Dwight B 11.8.1963 Tallahassee, FL BL/TR 5-11/175# d5.1																								
1989	†Chi N	109	343	52	111	19	6	9	52	31-0	2	51	.324	.382	.493	138	17	9-4	.975	4	104	141	*O-102(75-0-32)	2.0
1990	Chi N	117	290	34	76	15	0	6	27	28-2	2	46	.262	.329	.376	88	-4	11-6	.986	-0	98	82	O-81(59-3-22)	-0.6
1991	Chi N	90	167	16	38	7	2	3	21	11-2	1	32	.228	.279	.347	72	-7	2-3	.962	0	100	126	O-42(5-13-28)	-0.8
1992	Chi N	109	217	28	60	10	3	3	24	13-0	1	40	.276	.318	.392	98	-1	9-8	.979	-3	86	76	O-63(20-27-22)	-0.6
1993	Chi N	111	310	51	93	17	5	11	35	25-1	3	51	.300	.355	.494	127	11	8-6	.955	-2	95	115	O-89(14-53-28)	0.8
1994	Cal A	45	122	19	32	5	1	5	18	7-0	0	20	.262	.300	.443	88	-3	2-3	.912	-1	98	107	O-31(LF)/D-2	-0.5
	Bal A	28	74	12	23	2	1	3	12	5-1	1	17	.311	.363	.486	111	1	0-1	.939	-3	81	0	O-22(20-2-1)/D-3	-0.3

Year	Tm Lg	G	AB	R	H	2B	3B	HR	RBI	BB-IB	HP	SO	AVG	OBP	SLG	AOPS	ABR	SB-CS	FA	FR	Rng	Thr	G at Pos	BFW
	Year	73	196	31	55	7	2	8	30	12-1	1	37	.281	.324	.459	97	-2	2-4	.922	-4	91	63	O-53(51-2-1)/D-5	-0.8
1995	†Atl N	103	131	16	33	8	2	3	21	13-1	2	35	.252	.327	.412	91	-2	0-3	.923	-2	80	0	O-25(11-0-14)	-0.6
1996	Atl N	101	153	16	31	5	0	3	16	17-1	1	42	.203	.285	.294	51	-11	1-3	.962	2	124	73	O-29(3-0-26)	-1.1
Total	8	813	1807	244	497	88	20	46	226	150-8	13	334	.275	.333	.422	101	1	42-37	.964	-5	97	98	O-484(238-98-173)/D-5	-1.7
SMITH, JOHN John Joseph B 1858 New York, NY D 1.6.1899 San Francisco, CA 5-11/210# d5.1																								
1882	Tro N	35	149	27	36	4	3	0	14	3		24	.242	.257	.309	84	-3		.960	-0	95	95	1-35	-0.5
	Wor N	19	70	10	17	3	2	0	5	5		10	.243	.293	.343	101	0		.939	1	199	101	1-19	-0.1
	Year	54	219	37	53	7	5	0	19	8		34	.242	.269	.320	90	-3		.952	1	131	97	1-54	-0.6
SMITH, JACK John Joseph (born John Joseph Coffey) B 8.8.1893 Oswayo, PA D 12.4.1962 New York, NY BR/TR 5-9/?# d5.18																								
1912	Det A	1	0	0	0	0	0	0	0	0	0		—	—	—	—	0	0	1.000	0	86	1159	/3	0.0
SMITH, JOHN John Marshall B 9.27.1906 Washington, DC D 5.9.1982 Silver Spring, MD BB/TR 6-1/180# d9.17																								
1931	Bos A	4	15	2	2	0	0	0	1	2	0	1	.133	.235	.133	-1	-2	1-0	1.000	-1	0	31	/1-4	-0.3
SMITH, KEITH Keith Lavarne B 5.3.1953 Palmetto, FL BR/TR 5-9/178# d8.2																								
1977	Tex A	23	67	13	16	4	0	2	6	4-0	2	7	.239	.301	.388	85	-1	2-0	.975	-0	97	70	O-22(LF)	-0.2
1979	StL N	6	13	1	3	0	0	0	0	0-0	0	1	.231	.231	.231	26	-1	0-1	1.000	2	197	365	/O-5(LF)	0.0
1980	StL N	24	31	3	4	1	0	0	2	2-1	0	2	.129	.182	.161	-3	-4	0-0	1.000	-0	109	0	/O-7(4-1-2)	-0.5
Total	3	53	111	17	23	5	0	2	8	6-1	2	10	.207	.261	.306	54	-6	2-1	.985	2	112	96	/O-34(31-1-2)	-0.7
SMITH, KEN Kenneth Earl B 2.12.1958 Youngstown, OH BL/TR 6-1/195# d9.22																								
1981	Atl N	5	3	0	1	1	0	0	0	0-0	0	1	.333	.333	.667	174	0	0-0	1.000	0	118	0	/1-4	0.0
1982	Atl N	48	41	6	12	1	0	0	3	6-0	0	13	.293	.383	.317	94	0	0-0	1.000	-1	88	0	/1-6,O-3(LF)	-0.1
1983	Atl N	30	12	2	2	0	0	1	2	1-0	0	5	.167	.231	.417	71	-1	1-0	1.000	2	277	132	1-13	0.1
Total	3	83	56	8	15	2	0	1	5	7-0	0	19	.268	.349	.357	93	-1	1-0	1.000	1	193	69	/1-23,O-3(LF)	0.0
SMITH, L. L. d9.7																								
1882	Bal AA	1	3	0	0	0	0	0		0			.000	.000	.000	-99	-1		.500	-1	0	0	/O(CF)	-0.1
SMITH, PADDY Lawrence Patrick B 5.16.1894 Pelham, NY D 12.2.1990 New Rochelle, NY BL/TR 6/195# d7.6																								
1920	Bos A	2	2	0	0	0	0	0	0	0	0	1	.000	.000	.000	-99	-1	0-0	—	-0	*0*	*0*	/C	-0.1
SMITH, BULL Lewis Oscar B 8.20.1880 Plum, WV D 5.1.1928 Charleston, WV BR/TR 6/180# d8.30																								
1904	Pit N	13	42	2	6	0	1	0	0	1	0		.143	.163	.190	9	-5	0	.857	-0	123	0	O-13(11-0-2)	-0.6
1906	Chi N	1	1	0	0	0	0	0	0	0	0		.000	.000	.000	-95	0	0	—	0			H	0.0
1911	Was A	1	0	0	0	0	0	0	0	0	0		—	—	—	—	0	0	—	0			R	0.0
Total	3	15	43	2	6	0	1	0	0	1	0		.140	.159	.186	6	-5	0	.857	-0	123	0	/O-13(11-0-2)	-0.6
SMITH, LEO Lionel H. B 5.13.1859 Brooklyn, NY D 8.30.1935 Brooklyn, NY 5-6/142# d8.28																								
1890	Roc AA	35	112	11	21	1	3	0	11	14	1		.188	.283	.250	62	-5	1	.948	6	104	146	S-35	0.2
SMITH, LONNIE Lonnie B 12.22.1955 Chicago, IL BR/TR 5-9/170# d9.2																								
1978	Phi N	17	4	6	0	0	0	0	0	4-0	0	3	.000	.500	.000	50	0	4-0	1.000	1	94	529	O-11(10-1-1)	0.2
1979	Phi N	17	30	4	5	2	0	0	3	1-0	0	7	.167	.194	.233	15	-4	2-1	1.000	1	113	180	O-11(3-5-4)	-0.3
1980	†Phi N	100	298	69	101	14	4	3	20	26-2	4	48	.339	.397	.443	128	12	33-13	.969	-7	88	37	O-82(52-9-23)	0.5
1981	†Phi N	62	176	40	57	14	3	2	11	18-1	5	14	.324	.402	.472	141	10	21-10	.971	6	104	338	O-51(8-23-24)	1.8
1982	†StL N★	156	592	**120**	182	35	8	8	69	64-2	**9**	74	.307	.381	.434	127	24	68-26	.970	2	95	135	*O-149(135-36-0)	2.7
1983	StL N	130	492	83	158	31	5	8	45	41-2	**9**	55	.321	.381	.453	131	22	43-18	.941	1	93	148	*O-126(LF)	2.1
1984	StL N	145	504	77	126	20	4	6	49	70-0	**9**	90	.250	.349	.341	98	1	50-13	.948	-5	76	**179**	*O-140(LF)	-0.3
1985	StL N	28	96	15	25	2	2	0	7	15-0	3	20	.260	.377	.323	98	1	12-6	1.000	-1	94	57	O-28(LF)	0.0
	†KC A	120	448	77	115	23	4	6	41	41-0	4	69	.257	.321	.366	88	-7	40-7	.958	-4	88	143	*O-119(LF)	-0.9
1986	KC A	134	508	80	146	25	7	8	44	46-0	10	78	.287	.357	.411	107	6	26-9	.965	-0	105	68	*O-118(LF),D-10	0.3
1987	KC A	48	167	26	42	7	1	3	8	24-0	4	31	.251	.355	.359	89	-2	9-4	.915	-3	85	94	O-32(LF),D-15	-0.6
1988	Atl N	43	114	14	27	3	0	3	9	10-0	0	25	.237	.296	.342	79	-3	4-2	.968	1	104	113	O-35(LF)	-0.3
1989	Atl N	134	482	89	152	34	4	21	79	76-3	11	95	.315	**.415**	.533	166	46	25-12	.993	3	110	41	*O-132(LF)	4.8
1990	Atl N	135	466	72	142	27	9	9	42	58-3	6	69	.305	.384	.459	125	18	10-10	.956	2	110	73	*O-122(LF)	1.5
1991	†Atl N	122	353	58	97	19	1	7	44	50-3	9	64	.275	.377	.394	111	8	9-5	.965	-7	81	103	O-99(LF)	-0.1
1992	†Atl N	84	158	23	39	8	2	6	33	17-1	3	37	.247	.324	.437	109	2	4-0	.954	1	110	153	O-35(LF)	0.3
1993	Pit N	94	199	35	57	5	4	6	24	43-2	5	42	.286	.422	.442	133	12	9-4	.981	-0	112	28	O-60(58-3-0)	1.1
	Bal A	9	24	8	5	1	0	2	3	8-0	0	10	.208	.406	.500	136	2	0-0	1.000	0	66	442	/O-4(LF),D-5	0.2
1994	Bal A	35	59	13	12	3	0	0	2	11-0	1	18	.203	.333	.254	53	-4	1-0	1.000	1	61	839	D-30/O-2(RF)	-0.5
Total	17	1613	5170	909	1488	273	58	98	533	623-19	92	849	.288	.371	.420	117	144	370-140	.964	-9	96	114	*O-1356(1257-77-54)/D-60	12.5
SMITH, MARK Mark Edward B 5.7.1970 Pasadena, CA BR/TR 6-3/205# d5.14																								
1994	Bal A	3	7	0	1	0	0	0	2	0-0	0	2	.143	.143	.143	-25	-1	0-0	1.000	1	190	0	/O-3(RF)	-0.1
1995	Bal A	37	104	11	24	5	0	3	15	12-2	1	22	.231	.314	.365	76	-4	3-0	1.000	1	107	105	O-32(15-0-17)/D-3	-0.3
1996	Bal A	27	78	9	19	2	0	4	10	3-0	3	20	.244	.298	.423	80	-3	0-2	.980	2	137	0	O-20(12-0-8)/D-6	-0.2
1997	Pit N	71	193	29	55	13	1	9	35	28-1	0	36	.285	.374	.503	125	8	3-1	1.000	-0	83	169	O-42(21-0-22)/1-9,D-5	0.6
1998	Pit N	59	128	18	25	6	0	2	13	10-0	3	26	.195	.264	.289	46	-10	7-0	.977	0	110	0	O-24(16-0-9)/1-6,D-3	-1.0
2000	Fla N	104	192	22	47	8	1	5	27	17-1	2	54	.245	.310	.375	76	-8	2-0	1.000	2	95	183	O-49(29-0-25)/D	-0.7
2001	Mon N	80	194	28	47	13	1	6	18	23-0	2	38	.242	.326	.412	88	-3	0-2	1.000	1	105	62	O-60(54-6-4)/1	-0.5
2003	Mil N	33	63	8	15	4	0	3	10	4-0	0	13	.238	.275	.444	88	-1	0-0	.960	-1	104	0	O-15(12-0-3)	-0.2
Total	8	414	959	125	233	51	3	32	130	97-4	11	211	.243	.316	.403	85	-22	15-5	.993	6	104	91	O-245(159-6-91)/D-18,1-16	-2.4
SMITH, RED Marvin Harold B 7.17.1899 Ashley, IL D 2.19.1961 Los Angeles, CA BL/TR 5-7/165# d4.14																								
1925	Phi A	20	14	1	4	0	0	0	1	2	0	5	.286	.375	.286	65	-1	0-0	.864	-1	113	0	S-16/3-2	-0.1
SMITH, MILT Milton B 3.27.1929 Columbus, GA D 4.11.1997 San Diego, CA BR/TR 5-10/165# d7.21																								
1955	Cin N	36	102	15	20	3	1	3	8	13-0	1	24	.196	.293	.333	62	-6	2-2	.915	-1	105	87	3-28/2-5	-0.7
SMITH, NATE Nathaniel Beverly B 4.26.1935 Chicago, IL BR/TR 5-11/170# d9.19																								
1962	Bal A	5	9	3	2	1	0	0	0	1-0	1	4	.222	.364	.333	95	0	0-0	1.000	0	*91*	*0*	/C-3	0.1
SMITH, OLLIE Oliver H. B 1868 Mt.Vernon, OH BL/TL d7.11																								
1894	Lou N	39	137	27	41	6	1	3	20	29	3	15	.299	.432	.423	115	6	13	.883	-3	78	0	O-39(RF)	0.1
SMITH, OZZIE Osborne Earl B 12.26.1954 Mobile, AL BB/TR 5-11/150# d4.7 HF2001																								
1978	SD N	159	590	69	152	17	6	1	46	47-0	0	43	.258	.311	.312	81	-16	40-12	.970	30	**113**	115	*S-159	3.5
1979	SD N	156	587	77	124	18	6	0	27	37-5	2	37	.211	.260	.262	46	-46	28-7	.976	20	112	96	*S-155	-0.7
1980	SD N	158	609	67	140	18	5	0	35	71-1	5	49	.230	.313	.276	70	-23	57-15	.974	**39**	117	117	*S-158	4.1
1981	SD N★	**110**	450	53	100	11	2	0	21	41-1	5	37	.222	.294	.256	62	-23	22-12	**.976**	22	**115**	98	*S-110	1.3
1982	†StL N★	140	488	58	121	24	1	2	43	68-12	2	32	.248	.339	.314	84	-8	25-5	**.984**	**36**	**119**	125	*S-139	4.8
1983	StL N★	159	552	69	134	30	6	3	50	64-9	1	36	.243	.321	.335	82	-12	34-7	.975	16	110	107	*S-158	2.6
1984	StL N★	124	412	53	106	20	5	1	44	56-5	2	17	.257	.347	.337	96	0	35-7	**.982**	**32**	**116**	**132**	*S-124	5.1
1985	†StL N★	158	537	70	148	22	3	6	54	65-11	2	27	.276	.355	.361	102	3	31-8	**.983**	18	109	124	*S-158	4.4
1986	StL N★	153	514	67	144	19	4	0	54	79-13	2	27	.280	.376	.333	99	3	31-7	**.978**	-12	101	**122**	*S-144	1.2
1987	†StL N★	158	600	104	182	40	4	0	75	89-3	1	36	.303	.392	.383	105	10	43-9	**.987**	12	**108**	**122**	*S-158	4.3
1988	StL N★	153	575	80	155	27	1	3	51	74-2	1	43	.270	.350	.336	98	2	57-9	.972	**21**	**115**	96	*S-150	4.6
1989	StL N★	155	593	82	162	30	8	2	50	55-3	2	37	.273	.335	.361	96	-2	29-7	.976	12	112	99	*S-153	2.7
1990	StL N★	143	512	61	130	21	1	1	50	61-4	2	33	.254	.330	.305	77	-14	32-6	.980	-12	96	90	*S-140	-1.1
1991	StL N★	150	550	96	157	30	3	3	50	83-2	1	36	.285	.380	.367	110	12	35-9	**.987**	-7	95	114	*S-150	2.1
1992	StL N★	132	518	73	153	20	2	0	31	59-4	0	34	.295	.367	.342	105	6	43-9	.985	16	111	**125**	*S-132	4.0
1993	StL N	141	545	75	157	22	6	1	53	43-1	1	18	.288	.337	.356	89	-9	21-8	.974	**23**	**113**	**129**	*S-134	2.6
1994	StL N★	98	381	51	100	18	3	3	30	38-3	0	26	.262	.326	.349	79	-12	6-3	**.982**	2	103	110	S-96	-0.2
1995	StL N✳	44	156	16	31	5	1	0	11	17-0	2	12	.199	.282	.244	41	-13	4-3	.964	5	109	123	S-41	-0.5
1996	†StL N★	82	227	36	64	10	2	2	18	25-0	2	9	.282	.358	.370	93	-2	7-5	.969	7	106	121	S-52	0.9
Total	19	2573	9396	1257	2460	402	69	28	793	1072-79	33	589	.262	.337	.328	87	-144	580-148	.978	279	110	113	*S-2511	45.7

Year	Tm Lg	G	AB	R	H	2B	3B	HR	RBI	BB-IB	HP	SO	AVG	OBP	SLG	AOPS	ABR	SB-CS	FA	FR	Rng	Thr	G at Pos	BFW
SMITH, KEITH Patrick Keith B 10.20.1961 Los Angeles, CA BB/TR 6-1/175# d4.12																								
1984	NY A	2	4	0	0	0	0	0	0	0-0	1	2	.000	.200	.000	-41	-1	0-0	.923	1	167	83	/S-2	0.1
1985	NY A	4	0	1	0	0	0	0	0	0-0	0	0	—	—	—	—	0	0-0	1.000	-0	100	0	/S-3	0.0
Total	2	6	4	1	0	0	0	0	0	0-0	1	2	.000	.200	.000	-41	-1	0-0	.929	1	157	71	/S-5	0.1
SMITH, PAUL Paul Leslie B 3.19.1931 New Castle, PA BL/TL 5-8/165# d4.14 Mil 1955																								
1953	Pit N	118	389	41	110	12	7	4	44	24	3	23	.283	.329	.380	85	-9	3-0	.985	-1	100	75	1-74,O-19(LF)	-1.4
1957	Pit N	81	150	12	38	4	0	3	11	12-1	1	17	.253	.313	.340	78	-5	0-2	1.000	1	102	106	O-33(16-1-20)/1	-0.6
1958	Pit N	6	3	0	1	0	0	0	0	3-0	0	0	.333	.667	.333	180	1	0-0	—	0			H	0.1
	Chi N	18	20	1	3	0	0	0	1	3-0	0	4	.150	.261	.150	13	-3	0-0	.941	0	142	0	/1-4	-0.3
	Year	24	23	1	4	0	0	0	1	6-0	0	4	.174	.345	.174	44	-2	0-0	.941	0	142	0	/1-4	-0.2
Total	3	223	562	54	152	16	7	7	56	42-1	4	44	.270	.326	.361	81	-16	3-2	.984	-0	101	73	/1-79,O-52(35-1-20)	-2.2
SMITH, PAUL Paul Stoner B 5.7.1888 Mt.Zion, IL D 7.3.1958 Decatur, IL BL/TR 6-1/190# d9.19																								
1916	Cin N	10	44	5	10	0	1	0	1	1	0	8	.227	.244	.273	60	-2	3	1.000	-1	79	111	O-10(LF)	-0.4
SMITH, RAY Raymond Edward B 9.18.1955 Glendale, CA BR/TR 6-1/185# d4.9																								
1981	Min A	15	40	4	8	1	0	1	1	0-0	0	3	.200	.200	.300	40	-3	0-0	1.000	-0	158	63	C-15	-0.3
1982	Min A	9	23	1	5	0	1	0	1	1-0	0	3	.217	.250	.304	50	-2	0-0	1.000	-0	167	71	/C-9	-0.1
1983	Min A	59	152	11	34	5	0	0	8	10-0	1	12	.224	.274	.257	46	-11	1-0	.984	8	92	150	C-59	0.0
Total	3	83	215	16	47	6	1	1	10	11-0	1	18	.219	.259	.270	45	-16	1-0	.988	8	113	125	/C-83	-0.4
SMITH, DICK Richard Arthur B 5.17.1939 Lebanon, OR BR/TR 6-2/205# d7.20																								
1963	NY N	20	42	4	10	0	1	0	3	5-2	0	10	.238	.319	.286	74	-1	3-2	1.000	-1	92	0	O-10(3-7-0)/1-2	-0.3
1964	NY N	46	94	14	21	6	1	0	3	1-0	2	29	.223	.247	.309	57	-5	6-2	.987	-2	102	84	1-18,O-13(12-1-1)	-0.9
1965	LA N	10	6	0	0	0	0	0	1	0-0	0	3	.000	.000	.000	-99	-2	0-0	1.000	0	483	0	/O-9(5-4-1)	-0.2
Total	3	76	142	18	31	6	2	0	7	6-2	2	42	.218	.260	.289	56	-8	9-4	1.000	-3	68	0	/O-32(20-12-2),1-20	-1.4
SMITH, DICK Richard Harrison B 7.21.1927 Blandburg, PA BR/TR 5-8/160# d9.14																								
1951	Pit N	12	46	2	8	0	0	0	4	8	0	8	.174	.296	.174	29	-4	0-2	.936	2	115	188	3-12	-0.3
1952	Pit N	29	66	8	7	1	0	0	5	9	0	3	.106	.213	.121	-5	-9	0-0	.958	3	111	118	3-16/2-4,S-4	-0.6
1953	Pit N	13	43	4	7	0	1	0	2	6	0	6	.163	.265	.209	26	-5	0-1	.961	3	131	101	S-13	-0.1
1954	Pit N	12	31	2	3	1	1	0	0	6	0	5	.097	.243	.194	16	-4	0-0	.933	1	121	171	/3-9	-0.3
1955	Pit N	4	0	1	0	0	0	0	0	1-0	0	0	—	1.000	—	198	0	0-0	—	-0	0	0	/S	0.0
Total	5	70	186	17	25	2	2	0	11	30-0	0	22	.134	.255	.167	15	-22	0-3	.944	10	115	156	/3-37,S-18,2-4	-1.3
SMITH, DICK Richard Kelly B 8.25.1944 Lincolnton, NC BR/TR 6-5/200# d8.20																								
1969	Was A	21	28	2	3	0	0	0	0	4-1	1	7	.107	.242	.107	1	-4	0-0	.909	-1	82	0	/O-9(LF)	-0.5
SMITH, RED Richard Paul B 5.18.1904 Brokaw, WI D 3.8.1978 Sylvania, OH BR/TR 5-10/185# d5.31 C4																								
1927	NY N	1	0	0	0	0	0	0	0	0	0	0	—	—	—	—	0	0	1.000	-0	*0*	*0*	/C	0.0
SMITH, BOB Robert Eldridge B 4.22.1895 Rogersville, TN D 7.19.1987 Waycross, GA BR/TR 5-10/175# d4.19 ▲																								
1923	Bos N	115	375	30	94	16	3	0	40	17	1	35	.251	.285	.309	59	-23	4-9	.944	12	106	110	*S-101/2-8	-0.3
1924	Bos N	106	347	32	79	12	3	2	38	15	0	26	.228	.260	.297	51	-25	5-2	.958	4	103	103	S-80,3-23	-1.1
1925	Bos N	58	174	17	49	9	4	0	23	5	0	6	.282	.302	.379	80	-6	2-2	.906	-1	111	110	S-21,2-15,P-13/O(CF)	-0.3
1926	Bos N	40	84	10	25	6	2	0	13	2	0	4	.298	.314	.417	105	8	0	.972	2	120	207	P-33	0.0
1927	Bos N	54	109	10	27	3	1	1	10	2	0	4	.248	.261	.321	60	5	0	.966	2	110	101	P-41	0.0
1928	Bos N	39	92	11	23	2	0	1	8	1	0	6	.250	.258	.304	49	3	2	.965	2	116	142	P-38	0.0
1929	Bos N	39	99	12	17	4	2	1	8	2	0	8	.172	.188	.283	16	-14	1	.986	3	109	96	P-34/S-5	0.1
1930	Bos N	39	81	7	19	2	0	0	4	0	0	5	.235	.235	.259	20	-1	0	.984	1	106	100	P-38	0.0
1931	Chi N	36	87	7	19	2	0	0	4	5	0	2	.218	.261	.241	35	1	0	**1.000**	1	109	118	P-36	0.0
1932	†Chi N	36	42	5	10	4	1	0	4	0	0	2	.238	.238	.381	64	-2	1	1.000	2	105	206	P-34/2-2	0.2
1933	Cin N	23	25	2	5	1	0	0	1	1	0	0	.200	.231	.240	35	-2	1	.882	-1	92	471	P-16/S	-0.1
	Bos N	14	20	1	4	0	1	0	2	0	0	1	.200	.200	.300	45	0	0	1.000	1	146	0	P-14	0.0
	Year	37	45	3	9	1	1	0	3	1	0	1	.200	.217	.267	39	-4	1	.946	0	116	262	P-30/S	-0.1
1934	Bos N	42	36	5	9	1	0	0	3	0	0	1	.250	.250	.278	44	1	0	1.000	1	119	139	P-39	0.0
1935	Bos N	47	63	3	17	0	0	0	4	1	0	5	.270	.281	.270	53	3	0	.980	-1	91	40	P-46	0.0
1936	Bos N	35	45	1	10	2	0	0	4	0	0	4	.222	.222	.267	33	0	0	1.000	1	118	105	P-35	0.0
1937	Bos N	19	10	1	2	0	0	0	0	1	0	1	.200	.273	.200	33	0	0	1.000	-1	63	0	P-18	0.0
Total	15	742	1689	154	409	64	17	5	166	52	1	110	.242	.265	.309	53	-52	16-13	.981	29	109	125	P-435,S-208/2-25,3-23,O(CF)	-1.5
SMITH, BOBBY Robert Eugene B 4.10.1974 Oakland, CA BR/TR 6-3/190# d4.3 OF Total (1-LF 1-RF)																								
1998	TB A	117	370	44	102	15	3	11	55	34-0	6	110	.276	.343	.422	97	-2	5-3	.963	10	109	85	3-97/S-7,2-6,D-7	0.9
1999	TB A	68	199	18	36	4	1	3	19	16-0	1	64	.181	.244	.256	28	-23	4-4	.933	5	115	149	3-59,2-13	-1.6
2000	TB A	49	175	21	41	8	0	6	26	14-1	1	59	.234	.293	.383	70	-8	2-2	.970	2	107	86	2-45/3-5	-0.4
2001	TB A	6	19	1	2	0	0	0	1	3-0	0	10	.105	.227	.105	-8	-3	0-0	.958	-2	66	77	/2-6	-0.5
2002	TB A	18	63	4	11	2	0	1	6	3-0	0	25	.175	.212	.254	24	-7	0-0	.897	1	101	159	3-10/1-6,O-2(1-0-1),D	-0.6
Total	5	258	826	88	192	29	4	21	107	70-1	8	268	.232	.297	.354	67	-43	11-9	.947	15	111	110	3-171/2-70,D-8,S-7,1-6,O-2L	-2.2
SMITH, JOE Salvatore (born Salvatore Persico) B 12.29.1893 New York, NY D 1.12.1974 Yonkers, NY BR/TR 5-7/170# d7.7																								
1913	NY A	14	32	1	5	0	0	0	2	1	0	14	.156	.182	.156	-1	-4	1	.952	-1	*71*	*126*	C-14	-0.5
SMITH, SKYROCKET Samuel J. B 3.19.1868 St.Louis, MO D 4.26.1916 St.Louis, MO BR 6-2/170# d4.18																								
1888	Lou AA	58	206	27	49	9	4	1	31	24	11		.238	.349	.335	122	7	5	.970	-0	105	56	1-58	0.2
SMITH, SYD Sydney E. B 8.31.1883 Smithville, SC D 6.5.1961 Orangeburg, SC BR/TR 5-10/190# d4.14																								
1908	Phi A	46	128	8	26	8	0	1	10	4	1		.203	.233	.289	65	-5	0	.975	-2	*70*	*102*	C-31/1-6,O(CF)	-0.5
	StL A	27	76	6	14	4	0	0	5	4	0		.184	.225	.237	50	-4	2	.977	6	*142*	*89*	C-24	0.4
	Year	73	204	14	40	12	0	1	15	8	1		.196	.230	.270	60	-9	2	.976	4	*103*	*96*	C-55/1-6,O(CF)	-0.1
1910	Cle A	9	27	1	9	1	0	0	3	3	0		.333	.400	.370	140	1	0	.958	-1	*82*	*114*	/C-9	0.2
1911	Cle A	58	154	8	46	8	1	1	21	11	2		.299	.353	.383	104	1	0	.979	5	*93*	*94*	C-48/13	0.9
1914	Pit N	5	11	1	3	0	0	0	1	0	0	1	.273	.273	.273	65	-1	0	1.000	-0	*101*	*82*	/C-3	0.0
1915	Pit N	1	1	0	0	0	0	0	0	0	0	0	.000	.000	.000	-99	0	0	—	0			H	0.0
Total	5	146	397	24	98	21	1	2	40	22	3	1	.247	.291	.320	83	-8	2	.977	8	*97*	*96*	C-115/1-7,3O(CF)	1.0
SMITH, TOM Thomas N. B 1851 Guelph, ON, CAN D 3.28.1889 Detroit, MI 5-8/141# d9.15																								
1875	Atl NA	3	13	0	1	0	0	0	1	0		0	.077	.077	.077	-53	-2	0-0	.783	-0	116	0	/2-3	-0.2
SMITH, TOMMY Tommy Alexander B 8.1.1948 Albemarle, NC BL/TR 6-3/215# d9.6																								
1973	Cle A	14	41	6	10	2	0	2	3	1-0	0	2	.244	.262	.439	93	-1	1-0	1.000	-1	93	0	O-13(1-11-1)	-0.2
1974	Cle A	23	31	4	3	1	0	0	0	2-1	1	7	.097	.176	.129	-11	-4	0-0	.938	2	133	141	O-17(9-4-4)/D	-0.4
1975	Cle A	8	8	0	1	0	0	0	2	0-0	0	1	.125	.111	.125	-29	-1	0-0	1.000	0	135	0	/O-3(1-0-2),D-3	-0.1
1976	Cle A	55	164	17	42	3	1	2	12	8-2	0	8	.256	.289	.323	80	-5	8-0	.979	1	104	131	O-50(12-0-38)/D-2	-0.4
1977	Sea A	21	27	1	7	1	1	0	4	0-0	0	6	.259	.259	.370	70	-1	0-1	1.000	2	86	711	O-14(1-0-14)	0.0
Total	5	121	271	28	63	7	2	4	21	11-3	1	24	.232	.263	.317	68	-12	9-1	.977	4	105	156	/O-97(24-15-59),D-6	-1.1
SMITH, VINNIE Vincent Ambrose B 12.7.1915 Richmond, VA D 12.14.1979 Virginia Beach, VA BR/TR 6-1/176# d9.10 Mil 1942-45 U9																								
1941	Pit N	9	33	3	10	1	0	0	5	1	0	5	.303	.324	.333	86	-1	0	.941	-1	*92*	*84*	/C-9	-0.1
1946	Pit N	7	21	2	4	0	0	0	0	1	0	5	.190	.227	.190	19	-2	0	.967	0	*80*	*109*	/C-7	-0.2
Total	2	16	54	5	14	1	0	0	5	2	0	10	.259	.286	.278	59	-3	0	.953	-1	*87*	*94*	/C-16	-0.3
SMITH, WALLY Wallace H. B 3.13.1888 Philadelphia, PA D 6.10.1930 Florence, AZ BR/TR 5-11.5/180# d4.17																								
1911	StL N	81	194	23	42	6	5	2	19	21	3	33	.216	.303	.330	79	-6	5	.936	2	108	30	3-26,S-25/2-8,O(CF)	-0.2
1912	StL N	75	219	22	56	5	5	0	26	29	3	27	.256	.351	.324	87	-3	4	.949	1	106	69	3-32,S-22/1-6	-0.1
1914	Was A	45	97	11	19	4	1	0	8	3	2	12	.196	.235	.258	46	-7	3-4	.955	-3	57	99	2-12/1-7,S-7,3-5,O(RF)	-1.2
Total	3	201	510	56	117	15	11	2	53	53	8	72	.229	.312	.314	77	-16	12-4	.947	-1	107	63	/3-63,S-54,2-20,1-13,O-2(0-1-1)	-1.5

Year	Tm Lg	G	AB	R	H	2B	3B	HR	RBI	BB-IB	HP	SO	AVG	OBP	SLG	AOPS	ABR	SB-CS	FA	FR	Rng	Thr	G at Pos	BFW
SMITH, WIB Wilbur Floyd B 8.30.1886 Evart, MI D 11.18.1959 Fargo, ND BL/TR 5-10.5/165# d5.31																								
1909	StL A	17	42	3	8	0	0	0	2	0	0		.190	.190	.190	22	-4	0	.836	-7	*82*	*78*	C-13/1	-1.1
SMITH, RED Willard Jehu B 4.11.1892 Logansport, IN D 7.17.1972 Noblesville, IN BR/TR 5-8/165# d9.17																								
1917	Pit N	11	21	1	3	1	0	0	2	3	0	4	.143	.250	.190	35	-1	1	1.000	1	*79*	*163*	/C-6	0.0
1918	Pit N	15	24	1	4	1	0	0	3	3	0	0	.167	.259	.208	42	-2	0	.939	0	*142*	*45*	C-10	-0.1
Total	2	26	45	2	7	2	0	0	5	6	0	4	.156	.255	.200	39	-3	1	.969	1	*113*	*99*	/C-16	-0.1
SMITH, BILL William E. B 3.1860 E.Liverpool, OH D 8.9.1886 Toronto, ON, CAN 5-11/178# d9.17																								
1884	Cle N	1	3	0	0	0	0	0	0	0		2	.000	.000	.000	-97	-1		—	0	0	0	/O(LF)	-0.1
SMITH, BILL William J. B Baltimore, MD D 8.9.1886 d4.14 M1																								
1873	Mar NA	**6**	23	2	4	0	0	0	1	0		0	.174	.174	.174	5	-2	0-0	.500	-3	0	0	/O-3(CF),C-2,2M	-0.3
SMITH, WILLIE Willie B 2.11.1939 Anniston, AL BL/TL 6/190# d6.18 ▲																								
1963	Det A	17	8	2	1	0	0	0	0	0-0	0	1	.125	.125	.125	-29	0	0-0	1.000	0	118	0	P-11	0.0
1964	LA A	118	359	46	108	14	6	11	51	8-1	2	39	.301	.317	.465	128	10	7-5	.977	-5	88	45	O-87(58-3-31),P-15	-0.1
1965	Cal A	136	459	52	120	14	9	14	57	32-10	1	60	.261	.308	.423	109	3	9-8	.980	3	94	148	*O-123(123-0-1)/1-2	-0.2
1966	Cal A	90	195	18	36	3	2	1	20	12-2	3	37	.185	.239	.236	39	-16	1-0	.974	-0	90	150	O-52(32-0-22)	-2.0
1967	Cle A	21	32	0	7	2	0	0	2	1-0	0	10	.219	.242	.281	54	-2	0-2	.800	-1	74	0	/O-4(LF),1-3	-0.4
1968	Cle A	33	42	1	6	2	0	0	3	3-2	1	14	.143	.213	.190	25	-4	0-0	1.000	-0	65	149	/1-7,P-2,O(LF)	-0.5
	Chi N	55	142	13	39	8	2	5	25	12-2	1	33	.275	.333	.465	129	5	0-0	1.000	-1	88	53	O-38(LF)/1-4,P	0.2
1969	Chi N	103	195	21	48	9	1	9	25	25-3	0	49	.246	.330	.441	102	1	1-0	.929	-5	64	0	O-33(32-0-1),1-24	-0.7
1970	Chi N	87	167	15	36	9	1	5	24	11-0	1	32	.216	.267	.371	62	-9	2-1	.994	-5	45	120	1-43/O(RF)	-1.7
1971	Cin N	31	55	3	9	2	0	1	4	3-0	0	9	.164	.207	.255	31	-5	0-0	1.000	1	150	138	1-10	-0.5
Total	9	691	1654	171	410	63	21	46	211	107-20	9	284	.248	.295	.395	94	-17	20-16	.975	-13	88	95	O-339(288-3-56)/1-93,P-29	-5.9
SMITHERMAN, STEPHEN Stephen Lydell B 9.1.1978 McAlester, OK BR/TR 6-4/230# d7.1																								
2003	Cin N	21	44	3	7	2	0	1	6	3-0	0	9	.159	.213	.273	26	-5	1-0	1.000	-1	83	0	O-14(LF)	-0.6
SMOOT, HOMER Homer Vernon "Doc" B 3.23.1878 Galestown, MD D 3.25.1928 Salisbury, MD BL/TR 5-10/180# d4.17																								
1902	StL N	129	518	58	161	19	4	3	48	23	8		.311	.350	.380	131	18	20	.931	-2	80	102	*O-129(CF)	1.0
1903	StL N	129	500	67	148	22	8	4	49	32	3		.296	.342	.396	114	8	17	.942	-7	82	67	*O-129(CF)	-0.5
1904	StL N	137	520	58	146	23	6	3	66	37	2		.281	.331	.365	120	12	23	.966	-2	98	125	*O-137(CF)	0.4
1905	StL N	139	534	73	166	21	16	4	58	33	7		.311	.359	.433	140	24	21	.975	-0	101	134	*O-138(CF)	1.8
1906	StL N	86	343	41	85	9	10	0	31	11	9		.248	.289	.332	98	-3	3	.953	-2	70	140	O-86(0-55-31)	-1.1
	Cin N	60	220	11	57	8	1	1	17	13	5		.259	.315	.318	93	-2	0	.944	1	145	0	O-59(4-55-0)	-0.3
	Year	146	563	52	142	17	11	1	48	24	14		.252	.300	.327	96	-5	3	.950	-1	98	87	*O-145(4-110-31)	-1.4
Total	5	680	2635	308	763	102	45	15	269	149	34		.290	.336	.380	120	57	84	.953	-12	92	103	O-678(4-643-31)	1.3
SMOYER, HENRY Henry Neitz "Hennie" (born Henry Neitz Smowery) B 4.24.1890 Fredericksburg, PA D 2.28.1958 DuBois, PA BR/TR 5-6/?# d8.14																								
1912	StL A	6	14	1	3	0	0	0	0	2	0		.214	.313	.214	53	-1	0	1.000	0	125	0	/S-4,3-2	0.0
SMYKAL, FRANK Frank John (born Frank John Smejkal) B 10.13.1889 Chicago, IL D 8.11.1950 Chicago, IL BR/TR 5-7/150# d8.30																								
1916	Pit N	6	10	1	3	0	0	0	2	3	1	1	.300	.500	.300	147	1	1	.842	-1	114	66	/S-5,3	0.1
SMYRES, CLANCY Clarence Melvin B 5.24.1922 Culver City, CA BB/TR 5-11.5/175# d4.18																								
1944	Bro N	5	2	1	0	0	0	0	0	0	0	0	.000	.000	.000	-99	-1	0	—	0			H	-0.1
SMYTH, RED James Daniel B 1.30.1891 Holly Springs, MS D 4.14.1958 Inglewood, CA BL/TR 5-9/152# d8.11																								
1915	Bro N	19	22	3	3	1	0	0	3	4	0	2	.136	.269	.182	37	-1	1-2	1.000	1	126	154	/O-9(6-2-1)	-0.1
1916	Bro N	2	5	0	0	0	0	0	0	0	0	3	.000	.000	.000	-97	-1	0	1.000	-0	60	240	/2-2	-0.2
1917	Bro N	29	24	5	3	0	0	0	1	4	0	6	.125	.250	.125	16	-2	0	.667	-1	47	297	/3-4,O-2(CF)	-0.4
	StL N	38	72	5	15	0	2	0	4	4	2	9	.208	.269	.264	66	-3	3	.889	-3	73	50	O-23(12-4-5)	-0.8
	Year	67	96	10	18	0	2	0	5	8	2	15	.188	.264	.229	52	-5	3	.871	-4	77	48	O-25(12-6-5)/3-4	-1.2
1918	StL N	40	113	19	24	1	2	0	4	16	1	11	.212	.315	.257	78	-2	3	.956	-1	86	99	O-25(2-0-22),2-11	-0.5
Total	4	128	236	32	45	2	4	0	12	28	3	31	.191	.285	.233	60	-9	7-2	.934	-4	87	88	/O-59(20-8-28),2-13,3-4	-2.0
SNEAD, ESIX Esix B 6.7.1976 Fort Myers, FL BB/TR 5-10/175# d9.3																								
2002	NY N	17	13	3	4	0	0	1	3	1-0	0	4	.308	.357	.538	141	1	4-3	1.000	-0	88	0	/O-6(1-5-0)	0.0
SNEED, JOHN Jon Law B 1861 Shelby Co., TN D 1.4.1899 Memphis, TN BL 5-8/160# d5.1																								
1884	Ind AA	27	102	14	22	4	0	1		6	0		.216	.259	.284	79	-2		.817	-1	79	0	O-27(0-21-6)	-0.3
1890	Tol AA	9	30	3	6	0	0	0	4	8	0		.200	.368	.200	66	-1	5	.889	2	332	315	/O-9(RF)	0.1
	Col AA	128	484	114	141	13	15	2	65	63	9		.291	.383	.393	138	26	39	.883	-9	92	121	*O-126(26-3-97)/S-2	1.3
	Year	137	514	117	147	13	15	2	69	71	9		.286	.382	.381	133	25	44	.883	-7	108	134	*O-135(26-3-106)/S-2	1.4
1891	Col AA	99	366	66	94	9	6	1	61	55	8	29	.257	.366	.322	103	5	24	.894	-5	59	114	*O-99(RF)	-0.1
Total	3	263	982	197	263	26	21	4	130	132	17	29	.268	.364	.349	117	28	68	.879	-13	86	113	O-261(26-24-211)/S-2	1.0
SNELL, CHARLIE Charles Anthony (born Charles Anthony Schnell) B 11.29.1893 Hampstead, MD D 4.4.1988 Reading, PA BR/TR 5-11/160# d7.19																								
1912	StL A	8	19	0	4	1	0	0	0	3	1		.211	.348	.263	78	0	0	.941	0	*98*	*116*	/C-8	0.1
SNELL, WALLY Walter Henry "Doc" B 5.19.1889 W.Bridgewater, MA D 7.23.1980 Providence, RI BR/TR 5-10/170# d8.1																								
1913	Bos A	6	12	1	3	0	0	0	0	0	0	1	.250	.250	.250	45	-1	1	.923	-0	*140*	*88*	/C-2	-0.1
SNELLING, CHRIS Christopher Doyle B 12.3.1981 North Miami, FL BL/TL 5-10/165# d5.25																								
2002	Sea A	8	27	2	4	0	0	1	3	2-0	0	4	.148	.207	.259	24	-3	0-0	1.000	0	113	0	/O-8(6-0-2)	-0.3
SNIDER, DUKE Edwin Donald "The Silver Fox" B 9.19.1926 Los Angeles, CA BL/TR 6/190# d4.17 C2 HF1980																								
1947	Bro N	40	83	6	20	3	1	0	5	3	1	24	.241	.276	.301	51	-6	2	.980	-1	108	0	O-25(4-13-7)	-0.7
1948	Bro N	53	160	22	39	6	6	5	21	12	0	27	.244	.297	.450	96	-2	4	.989	1	93	188	O-47(0-41-7)	-0.3
1949	†Bro N	146	552	100	161	28	7	23	92	56	4	92	.292	.361	.493	122	16	12	.984	-4	93	120	*O-145(CF)	0.8
1950	Bro N★	152	620	109	**199**	31	10	31	107	58	0	79	.321	.379	.553	139	33	16	.983	-1	96	121	*O-151(CF)	2.7
1951	Bro N★	150	606	96	168	26	6	29	101	62	0	97	.277	.344	.483	118	14	14-10	.987	-6	95	92	*O-150(CF)	0.3
1952	†Bro N☆	144	534	80	162	25	7	21	92	55	0	77	.303	.368	.494	136	25	7-4	.992	-5	94	95	*O-141(CF)	1.7
1953	†Bro N★	153	590	**132**	198	38	4	42	126	82	3	90	.336	.419	**.627**	165	58	16-7	.987	-11	91	52	*O-151(CF)	3.9
1954	Bro N★	149	584	**120**	199	39	10	40	130	84	4	96	.341	.423	.647	170	**61**	6-6	.981	-10	91	72	*O-148(CF)	4.3
1955	†Bro N★	148	538	**126**	166	34	6	42	**136**	104-19	1	87	.309	.418	.628	169	57	9-7	.989	-3	97	85	*O-146(CF)	4.5
1956	†Bro N★	151	542	112	158	33	2	**43**	101	**99-26**	1	101	.292	**.399**	**.598**	152	**43**	3-3	.984	-4	94	104	*O-150(CF)	3.2
1957	Bro N	139	508	91	139	25	7	40	92	77-12	1	104	.274	.368	.587	139	28	3-4	.990	-12	87	63	*O-136(CF)	0.9
1958	LA N	106	327	45	102	12	3	15	58	32-4	1	49	.312	.371	.505	126	12	2-2	.987	-9	81	66	O-92(6-78-11)	-0.1
1959	†LA N	126	370	59	114	11	2	23	88	58-13	0	71	.308	.400	.535	137	21	1-5	.975	-10	84	33	*O-107(0-53-71)	0.6
1960	LA N	101	235	38	57	13	5	14	36	46-8	1	54	.243	.366	.519	131	11	1-0	.965	-5	86	64	O-75(0-48-35)	0.3
1961	LA N	85	233	35	69	8	3	16	56	29-3	1	43	.296	.375	.562	133	11	1-1	.975	2	104	129	O-66(0-24-51)	0.9
1962	LA N	80	158	28	44	11	3	5	30	36-6	2	32	.278	.418	.481	150	14	2-0	.967	-1	94	115	O-39(15-2-24)	1.1
1963	NY N★	129	354	44	86	8	3	14	45	56-9	1	74	.243	.345	.401	113	7	0-1	.986	-4	90	82	*O-106(34-13-62)	-0.2
1964	SF N	91	167	16	35	7	0	4	17	22-4	0	40	.210	.302	.323	74	-5	0-0	.979	-2	84	95	O-43(19-0-25)	-0.9
Total	18	2143	7161	1259	2116	358	85	407	1333	971-104	21	1237	.295	.380	.540	138	398	99-50	.985	-84	92	87	*O-1918(78-1590-293)	23.0
SNIDER, VAN Van Voorhees B 8.11.1963 Birmingham, AL BL/TR 6-3/185# d9.2																								
1988	Cin N	11	28	4	6	1	0	1	6	0-0	0	13	.214	.207	.357	59	-2	0-1	1.000	0	111	0	/O-8(6-0-3)	-0.2
1989	Cin N	8	7	1	1	0	0	0	0	0-0	0	5	.143	.143	.143	-17	-1	0-0	1.000	0	138	0	/O-6(5-0-2)	-0.1
Total	2	19	35	5	7	1	0	1	6	0-0	0	18	.200	.194	.314	44	-3	0-1	1.000	0	117	0	/O-14(11-0-5)	-0.3
SNIPES, ROXY Wyatt Eure "Rock" B 10.28.1896 Marion, SC D 5.1.1941 Fayetteville, NC BL/TR 6/185# d7.15																								
1923	Chi A	1	1	0	0	0	0	0	0	0	0	0	.000	.000	.000	-99	0	0-0	—	0			H	0.0
SNODGRASS, CHAPPIE Amzie Beal B 3.18.1870 Springfield, OH D 9.9.1951 New York, NY BR/TR 5-10/165# d5.15																								
1901	Bal A	3	10	0	1	0	0	0	1	0	0		.100	.100	.100	-43	-2	0	.500	-1	0	0	/O-2(LF)	-0.3

Year	Tm Lg	G	AB	R	H	2B	3B	HR	RBI	BB-IB	HP	SO	AVG	OBP	SLG	AOPS	ABR	SB-CS	FA	FR	Rng	Thr	G at Pos	BFW
SNODGRASS, FRED Frederick Carlisle "Snow" B 10.19.1887 Ventura, CA D 4.5.1974 Ventura, CA BR/TR 5-11.5/175# d6.4 OF Total (108-LF 666-CF 73-RF)																								
1908	NY N	6	4	2	1	0	0	0	1	0	0		.250	.250	.250	57	0	1	1.000	1	0	192	/C-3	0.0
1909	NY N	28	70	10	21	5	0	1	6	7	3		.300	.387	.414	146	4	7	.921	0	153	181	O-20(15-3-1)/C-2,1	0.4
1910	NY N	123	396	69	127	22	8	2	44	71	13	52	.321	.440	.432	154	33	33	.970	-2	97	85	*O-101(31-70-22)/1-9,C3	2.7
1911	†NY N	151	534	83	157	27	10	1	77	72	15	59	.294	.393	.388	115	14	51	.973	6	91	**153**	*O-149(1-149-0)/13	1.0
1912	†NY N	146	535	91	144	24	9	3	69	70	8	65	.269	.362	.364	96	-1	43	.948	-3	88	140	*O-116(52-66-5),1-27/2	-1.2
1913	†NY N	141	457	65	133	21	6	3	49	53	7	44	.291	.373	.383	115	11	27-18	.968	-2	97	100	*O-133(CF)/1-3,2	-0.1
1914	NY N	113	392	54	103	20	4	0	44	37	6	43	.263	.336	.334	103	2	25	.977	4	109	87	O-96(9-47-40),1-14/23	0.0
1915	NY N	80	252	36	49	9	0	0	20	35	6	33	.194	.307	.230	68	-8	11-12	.935	-0	94	136	O-75(0-68-5)	-1.7
	Bos N	23	79	10	22	2	0	0	9	7	2	9	.278	.352	.304	104	1	0-4	.938	-2	104	46	O-18(CF)/1-5	-0.4
	Year	103	331	46	71	11	0	0	29	42	8	42	.215	.318	.248	76	-7	11-16	.935	-2	96	118	O-93(0-88-5)/1-5	-2.1
1916	Bos N	112	382	33	95	13	5	1	32	34	5	54	.249	.318	.317	100	0	14	.983	9	106	142	*O-110(CF)	0.2
Total	9	923	3101	453	852	143	42	11	351	386	65	359	.275	.367	.359	110	56	212-34	.965	10	98	121	O-818C/1-60,C-6,2-3,3-3	0.9
SNOPEK, CHRIS Christopher Charles B 9.20.1970 Cynthiana, KY BR/TR 6-1/185# d7.31																								
1995	Chi A	22	68	12	22	4	0	1	7	9-0	0	12	.324	.403	.426	121	3	1-0	1.000	-3	50	0	3-17/S-6	0.1
1996	Chi A	46	104	18	27	6	1	6	18	6-0	1	16	.260	.304	.510	106	0	0-1	.939	2	103	152	3-27,S-12/D-3	0.3
1997	Chi A	86	298	27	65	15	0	5	35	18-0	1	51	.218	.263	.319	54	-21	3-2	.915	-15	79	80	3-82/S-4	-3.4
1998	Chi A	53	125	17	26	2	0	1	4	14-0	1	24	.208	.291	.248	44	-10	3-0	.972	1	111	87	S-33,2-12/3-3,10(RF)D	-0.6
	Bos A	8	12	2	2	0	0	0	2	2-0	0	5	.167	.286	.167	21	-1	0-0	.750	-1	120	0	/2-3,3-3,D-2	-0.2
	Year	61	137	19	28	2	0	1	6	16-0	1	29	.204	.290	.241	42	-12	3-0	.972	0	111	87	S-33,2-15/3-6,D-4,10(RF)	-0.8
Total	4	215	607	76	142	27	1	13	66	49-0	3	108	.234	.293	.346	68	-29	7-3	.928	-15	79	81	3-132/S-55,2-15,D-6,O(RF)1	-3.8
SNOW, CHARLIE Charles M. B 8.3.1849 Lowell, MA d10.1																								
1874	Atl NA	1	1	0	1	0	0	0	0	0		0	1.000	1.000	1.000	615	1	0-0	.000	-1			/C	0.0
SNOW, J. T. Jack Thomas B 2.26.1968 Long Beach, CA BB/TL (BL 1999-2003) 6-2/202# d9.20																								
1992	NY A	7	14	1	2	1	0	0	2	5-1	0	5	.143	.368	.214	67	0	0-0	1.000	-0	62	177	/1-6,D	-0.1
1993	Cal A	129	419	60	101	18	2	16	57	55-4	2	88	.241	.328	.408	95	-3	3-0	.995	2	106	98	*1-129	-1.2
1994	Cal A	61	223	22	49	4	0	8	30	19-1	3	48	.220	.289	.345	62	-14	0-1	.996	1	103	105	1-61	-1.8
1995	Cal A	143	544	80	157	22	1	24	102	52-4	3	91	.289	.353	.465	112	9	2-1	.997	-13	61	88	*1-143	-1.7
1996	Cal A	155	575	69	148	20	1	17	67	56-6	5	96	.257	.327	.384	79	-19	1-6	.993	3	106	95	*1-154	-3.0
1997	†SF N	157	531	81	149	36	1	28	104	96-13	1	124	.281	.387	.510	138	33	6-4	.995	1	104	108	*1-156	1.9
1998	SF N	138	435	65	108	29	1	15	79	58-3	0	84	.248	.332	.423	104	3	1-2	**.999**	4	110	105	*1-136	-0.4
1999	SF N	161	570	93	156	25	2	24	98	86-7	5	121	.274	.370	.451	116	15	0-4	.996	11	**127**	99	*1-160	0.9
2000	†SF N	155	536	82	152	33	2	19	96	66-6	11	129	.284	.365	.459	118	16	1-3	.995	-0	98	**114**	*1-153	0.1
2001	SF N	101	285	43	70	12	1	8	34	55-10	4	81	.246	.371	.379	103	4	0-0	.999	-0	98	120	1-92	-0.4
2002	†SF N	143	422	47	104	26	2	6	53	59-5	7	90	.246	.344	.360	95	-3	0-0	.993	1	105	**112**	*1-135	-1.3
2003	†SF N	103	330	48	90	18	3	8	51	55-0	8	55	.273	.387	.418	114	9	1-2	.994	5	122	110	1-97	0.5
Total	12	1453	4884	691	1286	244	16	173	773	662-60	49	1012	.263	.353	.426	105	50	15-23	.995	15	103	104	*1-1422/D	-6.5
SNYDER, BERNIE Bernard Austin B 8.25.1913 Philadelphia, PA D 4.15.1999 Havertown, PA BR/TR 6/165# d9.15																								
1935	Phi A	10	32	5	11	1	0	0	3	1	0	2	.344	.364	.375	92	0	0-0	.880	-3	66	33	/2-5,S-4	-0.3
SNYDER, CHARLES Charles B Camden, NJ D 3.3.1901 Philadelphia, PA BR/TR d9.19																								
1890	Phi AA	9	33	5	9	1	0	0	4	2	0		.273	.314	.303	82	-1	0	.583	-4	95	0	/O-5(1-0-4),C-5	-0.4
SNYDER, POP Charles N. B 10.6.1854 Washington, DC D 10.29.1924 Washington, DC BR/TR 5-11.5/184# d6.16 M4 U7																								
1873	Was NA	28	107	16	21	2	0	0	3	3		4	.196	.218	.215	30	-9	0-1	.819	-2			C-28/O-3(CF)	-0.8
1874	Bal NA	39	151	24	33	4	0	1	17	1		2	.219	.224	.265	56	-7	0-0	.789	-2			C-39	-0.7
1875	Phi NA	66	263	38	64	8	2	1	25	4		4	.243	.255	.300	89	-3	3-8	.825	4			*C-66/1	-0.1
1876	Lou N	56	224	21	44	4	1	1	9	2		7	.196	.204	.237	39	-16		.833	12			*C-55/O-4(0-3-1)	-0.2
1877	Lou N	**61**	248	23	64	7	2	2	28	3		14	.258	.267	.327	73	-9		**.910**	15			*C-61/O(RF)S	0.6
1878	Bos N	**60**	226	21	48	5	0	0	14	1		19	.212	.216	.235	44	-14		**.912**	7			*C-58/O-2(RF)	-0.5
1879	Bos N	81	329	42	78	16	3	2	35	5		31	.237	.249	.322	85	-5		**.925**	**25**			*C-80/O-2(RF)	2.0
1881	Bos N	62	219	14	50	8	0	0	16	3		23	.228	.239	.265	61	-9		.897	3			*C-60/O(RF)S2	-0.5
1882	Cin AA	72	309	49	90	12	2	1	50	9			.291	.311	.353	117	5		.916	18			*C-70/1-2,O(RF)M	2.6
1883	Cin AA	58	250	38	64	14	6	0	34	8			.256	.279	.360	99	-1		.919	13			C-57/S-2,M	1.5
1884	Cin AA	67	268	32	69	9	9	0	39	7	0		.257	.276	.358	101	-1		.922	26			C-65/1-2,O(RF)M	2.7
1885	Cin AA	39	152	13	36	4	3	1	19	6	1		.237	.270	.322	85	-3		.880	2			C-38/1	0.2
1886	Cin AA	60	220	33	41	8	3	0	28	13	3		.186	.242	.250	52	-13	11	.874	-4			C-41,1-19/O(CF)	-1.3
1887	Cle AA	74	282	33	72	12	6	0	27	9	1		.255	.281	.340	75	-11	5	.905	16			C-63,1-13	0.8
1888	Cle AA	64	237	22	51	7	3	0	14	6	1		.215	.238	.270	64	-10	9	.901	10			C-58/1-4,O-3(RF)	0.4
1889	Cle N	22	83	5	16	3	0	0	12	2	1	12	.193	.221	.229	26	-9	4	.907	3			C-22	-0.3
1890	Cle P	13	48	5	9	1	0	0	12	1	1	9	.188	.220	.208	16	-6	1	.958	-1	71	108	C-13	-0.4
1891	Was AA	8	27	4	5	0	1	0	2	0	2	3	.185	.241	.259	45	-2	0	1.000	0	73	0	/1-4,C-3,O(RF)M	-0.2
Total	3 NA	133	521	78	118	14	2	2	45	8	0	10	.226	.238	.273	66	-19	3-9	.000	-0			C-133/O-3(CF),1	-1.6
Total	15	797	3122	355	737	110	39	7	339	75	10	118	.236	.256	.303	73	-104	30-0	.904	144	2	2	C-744/1-45,O-17(0-4-13),S-4,2	7.4
SNYDER, EARL Earl Clifford B 5.6.1976 New Britain, CT BR/TR 6/207# d4.28																								
2002	Cle A	18	55	5	11	2	0	1	4	6-0	0	21	.200	.279	.291	53	-4	0-0	.981	0	119	31	1-12/3-2,D	-0.4
SNYDER, REDLEG Emanuel Sebastian (born Emanuel Sebastian Schneider) B 12.12.1854 Camden, NJ D 11.24.1932 Camden, NJ BR/TR 5-10/175# d4.25																								
1876	Cin N	55	205	10	31	3	1	0	12	1		19	.151	.155	.176	12	-17		.825	4	62	39	*O-55(54-0-1)	-1.5
1884	Wil U	**17**	52	4	10	0	0	0		1			.192	.208	.192	21	-7		.976	1	111	136	1-16/O(LF)	-0.6
Total	2	72	257	14	41	3	1	0	12	2		19	.160	.166	.179	14	-24		.825	5	62	39	/O-56(55-0-1),1-16	-2.1
SNYDER, COONEY Frank C. B Toronto, ON, CAN D 3.9.1917 Toronto, ON, CAN 6-3/180# d5.19																								
1898	Lou N	17	61	4	10	0	0	0	6	3	1		.164	.215	.164	9	-7	0	.935	-5	83	100	C-17	-1.0
SNYDER, FRANK Frank Elton "Pancho" B 5.27.1893 San Antonio, TX D 1.5.1962 San Antonio, TX BR/TR 6-2/185# d8.25 Mil 1918 C9																								
1912	StL N	11	18	2	2	0	0	0	0	2	0	7	.111	.200	.111	-14	-3		.919	-1	80	122	C-11	-0.3
1913	StL N	7	21	1	4	0	1	0	2	0	0	4	.190	.190	.286	35	-2	0	.956	0	85	126	/C-7	-0.1
1914	StL N	100	326	19	75	15	4	1	25	13	1	28	.230	.262	.310	71	-13	1	**.979**	4	104	96	C-98	-0.1
1915	StL N	144	473	41	141	22	7	2	55	39	1	49	.298	.353	.387	124	13	3-6	.983	11	111	109	*C-142	3.8
1916	StL N	132	406	23	105	12	4	0	39	18	0	31	.259	.290	.308	84	-9	7	.973	7	83	100	C-72,1-46/S	0.4
1917	StL N	115	313	18	74	9	2	1	33	27	2	43	.236	.301	.288	83	-6	4	.975	3	**121**	**117**	C-94/2	0.5
1918	StL N	39	112	5	28	7	1	0	10	6	0	13	.250	.288	.330	92	-1	4	.959	-1	86	112	C-27/1-3	0.1
1919	StL N	50	154	7	28	4	2	0	14	5	1	13	.182	.213	.234	36	-12	2	.983	4	103	143	C-48/1	-0.5
	NY N	32	92	7	21	6	0	0	11	8	1	9	.228	.297	.293	79	-2	1	.983	-3	93	93	C-31	-0.3
	Year	82	246	14	49	10	2	0	25	13	2	22	.199	.245	.256	53	-14	3	**.983**	1	99	**123**	C-79/1	-0.8
1920	NY N	87	264	26	66	13	4	3	27	17	0	18	.250	.295	.364	89	-4	2-2	.978	4	**128**	90	C-84	0.7
1921	†NY N	108	309	36	99	13	2	8	45	27	4	24	.320	.382	.453	120	10	3-4	.985	4	121	112	*C-101	1.9
1922	†NY N	104	318	34	109	21	5	5	51	23	0	25	.343	.387	.487	123	11	1-5	.980	2	**129**	74	C-97	1.6
1923	†NY N	120	402	37	103	13	6	5	63	24	0	29	.256	.298	.356	73	-17	5-3	**.990**	7	**164**	85	*C-112	-0.3
1924	†NY N	118	354	37	107	18	3	5	53	30	0	43	.302	.357	.412	109	5	3-0	.987	-11	95	84	*C-110	0.1
1925	NY N	107	325	21	78	9	1	11	51	20	1	49	.240	.286	.375	70	-16	0-0	**.985**	2	93	108	C-96	-0.8
1926	NY N	55	148	10	32	3	2	5	16	13	0	13	.216	.280	.365	73	-6	0	.981	-1	85	105	C-55	-0.4
1927	StL N	63	194	7	50	5	0	1	30	9	0	18	.258	.291	.299	56	-12	0	.981	-0	90	108	C-62	-0.9
Total	16	1392	4229	331	1122	170	44	47	525	281	11	416	.265	.313	.360	90	-64	37-20	.981	32	111	101	*C-1247/1-50,2S	5.4
SNYDER, JERRY Gerald George B 7.21.1929 Jenks, OK BR/TR 6/170# d5.8																								
1952	Was A	36	57	5	9	2	0	0	2	5	0	8	.158	.226	.193	18	-6	1-0	.965	2	118	117	2-19/S-4	-0.4
1953	Was A	29	62	10	21	4	0	0	4	5	0	8	.339	.388	.403	117	2	1-1	.988	3	117	109	S-17/2-4	0.5
1954	Was A	64	154	17	36	3	1	0	17	15	0	18	.234	.298	.266	60	-9	3-0	.978	3	107	106	S-48/2-3	-0.1
1955	Was A	46	107	7	24	5	0	0	5	6-0	0	6	.224	.265	.271	47	-8	1-1	.977	1	108	122	2-22,S-20	-0.5
1956	Was A	43	148	14	40	3	1	2	14	10-0	1	9	.270	.321	.345	76	-6	1-0	.968	-1	106	93	S-35/2-7	-0.3

Year	Tm Lg	G	AB	R	H	2B	3B	HR	RBI	BB-IB	HP	SO	AVG	OBP	SLG	AOPS	ABR	SB-CS	FA	FR	Rng	Thr	G at Pos	BFW
1957	Was A	42	93	6	14	1	0	1	4	4-0	0	9	.151	.186	.194	4	-13	0-1	.966	1	112	96	S-15,2-13/3	-1.1
1958	Was A	6	9	1	1	0	0	0	1	1-0	0	1	.111	.200	.111	-12	-1	0-0	1.000	-1	37	62	/2-2,S	-0.2
Total	7	266	630	60	145	18	2	3	47	46-0	1	59	.230	.283	.279	54	-41	7-3	.971	8	106	96	S-140/2-70,3	-2.1
SNYDER, JIM James C. A. B 9.15.1847 Brooklyn, NY D 12.1.1922 Rockaway Beach, NY 5-7/130# d5.7																								
1872	Eck NA	25	103	16	30	2	3	0	11	0		1	.291	.291	.369	120	4	0-2	.755	3	123	62	S-24/CO(RF)	0.4
SNYDER, CORY James Cory B 11.11.1962 Inglewood, CA BR/TR 6-3/185# d6.13 OF Total (99-LF 17-CF 793-RF)																								
1986	Cle A	103	416	58	113	21	1	24	69	16-0	0	123	.272	.299	.500	115	6	2-3	.987	-5	106	82	O-74(6-0-70),S-34,3-11/D	-0.1
1987	Cle A	157	577	74	136	24	2	33	82	31-4	1	166	.236	.273	.456	89	-12	5-1	.971	3	105	165	*O-139(15-0-134),S-18	-1.4
1988	Cle A	142	511	71	139	24	3	26	75	42-7	1	101	.272	.326	.483	121	13	5-1	.985	10	105	**187**	*O-141(1-3-139)/D	1.9
1989	Cle A	132	489	49	105	17	0	18	59	23-1	2	134	.215	.251	.360	70	-22	6-5	**.997**	16	107	**184**	*O-125(RF)/S-7,D-2	-1.1
1990	Cle A	123	438	46	102	27	3	14	55	21-3	2	118	.233	.268	.404	87	-10	1-4	.975	-2	96	133	*O-120(RF)/S-5	-1.7
1991	Chi A	50	117	10	22	4	0	3	11	6-1	0	41	.188	.228	.299	46	-9	0-0	.981	-1	104	65	O-29(13-0-17),1-18	-1.2
	Tor A	21	49	4	7	0	1	0	6	3-0	0	19	.143	.189	.184	4	-7	0-0	1.000	-0	62	145	O-14(RF)/1-4,3-3,D-3	-0.8
	Year	71	166	14	29	4	1	3	17	9-1	0	60	.175	.216	.265	33	-16	0-0	.985	-1	92	88	O-43(13-0-31),1-22/3-3,D-3	-2.0
1992	SF N	124	390	48	105	22	2	14	57	23-2	2	96	.269	.311	.444	119	8	4-4	.992	-0	93	181	O-70(22-13-48),1-27,3-14/2-4,S-3	0.4
1993	LA N	143	516	61	137	33	1	11	56	47-3	4	147	.266	.331	.397	100	0	4-1	.979	-11	81	170	*O-115(2-1-113),3-23,1-12/S-2	-1.6
1994	LA N	73	153	18	36	6	0	6	18	14-4	1	47	.235	.300	.392	85	-4	1-0	.967	-2	94	50	O-50(40-0-13)/1-9,3-6,S-4,2-3	-0.6
Total	9	1068	3656	439	902	178	13	149	488	226-25	13	992	.247	.291	.425	95	-37	28-19	.983	7	99	155	O-877R/S-73,1-70,3-57,2-7,D-7	-6.2
SNYDER, JIM James Robert B 8.15.1932 Dearborn, MI BR/TR 6-1/185# d9.15 M1 C4																								
1961	Min A	3	5	0	0	0	0	0	0	0-0	0	1	.000	.000	.000	-95	-1	0-0	1.000	0	85	105	/2-3	-0.1
1962	Min A	12	10	1	1	0	0	0	1	0-0	0	0	.100	.100	.100	-44	-2	0-1	.941	-3	59	93	/2-5,1	-0.5
1964	Min A	26	71	3	11	2	0	1	9	4-0	1	11	.155	.208	.225	21	-8	0-0	.990	-2	89	115	2-25	-0.8
Total	3	41	86	4	12	2	0	1	10	4-0	1	12	.140	.185	.198	6	-11	0-1	.984	-5	83	110	/2-33,1	-1.4
SNYDER, JACK John William B 10.6.1886 Lincoln, PA D 12.13.1981 Brownsville, PA BR/TR 5-9/168# d6.13																								
1914	Buf F	1	0	0	0	0	0	0	0	1	0	0	—	1.000	—	183	0	0	—	-0	*0*	*0*	/C	0.0
1917	Bro N	7	11	1	3	0	0	0	1	0	0	2	.273	.273	.273	66	0	0	1.000	0	*114*	*113*	/C-5	0.0
Total	2	8	11	1	3	0	0	0	1	1	0	2	.273	.333	.273	84	0	0	1.000	0	*109*	*108*	/C-6	0.0
SNYDER, JOSH Joshua M. B 3.1844 Brooklyn, NY D 4.21.1881 Brooklyn, NY d5.18																								
1872	Eck NA	9	37	4	6	2	0	0	1	1		3	.162	.184	.216	27	-2	0-0	.788	2	291	0	/O-9(LF)	0.0
SNYDER, RUSS Russell Henry B 6.22.1934 Oak, NE BL/TR 6-1/190# d4.18																								
1959	KC A	73	243	41	76	13	2	3	21	19-0	2	29	.313	.367	.420	113	5	6-2	.986	5	100	241	O-64(27-30-12)	0.7
1960	KC A	125	304	45	79	10	5	4	26	20-1	1	28	.260	.306	.365	81	-9	7-3	.986	-1	96	88	O-91(21-16-62)	-1.3
1961	Bal A	115	312	46	91	13	5	1	13	20-0	0	32	.292	.333	.375	92	-4	5-3	.966	-5	94	49	*O-108(75-28-22)	-1.3
1962	Bal A	139	416	47	127	19	4	9	40	17-0	2	46	.305	.335	.435	113	5	7-4	.974	2	102	141	*O-121(43-41-45)	0.3
1963	Bal A	148	429	51	110	21	2	7	36	40-1	2	48	.256	.321	.364	95	-2	18-5	.988	0	106	71	*O-130(32-74-57)	-0.5
1964	Bal A	56	93	11	27	3	0	1	7	11-1	0	22	.290	.362	.355	102	1	0-2	.971	-1	95	0	O-40(31-8-3)	-0.2
1965	Bal A	132	345	49	93	11	2	1	29	27-1	1	38	.270	.323	.322	83	-8	3-4	1.000	3	109	78	*O-106(36-36-52)	-1.1
1966	†Bal A	117	373	66	114	21	5	3	41	38-1	0	37	.306	.368	.413	127	14	2-1	.986	-0	100	98	*O-104(59-86-4)	1.0
1967	Bal A	108	275	40	65	8	2	4	23	32-0	1	48	.236	.314	.324	91	-3	5-2	.985	-0	103	73	O-69(24-25-27)	-0.7
1968	Chi A	38	82	2	11	2	0	1	5	4-1	0	16	.134	.172	.195	12	-9	0-0	1.000	-3	71	0	O-22(9-1-16)	-1.5
	Cle A	68	217	30	61	8	2	2	23	25-0	0	21	.281	.354	.364	120	6	1-1	.991	5	121	142	O-54(5-11-43)/1	0.8
	Year	106	299	32	72	10	2	3	28	29-1	0	37	.241	.306	.318	90	-3	1-1	.992	2	108	106	O-76(14-12-59)/1	-0.7
1969	Cle A	122	266	26	66	10	0	2	24	25-3	0	33	.248	.312	.308	72	-10	3-2	.961	2	120	46	O-84(37-28-21)	-1.1
1970	Mil A	124	276	34	64	11	0	4	31	16-1	0	40	.232	.270	.315	62	-15	1-3	.966	-3	99	23	*O-106(43-40-26)	-2.3
Total	12	1365	3631	488	984	150	29	42	319	294-10	9	438	.271	.325	.363	94	-29	58-32	.981	4	103	89	*O-1099(442-424-390)/1	-7.2
SOCKALEXIS, CHIEF Louis Francis B 10.24.1871 Old Town, ME D 12.24.1913 Burlington, ME BL/TR 5-11/185# d4.22																								
1897	Cle N	66	278	43	94	9	8	3	42	18	3		.338	.385	.460	116	5	16	.888	-0	103	173	O-66(0-1-66)	0.1
1898	Cle N	21	67	11	15	2	0	0	10	1	1		.224	.246	.254	44	-5	0	.964	3	299	693	O-16(4-4-8)	-0.3
1899	Cle N	7	22	0	6	1	0	0	3	1	0		.273	.304	.318	76	-1	0	.818	0	228	323	/O-5(RF)	-0.1
Total	3	94	367	54	115	12	8	3	55	20	4		.313	.355	.414	103	-1	16	.896	3	143	267	/O-87(4-5-79)	-0.3
SODD, BILL William B 9.18.1914 Ft.Worth, TX D 5.14.1998 Fort Worth, TX BR/TR 6-2/210# d9.27																								
1937	Cle A	1	1	0	0	0	0	0	0	0	0	1	.000	.000	.000	-99	0	0-0	—	0			H	0.0
SODERHOLM, ERIC Eric Thane B 9.24.1948 Cortland, NY BR/TR 5-11/187# d9.3																								
1971	Min A	21	64	9	10	4	0	1	4	10-1	3	17	.156	.299	.266	59	-3	0-1	.942	2	112	47	3-20	-0.2
1972	Min A	93	287	28	54	10	0	13	39	19-2	3	48	.188	.245	.359	75	-10	3-3	.942	1	104	116	3-79	-1.1
1973	Min A	35	111	22	33	7	2	1	9	21-0	1	16	.297	.414	.423	131	6	1-2	.921	2	110	86	3-33/S	0.7
1974	Min A	141	464	63	128	18	3	10	51	48-1	5	68	.276	.349	.392	110	7	7-3	.956	4	101	68	*3-130/S	1.1
1975	Min A	117	419	62	120	17	2	11	58	53-1	0	66	.286	.365	.415	119	11	3-5	.969	15	114	61	*3-113/D-3	2.5
1977	Chi A	130	460	77	129	20	3	25	67	47-5	4	47	.280	.350	.500	129	18	2-4	**.978**	-1	98	73	*3-126/D-3	1.4
1978	Chi A	143	457	57	118	17	1	20	67	39-2	4	44	.258	.318	.431	109	4	2-2	.964	5	96	73	*3-128,D-11/2	0.7
1979	Chi A	56	210	31	53	8	2	6	34	19-1	0	19	.252	.313	.395	90	-3	0-1	.986	13	118	109	3-56	0.8
	Tex A	63	147	15	40	6	0	4	19	12-0	1	9	.272	.325	.395	96	-1	0-0	.944	0	99	116	3-37,D-14/1-2	-0.2
	Year	119	357	46	93	14	2	10	53	31-1	1	28	.261	.318	.395	93	-4	0-1	.975	13	112	111	3-93,D-14/1-2	0.6
1980	†NY A	95	275	38	79	13	1	11	35	27-2	1	25	.287	.353	.462	123	9	0-0	.952	-1	100	71	D-51,3-37	0.6
Total	9	894	2894	402	764	120	14	102	383	295-15	22	359	.264	.335	.421	110	38	18-21	.962	39	104	79	3-759/D-82,1-2,S-2,2	6.3
SOFIELD, RICK Richard Michael B 12.16.1956 Cheyenne, WY BL/TR 6-1/195# d4.6																								
1979	Min A	35	93	8	28	5	0	0	12	12-0	0	27	.301	.381	.355	96	0	2-3	.954	-1	99	48	O-35(7-6-22)	-0.3
1980	Min A	131	417	52	103	18	4	9	49	24-2	2	92	.247	.287	.374	75	-15	4-5	.979	-2	100	84	*O-126(74-49-9)/D-2	-2.1
1981	Min A	41	102	9	18	2	0	0	5	8-0	0	22	.176	.234	.196	24	-10	3-2	.983	1	85	242	O-34(33-0-1)	-1.1
Total	3	207	612	69	149	25	4	9	66	44-2	2	141	.243	.293	.342	71	-25	9-10	.975	-2	97	105	O-195(114-55-32)/D-2	-3.5
SOJO, LUIS Luis Beltran (Sojo) B 1.3.1965 Caracas, Venezuela BR/TR 5-11/174# d7.14 OF Total (LF)																								
1990	Tor A	33	80	14	18	3	0	1	9	5-0	0	5	.225	.271	.300	58	-5	1-1	.969	-4	62	57	2-15/S-5,O-5(LF),3-4,D-3	-0.9
1991	Cal A	113	364	38	94	14	1	3	20	14-0	5	26	.258	.295	.327	72	-15	4-2	.981	**27**	115	118	*2-107/S-2,3O(LF)D	1.5
1992	Cal A	106	368	37	100	12	3	7	43	14-0	1	24	.272	.299	.378	88	-8	7-11	.985	14	112	121	2-96/3-9,S-5	0.7
1993	Tor A	19	47	5	8	2	0	0	6	4-0	0	2	.170	.231	.213	21	-5	0-0	1.000	-0	81	67	/2-8,S-8,3-3	-0.5
1994	Sea A	63	213	32	59	9	2	6	22	8-0	2	25	.277	.308	.423	85	-6	2-1	.973	18	117	97	2-40,S-24/3D	1.4
1995	†Sea A	102	339	50	98	18	2	7	39	23-0	1	19	.289	.335	.416	93	-4	4-2	.983	-14	82	70	S-80,2-19/O-6(LF)	-1.1
1996	Sea A	77	247	20	52	8	1	1	16	10-0	1	13	.211	.244	.263	28	-28	2-2	.940	5	113	147	3-33,2-27,S-19	-1.9
	†NY A	18	40	3	11	2	0	0	5	1-0	0	4	.275	.286	.325	56	-3	0-0	1.000	3	127	147	2-14/S-4,3	0.0
	Year	95	287	23	63	10	1	1	21	11-0	1	17	.220	.250	.272	32	-31	2-2	.986	7	104	111	2-41,3-34,S-23	-1.9
1997	NY A	77	215	27	66	6	1	2	25	16-0	1	14	.307	.355	.372	92	-3	3-1	.982	4	101	104	2-72/S-4,3-1,2	0.5
1998	†NY A	54	147	16	34	3	1	0	14	4-0	0	15	.231	.252	.265	36	-14	1-0	.973	0	91	132	S-20,1-19/2-8,3-6,D-2	-1.3
1999	†NY A	49	127	20	32	6	0	2	16	4-0	0	17	.252	.275	.346	58	-9	1-0	.974	1	71	108	3-20,2-16/S-6,1-4,D-2	-0.6
2000	Pit N	61	176	14	50	11	0	5	20	11-3	1	16	.284	.328	.432	91	-3	1-0	.960	4	120	58	3-50/2	0.2
	†NY A	34	125	19	36	7	1	2	17	6-0	0	6	.288	.321	.408	83	-3	1-0	.989	-3	100	51	2-25,3-10/1-7,S-2	-0.4
2001	NY A	39	79	5	13	2	0	0	9	4-0	1	12	.165	.214	.190	8	-11	1-0	.933	-0	100	119	3-17/1-8,2-7,S-5,D	-1.0
2003	NY A	3	4	0	0	0	0	0	0	0-0	0	0	.000	.000	.000	-99	-1	0-0	—	-0	0	0	/12D	-0.1
Total	13	848	2571	300	671	103	12	36	261	124-3	13	198	.261	.297	.352	71	-118	28-20	.982	53	108	106	2-456,S-184,3-158/1-41,D-12,O	-3.5
SOLAITA, TONY Tolia B 1.15.1947 Nuuuli, American Samoa D 2.10.1990 Tafuna, American Samoa BL/TL 6/215# d9.16																								
1968	NY A	1	1	0	0	0	0	0	0	0-0	0	1	.000	.000	.000	-99	0	0-0	1.000	-0	0	407	/1	0.0
1974	KC A	96	239	31	64	12	0	7	30	35-5	1	70	.268	.361	.406	115	6	0-3	.991	1	113	72	1-65,D-14/O(RF)	0.1
1975	KC A	93	231	35	60	11	0	16	44	39-1	2	79	.260	.369	.515	145	14	0-1	.994	3	130	99	D-37,1-35	1.4
1976	KC A	31	68	4	16	4	0	0	9	6-0	0	17	.235	.286	.294	73	-2	0-0	.974	0	126	38	D-14/1-5	-0.3
	Cal A	63	215	25	58	9	0	9	33	34-3	0	44	.270	.367	.437	145	13	1-1	.998	8	147	76	1-54/D-7	1.8
	Year	94	283	29	74	13	0	9	42	40-3	0	61	.261	.348	.403	126	10	1-1	.996	8	146	74	1-59,D-21	1.5

Year	Tm Lg	G	AB	R	H	2B	3B	HR	RBI	BB-IB	HP	SO	AVG	OBP	SLG	AOPS	ABR	SB-CS	FA	FR	Rng	Thr	G at Pos	BFW
1977	Cal A	116	324	40	78	15	0	14	53	56-6	0	77	.241	.349	.417	113	8	1-3	.990	3	108	77	1-91/D-6	0.5
1978	Cal A	60	94	10	21	3	0	1	14	16-3	0	25	.223	.336	.287	80	-2	0-0	1.000	1	127	106	D-18,1-11	-0.2
1979	Mon N	29	42	5	12	4	0	1	7	11-0	0	16	.286	.434	.452	143	3	0-0	.989	0	108	100	1-13	0.3
	Tor A	36	102	14	27	8	1	2	13	17-0	0	16	.265	.364	.422	112	2	0-0	1.000	0	133	195	D-26/1-6	0.2
Total	7	525	1316	164	336	66	1	50	203	214-18	3	345	.255	.357	.421	120	42	2-8	.993	16	122	82	1-281,D-122/O(RF)	3.8
SOLOMON, MOSE Mose Hirsch "The Rabbi Of Swat" B 12.8.1900 New York, NY D 6.25.1966 Miami, FL BL/TL 5-9.5/180# d9.30																								
1923	NY N	2	8	0	3	1	0	0	1	0	0	1	.375	.375	.500	131	0	0-0	.833	-1	70	0	/O-2(RF)	-0.1
SOLTERS, MOOSE Julius Joseph (born Julius Joseph Soltesz) B 3.22.1906 Pittsburgh, PA D 9.28.1975 Pittsburgh, PA BR/TR 6/190# d4.17																								
1934	Bos A	101	365	61	109	25	4	7	58	18	1	50	.299	.333	.447	93	-5	9-4	.933	-1	94	155	O-89(6-57-26)	-0.9
1935	Bos A	24	79	15	19	6	1	0	8	2	1	7	.241	.268	.342	53	-6	1-1	.966	2	120	108	O-21(10-0-11)	-0.5
	StL A	127	552	79	182	39	6	18	104	34	0	35	.330	.369	.520	122	16	10-1	.989	12	107	158	*O-127(116-12-0)	2.0
	Year	151	631	94	201	45	7	18	112	36	1	42	.319	.356	.498	113	10	11-2	.985	13	109	151	*O-148(126-12-11)	1.5
1936	StL A	152	628	100	183	45	7	17	134	41	1	76	.291	.336	.467	93	-10	3-0	.956	13	**118**	125	*O-147(145-6-0)	-0.4
1937	Cle A	152	589	90	190	42	11	20	109	42	4	56	.323	.372	.533	125	20	6-9	.953	2	93	171	*O-149(LF)	1.0
1938	Cle A	67	199	30	40	6	3	2	22	13	0	28	.201	.250	.291	36	-21	4-1	.969	2	104	126	O-46(40-0-6)	-2.0
1939	Cle A	41	102	19	28	7	2	2	19	9	0	15	.275	.333	.441	100	0	2-1	.915	-2	93	67	O-25(17-0-8)	-0.3
	StL A	40	131	14	27	6	1	0	14	10	0	20	.206	.262	.267	35	-13	1-0	.935	-1	101	89	O-30(22-1-7)	-1.4
	Year	81	233	33	55	13	3	2	33	19	0	35	.236	.294	.343	63	-14	3-1	.927	-2	98	80	O-55(39-1-15)	-1.7
1940	Chi A	116	428	65	132	28	3	12	80	27	1	54	.308	.351	.472	110	5	3-3	.971	6	**115**	77	*O-107(LF)	0.5
1941	Chi A	76	251	24	65	9	4	4	43	18	1	31	.259	.311	.375	82	-8	3-2	.966	-0	95	123	O-63(62-0-1)	-1.2
1943	Chi A	42	97	6	15	0	0	1	8	7	0	5	.155	.212	.186	17	-11	0-1	.941	-1	81	152	O-21(13-0-8)	-1.4
Total	9	938	3421	503	990	213	42	83	599	221	9	377	.289	.334	.449	96	-33	42-23	.960	31	104	133	O-825(687-76-67)	-4.6
SOMERLOTT, JOCK John Wesley B 10.26.1882 Flint, IN D 4.21.1965 Butler, IN BR/TR 6/160# d9.19																								
1910	Was A	16	63	6	14	0	0	0	2	3	0		.222	.258	.222	53	-4	2	.994	0	91	59	1-16	-0.4
1911	Was A	13	40	2	7	0	0	0	2	0	1		.175	.195	.175	4	-5	2	.992	2	140	135	1-12	-0.4
Total	2	29	103	8	21	0	0	0	4	3	1		.204	.234	.204	32	-9	4	.993	2	111	91	/1-28	-0.8
SOMERVILLE, ED Edward G. B 3.1.1853 Philadelphia, PA D 10.1.1877 London, ON, CAN BR/TR 5-7/158# d4.30																								
1875	Cen NA	**14**	57	6	13	3	0	0	6	1		3	.228	.241	.281	88	0	1-0	.771	-6	84	34	2-14/S	-0.6
	NH NA	33	136	14	29	5	0	0	7	1		3	.213	.219	.250	72	-2	1-2	.802	13	139	123	2-29/3-2,1S	0.7
	Year	47	193	20	42	8	0	0	13	2		6	.218	.226	.259	77	-2	2-2	.794	7	121	94	2-43/S-2,3-2,1	0.1
1876	Lou N	64	256	29	48	5	1	0	14	1		6	.188	.191	.215	30	-20		.870	**28**	**131**	115	*2-64	0.9
SOMMER, JOE Joseph John B 11.20.1858 Covington, KY D 1.16.1938 Cincinnati, OH BR/TR d7.8 ▲ OF Total (567-LF 15-CF 132-RF)																								
1880	Cin N	24	88	10	16	1	0	0	6	0		2	.182	.182	.193	28	-7		.913	1	88	110	O-22(14-8-0)/S3C	-0.7
1882	Cin AA	**80**	354	82	102	12	6	1	29	24			.288	.333	.364	128	10		**.925**	3	47	121	*O-80(LF)	1.0
1883	Cin AA	97	413	79	115	5	7	3	52	20			.278	.312	.346	106	1		.854	-3	58	53	*O-94(82-0-12)/3-3,P	-0.3
1884	Bal AA	107	479	96	129	11	10	4		8	8		.269	.293	.359	107	2		.841	3	94	95	*3-97/O-9(0-2-7),2	0.6
1885	Bal AA	**110**	471	84	118	23	6	1	44	24	3		.251	.291	.331	98	0		.920	12	77	54	*O-107(105-2-0)/S-2,3-2,P-2,1	0.8
1886	Bal AA	**139**	560	79	117	18	4	1	52	24	3		.209	.245	.261	60	-26	31	.900	7	73	131	*O-95(LF),2-32,3-11/S-3,P	-1.8
1887	Bal AA	131	463	88	123	11	5	0	65	63	4		.266	.358	.311	93	0	29	.902	-3	81	102	*O-110(LF),2-13,3-10/S-2,P	-0.4
1888	Bal AA	79	297	31	65	10	0	0	35	18	1		.219	.266	.253	68	-10	13	.871	-2	106	65	O-44(30-0-14),S-34/2-2,1	-1.1
1889	Bal AA	106	386	51	85	13	2	1	36	42	1	49	.220	.298	.272	62	-19	18	.929	9	119	157	*O-105(4-3-99)/S	-0.9
1890	Cle N	9	35	4	8	1	0	0	0	2	0	2	.229	.270	.257	55	-2	0	.789	-2	0	0	/O-9(LF),P	-0.3
	Bal AA	**38**	129	13	33	4	2	0	23	13	0		.256	.324	.318	85	-3	10	.892	2	80	221	O-38(LF)	-0.2
Total	10	920	3675	617	911	109	42	11	342	238	20	53	.248	.297	.309	88	-54	101	.901	27	83	108	O-713L,3-124/2-48,S-43,P-6,1-2,C	-3.3
SOMMERS, PETE Joseph Andrews B 10.26.1866 Cleveland, OH D 7.22.1908 Cleveland, OH BR/TR 5-11.5/181# d4.27																								
1887	NY AA	33	116	9	21	3	0	1	12	7	1		.181	.234	.233	32	-11	6	.830	-7			C-31/O(RF)1	-1.3
1888	Bos N	4	13	1	3	1	0	0	0	0	0	3	.231	.231	.308	69	0	0	.880	-1			/C-4	-0.1
1889	Chi N	12	45	5	10	5	0	0	8	2	1	8	.222	.271	.333	65	-2	0	.836	-4			C-11/O(RF)	-0.5
	Ind N	23	84	12	21	2	2	2	14	1	1	16	.250	.267	.393	82	-3	2	.905	-4			C-21/O-2(CF)	-0.4
	Year	35	129	17	31	7	2	2	22	3	2	24	.240	.269	.372	76	-5	2	.882	-8	*0*	*0*	C-32/O-3(0-2-1)	-0.9
1890	NY N	17	47	4	5	1	1	0	1	4	1	13	.106	.192	.170	6	-6	0	.837	-1	*98*	*148*	C-11/1-5,O-2(RF)	-0.5
	Cle N	9	34	4	7	1	1	0	1	2	0	3	.206	.250	.294	60	-2	0	.906	1	*119*	*117*	/C-8,O(CF)	0.0
	Year	26	81	8	12	2	2	0	2	6	1	16	.148	.216	.222	28	-8	0	.865	1	*108*	*133*	C-19/1-5,O-3(0-1-2)	-0.5
Total	4	98	339	35	67	13	4	3	36	16	4	43	.198	.242	.286	50	-24	8	.860	-15	*23*	*29*	/C-86,O-7(0-3-4),1-6	-2.8
SOMMERS, BILL William Dunn B 2.17.1923 Brooklyn, NY D 9.22.2000 Palm City, FL BR/TR 6/180# d4.25																								
1950	StL A	65	137	24	35	5	1	0	14	25	0	14	.255	.370	.307	72	-5	0-1	.917	-7	95	76	3-37,2-21	-1.1
SORENSEN, ZACH Zach Hart B 1.3.1977 Salt Lake City, UT BB/TR 6/190# d6.3																								
2003	Cle A	36	37	2	5	1	0	1	2	7-0	0	13	.135	.273	.243	39	-3	0-3	.944	-1	90	96	2-14/S-3,3O(LF)D	-0.5
SORIANO, ALFONSO Alfonso Guilleard B 1.7.1978 San Pedro De Macoris, D.R. BR/TR 6-1/160# d9.14																								
1999	NY A	9	8	2	1	0	0	1	1	0-0	0	3	.125	.125	.500	50	-1	0-1	.500	-1	37	166	/SD	-0.2
2000	NY A	22	50	5	9	3	0	2	3	1-0	0	15	.180	.196	.360	37	-5	2-0	.846	-6	77	153	3-10/S-9,2D	-0.9
2001	†NY A	158	574	77	154	34	3	18	73	29-0	3	125	.268	.304	.432	91	-9	43-14	.973	-12	84	99	*2-156/D-2	-0.8
2002	†NY A★	156	696	**128**	**209**	51	2	39	102	23-1	14	157	.300	.332	.547	130	28	**41**-13	.968	-13	92	90	*2-155/D	2.6
2003	†NY A★	156	682	114	198	36	5	38	91	38-7	12	130	.290	.338	.525	125	22	35-8	.975	3	100	91	*2-155	3.6
Total	5	501	2010	326	571	124	10	98	270	91-8	29	430	.284	.322	.502	114	35	121-36	.972	-28	92	93	2-467/3-10,D-10,S-10	4.3
SORRELL, BILL William B 10.14.1940 Morehead, KY BL/TR 6/190# d9.2																								
1965	Phi N	10	13	2	5	0	0	1	2	2-0	0	1	.385	.467	.615	206	2	0-0	—	-0	0	0	/3	0.2
1967	SF N	18	17	1	3	1	0	0	1	3-0	0	2	.176	.300	.235	56	-1	0-0	1.000	-0	44	0	/O-5(LF)	-0.1
1970	KC A	57	135	12	36	2	0	4	14	10-4	0	13	.267	.317	.370	89	-2	1-0	.873	-6	87	57	3-29/O-4(2-0-2),1-3	-0.9
Total	3	85	165	15	44	3	0	5	17	15-4	0	16	.267	.328	.376	95	-1	1-0	.873	-6	87	57	/3-30,O-9(7-0-2),1-3	-0.8
SORRELLS, CHICK Raymond Edwin B 7.31.1896 Stringtown, OK D 7.20.1983 Terrell, TX BR/TR 5-9/155# d9.18																								
1922	Cle A	2	1	0	0	0	0	0	0	0	0	0	.000	.000	.000	-99	0	0-0	1.000	0	205	0	/S	0.0
SORRENTO, PAUL Paul Anthony B 11.17.1965 Somerville, MA BL/TR 6-2/200# d9.8																								
1989	Min A	14	21	2	5	0	0	0	1	5-1	0	4	.238	.370	.238	74	0	0-0	1.000	-0	0	82	/1-5,D-5	-0.1
1990	Min A	41	121	11	25	4	1	5	13	12-0	1	31	.207	.281	.380	79	-4	1-1	.992	-1	71	109	D-23,1-15	-0.7
1991	†Min A	26	47	6	12	2	0	4	13	4-2	0	11	.255	.314	.553	129	2	0-0	1.000	1	119	106	1-13/D-2	0.1
1992	Cle A	140	458	52	123	24	1	18	60	51-7	1	89	.269	.341	.443	121	13	0-3	.993	-2	96	107	*1-121,D-11	0.1
1993	Cle A	148	463	75	119	26	1	18	65	58-11	2	121	.257	.340	.434	108	5	3-1	.995	-1	98	95	*1-144/O-3(RF),D	-0.7
1994	Cle A	95	322	43	90	14	0	14	62	34-6	0	68	.280	.345	.453	104	2	0-1	.995	-1	95	104	1-86/D-8	-0.7
1995	†Cle A	104	323	50	76	14	0	25	79	51-6	0	71	.235	.336	.511	116	7	1-1	.992	-4	88	128	1-91,D-11	-0.6
1996	Sea A	143	471	67	136	32	1	23	93	57-10	7	103	.289	.370	.507	120	15	0-2	.990	-0	100	100	*1-138	0.2
1997	†Sea A	146	457	68	123	19	0	31	80	51-9	3	112	.269	.345	.514	122	13	0-2	.996	8	120	86	*1-139/D	0.9
1998	TB A	137	435	40	98	27	0	17	57	54-1	3	133	.225	.313	.405	84	-10	2-3	1.000	3	138	102	D-86,1-27,O-18(4-0-14)	-1.6
1999	TB A	99	294	40	69	14	1	11	42	49-1	4	101	.235	.351	.401	91	-3	1-1	.957	-5	89	63	O-57(LF),1-27/D-9	-1.2
Total	11	1093	3412	454	876	176	5	166	565	426-54	21	844	.257	.340	.457	108	40	8-15	.994	-2	100	102	1-806,D-157/O-78(61-0-17)	-4.3
SOSA, JUAN Juan Luis (Encarnacion) B 8.19.1975 San Francisco De Macoris, D.R. BR/TR 6-1/175# d9.10																								
1999	Col N	11	9	3	2	0	0	0	0	2-0	0	2	.222	.364	.222	42	-1	0-0	1.000	0	81	0	/O-6(1-5-0),S-2	0.0
2001	Ari N	2	1	0	0	0	0	0	0	0-0	0	1	.000	.000	.000	-94	0	0-0	1.000	0	454	0	/3	0.0
Total	2	13	10	3	2	0	0	0	0	2-0	0	3	.200	.333	.200	32	-1	0-0	1.000	1	81	0	/O-6(1-5-0),S-2,3	0.0
SOSA, SAMMY Samuel Peralta B 11.12.1968 San Pedro De Macoris, D.R. BR/TR 6/185# d6.16																								
1989	Tex A	25	84	8	20	3	0	1	3	0-0	0	20	.238	.238	.310	52	-6	0-2	.944	-1	96	116	O-19(12-8-1)/D-6	-0.7
	Chi A	33	99	19	27	5	0	3	10	11-2	2	27	.273	.351	.414	120	3	7-3	.969	-4	81	55	O-33(1-25-9)	-0.1
	Year	58	183	27	47	8	0	4	13	11-2	2	47	.257	.303	.366	89	-3	7-5	.960	-4	86	77	O-52(13-33-10)/D-6	-0.8
1990	Chi A	153	532	72	124	26	10	15	70	33-4	6	150	.233	.282	.404	93	-8	32-16	.962	4	106	133	*O-152(0-1-152)	-0.7

Year	Tm Lg	G	AB	R	H	2B	3B	HR	RBI	BB-IB	HP	SO	AVG	OBP	SLG	AOPS	ABR	SB-CS	FA	FR	Rng	Thr	G at Pos	BFW
1991	Chi A	116	316	39	64	10	1	10	33	14-2	2	98	.203	.240	.335	59	-19	13-6	.973	3	110	92	*O-111(0-13-102)/D-2	-1.8
1992	Chi N	67	262	41	68	7	2	8	25	19-1	4	63	.260	.317	.393	98	-1	15-7	.961	-8	83	105	O-67(CF)	-0.9
1993	Chi N	159	598	92	156	25	5	33	93	38-6	4	135	.261	.309	.485	111	5	36-11	.976	3	97	160	*O-158(0-70-114)	0.8
1994	Chi N	105	426	59	128	17	6	25	70	25-1	2	92	.300	.339	.545	128	15	22-13	.973	3	114	63	*O-105(0-15-98)	1.3
1995	Chi N★	**144**	564	89	151	17	3	36	119	58-11	5	134	.268	.340	.500	121	14	34-7	.962	8	113	121	*O-143(RF)	2.0
1996	Chi N	124	498	84	136	21	2	40	100	34-6	5	134	.273	.323	.564	126	15	18-5	.964	6	105	174	*O-124(RF)	1.7
1997	Chi N	**162**	642	90	161	31	4	36	119	45-9	2	174	.251	.300	.480	98	-5	22-12	.977	7	108	134	*O-161(RF)	-0.6
1998	†Chi N✷	159	643	**134**	198	20	0	66	**158**	73-14	1	171	.308	.377	.647	158	51	18-9	.975	7	110	130	*O-159(0-7-156)	5.0
1999	Chi N★	**162**	625	114	180	24	2	63	141	78-8	3	171	.288	.367	.635	150	44	7-8	.978	9	118	75	*O-162(0-25-146)	4.2
2000	Chi N★	156	604	106	193	38	1	**50**	138	91-19	2	168	.320	.406	.634	162	59	7-4	.970	-6	100	30	*O-156(0-2-156)	4.2
2001	Chi N★	160	577	**146**	189	34	5	64	**160**	116-**37**	6	153	.328	.437	.737	208	97	0-2	.982	6	112	82	*O-160(RF)	8.9
2002	Chi N★	150	556	**122**	160	19	2	**49**	108	103-15	3	144	.288	.399	.594	165	51	2-0	.980	2	108	77	*O-150(RF)	4.5
2003	†Chi N	137	517	99	144	22	0	40	103	62-9	5	143	.279	.358	.553	136	26	0-1	.977	-10	90	25	*O-137(RF)	0.9
Total	15	2012	7543	1314	2099	319	43	539	1450	800-144	52	1977	.278	.349	.546	134	341	233-106	.972	31	106	100	*O-1997(13-233-1809)/D-8	28.7
SOTHERN, DENNY Dennis Elwood B 1.20.1904 Washington, DC D 12.7.1977 Durham, NC BR/TR 5-11/175# d9.10																								
1926	Phi N	14	53	5	13	1	0	3	10	4	1	10	.245	.310	.434	94	-1	0	.975	1	117	70	O-13(11-3-0)	-0.1
1928	Phi N	141	579	82	165	27	5	5	38	34	2	53	.285	.327	.375	80	-17	17	.964	5	101	**161**	*O-136(8-127-1)	-1.8
1929	Phi N	76	294	52	90	21	3	5	27	16	2	24	.306	.346	.449	90	-5	13	.967	2	102	132	O-71(2-63-6)	-0.6
1930	Phi N	90	347	66	97	26	1	5	36	22	2	37	.280	.326	.403	70	-17	6	.967	7	100	226	O-84(3-81-0)	-1.2
	Pit N	17	51	4	9	4	0	1	4	3	0	4	.176	.222	.314	28	-6	2	.971	0	114	0	O-13(0-12-1)	-0.6
	Year	107	398	70	106	30	1	6	40	25	2	41	.266	.313	.392	65	-23	8	.967	7	102	199	O-97(3-93-1)	-1.8
1931	Bro N	19	31	10	5	1	0	0	0	4	0	8	.161	.257	.194	23	-3	0	.958	0	120	0	O-10(3-7-0)	-0.3
Total	5	357	1355	219	379	80	9	19	115	83	7	136	.280	.325	.394	77	-49	38	.966	15	103	158	O-327(27-293-8)	-4.6
SOUCHOCK, STEVE Stephen "Bud" B 3.3.1919 Yatesboro, PA D 7.28.2002 Westland, MI BR/TR 6-2.5/203# d5.25																								
1946	NY A	47	86	15	26	3	3	2	10	7	1	13	.302	.362	.477	131	3	0-3	.964	-2	71	123	1-20	-0.1
1948	NY A	44	118	11	24	3	1	3	11	7	0	13	.203	.248	.322	51	-9	3-0	.988	-2	73	101	1-32	-1.1
1949	Chi A	84	252	29	59	13	5	7	37	25	0	38	.234	.303	.409	90	-6	5-2	.951	1	108	33	O-39(LF),1-30	-0.8
1951	Det A	91	188	33	46	10	3	11	28	18	1	27	.245	.314	.505	118	3	0-2	.941	-1	101	94	O-59(30-0-29)/3-3,12	-0.1
1952	Det A	92	265	40	66	16	4	13	45	21	0	28	.249	.304	.487	117	4	1-0	.964	2	110	106	O-56(16-1-41),3-13/1-9	0.4
1953	Det A	89	278	29	84	13	3	11	46	8	2	35	.302	.326	.489	119	5	5-1	.962	2	105	122	O-80(39-0-44)/1	0.5
1954	Det A	25	39	6	7	0	1	3	8	2	0	10	.179	.220	.462	84	-2	1-1	1.000	0	115	0	/O-9(LF),3-2	-0.2
1955	Det A	1	1	0	1	0	0	0	1	0-0	0	0	1.000	1.000	1.000	449	0	0-0	—	0			H	0.0
Total	8	473	1227	163	313	58	20	50	186	88-0	4	164	.255	.307	.457	106	-2	15-9	.957	0	106	92	O-243(133-1-114)/1-93,3-18,2	-1.4
SOUTHWICK, CLYDE Clyde Aubra B 11.3.1886 Maxwell, IA D 10.14.1961 Freeport, IL BL/TR 6/180# d8.22																								
1911	StL A	4	12	3	3	0	0	0	0	1	0		.250	.308	.250	58	-1	0	.938	-1	*75*	*82*	/C-4	-0.1
SOUTHWORTH, BILL William Frederick B 11.10.1945 Madison, WI BR/TR 6-2/205# d10.2																								
1964	Mil N	3	7	2	2	0	0	1	2	0-0	2	3	.286	.444	.714	219	1	0-0	1.000	-0	79	0	/3-2	0.1
SOUTHWORTH, BILLY William Harrison B 3.9.1893 Harvard, NE D 11.15.1969 Columbus, OH BL/TR 5-9/170# d8.4 M13 C1																								
1913	Cle A	1	0	0	0	0	0	0	0	0	0	0	—	—	—	—	0	0	—	0	0	0	/O	0.0
1915	Cle A	60	177	25	39	2	5	0	8	36	0	12	.220	.352	.288	90	-1	2-4	.942	0	96	117	O-44(10-30-4)	-0.5
1918	Pit N	64	246	37	84	5	7	2	43	26	2	9	.341	.409	.443	154	16	19	.980	6	119	112	O-64(RF)	2.1
1919	Pit N	121	453	56	127	14	**14**	4	61	32	1	22	.280	.329	.400	114	6	23	.968	6	110	105	*O-121(75-0-46)	0.7
1920	Pit N	146	546	64	155	17	13	2	53	52	2	20	.284	.348	.374	104	3	23-25	**.991**	7	121	64	*O-142(RF)	-0.1
1921	Bos N	141	569	86	175	25	15	7	79	36	2	13	.308	.351	.441	115	10	22-20	.975	5	101	123	*O-141(RF)	0.2
1922	Bos N	43	158	27	51	4	4	4	18	18	0	1	.323	.392	.475	128	7	4-1	.955	4	118	126	O-41(RF)	0.7
1923	Bos N	153	611	95	195	29	16	6	78	61	2	23	.319	.383	.448	124	21	14-16	.943	3	103	122	*O-151(RF)/2-2	0.9
1924	†NY N	94	281	40	72	13	0	3	36	32	0	16	.256	.332	.335	81	-6	1-6	.935	-6	94	63	O-75(1-51-19)	-1.8
1925	NY N	123	473	79	138	19	5	6	44	51	2	11	.292	.363	.391	97	-1	6-13	.964	-15	85	59	*O-119(0-117-2)	-2.3
1926	NY N	36	116	23	38	6	1	5	30	7	0	1	.328	.366	.526	139	6	1	.970	-2	93	67	O-29(7-16-8)	0.3
	†StL N	99	391	76	124	22	6	11	69	26	3	9	.317	.364	.488	123	12	13	.971	-3	109	36	O-99(RF)	0.1
	Year	135	507	99	162	28	7	16	99	33	3	10	.320	.365	.497	127	18	14	.971	-5	105	43	*O-128(7-16-107)	0.4
1927	StL N	92	306	52	92	15	5	2	39	23	0	7	.301	.350	.402	98	-1	10	.970	-4	95	64	O-83(RF)	-1.1
1929	StL N	19	32	1	6	2	0	0	3	2	0	4	.188	.235	.250	20	-4	0	1.000	0	118	0	/O-5(RF),M	-0.4
Total	13	1192	4359	661	1296	173	91	52	561	402	14	148	.297	.359	.415	111	68	138-85	.965	3	104	88	*O-1115(93-214-805)/2-2	-1.2
SOWDERS, LEN Leonard B 6.29.1861 Louisville, KY D 11.19.1888 Indianapolis, IN 5-11.5/172# d9.10 b-John b-Bill																								
1886	Bal AA	23	76	10	20	3	1	0	14	12	0		.263	.364	.329	121	3	6	.889	0	121	0	O-23(CF)/1	0.2
SPALDING, AL Albert Goodwill B 9.2.1850 Byron, IL D 9.9.1915 San Diego, CA BR/TR 6-1/170# d5.5 M2 HF1939 ▲ OF Total (9-LF 1-CF)																								
1871	Bos NA	**31**	144	43	39	10	1	1	31	8		1	.271	.309	.375	93	-1	2-0	.776	-1	108	105	*P-31/O-9(CF)	0.0
1872	Bos NA	**48**	237	60	84	12	5	0	47	3		1	.354	.363	.447	140	10	3-0	.902	8	**148**	111	*P-48/O-7(CF)	0.3
1873	Bos NA	**60**	323	83	106	15	1	1	71	3		2	.328	.334	.390	106	0	9-0	**.885**	10	154	197	*P-60,O-14(CF)	0.3
1874	Bos NA	**71**	362	80	119	13	1	0	54	3		0	.329	.334	.370	119	6	2-1	**.854**	5	124	144	*P-71/O-6(CF)	0.2
1875	Bos NA	74	343	68	107	15	3	0	56	3		3	.312	.318	.373	134	11	2-2	.906	3	112	**223**	*P-72,O-18(1-9-9)/1-4	0.2
1876	Chi N	**66**	292	54	91	14	2	0	44	6		3	.312	.326	.373	118	4		.951	4	110	**306**	*P-61,O-10(9-1-0)/1-3,SM	0.2
1877	Chi N	**60**	254	29	65	7	6	0	35	3		16	.256	.265	.331	77	-8		.959	5	**155**	**116**	*1-45,2-13/P-4,3-2,M	-0.4
1878	Chi N	1	4	0	2	0	0	0	0	0		0	.500	.500	.500	215	0		.429	-2	0	0	/2	-0.2
Total	5 NA	284	1409	334	455	65	11	2	259	20		7	.323	.332	.389	120	26	18-3	.000	25	130	164	P-282/O-54(1-45-9),1-4	1.0
Total	3	127	550	83	158	21	8	0	79	9		19	.287	.299	.355	99	-4		.948	7	114	300	/P-65,1-48,2-14,O-10L,3-2,S	-0.4
SPALDING, DICK Charles Harry B 10.13.1893 Philadelphia, PA D 2.3.1950 Philadelphia, PA BL/TL 5-11/185# d4.18 C6																								
1927	Phi N	115	442	68	131	16	3	0	25	38	0	40	.296	.352	.346	86	-8	5	**.992**	2	109	68	*O-113(LF)	-1.4
1928	Was A	16	23	1	8	0	0	0	0	0	0	4	.348	.348	.348	84	-1	0-2	1.000	-0	105	0	O-11(8-0-3)	-0.2
Total	2	131	465	69	139	16	3	0	25	38	0	44	.299	.352	.346	86	-9	5-2	.993	2	109	66	O-124(121-0-3)	-1.6
SPANGLER, AL Albert Donald B 7.8.1933 Philadelphia, PA BL/TL 6/175# d9.16 C3																								
1959	Mil N	6	12	3	5	0	1	0	0	1-0	0	1	.417	.462	.583	192	1	1-0	1.000	-0	98	0	/O-4(1-3-0)	0.1
1960	Mil N	101	105	26	28	5	2	0	6	14-1	1	17	.267	.355	.352	103	1	6-2	.989	5	126	130	O-92(90-1-1)	0.4
1961	Mil N	68	97	23	26	2	0	0	6	28-2	0	9	.268	.432	.289	102	3	4-2	1.000	-0	98	95	O-44(23-21-1)	0.2
1962	Hou N	129	418	51	119	10	9	5	35	70-6	3	46	.285	.389	.388	119	14	7-6	.960	-4	90	96	*O-121(93-28-0)	0.4
1963	Hou N	120	430	52	121	25	4	4	27	50-5	1	38	.281	.355	.386	122	14	5-8	.987	1	103	71	*O-113(87-33-3)	0.8
1964	Hou N	135	449	51	110	18	5	4	38	41-1	4	43	.245	.311	.334	88	-7	7-8	.964	-6	90	42	*O-127(113-18-0)	-2.2
1965	Hou N	38	112	18	24	1	1	1	7	14-2	0	8	.214	.299	.268	66	-5	1-1	.956	-0	85	200	O-33(31-1-1)	-0.7
	Cal A	51	96	17	25	1	0	0	1	8-0	0	9	.260	.317	.271	70	-4	4-0	.973	-1	97	0	O-24(4-17-6)	-0.5
1966	Cal A	6	9	2	6	0	0	0	0	2-0	0	2	.667	.727	.667	312	3	0-0	1.000	-0	88	0	/O-3(RF)	0.3
1967	Chi N	62	130	18	33	7	0	0	13	23-4	0	17	.254	.361	.308	91	0	2-2	.986	-2	102	0	O-41(0-7-34)	-0.5
1968	Chi N	88	177	21	48	9	3	2	18	20-2	1	24	.271	.343	.390	114	4	0-1	.973	-2	93	61	O-48(1-7-42)	-0.1
1969	Chi N	82	213	23	45	8	1	4	23	21-0	1	16	.211	.284	.315	60	-11	0-2	.950	-6	84	26	O-58(0-1-57)	-2.1
1970	Chi N	21	14	2	2	1	0	1	1	3-0	0	3	.143	.294	.429	81	0	0-0	1.000	0	164	0	/O-6(3-0-3)	0.0
1971	Chi N	5	5	0	2	0	0	0	0	0-0	0	1	.400	.400	.400	111	0	0-0	—	0			H	0.0
Total	13	912	2267	307	594	87	26	21	175	295-23	11	234	.262	.347	.351	100	13	37-32	.973	-15	96	69	O-714(446-137-151)	-3.9
SPEAKE, BOB Robert Charles "Spook" B 8.22.1930 Springfield, MO BL/TL 6-1/178# d4.16																								
1955	Chi N	95	261	36	57	9	5	12	43	28-4	3	71	.218	.300	.429	91	-4	3-4	.959	-1	94	110	O-55(49-0-8)/1-8	-0.9
1957	Chi N	129	418	65	97	14	5	16	50	38-1	3	68	.232	.299	.404	89	-8	5-6	.974	0	92	111	O-60(20-40-0),1-39	-1.5
1958	SF N	66	71	9	15	3	0	3	10	13-1	0	15	.211	.333	.380	90	-1	0-1	.938	1	91	363	O-10(LF)	-0.1
1959	SF N	15	11	0	1	0	0	0	1	1-0	0	4	.091	.167	.091	-30	-2	0-0	—	0			H	-0.2
Total	4	305	761	110	170	26	10	31	104	80-6	6	158	.223	.301	.406	88	-15	8-11	.966	0	93	126	O-125(79-40-8)/1-47	-2.7
SPEAKER, TRIS Tristram E "The Grey Eagle" B 4.4.1888 Hubbard, TX D 12.8.1958 Lake Whitney, TX BL/TL 5-11.5/193# d9.12 M8 HF1937																								
1907	Bos A	7	19	0	3	0	0	0	1	1	0		.158	.200	.158	14	-2	0	1.000	1	394	930	/O-4(RF)	-0.1
1908	Bos A	31	116	12	26	2	2	0	9	4	2		.224	.262	.276	73	-4	3	1.000	4	254	314	O-31(1-30-0)	-0.1

Year	Tm Lg	G	AB	R	H	2B	3B	HR	RBI	BB-IB	HP	SO	AVG	OBP	SLG	AOPS	ABR	SB-CS	FA	FR	Rng	Thr	G at Pos	BFW
1909	Bos A	143	544	73	168	26	13	7	77	38	7		.309	.362	.443	151	30	35	.973	19	**195**	**298**	*O-142(CF)	4.6
1910	Bos A	141	538	92	183	20	14	7	65	52	6		.340	.404	.468	169	43	35	.957	9	**117**	96	*O-140(CF)	4.8
1911	Bos A	141	500	88	167	34	13	8	70	59	13		.334	.418	.502	158	41	25	.956	3	100	118	*O-138(CF)	3.3
1912	†Bos A	153	580	136	222	**53**	12	**10**	90	82	6		.383	**.464**	.567	185	68	52	.958	16	110	**157**	*O-153(CF)	**7.2**
1913	Bos A	141	520	94	189	35	22	3	71	65	7	22	.363	.441	.533	180	54	46	.942	19	**122**	137	*O-139(CF)	6.5
1914	Bos A	158	571	101	**193**	**46**	18	4	90	77	7	25	.338	.423	.503	178	57	42-29	.968	23	**121**	142	*O-156(CF)/P1	**7.3**
1915	†Bos A	150	547	108	176	25	12	0	69	81	7	14	.322	.416	.411	152	39	29-25	.976	8	108	97	*O-150(CF)	3.6
1916	Cle A	151	546	102	**211**	**41**	8	2	79	82	4	20	**.386**	**.470**	**.502**	**181**	**60**	35-27	.975	6	103	117	*O-151(CF)	**5.7**
1917	Cle A	142	523	90	184	42	11	2	60	67	7	14	.352	.432	.486	168	45	30	.980	2	101	107	*O-142(CF)	4.1
1918	Cle A	127	471	73	150	**33**	11	0	61	64	3	9	.318	.403	.435	140	25	27	.973	8	**118**	83	*O-127(CF)	2.7
1919	Cle A	134	494	83	146	38	12	2	63	73	8	12	.296	.395	.433	125	20	19	.983	15	112	130	*O-134(CF),M	2.6
1920	†Cle A	150	552	137	214	**50**	11	8	107	97	5	13	.388	.483	.562	171	64	10-13	.977	6	102	130	*O-148(CF),M	5.4
1921	Cle A	132	506	107	183	**52**	14	3	75	68	2	12	.362	.439	.538	146	38	2-4	**.984**	9	**115**	98	*O-128(CF),M	3.8
1922	Cle A	131	426	85	161	**48**	8	11	71	77	1	11	.378	**.474**	.606	178	55	8-3	**.983**	3	101	114	*O-109(CF),M	5.1
1923	Cle A	150	574	133	218	**59**	11	17	130	93	4	15	.380	.469	.610	183	74	8-9	.968	3	94	**148**	*O-150(CF),M	6.5
1924	Cle A	135	486	94	167	36	9	9	65	72	4	13	.344	.432	.510	141	32	5-7	.963	1	94	164	*O-128(0-127-1),M	2.5
1925	Cle A	117	429	79	167	35	5	12	87	70	4	12	.389	**.479**	.578	166	48	5-2	.967	4	99	130	*O-109(CF),M	**4.3**
1926	Cle A	150	539	96	164	52	8	7	86	94	0	15	.304	.408	.469	127	26	6-1	.981	-2	98	130	*O-149(CF),M	1.8
1927	Was A	141	523	71	171	43	6	2	73	55	4	8	.327	.395	.444	119	17	9-8	.967	-3	94	103	*O-120(0-119-1),1-17	0.7
1928	Phi A	64	191	28	51	22	2	3	30	10	2	5	.267	.310	.450	95	-2	5-1	.975	1	94	162	O-50(1-49-0)	-0.2
Total	22	2789	10195	1882	3514	792	222	117	1529	1381	103	220	.345	.428	.500	156	828	436-129	.970	155	113	136	*O-2698(2-2690-6)/1-18,P	82.1
SPEED, HORACE Horace Arthur B 10.4.1951 Los Angeles, CA BR/TR 6-1/180# d4.10																								
1975	SF N	17	15	2	2	1	0	0	1	1-0	1	8	.133	.235	.200	21	-2	0-0	.900	-0	105	0	/O-9(5-0-5)	-0.2
1978	Cle A	70	106	13	24	4	1	0	4	14-1	1	31	.226	.320	.283	72	-3	2-4	.977	-1	99	39	O-61(12-23-30)/D-3	-0.7
1979	Cle A	26	14	6	2	0	0	0	1	5-0	0	7	.143	.368	.143	44	-1	2-1	.875	-1	102	0	O-16(10-3-3)/D-4	-0.2
Total	3	113	135	21	28	5	1	0	6	20-1	2	46	.207	.316	.259	63	-6	4-5	.956	-2	100	30	/O-86(27-26-38),D-7	-1.1
SPEHR, TIM Timothy Joseph B 7.2.1966 Excelsior Springs, MO BR/TR 6-2/200# d7.18																								
1991	KC A	37	74	7	14	5	0	3	14	9-0	1	18	.189	.282	.378	82	-2	1-0	.986	9	126	167	C-37	0.9
1993	Mon N	53	87	14	20	6	0	2	10	6-1	1	20	.230	.281	.368	71	-4	2-0	.954	1	49	170	C-49	-0.1
1994	Mon N	52	36	8	9	3	1	0	5	4-0	0	11	.250	.325	.389	84	-1	2-0	1.000	5	108	27	C-46/O-2(LF)	0.6
1995	Mon N	41	35	4	9	5	0	1	3	6-0	0	7	.257	.366	.486	118	1	0-0	.990	4	69	147	C-38	0.6
1996	Mon N	63	44	4	4	1	0	1	3	3-0	1	15	.091	.167	.182	-8	-7	1-0	.985	-1	79	39	C-58/O(RF)	-0.7
1997	KC A	17	35	3	6	0	0	1	2	2-0	1	12	.171	.237	.257	28	-4	0-0	1.000	3	59	118	C-17	-0.1
	Atl N	8	14	2	3	1	0	1	4	0-0	0	4	.214	.214	.500	78	-1	1-0	.947	1	159	273	/C-7	0.1
1998	NY N	21	51	3	7	1	0	0	3	7-1	2	16	.137	.267	.157	15	-6	1-0	1.000	2	89	147	C-21/1	-0.3
	KC A	11	25	5	6	2	0	1	2	8-0	2	3	.240	.457	.440	131	2	0-0	1.000	-2	150	58	C-11	0.1
1999	KC A	60	155	26	32	7	0	9	26	22-0	6	47	.206	.324	.426	88	-3	1-0	.990	-9	93	49	C-59	-0.8
Total	8	363	556	76	110	31	1	19	72	67-2	14	153	.198	.298	.360	71	-25	9-0	.985	11	92	106	C-343/O-3(2-0-1),1	0.3
SPEIER, CHRIS Chris Edward B 6.28.1950 Alameda, CA BR/TR (BB 1972 (part)) 6-1/182# d4.7 C2 s-Justin																								
1971	†SF N	157	601	74	141	17	6	8	46	56-6	7	90	.235	.307	.323	80	-16	4-7	.958	-4	103	102	*S-156	-0.4
1972	SF N★	150	562	74	151	25	2	15	71	82-2	3	92	.269	.361	.400	116	14	9-4	.974	3	107	76	*S-150	3.8
1973	SF N★	153	542	58	135	17	4	11	71	66-4	2	69	.249	.332	.356	87	-8	4-5	.956	0	102	103	*S-150/2	0.9
1974	SF N☆	141	501	55	125	19	5	9	53	62-8	4	64	.250	.336	.361	91	-5	3-2	.969	10	107	105	*S-135/2-4	2.1
1975	SF N	141	487	60	132	30	5	10	69	70-7	1	50	.271	.362	.415	111	9	4-5	**.982**	9	98	96	*S-136/3	3.5
1976	SF N	145	495	51	112	18	4	3	40	60-1	4	52	.226	.311	.297	72	-17	2-2	.974	3	104	95	*S-135/2-7,3-5,1	0.2
1977	SF N	6	17	1	3	1	0	0	0	0-0	0	3	.176	.176	.235	9	-2	0-0	.920	2	153	82	/S-5	0.0
	Mon N	139	531	58	125	30	6	5	38	67-3	1	78	.235	.321	.343	81	-13	1-2	.970	-8	99	94	*S-138	-0.7
	Year	145	548	59	128	31	6	5	38	67-3	1	81	.234	.317	.339	79	-16	1-2	.968	-6	101	94	*S-143	-0.7
1978	Mon N	150	501	47	126	18	3	5	51	60-10	1	75	.251	.329	.329	87	-8	1-0	.975	-2	99	114	*S-148	0.6
1979	Mon N	113	344	31	78	13	1	7	26	43-10	3	45	.227	.317	.331	78	-10	0-0	.970	1	101	88	*S-112	0.3
1980	Mon N	128	388	35	103	14	4	1	32	52-18	0	38	.265	.351	.330	91	-3	0-3	.965	0	102	88	*S-127/3	0.9
1981	†Mon N	96	307	33	69	10	2	2	25	38-10	0	29	.225	.310	.290	70	-11	1-2	.964	-6	94	108	S-96	-0.9
1982	Mon N	156	530	41	136	26	4	7	60	47-12	1	67	.257	.316	.360	88	-8	1-6	.982	-14	86	94	*S-155	-0.9
1983	Mon N	88	261	31	67	12	2	2	22	29-4	2	37	.257	.332	.341	88	-3	2-1	.962	-6	99	83	S-74,3-12/2-2	-0.3
1984	Mon N	25	40	1	6	0	0	0	1	1-0	0	8	.150	.171	.150	-10	-6	0-0	.960	1	98	126	S-13/3-4	-0.5
	StL N	38	118	9	21	7	1	3	8	9-1	1	19	.178	.242	.331	61	-7	0-0	.983	7	121	129	S-34/3-2	0.4
	Year	63	158	10	27	7	1	3	9	10-1	1	27	.171	.225	.285	44	-12	0-0	.980	8	118	129	S-47/3-6	-0.1
	Min A	12	33	2	7	0	0	0	1	3-0	0	7	.212	.278	.212	36	-3	0-0	.977	-3	85	93	S-12	-0.5
1985	Chi N	106	218	16	53	11	0	4	24	17-0	0	34	.243	.295	.349	72	-8	1-3	.964	5	113	151	S-58,3-31,2-13	0.0
1986	Chi N	95	155	21	44	8	0	6	23	15-3	1	32	.284	.349	.452	111	2	2-2	.984	3	92	71	3-53,S-23/2-7	0.7
1987	†SF N	111	317	39	79	13	0	11	39	42-5	3	51	.249	.342	.394	99	0	4-7	.989	4	90	94	2-55,3-44,S-22	0.5
1988	SF N	82	171	26	37	9	1	3	18	23-2	1	39	.216	.311	.333	89	-2	3-3	.985	4	105	117	2-45,3-22,S-12	0.3
1989	SF N	28	37	7	9	4	0	0	2	5-0	0	9	.243	.333	.351	99	0	0-0	1.000	-1	82	0	/3-9,S-9,2-4,1	0.0
Total	19	2260	7156	770	1759	302	50	112	720	847-106	35	988	.246	.327	.349	88	-105	42-54	.970	6	101	99	*S-1900,3-184,2-138/1-2	10.0
SPENCE, BOB John Robert B 2.10.1946 San Diego, CA BL/TR 6-4/215# d9.5																								
1969	Chi A	12	26	0	4	1	0	0	3	0-0	0	9	.154	.148	.192	-4	-4	0-0	1.000	-0	73	130	/1-6	-0.5
1970	Chi A	46	130	11	29	4	1	4	15	11-0	1	32	.223	.285	.362	75	-5	0-0	.994	3	133	122	1-37	-0.5
1971	Chi A	14	27	2	4	0	0	0	1	5-0	0	6	.148	.273	.148	24	-3	0-0	.986	-1	50	109	/1-7	-0.4
Total	3	72	183	13	37	5	1	4	19	16-0	1	47	.202	.265	.306	57	-12	0-0	.993	2	114	121	/1-50	-1.4
SPENCE, STAN Stanley Orville B 3.20.1915 S.Portsmouth, KY D 1.9.1983 Kinston, NC BL/TL 5-10.5/180# d6.8 Mil 1945																								
1940	Bos A	51	68	5	19	2	1	2	13	4	0	9	.279	.319	.426	88	-2	0-1	1.000	-1	97	0	O-15(6-0-9)	-0.3
1941	Bos A	86	203	22	47	10	3	2	28	18	3	14	.232	.304	.340	68	-10	1-0	1.000	3	103	161	O-52(27-10-16)/1	-0.8
1942	Was A☆	149	629	94	203	27	**15**	4	79	62	1	16	.323	.384	.432	131	25	5-2	.973	-7	97	63	*O-149(CF)	1.5
1943	Was A	149	570	72	152	23	10	12	88	84	5	39	.267	.366	.405	130	23	8-1	.983	-1	99	104	*O-148(CF)	2.1
1944	Was A★	153	592	83	187	31	8	18	100	69	4	28	.316	.391	.486	157	44	3-7	.989	15	103	197	*O-150(CF)/1-3	5.4
1946	Was A★	152	578	83	169	50	10	16	87	62	4	31	.292	.365	.497	148	36	1-7	.982	2	99	142	*O-150(CF)	3.3
1947	Was A★	147	506	62	141	22	6	16	73	81	0	41	.279	.378	.441	131	22	2-2	.984	6	105	131	*O-142(CF)	2.5
1948	Bos A	114	391	71	92	17	4	12	61	82	0	33	.235	.368	.391	97	0	0-2	.977	-3	101	57	O-92(24-0-70),1-14	-0.8
1949	Bos A	7	20	3	3	1	0	0	1	6	0	1	.150	.346	.200	43	-1	0-0	1.000	1	102	196	/O-5(0-2-3)	-0.1
	StL A	104	314	46	77	13	3	13	45	52	2	36	.245	.356	.430	103	1	1-1	.995	4	100	168	O-87(33-50-6)/1	0.1
	Year	111	334	49	80	14	3	13	46	58	2	37	.240	.355	.416	99	-1	1-1	.996	4	100	170	O-92(33-52-9)/1	0.0
Total	9	1112	3871	541	1090	196	60	95	575	520	19	248	.282	.369	.437	126	138	21-23	.984	19	101	125	O-990(90-801-104)/1-19	12.9
SPENCER d6.3																								
1872	Nat NA	1	4	1	0	0	0	0	0	0		0	.000	.000	.000	-86	-1	0-0	.429	-1	99	0	/S	-0.1
SPENCER, CHET Chester Arthur B 3.4.1883 S.Webster, OH D 11.10.1938 Portsmouth, OH BL/TR 6/180# d8.22																								
1906	Bos N	8	27	1	4	1	0	0	0	0	0		.148	.148	.185	4	-3	0	.875	-1	144	0	/O-8(1-3-3)	-0.5
SPENCER, DARYL Daryl Dean "Big Dee" B 7.13.1929 Wichita, KS BR/TR 6-2/190# d9.17 Mil 1954																								
1952	NY N	7	17	0	5	0	1	0	3	1	0	4	.294	.333	.412	105	0	0-0	1.000	1	116	59	/S-3,3-3	0.1
1953	NY N	118	408	55	85	18	5	20	56	42	3	74	.208	.287	.424	81	-13	0-1	.927	-8	103	86	S-53,3-36,2-32	-1.6
1956	NY N	146	489	46	108	13	2	14	42	35-2	3	65	.221	.275	.342	66	-25	1-3	.974	-8	95	80	2-70,S-66,3-12	-2.5
1957	NY N	148	534	65	133	31	2	11	50	50-0	1	50	.249	.313	.376	85	-11	3-1	.950	11	105	**132**	*S-110,2-36/3-6	1.2
1958	SF N	148	539	71	138	20	5	17	74	73-4	3	60	.256	.343	.406	101	2	1-0	.955	-5	104	100	*S-134,2-17	1.0
1959	SF N	152	555	59	147	20	1	12	62	58-4	0	67	.265	.332	.369	89	-8	5-0	.970	-1	100	89	*2-151/S-4	0.4
1960	StL N	148	507	70	131	20	3	16	58	81-7	5	74	.258	.365	.404	102	4	1-1	.946	-16	87	90	*S-138,2-16	0.0
1961	StL N	37	130	19	33	4	0	4	21	23-3	0	17	.254	.366	.377	89	-1	1-0	.956	0	99	107	S-37	0.2
	LA N	60	189	27	46	7	0	8	27	20-1	4	35	.243	.327	.407	86	-3	0-1	.964	4	96	149	3-57/S-3	0.0
	Year	97	319	46	79	11	0	12	48	43-4	4	52	.248	.343	.395	88	-5	1-1	.964	4	96	149	3-57,S-40	0.2
1962	LA N	77	157	24	37	5	1	2	12	32-4	0	31	.236	.365	.318	91	0	0-0	.925	2	104	52	3-57,S-10	0.2

Year	Tm Lg	G	AB	R	H	2B	3B	HR	RBI	BB-IB	HP	SO	AVG	OBP	SLG	AOPS	ABR	SB-CS	FA	FR	Rng	Thr	G at Pos	BFW
1963	LA N	7	9	0	1	0	0	0	0	3-0	0	2	.111	.333	.111	37	-1	0-0	1.000	-0	74	0	/3-3	-0.1
	Cin N	50	155	21	37	7	0	1	23	31-0	1	37	.239	.359	.303	93	1	1-0	.979	2	95	130	3-48	0.3
	Year	57	164	21	38	7	0	1	23	34-0	1	39	.232	.358	.293	91	0	1-0	.979	1	94	125	3-51	0.2
Total	10	1098	3689	457	901	145	20	105	428	449-25	20	516	.244	.327	.380	88	-55	13-7	.953	-17	99	103	S-558,2-322,3-222	-0.8
SPENCER, TUBBY Edward Russell B 1.26.1884 Oil City, PA D 2.1.1945 San Francisco, CA BR/TR 5-10/215# d7.23																								
1905	StL A	35	115	6	27	1	2	0	11	7	1		.235	.285	.278	83	-3	2	.962	-6	*71*	*107*	C-34	-0.6
1906	StL A	58	188	15	33	6	1	0	17	7	0		.176	.205	.218	34	-15	4	.935	-6	*88*	*100*	C-54	-1.7
1907	StL A	71	230	27	61	11	1	1	25	7	4		.265	.299	.335	102	0	1	.957	-5	*93*	*99*	C-63	0.2
1908	StL A	91	286	19	60	6	1	0	28	17	0		.210	.254	.238	60	-13	1	.983	5	*121*	*91*	C-88	0.1
1909	Bos A	28	74	6	12	1	0	0	9	6	0		.162	.225	.176	26	-6	2	.992	-1	*108*	*82*	C-26	-0.6
1911	Phi N	11	32	2	5	1	0	1	3	3	0	7	.156	.229	.281	42	-3	0	.925	-2	*88*	*114*	C-11	-0.4
1916	Det A	19	54	7	20	1	1	1	10	6	1	6	.370	.443	.481	172	5	2	.988	-5	77	114	C-19	0.1
1917	Det A	70	192	13	46	8	3	0	22	15	**9**	15	.240	.324	.313	95	-1	0	.978	-4	*89*	*89*	C-62	0.1
1918	Det A	66	155	11	34	8	1	0	8	19	2	18	.219	.313	.284	83	-3	1	.966	-11	*73*	*91*	C-48/1	-1.1
Total	9	449	1326	106	298	43	10	3	133	87	17	46	.225	.281	.279	76	-39	13	.966	-33	*94*	*96*	C-405/1	-3.9
SPENCER, TOM Hubert Thomas B 2.28.1951 Gallipolis, OH BR/TR 6/170# d7.17 C5																								
1978	Chi A	29	65	3	12	1	0	0	4	2-0	0	9	.185	.209	.200	15	-7	0-1	1.000	2	115	173	O-27(6-19-2)/D-2	-0.6
SPENCER, JIM James Lloyd B 7.30.1947 Hanover, PA D 2.10.2002 Ft.Lauderdale, FL BL/TL 6-2/195# d9.7 gf-Ben																								
1968	Cal A	19	68	2	13	1	0	0	5	3-0	1	10	.191	.233	.206	36	-5	0-0	.994	3	155	107	1-19	-0.5
1969	Cal A	113	386	39	98	14	3	10	31	26-6	2	53	.254	.304	.383	96	-4	1-0	.991	-1	94	100	*1-107	-1.4
1970	Cal A	146	511	61	140	20	4	12	68	28-6	0	61	.274	.309	.399	98	-4	0-2	**.995**	-0	97	**123**	*1-142	-1.7
1971	Cal A	148	510	50	121	21	2	18	59	48-7	3	63	.237	.304	.392	104	1	0-1	**.996**	2	104	99	*1-145	-1.0
1972	Cal A	82	212	13	47	5	0	1	14	12-1	0	25	.222	.262	.259	59	-11	0-1	.990	0	126	98	1-35,O-24(LF)	-1.8
1973	Cal A	29	87	10	21	4	2	2	11	9-1	1	9	.241	.316	.402	111	1	0-0	1.000	-3	46	109	1-26/D-2	-0.4
	Tex A★	102	352	35	94	12	3	4	43	34-6	1	41	.267	.332	.352	97	-1	0-3	.999	5	113	93	1-99/D	-0.5
	Year	131	439	45	115	16	5	6	54	43-7	2	50	.262	.329	.362	100	0	0-3	**.999**	2	99	96	*1-125/D-3	-0.9
1974	Tex A	118	352	36	98	11	4	7	44	22-3	3	27	.278	.323	.392	109	3	1-2	.998	0	93	94	1-60,D-54	-0.3
1975	Tex A	132	403	50	107	18	1	11	47	35-6	2	43	.266	.327	.397	105	2	0-1	.995	3	111	124	1-99,D-25	-0.3
1976	Chi A	150	518	53	131	13	2	14	70	49-**19**	1	52	.253	.315	.367	100	-1	6-4	**.998**	9	119	96	*1-143/D-2	-0.3
1977	Chi A	128	470	56	116	16	1	18	69	36-11	2	50	.247	.300	.400	90	-8	1-2	.991	2	105	70	*1-125	-1.4
1978	†NY A	71	150	12	34	9	1	7	24	15-3	0	32	.227	.295	.440	107	1	0-1	1.000	0	106	55	D-35,1-15	-0.1
1979	NY A	106	295	60	85	15	3	23	53	38-11	0	25	.288	.367	.593	158	23	0-2	.992	-0	96	155	D-71,1-26	1.8
1980	†NY A	97	259	38	61	9	0	13	43	30-2	1	44	.236	.313	.421	102	0	1-0	.990	2	109	91	1-75,D-15	-0.2
1981	NY A	25	63	6	9	2	0	2	4	9-2	0	7	.143	.250	.270	50	-4	0-0	1.000	3	140	107	1-25	-0.3
	†Oak A	54	171	14	35	6	0	2	9	10-1	0	20	.205	.246	.275	53	-11	1-0	.997	1	107	79	1-48	-1.3
	Year	79	234	20	44	8	0	4	13	19-3	0	27	.188	.247	.274	52	-15	1-0	.998	4	117	88	1-73	-1.6
1982	Oak A	33	101	6	17	3	1	2	5	3-1	0	20	.168	.190	.277	28	-10	0-0	.992	1	120	82	1-32	-1.1
Total	15	1553	4908	541	1227	179	27	146	599	407-86	17	582	.250	.307	.387	98	-28	11-19	.995	26	106	100	*1-1221,D-205/O-24(LF)	-10.8
SPENCER, BEN Lloyd Benjamin B 5.15.1890 Patapsco, MD D 9.1.1970 Finksburg, MD BL/TL 5-8/160# d9.8 gs-Jim																								
1913	Was A	8	21	2	6	1	1	0	2	2	0	4	.286	.348	.429	124	1	0	.917	-0	87	120	/O-8(7-1-0)	0.0
SPENCER, SHANE Michael Shane B 2.20.1972 Key West, FL BR/TR 5-11/210# d4.10																								
1998	†NY A	27	67	18	25	6	0	10	27	5-0	0	12	.373	.411	.910	241	13	0-1	1.000	-1	83	94	O-22(9-0-15)/1D	1.1
1999	†NY A	71	205	25	48	8	0	8	20	18-0	2	51	.234	.301	.390	76	-8	0-4	1.000	3	104	146	O-64(46-0-22)/D-3	-0.8
2000	NY A	73	248	33	70	11	3	9	40	19-0	2	45	.282	.330	.460	100	-1	1-2	.989	4	118	142	O-40(33-0-7),D-33	-0.1
2001	†NY A	80	283	40	73	14	2	10	46	21-0	4	58	.258	.315	.428	93	-3	4-1	.993	7	117	183	O-68(44-0-28),D-14	0.0
2002	†NY A	94	288	32	71	15	2	6	34	31-4	4	62	.247	.324	.375	87	-5	0-3	.975	-1	97	105	O-91(40-0-55)/D	-1.0
2003	Cle A	64	210	23	57	10	0	8	26	18-0	1	52	.271	.328	.433	103	1	2-0	.987	-3	92	84	O-43(16-0-30),1-11/D-7	-0.4
	Tex A	55	185	16	42	10	0	4	23	27-0	2	40	.227	.329	.346	73	-7	0-0	.982	0	102	65	O-54(50-0-12)/D	-0.8
	Year	119	395	39	99	20	0	12	49	45-0	3	92	.251	.328	.392	88	-6	2-0	.984	-3	98	73	O-97(66-0-42),1-11/D-8	-1.2
Total	6	464	1486	187	386	74	7	55	216	139-4	15	320	.260	.325	.430	96	-10	7-11	.988	9	104	121	O-382(238-0-169)/D-63,1-12	-2.0
SPENCER, ROY Roy Hampton B 2.22.1900 Scranton, NC D 2.8.1973 Port Charlotte, FL BR/TR 5-10/168# d4.19																								
1925	Pit N	14	28	1	6	1	0	0	2	1	0	3	.214	.241	.250	24	-3	1-0	.905	-1	*138*	*0*	C-11	-0.3
1926	Pit N	28	43	5	17	3	0	0	4	1	0	0	.395	.409	.465	128	2	0	.970	-0	*125*	*34*	C-12	0.2
1927	†Pit N	38	92	9	26	3	1	0	13	3	0	3	.283	.305	.337	67	-4	0	.974	2	*134*	*58*	C-34	-0.1
1929	Was A	50	116	18	18	4	0	1	9	8	2	15	.155	.222	.216	13	-15	0-0	.967	-0	*116*	*99*	C-41	-1.3
1930	Was A	93	321	32	82	11	4	0	36	18	4	27	.255	.303	.315	57	-22	3-0	.989	6	*127*	*97*	C-93	-0.8
1931	Was A	145	483	48	133	16	3	1	60	35	2	21	.275	.327	.327	72	-20	0-0	.985	7	*126*	*82*	*C-145	-0.4
1932	Was A	102	317	28	78	9	0	1	41	24	1	17	.246	.301	.284	53	-22	0-1	.978	-4	***152***	*87*	C-98	-2.0
1933	Cle A	75	227	26	46	5	2	0	23	23	2	17	.203	.282	.242	38	-20	0-0	.990	6	*136*	*116*	C-72	-1.0
1934	Cle A	5	7	0	1	1	0	0	2	0	0	1	.143	.143	.286	8	-1	0-0	1.000	0	*78*	*224*	/C-4	-0.1
1936	NY N	19	18	3	5	1	0	0	3	2	0	3	.278	.350	.333	86	0	0	1.000	1	*141*	*82*	C-14	0.1
1937	Bro N	51	117	5	24	2	2	0	4	8	0	17	.205	.256	.256	39	-10	0	1.000	6	*85*	*115*	C-45	-0.2
1938	Bro N	16	45	2	12	1	1	0	6	5	0	6	.267	.340	.333	84	-1	0	.968	-1	*84*	*73*	C-16	-0.1
Total	12	636	1814	177	448	57	13	3	203	128	11	130	.247	.301	.298	56	-116	4-1	.984	21	*128*	*91*	C-585	-6.0
SPENCER, VERN Vernon Murray B 2.4.1894 Wixom, MI D 6.3.1971 Wixom, MI BL/TR 5-7/165# d7.4																								
1920	NY N	45	140	15	28	2	3	0	19	11	0	17	.200	.258	.257	49	-10	4-3	.932	4	119	169	O-40(38-1-2)	-0.8
SPERAW, PAUL Paul Bachman "Polly" or "Birdie" B 10.5.1893 Annville, PA D 2.22.1962 Cedar Rapids, IA BR/TR 5-8.5/145# d9.15																								
1920	StL A	1	2	0	0	0	0	0	0	0	0	0	.000	.000	.000	-97	-1	0-0	1.000	-0	76	0	/3	-0.1
SPERBER, ED Edwin George B 1.21.1895 Cincinnati, OH D 1.5.1976 Cincinnati, OH BL/TL 5-11/175# d4.16																								
1924	Bos N	24	59	8	17	2	0	1	12	10	1	9	.288	.400	.373	113	2	3-1	.897	-2	82	56	O-17(2-1-14)	-0.1
1925	Bos N	2	2	0	0	0	0	0	0	0	0	0	.000	.000	.000	-99	-1	0-0	—	0			H	-0.1
Total	2	26	61	8	17	2	0	1	12	10	1	9	.279	.389	.361	106	1	3-1	.897	-2	82	56	/O-17(2-1-14)	-0.2
SPERRING, ROB Robert Walter B 10.10.1949 San Francisco, CA BR/TR 6-1/185# d8.11																								
1974	Chi N	42	107	9	22	3	0	1	5	9-1	0	28	.206	.267	.262	46	-8	1-2	.952	-4	104	83	2-35/S-8	-1.0
1975	Chi N	65	144	25	30	4	1	1	9	16-3	1	31	.208	.288	.271	54	-9	0-2	.946	4	124	60	3-22,2-17,S-16/O-8(2-0-6)	-0.4
1976	Chi N	43	93	8	24	3	0	0	7	9-0	0	25	.258	.320	.290	69	-4	0-2	.955	-11	36	34	3-20,S-15/2-4,O-3(LF)	-1.5
1977	Hou N	58	129	6	24	3	0	1	9	12-2	0	23	.186	.254	.233	35	-12	0-0	.940	-5	65	113	S-22,2-20,3-11	-1.5
Total	4	208	473	48	100	13	1	3	30	46-6	1	107	.211	.281	.262	51	-33	1-6	.964	-15	102	66	/2-76,S-61,3-53,O-11(5-0-6)	-4.4
SPERRY, STAN Stanley Kenneth B 2.19.1914 Evansville, WI D 9.27.1962 Evansville, WI BL/TR 5-10.5/164# d7.28																								
1936	Phi N	20	37	2	5	3	0	0	4	3	0	5	.135	.200	.216	11	-5	0	.900	-3	78	72	2-15	-0.7
1938	Phi A	60	253	28	69	6	3	0	27	15	0	9	.273	.313	.320	61	-16	1-2	.959	-5	105	60	2-60	-1.6
Total	2	80	290	30	74	9	3	0	31	18	0	14	.255	.299	.307	54	-21	1-2	.951	-8	102	62	/2-75	-2.3
SPIERS, BILL William James B 6.5.1966 Orangeburg, SC BL/TR 6-2/190# d4.7 OF Total (33-LF 11-CF 20-RF)																								
1989	Mil A	114	345	44	88	9	3	4	33	21-1	1	63	.255	.298	.333	79	-11	10-2	.962	10	107	110	S-89,3-12/2-4,1-2,D-4	0.7
1990	Mil A	112	363	44	88	15	3	2	36	16-0	1	45	.242	.274	.317	66	-18	11-6	.976	-7	103	99	*S-111	-1.6
1991	Mil A	133	414	71	117	13	6	8	54	34-0	2	55	.283	.337	.401	107	3	14-8	.970	-12	93	116	*S-128/O(CF)D	0.0
1992	Mil A	12	16	2	5	2	0	0	2	1-0	0	4	.313	.353	.438	123	1	1-1	1.000	-4	19	0	/S-5,2-4,3D	-0.3
1993	Mil A	113	340	43	81	8	4	2	36	29-2	4	51	.238	.302	.303	65	-17	9-8	.971	-23	83	86	*2-104/O-7(2-2-4),S-4,D	-3.6
1994	Mil A	73	214	27	54	10	1	0	17	19-1	1	42	.252	.316	.308	59	-13	7-1	.947	4	104	96	3-35,S-35/O-2(RF),1D	-0.5
1995	NY N	63	72	5	15	2	1	0	11	12-1	0	15	.208	.314	.264	58	-4	0-1	.794	3	128	180	3-11/2-6	-0.1
1996	Hou N	122	218	27	55	10	1	6	26	20-4	2	34	.252	.320	.390	94	-2	7-0	.959	-0	109	119	3-77/2-7,1-4,S-4,O-2(0-1-1)	0.0
1997	†Hou N	132	291	51	93	27	4	4	48	61-6	1	42	.320	.438	.481	146	24	10-5	.935	18	119	130	3-84,S-28/1-8,2-4	4.3
1998	†Hou N	123	384	66	105	27	4	4	43	45-0	5	62	.273	.356	.396	101	2	11-2	.966	-5	97	64	3-99/2-9,1-7,S-2	0.0
1999	†Hou N	127	393	56	113	18	5	4	39	47-2	0	45	.288	.363	.389	92	-4	10-5	.958	13	128	118	3-71,O-31(25-7-9),S-13/2-4,1	1.0
2000	Hou N	124	355	41	107	17	3	3	43	49-3	1	38	.301	.386	.392	93	-2	7-4	.959	9	124	108	3-51,S-27,2-26,O-10(6-0-4)	0.9

Year	Tm Lg	G	AB	R	H	2B	3B	HR	RBI	BB-IB	HP	SO	AVG	OBP	SLG	AOPS	ABR	SB-CS	FA	FR	Rng	Thr	G at Pos	BFW
2001	Hou N	4	3	0	1	0	0	0	0	1-1	0	0	.333	.500	.333	116	0	0-0	—	0			/H	0.0
Total	13	1252	3408	477	922	158	35	37	388	355-21	18	496	.271	.341	.370	90	-41	97-43	.970	7	101	113	S-446,3-441,2-168/O-53L,1-23,D	0.8

SPIES, HARRY Henry B 6.12.1866 New Orleans, LA D 7.7.1942 Los Angeles, CA BL/TR 5-9/170# d4.20

Year	Tm Lg	G	AB	R	H	2B	3B	HR	RBI	BB-IB	HP	SO	AVG	OBP	SLG	AOPS	ABR	SB-CS	FA	FR	Rng	Thr	G at Pos	BFW
1895	Cin N	14	50	2	11	0	1	0	5	3	0	2	.220	.264	.260	34	-5	0	.867	2	*103*	*165*	C-12/1-2	-0.2
	Lou N	72	276	42	74	14	7	2	35	11	7	19	.268	.313	.391	86	-7	4	.981	-6	90	98	1-47,C-26/S	-0.8
	Year	86	326	44	85	14	8	2	40	14	7	21	.261	.305	.371	78	-12	4	.979	-4	96	106	1-49,C-38/S	-1.0

SPIEZIO, ED Edward Wayne B 10.31.1941 Joliet, IL BR/TR 5-11/180# d7.23 s-Scott

Year	Tm Lg	G	AB	R	H	2B	3B	HR	RBI	BB-IB	HP	SO	AVG	OBP	SLG	AOPS	ABR	SB-CS	FA	FR	Rng	Thr	G at Pos	BFW
1964	StL N	12	12	0	4	0	0	0	0	0-0	0	1	.333	.333	.333	81	0	0-0	—	0			H	0.0
1965	StL N	10	18	0	3	0	0	0	5	1-0	1	4	.167	.250	.167	18	-2	0-0	1.000	0	119	0	/3-3	-0.2
1966	StL N	26	73	4	16	5	1	2	10	5-1	0	11	.219	.269	.397	82	-2	1-0	.885	-4	82	89	3-19	-0.6
1967	†StL N	55	105	9	22	2	0	3	10	7-0	1	18	.210	.265	.314	66	-5	2-1	.962	-0	96	145	3-19/O-7(2-0-6)	-0.6
1968	†StL N	29	51	1	8	0	0	0	2	5-0	0	6	.157	.228	.157	19	-5	1-1	1.000	1	113	135	O-11(3-0-9)/3-2	-0.6
1969	SD N	121	355	29	83	9	0	13	43	38-3	4	64	.234	.313	.369	95	-3	1-2	.939	0	105	55	3-98/O(LF)	-0.4
1970	SD N	110	316	45	90	18	1	12	42	43-2	4	42	.285	.373	.462	129	14	4-0	.953	2	108	59	3-93	1.6
1971	SD N	97	308	16	71	10	1	7	36	22-3	4	50	.231	.286	.338	83	-8	6-5	.962	1	101	83	3-91/O(LF)	-0.8
1972	SD N	20	29	2	4	2	0	0	4	1-0	0	6	.138	.161	.207	6	-4	1-0	1.000	-1	57	158	/3-5	-0.5
	Chi A	74	277	20	66	10	1	2	22	13-3	2	43	.238	.276	.303	71	-10	0-1	.952	6	106	75	3-74	-0.6
Total	9	554	1544	126	367	56	4	39	174	135-12	16	245	.238	.303	.355	88	-25	16-10	.949	4	103	72	3-404/O-20(7-0-15)	-2.7

SPIEZIO, SCOTT Scott Edward B 9.21.1972 Joliet, IL BB/TR 6-2/205# d9.14 f-Ed OF Total (29-LF 19-RF)

Year	Tm Lg	G	AB	R	H	2B	3B	HR	RBI	BB-IB	HP	SO	AVG	OBP	SLG	AOPS	ABR	SB-CS	FA	FR	Rng	Thr	G at Pos	BFW
1996	Oak A	9	29	6	9	2	0	2	8	4-1	0	4	.310	.394	.586	146	2	0-1	.846	-1	67	0	/3-5,D-4	0.1
1997	Oak A	147	538	58	131	28	4	14	65	44-2	1	75	.243	.300	.388	80	-17	9-3	**.990**	-8	99	88	*2-146/3	-1.7
1998	Oak A	114	406	54	105	19	1	9	50	44-3	2	56	.259	.333	.377	87	-8	1-3	.975	-3	101	103	*2-112/D	-0.6
1999	Oak A	89	247	31	60	24	0	8	33	29-3	2	36	.243	.324	.437	97	-1	0-0	.984	5	127	111	2-42,3-31,1-10/D-6	0.5
2000	Ana A	123	297	47	72	11	2	17	49	40-2	3	56	.242	.334	.465	98	-2	1-2	.993	-2	35	74	D-50,1-29,3-15,O-10(8-0-2)/2-2	-0.9
2001	Ana A	139	457	57	124	29	4	13	54	34-4	5	65	.271	.326	.438	97	-2	5-2	.999	6	125	86	*1-105,D-20,O-18(10-0-8),3-10	-0.6
2002	†Ana A	153	491	80	140	34	2	12	82	67-7	4	52	.285	.371	.436	115	13	6-7	**.997**	-8	72	106	*1-143,3-20,O-10(8-0-2)/2	-0.8
2003	Ana A	158	521	69	138	36	7	16	83	46-8	5	66	.265	.326	.453	108	6	6-3	.994	-10	89	83	*1-114,3-52,O-10(3-0-7)	-1.2
Total	8	932	2986	402	779	183	20	91	424	308-30	22	410	.261	.331	.427	98	-9	28-21	.997	-23	88	93	1-401,2-303,3-134/D-81,O-48L	-5.2

SPIKES, CHARLIE Leslie Charles B 1.23.1951 Bogalusa, LA BR/TR 6-3/220# d9.1

Year	Tm Lg	G	AB	R	H	2B	3B	HR	RBI	BB-IB	HP	SO	AVG	OBP	SLG	AOPS	ABR	SB-CS	FA	FR	Rng	Thr	G at Pos	BFW
1972	NY A	14	34	2	5	1	0	0	3	1-0	0	13	.147	.171	.176	4	-4	0-1	1.000	0	91	176	/O-9(RF)	-0.5
1973	Cle A	140	506	68	120	12	3	23	73	45-1	5	103	.237	.303	.409	98	-3	5-3	.964	3	94	**174**	*O-111(90-0-22),D-26	-0.8
1974	Cle A	155	568	63	154	23	1	22	80	34-2	7	100	.271	.319	.431	116	9	10-7	.968	-2	94	135	*O-154(RF)	0.0
1975	Cle A	111	345	41	79	13	3	11	33	30-3	0	51	.229	.291	.380	88	-7	7-6	.974	4	96	176	*O-103(31-0-72)/D-2	-0.9
1976	Cle A	101	334	34	79	11	5	3	31	23-3	5	50	.237	.294	.326	83	-8	5-6	.985	1	102	108	O-98(2-0-96)/D-2	-1.4
1977	Cle A	32	95	13	22	2	0	3	11	11-0	2	17	.232	.321	.347	86	-2	0-2	.972	-3	74	60	O-27(RF)/D-2	-0.6
1978	Det A	10	28	1	7	1	0	0	2	2-1	2	6	.250	.344	.286	77	-1	0-0	.909	-1	58	178	/O-9(RF)	-0.2
1979	Atl N	66	93	12	26	8	0	3	21	5-1	0	30	.280	.310	.462	102	0	0-0	.842	-2	72	0	O-15(12-0-3)	-0.3
1980	Atl N	41	36	6	10	1	0	0	2	3-2	1	18	.278	.350	.306	82	-1	0-0	1.000	-0	91	0	/O-7(1-0-6)	-0.1
Total	9	670	2039	240	502	72	12	65	256	154-13	22	388	.246	.304	.389	96	-17	27-25	.969	0	94	140	O-533(136-0-398)/D-32	-4.8

SPILMAN, HARRY William Harry B 7.18.1954 Albany, GA BL/TR 6-1/190# d9.11 C4

Year	Tm Lg	G	AB	R	H	2B	3B	HR	RBI	BB-IB	HP	SO	AVG	OBP	SLG	AOPS	ABR	SB-CS	FA	FR	Rng	Thr	G at Pos	BFW
1978	Cin N	4	4	1	1	0	0	0	0	0-0	0	1	.250	.250	.250	40	0	0-0	—	0			H	0.0
1979	†Cin N	43	56	7	12	3	0	0	5	7-2	2	5	.214	.323	.268	63	-3	0-0	1.000	-0	42	54	1-12/3-4	-0.3
1980	Cin N	65	101	14	27	4	0	4	19	9-1	1	19	.267	.327	.426	110	1	0-0	.986	1	131	99	1-18/O-2(LF),C3	0.1
1981	Cin N	23	24	4	4	1	0	0	3	3-0	0	7	.167	.259	.208	33	-2	0-0	1.000	-0	58	0	/3-3,1-2	-0.2
	†Hou N	28	34	5	10	0	0	0	1	2-0	0	3	.294	.333	.294	83	-1	0-1	1.000	-1	54	81	1-13	-0.2
	Year	51	58	9	14	1	0	0	4	5-0	0	10	.241	.302	.259	61	-3	0-1	.984	-1	64	65	1-15/3-3	-0.4
1982	Hou N	38	61	7	17	2	0	3	11	5-0	0	10	.279	.333	.459	129	2	0-0	.989	-1	71	73	1-11	0.1
1983	Hou N	42	78	7	13	3	0	1	9	5-0	0	12	.167	.212	.244	29	-8	0-0	1.000	-2	75	52	1-19/C-6	-1.1
1984	Hou N	32	72	14	19	2	0	2	15	12-0	0	10	.264	.356	.375	118	2	0-0	.978	-4	62	127	1-18/C-8	-0.3
1985	Hou N	44	66	3	9	1	0	1	4	3-0	0	7	.136	.174	.197	4	-9	0-0	1.000	-1	45	141	1-19/C-2	-1.2
1986	Det A	24	49	6	12	2	0	3	8	3-0	0	8	.245	.288	.469	102	0	0-0	1.000	-0	66	0	D-11/3-2,C1	-0.1
	SF N	58	94	12	27	7	0	2	22	12-3	0	13	.287	.368	.426	124	4	0-0	.994	1	126	70	1-19/3-5,C20(LF)	0.3
1987	†SF N	83	90	5	24	5	0	1	14	9-0	0	20	.267	.327	.356	87	-2	1-1	.875	-2	75	152	3-10/1-9,C	-0.4
1988	SF N	40	40	4	7	1	1	1	3	4-1	0	6	.175	.250	.325	67	-2	0-0	1.000	0	68	218	/1-6,C-2,O(LF)	-0.2
	Hou N	7	5	0	0	0	0	0	0	0-0	0	3	.000	.000	.000	-99	-1	0-0	1.000	-0	0	0	/1	-0.2
	Year	47	45	4	7	1	1	1	3	4-1	0	9	.156	.224	.289	48	-3	0-0	1.000	0	56	178	/1-7,C-2,O(LF)	-0.4
1989	Hou N	32	36	7	10	3	0	0	3	7-1	0	2	.278	.395	.361	122	2	0-0	1.000	0	120	58	/1-9,C	0.1
Total	12	563	810	96	192	34	1	18	117	81-8	3	126	.237	.306	.348	85	-17	1-2	.991	-11	82	91	1-157/3-25,C-23,D-11,O-4(LF),2	-3.6

SPINDEL, HAL Harold Stewart B 5.27.1913 Chandler, OK D 7.28.2002 San Clemente, CA BR/TR 6/185# d4.23

Year	Tm Lg	G	AB	R	H	2B	3B	HR	RBI	BB-IB	HP	SO	AVG	OBP	SLG	AOPS	ABR	SB-CS	FA	FR	Rng	Thr	G at Pos	BFW
1939	StL A	48	119	13	32	3	1	0	11	8	0	7	.269	.315	.311	59	-7	0-2	.993	-2	*82*	*100*	C-32	-0.8
1945	Phi N	36	87	7	20	3	0	0	8	6	0	7	.230	.280	.264	53	-6	0	.964	-1	*68*	*119*	C-31	-0.5
1946	Phi N	1	3	0	1	0	0	0	0	1	0	0	.333	.333	.333	92	0	0	1.000	0	*0*	*0*	/C	0.0
Total	3	85	209	20	53	6	1	0	20	14	0	14	.254	.300	.292	57	-13	0-2	.980	-3	*75*	*107*	/C-64	-1.3

SPIVEY, JUNIOR Ernest Lee B 1.28.1975 Oklahoma City, OK BR/TR 6/185# d6.2

Year	Tm Lg	G	AB	R	H	2B	3B	HR	RBI	BB-IB	HP	SO	AVG	OBP	SLG	AOPS	ABR	SB-CS	FA	FR	Rng	Thr	G at Pos	BFW
2001	Ari N	72	163	33	42	6	3	5	21	23-0	2	47	.258	.354	.423	95	-1	3-0	.985	-2	88	112	2-66/S	0.0
2002	†Ari N★	143	538	103	162	34	6	16	78	65-5	16	100	.301	.389	.476	120	16	11-6	.977	1	94	78	*2-143	2.4
2003	Ari N	106	365	52	93	22	2	13	50	33-1	7	95	.255	.326	.433	88	-6	4-3	.982	2	98	89	2-98/O(CF)	0.0
Total	3	321	1066	188	297	62	11	34	149	121-6	25	242	.279	.363	.453	105	9	18-9	.980	2	94	87	2-307/O(CF)S	2.4

SPOGNARDI, ANDY Andrea Ettore B 10.18.1908 Boston, MA D 1.1.2000 Dedham, MA BR/TR 5-9.5/160# d9.2

Year	Tm Lg	G	AB	R	H	2B	3B	HR	RBI	BB-IB	HP	SO	AVG	OBP	SLG	AOPS	ABR	SB-CS	FA	FR	Rng	Thr	G at Pos	BFW
1932	Bos A	17	34	9	10	1	0	0	1	6	0	6	.294	.400	.324	92	0	0-0	.979	2	130	110	/2-9,S-3,3-2	0.3

SPOHRER, AL Alfred Ray B 12.3.1902 Philadelphia, PA D 7.17.1972 Plymouth, NH BR/TR 5-10.5/175# d4.13

Year	Tm Lg	G	AB	R	H	2B	3B	HR	RBI	BB-IB	HP	SO	AVG	OBP	SLG	AOPS	ABR	SB-CS	FA	FR	Rng	Thr	G at Pos	BFW
1928	NY N	2	2	0	0	0	0	0	0	0	0	0	.000	.000	.000	-99	-1	0	1.000	0	*0*	*0*	/C-2	0.0
	Bos N	51	124	15	27	3	0	0	9	5	1	11	.218	.254	.242	32	-13	1	.976	-5	*90*	*89*	C-48	-1.5
	Year	53	126	15	27	3	0	0	9	5	1	11	.214	.250	.238	30	-13	1	.977	-5	*89*	*88*	C-50	-1.5
1929	Bos N	114	342	42	93	21	8	2	48	26	2	35	.272	.327	.398	82	-11	1	.954	-5	*105*	*90*	*C-109	-0.9
1930	Bos N	112	356	44	113	22	8	2	37	22	2	24	.317	.361	.441	96	-3	3	.957	-10	*115*	*61*	*C-108	-0.6
1931	Bos N	114	350	23	84	17	5	0	27	22	0	27	.240	.285	.317	64	-19	2	.982	1	*106*	*79*	*C-111	-1.1
1932	Bos N	104	335	31	90	12	2	0	33	15	0	26	.269	.300	.316	69	-15	2	.991	8	*138*	*101*	*C-100	-0.1
1933	Bos N	67	184	11	46	6	1	1	12	11	0	13	.250	.292	.310	78	-6	3	.972	-3	*196*	*73*	C-65	-0.6
1934	Bos N	100	265	25	59	15	0	0	17	14	0	18	.223	.262	.279	49	-20	1	.977	-1	*112*	*106*	C-98	-1.6
1935	Bos N	92	260	22	63	7	1	1	16	9	2	12	.242	.273	.288	55	-17	0	.958	-10	*88*	*100*	C-90	-2.2
Total	8	756	2218	213	575	103	25	6	199	124	7	166	.259	.301	.336	70	-105	13	.972	-25	*117*	*87*	C-731	-8.6

SPOTTS, JIM James Russell B 4.10.1909 Honey Brook, PA D 6.15.1964 Medford, NJ BR/TR 5-10.5/175# d4.23

Year	Tm Lg	G	AB	R	H	2B	3B	HR	RBI	BB-IB	HP	SO	AVG	OBP	SLG	AOPS	ABR	SB-CS	FA	FR	Rng	Thr	G at Pos	BFW
1930	Phi N	3	2	1	0	0	0	0	0	0	0	1	.000	.000	.000	-93	-1	0	1.000	0	*0*	*0*	/C-2	0.0

SPRAGUE, CHARLIE Charles Wellington B 10.10.1864 Cleveland, OH D 12.31.1912 Des Moines, IA BL/TL 5-11/150# d9.17 ▲

Year	Tm Lg	G	AB	R	H	2B	3B	HR	RBI	BB-IB	HP	SO	AVG	OBP	SLG	AOPS	ABR	SB-CS	FA	FR	Rng	Thr	G at Pos	BFW
1887	Chi N	3	13	0	2	0	0	0	0	0	0	2	.154	.154	.154	-13	-2	0	.667	-1	48	0	/P-3,O(CF)	0.0
1889	Cle N	2	7	2	1	0	0	0	1	1	0	0	.143	.250	.143	11	0	1	.857	1	180	780	/P-2	0.0
1890	Tol AA	55	199	25	47	5	6	1	19	16	3		.236	.303	.337	86	-5	10	.892	-4	84	79	O-40(24-10-6),P-19	-0.6
Total	3	60	219	27	50	5	6	1	20	17	3	2	.228	.293	.320	77	-7	11	.892	-4	83	78	/O-41(24-11-6),P-24	-0.6

SPRAGUE, ED Edward Nelson Jr. B 7.25.1967 Castro Valley, CA BR/TR 6-2/210# d5.8 f-Ed OF Total (14-LF 2-RF)

Year	Tm Lg	G	AB	R	H	2B	3B	HR	RBI	BB-IB	HP	SO	AVG	OBP	SLG	AOPS	ABR	SB-CS	FA	FR	Rng	Thr	G at Pos	BFW
1991	Tor A	61	160	17	44	7	0	4	20	19-2	3	43	.275	.361	.394	105	2	0-3	.870	-2	101	38	3-35,1-22/C-2,D-2	-0.3
1992	†Tor A	22	47	6	11	2	0	1	7	3-0	0	7	.234	.280	.340	70	-2	0-0	.985	0	104	26	C-15/1-4,3D	-0.1
1993	†Tor A	150	546	50	142	31	1	12	73	32-1	10	85	.260	.310	.386	86	-11	1-0	.955	-6	88	79	*3-150	-1.5
1994	Tor A	109	405	38	97	19	1	11	44	23-1	11	95	.240	.296	.373	71	-18	1-0	.946	-10	74	107	*3-107/1-3	-2.5
1995	Tor A	**144**	521	77	127	27	2	18	74	58-3	**15**	96	.244	.333	.407	93	-5	0-0	.958	-1	94	78	*3-139/1-7,D-2	-0.5

Year	Tm Lg	G	AB	R	H	2B	3B	HR	RBI	BB-IB	HP	SO	AVG	OBP	SLG	AOPS	ABR	SB-CS	FA	FR	Rng	Thr	G at Pos	BFW
1996	Tor A	159	591	88	146	35	2	36	101	60-3	12	146	.247	.325	.496	105	3	0-0	.956	-10	87	115	*3-148,D-10	-0.6
1997	Tor A	138	504	63	115	29	4	14	48	51-0	6	102	.228	.306	.385	79	-17	0-1	.945	-4	90	93	*3-129/D-8	-1.8
1998	Tor A	105	382	49	91	20	0	17	51	24-1	11	73	.238	.301	.424	86	-9	0-2	.924	-6	90	52	*3-105	-1.3
	Oak A	27	87	8	13	5	0	3	7	2-1	2	17	.149	.187	.310	27	-10	1-0	.909	-1	95	59	3-23/1	-1.0
	Year	132	469	57	104	25	0	20	58	26-2	13	90	.222	.280	.403	75	-19	1-2	.921	-6	91	53	*3-128/1	-2.3
1999	Pit N★	137	490	71	131	27	2	22	81	50-6	**17**	93	.267	.352	.465	106	4	3-6	.920	-1	103	99	*3-134	0.3
2000	SD N	53	117	17	32	10	0	10	25	10-2	2	28	.274	.336	.615	145	7	0-0	.964	-8	69	83	1-24/3-5,O-5(4-0-1)	-0.2
	Bos A	33	111	11	24	4	0	2	9	12-0	0	18	.216	.293	.306	50	-9	0-0	.972	0	96	22	3-30/1-3,D	-0.8
	SD N	20	40	2	9	2	0	0	2	3-0	1	12	.225	.295	.275	49	-3	0-0	1.000	-9	27	0	/3-5,O-2(LF),12	-1.4
2001	†Sea A	45	94	9	28	7	0	2	16	11-1	1	18	.298	.374	.436	121	3	0-0	.981	-2	43	79	1-12/O-9(8-0-1),3-8,CD	0.0
Total	11	1203	4095	506	1010	225	12	152	558	358-21	91	833	.247	.318	.419	90	-65	6-12	.942	-59	90	85	*3-1019/1-77,D-34,C-18,O-16L,2	-11.7
SPRATT, HARRY Henry Lee B 7.10.1887 Broadford, VA D 7.3.1969 Washington, DC BL/TR 5-8.5/175# d4.13																								
1911	Bos N	62	154	22	37	4	4	2	13	13	0	25	.240	.299	.357	77	-6	1	.892	-9	82	70	S-26/2-5,3-4,O-4(0-3-1)	-1.3
1912	Bos N	27	89	6	23	3	2	3	15	7	0	11	.258	.313	.438	102	0	2	.842	-10	88	65	S-23	-0.9
Total	2	89	243	28	60	7	6	5	28	20	0	36	.247	.304	.387	86	-6	3	.871	-18	85	68	/S-49,2-5,O-4(0-3-1),3-4	-2.2
SPRIGGS, GEORGE George Herman B 5.22.1941 Jewell, MD BL/TR 5-11/175# d9.15																								
1965	Pit N	9	2	5	1	0	0	0	0	0-0	0	0	.500	.500	.500	182	0	2-0	—	-0	0	0	/O(RF)	0.1
1966	Pit N	9	7	0	1	0	0	0	0	0-0	0	3	.143	.143	.143	-20	-1	0-0	—	0			H	-0.1
1967	Pit N	38	57	14	10	1	1	0	5	6-0	0	20	.175	.246	.228	39	-5	3-0	1.000	-1	98	0	O-13(10-0-3)	-0.5
1969	KC A	23	29	4	4	2	1	0	0	3-0	1	8	.138	.242	.276	44	-2	0-0	1.000	-1	82	0	/O-6(4-1-1)	-0.3
1970	KC A	51	130	12	27	2	3	1	7	14-0	0	32	.208	.283	.292	59	-8	4-3	.953	1	98	188	O-36(RF)	-0.9
Total	5	130	225	35	43	5	5	1	12	23-0	1	63	.191	.266	.271	51	-16	9-3	.965	-1	96	132	/O-56(14-1-41)	-1.7
SPRINGER, STEVE Steven Michael B 2.11.1961 Long Beach, CA BR/TR 6/190# d5.22																								
1990	Cle A	4	12	1	2	0	0	0	1	0-0	0	6	.167	.154	.167	-7	-2	0-0	1.000	-1	57	0	/3-3,D	-0.3
1992	NY N	4	5	0	2	1	0	0	0	0-0	0	1	.400	.400	.600	182	1	0-0	1.000	-0	37	182	/23	0.0
Total	2	8	17	1	4	1	0	0	1	0-0	0	7	.235	.222	.294	48	-1	0-0	1.000	-1	55	0	/3-4,2D	-0.3
SPRINZ, JOE Joseph Conrad "Mule" B 8.3.1902 St.Louis, MO D 1.11.1994 Fremont, CA BR/TR 5-11/185# d7.16																								
1930	Cle A	17	45	5	8	1	0	0	2	4	0	4	.178	.245	.200	14	-6	0-0	1.000	4	*108*	*116*	C-17	-0.1
1931	Cle A	1	3	0	0	0	0	0	0	0	0	0	.000	.000	.000	-95	-1	0-0	1.000	0	*0*	*411*	/C	-0.1
1933	StL N	3	5	1	1	0	0	0	0	1	0	1	.200	.333	.200	53	0	0	1.000	1	*74*	*159*	/C-3	0.1
Total	3	21	53	6	9	1	0	0	2	5	0	5	.170	.241	.189	12	-7	0-0	1.000	4	*99*	*133*	/C-21	-0.1
SPURGEON, FREDDY Fred B 10.9.1900 Wabash, IN D 11.5.1970 Kalamazoo, MI BR/TR 5-11.5/160# d9.19																								
1924	Cle A	3	7	0	1	1	0	0	0	0	1	0	.143	.250	.286	37	-1	0-0	.882	-0	125	0	/2-3	-0.1
1925	Cle A	107	376	50	108	9	3	0	32	15	0	21	.287	.315	.327	62	-23	8-5	.927	-3	110	119	3-56,2-46/S-3	-2.0
1926	Cle A	149	614	101	181	31	3	0	49	27	2	36	.295	.327	.355	77	-22	7-2	.962	-6	100	**119**	*2-149	-2.3
1927	Cle A	57	179	30	45	6	1	1	19	18	1	14	.251	.323	.313	65	-9	8-1	.938	-6	93	91	2-52	-1.2
Total	4	316	1176	181	335	47	7	1	100	60	4	71	.285	.322	.339	70	-55	23-8	.958	-16	99	104	2-250/3-56,S-3	-5.6
SPURNEY, ED Edward Frederick B 1.19.1872 Cleveland, OH D 10.12.1932 Cleveland, OH d6.26																								
1891	Pit N	3	7	2	2	1	0	0	0	2	0	1	.286	.444	.429	158	1	0	.889	-0	109	0	/S-3	0.0
SQUIRES, MIKE Michael Lynn B 3.5.1952 Kalamazoo, MI BL/TL 5-11/185# d9.1 C4																								
1975	Chi A	20	65	5	15	0	0	0	4	8-2	0	5	.231	.311	.231	55	-4	3-0	.988	0	108	82	1-20	-0.4
1977	Chi A	3	3	0	0	0	0	0	0	0-0	0	1	.000	.000	.000	-99	-1	0-0	1.000	0	418	0	/1	-0.1
1978	Chi A	46	150	25	42	9	2	0	19	16-0	0	21	.280	.343	.367	101	1	4-4	.997	-2	75	83	1-45	-0.5
1979	Chi A	122	295	44	78	10	1	2	22	22-3	2	9	.264	.318	.325	74	-10	15-5	.995	5	123	84	*1-110/O(LF)	-0.9
1980	Chi A	131	343	38	97	11	3	2	33	33-1	1	24	.283	.347	.350	92	-3	8-9	.995	6	123	90	*1-114/C-2	-0.5
1981	Chi A	92	294	35	78	9	0	0	25	22-0	0	17	.265	.312	.296	79	-8	7-2	.992	4	118	101	1-88/O(LF)	-0.8
1982	Chi A	116	195	33	52	9	3	1	21	14-3	0	13	.267	.316	.359	85	-4	3-3	.995	5	**134**	**119**	*1-109	-0.3
1983	†Chi A	143	153	21	34	4	1	1	11	22-3	2	11	.222	.326	.281	67	-6	3-3	**.996**	3	119	**131**	*1-124/3D	-0.7
1984	Chi A	104	82	9	15	1	0	0	6	6-1	0	7	.183	.239	.195	21	-9	2-2	1.000	1	93	155	1-77,3-13/O-3(0-1-1),P	-1.0
1985	Chi A	2	0	1	0	0	0	0	0	0-0	0	0	—	—	—	—	0	0-0	—	0			/R	0.0
Total	10	779	1580	211	411	53	10	6	141	143-13	5	108	.260	.321	.318	78	-44	45-28	.995	23	117	102	1-688/3-14,D-5,O-5(2-1-1),C-2,P	-5.2
STABELL, JOE Joseph F. B Buffalo, NY D 7.10.1923 Buffalo, NY d9.19																								
1885	Buf N	7	22	0	1	0	0	0	0	0		9	.045	.045	.045	-68	-4		.545	-2	0	0	/O-6(0-6-1),2	-0.6
STAEHLE, MARV Marvin Gustave B 3.13.1942 Oak Park, IL BL/TR 5-10/172# d9.15																								
1964	Chi A	6	5	0	2	0	0	0	2	0-0	0	0	.400	.400	.400	127	0	1-0	—	0			H	0.0
1965	Chi A	7	7	0	3	0	0	0	2	0-0	0	0	.429	.429	.429	154	0	0-0	—	0			H	0.0
1966	Chi A	8	15	2	2	0	0	0	0	4-0	0	2	.133	.316	.133	37	-1	1-0	1.000	1	118	197	/2-6	0.1
1967	Chi A	32	54	1	6	1	0	0	1	4-0	0	8	.111	.172	.130	-10	-7	1-1	1.000	-3	107	48	2-17/S-5	-1.0
1969	Mon N	6	17	4	7	2	0	1	1	2-0	0	0	.412	.474	.706	226	3	0-0	.944	-1	103	73	/2-4	0.3
1970	Mon N	104	321	41	70	9	1	0	26	39-1	3	21	.218	.306	.252	52	-21	1-3	.963	-17	89	94	2-91/S	-3.4
1971	Atl N	22	36	5	4	0	0	0	1	5-0	1	4	.111	.238	.111	2	-5	0-0	1.000	4	132	113	/2-7,3	0.0
Total	7	185	455	53	94	12	1	1	33	54-1	4	35	.207	.295	.244	50	-31	4-4	.971	-16	95	93	2-125/S-6,3	-4.0
STAFFORD, HEINIE Henry Alexander B 11.1.1891 Orleans, VT D 1.29.1972 Lake Worth, FL BR/TR 5-7/160# d10.5																								
1916	NY N	1	1	0	0	0	0	0	0	0	0	0	.000	.000	.000	-99	0	0	—	0			H	0.0
STAFFORD, GENERAL James Joseph "Jamsey" B 7.9.1868 Webster, MA D 9.18.1923 Worcester, MA BR/TR 5-8/165# d8.27 b-John ▲ OF Total (96-LF 111-CF 44-RF)																								
1890	Buf P	15	49	11	7	1	0	0	3	7	0	8	.143	.250	.163	13	-6	2	.893	-2	82	207	P-12/O-4(1-1-2)	-0.2
1893	NY N	67	281	58	79	7	4	5	27	25	2	31	.281	.344	.388	94	-4	19	.901	-7	72	173	O-67(CF)	-1.3
1894	NY N	14	46	10	10	1	1	0	4	10	1	7	.217	.368	.283	59	-3	2	.750	-4	75	104	/3-6,O-5(RF),21	-0.5
1895	NY N	124	463	79	129	12	5	3	73	40	6	32	.279	.344	.346	80	-14	42	.911	-7	99	97	*2-110,O-12(LF)/3-2	-1.4
1896	NY N	59	230	28	66	9	1	0	40	13	3	18	.287	.333	.335	79	-7	15	.897	-3	131	114	O-53(LF)/S-6	-1.2
1897	NY N	7	23	0	2	0	0	0	3	3	0		.087	.192	.087	-26	-4	0	1.000	-3	0	0	/O-5(LF),S-2	-0.6
	Lou N	113	441	68	122	16	5	7	54	31	3		.277	.328	.383	91	-7	15	.886	-10	101	82	*S-105/O-7(4-2-1),3	-1.1
	Year	120	464	68	124	16	5	7	57	34	3		.267	.321	.369	85	-11	15	.881	-12	100	83	*S-107,O-12(9-2-1)/3	-1.7
1898	Lou N	49	181	26	54	3	0	1	25	19	1		.298	.368	.331	102	1	7	.901	-5	95	56	2-28,O-22(6-7-9)/3	-0.4
	Bos N	37	123	21	32	2	0	1	8	4	1		.260	.289	.301	66	-6	3	.909	-3	22	0	O-35(9-1-25)/1	-1.0
	Year	86	304	47	86	5	0	2	33	23	2		.283	.337	.319	87	-5	10	.924	-8	69	170	O-57(15-8-34),2-28/31	-1.4
1899	Bos N	55	182	29	55	4	2	3	40	7	0		.302	.328	.396	89	-4	9	.956	-8	0	0	O-41(6-33-2)/2-5,S-5	-1.3
	Was N	31	118	11	29	5	1	1	14	5	0		.246	.276	.331	67	-6	4	.951	-4	85	39	2-17,S-13/3-2	-0.8
	Year	86	300	40	84	9	3	4	54	12	0		.280	.308	.370	81	-10	13	.956	-12	0	0	O-41(6-33-2),2-22,S-18/3-2	-2.1
Total	8	571	2137	341	585	60	19	21	291	164	17	96	.274	.330	.349	82	-60	118	.911	-55	69	110	O-251C,2-161,S-131/3-12,P-12,1-2	-9.8
STAFFORD, BOB Robert M. B 6.26.1872 Oak Ridge, NC D 8.20.1916 Moores Springs, NC 6/180# d10.12																								
1890	Phi AA	1	2	0	0	0	0	0	0	0	0		.000	.000	.000	-99	-1	0	—	-0	0	0	/O(RF)	-0.1
STAGGS, STEVE Stephen Robert B 5.6.1951 Anchorage, AK BR/TR 5-9/150# d7.1																								
1977	Tor A	72	290	37	75	11	6	2	28	36-0	0	38	.259	.339	.359	90	-4	5-9	.965	-13	88	67	2-72	-1.5
1978	Oak A	47	78	10	19	2	2	0	0	19-0	0	17	.244	.392	.321	108	2	2-3	.976	-3	90	64	2-40/S-2,3-2,D-2	0.0
Total	2	119	368	47	94	13	8	2	28	55-0	0	55	.255	.351	.351	94	-2	7-12	.968	-16	88	66	2-112/D-2,3-2,S-2	-1.5
STAHL, CHICK Charles Sylvester B 1.10.1873 Avilla, IN D 3.28.1907 W.Baden, IN BL/TL 5-10/160# d4.19 M1																								
1897	†Bos N	114	469	112	166	30	13	4	97	38	3		.354	.406	.499	130	19	18	.928	-5	104	141	*O-111(1-0-110)	0.8
1898	Bos N	125	467	72	144	21	8	3	52	46	4		.308	.375	.407	118	11	6	.968	-3	79	110	*O-125(8-0-118)	0.2
1899	Bos N	148	576	122	202	23	19	7	52	72	4		.351	.426	.493	138	31	33	.969	3	112	110	*O-148(1-1-146)/P	2.4
1900	Bos N	136	553	88	163	23	16	5	82	34	0		.295	.336	.421	96	-6	27	**.968**	5	110	80	*O-135(64-1-71)	-1.0
1901	Bos A	131	515	105	156	20	16	6	72	54	7		.303	.377	.439	128	20	29	.957	-5	70	89	*O-131(0-130-1)	0.8
1902	Bos A	127	508	92	164	22	11	2	58	37	5		.323	.375	.421	117	12	24	.953	-6	119	68	*O-125(CF)	0.0
1903	†Bos A	77	299	60	82	12	6	2	44	28	1		.274	.338	.375	108	3	10	.961	-3	134	106	O-74(CF)	-0.3

Year	Tm Lg	G	AB	R	H	2B	3B	HR	RBI	BB-IB	HP	SO	AVG	OBP	SLG	AOPS	ABR	SB-CS	FA	FR	Rng	Thr	G at Pos	BFW
1904	Bos A	**157**	587	83	170	27	**19**	3	67	64	7		.290	.366	.416	139	28	11	.961	-18	34	0	*O-157(CF)	0.3
1905	Bos A	134	500	61	129	17	4	0	47	50	5		.258	.332	.308	102	3	18	.977	-6	77	133	*O-134(CF)	-1.1
1906	Bos A	**155**	595	63	170	24	6	4	51	47	8		.286	.346	.366	123	17	13	.961	7	124	**216**	*O-155(CF),M	1.8
Total	10	1304	5069	858	1546	219	118	36	622	470	44		.305	.369	.416	121	138	189	.961	-31	94	104	*O-1295(74-777-446)/P	3.9

STAHL, JAKE Garland B 4.13.1879 Elkhart, IL D 9.18.1922 Monrovia, CA BR/TR 6-2/195# d4.20 M4

Year	Tm Lg	G	AB	R	H	2B	3B	HR	RBI	BB-IB	HP	SO	AVG	OBP	SLG	AOPS	ABR	SB-CS	FA	FR	Rng	Thr	G at Pos	BFW
1903	Bos A	40	92	14	22	3	5	2	8	4	2		.239	.286	.446	111	1	1	.956	0	*119*	*89*	C-28/O(LF)	0.3
1904	Was A	142	520	54	136	29	12	3	50	21	15		.262	.309	.381	119	11	25	.978	4	115	90	*1-119,O-23(CF)	1.3
1905	Was A	141	501	66	125	22	12	5	66	28	**17**		.250	.311	.371	121	11	41	.986	2	104	86	*1-140,M	1.1
1906	Was A	137	482	38	107	9	8	0	51	21	8		.222	.266	.274	73	-17	30	.983	-2	93	82	*1-136,M	-2.3
1908	NY A	75	274	34	70	18	5	2	42	11	8		.255	.304	.380	120	6	17	.933	4	177	123	O-68(64-4-0)/1-6	0.7
	Bos A	78	262	29	64	9	11	0	23	20	15		.244	.333	.363	123	7	13	.984	-2	88	98	1-78	0.4
	Year	153	536	63	134	27	16	2	65	31	**23**		.250	.319	.371	122	13	30	.984	2	87	91	1-84,O-68(64-4-0)	1.1
1909	Bos A	127	435	62	128	19	12	6	60	43	15		.294	.377	.434	153	27	16	.986	-12	64	93	*1-126	1.5
1910	Bos A	144	531	68	144	19	16	**10**	77	42	8		.271	.334	.424	134	18	22	.985	-7	75	75	*1-142	0.9
1912	†Bos A	95	326	40	98	21	6	3	60	31	6		.301	.372	.429	123	10	13	.980	-2	92	96	1-92,M	0.6
1913	Bos A	2	2	0	0	0	0	0	0	0	0	1	.000	.000	.000	-98	-1	0	—	0			HM	-0.1
Total	9	981	3425	405	894	149	87	31	437	221	94	1	.261	.323	.382	120	73	178	.983	-13	90	87	1-839/O-92(65-27-0),C-28	4.4

STAHL, LARRY Larry Floyd B 6.29.1941 Belleville, IL BL/TL 6-1/185# d9.11

Year	Tm Lg	G	AB	R	H	2B	3B	HR	RBI	BB-IB	HP	SO	AVG	OBP	SLG	AOPS	ABR	SB-CS	FA	FR	Rng	Thr	G at Pos	BFW
1964	KC A	15	46	7	12	1	0	3	6	1-0	0	10	.261	.277	.478	102	0	0-0	.955	0	93	156	O-10(5-4-1)	-0.1
1965	KC A	28	81	9	16	2	1	4	14	5-0	1	16	.198	.250	.395	82	-2	1-0	1.000	1	115	95	O-21(8-12-4)	-0.2
1966	KC A	119	312	37	78	11	5	5	34	17-3	1	63	.250	.289	.365	90	-5	5-3	.980	2	102	129	O-94(69-2-27)	-0.8
1967	NY N	71	155	9	37	5	0	1	18	8-0	2	25	.239	.283	.290	66	-7	2-2	.969	2	107	170	O-43(3-32-8)	-0.7
1968	NY N	53	183	15	43	7	2	3	10	21-1	0	38	.235	.314	.344	97	0	3-0	.983	4	112	147	O-47(13-30-19)/1-9	0.1
1969	SD N	95	162	10	32	6	2	3	10	17-3	1	31	.198	.278	.315	68	-7	3-3	.981	4	99	192	O-37(27-4-5),1-13	-0.6
1970	SD N	52	66	5	12	2	0	0	3	2-0	0	14	.182	.206	.212	13	-8	2-2	1.000	-0	82	129	O-20(17-0-4)	-1.0
1971	SD N	114	308	27	78	13	4	8	36	26-4	0	59	.253	.310	.399	107	2	4-3	.987	7	94	208	O-75(46-8-26)/1-7	0.4
1972	SD N	107	297	31	67	9	3	7	20	31-3	0	67	.226	.298	.347	89	-5	1-3	.986	-1	98	78	O-76(26-10-42)/1	-1.2
1973	†Cin N	76	111	17	25	2	2	2	12	14-3	1	34	.225	.315	.333	85	-2	1-0	1.000	-1	68	176	O-29(3-4-24)/1-2	-0.4
Total	10	730	1721	167	400	58	19	36	163	142-17	6	357	.232	.292	.351	86	-34	22-16	.983	18	100	145	O-452(217-106-160)/1-32	-4.5

STAHOVIAK, SCOTT Scott Edmund B 3.6.1970 Waukegan, IL BL/TR 6-5/210# d9.10

Year	Tm Lg	G	AB	R	H	2B	3B	HR	RBI	BB-IB	HP	SO	AVG	OBP	SLG	AOPS	ABR	SB-CS	FA	FR	Rng	Thr	G at Pos	BFW
1993	Min A	20	57	1	11	4	0	0	1	3-0	0	22	.193	.233	.263	33	-5	0-2	.922	2	129	35	3-19	-0.4
1995	Min A	94	263	28	70	19	0	3	23	30-1	1	61	.266	.341	.373	86	-4	5-1	.998	7	144	94	1-69,3-22/D	-0.2
1996	Min A	130	405	72	115	30	3	13	61	59-7	2	114	.284	.376	.469	111	8	3-3	.994	10	**134**	89	*1-114/D-9	0.7
1997	Min A	91	275	33	63	17	0	10	33	24-1	6	73	.229	.301	.400	81	-8	5-2	.990	4	124	110	1-81/D-5	-1.0
1998	Min A	9	19	1	2	0	0	1	1	0-0	0	7	.105	.105	.263	-8	-3	0-0	.975	0	145	117	/1-4,O(RF)	-0.3
Total	5	344	1019	135	261	70	3	27	119	116-9	9	277	.256	.335	.410	91	-12	13-8	.994	23	134	97	1-268/3-41,D-15,O(RF)	-1.2

STAIGER, ROY Roy Joseph B 1.6.1950 Tulsa, OK BR/TR 6/195# d9.12

Year	Tm Lg	G	AB	R	H	2B	3B	HR	RBI	BB-IB	HP	SO	AVG	OBP	SLG	AOPS	ABR	SB-CS	FA	FR	Rng	Thr	G at Pos	BFW
1975	NY N	13	19	2	3	1	0	0	0	0-0	0	4	.158	.158	.211	2	-3	0-0	1.000	-1	79	0	3-13	-0.4
1976	NY N	95	304	23	67	8	1	2	26	25-6	1	35	.220	.278	.273	62	-16	3-3	.967	13	111	132	3-93/S	-0.4
1977	NY N	40	123	16	31	9	0	2	11	4-0	0	20	.252	.276	.374	76	-5	1-0	.934	4	116	85	3-36/S	-0.1
1979	NY A	4	11	1	3	1	0	0	1	1-0	0	0	.273	.308	.364	90	0	0-0	1.000	-0	90	158	/3-4	0.0
Total	4	152	457	42	104	19	1	4	38	30-6	1	59	.228	.274	.300	64	-24	4-3	.960	16	110	115	3-146/S-2	-0.9

STAINBACK, TUCK George Tucker B 8.4.1911 Los Angeles, CA D 11.29.1992 Camarillo, CA BR/TR 5-11.5/175# d4.17

Year	Tm Lg	G	AB	R	H	2B	3B	HR	RBI	BB-IB	HP	SO	AVG	OBP	SLG	AOPS	ABR	SB-CS	FA	FR	Rng	Thr	G at Pos	BFW
1934	Chi N	104	359	47	110	14	3	2	46	8	3	42	.306	.327	.379	90	-6	7	.955	-3	97	64	O-96(60-22-15)/3	-1.3
1935	Chi N	47	94	16	24	4	0	3	11	0	2	13	.255	.271	.394	76	-4	1	.932	-1	99	49	O-28(1-1-26)	-0.6
1936	Chi N	44	75	13	13	3	0	1	5	6	0	14	.173	.235	.253	31	-7	1	1.000	1	110	79	O-26(15-6-5)	-0.7
1937	Chi N	72	160	18	37	7	1	0	14	7	1	16	.231	.268	.287	49	-11	3	.981	2	105	126	O-49(9-39-1)	-1.1
1938	StL N	6	10	2	0	0	0	0	0	0	0	3	.000	.000	.000	-95	-3	0	1.000	0	133	0	/O-2(1-1-0)	-0.3
	Phi N	30	81	9	21	3	0	1	11	3	1	3	.259	.294	.333	74	-3	1	.980	1	117	63	O-25(13-4-9)	-0.3
	Bro N	35	104	15	34	6	3	0	20	2	1	4	.327	.346	.442	113	1	1	.981	-1	99	56	O-23(2-21-0)	0.0
	Year	71	195	26	55	9	3	1	31	5	2	10	.282	.307	.374	86	-4	2	.982	0	109	56	O-50(16-26-9)	-0.6
1939	Bro N	68	201	22	54	7	0	3	19	4	2	23	.269	.290	.348	68	-10	0	.938	-4	103	0	O-55(10-39-7)	-1.5
1940	Det A	15	40	4	9	2	0	0	1	1	1	9	.225	.262	.275	36	-4	0-0	.968	2	99	542	/O-9(1-8-0)	-0.2
1941	Det A	94	200	19	49	8	1	2	10	3	1	21	.245	.260	.325	49	-15	6-3	.948	-1	103	69	O-80(39-6-36)	-1.9
1942	†NY A	15	10	0	2	0	0	0	0	0	0	2	.200	.200	.200	13	-1	0-0	1.000	0	122	0	/O-3(2-0-1)	-0.1
1943	†NY A	71	231	31	60	11	2	0	10	7	1	16	.260	.285	.325	77	-8	3-3	.993	-0	101	71	O-60(12-43-5)	-1.1
1944	NY A	30	78	13	17	3	0	0	5	3	0	7	.218	.247	.256	42	-6	1-0	.957	-0	104	68	O-24(4-4-17)	-0.8
1945	NY A	95	327	40	84	12	2	5	32	13	2	20	.257	.289	.352	82	-9	0-4	.968	5	107	137	O-83(2-72-9)	-0.9
1946	Phi A	91	291	35	71	10	2	0	20	7	1	20	.244	.264	.292	56	-19	3-2	.963	2	110	98	O-66(11-18-37)	-2.0
Total	13	817	2261	284	585	90	14	17	204	64	16	213	.259	.284	.333	68	-105	27-12	.965	3	104	88	O-629(182-284-168)/3	-12.8

STAIRS, MATT Matthew Wade B 2.27.1968 St.John, NB, CAN BL/TR 5-9/175# d5.29

Year	Tm Lg	G	AB	R	H	2B	3B	HR	RBI	BB-IB	HP	SO	AVG	OBP	SLG	AOPS	ABR	SB-CS	FA	FR	Rng	Thr	G at Pos	BFW
1992	Mon N	13	30	2	5	2	0	0	5	7-0	0	7	.167	.316	.233	61	-1	0-0	.933	-1	93	0	O-10(LF)	-0.2
1993	Mon N	6	8	1	3	1	0	0	2	0-0	0	1	.375	.375	.500	126	0	0-0	1.000	-0	88	0	/O(LF)	0.0
1995	†Bos A	39	88	8	23	7	1	1	17	4-0	1	14	.261	.298	.398	77	-3	0-1	.913	-4	48	150	O-23(17-0-6)/D-2	-0.8
1996	Oak A	61	137	21	38	5	1	10	23	19-2	1	23	.277	.367	.547	130	6	1-1	.985	4	86	339	O-44(16-0-29)/1D	0.8
1997	Oak A	133	352	62	105	19	0	27	73	50-1	3	60	.298	.386	.582	152	27	3-2	.977	-3	83	129	O-89(28-0-63),D-16/1-7	1.8
1998	Oak A	149	523	88	154	33	1	26	106	59-4	6	93	.294	.370	.511	130	24	8-3	1.000	4	102	449	*D-120,O-12(11-0-2)/1-6	1.8
1999	Oak A	146	531	94	137	26	3	38	102	89-6	2	124	.258	.366	.533	131	25	2-7	.981	-4	89	133	*O-139(0-1-139)/1D	1.1
2000	†Oak A	143	476	74	108	26	0	21	81	78-4	1	122	.227	.333	.414	91	-6	5-2	.979	-4	94	73	*O-103(0-1-102),D-37/1	-1.6
2001	Chi N	128	340	48	85	21	0	17	61	52-7	7	76	.250	.358	.462	117	10	2-3	.993	3	105	69	1-89,O-22(22-0-1)/2D	0.5
2002	Mil N	107	270	41	66	15	0	16	41	36-4	8	50	.244	.349	.478	120	7	2-0	.993	1	98	134	O-84(35-0-51)	0.5
2003	Pit N	121	305	49	89	20	1	20	57	45-3	5	64	.292	.389	.561	142	20	0-1	.987	-6	81	131	O-55(8-0-47),1-31/D-2	0.9
Total	11	1046	3060	488	813	175	7	176	568	439-31	34	634	.266	.362	.500	123	109	23-20	.981	-9	89	138	O-582(148-2-440),D-189,1-136/2	4.8

STALEY, GALE George Gaylord B 5.2.1899 DePere, WI D 4.19.1989 Walnut Creek, CA BL/TR 5-8.5/167# d9.16

Year	Tm Lg	G	AB	R	H	2B	3B	HR	RBI	BB-IB	HP	SO	AVG	OBP	SLG	AOPS	ABR	SB-CS	FA	FR	Rng	Thr	G at Pos	BFW
1925	Chi N	7	26	2	11	2	0	0	3	2	0	1	.423	.464	.500	144	2	0-1	.979	3	117	171	/2-7	0.4

STALLCUP, VIRGIL Thomas Virgil "Red" B 1.3.1922 Ravensford, NC D 5.2.1989 Greenville, SC BR/TR 6-3/185# d4.18

Year	Tm Lg	G	AB	R	H	2B	3B	HR	RBI	BB-IB	HP	SO	AVG	OBP	SLG	AOPS	ABR	SB-CS	FA	FR	Rng	Thr	G at Pos	BFW
1947	Cin N	8	1	1	0	0	0	0	0	0	0	1	.000	.000	.000	-99	0	0	—	-0	0	0	/S	0.0
1948	Cin N	149	539	40	123	30	4	3	65	18	0	52	.228	.253	.315	55	-36	2	.956	-0	98	99	*S-148	-2.8
1949	Cin N	141	575	49	146	28	5	3	45	9	2	44	.254	.268	.336	60	-34	1	.962	-14	96	97	*S-141	-3.9
1950	Cin N	136	483	44	121	23	2	8	54	17	0	39	.251	.276	.356	65	-26	4	**.973**	-5	95	89	*S-136	-2.3
1951	Cin N	121	428	33	103	17	2	8	49	6	0	40	.241	.251	.346	58	-27	2-4	**.969**	-6	99	87	*S-117	-2.7
1952	Cin N	2	1	0	0	0	0	0	0	0	0	0	.000	.000	.000	-99	0	0-0	—	-0	0	0	/S	0.0
	StL N	29	31	4	4	1	0	0	1	1	0	5	.129	.156	.161	-12	-5	0-0	1.000	2	134	159	S-12	-0.3
	Year	31	32	4	4	1	0	0	1	1	0	5	.125	.152	.156	-15	-5	0-0	1.000	2	130	155	S-13	-0.3
1953	StL N	1	1	0	0	0	0	0	0	0	0	0	.000	.000	.000	-99	0	0-0	—	0			H	0.0
Total	7	587	2059	171	497	99	13	22	214	51	2	181	.241	.260	.334	58	-128	9-4	.965	-23	97	94	S-556	-12.0

STALLER, GEORGE George Walborn "Stopper" B 4.1.1916 Rutherford Heights, PA D 7.3.1992 Harrisburg, PA BL/TL 5-11/190# d9.14 Mil 1944-45 C8

Year	Tm Lg	G	AB	R	H	2B	3B	HR	RBI	BB-IB	HP	SO	AVG	OBP	SLG	AOPS	ABR	SB-CS	FA	FR	Rng	Thr	G at Pos	BFW
1943	Phi A	21	85	14	23	1	3	3	12	5	2	6	.271	.326	.459	129	2	1-0	.977	-0	101	68	O-20(RF)	0.1

STALLINGS, GEORGE George Tweedy "Gentleman George" B 11.17.1867 Augusta, GA D 5.13.1929 Haddock, GA BR/TR 6-1/187# d5.22 M13

Year	Tm Lg	G	AB	R	H	2B	3B	HR	RBI	BB-IB	HP	SO	AVG	OBP	SLG	AOPS	ABR	SB-CS	FA	FR	Rng	Thr	G at Pos	BFW
1890	Bro N	4	11	1	0	0	0	0	0	1	1	3	.000	.154	.000	-54	-2	0	.933	-1	*85*	*29*	/C-4	-0.3
1897	Phi N	2	9	1	2	1	0	0	0	0	0		.222	.222	.333	47	-1	0	1.000	0	431	0	/O(RF)1M	0.0
1898	Phi N	1	0	1	0	0	0	0	0	0	0		—	—	—	—	-0	0	—	0			/HM	0.0
Total	3	7	20	3	2	1	0	0	0	1	1	3	.100	.182	.150	-7	-3	0	.933	-1	*85*	*29*	/C-4,1O(RF)	-0.3

STANAGE, OSCAR Oscar Harland B 3.17.1883 Tulare, CA D 11.11.1964 Detroit, MI BR/TR 5-9.5/185# d5.19 C5

Year	Tm Lg	G	AB	R	H	2B	3B	HR	RBI	BB-IB	HP	SO	AVG	OBP	SLG	AOPS	ABR	SB-CS	FA	FR	Rng	Thr	G at Pos	BFW
1906	Cin N	1	1	0	0	0	0	0	0	0	0		.000	.000	.000	-96	0	0	1.000	-0	*0*	*0*	/C	0.0
1909	†Det A	77	252	17	66	8	6	0	21	11	2		.262	.298	.341	98	-2	2	.964	-5	*98*	*88*	C-77	0.1

Year	Tm Lg	G	AB	R	H	2B	3B	HR	RBI	BB-IB	HP	SO	AVG	OBP	SLG	AOPS	ABR	SB-CS	FA	FR	Rng	Thr	G at Pos	BFW
1910	Det A	88	275	24	57	7	4	2	25	20	2		.207	.266	.284	68	-11	1	.952	-1	*103*	***113***	C-84	-0.4
1911	Det A	141	503	45	133	13	7	3	51	20	3		.264	.297	.336	73	-21	3	.952	-10	*103*	*105*	*C-141	-1.8
1912	Det A	121	394	35	103	9	4	0	41	34	4		.261	.326	.305	83	-8	3	.950	-34	*75*	*106*	*C-120	-3.3
1913	Det A	80	241	19	54	13	2	0	21	21	2	35	.224	.292	.295	73	-8	5	.960	-12	*81*	*108*	C-77	-1.5
1914	Det A	122	400	16	77	8	4	0	25	24	2	58	.192	.242	.233	41	-30	2-1	.960	-13	*91*	*104*	*C-122	-3.6
1915	Det A	100	300	27	67	9	2	1	31	20	1	41	.223	.274	.277	62	-15	5-1	.964	-9	*97*	*92*	*C-100	-1.7
1916	Det A	94	291	16	69	17	3	0	30	17	3	48	.237	.286	.316	78	-8	3	.969	-13	88	87	C-94	-1.5
1917	Det A	99	297	19	61	14	1	0	30	20	3	35	.205	.262	.259	59	-15	3	.977	-6	*88*	*88*	C-95	-1.5
1918	Det A	54	186	9	47	4	0	1	14	11	0	18	.253	.294	.290	80	-5	2	.980	-9	*76*	*90*	C-47/1-5,S	-1.2
1919	Det A	38	120	9	29	4	1	1	15	7	2	12	.242	.295	.317	73	-5	1	.974	-0	*89*	*90*	C-36/1	-0.2
1920	Det A	78	238	12	55	17	0	0	17	14	1	21	.231	.277	.303	55	-16	0-0	.958	-9	*87*	*105*	C-77	-1.9
1925	Det A	3	5	0	1	0	0	0	0	0	0	0	.200	.200	.200	2	-1	0-0	1.000	-1	*52*	*0*	/C-3	-0.1
Total	14	1096	3503	248	819	123	34	8	321	219	25	268	.234	.284	.295	69	-145	30-2	.961	-123	*91*	*99*	*C-1074/1-6,S	-18.6
STANDAERT, JERRY Jerome John B 11.2.1901 Chicago, IL D 8.4.1964 Chicago, IL BR/TR 5-10/168# d4.16																								
1925	Bro N	1	1	0	0	0	0	0	0	0	0	1	.000	.000	.000	-99	0	0-0	—	0			H	0.0
1926	Bro N	66	113	13	39	8	2	0	14	5	1	7	.345	.378	.451	124	4	0	.918	-7	72	57	2-21,3-14/S-6	-0.3
1929	Bos A	19	18	1	3	2	0	0	4	3	0	2	.167	.286	.278	47	-1	0-0	.958	0	121	90	1-10	-0.1
Total	3	86	132	14	42	10	2	0	18	8	1	10	.318	.362	.424	111	3	0-0	.918	-7	72	57	/2-21,3-14,1-10,S-6	-0.4
STANICEK, PETE Peter Louis B 4.18.1963 Harvey, IL BB/TR 5-11/175# d9.1 b-Steve																								
1987	Bal A	30	113	9	31	3	0	0	9	8-1	2	19	.274	.333	.301	72	-4	8-1	.975	-4	83	129	2-19,D-10/3-2	-0.6
1988	Bal A	83	261	29	60	7	1	4	17	28-0	4	45	.230	.313	.310	78	-7	12-6	.985	-1	100	114	O-65(LF),2-16/D	-1.0
Total	2	113	374	38	91	10	1	4	26	36-1	6	64	.243	.319	.307	76	-11	20-7	.985	-5	100	114	/O-65(LF),2-35,D-11,3-2	-1.6
STANICEK, STEVE Stephen Blair B 6.19.1961 Lake Forest, IL BR/TR 6- /190# d9.16 b-Pete																								
1987	Mil A	4	7	2	2	0	0	0	0	0-0	0	2	.286	.286	.286	51	-1	0-0	—	0			/D	-0.1
1989	Phi N	9	9	0	1	0	0	0	1	0-0	0	3	.111	.111	.111	-36	-2	0-0	—	0			H	-0.2
Total	2	13	16	2	3	0	0	0	1	0-0	0	5	.188	.188	.188	4	-3	0-0	.985	0	0	0	/D	-0.3
STANKARD, TOM Thomas Francis B 3.20.1882 Waltham, MA D 6.13.1958 Waltham, MA BR/TR 6/190# d7.2																								
1904	Pit N	2	2	0	0	0	0	0	0	0	0		.000	.000	.000	-97	0	0	1.000	-0	69	0	/S3	-0.1
STANKIEWICZ, ANDY Andrew Neal B 8.10.1964 Inglewood, CA BR/TR 5-9/165# d4.11																								
1992	NY A	116	400	52	107	22	2	2	25	38-0	5	42	.268	.338	.348	93	-3	9-5	.973	11	108	102	S-81,2-34/D	1.5
1993	NY A	16	9	5	0	0	0	0	0	1-0	0	1	.000	.100	.000	-73	-2	0-0	1.000	2	143	245	/2-6,3-4,SD	0.0
1994	Hou N	37	54	10	14	3	0	1	5	12-0	1	12	.259	.403	.370	109	2	1-1	1.000	-2	107	77	S-17/2-6,3	0.1
1995	Hou N	43	52	6	6	1	0	0	7	12-2	0	19	.115	.281	.135	15	-6	4-2	.985	4	137	81	S-14/2-6,3-3	0.0
1996	Mon N	64	77	12	22	5	1	0	9	6-1	3	12	.286	.356	.377	92	-1	1-0	.969	-2	111	54	2-19,S-13/3	-0.1
1997	Mon N	76	107	11	24	9	0	1	5	4-0	0	22	.224	.250	.336	53	-8	1-1	.957	1	118	109	2-25,S-14/3-3,D-2	-0.5
1998	Ari N	77	145	9	30	5	0	0	8	7-0	2	33	.207	.252	.241	31	-15	1-0	.994	-6	98	80	2-61	-1.9
Total	7	429	844	105	203	45	3	4	59	80-3	11	141	.241	.313	.315	72	-33	17-9	.986	9	107	93	2-157,S-140/3-12,D-4	-0.9
STANKY, EDDIE Edward Raymond "The Brat" or "Muggsy" B 9.3.1916 Philadelphia, PA D 6.6.1999 Fairhope, AL BR/TR 5-8/170# d4.21 M8 C2																								
1943	Chi N	142	510	92	125	15	1	0	47	92	2	42	.245	.363	.278	88	-3	4	.966	12	104	102	*2-131,S-12/3-2	1.8
1944	Chi N	13	25	4	6	0	1	0	0	2	0	2	.240	.296	.320	74	-1	1	.875	1	67	344	/2-3,S-3,3-3	0.0
	Bro N	89	261	32	72	9	2	0	16	44	1	13	.276	.382	.326	102	3	3	.961	-16	89	81	2-58,S-35/3	-0.7
	Year	102	286	36	78	9	3	0	16	46	1	15	.273	.375	.325	100	2	4	.958	-15	88	88	2-61,S-38/3-4	-0.7
1945	Bro N	153	555	**128**	143	29	5	1	39	**148**	4	42	.258	.417	.333	111	21	6	.962	9	97	117	*2-153/S	3.7
1946	Bro N	144	483	98	132	24	7	0	36	**137**	2	56	.273	**.436**	.352	124	27	8	.977	-6	92	110	*2-141	2.9
1947	†Bro N★	146	559	97	141	24	5	3	53	103	5	39	.252	.373	.329	85	-7	3	**.985**	8	98	**130**	*2-146	0.9
1948	†Bos N✳	67	247	49	79	14	2	2	29	61	0	13	.320	.455	.417	140	19	3	.981	3	106	123	2-66	2.5
1949	Bos N	138	506	90	144	24	5	1	42	113	2	41	.285	.417	.358	116	20	3	.979	-7	95	100	*2-135	2.0
1950	NY N☆	152	527	115	158	25	5	8	51	**144**	**12**	50	.300	**.460**	.412	131	37	9	.976	4	99	124	*2-151	4.6
1951	†NY N	145	515	88	127	17	2	14	43	127	6	63	.247	.401	.369	108	13	8-5	.977	0	100	118	*2-140	2.1
1952	StL N	53	83	13	19	4	0	0	7	19	0	9	.229	.373	.277	83	-1	0-0	1.000	2	103	90	2-20,M	0.2
1953	StL N	17	30	5	8	0	0	0	1	6	1	4	.267	.405	.267	80	0	0-0	1.000	1	117	85	/2-8,M	0.1
Total	11	1259	4301	811	1154	185	35	29	364	996	35	374	.268	.410	.348	109	128	48-5	.975	11	98	114	*2-1152/S-51,3-6	20.1
STANLEY, FRED Frederick Blair B 8.13.1947 Farnhamville, IA BR/TR (BB 1969-71) 5-10/167# d9.11 C1																								
1969	Sea A	17	43	2	12	2	1	0	4	3-0	0	8	.279	.319	.372	96	0	1-0	.962	-6	70	94	S-15/2	-0.5
1970	Mil A	6	0	1	0	0	0	0	0	0-0	0	0	—	—	—	—	0	0-0	1.000	0	147	0	/2-2	0.0
1971	Cle A	60	129	14	29	4	0	2	12	27-3	1	25	.225	.361	.302	83	-2	1-0	.971	4	110	99	S-55/2-3	0.9
1972	Cle A	6	12	1	2	1	0	0	0	2-0	0	3	.167	.286	.250	58	-1	0-0	.917	-2	56	0	/S-5,2	-0.3
	SD N	39	85	15	17	2	0	0	2	12-1	1	19	.200	.306	.224	57	-4	1-0	.989	0	106	124	2-21,S-17/3-4	-0.2
1973	NY A	26	66	6	14	0	1	1	5	7-0	0	16	.212	.288	.288	65	-3	0-0	.981	2	107	95	S-21/2-3	0.1
1974	NY A	33	38	2	7	0	0	0	3	3-0	0	2	.184	.244	.184	25	-4	1-2	.973	6	117	90	S-19,2-15	0.3
1975	NY A	117	252	34	56	5	1	0	15	21-0	1	27	.222	.283	.250	53	-16	3-1	.977	-3	91	95	S-83,2-33/3	-1.0
1976	†NY A	110	260	32	62	2	2	1	20	34-0	1	29	.238	.329	.273	78	-6	1-0	.983	-23	88	74	*S-110/2-3	-2.0
1977	†NY A	48	46	6	12	0	0	1	7	8-0	0	6	.261	.370	.326	93	0	1-1	.958	-3	91	65	S-42/3-3,2-2	-0.2
1978	†NY A	81	160	14	35	7	0	1	9	25-0	0	31	.219	.324	.281	73	-5	0-0	.959	-8	89	84	S-71,2-11/3-4	-0.7
1979	NY A	57	100	9	20	1	0	2	14	5-0	0	17	.200	.236	.270	38	-9	0-1	.978	4	114	152	S-31,3-16/2-8,1O(LF)	-0.4
1980	NY A	49	86	13	18	3	0	0	5	5-0	2	5	.209	.266	.244	42	-7	0-0	.923	-0	105	110	S-19,2-17,3-12	-0.5
1981	†Oak A	66	145	15	28	4	0	0	7	15-0	0	23	.193	.269	.221	44	-10	2-0	.986	-18	75	78	S-62/2-6	-2.4
1982	Oak A	101	228	33	44	7	0	2	17	29-0	1	32	.193	.287	.250	51	-15	0-1	.963	-19	91	81	S-98/2-2	-2.6
Total	14	816	1650	197	356	38	5	10	120	196-4	7	243	.216	.301	.263	62	-82	11-6	.971	-66	91	87	S-648,2-128/3-40,O(LF)1	-9.5
STANLEY, JIM James F. B 1889 BB/TR 5-6/148# d4.19																								
1914	Chi F	54	98	13	19	3	0	0	4	19	4	14	.194	.347	.224	61	-6	2	.878	-8	85	110	S-40/3-3,2O(LF)	-1.2
STANLEY, JOE Joseph B , NJ d4.24																								
1884	Bal U	6	21	3	5	1	0	0		0			.238	.238	.286	53	-2		.444	-2	77	0	/O-6(0-4-2)	-0.3
STANLEY, JOE Joseph Bernard B 4.2.1881 Washington, DC D 9.13.1967 Detroit, MI BB/TR 5-9.5/150# d9.11 b-Buck																								
1897	Was N	1	1	0	0	0	0	0	0	0	0		.000	.000	.000	-99	0	0	—	-0	0	0	/P	0.0
1902	Was A	3	12	2	4	0	0	0	1	0	0		.333	.333	.333	85	0	0	.833	-1	0	0	/O-3(LF)	-0.1
1903	Bos N	86	308	40	77	12	5	1	47	18	7		.250	.306	.331	85	-7	10	.902	2	197	74	O-77(11-32-34)/PS	-0.8
1904	Bos N	3	8	0	0	0	0	0	0	0	0		.000	.000	.000	-99	-2	0	.800	1	633	0	/O-3(1-0-2)	-0.1
1905	Was A	28	92	13	24	2	1	1	17	7	0		.261	.313	.337	111	1	4	.944	1	140	0	O-27(13-9-5)	0.0
1906	Was A	73	221	18	36	0	4	0	9	20	1		.163	.236	.199	38	-16	6	.934	-3	97	0	O-63(0-7-56)/P	-2.4
1909	Chi N	22	52	4	7	1	0	0	2	6	0		.135	.224	.154	17	-5	0	.947	-1	60	0	O-16(5-4-9)	-0.8
Total	7	216	694	77	148	15	10	2	76	51	8		.213	.275	.272	66	-29	20	.918	-2	150	32	O-189(33-52-106)/P-3,S	-4.2
STANLEY, MICKEY Mitchell Jack B 7.20.1942 Grand Rapids, MI BR/TR 6-1/195# d9.13 OF Total (44-LF 1171-CF 82-RF)																								
1964	Det A	4	11	3	3	0	0	0	1	0-0	0	1	.273	.273	.273	52	-1	0-0	1.000	-0	104	0	/O-4(3-1-1)	-0.1
1965	Det A	30	117	14	28	6	0	3	13	3-0	0	12	.239	.256	.368	75	-4	1-0	.986	-0	105	80	O-29(CF)	-0.5
1966	Det A	92	235	28	68	15	4	3	19	17-4	0	20	.289	.336	.426	115	5	2-1	1.000	6	118	166	O-82(CF)	1.0
1967	Det A	145	333	38	70	7	3	7	24	29-2	0	46	.210	.273	.312	71	-13	9-2	.982	2	114	59	*O-129(2-126-2)/1-8	-1.4
1968	†Det A	153	583	88	151	16	6	11	60	42-1	4	57	.259	.311	.364	102	0	4-3	**1.000**	-1	101	83	*O-130(CF),1-15/S-9,2	-0.6
1969	Det A	149	592	73	139	28	1	16	70	52-1	2	56	.235	.299	.367	82	-15	8-4	.985	-13	103	39	*O-101(0-98-3),S-59/1-4	-2.5
1970	Det A	142	568	83	143	21	11	13	47	45-1	0	56	.252	.305	.396	92	-9	10-1	**1.000**	-2	106	37	*O-132(CF)/1-9	-1.3
1971	Det A	139	401	43	117	14	5	7	41	24-5	0	44	.292	.329	.404	103	1	1-3	.988	9	114	142	*O-139(CF)	0.7
1972	†Det A	142	435	45	102	16	6	14	55	29-8	0	49	.234	.278	.395	97	-4	1-0	.994	2	103	114	*O-139(CF)	-0.6
1973	Det A	157	602	81	147	23	5	17	57	48-4	0	65	.244	.297	.384	86	-13	0-4	.993	5	109	91	*O-157(CF)	-1.4
1974	Det A	99	394	40	87	13	2	8	34	26-1	1	63	.221	.270	.325	68	-17	5-3	.992	2	107	63	O-91(1-90-0),1-12/2	-1.9
1975	Det A	52	164	26	42	7	3	3	19	15-2	1	27	.256	.320	.390	96	-1	1-1	.983	0	102	58	O-28(14-15-0),1-14/3-7,D	-0.3
1976	Det A	84	214	34	55	17	1	4	29	14-1	0	19	.257	.301	.402	101	0	2-0	.969	3	90	101	O-38(15-19-4),1-17,3-11/S-3,2-2,D-2	-2

Year	Tm Lg	G	AB	R	H	2B	3B	HR	RBI	BB-IB	HP	SO	AVG	OBP	SLG	AOPS	ABR	SB-CS	FA	FR	Rng	Thr	G at Pos	BFW
0.2																								
1977	Det A	75	222	30	51	9	1	8	23	18-2	0	30	.230	.284	.387	78	-7	0-0	.972	-5	89	51	O-57(7-10-44)/1-3,S-3,D-2	-1.5
1978	Det A	53	151	15	40	9	0	3	8	9-0	0	19	.265	.306	.384	90	-2	0-1	.960	-4	79	49	O-34(2-4-28),1-12	-0.8
Total	15	1516	5022	641	1243	201	48	117	500	371-32	8	564	.248	.298	.377	89	-80	44-23	.991	4	105	83	*O-1290C/1-94,S-74,3-18,D-5,2-4	-11.0
STANLEY, MIKE Robert Michael B 6.25.1963 Ft.Lauderdale, FL BR/TR 6-1/185# d6.24 C1																								
1986	Tex A	15	30	4	10	3	0	1	1	3-0	0	7	.333	.394	.533	146	2	1-0	.857	-2	86	143	/3-7,C-4,O(LF)D	0.1
1987	Tex A	78	216	34	59	8	1	6	37	31-0	1	48	.273	.361	.403	104	2	3-0	.980	-21	53	57	C-61,1-12/O(LF)D	-1.6
1988	Tex A	94	249	21	57	8	0	3	27	37-0	0	62	.229	.323	.297	75	-7	0-0	.991	-8	58	73	C-64,D-18/1-6,3-2	-1.3
1989	Tex A	67	122	9	30	3	1	1	11	12-1	2	29	.246	.324	.311	78	-3	1-0	.978	-8	122	60	C-25,D-21/1-7,3-3	-1.1
1990	Tex A	103	189	21	47	8	1	2	19	30-2	0	25	.249	.350	.333	92	-1	1-0	.985	-8	65	85	C-63,D-14/3-8,1-6	-0.7
1991	Tex A	95	181	25	45	13	1	3	25	34-0	2	44	.249	.372	.381	111	5	0-0	.980	-13	75	53	C-58,1-12/3-6,O(LF)D	-0.6
1992	NY A	68	173	24	43	7	0	8	27	33-0	1	45	.249	.372	.428	124	7	0-0	.980	-2	90	102	C-55/1-4,D-6	0.8
1993	NY A	130	423	70	129	17	1	26	84	57-4	5	85	.305	.389	.534	152	32	1-1	**.996**	-5	124	65	*C-122/D-2	3.3
1994	NY A	82	290	54	87	20	0	17	57	39-2	2	56	.300	.384	.545	142	19	0-0	.993	4	162	102	C-72/1-7,D-4	2.4
1995	†NY A★	118	399	63	107	29	1	18	83	57-1	5	106	.268	.360	.481	120	13	1-1	.993	-4	93	101	*C-107,D-10	1.3
1996	Bos A	121	397	73	107	20	1	24	69	69-3	5	62	.270	.383	.506	120	14	2-0	.985	-28	65	72	*C-105,D-10	-0.8
1997	Bos A	97	260	45	78	17	0	13	53	39-0	6	50	.300	.394	.515	135	15	0-1	.996	-3	103	110	D-53,1-31,C-15	0.6
	†NY A	28	87	16	25	8	0	3	12	15-4	0	22	.287	.388	.483	128	4	0-0	1.000	-1	55	110	D-16,1-12	0.1
	Year	125	347	61	103	25	0	16	65	54-4	6	72	.297	.393	.507	133	19	0-1	.997	-4	91	110	D-69,1-43,C-15	0.7
1998	Tor A	98	341	49	82	13	0	22	47	56-3	5	86	.240	.353	.472	112	7	2-1	.995	-2	74	78	D-73,1-22/O(LF)	-0.2
	†Bos A	47	156	25	45	12	0	7	32	26-2	2	43	.288	.388	.500	129	8	1-0	1.000	-1	70	150	D-34,1-13	0.3
	Year	145	497	74	127	25	0	29	79	82-5	7	129	.256	.364	.481	118	15	3-1	.997	-2	73	103	*D-107,1-35/O(LF)	0.1
1999	†Bos A	136	427	59	120	22	0	19	72	70-3	11	94	.281	.393	.466	115	13	0-0	.988	-1	94	88	*1-111,D-20	0.0
2000	Bos A	58	185	22	41	5	0	10	28	30-0	0	44	.222	.327	.411	84	-5	0-0	.997	4	138	93	1-39,D-18	-0.5
	Oak A	32	97	11	26	7	0	4	18	14-0	1	21	.268	.363	.464	111	2	0-0	.988	0	111	109	1-19/D-8	0.0
	Year	90	282	33	67	12	0	14	46	44-0	1	65	.238	.339	.429	93	-3	0-0	.993	4	129	98	1-58,D-26	-0.5
Total	15	1467	4222	625	1138	220	7	187	702	652-25	48	929	.270	.370	.458	117	127	13-4	.988	-98	93	80	C-751,D-321,1-301/3-26,O-4(LF)	2.1
STANSBURY, JACK John James B 12.6.1885 Phillipsburg, NJ D 12.26.1970 Easton, PA BR/TR 5-9/165# d6.30																								
1918	Bos A	20	47	3	6	1	0	0	2	6	1	3	.128	.241	.149	18	-5	0	.980	2	118	192	3-18/O-2(CF)	-0.2
STANTON, BUCK George Washington B 6.19.1906 Stantonsburg, NC D 1.1.1992 San Antonio, TX BL/TL 5-10/150# d9.5																								
1931	StL A	13	15	3	3	2	0	0	0	0	0	6	.200	.200	.333	37	-1	0-0	.750	-0	100	0	/O(RF)	-0.2
STANTON, HARRY Harry Andrew B St.Louis, MO TR d10.14																								
1900	StL N	1	0	0	0	0	0	0	0	0	0		—	—	—	—	0	0	—	0	*0*	*0*	/C	0.0
STANTON, LEROY Leroy Bobby B 4.10.1946 Latta, SC BR/TR 6-1/195# d9.10																								
1970	NY N	4	4	0	1	0	1	0	0	0-0	0	0	.250	.250	.750	157	0	0-0	1.000	0	404	0	/O(CF)	0.0
1971	NY N	5	21	2	4	1	0	0	2	2-1	0	4	.190	.261	.238	43	-2	0-0	1.000	-1	90	0	/O-5(RF)	-0.3
1972	Cal A	127	402	44	101	15	3	12	39	22-4	4	100	.251	.295	.393	110	3	2-3	.983	2	109	78	*O-124(0-2-123)	-0.2
1973	Cal A	119	306	41	72	9	2	8	34	27-2	2	88	.235	.300	.356	92	-4	3-3	.965	-1	99	89	*O-107(36-0-76)	-1.0
1974	Cal A	118	415	48	111	21	2	11	62	33-3	5	107	.267	.325	.407	117	9	10-8	.975	5	107	139	*O-114(0-10-110)	0.8
1975	Cal A	137	440	67	115	20	3	14	82	52-4	6	85	.261	.345	.416	124	14	18-6	.961	3	98	**165**	*O-131(0-5-127)/D	1.3
1976	Cal A	93	231	12	44	13	1	2	25	24-1	1	57	.190	.266	.281	66	-10	2-6	.985	-6	90	22	O-79(33-31-27)/D-4	-2.2
1977	Sea A	133	454	56	125	24	1	27	90	42-2	5	115	.275	.341	.511	131	18	0-1	.953	4	105	148	O-91(8-0-84),D-33	1.6
1978	Sea A	93	302	24	55	11	0	3	24	34-1	1	80	.182	.265	.248	46	-21	1-0	1.000	2	117	62	D-59,O-30(30-0-1)	-2.3
Total	9	829	2575	294	628	114	13	77	358	236-18	24	636	.244	.311	.388	103	7	36-27	.972	8	103	110	O-682(107-49-553)/D-97	-2.3
STANTON, TOM Thomas Patrick B 10.25.1874 St.Louis, MO D 1.17.1957 St.Louis, MO BB/TR 5-10/175# d4.19																								
1904	Chi N	1	3	0	0	0	0	0	0	0	0		.000	.000	.000	-99	-1	0	1.000	-0	*99*	*118*	/C	-0.1
STAPLETON, DAVE David Leslie B 1.16.1954 Fairhope, AL BR/TR 6-1/178# d5.30 OF Total (5-LF 2-RF)																								
1980	Bos A	106	449	61	144	33	5	7	45	13-1	1	32	.321	.338	.463	112	7	3-2	.979	11	111	132	2-94/1-8,O-6(4-0-2),3-2,D-3	2.2
1981	Bos A	93	355	45	101	17	1	10	42	21-1	1	22	.285	.325	.423	108	3	0-4	.948	-7	89	82	S-33,3-25,2-23,1-12/D-3	-0.2
1982	Bos A	150	538	66	142	28	1	14	65	31-5	3	40	.264	.305	.398	87	-10	2-4	.991	5	113	108	*1-106,S-27/2-9,3-5,O(LF)D	-1.0
1983	Bos A	151	542	54	134	31	1	10	66	40-2	2	44	.247	.297	.363	76	-17	1-1	.993	-0	102	97	*1-145/2-5	-2.7
1984	Bos A	13	39	4	9	2	0	0	1	3-1	0	3	.231	.286	.282	55	-2	0-0	1.000	1	111	57	1-10/D	-0.2
1985	Bos A	30	66	4	15	6	0	0	2	4-0	0	11	.227	.271	.318	58	-4	0-0	1.000	-1	91	88	2-14/1-8,D-5	-0.4
1986	†Bos A	39	39	4	5	1	0	0	3	2-0	0	10	.128	.171	.154	-11	-6	0-0	1.000	0	89	126	1-29/2-6,3-2	-0.7
Total	7	582	2028	238	550	118	8	41	224	114-10	7	162	.271	.310	.398	90	-29	6-11	.993	9	105	102	1-318,2-151/S-60,3-34,D-16,O-7L	-3.0
STARGELL, WILLIE Wilver Dornel B 3.6.1940 Earlsboro, OK D 4.9.2001 Wilmington, NC BL/TL 6-2.5/225# d9.16 C4 HF1988																								
1962	Pit N	10	31	1	9	3	1	0	4	3-1	0	10	.290	.353	.452	114	1	0-1	.929	-1	68	130	/O-9(2-1-6)	-0.1
1963	Pit N	108	304	34	74	11	6	11	47	19-0	2	85	.243	.290	.428	104	0	0-2	.953	-6	83	83	O-65(35-6-24),1-16	-1.1
1964	Pit N★	117	421	53	115	19	7	21	78	17-2	2	92	.273	.304	.501	123	10	1-1	.900	-10	76	51	O-59(57-1-2),1-50	-0.6
1965	Pit N★	144	533	68	145	25	8	27	107	39-13	7	127	.272	.328	.501	130	19	1-1	.965	1	94	162	*O-137(125-0-19)/1-7	1.3
1966	Pit N★	140	485	84	153	30	0	33	102	48-16	6	109	.315	.381	.581	164	42	2-3	.945	-5	89	111	*O-127(121-0-7),1-15	3.1
1967	Pit N	134	462	54	125	18	6	20	73	67-25	3	103	.271	.365	.465	136	23	1-0	.938	-1	91	207	O-98(92-0-6),1-37	1.6
1968	Pit N	128	435	57	103	15	1	24	67	47-11	6	105	.237	.315	.441	129	15	5-0	.945	-3	82	172	*O-113(108-0-5),1-13	0.7
1969	Pit N	145	522	89	160	31	6	29	92	61-14	6	120	.307	.382	.556	164	45	1-0	.970	-5	90	69	*O-116(115-0-1),1-23	3.3
1970	†Pit N	136	474	70	125	18	3	31	85	44-11	5	119	.264	.329	.511	125	14	0-1	.976	3	90	**187**	*O-125(123-0-2)/1	0.9
1971	†Pit N★	141	511	104	151	26	0	**48**	125	83-20	7	154	.295	.398	.628	188	**61**	0-0	.984	-4	88	85	*O-138(LF)	**5.1**
1972	†Pit N★	138	495	75	145	28	2	33	112	65-15	2	129	.293	.373	.558	166	43	1-1	.984	-12	67	133	*1-101,O-32(LF)	2.2
1973	Pit N★	148	522	106	156	**43**	3	**44**	**119**	80-22	3	129	.299	.392	**.646**	**189**	**63**	0-0	.975	2	91	145	*O-142(LF)	5.8
1974	†Pit N	140	508	90	153	37	4	25	96	87-21	6	106	.301	.407	.537	**169**	**51**	0-2	.967	-4	95	80	*O-135(LF)/1	3.9
1975	†Pit N	124	461	71	136	32	2	22	90	58-6	3	109	.295	.375	.516	147	30	0-0	.992	-7	75	**116**	*1-122	1.3
1976	Pit N	117	428	54	110	20	3	20	65	50-6	5	101	.257	.339	.458	124	13	2-0	.988	-8	76	86	*1-111	-0.3
1977	Pit N	63	186	29	51	12	0	13	35	31-10	3	55	.274	.383	.548	144	12	0-1	.986	-1	98	73	1-55	0.8
1978	Pit N★	122	390	60	115	18	2	28	97	50-10	7	93	.295	.382	.567	156	29	3-2	.994	-2	91	95	*1-112	2.2
1979	†Pit N	126	424	60	119	19	0	32	82	47-12	3	105	.281	.352	.552	138	21	0-1	**.997**	-8	68	**124**	*1-113	0.6
1980	Pit N	67	202	28	53	10	1	11	38	26-10	2	52	.262	.351	.485	129	8	0-0	.992	0	100	143	1-54	0.5
1981	Pit N	38	60	2	17	4	0	0	9	5-1	0	9	.283	.333	.350	93	0	0-0	1.000	-2	0	143	/1-9	-0.4
1982	Pit N	74	73	6	17	4	0	3	17	10-1	0	24	.233	.318	.411	102	0	0-0	1.000	0	104	65	/1-8	0.0
Total	21	2360	7927	1195	2232	423	55	475	1540	937-227	78	1936	.282	.360	.529	147	500	17-16	.961	-72	89	124	*O-1296(1225-8-72),1-848	30.8
STARK, MATT Matthew Scott B 1.21.1965 Whittier, CA BR/TR 6-4/225# d4.8																								
1987	Tor A	5	12	0	1	0	0	0	0	0-0	0	0	.083	.083	.083	-55	-3	0-0	1.000	-0	41	89	/C-5	-0.3
1990	Chi A	8	16	0	4	1	0	0	3	1-0	0	6	.250	.294	.313	71	-1	0-0	—	0			/D-6	-0.1
Total	2	13	28	0	5	1	0	0	3	1-0	0	6	.179	.207	.214	15	-4	0-0	1.000	-0	41	89	/D-6,C-5	-0.4
STARK, DOLLY Monroe Randolph B 1.19.1885 Ripley, MS D 12.1.1924 Memphis, TN BR/TR 5-9/160# d9.12																								
1909	Cle A	19	60	4	12	0	0	0	1	6	0		.200	.273	.200	48	-3	4	.875	-7	73	52	S-19	-1.2
1910	Bro N	30	103	7	17	3	0	0	8	7	1	19	.165	.225	.194	23	-10	2	.893	-2	98	106	S-30	-1.2
1911	Bro N	70	193	25	57	4	1	0	19	20	3	24	.295	.370	.326	100	1	6	.910	-4	96	101	S-34,2-18/3-3	-0.1
1912	Bro N	8	22	2	4	0	0	0	2	1	0	3	.182	.217	.182	10	-3	2	.892	-1	98	113	/S-7	-0.3
Total	4	127	378	38	90	7	1	0	30	34	4	46	.238	.308	.262	66	-15	14	.896	-14	92	94	/S-90,2-18,3-3	-2.8
STARNAGLE, GEORGE George Henry (born George Henry Steuernagel) B 10.6.1873 Belleville, IL D 2.15.1946 Belleville, IL BR/TR 5-11/175# d9.14																								
1902	Cle A	1	3	0	0	0	0	0	0	0	0		.000	.000	.000	-99	-1	0	.667	-1	*83*	*0*	/C	-0.1
STARR, CHARLIE Charles Watkin B 8.30.1878 Pike Co., OH D 10.18.1937 Pasadena, CA TR 5-10.5/165# d4.29																								
1905	StL A	26	97	9	20	0	0	0	6	7	0		.206	.260	.206	51	-5	0	.938	-2	109	27	2-18/3-6	-0.8
1908	Pit N	20	59	8	11	2	0	0	8	13	1		.186	.342	.220	80	0	6	.926	-4	99	95	2-12/S-5,3-2	-0.5
1909	Bos N	61	216	16	48	2	3	0	6	31	5		.222	.333	.259	80	-4	7	.931	-4	100	99	2-54/S-6,3-3	-0.8
	Phi N	3	3	0	0	0	0	0	0	0	0		.000	.000	.000	-99	-1	0	—	0			H	-0.1

Year	Tm Lg	G	AB	R	H	2B	3B	HR	RBI	BB-IB	HP	SO	AVG	OBP	SLG	AOPS	ABR	SB-CS	FA	FR	Rng	Thr	G at Pos	BFW
	Year	64	219	16	48	2	3	0	6	31	5		.219	.329	.256	78	-4	7	.931	-4	100	99	2-54/S-6,3-3	-0.9
Total	3	110	375	33	79	4	3	0	20	51	6		.211	.315	.237	72	-10	13	.931	-10	102	85	/2-84,S-11,3-11	-2.2
STARR, BILL William B 2.26.1911 Brooklyn, NY D 8.12.1991 LaJolla, CA BR/TR 6-1/175# d8.23																								
1935	Was A	12	24	1	5	0	0	0	1	0	0	1	.208	.208	.208	8	-3	0-0	.971	0	*92*	*157*	C-12	-0.3
1936	Was A	1	0	0	0	0	0	0	0	0	0	0	—	—	—	—	0	0-0	—	0	*0*	*0*	/C	0.0
Total	2	13	24	1	5	0	0	0	1	0	0	1	.208	.208	.208	8	-3	0-0	.971	0	*91*	*155*	/C-13	-0.3
START, JOE Joseph "Old Reliable" or "Rocks" B 10.14.1842 New York, NY D 3.27.1927 Providence, RI BL/TL 5-9/165# d5.18 M1																								
1871	Mut NA	**33**	161	35	58	5	1	1	34	3		0	.360	.372	.422	140	10	4-2	.921	-2	38	82	*1-33	0.6
1872	Mut NA	54	277	60	75	5	0	0	48	0		0	.271	.271	.289	77	-6	3-3	**.958**	2	0	139	*1-54	-0.2
1873	Mut NA	**53**	252	42	67	8	3	1	29	4		0	.266	.277	.333	81	-6	1-0	.943	6	**150**	88	*1-53/O-2(RF),M	0.1
1874	Mut NA	63	306	67	96	13	3	2	46	4		0	.314	.323	.395	125	8	5-0	**.961**	5	**108**	67	*1-63/O-2(1-1-0)	1.2
1875	Mut NA	69	314	58	90	10	5	4	30	3		0	.287	.293	.389	128	7	1-4	.948	2	88	72	*1-69	0.8
1876	NY N	56	264	40	73	6	0	0	21	1		2	.277	.279	.299	107	3		**.964**	3	99	48	*1-56	0.4
1877	Har N	**60**	271	55	90	3	6	1	21	6		2	.332	.347	.399	150	16		**.964**	-2	52	98	*1-60	0.9
1878	Chi N	**61**	285	58	**100**	12	5	1	27	2		3	.351	.355	.439	150	14		.957	-2	75	103	*1-61	0.8
1879	Pro N	66	317	70	101	11	5	2	37	7		4	.319	.333	.404	144	14		**.973**	0	65	88	*1-65/O(RF)	1.1
1880	Pro N	82	345	53	96	14	6	0	27	13		20	.278	.304	.354	126	10		.971	-3	45	93	*1-82	0.3
1881	Pro N	79	348	56	114	12	6	0	29	9		7	.328	.345	.397	135	13		.963	-4	59	111	*1-79	0.5
1882	Pro N	82	356	58	117	8	10	0	48	11		7	.329	.349	.407	142	15		.974	2	92	**144**	*1-82	0.9
1883	Pro N	87	370	63	105	16	7	1	57	22		16	.284	.324	.373	108	3		.957	-1	102	**126**	*1-87	-0.5
1884	†Pro N	93	381	80	105	10	5	2	32	35		25	.276	.337	.344	117	9		**.980**	1	75	91	*1-93	0.1
1885	Pro N	101	374	47	103	11	4	0	41	39		10	.275	.344	.326	121	11		.972	1	104	83	*1-101	0.3
1886	Was N	31	122	10	27	4	1	0	17	5		13	.221	.252	.270	64	-5	4	.973	-2	58	92	1-31	-0.9
Total	5 NA	272	1310	262	386	41	12	8	187	14		0	.295	.302	.363	109	13	14-9	.000	13	81	89	1-272/O-4(1-1-2)	2.5
Total	11	798	3433	590	1031	107	55	7	357	150		109	.300	.330	.370	127	103	4-0	.968	-7	77	100	1-797/O(RF)	3.9
STATON, DAVE David Alan B 4.12.1968 Seattle, WA BR/TR 6-5/215# d9.8																								
1993	SD N	17	42	7	11	3	0	5	9	3-0	1	12	.262	.326	.690	161	3	0-0	1.000	3	200	137	1-12	0.5
1994	SD N	29	66	6	12	2	0	4	6	10-0	0	18	.182	.289	.394	78	-2	0-0	1.000	3	150	65	1-20	-0.1
Total	2	46	108	13	23	5	0	9	15	13-0	1	30	.213	.303	.509	110	1	0-0	1.000	6	167	90	/1-32	0.4
STATON, JOE Joseph B 3.8.1948 Seattle, WA BL/TL 6-3/175# d9.5																								
1972	Det A	6	2	1	0	0	0	0	0	0-0	0	1	.000	.000	.000	-97	0	0-1	1.000	-0	0	0	/1-2	-0.1
1973	Det A	9	17	2	4	0	0	0	3	0-0	0	3	.235	.235	.235	31	-2	1-0	.969	1	257	30	/1-5	0.0
Total	2	15	19	3	4	0	0	0	3	0-0	0	4	.211	.211	.211	18	-2	1-1	.973	1	213	25	/1-7	-0.1
STATZ, JIGGER Arnold John B 10.20.1897 Waukegan, IL D 3.16.1988 Corona Del Mar, CA BR/TR (BB 1922 (part)) 5-7.5/150# d7.30																								
1919	NY N	21	60	7	18	2	1	0	6	3	0	8	.300	.333	.367	112	1	2	.977	-1	115	0	O-18(3-7-8)/2-5	-0.1
1920	NY N	16	30	0	4	0	1	0	5	2	0	9	.133	.188	.200	11	-4	0-1	.944	-2	69	76	O-12(CF)	-0.7
	Bos A	2	3	0	0	0	0	0	0	0	0	0	.000	.000	.000	-99	-1	0-0	1.000	-0	98	0	/O-2(RF)	-0.1
1922	Chi N	110	462	77	137	19	5	1	34	41	1	31	.297	.355	.366	85	-10	16-13	.959	1	100	113	*O-110(CF)	-1.4
1923	Chi N	**154**	655	110	209	33	8	10	70	56	3	42	.319	.375	.440	114	14	29-23	.975	11	106	128	*O-154(CF)	1.6
1924	Chi N	135	549	69	152	22	5	3	49	37	2	50	.277	.325	.352	80	-15	13-9	.961	8	104	**154**	*O-131(CF)/2	-1.3
1925	Chi N	38	148	21	38	6	3	2	14	11	2	16	.257	.317	.378	76	-6	4-0	.943	-1	104	82	O-37(CF)	-0.7
1927	Bro N	130	507	64	139	24	7	1	21	26	0	43	.274	.310	.355	77	-17	10	.990	10	**111**	108	*O-122(3-118-1)/2	-1.3
1928	Bro N	77	171	28	40	8	1	0	16	18	1	12	.234	.311	.292	59	-10	3	.965	-1	99	83	O-52(2-49-1)/2	-1.3
Total	8	683	2585	376	737	114	31	17	215	194	9	211	.285	.337	.373	87	-48	77-46	.969	25	105	117	O-638(8-618-12)/2-8	-5.3
STAUB, RUSTY Daniel Joseph B 4.1.1944 New Orleans, LA BL/TR 6-2/200# d4.9 C1																								
1963	Hou N	150	513	43	115	17	4	6	45	59-8	5	58	.224	.309	.308	84	-10	0-0	.989	-4	82	72	*1-109,O-49(0-1-48)	-2.5
1964	Hou N	89	292	26	63	10	2	8	35	21-4	3	31	.216	.272	.346	78	-9	1-1	.992	-3	82	99	1-49,O-38(0-7-31)	-1.9
1965	Hou N	131	410	43	105	20	1	14	63	52-5	2	57	.256	.339	.412	120	12	3-0	.951	0	95	149	*O-112(1-2-110)/1	0.5
1966	Hou N	153	554	60	155	28	3	13	81	58-13	1	61	.280	.345	.412	119	15	2-1	.962	6	109	123	*O-148(55-1-105)/1	1.2
1967	Hou N★	149	546	71	182	**44**	1	10	74	60-21	3	47	.333	.398	.473	155	42	0-4	.962	1	103	96	*O-144(RF)	3.3
1968	Hou N★	161	591	54	172	37	1	6	72	73-24	7	57	.291	.373	.387	132	28	2-0	.992	1	101	85	*1-147,O-15(RF)	2.1
1969	Mon N☆	158	549	89	166	26	5	29	79	110-11	9	61	.302	.426	.526	165	54	3-4	.966	2	99	140	*O-156(RF)	4.9
1970	Mon N★	160	569	98	156	23	7	30	94	112-11	3	93	.274	.394	.497	138	34	12-11	.985	6	105	130	*O-160(RF)	3.0
1971	Mon N☆	**162**	599	94	186	34	6	19	97	74-13	9	42	.311	.392	.482	147	39	9-5	.945	2	96	173	*O-162(1-0-162)	3.6
1972	NY N	66	239	32	70	11	0	9	38	31-7	2	13	.293	.372	.452	139	13	0-1	.982	-3	91	86	O-65(RF)	0.7
1973	†NY N	152	585	77	163	36	1	15	76	74-10	3	52	.279	.361	.421	118	17	1-1	.978	5	102	126	*O-152(RF)	1.4
1974	NY N	151	561	65	145	22	2	19	78	77-12	3	39	.258	.347	.406	113	11	2-1	.983	3	92	**185**	*O-147(RF)	0.7
1975	NY N	155	574	93	162	30	4	19	105	77-14	9	55	.282	.371	.448	134	28	2-0	.986	1	92	146	*O-153(RF)	2.1
1976	Det A★	**161**	589	73	176	28	3	15	96	83-11	7	49	.299	.386	.433	136	30	3-1	.970	-10	82	86	*O-126(RF),D-36	1.4
1977	Det A	158	623	84	173	34	3	22	101	59-4	1	47	.278	.336	.448	107	7	1-1	—	0	0	0	*D-156	0.2
1978	Det A	162	642	75	175	30	1	24	121	76-5	3	35	.273	.347	.435	117	15	3-1	—	0	0	0	*D-162	1.1
1979	Det A	68	246	32	58	12	1	9	40	32-1	5	18	.236	.331	.402	95	-1	1-0	—	0	0	0	D-66	-0.3
	Mon N	38	86	9	23	3	0	3	14	14-3	0	10	.267	.366	.407	113	2	0-0	.994	-2	64	79	1-22/O(RF)	-0.1
1980	Tex A	109	340	42	102	23	2	9	55	39-3	2	18	.300	.370	.459	131	16	1-1	.977	-0	58	109	D-57,1-30,O-14(3-0-11)	1.2
1981	NY N	70	161	9	51	9	0	5	21	22-3	1	12	.317	.398	.466	148	11	1-0	.989	-2	77	87	1-41	0.7
1982	NY N	112	219	11	53	9	0	3	27	24-1	0	10	.242	.309	.324	80	-5	0-0	.959	2	91	212	O-27(12-0-15),1-18	-0.6
1983	NY N	104	115	5	34	6	0	3	28	14-3	1	10	.296	.371	.426	123	4	0-0	.976	-1	132	148	/1-5,O-5(3-0-2)	0.3
1984	NY N	78	72	2	19	4	0	1	18	4-3	0	9	.264	.291	.361	87	-1	0-0	1.000	-0	0	168	/1-3	-0.2
1985	NY N	54	45	2	12	3	0	1	8	10-3	0	4	.267	.400	.400	128	2	0-0	1.000	-0	68	0	/O(RF)	0.2
Total	23	2951	9720	1189	2716	499	47	292	1466	1255-193	79	888	.279	.362	.431	125	354	47-33	.969	6	98	136	*O-1675(75-11-1604),D-477,1-426	23.0
STEARNS, ECKY Daniel Eckford B 10.17.1861 Buffalo, NY D 6.28.1944 Glendale, CA BL/TR 6-1/185# d8.17 U1 OF Total (7-LF 3-CF 28-RF)																								
1880	Buf N	28	104	8	19	6	1	0	13	3		23	.183	.206	.260	55	-5		.774	-5	88	142	O-20(6-1-15)/C-8,3-5,S	-1.0
1881	Det N	3	11	1	1	1	0	0	0	0		2	.091	.091	.182	-16	-1		.714	-1	100	115	/S-3	-0.2
1882	Cin AA	49	214	28	55	10	2	0	35	6			.257	.277	.322	96	-1		.931	-3	57	126	1-35,O-12(RF)/2-2,S	-0.7
1883	Bal AA	93	382	54	94	10	9	1		**34**			.246	.308	.327	101	1		.947	3	**141**	79	*1-92/O(LF)	-0.4
1884	Bal AA	100	396	61	94	12	3	3		28	6		.237	.298	.306	94	-2		.949	4	139	78	*1-100/2	-0.7
1885	Bal AA	67	253	40	47	3	8	1	29	38	6		.186	.306	.273	85	-2		.973	2	115	102	1-63/O-3(0-2-1),C-2	-0.5
	Buf N	30	105	7	21	6	1	0	9	8		23	.200	.257	.276	70	-3		.821	-7	75	59	S-19,1-12/C-2	-1.0
1889	KC AA	**139**	560	96	160	24	12	3	87	56	0	69	.286	.351	.387	104	1	67	.967	0	117	91	*1-135/3-4	-0.9
Total	7	509	2025	295	491	72	36	8	173	173	12	117	.242	.306	.325	94	-12	67	.956	-7	122	89	1-437/O-36R,S-24,C-12,3-9,2-3	-5.4
STEARNS, JOHN John Hardin B 8.21.1951 Denver, CO BR/TR 6/185# d9.22 C5																								
1974	Phi N	1	2	0	1	0	0	0	0	0-0	0	0	.500	.500	.500	173	0	0-0	1.000	0	0	0	/C	0.0
1975	NY N	59	169	25	32	5	1	3	10	17-4	2	15	.189	.268	.284	57	-10	4-1	.994	3	76	167	C-54	-0.5
1976	NY N	32	103	13	27	6	0	2	10	16-0	1	11	.262	.364	.379	119	3	1-2	.987	6	138	172	C-30	1.1
1977	NY N★	139	431	52	108	25	1	12	55	77-7	7	76	.251	.370	.397	112	11	9-8	.982	10	117	103	*C-127/1-6	2.5
1978	NY N	143	477	65	126	24	1	15	73	70-4	8	57	.264	.364	.413	122	17	25-13	.985	3	126	106	*C-141/3	2.8
1979	NY N☆	155	538	58	131	29	2	9	66	52-5	4	57	.243	.312	.355	86	-11	15-15	.983	-0	87	117	*C-121,1-16,3-11/O-6(LF)	-0.9
1980	NY N★	91	319	42	91	25	1	0	45	33-1	1	24	.285	.346	.370	105	4	7-3	.985	9	108	92	C-74,1-16/3	1.6
1981	NY N	80	273	25	74	12	1	1	24	24-2	0	17	.271	.329	.333	90	-3	12-2	.983	1	123	93	C-66/1-9,3-4	0.2
1982	NY N★	98	352	46	103	25	3	4	28	30-2	2	35	.293	.349	.415	114	7	17-7	.987	-4	100	**146**	C-81,3-12	0.8
1983	NY N	4	0	2	0	0	0	0	0	0-0	0	0	—	—	—	—	0	0-0	—	—	—	—	/R	0.0
1984	NY N	8	17	6	3	1	0	0	1	4-0	0	2	.176	.333	.235	63	-1	1-0	1.000	-0	89	0	/C-4,1-2	-0.1
Total	11	810	2681	334	696	152	10	46	312	323-25	25	294	.260	.341	.375	102	17	91-51	.985	27	109	116	C-699/1-49,3-29,O-6(LF)	7.5
STEDRONSKY, JOHN John B Troy, NY d9.26																								
1879	Chi N	4	12	0	1	0	0	0	0	0		3	.083	.083	.083	-42	-2		.789	1	144	233	/3-4	-0.1

Year	Tm Lg	G	AB	R	H	2B	3B	HR	RBI	BB-IB	HP	SO	AVG	OBP	SLG	AOPS	ABR	SB-CS	FA	FR	Rng	Thr	G at Pos	BFW
STEELMAN, FARMER Morris James B 6.29.1875 Millville, NJ D 9.16.1944 Merchantville, NJ TR d9.15																								
1899	Lou N	4	15	2	1	0	1	0	2	2	0		.067	.176	.200	3	-2	0	.929	-1	*111*	*46*	/C-4	-0.3
1900	Bro N	1	4	0	0	0	0	0	0	0	0		.000	.000	.000	-94	-1	0	1.000	0	*81*	*153*	/C	-0.1
1901	Bro N	1	3	0	1	0	0	0	0	0	0		.333	.333	.333	91	0	0	.875	0	*126*	*199*	/C	0.0
	Phi A	27	88	5	23	2	0	0	7	10	2		.261	.350	.284	74	-3	4	1.000	3	*100*	*132*	C-14,O-12(RF)	0.1
1902	Phi A	10	32	1	6	1	0	0	6	2	0		.188	.235	.219	25	-3	2	1.000	1	*94*	*80*	/C-5,O-5(RF)	-0.2
Total	4	42	142	8	31	3	1	0	15	14	2		.218	.297	.254	52	-9	6	.985	3	*101*	*114*	/C-25,O-17(RF)	-0.5
STEELS, JAMES James Earl B 5.30.1961 Jackson, MS BL/TL 5-10/185# d4.6																								
1987	SD N	62	68	9	13	1	1	0	6	11-0	0	14	.191	.300	.235	47	-5	3-2	.960	-0	95	129	O-28(17-6-7)	-0.6
1988	Tex A	36	53	4	10	1	0	0	5	0-0	0	15	.189	.185	.208	11	-6	2-0	1.000	-1	79	0	O-17(9-1-7)/1-7,D-7	-0.7
1989	SF N	13	12	0	1	0	0	0	0	2-1	0	4	.083	.214	.083	-12	-2	0-0	1.000	1	177	0	/1-3,O(RF)	-0.1
Total	3	111	133	13	24	2	1	0	11	13-1	0	33	.180	.250	.211	28	-13	5-2	.973	-0	91	82	/O-46(26-7-15),1-10,D-7	-1.4
STEERE, GENE Frederick Eugene B 8.16.1872 S.Scituate, RI D 3.13.1942 San Francisco, CA d8.29																								
1894	Pit N	10	39	3	8	0	0	0	4	2	0	1	.205	.244	.205	9	-6	2	.896	-2	93	105	S-10	-0.6
STEFERO, JOHN John Robert B 9.22.1959 Sumter, SC BL/TR 5-8/185# d6.24																								
1983	Bal A	9	11	2	5	1	0	0	4	3-0	0	2	.455	.571	.545	213	2	0-0	.920	0	84	164	/C-9	0.3
1986	Bal A	52	120	14	28	2	0	2	13	16-0	0	25	.233	.321	.300	72	-4	0-1	.984	-4	65	145	C-50/2	-0.7
1987	Mon N	18	56	4	11	0	0	1	3	3-1	0	17	.196	.237	.250	28	-6	0-0	.981	1	76	57	C-17	-0.5
Total	3	79	187	20	44	3	0	3	20	22-1	0	44	.235	.314	.299	67	-8	0-1	.979	-2	69	124	/C-76,2	-0.9
STEGMAN, DAVE David William B 1.30.1954 Inglewood, CA BR/TR 5-11/190# d9.4																								
1978	Det A	8	14	3	4	2	0	1	3	1-0	0	2	.286	.313	.643	164	1	0-0	1.000	-1	91	0	/O-7(0-5-3)	0.0
1979	Det A	12	31	6	6	0	0	3	5	2-0	0	3	.194	.242	.484	88	-1	1-1	1.000	1	131	0	O-12(0-11-1)	0.0
1980	Det A	65	130	12	23	5	0	2	9	14-0	0	23	.177	.255	.262	41	-10	1-1	.988	-4	85	34	O-57(14-27-23)/D-2	-1.6
1982	NY A	2	0	0	0	0	0	0	0	0-0	0	0	—	—	—	—	0	0-0	—	0			/D	0.0
1983	Chi A	30	53	5	9	2	0	0	4	10-0	0	9	.170	.292	.208	42	-4	0-1	1.000	-2	74	93	O-29(5-19-5)	-0.7
1984	Chi A	55	92	13	24	1	2	2	11	4-0	2	18	.261	.306	.380	85	-2	3-0	.985	-2	89	54	O-46(11-27-8)/D-3	-0.4
Total	6	172	320	39	66	10	2	8	32	31-0	2	55	.206	.277	.325	64	-16	5-3	.991	-8	89	44	O-151(30-89-40)/D-6	-2.7
STEIN, JUSTIN Justin Marion "Ott" B 8.9.1911 St.Louis, MO D 5.1.1992 Creve Coeur, MO BR/TR 5-11/180# d5.28																								
1938	Phi N	11	39	6	10	0	1	0	2	2	0	4	.256	.293	.308	67	-2	0	.880	-1	104	199	/3-7,2-3	-0.2
	Cin N	11	18	3	6	1	0	0	1	0	0	1	.333	.333	.389	101	0	0	.857	-0	117	97	/S-7,2-2	0.0
	Year	22	57	9	16	1	1	0	3	2	0	5	.281	.305	.333	78	-2	0	.857	-1	104	199	/3-7,S-7,2-5	-0.2
STEIN, BILL William Allen B 1.21.1947 Battle Creek, MI BR/TR 5-10/170# d9.6 OF Total (15-LF 14-RF)																								
1972	StL N	14	35	2	11	0	1	2	3	0-0	0	7	.314	.314	.543	141	1	1-0	1.000	-3	48	0	/3-4,O-4(4-0-1)	-0.1
1973	StL N	32	55	4	12	2	0	0	2	7-0	0	18	.218	.306	.255	57	-3	0-0	1.000	-1	105	0	O-10(2-0-8)/1-2,3	-0.4
1974	Chi A	13	43	5	12	1	0	0	5	7-2	0	8	.279	.380	.302	96	0	0-0	.871	-3	80	0	3-11/D-2	-0.3
1975	Chi A	76	226	23	61	7	1	3	21	18-0	1	32	.270	.327	.350	90	-3	2-2	.974	-1	115	82	2-28,3-24,D-18/O(LF)	-0.4
1976	Chi A	117	392	32	105	15	2	4	36	22-3	2	67	.268	.310	.347	92	-5	4-2	.960	-5	96	95	2-58,3-58/1SO(RF)D	-0.7
1977	Sea A	151	556	53	144	26	5	13	67	29-2	5	79	.259	.299	.394	89	-10	3-4	.964	-9	89	70	*3-147/S-2,D-3	-2.2
1978	Sea A	114	403	41	105	24	4	4	37	37-3	0	56	.261	.318	.370	95	-3	1-0	.929	-1	108	91	*3-111/D	-0.5
1979	Sea A	88	250	28	62	9	2	7	27	17-1	2	28	.248	.297	.384	82	-7	1-2	.959	-1	99	113	3-67,2-17/S-3	-0.8
1980	Sea A	67	198	16	53	5	1	5	27	16-4	1	25	.268	.321	.379	92	-3	1-1	.972	6	112	60	3-34,2-14/1-8,D-5	0.3
1981	Tex A	53	115	21	38	6	0	2	22	7-3	0	15	.330	.360	.435	138	5	1-2	1.000	0	109	82	1-20/O-8(7-0-1),3-7,2-3,S	0.4
1982	Tex A	85	184	14	44	8	0	1	16	12-0	2	23	.239	.293	.299	66	-8	0-0	.957	7	117	149	2-34,3-28/S-6,1-2,O(LF)D	-0.1
1983	Tex A	78	232	21	72	15	1	2	33	8-0	0	31	.310	.331	.409	105	1	2-3	.975	1	84	122	2-32,1-23,3-10/D-6	0.1
1984	Tex A	27	43	3	12	1	0	0	3	5-2	0	9	.279	.354	.302	81	-1	0-0	.967	-2	91	74	2-11/1-3,3-3,D-4	-0.3
1985	Tex A	44	79	5	20	3	1	1	12	1-1	1	15	.253	.272	.354	69	-4	0-0	.952	2	109	73	3-11/1-8,2-3,O-3(RF),D-6	-0.3
Total	14	959	2811	268	751	122	18	44	311	186-21	14	413	.267	.313	.370	91	-40	16-16	.950	-9	98	80	3-516,2-200/1-67,D-49,O-28L,S-13	-5.3
STEINBACH, TERRY Terry Lee B 3.2.1962 New Ulm, MN BR/TR 6-1/195# d9.12 OF Total (7-LF 8-RF)																								
1986	Oak A	6	15	3	5	0	0	2	4	1-0	0	0	.333	.375	.733	208	2	0-0	.962	0	35	357	/C-5	0.2
1987	Oak A	122	391	66	111	16	3	16	56	32-2	9	66	.284	.349	.463	122	12	1-2	.986	-4	115	**118**	*C-107,3-10/1D	1.2
1988	†Oak A★	104	351	42	93	19	1	9	51	33-2	6	47	.265	.334	.402	110	5	3-0	.983	7	104	**161**	C-84/3-9,1-8,O(LF)D	1.7
1989	†Oak A★	130	454	37	124	13	1	7	42	30-2	2	66	.273	.319	.352	93	-5	1-2	.985	2	**166**	88	*C-103,O-14(6-0-8),1-10/3-3,D-4	0.1
1990	†Oak A	114	379	32	95	15	2	9	57	19-1	4	66	.251	.291	.372	89	-7	0-1	.988	-2	115	75	C-83,D-25/1-3	-0.6
1991	Oak A	129	456	50	125	31	1	6	67	22-4	7	70	.274	.312	.386	99	-1	2-2	.980	-16	87	101	*C-117/1-9,D-2	-1.1
1992	†Oak A	128	438	48	122	20	1	12	53	45-3	1	58	.279	.345	.411	118	10	2-3	.985	1	122	125	*C-124/1-5,D-2	1.7
1993	Oak A★	104	389	47	111	19	1	10	43	25-1	3	65	.285	.333	.416	107	2	3-3	.989	-15	86	111	C-86,1-15/D-6	-0.9
1994	Oak A	103	369	51	105	21	2	11	57	26-4	0	62	.285	.327	.442	106	2	2-1	**.998**	9	119	144	C-93/1-6,D-6	1.5
1995	Oak A	114	406	43	113	26	1	15	65	25-4	3	74	.278	.322	.458	107	3	1-3	.993	7	112	**132**	*C-111/1-2	1.5
1996	Oak A	145	514	79	140	25	1	35	100	49-5	6	115	.272	.342	.529	118	12	0-1	.991	-7	102	94	*C-137/1D	1.3
1997	Min A	122	447	60	111	27	1	12	54	35-2	1	106	.248	.302	.394	79	-14	6-1	.993	-0	124	80	*C-116/1-2,D	-0.6
1998	Min A	124	422	45	102	25	2	14	54	38-0	4	89	.242	.310	.410	84	-11	0-1	.990	-1	131	91	*C-119/D-3	-0.4
1999	Min A	101	338	35	96	16	4	4	42	38-1	2	54	.284	.358	.391	88	-5	2-2	.991	-5	124	53	C-96/D	-0.4
Total	14	1546	5369	638	1453	273	21	162	745	418-31	48	938	.271	.326	.420	102	5	23-22	.989	-24	116	105	*C-1381/D-69,1-62,3-22,O-15R	5.2
STEINBACHER, HANK Henry John B 3.22.1913 Sacramento, CA D 4.3.1977 Sacramento, CA BL/TR 5-11/180# d4.21																								
1937	Chi A	26	73	13	19	4	1	1	9	4	0	7	.260	.299	.384	71	-4	2-0	.960	-1	90	0	O-15(LF)	-0.5
1938	Chi A	106	399	59	132	23	8	4	61	41	0	19	.331	.393	.459	110	6	1-3	.963	-4	96	74	*O-101(0-8-93)	-0.4
1939	Chi A	71	111	16	19	2	1	1	15	21	0	8	.171	.303	.234	38	-10	0-0	1.000	-1	95	64	O-22(1-0-21)	-1.1
Total	3	203	583	88	170	29	10	6	85	66	0	34	.292	.364	.407	92	-8	3-3	.968	-6	95	65	O-138(16-8-114)	-2.0
STEINBRENNER, GENE Eugene Gass B 11.17.1892 Pittsburgh, PA D 4.25.1970 Pittsburgh, PA BR/TR 5-8.5/155# d4.25																								
1912	Phi N	3	9	0	2	1	0	0	1	0	0	3	.222	.222	.333	48	-1	0	.900	-0	87	122	/2-3	-0.1
STEINECKE, BILL William Robert B 2.7.1907 Cincinnati, OH D 7.20.1986 St.Augustine, FL BR/TR 5-8.5/175# d9.16																								
1931	Pit N	4	4	0	0	0	0	0	0	0	0	1	.000	.000	.000	-99	-1	0	—	0	*0*	*0*	/C	-0.1
STEINER, BEN Benjamin Saunders B 7.28.1921 Alexandria, VA D 10.27.1988 Venice, FL BL/TR 5-11/165# d4.17																								
1945	Bos A	78	304	39	78	8	3	3	20	31	1	29	.257	.327	.332	89	-4	10-6	.967	-2	96	118	2-77	-0.2
1946	Bos A	3	4	1	1	0	0	0	0	0	0	0	.250	.250	.250	38	0	0-0	.750	-0	54	0	/3	-0.1
1947	Det A	1	0	1	0	0	0	0	0	0	0	0	—	—	—	—	0	0-0	—	0			R	0.0
Total	3	82	308	41	79	8	3	3	20	31	1	29	.256	.326	.331	89	-4	10-6	.967	-2	96	118	/2-77,3	-0.3
STEINER, RED James Harry B 1.7.1915 Los Angeles, CA D 11.16.2001 Gardena, CA BL/TR 6/185# d5.11																								
1945	Cle A	12	20	0	3	0	0	0	2	1	0	4	.150	.190	.150	-1	-3	0-0	1.000	1	*68*	*95*	/C-4	-0.2
	Bos A	26	59	6	12	1	0	0	4	14	0	2	.203	.356	.220	67	-2	0-0	.986	-3	*90*	*94*	C-24	-0.3
	Year	38	79	6	15	1	0	0	6	15	0	6	.190	.319	.203	52	-4	0-0	.989	-2	*86*	*94*	C-28	-0.5
STEINFELDT, HARRY Harry M. B 9.29.1877 St.Louis, MO D 8.17.1914 Bellevue, KY BR/TR 5-9.5/180# d4.22 OF Total (15-LF 16-CF 4-RF)																								
1898	Cin N	88	308	47	91	18	6	0	43	27	1		.295	.354	.393	107	2	9	.917	-7	96	97	2-31,O-29(14-15-0),3-22/S-5,1-4	-0.5
1899	Cin N	108	390	63	96	16	8	0	43	40	6		.246	.326	.328	78	-11	19	.888	-8	94	67	3-60,2-40/S-8,O-2(0-1-1)	-1.5
1900	Cin N	134	510	57	125	29	7	2	66	27	7		.245	.292	.341	76	-17	14	.922	16	100	110	3-67,2-64/O-2(RF),S-2	0.3
1901	Cin N	105	382	40	95	18	7	6	47	28	2		.249	.303	.380	104	1	10	.886	7	116	76	3-55,2-50	1.0
1902	Cin N	129	479	53	133	20	7	1	49	24	3		.278	.316	.355	98	-2	12	.912	22	**118**	**174**	*3-129/O(RF)	2.4
1903	Cin N	118	439	71	137	**32**	12	6	83	47	6		.312	.386	.481	132	18	13	.937	6	101	104	*3-104,S-14	2.6
1904	Cin N	99	349	35	85	11	6	1	52	29	6		.244	.313	.318	87	-5	17	.887	-10	85	128	3-98	-1.3
1905	Cin N	114	384	49	104	16	9	1	39	30	3		.271	.329	.367	97	-2	15	.919	12	**111**	**122**	*3-103/12O(LF)	1.3
1906	†Chi N	151	539	81	**176**	27	10	3	**83**	47	14		.327	.395	.430	149	31	29	**.954**	-20	84	88	*3-150/2	1.7
1907	†Chi N	152	542	52	144	25	5	1	70	37	9		.266	.323	.336	100	0	19	**.967**	-7	96	104	*3-151	-0.3
1908	†Chi N	150	539	63	130	20	6	1	62	36	4		.241	.294	.306	88	-8	12	.940	-13	91	89	*3-150	-1.9
1909	Chi N	151	528	73	133	27	6	2	59	57	5		.252	.331	.337	105	4	22	.940	1	99	101	*3-151	1.0

Year	Tm Lg	G	AB	R	H	2B	3B	HR	RBI	BB-IB	HP	SO	AVG	OBP	SLG	AOPS	ABR	SB-CS	FA	FR	Rng	Thr	G at Pos	BFW
1910	†Chi N	129	448	70	113	21	1	2	58	36	11	29	.252	.323	.317	88	-6	10	**.946**	1	102	97	*3-128	-0.3
1911	Bos N	19	63	5	16	4	0	1	8	6	2	3	.254	.338	.365	89	-1	1	.810	-5	77	70	3-19	-0.5
Total	14	1647	5900	759	1578	284	90	27	762	471	79	32	.267	.330	.360	101	4	202	.926	-5	98	106	*3-1387,2-187/O-35C,S-29,1-5	4.0
STELLBAUER, BILL William Jennings B 3.20.1894 Bremond, TX D 2.16.1974 New Braunfels, TX BR/TR 5-10/175# d4.12																								
1916	Phi A	25	48	2	13	2	1	0	5	6	0	7	.271	.352	.354	118	1	2	.857	-3	79	0	O-14(LF)	-0.2
STELMASZEK, RICK Richard Francis B 10.8.1948 Chicago, IL BL/TR 6-1/195# d6.25 C23																								
1971	Was A	6	9	0	0	0	0	0	0	0-0	0	3	.000	.000	.000	-99	-2	0-0	1.000	-1	0	243	/C-3	-0.3
1973	Tex A	7	9	0	1	0	0	0	0	1-0	0	2	.111	.200	.111	-11	-1	0-0	1.000	-1	157	0	/C-7	-0.2
	Cal A	22	26	2	4	1	0	0	3	6-0	0	7	.154	.313	.192	49	-1	0-0	1.000	-4	124	105	C-22	-0.5
	Year	29	35	2	5	1	0	0	3	7-0	0	9	.143	.286	.171	34	-3	0-0	1.000	-4	131	83	C-29	-0.7
1974	Chi N	25	44	2	10	2	0	1	7	10-0	0	6	.227	.364	.341	96	0	0-0	.983	-5	70	61	C-16	-0.4
Total	3	60	88	4	15	3	0	1	10	17-0	0	18	.170	.302	.239	55	-4	0-0	.993	-10	99	83	/C-48	-1.4
STEM, FRED Frederick Boothe B 9.22.1885 Oxford, NC D 9.5.1964 Darlington, SC BL/TR 6-2/160# d9.15																								
1908	Bos N	20	72	9	20	0	1	0	3	2	0		.278	.297	.306	94	-1	1	.995	-1	80	111	1-19	-0.2
1909	Bos N	73	245	13	51	2	3	0	11	12	3		.208	.254	.241	51	-15	5	.989	11	172	86	1-68	-0.6
Total	2	93	317	22	71	2	4	0	14	14	3		.224	.263	.256	60	-16	6	.990	10	152	91	/1-87	-0.8
STENGEL, CASEY Charles Dillon "The Old Professor" B 7.30.1890 Kansas City, MO D 9.29.1975 Glendale, CA BL/TL 5-11/175# d9.17 Mil 1918 M25 C2 HF1966																								
1912	Bro N	17	57	9	18	1	0	1	13	15	1	9	.316	.466	.386	140	5	5	.902	-2	94	40	O-17(CF)	0.1
1913	Bro N	124	438	60	119	16	8	7	43	56	1	58	.272	.356	.393	110	7	19-17	.960	-4	95	95	*O-119(0-117-2)	-0.8
1914	Bro N	126	412	55	130	13	10	4	60	56	5	55	.316	**.404**	.425	143	24	19	.964	-7	89	81	*O-121(0-2-119)	1.2
1915	Bro N	132	459	52	109	20	12	3	50	34	3	46	.237	.294	.353	94	-5	5-10	.959	-1	102	86	*O-129(1-0-128)	-1.7
1916	†Bro N	127	462	66	129	27	8	8	53	33	1	51	.279	.329	.424	127	14	11	.965	5	112	101	*O-121(RF)	1.5
1917	Bro N	150	549	69	141	23	12	6	73	60	5	62	.257	.336	.375	115	11	18	.969	11	102	**157**	*O-150(0-1-149)	1.6
1918	Pit N	39	122	18	30	4	1	1	12	16	2	14	.246	.343	.320	99	1	11	.973	3	112	133	O-37(RF)	0.2
1919	Pit N	89	321	38	94	10	10	4	43	35	1	35	.293	.364	.424	131	12	12	.957	1	118	53	O-87(RF)	0.9
1920	Phi N	129	445	53	130	25	6	9	50	38	6	35	.292	.356	.436	121	13	7-13	.954	-2	97	110	*O-118(1-5-113)	0.2
1921	Phi N	24	59	7	18	3	1	0	4	6	0	7	.305	.369	.390	94	0	1-1	.969	2	93	251	O-15(RF)	0.1
	NY N	18	22	4	5	1	0	0	2	1	0	5	.227	.261	.273	41	-2	0-1	.875	-0	107	0	/O-8(0-2-6)	-0.3
	Year	42	81	11	23	4	1	0	6	7	0	12	.284	.341	.358	81	-2	1-2	.950	2	95	207	O-23(0-2-21)	-0.2
1922	†NY N	84	250	48	92	8	10	7	48	21	**9**	17	.368	.436	.564	155	20	4-2	.969	-4	94	79	O-77(0-75-2)	1.3
1923	†NY N	75	218	39	74	11	5	5	43	20	2	18	.339	.400	.505	139	12	6-2	.983	-6	83	59	O-57(6-51-0)	0.4
1924	Bos N	131	461	57	129	20	6	5	39	45	3	39	.280	.348	.382	100	0	13-13	.978	-6	89	84	*O-126(0-5-121)	-1.7
1925	Bos N	12	13	0	1	0	0	0	2	1	0	2	.077	.143	.077	-46	-3	0-1	1.000	-0	68	0	/O(RF)	-0.3
Total	14	1277	4288	575	1219	182	89	60	535	437	39	453	.284	.356	.410	119	109	131-60	.964	-10	99	98	*O-1183(8-275-901)	2.7
STENHOUSE, MIKE Michael Steven B 5.29.1958 Pueblo, CO BL/TR 6-1/195# d10.3 f-Dave																								
1982	Mon N	1	1	0	0	0	0	0	0	0-0	0	1	.000	.000	.000	-98	0	0-0	—	0			/H	0.0
1983	Mon N	24	40	2	5	1	0	0	2	4-0	0	10	.125	.205	.150	-0	-5	0-0	1.000	-1	99	0	/O-9(3-0-7),1-5	-0.7
1984	Mon N	80	175	14	32	8	0	4	16	26-4	1	32	.183	.289	.297	69	-7	0-0	.986	-1	90	139	O-48(30-0-19),1-14	-1.1
1985	Min A	81	179	23	40	5	0	5	21	29-1	0	18	.223	.330	.335	79	-5	1-0	.929	2	95	248	D-27,O-16(8-0-9)/1-8	-0.5
1986	Bos A	21	21	1	2	1	0	0	1	12-0	0	5	.095	.424	.143	63	0	0-0	1.000	1	105	0	/O-4(2-0-2),1-3	0.0
Total	5	207	416	40	79	15	0	9	40	71-5	1	66	.190	.308	.291	67	-17	1-0	.973	0	92	146	/O-77(43-0-37),1-30,D-27	-2.3
STENNETT, RENNIE Renaldo Antonio (Porte) B 4.5.1951 Colon, Panama BR/TR 5-11/175# d7.10																								
1971	Pit N	50	153	24	54	5	4	1	15	7-0	0	9	.353	.377	.458	137	7	1-1	.954	6	114	106	2-36	1.5
1972	†Pit N	109	370	43	106	14	5	3	30	9-1	2	43	.286	.307	.376	95	-4	4-3	.977	11	110	145	2-49,O-41(31-5-10)/S-6	0.9
1973	Pit N	128	466	45	113	18	3	10	55	16-3	0	63	.242	.265	.358	74	-19	2-3	.981	17	107	119	2-84,S-43/O-5(3-0-2)	0.6
1974	†Pit N	157	673	84	196	29	3	7	56	32-8	2	51	.291	.322	.374	99	-3	8-9	.980	21	**112**	113	*2-154/O-2(RF)	2.7
1975	†Pit N	148	616	89	176	25	7	7	62	33-1	4	42	.286	.324	.383	97	-5	5-4	.979	26	**114**	107	*2-144	3.1
1976	Pit N	157	654	59	168	31	9	2	60	19-2	1	32	.257	.277	.341	75	-24	18-6	.981	24	**111**	111	*2-157/S-4	1.3
1977	Pit N	116	453	53	152	20	4	5	51	29-4	2	24	.336	.376	.430	113	9	28-18	.982	1	103	109	*2-113	1.6
1978	Pit N	106	333	30	81	9	2	3	35	13-6	2	22	.243	.274	.309	60	-18	2-1	.971	-4	99	91	2-80/3-6	-2.0
1979	†Pit N	108	319	31	76	13	2	0	24	24-6	0	25	.238	.289	.292	57	-19	1-4	.974	0	107	115	*2-102	-1.6
1980	SF N	120	397	34	97	13	2	2	37	22-10	2	31	.244	.286	.302	66	-19	4-4	.973	-7	98	80	*2-111	-2.2
1981	SF N	38	87	8	20	0	0	1	7	3-0	1	6	.230	.264	.264	51	-6	2-1	1.000	-3	81	77	2-19	-0.9
Total	11	1237	4521	500	1239	177	41	41	432	207-41	16	348	.274	.306	.359	85	-101	75-54	.978	91	107	108	*2-1049/S-53,O-48(34-5-14),3-6	5.0
STENSON, DERNELL Dernell Renauld B 6.17.1978 Lagrange, GA D 11.5.2003 Chandler, AZ BL/TL 6-1/230# d8.13																								
2003	Cin N	37	81	14	20	5	0	3	13	11-0	0	24	.247	.333	.420	98	0	0-0	.979	2	114	156	O-22(18-0-7)/1	0.1
STENZEL, JAKE Jacob Charles (born Jacob Charles Stelzle) B 6.24.1867 Cincinnati, OH D 1.6.1919 Cincinnati, OH BR/TR 5-10/168# d6.16																								
1890	Chi N	11	41	3	11	1	0	0	3	1	0	0	.268	.286	.293	66	-2	0	.857	-1	0	0	/O-6(RF),C-6	-0.2
1892	Pit N	3	9	0	0	0	0	0	0	1	0	3	.000	.100	.000	-69	-2	1	1.000	0	270	0	/O-2(1-1-0),C	-0.2
1893	Pit N	60	224	57	81	13	4	4	37	24	0	17	.362	.423	.509	150	16	16	.905	-7	55	138	O-45(4-18-23),C-12/S2	0.6
1894	Pit N	132	525	150	185	39	20	13	121	76	6	13	.352	.440	.577	145	40	61	.926	-3	104	112	*O-132(5-127-0)	2.2
1895	Pit N	130	518	114	192	38	13	7	97	57	11	25	.371	.444	.535	160	50	53	.909	-10	116	137	*O-130(CF)	2.6
1896	Pit N	114	479	104	173	26	14	2	82	32	8	13	.361	.410	.486	142	29	57	.922	-8	78	119	*O-114(CF)/1	1.2
1897	†Bal N	131	536	113	189	**43**	7	4	116	36	10		.353	.404	.481	133	26	69	.932	-15	63	58	*O-131(CF)	0.3
1898	Bal N	35	138	33	35	5	2	0	22	12	6		.254	.340	.319	87	-2	4	.926	-1	139	111	O-35(CF)	-0.4
	StL N	108	404	64	114	15	11	1	33	41	13		.282	.367	.381	112	7	21	.943	-3	53	54	*O-108(CF)	-0.2
	Year	143	542	97	149	20	13	1	55	53	19		.275	.360	.365	106	5	25	.940	-3	72	67	*O-143(CF)	-0.6
1899	StL N	35	128	21	35	9	0	1	19	16	3		.273	.367	.367	99	1	8	.949	-2	56	74	O-33(8-21-4)	-0.3
	Cin N	9	29	5	9	1	0	0	3	4	1		.310	.412	.345	106	1	2	1.000	-1	0	0	/O-7(CF)	0.0
	Year	44	157	26	44	10	0	1	22	20	4		.280	.376	.363	101	1	10	.957	-3	48	63	O-40(8-28-4)	-0.3
Total	9	768	3031	664	1024	190	71	32	533	300	58	71	.338	.408	.479	135	164	292	.927	-49	83	97	O-743(18-692-33)/C-19,12S	5.6
STEPHENS, RAY Carl Ray B 9.22.1962 Houston, TX BR/TR 6/190# d9.20																								
1990	StL N	5	15	2	2	1	0	1	1	0-0	0	3	.133	.133	.400	41	-1	0-0	1.000	-1	35	0	/C-5	-0.2
1991	StL N	6	7	0	2	0	0	0	0	1-0	0	3	.286	.375	.286	88	0	0-0	1.000	-1	51	81	/C-6	0.0
1992	Tex A	8	13	0	2	0	0	0	0	0-0	0	5	.154	.154	.154	-14	-2	0-0	1.000	-2	120	248	/C-6,D	-0.4
Total	3	19	35	2	6	1	0	1	1	1-0	0	11	.171	.194	.286	32	-3	0-0	1.000	-3	65	97	/C-17,D	-0.6
STEPHENS, GENE Glen Eugene B 1.20.1933 Gravette, AR BL/TR 6-3.5/175# d4.16																								
1952	Bos A	21	53	10	12	5	0	0	5	3	0	8	.226	.268	.321	59	-3	4-2	.962	0	107	104	O-13(2-0-11)	-0.3
1953	Bos A	78	221	30	45	6	2	3	18	29	2	56	.204	.302	.290	57	-13	3-3	.966	-3	95	46	O-72(71-0-3)	-2.0
1955	Bos A	109	157	25	46	9	4	3	18	20-0	2	34	.293	.374	.459	114	3	0-0	.947	3	100	220	O-75(71-4-0)	0.4
1956	Bos A	104	63	22	17	2	0	1	7	12-0	0	12	.270	.387	.349	85	-1	0-1	.983	4	137	130	O-71(69-2-2)	0.1
1957	Bos A	120	173	25	46	6	4	3	26	26-1	0	20	.266	.353	.399	102	1	0-2	.987	-0	85	174	O-90(75-6-11)	-0.2
1958	Bos A	134	270	38	59	10	1	9	25	22-1	1	46	.219	.279	.363	71	-11	1-2	.975	1	100	115	*O-110(92-26-3)	-1.6
1959	Bos A	92	270	34	75	13	1	3	39	29-0	4	33	.278	.353	.367	95	-1	5-2	.981	4	93	236	O-85(62-17-7)	-0.1
1960	Bos A	35	109	9	25	4	0	2	11	14-0	0	22	.229	.312	.321	71	-4	5-1	.951	-0	98	107	O-31(21-4-8)	-0.5
	Bal A	84	193	38	46	11	0	5	11	25-0	1	25	.238	.327	.373	91	-2	4-2	.992	3	107	135	O-77(36-19-42)	-0.2
	Year	119	302	47	71	15	0	7	22	39-0	1	47	.235	.322	.354	83	-6	9-3	.979	3	104	126	*O-108(57-23-50)	-0.7
1961	Bal A	32	58	4	11	2	0	0	2	14-0	0	7	.190	.347	.224	58	-3	1-1	1.000	1	93	152	O-30(27-5-5)	-0.3
	KC A	62	183	22	38	6	1	4	26	16-0	2	27	.208	.279	.317	58	-11	3-2	.968	3	101	179	O-54(6-28-25)	-1.1
	Year	94	241	26	49	8	1	4	28	30-0	2	34	.203	.297	.295	59	-14	4-3	.975	3	99	172	O-84(33-33-30)	-1.4
1962	KC A	5	4	0	0	0	0	0	0	1-0	0	1	.000	.200	.000	-39	-1	0-0	—	0			H	-0.1
1963	Chi A	6	18	5	7	0	0	1	2	1-0	0	3	.389	.421	.556	174	2	0-0	.909	1	88	614	/O-5(2-0-3)	0.2
1964	Chi A	82	141	21	33	4	2	3	17	21-3	2	28	.234	.335	.355	97	0	1-2	.969	1	110	80	O-59(32-25-6)	-0.1
Total	12	964	1913	283	460	78	15	37	207	233-5	14	322	.240	.325	.355	82	-44	27-20	.973	16	100	148	O-772(566-136-126)	-5.8
STEPHENS, JIM James Walter "Little Nemo" B 12.10.1883 Salineville, OH D 1.2.1965 Oxford, AL BR/TR 5-6.5/157# d4.11																								
1907	StL A	58	173	15	35	6	3	0	11	15	1		.202	.270	.272	73	-5	3	.967	-5	*91*	*96*	C-56	-0.5

Year	Tm Lg	G	AB	R	H	2B	3B	HR	RBI	BB-IB	HP	SO	AVG	OBP	SLG	AOPS	ABR	SB-CS	FA	FR	Rng	Thr	G at Pos	BFW
1908	StL A	47	150	14	30	4	1	0	6	9	2		.200	.255	.240	61	-6	0	.960	2	*121*	*107*	C-45	0.0
1909	StL A	79	223	18	49	5	0	3	18	13	5		.220	.278	.283	83	-5	5	.980	2	*96*	*109*	C-72	0.4
1910	StL A	99	289	24	62	3	7	0	23	16	2		.215	.261	.273	72	-11	2	.971	-1	*82*	***113***	C-96	-0.3
1911	StL A	70	212	11	49	5	5	0	17	17	4		.231	.300	.302	71	-9	1	.949	-8	*75*	*102*	C-66	-1.1
1912	StL A	75	205	13	51	7	5	0	22	7	0		.249	.274	.332	76	-8	3	.954	-1	*88*	*119*	C-66	-0.4
Total	6	428	1252	95	276	30	21	3	97	77	14		.220	.273	.285	73	-44	14	.965	-11	*90*	*108*	C-401	-1.9

STEPHENS, VERN Vernon Decatur "Junior" or "Buster" B 10.23.1920 McAlister, NM D 11.4.1968 Long Beach, CA BR/TR 5-10/185# d9.13

Year	Tm Lg	G	AB	R	H	2B	3B	HR	RBI	BB-IB	HP	SO	AVG	OBP	SLG	AOPS	ABR	SB-CS	FA	FR	Rng	Thr	G at Pos	BFW
1941	StL A	3	2	0	1	0	0	0	0	0	0	0	.500	.500	.500	160	0	0-0	.500	-0	103	0	/S	0.0
1942	StL A	145	575	84	169	26	6	14	92	41	0	53	.294	.341	.433	115	9	1-3	.944	-13	98	92	*S-144	0.6
1943	StL A★	137	512	75	148	27	3	22	91	54	0	73	.289	.357	.482	142	25	3-2	.943	-22	91	62	*S-123,O-11(9-0-3)	1.3
1944	†StL A★	145	559	91	164	32	1	20	**109**	62	1	54	.293	.365	.462	128	21	2-2	.954	-5	102	76	*S-143	2.8
1945	StL A✳	149	571	90	165	27	3	**24**	89	55	1	70	.289	.352	.473	132	21	2-1	**.961**	-18	94	80	*S-144/3-4	1.6
1946	StL A★	115	450	67	138	19	4	14	64	35	0	49	.307	.357	.460	121	11	0-1	.950	-1	103	93	*S-112	1.7
1947	StL A	150	562	74	157	18	4	15	83	70	0	61	.279	.359	.406	110	8	8-4	.970	13	**108**	103	*S-149	3.1
1948	Bos A★	**155**	635	114	171	25	8	29	137	77	2	56	.269	.350	.471	112	7	1-0	.971	9	**110**	99	*S-155	2.5
1949	Bos A★	**155**	610	113	177	31	2	39	**159**	101	0	73	.290	.391	.539	135	30	2-2	.966	2	**105**	108	*S-155	3.9
1950	Bos A☆	149	628	125	185	34	6	30	**144**	65	0	43	.295	.361	.511	110	7	1-0	.981	1	97	102	*S-146	1.6
1951	Bos A★	109	377	62	113	21	2	17	78	38	0	33	.300	.364	.501	120	10	1-2	.978	12	111	102	3-89/S-2	2.0
1952	Bos A	92	295	35	75	13	2	7	44	39	1	31	.254	.343	.383	95	-2	2-2	.957	4	104	119	S-53,3-29	0.5
1953	Chi A	44	129	14	24	6	0	1	14	13	0	18	.186	.261	.256	39	-11	2-0	.990	-0	99	97	3-38/S-3	-1.1
	StL A	46	165	16	53	8	0	4	17	18	0	24	.321	.388	.442	121	5	0-0	.954	-2	95	77	3-46	0.3
	Year	90	294	30	77	14	0	5	31	31	0	42	.262	.332	.361	85	-6	2-0	.968	-2	97	85	3-84/S-3	-0.8
1954	Bal A	101	365	31	104	17	1	8	46	17	0	36	.285	.311	.403	104	0	0-3	.966	-2	98	101	3-96	-0.3
1955	Bal A	3	6	0	1	0	0	0	0	0-0	1	0	.167	.286	.167	26	-1	0-0	1.000	-0	96	0	/3-2	-0.1
	Chi A	22	56	10	14	3	0	3	7	7-0	0	11	.250	.328	.464	110	1	0-0	1.000	2	113	137	3-18	0.3
	Year	25	62	10	15	3	0	3	7	7-0	1	11	.242	.324	.435	102	0	0-0	1.000	2	112	129	3-20	0.2
Total	15	1720	6497	1001	1859	307	42	247	1174	692-0	6	685	.286	.355	.460	118	141	25-22	.960	-20	101	92	*S-1330,3-322/O-11(9-0-3)	20.7

STEPHENSON, RIGGS Jackson Riggs "Old Hoss" B 1.5.1898 Akron, AL D 11.15.1985 Tuscaloosa, AL BR/TR 5-10/185# d4.13

Year	Tm Lg	G	AB	R	H	2B	3B	HR	RBI	BB-IB	HP	SO	AVG	OBP	SLG	AOPS	ABR	SB-CS	FA	FR	Rng	Thr	G at Pos	BFW
1921	Cle A	65	206	45	68	17	2	2	34	23	4	15	.330	.408	.461	119	7	4-1	.942	-4	95	115	2-54/3-2	0.5
1922	Cle A	86	233	47	79	24	5	2	32	27	6	18	.339	.421	.511	141	16	3-0	.952	-4	96	75	3-34,2-25/O-3(2-0-1)	1.4
1923	Cle A	91	301	48	96	20	6	5	65	15	3	25	.319	.357	.475	118	6	5-5	.970	11	106	124	2-66/O-3(RF),3-2	1.8
1924	Cle A	71	240	33	89	20	0	4	44	27	2	10	.371	.439	.504	141	16	1-2	.961	-11	102	58	2-58/O-7(RF)	0.6
1925	Cle A	19	54	8	16	3	1	1	9	7	1	3	.296	.387	.444	110	1	1-1	.946	1	112	124	O-16(RF)	0.0
1926	Chi N	82	281	40	95	18	3	3	44	31	0	16	.338	.404	.456	129	13	2	.950	-4	90	105	O-74(73-0-1)	0.4
1927	Chi N	152	579	101	199	**46**	9	7	82	65	6	28	.344	.415	.491	142	37	8	.975	0	96	129	*O-146(LF)/3-6	2.5
1928	Chi N	137	512	75	166	36	9	8	90	68	3	29	.324	.407	.477	132	26	8	.982	-2	97	98	*O-135(LF)	1.4
1929	†Chi N	136	495	91	179	36	6	17	110	67	7	21	.362	.445	.562	147	40	10	.984	-2	93	105	*O-130(LF)	2.5
1930	Chi N	109	341	56	125	21	1	5	68	32	0	20	.367	.421	.478	116	11	2	.958	-3	91	99	O-80(LF)	0.2
1931	Chi N	80	263	34	84	14	4	1	52	37	1	14	.319	.405	.414	119	9	1	.985	-2	98	29	O-66(LF)	0.3
1932	†Chi N	147	583	86	189	49	4	4	85	54	2	27	.324	.383	.443	123	21	3	.984	-7	92	77	*O-147(LF)	0.7
1933	Chi N	97	346	45	114	17	4	4	51	34	5	16	.329	.397	.436	138	19	5	.985	-1	99	73	O-91(LF)	1.3
1934	Chi N	38	74	5	16	0	0	0	7	7	1	5	.216	.293	.216	39	-6	0	1.000	2	93	327	O-15(LF)	-0.5
Total	14	1310	4508	714	1515	321	54	63	773	494	41	247	.336	.407	.473	130	216	53-9	.978	-25	95	98	O-913(885-0-28),2-203/3-44	13.1

STEPHENSON, JOHN John Herman B 4.13.1941 S.Portsmouth, KY BL/TR 5-11/180# d4.14

Year	Tm Lg	G	AB	R	H	2B	3B	HR	RBI	BB-IB	HP	SO	AVG	OBP	SLG	AOPS	ABR	SB-CS	FA	FR	Rng	Thr	G at Pos	BFW
1964	NY N	37	57	2	9	0	0	1	2	4-0	1	18	.158	.226	.211	24	-6	0-0	.800	-2	104	64	3-14/O-8(5-3-0)	-0.8
1965	NY N	62	121	9	26	5	0	4	15	8-2	0	19	.215	.264	.355	75	-4	0-1	.981	-5	*79*	*79*	C-47/O-2(RF)	-0.9
1966	NY N	63	143	17	28	1	1	1	11	8-0	2	28	.196	.248	.238	37	-13	0-0	.973	-2	*86*	*133*	C-52/O(LF)	-1.3
1967	Chi N	18	49	3	11	3	1	0	5	1-1	1	6	.224	.255	.327	62	-2	0-0	1.000	1	*127*	*117*	C-13	-0.1
1968	Chi N	2	2	0	0	0	0	0	0	0-0	0	0	.000	.000	.000	-94	0	0-0	—	0			H	-0.1
1969	SF N	22	27	2	6	2	0	0	3	0-0	0	4	.222	.214	.296	45	-2	0-0	.941	-3	35	0	/C-9,3	-0.5
1970	SF N	23	43	3	3	1	0	0	6	2-0	0	7	.070	.109	.093	-45	-9	0-0	1.000	1	74	90	/C-9,O(LF)	-0.7
1971	Cal A	98	279	24	61	17	0	3	25	22-6	3	21	.219	.281	.312	74	-10	0-0	.992	-2	106	61	C-88	-0.9
1972	Cal A	66	146	14	40	3	1	2	17	11-5	4	8	.274	.342	.349	112	2	0-0	.993	-4	67	79	C-56	0.0
1973	Cal A	60	122	9	30	5	0	1	9	7-1	1	7	.246	.292	.311	76	-4	0-0	.980	-4	94	58	C-56	-0.7
Total	10	451	989	83	214	37	3	12	93	63-15	12	118	.216	.271	.296	64	-48	0-1	.986	-20	*90*	*80*	C-330/3-15,O-12(7-3-2)	-6.0

STEPHENSON, JOE Joseph Chester B 6.30.1921 Detroit, MI D 9.20.2001 Fullerton, CA BR/TR 6-2/185# d9.19 Mil 1944-45 s-Jerry

Year	Tm Lg	G	AB	R	H	2B	3B	HR	RBI	BB-IB	HP	SO	AVG	OBP	SLG	AOPS	ABR	SB-CS	FA	FR	Rng	Thr	G at Pos	BFW
1943	NY N	9	24	4	6	1	0	0	1	0	0	5	.250	.250	.292	56	-1	0	.973	1	*98*	*194*	/C-6	0.0
1944	Chi N	4	8	1	1	0	0	0	0	1	0	3	.125	.222	.125	-1	-1	1	1.000	1	*77*	*174*	/C-3	0.0
1947	Chi A	16	35	3	5	0	0	0	3	1	2	7	.143	.211	.143	-1	-5	0-0	.959	-1	*94*	*118*	C-13	-0.5
Total	3	29	67	8	12	1	0	0	4	2	2	15	.179	.225	.194	19	-7	1-0	.970	1	*93*	*151*	/C-22	-0.5

STEPHENSON, PHIL Phillip Raymond B 9.19.1960 Guthrie, OK BL/TL 6-1/195# d4.5

Year	Tm Lg	G	AB	R	H	2B	3B	HR	RBI	BB-IB	HP	SO	AVG	OBP	SLG	AOPS	ABR	SB-CS	FA	FR	Rng	Thr	G at Pos	BFW
1989	Chi N	17	21	0	3	0	0	0	0	2-0	0	3	.143	.217	.143	5	-3	1-0	1.000	-1	57	0	/O-3(LF)	-0.3
	SD N	10	17	4	6	0	0	2	2	3-0	0	2	.353	.450	.706	225	3	0-0	.977	0	121	90	/1-8	0.3
	Year	27	38	4	9	0	0	2	2	5-0	0	5	.237	.326	.395	100	0	1-0	.977	-0	121	90	/1-8,O-3(LF)	0.0
1990	SD N	103	182	26	38	9	1	4	19	30-1	0	43	.209	.319	.335	80	-4	2-1	.997	2	116	111	1-60	-0.5
1991	SD N	11	7	0	2	0	0	0	0	2-0	0	3	.286	.444	.286	106	0	0-0	—	0			/H	0.0
1992	SD N	53	71	5	11	2	1	0	8	10-0	0	11	.155	.259	.211	34	-6	0-0	1.000	-1	79	0	O-15(10-0-6)/1-7	-0.9
Total	4	194	298	35	60	11	2	6	29	47-1	0	62	.201	.309	.312	73	-10	3-1	.993	1	117	107	/1-75,O-18(13-0-6)	-1.4

STEPHENSON, DUMMY Reuben Crandol B 9.22.1869 Petersburg, NJ D 12.1.1924 Trenton, NJ BR/TR 5-11.5/180# d9.9

Year	Tm Lg	G	AB	R	H	2B	3B	HR	RBI	BB-IB	HP	SO	AVG	OBP	SLG	AOPS	ABR	SB-CS	FA	FR	Rng	Thr	G at Pos	BFW
1892	Phi N	8	37	4	10	3	0	0	5	0	1	2	.270	.289	.351	94	0	0	.800	-2	83	0	/O-8(CF)	-0.2

STEPHENSON, BOB Robert Lloyd B 8.11.1928 Blair, OK BR/TR 6/165# d4.14

Year	Tm Lg	G	AB	R	H	2B	3B	HR	RBI	BB-IB	HP	SO	AVG	OBP	SLG	AOPS	ABR	SB-CS	FA	FR	Rng	Thr	G at Pos	BFW
1955	StL N	67	111	19	27	3	0	0	6	5-0	0	18	.243	.274	.270	46	-9	2-1	.938	-2	89	122	S-48/2-7,3	-0.8

STEPHENSON, WALTER Walter McQueen "Tarzan" B 3.27.1911 Saluda, NC D 7.4.1993 Shreveport, LA BR/TR 6/180# d4.29

Year	Tm Lg	G	AB	R	H	2B	3B	HR	RBI	BB-IB	HP	SO	AVG	OBP	SLG	AOPS	ABR	SB-CS	FA	FR	Rng	Thr	G at Pos	BFW
1935	†Chi N	16	26	2	10	1	1	0	2	1	0	5	.385	.407	.500	142	1	0	1.000	1	*126*	*299*	/C-6	0.3
1936	Chi N	6	12	0	1	0	0	0	1	0	0	5	.083	.083	.083	-54	-3	0	1.000	0	*65*	*0*	/C-4	-0.2
1937	Phi N	10	23	1	6	0	0	0	2	2	0	3	.261	.320	.261	55	-1	0	.967	0	*102*	*112*	/C-7	-0.1
Total	3	32	61	3	17	1	1	0	5	3	0	13	.279	.313	.328	70	-3	0	.984	2	*104*	*156*	/C-17	0.0

STERRETT, DUTCH Charles Hurlbut B 10.1.1889 Milroy, PA D 12.9.1965 Baltimore, MD BR/TR 5-11.5/165# d6.20

Year	Tm Lg	G	AB	R	H	2B	3B	HR	RBI	BB-IB	HP	SO	AVG	OBP	SLG	AOPS	ABR	SB-CS	FA	FR	Rng	Thr	G at Pos	BFW
1912	NY A	66	230	30	61	4	7	1	32	11	4		.265	.310	.357	85	-6	8	.972	-5	96	63	O-37(0-31-6),1-17,C-10/2	-1.3
1913	NY A	21	35	0	6	0	0	0	3	1	1	5	.171	.216	.171	14	-4	1	1.000	-1	68	38	/1-6,C	-0.5
Total	2	87	265	30	67	4	7	1	35	12	5	5	.253	.298	.332	77	-10	9	.972	-5	96	63	/O-37(0-31-6),1-23,C-11,2	-1.8

STEVENS, CHUCK Charles Augustus B 7.10.1918 Van Houten, NM BB/TL 6-1/180# d9.16 Mil 1943-45

Year	Tm Lg	G	AB	R	H	2B	3B	HR	RBI	BB-IB	HP	SO	AVG	OBP	SLG	AOPS	ABR	SB-CS	FA	FR	Rng	Thr	G at Pos	BFW
1941	StL A	4	13	2	2	0	0	0	2	0	0	1	.154	.154	.154	-18	-2	0-0	.966	-1	0	121	/1-4	-0.4
1946	StL A	122	432	53	107	17	4	3	27	47	2	62	.248	.324	.326	78	-12	4-6	**.995**	4	110	90	*1-120	-1.4
1948	StL A	85	287	34	75	12	4	1	26	41	0	26	.261	.354	.341	83	-6	2-2	.991	1	103	101	1-85	-0.9
Total	3	211	732	89	184	29	8	4	55	88	2	89	.251	.333	.329	79	-20	6-8	.993	3	106	95	1-209	-2.7

STEVENS, LEE De Wain Lee B 7.10.1967 Kansas City, MO BL/TL 6-4/219# d7.16

Year	Tm Lg	G	AB	R	H	2B	3B	HR	RBI	BB-IB	HP	SO	AVG	OBP	SLG	AOPS	ABR	SB-CS	FA	FR	Rng	Thr	G at Pos	BFW
1990	Cal A	67	248	28	53	10	0	7	32	22-3	0	75	.214	.275	.339	73	-10	1-1	.994	-2	85	105	1-67	-1.7
1991	Cal A	18	58	8	17	7	0	0	9	6-2	0	12	.293	.354	.414	113	1	1-2	.989	-0	113	72	1-11/O-9(1-0-8)	0.0
1992	Cal A	106	312	25	69	19	0	7	37	29-6	1	64	.221	.288	.349	78	-9	1-4	.995	-1	92	121	1-91/D-2	-1.8
1996	Tex A	27	78	6	18	2	3	3	12	6-0	1	22	.231	.291	.449	80	-3	0-0	.994	0	122	143	1-18/O-5(LF)	-0.4
1997	Tex A	137	426	58	128	24	2	21	74	23-2	1	83	.300	.336	.514	112	6	1-3	.994	-4	89	93	1-62,D-38,O-22(3-0-19)	-0.7
1998	†Tex A	120	344	52	91	17	4	20	59	31-4	0	93	.265	.324	.512	109	3	0-2	.996	0	94	56	D-72,1-37/O-7(RF)	-0.4
1999	†Tex A	146	517	76	146	31	1	24	81	52-10	0	132	.282	.344	.485	105	3	2-3	.994	-9	73	**109**	*1-133/D-8	-1.7
2000	Mon N	123	449	60	119	27	2	22	75	48-6	2	105	.265	.337	.481	101	0	0-0	.991	0	102	97	*1-123	-1.1
2001	Mon N	152	542	77	133	35	1	25	95	74-12	5	157	.245	.338	.452	101	1	2-1	.986	-4	94	94	*1-152	-1.6

Year	Tm Lg	G	AB	R	H	2B	3B	HR	RBI	BB-IB	HP	SO	AVG	OBP	SLG	AOPS	ABR	SB-CS	FA	FR	Rng	Thr	G at Pos	BFW
2002	Mon N	63	205	28	39	6	1	10	31	39-5	0	57	.190	.318	.376	79	-7	1-0	.993	4	125	101	1-58	-0.9
	Cle A	53	153	22	34	7	1	5	26	15-0	0	32	.222	.285	.379	78	-5	0-0	.987	-1	58	96	1-25,O-16(11-0-5)/D-3	-0.9
Total	10	1012	3332	440	847	185	15	144	531	345-50	10	832	.254	.323	.448	97	-20	9-16	.992	-17	92	102	1-777,D-123/O-59(20-0-39)	-11.2
STEVENS, ED Edward Lee "Big Ed" B 1.12.1925 Galveston, TX BL/TL 6-1/190# d8.9 C1																								
1945	Bro N	55	201	29	55	14	3	4	29	32	1	20	.274	.376	.433	125	8	0	.987	0	103	97	1-55	0.5
1946	Bro N	103	310	34	75	13	7	10	60	27	0	44	.242	.303	.426	104	0	2	.986	-4	84	90	1-99	-0.8
1947	Bro N	5	13	0	2	1	0	0	0	1	0	5	.154	.214	.231	18	-2	0	.971	1	193	79	/1-4	-0.1
1948	Pit N	128	429	47	109	19	6	10	69	35	2	53	.254	.313	.396	89	-8	4	**.996**	4	112	**114**	*1-117	-0.7
1949	Pit N	67	221	22	58	10	1	4	32	22	1	24	.262	.332	.371	86	-4	1	.995	10	167	131	1-58	0.4
1950	Pit N	17	46	2	9	2	0	0	3	4	0	5	.196	.260	.239	31	-5	0	1.000	1	115	109	1-12	-0.4
Total	6	375	1220	134	308	59	17	28	193	121	4	151	.252	.322	.398	95	-11	7	.992	12	114	107	1-345	-1.1
STEVENS, R C R C B 7.22.1934 Moultrie, GA BL/TR 6-5/219# d4.15																								
1958	Pit N	59	90	16	24	3	1	7	18	5-0	2	25	.267	.320	.556	129	3	0-0	.991	2	128	138	1-52	0.4
1959	Pit N	3	7	2	2	0	0	1	1	0-0	0	0	.286	.286	.714	157	0	0-0	1.000	0	113	100	/1	0.0
1960	Pit N	9	3	1	0	0	0	0	0	0-0	0	1	.000	.000	.000	-99	-1	0-0	1.000	1	361	340	/1-7	0.0
1961	Was A	33	62	2	8	1	0	0	2	7-0	0	15	.129	.217	.145	-1	-9	1-0	1.000	3	170	131	1-25	-0.6
Total	4	104	162	21	34	4	1	8	21	12-0	2	41	.210	.273	.395	77	-7	1-0	.995	6	148	138	/1-85	-0.2
STEVENS, ROBERT Robert d5.4																								
1875	Was NA	1	4	0	1	0	0	0	0	0		0	.250	.250	.250	77	0	0-0	.000	-0	0	0	/O(RF)	0.0
STEVENS, BOBBY Robert Jordan B 4.17.1907 Chevy Chase, MD BL/TR 5-8/149# d7.3																								
1931	Phi N	12	35	3	12	0	0	0	4	2	2	2	.343	.410	.343	97	0	0	.870	-4	73	77	S-10	-0.3
STEVERSON, TODD Todd Anthony B 11.15.1971 Los Angeles, CA BR/TR 6-2/195# d4.28																								
1995	Det A	30	42	11	11	0	0	2	6	6-0	0	10	.262	.340	.405	97	0	2-0	1.000	-2	73	100	O-27(17-1-10)/D	-0.2
1996	SD N	1	1	0	0	0	0	0	0	0-0	0	1	.000	.000	.000	-99	0	0-0	—	0			/H	0.0
Total	2	31	43	11	11	0	0	2	6	6-0	0	11	.256	.333	.395	93	0	2-0	1.000	-2	73	100	/O-27(17-1-10),D	-0.2
STEWART, ANDY Andrew David B 12.5.1970 Oshawa, ON, CAN BR/TR 5-11/205# d9.6																								
1997	KC A	5	8	1	2	1	0	0	0	0-0	0	0	.250	.250	.375	59	0	0-0	1.000	0	113	185	/C-4,D	0.0
STEWART, ACE Asa B 2.14.1869 Terre Haute, IN D 4.17.1912 Terre Haute, IN BR/TR 5-10/176# d4.18																								
1895	Chi N	97	365	52	88	8	10	8	76	39	0	40	.241	.314	.384	75	-17	14	.911	-9	94	124	*2-97	-1.7
STEWART, TUFFY Charles Eugene B 7.31.1883 Chicago, IL D 11.18.1934 Chicago, IL BL/TL 5-10/167# d8.8																								
1913	Chi N	9	8	1	1	1	0	0	2	2	0	5	.125	.300	.250	58	0	1	1.000	0	152	0	/O(RF)	0.0
1914	Chi N	2	1	0	0	0	0	0	0	0	0	0	.000	.000	.000	-99	0	0	—	0			H	0.0
Total	2	11	9	1	1	1	0	0	2	2	0	5	.111	.273	.222	43	0	1	1.000	0	152	0	/O(RF)	0.0
STEWART, BUD Edward Perry B 6.15.1916 Sacramento, CA D 6.21.2000 Palo Alto, CA BL/TR 5-11/170# d4.19 Def 1943 Mil 1944-45																								
1941	Pit N	73	172	27	46	7	0	0	10	12	0	17	.267	.315	.308	76	-5	3	.962	1	97	176	O-41(15-4-24)	-0.6
1942	Pit N	82	183	21	40	8	4	0	20	22	0	16	.219	.302	.306	76	-5	2	1.000	-1	110	42	O-34(19-0-16),3-10/2-6	-0.9
1948	NY A	6	5	1	1	1	0	0	0	0	0	0	.200	.200	.400	58	0	0-0	—	0			H	0.0
	Was A	118	401	56	112	17	13	7	69	49	2	27	.279	.361	.439	115	7	8-9	.975	-1	104	60	*O-114(10-37-72)	0.1
	Year	124	406	57	113	18	13	7	69	49	2	27	.278	.359	.438	115	7	8-9	.975	-1	104	60	*O-114(10-37-72)	0.1
1949	Was A	118	388	58	110	23	4	8	43	49	3	33	.284	.368	.425	112	7	6-4	.982	-3	91	103	*O-105(75-16-20)	-0.3
1950	Was A	118	378	46	101	15	6	4	35	46	1	33	.267	.348	.370	88	-7	5-4	.991	2	99	126	*O-100(42-0-66)	-0.9
1951	Chi A	95	217	40	60	13	5	6	40	29	2	9	.276	.367	.465	127	8	1-6	.983	-1	93	97	O-63(52-1-14)	0.1
1952	Chi A	92	225	23	60	10	0	5	30	28	1	17	.267	.350	.378	102	1	3-0	.982	-1	102	31	O-60(57-0-3)	-0.3
1953	Chi A	53	59	16	16	2	0	2	13	14	0	3	.271	.411	.407	118	2	1-0	1.000	-1	83	0	O-16(11-0-5)	0.1
1954	Chi A	18	13	0	1	0	0	0	0	3	0	2	.077	.250	.077	-7	-2	0-0	1.000	0	175	0	/O-2(RF)	-0.2
Total	9	773	2041	288	547	96	32	32	260	252	9	157	.268	.351	.393	102	6	29-23	.982	-6	99	89	O-535(281-58-222)/3-10,2-6	-2.9
STEWART, GLEN Glen Weldon "Gabby" B 9.29.1912 Tullahoma, TN D 2.11.1997 Memphis, TN BR/TR 6/175# d6.26																								
1940	NY N	15	29	1	4	1	0	0	0	1	0	2	.138	.167	.172	-6	-4	0	.875	0	133	0	/3-6,S-5	-0.4
1943	Phi N	110	336	23	71	10	1	2	24	32	2	41	.211	.284	.265	61	-17	1	.947	-12	94	90	S-77,2-18/1-8,C	-2.4
1944	Phi N	118	377	32	83	11	5	0	29	28	0	40	.220	.274	.276	57	-23	0	.963	1	105	88	3-83,S-32/2	-1.9
Total	3	243	742	56	158	22	6	2	53	61	2	83	.213	.275	.267	56	-44	1	.953	-11	97	90	S-114/3-89,2-19,1-8,C	-4.7
STEWART, JIMMY James Franklin B 6.11.1939 Opelika, AL BB/TR 6/165# d9.3 OF Total (176-LF 43-CF 11-RF)																								
1963	Chi N	13	37	1	11	2	0	0	1	1-0	0	7	.297	.316	.351	87	-1	1-1	.973	1	109	161	/S-9,2	0.1
1964	Chi N	132	415	59	105	17	0	3	33	49-0	2	61	.253	.331	.316	81	-8	10-8	.981	2	110	116	2-61,S-45/O-4(CF),3	0.1
1965	Chi N	116	282	26	63	9	4	0	19	30-1	2	53	.223	.301	.284	65	-13	13-3	.955	-5	93	149	O-55(47-8-0),S-48	-1.8
1966	Chi N	57	90	4	16	4	1	0	4	7-0	2	12	.178	.253	.244	38	-7	1-1	1.000	-1	101	99	O-15(4-11-1)/2-4,S-2,3-2	-1.0
1967	Chi N	6	6	1	1	0	0	0	1	0-0	0	0	.167	.167	.167	-4	-1	0-0	—	0			H	-0.1
	Chi A	24	18	5	3	0	0	0	1	1-0	0	6	.167	.211	.167	13	-2	1-0	1.000	1	0	1192	/O-6(LF),2-5,S-2	-0.1
1969	Cin N	119	221	26	56	3	4	4	24	19-3	0	33	.253	.311	.357	83	-6	4-2	.973	1	93	176	O-66(55-10-1),2-18/3-6,S	-0.6
1970	†Cin N	101	105	15	28	3	1	1	8	8-1	1	13	.267	.322	.343	79	-3	5-3	1.000	2	73	120	O-48(41-2-5),2-18/3-9,C1	-0.1
1971	Cin N	80	82	7	19	2	2	0	9	9-1	0	12	.232	.308	.305	76	-3	3-1	1.000	-2	45	0	O-19(11-6-3)/3-9,2-6	-0.4
1972	Hou N	68	96	14	21	5	2	0	9	6-2	0	9	.219	.257	.313	65	-5	0-1	1.000	-2	80	0	O-11(9-2-1)/1-9,2-8,3-2	-0.8
1973	Hou N	61	68	6	13	0	0	0	3	9-1	1	12	.191	.295	.191	37	-6	0-0	1.000	1	118	151	/3-8,O-3(LF),2	-0.5
Total	10	777	1420	164	336	45	14	8	112	139-9	8	218	.237	.306	.305	71	-55	38-20	.969	-3	89	146	O-227L,2-122,S-107/3-37,1-10,C	-5.2
STEWART, STUFFY John Franklin B 1.31.1894 Jasper, FL D 12.30.1980 Lake City, FL BR/TR 5-9.5/160# d9.3																								
1916	StL N	9	17	0	3	0	0	0	1	0	0	3	.176	.176	.176	9	-2	0	.833	-1	75	112	/2-8	-0.4
1917	StL N	13	9	4	0	0	0	0	0	0	0	4	.000	.000	.000	-99	-2	0	1.000	0	64	511	/O-7(2-3-2),2-2	-0.2
1922	Pit N	3	13	3	2	0	0	0	0	0	0	1	.154	.154	.154	-20	-2	0-0	.875	-1	84	122	/2-3	-0.4
1923	Bro N	4	11	3	4	1	0	1	1	1	0	1	.364	.417	.727	202	2	0-0	.786	-1	86	68	/2-3	0.0
1925	Was A	7	17	3	6	1	0	0	3	1	0	2	.353	.389	.412	105	0	1-0	.929	0	112	133	/3-5,2	0.1
1926	Was A	62	63	27	17	6	1	0	9	6	0	6	.270	.333	.397	92	-1	8-4	.975	4	112	111	2-25/3	0.3
1927	Was A	56	129	24	31	6	2	0	4	8	0	15	.240	.285	.318	57	-9	12-2	.939	-0	102	96	2-37/3-2	-0.6
1929	Was A	22	6	10	0	0	0	0	0	1	0	0	.000	.143	.000	-60	-1	0-1	1.000	1	176	0	/2-3	-0.1
Total	8	176	265	74	63	14	3	1	18	17	0	32	.238	.284	.325	61	-15	21-7	.932	1	101	99	/2-82,3-8,O-7(2-3-2)	-1.3
STEWART, MARK Mark "Big Slick" B 10.11.1889 Whitlock, TN D 1.17.1932 Memphis, TN BL/TR 6-1/180# d10.4																								
1913	Cin N	1	1	0	0	0	0	0	0	0	0	0	.000	.000	.000	-99	0	0	—	-0	0	0	/C	0.0
STEWART, SHANNON Shannon Harold B 2.25.1974 Cincinnati, OH BR/TR 6/175# d9.2																								
1995	Tor A	12	38	2	8	0	0	0	1	5-0	1	5	.211	.318	.211	41	-3	2-0	.955	-1	76	196	O-12(CF)	-0.4
1996	Tor A	7	17	2	3	1	0	0	2	1-0	0	4	.176	.222	.235	16	-2	1-0	.800	-2	43	0	/O-6(CF)	-0.3
1997	Tor A	44	168	25	48	13	7	0	22	19-1	4	24	.286	.368	.446	112	3	10-3	.980	-2	99	50	O-41(2-39-0)/D	0.3
1998	Tor A	144	516	90	144	29	3	12	55	67-1	15	77	.279	.377	.417	106	7	51-18	.980	0	104	51	*O-144(110-44-0)	0.9
1999	Tor A	145	608	102	185	28	2	11	67	59-0	8	83	.304	.371	.411	98	0	37-14	.981	-10	91	44	*O-142(140-7-0)/D-2	-1.1
2000	Tor A	136	583	107	186	43	5	21	69	37-1	6	79	.319	.363	.518	117	14	20-5	.993	2	106	61	*O-136(136-1-0)	1.2
2001	Tor A	155	640	103	202	44	7	12	60	46-1	11	72	.316	.371	.463	115	15	27-10	.981	-7	88	79	*O-142(LF),D-13	0.4
2002	Tor A	141	577	103	175	38	6	10	45	54-2	9	60	.303	.371	.442	111	11	14-2	.990	-4	92	51	O-99(LF),D-38	0.3
2003	Tor A	71	303	47	89	22	2	7	35	27-2	2	30	.294	.347	.449	108	4	1-2	.974	0	103	72	O-69(LF)/D-2	0.1
	†Min A	65	270	43	87	22	0	6	38	25-1	4	36	.322	.384	.470	124	11	3-4	.993	4	115	113	O-58(46-0-14)/D-6	1.1
	Year	136	573	90	176	44	2	13	73	52-3	6	66	.307	.364	.459	116	15	4-6	.983	5	108	91	*O-127(115-0-14)/D-8	1.2
Total	9	920	3720	624	1127	240	32	79	394	340-9	60	470	.303	.368	.448	110	60	166-58	.984	-18	98	64	O-849(744-109-14)/D-62	2.5
STEWART, NEB Walter Nesbitt B 5.21.1918 S.Charleston, OH D 6.8.1990 London, OH BR/TR 6-1/195# d9.8																								
1940	Phi N	10	31	3	4	0	0	0	0	1	0	5	.129	.156	.129	-21	-5	0	.944	1	86	342	/O-9(8-1-0)	-0.5
STEWART, BILL William Wayne B 4.15.1928 Bay City, MI BR/TR 5-11/200# d4.17																								
1955	KC A	11	18	2	2	1	0	0	0	1-0	0	6	.111	.158	.167	-13	-3	0-0	1.000	1	103	361	/O-6(4-0-2)	-0.2

Year	Tm Lg	G	AB	R	H	2B	3B	HR	RBI	BB-IB	HP	SO	AVG	OBP	SLG	AOPS	ABR	SB-CS	FA	FR	Rng	Thr	G at Pos	BFW
STILLMAN, ROYLE Royle Eldon B 1.2.1951 Santa Monica, CA BL/TL 5-11/180# d6.22																								
1975	Bal A	13	14	1	6	0	0	0	1	1-0	0	3	.429	.467	.429	165	1	0-0	1.000	0	141	0	/O-2(0-1-1)	0.1
1976	Bal A	20	22	0	2	0	0	0	1	3-1	0	4	.091	.200	.091	-14	-3	0-0	1.000	-0	0	0	/1-2,D-5	-0.3
1977	Chi A	56	119	18	25	7	1	3	13	17-1	0	21	.210	.307	.361	82	-3	2-1	.977	0	122	0	O-26(19-0-8),D-13/1	-0.4
Total	3	89	155	19	33	7	1	3	15	21-2	0	28	.213	.305	.329	77	-5	2-1	.978	0	123	0	/O-28(19-1-9),D-18,1-3	-0.6
STILLWELL, KURT Kurt Andrew B 6.4.1965 Glendale, CA BB/TR 5-11/175# d4.13 f-Ron																								
1986	Cin N	104	279	31	64	6	1	0	26	30-1	2	47	.229	.309	.258	56	-16	6-2	.951	-5	99	100	S-80	-1.4
1987	Cin N	131	395	54	102	20	7	4	33	32-2	2	50	.258	.316	.375	79	-12	4-6	.914	-19	80	80	S-51,2-37,3-20	-2.6
1988	KC A★	128	459	63	115	28	5	10	53	47-0	3	76	.251	.322	.399	100	0	6-5	.976	-10	97	78	*S-124	-0.1
1989	KC A	130	463	52	121	20	7	7	54	42-2	3	64	.261	.325	.380	99	-1	9-6	.970	-19	89	84	*S-130	-1.0
1990	KC A	144	506	60	126	35	4	3	51	39-1	4	60	.249	.304	.352	85	-10	0-2	.957	-12	94	88	*S-141	-1.3
1991	KC A	122	385	44	102	17	1	6	51	33-5	1	56	.265	.322	.361	89	-6	3-4	.959	-14	87	99	*S-118	-1.3
1992	SD N	114	379	35	86	15	3	2	24	26-9	1	58	.227	.274	.298	62	-19	4-1	.970	-12	87	105	*2-111	-3.0
1993	SD N	57	121	9	26	4	0	1	11	11-2	1	22	.215	.286	.273	49	-9	4-3	.921	-5	82	77	S-30/3-3	-1.2
	Cal A	22	61	2	16	2	2	0	3	4-0	0	11	.262	.299	.361	76	-2	2-0	.952	1	106	62	2-18/S-7	0.0
1996	Tex A	46	77	12	21	4	0	1	4	10-0	1	11	.273	.364	.364	81	-2	0-0	.964	-9	68	40	2-21/S-9,3-6,1D	-0.9
Total	9	998	3125	362	779	151	30	34	310	274-22	18	455	.249	.311	.349	82	-77	38-29	.958	-104	92	87	S-690,2-187/3-29,D1	-12.8
STILLWELL, RON Ronald Roy B 12.3.1939 Los Angeles, CA BR/TR 5-11/165# d7.3 s-Kurt																								
1961	Was A	8	16	3	2	1	0	0	1	1-0	0	4	.125	.176	.188	-3	-2	0-0	.929	-0	102	205	/S-5	-0.2
1962	Was A	6	22	5	6	0	0	0	2	2-0	0	2	.273	.333	.273	66	-1	0-0	1.000	-1	81	82	/2-6,S	-0.2
Total	2	14	38	8	8	1	0	0	3	3-0	0	6	.211	.268	.237	37	-3	0-0	1.000	-1	81	82	/2-6,S-6	-0.4
STIMAC, CRAIG Craig Steven B 11.18.1954 Oak Park, IL BR/TR 6-2/185# d8.12																								
1980	SD N	20	50	5	11	2	0	0	7	1-0	0	6	.220	.222	.260	40	-4	0-0	.982	1	52	151	C-11/3-2	-0.3
1981	SD N	9	9	0	1	0	0	0	0	0-0	0	3	.111	.111	.111	-40	-2	0-0	—	0			/H	-0.2
Total	2	29	59	5	12	2	0	0	7	1-0	0	9	.203	.206	.237	29	-6	0-0	.982	1	52	151	/C-11,3-2	-0.5
STINNETT, KELLY Kelly Lee B 2.14.1970 Lawton, OK BR/TR 5-11/195# d4.5																								
1994	NY N	47	150	20	38	6	2	2	14	11-1	5	28	.253	.323	.360	79	-5	2-0	.979	-6	122	87	C-44	-0.8
1995	NY N	77	196	23	43	8	1	4	18	29-3	6	65	.219	.338	.332	80	-5	2-0	.983	-10	67	86	C-67	-1.1
1996	Mil A	14	26	1	2	0	0	0	0	2-0	1	11	.077	.172	.077	-33	-5	0-0	.960	-1	75	44	C-14/D	-0.6
1997	Mil A	30	36	2	9	4	0	0	3	3-0	0	9	.250	.308	.361	73	-1	0-0	.989	3	250	84	C-25/D	0.3
1998	Ari N	92	274	35	71	14	1	11	34	35-3	6	74	.259	.353	.438	108	4	0-1	.984	-6	104	124	C-86/D	0.3
1999	†Ari N	88	284	36	66	13	0	14	38	24-2	5	83	.232	.302	.426	81	-9	2-1	.990	-8	86	120	C-86	-1.1
2000	Ari N	76	240	22	52	7	0	8	33	19-4	6	56	.217	.291	.346	58	-16	0-1	.990	5	81	117	C-74	-0.7
2001	Cin N	63	187	27	48	11	0	9	25	17-3	5	61	.257	.333	.460	98	0	2-2	.966	-7	72	84	C-59/D	-0.4
2002	Cin N	34	93	10	21	5	0	3	13	15-1	0	25	.226	.333	.376	87	-2	2-0	.990	2	83	95	C-30	0.2
2003	Cin N	60	179	14	41	13	0	3	19	13-3	4	51	.229	.294	.352	69	-8	0-0	.993	-6	116	86	C-50	-1.1
	Phi N	7	7	0	3	0	0	0	0	1-0	0	1	.429	.500	.429	155	1	0-0	1.000	1	0	0	/C	0.1
	Year	67	186	14	44	13	0	3	19	14-3	4	52	.237	.302	.355	73	-7	0-0	.993	-5	115	85	C-51	-1.0
Total	10	588	1672	190	394	81	4	54	197	169-20	38	464	.236	.319	.386	81	-46	10-5	.985	-33	94	102	C-536/D-4	-4.9
STINSON, BOB Gorrell Robert B 10.11.1945 Elkin, NC BB/TR (BR 1969 BL 1980 (part)) 5-11.5/185# d9.23																								
1969	LA N	4	8	1	3	0	0	0	2	0-0	0	2	.375	.375	.375	119	0	0-1	.952	-1	65	115	/C-4	-0.1
1970	LA N	4	3	1	0	0	0	0	0	0-0	0	1	.000	.000	.000	-99	-1	0-0	1.000	-1	0	0	/C-3	-0.1
1971	StL N	17	19	3	4	1	0	0	1	1-0	0	7	.211	.250	.263	44	-1	0-0	.971	0	63	189	/C-6,O-3(1-0-2)	-0.1
1972	Hou N	27	35	3	6	1	0	0	2	1-0	1	6	.171	.211	.200	19	-4	0-0	.964	-2	40	0	C-12/O-3(2-0-1)	-0.6
1973	Mon N	48	111	12	29	6	1	3	12	17-2	3	15	.261	.374	.414	114	3	0-1	.979	-4	98	71	C-35/3	0.0
1974	Mon N	38	87	4	15	2	0	1	6	15-3	0	16	.172	.294	.230	45	-6	1-1	1.000	3	140	98	C-29	-0.2
1975	KC A	63	147	18	39	9	1	1	9	18-1	1	29	.265	.345	.361	98	0	1-0	.993	7	110	105	C-59/120(RF)D	1.0
1976	†KC A	79	209	26	55	7	1	2	25	25-2	1	29	.263	.342	.335	99	0	3-1	.979	-3	98	80	C-79	0.1
1977	Sea A	105	297	27	80	11	1	8	32	37-4	6	50	.269	.360	.394	107	4	0-3	.984	-8	68	73	C-99/D	-0.1
1978	Sea A	124	364	46	94	14	3	11	55	45-1	6	42	.258	.346	.404	112	7	2-1	.987	-18	71	117	*C-123/D	-0.6
1979	Sea A	95	247	19	60	8	0	6	28	33-3	4	38	.243	.338	.348	85	-4	1-2	.978	-10	71	71	C-91	-1.1
1980	Sea A	48	107	6	23	2	0	1	8	9-0	1	19	.215	.277	.262	50	-7	0-0	.979	-8	55	78	C-45	-1.5
Total	12	652	1634	166	408	61	7	33	180	201-16	23	254	.250	.337	.356	93	-9	8-10	.984	-46	81	89	C-585/O-7(3-0-4),D-3,213	-3.3
STIRES, GAT Garrett B 10.13.1849 Hunterdon Co., NJ D 6.13.1933 Byron, IL BL/TR 5-8/180# d5.6																								
1871	Rok NA	**25**	110	23	30	4	6	2	24	7		5	.273	.316	.473	129	4	3-0	.837	-0	101	0	*O-25(RF)	0.4
STIRNWEISS, SNUFFY George Henry B 10.26.1918 New York, NY D 9.15.1958 Newark Bay, NJ BR/TR 5-8.5/175# d4.22																								
1943	†NY A	83	274	34	60	8	4	1	25	47	0	37	.219	.333	.288	82	-5	11-9	.938	-2	99	129	S-68/2-4	-0.2
1944	NY A	**154**	643	**125**	**205**	35	**16**	8	43	73	1	87	.319	.389	.460	137	32	**55**-11	**.982**	18	105	104	*2-154	6.8
1945	NY A✳	**152**	632	**107**	**195**	32	**22**	10	64	78	1	62	**.309**	.385	**.476**	**143**	**34**	**33**-17	.970	**25**	110	**126**	*2-152	**7.2**
1946	NY A★	129	487	75	122	19	7	0	37	66	0	58	.251	.340	.318	83	-9	18-6	.991	6	103	118	3-79,2-46/S-4	0.1
1947	†NY A	148	571	102	146	18	8	5	41	89	2	47	.256	.358	.342	96	-1	5-3	.983	-9	92	107	*2-148	-0.1
1948	NY A	141	515	90	130	20	7	3	32	86	1	62	.252	.360	.336	87	-8	5-4	**.993**	-8	88	107	*2-141	-0.8
1949	†NY A	70	157	29	41	8	2	0	11	29	1	20	.261	.380	.338	90	-1	3-2	.974	2	91	105	2-51/3-4	0.3
1950	NY A	7	2	0	0	0	0	0	0	0	0	0	.000	.000	.000	-99	-1	0-0	1.000	0	203	0	/2-4	0.0
	StL A	93	326	32	71	16	2	1	24	51	0	49	.218	.324	.288	56	-21	3-3	.975	-17	90	83	2-62,3-31/S-5	-3.3
	Year	100	328	32	71	16	2	1	24	51	0	49	.216	.322	.287	55	-22	3-3	.975	-16	91	82	2-66,3-31/S-5	-3.3
1951	Cle A	50	88	10	19	1	0	1	4	22	0	25	.216	.373	.261	78	-1	1-0	.992	5	116	116	2-25/3-2	0.5
1952	Cle A	1	0	0	0	0	0	0	0	0	0	0	—	—	—	—	0	0-0	—	-0	0	0	/3	0.0
Total	10	1028	3695	604	989	157	68	29	281	541	6	447	.268	.362	.371	102	19	134-55	.980	21	99	109	2-787,3-117/S-77	10.5
STIVETTS, JACK John Elmer "Happy Jack" B 3.31.1868 Ashland, PA D 4.18.1930 Ashland, PA BR/TR 6-2/185# d6.26 ▲ OF Total (41-LF 33-CF 69-RF)																								
1889	StL AA	27	79	12	18	2	2	0	7	3	1	13	.228	.265	.304	55	-5	0	.896	-1	81	0	P-26/O(RF)	-0.1
1890	StL AA	67	226	36	65	15	6	7	43	16	1		.288	.337	.500	128	5	2	.894	3	102	119	P-54,O-10(CF)/1-3	0.2
1891	StL AA	85	302	45	92	10	2	7	54	10	2	32	.305	.331	.421	100	-3	4	.898	4	104	63	P-64,O-24(1-0-23)	0.1
1892	†Bos N	71	240	40	71	14	2	3	36	27	1	28	.296	.369	.408	124	7	8	.904	1	103	177	P-54,O-18(16-2-0)/1	0.1
1893	Bos N	50	172	32	51	5	6	3	25	12	0	14	.297	.342	.448	101	-2	6	.955	-4	79	105	P-38/O-8(3-0-5),3-3	-0.3
1894	Bos N	68	244	55	80	12	7	8	64	16	0	21	.328	.369	.533	107	0	3	.943	-4	74	46	P-45,O-16(8-2-6)/1-4	-0.2
1895	Bos N	46	158	20	30	6	4	0	24	6	0	18	.190	.220	.278	26	-19	1	.961	-2	76	49	P-38/1-5,O-2(0-1-1)	-0.4
1896	Bos N	67	222	43	77	9	6	3	49	12	1	10	.347	.383	.482	120	5	4	.946	-7	70	113	P-42,O-12(3-2-7)/1-5,3	-0.4
1897	†Bos N	61	199	41	73	9	9	2	37	15	2		.367	.417	.533	141	11	2	.926	-3	75	144	O-29(6-10-14),P-18/2-2,1-2	0.2
1898	Bos N	41	111	16	28	1	1	2	16	10	0		.252	.314	.333	81	-3	1	.909	-4	59	0	O-14(2-5-8),1-10/S-4,2-2,P-2	-0.7
1899	Cle N	18	39	8	8	1	1	0	2	6	1		.205	.326	.282	73	-1	0	1.000	1	112	0	/O-7(2-1-4),P-7,S3	0.0
Total	11	601	1992	348	593	84	46	35	357	133	9	136	.298	.344	.439	104	-5	31	.924	-16	91	86	P-388,O-141R/1-30,S-5,3-5,2-4	-1.5
STOCK, MILT Milton Joseph B 7.11.1893 Chicago, IL D 7.16.1977 Fairhope, AL BR/TR 5-8/154# d9.29 C9																								
1913	NY N	7	17	2	3	1	0	0	1	2	0	1	.176	.263	.235	43	-1	2	.838	0	108	223	/S-7	0.0
1914	NY N	115	365	52	96	17	1	3	41	34	4	21	.263	.333	.340	103	2	11	.939	13	**122**	122	*3-113/S	1.9
1915	†Phi N	69	227	37	59	7	3	1	15	22	0	26	.260	.325	.330	98	0	6-2	.971	-0	96	102	3-55/S-4	0.2
1916	Phi N	132	509	61	143	25	6	1	43	27	2	33	.281	.320	.360	105	3	21-26	.955	-2	93	142	*3-117,S-15	0.1
1917	Phi N	150	564	76	149	27	6	3	53	51	1	34	.264	.326	.349	103	3	25	.942	-8	92	76	*3-133,S-19	0.0
1918	Phi N	123	481	62	132	14	1	1	42	35	1	22	.274	.325	.314	89	-5	20	.946	-5	102	74	*3-123	-0.8
1919	StL N	135	492	56	151	16	4	0	52	49	1	21	.307	.371	.356	127	18	17	.966	19	109	98	2-77,3-58	4.4
1920	StL N	**155**	639	85	204	28	6	0	76	40	1	27	.319	.360	.382	117	15	15-17	.939	-10	97	78	*3-155	0.7
1921	StL N	149	587	96	180	27	6	3	84	48	1	26	.307	.360	.388	100	2	11-3	.940	-20	83	77	*3-149	-0.8
1922	StL N	151	581	85	177	33	9	5	79	42	0	29	.305	.352	.418	103	2	7-12	.950	-8	89	90	*3-149/S	0.1
1923	StL N	151	603	63	174	33	3	2	96	40	1	21	.289	.334	.363	86	-12	9-6	.955	-15	91	90	*3-150/2	-1.7
1924	Bro N	142	561	66	136	14	4	2	52	26	1	32	.242	.277	.292	54	-37	3-8	.931	-21	78	61	*3-142	-5.2
1925	Bro N	146	615	98	202	28	9	1	62	38	0	28	.328	.368	.408	101	1	8-1	.978	-1	98	85	*2-141/3-5	0.5
1926	Bro N	3	8	0	0	0	0	0	0	1	0	0	.000	.111	.000	-69	-2	0	.923	-0	98	70	/2-3	-0.2

Year	Tm Lg	G	AB	R	H	2B	3B	HR	RBI	BB-IB	HP	SO	AVG	OBP	SLG	AOPS	ABR	SB-CS	FA	FR	Rng	Thr	G at Pos	BFW
Total	14	1628	6249	839	1806	270	58	22	696	455	13	321	.289	.339	.361	98	-11	155-75	.945	-57	94	92	*3-1349,2-222/S-47	-0.8
STOCKER, KEVIN Kevin Douglas B 2.13.1970 Spokane, WA BB/TR 6-1/175# d7.7																								
1993	†Phi N	70	259	46	84	12	3	2	31	30-11	8	43	.324	.409	.417	124	11	5-0	.958	-4	91	101	S-70	1.3
1994	Phi N	82	271	38	74	11	2	2	28	44-8	7	41	.273	.383	.351	92	-1	2-2	.959	-1	102	90	S-82	0.5
1995	Phi N	125	412	42	90	14	3	1	32	43-9	9	75	.218	.304	.274	54	-27	6-1	.969	5	106	100	*S-125	-1.1
1996	Phi N	119	394	46	100	22	6	5	41	43-9	8	89	.254	.336	.378	88	-6	6-4	.975	7	102	112	*S-119	0.9
1997	Phi N	149	504	51	134	23	5	4	40	51-7	2	91	.266	.335	.355	81	-14	11-6	.981	-12	90	83	*S-147	-1.4
1998	TB A	112	336	37	70	11	3	6	25	27-1	8	80	.208	.282	.313	54	-24	5-3	.979	11	106	**117**	*S-110	-0.4
1999	TB A	79	254	39	76	11	2	1	27	24-0	4	41	.299	.369	.370	88	-4	9-7	.957	4	100	97	S-76	0.5
2000	TB A	40	114	20	30	7	1	2	8	19-0	2	27	.263	.378	.395	97	0	1-2	.933	-5	102	99	S-40	-0.2
	Ana A	70	229	21	45	13	3	0	16	32-0	2	54	.197	.299	.279	47	-18	0-3	.978	3	110	112	S-69	-1.1
	Year	110	343	41	75	20	4	2	24	51-0	4	81	.219	.326	.318	63	-18	1-5	.962	-2	107	107	*S-109	-1.3
Total	8	846	2773	340	703	124	28	23	248	313-45	50	541	.254	.338	.343	78	-83	45-28	.969	9	100	101	S-838	-1.0
STOCKWELL, LEN Leonard Clark B 8.25.1859 Cordova, IL D 1.28.1905 Niles, CA BR/TR 5-11/165# d5.17																								
1879	Cle N	2	6	0	0	0	0	0	0	0		2	.000	.000	.000	-99	-1		1.000	1	471	1934	/O-2(0-1-1)	0.0
1884	Lou AA	2	9	0	1	0	0	0		0	0		.111	.111	.111	-29	-1		.667	-1	0	0	/O-2(1-1-0),C	-0.2
1890	Cle N	2	7	2	2	1	0	0	0	0	0	3	.286	.286	.429	110	0	0	1.000	0	518	0	/O(LF)1	0.0
Total	3	6	22	2	3	1	0	0	0	0	0	5	.136	.136	.182	-1	-2	0	.900	1	307	765	/O-5(2-2-1),1C	-0.2
STODDARD d9.25																								
1875	Atl NA	2	9	1	1	1	0	0	0	0		1	.111	.111	.222	15	-1	0-0	.800	-1	0	0	/O-2(1-1-0)	-0.1
STOKES, AL Albert John (born Albert John Stocek) B 1.1.1900 Chicago, IL D 12.19.1986 Grantham, NH BR/TR 5-9/175# d5.10																								
1925	Bos A	17	52	7	11	0	1	0	1	4	0	8	.212	.268	.250	32	-6	0-0	.969	1	*76*	*153*	C-17	-0.3
1926	Bos A	30	86	7	14	3	3	0	6	8	0	28	.163	.234	.267	32	-9	0-0	.931	-5	*61*	*106*	C-29	-1.3
Total	2	47	138	14	25	3	4	0	7	12	0	36	.181	.247	.261	32	-15	0-0	.946	-4	*67*	*124*	/C-46	-1.6
STONE, GENE Eugene Daniel B 1.16.1944 Burbank, CA BL/TL 5-11/190# d5.13																								
1969	Phi N	18	28	4	6	0	1	0	0	4-1	0	9	.214	.313	.286	70	-1	0-0	1.000	-1	33	69	/1-5	-0.2
STONE, GEORGE George Robert B 9.3.1877 Lost Nation, IA D 1.3.1945 Clinton, IA BL/TL 5-9/175# d4.20																								
1903	Bos A	2	2	0	0	0	0	0	0	0	0		.000	.000	.000	-95	0	0	—	0			H	0.0
1905	StL A	154	632	76	**187**	25	13	7	52	44	5		.296	.347	.410	147	32	26	.954	2	88	127	*O-154(LF)	2.8
1906	StL A	**154**	581	91	208	25	20	6	71	52	7		**.358**	**.417**	**.501**	**195**	**63**	35	.968	0	52	79	*O-154(LF)	5.9
1907	StL A	**155**	596	77	191	13	11	4	59	59	6		.320	.387	.399	151	36	23	.970	-3	60	112	*O-155(LF)	2.6
1908	StL A	148	588	89	165	21	8	5	31	55	3		.281	.345	.369	131	21	20	.947	0	64	67	*O-148(LF)	1.4
1909	StL A	83	310	33	89	5	4	1	15	24	1		.287	.340	.339	123	8	8	.928	-1	70	149	O-81(63-0-18)	0.2
1910	StL A	152	562	60	144	17	12	0	40	48	0		.256	.315	.329	108	4	20	.972	-1	92	107	*O-145(139-1-5)	-0.5
Total	7	848	3271	426	984	106	68	23	268	282	22		.301	.360	.396	145	164	132	.958	-2	71	104	O-837(813-1-23)	12.4
STONE, RON Harry Ronald B 9.9.1942 Corning, CA BL/TL 6-2/195# d4.13																								
1966	KC A	26	22	2	6	1	0	0	0	0-0	0	2	.273	.273	.318	71	-1	1-1	1.000	0	120	0	/O-4(2-2-1),1-3	-0.1
1969	Phi N	103	222	22	53	7	1	1	24	29-8	3	28	.239	.332	.293	79	-5	3-1	.978	-1	86	164	O-69(37-2-32)	-0.9
1970	Phi N	123	321	30	84	12	5	3	39	38-1	1	45	.262	.338	.358	90	-4	5-6	.968	-1	102	87	O-99(51-0-48)/1-6	-1.1
1971	Phi N	95	185	16	42	8	1	2	23	25-3	0	36	.227	.315	.314	80	-4	2-2	.964	1	100	179	O-51(22-1-33)/1-3	-0.6
1972	Phi N	41	54	3	9	0	1	0	3	9-1	0	11	.167	.286	.204	40	-4	0-0	1.000	3	143	464	O-15(6-1-9)	-0.1
Total	5	388	804	73	194	28	8	6	89	101-13	4	122	.241	.326	.318	81	-18	11-10	.973	3	99	147	O-238(118-6-123)/1-12	-2.8
STONE, JEFF Jeffrey Glen B 12.26.1960 Kennett, MO BL/TR 6/175# d9.9																								
1983	Phi N	9	4	2	3	0	2	0	3	0-0	0	1	.750	.750	1.750	580	2	4-0	—	-0	0	0	/O(CF)	0.3
1984	Phi N	51	185	27	67	4	6	1	15	9-0	2	26	.362	.394	.465	139	9	27-5	.916	-4	94	29	O-46(LF)	0.8
1985	Phi N	88	264	36	70	4	3	3	11	15-0	1	50	.265	.307	.337	78	-9	15-5	.966	-4	78	98	O-69(LF)	-1.5
1986	Phi N	82	249	32	69	6	4	6	19	20-0	4	52	.277	.341	.406	101	0	19-6	.982	1	89	224	O-58(37-25-0)	0.1
1987	Phi N	66	125	19	32	7	1	1	16	8-0	3	38	.256	.316	.352	74	-5	3-1	1.000	0	80	221	O-25(20-5-1)	-0.5
1988	Bal A	26	61	4	10	1	0	0	1	4-0	0	11	.164	.215	.180	12	-7	4-1	.963	0	70	331	O-21(18-0-3)/D	-0.7
1989	Tex A	22	36	5	6	1	2	0	5	3-0	1	5	.167	.250	.306	55	-2	2-1	—	-1	0	0	D-15/O-3(1-1-1)	-0.4
	Bos A	18	15	3	3	0	0	0	1	1-1	0	2	.200	.235	.200	27	-1	1-0	1.000	-0	106	0	O-11(0-4-7)/D-3	-0.1
	Year	40	51	8	9	1	2	0	6	4-1	1	7	.176	.246	.275	46	-4	3-1	1.000	-1	75	0	D-18,O-14(1-5-8)	-0.5
1990	Bos A	10	2	1	1	0	0	0	1	0-0	0	1	.500	.500	.500	173	0	0-1	—	0			/D-2	0.0
Total	8	372	941	129	261	23	18	11	72	60-1	11	186	.277	.327	.375	92	-13	75-20	.963	-8	84	146	O-234(191-36-12)/D-21	-2.0
STONE, JOHN John Thomas "Rocky" B 10.10.1905 Mulberry, TN D 11.30.1955 Shelbyville, TN BL/TR 6-1/178# d8.31																								
1928	Det A	26	113	20	40	10	3	2	21	5	1	8	.354	.387	.549	141	6	1-0	.962	-1	90	83	O-26(LF)	0.3
1929	Det A	51	150	23	39	11	2	2	15	11	0	13	.260	.311	.400	81	-5	1-1	.986	2	104	132	O-36(35-0-2)	-0.5
1930	Det A	127	425	60	132	29	11	3	56	32	1	49	.311	.360	.452	102	1	6-9	.966	-1	102	63	*O-109(93-11-6)	-0.9
1931	Det A	147	584	86	191	28	11	10	76	56	2	48	.327	.388	.464	119	16	13-13	.959	5	108	107	*O-147(143-5-0)	1.1
1932	Det A	145	582	106	173	35	12	17	108	58	0	64	.297	.361	.486	113	10	2-1	.961	-1	99	99	*O-142(90-53-0)	0.2
1933	Det A	148	574	86	161	33	11	11	80	54	2	37	.280	.344	.434	103	1	1-4	.970	-2	100	84	*O-141(18-0-124)	-1.0
1934	Was A	113	419	77	132	28	7	7	67	52	3	26	.315	.395	.465	126	17	1-2	.966	5	103	144	*O-112(0-16-98)	1.4
1935	Was A	125	455	78	143	27	18	1	78	39	3	29	.314	.372	.459	118	10	4-5	.955	2	100	130	*O-114(19-7-90)	0.5
1936	Was A	123	437	95	149	22	11	15	90	60	0	26	.341	.421	.545	145	31	8-0	.967	6	108	121	*O-114(109-0-6)	2.8
1937	Was A	139	542	84	179	33	15	6	88	66	0	36	.330	.403	.480	127	23	6-4	.984	7	107	121	*O-137(37-7-95)	2.1
1938	Was A	56	213	24	52	12	4	3	28	30	0	16	.244	.337	.380	85	-5	2-1	.974	-1	95	110	O-53(29-1-26)	-0.8
Total	11	1200	4494	739	1391	268	105	77	707	463	12	352	.310	.376	.467	116	105	45-40	.967	20	103	108	*O-1131(599-100-447)	5.2
STONE, TIGE William Arthur B 9.18.1901 Macon, GA D 1.1.1960 Jacksonville, FL BR/TR 5-8/145# d8.23																								
1923	StL N	5	1	0	1	0	0	0	0	2	0	0	1.000	1.000	1.000	438	1	0-0	—	0	0	0	/O-4(2-2-0),P	0.0
STONEHAM, JOHN John Andrew B 11.8.1908 Wood River, IL BL/TR 5-9.5/168# d9.18																								
1933	Chi A	10	25	4	3	0	0	1	3	2	0	2	.120	.185	.240	12	-3	0-0	1.000	-0	100	0	/O-9(1-1-7)	-0.4
STORIE, HOWIE Howard Edward "Sponge" B 5.15.1911 Pittsfield, MA D 7.27.1968 Pittsfield, MA BR/TR 5-10/175# d9.7																								
1931	Bos A	6	17	2	2	0	0	0	0	3	0	2	.118	.250	.118	-1	-2	0-0	1.000	0	*145*	*49*	/C-6	-0.2
1932	Bos A	6	8	0	3	0	0	0	0	0	0	0	.375	.375	.375	98	0	0-0	1.000	0	*97*	*0*	/C-5	0.0
Total	2	12	25	2	5	0	0	0	0	3	0	2	.200	.286	.200	31	-2	0-0	1.000	0	*131*	*35*	/C-11	-0.2
STORKE, ALAN Alan Marshall B 9.27.1884 Auburn, NY D 3.18.1910 Newton, MA BR/TR 6-1/?# d9.24																								
1906	Pit N	5	12	1	3	1	0	0	1	1	0		.250	.308	.333	96	0	1	1.000	0	121	770	/3-2,S	0.0
1907	Pit N	112	357	24	92	6	6	1	39	16	3		.258	.295	.317	90	-6	6	.925	-9	94	128	3-67,1-23/2-7,S-5	-1.4
1908	Pit N	64	202	20	51	5	3	1	12	9	0		.252	.284	.322	93	-2	4	.988	-6	56	96	1-49/3-6,2	-1.1
1909	Pit N	37	118	12	30	5	2	0	12	7	1		.254	.302	.331	89	-2	1	.994	-1	75	137	1-18,3-14	-0.3
	StL N	48	174	11	49	5	0	0	10	12	0		.282	.328	.310	105	1	5	.958	-1	99	81	S-44/2-4,1	0.2
	Year	85	292	23	79	10	2	0	22	19	1		.271	.317	.318	97	-1	6	.958	-1	99	81	S-44,1-19,3-14/2-4	-0.1
Total	4	266	863	68	225	22	11	2	74	45	4		.261	.300	.319	94	-9	17	.990	-15	68	99	/1-91,3-89,S-50,2-12	-2.6
STORTI, LIN Lindo Ivan B 12.5.1906 Santa Monica, CA D 7.24.1982 Ontario, CA BB/TR 5-11/165# d9.18																								
1930	StL A	7	28	6	9	1	1	0	2	2	0	6	.321	.367	.429	98	0	0-0	.975	1	96	201	/2-6	0.1
1931	StL A	86	273	32	60	15	4	3	26	15	1	50	.220	.263	.337	55	-19	0-2	.926	5	105	168	3-67/2-7	-1.2
1932	StL A	53	193	19	50	11	2	3	26	5	0	20	.259	.278	.383	66	-11	1-0	.956	-0	96	104	3-51	-0.8
1933	StL A	70	210	26	41	7	4	3	21	25	0	31	.195	.281	.310	53	-15	2-2	.934	1	102	198	3-32,2-24	-1.1
Total	4	216	704	83	160	34	11	9	75	47	1	107	.227	.277	.345	59	-45	3-4	.936	7	102	154	3-150/2-37	-3.0
STOUCH, TOM Thomas Carl B 12.2.1869 Perrysville, OH D 10.7.1956 Lancaster, PA BR/TR 6-2/165# d7.7																								
1898	Lou N	4	16	4	5	1	0	0	6	1	0		.313	.353	.375	110	0	0	.850	-2	78	66	/2-4	-0.1
STOVALL, DA ROND Da Rond Tyrone B 1.3.1973 St.Louis, MO BB/TL 6-1/185# d4.1																								
1998	Mon N	62	78	11	16	2	1	2	6	6-0	0	29	.205	.262	.333	56	-5	1-0	.925	-1	91	157	O-47(27-14-7)	-0.6

Year	Tm Lg	G	AB	R	H	2B	3B	HR	RBI	BB-IB	HP	SO	AVG	OBP	SLG	AOPS	ABR	SB-CS	FA	FR	Rng	Thr	G at Pos	BFW
STOVALL, GEORGE George Thomas "Firebrand" B 11.23.1877 Leeds, MO D 11.5.1951 Burlington, IA BR/TR 6-2/180# d7.4 M5 b-Jesse																								
1904	Cle A	52	181	18	54	10	1	1	31	2	3		.298	.317	.381	121	4	3	.978	-1	93	115	1-38/2-9,O-3(2-1-0),3	0.3
1905	Cle A	112	423	41	115	31	1	1	47	13	1		.272	.295	.357	105	2	13	.973	-3	133	115	1-60,2-46/O-4(CF)	-0.2
1906	Cle A	116	443	54	121	19	5	0	37	8	1		.273	.288	.339	97	-3	15	.985	-1	111	214	1-55,3-30,2-19	-0.6
1907	Cle A	124	466	38	110	17	6	1	36	18	2		.236	.267	.305	82	-11	13	.983	-3	89	**168**	*1-122/3-2	-1.8
1908	Cle A	138	534	71	156	29	6	2	45	17	2		.292	.316	.380	126	13	14	**.990**	2	104	**146**	*1-132/O-5(CF),S	1.4
1909	Cle A	145	565	60	139	17	10	2	49	6	4		.246	.259	.322	80	-16	25	**.988**	10	**126**	**119**	*1-145	-1.0
1910	Cle A	142	521	49	136	19	4	0	52	14	3		.261	.284	.313	86	-11	16	**.988**	7	**121**	94	*1-132/2-2	-0.7
1911	Cle A	126	458	48	124	17	7	0	79	21	2		.271	.306	.338	79	-15	11	**.986**	7	**118**	103	*1-118/2-2,M	-1.1
1912	StL A	116	398	35	101	17	5	0	45	14	4		.254	.286	.322	76	-14	11	.983	5	125	139	1-94,M	-1.1
1913	StL A	89	303	34	87	14	3	1	24	7	1	23	.287	.305	.363	98	-3	7	.988	8	143	91	1-76,M	0.3
1914	KC F	124	450	51	128	20	5	7	75	23	4	35	.284	.325	.398	100	-9	6	.989	5	117	**131**	*1-116/3M	-0.8
1915	KC F	130	480	48	111	21	3	0	44	31	6	36	.231	.286	.287	64	-31	8	.987	5	**121**	91	*1-129,M	-3.2
Total	12	1414	5222	547	1382	231	56	15	564	174	33	94	.265	.293	.339	91	-94	142	.986	40	117	125	*1-1217/2-78,3-34,O-12(2-9-0),S	-8.5
STOVEY, HARRY Harry Duffield (born Harry Duffield Stowe) B 12.20.1856 Philadelphia, PA D 9.20.1937 New Bedford, MA BR/TR 5-11.5/175# d5.1 M2 ▲																								
1880	Wor N	83	355	76	94	21	**14**	**6**	28	12		46	.265	.289	.454	136	12		.860	-6	54	54	O-46(5-42-0),1-37/P-2	0.2
1881	Wor N	75	341	57	92	25	7	2	30	12		23	.270	.295	.402	111	4		.955	-5	79	75	*1-57,O-18(1-0-17),M	-0.4
1882	Wor N	**84**	360	90	104	13	10	5	26	22		34	.289	.330	.422	136	14		.956	3	111	91	1-43,O-41(LF)	1.1
1883	Phi AA	94	421	**110**	128	**31**	6	**14**	66	27			.304	.346	**.506**	156	25		**.965**	1	81	74	*1-93/O-3(CF),P	1.5
1884	Phi AA	104	448	**124**	146	22	**23**	10	83	26	4		.326	.368	.545	182	38		.960	-1	90	99	*1-104	2.5
1885	Phi AA	112	486	**130**	153	27	9	**13**	75	39	4		.315	.371	.488	160	32		.967	4	**128**	**106**	*1-82,O-30(CF),M	2.5
1886	Phi AA	123	489	115	144	28	11	7	59	64	1		.294	.377	.440	154	32	**68**	.870	-1	106	178	O-63(0-46-17),1-62/P	2.0
1887	Phi AA	124	497	125	142	31	12	4	77	56	7		.286	.366	.421	119	14	74	.902	7	109	32	O-80(49-29-2),1-46	1.1
1888	Phi AA	130	530	127	152	25	**20**	9	65	62	3		.287	.365	.460	165	**39**	87	.943	4	61	102	*O-118(LF),1-13	**3.5**
1889	Phi AA	137	556	**152**	171	38	13	**19**	**119**	77	1	68	.308	.393	**.525**	162	46	63	.897	18	146	153	*O-137(LF)/1	**5.0**
1890	Bos P	118	481	142	144	25	11	12	84	81	5	38	.299	.406	.472	126	18	**97**	.921	0	109	69	*O-117(1-0-116)/1	1.3
1891	Bos N	134	544	118	152	31	**20**	**16**	95	79	2	69	.279	.373	**.498**	137	23	57	.910	7	101	123	*O-134(39-0-96)/1	2.4
1892	Bos N	38	146	21	24	8	1	0	12	14	3	19	.164	.252	.233	43	-10	20	.901	0	48	84	O-38(LF)	-1.3
	Bal N	74	283	58	77	14	11	4	55	40	1	32	.272	.364	.442	140	13	20	.913	-2	60	80	O-64(LF),1-10	0.5
	Year	112	429	79	101	22	12	4	67	54	4	51	.235	.326	.371	105	2	40	.908	-2	55	82	*O-102(LF),1-10	-0.8
1893	Bal N	8	26	4	4	2	0	0	5	8	0	3	.154	.353	.231	55	-1	1	.864	-0	71	0	/O-7(LF)	-0.2
	Bro N	48	175	43	44	6	6	1	29	44	0	11	.251	.402	.371	111	5	22	.901	-4	35	0	O-48(19-26-3)	-0.2
	Year	56	201	47	48	8	6	1	34	52	0	14	.239	.395	.353	103	4	23	.895	-4	40	0	O-55(26-26-3)	-0.4
Total	14	1486	6138	1492	1771	347	174	122	908	663	31	343	.289	.361	.461	141	304	509	.896	23	95	97	O-944(519-176-251),1-550/P-4	21.5
STOVIAK, RAY Raymond Thomas B 6.6.1915 Scottdale, PA D 2.23.1998 Nicoya, Costa Rica BL/TL 6-1/195# d6.5																								
1938	Phi N	10	10	1	0	0	0	0	0	0	0	3	.000	.000	.000	-99	-3	0	1.000	1	57	1233	/O-4(RF)	-0.2
STOWERS, CHRIS Christopher James B 8.18.1974 St.Louis, MO BL/TL 6-3/195# d7.10																								
1999	Mon N	4	2	0	0	0	0	0	0	0-0	0	0	.000	.000	.000	-99	-1	0-0	1.000	0	127	0	/O-2(0-1-1)	-0.1
STRAIN, JOE Joseph Allan B 4.30.1954 Denver, CO BR/TR 5-10/169# d6.28																								
1979	SF N	67	257	27	62	8	1	1	12	13-0	3	21	.241	.285	.292	62	-14	8-4	.982	7	110	75	2-67/3	-0.4
1980	SF N	77	189	26	54	6	0	0	16	10-0	0	10	.286	.320	.317	81	-5	1-2	.989	-5	95	63	2-42/3-6,S	-0.9
1981	Chi N	25	74	7	14	1	0	0	1	5-0	1	7	.189	.250	.203	28	-7	0-0	.975	9	142	83	2-20	0.3
Total	3	169	520	60	130	15	1	1	29	28-0	4	38	.250	.292	.288	64	-26	9-6	.983	11	110	72	2-129/3-7,S	-1.0
STRAND, PAUL Paul Edward B 12.19.1893 Carbonado, WA D 7.2.1974 Salt Lake City, UT BR/TL 6-0.5/190# d5.15 ▲																								
1913	Bos N	7	6	0	1	0	0	0	0	0	0	0	.167	.167	.167	-5	0	0	.875	0	137	0	/P-7	0.0
1914	Bos N	18	24	2	8	2	0	0	3	0	0	2	.333	.333	.417	123	2	0	.813	-0	89	237	P-16	0.0
1915	Bos N	24	22	3	2	0	0	0	2	0	0	4	.091	.091	.091	-47	-4	0	.750	-1	32	0	/P-6,O-5(2-1-0)	-0.2
1924	Phi A	47	167	15	38	9	4	0	13	4	2	9	.228	.254	.329	49	-14	3-3	.988	-3	83	81	O-44(0-39-5)	-1.9
Total	4	96	219	20	49	11	4	0	18	4	2	15	.224	.244	.311	47	-16	3-3	.989	-4	82	98	/O-49(2-40-5),P-29	-2.1
STRANDS, LARRY John Lawrence B 12.5.1885 Chicago, IL D 1.19.1957 Forest Park, IL BR/TR 5-10.5/165# d4.25																								
1915	New F	35	75	7	14	3	1	1	11	6	0	11	.187	.247	.293	55	-6	1	.852	-4	83	161	3-12/2-9,O-2(RF)	-1.1
STRANG, SAMMY Samuel Nicklin "The Dixie Thrush" (born Samuel Strang Nicklin) B 12.16.1876 Chattanooga, TN D 3.13.1932 Chattanooga, TN BB/TR 5-8/160# d7.10 OF Total (11-LF 63-CF 92-RF)																								
1896	Lou N	14	46	6	12	0	0	0	7	6	0	6	.261	.346	.261	64	-2	4	.803	-6	78	90	S-14	-0.6
1900	Chi N	27	102	15	29	3	0	0	9	8	2		.284	.348	.314	86	-1	1	.887	-7	93	160	3-16/S-9,2-2	-0.7
1901	NY N	135	493	55	139	14	6	1	34	59	5		.282	.364	.341	109	9	40	.877	8	113	155	3-91,2-37/O-5(RF),S-4	1.9
1902	Chi A	137	536	108	158	18	5	3	46	76	5		.295	.387	.364	114	15	38	.890	5	**109**	109	*3-137	2.2
	Chi N	3	11	1	4	0	0	0	0	0	0		.364	.364	.364	128	0	1	1.000	-1	59	996	/2-2,3-2	0.0
1903	Bro N	135	508	101	138	21	5	0	38	75	10		.272	.376	.333	106	9	46	.914	-5	100	105	*3-124/O-8(CF),2-3	0.7
1904	Bro N	77	271	28	52	11	0	1	9	45	4		.192	.316	.244	75	-5	16	.910	-29	84	65	2-63,3-12/S	-3.6
1905	†NY N	111	294	51	76	9	4	3	29	58	5		.259	.389	.347	117	10	23	.915	-7	97	81	2-47,O-38(4-7-27)/S-9,13	0.3
1906	NY N	113	313	50	100	16	4	4	49	54	2		.319	.423	.435	164	26	21	.944	6	111	78	2-57,O-39(5-17-17)/S-4,3-3,1	3.4
1907	NY N	123	306	56	77	20	4	4	30	60	8		.252	.388	.382	137	18	21	.947	-0	138	229	O-70(1-28-41),2-13/3-7,1-5,S	1.6
1908	NY N	28	53	8	5	0	0	0	2	23	2		.094	.385	.094	52	0	5	.863	-3	98	138	2-14/O-5(1-3-2),S-3	-0.4
Total	10	903	2933	479	790	112	28	16	253	464	43	6	.269	.377	.343	113	79	216	.891	-38	106	119	3-393,2-238,O-165R/S-45,1-7	4.8
STRANGE, ALAN Alan Cochrane "Inky" B 11.7.1906 Philadelphia, PA D 6.27.1994 Seattle, WA BR/TR 5-9/162# d4.17																								
1934	StL A	127	430	39	100	17	2	1	45	48	0	28	.233	.310	.288	51	-31	3-1	.955	5	100	104	*S-125	-1.6
1935	StL A	49	147	8	34	6	1	0	17	17	0	7	.231	.311	.286	53	-10	0-0	.960	3	101	96	S-49	-0.4
	Was A	20	54	3	10	2	1	0	5	4	0	1	.185	.241	.259	30	-6	0-0	.974	2	113	119	S-16	-0.3
	Year	69	201	11	44	8	2	0	22	21	0	8	.219	.293	.279	47	-16	0-0	.963	5	104	102	S-65	-0.7
1940	StL A	54	167	26	31	8	3	0	6	22	1	12	.186	.284	.269	43	-14	2-1	.962	5	115	105	S-35/2-4	-0.6
1941	StL A	45	112	14	26	4	0	0	11	15	0	5	.232	.323	.268	56	-7	1-0	.973	0	98	91	S-32/1-2,3	-0.4
1942	StL A	19	37	3	10	2	0	0	5	3	0	1	.270	.325	.324	82	-1	0-1	.935	2	142	218	3-10/S-3,2	0.1
Total	5	314	947	93	211	39	7	1	89	109	1	54	.223	.304	.282	50	-69	6-3	.959	17	103	101	S-260/3-11,2-5,1-2	-3.2
STRANGE, DOUG Joseph Douglas B 4.13.1964 Greenville, SC BB/TR 6-1/185# d7.13 OF Total (18-LF 2-RF)																								
1989	Det A	64	196	16	42	4	1	1	14	17-0	1	36	.214	.280	.260	54	-12	3-3	.878	-1	100	118	3-54/2-9,S-9,D	-1.4
1991	Chi N	3	9	0	4	1	0	0	1	0-0	1	1	.444	.455	.556	188	1	1-0	.800	-2	53	0	/3-3	0.0
1992	Chi N	52	94	7	15	1	0	1	5	10-2	0	15	.160	.240	.202	26	-9	1-0	.900	-2	93	57	3-33,2-12	-1.2
1993	Tex A	145	484	58	124	29	0	7	60	43-3	3	69	.256	.318	.360	86	-9	6-4	.980	4	102	95	*2-135/3-9,S	0.1
1994	Tex A	73	226	26	48	12	1	5	26	15-0	3	38	.212	.268	.341	56	-15	1-3	.970	3	107	114	2-53,3-13/O-3(2-0-1)	-1.0
1995	†Sea A	74	155	19	42	9	2	2	21	10-0	2	25	.271	.323	.394	85	-4	0-3	.948	6	120	39	3-41/2-5,O-4(LF),D	0.2
1996	Sea A	88	183	19	43	7	1	3	23	14-0	1	31	.235	.290	.333	58	-12	1-0	.961	-6	80	65	3-39,O-11(10-0-1),D-10/1-3,2-3	-1.7
1997	Mon N	118	327	40	84	16	2	12	47	36-9	2	76	.257	.332	.428	98	-1	0-2	.947	0	99	85	*3-105/2-3,O-2(LF),1	-0.1
1998	Pit N	90	185	9	32	8	0	0	14	10-1	1	39	.173	.217	.216	15	-23	1-0	.940	-4	83	51	3-42/2-9,1-3	-2.6
Total	9	707	1859	194	434	87	7	31	211	155-15	14	330	.233	.295	.338	69	-84	14-15	.927	-1	98	82	3-339,2-229/O-20L,D-12,S-10,1-7	-7.7
STRATTON, ASA Asa Evans B 2.10.1853 Grafton, MA D 8.14.1925 Fitchburg, MA d6.17																								
1881	Wor N	1	4	0	1	0	0	0	0	0		2	.250	.250	.250	55	0		.333	-1	38	0	/S	-0.1
STRATTON, SCOTT C. Scott B 10.2.1869 Campbellsburg, KY D 3.8.1939 Louisville, KY BL/TR 6/180# d4.21 ▲																								
1888	Lou AA	67	249	35	64	8	1	1	29	12	7		.257	.310	.309	101	1	10	.825	-1	146	0	O-38(28-7-3),P-33	-0.1
1889	Lou AA	62	229	30	66	7	5	4	34	13	2	36	.288	.332	.415	114	3	10	.915	6	173	75	O-29(10-4-15),P-19,1-17	0.4
1890	†Lou AA	55	189	29	61	3	5	0	24	16	3		.323	.385	.392	132	7	8	**.977**	5	128	88	P-50/O-5(CF)	0.2
1891	Pit N	2	8	1	1	0	0	0	0	0	0	3	.125	.125	.125	-28	-1	0	.900	1	242	0	/P-2	0.0
	Lou AA	34	115	9	27	2	0	0	8	11	1	13	.235	.307	.252	61	-6	8	.939	3	133	**378**	P-20/1-8,O-6(2-3-1)	-0.1
1892	Lou N	63	219	22	56	2	9	0	23	17	3	21	.256	.318	.347	110	2	9	.915	2	109	152	P-42,O-17(1-0-16)/1-6	0.1
1893	Lou N	61	221	34	50	8	5	0	16	25	1	15	.226	.308	.308	69	-10	6	.975	6	**131**	79	P-37,O-24(RF)/1	-0.1
1894	Lou N	13	37	9	12	1	2	0	4	4	0	2	.324	.390	.459	112	1	1	.929	2	123	0	/P-7,O-5(RF)	0.1

Year	Tm Lg	G	AB	R	H	2B	3B	HR	RBI	BB-IB	HP	SO	AVG	OBP	SLG	AOPS	ABR	SB-CS	FA	FR	Rng	Thr	G at Pos	BFW
	Chi N	24	99	30	37	5	4	3	23	7	1	1	.374	.421	.596	135	5	3	.938	-0	98	230	P-16/O-5(RF),1-2	0.1
	Year	37	136	39	49	6	6	3	27	11	1	3	.360	.412	.559	131	6	4	.935	1	105	169	P-23,O-10(RF)/1-2	0.2
1895	Chi N	10	24	3	7	1	1	0	2	4	0	2	.292	.393	.417	102	0	1	.833	-0	147	0	/P-5,O-4(CF)	-0.1
Total	8	391	1390	202	381	37	32	8	163	109	18	93	.274	.335	.364	103	2	56	.938	22	120	143	P-231,O-133(41-23-68)/1-34	0.5
STRAUB, JOE Joseph B 1.19.1858 , Germany D 2.13.1929 Pueblo, CO BR/TR 5-10/160# d6.24																								
1880	Tro N	3	12	1	3	0	0	0	3	1		3	.250	.308	.250	87	0		.815	0			/C-3	0.0
1882	Phi AA	8	32	2	6	2	0	0	1	1			.188	.212	.250	52	-2		.830	-1			/C-7,O(RF)	-0.2
1883	Col AA	27	100	4	13	0	0	0		4			.130	.163	.130	-5	-11		.860	-2			C-14,1-12/O(CF)	-1.1
Total	3	38	144	7	22	2	0	0	4	6		3	.153	.187	.167	17	-13		.843	-3			/C-24,1-12,O-2(0-1-1)	-1.3
STRAUSS, JOE Joseph "Dutch" or "The Socker" (born Joseph Strasser) B 11.16.1858 Cincinnati, OH D 6.24.1906 Cincinnati, OH BR/TR d7.27																								
1884	KC U	16	60	4	12	3	0	0		1			.200	.213	.250	46	-6		.833	-2	81	0	O-10(8-2-0)/C-3,2-2,3	-0.7
1885	Lou AA	2	6	0	1	0	0	0	0	0	0		.167	.167	.167	6	-1		—	-1	0	0	/O(LF)C	-0.2
1886	Lou AA	74	297	36	64	5	6	1	31	8	1		.215	.239	.283	60	-16	25	.857	3	158	0	O-73(67-6-1)/P-2,C	-1.3
	Bro AA	9	36	6	9	1	1	0	5	1	0		.250	.270	.333	88	-1	4	1.000	1	108	0	/O-7(LF),C-2	0.0
	Year	83	333	42	73	6	7	1	36	9	1		.219	.242	.288	63	-17	29	.866	4	154	0	O-80(74-6-1)/C-3,P-2	-1.3
Total	3	101	399	46	86	9	7	1	36	10	1		.216	.237	.281	59	-24	29	.861	1	146	0	/O-91(83-8-1),C-7,P-2,2-2,3	-2.2
STRAWBERRY, DARRYL Darryl Eugene B 3.12.1962 Los Angeles, CA BL/TL 6-6/200# d5.6																								
1983	NY N	122	420	63	108	15	7	26	74	47-9	4	128	.257	.336	.512	134	17	19-6	.984	0	104	94	*O-117(RF)	1.4
1984	NY N★	147	522	75	131	27	4	26	97	75-15	0	131	.251	.343	.467	128	20	27-8	.980	0	101	120	*O-146(0-21-134)	1.7
1985	NY N★	111	393	78	109	15	4	29	79	73-13	1	96	.277	.389	.557	167	36	26-11	.991	-4	95	68	*O-110(0-27-100)	3.1
1986	†NY N★	136	475	76	123	27	5	27	93	72-9	6	141	.259	.358	.507	142	28	28-12	.975	-3	93	95	*O-131(1-0-130)	2.0
1987	NY N★	154	532	108	151	32	5	39	104	97-13	7	122	.284	.398	.583	165	53	36-12	.972	-4	99	60	*O-151(RF)	4.4
1988	†NY N★	153	543	101	146	27	3	**39**	101	85-21	3	127	.269	.366	**.545**	**168**	49	29-14	.971	3	109	58	*O-150(RF)	**5.1**
1989	NY N✳	134	476	69	107	26	1	29	77	61-13	1	105	.225	.312	.466	126	15	11-4	.972	5	**114**	61	*O-131(RF)	1.8
1990	NY N★	152	542	92	150	18	1	37	108	70-15	4	110	.277	.361	.518	140	29	15-8	.989	1	97	106	*O-149(RF)	2.7
1991	LA N✳	139	505	86	134	22	4	28	99	75-4	3	125	.265	.361	.491	141	28	10-8	.978	-9	81	109	*O-136(RF)	1.5
1992	LA N	43	156	20	37	8	0	5	25	19-4	1	34	.237	.322	.385	101	1	3-1	.986	-2	88	77	O-42(2-0-40)	-0.3
1993	LA N	32	100	12	14	2	0	5	12	16-1	2	19	.140	.267	.310	59	-6	1-0	.905	-5	69	48	O-29(4-0-25)	-1.2
1994	SF N	29	92	13	22	3	1	4	17	19-4	0	22	.239	.363	.424	111	2	0-3	.969	2	126	54	O-27(RF)	0.1
1995	†NY A	32	87	15	24	4	1	3	13	10-1	2	22	.276	.364	.448	111	1	0-0	.909	1	110	358	D-15,O-11(1-0-10)	0.1
1996	†NY A	63	202	35	53	13	0	11	36	31-5	1	55	.262	.359	.490	113	4	6-5	1.000	-2	82	53	O-34(26-0-8),D-26	-0.1
1997	NY A	11	29	1	3	1	0	0	2	3-0	0	9	.103	.188	.138	-13	-5	0-0	1.000	-1	78	0	/O-4(LF),D-4	-0.5
1998	NY A	101	295	44	73	11	2	24	57	46-4	3	90	.247	.354	.542	134	14	8-7	.905	-2	88	0	D-81,O-16(LF)	0.6
1999	†NY A	24	49	10	16	5	0	3	6	17-0	0	16	.327	.500	.612	184	8	2-0	—	0	0	0	D-17	0.7
Total	17	1583	5418	898	1401	256	38	335	1000	816-131	38	1352	.259	.357	.505	139	294	221-99	.977	-18	98	84	*O-1384(54-48-1308),D-143	23.1
STREET, GABBY Charles Evard "Old Sarge" B 9.30.1882 Huntsville, AL D 2.6.1951 Joplin, MO BR/TR 5-11/180# d9.13 M6 C2																								
1904	Cin N	11	33	1	4	1	0	0	0	1	0		.121	.147	.152	-7	-4	2	.973	3	*127*	*109*	C-11	0.0
1905	Cin N	2	2	0	0	0	0	0	0	2	0		.000	.500	.000	48	0	0	1.000	0	*118*	*207*	/C	0.1
	Bos N	3	12	0	2	0	0	0	0	0	0		.167	.167	.167	-1	-2	1	.778	-2	*69*	*89*	/C-3	-0.4
	Cin N	29	91	8	23	5	1	0	8	6	1		.253	.306	.330	81	-2	1	.975	2	*118*	*207*	C-26	0.3
	Year	34	105	8	25	5	1	0	8	8	1		.238	.298	.305	73	-3	2	.957	1	*96*	*120*	C-30	0.0
1908	Was A	131	394	31	81	12	7	1	32	40	6		.206	.289	.279	92	-2	5	.973	4	*109*	*103*	*C-128	1.5
1909	Was A	137	407	25	86	12	1	0	29	26	2		.211	.262	.246	63	-17	2	.981	1	*88*	*100*	*C-137	-0.3
1910	Was A	89	257	13	52	6	0	1	16	23	2		.202	.273	.237	63	-11	1	**.978**	8	*103*	*111*	C-86	0.6
1911	Was A	72	216	16	48	7	1	0	14	14	3		.222	.279	.264	53	-14	4	.973	9	*105*	*92*	C-71	0.1
1912	NY A	29	88	4	16	1	1	0	6	7	2		.182	.258	.216	34	-8	1	.958	-1	*89*	*109*	C-29	-0.7
1931	StL N	1	1	0	0	0	0	0	0	0	0	0	.000	.000	.000	-96	0	0	1.000	0	*0*	*0*	/CM	0.0
Total	8	504	1501	98	312	44	11	2	105	119	16	0	.208	.273	.256	66	-60	17	.974	25	*100*	*103*	C-493	1.2
STREULI, WALT Walter Herbert B 9.26.1935 Memphis, TN BR/TR 6-2/195# d9.25																								
1954	Det A	1	0	0	0	0	0	0	0	1	0	0	—	1.000	—	195	0	0-0	1.000	-0	*0*	*0*	/C	0.0
1955	Det A	2	4	1	1	1	0	0	1	0-0	0	0	.250	.200	.500	100	0	0-0	1.000	0	*0*	*0*	/C-2	0.0
1956	Det A	3	8	0	2	1	0	0	1	1-0	0	2	.250	.333	.375	87	0	0-0	.933	-0	*0*	*204*	/C-3	0.0
Total	3	6	12	1	3	2	0	0	2	2-0	0	2	.250	.333	.417	106	0	0-0	.957	-0	*0*	*122*	/C-6	0.0
STRICK, CHARLES Charles E. (born Charles E. Streck) B 9.15.1858 Erie, PA D 11.18.1933 Erie, PA d5.18																								
1882	Lou AA	32	110	17	18	6	1	0		9			.164	.227	.236	60	-4		.898	1			C-21/O-6(CF),2-6,S1	-0.1
STRICKER, CUB John A. (born John A. Streaker) B 2.15.1860 Philadelphia, PA D 11.19.1937 Philadelphia, PA BR/TR 5-3/138# d5.2 M1 ▲ OF Total (1-CF 19-RF)																								
1882	Phi AA	72	272	34	59	6	1	0	18	15			.217	.258	.246	66	-10		.904	**23**	**123**	101	*2-72/P-2,O(RF)	1.4
1883	Phi AA	89	330	67	90	8	0	1	40	19			.273	.312	.306	91	-4		.837	-22	86	68	*2-88/C-2	-2.0
1884	Phi AA	107	399	59	92	16	11	1		19	1		.231	.267	.333	89	-6		.870	-36	77	92	*2-107/O(CF)CP	-3.5
1885	Phi AA	106	398	71	93	9	3	1	41	21	7		.234	.284	.279	74	-12		.879	-14	92	86	*2-106	-2.0
1887	Cle AA	131	534	122	141	19	4	2	53	53	3		.264	.334	.326	87	-7	86	.912	11	97	97	*2-126/S-6,P-3	0.7
1888	Cle AA	127	493	80	115	13	6	1	33	50	6		.233	.311	.290	96	0	60	.929	24	102	121	*2-122/O-6(RF),P-2	2.6
1889	Cle N	**136**	566	83	142	10	4	1	47	58	2	18	.251	.323	.288	73	-21	32	.932	8	96	108	*2-135/S	-0.7
1890	Cle P	127	544	93	133	19	8	2	65	54	5	16	.244	.318	.320	77	-16	24	.905	3	104	98	*2-109,S-20	-0.7
1891	Bos AA	**139**	514	96	111	15	4	0	46	63	6	34	.216	.309	.261	64	-22	54	.942	24	101	**148**	*2-139	0.5
1892	StL N	28	98	12	20	1	0	0	11	10	3	7	.204	.297	.214	58	-4	5	.939	-2	92	70	2-27/SM	-0.5
	Bal N	75	269	45	71	5	5	3	37	32	1	18	.264	.344	.353	108	3	13	.918	2	98	85	2-75	0.7
	Year	103	367	57	91	6	5	3	48	42	4	25	.248	.332	.316	95	-2	18	.923	-1	96	81	*2-102/S	0.2
1893	Was N	59	218	28	39	7	1	0	20	20	0	12	.179	.248	.220	25	-24	4	.903	6	104	105	2-39,O-12(RF)/S-4,3-4	-1.4
Total	11	1196	4635	790	1106	128	47	12	411	414	34	105	.239	.306	.294	78	-123	278	.907	26	97	103	*2-1145/S-32,O-20R,P-8,3-4,C-3	-4.9
STRICKLAND, GEORGE George Bevan "Bo" B 1.10.1926 New Orleans, LA BR/TR 6-1/180# d5.7 M2 C11																								
1950	Pit N	23	27	0	3	0	0	0	2	3	1	8	.111	.226	.111	-8	-4	0	.978	1	93	126	S-19/3	-0.3
1951	Pit N	138	454	59	98	12	7	9	47	65	3	83	.216	.318	.333	73	-17	4-2	.943	9	105	104	*S-125,2-13	0.0
1952	Pit N	76	232	17	41	6	2	5	22	21	1	45	.177	.248	.284	46	-18	4-2	.953	11	112	103	2-45,S-28/13	-0.3
	Cle A	31	88	8	19	4	0	1	8	14	0	15	.216	.324	.295	78	-2	0-0	.964	6	115	103	S-30/2	0.6
1953	Cle A	123	419	43	119	17	4	5	47	51	0	52	.284	.362	.379	103	3	0-0	.974	**21**	**109**	**135**	*S-122/1	3.3
1954	†Cle A	112	361	42	77	12	3	6	37	55	1	62	.213	.314	.313	72	-13	2-1	.961	-13	95	95	*S-112	-1.7
1955	Cle A	130	388	34	81	9	5	2	34	49-0	3	60	.209	.302	.273	54	-25	1-0	**.976**	7	95	**115**	*S-128	-0.7
1956	Cle A	85	171	22	36	1	2	3	17	22-0	0	27	.211	.299	.292	56	-11	0-1	.986	8	106	128	2-28,S-28,3-26	-0.1
1957	Cle A	89	201	21	47	8	2	1	19	26-1	1	29	.234	.323	.308	75	-7	0-3	.980	7	99	78	2-48,S-23,3-19	0.3
1959	Cle A	132	441	55	105	15	2	3	48	51-2	0	64	.238	.313	.302	74	-15	1-1	.971	-8	90	89	3-80,S-50/2-4	-1.9
1960	Cle A	32	42	4	7	0	0	1	3	4-1	1	8	.167	.255	.238	35	-4	0-0	.962	1	117	143	S-14,3-12/2-2	-0.3
Total	10	971	2824	305	633	84	27	36	284	361-4	11	453	.224	.313	.311	70	-113	12-10	.963	49	102	115	S-679,2-141,3-139/1-2	-1.1
STRIEF, GEORGE George Andrew B 10.16.1856 Cincinnati, OH D 4.1.1946 Cleveland, OH BR/TR 5-7/172# d5.1 U1 OF Total (61-LF 60-CF 8-RF)																								
1879	Cle N	71	264	24	46	7	1	0	15	10		23	.174	.204	.208	37	-17		.918	-8	64	0	O-55(1-54-1),2-16	-2.5
1882	Pit AA	**79**	297	45	58	9	6	2		13			.195	.229	.286	76	-7		.917	0	91	93	*2-78/S	-0.3
1883	StL AA	82	302	22	68	9	0	1	22	12			.225	.255	.265	64	-12		.899	5	104	127	*2-67,O-15(11-1-3)	-0.5
1884	StL AA	48	184	22	37	5	2	2		13	0		.201	.254	.283	72	-6		.848	-4	57	0	O-44(43-1-0)/2-3,1	-1.0
	KC U	15	56	5	6	5	0	0		4			.107	.167	.196	11	-8		.900	5	119	153	2-15	-0.2
	CP U	15	53	6	11	5	0	0		3			.208	.250	.302	67	-4		.905	-1	88	25	2-15	-0.3
	Year	30	109	11	17	10	0	0		7			.156	.207	.248	40	-11		.902	4	105	94	2-30	-0.5
	Cle N	8	29	2	7	2	0	0	0	0		5	.241	.241	.310	70	-1		1.000	1	240	0	/O-6(LF),3-2	0.0
1885	Phi AA	44	175	19	48	8	5	0	27	9	0		.274	.310	.377	110	1		.828	0	98	0	3-19,S-10/O-8(0-4-4),2-7	0.2
Total	5	362	1360	145	281	50	14	5	64	64	0	28	.207	.242	.275	67	-54		.899	-2	96	108	2-201,O-128L/3-21,S-11,1	-4.6
STRINGER, LOU Louis Bernard B 5.13.1917 Grand Rapids, MI BR/TR 5-11/173# d4.15 Mil 1943-45																								
1941	Chi N	145	512	59	126	31	4	5	53	59	0	86	.246	.324	.352	94	-4	3	.960	24	**114**	101	*2-137/S-7	2.9

Year	Tm Lg	G	AB	R	H	2B	3B	HR	RBI	BB-IB	HP	SO	AVG	OBP	SLG	AOPS	ABR	SB-CS	FA	FR	Rng	Thr	G at Pos	BFW
1942	Chi N	121	406	45	96	10	5	9	41	31	1	55	.236	.292	.352	92	-7	3	.955	-1	**106**	85	*2-113/3	0.0
1946	Chi N	80	209	26	51	3	1	3	19	26	0	34	.244	.328	.311	83	-5	0	.956	-9	95	54	2-62/S3	-1.1
1948	Bos A	4	11	1	1	0	0	1	1	0	0	3	.091	.091	.364	17	-2	0-0	.947	2	146	231	/2-2	0.0
1949	Bos A	35	41	10	11	4	0	1	6	5	0	10	.268	.348	.439	100	0	0-0	.978	2	96	208	/2-9	0.3
1950	Bos A	24	17	7	5	1	0	0	2	0	0	4	.294	.294	.353	59	-1	1-0	.778	1	141	334	/3-3,2S	0.0
Total	6	409	1196	148	290	49	10	19	122	121	1	192	.242	.313	.348	90	-19	7-0	.958	20	108	91	2-324/S-9,3-5	2.1
STRIPP, JOE Joseph Valentine "Jersey Joe" B 2.3.1903 Harrison, NJ D 6.10.1989 Orlando, FL BR/TR 5-11.5/175# d7.2 OF Total (10-LF 12-RF)																								
1928	Cin N	42	139	18	40	7	3	1	17	8	3	8	.288	.340	.403	95	-1	0	.931	-4	92	0	O-21(10-0-11),3-17/S	-0.5
1929	Cin N	64	187	24	40	3	2	3	20	24	3	15	.214	.313	.299	55	-13	2	.960	3	115	52	3-55/2-2	-0.6
1930	Cin N	130	464	74	142	37	6	3	64	51	2	37	.306	.377	.431	100	2	15	.996	-0	83	113	1-75,3-48	0.0
1931	Cin N	105	426	71	138	26	2	3	42	21	2	31	.324	.359	.415	114	8	5	.957	6	108	126	3-96/1-9	1.7
1932	Bro N	138	534	94	162	36	9	6	64	36	2	30	.303	.350	.438	113	9	14	.954	16	115	133	3-93,1-43	2.4
1933	Bro N	141	537	69	149	20	7	1	51	26	1	23	.277	.312	.346	92	-7	5	.967	7	99	86	*3-140	0.5
1934	Bro N	104	384	50	121	19	6	1	40	22	1	20	.315	.354	.404	108	4	2	.941	-4	90	159	3-96/1-7,S	0.2
1935	Bro N	109	373	44	114	13	5	3	43	22	0	15	.306	.344	.391	99	-1	2	.962	7	116	142	3-88,1-15/O(RF)	0.7
1936	Bro N	110	439	51	139	31	1	1	60	22	1	12	.317	.351	.399	100	1	2	**.968**	7	97	99	*3-106	1.1
1937	Bro N	90	300	37	73	10	2	1	26	20	0	18	.243	.291	.300	60	-17	1	.971	-4	89	52	3-66,1-14/S-3	-2.0
1938	StL N	54	199	24	57	7	0	0	18	18	1	10	.286	.349	.322	81	-5	0	.977	-4	82	113	3-51	-0.7
	Bos N	59	229	19	63	10	0	1	19	10	0	7	.275	.305	.332	84	-6	2	.966	-1	100	126	3-58	-0.4
	Year	113	428	43	120	17	0	1	37	28	1	17	.280	.326	.327	82	-10	2	**.971**	-4	92	**120**	*3-109	-1.1
Total	11	1146	4211	575	1238	219	43	24	464	280	16	226	.294	.340	.384	96	-26	50	.961	30	102	108	3-914,1-163/O-22R,S-5,2-2	2.4
STRITTMATTER, MARK Mark Arthur B 4.4.1969 Huntington, NY BR/TR 6-1/210# d9.3																								
1998	Col N	4	4	0	0	0	0	0	0	0-0	0	3	.000	.000	.000	-82	-1	0-0	1.000	1	72	0	/C-3	0.0
STROBEL, ALLIE Albert Irving B 6.11.1884 Boston, MA D 2.10.1955 Hollywood, FL BR/TR 6/160# d8.29																								
1905	Bos N	5	19	1	2	0	0	0	2	0	0		.105	.105	.105	-38	-3	0	1.000	0	101	228	/3-4,O(LF)	-0.3
1906	Bos N	100	317	28	64	10	3	1	24	29	2		.202	.273	.262	69	-12	2	.946	-6	95	98	2-93/S-6,O(CF)	-1.8
Total	2	105	336	29	66	10	3	1	26	29	2		.196	.264	.253	63	-15	2	.946	-6	95	98	/2-93,S-6,3-4,O-2(1-1-0)	-2.1
STRONER, JIM James Melvin B 5.29.1901 Chicago, IL D 12.6.1975 Tarboro, NC BR/TR 5-10/175# d5.1																								
1929	Pit N	6	8	0	3	1	0	0	0	1	0	0	.375	.444	.500	130	0	0	.571	-1	88	0	/3-2	0.0
STRONG, JAMAL Jamal Najar B 8.5.1978 Pasadena, CA BR/TR 5-10/180# d9.2																								
2003	Sea A	12	2	2	0	0	0	0	0	0-0	0	0	.000	.000	.000	-99	-1	0-0	—	-0	0	0	/O-2(CF),D-7	-0.1
STROUD, ED Edwin Marvin B 10.31.1939 Lapine, AL BL/TR 5-11/180# d9.11																								
1966	Chi A	12	36	3	6	2	0	0	1	2-0	1	8	.167	.231	.222	33	-3	3-0	1.000	-0	102	0	O-11(4-0-7)	-0.4
1967	Chi A	20	27	6	8	0	1	0	3	1-0	1	5	.296	.345	.370	116	0	7-2	1.000	2	106	395	O-12(11-0-5)	0.3
	Was A	87	204	36	41	5	3	1	10	25-0	1	29	.201	.289	.270	69	-8	8-6	.983	-7	88	28	O-79(1-79-0)	-1.8
	Year	107	231	42	49	5	4	1	13	26-0	2	34	.212	.295	.281	75	-7	15-8	.985	-5	90	69	O-91(12-79-5)	-1.5
1968	Was A	105	306	41	73	10	10	4	23	20-1	0	50	.239	.284	.376	102	-1	9-3	.979	-1	105	45	O-84(25-7-58)	-0.7
1969	Was A	123	206	35	52	5	6	4	29	30-1	2	33	.252	.353	.393	114	4	12-2	.982	1	117	25	O-85(28-1-58)	0.4
1970	Was A	129	433	69	115	11	5	5	32	40-2	3	79	.266	.331	.349	92	-5	29-8	.993	3	105	113	*O-118(9-106-9)	-0.2
1971	Chi A	53	141	19	25	4	3	0	2	11-0	0	20	.177	.237	.248	36	-12	4-5	1.000	-6	72	0	O-44(8-22-20)	-2.2
Total	6	529	1353	209	320	37	28	14	100	129-4	8	224	.237	.306	.336	87	-25	72-26	.988	-8	101	62	O-433(86-215-157)	-4.6
STROUGHTER, STEVE Stephen Lewis B 3.15.1952 Visalia, CA BL/TR 6-2/190# d4.7																								
1982	Sea A	26	47	4	8	1	0	1	3	3-1	1	9	.170	.235	.255	34	-4	0-0	1.000	1	194	975	/O-3(LF),D-9	-0.3
STRUEVE, AL Albert Frederick B 6.26.1860 Cincinnati, OH D 1.28.1929 Buckskin Township, OH d6.22																								
1884	StL AA	2	7	2	2	0	0	0		0	0		.286	.286	.286	84	0		—	1	0	0	/O(CF)C	0.1
STRUNK, AMOS Amos Aaron B 1.22.1889 Philadelphia, PA D 7.22.1979 Llanerch, PA BL/TL 5-11.5/175# d9.24																								
1908	Phi A	12	34	4	8	1	0	0	0	4	0		.235	.316	.265	83	0	0	.903	0	74	271	O-11(1-10-0)	-0.1
1909	Phi A	11	35	1	4	0	0	0	2	1	0		.114	.139	.114	-20	-5	2	1.000	0	245	0	/O-9(1-8-0)	-0.6
1910	†Phi A	16	48	9	16	0	1	0	2	3	0		.333	.373	.375	135	2	4	1.000	1	121	51	O-14(CF)	0.2
1911	†Phi A	74	215	42	55	7	2	1	21	35	1		.256	.363	.321	93	0	13	.958	2	104	116	O-62(19-43-0)/1-2	-0.2
1912	Phi A	122	412	58	119	13	12	3	63	47	3		.289	.366	.400	123	13	29	**.990**	8	112	99	*O-116(65-51-0)	1.4
1913	†Phi A	94	292	30	89	11	12	0	46	29	0	23	.305	.368	.425	135	12	14	.962	-2	100	74	O-81(CF)	0.4
1914	†Phi A	122	404	58	111	15	3	2	45	57	0	38	.275	.364	.342	117	11	25-22	**.987**	6	111	93	*O-120(12-108-0)	0.8
1915	Phi A	132	485	76	144	28	16	1	45	56	1	45	.297	.371	.427	144	25	17-19	.980	10	106	**165**	*O-111(0-59-52),1-19	2.6
1916	Phi A	150	544	71	172	30	9	3	49	66	3	59	.316	.393	.421	152	36	21-23	.978	0	98	108	*O-143(6-119-18)/1-7	2.5
1917	Phi A	148	540	83	152	26	7	1	45	68	1	37	.281	.363	.361	123	17	16	**.986**	-5	100	63	*O-146(CF)	0.1
1918	†Bos A	114	413	50	106	18	9	0	35	36	0	13	.257	.316	.344	101	-1	20	**.988**	-6	90	85	*O-113(1-112-0)	-1.6
1919	Bos A	48	184	27	50	11	3	0	17	13	1	13	.272	.323	.364	98	-1	3	.968	-4	94	55	O-48(CF)	-0.9
	Phi A	60	194	15	41	6	4	0	13	23	1	15	.211	.298	.284	63	-10	3	.981	-1	97	95	O-52(0-10-42)	-1.4
	Year	108	378	42	91	17	7	0	30	36	2	28	.241	.310	.323	79	-11	6	.974	-5	96	75	*O-100(0-58-42)	-2.3
1920	Phi A	58	202	23	60	9	3	0	20	21	0	9	.297	.363	.371	94	-1	0-6	.990	-4	97	29	O-54(6-10-38)	-1.0
	Chi A	53	188	33	45	8	1	1	16	28	0	15	.239	.338	.309	72	-7	1-0	.981	-1	109	47	O-49(3-7-38)	-1.0
	Year	111	390	56	105	17	4	1	36	49	0	24	.269	.351	.341	83	-8	1-6	.985	-5	103	38	*O-103(9-17-76)	-2.0
1921	Chi A	121	401	68	133	19	10	3	69	38	1	27	.332	.391	.451	116	10	7-10	.970	-6	93	76	*O-111(9-69-33)	-0.4
1922	Chi A	92	311	36	90	11	4	0	33	33	0	28	.289	.358	.350	85	-6	9-6	.989	1	99	117	O-74(14-56-4)/1-7	-0.9
1923	Chi A	54	54	7	17	0	0	0	8	8	0	5	.315	.403	.315	92	0	1-0	1.000	0	136	0	/O-5(2-3-0),1-2	0.0
1924	Chi A	1	1	0	0	0	0	0	0	0	0	0	.000	.000	.000	-99	0	0-0	—	0			H	0.0
	Phi A	30	42	5	6	0	0	0	1	7	0	4	.143	.265	.143	7	-6	0-0	1.000	-1	62	0	/O-8(4-1-3)	-0.7
	Year	31	43	5	6	0	0	0	1	7	0	4	.140	.260	.140	5	-6	0-0	1.000	-1	62	0	/O-8(4-1-3)	-0.7
Total	17	1512	4999	696	1418	213	96	15	530	573	12	331	.284	.359	.374	112	89	185-86	.980	-2	102	92	*O-1327(143-955-228)/1-37	-0.8
STUART, LUKE Luther Lane B 5.23.1892 Alamance Co., NC D 6.15.1947 Winston-Salem, NC BR/TR 5-8/165# d7.28																								
1921	StL A	3	3	2	1	0	0	1	2	0	0	1	.333	.333	1.333	291	1	0-0	1.000	-0	58	0	/2-3	0.0
STUART, DICK Richard Lee "Dr. Strangeglove" B 11.7.1932 San Francisco, CA D 12.15.2002 Redwood City, CA BR/TR 6-4/212# d7.10																								
1958	Pit N	67	254	38	68	12	5	16	48	11-1	5	75	.268	.310	.543	124	7	0-0	.973	-1	109	124	1-64	0.2
1959	Pit N	118	397	64	118	15	2	27	78	42-7	2	86	.297	.362	.549	141	23	1-1	.976	0	**113**	108	*1-105/O(LF)	1.7
1960	†Pit N	122	438	48	114	17	5	23	83	39-5	0	107	.260	.317	.479	115	7	0-0	.986	-1	103	113	*1-108	0.0
1961	Pit N★	138	532	83	160	28	8	35	117	34-1	4	121	.301	.344	.581	140	28	0-3	.983	1	107	**122**	*1-132/O(LF)	1.9
1962	Pit N	114	394	52	90	11	4	16	64	32-1	2	94	.228	.286	.398	83	-11	0-1	.982	1	109	117	*1-101	-1.7
1963	Bos A	157	612	81	160	25	4	42	**118**	44-2	1	144	.261	.312	.521	125	17	0-0	.979	7	**118**	81	*1-155	1.5
1964	Bos A	156	603	73	168	27	1	33	114	37-7	3	130	.279	.320	.491	117	12	0-0	.981	-0	100	80	*1-155	0.3
1965	Phi N	149	538	53	126	19	1	28	95	39-8	3	136	.234	.287	.429	101	-1	1-0	.986	3	109	92	*1-143/3	-0.7
1966	NY N	31	87	7	19	0	0	4	13	9-2	0	26	.218	.292	.356	81	-2	0-1	.974	-1	93	105	1-23	-0.6
	†LA N	38	91	4	24	1	0	3	9	11-0	2	17	.264	.356	.374	112	2	0-1	.991	3	158	99	1-25	0.4
	Year	69	178	11	43	1	0	7	22	20-2	2	43	.242	.325	.365	97	-1	0-2	.982	2	126	102	1-48	-0.2
1969	Cal A	22	51	3	8	2	0	1	4	3-0	0	21	.157	.204	.255	29	-5	0-0	.991	-1	54	128	1-13	-0.8
Total	10	1112	3997	506	1055	157	30	228	743	301-34	22	957	.264	.316	.489	117	77	2-7	.982	11	109	102	*1-1024/O-2(LF),3	2.2
STUART, BILL William Alexander "Chauncey" B 8.28.1873 Boalsburg, PA D 10.14.1928 Fort Worth, TX 5-11/170# d8.15																								
1895	Pit N	19	77	5	19	3	0	0	10	2	1	6	.247	.275	.286	47	-6	2	.913	-1	99	72	S-17/2-2	-0.5
1899	NY N	1	3	0	0	0	0	0	0	0	0		.000	.000	.000	-99	-1	0	1.000	0	93	0	/2	-0.1
Total	2	20	80	5	19	3	0	0	10	2	1	6	.237	.265	.275	42	-7	2	.913	-1	99	72	/S-17,2-3	-0.6
STUBBS, FRANKLIN Franklin Lee B 10.21.1960 Richlands, NC BL/TL 6-2/215# d4.28																								
1984	LA N	87	217	22	42	2	3	8	17	24-3	0	63	.194	.273	.341	73	-9	2-2	.993	2	138	94	1-51,O-20(6-3-13)	-1.1
1985	LA N	10	9	0	2	0	0	0	2	0-0	0	3	.222	.222	.222	25	-1	0-0	1.000	-0	0	117	/1-4	-0.1
1986	LA N	132	420	55	95	11	1	23	58	37-11	2	107	.226	.291	.421	101	-2	7-1	.969	3	101	140	*O-124(108-23-15),1-13	-0.3
1987	LA N	129	386	48	90	16	3	16	52	31-9	1	85	.233	.290	.415	87	-9	8-1	**.994**	6	117	90	*1-111,O-18(13-0-6)	-0.8

Year	Tm Lg	G	AB	R	H	2B	3B	HR	RBI	BB-IB	HP	SO	AVG	OBP	SLG	AOPS	ABR	SB-CS	FA	FR	Rng	Thr	G at Pos	BFW
1988	†LA N	115	242	30	54	13	0	8	34	23-3	1	61	.223	.288	.376	94	-2	11-3	.978	4	126	99	1-84,O-13(7-1-6)	-0.2
1989	LA N	69	103	11	30	6	0	4	15	16-2	0	27	.291	.387	.466	145	7	3-2	.948	4	117	262	O-28(22-5-3)/1-7	1.0
1990	Hou N	146	448	59	117	23	2	23	71	48-3	2	114	.261	.334	.475	124	14	19-6	.991	-7	89	100	1-72,O-71(67-0-5)	0.3
1991	Mil A	103	362	48	77	16	2	11	38	35-3	2	71	.213	.282	.359	79	-11	13-4	.991	4	124	100	1-92/O-4(LF),D-4	-1.2
1992	Mil A	92	288	37	66	11	1	9	42	27-3	1	68	.229	.297	.368	87	-6	11-8	.987	5	134	92	1-68,D-16/O(RF)	-0.6
1995	Det A	62	116	13	29	11	0	2	19	19-1	1	27	.250	.358	.397	97	0	0-1	.972	-4	56	111	1-20,O-20(LF)/D-3	-0.5
Total	10	945	2591	323	602	109	12	104	348	260-38	10	626	.232	.303	.404	97	-19	74-28	.989	16	118	96	1-522,O-299(247-32-49)/D-23	-3.5
STUBING, MOOSE Lawrence George B 3.31.1938 Bronx, NY BL/TL 6-3/220# d8.14 M1 C6																								
1967	Cal A	5	5	0	0	0	0	0	0	0-0	0	4	.000	.000	.000	-99	-1	0-0	—	0			H	-0.1
STUDLEY, SEEM Seymour L. "Warhorse" B 5.1841 Byron, NY D 7.19.1901 Grand Island, NE 5-7.5/180# d4.20																								
1872	Nat NA	5	21	3	2	0	0	0	2	0		1	.095	.095	.095	-35	-4	0-0	.571	-2	0	0	/O-5(CF)	-0.4
STUMPF, GEORGE George Frederick B 12.15.1910 New Orleans, LA D 3.6.1993 Metairie, LA BL/TL 5-8/155# d9.19																								
1931	Bos A	7	28	2	7	1	1	0	4	1	0	2	.250	.276	.357	69	-2	0-0	1.000	-0	96	0	/O-7(6-2-0)	-0.2
1932	Bos A	79	169	18	34	2	2	1	18	18	0	21	.201	.278	.254	40	-16	1-1	.952	-2	95	65	O-51(17-2-32)	-1.9
1933	Bos A	22	41	8	14	3	0	0	5	4	0	2	.341	.400	.415	117	1	4-0	1.000	-0	110	0	O-15(3-8-4)	0.2
1936	Chi A	10	22	3	6	1	0	0	5	2	0	1	.273	.333	.318	59	-1	0-0	1.000	0	93	243	/O-4(LF)	-0.1
Total	4	118	260	31	61	7	3	1	32	25	0	26	.235	.302	.296	57	-18	5-1	.969	-2	97	63	/O-77(30-12-36)	-2.0
STUMPF, BILL William Frederick B 3.21.1892 Baltimore, MD D 2.14.1966 Crownsville, MD BR/TR 6-0.5/175# d5.11																								
1912	NY A	42	129	8	31	0	0	0	10	6	1		.240	.279	.240	46	-9	5	.892	-6	95	109	S-26/2-8,3-5,1O(CF)	-1.3
1913	NY A	12	29	5	6	1	0	0	1	3	0	3	.207	.281	.241	53	-2	0	.818	-3	96	0	/S-6,2-4,O(RF)	-0.4
Total	2	54	158	13	37	1	0	0	11	9	1	3	.234	.280	.241	47	-11	5	.877	-8	95	87	/S-32,2-12,3-5,O-2(0-1-1),1	-1.7
STURDY, GUY Guy R. B 8.7.1899 Sherman, TX D 5.4.1965 Marshall, TX BL/TL 6-0.5/180# d9.30																								
1927	StL A	5	21	5	9	1	0	0	5	1	0	0	.429	.455	.476	137	1	2-0	.974	-0	69	54	/1-5	0.1
1928	StL A	54	45	3	10	1	0	1	8	8	0	4	.222	.340	.311	70	-2	1-0	1.000	-0	0	0	/1	-0.2
Total	2	59	66	8	19	2	0	1	13	9	0	4	.288	.373	.364	91	-1	3-0	.975	-1	66	51	/1-6	-0.1
STURGEON, BOBBY Robert Howard B 8.6.1919 Clinton, IN BR/TR 6/175# d4.16 Mil 1943-45																								
1940	Chi N	7	21	1	4	1	0	0	2	0	0	1	.190	.190	.238	18	-2	0	.848	-1	91	123	/S-7	-0.3
1941	Chi N	129	433	45	106	15	3	0	25	9	0	30	.245	.260	.293	58	-26	5	.956	-0	101	98	*S-126/23	-1.9
1942	Chi N	63	162	8	40	7	1	0	7	4	1	13	.247	.269	.302	70	-7	2	.988	13	125	106	2-32,S-29/3-2	1.0
1946	Chi N	100	294	26	87	12	2	1	21	10	0	18	.296	.319	.361	94	-4	0	.934	-10	90	92	S-72,2-21	-1.0
1947	Chi N	87	232	16	59	10	5	0	21	7	0	12	.254	.276	.341	66	-13	0	.975	11	108	104	S-45,2-30/3-5	0.1
1948	Bos N	34	78	10	17	3	1	0	4	4	0	5	.218	.256	.282	46	-6	0	.938	-4	97	113	2-18/S-4,3-4	-0.9
Total	6	420	1220	106	313	48	12	1	80	34	1	79	.257	.277	.318	68	-58	7	.951	9	100	100	S-283,2-102/3-12	-3.0
STURGIS, DEAN Dean Donnell B 12.1.1892 Beloit, KS D 6.4.1950 Uniontown, PA BR/TR 6-1/180# d5.1																								
1914	Phi A	4	4	1	1	0	0	0	0	1	0	2	.250	.400	.250	100	0	0	1.000	0	*87*	*138*	/C	0.0
STURM, JOHNNY John Peter Joseph B 1.23.1916 St.Louis, MO BL/TL 6-1/185# d4.14 Mil 1942-45																								
1941	†NY A	124	524	58	125	17	3	3	36	37	3	50	.239	.293	.300	58	-33	3-5	.990	-2	94	**117**	*1-124	-4.7
STUTZ, GEORGE George "Kid" or "Satan" B 2.12.1893 Philadelphia, PA D 12.29.1930 Philadelphia, PA BL/TR 5-5/150# d8.17																								
1926	Phi N	6	9	0	0	0	0	0	0	0	0	2	.000	.000	.000	-95	-2	0	.938	0	95	127	/S-5	-0.2
STYLES, LENA William Graves B 11.27.1899 Gurley, AL D 3.14.1956 Hunstville, AL BR/TR 6-1/185# d9.10																								
1919	Phi A	8	22	0	6	1	0	0	5	1	0	6	.273	.304	.318	74	-1	0	.974	-0	*76*	*93*	/C-8	-0.1
1920	Phi A	24	50	5	13	3	1	0	5	6	0	7	.260	.339	.360	84	-1	1-0	.966	1	*111*	*195*	/C-9,1-7	0.0
1921	Phi A	4	5	0	1	0	0	0	0	0	0	2	.200	.200	.200	2	-1	0-0	.333	-1	*0*	*237*	/C-2	-0.2
1930	Cin N	7	12	2	3	0	1	0	1	1	1	2	.250	.357	.417	91	0	0	.875	-0	*70*	*184*	/C-5,1	0.0
1931	Cin N	34	87	7	21	3	0	0	5	8	1	7	.241	.313	.276	63	-4	0	.949	-5	*84*	*51*	C-31	-0.8
Total	5	77	176	14	44	7	2	0	16	16	2	24	.250	.320	.313	71	-7	1-0	.929	-6	*83*	*93*	/C-55,1-8	-1.1
STYNES, CHRIS Christopher Desmond B 1.19.1973 Queens, NY BR/TR 5-9/170# d5.19 OF Total (134-LF 2-CF 22-RF)																								
1995	KC A	22	35	7	6	1	0	0	2	4-0	0	3	.171	.256	.200	20	-4	0-0	.982	2	111	204	2-17/D-2	-0.1
1996	KC A	36	92	8	27	6	0	0	6	2-0	0	5	.293	.309	.359	68	-5	5-2	.939	-3	93	91	O-19(LF)/2-5,3-2,D-3	-0.7
1997	Cin N	49	198	31	69	7	1	6	28	11-1	4	13	.348	.394	.485	127	8	11-2	.976	3	112	204	O-38(LF)/2-8,3-3	1.1
1998	Cin N	123	347	52	88	10	1	6	27	32-1	4	36	.254	.323	.340	74	-13	15-1	1.000	5	108	100	O-80(64-2-20),3-22,2-11/S-2	-0.8
1999	Cin N	73	113	18	27	1	0	2	14	12-1	0	13	.239	.310	.301	55	-8	5-2	.956	-9	82	70	2-43/3-8,O-4(LF)	-1.4
2000	Cin N	119	380	71	127	24	1	12	40	32-2	2	54	.334	.386	.497	119	12	5-2	.966	-4	88	106	3-77,2-15/O-8(6-0-2)	0.8
2001	Bos A	96	361	52	101	19	2	8	33	20-0	3	56	.280	.322	.410	91	-5	4-5	.949	-4	81	68	3-46,2-43/O-3(LF)	-0.8
2002	Chi N	98	195	25	47	9	1	5	26	21-1	1	29	.241	.314	.374	86	-5	1-1	.921	-3	74	48	3-40,2-20	-0.7
2003	Col N	138	443	71	113	31	3	11	73	48-1	6	76	.255	.335	.413	82	-10	3-1	.972	3	104	99	*3-119/2-5	-0.5
Total	9	754	2164	335	605	108	9	50	249	182-7	20	285	.280	.340	.407	90	-30	49-16	.960	-10	94	91	3-317,2-167,O-152L/D-5,S-2	-3.1
STYNES, NEIL Cornelius William B 12.10.1868 Arlington, MA D 3.26.1944 Somerville, MA BR/TR 6/165# d9.8																								
1890	Cle P	2	8	0	0	0	0	0	0	0	0	0	.000	.000	.000	-99	-2	0	.786	-1	*70*	*0*	/C-2	-0.3
SUAREZ, KEN Kenneth Raymond B 4.12.1943 Tampa, FL BR/TR 5-9/175# d4.14																								
1966	KC A	35	69	5	10	0	1	0	2	15-0	0	26	.145	.298	.174	41	-5	2-0	.954	2	*82*	*157*	C-34	-0.1
1967	KC A	39	63	7	15	5	0	2	9	16-1	0	21	.238	.387	.413	143	5	1-0	.979	5	93	175	C-36	1.2
1968	Cle A	17	10	1	1	0	0	0	0	1-0	0	3	.100	.182	.100	-13	-1	0-0	1.000	0	0	0	C-12/23O(LF)	-0.1
1969	Cle A	36	85	7	25	5	0	1	9	15-5	0	12	.294	.400	.388	117	3	1-0	.991	1	176	123	C-36	0.6
1971	Cle A	50	123	10	25	7	0	1	9	18-3	2	15	.203	.310	.285	65	-5	0-1	.993	1	121	113	C-48	-0.3
1972	Tex A	25	33	2	5	1	0	0	4	1-0	0	4	.152	.167	.182	7	-4	0-0	.965	1	318	147	C-17	-0.3
1973	Tex A	93	278	25	69	11	0	1	27	33-0	5	16	.248	.334	.299	84	-4	1-2	.989	-2	91	111	C-90	-0.2
Total	7	295	661	57	150	29	1	5	60	99-9	7	97	.227	.330	.297	81	-11	5-3	.984	9	*115*	*125*	C-273/O(LF)32	0.8
SUAREZ, LUIS Luis Abelardo B 8.24.1916 Alto Songo, Cuba D 6.5.1991 Havana, Cuba BR/TR 5-11/170# d5.28																								
1944	Was A	1	2	0	0	0	0	0	0	0	0	0	.000	.000	.000	-99	-1	0-0	1.000	0	159	0	/3	0.0
SUCK, TONY Anthony (born Charles Anthony Zuck) B 6.11.1858 Chicago, IL D 1.29.1895 Chicago, IL 5-9/164# d8.9																								
1883	Buf N	2	7	1	0	0	0	0	0	1		4	.000	.125	.000	-56	-1		—	-2	0	0	/O(LF)C	-0.3
1884	CP U	53	188	18	28	2	0	0		13			.149	.204	.160	12	-26		.904	-4			C-28,S-15,O-12(1-10-1)/3	-2.5
	Bal U	3	10	2	3	0	0	0		0			.300	.300	.300	75	-1		.882	1			/C-3	0.0
	Year	56	198	20	31	2	0	0		13			.157	.209	.167	15	-27		.901	-4			C-31,S-15,O-12(1-10-1)/3	-2.5
Total	2	58	205	21	31	2	0	0	0	14		4	.151	.205	.161	12	-28		.894	-5			/C-32,S-15,O-13(2-10-1),3	-2.8
SUDAKIS, BILL William Paul "Suds" B 3.27.1946 Joliet, IL BB/TR 6-1/190# d9.3																								
1968	LA N	24	87	11	24	4	2	3	12	15-1	0	14	.276	.382	.471	168	8	1-0	.953	2	107	63	3-24	1.1
1969	LA N	132	462	50	108	17	5	14	53	40-5	1	94	.234	.294	.383	96	-5	3-2	.946	10	**110**	136	*3-121	0.5
1970	LA N	94	269	37	71	11	0	14	44	35-4	3	46	.264	.352	.461	122	9	4-0	.983	-4	54	24	C-38,3-37/O-3(RF),1	0.6
1971	LA N	41	83	10	16	3	0	3	7	12-2	1	22	.193	.302	.337	86	-1	0-1	1.000	2	143	128	C-19/3-3,1O(1-0-1)	0.1
1972	NY N	18	49	3	7	0	0	1	7	6-0	0	14	.143	.236	.204	27	-5	0-0	.967	1	186	59	/1-7,C-5	-0.5
1973	Tex A	82	235	32	60	11	0	15	43	23-1	0	53	.255	.320	.494	132	9	0-1	.962	-2	89	19	3-29,1-24/C-9,O-2(RF),D-8	0.6
1974	NY A	89	259	26	60	8	0	7	39	25-1	1	48	.232	.296	.344	87	-5	0-0	.990	1	126	120	D-39,1-33/3-3,C	-0.8
1975	Cal A	30	58	4	7	2	0	1	6	12-3	1	15	.121	.274	.207	43	-4	1-1	.941	-0	14	186	D-13/C-5,1-2	-0.5
	Cle A	20	46	4	9	0	0	1	3	4-1	0	7	.196	.260	.261	48	-3	0-1	1.000	-0	58	118	1-12/C-6	-0.5
	Year	50	104	8	16	2	0	2	9	16-4	1	22	.154	.268	.231	45	-7	1-2	1.000	-1	50	102	1-14,D-13,C-11	-1.0
Total	8	530	1548	177	362	56	7	59	214	172-18	7	313	.234	.311	.393	102	3	9-6	.942	9	111	114	3-217/C-83,1-80,D-60,O-6(1-0-6)	0.6
SUDER, PETE Peter "Pecky" B 4.16.1916 Aliquippa, PA BR/TR 6/175# d4.15 Mil 1944-45																								
1941	Phi A	139	531	45	130	20	9	4	52	19	0	47	.245	.271	.339	62	-33	1-3	.957	-6	97	95	*3-136/S-3	-3.3
1942	Phi A	128	476	46	122	20	4	4	54	24	1	39	.256	.293	.340	78	-16	4-4	.954	-1	97	69	S-69,3-34,2-31	-0.9
1943	Phi A	131	475	30	105	14	5	3	41	14	0	40	.221	.243	.291	56	-29	1-1	.971	-9	95	84	2-95,3-32/S-5	-3.6

Year	Tm Lg	G	AB	R	H	2B	3B	HR	RBI	BB-IB	HP	SO	AVG	OBP	SLG	AOPS	ABR	SB-CS	FA	FR	Rng	Thr	G at Pos	BFW
1946	Phi A	128	455	38	128	20	3	2	50	18	0	37	.281	.309	.352	85	-11	1-1	.959	2	102	85	S-67,3-33,2-12/1-3,O-2(RF)	-0.4
1947	Phi A	145	528	45	127	28	4	5	60	35	2	44	.241	.290	.337	73	-21	0-3	**.986**	-21	97	96	*2-140/S-3,3-2	-3.7
1948	Phi A	148	519	64	125	23	5	7	60	60	1	60	.241	.321	.345	77	-18	1-3	.988	-4	101	103	*2-148	-1.4
1949	Phi A	118	445	44	119	24	6	10	75	23	2	35	.267	.306	.416	93	-9	0-1	.975	5	107	122	2-89,3-36/S-2	0.0
1950	Phi A	77	248	34	61	10	0	8	35	23	0	31	.246	.310	.383	78	-9	2-2	.979	2	106	120	2-47,3-11,S-10/1-4	-0.4
1951	Phi A	123	440	46	108	18	1	1	42	30	1	42	.245	.295	.298	59	-26	5-5	**.987**	11	**107**	**119**	*2-103,S-18/3-3	-0.9
1952	Phi A	74	228	22	55	7	2	1	20	16	0	17	.241	.291	.303	61	-12	1-1	.991	1	98	109	2-43,S-17,3-16	-0.9
1953	Phi A	115	454	44	130	11	3	4	35	17	0	35	.286	.312	.350	76	-17	3-3	.974	3	109	103	3-72,2-38/S-7	-1.2
1954	Phi A	69	205	8	41	11	1	0	16	7	0	16	.200	.225	.263	34	-19	0-0	.961	4	105	102	2-35,3-20/S-2	-1.4
1955	KC A	26	81	3	17	4	1	0	1	2-0	0	13	.210	.229	.284	37	-8	0-1	.990	-2	88	106	2-24	-0.9
Total	13	1421	5085	469	1268	210	44	49	541	288-0	7	456	.249	.290	.337	71	-228	19-28	.982	-15	101	103	2-805,3-395,S-203/1-7,O-2(RF)	-19.0
SUERO, WILLIAM Williams (Urban) B 11.7.1966 Santo Domingo, D.R. D 11.30.1995 Santo Domingo, D.R. BR/TR 5-9/175# d4.9																								
1992	Mil A	18	16	4	3	1	0	0	0	2-0	1	1	.188	.316	.250	62	-1	1-1	.971	2	134	154	2-15/SD	0.1
1993	Mil A	15	14	0	4	0	0	0	0	1-0	0	3	.286	.333	.286	69	-1	0-1	.944	1	137	50	/2-8,3	0.0
Total	2	33	30	4	7	1	0	0	0	3-0	1	4	.233	.324	.267	65	-2	1-2	.962	3	135	117	/2-23,D-2,3S	0.1
SUGDEN, JOE Joseph B 7.31.1870 Philadelphia, PA D 6.28.1959 Philadelphia, PA BB/TR 5-10/180# d7.20 C7 OF Total (6-CF 18-RF)																								
1893	Pit N	27	92	20	24	4	3	0	12	10	1	11	.261	.340	.370	90	-1	1	.956	1	*99*	*103*	C-27	0.1
1894	Pit N	39	139	23	46	13	2	2	23	14	3	2	.331	.404	.496	117	4	3	.910	-5	*103*	*89*	C-31/3-4,S-3,O(CF)	0.2
1895	Pit N	50	158	28	48	4	1	1	17	16	3	12	.304	.379	.361	97	0	4	.901	-3	*88*	*122*	C-50	0.1
1896	Pit N	80	301	42	89	5	7	0	36	19	5	9	.296	.348	.359	90	-5	5	.952	-5	*84*	*100*	C-70/1-7,O-4(CF)	-0.3
1897	Pit N	84	288	31	64	6	4	0	38	18	3		.222	.275	.271	46	-23	9	.941	-12	*83*	*94*	C-81/1-3	-2.4
1898	StL N	89	289	29	73	7	1	0	34	23	3		.253	.314	.284	70	-11	5	.937	-6	*74*	*137*	C-60,O-15(0-1-14)/1-8	-1.2
1899	Cle N	76	250	19	69	5	1	0	14	11	0		.276	.307	.304	73	-10	2	.935	-18	*59*	*129*	C-66/O-4(RF),1-3,3	-2.0
1901	Chi A	48	153	21	42	7	1	0	19	13	2		.275	.339	.333	89	-2	4	.970	5	*115*	*103*	C-42/1-5	0.7
1902	StL A	68	200	25	50	7	2	0	15	20	4		.250	.330	.305	78	-5	2	.956	-0	*110*	*100*	C-61/1-4,P	0.0
1903	StL A	79	241	18	51	4	0	0	22	25	1		.212	.288	.228	58	-11	4	.983	7	*121*	*102*	C-66/1-8	0.3
1904	StL A	105	348	25	93	6	3	0	30	28	5		.267	.331	.302	107	4	6	**.989**	-3	*94*	*100*	C-79,1-28	0.9
1905	StL A	90	266	21	46	4	0	0	23	23	3		.173	.247	.188	41	-17	3	.983	7	*81*	*118*	C-76/1-9	-0.3
1912	Det A	1	4	1	1	0	0	0	0	0	0		.250	.250	.250	44	0	0	.941	1	410	0	/1	0.0
Total	13	836	2729	303	696	72	25	3	283	220	33	34	.255	.318	.303	78	-77	48	.957	-32	*91*	*109*	C-709/1-76,O-24R,3-5,S-3,P	-3.9
SUHR, GUS August Richard B 1.3.1906 San Francisco, CA BL/TR 6/180# d4.15																								
1930	Pit N	151	542	93	155	26	14	17	107	80	2	56	.286	.380	.480	106	5	11	.992	-7	83	97	*1-151	-1.0
1931	Pit N	87	270	26	57	13	4	4	32	38	0	25	.211	.308	.333	73	-10	4	.993	-0	100	118	1-76	-1.7
1932	Pit N	**154**	581	78	153	31	16	5	81	63	2	39	.263	.337	.398	99	-1	7	.988	-10	79	92	*1-154	-2.6
1933	Pit N	**154**	566	72	151	31	11	10	75	72	0	52	.267	.350	.413	117	14	2	.991	-3	91	97	*1-154	-0.4
1934	Pit N	**151**	573	67	162	36	13	13	103	66	3	52	.283	.360	.459	115	13	4	.994	-4	85	94	*1-151	-0.5
1935	Pit N	**153**	529	68	144	33	12	10	81	70	0	54	.272	.357	.437	109	8	6	.989	-7	80	86	*1-149/O-2(RF)	-1.2
1936	Pit N☆	**156**	583	111	182	33	12	11	118	95	2	34	.312	.410	.467	133	31	8	**.993**	-5	86	86	*1-156	1.1
1937	Pit N	151	575	69	160	28	14	5	97	83	0	42	.278	.369	.402	109	10	2	.993	-4	85	94	*1-151	-0.9
1938	Pit N	145	530	82	156	35	14	3	64	87	0	37	.294	.394	.430	126	22	4	.993	-10	77	**124**	*1-145	-0.2
1939	Pit N	63	204	23	59	10	2	1	31	25	0	23	.289	.367	.373	101	1	4	.993	-5	66	88	1-52	-0.9
	Phi N	60	198	21	63	12	2	3	24	34	1	14	.318	.421	.444	137	12	1	.995	0	98	90	1-60	0.7
	Year	123	402	44	122	22	4	4	55	59	1	37	.303	.394	.408	118	13	5	.994	-4	83	89	*1-112	-0.2
1940	Phi N	10	25	4	4	0	0	2	5	5	0	5	.160	.300	.400	95	0	0	.967	-2	25	96	/1-7	-0.2
Total	11	1435	5176	714	1446	288	114	84	818	718	10	433	.279	.368	.428	112	105	53	.992	-56	84	97	*1-1406/O-2(RF)	-7.8
SUKEFORTH, CLYDE Clyde Leroy "Sukey" B 11.30.1901 Washington, ME D 9.3.2000 Waldoboro, ME BL/TR 5-10/155# d5.23 M1 C15																								
1926	Cin N	1	1	0	0	0	0	0	0	0	0	1	.000	.000	.000	-99	0	0	—	0			H	0.0
1927	Cin N	38	58	12	11	2	0	0	2	7	0	2	.190	.277	.224	37	-5	2	.970	-0	*81*	*77*	C-24	-0.4
1928	Cin N	33	53	5	7	2	1	0	3	3	0	5	.132	.179	.208	1	-8	0	.966	0	*99*	*83*	C-26	-0.7
1929	Cin N	84	237	31	84	16	2	1	33	17	0	6	.354	.398	.451	115	6	8	.981	-2	*109*	*100*	C-76	0.8
1930	Cin N	94	296	30	84	9	3	1	19	17	1	12	.284	.325	.345	65	-17	1	.976	-2	*92*	*109*	C-82	-1.2
1931	Cin N	112	351	22	90	15	4	0	25	38	3	13	.256	.334	.322	82	-8	0	.965	-9	*84*	*97*	*C-106	-1.1
1932	Bro N	59	111	14	26	4	4	0	12	6	1	10	.234	.280	.342	68	-6	1	.991	-2	*93*	*89*	C-36	-0.6
1933	Bro N	20	36	1	2	0	0	0	0	2	0	1	.056	.105	.056	-55	-7	0	.983	2	*85*	*103*	C-18	-0.5
1934	Bro N	27	43	5	7	1	0	0	1	1	0	6	.163	.182	.186	-1	-6	0	1.000	-0	*83*	*112*	C-18	-0.6
1945	Bro N	18	51	2	15	1	0	0	1	4	0	1	.294	.345	.314	85	-1	0	.947	-2	*98*	*0*	C-13	-0.3
Total	10	486	1237	122	326	50	14	2	96	95	5	57	.264	.319	.331	71	-52	12	.974	-16	*92*	*95*	C-399	-4.6
SULARZ, GUY Guy Patrick B 11.7.1955 Minneapolis, MN BR/TR 5-11/165# d9.2																								
1980	SF N	25	65	3	16	1	1	0	3	9-1	0	6	.246	.333	.292	79	-2	1-0	.975	7	125	114	2-21/3-5	0.7
1981	SF N	10	20	0	4	0	0	0	2	2-0	1	4	.200	.292	.200	46	-1	0-1	1.000	2	118	95	/2-6,3	0.1
1982	SF N	63	101	15	23	3	0	1	7	9-0	0	11	.228	.291	.287	62	-5	3-0	.961	6	111	166	S-37,3-14/2-9	0.4
1983	SF N	10	20	3	2	0	0	0	0	3-0	0	2	.100	.217	.100	-10	-3	0-0	.917	1	98	83	/S-6,3-4	-0.1
Total	4	108	206	21	45	4	1	1	12	23-1	1	23	.218	.297	.262	59	-11	4-1	.954	16	109	153	/S-43,2-36,3-24	1.1
SULIK, ERNIE Ernest Richard "Dave" B 7.7.1910 San Francisco, CA D 5.31.1963 Oakland, CA BL/TL 5-10/178# d4.15																								
1936	Phi N	122	404	69	116	14	4	6	36	40	1	22	.287	.353	.386	90	-5	4	.971	-3	97	85	*O-105(41-65-1)	-1.1
SULLIVAN B Bristol, RI d5.15																								
1875	NH NA	2	8	3	3	0	0	0	2	0		1	.375	.375	.375	185	1	1-0	1.000	-0	0	0	/O-2(RF)	0.1
SULLIVAN, ANDY Andrew R. B 8.30.1884 Southborough, MA D 2.14.1920 Framingham, MA TR d9.13																								
1904	Bos N	1	1	0	0	0	0	0	0	1	0		.000	.500	.000	61	0	0	1.000	-0	0	0	/S	0.0
SULLIVAN, JACKIE Carl Mancel B 2.22.1918 Princeton, TX D 10.15.1992 Dallas, TX BR/TR 5-11/172# d7.6																								
1944	Det A	1	1	0	0	0	0	0	0	0	0	0	.000	.000	.000	-95	0	0-0	1.000	-0	0	0	/2	0.0
SULLIVAN, DAN Daniel C. "Link" B 5.9.1857 Providence, RI D 10.26.1893 Providence, RI TR 5-11/194# d5.2																								
1882	Lou AA	67	286	44	78	8	2	0		9			.273	.295	.315	112	4		.878	5			*C-54,3-10/O-4(0-3-1),S	1.3
1883	Lou AA	36	145	8	31	5	2	0		3			.214	.230	.276	67	-5		.900	-6			C-31/O-2(CF),3-2,S	-0.7
1884	Lou AA	63	247	27	59	8	6	0	26	9	1		.239	.268	.320	95	-1		.930	-14			C-63/O(LF)	-0.9
1885	Lou AA	13	44	3	8	1	0	0	4	2	1		.182	.234	.205	40	-3		.948	-2			C-13	-0.4
	StL AA	17	60	4	7	2	0	0	3	6	0		.117	.197	.150	10	-6		.956	2			C-13/1-4	-0.3
	Year	30	104	7	15	3	0	0	7	8	1		.144	.212	.173	22	-9		.952	-0			C-26/1-4	-0.7
1886	Pit AA	1	4	0	0	0	0	0	0	0	0		.000	.000	.000	-99	-1	0	.600	-1			/C	-0.2
Total	5	197	786	86	183	24	10	0	33	29	2		.233	.262	.289	84	-12	0	.909	-16			C-175/3-12,O-7(1-5-1),1-4,S-2	-1.2
SULLIVAN, DENNY Dennis J. B 6.26.1858 Boston, MA D 12.31.1925 Boston, MA TR 5-9/170# d8.25																								
1879	Pro N	5	19	5	5	2	0	0	2	1		1	.263	.300	.368	121	1		.429	-3	63	0	/3-4,O(RF)	-0.2
1880	Bos N	1	4	1	1	0	0	0	2	0		1	.250	.250	.250	72	0		.857	-0			/C	-0.1
Total	2	6	23	6	6	2	0	0	4	1		2	.261	.292	.348	113	1		.429	-4			/3-4,CO(RF)	-0.3
SULLIVAN, DENNY Dennis William B 9.28.1882 Hillsboro, WI D 6.2.1956 W.Los Angeles, CA BL/TR 5-10/?# d4.22																								
1905	Was A	3	11	0	0	0	0	0	0	1	0		.000	.083	.000	-76	-2	0	1.000	-0	0	0	/O-3(RF)	-0.3
1907	Bos A	144	551	73	135	18	0	1	26	44	12		.245	.315	.283	92	-3	16	.975	-1	89	79	*O-143(CF)	-1.2
1908	Bos A	101	355	33	85	7	8	0	25	14	4		.239	.276	.304	86	-7	4	.981	5	152	132	O-97(0-92-5)	-0.8
	Cle A	4	6	0	0	0	0	0	0	0	0		.000	.000	.000	-99	-1	0	1.000	-0	0	0	/O-2(1-0-1)	-0.2
	Year	105	361	33	85	7	8	0	25	14	4		.235	.272	.299	83	-8	4	.982	4	150	130	O-99(1-92-6)	-1.0
1909	Cle A	3	2	0	1	0	0	0	0	0	0		.500	.500	.500	207	0	0	—	0	0	0	/O-2(RF)	0.0
Total	4	255	925	106	221	25	8	1	51	59	16		.239	.296	.286	87	-13	20	.978	3	113	99	O-247(1-235-11)	-2.5
SULLIVAN, HAYWOOD Haywood Cooper B 12.15.1930 Donalsonville, GA D 2.12.2003 Fort Myers, FL BR/TR 6-4/215# d9.20 M1 s-Marc																								
1955	Bos A	2	6	1	0	0	0	0	0	0-0	0	1	.000	.000	.000	-92	-2	0-0	1.000	1	*0*	*0*	/C-2	-0.1
1957	Bos A	2	1	0	0	0	0	0	0	0-0	0	0	.000	.000	.000	-95	0	0-0	1.000	0	*0*	*0*	/C	0.0

Batter Register SULLIVAN—SULLIVAN 645

Year	Tm Lg	G	AB	R	H	2B	3B	HR	RBI	BB-IB	HP	SO	AVG	OBP	SLG	AOPS	ABR	SB-CS	FA	FR	Rng	Thr	G at Pos	BFW
1959	Bos A	4	2	0	0	0	0	0	0	1-0	0	1	.000	.333	.000	-0	0	0-0	1.000	0	0	0	/C-2	0.0
1960	Bos A	52	124	9	20	1	0	3	10	16-2	0	24	.161	.255	.242	35	-12	0-0	.992	3	122	84	C-50	-0.6
1961	KC A	117	331	42	80	16	2	6	40	46-0	0	45	.242	.333	.356	83	-7	1-0	.984	-2	109	79	C-88,1-16/O-5(2-0-3)	-0.6
1962	KC A	95	274	33	68	7	2	4	29	31-5	1	54	.248	.325	.332	74	-10	1-0	.980	-7	80	69	C-94/1	-1.3
1963	KC A	40	113	9	24	6	1	0	8	15-2	0	15	.212	.300	.283	62	-5	0-0	.992	4	40	130	C-37	0.0
Total	7	312	851	94	192	30	5	13	87	109-9	1	140	.226	.312	.318	69	-36	2-0	.985	-1	90	83	C-274/1-17,O-5(2-0-3)	-2.6
SULLIVAN, JOHN John Eugene B 2.16.1873 , IL D 6.5.1924 St.Paul, MN BR/TR 5-10/170# d4.19																								
1905	Det A	13	32	4	5	0	0	0	4	4	0		.156	.250	.156	29	-2	0	.964	1	80	165	C-12	-0.1
1908	Pit N	1	1	0	0	0	0	0	0	0	0		.000	.000	.000	-99	0	0	1.000	0	0	321	/C	0.0
Total	2	14	33	4	5	0	0	0	4	4	0		.152	.243	.152	26	-2	0	.965	1	78	169	/C-13	-0.1
SULLIVAN, CHUB John Frank B 1.12.1856 Boston, MA D 9.12.1881 Boston, MA BR/TR 6/164# d9.24																								
1877	Cin N	8	32	4	8	0	0	0	4	1		0	.250	.273	.250	74	-1		.944	-1	44	24	/1-8	-0.1
1878	Cin N	**61**	244	29	63	4	2	0	20	2		9	.258	.264	.291	91	-2		**.975**	5	133	125	*1-61	0.0
1880	Wor N	43	166	22	43	6	3	0	0	4		6	.259	.276	.331	97	-1		.983	3	108	104	1-43	0.0
Total	3	112	442	55	114	10	5	0	24	7		15	.258	.269	.303	92	-4		.976	7	118	110	1-112	-0.1
SULLIVAN, JOHN John Lawrence B 3.21.1890 Williamsport, PA D 4.1.1966 Milton, PA BR/TR 5-11/180# d4.18																								
1920	Bos N	81	250	36	74	14	4	1	28	29	2	29	.296	.374	.396	126	10	3-2	.977	-2	89	123	O-66(16-5-45)/1-6	0.5
1921	Bos N	5	5	0	0	0	0	0	0	0	0	0	.000	.000	.000	-99	-1	0-0	—	0			H	-0.1
	Chi N	76	240	28	79	14	4	4	41	19	1	26	.329	.381	.471	124	9	3-5	.962	-5	94	40	O-66(63-1-1)	-0.2
	Year	81	245	28	79	14	4	4	41	19	1	26	.322	.374	.461	120	7	3-5	.962	-5	94	40	O-66(63-1-1)	-0.3
Total	2	162	495	64	153	28	8	5	69	48	3	55	.309	.374	.428	123	18	6-7	.969	-7	91	83	O-132(79-6-46)/1-6	0.2
SULLIVAN, JOHN John Paul B 11.2.1920 Chicago, IL BR/TR 5-10/170# d6.7 Mil 1945-46 C15																								
1942	Was A	94	357	38	84	16	1	0	42	25	0	30	.235	.285	.286	61	-19	2-0	.936	-10	90	81	S-92	-2.3
1943	Was A	134	456	49	95	12	2	1	55	57	1	59	.208	.298	.250	63	-20	6-2	.946	9	**109**	99	*S-133	0.0
1944	Was A	138	471	49	118	12	1	0	30	52	0	43	.251	.325	.280	77	-13	3-3	.934	-13	94	94	*S-138	-1.5
1947	Was A	49	133	13	34	0	1	0	5	22	0	14	.256	.361	.271	79	-3	0-2	.963	2	104	91	S-40/2	0.1
1948	Was A	85	173	25	36	4	1	0	12	22	0	25	.208	.297	.243	46	-13	2-2	.951	-3	98	91	S-57/2-4	-1.3
1949	StL A	105	243	29	55	8	3	0	18	38	0	35	.226	.331	.284	61	-13	5-2	.942	-7	91	78	S-71,3-23/2-6	-1.6
Total	6	605	1833	203	422	52	9	1	162	216	1	206	.230	.312	.270	66	-81	18-11	.942	-22	98	91	S-531/3-23,2-11	-6.6
SULLIVAN, JOHN John Peter B 1.3.1941 Somerville, NJ BL/TR 6/195# d9.20																								
1963	Det A	3	5	0	0	0	0	0	0	2-0	0	1	.000	.286	.000	-11	-1	0-0	1.000	-0	51	0	/C-2	-0.1
1964	Det A	2	3	0	0	0	0	0	0	0-0	0	1	.000	.000	.000	-99	-1	0-0	1.000	0	0	804	/C-2	-0.1
1965	Det A	34	86	5	23	0	0	2	11	9-0	1	13	.267	.340	.337	93	-1	0-0	.994	2	148	118	C-29	0.3
1967	NY N	65	147	4	32	5	0	0	6	6-3	0	26	.218	.248	.252	44	-11	0-2	.991	-6	74	95	C-57	-1.8
1968	Phi N	12	18	0	4	0	0	0	1	2-0	0	4	.222	.300	.222	59	-1	0-0	.967	0	190	166	/C-8	-0.1
Total	5	116	259	9	59	5	0	2	18	19-3	1	45	.228	.282	.270	59	-15	0-2	.991	-4	107	113	/C-98	-1.8
SULLIVAN, JOE Joseph Daniel B 1.6.1870 Charlestown, MA D 11.2.1897 Charlestown, MA 5-10/178# d4.27																								
1893	Was N	128	508	72	134	16	13	2	64	36	8	24	.264	.322	.358	83	-14	7	.860	-29	91	56	*S-128	-3.0
1894	Was N	17	60	7	15	3	0	0	5	6	4	2	.250	.357	.300	62	-3	3	.900	-2	106	24	/2-8,S-6,3O(RF)	-0.4
	Phi N	77	312	65	110	10	8	3	63	24	5	10	.353	.408	.465	112	6	12	.886	-18	85	99	S-77	-0.6
	Year	94	372	72	125	13	8	3	68	30	9	12	.336	.399	.438	104	3	15	.883	-20	84	96	S-83/2-8,3O(RF)	-1.0
1895	Phi N	94	373	75	126	7	3	2	50	24	11	20	.338	.395	.389	102	2	15	.879	-19	89	83	*S-89/O-6(3-2-1)	-1.1
1896	Phi N	48	191	45	48	5	3	2	24	18	10	12	.251	.347	.340	82	-4	9	.962	-3	51	0	O-45(8-37-0)/S-2,3	-0.8
	StL N	51	212	25	62	4	2	2	21	9	10	12	.292	.351	.358	91	-3	5	.955	-4	65	59	O-45(LF)/2-7,3	-0.9
	Year	99	403	70	110	9	5	4	45	27	20	24	.273	.349	.350	87	-7	14	.959	-7	58	30	O-90(53-37-0)/2-7,S-2,3-2	-1.7
Total	4	415	1656	289	495	45	29	11	227	117	48	80	.299	.362	.381	93	-16	51	.871	-75	88	75	S-302/O-97(56-39-2),2-15,3-3	-6.8
SULLIVAN, MARC Marc Cooper B 7.25.1958 Quincy, MA BR/TR 6-4/205# d10.1 f-Haywood																								
1982	Bos A	2	6	0	2	0	0	0	0	0-0	0	2	.333	.333	.333	79	0	0-0	1.000	1	0	166	/C-2	0.1
1984	Bos A	2	6	1	3	0	0	0	1	1-0	0	0	.500	.571	.500	191	1	0-0	.950	1	114	0	/C-2	0.2
1985	Bos A	32	69	10	12	2	0	2	3	6-0	0	15	.174	.240	.290	43	-6	0-0	.993	-2	140	105	C-32	-0.6
1986	Bos A	41	119	15	23	4	0	1	14	7-0	4	32	.193	.260	.252	40	-10	0-0	.986	-7	102	59	C-41	-1.5
1987	Bos A	60	160	11	27	5	0	2	10	4-0	2	43	.169	.198	.237	15	-20	0-0	.994	-3	109	140	C-60	-2.0
Total	5	137	360	37	67	11	0	5	28	18-0	6	92	.186	.236	.258	33	-35	0-0	.990	-10	112	105	C-137	-3.8
SULLIVAN, MARTY Martin C. B 10.20.1862 Lowell, MA D 1.6.1894 Lowell, MA BR/TR d4.30																								
1887	Chi N	115	472	98	134	13	16	7	77	36	4	53	.284	.340	.424	98	-4	35	.847	-9	47	0	*O-115(111-3-1)/P	-1.4
1888	Chi N	75	314	40	74	12	6	7	39	15	1	32	.236	.273	.379	99	-2	9	.927	3	102	272	O-75(74-1-0)	-0.1
1889	Ind N	69	256	45	73	11	3	4	35	50	1	31	.285	.404	.398	122	10	15	.910	-6	74	176	O-64(0-63-1)/1-5	0.1
1890	Bos N	121	505	82	144	19	7	6	61	56	0	48	.285	.357	.386	108	4	33	.951	4	64	26	*O-120(LF)/3	0.4
1891	Bos N	17	67	15	15	1	0	2	7	5	1	3	.224	.288	.328	71	-3	7	.926	-1	43	0	O-17(LF)	-0.4
	Cle N	1	4	0	1	0	0	0	1	0	0	1	.250	.250	.250	44	0	0	—	0	0	0	/O(RF)	0.0
	Year	18	71	15	16	1	0	2	8	5	1	4	.225	.286	.324	69	-3	7	.926	-1	43	0	O-18(17-0-1)	-0.4
Total	5	398	1618	280	441	56	32	26	220	162	7	168	.273	.341	.395	104	5	99	.909	-9	67	89	O-392(322-67-3)/1-5,3P	-1.4
SULLIVAN, MIKE Michael Joseph B 6.10.1860 Webster, MA D 6.16.1929 Webster, MA BR/TR 5-8.5/165# d4.26																								
1888	Phi AA	28	112	20	31	5	6	1	19	3	0		.277	.296	.455	140	4	10	.742	-7	36	0	O-18(16-0-2),3-10	-0.3
SULLIVAN, PAT Patrick J. B 12.22.1862 Milwaukee, WI TR 5-11/165# d8.30																								
1884	KC U	31	114	15	22	3	1	0		4			.193	.220	.237	44	-11		.767	1	108	231	3-21/O-9(1-8-0),CP	-0.8
SULLIVAN, RUSS Russell Guy B 2.19.1923 Fredericksburg, VA BL/TR 6/196# d9.8																								
1951	Det A	7	26	2	5	1	0	1	1	2	0	1	.192	.250	.346	60	-2	0-0	.938	0	91	187	/O-7(6-0-1)	-0.2
1952	Det A	15	52	7	17	2	1	3	5	3	1	5	.327	.375	.577	161	4	1-0	.826	-1	75	227	O-14(6-0-9)	0.2
1953	Det A	23	72	7	18	5	1	1	6	13	2	5	.250	.379	.389	109	2	0-0	.958	2	98	261	O-20(LF)	0.2
Total	3	45	150	16	40	8	2	5	12	18	3	11	.267	.357	.447	118	4	1-0	.920	1	90	238	/O-41(32-0-10)	0.2
SULLIVAN, SUTER Suter G. B 10.14.1872 Baltimore, MD D 4.19.1925 Baltimore, MD 6/170# d7.24 OF Total (1-LF 30-RF)																								
1898	StL N	42	144	10	32	3	0	0	12	13	3		.222	.300	.243	55	-8	1	.875	-10	78	59	S-23,O-10(RF)/2-6,1P	-1.6
1899	Cle N	127	473	37	116	16	3	0	55	25	10		.245	.297	.292	67	-21	16	.938	12	115	118	*3-101,O-20(1-0-20)/S-3,1-3,2-2	-0.8
Total	2	169	617	47	148	19	3	0	67	38	13		.240	.298	.280	64	-29	17	.938	2	115	118	3-101/O-30R,S-26,2-8,1-4,P	-2.4
SULLIVAN, TOM Thomas Brandon B 12.19.1906 Nome, AK D 8.16.1944 Seattle, WA BR/TR 6/190# d6.14																								
1925	Cin N	1	1	0	0	0	0	0	0	0	0	0	.000	.000	.000	-99	0	0-0	1.000	-0	0	0	/C	0.0
SULLIVAN, SLEEPER Thomas Jefferson "Old Iron Hands" B 1850 , Ireland D 10.13.1909 St.Louis, MO BR/TR ?/175# d5.3																								
1881	Buf N	35	121	13	23	4	0	0	15	1		21	.190	.197	.223	32	-9		.853	-11			C-31/O-5(0-2-4)	-1.9
1882	StL AA	51	188	24	34	3	3	0		3			.181	.194	.229	40	-12		.840	-18			C-51	-2.4
1883	StL AA	8	27	2	6	0	1	0		0			.222	.222	.296	62	-1		.939	3			/C-6,O-2(0-1-1)	0.2
	Lou AA	1	2	0	0	0	0	0		0			.000	.000	.000	-99	0		.667	-0			/C	-0.1
	Year	9	29	2	6	0	1	0		0			.207	.207	.276	52	-2		.923	3			/C-7,O-2(0-1-1)	0.1
1884	StL U	2	9	0	1	0	0	0		0			.111	.111	.111	-31	-2		—	-1	0	0	/O(RF)CP	-0.1
Total	4	97	347	39	64	7	4	0	15	4		21	.184	.194	.228	36	-24		.851	-27			/C-90,O-8(0-3-6),P	-4.3
SULLIVAN, TED Timothy Paul B 1851 County Clare, Ireland D 7.5.1929 Washington, DC d9.9 M3 U2																								
1884	KC U	3	9	0	3	0	0	0		1			.333	.400	.333	143	0		1.000	-1	0	0	/O-2(RF),SM	-0.1
SULLIVAN, BILL William B 7.4.1853 Holyoke, MA D 11.13.1884 Holyoke, MA d8.9																								
1878	Chi N	2	6	1	1	0	0	0	0	0		0	.167	.167	.167	9	-1		1.000	-0	0	0	/O-2(LF)	-0.1
SULLIVAN, BILLY William Joseph Jr. B 10.23.1910 Chicago, IL D 1.4.1994 Sarasota, FL BL/TR 6/170# d6.9 Mil 1944-46 f-Billy OF Total (33-LF 33-RF)																								
1931	Chi A	92	363	48	100	16	5	2	33	20	1	14	.275	.315	.364	83	-10	4-4	.912	-6	97	58	3-83/O-2(RF),1	-1.3
1932	Chi A	93	307	31	97	16	1	1	45	20	0	9	.316	.358	.384	99	-1	1-3	.990	-2	114	95	1-52,3-17/C-5,O-3(1-0-2)	-0.7

Year	Tm Lg	G	AB	R	H	2B	3B	HR	RBI	BB-IB	HP	SO	AVG	OBP	SLG	AOPS	ABR	SB-CS	FA	FR	Rng	Thr	G at Pos	BFW
1933	Chi A	54	125	9	24	0	1	0	13	10	0	5	.192	.252	.208	24	-14	0-0	.982	-3	108	138	1-22/C-8	-1.8
1935	Cin N	85	241	29	64	9	4	2	36	19	2	16	.266	.324	.361	87	-5	4	.992	3	135	125	1-40,3-15/2-6	-0.4
1936	Cle A	93	319	39	112	32	6	2	48	16	0	9	.351	.382	.508	117	8	5-2	.968	-1	*96*	*117*	C-72/3-5,1-3,O(1-0-1)	1.1
1937	Cle A	72	168	26	48	12	3	3	22	17	1	7	.286	.355	.446	100	0	1-4	.949	-5	*81*	*116*	C-38/1-5,3	-0.4
1938	StL A	111	375	35	104	16	1	7	49	20	1	10	.277	.316	.381	74	-17	8-5	**.990**	0	*77*	***123***	C-99/1-6	-1.0
1939	StL A	118	332	53	96	17	5	5	50	34	4	18	.289	.362	.416	96	-2	3-3	.954	1	104	152	O-59(31-0-28),C-19/1-4	-0.4
1940	†Det A	78	220	36	68	14	4	3	41	31	2	11	.309	.399	.450	109	4	2-0	.976	3	*104*	*99*	C-57/3-6	1.0
1941	Det A	85	234	29	66	15	1	3	29	35	0	11	.282	.375	.393	94	-1	0-3	.976	3	*90*	*77*	C-63	0.5
1942	Bro N	43	101	11	27	2	1	1	14	12	0	6	.267	.345	.337	98	0	1	.962	0	*153*	*77*	C-41	0.2
1947	Pit N	38	55	1	14	3	0	0	8	6	0	3	.255	.328	.309	68	-2	1	1.000	0	*93*	*90*	C-12	-0.1
Total	12	962	2840	347	820	152	32	29	388	240	11	119	.289	.346	.395	91	-40	30-24	.972	-7	*94*	*102*	C-414,1-133,3-127/O-65L,2-6	-3.3

SULLIVAN, BILLY William Joseph Sr. B 2.1.1875 Oakland, WI D 1.28.1965 Newberg, OR BR/TR 5-9/155# d9.13 M1 s-Billy

Year	Tm Lg	G	AB	R	H	2B	3B	HR	RBI	BB-IB	HP	SO	AVG	OBP	SLG	AOPS	ABR	SB-CS	FA	FR	Rng	Thr	G at Pos	BFW
1899	Bos N	22	74	10	20	2	0	2	12	1	3		.270	.308	.378	80	-2	2	.952	4	*120*	*87*	C-22	0.3
1900	Bos N	72	238	36	65	6	0	8	41	9	1		.273	.302	.399	83	-7	4	.974	4	*101*	*85*	C-66/S2	0.2
1901	Chi A	98	367	54	90	15	6	4	56	10	3		.245	.271	.351	74	-15	12	**.967**	5	***110***	*98*	C-97/3	0.0
1902	Chi A	76	263	36	64	12	3	1	26	6	3		.243	.268	.323	66	-13	11	.967	4	*121*	*106*	C-70/1-2,O-2(1-0-1)	-0.2
1903	Chi A	32	111	10	21	4	0	1	7	5	0		.189	.224	.252	45	-7	3	.988	-1	*108*	*104*	C-31	-0.5
1904	Chi A	108	371	29	85	18	4	1	44	12	1		.229	.255	.307	81	-9	11	.964	6	*128*	*107*	*C-107	0.9
1905	Chi A	98	323	25	65	10	3	2	26	13	3		.201	.239	.269	64	-14	14	.974	3	***127***	*94*	C-92/1-2,3	-0.3
1906	†Chi A	118	387	37	83	18	4	2	33	22	3		.214	.262	.297	77	-11	10	**.974**	6	***145***	*92*	*C-118	0.7
1907	Chi A	112	329	30	59	8	4	0	36	21	3		.179	.235	.228	49	-19	6	.983	2	***118***	*92*	*C-108/2	-0.8
1908	Chi A	137	430	40	82	8	4	0	29	22	3		.191	.235	.228	51	-24	15	**.985**	-12	*109*	*97*	*C-137	-2.7
1909	Chi A	97	265	11	43	3	0	0	16	17	5		.162	.226	.174	28	-22	9	.983	1	*96*	*98*	C-97,M	-1.3
1910	Chi A	45	142	10	26	4	1	0	6	7	1		.183	.227	.225	43	-10	0	.976	9	*130*	*92*	C-45	0.4
1911	Chi A	89	256	26	55	9	3	0	31	16	2		.215	.266	.273	52	-17	1	**.986**	7	***147***	*91*	C-89	-0.3
1912	Chi A	41	91	9	19	2	1	0	15	9	1		.209	.287	.253	57	-5	0	.975	1	*97*	*105*	C-41	-0.1
1914	Chi A	1	0	0	0	0	0	0	0	0	0	0	—	—	—	—	0	0	1.000	-0	*0*	*0*	/C	0.0
1916	Det A	1	0	0	0	0	0	0	0	0	0	0	—	—	—	—	0	0	—	-0	0	0	/C	0.0
Total	16	1147	3647	363	777	119	33	21	378	170	32	0	.213	.254	.281	63	-175	98	.976	39	*120*	*96*	*C-1122/1-4,O-2(1-0-1),3-2,2-2,S	-3.7

SUMMA, HOMER Homer Wayne B 11.3.1898 Gentry, MO D 1.29.1966 Los Angeles, CA BL/TR 5-10.5/170# d9.13

Year	Tm Lg	G	AB	R	H	2B	3B	HR	RBI	BB-IB	HP	SO	AVG	OBP	SLG	AOPS	ABR	SB-CS	FA	FR	Rng	Thr	G at Pos	BFW
1920	Pit N	10	22	1	7	1	1	0	1	3	0	1	.318	.400	.455	141	1	1-0	.950	0	112	110	/O-6(1-5-0)	0.2
1922	Cle A	12	46	9	16	3	3	1	6	1	3	1	.348	.400	.609	159	4	1-2	1.000	1	78	271	O-12(RF)	0.3
1923	Cle A	137	525	92	172	27	6	3	69	33	6	20	.328	.374	.419	109	6	9-13	.951	-12	81	84	*O-136(0-3-133)	-1.9
1924	Cle A	111	390	55	113	21	6	2	38	11	1	16	.290	.311	.390	79	-15	4-2	.941	-3	101	81	O-95(0-3-92)	-2.3
1925	Cle A	75	224	28	74	10	1	0	25	13	3	6	.330	.375	.384	92	-2	3-2	.966	-5	94	42	O-54(18-1-35)/3-2	-1.0
1926	Cle A	**154**	581	74	179	31	6	4	76	47	8	9	.308	.368	.403	100	0	15-8	.975	6	109	102	*O-154(RF)	-0.6
1927	Cle A	145	574	72	164	41	7	4	74	32	7	18	.286	.331	.402	89	-11	6-5	.955	-9	89	78	*O-145(0-1-144)	-3.0
1928	Cle A	134	504	60	143	26	3	3	57	20	6	15	.284	.319	.365	78	-17	4-2	.971	-6	90	88	*O-132(RF)	-3.3
1929	†Phi A	37	81	12	22	4	0	0	10	2	1	1	.272	.298	.321	57	-5	1-1	.980	1	126	53	O-24(18-0-16)	-0.5
1930	Phi A	25	54	10	15	2	1	1	5	4	1	1	.278	.339	.407	85	-1	0-0	.938	0	117	87	O-15(3-0-12)	-0.2
Total	10	840	3001	413	905	166	34	18	361	166	36	88	.302	.346	.398	92	-40	44-35	.961	-27	95	87	O-773(40-13-730)/3-2	-12.3

SUMMERS, CHAMP John Junior B 6.15.1946 Bremerton, WA BL/TR 6-2/205# d5.4 C2

Year	Tm Lg	G	AB	R	H	2B	3B	HR	RBI	BB-IB	HP	SO	AVG	OBP	SLG	AOPS	ABR	SB-CS	FA	FR	Rng	Thr	G at Pos	BFW
1974	Oak A	20	24	2	3	1	0	0	3	1-0	0	5	.125	.160	.167	-6	-3	0-0	1.000	-1	78	0	O-12(8-0-4)/D-2	-0.4
1975	Chi N	76	91	14	21	5	1	1	16	10-0	1	13	.231	.311	.341	78	-3	0-0	.889	-2	80	0	O-18(15-0-3)	-0.5
1976	Chi N	83	126	11	26	2	0	3	13	13-1	1	31	.206	.284	.294	59	-7	1-0	.964	-1	87	90	O-26(19-0-7),1-10/C	-1.0
1977	Cin N	59	76	11	13	4	0	3	6	6-1	1	16	.171	.238	.342	53	-5	0-0	1.000	1	113	127	O-16(3-0-13)/3	-0.5
1978	Cin N	13	35	4	9	2	0	1	3	7-1	0	4	.257	.381	.400	118	1	2-1	.933	-2	67	0	O-12(RF)	-0.2
1979	Cin N	27	60	10	12	2	1	1	11	13-0	1	15	.200	.351	.317	83	-1	0-1	.941	-1	74	119	O-13(4-0-9)/1-6	-0.3
	Det A	90	246	47	77	12	1	20	51	40-4	3	33	.313	.414	.614	168	24	7-6	.989	-8	75	70	O-69(2-0-67),D-10/1-4	1.2
1980	Det A	120	347	61	103	19	1	17	60	52-6	5	52	.297	.393	.504	142	22	4-3	.953	-5	81	37	D-64,O-47(21-0-26)/1	1.3
1981	Det A	64	165	16	42	8	0	3	21	19-3	3	35	.255	.339	.358	98	0	1-1	.964	-1	92	99	D-37,O-18(RF)	-0.2
1982	SF N	70	125	15	31	5	0	4	19	16-0	3	17	.248	.342	.384	105	1	0-1	.913	-3	74	89	O-31(30-0-1)/1-3	-0.4
1983	SF N	29	22	3	3	0	0	0	3	7-0	0	8	.136	.333	.136	39	-1	0-0	1.000	0	179	0	/O(LF)	-0.1
1984	†SD N	47	54	5	10	3	0	1	12	4-1	1	15	.185	.254	.296	54	-3	0-0	1.000	-1	30	196	/1-8	-0.5
Total	11	698	1371	199	350	63	4	54	218	188-17	19	244	.255	.350	.425	111	25	15-13	.959	-22	80	67	O-263(103-0-160),D-113/1-32,3C	-1.6

SUMMERS, KID William B Toronto, ON, CAN D 10.16.1895 Toronto, ON, CAN TR 5-10/169# d8.5

Year	Tm Lg	G	AB	R	H	2B	3B	HR	RBI	BB-IB	HP	SO	AVG	OBP	SLG	AOPS	ABR	SB-CS	FA	FR	Rng	Thr	G at Pos	BFW
1893	StL N	2	1	1	0	0	0	0	0	0	1	0	.000	.500	.000	37	0	0	.500	-1	0	0	/O(LF)C	0.0

SUMNER, CARL Carl Ringdahl "Lefty" B 9.28.1908 Cambridge, MA D 2.8.1999 Chatham, MA BL/TL 5-8/170# d7.28

Year	Tm Lg	G	AB	R	H	2B	3B	HR	RBI	BB-IB	HP	SO	AVG	OBP	SLG	AOPS	ABR	SB-CS	FA	FR	Rng	Thr	G at Pos	BFW
1928	Bos A	16	29	6	8	1	1	0	3	5	0	6	.276	.382	.379	103	0	0-0	.923	-1	86	0	O-10(5-4-1)	-0.1

SUNDAY, ART Arthur (born August Hawker) B 1.21.1862 Springfield, IL D 10.2.1926 Reno, NV BL/TL 5-9/193# d5.5

Year	Tm Lg	G	AB	R	H	2B	3B	HR	RBI	BB-IB	HP	SO	AVG	OBP	SLG	AOPS	ABR	SB-CS	FA	FR	Rng	Thr	G at Pos	BFW
1890	Bro P	24	83	26	22	5	1	0	13	15	7	9	.265	.419	.349	100	1	0	.909	-3	57	0	O-24(0-5-20)	-0.1

SUNDAY, BILLY William Ashley "Parson" or "The Evangelist" B 11.19.1862 Ames, IA D 11.6.1935 Chicago, IL BL/TR 5-10/160# d5.22

Year	Tm Lg	G	AB	R	H	2B	3B	HR	RBI	BB-IB	HP	SO	AVG	OBP	SLG	AOPS	ABR	SB-CS	FA	FR	Rng	Thr	G at Pos	BFW
1883	Chi N	14	54	6	13	4	0	0	5	1		18	.241	.255	.315	66	-2		.647	-3	43	0	O-14(1-0-13)	-0.5
1884	Chi N	43	176	25	39	4	1	4	28	4		36	.222	.239	.324	70	-7		.663	-9	94	72	O-43(0-9-34)	-1.5
1885	†Chi N	46	172	36	44	3	3	2	20	12		33	.256	.304	.343	96	-2		.825	-5	81	222	O-46(1-4-43)	-0.7
1886	Chi N	28	103	16	25	2	2	0	6	7		26	.243	.291	.301	70	-4	10	.914	-1	49	0	O-28(1-0-27)	-0.5
1887	Chi N	50	199	41	58	6	6	3	32	21	1	20	.291	.362	.427	105	0	34	.766	-10	42	119	O-50(2-23-25)	-0.9
1888	Pit N	120	505	69	119	14	3	0	15	12	2	36	.236	.256	.275	76	-13	71	.939	15	133	125	*O-120(1-117-3)	-0.2
1889	Pit N	81	321	62	77	10	6	2	25	27	4	33	.240	.307	.327	85	-7	47	.946	8	110	73	O-81(1-0-80)	0.0
1890	Pit N	86	358	58	92	9	2	1	33	32	5	20	.257	.327	.302	94	-1	56	.883	8	150	217	O-86(0-51-35)/P	0.5
	Phi N	31	119	26	31	3	1	0	6	18	2	7	.261	.367	.303	93	0	28	.950	2	129	174	O-31(CF)	0.1
	Year	117	477	84	123	12	3	1	39	50	7	27	.258	.337	.302	94	-1	84	.900	10	145	**206**	*O-117(0-82-35)/P	0.6
Total	8	499	2007	339	498	55	24	12	170	134	14	229	.248	.300	.317	86	-36	246	.883	4	108	129	O-499(7-235-260)/P	-3.7

SUNDBERG, JIM James Howard B 5.18.1951 Galesburg, IL BR/TR 6/195# d4.4

Year	Tm Lg	G	AB	R	H	2B	3B	HR	RBI	BB-IB	HP	SO	AVG	OBP	SLG	AOPS	ABR	SB-CS	FA	FR	Rng	Thr	G at Pos	BFW
1974	Tex A☆	132	368	45	91	13	3	3	36	62-0	0	61	.247	.354	.323	99	2	2-4	.990	6	114	93	*C-132	1.3
1975	Tex A	155	472	45	94	9	0	6	36	51-0	4	77	.199	.283	.256	54	-29	3-1	.981	10	135	104	*C-155	-1.2
1976	Tex A	140	448	33	102	24	2	3	34	37-0	0	61	.228	.285	.310	73	-15	0-0	**.991**	**20**	127	112	*C-140	1.2
1977	Tex A	149	453	61	132	20	3	6	65	53-0	2	77	.291	.365	.389	105	5	2-3	**.994**	**32**	**197**	100	*C-149	4.2
1978	Tex A★	149	518	54	144	23	6	6	58	64-6	3	70	.278	.358	.380	108	8	2-5	**.997**	17	118	126	*C-148/D	3.1
1979	Tex A	150	495	50	136	23	4	5	64	51-5	5	51	.275	.345	.368	94	-3	3-3	**.995**	15	127	100	*C-150	1.8
1980	Tex A	151	505	59	138	24	1	10	63	64-3	1	67	.273	.353	.384	106	6	2-2	.993	-1	92	104	*C-151	1.2
1981	Tex A	102	339	42	94	17	2	3	28	50-6	1	48	.277	.369	.366	120	11	2-5	.996	3	146	107	C-98/O-2(LF)	1.8
1982	Tex A	139	470	37	118	22	5	10	47	49-2	1	57	.251	.322	.383	98	-1	2-6	.991	3	104	113	*C-132/O(LF)	0.6
1983	Tex A	131	378	30	76	14	0	2	28	35-0	2	64	.201	.272	.254	47	-27	0-4	.993	4	101	**132**	*C-131	-2.0
1984	Mil A★	110	348	43	91	19	4	7	43	38-2	0	63	.261	.332	.399	106	3	1-1	**.995**	12	142	129	*C-109	1.9
1985	†KC A	115	367	38	90	12	4	10	35	33-3	1	67	.245	.308	.381	88	-7	0-2	.992	2	114	73	*C-112	-0.1
1986	KC A	140	429	41	91	9	1	12	42	57-1	0	91	.212	.303	.322	69	-18	1-1	**.995**	-1	118	102	*C-134	-1.4
1987	Chi N	61	139	9	28	2	0	4	15	19-3	2	40	.201	.306	.302	60	-8	0-0	.994	4	90	108	C-57	-0.2
1988	Chi N	24	54	8	13	1	0	2	9	8-0	0	15	.241	.333	.370	99	0	0-0	1.000	-2	99	116	C-20	-0.1
	Tex A	38	91	13	26	4	0	4	13	5-0	0	17	.286	.323	.462	114	1	0-0	1.000	-4	95	76	C-36	-0.1
1989	Tex A	76	147	13	29	7	1	2	8	23-0	0	37	.197	.304	.299	70	-5	0-0	.992	-1	107	127	C-73/D	-0.3
Total	16	1962	6021	621	1493	243	36	95	624	699-31	22	963	.248	.327	.348	89	-77	20-37	.993	120	123	108	*C-1927/O-3(LF),D-2	11.7

SURHOFF, B.J. William James B 8.4.1964 Bronx, NY BL/TR 6-1/200# d4.8 b-Rich OF Total (824-LF 5-CF 40-RF)

Year	Tm Lg	G	AB	R	H	2B	3B	HR	RBI	BB-IB	HP	SO	AVG	OBP	SLG	AOPS	ABR	SB-CS	FA	FR	Rng	Thr	G at Pos	BFW
1987	Mil A	115	395	50	118	22	3	7	68	36-1	0	30	.299	.350	.423	103	2	11-10	.984	8	105	116	C-98,3-10/1D	1.3
1988	Mil A	139	493	47	121	21	0	5	38	31-9	3	49	.245	.292	.318	71	-19	21-6	.990	0	113	89	*C-106,3-31/1-2,SO(LF)	-1.1
1989	Mil A	126	436	42	108	17	4	5	55	25-1	3	29	.248	.287	.339	79	-14	14-12	.985	-4	84	88	*C-106,D-12/3-6	-1.3
1990	Mil A	135	474	55	131	21	4	6	59	41-5	1	37	.276	.331	.376	99	-1	18-7	.985	-5	84	78	*C-125,3-11	0.3

Year	Tm Lg	G	AB	R	H	2B	3B	HR	RBI	BB-IB	HP	SO	AVG	OBP	SLG	AOPS	ABR	SB-CS	FA	FR	Rng	Thr	G at Pos	BFW
1991	Mil A	143	505	57	146	19	4	5	68	26-2	0	33	.289	.319	.372	94	-5	5-8	.995	0	88	91	*C-127/3-5,O-2(0-1-1),2D	0.1
1992	Mil A	139	480	63	121	19	1	4	62	46-8	2	41	.252	.314	.321	82	-11	14-8	.990	13	122	107	*C-109,1-17/O-7(5-1-1),3-3,D-9	0.7
1993	Mil A	148	552	66	151	38	3	7	79	36-5	2	47	.274	.318	.391	92	-7	12-9	.949	-2	100	92	*3-121,O-24(12-0-14)/1-8,C-3,D	-0.9
1994	Mil A	40	134	20	35	11	2	5	22	16-0	0	14	.261	.336	.485	105	1	0-1	.923	-9	53	0	3-18,C-12/1-8,O-3(RF),D	-0.8
1995	Mil A	117	415	72	133	26	3	13	73	37-4	4	43	.320	.378	.492	118	12	7-3	.993	6	107	232	O-60(54-3-9),1-55,C-18/D-3	1.2
1996	†Bal A	143	537	74	157	27	6	21	82	47-8	3	79	.292	.352	.482	109	6	0-1	.948	-7	90	118	*3-106,O-27(LF),D-10/1-2	-0.2
1997	†Bal A	147	528	80	150	30	4	18	88	49-14	5	60	.284	.345	.458	112	9	1-1	.992	4	99	136	*O-133(LF)/1-3,3-3,D-9	0.7
1998	Bal A	**162**	573	79	160	34	1	22	92	49-9	1	81	.279	.332	.457	106	4	9-7	.989	-4	87	137	*O-157(LF)/1	-0.6
1999	Bal A★	**162**	673	104	207	38	1	28	107	43-1	2	78	.308	.347	.492	116	14	5-1	**1.000**	7	96	171	*O-148(LF),D-13/3-2	1.4
2000	Bal A	103	411	56	120	27	0	13	57	29-3	2	46	.292	.341	.453	104	2	7-2	.987	4	107	83	*O-102(LF)/D	0.2
	†Atl N	44	128	13	37	9	2	1	11	12-0	1	12	.289	.352	.414	93	-1	3-0	1.000	-2	87	52	O-32(LF)	-0.3
2001	†Atl N	141	484	68	131	33	1	10	58	38-5	1	48	.271	.321	.405	85	-10	9-3	.986	-3	91	99	*O-129(LF)/D-3	-1.7
2002	Atl N	25	75	5	22	5	0	0	9	9-0	0	5	.293	.369	.360	96	0	1-3	1.000	3	105	140	1-11/O-9(RF)	0.0
2003	Bal A	93	319	32	94	20	0	5	41	29-3	1	29	.295	.353	.404	104	3	2-2	.978	-4	80	0	D-39,O-27(24-0-3),1-22	-0.7
Total	17	2122	7612	983	2142	417	39	175	1069	599-78	31	761	.281	.332	.415	99	-15	139-84	.990	4	95	129	O-861L,C-704,3-316,1-130,D/2S	-1.7
SUSCE, GEORGE George Cyril Methodius "Good Kid" B 8.13.1907 Pittsburgh, PA D 2.25.1986 Sarasota, FL BR/TR 5-11.5/200# d4.23 C29 s-George																								
1929	Phi N	17	17	5	5	3	0	1	1	1	1	2	.294	.368	.647	137	1	0	.900	-2	82	0	C-11	0.0
1932	Det A	2	0	0	0	0	0	0	0	0	0	0	—	—	—	—	0	0-0	1.000	-0	0	0	/C-2	0.0
1939	Pit N	31	75	8	17	3	1	1	4	12	0	5	.227	.333	.333	81	-2	0	.984	1	111	92	C-31	0.1
1940	StL A	61	113	6	24	4	0	0	13	9	2	9	.212	.282	.248	38	-10	1-0	.984	1	111	84	C-61	-0.6
1941	Cle A	1	0	0	0	0	0	0	0	0	0	0	—	—	—	—	0	0-0	1.000	-0	0	0	/C	0.0
1942	Cle A	2	1	1	1	0	0	0	0	1	0	0	1.000	1.000	1.000	492	1	0-0	1.000	-0	0	0	/C-2	0.1
1943	Cle A	3	1	0	0	0	0	0	0	0	0	0	.000	.000	.000	-99	0	0-0	1.000	-0	0	838	/C-3	0.0
1944	Cle A	29	61	3	14	1	0	0	4	2	0	5	.230	.254	.246	45	-5	0-0	.948	-0	103	121	C-29	-0.4
Total	8	146	268	23	61	11	1	2	22	25	3	21	.228	.301	.299	60	-15	1-0	.974	0	107	93	C-140	-0.8
SUSKO, PETE Peter Jonathan B 7.2.1904 Laura, OH D 5.22.1978 Jacksonville, FL BL/TL 5-11/172# d8.1																								
1934	Was A	58	224	25	64	5	3	2	25	18	1	10	.286	.342	.362	85	-6	3-4	.988	3	129	112	1-58	-0.9
SUTCLIFFE, BUTCH Charles Inigo B 7.22.1915 Fall River, MA D 3.2.1994 Fall River, MA BR/TR 5-8.5/165# d8.28																								
1938	Bos N	4	4	1	1	0	0	0	2	2	0	1	.250	.500	.250	124	0	0	.800	-0	0	0	/C-3	0.0
SUTCLIFFE, SY Elmer Ellsworth B 4.15.1862 Wheaton, IL D 2.13.1893 Wheaton, IL BL/TL 6-2/170# d10.2 OF Total (10-LF 5-CF 43-RF)																								
1884	Chi N	4	15	4	3	1	0	0	2	2		4	.200	.294	.267	72	0		.976	1			/C-4	0.1
1885	Chi N	11	43	5	8	1	1	0	4	2		5	.186	.222	.256	48	-3		.838	-4			C-11/O(RF)	-0.5
	StL N	16	49	2	6	1	0	0	4	5		10	.122	.204	.143	15	-4		.881	-3			C-14/O-2(RF)	-0.6
	Year	27	92	7	14	2	1	0	8	7		15	.152	.212	.196	32	-7		.862	-7			C-25/O-3(RF)	-1.1
1888	Det N	49	191	17	49	5	3	0	23	5	0	14	.257	.276	.314	87	-3	6	.901	3	111	85	S-24,C-14/1-5,O-4(RF),2-2	0.1
1889	Cle N	46	161	17	40	3	2	1	21	14	0	6	.248	.309	.311	75	-6	5	.892	6			C-37/1-8,O(RF)	0.3
1890	Cle P	99	386	62	127	14	8	2	60	33	0	16	.329	.382	.422	125	14	10	.883	-19	70	124	C-84,O-15(1-0-14)/S-4,3-2	0.2
1891	Was AA	53	201	29	71	8	3	2	33	17	2	17	.353	.409	.453	154	14	8	.918	-4	107	71	O-35(9-5-21),C-22/S-3,3	1.0
1892	Bal N	66	276	41	77	10	7	1	27	14	1	15	.279	.316	.377	106	0	12	.958	-7	71	92	1-66	-0.6
Total	7	344	1322	177	381	43	24	6	174	92	3	87	.288	.336	.371	107	12	41	.887	-25	39	68	C-186/1-79,O-58R,S-31,3-3,2-2	0.0
SUTHERLAND, GARY Gary Lynn B 9.27.1944 Glendale, CA BR/TR 6/185# d9.17 b-Darrell OF Total (31-LF 6-RF)																								
1966	Phi N	3	3	0	0	0	0	0	0	0-0	0	0	.000	.000	.000	-99	-1	0-0	1.000	0	141	373	/S	0.0
1967	Phi N	103	231	23	57	12	1	1	19	17-5	0	22	.247	.298	.320	76	-7	0-3	.928	-7	85	134	S-66,O-25(LF)	-1.3
1968	Phi N	67	138	16	38	7	0	0	15	8-0	0	15	.275	.313	.326	93	-1	0-0	.968	0	107	79	2-17,S-10,3-10/O-7(2-0-5)	0.0
1969	Mon N	141	544	63	130	26	1	3	35	37-5	2	31	.239	.289	.307	67	-24	5-7	.971	11	101	**114**	*2-139,S-15/O(RF)	-0.6
1970	Mon N	116	359	37	74	10	0	3	26	31-1	2	22	.206	.271	.259	43	-29	2-2	.975	3	105	123	2-97,S-15/3	-2.1
1971	Mon N	111	304	25	78	7	2	4	26	18-3	2	12	.257	.302	.332	79	-9	3-4	.963	-1	108	121	2-56,S-46/O-4(LF),3-2	-0.3
1972	Hou N	5	8	0	1	0	0	0	1	0-0	0	0	.125	.125	.125	-29	-1	0-0	—	0	0	0	/23	-0.1
1973	Hou N	16	54	8	14	5	0	0	3	3-0	0	5	.259	.298	.352	80	-1	0-0	.971	-2	81	123	2-14/S	-0.3
1974	Det A	149	619	60	157	20	1	5	49	26-1	0	37	.254	.282	.313	69	-26	1-3	.976	-11	94	90	*2-147,S-10/3-4	-2.9
1975	Det A	129	503	51	130	12	3	6	39	45-3	3	41	.258	.321	.330	81	-12	0-2	.968	-3	98	91	*2-128	-0.8
1976	Det A	42	117	10	24	5	2	0	6	7-0	0	12	.205	.248	.282	53	-7	0-1	.984	5	112	125	2-42	0.0
	Mil A	59	115	9	25	2	0	1	9	8-2	1	7	.217	.268	.261	58	-6	0-2	.955	-0	96	101	2-45/1-2,D-8	-0.6
	Year	101	232	19	49	7	2	1	15	15-2	1	19	.211	.258	.272	56	-13	0-3	.970	4	105	114	2-87/D-8,1-2	-0.6
1977	SD N	80	103	5	25	3	0	1	11	7-0	0	15	.243	.291	.301	66	-5	0-0	.943	-3	98	100	2-30,3-21/1-4	-0.8
1978	StL N	10	6	1	1	0	0	0	0	0-0	0	0	.167	.167	.167	-7	-1	0-0	1.000	1	437	0	/2	0.0
Total	13	1031	3104	308	754	109	10	24	239	207-20	10	219	.243	.291	.308	69	-130	11-24	.971	-6	100	105	2-717,S-164/3-39,O-37L,D-8,1-6	-9.8
SUTHERLAND, LEO Leonardo (Cantin) B 4.6.1958 Santiago De Cuba, Cuba BL/TL 5-10/165# d8.11																								
1980	Chi A	34	89	9	23	3	0	0	5	1-1	0	11	.258	.264	.292	53	-6	4-1	.943	-1	110	0	O-23(16-7-0)	-0.7
1981	Chi A	11	12	6	2	0	0	0	0	3-0	0	1	.167	.333	.167	49	-1	2-1	1.000	-1	66	0	/O-7(4-4-0)	-0.2
Total	2	45	101	15	25	3	0	0	5	4-1	0	12	.248	.274	.277	53	-7	6-2	.949	-2	103	0	/O-30(20-11-0)	-0.9
SUTKO, GLENN Glenn Edward B 5.9.1968 Atlanta, GA BR/TR 6-3/225# d10.3																								
1990	Cin N	1	1	0	0	0	0	0	0	0-0	0	1	.000	.000	.000	-96	0	0-0	1.000	0	0	0	/C	0.0
1991	Cin N	10	10	0	1	0	0	0	1	2-0	0	6	.100	.250	.100	2	-1	0-0	.875	-1	61	265	/C-9	-0.2
Total	2	11	11	0	1	0	0	0	1	2-0	0	7	.091	.231	.091	-6	-1	0-0	.889	-1	54	236	/C-10	-0.2
SUTTON, EZRA Ezra Ballou B 9.17.1850 Palmyra, NY D 6.20.1907 Braintree, MA BR/TR 5-8.5/153# d5.4 OF NA (1-CF 2-RF) OF Total (29-LF 7-CF 30-RF)																								
1871	Cle NA	**29**	128	35	45	3	7	3	23	1		0	.352	.357	.555	166	11	3-1	**.795**	-0	89	89	*3-29/O-2(0-1-1),C	0.6
1872	Cle NA	**22**	107	30	30	6	1	0	10	1		1	.280	.287	.355	102	1	1-0	.718	-6	77	67	3-22	-0.4
1873	Ath NA	51	243	51	81	7	6	0	34	2		2	.333	.339	.412	113	2	2-3	.803	-1	103	53	*3-43/S-8,2-2	-0.1
1874	Ath NA	**55**	243	54	71	10	3	0	28	0		2	.292	.292	.358	99	-2	6-4	.827	0	87	97	3-36,S-20	-0.2
1875	Ath NA	75	358	83	116	11	7	1	59	1		3	.324	.326	.402	136	10	13-10	.803	13	**115**	**147**	*3-73/P-2,1-2,SO(RF)	1.7
1876	Phi N	54	236	45	70	12	7	1	31	3		2	.297	.305	.419	141	10		.915	-5	201	47	1-29,2-15/3-8,O-4(RF)	0.3
1877	Bos N	58	253	43	74	10	6	0	39	4		10	.292	.304	.379	110	2		.882	-11	78	106	S-36,3-22	-0.6
1878	Bos N	**60**	239	31	54	9	3	1	29	2		14	.226	.232	.301	69	-9		.888	-2	93	121	*3-59/S	-0.8
1879	Bos N	**84**	339	54	84	13	4	0	34	2		18	.248	.252	.310	82	-7		.884	-9	99	147	S-51,3-33	-1.1
1880	Bos N	76	288	41	72	9	2	0	25	7		7	.250	.268	.295	94	-2		.896	2	101	132	S-39,3-37	0.3
1881	Bos N	**83**	333	42	97	12	4	0	31	13		9	.291	.318	.351	116	6		.877	-1	99	82	*3-81/S-2	0.7
1882	Bos N	81	319	44	80	8	1	2	38	24		25	.251	.303	.301	94	-1		.856	-5	89	67	*3-77/S-4	-0.4
1883	Bos N	94	414	101	134	28	15	3	73	17		12	.324	.350	.486	147	22		.866	-0	83	131	*3-93/O(RF)S	2.0
1884	Bos N	110	468	102	**162**	28	7	3	61	29		22	.346	.384	.455	164	35		**.908**	-5	86	63	*3-110	2.8
1885	Bos N	110	457	78	143	23	8	4	47	17		25	.313	.338	.425	151	25		.875	3	93	150	*3-91,S-16/2-2,1	2.8
1886	Bos N	116	499	83	138	21	6	3	48	26		21	.277	.312	.361	107	4	18	.859	-9	55	71	O-43(20-7-16),S-28,3-28,2-18	-0.3
1887	Bos N	77	326	61	99	14	9	3	46	13	6	6	.304	.342	.429	112	4	17	.875	10	124	71	S-37,O-18(9-0-9),2-13,3-11	1.4
1888	Bos N	28	110	16	24	3	1	1	16	7	2	3	.218	.277	.291	79	-2	10	.859	-3	92	116	3-27/S	-0.5
Total	5 NA	232	1079	253	343	37	24	4	154	5	0	8	.318	.321	.408	122	22	25-18	.000	5	100	101	3-203/S-29,O-3R,1-2,P-2,2-2,C	1.6
Total	13	1031	4281	741	1231	190	73	21	518	164	8	174	.288	.315	.381	118	87	45-0	.871	-34	88	102	3-677,S-216/O-66R,2-48,1-30	6.6
SUTTON, LARRY Larry James B 5.14.1970 West Covina, CA BL/TL 5-11/175# d8.17																								
1997	KC A	27	69	9	20	2	0	2	8	5-0	0	12	.290	.338	.406	91	-1	0-0	1.000	0	99	105	1-12/O(LF)D	-0.2
1998	KC A	111	310	29	76	14	2	5	42	29-3	3	46	.245	.311	.352	71	-13	3-3	.987	-0	100	80	O-79(39-0-47)/1-6,D-3	-1.7
1999	KC A	43	102	14	23	6	0	2	15	13-0	0	17	.225	.308	.343	66	-5	1-0	.987	-1	97	88	1-30/O(RF)D	-0.8
2000	StL N	23	25	5	8	0	0	1	6	5-0	0	7	.320	.406	.440	121	1	0-0	1.000	0	101	89	/1-6,O-4(3-0-1)	0.1
2001	StL N	33	42	3	5	1	0	1	3	1-0	0	10	.119	.140	.214	-11	-7	0-0	1.000	1	214	108	1-11/O-3(RF)	-0.7
2002	Oak A	7	19	3	2	0	0	1	3	1-0	0	8	.105	.150	.263	7	-3	0-0	1.000	0	0	0	/1-6,O-3(2-0-1)	-0.3
Total	6	244	567	63	134	23	2	12	77	54-3	3	100	.236	.302	.347	67	-28	4-3	.988	-0	99	94	/O-91(45-0-53),1-71,D-11	-3.6
SUZUKI, ICHIRO Ichiro B 10.22.1973 Kasugai, Japan BL/TR 5-9/160# d4.2																								
2001	†Sea A★	157	692	127	**242**	34	8	8	69	30-10	8	53	**.350**	.381	.457	128	27	**56**-14	.997	7	113	80	*O-152(RF)/D-4	3.2

Year	Tm Lg	G	AB	R	H	2B	3B	HR	RBI	BB-IB	HP	SO	AVG	OBP	SLG	AOPS	ABR	SB-CS	FA	FR	Rng	Thr	G at Pos	BFW
2002	Sea A★	157	647	111	208	27	8	8	51	68-**27**	5	62	.321	.388	.425	121	21	31-15	.991	7	113	87	*O-152(0-3-150)/D-4	2.1
2003	Sea A★	159	679	111	212	29	8	13	62	36-7	6	69	.312	.352	.436	110	8	34-8	.994	9	109	135	*O-159(RF)	1.3
Total	3	473	2018	349	662	90	24	29	182	134-44	19	184	.328	.374	.440	120	56	121-37	.994	23	112	101	O-463(0-3-461)/D-8	6.6

SVEUM, DALE Dale Curtis B 11.23.1963 Richmond, CA BB/TR 6-3/185# d5.12 OF Total (LF)

Year	Tm Lg	G	AB	R	H	2B	3B	HR	RBI	BB-IB	HP	SO	AVG	OBP	SLG	AOPS	ABR	SB-CS	FA	FR	Rng	Thr	G at Pos	BFW
1986	Mil A	91	317	35	78	13	2	7	35	32-0	1	63	.246	.316	.366	83	-8	4-3	.865	-12	95	70	3-65,2-13,S-13	-1.8
1987	Mil A	153	535	86	135	27	3	25	95	40-4	1	133	.252	.303	.454	95	-5	2-6	.965	-20	88	96	*S-142,2-13	-1.1
1988	Mil A	129	467	41	113	14	4	9	51	21-0	1	122	.242	.274	.347	73	-19	1-0	.955	-2	99	**125**	*S-127/2D	-1.2
1990	Mil A	48	117	15	23	7	0	1	12	12-0	2	30	.197	.278	.282	59	-6	0-1	.918	-7	77	57	3-22,2-16/1-5,S-5	-1.4
1991	Mil A	90	266	33	64	19	1	4	43	32-0	1	78	.241	.320	.365	93	-2	2-4	.968	-5	104	92	S-51,3-38/2-2,D-3	-0.5
1992	Phi N	54	135	13	24	4	0	2	16	16-4	0	39	.178	.261	.252	47	-9	0-0	.948	5	109	105	S-34/3-5,1-4	-0.2
	Chi A	40	114	15	25	9	0	2	12	12-0	0	29	.219	.287	.351	81	-3	1-1	.944	-6	97	90	S-37/1-2,3-2	-0.7
1993	Oak A	30	79	12	14	2	1	2	6	16-1	0	21	.177	.316	.304	72	-3	0-0	.976	-5	53	95	1-14/3-7,2-4,SO(LF)D	-0.9
1994	Sea A	10	27	3	5	0	0	1	2	2-0	0	10	.185	.241	.296	37	-3	0-0	.909	2	181	0	/3-3,D-4	-0.1
1996	Pit N	12	34	9	12	5	0	1	5	6-0	0	6	.353	.450	.588	167	4	0-0	.913	-1	100	73	3-10	0.3
1997	Pit N	126	306	30	80	20	1	12	47	27-2	0	81	.261	.319	.451	98	-2	0-3	.941	1	107	58	3-47,S-28,1-21/2-2	-0.1
1998	NY A	30	58	6	9	0	0	0	3	4-0	0	16	.155	.203	.155	-3	-9	0-0	.975	-1	125	110	1-21/3-6,D-3	-1.1
1999	Pit N	49	71	7	15	5	1	3	13	7-1	0	28	.211	.278	.437	78	-3	0-0	.944	0	109	0	3-12/1-4,S-4,2-2,O(LF)	-0.2
Total	12	862	2526	305	597	125	13	69	340	227-12	6	656	.236	.298	.378	82	-68	10-18	.960	-51	97	105	S-442,3-217/1-71,2-53,D-13,O-2L	-9.0

SWACINA, HARRY Harry Joseph "Swats" B 8.22.1881 St.Louis, MO D 6.21.1944 Birmingham, AL BR/TR 6-2/190# d9.13

Year	Tm Lg	G	AB	R	H	2B	3B	HR	RBI	BB-IB	HP	SO	AVG	OBP	SLG	AOPS	ABR	SB-CS	FA	FR	Rng	Thr	G at Pos	BFW
1907	Pit N	26	95	9	19	1	1	0	10	4	1		.200	.240	.232	47	-6	1	.996	-1	76	73	1-26	-0.9
1908	Pit N	53	176	7	38	6	1	0	13	5	0		.216	.238	.261	59	-9	4	.983	-5	63	95	1-50	-1.7
1914	Bal F	158	617	70	173	26	8	0	90	14	1	23	.280	.297	.348	73	-34	15	.985	10	**128**	93	*1-158	-2.9
1915	Bal F	85	301	24	74	13	1	1	38	9	0	11	.246	.268	.306	59	-21	9	.986	6	137	111	1-75/2	-1.9
Total	4	322	1189	110	304	46	11	1	151	32	2	34	.256	.276	.315	66	-70	29	.986	10	115	96	1-309/2	-7.4

SWAN, ANDY Andrew J. d7.23

Year	Tm Lg	G	AB	R	H	2B	3B	HR	RBI	BB-IB	HP	SO	AVG	OBP	SLG	AOPS	ABR	SB-CS	FA	FR	Rng	Thr	G at Pos	BFW
1884	Was AA	5	21	3	3	1	0	0		0	0		.143	.143	.190	9	-2		.824	-2	0	0	/1-3,3-2	-0.4
	Ric AA	3	10	2	5	0	0	0		0	0		.500	.500	.500	230	1		1.000	-0	0	0	/1-3	0.1
	Year	8	31	5	8	1	0	0		0	0		.258	.258	.290	85	0		.902	-2	0	0	/1-6,3-2	-0.3

SWANDELL, MARTY John Martin (born Martin Schwendel) B 1841 Baden, Germany D 10.25.1906 Brooklyn, NY TL 5-10.5/146# d5.7 U1

Year	Tm Lg	G	AB	R	H	2B	3B	HR	RBI	BB-IB	HP	SO	AVG	OBP	SLG	AOPS	ABR	SB-CS	FA	FR	Rng	Thr	G at Pos	BFW
1872	Eck NA	14	52	8	12	1	0	0	4	4		1	.231	.286	.250	78	0	0-1	.564	-5	69	100	/3-6,O-5(0-4-1),2-2,1	-0.4
1873	Res NA	2	9	1	1	0	0	0	1	0		0	.111	.111	.111	-37	-1	0-0	.909	-0	0	0	/1-2	-0.1
Total	2 NA	16	61	9	13	1	0	0	5	4		1	.213	.262	.230	60	-1	0-1	.564	-5	69	100	/3-6,O-5(0-4-1),1-3,2-2	-0.5

SWANDER, PINKY Edward O. B 7.4.1880 Portsmouth, OH D 10.24.1944 Springfield, MA BL/TL 5-9/180# d9.18

Year	Tm Lg	G	AB	R	H	2B	3B	HR	RBI	BB-IB	HP	SO	AVG	OBP	SLG	AOPS	ABR	SB-CS	FA	FR	Rng	Thr	G at Pos	BFW
1903	StL A	14	51	9	14	2	2	0	6	10	2		.275	.413	.392	146	4	0	.833	-1	142	0	O-14(RF)	0.2
1904	StL A	1	1	0	0	0	0	0	0	0	0		.000	.000	.000	-99	0	0	—	0			H	0.0
Total	2	15	52	9	14	2	2	0	6	10	2		.269	.406	.385	142	4	0	.833	-1	142	0	/O-14(RF)	0.2

SWANN, PEDRO Pedro Maurice B 10.27.1970 Wilmington, DE BL/TR 6/195# d9.9

Year	Tm Lg	G	AB	R	H	2B	3B	HR	RBI	BB-IB	HP	SO	AVG	OBP	SLG	AOPS	ABR	SB-CS	FA	FR	Rng	Thr	G at Pos	BFW
2000	Atl N	4	2	0	0	0	0	0	0	0-0	0	2	.000	.000	.000	-99	-1	0-0	—	-0	0	0	/O-3(1-1-2)	-0.1
2002	Tor A	13	12	3	1	0	0	0	1	1-0	0	6	.083	.154	.083	-33	-2	0-0	—	-0	0	0	/O(RF)D	-0.2
2003	Bal A	8	14	3	3	1	0	1	2	1-0	0	4	.214	.267	.500	100	0	0-0	1.000	-0	94	0	/O-6(LF),D	0.0
Total	3	25	28	6	4	1	0	1	3	2-0	0	12	.143	.200	.286	26	-3	0-0	1.000	-1	75	0	/O-10(7-1-3),D-4	-0.3

SWANSON, EVAR Ernest Evar B 10.15.1902 DeKalb, IL D 7.17.1973 Galesburg, IL BR/TR 5-9/170# d4.18

Year	Tm Lg	G	AB	R	H	2B	3B	HR	RBI	BB-IB	HP	SO	AVG	OBP	SLG	AOPS	ABR	SB-CS	FA	FR	Rng	Thr	G at Pos	BFW
1929	Cin N	148	574	100	172	35	12	4	43	41	6	47	.300	.353	.423	96	-5	33	.970	-4	97	82	*O-142(91-51-0)	-1.6
1930	Cin N	95	301	43	93	15	3	2	22	11	1	17	.309	.335	.399	81	-10	4	.963	-1	101	92	O-71(3-68-0)	-1.2
1932	Chi A	14	52	9	16	3	1	0	8	8	0	3	.308	.400	.404	116	2	3-1	.960	-2	87	0	O-14(LF)	0.0
1933	Chi A	144	539	102	165	25	7	1	63	93	3	35	.306	.411	.384	117	19	19-11	.973	-10	93	51	*O-139(6-8-129)	0.1
1934	Chi A	117	426	71	127	9	5	0	34	59	1	31	.298	.385	.343	86	-7	10-3	.980	-3	98	51	*O-105(4-1-100)	-1.4
Total	5	518	1892	325	573	87	28	7	170	212	11	133	.303	.376	.390	98	-1	69-15	.971	-19	96	65	O-471(118-128-229)	-4.1

SWANSON, KARL Karl Edward B 12.17.1900 N.Henderson, IL D 4.3.2002 Rock Island, IL BL/TR 5-10/155# d8.12

Year	Tm Lg	G	AB	R	H	2B	3B	HR	RBI	BB-IB	HP	SO	AVG	OBP	SLG	AOPS	ABR	SB-CS	FA	FR	Rng	Thr	G at Pos	BFW
1928	Chi A	22	64	2	9	1	0	0	6	4	0	7	.141	.191	.156	-8	-10	3-0	.943	-1	110	81	2-21	-1.0
1929	Chi A	2	1	0	0	0	0	0	0	0	0	0	.000	.000	.000	-99	0	0-0	—	0			H	0.0
Total	2	24	65	2	9	1	0	0	6	4	0	7	.138	.188	.154	-9	-10	3-0	.943	-1	110	81	/2-21	-1.0

SWANSON, STAN Stanley Lawrence B 5.19.1944 Yuba City, CA BR/TR 5-11/168# d6.23

Year	Tm Lg	G	AB	R	H	2B	3B	HR	RBI	BB-IB	HP	SO	AVG	OBP	SLG	AOPS	ABR	SB-CS	FA	FR	Rng	Thr	G at Pos	BFW
1971	Mon N	49	106	14	26	3	0	2	11	10-1	0	13	.245	.310	.330	81	-3	1-3	1.000	-1	95	0	O-38(24-16-2)	-0.6

SWANSON, BILL William Andrew B 10.12.1888 New York, NY D 10.14.1954 New York, NY BB/TR 5-6/156# d9.2

Year	Tm Lg	G	AB	R	H	2B	3B	HR	RBI	BB-IB	HP	SO	AVG	OBP	SLG	AOPS	ABR	SB-CS	FA	FR	Rng	Thr	G at Pos	BFW
1914	Bos A	11	20	0	4	2	0	0	0	3	0	4	.200	.304	.300	82	0	0-1	.875	-3	81	0	/2-6,3-3,S	-0.4

SWARTWOOD, ED Cyrus Edward B 1.12.1859 Rockford, IL D 5.15.1924 Pittsburgh, PA BL/TR 5-11/198# d8.11 U4 OF Total (47-LF 89-CF 502-RF)

Year	Tm Lg	G	AB	R	H	2B	3B	HR	RBI	BB-IB	HP	SO	AVG	OBP	SLG	AOPS	ABR	SB-CS	FA	FR	Rng	Thr	G at Pos	BFW
1881	Buf N	1	3	0	1	0	0	0	0	1		0	.333	.500	.333	170	0		.500	-1	0	0	/O(RF)	0.0
1882	Pit AA	76	325	**86**	107	**18**	11	4		21			.329	.370	.489	197	33		.788	-12	49	112	*O-73(0-29-44)/1-4	1.8
1883	Pit AA	94	412	86	**147**	24	8	3		25			**.357**	**.394**	.476	**186**	**41**		.936	-1	131	87	1-60,O-37(0-31-6)/C-3	2.8
1884	Pit AA	102	399	74	115	19	6	0		33	**15**		.288	.365	.366	141	21		.804	-5	141	71	*O-79(0-2-77),1-22/3P	1.2
1885	Bro AA	99	399	80	106	8	9	0	49	36	5		.266	.334	.331	110	5		.851	-12	47	0	*O-95(47-0-48)/1-4,SC	-0.8
1886	Bro AA	122	471	95	132	13	10	3	58	**70**	3		.280	.377	.369	133	21	37	.884	5	154	101	*O-122(0-20-103)/C	2.1
1887	Bro AA	91	363	72	92	14	8	1	54	46	3		.253	.342	.344	91	-4	29	.835	1	155	149	O-91(RF)	-0.3
1890	Tol AA	126	462	106	151	23	11	3	64	80	17		.327	.444	.444	157	38	53	.925	6	105	43	*O-126(0-7-119)/P	3.8
1892	Pit N	13	42	8	10	1	0	0	4	13	0	11	.238	.418	.262	106	2	1	.933	3	259	400	O-13(RF)	0.4
Total	9	724	2876	607	861	120	63	14	229	325	43	11	.299	.379	.400	142	157	120	.856	-15	114	78	0-637R/1-90,C-5,P-2,S3	11.0

SWEASY, CHARLIE Charles James (born Charles James Swasey) B 11.2.1847 Newark, NJ D 3.30.1908 Newark, NJ BR/TR 5-9/172# d5.19 M1

Year	Tm Lg	G	AB	R	H	2B	3B	HR	RBI	BB-IB	HP	SO	AVG	OBP	SLG	AOPS	ABR	SB-CS	FA	FR	Rng	Thr	G at Pos	BFW
1871	Oly NA	5	19	5	4	1	0	0	4	1		0	.211	.250	.263	50	-1	0-0	.788	-1	95	0	/2-5	-0.2
1872	Cle NA	12	57	8	16	0	0	0	6	2		1	.281	.305	.281	86	-1	1-0	.833	2	116	74	2-11/O(RF)	0.1
1873	Bos NA	1	4	0	1	0	0	0	0	0		0	.250	.250	.250	45	0	0-0	.714	0	140	244	/2	0.0
1874	Bal NA	8	33	2	8	0	0	0	4	2		0	.242	.286	.242	72	-1	0-0	.646	-6	53	96	/2-8,O(RF)	-0.6
	Atl NA	10	44	4	5	1	0	0	3	0		0	.114	.114	.136	-23	-5	0-0	.879	6	174	106	2-10	0.0
	Year	18	77	6	13	1	0	0	7	2		0	.169	.190	.182	21	-6	0-0	.781	-0	117	101	2-18/O(RF)	-0.6
1875	RS NA	**19**	76	7	13	1	0	0	4	3		1	.171	.203	.184	39	-4	2-4	.828	-5	78	76	2-19,M	-1.0
1876	Cin N	56	225	18	46	5	2	0	10	2		5	.204	.211	.244	60	-8		.864	1	98	**130**	*2-55/O(RF)	-0.3
1878	Pro N	55	212	23	37	3	0	0	8	7		23	.175	.201	.189	29	-16		.846	-8	97	87	*2-55	-2.1
Total	5 NA	55	233	26	47	3	0	0	21	8		2	.202	.228	.215	47	-12	3-4	.000	-4	101	80	/2-54,O-2(RF)	-1.7
Total	2	111	437	41	83	8	2	0	18	9		28	.190	.206	.217	44	-24		.855	-7	98	109	2-110/O(RF)	-2.4

SWEENEY, BUCK Charles Francis B 4.15.1890 Pittsburgh, PA D 3.13.1955 Pittsburgh, PA d9.28

Year	Tm Lg	G	AB	R	H	2B	3B	HR	RBI	BB-IB	HP	SO	AVG	OBP	SLG	AOPS	ABR	SB-CS	FA	FR	Rng	Thr	G at Pos	BFW
1914	Phi A	1	1	0	0	0	0	0	0	0	0	1	.000	.000	.000	-99	0	0	1.000	0	161	0	/O(LF)	0.0

SWEENEY, CHARLIE Charles J. B 4.13.1863 San Francisco, CA D 4.4.1902 San Francisco, CA BR/TR 5-10.5/181# d5.11 ▲ OF Total (30-LF 31-CF 31-RF)

Year	Tm Lg	G	AB	R	H	2B	3B	HR	RBI	BB-IB	HP	SO	AVG	OBP	SLG	AOPS	ABR	SB-CS	FA	FR	Rng	Thr	G at Pos	BFW
1882	Pro N	1	4	0	0	0	0	0	0	0		1	.000	.000	.000	-99	-1		.500	0	443	0	/O(RF)	-0.1
1883	Pro N	22	87	9	19	3	0	0	15	2		10	.218	.236	.253	47	-5		.863	1	128	144	P-20/O-7(2-3-2)	-0.2
1884	Pro N	41	168	24	50	9	0	1	19	11		17	.298	.341	.369	126	6		.940	0	104	89	P-27,O-17(0-5-13)/1	0.1
	StL U	45	171	31	54	14	2	1		10			.316	.354	.439	134	3		**.943**	5	124	**267**	P-33,O-13(LF)/1	0.3
1885	StL N	71	267	27	55	7	1	0	24	12		33	.206	.240	.240	59	-11		.827	-4	70	100	O-39(14-19-6),P-35	-1.0
1886	StL N	17	64	4	16	2	0	0	7	3		10	.250	.284	.281	77	-2	0	.929	-0	104	159	P-11/O-4(CF),S-2	-0.1
1887	Cle AA	36	133	22	30	4	4	0	19	21	0		.226	.331	.316	83	-2	11	.936	-4	79	35	1-20,O-10(1-0-9)/P-3,S-2,3-2	-0.6
Total	6	233	894	117	224	39	7	2	84	59	0	71	.251	.297	.317	90	-12	11	.909	-1	111	155	P-129/O-91C,1-22,S-4,3-2	-1.6

SWEENEY, DAN Daniel J. B 1.28.1868 Philadelphia, PA D 7.13.1913 Louisville, KY 5-5/160# d4.18

Year	Tm Lg	G	AB	R	H	2B	3B	HR	RBI	BB-IB	HP	SO	AVG	OBP	SLG	AOPS	ABR	SB-CS	FA	FR	Rng	Thr	G at Pos	BFW
1895	Lou N	22	90	18	24	5	0	1	16	17	1	2	.267	.389	.356	99	1	2	.800	-3	65	0	O-22(0-1-21)	-0.2

Year	Tm Lg	G	AB	R	H	2B	3B	HR	RBI	BB-IB	HP	SO	AVG	OBP	SLG	AOPS	ABR	SB-CS	FA	FR	Rng	Thr	G at Pos	BFW
SWEENEY, ED Edward Francis "Jeff" B 7.19.1888 Chicago, IL D 7.4.1947 Chicago, IL BR/TR 6-1/200# d5.16																								
1908	NY A	32	82	4	12	2	0	0	2	5	0		.146	.195	.171	19	-7	0	.955	-3	*84*	*92*	C-25/1O(RF)	-0.9
1909	NY A	67	176	18	47	3	0	0	21	16	0		.267	.328	.284	93	-1	3	.947	-1	*94*	*114*	C-62/1-3	0.4
1910	NY A	78	215	25	43	4	4	0	13	17	4		.200	.271	.256	62	-10	12	.974	2	*105*	*104*	C-77	0.0
1911	NY A	83	229	17	53	6	5	0	18	14	8		.231	.299	.301	63	-12	8	.964	-3	*94*	*95*	C-83	-0.8
1912	NY A	110	351	37	94	12	1	0	30	27	3		.268	.325	.308	77	-10	6	.955	-5	*89*	***109***	*C-108	-0.6
1913	NY A	117	351	35	93	10	2	2	40	37	8	41	.265	.348	.322	96	0	11	.964	-7	*72*	***114***	*C-112/1O(CF)	0.3
1914	NY A	87	258	25	55	8	1	1	22	35	4	30	.213	.316	.264	75	-7	19-6	.980	2	*92*	*98*	C-78	0.5
1915	NY A	53	137	12	26	2	0	0	5	25	1	12	.190	.319	.204	57	-6	3-3	.975	-4	*91*	*92*	C-53	-0.6
1919	Pit N	17	42	0	4	1	0	0	0	5	0	6	.095	.191	.119	-5	-5	1	.944	-1	*113*	*111*	C-15	-0.6
Total	9	644	1841	173	427	48	13	3	151	181	28	89	.232	.310	.277	73	-58	63-9	.964	-19	*90*	*104*	C-613/1-5,O-2(0-1-1)	-2.3
SWEENEY, HANK Henry Leon B 12.28.1915 Franklin, TN D 5.6.1980 Columbia, TN BL/TL 6/185# d10.1																								
1944	Pit N	1	2	0	0	0	0	0	0	0	0	1	.000	.000	.000	-96	-1	0	1.000	0	197	0	/1	0.0
SWEENEY, JERRY Jeremiah H. B 1860 Boston, MA D 8.25.1891 Boston, MA 5-9.5/157# d8.22																								
1884	KC U	31	129	16	34	3	0	0		4			.264	.286	.287	85	-6		.958	3	156	119	1-31	-0.5
SWEENEY, ROONEY John J. B 1860 New York, NY 5-8/155# d7.25																								
1883	Bal AA	25	101	13	21	5	2	0		4			.208	.238	.297	69	-3		.878	-0			C-23/O-3(RF)	-0.2
1884	Bal U	48	186	37	42	7	1	0		15			.226	.284	.274	63	-14		.917	-5			C-33,O-16(0-6-10)/3	-1.5
1885	StL N	3	11	1	1	0	0	0	0	0		4	.091	.091	.091	-44	-2		.750	-0	0	0	/O-2(1-1-0),C	-0.2
Total	3	76	298	51	64	12	3	0	0	19		4	.215	.262	.275	62	-19		.905	-6			/C-57,O-21(1-7-13),3	-1.9
SWEENEY, MARK Mark Patrick B 10.26.1969 Framingham, MA BL/TL 6-1/195# d8.4																								
1995	StL N	37	77	5	21	2	0	2	13	10-0	0	15	.273	.348	.377	94	-1	1-1	.994	-1	90	145	1-19/O(LF)	-0.3
1996	†StL N	98	170	32	45	9	0	3	22	33-2	1	29	.265	.387	.371	102	2	3-0	.984	-1	106	55	O-43(36-0-7),1-15	0.0
1997	StL N	44	61	5	13	3	0	0	4	9-1	1	14	.213	.319	.262	56	-4	0-1	1.000	-1	100	0	O-25(10-0-15)/1-4	-0.5
	SD N	71	103	11	33	4	0	2	19	11-0	0	18	.320	.383	.417	119	3	2-2	.944	-2	74	0	O-20(6-1-13)/1-7	0.0
	Year	115	164	16	46	7	0	2	23	20-1	1	32	.280	.358	.360	94	-1	2-3	.976	-3	87	0	O-45(16-1-28),1-11	-0.5
1998	†SD N	122	192	17	45	8	3	2	15	26-0	1	37	.234	.324	.339	82	-5	1-2	1.000	-3	99	0	O-34(5-0-29),1-21/D	-1.1
1999	Cin N	37	31	6	11	3	0	2	7	4-1	0	9	.355	.429	.645	162	3	0-0	1.000	0	0	601	/1O(LF)	0.3
2000	Mil N	71	73	9	16	6	0	1	6	12-1	1	18	.219	.337	.342	74	-3	0-0	1.000	1	315	0	/O-3(LF),1-2,D-4	-0.2
2001	Mil N	48	89	9	23	3	1	3	11	12-0	0	23	.258	.347	.416	98	0	2-1	.968	-2	86	0	O-20(20-0-3)/1-2	-0.3
2002	SD N	48	65	3	11	3	0	1	4	4-0	0	19	.169	.217	.262	30	-7	0-0	.946	0	95	116	1-11/O-5(RF),D	-0.8
2003	Col N	67	97	13	25	9	0	2	14	9-1	0	27	.258	.321	.412	78	-3	0-1	1.000	-2	77	0	O-17(7-0-11)/1-8,D	-0.6
Total	9	643	958	110	243	50	4	18	115	130-6	4	209	.254	.343	.371	89	-15	9-8	.981	-11	98	15	O-169(89-1-83)/1-90,D-7	-3.5
SWEENEY, MIKE Michael John B 7.22.1973 Orange, CA BR/TR 6-1/195# d9.14																								
1995	KC A	4	4	1	1	0	0	0	0	0-0	0	0	.250	.250	.250	30	0	0-0	.875	0	0	0	/C-4	0.0
1996	KC A	50	165	23	46	10	0	4	24	18-0	4	21	.279	.358	.412	96	0	1-2	.994	2	139	120	C-26,D-22	0.1
1997	KC A	84	240	30	58	8	0	7	31	17-0	6	33	.242	.306	.363	72	-10	3-2	.993	9	136	110	C-76/D-3	0.3
1998	KC A	92	282	32	73	18	0	8	35	24-1	2	38	.259	.320	.408	86	-6	2-3	.984	-3	114	80	C-91	-0.4
1999	KC A	150	575	101	185	44	2	22	102	54-0	10	48	.322	.387	.520	127	24	6-1	.981	-4	95	110	D-71,1-74/C-4	0.9
2000	KC A★	159	618	105	206	30	0	29	144	71-5	**15**	67	.333	.407	.523	131	32	8-3	.991	3	112	103	*1-114,D-45	2.0
2001	KC A★	147	559	97	170	46	0	29	99	64-13	2	64	.304	.374	.542	127	24	10-3	.989	3	115	**136**	*1-108,D-38	1.4
2002	KC A★	126	471	81	160	31	1	24	86	61-10	6	46	.340	.417	.563	142	31	9-7	.991	14	159	107	*1-102,D-24	3.2
2003	KC A✳	108	392	62	115	18	1	16	83	64-5	2	56	.293	.391	.467	111	8	3-2	.990	2	126	78	D-62,1-45	0.2
Total	9	920	3306	532	1014	205	4	139	604	373-34	47	373	.307	.381	.497	119	103	42-23	.989	26	122	111	1-443,D-265,C-201	7.7
SWEENEY, PETE Peter Jay B 12.31.1863 , CA D 8.22.1901 San Francisco, CA BR/TR d9.28																								
1888	Was N	11	44	3	8	0	1	0	5	0	0	4	.182	.182	.227	32	-4	0	.784	-1	68	77	/3-8,O-3(LF)	-0.5
1889	Was N	49	193	13	44	7	3	1	23	11	4	26	.228	.284	.311	70	-8	8	.802	-10	87	65	3-47/2O(RF)	-1.5
	StL AA	9	38	8	14	2	0	0	8	1	2	5	.368	.415	.421	122	1	2	.780	-2	81	71	/3-8,O(CF)	0.0
1890	StL AA	49	190	23	34	3	2	0	10	17	7		.179	.271	.216	38	-16	8	.880	-6	94	71	2-23,3-21/1-3,O-2(RF)	-1.9
	Lou AA	2	7	1	1	1	0	0	1	1	0		.143	.250	.286	59	0	1	.889	-1	33	0	/S-2	-0.1
	Phi AA	14	49	5	8	1	1	0	0	7	1		.163	.281	.224	49	-3	0	.915	-4	79	23	/2-9,O-4(CF),3-2	-0.6
	Year	65	246	29	43	5	3	0	11	25	8		.175	.272	.220	41	-19	9	.889	-11	90	58	2-32,3-23/O-6(0-4-2),1-3,S-2	-2.6
Total	3	134	521	53	109	14	7	1	47	37	14	35	.209	.280	.269	57	-30	19	.799	-24	77	79	/3-86,2-33,O-11(3-5-3),1-3,S-2	-4.6
SWEENEY, BILL William John B 3.6.1886 Covington, KY D 5.26.1948 Cambridge, MA BR/TR 5-11/175# d6.14 OF Total (9-LF 1-CF 1-RF)																								
1907	Chi N	3	10	1	1	0	0	0	1	1	0		.100	.182	.100	-11	-1	1	.571	-3	66	0	/S-3	-0.6
	Bos N	58	191	24	50	2	0	0	18	15	0		.262	.316	.272	85	-3	8	.871	-0	108	153	3-23,S-15,O-11(9-1-1)/2-5,1	-0.4
	Year	61	201	25	51	2	0	0	19	16	0		.254	.309	.264	79	-5	9	.871	-4	108	153	3-23,S-18,O-11(9-1-1)/2-5,1	-1.0
1908	Bos N	127	418	44	102	15	3	0	40	45	0		.244	.317	.294	97	0	17	.930	12	**114**	92	*3-123/S-3,2	1.8
1909	Bos N	138	493	44	120	19	3	1	36	37	0		.243	.296	.300	81	-11	25	.903	7	109	90	*3-112,S-26	0.0
1910	Bos N	150	499	43	133	22	4	5	46	61	2	28	.267	.349	.357	101	2	25	.903	-4	91	113	*S-110,3-21,1-17	0.2
1911	Bos N	137	523	92	164	33	6	3	63	77	2	26	.314	.404	.417	120	17	33	.944	11	104	87	*2-136	3.1
1912	Bos N	153	593	84	204	31	13	1	100	68	5	34	.344	.416	.445	133	30	27	.959	26	**104**	108	*2-153	5.6
1913	Bos N	139	502	65	129	17	6	0	47	66	3	50	.257	.347	.315	88	-5	18-18	.939	1	101	79	*2-137	-0.5
1914	Chi N	134	463	45	101	14	5	1	38	53	0	15	.218	.298	.276	71	-16	18	.954	16	**107**	79	*2-134	0.3
Total	8	1039	3692	442	1004	153	40	11	389	423	12	153	.272	.349	.344	100	13	172-18	.949	66	104	88	2-566,3-279,S-157/1-18,O-11L	9.5
SWEENEY, BILL William Joseph B 12.29.1904 Cleveland, OH D 4.18.1957 San Diego, CA BR/TR 5-11/180# d4.13 C2																								
1928	Det A	89	309	47	78	15	5	0	19	15	0	28	.252	.287	.333	62	-18	12-8	.993	4	120	88	1-75/O-3(LF)	-1.9
1930	Bos A	88	243	32	75	13	0	4	30	9	0	15	.309	.333	.412	91	-4	5-3	.997	-1	93	113	1-56/3	-0.7
1931	Bos A	131	498	48	147	30	3	1	58	20	0	30	.295	.322	.373	87	-10	5-12	**.993**	8	132	92	*1-124	-1.6
Total	3	308	1050	127	300	58	8	5	107	44	0	73	.286	.314	.370	80	-32	22-23	.994	12	120	95	1-255/O-3(LF),3	-4.2
SWEET, RICK Ricky Joe B 9.7.1952 Longview, WA BB/TR (BL 1978 (part)) 6-1/200# d4.8 C2																								
1978	SD N	88	226	15	50	8	0	1	11	27-7	1	22	.221	.306	.270	68	-9	1-4	.984	6	164	111	C-76	-0.2
1982	NY N	3	3	0	1	0	0	0	0	0-0	0	1	.333	.333	.333	88	0	0-0	—	0			/H	0.0
	Sea A	88	258	29	66	6	1	4	24	20-0	2	24	.256	.311	.333	76	-9	3-0	.993	1	116	92	C-83	-0.4
1983	Sea A	93	249	18	55	9	0	1	22	13-1	0	26	.221	.259	.269	44	-19	2-2	.987	5	81	131	C-85	-1.2
Total	3	272	736	62	172	23	1	6	57	60-8	3	73	.234	.292	.292	63	-37	6-6	.988	11	119	111	C-244	-1.8
SWEIGERT, HAM Hampton d10.12																								
1890	Phi AA	1	1	0	0	0	0	0	0	1	0		.000	.500	.000	48	0	1	1.000	1	722	0	/O(LF)	0.1
SWENTOR, AUGIE August William B 11.21.1899 Seymour, CT D 11.10.1969 Waterbury, CT BR/TR 6/185# d9.12																								
1922	Chi A	1	1	0	0	0	0	0	0	0	0	1	.000	.000	.000	-99	0	0-0	—	0			H	0.0
SWETT, POP William E. B 4.16.1870 San Francisco, CA D 11.22.1934 San Francisco, CA 6/175# d5.3																								
1890	Bos P	37	94	16	18	4	3	1	12	16	2	26	.191	.321	.330	69	-4	4	.820	-2	*151*	*44*	C-34/O-3(RF)	-0.4
SWIFT, BOB Robert Virgil B 3.6.1915 Salina, KS D 10.17.1966 Detroit, MI BR/TR 5-11.5/180# d4.16 M2 C10																								
1940	StL A	130	398	37	97	20	1	0	39	28	1	39	.244	.295	.299	53	-27	1-0	.980	-15	*93*	*79*	*C-128	-3.4
1941	StL A	63	170	13	44	7	0	0	21	22	0	11	.259	.344	.300	69	-7	2-0	.985	-4	*96*	*81*	C-58	-0.7
1942	StL A	29	76	3	15	4	0	1	8	3	0	5	.197	.228	.289	44	-6	0-2	1.000	-1	*78*	*76*	C-28	-0.7
	Phi A	60	192	9	44	3	0	0	15	13	0	17	.229	.278	.245	48	-14	1-2	.970	-2	*76*	*132*	C-60	-1.3
	Year	89	268	12	59	7	0	1	23	16	0	22	.220	.264	.257	47	-20	1-4	.977	-4	*77*	*117*	C-88	-2.0
1943	Phi A	77	224	16	43	5	1	1	11	35	0	16	.192	.301	.237	58	-11	0-0	.976	-5	*76*	*98*	C-77	-1.3
1944	Det A	80	247	15	63	11	1	1	19	27	1	27	.255	.331	.320	82	-5	2-0	.982	7	*172*	*151*	C-76	0.7
1945	†Det A	95	279	19	65	5	0	0	24	26	0	22	.233	.298	.251	56	-15	1-0	.988	5	*115*	***120***	C-94	-0.6
1946	Det A	42	107	13	25	2	0	2	10	14	0	7	.234	.322	.308	72	-4	0-0	.980	-3	*98*	*59*	C-42	-0.5
1947	Det A	97	279	23	70	11	0	1	21	33	0	16	.251	.330	.301	74	-9	2-2	.989	3	*120*	*95*	C-97	-0.2
1948	Det A	113	292	23	65	6	0	4	33	51	0	29	.223	.338	.284	65	-14	1-0	.991	3	*100*	*89*	*C-112	-0.5

Year	Tm Lg	G	AB	R	H	2B	3B	HR	RBI	BB-IB	HP	SO	AVG	OBP	SLG	AOPS	ABR	SB-CS	FA	FR	Rng	Thr	G at Pos	BFW
1949	Det A	74	189	16	45	6	0	2	18	26	0	20	.238	.330	.302	68	-9	0-0	.989	-1	105	110	C-69	-0.6
1950	Det A	67	132	14	30	4	0	2	9	25	0	6	.227	.350	.303	66	-6	0-0	.995	5	149	90	C-66	0.1
1951	Det A	44	104	8	20	0	0	0	5	12	0	10	.192	.276	.192	28	-11	0-0	.982	-0	76	89	C-43	-0.9
1952	Det A	28	58	3	8	1	0	0	4	7	1	7	.138	.242	.155	12	-7	0-0	.977	3	124	120	C-28	-0.3
1953	Det A	2	3	0	1	1	0	0	1	2	0	1	.333	.600	.667	245	1	0-0	1.000	0	0	0	/C-2	0.1
Total	14	1001	2750	212	635	86	3	14	238	324	3	233	.231	.313	.280	61	-144	10-6	.985	-5	107	100	C-980	-10.1
SWINDELLS, CHARLIE Charles Jay "Swin" B 10.26.1878 Rockford, IL D 7.22.1940 Portland, OR BR/TR 5-11.5/180# d9.7																								
1904	StL N	3	8	0	1	0	0	0	0	0	0		.125	.125	.125	-24	-1	0	1.000	0	101	39	/C-3	-0.1
SWISHER, STEVE Steven Eugene B 8.9.1951 Parkersburg, WV BR/TR 6-2/205# d6.14 C4																								
1974	Chi N	90	280	21	60	5	0	5	27	37-1	2	63	.214	.307	.286	65	-13	0-3	.987	-3	113	96	C-90	-1.3
1975	Chi N	93	254	20	54	16	2	1	22	30-7	4	57	.213	.301	.303	66	-11	1-0	.979	-11	104	95	C-93	-1.9
1976	Chi N☆	109	377	25	89	13	3	5	42	20-3	2	82	.236	.275	.326	65	-18	2-1	.983	-4	119	104	*C-107	-1.8
1977	Chi N	74	205	21	39	7	0	5	15	9-5	2	47	.190	.229	.298	37	-19	0-0	.976	-4	100	103	C-72	-2.1
1978	StL N	45	115	11	32	5	1	1	10	8-0	1	14	.278	.331	.365	96	-1	1-0	.991	-2	84	86	C-42	-0.1
1979	StL N	38	73	4	11	1	1	1	3	6-0	0	17	.151	.213	.233	22	-8	0-0	.974	-4	140	58	C-33	-1.1
1980	StL N	18	24	2	6	1	0	0	2	1-0	0	7	.250	.280	.292	58	-1	0-0	.957	-1	86	103	/C-8	-0.2
1981	SD N	16	28	2	4	0	0	0	0	2-0	0	11	.143	.200	.143	-2	-4	0-0	.971	-1	110	39	C-10	-0.5
1982	SD N	26	58	2	10	1	0	2	3	5-0	0	24	.172	.238	.293	50	-4	0-0	.981	-3	89	64	C-26	-0.6
Total	9	509	1414	108	305	49	7	20	124	118-16	11	322	.216	.279	.303	59	-79	4-4	.982	-32	109	94	C-481	-9.6
SWOBODA, RON Ronald Alan "Rocky" B 6.30.1944 Baltimore, MD BR/TR 6-2/205# d4.12																								
1965	NY N	135	399	52	91	15	3	19	50	33-3	3	102	.228	.291	.424	102	0	2-3	.947	1	99	150	*O-112(73-26-15)	-0.5
1966	NY N	112	342	34	76	9	4	8	50	31-4	5	76	.222	.296	.342	79	-10	4-2	.987	1	96	118	O-97(88-0-10)	-1.5
1967	NY N	134	449	47	126	17	3	13	53	41-4	1	96	.281	.340	.419	119	11	3-1	.957	3	103	107	*O-108(RF),1-20	0.6
1968	NY N	132	450	46	109	14	6	11	59	52-1	4	113	.242	.325	.373	109	6	8-1	.975	3	98	139	*O-125(RF)	0.2
1969	†NY N	109	327	38	77	10	2	9	52	43-4	2	90	.235	.326	.361	91	-3	1-1	.988	-1	100	76	O-97(22-0-77)	-1.0
1970	NY N	115	245	29	57	8	2	9	40	40-0	1	72	.233	.340	.392	96	-1	2-4	.984	-2	93	66	*O-100(1-0-100)	-0.8
1971	Mon N	39	75	7	19	4	3	0	6	11-0	2	16	.253	.364	.387	112	2	0-1	.977	2	98	286	O-26(10-17-3)	0.2
	NY A	54	138	17	36	2	1	2	20	27-1	3	35	.261	.391	.333	114	4	0-0	.965	-1	97	71	O-47(7-1-39)	0.1
1972	NY A	63	113	9	28	8	0	1	12	17-1	0	29	.248	.341	.345	110	2	0-1	.983	-0	96	99	O-35(0-5-35)/1-2	0.0
1973	NY A	35	43	6	5	0	0	1	2	4-0	0	18	.116	.191	.186	7	-6	0-0	1.000	-1	98	0	O-20(0-8-12)/D-4	-0.7
Total	9	928	2581	285	624	87	24	73	344	299-18	21	647	.242	.324	.379	101	5	20-14	.972	4	98	113	O-767(201-57-524)/1-22,D-4	-3.4
SYLVESTER, LOU Louis J. B 2.14.1855 Springfield, IL D 5.5.1936 Brooklyn, NY BR/TR 5-6/165# d4.18 ▲																								
1884	Cin U	82	333	67	89	13	8	2		18			.267	.305	.372	97	-12		.792	-3	110	70	*O-81(54-6-22)/P-6,S-2	-1.3
1886	Lou AA	45	154	41	35	5	3	0	17	29	0		.227	.350	.299	98	1	3	.913	1	140	258	O-45(CF)	0.0
	Cin AA	17	55	10	10	0	0	3	8	7	1		.182	.286	.345	94	0	2	.909	1	144	367	O-17(7-7-3)	0.0
	Year	62	209	51	45	5	3	3	25	36	1		.215	.333	.311	97	0	5	.912	2	141	291	O-62(7-52-3)	0.0
1887	StL AA	29	112	20	25	4	3	1	18	13	1		.223	.310	.339	73	-5	13	.923	2	148	323	O-29(12-4-13)/2	-0.3
Total	3	173	654	138	159	22	14	6	43	67	2		.243	.315	.347	93	-16	18	.854	2	127	186	O-172(73-62-38)/P-6,S-2,2	-1.6
SZEKELY, JOE Joseph B 2.2.1925 Cleveland, OH BR/TR 5-11/180# d9.13																								
1953	Cin N	5	13	0	1	0	0	0	0	0	0	3	.077	.077	.077	-59	-3	0-0	1.000	1	72	942	/O-3(RF)	-0.2
SZOTKIEWICZ, KEN Kenneth John B 2.25.1947 Wilmington, DE BL/TR 6/165# d4.7																								
1970	Det A	47	84	9	9	1	0	3	9	12-2	0	29	.107	.216	.226	23	-9	0-0	.971	3	111	106	S-44	-0.3
TABB, JERRY Jerry Lynn B 3.17.1952 Altus, OK BL/TR 6-2/195# d9.8																								
1976	Chi N	11	24	2	7	0	0	0	0	3-0	0	2	.292	.370	.292	82	0	0-0	1.000	-0	64	112	/1-6	-0.1
1977	Oak A	51	144	8	32	3	0	6	19	10-2	0	26	.222	.269	.368	74	-6	0-1	.993	-2	77	98	1-36/D-5	-1.0
1978	Oak A	12	9	0	1	0	0	0	1	2-1	0	5	.111	.273	.111	12	-1	0-0	1.000	-0	0	0	/1-2,D-2	-0.1
Total	3	74	177	10	40	3	0	6	20	15-3	0	33	.226	.284	.345	72	-7	0-1	.994	-2	74	98	/1-44,D-7	-1.2
TABLER, PAT Patrick Sean B 2.2.1958 Hamilton, OH BR/TR 6-2/200# d8.21 OF Total (204-LF 80-RF)																								
1981	Chi N	35	101	11	19	3	1	1	5	13-0	0	26	.188	.281	.267	54	-6	0-1	.982	-2	94	82	2-35	-0.7
1982	Chi N	25	85	9	20	4	2	1	7	6-0	1	20	.235	.287	.365	81	-2	0-0	.949	-5	72	75	3-25	-0.8
1983	Cle A	124	430	56	125	23	5	6	65	56-1	1	63	.291	.370	.409	111	8	2-4	.948	-5	95	59	O-88(87-0-1),3-25/2-2,D-6	-0.1
1984	Cle A	144	473	66	137	21	3	10	68	47-2	3	62	.290	.354	.410	110	7	3-1	.998	-6	93	95	1-67,O-43(LF),3-36/2D	-0.4
1985	Cle A	117	404	47	111	18	3	5	59	27-2	2	55	.275	.321	.371	90	-6	0-6	.983	3	119	99	1-92,D-18/3-4,2	-1.0
1986	Cle A	130	473	61	154	29	2	6	48	29-3	3	75	.326	.368	.433	119	13	3-1	.990	-1	103	93	*1-107,D-18	0.6
1987	Cle A★	151	553	66	170	34	3	11	86	51-6	6	84	.307	.369	.439	113	12	5-2	.984	6	134	72	1-82,D-66	1.1
1988	Cle A	41	143	16	32	5	1	1	17	23-1	1	27	.224	.333	.294	76	-4	1-0	1.000	-0	80	66	D-29,1-10	-0.6
	KC A	89	301	37	93	17	2	1	49	23-0	2	41	.309	.358	.389	109	4	2-3	.986	-1	101	52	D-40,O-37(28-0-9)/1-7,3	0.0
	Year	130	444	53	125	22	3	2	66	46-1	3	68	.282	.349	.358	98	0	3-3	.986	-2	101	52	D-69,O-37(28-0-9),1-17/3	-0.6
1989	KC A	123	390	36	101	11	1	2	42	37-0	2	42	.259	.325	.308	80	-10	0-0	.970	5	94	258	O-55(26-0-28),D-39,1-20/2-3,3	-0.8
1990	KC A	75	195	12	53	14	0	1	19	20-2	1	21	.272	.338	.359	98	0	0-2	.986	1	105	179	O-42(11-0-31),D-15/3-6,1-5	-0.1
	NY N	17	43	6	12	1	1	1	10	3-0	1	8	.279	.340	.419	108	0	0-0	1.000	1	116	168	O-10(3-0-8)	0.1
1991	†Tor A	82	185	20	40	5	1	1	21	29-5	1	21	.216	.318	.270	64	-8	0-0	.985	0	103	70	D-57,1-20/O(LF)	-1.2
1992	†Tor A	49	135	11	34	5	0	0	16	11-0	0	14	.252	.306	.289	65	-6	0-0	1.000	0	98	81	1-34/O-8(5-0-3),3D	-0.8
Total	12	1202	3911	454	1101	190	25	47	512	375-22	24	559	.282	.345	.379	99	2	16-20	.988	-3	111	90	1-444,D-291,O-284L/3-99,2-42	-4.7
TABOR, GREG Gregory Steven B 5.21.1961 Castro Valley, CA BR/TR 6- /165# d9.10																								
1987	Tex A	9	9	4	1	1	0	0	1	0-0	0	4	.111	.111	.222	-15	-1	0-0	.938	1	146	113	/2-4,D	0.0
TABOR, JIM James Reubin "Rawhide" B 11.5.1916 New Hope, AL D 8.22.1953 Sacramento, CA BR/TR 6-2/175# d8.2 Mil 1944-45																								
1938	Bos A	19	57	8	18	3	2	1	8	1	0	6	.316	.328	.491	98	-1	0-1	.889	-1	100	91	3-11/S-2	-0.1
1939	Bos A	149	577	76	167	33	8	14	95	40	1	54	.289	.337	.447	95	-7	16-10	.923	4	108	107	*3-148	0.3
1940	Bos A	120	459	73	131	28	6	21	81	42	0	58	.285	.345	.510	114	8	14-10	.926	3	103	99	*3-120	1.4
1941	Bos A	126	498	65	139	29	3	16	101	36	0	48	.279	.328	.446	100	-2	17-9	.930	0	104	99	*3-125	0.4
1942	Bos A	139	508	56	128	18	2	12	75	37	0	47	.252	.303	.366	85	-12	6-13	.924	-8	90	103	*3-138	-1.9
1943	Bos A	137	537	57	130	26	3	13	85	43	1	54	.242	.299	.374	95	-5	7-7	.938	-7	100	**125**	*3-133/O-2(LF)	-1.3
1944	Bos A	116	438	58	125	25	3	13	72	31	1	38	.285	.334	.445	123	11	4-4	.950	4	105	63	*3-114	1.7
1946	Phi N	124	463	53	124	15	2	10	50	36	1	51	.268	.322	.374	100	-2	3	.954	-2	**94**	89	*3-124	-0.5
1947	Phi N	75	251	27	59	14	0	4	31	20	2	21	.235	.297	.339	71	-11	2	.916	-12	79	73	3-67	-2.3
Total	9	1005	3788	473	1021	191	29	104	598	286	6	377	.270	.322	.418	99	-21	69-54	.933	-18	99	97	3-980/O-2(LF),S-2	-2.3
TACKETT, JEFF Jeffrey Wilson B 12.1.1965 Fresno, CA BR/TR 6-2/200# d9.11																								
1991	Bal A	6	8	1	1	0	0	0	0	2-0	0	2	.125	.300	.125	23	-1	0-0	1.000	-1	75	0	/C-6	-0.1
1992	Bal A	65	179	21	43	8	1	5	24	17-1	2	28	.240	.307	.380	91	-2	0-0	.997	3	134	81	C-64/3	0.4
1993	Bal A	39	87	8	15	3	0	0	9	13-0	0	28	.172	.277	.207	32	-8	0-0	.989	-1	93	150	C-38/P	-0.7
1994	Bal A	26	53	5	12	3	1	2	9	5-0	2	13	.226	.317	.434	87	-1	0-0	.980	-3	114	68	C-26	-0.3
Total	4	136	327	35	71	14	2	7	42	37-1	4	71	.217	.300	.336	72	-12	0-0	.992	-1	118	95	C-134/P3	-0.7
TAGUCHI, SO So B 7.22.1969 Hyogo, Japan BR/TR 5-10/163# d6.10																								
2002	StL N	19	15	4	6	0	0	0	2	2-0	0	1	.400	.471	.400	140	1	1-0	.929	2	115	803	O-14(8-6-0)	0.3
2003	StL N	43	54	9	14	3	1	3	13	4-1	0	11	.259	.310	.519	116	1	0-0	1.000	1	102	246	O-38(11-16-13)/2	0.2
Total	2	62	69	13	20	3	1	3	15	6-1	0	12	.290	.347	.493	121	2	1-0	.978	3	105	382	/O-52(19-22-13),2	0.5
TAITT, DOUG Douglas John "Poco" B 8.3.1902 Bay City, MI D 12.12.1970 Portland, OR BL/TR 6/176# d4.10																								
1928	Bos A	143	482	51	144	28	14	3	61	36	2	32	.299	.350	.434	107	3	13-6	.975	6	102	140	*O-139(9-0-130)/P	-0.1
1929	Bos A	26	65	6	18	4	0	0	6	8	1	5	.277	.365	.338	84	-1	0-1	.955	1	106	163	O-21(11-0-11)	-0.1
	Chi A	47	124	11	21	7	0	0	12	8	0	13	.169	.220	.226	15	-16	0-0	.966	1	101	141	O-30(RF)	-1.6
	Year	73	189	17	39	11	0	0	18	16	1	18	.206	.272	.265	39	-17	0-1	.961	2	103	150	O-51(11-0-41)	-1.7
1931	Phi N	38	151	13	34	4	2	1	15	4	0	14	.225	.245	.298	42	-13	0	.990	4	113	190	O-38(LF)	-1.1
1932	Phi N	4	2	0	0	0	0	0	1	2	0	0	.000	.500	.000	43	0	0	—	0			H	0.0
Total	4	258	824	81	217	43	16	4	95	58	3	64	.263	.314	.369	79	-27	13-7	.975	12	104	151	O-228(58-0-171)/P	-2.9

Year	Tm Lg	G	AB	R	H	2B	3B	HR	RBI	BB-IB	HP	SO	AVG	OBP	SLG	AOPS	ABR	SB-CS	FA	FR	Rng	Thr	G at Pos	BFW
TALBOT, BOB Robert Dale B 6.6.1927 Visalia, CA BR/TR 6/170# d9.16																								
1953	Chi N	8	30	5	10	0	1	0	0	0	0	4	.333	.333	.400	88	-1	1-0	1.000	2	98	442	/O-7(CF)	0.1
1954	Chi N	114	403	45	97	15	4	1	19	16	3	25	.241	.274	.305	50	-30	3-6	.985	-3	91	132	*O-111(CF)	-4.0
Total	2	122	433	50	107	15	5	1	19	16	3	29	.247	.278	.312	53	-31	4-6	.986	-1	91	153	O-118(CF)	-3.9
TALTON, TIM Marion Lee B 1.14.1939 Pikeville, NC BL/TR 6-3/200# d7.8																								
1966	KC A	37	53	8	18	3	1	2	6	1-0	1	5	.340	.364	.547	163	4	0-1	1.000	-1	*64*	*80*	C-14/1-9	0.3
1967	KC A	46	59	7	15	3	1	0	5	7-1	0	13	.254	.328	.339	102	0	0-0	.971	-1	37	79	C-22/1	-0.1
Total	2	83	112	15	33	6	2	2	11	8-1	1	18	.295	.344	.438	131	4	0-1	.980	-2	*46*	79	/C-36,1-10	0.2
TAMARGO, JOHN John Felix B 11.7.1951 Tampa, FL BB/TR 5-10/180# d9.3 C5																								
1976	StL N	10	10	2	3	0	0	0	1	3-0	0	0	.300	.429	.300	118	1	0-0	1.000	-1	70	0	/C	0.0
1977	StL N	4	4	0	0	0	0	0	0	0-0	0	2	.000	.000	.000	-99	-1	0-0	1.000	0	0	0	/C	-0.1
1978	StL N	6	6	0	0	0	0	0	0	0-0	0	2	.000	.000	.000	-99	-2	0-0	—	-0	0	0	/C	-0.2
	SF N	36	92	6	22	4	1	1	8	18-5	0	7	.239	.360	.337	101	1	1-1	.965	-5	63	29	C-31	-0.3
	Year	42	98	6	22	4	1	1	8	18-5	0	9	.224	.342	.316	89	-1	1-1	.965	-5	63	29	C-32	-0.5
1979	SF N	30	60	7	12	3	0	2	6	4-0	0	8	.200	.239	.350	66	-3	0-0	.985	-3	101	128	C-17	-0.5
	Mon N	12	21	0	8	2	0	0	5	3-0	0	3	.381	.440	.476	157	2	0-0	1.000	-2	45	61	/C-4	0.0
	Year	42	81	7	20	5	0	2	11	7-0	0	11	.247	.293	.383	92	-1	0-0	.989	-5	87	111	C-21	-0.5
1980	Mon N	37	51	4	14	3	0	1	13	6-0	0	5	.275	.345	.392	107	1	0-0	.975	-2	45	72	C-12	-0.1
Total	5	135	244	19	59	12	1	4	33	34-5	0	27	.242	.326	.348	92	-1	1-1	.974	-12	68	60	/C-67	-1.2
TANKERSLEY, LEO Lawrence William B 6.8.1901 Terrell, TX D 9.18.1980 Dallas, TX BR/TR 6/176# d7.2																								
1925	Chi A	1	3	0	0	0	0	0	0	0	0	0	.000	.000	.000	-99	-1	0-0	1.000	-0	*0*	*0*	/C	-0.1
TANNEHILL, JESSE Jesse Niles "Powder" B 7.14.1874 Dayton, KY D 9.22.1956 Dayton, KY BB/TL (BL 1903) 5-8/150# d6.17 C1 b-Lee ▲																								
1894	Cin N	5	11	0	0	0	0	0	1	1	0	2	.000	.083	.000	-76	-2	0	.600	-1	37	0	/P-5	0.0
1897	Pit N	56	184	22	49	8	2	0	22	18	2		.266	.338	.332	80	-5	4	.900	4	151	0	O-33(4-27-2),P-21	-0.2
1898	Pit N	60	152	25	44	9	3	1	17	7	0		.289	.321	.408	110	1	4	.956	3	116	81	P-43/O-7(3-4-0)	0.1
1899	Pit N	48	136	18	34	5	3	0	11	8	2		.250	.301	.331	74	-5	2	.955	3	124	311	P-41/O(LF)	0.1
1900	Pit N	34	110	19	37	7	0	0	17	5	0		.336	.365	.400	110	2	2	.924	1	109	0	P-29/O-4(RF)	0.1
1901	Pit N	42	135	19	33	3	3	1	12	6	0		.244	.277	.333	74	-5	0	.917	-2	78	0	P-32,O-10(9-0-1)	-0.2
1902	Pit N	44	148	27	43	6	1	1	17	12	1		.291	.348	.365	116	3	3	.969	-1	96	197	P-26,O-16(5-0-11)	-0.1
1903	NY A	40	111	18	26	6	2	1	13	8	1		.234	.292	.351	87	-2	1	.969	2	115	124	P-32/O-5(4-1-0)	0.1
1904	Bos A	45	122	14	24	2	6	0	6	9	0		.197	.252	.311	73	-4	1	.991	2	117	173	P-33/O-2(LF)	0.1
1905	Bos A	37	93	11	21	2	0	1	12	16	0		.226	.339	.280	96	6	1	.946	2	117	141	P-37	0.0
1906	Bos A	31	79	12	22	2	2	0	4	6	0		.278	.329	.354	114	6	1	.948	0	98	63	P-27	0.0
1907	Bos A	21	51	2	10	3	1	0	6	2	1		.196	.241	.294	71	1	0	.981	0	103	285	P-18	0.0
1908	Bos A	1	2	0	1	0	0	0	0	0	0		.500	.500	.500	219	0	0	1.000	0	196	0	/P	0.0
	Was A	26	43	1	11	1	0	0	3	2	0		.256	.289	.279	92	2	0	.897	1	141	339	P-10	0.0
	Year	27	45	1	12	1	0	0	3	2	0		.267	.298	.289	99	3	0	.907	2	145	317	P-11	0.0
1909	Was A	16	36	2	6	1	0	0	1	5	1		.167	.286	.194	55	-2	0	1.000	0	0	0	/O-9(RF),P-3	-0.2
1911	Cin N	1	1	0	0	0	0	0	0	0	0	1	.000	.000	.000	-99	0	0	1.000	-0	93	0	/P	0.0
Total	15	507	1414	190	361	55	23	5	142	105	8	3	.255	.310	.337	89	-4	19	.953	15	111	140	P-359/O-87(28-32-27)	-0.2
TANNEHILL, LEE Lee Ford B 10.26.1880 Dayton, KY D 2.16.1938 Live Oak, FL BR/TR 5-11/170# d4.22 b-Jesse																								
1903	Chi A	**138**	503	48	113	14	3	2	50	25	1		.225	.263	.276	65	-22	10	.908	-9	103	118	*S-138	-2.7
1904	Chi A	153	547	50	125	31	5	0	61	20	3		.229	.260	.303	81	-12	14	.947	**27**	**123**	**172**	*3-153	2.1
1905	Chi A	142	480	38	96	17	2	0	39	45	4		.200	.274	.244	67	-16	8	.931	25	**124**	**156**	*3-142	1.4
1906	†Chi A	116	378	26	69	8	3	0	33	31	5		.183	.254	.220	50	-21	7	.951	**32**	136	139	3-99,S-17	1.6
1907	Chi A	33	108	9	26	2	0	0	11	8	0		.241	.293	.259	79	-2	3	.912	4	125	97	3-31/S-2	0.3
1908	Chi A	141	482	44	104	15	3	0	35	25	2		.216	.257	.259	69	-17	6	.935	17	**122**	112	*3-136/S-5	0.4
1909	Chi A	155	531	39	118	21	5	0	47	31	3		.222	.269	.281	77	-15	12	.941	7	92	112	3-91,S-64	-0.4
1910	Chi A	67	230	17	51	10	0	1	21	11	2		.222	.263	.278	73	-8	3	.947	7	114	134	S-38,1-23/3-6	0.1
1911	Chi A	141	516	60	131	17	6	0	49	32	2		.254	.300	.310	73	-20	0	.957	**36**	114	109	*S-102,2-27/3-7,1-5	2.3
1912	Chi A	4	3	0	0	0	0	0	0	1	1		.000	.400	.000	18	0	0	.667	-1	66	504	/3-3,S	-0.1
Total	10	1090	3778	331	833	135	27	3	346	229	23		.220	.269	.273	70	-133	63	.938	147	120	141	3-668,S-367/1-28,2-27	5.0
TANNER, CHUCK Charles William B 7.4.1929 New Castle, PA BL/TL 6/185# d4.12 M19 s-Bruce																								
1955	Mil N	97	243	27	60	9	3	6	27	27-3	0	32	.247	.319	.383	91	-4	0-0	.981	-2	91	94	O-62(52-0-11)	-0.9
1956	Mil N	60	63	6	15	2	0	1	4	10-2	0	10	.238	.342	.317	84	-1	0-0	.800	-1	53	0	/O-8(7-0-1)	-0.3
1957	Mil N	22	69	5	17	3	0	2	6	5-0	0	4	.246	.297	.377	86	-2	0-0	1.000	-1	103	0	O-18(LF)	-0.3
	Chi N	95	318	42	91	16	2	7	42	23-2	2	20	.286	.336	.415	103	1	0-2	.988	-2	93	95	O-82(59-25-0)	-0.6
	Year	117	387	47	108	19	2	9	48	28-2	2	24	.279	.329	.408	100	0	0-2	.990	-2	95	78	*O-100(77-25-0)	-0.9
1958	Chi N	73	103	10	27	6	0	4	17	9-2	0	10	.262	.321	.437	100	0	1-0	.955	-2	86	0	O-15(2-3-10)	-0.2
1959	Cle A	14	48	6	12	2	0	1	5	2-0	0	9	.250	.280	.354	76	-2	0-0	1.000	-1	84	0	O-10(3-7-0)	-0.3
1960	Cle A	21	25	2	7	1	0	0	4	4-0	0	6	.280	.367	.320	94	0	1-0	1.000	-0	91	0	/O-4(LF)	0.0
1961	LA A	7	8	0	1	0	0	0	0	2-0	0	2	.125	.300	.125	16	-1	0-0	—	-0	0	0	/O(RF)	-0.1
1962	LA A	7	8	0	1	0	0	0	0	0-0	0	0	.125	.125	.125	-34	-2	0-0	—	-0	0	0	/O-2(1-0-1)	-0.2
Total	8	396	885	98	231	39	5	21	105	82-9	2	93	.261	.323	.388	93	-11	2-2	.983	-8	91	71	O-202(146-35-24)	-2.9
TAPPAN, WALTER Walter Van Dorn "Tap" B 10.8.1890 Carlinville, IL D 12.19.1967 Lynwood, CA BR/TR 5-8/158# d4.16																								
1914	KC F	18	39	1	8	1	0	1	3	1	0	0	.205	.225	.308	46	-4	1	.875	-2	126	80	/S-8,3-6,2	-0.5
TAPPE, EL Elvin Walter B 5.21.1927 Quincy, IL D 10.10.1998 Quincy, IL BR/TR 5-11/180# d4.24 M2 C8																								
1954	Chi N	46	119	5	22	3	0	0	4	10	0	9	.185	.246	.210	21	-14	0-0	.986	1	*62*	*113*	C-46	-1.1
1955	Chi N	2	0	0	0	0	0	0	0	0-0	0	0	—	—	—	—	0	0-0	1.000	1	*0*	*0*	/C-2	0.1
1956	Chi N	3	1	0	0	0	0	0	0	1-0	0	0	.000	.500	.000	51	0	0-0	1.000	0	*0*	*0*	/C-3	0.0
1958	Chi N	17	28	2	6	0	0	0	4	3-2	0	1	.214	.290	.214	37	-3	0-0	.962	-1	*88*	*123*	C-16	-0.3
1960	Chi N	51	103	11	24	7	0	0	3	11-1	1	12	.233	.313	.301	70	-4	0-1	.992	3	*77*	*167*	C-49	0.1
1962	Chi N	26	53	3	11	0	0	0	6	4-0	2	3	.208	.288	.208	34	-5	0-0	1.000	3	*86*	*160*	C-26,M	-0.1
Total	6	145	304	21	63	10	0	0	17	29-3	3	25	.207	.282	.240	41	-26	0-1	.989	6	*73*	*140*	C-142	-1.3
TAPPE, TED Theodore Nash B 2.2.1931 Seattle, WA BL/TR 6-3/185# d9.14																								
1950	Cin N	7	5	1	1	0	0	1	1	1	0	1	.200	.333	.800	187	1	0	—	0			H	0.1
1951	Cin N	4	3	0	1	0	0	0	0	0	0	0	.333	.333	.333	79	0	0-0	—	0			H	0.0
1955	Chi N	23	50	12	13	2	0	4	10	11-3	2	11	.260	.413	.540	151	4	0-0	1.000	-1	81	101	O-15(RF)	0.3
Total	3	34	58	13	15	2	0	5	11	12-3	2	12	.259	.403	.552	151	5	0-0	1.000	-1	81	101	/O-15(RF)	0.4
TARASCO, TONY Anthony Giacinto B 12.9.1970 New York, NY BL/TR 6-1/205# d4.30																								
1993	†Atl N	24	35	6	8	2	0	0	2	0-0	1	5	.229	.243	.286	43	-3	0-1	1.000	-1	82	0	O-12(4-0-8)	-0.4
1994	Atl N	87	132	16	36	6	0	5	19	9-1	0	17	.273	.313	.432	91	-2	5-0	1.000	-1	94	63	O-45(26-0-22)	-0.3
1995	Mon N	126	438	64	109	18	4	14	40	51-12	2	78	.249	.329	.404	89	-7	24-3	.979	2	103	86	*O-116(11-0-105)	-0.7
1996	†Bal A	31	84	14	20	3	0	1	9	7-0	0	15	.238	.297	.310	54	-6	5-3	1.000	2	126	75	O-23(0-1-22)/D-6	-0.4
1997	Bal A	100	166	26	34	8	1	7	26	25-1	1	33	.205	.313	.392	85	-4	2-2	.991	2	105	132	O-81(7-8-68)/D-2	-0.4
1998	Cin N	15	24	5	5	2	0	1	4	3-0	0	5	.208	.296	.417	84	-1	0-0	1.000	0	114	0	/O-7(4-1-2)	-0.1
1999	NY A	14	31	5	5	2	0	0	3	3-0	0	5	.161	.229	.226	19	-4	1-0	1.000	-2	66	0	O-12(9-0-5)	-0.5
2002	NY N	60	96	15	24	5	0	6	15	8-0	0	13	.250	.305	.490	113	1	2-1	.977	3	128	286	O-29(18-2-13)/1-7,D-2	0.3
Total	8	457	1006	151	241	46	5	34	118	106-14	4	171	.240	.313	.397	84	-26	39-10	.987	7	104	98	O-325(79-12-245)/D-10,1-7	-2.5
TARBERT, ARLIE Wilbur Arlington B 9.10.1904 Cleveland, OH D 11.27.1946 Cleveland, OH BR/TR 6/160# d6.18																								
1927	Bos A	33	69	5	13	1	0	0	5	3	3	12	.188	.253	.203	20	-8	0-0	.944	1	85	222	O-27(10-3-14)	-0.9
1928	Bos A	6	17	1	3	1	0	0	2	1	0	1	.176	.222	.235	21	-2	1-0	.900	0	91	202	/O-6(RF)	-0.2
Total	2	39	86	6	16	2	0	0	7	4	3	13	.186	.247	.209	20	-10	1-0	.935	1	86	218	/O-33(10-3-20)	-1.1
TARTABULL, DANNY Danilo (Mora) B 10.30.1962 San Juan, P.R. BR/TR 6-1/205# d9.7 f-Jose OF Total (15-LF 904-RF)																								
1984	Sea A	10	20	3	6	1	0	2	7	2-0	1	3	.300	.375	.650	185	2	0-0	.931	2	120	109	/S-8,2	0.5

Year	Tm Lg	G	AB	R	H	2B	3B	HR	RBI	BB-IB	HP	SO	AVG	OBP	SLG	AOPS	ABR	SB-CS	FA	FR	Rng	Thr	G at Pos	BFW
1985	Sea A	19	61	8	20	7	1	1	7	8-0	0	14	.328	.406	.525	152	5	1-0	.940	2	100	127	S-16/3-4	0.8
1986	Sea A	137	511	76	138	25	6	25	96	61-2	1	157	.270	.347	.489	124	17	4-8	.953	-3	77	100	*O-101(14-0-87),2-31/3D	0.8
1987	KC A	158	582	95	180	27	3	34	101	79-2	1	136	.309	.390	.541	141	35	9-4	.976	-13	78	105	*O-149(RF)/D-6	1.5
1988	KC A	146	507	80	139	38	3	26	102	76-4	4	119	.274	.369	.515	145	32	8-5	.963	-8	84	103	*O-130(RF),D-13	2.0
1989	KC A	133	441	54	118	22	0	18	62	69-2	3	123	.268	.369	.440	128	19	4-2	.982	-9	75	57	O-71(RF),D-55	0.6
1990	KC A	88	313	41	84	19	0	15	60	36-0	0	93	.268	.341	.473	128	12	1-1	.965	-5	88	30	O-52(RF),D-32	0.4
1991	KC A★	132	484	78	153	35	3	31	100	65-6	3	121	.316	.397	**.593**	170	47	6-3	.965	-14	80	46	*O-124(RF)/D-6	2.9
1992	NY A	123	421	72	112	19	0	25	85	103-14	0	115	.266	.409	.489	152	35	2-2	.980	-3	97	62	O-69(1-0-68),D-53	2.8
1993	NY A	138	513	87	128	33	2	31	102	92-9	2	156	.250	.363	.503	135	27	0-0	.978	-4	83	80	D-88,O-50(RF)	1.5
1994	NY A	104	399	68	102	24	1	19	67	66-3	1	111	.256	.360	.464	115	11	1-1	1.000	-3	79	51	D-78,O-26(RF)	0.1
1995	NY A	59	192	25	43	12	0	6	28	33-1	1	54	.224	.335	.380	88	-3	0-0	1.000	-0	90	98	D-39,O-18(RF)	-0.6
	Oak A	24	88	9	23	4	0	2	7	10-0	0	28	.261	.337	.375	90	-1	0-2	1.000	0	115	0	D-22/O(RF)	-0.3
	Year	83	280	34	66	16	0	8	35	43-1	1	82	.236	.335	.379	89	-4	0-2	.911	-0	91	95	D-61,O-19(RF)	-0.9
1996	Chi A	132	472	58	120	23	3	27	101	64-4	0	128	.254	.340	.487	112	8	1-2	.973	1	109	49	*O-122(RF),D-10	0.1
1997	Phi N	3	7	2	0	0	0	0	0	4-0	0	4	.000	.364	.000	5	-1	0-0	1.000	-1	47	0	/O-3(RF)	-0.1
Total	14	1406	5011	756	1366	289	22	262	925	768-47	17	1362	.273	.368	.496	133	245	37-30	.971	-58	85	75	O-916R,D-405/2-32,S-24,3-5	13.0
TARTABULL, JOSE Jose Milages (Guzman) B 11.27.1938 Cienfuegos, Cuba BL/TL 5-11/165# d4.10 s-Danny																								
1962	KC A	107	310	49	86	6	5	0	22	20-0	1	19	.277	.321	.329	73	-12	19-5	.974	3	110	174	O-85(1-85-0)	-0.9
1963	KC A	79	242	27	58	8	5	1	19	17-0	0	17	.240	.290	.326	68	-11	16-1	.986	-4	95	78	O-71(1-70-0)	-1.4
1964	KC A	104	100	9	20	2	0	0	3	5-0	0	12	.200	.238	.220	28	-10	4-0	.978	3	115	280	O-59(44-13-5)	-0.7
1965	KC A	68	218	28	68	11	4	1	19	18-0	0	20	.312	.361	.413	122	6	11-5	.986	5	114	162	O-54(26-27-8)	1.0
1966	KC A	37	127	13	30	2	3	0	4	11-0	0	13	.236	.297	.299	74	-5	8-1	1.000	-2	94	51	O-32(1-32-0)	-0.6
	Bos A	68	195	28	54	7	4	0	11	6-0	0	11	.277	.297	.354	79	-6	11-3	.989	-4	90	38	O-47(CF)	-1.0
	Year	105	322	41	84	9	7	0	15	17-0	0	24	.261	.297	.332	77	-10	19-4	.994	-6	92	43	O-79(1-79-0)	-1.6
1967	†Bos A	115	247	36	55	1	2	0	10	23-0	0	26	.223	.287	.243	54	-14	6-6	.989	-3	87	83	O-83(12-19-55)	-2.4
1968	Bos A	72	139	24	39	6	0	0	6	6-0	0	5	.281	.306	.324	87	-2	2-3	.984	1	111	58	O-43(12-11-20)	-0.4
1969	Oak A	75	266	28	71	11	1	0	11	9-0	0	11	.267	.290	.316	73	-11	3-4	.993	-1	101	47	O-63(28-36-0)	-1.6
1970	Oak A	24	13	5	3	2	0	0	2	0-0	0	2	.231	.231	.385	69	-1	1-0	1.000	-0	66	0	/O-6(4-2-0)	-0.1
Total	9	749	1857	247	484	56	24	2	107	115-0	1	136	.261	.303	.320	74	-66	81-28	.986	-2	101	103	O-543(129-342-88)	-8.1
TARVER, LA SCHELLE La Schelle B 1.30.1959 Modesto, CA BL/TL 5-11/165# d7.12																								
1986	Bos A	13	25	3	3	0	0	0	1	1-0	0	4	.120	.154	.120	-24	-4	0-1	1.000	-0	98	0	/O-9(3-7-0)	-0.5
TASBY, WILLIE Willie B 1.8.1933 Shreveport, LA BR/TR 5-11/175# d9.9																								
1958	Bal A	18	50	6	10	3	0	1	1	7-0	1	15	.200	.310	.320	78	-1	1-1	1.000	-1	102	0	O-16(6-12-5)	-0.3
1959	Bal A	142	505	69	126	16	5	13	48	34-0	6	80	.250	.303	.378	88	-10	3-5	.968	-4	92	137	*O-137(5-132-1)	-2.2
1960	Bal A	39	85	9	18	2	1	0	3	9-1	1	12	.212	.295	.259	52	-6	1-0	.980	-0	101	67	O-36(17-9-18)	-0.7
	Bos A	105	385	68	108	17	1	7	37	51-0	5	54	.281	.371	.384	101	3	3-1	.979	-4	96	100	*O-102(CF)	-0.6
	Year	144	470	77	126	19	2	7	40	60-1	6	66	.268	.358	.362	93	-2	4-1	.979	-4	97	94	*O-138(17-111-18)	-1.3
1961	Was A	141	494	54	124	13	2	17	63	58-2	2	94	.251	.330	.389	93	-5	4-10	.985	-7	96	66	*O-139(0-138-1)	-1.9
1962	Was A	11	34	4	7	0	0	0	0	2-0	0	6	.206	.250	.206	24	-4	0-0	.933	-1	85	0	O-10(7-3-0)	-0.5
	Cle A	75	199	25	48	7	0	4	17	25-0	0	41	.241	.326	.337	81	-5	0-2	1.000	-3	95	40	O-66(12-57-10)/3	-1.0
	Year	86	233	29	55	7	0	4	17	27-0	0	47	.236	.315	.318	73	-9	0-2	.992	-3	94	34	O-76(19-60-10)/3	-1.5
1963	Cle A	52	116	11	26	3	1	4	5	15-4	1	25	.224	.318	.371	93	-1	0-1	.981	-3	86	0	O-37(18-7-13)/2	-0.7
Total	6	583	1868	246	467	61	10	46	174	201-7	16	327	.250	.327	.367	89	-29	12-20	.980	-23	94	83	O-543(65-460-48)/23	-7.9
TATE, POP Edward Christopher "Dimples" B 12.22.1860 Richmond, VA D 6.25.1932 Richmond, VA BR/TL 5-10/178# d9.26																								
1885	Bos N	4	13	1	2	0	0	0	2	1		3	.154	.214	.154	21	-1		.865	1			/C-4	0.0
1886	Bos N	31	106	13	24	3	1	0	3	7		17	.226	.274	.274	69	-4	0	.885	-5			C-31	-0.6
1887	Bos N	60	231	34	60	5	3	0	27	8	4	9	.260	.296	.307	67	-11	7	.924	13			C-53/O-8(RF)	0.6
1888	Bos N	41	148	18	34	7	1	1	6	8	2	7	.230	.278	.311	85	-2	3	.854	-4			C-41/O(RF)	-0.2
1889	Bal AA	72	253	28	46	6	3	1	27	13	5	37	.182	.236	.241	35	-22	4	.938	0			C-62,1-10	-1.5
1890	Bal AA	19	71	7	13	1	1	0	6	4	6		.183	.284	.225	48	-5	3	.923	0	*118*	*124*	C-11/1-8	-0.4
Total	6	227	822	101	179	22	9	2	71	41	17	73	.218	.269	.274	58	-45	17	.905	5	*5*	*5*	C-202/1-18,O-9(RF)	-2.1
TATE, BENNIE Henry Bennett B 12.3.1901 Whitwell, TN D 10.27.1973 W.Frankfort, IL BL/TR 5-8/165# d4.29																								
1924	†Was A	21	43	2	13	2	0	0	7	1	0	2	.302	.318	.349	74	-2	0-0	.841	-2	*129*	*48*	C-14	-0.3
1925	Was A	16	27	0	13	3	0	0	7	2	0	2	.481	.517	.593	185	4	0-0	.955	2	*137*	*85*	C-14	0.5
1926	Was A	59	142	17	38	5	2	1	13	15	0	1	.268	.338	.352	82	-4	0-0	.960	-3	*89*	*134*	C-45	-0.5
1927	Was A	61	131	12	41	5	1	1	24	8	1	4	.313	.357	.389	95	-1	0-3	.977	3	*123*	*81*	C-39	0.2
1928	Was A	57	122	10	30	6	0	0	15	10	0	4	.246	.303	.295	58	-7	0-4	.985	2	*123*	*100*	C-30	-0.4
1929	Was A	81	265	26	78	12	3	0	30	16	0	8	.294	.335	.362	79	-9	2-6	.971	1	*116*	*107*	C-74	-0.5
1930	Was A	14	20	1	5	0	0	0	2	0	0	1	.250	.250	.250	27	-2	0-0	.933	-1	*157*	*89*	/C-9	-0.2
	Chi A	72	230	26	73	11	2	0	27	18	0	10	.317	.367	.383	94	-2	2-1	.981	-6	*90*	*92*	C-70	-0.3
	Year	86	250	27	78	11	2	0	29	18	0	11	.312	.358	.372	88	-4	2-1	.978	-6	*94*	*92*	C-79	-0.5
1931	Chi A	89	273	27	73	12	3	0	22	26	0	10	.267	.331	.333	80	-8	1-1	.987	-0	*71*	*105*	C-85	-0.3
1932	Chi A	4	10	1	1	0	0	0	0	1	0	0	.100	.182	.100	-27	-2	0-0	1.000	0	*117*	*223*	/C-4	-0.2
	Bos A	81	273	21	67	12	5	2	26	20	0	6	.245	.297	.348	68	-14	0-1	.974	-6	*63*	*110*	C-76	-1.5
	Year	85	283	22	68	12	5	2	26	21	0	6	.240	.293	.339	65	-16	0-1	.975	-6	*65*	*114*	C-80	-1.7
1934	Chi N	11	24	1	3	0	0	0	0	1	0	3	.125	.160	.125	-23	-4	0	1.000	-1	*116*	*119*	/C-8	-0.5
Total	10	566	1560	144	435	68	16	4	173	118	1	51	.279	.330	.351	78	-51	5-16	.974	-12	*93*	*104*	C-468	-4.0
TATE, HUGHIE Hugh Henry B 5.19.1880 Everett, PA D 8.7.1956 Greenville, PA BR/TR 5-11/190# d9.21																								
1905	Was A	4	13	1	4	0	1	0	2	0	0		.308	.308	.462	149	0	1	1.000	0	0	0	/O-3(LF)	0.0
TATE, LEE Lee Willie "Skeeter" B 3.18.1932 Black Rock, AR BR/TR 5-10/165# d9.12																								
1958	StL N	10	35	4	7	2	0	0	1	4-0	0	3	.200	.282	.257	42	-3	0-0	.950	-3	78	74	/S-9	-0.5
1959	StL N	41	50	5	7	1	1	1	4	5-1	1	7	.140	.232	.260	29	-5	0-0	.927	-1	93	88	S-39/2-2,3-2	-0.5
Total	2	51	85	9	14	3	1	1	5	9-1	1	10	.165	.253	.259	34	-8	0-0	.934	-4	87	83	/S-48,3-2,2-2	-1.0
TATIS, FERNANDO Fernando B 1.1.1975 San Pedro De Macoris, D.R. BR/TR 6-1/175# d7.26																								
1997	Tex A	60	223	29	57	9	0	8	29	14-0	0	42	.256	.297	.404	77	-8	3-0	.951	-10	81	46	3-60	-1.7
1998	Tex A	95	330	41	89	17	2	3	32	12-2	4	66	.270	.303	.361	69	-16	6-2	.945	11	116	102	3-94	-0.3
	StL N	55	202	28	58	16	2	8	26	24-1	2	57	.287	.367	.505	128	9	7-3	.928	1	114	71	3-55/S-3	1.1
1999	StL N	149	537	104	160	31	2	34	107	82-4	16	128	.298	.404	.553	139	34	21-9	.958	-9	94	115	*3-147	2.7
2000	†StL N	96	324	59	82	21	1	18	64	57-1	10	94	.253	.379	.491	118	10	2-3	.953	-12	85	102	3-91/1D	-0.1
2001	Mon N	41	145	20	37	9	0	2	11	16-0	4	43	.255	.339	.359	81	-3	0-0	.889	-9	78	29	3-41	-1.2
2002	Mon N	114	381	43	87	18	1	15	55	35-1	8	90	.228	.303	.399	80	-13	2-2	.948	-2	102	91	3-99/D-4	-1.4
2003	Mon N	53	175	15	34	6	0	2	15	18-0	3	40	.194	.281	.263	39	-16	2-1	.968	1	102	110	3-49	-1.4
Total	7	663	2317	339	604	127	8	90	339	258-9	47	560	.261	.344	.439	98	-3	43-20	.947	-29	97	91	3-636/D-6,S-3,1	-2.3
TATUM, JIM James Ray B 10.9.1967 Grossmont, CA BR/TR 6-2/200# d9.18																								
1992	Mil A	5	8	0	1	0	0	0	0	1-0	0	2	.125	.222	.125	-0	-1	0-0	1.000	-1	39	0	/3-5	-0.2
1993	Col N	92	98	7	20	5	0	1	12	5-0	1	27	.204	.245	.286	37	-9	0-0	.978	-2	111	136	1-12/3-6,O-3(2-0-1)	-1.1
1995	Col N	34	34	4	8	1	1	0	4	1-0	0	7	.235	.257	.324	40	-3	0-0	1.000	-1	95	0	/O-2(LF),C	-0.3
1996	Bos A	2	8	1	1	0	0	0	0	0-0	0	2	.125	.125	.125	-36	-2	0-0	1.000	-0	53	0	/3-2	-0.2
	SD N	5	3	0	0	0	0	0	0	0-0	0	1	.000	.000	.000	-99	-1	0-0	—	-0	0	0	/3	-0.1
1998	NY N	35	50	4	9	1	2	2	13	3-0	0	19	.180	.211	.400	61	-3	0-0	1.000	0	35	33	/1-9,C-4,O-4(LF),3-3,D	-0.4
Total	5	173	201	16	39	7	3	3	29	10-0	1	58	.194	.229	.303	37	-19	0-0	.987	-4	77	91	/1-21,3-17,O-9(8-0-1),C-5,D	-2.3
TATUM, JARVIS Jarvis B 10.11.1946 Fresno, CA D 1.6.2003 Los Angeles, CA BR/TR 6/185# d9.7																								
1968	Cal A	17	51	7	9	1	0	0	2	0-0	0	9	.176	.176	.196	13	-6	0-0	1.000	-1	94	0	O-11(CF)	-0.8
1969	Cal A	10	22	2	7	0	0	0	0	0-0	0	6	.318	.318	.318	83	-1	0-1	.857	-1	86	0	/O-5(RF)	-0.2
1970	Cal A	75	181	28	43	7	0	0	6	17-1	0	35	.238	.302	.276	63	-9	1-0	.982	0	105	68	O-58(8-43-12)	-1.1
Total	3	102	254	37	59	8	0	0	8	17-1	0	50	.232	.279	.264	56	-16	1-1	.979	-2	102	51	/O-74(8-54-17)	-2.1

TATUM, TOMMY V T B 7.16.1919 Decatur, TX D 11.7.1989 Oklahoma City, OK BR/TR 6/185# d8.1 Mil 1942-45

Year	Tm Lg	G	AB	R	H	2B	3B	HR	RBI	BB-IB	HP	SO	AVG	OBP	SLG	AOPS	ABR	SB-CS	FA	FR	Rng	Thr	G at Pos	BFW
1941	Bro N	8	12	1	2	1	0	0	1	1	0	3	.167	.231	.250	34	-1	0	1.000	-0	90	0	/O-4(1-3-0)	-0.1
1947	Bro N	4	6	0	0	0	0	0	0	0	0	1	.000	.000	.000	-96	-2	0	1.000	-0	90	0	/O-3(2-0-1)	-0.2
	Cin N	69	176	19	48	5	2	1	16	16	0	16	.273	.333	.341	80	-5	7	1.000	6	112	198	O-49(9-37-4)/2	-0.1
	Year	73	182	19	48	5	2	1	16	16	0	17	.264	.323	.330	74	-7	7	1.000	5	111	193	O-52(11-37-5)/2	-0.3
Total	2	81	194	20	50	6	2	1	17	17	0	20	.258	.318	.325	72	-8	7	1.000	5	111	185	/O-56(12-40-5),2	-0.4

TAUBENSEE, EDDIE Edward Kenneth B 10.31.1968 Beeville, TX BL/TR 6-4/205# d5.18

Year	Tm Lg	G	AB	R	H	2B	3B	HR	RBI	BB-IB	HP	SO	AVG	OBP	SLG	AOPS	ABR	SB-CS	FA	FR	Rng	Thr	G at Pos	BFW
1991	Cle A	26	66	5	16	2	1	0	8	5-1	0	16	.242	.288	.303	66	-3	0-0	.979	-8	70	45	C-25	-1.1
1992	Hou N	104	297	23	66	15	0	5	28	31-3	2	78	.222	.299	.323	80	-8	2-1	.992	3	106	102	*C-103	0.1
1993	Hou N	94	288	26	72	11	1	9	42	21-5	0	44	.250	.299	.389	86	-7	1-0	.992	5	122	78	C-90	0.4
1994	Hou N	5	10	0	1	0	0	0	0	0-0	0	3	.100	.100	.100	-50	-2	0-0	1.000	1	183	114	/C-5	-0.2
	Cin N	61	177	29	52	8	2	8	21	15-2	0	28	.294	.345	.497	118	4	2-0	.990	-4	82	99	C-61	0.4
	Year	66	187	29	53	8	2	8	21	15-2	0	31	.283	.333	.476	110	2	2-0	.990	-3	87	100	C-66	0.2
1995	†Cin N	80	218	32	62	14	2	9	44	22-2	2	52	.284	.354	.491	121	6	2-2	.983	-8	95	64	C-65/1-3	0.2
1996	Cin N	108	327	46	95	20	0	12	48	26-5	0	64	.291	.338	.462	109	4	3-4	.981	-5	68	109	C-94	0.4
1997	Cin N	108	254	26	68	18	0	10	34	22-2	1	66	.268	.323	.457	102	0	0-1	.987	-1	76	67	C-64,O-11(6-0-5)/1-7,D-3	0.2
1998	Cin N	130	431	61	120	27	0	11	72	52-6	0	93	.278	.352	.418	101	2	1-0	.988	-9	89	71	*C-126	0.1
1999	Cin N	126	424	58	132	22	2	21	87	30-1	1	67	.311	.354	.521	116	9	0-2	.989	-3	83	50	*C-124	1.1
2000	Cin N	81	266	29	71	12	0	6	24	21-1	2	44	.267	.324	.380	76	-10	0-0	.989	-3	81	73	C-76	-0.9
2001	Cle A	52	116	16	29	2	1	3	11	10-1	1	19	.250	.315	.362	77	-4	0-0	.986	-8	72	82	C-38/D-5	-1.0
Total	11	975	2874	351	784	151	9	94	419	255-29	9	574	.273	.331	.430	99	-9	11-10	.988	-40	89	78	C-871/O-11(6-0-5),1-10,D-8	-0.3

TAUBY, FRED Frederick Joseph (born Frederick Joseph Taubensee) B 3.27.1906 Canton, OH D 11.23.1955 Concord, CA BR/TR 5-9.5/168# d9.1

Year	Tm Lg	G	AB	R	H	2B	3B	HR	RBI	BB-IB	HP	SO	AVG	OBP	SLG	AOPS	ABR	SB-CS	FA	FR	Rng	Thr	G at Pos	BFW
1935	Chi A	13	32	5	4	1	0	0	2	2	0	3	.125	.176	.156	-13	-6	0-0	1.000	1	97	323	/O-7(1-1-5)	-0.4
1937	Phi N	11	20	2	0	0	0	0	3	0	0	5	.000	.000	.000	-93	-5	1	1.000	-0	105	0	/O-7(3-3-1)	-0.6
Total	2	24	52	7	4	1	0	0	5	2	0	8	.077	.111	.096	-43	-11	1-0	1.000	1	100	221	/O-14(4-4-6)	-1.0

TAUSSIG, DON Donald Franklin B 2.19.1932 New York, NY BR/TR 6/180# d4.23

Year	Tm Lg	G	AB	R	H	2B	3B	HR	RBI	BB-IB	HP	SO	AVG	OBP	SLG	AOPS	ABR	SB-CS	FA	FR	Rng	Thr	G at Pos	BFW
1958	SF N	39	50	10	10	0	0	1	4	3-1	0	8	.200	.245	.260	35	-5	0-0	1.000	0	112	0	O-36(27-0-11)	-0.6
1961	StL N	98	188	27	54	14	5	2	25	16-0	0	34	.287	.338	.447	98	0	2-2	.992	6	119	137	O-87(48-20-30)	0.2
1962	Hou N	16	25	1	5	0	0	1	1	2-0	0	11	.200	.259	.320	59	-2	0-0	1.000	0	128	0	/O-4(LF)	-0.2
Total	3	153	263	38	69	14	5	4	30	21-1	0	53	.262	.314	.399	84	-7	2-2	.994	6	118	103	O-127(79-20-41)	-0.6

TAVAREZ, JESUS Jesus Rafael (Alcantaras) B 3.26.1971 Santo Domingo, D.R. BB/TR 6/170# d5.23

Year	Tm Lg	G	AB	R	H	2B	3B	HR	RBI	BB-IB	HP	SO	AVG	OBP	SLG	AOPS	ABR	SB-CS	FA	FR	Rng	Thr	G at Pos	BFW
1994	Fla N	17	39	4	7	0	0	0	4	1-0	0	5	.179	.200	.179	-0	-6	1-1	1.000	3	168	177	O-11(1-2-8)	-0.4
1995	Fla N	63	190	31	55	6	2	2	13	16-1	1	27	.289	.346	.374	90	-3	7-5	1.000	0	102	34	O-61(4-47-32)	-0.4
1996	Fla N	98	114	14	25	3	0	0	6	7-0	0	18	.219	.264	.246	37	-11	5-1	1.000	0	105	0	O-65(25-30-12)	-1.0
1997	Bos A	42	69	12	12	3	1	0	9	4-0	0	9	.174	.216	.246	21	-8	0-0	.980	-0	99	89	O-35(4-29-4)/D-2	-0.8
1998	Bal A	8	11	2	2	0	0	1	1	2-0	0	3	.182	.308	.455	96	0	0-1	1.000	-1	77	0	/O-8(0-5-4)	-0.1
Total	5	228	423	63	101	12	3	3	33	30-1	1	62	.239	.289	.303	56	-28	13-8	.996	2	106	45	O-180(34-113-60)/D-2	-2.7

TAVENER, JACKIE John Adam "Rabbit" B 12.27.1897 Celina, OH D 9.14.1969 Fort Worth, TX BL/TR 5-5/138# d9.24

Year	Tm Lg	G	AB	R	H	2B	3B	HR	RBI	BB-IB	HP	SO	AVG	OBP	SLG	AOPS	ABR	SB-CS	FA	FR	Rng	Thr	G at Pos	BFW
1921	Det A	2	4	0	0	0	0	0	0	0	0	1	.000	.000	.000	-99	-1	0-0	1.000	0	113	0	/S-2	-0.1
1925	Det A	134	453	45	111	11	11	0	47	39	3	60	.245	.309	.318	60	-30	5-4	.963	3	104	96	*S-134	-1.2
1926	Det A	156	532	65	141	22	14	1	58	52	1	53	.265	.332	.365	80	-17	8-7	.952	7	103	106	*S-156	0.6
1927	Det A	116	419	60	115	22	9	5	59	36	1	38	.274	.333	.406	90	-8	19-8	.948	2	100	116	*S-114	0.8
1928	Det A	132	473	59	123	24	15	5	52	33	4	51	.260	.314	.406	86	-12	13-8	.944	12	106	101	*S-131	1.4
1929	Cle A	92	250	25	53	9	4	2	27	26	1	28	.212	.289	.304	51	-19	1-4	.945	22	123	125	S-89	0.9
Total	6	632	2131	254	543	88	53	13	243	186	10	231	.255	.318	.364	75	-87	46-31	.951	46	106	107	S-626	2.4

TAVERAS, ALEX Alejandro Antonio (Betances) B 10.9.1955 Santiago, D.R. BR/TR 5-10/155# d9.9

Year	Tm Lg	G	AB	R	H	2B	3B	HR	RBI	BB-IB	HP	SO	AVG	OBP	SLG	AOPS	ABR	SB-CS	FA	FR	Rng	Thr	G at Pos	BFW
1976	Hou N	14	46	3	10	0	0	0	2	2-0	0	1	.217	.250	.217	37	-4	1-2	.923	3	116	50	/2-7,S-7	-0.1
1982	LA N	11	3	1	1	1	0	0	2	0-0	0	1	.333	.333	.667	178	0	0-0	1.000	2	102	0	/2-4,3-4,S-2	0.2
1983	LA N	10	4	0	0	0	0	0	0	0-0	0	1	.000	.000	.000	-99	-1	0-0	—	0	0	0	/S-3,2-2,3	-0.1
Total	3	35	53	4	11	1	0	0	4	2-0	0	3	.208	.236	.226	34	-5	1-2	.938	4	109	38	/2-13,S-12,3-5	0.0

TAVERAS, FRANK Franklin Crisostomo (Fabian) B 12.24.1949 Las Matas De Santa Cruz, D.R. BR/TR 6/168# d9.25

Year	Tm Lg	G	AB	R	H	2B	3B	HR	RBI	BB-IB	HP	SO	AVG	OBP	SLG	AOPS	ABR	SB-CS	FA	FR	Rng	Thr	G at Pos	BFW
1971	Pit N	1	0	0	0	0	0	0	0	0-0	0	0	—	—	—	—	0	0-0	—	0			R	0.0
1972	Pit N	4	3	0	0	0	0	0	0	1-0	0	1	.000	.250	.000	-24	0	0-0	1.000	-1	56	155	/S-4	-0.1
1974	†Pit N	126	333	33	82	4	2	0	26	25-2	2	41	.246	.300	.270	63	-17	13-4	.941	-18	93	97	*S-124	-2.2
1975	†Pit N	134	378	44	80	9	4	0	23	37-0	2	42	.212	.284	.257	52	-25	17-6	.953	-6	95	110	*S-132	-1.6
1976	Pit N	144	519	76	134	8	6	0	24	44-1	4	79	.258	.321	.297	75	-17	58-11	.952	4	**108**	94	*S-141	1.3
1977	Pit N	147	544	72	137	20	10	1	29	38-2	6	71	.252	.306	.331	69	-24	**70**-18	.962	-22	97	84	*S-146	-2.3
1978	Pit N	157	654	81	182	31	9	0	38	29-3	5	60	.278	.313	.353	82	-16	46-25	.946	-26	91	92	*S-157	-2.6
1979	Pit N	11	45	4	11	3	0	0	1	0-0	0	2	.244	.244	.311	48	-3	2-1	.935	-3	80	70	S-11	-0.6
	NY N	153	635	89	167	26	9	1	33	33-1	2	72	.263	.301	.337	77	-22	42-19	.966	-20	91	95	*S-153	-2.5
	Year	164	680	93	178	29	9	1	34	33-1	2	74	.262	.298	.335	75	-26	44-20	.964	-24	90	93	*S-164	-3.1
1980	NY N	141	562	65	157	27	0	0	25	23-0	1	64	.279	.308	.327	80	-16	32-18	.959	-25	82	79	*S-140	-2.8
1981	NY N	84	283	30	65	11	3	0	11	12-0	2	36	.230	.263	.290	58	-16	16-4	.931	-12	89	99	S-79	-2.0
1982	Mon N	48	87	9	14	5	1	0	4	7-0	0	6	.161	.221	.241	29	-8	4-0	.947	-2	56	103	S-26,2-19	-0.8
Total	11	1150	4043	503	1029	144	44	2	214	249-9	24	474	.255	.301	.313	71	-164	300-106	.953	-131	93	93	*S-1113/2-19	-16.2

TAYLOR, TONY Antonio Nemesio (Sanchez) B 12.19.1935 Central Alara, Cuba BR/TR 5-9/179# d4.15 C8 OF Total (LF)

Year	Tm Lg	G	AB	R	H	2B	3B	HR	RBI	BB-IB	HP	SO	AVG	OBP	SLG	AOPS	ABR	SB-CS	FA	FR	Rng	Thr	G at Pos	BFW
1958	Chi N	140	497	63	117	15	3	6	27	40-0	7	93	.235	.299	.314	64	-26	21-6	.968	12	104	106	*2-137/3	-0.2
1959	Chi N	150	624	96	175	30	8	8	38	45-0	6	86	.280	.331	.393	94	-6	23-9	.970	7	**107**	113	*2-149/S-2	1.5
1960	Chi N	19	76	14	20	3	3	1	9	8-0	1	12	.263	.337	.421	108	1	2-0	.977	1	102	177	2-19	0.3
	Phi N★	127	505	66	145	22	4	4	35	33-2	2	86	.287	.330	.370	92	-5	24-11	.968	-6	101	87	*2-123/3-4	-0.1
	Year	146	581	80	165	25	7	5	44	41-2	3	98	.284	.331	.377	94	-5	26-11	.969	-5	101	98	*2-142/3-4	0.2
1961	Phi N	106	400	47	100	17	3	2	26	29-4	2	59	.250	.304	.322	67	-19	11-5	.980	1	99	106	2-91/3-3	-1.0
1962	Phi N	152	625	87	162	21	5	7	43	68-4	5	82	.259	.336	.342	85	-12	20-9	.972	-15	90	98	*2-150/S-2	-1.2
1963	Phi N	157	640	102	180	20	10	5	49	42-1	7	99	.281	.330	.367	102	1	23-9	**.986**	-4	94	98	*2-149,3-13	1.3
1964	Phi N	154	570	62	143	13	6	4	46	46-8	**13**	74	.251	.320	.316	81	-14	13-7	.977	-22	85	107	*2-150	-2.4
1965	Phi N	106	323	41	74	14	3	3	27	22-0	12	58	.229	.302	.319	77	-10	5-4	.958	-4	94	99	2-86/3-5	-0.8
1966	Phi N	125	434	47	105	14	8	5	40	31-0	1	56	.242	.294	.346	77	-14	8-4	.988	1	101	91	2-68,3-52	-0.9
1967	Phi N	132	462	55	110	16	6	2	34	42-8	5	74	.238	.308	.312	77	-13	10-9	.991	-5	83	120	1-58,3-44,2-42/S-3	-2.1
1968	Phi N	145	547	59	137	20	2	3	38	39-7	3	60	.250	.302	.311	85	-10	22-5	.966	13	110	95	*3-138/2-5,1	0.7
1969	Phi N	138	557	68	146	24	5	3	30	42-1	4	62	.262	.317	.339	87	-10	19-10	.967	-1	112	66	3-71,2-57,1-10	-0.9
1970	Phi N	124	439	74	132	26	9	9	55	50-9	3	67	.301	.374	.462	127	17	9-11	.996	6	88	114	2-59,3-38,O-18(LF)/S	2.4
1971	Phi N	36	107	9	25	2	1	1	5	9-2	0	10	.234	.291	.299	68	-5	2-2	1.000	3	106	146	2-14,3-11/1-2	-0.1
	Det A	55	181	27	52	10	2	3	19	12-1	1	11	.287	.335	.414	107	1	5-1	.995	0	95	97	2-51/3-3	0.5
1972	†Det A	78	228	33	69	12	4	1	20	14-0	2	34	.303	.346	.404	119	5	5-1	.966	-2	87	84	2-67/3-8,1	0.8
1973	Det A	84	275	35	63	9	3	5	24	17-0	1	29	.229	.276	.338	68	-13	9-5	.987	-6	95	85	2-72/1-6,3-4,O(LF)D	-1.5
1974	Phi N	62	64	5	21	4	0	2	13	6-0	1	6	.328	.389	.484	139	3	0-0	1.000	-1	63	0	/1-7,3-5,2-4	0.2
1975	Phi N	79	103	13	25	5	1	1	17	17-2	1	18	.243	.350	.340	90	-1	3-3	.913	2	125	52	3-16/1-4,2-3	0.1
1976	Phi N	26	23	2	6	1	0	0	3	1-0	1	7	.261	.320	.304	76	-1	0-0	—	-0	0	0	/2-2,3	-0.1
Total	19	2195	7680	1005	2007	298	86	75	598	613-49	78	1083	.261	.321	.352	88	-131	234-111	.976	-21	96	103	*2-1498,3-417/1-89,O-19L,S-8,D-2	-3.5

TAYLOR, BEN Benjamin Eugene B 9.30.1924 Metropolis, IL D 5.11.1999 Alma, OK BL/TL 6/185# d7.29

Year	Tm Lg	G	AB	R	H	2B	3B	HR	RBI	BB-IB	HP	SO	AVG	OBP	SLG	AOPS	ABR	SB-CS	FA	FR	Rng	Thr	G at Pos	BFW
1951	StL A	33	93	14	24	2	1	3	6	9	2	22	.258	.337	.398	95	-1	1-1	.972	-2	82	78	1-25	-0.4
1952	Det A	7	18	0	3	0	0	0	0	0	0	5	.167	.167	.167	-7	-3	0-0	1.000	-0	78	112	/1-4	-0.3
1955	Mil N	12	10	2	1	0	0	0	0	2-0	0	4	.100	.250	.100	-3	-1	0-0	1.000	-0	0	0	/1	-0.2
Total	3	52	121	16	28	2	1	3	6	11-0	2	31	.231	.306	.339	73	-5	1-1	.976	-2	81	82	/1-30	-0.9

TAYLOR, CHINK C L B 2.9.1898 Burnet, TX D 7.7.1980 Temple, TX BR/TR 5-9/160# d4.18

Year	Tm Lg	G	AB	R	H	2B	3B	HR	RBI	BB-IB	HP	SO	AVG	OBP	SLG	AOPS	ABR	SB-CS	FA	FR	Rng	Thr	G at Pos	BFW
1925	Chi N	8	6	2	0	0	0	0	0	0	0	0	.000	.000	.000	-99	-2	0-0	1.000	0	138	0	/O-2(1-0-1)	-0.2

Year	Tm Lg	G	AB	R	H	2B	3B	HR	RBI	BB-IB	HP	SO	AVG	OBP	SLG	AOPS	ABR	SB-CS	FA	FR	Rng	Thr	G at Pos	BFW
TAYLOR, CARL Carl Means B 1.20.1944 Sarasota, FL BR/TR 6-2/207# d4.11																								
1968	Pit N	44	71	5	15	1	0	0	7	10-3	0	10	.211	.309	.225	63	-3	1-0	.979	-3	*89*	*115*	C-29/O-2(1-0-1)	-0.6
1969	Pit N	104	221	30	77	10	1	4	33	31-0	3	36	.348	.432	.457	153	18	0-1	.914	1	107	171	O-36(19-0-19),1-24	1.6
1970	StL N	104	245	39	61	12	2	6	45	41-0	1	30	.249	.358	.388	98	1	5-2	.986	-3	85	106	O-46(RF),1-15/3	-0.5
1971	Pit N	7	12	1	2	0	1	0	0	0-0	0	5	.167	.167	.333	39	-1	0-0	1.000	0	121	0	/O(RF)	-0.1
	KC A	20	39	3	7	0	0	0	3	5-0	0	13	.179	.261	.179	30	-4	0-1	.964	1	145	0	O-12(6-0-6)	-0.4
1972	KC A	63	113	17	30	2	1	0	11	17-1	1	16	.265	.361	.301	101	1	4-1	.982	-2	78	60	C-21/O-7(1-0-6),1-6,3-5	0.0
1973	KC A	69	145	18	33	6	1	0	16	32-0	0	20	.228	.363	.283	79	-2	2-2	.980	-2	84	56	C-63/1-2,D	-0.2
Total	6	411	846	113	225	31	6	10	115	136-4	5	130	.266	.367	.352	103	10	12-7	.980	-7	*84*	*68*	C-113,O-104(27-0-79)/1-47,3-6,D	-0.2
TAYLOR, DANNY Daniel Turney B 12.23.1900 Lash, PA D 10.11.1972 Latrobe, PA BR/TR 5-10/190# d6.30																								
1926	Was A	21	50	10	15	0	1	1	5	5	0	7	.300	.364	.400	102	0	1-2	1.000	-0	95	98	O-12(0-1-11)	-0.1
1929	Chi N	2	3	0	0	0	0	0	0	1	0	1	.000	.250	.000	-32	-1	0	1.000	-0	82	0	/O(RF)	-0.1
1930	Chi N	74	219	43	62	14	3	2	37	27	1	34	.283	.364	.402	84	-5	6	.971	-1	97	86	O-52(LF)	-0.9
1931	Chi N	88	270	48	81	13	6	5	41	31	0	46	.300	.372	.448	117	7	4	.989	0	105	64	O-67(39-22-4)	0.4
1932	Chi N	6	22	3	5	2	0	0	3	3	0	1	.227	.320	.318	73	-1	1	.900	-1	96	0	/O-6(0-4-2)	-0.2
	Bro N	105	395	84	128	22	7	11	48	33	1	41	.324	.378	.499	136	20	13	.989	-1	100	91	O-96(CF)	1.7
	Year	111	417	87	133	24	7	11	51	36	1	42	.319	.374	.489	133	19	14	.983	-2	100	85	*O-102(0-100-2)	1.5
1933	Bro N	103	358	75	102	21	9	9	40	47	0	45	.285	.368	.469	144	21	11	.977	-2	101	62	O-91(CF)	1.7
1934	Bro N	120	405	62	121	24	6	7	57	63	2	47	.299	.396	.440	130	20	12	.975	-2	90	121	*O-108(89-21-0)	1.3
1935	Bro N	112	352	51	102	19	5	7	59	46	0	32	.290	.372	.432	118	10	6	.970	-3	96	60	O-99(LF)	0.2
1936	Bro N	43	116	12	34	6	0	2	15	11	1	14	.293	.359	.397	102	1	2	.981	-0	94	107	O-31(LF)	-0.1
Total	9	674	2190	388	650	121	37	44	305	267	5	268	.297	.374	.446	121	72	56-2	.979	-11	98	82	O-563(310-235-18)	3.9
TAYLOR, DWIGHT Dwight Bernard B 3.24.1960 Los Angeles, CA BL/TL 5-9/166# d4.14																								
1986	KC A	4	2	1	0	0	0	0	0	0-0	0	0	.000	.000	.000	-98	-1	0-0	—	-0	0	0	/O(CF)D	-0.1
TAYLOR, ED Edward James B 11.17.1901 Chicago, IL D 1.30.1992 Chula Vista, CA BR/TR 5-6.5/160# d4.14																								
1926	Bos N	92	272	37	73	8	2	0	33	38	5	26	.268	.368	.313	93	0	4	.945	-1	98	102	3-62,S-33	0.4
TAYLOR, LIVE OAK Edward S. d8.21																								
1877	Har N	2	8	0	3	0	0	0	0	0		2	.375	.375	.375	153	0		1.000	-0	0	0	/O-2(LF)	0.0
1884	Pit AA	41	152	22	32	4	1	0		6	3		.211	.255	.250	66	-5		.798	-2	87	0	O-41(CF)	-0.8
Total	2	43	160	22	35	4	1	0	0	6	3	2	.219	.260	.256	70	-5		.802	-3	83	0	/O-43(2-41-0)	-0.8
TAYLOR, FRED Frederick Rankin B 12.3.1924 Zanesville, OH D 1.6.2002 Columbus, OH BL/TR 6-3/201# d9.12																								
1950	Was A	6	16	1	2	0	0	0	0	1	0	2	.125	.176	.125	-23	-3	0-0	.968	0	144	147	/1-3	-0.3
1951	Was A	6	12	1	2	1	0	0	0	0	0	4	.167	.167	.250	12	-2	0-0	.962	-1	57	165	/1-2	-0.2
1952	Was A	10	19	3	5	1	0	0	4	3	0	2	.263	.364	.316	93	0	0-0	1.000	1	177	99	/1-5	0.1
Total	3	22	47	5	9	2	0	0	4	4	0	8	.191	.255	.234	33	-5	0-0	.979	1	137	130	/1-10	-0.4
TAYLOR, HARRY Harry Leonard B 4.4.1866 Halsey Valley, NY D 7.12.1955 Buffalo, NY BL 6-2/160# d4.18 OF Total (23-LF 50-RF)																								
1890	†Lou AA	**134**	553	115	169	7	7	0	53	68	1		.306	.383	.344	117	14	45	.982	3	104	100	*1-118,S-12/2-4,C	0.6
1891	Lou AA	91	348	80	103	7	3	2	35	55	4	30	.296	.398	.351	116	10	15	.978	2	118	106	1-90/32C	0.4
1892	Lou N	125	493	66	128	7	1	0	34	58	4	23	.260	.342	.278	96	1	24	.923	-6	80	114	O-73(23-0-50),1-34,2-14/3-5,S-2	-0.8
1893	Bal N	88	360	50	102	9	1	1	54	32	3	11	.283	.347	.322	77	-12	24	.976	-3	88	100	*1-88	-1.2
Total	4	438	1754	311	502	30	12	3	176	213	12	64	.286	.367	.322	102	13	108	.979	-3	104	104	1-330/O-73R,2-19,S-14,3-6,C-2	-1.0
TAYLOR, HARRY Harry Warren B 12.26.1907 McKeesport, PA D 4.27.1969 Toledo, OH BL/TL 6-1.5/185# d4.14																								
1932	Chi N	10	8	1	1	0	0	0	0	1	0	1	.125	.222	.125	-4	-1	0	1.000	-0	0	0	/1	-0.1
TAYLOR, SANDY James B. 5-10.5/175# d8.11																								
1879	Tro N	24	97	10	21	4	0	0	8	1		8	.216	.224	.258	63	-3		.765	-3	37	0	O-24(LF)	-0.8
TAYLOR, ZACK James Wren B 7.27.1898 Yulee, FL D 9.19.1974 Orlando, FL BR/TR 5-11.5/180# d6.15 M5 C8																								
1920	Bro N	9	13	3	5	2	0	0	5	0	0	2	.385	.385	.538	158	1	0-1	.882	-1	*86*	*89*	/C-9	0.0
1921	Bro N	30	102	6	20	0	2	0	8	1	1	8	.196	.212	.235	17	-12	2-0	.965	-0	*86*	*96*	C-30	-1.0
1922	Bro N	7	14	0	3	0	0	0	2	1	0	1	.214	.267	.214	26	-2	0-0	.950	-1	*79*	*99*	/C-6	-0.2
1923	Bro N	96	337	29	97	11	6	0	46	9	3	13	.288	.312	.356	78	-12	2-5	.967	7	*84*	*136*	C-84	-0.1
1924	Bro N	99	345	36	100	9	4	1	39	14	1	14	.290	.319	.348	81	-10	0-1	**.988**	-4	*88*	*121*	C-93	-0.9
1925	Bro N	109	352	33	109	16	4	3	44	17	1	19	.310	.343	.403	92	-5	0-0	.959	-10	*68*	***173***	C-96	-0.8
1926	Bos N	125	432	36	110	22	3	0	42	28	2	27	.255	.303	.319	74	-16	1	.985	-0	*81*	***134***	*C-123	-0.8
1927	Bos N	30	96	8	23	2	1	1	14	8	0	5	.240	.298	.313	69	-5	0	.988	6	*100*	*127*	C-27	0.3
	NY N	83	258	18	60	7	3	0	21	17	1	20	.233	.283	.283	52	-18	2	.972	-3	*119*	*92*	C-81	-1.6
	Year	113	354	26	83	9	4	1	35	25	1	25	.234	.287	.291	56	-23	2	**.978**	3	*113*	***102***	*C-108	-1.3
1928	Bos N	125	399	36	100	15	1	2	30	33	3	29	.251	.313	.308	66	-20	2	.985	-12	*90*	*99*	*C-124	-2.4
1929	Bos N	34	101	8	25	7	0	0	10	7	1	9	.248	.303	.317	56	-7	0	.965	4	*104*	*164*	C-31	-0.1
	†Chi N	64	215	29	59	16	3	1	31	19	1	18	.274	.336	.391	79	-7	0	.979	2	*129*	*89*	C-64	-0.1
	Year	98	316	37	84	23	3	1	41	26	2	27	.266	.326	.367	72	-14	0	.974	6	*120*	*115*	C-95	-0.2
1930	Chi N	32	95	12	22	2	1	1	11	2	1	12	.232	.255	.305	34	-11	0	1.000	0	*121*	*137*	C-28	-0.8
1931	Chi N	8	4	0	1	0	0	0	0	2	0	1	.250	.500	.250	106	0	0	1.000	0	*0*	*229*	/C-5	0.1
1932	Chi N	21	30	2	6	1	0	0	3	1	0	4	.200	.226	.233	24	-3	0	1.000	2	*269*	*92*	C-14	-0.1
1933	Chi N	16	11	0	0	0	0	0	0	0	0	1	.000	.000	.000	-99	-3	0	1.000	0	*0*	*0*	C-12	-0.3
1934	NY A	4	7	0	1	0	0	0	0	0	0	1	.143	.143	.143	-28	-1	0-0	1.000	-0	*55*	*321*	/C-3	-0.1
1935	Bro N	26	54	2	7	3	0	0	5	2	1	8	.130	.175	.185	-3	-8	0	.970	1	*111*	*170*	C-26	-0.6
Total	16	918	2865	258	748	113	28	9	311	161	16	192	.261	.304	.329	68	-139	9-7	.977	-10	*95*	*124*	C-856	-9.5
TAYLOR, JOE Joe Cephus B 3.2.1926 Chapman, AL D 3.18.1993 Pittsburgh, PA BR/TR 6-1/185# d8.26																								
1954	Phi A	18	58	5	13	1	1	1	8	2	0	9	.224	.250	.328	57	-4	0-1	.943	0	110	99	O-16(9-0-8)	-0.5
1957	Cin N	33	107	14	28	7	0	4	9	6-0	0	24	.262	.301	.439	89	-2	0-1	.971	3	121	159	O-27(19-0-8)	0.0
1958	StL N	18	23	2	7	3	0	1	3	2-0	0	4	.304	.346	.565	135	1	0-0	1.000	0	120	0	/O-5(2-2-1)	0.1
	Bal A	36	77	11	21	4	0	2	9	7-1	0	19	.273	.333	.403	107	1	0-0	.972	-0	101	78	O-21(3-4-15)	0.0
1959	Bal A	14	32	2	5	1	0	1	2	11-0	0	5	.156	.372	.281	84	0	0-0	1.000	-1	70	0	O-12(2-0-10)	-0.2
Total	4	119	297	34	74	16	1	9	31	28-1	0	61	.249	.313	.401	92	-4	0-2	.969	2	108	101	/O-81(35-6-42)	-0.6
TAYLOR, LEO Leo Thomas "Chink" B 5.13.1901 Walla Walla, WA D 5.20.1982 Seattle, WA BR/TR 5-10.5/150# d5.3																								
1923	Chi A	1	0	0	0	0	0	0	0	0	0	0	—	—	—	—	0	0-0	—	0			R	0.0
TAYLOR, REGGIE Reginald Tremain B 1.12.1977 Newberry, SC BL/TR 6-1/175# d9.17																								
2000	Phi N	9	11	1	1	0	0	0	0	0-0	0	8	.091	.091	.091	-54	-3	1-0	.800	-1	76	0	/O-3(CF)	-0.3
2001	Phi N	5	7	1	0	0	0	0	0	1-0	0	1	.000	.125	.000	-65	-2	0-0	1.000	-0	96	0	/O-2(CF)	-0.2
2002	Cin N	135	287	41	73	15	4	9	38	14-3	2	79	.254	.291	.429	88	-8	11-8	.973	1	109	49	*O-103(34-68-5)	-0.8
2003	Cin N	100	180	17	39	5	2	5	19	11-0	1	68	.217	.266	.350	60	-12	7-0	.990	1	107	89	O-60(13-49-3)	-0.9
Total	4	249	485	60	113	20	6	14	57	26-3	3	156	.233	.275	.386	72	-25	19-8	.976	2	107	61	O-168(47-122-8)	-2.2
TAYLOR, HAWK Robert Dale B 4.3.1939 Metropolis, IL BR/TR 6-2/190# d6.9																								
1957	Mil N	7	1	2	0	0	0	0	0	0-0	0	0	.000	.000	.000	-99	0	0-0	—	0	*0*	*0*	/C	0.0
1958	Mil N	4	8	1	1	1	0	0	0	0-0	0	3	.125	.125	.250	-4	-1	0-0	1.000	0	119	0	/O-4(LF)	-0.1
1961	Mil N	20	26	1	5	0	0	1	1	3-0	0	11	.192	.276	.308	58	-2	0-1	1.000	0	104	287	/O-5(4-0-1),C	-0.2
1962	Mil N	20	47	3	12	0	0	0	2	2-0	0	10	.255	.286	.255	48	-4	0-1	.960	1	118	119	O-11(7-0-4)	-0.4
1963	Mil N	16	29	1	2	0	0	0	0	1-0	0	12	.069	.100	.069	-51	-6	0-0	1.000	0	115	0	/O-8(4-3-1)	-0.7
1964	NY N	92	225	20	54	8	0	4	23	8-1	2	33	.240	.272	.329	70	-9	0-0	.981	0	*83*	*154*	C-45,O-16(LF)	-0.8
1965	NY N	25	46	5	7	0	0	4	10	1-0	0	8	.152	.167	.413	61	-3	0-0	.962	-2	*75*	*83*	C-15/1	-0.5
1966	NY N	53	109	5	19	2	0	3	12	3-0	1	19	.174	.204	.275	32	-10	0-1	1.000	-2	*80*	*114*	C-29,1-13	-1.3
1967	NY N	13	37	3	9	3	0	0	4	2-1	0	8	.243	.282	.324	74	-1	0-0	.955	2	*114*	*217*	C-12	0.2
	Cal A	23	52	5	16	3	0	1	3	4-0	0	8	.308	.357	.423	135	2	0-0	1.000	3	291	177	C-19	0.6
1969	KC A	64	89	7	24	5	0	3	21	6-0	0	18	.270	.313	.427	105	0	0-0	.909	1	122	148	O-18(2-0-16)/C-6	0.1

Year	Tm Lg	G	AB	R	H	2B	3B	HR	RBI	BB-IB	HP	SO	AVG	OBP	SLG	AOPS	ABR	SB-CS	FA	FR	Rng	Thr	G at Pos	BFW
1970	KC A	57	55	3	9	3	0	0	6	6-2	1	16	.164	.258	.218	33	-5	0-0	1.000	-1	67	0	/C-3,1	-0.6
Total	11	394	724	56	158	25	0	16	82	36-4	4	146	.218	.258	.319	62	-39	0-3	.984	3	114	144	C-131/O-62(37-3-22),1-15	-3.7
TAYLOR, BOB Robert Lee B 3.20.1944 Leland, MS BL/TR 5-9/170# d4.9																								
1970	SF N	63	84	12	16	0	0	2	10	12-0	4	13	.190	.320	.262	58	-5	0-0	1.000	-1	85	80	O-26(22-0-5)/C	-0.6
TAYLOR, SAMMY Samuel Douglas B 2.27.1933 Woodruff, SC BL/TR 6-2/185# d4.20																								
1958	Chi N	96	301	30	78	12	2	6	36	27-4	0	46	.259	.319	.372	84	-7	2-1	.988	-9	78	63	C-87	-1.2
1959	Chi N	110	353	41	95	13	2	13	43	35-13	1	47	.269	.336	.428	103	1	1-0	.982	-20	53	80	*C-109	-1.4
1960	Chi N	74	150	14	31	9	0	3	17	6-0	1	18	.207	.241	.327	55	-10	0-1	.978	-7	65	161	C-43	-1.6
1961	Chi N	89	235	26	56	8	2	8	23	23-7	4	39	.238	.316	.391	86	-5	0-0	.989	-6	98	67	C-75	-0.7
1962	Chi N	7	15	0	2	1	0	0	1	3-1	0	3	.133	.278	.200	30	-1	0-0	1.000	-1	71	92	/C-6	-0.2
	NY N	68	158	12	35	4	2	3	20	23-1	2	17	.222	.323	.329	76	-5	0-0	.991	-6	80	130	C-50	-0.9
	Year	75	173	12	37	5	2	3	21	26-2	2	20	.214	.319	.318	72	-6	0-0	.992	-7	79	126	C-56	-1.1
1963	NY N	22	35	3	9	0	1	0	6	5-1	0	7	.257	.341	.314	91	0	0-0	1.000	1	127	76	C-13	0.1
	Cin N	3	6	0	0	0	0	0	0	0-0	0	2	.000	.000	.000	-97	-2	0-0	.833	-1	41	0	/C-2	-0.3
	Year	25	41	3	9	0	1	0	6	5-1	0	9	.220	.298	.268	65	-2	0-0	.984	-0	118	68	C-15	-0.2
	Cle A	4	10	1	3	0	0	0	1	0-0	0	2	.300	.300	.300	69	0	0-0	1.000	0	0	375	/C-2	0.0
Total	6	473	1263	127	309	47	9	33	147	122-27	8	181	.245	.313	.375	84	-29	3-2	.986	-48	74	89	C-387	-6.2
TAYLOR, TOMMY Thomas Livingstone Carlton B 9.17.1892 Mexia, TX D 4.5.1956 Greenville, MS BR/TR 5-8.5/160# d7.9																								
1924	†Was A	26	73	11	19	3	1	0	10	2	1	8	.260	.289	.329	61	-5	2-0	.923	-4	60	191	3-16/2-2,O(CF)	-0.8
TAYLOR, BILLY William H. B 12.1870 Butler, KY D 9.12.1905 Cincinnati, OH 5-10/160# d9.19																								
1898	Lou N	9	24	2	6	1	0	0	2	1	1		.250	.308	.292	73	-1	1	.909	-1	115	0	/3-7,2	-0.2
TAYLOR, BILLY William Henry "Bollicky Bill" B 1855 Washington, DC D 5.14.1900 Jacksonville, FL BR/TR 5-11.5/204# d5.21 ▲ OF Total (24-LF 15-CF 38-RF)																								
1881	Wor N	6	28	3	3	1	0	0	2	0		2	.107	.107	.143	-21	-4		.882	0	59	0	/O-5(RF),P	-0.3
	Det N	1	4	0	2	2	0	0	1	0		0	.500	.500	1.000	346	1		.750	-0	99	0	/3	0.1
	Cle N	24	103	6	25	1	0	0	12	0		8	.243	.243	.252	59	-5		.859	-2	61	108	O-23(LF)/P3	-0.8
	Year	31	135	9	30	4	0	0	15	0		10	.222	.222	.252	50	-8		.864	-2	61	86	O-28(23-0-5)/P-2,3-2	-1.0
1882	Pit AA	70	299	40	84	16	13	3		7			.281	.297	.452	157	17		.862	-8			C-27,1-23,3-14/O-8(0-6-2),P	0.8
1883	Pit AA	83	369	43	96	13	7	2		9			.260	.278	.350	105	2		.747	-16	135	0	O-37(0-8-29),C-33,P-19/1-9	-1.0
1884	StL U	43	186	44	68	23	1	3		7			.366	.389	.548	175	12		.872	-2	86	138	P-33,1-10/O-4(1-1-2)	0.2
	Phi AA	30	111	8	28	6	2	0		2	1		.252	.272	.342	93	3		.788	2	126	95	P-30	0.0
1885	Phi AA	6	21	0	4	0	0	0	2	0	0		.190	.190	.190	19	-1		.556	-1	58	0	/P-6	0.0
1886	Bal AA	10	39	4	12	0	1	0	8	1	0		.308	.325	.359	117	0	1	.800	-1	97	0	/P-8,1C	-0.1
1887	Phi AA	1	4	0	1	0	0	0	1	0	0		.250	.250	.250	40	0	0	1.000	-0	55	0	/P	0.0
Total	7	274	1164	148	323	62	24	8	26	26	1	10	.277	.294	.393	121	25	1	.822	-28			P-100/O-77R,C-61,1-43,3-16	-1.1
TAYLOR, BILL William Michael B 12.30.1929 Alhambra, CA BL/TR 6-3/212# d4.14																								
1954	NY N	55	65	4	12	1	0	2	10	3	2	15	.185	.239	.292	38	-6	0-0	1.000	-1	66	0	/O-9(7-0-2)	-0.7
1955	NY N	65	64	9	17	4	0	4	12	1-0	0	16	.266	.273	.516	104	0	0-0	—	-0	0	0	/O-2(RF)	0.0
1956	NY N	1	4	0	1	1	0	0	0	0-0	0	1	.250	.250	.500	96	0	0-0	1.000	-0	67	0	/O(RF)	0.0
1957	NY N	11	9	0	0	0	0	0	0	1-0	0	2	.000	.100	.000	-70	-2	0-0	—	0			H	-0.2
	Det A	9	23	4	8	2	0	1	3	0-0	0	3	.348	.348	.565	142	1	0-0	1.000	-0	74	0	/O-5(LF)	0.1
1958	Det A	8	8	0	3	0	0	0	1	0-0	0	2	.375	.375	.375	100	0	0-0	1.000	0	155	0	/O(RF)	0.0
Total	5	149	173	17	41	8	0	7	26	5-0	2	39	.237	.264	.405	74	-7	0-0	1.000	-1	72	0	/O-18(12-0-6)	-0.8
TAYLOR, ZACHARY Zachary H. d9.10																								
1874	Bal NA	13	48	3	12	0	0	0	3	0		1	.250	.250	.250	61	-2	0-0	.914	-1	112	17	1-13	-0.2
TEBBETTS, BIRDIE George Robert B 11.10.1912 Burlington, VT D 3.24.1999 Manatee, FL BR/TR 5-11.5/170# d9.16 Mil 1943-45 M11																								
1936	Det A	10	33	7	10	1	2	1	4	5	0	3	.303	.395	.545	129	1	0-0	.982	1	158	76	C-10	0.2
1937	Det A	50	162	15	31	4	3	2	16	10	0	13	.191	.238	.290	32	-18	0-0	.963	-4	89	91	C-48	-1.9
1938	Det A	53	143	16	42	6	2	1	25	12	0	13	.294	.348	.385	79	-5	1-2	.985	-1	131	89	C-53	-0.4
1939	Det A	106	341	37	89	22	2	4	53	25	2	20	.261	.315	.372	70	-16	2-1	.970	11	114	126	*C-100	0.1
1940	†Det A	111	379	46	112	24	4	4	46	35	1	14	.296	.357	.412	90	-5	4-5	.975	15	112	**149**	*C-107	1.5
1941	Det A☆	110	359	28	102	19	4	2	47	38	1	29	.284	.354	.376	85	-7	1-2	.977	6	88	**130**	C-98	0.4
1942	Det A★	99	308	24	76	11	0	1	27	39	2	17	.247	.335	.292	71	-10	4-0	.977	7	102	107	C-97	0.3
1946	Det A	87	280	20	68	11	2	1	34	28	0	23	.243	.312	.307	69	-11	1-3	.982	-0	105	86	C-87	-0.8
1947	Det A	20	53	1	5	1	0	0	2	3	0	3	.094	.143	.113	-27	-9	0-1	1.000	5	139	158	C-20	-0.4
	Bos A	90	291	22	87	10	0	1	28	21	0	30	.299	.346	.344	86	-5	2-4	.974	-1	88	75	C-89	-0.3
	Year	110	344	23	92	11	0	1	30	24	0	33	.267	.315	.308	69	-14	2-5	.980	4	97	90	*C-109	-0.7
1948	Bos A★	128	446	54	125	26	2	5	68	62	2	32	.280	.371	.381	95	-1	5-2	.981	-8	116	68	*C-126	-0.1
1949	Bos A★	122	403	42	109	14	0	5	48	62	1	22	.270	.369	.342	83	-8	8-1	.980	-2	130	67	*C-118	-0.2
1950	Bos A	79	268	33	83	10	1	8	45	29	0	26	.310	.377	.444	100	0	1-1	.988	-3	110	90	C-74	0.0
1951	Cle A	55	137	8	36	6	0	2	18	8	1	7	.263	.308	.350	82	-4	0-0	.977	1	93	118	C-44	-0.1
1952	Cle A	42	101	4	25	4	0	1	8	12	2	9	.248	.339	.317	89	-1	0-1	.986	-2	93	98	C-37	-0.2
Total	14	1162	3704	357	1000	169	22	38	469	389	12	261	.270	.341	.358	81	-99	29-23	.978	23	108	100	*C-1108	-1.9
TEBEAU, PUSSY Charles Alston B 2.22.1870 Worcester, MA D 3.25.1950 Pittsfield, MA BR/TR 5-10/175# d7.22																								
1895	Cle N	2	6	3	3	0	0	0	1	2	0	1	.500	.625	.500	182	1	1	1.000	1	303	0	/O-2(RF)	0.1
TEBEAU, GEORGE George E. "White Wings" B 12.26.1861 St.Louis, MO D 2.4.1923 Denver, CO BR/TR 5-9/175# d4.16 b-Patsy ▲																								
1887	Cin AA	85	318	57	94	12	5	4	33	31	3		.296	.364	.403	111	5	37	.887	1	95	68	O-84(80-1-3)/P	0.3
1888	Cin AA	121	411	72	94	12	12	3	51	61	7		.229	.338	.338	111	6	37	.911	2	99	72	*O-121(LF)	0.5
1889	Cin AA	135	496	110	125	21	11	7	70	69	6	62	.252	.350	.381	105	3	61	.887	-7	69	53	*O-134(LF)/1	-0.6
1890	Tol AA	94	381	71	102	16	10	1	36	51	3		.268	.359	.370	112	6	55	.951	1	87	30	*O-94(1-93-0)/P	0.3
1894	Was N	61	222	41	50	10	6	0	28	37	2	20	.225	.341	.324	63	-13	17	.857	-5	90	43	O-61(8-53-0)	-1.7
	Cle N	40	150	32	47	9	4	0	25	25	0	18	.313	.411	.427	98	0	9	.928	-5	24	213	O-27(4-23-0),1-12/3	-0.5
	Year	101	372	73	97	19	10	0	53	62	2	38	.261	.369	.366	78	-12	26	.880	-10	69	97	O-88(12-76-0),1-12/3	-2.2
1895	Cle N	92	341	58	111	16	6	0	68	50	1	29	.326	.413	.408	106	5	12	.873	-7	48	0	O-49(1-0-48),1-43	-0.4
Total	6	628	2319	441	623	96	54	15	311	324	22	129	.269	.364	.376	103	12	228	.900	-20	81	58	O-570(349-170-51)/1-56,P-2,3	-2.1
TEBEAU, PATSY Oliver Wendell B 12.5.1864 St.Louis, MO D 5.15.1918 St.Louis, MO BR/TR 5-8/163# d9.20 M11 b-George																								
1887	Chi N	20	68	8	11	3	0	0	10	4	0	4	.162	.208	.206	14	-8	8	.855	-1	96	147	3-20	-0.8
1889	Cle N	**136**	521	72	147	20	6	8	76	37	2	41	.282	.332	.390	103	0	26	.897	1	100	110	*3-136	0.3
1890	Cle P	110	450	86	134	26	6	5	74	34	3	20	.298	.351	.416	114	9	14	**.872**	13	103	120	*3-110,M	1.9
1891	Cle N	61	249	38	65	8	3	1	41	16	3	13	.261	.313	.329	84	-6	12	.884	6	107	137	3-61/O(LF)M	0.1
1892	†Cle N	86	340	47	83	13	3	2	49	23	8	34	.244	.307	.318	86	-6	6	.911	-3	94	172	3-74/2-5,1-4,S-3,M	-0.7
1893	Cle N	116	486	90	160	32	8	2	102	32	4	11	.329	.375	.440	110	5	19	.980	5	128	82	1-57,3-56/2-3,M	0.8
1894	Cle N	125	523	82	158	23	7	3	89	35	1	35	.302	.347	.390	74	-24	30	.977	-5	75	100	*1-115,2-10/3-2,SM	-2.2
1895	†Cle N	63	264	50	84	13	2	2	52	16	2	18	.318	.362	.405	92	-4	8	.992	3	76	113	1-49/2-9,3-6,M	0.0
1896	†Cle N	132	543	56	146	22	6	2	94	21	3	22	.269	.300	.343	65	-30	20	.985	3	112	**130**	*1-122/3-7,2-5,SPM	-2.3
1897	Cle N	109	412	62	110	15	9	0	59	30	4		.267	.323	.347	73	-17	11	**.994**	1	89	107	*1-92,2-18/3-2,SM	-1.4
1898	Cle N	131	477	53	123	11	4	1	63	53	7		.258	.341	.304	86	-7	5	.984	3	97	85	1-91,2-34/S-7,3-3,M	-0.2
1899	StL N	77	281	27	69	10	3	1	26	18	5		.246	.303	.313	67	-13	5	.980	-3	73	96	1-65,S-11/32M	-1.4
1900	StL N	1	4	0	0	0	0	0	0	0	0		.000	.000	.000	-99	-1	0	.700	-1	65	0	/SM	-0.2
Total	13	1167	4618	671	1290	196	57	27	735	319	42	198	.279	.332	.364	86	-102	164	.984	23	94	104	1-595,3-478/2-85,S-25,PO(LF)	-6.1
TEED, DICK Richard Leroy B 3.8.1926 Springfield, MA BB/TR 5-11/180# d7.24																								
1953	Bro N	1	1	0	0	0	0	0	0	0	0	1	.000	.000	.000	-98	0	0-0	—	0			H	0.0
TEIXEIRA, MARK Mark Charles B 4.11.1980 Annapolis, MD BB/TR 6-3/220# d4.1																								
2003	Tex A	146	529	66	137	29	5	26	84	44-5	14	120	.259	.331	.480	102	1	1-2	.996	-3	96	96	*1-116,O-25(14-0-11),3-15/D-5	-1.3

Year	Tm Lg	G	AB	R	H	2B	3B	HR	RBI	BB-IB	HP	SO	AVG	OBP	SLG	AOPS	ABR	SB-CS	FA	FR	Rng	Thr	G at Pos	BFW
TEJADA, MIGUEL Miguel Odalis (Martinez) B 5.25.1976 Bani, D.R. BR/TR 5-10/170# d8.27																								
1997	Oak A	26	99	10	20	3	2	2	10	2-0	3	22	.202	.240	.333	48	-8	2-0	.968	-1	93	94	S-26	-0.6
1998	Oak A	105	365	53	85	20	1	11	45	28-0	7	86	.233	.298	.384	78	-13	5-6	.951	3	106	110	*S-104	-0.2
1999	Oak A	159	593	93	149	33	4	21	84	57-3	10	94	.251	.325	.427	94	-6	8-7	.973	9	103	100	*S-159	1.3
2000	†Oak A	160	607	105	167	32	1	30	115	66-6	4	102	.275	.349	.479	110	8	6-0	.972	2	105	101	*S-160	2.2
2001	†Oak A	**162**	622	107	166	31	3	31	113	43-5	13	89	.267	.326	.476	108	5	11-5	.973	7	102	102	*S-162	2.4
2002	†Oak A★	**162**	662	108	204	30	0	34	131	38-3	11	84	.308	.354	.508	126	23	7-2	.975	8	107	107	*S-162	4.2
2003	†Oak A	**162**	636	98	177	42	0	27	106	53-7	6	65	.278	.336	.472	110	9	10-0	.972	7	104	97	*S-162	3.0
Total	7	936	3584	574	968	191	11	156	604	287-24	54	542	.270	.331	.460	105	18	49-20	.970	35	104	102	S-935	12.3
TEJADA, WILFREDO Wilfredo Aristides (Andujar) B 11.12.1962 Santo Domingo, D.R. BR/TR 6/175# d9.9																								
1986	Mon N	10	25	1	6	1	0	0	2	2-1	0	8	.240	.296	.280	60	-1	0-0	1.000	-2	93	117	C-10	-0.3
1988	Mon N	8	15	1	4	2	0	0	2	0-0	0	4	.267	.250	.400	85	0	0-0	1.000	0	94	0	/C-7	0.0
Total	2	18	40	2	10	3	0	0	4	2-1	0	12	.250	.279	.325	70	-1	0-0	1.000	-1	93	71	/C-17	-0.3
TEMPLE, JOHNNY John Ellis B 8.8.1927 Lexington, NC D 1.9.1994 Anderson, SC BR/TR 5-11/175# d4.15 C1																								
1952	Cin N	30	97	8	19	3	0	1	5	5	0	1	.196	.235	.258	37	-9	2-1	.984	-0	92	117	2-22	-0.8
1953	Cin N	63	110	14	29	4	0	1	9	7	1	12	.264	.314	.327	67	-5	1-0	.964	7	127	110	2-44	0.4
1954	Cin N	146	505	60	155	14	8	0	44	62	2	24	.307	.384	.366	94	-2	21-7	.973	-4	93	107	*2-144	0.6
1955	Cin N	150	588	94	165	20	3	0	50	80-0	1	32	.281	.365	.325	81	-12	19-4	.971	2	99	**118**	*2-149/S	0.3
1956	Cin N★	154	632	88	180	18	3	2	41	58-0	1	40	.285	.344	.332	78	-17	14-4	.981	-7	99	87	*2-154/O(RF)	-1.1
1957	Cin N★	145	557	85	158	24	4	0	37	**94**-0	4	34	.284	.387	.341	92	0	19-5	.974	-19	89	85	*2-145	-0.6
1958	Cin N	141	542	82	166	31	6	3	47	91-0	0	41	.306	.405	.402	109	13	15-8	.979	-14	90	91	*2-141/1	0.9
1959	Cin N★	149	598	102	186	35	6	8	67	72-2	2	40	.311	.380	.430	114	15	14-3	.974	-25	92	98	*2-149	0.3
1960	Cle A	98	381	50	102	13	1	2	19	32-0	1	20	.268	.326	.323	79	-11	11-5	.974	-23	78	97	2-77,3-17	-2.9
1961	Cle A★	129	518	73	143	22	3	3	30	61-1	0	36	.276	.351	.347	90	-6	9-5	.969	-29	92	91	*2-129	-2.4
1962	Bal A	78	270	28	71	8	1	1	17	36-0	1	22	.263	.352	.311	85	-4	7-4	.981	-10	91	97	2-71	-0.9
	Hou N	31	95	14	25	4	0	0	12	7-0	0	11	.263	.311	.305	72	-4	1-0	.941	-6	92	42	2-26/3	-0.8
1963	Hou N	100	322	22	85	12	1	1	17	41-1	0	24	.264	.347	.317	99	1	7-2	.970	-19	85	55	2-61,3-29	-1.3
1964	Cin N	6	3	0	0	0	0	0	0	2-1	0	1	.000	.400	.000	23	0	0-0	—	0			H	0.0
Total	13	1420	5218	720	1484	208	36	22	395	648-5	13	338	.284	.363	.351	91	-41	140-48	.974	-146	93	95	*2-1312/3-47,1O(RF)S	-8.3
TEMPLETON, GARRY Garry Lewis B 3.24.1956 Lockney, TX BB/TR 5-11/190# d8.9																								
1976	StL N	53	213	32	62	8	2	1	17	7-0	1	33	.291	.314	.362	91	-3	11-7	.922	5	104	127	S-53	0.9
1977	StL N★	153	621	94	200	19	**18**	8	79	15-3	1	70	.322	.336	.449	111	5	28-24	.958	3	99	121	*S-151	2.2
1978	StL N	155	647	82	181	31	**13**	2	47	22-3	1	87	.280	.303	.377	91	-11	34-11	.953	**33**	111	124	*S-155	4.3
1979	StL N✱	154	672	105	**211**	32	**19**	9	62	18-4	1	91	.314	.331	.458	113	8	26-10	.960	24	113	121	*S-150	5.0
1980	StL N	118	504	83	161	19	9	4	43	18-6	0	43	.319	.342	.417	108	3	31-15	.959	36	**122**	**125**	*S-115	5.4
1981	StL N	80	333	47	96	16	8	1	33	14-3	0	55	.288	.315	.393	98	-2	8-12	.960	11	113	**123**	S-76	1.5
1982	SD N	141	563	76	139	25	8	6	64	26-7	1	82	.247	.279	.352	80	-18	27-16	.961	-23	94	95	*S-136	-2.8
1983	SD N	126	460	39	121	20	2	3	40	21-7	0	57	.263	.294	.335	77	-16	16-6	.960	-7	95	98	*S-123	-0.9
1984	†SD N	148	493	40	127	19	3	2	35	39-**23**	1	81	.258	.312	.320	79	-14	8-3	.960	-24	92	99	*S-146	-2.4
1985	SD N★	148	546	63	154	30	2	6	55	41-**24**	1	88	.282	.332	.377	100	0	16-6	.968	-4	101	115	*S-148	1.3
1986	SD N	147	510	42	126	21	2	2	44	35-21	1	86	.247	.296	.308	68	-23	10-5	.966	-25	88	74	*S-144	-3.5
1987	SD N	148	510	42	113	13	5	5	48	42-11	1	92	.222	.281	.296	55	-34	14-3	.972	13	106	92	*S-146	-0.4
1988	SD N	110	362	35	90	15	7	3	36	20-10	0	50	.249	.286	.354	85	-9	8-2	.968	9	106	118	*S-105/3-2	1.0
1989	SD N	142	506	43	129	26	3	6	40	23-12	0	80	.255	.286	.354	82	-13	1-3	.970	13	105	112	*S-140	1.0
1990	SD N	144	505	45	125	25	3	9	59	24-7	0	59	.248	.280	.362	75	-19	1-4	.957	-9	96	107	*S-135	-1.9
1991	SD N	32	57	5	11	1	1	1	6	1-0	0	9	.193	.203	.298	39	-5	0-1	.950	-3	86	131	3-15/S	-0.8
	NY N	80	219	20	50	9	1	2	20	9-3	0	29	.228	.257	.306	59	-13	3-1	.963	8	112	117	S-40,1-25/3-2,O-2(RF)	-0.4
	Year	112	276	25	61	10	2	3	26	10-3	0	38	.221	.246	.304	54	-18	3-2	.963	5	110	115	S-41,1-25,3-17/O-2(RF)	-1.2
Total	16	2079	7721	893	2096	329	106	70	728	375-144	9	1092	.271	.304	.369	87	-164	242-129	.961	61	103	109	*S-1964/1-25,3-19,O-2(RF)	9.5
TENACE, GENE Fury Gene (born Fiore Gino Tennaci) B 10.10.1946 Russellton, PA BR/TR 6/190# d5.29 M1 C10 OF Total (1-LF 10-RF)																								
1969	Oak A	16	38	1	6	0	0	1	2	1-0	1	15	.158	.200	.237	23	-4	0-0	1.000	1	99	70	C-13	-0.3
1970	Oak A	38	105	19	32	6	0	7	20	23-2	0	30	.305	.430	.562	178	12	0-2	.990	4	51	127	C-30	1.7
1971	†Oak A	65	179	26	49	7	0	7	25	29-0	2	34	.274	.381	.430	132	9	2-1	.994	-2	132	67	C-52/O(LF)	0.9
1972	†Oak A	82	227	22	51	5	3	5	32	24-2	3	42	.225	.307	.339	97	-1	0-0	.979	-5	102	69	C-49/O-9(RF),1-7,2-2,3-2	-0.5
1973	†Oak A	160	510	83	132	18	2	24	84	101-8	10	94	.259	.387	.443	142	34	2-2	.989	-6	86	107	*1-134,C-33/2D	1.9
1974	†Oak A	158	484	71	102	17	1	26	73	**110**-6	12	105	.211	.367	.411	133	27	2-9	.995	5	80	107	*1-106,C-79/2-3	2.5
1975	†Oak A★	158	498	83	127	17	0	29	87	106-2	12	127	.255	.395	.464	146	36	7-4	.984	2	104	79	*C-125,1-68/D	4.0
1976	Oak A	128	417	64	104	19	1	22	66	81-2	4	91	.249	.373	.458	150	30	5-4	.995	-12	69	95	1-70,C-65/D-2	1.6
1977	SD N	147	437	66	102	24	4	15	61	**125**-10	**13**	119	.233	.415	.410	137	34	5-3	.980	1	96	129	C-99,1-36,3-14	3.7
1978	SD N	142	401	60	90	18	4	16	61	101-8	11	98	.224	.392	.409	135	26	6-5	.993	4	95	118	1-80,C-71/3	2.9
1979	SD N	151	463	61	122	16	4	20	67	105-4	7	106	.263	.403	.445	141	32	2-6	**.998**	8	140	**126**	C-94,1-72	3.9
1980	SD N	133	316	46	70	11	1	17	50	92-11	4	63	.222	.399	.424	139	23	4-4	.979	-4	94	109	*C-104,1-19	2.2
1981	StL N	58	129	26	30	7	0	5	22	38-2	4	26	.233	.416	.403	131	8	0-0	.980	-6	94	82	C-38/1-7	0.4
1982	†StL N	66	124	18	32	9	0	7	18	36-1	4	31	.258	.436	.500	160	13	1-1	.994	2	92	118	C-37/1-7	1.7
1983	Pit N	53	62	7	11	5	0	0	6	12-0	4	17	.177	.346	.258	68	-2	0-1	.989	-0	76	83	1-19/C-3,O(RF)	-0.3
Total	15	1555	4390	653	1060	179	20	201	674	984-58	91	998	.241	.388	.429	137	277	36-42	.986	-8	105	100	C-892,1-625/3-17,O-11R,D-6,2-6	26.3
TENNANT, TOM Thomas Francis B 7.3.1882 Monroe, WI D 2.15.1955 San Carlos, CA BL/TL 5-11/165# d4.18																								
1912	StL A	2	2	1	0	0	0	0	0	0	0		.000	.000	.000	-99	-1	0	—	0			H	-0.1
TENNEY, FRED Fred Clay B 7.9.1859 Marlborough, NH D 6.15.1919 Fall River, MA d4.28 ▲																								
1884	Was U	32	119	17	28	3	1	0		6			.235	.272	.277	69	-8		.867	-0	85	209	O-27(0-1-26)/1-6	-0.8
	Bos U	4	17	1	2	0	0	0		0			.118	.118	.118	-29	-3		.750	-1	51	0	/P-4	0.0
	Wil U	1	3	0	0	0	0	0		0			.000	.000	.000	-97	-1		1.000	0	55	1698	/P	0.0
	Year	37	139	18	30	3	1	0		6			.216	.248	.252	53	-12		.867	-1	85	209	O-27(0-1-26)/1-6,P-5	-0.8
TENNEY, FRED Frederick B 11.26.1871 Georgetown, MA D 7.3.1952 Boston, MA BL/TL 5-9/155# d6.16 M4																								
1894	Bos N	27	86	23	34	7	1	2	21	12	0	9	.395	.469	.570	139	6	6	.893	2	*120*	*108*	C-20/O-6(3-2-1),1	0.7
1895	Bos N	49	173	35	47	9	1	1	21	24	0	5	.272	.360	.353	78	-5	6	.885	2	160	129	O-28(25-3-0),C-21	-0.3
1896	Bos N	88	348	64	117	14	3	2	49	36	1	12	.336	.400	.411	108	4	18	.957	4	119	56	O-60(7-0-53),C-27	0.7
1897	†Bos N	132	566	125	180	24	3	1	85	49	4		.318	.376	.376	93	-5	34	.988	5	111	109	*1-128/O-4(RF)	0.0
1898	Bos N	117	488	106	160	25	5	0	62	33	0		.328	.370	.400	114	9	23	.980	5	115	115	*1-117/C	1.2
1899	Bos N	150	603	115	209	19	17	1	67	63	3		.347	.411	.439	122	18	28	.978	10	131	**134**	*1-150	2.4
1900	Bos N	112	437	77	122	13	5	1	56	39	6		.279	.346	.339	80	-12	17	.981	9	**131**	85	*1-111	-0.4
1901	Bos N	115	451	66	127	13	1	1	22	37	3		.282	.340	.322	85	-8	15	.976	7	**132**	112	*1-113/C-2	-0.2
1902	Bos N	134	489	88	154	18	3	2	30	73	5		.315	.409	.376	141	29	21	**.985**	12	**135**	104	*1-134	**4.0**
1903	Bos N	122	447	79	140	22	3	3	41	70	8		.313	.415	.396	137	28	21	.974	9	**131**	93	*1-122	3.2
1904	Bos N	147	533	76	144	17	9	1	37	57	9		.270	.351	.341	118	14	17	.986	8	120	95	*1-144/O-4(0-1-3)	2.0
1905	Bos N	149	549	84	158	18	3	0	28	67	3		.288	.368	.332	111	12	17	.982	22	**160**	87	*1-148/PM	3.2
1906	Bos N	143	544	61	154	12	8	1	28	58	5		.283	.357	.340	121	14	17	.983	11	**130**	107	*1-143,M	2.4
1907	Bos N	150	554	83	151	18	8	0	26	82	5		.273	.371	.334	121	18	15	.989	9	**122**	104	*1-149,M	2.7
1908	NY N	156	583	**101**	149	20	1	2	49	72	7		.256	.344	.304	102	6	17	.990	10	121	111	*1-156	1.5
1909	NY N	101	375	43	88	8	2	3	30	52	3		.235	.333	.291	92	-2	8	.986	8	131	115	1-98	0.5
1911	Bos N	102	369	52	97	13	4	1	36	50	1	17	.263	.352	.328	84	-7	5	.985	4	120	74	1-96/O-2(0-1-1),M	-0.6
Total	17	1994	7595	1278	2231	270	77	22	688	874	63	43	.294	.371	.358	109	119	285	.983	135	128	104	*1-1810,O-104(35-7-62)/C-71,P	23.0
TEPEDINO, FRANK Frank Ronald B 11.23.1947 Brooklyn, NY BL/TL 5-11/192# d5.12																								
1967	NY A	9	5	0	2	0	0	0	0	1-0	0	1	.400	.500	.400	175	1	0-0	1.000	-0	0	0	/1	0.1
1969	NY A	13	39	6	9	0	0	0	4	4-0	0	4	.231	.302	.231	53	-2	1-0	.950	-1	99	0	O-13(RF)	-0.4
1970	NY A	16	19	2	6	2	0	0	2	1-0	0	2	.316	.350	.421	118	0	0-1	1.000	-1	0	0	/1O(LF)	-0.1
1971	NY A	6	6	0	0	0	0	0	0	0-0	0	0	.000	.000	.000	-99	-2	0-0	1.000	0	224	0	/O(LF)	-0.2
	Mil A	53	106	11	21	1	0	2	7	4-0	1	17	.198	.234	.264	41	-9	2-2	.986	2	144	96	1-28	-0.9

Year	Tm Lg	G	AB	R	H	2B	3B	HR	RBI	BB-IB	HP	SO	AVG	OBP	SLG	AOPS	ABR	SB-CS	FA	FR	Rng	Thr	G at Pos	BFW
	Year	59	112	11	21	1	0	2	7	4-0	1	17	.188	.222	.250	34	-10	2-2	.986	3	144	96	1-28/O(LF)	-1.1
1972	NY A	8	8	0	0	0	0	0	0	0-0	0	1	.000	.000	.000	-99	-2	0-0	—	0			H	-0.2
1973	Atl N	74	148	20	45	5	0	4	29	13-3	0	21	.304	.354	.419	107	2	0-0	.992	1	108	91	1-58	-0.1
1974	Atl N	78	169	11	39	5	1	0	16	9-2	1	13	.231	.272	.272	51	-11	1-2	.988	-0	103	128	1-46	-1.6
1975	Atl N	8	7	0	0	0	0	0	0	1-0	0	2	.000	.125	.000	-61	-2	0-0	—	0			H	-0.2
Total	8	265	507	50	122	13	1	6	58	33-5	2	61	.241	.288	.306	65	-25	4-5	.989	2	113	105	1-134/O-15(2-0-13)	-3.6
TEPSIC, JOE Joseph John B 9.18.1923 Slovan, PA BR/TR 5-9/170# d7.12																								
1946	Bro N	15	5	2	0	0	0	0	0	1	0	1	.000	.167	.000	-50	-1	0	1.000	0	138	0	/O(LF)	-0.1
TERRELL, JERRY Jerry Wayne B 7.13.1946 Waseca, MN BR/TR (BB 1974 (part)) 6/170# d4.14 OF Total (12-LF 1-CF 11-RF)																								
1973	Min A	124	438	43	116	15	2	1	32	21-0	1	56	.265	.297	.315	71	-18	13-7	.962	-12	87	74	S-81,3-30,2-14/O(RF)D	-2.0
1974	Min A	116	229	43	56	4	6	0	19	11-1	0	27	.245	.279	.314	68	-10	3-2	.960	12	109	105	S-34,2-26,3-21,D-12/O-3(LF),1-2	0.5
1975	Min A	108	385	48	110	16	2	1	36	19-0	3	27	.286	.324	.345	88	-6	4-4	.947	2	98	131	S-41,2-39,1-15,3-12/O-6(RF),D-2	0.0
1976	Min A	89	171	29	42	3	1	0	8	9-0	1	15	.246	.286	.275	64	-8	11-2	.988	2	88	101	2-31,3-26,S-16,D-12/O-6(3-1-2)	-0.3
1977	Min A	93	214	32	48	6	0	1	20	11-1	1	21	.224	.263	.266	46	-16	10-4	.953	1	101	115	3-59,2-14/S-7,1O(RF)D	-1.5
1978	KC A	73	133	14	27	1	0	0	8	4-0	0	13	.203	.225	.211	23	-14	8-4	1.000	-2	95	68	2-31,3-25,S-11/1-5	-1.5
1979	KC A	31	40	5	12	3	0	1	2	1-0	0	1	.300	.317	.450	102	0	1-0	.963	-1	97	54	3-19/2-7,PSD	0.0
1980	KC A	23	16	4	1	0	0	0	0	0-0	0	0	.063	.063	.063	-65	-4	0-0	1.000	1	112	0	/O-7(6-0-1),1-3,2-3,PD	-0.3
Total	8	657	1626	218	412	48	11	4	125	76-2	6	160	.253	.288	.304	66	-76	50-23	.961	3	102	132	3-192,S-191,2-165/D-39,1-26,OL,P	-5.1
TERRELL, TOM John Thomas B 6.19.1867 Louisville, KY D 7.9.1893 Louisville, KY d10.5																								
1886	Lou AA	1	4	0	1	0	0	0	0	0	0		.250	.250	.250	54	0	0	—	-1	0	0	/O(LF)C	-0.1
TERRERO, LUIS Luis Enrique B 5.18.1980 Barahona, D.R. BR/TR 6-2/206# d7.10																								
2003	Ari N	5	4	0	1	0	0	0	0	0-0	1	1	.250	.400	.250	68	0	0-0	1.000	-0	68	0	/O-3(0-2-1)	0.0
TERRY, WALLACE Wallace W. B 10.1850 Attleborough, PA D 1.21.1916 Philadelphia, PA d4.26																								
1875	Was NA	6	22	0	4	0	1	0	2	0		1	.182	.182	.273	58	-1	0-0	.810	-3	0	0	/1-4,O-3(0-1-2)	-0.3
TERRY, ADONIS William H B 8.7.1864 Westfield, MA D 2.24.1915 Milwaukee, WI BR/TR 5-11.5/168# d5.1 U1 ▲ OF Total (94-LF 43-CF 79-RF)																								
1884	Bro AA	67	236	15	55	10	3	0		8	0		.233	.258	.301	81	-5		.764	-2	83	0	P-56,O-13(2-7-4)	-0.1
1885	Bro AA	71	264	23	45	1	3	1	20	10	0		.170	.201	.208	29	-22		.883	1	120	133	O-47(26-11-10),P-25/3	-1.4
1886	Bro AA	75	299	34	71	8	9	2	39	10	1		.237	.265	.344	89	-6	17	.934	1	**128**	127	P-34,O-32(10-11-11),S-13	-0.4
1887	Bro AA	86	352	56	103	6	10	3	65	16	0		.293	.323	.392	98	-4	27	.895	2	62	55	O-49(12-4-33),P-40/S-2	-0.3
1888	Bro AA	30	115	13	29	6	0	0	8	5	0		.252	.283	.304	89	-1	7	.909	2	93	203	P-23/O-7(2-4-1),1-2	0.1
1889	†Bro AA	49	160	29	48	6	6	2	26	14	0	14	.300	.356	.450	129	5	8	.963	5	125	113	P-41,1-10	0.2
1890	†Bro N	99	363	63	101	17	9	4	59	40	4	34	.278	.356	.408	122	10	32	.930	-3	40	103	O-54(42-5-7),P-46/1	0.1
1891	Bro N	30	91	10	19	7	1	0	6	9	3	26	.209	.301	.308	78	-2	4	.957	-1	85	70	P-25/O-5(RF)	-0.1
1892	Bal N	1	4	0	0	0	0	0	0	0	0	1	.000	.000	.000	-97	-1	0	1.000	0	149	0	/P	0.0
	Pit N	31	100	10	16	0	4	2	11	10	0	11	.160	.236	.300	62	-6	2	.938	-1	90	0	P-30/O(CF)	-0.1
	Year	32	104	10	16	0	4	2	11	10	0	12	.154	.228	.288	56	-7	2	.940	-1	92	0	P-31/O(CF)	-0.1
1893	Pit N	26	71	9	18	4	3	0	11	3	1	12	.254	.293	.394	84	2	1	.920	0	98	170	P-26	0.0
1894	Pit N	1	0	0	0	0	0	0	0	0	0	0	—	—	—	—	0	0	—	-0	0	0	/P	0.0
	Chi N	30	95	19	33	4	2	0	17	11	0	12	.347	.415	.432	99	0	3	.875	-1	85	0	P-23/O-7(RF),1-2	0.0
	Year	31	95	19	33	4	2	0	17	11	0	12	.347	.415	.432	99	0	3	.875	-1	84	0	P-24/O-7(RF),1-2	0.0
1895	Chi N	40	137	18	30	3	2	1	10	2	1	17	.219	.236	.292	33	-15	1	.895	1	115	123	P-38/O(RF)S	0.0
1896	Chi N	30	99	14	26	4	2	0	15	8	1	12	.263	.324	.343	73	2	4	.968	-2	74	0	P-30	0.0
1897	Chi N	1	3	1	0	0	0	0	0	0	0		.000	.000	.000	-96	-1	0	.750	0	164	0	/P	0.0
Total	14	667	2389	314	594	76	54	15	287	146	11	139	.249	.295	.344	85	-44	106	.903	1	101	69	P-440,O-216L/S-16,1-15,3	-2.0
TERRY, BILL William Harold "Memphis Bill" B 10.30.1898 Atlanta, GA D 1.9.1989 Jacksonville, FL BL/TL 6-1/200# d9.24 M10 HF1954																								
1923	NY N	3	7	1	1	0	0	0	0	2	0	2	.143	.333	.143	30	-1	0-0	1.000	0	94	67	/1-2	-0.1
1924	†NY N	77	163	26	39	7	2	5	24	17	0	18	.239	.311	.399	91	-2	1-1	.988	-1	82	120	1-35	-0.6
1925	NY N	133	489	75	156	31	6	11	70	42	1	52	.319	.374	.474	120	15	4-5	.990	4	**113**	84	*1-126	0.9
1926	NY N	98	225	26	65	12	5	5	43	22	0	17	.289	.352	.453	117	5	3	.979	4	140	124	1-38,O-14(1-0-13)	0.5
1927	NY N	150	580	101	189	32	13	20	121	46	2	53	.326	.377	.529	141	31	1	.993	5	**111**	111	*1-150	2.6
1928	NY N	149	568	100	185	36	11	17	101	64	0	36	.326	.394	.518	136	30	7	.993	-2	93	**123**	*1-149	1.8
1929	NY N	150	607	103	226	39	5	14	117	48	0	35	.372	.418	.522	132	31	10	.994	7	**118**	**129**	*1-149/O(LF)	2.5
1930	NY N	**154**	633	139	**254**	39	15	23	129	57	1	33	**.401**	.452	.619	159	61	8	.990	14	**137**	94	*1-154	5.6
1931	NY N	**153**	611	**121**	213	43	**20**	9	112	47	2	36	.349	.397	.529	150	**42**	8	.990	10	129	89	*1-153	**3.7**
1932	NY N	**154**	643	124	225	42	11	28	117	32	1	23	.350	.382	.580	158	49	4	.991	15	**135**	99	*1-154,M	4.8
1933	†NY N★	123	475	68	153	20	5	6	58	40	0	23	.322	.375	.423	129	19	3	.992	1	101	**120**	*1-117,M	0.9
1934	NY N★	**153**	602	109	213	30	6	8	83	60	2	47	.354	.414	.463	138	35	0	**.994**	6	115	**123**	*1-153,M	2.5
1935	NY N★	145	596	91	203	32	8	6	64	41	0	55	.341	.383	.451	126	22	7	**.996**	6	**113**	109	*1-143,M	1.4
1936	†NY N	79	229	36	71	10	5	2	39	19	0	19	.310	.363	.424	112	4	0	.996	3	120	142	1-56,M	0.2
Total	14	1721	6428	1120	2193	373	112	154	1078	537	9	449	.341	.393	.506	137	341	56-6	.992	72	117	110	*1-1579/O-15(2-0-13)	26.7
TERRY, ZEB Zebulon Alexander B 6.17.1891 Denison, TX D 3.14.1988 Los Angeles, CA BR/TR 5-8/129# d4.12 Mil 1918																								
1916	Chi A	94	269	20	51	8	4	0	17	33	6	36	.190	.292	.249	62	-12	4	.935	-9	93	130	S-93	-1.7
1917	Chi A	2	1	0	0	0	0	0	0	2	0	0	.000	.667	.000	102	0	0	1.000	-0	74	0	/S	0.0
1918	Bos N	28	105	17	32	2	2	0	8	8	1	14	.305	.360	.362	125	3	1	.977	7	115	116	S-27	1.3
1919	Pit N	129	472	46	107	12	6	0	27	31	4	26	.227	.280	.278	65	-20	12	**.960**	-31	90	84	*S-127	-4.7
1920	Chi N	133	496	56	139	26	9	0	52	44	2	22	.280	.341	.369	102	2	12-16	.962	17	107	99	S-70,2-63	2.4
1921	Chi N	123	488	59	134	18	1	2	45	27	4	19	.275	.318	.328	71	-20	1-13	.972	8	103	94	*2-122	-1.2
1922	Chi N	131	496	56	142	24	2	0	67	34	2	16	.286	.335	.343	74	-19	2-11	.964	5	102	**111**	*2-125/S-4,3-3	-1.2
Total	7	640	2327	254	605	90	24	2	216	179	19	133	.260	.318	.322	78	-66	32-40	.956	-3	97	103	S-322,2-310/3-3	-5.1
TERWILLIGER, WAYNE Willard Wayne "Twig" B 6.27.1925 Clare, MI BR/TR 5-11/170# d8.6 C18																								
1949	Chi N	36	112	11	25	2	1	2	10	16	1	22	.223	.326	.313	74	-4	0	.978	4	119	48	2-34	0.2
1950	Chi N	133	480	63	116	22	3	10	32	43	5	63	.242	.311	.363	77	-16	13	.967	-7	**106**	78	*2-126/13O(CF)	-1.6
1951	Chi N	50	192	26	41	6	0	0	10	29	0	21	.214	.317	.245	52	-12	3-1	.969	-2	99	93	2-49	-1.1
	Bro N	37	50	11	14	1	0	0	4	8	1	7	.280	.390	.300	87	0	1-0	.949	4	126	102	2-24/3	0.4
	Year	87	242	37	55	7	0	0	14	37	1	28	.227	.332	.256	59	-12	4-1	.964	1	104	95	2-73/3	-0.7
1953	Was A	134	464	62	117	24	4	4	46	64	0	65	.252	.343	.347	89	-6	7-4	.982	7	**107**	112	*2-133	1.1
1954	Was A	106	337	42	70	10	1	3	24	32	3	40	.208	.282	.270	55	-22	3-3	.972	10	117	115	2-90,3-10/S-3	-0.6
1955	NY N	80	257	29	66	16	1	1	18	36-1	1	42	.257	.348	.339	84	-4	2-4	.985	17	112	128	2-78/S3	1.7
1956	NY N	14	18	0	4	1	0	0	0	0-0	0	5	.222	.222	.278	34	-2	0-0	.958	1	88	121	/2-6	-0.1
1959	KC A	74	180	27	48	11	0	2	18	19-0	0	31	.267	.335	.361	90	-2	2-2	.972	12	115	109	2-63/S-2,3	1.4
1960	KC A	2	1	0	0	0	0	0	0	0-0	0	0	.000	.000	.000	-99	0	0-0	1.000	0	103	376	/2-2	0.0
Total	9	666	2091	271	501	93	10	22	162	247-1	11	296	.240	.323	.325	76	-68	31-14	.974	45	110	102	2-605/3-14,S-6,O(CF)1	1.4
TESCH, AL Albert John "Tiny" B 1.27.1891 Jersey City, NJ D 8.3.1947 Jersey City, NJ BB/TR 5-10/155# d8.21																								
1915	Bro F	8	7	2	2	1	0	0	2	0	0	0	.286	.286	.429	100	0	0	.867	1	176	151	/2-3	0.1
TESTA, NICK Nicholas B 6.29.1928 New York, NY BR/TR 5-8/180# d4.23 C1																								
1958	SF N	1	0	0	0	0	0	0	0	0-0	0	0	—	—	—	—	0	0-0	.000	-0	*0*	*0*	/C	0.0
TETTELBACH, DICK Richard Morley "Tut" B 6.26.1929 New Haven, CT D 1.26.1995 E.Harwich, MA BR/TR 6/195# d9.25																								
1955	NY A	2	5	0	0	0	0	0	0	0-0	0	0	.000	.000	.000	-99	-1	0-0	1.000	0	0	1288	/O-2(LF)	-0.1
1956	Was A	18	64	10	10	1	2	1	9	14-0	0	15	.156	.304	.281	56	-4	0-1	1.000	1	98	137	O-18(LF)	-0.5
1957	Was A	9	11	2	2	0	0	0	1	4-0	0	2	.182	.375	.182	65	0	0-0	.900	0	124	0	/O-3(2-2-0)	0.0
Total	3	29	80	12	12	1	2	1	10	18-0	0	17	.150	.300	.250	49	-5	0-1	.980	1	98	164	/O-23(22-2-0)	-0.6
TETTLETON, MICKEY Mickey Lee B 9.16.1960 Oklahoma City, OK BB/TR 6-2/212# d6.30 OF Total (24-LF 120-RF)																								
1984	Oak A	33	76	10	20	2	1	1	5	11-0	0	21	.263	.352	.355	105	1	0-0	.992	1	155	97	C-32	0.2
1985	Oak A	78	211	23	53	12	0	3	15	28-0	2	59	.251	.344	.351	98	1	2-2	.989	-9	72	107	C-76/D	-0.5
1986	Oak A	90	211	26	43	9	0	10	35	39-0	1	51	.204	.325	.389	103	2	7-1	.984	-8	80	111	C-89	-0.2

Year	Tm Lg	G	AB	R	H	2B	3B	HR	RBI	BB-IB	HP	SO	AVG	OBP	SLG	AOPS	ABR	SB-CS	FA	FR	Rng	Thr	G at Pos	BFW
1987	Oak A	82	211	19	41	3	0	8	26	30-0	0	65	.194	.292	.322	68	-10	1-1	.987	-6	94	72	C-80/1D	-1.2
1988	Bal A	86	283	31	74	11	1	11	37	28-2	2	70	.261	.330	.424	113	5	0-1	.992	-7	80	101	C-80	0.2
1989	Bal A★	117	411	72	106	21	2	26	65	73-4	1	117	.258	.369	.509	150	29	3-2	.994	-6	91	95	C-75,D-43	2.6
1990	Bal A	135	444	68	99	21	2	15	51	106-3	5	160	.223	.376	.381	117	16	2-4	.991	-6	103	71	C-90,D-40/1-5,O(RF)	1.3
1991	Det A	154	501	85	132	17	2	31	89	101-9	2	131	.263	.387	.491	140	30	3-3	.990	-2	114	100	*C-125,D-24/O-3(2-0-1),1	3.3
1992	Det A	157	525	82	125	25	0	32	83	**122**-18	1	137	.238	.379	.469	137	30	0-6	**.996**	-9	111	96	*C-113,D-40/1-3,O-2(1-0-1)	2.5
1993	Det A	152	522	79	128	25	4	32	110	109-12	0	139	.245	.372	.492	132	26	3-7	.992	-9	84	113	1-59,C-56,O-55(18-0-39)/D-4	1.2
1994	Det A★	107	339	57	84	18	2	17	51	97-10	5	98	.248	.419	.463	127	20	0-1	.992	-14	66	72	C-53,1-24,D-22,O-18(1-0-17)	0.5
1995	Tex A	134	429	76	102	19	1	32	78	107-5	7	110	.238	.396	.510	131	23	0-0	.972	-3	92	81	O-63(2-0-61),D-58/1-9,C-3	1.2
1996	†Tex A	143	491	78	121	26	1	24	83	95-8	3	137	.246	.366	.450	101	3	2-1	.977	-2	77	76	*D-115,1-23	-0.8
1997	Tex A	17	44	5	4	1	0	3	4	3-1	1	12	.091	.167	.318	22	-6	0-0	—	0	0	0	D-13	-0.6
Total	14	1485	4698	711	1132	210	16	245	732	949-72	30	1307	.241	.369	.449	122	170	23-29	.991	-80	95	90	C-872,D-361,O-142R,1-125	9.7

TEUFEL, TIM Timothy Shawn B 7.7.1958 Greenwich, CT BR/TR 6/175# d9.3

Year	Tm Lg	G	AB	R	H	2B	3B	HR	RBI	BB-IB	HP	SO	AVG	OBP	SLG	AOPS	ABR	SB-CS	FA	FR	Rng	Thr	G at Pos	BFW
1983	Min A	21	78	11	24	7	1	3	6	2-0	0	8	.308	.325	.538	128	3	0-0	.990	2	105	102	2-18/SD	0.6
1984	Min A	157	568	76	149	30	3	14	61	76-8	2	73	.262	.349	.400	103	4	1-3	.984	-6	103	82	*2-157	0.6
1985	Min A	138	434	58	113	24	3	10	50	48-2	3	70	.260	.335	.399	95	-2	4-2	.980	-24	91	78	*2-137/D	-1.9
1986	†NY N	93	279	35	69	20	1	4	31	32-1	1	42	.247	.324	.369	94	-2	1-2	.971	-22	80	69	2-84/1-3,3	-2.2
1987	NY N	97	299	55	92	29	0	14	61	44-2	2	53	.308	.398	.545	155	26	3-2	.972	-7	96	93	2-92/1	2.3
1988	†NY N	90	273	35	64	20	0	4	31	29-1	1	41	.234	.306	.352	94	-1	0-1	.981	16	107	133	2-84/1-3	1.7
1989	NY N	83	219	27	56	7	2	2	15	32-1	1	50	.256	.350	.333	102	2	1-3	.960	-0	95	80	2-40,1-33	-0.1
1990	NY N	80	175	28	43	11	0	10	24	15-1	0	33	.246	.304	.480	113	2	0-0	.991	-6	93	125	1-24,2-24,3-10	-0.5
1991	NY N	20	34	2	4	0	0	1	2	2-0	0	8	.118	.167	.206	4	-5	1-1	1.000	0	59	32	/1-6,3-5,2	-0.5
	SD N	97	307	39	70	16	0	11	42	49-4	1	69	.228	.334	.388	100	1	8-2	.987	-15	81	84	2-65,3-48	-1.2
	Year	117	341	41	74	16	0	12	44	51-4	1	77	.217	.319	.370	91	-3	9-3	.987	-15	82	83	2-66,3-53/1-6	-1.7
1992	SD N	101	246	23	55	10	0	6	25	31-3	1	45	.224	.312	.337	83	-5	2-1	.987	-3	98	77	2-52,3-26/1-5	-0.7
1993	SD N	96	200	26	50	11	2	7	31	27-0	0	39	.250	.338	.430	102	1	2-2	.990	-4	94	86	2-52/3-9,1-8	-0.1
Total	11	1073	3112	415	789	185	12	86	379	387-23	12	531	.254	.336	.404	104	24	23-19	.980	-69	94	86	2-806/3-99,1-83,D-2,S	-2.0

TEXTOR, GEORGE George Bernhardt B 12.27.1888 Newport, KY D 3.10.1954 Massillon, OH BB/TR 5-10.5/174# d4.19

Year	Tm Lg	G	AB	R	H	2B	3B	HR	RBI	BB-IB	HP	SO	AVG	OBP	SLG	AOPS	ABR	SB-CS	FA	FR	Rng	Thr	G at Pos	BFW
1914	Ind F	22	57	2	10	0	0	0	4	2	2	9	.175	.230	.175	10	-8	0	.955	1	*87*	*141*	C-21	-0.6
1915	New F	3	6	1	2	0	0	0	0	0	0	0	.333	.333	.333	93	0	0	1.000	-1	*73*	*85*	/C-3	-0.1
Total	2	25	63	3	12	0	0	0	4	2	2	9	.190	.239	.190	17	-8	0	.957	1	*86*	*137*	/C-24	-0.7

THACKER, MOE Morris Benton B 5.21.1934 Louisville, KY D 11.13.1997 Louisville, KY BR/TR 6-3/210# d8.3

Year	Tm Lg	G	AB	R	H	2B	3B	HR	RBI	BB-IB	HP	SO	AVG	OBP	SLG	AOPS	ABR	SB-CS	FA	FR	Rng	Thr	G at Pos	BFW
1958	Chi N	11	24	4	6	1	0	2	3	1-1	0	7	.250	.269	.542	113	0	0-0	.952	0	*105*	*233*	/C-9	0.1
1960	Chi N	54	90	5	14	1	0	0	6	14-5	0	20	.156	.269	.167	23	-9	1-1	.980	1	*75*	*175*	C-50	-0.7
1961	Chi N	25	35	3	6	0	0	0	2	11-1	1	11	.171	.383	.171	53	-2	0-0	.973	-1	*98*	*67*	C-25	-0.2
1962	Chi N	65	107	8	20	5	0	0	9	14-1	1	40	.187	.287	.234	40	-9	0-1	.996	8	*87*	*193*	C-65	0.1
1963	StL N	3	4	0	0	0	0	0	0	0-0	0	3	.000	.000	.000	-91	-1	0-0	1.000	0	*51*	*263*	/C-3	-0.1
Total	5	158	260	20	46	7	0	2	20	40-8	2	81	.177	.290	.227	41	-21	1-2	.984	8	*85*	*173*	C-152	-0.8

THAKE, AL Albert B 9.21.1849 Wymondham, England D 9.1.1872 Brooklyn, NY 6/?# d6.13

Year	Tm Lg	G	AB	R	H	2B	3B	HR	RBI	BB-IB	HP	SO	AVG	OBP	SLG	AOPS	ABR	SB-CS	FA	FR	Rng	Thr	G at Pos	BFW
1872	Atl NA	18	78	14	23	2	2	0	15	0		2	.295	.295	.372	88	-2	2-0	.808	-1	50	0	O-18(LF)/2	-0.2

THAMES, MARCUS Marcus Markley B 3.6.1977 Louisville, MS BR/TR 6-2/205# d6.10

Year	Tm Lg	G	AB	R	H	2B	3B	HR	RBI	BB-IB	HP	SO	AVG	OBP	SLG	AOPS	ABR	SB-CS	FA	FR	Rng	Thr	G at Pos	BFW
2002	NY A	7	13	2	3	1	0	1	2	0-0	0	4	.231	.231	.538	96	0	0-0	1.000	-0	104	0	/O-7(3-0-4)	0.0
2003	Tex A	30	73	12	15	2	0	1	4	8-0	2	18	.205	.298	.274	49	-5	0-1	1.000	-1	91	85	O-24(4-0-20)/D-4	-0.7
Total	2	37	86	14	18	3	0	2	6	8-0	2	22	.209	.289	.314	56	-5	0-1	1.000	-1	93	73	/O-31(7-0-24),D-4	-0.7

THEOBALD, RON Ronald Merrill B 7.28.1943 Oakland, CA BR/TR 5-8/165# d4.12

Year	Tm Lg	G	AB	R	H	2B	3B	HR	RBI	BB-IB	HP	SO	AVG	OBP	SLG	AOPS	ABR	SB-CS	FA	FR	Rng	Thr	G at Pos	BFW
1971	Mil A	126	388	50	107	12	2	1	23	38-0	3	39	.276	.342	.325	92	-3	11-8	.973	7	105	117	*2-111/S3	1.1
1972	Mil A	125	391	45	86	11	0	1	19	68-2	5	38	.220	.342	.256	81	-5	0-7	.988	-9	104	99	*2-113	-1.1
Total	2	251	779	95	193	23	2	2	42	106-2	8	77	.248	.342	.290	87	-8	11-15	.980	-2	104	108	2-224/3S	0.0

THEODORE, GEORGE George Basil B 11.13.1947 Salt Lake City, UT BR/TR 6-4/190# d4.14

Year	Tm Lg	G	AB	R	H	2B	3B	HR	RBI	BB-IB	HP	SO	AVG	OBP	SLG	AOPS	ABR	SB-CS	FA	FR	Rng	Thr	G at Pos	BFW
1973	†NY N	45	116	14	30	4	0	1	15	10-0	1	13	.259	.320	.319	80	-3	1-0	.984	3	118	169	O-33(28-4-1)/1-4	-0.2
1974	NY N	60	76	7	12	1	0	1	1	8-0	1	14	.158	.247	.211	29	-7	0-0	.990	-2	35	87	1-14,O-12(8-0-4)	-1.1
Total	2	105	192	21	42	5	0	2	16	18-0	2	27	.219	.291	.276	60	-10	1-0	.958	1	107	188	/O-45(36-4-5),1-18	-1.3

THEVENOW, TOMMY Thomas Joseph B 9.6.1903 Madison, IN D 7.29.1957 Madison, IN BR/TR 5-10/155# d9.4

Year	Tm Lg	G	AB	R	H	2B	3B	HR	RBI	BB-IB	HP	SO	AVG	OBP	SLG	AOPS	ABR	SB-CS	FA	FR	Rng	Thr	G at Pos	BFW
1924	StL N	23	89	4	18	4	1	0	7	1	0	6	.202	.211	.270	28	-9	1-3	.951	4	110	87	S-23	-0.3
1925	StL N	50	175	17	47	7	2	0	17	7	1	12	.269	.301	.331	60	-11	3-0	.950	1	104	60	S-50	-0.4
1926	†StL N	**156**	563	64	144	15	5	2	63	27	1	26	.256	.291	.311	60	-33	8	.956	16	**111**	106	*S-156	0.0
1927	StL N	59	191	23	37	6	1	0	4	14	0	8	.194	.249	.236	29	-19	2	.945	5	111	124	S-59	-0.8
1928	†StL N	69	171	11	35	8	3	0	13	20	0	12	.205	.288	.287	50	-13	0	.931	-8	96	99	S-64/3-3,1	-1.5
1929	Phi N	90	317	30	72	11	0	0	35	25	2	25	.227	.288	.262	35	-32	3	.953	-1	101	87	S-90	-2.2
1930	Phi N	**156**	573	57	164	21	1	0	78	23	2	26	.286	.316	.326	52	-44	1	.941	-6	104	84	*S-156	-3.0
1931	Pit N	120	404	35	86	12	1	0	38	28	1	22	.213	.266	.248	39	-35	0	.964	5	**109**	114	*S-120	-2.2
1932	Pit N	59	194	12	46	3	3	0	26	7	0	12	.237	.264	.284	48	-15	0	.918	-1	91	111	S-29,3-22	-1.4
1933	Pit N	73	253	20	79	5	1	0	34	3	0	5	.312	.320	.340	89	-5	2	.975	-8	94	94	2-61/S-3,3	-1.0
1934	Pit N	122	446	37	121	16	2	0	54	20	2	20	.271	.306	.316	65	-22	0	.969	-14	89	82	2-75,3-44/S	-3.0
1935	Pit N	110	408	38	97	9	9	0	47	12	1	23	.238	.261	.304	50	-30	1	.951	4	107	93	3-82,S-13/2-8	-2.2
1936	Cin N	106	321	25	75	7	2	0	36	15	0	23	.234	.268	.268	48	-25	2	.945	-3	96	87	S-68,2-33,3-12	-2.1
1937	Bos N	21	34	5	4	0	1	0	2	4	0	2	.118	.211	.176	7	-5	0	.969	0	120	69	S-12/3-6,2-2	-0.4
1938	Pit N	15	25	2	5	0	0	0	2	4	1	0	.200	.333	.200	49	-2	0	1.000	2	129	44	/2-9,S-4,3	0.1
Total	15	1229	4164	380	1030	124	32	2	456	210	11	222	.247	.285	.294	52	-300	23-3	.950	-4	105	98	S-848,2-188,3-171/1	-20.4

THOMAS, ANDRES Andres Perez (born Andres Perez (Thomas)) B 11.10.1963 Boca Chica, D.R. BR/TR 6-1/185# d9.3

Year	Tm Lg	G	AB	R	H	2B	3B	HR	RBI	BB-IB	HP	SO	AVG	OBP	SLG	AOPS	ABR	SB-CS	FA	FR	Rng	Thr	G at Pos	BFW
1985	Atl N	15	18	6	5	0	0	0	2	0-0	0	2	.278	.278	.278	53	-1	0-0	.920	1	128	69	S-10	0.0
1986	Atl N	102	323	26	81	17	2	6	32	8-2	0	49	.251	.267	.372	71	-14	4-6	.958	25	121	124	S-97	1.9
1987	Atl N	82	324	29	75	11	0	5	39	14-0	2	50	.231	.268	.312	50	-24	6-5	.953	11	115	111	S-81	-0.5
1988	Atl N	153	606	54	153	22	2	13	68	14-6	1	95	.252	.268	.360	76	-21	7-3	.959	-8	101	98	*S-150	-1.9
1989	Atl N	141	554	41	118	18	0	13	57	12-3	0	62	.213	.228	.316	53	-36	3-3	.956	9	102	119	*S-138	-1.9
1990	Atl N	84	278	26	61	8	0	5	30	11-2	0	43	.219	.248	.302	48	-20	2-1	.967	-1	97	101	S-72/3-5	-1.7
Total	6	577	2103	182	493	76	4	42	228	59-13	3	301	.234	.255	.334	61	-116	22-18	.958	36	106	110	S-548/3-5	-4.1

THOMAS, PINCH Chester David B 1.24.1888 Camp Point, IL D 12.24.1953 Modesto, CA BL/TR 5-9.5/173# d4.24

Year	Tm Lg	G	AB	R	H	2B	3B	HR	RBI	BB-IB	HP	SO	AVG	OBP	SLG	AOPS	ABR	SB-CS	FA	FR	Rng	Thr	G at Pos	BFW
1912	Bos A	13	30	0	6	0	0	0	5	2	0		.200	.250	.200	28	-3	1	.966	1	*129*	*118*	/C-8	-0.1
1913	Bos A	38	91	6	26	1	2	1	15	2	1	11	.286	.309	.374	97	-1	1	.983	0	*92*	*108*	C-31	0.1
1914	Bos A	66	130	9	25	1	0	0	5	18	0	17	.192	.291	.200	48	-8	1	.966	2	*127*	*72*	C-64/1	-0.2
1915	†Bos A	86	203	21	48	4	4	0	21	13	1	20	.236	.286	.296	76	-7	3-2	.969	7	*122*	*89*	C-82	0.5
1916	†Bos A	99	216	21	57	10	1	1	21	33	1	13	.264	.364	.333	109	4	4	.981	0	135	75	C-90	1.1
1917	Bos A	83	202	24	48	7	0	0	24	27	2	9	.238	.333	.272	86	-2	2	**.986**	4	*127*	*80*	C-77	0.9
1918	Cle A	32	73	2	18	0	1	0	5	6	0	6	.247	.304	.274	68	-3	0	.948	1	*130*	*83*	C-24	0.0
1919	Cle A	34	46	2	5	0	0	0	2	4	0	3	.109	.180	.109	-17	-7	0	.980	-1	*131*	*79*	C-21	-0.7
1920	†Cle A	9	9	2	3	1	0	0	0	3	0	1	.333	.500	.444	147	1	0-0	1.000	1	*183*	*60*	/C-7	0.2
1921	Cle A	21	35	1	9	3	0	0	4	10	0	2	.257	.422	.343	96	1	0-0	.882	-4	*72*	*24*	C-19	-0.3
Total	10	481	1035	88	245	27	8	2	102	118	5	82	.237	.318	.284	78	-25	12-2	.973	11	*124*	*81*	C-423/1	1.5

THOMAS, DAN Danny Lee B 5.9.1951 Birmingham, AL D 6.12.1980 Mobile, AL BR/TR 6-2/190# d9.2

Year	Tm Lg	G	AB	R	H	2B	3B	HR	RBI	BB-IB	HP	SO	AVG	OBP	SLG	AOPS	ABR	SB-CS	FA	FR	Rng	Thr	G at Pos	BFW
1976	Mil A	32	105	13	29	5	1	4	15	14-1	2	28	.276	.372	.457	145	6	1-2	.955	-1	92	132	O-32(LF)	0.3
1977	Mil A	22	70	11	19	3	2	2	11	8-2	1	11	.271	.350	.457	119	2	0-2	1.000	1	126	0	/O-9(LF),D-9	0.1
Total	2	54	175	24	48	8	3	6	26	22-3	3	39	.274	.363	.457	134	8	1-4	.966	-0	100	103	/O-41(LF),D-9	0.4

THOMAS, DERREL Derrel Osbon B 1.14.1951 Los Angeles, CA BB/TR 6/160# d9.14 OF Total (93-LF 394-CF 65-RF)

Year	Tm Lg	G	AB	R	H	2B	3B	HR	RBI	BB-IB	HP	SO	AVG	OBP	SLG	AOPS	ABR	SB-CS	FA	FR	Rng	Thr	G at Pos	BFW
1971	Hou N	5	5	0	0	0	0	0	0	0-0	0	2	.000	.000	.000	-99	-1	0-1	1.000	-0	64	148	/2	-0.2

Year	Tm Lg	G	AB	R	H	2B	3B	HR	RBI	BB-IB	HP	SO	AVG	OBP	SLG	AOPS	ABR	SB-CS	FA	FR	Rng	Thr	G at Pos	BFW
1972	SD N	130	500	48	115	15	5	5	36	41-1	2	73	.230	.290	.310	76	-17	9-9	.967	-6	99	91	2-83,S-49/O-3(0-2-1)	-1.4
1973	SD N	113	404	41	96	7	1	0	22	34-3	2	52	.238	.299	.260	61	-21	15-5	.914	4	106	91	S-74,2-47	-0.6
1974	SD N	141	523	48	129	24	6	3	41	51-7	1	58	.247	.313	.333	85	-11	7-8	.976	2	103	62	*2-104,3-22,O-20(1-19-0)/S-5	-0.5
1975	SF N	144	540	99	149	21	9	6	48	57-0	3	56	.276	.347	.381	98	-1	28-13	.974	0	92	108	*2-141/O(RF)	1.0
1976	SF N	81	272	38	63	5	4	2	19	29-0	4	26	.232	.313	.301	73	-9	10-11	.964	6	108	118	2-69/O-2(0-1-1),S3	-0.1
1977	SF N	148	506	75	135	13	10	8	44	46-1	2	70	.267	.328	.379	90	-8	15-13	.991	8	111	208	O-78(4-74-0),2-27,S-26/3-6,1-3	0.1
1978	SD N	128	352	36	80	10	2	3	26	35-3	3	37	.227	.301	.293	73	-13	11-6	.991	19	119	246	O-77(12-67-0),2-40,3-26,1-14	0.6
1979	LA N	141	406	47	104	15	4	5	44	41-7	5	49	.256	.330	.350	87	-7	18-5	.996	2	106	139	*O-119(CF),3-18/2-5,S-3,1	-0.3
1980	LA N	117	297	32	79	18	3	1	22	26-3	1	48	.266	.326	.357	93	-3	7-9	.987	-1	119	114	O-52(4-40-8),S-49,2-18/C-5,3-4	-0.1
1981	†LA N	80	218	25	54	4	0	4	24	25-2	0	23	.248	.322	.321	87	-4	7-2	.986	-6	86	102	2-30,S-26,O-18(3-10-6),3-10	-0.6
1982	LA N	66	98	13	26	2	1	0	2	10-1	0	12	.265	.333	.306	82	-2	2-3	1.000	-4	134	0	O-28(6-16-8),2-18,3-14/S-6	-0.6
1983	†LA N	118	192	38	48	6	6	2	8	27-2	2	36	.250	.345	.375	101	0	9-3	.990	0	108	142	O-82(15-42-29),S-13/2-9,3-7	0.2
1984	Mon N	108	243	26	62	12	2	0	20	20-1	0	33	.255	.308	.321	82	-6	0-4	.963	-11	83	111	S-62,O-48(41-0-7),2-15/3-4,1	-1.5
	Cal A	14	29	3	4	0	1	0	2	3-0	0	4	.138	.219	.207	19	-3	0-0	.889	-3	75	0	/O-7(2-2-4),S-4,3-3	-0.6
1985	Phi N	63	92	16	19	2	0	4	12	11-1	0	14	.207	.291	.359	79	-3	2-0	.906	-2	92	50	S-21/O-7(5-2-0),C23	-0.3
Total	15	1597	4677	585	1163	154	54	43	370	456-32	25	593	.249	.317	.332	83	-109	140-92	.970	8	99	98	2-608,O-542C,S-339,3-116/1-19,C	-4.9
THOMAS, FRANK Frank Edward "The Big Hurt" B 5.27.1968 Columbus, GA BR/TR 6-5/257# d8.2																								
1990	Chi A	60	191	39	63	11	3	7	31	44-0	2	54	.330	.454	.529	180	24	0-1	.989	-4	77	133	1-51/D-8	1.6
1991	Chi A	158	559	104	178	31	2	32	109	**138**-13	1	112	.318	**.453**	.553	**181**	**72**	1-2	.996	-4	70	100	*D-101,1-56	5.9
1992	Chi A	160	573	108	185	**46**	2	24	115	**122**-6	5	88	.323	**.439**	.536	176	**67**	6-3	.992	-11	80	82	*1-158/D-2	4.5
1993	†Chi A★	153	549	106	174	36	0	41	128	112-23	2	54	.317	.426	.607	180	68	4-2	.989	-11	77	104	*1-150/D-4	4.1
1994	Chi A★	**113**	399	**106**	141	34	1	38	101	**109**-12	2	61	.353	**.487**	**.729**	**214**	**77**	2-3	.991	-8	68	99	1-99,D-13	**5.2**
1995	Chi A★	**145**	493	102	152	27	0	40	111	**136-29**	6	74	.308	.454	.606	184	71	3-2	.991	-11	56	82	1-90,D-54	4.5
1996	Chi A✳	141	527	110	184	26	0	40	134	109-**26**	5	70	.349	.459	.626	181	**73**	1-1	.992	-4	89	90	*1-139	4.9
1997	Chi A✳	146	530	110	184	35	0	35	125	109-9	3	69	**.347**	**.456**	.611	**184**	**73**	1-1	.986	-6	79	87	1-97,D-49	5.1
1998	Chi A	160	585	109	155	35	2	29	109	110-2	6	93	.265	.381	.480	127	28	7-0	.984	-1	72	107	*D-146,1-14	1.6
1999	Chi A	135	486	74	148	36	0	15	77	87-13	9	66	.305	.414	.471	126	25	3-3	.990	-4	65	90	D-82,1-49	1.0
2000	†Chi A	159	582	115	191	44	0	43	143	112-18	5	94	.328	.436	.625	163	62	1-3	.996	-1	83	145	*D-127,1-30	4.4
2001	Chi A	20	68	8	15	3	0	4	10	10-2	0	12	.221	.316	.441	95	-1	0-0	.955	-0	66	106	D-16/1-3	-0.2
2002	Chi A	148	523	77	132	29	1	28	92	88-2	7	115	.252	.361	.472	119	17	3-0	.955	0	176	175	*D-140/1-4	0.8
2003	Chi A	153	546	87	146	35	0	42	105	100-4	12	115	.267	.390	.562	146	40	0-0	.995	-3	56	101	*D-124,1-27	2.6
Total	14	1851	6611	1255	2048	428	11	418	1390	1386-159	65	1077	.310	.428	.568	164	696	32-21	.991	-67	76	96	1-967,D-866	46.0
THOMAS, FRANK Frank Joseph B 6.11.1929 Pittsburgh, PA BR/TR 6-3/205# d8.17 OF Total (709-LF 308-CF 48-RF)																								
1951	Pit N	39	148	21	39	9	2	2	16	9	0	15	.264	.306	.392	84	-4	0-2	1.000	0	92	163	O-37(CF)	-0.5
1952	Pit N	6	21	1	2	0	0	0	0	1	0	1	.095	.136	.095	-34	-4	0-0	1.000	0	77	254	/O-5(CF)	-0.4
1953	Pit N	128	455	68	116	22	1	30	102	50	2	93	.255	.331	.505	115	9	1-2	.976	6	102	**166**	*O-118(6-96-16)	0.9
1954	Pit N★	153	577	81	172	32	7	23	94	51	**10**	74	.298	.359	.497	124	20	3-2	.989	7	106	122	*O-153(48-109-0)	1.8
1955	Pit N★	142	510	72	125	16	2	25	72	60-10	2	76	.245	.324	.431	101	0	2-0	.984	-2	99	77	*O-139(86-59-0)	-0.9
1956	Pit N	**157**	588	69	166	24	3	25	80	36-5	5	61	.282	.326	.461	112	8	0-5	.942	-5	91	117	*3-111,O-56(LF)/2-4	-0.2
1957	Pit N	151	594	72	172	30	1	23	89	44-9	3	66	.290	.335	.460	116	13	3-1	.977	4	99	93	1-71,O-59(46-2-19),3-31	1.0
1958	Pit N★	149	562	89	158	26	4	35	109	42-2	7	79	.281	.334	.528	129	21	0-1	.926	-26	86	78	*3-139/O-8(5-0-3),1-2	-0.6
1959	Cin N	108	374	41	84	18	2	12	47	27-6	3	56	.225	.278	.380	72	-16	0-2	.927	-5	95	82	3-64,O-33(LF),1-14	-2.4
1960	Chi N	135	479	54	114	12	1	21	64	28-4	0	74	.238	.280	.399	84	-13	1-0	.983	-8	100	93	1-50,O-49(44-0-6),3-33	-2.7
1961	Chi N	15	50	7	13	2	0	2	6	2-0	0	8	.260	.288	.420	84	-1	0-0	1.000	0	73	367	O-10(LF)/1-6	-0.2
	Mil N	124	423	58	120	13	3	25	67	29-7	6	70	.284	.335	.506	128	15	2-4	.954	-4	99	45	*O-109(LF),1-11	0.3
	Year	139	473	65	133	15	3	27	73	31-7	6	78	.281	.331	.497	123	13	2-4	.956	-4	97	64	*O-119(LF),1-17	0.1
1962	NY N	156	571	69	152	23	3	34	94	48-4	8	95	.266	.329	.496	117	12	2-1	.962	2	101	164	*O-126(LF),1-11,3-10	0.6
1963	NY N	126	420	34	109	9	1	15	60	33-5	3	48	.260	.317	.393	102	0	0-0	.988	3	104	142	O-96(LF),1-15/3	-0.2
1964	NY N	60	197	19	50	6	1	3	19	10-1	2	29	.254	.295	.340	81	-5	1-1	1.000	4	114	106	O-31(LF),1-19/3-2	-0.5
	Phi N	39	143	20	42	11	0	7	26	5-2	0	12	.294	.311	.517	132	6	0-1	.976	1	117	134	1-36	0.4
	Year	99	340	39	92	17	1	10	45	15-3	2	41	.271	.302	.415	103	0	1-2	.982	5	119	117	1-55,O-31(LF)/3-2	-0.1
1965	Phi N	35	77	7	20	4	0	1	7	4-0	0	10	.260	.289	.351	83	-2	0-0	1.000	-1	99	289	O-12(9-0-4),1-11/3	-0.4
	Hou N	23	58	7	10	2	0	3	9	3-0	0	15	.172	.210	.362	63	-3	0-0	.984	-2	64	107	1-16/3-2,O(LF)	-0.6
	Mil N	15	33	3	7	3	0	0	1	2-0	0	11	.212	.250	.303	57	-2	0-0	.979	-0	86	71	/1-6,O-3(LF)	-0.3
	Year	73	168	17	37	9	0	4	17	9-0	0	36	.220	.254	.345	71	-7	0-0	.985	-3	66	106	1-33,O-16(13-0-4)/3-3	-1.3
1966	Chi N	5	5	0	0	0	0	0	0	0-0	0	1	.000	.000	.000	-99	-1	0-0	—	0			H	-0.1
Total	16	1766	6285	792	1671	262	31	286	962	484-55	51	894	.266	.320	.454	108	53	15-22	.978	-25	101	131	*O-1045L,3-394,1-268/2-4	-5.0
THOMAS, FRED Frederick Harvey "Tommy" B 12.19.1892 Milwaukee, WI D 1.15.1986 Rice Lake, WI BR/TR 5-10/160# d4.22 Mil 1918																								
1918	†Bos A	44	144	19	37	2	1	1	11	15	1	20	.257	.331	.306	94	-1	4	.968	2	105	52	3-41/S	0.3
1919	Phi A	124	453	42	96	11	10	2	23	43	2	52	.212	.283	.294	61	-25	12	.945	-3	94	63	*3-124	-2.6
1920	Phi A	76	255	27	59	6	3	1	11	26	2	17	.231	.307	.290	58	-15	8-4	.960	2	101	86	3-61,S-12	-1.0
	Was A	3	7	0	1	0	0	0	0	0	0	1	.143	.143	.143	-25	-1	0-1	1.000	1	189	0	/3-2	0.0
	Year	79	262	27	60	6	3	1	11	26	2	18	.229	.303	.286	56	-17	8-5	.962	4	104	83	3-63,S-12	-1.0
Total	3	247	859	88	193	19	14	4	45	84	5	90	.225	.297	.293	65	-42	24-5	.954	3	99	66	3-228/S-13	-3.3
THOMAS, GEORGE George Edward B 11.29.1937 Minneapolis, MN BR/TR 6-3.5/190# d9.11 C1 OF Total (136-LF 170-CF 186-RF)																								
1957	Det A	1	1	0	0	0	0	0	0	0-0	0	1	.000	.000	.000	-97	0	0-0	.000	-1	0	0	/3	-0.1
1958	Det A	1	0	0	0	0	0	0	0	0-0	0	0	—	—	—	—	0	0-0	—	-0	0	0	/O(RF)	0.0
1961	Det A	17	6	2	0	0	0	0	0	0-0	0	4	.000	.000	.000	-97	-2	0-0	—	0	0	0	/O-2(RF),S	-0.1
	LA A	79	282	39	79	12	1	13	59	21-1	3	66	.280	.334	.468	101	0	3-6	.986	-7	95	0	O-45(24-17-4),3-38	-1.0
	Year	96	288	41	79	12	1	13	59	21-1	3	70	.274	.328	.458	99	-1	3-6	.986	-6	94	0	O-47(24-17-6),3-38/S	-1.1
1962	LA A	56	181	13	43	10	2	4	12	21-0	1	37	.238	.320	.381	91	-2	0-0	.957	1	104	133	O-51(3-8-45)	-0.5
1963	LA A	53	167	14	35	7	1	4	15	9-1	1	32	.210	.254	.335	68	-8	0-0	.941	-1	101	45	O-39(3-1-35),3-10/1-4	-1.2
	Det A	49	109	13	26	4	1	1	11	11-0	1	22	.239	.306	.321	76	-3	2-1	1.000	1	122	0	O-40(2-30-9)/2	-0.4
	Year	102	276	27	61	11	2	5	26	20-1	2	54	.221	.276	.330	71	-11	2-1	.974	-0	111	23	O-79(5-31-44),3-10/1-4,2	-1.6
1964	Det A	105	308	39	88	15	2	12	44	18-0	3	53	.286	.329	.464	117	6	4-1	.988	0	103	81	O-90(17-57-19)/3	0.4
1965	Det A	79	169	19	36	5	1	3	10	12-1	2	39	.213	.269	.308	64	-8	2-3	.948	1	103	172	O-59(5-26-28)/2	-1.1
1966	Bos A	69	173	25	41	4	0	5	20	23-1	2	33	.237	.332	.347	87	-2	1-0	1.000	2	99	163	O-48(10-25-15)/3-6,C-2,1-2	-0.3
1967	†Bos A	65	89	10	19	2	0	1	6	3-0	2	23	.213	.255	.270	51	-5	0-1	.973	-1	93	0	O-43(20-3-20)/1-3,C	-0.9
1968	Bos A	12	10	3	2	0	0	1	1	1-0	0	3	.200	.273	.500	122	0	1-0	1.000	0	144	0	/O-9(5-2-2)	0.1
1969	Bos A	29	51	9	18	3	1	0	8	3-0	1	11	.353	.400	.451	131	2	0-0	1.000	0	154	0	O-12(8-1-3),1-10/C3	0.1
1970	Bos A	38	99	13	34	8	0	2	13	11-0	2	12	.343	.420	.485	139	6	0-0	.972	-4	109	0	O-26(25-0-1)/3-6	0.1
1971	Bos A	9	13	0	1	0	0	0	1	1-0	0	4	.077	.143	.077	-34	-2	0-0	1.000	-1	37	0	/O-5(3-0-2)	-0.4
	Min A	23	30	4	8	1	0	0	2	4-0	0	3	.267	.353	.300	84	0	0-0	1.000	-2	51	0	O-11(LF)/13	-0.3
	Year	32	43	4	9	1	0	0	3	5-0	0	7	.209	.292	.233	48	-3	0-0	1.000	-2	45	0	O-16(14-0-2)/13	-0.7
Total	13	685	1688	203	430	71	9	46	202	138-4	18	343	.255	.316	.389	92	-18	13-12	.976	-11	103	79	O-481R/3-64,1-20,C-4,2-2,S	-5.6
THOMAS, HERB Herbert Mark B 5.26.1902 Sampson City, FL D 12.4.1991 Starke, FL BR/TR 5-4.5/157# d8.28																								
1924	Bos N	32	127	12	28	4	1	1	8	9	3	8	.220	.288	.291	58	-8	5-2	.983	6	119	165	O-32(CF)	-0.3
1925	Bos N	5	17	2	4	0	1	0	0	2	1	0	.235	.350	.353	88	0	0-1	.963	-1	97	35	/2-5	-0.2
1927	Bos N	24	74	11	17	6	1	0	6	3	1	9	.230	.269	.338	67	-4	2	.972	-7	80	75	2-17/S-2	-1.0
	NY N	13	17	2	3	1	1	0	1	1	1	1	.176	.263	.353	64	-1	0	.900	-0	125	0	/O-3(1-0-2),S	-0.1
	Year	37	91	13	20	7	2	0	7	4	2	10	.220	.268	.341	65	-5	2	.972	-7	80	75	2-17/S-3,O-3(1-0-2)	-1.1
Total	3	74	235	27	52	11	4	1	15	15	6	18	.221	.285	.315	63	-13	7-3	.976	-2	120	150	/O-35(1-32-2),2-22,S-3	-1.6
THOMAS, IRA Ira Felix B 1.22.1881 Ballston Spa, NY D 10.11.1958 Philadelphia, PA BR/TR 6-2/200# d5.18 C6																								
1906	NY A	44	115	12	23	1	2	0	15	8	1		.200	.258	.243	52	-6	2	.938	-3	*103*	*97*	C-42	-0.7
1907	NY A	80	208	20	40	5	4	1	24	10	3		.192	.240	.269	58	-10	5	.953	5	*95*	*127*	C-61/1-2	0.0
1908	†Det A	40	101	6	31	1	0	0	8	5	1		.307	.346	.317	111	1	0	.972	-3	*90*	*51*	C-29	0.1
1909	Phi A	84	256	22	57	9	3	0	31	18	7		.223	.292	.281	79	-6	4	**.985**	14	***127***	*91*	C-84	1.9
1910	†Phi A	60	180	14	50	8	2	1	19	6	0		.278	.301	.361	108	1	2	.967	7	*114*	*96*	C-60	1.4
1911	†Phi A	103	297	33	81	14	3	0	39	23	8		.273	.341	.340	92	-3	4	.974	6	*116*	***110***	*C-103	1.1

Year	Tm Lg	G	AB	R	H	2B	3B	HR	RBI	BB-IB	HP	SO	AVG	OBP	SLG	AOPS	ABR	SB-CS	FA	FR	Rng	Thr	G at Pos	BFW
1912	Phi A	48	139	14	30	4	2	1	13	8	2		.216	.268	.295	63	-7	3	.971	2	131	89	C-48	-0.1
1913	Phi A	22	53	3	15	4	1	0	6	4	0	8	.283	.333	.396	116	1	0	.983	2	120	97	C-21	0.4
1914	Phi A	2	3	0	0	0	0	0	0	0	0	0	.000	.000	.000	-99	-1	0	1.000	0	101	118	/C	-0.1
1915	Phi A	1	0	0	0	0	0	0	0	0	0	0	—	—	—	—	0	0	1.000	0	0	498	/C	0.0
Total	10	484	1352	124	327	46	17	3	155	82	22	8	.242	.296	.308	82	-30	20	.970	29	114	99	C-450/1-2	4.0

THOMAS, GORMAN James Gorman B 12.12.1950 Charleston, SC BR/TR 6-2/210# d4.6 OF Total (66-LF 967-CF 133-RF)

Year	Tm Lg	G	AB	R	H	2B	3B	HR	RBI	BB-IB	HP	SO	AVG	OBP	SLG	AOPS	ABR	SB-CS	FA	FR	Rng	Thr	G at Pos	BFW
1973	Mil A	59	155	16	29	7	1	2	11	14-1	0	61	.187	.254	.284	53	-10	5-5	.957	-3	99	32	O-50(4-1-46)/3D	-1.6
1974	Mil A	17	46	10	12	4	0	2	11	8-0	0	15	.261	.357	.478	143	3	4-0	1.000	-1	101	0	O-13(4-1-8)/D-2	0.3
1975	Mil A	121	240	34	43	12	2	10	28	31-0	0	84	.179	.268	.371	80	-7	4-2	.961	-1	102	86	*O-113(23-92-1)/D-6	-1.0
1976	Mil A	99	227	27	45	9	2	8	36	31-1	1	67	.198	.294	.361	94	-2	2-3	.986	5	114	76	O-94(1-66-29)/3D	0.0
1978	Mil A	137	452	70	111	24	1	32	86	73-4	2	133	.246	.351	.515	141	25	3-4	.983	-13	90	55	*O-137(CF)	1.1
1979	Mil A	156	557	97	136	29	0	**45**	123	98-6	2	175	.244	.356	.539	138	31	1-5	.991	-7	98	37	*O-152(CF)/D-4	2.0
1980	Mil A	**162**	628	78	150	26	3	38	105	58-4	2	170	.239	.303	.471	113	8	8-5	.985	-9	97	51	*O-160(CF)/D-2	-0.2
1981	†Mil A★	103	363	54	94	22	0	21	65	50-8	2	85	.259	.348	.493	149	23	4-5	.979	-1	95	122	O-97(0-49-49)/D-6	1.9
1982	†Mil A	158	567	96	139	29	1	**39**	112	84-5	4	143	.245	.343	.506	139	31	3-7	.991	-2	97	101	*O-157(CF)	2.6
1983	Mil A	46	164	21	30	6	1	5	18	23-0	1	50	.183	.284	.323	73	-6	2-1	.992	-4	94	0	O-46(CF)	-1.0
	Cle A	106	371	51	82	17	0	17	51	57-2	1	98	.221	.322	.404	96	-1	8-3	.982	4	108	107	*O-106(CF)	0.3
	Year	152	535	72	112	23	1	22	69	80-2	2	148	.209	.310	.379	90	-7	10-4	.985	0	104	74	*O-152(CF)	-0.7
1984	Sea A	35	108	6	17	3	0	1	13	28-0	1	27	.157	.322	.213	56	-5	0-3	1.000	-3	73	99	O-34(LF)/D	-1.1
1985	Sea A	135	484	76	104	16	1	32	87	84-6	1	126	.215	.330	.450	111	8	3-2	—	0	0	0	*D-133	0.4
1986	Sea A	57	170	24	33	4	0	10	26	27-3	1	55	.194	.308	.394	89	-3	1-2	—	0	0	0	D-52	-0.5
	Mil A	44	145	21	26	4	1	6	10	31-1	0	50	.179	.324	.345	80	-4	2-2	.980	-1	71	63	D-36/1-6	-0.6
	Year	101	315	45	59	8	1	16	36	58-4	1	105	.187	.316	.371	85	-6	3-4	.980	-1	71	63	D-88/1-6	-1.1
Total	13	1435	4677	681	1051	212	13	268	782	697-41	18	1339	.225	.324	.448	114	91	50-49	.984	-35	98	70	*O-1159C,D-246/1-6,3-2	2.6

THOMAS, LEE James Leroy B 2.5.1936 Peoria, IL BL/TR 6-2/198# d4.22 C2

Year	Tm Lg	G	AB	R	H	2B	3B	HR	RBI	BB-IB	HP	SO	AVG	OBP	SLG	AOPS	ABR	SB-CS	FA	FR	Rng	Thr	G at Pos	BFW
1961	NY A	2	2	0	1	0	0	0	0	0-0	0	0	.500	.500	.500	177	0	0-0	—	0			H	0.0
	LA A	130	450	77	128	11	5	24	70	47-2	2	74	.284	.353	.491	111	6	0-5	.966	-3	99	144	O-86(26-0-65),1-34	-0.6
	Year	132	452	77	129	11	5	24	70	47-2	2	74	.285	.353	.491	111	6	0-5	.966	-3	99	144	O-86(26-0-65),1-34	-0.6
1962	LA A★	160	583	88	169	21	2	26	104	55-3	6	74	.290	.355	.467	124	19	6-1	.982	-10	70	91	1-90,O-74(17-18-42)	0.0
1963	LA A	149	528	52	116	12	6	9	55	53-6	9	82	.220	.301	.316	78	-16	6-0	.996	3	113	106	*1-104,O-43(2-0-41)	-2.2
1964	LA A	47	172	14	47	8	1	2	24	18-1	0	22	.273	.340	.366	108	2	1-0	.949	-2	87	140	O-47(1-0-46)/1	-0.3
	Bos A	107	401	44	103	19	2	13	42	34-4	4	29	.257	.319	.411	97	-1	2-1	.995	1	104	101	*O-107(RF)/1	-0.8
	Year	154	573	58	150	27	3	15	66	52-5	4	51	.262	.325	.398	100	0	3-1	.981	-0	99	113	*O-154(1-0-153)/1-2	-1.1
1965	Bos A	151	521	74	141	27	4	22	75	72-8	3	42	.271	.361	.464	126	19	6-2	.984	4	**114**	82	*1-127,O-20(14-0-6)	1.6
1966	Atl N	39	126	11	25	1	1	6	15	10-1	1	15	.198	.261	.365	71	-5	1-1	.987	2	125	83	1-36	-0.6
	Chi N	75	149	15	36	4	0	1	9	14-1	3	15	.242	.319	.289	70	-6	0-0	.992	-0	101	114	1-20,O-17(16-1-0)	-0.8
	Year	114	275	26	61	5	1	7	24	24-2	4	30	.222	.293	.324	71	-11	1-1	.989	2	118	92	1-56,O-17(16-1-0)	-1.4
1967	Chi N	77	191	16	42	4	1	2	23	15-5	3	22	.220	.284	.283	61	-10	1-0	.969	-3	85	72	O-43(0-1-43),1-10	-1.6
1968	Hou N	90	201	14	39	4	0	1	11	14-4	1	22	.194	.249	.229	45	-13	2-1	.973	1	90	150	O-48(7-0-42)/1-2	-1.8
Total	8	1027	3324	405	847	111	22	106	428	332-35	32	397	.255	.327	.397	99	-5	25-11	.975	-7	96	114	O-485(83-20-392),1-425	-7.1

THOMAS, BUD John Tillman B 3.10.1929 Sedalia, MO BR/TR 6/180# d9.2

Year	Tm Lg	G	AB	R	H	2B	3B	HR	RBI	BB-IB	HP	SO	AVG	OBP	SLG	AOPS	ABR	SB-CS	FA	FR	Rng	Thr	G at Pos	BFW
1951	StL A	14	20	3	7	0	0	1	1	0	0	3	.350	.350	.500	124	0	2-0	1.000	1	108	82	S-14	0.2

THOMAS, KITE Keith Marshall B 4.27.1923 Kansas City, KS D 1.7.1995 Rocky Mount, NC BR/TR 6-1.5/195# d4.19

Year	Tm Lg	G	AB	R	H	2B	3B	HR	RBI	BB-IB	HP	SO	AVG	OBP	SLG	AOPS	ABR	SB-CS	FA	FR	Rng	Thr	G at Pos	BFW
1952	Phi A	75	116	24	29	6	1	6	18	20	1	27	.250	.365	.474	124	4	0-1	.957	-1	101	60	O-29(12-0-17)	0.2
1953	Phi A	24	49	1	6	0	0	0	2	3	0	6	.122	.173	.122	-18	-8	0-0	1.000	0	121	0	O-15(6-0-9)	-0.9
	Was A	38	58	10	17	3	2	1	12	11	1	7	.293	.414	.466	141	4	0-0	1.000	-1	84	0	/O-8(3-0-5),C	0.2
	Year	62	107	11	23	3	2	1	14	14	1	13	.215	.311	.308	68	-5	0-0	1.000	-1	108	0	O-23(9-0-14)/C	-0.7
Total	2	137	223	35	52	9	3	7	32	34	2	40	.233	.340	.395	98	0	0-1	.978	-2	104	32	/O-52(21-0-31),C	-0.5

THOMAS, LEO Leo Raymond "Tommy" B 7.26.1923 Turlock, CA D 3.5.2001 Concord, CA BR/TR 5-11.5/178# d4.29

Year	Tm Lg	G	AB	R	H	2B	3B	HR	RBI	BB-IB	HP	SO	AVG	OBP	SLG	AOPS	ABR	SB-CS	FA	FR	Rng	Thr	G at Pos	BFW
1950	StL A	35	121	19	24	6	0	1	9	20	0	14	.198	.312	.273	49	-9	0-1	.964	-2	102	83	3-35	-1.1
1952	StL A	41	124	12	29	5	1	0	12	17	2	7	.234	.336	.290	73	-4	2-0	.934	2	106	106	3-37/S-3,2	-0.2
	Chi A	19	24	1	4	0	0	0	6	6	0	4	.167	.333	.167	42	-2	0-0	.952	1	116	75	/3-9	-0.1
	Year	60	148	13	33	5	1	0	18	23	2	11	.223	.335	.270	68	-5	2-0	.936	2	107	101	3-46/S-3,2	-0.3
Total	2	95	269	32	57	11	1	1	27	43	2	25	.212	.325	.271	59	-15	2-1	.948	-0	105	93	/3-81,S-3,2	-1.4

THOMAS, RAY Raymond Joseph B 7.9.1910 Dover, NH D 12.6.1993 Wilson, NC BR/TR 5-10.5/175# d7.22

Year	Tm Lg	G	AB	R	H	2B	3B	HR	RBI	BB-IB	HP	SO	AVG	OBP	SLG	AOPS	ABR	SB-CS	FA	FR	Rng	Thr	G at Pos	BFW
1938	Bro N	1	3	1	1	0	0	0	0	0	0	0	.333	.333	.333	82	0	0	1.000	0	0	0	/C	0.0

THOMAS, RED Robert William B 4.25.1898 Hargrove, AL D 3.22.1962 Fremont, OH BR/TR 5-11/165# d9.13

Year	Tm Lg	G	AB	R	H	2B	3B	HR	RBI	BB-IB	HP	SO	AVG	OBP	SLG	AOPS	ABR	SB-CS	FA	FR	Rng	Thr	G at Pos	BFW
1921	Chi N	8	30	5	8	3	0	1	5	4	1	5	.267	.371	.467	120	1	0-1	.962	-0	103	76	/O-8(CF)	0.0

THOMAS, ROY Roy Allen B 3.24.1874 Norristown, PA D 11.20.1959 Norristown, PA BL/TL 5-11/150# d4.14 C1 b-Bill

Year	Tm Lg	G	AB	R	H	2B	3B	HR	RBI	BB-IB	HP	SO	AVG	OBP	SLG	AOPS	ABR	SB-CS	FA	FR	Rng	Thr	G at Pos	BFW
1899	Phi N	150	547	137	178	12	4	0	47	115	17		.325	.457	.362	130	37	42	.952	1	107	150	*O-135(CF),1-14	2.6
1900	Phi N	140	531	**132**	168	4	3	0	33	**115**	15		.316	.451	.335	119	27	37	.958	-6	98	110	*O-139(CF)/P	1.1
1901	Phi N	129	479	102	148	5	2	1	28	**100**	9		.309	.437	.334	123	23	27	.967	-3	56	55	*O-129(CF)	1.4
1902	Phi N	**138**	500	89	143	4	7	0	24	**107**	2		.286	**.414**	.322	127	25	17	.974	5	126	60	*O-138(CF)	2.4
1903	Phi N	130	477	88	156	11	2	1	27	**107**	3		.327	**.453**	.365	139	35	17	.963	12	106	65	*O-130(CF)	3.9
1904	Phi N	139	496	92	144	6	6	3	29	**102**	5		.290	.416	.345	141	33	28	.974	13	123	70	*O-139(CF)	4.1
1905	Phi N	147	562	118	178	11	6	0	31	93	4		.317	.417	.358	137	33	23	.983	15	137	128	*O-147(CF)	4.1
1906	Phi N	142	493	81	125	10	7	0	16	**107**	6		.254	.393	.302	117	18	22	**.986**	8	69	167	*O-142(CF)	2.2
1907	Phi N	121	419	70	102	15	3	1	23	**83**	4		.243	.374	.301	113	13	11	.980	2	89	100	*O-121(CF)	1.0
1908	Phi N	6	24	2	4	0	0	0	0	2	0		.167	.231	.167	26	-2	0	1.000	-1	0	0	/O-6(CF)	-0.3
	Pit N	102	386	52	99	11	10	1	24	49	5		.256	.348	.345	121	11	11	.975	1	54	136	*O-101(CF)	0.8
	Year	108	410	54	103	11	10	1	24	51	5		.251	.341	.334	116	9	11	.976	0	51	129	*O-107(CF)	0.5
1909	Bos N	82	281	36	74	9	1	0	11	47	0		.263	.369	.302	104	4	5	.976	1	88	39	O-76(75-2-0)	0.1
1910	Phi N	23	71	7	13	0	2	0	4	7	1	5	.183	.266	.239	46	-5	4	.952	-1	98	87	O-20(CF)	-0.7
1911	Phi N	21	30	5	5	2	0	0	2	8	0	6	.167	.342	.233	61	-1	0	1.000	1	96	249	O-11(RF)	0.0
Total	13	1470	5296	1011	1537	100	53	7	299	1042	71	11	.290	.413	.333	124	251	244	.972	49	97	101	*O-1434(75-1349-11)/1-14,P	22.7

THOMAS, VALMY Valmy B 10.21.1928 Santurce, P.R. BR/TR 5-9/165# d4.16

Year	Tm Lg	G	AB	R	H	2B	3B	HR	RBI	BB-IB	HP	SO	AVG	OBP	SLG	AOPS	ABR	SB-CS	FA	FR	Rng	Thr	G at Pos	BFW
1957	NY N	88	241	30	60	10	3	6	31	16-1	1	29	.249	.296	.390	83	-6	0-0	.991	2	129	80	C-88	0.0
1958	SF N	63	143	14	37	5	0	3	16	13-0	1	24	.259	.321	.357	82	-4	1-0	.992	1	116	110	C-61	-0.1
1959	Phi N	66	140	5	28	2	0	1	7	9-2	1	19	.200	.253	.236	31	-14	1-0	.980	8	89	150	C-65/3	-0.4
1960	Bal A	8	16	0	1	0	0	0	0	1-0	0	0	.063	.118	.063	-51	-3	0-1	1.000	1	81	113	/C-8	-0.3
1961	Cle A	27	86	7	18	3	0	2	6	6-0	0	7	.209	.261	.314	54	-6	0-0	.988	5	134	174	C-27	0.0
Total	5	252	626	56	144	20	3	12	60	45-3	3	79	.230	.283	.329	64	-33	2-1	.988	16	116	116	C-249/3	-0.8

THOMAS, BILL William Miskey B 12.8.1877 Norristown, PA D 1.14.1950 Evansburg, PA BR/TR 5-10/190# d5.1 b-Roy

Year	Tm Lg	G	AB	R	H	2B	3B	HR	RBI	BB-IB	HP	SO	AVG	OBP	SLG	AOPS	ABR	SB-CS	FA	FR	Rng	Thr	G at Pos	BFW
1902	Phi N	6	17	1	2	0	0	0	0	1	0		.118	.167	.118	-12	-2	0	.500	-1	0	1195	/O-3(2-0-1),12	-0.3

THOMAS, WALT William Walter "Tommy" B 4.28.1884 Foot Of Ten, PA D 6.6.1950 Altoona, PA BR/TR 5-8/156# d9.18

Year	Tm Lg	G	AB	R	H	2B	3B	HR	RBI	BB-IB	HP	SO	AVG	OBP	SLG	AOPS	ABR	SB-CS	FA	FR	Rng	Thr	G at Pos	BFW
1908	Bos N	5	13	2	2	0	0	0	1	3	0		.154	.313	.154	51	-1	2	.864	-1	96	83	/S-5	-0.1

THOMASON, ART Arthur Wilson B 2.12.1889 Liberty, MO D 5.2.1944 Kansas City, MO BL/TL 5-8/150# d8.10

Year	Tm Lg	G	AB	R	H	2B	3B	HR	RBI	BB-IB	HP	SO	AVG	OBP	SLG	AOPS	ABR	SB-CS	FA	FR	Rng	Thr	G at Pos	BFW
1910	Cle A	20	70	4	12	0	1	0	2	5	0		.171	.227	.200	33	-6	3	.944	2	98	174	O-20(0-1-19)	-0.6

THOMASSON, GARY Gary Leah B 7.29.1951 San Diego, CA BL/TL 6-1/180# d9.5

Year	Tm Lg	G	AB	R	H	2B	3B	HR	RBI	BB-IB	HP	SO	AVG	OBP	SLG	AOPS	ABR	SB-CS	FA	FR	Rng	Thr	G at Pos	BFW
1972	SF N	10	27	5	9	1	1	0	1	1-0	0	7	.333	.357	.444	125	1	0-0	1.000	-1	28	146	/1-7,O-2(LF)	-0.1
1973	SF N	112	235	35	67	10	4	4	30	22-2	0	43	.285	.345	.413	105	2	2-0	.992	-3	76	64	1-47,O-43(23-11-9)	-0.5
1974	SF N	120	315	41	77	14	3	2	29	38-2	0	56	.244	.325	.327	79	-8	7-1	.981	2	102	89	O-76(20-32-26),1-15	-0.9
1975	SF N	114	326	44	74	12	3	7	32	37-1	1	48	.227	.304	.347	78	-10	9-3	.978	8	115	194	O-74(27-34-18),1-17	-0.5
1976	SF N	103	328	45	85	20	5	8	38	30-7	1	45	.259	.321	.424	107	3	8-3	.959	-4	106	64	O-54(5-35-19),1-39	-0.5
1977	SF N	145	446	63	114	24	6	17	71	75-8	1	102	.256	.358	.451	118	13	16-4	.959	-1	108	27	*O-113(62-49-20),1-31	0.9

Year	Tm Lg	G	AB	R	H	2B	3B	HR	RBI	BB-IB	HP	SO	AVG	OBP	SLG	AOPS	ABR	SB-CS	FA	FR	Rng	Thr	G at Pos	BFW
1978	Oak A	47	154	17	31	4	1	5	16	15-2	0	44	.201	.272	.338	74	-6	4-1	.969	1	101	126	O-44(RF)/1-5	-0.7
	†NY A	55	116	20	32	4	1	3	20	13-0	0	22	.276	.346	.405	114	2	0-2	.972	6	126	173	O-50(24-16-12)/D	0.6
	Year	102	270	37	63	8	2	8	36	28-2	0	66	.233	.304	.367	92	-4	4-3	.971	7	112	147	O-94(24-16-56)/1-5,D	-0.1
1979	LA N	115	315	39	78	11	1	14	45	43-4	1	70	.248	.339	.422	108	4	4-2	.980	-3	99	62	*O-100(10-61-43)/1	-0.1
1980	LA N	80	111	6	24	3	0	1	12	17-3	1	26	.216	.326	.270	69	-4	0-0	.974	-1	90	71	O-31(9-9-15)/1	-0.6
Total	9	901	2373	315	591	103	25	61	294	291-29	5	463	.249	.330	.391	98	-3	50-16	.970	3	106	90	O-587(182-247-206),1-163/D	-2.4
THOME, JIM James Howard B 8.27.1970 Peoria, IL BL/TR 6-4/220# d9.4																								
1991	Cle A	27	98	7	25	4	2	1	9	5-1	1	16	.255	.298	.367	82	-3	1-1	.900	-1	108	109	3-27	-0.4
1992	Cle A	40	117	8	24	3	1	2	12	10-2	2	34	.205	.275	.299	63	-6	2-0	.882	-7	86	48	3-40	-1.3
1993	Cle A	47	154	28	41	11	0	7	22	29-1	4	36	.266	.385	.474	133	9	2-1	.950	1	105	122	3-47	1.0
1994	Cle A	98	321	58	86	20	1	20	52	46-5	0	84	.268	.359	.523	124	11	3-3	.940	7	115	83	3-94	1.7
1995	†Cle A	137	452	92	142	29	3	25	73	97-3	5	113	.314	.438	.558	155	42	4-3	.948	-9	94	106	*3-134/D	3.2
1996	†Cle A	151	505	122	157	28	5	38	116	123-8	6	141	.311	.450	.612	166	58	2-2	.953	2	106	98	*3-150/D	5.4
1997	†Cle A★	147	496	104	142	25	0	40	102	**120**-9	3	146	.286	.423	.579	154	45	1-1	.993	-0	98	101	*1-145	2.9
1998	†Cle A★	123	440	89	129	34	2	30	85	89-8	4	141	.293	.413	.584	151	37	1-0	.991	-0	101	98	*1-117/D-6	2.4
1999	†Cle A★	146	494	101	137	27	2	33	108	**127**-13	4	171	.277	.426	.540	139	35	0-0	.994	7	**123**	96	*1-111,D-34	2.7
2000	Cle A	158	557	106	150	33	1	37	106	118-4	4	171	.269	.398	.531	131	30	1-0	.995	10	130	105	*1-107,D-48	2.5
2001	†Cle A	156	526	101	153	26	1	49	124	111-14	4	185	.291	.416	.624	167	55	0-1	.992	-5	81	83	*1-148/D-6	3.4
2002	Cle A	147	480	101	146	19	2	52	118	**122**-18	5	139	.304	.445	**.677**	**197**	**74**	1-2	.991	-1	94	104	*1-128,D-18	5.5
2003	Phi N	159	578	111	154	30	3	**47**	131	111-11	4	182	.266	.385	.573	156	50	0-3	.997	-6	83	103	*1-156/D-2	2.7
Total	13	1536	5218	1028	1486	289	23	381	1058	1108-97	46	1559	.285	.411	.568	151	437	18-17	.993	-3	99	98	1-912,3-492,D-116	31.7
THOMPSON, ANDREW Andrew d4.26																								
1875	Was NA	11	41	3	4	0	1	0	3	0		1	.098	.098	.146	-17	-5	0-0	.624	-8			C-11/O(RF)	-1.1
THOMPSON, ANDY Andrew John B 10.8.1975 Oconomowoc, WI BR/TR 6-3/210# d5.2																								
2000	Tor A	2	6	2	1	0	0	0	1	3-0	0	2	.167	.444	.167	62	0	0-0	1.000	-1	47	0	/O-2(LF)	-0.1
THOMPSON, BOBBY Bobby La Rue B 11.3.1953 Charlotte, NC BB/TR 5-11/175# d4.16																								
1978	Tex A	64	120	23	27	3	3	2	12	9-1	2	26	.225	.284	.350	79	-4	7-2	.982	1	109	40	O-52(8-37-10)/D-3	-0.3
THOMPSON, TIM Charles Lemoine B 3.1.1924 Coalport, PA BL/TR 5-11/190# d4.28 C1																								
1954	Bro N	10	13	2	2	1	0	0	1	1	0	1	.154	.214	.231	15	-2	0-0	.909	-1	*0*	*0*	/C-2,O(LF)	-0.2
1956	KC A	92	268	21	73	13	2	1	27	17-1	2	23	.272	.319	.347	76	-10	2-4	.981	1	*88*	*120*	C-68	-0.6
1957	KC A	81	230	25	47	10	0	7	19	18-6	0	26	.204	.262	.339	62	-13	0-0	.993	-1	*87*	*70*	C-62	-1.1
1958	Det A	4	6	1	1	0	0	0	0	3-0	0	2	.167	.444	.167	70	0	0-0	1.000	-1	*54*	*229*	/C-4	-0.1
Total	4	187	517	49	123	24	2	8	47	39-7	2	52	.238	.293	.338	68	-25	2-4	.986	-1	*86*	*97*	C-136/O(LF)	-2.0
THOMPSON, DANNY Danny Leon B 2.1.1947 Wichita, KS D 12.10.1976 Rochester, MN BR/TR 6/183# d6.25																								
1970	†Min A	96	302	25	66	9	0	0	22	7-0	0	39	.219	.234	.248	33	-28	0-0	.986	-0	105	83	2-81,3-37/S-6	-2.4
1971	Min A	48	57	10	15	2	0	0	7	7-0	0	12	.263	.338	.298	81	-1	0-0	.897	-2	95	113	3-17/2-3,S	-0.3
1972	Min A	144	573	54	158	22	6	4	48	34-1	2	57	.276	.318	.356	96	-4	3-4	.957	-5	102	90	*S-144	0.9
1973	Min A	99	347	29	78	13	2	1	36	16-3	2	41	.225	.259	.282	52	-23	1-0	.950	8	111	85	S-95/3D	-0.4
1974	Min A	97	264	25	66	6	1	4	25	22-0	2	29	.250	.311	.326	81	-6	1-1	.963	-9	83	91	S-88/3-5,D	-0.7
1975	Min A	112	355	25	96	11	2	5	37	18-2	0	30	.270	.302	.355	85	-8	0-3	.941	-7	95	76	*S-100/3-7,2D	-0.6
1976	Min A	34	124	9	29	4	0	0	6	3-0	1	8	.234	.256	.266	53	-8	1-1	.988	-0	97	106	S-34	-0.4
	Tex A	64	196	12	42	3	0	1	13	13-0	1	19	.214	.264	.245	49	-13	2-2	.976	-8	84	56	3-39,2-14,S-10/D	-2.1
	Year	98	320	21	71	7	0	1	19	16-0	2	27	.222	.261	.253	51	-20	3-3	.981	-9	95	102	S-44,3-39,2-14/D	-2.5
Total	7	694	2218	189	550	70	11	15	194	120-6	8	235	.248	.287	.310	70	-91	8-11	.956	-24	99	87	S-478,3-106/2-99,D-6	-6.0
THOMPSON, DON Donald Newlin B 12.28.1923 Swepsonville, NC BL/TL 6/185# d4.24																								
1949	Bos N	7	11	0	2	0	0	0	0	0	0	2	.182	.182	.182	-2	-2	0	.800	-0	116	0	/O-2(RF)	-0.2
1951	Bro N	80	118	25	27	3	0	0	6	12	1	12	.229	.305	.254	51	-8	2-8	.987	2	110	110	O-61(56-6-0)	-1.0
1953	†Bro N	96	153	25	37	5	0	1	12	14	1	13	.242	.310	.294	57	-9	2-3	.989	2	105	155	O-81(51-8-25)	-0.9
1954	Bro N	34	25	2	1	0	0	0	1	5	1	5	.040	.226	.040	-25	-5	0-0	1.000	1	99	230	O-29(27-2-0)	-0.5
Total	4	217	307	52	67	8	0	1	19	31	3	32	.218	.296	.254	46	-24	4-11	.984	5	107	140	O-173(134-16-27)	-2.6
THOMPSON, FRANK Frank d9.11																								
1875	Atl NA	1	5	1	2	0	0	0	1	0		0	.400	.400	.400	205	1	0-0	.000	-1	0	0	/O(RF)	0.0
THOMPSON, FRANK Frank E B 7.2.1895 Springfield, MO D 6.27.1940 Jasper Co., MO BR/TR 5-8/155# d5.6																								
1920	StL A	22	53	7	9	0	0	0	5	13	1	10	.170	.343	.170	38	-4	1-1	.878	-4	88	44	3-14/2-2	-0.7
THOMPSON, HANK Henry Curtis B 12.8.1925 Oklahoma City, OK D 9.30.1969 Fresno, CA BL/TR 5-9/174# d7.17																								
1947	StL A	27	78	10	20	1	1	0	5	10	0	7	.256	.341	.295	76	-2	2-1	.957	0	97	104	2-19	-0.1
1949	NY N	75	275	51	77	10	4	9	34	42	1	30	.280	.377	.444	120	8	5	.961	-6	91	97	2-69/3	0.6
1950	NY N	148	512	82	148	17	6	20	91	83	3	60	.289	.391	.463	123	19	8	.944	10	**108**	**165**	*3-138,O-10(0-2-9)	2.7
1951	†NY N	87	264	37	62	8	4	8	33	43	0	23	.235	.342	.386	95	-2	1-2	.925	-9	88	111	3-71	-1.2
1952	NY N	128	423	67	110	13	9	17	67	50	4	38	.260	.344	.454	119	10	4-4	.979	1	102	74	O-72(20-51-1),3-46/2-4	0.7
1953	NY N	114	388	80	117	15	8	24	74	60	4	39	.302	.400	.567	146	27	6-5	.956	3	108	83	*3-101/O-9(1-0-8),2	2.8
1954	†NY N	136	448	76	118	18	1	26	86	90	5	58	.263	.389	.482	126	20	3-0	.945	-2	98	114	*3-130/2-2,O(LF)	1.8
1955	NY N	135	432	65	106	13	1	17	63	84-4	4	56	.245	.367	.398	105	6	2-2	.943	1	**106**	99	*3-124/2-7,S	0.7
1956	NY N	83	183	24	43	9	0	8	29	31-2	1	26	.235	.346	.415	105	2	2-1	.908	1	117	104	3-44,O-10(8-0-3)/S	0.2
Total	9	933	3003	492	801	104	34	129	482	493-6	22	337	.267	.372	.453	118	88	33-15	.941	-2	104	116	3-655,O-102(30-53-21),2-102/S-2	8.2
THOMPSON, HOMER Homer Thomas B 6.1.1891 Spring City, TN D 9.12.1957 Atlanta, GA BR/TR 5-9/160# d10.5 b-Tommy																								
1912	NY A	1	0	0	0	0	0	0	0	0	0		—	—	—	—	0	0	.500	-0	*0*	*0*	/C	0.0
THOMPSON, SHAG James Alfred B 4.29.1893 Haw River, NC D 1.7.1990 Black Mountain, NC BL/TR 5-8.5/165# d6.8																								
1914	Phi A	16	29	3	5	0	1	0	2	7	1	8	.172	.351	.241	82	0	1	.941	2	90	335	/O-8(2-6-0)	0.1
1915	Phi A	17	33	5	11	2	0	0	2	4	0	6	.333	.405	.394	144	2	0-1	1.000	1	87	257	/O-7(CF)	0.2
1916	Phi A	15	17	4	0	0	0	0	0	7	0	6	.000	.292	.000	-12	-2	1	1.000	0	136	0	/O-8(1-6-1)	-0.2
Total	3	48	79	12	16	2	1	0	4	18	1	20	.203	.357	.253	87	0	2-1	.978	3	103	206	/O-23(3-19-1)	0.1
THOMPSON, JASON Jason Dolph B 7.6.1954 Hollywood, CA BL/TL 6-3/210# d4.23																								
1976	Det A	123	412	45	90	12	1	17	54	68-6	1	72	.218	.328	.376	103	3	2-4	.994	4	112	103	*1-117	-0.4
1977	Det A☆	158	585	87	158	24	5	31	105	73-2	1	91	.270	.347	.487	120	16	0-1	.991	-6	88	101	*1-158	-0.1
1978	Det A★	153	589	79	169	25	3	26	96	74-3	0	96	.287	.364	.472	130	24	0-0	.993	-9	82	**123**	*1-151	0.6
1979	Det A	145	492	58	121	16	1	20	79	70-8	1	90	.246	.338	.404	97	-1	2-0	.994	-1	94	115	*1-140/D-2	-1.0
1980	Det A	36	126	10	27	5	0	4	20	13-1	1	26	.214	.289	.349	73	-5	0-1	1.000	3	128	103	1-36	-0.4
	Cal A	102	312	59	99	14	0	17	70	70-9	0	60	.317	.439	.526	168	34	2-0	1.000	-3	71	76	1-47,D-45	2.7
	Year	138	438	69	126	19	0	21	90	83-10	1	86	.288	.398	.475	141	29	2-1	1.000	0	96	88	1-83,D-45	2.3
1981	Pit N	86	223	36	54	13	0	15	42	59-1	0	49	.242	.396	.502	150	18	0-0	.989	-2	93	115	1-78	1.2
1982	Pit N★	156	550	87	156	32	0	31	101	101-7	2	107	.284	.391	.511	148	39	1-0	.993	-0	97	98	*1-155	3.1
1983	Pit N	152	517	70	134	20	1	18	76	99-7	1	128	.259	.376	.406	115	14	1-0	.993	-5	84	113	*1-151	0.1
1984	Pit N	154	543	61	138	22	0	17	74	87-14	2	73	.254	.357	.389	110	10	0-0	.990	-8	79	99	*1-152	-0.8
1985	Pit N	123	402	42	97	17	1	12	61	84-10	0	58	.241	.369	.378	111	10	0-0	.992	1	101	69	*1-114	0.4
1986	Mon N	30	51	6	10	4	0	0	4	18-2	0	12	.196	.406	.275	92	1	0-1	.962	-3	45	81	1-15	-0.3
Total	11	1418	4802	640	1253	204	12	208	782	816-70	9	862	.261	.366	.438	121	163	8-7	.992	-28	91	103	*1-1314/D-47	5.1
THOMPSON, JASON Jason Michael B 6.13.1971 Orlando, FL BL/TL 6-4/200# d6.9																								
1996	SD N	13	49	4	11	4	0	2	6	1-0	0	14	.224	.235	.429	76	-2	0-0	.964	1	136	63	1-13	-0.2
THOMPSON, TUG John P. F. B London, ON, CAN BL/TR 5-8/160# d8.31																								
1882	Cin AA	1	5	0	1	0	0	0		0			.200	.200	.200	33	0		.000	-1	0	0	/O(CF)	-0.1
1884	Ind AA	24	97	10	20	3	0	0		2	0		.206	.222	.237	51	-5		.429	-9	95	0	O-12(0-7-5),C-12	-1.2
Total	2	25	102	10	21	3	0	0		2	0		.206	.221	.235	50	-5		.409	-9	88	0	/O-13(0-8-5),C-12	-1.3

THOMPSON, FRESCO Lafayette Fresco "Tommy" B 6.6.1902 Centreville, AL D 11.20.1968 Fullerton, CA BR/TR 5-8/150# d9.5

Year	Tm Lg	G	AB	R	H	2B	3B	HR	RBI	BB-IB	HP	SO	AVG	OBP	SLG	AOPS	ABR	SB-CS	FA	FR	Rng	Thr	G at Pos	BFW
1925	Pit N	14	37	4	9	2	1	0	8	4	0	1	.243	.317	.351	66	-2	2-1	.977	-1	88	135	2-12	-0.2
1926	NY N	2	8	1	5	0	0	0	1	2	0	0	.625	.700	.625	262	2	1	1.000	-0	113	0	/2-2	0.2
1927	Phi N	153	597	78	181	32	14	1	70	34	2	36	.303	.343	.409	99	-2	19	.963	1	94	98	*2-153	0.3
1928	Phi N	**152**	634	99	182	34	11	3	50	42	1	27	.287	.332	.390	85	-15	19	.966	8	101	91	*2-152	-0.3
1929	Phi N	148	623	115	202	41	3	4	53	75	1	34	.324	.398	.419	96	0	16	.965	11	103	98	*2-148	1.4
1930	Phi N	122	478	77	135	34	4	4	46	35	0	29	.282	.331	.395	70	-23	7	.955	-3	100	101	*2-112	-2.1
1931	Bro N	74	181	26	48	6	1	1	21	23	1	16	.265	.351	.326	84	-3	5	.946	-2	94	138	2-43,S-10/3-5	-0.2
1932	Bro N	3	1	0	0	0	0	0	0	0	0	0	.000	.000	.000	-99	0	0	—	0			H	0.0
1934	NY N	1	1	0	0	0	0	0	0	0	0	0	.000	.000	.000	-99	0	0	—	0			H	0.0
Total	9	669	2560	400	762	149	34	13	249	215	5	143	.298	.353	.398	88	-43	69-1	.962	13	99	100	2-622/S-10,3-5	-0.9

THOMPSON, MILT Milton Bernard B 1.5.1959 Washington, DC BL/TR 5-11/170# d9.4

Year	Tm Lg	G	AB	R	H	2B	3B	HR	RBI	BB-IB	HP	SO	AVG	OBP	SLG	AOPS	ABR	SB-CS	FA	FR	Rng	Thr	G at Pos	BFW
1984	Atl N	25	99	16	30	1	0	2	4	11-1	0	11	.303	.373	.374	103	1	14-2	.956	1	75	302	O-25(LF)	0.3
1985	Atl N	73	182	17	55	7	2	0	6	7-0	3	36	.302	.339	.363	91	-2	9-4	.964	1	112	78	O-49(23-5-27)	-0.3
1986	Phi N	96	299	38	75	7	1	6	23	26-1	1	62	.251	.311	.341	78	-10	19-4	.991	2	117	22	O-89(CF)	-0.6
1987	Phi N	150	527	86	159	26	9	7	43	42-2	0	87	.302	.351	.425	102	1	46-10	.989	4	114	54	*O-146(1-145-1)	1.0
1988	Phi N	122	378	53	109	16	2	2	33	39-6	1	59	.288	.354	.357	103	3	17-9	.983	7	**114**	116	*O-112(0-112-5)	1.0
1989	StL N	155	545	60	158	28	8	4	68	39-5	4	91	.290	.340	.393	106	4	27-8	.978	-4	99	66	*O-147(23-123-3)	0.1
1990	StL N	135	418	42	91	14	7	6	30	39-5	5	60	.218	.292	.328	70	-18	25-5	.971	-4	100	52	*O-116(12-14-96)	-2.2
1991	StL N	115	326	55	100	16	5	6	34	32-7	0	53	.307	.368	.442	126	11	16-9	.991	9	116	160	O-91(72-12-12)	1.9
1992	StL N	109	208	31	61	9	1	4	17	16-3	2	39	.293	.350	.404	116	4	18-6	.974	-3	89	47	O-45(35-1-11)	0.3
1993	†Phi N	129	340	42	89	14	2	4	44	40-9	2	57	.262	.341	.350	87	-5	9-4	.994	-1	97	93	*O-106(102-4-0)	-0.9
1994	Phi N	87	220	29	60	7	0	3	30	23-4	3	28	.273	.348	.345	80	-6	7-2	1.000	-1	100	27	O-79(72-12-0)	-0.8
	Hou N	9	21	5	6	0	0	1	3	1-0	0	2	.286	.318	.429	97	0	2-0	1.000	0	82	306	/O-6(RF)	0.0
	Year	96	241	34	66	7	0	4	33	24-4	3	30	.274	.346	.353	82	-6	9-2	1.000	-1	99	46	O-85(72-12-6)	-0.8
1995	Hou N	92	132	14	29	9	0	2	19	14-3	1	37	.220	.297	.333	71	-5	4-2	.979	2	109	137	O-34(15-1-21)	-0.5
1996	LA N	48	51	2	6	1	0	0	1	6-0	0	10	.118	.211	.137	-6	-8	1-1	1.000	-1	87	0	O-17(LF)	-0.9
	Col N	14	15	1	1	1	0	0	2	1-0	0	3	.067	.125	.133	-26	-3	0-0	1.000	0	135	0	/O(LF)	-0.3
	Year	62	66	3	7	2	0	0	3	7-0	0	13	.106	.192	.136	-12	-11	1-1	1.000	-1	91	0	O-18(LF)	-1.2
Total	13	1359	3761	491	1029	156	37	47	357	336-46	22	635	.274	.335	.372	94	-33	214-66	.984	13	105	81	*O-1063(398-518-182)	-1.9

THOMPSON, ROBBY Robert Randall B 5.10.1962 W.Palm Beach, FL BR/TR 5-11/170# d4.8 C3

Year	Tm Lg	G	AB	R	H	2B	3B	HR	RBI	BB-IB	HP	SO	AVG	OBP	SLG	AOPS	ABR	SB-CS	FA	FR	Rng	Thr	G at Pos	BFW
1986	SF N	149	549	73	149	27	3	7	47	42-0	5	112	.271	.328	.370	97	-3	12-15	.976	-3	101	116	*2-149/S	0.0
1987	†SF N	132	420	62	110	26	5	10	44	40-3	8	91	.262	.338	.419	104	2	16-11	.972	4	99	**138**	*2-126	1.2
1988	SF N✱	138	477	66	126	24	6	7	48	40-0	4	111	.264	.323	.384	108	4	14-5	.978	-3	99	**128**	*2-134	0.7
1989	†SF N	148	547	91	132	26	**11**	13	50	51-0	**13**	133	.241	.321	.400	108	5	12-2	.989	-2	100	116	*2-148	0.9
1990	SF N	144	498	67	122	22	3	15	56	34-1	6	96	.245	.299	.392	92	-7	14-4	.989	20	112	127	*2-142	1.9
1991	SF N	144	492	74	129	24	5	19	48	63-2	6	95	.262	.352	.447	128	19	14-7	.985	12	102	**133**	*2-144	3.6
1992	SF N	128	443	54	115	25	1	14	49	43-1	8	75	.260	.333	.415	118	11	5-9	.978	**26**	109	**144**	*2-120	4.0
1993	SF N✱	128	494	85	154	30	2	19	65	45-0	7	97	.312	.375	.496	136	25	10-4	.988	17	106	**138**	*2-128	4.8
1994	SF N	35	129	13	27	8	2	2	7	15-0	0	32	.209	.290	.349	69	-6	3-1	.989	5	114	114	2-35	0.0
1995	SF N	95	336	51	75	15	0	8	23	42-1	4	76	.223	.317	.339	75	-12	1-2	.993	-19	93	87	2-91	-2.6
1996	SF N	63	227	35	48	11	1	5	21	24-0	5	69	.211	.301	.335	70	-10	2-2	.976	-6	94	99	2-62	-1.3
Total	11	1304	4612	671	1187	238	39	119	458	439-8	66	987	.257	.329	.403	105	28	103-62	.983	50	103	124	*2-1279/S	13.2

THOMPSON, TOMMY Rupert Lockhart B 5.19.1910 Elkhart, IL D 5.24.1971 Auburn, CA BL/TR 5-9.5/155# d9.3

Year	Tm Lg	G	AB	R	H	2B	3B	HR	RBI	BB-IB	HP	SO	AVG	OBP	SLG	AOPS	ABR	SB-CS	FA	FR	Rng	Thr	G at Pos	BFW
1933	Bos N	24	97	6	18	1	0	0	6	4	0	6	.186	.218	.196	21	-10	0	1.000	2	105	146	O-24(1-13-10)	-1.1
1934	Bos N	105	343	40	91	12	3	0	37	13	4	19	.265	.300	.318	71	-15	2	.964	8	113	152	O-82(6-1-75)	-1.2
1935	Bos N	112	297	34	81	7	1	4	30	36	1	17	.273	.353	.343	96	-1	2	.965	5	111	120	O-85(12-12-62)	0.0
1936	Bos N	106	266	37	76	9	0	4	36	31	1	12	.286	.362	.365	103	2	3	1.000	-1	99	96	O-39(10-22-7),1-25	-0.3
1938	Chi A	19	18	2	2	0	0	0	2	1	0	2	.111	.158	.111	-31	-4	0-0	1.000	-0	0	483	/1	-0.4
1939	Chi A	1	0	0	0	0	0	0	1	0	0	0	—	—	—	—	0	0-0	—	0			H	0.0
	StL A	30	86	23	26	5	0	1	7	23	1	7	.302	.455	.395	117	4	0-0	.977	0	90	172	O-23(RF)	0.3
	Year	31	86	23	26	5	0	1	8	23	1	7	.302	.455	.395	117	4	0-0	.977	0	90	172	O-23(RF)	0.3
Total	6	397	1107	142	294	34	4	9	119	108	7	63	.266	.335	.328	84	-24	7-0	.975	13	107	135	O-253(29-48-177)/1-26	-2.7

THOMPSON, RYAN Ryan Orlando B 11.4.1967 Chestertown, MD BR/TR 6-3/200# d9.1

Year	Tm Lg	G	AB	R	H	2B	3B	HR	RBI	BB-IB	HP	SO	AVG	OBP	SLG	AOPS	ABR	SB-CS	FA	FR	Rng	Thr	G at Pos	BFW
1992	NY N	30	108	15	24	7	1	3	10	8-0	0	24	.222	.274	.389	88	-2	2-2	.988	2	117	126	O-29(0-26-10)	0.0
1993	NY N	80	288	34	72	19	2	11	26	19-4	3	81	.250	.302	.444	98	-2	2-7	.987	5	114	100	O-76(CF)	0.2
1994	NY N	98	334	39	75	14	1	18	59	28-7	10	94	.225	.301	.434	90	-6	1-1	.989	3	108	90	O-98(CF)	-0.2
1995	NY N	75	267	39	67	13	0	7	31	19-1	4	77	.251	.306	.378	83	-7	3-1	.985	7	123	86	O-74(11-38-31)	-0.2
1996	Cle A	8	22	2	7	0	0	1	5	1-0	0	6	.318	.348	.455	101	0	0-0	1.000	-2	37	0	/O-8(CF)	-0.2
1999	Hou N	12	20	2	4	1	0	1	5	2-0	0	7	.200	.273	.400	68	-1	0-0	.800	-1	32	394	O-10(2-5-3)	-0.2
2000	NY A	33	50	12	13	3	0	3	14	5-0	1	12	.260	.339	.500	110	1	0-1	1.000	-0	104	0	O-31(20-9-6)	-0.1
2001	Fla N	18	31	6	9	5	0	0	2	1-0	0	8	.290	.313	.452	97	0	0-0	.923	-1	62	193	O-16(1-4-12)	-0.1
2002	Mil N	62	137	16	34	9	2	8	24	7-0	2	38	.248	.295	.518	113	1	1-0	.985	0	101	99	O-51(34-5-14)	0.0
Total	9	416	1257	165	305	71	6	52	176	90-12	20	347	.243	.301	.433	94	-16	9-12	.986	13	109	96	O-393(68-269-76)	-0.8

THOMPSON, SAM Samuel Luther "Big Sam" B 3.5.1860 Danville, IN D 11.7.1922 Detroit, MI BL/TL 6-2/207# d7.2 HF1974

Year	Tm Lg	G	AB	R	H	2B	3B	HR	RBI	BB-IB	HP	SO	AVG	OBP	SLG	AOPS	ABR	SB-CS	FA	FR	Rng	Thr	G at Pos	BFW
1885	Det N	63	254	58	77	11	9	7	44	16		22	.303	.344	.500	170	19		.885	6	203	0	O-63(RF)	2.3
1886	Det N	122	503	101	156	18	13	8	89	35		31	.310	.355	.445	137	21	13	.945	8	117	**329**	*O-122(RF)	2.5
1887	†Det N	**127**	545	118	**203**	29	**23**	10	**166**	32	9	19	.372	.416	**.565**	164	45	22	.909	6	107	179	*O-127(RF)	4.2
1888	Det N	56	238	51	67	10	8	6	40	23	3	10	.282	.352	.466	157	16	5	.882	-8	41	0	O-56(RF)	0.7
1889	Phi N	128	533	103	158	36	4	**20**	111	36	6	22	.296	.348	.492	123	12	24	.901	-8	78	150	*O-128(RF)	0.2
1890	Phi N	132	549	116	**172**	**41**	9	4	102	42	8	29	.313	.371	.443	133	22	25	.939	0	126	103	*O-132(RF)	1.9
1891	Phi N	133	554	108	163	23	10	7	90	52	8	20	.294	.363	.410	122	15	29	.937	18	153	164	*O-133(0-2-131)	2.8
1892	Phi N	153	609	109	186	28	11	9	104	59	11	19	.305	.377	.432	145	33	28	.937	1	110	136	*O-153(3-0-150)	2.5
1893	Phi N	131	600	130	**222**	**37**	13	11	126	50	6	17	.370	.424	.530	153	44	18	.931	-12	78	65	*O-131(RF)/1	2.1
1894	Phi N	102	451	114	187	32	28	13	**147**	41	1	13	.415	.465	**.696**	**181**	57	27	**.972**	-4	73	50	*O-102(RF)	3.6
1895	Phi N	119	538	131	211	45	21	**18**	**165**	31	5	11	.392	.430	**.654**	177	57	27	.943	12	**179**	49	*O-118(RF)	5.0
1896	Phi N	119	517	103	154	28	7	12	100	28	6	13	.298	.341	.449	108	4	12	**.974**	18	166	**238**	*O-119(RF)	1.3
1897	Phi N	3	13	2	3	0	1	0	3	1	0		.231	.286	.385	78	-1	0	.833	0	224	0	/O-3(RF)	-0.1
1898	Phi N	14	63	14	22	5	3	1	15	4	0		.349	.388	.571	182	6	2	1.000	3	281	0	O-14(RF)	0.7
1906	Det A	8	31	4	7	0	1	0	3	1	0		.226	.250	.290	67	-1	0	1.000	-0	0	0	/O-8(RF)	-0.2
Total	15	1410	5998	1262	1988	343	161	126	1305	451	63	226	.331	.384	.505	146	349	232	.934	41	120	133	*O-1409(3-2-1404)/1	29.5

THOMPSON, SCOT Vernon Scot B 12.7.1955 Grove City, PA BL/TL 6-3/195# d9.3

Year	Tm Lg	G	AB	R	H	2B	3B	HR	RBI	BB-IB	HP	SO	AVG	OBP	SLG	AOPS	ABR	SB-CS	FA	FR	Rng	Thr	G at Pos	BFW
1978	Chi N	19	36	7	15	3	0	0	2	2-0	0	4	.417	.447	.500	147	2	0-0	1.000	-1	50	0	/O-5(0-5-1),1-2	0.1
1979	Chi N	128	346	36	100	13	5	2	29	17-1	1	37	.289	.322	.373	82	-9	4-3	.971	-1	98	112	*O-100(12-26-72)	-1.4
1980	Chi N	102	226	26	48	10	1	2	13	28-3	1	31	.212	.301	.292	62	-11	6-6	.963	-3	89	90	O-66(1-14-52),1-12	-1.9
1981	Chi N	57	115	8	19	5	0	0	8	7-1	0	8	.165	.208	.209	19	-12	2-0	.980	-4	78	54	O-30(3-20-8)/1-3	-1.7
1982	Chi N	49	74	11	27	5	1	0	7	5-0	0	4	.365	.405	.459	138	4	0-1	1.000	3	130	186	O-23(20-1-4)/1-4	0.6
1983	Chi N	53	88	4	17	3	1	0	10	3-0	0	14	.193	.220	.250	28	-9	0-0	1.000	-2	88	0	O-29(23-0-6)/1	-1.2
1984	SF N	120	245	30	75	7	1	1	31	30-5	0	26	.306	.376	.355	112	5	5-3	.998	-2	92	93	1-87/O-6(2-0-4)	-0.1
1985	SF N	64	111	8	23	5	0	0	6	2-0	0	10	.207	.221	.252	34	-10	0-0	.995	2	146	94	1-24	-1.0
	Mon N	34	32	2	9	1	0	0	4	3-0	0	7	.281	.333	.313	90	0	0-0	1.000	1	114	100	/1-3,O-3(RF)	0.0
	Year	98	143	10	32	6	0	0	10	5-0	0	17	.224	.248	.266	47	-11	0-0	.995	3	144	94	1-27/O-3(RF)	-1.0
Total	8	626	1273	132	333	52	9	5	110	97-10	2	141	.262	.312	.328	76	-40	17-13	.973	-6	92	96	O-262(61-66-150),1-136	-6.6

THOMSON, BOBBY Robert Brown "The Staten Island Scot" B 10.25.1923 Glasgow, Scotland BR/TR 6-2/185# d9.9

Year	Tm Lg	G	AB	R	H	2B	3B	HR	RBI	BB-IB	HP	SO	AVG	OBP	SLG	AOPS	ABR	SB-CS	FA	FR	Rng	Thr	G at Pos	BFW
1946	NY N	18	54	8	17	4	1	2	9	4	0	5	.315	.362	.537	152	3	0	.935	-0	94	0	3-16	0.3
1947	NY N	138	545	105	154	26	5	29	85	40	4	78	.283	.336	.508	121	13	1	.980	-3	96	132	*O-127(CF)/2-9	0.7
1948	NY N★	138	471	75	117	20	2	16	63	30	2	77	.248	.296	.401	87	-11	2	.970	3	105	105	*O-125(64-57-4)	-1.4
1949	NY N★	**156**	641	99	198	35	9	27	109	44	2	45	.309	.355	.518	132	25	10	.982	8	111	87	*O-156(CF)	2.8

Year	Tm Lg	G	AB	R	H	2B	3B	HR	RBI	BB-IB	HP	SO	AVG	OBP	SLG	AOPS	ABR	SB-CS	FA	FR	Rng	Thr	G at Pos	BFW
1950	NY N	149	563	79	142	22	7	25	85	55	5	45	.252	.324	.449	101	-2	3	.978	3	101	121	*O-149(CF)	-0.3
1951	†NY N	148	518	89	152	27	8	32	101	73	4	57	.293	.385	.562	150	37	5-5	.966	-10	97	48	O-77(33-43-3),3-69	2.2
1952	NY N★	153	608	89	164	29	**14**	24	108	52	4	74	.270	.331	.482	122	15	5-2	.940	-5	104	87	3-91,O-63(CF)	0.9
1953	NY N	154	608	80	175	22	6	26	106	43	3	57	.288	.338	.472	106	4	4-2	.983	-4	92	114	*O-154(0-153-1)	-0.7
1954	Mil N	43	99	7	23	3	0	2	15	12	0	29	.232	.315	.323	71	-4	0-0	.980	1	93	198	O-26(LF)	-0.5
1955	Mil N	101	343	40	88	12	3	12	56	34-4	0	52	.257	.319	.414	99	-1	2-1	.969	-3	97	72	O-91(88-3-0)	-0.9
1956	Mil N	142	451	59	106	10	4	20	74	43-4	2	75	.235	.302	.408	95	-5	2-4	.974	-4	100	84	*O-136(128-18-0)/3-3	-1.8
1957	Mil N	41	148	15	35	5	3	4	23	8-0	2	27	.236	.285	.392	86	-4	2-1	.988	-0	99	75	O-38(36-5-1)	-0.7
	NY N	81	215	24	52	7	4	8	38	19-2	0	39	.242	.302	.423	93	-3	1-2	.992	-0	103	47	O-71(54-3-17)/3	-0.7
	Year	122	363	39	87	12	7	12	61	27-2	2	66	.240	.295	.410	90	-7	3-3	.990	-1	101	58	*O-109(90-8-18)/3	-1.4
1958	Chi N	152	547	67	155	27	5	21	82	56-7	4	76	.283	.351	.466	117	13	0-2	.989	-5	94	111	*O-148(7-143-1)/3-4	0.1
1959	Chi N	122	374	55	97	15	2	11	52	35-6	2	50	.259	.322	.398	93	-4	1-0	.987	3	102	120	*O-116(62-49-29)	-0.6
1960	Bos A	40	114	12	30	3	1	5	20	11-0	0	15	.263	.323	.439	102	0	0-1	.971	-0	108	57	O-27(12-13-2)/1	-0.2
	Bal A	3	6	0	0	0	0	0	0	0-0	0	3	.000	.000	.000	-99	-2	0-0	—	-0	0	0	/O-2(1-0-1)	-0.2
	Year	43	120	12	30	3	1	5	20	11-0	0	18	.250	.308	.417	93	-2	0-1	.971	-1	108	57	O-29(13-13-3)/1	-0.4
Total	15	1779	6305	903	1705	267	74	264	1026	559-23	34	804	.270	.332	.462	111	74	38-20	.980	-17	100	98	*O-1506(511-982-59),3-184/2-9,1	-1.0

THON, DICKIE Richard William B 6.20.1958 South Bend, IN BR/TR 5-11/175# d5.22

Year	Tm Lg	G	AB	R	H	2B	3B	HR	RBI	BB-IB	HP	SO	AVG	OBP	SLG	AOPS	ABR	SB-CS	FA	FR	Rng	Thr	G at Pos	BFW
1979	†Cal A	35	56	6	19	3	0	0	8	5-0	0	10	.339	.393	.393	117	2	0-0	.923	-3	84	114	2-24/S-8,3D	0.0
1980	Cal A	80	267	32	68	12	2	0	15	10-0	1	28	.255	.282	.315	65	-13	7-5	.928	-11	99	80	S-22,2-21,D-15,3-10/1	-2.2
1981	†Hou N	49	95	13	26	6	0	0	3	9-1	0	13	.274	.337	.337	96	0	6-1	.950	-10	63	93	2-28,S-13/3-5	-0.8
1982	Hou N	136	496	73	137	31	**10**	3	36	37-2	1	48	.276	.327	.397	110	5	37-8	.975	18	109	125	*S-119/3-8,2	4.3
1983	Hou N★	154	619	81	177	28	9	20	79	54-10	2	73	.286	.341	.457	128	21	34-16	.966	22	111	**128**	*S-154	6.3
1984	Hou N	5	17	3	6	0	1	0	1	0-0	1	4	.353	.389	.471	151	1	0-1	1.000	-0	94	40	/S-5	0.1
1985	Hou N	84	251	26	63	6	1	6	29	18-4	0	50	.251	.299	.355	85	-6	8-3	.967	2	101	115	S-79	0.4
1986	†Hou N	106	278	24	69	13	1	3	21	29-5	0	49	.248	.318	.335	83	-6	6-5	.972	-2	87	95	*S-104	0.0
1987	Hou N	32	66	6	14	1	0	1	3	16-3	0	13	.212	.366	.273	75	-2	3-0	.925	-5	87	62	S-31	-0.4
1988	SD N	95	258	36	68	12	2	1	18	33-0	1	49	.264	.347	.337	100	1	19-4	.954	-11	92	87	S-70/2-2,3	-0.3
1989	Phi N	136	435	45	118	18	4	15	60	33-6	0	81	.271	.321	.434	115	7	6-3	.972	20	**113**	102	*S-129	3.7
1990	Phi N	149	552	54	141	20	4	8	48	37-10	3	77	.255	.305	.350	80	-16	12-5	.964	2	105	108	*S-148	-0.3
1991	Phi N	146	539	44	136	18	4	9	44	25-6	0	84	.252	.283	.351	79	-17	11-5	.969	-9	96	85	*S-146	-1.5
1992	Tex A	95	275	30	68	15	3	4	37	20-1	0	40	.247	.293	.367	89	-5	12-2	.958	-2	98	72	S-87	0.1
1993	Mil A	85	245	23	66	10	1	1	33	22-3	0	39	.269	.324	.331	79	-7	6-5	.966	-9	96	62	S-28,3-25,2-22,D-14	-1.5
Total	15	1387	4449	496	1176	193	42	71	435	348-51	9	658	.264	.317	.374	95	-35	167-63	.965	1	102	101	*S-1143/2-98,3-50,D-30,1	7.9

THONEY, JACK John "Bullet Jack" (born John Thoeny) B 12.8.1879 Ft.Thomas, KY D 10.24.1948 Covington, KY BR/TR 5-10/175# d4.26

Year	Tm Lg	G	AB	R	H	2B	3B	HR	RBI	BB-IB	HP	SO	AVG	OBP	SLG	AOPS	ABR	SB-CS	FA	FR	Rng	Thr	G at Pos	BFW
1902	Cle A	28	105	14	30	7	1	0	11	9	0		.286	.342	.371	102	1	4	.891	-11	102	21	2-14,S-11/O-2(RF)	-1.0
	Bal A	3	11	1	0	0	0	0	0	1	0		.000	.083	.000	-72	-3	1	.778	-1	68	0	/3-3	-0.4
	Year	31	116	15	30	7	1	0	11	10	0		.259	.317	.336	84	-2	5	.891	-12	102	21	2-14,S-11/3-3,O-2(RF)	-1.4
1903	Cle A	32	122	10	25	3	0	1	9	2	0		.205	.218	.254	42	-9	7	.889	-1	217	148	O-24(0-23-1)/2-5,3-2	-1.1
1904	Was A	17	70	6	21	3	0	0	6	1	0		.300	.310	.343	108	0	2	.860	0	180	299	O-17(0-8-9)	0.0
	NY A	36	128	17	24	4	2	0	12	8	1		.188	.241	.250	53	-7	9	.826	-2	82	100	3-26,O-10(CF)	-1.0
	Year	53	198	23	45	7	2	0	18	9	1		.227	.264	.283	71	-7	11	.886	-2	234	194	O-27(0-18-9),3-26	-1.0
1908	Bos A	109	416	58	106	5	9	2	30	13	3		.255	.282	.325	94	-5	16	.948	4	94	58	*O-101(87-11-3)	-0.8
1909	Bos A	13	40	1	5	1	0	0	3	2	0		.125	.167	.150	0	-5	2	.960	1	67	297	O-10(LF)	-0.6
1911	Bos A	26	20	5	5	0	0	0	2	0	0		.250	.250	.250	40	-2	1	—	0			H	-0.2
Total	6	264	912	112	216	23	12	3	73	36	4		.237	.269	.298	75	-30	42	.929	-10	132	108	O-164(97-52-15)/3-31,2-19,S-11	-5.1

THORNTON, ANDY Andre B 8.13.1949 Tuskegee, AL BR/TR 6-2/205# d7.28

Year	Tm Lg	G	AB	R	H	2B	3B	HR	RBI	BB-IB	HP	SO	AVG	OBP	SLG	AOPS	ABR	SB-CS	FA	FR	Rng	Thr	G at Pos	BFW
1973	Chi N	17	35	3	7	3	0	0	2	7-0	0	9	.200	.333	.286	68	-1	0-0	.989	2	177	44	/1-9	0.0
1974	Chi N	107	303	41	79	16	4	10	46	48-4	4	50	.261	.368	.439	120	9	2-1	.992	7	131	84	1-90/3	1.0
1975	Chi N	120	372	70	109	21	4	18	60	88-12	4	63	.293	.428	.516	156	33	3-2	.988	0	102	90	*1-113/3-2	2.5
1976	Chi N	27	85	8	17	6	0	2	14	20-1	2	14	.200	.361	.341	93	0	2-0	.987	1	114	89	1-25	0.0
	Mon N	69	183	20	35	5	2	9	24	28-0	3	32	.191	.304	.388	93	-2	2-1	.994	-0	103	126	1-43,O-11(RF)	-0.6
	Year	96	268	28	52	11	2	11	38	48-1	5	46	.194	.323	.373	93	-1	4-1	.991	1	107	112	1-68,O-11(RF)	-0.6
1977	Cle A	131	433	77	114	20	5	28	70	70-1	11	82	.263	.378	.527	149	31	3-4	.995	-4	84	100	*1-117/D-9	1.9
1978	Cle A	145	508	97	133	22	4	33	105	93-4	6	72	.262	.377	.516	152	38	4-7	.995	7	116	87	*1-145	3.5
1979	Cle A	143	515	89	120	31	1	26	93	90-2	4	93	.233	.347	.449	114	12	5-4	.994	-3	88	82	*1-130,D-13	0.0
1981	Cle A	69	226	22	54	12	0	6	30	23-1	0	37	.239	.303	.372	97	-1	3-1	.986	-1	74	78	D-53,1-11	-0.4
1982	Cle A★	161	589	90	161	26	1	32	116	109-**18**	2	81	.273	.386	.484	139	35	6-7	1.000	-0	78	63	*D-152/1-8	2.9
1983	Cle A	141	508	78	143	27	1	17	77	87-14	2	72	.281	.383	.439	123	20	4-2	.991	1	114	83	*D-114,1-27	1.6
1984	Cle A★	155	587	91	159	26	0	33	99	91-11	2	79	.271	.366	.484	132	28	6-5	.979	0	108	113	*D-144,1-11	2.2
1985	Cle A	124	461	49	109	13	0	22	88	47-1	0	75	.236	.304	.408	94	-5	3-2	—	0	0	0	*D-122	-0.8
1986	Cle A	120	401	49	92	14	0	17	66	65-0	1	67	.229	.333	.392	100	1	4-1	—	0	0	0	*D-110	-0.2
1987	Cle A	36	85	8	10	2	0	0	5	10-0	0	25	.118	.206	.141	-4	-13	1-0	—	0	0	0	D-21	-1.3
Total	14	1565	5291	792	1342	244	22	253	895	876-69	41	851	.254	.360	.452	123	185	48-37	.992	9	104	90	D-738,1-729/O-11(RF),3-3	12.3

THORNTON, LOU Louis B 4.26.1963 Montgomery, AL BL/TR 6-2/185# d4.8

Year	Tm Lg	G	AB	R	H	2B	3B	HR	RBI	BB-IB	HP	SO	AVG	OBP	SLG	AOPS	ABR	SB-CS	FA	FR	Rng	Thr	G at Pos	BFW
1985	†Tor A	56	72	18	17	1	1	1	8	2-0	1	24	.236	.267	.319	58	-4	1-0	.957	-2	99	0	O-35(16-0-20),D-16	-0.7
1987	Tor A	12	2	5	1	0	0	0	0	1-1	0	0	.500	.667	.500	212	0	0-1	—	-0	0	0	/O-4(LF),D-6	0.0
1988	Tor A	11	2	1	0	0	0	0	0	0-0	0	0	.000	.000	.000	-99	-1	0-0	1.000	-1	30	0	O-10(9-0-1)/D	-0.1
1989	NY N	13	13	5	4	1	0	0	1	0-0	0	1	.308	.308	.385	102	0	2-0	1.000	1	149	0	/O-6(3-1-2)	0.1
1990	NY N	3	0	0	0	0	0	0	0	0-0	0	0	—	—	—	—	0	0-0	1.000	0	134	0	/O-2(0-1-1)	0.0
Total	5	95	89	29	22	2	1	1	9	3-1	1	25	.247	.280	.326	65	-5	3-1	.965	-2	98	0	/O-57(32-2-24),D-23	-0.7

THORNTON, OTIS Otis Benjamin B 6.30.1945 Docena, AL BR/TR 6-1/186# d7.6

Year	Tm Lg	G	AB	R	H	2B	3B	HR	RBI	BB-IB	HP	SO	AVG	OBP	SLG	AOPS	ABR	SB-CS	FA	FR	Rng	Thr	G at Pos	BFW
1973	Hou N	2	3	0	0	0	0	0	1	0-0	0	2	.000	.000	.000	-99	-1	0-0	1.000	0	27	0	/C-2	-0.1

THORNTON, WALTER Walter Miller B 2.18.1875 Lewiston, ME D 7.14.1960 Los Angeles, CA BL/TL 6-1/180# d7.1 ▲

Year	Tm Lg	G	AB	R	H	2B	3B	HR	RBI	BB-IB	HP	SO	AVG	OBP	SLG	AOPS	ABR	SB-CS	FA	FR	Rng	Thr	G at Pos	BFW
1895	Chi N	8	22	4	7	1	0	1	7	3	0	1	.318	.400	.500	123	1	0	.900	-1	55	0	/P-7,1	0.0
1896	Chi N	9	22	6	8	0	1	0	1	5	0	2	.364	.481	.455	142	2	2	.800	-1	50	0	/P-5,O-3(0-2-1)	0.0
1897	Chi N	75	265	39	85	9	6	0	55	30	6		.321	.402	.400	108	4	13	.781	-9	102		O-59(48-8-3),P-16	-0.9
1898	Chi N	62	210	34	62	5	2	0	14	22	0		.295	.362	.338	101	1	8	.877	-3	111	199	O-34(2-26-6),P-28	-0.3
Total	4	154	519	83	162	15	9	1	77	60	6	3	.312	.390	.382	108	8	23	.821	-14	101	71	/O-96(50-36-10),P-56,1	-1.2

THORPE, BOB Benjamin Robert B 11.19.1926 Caryville, FL D 10.30.1996 Waveland, MS BR/TR 6-1.5/190# d4.19

Year	Tm Lg	G	AB	R	H	2B	3B	HR	RBI	BB-IB	HP	SO	AVG	OBP	SLG	AOPS	ABR	SB-CS	FA	FR	Rng	Thr	G at Pos	BFW
1951	Bos N	2	2	1	1	0	1	0	1	0	0	0	.500	.500	1.500	448	1	0-0	—	0			H	0.1
1952	Bos N	81	292	20	76	8	2	3	26	5	1	42	.260	.275	.332	70	-13	3-1	.972	2	98	140	O-72(8-0-70)	-1.5
1953	Mil N	27	37	1	6	1	0	0	5	1	0	6	.162	.184	.189	-3	-6	0-1	1.000	-1	96	0	O-18(10-0-8)	-0.7
Total	3	110	331	22	83	9	3	3	32	6	1	48	.251	.266	.323	64	-18	3-2	.975	1	98	128	/O-90(18-0-78)	-2.1

THORPE, JIM James Francis B 5.28.1887 Prague, OK D 3.28.1953 Long Beach, CA BR/TR (BB 1915) 6-1/185# d4.14

Year	Tm Lg	G	AB	R	H	2B	3B	HR	RBI	BB-IB	HP	SO	AVG	OBP	SLG	AOPS	ABR	SB-CS	FA	FR	Rng	Thr	G at Pos	BFW
1913	NY N	19	35	6	5	0	0	1	2	1	0	9	.143	.167	.229	12	-4	2-1	.944	1	92	202	/O-9(3-7-0)	-0.4
1914	NY N	30	31	5	6	1	0	0	2	0	0	4	.194	.194	.226	25	-3	1	.750	-0	101	0	/O-4(0-2-2)	-0.4
1915	NY N	17	52	8	12	3	1	0	1	2	0	16	.231	.259	.327	82	-1	4-2	.933	-2	99	0	O-15(0-13-2)	-0.4
1917	Cin N	77	251	29	62	2	8	4	36	6	1	35	.247	.267	.367	98	-3	11	.962	2	111	80	O-69(38-0-33)	-0.6
	†NY N	26	57	12	11	3	2	0	4	8	1	10	.193	.303	.316	93	0	1	.939	-1	111	0	O-18(6-1-13)	-0.2
	Year	103	308	41	73	5	10	4	40	14	2	45	.237	.275	.357	97	-3	12	.958	1	111	66	O-87(44-1-46)	-0.8
1918	NY N	58	113	15	28	4	4	1	11	4	2	18	.248	.286	.381	105	0	3	.983	-2	92	53	O-44(2-33-12)	-0.5
1919	NY N	2	3	0	1	0	0	0	1	0	0	0	.333	.333	.333	102	0	0	1.000	-0	98	0	/O-2(1-1-0)	0.0
	Bos N	60	156	16	51	7	3	1	25	6	2	30	.327	.360	.429	143	7	7	.926	-4	98	43	O-38(22-12-7)/1-2	0.2
	Year	62	159	16	52	7	3	1	26	6	2	30	.327	.359	.428	142	7	7	.928	-4	98	42	O-40(23-13-7)/1-2	0.2
Total	6	289	698	91	176	20	18	7	82	27	6	122	.252	.286	.362	99	-4	29-3	.951	-7	103	59	O-199(72-69-69)/1-2	-2.3

THRASHER, BUCK Frank Edward B 8.6.1889 Watkinsville, GA D 6.12.1938 Cleveland, OH BL/TR 5-11/182# d9.27

Year	Tm Lg	G	AB	R	H	2B	3B	HR	RBI	BB-IB	HP	SO	AVG	OBP	SLG	AOPS	ABR	SB-CS	FA	FR	Rng	Thr	G at Pos	BFW
1916	Phi A	7	29	4	9	2	1	0	4	2	0	1	.310	.355	.448	148	1	0	1.000	-1	98	0	/O-7(RF)	0.1

Year	Tm Lg	G	AB	R	H	2B	3B	HR	RBI	BB-IB	HP	SO	AVG	OBP	SLG	AOPS	ABR	SB-CS	FA	FR	Rng	Thr	G at Pos	BFW
1917	Phi A	23	77	5	18	2	1	0	2	3	1	12	.234	.272	.286	71	-3	0	.938	-3	85	36	O-22(RF)	-0.8
Total	2	30	106	9	27	4	2	0	6	5	1	13	.255	.295	.330	92	-2	0	.951	-3	88	28	/O-29(RF)	-0.7
THRONEBERRY, MARV Marvin Eugene "Marvelous Marv" B 9.2.1933 Collierville, TN D 6.23.1994 Fisherville, TN BL/TL 6/197# d9.25 b-Maynard																								
1955	NY A	1	2	1	2	1	0	0	3	0-0	0	0	1.000	.667	1.500	574	1	1-0	1.000	0	281	0	/1	0.2
1958	†NY A	60	150	30	34	5	2	7	19	19-0	1	40	.227	.316	.427	107	1	1-1	.991	-1	99	134	1-40/O-5(RF)	-0.2
1959	NY A	80	192	27	46	5	0	8	22	18-1	0	51	.240	.302	.391	93	-3	0-0	.989	2	111	123	1-54,O-13(1-0-12)	-0.3
1960	KC A	104	236	29	59	9	2	11	41	23-1	0	60	.250	.315	.445	103	0	0-0	.991	1	106	106	1-71	-0.3
1961	KC A	40	130	17	31	2	1	6	24	19-1	0	30	.238	.336	.408	96	-1	0-0	.996	2	128	117	1-30,O-10(RF)	-0.1
	Bal A	56	96	9	20	3	0	5	11	12-0	0	20	.208	.296	.396	86	-2	0-0	.923	0	79	0	O-15(RF),1-11	-0.3
	Year	96	226	26	51	5	1	11	35	31-1	0	50	.226	.319	.403	93	-3	0-0	.991	2	136	110	1-41,O-25(RF)	-0.4
1962	Bal A	9	9	1	0	0	0	0	0	4-0	0	6	.000	.308	.000	-9	-1	0-0	1.000	0	110	0	/O-2(RF)	-0.1
	NY N	116	357	29	87	11	3	16	49	34-4	0	83	.244	.306	.426	94	-4	1-3	.981	4	126	105	1-97	-0.7
1963	NY N	14	14	0	2	1	0	0	1	1-0	0	5	.143	.200	.214	19	-1	0-0	1.000	-0	0	114	/1-3	-0.2
Total	7	480	1186	143	281	37	8	53	170	130-7	1	295	.237	.311	.416	96	-10	3-4	.987	8	117	112	1-307/O-45(1-0-44)	-2.0
THRONEBERRY, FAYE Maynard Faye B 6.22.1931 Fisherville, TN D 4.26.1999 Memphis, TN BL/TR 6/190# d4.15 Mil 1953 b-Marv																								
1952	Bos A	98	310	38	80	11	3	5	23	33	1	67	.258	.331	.361	86	-6	16-7	.955	1	98	148	O-86(11-4-71)	-0.7
1955	Bos A	60	144	20	37	7	3	6	27	14-1	1	31	.257	.323	.472	104	0	0-0	.960	0	101	110	O-34(32-0-3)	-0.2
1956	Bos A	24	50	6	11	2	0	1	3	3-0	0	16	.220	.264	.320	48	-4	0-0	.909	-2	86	0	O-13(8-2-3)	-0.6
1957	Bos A	1	1	0	0	0	0	0	0	0-0	0	1	.000	.000	.000	-95	0	0-0	—	0			H	0.0
	Was A	68	195	21	36	8	2	2	12	17-0	1	37	.185	.252	.277	45	-15	0-1	.983	-1	99	62	O-58(14-48-2)	-2.0
	Year	69	196	21	36	8	2	2	12	17-0	1	38	.184	.251	.276	45	-15	0-1	.983	-1	99	62	O-58(14-48-2)	-2.0
1958	Was A	44	87	12	16	1	1	4	7	4-0	3	28	.184	.245	.356	64	-5	0-1	1.000	-1	93	88	O-26(5-13-8)	-0.7
1959	Was A	117	327	36	82	11	2	10	42	33-3	3	61	.251	.322	.388	95	-2	6-4	.953	-2	92	151	O-86(16-1-71)	-0.8
1960	Was A	85	157	18	39	7	1	1	23	18-3	1	33	.248	.326	.325	78	-4	1-1	.947	-1	90	108	O-34(12-7-17)	-0.7
1961	LA A	24	31	1	6	1	0	0	0	5-0	0	10	.194	.306	.226	40	-3	0-0	1.000	1	98	317	/O-5(3-0-2)	-0.2
Total	8	521	1302	152	307	48	12	29	137	127-7	10	284	.236	.307	.358	79	-39	23-14	.962	-5	95	121	O-342(101-75-177)	-5.9
THURMAN, GARY Gary Montez B 11.12.1964 Indianapolis, IN BR/TR 5-10/175# d8.30																								
1987	KC A	27	81	12	24	2	0	0	5	8-0	0	20	.296	.360	.321	81	-2	7-2	.971	5	120	320	O-27(22-6-0)	0.2
1988	KC A	35	66	6	11	1	0	0	2	4-0	0	20	.167	.214	.182	12	-8	5-1	.949	-2	77	93	O-32(22-11-0)/D	-1.0
1989	KC A	72	87	24	17	2	1	0	5	15-0	0	26	.195	.311	.241	59	-4	16-0	.949	-4	73	104	O-60(12-28-24)/D-4	-0.6
1990	KC A	23	60	5	14	3	0	0	3	2-0	0	12	.233	.258	.283	52	-4	1-1	1.000	-1	98	0	O-21(5-2-15)	-0.6
1991	KC A	80	184	24	51	9	0	2	13	11-0	1	42	.277	.320	.359	87	-3	15-5	.970	4	122	67	O-72(39-9-29)	0.1
1992	KC A	88	200	25	49	6	3	0	20	9-0	1	34	.245	.281	.305	62	-11	9-6	.986	5	117	132	O-67(7-2-59)/D-9	-0.8
1993	Det A	75	89	22	19	2	2	0	13	11-0	0	30	.213	.297	.281	58	-5	7-0	.950	-3	77	161	O-53(17-21-15)/D-9	-0.7
1995	Sea A	13	25	3	8	2	0	0	3	1-0	0	3	.320	.333	.400	93	0	5-2	1.000	0	113	0	/O-9(5-1-4)	0.0
1997	NY N	11	6	0	1	0	0	0	0	0-0	0	0	.167	.167	.167	-13	-1	0-1	1.000	0	157	0	/O-7(3-4-1)	-0.1
Total	9	424	798	121	194	27	6	2	64	61-0	2	187	.243	.297	.299	65	-38	65-18	.971	3	103	121	O-348(132-84-147)/D-23	-3.5
THURMAN, BOB Robert Burns B 5.14.1917 Wichita, KS D 10.31.1998 Wichita, KS BL/TL 6-1/205# d4.14																								
1955	Cin N	82	152	19	33	2	3	7	22	17-2	0	26	.217	.296	.408	80	-5	0-2	.949	-0	99	98	O-36(LF)	-0.8
1956	Cin N	80	139	25	41	5	2	8	22	10-2	0	14	.295	.340	.532	123	4	0-0	.953	-1	92	109	O-29(9-0-20)	0.2
1957	Cin N	74	190	38	47	4	2	16	40	15-0	1	33	.247	.306	.542	114	3	0-0	.987	1	104	115	O-44(29-0-15)	0.2
1958	Cin N	94	178	23	41	7	4	4	20	20-1	4	38	.230	.320	.382	81	-5	1-2	.976	1	110	69	O-41(33-0-8)	-0.6
1959	Cin N	4	4	1	1	0	0	0	2	0-0	0	1	.250	.250	.250	33	0	0-0	—	0			H	0.0
Total	5	334	663	106	163	18	11	35	106	62-5	5	112	.246	.314	.465	99	-3	1-4	.970	1	103	96	O-150(107-0-43)	-1.0
THURSTON, JOE Joseph William B 9.29.1979 Fairfield, CA BL/TR 5-11/175# d9.2																								
2002	LA N	8	13	1	6	1	0	0	1	0-0	0	1	.462	.429	.538	179	1	0-0	1.000	0	104	229	/2-4	0.2
2003	LA N	12	10	2	2	0	0	0	0	1-0	0	1	.200	.273	.200	28	-1	0-0	.857	1	206	478	/2-3	0.0
Total	2	20	23	3	8	1	0	0	1	1-0	0	2	.348	.360	.391	110	0	0-0	.941	2	128	289	/2-7	0.2
TIEMEYER, EDDIE Edward Carl B 5.9.1885 Cincinnati, OH D 9.27.1946 Cincinnati, OH BR/TR 5-11.5/185# d8.19																								
1906	Cin N	5	11	3	2	0	0	0	0	1	0		.182	.250	.182	33	-1	0	1.000	0	133	377	/3-3,P	0.0
1907	Cin N	1	0	1	0	0	0	0	0	1	0		—	1.000	—	206	0	0	—	0			H	0.0
1909	NY A	3	8	1	3	1	0	0	0	1	0		.375	.444	.500	197	1	0	.962	-1	0	0	/1-3	0.0
Total	3	9	19	5	5	1	0	0	0	3	0		.263	.364	.316	110	0	0	.962	-0	0	0	/1-3,3-3,P	0.0
TIERNAN, MIKE Michael Joseph "Silent Mike" B 1.21.1867 Trenton, NJ D 11.9.1918 New York, NY BL/TL 5-11/165# d4.30 ▲																								
1887	NY N	103	407	82	117	13	12	10	62	32	3	31	.287	.344	.452	125	13	28	.865	-7	58	101	*O-103(34-11-58)/P-5	0.4
1888	†NY N	113	443	75	130	16	8	9	52	42	7	42	.293	.364	.427	153	28	52	**.960**	-1	83	60	*O-113(0-1-112)	2.5
1889	†NY N	122	499	**147**	167	23	14	10	73	**96**	5	32	.335	.447	.497	163	47	33	.896	-3	82	48	*O-122(0-1-122)	3.7
1890	NY N	133	553	132	168	25	21	**13**	59	68	5	53	.304	.385	**.495**	**156**	**37**	56	.896	-15	59	105	*O-133(2-131-1)	1.6
1891	NY N	134	542	111	166	30	12	**16**	73	69	3	32	.306	.388	.494	**163**	**44**	53	.901	-8	78	116	*O-134(0-4-130)	3.0
1892	NY N	116	450	79	130	16	10	5	66	57	2	46	.289	.371	.402	136	21	20	.899	-4	80	49	*O-116(RF)	1.0
1893	NY N	125	511	114	158	19	12	14	102	72	4	24	.309	.399	.476	131	23	26	.927	-11	56	45	*O-125(RF)	0.4
1894	†NY N	113	429	87	120	20	13	5	79	55	1	21	.280	.363	.422	89	-8	28	.923	-12	48	24	*O-112(RF)	-2.0
1895	NY N	120	476	127	165	23	21	7	70	66	1	19	.347	.427	.527	149	35	36	.946	-5	46	51	*O-119(RF)	1.9
1896	NY N	**133**	521	132	192	24	16	7	89	77	2	18	.369	.452	.516	159	48	35	.970	-2	81	84	*O-133(RF)	3.4
1897	NY N	128	532	123	174	29	10	5	72	61	1		.327	.397	.447	126	22	40	.931	-13	59	57	*O-128(38-0-90)	0.1
1898	NY N	103	415	90	116	15	11	5	49	43	7		.280	.357	.405	122	12	19	.973	-10	85	57	*O-103(96-0-7)	-0.6
1899	NY N	35	137	17	35	4	2	0	7	10	0		.255	.306	.314	73	-5	2	.938	-4	58	61	O-35(RF)	-1.0
Total	13	1478	5915	1316	1838	257	162	106	853	748	41	318	.311	.392	.463	138	317	428	.924	-96	68	67	*O-1476(170-148-1160)/P-5	14.4
TIERNEY, COTTON James Arthur B 2.10.1894 Kansas City, KS D 4.18.1953 Kansas City, MO BR/TR 5-8/175# d9.23																								
1920	Pit N	12	46	4	11	5	0	0	8	3	0	4	.239	.286	.348	79	-1	1-1	.964	-1	104	91	2-10/S-2	-0.2
1921	Pit N	117	442	49	132	22	8	3	52	24	2	31	.299	.338	.405	93	-5	4-6	.965	-28	78	108	2-72,3-32/O-4(RF),S-3	-3.0
1922	Pit N	122	441	58	152	26	14	7	86	22	2	40	.345	.378	.515	127	16	7-8	.964	-30	86	97	*2-105/O-2(RF),S3	-1.2
1923	Pit N	29	120	22	35	5	2	2	23	2	1	10	.292	.309	.417	88	-3	2-1	.941	-2	95	130	2-29	-0.4
	Phi N	121	480	68	152	31	1	11	65	24	2	42	.317	.352	.454	100	0	3-4	.975	19	112	106	*2-115/O-7(3-0-4),3-2	2.0
	Year	150	600	90	187	36	3	13	88	26	3	52	.312	.343	.447	97	-3	5-5	**.968**	**17**	**108**	**111**	*2-144/O-7(3-0-4),3-2	1.6
1924	Bos N	136	505	38	131	16	1	6	58	22	4	37	.259	.296	.331	71	-22	11-8	.964	-8	99	112	*2-115,3-22	-2.6
1925	Bro N	93	265	27	68	14	4	2	39	12	2	23	.257	.294	.362	68	-13	0-3	.963	-3	94	54	3-61/12	-1.3
Total	6	630	2299	266	681	119	30	31	331	109	13	187	.296	.332	.415	93	-28	28-31	.966	-52	96	107	2-447,3-118/O-13(3-0-10),S-6,1	-6.7
TIERNEY, BILL William J. B 5.14.1858 Boston, MA D 9.21.1898 Boston, MA d5.2																								
1882	Cin AA	1	5	1	0	0	0	0		0			.000	.000	.000	-95	-1		.917	0	317	0	/1	-0.1
1884	Bal U	1	3	0	1	0	0	0		1			.333	.500	.333	142	0		1.000	-0	0	0	/O(RF)	0.0
Total	2	2	8	1	1	0	0	0		1			.125	.222	.125	13	-1		1.000	0	0	0	/O(RF)1	-0.1
TILLEY, JOHN John C. B New York, NY BR 5-7/154# d8.23																								
1882	Cle N	15	56	2	5	1	1	0	4	2		11	.089	.121	.143	-16	-7		.857	1	110	135	O-15(14-1-0)	-0.6
1884	Tol AA	17	56	5	10	2	0	0		4	1		.179	.246	.214	50	-3		.632	-3	0	0	O-17(LF)	-0.6
	StP U	**9**	26	2	4	1	0	0		3			.154	.241	.192	61	-1		.938	1	50	0	/O-9(LF)	-0.1
Total	2	41	138	9	19	4	1	0	4	9		11	.138	.196	.181	23	-11		.818	-1	58	58	/O-41(40-1-0)	-1.3
TILLMAN, BOB John Robert B 3.24.1937 Nashville, TN D 6.23.2000 Gallatin, TN BR/TR 6-4/205# d4.15																								
1962	Bos A	81	249	28	57	6	4	14	38	19-0	1	65	.229	.283	.454	93	-4	0-0	.983	-6	*81*	*55*	C-66	-0.8
1963	Bos A	96	307	24	69	10	2	8	32	34-8	1	64	.225	.304	.349	80	-8	0-0	.992	-7	75	52	C-95	-1.1
1964	Bos A	131	425	43	118	18	1	17	61	49-11	0	74	.278	.352	.445	114	9	0-0	.989	-9	*75*	*90*	*C-131	0.7
1965	Bos A	111	368	20	79	10	3	6	35	40-3	0	69	.215	.288	.307	66	-16	0-0	.988	-10	*71*	*96*	*C-106	-2.2
1966	Bos A	78	204	12	47	8	0	3	24	22-3	0	35	.230	.303	.314	71	-7	0-0	.990	-6	*66*	*99*	C-72	-1.1
1967	Bos A	30	64	4	12	1	0	1	4	3-0	0	18	.188	.224	.250	37	-5	0-0	.977	-3	42	78	C-26	-0.7
	NY A	22	63	5	16	1	0	2	9	7-1	0	17	.254	.324	.365	109	1	0-0	.970	-2	62	124	C-15	-0.1
	Year	52	127	9	28	2	0	3	13	10-1	0	35	.220	.275	.307	70	-5	0-0	.974	-5	*51*	*100*	C-41	-0.8

Year	Tm Lg	G	AB	R	H	2B	3B	HR	RBI	BB-IB	HP	SO	AVG	OBP	SLG	AOPS	ABR	SB-CS	FA	FR	Rng	Thr	G at Pos	BFW
1968	Atl N	86	.236	16	52	4	0	5	20	16-2	3	55	.220	.278	.301	74	-8	1-0	.990	-3	*79*	*75*	C-75	-0.8
1969	†Atl N	69	190	18	37	5	0	12	29	18-1	0	47	.195	.263	.411	86	-5	0-0	.988	-9	90	26	C-69	-1.1
1970	Atl N	71	223	19	53	5	0	11	30	20-4	0	66	.238	.299	.408	83	-6	0-0	.988	-5	72	54	C-70	-0.8
Total	9	775	2329	189	540	68	10	79	282	228-33	5	510	.232	.300	.371	85	-49	1-0	.988	-58	*74*	*73*	C-725	-8.0
TILLMAN, RUSTY Kerry Jerome B 8.29.1960 Jacksonville, FL BR/TR 6/185# d6.6																								
1982	NY N	12	13	4	2	1	0	0	0	0-0	0	4	.154	.154	.231	6	-2	1-0	1.000	-1	51	0	/O-3(RF)	-0.2
1986	Oak A	22	39	6	10	1	0	1	6	3-0	0	11	.256	.310	.359	88	-1	2-0	.952	-1	97	0	O-17(8-0-10)	-0.2
1988	SF N	4	4	1	1	0	0	1	3	2-0	0	1	.250	.500	1.000	335	1	0-0	1.000	0	143	0	/O(LF)	0.1
Total	3	38	56	11	13	2	0	2	9	5-0	0	16	.232	.295	.375	88	-2	3-0	.958	-1	91	0	/O-21(9-0-13)	-0.3
TIMMONS, OZZIE Osborne Llewellyn B 9.18.1970 Tampa, FL BR/TR 6-2/205# d4.26																								
1995	Chi N	77	171	30	45	10	1	8	28	13-2	0	32	.263	.314	.474	107	1	3-0	.970	-3	88	41	O-55(49-0-6)	-0.3
1996	Chi N	65	140	18	28	4	0	7	16	15-0	1	30	.200	.282	.379	70	-7	1-0	1.000	1	111	50	O-47(25-0-22)	-0.6
1997	Cin N	6	9	1	3	1	0	0	0	0-0	0	1	.333	.333	.444	100	0	0-0	.000	-1	0	0	/O(LF)	-0.1
1999	Sea A	26	44	4	5	2	0	1	3	4-0	0	12	.114	.188	.227	5	-7	0-1	1.000	-2	69	0	O-17(12-0-5)/1D	-0.8
2000	TB A	12	41	9	14	3	0	4	13	1-0	0	7	.341	.357	.707	162	3	0-0	1.000	-2	45	0	/O-9(2-0-7),D	0.1
Total	5	186	405	62	95	20	1	20	60	33-2	1	82	.235	.293	.437	88	-10	4-1	.980	-6	89	35	O-129(89-0-40)/D-6,1	-1.7
TINGLEY, RON Ronald Irvin B 5.27.1959 Presque Isle, ME BR/TR 6-2/194# d9.25																								
1982	SD N	8	20	0	2	0	0	0	0	0-0	0	7	.100	.100	.100	-46	-4	0-0	.957	-1	40	72	/C-8	-0.5
1988	Cle A	9	24	1	4	0	0	1	2	2-0	0	8	.167	.231	.292	44	-2	0-0	1.000	2	55	133	/C-9	0.1
1989	Cal A	4	3	0	1	0	0	0	0	1-0	0	0	.333	.500	.333	142	0	0-0	.889	-1	32	0	/C-4	0.0
1990	Cal A	5	3	0	0	0	0	0	0	1-0	0	1	.000	.250	.000	-25	0	0-0	1.000	-0	0	0	/C-5	0.0
1991	Cal A	45	115	11	23	7	0	1	13	8-0	1	34	.200	.258	.287	51	-8	1-1	.988	6	117	184	C-45	0.1
1992	Cal A	71	127	15	25	2	1	3	8	13-0	2	35	.197	.282	.299	62	-7	0-1	.987	7	121	139	C-69	0.3
1993	Cal A	58	90	7	18	7	0	0	12	9-0	1	22	.200	.277	.278	49	-6	1-2	.995	4	155	84	C-58	0.0
1994	Fla N	19	52	4	9	3	1	1	2	5-0	0	18	.173	.246	.327	46	-4	0-0	.990	2	173	144	C-18	-0.1
	Chi A	5	5	0	0	0	0	0	0	0-0	0	2	.000	.000	.000	-99	-2	0-0	1.000	-0	50	0	/C-5	-0.2
1995	Det A	54	124	14	28	8	1	4	18	15-0	0	38	.226	.307	.403	84	-3	0-1	.991	-5	113	118	C-53/1	-0.5
Total	9	278	563	52	110	27	3	10	55	54-0	4	165	.195	.270	.307	56	-36	2-5	.989	15	121	127	C-274/1	-0.8
TINKER, JOE Joseph Bert B 7.27.1880 Muscotah, KS D 7.27.1948 Orlando, FL BR/TR 5-9/175# d4.17 M4 HF1946																								
1902	Chi N	133	501	55	132	19	5	2	55	26	0		.263	.300	.333	98	-3	27	.908	1	108	113	*S-126/3-8	0.3
1903	Chi N	124	460	67	134	21	7	2	70	37	1		.291	.345	.380	110	5	27	.906	0	105	106	*S-107,3-19	0.9
1904	Chi N	141	488	55	108	12	13	3	41	29	2		.221	.268	.318	80	-13	41	.925	16	105	120	*S-140/O(RF)	0.7
1905	Chi N	149	547	70	135	18	8	2	66	34	1		.247	.292	.320	79	-15	31	.940	12	105	**130**	*S-149	0.2
1906	†Chi N	148	523	75	122	18	4	1	64	43	1		.233	.293	.289	77	-14	30	**.944**	-0	100	131	*S-147/3	-1.1
1907	†Chi N	117	402	36	89	11	3	1	36	25	1		.221	.269	.271	65	-17	20	.939	13	**111**	**135**	*S-113	0.1
1908	†Chi N	157	548	67	146	22	14	6	68	32	0		.266	.307	.391	117	8	30	**.958**	26	109	106	*S-157	4.5
1909	Chi N	143	516	56	132	26	11	4	57	17	0		.256	.280	.372	100	-4	23	**.940**	18	**105**	112	*S-143	2.1
1910	†Chi N	134	473	48	136	25	9	3	69	24	0	35	.288	.322	.397	110	3	20	.942	14	104	113	*S-132	2.3
1911	Chi N	144	536	61	149	24	12	4	69	39	0	31	.278	.327	.390	100	-2	30	**.937**	**22**	**109**	103	*S-143	2.9
1912	Chi N	142	550	80	155	24	7	0	75	38	2	21	.282	.331	.351	87	-11	25	.943	**26**	106	132	*S-142	2.5
1913	Cin N	110	382	47	121	20	13	1	57	20	1	26	.317	.352	.445	127	12	10-12	.968	21	111	95	*S-101/3-9,M	**3.8**
1914	Chi F	126	438	50	112	21	7	2	46	38	1	30	.256	.317	.349	86	-17	19	.947	12	109	**123**	*S-125,M	0.5
1915	Chi F	31	67	7	18	2	1	0	9	13	0	5	.269	.387	.328	109	1	3	.914	-2	109	50	S-16/2-5,3-4,M	0.0
1916	Chi N	7	10	0	1	0	0	0	1	1	0	1	.100	.182	.100	-11	-1	0	.909	-0	106	0	/S-4,3-2,M	-0.2
Total	15	1806	6441	774	1690	263	114	31	783	416	10	149	.262	.308	.353	95	-68	336-12	.938	180	107	117	*S-1745/3-43,2-5,O(RF)	19.5
TINSLEY, LEE Lee Owen B 3.4.1969 Shelbyville, KY BB/TR 5-10/185# d4.6																								
1993	Sea A	11	19	2	3	1	0	1	2	2-0	0	9	.158	.238	.368	60	-1	0-0	.900	0	147	0	/O-6(5-1-1),D-2	-0.1
1994	Bos A	78	144	27	32	4	0	2	14	19-1	1	36	.222	.315	.292	56	-9	13-0	.991	1	111	35	O-60(27-26-11),D-10	-0.6
1995	†Bos A	100	341	61	97	17	1	7	41	39-1	1	74	.284	.359	.402	95	-2	18-8	.979	-0	103	93	O-97(CF)	0.0
1996	Phi N	31	52	1	7	0	0	0	2	4-0	0	22	.135	.196	.135	-11	-9	2-4	.960	0	107	0	O-22(18-7-0)	-1.0
	Bos A	92	192	28	47	6	1	3	14	13-0	2	56	.245	.298	.333	59	-13	6-8	.993	1	94	237	O-83(4-79-0)	-1.1
1997	Sea A	49	122	12	24	6	2	0	6	11-0	0	34	.197	.263	.279	42	-11	2-0	1.000	1	105	98	O-41(34-6-2)/D-5	-1.0
Total	5	361	870	131	210	34	4	13	79	88-2	4	231	.241	.313	.334	66	-45	41-20	.985	3	103	112	O-309(88-216-14)/D-17	-3.8
TIPPER, JIM James B 6.18.1849 Middletown, CT D 4.21.1895 New Haven, CT 5-5.5/148# d4.26																								
1872	Man NA	**24**	110	24	29	4	0	0	18	0		1	.264	.264	.300	77	-2	0-0	.773	-2	141	0	O-20(LF)/3-5	-0.3
1874	Har NA	45	197	36	60	8	0	0	19	1		7	.305	.308	.345	104	0	0-1	.812	-1	78	77	*O-45(LF)	0.1
1875	NH NA	41	159	10	25	1	0	0	4	1		6	.157	.162	.164	16	-12	1-0	.790	-3	94	73	O-41(8-32-3)	-1.2
Total	3 NA	110	466	70	114	13	0	0	41	2		14	.245	.248	.273	72	-14	1-1	.000	-6	96	61	O-106(73-32-3)/3-5	-1.4
TIPTON, ERIC Eric Gordon "Dukie" or "Blue Devil" B 4.20.1915 Petersburg, VA D 8.29.2001 Newport News, VA BR/TR 5-11/190# d6.9																								
1939	Phi A	47	104	12	24	4	2	1	14	13	0	7	.231	.316	.337	68	-5	2-0	.942	-0	114	0	O-34(33-0-2)	-0.6
1940	Phi A	2	8	2	1	0	1	0	0	1	0	1	.125	.222	.375	53	-1	0-0	1.000	-0	85	0	/O-2(LF)	-0.1
1941	Phi A	1	4	0	2	0	0	0	0	0	0	0	.500	.500	.500	169	0	0-0	1.000	-0	96	0	/O(LF)	0.0
1942	Cin N	63	207	22	46	5	5	4	18	25	1	14	.222	.309	.353	94	-2	1	.977	-2	97	67	O-58(38-20-1)	-0.8
1943	Cin N	140	493	82	142	26	7	9	49	85	2	36	.288	.395	.424	138	28	1	.984	-5	99	57	*O-139(LF)	1.6
1944	Cin N	140	479	62	144	28	3	3	36	59	2	32	.301	.380	.390	121	16	5	.983	2	107	73	*O-139(LF)	1.0
1945	Cin N	108	331	32	80	17	1	5	34	40	2	37	.242	.327	.344	89	-4	11	.970	-2	102	32	O-83(LF)	-1.2
Total	7	501	1626	212	439	80	19	22	151	223	7	127	.270	.360	.383	112	32	20-0	.977	-8	103	55	O-456(435-20-3)	-0.1
TIPTON, JOE Joe Hicks B 2.18.1922 McCaysville, GA D 3.1.1994 Birmingham, AL BR/TR 5-11/185# d5.2																								
1948	†Cle A	47	90	11	26	3	0	1	13	4	2	10	.289	.333	.356	85	-2	0-0	.971	2	*125*	*123*	C-40	0.1
1949	Chi A	67	191	20	39	5	3	3	19	27	1	17	.204	.306	.309	65	-10	1-1	.992	1	*85*	*113*	C-53	-0.6
1950	Phi A	64	184	15	49	5	1	6	20	19	0	16	.266	.335	.402	90	-4	0-0	.987	-4	*88*	*71*	C-59	-0.5
1951	Phi A	72	213	23	51	9	0	3	20	51	1	25	.239	.389	.324	92	1	1-1	.969	5	*149*	*149*	C-72	0.9
1952	Phi A	23	68	6	13	4	0	3	8	15	0	10	.191	.337	.382	94	0	0-0	.990	-1	*121*	*174*	C-23	0.0
	Cle A	43	105	15	26	2	0	6	22	21	2	21	.248	.383	.438	137	6	1-0	.971	-5	*85*	*110*	C-35	0.3
	Year	66	173	21	39	6	0	9	30	36	2	31	.225	.365	.416	119	6	1-0	.979	-6	*100*	*137*	C-58	0.3
1953	Cle A	47	109	17	25	2	0	6	13	19	3	13	.229	.359	.413	111	2	0-0	1.000	-3	*82*	*91*	C-46	0.0
1954	Was A	54	157	9	35	6	1	1	10	30	2	30	.223	.353	.293	83	-2	0-1	.992	0	*93*	*98*	C-52	0.1
Total	7	417	1117	116	264	36	5	29	125	186	11	142	.236	.351	.355	91	-9	3-3	.984	-5	*105*	*114*	C-380	0.3
TISCHINSKI, TOM Thomas Arthur B 7.12.1944 Kansas City, MO BR/TR 5-10/190# d4.11																								
1969	Min A	37	47	2	9	0	0	0	2	8-0	0	8	.191	.309	.191	42	-3	0-0	1.000	-3	198	69	C-32	-0.6
1970	Min A	24	46	6	9	0	0	1	2	9-1	0	6	.196	.327	.261	63	-2	0-0	.990	-2	120	110	C-22	-0.3
1971	Min A	21	23	0	3	2	0	0	2	1-0	1	4	.130	.200	.217	18	-2	0-0	.982	-0	55	124	C-21	-0.3
Total	3	82	116	8	21	2	0	1	6	18-1	1	18	.181	.296	.224	46	-7	0-0	.992	-5	136	97	/C-75	-1.2
TITUS, JOHN John Franklin "Silent John" B 2.21.1876 St.Clair, PA D 1.8.1943 St.Clair, PA BL/TL 5-9/156# d6.8																								
1903	Phi N	72	280	38	80	15	6	2	34	19	4		.286	.340	.404	115	5	5	.952	3	129	77	O-72(34-2-36)	0.4
1904	Phi N	146	504	60	148	25	5	4	55	46	8		.294	.362	.387	136	23	15	.952	10	122	122	*O-140(105-2-33)	2.7
1905	Phi N	147	548	99	169	36	14	2	89	69	12		.308	.397	.436	154	40	11	.962	7	122	86	*O-147(RF)	4.1
1906	Phi N	145	484	67	129	22	5	1	57	78	9		.267	.378	.339	124	19	12	.974	7	131	118	*O-142(0-8-134)	2.1
1907	Phi N	145	523	72	144	23	12	3	63	47	9		.275	.345	.382	130	18	9	.928	-5	107	64	*O-142(RF)	0.7
1908	Phi N	149	539	75	154	24	5	2	48	53	14		.286	.365	.360	127	19	27	.963	-4	116	69	*O-149(RF)	1.0
1909	Phi N	151	540	69	146	22	6	3	46	66	**16**		.270	.367	.350	121	17	23	.971	4	108	130	*O-149(RF)	1.5
1910	Phi N	143	535	91	129	26	5	3	35	93	4	44	.241	.358	.325	96	2	20	.976	-1	94	107	*O-142(1-0-142)	-0.6
1911	Phi N	76	236	35	67	14	1	8	26	32	1	16	.284	.372	.453	129	9	3	.979	-1	87	125	O-60(1-0-59)	0.6
1912	Phi N	45	157	43	43	9	5	3	22	33	1	14	.274	.403	.452	125	7	6	.917	-5	85	36	O-42(RF)	-0.1
	Bos N	96	345	56	112	23	6	2	48	49	9	20	.325	.422	.443	134	20	5	.965	-3	96	86	O-96(1-0-96)	1.1
	Year	141	502	99	155	32	11	5	70	82	10	34	.309	.416	.446	131	26	11	.952	-9	93	72	*O-138(1-0-138)	1.0

Year	Tm Lg	G	AB	R	H	2B	3B	HR	RBI	BB-IB	HP	SO	AVG	OBP	SLG	AOPS	ABR	SB-CS	FA	FR	Rng	Thr	G at Pos	BFW
1913	Bos N	87	269	33	80	14	2	5	38	35	7	22	.297	.392	.420	129	12	4-7	.919	-5	85	93	O-75(RF)	0.2
Total	11	1402	4960	738	1401	253	72	38	561	620	94	116	.282	.373	.385	127	191	140-7	.959	5	110	96	*O-1356(142-12-1204)	13.7
TOBIN, JOHNNY John Martin "Tip" B 9.15.1906 Jamaica Plain, MA D 8.6.1983 Rhinebeck, NY BR/TR 6-3/187# d9.22																								
1932	NY N	1	1	0	0	0	0	0	0	0	0	0	.000	.000	.000	-99	0	0	—	0			H	0.0
TOBIN, JOHNNY John Patrick "Jackie" B 1.8.1921 Oakland, CA D 1.18.1982 Oakland, CA BL/TR 6/165# d4.20 b-Jim																								
1945	Bos A	84	278	25	70	6	2	0	21	26	2	24	.252	.320	.288	75	-9	2-6	.951	7	112	121	3-72/2-5,O(CF)	-0.2
TOBIN, JACK John Thomas B 5.4.1892 St.Louis, MO D 12.10.1969 St.Louis, MO BL/TL 5-8/142# d4.16 C3																								
1914	StL F	139	529	81	143	24	10	7	35	51	5	53	.270	.340	.393	94	-12	20	.952	6	94	151	*O-132(12-7-113)	-1.4
1915	StL F	158	625	92	**184**	26	13	6	51	68	3	42	.294	.366	.406	111	2	31	.965	-1	100	99	*O-158(0-31-128)	-0.9
1916	StL A	77	150	16	32	4	1	0	10	12	0	13	.213	.272	.253	61	-8	7	.842	-5	86	51	O-41(0-6-35)	-1.6
1918	StL A	122	480	59	133	19	5	0	36	48	5	26	.277	.349	.338	111	7	13	.971	-5	86	114	*O-122(43-78-1)	-0.6
1919	StL A	127	486	54	159	22	7	6	57	36	2	24	.327	.376	.438	125	15	8	.953	1	97	124	*O-123(LF)	1.1
1920	StL A	147	593	94	202	34	10	4	62	39	2	23	.341	.383	.452	117	14	21-13	.960	3	109	91	*O-147(34-0-113)	0.9
1921	StL A	150	671	132	236	31	**18**	8	59	45	3	22	.352	.395	.487	117	16	7-12	.956	5	98	134	*O-150(0-8-143)	0.5
1922	StL A	146	625	122	207	34	8	13	66	56	2	22	.331	.388	.474	119	18	7-9	.940	-9	85	94	*O-145(0-1-144)	-0.5
1923	StL A	151	637	91	202	32	15	13	73	42	4	13	.317	.363	.476	113	9	8-7	.969	-10	90	69	*O-151(RF)	-1.4
1924	StL A	136	569	87	170	30	8	2	48	50	2	12	.299	.357	.390	87	-11	6-10	.957	-1	101	101	*O-132(1-1-130)	-2.3
1925	StL A	77	193	25	58	11	0	2	27	9	1	5	.301	.335	.389	79	-6	8-2	1.000	-3	98	29	O-39(1-1-38)/1-3	-1.0
1926	Was A	27	33	5	7	0	1	0	3	0	0	0	.212	.212	.273	26	-4	0-0	1.000	-0	118	0	/O-7(0-4-3)	-0.4
	Bos A	51	209	26	57	9	0	1	14	16	0	3	.273	.324	.330	73	-8	6-5	.966	-4	79	118	O-51(1-0-51)	-1.6
	Year	78	242	31	64	9	1	1	17	16	0	3	.264	.310	.322	67	-12	6-5	.970	-4	82	110	O-58(1-4-54)	-2.0
1927	Bos A	111	374	52	116	18	3	2	40	36	0	9	.310	.371	.390	100	0	5-4	.947	-3	89	103	O-93(5-0-89)	-1.0
Total	13	1619	6174	936	1906	294	99	64	581	508	29	267	.309	.364	.420	106	32	147-62	.957	-26	95	104	*O-1491(220-137-1139)/1-3	-10.2
TOBIN, BILL William F. B 10.10.1854 Hartford, CT D 10.10.1912 Hartford, CT BL d7.21																								
1880	Wor N	5	16	1	2	0	0	0	3	0		5	.125	.125	.125	-14	-2		1.000	-0	0	99	/1-5	-0.2
	Tro N	33	136	14	22	1	1	0	8	4		20	.162	.186	.184	24	-11		.950	-1	94	160	1-33	-1.3
	Year	38	152	15	24	1	1	0	11	4		25	.158	.179	.178	20	-13		.958	-1	82	152	1-38	-1.5
TOCA, JORGE Jorge Luis B 1.7.1975 Remedios, Cuba BR/TR 6-3/220# d9.12																								
1999	NY N	4	3	0	1	0	0	0	0	0-0	0	2	.333	.333	.333	72	0	0-0	1.000	0	0	0	/1	0.0
2000	NY N	8	7	1	3	1	0	0	4	0-0	0	1	.429	.429	.571	156	1	0-0	1.000	-0	0	0	/1-5,O(LF)	0.0
2001	NY N	13	17	3	3	0	0	0	1	0-0	0	8	.176	.176	.176	-9	-3	0-0	1.000	0	113	93	/1-3,O-2(LF)	-0.3
Total	3	25	27	4	7	1	0	0	5	0-0	0	11	.259	.259	.296	44	-2	0-0	1.000	-0	64	53	/1-9,O-3(LF)	-0.3
TODD, AL Alfred Chester B 1.7.1902 Troy, NY D 3.8.1985 Elmira, NY BR/TR 6-1/198# d4.25																								
1932	Phi N	33	70	8	16	5	0	0	9	1	2	9	.229	.260	.300	45	-5	1	.899	-4	*90*	*46*	C-25	-0.8
1933	Phi N	73	136	13	28	4	0	0	10	4	2	18	.206	.239	.235	32	-12	1	.983	1	*72*	*150*	C-34/O-2(LF)	-0.9
1934	Phi N	91	302	33	96	22	2	4	41	10	2	39	.318	.344	.444	96	-1	3	.976	1	*119*	*84*	C-82	0.4
1935	Phi N	107	328	40	95	18	3	3	42	19	3	35	.290	.334	.390	85	-6	3	.968	-7	*99*	*82*	C-87	-0.8
1936	Pit N	76	267	28	73	10	5	2	28	11	2	24	.273	.307	.371	80	-9	4	.976	-1	*76*	*88*	C-70	-0.5
1937	Pit N	133	514	51	158	18	10	8	86	16	1	36	.307	.330	.428	104	0	2	.972	-7	*61*	*104*	*C-128	0.1
1938	Pit N	133	491	52	130	19	7	7	75	18	4	31	.265	.296	.375	83	-14	2	.985	8	*101*	*121*	*C-132	0.3
1939	Bro N	86	245	28	68	10	0	5	32	13	1	16	.278	.317	.380	83	-6	1	.985	6	*107*	*104*	C-73	0.4
1940	Chi N	104	381	31	97	13	2	6	42	11	4	29	.255	.283	.346	74	-15	1	.984	-4	*101*	*95*	*C-104	-1.3
1941	Chi N	6	6	1	1	0	0	0	0	0	0	1	.167	.167	.167	-6	-1	0	—	0			H	-0.1
1943	Chi N	21	45	1	6	0	0	0	1	1	0	5	.133	.152	.133	-17	-7	0	.986	1	*133*	*64*	C-17	-0.5
Total	11	863	2785	286	768	119	29	35	366	104	21	243	.276	.307	.377	82	-76	18	.977	-5	*93*	*99*	C-752/O-2(LF)	-3.7
TODT, PHIL Philip Julius "Hook" B 8.9.1901 St.Louis, MO D 11.15.1973 St.Louis, MO BL/TL 6/175# d4.25																								
1924	Bos A	52	103	17	27	8	2	1	14	6	1	9	.262	.309	.408	84	-3	0-1	.983	-1	91	63	1-18/O-4(0-2-2)	-0.5
1925	Bos A	141	544	62	151	29	13	11	75	44	10	29	.278	.343	.439	97	-5	3-2	.991	3	105	103	*1-140	-1.1
1926	Bos A	**154**	599	56	153	19	12	7	69	40	4	38	.255	.306	.362	76	-25	3-2	.988	10	**130**	97	*1-154	-2.4
1927	Bos A	140	516	55	122	22	6	6	52	28	3	23	.236	.280	.337	61	-33	6-2	.991	8	121	106	*1-139	-3.1
1928	Bos A	144	539	61	136	31	8	12	73	26	3	47	.252	.290	.406	83	-17	6-5	**.997**	3	102	87	*1-144	-2.3
1929	Bos A	153	534	49	140	38	10	4	64	31	2	28	.262	.305	.393	80	-18	6-7	.991	3	108	101	*1-153	-2.5
1930	Bos A	111	383	49	103	22	5	11	62	24	0	33	.269	.312	.439	92	-7	4-1	.993	2	**109**	105	*1-104	-1.0
1931	†Phi A	62	197	23	48	14	2	5	44	8	0	22	.244	.273	.411	73	-9	1-1	.995	-4	53	117	1-52	-1.6
Total	8	957	3415	372	880	183	58	57	453	207	23	229	.258	.305	.395	81	-117	29-21	.992	23	109	100	1-904/O-4(0-2-2)	-14.5
TOLAN, BOBBY Robert B 11.19.1945 Los Angeles, CA BL/TL 5-11/170# d9.3 C5																								
1965	StL N	17	69	8	13	2	0	0	6	0-0	1	4	.188	.197	.217	16	-8	2-1	.970	-1	104	0	O-17(RF)	-1.0
1966	StL N	43	93	10	16	5	1	1	6	6-2	2	15	.172	.233	.280	43	-7	1-2	.952	-1	103	67	O-26(10-0-16)/1	-1.0
1967	†StL N	110	265	35	67	7	3	6	32	19-0	4	43	.253	.309	.370	96	-2	12-7	.992	2	110	126	O-80(6-54-25),1-13	-0.3
1968	†StL N	92	278	28	64	12	1	5	17	13-3	3	42	.230	.272	.335	82	-7	9-5	.967	1	104	63	O-67(2-9-57)/1-9	-1.2
1969	Cin N	152	637	104	194	25	10	21	93	27-2	15	92	.305	.347	.474	122	16	26-12	.974	2	112	55	*O-150(0-88-62)	1.4
1970	†Cin N	152	589	112	186	34	6	16	80	62-3	8	94	.316	.384	.475	130	26	**57**-20	.978	-2	103	82	*O-150(CF)	2.6
1972	†Cin N	149	604	88	171	28	5	8	82	44-5	6	88	.283	.334	.386	112	8	42-15	.990	3	103	94	*O-149(CF)	1.2
1973	Cin N	129	457	42	94	14	2	9	51	27-2	3	68	.206	.251	.304	57	-29	15-10	.966	1	103	99	*O-120(0-76-65)	-3.5
1974	SD N	95	357	45	95	16	1	8	40	20-4	9	41	.266	.320	.384	101	-1	7-9	.971	-3	98	86	O-88(1-9-81)	-0.9
1975	SD N	147	506	58	129	19	4	5	43	28-3	10	45	.255	.306	.338	84	-13	11-13	.971	-3	96	56	*O-120(90-16-19),1-27	-2.7
1976	†Phi N	110	272	32	71	7	0	5	35	7-3	4	39	.261	.285	.342	76	-9	10-5	.992	-6	50	114	1-50,O-35(20-10-5)	-2.1
1977	Phi N	15	16	1	2	0	0	0	1	1-0	0	4	.125	.176	.125	-17	-3	0-0	.944	-0	104	79	/1-5	-0.3
	Pit N	49	74	7	15	4	0	2	9	4-0	0	10	.203	.241	.338	53	-5	1-1	1.000	0	93	109	1-20/O-2(LF)	-0.6
	Year	64	90	8	17	4	0	2	10	5-0	0	14	.189	.229	.300	40	-8	1-1	.992	0	94	105	1-25/O-2(LF)	-0.9
1979	SD N	22	21	2	4	0	1	0	2	0-0	0	2	.190	.190	.286	30	-2	0-0	1.000	0	232	172	/1-5,O(RF)	-0.2
Total	13	1282	4238	572	1121	173	34	86	497	258-27	65	587	.265	.314	.382	96	-36	193-100	.976	-7	103	78	*O-1005(131-561-348),1-130	-8.6
TOLENTINO, JOSE Jose (Franco) B 6.3.1961 Mexico City, Mexico BL/TL 6-1/195# d7.28																								
1991	Hou N	44	54	6	14	4	0	1	6	4-0	0	9	.259	.305	.389	101	0	0-0	.982	1	112	74	1-10/O(LF)	0.0
TOLLESON, WAYNE Jimmy Wayne B 11.22.1955 Spartanburg, SC BB/TR 5-9/160# d9.1 OF Total (1-LF 2-CF)																								
1981	Tex A	14	24	6	4	0	0	0	1	1-0	0	5	.167	.200	.167	7	-3	2-0	1.000	-2	71	0	/3-6,S-2	-0.5
1982	Tex A	38	70	6	8	1	0	0	2	5-0	0	14	.114	.173	.129	-16	-11	1-1	.958	1	96	140	S-26/3-4,2	-0.8
1983	Tex A	134	470	64	122	13	2	3	20	40-0	2	68	.260	.319	.315	77	-14	33-10	.972	-6	97	95	*2-112,S-26/D	-0.8
1984	Tex A	118	338	35	72	9	2	0	9	27-0	3	47	.213	.276	.251	46	-25	22-4	.979	-9	94	96	*2-109/S-7,3-5,O(CF)D	-2.5
1985	Tex A	123	323	45	101	9	5	1	18	21-0	0	46	.313	.353	.381	100	0	21-12	.972	-3	95	86	S-81,2-29,3-12/D-6	0.5
1986	Chi A	81	260	39	65	7	3	3	29	38-0	0	43	.250	.342	.335	84	-5	13-6	.955	-6	99	85	3-65,S-18/O-2(1-1-0),D-2	-1.1
	NY A	60	215	22	61	9	2	0	14	14-0	2	33	.284	.332	.344	86	-4	4-4	.981	9	115	108	S-56/3-7,2-3	1.0
	Year	141	475	61	126	16	5	3	43	52-0	2	76	.265	.338	.339	85	-9	17-10	.981	3	110	98	S-74,3-72/2-3,O-2(1-1-0),D-2	-0.1
1987	NY A	121	349	48	77	4	0	1	22	43-0	0	72	.221	.306	.241	48	-25	5-3	.970	-3	100	100	*S-119/3-3	-1.7
1988	NY A	21	59	8	15	2	0	0	5	8-0	0	12	.254	.338	.288	79	-1	1-0	.981	6	136	120	2-12,3-10/S	0.5
1989	NY A	80	140	16	23	5	2	1	9	16-0	1	23	.164	.255	.250	43	-11	5-1	.912	2	89	130	3-28,S-28,2-13,D-10	-0.7
1990	NY A	73	74	12	11	1	1	0	4	6-0	0	21	.149	.210	.189	13	-9	1-0	.983	7	129	176	S-45,2-13/3-3,D-5	0.0
Total	10	863	2322	301	559	60	17	9	133	219-0	8	384	.241	.307	.293	66	-108	108-41	.974	-3	103	104	S-409,2-292,3-143/D-25,O-3C	-6.1
TOLMAN, TIM Timothy Lee B 4.20.1956 Santa Monica, CA BR/TR 6/195# d9.9																								
1981	Hou N	4	8	0	1	0	0	0	0	0-0	0	0	.125	.125	.125	-30	-1	0-0	1.000	-0	65	0	/O-3(3-0-1)	-0.2
1982	Hou N	15	26	4	5	2	0	1	3	4-0	0	3	.192	.300	.385	98	0	0-0	1.000	-1	77	0	/O-5(4-0-1),1	-0.1
1983	Hou N	43	56	4	11	4	0	2	10	6-0	0	9	.196	.270	.375	83	-1	0-1	1.000	-1	48	141	/1-7,O-3(LF)	-0.3
1984	Hou N	14	17	2	3	1	0	0	0	0-0	0	3	.176	.176	.235	16	-2	0-0	1.000	0	123	0	/O-3(1-0-2),1	-0.2
1985	Hou N	31	43	4	6	1	0	2	8	1-0	1	10	.140	.178	.302	33	-4	0-1	1.000	1	122	0	/O-9(6-0-3),1-6	-0.5
1986	Det A	16	34	4	6	1	0	0	2	6-0	0	4	.176	.293	.206	41	-3	1-1	1.000	-0	138	0	/O-4(RF),1-3,D-9	-0.3
1987	Det A	9	12	3	1	1	0	0	1	7-1	1	2	.083	.429	.167	77	0	0-0	1.000	-1	80	0	/O-7(2-0-5),D-2	0.0

Year	Tm Lg	G	AB	R	H	2B	3B	HR	RBI	BB-IB	HP	SO	AVG	OBP	SLG	AOPS	ABR	SB-CS	FA	FR	Rng	Thr	G at Pos	BFW
Total	7	132	196	21	33	10	0	5	24	24-1	2	31	.168	.262	.296	58	-11	1-3	1.000	-2	97	0	/O-34(19-0-16),1-18,D-11	-1.6
TOLSON, CHICK Charles Julius "Toby" B 11.6.1898 Washington, DC D 4.16.1965 Washington, DC BR/TR 6/185# d7.3																								
1925	Cle A	3	12	0	3	0	0	0	0	2	0	1	.250	.357	.250	56	-1	0-0	1.000	0	93	36	/1-3	-0.1
1926	Chi N	57	80	4	25	6	1	1	8	5	0	8	.313	.353	.450	113	1	0	.991	0	112	128	1-13	0.1
1927	Chi N	39	54	6	16	4	0	2	17	4	0	9	.296	.345	.481	119	1	0	1.000	0	106	49	/1-8	0.1
1929	†Chi N	32	109	13	28	5	0	1	19	9	2	16	.257	.325	.330	63	-6	0	.978	-2	83	88	1-31	-0.9
1930	Chi N	13	20	0	6	1	0	0	1	6	0	5	.300	.462	.350	99	1	1	.979	0	141	145	/1-5	0.1
Total	5	144	275	23	78	16	1	4	45	26	2	39	.284	.350	.393	90	-4	1-0	.985	-1	97	92	/1-60	-0.7
TOMBERLIN, ANDY Andy Lee B 11.7.1966 Monroe, NC BL/TL 5-11/160# d8.12																								
1993	Pit N	27	42	4	12	0	1	1	5	2-0	1	14	.286	.333	.405	97	0	0-0	1.000	-0	68	194	/O-7(6-0-1)	-0.1
1994	Bos A	18	36	1	7	0	1	1	1	6-0	0	12	.194	.310	.333	63	-2	1-0	1.000	1	75	345	O-11(5-0-6)/PD	-0.2
1995	Oak A	46	85	15	18	0	0	4	10	5-0	0	22	.212	.256	.353	60	-6	4-1	.979	-2	80	74	O-42(5-18-20)/D-2	-0.8
1996	NY N	63	66	12	17	4	0	3	10	9-0	1	27	.258	.355	.455	117	2	0-0	1.000	-1	58	214	O-17(9-0-8)/1	0.1
1997	NY N	6	7	0	2	0	0	0	0	1-0	0	3	.286	.375	.286	79	0	0-0	1.000	0	111	0	/O-2(1-0-1)	0.0
1998	Det A	32	69	8	15	2	0	2	12	3-1	3	25	.217	.280	.333	58	-4	1-0	1.000	1	237	0	D-22/O-5(4-0-1)	-0.5
Total	6	192	305	40	71	6	2	11	38	26-1	5	103	.233	.304	.374	77	-10	6-1	.989	-2	78	154	/O-84(30-18-37),D-29,1P	-1.5
TOMER, GEORGE George Clarence B 11.26.1895 Perry, IA D 12.15.1984 Perry, IA BL/TR 6/180# d9.17																								
1913	StL A	1	1	0	0	0	0	0	0	0	0	1	.000	.000	.000	-99	0	0	—	0			H	0.0
TOMNEY, PHIL Philip Howard "Buster" B 7.17.1863 Reading, PA D 3.18.1892 Reading, PA BR/TR 5-7/155# d9.7																								
1888	Lou AA	34	120	15	18	3	0	0	4	7	0		.150	.197	.175	20	-11	11	.882	6	114	87	S-34	-0.3
1889	Lou AA	112	376	61	80	8	5	4	38	46	3	47	.213	.304	.293	71	-14	26	.857	22	**115**	121	*S-112	0.9
1890	†Lou AA	108	386	72	107	21	7	1	58	43	5		.277	.357	.376	119	10	27	**.902**	15	**112**	**111**	*S-108	2.4
Total	3	254	882	148	205	32	12	5	100	96	8	47	.232	.313	.313	86	-15	64	.878	43	114	112	S-254	3.0
TONNEMAN, TONY Charles Richard B 9.10.1881 Chicago, IL D 8.7.1951 Prescott, AZ BR/TR 5-10.5/175# d9.19																								
1911	Bos A	2	5	0	1	1	0	0	3	1	0		.200	.333	.400	105	0	0	.900	0	*106*	*77*	/C-2	0.0
TOOLEY, BERT Albert R. B 8.30.1886 Howell, MI D 8.17.1976 Marshall, MI BR/TR 5-10/155# d4.12																								
1911	Bro N	119	433	55	89	11	3	1	29	53	2	63	.206	.295	.252	56	-25	18	.925	-6	98	94	*S-114	-2.4
1912	Bro N	77	265	34	62	6	5	2	37	19	0	21	.234	.285	.317	67	-13	12	.885	-17	90	74	S-76	-2.5
Total	2	196	698	89	151	17	8	3	66	72	2	84	.216	.291	.277	60	-38	30	.909	-23	95	86	S-190	-4.9
TOPORCER, SPECS George B 2.9.1899 New York, NY D 5.17.1989 Huntington Station, NY BL/TR 5-10.5/165# d4.13																								
1921	StL N	22	53	4	14	1	0	0	2	3	0	4	.264	.304	.283	57	-3	1-0	.938	-0	98	111	2-12/S-2	-0.3
1922	StL N	116	352	56	114	25	6	3	36	24	2	18	.324	.370	.455	117	9	2-1	.939	-14	91	71	S-91/3-6,2O(RF)	0.3
1923	StL N	97	303	45	77	11	3	3	35	41	3	14	.254	.349	.340	84	-6	4-3	.945	-14	88	120	2-52,S-33/13	-1.5
1924	StL N	70	198	30	62	10	3	1	24	11	4	14	.313	.362	.409	108	2	2-3	.974	-8	96	36	3-33,S-25/2-3	-0.3
1925	StL N	83	268	38	76	13	4	2	26	36	2	15	.284	.373	.384	92	-2	7-2	.960	-1	97	97	S-66/2-7	0.5
1926	†StL N	64	88	13	22	3	2	0	9	8	2	9	.250	.327	.330	74	-3	1	.983	-6	81	44	2-27/S-5,3	-0.9
1927	StL N	86	290	37	72	13	4	0	19	27	1	16	.248	.314	.321	68	-13	5	.980	-8	92	101	3-54,S-27/2-2,1	-1.5
1928	StL N	8	14	0	0	0	0	0	0	0	0	3	.000	.000	.000	-98	-4	0	1.000	0	536	0	/12	-0.4
Total	8	546	1566	223	437	76	22	9	151	150	14	93	.279	.347	.373	90	-20	22-9	.946	-51	93	87	S-249,2-105/3-95,1-3,O(RF)	-4.1
TORBORG, JEFF Jeffrey Allen B 11.26.1941 Plainfield, NJ BR/TR 6-0.5/195# d5.10 M11 C13																								
1964	LA N	28	43	4	10	1	1	0	4	3-1	1	8	.233	.292	.302	75	-2	0-0	.977	-1	*134*	*68*	C-27	-0.2
1965	LA N	56	150	8	36	5	1	3	13	10-4	1	26	.240	.290	.347	85	-3	0-0	.991	3	*125*	*81*	C-53	0.1
1966	LA N	46	120	4	27	3	0	1	13	10-3	0	23	.225	.278	.275	61	-6	0-0	.986	5	*143*	*86*	C-45	0.1
1967	LA N	76	196	11	42	4	1	2	12	13-3	1	31	.214	.265	.276	60	-11	1-3	.989	6	*135*	*88*	C-75	-0.2
1968	LA N	37	93	2	15	2	0	0	4	6-2	0	10	.161	.212	.183	21	-9	0-0	.991	6	*122*	*152*	C-37	-0.1
1969	LA N	51	124	7	23	4	0	0	7	9-5	0	17	.185	.241	.218	31	-12	1-0	.996	3	102	100	C-50	-0.7
1970	LA N	64	134	11	31	8	0	1	17	14-6	0	15	.231	.300	.313	69	-6	1-1	.983	4	128	91	C-63	0.0
1971	Cal A	55	123	6	25	5	0	0	5	3-1	0	6	.203	.220	.244	34	-11	0-0	.987	-4	76	92	C-49	-1.4
1972	Cal A	59	153	5	32	3	0	0	8	14-4	1	21	.209	.280	.229	56	-8	0-0	.998	6	67	115	C-58	0.0
1973	Cal A	102	255	20	56	7	0	1	18	21-0	0	32	.220	.278	.259	57	-15	0-2	.991	2	80	77	*C-102	-0.9
Total	10	574	1391	78	297	42	3	8	101	103-29	4	189	.214	.268	.265	56	-83	3-6	.990	30	*106*	*93*	C-559	-3.3
TORCATO, TONY Anthony Dale B 10.25.1979 Woodland, CA BL/TR 6-1/195# d7.26																								
2002	SF N	5	11	0	3	1	0	0	0	0-0	0	2	.273	.273	.364	72	-1	0-0	1.000	-1	40	0	/O-3(RF)	-0.1
2003	SF N	14	16	0	3	1	0	0	1	0-0	1	4	.188	.235	.250	27	-2	0-0	.833	-0	106	0	/O-6(4-0-2)	-0.2
Total	2	19	27	0	6	2	0	0	1	0-0	1	6	.222	.250	.296	45	-3	0-0	.875	-1	73	0	/O-9(4-0-5)	-0.3
TORGESON, EARL Clifford Earl "The Earl Of Snohomish" B 1.1.1924 Snohomish, WA D 11.8.1990 Everett, WA BL/TL 6-3/180# d4.15 C1																								
1947	Bos N	128	399	73	112	20	6	16	78	82	0	59	.281	.403	.481	137	24	11	.984	-1	106	100	*1-117	1.9
1948	†Bos N	134	438	70	111	23	5	10	67	81	2	54	.253	.372	.397	110	9	19	.993	0	101	103	*1-129	0.5
1949	Bos N	25	100	17	26	5	1	4	19	13	0	4	.260	.345	.450	118	2	4	.988	-3	50	94	1-25	-0.2
1950	Bos N	**156**	576	**120**	167	30	3	23	87	119	1	69	.290	.412	.472	141	41	15	.986	0	**104**	87	*1-156	3.5
1951	Bos N	**155**	581	99	153	21	4	24	92	102	2	70	.263	.375	.437	127	25	20-11	.988	0	100	90	*1-155	2.0
1952	Bos N	122	382	49	88	17	0	5	34	81	1	38	.230	.366	.314	94	1	11-7	.989	-1	99	90	*1-105/O-5(2-0-3)	-0.3
1953	Phi N	111	379	58	104	25	8	11	64	53	2	57	.274	.366	.470	117	10	7-1	.987	-4	89	98	*1-105	0.2
1954	Phi N	135	490	63	133	22	6	5	54	75	0	52	.271	.364	.371	93	-2	7-1	.990	-11	74	93	*1-133	-2.0
1955	Phi N	47	150	29	40	5	3	1	17	32-1	0	20	.267	.393	.360	104	3	2-3	.995	-2	84	78	1-43	-0.2
	Det A	89	300	58	85	10	1	9	50	61-2	0	29	.283	.397	.413	123	13	9-0	.992	-1	98	111	1-83	0.9
1956	Det A	117	318	61	84	9	3	12	42	78-0	0	47	.264	.406	.425	120	13	6-4	.992	-6	65	84	1-83	0.2
1957	Det A	30	50	5	12	2	1	1	5	12-0	0	10	.240	.387	.380	108	1	0-0	1.000	0	95	107	1-17	0.0
	Chi A	86	251	53	74	11	2	7	46	49-0	0	44	.295	.406	.438	131	13	7-3	.998	-4	72	126	1-70/O(RF)	0.6
	Year	116	301	58	86	13	3	8	51	61-0	0	54	.286	.403	.429	127	14	7-3	.999	-4	75	123	1-87/O(RF)	0.6
1958	Chi A	96	188	37	50	8	0	10	30	48-1	0	29	.266	.415	.468	146	15	7-2	.978	-3	91	116	1-73	1.0
1959	†Chi A	127	277	40	61	5	3	9	45	62-1	0	55	.220	.359	.357	100	2	7-6	.983	-7	74	92	*1-103	-1.0
1960	Chi A	68	57	12	15	2	0	2	9	21-2	0	8	.263	.462	.404	137	5	1-0	.983	0	121	64	1-10	0.5
1961	Chi A	20	15	1	1	0	0	0	1	3-0	0	5	.067	.211	.067	-19	-3	0-0	1.000	-0	0	0	/1	-0.3
	NY A	22	18	3	2	0	0	0	0	8-0	0	3	.111	.385	.111	42	-1	0-1	.969	-0	87	270	/1-8	-0.2
	Year	42	33	4	3	0	0	0	1	11-0	0	8	.091	.311	.091	16	-3	0-1	.970	-0	81	253	/1-9	-0.5
Total	15	1668	4969	848	1318	215	46	149	740	980-7	8	653	.265	.385	.417	118	171	133-39	.989	-41	91	97	*1-1416/O-6(2-0-4)	7.1
TORPHY, RED Walter Anthony B 11.6.1891 Fall River, MA D 2.11.1980 Fall River, MA BR/TR 5-11/169# d9.25																								
1920	Bos N	3	15	1	3	2	0	0	2	0	0	1	.200	.200	.333	54	-1	0-0	.969	-1	0	95	/1-3	-0.2
TORRE, FRANK Frank Joseph B 12.30.1931 Brooklyn, NY BL/TL 6-3/205# d4.20 b-Joe																								
1956	Mil N	111	159	17	41	6	0	0	16	11-2	0	4	.258	.304	.296	67	-7	1-0	.993	5	142	108	1-89	-0.5
1957	†Mil N	129	364	46	99	19	5	5	40	29-1	9	19	.272	.339	.393	104	2	0-0	**.996**	2	106	116	*1-117	-0.1
1958	†Mil N	138	372	41	115	22	5	6	55	42-7	7	14	.309	.386	.444	131	18	2-0	**.994**	6	118	104	*1-122	1.9
1959	Mil N	115	263	23	60	15	1	1	33	35-6	3	12	.228	.321	.304	75	-8	0-0	.994	-0	98	81	1-87	-1.2
1960	Mil N	21	44	2	9	1	0	0	5	3-1	0	2	.205	.245	.227	36	-4	0-0	1.000	-1	50	135	1-17	-0.6
1962	Phi N	108	168	13	52	8	2	0	20	24-1	4	6	.310	.404	.381	117	6	1-1	.980	3	130	110	1-76	0.6
1963	Phi N	92	112	8	28	7	2	1	10	11-2	3	7	.250	.333	.375	105	1	0-0	.989	4	155	130	1-56	0.4
Total	7	714	1482	150	404	78	15	13	179	155-20	26	64	.273	.349	.372	101	8	4-1	.993	18	116	107	1-564	0.5
TORRE, JOE Joseph Paul B 7.18.1940 Brooklyn, NY BR/TR 6-2/212# d9.25 M22 b-Frank																								
1960	Mil N	2	2	0	1	0	0	0	0	0-0	0	1	.500	.500	.500	189	0	0-0	—	0			H	0.0
1961	Mil N	113	406	40	113	21	4	10	42	28-4	4	60	.278	.330	.424	105	2	3-5	.982	-4	***136***	*102*	*C-112	0.2
1962	Mil N	80	220	23	62	8	1	5	26	24-2	2	24	.282	.355	.395	105	2	1-0	.986	7	*171*	*111*	C-63	1.2
1963	Mil N☆	142	501	57	147	19	4	14	71	42-4	5	79	.293	.350	.431	126	17	1-5	.994	-2	*108*	*83*	*C-105,1-37/O-2(LF)	1.7
1964	Mil N★	154	601	87	193	36	5	20	109	36-4	7	67	.321	.365	.498	140	31	2-4	**.995**	-3	*128*	*89*	C-96,1-70	3.0

Year	Tm Lg	G	AB	R	H	2B	3B	HR	RBI	BB-IB	HP	SO	AVG	OBP	SLG	AOPS	ABR	SB-CS	FA	FR	Rng	Thr	G at Pos	BFW
1965	Mil N★	148	523	68	152	21	1	27	80	61-7	8	79	.291	.372	.489	140	29	0-1	.991	-4	*88*	*120*	*C-100,1-49	2.8
1966	Atl N★	148	546	83	172	20	3	36	101	60-8	2	61	.315	.382	.560	157	42	0-4	.984	1	*108*	**135**	*C-114,1-36	4.6
1967	Atl N★	135	477	67	132	18	1	20	68	49-7	3	75	.277	.345	.444	127	17	2-2	.991	-3	*80*	*110*	*C-114,1-23	1.8
1968	Atl N	115	424	45	115	11	2	10	55	34-7	5	72	.271	.332	.377	112	6	1-0	**.996**	-10	*76*	*69*	C-92,1-29	0.0
1969	StL N	159	602	72	174	29	6	18	101	66-13	5	85	.289	.361	.447	126	21	0-0	.996	-5	91	**108**	*1-144,C-17	0.6
1970	StL N★	161	624	89	203	27	9	21	100	70-10	7	91	.325	.398	.498	136	33	2-2	.987	-10	93	96	C-90,3-73/1	2.6
1971	StL N★	161	634	97	**230**	34	8	24	**137**	63-20	4	70	**.363**	.421	.555	169	58	4-1	.951	-22	82	73	*3-161	3.8
1972	StL N★	149	544	71	157	26	6	11	81	54-13	8	64	.289	.357	.419	123	17	3-0	.963	-9	86	88	*3-117,1-27	0.6
1973	StL N★	141	519	67	149	17	2	13	69	65-14	10	78	.287	.376	.403	116	14	2-0	.993	-10	96	108	*1-114,3-58	-0.4
1974	StL N	147	529	59	149	28	1	11	70	69-9	8	88	.282	.371	.401	117	15	1-2	.992	2	**119**	**130**	*1-139,3-18	0.6
1975	NY N	114	361	33	89	16	3	6	35	35-3	2	55	.247	.317	.357	91	-5	0-0	.950	1	95	115	3-83,1-24	-0.6
1976	NY N	114	310	36	95	10	3	5	31	21-1	5	35	.306	.358	.406	124	9	1-3	.989	3	116	82	1-78/3-4	0.6
1977	NY N	26	51	2	9	3	0	1	9	2-1	0	10	.176	.204	.294	34	-5	0-0	.988	-2	35	128	1-16/3M	-0.8
Total	18	2209	7874	996	2342	344	59	252	1185	779-127	85	1094	.297	.365	.452	129	303	23-29	.990	-71	*110*	*103*	C-903,1-787,3-515/O-2(LF)	22.3

TORREALBA, STEVE Steven Alexander B 2.24.1978 Barquisimeto, Venezuela BR/TR 6/175# d10.6 f-Pablo

Year	Tm Lg	G	AB	R	H	2B	3B	HR	RBI	BB-IB	HP	SO	AVG	OBP	SLG	AOPS	ABR	SB-CS	FA	FR	Rng	Thr	G at Pos	BFW
2001	†Atl N	2	2	0	1	0	0	0	0	0-0	0	0	.500	.500	.500	157	0	0-0	1.000	0	0	0	/C-2	0.0
2002	Atl N	13	17	1	1	0	0	0	1	3-0	0	4	.059	.200	.059	-26	-3	0-0	1.000	-1	75	57	C-12	-0.4
Total	2	15	19	1	2	0	0	0	1	3-0	0	4	.105	.227	.105	-7	-3	0-0	1.000	-1	71	54	/C-14	-0.4

TORREALBA, YORVIT Yorvit Adolfo B 7.19.1978 Caracas, Venezuela BR/TR 5-11/190# d9.5

Year	Tm Lg	G	AB	R	H	2B	3B	HR	RBI	BB-IB	HP	SO	AVG	OBP	SLG	AOPS	ABR	SB-CS	FA	FR	Rng	Thr	G at Pos	BFW
2001	SF N	3	4	0	2	0	1	0	2	0-0	0	0	.500	.500	1.000	296	1	0-0	1.000	-0	0	0	/C-3	0.1
2002	SF N	53	136	17	38	10	0	2	14	14-2	2	20	.279	.355	.397	106	1	0-0	.993	2	86	96	C-53	0.6
2003	†SF N	66	200	22	52	10	2	4	29	14-1	2	39	.260	.312	.390	85	-5	1-0	.997	7	130	151	C-66/O(LF)	0.6
Total	3	122	340	39	92	20	3	6	45	28-3	4	59	.271	.332	.400	96	-3	1-0	.996	9	110	126	C-122/O(LF)	1.3

TORRES, ANDRES Andres Vungo (Feliciano) B 1.26.1978 Aguadilla, P.R. BB/TR 5-10/175# d4.7

Year	Tm Lg	G	AB	R	H	2B	3B	HR	RBI	BB-IB	HP	SO	AVG	OBP	SLG	AOPS	ABR	SB-CS	FA	FR	Rng	Thr	G at Pos	BFW
2002	Det A	19	70	7	14	1	1	0	3	6-0	1	16	.200	.266	.243	41	-6	2-2	.981	-1	104	0	O-19(CF)	-0.7
2003	Det A	59	168	23	37	4	3	1	9	10-0	0	35	.220	.263	.298	52	-13	5-5	.991	-0	91	179	O-50(1-36-16)/D-3	-1.4
Total	2	78	238	30	51	5	4	1	12	16-0	1	51	.214	.264	.282	49	-19	7-7	.987	-1	95	126	/O-69(1-55-16),D-3	-2.1

TORRES, GIL Don Gilberto (Nunez) B 8.23.1915 Regla, Cuba D 1.10.1983 Regla, Cuba BR/TR 6/155# d4.25 f-Ricardo ▲

Year	Tm Lg	G	AB	R	H	2B	3B	HR	RBI	BB-IB	HP	SO	AVG	OBP	SLG	AOPS	ABR	SB-CS	FA	FR	Rng	Thr	G at Pos	BFW
1940	Was A	2	0	0	0	0	0	0	0	0	0	0	—	—	—	—	0	0-0	1.000	0	184	0	/P-2	0.0
1944	Was A	134	524	42	140	20	6	0	58	21	1	24	.267	.297	.328	82	-15	10-7	.952	8	**110**	107	*3-123,2-10/1-4	-0.5
1945	Was A	147	562	39	133	12	5	0	48	21	0	29	.237	.264	.276	62	-31	7-4	.953	-24	93	76	*S-145/3-2	-4.7
1946	Was A	63	185	18	47	8	0	0	13	11	0	12	.254	.296	.297	70	-8	3-2	.939	-2	97	88	S-31,3-18/2-7,P-3	-0.9
Total	4	346	1271	99	320	40	11	0	119	53	1	65	.252	.282	.301	72	-54	20-13	.951	-18	94	78	S-176,3-143/2-17,P-5,1-4	-6.1

TORRES, FELIX Felix (Sanchez) B 5.1.1932 Ponce, P.R. BR/TR 5-11/165# d4.10

Year	Tm Lg	G	AB	R	H	2B	3B	HR	RBI	BB-IB	HP	SO	AVG	OBP	SLG	AOPS	ABR	SB-CS	FA	FR	Rng	Thr	G at Pos	BFW
1962	LA A	127	451	44	117	19	4	11	74	28-5	4	73	.259	.306	.392	90	-8	0-0	.938	-4	102	85	*3-123	-1.2
1963	LA A	138	463	40	121	32	1	4	51	30-0	3	73	.261	.307	.361	93	-4	1-0	.939	3	**109**	131	*3-122/1-2	-0.1
1964	LA A	100	277	25	64	10	0	12	28	13-0	1	56	.231	.266	.397	91	-5	1-3	.970	1	98	87	3-72/1-3	-0.6
Total	3	365	1191	109	302	61	5	27	153	71-5	8	202	.254	.297	.381	91	-17	2-3	.945	1	104	103	3-317/1-5	-1.9

TORRES, HECTOR Hector Epitacio (Marroquin) B 9.16.1945 Monterrey, Mexico BR/TR 6/175# d4.10 C1

Year	Tm Lg	G	AB	R	H	2B	3B	HR	RBI	BB-IB	HP	SO	AVG	OBP	SLG	AOPS	ABR	SB-CS	FA	FR	Rng	Thr	G at Pos	BFW
1968	Hou N	128	466	44	104	11	1	1	24	18-2	0	64	.223	.252	.258	54	-27	2-3	.958	-5	99	76	*S-127/2	-2.6
1969	Hou N	34	69	5	11	1	0	1	8	2-0	0	12	.159	.183	.217	12	-8	0-0	.944	-3	74	71	S-22	-1.1
1970	Hou N	31	65	6	16	1	2	0	5	6-0	0	8	.246	.310	.323	73	-3	0-0	.947	-4	92	71	S-22/2-6	-0.4
1971	Chi N	31	58	4	13	3	0	0	2	4-0	0	10	.224	.274	.276	49	-4	0-0	.962	-4	97	76	S-18/2-4	-0.7
1972	Mon N	83	181	14	28	4	1	2	7	13-1	1	26	.155	.215	.221	24	-19	0-2	.965	-7	95	94	2-60,S-16/O-2(1-0-1),P3	-2.4
1973	Hou N	38	66	3	6	1	0	0	2	7-0	1	13	.091	.189	.106	-16	-11	0-1	.952	1	124	73	S-22,2-13	-0.8
1975	SD N	112	352	31	91	12	0	5	26	22-3	0	32	.259	.297	.335	82	-10	2-3	.971	8	124	109	S-75,3-42,2-16	0.6
1976	SD N	74	215	8	42	6	0	4	15	16-3	1	31	.195	.254	.279	56	-13	2-1	.949	-20	86	84	S-63/3-4,2-3	-2.8
1977	Tor A	91	266	33	64	7	3	5	26	16-1	1	33	.241	.282	.346	70	-12	1-1	.980	-0	99	79	S-68,2-23/3-2	-0.5
Total	9	622	1738	148	375	46	7	18	115	104-10	4	229	.216	.260	.281	55	-107	7-11	.962	-34	101	83	S-433,2-126/3-49,O-2(1-0-1),P	-10.7

TORRES, RICARDO Ricardo J. (Martinez) B 4.16.1891 Regla, Cuba D 4.17.1960 Regla, Cuba BR/TR 5-11/160# d5.18 s-Gil

Year	Tm Lg	G	AB	R	H	2B	3B	HR	RBI	BB-IB	HP	SO	AVG	OBP	SLG	AOPS	ABR	SB-CS	FA	FR	Rng	Thr	G at Pos	BFW
1920	Was A	16	30	8	10	1	0	0	3	1	0	4	.333	.355	.367	94	0	0-0	1.000	-1	42	45	/1-7,C-5	-0.1
1921	Was A	2	3	1	1	0	0	0	0	1	0	1	.333	.500	.333	122	0	0-0	.750	-1	*0*	*0*	/C-2	0.0
1922	Was A	4	4	0	0	0	0	0	0	0	0	1	.000	.000	.000	-99	-1	0-0	1.000	1	*0*	*256*	/C-3	0.0
Total	3	22	37	9	11	1	0	0	3	2	0	6	.297	.333	.324	76	-1	0-0	.955	-1	*44*	*91*	/C-10,1-7	-0.1

TORRES, RUSTY Rosendo (Hernandez) B 9.30.1948 Aguadilla, P.R. BB/TR 5-10/180# d9.20

Year	Tm Lg	G	AB	R	H	2B	3B	HR	RBI	BB-IB	HP	SO	AVG	OBP	SLG	AOPS	ABR	SB-CS	FA	FR	Rng	Thr	G at Pos	BFW
1971	NY A	9	26	5	10	3	0	2	3	0-0	0	8	.385	.385	.731	223	4	0-1	1.000	0	122	0	/O-5(0-1-4)	0.4
1972	NY A	80	199	15	42	7	0	3	13	18-3	1	44	.211	.280	.291	73	-7	0-4	.978	-3	83	105	O-62(1-1-60)	-1.6
1973	Cle A	122	312	31	64	8	1	7	28	50-5	3	62	.205	.317	.304	76	-9	6-5	.976	-2	92	136	*O-114(1-37-77)	-1.6
1974	Cle A	108	150	19	28	2	0	3	12	13-1	0	24	.187	.248	.260	48	-10	2-1	.959	2	92	220	O-94(35-38-24)/D	-1.1
1976	Cal A	120	264	37	54	16	3	6	27	36-3	0	39	.205	.299	.356	98	0	4-4	.990	-4	92	88	*O-105(0-104-1)/3D	-0.8
1977	Cal A	58	77	9	12	1	1	3	10	10-0	0	18	.156	.250	.312	55	-5	0-1	.984	-1	92	55	O-54(4-40-10)	-0.7
1978	Chi A	16	44	7	14	3	0	3	6	6-0	0	7	.318	.400	.591	174	4	0-1	.964	-1	98	0	O-14(4-5-8)	0.3
1979	Chi A	90	170	26	43	5	0	8	24	23-1	2	37	.253	.349	.424	107	2	0-0	.976	-0	98	103	O-85(36-17-35)	0.0
1980	KC A	51	72	10	12	0	0	0	3	8-0	0	7	.167	.250	.167	16	-8	1-3	.973	5	130	221	O-40(15-8-21)/D	-0.6
Total	9	654	1314	159	279	45	5	35	126	164-13	6	246	.212	.301	.334	82	-29	13-20	.977	-5	94	122	O-573(96-251-240)/D-8,3	-5.7

TORVE, KELVIN Kelvin Curtis B 1.10.1960 Rapid City, SD BL/TR 6-3/205# d6.25

Year	Tm Lg	G	AB	R	H	2B	3B	HR	RBI	BB-IB	HP	SO	AVG	OBP	SLG	AOPS	ABR	SB-CS	FA	FR	Rng	Thr	G at Pos	BFW
1988	Min A	12	16	1	3	0	0	1	2	1-0	0	2	.188	.235	.375	66	-1	0-1	1.000	-0	58	50	/1-4,D	-0.2
1990	NY N	20	38	0	11	4	0	0	2	4-0	2	9	.289	.386	.395	116	1	0-0	1.000	-2	0	118	/1-9,O(LF)	-0.1
1991	NY N	10	8	0	0	0	0	0	0	0-0	0	1	.000	.000	.000	-99	-2	0-0	1.000	1	2399	0	/1	-0.1
Total	3	42	62	1	14	4	0	1	4	5-0	2	12	.226	.304	.339	78	-2	0-1	1.000	-1	40	101	/1-14,O(LF)D	-0.4

TOVAR, CESAR Cesar Leonardo "Pepito" (born Cesar Leonard Perez (Tovar)) B 7.3.1940 Caracas, Venezuela
D 7.14.1994 Caracas, Venezuela BR/TR 5-9/155# d4.12 OF Total (378-LF 471-CF 205-RF)

Year	Tm Lg	G	AB	R	H	2B	3B	HR	RBI	BB-IB	HP	SO	AVG	OBP	SLG	AOPS	ABR	SB-CS	FA	FR	Rng	Thr	G at Pos	BFW
1965	Min A	18	25	3	5	1	0	0	2	2-0	0	3	.200	.259	.240	41	-2	2-0	.800	-0	128	184	/2-4,3-2,O-2(CF),S	-0.1
1966	Min A	134	465	57	121	19	5	2	41	44-1	4	50	.260	.325	.335	86	-7	16-6	.978	-6	100	76	2-76,S-31,O-24(4-20-0)	-0.3
1967	Min A	**164**	649	98	173	32	7	6	47	46-0	13	51	.267	.325	.365	97	-2	19-11	.994	-7	118	124	O-74(10-64-5),3-70,2-36/S-9	-0.9
1968	Min A	157	613	89	167	31	6	6	47	34-0	17	41	.272	.326	.372	106	5	35-13	.966	6	123	110	O-78(39-34-10),3-75,S-35,2-18/PC1	1.6
1969	†Min A	158	535	99	154	25	5	11	52	37-3	9	37	.288	.342	.415	109	6	45-12	.983	3	**117**	152	*O-113(39-70-8),2-41,3-20	1.4
1970	†Min A	161	650	120	195	**36**	**13**	10	54	52-5	8	47	.300	.356	.442	118	15	30-15	.977	1	111	127	*O-151(39-134-2)/2-8,3-4	1.4
1971	Min A	157	657	94	**204**	29	3	1	45	45-5	3	39	.311	.356	.368	103	3	18-14	.986	13	**118**	150	*O-154(98-44-47)/3-7,2-2	0.8
1972	Min A	141	548	86	145	20	6	2	31	39-6	**14**	39	.265	.329	.334	93	-4	21-10	.983	4	108	97	*O-139(38-5-101)	-0.7
1973	Phi N	97	328	49	88	18	4	1	21	29-2	5	35	.268	.335	.357	90	-4	6-4	.928	1	71	90	3-46,O-24(6-3-16),2-22	-0.3
1974	Tex A	138	562	78	164	24	6	4	58	47-0	9	33	.292	.354	.377	114	11	13-9	.980	6	103	137	*O-135(66-87-11)/D-3	1.1
1975	Tex A	102	427	53	110	16	0	3	28	27-0	3	25	.258	.306	.316	77	-13	16-11	.919	-4	84	46	D-66,O-31(25-6-1)/2	-2.2
	†Oak A	19	26	5	6	1	0	0	3	3-0	0	3	.231	.310	.269	66	-1	4-0	1.000	-1	29	0	/2-4,3-3,SD	-0.2
	Year	121	453	58	116	17	0	3	31	30-0	3	28	.256	.306	.313	76	-14	20-11	.896	-6	84	46	D-73,O-31(25-6-1)/2-5,3-3,S	-2.4
1976	Oak A	29	45	1	8	0	0	0	4	4-0	2	4	.178	.275	.178	36	-4	1-2	.958	-1	88	0	O-20(14-2-4)/D-4	-0.7
	NY A	13	39	2	6	1	0	0	2	4-1	1	3	.154	.250	.179	27	-3	0-1	1.000	1	149	189	D-10/2-3	-0.3
	Year	42	84	3	14	1	0	0	6	8-1	3	7	.167	.263	.179	32	-7	1-3	.958	-0	88	0	O-20(14-2-4),D-14/2-3	-1.0
Total	12	1488	5569	834	1546	253	55	46	435	413-23	88	410	.278	.335	.368	99	0	226-108	.980	15	111	124	O-945C,3-227,2-215/D-90,S-77,1CP	0.6

TOWNE, BABE Jay King B 3.12.1880 Coon Rapids, IA D 10.29.1938 Des Moines, IA BR/TR 5-10/180# d8.1

Year	Tm Lg	G	AB	R	H	2B	3B	HR	RBI	BB-IB	HP	SO	AVG	OBP	SLG	AOPS	ABR	SB-CS	FA	FR	Rng	Thr	G at Pos	BFW
1906	†Chi A	14	36	3	10	0	0	0	6	7	0		.278	.395	.278	115	1	0	.923	-2	*141*	*69*	C-13	0.0

TOWNSEND, GEORGE George Hodgson "Sleepy" B 6.4.1867 Hartsdale, NY D 3.15.1930 New Haven, CT BR/TR 5-7.5/180# d6.25

Year	Tm Lg	G	AB	R	H	2B	3B	HR	RBI	BB-IB	HP	SO	AVG	OBP	SLG	AOPS	ABR	SB-CS	FA	FR	Rng	Thr	G at Pos	BFW
1887	Phi AA	31	109	12	21	3	0	0	14	3	0		.193	.214	.220	21	-12	8	.865	-5			C-28/O-3(1-0-2)	-1.2
1888	Phi AA	42	161	13	25	6	0	0	12	4	1		.155	.181	.193	20	-14	2	.912	1			C-42	-0.9
1890	Bal AA	18	67	6	16	4	1	0	9	4	0		.239	.282	.328	76	-2	3	.930	4	*116*	*139*	C-18	0.3

Year	Tm Lg	G	AB	R	H	2B	3B	HR	RBI	BB-IB	HP	SO	AVG	OBP	SLG	AOPS	ABR	SB-CS	FA	FR	Rng	Thr	G at Pos	BFW
1891	Bal AA	61	204	29	39	5	4	0	18	20	5	21	.191	.279	.255	53	-13	3	.909	2	*141*	*94*	C-58/O-3(0-1-2)	-0.6
Total	4	152	541	60	101	18	5	0	53	31	6	21	.187	.239	.238	40	-41	16	.905	3	*70*	*54*	C-146/O-6(1-1-4)	-2.4
TOY, JIM James Madison B 2.20.1858 Beaver Falls, PA D 3.13.1919 Cresson, PA 5-6/160# d4.20																								
1887	Cle AA	109	423	56	94	20	5	1	56	17	2		.222	.256	.300	56	-26	8	.975	4	113	111	1-82,O-11(2-2-7),C-10/3-8,S-3	-2.4
1890	Bro AA	44	160	11	29	3	0	0	7	11	1		.181	.238	.200	30	-14	2	.867	-7	*82*	*121*	C-44	-1.6
Total	2	153	583	67	123	23	5	1	63	28	3		.211	.251	.273	50	-40	10	.975	-4	113	111	/1-82,C-54,O-11(2-2-7),3-8,S-3	-4.0
TRABER, JIM James Joseph B 12.26.1961 Columbus, OH BL/TL 6/194# d9.21																								
1984	Bal A	10	21	3	5	0	0	0	2	2-0	0	4	.238	.292	.238	54	-1	0-0	—	0			/D-9	-0.2
1986	Bal A	65	212	28	54	7	0	13	44	18-2	5	31	.255	.321	.472	116	4	0-0	.988	2	98	121	1-29,D-21/O-8(7-0-1)	0.3
1988	Bal A	103	352	25	78	6	0	10	45	19-3	1	42	.222	.261	.324	65	-18	1-2	.990	7	141	105	1-57,D-30,O-11(2-0-8)	-1.7
1989	Bal A	86	234	14	49	8	0	4	26	19-1	0	41	.209	.266	.295	61	-13	4-3	.998	5	132	119	1-69/D-5	-1.2
Total	4	264	819	70	186	21	0	27	117	58-6	6	118	.227	.279	.352	77	-28	5-5	.993	13	129	114	1-155/D-65,O-19(9-0-9)	-2.8
TRACEWSKI, DICK Richard Joseph B 2.3.1935 Eynon, PA BR/TR 5-11/167# d4.12 M1 C24																								
1962	LA N	15	2	3	0	0	0	0	0	2-0	0	0	.000	.500	.000	50	0	0-0	1.000	1	223	0	/S-4	0.1
1963	†LA N	104	217	23	49	2	1	1	10	19-1	0	39	.226	.287	.258	63	-11	2-3	.957	11	113	102	S-81,2-23	0.6
1964	LA N	106	304	31	75	13	4	1	26	31-4	0	61	.247	.315	.326	88	-5	3-3	.970	-6	95	87	2-56,3-30,S-19	-0.6
1965	†LA N	78	186	17	40	6	0	1	20	25-4	2	30	.215	.313	.263	69	-7	2-6	.950	1	108	95	3-53,2-14/S-7	-0.7
1966	Det A	81	124	15	24	1	1	0	7	10-0	0	32	.194	.252	.218	36	-10	1-1	.947	5	109	129	2-70/S-3	-0.3
1967	Det A	74	107	19	30	4	2	1	9	8-0	0	20	.280	.325	.383	107	1	1-1	.965	6	107	139	S-44,2-12,3-10	0.9
1968	†Det A	90	212	30	33	3	1	4	15	24-0	0	51	.156	.239	.236	44	-14	3-0	.982	-8	94	102	S-51,3-16,2-14	-2.0
1969	Det A	66	79	10	11	2	0	0	4	15-1	0	20	.139	.277	.165	25	-8	3-0	.957	5	97	153	S-41,2-13/3-6	0.0
Total	8	614	1231	148	262	31	9	8	91	134-10	2	253	.213	.289	.272	65	-54	15-14	.958	14	105	111	S-250,2-202,3-115	-2.0
TRACY, ANDY Andrew Michael B 12.11.1973 Bowling Green, OH BL/TR 6-3/220# d4.25																								
2000	Mon N	83	192	29	50	8	1	11	32	22-1	2	61	.260	.339	.484	103	0	1-0	.882	-5	86	46	3-34,1-27	-0.6
2001	Mon N	38	55	4	6	1	0	2	8	6-0	0	26	.109	.190	.236	11	-8	0-0	1.000	-1	88	0	3-11/1-3,D-2	-0.9
Total	2	121	247	33	56	9	1	13	40	28-1	2	87	.227	.306	.429	83	-8	1-0	.912	-6	87	34	/3-45,1-30,D-2	-1.5
TRACY, JIM James Edwin B 12.31.1955 Hamilton, OH BL/TR 6/185# d7.20 M3 C6																								
1980	Chi N	42	122	12	31	3	3	3	9	13-1	0	37	.254	.326	.402	95	-1	2-2	.950	-6	66	0	O-31(22-0-14)/1	-1.0
1981	Chi N	45	63	6	15	2	1	0	5	12-0	0	14	.238	.355	.302	85	-1	1-0	1.000	-2	76	0	O-11(10-0-1)	-0.3
Total	2	87	185	18	46	5	4	3	14	25-1	0	51	.249	.336	.368	92	-2	3-2	.964	-8	69	0	/O-42(32-0-15),1	-1.3
TRAFFLEY, JOHN John M. B 1862 Chicago, IL D 5.15.1900 Baltimore, MD 5-9/180# d6.15 b-Bill																								
1889	Lou AA	1	2	0	1	0	0	0	0	0	0	0	.500	.500	.500	189	0	0	.000	-0	0	0	/O(RF)	0.0
TRAFFLEY, BILL William Franklin B 12.21.1859 Staten Island, NY D 6.23.1908 Des Moines, IA BR/TR 5-11.5/185# d7.27 b-John																								
1878	Chi N	2	9	1	1	0	0	0	1	0		1	.111	.111	.111	-25	-1		1.000	-1			/C-2	-0.2
1883	Cin AA	30	105	17	21	5	0	0	8	4			.200	.229	.248	51	-6		.851	0			C-29/S-2	-0.3
1884	Bal AA	53	210	25	37	4	6	0		3	1		.176	.192	.252	42	-14		.926	-4			C-47/O-6(RF),1	-1.3
1885	Bal AA	69	254	27	39	4	5	1	20	17	3		.154	.215	.220	38	-18		**.943**	4			C-61,O-10(0-5-5)/2-3	-0.8
1886	Bal AA	25	85	15	18	0	1	0	7	10	0		.212	.295	.235	68	-3	8	.952	-3			C-25	-0.3
Total	5	179	663	85	116	13	12	1	36	34	4	1	.175	.220	.235	45	-42	8	.927	-3			C-164/O-16(0-5-11),2-3,S-2,1	-2.9
TRAGESSER, WALT Walter Joseph B 6.14.1887 Lafayette, IN D 12.14.1970 Lafayette, IN BR/TR 6/175# d7.30 Mil 1918																								
1913	Bos N	2	0	0	0	0	0	0	0	0	0	0	—	—	—	—	0	0	1.000	-0	0	0	/C-2	0.0
1915	Bos N	7	7	1	0	0	0	0	0	0	0	2	.000	.000	.000	-99	-2	0	.944	1	*231*	*51*	/C-7	-0.1
1916	Bos N	41	54	3	11	1	0	0	4	5	1	10	.204	.283	.222	59	-2	0	.971	4	178	113	C-29	0.3
1917	Bos N	98	297	23	66	10	2	0	25	15	2	36	.222	.264	.269	68	-12	5	.971	0	*113*	*91*	C-94	-0.4
1918	Bos N	7	1	0	0	0	0	0	0	0	0	0	.000	.000	.000	-99	0	0	.833	0	*0*	*156*	/C-7	0.0
1919	Bos N	20	40	3	7	2	0	0	3	2	1	10	.175	.233	.225	39	-3	1	.959	-1	*92*	*150*	C-14	-0.3
	Phi N	35	114	7	27	7	0	0	8	9	1	31	.237	.298	.298	74	-3	4	.953	-2	*90*	*106*	C-34	-0.2
	Year	55	154	10	34	9	0	0	11	11	2	41	.221	.281	.279	67	-6	5	.954	-3	*90*	*115*	C-48	-0.5
1920	Phi N	62	176	17	37	11	1	6	26	4	2	36	.210	.236	.386	73	-7	4-0	.944	-10	*76*	*77*	C-52	-1.2
Total	7	272	689	54	148	31	3	6	66	35	7	125	.215	.260	.295	67	-29	14-0	.961	-7	*105*	*95*	C-239	-1.9
TRAMBACK, RED Stephen Joseph B 11.1.1915 Iselin, PA D 12.28.1979 Buffalo, NY BL/TL 6/175# d9.15																								
1940	NY N	2	4	0	1	0	0	0	0	1	0	1	.250	.400	.250	82	0	1	.667	-0	79	0	/O(RF)	-0.1
TRAMMELL, ALAN Alan Stuart B 2.21.1958 Garden Grove, CA BR/TR 6/175# d9.9 M1 C4 OF Total (5-LF 4-CF)																								
1977	Det A	19	43	6	8	0	0	0	0	4-0	0	12	.186	.255	.186	21	-5	0-0	.961	-8	74	57	S-19	-1.1
1978	Det A	139	448	49	120	14	6	2	34	45-0	2	56	.268	.335	.339	88	-6	3-1	.979	5	103	118	*S-139	1.3
1979	Det A	142	460	68	127	11	4	6	50	43-0	0	55	.276	.335	.357	85	-10	17-14	.961	-4	92	109	*S-142	-0.1
1980	Det A★	146	560	107	168	21	5	9	65	69-2	3	63	.300	.376	.404	112	12	12-12	.980	-18	92	92	*S-144	0.7
1981	Det A	105	392	52	101	15	3	2	31	49-2	3	31	.258	.342	.327	91	-3	10-3	.983	13	107	102	*S-105	2.2
1982	Det A	157	489	66	126	34	3	9	57	52-0	0	47	.258	.325	.395	97	-1	19-8	.978	1	99	111	*S-157	1.7
1983	Det A	142	505	83	161	31	2	14	66	57-2	0	64	.319	.385	.471	139	29	30-10	.979	-8	90	92	*S-140	3.7
1984	†Det A✳	139	555	85	174	34	5	14	69	60-2	3	63	.314	.382	.468	135	28	19-13	.980	-3	95	110	*S-114,D-22	3.6
1985	Det A★	149	605	79	156	21	7	13	57	50-4	2	71	.258	.312	.380	90	-9	14-5	.977	-13	93	98	*S-149	-0.5
1986	Det A	151	574	107	159	33	7	21	75	59-4	5	57	.277	.347	.469	121	16	25-12	.969	14	110	113	*S-149/D-2	4.6
1987	†Det A★	151	597	109	205	34	3	28	105	60-8	3	47	.343	.402	.551	157	50	21-2	.971	-4	99	109	*S-149	6.1
1988	Det A✳	128	466	73	145	24	1	15	69	46-8	4	46	.311	.373	.464	140	25	7-4	.980	-1	100	91	*S-125	3.4
1989	Det A	121	449	54	109	20	3	5	43	45-1	4	45	.243	.314	.334	86	-8	10-2	.985	16	**112**	85	*S-117/D-2	1.9
1990	Det A★	146	559	71	170	37	1	14	89	68-7	1	55	.304	.377	.449	130	25	12-10	.979	1	99	107	*S-142/D-3	3.5
1991	Det A	101	375	57	93	20	0	9	55	37-1	3	39	.248	.320	.373	90	-5	11-2	.979	4	111	101	S-92/D-6	0.8
1992	Det A	29	102	11	28	7	1	1	11	15-0	1	4	.275	.370	.392	114	3	2-2	.977	-0	101	90	S-27/D	0.4
1993	Det A	112	401	72	132	25	3	12	60	38-2	2	38	.329	.388	.496	137	21	12-8	.989	-6	104	64	S-63,3-35/O-8(4-4-0),D-6	2.0
1994	Det A	76	292	38	78	17	1	8	28	16-1	1	35	.267	.307	.414	84	-8	3-0	.968	0	101	108	S-63,D-11	-0.3
1995	Det A	74	223	28	60	12	0	2	23	27-4	0	19	.269	.345	.350	83	-5	3-1	.980	-4	100	87	S-60/D-6	-0.4
1996	Det A	66	193	16	45	2	0	1	16	10-0	0	27	.233	.267	.259	35	-20	6-0	.976	-4	101	51	S-43,2-11/3-8,O(LF)	-1.8
Total	20	2293	8288	1231	2365	412	55	185	1003	850-48	37	874	.285	.352	.415	110	129	236-109	.977	-19	100	100	*S-2139/D-59,3-43,2-11,O-9L	31.7
TRAMMELL, BUBBA Thomas Bubba B 11.6.1971 Knoxville, TN BR/TR 6-3/205# d4.1																								
1997	Det A	44	123	14	28	5	0	4	13	15-0	0	35	.228	.307	.366	77	-4	3-1	1.000	0	104	63	O-28(13-0-16),D-15	-0.6
1998	TB A	59	199	28	57	18	1	12	35	16-0	0	45	.286	.338	.568	128	8	0-2	1.000	-2	77	140	O-37(23-0-16),D-19	0.2
1999	TB A	82	283	49	82	19	0	14	39	43-1	1	37	.290	.384	.505	123	11	0-2	.993	-1	103	44	O-74(61-0-20)/D-6	0.6
2000	TB A	66	189	19	52	11	2	7	33	21-0	2	30	.275	.352	.466	106	2	3-0	1.000	-4	78	75	O-48(26-0-24)/D-9	-0.3
	†NY N	36	56	9	13	2	0	3	12	8-0	0	19	.232	.323	.429	93	-1	1-0	.963	0	96	121	O-25(11-0-16)	-0.1
2001	SD N	142	490	66	128	20	3	25	92	48-2	4	78	.261	.330	.467	113	8	2-2	.985	2	108	61	*O-132(34-0-102)/D-3	0.3
2002	SD N	133	403	54	98	16	1	17	56	53-2	3	71	.243	.333	.414	109	3	1-3	.973	-6	90	60	*O-122(23-0-104)/D-2	-0.9
2003	NY A	22	55	4	11	5	0	0	5	6-0	0	10	.200	.279	.291	51	-4	0-0	1.000	1	184	0	D-15/O-3(LF)	-0.4
Total	7	584	1798	243	469	96	7	82	285	210-5	10	325	.261	.339	.459	110	23	10-10	.986	-10	97	67	O-469(194-0-298)/D-69	-1.2
TRAVIS, CECIL Cecil Howell B 8.8.1913 Riverdale, GA BL/TR 6-1.5/185# d5.16 Mil 1942-45																								
1933	Was A	18	43	7	13	1	0	0	2	2	1	5	.302	.348	.326	80	-1	0-0	.974	2	132	52	3-15	0.1
1934	Was A	109	392	48	125	22	4	1	53	24	2	37	.319	.361	.403	101	0	1-5	.937	4	113	128	3-99	0.5
1935	Was A	138	534	85	170	27	8	0	61	41	**9**	28	.318	.377	.399	104	4	4-2	.963	21	**118**	**173**	*3-114,O-16(LF)	2.6
1936	Was A	138	517	77	164	34	10	2	92	39	1	21	.317	.366	.433	102	1	4-4	.938	-5	98	119	S-71,O-53(1-0-52)/2-4,3-2	-0.1
1937	Was A	135	526	72	181	27	7	3	66	39	5	34	.344	.395	.439	115	12	3-2	.965	-8	98	**122**	*S-129	1.3
1938	Was A☆	146	567	96	190	30	5	5	67	58	4	22	.335	.401	.432	117	16	6-5	.950	-4	102	110	*S-143	2.1
1939	Was A	130	476	55	139	20	9	5	63	34	2	25	.292	.342	.403	97	-4	0-3	.958	-5	101	106	*S-118	-0.1
1940	Was A★	136	528	60	170	37	11	2	76	48	2	23	.322	.381	.445	121	17	0-1	.934	11	108	**127**	*3-113,S-23	3.1
1941	Was A★	152	608	106	**218**	39	19	7	101	52	1	25	.359	.410	.520	152	44	2-2	.964	-0	98	104	*S-136,3-16	5.1
1945	Was A	15	54	4	13	2	1	0	10	4	0	5	.241	.293	.315	83	-1	0-1	.920	-1	94	154	3-14	-0.2

Year	Tm Lg	G	AB	R	H	2B	3B	HR	RBI	BB-IB	HP	SO	AVG	OBP	SLG	AOPS	ABR	SB-CS	FA	FR	Rng	Thr	G at Pos	BFW
1946	Was A	137	465	45	117	22	3	1	56	45	4	47	.252	.323	.318	85	-9	2-4	.959	-18	95	95	S-75,3-56	-2.5
1947	Was A	74	204	10	44	4	1	1	10	16	0	19	.216	.273	.260	50	-14	1-3	.932	-2	104	95	3-39,S-15	-1.7
Total	12	1328	4914	665	1544	265	78	27	657	402	31	291	.314	.370	.416	109	65	23-32	.955	-4	99	110	S-710,3-468/O-69(17-0-52),2-4	10.2

TRAXLER, BRIAN Brian Lee B 9.26.1967 Waukegan, IL BL/TL 5-10/200# d4.24

Year	Tm Lg	G	AB	R	H	2B	3B	HR	RBI	BB-IB	HP	SO	AVG	OBP	SLG	AOPS	ABR	SB-CS	FA	FR	Rng	Thr	G at Pos	BFW
1990	LA N	9	11	0	1	1	0	0	0	0-0	0	4	.091	.091	.182	-28	-2	0-0	1.000	1	226	0	/1-3	-0.2

TRAY, JIM James (born James Trahey) B 2.14.1860 Jackson, MI D 7.28.1905 Jackson, MI 5-11/180# d9.6

Year	Tm Lg	G	AB	R	H	2B	3B	HR	RBI	BB-IB	HP	SO	AVG	OBP	SLG	AOPS	ABR	SB-CS	FA	FR	Rng	Thr	G at Pos	BFW
1884	Ind AA	6	21	2	6	0	0	0		2	0		.286	.348	.286	112	0		.857	-2			/C-4,1-2	-0.1

TRAYNOR, PIE Harold Joseph B 11.11.1899 Framingham, MA D 3.16.1972 Pittsburgh, PA BR/TR 6/170# d9.15 M6 HF1948

Year	Tm Lg	G	AB	R	H	2B	3B	HR	RBI	BB-IB	HP	SO	AVG	OBP	SLG	AOPS	ABR	SB-CS	FA	FR	Rng	Thr	G at Pos	BFW
1920	Pit N	17	52	6	11	3	1	0	2	3	1	6	.212	.268	.308	63	-2	1-3	.860	-7	74	61	S-17	-1.1
1921	Pit N	7	19	0	5	0	0	0	2	1	0	2	.263	.300	.263	49	-1	0-0	.917	-0	104	0	/3-3,S	-0.1
1922	Pit N	142	571	89	161	17	12	4	81	27	4	28	.282	.319	.375	77	-21	17-3	.945	-8	89	105	*3-124,S-18	-1.6
1923	Pit N	153	616	108	208	19	**19**	12	101	34	5	19	.338	.377	.489	124	19	28-13	.950	9	103	115	*3-152/S	3.6
1924	Pit N	142	545	86	160	26	13	5	82	37	1	26	.294	.340	.417	100	-1	24-18	.968	6	102	**144**	*3-141	1.3
1925	†Pit N	150	591	114	189	39	14	6	106	52	2	19	.320	.377	.464	106	6	15-9	**.957**	23	107	**154**	*3-150/S	3.6
1926	Pit N	152	574	83	182	25	17	3	92	38	1	14	.317	.361	.436	108	5	8	.952	6	99	**128**	*3-148/S-3	2.0
1927	†Pit N	149	573	93	196	32	9	5	106	22	3	11	.342	.370	.455	112	9	11	.962	14	100	109	*3-143/S-9	3.2
1928	Pit N	144	569	91	192	38	12	3	124	28	1	10	.337	.370	.462	112	9	12	.946	6	103	57	*3-144	2.3
1929	Pit N	130	540	94	192	27	12	4	108	30	3	7	.356	.393	.472	111	8	13	.951	-3	95	127	*3-130	1.3
1930	Pit N	130	497	90	182	22	11	9	119	48	1	19	.366	.423	.509	124	20	7	.941	5	109	74	*3-130	2.9
1931	Pit N	**155**	615	81	183	37	15	2	103	54	0	28	.298	.354	.416	107	6	6	.925	-10	97	76	*3-155	0.2
1932	Pit N	135	513	74	169	27	10	2	68	32	4	20	.329	.373	.433	118	13	6	.936	-2	94	66	*3-127	1.6
1933	Pit N★	**154**	624	85	190	27	6	1	82	35	1	24	.304	.342	.372	104	3	5	.946	-2	98	77	*3-154	0.7
1934	Pit N★	119	444	62	137	22	10	1	61	21	1	27	.309	.341	.410	98	-2	3	.954	-10	84	**108**	*3-110,M	-0.8
1935	Pit N	57	204	24	57	10	3	1	36	10	3	17	.279	.323	.373	84	-5	2	.888	-3	94	28	3-49/1M	-0.6
1937	Pit N	5	12	3	2	0	0	0	0	0	0	1	.167	.167	.167	-9	-2	0	1.000	1	152	0	/3-3,M	-0.1
Total	17	1941	7559	1183	2416	371	164	58	1273	472	31	278	.320	.362	.435	107	64	158-46	.947	25	99	101	*3-1863/S-50,1	18.4

TREACEY, FRED Frederick S. B 1847 Brooklyn, NY 5-9.5/145# d5.16 b-Pete

Year	Tm Lg	G	AB	R	H	2B	3B	HR	RBI	BB-IB	HP	SO	AVG	OBP	SLG	AOPS	ABR	SB-CS	FA	FR	Rng	Thr	G at Pos	BFW
1871	Chi NA	25	124	39	42	7	5	**4**	33	2		5	.339	.349	.573	144	5	13-5	**.918**	7	**229**	201	*O-25(LF)	0.9
1872	Ath NA	**47**	236	53	65	7	3	2	31	5		10	.275	.290	.356	97	-1	7-5	.814	-2	59	108	*O-47(CF)	-0.2
1873	Phi NA	51	243	49	62	7	2	1	31	5		7	.255	.270	.313	70	-10	4-3	.761	2	140	**316**	*O-51(2-50-0)	-0.6
1874	Chi NA	35	148	18	28	5	0	0	12	2		6	.189	.200	.223	35	-10	4-4	.790	7	302	350	O-35(2-11-24)	-0.2
1875	Cen NA	11	46	9	12	3	0	0	2	2		0	.261	.292	.326	124	2	1-0	.848	1	108	214	O-11(LF)	0.3
	Phi NA	43	179	23	38	3	3	0	15	1		3	.212	.217	.263	63	-7	6-3	.858	1	40	75	O-43(42-1-0)	-0.3
	Year	54	225	32	50	6	3	0	17	3		3	.222	.232	.276	75	-6	7-3	.856	3	54	103	O-54(53-1-0)	0.0
1876	NY N	**57**	256	47	54	5	1	0	18	1		5	.211	.214	.238	58	-9		.844	9	84	36	*O-57(52-0-5)	-0.4
Total	5 NA	212	976	191	247	32	13	7	124	17		31	.253	.266	.334	84	-21	35-20	.000	16	135	205	O-212(82-109-24)	-0.1

TREACEY, PETE Peter B 1852 Brooklyn, NY d8.5 b-Fred

Year	Tm Lg	G	AB	R	H	2B	3B	HR	RBI	BB-IB	HP	SO	AVG	OBP	SLG	AOPS	ABR	SB-CS	FA	FR	Rng	Thr	G at Pos	BFW
1876	NY N	2	5	1	0	0	0	0	0	1		0	.000	.167	.000	-46	-1		.750	-1	84	0	/S-2	-0.1

TREADAWAY, RAY Edgar Raymond B 10.31.1907 Ragland, AL D 10.12.1935 Chattanooga, TN BL/TR 5-7/150# d9.17

Year	Tm Lg	G	AB	R	H	2B	3B	HR	RBI	BB-IB	HP	SO	AVG	OBP	SLG	AOPS	ABR	SB-CS	FA	FR	Rng	Thr	G at Pos	BFW
1930	Was A	6	19	1	4	2	0	0	1	0	0	3	.211	.211	.316	31	-2	0-0	.833	-1	63	147	/3-4	-0.3

TREADWAY, GEORGE George B. B 11.11.1866 Greenup County, KY BL/TL 6/185# d4.27

Year	Tm Lg	G	AB	R	H	2B	3B	HR	RBI	BB-IB	HP	SO	AVG	OBP	SLG	AOPS	ABR	SB-CS	FA	FR	Rng	Thr	G at Pos	BFW
1893	Bal N	115	458	78	119	16	17	1	67	58	4	50	.260	.348	.376	91	-7	24	.901	8	141	94	*O-115(1-0-114)	-0.4
1894	Bro N	124	482	125	159	28	26	4	102	73	2	43	.330	.420	.521	135	29	27	.893	-1	75	39	*O-123(121-0-2)/1	1.4
1895	Bro N	87	343	56	89	14	3	8	57	33	2	22	.259	.328	.388	91	-4	9	.886	-8	58	157	O-87(RF)	-1.3
1896	Lou N	2	7	0	1	0	0	0	0	1	0	0	.143	.250	.143	5	-1	0	.500	-1	0	0	/O(RF)1	-0.2
Total	4	328	1290	259	368	58	46	13	227	165	8	115	.285	.370	.432	108	17	60	.891	-2	94	87	O-326(122-0-204)/1-2	-0.5

TREADWAY, JEFF Hugh Jeffery B 1.22.1963 Columbus, GA BL/TR 5-11/170# d9.4

Year	Tm Lg	G	AB	R	H	2B	3B	HR	RBI	BB-IB	HP	SO	AVG	OBP	SLG	AOPS	ABR	SB-CS	FA	FR	Rng	Thr	G at Pos	BFW
1987	Cin N	23	84	9	28	4	0	2	4	2-0	1	6	.333	.356	.452	108	1	1-0	.958	-4	85	113	2-21	-0.2
1988	Cin N	103	301	30	76	19	4	2	23	27-7	3	30	.252	.315	.362	92	-3	2-0	.984	7	109	104	2-97/3-2	0.8
1989	Atl N	134	473	58	131	18	3	8	40	30-3	0	38	.277	.317	.378	96	-3	3-2	.981	6	98	121	*2-123/3-6	0.7
1990	Atl N	128	474	56	134	20	2	11	59	25-1	3	42	.283	.320	.403	93	-5	3-4	.976	24	**116**	107	*2-122	2.1
1991	†Atl N	106	306	41	98	17	2	3	32	23-1	2	19	.320	.368	.418	115	7	2-2	.960	1	105	92	2-93	1.0
1992	†Atl N	61	126	5	28	6	1	0	5	9-4	0	16	.222	.274	.286	55	-7	1-2	.993	1	103	145	2-45/3	-0.6
1993	Cle A	97	221	25	67	14	1	2	27	14-2	2	21	.303	.347	.403	102	1	1-1	.933	-1	109	83	3-42,2-19/D-4	0.1
1994	LA N	52	67	14	20	3	0	0	5	5-0	1	8	.299	.351	.343	89	-1	1-1	.950	1	106	104	2-24/3-3	0.0
1995	LA N	17	17	2	2	0	1	0	3	0-0	0	2	.118	.118	.235	-11	-3	0-0	—	0	0	0	/3-2,2	-0.3
	Mon N	41	50	4	12	2	0	0	10	5-1	0	2	.240	.309	.280	55	-3	0-1	1.000	-0	97	57	2-11/3	-0.4
	Year	58	67	6	14	2	1	0	13	5-1	0	4	.209	.264	.269	41	-6	0-1	1.000	-0	99	83	2-12/3-3	-0.7
Total	9	762	2119	244	596	103	14	28	208	140-19	12	184	.281	.326	.383	94	-16	14-13	.975	36	106	109	2-556/3-57,D-4	3.2

TREADWAY, RED Thadford Leon B 4.28.1920 Athlone, NC D 5.26.1994 Atlanta, GA BL/TR 5-10/175# d7.25

Year	Tm Lg	G	AB	R	H	2B	3B	HR	RBI	BB-IB	HP	SO	AVG	OBP	SLG	AOPS	ABR	SB-CS	FA	FR	Rng	Thr	G at Pos	BFW
1944	NY N	50	170	23	51	5	2	0	5	13	0	11	.300	.350	.353	98	0	2	.957	-0	106	77	O-38(10-2-27)	-0.3
1945	NY N	88	224	31	54	4	2	4	23	20	0	13	.241	.303	.330	75	-8	3	.940	-4	91	72	O-60(27-18-18)	-1.5
Total	2	138	394	54	105	9	4	4	28	33	0	24	.266	.323	.340	85	-8	5	.948	-4	98	74	/O-98(37-20-45)	-1.8

TRECHOCK, FRANK Frank Adam B 12.24.1915 Windber, PA D 1.16.1989 Minneapolis, MN BR/TR 5-10/175# d9.19

Year	Tm Lg	G	AB	R	H	2B	3B	HR	RBI	BB-IB	HP	SO	AVG	OBP	SLG	AOPS	ABR	SB-CS	FA	FR	Rng	Thr	G at Pos	BFW
1937	Was A	1	4	0	2	0	0	0	0	0	0	1	.500	.500	.500	160	0	0-0	.750	-0	100	249	/S	0.0

TREMARK, NICK Nicholas Joseph B 10.15.1912 Yonkers, NY D 9.7.2000 Tomball, TX BL/TL 5-5/150# d8.9

Year	Tm Lg	G	AB	R	H	2B	3B	HR	RBI	BB-IB	HP	SO	AVG	OBP	SLG	AOPS	ABR	SB-CS	FA	FR	Rng	Thr	G at Pos	BFW
1934	Bro N	17	28	3	7	1	0	0	6	2	0	2	.250	.300	.286	61	-2	0	1.000	0	123	0	/O-9(8-1-0)	-0.1
1935	Bro N	10	13	1	3	1	0	0	3	1	0	1	.231	.286	.308	61	-1	0	1.000	0	129	0	/O-4(RF)	-0.1
1936	Bro N	8	32	6	8	2	0	0	1	3	1	2	.250	.333	.313	74	-1	0	1.000	1	97	261	/O-8(0-2-6)	0.0
Total	3	35	73	10	18	4	0	0	10	6	1	5	.247	.313	.301	67	-4	0	1.000	1	111	128	/O-21(8-3-10)	-0.2

TREMIE, CHRIS Christopher James B 10.17.1969 Houston, TX BR/TR 6/200# d7.1

Year	Tm Lg	G	AB	R	H	2B	3B	HR	RBI	BB-IB	HP	SO	AVG	OBP	SLG	AOPS	ABR	SB-CS	FA	FR	Rng	Thr	G at Pos	BFW
1995	Chi A	10	24	0	4	0	0	0	0	1-0	0	2	.167	.200	.167	-3	-4	0-0	.976	-4	48	94	/C-9,D	-0.7
1998	Tex A	2	3	2	1	1	0	0	0	1-0	0	1	.333	.500	.667	192	1	0-0	—	0			/D-2	0.0
1999	Pit N	9	14	1	1	0	0	0	1	2-0	0	4	.071	.188	.071	-31	-3	0-0	1.000	0	61	159	/C-8	-0.3
Total	3	21	41	3	6	1	0	0	1	4-0	0	7	.146	.222	.171	3	-6	0-0	.986	-4	53	117	/C-17,D-3	-1.0

TREMPER, OVERTON Carlton Overton B 3.22.1906 Brooklyn, NY D 1.9.1996 Clearwater, FL BR/TR 5-10/163# d6.16

Year	Tm Lg	G	AB	R	H	2B	3B	HR	RBI	BB-IB	HP	SO	AVG	OBP	SLG	AOPS	ABR	SB-CS	FA	FR	Rng	Thr	G at Pos	BFW
1927	Bro N	26	60	4	14	0	0	0	4	0	1	2	.233	.246	.233	29	-6	0	1.000	-1	62	210	O-18(LF)	-0.8
1928	Bro N	10	31	1	6	2	1	0	1	0	0	1	.194	.194	.323	33	-3	0	1.000	1	79	378	/O-9(7-1-1)	-0.3
Total	2	36	91	5	20	2	1	0	5	0	1	3	.220	.228	.264	30	-9	0	1.000	-0	69	275	/O-27(25-1-1)	-1.1

TRENWITH, GEORGE George W. B 1851 Philadelphia, PA D 2.1.1890 Philadelphia, PA d4.30

Year	Tm Lg	G	AB	R	H	2B	3B	HR	RBI	BB-IB	HP	SO	AVG	OBP	SLG	AOPS	ABR	SB-CS	FA	FR	Rng	Thr	G at Pos	BFW
1875	Cen NA	10	45	5	8	2	0	0	4	1		2	.178	.196	.222	49	-2	0-0	.583	-6	58	0	3-10	-0.7
	NH NA	6	25	1	6	2	0	0	3	0		1	.240	.240	.320	106	0	0-0	.692	-2	78	0	/3-6	-0.1
	Year	16	70	6	14	4	0	0	7	1		3	.200	.211	.257	69	-1	0-0	.629	-7	66	0	3-16	-0.8

TRESH, MIKE Michael B 2.23.1914 Hazleton, PA D 10.4.1966 Detroit, MI BR/TR 5-11/170# d9.4 s-Tom

Year	Tm Lg	G	AB	R	H	2B	3B	HR	RBI	BB-IB	HP	SO	AVG	OBP	SLG	AOPS	ABR	SB-CS	FA	FR	Rng	Thr	G at Pos	BFW
1938	Chi A	10	29	3	7	2	0	0	2	8	0	4	.241	.405	.310	80	0	0-0	.978	1	*114*	*110*	C-10	0.1
1939	Chi A	119	352	49	91	5	2	0	38	64	3	30	.259	.377	.284	70	-13	3-2	.985	2	*94*	*100*	*C-119	-0.3
1940	Chi A	135	480	62	135	15	5	1	64	49	1	40	.281	.349	.340	78	-15	3-10	.983	9	*111*	*80*	*C-135	0.0
1941	Chi A	115	390	38	98	10	1	0	33	38	1	27	.251	.319	.282	61	-22	1-0	.981	10	*103*	*125*	*C-115	-0.4
1942	Chi A	72	233	21	54	8	1	0	15	28	0	24	.232	.314	.275	68	-9	2-0	.977	-3	*100*	*69*	C-72	-0.8
1943	Chi A	86	279	20	60	3	0	0	20	37	0	20	.215	.307	.226	57	-14	2-1	.982	1	*99*	*90*	C-85	-0.8
1944	Chi A	93	312	22	81	8	1	0	25	37	2	15	.260	.342	.292	83	-6	0-3	.981	-1	*119*	*92*	C-93	-0.2
1945	Chi A✶	**150**	458	50	114	12	0	0	47	65	0	37	.249	.342	.275	82	-8	6-3	.984	2	***148***	*114*	*C-150	0.3
1946	Chi A	80	217	28	47	5	2	0	21	36	3	24	.217	.336	.258	70	-7	0-2	.995	10	*91*	*109*	C-79	0.7

Year	Tm Lg	G	AB	R	H	2B	3B	HR	RBI	BB-IB	HP	SO	AVG	OBP	SLG	AOPS	ABR	SB-CS	FA	FR	Rng	Thr	G at Pos	BFW
1947	Chi A	90	274	19	66	6	2	0	20	26	2	26	.241	.311	.277	67	-12	2-0	.975	-6	*74*	*94*	C-89	-1.4
1948	Chi A	39	108	10	27	1	0	1	11	9	0	9	.250	.308	.287	61	-6	0-0	.983	-2	*83*	*112*	C-34	-0.6
1949	Cle A	38	37	4	8	0	0	0	1	5	0	7	.216	.310	.216	41	-3	0-0	1.000	4	*203*	*123*	C-38	0.2
Total	12	1027	3169	326	788	75	14	2	297	402	12	263	.249	.335	.283	71	-115	19-21	.983	28	*108*	*99*	*C-1019	-3.2
TRESH, TOM Thomas Michael B 9.20.1937 Detroit, MI BB/TR 6/191# d9.3 f-Mike																								
1961	NY A	9	8	1	2	0	0	0	0	0-0	0	1	.250	.250	.250	36	-1	0-0	1.000	2	189	141	/S-3	0.1
1962	†NY A★	157	622	94	178	26	5	20	93	67-3	8	74	.286	.359	.441	119	17	4-8	.970	-12	96	79	*S-111,O-43(LF)	1.1
1963	†NY A★	145	520	91	140	28	5	25	71	83-5	4	79	.269	.371	.487	140	31	3-3	.981	-6	99	65	*O-144(46-101-0)	2.0
1964	†NY A	153	533	75	131	25	5	16	73	73-3	7	110	.246	.342	.402	105	5	13-0	**.996**	-6	90	81	*O-146(106-69-6)	-0.5
1965	NY A	156	602	94	168	29	6	26	74	59-4	5	92	.279	.348	.477	133	25	5-2	.970	-4	91	135	*O-154(100-105-18)	1.5
1966	NY A	151	537	76	125	12	4	27	68	86-5	6	89	.233	.341	.421	123	18	5-4	.985	**22**	102	204	O-84(69-18-0),3-64	3.7
1967	NY A	130	448	45	98	23	3	14	53	50-0	4	86	.219	.301	.377	104	2	1-0	.972	-1	91	106	*O-118(LF)	-0.6
1968	NY A	152	507	60	99	18	3	11	52	76-8	4	97	.195	.304	.308	89	-5	10-5	.951	14	**117**	**114**	*S-119,O-27(LF)	2.1
1969	NY A	45	143	13	26	5	2	1	9	17-2	0	23	.182	.269	.266	52	-9	2-1	.980	1	100	94	S-41	-0.4
	Det A	94	331	46	74	13	1	13	37	39-0	2	47	.224	.305	.387	90	-5	2-2	.965	-11	84	95	S-77,O-11(7-0-4)/3	-0.9
	Year	139	474	59	100	18	3	14	46	56-2	2	70	.211	.294	.350	79	-14	4-3	.971	-10	90	95	*S-118,O-11(7-0-4)/3	-1.3
Total	9	1192	4251	595	1041	179	34	153	530	550-30	40	698	.245	.335	.411	113	78	45-25	.979	-1	94	110	O-727(516-293-28),S-351/3-65	8.1
TREVINO, ALEX Alejandro (Castro) B 8.26.1957 Monterrey, Mexico BR/TR 5-11/170# d9.11 b-Bobby																								
1978	NY N	6	12	3	3	0	0	0	0	1-0	0	2	.250	.308	.250	60	-1	0-0	1.000	1	0	368	/C-5,3	0.0
1979	NY N	79	207	24	56	11	1	0	20	20-2	1	27	.271	.338	.333	87	-3	2-2	.976	8	111	162	C-36,3-27/2-8	0.6
1980	NY N	106	355	26	91	11	2	0	37	13-1	1	41	.256	.281	.299	65	-18	0-3	.977	-1	128	143	C-86,3-14/2	-1.8
1981	NY N	56	149	17	39	2	0	0	10	13-0	1	19	.262	.323	.275	73	-5	3-0	.963	5	164	83	C-45/2-4,O-2(2-0-1),3	0.2
1982	Cin N	120	355	24	89	10	3	1	33	34-11	3	34	.251	.318	.304	74	-12	3-1	.979	9	110	80	*C-116/3-2	0.3
1983	Cin N	74	167	14	36	8	1	1	13	17-6	0	20	.216	.285	.293	59	-9	0-0	.987	12	143	93	C-63/3-4,2	0.6
1984	Cin N	6	6	0	1	0	0	0	0	0-0	0	2	.167	.167	.167	-6	-1	0-0	1.000	-0	29	0	/C-4	-0.1
	Atl N	79	266	36	65	16	0	3	28	16-1	1	27	.244	.289	.338	71	-10	5-2	.989	13	92	143	C-79	0.6
	Year	85	272	36	66	16	0	3	28	16-1	1	29	.243	.286	.335	69	-11	5-2	**.989**	13	91	**142**	C-83	0.5
1985	SF N	57	157	17	34	10	1	6	19	20-0	0	24	.217	.303	.408	103	0	0-0	.978	-7	105	74	C-55/3	-0.4
1986	LA N	89	202	31	53	13	0	4	26	27-2	1	35	.262	.351	.386	111	4	0-0	.969	-3	123	138	C-63/1	0.4
1987	LA N	72	144	16	32	7	1	3	16	6-2	4	28	.222	.271	.347	65	-8	1-0	.987	-2	125	103	C-45/O-2(1-0-1),3	-0.8
1988	Hou N	78	193	19	48	17	0	2	13	24-4	3	29	.249	.341	.368	108	3	5-2	.977	-16	73	60	C-74/O(LF)	-0.9
1989	Hou N	59	131	15	38	7	1	2	16	7-0	1	18	.290	.329	.405	113	2	0-0	.989	-2	148	72	C-32/1-2,3-2	0.2
1990	Hou N	42	69	3	13	3	0	1	10	6-1	2	11	.188	.266	.275	53	-4	0-1	.992	4	106	94	C-30/1	0.1
	NY N	9	10	0	3	1	0	0	2	1-0	0	0	.300	.333	.400	110	0	0-0	.929	-0	88	92	/C-7	0.0
	Cin N	7	7	0	3	1	0	0	1	0-0	1	0	.429	.500	.571	186	1	0-0	1.000	0	0	0	/C-2	0.1
	Year	58	86	3	19	5	0	1	13	7-1	3	11	.221	.293	.314	71	-3	0-1	.982	5	98	89	C-39/1	0.2
Total	13	939	2430	245	604	117	10	23	244	205-30	19	317	.249	.310	.333	81	-61	19-11	.979	23	115	106	C-742/3-53,2-14,O-5(4-0-2),1-4	-0.9
TREVINO, BOBBY Carlos (Castro) B 8.15.1943 Monterrey, Mexico BR/TR 6-2/185# d5.22 b-Alex																								
1968	Cal A	17	40	1	9	1	0	0	1	2-0	0	9	.225	.262	.250	58	-2	0-1	.962	1	123	169	O-11(1-7-5)	-0.2
TRIANDOS, GUS Gus B 7.30.1930 San Francisco, CA BR/TR 6-3/215# d8.13																								
1953	NY A	18	51	5	8	2	0	1	6	3	0	9	.157	.204	.255	24	-6	0-0	.991	-0	90	85	1-12/C-5	-0.6
1954	NY A	2	1	0	0	0	0	0	0	0	0	1	.000	.000	.000	-99	0	0-0	—	0	*0*	*0*	/C	0.0
1955	Bal A	140	481	47	133	17	3	12	65	40-4	2	55	.277	.333	.399	104	1	0-0	.989	-1	109	102	*1-103,C-36/3	-0.4
1956	Bal A	131	452	47	126	18	1	21	88	48-4	2	73	.279	.348	.462	122	13	0-0	.989	9	*76*	*120*	C-89,1-52	2.2
1957	Bal A☆	129	418	44	106	21	1	19	72	38-7	3	73	.254	.317	.445	114	6	0-0	.992	-2	*107*	*135*	*C-120	1.0
1958	Bal A★	137	474	59	116	10	0	30	79	60-4	1	65	.245	.327	.456	120	12	1-0	.987	7	***164***	*77*	*C-132	2.6
1959	Bal A★	126	393	43	85	7	1	25	73	65-6	3	56	.216	.330	.430	110	5	0-0	.981	3	***135***	***133***	*C-125	1.4
1960	Bal A	109	364	36	98	18	0	12	54	41-5	1	62	.269	.343	.418	107	4	0-0	.989	-3	*97*	*76*	*C-105	0.6
1961	Bal A	115	397	35	97	21	0	17	63	44-7	1	60	.244	.320	.426	101	0	0-0	.989	5	*117*	*96*	*C-114	1.0
1962	Bal A	66	207	20	33	7	0	6	23	29-2	0	43	.159	.262	.280	49	-15	0-0	.985	-4	*73*	*122*	C-63	-1.7
1963	Det A	106	327	28	78	13	0	14	41	32-4	6	67	.239	.315	.407	98	-1	0-0	**.998**	-4	143	85	C-90	0.0
1964	Phi N	73	188	17	47	9	0	8	33	26-5	1	41	.250	.339	.426	117	5	0-0	.985	1	*117*	*92*	C-64/1	0.9
1965	Phi N	30	82	3	14	2	0	0	4	9-1	0	17	.171	.253	.195	29	-8	0-0	.975	-3	*103*	*86*	C-28	-1.1
	Hou N	24	72	5	13	2	0	2	7	5-0	1	14	.181	.244	.292	54	-5	0-0	.970	-3	*106*	*40*	C-20	-0.7
	Year	54	154	8	27	4	0	2	11	14-1	1	31	.175	.249	.240	40	-12	0-0	.973	-6	*104*	*64*	C-48	-1.8
Total	13	1206	3907	389	954	147	6	167	608	440-49	21	636	.244	.322	.413	103	11	1-0	.987	3	*117*	*102*	C-992,1-168/3	5.2
TRILLO, MANNY Jesus Manuel Marcano (born Jesus Manuel Marcano (Trillo)) B 12.25.1950 Caripito, Venezuela BR/TR 6-1/164# d6.28																								
1973	Oak A	17	12	0	3	2	0	0	3	0-0	0	4	.250	.250	.417	90	0	0-0	.941	1	111	137	2-16	0.1
1974	†Oak A	21	33	3	5	0	0	0	2	2-0	1	8	.152	.222	.152	10	-4	0-0	.949	4	133	118	2-21	0.1
1975	Chi N	154	545	55	135	12	2	7	70	45-3	3	78	.248	.306	.316	70	-22	1-7	.967	18	108	95	*2-153/S	0.4
1976	Chi N	158	582	42	139	24	3	4	59	53-4	3	70	.239	.304	.311	69	-23	17-6	.981	9	105	97	*2-156/S	-0.2
1977	Chi N★	152	504	51	141	18	5	7	57	44-6	5	58	.280	.339	.377	84	-11	3-5	.970	30	114	98	*2-149	2.6
1978	Chi N	152	552	53	144	17	5	4	55	50-3	2	67	.261	.320	.332	75	-18	0-7	.978	29	**117**	109	*2-149	1.8
1979	Phi N	118	431	40	112	22	1	6	42	20-3	4	59	.260	.296	.357	76	-15	4-7	.985	18	**112**	**116**	*2-118	0.8
1980	†Phi N	141	531	68	155	25	9	7	43	32-8	3	46	.292	.334	.412	102	1	8-3	.987	24	111	101	*2-140	3.5
1981	†Phi N★	94	349	37	100	14	3	6	36	26-3	3	37	.287	.338	.395	104	2	10-4	.987	18	104	107	2-94	2.7
1982	Phi N★	149	549	52	149	24	1	0	39	33-3	3	53	.271	.316	.319	76	-17	8-10	**.994**	14	97	114	*2-149	0.3
1983	Cle A★	88	320	33	87	13	1	1	29	21-2	0	46	.272	.315	.328	75	-11	1-3	.989	8	107	95	2-87	0.0
	Mon N	31	121	16	32	8	0	2	16	10-0	2	18	.264	.331	.380	97	0	0-0	.979	-4	92	126	2-31	-0.2
1984	SF N	98	401	45	102	21	1	4	36	25-0	3	55	.254	.300	.342	84	-9	0-0	.988	-0	101	101	2-96/3-4	-0.5
1985	SF N	125	451	36	101	16	2	3	25	40-0	1	44	.224	.287	.288	65	-22	2-0	.981	12	106	94	*2-120/3	-0.3
1986	Chi N	81	152	22	45	10	0	1	19	16-0	0	21	.296	.359	.382	98	0	0-2	.949	-3	89	59	3-53,1-11/2-6	-0.4
1987	Chi N	108	214	27	63	8	0	8	26	25-0	0	37	.294	.367	.444	110	3	0-3	.994	-5	89	106	1-47,3-35,2-10/S-6	-0.5
1988	Chi N	76	164	15	41	5	0	1	14	8-0	0	32	.250	.283	.299	65	-8	2-0	.994	-1	54	61	1-24,3-17,2-13/S-7	-0.9
1989	Cin N	17	39	3	8	0	0	0	0	2-0	1	9	.205	.262	.205	34	-3	0-0	1.000	-4	72	39	2-10/1-3,S	-0.8
Total	17	1780	5950	598	1562	239	33	61	571	452-35	34	742	.263	.316	.345	80	-157	56-57	.981	167	107	103	*2-1518,3-110/1-85,S-16	8.5
TRIPLETT, COAKER Herman Coaker B 12.18.1911 Boone, NC D 1.30.1992 Boone, NC BR/TR 5-11/185# d4.19																								
1938	Chi N	12	36	4	9	2	1	0	2	0	0	1	.250	.250	.361	65	-2	0	1.000	0	94	169	/O-9(6-2-1)	-0.2
1941	StL N	76	185	29	53	6	3	3	21	18	0	27	.286	.350	.400	104	1	0	.965	-0	93	140	O-46(38-0-8)	-0.2
1942	StL N	64	154	18	42	7	4	1	23	17	0	15	.273	.345	.390	107	1	1	.966	2	114	86	O-46(45-0-1)	0.1
1943	StL N	9	25	1	2	0	0	1	4	1	0	6	.080	.115	.200	-9	-4	0	1.000	-0	116	0	/O-6(2-0-4)	-0.5
	Phi N	105	360	45	98	16	4	14	52	28	0	28	.272	.325	.456	129	11	2	.970	3	103	133	O-90(LF)	0.9
	Year	114	385	46	100	16	4	15	56	29	0	34	.260	.312	.439	120	7	2	.972	3	104	125	O-96(92-0-4)	0.4
1944	Phi N	84	184	15	43	5	1	1	25	19	0	10	.234	.305	.288	70	-7	1	.989	0	100	92	O-44(41-1-2)	-1.0
1945	Phi N	120	363	36	87	11	1	7	46	40	0	27	.240	.315	.333	83	-9	6	.945	-3	103	46	O-92(92-0-2)	-1.7
Total	6	470	1307	148	334	47	14	27	173	123	0	114	.256	.320	.375	97	-9	10	.965	2	103	95	O-333(314-3-18)	-2.6
TROSKY, HAL Harold Arthur Sr. (born Harold Arthur Troyavesky Sr.) B 11.11.1912 Norway, IA D 6.18.1979 Cedar Rapids, IA BL/TR (BB 1935 (part)) 6-2/207# d9.11 s-Hal																								
1933	Cle A	11	44	6	13	1	2	1	8	2	1	12	.295	.340	.477	110	0	0-0	.990	-1	73	82	1-11	-0.1
1934	Cle A	**154**	625	117	206	45	9	35	142	58	2	49	.330	.388	.598	149	42	2-2	.986	0	104	**110**	*1-154	2.5
1935	Cle A	154	632	84	171	33	7	26	113	46	1	60	.271	.321	.468	100	-4	1-2	.993	1	102	106	*1-153	-1.7
1936	Cle A	151	629	124	216	45	9	42	**162**	36	3	58	.343	.382	.644	148	41	6-5	.985	1	107	96	*1-151/2	2.4
1937	Cle A	153	601	104	179	36	9	32	128	65	1	60	.298	.367	.547	127	22	3-1	.993	-2	89	99	*1-152	0.5
1938	Cle A	150	554	106	185	40	9	19	110	67	1	40	.334	.407	.542	138	33	5-1	.993	4	103	88	*1-148	2.1
1939	Cle A	122	448	89	150	31	4	25	104	52	1	28	.335	.405	.589	157	38	2-3	.992	12	**137**	100	*1-118	3.4
1940	Cle A	140	522	85	154	39	4	25	93	79	4	45	.295	.392	.529	140	33	1-2	.991	-6	79	**117**	*1-139	1.3
1941	Cle A	89	310	43	91	17	0	11	51	44	1	21	.294	.383	.455	127	13	1-2	.989	-1	93	108	1-85	0.3
1944	Chi A	135	497	55	120	32	2	10	70	62	1	30	.241	.327	.374	101	2	3-2	.993	-9	71	107	*1-130	-1.5
1946	Chi A	88	299	22	76	12	3	2	31	34	0	37	.254	.330	.334	89	-4	4-3	.991	-7	68	97	1-80	-1.5

Year	Tm Lg	G	AB	R	H	2B	3B	HR	RBI	BB-IB	HP	SO	AVG	OBP	SLG	AOPS	ABR	SB-CS	FA	FR	Rng	Thr	G at Pos	BFW
Total	11	1347	5161	835	1561	331	58	228	1012	545	16	440	.302	.371	.522	130	216	28-23	.991	-8	96	103	*1-1321/2	7.7
TROST, MIKE Michael J. B 1866 Philadelphia, PA D 3.24.1901 Philadelphia, PA TR 6-0.5/180# d8.21																								
1890	StL AA	17	51	10	13	2	0	1	7	6	1		.255	.345	.353	93	-1	4	.890	-1	*99*	*84*	C-13/O-4(0-3-1)	-0.1
1895	Lou N	3	12	1	1	0	0	0	1	0	0	1	.083	.083	.083	-61	-3	1	1.000	-0	0	63	/1-3	-0.3
Total	2	20	63	11	14	2	0	1	8	6	1	1	.222	.300	.302	66	-4	5	.890	-2	*99*	*84*	/C-13,O-4(0-3-1),1-3	-0.4
TROTT, SAM Samuel W. B 3.1859 , MD D 6.5.1925 Catonsville, MD BL/TL 5-9/190# d5.29 M1 OF Total (8-LF 5-CF 14-RF)																								
1880	Bos N	39	125	14	26	4	1	0	9	3		5	.208	.227	.256	65	-4		.893	5			C-36/O-4(1-3-0)	0.1
1881	Det N	6	25	3	5	2	1	0	2	1		3	.200	.231	.360	80	-1		.868	-1			/C-6	-0.2
1882	Det N	32	129	11	31	7	1	0	12	0		13	.240	.240	.310	75	-4		.890	2			C-23/S-3,2-3,1-3,O-2(LF),3	0.1
1883	Det N	75	295	27	72	14	1	0	29	10		23	.244	.269	.298	76	-8		.882	-15	82	97	2-42,C-34/O-6(0-1-5),1	-1.6
1884	Bal AA	71	284	36	73	17	9	3		4	2		.257	.272	.412	116	4		.931	11			C-60/2-6,O-5(1-1-3)	1.8
1885	Bal AA	21	88	12	24	2	2	0	12	5	0		.273	.312	.341	108	1		.882	-3			C-17/O-4(RF),2-2,S	-0.1
1887	Bal AA	85	300	44	77	16	3	0	37	27	2		.257	.322	.330	87	-4	8	.915	2			C-69,2-11/O-3(LF),1-2,S	0.3
1888	Bal AA	31	108	19	30	11	4	0	22	4	0		.278	.304	.454	145	5	1	.908	-5			C-27/O-3(1-0-2),21	0.2
Total	8	360	1354	166	338	73	22	3	123	54	4	44	.250	.280	.343	93	-11	9	.906	-4			C-272/2-65,O-27R,1-7,S-5,3	0.6
TROUPPE, QUINCY Quincy Thomas B 12.25.1912 Dublin, GA D 8.12.1993 Creve Coeur, MO BB/TR 6-2.5/225# d4.30																								
1952	Cle A	6	10	1	1	0	0	0	0	1	0	3	.100	.182	.100	-22	-2	0-0	1.000	1	*110*	*106*	/C-6	0.0
TROY, DASHER John Joseph B 5.8.1856 New York, NY D 3.30.1938 Ozone Park, NY BR/TR 5-5/154# d8.23																								
1881	Det N	11	44	2	15	3	0	0	4	3		8	.341	.383	.409	143	2		.792	-1	103	0	/3-7,2-4	0.1
1882	Det N	40	152	22	37	7	2	0	14	5		10	.243	.268	.316	86	-2		.847	-17	80	65	2-31,S-11	-1.7
	Pro N	4	17	1	4	0	0	0	1	0		1	.235	.235	.235	52	-1		.750	-1	96	93	/S-4	-0.2
	Year	44	169	23	41	7	2	0	15	5		11	.243	.264	.308	83	-3		.847	-19	80	65	2-31,S-15	-1.9
1883	NY N	85	316	37	68	7	5	0	20	9		33	.215	.237	.269	54	-18		.879	-12	97	71	*2-73,S-12	-2.4
1884	†NY AA	107	421	80	111	22	10	2		19	3		.264	.300	.378	123	11		.879	-20	93	66	*2-107	-0.5
1885	NY AA	45	177	24	39	3	3	2	12	5	4		.220	.258	.305	81	-4		.866	-12	80	90	2-42/O-2(RF),S	-1.3
Total	5	292	1127	166	274	42	20	4	51	41	7	52	.243	.274	.327	91	-12		.873	-64	90	73	2-257/S-28,3-7,O-2(RF)	-6.0
TRUAX, FRED Frederick W. B 1868 D 12.18.1899 Omaha, NE d8.18																								
1890	Pit N	1	3	0	1	0	0	0	1	1	0	1	.333	.500	.333	163	0	0	1.000	0	0	3185	/O(LF)	0.0
TRUBY, CHRIS Christopher John B 12.9.1973 Palm Springs, CA BR/TR 6-2/190# d6.16																								
2000	Hou N	78	258	28	67	15	4	11	59	10-1	5	56	.260	.295	.477	87	-6	2-1	.926	3	105	116	3-74	-0.3
2001	†Hou N	48	136	11	28	6	1	8	23	13-2	1	38	.206	.276	.441	78	-5	1-2	.923	-4	91	72	3-35/1	-0.9
2002	Mon N	35	105	12	27	5	2	2	7	5-1	1	27	.257	.297	.400	78	-4	1-1	.924	-3	95	75	3-31/1-2,O(LF)	-0.8
	Det A	89	277	23	55	13	2	2	15	5-0	2	71	.199	.215	.282	33	-27	1-1	.958	10	116	147	3-89	-1.6
2003	TB A	13	43	4	12	3	0	0	3	5-0	0	13	.279	.354	.349	88	-1	0-0	.976	4	138	170	3-13	0.3
Total	4	263	819	78	189	42	9	23	107	38-4	9	205	.231	.269	.388	68	-43	5-5	.942	9	108	119	3-242/1-3,O(LF)	-3.3
TRUBY, HARRY Harry Garvin "Bird Eye" B 5.12.1870 Ironton, OH D 3.21.1953 Ironton, OH TR 5-11/185# d8.21 U1																								
1895	Chi N	33	119	17	40	3	0	0	16	10	3	7	.336	.402	.361	92	-1	7	.950	-0	90	143	2-33	0.0
1896	Chi N	29	109	13	28	2	2	2	31	6	3	5	.257	.314	.367	76	-4	4	.935	0	93	141	2-28	-0.3
	Pit N	8	32	1	5	0	0	0	3	2	0	4	.156	.206	.156	-4	-5	1	.949	-2	69	215	/2-8	-0.6
	Year	37	141	14	33	2	2	2	34	8	3	9	.234	.289	.319	59	-9	5	.938	-2	88	157	2-36	-0.9
Total	2	70	260	31	73	5	2	2	50	18	6	16	.281	.342	.338	75	-10	12	.944	-2	89	150	/2-69	-0.9
TRUESDALE, FRANK Frank Day B 3.31.1884 St.Louis, MO D 8.27.1943 Albuquerque, NM BB/TR 5-8/145# d4.27																								
1910	StL A	123	415	39	91	7	2	1	25	48	2		.219	.303	.253	79	-8	29	.914	-2	100	91	*2-122	-1.1
1911	StL A	1	0	1	0	0	0	0	0	0	0		—	—	—	—	0	0	—	0			R	0.0
1914	NY A	77	217	22	46	4	0	0	13	39	3	35	.212	.340	.230	72	-5	11-11	.947	3	109	106	2-67/3-4	-0.2
1918	Bos A	15	36	6	10	1	0	0	2	4	0	5	.278	.350	.306	99	0	1	.913	-1	106	59	2-10	-0.1
Total	4	216	668	68	147	12	2	1	40	91	5	40	.220	.318	.249	78	-13	41-11	.924	0	103	94	2-199/3-4	-1.4
TRUMBULL, ED Edward J. (born Edward J. Trembly) B 11.3.1860 Chicopee, MA D 1.14.1937 Kingston, PA d5.10 ▲																								
1884	Was AA	25	86	5	10	2	0	0		2	0		.116	.136	.140	-11	-10		.828	0	154	202	O-15(2-8-5),P-10	-0.5
TUBBS, GREG Gregory Alan B 8.31.1962 Smithville, TN BR/TR 5-9/185# d8.1																								
1993	Cin N	35	59	10	11	0	0	1	2	14-0	1	10	.186	.351	.237	61	-3	3-1	.975	1	105	109	O-21(11-14-2)	-0.2
TUCKER, EDDIE Eddie Jack "Scooter" B 11.18.1966 Greenville, MS BR/TR 6-2/205# d6.14																								
1992	Hou N	20	50	5	6	1	0	0	3	3-0	2	13	.120	.200	.140	-2	-7	1-1	.976	-6	83	71	C-19	-1.3
1993	Hou N	9	26	1	5	1	0	0	3	2-0	0	3	.192	.250	.231	31	-3	0-0	1.000	3	171	86	/C-8	0.0
1995	Hou N	5	7	1	2	0	0	1	1	0-0	0	0	.286	.286	.714	164	1	0-0	1.000	0	85	274	/C-3	0.1
	Cle A	17	20	2	0	0	0	0	0	5-0	1	4	.000	.231	.000	-33	-4	0-0	.982	-0	108	125	C-17	-0.3
Total	3	51	103	9	13	2	0	1	7	10-0	3	20	.126	.224	.175	11	-13	1-1	.986	-3	109	96	/C-47	-1.5
TUCKER, MICHAEL Michael Anthony B 6.25.1971 S.Boston, VA BL/TR 6-2/185# d4.26																								
1995	KC A	62	177	23	46	10	0	4	17	18-2	1	51	.260	.332	.384	84	-4	2-3	.986	1	98	133	O-36(30-1-5),D-22	-0.6
1996	KC A	108	339	55	88	18	4	12	53	40-1	7	69	.260	.346	.442	99	-1	10-4	.989	-2	97	77	O-98(28-0-73)/1-9,D-5	-0.6
1997	†Atl N	138	499	80	141	25	7	14	56	44-0	6	116	.283	.347	.445	104	2	12-7	.980	1	104	68	*O-129(53-0-102)	-0.3
1998	†Atl N	130	414	54	101	27	3	13	46	49-10	3	112	.244	.327	.418	94	-3	8-3	.995	-1	97	72	*O-118(RF)	-0.9
1999	Cin N	133	296	55	75	8	5	11	44	37-3	3	81	.253	.338	.426	90	-5	11-4	.990	7	115	158	*O-114(0-13-107)	0.0
2000	Cin N	148	270	55	72	13	4	15	36	44-1	7	64	.267	.381	.511	121	9	13-6	.969	-0	99	109	*O-120(41-28-67)/2	0.7
2001	Cin N	86	231	31	56	10	1	7	30	23-1	1	55	.242	.308	.385	76	-8	12-5	.978	3	100	188	O-70(37-32-19)	-0.6
	Chi N	63	205	31	54	9	7	5	31	23-3	1	47	.263	.339	.449	107	1	4-3	.991	2	103	72	O-57(38-44-6)/1-4	0.2
	Year	149	436	62	110	19	8	12	61	46-4	2	102	.252	.322	.415	90	-8	16-8	.984	5	101	133	*O-127(75-76-25)/1-4	-0.4
2002	KC A	144	475	65	118	27	6	12	56	56-1	3	105	.248	.330	.406	85	-10	23-9	.991	4	102	142	*O-108(33-14-67),D-23/1-5,2-2	-1.0
2003	KC A	104	389	61	102	20	5	13	55	39-3	2	88	.262	.331	.440	89	-6	8-10	.989	-3	88	145	O-85(21-30-47),D-15	-1.4
Total	9	1116	3295	510	853	167	42	106	424	373-25	34	788	.259	.338	.432	95	-25	103-54	.986	11	100	111	O-935(281-162-611)/D-65,1-18,2-3	-4.5
TUCKER, OLLIE Oliver Dinwiddie B 1.27.1902 Radiant, VA D 7.13.1940 Radiant, VA BL/TR 5-11/180# d4.17																								
1927	Was A	20	24	1	5	2	0	0	8	4	0	2	.208	.321	.292	61	-1	0-0	1.000	0	122	0	/O-5(RF)	-0.1
1928	Cle A	14	47	5	6	0	0	1	2	7	1	3	.128	.255	.191	19	-6	0-2	1.000	0	77	231	O-14(RF)	-0.7
Total	2	34	71	6	11	2	0	1	10	11	1	5	.155	.277	.225	33	-7	0-2	1.000	0	88	175	/O-19(RF)	-0.8
TUCKER, TOMMY Thomas Joseph "Foghorn" B 10.28.1863 Holyoke, MA D 10.22.1935 Montague, MA BB/TR 5-11/165# d4.16																								
1887	Bal AA	136	524	114	144	15	9	6	84	29	**29**		.275	.347	.372	107	7	85	.976	4	113	75	*1-136	-0.1
1888	Bal AA	136	520	74	149	17	12	6	61	16	18		.287	.330	.400	137	20	43	.975	3	**126**	105	*1-129/O-7(2-0-5),P	1.1
1889	Bal AA	134	527	103	**196**	22	11	5	99	42	**33**	26	**.372**	**.450**	.484	**163**	**46**	63	.964	-1	103	93	*1-123,O-12(0-11-1)	2.8
1890	Bos N	132	539	104	159	17	8	1	62	56	**25**	22	.295	.387	.362	110	8	43	**.979**	-2	85	85	*1-132	-0.5
1891	Bos N	**140**	548	103	148	16	5	2	69	37	**29**	30	.270	.349	.328	87	-9	26	.976	-3	87	100	*1-140/P	-2.3
1892	†Bos N	149	542	85	153	15	7	1	62	45	**26**	35	.282	.365	.341	104	4	22	.972	-12	65	129	*1-149	-0.8
1893	Bos N	121	486	83	138	13	2	7	91	27	20	31	.284	.347	.362	82	-14	8	.980	-11	58	**128**	*1-121	-2.1
1894	Bos N	123	500	112	165	24	6	3	100	53	17	21	.330	.412	.420	94	-4	18	**.985**	2	99	108	*1-123/O(CF)	-0.2
1895	Bos N	126	465	87	115	19	6	3	73	63	19	29	.247	.360	.333	74	-17	15	.978	5	118	111	*1-126	-1.0
1896	Bos N	122	474	74	144	27	5	2	72	30	14	29	.304	.363	.395	94	-4	6	.985	3	108	102	*1-122	-0.1
1897	Bos N	4	14	0	3	2	0	0	4	2	0		.214	.313	.357	72	-1	0	.957	0	172	0	/1-4	0.0
	Was N	93	352	52	119	18	5	5	61	27	11		.338	.403	.460	128	15	18	.984	-3	81	110	*1-93	1.0
	Year	97	366	52	122	20	5	5	65	29	11		.333	.399	.456	126	14	18	.982	-2	85	105	1-97	1.0
1898	Bro N	73	283	35	79	9	4	1	34	12	7		.279	.325	.350	94	-3	1	.991	7	138	97	1-73	0.4
	StL N	72	252	18	60	7	2	0	20	18	12		.238	.319	.282	71	-9	1	.973	-0	105	89	1-72	-0.9
	Year	145	535	53	139	16	6	1	54	30	19		.260	.322	.318	83	-12	2	.982	7	122	93	*1-145	-0.5
1899	Cle N	127	456	40	110	19	3	0	40	24	12		.241	.297	.296	68	-20	3	.977	0	99	77	*1-127	-1.8
Total	13	1688	6482	1084	1882	240	85	42	932	481	272	223	.290	.364	.373	101	19	352	.978	-8	98	101	*1-1670/O-20(2-12-6),P-2	-4.5

Year	Tm Lg	G	AB	R	H	2B	3B	HR	RBI	BB-IB	HP	SO	AVG	OBP	SLG	AOPS	ABR	SB-CS	FA	FR	Rng	Thr	G at Pos	BFW
TUCKER, THURMAN Thurman Lowell "Joe E." B 9.26.1917 Gordon, TX D 5.7.1993 Oklahoma City, OK BL/TR 5-11/170# d4.14 Mil 1945																								
1942	Chi A	7	24	2	3	0	1	0	1	0	0	4	.125	.125	.208	-7	-4	0-0	.900	-0	71	326	/O-5(CF)	-0.4
1943	Chi A	139	528	81	124	15	6	3	39	79	1	72	.235	.336	.303	87	-6	29-17	.988	9	109	133	*O-132(CF)	-0.1
1944	Chi A★	124	446	59	128	15	6	2	46	57	0	40	.287	.368	.361	110	7	13-12	**.991**	11	**115**	96	*O-120(CF)	1.4
1946	Chi A	121	438	62	126	20	3	1	36	54	1	45	.288	.367	.354	106	5	9-10	.990	-2	93	145	*O-110(CF)	-0.1
1947	Chi A	89	254	28	60	9	4	1	17	38	0	25	.236	.336	.315	85	-5	10-4	.978	-1	96	119	O-65(CF)	-0.7
1948	†Cle A	83	242	52	63	13	2	1	19	31	1	17	.260	.347	.343	86	-4	11-2	1.000	-0	97	98	O-66(CF)	-0.4
1949	Cle A	80	197	28	48	5	2	0	14	18	0	19	.244	.307	.289	59	-12	4-2	.984	-2	98	64	O-42(4-38-0)	-1.5
1950	Cle A	57	101	13	18	2	0	1	7	14	1	14	.178	.284	.228	34	-10	1-0	.968	1	103	107	O-34(15-16-4)	-1.0
1951	Cle A	1	1	0	0	0	0	0	0	0	0	1	.000	.000	.000	-99	0	0-0	—	0			H	0.0
Total	9	701	2231	325	570	79	24	9	179	291	4	237	.255	.342	.325	89	-29	77-47	.988	16	103	117	O-574(19-552-4)	-2.8
TURANG, BRIAN Brian Craig B 6.14.1967 Long Beach, CA BR/TR 5-10/170# d8.13																								
1993	Sea A	40	140	22	35	11	1	0	7	17-0	2	20	.250	.340	.343	83	-3	6-2	.986	-2	91	98	O-38(26-14-1)/3-2,2D	-0.5
1994	Sea A	38	112	9	21	5	1	1	8	7-0	1	25	.188	.242	.277	33	-12	3-1	.978	-2	98	77	O-30(20-12-0)/2-5,D-4	-1.2
Total	2	78	252	31	56	16	2	1	15	24-0	3	45	.222	.297	.313	60	-15	9-3	.983	-4	94	90	/O-68(46-26-1),2-6,D-5,3-2	-1.7
TURBIDY, JERRY Jeremiah B 7.4.1852 Dudley, MA D 9.5.1920 Webster, MA 5-8/165# d7.27																								
1884	KC U	13	49	5	11	4	0	0		3			.224	.269	.306	85	-2		.830	4	125	141	S-13	0.2
TURCHIN, EDDIE Edward Lawrence "Smiley" B 2.10.1917 New York, NY D 2.8.1982 Brookhaven, NY BR/TR 5-10/165# d5.9																								
1943	Cle A	11	13	4	3	0	0	0	1	3	0	1	.231	.375	.231	84	0	0-0	1.000	1	118	257	/3-4,S-2	0.1
TURGEON, PETE Eugene Joseph B 1.3.1897 Minneapolis, MN D 1.24.1977 Wichita Falls, TX BR/TR 5-6/145# d9.20																								
1923	Chi N	3	6	1	1	0	0	0	0	0	0	0	.167	.167	.167	-12	-1	0-0	.875	-0	64	258	/S-2	-0.1
TURNER, CHRIS Christopher Wan B 3.23.1969 Bowling Green, KY BR/TR 6-1/190# d8.27																								
1993	Cal A	25	75	9	21	5	0	1	13	9-0	1	16	.280	.360	.387	99	0	1-1	.992	-1	62	63	C-25	0.0
1994	Cal A	58	149	23	36	7	1	1	12	10-0	1	29	.242	.290	.322	58	-10	3-0	.997	1	91	91	C-57	-0.5
1995	Cal A	5	10	0	1	0	0	0	1	0-0	0	3	.100	.100	.100	-48	-2	0-0	1.000	1	0	0	/C-4,D	-0.1
1996	Cal A	4	3	1	1	0	0	0	1	1-0	0	0	.333	.400	.333	116	0	0-0	1.000	1	0	791	/C-3,O(LF)	0.1
1997	Ana A	13	23	4	6	1	1	1	2	5-0	0	8	.261	.393	.522	136	1	0-0	1.000	-4	53	0	/C-8,1-2,O(RF)D	-0.2
1998	KC A	4	9	0	0	0	0	0	0	0-0	1	4	.000	.100	.000	-69	-2	0-0	1.000	-0	177	0	/C-4	-0.2
1999	Cle A	12	21	3	4	0	0	0	0	1-0	0	8	.190	.227	.190	8	-3	1-0	.964	-1	87	90	C-12	-0.3
2000	NY A	37	89	9	21	3	0	1	7	10-0	1	21	.236	.320	.303	60	-5	0-1	1.000	-3	78	47	C-36/1	-0.7
Total	8	158	379	49	90	16	2	4	36	36-0	4	89	.237	.307	.322	63	-21	5-2	.994	-7	79	69	C-149/1-3,O-2(1-0-1),D-2	-1.9
TURNER, EARL Earl Edwin B 5.6.1923 Pittsfield, MA D 10.20.1999 Lee, MA BR/TR 5-9/170# d9.25																								
1948	Pit N	2	1	0	0	0	0	0	0	0	0	0	.000	.000	.000	-98	0	0	—	0	*0*	*0*	/C	0.0
1950	Pit N	40	74	10	18	0	0	3	5	4	0	13	.243	.282	.365	66	-4	1	.974	1	*127*	*99*	C-34	-0.2
Total	2	42	75	10	18	0	0	3	5	4	0	13	.240	.278	.360	64	-4	1	.974	1	*126*	*98*	/C-35	-0.2
TURNER, TUCK George A. B 2.13.1873 W.New Brighton, NY D 7.16.1945 Staten Island, NY BB/TL 5-6.5/155# d8.18																								
1893	Phi N	36	155	32	50	4	3	1	13	9	1	19	.323	.364	.406	105	0	7	.933	1	94	178	O-36(1-35-0)	-0.1
1894	Phi N	82	347	95	145	21	9	1	84	24	2	13	.418	.458	.539	143	25	11	.902	-5	58	34	O-80(56-3-22)/P	1.1
1895	Phi N	59	210	51	81	8	6	2	43	25	1	11	.386	.453	.510	147	16	14	.847	-4	70	0	O-55(31-9-15)	0.6
1896	Phi N	13	32	12	7	2	0	0	0	8	0	5	.219	.375	.281	75	-1	6	.905	2	382	0	/O-8(1-7-0)	0.1
	StL N	51	203	30	50	7	8	1	27	14	1	21	.246	.298	.374	80	-7	6	.961	-3	63	56	O-51(RF)	-1.1
	Year	64	235	42	57	9	8	1	27	22	1	26	.243	.310	.362	79	-8	12	.948	-1	108	48	O-59(1-7-51)	-1.0
1897	StL N	103	416	58	121	17	12	2	41	35	3		.291	.350	.404	101	-1	8	.945	-4	75	98	*O-102(RF)	-0.8
1898	StL N	35	141	20	28	8	0	0	7	14	2		.199	.280	.255	53	-8	1	.929	-3	42	85	O-34(RF)	-1.3
Total	6	379	1504	298	482	67	38	7	215	129	10	69	.320	.378	.430	111	24	53	.916	-18	74	69	O-366(89-54-224)/P	-1.5
TURNER, JERRY John Webber B 1.17.1954 Texarkana, AR BL/TL 5-9/180# d9.2																								
1974	SD N	17	48	4	14	1	0	0	2	3-0	0	5	.292	.333	.313	85	-1	2-1	1.000	-1	68	135	O-13(LF)	-0.2
1975	SD N	11	22	1	6	0	0	0	0	2-1	0	1	.273	.333	.273	74	-1	0-0	.909	0	131	0	/O-4(LF)	-0.1
1976	SD N	105	281	41	75	16	5	5	37	32-3	0	38	.267	.339	.413	123	8	12-6	.960	-2	89	128	O-74(LF)	0.3
1977	SD N	118	289	43	71	16	1	10	48	31-1	0	43	.246	.316	.412	105	1	12-4	.947	4	97	246	O-69(65-4-2)	0.4
1978	SD N	106	225	28	63	9	1	8	37	21-5	3	32	.280	.348	.436	128	8	6-4	.970	-1	90	137	O-58(28-17-24)	0.5
1979	SD N	138	448	55	111	23	2	9	61	34-0	2	58	.248	.301	.368	88	-9	4-2	.958	-2	97	85	*O-115(114-0-2)	-1.6
1980	SD N	85	153	22	44	5	0	3	18	10-4	2	18	.288	.335	.379	106	1	8-3	1.000	-1	91	93	O-34(5-0-30)	0.0
1981	SD N	33	31	5	7	0	0	2	6	4-1	0	3	.226	.314	.419	115	0	0-1	.833	-0	107	0	/O-4(RF)	0.0
	Chi A	10	12	1	2	0	0	0	2	1-0	0	2	.167	.231	.167	16	-1	0-0	1.000	0	106	0	/O(RF)	-0.1
1982	Det A	85	210	21	52	3	0	8	27	20-1	0	37	.248	.310	.376	88	-4	1-3	.909	-2	58	0	D-50,O-13(2-0-12)	-0.9
1983	SD N	25	23	1	3	0	0	0	0	1-1	0	8	.130	.167	.130	-17	-4	0-0	—	-0	0	0	/O(RF)	-0.4
Total	10	733	1742	222	448	73	9	45	238	159-17	7	245	.257	.319	.387	101	-2	45-24	.959	-5	93	129	O-386(305-21-76)/D-50	-2.1
TURNER, SHANE Shane Lee B 1.8.1963 Los Angeles, CA BL/TR 5-10/180# d8.19																								
1988	Phi N	18	35	1	6	0	0	0	1	5-0	0	9	.171	.275	.171	30	-3	0-0	.941	-3	83	76	/3-8,S-5	-0.6
1991	Bal A	4	1	0	0	0	0	0	0	0-0	0	0	.000	.000	.000	-99	0	0-0	1.000	0	290	0	/2D	0.0
1992	Sea A	34	74	8	20	5	0	0	5	9-0	0	15	.270	.341	.338	93	0	2-1	.881	-1	99	193	3-18,O-15(15-0-1)	-0.1
Total	3	56	110	9	26	5	0	0	6	14-0	0	24	.236	.317	.282	71	-3	2-1	.898	-3	94	153	/3-26,O-15(15-0-1),S-5,D2	-0.7
TURNER, TERRY Terrence Lamont "Cotton Top" B 2.28.1881 Sandy Lake, PA D 7.18.1960 Cleveland, OH BR/TR 5-8/149# d8.25 C1																								
1901	Pit N	2	7	0	3	0	0	0	1	0	0		.429	.429	.429	145	0	0	.833	1	151	0	/3-2	0.1
1904	Cle A	111	404	41	95	9	6	1	45	11	0		.235	.255	.295	74	-13	5	.940	3	106	85	*S-111	-0.8
1905	Cle A	**155**	586	49	155	16	14	4	72	14	6		.265	.289	.360	104	-1	17	.946	-25	94	106	*S-155	-2.4
1906	Cle A	147	584	85	170	27	7	2	62	35	6		.291	.338	.372	124	16	27	**.960**	19	**114**	**141**	*S-147	4.2
1907	Cle A	140	524	57	127	20	7	0	46	19	2		.242	.272	.307	84	-11	27	**.950**	-2	100	**155**	*S-139	-1.0
1908	Cle A	60	201	21	48	11	1	0	19	15	2		.239	.298	.303	95	-1	18	.952	-3	57	0	O-36(0-2-34),S-17	-0.5
1909	Cle A	53	208	25	52	7	4	0	16	14	2		.250	.304	.322	94	-2	14	.969	10	125	78	2-26,S-26	1.0
1910	Cle A	150	574	71	132	14	6	0	33	53	5		.230	.301	.275	79	-13	31	.973	-1	102	113	S-94,3-46/2-9	-1.1
1911	Cle A	117	417	59	105	16	9	0	28	34	1		.252	.310	.333	78	-13	29	.970	1	108	72	3-94,2-14,S-10	-0.9
1912	Cle A	103	370	54	114	14	4	0	33	31	1		.308	.363	.368	106	3	19	**.951**	3	97	**144**	*3-103	0.8
1913	Cle A	120	388	60	96	13	4	0	44	55	5	35	.247	.348	.302	88	-4	13	.954	13	99	272	3-71,2-25,S-21	1.4
1914	Cle A	121	428	43	105	14	9	1	33	44	2	36	.245	.319	.327	91	-5	17-13	**.963**	22	113	**140**	*3-104,2-17	2.1
1915	Cle A	75	262	35	66	14	1	0	14	29	1	13	.252	.329	.313	90	-2	12-11	.965	-4	94	58	2-51,3-20	-0.7
1916	Cle A	124	428	52	112	15	3	0	38	40	0	29	.262	.325	.311	86	-7	15	.963	9	112	70	3-77,2-42	0.5
1917	Cle A	69	180	16	37	7	0	0	15	14	0	19	.206	.263	.244	51	-10	4	.980	-0	91	68	3-40,2-23/S	-1.1
1918	Cle A	74	233	24	58	7	2	0	23	22	1	15	.249	.316	.296	77	-6	6	.969	2	110	39	3-46,2-26/S	-0.4
1919	Phi A	38	127	7	24	3	0	0	6	5	0	9	.189	.220	.213	21	-14	2	.946	3	117	155	S-19,2-17/3	-0.9
Total	17	1659	5921	699	1499	207	77	8	528	435	34	156	.253	.308	.318	89	-83	256-24	.952	49	103	123	S-741,3-604,2-250/O-36(0-2-34)	0.3
TURNER, TOM Thomas Richard B 9.8.1916 Custer Co., OK D 5.14.1986 Kennewick, WA BR/TR 6-2/195# d4.25 Mil 1945																								
1940	Chi A	37	96	11	20	1	2	0	6	3	1	12	.208	.240	.260	29	-11	1-0	.969	2	*116*	*83*	C-29	-0.7
1941	Chi A	38	126	7	30	5	0	0	8	9	0	15	.238	.289	.278	51	-9	2-0	.979	3	*104*	*101*	C-35	-0.3
1942	Chi A	56	182	18	44	9	1	3	21	19	0	15	.242	.313	.352	89	-3	0-1	.971	-0	*101*	*81*	C-54	0.0
1943	Chi A	51	154	16	37	7	1	2	11	13	0	21	.240	.299	.338	86	-3	1-0	.978	3	*105*	*92*	C-49	0.3
1944	Chi A	36	113	9	26	6	0	2	13	5	0	16	.230	.263	.336	71	-5	0-1	.958	-2	*119*	*87*	C-36	-0.5
	†StL A	15	25	2	8	1	0	0	4	2	0	5	.320	.370	.360	103	0	0-0	.969	-1	*97*	*56*	C-11	0.0
	Year	51	138	11	34	7	0	2	17	7	0	21	.246	.283	.341	77	-5	0-1	.960	-2	*115*	*82*	C-47	-0.5
Total	5	233	696	63	165	29	4	7	63	51	1	84	.237	.290	.320	70	-31	4-2	.972	5	*107*	*88*	C-214	-1.2
TUTTLE, BILL William Robert B 7.4.1929 Elwood, IL D 7.27.1998 Anoka, MN BR/TR 6/190# d9.10																								
1952	Det A	7	25	2	6	0	0	0	2	0	0	1	.240	.240	.240	34	-2	0-0	1.000	0	115	0	/O-6(3-3-0)	-0.3
1954	Det A	147	530	64	141	20	11	7	58	62	2	60	.266	.343	.385	102	1	5-8	.985	-2	93	133	*O-145(1-144-0)	-1.0
1955	Det A	**154**	603	102	168	23	4	14	78	76-2	1	54	.279	.358	.400	107	6	6-3	.985	5	104	127	*O-154(CF)	0.4

Year	Tm Lg	G	AB	R	H	2B	3B	HR	RBI	BB-IB	HP	SO	AVG	OBP	SLG	AOPS	ABR	SB-CS	FA	FR	Rng	Thr	G at Pos	BFW
1956	Det A	140	546	61	138	22	4	9	65	38-1	1	48	.253	.301	.357	73	-23	5-4	.976	3	102	149	*O-137(CF)	-2.6
1957	Det A	133	451	49	113	12	4	5	47	44-4	1	41	.251	.316	.328	75	-16	2-6	.982	-1	105	57	*O-128(CF)	-2.5
1958	KC A	148	511	77	118	14	9	11	51	74-1	1	58	.231	.327	.358	88	-8	7-9	.988	-4	93	125	*O-145(0-107-46)	-2.1
1959	KC A	126	463	74	139	19	6	7	43	48-2	4	38	.300	.369	.413	113	9	10-6	.984	9	103	**221**	*O-121(CF)	1.3
1960	KC A	151	559	75	143	21	3	8	40	66-2	2	52	.256	.336	.347	85	-11	1-5	.988	7	104	**177**	*O-148(CF)	-1.2
1961	KC A	25	84	15	22	2	2	0	8	9-0	0	9	.262	.333	.333	77	-3	0-0	.951	-2	102	0	O-25(CF)	-0.5
	Min A	113	370	38	91	12	3	5	38	43-4	0	41	.246	.321	.335	73	-14	1-3	.943	-3	97	93	3-85,O-64(0-63-6)/2-2	-1.9
	Year	138	454	53	113	14	5	5	46	52-4	0	50	.249	.323	.335	73	-17	1-3	.970	-4	103	35	O-89(0-88-6),3-85/2-2	-2.4
1962	Min A	110	123	21	26	4	1	1	13	19-1	1	14	.211	.317	.285	62	-6	1-0	.973	-1	94	123	*O-104(0-95-15)	-0.8
1963	Min A	16	3	0	0	0	0	0	0	1-1	0	0	.000	.250	.000	-22	0	0-0	1.000	1	156	823	O-14(CF)	0.1
Total	11	1270	4268	578	1105	149	47	67	443	480-18	13	416	.259	.334	.363	88	-67	38-44	.983	13	101	135	*O-1191(4-1139-67)/3-85,2-2	-11.1
TUTWILER, GUY Guy Isbel "King Tut" B 7.17.1888 Coalburg, AL D 8.15.1930 Birmingham, AL BL/TR 6/175# d8.29																								
1911	Det A	13	32	3	6	2	0	0	3	2	0		.188	.235	.250	34	-3	0	.778	-4	75	0	/2-6,O-3(LF)	-0.6
1913	Det A	14	47	4	10	0	1	0	7	4	0	12	.213	.275	.255	56	-3	2	.987	1	127	135	1-14	-0.3
Total	2	27	79	7	16	2	1	0	10	6	0	12	.203	.259	.253	47	-6	2	.987	-3	127	135	/1-14,2-6,O-3(LF)	-0.9
TWINEHAM, ART Arthur S. "Old Hoss" B 11.26.1866 Galesburg, IL BL/TL 6-1.5/190# d9.11																								
1893	StL N	14	48	8	15	2	0	0	11	1	1	2	.313	.340	.354	84	-1	0	.928	1	*85*	*120*	C-14	0.0
1894	StL N	38	127	22	40	4	1	1	16	9	6	11	.315	.387	.386	87	-2	2	.939	3	*106*	*103*	C-38	0.3
Total	2	52	175	30	55	6	1	1	27	10	7	13	.314	.375	.377	86	-3	2	.936	3	*100*	*107*	/C-52	0.3
TWITCHELL, LARRY Lawrence Grant B 2.18.1864 Cleveland, OH D 8.23.1930 Cleveland, OH BR/TR 6/185# d4.30 ▲																								
1886	Det N	4	16	0	1	0	0	0	0	0		2	.063	.063	.063	-60	-3	0	1.000	0	155	693	/P-4,O-2(1-1-0)	-0.1
1887	†Det N	65	264	44	88	14	6	0	51	8	2	19	.333	.358	.432	114	4	12	.871	-5	45	64	O-53(44-9-0),P-15	-0.2
1888	Det N	131	524	71	128	19	4	5	67	28	3	45	.244	.286	.324	93	-4	14	.885	-9	59	98	*O-131(LF)/P-2	-1.6
1889	Cle N	134	549	73	151	16	11	4	95	29	3	37	.275	.315	.366	92	-10	17	.916	-10	39	0	*O-134(LF)/P	-1.9
1890	Cle P	56	233	33	52	6	3	2	36	17	1	17	.223	.279	.300	60	-14	4	.821	-7	86	49	O-56(1-0-56)	-1.7
	Buf P	44	172	24	38	3	1	2	17	23	1	12	.221	.316	.285	67	-7	4	.918	1	64	90	O-32(4-0-28),P-13/1-3	-0.4
	Year	100	405	57	90	9	4	4	53	40	2	29	.222	.295	.294	63	-21	8	.857	-5	79	63	O-88(5-0-84),P-13/1-3	-2.1
1891	Col AA	57	224	32	62	9	4	2	35	20	2	28	.277	.341	.379	113	3	10	.887	-7	46	0	O-56(LF)/P-6	-0.4
1892	Was N	51	192	20	42	9	5	0	20	11	4	31	.219	.275	.318	82	-5	8	.897	-3	72	64	O-48(46-0-2)/S-3,3	-1.0
1893	Lou N	45	187	37	58	11	3	2	31	17	3	20	.310	.377	.433	125	7	7	.874	-2	77	0	O-45(43-0-2)	0.1
1894	Lou N	52	210	28	56	16	3	2	32	15	0	20	.267	.316	.400	77	-8	8	.908	7	179	189	O-51(LF)/P	-0.4
Total	9	639	2571	362	676	103	40	19	384	168	19	231	.263	.313	.356	91	-37	84	.890	-34	67	57	O-608(511-10-88)/P-42,S-3,1-3,3	-7.6
TWOMBLY, BABE Clarence Edward B 1.18.1896 Jamaica Plain, MA D 11.23.1974 San Clemente, CA BL/TR 5-10/165# d4.14 b-George																								
1920	Chi N	78	183	25	43	1	1	2	14	17	1	20	.235	.303	.284	68	-7	5-9	.970	0	101	107	O-45(5-15-25)/2-2	-1.3
1921	Chi N	87	175	22	66	8	1	1	18	11	0	10	.377	.414	.451	129	8	4-6	.968	4	94	220	O-45(10-29-6)	0.8
Total	2	165	358	47	109	9	2	3	32	28	1	30	.304	.357	.366	98	1	9-15	.969	4	98	158	/O-90(15-44-31),2-2	-0.5
TWOMBLY, GEORGE George Frederick "Silent George" B 6.4.1892 Boston, MA D 2.17.1975 Lexington, MA BR/TR 5-9/165# d7.9 b-Babe																								
1914	Cin N	68	240	22	56	0	5	0	19	14	3	27	.233	.284	.275	64	-11	12	.968	1	91	138	O-68(68-0-1)	-1.5
1915	Cin N	46	66	5	13	0	1	0	5	8	1	8	.197	.293	.227	57	-3	5-3	1.000	1	106	129	O-24(10-13-1)	-0.3
1916	Cin N	3	5	0	0	0	0	0	0	1	0	1	.000	.167	.000	-48	-1	0	1.000	-0	101	0	/O(LF)	-0.1
1917	Bos N	32	102	8	19	1	1	0	9	18	1	5	.186	.314	.216	68	-3	4	.943	-4	87	30	O-29(1-21-7)/1	-1.0
1919	Was A	1	4	0	0	0	0	0	0	0	0	0	.000	.000	.000	-99	-1	0	—	-0	0	0	/O(LF)	-0.1
Total	5	150	417	35	88	1	7	0	33	41	5	41	.211	.289	.247	62	-19	21-3	.967	-2	92	109	O-123(81-34-9)/1	-3.0
TYACK, JIM James Frederick B 1.9.1911 Florence, MT D 1.3.1995 Bakersfield, CA BL/TR 6-2/195# d4.20																								
1943	Phi A	54	155	11	40	8	1	0	23	14	0	9	.258	.320	.323	88	-2	1-1	.977	1	103	144	O-38(9-2-27)	-0.4
TYLER, FRED Frederick Franklin "Clancy" B 12.16.1891 Derry, NH D 10.14.1945 E.Derry, NH BR/TR 5-10.5/180# d10.3 b-Lefty																								
1914	Bos N	6	19	2	2	0	0	0	2	1	0	5	.105	.150	.105	-24	-3	0	1.000	-0	*117*	*107*	/C-6	-0.3
TYLER, JOHNNIE John Anthony "Ty Ty" or "Katz" (born John Tylka) B 7.30.1906 Mt.Pleasant, PA D 7.11.1972 Mt.Pleasant, PA BB/TR 6/175# d9.16																								
1934	Bos N	3	6	0	1	0	0	0	1	0	0	3	.167	.167	.167	-11	-1	0	1.000	1	82	989	/O(CF)	0.0
1935	Bos N	13	47	7	16	2	1	2	11	4	1	3	.340	.404	.553	168	4	0	.893	-0	100	127	O-11(LF)	0.3
Total	2	16	53	7	17	2	1	2	12	4	1	6	.321	.379	.509	148	3	0	.906	0	98	225	/O-12(11-1-0)	0.3
TYNER, JASON Jason Renyt B 4.23.1977 Bedford, TX BL/TL 6-1/170# d6.5																								
2000	NY N	13	41	3	8	2	0	0	5	1-0	1	4	.195	.222	.244	21	-5	1-1	.920	1	124	167	O-12(12-2-0)	-0.4
	TB A	37	83	6	20	2	0	0	8	4-0	1	12	.241	.281	.265	41	-8	6-1	1.000	2	97	286	O-31(27-4-0)/D	-0.5
2001	TB A	105	396	51	111	8	5	0	21	15-0	3	42	.280	.311	.326	69	-19	31-6	.978	4	106	147	*O-100(57-47-3)	-1.1
2002	TB A	44	168	17	36	2	1	0	9	7-0	1	19	.214	.249	.238	31	-17	7-1	.990	2	113	80	O-42(41-1-0)/D	-1.5
2003	TB A	46	90	12	25	7	0	0	6	10-0	0	12	.278	.350	.356	88	-1	2-1	.962	-0	101	72	O-32(9-2-23)/D-4	-0.2
Total	4	245	778	89	200	21	6	0	49	37-0	6	89	.257	.294	.299	58	-50	47-10	.978	9	107	142	O-217(146-56-26)/D-6	-3.7
TYREE, EARL Earl Carlton "Ty" B 3.4.1890 Huntsville, IL D 5.17.1954 Rushville, IL BR/TR 5-8/160# d10.5																								
1914	Chi N	1	4	1	0	0	0	0	0	0	0	0	.000	.000	.000	-99	-1	0	1.000	-1	*91*	*137*	/C	-0.2
TYRONE, JIM James Vernon B 1.29.1949 Alice, TX BR/TR 6-1/185# d8.27 b-Wayne																								
1972	Chi N	13	8	1	0	0	0	0	0	0-0	0	3	.000	.000	.000	-90	-2	1-0	1.000	1	180	839	/O-4(3-0-1)	-0.1
1974	Chi N	57	81	19	15	0	1	3	3	6-0	0	8	.185	.241	.321	54	-6	1-1	.962	-1	85	98	O-32(21-1-12)/3	-0.8
1975	Chi N	11	22	0	5	0	1	0	3	1-0	0	4	.227	.250	.318	58	-1	1-1	1.000	0	73	271	/O-8(LF)	-0.2
1977	Oak A	96	294	32	72	11	1	5	26	25-2	0	62	.245	.300	.340	76	-10	3-1	.950	1	107	90	O-81(10-4-70)/1SD	-1.3
Total	4	177	405	52	92	11	3	8	32	32-2	0	77	.227	.281	.328	67	-19	6-3	.955	1	103	113	O-125(42-5-83)/D-4,S13	-2.4
TYRONE, WAYNE Oscar Wayne B 8.1.1950 Alice, TX BR/TR 6-1/185# d7.15 b-Jim																								
1976	Chi N	30	57	3	13	1	0	1	8	3-2	0	21	.228	.262	.298	55	-3	0-0	1.000	-1	35	0	/O-7(6-0-1),1-5,3-5	-0.5
TYSON, TY Albert Thomas B 6.1.1892 Wilkes-Barre, PA D 8.16.1953 Buffalo, NY BR/TR 5-11/169# d4.13																								
1926	NY N	97	335	40	98	16	1	3	35	15	3	28	.293	.329	.373	90	-5	6	.980	1	99	105	O-92(12-83-0)	-0.9
1927	NY N	43	159	24	42	7	2	1	17	10	0	19	.264	.308	.352	76	-6	5	.929	-2	87	132	O-41(40-1-2)	-1.1
1928	Bro N	59	210	25	57	11	1	1	21	10	4	14	.271	.317	.348	75	-8	3	.965	-0	97	123	O-55(1-41-14)	-1.1
Total	3	199	704	89	197	34	4	5	73	35	7	61	.280	.320	.361	82	-19	14	.966	-1	96	116	O-188(53-125-16)	-3.1
TYSON, TURKEY Cecil Washington "Slim" B 12.6.1914 Elm City, NC D 2.17.2000 Elm City, NC BL/TR 6-5.5/225# d4.23																								
1944	Phi N	1	1	0	0	0	0	0	0	0	0	0	.000	.000	.000	-99	0	0	—	0			H	0.0
TYSON, MIKE Michael Ray B 1.13.1950 Rocky Mount, NC BR/TR (BB 1972, 76, 79, 80 (partS)) 5-9/170# d9.5																								
1972	StL N	13	37	1	7	1	0	0	0	1-0	0	9	.189	.211	.216	22	-4	0-1	.981	2	121	56	2-11/S-2	-0.2
1973	StL N	144	469	48	114	15	4	1	33	23-10	2	66	.243	.279	.299	61	-26	2-5	.944	-10	94	94	*S-128,2-16	-2.3
1974	StL N	151	422	35	94	14	5	1	37	22-9	3	70	.223	.264	.287	55	-27	4-2	.955	7	103	**145**	*S-143,2-12	-0.4
1975	StL N	122	368	45	98	16	3	2	37	24-4	3	39	.266	.316	.342	80	-10	5-2	.971	-8	91	83	S-95,2-24/3-5	-0.7
1976	StL N	76	245	26	70	12	9	3	28	16-5	0	34	.286	.326	.445	117	4	3-1	.971	10	116	113	2-74	1.9
1977	StL N	138	418	42	103	15	2	7	57	30-11	2	48	.246	.299	.342	73	-17	3-4	.979	24	**118**	**134**	*2-135	1.3
1978	StL N	125	377	26	88	16	0	3	26	24-7	0	41	.233	.277	.300	63	-19	2-0	.977	-8	90	**116**	*2-124	-2.2
1979	StL N	75	190	18	42	8	2	5	20	13-6	1	28	.221	.272	.363	72	-8	2-1	.975	2	106	120	2-71	-0.3
1980	Chi N	123	341	34	81	19	3	3	23	15-3	2	61	.238	.273	.337	65	-16	1-2	.968	10	106	103	*2-117	-0.2
1981	Chi N	50	92	6	17	2	0	2	8	7-1	1	15	.185	.248	.272	46	-7	1-0	.940	-3	97	85	2-36/S	-0.9
Total	10	1017	2959	281	714	118	28	27	269	175-56	14	411	.241	.285	.327	69	-130	23-18	.973	25	107	115	2-620,S-369/3-5	-4.0
UECKER, BOB Robert George B 1.26.1935 Milwaukee, WI BR/TR 6-1/190# d4.13																								
1962	Mil N	33	64	5	16	2	0	1	8	7-0	0	15	.250	.324	.328	78	-2	0-0	.982	3	*167*	*91*	C-24	0.2
1963	Mil N	13	16	3	4	2	0	0	0	2-0	0	5	.250	.333	.375	105	0	0-0	.958	0	*130*	*106*	/C-6	0.1
1964	StL N	40	106	8	21	1	0	1	6	17-0	1	24	.198	.315	.236	53	-6	0-1	.987	3	*116*	*107*	C-40	-0.2
1965	StL N	53	145	17	33	7	0	2	10	24-1	2	27	.228	.345	.317	80	-3	0-1	.985	-1	*87*	*132*	C-49	-0.2
1966	Phi N	78	207	15	43	6	0	7	30	22-6	0	36	.208	.279	.338	72	-8	0-0	.985	-0	*111*	*108*	C-76	-0.5

Year	Tm Lg	G	AB	R	H	2B	3B	HR	RBI	BB-IB	HP	SO	AVG	OBP	SLG	AOPS	ABR	SB-CS	FA	FR	Rng	Thr	G at Pos	BFW
1967	Phi N	18	35	3	6	2	0	0	7	5-1	0	9	.171	.275	.229	45	-2	0-0	.973	-0	*107*	*70*	C-17	-0.2
	Atl N	62	158	14	23	2	0	3	13	19-4	0	51	.146	.236	.215	31	-14	0-1	.972	-0	*87*	*119*	C-59	-1.4
	Year	80	193	17	29	4	0	3	20	24-5	0	60	.150	.243	.218	33	-17	0-1	.972	-0	*91*	*110*	C-76	-1.6
Total	6	297	731	65	146	22	0	14	74	96-12	3	167	.200	.293	.287	63	-35	0-3	.981	5	*106*	*112*	C-271	-2.2
UGUETO, LUIS Luis Enrique B 2.15.1979 Caracas, Venezuela BB/TR 5-11/170# d4.3																								
2002	Sea A	62	23	19	5	0	0	1	1	2-0	0	8	.217	.280	.348	68	-1	8-4	.960	2	118	119	D-16,2-11/S-8,3	0.0
2003	Sea A	12	5	4	1	0	0	0	1	1-0	0	0	.200	.333	.200	47	0	2-0	1.000	-0	98	334	/2-4,3SD	0.0
Total	2	74	28	23	6	0	0	1	2	3-0	0	8	.214	.290	.321	64	-1	10-4	.967	1	114	161	/D-19,2-15,S-9,3-2	0.0
UHALT, FRENCHY Bernard Bartholomew B 4.27.1910 Bakersfield, CA BL/TR 5-10/180# d4.17																								
1934	Chi A	57	165	28	40	5	1	0	16	29	1	12	.242	.359	.285	66	-7	6-5	.935	-2	96	62	O-40(4-14-22)	-1.1
UHLAENDER, TED Theodore Otto B 10.21.1940 Chicago Heights, IL BL/TR 6-2/190# d9.4 C2																								
1965	Min A	13	22	1	4	0	0	0	1	0-0	0	2	.182	.182	.182	3	-3	1-0	1.000	1	111	464	/O-4(LF)	-0.2
1966	Min A	105	367	39	83	12	2	2	22	27-1	1	33	.226	.280	.286	60	-19	10-2	.985	3	114	67	*O-100(4-96-0)	-1.9
1967	Min A	133	415	41	107	19	7	6	49	13-1	3	45	.258	.285	.381	88	-7	4-4	**.996**	2	107	95	*O-118(CF)	-1.1
1968	Min A	140	488	52	138	21	5	7	52	28-3	3	46	.283	.324	.389	110	5	16-7	.986	-7	96	36	*O-129(CF)	-0.5
1969	†Min A	152	554	93	151	18	2	8	62	44-4	4	52	.273	.328	.356	90	-8	15-9	.997	-8	89	85	*O-150(44-108-1)	-2.1
1970	Cle A	141	473	56	127	21	2	11	46	39-3	1	44	.268	.321	.391	92	-5	3-6	.991	-11	83	66	*O-134(24-116-8)	-2.3
1971	Cle A	141	500	52	144	20	3	2	47	38-5	0	44	.288	.336	.352	88	-7	3-6	.992	-1	99	79	*O-131(87-33-13)	-1.7
1972	†Cin N	73	113	9	18	3	0	0	6	13-3	0	11	.159	.246	.186	26	-11	0-1	.976	-0	86	185	O-27(3-2-23)	-1.4
Total	8	898	2932	343	772	114	21	36	285	202-20	12	277	.263	.311	.353	86	-55	52-35	.991	-21	97	76	O-793(166-602-45)	-11.2
UHLE, GEORGE George Ernest "The Bull" B 9.18.1898 Cleveland, OH D 2.26.1985 Lakewood, OH BR/TR 6/190# d4.30 C4 ▲																								
1919	Cle A	26	43	7	13	2	1	0	6	1	0	5	.302	.318	.395	94	3	0	.915	0	97	67	P-26	0.0
1920	†Cle A	27	32	4	11	0	0	0	2	2	0	2	.344	.382	.344	91	2	1-0	1.000	0	96	0	P-27	0.0
1921	Cle A	48	94	21	23	2	3	1	18	6	0	9	.245	.290	.362	64	3	0-0	.938	-3	75	102	P-41	0.0
1922	Cle A	56	109	21	29	8	2	0	14	13	1	6	.266	.350	.376	88	9	1-2	.932	-3	75	153	P-50	0.0
1923	Cle A	58	144	23	52	10	3	0	22	7	0	10	.361	.391	.472	127	17	2-1	.982	-0	96	184	P-54	0.0
1924	Cle A	59	107	10	33	6	1	1	19	4	1	8	.308	.339	.411	92	7	0-1	**1.000**	1	92	220	P-28	0.0
1925	Cle A	55	101	10	29	3	3	0	13	7	1	7	.287	.339	.376	81	6	0-0	.943	-3	72	80	P-29	0.0
1926	Cle A	50	132	16	30	3	0	1	11	10	1	12	.227	.287	.273	46	4	2-2	.933	-0	84	77	P-39	0.0
1927	Cle A	43	79	4	21	7	1	0	14	5	0	12	.266	.310	.380	78	5	0-1	.974	-1	82	159	P-25	0.0
1928	Cle A	55	98	9	28	3	2	1	17	8	0	4	.286	.340	.388	90	7	0-0	.972	2	122	127	P-31	0.0
1929	Det A	40	108	18	37	1	1	0	13	6	0	6	.343	.377	.370	93	8	0-0	.929	-3	73	64	P-32	0.0
1930	Det A	59	117	15	36	4	2	2	21	8	0	13	.308	.352	.427	95	8	0-0	.975	-3	60	75	P-33	0.0
1931	Det A	53	90	8	22	6	0	2	7	8	0	8	.244	.306	.378	76	5	0-1	**1.000**	-1	97	47	P-29	0.0
1932	Det A	38	55	2	10	3	1	0	4	6	0	5	.182	.262	.273	37	1	0-0	1.000	-1	84	111	P-33	0.0
1933	Det A	1	0	0	0	0	0	0	0	0	0	0	—	—	—	—	0	0-0	—	0	0	0	/P	0.0
	NY N	8	5	1	0	0	0	0	0	1	0	3	.000	.167	.000	-50	0	0	1.000	0	130	0	/P-6	0.0
	NY A	12	20	1	8	1	0	0	1	4	0	2	.400	.500	.450	163	4	0-0	1.000	-1	69	137	P-12	0.0
1934	NY A	10	5	1	3	0	1	0	1	0	0	0	.600	.600	1.000	329	2	0-0	1.000	-0	32	0	P-10	0.0
1936	Cle A	24	21	1	8	1	0	1	4	2	0	0	.381	.435	.571	145	4	0-0	—	-1	0	0	/P-7	0.0
Total	17	722	1360	172	393	60	21	9	187	98	4	112	.289	.339	.384	86	95	6-8	.960	-16	84	111	P-513	0.0
UHLER, MAURY Maurice William B 12.14.1886 Pikesville, MD D 5.4.1918 Baltimore, MD BR/TR 5-11/165# d4.14																								
1914	Cin N	46	56	12	12	2	0	0	3	5	0	11	.214	.279	.250	56	-3	4	.932	0	118	47	O-36(22-11-3)	-0.4
UHLIR, CHARLIE Charles Karel B 7.30.1912 Chicago, IL D 7.9.1984 Spirit Lake, IA BL/TL 5-7.5/150# d8.3																								
1934	Chi A	14	27	3	4	0	0	0	3	2	0	6	.148	.207	.148	-7	-4	0-0	1.000	-0	96	0	/O-6(LF)	-0.5
ULISNEY, MIKE Michael Edward "Slugs" B 9.28.1917 Greenwald, PA BR/TR 5-9/165# d5.5																								
1945	Bos N	11	18	4	7	1	0	1	4	1	0	0	.389	.421	.611	184	2	0	.714	-1	*92*	*165*	/C-4	0.1
ULLGER, SCOTT Scott Matthew B 6.10.1956 New York, NY BR/TR 6-2/186# d4.17 C9																								
1983	Min A	35	79	8	15	4	0	0	5	5-0	1	21	.190	.247	.241	34	-7	0-2	.990	-2	57	69	1-30/3-3,D	-1.1
ULRICH, GEORGE George T. B 6.5.1869 Philadelphia, PA d5.1																								
1892	Was N	6	24	1	7	1	0	0	0	0	0	4	.292	.292	.333	91	0	2	.889	0	71	0	/3-3,S-2,C-2	0.0
1893	Cin N	1	3	0	0	0	0	0	0	0	1	0	.000	.250	.000	-31	-1	1	1.000	-0	0	0	/O(CF)	-0.1
1896	NY N	14	45	4	8	1	0	0	1	1	2	1	.178	.229	.200	14	-6	0	.920	-0	191	249	O-11(LF)/3-3	-0.6
Total	3	21	72	5	15	2	0	0	1	1	3	5	.208	.250	.236	35	-7	3	.923	-0	180	234	/O-12(11-1-0),3-6,C-2,S-2	-0.7
UMPHLETT, TOM Thomas Mullen B 5.12.1930 Scotland Neck, NC BR/TR 6-2/180# d4.16																								
1953	Bos A	137	495	53	140	27	5	3	59	34	2	30	.283	.331	.376	86	-10	4-2	.983	-1	100	100	*O-136(CF)	-1.7
1954	Was A	114	342	21	75	8	3	1	33	17	0	42	.219	.255	.269	46	-27	1-2	.989	3	92	190	*O-101(12-4-86)	-3.0
1955	Was A	110	323	34	70	10	0	2	19	24-0	0	35	.217	.271	.266	47	-25	2-1	.988	5	108	128	*O-103(18-62-23)	-2.5
Total	3	361	1160	108	285	45	8	6	111	75-0	2	107	.246	.292	.314	65	-62	7-5	.986	7	100	133	O-340(30-202-109)	-7.2
UNGLAUB, BOB Robert Alexander B 7.31.1881 Baltimore, MD D 11.29.1916 Baltimore, MD BR/TR 5-11/178# d4.15 M1 OF Total (8-LF 34-RF)																								
1904	NY A	6	19	2	4	0	0	0	2	0	0		.211	.211	.211	32	-2	0	.786	-1	88	290	/3-4,S	-0.3
	Bos A	9	13	1	2	1	0	0	2	1	0		.154	.214	.231	39	-1	0	.625	-2	21	0	/2-3,3-2,S	-0.4
	Year	15	32	3	6	1	0	0	4	1	0		.188	.212	.219	35	-2	0	.842	-3	85	218	/3-6,2-3,S-2	-0.7
1905	Bos A	43	121	18	27	5	1	0	11	6	0		.223	.260	.281	71	-4	2	.928	-1	102	131	3-21/2-7,1-2	-0.5
1907	Bos A	139	544	49	138	17	13	1	62	23	0		.254	.284	.338	99	-3	14	.986	-1	96	117	*1-139,M	-0.8
1908	Bos A	72	266	23	70	11	3	1	25	7	2		.263	.287	.338	100	-1	6	.980	2	112	69	1-72	-0.1
	Was A	72	276	23	85	10	5	0	29	8	0		.308	.327	.380	142	11	8	.928	6	115	43	3-39,2-27/1-4	2.0
	Year	144	542	46	155	21	8	1	54	15	2		.286	.308	.360	120	9	14	.981	7	115	78	1-76,3-39,2-27	1.9
1909	Was A	130	480	43	127	14	9	3	41	22	3		.265	.301	.350	111	3	15	.992	2	109	111	1-57,O-42(8-0-34),2-25/3-4	0.3
1910	Was A	124	431	29	101	9	4	0	44	21	0		.234	.270	.274	74	-15	21	.985	6	119	99	*1-124	-1.2
Total	6	595	2150	188	554	67	35	5	216	88	5		.258	.288	.328	99	-12	66	.986	10	108	103	1-398/3-70,2-62,O-42R,S-2	-1.0
UNROE, TIM Timothy Brian B 10.7.1970 Round Lake Beach, IL BR/TR 6-3/200# d5.30																								
1995	Mil A	2	4	0	1	0	0	0	0	0-0	0	0	.250	.250	.250	29	0	0-0	1.000	-0	0	233	/1-2	-0.1
1996	Mil A	14	16	5	3	0	0	0	0	4-0	0	5	.188	.350	.188	40	-1	0-1	.976	2	0	117	1-11/3-3,O(LF)D	0.0
1997	Mil A	32	16	3	4	1	0	2	5	2-0	0	9	.250	.333	.688	156	1	2-0	.969	1	129	88	1-23/3-2,O-2(1-0-1),2	0.2
1999	Ana A	27	54	5	13	2	0	1	6	4-0	1	16	.241	.305	.333	63	-3	0-0	1.000	-2	67	150	O-12(4-0-8)/3-3,2D	-0.5
2000	Atl N	4	5	0	0	0	0	0	0	1-0	0	2	.000	.167	.000	-53	-1	0-0	1.000	1	278	0	/1-2,O(LF)	-0.1
Total	5	79	95	13	21	3	0	3	11	11-0	1	32	.221	.308	.347	67	-4	2-1	.977	1	92	104	/1-38,O-16(7-0-9),D-9,3-8,2-2	-0.5
UNSER, AL Albert Bernard B 10.12.1912 Morrisonville, IL D 7.7.1995 Decatur, IL BR/TR 6-1/175# d9.14 s-Del																								
1942	Det A	4	8	2	3	0	0	0	0	0	0	2	.375	.375	.375	103	0	0-0	1.000	1	*110*	*130*	/C-4	0.1
1943	Det A	38	101	14	25	5	0	0	4	15	1	15	.248	.350	.297	84	-1	0-1	.982	-1	*90*	*113*	C-37	0.0
1944	Det A	11	25	2	3	0	1	1	5	3	0	2	.120	.214	.320	49	-2	0-0	.864	-3	57	66	/2-5,C	-0.5
1945	Cin N	67	204	23	54	10	3	3	21	14	2	24	.265	.318	.387	98	-1	0	.956	-2	*86*	*85*	C-61	0.0
Total	4	120	338	41	85	15	4	4	30	32	3	43	.251	.322	.355	90	-4	0-1	.967	-5	*88*	*95*	C-103/2-5	-0.4
UNSER, DEL Delbert Bernard B 12.9.1944 Decatur, IL BL/TL 6-1/180# d4.10 C4 f-Al																								
1968	Was A	156	635	66	146	13	7	1	30	46-1	2	66	.230	.282	.277	73	-22	11-6	.988	10	100	**200**	*O-156(CF)/1	-1.9
1969	Was A	153	581	69	166	19	**8**	7	57	58-3	0	54	.286	.349	.382	111	7	8-10	.972	-3	102	89	*O-149(CF)	0.0
1970	Was A	119	322	37	83	5	1	5	30	30-3	0	29	.258	.319	.326	83	-8	1-1	.984	3	102	151	*O-103(11-43-50)	-0.9
1971	Was A	153	581	63	148	19	6	9	41	59-10	2	68	.255	.325	.355	98	-2	11-6	.981	10	113	103	*O-151(8-105-68)	0.2
1972	Cle A	132	383	29	91	12	0	1	17	28-4	1	46	.238	.288	.277	67	-15	5-9	.989	4	104	146	*O-119(14-85-23)	-1.9
1973	Phi N	136	440	64	127	20	4	11	52	47-7	1	55	.289	.354	.427	114	9	5-8	.988	14	**119**	**194**	*O-132(CF)	1.9
1974	Phi N	142	454	72	120	18	5	11	61	50-9	1	62	.264	.337	.399	101	1	6-4	.981	1	98	173	*O-135(CF)	-0.2
1975	NY N	147	531	65	156	18	2	10	53	37-6	0	76	.294	.337	.392	107	3	4-3	.987	9	109	158	*O-144(CF)	0.9
1976	NY N	77	276	28	63	13	2	5	25	18-1	1	40	.228	.275	.344	80	-8	4-4	.995	-1	98	112	O-77(2-75-0)	-1.3

Year	Tm Lg	G	AB	R	H	2B	3B	HR	RBI	BB-IB	HP	SO	AVG	OBP	SLG	AOPS	ABR	SB-CS	FA	FR	Rng	Thr	G at Pos	BFW
	Mon N	69	220	29	50	6	2	7	15	11-1	0	44	.227	.261	.368	75	-9	3-3	.983	-2	89	116	O-65(29-13-34)	-1.4
	Year	146	496	57	113	19	4	12	40	29-2	1	84	.228	.269	.355	78	-17	7-7	.990	-3	94	114	*O-142(31-88-34)	-2.7
1977	Mon N	113	289	33	79	14	1	12	40	33-7	0	41	.273	.346	.453	116	7	2-5	.976	-6	86	45	O-72(11-34-27),1-27	-0.4
1978	Mon N	130	179	16	35	5	0	2	15	24-5	1	29	.196	.293	.257	56	-10	2-0	.994	2	93	111	1-64,O-33(7-12-14)	-1.0
1979	Phi N	95	141	26	42	8	0	6	29	14-2	0	33	.298	.354	.482	124	5	2-0	.978	-1	102	0	O-30(16-11-3),1-22	0.3
1980	†Phi N	96	110	15	29	6	4	0	10	10-1	0	21	.264	.320	.391	94	-1	0-1	1.000	5	268	114	1-31,O-23(13-12-1)	0.3
1981	Phi N	62	59	5	9	3	0	0	6	13-1	0	9	.153	.301	.203	45	-4	0-0	1.000	1	146	96	1-18,O-16(7-6-4)	-0.3
1982	Phi N	19	14	0	0	0	0	0	0	3-1	0	2	.000	.176	.000	-46	-3	0-0	1.000	0	177	171	/1-5,O-2(RF)	-0.3
Total	15	1799	5215	617	1344	179	42	87	481	481-62	9	675	.258	.319	.358	93	-50	64-60	.984	46	104	136	*O-1407(118-1112-226),1-168	-6.0
UPHAM, JOHN John Leslie B 12.29.1941 Windsor, ON, CAN BL/TL 6/180# d4.16																								
1967	Chi N	8	3	1	2	0	0	0	0	0-0	0	0	.667	.667	.667	270	1	0-0	—	0	0	0	/P-5	0.0
1968	Chi N	13	10	0	2	0	0	0	0	0-0	0	3	.200	.200	.200	19	-1	0-0	1.000	0	262	0	/P-2,O-2(1-1-0)	0.0
Total	2	21	13	1	4	0	0	0	0	0-0	0	3	.308	.308	.308	78	0	0-0	1.000	0	229	0	/P-7,O-2(1-1-0)	0.0
UPRIGHT, DIXIE Roy T. B 5.30.1926 Kannapolis, NC D 11.13.1986 Concord, NC BL/TL 6/175# d4.18																								
1953	StL A	9	8	3	2	0	0	1	1	1	0	3	.250	.333	.625	151	0	0-0	—	0			H	0.0
UPSHAW, WILLIE Willie Clay B 4.27.1957 Blanco, TX BL/TL 6/185# d4.9 C4																								
1978	Tor A	95	224	26	53	8	2	1	17	21-0	0	35	.237	.298	.304	69	-9	4-6	.943	-5	86	68	O-52(46-6-1),D-18,1-10	-1.9
1980	Tor A	34	61	10	13	3	1	1	5	6-1	0	14	.213	.284	.344	68	-3	1-0	.983	1	160	178	1-14,D-12/O(LF)	-0.3
1981	Tor A	61	111	15	19	3	1	4	10	11-0	1	16	.171	.252	.324	61	-6	2-1	1.000	-1	105	119	D-15,1-14,O-14(6-0-8)	-0.8
1982	Tor A	160	580	77	155	25	7	21	75	52-8	1	91	.267	.327	.443	100	-1	8-8	.989	-6	89	95	*1-155/D-5	-1.7
1983	Tor A	160	579	99	177	26	7	27	104	61-8	5	98	.306	.373	.515	134	27	10-7	.985	-2	98	95	*1-159/D	1.5
1984	Tor A	152	569	79	158	31	9	19	84	55-14	5	86	.278	.345	.464	118	14	10-4	.990	-8	84	105	*1-151/D	-0.3
1985	†Tor A	148	501	79	138	31	5	15	65	48-7	4	71	.275	.342	.447	112	8	8-8	.992	-0	100	106	*1-147/D	-0.1
1986	Tor A	155	573	85	144	28	6	9	60	78-4	2	87	.251	.341	.368	91	-5	23-5	.992	4	107	95	*1-154/D	-0.8
1987	Tor A	150	512	68	125	22	4	15	58	58-4	3	78	.244	.324	.391	87	-10	10-11	.993	13	**129**	107	*1-146	-0.7
1988	Cle A	149	493	58	121	22	3	11	50	62-4	2	66	.245	.330	.369	94	-3	12-9	.991	2	108	81	*1-144	-1.1
Total	10	1264	4203	596	1103	199	45	123	528	452-50	23	642	.262	.335	.419	102	12	88-59	.990	-2	102	98	*1-1094/O-67(53-6-9),D-54	-6.2
UPTON, TOM Thomas Herbert "Muscles" B 12.29.1926 Esther, MO BR/TR 6/160# d4.19 b-Bill																								
1950	StL A	124	389	50	92	5	6	2	30	52	1	45	.237	.328	.296	58	-25	7-2	.946	-9	103	73	*S-115/2-2,3	-2.5
1951	StL A	52	131	9	26	4	3	0	12	12	1	22	.198	.271	.275	46	-10	1-1	.949	-4	93	100	S-47	-1.2
1952	Was A	5	5	1	0	0	0	0	0	1	0	0	.000	.167	.000	-53	-1	0-0	1.000	1	156	85	/S-3	0.0
Total	3	181	525	60	118	9	9	2	42	65	2	67	.225	.313	.288	55	-36	8-3	.948	-12	101	80	S-165/2-2,3	-3.7
URBAN, LUKE Louis John B 3.22.1898 Fall River, MA D 12.7.1980 Somerset, MA BR/TR 5-8/168# d7.19																								
1927	Bos N	35	111	11	32	5	0	0	10	3	1	6	.288	.313	.333	79	-3	1	.947	-4	*98*	*172*	C-34	-0.5
1928	Bos N	15	17	0	3	0	0	0	2	0	1	1	.176	.222	.176	6	-2	0	1.000	0	*92*	*202*	C-10	-0.2
Total	2	50	128	11	35	5	0	0	12	3	2	7	.273	.301	.313	69	-5	1	.955	-4	*97*	*176*	/C-44	-0.7
URBANSKI, BILLY William Michael B 6.5.1903 Linoleumville, NY D 7.12.1973 Perth Amboy, NJ BR/TR 5-8/165# d7.4																								
1931	Bos N	82	303	22	72	13	4	0	17	10	5	32	.238	.274	.307	58	-19	3	.961	6	111	131	3-68,S-19	-0.9
1932	Bos N	136	563	80	153	25	8	8	46	28	1	60	.272	.307	.387	89	-11	8	.946	-6	98	107	*S-136	-0.6
1933	Bos N	144	566	65	142	21	4	0	35	33	5	48	.251	.298	.302	78	-17	4	.953	-5	101	108	*S-143	-1.2
1934	Bos N	146	605	104	177	30	6	7	53	56	5	37	.293	.357	.397	110	9	4	**.961**	-10	98	101	*S-146	1.0
1935	Bos N	132	514	53	118	17	0	4	30	40	1	32	.230	.286	.286	59	-30	3	.939	-22	94	69	*S-129	-4.2
1936	Bos N	122	494	55	129	17	5	0	26	31	4	42	.261	.310	.316	74	-19	2	.937	-12	87	114	S-80,3-38	-2.4
1937	Bos N	1	1	0	0	0	0	0	0	0	0	1	.000	.000	.000	-99	0	0	—	0			H	0.0
Total	7	763	3046	379	791	123	27	19	207	198	21	252	.260	.309	.337	81	-87	24	.949	-49	96	99	S-653,3-106	-8.3
URIBE, JOSE Jose Altagracia (Played Under Real Name Of Jose Altagracia Gonzalez (Uribe) In 1984) B 1.21.1959 San Cristobal, D.R. BB/TR (BR 1984, 89 (part)) 5-10/165# d9.13																								
1984	StL N	8	19	4	4	0	0	0	3	0-0	0	2	.211	.211	.211	19	-2	1-0	.955	-0	99	149	/S-5,2	-0.2
1985	SF N	147	476	46	113	20	4	3	26	30-8	2	57	.237	.285	.315	71	-20	8-2	.961	-1	98	91	*S-145/2	-0.5
1986	SF N	157	453	46	101	15	1	3	43	61-19	0	76	.223	.315	.280	69	-18	22-11	.977	13	103	118	*S-156	1.2
1987	†SF N	95	309	44	90	16	5	5	30	24-9	1	35	.291	.343	.424	107	3	12-2	.971	9	105	121	S-95	2.2
1988	SF N	141	493	47	124	10	7	3	35	36-10	0	69	.252	.301	.318	82	-13	14-10	.970	-6	98	108	*S-140	-1.0
1989	†SF N	151	453	34	100	12	6	1	30	34-12	0	74	.221	.273	.280	61	-24	6-6	.973	17	**113**	**130**	*S-150	0.3
1990	SF N	138	415	35	103	8	6	1	24	29-13	0	49	.248	.297	.304	68	-19	5-9	.965	9	**113**	**113**	*S-134	-0.4
1991	SF N	90	231	23	51	8	4	1	12	20-6	0	33	.221	.283	.303	67	-11	3-4	.966	-0	105	98	S-87	-0.6
1992	SF N	66	162	24	39	9	1	2	13	14-3	0	25	.241	.299	.346	88	-3	2-2	.971	4	107	138	S-62	0.5
1993	Hou N	45	53	4	13	1	0	0	3	8-4	1	5	.245	.355	.264	71	-2	1-0	.944	2	92	187	S-41	0.1
Total	10	1038	3064	307	738	99	34	19	219	256-84	4	425	.241	.300	.314	75	-109	74-46	.969	47	105	115	*S-1015/2-2	1.6
URIBE, JUAN Juan C. (Tena) B 7.22.1979 Bani, D.R. BR/TR 5-11/173# d4.8																								
2001	Col N	72	273	32	82	15	11	8	53	8-1	2	55	.300	.325	.524	93	-3	3-0	.983	-5	92	103	S-69	-0.2
2002	Col N	155	566	69	136	25	7	6	49	34-1	5	120	.240	.286	.341	59	-36	9-2	.966	27	114	115	*S-155	0.4
2003	Col N	87	316	45	80	19	3	10	33	17-0	3	60	.253	.297	.427	76	-12	7-2	.972	27	121	118	S-74,2-11/O(CF)	2.2
Total	3	314	1155	146	298	59	21	24	135	59-2	10	235	.258	.298	.408	72	-51	19-4	.971	49	110	113	S-298/2-11,O(CF)	2.4
URY, LON Louis Newton "Old Sleep" B 1877 Ft.Scott, KS D 3.4.1918 Kansas City, MO TR 6/?# d9.9																								
1903	StL N	2	7	0	1	0	0	0	0	0	0		.143	.143	.143	-19	-1	0	1.000	0	88	95	/1-2	-0.1
USHER, BOB Robert Royce B 3.1.1925 San Diego, CA BR/TR 6-1.5/180# d4.16																								
1946	Cin N	92	152	16	31	5	1	1	14	13	1	27	.204	.271	.270	56	-9	2	.982	3	100	190	O-80(23-32-25)/3	-0.8
1947	Cin N	9	22	2	4	0	0	1	1	2	0	2	.182	.250	.318	50	-2	0	1.000	1	116	249	/O-8(3-5-0)	-0.1
1950	Cin N	106	321	51	83	17	0	6	35	27	0	38	.259	.316	.368	79	-10	3	.985	-1	96	108	O-93(4-80-12)	-1.3
1951	Cin N	114	303	27	63	12	2	5	25	19	1	36	.208	.257	.310	51	-22	4-5	.974	2	102	125	O-98(14-82-2)	-2.4
1952	Chi N	1	0	0	0	0	0	0	0	1	0	0	—	1.000	—	197	0	0-0	—	0			H	0.0
1957	Cle A	10	8	1	1	0	0	0	0	1-0	0	3	.125	.222	.125	-3	-1	0-0	1.000	-0	102	0	/O-4(1-3-0),3	-0.2
	Was A	96	295	36	77	7	1	5	27	27-2	2	30	.261	.324	.342	84	-7	0-0	.979	2	105	116	O-95(1-93-2)	-0.9
	Year	106	303	37	78	7	1	5	27	28-2	2	33	.257	.321	.337	82	-8	0-0	.979	2	105	114	O-99(2-96-2)/3	-1.1
Total	6	428	1101	133	259	41	4	18	102	90-2	4	136	.235	.295	.329	69	-51	9-5	.980	7	101	129	O-378(46-295-41)/3-2	-5.7
USSAT, DUTCH William August B 4.11.1904 Dayton, OH D 5.29.1959 Dayton, OH BR/TR 6-1/170# d9.13																								
1925	Cle A	1	1	0	0	0	0	0	0	0	0	0	.000	.000	.000	-99	0	0-0	1.000	0	142	0	/2	0.0
1927	Cle A	4	16	4	3	0	1	0	2	2	0	1	.188	.278	.313	53	-1	0-0	1.000	-0	82	134	/3-4	-0.1
Total	2	5	17	4	3	0	1	0	2	2	0	1	.176	.263	.294	44	-1	0-0	1.000	-0	82	134	/3-4,2	-0.1
UTLEY, CHASE Chase Cameron B 12.17.1978 Pasadena, CA BL/TR 6-1/170# d4.4																								
2003	Phi N	43	134	13	32	10	1	2	21	11-0	6	22	.239	.322	.373	87	-2	2-0	.983	3	106	134	2-37	0.2
VACHE, TEX Ernest Lewis B 11.17.1889 Santa Monica, CA D 6.11.1953 Los Angeles, CA BR/TR 6-1/200# d4.16																								
1925	Bos A	110	252	41	79	15	7	3	48	21	7	33	.313	.382	.464	114	5	2-2	.908	-7	84	37	O-53(52-0-1)	-0.6
VADEBONCOEUR, GENE Onesime Eugene B 7.15.1858 Louiseville, PQ, CAN D 10.16.1935 Haverhill, MA BR/TR 5-6/150# d7.11																								
1884	Phi N	4	14	1	3	0	0	0	3	1		2	.214	.267	.214	56	-1		.846	-1			/C-4	-0.1
VAHRENHORST, HARRY Harry Henry "Van" B 2.13.1885 St.Louis, MO D 10.10.1943 St.Louis, MO BR/TR 6-1/175# d9.21																								
1904	StL A	1	1	0	0	0	0	0	0	0	0		.000	.000	.000	-99	0	0	—	0			H	0.0
VAIL, MIKE Michael Lewis B 11.10.1951 San Francisco, CA BR/TR 6/185# d8.18																								
1975	NY N	38	162	17	49	8	1	3	17	9-1	0	37	.302	.339	.420	115	3	0-0	.971	9	127	315	O-36(35-1-0)	0.9
1976	NY N	53	143	8	31	5	1	0	9	6-0	0	19	.217	.243	.266	49	-10	0-1	.941	-1	103	40	O-35(2-0-33)	-1.5
1977	NY N	108	279	29	73	12	1	8	35	19-0	2	58	.262	.310	.398	94	-3	0-7	.965	5	123	98	O-85(2-0-83)	-0.4
1978	Cle A	14	34	2	8	2	1	0	2	1-1	0	9	.235	.250	.353	71	-1	1-1	1.000	1	142	0	/O-9(2-0-7),D	-0.1

Year	Tm Lg	G	AB	R	H	2B	3B	HR	RBI	BB-IB	HP	SO	AVG	OBP	SLG	AOPS	ABR	SB-CS	FA	FR	Rng	Thr	G at Pos	BFW
	Chi N	74	180	15	60	6	2	4	33	3-0	0	24	.333	.341	.456	109	1	0-1	.981	-5	74	34	O-45(7-0-39)/3	-0.6
1979	Chi N	87	179	28	60	8	2	7	35	14-1	0	27	.335	.379	.520	131	8	0-2	.964	-3	81	112	O-39(1-0-38)/3-2	0.3
1980	Chi N	114	312	30	93	17	2	6	47	14-1	1	77	.298	.330	.423	101	0	2-5	.963	-1	101	91	O-77(19-0-61)	-0.5
1981	Cin N	31	31	1	5	0	0	0	3	0-0	0	9	.161	.161	.161	-8	-4	0-0	1.000	0	130	0	/O-3(RF)	-0.5
1982	Cin N	78	189	9	48	10	1	4	29	6-1	0	33	.254	.274	.381	81	-6	0-0	.988	3	95	227	O-52(50-0-2)	-0.4
1983	SF N	18	26	1	4	1	0	0	3	0-0	1	7	.154	.185	.192	5	-3	0-0	1.000	-1	0	0	/1-4,O-2(LF)	-0.5
	Mon N	34	53	5	15	2	0	2	4	8-0	1	10	.283	.387	.434	128	2	0-0	.958	2	91	501	O-15(3-0-12)/13	0.4
	Year	52	79	6	19	3	0	2	7	8-0	2	17	.241	.326	.354	90	-1	0-0	.960	1	88	463	O-17(5-0-12)/1-5,3	-0.1
1984	LA N	16	16	1	1	0	0	0	2	1-0	0	7	.063	.118	.063	-49	-3	0-0	—	-0	0	0	/O(LF)	-0.4
Total	10	665	1604	146	447	71	11	34	219	81-5	5	317	.279	.313	.400	95	-16	3-17	.968	10	103	137	O-399(124-1-278)/1-5,3-4,D	-3.3
VALDERRAMA, CARLOS Carlos Alberto B 11.30.1977 Bachaquero, Venezuela BR/TR 6/180# d6.21																								
2003	SF N	7	7	0	1	0	0	0	0	0-0	0	3	.143	.143	.143	-26	-1	1-0	1.000	0	147	0	/O-5(4-2-0),D	-0.1
VALDES, PEDRO Pedro Jose (Manzo) B 6.29.1973 Fajardo, P.R. BL/TL 6-1/180# d5.15																								
1996	Chi N	9	8	2	1	1	0	0	1	1-0	0	5	.125	.222	.250	24	-1	0-0	1.000	0	150	0	/O-2(RF)	-0.1
1998	Chi N	14	23	1	5	1	1	0	2	1-0	0	3	.217	.250	.348	53	-2	0-1	1.000	0	134	0	/O-7(6-0-1)	-0.2
2000	Tex A	30	54	4	15	5	0	1	5	6-0	0	7	.278	.350	.426	94	0	0-0	1.000	-1	92	0	O-14(1-0-13)/D-5	-0.1
Total	3	53	85	7	21	7	1	1	8	8-0	0	15	.247	.312	.388	77	-3	0-1	1.000	-0	106	0	/O-23(7-0-16),D-5	-0.4
VALDES, ROY Rogelio Lazaro (Rojas) B 2.20.1920 Havana, Cuba BR/TR 5-11/185# d5.3																								
1944	Was A	1	1	0	0	0	0	0	0	0-0	0	0	.000	.000	.000	-99	0	0-0	—	0			H	0.0
VALDESPINO, SANDY Hilario (Borroto) B 1.14.1939 San Jose De Las Lajas, Cuba BL/TL 5-8/170# d4.12																								
1965	†Min A	108	245	38	64	8	2	1	22	20-3	2	28	.261	.319	.322	80	-6	7-4	.990	3	105	129	O-57(43-0-17)	-0.7
1966	Min A	52	108	11	19	1	1	2	9	4-0	1	24	.176	.211	.259	33	-10	2-2	1.000	-0	103	0	O-23(22-1-0)	-1.3
1967	Min A	99	97	9	16	2	0	1	3	5-1	0	22	.165	.204	.216	23	-9	3-1	.977	1	96	186	O-65(64-0-1)	-1.0
1968	Atl N	36	86	8	20	1	0	1	4	10-5	1	20	.233	.320	.279	81	-2	0-0	.976	-0	112	0	O-20(LF)	-0.4
1969	Hou N	41	119	17	29	4	0	0	12	15-0	0	19	.244	.326	.277	73	-4	2-2	.976	1	91	228	O-29(LF)	-0.5
	Sea A	20	38	3	8	1	0	0	2	1-0	1	7	.211	.250	.237	37	-3	0-1	.889	2	166	177	/O-7(LF)	-0.2
1970	Mil A	8	9	0	0	0	0	0	0	0-0	0	4	.000	.000	.000	-99	-2	0-0	—	-0	0	0	/O(LF)	-0.3
1971	KC A	18	63	10	20	6	0	2	15	2-0	0	5	.317	.338	.508	138	3	0-0	.950	-2	65	109	O-15(13-0-2)	0.0
Total	7	382	765	96	176	23	3	7	67	57-9	5	129	.230	.286	.295	66	-33	14-10	.974	4	101	121	O-217(199-1-20)	-4.4
VALDEZ, JULIO Julio Julian (born Julio Julian Castillo (Valdez) B 6.3.1956 San Cristobal, D.R. BB/TR (BR 1980) 6-2/160# d9.2																								
1980	Bos A	8	19	4	5	1	0	1	4	0-0	1	5	.263	.300	.474	103	0	2-0	.935	4	132	225	/S-8	0.5
1981	Bos A	17	23	1	5	0	0	0	3	0-0	0	2	.217	.208	.217	24	-2	0-1	.955	0	114	54	S-17	-0.1
1982	Bos A	28	20	3	5	1	0	0	1	0-0	0	7	.250	.250	.300	48	-1	1-0	.976	1	102	108	S-22/D-3	0.1
1983	Bos A	12	25	3	3	0	0	0	0	1-0	1	4	.120	.185	.120	-13	-4	0-0	.939	-3	74	57	/2-9,S-2,D	-0.7
Total	4	65	87	11	18	2	0	1	8	1-0	2	18	.207	.231	.264	36	-7	3-1	.955	3	115	120	/S-49,2-9,D-4	-0.2
VALDEZ, MARIO Mario A. B 11.19.1974 Obregon, Mexico BL/TL 6-2/190# d6.15																								
1997	Chi A	54	115	11	28	7	0	1	13	17-0	3	39	.243	.350	.330	84	-2	1-0	1.000	-4	51	62	1-47/3D	-0.9
2000	Oak A	5	12	0	0	0	0	0	0	0-0	0	3	.000	.000	.000	-99	-4	0-0	1.000	0	96	68	/1-4	-0.4
2001	Oak A	32	54	7	15	1	0	1	8	12-1	1	18	.278	.418	.352	106	1	0-0	1.000	0	98	312	D-12/O-7(LF),1-6	0.0
Total	3	91	181	18	43	8	0	2	21	29-1	4	60	.238	.352	.315	79	-5	1-0	1.000	-4	53	67	/1-57,D-14,O-7(LF),3	-1.3
VALDIVIELSO, JOSE Jose (Lopez) (born Jose Martinez De Valdivielso (Lopez)) B 5.22.1934 Matanzas, Cuba BR/TR 6-1/175# d6.21																								
1955	Was A	94	294	32	65	12	5	2	28	21-1	3	38	.221	.277	.316	63	-17	1-2	.956	11	110	106	S-94	0.1
1956	Was A	90	246	18	58	8	2	4	29	29-1	1	36	.236	.318	.333	72	-10	3-1	.947	9	110	97	S-90	0.5
1959	Was A	24	14	1	4	0	0	0	0	1-1	0	3	.286	.333	.286	72	-1	0-0	1.000	3	128	205	S-21	0.3
1960	Was A	117	268	23	57	1	1	2	19	20-0	4	36	.213	.276	.246	43	-22	1-2	.954	2	102	110	*S-115/3	-1.3
1961	Min A	76	149	15	29	5	0	1	9	8-0	0	19	.195	.234	.248	28	-15	1-1	.971	-2	98	96	S-43,2-15,3-14	-1.4
Total	5	401	971	89	213	26	8	9	85	79-3	8	132	.219	.282	.290	55	-65	6-6	.955	23	107	105	S-363/2-15,3-15	-1.8
VALENT, ERIC Eric Christian B 4.4.1977 LaMirada, CA BL/TL 6/191# d6.8																								
2001	Phi N	22	41	3	4	2	0	0	1	4-0	1	11	.098	.196	.146	-10	-7	0-0	1.000	3	191	517	/O-8(7-0-1),D-4	-0.4
2002	Phi N	7	10	1	2	0	0	0	0	0-0	0	3	.200	.200	.200	8	-1	0-0	—	-1	0	0	/O-2(RF),1	-0.2
2003	Cin N	18	42	3	9	0	0	0	1	2-0	0	9	.214	.250	.214	23	-5	0-0	1.000	1	122	181	/O-8(RF)	-0.4
Total	3	47	93	7	15	2	0	0	2	6-0	1	23	.161	.220	.183	7	-13	0-0	1.000	4	141	300	/O-18(7-0-11),D-4,1	-1.0
VALENTIN, JOHN John William B 2.18.1967 Mineola, NY BR/TR 6/185# d7.27																								
1992	Bos A	58	185	21	51	13	0	5	25	20-0	2	17	.276	.351	.427	110	3	1-0	.963	6	106	125	S-58	1.4
1993	Bos A	144	468	50	130	40	3	11	66	49-2	2	77	.278	.346	.447	106	4	3-4	.971	16	**105**	**113**	*S-144	3.0
1994	Bos A	84	301	53	95	26	2	9	49	42-1	3	38	.316	.400	.505	127	14	3-1	.979	4	100	104	S-83/D	2.2
1995	†Bos A	135	520	108	155	37	2	27	102	81-2	10	67	.298	.399	.533	136	31	20-5	.973	6	103	107	*S-135	4.6
1996	Bos A	131	527	84	156	29	3	13	59	63-0	7	59	.296	.374	.436	103	4	9-10	.971	6	102	100	*S-118,3-12/D	1.7
1997	Bos A	143	575	95	176	**47**	5	18	77	58-5	5	66	.306	.372	.499	123	21	7-4	.976	18	111	120	2-79,3-64	4.0
1998	†Bos A	153	588	113	145	44	1	23	73	77-3	9	82	.247	.340	.442	100	1	4-5	.965	18	**112**	132	*3-153/2	1.9
1999	†Bos A	113	450	58	114	27	1	12	70	40-2	4	68	.253	.315	.398	79	-15	0-1	.954	12	109	100	*3-111/D-2	-0.1
2000	Bos A	10	35	6	9	1	0	2	2	2-0	0	5	.257	.297	.457	85	-1	0-1	1.000	-3	52	0	3-10	-0.4
2001	Bos A	20	60	8	12	2	0	1	5	9-0	1	8	.200	.314	.283	59	-3	0-0	.970	-1	98	92	S-18/3-3	-0.3
2002	NY N	114	208	18	50	15	0	3	30	22-0	10	37	.240	.339	.356	91	-3	0-0	.971	-1	108	93	S-24,1-22,3-18/2-3,D-2	-0.4
Total	11	1105	3917	614	1093	281	17	124	558	463-15	53	524	.279	.360	.454	108	56	47-31	.972	82	103	108	S-580,3-371/2-83,1-22,D-6	17.6
VALENTIN, JOSE Jose Antonio B 10.12.1969 Manati, P.R. BB/TR 5-10/175# d9.17 b-Javier OF Total (24-CF 1-RF)																								
1992	Mil A	4	3	1	0	0	0	0	1	0-0	0	0	.000	.000	.000	-99	-1	0-0	.667	-2	36	0	/2S	-0.3
1993	Mil A	19	53	10	13	1	2	1	7	7-1	1	16	.245	.344	.396	100	0	1-0	.922	-5	97	79	S-19	-0.3
1994	Mil A	97	285	47	68	19	0	11	46	38-1	2	75	.239	.330	.421	89	-5	12-3	.954	**21**	**123**	**119**	S-83,2-18/3	2.3
1995	Mil A	112	338	62	74	23	3	11	49	37-0	0	83	.219	.293	.402	75	-13	16-8	.971	6	111	**119**	*S-104/3D	0.2
1996	Mil A	154	552	90	143	33	7	24	95	66-9	0	145	.259	.336	.475	99	-2	17-4	.950	1	107	112	*S-151	1.1
1997	Mil A	136	494	58	125	23	1	17	58	39-4	4	109	.253	.310	.407	85	-12	19-8	.967	5	102	106	*S-134/D	0.5
1998	Mil N	151	428	65	96	24	0	16	49	63-8	1	105	.224	.323	.393	88	-7	10-7	.963	0	103	91	*S-139/D	0.2
1999	Mil N	89	256	45	58	9	5	10	38	48-7	2	52	.227	.347	.418	95	-2	3-2	.937	-8	100	78	S-85	-0.3
2000	†Chi A	144	568	107	155	37	6	25	92	59-1	4	106	.273	.343	.491	107	5	19-2	.950	17	108	124	*S-141/O(RF)	3.3
2001	Chi A	124	438	74	113	22	2	28	68	50-2	3	114	.258	.336	.509	115	9	9-6	.926	12	106	97	3-66,S-43,O-24(CF)	2.3
2002	Chi A	135	474	70	118	26	4	25	75	43-2	2	99	.249	.311	.479	105	2	3-3	.952	5	107	112	3-83,S-50/D	1.0
2003	Chi A	144	503	79	119	26	2	28	74	54-4	3	114	.237	.313	.463	100	-1	8-3	.969	14	102	**114**	*S-143	2.3
Total	12	1309	4392	708	1082	243	32	196	652	504-39	22	1018	.246	.324	.450	97	-27	117-46	.958	67	106	111	*S-1093,3-151/O-25C,2-19,D-7	12.3
VALENTIN, JAVIER Jose Javier (Rosario) B 9.19.1975 Manati, P.R. BB/TR 5-10/198# d9.13 b-Jose																								
1997	Min A	4	7	1	2	0	0	0	0	0-0	0	3	.286	.286	.286	49	-1	0-0	1.000	1	111	363	/C-4	0.0
1998	Min A	55	162	11	32	7	1	3	18	11-1	0	30	.198	.247	.309	43	-14	0-0	.983	-3	97	67	C-53/D	-1.3
1999	Min A	78	218	22	54	12	1	5	28	22-0	1	39	.248	.313	.381	75	-8	0-0	.998	6	159	108	C-76	0.2
2002	Min A	4	4	0	2	0	0	0	0	0-0	0	0	.500	.500	.500	165	0	0-0	1.000	2	0	0	/C-4	0.2
2003	TB A	49	135	13	30	7	1	3	15	5-0	1	31	.222	.254	.356	60	-8	0-0	1.000	2	115	85	C-42/D-6	-0.4
Total	5	190	526	47	120	26	3	11	61	38-1	2	103	.228	.279	.352	62	-31	0-0	.994	7	127	92	C-179/D-7	-1.3
VALENTINE, ELLIS Ellis Clarence B 7.30.1954 Helena, AR BR/TR 6-4/207# d9.3																								
1975	Mon N	12	33	2	12	4	0	1	3	2-0	0	4	.364	.400	.576	161	3	0-0	.867	-1	67	158	O-11(RF)	0.1
1976	Mon N	94	305	36	85	15	2	7	39	30-0	0	51	.279	.339	.410	108	3	14-1	.972	-2	82	210	O-88(2-55-31)	0.1
1977	Mon N★	127	508	63	149	28	2	25	76	30-3	0	58	.293	.331	.504	124	15	13-5	.972	-5	95	91	*O-126(RF)	0.5
1978	Mon N	151	570	75	165	35	2	25	76	35-3	2	88	.289	.330	.489	129	19	13-8	.970	11	103	**198**	*O-146(0-3-145)	2.4
1979	Mon N	146	548	73	151	29	3	21	82	22-3	1	74	.276	.303	.454	105	1	11-9	.983	-4	96	82	*O-144(RF)	-1.1
1980	Mon N	86	311	40	98	22	2	13	67	25-0	3	44	.315	.367	.524	147	19	5-5	.970	-1	102	86	O-83(RF)	1.4
1981	Mon N	22	76	8	16	3	0	3	15	6-0	0	11	.211	.259	.368	78	-2	0-1	1.000	-1	87	125	O-21(RF)	-0.5
	NY N	48	169	15	35	8	1	5	21	5-0	0	38	.207	.227	.355	65	-9	0-3	.957	1	97	163	O-47(RF)	-1.3

Year	Tm Lg	G	AB	R	H	2B	3B	HR	RBI	BB-IB	HP	SO	AVG	OBP	SLG	AOPS	ABR	SB-CS	FA	FR	Rng	Thr	G at Pos	BFW
	Year	70	245	23	51	11	1	8	36	11-0	0	49	.208	.238	.359	69	-11	0-4	.969	0	94	152	O-68(RF)	-1.8
1982	NY N	111	337	33	97	14	1	8	48	5-0	1	38	.288	.294	.407	97	-3	1-3	.983	4	101	167	O-98(14-4-82)	-0.5
1983	Cal A	86	271	30	65	10	2	13	43	18-0	0	48	.240	.283	.435	97	-3	2-1	.963	-4	92	82	O-85(11-0-80)	-1.1
1985	Tex A	11	38	5	8	1	0	2	4	2-0	0	8	.211	.250	.395	72	-2	0-1	1.000	-1	64	0	/O-7(RF),D-4	-0.3
Total	10	894	3166	380	881	169	15	123	474	180-9	7	462	.278	.315	.458	113	41	59-37	.972	-3	96	132	O-856(27-62-777)/D-4	-0.3
VALENTINE, FRED Fred Lee "Squeaky" B 1.19.1935 Clarksdale, MS BB/TR 6-1/190# d9.7																								
1959	Bal A	12	19	0	6	0	0	0	1	3-0	0	4	.316	.409	.316	104	0	0-1	.889	0	81	368	/O-8(3-0-6)	0.0
1963	Bal A	26	41	5	11	1	0	0	1	8-0	0	5	.268	.388	.293	98	0	0-0	1.000	-0	98	0	O-10(1-0-10)	-0.1
1964	Was A	102	212	20	48	5	0	4	20	21-0	3	44	.226	.304	.307	71	-8	4-2	.978	-0	101	75	O-57(22-14-22)	-1.1
1965	Was A	12	29	6	7	0	0	0	1	4-0	1	5	.241	.353	.241	73	-1	3-0	1.000	1	124	0	O-11(5-6-1)	0.0
1966	Was A	146	508	77	140	29	7	16	59	51-1	10	63	.276	.351	.455	132	22	22-10	.980	2	108	75	*O-138(32-63-70)/1-2	1.9
1967	Was A	151	457	52	107	16	1	11	44	56-1	10	76	.234	.330	.346	104	4	17-3	.989	-2	100	85	*O-136(26-70-55)	-0.1
1968	Was A	37	101	11	24	2	0	3	7	6-0	2	11	.238	.291	.347	96	-1	1-0	1.000	-1	81	145	O-27(0-1-26)	-0.4
	Bal A	47	91	9	17	3	2	2	5	7-0	1	20	.187	.253	.330	75	-3	0-0	.972	1	97	183	O-26(6-6-14)	-0.4
	Year	84	192	20	41	5	2	5	12	13-0	3	31	.214	.273	.339	86	-4	1-0	.986	-0	88	162	O-53(6-7-40)	-0.8
Total	7	533	1458	180	360	56	10	36	138	156-2	27	228	.247	.330	.373	106	13	47-16	.983	-0	102	89	O-413(95-160-204)/1-2	-0.2
VALENTINE, BOB Robert d5.20																								
1876	NY N	1	3	0	0	0	0	0	0	0		0	.000	.000	.000	-99	-1		.333	-1			/C	-0.2
VALENTINE, BOBBY Robert John B 5.13.1950 Stamford, CT BR/TR 5-10/189# d9.2 M15 C4 OF Total (87-LF 18-CF 26-RF)																								
1969	LA N	5	0	3	0	0	0	0	0	0-0	0	0	—	—	—	—	0	0-0	—	0			R	0.0
1971	LA N	101	281	32	70	10	2	1	25	15-0	2	20	.249	.287	.310	75	-10	5-3	.961	-6	99	119	S-37,3-23,2-21,O-11(0-3-8)	-1.4
1972	LA N	119	391	42	107	11	2	3	32	27-2	2	33	.274	.319	.335	90	-6	5-5	.976	1	110	107	2-49,3-39,O-16(5-8-4),S-10	-0.2
1973	Cal A	32	126	12	38	5	2	1	13	5-0	0	9	.302	.323	.397	112	1	6-1	.948	-2	84	65	S-25/O-8(1-7-0)	0.3
1974	Cal A	117	371	39	97	10	3	3	39	25-0	3	25	.261	.308	.329	90	-5	8-5	.950	2	116	59	O-62(LF),S-36,3-15/2D	-0.3
1975	Cal A	26	57	5	16	2	0	0	5	4-0	1	3	.281	.323	.316	92	0	0-2	.958	-1	0	108	D-13/1-3,3-2,O-2(1-0-1)	-0.3
	SD N	7	15	1	2	0	0	1	1	4-0	0	0	.133	.316	.333	86	0	1-0	1.000	-1	54	0	/O-4(LF)	-0.1
1976	SD N	15	49	3	18	4	0	0	4	6-0	0	2	.367	.436	.449	165	5	0-1	1.000	2	104	297	O-10(7-0-5)/1-4	0.6
1977	SD N	44	67	5	12	3	0	1	10	7-1	0	10	.179	.253	.269	46	-5	0-0	.962	-1	94	34	S-10,3-10/1	-0.6
	NY N	42	83	8	11	1	0	1	3	6-0	0	9	.133	.191	.181	0	-12	0-0	1.000	-1	72	73	1-15,S-14/3-4	-1.3
	Year	86	150	13	23	4	0	2	13	13-1	0	19	.153	.220	.220	20	-18	0-0	.969	-2	98	92	S-24,1-16,3-14	-1.9
1978	NY N	69	160	17	43	7	0	1	18	19-1	1	18	.269	.346	.331	95	0	1-1	.977	-2	100	67	2-45/3-9	-0.1
1979	Sea A	62	98	9	27	6	0	0	7	22-1	0	5	.276	.405	.337	102	2	1-2	.971	-4	73	42	S-29,O-15(7-0-8)/2-4,3-4,C-2,D	-0.2
Total	10	639	1698	176	441	59	9	12	157	140-5	9	134	.260	.315	.326	86	-30	27-20	.957	-12	93	76	S-161,O-128L,2-120,3-106/1-23,DC	-3.6
VALENZUELA, BENNY Benjamin Beltran "Papelero" B 6.2.1933 Los Mochis, Mexico BR/TR 5-10/175# d4.27																								
1958	StL N	10	14	0	3	1	0	0	0	1-0	0	0	.214	.267	.286	45	-1	0-0	.875	-0	89	0	/3-3	-0.1
VALERA, YOHANNY Yohanny B 8.17.1976 Santo Domingo, D.R. BR/TR 6-1/205# d9.13																								
2000	Mon N	7	10	1	0	0	0	0	1	1-0	1	5	.000	.167	.000	-52	-2	0-0	1.000	1	99	112	/C-7	-0.1
VALLE, DAVE David B 10.30.1960 Bayside, NY BR/TR 6-2/200# d9.7																								
1984	Sea A	13	27	4	8	1	0	1	4	1-0	0	5	.296	.321	.444	111	0	0-0	1.000	1	113	116	C-13	0.2
1985	Sea A	31	70	2	11	1	0	0	4	1-0	1	17	.157	.181	.171	-3	-10	0-0	.976	-2	93	31	C-31	-1.1
1986	Sea A	22	53	10	18	3	0	5	15	7-0	0	7	.340	.417	.679	191	7	0-0	.982	-4	104	32	C-12/1-4	0.3
1987	Sea A	95	324	40	83	16	3	12	53	15-2	3	46	.256	.292	.435	86	-8	2-0	.989	6	134	98	C-75,D-14/1-2,O(RF)	0.2
1988	Sea A	93	290	29	67	15	2	10	50	18-0	9	38	.231	.295	.400	89	-5	0-1	.989	9	106	120	C-84/1D	0.9
1989	Sea A	94	316	32	75	10	3	7	34	29-2	6	32	.237	.311	.354	85	-6	0-0	.993	7	131	**125**	C-93	0.6
1990	Sea A	107	308	37	66	15	0	7	33	45-0	7	48	.214	.328	.331	84	-5	1-2	**.997**	1	97	85	*C-104/1	0.1
1991	Sea A	132	324	38	63	8	1	8	32	34-0	9	49	.194	.286	.299	63	-17	0-2	.992	10	**149**	89	*C-129/1-2	-0.1
1992	Sea A	124	367	39	88	16	1	9	30	27-1	8	58	.240	.305	.362	86	-7	0-0	.990	-7	98	96	*C-122	-0.8
1993	Sea A	135	423	48	109	19	0	13	63	48-4	**17**	56	.258	.354	.395	100	2	1-0	.995	12	129	118	*C-135	2.2
1994	Bos A	30	76	6	12	2	1	1	5	9-1	1	18	.158	.256	.250	30	-8	0-1	.982	-3	98	67	C-28/1-2	-1.0
	Mil A	16	36	8	14	6	0	1	5	9-1	1	4	.389	.522	.639	189	6	0-1	1.000	-2	84	67	C-12/D-2	0.4
	Year	46	112	14	26	8	1	2	10	18-2	2	22	.232	.348	.375	83	-2	0-2	.986	-5	94	67	C-40/1-2,D-2	-0.6
1995	Tex A	36	75	7	18	3	0	0	5	6-0	1	18	.240	.305	.280	52	-5	1-0	.993	2	122	94	C-29/1-7	-0.2
1996	Tex A	42	86	14	26	6	1	3	17	9-0	0	17	.302	.368	.500	111	1	0-0	.994	2	96	102	C-35/1-5,D	0.4
Total	13	970	2775	314	658	121	12	77	350	258-11	63	413	.237	.314	.373	86	-55	5-7	.992	32	118	100	C-902/1-24,D-20,O(RF)	2.1
VALLE, HECTOR Hector Jose B 10.27.1940 Vega Baja, P.R. BR/TR 5-9/180# d6.6																								
1965	LA N	9	13	1	4	0	0	0	2	2-0	0	3	.308	.400	.308	110	0	0-0	1.000	0	*113*	*0*	/C-6	0.0
VALO, ELMER Elmer William B 3.5.1921 Ribnik, Czechoslovakia D 7.19.1998 Palmerton, PA BL/TR 5-11/190# d9.22 Mil 1943-45 C2																								
1940	Phi A	6	23	6	8	0	0	0	0	3	0	0	.348	.423	.348	104	0	2-0	1.000	0	123	0	/O-6(LF)	0.1
1941	Phi A	15	50	13	21	0	1	2	6	4	0	2	.420	.463	.580	179	5	0-0	1.000	-0	103	0	O-10(LF)	0.4
1942	Phi A	133	459	64	115	13	10	2	40	70	4	21	.251	.355	.336	95	-1	13-8	.964	-1	**108**	55	*O-122(1-1-120)	-1.0
1943	Phi A	77	249	31	55	6	2	3	18	35	1	13	.221	.319	.297	81	-5	2-6	.986	-0	101	85	O-63(9-0-54)	-1.3
1946	Phi A	108	348	59	107	21	6	1	31	60	1	18	.307	.411	.411	131	18	9-8	.974	2	108	92	O-90(5-0-85)	1.6
1947	Phi A	112	370	60	111	12	6	5	36	64	2	21	.300	.406	.405	123	14	11-3	.973	0	101	120	*O-104(RF)	1.3
1948	Phi A	113	383	72	117	17	4	3	46	81	4	13	.305	.432	.394	120	17	10-6	.983	-4	99	48	*O-109(RF)	0.9
1949	Phi A	150	547	86	155	27	12	5	85	119	2	32	.283	.413	.404	121	22	14-11	.981	10	**118**	71	*O-150(LF)	1.9
1950	Phi A	129	446	62	125	16	5	10	46	82	7	22	.280	.400	.406	109	9	12-7	.982	2	106	91	*O-117(33-0-85)	0.6
1951	Phi A	123	444	75	134	27	8	7	55	75	8	20	.302	.412	.446	129	22	11-6	.981	-3	101	57	*O-116(1-22-95)	1.5
1952	Phi A	129	388	69	109	26	4	5	47	101	2	16	.281	.432	.407	126	21	12-11	.962	-4	100	73	*O-121(2-11-108)	1.3
1953	Phi A	50	85	15	19	3	0	0	9	22	0	7	.224	.383	.259	73	-2	0-1	1.000	0	107	55	O-25(10-0-15)	-0.3
1954	Phi A	95	224	28	48	11	6	1	33	51	0	18	.214	.356	.330	90	-1	2-1	.965	1	111	72	O-62(34-0-30)	-0.3
1955	KC A	112	283	50	103	17	4	3	37	52-2	0	18	.364	.460	.484	153	25	5-3	.987	1	104	90	O-72(46-4-23)	2.3
1956	KC A	9	9	1	2	0	0	0	2	1-0	0	1	.222	.273	.222	40	-1	0-0	—	-0	0	0	/O(LF)	-0.1
	Phi N	98	291	40	84	13	3	5	37	48-6	3	21	.289	.392	.405	118	10	7-6	.966	-1	107	54	O-87(RF)	0.5
1957	Bro N	81	161	14	44	10	1	4	26	25-2	1	16	.273	.370	.422	104	2	0-1	1.000	-2	94	0	O-36(26-0-14)	-0.2
1958	LA N	65	101	9	25	2	1	1	14	12-0	0	11	.248	.322	.317	69	-4	0-1	1.000	-2	84	0	O-26(16-0-13)	-0.7
1959	Cle A	34	24	3	7	0	0	0	5	7-1	0	0	.292	.424	.292	113	1	0-0	1.000	0	165	0	/O-2(RF)	0.1
1960	NY A	8	5	1	0	0	0	0	0	2-0	0	1	.000	.286	.000	-17	-1	0-0	—	-0	0	0	/O-2(RF)	-0.1
	Was A	76	64	6	18	3	0	0	16	17-0	1	4	.281	.424	.328	112	3	0-0	1.000	1	86	497	/O-6(1-0-5)	0.3
	Year	84	69	7	18	3	0	0	16	19-0	1	5	.261	.413	.304	103	2	0-0	1.000	0	83	479	/O-8(1-0-7)	0.2
1961	Min A	33	32	0	5	2	0	0	4	3-1	1	3	.156	.250	.219	25	-3	0-0	1.000	0	118	0	/O(LF)	-0.3
	Phi N	50	43	4	8	2	0	1	8	8-0	1	6	.186	.327	.302	69	-2	0-0	—	-0	0	0	/O(RF)	-0.2
Total	20	1806	5029	768	1420	228	73	58	601	942-12	38	284	.282	.398	.391	114	149	110-79	.977	-0	105	71	*O-1329(352-38-952)	8.3
Van BUREN, DEACON Edward Eugene B 12.14.1870 LaSalle Co., IL D 6.29.1957 Portland, OR BL/TR 5-10/175# d4.21																								
1904	Bro N	1	1	0	1	0	0	0	0	0	0		1.000	1.000	1.000	531	0	0	—	0			H	0.0
	Phi N	12	43	2	10	2	0	0	3	3	0		.233	.283	.279	76	-1	2	.962	1	131	197	O-12(LF)	-0.1
	Year	13	44	2	11	2	0	0	3	3	0		.250	.298	.295	86	-1	2	.962	1	131	197	O-12(LF)	-0.1
Van BURKLEO, TY Tyler Lee B 10.7.1963 Oakland, CA BL/TL 6-5/225# d7.28																								
1993	Cal A	12	33	2	5	3	0	1	1	6-0	0	9	.152	.282	.333	63	-2	1-0	1.000	-1	46	90	1-12	-0.4
1994	Col N	2	5	0	0	0	0	0	0	0-0	0	1	.000	.000	.000	-86	-1	0-0	1.000	0	127	104	/1-2	-0.1
Total	2	14	38	2	5	3	0	1	1	6-0	0	10	.132	.250	.289	42	-3	1-0	1.000	-1	53	91	/1-14	-0.5
Van CAMP, AL Albert Joseph B 9.7.1903 Moline, IL D 2.2.1981 Davenport, IA BR/TR 5-11.5/175# d9.11																								
1928	Cle A	5	17	0	4	1	0	0	2	0	0	1	.235	.235	.294	38	-2	1-0	.980	-1	37	27	/1-5	-0.2
1931	Bos A	101	324	34	89	15	4	0	33	20	1	24	.275	.319	.346	79	-11	3-2	.973	-2	89	73	O-59(58-3-2),1-25	-1.6
1932	Bos A	34	103	10	23	4	2	0	6	4	0	17	.223	.252	.301	44	-9	0-0	.985	1	118	88	1-25	-1.0
Total	3	140	444	44	116	20	6	0	41	24	1	42	.261	.301	.333	69	-22	4-2	.973	-2	89	73	/O-59(58-3-2),1-55	-2.8

Year	Tm Lg	G	AB	R	H	2B	3B	HR	RBI	BB-IB	HP	SO	AVG	OBP	SLG	AOPS	ABR	SB-CS	FA	FR	Rng	Thr	G at Pos	BFW
VANDAGRIFT, CARL Carl William B 4.22.1883 Cantrall, IL D 10.9.1920 Fort Wayne, IN BR/TR 5-8/155# d5.19																								
1914	Ind F	43	136	25	34	4	0	0	9	9	1	15	.250	.301	.279	53	-11	7	.925	-5	83	72	2-28,3-12/S-5	-1.6
VANDER WAL, JOHN John Henry B 4.29.1966 Grand Rapids, MI BL/TL 6-2/190# d9.6																								
1991	Mon N	21	61	4	13	4	1	1	8	1-0	0	18	.213	.222	.361	63	-3	0-0	1.000	-1	99	0	O-17(LF)	-0.5
1992	Mon N	105	213	21	51	8	2	4	20	24-2	0	36	.239	.316	.352	90	-3	3-0	.981	3	112	96	O-57(55-0-4)/1-7	-0.1
1993	Mon N	106	215	34	50	7	4	5	30	27-2	1	30	.233	.320	.372	81	-6	6-3	.988	-6	74	90	1-42,O-38(27-2-10)	-1.4
1994	Col N	91	110	12	27	3	1	5	15	16-0	0	31	.245	.339	.427	85	-2	2-1	1.000	-2	37	111	1-14/O-7(5-0-2)	-0.5
1995	†Col N	105	101	15	35	8	1	5	21	16-5	0	23	.347	.432	.594	131	5	1-1	.957	1	95	85	1-10,O-10(7-0-3)	0.5
1996	Col N	104	151	20	38	6	2	5	31	19-2	1	38	.252	.335	.417	79	-4	2-2	1.000	-2	91	0	O-26(25-0-1),1-10	-0.8
1997	Col N	76	92	7	16	2	0	1	11	10-0	0	33	.174	.255	.228	23	-10	1-1	.923	-1	104	0	/O-9(2-0-7),1-5,D-2	-1.2
1998	Col N	89	104	18	30	10	1	5	20	16-0	0	29	.288	.380	.548	116	3	0-0	1.000	1	88	237	O-25(3-0-22)/1-2	0.3
	†SD N	20	25	3	6	3	0	0	0	6-0	0	5	.240	.387	.360	106	1	0-0	1.000	1	169	0	/O-5(2-0-3),1-3,D-3	0.1
	Year	109	129	21	36	13	1	5	20	22-0	0	34	.279	.382	.512	114	4	0-0	1.000	1	101	200	O-30(5-0-25)/1-5,D-3	0.4
1999	SD N	132	246	26	67	18	0	6	41	37-1	2	59	.272	.368	.419	108	5	2-1	1.000	0	109	96	O-48(45-0-3),1-28/D	0.2
2000	Pit N	134	384	74	115	29	0	24	94	72-5	2	92	.299	.410	.563	144	29	11-2	.965	-6	96	45	O-78(13-0-65),1-33/D-3	1.8
2001	Pit N	97	313	39	87	22	3	11	50	42-6	1	84	.278	.361	.473	112	6	7-4	.973	-8	78	44	O-73(20-0-56),1-13/D-7	-0.6
	SF N	49	139	19	35	6	1	3	20	26-3	0	38	.252	.370	.374	101	1	1-2	1.000	2	115	43	O-41(3-0-38)/1	0.0
	Year	146	452	58	122	28	4	14	70	68-9	1	122	.270	.364	.442	109	8	8-6	.985	-7	91	44	*O-114(23-0-94),1-14/D-7	-0.6
2002	†NY A	84	219	30	57	17	1	6	20	23-3	0	58	.260	.327	.429	101	0	1-1	.978	-4	99	0	O-57(8-0-49),D-16/1-6	-0.7
2003	Mil N	117	327	50	84	25	1	14	45	46-3	1	104	.257	.350	.468	113	7	1-2	.984	3	110	75	O-89(6-0-83)	0.5
Total	13	1330	2700	372	711	168	18	95	426	381-32	8	678	.263	.354	.444	104	29	38-20	.982	-20	99	58	0-580(238-2-346),1-174/D-32	-2.4
Van DUSEN, FRED Frederick William B 7.31.1937 Jackson Heights, NY BL/TL 6-3/180# d9.11																								
1955	Phi N	1	0	0	0	0	0	0	0	0-0	1	0	—	1.000	—	199	0	0-0	—	0			H	0.0
Van DYKE, BILL William Jennings B 12.15.1863 Paris, IL D 5.5.1933 ElPaso, TX BR/TR 5-8/170# d4.17																								
1890	Tol AA	129	502	74	129	14	11	2	54	25	3		.257	.296	.341	85	-13	73	.924	-6	80	0	*O-110(109-1-0),3-18/2-2,C	-1.9
1892	StL N	4	16	2	2	0	0	0	1	0	0	1	.125	.125	.125	-26	-2	0	.875	-1	0	0	/O-4(CF)	-0.3
1893	Bos N	3	12	2	3	1	0	0	1	0	0	1	.250	.250	.333	50	-1	1	1.000	-0	0	0	/O-3(LF)	-0.1
Total	3	136	530	78	134	15	11	2	56	25	3	2	.253	.290	.334	81	-16	74	.924	-7	76	0	O-117(112-5-0)/3-18,2-2,C	-2.3
Van GORDER, DAVE David Thomas B 3.27.1957 Los Angeles, CA BR/TR 6-2/205# d6.15																								
1982	Cin N	51	137	4	25	3	1	0	7	14-2	1	19	.182	.263	.219	35	-12	1-0	.986	-8	78	49	C-51	-1.9
1984	Cin N	38	101	10	23	2	0	0	6	12-2	0	17	.228	.310	.248	56	-6	0-0	1.000	-1	97	67	C-36/1	-0.6
1985	Cin N	73	151	12	36	7	0	2	24	9-2	1	19	.238	.280	.325	67	-7	0-0	.989	-8	111	61	C-70	-1.3
1986	Cin N	9	10	0	0	0	0	0	0	1-0	0	2	.000	.091	.000	-70	-2	0-0	1.000	0	135	0	/C-7	-0.2
1987	Bal A	12	21	4	5	0	0	1	1	3-0	0	6	.238	.333	.381	91	0	0-0	.978	-3	55	0	C-12	-0.3
Total	5	183	420	30	89	12	1	3	38	39-6	2	63	.212	.280	.267	52	-27	1-0	.990	-19	94	53	C-176/1	-4.3
Van HALTREN, GEORGE George Edward Martin "Rip" B 3.30.1866 St.Louis, MO D 9.29.1945 Oakland, CA BL/TL 5-11/170# d6.27 M1 ▲ OF Total (313-LF 1376-CF 149-RF)																								
1887	Chi N	45	172	30	35	4	0	3	17	15	1	15	.203	.271	.279	47	-13	12	.927	-3	23	131	O-27(4-0-23),P-20	-0.9
1888	Chi N	81	318	46	90	9	14	4	34	22	0	34	.283	.329	.437	133	10	21	.872	0	102	0	O-57(47-4-7),P-30	0.4
1889	Chi N	134	543	126	175	20	10	9	81	82	5	41	.322	.416	.446	134	26	28	.898	-5	98	68	*O-130(115-15-0)/S-3,2	1.5
1890	Bro P	92	376	84	126	8	9	5	54	41	3	23	.335	.405	.444	119	9	35	.896	4	130	39	O-67(6-12-49),P-28/S-3	0.7
1891	Bal AA	**139**	566	136	180	14	15	9	83	71	4	46	.318	.398	.443	139	28	75	.882	-15	146	234	O-81(79-0-2),S-59/P-6,2-2	1.1
1892	Bal N	135	556	105	168	20	12	7	57	70	2	34	.302	.382	.419	138	26	49	.850	-4	126	93	*O-129(16-62-53)/P-4,3-3,1-2,S-2,M	1.3
	Pit N	13	55	10	11	2	2	0	5	6	0	0	.200	.279	.309	77	-2	6	.905	-2	56	258	O-13(CF)	-0.4
	Year	148	611	115	179	22	14	7	62	76	2	34	.293	.373	.409	133	25	55	.854	-5	121	106	*O-142(16-75-53)/P-4,3-3,1-2,S-2	0.9
1893	Pit N	124	529	129	179	14	11	3	79	75	2	25	.338	.422	.423	128	24	37	.869	-11	126	78	*O-111(CF),S-12/2-2	0.5
1894	†NY N	**139**	528	109	175	22	4	7	105	55	4	23	.331	.399	.428	100	1	43	.915	-6	125	96	*O-139(CF)	-1.0
1895	NY N	131	521	113	177	23	19	8	103	57	3	29	.340	.408	.503	137	28	32	.914	-5	134	69	*O-131(CF)/P	1.2
1896	NY N	**133**	562	136	197	18	**21**	5	74	55	2	36	.351	.410	.484	139	31	39	.952	4	137	86	*O-133(CF)/P-2	2.3
1897	NY N	130	566	119	186	22	9	3	64	42	1		.329	.376	.415	112	9	50	.938	7	**166**	114	*O-130(CF)	0.7
1898	NY N	**156**	654	129	204	28	16	2	68	59	4		.312	.372	.413	129	24	36	.917	-8	97	88	*O-156(17-138-3)	0.5
1899	NY N	**152**	607	118	183	22	3	2	58	75	1		.301	.379	.357	106	9	31	.932	-0	134	110	*O-152(23-129-0)	-0.1
1900	NY N	**141**	571	114	180	30	7	1	51	50	1		.315	.371	.398	118	15	**45**	.939	8	**148**	123	*O-141(CF)/P	1.3
1901	NY N	135	543	82	182	23	6	1	47	51	4		.335	.396	.405	138	29	24	.941	5	139	109	*O-135(CF)/P	2.6
1902	NY N	26	96	14	24	1	2	0	7	17	0		.250	.363	.302	107	2	6	.929	1	164	108	O-26(3-13-10)	0.1
1903	NY N	84	280	42	72	6	1	0	28	28	1		.257	.327	.286	72	-9	14	.959	-5	31	46	O-75(3-70-2)	-1.7
Total	17	1990	8043	1642	2544	286	161	69	1015	871	38	306	.316	.386	.418	122	247	583	.915	-34	124	96	*O-1833C/P-93,S-79,2-5,3-3,1-2	10.1
VANN, JOHN John Silas B 6.7.1893 Fairland, OK D 6.10.1958 Shreveport, LA BR/TR d6.11																								
1913	StL N	1	1	0	0	0	0	0	0	0	0	1	.000	.000	.000	-99	0	0	—	0			H	0.0
Van NOY, JAY Jay Lowell B 11.4.1928 Garland, UT BL/TR 6-1/200# d6.18																								
1951	StL N	6	7	1	0	0	0	0	0	1	0	6	.000	.125	.000	-63	-2	0-0	1.000	0	126	0	/O(RF)	-0.2
Van ROBAYS, MAURICE Maurice Rene "Bomber" B 11.15.1914 Detroit, MI D 3.1.1965 Detroit, MI BR/TR 6-0.5/190# d9.7 Mil 1944-45																								
1939	Pit N	27	105	13	33	9	0	2	16	6	0	10	.314	.351	.457	118	3	0	.919	-2	76	78	O-25(LF)/3	-0.1
1940	Pit N	145	572	82	156	27	7	11	116	33	3	58	.273	.316	.402	98	-4	2	.963	-5	90	96	*O-143(137-0-6)/1	-1.7
1941	Pit N	129	457	62	129	23	5	4	78	41	1	29	.282	.343	.381	104	2	0	.974	6	108	105	*O-121(LF)	0.2
1942	Pit N	100	328	29	76	13	5	1	46	30	1	24	.232	.298	.311	76	-10	0	.986	4	108	103	O-84(LF)	-1.1
1943	Pit N	69	236	32	68	17	7	1	35	18	2	19	.288	.344	.432	119	5	0	.940	-3	97	80	O-60(15-0-45)	-0.1
1946	Pit N	59	146	14	31	5	3	1	12	11	1	15	.212	.272	.308	63	-8	0	.955	-2	95	34	O-37(21-3-13)/1-2	-1.3
Total	6	529	1844	232	493	94	27	20	303	139	8	155	.267	.321	.380	97	-12	2	.966	-2	99	93	O-470(403-3-64)/1-3,3	-4.1
Van SLYKE, ANDY Andrew James B 12.21.1960 Utica, NY BL/TR 6-2/192# d6.17																								
1983	StL N	101	309	51	81	15	5	8	38	46-5	1	64	.262	.357	.421	115	7	21-7	.974	-1	97	99	O-69(50-7-23),3-30/1-9	0.5
1984	StL N	137	361	45	88	16	4	7	50	63-9	0	71	.244	.354	.368	107	5	28-5	1.000	2	79	133	O-81(34-15-35),3-32,1-30	0.8
1985	†StL N	146	424	61	110	25	6	13	55	47-6	2	54	.259	.335	.439	116	9	34-6	.996	6	101	160	*O-142(4-10-133)/1-2	1.5
1986	StL N	137	418	48	113	23	7	13	61	47-5	1	85	.270	.343	.452	119	10	21-8	.969	8	108	148	*O-110(1-27-87),1-38	1.5
1987	Pit N	157	564	93	165	36	11	21	82	56-4	4	122	.293	.359	.507	126	20	34-8	.988	1	101	118	*O-150(0-114-37)/1	2.3
1988	Pit N★	154	587	101	169	23	**15**	25	100	57-2	1	126	.288	.345	.506	146	32	30-9	.991	5	102	170	*O-152(CF)	4.1
1989	Pit N	130	476	64	113	18	9	9	53	47-3	3	100	.237	.308	.370	97	-3	16-4	.989	4	104	135	*O-123(CF)/1-2	0.2
1990	†Pit N	136	493	67	140	26	6	17	77	66-2	1	89	.284	.367	.465	133	23	14-4	.976	-8	96	82	*O-133(CF)	1.7
1991	†Pit N	138	491	87	130	24	7	17	83	71-1	4	85	.265	.355	.446	128	20	10-3	.996	-11	86	110	*O-135(CF)	0.9
1992	†Pit N★	154	614	103	**199**	**45**	12	14	89	58-4	4	99	.324	.381	.505	152	42	12-3	.989	-3	98	117	*O-154(CF)	4.2
1993	Pit N✳	83	323	42	100	13	4	8	50	24-5	2	40	.310	.357	.449	116	7	11-2	.995	-3	98	48	O-78(CF)	0.6
1994	Pit N	105	374	41	92	18	3	6	30	52-7	2	72	.246	.340	.358	82	-9	7-0	.992	2	99	170	O-99(CF)	-0.5
1995	Bal A	17	63	6	10	1	0	3	8	5-1	0	15	.159	.221	.317	37	-6	0-0	.978	1	104	247	O-17(0-16-1)	-0.5
	Phi N	63	214	26	52	10	2	3	16	28-1	2	41	.243	.333	.350	81	-5	7-0	.984	-1	91	171	O-56(CF)	-0.4
Total	13	1658	5711	835	1562	293	91	164	792	667-55	27	1063	.274	.349	.443	120	152	245-59	.988	3	98	130	*O-1499(89-1119-316)/1-82,3-62	16.9
Van ZANDT, IKE Charles Isaac B 2.1876 Brooklyn, NY D 9.14.1908 Nashua, NH BL/TL d8.5 ▲																								
1901	NY N	3	6	1	1	0	0	0	0	0	0		.167	.167	.167	-3	-1	0	.333	-1	0	0	/P-2,O(LF)	-0.1
1904	Chi N	3	11	0	0	0	0	0	0	0	0		.000	.000	.000	-99	-3	0	1.000	-0	0	0	/O-3(RF)	-0.3
1905	StL A	94	322	31	75	15	1	1	20	7	1		.233	.252	.295	77	-9	7	.874	-11	93	0	O-75(0-29-45)/P1	-2.6
Total	3	100	339	32	76	15	1	1	20	7	1		.224	.242	.283	69	-13	7	.868	-13	89	0	/O-79(1-29-46),P-3,1	-3.0
Van ZANT, DICK Richard "Foghorn Dick" B 11.1864 , IN D 8.6.1912 Wayne Co., IN 6/?# d10.4																								
1888	Cle AA	10	31	1	8	1	0	0	1	1	1		.258	.303	.290	93	0	1	.784	0	122	150	3-10	0.0
VARGAS, EDDIE Hediberto (Rodriguez) B 2.23.1959 Guanica, P.R. BR/TR 6-4/205# d9.8																								
1982	Pit N	8	8	1	3	1	0	0	3	0-0	0	2	.375	.333	.500	139	0	0-0	1.000	-0	69	65	/1-5	0.0
1984	Pit N	18	31	3	7	2	0	0	2	3-0	0	5	.226	.294	.290	65	-1	0-0	.982	-0	91	115	1-13	-0.2

Year	Tm Lg	G	AB	R	H	2B	3B	HR	RBI	BB-IB	HP	SO	AVG	OBP	SLG	AOPS	ABR	SB-CS	FA	FR	Rng	Thr	G at Pos	BFW
Total	2	26	39	4	10	3	0	0	5	3-0	0	7	.256	.302	.333	80	-1	0-0	.986	-0	86	104	/1-18	-0.2
VARITEK, JASON Jason Andrew B 4.11.1972 Rochester, MN BB/TR 6-2/210# d9.24																								
1997	Bos A	1	1	0	1	0	0	0	0	0-0	0	0	1.000	1.000	1.000	416	0	0-0	1.000	0	0	0	/C	0.0
1998	†Bos A	86	221	31	56	13	0	7	33	17-1	2	45	.253	.309	.407	84	-6	2-2	.988	-1	88	97	C-75/D-3	-0.3
1999	†Bos A	144	483	70	130	39	2	20	76	46-2	2	85	.269	.330	.482	102	1	1-2	.990	9	69	110	*C-140/D-2	1.7
2000	Bos A	139	448	55	111	31	1	10	65	60-3	6	84	.248	.342	.388	83	-11	1-1	.992	0	71	107	*C-128/D	-0.2
2001	Bos A	51	174	19	51	11	1	7	25	21-3	1	35	.293	.371	.489	123	6	0-0	.996	11	72	122	C-50	1.9
2002	Bos A	132	467	58	124	27	1	10	61	41-3	7	95	.266	.332	.392	90	-6	4-3	.996	12	82	99	*C-127/D	1.4
2003	†Bos A☆	142	451	63	123	31	1	25	85	51-8	7	106	.273	.351	.512	122	15	3-2	.990	-7	111	79	*C-137/D-4	1.5
Total	7	695	2245	296	596	152	6	79	345	236-20	25	450	.265	.338	.444	100	-1	11-10	.992	23	83	101	C-658/D-11	6.0
VARNER, BUCK Glen Gann B 8.17.1930 Hixson, TN BL/TR 5-10/170# d9.19																								
1952	Was A	2	4	0	0	0	0	0	0	1	0	1	.000	.200	.000	-43	-1	0-0	1.000	-0	78	0	/O(RF)	-0.1
VARNEY, PETE Richard Fred B 4.10.1949 Roxbury, MA BR/TR 6-3/235# d8.26																								
1973	Chi A	5	4	0	0	0	0	0	0	1-0	0	0	.000	.200	.000	-38	-1	0-0	1.000	0	0	0	/C-5	0.0
1974	Chi A	9	28	1	7	0	0	0	2	1-0	0	8	.250	.267	.250	51	-2	0-0	.981	2	245	169	/C-9	0.0
1975	Chi A	36	107	12	29	5	1	2	8	6-1	1	28	.271	.316	.393	98	-1	2-0	.988	-2	100	114	C-34/D-2	-0.1
1976	Chi A	14	41	5	10	2	0	3	5	2-0	0	9	.244	.279	.512	128	1	0-0	.988	-1	57	57	C-14	0.0
	Atl N	5	10	0	1	0	0	0	0	0-0	0	2	.100	.100	.100	-41	-2	0-0	1.000	-1	27	153	/C-5	-0.2
Total	4	69	190	18	47	7	1	5	15	10-1	1	47	.247	.287	.374	86	-5	2-0	.988	-2	106	107	/C-67,D-2	-0.3
VARSHO, GARY Gary Andrew B 6.20.1961 Marshfield, WI BL/TR 5-11/190# d7.6 C2																								
1988	Chi N	46	73	6	20	3	0	0	5	1-0	0	6	.274	.280	.315	69	-3	5-0	.906	-0	116	0	O-18(10-0-8)	-0.3
1989	Chi N	61	87	10	16	4	2	0	6	4-1	0	13	.184	.220	.276	38	-7	3-0	.929	-1	86	125	O-21(17-0-4)	-0.8
1990	Chi N	46	48	10	12	4	0	0	1	1-1	0	6	.250	.265	.333	59	-3	2-0	1.000	-0	83	0	/O-3(2-0-1)	-0.2
1991	†Pit N	99	187	23	51	11	2	4	23	19-2	2	34	.273	.344	.417	115	4	9-2	.989	-0	100	67	O-54(5-5-45)/1-3	0.4
1992	†Pit N	103	162	22	36	6	3	4	22	10-1	0	32	.222	.266	.370	80	-5	5-2	.984	-1	101	54	O-44(14-2-28)	-0.7
1993	Cin N	77	95	8	22	6	0	2	11	9-0	1	19	.232	.302	.358	77	-3	1-0	1.000	0	99	96	O-22(13-0-9)	-0.3
1994	Pit N	67	82	15	21	6	3	0	5	4-1	2	19	.256	.307	.402	82	-2	0-1	.926	-2	85	0	O-36(18-2-18)/1	-0.6
1995	Phi N	72	103	7	26	1	1	0	11	7-1	2	17	.252	.310	.282	58	-6	2-0	.939	-0	113	0	O-25(9-0-16)	-0.7
Total	8	571	837	101	204	41	11	10	84	55-7	7	146	.244	.294	.355	78	-25	27-5	.963	-4	100	52	O-223(88-9-129)/1-4	-3.2
VATCHER, JIM James Ernest B 5.27.1965 Santa Monica, CA BR/TR 5-9/165# d5.30																								
1990	Phi N	36	46	5	12	1	0	1	4	4-0	0	6	.261	.320	.348	84	-1	0-0	1.000	-1	96	0	O-24(12-0-12)	-0.2
	Atl N	21	27	2	7	1	1	0	3	1-0	0	9	.259	.286	.370	75	-1	0-0	1.000	0	129	0	/O-6(2-0-4)	-0.1
	Year	57	73	7	19	2	1	1	7	5-0	0	15	.260	.308	.356	80	-2	0-0	1.000	-0	103	0	O-30(14-0-16)	-0.3
1991	SD N	17	20	3	4	0	0	0	2	4-0	0	6	.200	.333	.200	52	-1	1-0	.900	-0	76	253	O-11(2-0-9)	-0.1
1992	SD N	13	16	1	4	1	0	0	2	3-0	0	6	.250	.368	.313	93	0	0-0	1.000	1	95	229	O-13(0-1-12)	0.0
Total	3	87	109	11	27	3	1	1	11	12-0	0	27	.248	.322	.321	77	-3	1-0	.980	-0	95	117	/O-54(16-1-37)	-0.4
VAUGHAN, GLENN Glenn Edward "Sparky" B 2.15.1944 Compton, CA BB/TR 5-11/170# d9.20																								
1963	Hou N	9	30	1	5	0	0	0	0	2-0	0	5	.167	.219	.167	14	-3	1-0	.914	-3	84	23	/S-9,3	-0.6
VAUGHAN, ARKY Joseph Floyd B 3.9.1912 Clifty, AR D 8.30.1952 Eagleville, CA BL/TR 5-10.5/175# d4.17 HF1985																								
1932	Pit N	129	497	71	158	15	10	4	61	39	6	26	.318	.375	.412	113	10	10	.934	-16	96	101	*S-128	0.3
1933	Pit N	152	573	85	180	29	**19**	9	97	64	5	23	.314	.388	.478	146	35	3	.945	-10	98	104	*S-152	3.8
1934	Pit N★	149	558	115	186	41	11	12	94	**94**	2	38	.333	**.431**	.511	148	43	10	.952	3	101	91	*S-149	**5.5**
1935	Pit N★	137	499	108	192	34	10	19	99	**97**	7	18	**.385**	**.491**	**.607**	**187**	**69**	4	.950	-9	101	79	*S-137	**6.6**
1936	Pit N☆	**156**	568	**122**	190	30	11	9	78	**118**	5	21	.335	**.453**	.474	146	46	6	.945	-9	97	93	*S-156	4.7
1937	Pit N★	126	469	71	151	17	**17**	5	72	54	2	22	.322	.394	.463	132	21	7	.956	5	100	93	*S-108,O-12(LF)	3.2
1938	Pit N☆	148	541	88	174	35	5	7	68	104	2	21	.322	.433	.444	140	38	14	.961	17	108	**118**	*S-147	6.4
1939	Pit N★	152	595	94	182	30	11	6	62	70	6	20	.306	.385	.424	119	18	12	.962	11	**107**	96	*S-152	4.0
1940	Pit N★	**156**	594	**113**	178	40	**15**	7	95	88	3	25	.300	.393	.453	134	31	12	.942	9	**109**	89	*S-155/3-2	**5.1**
1941	Pit N★	106	374	69	118	20	7	6	38	50	2	13	.316	.399	.455	141	21	8	.958	-8	100	77	S-97/3-3	2.1
1942	Bro N★	128	495	82	137	18	4	2	49	51	3	17	.277	.348	.341	100	1	8	.959	-10	88	89	*3-119/S-5,2	-0.5
1943	Bro N	149	610	**112**	186	39	6	5	66	60	3	13	.305	.370	.413	126	21	**20**	.965	-15	93	89	S-99,3-55	1.6
1947	†Bro N	64	126	24	41	5	2	2	25	27	0	11	.325	.444	.444	132	7	4	1.000	1	112	0	O-22(LF),3-10	0.7
1948	Bro N	65	123	19	30	3	0	3	22	21	0	8	.244	.354	.341	86	-2	0	1.000	2	93	210	O-26(LF)/3-8	-0.2
Total	14	1817	6622	1173	2103	356	128	96	926	937	46	276	.318	.406	.453	136	359	118	.951	-29	101	95	*S-1485,3-197/O-60(LF),2	43.3
VAUGHN, FRED Frederick Thomas "Muscles" B 10.18.1918 Coalinga, CA D 3.2.1964 Near Lake Wales, FL BR/TR 5-10/185# d8.20																								
1944	Was A	30	109	10	28	2	1	1	21	9	1	24	.257	.319	.321	87	-2	2-2	.942	-2	100	90	2-26/3-3	-0.3
1945	Was A	80	268	28	63	7	4	1	25	23	1	48	.235	.298	.302	81	-7	0-3	.946	-11	94	84	2-76/S	-1.8
Total	2	110	377	38	91	9	5	2	46	32	2	72	.241	.304	.308	83	-9	2-5	.945	-13	96	86	2-102/3-3,S	-2.1
VAUGHN, GREG Gregory Lamont B 7.3.1965 Sacramento, CA BR/TR 6/193# d8.10																								
1989	Mil A	38	113	18	30	3	0	5	23	13-0	0	23	.265	.336	.425	116	2	4-1	.943	-2	83	90	O-24(LF),D-13	0.0
1990	Mil A	120	382	51	84	26	2	17	61	33-1	1	91	.220	.280	.432	98	-2	7-4	.967	-1	95	124	*O-106(LF)/D-8	-0.7
1991	Mil A	145	542	81	132	24	5	27	98	62-2	1	125	.244	.319	.456	116	10	2-2	.994	6	110	65	*O-135(134-0-1),D-10	1.1
1992	Mil A	141	501	77	114	18	2	23	78	60-1	5	123	.228	.313	.409	104	2	15-15	.990	-2	99	65	*O-131(131-0-1)/D-7	-0.6
1993	Mil A★	154	569	97	152	28	2	30	97	89-14	5	118	.267	.369	.482	129	25	10-7	.986	-1	106	17	O-94(LF),D-58	1.6
1994	Mil A	95	370	59	94	24	1	19	55	51-6	1	93	.254	.345	.478	105	3	9-5	.982	-3	92	82	O-81(81-1-0),D-14	-0.4
1995	Mil A	108	392	67	88	19	1	17	59	55-3	0	89	.224	.317	.408	83	-10	10-4	—	0	0	0	*D-104	-1.6
1996	Mil A☆	102	375	78	105	16	0	31	95	58-4	4	99	.280	.378	.571	132	18	5-2	.980	-4	94	72	*O-100(98-3-0)/D	1.0
	†SD N	43	141	20	29	3	1	10	22	24-2	2	31	.206	.329	.454	110	2	4-1	.974	1	109	92	O-39(LF)	0.2
1997	SD N	120	361	60	78	10	0	18	57	56-1	2	110	.216	.322	.393	94	-4	7-4	.994	0	92	120	O-94(LF)/D-3	-0.7
1998	†SD N★	158	573	112	156	28	4	50	119	79-6	5	121	.272	.363	.597	160	48	11-4	.993	1	100	53	*O-151(LF)/D-4	4.2
1999	Cin N	153	550	104	135	20	2	45	118	85-3	3	137	.245	.347	.535	116	12	15-2	.986	1	100	93	*O-144(LF)/D-6	1.0
2000	TB A	127	461	83	117	27	1	28	74	80-3	2	128	.254	.365	.499	117	13	8-1	.993	1	95	138	O-72(LF),D-52	0.9
2001	TB A✱	136	485	74	113	25	0	24	82	71-7	3	130	.233	.333	.433	102	2	11-5	.978	6	120	124	D-76,O-57(LF)	0.1
2002	TB A	69	251	28	41	10	2	8	29	41-1	3	82	.163	.286	.315	61	-14	3-2	.987	3	119	110	D-38,O-31(LF)	-1.5
2003	Col N	22	37	8	7	3	0	3	5	8-0	0	13	.189	.326	.514	102	0	0-0	1.000	1	144	0	/O-7(6-0-1),D-3	0.1
Total	15	1731	6103	1017	1475	284	23	355	1072	865-54	37	1513	.242	.337	.470	112	107	121-59	.986	7	101	82	*O-1266(1261-4-3),D-397	4.7
VAUGHN, FARMER Harry Francis B 3.1.1864 Ruraldale, OH D 2.21.1914 Cincinnati, OH BR/TR 6-3/177# d10.7 OF Total (59-LF 14-CF 35-RF)																								
1886	Cin AA	1	3	0	0	0	0	0	0	0	1		.000	.250	.000	-19	0	0	.917	0			/C	0.0
1888	Lou AA	51	189	15	37	4	2	1	21	4	1		.196	.216	.254	52	-11	4	.863	-1	95	207	O-28(22-1-5),C-25	-1.0
1889	Lou AA	90	360	39	86	11	5	3	45	7	0	41	.239	.253	.322	65	-19	13	.900	-2			C-54,O-20(5-9-4),1-18/3-3	-1.6
1890	NY P	44	166	27	44	7	0	1	22	10	0	9	.265	.307	.325	63	-9	6	.877	-8	*99*	*66*	C-30,O-12(8-1-3)/32	-1.2
1891	Cin AA	51	175	21	45	7	1	1	14	14	1	15	.257	.316	.326	77	-6	7	.923	4	*89*	*129*	C-44/O-6(3-1-2),1-2,3-2,P	0.1
	Mil AA	25	99	13	33	7	0	0	9	4	0	5	.333	.359	.404	98	-1	1	.924	5	*120*	*67*	C-20/1-4,O(LF)	0.4
	Year	76	274	34	78	14	1	1	23	18	1	20	.285	.331	.354	86	-7	8	.923	9	*100*	*107*	C-64/O-7(4-1-2),1-6,3-2,P	0.5
1892	Cin N	91	346	45	88	10	5	2	50	16	4	13	.254	.295	.329	90	-6	10	.929	-6	*118*	*73*	C-67,1-14,O-11(4-0-7)/3-6	-0.6
1893	Cin N	121	483	68	135	17	12	1	108	35	3	17	.280	.332	.371	85	-13	16	**.969**	1	*110*	*84*	C-80,O-23(12-1-10),1-21	-0.5
1894	Cin N	72	284	50	88	15	5	8	64	12	0	11	.310	.338	.482	93	-6	5	.918	-3	*98*	*87*	C-43,1-27/O-8(4-1-3),S-3	-0.4
1895	Cin N	92	334	60	102	23	5	1	48	17	0	10	.305	.339	.413	90	-6	15	.934	10	*102*	*107*	C-77,1-15/32	0.9
1896	Cin N	114	433	71	127	20	9	2	66	16	1	7	.293	.320	.395	82	-14	7	.984	12	98	114	1-57,C-57	0.3
1897	Cin N	54	199	21	58	13	5	0	30	2	0		.291	.299	.407	80	-7	2	.986	1	85	101	1-35,C-15	-0.4
1898	Cin N	78	275	35	84	12	4	1	46	11	3		.305	.339	.389	101	-1	4	.979	0	51	111	1-39,C-33	0.3
1899	Cin N	31	108	9	19	1	0	0	2	3	0		.176	.198	.185	5	-14	2	.982	3	124	82	1-21/C-7,O(RF)	-1.0
Total	13	915	3454	474	946	147	53	21	525	151	14	128	.274	.307	.365	80	-113	92	.926	17	*100*	*78*	C-553,1-253,O-110L/3-13,S-3,2-2,P	-4.7
VAUGHN, MO Maurice Samuel B 12.15.1967 Norwalk, CT BL/TR 6-1/230# d6.27																								
1991	Bos A	74	219	21	57	12	0	4	32	26-2	2	43	.260	.339	.370	93	-1	2-1	.985	-1	93	127	1-49,D-16	-0.6
1992	Bos A	113	355	42	83	16	2	13	57	47-7	3	67	.234	.326	.400	97	-1	3-3	.982	-1	102	108	1-85,D-20	-1.0

Year	Tm Lg	G	AB	R	H	2B	3B	HR	RBI	BB-IB	HP	SO	AVG	OBP	SLG	AOPS	ABR	SB-CS	FA	FR	Rng	Thr	G at Pos	BFW
1993	Bos A	152	539	86	160	34	1	29	101	79-23	8	130	.297	.390	.525	136	30	4-3	.987	-11	75	98	*1-131,D-19	0.5
1994	Bos A	111	394	65	122	25	1	26	82	57-**20**	10	112	.310	.408	.576	144	27	4-4	.989	-5	82	112	*1-106/D	1.1
1995	†Bos A★	140	550	98	165	28	3	39	**126**	68-17	14	150	.300	.388	.575	142	35	11-4	.992	-3	94	106	*1-138/D-2	1.8
1996	Bos A★	161	635	118	207	29	1	44	143	95-19	14	154	.326	.420	.583	148	50	2-0	.988	-12	71	86	*1-146,D-15	2.1
1997	Bos A	141	527	91	166	24	0	35	96	86-17	12	154	.315	.420	.560	151	43	2-2	.988	-7	85	99	*1-131/D-9	2.2
1998	†Bos A✳	154	609	107	205	31	2	40	115	61-13	8	144	.337	.402	.591	151	46	0-0	.991	-4	90	83	*1-142,D-12	2.6
1999	Ana A	139	524	63	147	20	0	33	108	54-7	11	127	.281	.358	.508	119	14	0-0	.995	-2	88	102	1-72,D-67	0.1
2000	Ana A	161	614	93	167	31	0	36	117	79-11	14	181	.272	.365	.498	114	13	2-0	.990	-12	74	**120**	*1-147,D-14	-1.2
2002	NY N	139	487	67	126	18	0	26	72	59-6	10	145	.259	.349	.456	118	10	0-1	.984	-15	59	89	*1-134	-1.7
2003	NY N	27	79	10	15	2	0	3	15	14-2	2	22	.190	.323	.329	74	-3	0-0	.974	-3	64	117	1-24	-0.7
Total	12	1512	5532	861	1620	270	10	328	1064	725-144	108	1429	.293	.383	.523	131	263	30-18	.988	-74	81	101	*1-1305,D-175	5.2
VAUGHN, BOBBY Robert B 6.4.1885 Stamford, NY D 4.11.1965 Seattle, WA BR/TR 5-9/150# d6.12																								
1909	NY A	5	14	1	2	0	0	0	0	1	0		.143	.200	.143	8	-1	1	.882	-3	46	0	/2-4,S	-0.5
1915	StL F	144	521	69	146	19	9	0	32	58	3	38	.280	.356	.351	94	-10	24	.953	-7	97	94	*2-127,S-12/3-8	-1.5
Total	2	149	535	70	148	19	9	0	32	59	3	38	.277	.352	.346	92	-11	25	.951	-10	96	91	2-131/S-13,3-8	-2.0
VAZQUEZ, RAMON Ramon Luis B 8.21.1976 Aibonito, P.R. BL/TR 5-11/170# d9.7																								
2001	†Sea A	17	35	5	8	0	0	0	4	0-0	0	3	.229	.222	.229	22	-4	0-0	1.000	-5	56	99	S-10/2-6,3-2	-0.8
2002	SD N	128	423	50	116	21	5	2	32	45-3	1	79	.274	.344	.362	99	-3	7-2	.985	9	102	99	2-81,S-41,3-20	1.3
2003	SD N	116	422	56	110	17	4	3	30	52-2	2	88	.261	.342	.341	88	-7	10-3	.969	-13	92	85	*S-108/3-4,2-3	-1.0
Total	3	261	880	111	234	38	9	5	66	97-5	3	170	.266	.339	.347	90	-14	17-5	.974	-8	96	84	S-159/2-90,3-26	-0.5
VEACH, BOBBY Robert Hayes B 6.29.1888 Island, KY D 8.7.1945 Detroit, MI BL/TR 5-11/160# d9.6																								
1912	Det A	23	79	8	27	5	1	0	15	5	1		.342	.388	.430	138	4	2	.927	1	97	162	O-22(LF)	0.4
1913	Det A	137	491	54	132	22	10	0	64	53	5	31	.269	.346	.354	107	5	22	.917	-5	98	86	*O-135(LF)	-0.7
1914	Det A	149	531	56	146	19	14	1	72	50	3	29	.275	.341	.369	110	5	20-20	.965	3	100	103	*O-145(LF)	-0.1
1915	Det A	152	569	81	178	**40**	10	3	**112**	68	4	43	.313	.390	.434	140	29	16-19	.975	2	100	97	*O-152(LF)	2.2
1916	Det A	150	566	92	173	33	15	3	91	52	3	41	.306	.367	.433	135	23	24-15	.967	3	109	70	*O-150(LF)	2.1
1917	Det A	**154**	571	79	182	31	12	8	**103**	61	**9**	44	.319	.393	.457	160	41	21	.956	2	111	77	*O-154(LF)	4.0
1918	Det A	127	499	59	139	21	13	3	**78**	35	4	23	.279	.331	.391	123	11	21	.977	2	107	83	*O-127(124-1-2)/P	0.8
1919	Det A	139	538	87	**191**	**45**	**17**	3	101	33	5	33	.355	.398	.519	160	41	19	.967	9	**117**	95	*O-138(LF)	4.5
1920	Det A	154	612	92	188	39	15	11	113	36	7	22	.307	.353	.474	121	15	11-7	.967	14	112	129	*O-154(LF)	2.1
1921	Det A	150	612	110	207	43	13	16	128	48	1	31	.338	.387	.529	133	29	14-10	.974	13	**115**	108	*O-149(LF)	2.7
1922	Det A	**155**	618	96	202	34	13	9	126	42	8	27	.327	.377	.468	123	20	9-1	.982	10	**116**	84	*O-154(LF)	1.8
1923	Det A	114	293	45	94	13	3	2	39	29	3	21	.321	.388	.406	111	5	10-3	.943	-6	88	72	O-85(46-13-26)	-0.4
1924	Bos A	142	519	77	153	35	9	5	99	47	5	18	.295	.359	.426	102	1	5-5	.956	-4	97	82	*O-130(LF)	-1.3
1925	Bos A	1	5	0	1	0	0	0	2	1	0	1	.200	.333	.200	38	0	0-0	1.000	-0	101	0	/O(LF)	-0.1
	NY A	56	116	13	41	10	2	0	15	8	1	0	.353	.400	.474	123	4	1-4	.957	2	87	253	O-33(13-0-30)	0.3
	†Was A	18	37	4	9	3	0	0	8	3	0	3	.243	.300	.324	60	-2	0-0	.923	-1	90	0	O-11(4-0-7)	-0.4
	Year	75	158	17	51	13	2	0	25	12	1	4	.323	.374	.430	106	1	1-4	.952	1	88	186	O-45(18-0-37)	-0.2
Total	14	1821	6656	953	2063	393	147	64	1166	571	59	367	.310	.370	.442	127	231	195-84	.964	43	106	94	*O-1740(1671-14-65)/P	17.9
VEACH, PEEK-A-BOO William Walter B 6.15.1862 Indianapolis, IN D 11.12.1937 Indianapolis, IN 6/175# d8.24 ▲																								
1884	KC U	27	82	9	11	1	0	1		9			.134	.220	.183	27	-10		.833	2	149	267	O-14(11-2-1),P-12/21	-0.3
1887	Lou AA	1	3	0	0	0	0	0	0	1	0		.000	.250	.000	-26	0	0	.750	-0	55	0	/P	0.0
1890	Cle N	64	238	24	56	10	5	0	32	33	3	28	.235	.336	.319	93	-1	9	.971	6	184	105	1-64	0.0
	Pit N	8	30	6	9	1	1	2	5	8	0	3	.300	.447	.600	231	6	0	.968	0	136	17	/1-8	0.4
	Year	72	268	30	65	11	6	2	37	41	3	31	.243	.349	.351	107	4	9	.971	7	178	95	1-72	0.4
Total	3	100	353	39	76	12	6	3	37	51	3	31	.215	.319	.309	90	-5	9	.971	8	175	93	/1-73,O-14(11-2-1),P-13,2	0.1
VEAL, COOT Orville Inman B 7.9.1932 Sandersville, GA BR/TR 6-1/165# d7.30																								
1958	Det A	58	207	29	53	10	2	0	16	14-0	1	21	.256	.304	.324	69	-9	1-1	.981	-5	92	82	S-58	-1.0
1959	Det A	77	89	12	18	1	0	1	15	8-1	1	7	.202	.273	.247	42	-7	0-0	.962	5	107	94	S-72	0.1
1960	Det A	27	64	8	19	5	1	0	8	11-0	0	7	.297	.400	.406	115	2	0-0	.988	-1	103	97	S-22/3-3,2	0.3
1961	Was A	69	218	21	44	10	0	0	8	19-0	3	29	.202	.273	.248	41	-18	1-8	.974	3	100	113	S-63	-1.3
1962	Pit N	1	1	0	0	0	0	0	0	0-0	0	1	.000	.000	.000	-99	0	0-0	—	0			H	0.0
1963	Det A	15	32	5	7	0	0	0	4	4-0	0	4	.219	.297	.219	48	-2	0-0	.980	2	126	19	S-12	0.0
Total	6	247	611	75	141	26	3	1	51	56-1	5	69	.231	.298	.288	59	-34	2-9	.976	4	100	93	S-227/3-3,2	-1.9
VEGA, JESUS Jesus Anthony (Morales) B 10.14.1955 Bayamon, P.R. BR/TR 6-1/176# d9.5																								
1979	Min A	4	7	0	0	0	0	0	0	0-0	0	2	.000	.000	.000	-96	-2	0-0	—	0			/D-3	-0.2
1980	Min A	12	30	3	5	0	0	0	4	3-0	0	7	.167	.242	.167	13	-4	1-0	1.000	0	697	0	/1-2,D-9	-0.3
1982	Min A	71	199	23	53	6	0	5	29	8-1	0	19	.266	.289	.372	80	-6	6-1	.974	-2	78	63	D-39,1-18/O(LF)	-0.9
Total	3	87	236	26	58	6	0	5	33	11-1	0	28	.246	.275	.335	65	-12	7-1	.975	-1	87	62	/D-51,1-20,O(LF)	-1.4
VELANDIA, JORGE Jorge Luis (Macias) B 1.12.1975 Caracas, Venezuela BR/TR 5-9/160# d6.20																								
1997	SD N	14	29	0	3	2	0	0	0	1-0	0	7	.103	.133	.172	-22	-5	0-0	.941	-2	92	139	/S-6,2-5,3-3	-0.6
1998	Oak A	8	4	0	1	0	0	0	0	0-0	0	1	.250	.250	.250	31	0	0-0	.909	1	173	112	/S-7,2	0.1
1999	Oak A	63	48	4	9	1	0	0	2	2-0	1	13	.188	.235	.208	15	-6	2-0	.989	8	118	119	2-52/S-8,3-2,D	0.3
2000	Oak A	18	24	1	3	1	0	0	2	0-0	1	6	.125	.160	.167	-17	-4	0-0	1.000	1	111	124	2-14/S-4	-0.2
	NY N	15	7	1	0	0	0	0	0	2-0	0	2	.000	.222	.000	-39	-2	0-0	1.000	-2	35	0	/2-7,S-7,3-3	-0.3
2001	NY N	9	9	1	0	0	0	0	0	2-0	0	1	.000	.182	.000	-50	-2	0-0	1.000	-2	77	100	/S-8,3	-0.3
2003	NY N	23	58	6	11	3	1	0	8	10-1	0	15	.190	.304	.276	56	-4	0-0	.972	3	110	96	S-23	0.1
Total	6	150	179	13	27	7	1	0	12	17-1	2	45	.151	.231	.201	14	-23	2-0	.987	8	108	104	/2-79,S-63,3-9,D	-0.9
VELARDE, RANDY Randy Lee B 11.24.1962 Midland, TX BR/TR 6/190# d8.20 OF Total (97-LF 4-CF 12-RF)																								
1987	NY A	8	22	1	4	0	0	0	1	0-0	0	6	.182	.182	.182	-3	-3	0-0	.933	-1	100	76	/S-8	-0.4
1988	NY A	48	115	18	20	6	0	5	12	8-0	2	24	.174	.240	.357	65	-6	1-1	.967	3	109	168	2-24,S-14,3-11	-0.2
1989	NY A	33	100	12	34	4	2	2	11	7-0	1	14	.340	.389	.480	145	6	0-3	.954	-0	87	154	3-27/S-9	0.5
1990	NY A	95	229	21	48	6	2	5	19	20-0	1	53	.210	.275	.319	66	-11	0-3	.945	8	113	105	3-74,S-15/O-5(LF),2-3,D-3	-0.3
1991	NY A	80	184	19	45	11	1	1	15	18-0	3	43	.245	.322	.332	81	-4	3-1	.935	10	118	114	3-50,S-31/O-2(LF)	0.8
1992	NY A	121	412	57	112	24	1	7	46	38-1	2	78	.272	.333	.386	103	2	7-2	.974	-1	103	91	S-75,3-26,O-23(14-2-7)/2-3	0.7
1993	NY A	85	226	28	68	13	2	7	24	18-2	4	39	.301	.360	.469	126	8	2-2	.932	1	101	103	O-50(48-2-0),S-26,3-16/D	1.0
1994	NY A	77	280	47	78	16	1	9	34	22-0	4	61	.279	.338	.439	103	1	4-2	.944	2	107	116	S-49,3-27/O-7(6-0-1),2-5	0.6
1995	†NY A	111	367	60	102	19	1	7	46	55-0	4	64	.278	.375	.392	102	3	5-1	.976	-2	89	72	2-62,S-28,O-20(20-0-1),3-19	0.6
1996	Cal A	136	530	82	151	27	3	14	54	70-0	5	118	.285	.372	.426	101	3	7-7	.982	-17	81	99	*2-114,3-28/S-7	-0.9
1997	Ana A	1	0	0	0	0	0	0	0	0-0	0	0	—	—	—	—	0	0-0	—	0			/R	0.0
1998	Ana A	51	188	29	49	13	1	4	26	34-0	1	42	.261	.375	.404	103	2	7-2	.982	-4	95	79	2-51	0.2
1999	Ana A	95	376	57	115	15	4	9	48	43-1	4	56	.306	.383	.439	110	6	13-4	.986	6	110	94	2-95	1.7
	Oak A	61	255	48	85	10	3	7	28	27-1	2	42	.333	.401	.478	129	11	11-4	.977	-3	100	102	2-61	1.1
	Year	156	631	105	200	25	7	16	76	70-2	6	98	.317	.390	.455	117	17	24-8	.983	2	106	97	*2-156	2.8
2000	†Oak A	122	485	82	135	23	0	12	41	54-0	3	95	.278	.354	.400	93	-5	9-3	.982	**22**	**115**	111	*2-122	2.2
2001	Tex A	78	296	46	88	16	2	9	31	29-0	5	73	.297	.369	.456	112	6	4-2	.988	0	100	109	2-52/1-9,3-7,O-2(RF),D-6	0.7
	†NY A	15	46	4	7	3	0	0	1	5-0	3	13	.152	.278	.217	33	-4	2-0	.952	2	135	106	/3-7,O-3(2-0-1),1D	-0.2
	Year	93	342	50	95	19	2	9	32	34-0	8	86	.278	.356	.424	101	2	6-2	.988	3	100	109	2-52,3-14,D-11,1-10/O-5(2-0-3)	0.5
2002	†Oak A	56	133	22	30	8	0	2	8	15-1	5	32	.226	.325	.331	75	-4	3-0	.981	4	108	121	2-38/1-5,3D	0.2
Total	16	1273	4244	633	1171	214	23	100	445	463-6	49	853	.276	.352	.408	100	11	78-37	.980	31	101	102	2-630,3-293,S-262,O-112L/D-20,1	8.3
VELASQUEZ, GUILLERMO Guillermo (Burgara) B 4.23.1968 Mexicali, Mexico BL/TR 6-3/220# d9.14																								
1992	SD N	15	23	1	7	0	0	1	5	1-0	0	7	.304	.333	.435	114	0	0-0	.933	-0	82	83	/1-3,O-2(LF)	0.0
1993	SD N	79	143	7	30	2	0	3	20	13-2	0	35	.210	.274	.287	50	-10	0-0	.984	-1	99	91	1-38/O-6(4-0-2)	-1.4
Total	2	94	166	8	37	2	0	4	25	14-2	0	42	.223	.282	.307	58	-10	0-0	.981	-1	98	91	/1-41,O-8(6-0-2)	-1.4
VELAZQUEZ, FREDDIE Federico Antonio (Velasquez) B 12.6.1937 Santo Domingo, D.R. BR/TR 6-1/185# d4.20																								
1969	Sea A	6	16	1	2	2	0	0	2	1-0	0	3	.125	.176	.250	18	-2	0-0	1.000	-2	40	0	/C-5	-0.3

Year	Tm Lg	G	AB	R	H	2B	3B	HR	RBI	BB-IB	HP	SO	AVG	OBP	SLG	AOPS	ABR	SB-CS	FA	FR	Rng	Thr	G at Pos	BFW
1973	Atl N	15	23	2	8	1	0	0	3	1-0	0	3	.348	.375	.391	105	0	0-0	.975	1	146	60	C-11	0.1
Total	2	21	39	3	10	3	0	0	5	2-0	0	6	.256	.293	.333	71	-2	0-0	.985	-1	102	35	/C-16	-0.2
VELEZ, OTTO Otoniel (Franceschi) B 11.29.1950 Ponce, P.R. BR/TR 6/195# d9.4																								
1973	NY A	23	77	9	15	4	0	2	7	15-0	0	24	.195	.326	.325	87	-1	0-1	.959	-0	99	128	O-23(RF)	-0.3
1974	NY A	27	67	9	14	1	1	2	10	15-1	0	24	.209	.345	.343	103	1	0-0	.986	-3	48	54	1-21/O-3(RF),3-2	-0.4
1975	NY A	6	8	0	2	0	0	0	1	2-0	0	0	.250	.400	.250	89	0	0-0	1.000	-0	0	124	/1D	0.0
1976	†NY A	49	94	11	25	6	0	2	10	23-1	0	26	.266	.410	.394	137	6	0-0	.979	-1	107	66	O-24(6-0-19)/1-8,3D	0.4
1977	Tor A	120	360	50	92	19	3	16	62	65-1	1	87	.256	.366	.458	123	13	4-2	.973	0	100	98	O-79(RF),D-28	0.9
1978	Tor A	91	248	29	66	14	2	9	38	45-1	2	41	.266	.380	.448	130	12	1-3	.982	9	112	220	O-74(39-0-39)/1D	1.7
1979	Tor A	99	274	45	79	21	0	15	48	46-2	3	45	.288	.396	.529	145	20	0-1	.971	-1	102	65	O-73(43-0-34)/1-6,D-9	1.5
1980	Tor A	104	357	54	96	12	3	20	62	54-8	2	86	.269	.365	.487	126	14	0-0	.975	0	118	55	D-97/1-3	1.0
1981	Tor A	80	240	32	51	9	2	11	28	55-3	3	60	.213	.363	.404	114	7	0-3	1.000	-0	0	0	D-74/1	0.3
1982	Tor A	28	52	4	10	1	0	1	5	13-0	0	15	.192	.354	.269	68	-2	1-0	—	0	0	0	D-24	-0.2
1983	Cle A	10	25	1	2	0	0	0	1	3-0	0	6	.080	.179	.080	-25	-4	0-0	—	0			/D-8	-0.5
Total	11	637	1802	244	452	87	11	78	272	336-17	11	414	.251	.369	.441	122	66	6-10	.973	3	104	122	O-276(88-0-197),D-255/1-41,3-3	4.4
VELTMAN, PAT Arthur Patrick B 3.24.1906 Mobile, AL D 10.1.1980 San Antonio, TX BR/TR 6/175# d4.17																								
1926	Chi A	5	4	1	1	0	0	0	0	1	0	1	.250	.400	.250	75	0	0-0	1.000	0	151	0	/S	0.0
1928	NY N	1	3	1	1	0	1	0	0	1	0	0	.333	.500	1.000	282	1	0	1.000	-0	95	0	/O(CF)	0.1
1929	NY N	2	1	1	0	0	0	0	0	2	0	0	.000	.667	.000	81	0	0	1.000	-0	*0*	*0*	/C	0.0
1931	Bos N	1	1	0	0	0	0	0	0	0	0	0	.000	.000	.000	-99	0	0	—	0			H	0.0
1932	NY N	2	1	0	0	0	0	0	0	0	0	1	.000	.000	.000	-99	0	0	—	0			H	0.0
1934	Pit N	12	28	1	3	0	0	0	2	0	0	1	.107	.107	.107	-41	-6	0	1.000	-1	*65*	*0*	C-11	-0.6
Total	6	23	38	4	5	0	1	0	2	4	0	3	.132	.214	.184	7	-5	0-0	1.000	-1	*62*	*0*	/C-12,O(CF)S	-0.5
VENABLE, MAX William McKinley B 6.6.1957 Phoenix, AZ BL/TR 5-10/185# d4.8																								
1979	SF N	55	85	12	14	1	1	0	3	10-1	1	18	.165	.260	.200	29	-8	3-3	.914	-2	78	127	O-25(6-2-21)	-1.2
1980	SF N	64	138	13	37	5	0	0	10	15-0	0	22	.268	.333	.304	83	-3	8-2	1.000	-3	94	0	O-40(16-14-11)	-0.6
1981	SF N	18	32	2	6	0	2	0	1	4-0	0	3	.188	.278	.313	68	-2	3-1	1.000	-0	102	0	/O-5(0-2-3)	-0.2
1982	SF N	71	125	17	28	2	1	1	7	7-0	0	16	.224	.265	.280	53	-8	9-3	.986	4	102	258	O-53(33-12-8)	-0.5
1983	SF N	94	228	28	50	7	4	6	27	22-1	3	34	.219	.295	.364	85	-6	15-2	.993	6	117	139	O-66(32-25-14)	0.1
1984	Mon N	38	71	7	17	2	0	2	7	3-1	1	7	.239	.276	.352	80	-2	1-0	1.000	-0	107	0	O-27(23-3-3)	-0.3
1985	Cin N	77	135	21	39	12	3	0	10	6-0	0	17	.289	.315	.422	101	0	11-3	1.000	3	116	157	O-39(31-7-3)	0.3
1986	Cin N	108	147	17	31	7	1	2	15	17-2	0	24	.211	.289	.313	64	-7	7-2	.969	-0	111	0	O-57(49-8-3)	-0.8
1987	Cin N	7	7	2	1	0	0	0	2	0-0	0	0	.143	.143	.143	-23	-1	0-0	1.000	-0	72	0	/O-4(CF)	-0.2
1989	Cal A	20	53	7	19	4	0	0	4	1-0	0	16	.358	.370	.434	128	2	0-0	1.000	-1	86	0	O-13(4-4-7)	0.0
1990	Cal A	93	189	26	49	9	3	4	21	24-2	0	31	.259	.340	.402	110	3	5-1	.975	-1	96	101	O-77(40-33-10)/D	0.2
1991	Cal A	82	187	24	46	8	2	3	21	11-2	2	30	.246	.292	.358	80	-6	2-1	.967	-5	76	101	O-65(13-27-30)/D-3	-1.2
Total	12	727	1397	176	337	57	17	18	128	120-9	7	218	.241	.302	.345	81	-38	64-18	.982	-1	99	100	O-471(247-141-113)/D-4	-4.4
VENTURA, ROBIN Robin Mark B 7.14.1967 Santa Maria, CA BL/TR 6-1/198# d9.12																								
1989	Chi A	16	45	5	8	3	0	0	7	8-0	1	6	.178	.298	.244	61	-2	0-0	.962	2	110	73	3-16	0.0
1990	Chi A	150	493	48	123	17	1	5	54	55-2	1	53	.249	.324	.318	83	-10	1-4	.939	3	100	**133**	*3-147/1	-0.8
1991	Chi A	157	606	92	172	25	1	23	100	80-3	4	67	.284	.367	.442	127	24	2-4	.959	1	99	111	*3-151,1-31	2.3
1992	Chi A★	157	592	85	167	38	1	16	93	93-9	0	71	.282	.375	.431	128	26	2-4	.957	26	**119**	106	*3-157/1-2	**5.1**
1993	†Chi A	157	554	85	145	27	1	22	94	105-16	3	82	.262	.379	.433	121	21	1-6	.965	-2	97	97	*3-155/1-4	1.8
1994	Chi A	109	401	57	113	15	1	18	78	61-15	2	69	.282	.373	.459	117	11	3-1	.935	-3	90	**143**	*3-108/1-3,S	0.9
1995	Chi A	135	492	79	145	22	0	26	93	75-11	1	98	.295	.384	.498	135	27	4-3	.948	-0	94	70	*3-121,1-18/D	2.5
1996	Chi A	158	586	96	168	31	2	34	105	78-10	2	81	.287	.368	.520	129	26	1-3	.974	3	93	**132**	*3-150,1-14	2.6
1997	Chi A	54	183	27	48	10	1	6	26	34-5	0	21	.262	.373	.426	114	5	0-0	.956	3	101	120	3-54	0.8
1998	Chi A	161	590	84	155	31	4	21	91	79-**15**	1	111	.263	.349	.436	106	6	1-1	.966	14	**112**	**154**	*3-161	2.0
1999	†NY N	161	588	88	177	38	0	32	120	74-10	3	109	.301	.379	.529	131	29	1-1	**.980**	19	107	**137**	*3-160/1	4.5
2000	†NY N	141	469	61	109	23	1	24	84	75-12	2	91	.232	.338	.439	99	-1	3-5	.954	5	99	122	*3-137/1	0.4
2001	NY N	142	456	70	108	20	0	21	61	88-10	1	101	.237	.359	.419	106	7	2-5	.957	9	105	117	*3-139	1.6
2002	†NY A★	141	465	68	115	17	0	27	93	90-9	2	101	.247	.368	.458	120	16	3-1	.941	11	105	109	*3-137/1-5	2.6
2003	NY A	89	283	31	71	13	0	9	42	40-2	0	62	.251	.344	.392	95	-1	0-0	.974	-0	100	74	3-80/2D	-0.1
	LA N	49	109	11	24	5	1	5	13	18-2	0	25	.220	.331	.422	100	0	0-0	.993	-2	92	118	1-42/3-3	-0.4
Total	15	1977	6912	987	1848	335	14	289	1154	1053-131	23	1148	.267	.363	.445	116	184	24-38	.958	88	102	117	*3-1876,1-122/D-5,2S	25.8
VENTURA, VINCE Vincent B 4.18.1917 New York, NY D 9.11.2001 Lake Worth, FL BR/TR 6-1.5/190# d5.8																								
1945	Was A	18	58	4	12	0	0	0	2	4	0	4	.207	.258	.207	39	-5	0-0	.886	-1	99	78	O-15(LF)	-0.7
VERAS, QUILVIO Quilvio Alberto (Perez) B 4.3.1971 Santo Domingo, D.R. BB/TR 5-9/170# d4.25																								
1995	Fla N	124	440	86	115	20	7	5	32	80-0	9	68	.261	.384	.373	101	4	**56**-21	.986	5	93	110	*2-122/O-2(0-1-1)	1.9
1996	Fla N	73	253	40	64	8	1	4	14	51-1	2	42	.253	.381	.340	96	1	8-8	.986	10	102	126	2-67	1.3
1997	SD N	145	539	74	143	23	1	3	45	72-0	7	84	.265	.357	.328	88	-7	33-12	.984	-5	103	71	*2-142	-0.1
1998	†SD N	138	517	79	138	24	2	6	45	84-2	6	78	.267	.373	.356	102	5	24-9	.987	20	**108**	113	*2-131	3.3
1999	SD N	132	475	95	133	25	2	6	41	65-0	2	88	.280	.368	.379	97	0	30-17	.981	16	103	110	*2-118	2.1
2000	Atl N	84	298	56	92	15	0	5	37	51-0	5	50	.309	.413	.409	110	8	25-12	.984	4	109	91	2-82	1.6
2001	Atl N	71	258	39	65	14	2	3	25	24-1	7	52	.252	.330	.357	77	-9	7-4	.991	5	106	102	2-67	0.0
Total	7	767	2780	469	750	129	15	32	239	427-4	38	462	.270	.372	.362	96	2	183-83	.985	55	103	102	2-729/O-2(0-1-1)	10.1
VERAS, WILTON Wilton Andres B 1.19.1978 Monte Cristi, D.R. BR/TR 6-2/186# d7.1																								
1999	Bos A	36	118	14	34	5	1	2	13	5-0	2	14	.288	.323	.398	82	-4	0-2	.929	0	95	141	3-35	-0.4
2000	Bos A	49	164	21	40	7	1	0	14	7-0	2	20	.244	.278	.299	46	-14	0-0	.907	4	109	145	3-49	-0.9
Total	2	85	282	35	74	12	2	2	27	12-0	4	34	.262	.297	.340	61	-18	0-2	.916	4	103	143	/3-84	-1.3
VERBAN, EMIL Emil Matthew "Dutch" or "Antelope" B 8.27.1915 Lincoln, IL D 6.8.1989 Quincy, IL BR/TR 5-11/165# d4.18																								
1944	†StL N	146	498	51	128	14	2	0	43	19	2	14	.257	.287	.293	62	-26	0	.968	-5	94	**150**	*2-146	-2.4
1945	StL N✱	**155**	597	59	166	22	8	0	72	19	3	15	.278	.304	.342	77	-21	4	**.978**	-21	88	118	*2-155	-3.4
1946	StL N	1	1	0	0	0	0	0	0	0	0	0	.000	.000	.000	-96	0	0	—	0			H	0.0
	Phi N★	138	473	44	130	17	5	0	34	21	0	18	.275	.306	.332	83	-13	5	.963	-2	100	100	*2-138	-0.8
	Year	139	474	44	130	17	5	0	34	21	0	18	.274	.305	.331	83	-13	5	.963	-2	100	100	*2-138	-0.8
1947	Phi N★	**155**	540	50	154	14	8	0	42	23	1	8	.285	.316	.341	77	-20	5	.982	**18**	**104**	111	*2-155	0.6
1948	Phi N	55	169	14	39	5	1	0	11	11	1	5	.231	.282	.272	51	-12	0	.975	-2	100	91	2-54	-1.2
	Chi N	56	248	37	73	15	1	1	16	4	1	7	.294	.308	.375	88	-5	4	.964	5	106	134	2-56	0.3
	Year	111	417	51	112	20	2	1	27	15	2	12	.269	.297	.333	72	-17	4	**.969**	3	**103**	**115**	*2-110	-0.9
1949	Chi N	98	343	38	99	11	1	0	22	8	2	2	.289	.309	.327	72	-14	3	.965	6	107	98	2-88	-0.4
1950	Chi N	45	37	7	4	1	0	0	1	3	0	5	.108	.175	.135	-17	-6	0	.966	3	165	202	/2-8,S-3,3O(CF)	-0.3
	Bos N	4	5	1	0	0	0	0	0	0	0	0	.000	.000	.000	-99	-2	0	.833	-0	72	175	/2-2	-0.2
	Year	49	42	8	4	1	0	0	1	3	0	5	.095	.156	.119	-27	-8	0	.927	3	138	194	2-10/S-3,3O(CF)	-0.5
Total	7	853	2911	301	793	99	26	1	241	108	10	74	.272	.301	.325	73	-119	21	.971	1	99	117	2-802/S-3,O(CF)3	-7.8
VERBLE, GENE Gene Kermit "Satchel" B 6.29.1928 Concord, NC BR/TR 5-10/163# d4.17																								
1951	Was A	68	177	16	36	3	2	0	15	18	0	10	.203	.277	.243	42	-15	1-1	.978	-3	99	99	S-28,2-19/3	-1.5
1953	Was A	13	21	4	4	0	0	0	2	2	0	1	.190	.261	.190	24	-2	0-0	1.000	1	113	126	/S-8	-0.1
Total	2	81	198	20	40	3	2	0	17	20	0	11	.202	.275	.237	40	-17	1-1	.981	-2	101	104	/S-36,2-19,3	-1.6
VERDI, FRANK Frank Michael B 6.2.1926 Brooklyn, NY BR/TR 5-10.5/170# d5.10																								
1953	NY A	1	0	0	0	0	0	0	0	0	0	0	—	—	—	—	0	0-0	—	-0	0	0	/S	0.0
VERGEZ, JOHNNY John Louis B 7.9.1906 Oakland, CA D 7.15.1991 Davis, CA BR/TR 5-8/165# d4.14																								
1931	NY N	152	565	67	157	24	2	13	81	29	6	65	.278	.320	.396	94	-7	11	.932	-6	92	95	*3-152	-0.7
1932	NY N	118	376	42	98	21	3	6	43	25	2	36	.261	.310	.380	86	-8	1	.935	5	**107**	**123**	*3-111/S	0.1
1933	NY N	123	458	57	124	21	6	16	72	39	3	66	.271	.332	.448	123	13	1	.928	-13	91	108	*3-123	0.4
1934	NY N	108	320	31	64	18	1	7	27	28	2	55	.200	.269	.328	60	-18	1	.943	9	**116**	102	*3-104	-0.6

Year	Tm Lg	G	AB	R	H	2B	3B	HR	RBI	BB-IB	HP	SO	AVG	OBP	SLG	AOPS	ABR	SB-CS	FA	FR	Rng	Thr	G at Pos	BFW
1935	Phi N	148	546	56	136	27	4	9	63	46	4	67	.249	.312	.363	73	-20	8	**.953**	-4	88	102	*3-148/S-2	-1.9
1936	Phi N	15	40	4	11	2	0	1	5	3	0	11	.275	.326	.400	86	-1	0	.964	1	98	154	3-12	0.0
	StL N	8	18	1	3	1	0	0	1	1	0	3	.167	.211	.222	17	-2	0	.929	-0	76	166	/3-8	-0.2
	Year	23	58	5	14	3	0	1	6	4	0	14	.241	.290	.345	66	-3	0	.952	0	91	158	3-20	-0.2
Total	6	672	2323	258	593	114	16	52	292	171	17	303	.255	.311	.385	87	-43	22	.939	-8	97	106	3-658/S-3	-2.9
VERNON, MICKEY James Barton B 4.22.1918 Marcus Hook, PA BL/TL 6-2/180# d7.8 Mil 1944-45 M3 C6																								
1939	Was A	76	276	23	71	15	4	1	30	24	0	28	.257	.317	.351	76	-10	1-1	.985	-3	91	119	1-75	-1.9
1940	Was A	5	19	0	3	0	0	0	0	0	0	3	.158	.158	.158	-19	-3	0-0	1.000	-0	72	122	/1-4	-0.4
1941	Was A	138	531	73	159	27	11	9	93	43	0	51	.299	.352	.443	114	9	9-3	.992	-7	81	101	*1-132	-1.0
1942	Was A	**151**	621	76	168	34	6	9	86	59	3	63	.271	.337	.388	104	3	25-6	.982	-9	84	76	*1-151	-1.8
1943	Was A	145	553	89	148	29	8	7	70	67	**10**	55	.268	.357	.387	122	17	24-8	.990	-11	75	99	*1-143	0.1
1946	Was A★	148	587	88	207	**51**	8	8	85	49	0	64	**.353**	.403	.508	163	49	14-10	.990	-2	100	96	*1-147	4.3
1947	Was A	**154**	600	77	159	29	12	7	85	49	0	42	.265	.320	.388	99	-4	12-12	.987	-3	94	83	*1-154	-1.4
1948	Was A★	150	558	78	135	27	7	3	48	54	1	43	.242	.310	.332	73	-23	15-11	.989	5	114	83	*1-150	-2.4
1949	Cle A	153	584	72	170	27	4	18	83	58	2	51	.291	.357	.443	113	8	9-7	.991	16	**134**	116	*1-153	1.8
1950	Cle A	28	90	8	17	0	0	0	10	12	0	10	.189	.284	.189	24	-10	2-0	.996	1	102	126	1-25	-1.0
	Was A	90	327	47	100	17	3	9	65	50	4	29	.306	.404	.459	127	15	6-1	.990	2	111	104	1-85	1.4
	Year	118	417	55	117	17	3	9	75	62	4	39	.281	.379	.400	104	4	8-1	**.991**	3	109	109	*1-110	0.4
1951	Was A	141	546	69	160	30	7	9	87	53	2	45	.293	.358	.423	112	9	7-6	**.994**	-5	86	87	*1-137	-0.1
1952	Was A	154	569	71	143	33	9	10	80	89	0	66	.251	.353	.394	111	10	7-7	**.993**	-4	93	94	*1-153	0.0
1953	Was A★	**152**	608	101	205	**43**	11	15	115	63	4	57	**.337**	.403	.518	151	43	4-6	.992	-3	93	116	*1-152	3.0
1954	Was A★	151	597	90	173	**33**	14	20	97	61	5	61	.290	.357	.492	140	30	1-4	**.992**	-6	84	105	*1-148	1.4
1955	Was A★	150	538	74	162	23	8	14	85	74-9	3	50	.301	.384	.452	133	26	0-4	.994	-6	81	97	*1-144	1.0
1956	Bos A★	119	403	67	125	28	4	15	84	57-6	7	40	.310	.403	.511	125	16	1-0	.989	-5	85	99	*1-108	0.6
1957	Bos A	102	270	36	65	18	1	7	38	41-2	5	35	.241	.350	.393	97	1	0-0	.992	3	115	74	1-70	-0.1
1958	Cle A★	119	355	49	104	22	3	8	55	44-3	2	56	.293	.372	.439	126	14	0-4	.987	-2	93	104	1-96	0.5
1959	Mil N	74	91	8	20	4	0	3	14	7-1	1	20	.220	.283	.363	77	-3	0-0	.983	-0	108	71	1-10/O-4(2-0-2)	-0.4
1960	Pit N	9	8	0	1	0	0	0	1	1-1	0	0	.125	.222	.125	-2	-1	0-0	—	0			H	-0.1
Total	20	2409	8731	1196	2495	490	120	172	1311	955-22	49	869	.286	.359	.428	116	196	137-90	.990	-39	94	97	*1-2237/O-4(2-0-2)	3.5
VERSALLES, ZOILO Zoilo Casanova (Rodriguez) "Zorro" B 12.18.1939 Veldado, Cuba D 6.9.1995 Bloomington, MN BR/TR 5-10/150# d8.1																								
1959	Was A	29	59	4	9	0	0	1	1	4-0	1	15	.153	.219	.203	17	-7	1-0	.943	2	102	108	S-29	-0.3
1960	Was A	15	45	2	6	2	2	0	4	2-0	0	5	.133	.170	.267	16	-6	0-0	.935	-2	93	62	S-15	-0.7
1961	Min A	129	510	65	143	25	5	7	53	25-2	1	61	.280	.314	.390	83	-13	16-9	.952	-6	95	90	*S-129	-0.7
1962	Min A	160	568	69	137	18	3	17	67	37-8	2	71	.241	.287	.373	74	-22	5-5	.970	30	104	**134**	*S-160	2.1
1963	Min A★	159	621	74	162	31	**13**	10	54	33-2	5	66	.261	.303	.401	94	-7	7-4	.961	-4	95	100	*S-159	0.4
1964	Min A	160	659	94	171	33	**10**	20	64	42-1	**8**	88	.259	.311	.431	103	1	14-4	.957	-21	89	95	*S-160	-0.4
1965	†Min A★	160	666	**126**	182	**45**	**12**	19	77	41-3	7	122	.273	.319	.462	115	12	27-5	.950	0	104	**123**	*S-160	3.2
1966	Min A	137	543	73	135	20	6	7	36	40-2	7	85	.249	.307	.346	82	-12	10-12	.942	-14	93	95	*S-135	-1.7
1967	Min A	160	581	63	116	16	7	6	50	33-2	6	113	.200	.249	.282	53	-35	5-3	.958	7	101	101	*S-159	-1.6
1968	LA N	122	403	29	79	16	3	2	24	26-4	0	84	.196	.244	.266	57	-22	6-4	.954	7	100	97	*S-119	-0.6
1969	Cle A	72	217	21	49	11	1	1	13	21-1	2	47	.226	.298	.300	66	-10	3-1	.975	-7	89	66	2-46,3-30/S-3	-1.4
	Was A	31	75	9	20	2	1	0	6	3-0	1	13	.267	.304	.320	79	-2	1-0	.935	-1	110	34	S-13/2-6,3-5	-0.2
	Year	103	292	30	69	13	2	1	19	24-1	3	60	.236	.299	.305	69	-12	4-1	.978	-8	91	64	2-52,3-35,S-16	-1.6
1971	Atl N	66	194	21	37	11	0	5	22	11-1	0	40	.191	.233	.325	53	-12	2-1	.902	-14	84	41	3-30,S-24/2	-2.6
Total	12	1400	5141	650	1246	230	63	95	471	318-26	40	810	.242	.290	.367	82	-135	97-48	.956	-22	97	104	*S-1265/3-65,2-53	-4.5
VERYZER, TOM Thomas Martin B 2.11.1953 Port Jefferson, NY BR/TR 6-1/185# d8.14																								
1973	Det A	18	20	1	6	0	1	0	2	2-0	0	4	.300	.364	.400	108	0	0-0	.857	-4	63	28	S-18	-0.3
1974	Det A	22	55	4	13	2	0	2	9	5-0	0	8	.236	.300	.382	92	-1	1-0	.927	-8	69	43	S-20	-0.7
1975	Det A	128	404	37	102	13	1	5	48	23-1	5	76	.252	.297	.327	74	-14	2-6	.960	-3	96	79	*S-128	-0.5
1976	Det A	97	354	31	83	8	2	1	25	21-1	6	44	.234	.286	.277	64	-16	1-4	.966	4	102	89	S-97	-0.3
1977	Det A	125	350	31	69	12	1	2	28	16-0	0	44	.197	.230	.254	31	-34	0-1	.969	12	112	95	*S-124	-1.0
1978	Cle A	130	421	48	114	18	4	1	32	13-0	5	36	.271	.298	.340	81	-12	1-2	.963	-11	98	75	*S-129	-1.1
1979	Cle A	149	449	41	99	9	3	0	34	34-0	4	54	.220	.279	.254	45	-35	2-5	.974	2	100	90	*S-148	-1.9
1980	Cle A	109	358	28	97	12	0	2	28	10-1	8	25	.271	.303	.321	72	-14	0-5	.971	4	100	81	*S-108	-0.1
1981	Cle A	75	221	13	54	4	0	0	14	10-1	1	10	.244	.278	.262	58	-12	1-0	.970	-1	94	98	S-75	-0.6
1982	NY N	40	54	6	18	2	0	0	4	3-2	0	4	.333	.362	.370	108	1	1-0	.962	-11	107	66	2-26,S-16	-0.9
1983	Chi N	59	88	5	18	3	0	1	3	3-1	0	13	.205	.231	.273	37	-8	0-0	.978	1	115	140	S-28,3-17	-0.5
1984	†Chi N	44	74	5	14	1	0	0	4	3-1	4	11	.189	.259	.203	29	-7	0-0	.966	-3	82	89	S-36/3-5,2-4	-0.8
Total	12	996	2848	250	687	84	12	14	231	143-8	33	329	.241	.283	.294	61	-152	9-23	.966	-17	99	85	S-927/2-30,3-22	-8.7
VICK, ERNIE Henry Arthur B 7.2.1900 Toledo, OH D 7.16.1980 Ann Arbor, MI BR/TR 5-9.5/185# d6.29																								
1922	StL N	3	6	1	2	2	0	0	0	0	0	0	.333	.333	.667	159	1	0-0	.875	-0	*92*	*0*	/C-3	0.0
1924	StL N	16	23	2	8	1	0	0	0	3	0	3	.348	.423	.391	122	1	0-0	.974	2	*115*	*153*	C-16	0.3
1925	StL N	14	32	3	6	2	1	0	3	3	0	1	.188	.257	.313	44	-3	0-0	.929	-0	*115*	*56*	/C-9	-0.2
1926	StL N	24	51	6	10	2	0	0	4	3	0	4	.196	.241	.235	27	-5	0	.944	0	*128*	*101*	C-23	-0.4
Total	4	57	112	12	26	7	1	0	7	9	0	8	.232	.289	.313	58	-6	0-0	.944	1	*120*	*97*	/C-51	-0.3
VICK, SAMMY Samuel Bruce B 4.12.1895 Batesville, MS D 8.17.1986 Memphis, TN BR/TR 5-10.5/163# d9.20 Mil 1918																								
1917	NY A	10	36	4	10	3	0	0	2	1	0	6	.278	.297	.361	100	0	2	.882	-1	95	83	O-10(RF)	-0.1
1918	NY A	2	3	1	2	0	0	0	1	0	0	0	.667	.667	.667	296	1	0	—	-0	0	0	/O(RF)	0.1
1919	NY A	106	407	59	101	15	9	2	27	35	0	55	.248	.308	.344	82	-11	9	.952	-6	92	78	*O-100(RF)	-2.3
1920	NY A	51	118	21	26	7	1	0	11	14	2	20	.220	.313	.297	60	-6	1-1	.949	-2	113	0	O-33(4-1-28)	-1.0
1921	Bos A	44	77	5	20	3	1	0	9	1	0	10	.260	.269	.325	52	-6	0-1	1.000	-0	104	65	O-14(RF)	-0.7
Total	5	213	641	90	159	28	11	2	50	51	2	91	.248	.305	.335	76	-22	12-2	.951	-8	97	63	O-158(4-1-153)	-4.0
VICO, GEORGE George Steve "Sam" B 8.9.1923 San Fernando, CA D 1.14.1994 Redondo Beach, CA BL/TR 6-4/200# d4.20																								
1948	Det A	144	521	50	139	23	9	8	58	39	7	39	.267	.326	.392	88	-11	2-2	.988	-2	94	88	*1-142	-1.7
1949	Det A	67	142	15	27	5	2	4	18	21	4	17	.190	.311	.338	72	-6	0-0	.985	1	112	93	1-53	-0.6
Total	2	211	663	65	166	28	11	12	76	60	11	56	.250	.323	.380	85	-17	2-2	.987	-0	98	89	1-195	-2.3
VICTORINO, SHANE Shane Patrick B 11.30.1980 Wailuku, HI BB/TR 5-9/160# d4.2																								
2003	SD N	36	73	8	11	2	0	0	4	7-0	1	17	.151	.232	.178	11	-10	7-2	1.000	1	91	241	O-32(15-16-3)	-0.9
VIDAL, JOSE Jose (Nicolas) "Papito" B 4.3.1940 Batey Lechuga, D.R. BR/TR 6/190# d9.5																								
1966	Cle A	17	32	4	6	1	1	0	3	5-0	0	11	.188	.297	.281	67	-1	0-1	1.000	0	112	0	O-11(0-3-8)	-0.2
1967	Cle A	16	34	4	4	0	0	0	0	7-0	0	12	.118	.268	.118	17	-3	0-1	1.000	1	106	162	O-10(8-6-1)	-0.4
1968	Cle A	37	54	5	9	0	0	2	5	2-0	0	15	.167	.196	.278	43	-4	3-0	1.000	-1	75	0	O-26(11-0-15)/1	-0.6
1969	Sea A	18	26	7	5	0	1	1	2	4-0	1	8	.192	.323	.385	99	0	1-1	.917	-0	107	0	/O-6(1-0-5)	-0.1
Total	4	88	146	20	24	1	2	3	10	18-0	1	46	.164	.261	.260	53	-8	4-3	.985	-1	96	44	/O-53(20-9-29),1	-1.3
VIDRO, JOSE Jose Angel (Cetty) B 8.27.1974 Mayaguez, P.R. BB/TR 5-11/175# d6.8																								
1997	Mon N	67	169	19	42	12	1	2	17	11-0	2	20	.249	.297	.367	74	-6	1-0	.958	-2	90	123	3-36/2-5,D-5	-0.8
1998	Mon N	83	205	24	45	12	0	0	18	27-0	4	33	.220	.318	.278	61	-11	2-2	.975	-11	91	82	2-56/3-7	-1.9
1999	Mon N	140	494	67	150	45	2	12	59	29-2	4	51	.304	.346	.476	108	6	0-4	.982	-16	91	84	*2-121,1-14/O-3(LF),3-2	-0.7
2000	Mon N★	153	606	101	200	51	2	24	97	49-4	2	69	.330	.379	.540	126	24	5-4	.986	-1	105	101	*2-153	2.9
2001	Mon N	124	486	82	155	34	1	15	59	31-2	10	49	.319	.371	.486	117	13	4-1	.983	-13	95	85	*2-121/D-2	0.6
2002	Mon N★	152	604	103	190	43	3	19	96	60-1	3	70	.315	.378	.490	120	17	2-1	.986	6	103	94	*2-152	3.0
2003	Mon N★	144	509	77	158	36	0	15	65	69-6	7	50	.310	.397	.470	115	15	3-2	.983	-18	98	87	*2-137	0.3
Total	7	863	3073	473	940	233	9	87	411	276-15	32	342	.306	.367	.473	112	58	17-14	.984	-54	99	90	2-745/3-45,1-14,D-7,O-3(LF)	3.4
VILLANUEVA, HECTOR Hector (Balasquide) B 10.2.1964 Rio Piedras, P.R. BR/TR 6-1/220# d6.1																								
1990	Chi N	52	114	14	31	4	1	7	18	4-2	2	27	.272	.308	.509	112	1	1-0	.991	3	729	50	C-23,1-14	0.5
1991	Chi N	71	192	23	53	10	1	13	32	21-1	0	30	.276	.346	.542	140	10	0-0	.979	-5	91	86	C-55/1-6	0.7

Year	Tm Lg	G	AB	R	H	2B	3B	HR	RBI	BB-IB	HP	SO	AVG	OBP	SLG	AOPS	ABR	SB-CS	FA	FR	Rng	Thr	G at Pos	BFW
1992	Chi N	51	112	9	17	6	0	2	13	11-2	0	24	.152	.228	.259	37	-9	0-0	.978	5	97	116	C-28/1-6	-0.4
1993	StL N	17	55	7	8	1	0	3	9	4-1	0	17	.145	.203	.327	40	-5	0-0	1.000	-3	70	92	C-17	-0.7
Total	4	191	473	53	109	21	2	25	72	40-6	2	98	.230	.293	.442	98	-3	1-0	.984	0	189	89	C-123/1-26	0.1
VINA, FERNANDO Fernando B 4.16.1969 Sacramento, CA BL/TR 5-9/170# d4.10																								
1993	Sea A	24	45	5	10	2	0	0	2	4-0	3	3	.222	.327	.267	61	-2	6-0	1.000	1	108	144	2-16/S-4,D-2	0.1
1994	NY N	79	124	20	31	6	0	0	6	12-0	**12**	11	.250	.372	.298	78	-3	3-1	.979	1	118	105	2-13,3-12/S-9,O-6(LF)	-0.1
1995	Mil A	113	288	46	74	7	7	3	29	22-0	9	28	.257	.327	.361	75	-11	6-3	.983	12	107	**136**	2-99/S-6,3-2	0.5
1996	Mil A	140	554	94	157	19	10	7	46	38-3	13	35	.283	.342	.392	82	-16	16-7	.979	18	108	**121**	*2-137	0.9
1997	Mil A	79	324	37	89	12	2	4	28	12-1	7	23	.275	.312	.361	75	-12	8-7	.982	8	106	114	2-77/D	-0.2
1998	Mil N★	159	637	101	198	39	7	7	45	54-2	25	46	.311	.386	.427	114	15	22-16	.986	28	107	**128**	*2-158	4.9
1999	Mil N	37	154	17	41	7	0	1	16	14-0	4	6	.266	.339	.331	73	-6	5-2	.995	2	103	122	2-37	-0.2
2000	†StL N	123	487	81	146	24	6	4	31	36-0	**28**	36	.300	.380	.398	97	0	10-8	**.988**	11	100	118	*2-122	1.5
2001	†StL N	154	631	95	191	30	8	9	56	32-3	22	35	.303	.357	.418	101	0	17-7	**.987**	-4	94	114	*2-151	0.5
2002	†StL N	150	622	75	168	29	5	1	54	44-2	18	36	.270	.333	.338	84	-17	17-11	.981	-16	94	109	*2-150	-2.7
2003	StL N	61	259	35	65	14	4	4	23	11-0	11	24	.251	.309	.382	82	-7	4-4	.974	-9	87	108	2-60	-1.4
Total	11	1119	4125	606	1170	189	49	40	336	279-11	152	283	.284	.350	.382	90	-59	114-66	.984	51	101	119	*2-1020/S-19,3-14,O-6(LF),D-3	3.8
VINSON, CHARLIE Charles Anthony "Chuck" B 1.5.1944 Washington, DC BL/TL 6-3/207# d9.19																								
1966	Cal A	13	22	3	4	2	0	1	6	5-0	1	9	.182	.357	.409	123	1	0-0	1.000	-1	45	146	1-11	0.0
VINSON, RUBE Ernest Augustus B 3.20.1879 Dover, DE D 10.12.1951 Chester, PA BL/TR 5-9/168# d9.27																								
1904	Cle A	15	49	12	15	1	0	0	2	10	1		.306	.433	.327	143	3	2	1.000	4	370	0	O-15(LF)	0.7
1905	Cle A	39	134	12	26	3	1	0	9	7	2		.194	.245	.231	51	-8	4	.930	-2	27	0	O-36(27-9-0)	-1.3
1906	Chi A	10	24	2	6	0	0	0	3	2	0		.250	.308	.250	77	-1	1	.600	-2	0	0	/O-7(LF)	-0.4
Total	3	64	207	26	47	4	1	0	14	19	3		.227	.301	.256	77	-6	7	.919	-1	116	0	/O-58(49-9-0)	-1.0
VIOX, JIM James Harry B 12.30.1890 Lockland, OH D 1.6.1969 Erlanger, KY BR/TR 5-7/150# d5.9																								
1912	Pit N	33	70	8	13	2	3	1	7	3	0	9	.186	.219	.343	53	-5	2	.957	-3	114	0	3-10/S-8,O-3(RF),2	-0.8
1913	Pit N	137	492	86	156	32	8	2	65	64	3	28	.317	.399	.427	142	30	14-14	.959	-40	85	59	*2-124,S-10	-0.9
1914	Pit N	143	506	52	134	18	5	1	57	63	4	33	.265	.351	.326	106	6	9	.939	-22	99	88	*2-138/S-2,O-2(RF)	-1.4
1915	Pit N	150	503	56	129	17	8	2	45	75	4	31	.256	.357	.334	111	10	12-8	.954	-20	95	69	*2-134,3-13/O-2(CF)	-0.9
1916	Pit N	43	132	12	33	7	0	1	17	17	1	11	.250	.340	.326	104	2	2	.937	-11	82	64	2-25,3-11	-1.0
Total	5	506	1703	214	465	76	24	7	191	222	12	112	.273	.361	.358	116	43	39-22	.949	-96	93	72	2-422/3-34,S-20,O-7(0-2-5)	-5.0
VIRDON, BILL William Charles B 6.9.1931 Hazel Park, MI BL/TR 6/175# d4.12 M13 C8																								
1955	StL N	144	534	58	150	18	6	17	68	36-3	1	64	.281	.322	.433	100	-2	2-4	.966	-5	99	63	*O-142(1-109-34)	-1.5
1956	StL N	24	71	10	15	2	0	2	9	5-2	1	8	.211	.269	.324	60	-4	0-1	.982	-1	90	121	O-24(CF)	-0.7
	Pit N	133	509	67	170	21	10	8	37	33-7	1	63	.334	.374	.462	126	18	6-6	.989	2	102	110	*O-130(CF)	1.4
	Year	157	580	77	185	23	10	10	46	38-9	2	71	.319	.361	.445	118	14	6-7	.988	1	100	112	*O-154(CF)	0.7
1957	Pit N	144	561	59	141	28	11	8	50	33-5	0	69	.251	.291	.383	82	-16	3-3	.986	7	108	127	*O-141(CF)	-1.6
1958	Pit N	144	604	75	161	24	11	9	46	52-5	1	70	.267	.324	.387	90	-10	5-3	.993	2	105	93	*O-143(CF)	-1.5
1959	Pit N	144	519	67	132	24	2	8	41	55-11	2	65	.254	.327	.355	83	-12	7-4	.979	14	**114**	**190**	*O-144(CF)	-0.5
1960	†Pit N	120	409	60	108	16	9	8	40	40-2	0	44	.264	.326	.406	99	-1	8-2	.983	4	106	130	*O-109(CF)	-0.1
1961	Pit N	146	599	81	156	22	8	9	58	49-1	0	45	.260	.313	.369	81	-17	5-8	.985	-0	107	55	*O-145(CF)	-2.3
1962	Pit N	156	663	82	164	27	**10**	6	47	36-0	1	65	.247	.286	.345	69	-31	5-13	.976	-1	99	108	*O-156(CF)	-4.1
1963	Pit N	142	554	58	149	22	6	8	53	43-4	0	55	.269	.321	.374	99	-1	1-2	.988	-5	97	64	*O-142(CF)	-1.2
1964	Pit N	145	473	59	115	11	3	3	27	30-1	0	48	.243	.287	.298	66	-22	1-5	.976	-5	98	70	*O-134(CF)	-3.4
1965	Pit N	135	481	58	134	22	5	4	24	30-0	1	49	.279	.322	.370	94	-4	4-3	.970	-9	93	42	*O-128(1-127-0)	-1.8
1968	Pit N	6	3	1	1	0	0	1	2	0-0	0	2	.333	.333	1.333	388	1	0-0	1.000	0	120	0	/O-4(1-0-3)	0.1
Total	12	1583	5980	735	1596	237	81	91	502	442-41	8	647	.267	.316	.379	89	-101	47-54	.982	4	102	96	*O-1542(3-1504-37)	-17.2
VIRGIL, OZZIE Osvaldo Jose Jr. B 12.7.1956 Mayaguez, P.R. BR/TR 6-1/205# d10.5 f-Ozzie																								
1980	Phi N	1	5	1	1	1	0	0	0	0-0	0	1	.200	.200	.400	60	0	0-0	1.000	-2	21	0	/C	-0.2
1981	Phi N	6	6	0	0	0	0	0	0	0-0	0	2	.000	.000	.000	-96	-2	0-0	1.000	0	0	0	/C	-0.1
1982	Phi N	49	101	11	24	6	0	3	8	10-0	0	26	.238	.306	.386	91	-1	0-1	.964	1	80	59	C-35	0.0
1983	†Phi N	55	140	11	30	7	0	6	23	8-0	3	34	.214	.272	.393	83	-4	0-2	.966	-11	63	97	C-51	-1.5
1984	Phi N	141	456	61	119	21	2	18	68	45-5	5	91	.261	.331	.434	113	7	1-1	.992	-3	107	77	*C-137	1.1
1985	Phi N★	131	426	47	105	16	3	19	55	49-6	5	85	.246	.330	.432	109	5	0-0	**.994**	-9	81	84	*C-120	0.1
1986	Atl N	114	359	45	80	9	0	15	48	63-5	4	73	.223	.343	.373	93	-2	1-0	.984	13	75	132	*C-111	1.7
1987	Atl N★	123	429	57	106	13	1	27	72	47-4	7	81	.247	.331	.471	104	2	0-1	.989	-4	85	93	*C-122	0.2
1988	Atl N	107	320	23	82	10	0	9	31	22-1	5	54	.256	.313	.372	92	-4	2-0	.990	-6	102	93	C-96	-0.4
1989	Tor A	9	11	2	2	1	0	1	2	4-0	0	3	.182	.400	.545	167	1	0-0	1.000	0	0	0	/CD	0.1
1990	Tor A	3	5	0	0	0	0	0	0	0-0	0	3	.000	.000	.000	-98	-1	0-0	1.000	-1	0	0	/C-2,D	-0.2
Total	11	739	2258	258	549	84	6	98	307	248-21	29	453	.243	.324	.416	101	1	4-5	.987	-21	88	93	C-677/D-7	0.8
VIRGIL, OZZIE Osvaldo Jose Sr. (Pichardo) B 5.17.1933 Monte Cristi, D.R. BR/TR 6/175# d9.23 C19 s-Ozzie OF Total (8-LF 18-RF)																								
1956	NY N	3	12	2	5	1	1	0	2	0-0	0	0	.417	.417	.667	186	1	1-0	.800	-1	22	259	/3-3	0.0
1957	NY N	96	226	26	53	0	2	4	24	14-1	0	27	.235	.278	.305	57	-15	2-3	.926	8	142	133	3-62,O-24(8-0-16)/S	-0.9
1958	Det A	49	193	19	47	10	2	3	19	8-0	0	20	.244	.272	.363	69	-9	1-0	.981	4	102	73	3-49	-0.5
1960	Det A	62	132	16	30	4	2	3	13	4-1	0	14	.227	.248	.356	60	-8	1-1	.974	3	98	153	3-42/2-8,S-5,C	-0.5
1961	Det A	20	30	1	4	0	0	1	1	1-0	0	5	.133	.161	.233	4	-4	0-0	.938	-2	55	202	/3-9,C-3,2S	-0.6
	KC A	11	21	1	3	0	0	0	0	0-0	0	3	.143	.143	.143	-23	-4	0-0	.818	0	115	152	/3-4,C-3	-0.4
	Year	31	51	2	7	0	0	1	1	1-0	0	8	.137	.154	.196	-7	-8	0-0	.889	-2	76	184	3-13/C-6,2S	-1.0
1962	Bal A	1	0	0	0	0	0	0	0	1-1	0	0	—	1.000	—	209	0	0-0	—	0			H	0.0
1965	Pit N	39	49	3	13	2	0	1	5	2-0	0	10	.265	.294	.367	85	-1	0-0	1.000	1	*118*	*76*	C-15/3-7,2-5	0.0
1966	SF N	42	89	7	19	2	0	2	9	4-1	0	12	.213	.245	.303	51	-6	1-1	.984	-1	*107*	*72*	C-13,3-13/1-5,2-2,O-2(RF)	-0.7
1969	SF N	1	1	0	0	0	0	0	0	0-0	0	0	.000	.000	.000	-99	0	0-0	—	0			H	0.0
Total	9	324	753	75	174	19	7	14	73	34-4	0	91	.231	.263	.331	59	-46	6-5	.951	11	112	112	3-189/C-35,O-26R,2-16,S-7,1-5	-3.6
VIRTUE, JAKE Jacob Kitchline "Guesses" B 3.2.1865 Philadelphia, PA D 2.3.1943 Camden, NJ BB/TL 5-9.5/165# d7.21 OF Total (25-CF 9-RF)																								
1890	Cle N	62	223	39	68	6	5	2	25	49	1	15	.305	.432	.404	147	17	9	.982	0	99	96	1-62	1.0
1891	Cle N	139	517	82	135	19	14	2	72	75	8	40	.261	.363	.364	107	6	15	.972	-10	71	89	*1-139	-1.4
1892	†Cle N	147	557	98	157	15	20	2	89	84	4	68	.282	.380	.391	128	20	14	.984	-4	78	85	*1-147	1.4
1893	Cle N	97	378	87	100	16	10	1	60	54	1	14	.265	.358	.368	88	-7	11	.975	1	115	108	1-73,O-13(0-9-4)/S-5,3-5,P	-0.6
1894	Cle N	29	89	15	23	4	1	0	10	13	1	3	.258	.359	.326	64	-5	1	.885	-2	93	0	O-21(0-16-5)/2-3,1-2,P	-0.6
Total	5	474	1764	321	483	60	50	7	256	275	15	140	.274	.376	.376	111	31	50	.978	-15	85	92	1-423/O-34C,3-5,S-5,2-3,P-2	-0.2
VISNER, JOE Joseph Paul (born Joseph Paul Vezina) B 9.27.1859 Minneapolis, MN D 6.17.1945 Fosston, MN BL/TR 5-11/180# d7.4																								
1885	Bal AA	4	13	2	3	0	0	0	2	2	0		.231	.333	.231	82	0		.750	-1	0	0	/O-4(0-2-2)	-0.1
1889	†Bro AA	80	295	56	76	12	10	8	68	36	4	36	.258	.346	.447	125	9	13	.871	-11			C-53,O-29(2-0-27)	0.1
1890	Pit P	127	521	110	139	15	**22**	3	71	76	8	44	.267	.369	.397	114	13	18	.893	-7	78	91	*O-127(RF)	0.4
1891	Was AA	18	68	13	19	2	3	1	7	8	0	7	.279	.355	.441	134	3	2	.806	-3	67	0	O-17(RF)/C3	0.0
	StL AA	6	27	2	4	0	1	0	1	0	0	3	.148	.148	.222	5	-4	0	1.000	0	112	0	/O-6(RF)	-0.3
	Year	24	95	15	23	2	4	1	8	8	0	10	.242	.301	.379	94	-2	2	.846	-2	77	0	O-23(RF)/C3	-0.3
Total	4	235	924	183	241	29	36	12	149	122	12	90	.261	.354	.409	115	21	33	.892	-20			O-183(2-2-179)/C-54,3	0.1
VITIELLO, JOE Joseph David B 4.11.1970 Cambridge, MA BR/TR 6-2/215# d4.29																								
1995	KC A	53	130	13	33	4	0	7	21	8-0	4	25	.254	.317	.446	95	-2	0-0	.982	-1	80	69	D-38/1-8	-0.5
1996	KC A	85	257	29	62	15	1	8	40	38-2	3	69	.241	.342	.401	88	-4	2-0	1.000	0	120	76	D-70/1-9,O(RF)	-0.8
1997	KC A	51	130	11	31	6	0	5	18	14-1	2	37	.238	.322	.400	85	-3	0-0	.980	-0	111	0	O-28(12-0-16),D-12/1	-0.5
1998	KC A	3	7	0	1	0	0	0	0	1-0	0	2	.143	.250	.143	6	-1	0-0	—	0			/D-2	-0.1
1999	KC A	13	41	4	6	1	0	1	4	2-0	2	9	.146	.222	.244	18	-5	0-0	1.000	1	132	128	1-10/D-2	-0.5
2000	SD N	39	52	7	13	3	0	2	8	10-0	0	9	.250	.365	.423	107	1	0-0	.966	-1	95	128	1-17/O(RF)	-0.1
2003	Mon N	38	76	12	26	6	0	3	13	7-0	2	14	.342	.407	.539	133	4	0-0	1.000	-1	76	0	O-15(LF),1-12/D	0.2
Total	7	282	693	76	172	35	1	26	104	80-3	13	165	.248	.335	.414	90	-10	2-0	.983	-1	112	108	D-125/1-57,O-45(27-0-18)	-2.3

VITT, OSSIE Oscar Joseph B 1.4.1890 San Francisco, CA D 1.31.1963 Oakland, CA BR/TR 5-10/150# d4.11 M3 OF Total (31-LF 6-CF 1-RF)

Year	Tm Lg	G	AB	R	H	2B	3B	HR	RBI	BB-IB	HP	SO	AVG	OBP	SLG	AOPS	ABR	SB-CS	FA	FR	Rng	Thr	G at Pos	BFW
1912	Det A	76	273	39	67	4	4	0	19	18	2		.245	.297	.289	70	-11	17	.929	0	87	53	O-28(26-1-1),3-24,2-15	-1.2
1913	Det A	99	359	45	86	11	3	2	33	31	2	18	.240	.304	.304	79	-10	5	.960	2	107	84	2-78,3-17/O-2(CF)	-0.7
1914	Det A	66	195	35	49	7	0	0	8	31	0	8	.251	.354	.287	90	-1	10-8	.964	3	117	90	2-36,3-16/O-2(LF),S	0.3
1915	Det A	152	560	116	140	18	13	1	48	80	4	22	.250	.348	.334	99	1	26-18	**.964**	13	**112**	81	*3-151/2-2	1.8
1916	Det A	153	597	88	135	17	12	0	42	75	1	28	.226	.314	.295	80	-14	18	**.964**	26	**118**	**107**	*3-151/S-2	1.8
1917	Det A	140	512	65	130	13	6	0	47	56	1	15	.254	.329	.303	93	-4	18	.940	-17	88	86	*3-140	-1.8
1918	Det A	81	267	29	64	5	2	0	17	32	0	6	.240	.321	.273	83	-5	5	.953	3	97	108	3-66/2-9,O-3(CF)	-0.1
1919	Bos A	133	469	64	114	10	3	0	40	44	1	11	.243	.309	.277	69	-19	9	**.970**	18	**113**	115	*3-133	0.3
1920	Bos A	87	296	50	65	10	4	1	28	43	1	10	.220	.321	.291	65	-14	5-4	.986	-1	104	51	3-64,2-21	-1.3
1921	Bos A	78	232	29	44	11	1	0	13	45	0	13	.190	.321	.246	48	-17	1-2	.962	-3	99	122	3-71/O-3(LF),1-2	-1.5
Total	10	1065	3760	560	894	106	48	4	295	455	12	131	.238	.322	.295	80	-94	114-32	.960	45	107	96	3-833,2-161/O-38L,S-3,1-2	-2.4

VIZCAINO, JOSE Jose Luis (Pimental) B 3.26.1968 San Cristobal, D.R. BB/TR 6-1/180# d9.10

Year	Tm Lg	G	AB	R	H	2B	3B	HR	RBI	BB-IB	HP	SO	AVG	OBP	SLG	AOPS	ABR	SB-CS	FA	FR	Rng	Thr	G at Pos	BFW
1989	LA N	7	10	2	2	0	0	0	0	0-0	0	1	.200	.200	.200	15	-1	0-0	.882	1	114	148	/S-5	0.0
1990	LA N	37	51	3	14	1	1	0	2	4-1	0	8	.275	.327	.333	85	-1	1-1	.956	1	104	120	S-11/2-6	0.0
1991	Chi N	93	145	7	38	5	0	0	10	5-0	0	18	.262	.283	.297	61	-8	2-1	.947	1	86	37	3-57,S-33/2-9	-0.5
1992	Chi N	86	285	25	64	10	4	1	17	14-2	0	35	.225	.260	.298	57	-17	3-0	.969	7	115	117	S-50,3-29/2-5	-0.6
1993	Chi N	151	551	74	158	19	4	4	54	46-2	3	71	.287	.340	.358	90	-8	12-9	.968	15	114	93	S-81,3-44,2-34	1.5
1994	NY N	103	410	47	105	13	3	3	33	33-3	2	62	.256	.310	.324	68	-20	1-11	.970	-10	100	92	*S-102	-2.5
1995	NY N	135	509	66	146	21	5	3	56	35-4	1	76	.287	.332	.365	87	-10	8-3	**.984**	15	**109**	112	*S-134/2	1.6
1996	NY N	96	363	47	110	12	6	1	32	28-0	3	58	.303	.356	.377	99	-1	9-5	.986	1	100	123	2-93	0.5
	†Cle A	48	179	23	51	5	2	0	13	7-0	0	24	.285	.310	.335	64	-10	6-2	.981	-4	92	92	2-45/S-4,D	-1.1
1997	†SF N	151	568	77	151	19	7	5	50	48-1	0	87	.266	.323	.350	78	-19	8-8	.976	6	106	110	*S-147/2-5	-0.3
1998	LA N	67	237	30	62	9	0	3	29	17-0	1	35	.262	.311	.338	76	-9	7-3	.985	-3	93	88	S-66	-0.6
1999	LA N	94	266	27	67	9	0	1	29	20-0	1	23	.252	.304	.297	57	-18	2-1	.966	4	100	85	S-44,2-30/3-9,O(LF)	-0.9
2000	LA N	40	93	9	19	2	1	0	4	10-3	1	15	.204	.288	.247	39	-9	1-0	1.000	1	105	68	S-19,3-12/2-3,1D	-0.6
	†NY A	73	174	23	48	8	1	0	10	12-0	0	28	.276	.319	.333	67	-9	5-7	.990	-2	94	94	2-62/3-6,S-2,D-4	-0.9
2001	†Hou N	107	256	38	71	8	3	1	14	15-0	2	33	.277	.322	.344	69	-12	3-2	.937	-3	102	90	S-53,2-18/3-7	-1.2
2002	Hou N	125	406	53	123	19	2	5	37	24-2	1	40	.303	.342	.397	93	-6	3-5	.980	2	96	112	S-58,3-30,2-25/1-5	0.0
2003	Hou N	91	189	14	47	7	3	3	26	8-3	1	22	.249	.281	.365	64	-11	0-1	.963	-1	86	103	S-32,2-20/3-2,1	-1.0
Total	15	1504	4692	565	1276	167	42	30	416	326-21	16	636	.272	.319	.345	76	-169	71-59	.973	30	105	103	S-841,2-356,3-196/1-7,D-6,O(LF)	-6.6

VIZQUEL, OMAR Omar Enrique (Gonzalez) B 4.24.1967 Caracas, Venezuela BB/TR 5-9/165# d4.3

Year	Tm Lg	G	AB	R	H	2B	3B	HR	RBI	BB-IB	HP	SO	AVG	OBP	SLG	AOPS	ABR	SB-CS	FA	FR	Rng	Thr	G at Pos	BFW
1989	Sea A	143	387	45	85	7	3	1	20	28-0	1	40	.220	.273	.261	50	-26	1-4	.971	5	100	**119**	*S-143	-1.3
1990	Sea A	81	255	19	63	3	2	2	18	18-0	0	22	.247	.295	.298	66	-12	4-1	.980	4	103	95	S-81	-0.2
1991	Sea A	142	426	42	98	16	4	1	41	45-0	0	37	.230	.302	.293	66	-20	7-2	.980	26	108	128	*S-138/2	1.7
1992	Sea A	136	483	49	142	20	4	0	21	32-0	2	38	.294	.340	.352	94	-4	15-13	**.989**	8	99	100	*S-136	1.2
1993	Sea A	158	560	68	143	14	2	2	31	50-2	4	71	.255	.319	.298	67	-26	12-14	.980	20	103	112	*S-155/D-2	0.3
1994	Cle A	69	286	39	78	10	1	1	33	23-0	0	23	.273	.325	.325	69	-13	13-4	.981	2	102	117	S-69	-0.4
1995	†Cle A	136	542	87	144	28	0	6	56	59-0	1	59	.266	.333	.351	79	-16	29-11	.986	5	104	103	*S-136	0.2
1996	†Cle A	151	542	98	161	36	1	9	64	56-0	4	42	.297	.362	.417	98	0	35-9	.971	4	105	97	*S-150	1.8
1997	†Cle A	153	565	89	158	23	6	5	49	57-1	2	58	.280	.347	.368	84	-13	43-12	.985	10	102	100	*S-152	1.3
1998	†Cle A★	151	576	86	166	30	6	2	50	62-1	4	64	.288	.358	.372	88	-8	37-12	**.993**	8	102	96	*S-151	1.4
1999	†Cle A★	144	574	112	191	36	4	5	66	65-0	1	50	.333	.397	.436	109	10	42-9	.976	-0	98	92	*S-143/O(RF)	2.5
2000	Cle A	156	613	101	176	27	3	7	66	87-0	5	72	.287	.377	.375	90	-6	22-10	**.995**	-0	92	94	*S-156	0.7
2001	†Cle A	155	611	84	156	26	8	2	50	61-0	2	72	.255	.323	.334	73	-23	13-9	**.989**	6	98	90	*S-154	-0.6
2002	Cle A★	151	582	85	160	31	5	14	72	56-3	8	64	.275	.341	.418	104	4	18-10	.990	13	102	95	*S-150	2.7
2003	Cle A	64	250	43	61	13	2	2	19	29-0	0	20	.244	.321	.336	77	-8	8-3	.978	13	111	146	S-64	1.0
Total	15	1990	7252	1047	1982	320	51	59	656	728-7	34	732	.273	.340	.356	84	-161	299-123	.983	121	101	103	*S-1978/D-2,O(RF)2	12.3

VOGEL, OTTO Otto Henry B 10.26.1899 Mendota, IL D 7.19.1969 Iowa City, IA BR/TR 6/195# d6.5

Year	Tm Lg	G	AB	R	H	2B	3B	HR	RBI	BB-IB	HP	SO	AVG	OBP	SLG	AOPS	ABR	SB-CS	FA	FR	Rng	Thr	G at Pos	BFW
1923	Chi N	41	81	10	17	0	1	1	6	7	3	11	.210	.297	.272	51	-6	2-3	.929	0	96	143	O-24(3-0-21)/3	-0.7
1924	Chi N	70	172	28	46	11	2	1	24	10	3	26	.267	.319	.372	84	-4	4-4	.956	3	107	128	O-53(12-1-40)/3-2	-0.5
Total	2	111	253	38	63	11	3	2	30	17	6	37	.249	.312	.340	73	-10	6-7	.948	3	104	132	/O-77(15-1-61),3-3	-1.2

VOIGT, JACK John David B 5.17.1966 Sarasota, FL BR/TR 6-1/175# d8.3

Year	Tm Lg	G	AB	R	H	2B	3B	HR	RBI	BB-IB	HP	SO	AVG	OBP	SLG	AOPS	ABR	SB-CS	FA	FR	Rng	Thr	G at Pos	BFW
1992	Bal A	1	0	0	0	0	0	0	0	0-0	0	0	—	—	—	—	0	0-0	—	0			/R	0.0
1993	Bal A	64	152	32	45	11	1	6	23	25-0	0	33	.296	.395	.500	133	8	1-0	.987	-0	99	121	O-43(22-0-23)/1-5,3-3,D-9	0.6
1994	Bal A	59	141	15	34	5	0	3	20	18-1	1	25	.241	.327	.340	70	-6	0-0	.989	1	107	68	O-54(17-1-37)/1-6,D-2	-0.7
1995	Bal A	3	1	1	1	0	0	0	0	0-0	0	0	1.000	1.000	1.000	416	0	0-0	1.000	0	409	0	/1D	0.1
	Tex A	33	62	8	10	3	0	2	8	10-0	0	14	.161	.274	.306	51	-5	0-0	1.000	-0	103	84	O-25(8-0-17)/1-5,D-2	-0.6
	Year	36	63	9	11	3	0	2	8	10-0	0	14	.175	.284	.317	56	-4	0-0	1.000	-0	103	84	O-25(8-0-17)/1-6,D-3	-0.5
1996	Tex A	5	9	1	1	0	0	0	0	0-0	0	2	.111	.111	.111	-41	-2	0-0	1.000	0	151	0	/O-3(2-0-1),3	-0.2
1997	Mil A	72	151	20	37	9	2	8	22	19-2	1	36	.245	.331	.490	110	2	1-2	.985	-0	103	266	O-40(35-2-5),1-19/3-6,D	-0.1
1998	Oak A	57	72	7	10	4	0	1	10	6-0	0	19	.139	.205	.236	15	-9	5-1	.987	-0	40	128	1-27,O-20(9-10-2)/3-2,D-3	-0.9
Total	7	294	588	84	138	32	3	20	83	78-3	2	129	.235	.324	.401	87	-12	7-3	.990	1	103	143	O-185(93-13-85)/1-63,D-18,3-12	-1.8

VOLLMER, CLYDE Clyde Frederick B 9.24.1921 Cincinnati, OH BR/TR 6-1/190# d5.31 Mil 1943-45

Year	Tm Lg	G	AB	R	H	2B	3B	HR	RBI	BB-IB	HP	SO	AVG	OBP	SLG	AOPS	ABR	SB-CS	FA	FR	Rng	Thr	G at Pos	BFW
1942	Cin N	12	43	2	4	0	0	1	4	1	0	5	.093	.114	.163	-20	-7	0	1.000	1	113	0	O-11(10-1-0)	-0.8
1946	Cin N	9	22	1	4	0	0	0	1	1	0	3	.182	.217	.182	14	-3	2	1.000	-1	75	0	/O-7(5-3-1)	-0.4
1947	Cin N	78	155	19	34	10	0	1	13	9	1	18	.219	.267	.303	51	-11	0	.984	4	123	72	O-66(8-58-0)	-0.8
1948	Cin N	7	9	0	1	0	0	0	0	1	0	1	.111	.200	.111	-14	-1	0	—	-0	0		/O-2(0-1-1)	-0.2
	Was A	1	5	1	2	0	0	0	0	0	0	1	.400	.400	.400	116	0	0-0	1.000	-0	74	0	/O(CF)	0.0
1949	Was A	129	443	58	112	17	1	14	59	53	2	62	.253	.335	.391	94	-6	1-2	.982	1	109	37	*O-114(0-99-15)	-0.8
1950	Was A	6	14	4	4	0	0	0	1	2	0	3	.286	.375	.286	75	0	1-0	1.000	0	79	458	/O-3(LF)	0.0
	Bos A	57	169	35	48	10	0	7	37	21	0	35	.284	.363	.467	102	0	1-0	.954	-2	93	98	O-39(17-11-11)	-0.3
	Year	63	183	39	52	10	0	7	38	23	0	38	.284	.364	.454	100	0	2-0	.957	-1	92	123	O-42(20-11-11)	-0.3
1951	Bos A	115	386	66	97	9	2	22	85	55	1	66	.251	.346	.456	105	2	0-0	.986	-4	97	66	*O-106(2-8-97)	-0.5
1952	Bos A	90	250	35	66	12	4	11	50	39	3	47	.264	.370	.476	124	9	2-2	1.000	1	104	66	O-70(43-9-21)	0.5
1953	Bos A	1	0	0	0	0	0	0	0	1	0	0	—	1.000	—	180	0	0-0	—	0			H	0.0
	Was A	118	408	54	106	15	3	11	74	48	3	59	.260	.342	.392	100	0	0-2	.979	3	103	102	*O-106(104-0-2)	-0.5
	Year	119	408	54	106	15	3	11	74	49	3	59	.260	.343	.392	101	0	0-2	.979	3	103	102	*O-106(104-0-2)	-0.5
1954	Was A	62	117	8	30	4	0	2	15	12	1	28	.256	.331	.342	89	-2	0-0	1.000	-1	80	131	O-26(5-0-21)	-0.4
Total	10	685	2021	283	508	77	10	69	339	243	11	328	.251	.335	.402	95	-19	7-6	.984	0	103	72	O-551(197-191-169)	-4.2

Von KOLNITZ, FRITZ Alfred Holmes B 5.20.1893 Charleston, SC D 3.18.1948 Mount Pleasant, SC BR/TR 5-10.5/175# d4.18

Year	Tm Lg	G	AB	R	H	2B	3B	HR	RBI	BB-IB	HP	SO	AVG	OBP	SLG	AOPS	ABR	SB-CS	FA	FR	Rng	Thr	G at Pos	BFW
1914	Cin N	41	104	8	23	2	0	0	6	6	1	16	.221	.270	.240	51	-6	4	.914	-1	112	72	3-20,O-11(2-7-2)/C-2,1	-0.8
1915	Cin N	50	78	6	15	4	1	0	6	7	0	11	.192	.259	.269	59	-4	1-3	.933	-3	85	191	3-18/S-6,1-3,C-2,O(RF)	-0.8
1916	Chi A	24	44	1	10	3	0	0	7	2	0	6	.227	.261	.295	66	-2	0	.909	-3	64	74	3-13	-0.5
Total	3	115	226	15	48	9	1	0	19	15	1	33	.212	.264	.261	56	-12	5-3	.918	-7	94	107	/3-51,O-12(2-7-3),S-6,1-4,C-4	-2.1

VOSMIK, JOE Joseph Franklin B 4.4.1910 Cleveland, OH D 1.27.1962 Cleveland, OH BR/TR 6/185# d9.13

Year	Tm Lg	G	AB	R	H	2B	3B	HR	RBI	BB-IB	HP	SO	AVG	OBP	SLG	AOPS	ABR	SB-CS	FA	FR	Rng	Thr	G at Pos	BFW
1930	Cle A	9	26	1	6	2	0	0	4	1	0	1	.231	.259	.308	42	-2	0-0	.933	0	88	237	/O-5(1-4-0)	-0.2
1931	Cle A	149	591	80	189	36	14	7	117	38	2	30	.320	.363	.464	110	7	7-7	.970	4	104	116	*O-147(147-1-0)	0.1
1932	Cle A	**153**	621	106	194	39	12	10	97	58	5	42	.312	.376	.462	109	8	2-3	**.989**	19	**124**	99	*O-153(LF)	1.6
1933	Cle A	119	438	53	115	20	10	4	56	42	3	13	.263	.331	.381	84	-11	0-2	.985	3	97	130	*O-113(LF)	-1.4
1934	Cle A	104	405	71	138	33	2	6	78	35	0	10	.341	.393	.477	122	14	1-1	.976	-4	93	80	*O-104(LF)	0.4
1935	Cle A★	152	620	93	**216**	**47**	**20**	10	110	59	4	30	.348	.408	.537	140	36	2-1	.986	3	110	41	*O-150(LF)	2.8
1936	Cle A	138	506	76	145	29	7	7	94	79	0	21	.287	.383	.413	96	-2	5-1	.978	-3	95	95	*O-136(136-0-1)	-1.0
1937	StL A	144	594	81	193	47	9	4	93	49	1	38	.325	.377	.455	108	8	2-3	.972	7	109	107	*O-143(LF)	0.6
1938	Bos A	146	621	121	**201**	37	6	9	86	59	2	26	.324	.384	.446	103	3	0-3	.978	4	100	131	*O-146(146-1-0)	-0.2
1939	Bos A	145	554	89	153	29	6	7	84	66	3	33	.276	.356	.388	87	-10	4-3	.974	-6	92	90	*O-144(LF)	-2.2
1940	Bro N	116	404	45	114	14	6	1	42	22	1	21	.282	.321	.354	81	-11	0	.976	1	98	123	O-99(39-9-51)	-1.6
1941	Bro N	25	56	0	11	0	0	0	4	4	0	4	.196	.250	.196	26	-6	0	1.000	-2	71	0	O-18(2-0-16)	-0.8

Year	Tm Lg	G	AB	R	H	2B	3B	HR	RBI	BB-IB	HP	SO	AVG	OBP	SLG	AOPS	ABR	SB-CS	FA	FR	Rng	Thr	G at Pos	BFW
1944	Was A	14	36	2	7	2	0	0	9	2	0	3	.194	.237	.250	41	-3	0-0	1.000	-0	102	0	O-12(5-0-7)	-0.4
Total	13	1414	5472	818	1682	335	92	65	874	514	21	272	.307	.369	.438	104	31	23-24	.979	26	103	100	*O-1370(1283-15-75)	-2.3
VOSS, ALEX Alexander B 5.16.1858 Roswell, GA D 8.31.1906 Cincinnati, OH BR/TR 6-1/180# d4.17 ▲																								
1884	Was U	63	245	33	47	9	0	0		5			.192	.208	.229	33	-27		.848	6	126	156	P-27,3-16,1-15,O-13(0-7-6)/S	-1.3
	KC U	14	45	1	4	0	0	0		0			.089	.089	.089	-53	-10		.867	2	133	358	/O-8(5-3-0),P-7	-0.3
	Year	77	290	34	51	9	0	0		5			.176	.190	.207	21	-37		.859	7	126	174	P-34,O-21(5-10-6),3-16,1-15/S	-1.6
VOSS, BILL William Edward B 10.31.1943 Glendale, CA BL/TL 6-2/160# d9.14																								
1965	Chi A	11	33	4	6	0	1	1	3	3-1	0	5	.182	.250	.333	68	-2	0-0	1.000	-1	83	0	O-10(RF)	-0.3
1966	Chi A	2	2	0	0	0	0	0	0	0-0	0	2	.000	.000	.000	-99	-1	0-0	1.000	0	119	0	/O(LF)	-0.1
1967	Chi A	13	22	4	2	0	0	0	0	0-0	0	1	.091	.091	.091	-48	-4	1-1	1.000	0	113	0	O-11(1-2-9)	-0.5
1968	Chi A	61	167	14	26	2	1	2	15	16-1	2	34	.156	.238	.216	38	-13	5-3	.963	-1	86	179	O-55(5-2-53)	-1.9
1969	Cal A	133	349	33	91	11	4	2	40	35-6	0	40	.261	.327	.332	90	-5	5-3	.995	7	110	**161**	*O-111(6-4-104)/1-2	-0.3
1970	Cal A	80	181	21	44	4	3	3	30	23-2	2	18	.243	.327	.348	92	-2	2-1	.979	3	99	224	O-55(RF)	-0.1
1971	Mil A	97	275	31	69	4	0	10	30	24-1	1	45	.251	.312	.375	95	-3	2-2	.987	-1	109	22	O-79(4-13-67)	-0.7
1972	Mil A	27	36	1	3	1	0	0	1	5-0	0	4	.083	.195	.111	-7	-5	0-1	.929	-1	97	0	O-11(3-0-9)	-0.7
	Oak A	40	97	10	22	5	1	1	5	9-3	1	16	.227	.296	.330	92	-1	0-0	1.000	1	102	158	O-34(1-13-21)	-0.1
	Year	67	133	11	25	6	1	1	6	14-3	1	20	.188	.268	.271	64	-6	0-1	.987	0	101	126	O-45(4-13-30)	-0.8
	StL N	11	15	1	4	2	0	0	3	2-0	0	2	.267	.333	.400	115	0	0-0	1.000	-0	92	0	/O-2(CF)	0.0
Total	8	475	1177	119	267	29	10	19	127	117-14	6	167	.227	.298	.317	78	-36	15-11	.986	8	103	129	O-369(21-36-328)/1-2	-4.7
VOYLES, PHIL Philip Vance B 5.12.1900 Murphy, NC D 11.3.1972 Marlborough, MA BL/TR 5-11.5/175# d9.4																								
1929	Bos N	20	68	9	16	0	2	0	14	6	0	8	.235	.297	.294	49	-6	0	.922	-1	92	116	O-20(1-19-0)	-0.7
VUKOVICH, GEORGE George Stephen B 6.24.1956 Chicago, IL BL/TR 6/198# d4.13																								
1980	†Phi N	78	58	6	13	1	1	0	8	6-0	0	9	.224	.297	.276	58	-3	0-0	.933	-0	112	0	O-28(13-0-15)	-0.4
1981	†Phi N	20	26	5	10	0	0	1	4	1-0	0	0	.385	.407	.500	150	2	1-0	1.000	0	118	0	/O-9(3-1-5)	0.2
1982	Phi N	123	335	41	91	18	2	6	42	32-14	0	47	.272	.334	.391	100	0	2-9	.977	1	108	67	*O-102(15-0-100)	-0.6
1983	Cle A	124	312	31	77	13	2	3	44	24-4	2	37	.247	.301	.330	72	-12	3-4	.986	0	111	44	*O-122(20-3-107)	-1.7
1984	Cle A	134	437	38	133	22	5	9	60	34-3	1	61	.304	.354	.439	117	10	1-4	.994	19	**128**	172	*O-130(16-0-124)	2.1
1985	Cle A	149	434	43	106	22	0	8	45	30-6	1	75	.244	.292	.350	76	-14	2-2	.988	-0	105	51	*O-137(10-0-131)	-2.1
Total	6	628	1602	164	430	76	10	27	203	127-27	4	229	.268	.322	.379	92	-17	9-19	.987	20	114	86	O-528(77-4-482)	-2.5
VUKOVICH, JOHN John Christopher B 7.31.1947 Sacramento, CA BR/TR 6-1/190# d9.11 M2 C22																								
1970	Phi N	3	8	1	1	0	0	0	0	1-0	0	0	.125	.222	.125	-5	-1	0-0	.778	0	72	95	/S-2,3	-0.1
1971	Phi N	74	217	11	36	5	0	0	14	12-1	1	34	.166	.211	.189	15	-25	2-1	.956	4	107	75	3-74	-2.3
1973	Mil A	55	128	10	16	3	0	2	9	9-0	0	40	.125	.182	.195	7	-16	0-2	.948	-4	94	42	3-40,1-13/S	-2.3
1974	Mil A	38	80	5	15	1	0	3	11	1-0	0	16	.188	.193	.313	45	-6	2-1	.945	-5	102	92	S-12,3-12,2-11/1-4	-1.0
1975	Cin N	31	38	4	8	3	0	0	2	4-1	0	5	.211	.286	.289	59	-2	0-0	.925	0	109	148	3-31	-0.2
1976	Phi N	4	8	2	1	0	0	1	2	0-0	0	2	.125	.125	.500	69	0	0-0	1.000	-1	48	0	/3-4,1	-0.2
1977	Phi N	2	2	0	0	0	0	0	0	0-0	0	1	.000	.000	.000	-96	-1	0-0	—	0			H	-0.1
1979	Phi N	10	15	0	3	1	0	0	1	0-0	0	3	.200	.200	.267	25	-2	0-0	1.000	-0	164	218	/3-7,2-3	-0.2
1980	Phi N	49	62	4	10	1	1	0	5	2-1	1	7	.161	.197	.210	14	-7	0-1	.958	-4	84	0	3-34/2-9,S-5,1	-1.3
1981	Phi N	11	1	0	0	0	0	0	0	0-0	0	1	.000	.000	.000	-96	0	0-0	.800	-1	105	0	/3-9,12	-0.1
Total	10	277	559	37	90	14	1	6	44	29-3	2	109	.161	.203	.222	20	-60	4-5	.951	-12	103	62	3-212/2-24,1-20,S-20	-7.8
WADDEY, FRANK Frank Orum B 8.21.1905 Memphis, TN D 10.21.1990 Knoxville, TN BL/TL 5-10.5/185# d4.16																								
1931	StL A	14	22	3	6	1	0	0	2	2	0	3	.273	.333	.318	70	-1	0-0	1.000	-1	71	0	/O-7(1-5-1)	-0.2
WADE, HAM Abraham Lincoln B 12.20.1880 Spring City, PA D 7.21.1968 Riverside, NJ BR/TR 5-8/155# d9.9																								
1907	NY N	1	0	0	0	0	0	0	0	0	1		—	1.000	—	208	0	0	1.000	0	0	0	/O(LF)	0.0
WADE, GALE Galeard Lee B 1.20.1929 Hollister, MO BL/TR 6-1.5/185# d4.11																								
1955	Chi N	9	33	5	6	1	0	1	1	4-0	0	3	.182	.270	.303	52	-2	0-0	.867	-2	62	175	/O-9(CF)	-0.4
1956	Chi N	10	12	0	0	0	0	0	0	1-0	0	0	.000	.077	.000	-78	-3	0-0	.875	-0	119	0	/O-3(CF)	-0.3
Total	2	19	45	5	6	1	0	1	1	5-0	0	3	.133	.220	.222	18	-5	0-0	.870	-2	75	134	/O-12(CF)	-0.7
WADE, RIP Richard Frank B 1.12.1898 Duluth, MN D 7.15.1957 Duluth, MN BL/TR 5-11/174# d4.19																								
1923	Was A	33	69	8	16	2	2	2	14	5	0	10	.232	.284	.406	84	-2	0-0	.967	0	82	190	O-19(5-12-2)	-0.3
WAGENHORST, WOODY Ellwood Otto B 6.3.1863 Kutztown, PA D 2.12.1946 Washington, DC 5-11/165# d6.25																								
1888	Phi N	2	8	2	1	0	0	0	0	0	0	1	.125	.125	.125	-19	-1	0	.800	-1	53	414	/3-2	-0.2
WAGNER, BUTTS Albert B 9.17.1871 Chartiers, PA D 11.26.1928 Pittsburgh, PA BR/TR 5-10/170# d4.27 b-Honus																								
1898	Was N	63	223	20	50	11	2	1	31	14	3		.224	.279	.305	67	-10	4	.833	-9	84	79	3-39,O-10(1-9-0)/S-8,2-5	-1.7
	Bro N	11	38	2	9	1	1	0	3	2	0		.237	.275	.316	69	-2	0	.813	-3	88	53	3-11	-0.4
	Year	74	261	22	59	12	3	1	34	16	3		.226	.279	.307	68	-11	4	.828	-12	85	73	3-50,O-10(1-9-0)/S-8,2-5	-2.1
WAGNER, HEINIE Charles F. B 9.23.1880 New York, NY D 3.20.1943 New Rochelle, NY BR/TR 5-9/183# d7.1 M1 C7																								
1902	NY N	17	56	4	12	1	0	0	2	0	0		.214	.214	.232	38	-4	3	.862	-4	86	91	S-17	-0.8
1906	Bos A	9	32	1	9	0	0	0	4	1	0		.281	.303	.281	83	-1	2	.943	1	129	65	/2-9	0.1
1907	Bos A	111	385	29	82	10	4	2	21	31	2		.213	.275	.275	76	-10	20	.931	-6	99	92	*S-109/23	-1.4
1908	Bos A	153	526	62	130	11	5	1	46	27	3		.247	.288	.293	86	-9	20	.939	32	**108**	108	*S-153	3.2
1909	Bos A	124	430	53	110	16	7	1	49	35	3		.256	.316	.333	103	1	18	.933	10	105	97	*S-123/2	1.7
1910	Bos A	142	491	61	134	26	7	1	52	44	2		.273	.335	.360	115	9	26	.927	-13	94	83	*S-140	0.0
1911	Bos A	80	261	34	67	13	8	1	38	29	4		.257	.340	.379	101	0	15	.946	-6	92	81	2-40,S-32	-0.3
1912	†Bos A	144	504	75	138	25	6	2	68	62	4		.274	.358	.359	100	2	21	.922	-13	87	102	*S-144	-0.1
1913	Bos A	110	365	43	83	14	8	2	34	40	7	29	.227	.316	.326	86	-7	9	.937	-0	91	85	*S-103/2-5,3	0.0
1915	Bos A	84	267	38	64	11	2	0	29	37	3	34	.240	.339	.296	93	-1	8-4	.927	-15	87	70	2-79/3O(LF)	-1.6
1916	Bos A	6	8	2	4	1	0	0	0	3	0	0	.500	.636	.625	278	2	2	1.000	1	149	0	/3-4,2S	0.4
1918	Bos A	3	8	0	1	0	0	0	0	1	0	0	.125	.222	.125	5	-1	0	.900	-0	113	254	/2-2,3	-0.1
Total	12	983	3333	402	834	128	47	10	343	310	28	63	.250	.319	.326	95	-19	144-4	.928	-14	97	96	S-822,2-138/3-8,O(LF)	1.1
WAGNER, HAL Harold Edward B 7.2.1915 E.Riverton, NJ D 8.7.1979 Riverside, NJ BL/TR 6/165# d10.3 Mil 1944-45																								
1937	Phi A	1	0	0	0	0	0	0	0	0	0	0	—	—	—	—	0	0-0	1.000	0	*0*	*0*	/C	0.0
1938	Phi A	33	88	10	20	2	1	0	8	8	1	9	.227	.299	.273	45	-8	0-0	.972	-2	*78*	*136*	C-30	-0.7
1939	Phi A	5	8	0	1	0	0	0	0	0	0	3	.125	.125	.125	-37	-2	0-0	1.000	1	*127*	*264*	/C-5	-0.1
1940	Phi A	34	75	9	19	5	1	0	10	11	1	6	.253	.356	.347	85	-1	0-0	.964	1	*69*	*121*	C-28	0.1
1941	Phi A	46	131	18	29	8	2	1	15	19	0	9	.221	.320	.336	75	-4	1-0	.976	-1	*89*	*91*	C-42	-0.2
1942	Phi A☆	104	288	26	68	17	1	1	30	24	4	29	.236	.304	.313	74	-10	1-0	.986	-6	*74*	*110*	C-94	-1.0
1943	Phi A	111	289	22	69	17	1	1	26	36	2	17	.239	.327	.315	89	-3	3-3	.980	-10	*75*	*88*	C-99	-0.9
1944	Phi A	5	4	0	1	0	0	0	0	0	0	0	.250	.250	.250	44	0	0-0	1.000	0	*0*	*1076*	/C	0.0
	Bos A	66	223	21	74	13	4	1	38	29	4	14	.332	.418	.439	147	15	1-1	.970	-2	*101*	*80*	C-64	1.8
	Year	71	227	21	75	13	4	1	38	29	4	14	.330	.415	.436	145	15	1-1	.971	-2	*100*	*85*	C-65	1.8
1946	†Bos A★	117	370	39	85	12	2	6	52	69	2	32	.230	.354	.322	85	-5	3-1	.983	-5	***133***	*61*	*C-116	-0.4
1947	Bos A	21	65	5	15	3	0	0	6	9	0	5	.231	.324	.277	63	-3	0-0	.978	-1	*87*	*59*	C-21	-0.3
	Det A	71	191	19	55	10	0	5	33	28	1	16	.288	.382	.419	119	6	0-1	.990	-0	*119*	*70*	C-71	0.9
	Year	92	256	24	70	13	0	5	39	37	1	21	.273	.367	.383	105	3	0-1	.987	-1	*111*	*67*	C-92	0.6
1948	Det A	54	109	10	22	3	0	0	10	20	0	11	.202	.326	.229	48	-8	1-0	.989	-2	*95*	*51*	C-52	-0.7
	Phi N	3	4	0	0	0	0	0	0	0	0	0	.000	.000	.000	-99	-1	0	1.000	1	*0*	*540*	/C	-0.1
1949	Phi N	1	4	0	0	0	0	0	0	0	0	1	.000	.000	.000	-99	-1	0	.750	-0	*0*	*0*	/C	-0.2
Total	12	672	1849	179	458	90	12	15	228	253	15	152	.248	.343	.334	87	-25	10-6	.981	-26	*97*	*85*	C-626	-1.8
WAGNER, HONUS John Peter "The Flying Dutchman" B 2.24.1874 Chartiers, PA D 12.6.1955 Carnegie, PA BR/TR (BB 1909 (part)) 5-11/200# d7.19 M1 C19 HF1936 b-Butts OF Total (35-LF 67-CF 272-RF)																								
1897	Lou N	62	242	38	81	18	4	2	39	15	1		.335	.376	.467	126	9	20	.912	4	233	330	O-53(1-53-0)/2-9	0.8
1898	Lou N	151	588	80	176	29	3	10	105	31	6		.299	.341	.410	117	11	27	.972	-1	113	95	1-75,3-65,2-10	1.1

Year	Tm Lg	G	AB	R	H	2B	3B	HR	RBI	BB-IB	HP	SO	AVG	OBP	SLG	AOPS	ABR	SB-CS	FA	FR	Rng	Thr	G at Pos	BFW
1899	Lou N	148	575	100	196	45	13	7	114	40	11		.341	.395	.501	145	35	37	.920	4	104	97	3-76,O-61(3-0-58)/2-7,1-4	3.4
1900	†Pit N	135	527	107	201	**45**	**22**	4	100	41	8		**.381**	.434	**.573**	**175**	53	38	.965	-3	71	109	*O-118(RF)/3-9,2-7,1-3,P	4.1
1901	Pit N	**140**	549	101	194	37	11	6	**126**	53	7		.353	.417	.494	159	43	**49**	.918	3	99	139	S-61,O-54(1-0-53),3-24/2	4.4
1902	Pit N	136	534	**105**	176	**30**	16	3	**91**	43	**14**		.330	.394	**.463**	**159**	**37**	**42**	1.000	3	119	97	0-61(20-11-30),S-44,1-32/P2	3.8
1903	†Pit N	129	512	97	182	30	**19**	5	101	44	7		**.355**	.414	.518	160	39	46	.933	18	106	**132**	*S-111,O-12(1-0-11)/1-6	5.6
1904	Pit N	132	490	97	171	**44**	14	4	75	59	4		**.349**	**.423**	**.520**	**186**	**52**	**53**	.929	-4	97	110	*S-121/O-8(6-2-0),1-3,2-2	**5.3**
1905	Pit N	147	548	114	199	32	14	6	101	54	7		.363	.427	.505	173	50	57	.935	19	**108**	117	*S-145/O-2(LF)	**7.5**
1906	Pit N	142	516	**103**	175	**38**	9	2	71	58	10		**.339**	.416	.459	166	42	53	.941	20	**109**	**137**	*S-137/O-2(RF),3	**7.2**
1907	Pit N	142	515	98	180	**38**	14	6	82	46	5		**.350**	**.408**	**.513**	**186**	**50**	**61**	.938	6	102	73	*S-138/1-4	**6.7**
1908	Pit N	151	568	100	**201**	**39**	**19**	10	**109**	54	5		**.354**	**.415**	**.542**	**205**	**66**	**53**	.943	-11	93	106	*S-151	**6.9**
1909	†Pit N	137	495	92	168	**39**	10	5	**100**	66	3		**.339**	**.420**	**.489**	**168**	**42**	35	.940	5	99	**134**	*S-136/O(LF)	**5.6**
1910	Pit N	150	556	90	**178**	34	8	4	81	59	5	47	.320	.390	.432	132	24	24	.935	5	97	**119**	*S-138,1-11/2-2	3.5
1911	Pit N	130	473	87	158	23	16	9	89	67	6	34	**.334**	.423	.507	154	35	20	.932	-0	97	153	*S-101,1-28/O(CF)	4.1
1912	Pit N	145	558	91	181	35	20	7	**102**	59	6	38	.324	.395	.496	145	34	26	**.962**	17	100	**137**	*S-143	**5.9**
1913	Pit N	114	413	51	124	18	4	3	56	26	5	40	.300	.349	.385	114	7	21-11	**.962**	9	96	120	*S-105	2.5
1914	Pit N	150	552	60	139	15	9	1	50	51	2	51	.252	.317	.317	93	-5	23	**.950**	8	102	102	*S-132,3-17/1	1.2
1915	Pit N	**156**	566	68	155	32	17	6	78	39	4	64	.274	.325	.422	127	16	22-15	**.948**	1	97	105	*S-131,2-12,1-10	2.8
1916	Pit N	123	432	45	124	15	9	1	39	34	8	36	.287	.350	.370	120	11	11	.942	-14	86	79	S-92,1-24/2-4	0.3
1917	Pit N	74	230	15	61	7	1	0	24	24	1	17	.265	.337	.304	94	0	5	.985	-4	89	93	1-47,3-18/2-2,SM	-0.6
Total	21	2794	10439	1739	3420	643	252	101	1733	963	125	<u>327</u>	.328	.391	.467	150	651	723-<u>26</u>	.940	84	100	116	*S-1887,O-373R,1-248,3-210/2P	82.1

WAGNER, JOE Joseph Bernard B 4.24.1889 New York, NY D 11.15.1948 Bronx, NY BR/TR 5-11/165# d4.25

Year	Tm Lg	G	AB	R	H	2B	3B	HR	RBI	BB-IB	HP	SO	AVG	OBP	SLG	AOPS	ABR	SB-CS	FA	FR	Rng	Thr	G at Pos	BFW
1915	Cin N	75	197	17	35	5	2	0	13	8	0	35	.178	.210	.223	31	-17	4-6	.961	6	101	162	2-46,S-12/3-2	-1.3

WAGNER, LEON Leon Lamar "Daddy Wags" B 5.13.1934 Chattanooga, TN D 1.03.2004 Los Angeles, CA BL/TR 6-1/195# d6.22

Year	Tm Lg	G	AB	R	H	2B	3B	HR	RBI	BB-IB	HP	SO	AVG	OBP	SLG	AOPS	ABR	SB-CS	FA	FR	Rng	Thr	G at Pos	BFW
1958	SF N	74	221	31	70	9	0	13	35	18-3	1	34	.317	.371	.534	139	12	1-0	.949	-1	89	130	O-57(LF)	0.8
1959	SF N	87	129	20	29	4	3	5	22	25-6	3	24	.225	.361	.419	110	2	0-0	.941	-1	105	0	O-28(LF)	0.0
1960	StL N	39	98	12	21	2	0	4	11	17-3	1	17	.214	.333	.357	83	-2	0-1	.963	1	96	179	O-32(29-0-4)	-0.3
1961	LA A	133	453	74	127	19	2	28	79	48-2	3	65	.280	.348	.517	116	10	5-1	.971	1	93	154	*O-116(104-0-14)	0.5
1962	LA A★	160	612	96	164	21	5	37	107	50-4	5	87	.268	.326	.500	123	16	7-5	.972	-6	90	78	*O-156(102-0-62)	0.1
1963	LA A★	149	550	73	160	11	1	26	90	49-8	7	73	.291	.352	.456	134	24	5-7	.960	-4	93	72	*O-141(136-0-7)	1.1
1964	Cle A	163	641	94	162	19	2	31	100	56-12	6	121	.253	.316	.434	108	5	14-2	.959	-6	94	64	*O-163(LF)	-0.8
1965	Cle A	144	517	91	152	18	1	28	79	60-8	3	52	.294	.369	.495	143	29	12-2	.957	-10	82	42	*O-134(LF)	1.5
1966	Cle A	150	549	70	153	20	0	23	66	46-9	1	69	.279	.334	.441	121	14	5-2	.990	-12	78	48	*O-139(LF)	-0.5
1967	Cle A	135	433	56	105	15	1	15	54	37-6	12	76	.242	.317	.386	107	4	3-3	.980	-7	79	58	*O-117(LF)	-1.1
1968	Cle A	38	49	5	9	4	0	0	6	6-0	0	6	.184	.273	.265	65	-2	0-0	.500	-3	27	0	O-10(7-0-3)	-0.5
	Chi A	69	162	14	46	8	0	1	18	21-2	0	31	.284	.366	.352	117	4	2-1	.941	-6	72	0	O-46(9-1-36)	-0.5
	Year	107	211	19	55	12	0	1	24	27-2	0	37	.261	.345	.332	106	3	2-1	.895	-9	65	0	O-56(16-1-39)	-1.0
1969	SF N	11	12	0	4	0	0	0	2	2-1	1	1	.333	.467	.333	130	1	0-0	1.000	0	164	0	/O(LF)	0.1
Total	12	1352	4426	636	1202	150	15	211	669	435-64	43	656	.272	.340	.455	121	117	54-24	.964	-53	87	73	*O-1140(1026-1-126)	0.4

WAGNER, MARK Mark Duane B 3.4.1954 Conneaut, OH BR/TR 6-1/175# d8.20

Year	Tm Lg	G	AB	R	H	2B	3B	HR	RBI	BB-IB	HP	SO	AVG	OBP	SLG	AOPS	ABR	SB-CS	FA	FR	Rng	Thr	G at Pos	BFW
1976	Det A	39	115	9	30	2	3	0	12	6-0	0	18	.261	.298	.330	81	-3	0-2	.947	7	116	110	S-39	0.8
1977	Det A	22	48	4	7	0	1	1	3	4-0	1	12	.146	.222	.250	28	-5	0-1	.923	-1	118	107	S-21/2	-0.4
1978	Det A	39	109	10	26	1	2	0	6	3-0	2	11	.239	.272	.284	55	-7	1-0	.964	-3	92	107	S-35/2-4	-0.7
1979	Det A	75	146	16	40	3	0	1	13	16-0	0	25	.274	.341	.315	77	-4	3-2	.974	-6	96	98	S-41,2-29/3-2,D	-0.6
1980	Det A	45	72	5	17	1	0	0	3	7-0	0	11	.236	.304	.250	52	-5	0-1	.935	-10	71	49	S-28/3-9,2-6	-1.3
1981	Tex A	50	85	15	22	4	1	1	14	8-0	0	13	.259	.323	.365	103	0	1-1	.964	0	92	89	S-43/2-4,3-2	0.3
1982	Tex A	60	179	14	43	4	1	0	8	10-0	0	28	.240	.280	.274	56	-11	1-0	.955	2	110	88	S-60	-0.3
1983	Tex A	2	2	0	0	0	0	0	0	0-0	0	1	.000	.000	.000	-99	-1	0-0	1.000	1	193	0	/S-2	0.0
1984	Oak A	82	87	8	20	5	1	0	12	7-0	0	11	.230	.284	.310	70	-4	2-0	.951	-4	86	84	S-57,3-15/2-8,PD	-0.4
Total	9	414	843	81	205	20	9	3	71	61-0	3	130	.243	.295	.299	66	-40	8-7	.953	-13	100	92	S-326/2-52,3-28,D-4,P	-2.6

WAGNER, BILL William Joseph B 1.2.1894 Jesup, IA D 1.11.1951 Waterloo, IA BR/TR 6/187# d7.16

Year	Tm Lg	G	AB	R	H	2B	3B	HR	RBI	BB-IB	HP	SO	AVG	OBP	SLG	AOPS	ABR	SB-CS	FA	FR	Rng	Thr	G at Pos	BFW
1914	Pit N	3	1	0	0	0	0	0	0	0	0	0	.000	.000	.000	-99	0	0	1.000	0	*0*	*316*	/C-3	0.0
1915	Pit N	5	5	0	0	0	0	0	0	1	0	2	.000	.167	.000	-48	-1	0	1.000	1	*135*	*252*	/C-3	0.0
1916	Pit N	19	38	2	9	0	2	0	2	5	0	8	.237	.326	.342	104	0	0	.936	0	93	139	C-15	0.1
1917	Pit N	53	151	15	31	7	2	0	9	11	1	22	.205	.264	.278	64	-6	1	.958	-6	*72*	*117*	C-37,1-12	-1.1
1918	Bos N	13	47	2	10	0	0	1	7	4	0	5	.213	.275	.277	71	-2	0	.917	-4	*88*	*78*	C-13	-0.5
Total	5	93	242	19	50	7	4	1	18	21	1	37	.207	.273	.281	69	-9	1	.947	-9	*81*	*117*	/C-71,1-12	-1.5

WAHL, KERMIT Kermit Emerson B 11.18.1922 Columbia, SD D 9.16.1987 Tucson, AZ BR/TR 5-11/170# d6.23

Year	Tm Lg	G	AB	R	H	2B	3B	HR	RBI	BB-IB	HP	SO	AVG	OBP	SLG	AOPS	ABR	SB-CS	FA	FR	Rng	Thr	G at Pos	BFW
1944	Cin N	4	1	0	0	0	0	0	0	0	0	0	.000	.000	.000	-99	0	0	—	-0	0	0	/3	0.0
1945	Cin N	71	194	18	39	8	2	0	10	23	0	22	.201	.286	.263	54	-12	2	.948	-1	101	82	2-32,S-31/3-7	-0.9
1947	Cin N	39	81	8	14	0	0	1	4	6	1	12	.173	.239	.210	20	-10	0	.964	3	97	70	3-20/S-9,2-2	-0.7
1950	Phi A	89	280	26	72	12	3	2	27	30	1	30	.257	.331	.343	74	-11	1-1	.946	4	108	77	3-61,S-18/2-2	-0.6
1951	Phi A	20	59	4	11	2	0	0	6	9	0	5	.186	.294	.220	40	-5	0-0	.967	2	110	117	3-18	-0.3
	StL A	8	27	2	9	1	1	0	3	0	0	3	.333	.333	.444	106	0	0-0	.950	1	103	205	/3-6	0.0
	Year	28	86	6	20	3	1	0	9	9	0	8	.233	.305	.291	60	-5	0-0	.962	2	108	141	3-24	-0.3
Total	5	231	642	58	145	23	6	3	50	68	2	72	.226	.302	.294	60	-38	3-<u>1</u>	.949	8	107	86	3-113/S-58,2-36	-2.5

WAITKUS, EDDIE Edward Stephen B 9.4.1919 Cambridge, MA D 9.16.1972 Jamaica Plain, MA BL/TL 6-1/175# d4.15 Mil 1942-45

Year	Tm Lg	G	AB	R	H	2B	3B	HR	RBI	BB-IB	HP	SO	AVG	OBP	SLG	AOPS	ABR	SB-CS	FA	FR	Rng	Thr	G at Pos	BFW
1941	Chi N	12	28	1	5	0	0	0	0	0	1	3	.179	.207	.179	10	-3	0	.949	-1	71	141	/1-9	-0.6
1946	Chi N	113	441	50	134	24	5	4	55	23	1	14	.304	.340	.408	114	6	3	.996	3	105	89	*1-106	0.6
1947	Chi N	130	514	60	150	28	6	2	35	32	2	17	.292	.336	.381	94	-6	3	.994	8	**124**	101	*1-126	-0.1
1948	Chi N★	139	562	87	166	27	10	7	44	43	2	19	.295	.348	.416	110	7	11	.992	7	**123**	84	*1-116,O-20(LF)	0.8
1949	Phi N✳	54	209	41	64	16	3	1	28	33	1	12	.306	.403	.426	126	10	3	.994	1	106	114	1-54	0.8
1950	†Phi N	154	641	102	182	32	5	2	44	55	1	29	.284	.341	.359	86	-13	3	.993	-3	91	107	*1-154	-2.1
1951	Phi N	145	610	65	157	27	4	1	46	53	0	22	.257	.317	.320	73	-23	0-3	.992	-2	92	91	*1-144	-3.2
1952	Phi N	146	499	51	144	29	4	2	49	64	1	23	.289	.371	.375	108	8	2-2	.991	-3	94	104	*1-146	0.0
1953	Phi N	81	247	24	72	9	2	1	16	13	1	23	.291	.330	.356	79	-8	1-1	.989	-1	94	141	1-59	-1.2
1954	Bal A	95	311	35	88	17	4	2	33	28	1	25	.283	.341	.383	107	2	0-1	1.000	-0	91	104	1-78	-0.3
1955	Bal A	38	85	2	22	1	1	0	9	11-3	0	10	.259	.344	.294	78	-2	2-0	.974	-3	68	80	1-26	-0.6
	Phi N	33	107	10	30	5	0	2	14	17-1	0	7	.280	.379	.383	105	2	0-1	.996	0	96	126	1-31	-0.1
Total	11	1140	4254	528	1214	215	44	24	373	372-<u>4</u>	11	204	.285	.344	.374	96	-20	28-<u>8</u>	.993	5	101	101	*1-1049/O-20(LF)	-6.0

WAITT, CHARLIE Charles C. B 10.14.1853 Hallowell, ME D 10.21.1912 San Francisco, CA TR 5-11/165# d5.25

Year	Tm Lg	G	AB	R	H	2B	3B	HR	RBI	BB-IB	HP	SO	AVG	OBP	SLG	AOPS	ABR	SB-CS	FA	FR	Rng	Thr	G at Pos	BFW
1875	StL NA	30	113	14	23	10	0	0	12	2		7	.204	.217	.292	83	0	3-2	.787	-2	72	284	O-28(2-7-23)/1-4	-0.1
1877	Chi N	10	41	2	4	0	0	0	2	0		3	.098	.098	.098	-34	-6		.793	1	135	264	O-10(RF)	-0.5
1882	Bal AA	72	250	19	39	4	0	0		13			.156	.198	.172	28	-17		.874	0	65	100	*O-72(60-0-12)	-1.7
1883	Phi N	1	3	0	1	0	0	0	0	0		1	.333	.333	.333	114	0		.333	-1	0	0	/O(CF)	-0.1
Total	3	83	294	21	44	4	0	0	<u>2</u>	13		<u>4</u>	.150	.186	.163	18	-23		.855	0	74	122	/O-83(60-1-22)	-2.3

WAKAMATSU, DON Wilbur Donald B 2.22.1963 Hood River, OR BR/TR 6-2/200# d5.22 C1

Year	Tm Lg	G	AB	R	H	2B	3B	HR	RBI	BB-IB	HP	SO	AVG	OBP	SLG	AOPS	ABR	SB-CS	FA	FR	Rng	Thr	G at Pos	BFW
1991	Chi A	18	31	2	7	0	0	0	0	1-0	0	6	.226	.250	.226	33	-3	0-0	1.000	-3	325	60	C-18	-0.5

WAKEFIELD, HOWARD Howard John B 4.2.1884 Bucyrus, OH D 4.16.1941 Chicago, IL BR/TR 6-1/185# d9.18 s-Dick

Year	Tm Lg	G	AB	R	H	2B	3B	HR	RBI	BB-IB	HP	SO	AVG	OBP	SLG	AOPS	ABR	SB-CS	FA	FR	Rng	Thr	G at Pos	BFW
1905	Cle A	10	26	3	4	0	0	0	1	0	1		.154	.185	.154	8	-3	0	.926	-2	*96*	*108*	/C-8	-0.4
1906	Was A	77	211	17	59	9	2	1	21	7	0		.280	.303	.355	111	2	6	.946	-13	*74*	92	C-60	-0.7
1907	Cle A	26	37	4	5	2	0	0	3	3	0		.135	.200	.189	24	-3	0	.930	-1	*111*	32	C-11	-0.3
Total	3	113	274	24	68	11	2	1	25	10	1		.248	.277	.314	89	-4	6	.943	-15	*80*	87	/C-79	-1.4

WAKEFIELD, DICK Richard Cummings B 5.6.1921 Chicago, IL D 8.26.1985 Redford, MI BL/TR 6-4/210# d6.26 Mil 1944-45 f-Howard

Year	Tm Lg	G	AB	R	H	2B	3B	HR	RBI	BB-IB	HP	SO	AVG	OBP	SLG	AOPS	ABR	SB-CS	FA	FR	Rng	Thr	G at Pos	BFW
1941	Det A	7	7	0	1	0	0	0	0	0	0	1	.143	.143	.143	-22	-1	0-0	1.000	0	114	0	/O(RF)	-0.1
1943	Det A★	**155**	633	91	**200**	**38**	8	7	79	62	0	60	.316	.377	.434	127	22	4-5	.959	-7	92	90	*O-155(140-0-15)	0.5
1944	Det A	78	276	53	98	15	5	12	53	55	1	29	.355	.464	.576	186	34	2-2	.963	-5	93	46	O-78(LF)	2.4

Year	Tm Lg	G	AB	R	H	2B	3B	HR	RBI	BB-IB	HP	SO	AVG	OBP	SLG	AOPS	ABR	SB-CS	FA	FR	Rng	Thr	G at Pos	BFW
1946	Det A	111	396	64	106	11	5	12	59	59	1	55	.268	.364	.412	110	6	3-5	.964	-2	96	87	*O-104(LF)	-0.6
1947	Det A	112	368	59	104	15	5	8	51	80	1	44	.283	.412	.416	127	17	1-4	.950	-2	90	148	*O-101(LF)	0.7
1948	Det A	110	322	50	89	20	5	11	53	70	0	55	.276	.406	.472	129	16	0-1	.948	-2	105	47	O-86(LF)	0.7
1949	Det A	59	126	17	26	3	1	6	19	32	0	24	.206	.367	.389	100	1	0-0	1.000	2	103	131	O-32(LF)	0.0
1950	NY A	3	2	0	1	0	0	0	1	1	0	1	.500	.667	.500	208	1	0-0	—	0			H	0.0
1952	NY N	3	2	0	0	0	0	0	0	1	0	1	.000	.333	.000	-0	0	0-0	—	0			H	0.0
Total	9	638	2132	334	625	102	29	56	315	360	3	270	.293	.396	.447	130	96	10-17	.959	-16	95	89	O-557(541-0-16)	3.6
WAKELAND, CHRIS Christopher Robert B 6.15.1974 Huntington Beach, CA BL/TL 6/185# d9.4																								
2001	Det A	10	36	5	9	2	0	2	6	0-0	0	13	.250	.250	.472	88	-1	0-0	.941	2	164	0	O-10(RF)	0.0
WALBECK, MATT Matthew Lovick B 10.2.1969 Sacramento, CA BB/TR 5-11/190# d4.7																								
1993	Chi N	11	30	2	6	2	0	1	6	1-0	0	6	.200	.226	.367	56	-2	0-0	1.000	-1	74	37	C-11	-0.2
1994	Min A	97	338	31	69	12	0	5	35	17-1	2	37	.204	.246	.284	36	-33	1-1	.993	-3	94	**149**	C-95/D	-2.9
1995	Min A	115	393	40	101	18	1	1	44	25-2	1	71	.257	.302	.316	61	-23	3-1	.991	-14	107	68	*C-113	-2.7
1996	Min A	63	215	25	48	10	0	2	24	9-0	0	34	.223	.252	.298	38	-21	3-1	.994	-3	106	93	C-61	-1.9
1997	Det A	47	137	18	38	3	0	3	10	12-0	0	19	.277	.331	.365	83	-3	3-3	.988	-3	94	98	C-44	-0.4
1998	Ana A	108	338	41	87	15	2	6	46	30-0	2	68	.257	.317	.367	78	-11	1-1	.990	2	72	131	*C-104/D-2	-0.3
1999	Ana A	107	288	26	69	8	1	3	22	26-1	3	46	.240	.308	.306	58	-19	2-3	.989	-9	91	116	C-97/D	-2.1
2000	Ana A	47	146	17	29	5	0	6	12	7-0	1	22	.199	.240	.356	47	-13	0-1	.991	-4	73	165	C-44/1-2,D	-1.3
2001	Phi N	1	1	0	1	0	0	0	0	0-0	0	0	1.000	1.000	1.000	431	0	0-0	—	0			/H	0.0
2002	Det A	27	85	4	20	2	0	0	3	3-0	0	14	.235	.258	.259	41	-7	0-0	.993	-1	229	32	C-27	-0.7
2003	Det A	59	138	11	24	4	1	1	6	3-0	1	26	.174	.197	.239	16	-18	0-1	.979	-11	66	115	C-55/D	-2.5
Total	11	682	2109	215	492	79	5	28	208	133-4	10	343	.233	.280	.315	54	-150	13-12	.991	-46	96	110	C-651/D-6,1-2	-15.0
WALCZAK, ED Edwin Joseph "Husky" B 9.21.1918 Arctic, RI D 3.10.1998 Norwich, CT BR/TR 5-11/180# d9.3																								
1945	Phi N	20	57	6	12	3	0	0	2	6	0	9	.211	.286	.263	55	-3	0	.966	0	91	134	2-17/S-2	-0.2
WALDEN, FRED Thomas Fred B 6.25.1890 Fayette, MO D 9.27.1955 Jefferson Barracks, MO BR/TR d6.3																								
1912	StL A	1	0	0	0	0	0	0	0	0	0		—	—	—	—	0	0	.000	-1	*34*	*0*	/C	-0.1
WALDRON, IRV Irving J. B 1.21.1876 Hillside, NY D 7.22.1944 Worcester, MA BL/TR 5-5.5/155# d4.25																								
1901	Mil A	62	266	48	79	8	6	0	29	16	2		.297	.342	.372	103	1	12	.883	-2	112	0	O-62(RF)	-0.4
	Was A	79	332	54	107	14	3	0	23	22	2		.322	.368	.383	110	5	8	.955	-3	76	0	O-78(0-69-9)	-0.1
	Year	141	598	102	186	22	9	0	52	38	4		.311	.356	.378	107	6	20	.923	-6	93	0	*O-140(0-69-71)	-0.5
WALEWANDER, JIM James B 5.2.1962 Chicago, IL BB/TR 5-10/160# d5.31																								
1987	Det A	53	54	24	13	3	1	1	4	7-0	0	6	.241	.328	.389	93	0	2-1	1.000	2	112	136	2-24,3-17/S-3,D-8	0.2
1988	Det A	88	175	23	37	5	0	0	6	12-0	0	26	.211	.261	.240	43	-13	11-4	.977	-5	93	109	2-61/S-8,3-3,D-9	-1.6
1990	NY A	9	5	1	1	1	0	0	1	0-0	0	0	.200	.200	.400	64	0	1-1	1.000	-0	50	0	/2-2,3-2,SD	0.0
1993	Cal A	12	8	2	1	0	0	0	3	5-0	0	1	.125	.429	.125	64	0	1-1	1.000	1	114	163	/S-6,2-2,D-3	0.1
Total	4	162	242	50	52	9	1	1	14	24-0	0	33	.215	.284	.273	57	-13	15-7	.982	-2	95	112	/2-89,D-22,3-22,S-18	-1.3
WALKER, RUBE Albert Bluford B 5.16.1926 Lenoir, NC D 12.12.1992 Morganton, NC BL/TR 6-1/185# d4.20 C21																								
1948	Chi N	79	171	17	47	8	0	5	26	24	2	17	.275	.371	.409	115	4	0	.980	-2	*97*	*123*	C-44	0.4
1949	Chi N	56	172	11	42	4	1	3	22	9	0	18	.244	.282	.331	66	-9	0	.964	-5	*64*	*124*	C-43	-1.2
1950	Chi N	74	213	19	49	7	1	6	16	18	0	34	.230	.290	.357	70	-10	0	.975	-2	*66*	*129*	C-62	-0.8
1951	Chi N	37	107	9	25	4	0	2	5	12	0	13	.234	.311	.327	71	-4	0-0	.969	-4	*57*	*107*	C-31	-0.7
	Bro N	36	74	6	18	4	0	2	9	6	0	14	.243	.300	.378	80	-2	0-0	.972	-2	*242*	*102*	C-23	-0.3
	Year	73	181	15	43	8	0	4	14	18	0	27	.238	.307	.348	74	-7	0-0	.970	-6	*121*	*105*	C-54	-1.0
1952	Bro N	46	139	9	36	8	0	1	19	8	1	17	.259	.304	.338	77	-4	0-0	.987	2	*169*	*105*	C-40	0.0
1953	Bro N	43	95	5	23	6	0	3	9	7	1	11	.242	.301	.400	79	-3	0-0	.978	1	*161*	*123*	C-28	-0.1
1954	Bro N	50	155	12	28	7	0	5	23	24	1	17	.181	.291	.323	59	-9	0-0	.996	1	*152*	*84*	C-47	-0.6
1955	Bro N	48	103	6	26	5	0	2	13	15-4	0	11	.252	.342	.359	86	-2	1-0	.987	2	*116*	*73*	C-35	0.1
1956	†Bro N	54	146	5	31	6	1	3	20	7-2	0	18	.212	.245	.329	50	-11	0-1	.986	1	*139*	*123*	C-43	-0.8
1957	Bro N	60	166	12	30	8	0	2	23	15-4	0	33	.181	.243	.265	35	-15	2-0	.992	-0	*115*	*97*	C-50	-1.3
1958	LA N	25	44	3	5	2	0	1	7	5-2	0	10	.114	.200	.227	14	-6	0-0	.985	-1	*156*	*158*	C-20	-0.6
Total	11	608	1585	114	360	69	3	35	192	150-12	5	213	.227	.294	.341	68	-71	3-1	.982	-8	*117*	*111*	C-466	-5.9
WALKER, TONY Anthony Bruce B 7.1.1959 San Diego, CA BR/TR 6-2/205# d4.8																								
1986	Hou N	84	90	19	20	7	0	2	10	11-2	0	15	.222	.307	.367	87	-1	11-3	.986	0	119	0	O-68(CF)	0.0
WALKER, FRANK Charles Franklin B 9.22.1894 Enoree, SC D 9.16.1974 Bristol, TN BR/TR 5-11/165# d9.6																								
1917	Det A	2	2	0	0	0	0	0	0	0	0	1	.000	.000	.000	-99	0	0	—	0			H	-0.1
1918	Det A	55	167	10	33	10	3	1	20	7	1	29	.198	.234	.311	67	-8	3	.922	-2	103	80	O-45(3-34-9)	-1.4
1920	Phi A	24	91	10	21	2	2	0	10	5	2	14	.231	.286	.297	54	-6	0-2	.983	-2	98	33	O-24(CF)	-1.1
1921	Phi A	19	66	6	15	3	0	1	6	8	0	11	.227	.311	.318	60	-4	1-0	.961	0	97	122	O-19(3-16-0)	-0.4
1925	NY N	39	81	12	18	1	0	1	5	9	1	11	.222	.308	.272	51	-6	1-1	.960	-1	86	162	O-21(0-21-1)	-0.7
Total	5	139	407	38	87	16	5	3	41	29	4	66	.214	.273	.300	58	-24	5-3	.949	-4	98	91	O-109(6-95-10)	-3.7
WALKER, TILLY Clarence William B 9.4.1887 Telford, TN D 9.20.1959 Unicoi, TN BR/TR 5-11/165# d6.10																								
1911	Was A	95	356	44	99	6	4	2	39	15	2		.278	.311	.334	82	-10	12	.917	-2	98	98	O-94(LF)	-1.6
1912	Was A	39	110	22	30	2	1	0	9	8	2		.273	.333	.309	83	-2	11	.837	-1	80	164	O-34(4-7-23)/2	-0.5
1913	StL A	23	85	7	25	4	1	0	11	2	0	9	.294	.310	.365	100	-1	5	.911	0	86	165	O-23(LF)	-0.2
1914	StL A	151	517	67	154	24	16	6	78	51	4	72	.298	.365	.441	148	28	29-17	.972	17	112	144	*O-145(LF)	4.2
1915	StL A	144	510	53	137	20	7	5	49	36	5	77	.269	.323	.365	110	4	20-17	.940	9	106	135	*O-139(1-119-19)	0.1
1916	†Bos A	128	467	68	124	29	11	3	46	23	2	45	.266	.303	.394	109	2	14	.959	-5	101	69	*O-128(3-125-0)	-1.3
1917	Bos A	106	337	41	83	18	7	2	37	25	1	38	.246	.300	.359	102	-1	6	.972	4	96	144	O-96(CF)	-0.4
1918	Phi A	114	414	56	122	20	0	**11**	48	41	1	44	.295	.360	.423	135	17	8	.953	3	94	155	*O-109(CF)	1.3
1919	Phi A	125	456	47	133	30	6	10	64	26	0	41	.292	.330	.450	116	8	8	.933	-4	98	89	*O-115(28-85-2)	-0.3
1920	Phi A	149	585	79	157	23	7	17	82	41	4	59	.268	.321	.419	94	-8	8-3	.940	-0	94	127	*O-149(123-26-0)	-1.5
1921	Phi A	142	556	89	169	32	5	23	101	73	4	41	.304	.389	.504	125	22	3-5	.955	5	102	125	*O-142(LF)	1.3
1922	Phi A	153	565	111	160	31	4	37	99	61	4	67	.283	.357	.549	130	22	4-3	.956	-2	95	103	*O-148(137-11-0)	0.8
1923	Phi A	52	109	12	30	5	2	2	16	14	2	11	.275	.368	.413	104	1	1-2	1.000	-1	102	34	O-26(LF)	-0.2
Total	13	1421	5067	696	1423	244	71	118	679	416	31	504	.281	.339	.427	115	82	129-47	.949	23	99	119	*O-1348(726-578-44)/2	1.7
WALKER, CHICO Cleotha B 11.25.1958 Jackson, MS BB/TR 5-9/179# d9.2																								
1980	Bos A	19	57	3	12	0	0	1	5	6-1	1	10	.211	.292	.263	52	-4	3-2	.958	-2	101	98	2-11/D-7	-0.5
1981	Bos A	6	17	3	6	0	0	0	2	1-0	0	2	.353	.389	.353	108	0	0-2	1.000	-2	81	35	/2-5	-0.3
1983	Bos A	4	5	2	2	0	2	0	1	0-0	0	0	.400	.400	1.200	299	1	0-0	1.000	1	146	977	/O-3(LF)	0.2
1984	Bos A	3	2	0	0	0	0	0	1	0-0	0	1	.000	.000	.000	-96	-1	0-0	1.000	0	146	0	/2	-0.1
1985	Chi N	21	12	3	1	0	0	0	0	0-0	0	5	.083	.083	.083	-48	-2	1-0	1.000	-0	92	0	/O-6(3-0-3),2-2	-0.3
1986	Chi N	28	101	21	28	3	2	1	7	10-0	0	20	.277	.339	.376	91	-1	15-4	.956	-3	83	56	O-26(1-11-22)	-0.3
1987	Chi N	47	105	15	21	4	0	0	7	12-1	0	23	.200	.277	.238	38	-9	11-4	.974	-4	74	0	O-33(25-3-5)/3-2	-1.4
1988	Cal A	33	78	8	12	1	0	0	2	6-0	0	15	.154	.214	.167	8	-10	2-1	.933	-2	76	149	O-17(5-12-0)/2-7,3-2	-1.2
1991	Chi N	124	374	51	96	10	1	6	34	33-2	0	57	.257	.315	.337	80	-10	13-5	.929	-7	87	99	3-57,O-53(20-36-8)/2-6	-1.7
1992	Chi N	19	26	2	3	0	0	0	2	3-0	0	4	.115	.200	.115	-6	-4	1-0	1.000	1	206	0	/O-6(6-0-1),2-2,3-2	-0.3
	NY N	107	227	24	70	12	1	4	36	24-3	0	46	.308	.369	.423	127	9	14-1	.971	-0	102	44	3-36,2-16,O-15(9-4-2)	1.2
	Year	126	253	26	73	12	1	4	38	27-3	0	50	.289	.351	.391	113	5	15-1	.960	1	105	42	3-38,O-21(15-4-3),2-18	0.9
1993	NY N	115	213	18	48	7	1	5	19	14-0	0	29	.225	.271	.338	63	-12	7-0	.976	4	113	98	2-24,3-23,O-15(15-0-1)	-0.6
Total	11	526	1217	150	299	37	7	17	116	109-7	1	212	.246	.305	.329	75	-43	67-19	.968	-14	84	127	O-174(87-66-42),3-122/2-74,D-7	-5.3
WALKER, DUANE Duane Allen B 3.13.1957 Pasadena, TX BL/TL 6/185# d5.25																								
1982	Cin N	86	239	26	52	10	0	5	22	27-0	2	58	.218	.298	.322	73	-8	9-3	.992	1	94	150	O-69(40-2-31)	-1.0
1983	Cin N	109	225	14	53	12	1	2	29	20-4	0	43	.236	.296	.324	70	-9	6-3	.956	3	113	114	O-60(35-0-26)	-0.9
1984	Cin N	83	195	35	57	10	3	10	28	33-2	0	35	.292	.391	.528	150	14	7-3	.950	-0	105	77	O-68(51-13-9)	1.3
1985	Cin N	37	48	5	8	2	1	2	6	6-1	0	18	.167	.259	.375	72	-2	1-0	.882	-0	120	0	O-10(8-0-2)	-0.2

Year	Tm Lg	G	AB	R	H	2B	3B	HR	RBI	BB-IB	HP	SO	AVG	OBP	SLG	AOPS	ABR	SB-CS	FA	FR	Rng	Thr	G at Pos	BFW
	Tex A	53	132	14	23	2	0	5	11	15-0	1	29	.174	.264	.303	54	-9	2-1	1.000	3	94	340	O-32(12-0-23),D-10	-0.7
1988	StL N	24	22	1	4	1	0	0	3	2-0	0	7	.182	.250	.227	38	-2	0-0	—	-1	0	0	/O-4(2-0-2),1	-0.3
Total	5	392	861	95	197	37	5	24	99	103-7	3	190	.229	.311	.367	86	-16	25-10	.967	6	102	142	O-243(148-15-93)/D-10,1	-1.8
WALKER, ERNIE Ernest Robert B 9.17.1890 Blossburg, AL D 4.1.1965 Pell City, AL BL/TR 6/165# d4.13 b-Dixie																								
1913	StL A	7	14	0	3	0	0	0	2	0	0	5	.214	.214	.214	26	-1	0	1.000	-0	113	0	/O-2(CF)	-0.2
1914	StL A	74	131	19	39	5	3	1	14	13	1	26	.298	.366	.405	137	6	6-4	.960	-1	96	87	O-38(21-9-10)	0.4
1915	StL A	50	109	15	23	4	2	0	9	23	0	32	.211	.348	.284	93	0	5-8	.881	-3	89	32	O-33(3-3-27)	-0.6
Total	3	131	254	34	65	9	5	1	25	36	1	63	.256	.351	.343	112	5	11-12	.928	-4	93	57	/O-73(24-14-37)	-0.4
WALKER, DIXIE Fred "The People's Cherce" B 9.24.1910 Villa Rica, GA D 5.17.1982 Birmingham, AL BL/TR 6-1/175# d4.28 C5 b-Harry f-Dixie																								
1931	NY A	2	10	1	3	2	0	0	1	0	0	4	.300	.300	.500	113	0	0-0	1.000	-0	74	0	/O-2(1-0-1)	0.0
1933	NY A	98	328	68	90	15	7	15	51	26	1	28	.274	.330	.500	125	9	2-2	.962	1	102	117	O-77(15-60-3)	0.6
1934	NY A	17	17	2	2	0	0	0	0	1	0	3	.118	.167	.118	-27	-3	0-0	1.000	-0	87	0	/O(LF)	-0.3
1935	NY A	8	13	1	2	1	0	0	1	0	0	1	.154	.154	.231	-2	-2	0-0	.750	-0	85	0	/O-2(LF)	-0.2
1936	NY A	6	20	3	7	0	2	1	5	1	0	3	.350	.381	.700	167	2	1-1	1.000	-0	90	0	/O-5(CF)	0.1
	Chi A	26	70	12	19	2	0	0	11	14	1	6	.271	.400	.300	73	-2	1-0	1.000	1	101	134	O-17(0-16-1)	-0.2
	Year	32	90	15	26	2	2	1	16	15	1	9	.289	.396	.389	92	-1	2-1	1.000	0	99	109	O-22(0-21-1)	-0.1
1937	Chi A	**154**	593	105	179	28	**16**	9	95	78	0	26	.302	.383	.449	109	8	1-2	.952	-10	92	70	*O-154(RF)	-1.0
1938	Det A	127	454	84	140	27	6	6	43	65	1	32	.308	.396	.434	102	3	5-4	.979	-3	94	96	*O-114(94-26-0)	-0.5
1939	Det A	43	154	30	47	4	5	4	19	15	0	8	.305	.367	.474	106	0	4-1	.970	2	105	138	O-37(23-4-11)	0.1
	Bro N	61	225	27	63	6	4	2	38	20	0	10	.280	.339	.369	87	-4	1	.968	-1	97	104	O-59(CF)	-0.7
1940	Bro N	143	556	75	171	37	8	6	66	42	1	21	.308	.357	.435	111	8	3	.973	-5	102	50	*O-136(14-112-20)	-0.1
1941	†Bro N	148	531	88	165	32	8	9	71	70	0	18	.311	.391	.452	131	24	4	.976	10	106	**160**	*O-146(22-22-105)	2.6
1942	Bro N	118	393	57	114	28	1	6	54	47	1	15	.290	.367	.412	126	14	1	.986	0	103	87	*O-110(0-7-104)	0.9
1943	Bro N★	138	540	83	163	32	6	5	71	49	3	24	.302	.363	.411	123	16	3	.969	4	99	**152**	*O-136(57-0-82)	1.3
1944	Bro N★	147	535	77	191	37	8	13	91	72	1	27	**.357**	.434	.529	173	55	6	.962	2	100	127	*O-140(19-0-125)	4.9
1945	Bro N✳	154	607	102	182	42	9	8	**124**	75	5	16	.300	.381	.438	128	25	6	.992	10	109	124	*O-153(RF)	2.4
1946	Bro N★	150	576	80	184	29	9	9	116	67	1	28	.319	.391	.448	136	28	14	.969	-9	85	103	*O-149(RF)	1.6
1947	†Bro N★	148	529	77	162	31	3	9	94	97	1	26	.306	.415	.427	119	20	6	.964	-8	92	74	*O-147(RF)	0.7
1948	Pit N	129	408	39	129	19	3	2	54	52	0	18	.316	.393	.392	111	9	1	.977	-6	91	57	*O-112(1-1-110)	0.0
1949	Pit N	88	181	26	51	4	1	1	18	26	0	11	.282	.372	.331	88	-2	0	.984	-2	93	69	O-39(RF)/1-3	-0.5
Total	18	1905	6740	1037	2064	376	96	105	1023	817	16	325	.306	.383	.437	121	208	59-10	.972	-14	98	102	*O-1736(249-312-1204)/1-3	11.7
WALKER, GEE Gerald Holmes B 3.19.1908 Gulfport, MS D 3.20.1981 Whitfield, MS BR/TR 5-11/188# d4.14 C1 b-Hub																								
1931	Det A	59	189	20	56	17	2	1	28	14	0	21	.296	.345	.423	98	-1	10-7	.953	-5	86	59	O-44(1-41-1)	-0.6
1932	Det A	127	480	71	155	32	6	8	78	13	3	38	.323	.345	.465	104	1	30-6	.949	1	105	96	*O-116(39-79-0)	0.2
1933	Det A	127	483	68	135	29	7	9	64	15	2	49	.280	.304	.424	89	-10	26-9	.942	-4	94	89	*O-113(92-8-13)	-1.7
1934	†Det A	98	347	54	104	19	2	6	39	19	2	20	.300	.340	.418	94	-4	20-9	.947	-0	104	80	O-80(9-48-23)	-0.6
1935	†Det A	98	362	52	109	22	6	7	53	15	0	21	.301	.329	.453	104	0	6-4	.954	-3	103	31	O-85(29-45-11)	-0.6
1936	Det A	134	550	105	194	55	5	12	93	23	8	30	.353	.387	.536	125	21	17-8	.948	1	101	117	*O-125(2-21-103)	1.4
1937	Det A✳	151	635	105	213	42	4	18	113	41	5	74	.335	.380	.499	117	16	23-7	.956	-5	98	69	*O-151(88-11-54)	0.4
1938	Chi A	120	442	69	135	23	6	16	87	38	0	32	.305	.360	.493	109	4	9-4	.958	-5	91	102	*O-107(50-0-57)	-0.5
1939	Chi A	149	598	95	174	30	11	13	111	28	7	43	.291	.330	.443	94	-9	17-6	.967	8	110	108	*O-147(LF)	-0.8
1940	Was A	140	595	87	175	29	7	13	96	24	3	58	.294	.325	.432	101	-3	21-4	.967	-2	96	100	*O-140(LF)	-0.8
1941	Cle A	121	445	56	126	26	11	6	48	18	1	46	.283	.313	.431	100	-4	12-6	.982	5	111	98	*O-105(103-2-0)	-0.4
1942	Cin N	119	422	40	97	20	2	5	50	31	5	44	.230	.290	.322	79	-12	11	.973	-2	103	68	*O-110(20-74-19)	-1.9
1943	Cin N	114	429	48	105	23	2	3	54	12	3	38	.245	.270	.329	74	-16	6	.980	-6	91	79	*O-106(15-75-17)	-2.9
1944	Cin N	121	478	56	133	21	3	5	62	23	5	48	.278	.318	.366	96	-4	7	.967	-9	100	24	*O-117(1-59-61)	-1.9
1945	Cin N	106	316	28	80	11	2	2	21	16	0	38	.253	.289	.320	71	-14	8	.962	-5	93	67	O-67(6-0-61)/3-3	-2.3
Total	15	1784	6771	954	1991	399	76	124	997	330	44	600	.294	.331	.430	99	-35	223-70	.961	-31	100	82	*O-1613(742-463-420)/3-3	-13.0
WALKER, GREG Gregory Lee B 10.6.1959 Douglas, GA BL/TR 6-3/210# d9.18 C1																								
1982	Chi A	11	17	3	7	2	1	2	7	2-0	0	3	.412	.474	1.000	292	4	0-0	—	0			/D-4	0.4
1983	†Chi A	118	307	32	83	16	3	10	55	28-3	2	57	.270	.332	.440	107	3	2-1	.985	-5	62	105	1-59,D-21	-0.6
1984	Chi A	136	442	62	130	29	2	24	75	35-3	2	66	.294	.346	.532	134	20	8-5	.995	-5	78	93	*1-101,D-21	0.8
1985	Chi A	**163**	601	77	155	38	4	24	92	44-6	2	100	.258	.309	.454	102	1	5-2	.994	-1	91	91	*1-151/D-7	-0.9
1986	Chi A	78	282	37	78	10	6	13	51	29-4	2	44	.277	.345	.493	122	8	1-2	.993	-1	94	93	1-77/D	0.1
1987	Chi A	157	566	85	145	33	2	27	94	75-7	5	112	.256	.346	.465	110	10	2-1	.994	-15	71	112	*1-154/D-3	-1.4
1988	Chi A	99	377	45	93	22	1	8	42	29-3	3	77	.247	.304	.374	90	-5	0-1	.993	-13	58	106	1-98	-2.6
1989	Chi A	77	233	25	49	14	0	5	26	23-2	3	50	.210	.286	.335	77	-7	0-0	.987	-5	59	101	1-48,D-23	-1.6
1990	Chi A	2	5	0	1	0	0	0	0	0-0	0	2	.200	.200	.200	12	-1	0-0	1.000	0	155	264	/1D	-0.1
	Bal A	14	34	2	5	0	0	0	2	3-0	1	9	.147	.237	.147	10	-4	1-0	—	0	0	0	D-11	-0.4
	Year	16	39	2	6	0	0	0	2	3-0	1	11	.154	.233	.154	10	-5	1-0	1.000	0	155	264	D-12/1	-0.5
Total	9	855	2864	368	746	164	19	113	444	268-28	20	520	.260	.326	.449	108	29	19-12	.993	-45	76	101	1-689/D-92	-6.3
WALKER, HARRY Harry William "Harry The Hat" B 10.22.1916 Pascagoula, MS D 8.8.1999 Birmingham, AL BL/TR 6-2/190# d9.25 Mil 1944-45 M9 C4 b-Dixie f-Dixie																								
1940	StL N	7	27	2	5	2	0	0	6	0	0	2	.185	.185	.259	20	-3	0	1.000	2	125	350	/O-7(2-5-1)	-0.1
1941	StL N	7	15	3	4	1	0	0	1	2	0	1	.267	.353	.333	88	0	0	.875	-0	94	0	/O-5(LF)	-0.1
1942	†StL N	74	191	38	60	12	2	0	16	11	1	14	.314	.355	.398	112	3	2	.968	2	104	145	O-56(12-43-3)/2-2	0.3
1943	†StL N★	148	564	76	166	28	6	2	53	40	0	24	.294	.341	.376	102	1	5	.965	-6	92	111	*O-144(0-143-1)/2	-0.9
1946	†StL N	112	346	53	82	14	6	3	27	30	1	29	.237	.300	.338	77	-11	12	.974	3	102	146	O-92(13-79-0)/1-8	-1.2
1947	StL N	10	25	2	5	1	0	0	0	4	0	2	.200	.310	.240	46	-2	0	.938	-1	87	0	O-10(2-7-0)	-0.3
	Phi N★	130	488	79	181	28	16	1	41	59	4	37	.371	.443	.500	156	41	13	.966	5	103	167	*O-127(CF)/1-4	4.1
	Year	140	513	81	186	29	**16**	1	41	63	4	39	**.363**	.436	.487	150	39	13	.964	4	102	**159**	*O-137(2-134-0)/1-4	3.8
1948	Phi N	112	332	34	97	11	2	2	23	33	1	30	.292	.358	.355	95	-2	4	.981	2	106	108	O-81(21-58-3)/1-4,3	-0.2
1949	Chi N	42	159	20	42	6	3	1	14	11	0	6	.264	.312	.358	81	-5	2	.947	-3	85	92	O-39(27-0-13)	-1.0
	Cin N	86	314	53	100	15	2	1	23	34	0	17	.318	.385	.389	107	4	4	.963	-2	97	106	O-77(22-26-29)/1	0.0
	Year	128	473	73	142	21	5	2	37	45	0	23	.300	.361	.378	99	0	6	.959	-4	93	101	*O-116(49-26-42)/1	-1.0
1950	StL N	60	150	17	31	5	0	0	7	18	0	12	.207	.292	.240	40	-13	0	.969	-0	101	101	O-46(9-30-3)/1-2	-1.4
1951	StL N	8	26	6	8	1	0	0	2	2	0	1	.308	.357	.346	90	0	0-0	1.000	-1	84	0	/O-6(2-4-0),1	-0.1
1955	StL N	11	14	2	5	2	0	0	1	1-0	0	0	.357	.400	.500	137	1	0-0	1.000	1	79	1064	/O(LF)M	0.2
Total	11	807	2651	385	786	126	37	10	214	245-0	7	175	.296	.358	.383	103	14	42-0	.968	2	99	128	O-691(116-522-53)/1-20,2-3,3	-0.7
WALKER, HUB Harvey Willos B 8.17.1906 Gulfport, MS D 11.26.1982 San Jose, CA BL/TR 5-10.5/175# d4.15 Mil 1942-44 b-Gee																								
1931	Det A	90	252	27	72	13	1	0	16	23	4	25	.286	.355	.345	82	-6	10-1	.961	-2	98	78	O-66(4-60-2)	-0.7
1935	Det A	9	25	4	4	3	0	0	1	3	0	4	.160	.250	.280	38	-2	0-0	1.000	0	112	0	/O-7(CF)	-0.2
1936	Cin N	92	258	49	71	18	1	4	23	35	2	32	.275	.366	.399	113	6	8	.970	-0	101	85	O-73(25-47-2)/C1	0.4
1937	Cin N	78	221	33	55	9	4	1	19	34	0	24	.249	.349	.339	92	-1	7	.993	1	101	110	O-58(17-40-1)/2-3	-0.2
1945	†Det A	28	23	4	3	0	0	0	1	9	0	4	.130	.375	.130	46	-1	1-0	1.000	-0	89	0	/O-7(5-0-2)	-0.1
Total	5	297	779	117	205	43	6	5	60	104	6	89	.263	.354	.353	92	-4	26-1	.975	-1	100	86	O-211(51-154-7)/2-3,1C	-0.8
WALKER, JOHNNY John Miles B 12.11.1896 Toulon, IL D 8.19.1976 Hollywood, FL BR/TR 6/175# d9.19																								
1919	Phi A	3	9	0	0	0	0	0	0	0	0	2	.000	.000	.000	-99	-2	0	.941	-1	*73*	*56*	/C-3	-0.3
1920	Phi A	9	22	0	5	1	0	0	5	0	0	1	.227	.227	.273	32	-2	0-0	.960	-0	*106*	*102*	/C-6	-0.2
1921	Phi A	113	423	41	109	14	5	2	46	9	3	29	.258	.278	.329	54	-31	5-0	.989	-7	75	99	1-99/C-7	-4.2
Total	3	125	454	41	114	15	5	2	51	9	3	32	.251	.270	.319	50	-35	5-0	.989	-8	75	99	/1-99,C-16	-4.7
WALKER, SPEED Joseph Richard B 1.23.1898 Munhall, PA D 6.20.1959 W.Mifflin, PA BR/TR 6/170# d9.15																								
1923	StL N	2	7	1	2	0	0	0	0	0	0	1	.286	.286	.286	52	-1	0-0	1.000	-0	0	69	/1-2	-0.1
WALKER, LARRY Larry Kenneth Robert B 12.1.1966 Maple Ridge, BC, CAN BL/TR 6-3/215# d8.16 OF Total (33-LF 68-CF 1558-RF)																								
1989	Mon N	20	47	4	8	0	0	0	4	5-0	1	13	.170	.264	.170	26	-4	1-1	1.000	0	78	292	O-15(2-0-13)	-0.5
1990	Mon N	133	419	59	101	18	3	19	51	49-5	5	112	.241	.326	.434	112	6	21-7	.985	6	105	145	*O-124(RF)	1.1
1991	Mon N	137	487	59	141	30	2	16	64	42-2	5	102	.290	.349	.458	128	18	14-9	.991	8	119	86	*O-102(0-5-99),1-39	2.1
1992	Mon N★	143	528	85	159	31	4	23	93	41-10	6	97	.301	.353	.506	143	29	18-6	.993	6	98	169	*O-139(RF)	3.4

Year	Tm Lg	G	AB	R	H	2B	3B	HR	RBI	BB-IB	HP	SO	AVG	OBP	SLG	AOPS	ABR	SB-CS	FA	FR	Rng	Thr	G at Pos	BFW
1993	Mon N	138	490	85	130	24	5	22	86	80-20	6	76	.265	.371	.469	119	15	29-7	.979	4	102	128	*O-132(RF)/1-4	1.6
1994	Mon N	103	395	76	127	**44**	2	19	86	47-5	4	74	.322	.394	.587	151	32	15-5	.973	0	102	97	O-68(RF),1-35	2.6
1995	†Col N	131	494	96	151	31	5	36	101	49-13	14	72	.306	.381	.607	121	16	16-3	.988	-1	91	140	*O-129(0-4-129)	1.1
1996	Col N	83	272	58	75	18	4	18	58	20-2	9	58	.276	.342	.570	110	4	18-2	.994	-1	97	101	O-83(0-54-33)	0.5
1997	Col N★	153	568	143	208	46	4	**49**	130	78-14	14	90	.366	**.452**	**.720**	164	56	33-8	.992	-9	83	107	*O-151(0-2-150)/1-3,D	4.3
1998	Col N★	130	454	113	165	46	3	23	67	64-2	4	61	**.363**	.445	.630	147	35	14-4	.984	2	104	100	*O-123(0-3-123)/23D	3.2
1999	Col N★	127	438	108	166	26	4	37	115	57-8	12	52	**.379**	**.458**	**.710**	151	36	11-4	.982	3	95	182	*O-114(RF)/D	3.2
2000	Col N	87	314	64	97	21	7	9	51	46-4	9	40	.309	.409	.506	104	4	5-5	.994	7	104	202	O-83(31-0-52)/D-3	0.6
2001	Col N★	142	497	107	174	35	3	38	123	82-6	14	103	**.350**	.449	.662	150	41	14-5	.984	-1	94	95	*O-129(RF)/D-5	3.4
2002	Col N	136	477	95	161	40	4	26	104	65-6	7	73	.338	.421	.602	147	33	6-5	.984	4	95	172	*O-123(RF)/D-7	3.0
2003	Col N	143	454	86	129	25	7	16	79	98-14	11	87	.284	.422	.476	118	17	7-4	.983	-5	90	93	*O-131(RF)/D-2	0.5
Total	15	1806	6334	1238	1992	435	57	351	1212	823-111	121	1110	.314	.400	.567	135	338	222-75	.986	24	97	131	*O-1646R/1-81,D-20,32	30.1
WALKER, FLEET Moses Fleetwood B 10.7.1856 Mt.Pleasant, OH D 5.11.1924 Cleveland, OH BR/TR ?/159# d5.1 b-Welday																								
1884	Tol AA	42	152	23	40	2	3	0		8	6		.263	.325	.316	106	1		.887	-5			C-41/O(LF)	0.0
WALKER, OSCAR Oscar B 3.18.1854 Brooklyn, NY D 5.20.1889 Brooklyn, NY BL/TL 5-10/166# d9.17																								
1875	Atl NA	1	2	0	0	0	0	0	0	1		0	.000	.333	.000	30	0	0-0	.400	-0	0	366	/1O(RF)	0.0
1879	Buf N	72	287	35	79	15	6	1	35	8		38	.275	.295	.380	118	5		.946	3	**165**	**181**	*1-72	0.4
1880	Buf N	34	126	12	29	4	2	1	15	6		18	.230	.265	.317	95	-1		.917	-1	115	130	1-24,O-11(3-7-1)	-0.4
1882	StL AA	76	318	48	76	15	7	**7**		10			.239	.262	.396	115	4		.846	6	101	212	*O-75(1-74-0)/21	0.6
1884	Bro AA	95	382	59	103	12	8	2		9	3		.270	.292	.359	110	3		.868	1	114	0	O-59(16-43-0),1-36	-0.1
1885	Bal AA	4	13	1	0	0	0	0	1	0	0		.000	.000	.000	-99	-3		.667	-1	0	0	/O-4(RF)	-0.4
Total	5	281	1126	155	287	46	23	11	<u>51</u>	33	3	<u>56</u>	.255	.278	.366	109	8		.850	7	105	126	O-149(20-124-5),1-133/2	0.1
WALKER, TODD Todd Arthur B 5.25.1973 Bakersfield, CA BL/TR 6/180# d8.30																								
1996	Min A	25	82	8	21	6	0	0	6	4-0	0	13	.256	.281	.329	55	-6	2-0	.956	-0	103	100	3-20/2-4,D	-0.5
1997	Min A	52	156	15	37	7	1	3	16	11-1	1	30	.237	.288	.353	66	-8	7-0	.969	-1	106	67	3-40/2-8,D-2	-0.6
1998	Min A	143	528	85	167	41	3	12	62	47-9	2	65	.316	.372	.473	117	14	19-7	.978	-20	96	86	*2-140/D	0.2
1999	Min A	143	531	62	148	37	4	6	46	52-5	1	83	.279	.343	.397	85	-11	18-10	.984	-12	97	86	*2-103,D-34	-1.8
2000	Min A	23	77	14	18	1	0	2	8	7-0	0	10	.234	.287	.325	55	-6	3-0	.946	-4	78	105	2-19/D-2	-0.7
	Col N	57	171	28	54	10	4	7	36	20-0	1	19	.316	.385	.544	106	2	4-1	.975	-6	96	84	2-52	-0.2
2001	Col N	85	290	52	86	18	2	12	43	25-1	0	40	.297	.349	.497	95	-2	1-3	.981	7	108	108	2-77	0.8
	Cin N	66	261	41	77	17	0	5	32	26-0	1	42	.295	.361	.418	96	-1	0-5	.987	-6	97	83	2-65/S	-0.5
	Year	151	551	93	163	35	2	17	75	51-1	1	82	.296	.355	.459	95	-3	1-8	.984	1	103	96	*2-142/S	0.3
2002	Cin N	155	612	79	183	42	3	11	64	50-7	3	81	.299	.353	.431	106	4	8-5	**.989**	-7	100	91	*2-154	0.4
2003	†Bos A	144	587	92	166	38	4	13	85	48-0	1	54	.283	.333	.428	98	-2	1-1	.975	-7	95	88	*2-139/D-2	-0.2
Total	8	893	3295	476	957	217	21	71	398	290-23	10	437	.290	.346	.434	97	-16	63-32	.981	-56	98	90	2-761/3-60,D-42,S	-3.1
WALKER, WALLIE Walter S. B 3.12.1860 Berlin, MI D 2.28.1922 Pontiac, MI TR 5-10.5/162# d5.8																								
1884	Det N	1	4	1	1	0	0	0	0	0		0	.250	.250	.250	61	0		.750	-1			C	-0.1
WALKER, WELDAY Welday Wilberforce B 6.1859 Steubenville, OH D 11.23.1937 Steubenville, OH d7.15 b-Fleet																								
1884	Tol AA	5	18	1	4	1	0	0	2	0	0		.222	.222	.278	60	-1		.667	-1	0	0	/O-5(4-1-0)	-0.2
WALKER, CURT William Curtis B 7.3.1896 Beeville, TX D 12.9.1955 Beeville, TX BL/TR 5-9.5/170# d9.17																								
1919	NY A	1	1	0	0	0	0	0	0	0	0	0	.000	.000	.000	-99	0	0	—	0			H	0.0
1920	NY N	8	14	0	1	0	0	0	0	1	0	3	.071	.133	.071	-41	-3	0-0	1.000	-1	80	0	/O-4(1-2-1)	-0.4
1921	NY N	64	192	30	55	13	5	3	35	15	0	8	.286	.338	.453	107	2	4-3	.978	3	98	150	O-58(0-46-13)	0.2
	Phi N	21	77	11	26	2	1	0	8	5	0	5	.338	.378	.390	96	0	0-2	.970	-2	79	85	O-21(7-7-10)	-0.4
	Year	85	269	41	81	15	6	3	43	20	0	13	.301	.349	.435	104	1	4-5	.976	1	93	133	O-79(7-53-23)	-0.2
1922	Phi N	148	581	102	196	36	11	12	89	56	4	46	.337	.399	.499	119	17	11-4	.955	5	100	125	*O-147(RF)	1.1
1923	Phi N	140	527	66	148	26	5	5	66	45	0	31	.281	.337	.378	79	-15	12-12	.947	3	102	121	*O-137(12-0-125)/1	-2.4
1924	Phi N	24	71	11	21	6	1	1	8	7	0	4	.296	.359	.451	103	1	0-1	.900	-2	84	53	O-20(RF)	-0.3
	Cin N	109	397	55	119	21	10	4	46	44	1	15	.300	.371	.433	117	10	7-5	.978	1	97	116	*O-109(3-23-86)	0.3
	Year	133	468	66	140	27	11	5	54	51	1	19	.299	.369	.436	114	10	7-6	.969	-1	95	108	*O-129(3-23-106)	0.0
1925	Cin N	145	509	86	162	22	16	6	71	57	0	31	.318	.387	.460	118	14	14-11	**.983**	0	109	61	*O-141(4-15-124)	0.3
1926	Cin N	155	571	83	175	24	20	6	78	60	0	31	.306	.372	.450	124	18	3	.961	-0	99	97	*O-152(1-0-151)	0.6
1927	Cin N	146	527	60	154	16	10	6	80	47	0	19	.292	.350	.395	102	1	5	.957	2	107	87	*O-141(RF)	-0.8
1928	Cin N	123	427	64	119	15	12	6	73	49	1	14	.279	.354	.412	101	0	19	.955	1	107	70	*O-122(RF)	-0.9
1929	Cin N	141	492	76	154	28	15	7	83	85	2	17	.313	.416	.474	126	23	17	.969	-4	98	75	*O-138(RF)	0.8
1930	Cin N	134	472	74	145	26	11	8	51	64	1	30	.307	.391	.460	110	9	4	.965	-3	102	49	*O-120(77-2-42)	-0.2
Total	12	1359	4858	718	1475	235	117	64	688	535	9	254	.304	.374	.440	110	77	96-<u>38</u>	.963	3	102	91	*O-1310(105-95-1120)/1	-2.1
WALKSUM d6.22																								
1872	Eck NA	1	2	0	0	0	0	0	0	0		1	.000	.000	.000	-99	0	0-0	.500	-1	122	0	/2	-0.1
WALL, HOWARD Howard Cornelius B 12.1854 Washington, DC D 3.15.1909 Washington, DC d9.13																								
1873	Was NA	1	3	1	1	0	0	0	0	1		0	.333	.500	.333	158	0	0-0	.000	-1	0	0	/S	-0.1
WALL, JOE Joseph Francis "Gummy" B 7.24.1873 Brooklyn, NY D 7.17.1936 Brooklyn, NY BL/TL d9.22																								
1901	NY N	4	8	0	4	0	0	0	1	0	0		.500	.500	.500	198	1	0	1.000	-1	*48*	*0*	/C-2,O(RF)	0.0
1902	NY N	6	14	2	5	2	0	0	0	2	0		.357	.438	.500	191	2	0	1.000	0	327	0	/O-3(RF)	0.2
	Bro N	5	18	0	3	0	0	0	0	3	1		.167	.318	.167	50	-1	0	.893	-3	*75*	*41*	/C-5	-0.3
	Year	11	32	2	8	2	0	0	0	5	1		.250	.368	.313	111	1	0	.893	-3	*75*	*41*	/C-5,O-3(RF)	-0.1
Total	2	15	40	2	12	2	0	0	1	5	1		.300	.391	.350	127	2	0	.903	-4	*70*	*33*	/C-7,O-4(RF)	-0.1
WALLACE, JACK Clarence Eugene B 8.6.1890 Winnfield, LA D 10.15.1960 Winnfield, LA BR/TR 5-10.5/175# d9.27																								
1915	Chi N	2	7	1	2	0	0	0	1	0	1	2	.286	.375	.286	101	0	0	1.000	1	*116*	*151*	/C-2	0.1
WALLACE, DON Donald Allen B 8.25.1940 Sapulpa, OK BL/TR 5-8/165# d4.12																								
1967	Cal A	23	6	2	0	0	0	0	0	3-0	0	2	.000	.333	.000	6	0	0-1	1.000	-0	81	122	/2-4,13	-0.1
WALLACE, DOC Frederick Renshaw "Jesse" B 9.30.1893 Church Hill, MD D 12.31.1964 Haverford, PA BR/TR 5-6.5/135# d5.2																								
1919	Phi N	2	4	0	1	0	0	0	0	0	0	1	.250	.250	.250	47	0	0	.875	-0	104	0	/S-2	0.0
WALLACE, JIM James L. B 11.14.1881 Boston, MA D 5.16.1953 Revere, MA BL/TL 5-9/150# d8.24																								
1905	Pit N	7	29	3	6	1	0	0	3	3	0		.207	.281	.241	55	-2	2	.929	1	291	0	/O-7(RF)	-0.1
WALLACE, BOBBY Rhoderick John B 11.4.1873 Pittsburgh, PA D 11.3.1960 Torrance, CA BR/TR 5-8/170# d9.15 M3 C1 U1 HF1953 ▲ OF Total (4-LF 6-CF 16-RF)																								
1894	Cle N	4	13	0	2	1	0	0	1	0	0	1	.154	.154	.231	-8	-1	0	1.000	1	184	0	/P-4	0.0
1895	Cle N	30	98	16	21	2	3	0	10	6	2	17	.214	.274	.296	44	-3	0	.910	3	127	129	P-30	0.0
1896	†Cle N	45	149	19	35	6	3	1	17	11	0	21	.235	.287	.336	60	-9	2	.950	-2	100	0	O-23(3-6-15),P-22/1	-0.7
1897	Cle N	**130**	516	99	173	33	21	4	112	48	2		.335	.394	.504	129	20	14	.928	4	99	68	*3-130/O(LF)	2.2
1898	Cle N	154	593	81	160	25	13	3	99	63	4		.270	.344	.371	106	5	7	.936	18	109	103	*3-141,2-13	2.4
1899	StL N	151	577	91	170	28	14	12	108	54	2		.295	.357	.454	119	13	17	.919	30	109	107	*S-100,3-52	4.4
1900	StL N	126	485	70	130	25	9	4	70	40	3		.268	.328	.381	96	-3	7	.934	6	98	64	*S-126/3	0.8
1901	StL N	134	550	69	178	34	15	2	91	20	3		.324	.351	.451	138	24	15	.929	**27**	**116**	**131**	*S-134	5.4
1902	StL A	133	494	71	141	32	9	1	63	45	4		.285	.350	.393	107	6	18	.948	7	104	118	*S-131/PO(RF)	1.6
1903	StL A	135	511	63	136	21	7	1	54	28	4		.266	.309	.341	97	-2	10	.924	18	**109**	117	*S-135	2.2
1904	StL A	139	541	57	149	29	4	2	69	42	2		.275	.330	.355	124	16	20	**.947**	3	105	84	*S-139	2.6
1905	StL A	**156**	587	67	159	25	9	1	59	45	1		.271	.324	.349	120	13	13	.935	21	108	82	*S-156	4.2
1906	StL A	139	476	64	123	21	7	2	67	58	4		.258	.344	.345	121	14	24	.949	2	99	115	*S-138	2.3
1907	StL A	147	538	56	138	20	7	0	70	54	3		.257	.328	.320	107	6	16	.941	8	105	116	*S-147	2.0
1908	StL A	137	487	59	123	24	4	1	60	52	2		.253	.327	.324	111	8	5	**.951**	15	107	108	*S-137	3.1
1909	StL A	116	403	36	96	12	2	0	35	38	4		.238	.310	.278	92	-2	7	.946	11	100	113	S-87,3-29	1.4
1910	StL A	138	508	47	131	19	7	0	37	49	1		.258	.324	.323	110	6	12	.948	23	108	91	S-99,3-39	3.6
1911	StL A	125	410	35	95	12	2	0	31	46	2		.232	.312	.271	66	-18	8	.943	4	107	101	*S-124/2M	-0.5

Year	Tm Lg	G	AB	R	H	2B	3B	HR	RBI	BB-IB	HP	SO	AVG	OBP	SLG	AOPS	ABR	SB-CS	FA	FR	Rng	Thr	G at Pos	BFW
1912	StL A	100	323	39	78	14	5	0	31	43	1		.241	.332	.316	89	-3	3	.942	8	104	102	S-87,3-10/2-2,M	1.1
1913	StL A	55	147	11	31	5	0	0	21	14	3	16	.211	.293	.245	59	-7	1	.931	-4	93	59	S-39/3-7	-0.9
1914	StL A	26	73	3	16	2	1	0	5	5	0	13	.219	.269	.274	66	-3	1-1	.889	-7	89	30	S-19/3-2	-1.0
1915	StL A	9	13	1	3	0	1	0	4	5	0	0	.231	.444	.385	154	1	0-1	.848	0	108	198	/S-9	0.2
1916	StL A	14	18	0	5	0	0	0	1	2	0	1	.278	.350	.278	93	0	0	.958	3	167	97	/3-9,S-5	0.3
1917	StL N	8	10	0	1	0	0	0	2	0	0	1	.100	.100	.100	-40	-2	0	1.000	-1	0	0	/3-5,S-2	-0.3
1918	StL N	32	98	3	15	1	0	0	4	6	0	9	.153	.202	.163	12	-10	1	.959	1	110	113	2-17,S-12/3	-1.0
Total	25	2383	8618	1057	2309	391	143	34	1121	774	47	79	.268	.332	.358	106	69	201-2	.938	201	105	102	*S-1826,3-426/P-57,2-33,O-25R,1	35.4
WALLACH, TIM Timothy Charles B 9.14.1957 Huntington Park, CA BR/TR 6-3/200# d9.6 OF Total (4-LF 36-RF)																								
1980	Mon N	5	11	1	2	0	0	1	2	1-0	0	5	.182	.250	.455	93	0	0-0	1.000	-1	57	0	/O-3(2-0-1),1	-0.1
1981	†Mon N	71	212	19	50	9	1	4	13	15-2	4	37	.236	.299	.344	81	-5	0-1	1.000	-2	92	116	O-35(1-0-34),1-16,3-15	-1.1
1982	Mon N	158	596	89	160	31	3	28	97	36-4	4	81	.268	.313	.471	115	9	6-4	.948	2	96	97	*3-156/O-2(1-0-1),1	0.9
1983	Mon N	156	581	54	156	33	3	19	70	55-8	6	97	.269	.335	.434	113	10	0-3	.956	-3	93	103	*3-156	0.4
1984	Mon N★	160	582	55	143	25	4	18	72	50-6	7	101	.246	.311	.395	102	0	3-7	.959	22	110	**118**	*3-160/S	1.9
1985	Mon N★	155	569	70	148	36	3	22	81	38-8	5	79	.260	.310	.450	117	11	9-9	.967	36	**123**	**132**	*3-154	4.4
1986	Mon N	134	480	50	112	22	1	18	71	44-8	**10**	72	.233	.308	.396	94	-4	8-4	.958	18	117	126	*3-132	1.2
1987	Mon N★	153	593	89	177	**42**	4	26	123	37-5	7	98	.298	.343	.514	121	17	9-5	.952	7	102	88	*3-150/P	2.1
1988	Mon N	159	592	52	152	32	5	12	69	38-7	3	88	.257	.302	.389	93	-6	2-6	.962	19	**114**	131	*3-153/2	1.3
1989	Mon N★	154	573	76	159	**42**	0	13	77	58-10	1	81	.277	.341	.419	116	13	3-7	.958	9	104	82	*3-153/P	2.2
1990	Mon N★	161	626	69	185	37	5	21	98	42-11	3	80	.296	.339	.471	126	20	6-9	.954	5	103	102	*3-161	2.4
1991	Mon N	151	577	60	130	22	1	13	73	50-8	6	100	.225	.292	.334	77	-18	2-4	**.968**	6	105	110	*3-149	-1.4
1992	Mon N	150	537	53	120	29	1	9	59	50-2	8	90	.223	.296	.331	79	-14	2-2	.964	19	122	133	3-85,1-71	-0.1
1993	LA N	133	477	42	106	19	1	12	62	32-2	3	70	.222	.271	.342	68	-23	0-2	.958	9	106	70	*3-130/1	-1.4
1994	LA N	113	414	68	116	21	1	23	78	46-2	4	80	.280	.356	.502	130	17	0-2	.959	-4	94	63	*3-113	1.4
1995	†LA N	97	327	24	87	22	2	9	38	27-4	4	69	.266	.326	.428	107	3	0-0	**.976**	-6	90	72	3-96/1	-0.2
1996	Cal A	57	190	23	45	7	0	8	20	18-2	1	47	.237	.306	.400	76	-8	1-0	.941	3	110	52	3-46/1-3,D-8	-0.4
	†LA N	45	162	14	37	3	1	4	22	12-0	1	32	.228	.286	.333	68	-8	0-1	.971	-6	74	44	3-45	-1.4
Total	17	2212	8099	908	2085	432	36	260	1125	649-89	77	1307	.257	.316	.416	103	14	51-66	.959	133	105	100	*3-2054/1-94,O-40R,D-8,P-2,2S	12.1
WALLAESA, JACK John B 8.31.1919 Easton, PA D 12.27.1986 Easton, PA BB/TR (BR 1940) 6-3/191# d9.22 Mil 1943-45																								
1940	Phi A	6	20	0	3	0	0	0	2	0	0	2	.150	.150	.150	-22	-4	0-0	.903	-0	113	81	/S-6	-0.3
1942	Phi A	36	117	13	30	4	1	2	13	8	2	26	.256	.315	.359	90	-2	0-1	.920	-6	86	80	S-36	-0.7
1946	Phi A	63	194	16	38	4	2	5	11	14	0	47	.196	.250	.314	57	-12	1-0	.916	-10	85	87	S-59	-2.1
1947	Chi A	81	205	25	40	9	1	7	32	23	1	51	.195	.279	.351	78	-7	2-2	.968	6	113	114	S-27,O-22(LF)/3	-0.2
1948	Chi A	33	48	2	9	0	0	1	3	1	0	12	.188	.204	.250	21	-6	0-0	1.000	1	107	124	/S-5,O(LF)	-0.5
Total	5	219	584	56	120	17	4	15	61	46	3	138	.205	.267	.325	65	-31	3-3	.933	-10	94	92	S-133/O-23(LF),3	-3.8
WALLEN, NORM Norman Edward (born Norman Edward Walentoski) B 2.13.1917 Milwaukee, WI D 6.20.1994 Milwaukee, WI BR/TR 5-11.5/175# d4.20																								
1945	Bos N	4	15	1	2	0	1	0	1	1	0	1	.133	.188	.267	25	-2	0	.800	-1	73	0	/3-4	-0.3
WALLER, TY Elliott Tyrone B 3.14.1957 Fresno, CA BR/TR 6/180# d9.6 C1																								
1980	StL N	5	12	3	1	0	0	0	0	1-0	0	5	.083	.154	.083	-31	-2	0-0	1.000	-3	27	0	/3-5	-0.5
1981	Chi N	30	71	10	19	2	1	3	13	4-1	0	18	.268	.303	.451	108	0	2-0	.978	0	100	68	3-22/2-3,O-3(CF)	0.1
1982	Chi N	17	21	4	5	0	0	0	1	2-0	0	5	.238	.304	.238	52	-1	0-0	1.000	-0	84	0	/O-7(1-5-1),3	-0.2
1987	Hou N	11	6	1	1	1	0	0	0	0-0	0	3	.167	.167	.333	30	-1	0-0	1.000	0	205	0	/O-3(1-2-0)	0.0
Total	4	63	110	18	26	3	1	3	14	7-1	0	31	.236	.280	.364	78	-4	2-0	.961	-2	89	55	/3-28,O-13(2-10-1),2-3	-0.6
WALLING, DENNY Dennis Martin B 4.17.1954 Neptune, NJ BL/TR 6-1/185# d9.7 C4																								
1975	Oak A	6	8	0	1	1	0	0	2	0-0	0	4	.125	.125	.250	4	-1	0-0	1.000	-0	88	0	/O-3(1-2-0)	-0.1
1976	Oak A	3	11	1	3	0	0	0	0	0-0	0	3	.273	.273	.273	63	-1	0-0	.889	-0	108	0	/O-3(2-2-0)	-0.1
1977	Hou N	6	21	1	6	0	1	0	6	2-0	0	4	.286	.348	.381	105	0	0-1	1.000	0	125	0	/O-5(2-1-2)	0.0
1978	Hou N	120	247	30	62	11	3	3	36	30-3	1	24	.251	.332	.356	101	0	9-2	.980	4	116	81	O-78(66-7-4)	0.3
1979	Hou N	82	147	21	48	8	4	3	31	17-2	0	21	.327	.394	.497	151	10	3-2	.985	-0	103	75	O-42(7-0-35)	0.8
1980	†Hou N	100	284	30	85	6	5	3	29	35-4	0	26	.299	.374	.387	123	9	4-3	.989	-5	81	114	1-63,O-19(1-0-18)	0.0
1981	†Hou N	65	158	23	37	6	0	5	23	28-1	0	17	.234	.346	.367	109	3	2-1	.990	-4	56	118	1-27,O-27(5-1-21)	-0.3
1982	Hou N	85	146	22	30	4	1	1	14	23-3	0	19	.205	.312	.267	69	-5	4-2	1.000	-0	89	218	O-32(4-11-18),1-20	-0.7
1983	Hou N	100	135	24	40	5	3	3	19	15-1	0	16	.296	.364	.444	132	6	2-2	.992	-1	76	112	1-42,3-13,O-13(2-0-12)	0.3
1984	Hou N	87	249	37	70	11	5	3	31	16-2	1	28	.281	.325	.402	112	3	7-1	.956	6	116	202	3-52,1-16/O-6(3-3-0)	0.9
1985	Hou N	119	345	44	93	20	1	7	45	25-2	0	26	.270	.316	.394	101	0	5-2	.938	2	111	112	3-51,1-46,O-13(6-0-7)	-0.1
1986	†Hou N	130	382	54	119	23	1	13	58	36-5	0	31	.312	.367	.479	136	19	1-1	.960	3	95	49	*3-102,O-11(6-0-5)/1-4	2.0
1987	Hou N	110	325	45	92	21	4	5	33	39-1	0	37	.283	.356	.418	110	5	5-1	.948	0	83	122	3-79,1-16/O-7(6-0-2)	0.4
1988	Hou N	65	176	19	43	10	2	1	20	15-3	0	18	.244	.304	.341	88	-3	1-0	.950	8	115	207	3-51/1-3,O(LF)	0.5
	StL N	19	58	3	13	3	0	0	1	2-0	0	7	.224	.250	.276	50	-4	1-0	1.000	-1	65	0	O-11(10-0-1)/3-5,1	-0.5
	Year	84	234	22	56	13	2	1	21	17-3	0	25	.239	.291	.325	79	-7	2-0	.941	7	118	218	3-56,O-12(11-0-1)/1-4	0.0
1989	StL N	69	79	9	24	7	0	1	11	14-2	0	12	.304	.409	.430	136	5	0-0	.969	-4	87	89	1-20/3-9,O-6(3-0-3)	0.1
1990	StL N	78	127	7	28	5	0	1	19	8-0	0	15	.220	.265	.283	51	-9	0-0	1.000	1	92	63	1-15,3-11/O-8(3-0-5)	-0.9
1991	Tex A	24	44	1	4	1	0	0	2	3-0	2	8	.091	.184	.114	-16	-7	0-0	.950	-1	97	0	3-14/O-5(3-0-2)	-0.8
1992	Hou N	3	3	1	1	0	0	0	0	0-0	0	0	.333	.333	.333	94	0	0-0	—	0			/H	0.0
Total	18	1271	2945	372	799	142	30	49	380	308-29	4	316	.271	.339	.390	107	30	44-18	.947	8	101	119	3-387,O-290(131-27-135),1-273	1.8
WALLIS, JOE Harold Joseph B 1.9.1952 E.St.Louis, IL BB/TR 5-10/195# d9.2																								
1975	Chi N	16	56	9	16	2	2	1	4	5-0	0	14	.286	.344	.446	113	1	2-0	1.000	-0	98	123	O-15(0-14-1)	0.1
1976	Chi N	121	338	51	86	11	5	5	21	33-3	1	62	.254	.322	.361	86	-6	3-9	.976	2	94	198	O-90(10-68-16)	-1.1
1977	Chi N	56	80	14	20	3	0	2	8	16-1	0	25	.250	.375	.363	89	-1	0-1	.974	-3	69	146	O-35(CF)	-0.4
1978	Chi N	28	55	7	17	2	1	1	6	5-1	0	13	.309	.367	.436	110	1	0-2	1.000	-1	86	110	O-25(CF)	-0.1
	Oak A	85	279	28	66	16	1	6	26	26-1	0	42	.237	.300	.366	91	-3	1-4	.980	3	102	146	O-80(5-55-23)/D	-0.3
1979	Oak A	23	78	6	11	2	0	1	3	10-1	1	18	.141	.247	.205	25	-8	1-0	1.000	-1	93	62	O-23(0-1-23)	-1.0
Total	5	329	886	115	216	36	9	16	68	95-7	2	174	.244	.317	.359	86	-16	7-16	.982	-1	94	153	O-268(15-198-63)/D	-2.8
WALLS, LEE Ray Lee B 1.6.1933 San Diego, CA D 10.11.1993 Los Angeles, CA BR/TR 6-3/205# d4.21 C5																								
1952	Pit N	32	80	6	15	0	1	2	5	8	0	22	.188	.261	.287	51	-6	0-0	1.000	0	96	116	O-19(1-18-0)	-0.6
1956	Pit N	143	474	72	130	20	11	11	54	50-0	2	83	.274	.345	.432	110	6	3-5	.967	2	109	101	*O-133(74-10-56)/3	0.1
1957	Pit N	8	22	3	4	1	0	0	0	2-0	0	5	.182	.250	.227	30	-2	1-0	1.000	1	111	250	/O-7(LF)	-0.2
	Chi N	117	366	42	88	10	5	6	33	27-1	1	67	.240	.292	.344	72	-15	5-3	.984	-2	94	102	O-94(67-29-6)/3	-2.3
	Year	125	388	45	92	11	5	6	33	29-1	1	72	.237	.290	.338	70	-18	6-3	.985	-1	95	111	*O-101(74-29-6)/3	-2.5
1958	Chi N★	136	513	80	156	19	3	24	72	47-0	**8**	62	.304	.370	.493	128	21	4-4	.992	-1	99	91	*O-132(RF)	1.4
1959	Chi N	120	354	43	91	18	3	8	33	42-1	5	73	.257	.342	.393	97	-1	0-2	.967	-6	102	12	*O-119(RF)	-1.1
1960	Cin N	29	84	12	23	3	2	1	7	17-1	0	20	.274	.392	.393	115	3	2-0	.960	-0	103	95	O-24(12-0-12)/1-2	0.2
	Phi N	65	181	19	36	6	1	3	19	14-1	0	32	.199	.253	.293	50	-13	3-2	.947	-4	92	82	3-34,O-13(8-0-5)/1-7	-1.9
	Year	94	265	31	59	9	3	4	26	31-2	0	52	.223	.300	.325	72	-10	5-2	.958	-5	102	66	O-37(20-0-17),3-34/1-9	-1.7
1961	Phi N	91	261	32	73	6	4	8	30	19-1	0	48	.280	.329	.425	99	-1	2-2	.987	-2	101	128	1-28,3-26,O-17(11-1-8)	-0.6
1962	LA N	60	109	9	29	3	1	0	17	10-0	0	21	.266	.325	.312	77	-3	1-0	.929	-1	92	184	O-17(15-0-3),1-11/3-4	-0.5
1963	LA N	64	86	12	20	1	0	3	11	7-1	0	25	.233	.290	.349	89	-2	0-0	1.000	1	111	0	O-18(10-0-8)/1-5,3-2	-0.1
1964	LA N	37	28	1	5	1	0	0	3	2-0	0	12	.179	.233	.214	29	-3	0-0	1.000	-0	75	0	/O-6(3-0-3),C	-0.3
Total	10	902	2558	331	670	88	31	66	284	245-6	16	470	.262	.329	.398	96	-16	21-18	.977	-12	101	81	O-599(208-58-352)/3-68,1-53,C	-5.9
WALSH, AUSTIN Austin Edward B 9.1.1891 Cambridge, MA D 1.26.1955 Glendale, CA BL/TL 5-11/175# d4.19																								
1914	Chi F	57	121	14	29	6	1	1	10	4	0	25	.240	.264	.331	65	-9	0	1.000	-0	98	83	O-30(21-1-8)	-1.0
WALSH, JIMMY James Charles B 9.22.1885 Kallila, Ireland D 7.3.1962 Syracuse, NY BL/TR 5-10.5/170# d8.26 Mil 1918																								
1912	Phi A	31	107	11	27	8	2	0	15	12	0		.252	.328	.364	101	0	7	.947	-0	115	25	O-30(LF)	-0.1
1913	Phi A	97	303	56	77	16	5	0	27	38	2	40	.254	.341	.340	102	2	15	.961	2	109	87	O-90(39-44-13)	-0.1
1914	NY A	43	136	13	26	1	3	1	11	29	0	21	.191	.333	.265	80	-2	6-9	.977	-1	103	69	O-41(37-4-0)	-0.7
	†Phi A	68	216	35	51	11	6	3	36	30	4	27	.236	.340	.384	123	6	6-12	.966	-0	101	97	O-56(25-26-6)/1-3,3-3,S	0.0
	Year	111	352	48	77	12	9	4	47	59	4	48	.219	.337	.338	106	4	12-21	.971	-1	102	85	O-97(62-30-6)/1-3,3-3,S	-0.7

Year	Tm Lg	G	AB	R	H	2B	3B	HR	RBI	BB-IB	HP	SO	AVG	OBP	SLG	AOPS	ABR	SB-CS	FA	FR	Rng	Thr	G at Pos	BFW
1915	Phi A	117	417	48	86	15	6	1	20	57	3	64	.206	.306	.278	78	-11	22-12	.976	5	110	105	*O-109(29-44-36)/3-2,1	-1.2
1916	Phi A	114	390	42	91	13	6	1	27	54	2	36	.233	.330	.305	95	-1	27-14	.939	-1	101	100	*O-113(0-6-107)/1	-0.8
	†Bos A	14	17	5	3	1	0	0	2	4	0	2	.176	.333	.235	71	0	3-2	1.000	-1	104	0	/O-6(1-3-2),3-2	-0.1
	Year	128	407	47	94	14	6	1	29	58	2	38	.231	.330	.302	94	-2	30-16	.940	-2	101	98	*O-119(1-9-109)/3-2,1	-0.9
1917	Bos A	57	185	25	49	6	3	0	12	25	0	14	.265	.352	.330	109	3	6	.982	-1	91	117	O-47(2-43-2)	-0.2
Total	6	541	1771	235	410	71	31	6	150	249	11	204	.232	.330	.317	96	-3	92-49	.964	3	105	92	O-492(163-170-166)/3-7,1-5,S	-3.2
WALSH, JOHN John Gabriel B 3.25.1879 Wilkes-Barre, PA D 4.25.1947 Jamaica, NY BR/TR 5-8.5/162# d6.22																								
1903	Phi N	1	3	0	0	0	0	0	0	0	0		.000	.000	.000	-99	-1	0	1.000	-0	123	0	/3	-0.1
WALSH, JOE Joseph Francis B 10.14.1886 Minersville, PA D 1.6.1967 Buffalo, NY BR/TR 6-2/170# d10.8																								
1910	NY A	1	4	0	2	1	0	0	2	0	0		.500	.500	.750	275	1	0	.900	-0	*167*	*74*	/C	0.1
1911	NY A	4	9	2	2	1	0	0	0	0	0		.222	.222	.333	51	-1	0	1.000	-2	*71*	*58*	/C-4	-0.2
Total	2	5	13	2	4	2	0	0	2	0	0		.308	.308	.462	114	0	0	.933	-2	*115*	*65*	/C-5	-0.1
WALSH, JOE Joseph Patrick "Tweet" B 3.13.1917 Boston, MA D 10.5.1996 Boston, MA BR/TR 5-10/155# d7.1																								
1938	Bos N	4	8	0	0	0	0	0	0	0	0	2	.000	.000	.000	-99	-2	0	.900	-1	50	86	/S-4	-0.3
WALSH, JOE Joseph R. "Reddy" B 11.5.1864 Chicago, IL D 8.8.1911 Omaha, NE BL/TR d9.3																								
1891	Bal AA	26	100	14	21	0	1	1	10	6	0	18	.210	.255	.260	47	-8	4	.865	1	85	215	S-13,2-13	-0.5
WALSH, DEE Leo Thomas B 3.28.1890 St.Louis, MO D 7.14.1971 St.Louis, MO BB/TR 5-9.5/165# d4.10																								
1913	StL A	23	53	8	9	0	1	0	5	6	4	11	.170	.302	.208	51	-3	3	.933	0	112	81	S-22/3	-0.2
1914	StL A	7	23	1	2	0	0	0	1	2	0	4	.087	.160	.087	-27	-4	1-1	.919	-0	97	188	/S-7	-0.4
1915	StL A	59	150	13	33	5	0	0	6	14	5	25	.220	.308	.253	71	-5	6-6	.951	4	95	227	O-45(0-21-24)/3-2,P2S	-0.4
Total	3	89	226	22	44	5	1	0	12	22	9	40	.195	.292	.226	56	-12	10-7	.951	4	95	227	/O-45(0-21-24),S-30,3-3,2P	-1.0
WALSH, JIMMY Michael Timothy "Runt" B 3.25.1886 Lima, OH D 1.21.1947 Baltimore, MD BR/TR 5-9/174# d4.25 OF Total (29-LF 16-CF 33-RF)																								
1910	Phi N	88	242	28	60	8	3	3	31	25	2	38	.248	.323	.343	91	-3	5	.947	-4	113	82	2-26,O-26(7-14-6)/S-9,3-5	-0.8
1911	Phi N	94	289	29	78	20	3	1	31	21	2	30	.270	.324	.370	93	-3	5	.962	-3	92	50	O-48(22-2-25),2-14/S-9,3-7,C-4,P1	-0.7
1912	Phi N	51	150	16	40	6	3	2	19	8	0	20	.267	.304	.387	83	-4	3	.944	1	108	81	2-31,3-12/C-5	-0.3
1913	Phi N	26	30	3	10	4	0	0	5	1	0	5	.333	.355	.467	128	1	1	1.000	-0	90	219	/2-6,S-3,3O(RF)	0.1
1914	Bal F	120	428	54	132	25	4	10	65	22	2	56	.308	.345	.456	113	0	18	.932	3	102	107	*3-113/2SO(RF)	0.7
1915	Bal F	106	401	43	121	20	1	9	60	21	2	44	.302	.340	.424	111	-1	12	.936	-5	94	91	*3-106	-0.4
	StL F	17	31	5	6	1	0	0	1	3	2	4	.194	.306	.226	48	-2	1	.913	-0	106	0	/3-9	-0.3
	Year	123	432	48	127	21	1	9	61	24	4	48	.294	.337	.410	106	-3	13	.934	-6	95	85	*3-115	-0.7
Total	6	502	1571	178	447	84	14	25	212	101	10	197	.285	.332	.404	102	-12	45	.925	-8	97	95	3-253/2-78,O-76R,S-22,C-9,1P	-1.7
WALSH, TOM Thomas Joseph B 2.28.1886 Davenport, IA D 3.16.1963 Naples, FL BR/TR 5-11/170# d8.15																								
1906	Chi N	2	1	0	0	0	0	0	0	0	0		.000	.000	.000	-95	0	0	1.000	-0	*0*	*323*	/C-2	0.0
WALSH, WALT Walter William B 4.30.1897 Newark, NJ D 1.15.1966 Avon By The Sea, NJ BR/TR 5-11/170# d5.4																								
1920	Phi N	2	0	0	0	0	0	0	0	0	0	0	—	—	—	—	0	0-0	—	0			R	0.0
WALTERS, ROXY Alfred John B 11.5.1892 San Francisco, CA D 6.3.1956 Alameda, CA BR/TR 5-8.5/160# d9.16																								
1915	NY A	2	3	0	1	0	0	0	0	0	0	0	.333	.333	.333	100	0	0	1.000	1	*141*	*189*	/C-2	0.1
1916	NY A	66	203	13	54	9	3	0	23	14	2	42	.266	.320	.340	96	-1	2	.974	12	143	139	C-65	1.8
1917	NY A	61	171	16	45	2	0	0	14	9	1	22	.263	.304	.275	76	-5	2	.968	8	*139*	*105*	C-57	0.9
1918	NY A	64	191	18	38	5	1	0	12	9	1	18	.199	.239	.236	42	-14	3	.953	-2	*120*	*76*	C-50/O-9(RF)	-1.4
1919	Bos A	48	135	7	26	2	0	0	9	7	5	15	.193	.259	.207	33	-12	1	.982	3	*105*	*109*	C-47	-0.6
1920	Bos A	88	258	25	51	11	1	0	28	30	9	21	.198	.303	.248	49	-18	2-2	.980	3	*77*	*100*	C-85/1-2	-0.8
1921	Bos A	54	169	17	34	4	1	0	14	10	2	11	.201	.254	.237	27	-19	3-0	.990	11	*128*	*111*	C-54	-0.4
1922	Bos A	38	98	4	19	2	0	0	6	6	0	8	.194	.240	.214	19	-12	0-0	.967	3	*99*	*90*	C-36	-0.7
1923	Bos A	40	104	9	26	4	0	0	5	2	0	6	.250	.264	.288	45	-9	0-2	.974	3	*90*	*135*	C-36/2	-0.4
1924	Cle A	32	74	10	19	2	0	0	5	10	0	6	.257	.345	.284	63	-4	0-1	.979	3	*104*	*129*	C-25/2-7	0.0
1925	Cle A	5	20	0	4	0	0	0	0	0	0	2	.200	.200	.200	2	-3	0-0	1.000	0	*124*	*197*	/C-5	-0.2
Total	11	498	1426	119	317	41	6	0	116	97	20	151	.222	.281	.259	51	-97	13-5	.975	46	*113*	*111*	C-462/O-9(RF),2-8,1-2	-1.7
WALTERS, DAN Daniel Gene B 8.15.1966 Brunswick, ME BR/TR 6-4/225# d6.1																								
1992	SD N	57	179	14	45	11	1	4	22	10-0	2	28	.251	.295	.391	92	-2	1-0	.992	3	85	97	C-55	0.5
1993	SD N	27	94	6	19	3	0	1	10	7-2	0	13	.202	.255	.266	40	-8	0-0	.970	-5	75	140	C-26	-1.2
Total	2	84	273	20	64	14	1	5	32	17-2	2	41	.234	.281	.348	73	-10	1-0	.985	-2	81	112	/C-81	-0.7
WALTERS, FRED Fred James "Whale" B 9.4.1912 Laurel, MS D 2.1.1980 Laurel, MS BR/TR 6-1/210# d4.17																								
1945	Bos A	40	93	2	16	2	0	0	5	10	0	9	.172	.252	.194	29	-8	1-1	.993	3	*115*	*196*	C-38	-0.4
WALTERS, KEN Kenneth Rogers B 11.11.1933 Fresno, CA BR/TR 6-1/180# d4.12																								
1960	Phi N	124	426	42	102	10	0	8	37	16-3	1	50	.239	.266	.319	60	-25	4-3	.988	12	**114**	**176**	*O-119(5-2-116)	-1.8
1961	Phi N	86	180	23	41	8	2	2	14	5-0	1	25	.228	.251	.328	53	-13	2-2	.975	1	104	116	O-56(0-4-53)/1-5,3	-1.5
1963	Cin N	49	75	6	14	2	0	1	7	4-1	1	14	.187	.237	.253	40	-6	0-2	.889	-2	89	0	O-21(11-0-10)/1	-1.0
Total	3	259	681	71	157	20	2	11	58	25-4	3	89	.231	.259	.314	56	-44	6-7	.979	11	110	148	O-196(16-6-179)/1-6,3	-4.3
WALTERS, BUCKY William Henry B 4.19.1909 Philadelphia, PA D 4.20.1991 Abington, PA BR/TR 6-1/180# d9.18 M2 C8 ▲																								
1931	Bos N	9	38	2	8	2	0	0	0	0	0	3	.211	.211	.263	28	-4	0	.947	1	113	0	/3-6,2-3	-0.3
1932	Bos N	22	75	8	14	3	1	0	4	2	0	18	.187	.208	.253	24	-8	0	.910	0	106	213	3-22	-0.8
1933	Bos A	52	195	27	50	8	3	4	28	19	1	24	.256	.326	.390	90	-3	1-1	.940	1	106	143	3-43/2-7	-0.1
1934	Bos A	23	88	10	19	4	4	4	18	3	0	12	.216	.242	.489	79	-4	0-0	.906	3	112	129	3-23	0.0
	Phi N	83	300	36	78	20	3	4	38	19	2	54	.260	.308	.387	75	-10	1	.950	-6	91	106	3-80/2-3,P-2	-1.4
1935	Phi N	49	96	14	24	2	1	0	6	9	0	12	.250	.314	.292	58	-6	0	1.000	2	126	211	P-24/O-5(LF),2-2,3	0.0
1936	Phi N	64	121	12	29	10	1	1	16	7	0	15	.240	.281	.364	66	-6	0	.974	8	**176**	149	P-40/23	0.4
1937	Phi N★	56	137	15	38	6	0	1	16	5	0	16	.277	.303	.343	69	-6	1	.988	5	143	**237**	P-37/3-8	0.2
1938	Phi N	15	35	6	10	2	0	1	3	1	0	5	.286	.306	.429	103	3	1	.955	0	107	250	P-12	0.0
	Cin N	36	64	10	9	1	0	0	5	7	1	18	.141	.236	.156	10	0	0	.981	2	141	100	P-27	0.0
	Year	51	99	16	19	3	0	1	8	8	1	23	.192	.259	.253	42	3	1	.973	3	130	150	P-39	0.0
1939	†Cin N☆	40	120	16	39	8	1	1	16	5	1	12	.325	.357	.433	111	13	1	.979	4	118	291	P-39	0.0
1940	†Cin N★	37	117	11	24	3	0	1	18	4	0	14	.205	.231	.256	34	2	2	.945	-1	91	233	P-36	0.0
1941	Cin N★	39	106	6	20	6	0	0	9	7	0	13	.189	.239	.245	36	2	0	.977	2	109	153	P-37	0.0
1942	Cin N★	40	99	13	24	6	1	2	13	3	0	13	.242	.265	.384	89	-2	0	.961	1	110	198	P-34/O(LF)	0.1
1943	Cin N	37	90	11	24	7	1	1	12	6	0	15	.267	.313	.400	107	8	1	.971	1	97	**206**	P-34	0.0
1944	Cin N★	37	107	9	30	4	0	0	13	8	0	18	.280	.330	.318	86	8	0	**1.000**	0	101	241	P-34	0.0
1945	Cin N	24	61	11	14	3	0	3	8	3	0	14	.230	.266	.426	93	5	2	.975	-0	100	165	P-22	0.0
1946	Cin N	24	55	6	7	2	0	0	5	4	0	12	.127	.186	.164	-0	-1	2	.940	2	123	371	P-22	0.0
1947	Cin N	20	45	3	12	2	0	0	4	2	0	13	.267	.298	.311	62	3	0	.962	-1	83	0	P-20	0.0
1948	Cin N	7	15	1	4	0	0	0	2	0	0	2	.267	.267	.267	46	1	0	1.000	1	169	0	/P-7,M	0.0
1950	Bos N	1	2	0	0	0	0	0	0	0	0	0	.000	.000	.000	-99	0	0	1.000	-0	0	0	/P	0.0
Total	19	715	1966	227	477	99	16	23	234	114	5	303	.243	.286	.344	69	-5	12-1	.974	24	117	205	P-428,3-184/2-16,O-6(LF)	-1.9
WALTON, DANNY Daniel James "Mickey" B 7.14.1947 Los Angeles, CA BR/TR (BB 1975-80) 6/200# d4.20 OF Total (172-LF 1-CF 6-RF)																								
1968	Hou N	2	2	0	0	0	0	0	0	0-0	0	1	.000	.000	.000	-99	0	0-0	—	0			H	-0.1
1969	Sea A	23	92	12	20	1	2	3	10	5-0	3	26	.217	.275	.370	82	-3	2-0	.976	-2	87	0	O-23(LF)	-0.7
1970	Mil A	117	397	32	102	20	1	17	66	51-4	6	126	.257	.349	.441	116	9	2-3	.965	-5	86	62	*O-114(LF)	-0.3
1971	Mil A	30	69	5	14	3	0	2	9	7-0	1	22	.203	.286	.333	76	-2	0-0	.923	-3	75	0	O-19(19-1-0)/3	-0.7
	NY A	5	14	1	2	0	0	1	2	0-0	0	7	.143	.143	.357	40	-1	0-0	1.000	-1	62	0	/O-4(1-0-3)	-0.2
	Year	35	83	6	16	3	0	3	11	7-0	1	29	.193	.264	.337	71	-4	0-0	.933	-3	73	0	O-23(20-1-3)/3	-0.9
1973	Min A	37	96	13	17	1	1	4	8	17-0	0	28	.177	.301	.333	75	-3	0-0	1.000	-2	61	0	O-18(15-0-3),D-11/3	-0.7
1975	Min A	42	63	4	11	2	0	1	8	4-2	0	18	.175	.224	.254	34	-6	0-0	.962	-0	52	169	/1-7,C-2,D-6	-0.6
1976	LA N	18	15	0	2	0	0	0	2	1-0	0	2	.133	.176	.133	-8	-2	0-0	—	0			H	-0.3
1977	Hou N	13	21	0	4	0	0	0	1	0-0	0	5	.190	.190	.190	3	-3	0-0	.956	-1	85	37	/1-5	-0.4

Year	Tm Lg	G	AB	R	H	2B	3B	HR	RBI	BB-IB	HP	SO	AVG	OBP	SLG	AOPS	ABR	SB-CS	FA	FR	Rng	Thr	G at Pos	BFW
1980	Tex A	10	10	2	2	0	0	0	1	3-0	0	5	.200	.385	.200	67	0	0-0	—	0			/D	0.0
Total	9	297	779	69	174	27	4	28	107	88-6	10	240	.223	.309	.376	90	-11	4-3	.966	-14	82	39	O-178L/D-18,1-12,C-2,3-2	-4.0

WALTON, JEROME Jerome O'Terrell B 7.8.1965 Newnan, GA BR/TR 6-1/175# d4.4

Year	Tm Lg	G	AB	R	H	2B	3B	HR	RBI	BB-IB	HP	SO	AVG	OBP	SLG	AOPS	ABR	SB-CS	FA	FR	Rng	Thr	G at Pos	BFW
1989	†Chi N	116	475	64	139	23	3	5	46	27-1	6	77	.293	.335	.385	99	0	24-7	.990	-5	99	34	*O-115(CF)	-0.3
1990	Chi N	101	392	63	103	16	2	2	21	50-1	4	70	.263	.350	.329	82	-7	14-7	.977	-5	99	56	O-98(CF)	-1.3
1991	Chi N	123	270	42	59	13	1	5	17	19-0	3	55	.219	.275	.330	67	-12	7-3	.983	-2	104	53	*O-101(0-100-1)	-1.4
1992	Chi N	30	55	7	7	0	1	0	1	9-0	2	13	.127	.273	.164	26	-5	1-2	.944	-1	94	0	O-24(22-1-1)	-0.8
1993	Cal A	5	2	2	0	0	0	0	0	1-0	0	2	.000	.333	.000	-2	0	1-0	1.000	0	174	0	/O(LF)D	0.0
1994	Cin N	46	68	10	21	4	0	1	9	4-0	0	12	.309	.347	.412	98	0	1-3	1.000	-0	107	166	O-26(16-5-6)/1-7	-0.2
1995	†Cin N	102	162	32	47	12	1	8	22	17-0	4	25	.290	.368	.525	134	8	10-7	.982	3	116	82	O-89(36-50-8)/1-3	1.0
1996	Atl N	37	47	9	16	5	0	1	4	5-0	0	10	.340	.389	.511	132	2	0-0	1.000	2	157	0	O-28(23-1-5)	0.4
1997	†Bal A	26	68	8	20	1	0	3	9	4-0	0	10	.294	.333	.441	103	0	0-0	1.000	-0	111	0	O-19(9-2-11)/1-5,D-2	-0.1
1998	TB A	12	34	4	11	3	0	0	3	2-0	0	6	.324	.361	.412	99	0	0-0	1.000	2	124	581	/O-8(4-0-4),D-3	0.2
Total	10	598	1573	241	423	77	8	25	132	138-2	19	280	.269	.333	.376	92	-14	58-29	.984	-6	105	56	O-509(111-373-36)/1-15,D-9	-2.5

WALTON, REGGIE Reginald Sherard B 10.24.1952 Kansas City, MO BR/TR 6-3/205# d6.13

Year	Tm Lg	G	AB	R	H	2B	3B	HR	RBI	BB-IB	HP	SO	AVG	OBP	SLG	AOPS	ABR	SB-CS	FA	FR	Rng	Thr	G at Pos	BFW
1980	Sea A	31	83	8	23	6	0	2	9	3-0	1	10	.277	.307	.422	98	0	2-2	.929	-0	118	0	O-17(6-0-11),D-11	-0.2
1981	Sea A	12	6	1	0	0	0	0	0	1-0	0	2	.000	.143	.000	-54	-1	0-0	—	-0	0	0	/O-4(3-0-1),D	-0.2
1982	Pit N	13	15	1	3	1	0	0	0	1-0	1	1	.200	.294	.267	56	-1	0-0	—	-1	0	0	/O-2(LF)	-0.1
Total	3	56	104	10	26	7	0	2	9	5-0	2	13	.250	.295	.375	83	-2	2-2	.929	-1	101	0	/O-23(11-0-12),D-12	-0.5

WAMBSGANSS, BILL William Adolph B 3.19.1894 Cleveland, OH D 12.8.1985 Lakewood, OH BR/TR 5-11/175# d8.4 Mil 1918

Year	Tm Lg	G	AB	R	H	2B	3B	HR	RBI	BB-IB	HP	SO	AVG	OBP	SLG	AOPS	ABR	SB-CS	FA	FR	Rng	Thr	G at Pos	BFW
1914	Cle A	43	143	12	31	6	2	0	12	8	4	24	.217	.277	.287	67	-6	2-7	.921	-2	103	105	S-36/2-4	-0.8
1915	Cle A	121	375	30	73	4	4	0	21	36	4	50	.195	.272	.227	48	-24	8-9	.938	-2	104	81	2-78,3-35	-2.7
1916	Cle A	136	475	57	117	14	4	0	45	41	5	40	.246	.313	.293	77	-13	13	.925	-5	100	95	*S-106,2-24/3-5	-1.1
1917	Cle A	141	499	52	127	17	6	0	43	37	7	42	.255	.315	.313	85	-9	16	.951	15	**111**	**126**	*2-137/1-3	0.9
1918	Cle A	87	315	34	93	15	2	0	40	21	3	21	.295	.345	.356	102	1	16	.952	-1	97	98	2-87	0.1
1919	Cle A	**139**	526	60	146	17	6	2	60	32	3	24	.278	.323	.344	82	-13	18	.963	11	103	109	*2-139	0.0
1920	†Cle A	153	565	83	138	16	11	1	55	54	5	26	.244	.316	.317	66	-28	9-18	.960	8	101	114	*2-153	-2.2
1921	Cle A	107	410	80	117	28	5	2	47	44	3	27	.285	.359	.393	90	-5	13-7	.963	-16	82	101	*2-103/3-2	-1.7
1922	Cle A	142	538	89	141	22	6	0	47	60	4	26	.262	.341	.325	74	-19	17-10	.961	-7	98	101	*2-125,S-16	-2.1
1923	Cle A	101	345	59	100	20	4	1	59	43	3	15	.290	.373	.380	99	1	10-9	.963	7	105	92	2-88/3-4	0.9
1924	Bos A	156	636	93	174	41	5	0	49	54	4	33	.274	.334	.354	77	-21	14-8	.963	13	100	110	*2-156	-0.3
1925	Bos A	111	360	50	83	12	4	1	41	52	1	21	.231	.329	.294	59	-22	3-5	.957	8	106	98	*2-103/1-6	-1.1
1926	Phi A	54	54	11	19	3	0	0	1	8	1	8	.352	.444	.407	117	2	1-1	.923	0	107	122	S-17/2-8	0.3
Total	13	1491	5241	710	1359	215	59	7	520	490	47	357	.259	.328	.327	78	-156	140-74	.958	29	101	105	*2-1205,S-175/3-46,1-9	-9.8

WANER, LLOYD Lloyd James "Little Poison" B 3.16.1906 Harrah, OK D 7.22.1982 Oklahoma City, OK BL/TR 5-9/150# d4.12 Def 1943 HF1967 b-Paul

Year	Tm Lg	G	AB	R	H	2B	3B	HR	RBI	BB-IB	HP	SO	AVG	OBP	SLG	AOPS	ABR	SB-CS	FA	FR	Rng	Thr	G at Pos	BFW
1927	†Pit N	150	629	**133**	223	17	6	2	27	37	6	23	.355	.396	.410	108	9	14	.976	-4	103	58	*O-150(42-109-0)/2	-0.3
1928	Pit N	**152**	659	121	221	22	14	5	61	40	4	13	.335	.377	.434	107	6	8	.980	-1	99	107	*O-152(10-143-0)	-0.2
1929	Pit N	151	662	134	234	28	**20**	5	74	37	9	20	.353	.395	.479	113	12	6	.987	7	101	140	*O-151(CF)	1.1
1930	Pit N	68	260	32	94	8	3	1	36	5	1	5	.362	.376	.427	93	-3	3	.983	3	105	125	O-65(CF)	-0.3
1931	Pit N	154	681	90	**214**	25	13	4	57	39	1	16	.314	.352	.407	104	2	7	.979	10	105	143	*O-153(CF)/2	0.9
1932	Pit N	134	565	90	188	27	11	2	38	31	0	11	.333	.367	.430	116	12	6	.986	9	116	76	*O-131(CF)	1.7
1933	Pit N	121	500	59	138	14	5	0	26	22	0	8	.276	.307	.324	80	-14	3	.982	1	101	107	*O-114(65-49-0)	-1.9
1934	Pit N	140	611	95	173	27	6	1	48	38	1	12	.283	.326	.352	80	-17	6	.979	7	113	81	*O-139(CF)	-1.3
1935	Pit N	122	537	83	166	22	14	0	46	22	0	10	.309	.336	.402	95	-6	1	.989	2	108	50	*O-121(CF)	-0.7
1936	Pit N	106	414	67	133	13	8	1	31	31	0	5	.321	.369	.399	104	2	1	.984	-3	100	30	O-92(CF)	-0.3
1937	Pit N	129	537	80	177	23	4	1	45	34	0	12	.330	.370	.393	107	6	3	.988	0	102	80	*O-123(CF)	0.3
1938	Pit N☆	147	619	79	194	25	7	5	57	28	0	11	.313	.343	.401	103	1	5	.986	-5	92	121	*O-144(CF)	-0.7
1939	Pit N	112	379	49	108	15	3	0	24	17	3	13	.285	.321	.340	79	-12	0	.992	5	105	130	O-92(CF)/3	-0.9
1940	Pit N	72	166	30	43	3	0	0	3	5	1	5	.259	.285	.277	56	-10	2	.989	0	101	102	O-42(1-41-0)	-1.1
1941	Pit N	3	4	2	1	0	0	0	1	2	0	0	.250	.500	.250	116	0	0	1.000	0	114	0	/O(CF)	0.0
	Bos N	19	51	7	21	1	0	0	4	2	0	0	.412	.434	.431	151	3	1	.969	0	104	106	O-15(3-11-1)	0.3
	Cin N	55	164	17	42	4	1	0	6	8	0	0	.256	.291	.293	64	-8	0	.986	-1	93	101	O-44(0-13-31)	-1.1
	Year	77	219	26	64	5	1	0	11	12	0	0	.292	.329	.324	85	-5	1	.981	-1	96	99	O-60(3-25-32)	-0.8
1942	Phi N	101	287	23	75	7	3	0	10	16	0	6	.261	.300	.307	82	-8	1	.967	-2	100	92	O-75(CF)	-1.2
1944	Bro N	15	14	3	4	0	0	0	1	3	0	0	.286	.412	.286	101	0	0	1.000	-0	97	0	/O-4(CF)	0.0
	Pit N	19	14	2	5	0	0	0	2	2	0	0	.357	.438	.357	120	1	0	1.000	1	162	0	/O-7(1-6-0)	0.1
	Year	34	28	5	9	0	0	0	3	5	0	0	.321	.424	.321	110	1	0	1.000	1	139	0	O-11(1-10-0)	0.1
1945	Pit N	23	19	5	5	0	0	0	1	1	0	3	.263	.300	.263	55	-1	0	1.000	1	104	1380	/O-3(2-0-1)	0.0
Total	18	1993	7772	1201	2459	281	118	27	598	420	26	173	.316	.353	.393	99	-25	67	.983	31	103	97	*O-1818(124-1663-33)/2-2,3	-5.6

WANER, PAUL Paul Glee "Big Poison" B 4.16.1903 Harrah, OK D 8.29.1965 Sarasota, FL BL/TL 5-8.5/153# d4.13 Mil 1945 C1 HF1952 b-Lloyd

Year	Tm Lg	G	AB	R	H	2B	3B	HR	RBI	BB-IB	HP	SO	AVG	OBP	SLG	AOPS	ABR	SB-CS	FA	FR	Rng	Thr	G at Pos	BFW
1926	Pit N	144	536	101	180	35	**22**	8	79	66	4	19	.336	**.413**	.528	144	34	11	.976	4	103	108	*O-139(6-0-133)	2.6
1927	†Pit N	155	623	114	**237**	42	**18**	9	**131**	60	3	14	**.380**	.437	.549	152	47	5	.980	5	107	112	*O-143(RF),1-14	3.9
1928	Pit N	**152**	602	**142**	223	**50**	19	6	86	77	5	16	.370	.446	.547	152	49	6	.975	3	107	105	*O-131(RF),1-24	3.9
1929	Pit N	151	596	131	200	43	15	15	100	89	3	24	.336	.424	.534	133	33	15	.986	1	101	95	*O-143(RF)/1-7	2.0
1930	Pit N	145	589	117	217	32	18	8	77	57	4	18	.368	.428	.525	128	28	18	.959	-4	106	50	*O-143(0-5-138)	1.2
1931	Pit N	150	559	88	180	35	10	6	70	73	4	21	.322	.404	.453	131	28	6	.976	**13**	**107**	**153**	*O-138(RF),1-10	3.1
1932	Pit N	**154**	630	107	215	**62**	10	8	82	56	2	24	.341	.397	.510	144	42	13	.974	1	105	81	*O-154(0-9-145)	3.3
1933	Pit N★	**154**	618	101	191	38	16	7	70	60	2	20	.309	.372	.456	136	29	3	.981	3	103	105	*O-154(RF)	2.4
1934	Pit N★	146	599	**122**	**217**	32	16	14	90	68	2	24	**.362**	.429	.539	154	47	8	.985	7	108	113	*O-145(RF)	4.3
1935	Pit N★	139	549	98	176	29	12	11	78	61	3	22	.321	.392	.477	128	23	2	.983	1	103	91	*O-136(RF)	1.5
1936	Pit N	148	585	107	218	53	9	5	94	74	3	29	**.373**	.446	.520	156	51	7	.960	7	**114**	95	*O-145(RF)	4.7
1937	Pit N★	**154**	619	94	219	30	9	2	74	63	0	34	.354	.413	.441	132	30	4	.970	-0	99	107	*O-150(RF)/1-3	2.0
1938	Pit N	148	625	77	175	31	6	6	69	47	1	28	.280	.331	.378	94	-6	2	.977	-6	95	79	*O-147(0-1-148)	-2.1
1939	Pit N	125	461	62	151	30	6	3	45	35	0	18	.328	.375	.438	120	13	0	.978	1	97	122	*O-106(RF)	0.7
1940	Pit N	89	238	32	69	16	1	1	32	23	0	14	.290	.352	.378	102	2	0	.985	-1	92	109	O-45(RF)/1-8	-0.2
1941	Bro N	11	35	5	6	0	0	0	4	8	0	0	.171	.326	.171	41	-2	0	.923	-1	83	0	/O-9(RF)	-0.4
	Bos N	95	294	40	82	10	2	2	46	47	0	14	.279	.378	.347	110	6	1	.965	-1	95	120	O-77(10-3-66)/1-7	0.1
	Year	106	329	45	88	10	2	2	50	55	0	14	.267	.372	.328	102	3	1	.961	-2	94	108	O-86(10-3-75)/1-7	-0.3
1942	Bos N	114	333	43	86	17	1	1	39	62	1	20	.258	.376	.324	108	7	2	.969	-5	90	78	O-94(RF)	-0.3
1943	Bro N	82	225	29	70	16	0	1	26	35	1	9	.311	.406	.396	132	12	0	.960	-1	106	70	O-57(1-0-56)	0.8
1944	Bro N	83	136	16	39	4	1	0	16	27	0	7	.287	.405	.331	111	4	0	.983	1	108	112	O-32(1-0-31)	0.3
	NY A	9	7	1	1	0	0	0	1	2	0	1	.143	.333	.143	37	0	1-0	—	0			H	0.0
1945	NY A	1	0	0	0	0	0	0	0	1	0	0	—	1.000	—	191	0	0-0	—	0			H	0.0
Total	20	2549	9459	1627	3152	605	191	113	1309	1091	38	376	.333	.404	.473	133	477	104-0	.975	29	103	99	*O-2288(18-18-2256)/1-73	33.8

WANNER, JACK Clarence Curtis "Johnny" B 11.29.1885 Geneseo, IL D 5.28.1919 Geneseo, IL BR/TR 5-11.5/190# d9.28

Year	Tm Lg	G	AB	R	H	2B	3B	HR	RBI	BB-IB	HP	SO	AVG	OBP	SLG	AOPS	ABR	SB-CS	FA	FR	Rng	Thr	G at Pos	BFW
1909	NY A	3	8	0	1	0	0	0	0	2	0		.125	.300	.125	35	0	1	.600	-2	80	143	/S-2	-0.2

WANNINGER, PEE-WEE Paul Louis B 12.12.1902 Birmingham, AL D 3.7.1981 N.Augusta, SC BL/TR 5-7/150# d4.22

Year	Tm Lg	G	AB	R	H	2B	3B	HR	RBI	BB-IB	HP	SO	AVG	OBP	SLG	AOPS	ABR	SB-CS	FA	FR	Rng	Thr	G at Pos	BFW
1925	NY A	117	403	35	95	13	6	1	22	11	0	34	.236	.256	.305	43	-38	3-5	.944	-5	93	98	*S-111/3-3,2	-3.1
1927	Bos A	18	60	4	12	0	0	0	1	6	1	2	.200	.284	.200	28	-6	2-4	.890	-1	104	125	S-15	-0.6
	Cin N	28	93	14	23	2	2	0	8	6	0	7	.247	.293	.312	64	-5	0	.953	3	107	131	S-28	0.1
Total	2	163	556	53	130	15	8	1	31	23	1	43	.234	.266	.295	45	-49	5-9	.941	-3	97	107	S-154/3-3,2	-3.6

WARD, AARON Aaron Lee B 8.28.1896 Booneville, AR D 1.30.1961 New Orleans, LA BR/TR 5-10.5/160# d8.14 Mil 1918

Year	Tm Lg	G	AB	R	H	2B	3B	HR	RBI	BB-IB	HP	SO	AVG	OBP	SLG	AOPS	ABR	SB-CS	FA	FR	Rng	Thr	G at Pos	BFW
1917	NY A	8	26	0	3	0	0	0	1	1	0	5	.115	.148	.115	-19	-4	0	.926	-1	75	126	/S-7	-0.6
1918	NY A	20	32	2	4	1	0	0	1	2	0	7	.125	.176	.156	0	-4	1	.941	3	121	186	S-12/O-4(CF),2-3	-0.1
1919	NY A	27	34	5	7	2	0	0	2	5	0	6	.206	.308	.265	61	-2	0	1.000	1	94	261	/1-5,3-3,S-2,2	0.0
1920	NY A	127	496	62	127	18	7	11	54	33	1	84	.256	.304	.387	79	-17	7-5	.965	17	**110**	127	*3-114,S-12	0.3
1921	†NY A	**153**	556	77	170	30	10	5	75	42	8	68	.306	.363	.423	98	-2	6-8	.961	19	110	58	*2-124,3-33	1.9
1922	†NY A	**154**	558	69	149	19	5	7	68	45	6	64	.267	.328	.357	77	-20	6-4	.974	1	103	99	*2-152/3-2	-1.4

Year	Tm Lg	G	AB	R	H	2B	3B	HR	RBI	BB-IB	HP	SO	AVG	OBP	SLG	AOPS	ABR	SB-CS	FA	FR	Rng	Thr	G at Pos	BFW
1923	†NY A	**152**	567	79	161	26	11	10	82	56	3	65	.284	.351	.422	101	-1	8-8	**.980**	10	**105**	107	*2-152	1.2
1924	NY A	120	400	42	101	13	10	8	66	40	2	45	.253	.324	.395	85	-12	1-4	.973	8	**104**	92	*2-120/S	-0.2
1925	NY A	125	439	41	108	22	3	4	38	49	3	49	.246	.326	.337	70	-20	1-4	.966	-14	91	92	*2-113,3-10	-2.9
1926	NY A	22	31	5	10	2	0	0	3	2	0	6	.323	.364	.387	97	0	0-0	1.000	-3	50	0	/2-4,3	-0.3
1927	Chi A	145	463	75	125	25	8	5	56	63	2	56	.270	.360	.391	97	-1	6-5	.963	-24	95	85	*2-139/3-6	-2.0
1928	Cle A	6	9	0	1	0	0	0	0	1	0	2	.111	.200	.111	-16	-2	0-0	.818	1	160	414	/3-3,S-2,2	-0.1
Total	12	1059	3611	457	966	158	54	50	446	339	25	457	.268	.335	.383	85	-85	36-38	.970	17	101	89	2-809,3-172/S-36,1-5,O-4(CF)	-4.2
WARD, CHUCK Charles William B 7.30.1894 St.Louis, MO D 4.4.1969 Indian Rocks, FL BR/TR 5-11.5/170# d4.11 Mil 1918																								
1917	Pit N	125	423	25	100	12	3	0	43	32	8	43	.236	.302	.279	76	-11	5	.912	-26	87	98	*S-112/2-8,3-5	-3.3
1918	Bro N	2	6	0	2	0	0	0	3	0	0	0	.333	.333	.333	104	0	0	1.000	-0	103	0	/3-2	0.0
1919	Bro N	45	150	7	35	1	2	0	8	7	2	11	.233	.277	.267	62	-7	0	.920	-7	88	0	3-45	-1.4
1920	Bro N	19	71	7	11	1	0	0	4	3	1	3	.155	.200	.169	6	-9	1-0	.928	-7	71	63	S-19	-1.5
1921	Bro N	12	28	1	2	1	0	0	0	4	0	2	.071	.188	.107	-19	-5	0-0	.937	2	110	143	S-12	-0.1
1922	Bro N	33	91	12	25	5	1	0	14	5	1	8	.275	.320	.352	74	-4	1-1	.934	-4	94	81	S-31/3-2	-0.4
Total	6	236	769	52	175	20	6	0	72	51	12	67	.228	.286	.269	63	-36	7-1	.919	-40	88	94	S-174/3-54,2-8	-6.7
WARD, CHRIS Chris Gilbert B 5.18.1949 Oakland, CA BL/TL 6/180# d9.10																								
1972	Chi N	1	1	0	0	0	0	0	0	0-0	0	0	.000	.000	.000	-90	0	0-0	—	0			H	0.0
1974	Chi N	92	137	8	28	4	0	1	15	18-3	0	13	.204	.293	.255	53	-8	0-2	.977	2	122	84	O-22(21-0-1)/1-6	-0.9
Total	2	93	138	8	28	4	0	1	15	18-3	0	13	.203	.291	.254	52	-8	0-2	.977	2	122	84	/O-22(21-0-1),1-6	-0.9
WARD, DARYLE Daryle Lamar B 6.27.1975 Lynwood, CA BL/TL 6-2/240# d5.14 f-Gary																								
1998	Hou N	4	3	1	1	0	0	0	0	1-0	0	2	.333	.500	.333	128	0	0-0	—	0			/H	0.0
1999	†Hou N	64	150	11	41	6	0	8	30	9-0	0	31	.273	.311	.473	97	-2	0-0	.944	-3	74	70	O-31(LF),1-10/D-3	-0.5
2000	Hou N	119	264	36	68	10	2	20	47	15-2	0	61	.258	.295	.538	100	-2	0-0	.986	-3	88	40	O-47(43-0-4),1-19/D-4	-0.7
2001	†Hou N	95	213	21	56	15	0	9	39	19-4	1	48	.263	.323	.460	95	-2	0-0	.985	-2	89	82	O-42(27-0-15)/1-9,D-3	-0.6
2002	Hou N	136	453	41	125	31	0	12	72	33-5	1	82	.276	.324	.424	94	-6	1-3	.981	-5	76	141	*O-122(LF)/D	-1.6
2003	LA N	52	109	6	20	1	0	0	9	3-0	1	19	.183	.211	.193	7	-15	0-0	.992	-0	146	171	1-13,O-11(LF)	-1.7
Total	6	470	1192	116	311	63	2	49	197	80-11	3	243	.261	.306	.440	89	-27	1-3	.979	-13	80	99	O-253(234-0-19)/1-51,D-11	-5.1
WARD, PIGGY Frank Gray B 4.16.1867 Chambersburg, PA D 10.24.1912 Altoona, PA BB/TR 5-9.5/196# d6.12 OF Total (21-LF 4-CF 85-RF)																								
1883	Phi N	1	5	0	0	0	0	0	0	0		2	.000	.000	.000	-99	-1		1.000	-0	111	0	/3	-0.1
1889	Phi N	7	25	0	4	1	0	0	4	0	0	7	.160	.160	.200	0	-3	1	.848	-2	98	0	/2-6,O(CF)	-0.5
1891	Pit N	6	18	3	6	0	0	0	2	3	1	3	.333	.455	.333	134	1	3	.833	-1	0	0	/O-5(LF)	0.0
1892	Bal N	56	186	28	54	6	5	1	33	31	4	18	.290	.403	.392	137	10	10	.892	3	202	248	O-43(RF)/2-7,S-5,C	1.1
1893	Bal N	11	49	11	12	1	3	0	5	5	1	2	.245	.327	.388	88	-1	4	.862	-1	55	0	/O-9(LF),1-2	-0.3
	Cin N	42	150	44	42	4	1	0	10	37	6	10	.280	.440	.320	101	4	27	.827	-2	125	295	O-40(1-0-39)/1	0.0
	Year	53	199	55	54	5	4	0	15	42	7	12	.271	.415	.337	99	2	31	.837	-3	110	230	O-49(10-0-39)/1-3	-0.3
1894	Was N	98	347	86	105	11	7	0	36	80	11	31	.303	.447	.375	103	9	41	.900	-14	99	54	2-79,O-12(6-3-3)/S-3,3	-0.2
Total	6	221	780	172	223	23	16	1	90	156	23	73	.286	.419	.360	105	19	86	.854	-17	133	222	O-110R/2-92,S-8,1-3,3-2,C	-0.0
WARD, GARY Gary Lamell B 12.6.1953 Los Angeles, CA BR/TR 6-2/202# d9.3 C2 s-Daryle OF Total (848-LF 181-CF 111-RF)																								
1979	Min A	10	14	2	4	0	0	0	1	3-0	0	3	.286	.412	.286	89	0	0-1	1.000	0	138	0	/O-5(1-0-4),D-3	0.0
1980	Min A	13	41	11	19	6	2	1	10	3-1	0	6	.463	.489	.780	228	7	0-0	1.000	-2	68	0	O-12(LF)	0.5
1981	Min A	85	295	42	78	7	6	3	29	28-4	0	48	.264	.325	.359	92	-3	5-2	.975	4	103	151	O-80(61-19-1)/D-2	-0.2
1982	Min A	152	570	85	165	33	7	28	91	37-4	1	105	.289	.330	.519	127	19	13-1	.989	11	111	142	*O-150(127-4-25)/D-2	2.5
1983	Min A★	157	623	76	173	34	5	19	88	44-2	3	98	.278	.326	.440	105	4	8-1	.978	19	112	194	*O-152(LF)/D-2	1.7
1984	Tex A	155	602	97	171	21	7	21	79	55-3	0	95	.284	.343	.447	113	10	7-5	.987	5	105	110	*O-148(58-59-36)/D-5	1.0
1985	Tex A★	154	593	77	170	28	7	15	70	39-3	1	97	.287	.329	.433	106	4	26-7	.969	-2	94	116	*O-153(139-21-1)/D	-0.1
1986	Tex A	105	380	54	120	15	2	5	51	31-3	4	72	.316	.372	.405	109	6	12-8	.996	10	116	128	*O-104(102-4-0)/D	1.1
1987	NY A	146	529	65	131	22	1	16	78	33-2	1	101	.248	.291	.384	78	-18	9-1	.985	0	109	38	O-94(69-30-5),D-36,1-15	-2.0
1988	NY A	91	231	26	52	8	0	4	24	24-4	2	41	.225	.302	.312	73	-8	0-1	.992	-1	109	0	O-54(17-39-3),1-11/3-2,D-9	-1.1
1989	NY A	8	17	3	5	1	0	0	1	3-1	0	5	.294	.400	.353	115	1	0-0	1.000	-1	64	0	/O-6(RF),D	-0.1
	Det A	105	275	24	69	10	2	9	29	21-1	0	54	.251	.300	.400	99	-1	1-3	.990	4	119	78	O-51(35-5-14),1-26,D-26	-0.1
	Year	113	292	27	74	11	2	9	30	24-2	0	59	.253	.306	.397	100	-1	1-3	.991	3	113	69	O-57(35-5-20),D-27,1-26	-0.2
1990	Det A	106	309	32	79	11	2	9	46	30-0	1	50	.256	.322	.392	98	-1	2-0	.988	-1	102	41	O-85(75-0-16),D-13/1-2	-0.5
Total	12	1287	4479	594	1236	196	41	130	597	351-28	13	775	.276	.328	.425	104	20	83-30	.984	45	107	114	*O-1094L,D-101/1-54,3-2	2.7
WARD, JIM James H. H. B 3.2.1855 Boston, MA D 6.4.1886 Boston, MA d8.3																								
1876	Phi N	1	4	1	2	0	0	0	1	0		1	.500	.500	.500	236	1		.750	-1			/C	0.0
WARD, RUBE John Andrew B 2.6.1879 New Lexington, OH D 1.17.1945 Akron, OH d4.28																								
1902	Bro N	13	31	4	9	1	0	0	2	2	0		.290	.333	.323	102	0	0	.850	-0	88	0	O-11(6-1-4)	-0.1
WARD, JOHN John E. B Washington, DC d5.23																								
1884	Was U	1	4	0	1	0	0	0		0			.250	.250	.250	54	0		.000	-1	0	0	/O(CF)	-0.1
WARD, JAY John Francis B 9.9.1938 Brookfield, MO BR/TR 6-1/185# d5.6 C3																								
1963	Min A	9	15	0	1	1	0	0	2	1-0	0	5	.067	.125	.133	-27	-3	0-0	1.000	-2	61	0	/3-4,O(LF)	-0.4
1964	Min A	12	31	4	7	2	0	0	2	6-1	0	13	.226	.351	.290	80	0	0-0	.977	0	97	77	/2-9,O-3(LF)	0.0
1970	Cin N	6	3	0	0	0	0	0	0	2-0	0	1	.000	.400	.000	17	0	0-0	1.000	0	114	0	/3-2,12	0.0
Total	3	27	49	4	8	3	0	0	4	9-1	0	19	.163	.293	.224	46	-3	0-0	.977	-1	96	76	/2-10,3-6,O-4(LF),1	-0.4
WARD, JOHN John Montgomery B 3.3.1860 Bellefonte, PA D 3.4.1925 Augusta, GA BL/TR (BB 1888) 5-9/165# d7.15 M7 HF1964 ▲ OF Total (4-LF 110-CF 100-RF)																								
1878	Pro N	37	138	14	27	5	4	1	15	2		13	.196	.207	.312	69	1		.866	2	107	179	P-37	0.0
1879	Pro N	83	364	71	104	9	4	2	41	7		14	.286	.299	.349	115	5		.938	4	109	86	*P-70,3-16/O-8(4-0-4)	0.3
1880	Pro N	86	356	53	81	12	2	0	27	6		16	.228	.240	.272	76	-9		.983	14	112	55	*P-70,3-25/O-2(RF),M	0.9
1881	Pro N	**85**	357	56	87	18	6	0	53	5		10	.244	.254	.328	83	-7		.887	3	126	0	O-40(0-4-36),P-39,S-13	-0.3
1882	Pro N	83	355	58	87	10	3	1	39	13		22	.245	.272	.299	83	-7		.824	5	174	142	O-49(0-2-47),P-34/S-4	-0.1
1883	NY N	88	380	76	97	18	7	7	54	8		25	.255	.271	.395	100	-1		.859	14	198	88	O-56(0-45-11),P-34/3-5,S-2,2	0.9
1884	NY N	113	482	98	122	11	8	2	51	28		47	.253	.294	.322	91	-6		.847	10	105	93	O-59(CF),2-47/P-9,M	0.4
1885	NY N	111	446	72	101	8	9	0	37	17		39	.226	.255	.285	75	-13		.904	4	95	**127**	*S-111	-0.6
1886	NY N	122	491	82	134	17	5	2	81	19		46	.273	.300	.340	93	-5	36	.890	11	99	113	*S-122	0.9
1887	NY N	**129**	545	114	184	16	5	1	53	29	4	12	.338	.375	.391	119	15	**111**	**.919**	32	109	**136**	*S-129	**4.3**
1888	†NY N	122	510	70	128	14	5	2	49	9	1	13	.251	.265	.310	84	-10	38	.857	-4	90	**129**	*S-122	-1.1
1889	†NY N	114	479	87	143	13	4	1	67	27	2	7	.299	.339	.349	92	-7	62	.890	9	95	104	*S-108/2-7	0.4
1890	Bro P	128	561	134	188	15	12	4	60	51	2	22	.335	.393	.426	112	7	63	.878	17	104	105	*S-128,M	2.2
1891	Bro N	105	441	85	122	13	5	0	39	36	3	10	.277	.335	.329	94	-3	57	.878	3	104	93	S-87,2-18,M	0.2
1892	Bro N	148	614	109	163	13	3	1	47	82	3	19	.265	.355	.301	103	6	**88**	.920	-2	101	79	*2-148,M	1.0
1893	NY N	135	588	129	193	27	9	2	77	47	1	5	.328	.379	.415	110	8	46	.918	4	105	65	*2-134,M	1.4
1894	†NY N	138	549	102	146	12	5	0	79	35	1	6	.266	.311	.306	49	-46	39	.923	1	104	90	*2-138,M	-3.1
Total	17	1827	7656	1410	2107	231	96	26	869	421	17	326	.275	.314	.341	93	-72	540	.887	123	99	115	S-826,2-493,P-293,O-214C/3-46	7.7
WARD, JOE Joseph A. B 9.2.1884 Philadelphia, PA D 8.11.1934 Philadelphia, PA TR d4.24																								
1906	Phi N	35	129	12	38	8	6	0	11	5	0		.295	.321	.450	140	5	2	.929	-5	80	66	3-27/2-3,S	0.0
1909	NY A	9	28	3	5	0	0	0	0	1	1		.179	.233	.179	30	-2	2	.846	-4	75	41	/2-7,1	-0.7
	Phi N	74	184	21	49	8	2	0	23	9	1		.266	.304	.332	96	-1	7	.944	-6	95	126	2-48/S-8,1-5,O-2(1-1-0)	-0.8
1910	Phi N	48	124	11	18	2	1	0	13	3	2	11	.145	.178	.177	4	-16	1	.975	2	133	62	1-32/S3	-1.6
Total	3	166	465	47	110	18	9	0	47	18	4	11	.237	.271	.314	78	-14	12	.929	-13	91	102	/2-58,1-38,3-28,S-10,O-2(1-1-0)	-3.1
WARD, HAP Joseph Nichols B 11.15.1885 Leesburg, NJ D 9.13.1979 Elmer, NJ d5.18																								
1912	Det A	1	2	0	0	0	0	0	0	0	0		.000	.000	.000	-99	-1	0	1.000	0	0	0	/O	0.0
WARD, KEVIN Kevin Michael B 9.28.1961 Lansdale, PA BR/TR 6-1/195# d5.10																								
1991	SD N	44	107	13	26	7	2	2	8	9-0	1	27	.243	.308	.402	95	-1	1-4	.982	-1	102	0	O-33(31-0-2)	-0.4
1992	SD N	81	147	12	29	5	0	3	12	14-0	2	38	.197	.274	.293	60	-8	2-3	.946	-1	96	116	O-51(36-9-8)	-1.1
Total	2	125	254	25	55	12	2	5	20	23-0	3	65	.217	.288	.339	75	-9	3-7	.961	-2	99	66	/O-84(67-9-10)	-1.5

Year	Tm Lg	G	AB	R	H	2B	3B	HR	RBI	BB-IB	HP	SO	AVG	OBP	SLG	AOPS	ABR	SB-CS	FA	FR	Rng	Thr	G at Pos	BFW
WARD, PETE Peter Thomas B 7.26.1939 Montreal, PQ, CAN BL/TR 6-1/200# d9.21 C1 OF Total (139-LF 54-RF)																								
1962	Bal A	8	21	1	3	2	0	0	2	4-0	0	5	.143	.280	.238	44	-2	0-0	1.000	-0	101	0	/O-6(2-0-4)	-0.2
1963	Chi A	157	600	80	177	34	6	22	84	52-1	5	77	.295	.353	.482	135	27	7-6	.923	-8	95	99	*3-154/2S	1.9
1964	Chi A	144	539	61	152	28	3	23	94	56-11	2	76	.282	.348	.473	131	22	1-1	.958	9	110	117	*3-138	3.1
1965	Chi A	138	507	62	125	25	3	10	57	56-11	6	83	.247	.327	.367	104	3	2-4	.952	4	113	91	*3-134/2	0.6
1966	Chi A	84	251	22	55	7	1	3	28	24-0	3	49	.219	.290	.291	74	-8	3-1	.989	1	88	93	O-59(44-0-18),3-16/1-5	-1.1
1967	Chi A	146	467	49	109	16	2	18	62	61-9	11	109	.233	.334	.392	119	12	3-2	.991	-10	72	52	O-89(74-0-19),1-39,3-22	-0.5
1968	Chi A	125	399	43	86	15	0	15	50	76-8	10	85	.216	.354	.366	117	13	4-3	.946	-2	105	57	3-77,1-31,O-22(16-0-7)	0.9
1969	Chi A	105	199	22	49	7	0	6	32	33-1	3	38	.246	.359	.372	101	1	0-0	.994	0	107	76	1-25,3-21/O-9(3-0-6)	0.0
1970	NY A	66	77	5	20	2	2	1	18	9-0	0	17	.260	.333	.377	102	0	0-0	1.000	-1	48	97	1-13	-0.2
Total	9	973	3060	345	776	136	17	98	427	371-41	40	539	.254	.339	.405	116	68	20-17	.945	-7	106	97	3-562,O-185L,1-113/2-2,S	4.5
WARD, PRESTON Preston Meyer B 7.24.1927 Columbia, MO BL/TR 6-3/198# d4.20 Mil 1951																								
1948	Bro N	42	146	9	38	9	2	1	21	15	0	23	.260	.329	.370	86	-3	0	.990	-1	86	79	1-38	-0.5
1950	Chi N	80	285	31	72	11	2	6	33	27	0	42	.253	.317	.368	81	-8	3	.995	9	142	106	1-76	-0.2
1953	Chi N	33	100	10	23	5	0	4	12	18	0	21	.230	.347	.400	92	-1	3-1	.961	-4	89	0	O-27(CF)/1-7	-0.5
	Pit N	88	281	35	59	7	1	8	27	44	1	39	.210	.319	.327	69	-12	1-3	.991	3	117	88	1-78	-1.4
	Year	121	381	45	82	12	1	12	39	62	1	60	.215	.327	.346	76	-13	4-4	.991	-1	110	93	1-85,O-27(CF)	-1.9
1954	Pit N	117	360	37	97	16	2	7	48	39	0	61	.269	.337	.383	90	-5	0-0	.984	6	141	80	1-48,O-42(RF),3-11	-0.3
1955	Pit N	84	179	16	38	7	4	5	25	22-4	0	28	.212	.296	.380	80	-6	0-0	.998	2	113	100	1-48/O(RF)	-0.6
1956	Pit N	16	30	3	10	0	1	1	11	6-0	0	4	.333	.432	.500	157	3	0-0	1.000	-2	47	0	/3-5,O-5(RF)	0.1
	Cle A	87	150	18	38	10	0	6	21	16-0	0	20	.253	.325	.440	98	-1	0-0	.988	3	127	91	1-60,O-17(14-0-3)	0.0
1957	Cle A	10	11	2	2	1	0	0	0	0-0	0	2	.182	.182	.273	23	-1	0-0	1.000	-0	0	0	/1	-0.1
1958	Cle A	48	148	22	50	3	1	4	21	10-1	1	27	.338	.379	.453	133	6	0-1	.957	-1	85	59	3-24,1-21	0.4
	KC A	81	268	28	68	10	1	6	24	27-2	0	36	.254	.319	.366	87	-5	0-1	.989	-6	92	77	1-39,3-34/O-2(LF)	-1.4
	Year	129	416	50	118	13	2	10	45	37-3	1	63	.284	.340	.397	103	1	0-2	.992	-8	98	75	1-60,3-58/O-2(LF)	-1.0
1959	KC A	58	109	8	27	4	1	2	19	7-1	0	12	.248	.286	.358	76	-4	0-0	.982	-3	60	83	1-22/O(LF)	-0.8
Total	9	744	2067	219	522	83	15	50	262	231-8	2	315	.253	.326	.380	88	-37	7-6	.992	6	115	90	1-438/O-95(17-27-51),3-74	-5.3
WARD, TURNER Turner Max B 4.11.1965 Orlando, FL BB/TR 6-2/200# d9.10																								
1990	Cle A	14	46	10	16	2	1	1	10	3-0	0	8	.348	.388	.500	147	3	3-0	.957	0	88	251	O-13(RF)/D	0.3
1991	Cle A	40	100	11	23	7	0	0	5	10-0	0	16	.230	.300	.300	66	-4	0-0	1.000	-1	101	45	O-38(0-2-36)	-0.6
	Tor A	8	13	1	4	0	0	0	2	1-0	0	2	.308	.357	.308	83	0	0-0	1.000	-1	64	0	/O-6(1-0-5)	-0.1
	Year	48	113	12	27	7	0	0	7	11-0	0	18	.239	.306	.301	68	-5	0-0	1.000	-1	97	40	O-44(1-2-41)	-0.7
1992	Tor A	18	29	7	10	3	0	1	3	4-0	0	4	.345	.424	.552	164	3	0-1	1.000	1	104	208	O-12(2-4-6)	0.3
1993	Tor A	72	167	20	32	4	2	4	28	23-2	1	26	.192	.287	.311	62	-9	3-3	.990	-2	93	65	O-65(33-10-22)/1	-1.3
1994	Mil A	102	367	55	85	15	2	9	45	52-4	3	68	.232	.328	.357	74	-14	6-2	.985	6	109	125	O-99(35-52-25)/3	-0.8
1995	Mil A	44	129	19	34	3	1	4	16	14-1	1	21	.264	.338	.395	86	-3	6-1	.989	3	106	202	O-40(26-7-19)/D	0.0
1996	Mil A	43	67	7	12	2	1	2	10	13-0	0	17	.179	.309	.328	60	-4	3-0	1.000	3	135	76	O-32(15-3-18)/D	-0.1
1997	Pit N	71	167	33	59	16	1	7	33	18-2	2	17	.353	.420	.587	158	15	4-1	1.000	-2	85	94	O-54(11-31-23)	1.2
1998	Pit N	123	282	33	74	13	3	9	46	27-1	4	40	.262	.328	.426	97	-1	5-4	.983	7	115	165	O-97(41-48-22)/D	0.4
1999	Pit N	49	91	2	19	2	0	0	8	13-0	1	9	.209	.311	.231	41	-8	2-2	.955	-2	82	78	O-34(5-22-13)	-1.0
	†Ari N	10	23	6	8	1	0	2	7	2-0	0	6	.348	.385	.652	159	2	0-0	1.000	0	113	0	/O-5(0-2-4)	0.2
	Year	59	114	8	27	3	0	2	15	15-0	1	15	.237	.326	.316	65	-6	2-2	.964	-2	87	65	O-39(5-24-17)	-0.8
2000	Ari N	15	52	5	9	4	0	0	4	5-0	0	7	.173	.241	.250	25	-6	1-1	1.000	1	121	0	O-15(0-1-14)	-0.6
2001	Phi N	17	15	1	4	1	0	0	2	1-1	1	6	.267	.353	.333	81	0	0-0	—	0			/H	-0.1
Total	12	626	1548	210	389	73	11	39	219	186-11	13	247	.251	.332	.388	87	-26	33-15	.988	13	104	115	O-510(169-182-220)/D-4,31	-2.2
WARES, BUZZY Clyde Ellsworth B 3.23.1886 Vandalia, MI D 5.26.1964 South Bend, IN BR/TR 5-10/150# d9.15 C22																								
1913	StL A	11	35	5	10	2	0	0	1	1	0	3	.286	.306	.343	92	0	2	.973	-2	71	139	/2-9	-0.3
1914	StL A	81	215	20	45	10	1	0	23	28	0	35	.209	.300	.265	73	-6	10-10	.903	-6	103	93	S-68/2-8	-1.0
Total	2	92	250	25	55	12	1	0	24	29	0	38	.220	.301	.276	76	-6	12-10	.903	-8	103	93	/S-68,2-17	-1.3
WARNER, FRED Frederick John Rodney B 1855 Philadelphia, PA D 2.13.1886 Philadelphia, PA 5-7/155# d4.30																								
1875	Cen NA	**14**	57	11	14	4	0	0	2	1		2	.246	.259	.316	107	1	0-0	.784	-1	86	0	O-14(CF)	0.0
1876	Phi N	1	3	0	0	0	0	0	0	0		0	.000	.000	.000	-99	-1		.600	-1	0	0	/O(CF)	-0.1
1878	Ind N	43	165	19	41	4	0	0	10	2		15	.248	.257	.273	86	-2		.907	-5	92	92	*S-41/O-2(LF)	-0.5
1879	Cle N	76	316	32	77	11	4	0	22	2		20	.244	.248	.304	82	-6		.827	1	99	72	3-54,O-21(13-7-1)/1	-0.5
1883	Phi N	39	141	13	32	6	1	0	13	5		21	.227	.253	.284	69	-5		.775	-6	82	70	3-38/O(RF)	-0.9
1884	Bro AA	84	352	40	78	4	0	1		17	1		.222	.259	.241	64	-14		.824	-6	97	133	*3-84	-1.7
Total	5	243	977	104	228	25	5	1	45	26	1	56	.233	.254	.272	73	-28		.815	-17	95	102	3-176/S-41,O-25(15-8-2),1	-3.7
WARNER, HOOKS Hoke Hayden B 5.22.1894 Del Rio, TX D 2.19.1947 San Francisco, CA BL/TR 5-10.5/170# d8.21 Mil 1918																								
1916	Pit N	44	168	12	40	1	1	2	14	6	0	19	.238	.264	.292	70	-7	6	.899	-10	67	82	3-42/2	-1.8
1917	Pit N	3	5	0	1	0	0	0	0	0	0	1	.200	.200	.200	22	0	0	1.000	0	65	0	/3	0.0
1919	Pit N	6	8	0	1	0	0	0	2	3	0	1	.125	.364	.125	48	0	0	.818	-0	104	0	/3-3	-0.1
1921	Chi N	14	38	4	8	1	0	0	3	2	1	1	.211	.268	.237	35	-4	1-1	.957	0	114	65	3-10	-0.3
Total	4	67	219	16	50	2	1	2	19	11	1	22	.228	.268	.274	61	-11	7-1	.906	-10	76	73	/3-56,2	-2.2
WARNER, JOHN John Joseph B 8.15.1872 New York, NY D 12.21.1943 Far Rockaway, NY BL/TR 5-11/165# d4.23																								
1895	Bos N	3	7	2	1	0	0	0	1	1	1	0	.143	.333	.143	24	-1	0	.917	1	*135*	*168*	/C-3	0.0
	Lou N	67	232	20	62	4	2	1	20	11	7	16	.267	.320	.315	68	-11	10	.931	-11	*91*	*80*	C-64/1-3,2	-1.4
	Year	70	239	22	63	4	2	1	21	12	8	16	.264	.320	.310	67	-12	10	.930	-11	*93*	*83*	C-67/1-3,2	-1.4
1896	Lou N	33	110	9	25	1	1	0	10	10	2	10	.227	.303	.255	50	-8	3	.939	2	*78*	*120*	C-32/1	-0.3
	NY N	19	54	9	14	1	0	0	3	3	1	7	.259	.310	.278	57	-3	1	.922	-2	*95*	*89*	C-19	-0.3
	Year	52	164	18	39	2	1	0	13	13	3	17	.238	.306	.262	52	-11	4	.934	-0	*84*	*109*	C-51/1	-0.6
1897	NY N	111	400	50	109	6	3	2	51	26	16		.273	.342	.318	77	-13	8	.953	**32**	***169***	*111*	*C-111	2.5
1898	NY N	110	373	40	96	14	5	0	42	22	10		.257	.316	.322	86	-7	9	.968	9	*91*	***111***	*C-109/O(RF)	1.0
1899	NY N	88	293	38	78	8	1	0	19	15	6		.266	.315	.300	72	-11	15	.952	0	*86*	***122***	C-82/1-3	-0.3
1900	NY N	34	108	15	27	4	0	0	13	8	3		.250	.319	.287	71	-4	1	.948	4	*111*	*109*	C-31	0.3
1901	NY N	87	291	19	70	6	1	0	20	3	8		.241	.268	.268	58	-16	3	.967	-4	*84*	*112*	C-84	-1.2
1902	Bos A	65	222	19	52	5	7	0	12	13	3		.234	.286	.320	66	-11	0	.979	8	*128*	*92*	C-64	0.3
1903	NY N	89	285	38	81	8	5	0	34	7	9		.284	.322	.347	88	-6	5	**.986**	12	*119*	*108*	C-85	1.3
1904	NY N	86	287	29	57	5	1	1	15	14	7		.199	.253	.233	48	-17	7	**.982**	8	*140*	*108*	C-86	-0.1
1905	StL N	41	137	9	35	2	2	1	12	6	3		.255	.301	.321	88	-2	2	.958	-2	*90*	*116*	C-41	0.0
	Det A	36	119	12	24	2	3	0	7	8	0		.202	.252	.269	65	-5	2	.974	-2	*75*	*98*	C-36	-0.4
1906	Det A	50	153	15	37	4	2	0	10	12	7		.242	.326	.294	92	-1	4	.978	9	*110*	*120*	C-49	1.3
	Was A	32	103	5	21	4	1	1	9	2	1		.204	.226	.291	65	-5	3	.968	3	*86*	*149*	C-32	0.2
	Year	82	256	20	58	8	3	1	19	14	8		.227	.288	.293	82	-5	7	**.974**	11	*100*	***132***	C-81	1.5
1907	Was A	72	207	11	53	5	0	0	17	12	3		.256	.306	.280	95	-1	3	.971	-8	*84*	*100*	C-64	-0.4
1908	Was A	51	116	8	28	2	1	0	8	8	4		.241	.313	.276	100	0	7	.982	2	*112*	*83*	C-41/1	0.6
Total	14	1074	3497	348	870	81	35	6	303	181	91	33	.249	.303	.297	73	-122	83	.966	60	*108*	*108*	*C-1033/1-8,O(RF)2	3.1
WARNER, JACKIE John Joseph B 8.1.1943 Monrovia, CA BR/TR 6/180# d4.12																								
1966	Cal A	45	123	22	26	4	1	7	16	9-0	0	55	.211	.263	.431	99	-1	0-0	.984	-1	98	53	O-37(RF)	-0.4
WARNER, JACK John Ralph B 8.29.1903 Evansville, IN D 3.13.1986 Mt.Vernon, IL BR/TR 5-9.5/165# d9.24																								
1925	Det A	10	39	7	13	0	0	0	2	3	0	6	.333	.381	.333	84	-1	0-0	1.000	-1	101	204	3-10	-0.1
1926	Det A	100	311	41	78	8	6	0	34	38	5	24	.251	.342	.315	71	-13	8-4	.956	-1	97	62	3-95/S-3	-0.8
1927	Det A	139	559	78	149	22	9	1	45	47	6	45	.267	.330	.343	74	-22	14-4	.947	-4	99	116	*3-138	-1.6
1928	Det A	75	206	33	44	4	4	0	13	16	1	15	.214	.274	.272	43	-18	4-5	.944	4	109	64	3-52/S-7	-1.1
1929	Bro N	17	62	3	17	2	0	0	4	7	0	6	.274	.348	.306	65	-3	3	.945	-2	93	72	S-17	-0.3
1930	Bro N	21	25	4	8	1	0	0	0	2	0	7	.320	.370	.360	79	-1	1	1.000	1	137	0	/3-8	0.1
1931	Bro N	9	4	2	2	0	0	0	0	1	0	1	.500	.600	.500	200	1	0	1.000	1	211	0	/S-2,3	0.2
1933	Phi N	107	340	31	76	15	1	0	22	28	1	33	.224	.285	.274	53	-20	1	.973	4	102	98	2-71,3-30/S	-1.1
Total	8	478	1546	199	387	52	20	1	120	142	13	137	.250	.319	.312	65	-77	31-13	.950	2	103	100	3-334/2-71,S-30	-4.7

WARNOCK, HAL Harold Charles B 1.6.1912 New York, NY D 2.8.1997 Tucson, AZ BL/TR 6-2/180# d9.2

Year	Tm Lg	G	AB	R	H	2B	3B	HR	RBI	BB-IB	HP	SO	AVG	OBP	SLG	AOPS	ABR	SB-CS	FA	FR	Rng	Thr	G at Pos	BFW
1935	StL A	6	7	1	2	2	0	0	0	0	0	3	.286	.286	.571	112	0	0-0	1.000	-0	59	0	/O-2(1-1-0)	0.0

WARREN, BENNIE Bennie Louis B 3.2.1912 Elk City, OK D 5.11.1994 Oklahoma City, OK BR/TR 6-1/184# d9.13 Mil 1943-45

Year	Tm Lg	G	AB	R	H	2B	3B	HR	RBI	BB-IB	HP	SO	AVG	OBP	SLG	AOPS	ABR	SB-CS	FA	FR	Rng	Thr	G at Pos	BFW
1939	Phi N	18	56	4	13	0	0	1	7	7	0	7	.232	.317	.286	65	-3	0	.958	-3	*53*	*100*	C-17	-0.5
1940	Phi N	106	289	33	71	6	1	12	34	40	1	46	.246	.339	.398	107	3	1	.975	-3	*92*	*110*	C-97/1	0.5
1941	Phi N	121	345	34	74	13	2	9	35	44	3	66	.214	.309	.342	86	-6	0	.973	-5	*73*	***140***	*C-110	-0.5
1942	Phi N	90	225	19	47	6	3	7	20	24	1	36	.209	.288	.356	92	-3	0	.972	-6	*67*	***132***	C-78/1	-0.5
1946	NY N	39	69	7	11	1	1	4	8	14	0	21	.159	.301	.377	91	-1	0	.965	-0	*86*	*67*	C-30	0.0
1947	NY N	3	5	0	1	0	0	0	0	0	0	1	.200	.200	.200	6	-1	0	1.000	-0	*0*	*0*	/C-3	-0.1
Total	6	377	989	97	217	26	7	33	104	129	5	177	.219	.313	.360	92	-11	1	.972	-17	*77*	*122*	C-335/1-2	-1.1

WARREN, BILL William Hackney "Hack" B 2.11.1883 , MO D 1.28.1960 Whiteville, TN BR/TR 5-8/165# d4.30

Year	Tm Lg	G	AB	R	H	2B	3B	HR	RBI	BB-IB	HP	SO	AVG	OBP	SLG	AOPS	ABR	SB-CS	FA	FR	Rng	Thr	G at Pos	BFW
1914	Ind F	26	50	5	12	2	0	0	5	5	0	7	.240	.309	.280	55	-4	2	.931	-3	*81*	*84*	C-23	-0.6
1915	New F	5	3	0	1	0	0	0	1	0	0	0	.333	.333	.333	93	0	0	1.000	-0	*0*	*0*	/C1	0.0
Total	2	31	53	5	13	2	0	0	6	5	0	7	.245	.310	.283	57	-4	2	.932	-3	*80*	*83*	/C-24,1	-0.6

WARSTLER, RABBIT Harold Burton B 9.13.1903 N.Canton, OH D 5.31.1964 N.Canton, OH BR/TR 5-7.5/150# d7.24

Year	Tm Lg	G	AB	R	H	2B	3B	HR	RBI	BB-IB	HP	SO	AVG	OBP	SLG	AOPS	ABR	SB-CS	FA	FR	Rng	Thr	G at Pos	BFW
1930	Bos A	54	162	16	30	2	3	1	13	20	0	21	.185	.275	.253	36	-16	0-2	.947	-1	103	103	S-54	-1.2
1931	Bos A	66	181	20	44	5	3	0	10	15	2	27	.243	.308	.304	65	-10	2-3	.933	-0	115	89	2-42,S-19/3	-0.7
1932	Bos A	115	388	26	82	15	5	0	34	22	3	43	.211	.259	.276	40	-36	9-6	.939	**23**	**115**	**114**	*S-107	-0.5
1933	Bos A	92	322	44	70	13	1	1	17	42	0	36	.217	.308	.273	55	-20	2-4	.951	-1	103	82	S-87	-1.5
1934	Phi A	117	419	56	99	19	3	1	36	51	1	30	.236	.321	.303	64	-22	9-3	.969	16	**117**	**116**	*2-107/S-2	0.1
1935	Phi A	138	496	62	124	20	7	3	59	56	0	53	.250	.326	.337	72	-21	8-4	.959	1	105	92	*2-136/3-2	-1.1
1936	Phi A	66	236	27	59	8	6	1	24	36	2	16	.250	.354	.347	75	-9	0-0	.973	10	121	94	2-66	0.5
	Bos N	74	304	27	64	6	0	0	17	22	1	33	.211	.266	.230	37	-27	2	.948	7	114	120	S-74	-1.4
1937	Bos N	149	555	57	124	20	0	3	36	51	2	62	.223	.291	.276	60	-30	4	.942	-9	106	104	*S-149	-2.8
1938	Bos N	142	467	37	108	10	4	0	40	48	0	38	.231	.303	.270	65	-22	3	.937	-7	103	94	*S-135/2-7	-2.0
1939	Bos N	114	342	34	83	11	3	0	24	24	0	31	.243	.292	.292	62	-19	2	.953	2	100	116	S-49,2-43,3-21	-1.1
1940	Bos N	33	57	6	12	0	0	0	4	10	0	5	.211	.328	.211	54	-3	0	.974	0	100	161	2-24/3-2,S	-0.2
	Chi N	45	159	19	36	4	1	1	18	8	0	19	.226	.263	.283	52	-11	1	.939	-0	104	81	S-28,2-17	-0.8
	Year	78	216	25	48	4	1	1	22	18	0	24	.222	.282	.264	53	-14	1	.960	-0	103	113	2-41,S-29/3-2	-1.0
Total	11	1205	4088	431	935	133	36	11	332	405	11	414	.229	.300	.287	59	-246	42-22	.942	41	106	102	S-705,2-442/3-26	-12.7

WARWICK, CARL Carl Wayne B 2.27.1937 Dallas, TX BR/TL 5-10/170# d4.11

Year	Tm Lg	G	AB	R	H	2B	3B	HR	RBI	BB-IB	HP	SO	AVG	OBP	SLG	AOPS	ABR	SB-CS	FA	FR	Rng	Thr	G at Pos	BFW
1961	LA N	19	11	2	1	0	0	0	1	2-0	0	3	.091	.231	.091	-9	-2	0-0	1.000	-0	77	0	O-12(6-5-1)	-0.2
	StL N	55	152	27	38	6	2	4	16	18-0	0	33	.250	.324	.395	83	-4	3-0	.970	-1	102	60	O-48(15-34-10)	-0.6
	Year	74	163	29	39	6	2	4	17	20-0	0	36	.239	.317	.374	77	-5	3-0	.970	-1	101	58	O-60(21-39-11)	-0.8
1962	StL N	13	23	4	8	0	0	1	4	2-0	0	2	.348	.385	.478	123	1	2-0	1.000	0	87	204	O-10(1-0-9)	0.1
	Hou N	130	477	63	124	17	1	16	60	38-1	0	77	.260	.312	.400	98	-3	2-3	.986	-1	94	143	*O-128(15-116-9)	-0.9
	Year	143	500	67	132	17	1	17	64	40-1	0	79	.264	.315	.404	98	-3	4-3	.986	-1	94	146	*O-138(16-116-18)	-0.8
1963	Hou N	150	528	49	134	19	5	7	47	49-4	2	70	.254	.319	.348	98	-1	3-3	.988	-1	103	71	*O-141(23-11-114)/1-2	-1.2
1964	†StL N	88	158	14	41	7	1	3	15	11-1	0	30	.259	.306	.373	83	-3	2-0	.933	-1	91	126	O-49(11-0-41)	-0.6
1965	StL N	50	77	3	12	2	1	0	6	4-0	0	18	.156	.198	.208	13	-9	1-0	.960	-0	104	128	O-21(4-2-15)/1-4	-1.1
	Bal A	9	14	3	0	0	0	0	0	3-0	0	2	.000	.176	.000	-44	-3	0-0	1.000	-0	76	0	/O-3(1-0-2)	-0.3
1966	Chi N	16	22	3	5	0	0	0	0	0-0	0	6	.227	.227	.227	27	-2	0-0	1.000	1	96	364	O-10(3-7-0)	-0.2
Total	6	530	1462	168	363	51	10	31	149	127-6	2	241	.248	.307	.360	87	-26	13-6	.980	-3	98	107	O-422(79-175-201)/1-6	-5.0

WARWICK, BILL Firmin Newton B 11.26.1897 Philadelphia, PA D 12.19.1984 San Antonio, TX BR/TR 6-0.5/180# d7.18

Year	Tm Lg	G	AB	R	H	2B	3B	HR	RBI	BB-IB	HP	SO	AVG	OBP	SLG	AOPS	ABR	SB-CS	FA	FR	Rng	Thr	G at Pos	BFW
1921	Pit N	1	1	0	0	0	0	0	0	0	0	0	.000	.000	.000	-97	0	0-0	.500	-0	*0*	*470*	/C	-0.1
1925	StL N	13	41	8	12	1	2	1	6	5	0	5	.293	.370	.488	114	1	0-1	1.000	-2	*91*	*47*	C-13	-0.1
1926	StL N	9	14	0	5	0	0	0	2	0	0	2	.357	.357	.357	89	0	0	.923	1	*120*	*107*	/C-9	0.1
Total	3	23	56	8	17	1	2	1	8	5	0	7	.304	.361	.446	105	1	0-1	.954	-1	*99*	*76*	/C-23	-0.1

WASDELL, JIMMY James Charles B 5.15.1914 Cleveland, OH D 8.6.1983 New Port Richey, FL BL/TL 5-11/185# d9.3

Year	Tm Lg	G	AB	R	H	2B	3B	HR	RBI	BB-IB	HP	SO	AVG	OBP	SLG	AOPS	ABR	SB-CS	FA	FR	Rng	Thr	G at Pos	BFW
1937	Was A	32	110	13	28	4	4	2	12	7	0	13	.255	.299	.418	82	-4	0-1	.995	0	85	99	1-21/O-7(3-0-4)	-0.6
1938	Was A	53	140	19	33	2	1	2	16	12	0	12	.236	.296	.307	55	-10	5-2	.996	-2	79	119	1-26/O-6(RF)	-1.3
1939	Was A	29	109	12	33	5	1	0	13	9	1	16	.303	.361	.367	94	-1	3-1	.964	-2	90	100	1-28	-0.5
1940	Was A	10	35	3	3	1	0	0	0	2	0	7	.086	.135	.114	-37	-7	0-0	1.000	-1	38	103	/1-8	-0.9
	Bro N	77	230	35	64	14	4	3	37	18	1	24	.278	.333	.413	99	-1	4	.947	-5	93	33	O-42(1-1-40),1-17	-1.0
1941	†Bro N	94	265	39	79	14	3	4	48	16	3	15	.298	.345	.419	110	3	2	.956	-3	97	54	O-54(8-0-46),1-15	-0.4
1942	Pit N	122	409	44	106	11	2	3	38	47	1	22	.259	.337	.318	90	-4	1	.957	-2	99	102	O-97(36-2-61)/1-7	-1.3
1943	Pit N	4	2	0	1	0	0	0	1	2	0	0	.500	.750	.500	256	1	0	—	0			H	0.1
	Phi N	141	522	54	136	19	6	4	67	46	2	22	.261	.323	.343	96	-4	6	.988	1	110	91	1-82,O-56(39-22-5)	-0.9
	Year	145	524	54	137	19	6	4	68	48	2	22	.261	.326	.344	97	-3	6	.988	1	110	91	1-82,O-56(39-22-5)	-0.8
1944	Phi N	133	451	47	125	20	3	3	40	45	1	17	.277	.344	.355	100	1	0	.980	-6	96	66	*O-121(118-5-3)/1-4	-1.2
1945	Phi N	134	500	65	150	19	8	7	60	32	3	11	.300	.346	.412	113	7	7	.967	-1	103	74	O-65(17-13-37),1-63	-0.1
1946	Phi N	26	51	7	13	0	2	1	5	3	1	2	.255	.309	.392	101	0	0	.923	-1	79	0	O-11(4-0-6)/1-2	-0.2
	Cle A	32	41	1	11	0	0	0	4	4	0	4	.268	.333	.268	74	-1	1-0	.939	-1	105	223	/1-4,O-3(1-0-2)	-0.2
1947	Cle A	1	1	0	0	0	0	0	0	0	0	0	.000	.000	.000	-99	0	0-0	—	0			H	0.0
Total	11	888	2866	339	782	109	34	29	341	243	13	165	.273	.332	.365	96	-20	29-4	.966	-22	98	75	O-462(227-43-210),1-277	-8.5

WASEM, LINK Lincoln William B 1.30.1911 Birmingham, OH D 3.6.1979 S.Laguna, CA BR/TR 5-9.5/180# d5.5

Year	Tm Lg	G	AB	R	H	2B	3B	HR	RBI	BB-IB	HP	SO	AVG	OBP	SLG	AOPS	ABR	SB-CS	FA	FR	Rng	Thr	G at Pos	BFW
1937	Bos N	2	1	0	0	0	0	0	0	0	0	0	.000	.000	.000	-99	0	0	1.000	0	*0*	*0*	/C-2	0.0

WASHBURN, LIBE Libeus B 6.16.1874 Lyme, NH D 3.22.1940 Malone, NY BB/TL 5-10/180# d5.30 ▲

Year	Tm Lg	G	AB	R	H	2B	3B	HR	RBI	BB-IB	HP	SO	AVG	OBP	SLG	AOPS	ABR	SB-CS	FA	FR	Rng	Thr	G at Pos	BFW
1902	NY N	6	9	1	4	0	0	0	0	2	2		.444	.615	.444	230	2	1	1.000	-0	0	0	/O-3(0-2-1)	0.2
1903	Phi N	8	18	1	3	0	0	0	1	1	0		.167	.211	.167	8	-2	0	1.000	-1	73	0	/P-4,O-2(LF)	-0.1
Total	2	14	27	2	7	0	0	0	1	3	2		.259	.375	.259	89	0	1	1.000	-1	0	0	/O-5(1-2-1),P-4	0.1

WASHINGTON, CLAUDELL Claudell B 8.31.1954 Los Angeles, CA BL/TL 6/190# d7.5

Year	Tm Lg	G	AB	R	H	2B	3B	HR	RBI	BB-IB	HP	SO	AVG	OBP	SLG	AOPS	ABR	SB-CS	FA	FR	Rng	Thr	G at Pos	BFW
1974	†Oak A	73	221	16	63	10	5	0	19	13-1	1	44	.285	.326	.376	109	2	6-8	.985	1	110	107	D-38,O-32(14-10-10)	-0.1
1975	†Oak A★	148	590	86	182	24	7	10	77	32-9	5	80	.308	.345	.424	120	14	40-15	.978	-5	96	73	*O-148(112-35-11)	0.4
1976	Oak A	134	490	65	126	20	6	5	53	30-1	3	90	.257	.302	.353	96	-4	37-20	.963	-3	97	105	*O-126(0-30-105)/D-6	-1.2
1977	Tex A	129	521	63	148	31	2	12	68	25-9	3	112	.284	.318	.420	99	-1	21-8	.978	-2	92	120	*O-127(93-41-4)/D	-0.6
1978	Tex A	12	42	1	7	0	0	0	2	1-0	0	12	.167	.186	.167	-0	-6	0-1	.917	-2	71	0	/O-7(1-0-6),D-4	-0.9
	Chi A	86	314	33	83	16	5	6	31	12-2	1	57	.264	.290	.404	94	-4	5-5	.959	-2	94	106	O-82(15-8-63)/D	-1.1
	Year	98	356	34	90	16	5	6	33	13-2	1	69	.253	.278	.376	83	-10	5-6	.957	-4	92	97	O-89(16-8-69)/D-5	-2.0
1979	Chi A	131	471	79	132	33	5	13	66	28-7	3	93	.280	.322	.454	108	4	19-11	.974	1	104	80	*O-122(0-1-121)/D-3	0.0
1980	Chi A	32	90	15	26	4	2	1	12	5-0	1	19	.289	.333	.411	103	0	4-2	.933	-1	101	67	O-23(21-0-3)/D-2	-0.1
	NY N	79	284	38	78	16	4	10	42	20-5	1	63	.275	.324	.465	121	7	17-5	.978	4	97	214	O-70(23-1-58)	1.0
1981	Atl N	85	320	37	93	22	3	5	37	15-1	4	47	.291	.328	.425	110	4	12-6	.993	-3	94	74	O-79(RF)	-0.4
1982	†Atl N	150	563	94	150	24	6	16	80	50-9	6	107	.266	.330	.416	104	3	33-10	.950	-11	84	88	*O-139(RF)	-1.3
1983	Atl N	134	496	75	138	24	8	9	44	35-6	0	103	.278	.322	.413	96	-3	31-9	.974	-3	97	94	*O-128(RF)	-0.9
1984	Atl N★	120	416	62	119	21	2	17	61	59-8	1	77	.286	.374	.469	127	16	21-9	.967	-10	86	57	*O-107(RF)	0.3
1985	Atl N	122	398	62	110	14	6	15	43	40-11	1	66	.276	.342	.455	115	7	14-4	.962	-15	67	45	O-99(RF)	-1.2
1986	Atl N	40	137	17	37	11	0	5	14	14-0	0	26	.270	.336	.460	112	2	4-7	.957	-5	75	39	O-38(RF)	-0.6
	NY A	54	135	19	32	5	0	6	16	7-0	2	33	.237	.285	.407	87	-3	6-1	.985	-2	100	0	O-39(11-20-9)	-0.4
1987	NY A	102	312	42	87	17	0	9	44	27-2	0	54	.279	.336	.420	100	0	10-1	.988	0	101	102	O-72(2-69-1),D-13	0.1
1988	NY A	126	455	62	140	22	3	11	64	24-2	2	74	.308	.342	.442	120	11	15-6	.984	2	103	93	*O-117(13-103-8)	1.3
1989	Cal A	110	418	53	114	18	4	13	42	27-3	2	84	.273	.319	.428	111	4	13-5	.975	-5	90	80	*O-100(0-2-99)/D-7	-0.3
1990	Cal A	12	34	3	6	1	0	1	3	2-0	0	8	.176	.222	.294	44	-3	1-0	1.000	1	111	168	/O-9(RF)	-0.2
	NY A	33	80	4	13	1	1	0	6	2-1	0	17	.162	.181	.200	7	-10	3-1	1.000	1	103	152	O-21(19-0-4)/D-2	-1.0
	Year	45	114	7	19	2	1	1	9	4-1	0	25	.167	.193	.228	18	-13	4-1	1.000	2	105	157	O-30(19-0-13)/D-2	-1.2
Total	17	1912	6787	926	1884	334	69	164	824	468-77	36	1266	.278	.325	.420	106	40	312-134	.973	-57	93	90	*O-1685(324-320-1101)/D-77	-7.2

Year	Tm Lg	G	AB	R	H	2B	3B	HR	RBI	BB-IB	HP	SO	AVG	OBP	SLG	AOPS	ABR	SB-CS	FA	FR	Rng	Thr	G at Pos	BFW
WASHINGTON, HERB Herbert Lee B 11.16.1951 Belzoni, MS BR/TR 6/170# d4.4																								
1974	†Oak A	92	0	29	0	0	0	0	0	0-0	0	0	—	—	—	—	0	29-16	—	0			R	-0.2
1975	Oak A	13	0	4	0	0	0	0	0	0-0	0	0	—	—	—	—	0	2-1	—	0			R	0.0
Total	2	105	0	33	0	0	0	0	0	0-0	0	0	—	—	—	—	0	31-17	.973	0				-0.2
WASHINGTON, LA RUE La Rue B 9.7.1953 Long Beach, CA BR/TR 6/170# d9.7																								
1978	Tex A	3	3	0	0	0	0	0	0	0-0	0	1	.000	.000	.000	-99	-1	0-0	1.000	1	202	399	/2-2,D	0.0
1979	Tex A	25	18	5	5	0	0	0	2	4-0	0	0	.278	.409	.278	90	0	2-1	1.000	-0	93	0	O-13(0-12-1)/3D	0.0
Total	2	28	21	5	5	0	0	0	2	4-0	0	1	.238	.360	.238	67	-1	2-1	1.000	1	93	0	/O-13(0-12-1),D-2,2-2,3	0.0
WASHINGTON, RON Ronald B 4.29.1952 New Orleans, LA BR/TR 5-11/163# d9.10 C8 OF Total (2-LF 2-CF)																								
1977	LA N	10	19	4	7	0	0	0	1	0-0	1	2	.368	.400	.368	108	0	1-1	.857	-3	83	73	S-10	-0.2
1981	Min A	28	84	8	19	3	1	0	5	4-0	1	14	.226	.270	.286	56	-5	4-1	.951	4	100	107	S-26/O-2(CF)	0.2
1982	Min A	119	451	48	122	17	6	5	39	14-0	0	79	.271	.291	.368	78	-15	3-3	.972	-22	77	79	S-91,2-37/3	-2.8
1983	Min A	99	317	28	78	7	3	4	26	22-1	1	50	.246	.296	.325	69	-14	10-5	.962	-11	89	100	S-81,2-14/3D	-1.6
1984	Min A	88	197	25	58	11	5	3	23	4-0	1	31	.294	.307	.447	102	0	1-1	.978	-8	91	78	S-71/2-9,3-2,D-4	-0.4
1985	Min A	70	135	24	37	6	4	1	14	8-0	0	15	.274	.308	.400	89	-2	5-1	.951	-2	102	62	S-31,2-24/3-7,1D	-0.1
1986	Min A	48	74	15	19	3	0	4	11	3-0	0	21	.257	.278	.459	96	-1	1-2	.917	-2	68	71	2-16,D-15/S-7,3-3	-0.3
1987	Bal A	26	79	7	16	3	1	1	6	1-0	0	15	.203	.213	.304	36	-8	0-1	1.000	2	123	93	3-20/2-3,O-2(LF),SD	-0.6
1988	Cle A	69	223	30	57	14	2	2	21	9-0	5	35	.256	.298	.363	82	-5	3-3	.933	-6	96	81	S-54/3-8,2-7,D	-0.8
1989	Hou N	7	7	1	1	1	0	0	0	0-0	0	4	.143	.143	.286	20	-1	0-0	—	-0	0	0	/23	-0.1
Total	10	564	1586	190	414	65	22	20	146	65-1	9	266	.261	.292	.368	79	-51	28-18	.958	-47	89	87	S-372,2-111/3-43,D-30,O-4L,1	-6.7
WASHINGTON, GEORGE Sloan Vernon "Vern" B 6.4.1907 Linden, TX D 2.17.1985 Linden, TX BL/TR 5-11.5/190# d4.17																								
1935	Chi A	108	339	40	96	22	3	8	47	10	3	18	.283	.310	.437	89	-7	1-0	.974	2	96	162	O-79(RF)	-0.9
1936	Chi A	20	49	6	8	2	0	1	5	1	0	4	.163	.180	.265	8	-7	0-0	.938	0	75	248	O-12(RF)	-0.7
Total	2	128	388	46	104	24	3	9	52	11	3	22	.268	.294	.415	78	-14	1-0	.970	2	94	171	/O-91(RF)	-1.6
WASHINGTON, U L U L B 10.27.1953 Stringtown, OK BB/TR 5-11/175# d9.6																								
1977	KC A	10	20	0	4	1	1	0	1	5-0	0	4	.200	.360	.350	94	0	1-0	.872	-1	98	101	/S-9	0.0
1978	KC A	69	129	10	34	2	1	0	9	10-0	0	20	.264	.314	.295	71	-5	12-6	.927	-14	69	55	S-49,2-19/D	-1.5
1979	KC A	101	268	32	68	12	5	2	25	20-1	0	44	.254	.299	.358	77	-9	10-7	.970	-2	101	114	S-50,2-46/3D	-0.5
1980	†KC A	153	549	79	150	16	11	6	53	53-0	0	78	.273	.336	.375	94	-5	20-7	.957	-20	98	88	*S-152	-0.7
1981	†KC A	98	339	40	77	19	1	2	29	41-1	0	43	.227	.310	.307	79	-8	10-10	.973	-20	93	92	S-98	-2.0
1982	KC A	119	437	64	125	19	3	10	60	38-0	0	48	.286	.338	.412	106	4	23-7	.961	-4	102	96	*S-117/D	1.4
1983	KC A	144	547	76	129	19	6	5	41	48-0	1	78	.236	.298	.320	70	-23	40-7	.947	-8	103	104	*S-140/D	-1.0
1984	†KC A	63	170	18	38	6	0	1	10	14-0	0	31	.224	.281	.276	55	-10	4-6	.961	-2	99	127	S-61	-0.8
1985	Mon N	68	193	24	48	9	4	1	17	15-1	0	33	.249	.301	.352	88	-4	6-3	.978	-5	96	96	2-43/S-9,3-3	-0.7
1986	Pit N	72	135	14	27	0	4	0	10	15-2	0	27	.200	.278	.259	49	-10	6-0	.947	-1	98	135	S-51/2-3	-0.6
1987	Pit N	10	10	1	3	0	0	0	0	2-1	0	3	.300	.417	.300	93	0	0-0	.833	-0	133	0	/S3	0.0
Total	11	907	2797	358	703	103	36	27	255	261-6	1	409	.251	.313	.343	82	-70	132-53	.956	-77	98	100	S-737,2-111/D-6,3-5	-6.4
WASINGER, MARK Mark Thomas B 8.4.1961 Monterey, CA BR/TR 6/165# d5.27																								
1986	SD N	3	8	0	0	0	0	0	1	0-0	0	2	.000	.000	.000	-99	-2	0-0	.500	-2	57	325	/3-3,2	-0.4
1987	SF N	44	80	16	22	3	0	1	3	8-0	0	14	.275	.341	.350	88	-1	2-0	.973	1	99	161	3-21,2-10/S-2	0.0
1988	SF N	3	2	1	0	0	0	0	0	0-0	0	0	.000	.000	.000	-99	-1	0-0	—	0	0	0	/3	-0.1
Total	3	50	90	17	22	3	0	1	4	8-0	0	16	.244	.306	.311	68	-4	2-0	.907	-0	94	179	/3-25,2-11,S-2	-0.5
WASZGIS, B.J. Robert Michael B 8.24.1970 Omaha, NE BR/TR 6-2/215# d7.29																								
2000	Tex A	24	45	6	10	1	0	0	4	4-0	1	10	.222	.294	.244	40	-4	0-0	1.000	-4	265	30	C-23/1-3	-0.7
WATERMAN, FRED Frederick A. B 12.1845 New York, NY D 12.16.1899 Cincinnati, OH 5-7.5/148# d5.5 M1																								
1871	Oly NA	**32**	158	46	50	7	4	0	17	10		0	.316	.357	.411	127	7	11-3	.695	2	117	**200**	*3-28/C-6	0.6
1872	Oly NA	**9**	45	13	17	1	2	0	6	0		0	.378	.378	.489	173	4	0-0	.843	4	170	260	/3-7,C-2,M	0.5
1873	Was NA	15	80	20	28	1	1	0	12	1		1	.350	.358	.387	125	2	0-0	.649	-6	70	0	/S-9,O-4(0-3-1),3-2	-0.3
1875	Chi NA	5	20	2	6	0	0	0	3	0		2	.300	.300	.300	108	0	0-1	.545	-3	72	221	/3-5	-0.3
Total	4 NA	61	303	81	101	9	7	0	38	11		3	.333	.357	.409	132	13	11-4	.000	-3	118	204	/3-42,S-9,C-8,O-4(0-3-1)	0.5
WATHAN, DUSTY Dustin James B 8.22.1973 Jacksonville, FL BR/TR 6-4/215# d9.24 f-John																								
2002	KC A	3	5	1	3	1	0	0	1	0-0	1	1	.600	.667	.800	257	1	0-0	1.000	1	82	0	/C-3	0.2
WATHAN, JOHN John David B 10.4.1949 Cedar Rapids, IA BR/TR 6-2/205# d5.26 M6 C4 s-Dusty																								
1976	†KC A	27	42	5	12	1	0	0	5	2-0	1	5	.286	.333	.310	88	-1	0-2	.984	-1	103	63	C-23/1-3	-0.1
1977	†KC A	55	119	18	39	5	3	2	21	5-1	0	8	.328	.346	.471	122	3	2-0	.993	-1	94	32	C-35/1-5,D-2	0.3
1978	†KC A	67	190	19	57	10	1	2	28	3-1	4	12	.300	.320	.395	99	-1	2-1	1.000	1	102	76	1-47,C-21	-0.1
1979	KC A	90	199	26	41	7	3	2	28	7-1	0	24	.206	.227	.302	42	-17	2-1	.993	-3	98	118	1-49,C-23,D-11/O-3(2-0-1)	-2.1
1980	†KC A	126	453	57	138	14	7	6	58	50-6	3	42	.305	.377	.406	114	10	17-3	.982	-9	76	83	C-77,O-35(19-0-17),1-12	0.4
1981	†KC A	89	301	24	76	9	3	1	19	19-1	2	23	.252	.298	.312	78	-9	11-6	.979	-5	89	73	C-73,O-16(3-0-13)/1	-1.2
1982	KC A	121	448	79	121	11	3	3	51	48-0	2	46	.270	.343	.328	85	-8	36-9	.980	-9	108	102	*C-120/1-3	-0.7
1983	KC A	128	437	49	107	18	3	2	32	27-0	1	56	.245	.289	.314	66	-21	28-7	.985	1	99	102	C-92,1-37/O-9(3-0-6)	-1.4
1984	†KC A	97	171	17	31	7	1	2	10	21-0	0	34	.181	.271	.269	50	-12	6-6	.975	-2	92	86	C-59,1-33/O(LF)D	-1.3
1985	†KC A	60	145	11	34	8	1	1	9	17-0	1	15	.234	.319	.324	76	-4	1-1	.986	12	126	121	C-49/1-6,D-2	0.9
Total	10	860	2505	305	656	90	25	21	261	199-10	14	265	.262	.318	.343	83	-60	105-36	.982	-17	100	88	C-572,1-196/O-64(28-0-37),D-19	-5.3
WATKINS, DAVE David Roger B 3.15.1944 Owensboro, KY BR/TR 5-10/185# d4.9																								
1969	Phi N	69	148	17	26	2	1	4	12	22-0	2	53	.176	.291	.284	63	-7	2-3	.981	-4	79	124	C-54/O-5(5-0-1),3	-1.1
WATKINS, GEORGE George Archibald B 6.4.1900 Freestone Co., TX D 6.1.1970 Houston, TX BL/TR 6/175# d4.15																								
1930	†StL N	119	391	85	146	32	7	17	87	24	4	49	.373	.415	.621	141	26	5	.956	-3	91	100	O-89(3-1-85),1-13/2	1.3
1931	†StL N	131	503	93	145	30	13	13	51	31	5	66	.288	.336	.477	112	6	15	.958	-3	99	83	*O-129(0-9-121)	-0.4
1932	StL N	127	458	67	143	35	3	9	63	45	**8**	46	.312	.384	.461	122	17	18	.949	-2	99	106	*O-120(38-19-62)	0.8
1933	StL N	138	525	66	146	24	5	5	62	39	**12**	62	.278	.342	.371	98	0	11	.953	1	109	74	*O-135(RF)	-0.7
1934	NY N	105	296	38	73	18	3	6	33	24	6	34	.247	.316	.389	90	-4	2	.944	-8	86	54	O-81(8-68-5)	-1.5
1935	Phi N	150	600	80	162	25	5	17	76	40	4	78	.270	.320	.413	87	-12	3	.958	3	96	163	*O-148(128-20-1)	-1.6
1936	Phi N	19	70	7	17	4	0	2	5	5	0	13	.243	.293	.386	74	-3	2	.889	-2	75	93	O-17(LF)	-0.5
	Bro N	105	364	54	93	24	6	4	43	38	5	34	.255	.334	.387	93	-3	5	.969	-3	99	67	O-98(72-1-25)	-1.1
	Year	124	434	61	110	28	6	6	48	43	5	47	.253	.328	.387	90	-6	7	.959	-4	96	70	*O-115(89-1-25)	-1.6
Total	7	894	3207	490	925	192	42	73	420	246	44	382	.288	.347	.443	105	27	61	.954	-16	98	97	O-817(266-118-434)/1-13,2	-3.7
WATKINS, ED James Edward B 6.21.1877 Philadelphia, PA D 3.29.1933 Kelvin, AZ d9.6																								
1902	Phi N	1	3	0	0	0	0	0	0	1	0		.000	.250	.000	-22	0	0	1.000	-0	0	0	/O(LF)	-0.1
WATKINS, BILL William Henry B 5.5.1858 Brantford, ON, CAN D 6.9.1937 Port Huron, MI 5-10/156# d8.1 M9																								
1884	Ind AA	34	127	16	26	4	0	0		5	1		.205	.241	.236	58	-5		.845	-4	74	40	3-23/2-9,S-2,M	-0.8
WATKINS, PAT William Patrick B 9.2.1972 Raleigh, NC BR/TR 6-2/185# d9.9																								
1997	Cin N	17	29	2	6	2	0	0	0	0-0	0	5	.207	.207	.276	25	-3	1-0	1.000	-1	69	299	O-15(CF)	-0.3
1998	Cin N	83	147	11	39	8	1	2	15	8-0	1	26	.265	.300	.374	77	-5	1-3	.971	0	111	38	O-77(13-39-28)	-0.6
1999	Col N	16	19	2	1	0	0	0	0	2-0	0	5	.053	.143	.053	-38	-4	0-0	1.000	0	113	0	O-10(4-1-5)	-0.4
Total	3	116	195	15	46	10	1	2	15	10-0	1	36	.236	.271	.328	55	-12	2-3	.976	0	106	70	O-102(17-55-33)	-1.3
WATLINGTON, NEAL Julius Neal B 12.25.1922 Yanceyville, NC BL/TR 6/195# d7.10																								
1953	Phi A	21	44	4	7	1	0	0	3	3	0	8	.159	.213	.182	7	-6	0-1	.978	0	*117*	*174*	/C-9	-0.5
WATSON, ART Arthur Stanhope "Watty" B 1.11.1884 Jeffersonville, IN D 5.9.1950 Buffalo, NY BL/TR 5-10/175# d5.19																								
1914	Bro F	22	46	7	13	4	1	1	3	1	0	6	.283	.298	.478	110	0	0	.977	-0	*89*	*113*	C-18	0.1
1915	Bro F	9	19	4	5	0	3	0	1	3	0	4	.263	.364	.579	164	1	0	.957	-2	*74*	*72*	/C-7	0.0
	Buf F	22	30	6	14	1	0	1	13	0	0	4	.467	.467	.600	195	3	0	.778	-3	*59*	*91*	/C-6,O(LF)	0.0

Year	Tm Lg	G	AB	R	H	2B	3B	HR	RBI	BB-IB	HP	SO	AVG	OBP	SLG	AOPS	ABR	SB-CS	FA	FR	Rng	Thr	G at Pos	BFW
	Year	31	49	10	19	1	3	1	14	3	0	8	.388	.423	.592	182	4	0	.878	-5	68	80	C-13/O(LF)	0.0
Total	2	53	95	17	32	5	4	2	17	4	0	14	.337	.364	.537	147	4	0	.946	-5	80	100	/C-31,O(LF)	0.1
WATSON, JOHNNY John Thomas B 1.16.1908 Tazewell, VA D 4.29.1965 Huntington, WV BL/TR 6/175# d9.26																								
1930	Det A	4	12	1	3	2	0	0	3	1	0	2	.250	.308	.417	80	0	0-0	.933	-1	73	151	/S-4	-0.1
WATSON, MATT Matthew Kyle B 9.5.1978 Lancaster, PA BL/TR 5-11/190# d9.12																								
2003	NY N	15	23	0	4	2	0	0	2	1-0	0	5	.174	.208	.261	22	-3	0-0	.846	0	181	0	/O-5(LF)	-0.2
WATSON, BOB Robert Jose "Bull" B 4.10.1946 Los Angeles, CA BR/TR 6-2/205# d9.9 C3																								
1966	Hou N	1	1	0	0	0	0	0	0	0-0	0	0	.000	.000	.000	-99	0	0-0	—	0			H	0.0
1967	Hou N	6	14	1	3	0	0	1	2	0-0	0	3	.214	.214	.429	82	0	0-0	.958	0	127	0	/1-3	-0.1
1968	Hou N	45	140	13	32	7	0	2	8	13-1	1	32	.229	.297	.321	88	-2	1-0	.885	-4	85	0	O-40(40-0-1)	-0.9
1969	Hou N	20	40	3	11	3	0	0	3	6-0	2	5	.275	.396	.350	113	1	0-0	1.000	1	90	0	/O-6(LF),1-5,C	0.1
1970	Hou N	97	327	48	89	19	2	11	61	24-1	4	59	.272	.324	.443	110	4	1-1	.992	-6	70	81	1-83/C-6,O(LF)	-0.9
1971	Hou N	129	468	49	135	17	3	9	67	41-5	2	56	.288	.347	.395	113	8	0-3	.985	-10	79	35	O-87(LF),1-45	-1.2
1972	Hou N	147	548	74	171	27	4	16	86	53-5	8	83	.312	.378	.464	142	31	1-1	.978	-10	80	61	*O-143(LF)/1-2	1.3
1973	Hou N★	158	573	97	179	24	3	16	94	85-8	4	73	.312	.403	.449	137	32	1-4	.969	-4	99	84	*O-142(LF),1-26/C-3	1.9
1974	Hou N	150	524	69	156	19	4	11	67	60-9	3	61	.298	.370	.412	125	18	3-4	.981	-7	83	79	*O-140(LF),1-35	0.2
1975	Hou N★	132	485	67	157	27	1	18	85	40-10	3	50	.324	.375	.495	152	32	3-5	.993	-2	92	107	*1-118/O-9(LF)	2.1
1976	Hou N	157	585	76	183	31	3	16	102	62-10	4	64	.313	.377	.458	151	40	3-3	.990	-6	88	95	*1-155	2.3
1977	Hou N	151	554	77	160	38	6	22	110	57-11	7	69	.289	.360	.498	141	31	5-0	.994	10	**126**	92	*1-146	3.4
1978	Hou N	139	461	51	133	25	4	14	79	51-16	4	57	.289	.357	.451	137	23	3-1	.992	8	**122**	68	*1-128	2.5
1979	Hou N	49	163	15	39	4	0	3	18	16-1	0	23	.239	.304	.319	75	-6	0-0	.993	3	121	77	1-44	-0.6
	Bos A	84	312	48	105	19	4	13	53	29-7	5	33	.337	.401	.548	145	20	3-2	.988	1	111	119	1-58,D-26	1.7
1980	†NY A	130	469	62	144	25	3	13	68	48-5	1	56	.307	.368	.456	128	19	2-1	.990	3	113	105	*1-104,D-21	1.5
1981	†NY A	59	156	15	33	3	3	6	12	24-2	0	17	.212	.317	.385	103	0	0-0	.997	1	101	130	1-50/D-6	-0.1
1982	NY A	7	17	3	4	3	0	0	3	3-0	0	0	.235	.350	.412	110	0	0-0	1.000	-1	0	144	/1-6,D	-0.1
	Atl N	57	114	16	28	3	1	5	22	14-2	0	20	.246	.323	.421	104	0	1-1	1.000	-4	49	110	1-27/O-2(LF)	-0.5
1983	Atl N	65	149	14	46	9	0	6	37	18-3	0	23	.309	.376	.490	131	7	0-2	.984	-2	81	93	1-34	0.2
1984	Atl N	49	85	4	18	4	0	2	12	9-2	0	12	.212	.287	.329	68	-4	0-0	.983	0	114	147	1-19	-0.5
Total	19	1832	6185	802	1826	307	41	184	989	653-98	48	796	.295	.364	.447	130	254	27-28	.991	-28	99	95	*1-1088,O-570(570-0-1)/D-54,C-10	12.3
WATT, ALLIE Albert Bailey B 12.12.1899 Philadelphia, PA D 3.15.1968 Norfolk, VA BR/TR 5-8/154# d10.3 b-Frank																								
1920	Was A	1	1	0	1	1	0	0	1	0	0	0	1.000	1.000	2.000	700	1	0-0	1.000	0	143	0	/2	0.1
WATWOOD, JOHNNY John Clifford "Lefty" B 8.17.1905 Alexander City, AL D 3.1.1980 Goodwater, AL BL/TL 6-1/186# d4.16																								
1929	Chi A	85	278	33	84	12	6	2	28	22	1	21	.302	.355	.410	98	-1	6-3	.942	-1	102	90	O-77(1-53-23)	-0.5
1930	Chi A	133	427	75	129	25	4	2	51	52	3	35	.302	.382	.393	100	3	5-7	.989	3	117	116	1-62,O-52(1-36-14)	-0.2
1931	Chi A	128	367	51	104	16	6	1	47	56	1	30	.283	.380	.368	103	4	9-3	.944	5	105	161	*O-102(4-76-24)/1-4	0.6
1932	Chi A	13	49	5	15	2	0	0	0	1	1	3	.306	.333	.347	82	-1	0-0	.960	-0	91	107	O-13(4-1-11)	-0.2
	Bos A	95	266	26	66	11	0	0	30	20	0	11	.248	.301	.289	55	-18	7-4	.945	-2	92	83	O-46(7-25-14),1-18	-2.1
	Year	108	315	31	81	13	0	0	30	21	1	14	.257	.306	.298	59	-19	7-4	.948	-2	92	88	O-59(11-26-25),1-18	-2.3
1933	Bos A	13	30	2	4	0	0	0	2	3	0	3	.133	.212	.133	-7	-5	0-0	.950	-0	119	0	/O-9(5-0-4)	-0.5
1939	Phi N	2	6	0	1	0	0	0	0	0	0	0	.167	.167	.167	-11	-1	0	.933	-1	0	0	/1-2	-0.2
Total	6	469	1423	192	403	66	16	5	158	154	6	103	.283	.356	.363	89	-19	27-17	.948	5	101	119	O-299(22-191-90)/1-86	-3.1
WAY, BOB Robert Clinton B 4.2.1906 Emlenton, PA D 6.20.1974 Pittsburgh, PA BR/TR 5-10.5/168# d4.12																								
1927	Chi A	5	3	3	1	0	0	0	1	0	0	0	.333	.333	.333	75	0	0-0	1.000	-0	0	0	/2	0.0
WEATHERLY, ROY Cyril Roy "Stormy" B 2.25.1915 Warren, TX D 1.19.1991 Woodville, TX BL/TR 5-6.5/170# d6.27 Mil 1944-45																								
1936	Cle A	84	349	64	117	28	6	8	53	16	0	29	.335	.364	.519	115	6	3-8	.973	5	97	197	O-84(3-5-80)	0.4
1937	Cle A	53	134	19	27	4	0	5	13	6	2	14	.201	.246	.343	47	-12	1-1	.964	1	84	227	O-38(7-0-32)/3	-1.2
1938	Cle A	83	210	32	55	14	3	2	18	14	0	14	.262	.308	.386	74	-9	8-5	.975	2	97	170	O-55(6-41-8)	-0.8
1939	Cle A	95	323	43	100	16	6	1	32	19	0	23	.310	.348	.406	95	-3	7-2	.961	-5	91	58	O-76(36-27-14)	-0.9
1940	Cle A	135	578	90	175	35	11	12	59	27	1	26	.303	.335	.464	108	4	9-8	.969	2	103	101	*O-135(1-134-0)	0.1
1941	Cle A	102	363	59	105	21	5	3	37	32	2	20	.289	.350	.399	103	1	2-5	.968	-8	94	15	O-88(0-87-1)	-0.9
1942	Cle A	128	473	61	122	23	7	5	39	35	1	25	.258	.310	.368	96	-5	8-13	.991	2	104	82	*O-117(CF)	-0.8
1943	†NY A	77	280	37	74	8	3	7	28	18	1	9	.264	.311	.389	104	0	4-7	.983	-4	97	39	O-68(CF)	-0.8
1946	NY A	2	2	0	1	0	0	0	0	0	0	0	.500	.500	.500	178	0	0-0	—	0			H	0.0
1950	NY N	52	69	10	18	3	3	0	11	13	0	10	.261	.378	.391	102	1	0	1.000	1	95	261	O-15(12-1-2)	0.1
Total	10	811	2781	415	794	152	44	43	290	180	7	170	.286	.331	.418	99	-17	42-49	.975	-3	98	101	O-676(65-480-137)/3	-4.8
WEAVER, ART Arthur Coggshall "Six O'Clock" B 4.7.1879 Wichita, KS D 3.23.1917 Denver, CO TR 6-1/160# d9.14																								
1902	StL N	11	33	2	6	2	0	0	3	1	0		.182	.206	.242	40	-2	0	.983	0	99	136	C-11	-0.1
1903	StL N	16	49	4	12	0	0	0	5	4	0		.245	.302	.245	58	-3	1	.969	1	94	124	C-16	0.0
	Pit N	16	48	8	11	0	1	0	3	2	0		.229	.260	.271	50	-3	0	.978	0	142	85	C-11/1-5	-0.3
	Year	32	97	12	23	0	1	0	8	6	0		.237	.282	.258	54	-6	1	.972	1	111	111	C-27/1-5	-0.3
1905	StL A	28	92	5	11	2	1	0	3	1	0		.120	.129	.163	-8	-12	0	.962	1	79	113	C-28	-0.8
1908	Chi A	15	35	1	7	1	0	0	1	1	0		.200	.222	.229	47	-2	0	.953	-3	92	78	C-15	-0.5
Total	4	86	257	20	47	5	2	0	15	9	0		.183	.211	.218	31	-22	1	.967	0	94	111	/C-81,1-5	-1.7
WEAVER, BUCK George Daniel B 8.18.1890 Pottstown, PA D 1.31.1956 Chicago, IL BB/TR (BR 1912) 5-11/170# d4.11																								
1912	Chi A	147	523	55	117	21	8	1	43	9	6		.224	.245	.300	58	-32	13	.915	-7	93	115	*S-147	-2.9
1913	Chi A	151	533	51	145	17	8	4	52	15	8	60	.272	.302	.356	94	-8	20	.929	**36**	**111**	**132**	*S-151	4.0
1914	Chi A	136	541	64	133	20	9	2	28	20	5	40	.246	.279	.327	83	-14	14-20	.928	6	96	108	*S-134	-0.3
1915	Chi A	148	563	83	151	18	11	3	49	32	7	58	.268	.316	.355	98	-5	24-20	.939	-1	103	112	*S-148	0.4
1916	Chi A	151	582	78	132	27	6	3	38	30	13	48	.227	.280	.309	76	-19	22-13	.941	-0	100	145	3-85,S-66	-1.3
1917	†Chi A	118	447	64	127	16	5	3	32	27	5	29	.284	.332	.362	110	4	19	**.949**	2	95	**120**	*3-107,S-10	1.0
1918	Chi A	112	420	37	126	12	5	0	29	11	3	24	.300	.323	.352	103	-1	20	.941	1	103	134	S-98,3-11/2	0.7
1919	†Chi A	**140**	571	89	169	33	9	3	75	11	5	21	.296	.315	.401	100	-3	22	.963	-3	97	96	3-97,S-43	0.0
1920	Chi A	151	629	102	208	34	8	2	74	28	6	23	.331	.365	.420	107	6	19-17	.933	-15	91	75	*3-127,S-25	-0.5
Total	9	1254	4809	623	1308	198	69	21	420	183	58	303	.272	.307	.355	92	-72	173-70	.935	19	100	121	S-822,3-427/2	1.1
WEAVER, JIM James Francis B 10.10.1959 Kingston, NY BL/TL 6-3/190# d4.10																								
1985	Det A	12	7	2	1	1	0	0	0	1-0	0	4	.143	.250	.286	47	0	0-1	1.000	-0	43	0	/O-4(0-3-1),D-4	-0.1
1987	Sea A	7	4	2	0	0	0	0	0	2-0	0	3	.000	.333	.000	-1	-1	1-1	1.000	1	83	751	/O-4(1-2-2)	0.0
1989	SF N	12	20	2	4	3	0	0	2	0-0	0	7	.200	.200	.350	56	-1	1-0	1.000	-1	73	0	/O-8(1-0-7)	-0.2
Total	3	31	31	6	5	4	0	0	2	3-0	0	14	.161	.235	.290	47	-2	2-2	1.000	-1	72	210	/O-16(2-5-10),D-4	-0.3
WEAVER, FARMER William B. B 3.23.1865 Parkersburg, WV D 1.23.1943 Akron, OH BL 5-10/170# d9.16 OF Total (132-LF 406-CF 111-RF)																								
1888	Lou AA	26	112	12	28	1	1	0	8	3	1		.250	.276	.277	79	-3	12	.878	-1	158	0	O-26(CF)	-0.4
1889	Lou AA	124	499	62	145	17	6	0	60	40	7	22	.291	.352	.349	102	2	21	.918	1	136	71	*O-123(CF)/C-2,32	-0.1
1890	†Lou AA	130	557	101	161	27	9	3	67	29	8		.289	.333	.386	114	8	45	.933	-6	101	96	*O-127(0-126-1)/S-2,3	-0.2
1891	Lou AA	133	556	74	157	25	7	1	53	33	11	23	.282	.335	.358	99	-2	30	**.958**	13	**139**	141	*O-130(CF)/C-4	0.6
1892	Lou N	138	551	58	140	15	4	0	57	40	9	17	.254	.315	.296	92	-4	30	.902	-10	93	74	*O-122(109-1-12),C-15/1	-2.1
1893	Lou N	106	439	79	128	17	7	2	49	27	11	12	.292	.348	.376	100	0	17	.913	2	119	60	O-85(20-0-65),C-21	0.0
1894	Lou N	64	244	19	54	5	2	3	24	7	2	11	.221	.249	.295	33	-28	3	.958	1	133	0	O-35(2-0-33),C-17,1-10/2	-2.1
	Pit N	30	115	16	40	7	2	0	24	6	5	1	.348	.405	.443	105	1	4	.943	-8	100	96	C-14,S-12/3-5,O(LF)	-0.4
	Year	94	359	35	94	12	4	3	48	13	7	12	.262	.301	.343	58	-26	7	.947	-7	128	0	O-36(3-0-33),C-31,S-12,1-10/3-5,2-2	-2.5
Total	7	751	3073	421	853	114	38	9	342	185	54	86	.278	.330	.348	95	-26	162	.927	-8	120	83	O-649C/C-73,S-14,1-11,3-7,2-2	-4.7
WEBB, SKEETER James Laverne B 11.4.1909 Meridian, MS D 7.8.1986 Meridian, MS BR/TR 5-9.5/150# d7.20																								
1932	StL N	1	0	0	0	0	0	0	0	0	0	0	—	—	—	—	0	0	—	-0	0	0	/S	0.0
1938	Cle A	20	58	11	16	2	0	0	2	8	0	7	.276	.364	.310	72	-2	1-0	.964	-2	85	94	S-13/3-3,2-2	-0.3
1939	Cle A	81	269	28	71	14	1	2	26	15	1	24	.264	.305	.346	68	-13	1-1	.932	-8	89	91	S-81	-1.4
1940	Chi A	84	334	33	79	11	2	1	29	30	0	33	.237	.299	.290	53	-23	3-6	.969	-9	100	95	2-74/S-7,3	-2.8

Year	Tm Lg	G	AB	R	H	2B	3B	HR	RBI	BB-IB	HP	SO	AVG	OBP	SLG	AOPS	ABR	SB-CS	FA	FR	Rng	Thr	G at Pos	BFW
1941	Chi A	29	84	7	16	2	0	0	6	3	1	9	.190	.227	.214	18	-10	1-0	.940	-0	103	121	2-18/S-5,3-3	-0.9
1942	Chi A	32	94	5	16	2	1	0	4	4	0	13	.170	.204	.213	18	-11	1-2	.961	1	111	85	2-29	-0.9
1943	Chi A	58	213	15	50	5	2	0	22	6	0	19	.235	.256	.277	56	-13	5-4	.953	0	111	95	2-54	-1.1
1944	Chi A	139	513	44	108	19	6	0	30	20	1	39	.211	.242	.271	47	-38	7-3	.944	-3	**106**	95	*S-135/2-5	-3.2
1945	†Det A	118	407	43	81	12	2	0	21	30	0	35	.199	.254	.238	41	-31	8-7	.957	16	106	115	*S-104,2-11	-0.8
1946	Det A	64	169	12	37	1	1	0	17	9	0	18	.219	.258	.237	37	-15	3-3	.972	8	112	100	2-50/S-8	-0.5
1947	Det A	50	79	13	16	3	0	0	6	7	0	9	.203	.267	.241	41	-6	3-0	.992	6	125	62	2-30/S-6	0.1
1948	Phi A	23	54	5	8	2	0	0	3	0	0	9	.148	.148	.185	-12	-9	0-0	1.000	2	97	199	/2-9,S-8	-0.6
Total	12	699	2274	216	498	73	15	3	166	132	3	215	.219	.263	.268	46	-171	33-26	.946	11	102	99	S-368,2-282/3-7	-12.4

WEBB, EARL William Earl B 9.17.1897 Bon Air, TN D 5.23.1965 Jamestown, TN BL/TR 6-1/185# d8.13

Year	Tm Lg	G	AB	R	H	2B	3B	HR	RBI	BB-IB	HP	SO	AVG	OBP	SLG	AOPS	ABR	SB-CS	FA	FR	Rng	Thr	G at Pos	BFW
1925	NY N	4	3	0	0	0	0	0	0	1	0	1	.000	.250	.000	-31	-1	0-0	—	0			H	-0.1
1927	Chi N	102	332	58	100	18	4	14	52	48	1	31	.301	.391	.506	138	19	3	.959	0	93	133	O-86(8-0-78)	1.2
1928	Chi N	62	140	22	35	7	3	3	23	14	0	17	.250	.318	.407	90	-3	0	.986	1	99	127	O-31(RF)	-0.4
1930	Bos A	127	449	61	145	30	6	16	66	44	1	56	.323	.385	.523	133	22	2-1	.959	-6	92	75	*O-116(RF)	0.7
1931	Bos A	151	589	96	196	**67**	3	14	103	70	0	51	.333	.404	.528	151	47	2-2	.948	-5	86	136	*O-151(RF)	3.0
1932	Bos A	52	192	23	54	9	1	5	27	25	0	15	.281	.364	.417	105	2	0-0	.964	-1	78	190	O-50(RF)/1-2	-0.2
	Det A	88	338	49	97	19	8	3	51	39	0	18	.287	.361	.417	97	-1	1-1	.955	0	98	125	O-85(RF)	-0.6
	Year	140	530	72	151	28	9	8	78	64	0	33	.285	.362	.417	100	0	1-1	.958	-1	91	148	*O-135(RF)/1-2	-0.8
1933	Det A	6	11	1	3	0	0	0	3	3	0	0	.273	.429	.273	87	0	0-0	1.000	-0	38	0	/O-2(RF)	0.0
	Chi A	58	107	16	31	5	0	1	8	16	0	13	.290	.382	.364	103	1	0-0	1.000	-2	92	197	O-16(5-0-11),1-10	-0.2
	Year	64	118	17	34	5	0	1	11	19	0	13	.288	.387	.356	101	1	0-0	1.000	-2	86	174	O-18(5-0-13),1-10	-0.2
Total	7	650	2161	326	661	155	25	56	333	260	2	202	.306	.381	.478	125	86	8-4	.958	-13	90	126	O-537(13-0-524)/1-12	3.4

WEBB, BILL William Joseph B 6.25.1895 Chicago, IL D 1.12.1943 Chicago, IL BR/TR 5-10/161# d9.17 Mil 1918 C5

Year	Tm Lg	G	AB	R	H	2B	3B	HR	RBI	BB-IB	HP	SO	AVG	OBP	SLG	AOPS	ABR	SB-CS	FA	FR	Rng	Thr	G at Pos	BFW
1917	Pit N	5	15	1	3	0	0	0	0	2	0	3	.200	.294	.200	51	-1	0	1.000	0	104	82	/2-4,S	-0.1

WEBER, HARRY Henry J. B 3.1862 , NY D 12.22.1926 Indianapolis, IN d7.22

Year	Tm Lg	G	AB	R	H	2B	3B	HR	RBI	BB-IB	HP	SO	AVG	OBP	SLG	AOPS	ABR	SB-CS	FA	FR	Rng	Thr	G at Pos	BFW
1884	Ind AA	3	8	0	0	0	0	0		0	1		.000	.111	.000	-62	-1		.794	-1			/C-3	-0.2

WEBER, JOE Joseph Edward B 2.15.1862 Hamilton, ON, CAN D 12.15.1921 Hamilton, ON, CAN d5.30

Year	Tm Lg	G	AB	R	H	2B	3B	HR	RBI	BB-IB	HP	SO	AVG	OBP	SLG	AOPS	ABR	SB-CS	FA	FR	Rng	Thr	G at Pos	BFW
1884	Det N	2	8	0	0	0	0	0	0	0		2	.000	.000	.000	-99	-2		.750	0	227	0	/O-2(1-0-1)	-0.2

WEBSTER, LENNY Leonard Irell B 2.10.1965 New Orleans, LA BR/TR 5-9/191# d9.1

Year	Tm Lg	G	AB	R	H	2B	3B	HR	RBI	BB-IB	HP	SO	AVG	OBP	SLG	AOPS	ABR	SB-CS	FA	FR	Rng	Thr	G at Pos	BFW
1989	Min A	14	20	3	6	2	0	0	1	3-0	0	2	.300	.391	.400	116	1	0-0	1.000	-3	50	0	C-14	-0.2
1990	Min A	2	6	1	2	1	0	0	0	1-0	0	1	.333	.429	.500	149	0	0-0	1.000	-1	68	0	/C-2	0.0
1991	Min A	18	34	7	10	1	0	3	8	6-0	0	10	.294	.390	.588	162	3	0-0	.986	4	128	62	C-17	0.7
1992	Min A	53	118	10	33	10	1	1	13	9-0	0	11	.280	.331	.407	102	0	0-2	.995	-6	91	69	C-49/D	-0.4
1993	Min A	49	106	14	21	2	0	1	8	11-1	0	8	.198	.274	.245	40	-9	1-0	1.000	-1	111	94	C-45/D	-0.8
1994	Mon N	57	143	13	39	10	0	5	23	16-1	6	24	.273	.370	.448	111	3	0-0	.996	-3	73	110	C-46	0.2
1995	Phi N	49	150	18	40	9	0	4	14	16-0	0	27	.267	.337	.407	94	-1	0-0	.990	-8	68	51	C-43	-0.6
1996	Mon N	78	174	18	40	10	0	2	17	25-2	2	21	.230	.332	.322	72	-6	0-0	.998	10	124	123	C-63	0.7
1997	†Bal A	98	259	29	66	8	1	7	37	22-0	2	46	.255	.317	.375	82	-7	0-1	.995	-3	78	112	C-97/D	-0.5
1998	Bal A	108	309	37	88	16	0	10	46	15-0	0	38	.285	.317	.434	94	-4	0-0	.993	-13	73	92	*C-102/D-4	-1.0
1999	Bal A	16	36	1	6	1	0	0	3	8-0	1	5	.167	.333	.194	41	-3	0-0	.986	2	88	131	C-12/D-2	0.0
	Bos A	6	14	0	0	0	0	0	1	2-0	1	2	.000	.176	.000	-48	-3	0-0	1.000	-1	71	73	/C-6	-0.3
	Year	22	50	1	6	1	0	0	4	10-0	2	7	.120	.290	.140	15	-6	0-0	.990	1	83	113	C-18/D-2	-0.3
2000	Mon N	39	81	6	17	3	0	0	5	6-1	0	14	.210	.264	.247	29	-9	0-0	1.000	-5	74	50	C-32	-1.2
Total	12	587	1450	157	368	73	2	33	176	140-5	12	209	.254	.324	.375	83	-35	1-3	.995	-26	85	91	C-528/D-9	-3.4

WEBSTER, MITCH Mitchell Dean B 5.16.1959 Larned, KS BB/TL 6-1/185# d9.2

Year	Tm Lg	G	AB	R	H	2B	3B	HR	RBI	BB-IB	HP	SO	AVG	OBP	SLG	AOPS	ABR	SB-CS	FA	FR	Rng	Thr	G at Pos	BFW
1983	Tor A	11	11	2	2	0	0	0	0	1-0	0	1	.182	.250	.182	20	-1	0-0	1.000	-1	52	0	/O-7(CF),D-2	-0.2
1984	Tor A	26	22	9	5	2	1	0	4	1-0	0	7	.227	.261	.409	79	-1	0-0	.875	-0	119	0	/O-10(3-7-0)/1D	-0.1
1985	Tor A	4	1	0	0	0	0	0	0	0-0	0	0	.000	.000	.000	-98	0	0-1	—	-0	0	0	/O-2(LF),D-2	-0.1
	Mon N	74	212	32	58	8	2	11	30	20-3	0	33	.274	.335	.486	135	9	15-9	.993	0	101	86	O-64(4-52-20)	0.8
1986	Mon N	151	576	89	167	31	**13**	8	49	57-4	4	78	.290	.355	.431	117	13	36-15	.977	0	100	130	*O-146(8-118-44)	1.4
1987	Mon N	156	588	101	165	30	8	15	63	70-5	6	95	.281	.361	.435	107	7	33-10	.982	-4	96	78	*O-153(RF)	-0.1
1988	Mon N	81	259	33	66	5	2	2	13	36-2	5	37	.255	.354	.313	90	-2	12-10	.994	-4	91	59	O-71(12-53-12)	-0.8
	Chi N	70	264	36	70	11	6	4	26	19-0	3	50	.265	.319	.398	101	0	10-4	.971	1	109	33	O-65(8-52-10)	0.0
	Year	151	523	69	136	16	8	6	39	55-2	8	87	.260	.337	.356	95	-2	22-14	.982	-3	100	47	*O-136(20-105-22)	-0.8
1989	†Chi N	98	272	40	70	12	4	3	19	30-5	1	55	.257	.331	.364	92	-2	14-2	.965	3	116	82	O-74(52-13-21)	0.2
1990	Cle A	128	437	58	110	20	6	12	55	20-1	3	61	.252	.285	.407	93	-6	22-6	.991	8	122	17	*O-118(25-95-0)/1-3,D-3	0.3
1991	Cle A	13	32	2	4	0	0	0	0	3-0	0	9	.125	.200	.125	-8	-5	2-2	1.000	0	115	0	O-10(6-1-6)	-0.5
	Pit N	36	97	9	17	3	4	1	9	9-1	0	31	.175	.245	.320	59	-6	0-0	.963	-1	94	116	O-29(2-9-20)	-0.8
	LA N	58	74	12	21	5	1	1	10	9-0	0	21	.284	.361	.419	122	2	0-1	1.000	1	120	0	O-36(29-4-7)/1	0.2
	Year	94	171	21	38	8	5	2	19	18-1	0	52	.222	.296	.363	86	-4	0-1	.978	0	103	74	O-65(31-13-27)/1	-0.6
1992	LA N	135	262	33	70	12	5	6	35	27-3	2	49	.267	.334	.420	116	5	11-5	.977	-2	103	0	O-90(36-8-56)	0.2
1993	LA N	88	172	26	42	6	2	2	14	11-2	2	24	.244	.293	.337	74	-7	4-6	.950	-2	97	35	O-56(32-2-27)	-1.2
1994	LA N	82	84	16	23	4	0	4	12	8-1	1	13	.274	.344	.464	116	2	1-2	1.000	-1	95	0	O-48(45-0-6)	0.0
1995	†LA N	54	56	6	10	1	1	1	3	4-1	1	14	.179	.246	.286	44	-5	0-0	1.000	-1	72	0	O-25(11-4-11)	-0.6
Total	13	1265	3419	504	900	150	55	70	342	325-28	28	578	.263	.330	.401	101	3	160-73	.980	-3	103	63	*O-1004(275-425-393)/D-16,1-5	-1.3

WEBSTER, RAY Ramon Alberto B 8.31.1942 Colon, Panama BL/TL 6/185# d4.11

Year	Tm Lg	G	AB	R	H	2B	3B	HR	RBI	BB-IB	HP	SO	AVG	OBP	SLG	AOPS	ABR	SB-CS	FA	FR	Rng	Thr	G at Pos	BFW
1967	KC A	122	360	41	92	15	4	11	51	32-1	2	44	.256	.320	.411	118	7	5-3	.989	-3	76	75	1-83,O-15(14-0-2)	-0.1
1968	Oak A	66	196	17	42	11	1	3	23	12-6	0	24	.214	.258	.327	81	-5	3-0	.988	-3	79	91	1-55	-1.2
1969	Oak A	64	77	5	20	0	1	1	13	12-5	1	8	.260	.359	.325	99	0	0-0	1.000	0	104	69	1-13	0.0
1970	SD N	95	116	12	30	3	0	2	11	11-0	0	12	.259	.323	.336	80	-3	1-1	.981	-1	83	134	1-15/O(LF)	-0.6
1971	SD N	10	8	0	1	0	0	0	0	2-0	0	1	.125	.300	.125	26	-1	0-0	—	0			H	-0.1
	Oak A	7	5	0	0	0	0	0	0	0-0	0	2	.000	.000	.000	-99	-1	0-0	1.000	-0	0	0	/1	-0.2
	Chi N	16	16	1	5	2	0	0	0	1-0	0	3	.313	.353	.438	107	0	0-0	1.000	0	316	266	/1	0.1
Total	5	380	778	76	190	31	6	17	98	70-12	3	94	.244	.308	.365	99	-3	9-4	.989	-7	80	85	1-168/O-16(15-0-2)	-2.1

WEBSTER, RAY Raymond George B 11.15.1937 Grass Valley, CA BR/TR 6/175# d4.17

Year	Tm Lg	G	AB	R	H	2B	3B	HR	RBI	BB-IB	HP	SO	AVG	OBP	SLG	AOPS	ABR	SB-CS	FA	FR	Rng	Thr	G at Pos	BFW
1959	Cle A	40	74	10	15	2	1	2	10	5-0	0	7	.203	.253	.338	63	-4	1-0	.929	-2	99	109	2-24/3-4	-0.5
1960	Bos A	7	3	1	0	0	0	0	1	1-0	0	0	.000	.200	.000	-25	-1	0-0	1.000	0	152	531	/2	0.0
Total	2	47	77	11	15	2	1	2	11	6-0	0	7	.195	.250	.325	59	-5	1-0	.931	-2	100	116	/2-25,3-4	-0.5

WECKBECKER, PETE Peter B 8.30.1864 Butler, PA D 5.16.1935 Hampton, VA 5-7/150# d10.5

Year	Tm Lg	G	AB	R	H	2B	3B	HR	RBI	BB-IB	HP	SO	AVG	OBP	SLG	AOPS	ABR	SB-CS	FA	FR	Rng	Thr	G at Pos	BFW
1889	Ind N	1	1	0	0	0	0	0	0	0	0	0	.000	.000	.000	-98	0	0	1.000	-0			/C	0.0
1890	†Lou AA	32	101	17	24	1	0	0	11	8	1		.238	.300	.248	63	-5	7	.941	4	*135*	73	C-32	0.2
Total	2	33	102	17	24	1	0	0	11	8	1	0	.235	.297	.245	61	-5	7	.941	4	*133*	72	/C-33	0.2

WEDGE, ERIC Eric Michael B 1.27.1968 Fort Wayne, IN BR/TR 6-3/215# d10.5 M1

Year	Tm Lg	G	AB	R	H	2B	3B	HR	RBI	BB-IB	HP	SO	AVG	OBP	SLG	AOPS	ABR	SB-CS	FA	FR	Rng	Thr	G at Pos	BFW
1991	Bos A	1	1	0	1	0	0	0	0	0-0	0	0	1.000	1.000	1.000	434	0	0-0	—	0			/D	0.0
1992	Bos A	27	68	11	17	2	0	5	11	13-0	0	18	.250	.370	.500	133	3	0-0	1.000	-1	77	0	D-20/C-5	0.2
1993	Col N	9	11	2	2	0	0	0	1	0-0	0	4	.182	.182	.182	-2	-2	0-0	1.000	0	75	300	/C	-0.1
1994	Bos A	2	6	0	0	0	0	0	0	1-0	0	3	.000	.143	.000	-56	-1	0-0	—	0			/D-2	-0.2
Total	4	39	86	13	20	2	0	5	12	14-0	0	25	.233	.340	.430	104	0	0-0	1.000	-1	77	61	/D-23,C-6	-0.1

WEEDEN, BERT Charles Albert B 12.21.1882 Northwood, NH D 1.7.1939 Northwood, NH BL/TR 6/200# d6.4

Year	Tm Lg	G	AB	R	H	2B	3B	HR	RBI	BB-IB	HP	SO	AVG	OBP	SLG	AOPS	ABR	SB-CS	FA	FR	Rng	Thr	G at Pos	BFW
1911	Bos N	1	1	0	0	0	0	0	0	0	0	0	.000	.000	.000	-93	0	0	—	0			H	0.0

WEEKLY, JOHNNY Johnny B 6.14.1937 Waterproof, LA D 11.24.1974 Walnut Creek, CA BR/TR 6- /200# d4.13

Year	Tm Lg	G	AB	R	H	2B	3B	HR	RBI	BB-IB	HP	SO	AVG	OBP	SLG	AOPS	ABR	SB-CS	FA	FR	Rng	Thr	G at Pos	BFW
1962	Hou N	13	26	3	5	1	0	2	2	7-0	0	4	.192	.364	.462	129	1	0-0	1.000	-1	88	0	/O-7(4-0-4)	0.1
1963	Hou N	34	80	4	18	3	0	3	14	7-0	1	14	.225	.292	.375	98	0	0-0	1.000	1	107	152	O-23(15-0-8)	0.0
1964	Hou N	6	15	0	2	0	0	0	3	1-0	0	3	.133	.167	.133	-8	-2	0-0	1.000	1	109	283	/O-5(RF)	-0.2
Total	3	53	121	7	25	4	0	5	19	15-0	1	21	.207	.293	.364	92	-1	0-0	1.000	1	104	146	/O-35(19-0-17)	-0.1

Year	Tm Lg	G	AB	R	H	2B	3B	HR	RBI	BB-IB	HP	SO	AVG	OBP	SLG	AOPS	ABR	SB-CS	FA	FR	Rng	Thr	G at Pos	BFW
WEEKS, RICKIE Rickie Darnell B 9.13.1982 Altamonte Springs, FL BR/TR 6/195# d9.15																								
2003	Mil N	7	12	1	2	1	0	0	0	1-0	1	6	.167	.286	.250	42	-1	0-0	.667	-4	15	0	/2-4	-0.5
WEHNER, JOHN John Paul B 6.29.1967 Pittsburgh, PA BR/TR 6-3/205# d7.17 OF Total (69-LF 29-CF 54-RF)																								
1991	Pit N	37	106	15	36	7	0	0	7	7-0	0	17	.340	.381	.406	123	3	3-0	.936	5	118	223	3-36	1.0
1992	†Pit N	55	123	11	22	6	0	0	4	12-2	0	22	.179	.252	.228	37	-10	3-0	.961	2	130	223	3-34,1-13/2-5	-0.9
1993	Pit N	29	35	3	5	0	0	0	0	6-1	0	10	.143	.268	.143	14	-4	0-0	1.000	2	121	294	O-13(4-8-2)/2-3,3-3	-0.2
1994	Pit N	2	4	1	1	1	0	0	3	0-0	0	1	.250	.250	.500	88	0	0-0	1.000	0	122	0	/3	0.0
1995	Pit N	52	107	13	33	0	3	0	5	10-1	0	17	.308	.361	.364	92	-1	3-1	1.000	0	104	137	O-23(18-2-3),3-19/CS	-0.1
1996	Pit N	86	139	19	36	9	1	2	13	8-1	0	22	.259	.299	.381	76	-5	1-5	.971	-1	100	113	O-29(9-13-8),3-24,2-12/C	-0.7
1997	†Fla N	44	36	8	10	2	0	0	2	2-0	1	5	.278	.333	.333	79	-1	1-0	1.000	-1	78	0	O-27(10-1-19)/3-6	-0.2
1998	Fla N	53	88	10	20	2	0	0	5	7-0	0	12	.227	.281	.250	44	-7	1-0	1.000	1	93	214	O-23(12-2-11)/3-8	-0.7
1999	Pit N	39	65	6	12	2	0	1	4	7-0	0	12	.185	.264	.262	34	-7	1-0	.958	-1	100	0	O-17(12-2-6)/3-2,S-2,2	-0.7
2000	Pit N	21	50	10	15	3	0	1	9	4-0	0	6	.300	.352	.420	95	0	0-0	.973	1	100	0	3-16/O(LF)	0.0
2001	Pit N	43	51	3	10	1	0	0	2	10-0	0	12	.196	.328	.216	44	-4	2-1	1.000	-0	37	52	1-11/O-8(3-1-5),3-6,C2	-0.4
Total	11	461	804	99	200	33	4	4	54	73-5	1	136	.249	.311	.315	68	-36	15-7	.964	8	112	154	3-155,O-141L/1-24,2-22,S-3,C-3	-2.9
WEIGEL, RALPH Ralph Richard "Wig" B 10.2.1921 Coldwater, OH D 4.15.1992 Memphis, TN BR/TR 6-1/180# d9.18																								
1946	Cle A	6	12	0	2	0	0	0	0	0	0	2	.167	.167	.167	-7	-2	1-0	1.000	-1	*90*	*0*	/C-6	-0.2
1948	Chi A	66	163	8	38	7	3	0	26	13	1	18	.233	.294	.313	64	-9	1-2	.969	-4	*78*	*105*	C-39/O-2(LF)	-1.2
1949	Was A	34	60	4	14	2	0	0	4	8	0	6	.233	.324	.267	58	-3	0-1	.985	-1	*89*	*137*	C-21	-0.3
Total	3	106	235	12	54	9	3	0	30	21	1	26	.230	.296	.294	59	-14	2-3	.976	-6	*82*	*108*	/C-66,O-2(LF)	-1.7
WEIHE, PODGE John Garibaldi B 11.13.1862 Cincinnati, OH D 4.15.1914 Cincinnati, OH BR/TR 5-11/175# d8.6																								
1883	Cin AA	1	4	1	1	0	0	0		0			.250	.250	.250	58	0		1.000	0	0	0	/O(CF)	0.0
1884	Ind AA	63	256	29	65	13	2	4		9	0		.254	.279	.367	112	4		.860	-0	124	105	O-58(1-23-35)/2-4,1-3	0.2
Total	2	64	260	30	66	13	2	4		9	0		.254	.279	.365	111	4		.864	-0	121	102	/O-59(1-24-35),2-4,1-3	0.2
WEINGARTNER, ELMER Elmer William "Dutch" B 8.13.1918 Cleveland, OH BR/TR 5-11/178# d4.19																								
1945	Cle A	20	39	5	9	1	0	0	1	4	0	11	.231	.302	.256	66	-2	0-0	.871	-3	81	90	S-20	-0.4
WEINTRAUB, PHIL Philip "Mickey" B 10.12.1907 Chicago, IL D 6.21.1987 Palm Springs, CA BL/TL 6-1/195# d9.5																								
1933	NY N	8	15	3	3	0	0	1	1	3	0	2	.200	.333	.400	110	0	0	.667	-1	58	0	/O-6(RF)	-0.1
1934	NY N	31	74	13	26	2	0	0	15	15	0	10	.351	.461	.378	130	5	0	.944	-3	82	0	O-20(12-9-0)	0.1
1935	NY N	64	112	18	27	3	3	1	6	17	0	13	.241	.341	.348	87	-2	0	.975	-0	107	79	1-19/O-7(1-0-6)	-0.4
1937	Cin N	49	177	27	48	10	4	3	20	19	1	25	.271	.345	.424	113	3	1	.976	-2	90	89	O-47(41-0-6)	-0.1
	NY N	6	9	3	3	2	0	0	1	1	0	1	.333	.400	.556	155	1	0	1.000	-0	51	0	/O(LF)	0.0
	Year	55	186	30	51	12	4	3	21	20	1	26	.274	.348	.430	115	4	1	.976	-2	89	87	O-48(42-0-6)	-0.1
1938	Phi N	100	351	51	109	23	2	4	45	64	4	43	.311	.422	.422	137	23	1	.988	3	112	73	1-98	1.6
1944	NY N	104	361	55	114	18	9	13	77	59	0	59	.316	.412	.524	162	31	0	.992	3	109	88	1-99	3.0
1945	NY N	82	283	45	77	9	1	10	42	54	0	29	.272	.389	.417	122	10	2	.993	2	107	84	1-77	0.8
Total	7	444	1382	215	407	67	19	32	207	232	5	182	.295	.398	.440	133	71	4	.990	2	109	81	1-293/O-81(55-9-18)	4.9
WEIS, AL Albert John B 4.2.1938 Franklin Square, NY BB/TR (BR 1969-71) 6/170# d9.15																								
1962	Chi A	7	12	2	1	0	0	0	0	2-0	1	3	.083	.267	.083	-1	-2	1-0	.882	-1	126	0	/S-4,23	-0.2
1963	Chi A	99	210	41	57	9	0	0	18	18-1	2	37	.271	.333	.314	85	-4	15-1	.990	6	110	139	2-48,S-27/3	1.1
1964	Chi A	133	328	36	81	4	4	2	23	22-0	3	41	.247	.299	.302	70	-14	22-7	.966	7	112	**135**	*2-116/S-9,O-2(CF)	0.3
1965	Chi A	103	135	29	40	4	3	1	12	12-1	2	22	.296	.360	.393	122	4	4-1	.975	15	126	128	2-74/S-7,3-2,O-2(CF)	2.4
1966	Chi A	129	187	20	29	4	1	0	9	17-3	2	50	.155	.233	.187	24	-19	3-5	.987	22	129	153	2-96,S-18	0.8
1967	Chi A	50	53	9	13	2	0	0	4	1-0	1	7	.245	.273	.283	67	-2	3-3	.986	-2	113	23	2-32,S-13	-0.3
1968	NY N	90	274	15	47	6	0	1	14	21-3	2	63	.172	.234	.204	33	-22	3-1	.958	2	99	94	S-59,2-29/3-2	-1.6
1969	†NY N	103	247	20	53	9	2	2	23	15-1	0	51	.215	.259	.291	53	-16	3-3	.960	-2	93	117	S-52,2-43/3	-1.2
1970	NY N	75	121	20	25	7	1	1	11	7-1	1	21	.207	.254	.306	50	-9	1-1	.952	-12	73	58	2-44,S-15	-1.8
1971	NY N	11	11	3	0	0	0	0	1	2-1	0	4	.000	.143	.000	-54	-2	0-0	1.000	-0	53	81	/2-5,3-2	-0.2
Total	10	800	1578	195	346	45	11	7	115	117-11	14	299	.219	.278	.275	59	-86	55-22	.975	35	111	123	2-488,S-204/3-9,O-4(CF)	-0.7
WEIS, BUTCH Arthur John B 3.2.1901 St.Louis, MO D 5.4.1997 St.Louis, MO BL/TL 5-11/180# d4.15																								
1922	Chi N	2	2	2	1	0	0	0	0	0	0	0	.500	.500	.500	156	0	0-0	—	0			H	0.0
1923	Chi N	22	26	2	6	1	0	0	2	5	0	8	.231	.355	.269	67	-1	0-1	1.000	-0	110	0	/O-6(4-0-2)	-0.2
1924	Chi N	37	133	19	37	8	1	0	23	15	1	14	.278	.356	.353	90	-1	4-5	.978	4	102	178	O-36(14-0-22)	-0.2
1925	Chi N	67	180	16	48	5	3	2	25	23	0	22	.267	.350	.361	81	-5	2-4	.964	-3	88	76	O-47(45-0-2)	-1.1
Total	4	128	341	39	92	14	4	2	50	43	1	44	.270	.353	.352	84	-7	6-10	.973	0	96	120	/O-89(63-0-26)	-1.5
WEISER, BUD Harry Budson B 1.8.1891 Shamokin, PA D 7.31.1961 Shamokin, PA BR/TR 5-11/165# d4.29																								
1915	Phi N	37	64	6	9	2	0	0	8	7	1	12	.141	.236	.172	24	-6	2-2	.897	-3	83	0	O-20(4-16-0)	-1.1
1916	Phi N	4	10	1	3	1	0	0	1	0	0	3	.300	.300	.400	110	0	0	1.000	-0	110	0	/O-4(LF)	0.0
Total	2	41	74	7	12	3	0	0	9	7	1	15	.162	.244	.203	36	-6	2-2	.912	-3	87	0	/O-24(8-16-0)	-1.1
WEISS, GARY Gary Lee B 12.27.1955 Brenham, TX BB/TR (BR 1980) 5-10/170# d9.13																								
1980	LA N	8	0	2	0	0	0	0	0	0-0	0	0	—	—	—	—	0	0-0	—	0			/R	0.0
1981	LA N	14	19	2	2	0	0	0	1	1-0	0	4	.105	.143	.105	-28	-3	0-0	.920	-4	49	209	S-13	-0.7
Total	2	22	19	4	2	0	0	0	1	1-0	0	4	.105	.143	.105	-28	-3	0-0	.920	-4	49	209	/S-13	-0.7
WEISS, JOE Joseph Harold B 1.27.1894 Chicago, IL D 7.7.1967 Cedar Rapids, IA BR/TR 6/165# d8.29																								
1915	Chi F	29	85	6	19	1	2	0	11	3	0	24	.224	.250	.282	53	-7	0	.992	-1	75	58	1-29	-1.0
WEISS, WALT Walter William B 11.28.1963 Tuxedo, NY BB/TR 6/175# d7.12																								
1987	Oak A	16	26	3	12	4	0	0	1	2-0	0	2	.462	.500	.615	208	4	1-2	.974	1	125	81	S-11/D-2	0.6
1988	†Oak A	147	452	44	113	17	3	3	39	35-1	9	56	.250	.312	.321	82	-11	4-4	.979	10	104	95	*S-147	0.9
1989	†Oak A	84	236	30	55	11	0	3	21	21-0	1	39	.233	.298	.318	76	-7	6-1	.953	-14	87	99	S-84	-1.5
1990	†Oak A	138	445	50	118	17	1	2	35	46-5	4	53	.265	.337	.321	89	-5	9-3	.979	-15	98	101	*S-137	-0.9
1991	Oak A	40	133	15	30	6	1	0	13	12-0	0	14	.226	.286	.286	63	-7	6-0	.970	-3	92	86	S-40	-0.6
1992	†Oak A	103	316	36	67	5	2	0	21	43-1	1	39	.212	.305	.241	59	-17	6-3	.956	-13	94	89	*S-103	-2.2
1993	Fla N	158	500	50	133	14	2	1	39	79-13	3	73	.266	.367	.308	79	-11	7-3	.977	-18	91	86	*S-153	-1.6
1994	Col N	110	423	58	106	11	4	1	32	56-0	0	58	.251	.336	.303	59	-24	12-7	.973	7	105	94	*S-110	-0.8
1995	†Col N	137	427	65	111	17	3	1	25	98-8	5	57	.260	.403	.321	73	-12	15-3	.974	14	107	**119**	*S-136	1.4
1996	Col N	155	517	89	146	20	2	8	48	80-5	6	78	.282	.381	.375	82	-11	10-2	.957	-2	104	87	*S-155	0.0
1997	Col N	121	393	52	106	23	5	4	38	66-3	2	56	.270	.377	.384	81	-8	5-2	.983	19	**117**	**118**	*S-119	1.9
1998	†Atl N★	96	347	64	97	18	2	0	27	59-0	3	53	.280	.386	.343	94	1	7-1	.967	-1	96	130	S-96	0.8
1999	†Atl N	110	279	38	63	13	4	2	29	35-1	3	48	.226	.315	.323	63	-16	7-3	.963	-10	90	95	*S-102	-1.8
2000	†Atl N	80	192	29	50	6	2	0	18	26-1	3	32	.260	.353	.313	71	-8	1-1	.949	7	113	110	S-69	0.4
Total	14	1495	4686	623	1207	182	31	25	386	658-38	40	658	.258	.351	.326	77	-132	96-35	.970	-16	101	100	*S-1462/D-2	-3.4
WELAJ, JOHNNY John Ludwig B 5.27.1914 Moss Creek, PA D 9.13.2003 Arlington, TX BR/TR 6/164# d5.2 Mil 1943-45																								
1939	Was A	63	201	23	55	11	2	1	33	13	0	20	.274	.318	.363	80	-7	13-2	.975	0	106	55	O-55(13-17-26)	-0.6
1940	Was A	88	215	31	55	9	0	3	21	19	2	20	.256	.322	.340	77	-7	8-7	.978	1	111	28	O-53(15-35-3)	-0.9
1941	Was A	49	96	16	20	4	0	0	5	6	0	16	.208	.255	.250	36	-9	3-1	.979	0	120	0	O-19(13-3-3)	-0.9
1943	Phi A	93	281	45	68	16	1	0	15	15	0	17	.242	.280	.306	72	-11	12-5	.960	0	110	54	O-72(15-27-32)	-1.4
Total	4	293	793	115	198	40	3	4	74	53	2	73	.250	.298	.323	71	-34	36-15	.970	1	110	42	O-199(56-82-64)	-3.8
WELCH, CURT Curtis Benton B 2.10.1862 Williamsport, OH D 8.29.1896 E.Liverpool, OH BR/TR 5-10/175# d5.1 OF Total (17-LF 1059-CF)																								
1884	Tol AA	**109**	425	61	95	24	5	0		10	4		.224	.248	.304	76	-11		.888	14	119	97	*O-107(1-106-0)/2-2,C-2,1	0.0
1885	†StL AA	**112**	432	84	117	18	8	3	69	23	7		.271	.318	.370	112	5		**.946**	12	130	159	*O-112(CF)	1.2
1886	†StL AA	138	563	114	158	31	13	2	95	29	14		.281	.332	.393	121	12	59	**.952**	10	83	109	*O-138(CF)/2-2	1.5
1887	†StL AA	131	544	98	151	32	7	3	108	25	11		.278	.322	.379	86	-13	89	.941	12	140	172	*O-123(CF)/2-8,1	-0.4
1888	Phi AA	**136**	549	125	155	22	8	1	61	33	**29**		.282	.355	.357	129	20	95	.952	1	104	135	*O-135(CF)/2-3	1.5
1889	Phi AA	125	516	134	140	**39**	6	0	39	67	19	30	.271	.375	.370	114	15	66	.923	5	124	183	*O-125(CF)	1.3

Year	Tm Lg	G	AB	R	H	2B	3B	HR	RBI	BB-IB	HP	SO	AVG	OBP	SLG	AOPS	ABR	SB-CS	FA	FR	Rng	Thr	G at Pos	BFW
1890	Phi AA	103	396	100	106	21	4	2	40	49	32		.268	.392	.356	121	16	64	.919	11	134	149	*O-103(CF)/P	2.0
	Bal AA	19	68	16	9	4	0	0	5	9	2		.132	.253	.191	30	-6	8	.974	1	97	149	O-17(CF)/1-2	-0.5
	Year	122	464	116	115	25	4	2	45	58	**34**		.248	.372	.332	107	9	72	.926	12	129	149	*O-120(CF)/1-2,P	1.5
1891	Bal AA	132	514	122	138	22	10	3	55	77	**36**	42	.268	.400	.368	119	18	50	.946	13	111	97	*O-113(1-112-0),2-21/S-2	2.4
1892	Bal N	63	237	42	56	1	3	1	22	36	11	9	.236	.363	.278	92	0	14	.905	-5	41	41	O-63(CF)	-0.8
	Cin N	25	94	14	19	0	2	1	7	7	6	8	.202	.299	.277	75	-3	7	.925	-2	46	112	O-25(1-25-0)	-0.6
	Year	88	331	56	75	1	5	2	29	43	17	17	.227	.345	.278	88	-3	21	.911	-7	43	63	O-88(1-88-0)	-1.4
1893	Lou N	14	47	5	8	1	0	0	2	16	2	4	.170	.400	.191	64	0	1	.912	0	84	0	O-14(LF)	-0.1
Total	10	1107	4385	915	1152	215	66	16	503	381	173	93	.263	.345	.353	107	53	453	.933	73	110	130	*O-1075C/2-36,1-4,S-2,C-2,P	7.5
WELCH, FRANK Frank Tiguer "Bugger" B 8.10.1897 Birmingham, AL D 7.25.1957 Birmingham, AL BR/TR 5-9/175# d9.9																								
1919	Phi A	15	54	5	9	1	1	2	7	7	0	10	.167	.262	.333	66	-3	0	.909	-0	103	95	O-15(CF)	-0.5
1920	Phi A	100	360	43	93	17	5	4	40	26	2	41	.258	.312	.367	78	-12	2-9	.937	-5	89	117	O-97(0-84-16)	-2.6
1921	Phi A	115	403	48	115	18	6	7	45	34	4	43	.285	.347	.412	92	-5	6-0	.943	-2	95	116	*O-104(3-93-8)	-1.1
1922	Phi A	114	375	43	97	17	3	11	49	40	3	40	.259	.335	.408	90	-6	3-4	.949	1	104	109	*O-104(4-6-94)	-1.3
1923	Phi A	125	421	56	125	19	9	4	55	48	4	40	.297	.374	.413	106	4	1-4	.967	6	**116**	88	*O-117(RF)	-0.1
1924	Phi A	94	293	47	85	13	2	5	31	35	3	27	.290	.372	.399	98	0	2-3	.985	1	88	147	O-74(0-2-72)	-0.6
1925	Phi A	85	202	40	56	5	4	4	41	29	2	14	.277	.373	.401	90	-3	2-1	.968	-2	86	110	O-57(RF)	-0.8
1926	Phi A	75	174	26	49	8	1	4	23	26	2	9	.282	.381	.408	100	1	2-5	.975	-1	92	96	O-49(28-3-20)	-0.5
1927	Bos A	15	28	2	5	2	0	0	4	5	0	1	.179	.303	.250	46	-2	0-2	1.000	2	80	466	/O-6(RF)	-0.1
Total	9	738	2310	310	634	100	31	41	295	250	20	225	.274	.350	.398	92	-26	18-28	.955	-2	98	115	O-623(35-203-390)	-7.6
WELCH, HERB Herbert M. "Dutch" B 10.19.1898 RoEllen, TN D 4.13.1967 Memphis, TN BL/TR 5-6/154# d9.15																								
1925	Bos A	13	38	2	11	0	1	0	2	0	0	6	.289	.289	.342	60	-3	0-0	.893	3	124	125	S-13	0.1
WELCH, TUB James T. B 7.3.1866 St.Louis, MO TR 5-11/230# d6.12																								
1890	Tol AA	35	108	15	31	3	1	1	14	8	4		.287	.358	.361	109	1	7	.930	1	*114*	*116*	C-25,1-10	0.3
1895	Lou N	47	153	18	37	4	1	1	8	13	2	7	.242	.310	.301	62	-9	2	.888	-3	*91*	*106*	C-28,1-20	-0.8
Total	2	82	261	33	68	7	2	2	22	21	6	7	.261	.330	.326	81	-8	9	.911	-2	*102*	*111*	/C-53,1-30	-0.5
WELCH, MILT Milton Edward B 7.26.1924 Farmersville, IL BR/TR 5-10/175# d6.5																								
1945	Det A	1	2	0	0	0	0	0	0	0	0	1	.000	.000	.000	-94	0	0-0	1.000	0	*0*	*0*	/C	0.0
WELCHONCE, HARRY Harry Monroe "Welch" B 11.20.1883 North Point, PA D 2.26.1977 Arcadia, CA BL/TR 6/170# d4.17																								
1911	Phi N	26	66	9	14	4	0	0	6	7	0	8	.212	.288	.273	56	-4	0	.929	-2	91	49	O-17(1-6-11)	-0.6
WELDAY, MIKE Lyndon Earl B 12.19.1879 Conway, IA D 5.28.1942 Leavenworth, KS BL/TL d4.21																								
1907	Chi A	24	35	2	8	1	1	0	0	6	0		.229	.341	.314	113	1	0	.938	0	177	0	O-15(4-8-3)	0.0
1909	Chi A	29	74	3	14	0	0	0	5	4	0		.189	.231	.189	34	-6	2	.886	-0	148	182	O-20(7-10-3)	-0.8
Total	2	53	109	5	22	1	1	0	5	10	0		.202	.269	.229	60	-5	2	.900	-0	157	128	/O-35(11-18-6)	-0.8
WELF, OLLIE Oliver Henry B 1.17.1889 Cleveland, OH D 6.15.1967 Cleveland, OH BR/TL 5-9/160# d8.30																								
1916	Cle A	1	0	0	0	0	0	0	0	0	0	0	—	—	—	—	0	0	—	0			R	0.0
WELLMAN, BRAD Brad Eugene B 8.17.1959 Lodi, CA BR/TR 6/170# d9.4																								
1982	SF N	6	4	1	1	0	0	0	0	0-0	0	1	.250	.250	.250	40	0	0-0	1.000	-1	48	0	/2-2	-0.1
1983	SF N	82	182	15	39	3	0	1	16	22-1	0	39	.214	.296	.247	55	-11	5-3	.965	-8	99	74	2-74/S-2	-1.6
1984	SF N	93	265	23	60	9	1	2	25	19-0	0	41	.226	.274	.291	62	-14	10-5	.977	6	109	71	2-54,S-34/3-9	-0.3
1985	SF N	71	174	16	41	11	1	0	16	4-1	4	33	.236	.268	.310	65	-9	5-2	.983	-7	79	63	2-36,3-25/S-3	-1.5
1986	SF N	12	13	0	2	0	0	0	1	1-0	0	2	.154	.214	.154	3	-2	0-0	1.000	-0	87	0	/S-8,23	-0.2
1987	LA N	3	4	1	1	0	0	0	1	0-0	0	1	.250	.250	.250	34	0	0-0	1.000	1	296	0	/2S3	0.0
1988	KC A	71	107	11	29	3	0	1	6	6-0	2	23	.271	.322	.327	81	-3	1-2	.972	2	111	118	2-46,S-15/3-4,D-3	0.0
1989	KC A	103	178	30	41	4	0	2	12	7-0	1	36	.230	.263	.287	55	-11	5-3	.995	1	107	109	2-64,S-34/3-3,D	-0.8
Total	8	441	927	97	214	30	2	6	77	59-2	7	176	.231	.280	.287	61	-50	26-15	.978	-6	102	85	2-278/S-97,3-43,D-4	-4.5
WELLMAN, BOB Robert Joseph B 7.15.1925 Norwood, OH D 12.20.1994 Villa Hills, KY BR/TR 6-4/210# d9.23																								
1948	Phi A	4	10	1	2	0	1	0	0	3	0	2	.200	.385	.400	109	0	0-0	1.000	-0	77	106	/1-2,O(RF)	0.0
1950	Phi A	11	15	1	5	0	0	1	1	0	0	3	.333	.333	.533	121	0	0-0	1.000	0	119	0	/O-2(RF)	0.0
Total	2	15	25	2	7	0	1	1	1	3	0	5	.280	.357	.480	117	0	0-0	.889	-0	110	0	/O-3(RF),1-2	0.0
WELLS, GREG Gregory De Wayne B 4.25.1954 McIntosh, AL BR/TR 6-5/218# d8.10																								
1981	Tor A	32	73	7	18	5	0	0	5	5-0	0	12	.247	.295	.315	71	-3	0-2	.994	-1	81	65	1-22/D-3	-0.6
1982	Min A	15	54	5	11	1	2	0	3	1-0	0	8	.204	.211	.296	39	-5	0-0	.962	-2	33	72	1-10/D-5	-0.8
Total	2	47	127	12	29	6	2	0	8	6-0	0	20	.228	.259	.307	58	-8	0-2	.983	-3	64	68	/1-32,D-8	-1.4
WELLS, JAKE Jacob B 8.9.1863 Memphis, TN D 3.16.1927 Hendersonville, NC BR/TR 5-11/167# d8.10																								
1888	Det N	16	57	5	9	1	0	0	2	0	0	5	.158	.158	.175	6	-6	0	.917	2			C-16	-0.3
1890	StL AA	30	105	17	25	3	0	0	12	10	5		.238	.333	.267	67	-4	1	.941	2	*99*	*102*	C-28/O-3(LF)	0.0
Total	2	46	162	22	34	4	0	0	14	10	5	5	.210	.277	.235	50	-10	1	.932	3	*62*	*64*	/C-44,O-3(LF)	-0.3
WELLS, LEO Leo Donald B 7.18.1917 Kansas City, KS BR/TR 5-9/170# d4.16 Mil 1943-45																								
1942	Chi A	35	62	8	12	2	0	1	4	4	0	5	.194	.242	.274	46	-5	1-0	1.000	7	149	157	S-12/3-6	0.3
1946	Chi A	45	127	11	24	4	1	1	11	12	0	34	.189	.259	.260	47	-9	3-4	.942	4	117	91	3-38/S-2	-0.7
Total	2	80	189	19	36	6	1	2	15	16	0	39	.190	.254	.265	47	-14	4-4	.938	11	119	104	/3-44,S-14	-0.4
WELLS, VERNON Vernon M. B 12.8.1978 Shreveport, LA BR/TR 6-1/195# d8.30																								
1999	Tor A	24	88	8	23	5	0	1	8	4-0	0	18	.261	.293	.352	63	-5	1-1	1.000	0	84	272	O-24(CF)	-0.4
2000	Tor A	3	2	0	0	0	0	0	0	0-0	0	0	.000	.000	.000	-97	-1	0-0	1.000	-0	96	0	/O-3(CF)	-0.1
2001	Tor A	30	96	14	30	8	0	1	6	5-0	1	15	.313	.350	.427	102	0	5-0	.969	-1	96	135	O-30(0-27-3)	0.1
2002	Tor A	159	608	87	167	34	4	23	100	27-0	3	85	.275	.305	.457	96	-5	9-4	.992	-3	96	120	*O-159(0-146-13)	-0.6
2003	Tor A★	161	678	118	**215**	**49**	5	33	117	42-2	7	80	.317	.359	.550	134	32	4-1	.990	-13	90	41	*O-161(CF)	2.0
Total	5	377	1472	227	435	96	9	58	231	78-2	11	198	.296	.332	.491	112	21	19-6	.990	-16	93	96	O-377(0-361-16)	1.0
WELSH, JIMMY James Daniel B 10.9.1902 Denver, CO D 10.30.1970 Oakland, CA BL/TR 6-1/174# d4.14																								
1925	Bos N	122	484	69	151	25	8	7	63	20	8	24	.312	.350	.440	110	6	7-4	.960	5	93	157	*O-116(7-1-109)/2-3	0.1
1926	Bos N	134	490	69	136	18	11	3	57	33	8	28	.278	.333	.378	100	-1	6	.965	8	105	129	*O-129(RF)	-0.3
1927	Bos N	131	497	72	143	26	7	9	54	23	8	27	.288	.330	.423	109	4	11	.969	8	101	161	*O-129(1-121-11)/1	0.6
1928	NY N	124	476	77	146	22	5	9	54	29	8	30	.307	.357	.431	104	2	4	.981	-3	98	76	*O-117(6-110-1)	-0.6
1929	NY N	38	129	25	32	7	0	2	8	9	7	3	.248	.331	.349	69	-6	3	.940	-3	65	181	O-35(30-7-0)	-1.1
	Bos N	53	186	24	54	8	7	2	16	13	4	9	.290	.350	.441	98	-1	1	.979	5	116	110	O-51(1-49-2)	0.1
	Year	91	315	49	86	15	7	4	24	22	**11**	12	.273	.342	.403	86	-8	4	.970	2	98	135	O-86(31-56-2)	-1.0
1930	Bos N	113	422	51	116	21	9	3	36	29	4	23	.275	.327	.389	75	-18	5	.980	7	113	90	*O-110(CF)	-1.4
Total	6	715	2684	387	778	127	47	35	288	156	47	144	.290	.340	.411	98	-14	37-4	.971	26	101	126	O-687(45-398-252)/2-3,1	-2.6
WENDELL, LEW Lewis Charles B 3.22.1892 New York, NY D 7.11.1953 Brooklyn, NY BR/TR 5-11/178# d6.10																								
1915	NY N	20	36	0	8	1	1	0	5	2	0	7	.222	.263	.306	76	-1	0	.920	-4	*76*	*115*	C-18	-0.5
1916	NY N	2	2	0	0	0	0	0	0	0	0	2	.000	.000	.000	-99	0	0	—	0			H	-0.1
1924	Phi N	21	32	3	8	1	0	0	2	3	0	5	.250	.314	.281	54	-2	0-0	1.000	-1	*93*	*77*	C-17	-0.2
1925	Phi N	18	26	0	2	0	0	0	3	1	0	3	.077	.111	.077	-47	-6	0-0	.909	-1	*99*	*92*	/C-9	-0.6
1926	Phi N	1	4	0	0	0	0	0	0	0	0	0	.000	.000	.000	-95	-1	0	.333	-1	*0*	*319*	/C	-0.2
Total	5	62	100	3	18	2	1	0	10	6	0	17	.180	.226	.220	23	-10	0-0	.925	-6	*84*	*104*	/C-45	-1.6
WENTZ, JACK John George (born John George Wernz) B 3.4.1863 Louisville, KY D 9.14.1907 Louisville, KY BR/TR 5-10.5/175# d4.15																								
1891	Lou AA	1	4	0	1	0	0	0	0	0	0	0	.250	.250	.250	44	0	0	.667	-1	59	0	/2	-0.1
WENTZEL, STAN Stanley Aaron B 1.13.1917 Lorane, PA D 11.28.1991 St.Lawrence, PA BR/TR 6-1/200# d9.23																								
1945	Bos N	4	19	3	4	0	1	0	6	0	0	3	.211	.211	.316	45	-2	1	1.000	-1	80	0	/O-4(CF)	-0.2

Year	Tm Lg	G	AB	R	H	2B	3B	HR	RBI	BB-IB	HP	SO	AVG	OBP	SLG	AOPS	ABR	SB-CS	FA	FR	Rng	Thr	G at Pos	BFW
WERA, JULIE Julian Valentine B 2.9.1902 Winona, MN D 12.12.1975 Rochester, MN BR/TR 5-8/164# d4.14																								
1927	NY A	38	42	7	10	3	0	1	8	1	1	5	.238	.273	.381	70	-2	0-0	1.000	0	86	0	3-19	-0.1
1929	NY A	5	12	1	5	0	0	0	2	1	0	1	.417	.462	.417	137	1	0-0	1.000	-0	114	0	/3-4	0.1
Total	2	43	54	8	15	3	0	1	10	2	1	6	.278	.316	.389	85	-1	0-0	1.000	-0	92	0	/3-23	0.0
WERBER, BILLY William Murray B 6.20.1908 Berwyn, MD BR/TR 5-10/170# d6.25																								
1930	NY A	4	14	5	4	0	0	0	2	3	0	1	.286	.412	.286	84	0	0-0	.955	0	82	133	/S-3,3	0.0
1933	NY A	3	2	0	0	0	0	0	0	0	0	0	.000	.000	.000	-99	-1	0-0	—	-0	0	0	/3	-0.1
	Bos A	108	425	64	110	30	6	3	39	33	0	39	.259	.312	.379	83	-11	15-5	.910	-14	90	90	S-71,3-38/2-2	-1.7
	Year	111	427	64	110	30	6	3	39	33	0	39	.258	.311	.377	82	-12	15-5	.910	-14	90	90	S-71,3-39/2-2	-1.8
1934	Bos A	152	623	129	200	41	10	11	67	77	1	37	.321	.397	.472	115	15	**40**-15	.941	17	**122**	97	*3-130,S-22	3.9
1935	Bos A	124	462	84	118	30	3	14	61	69	4	41	.255	.357	.424	95	-3	**29**-7	.942	14	109	118	*3-123	1.8
1936	Bos A	145	535	89	147	29	6	10	67	89	4	37	.275	.382	.407	90	-7	23-13	.935	-11	81	104	*3-101,O-45(38-0-7)/2	-1.5
1937	Phi A	128	493	85	144	31	4	7	70	74	1	39	.292	.386	.414	103	5	**35**-13	.958	4	104	99	*3-125/O-3(1-2-0)	1.5
1938	Phi A	134	499	92	129	22	7	11	69	93	2	37	.259	.377	.397	96	0	19-15	.935	4	100	82	*3-134	0.6
1939	†Cin N	147	599	**115**	173	35	5	5	57	91	6	46	.289	.388	.389	109	12	15	.933	9	104	**128**	*3-147	2.7
1940	†Cin N	143	584	105	162	35	5	12	48	68	8	40	.277	.361	.416	113	12	16	**.962**	6	107	**126**	*3-143	2.3
1941	Cin N	109	418	56	100	9	2	4	46	53	2	24	.239	.328	.299	77	-12	14	.959	10	108	**150**	*3-107	0.2
1942	NY N	98	370	51	76	9	2	1	13	51	4	22	.205	.308	.249	64	-15	9	.927	13	126	88	3-93	0.0
Total	11	1295	5024	875	1363	271	50	78	539	701	32	363	.271	.364	.392	97	-5	215-<u>68</u>	.944	50	106	111	*3-1143/S-96,O-48(39-2-7),2-3	9.7
WERDEN, PERRY Percival Wheritt B 7.21.1865 St.Louis, MO D 1.9.1934 Minneapolis, MN BR/TR 6-2/220# d4.24 ▲																								
1884	StL U	18	76	7	18	2	0	0		2			.237	.256	.263	56	-6		.893	0	113	128	P-16/O-6(4-1-1)	-0.1
1888	Was N	3	10	0	3	0	0	0	2	1	0	4	.300	.364	.300	121	0	0	.857	-0	0	0	/O-3(LF)	0.0
1890	Tol AA	128	498	113	147	22	**20**	6	72	78	13		.295	.404	.456	149	32	59	.972	5	121	93	*1-124/O-5(0-4-1)	2.3
1891	Bal AA	**139**	552	102	160	20	18	6	104	52	11	59	.290	.363	.424	124	15	46	.980	1	101	102	*1-139	0.3
1892	StL N	149	598	73	154	22	6	8	84	59	4	52	.258	.328	.355	112	9	20	.982	12	131	91	*1-149	1.9
1893	StL N	125	500	73	138	22	**29**	1	94	49	7	25	.276	.349	.442	109	3	11	.968	2	118	99	*1-124/O(RF)	0.4
1897	Lou N	133	512	76	154	21	14	5	83	41	12		.301	.366	.426	112	9	15	.984	19	**163**	94	*1-133	2.3
Total	7	695	2746	444	774	109	87	26	<u>439</u>	282	47	<u>140</u>	.282	.359	.413	119	62	151	.978	40	127	96	1-669/P-16,O-15(7-5-3)	7.1
WERHAS, JOHNNY John Charles "Peaches" B 2.7.1938 Highland Park, MI BR/TR 6-2/200# d4.14																								
1964	LA N	29	83	6	16	2	1	0	8	13-0	0	12	.193	.296	.241	59	-4	0-0	.952	0	91	100	3-28	-0.4
1965	LA N	4	3	1	0	0	0	0	0	1-0	0	2	.000	.250	.000	-24	0	0-0	1.000	-0	0	0	/1	-0.1
1967	LA N	7	7	0	1	0	0	0	0	0-0	0	3	.143	.143	.143	-20	-1	0-0	—	0			H	-0.1
	Cal A	49	75	8	12	1	1	2	6	10-0	1	22	.160	.264	.280	64	-3	0-0	.963	-0	98	0	3-30/1-4,O(LF)	-0.4
Total	3	89	168	15	29	3	2	2	14	24-0	1	39	.173	.276	.250	57	-8	0-0	.956	-0	94	62	/3-58,1-5,O(LF)	-1.0
WERNER, DON Donald Paul B 3.8.1953 Appleton, WI BR/TR 6-1/185# d9.2																								
1975	Cin N	7	8	0	1	0	0	0	0	0-0	1	0	.125	.222	.125	-2	-1	0-0	.923	-2	31	0	/C-7	-0.3
1976	Cin N	3	4	0	2	1	0	0	1	1-0	0	1	.500	.600	.750	275	1	0-0	1.000	-0	54	0	/C-3	0.1
1977	Cin N	10	23	3	4	0	0	2	4	2-1	0	3	.174	.231	.435	75	-1	0-1	1.000	0	88	68	C-10	-0.1
1978	Cin N	50	113	7	17	2	1	0	11	14-2	1	30	.150	.242	.186	23	-12	1-0	.987	-4	81	87	C-49	-1.5
1980	Cin N	24	64	2	11	2	0	0	5	7-0	1	10	.172	.260	.203	32	-6	1-0	.962	-5	64	46	C-24	-1.0
1981	Tex A	2	8	1	2	0	0	0	0	0-0	0	2	.250	.250	.250	47	-1	0-1	—	0			/D-2	-0.1
1982	Tex A	22	59	4	12	2	0	0	3	3-0	0	7	.203	.242	.237	34	-5	0-0	.980	-1	120	30	C-22	-0.6
Total	7	118	279	17	49	7	1	2	24	27-3	3	53	.176	.251	.229	36	-25	2-2	.979	-12	84	59	C-115/D-2	-3.5
WERRICK, JOE Joseph Abraham B 10.25.1861 St.Paul, MN D 5.10.1943 St.Peter, MN BR/TR 5-9/151# d9.27																								
1884	StP U	**9**	27	3	2	0	0	0		1			.074	.107	.074	-81	-7		.756	1	112	0	/S-9	-0.5
1886	Lou AA	136	561	75	140	20	14	3	62	33	2		.250	.294	.351	96	-6	19	.853	-2	94	47	*3-136	-0.5
1887	Lou AA	136	533	90	152	21	13	7	99	38	3		.285	.336	.413	106	2	49	.831	-2	103	61	*3-136	0.2
1888	Lou AA	111	413	49	89	12	7	0	51	30	3		.215	.274	.278	79	-10	15	.811	-15	92	69	3-89,S-11/2-8,O-3(LF)	-2.1
Total	4	392	1534	217	383	53	34	10	<u>212</u>	102	8		.250	.300	.348	94	-21	83	.834	-18	97	58	3-361/S-20,2-8,O-3(LF)	-2.9
WERT, DON Donald Ralph B 7.29.1938 Strasburg, PA BR/TR 5-9/165# d5.11																								
1963	Det A	78	251	31	65	6	2	7	25	24-2	2	51	.259	.326	.382	95	-2	3-3	.957	5	110	75	3-47,2-21/S-8	0.5
1964	Det A	148	525	63	135	18	5	9	55	50-5	6	74	.257	.325	.362	91	-6	3-4	.965	2	101	121	*3-142/S-4	-0.5
1965	Det A	**162**	609	81	159	22	2	12	54	73-4	3	71	.261	.341	.363	100	1	5-6	**.976**	4	96	106	*3-161/S-3,2	0.4
1966	Det A	150	559	56	150	20	2	11	70	64-3	2	69	.268	.342	.370	103	4	6-3	.972	-17	84	76	*3-150	-1.4
1967	Det A	142	534	60	137	23	2	6	40	44-2	7	59	.257	.320	.341	93	-4	1-1	.978	2	98	100	*3-140/S	-0.2
1968	†Det A★	150	536	44	107	15	1	12	37	37-7	5	79	.200	.258	.299	66	-23	0-3	.966	-6	92	90	*3-150/S-2	-3.5
1969	Det A	132	423	46	95	11	1	14	50	49-6	1	60	.225	.303	.355	81	-11	3-1	.966	1	97	81	*3-129	-1.1
1970	Det A	128	363	34	79	13	0	6	33	44-7	4	56	.218	.307	.303	69	-15	1-3	.953	-11	83	88	*3-117/2-2	-2.8
1971	Was A	20	40	2	2	1	0	0	2	4-1	1	10	.050	.156	.075	-35	-7	0-0	1.000	-4	92	30	/S-7,3-7,2	-1.1
Total	9	1110	3840	417	929	129	15	77	366	389-37	31	529	.242	.314	.343	87	-63	22-24	.968	-23	94	94	*3-1043/S-25,2-25	-9.7
WERTH, DENNIS Dennis Dean B 12.29.1952 Lincoln, IL BR/TR 6-1/200# d9.17 s-Jayson																								
1979	NY A	3	4	1	1	0	0	0	0	0-0	0	0	.250	.250	.250	36	0	0-0	1.000	0	329	0	/1	0.0
1980	NY A	39	65	15	20	3	0	3	12	12-0	0	19	.308	.416	.492	150	5	0-1	1.000	-1	63	126	1-12/O-8(3-0-5),C3D	0.3
1981	NY A	34	55	7	6	1	0	0	1	12-2	0	12	.109	.269	.127	18	-5	1-0	1.000	2	145	86	1-19/O-8(4-0-4),C-3,D-4	-0.5
1982	KC A	41	15	5	2	0	0	0	2	4-0	0	2	.133	.316	.133	29	-1	0-0	.990	1	169	135	1-35/C-2	-0.1
Total	4	117	139	28	29	4	0	3	15	28-2	0	33	.209	.341	.302	82	-1	1-1	.996	2	132	112	/1-67,O-16(7-0-9),D-12,C-6,3	-0.3
WERTH, JAYSON Jayson Richard B 5.20.1979 Springfield, IL BR/TR 6-5/215# d9.1 f-Dennis gf-John																								
2002	Tor A	15	46	4	12	2	1	0	6	6-0	0	11	.261	.340	.348	82	-1	1-0	1.000	1	117	118	O-15(4-1-10)	0.0
2003	Tor A	26	48	7	10	4	0	2	10	3-0	0	22	.208	.255	.417	72	-2	1-0	1.000	1	108	144	O-20(0-1-19)/D-3	-0.2
Total	2	41	94	11	22	6	1	2	16	9-0	0	33	.234	.298	.383	77	-3	2-0	1.000	2	113	130	/O-35(4-2-29),D-3	-0.2
WERTZ, DEL Dwight Lyman Moody B 10.11.1888 Canton, OH D 5.26.1958 Sarasota, FL BR/TR 5-10/160# d5.23																								
1914	Buf F	3	0	1	0	0	0	0	0	0	0	0	—	—	—	—	0	0	1.000	-0	0	0	/S	0.0
WERTZ, VIC Victor Woodrow B 2.9.1925 York, PA D 7.7.1983 Detroit, MI BL/TR 6/186# d4.15																								
1947	Det A	102	333	60	96	22	4	6	44	47	0	66	.288	.376	.432	121	11	2-0	.965	-2	95	106	O-83(38-2-43)	0.5
1948	Det A	119	391	49	97	19	9	7	67	48	3	70	.248	.335	.396	92	-6	0-0	.954	1	96	158	O-98(64-1-36)	-1.0
1949	Det A★	**155**	608	96	185	26	6	20	133	80	0	61	.304	.385	.465	124	20	2-3	.981	-2	98	95	*O-155(RF)	1.3
1950	Det A	149	559	99	172	37	4	27	123	91	4	55	.308	.408	.533	135	31	0-1	.967	-11	95	39	*O-145(RF)	1.4
1951	Det A★	138	501	86	143	24	4	27	94	78	1	61	.285	.383	.511	139	28	0-3	.989	0	103	79	*O-131(RF)	2.2
1952	Det A☆	85	285	46	70	15	3	17	51	46	1	44	.246	.352	.498	134	13	1-0	.986	2	103	136	O-79(RF)	1.3
	StL A	37	130	22	45	5	0	6	19	23	0	20	.346	.444	.523	164	12	0-0	.955	-3	103	0	O-36(RF)	0.9
	Year	122	415	68	115	20	3	23	70	69	1	64	.277	.381	.506	143	25	1-0	.976	-0	103	93	*O-115(RF)	2.2
1953	StL A	128	440	61	118	18	6	19	70	72	4	44	.268	.376	.466	124	16	1-4	.974	4	103	134	*O-121(0-1-120)	1.4
1954	Bal A	29	94	5	19	1	0	1	13	11	0	17	.202	.283	.245	50	-7	0-0	.963	3	103	277	O-27(RF)	-0.5
	†Cle A	94	295	33	81	14	2	14	48	34	0	40	.275	.344	.478	123	8	0-2	.989	1	109	108	1-83/O-5(2-0-3)	0.5
	Year	123	389	38	100	15	2	15	61	45	0	57	.257	.330	.422	106	2	0-2	.989	4	109	108	1-83,O-32(2-0-30)	0.0
1955	Cle A	74	257	30	65	11	2	14	55	32-3	1	33	.253	.332	.475	112	4	0-0	.984	-2	86	100	1-63/O-9(1-0-8)	-0.2
1956	Cle A	136	481	65	127	22	0	32	106	75-10	5	87	.264	.364	.509	127	19	0-0	.991	1	98	95	*1-133	1.2
1957	Cle A★	144	515	84	145	21	0	28	105	78-6	2	88	.282	.371	.485	136	27	2-3	.988	-1	98	89	*1-139	1.8
1958	Cle A	25	43	5	12	1	0	3	12	5-0	0	7	.279	.354	.512	139	2	0-0	.980	0	131	82	/1-8	0.2
1959	Bos A	94	247	38	68	13	0	7	49	22-5	2	32	.275	.337	.413	101	1	0-0	.992	2	116	94	1-64	0.0
1960	Bos A	131	443	45	125	22	0	19	103	37-4	1	54	.282	.335	.460	110	6	0-2	.987	3	109	86	*1-117	0.1
1961	Bos A	99	317	33	83	16	2	11	60	38-3	2	43	.262	.339	.429	103	2	0-0	.991	3	110	89	1-86	-0.1
	Det A	8	6	0	1	0	0	0	1	0-0	0	1	.167	.167	.167	-10	-1	0-0	—	0			H	-0.1
	Year	107	323	33	84	16	2	11	61	38-3	2	44	.260	.336	.424	101	1	0-0	.991	3	110	89	1-86	-0.2
1962	Det A	74	105	7	34	2	0	5	18	5-0	1	13	.324	.357	.486	121	3	0-0	.988	0	112	54	1-16	0.2
1963	Det A	6	5	0	0	0	0	0	0	0-0	0	1	.000	.000	.000	-97	-1	0-0	—	0			H	-0.1

Year	Tm Lg	G	AB	R	H	2B	3B	HR	RBI	BB-IB	HP	SO	AVG	OBP	SLG	AOPS	ABR	SB-CS	FA	FR	Rng	Thr	G at Pos	BFW
	Min A	35	44	3	6	0	0	3	7	6-2	0	5	.136	.240	.341	59	-3	0-0	1.000	1	148	53	/1-6	-0.2
	Year	41	49	3	6	0	0	3	7	6-2	0	6	.122	.218	.306	44	-4	0-0	1.000	1	148	53	/1-6	-0.3
Total	17	1862	6099	867	1692	289	42	266	1178	828-33	27	842	.277	.364	.469	121	185	9-19	.973	2	99	102	O-889(105-4-783),1-715	10.8
WESSINGER, JIM James Michael B 9.25.1955 Utica, NY BR/TR 5-10/165# d8.4																								
1979	Atl N	10	7	2	0	0	0	0	0	1-0	0	4	.000	.125	.000	-59	-2	0-0	.833	-1	66	0	/2-2	-0.3
WESSON, BARRY Barry Jarvis B 4.6.1977 Tupelo, MS BR/TR 6-2/195# d7.15																								
2002	Hou N	15	20	1	4	0	1	0	1	1-0	0	5	.200	.238	.300	41	-2	0-0	1.000	-1	81	0	O-15(3-9-3)	-0.3
2003	Ana A	10	11	2	2	0	0	1	3	0-0	0	4	.182	.182	.455	62	-1	1-0	1.000	0	130	0	/O-9(5-0-4),D	0.0
Total	2	25	31	3	6	0	1	1	4	1-0	0	9	.194	.219	.355	48	-3	1-0	1.000	-1	98	0	/O-24(8-9-7),D	-0.3
WEST, MAX Max Edward B 11.28.1916 Dexter, MO D 12.31.03 Sierra Madre, CA BL/TR 6-1.5/182# d4.19 Mil 1943-45																								
1938	Bos N	123	418	47	98	16	5	10	63	38	1	38	.234	.300	.368	92	-6	5	.986	-4	94	70	*O-109(75-0-36)/1-7	-1.7
1939	Bos N	130	449	67	128	26	6	19	82	51	5	55	.285	.364	.497	139	24	1	.974	1	104	80	*O-124(44-46-54)	1.9
1940	Bos N★	139	524	72	137	27	5	7	72	65	1	54	.261	.344	.372	103	4	2	.975	5	98	199	*O-102(4-59-49),1-36	0.1
1941	Bos N	138	484	63	134	28	4	12	68	72	2	68	.277	.373	.426	130	21	5	.981	5	101	135	*O-132(126-5-5)	2.0
1942	Bos N	134	452	54	115	22	0	16	56	68	2	59	.254	.354	.409	126	16	4	.991	-1	97	108	1-85,O-50(36-2-13)	0.6
1946	Bos N	1	1	0	0	0	0	0	0	0	0	1	.000	.000	.000	-99	0	0	1.000	-0	0	0	/1	0.0
	Cin N	72	202	16	43	13	0	5	18	32	1	36	.213	.323	.351	95	-1	1	.952	-3	86	112	O-58(54-3-1)	-0.8
	Year	73	203	16	43	13	0	5	18	32	1	37	.212	.322	.350	94	-1	1	.952	-3	86	112	O-58(54-3-1)/1	-0.8
1948	Pit N	87	146	19	26	4	0	8	21	27	1	29	.178	.310	.370	82	-4	1	.991	1	123	78	1-32,O-16(3-0-13)	-0.4
Total	7	824	2676	338	681	136	20	77	380	353	13	340	.254	.344	.407	114	54	19	.975	4	98	117	O-591(342-115-171),1-161	1.7
WEST, BUCK Milton Douglas B 8.29.1860 Spring Mill, OH D 1.13.1929 Mansfield, OH BL/TR 5-10/200# d8.24																								
1884	Cin AA	33	131	20	32	2	8	1	15	2	0		.244	.256	.405	107	0		.825	-4	19	0	O-33(CF)	-0.5
1890	Cle N	37	151	20	37	6	1	2	29	7	1	11	.245	.283	.338	82	-4	4	.831	-1	147	73	O-37(0-4-33)	-0.5
Total	2	70	282	40	69	8	9	3	44	9	1	11	.245	.271	.369	94	-4	4	.828	-5	92	42	/O-70(0-37-33)	-1.0
WEST, DICK Richard Thomas B 11.24.1915 Louisville, KY D 3.13.1996 Fort Wayne, IN BR/TR 6-2/180# d9.28 Mil 1944-45																								
1938	Cin N	1	1	0	0	0	0	0	0	0	0	0	.000	.000	.000	-99	0	0	—	0			H	0.0
1939	Cin N	8	19	1	4	0	0	0	4	1	0	4	.211	.250	.211	25	-2	0	1.000	-0	90	0	/O-5(LF),C	-0.3
1940	Cin N	7	28	4	11	2	0	1	6	0	0	2	.393	.393	.571	161	2	1	1.000	-1	*102*	*60*	/C-7	0.1
1941	Cin N	67	172	15	37	5	2	1	17	6	1	23	.215	.246	.285	49	-12	4	.970	-4	*77*	*84*	C-64	-1.4
1942	Cin N	33	79	9	14	3	0	1	8	5	0	13	.177	.226	.253	40	-6	1	.989	1	*92*	*150*	C-17/O-6(LF)	-0.4
1943	Cin N	3	0	1	0	0	0	0	0	0	0	0	—	—	—	—	0	0	—	0			R	0.0
Total	6	119	299	30	66	10	2	3	35	12	1	42	.221	.253	.298	55	-18	6	.977	-4	*82*	*97*	/C-89,O-11(LF)	-2.0
WEST, SAM Samuel Filmore B 10.5.1904 Longview, TX D 11.23.1985 Lubbock, TX BL/TL 5-11/165# d4.17 Mil 1943-45 C3																								
1927	Was A	38	67	9	16	4	1	0	6	8	0	8	.239	.320	.328	69	-3	1-0	.939	1	95	223	O-18(5-8-5)	-0.3
1928	Was A	125	378	59	114	30	7	3	40	20	1	23	.302	.338	.442	104	1	5-6	**.996**	2	97	138	*O-116(53-60-6)	-0.3
1929	Was A	142	510	60	136	16	8	3	75	45	0	41	.267	.326	.347	73	-22	10-8	.978	13	103	**178**	*O-139(4-136-0)	-1.4
1930	Was A	120	411	75	135	22	10	6	67	37	1	34	.328	.385	.474	116	10	5-5	.972	3	103	99	*O-118(1-117-0)	0.7
1931	Was A	132	526	77	175	43	13	3	91	30	0	37	.333	.369	.481	121	15	6-8	.990	14	**115**	128	*O-127(CF)	2.2
1932	Was A	146	554	88	159	27	12	6	83	48	1	57	.287	.345	.412	96	-4	4-5	.979	15	115	126	*O-143(CF)	0.6
1933	StL A★	133	517	93	155	25	12	11	48	59	1	49	.300	.373	.458	112	8	10-8	.988	5	102	157	*O-127(CF)	0.9
1934	StL A★	122	482	90	157	22	10	9	55	62	0	55	.326	.403	.469	115	11	3-5	.972	5	101	**151**	*O-120(CF)	1.1
1935	StL A☆	138	527	93	158	37	4	10	70	75	1	46	.300	.388	.442	109	9	1-6	**.989**	11	**118**	65	*O-135(CF)	1.4
1936	StL A	152	533	78	148	26	4	7	70	94	0	70	.278	.386	.381	87	-8	2-0	.983	6	110	77	*O-148(CF)	-0.4
1937	StL A★	122	457	68	150	37	4	7	58	46	0	28	.328	.390	.473	115	12	1-1	.987	9	103	169	*O-105(CF)	1.7
1938	StL A	44	165	17	51	8	2	1	27	14	0	9	.309	.363	.400	91	-2	1-0	.971	-3	102	0	O-41(CF)	-0.5
	Was A	92	344	51	104	19	5	5	47	33	0	21	.302	.363	.430	105	2	1-1	.983	-3	98	50	O-85(1-84-0)	-0.3
	Year	136	509	68	155	27	7	6	74	47	0	30	.305	.363	.420	100	0	2-1	.979	-6	99	34	*O-126(1-125-0)	-0.8
1939	Was A	115	390	52	110	20	8	3	52	67	0	29	.282	.387	.397	109	8	1-1	.992	1	104	98	O-89(23-55-11),1-17	0.4
1940	Was A	57	99	7	25	6	1	1	18	16	0	13	.253	.357	.364	93	0	0-2	.990	0	100	127	1-12/O-9(0-3-6)	-0.2
1941	Was A	26	37	3	10	0	0	0	6	11	0	2	.270	.438	.270	95	1	1-0	1.000	0	116	0	/O-8(4-1-3)	0.1
1942	Chi A	49	151	14	35	5	0	0	25	31	0	18	.232	.363	.265	80	-2	2-0	.983	-1	101	33	O-45(1-44-0)	-0.4
Total	16	1753	6148	934	1838	347	101	75	838	696	5	540	.299	.371	.425	103	36	54-56	.983	79	106	115	*O-1573(92-1454-31)/1-29	5.3
WEST, MAX Walter Maxwell B 7.14.1904 Sunset, TX D 4.25.1971 Houston, TX BR/TR 5-11/165# d9.18																								
1928	Bro N	7	21	4	6	1	1	0	1	4	0	1	.286	.400	.429	118	1	0	.882	1	78	544	/O-6(1-4-1)	0.1
1929	Bro N	5	8	1	2	1	0	0	1	1	0	0	.250	.333	.375	77	0	0	1.000	-0	68	0	/O-2(1-1-0)	-0.1
Total	2	12	29	5	8	2	1	0	2	5	0	1	.276	.382	.414	107	1	0	.895	1	76	453	/O-8(2-5-1)	0.0
WEST, BILLY William Nelson B 8.21.1840 Philadelphia, PA d5.22																								
1874	Atl NA	9	35	4	8	1	0	0	2	1		2	.229	.250	.257	71	-1	0-0	.707	-2	139	75	/2-9,CS	-0.2
1876	NY N	1	4	0	0	0	0	0	0	0		0	.000	.000	.000	-99	-1		1.000	0	118	281	/2	-0.1
WESTERBERG, OSCAR Oscar William B 7.8.1882 Alameda, CA D 4.17.1909 Alameda, CA BB/TR d9.5																								
1907	Bos N	2	6	0	2	0	0	0	1	1	0		.333	.429	.333	139	0	0	1.000	-0	72	199	/S-2	0.0
WESTLAKE, JIM James Patrick B 7.3.1930 Sacramento, CA D 1.3.2003 Sacramento, CA BL/TL 6-1/190# d4.16 b-Wally																								
1955	Phi N	1	1	0	0	0	0	0	0	0-0	0	1	.000	.000	.000	-99	0	0-0	—	0			H	0.0
WESTLAKE, WALLY Waldon Thomas B 11.8.1920 Gridley, CA BR/TR 6/186# d4.15 b-Jim																								
1947	Pit N	112	407	59	111	17	4	17	69	27	4	63	.273	.324	.459	103	0	5	.988	3	109	89	*O-109(0-12-97)	0.0
1948	Pit N	132	428	78	122	10	6	17	65	46	4	40	.285	.360	.456	117	9	2	.976	-2	98	91	*O-125(1-67-57)	0.4
1949	Pit N	147	525	77	148	24	8	23	104	45	6	69	.282	.345	.490	118	12	6	.982	3	104	103	*O-143(0-51-92)	1.0
1950	Pit N	139	477	69	136	15	6	24	95	48	7	78	.285	.359	.493	118	11	1	**.991**	1	108	40	*O-123(5-97-26)	0.8
1951	Pit N	50	181	28	51	4	0	16	45	9	2	26	.282	.323	.569	131	6	0-1	.908	5	120	136	3-34,O-11(10-1-0)	1.0
	StL N★	73	267	36	68	8	5	6	39	24	4	42	.255	.325	.390	91	-4	1-2	.982	-1	96	113	O-68(11-29-28)	-0.8
	Year	123	448	64	119	12	5	22	84	33	6	68	.266	.324	.462	107	2	1-3	.984	4	95	129	O-79(21-30-28),3-34	0.2
1952	StL N	21	74	7	16	3	0	0	10	8	0	11	.216	.293	.257	53	-4	1-1	1.000	3	122	161	O-15(CF)	-0.2
	Cin N	59	183	29	37	4	0	3	14	31	2	29	.202	.324	.273	67	-7	0-2	.992	-1	98	98	O-56(5-43-10)	-1.1
	Year	80	257	36	53	7	0	3	24	39	2	40	.206	.315	.268	63	-12	1-3	.995	2	104	115	O-71(5-58-10)	-1.3
	Cle A	29	69	11	16	4	1	1	9	8	0	16	.232	.312	.362	93	-1	1-0	1.000	2	100	245	O-28(12-4-20)	0.1
1953	Cle A	82	218	42	72	7	1	9	46	35	2	29	.330	.427	.495	153	18	2-0	.963	-2	99	59	O-72(38-12-36)	1.3
1954	†Cle A	85	240	36	63	9	2	11	42	26	2	37	.262	.337	.454	114	4	0-1	.964	-4	97	23	O-70(49-10-14)	-0.4
1955	Cle A	16	20	2	5	1	0	0	1	3-1	0	5	.250	.348	.300	73	-1	0-0	1.000	1	107	339	/O-7(4-3-0)	0.0
	Bal A	8	24	0	3	1	0	0	0	6-0	0	5	.125	.300	.167	30	-2	0-0	1.000	-1	76	0	/O-7(2-0-5)	-0.3
	Year	24	44	2	8	2	0	0	1	9-1	0	10	.182	.321	.227	49	-3	0-0	1.000	-0	90	151	O-14(6-3-5)	-0.3
1956	Phi N	5	4	0	0	0	0	0	0	1-0	0	3	.000	.200	.000	-41	-1	0-0	—	0			H	-0.1
Total	10	958	3117	474	848	107	33	127	539	317-1	33	453	.272	.345	.450	111	40	19-7	.983	8	102	88	O-834(137-344-385)/3-34	1.7
WESTON, AL Alfred John B 12.11.1905 Lynn, MA D 11.13.1997 San Diego, CA BR/TR 6/195# d7.7																								
1929	Bos N	3	3	0	0	0	0	0	0	0	0	2	.000	.000	.000	-99	-1	0	—	0			H	-0.1
WESTRUM, WES Wesley Noreen B 11.28.1922 Clearbrook, MN D 5.28.2002 Clearbrook, MN BR/TR 5-11/185# d9.17 M5 C12																								
1947	NY N	6	12	1	5	1	0	0	2	0	0	2	.417	.417	.500	142	1	0	1.000	0	*0*	*202*	/C-2	0.1
1948	NY N	66	125	14	20	3	1	4	16	20	0	36	.160	.276	.296	54	-8	3	.981	5	*120*	*104*	C-63	-0.1
1949	NY N	64	169	23	41	4	1	7	28	37	2	39	.243	.385	.402	111	4	1	.980	-0	*90*	*59*	C-62	0.7
1950	NY N	140	437	68	103	13	3	23	71	92	2	73	.236	.371	.437	111	9	2	**.999**	14	***153***	*98*	*C-139	2.9
1951	†NY N	124	361	59	79	12	0	20	70	104	5	93	.219	.400	.418	119	16	1-0	.987	8	*142*	*123*	*C-122	3.0
1952	NY N☆	114	322	47	71	11	0	14	43	76	3	68	.220	.374	.385	110	8	1-2	.978	2	***182***	*88*	*C-112	1.5
1953	NY N☆	107	290	40	65	5	0	12	30	56	1	73	.224	.352	.366	86	-5	2-0	.982	5	*138*	*109*	*C-106/3	0.5
1954	†NY N	98	246	25	46	3	1	8	27	45	3	60	.187	.315	.305	63	-13	0-1	.985	10	*157*	*116*	C-98	0.1
1955	NY N	69	137	11	29	1	0	4	18	24-3	1	18	.212	.327	.307	71	-5	0-1	.987	5	*130*	*105*	C-68	0.2
1956	NY N	68	132	10	29	5	2	3	8	25-5	1	28	.220	.346	.356	91	-1	0-0	.982	8	*132*	*111*	C-67	0.9

Year	Tm Lg	G	AB	R	H	2B	3B	HR	RBI	BB-IB	HP	SO	AVG	OBP	SLG	AOPS	ABR	SB-CS	FA	FR	Rng	Thr	G at Pos	BFW
1957	NY N	63	91	4	15	1	0	1	2	10-1	1	24	.165	.255	.209	27	-9	0-1	.966	1	*132*	*134*	C-63	-0.7
Total	11	919	2322	302	503	59	8	96	315	489-9	19	514	.217	.356	.373	95	-3	10-5	.985	58	*144*	*104*	C-902/3	9.1
WETHERBY, JEFF Jeffrey Barrett B 10.18.1963 Granada Hills, CA BL/TL 6-2/195# d6.7																								
1989	Atl N	52	48	5	10	2	1	1	7	4-0	0	6	.208	.264	.354	75	-2	1-0	1.000	-0	100	0	/O-9(7-0-2)	-0.2
WETZEL, DUTCH Franklin Burton B 7.7.1893 Columbus, IN D 3.5.1942 Hollywood, CA BR/TR 5-9.5/177# d9.15																								
1920	StL A	7	21	5	9	1	1	0	5	4	0	1	.429	.520	.571	183	3	0-1	.875	-0	96	121	/O-6(5-1-0)	0.2
1921	StL A	61	119	16	25	2	0	2	10	9	1	20	.210	.271	.277	38	-11	0-0	.981	0	115	35	O-27(12-4-11)	-1.2
Total	2	68	140	21	34	3	1	2	15	13	1	21	.243	.312	.321	59	-8	0-1	.957	-0	111	54	/O-33(17-5-11)	-1.0
WHALEY, BILL William Carl B 2.10.1899 Indianapolis, IN D 3.3.1943 Indianapolis, IN BR/TR 5-11/178# d4.18																								
1923	StL A	23	50	5	12	2	1	0	1	4	1	2	.240	.309	.320	62	-3	0-0	1.000	1	96	160	O-13(4-9-0)	-0.3
WHALING, BERT Albert James B 6.22.1888 Los Angeles, CA D 1.21.1965 Sawtelle, CA BR/TR 6/185# d4.22																								
1913	Bos N	79	211	22	51	8	2	0	25	10	2	32	.242	.283	.299	65	-10	3-3	**.990**	1	101	101	C-77	-0.4
1914	Bos N	60	172	18	36	7	0	0	12	21	2	28	.209	.303	.250	65	-6	2	.981	10	*142*	*106*	C-59	0.9
1915	Bos N	72	190	10	42	6	2	0	13	8	3	38	.221	.264	.274	66	-8	0-1	.986	5	*144*	*82*	C-69	0.1
Total	3	211	573	50	129	21	4	0	50	39	7	98	.225	.283	.276	65	-24	5-4	.986	15	*128*	*96*	C-205	0.6
WHEAT, MACK McKinley Davis B 6.9.1893 Polo, MO D 8.14.1979 Los Banos, CA BR/TR 5-11.5/167# d4.14 b-Zack																								
1915	Bro N	8	14	0	1	0	0	0	0	0	0	5	.071	.071	.071	-56	-3	0	.957	-1	*95*	*63*	/C-8	-0.3
1916	Bro N	2	2	0	0	0	0	0	0	0	0	1	.000	.000	.000	-97	0	0	1.000	-0	70	0	/C-2	-0.1
1917	Bro N	29	60	2	8	1	0	0	0	1	1	12	.133	.161	.150	-4	-7	1	.968	2	*108*	*130*	C-18/O-9(9-1-0)	-0.5
1918	Bro N	57	157	11	34	7	1	1	3	8	0	24	.217	.255	.293	67	-6	2	.966	-1	*87*	*109*	C-38/O-7(1-1-4)	-0.6
1919	Bro N	41	112	5	23	3	0	0	8	2	4	22	.205	.246	.232	43	-8	1	.944	-3	*86*	*100*	C-38	-0.9
1920	Phi N	78	230	15	52	10	3	3	20	8	3	35	.226	.261	.335	67	-10	3-1	.961	2	*87*	*114*	C-74	-0.2
1921	Phi N	10	27	1	5	2	1	0	4	0	2	3	.185	.241	.333	47	-2	0-0	.980	2	*90*	*119*	/C-9	0.0
Total	7	225	602	34	123	23	5	4	35	19	10	102	.204	.241	.279	52	-36	7-1	.961	0	*89*	*110*	C-187/O-16(10-2-4)	-2.6
WHEAT, ZACK Zachary Davis "Buck" B 5.23.1888 Hamilton, MO D 3.11.1972 Sedalia, MO BL/TR 5-10/170# d9.11 HF1959 b-Mack																								
1909	Bro N	26	102	15	31	7	3	0	4	6	0		.304	.343	.431	145	5	1	.952	1	126	105	O-26(25-1-0)	0.4
1910	Bro N	**156**	606	78	172	36	15	2	55	47	6	80	.284	.341	.403	120	14	16	.962	5	105	99	*O-156(LF)	0.9
1911	Bro N	140	534	55	153	26	13	5	76	29	7	58	.287	.332	.412	112	5	21	.955	-3	105	62	*O-136(135-1-0)	-0.4
1912	Bro N	123	453	70	138	28	7	8	65	39	6	40	.305	.367	.450	128	17	16	.968	1	108	70	*O-120(LF)	1.2
1913	Bro N	138	535	64	161	28	10	7	58	25	2	45	.301	.335	.430	114	8	19-20	.978	8	**117**	69	*O-135(LF)	0.7
1914	Bro N	145	533	66	170	26	9	9	89	47	3	50	.319	.377	.452	143	28	20	.962	15	**121**	118	*O-144(LF)	3.8
1915	Bro N	146	528	64	136	15	12	5	66	52	5	42	.258	.330	.360	107	4	21-14	.953	9	**115**	101	*O-144(LF)	0.7
1916	†Bro N	149	568	76	177	32	13	9	73	43	6	49	.312	.366	**.461**	149	**33**	19	.975	6	**114**	88	*O-149(149-1-0)	3.6
1917	Bro N	109	362	38	113	15	11	1	41	20	2	18	.312	.352	.423	133	13	5	.979	6	111	100	O-98(LF)	1.7
1918	Bro N	105	409	39	137	15	3	0	51	16	6	17	**.335**	.369	.386	131	15	9	.979	3	105	98	*O-105(LF)	1.4
1919	Bro N	137	536	70	159	23	11	5	62	33	6	27	.297	.344	.409	123	14	15	.971	-3	108	51	*O-137(LF)	0.6
1920	†Bro N	148	583	89	191	26	13	9	73	48	6	21	.328	.385	.463	138	29	8-10	.971	-4	100	63	*O-148(LF)	1.8
1921	Bro N	148	568	91	182	31	10	14	85	44	3	19	.320	.372	.484	121	17	11-8	.965	-3	92	103	*O-148(LF)	0.2
1922	Bro N	152	600	92	201	29	12	16	112	45	7	22	.335	.388	.503	129	25	9-6	**.991**	1	104	76	*O-152(LF)	1.3
1923	Bro N	98	349	63	131	13	5	8	65	23	2	12	.375	.417	.510	148	23	3-3	.908	-8	86	57	O-87(85-0-2)	0.8
1924	Bro N	141	566	92	212	41	8	14	97	49	4	18	.375	.428	.549	165	54	3-4	.965	4	106	97	*O-139(LF)	4.5
1925	Bro N	150	616	125	221	42	14	14	103	45	1	22	.359	.403	.541	143	39	3-1	.962	-2	106	54	*O-149(LF)	2.4
1926	Bro N	111	411	68	119	31	2	5	35	21	1	14	.290	.326	.411	99	-1	4	.955	1	105	99	*O-102(LF)	-0.8
1927	Phi A	88	247	34	80	12	1	1	38	18	4	5	.324	.379	.393	95	-1	2-3	.983	-1	86	137	O-62(57-2-3)	-0.7
Total	19	2410	9106	1289	2884	476	172	132	1248	650	77	559	.317	.367	.450	129	341	205-69	.966	34	107	84	*O-2337(2328-5-5)	24.1
WHEATON, WOODY Elwood Pierce B 10.3.1914 Philadelphia, PA D 12.11.1995 Lancaster, PA BL/TL 5-8.5/160# d9.28 ▲																								
1943	Phi A	7	30	2	6	2	0	0	2	3	1	2	.200	.294	.267	65	-1	0-0	1.000	1	103	178	/O-7(CF)	-0.1
1944	Phi A	30	59	1	11	2	0	0	5	5	0	3	.186	.250	.220	35	-5	1-2	1.000	0	56	0	P-11/O-8(CF)	-0.4
Total	2	37	89	3	17	4	0	0	7	8	1	5	.191	.265	.236	45	-6	1-2	.981	1	103	192	/O-15(CF),P-11	-0.5
WHEELER, DON Donald Wesley "Scott" B 9.29.1922 Minneapolis, MN D 12.10.2003 Minneapolis, MN BR/TR 5-10/175# d4.23																								
1949	Chi A	67	192	17	46	9	2	1	22	27	0	19	.240	.333	.323	76	-6	2-0	.976	1	*88*	*125*	C-58	-0.2
WHEELER, ED Edward B 6.15.1878 Sherman, MI D 8.15.1960 Ft.Worth, TX BB/TR 5-10/160# d5.10																								
1902	Bro N	30	96	4	12	0	0	0	5	3	0		.125	.152	.125	-14	-13	1	.863	-6	74	0	3-11,2-10/S-5	-2.0
WHEELER, ED Edward Raymond B 5.24.1915 Los Angeles, CA D 8.4.1983 Centralia, WA BR/TR 5-9/160# d4.19																								
1945	Cle A	46	72	12	14	2	0	0	2	8	0	13	.194	.275	.222	47	-5	1-1	.912	-6	56	0	3-14,S-11/2-3	-1.1
WHEELER, GEORGE George Harrison "Heavy" B 11.10.1881 Shelburn, IN D 6.13.1918 Clinton, IN BL/TR 5-9.5/180# d7.27																								
1910	Cin N	3	3	0	0	0	0	0	0	0	0	2	.000	.000	.000	-99	-1	0	—	0			H	-0.1
WHEELER, HARRY Harry Eugene B 3.3.1858 Versailles, IN D 10.9.1900 Cincinnati, OH BR/TR 5-11/165# d6.19 M1 ▲																								
1878	Pro N	7	27	7	4	0	0	0	1	2		15	.148	.207	.148	18	-1		.875	-2	39	0	/P-7	0.0
1879	Cin N	1	3	0	0	0	0	0	0	0		2	.000	.000	.000	-99	-1		1.000	-0	0	0	/O(RF)P	-0.1
1880	Cle N	1	4	0	1	0	0	0	0	0		0	.250	.250	.250	72	0		1.000	-0	0	0	/O(LF)	0.0
	Cin N	17	65	1	6	2	0	0	2	0		15	.092	.092	.123	-28	-8		.750	1	116	116	O-17(16-1-0)	-0.9
	Year	18	69	1	7	2	0	0	2	0		15	.101	.101	.130	-22	-8		.759	0	107	107	O-18(17-1-0)	-0.9
1882	Cin AA	76	344	59	86	11	11	1	29	7			.250	.265	.355	102	-1		.808	-7	72	76	*O-64(RF),1-12/P-4	-0.9
1883	Col AA	82	371	42	84	6	7	0		6			.226	.239	.280	72	-11		.803	-2	83	48	*O-82(LF)/2P	-1.3
1884	StL AA	5	19	0	5	2	0	0		1	0		.263	.300	.368	113	0		.600	-2	0	0	/O-5(4-1-0)	-0.1
	KC U	14	62	11	16	1	0	0		3			.258	.292	.274	83	-3		.769	-1	27	0	O-13(12-0-1)/PM	-0.4
	CP U	37	158	29	36	5	3	1		4			.228	.247	.316	70	-11		.774	-5	35	0	O-37(CF)	-1.6
	Bal U	17	69	3	18	2	0	0		0			.261	.261	.290	60	-5		.815	-1	99	0	O-17(0-1-16)	-0.6
	Year	68	289	43	70	8	3	1		7			.242	.260	.301	70	-20		.781	-7	49	0	O-67(12-38-17)/P	-2.6
Total	6	257	1122	152	256	29	21	2	32	23		32	.228	.244	.297	74	-41		.791	-19	70	46	O-237(115-40-82)/P-14,1-12,2	-5.9
WHEELER, DICK Richard (born Richard Wheeler Maynard) B 1.14.1898 Keene, NH D 2.12.1962 Lexington, MA BR/TR 5-11/185# d6.17																								
1918	StL N	3	6	0	0	0	0	0	0	0	0	3	.000	.000	.000	-99	-1	0	—	-0	0	0	/O-2(RF)	-0.2
WHEELOCK, BOBBY Warren H. B 8.6.1864 Charlestown, MA D 3.13.1928 Boston, MA BR/TR 5-8/160# d5.19																								
1887	Bos N	48	166	32	42	4	2	2	15	15	0	15	.253	.315	.337	80	-4	20	.878	-2	25	0	O-28(9-1-18),S-20/2-4	-0.5
1890	Col AA	52	190	24	45	6	1	1	16	25	0		.237	.326	.295	89	-2	34	.885	-0	95	89	S-52	0.0
1891	Col AA	136	498	82	114	15	1	0	39	78	2	55	.229	.336	.263	76	-11	52	.899	16	110	**144**	*S-136	0.8
Total	3	236	854	138	201	25	4	3	70	118	2	70	.235	.330	.285	80	-17	106	.894	14	107	125	S-208/O-28(9-1-18),2-4	0.3
WHELAN, JIMMY James Francis B 5.11.1890 Kansas City, MO D 11.29.1929 Dayton, OH BR/TR 5-8.5/165# d4.24																								
1913	StL N	1	1	0	0	0	0	0	0	0	0	0	.000	.000	.000	-99	0	0	—	0			H	0.0
WHELAN, TOM Thomas Joseph B 1.3.1894 Lynn, MA D 6.26.1957 Boston, MA BR/TR 5-11/175# d8.13																								
1920	Bos N	1	1	0	0	0	0	0	0	1	0	1	.000	.500	.000	54	0	0-0	1.000	-0	0	0	/1	0.0
WHISENANT, PETE Thomas Peter B 12.14.1929 Asheville, NC D 3.22.1996 Port Charlotte, FL BR/TR 6-2/200# d4.16 C2																								
1952	Bos N	24	52	3	10	2	0	0	7	4	0	13	.192	.250	.231	35	-5	1-1	.973	2	118	184	O-14(9-5-0)	-0.4
1955	StL N	58	115	10	22	5	1	2	9	5-0	0	29	.191	.223	.304	39	-11	2-0	.964	3	116	162	O-40(12-11-19)	-0.8
1956	Chi N	103	314	37	75	16	3	11	46	24-1	1	53	.239	.292	.414	89	-5	8-2	.992	2	105	93	O-93(6-84-0)	-0.7
1957	Cin N	67	90	18	19	3	2	5	11	5-0	0	24	.211	.250	.456	80	-3	0-1	.982	2	132	0	O-43(24-9-12)	-0.3
1958	Cin N	85	203	33	48	9	2	11	40	18-0	0	37	.236	.292	.463	93	-3	3-0	1.000	3	116	68	O-66(26-2-42)/2	-0.2
1959	Cin N	36	71	13	17	2	0	5	11	8-0	0	18	.239	.316	.479	105	0	0-0	.966	-0	97	86	O-21(5-0-16)	0.0
1960	Cin N	1	1	0	0	0	0	0	0	0-0	0	0	.000	.000	.000	-98	0	0-0	—	0			H	0.0
	Cle A	7	6	0	1	0	0	0	0	0-0	0	2	.167	.167	.167	-10	-1	0-0	1.000	0	139	0	/O-2(LF)	-0.1
	Was A	58	115	19	26	9	0	3	9	19-0	0	14	.226	.336	.383	95	0	2-1	1.000	0	100	103	O-47(23-31-1)	-0.1

Year	Tm Lg	G	AB	R	H	2B	3B	HR	RBI	BB-IB	HP	SO	AVG	OBP	SLG	AOPS	ABR	SB-CS	FA	FR	Rng	Thr	G at Pos	BFW
	Year	65	121	19	27	9	0	3	9	19-0	0	16	.223	.329	.372	90	-1	2-1	1.000	0	100	102	O-49(25-31-1)	-0.2
1961	Min A	10	6	1	0	0	0	0	0	1-0	0	2	.000	.143	.000	-55	-1	0-0	1.000	0	158	0	/O-5(LF)	-0.1
	Cin N	26	15	6	3	0	0	0	1	2-0	0	4	.200	.294	.200	34	-1	1-0	1.000	0	148	0	O-12(10-0-2)/C3	-0.1
Total	8	475	988	140	221	46	8	37	134	86-1	1	196	.224	.284	.399	80	-30	17-5	.988	11	111	94	O-343(122-142-92)/3C2	-2.8
WHISENTON, LARRY Larry B 7.3.1956 St.Louis, MO BL/TL 6-1/190# d9.17																								
1977	Atl N	4	4	1	1	0	0	0	1	0-0	0	3	.250	.250	.250	31	0	0-0	—	0			H	-0.1
1978	Atl N	6	16	1	3	1	0	0	2	1-0	0	2	.188	.235	.250	32	-1	0-0	1.000	-1	67	0	/O-4(RF)	-0.3
1979	Atl N	13	37	3	9	2	1	0	1	3-0	0	3	.243	.300	.351	72	-1	1-0	1.000	4	138	371	O-13(9-0-4)	0.2
1981	Atl N	9	5	1	1	0	0	0	0	2-0	0	1	.200	.429	.200	81	0	0-0	.000	-0	0	0	/O-2(1-0-1)	0.0
1982	†Atl N	84	143	21	34	7	2	4	17	23-3	0	33	.238	.339	.399	103	1	2-2	.964	-2	88	42	O-34(29-0-5)	-0.3
Total	5	116	205	27	48	10	3	4	21	29-3	0	42	.234	.326	.371	90	-1	3-2	.968	0	97	115	/O-53(39-0-14)	-0.5
WHISTLER, LEW Lewis W. (born Lewis Wissler) B 3.10.1868 St.Louis, MO D 12.30.1959 St.Louis, MO TR 5-10.5/178# d8.7 OF Total (15-LF 5-CF 12-RF)																								
1890	NY N	45	170	27	49	9	7	2	29	20	1	37	.288	.366	.459	140	8	8	.982	-2	62	111	1-45	0.2
1891	NY N	72	265	39	65	8	7	3	38	24	3	45	.245	.315	.362	101	0	4	.852	-14	91	60	S-33,O-22(14-5-3)/1-7,2-6,3-5	-1.2
1892	Bal N	52	209	32	47	6	6	2	21	18	3	22	.225	.296	.340	90	-4	12	.973	-1	97	62	1-51/O(LF)	-0.4
	Lou N	80	285	42	67	4	7	5	34	30	2	45	.235	.312	.351	109	3	14	.978	-2	84	131	1-72,2-10	0.1
	Year	132	494	74	114	10	13	7	55	48	5	67	.231	.305	.346	101	-1	26	.976	-3	89	102	*1-123,2-10/O(LF)	-0.3
1893	Lou N	13	47	5	10	1	1	0	9	5	1	5	.213	.302	.277	59	-3	1	.946	-1	116	93	1-13	-0.3
	StL N	10	38	5	9	1	0	0	2	3	0	2	.237	.293	.263	48	-3	0	.923	-1	82	0	/O-9(RF),1	-0.3
	Year	23	85	10	19	2	1	0	11	8	1	7	.224	.298	.271	54	-6	1	.949	-1	107	98	1-14/O-9(RF)	-0.6
Total	4	272	1014	150	247	29	28	12	133	100	10	156	.244	.318	.363	103	1	39	.976	-19	82	104	1-189/S-33,O-32L,2-16,3-5	-1.9
WHITAKER, LOU Louis Rodman B 5.12.1957 Brooklyn, NY BL/TR 5-11/160# d9.9																								
1977	Det A	11	32	5	8	1	0	0	2	4-0	0	6	.250	.333	.281	66	-1	2-2	1.000	-4	71	37	/2-9	-0.5
1978	Det A	139	484	71	138	12	7	3	58	61-0	1	65	.285	.361	.357	101	2	7-7	.978	20	111	115	*2-136/D-2	2.9
1979	Det A	127	423	75	121	14	8	3	42	78-2	1	66	.286	.395	.378	107	8	20-10	.986	17	102	**125**	*2-126	3.1
1980	Det A	145	477	68	111	19	1	1	45	73-0	0	79	.233	.331	.283	69	-17	8-4	.985	-1	97	92	*2-143	-1.0
1981	Det A	**109**	335	48	88	14	4	5	36	40-3	1	42	.263	.340	.373	103	2	5-3	.985	7	105	111	*2-108	1.6
1982	Det A	152	560	76	160	22	8	15	65	48-4	1	58	.286	.341	.434	111	8	11-3	**.988**	13	104	**125**	*2-149/D	3.0
1983	Det A★	161	643	94	206	40	6	12	72	67-8	0	70	.320	.380	.457	134	32	17-10	.983	-19	90	92	*2-160	2.1
1984	†Det A★	143	558	90	161	25	1	13	56	62-5	0	63	.289	.357	.407	112	11	6-5	.979	-5	94	100	*2-142	1.3
1985	Det A★	152	609	102	170	29	8	21	73	80-9	2	56	.279	.362	.456	124	21	6-4	.985	-14	89	103	*2-150	1.5
1986	Det A★	144	584	95	157	26	6	20	73	63-5	0	70	.269	.338	.437	110	8	13-8	.984	6	106	113	*2-141	2.1
1987	†Det A✱	149	604	110	160	38	6	16	59	71-2	1	108	.265	.341	.427	107	7	13-5	.976	-11	97	106	*2-148	0.5
1988	Det A	115	403	54	111	18	2	12	55	66-5	0	61	.275	.376	.419	128	17	2-0	.984	-9	93	82	*2-110	1.2
1989	Det A	148	509	77	128	21	1	28	85	89-6	3	59	.251	.361	.462	135	26	6-3	.985	6	98	99	*2-146/D-2	3.5
1990	Det A	132	472	75	112	22	2	18	60	74-7	0	71	.237	.338	.407	107	6	8-2	.991	18	**106**	114	*2-130/D	2.8
1991	Det A	138	470	94	131	26	2	23	78	90-6	2	45	.279	.391	.489	142	30	4-2	**.994**	-5	103	103	*2-135/D-3	2.9
1992	Det A	130	453	77	126	26	0	19	71	81-5	1	46	.278	.386	.461	137	25	6-4	.984	-13	94	90	*2-119,D-10	1.5
1993	Det A	119	383	72	111	32	1	9	67	78-4	4	46	.290	.412	.449	133	23	3-3	.981	18	**114**	112	*2-110	4.4
1994	Det A	92	322	67	97	21	2	12	43	41-4	1	47	.301	.377	.491	122	12	2-0	.970	-1	**110**	88	2-83/D-5	1.4
1995	Det A	84	249	36	73	14	0	14	44	31-4	2	41	.293	.372	.518	130	11	4-0	.985	-1	105	83	2-63/D-8	1.3
Total	19	2390	8570	1386	2369	420	65	244	1084	1197-79	20	1099	.276	.363	.426	117	231	143-75	.984	24	100	104	*2-2308/D-32	35.6
WHITAKER, STEVE Stephen Edward B 5.7.1943 Tacoma, WA BL/TR 6-1/187# d8.23																								
1966	NY A	31	114	15	28	3	2	7	15	9-0	1	24	.246	.306	.491	130	4	0-0	.955	-1	93	162	O-31(4-20-10)	0.2
1967	NY A	122	441	37	107	12	3	11	50	23-2	3	89	.243	.283	.358	92	-6	2-5	.982	2	94	153	*O-114(26-12-78)	-1.5
1968	NY A	28	60	3	7	2	0	0	3	8-0	0	18	.117	.221	.150	14	-6	0-1	.917	-2	66	209	O-14(6-7-2)	-1.0
1969	Sea A	69	116	15	29	2	1	6	13	12-1	1	29	.250	.323	.440	114	2	2-0	.962	1	87	227	O-39(22-0-18)	0.1
1970	SF N	16	27	3	3	1	0	0	4	2-0	0	14	.111	.167	.148	-13	-4	0-0	.857	-1	58	0	/O-9(LF)	-0.6
Total	5	266	758	73	174	20	6	24	85	54-3	5	174	.230	.283	.367	92	-10	4-6	.967	-1	90	165	O-207(67-39-108)	-2.8
WHITE, FUZZ Albert Eugene B 6.27.1918 Springfield, MO BL/TR 6/175# d9.17																								
1940	StL A	2	2	0	0	0	0	0	0	0	0	0	.000	.000	.000	-98	-1	0-0	—	0			H	-0.1
1947	NY N	7	13	3	3	0	0	0	0	0	0	0	.231	.231	.231	23	-1	0	1.000	1	153	0	/O-5(RF)	-0.1
Total	2	9	15	3	3	0	0	0	0	0	0	0	.200	.200	.200	6	-2	0-0	1.000	1	153	0	/O-5(RF)	-0.2
WHITE, C. B. C. B. B Wakeman, OH d6.1																								
1883	Phi N	1	1	0	0	0	0	0	0	0		0	.000	.000	.000	-99	0		.667	-0	0	0	/S3	0.0
WHITE, CHARLIE Charles B 8.12.1928 Kinston, NC D 5.26.1998 Seattle, WA BL/TR 5-11/192# d4.18																								
1954	Mil N	50	93	14	22	4	0	1	8	9	0	8	.237	.304	.312	65	-5	0-0	.981	-1	*101*	*27*	C-28	-0.5
1955	Mil N	12	30	3	7	1	0	0	4	5-0	1	7	.233	.361	.267	74	-1	0-0	1.000	-1	*127*	*50*	C-10	-0.2
Total	2	62	123	17	29	5	0	1	12	14-0	1	15	.236	.319	.301	67	-6	0-0	.986	-2	*109*	*34*	/C-38	-0.7
WHITE, DERRICK Derrick Ramon B 10.12.1969 San Rafael, CA BR/TR 6-1/220# d7.22																								
1993	Mon N	17	49	6	11	3	0	2	4	2-1	1	12	.224	.269	.408	75	-2	2-0	.993	-1	87	162	1-17	-0.3
1995	Det A	39	48	3	9	2	0	0	2	0-0	0	7	.188	.188	.229	8	-7	1-0	.981	-1	137	83	1-16,D-11/O-9(4-0-5)	-0.9
1998	Chi N	11	10	1	1	0	0	1	2	0-0	0	5	.100	.100	.400	23	-1	0-0	—	0	0	0	/O(LF)	-0.1
	Col N	9	9	0	0	0	0	0	0	0-0	0	4	.000	.000	.000	-82	-2	0-0	1.000	0	113	0	/O-2(LF),D	-0.2
	Year	20	19	1	1	0	0	1	2	0-0	0	9	.053	.053	.211	-31	-4	0-0	1.000	0	90	0	/O-3(LF),D	-0.3
Total	3	76	116	10	21	5	0	3	8	2-1	1	28	.181	.202	.302	30	-12	3-0	.990	-2	101	140	/1-33,O-12(8-0-5),D-12	-1.5
WHITE, DEVON Devon Markes B 12.29.1962 Kingston, Jamaica BB/TR 6-2/182# d9.2																								
1985	Cal A	21	7	7	1	0	0	0	0	1-0	1	3	.143	.333	.143	37	-1	3-1	1.000	1	100	350	O-16(14-1-3)	0.0
1986	†Cal A	29	51	8	12	1	1	1	3	6-0	0	8	.235	.316	.353	83	-1	6-0	.961	1	125	0	O-28(17-7-5)	0.1
1987	Cal A	159	639	103	168	33	5	24	87	39-2	2	135	.263	.306	.443	99	-3	32-11	.980	18	120	156	*O-159(6-64-120)	1.1
1988	Cal A	122	455	76	118	22	2	11	51	23-1	2	84	.259	.297	.389	93	-6	17-8	.976	9	113	128	*O-116(CF)	0.3
1989	Cal A★	156	636	86	156	18	13	12	56	31-3	2	129	.245	.282	.371	84	-17	44-16	.989	3	103	118	*O-154(CF)/D	-1.1
1990	Cal A	125	443	57	96	17	3	11	44	44-5	3	116	.217	.290	.343	79	-14	21-6	.972	3	100	**186**	*O-122(CF)	-0.9
1991	†Tor A	156	642	110	181	40	10	17	60	55-1	7	135	.282	.342	.455	115	13	33-10	**.998**	5	107	98	*O-156(CF)	2.0
1992	†Tor A	153	641	98	159	26	7	17	60	47-0	5	133	.248	.303	.390	89	-11	37-4	.985	7	111	98	*O-152(CF)/D	0.2
1993	†Tor A★	146	598	116	163	42	6	15	52	57-1	7	127	.273	.341	.438	108	7	34-4	.993	4	107	77	*O-145(CF)	1.7
1994	Tor A	100	403	67	109	24	6	13	49	21-3	5	80	.270	.313	.457	95	-5	11-3	.978	5	115	64	O-98(CF)	0.3
1995	Tor A	101	427	61	121	23	5	10	53	29-1	5	97	.283	.334	.431	99	-2	11-2	.989	2	102	142	O-99(CF)	0.2
1996	Fla N	146	552	77	151	37	6	17	84	38-6	8	99	.274	.325	.455	108	5	22-6	.987	-8	91	71	*O-139(CF)	0.1
1997	†Fla N	74	265	37	65	13	1	6	34	32-2	7	65	.245	.338	.370	90	-3	13-5	.987	0	102	128	O-71(CF)	-0.1
1998	Ari N★	146	563	84	157	32	1	22	85	42-4	9	102	.279	.335	.456	107	5	22-8	.987	-2	109	33	*O-144(CF)	0.6
1999	LA N	134	474	60	127	20	2	14	68	39-2	11	88	.268	.337	.407	93	-6	19-5	.986	-11	90	45	*O-128(CF)/D	-1.3
2000	LA N	47	158	26	42	5	1	4	13	9-0	1	30	.266	.310	.386	79	-6	3-6	.972	-4	84	99	O-40(CF)	-1.0
2001	Mil N	126	390	52	108	25	2	14	47	28-1	12	95	.277	.343	.459	108	4	18-3	1.000	-7	90	58	*O-100(13-86-2)	0.1
Total	17	1941	7344	1125	1934	378	71	208	846	541-32	87	1526	.263	.319	.419	98	-41	346-98	.986	25	105	100	*O-1867(50-1722-130)/D-3	2.3
WHITE, DON Donald William B 1.8.1919 Everett, WA D 6.15.1987 Carlsbad, CA BR/TR 6-1/195# d4.19																								
1948	Phi A	86	253	29	62	14	2	1	28	19	2	16	.245	.303	.328	68	-12	0-1	.957	0	100	84	O-54(33-7-17),3-17	-1.5
1949	Phi A	57	169	12	36	6	0	0	10	14	0	12	.213	.273	.249	40	-15	2-0	.989	1	106	103	O-48(6-0-43)/3-4	-1.5
Total	2	143	422	41	98	20	2	1	38	33	2	28	.232	.291	.296	57	-27	2-1	.971	1	103	93	O-102(39-7-60)/3-21	-3.0
WHITE, ED Edward Perry B 4.6.1926 Anniston, AL D 9.28.1982 Lakeland, FL BR/TR 6-2/200# d9.16																								
1955	Chi A	3	4	0	2	0	0	0	0	1-0	0	1	.500	.600	.500	193	1	0-0	1.000	0	115	0	/O-2(RF)	0.1
WHITE, ELDER Elder Lafayette B 12.23.1934 Colerain, NC BR/TR 5-11/165# d4.10																								
1962	Chi N	23	53	4	8	2	0	0	1	8-0	1	11	.151	.274	.189	26	-5	3-0	.986	1	107	66	S-15/3	-0.3
WHITE, ELMER Elmer B 5.23.1850 Caton, NY D 3.17.1872 Caton, NY d5.4																								
1871	Cle NA	15	70	13	18	2	0	0	9	1		6	.257	.268	.286	63	-3	0-1	.783	-1	62	0	O-15(RF)/C-3	-0.2

Year	Tm Lg	G	AB	R	H	2B	3B	HR	RBI	BB-IB	HP	SO	AVG	OBP	SLG	AOPS	ABR	SB-CS	FA	FR	Rng	Thr	G at Pos	BFW
WHITE, FRANK Frank B 9.4.1950 Greenville, MS BR/TR 5-11/170# d6.12 C8 OF Total (1-CF 1-RF)																								
1973	KC A	51	139	20	31	6	1	0	5	8-0	0	23	.223	.262	.281	50	-9	3-1	.937	5	103	139	S-37,2-11	0.0
1974	KC A	99	204	19	45	6	3	1	18	5-0	0	33	.221	.239	.294	50	-14	3-4	.962	7	102	106	2-50,S-29,3-16/D-3	-0.3
1975	KC A	111	304	43	76	10	2	7	36	20-0	1	39	.250	.297	.365	84	-7	11-3	.987	4	104	92	2-67,S-42/3-4,CD	0.5
1976	†KC A	152	446	39	102	17	6	2	46	19-0	3	42	.229	.263	.307	67	-20	20-11	.973	18	**114**	105	*2-130,S-37	1.0
1977	†KC A	152	474	59	116	21	5	5	50	25-0	2	67	.245	.284	.342	70	-21	23-5	**.989**	-1	101	95	*2-152/S-4	-1.1
1978	†KC A★	143	461	66	127	24	6	7	50	26-1	3	59	.275	.317	.399	98	-2	13-10	.978	-8	96	112	*2-140	-0.3
1979	KC A★	127	467	73	124	26	4	10	48	25-3	1	54	.266	.300	.403	87	-10	28-8	.982	-15	92	90	*2-125	-1.4
1980	†KC A	154	560	70	148	23	4	7	60	19-0	2	69	.264	.289	.357	76	-20	19-6	.988	-2	98	98	*2-153	-1.2
1981	†KC A★	94	364	35	91	17	1	9	38	19-0	0	50	.250	.285	.376	91	-6	4-2	.988	-10	93	109	2-93	-1.1
1982	KC A★	145	524	71	156	45	6	11	56	16-1	2	65	.298	.318	.469	114	9	10-7	.978	4	102	107	*2-144	2.0
1983	KC A	146	549	52	143	35	6	11	77	20-4	0	51	.260	.283	.406	88	-11	13-5	**.990**	22	109	**118**	*2-145	2.0
1984	†KC A	129	479	58	130	22	5	17	56	27-3	2	72	.271	.311	.445	106	2	5-5	.985	29	**118**	**124**	*2-129	3.7
1985	†KC A	149	563	62	140	25	1	22	69	28-2	1	86	.249	.284	.414	88	-11	10-4	.980	23	**114**	101	*2-149	2.0
1986	KC A★	151	566	76	154	37	3	22	84	43-5	2	88	.272	.322	.465	110	7	4-4	.987	13	107	98	*2-151/S3	2.6
1987	KC A	154	563	67	138	32	2	17	78	51-5	2	86	.245	.308	.400	84	-13	1-3	.987	22	**112**	91	*2-152/D	1.5
1988	KC A	150	537	48	126	25	1	8	58	21-3	4	67	.235	.266	.330	66	-26	7-3	**.994**	21	**110**	98	*2-148/D-3	-0.1
1989	KC A	135	418	34	107	22	1	2	36	30-0	2	52	.256	.307	.328	80	-11	3-2	.985	14	109	83	*2-132/O(CF)	0.6
1990	KC A	82	241	20	52	14	1	2	21	10-0	3	32	.216	.253	.307	58	-14	1-0	.978	1	96	98	2-79/O(RF)	-1.2
Total	18	2324	7859	912	2006	407	58	160	886	412-27	30	1035	.255	.293	.383	85	-177	178-83	.984	147	105	102	*2-2150,S-150/3-21,D-8,O-2C,C	9.2
WHITE, DOC Guy Harris B 4.9.1879 Washington, DC D 2.19.1969 Silver Spring, MD BL/TL 6-1/150# d4.22 ▲																								
1901	Phi N	31	98	15	27	3	1	1	10	2	1		.276	.297	.357	87	-2	1	.951	2	119	0	P-31/O(LF)	0.1
1902	Phi N	61	179	17	47	3	1	1	15	11	0		.263	.305	.307	89	-3	5	.931	0	107	0	P-36,O-19(17-0-2)	-0.3
1903	Chi A	38	99	10	20	3	0	0	5	19	0		.202	.331	.232	74	-2	1	.969	2	108	236	P-37/O(CF)	0.1
1904	Chi A	33	76	7	12	2	0	0	2	10	0		.158	.256	.184	42	-5	3	.951	1	92	101	P-30/O-2(CF)	0.0
1905	Chi A	37	90	7	15	4	1	0	7	4	0		.167	.202	.233	40	-6	3	.953	2	101	104	P-36/O(LF)	0.1
1906	†Chi A	29	65	11	12	1	1	0	3	13	0		.185	.321	.231	75	-1	3	.922	2	117	64	P-28/O(CF)	0.1
1907	Chi A	48	90	12	20	1	0	0	2	12	0		.222	.314	.233	77	-2	2	**.986**	5	113	43	P-46/O-2(RF),2	0.2
1908	Chi A	51	109	12	25	1	0	0	10	12	0		.229	.306	.239	79	-2	4	**.986**	7	128	**326**	P-41/O-3(0-2-1)	0.4
1909	Chi A	72	192	24	45	1	5	0	7	33	0		.234	.347	.292	106	3	7	.926	-3	158	0	O-40(1-35-4),P-24	-0.2
1910	Chi A	56	126	14	25	1	2	0	8	14	0		.198	.279	.238	65	-5	2	.972	3	100	222	P-33,O-14(0-10-4)	0.0
1911	Chi A	39	78	12	20	1	1	0	6	7	0		.256	.318	.295	74	-3	1	.919	-1	97	133	P-34/1-2,O(RF)	-0.1
1912	Chi A	32	56	5	7	1	1	0	0	7	0		.125	.222	.179	15	-2	0	**1.000**	-1	92	74	P-32	0.0
1913	Chi A	21	25	1	3	0	0	0	0	3	0	1	.120	.214	.120	-2	-3	0	.959	2	142	0	P-19/1	0.1
Total	13	548	1283	147	278	22	13	2	75	147	1	1	.217	.298	.259	74	-33	32	.959	20	108	111	P-427/O-85(20-51-14),1-3,2	0.5
WHITE, DEACON James Laurie B 12.7.1847 Caton, NY D 7.7.1939 Aurora, IL BL/TR 5-11/175# d5.4 M2 b-Will ▲ OF Total (8-LF 5-CF 101-RF)																								
1871	Cle NA	**29**	146	40	47	6	5	1	21	4		1	.322	.340	.452	132	7	2-2	.821	-4			*C-29/S-2,230(RF)	0.2
1872	Cle NA	**22**	109	21	37	2	2	0	22	4		1	.339	.363	.394	140	6	0-0	.882	1			C-14/2-7,O-5(2-1-3),M	0.4
1873	Bos NA	**60**	311	79	122	17	8	1	**77**	0		2	.392	.392	.508	153	17	19-3	.842	-0			*C-56,O-12(2-2-8)	1.4
1874	Bos NA	70	352	75	106	5	7	3	52	5		0	.301	.311	.381	114	3	1-1	.839	1			*C-58,O-21(RF)/1	0.4
1875	Bos NA	80	371	76	136	23	3	1	60	3		2	**.367**	.372	.453	178	28	2-3	.880	19			*C-75,O-14(RF)/1	3.9
1876	Chi N	**66**	303	66	104	18	1	1	**60**	7		3	.343	.358	.419	141	12		.844	8			*C-63/O-3(LF),1-3,3P	1.9
1877	Bos N	59	266	51	**103**	14	**11**	2	**49**	8		3	**.387**	.405	**.545**	**190**	**26**		.963	1	119	117	1-35,O-19(RF)/C-7	2.2
1878	Cin N	**61**	258	41	81	4	1	0	29	10		5	.314	.340	.337	136	11		.909	0			*C-48,O-16(RF)/3	1.1
1879	Cin N	78	333	55	110	16	6	1	52	6		9	.330	.342	.423	159	21		.901	6			*C-59,O-21(0-4-18)/1-2,M	2.5
1880	Cin N	35	141	21	42	4	2	0	7	9		7	.298	.340	.355	137	6		.738	-4	115	64	O-33(0-1-33)/1-3,2	0.2
1881	Buf N	78	319	58	99	24	4	0	53	9		8	.310	.329	.411	133	12		.943	-9	91	67	1-26,2-25,O-17(2-0-15)/3-7,C-4	0.4
1882	Buf N	83	337	51	95	17	0	1	33	15		16	.282	.313	.341	108	3		.837	-11	85	77	*3-63,C-20	-0.4
1883	Buf N	94	391	62	114	14	5	0	47	23		18	.292	.331	.353	106	3		.797	-14	85	82	*3-77,C-22	-0.7
1884	Buf N	110	452	82	147	16	11	5	74	32		13	.325	.370	.442	149	25		.825	-5	98	88	*3-108/C-3	1.9
1885	Buf N	98	404	54	118	6	6	0	57	12		11	.292	.313	.337	106	1		.888	2	103	83	*3-98	0.4
1886	Det N	124	491	65	142	19	5	1	76	31		35	.289	.331	.354	105	3	9	.847	-9	97	141	*3-124	-0.4
1887	†Det N	111	449	71	136	20	11	3	75	26	9	15	.303	.353	.416	109	5	20	.848	1	105	110	*3-106/O-3(LF),1-2	0.6
1888	Det N	125	527	75	157	22	5	4	71	21	9	24	.298	.336	.381	127	16	12	.857	-3	100	122	*3-125	1.4
1889	Pit N	55	225	35	57	10	1	0	26	16	4	18	.253	.314	.307	82	-5	2	.872	-8	88	79	3-52/1-3	-1.1
1890	Buf P	122	439	62	114	13	4	0	47	67	19	30	.260	.381	.308	93	3	3	.905	18	117	140	3-64,1-57/SP	1.3
Total	5 NA	261	1289	291	448	53	25	6	232	16	0	6	.348	.356	.441	146	61	24-9	.000	16			C-232/O-53(4-3-47),2-8,1-2,S-2,3	6.3
Total	15	1299	5335	849	1619	217	73	18	756	292	41	215	.303	.344	.382	122	142	46-0	.853	-27			3-826,C-226,1-131,O-112R/2-26,PS	11.3
WHITE, JERRY Jerome Cardell B 8.23.1952 Shirley, MA BB/TR 5-11/165# d9.16 C7																								
1974	Mon N	9	10	0	4	1	1	0	2	0-0	0	0	.400	.400	.700	193	1	3-0	1.000	-1	76	0	/O-7(5-2-0)	0.1
1975	Mon N	39	97	14	29	4	1	2	7	10-1	0	7	.299	.364	.423	113	2	5-2	.976	2	120	58	O-30(7-24-0)	0.4
1976	Mon N	114	278	32	68	11	1	2	21	27-2	2	31	.245	.316	.313	76	-8	15-7	.982	-3	94	90	O-92(27-67-0)	-1.4
1977	Mon N	16	21	4	4	0	0	0	1	1-0	0	3	.190	.227	.190	14	-3	1-0	1.000	-0	73	0	/O-8(7-0-1)	-0.3
1978	Mon N	18	10	2	2	0	0	0	0	1-0	0	3	.200	.273	.200	34	-1	1-0	—	-0	0	0	/O-3(1-0-2)	-0.1
	Chi N	59	136	22	37	6	0	1	10	23-1	0	16	.272	.373	.338	90	-1	4-3	.981	1	99	178	O-54(CF)	0.0
	Year	77	146	24	39	6	0	1	10	24-1	0	19	.267	.366	.329	89	-1	5-3	.981	1	98	176	O-57(1-54-2)	-0.1
1979	Mon N	88	138	30	41	7	1	3	18	21-2	1	23	.297	.391	.428	125	6	8-4	.983	-3	82	81	O-43(6-13-26)	0.2
1980	Mon N	110	214	22	56	9	3	7	23	30-0	1	37	.262	.351	.430	118	6	8-7	.946	-1	96	122	O-84(62-7-18)	0.2
1981	†Mon N	59	119	11	26	5	1	3	11	13-0	0	17	.218	.293	.353	82	-3	5-2	.952	-1	97	86	O-39(7-13-20)	-0.5
1982	Mon N	69	115	13	28	6	1	2	13	8-1	2	26	.243	.304	.365	85	-2	3-3	1.000	0	100	72	O-30(21-9-2)	-0.4
1983	Mon N	40	34	4	5	1	0	0	0	12-0	1	8	.147	.383	.176	60	-1	4-0	1.000	0	104	0	O-13(2-5-6)	0.0
1986	StL N	25	24	1	3	0	0	1	3	2-0	0	3	.125	.179	.250	21	-3	0-0	1.000	0	154	0	/O-6(3-0-3)	-0.3
Total	11	646	1196	155	303	50	9	21	109	148-7	7	174	.253	.337	.363	94	-7	57-28	.974	-5	97	98	O-409(148-194-78)	-2.1
WHITE, JACK John Peter B 8.31.1905 New York, NY D 6.19.1971 Flushing, NY BB/TR 5-7.5/150# d6.22																								
1927	Cin N	5	4	1	0	0	0	0	0	0	0	0	.000	.000	.000	-99	-1	0	1.000	0	117	146	/2-3,S-2	-0.1
1928	Cin N	1	3	0	0	0	0	0	0	0	0	1	.000	.000	.000	-99	-1	0	.833	-1	0	0	/2	-0.2
Total	2	6	7	1	0	0	0	0	0	0	0	1	.000	.000	.000	-99	-2	0	.929	-1	68	85	/2-4,S-2	-0.3
WHITE, JACK John Wallace B 1.19.1878 Traders Point, IN D 9.30.1963 Indianapolis, IN BR/TR 5-6/?# d6.26																								
1904	Bos N	1	5	1	0	0	0	0	0	0	0		.000	.000	.000	-99	-1	0	1.000	1	497	0	/O(LF)	-0.1
WHITE, JO-JO Joyner Clifford B 6.1.1909 Red Oak, GA D 10.9.1986 Tacoma, WA BL/TR 5-11/165# d4.15 M1 C10 s-Mike																								
1932	Det A	80	208	25	54	6	3	2	21	22	0	19	.260	.330	.346	73	-9	6-8	.962	2	96	176	O-48(16-17-16)	-1.0
1933	Det A	91	234	43	59	9	5	2	34	27	3	26	.252	.337	.359	83	-6	5-5	.977	-1	98	93	O-54(16-32-6)	-0.9
1934	†Det A	115	384	97	120	18	5	0	44	69	1	39	.313	.419	.385	108	9	28-6	.959	-0	98	123	*O-100(1-93-6)	0.9
1935	†Det A	114	412	82	99	13	12	2	32	68	0	42	.240	.348	.345	83	-10	19-10	.962	-4	94	94	O-98(CF)	-1.5
1936	Det A	58	51	11	14	3	0	0	6	9	0	10	.275	.383	.333	78	-1	2-0	.938	0	96	211	O-18(0-18-1)	-0.1
1937	Det A	94	305	50	75	5	7	0	21	50	1	40	.246	.354	.308	67	-15	12-7	.973	-5	96	51	O-82(3-79-0)	-2.0
1938	Det A	78	206	40	54	6	1	0	15	30	1	15	.262	.359	.301	63	-11	3-4	.967	1	106	85	O-55(21-34-1)	-1.2
1943	Phi A	139	500	69	124	17	7	1	30	61	4	51	.248	.335	.316	91	-5	12-4	.966	-5	97	80	*O-133(2-131-0)	-1.3
1944	Phi A	85	267	30	59	4	2	1	21	40	3	27	.221	.329	.262	71	-9	5-4	.949	0	106	93	O-74(10-9-57)/S	-1.4
	Cin N	24	85	9	20	2	0	0	5	10	0	7	.235	.316	.259	65	-4	0	1.000	1	99	177	O-23(4-11-10)	-0.3
Total	9	878	2652	456	678	83	42	8	229	386	13	276	.256	.353	.328	82	-61	92-48	.965	-11	98	98	O-685(73-522-97)/S	-8.8
WHITE, MIKE Joyner Michael B 12.18.1938 Detroit, MI BR/TR 5-8/160# d9.21 f-Jo-Jo																								
1963	Hou N	3	7	0	2	0	0	0	0	0-0	0	0	.286	.286	.286	69	0	0-0	1.000	-1	47	0	/2-2	-0.1
1964	Hou N	89	280	30	76	11	3	0	27	20-0	0	47	.271	.319	.332	89	-4	1-1	.978	2	103	105	O-72(9-55-8),2-10/3-3	-0.4
1965	Hou N	8	9	0	0	0	0	0	0	1-0	0	2	.000	.100	.000	-74	-2	0-0	1.000	-0	98	0	/3	-0.2
Total	3	100	296	30	78	11	3	0	27	21-0	0	49	.264	.311	.321	84	-6	1-1	.978	1	103	105	/O-72(9-55-8),2-12,3-4	-0.7
WHITE, MYRON Myron Alan B 8.1.1957 Long Beach, CA BL/TL 5-11/180# d9.4																								
1978	LA N	7	4	1	2	0	0	0	1	0-0	0	1	.500	.500	.500	181	0	0-1	1.000	-0	75	0	/O-4(1-0-3)	0.0

Year	Tm Lg	G	AB	R	H	2B	3B	HR	RBI	BB-IB	HP	SO	AVG	OBP	SLG	AOPS	ABR	SB-CS	FA	FR	Rng	Thr	G at Pos	BFW
WHITE, RONDELL Rondell Bernard B 2.23.1972 Milledgeville, GA BR/TR 6-1/205# d9.1																								
1993	Mon N	23	73	9	19	3	1	2	15	7-0	0	16	.260	.321	.411	91	-1	1-2	1.000	-2	88	0	O-21(19-5-0)	-0.4
1994	Mon N	40	97	16	27	10	1	2	13	9-0	3	18	.278	.358	.464	111	2	1-1	.946	-2	80	75	O-29(25-4-0)	-0.1
1995	Mon N	130	474	87	140	33	4	13	57	41-1	6	87	.295	.356	.464	111	8	25-5	.986	-3	99	78	*O-119(8-111-0)	1.0
1996	Mon N	88	334	35	98	19	4	6	41	22-0	2	53	.293	.340	.428	99	-1	14-6	.990	-0	98	121	O-86(CF)	0.0
1997	Mon N	151	592	84	160	29	5	28	82	31-3	10	111	.270	.316	.478	105	1	16-8	**.992**	3	109	83	*O-151(CF)	0.7
1998	Mon N	97	357	54	107	21	2	17	58	30-2	7	57	.300	.363	.513	130	15	16-7	.996	9	120	117	O-96(15-83-0)/D	2.5
1999	Mon N	138	539	83	168	26	6	22	64	32-2	11	85	.312	.359	.505	120	14	10-6	.964	-0	100	91	*O-135(102-73-0)	1.1
2000	Mon N	75	290	52	89	24	0	11	54	28-0	2	67	.307	.370	.503	115	7	5-1	.994	6	117	92	O-74(LF)	1.1
	Chi N	19	67	7	22	2	0	2	7	5-0	2	12	.328	.392	.448	114	2	0-2	1.000	2	133	0	O-18(LF)	0.2
	Year	94	357	59	111	26	0	13	61	33-0	4	79	.311	.374	.493	115	9	5-3	.995	8	120	75	O-92(LF)	1.3
2001	Chi N	95	323	43	99	19	1	17	50	26-4	7	56	.307	.371	.529	136	17	1-0	.979	-0	97	82	O-90(LF)	1.3
2002	†NY A	126	455	59	109	21	0	14	62	25-1	8	86	.240	.288	.378	76	-16	1-2	**1.000**	4	114	47	*O-113(113-1-0),D-11	-1.8
2003	SD N★	115	413	49	115	17	3	18	66	25-2	8	71	.278	.330	.465	115	7	1-4	.978	1	99	104	*O-104(LF)/D-3	0.3
	KC A	22	75	13	26	6	1	4	21	6-0	2	8	.347	.400	.613	145	5	0-0	.978	2	144	0	O-17(LF)/D-4	0.6
Total	11	1119	4089	591	1179	230	28	156	590	287-15	68	727	.288	.343	.473	111	60	91-44	.986	20	106	84	*O-1053(585-514-0)/D-19	6.5
WHITE, ROY Roy Hilton B 12.27.1943 Los Angeles, CA BB/TR 5-10/172# d9.7 C3 OF Total (1520-LF 63-CF 56-RF)																								
1965	NY A	14	42	7	14	2	0	0	3	4-0	1	7	.333	.404	.381	125	2	2-1	1.000	-1	82	0	O-10(0-1-9)/2	0.0
1966	NY A	115	316	39	71	13	2	7	20	37-1	1	43	.225	.308	.345	91	-3	14-7	.957	-0	105	61	O-82(72-12-0)/2-2	-0.8
1967	NY A	70	214	22	48	8	0	2	18	19-0	1	25	.224	.287	.290	75	-7	10-4	.968	-7	95	43	O-36(5-0-31),3-17	-1.7
1968	NY A	159	577	89	154	20	7	17	62	73-6	3	50	.267	.350	.414	136	26	20-11	.997	2	93	134	*O-154(119-25-12)	2.2
1969	NY A★	130	448	55	130	30	5	7	74	81-4	1	51	.290	.392	.426	136	26	18-10	.989	6	110	88	*O-126(LF)	2.6
1970	NY A☆	162	609	109	180	30	6	22	94	95-11	0	66	.296	.387	.473	144	39	24-10	.994	0	101	55	*O-161(161-0-1)	3.2
1971	NY A	147	524	86	153	22	7	19	84	86-7	7	66	.292	.388	.469	154	41	14-7	**1.000**	5	107	84	*O-145(LF)	3.9
1972	NY A	**155**	556	76	150	29	0	10	54	**99**-10	5	59	.270	.384	.376	131	28	23-7	.994	2	109	62	*O-155(LF)	2.6
1973	NY A	**162**	639	88	157	22	3	18	60	78-3	2	81	.246	.329	.374	101	1	16-9	.977	-1	104	35	*O-162(LF)	-0.9
1974	NY A	136	473	68	130	19	8	7	43	67-5	4	44	.275	.367	.393	121	15	15-6	.993	1	106	43	O-67(LF),D-53	1.3
1975	NY A	148	556	81	161	32	5	12	59	72-1	2	50	.290	.372	.430	129	23	16-15	.984	7	110	112	*O-135(LF)/1-7,D-2	2.0
1976	†NY A	156	626	**104**	179	29	3	14	65	83-1	0	52	.286	.365	.409	129	25	31-13	.987	-0	103	73	*O-156(140-21-1)	1.9
1977	†NY A	143	519	72	139	25	2	14	52	75-9	0	58	.268	.358	.405	109	9	18-11	.981	4	111	69	*O-135(133-1-2)/D-4	0.7
1978	†NY A	103	346	44	93	13	3	8	43	42-7	2	35	.269	.349	.393	112	6	10-4	.992	-6	89	22	O-74(73-3-0),D-23	-0.3
1979	NY A	81	205	24	44	6	0	3	27	23-1	0	21	.215	.290	.288	59	-12	2-2	1.000	-1	86	154	D-29,O-27(LF)	-1.4
Total	15	1881	6650	964	1803	300	51	160	758	934-66	29	708	.271	.360	.404	122	219	233-117	.988	10	104	74	*O-1625L,D-111/3-17,1-7,2-3	15.3
WHITE, SAMMY Samuel Charles B 7.7.1927 Wenatchee, WA D 8.5.1991 Princeville, HI BR/TR 6-3/195# d9.26																								
1951	Bos A	4	11	0	2	0	0	0	0	0	0	3	.182	.182	.182	-1	-2	0-0	1.000	1	*105*	*0*	/C-4	-0.1
1952	Bos A	115	381	35	107	20	2	10	49	16	0	43	.281	.310	.423	95	-4	2-3	.983	3	***124***	*93*	*C-110	0.4
1953	Bos A☆	136	476	59	130	34	2	13	64	29	2	48	.273	.318	.435	96	-4	3-2	.986	10	*106*	*93*	*C-131	1.3
1954	Bos A	137	493	46	139	25	2	14	75	21	0	50	.282	.307	.426	90	-8	1-3	.979	4	*81*	*99*	*C-133	0.2
1955	Bos A	143	544	65	142	30	4	11	64	44-4	7	58	.261	.323	.392	84	-12	1-2	.984	-2	*82*	*106*	*C-143	-0.7
1956	Bos A	114	392	28	96	15	2	5	44	35-7	0	40	.245	.304	.332	61	-22	2-1	.984	3	*124*	*102*	*C-114	-1.3
1957	Bos A	111	340	24	73	10	1	3	31	25-6	0	38	.215	.267	.276	46	-25	0-1	.985	-1	*139*	*87*	*C-111	-2.3
1958	Bos A	102	328	25	85	15	3	6	35	21-4	1	37	.259	.305	.378	81	-9	1-1	.988	-2	*128*	*103*	*C-102	-0.6
1959	Bos A	119	377	34	107	13	4	1	42	23-6	1	39	.284	.324	.347	81	-10	4-2	.990	4	*132*	*90*	*C-119	-0.1
1961	Mil N	21	63	1	14	1	0	1	5	2-0	0	9	.222	.242	.286	43	-5	0-0	.974	2	*177*	*68*	C-20	-0.3
1962	Phi N	41	97	7	21	4	0	2	12	2-0	1	16	.216	.238	.320	50	-7	0-0	.975	3	*123*	*142*	C-40	-0.3
Total	11	1043	3502	324	916	167	20	66	421	218-27	12	381	.262	.305	.377	79	-108	14-15	.984	24	*113*	*97*	*C-1027	-3.8
WHITE, SAM Samuel Lambeth B 8.23.1892 Greater Preston, England D 11.11.1929 Philadelphia, PA BL/TR 6/185# d9.8																								
1919	Bos N	1	1	0	0	0	0	0	0	0	0	0	.000	.000	.000	-99	0	0	1.000	1	*0*	*650*	/C	0.1
WHITE, BARNEY William Barney "Bear" B 6.25.1923 Paris, TX D 7.24.2002 Tyler, TX BR/TR 5-11/186# d6.5																								
1945	Bro N	4	1	2	0	0	0	0	0	1	0	1	.000	.500	.000	46	0	0	1.000	-0	93	0	/S3	0.0
WHITE, BILL William De Kova B 1.28.1934 Lakewood, FL BL/TL 6/195# d5.7 Mil 1957-58																								
1956	NY N	138	508	63	130	23	7	22	59	47-3	4	72	.256	.321	.459	108	5	15-8	.989	5	113	91	*1-138/O-2(1-0-1)	0.2
1958	SF N	26	29	5	7	1	0	1	4	7-1	0	5	.241	.389	.379	107	1	1-0	1.000	-0	69	100	/1-3,O-2(1-0-1)	0.0
1959	StL N☆	138	517	77	156	33	9	12	72	34-1	2	61	.302	.344	.470	108	6	15-10	.962	-3	108	32	O-92(86-9-0),1-71	-0.5
1960	StL N★	144	554	81	157	27	10	16	79	42-1	2	83	.283	.334	.455	105	3	12-6	.990	-7	80	**122**	*1-123,O-29(3-28-0)	-1.2
1961	StL N★	153	591	89	169	28	11	20	90	64-4	1	84	.286	.354	.472	107	6	8-11	.989	-2	95	93	*1-151	-0.7
1962	StL N	159	614	93	199	31	3	20	102	58-6	6	69	.324	.386	.482	120	19	9-7	.993	0	99	105	*1-146,O-27(8-0-19)	0.9
1963	StL N★	**162**	658	106	200	26	8	27	109	59-9	0	100	.304	.360	.491	131	26	10-9	.991	-1	96	100	*1-162	1.5
1964	†StL N★	160	631	92	191	37	4	21	102	52-7	1	103	.303	.355	.474	121	19	7-6	**.996**	1	99	103	*1-160	1.0
1965	StL N	148	543	82	157	26	3	24	73	63-11	4	86	.289	.364	.481	125	19	3-3	.992	6	**114**	102	*1-144	1.6
1966	Phi N	159	577	85	159	23	6	22	103	68-12	3	109	.276	.352	.451	122	18	16-6	**.994**	6	111	96	*1-158	1.6
1967	Phi N	110	308	29	77	6	2	8	33	52-9	3	61	.250	.359	.360	107	5	6-1	.993	0	98	129	1-95	0.1
1968	Phi N	127	385	34	92	16	2	9	40	39-6	2	79	.239	.309	.361	102	1	0-1	.994	5	118	**114**	*1-111	0.0
1969	StL N	49	57	7	12	1	0	0	4	11-0	0	15	.211	.338	.228	61	-2	1-0	1.000	1	126	106	1-15	-0.2
Total	13	1673	5972	843	1706	278	65	202	870	596-70	28	927	.286	.351	.455	115	126	103-68	.992	10	102	103	*1-1477,O-152(99-37-21)	4.3
WHITE, BILL William Dighton B 5.1.1860 Bridgeport, OH D 12.29.1924 Bellaire, OH TR d5.3																								
1884	Pit AA	74	291	25	66	7	10	0		13	1		.227	.262	.320	90	-4		.807	-9	102	72	S-60,3-10/O-4(RF)	-1.0
1886	Lou AA	135	557	96	143	17	10	1	66	37	1		.257	.304	.329	93	-7	14	.871	17	99	123	*S-135/P	1.2
1887	Lou AA	132	512	85	129	7	9	2	79	47	0		.252	.315	.313	74	-19	41	.869	18	103	**137**	*S-132	0.2
1888	Lou AA	49	198	35	55	6	5	1	30	7	3		.278	.313	.374	122	4	15	.816	1	105	51	S-38,3-11	0.5
	†StL AA	76	275	31	48	2	3	2	30	21	2		.175	.238	.225	44	-18	6	.892	-5	86	69	S-74/2-2	-2.0
	Year	125	473	66	103	8	8	3	60	28	5		.218	.269	.288	74	-16	21	.864	-5	93	63	*S-112,3-11/2-2	-1.5
Total	4	466	1833	272	441	39	37	6	205	125	7		.241	.292	.312	82	-44	76	.860	20	99	105	S-439/3-21,O-4(RF),2-2,P	-1.1
WHITE, BILL William Edward B Milner, GA d6.21																								
1879	Pro N	1	4	1	1	0	0	0	0	0		1	.250	.250	.250	67	0		1.000	0	0	242	/1	0.0
WHITE, WARREN William Warren (a/k/a William Warren) B 1844 Washington, DC 5-10.5/170# d6.17 M2																								
1871	Oly NA	1	4	0	0	0	0	0	0	0		0	.000	.000	.000	-99	-1	0-0	1.000	-0	54	0	/2	-0.1
1872	Nat NA	10	45	7	12	0	0	0	4	0		0	.267	.267	.267	55	-3	0-0	.861	7	148	120	/3-9,SM	0.2
1873	Was NA	**39**	158	29	43	3	4	0	20	0		1	.272	.272	.342	84	-3	2-1	.728	3	116	124	*3-37/S-3	-0.1
1874	Bal NA	45	211	21	57	1	0	0	17	2		2	.270	.277	.275	78	-5	1-0	.782	**25**	**175**	82	*3-45/C-3,M	1.4
1875	Chi NA	**69**	287	37	71	9	0	0	23	0		3	.247	.247	.279	82	-5	5-10	.813	5	111	70	*3-59/S-5,O-5(CF),2-2	-0.4
1884	Was U	4	18	2	1	0	0	0		0			.056	.056	.056	-68	-4		.692	-2	59	0	/3-2,S2	-0.5
Total	5 NA	164	705	94	183	13	4	0	64	2		6	.260	.262	.289	78	-17	8-11	.000	40	133	90	3-150/S-9,O-5(CF),C-3,2-3	1.0
WHITED, ED Edward Morris B 2.9.1964 Bristol, PA BR/TR 6-3/195# d7.5																								
1989	Atl N	36	74	5	12	3	0	1	4	6-2	0	15	.162	.222	.243	33	-7	1-0	.914	-3	78	59	3-29/1-3	-1.0
WHITEHEAD, BURGESS Burgess Urquhart "Whitey" B 6.29.1910 Tarboro, NC D 11.25.1993 Windsor, NC BR/TR 5-10.5/160# d4.30 Mil 1942-45																								
1933	StL N	12	7	2	2	0	0	0	1	0	0	1	.286	.286	.286	60	0	0	1.000	0	74	128	/S-9,2-3	0.0
1934	†StL N	100	332	55	92	13	5	1	24	12	4	19	.277	.310	.355	73	-13	5	.962	-1	106	119	2-48,S-29,3-28	-1.0
1935	StL N★	107	338	45	89	10	2	0	33	11	1	14	.263	.289	.305	57	-21	5	.980	1	97	119	2-80/3-8,S-6	-1.5
1936	†NY N	**154**	632	99	176	31	3	4	47	29	7	32	.278	.317	.356	82	-17	14	.969	32	111	125	*2-153	2.4
1937	†NY N★	**152**	574	64	164	15	6	5	52	28	4	20	.286	.323	.359	84	-14	7	**.974**	28	107	**126**	*2-152	2.4
1939	NY N	95	335	31	80	6	3	2	24	24	5	19	.239	.299	.293	59	-20	1	.970	23	116	100	2-91/S-4,3	0.9
1940	NY N	133	568	68	160	9	6	4	36	26	5	17	.282	.319	.340	81	-16	9	.947	11	91	46	3-74,2-57/S-4	0.1
1941	NY N	116	403	41	92	15	4	1	23	14	2	10	.228	.258	.293	54	-26	7	.970	3	97	97	*2-104/3	-1.7
1946	Pit N	55	127	10	28	1	2	0	5	6	1	6	.220	.261	.260	47	-9	3	.963	-3	92	92	2-30/3-4,S	-1.2
Total	9	924	3316	415	883	100	31	17	245	150	29	138	.266	.304	.331	72	-136	51	.972	94	106	116	2-718,3-116/S-53	0.4

Year	Tm Lg	G	AB	R	H	2B	3B	HR	RBI	BB-IB	HP	SO	AVG	OBP	SLG	AOPS	ABR	SB-CS	FA	FR	Rng	Thr	G at Pos	BFW
WHITEHEAD, MILT Milton P. B 1862 , , CAN D 8.15.1901 Highland, CA BB/TR d4.20																								
1884	StL U	99	393	61	83	15	1	1		8			.211	.227	.262	46	-38		.803	-12	98	151	*S-94/O-2(CF),P23	-4.1
	KC U	5	22	2	3	0	0	0		0			.136	.136	.136	-20	-4		.857	0	141	0	/2-3,CS3	-0.3
	Year	104	415	63	86	15	1	1		8			.207	.222	.255	43	-41		**.804**	-12	98	**150**	S-95/2-4,O-2(CF),3-2,PC	-4.4
WHITEHOUSE, GIL Gilbert Arthur B 10.15.1893 Somerville, MA D 2.14.1926 Brewer, ME BB/TR 5-10/170# d6.20																								
1912	Bos N	2	3	0	0	0	0	0	0	0	0	3	.000	.000	.000	-98	-1	0	.667	-1	*120*	*0*	/C-2	-0.2
1915	New F	35	120	16	27	6	2	0	9	6	1	16	.225	.268	.308	66	-8	3	.949	-0	70	206	O-28(0-2-26)/PC	-1.0
Total	2	37	123	16	27	6	2	0	9	6	1	19	.220	.262	.301	61	-9	3	.949	-1	70	206	/O-28(0-2-26),C-3,P	-1.2
WHITELEY, GURDON Gurdon W. B 10.5.1859 Ashaway, RI D 11.24.1924 Cranston, RI 5-11/190# d8.7																								
1884	Cle N	8	34	4	5	0	0	0	0	1		8	.147	.171	.147	1	-4		.800	1	196	764	/O-8(4-3-1)	-0.3
1885	Bos N	33	135	14	25	2	2	1	7	1		25	.185	.191	.252	44	-9		.781	-3	123	218	O-32(8-0-24)/C	-1.2
Total	2	41	169	18	30	2	2	1	7	2		33	.178	.187	.231	34	-13		.785	-2	136	316	/O-40(12-3-25),C	-1.5
WHITEMAN, GEORGE George "Lucky" B 12.23.1882 Peoria, IL D 2.10.1947 Houston, TX BR/TR 5-7/160# d9.13																								
1907	Bos A	4	12	0	2	0	0	0	1	0	0		.167	.167	.167	6	-1	0	1.000	-0	0	0	/O-2(LF)	-0.2
1913	NY A	11	32	8	11	3	1	0	2	7	0	2	.344	.462	.500	181	4	2	.938	-0	114	50	O-11(4-4-3)	0.3
1918	†Bos A	71	214	24	57	14	0	1	28	20	2	9	.266	.335	.346	107	2	9	.935	-5	86	68	O-69(65-0-4)	-0.6
Total	3	86	258	32	70	17	1	1	31	27	2	11	.271	.345	.357	113	5	11	.936	-6	89	63	/O-82(71-4-7)	-0.5
WHITEN, MARK Mark Anthony B 11.25.1966 Pensacola, FL BB/TR 6-3/215# d7.12																								
1990	Tor A	33	88	12	24	1	1	2	7	7-0	0	14	.273	.323	.375	94	-1	2-0	1.000	3	115	165	O-30(3-0-27)/D-2	0.1
1991	Tor A	46	149	12	33	4	3	2	19	11-1	1	35	.221	.274	.329	65	-8	0-1	1.000	1	107	67	O-42(RF)	-0.9
	Cle A	70	258	34	66	14	4	7	26	19-1	2	50	.256	.310	.422	100	-1	4-2	.962	10	119	230	O-67(0-8-63)/D-3	0.7
	Year	116	407	46	99	18	7	9	45	30-2	3	85	.243	.297	.388	87	-8	4-3	.975	11	**114**	168	*O-109(0-8-105)/D-3	-0.2
1992	Cle A	148	508	73	129	19	4	9	43	72-10	2	102	.254	.347	.360	101	2	16-12	.980	5	103	137	*O-144(RF)/D-2	0.2
1993	StL N	152	562	81	142	13	4	25	99	58-9	2	110	.253	.323	.423	100	-2	15-8	.971	-3	99	77	*O-148(0-22-138)	-1.0
1994	StL N	92	334	57	98	18	2	14	53	37-9	1	75	.293	.364	.485	122	11	10-5	.964	11	**128**	130	O-90(RF)	1.7
1995	Bos A	32	108	13	20	3	0	1	10	8-0	0	23	.185	.239	.241	25	-12	1-0	1.000	2	95	213	O-31(RF)/D	-1.1
	Phi N	60	212	38	57	10	1	11	37	31-1	1	63	.269	.365	.481	120	6	7-0	.965	-1	98	100	O-55(RF)	0.4
1996	Phi N	60	182	33	43	8	0	7	21	33-2	1	62	.236	.356	.396	97	0	13-3	.945	3	107	199	O-51(0-8-44)	0.3
	Atl N	36	90	12	23	5	1	3	17	16-0	0	25	.256	.364	.433	105	1	2-5	.933	-2	90	63	O-29(RF)	-0.3
	Year	96	272	45	66	13	1	10	38	49-2	1	87	.243	.359	.408	99	1	15-8	.942	1	101	153	O-80(0-8-73)	0.0
	Sea A	40	140	31	42	7	0	12	33	21-4	2	40	.300	.399	.607	149	11	2-1	.969	3	116	149	O-39(36-0-4)	1.1
1997	NY A	69	215	34	57	11	0	5	24	30-5	2	47	.265	.360	.386	96	0	4-2	.954	-2	100	60	O-57(44-0-16)/D-6	-0.4
1998	†Cle A	88	226	31	64	14	0	6	29	29-0	3	60	.283	.372	.425	103	2	2-1	.970	2	99	194	O-72(43-22-13)/PD	0.3
1999	Cle A	8	25	2	4	1	0	1	4	3-0	0	4	.160	.250	.320	42	-2	0-0	1.000	-0	77	238	/O-7(5-2-0)	-0.2
2000	Cle A	6	7	2	2	1	0	0	1	3-0	0	2	.286	.500	.429	136	1	0-0	1.000	-0	64	0	/O-5(CF)	0.0
Total	11	940	3104	465	804	129	20	105	423	378-42	17	712	.259	.341	.415	101	8	78-40	.970	32	106	132	O-867(131-67-696)/D-19,P	0.9
WHITFIELD, FRED Fred Dwight B 1.7.1938 Vandiver, AL BL/TL 6-1/190# d5.27																								
1962	StL N	73	158	20	42	7	1	8	34	7-1	1	30	.266	.299	.475	95	-2	1-0	.987	1	114	127	1-38	-0.2
1963	Cle A	109	346	44	87	17	3	21	54	24-5	4	61	.251	.302	.500	123	9	0-1	.987	-4	83	97	1-92	-0.1
1964	Cle A	101	293	29	79	13	1	10	29	12-3	2	58	.270	.301	.423	100	-1	0-5	.992	-3	79	110	1-79	-1.1
1965	Cle A	132	468	49	137	23	1	26	90	16-7	2	42	.293	.316	.513	131	16	2-2	.993	4	105	93	*1-122	1.3
1966	Cle A	137	502	59	121	15	2	27	78	27-9	4	76	.241	.283	.440	105	1	1-2	.991	-4	84	96	*1-132	-1.3
1967	Cle A	100	257	24	56	10	0	9	31	25-8	1	45	.218	.290	.362	91	-3	3-3	.993	4	120	119	1-66	-0.3
1968	Cin N	87	171	15	44	8	0	6	32	9-1	2	29	.257	.302	.409	105	1	0-3	.981	-1	98	107	1-41	-0.3
1969	Cin N	74	74	2	11	0	0	1	8	18-0	0	27	.149	.315	.189	42	-5	0-0	.985	1	181	82	1-14	-0.5
1970	Mon N	4	15	0	1	0	0	0	0	1-0	0	3	.067	.125	.067	-47	-3	0-0	.976	2	253	89	/1-4	-0.2
Total	9	817	2284	242	578	93	8	108	356	139-34	16	371	.253	.298	.443	107	13	7-16	.990	-1	97	102	1-588	-2.7
WHITFIELD, TERRY Terry Bertland B 1.12.1953 Blythe, CA BL/TR 6-1/197# d9.29																								
1974	NY A	2	5	0	1	0	0	0	0	0-0	0	1	.200	.200	.200	16	-1	0-0	—	-1	0	0	/O(CF)	-0.1
1975	NY A	28	81	9	22	1	1	0	7	1-0	0	17	.272	.274	.309	67	-4	1-0	.978	1	101	173	O-25(2-0-23)/D	-0.4
1976	NY A	1	0	0	0	0	0	0	0	0-0	0	0	—	—	—	—	0	0-0	—	-0	0	0	/O(LF)	0.0
1977	SF N	114	326	41	93	21	3	7	36	20-1	2	46	.285	.329	.433	103	1	2-3	.972	0	107	72	O-84(22-22-49)	-0.3
1978	SF N	149	488	70	141	20	2	10	32	33-5	2	69	.289	.335	.400	109	5	5-11	.988	-1	103	66	*O-140(138-5-0)	-0.4
1979	SF N	133	394	52	113	20	4	5	44	36-6	4	47	.287	.349	.396	111	6	5-4	.957	0	95	138	*O-106(105-1-0)	0.2
1980	SF N	118	321	38	95	16	2	4	26	20-3	1	44	.296	.337	.396	107	3	4-2	.987	2	94	188	O-95(LF)	0.2
1984	LA N	87	180	15	44	8	0	4	18	17-2	1	35	.244	.313	.356	88	-3	1-4	.988	-1	91	130	O-58(23-2-37)	-0.7
1985	†LA N	79	104	8	27	7	0	3	16	6-1	0	27	.260	.300	.413	101	0	0-0	.926	-1	83	188	O-28(21-1-7)	-0.2
1986	LA N	19	14	0	1	0	0	0	0	5-2	0	2	.071	.316	.071	14	-1	0-0	1.000	0	159	0	/O(LF)	-0.1
Total	10	730	1913	233	537	93	12	33	179	138-20	10	288	.281	.330	.394	103	6	18-24	.976	1	98	118	O-539(408-32-116)/D	-1.8
WHITING, ED Edward C. (a/k/a Harry Zieber) B 1860 Philadelphia, PA BL/TR ?/188# d5.2																								
1882	Bal AA	**74**	308	43	80	14	5	0		7			.260	.276	.338	115	6		.834	-6			*C-72/1-3,O-2(1-0-1)	0.4
1883	Lou AA	58	240	35	70	16	4	2		9			.292	.317	.417	145	13		.884	-9			C-50/O-6(3-3-0),2-2,31	0.7
1884	Lou AA	42	157	16	35	7	3	0	18	9	2		.223	.274	.306	93	-1		.891	-6			C-40/O-2(1-0-1),1-2	-0.3
1886	Was N	6	21	0	0	0	0	0	0	1		12	.000	.045	.000	-92	-5	0	.919	-2			/C-6	-0.6
Total	4	180	726	94	185	37	12	2	<u>18</u>	26		<u>12</u>	.255	.282	.347	114	13	0	.866	-24			C-168/O-10(5-3-2),1-6,2-2,3	0.2
WHITMAN, DICK Dick Corwin B 11.9.1920 Woodburn, OR D 2.12.2003 Peoria, AZ BL/TR 5-11/170# d4.16																								
1946	Bro N	104	265	39	69	15	3	2	31	22	0	19	.260	.317	.362	92	-3	5	1.000	3	110	83	O-85(30-54-1)	-0.4
1947	Bro N	4	10	1	4	0	0	0	2	1	0	0	.400	.455	.400	124	0	0	1.000	0	114	0	/O-3(2-0-1)	0.0
1948	Bro N	60	165	24	48	13	0	0	20	14	0	12	.291	.346	.370	91	-2	4	.990	1	108	95	O-48(12-4-34)	-0.2
1949	†Bro N	23	49	8	9	2	0	0	2	4	0	4	.184	.245	.224	26	-5	0	.952	-1	98	0	O-11(10-0-1)	-0.7
1950	†Phi N	75	132	21	33	7	0	0	12	10	3	10	.250	.317	.303	65	-6	1	.983	0	101	101	O-32(7-13-15)	-0.7
1951	Phi N	19	17	0	2	0	0	0	0	0	0	1	.118	.118	.118	-37	-3	0-0	—	-0	0	0	/O-6(5-1-0)	-0.3
Total	6	285	638	93	165	37	3	2	67	51	3	46	.259	.316	.335	78	-19	10-<u>0</u>	.992	3	107	82	O-185(66-72-52)	-2.3
WHITMAN, FRANK Walter Franklin "Hooker" B 8.15.1924 Marengo, IN D 2.6.1994 Maryville, IL BR/TR 6-2/175# d6.30																								
1946	Chi A	17	16	7	1	0	0	0	1	2	1	6	.063	.211	.063	-22	-3	0-1	1.000	1	153	0	/S-6,12	-0.2
1948	Chi A	3	6	0	0	0	0	0	0	0	0	3	.000	.000	.000	-99	-2	0-0	.500	-1	63	124	/S	-0.3
Total	2	20	22	7	1	0	0	0	1	2	1	9	.045	.160	.045	-43	-5	0-1	.885	-0	128	35	/S-7,21	-0.5
WHITMER, DAN Daniel Charles B 11.23.1955 Redlands, CA BR/TR 6-3/195# d7.20 C3																								
1980	Cal A	48	87	8	21	3	0	0	7	4-0	0	21	.241	.269	.276	53	-6	1-0	1.000	3	106	72	C-48	-0.1
1981	Tor A	7	9	0	1	1	0	0	0	1-0	0	2	.111	.200	.222	20	-1	0-0	1.000	1	95	0	/C-7	0.0
Total	2	55	96	8	22	4	0	0	7	5-0	0	23	.229	.262	.271	49	-7	1-0	1.000	3	105	66	/C-55	-0.1
WHITMORE, DARRELL Darrell Lamont B 11.18.1968 Front Royal, VA BL/TR 6-1/210# d6.25																								
1993	Fla N	76	250	24	51	8	2	4	19	10-0	5	72	.204	.249	.300	44	-21	4-2	.979	0	108	60	O-69(1-0-69)	-2.4
1994	Fla N	9	22	1	5	1	0	0	0	3-0	0	5	.227	.320	.273	55	-1	0-1	1.000	0	125	0	/O-6(5-0-1)	-0.2
1995	Fla N	27	58	6	11	2	0	1	2	5-0	0	15	.190	.250	.276	40	-5	0-0	.960	-2	85	0	O-16(0-14-3)	-0.7
Total	3	112	330	31	67	11	2	5	21	18-0	5	92	.203	.254	.294	44	-27	4-3	.978	-1	106	47	/O-91(6-14-73)	-3.3
WHITNEY, PINKY Arthur Carter B 1.2.1905 San Antonio, TX D 9.1.1987 Center, TX BR/TR 5-10/165# d4.11																								
1928	Phi N	151	585	73	176	35	4	10	103	36	1	30	.301	.342	.426	96	-4	3	.955	5	99	83	*3-149	1.0
1929	Phi N	**154**	612	89	200	43	14	8	115	61	2	35	.327	.390	.482	108	8	7	.967	**23**	**116**	113	*3-154	3.7
1930	Phi N	149	606	87	207	41	5	8	117	40	1	41	.342	.383	.465	97	-2	3	.965	21	**113**	91	*3-148	2.5
1931	Phi N	130	501	64	144	36	5	9	74	30	3	38	.287	.331	.433	96	-3	6	.948	-6	91	84	*3-128	-0.4
1932	Phi N	**154**	624	93	186	33	11	13	124	35	0	66	.298	.335	.449	97	-3	6	**.960**	3	97	110	*3-151/2-5	0.6
1933	Phi N	31	121	12	32	4	0	3	19	8	0	8	.264	.310	.372	83	-3	1	.963	-1	91	144	3-30	-0.3
	Bos N	100	382	42	94	17	2	8	49	25	2	23	.246	.296	.364	95	-3	2	.971	2	110	134	3-85,2-18	0.3
	Year	131	503	54	126	21	2	11	68	33	2	31	.250	.299	.366	92	-6	3	**.969**	1	105	**136**	*3-115,2-18	0.0

Year	Tm Lg	G	AB	R	H	2B	3B	HR	RBI	BB-IB	HP	SO	AVG	OBP	SLG	AOPS	ABR	SB-CS	FA	FR	Rng	Thr	G at Pos	BFW
1934	Bos N	146	563	58	146	26	2	12	79	25	3	54	.259	.294	.377	85	-14	7	**.968**	2	107	72	*3-111,2-36/S-2	-0.6
1935	Bos N	126	458	41	125	23	4	4	60	24	2	36	.273	.312	.367	89	-8	2	.958	3	110	65	3-74,2-49	0.1
1936	Bos N	10	40	1	7	0	0	0	5	2	1	4	.175	.233	.175	12	-5	0	.971	1	98	144	3-10	-0.4
	Phi N★	114	411	44	121	17	3	6	59	37	1	33	.294	.354	.394	92	-4	2	.955	12	120	100	*3-111/2	1.2
	Year	124	451	45	128	17	3	6	64	39	2	37	.284	.343	.375	86	-9	2	**.956**	13	**118**	104	*3-121/2	0.8
1937	Phi N	138	487	56	166	19	4	8	79	43	1	44	.341	.395	.446	118	13	6	**.982**	3	103	93	*3-130	2.1
1938	Phi N	102	300	27	83	9	1	3	38	27	0	22	.277	.336	.343	90	-4	0	.934	-4	95	60	3-75/1-4,2-2	-0.6
1939	Phi N	34	75	9	14	0	1	1	6	7	0	4	.187	.256	.253	38	-7	0	.991	1	131	98	1-12/2-8,3-2	-0.6
Total	12	1539	5765	696	1701	303	56	93	927	400	17	438	.295	.343	.415	96	-39	45	.961	67	105	95	*3-1358,2-119/1-16,S-2	8.6
WHITNEY, ART Arthur Wilson B 1.16.1858 Brockton, MA D 8.15.1943 Lowell, MA BR/TR 5-8/155# d5.1 b-Frank ▲																								
1880	Wor N	76	302	38	67	13	5	1	36	9		15	.222	.244	.308	79	-7		.860	-2	103	78	*3-76	-0.6
1881	Det N	58	214	23	39	7	5	0	9	7		15	.182	.208	.262	45	-14		.849	7	121	111	*3-58	-0.4
1882	Pro N	11	40	2	3	0	0	0	1	2		11	.075	.119	.075	-36	-6		.784	-3	97	75	S-11	-0.8
	Det N	31	115	10	21	0	0	0	4	1		12	.183	.190	.183	20	-10		.854	-2	82	97	3-22/S-8,P-3	-1.0
	Year	42	155	12	24	0	0	0	5	3		23	.155	.171	.155	5	-16		.854	-5	82	97	3-22,S-19/P-3	-1.8
1884	Pit AA	23	94	10	28	4	0	0		1	0		.298	.305	.340	112	1		.916	3	121	37	3-21/O(CF)S	0.4
1885	Pit AA	90	373	53	87	10	4	0	28	16	1		.233	.267	.282	74	-11		**.918**	-15	85	101	*S-75/3-8,2-4,O-3(LF)	-2.1
1886	Pit AA	136	511	70	122	13	4	0	55	51	6		.239	.315	.280	87	-5	15	**.906**	12	108	**139**	*3-95,S-42/P	0.8
1887	Pit N	119	431	57	112	11	4	0	51	55	2	18	.260	.346	.304	89	-2	10	**.924**	-8	96	68	*3-119	-0.7
1888	†NY N	90	328	28	72	1	4	1	28	8	1	22	.220	.240	.256	59	-16	7	.887	5	103	104	3-90	-1.0
1889	†NY N	129	473	71	103	12	2	1	59	56	2	39	.218	.303	.258	57	-27	19	.882	2	98	120	*3-129/P	-2.0
1890	NY P	119	442	71	97	12	3	0	45	64	3	19	.219	.322	.260	52	-31	8	.865	-12	89	74	3-88,S-31	-3.2
1891	Cin AA	93	347	42	69	6	1	3	33	31	3	20	.199	.270	.248	45	-27	8	.903	-6	95	74	3-93	-2.7
	StL AA	3	11	0	0	0	0	0	0	1	0	2	.000	.083	.000	-66	-2	0	.867	1	170	0	/3-3	-0.1
	Year	96	358	42	69	6	1	3	33	32	3	22	.193	.265	.240	41	-29	8	**.902**	-5	98	71	3-96	-2.8
Total	11	978	3681	475	820	89	32	6	349	302	18	173	.223	.285	.269	64	-157	67	.888	-18	101	94	3-802,S-168/P-5,2-4,O-4(3-1-0)	-13.4
WHITNEY, FRANK Frank Thomas "Jumbo" B 2.18.1856 Brockton, MA D 10.30.1943 Baltimore, MD BR/TR 5-7.5/152# d5.17 b-Art																								
1876	Bos N	34	139	27	33	7	1	0	15	1		3	.237	.243	.302	79	-3		.818	1	129	278	O-34(24-0-10)/2	-0.3
WHITT, ERNIE Leo Ernest B 6.13.1952 Detroit, MI BL/TR 6-2/200# d9.12																								
1976	Bos A	8	18	4	4	2	0	1	3	2-0	0	2	.222	.300	.500	117	0	0-0	1.000	-1	264	38	/C-8	0.0
1977	Tor A	23	41	4	7	3	0	0	6	2-0	0	12	.171	.200	.244	23	-4	0-0	1.000	1	94	96	C-14	-0.3
1978	Tor A	2	4	0	0	0	0	0	0	1-0	0	1	.000	.200	.000	-38	-1	0-0	1.000	1	0	279	/C	0.0
1980	Tor A	106	295	23	70	12	2	6	34	22-0	0	30	.237	.287	.353	72	-12	1-3	.986	6	87	107	*C-105	-0.3
1981	Tor A	74	195	16	46	9	0	1	16	20-3	0	30	.236	.307	.297	70	-7	5-2	.991	13	129	105	C-72	0.9
1982	Tor A	105	284	28	74	14	2	11	42	26-5	0	34	.261	.317	.440	98	-1	3-1	.982	4	105	81	C-98/D	0.6
1983	Tor A	123	344	53	88	15	2	17	56	50-5	0	55	.256	.346	.459	114	7	1-1	.992	14	118	108	*C-119	2.5
1984	Tor A	124	315	35	75	12	1	15	46	43-7	1	49	.238	.327	.425	104	2	0-3	.994	13	108	83	*C-118	1.8
1985	†Tor A★	139	412	55	101	21	2	19	64	47-9	1	59	.245	.323	.444	105	3	3-6	.988	13	121	80	*C-134	1.9
1986	Tor A	131	395	48	106	19	2	16	56	35-3	0	39	.268	.326	.448	106	3	0-1	.991	-1	114	89	*C-129	0.6
1987	Tor A	135	446	57	120	24	1	19	75	44-4	1	50	.269	.334	.455	105	3	0-1	.994	17	107	116	*C-131	2.3
1988	Tor A	127	398	63	100	11	2	16	70	61-4	1	38	.251	.348	.410	112	7	4-2	.994	-3	82	99	*C-123	1.2
1989	†Tor A	129	385	42	101	24	1	11	53	52-2	0	53	.262	.349	.416	117	10	5-4	.992	1	112	87	*C-115/D-8	1.7
1990	Atl N	67	180	14	31	8	0	2	10	23-1	0	27	.172	.265	.250	40	-14	0-2	.991	-3	67	166	C-59	-1.5
1991	Bal A	35	62	5	15	2	0	0	3	8-0	0	12	.242	.329	.274	71	-2	0-0	1.000	-1	80	133	C-20/D-2	-0.2
Total	15	1328	3774	447	938	176	15	134	534	436-43	4	491	.249	.324	.410	98	-6	22-26	.991	72	106	99	*C-1246/D-11	11.2
WHITTED, POSSUM George Bostic B 2.4.1890 Durham, NC D 10.16.1962 Wilmington, NC BR/TR 5-8.5/168# d9.16 OF Total (442-LF 94-CF 117-RF)																								
1912	StL N	12	46	7	12	3	0	0	7	3	0	5	.261	.306	.326	75	-2	1	.857	-3	71	56	3-12	-0.4
1913	StL N	123	404	44	89	10	5	0	38	31	4	44	.220	.282	.270	59	-22	9-16	.989	3	106	90	O-41(20-3-18),S-38,3-22/2-7,1-2	-2.3
1914	StL N	20	31	3	4	1	0	0	1	0	0	3	.129	.129	.161	-14	-4	1	.889	-2	97	148	/3-5,O-3(2-0-2),2	-0.6
	†Bos N	66	218	36	57	11	4	2	31	18	3	18	.261	.326	.376	109	2	10	.967	-2	100	76	O-38(4-25-10),2-15/1-4,3-4,S-3	-0.2
	Year	86	249	39	61	12	4	2	32	18	3	21	.245	.304	.349	95	-2	11	.957	-3	97	74	O-41(6-25-12),2-16/3-9,1-4,S-3	-0.8
1915	†Phi N	128	448	46	126	17	3	1	43	29	2	47	.281	.328	.339	101	0	24-15	.978	-1	100	48	*O-119(53-66-0)/1-7	-0.9
1916	Phi N	147	526	68	148	20	12	6	68	19	2	46	.281	.309	.399	113	5	29-17	.964	3	110	92	*O-136(LF),1-16	0.3
1917	Phi N	149	553	69	155	24	9	3	70	30	0	56	.280	.317	.373	107	3	10	.977	4	102	114	*O-141(LF),1-10/3-7,2	0.1
1918	Phi N	24	86	7	21	4	0	0	3	4	0	10	.244	.278	.291	69	-3	4	.982	1	104	112	O-22(LF)/1	-0.4
1919	Phi N	78	289	32	72	14	1	3	32	14	0	20	.249	.284	.336	80	-7	5	.955	-1	96	138	O-47(LF),2-26/1-2	-1.1
	Pit N	35	131	15	51	7	7	0	21	6	1	4	.389	.420	.550	183	12	7	.988	3	140	131	1-33/3-2,O(LF)	1.6
	Year	113	420	47	123	21	8	3	53	20	1	24	.293	.327	.402	112	5	12	.955	2	96	137	O-48(LF),1-35,2-26/3-2	0.5
1920	Pit N	134	494	53	129	11	12	1	74	35	3	36	.261	.314	.338	85	-10	11-11	.961	-4	92	81	*3-125,1-10/O(LF)	-1.4
1921	Pit N	108	403	60	114	23	7	7	63	26	1	21	.283	.328	.427	96	-3	5-10	.988	6	118	62	*O-102(15-0-87)/1-7	-0.9
1922	Bro N	1	1	0	0	0	0	0	0	0	0	0	.000	.000	.000	-99	0	0-0	—	0			H	0.0
Total	11	1025	3630	440	978	145	60	23	451	215	16	310	.269	.313	.361	95	-29	116-69	.975	5	105	87	O-651L,3-177/1-92,2-50,S-41	-6.2
WICKER, FLOYD Floyd Euliss B 9.12.1943 Burlington, NC BL/TR 6-2/175# d6.23																								
1968	StL N	5	4	2	2	0	0	0	0	0-0	0	0	.500	.500	.500	204	0	0-0	—	0			H	0.1
1969	Mon N	41	39	2	4	0	0	0	2	2-0	0	20	.103	.146	.103	-29	-7	0-0	1.000	1	149	0	O-11(2-7-2)	-0.7
1970	Mil A	15	41	3	8	1	0	1	3	1-0	0	8	.195	.214	.293	38	-4	0-0	1.000	-0	103	0	O-12(8-0-4)	-0.5
1971	Mil A	11	8	0	1	0	0	0	0	2-0	0	0	.125	.300	.125	24	-1	0-0	—	0			H	-0.1
	SF N	9	21	3	3	0	0	0	1	2-0	1	5	.143	.250	.143	14	-2	0-0	1.000	1	108	253	/O-7(LF)	-0.2
Total	4	81	113	10	18	1	0	1	6	7-0	1	33	.159	.215	.195	15	-14	0-0	1.000	1	114	83	/O-30(17-7-6)	-1.4
WICKLAND, AL Albert B 1.27.1888 Chicago, IL D 3.14.1980 Port Washington, WI BL/TL 5-7/155# d8.21																								
1913	Cin N	26	79	7	17	5	5	0	8	6	1	19	.215	.279	.405	94	-1	3-4	.983	1	111	66	O-24(CF)	-0.3
1914	Chi F	**157**	536	74	148	31	10	6	68	**81**	4	58	.276	.375	.405	119	9	17	.962	-2	101	88	*O-157(30-1-129)	-0.2
1915	Chi F	30	86	11	21	2	2	1	5	13	0	11	.244	.343	.349	101	-1	3	.946	-0	92	111	O-24(5-0-20)	-0.3
	Pit F	110	389	63	117	12	8	1	30	52	2	47	.301	.386	.380	117	5	23	.968	4	116	77	*O-109(109-0-1)	0.5
	Year	140	475	74	138	14	10	2	35	65	2	58	.291	.378	.375	114	4	26	.966	4	112	82	*O-133(114-0-21)	0.2
1918	Bos N	95	332	55	87	7	13	4	32	53	2	39	.262	.367	.398	139	17	12	.975	-0	109	71	O-95(1-0-94)	1.3
1919	NY A	26	46	2	7	1	0	0	1	2	0	10	.152	.188	.174	2	-6	0	1.000	-1	95	0	O-15(RF)	-0.8
Total	5	444	1468	212	397	58	38	12	144	207	9	184	.270	.364	.386	117	23	58-4	.968	1	107	79	O-424(145-25-259)	0.2
WIDGER, CHRIS Christopher Jon B 5.21.1971 Wilmington, DE BR/TR 6-3/195# d6.23																								
1995	†Sea A	23	45	2	9	0	0	1	2	3-0	0	11	.200	.245	.267	34	-5	0-0	1.000	-6	88	0	C-19/O-3(2-0-1),D	-1.0
1996	Sea A	8	11	1	2	0	0	0	0	0-0	1	5	.182	.250	.182	12	-2	0-0	.905	-2	224	0	/C-7	-0.3
1997	Mon N	91	278	30	65	20	3	7	37	22-1	1	59	.234	.290	.403	80	-9	2-0	.981	-24	54	80	C-85	-2.8
1998	Mon N	125	417	36	97	18	1	15	53	29-2	0	85	.233	.281	.388	75	-17	6-1	.983	4	88	**143**	*C-123	-0.4
1999	Mon N	124	383	42	101	24	1	14	56	28-0	7	86	.264	.325	.441	94	-4	1-4	.992	-5	77	94	*C-118	-0.4
2000	Mon N	86	281	31	67	17	2	12	34	29-3	1	61	.238	.311	.441	85	-7	1-2	.985	0	90	93	C-85	-0.3
	Sea A	10	11	1	1	0	0	1	1	1-0	0	2	.091	.167	.364	30	-1	0-0	1.000	-1	0	0	/C-6,1-2,O(RF)	-0.2
2002	NY A	21	64	4	19	5	0	0	5	2-0	2	9	.297	.338	.375	90	-1	0-0	.983	-3	120	66	C-21	-0.3
2003	StL N	44	102	9	24	9	0	0	14	6-1	1	20	.235	.279	.324	61	-6	0-0	.995	-3	131	84	C-41/1O(RF)	-0.6
Total	8	532	1592	156	385	93	7	50	202	120-7	13	338	.242	.299	.403	80	-52	10-7	.986	-39	85	99	C-505/O-5(2-0-3),1-3,D	-6.3
WIEDENBAUER, TOM Thomas John B 11.5.1958 Menomonie, WI BR/TR 6-1/180# d9.14																								
1979	Hou N	4	6	0	4	1	0	0	2	0-0	0	2	.667	.667	.833	326	2	0-0	1.000	-0	97	0	/O-3(1-1-1)	0.2
WIEDMAN, STUMP George Edward B 2.17.1861 Rochester, NY D 3.2.1905 New York, NY BR/TR 5-7.5/165# d8.26 U1 ▲																								
1880	Buf N	23	78	8	8	1	0	0	3	2		11	.103	.125	.115	-18	-9		.893	-1	79	0	P-17,O-13(1-11-1)	-0.4
1881	Det N	13	47	9	12	1	0	0	5	2		2	.255	.286	.277	75	0		**1.000**	-2	68	0	P-13	0.0
1882	Det N	50	193	20	42	7	1	0	20	2		19	.218	.226	.264	57	-9		.906	0	91	84	P-46/O-6(1-2-2),S	0.0
1883	Det N	79	313	34	58	6	1	1	24	4		38	.185	.196	.220	27	-27		.909	-4	91	43	P-52,O-35(1-5-29)/2-4	-1.4
1884	Det N	81	300	24	49	6	0	0	26	13		41	.163	.198	.183	22	-26		.846	-5	101	95	O-53(RF),P-26/S2	-2.1

Year	Tm Lg	G	AB	R	H	2B	3B	HR	RBI	BB-IB	HP	SO	AVG	OBP	SLG	AOPS	ABR	SB-CS	FA	FR	Rng	Thr	G at Pos	BFW
1885	Det N	44	153	7	24	2	1	1	14	8		32	.157	.199	.203	30	-12		.867	-6	78	0	P-38/O-7(6-1-0),2	-0.5
1886	KC N	51	179	13	30	2	0	0	7	5		46	.168	.190	.179	12	-19	3	.936	3	120	155	P-51/O-3(1-2-0)	0.1
1887	Det N	21	82	12	17	2	0	1	11	3	0	3	.207	.235	.268	38	-7	6	.837	-1	102	0	P-21/O-2(LF)	0.0
	NY AA	14	46	5	7	1	1	0	1	4	0		.152	.220	.217	23	-5	2	.882	2	106	0	P-12/O-3(1-0-2)	0.1
	NY N	1	3	0	1	0	0	0	0	0	0	0	.333	.333	.333	90	0	0	.500	-0	67	0	/P	0.0
1888	NY N	2	7	1	0	0	0	0	1	2	0	1	.000	.222	.000	-24	0	0	.714	-0	51	0	/P-2	0.0
Total	9	379	1401	133	248	28	4	3	112	45	0	193	.177	.203	.209	28	-114	11	.885	-12	95	57	P-279,O-122(13-21-87)/2-6,S-2	-4.2
WIEGHAUS, TOM Thomas Robert B 2.1.1957 Chicago Heights, IL BR/TR 6/195# d10.4																								
1981	Mon N	1	1	0	0	0	0	0	0	0-0	0	0	.000	.000	.000	-99	0	0-0	1.000	-0	9	0	/C	0.0
1983	Mon N	1	0	0	0	0	0	0	0	0-0	0	0	—	—	—	—	0	0-0	1.000	-0	0	0	/C	0.0
1984	Hou N	6	10	0	0	0	0	0	1	1-0	0	3	.000	.083	.000	-78	-2	0-0	1.000	-0	55	118	/C-6	-0.2
Total	3	8	11	0	0	0	0	0	1	1-0	0	3	.000	.077	.000	-80	-2	0-0	1.000	-0	50	107	/C-8	-0.2
WIETELMANN, WHITEY William Frederick B 3.15.1919 Zanesville, OH D 3.26.2002 San Diego, CA BB/TR (BR 1939-41) 6/170# d9.6 C13																								
1939	Bos N	23	69	2	14	1	0	0	5	2	0	9	.203	.225	.217	21	-8	1	.953	1	111	81	S-22/2	-0.6
1940	Bos N	35	41	3	8	1	0	0	1	5	0	5	.195	.283	.220	43	-3	0	.962	2	84	175	2-15/3-9,S-3	-0.1
1941	Bos N	16	33	1	3	0	0	0	0	1	0	2	.091	.118	.091	-43	-6	0	1.000	1	110	0	2-10/S-5,3-2	-0.5
1942	Bos N	13	34	4	7	2	0	0	0	4	0	5	.206	.289	.265	64	-1	0	.941	-1	101	107	S-11/2	-0.2
1943	Bos N	**153**	534	33	115	14	1	0	39	46	3	40	.215	.281	.245	53	-32	9	.957	18	**115**	101	*S-153	-0.1
1944	Bos N	125	417	46	100	18	1	2	32	33	3	25	.240	.300	.302	67	-18	0	.954	-2	96	108	*S-103,2-23/3	-1.2
1945	Bos N	123	428	53	116	15	3	4	33	39	2	27	.271	.335	.348	89	-6	4	.972	-5	94	124	2-87,S-39/3-2,P	-0.4
1946	Bos N	44	78	7	16	0	0	0	5	14	0	8	.205	.326	.205	52	-4	0	.915	-4	74	77	S-16/3-8,2-4,P-3	-0.8
1947	Pit N	48	128	21	30	4	1	1	7	12	0	10	.234	.300	.305	59	-8	0	.885	-12	77	59	S-22,2-14/3-6,1	-1.8
Total	9	580	1762	170	409	55	6	7	122	156	8	131	.232	.298	.282	63	-86	14	.952	-2	104	100	S-374,2-155/3-28,P-4,1	-5.7
WIGGINS, ALAN Alan Anthony B 2.17.1958 Los Angeles, CA D 1.6.1991 Los Angeles, CA BB/TR 6-2/160# d9.4																								
1981	SD N	15	14	4	5	0	0	0	0	1-0	0	0	.357	.400	.357	125	0	2-0	.750	-0	115	0	/O-4(LF)	0.0
1982	SD N	72	254	40	65	3	3	1	15	13-0	1	19	.256	.295	.303	71	-11	33-6	.967	4	104	167	O-68(51-19-6)/2	-0.5
1983	SD N	144	503	83	139	20	2	0	22	65-3	1	43	.276	.360	.324	94	-1	66-13	.992	7	115	100	*O-105(63-48-14),1-45	1.1
1984	†SD N	158	596	106	154	19	7	3	34	75-1	3	57	.258	.342	.329	90	-6	70-21	.962	-20	92	100	*2-157	-1.0
1985	SD N	10	37	3	2	1	0	0	0	2-0	0	4	.054	.103	.081	-49	-7	0-1	1.000	-4	74	67	/2-9	-1.2
	Bal A	76	298	43	85	11	4	0	21	29-0	2	16	.285	.353	.349	96	-1	30-13	.960	-19	82	109	2-76	-1.4
1986	Bal A	71	239	30	60	3	1	0	11	22-0	0	20	.251	.309	.272	62	-12	21-7	.978	-5	90	105	2-66/D	-1.2
1987	Bal A	85	306	37	71	4	2	1	15	28-0	1	34	.232	.298	.268	53	-21	20-7	.983	1	102	95	D-44,2-33/O-5(LF)	-1.7
Total	7	631	2247	346	581	61	19	5	118	235-4	8	193	.259	.330	.309	80	-59	242-68	.967	-37	90	101	2-342,O-182(123-67-20)/D-45,1-45	-5.9
WIGGINTON, TY Ty Allen B 10.11.1977 San Diego, CA BR/TR 6/200# d5.16																								
2002	NY N	46	116	18	35	8	0	6	18	8-0	2	19	.302	.354	.526	138	5	2-1	.900	2	87	133	3-14,1-13,2-12/O-2(1-0-1)	0.7
2003	NY N	156	573	73	146	36	6	11	71	46-2	9	124	.255	.318	.396	88	-11	12-2	.962	-10	93	91	*3-155	-1.7
Total	2	202	689	91	181	44	6	17	89	54-2	11	143	.263	.324	.418	96	-6	14-3	.958	-8	93	94	3-169/1-13,2-12,O-2(1-0-1)	-1.0
WILBER, DEL Delbert Quentin "Babe" B 2.24.1919 Lincoln Park, MI D 7.18.2002 St.Petersburg, FL BR/TR 6-3/200# d4.21 M1 C4																								
1946	StL N	4	4	0	0	0	0	0	0	1	0	0	.000	.200	.000	-39	-1	0	1.000	1	*0*	*0*	/C-4	0.0
1947	StL N	51	99	7	23	8	1	0	12	5	0	13	.232	.269	.333	57	-6	0	.983	0	*115*	*73*	C-34	-0.5
1948	StL N	27	58	5	11	2	0	0	10	4	0	9	.190	.242	.224	25	-6	0	.949	-1	*301*	*75*	C-26	-0.7
1949	StL N	2	4	0	1	0	0	0	0	0	0	0	.250	.250	.250	33	0	0	1.000	0	*0*	*0*	/C-2	0.0
1951	Phi N	84	245	30	68	7	3	8	34	17	0	26	.278	.324	.429	102	0	0-1	.978	2	*119*	*68*	C-73	0.5
1952	Phi N	2	2	0	0	0	0	0	0	0	0	1	.000	.000	.000	-99	-1	0-0	—	0			H	-0.1
	Bos A	47	135	7	36	10	1	3	23	7	1	20	.267	.308	.422	94	-1	1-0	.995	2	*122*	*106*	C-39	0.3
1953	Bos A	58	112	16	27	6	1	7	29	6	1	21	.241	.286	.500	103	0	0-0	.980	-1	*103*	*66*	C-28/1-2	-0.1
1954	Bos A	24	61	2	8	2	1	1	7	4	0	6	.131	.179	.246	15	-7	0-0	.950	-3	*70*	*102*	C-18	-1.0
Total	8	299	720	67	174	35	7	19	115	44	2	96	.242	.286	.389	79	-22	1-1	.978	-0	*128*	*78*	C-224/1-2	-1.6
WILBORN, CLAUDE Claude Edward B 9.1.1912 Woodsdale, NC D 11.13.1992 Roxboro, NC BL/TR 6-1/180# d9.8																								
1940	Bos N	5	7	0	0	0	0	0	0	0	0	1	.000	.000	.000	-99	-2	0	.500	-1	46	0	/O-3(RF)	-0.3
WILBORN, TED Thaddeaus Iglehart B 12.16.1958 Waco, TX BB/TR 6/165# d4.5																								
1979	Tor A	22	12	3	0	0	0	0	0	1-0	0	7	.000	.077	.000	-76	-3	0-1	.875	-1	73	0	/O-7(4-1-2),D-4	-0.4
1980	NY A	8	8	2	2	0	0	0	1	0-0	0	1	.250	.250	.250	38	-1	0-0	1.000	1	129	720	/O-3(1-1-1)	0.0
Total	2	30	20	5	2	0	0	0	1	1-0	0	8	.100	.143	.100	-33	-4	0-1	.933	0	91	227	/O-10(5-2-3),D-4	-0.4
WILEY, JOHN John d6.23																								
1884	Was U	1	4	0	0	0	0	0		0			.000	.000	.000	-99	-1		.333	-1	61	0	/3	-0.2
WILFONG, ROB Robert Donald B 9.1.1953 Pasadena, CA BL/TR 6-1/185# d4.10 OF Total (2-LF 9-CF 1-RF)																								
1977	Min A	73	171	22	42	1	1	1	13	17-0	2	26	.246	.321	.281	67	-8	10-4	.959	-1	102	112	2-66/D	-0.5
1978	Min A	92	199	23	53	8	0	1	11	19-1	2	27	.266	.336	.322	84	-4	8-4	.986	-8	94	82	2-80/D-5	-0.7
1979	Min A	140	419	71	131	22	6	9	59	29-3	2	54	.313	.352	.458	115	8	11-4	.979	19	111	111	*2-133/O-3(1-1-1)	3.3
1980	Min A	131	416	55	103	16	5	8	45	34-3	3	61	.248	.308	.368	79	-13	10-6	**.995**	4	104	110	*2-120/O-6(CF)	-0.2
1981	Min A	93	305	32	75	11	3	3	19	29-1	0	43	.246	.311	.331	80	-8	2-4	.980	0	102	82	2-93	-0.4
1982	Min A	25	81	7	13	1	0	0	5	7-0	1	13	.160	.236	.173	14	-10	0-2	.980	1	110	125	2-22	-0.9
	†Cal A	55	102	17	25	4	2	1	11	7-1	0	17	.245	.294	.353	77	-4	4-0	.982	6	133	106	2-28/3-5,O-3(1-2-0),S-2,D	0.4
	Year	80	183	24	38	5	2	1	16	14-1	1	30	.208	.268	.273	49	-13	4-2	.981	6	121	116	2-50/3-5,O-3(1-2-0),S-2,D	-0.5
1983	Cal A	65	177	17	45	7	1	2	17	10-1	0	25	.254	.293	.339	74	-7	0-2	.995	8	111	100	2-39,3-13/S-6,D	0.3
1984	Cal A	108	307	31	76	13	2	6	33	20-0	2	53	.248	.296	.362	82	-8	3-2	.975	6	112	94	2-97/S-4,D	0.2
1985	Cal A	83	217	16	41	3	0	4	13	16-1	0	32	.189	.243	.258	38	-19	4-1	.986	13	119	116	2-69/D-2	-0.2
1986	†Cal A	92	288	25	63	11	3	3	33	16-2	2	34	.219	.263	.309	56	-18	1-4	.982	4	109	102	2-90	-1.1
1987	SF N	2	8	2	1	0	0	1	2	1-0	0	2	.125	.222	.500	89	0	1-0	.833	-1	55	177	/2-2	-0.1
Total	11	959	2690	318	668	97	23	39	261	205-13	14	387	.248	.303	.345	77	-91	54-33	.982	51	108	102	2-839/3-18,S-12,O-12C,D-11	0.1
WILHELM, SPIDER Charles Ernest B 5.23.1929 Baltimore, MD D 10.20.1992 Venice, FL BR/TR 5-9/170# d9.6																								
1953	Phi A	7	7	1	2	1	0	0	0	0	0	3	.286	.286	.429	87	0	0-0	.875	-0	108	0	/S-6	0.0
WILHELM, JIM James Webster B 9.20.1952 San Rafael, CA BR/TR 6-3/190# d9.4																								
1978	SD N	10	19	2	7	2	0	0	4	0-0	1	2	.368	.381	.474	155	1	1-0	1.000	-1	59	0	O-10(3-7-0)	0.0
1979	SD N	39	103	8	25	4	3	0	8	2-0	0	12	.243	.255	.340	65	-6	1-1	.985	0	90	200	O-30(4-25-1)	-0.6
Total	2	49	122	10	32	6	3	0	12	2-0	1	14	.262	.276	.361	79	-5	2-1	.987	-1	84	164	/O-40(7-32-1)	-0.6
WILHOIT, JOE Joseph William B 12.20.1885 Hiawatha, KS D 9.25.1930 Santa Barbara, CA BL/TR 6-2/175# d4.12																								
1916	Bos N	116	383	44	88	13	4	2	38	27	1	45	.230	.282	.300	82	-8	18	.979	3	109	98	*O-108(1-1-106)	-1.2
1917	Bos N	54	186	20	51	5	0	1	10	17	0	15	.274	.335	.317	107	2	5	.928	-2	86	112	O-52(RF)	-0.3
	Pit N	9	10	0	2	0	0	0	0	1	0	1	.200	.273	.200	45	-1	0	1.000	1	49	686	/O-3(1-0-2),1	0.0
	†NY N	34	50	9	17	2	2	0	8	8	0	5	.340	.431	.460	179	5	0	1.000	0	104	97	O-11(0-2-10)	0.5
	Year	97	246	29	70	7	2	1	18	26	0	21	.285	.353	.341	118	6	5	.941	-2	88	121	O-66(1-2-64)/1	0.2
1918	NY N	64	135	13	37	3	3	0	15	17	0	14	.274	.355	.341	115	3	4	.975	-1	85	137	O-55(3-34-15)	0.0
1919	Bos A	6	18	7	6	0	0	0	2	5	0	2	.333	.478	.333	138	1	1	1.000	-1	81	0	/O-5(RF)	0.0
Total	4	283	782	93	201	23	9	3	73	75	1	82	.257	.323	.321	101	2	28	.969	1	98	109	O-234(5-37-190)/1	-1.0
WILIE, DENNEY Dennis Ernest B 9.22.1890 Mt.Calm, TX D 6.20.1966 Hayward, CA BL/TL 5-8/155# d7.27																								
1911	StL N	28	51	10	12	3	1	0	3	8	2	11	.235	.361	.333	97	0	3	1.000	0	90	140	O-15(11-3-2)	0.0
1912	StL N	30	48	2	11	0	1	0	6	7	2	9	.229	.351	.271	73	-1	0	.917	-1	101	58	O-16(3-1-12)	-0.3
1915	Cle A	45	131	14	33	4	1	2	10	26	2	18	.252	.384	.344	115	4	2-6	.910	-3	104	21	O-35(11-24-0)	-0.3
Total	3	103	230	26	56	7	3	2	19	41	6	38	.243	.372	.326	102	3	5-6	.925	-4	101	49	/O-66(25-28-14)	-0.6
WILKE, HARRY Henry Joseph B 12.14.1900 Cincinnati, OH D 6.21.1991 Hamilton, OH BR/TR 5-10.5/171# d5.12																								
1927	Chi N	3	9	0	0	0	0	0	0	0	0	1	.000	.000	.000	-99	-3	0	1.000	0	124	0	/3-3	-0.2

Year	Tm Lg	G	AB	R	H	2B	3B	HR	RBI	BB-IB	HP	SO	AVG	OBP	SLG	AOPS	ABR	SB-CS	FA	FR	Rng	Thr	G at Pos	BFW
WILKERSON, CURTIS Curtis Vernon B 4.26.1961 Petersburg, VA BB/TR 5-9/158# d9.10																								
1983	Tex A	16	35	7	6	0	1	0	1	2-0	0	5	.171	.216	.229	23	-4	3-0	1.000	1	111	70	/S-9,2-2,3-2	-0.1
1984	Tex A	153	484	47	120	12	0	1	26	22-0	2	72	.248	.282	.279	55	-30	12-10	.944	-25	92	79	*S-116,2-47	-4.4
1985	Tex A	129	360	35	88	11	6	0	22	22-0	4	63	.244	.293	.308	65	-18	14-7	.957	0	103	84	*S-110,2-19/D-2	-0.6
1986	Tex A	110	236	27	56	10	3	0	15	11-0	1	42	.237	.273	.305	56	-15	9-7	.968	-1	99	110	2-60,S-56/D-2	-1.1
1987	Tex A	85	138	28	37	5	3	2	14	6-0	2	16	.268	.308	.391	84	-4	6-3	.946	-2	89	67	S-33,2-28,3-18/D-4	-0.3
1988	Tex A	117	338	41	99	12	5	0	28	26-3	2	43	.293	.345	.358	95	-2	9-4	.970	5	106	98	2-87,S-24,3-11/D	0.7
1989	†Chi N	77	160	18	39	4	2	1	10	8-0	0	33	.244	.278	.313	64	-8	4-2	.881	4	103	63	3-26,2-15/S-7,O(LF)	-0.3
1990	Chi N	77	186	21	41	5	1	0	16	7-2	0	36	.220	.249	.258	37	-16	2-2	.888	-3	95	71	3-52,2-14/SO(LF)	-2.0
1991	†Pit N	85	191	20	36	9	1	2	18	15-0	0	40	.188	.243	.277	48	-14	2-1	.992	7	121	124	2-30,S-15,3-14	-0.5
1992	KC A	111	296	27	74	10	1	2	29	18-3	1	47	.250	.292	.311	68	-13	18-7	.968	-4	92	83	S-69,2-39/3-5,D	-1.1
1993	KC A	12	28	1	4	0	0	0	0	1-0	0	6	.143	.172	.143	-13	-5	2-0	1.000	-1	120	104	2-10/S-4	-0.4
Total	11	972	2452	272	600	78	23	8	179	138-8	12	403	.245	.286	.305	63	-129	81-43	.957	-19	95	84	S-444,2-351,3-128/D-10,O-2(LF)	-10.1
WILKERSON, BRAD Stephen Bradley B 6.1.1977 Owensboro, KY BL/TL 6/200# d7.12																								
2001	Mon N	47	117	11	24	7	2	1	5	17-1	0	41	.205	.304	.325	62	-7	2-1	.970	-0	97	88	O-38(LF)	-0.8
2002	Mon N	153	507	92	135	27	8	20	59	81-7	5	161	.266	.370	.469	114	10	7-8	.972	-0	88	**188**	*O-129(72-73-3),1-23	0.4
2003	Mon N	146	504	78	135	34	4	19	77	89-0	4	155	.268	.380	.464	109	10	13-10	.982	3	101	145	*O-135(95-42-16),1-27	0.7
Total	3	346	1128	181	294	68	14	40	141	187-8	9	357	.261	.368	.452	107	13	22-19	.976	3	95	156	O-302(205-115-19)/1-50	0.3
WILKINS, RICK Richard David B 6.4.1967 Jacksonville, FL BL/TR 6-2/210# d6.6																								
1991	Chi N	86	203	21	45	9	0	6	22	19-2	6	56	.222	.307	.355	82	-5	3-3	.993	5	112	119	C-82	0.4
1992	Chi N	83	244	20	66	9	1	8	22	28-7	0	53	.270	.344	.414	111	4	0-2	.993	11	111	114	C-73	2.0
1993	Chi N	136	446	78	135	23	1	30	73	50-13	3	99	.303	.376	.561	149	31	2-1	.996	16	140	**131**	*C-133	5.4
1994	Chi N	100	313	44	71	25	2	7	39	40-5	2	86	.227	.317	.387	84	-7	4-3	.993	0	119	111	C-95/1-2	-0.1
1995	Chi N	50	162	24	31	2	0	6	14	36-1	1	51	.191	.340	.315	76	-5	0-0	.988	-1	101	130	C-49/1-2	-0.2
	Hou N	15	40	6	10	1	0	1	5	10-1	0	10	.250	.392	.350	107	1	0-0	1.000	-1	112	78	C-13	0.1
	Year	65	202	30	41	3	0	7	19	46-2	1	61	.203	.351	.322	82	-4	0-0	.990	-2	103	119	C-62/1-2	-0.1
1996	Hou N	84	254	34	54	8	2	6	23	46-10	1	81	.213	.330	.331	83	-5	0-1	.990	-1	101	98	C-82	-0.1
	SF N	52	157	19	46	10	0	8	36	21-3	0	40	.293	.366	.510	136	9	0-2	.991	-5	85	164	C-42/1-7	0.5
	Year	136	411	53	100	18	2	14	59	67-13	1	121	.243	.344	.399	104	4	0-3	.990	-6	96	119	*C-124/1-7	0.4
1997	SF N	66	190	18	37	5	0	6	23	17-0	0	65	.195	.257	.316	51	-14	0-0	.986	2	126	153	C-57	-0.9
	†Sea A	5	12	2	3	1	0	1	4	1-0	0	2	.250	.286	.583	127	0	0-0	1.000	-1	31	167	/C-3,D-2	-0.1
1998	Sea A	19	41	5	8	1	1	1	4	4-0	0	14	.195	.261	.341	57	-3	0-0	1.000	-1	171	63	/C-6,1-6,D-2	-0.4
	NY N	5	15	3	2	0	0	0	1	2-0	0	2	.133	.235	.133	0	-2	0-0	.957	-2	82	90	/C-4	-0.4
1999	LA N	3	4	0	0	0	0	0	0	0-0	0	2	.000	.000	.000	-99	-1	0-0	1.000	0	0	0	/C	-0.1
2000	†StL N	4	11	3	3	0	0	0	1	2-0	0	2	.273	.385	.273	70	0	0-0	1.000	3	0	125	/C-3	0.2
2001	SD N	12	22	3	4	1	0	1	8	2-0	0	8	.182	.250	.364	61	-1	0-0	1.000	1	104	0	/C-7,1	0.0
Total	11	720	2114	280	515	95	7	81	275	278-42	13	571	.244	.332	.410	100	2	9-12	.992	26	116	122	C-650/1-18,D-4	6.3
WILKINS, BOBBY Robert Linwood B 8.11.1922 Denton, NC BR/TR 5-9/165# d4.18																								
1944	Phi A	24	25	7	6	0	0	0	3	1	1	4	.240	.296	.240	55	-1	0-0	.943	2	128	96	/S-9	0.1
1945	Phi A	62	154	22	40	6	0	0	4	10	0	17	.260	.305	.299	76	-5	2-4	.923	-1	102	96	S-40/O-4(LF)	-0.5
Total	2	86	179	29	46	6	0	0	7	11	1	21	.257	.304	.291	73	-6	2-4	.926	1	105	96	/S-49,O-4(LF)	-0.4
WILKINSON, ED Edward Henry B 6.20.1890 Jacksonville, OR D 4.9.1918 Tucson, AZ BR/TR 6/170# d7.4																								
1911	NY A	10	13	2	3	0	0	0	1	0	0		.231	.231	.231	27	-1	0	.800	-0	104	0	/O-3(LF),2	-0.2
WILL, BOB Robert Lee "Butch" B 7.15.1931 Berwyn, IL BL/TL 5-10.5/175# d4.16																								
1957	Chi N	70	112	13	25	3	0	1	10	5-0	0	21	.223	.254	.277	44	-9	1-0	.963	-2	94	67	O-30(CF)	-1.2
1958	Chi N	6	4	1	1	0	0	0	0	2-0	0	0	.250	.500	.250	108	0	0-0	—	-0	0	0	/O(RF)	0.0
1960	Chi N	138	475	58	121	20	9	6	53	47-3	1	54	.255	.321	.373	91	-6	1-5	.992	-1	101	89	*O-121(4-0-117)	-1.3
1961	Chi N	86	113	9	29	9	0	0	8	15-0	0	19	.257	.341	.336	80	-2	0-1	1.000	-1	104	0	O-30(9-0-22)/1	-0.5
1962	Chi N	87	92	6	22	3	0	2	15	13-2	0	22	.239	.327	.337	78	-3	0-0	1.000	-0	108	0	/O-9(RF)	-0.3
1963	Chi N	23	23	0	4	0	0	0	1	1-0	0	3	.174	.208	.174	11	-3	0-0	1.000	-0	0	199	/1	-0.3
Total	6	410	819	87	202	35	9	9	87	83-5	1	119	.247	.314	.344	80	-23	2-6	.988	-4	101	73	O-191(13-30-149)/1-2	-3.6
WILLARD, JERRY Gerald Duane B 3.14.1960 Oxnard, CA BL/TR 6-2/195# d4.11																								
1984	Cle A	87	246	21	55	8	1	10	37	26-0	0	55	.224	.295	.386	86	-5	1-0	.981	-5	85	109	C-76/D	-0.7
1985	Cle A	104	300	39	81	13	0	7	36	28-1	1	59	.270	.333	.383	97	-1	0-0	.990	3	76	109	C-96/D	0.6
1986	Oak A	75	161	17	43	7	0	4	26	22-0	2	28	.267	.354	.385	112	4	0-1	.994	-9	76	67	C-71/D	-0.3
1987	Oak A	7	6	1	1	0	0	0	0	2-0	0	1	.167	.375	.167	55	0	0-0	1.000	-0	0	0	/13D	-0.1
1990	Chi A	3	3	0	0	0	0	0	0	0-0	0	2	.000	.000	.000	-99	-1	0-0	—	-0	0	0	/C	-0.1
1991	†Atl N	17	14	1	3	0	0	1	4	2-0	0	5	.214	.313	.429	100	0	0-0	1.000	0	0	0	/C	0.0
1992	Atl N	26	23	2	8	1	0	2	7	1-1	0	3	.348	.375	.652	175	2	0-0	1.000	0	0	0	/C	0.2
	Mon N	21	25	0	3	0	0	0	1	1-0	0	7	.120	.154	.120	-22	-4	0-0	.952	0	139	0	/1-5	-0.4
	Year	47	48	2	11	1	0	2	8	2-1	0	10	.229	.260	.375	76	-2	0-0	.952	0	139	0	/1-5,C	-0.2
1994	Sea A	6	5	1	1	0	0	1	3	1-0	0	1	.200	.333	.800	177	0	0-0	—	-0	0	0	/CD	0.0
Total	8	346	783	82	195	29	1	25	114	83-2	3	161	.249	.320	.384	95	-5	1-1	.988	-11	79	98	C-247/D-7,1-6,3	-0.8
WILLIAMS, RIP Alva Mitchel "Buff" B 1.31.1882 Carthage, IL D 7.23.1933 Keokuk, IA BR/TR 6-0.5/187# d4.12																								
1911	Bos A	95	284	36	68	8	5	0	31	24	7		.239	.314	.303	73	-10	9	.975	-0	86	111	1-57,C-38	-0.9
1912	Was A	60	157	14	50	11	4	0	22	7	1		.318	.352	.439	125	4	2	.978	8	*131*	*106*	C-48	1.6
1913	Was A	66	106	9	30	6	2	1	12	9	0	16	.283	.339	.406	115	2	3	.985	-0	*100*	*95*	C-18/1-9,O-5(0-1-4)	0.2
1914	Was A	81	169	17	47	6	4	1	22	13	3	19	.278	.341	.379	112	2	2-2	.975	-3	*99*	*108*	C-44/1-8,O(RF)	0.2
1915	Was A	91	197	14	48	8	4	0	31	18	4	20	.244	.320	.325	91	-2	4-3	.967	7	*117*	*90*	C-40,1-15/3	0.8
1916	Was A	76	202	16	54	10	2	0	20	15	2	19	.267	.324	.337	100	0	5	.982	-6	60	108	1-34,C-23/3	-0.5
1918	Cle A	28	71	5	17	2	2	0	7	9	0	6	.239	.325	.324	87	-1	2	.980	-1	81	99	1-21/C	-0.3
Total	7	497	1186	111	314	51	23	2	145	95	17	80	.265	.328	.352	97	-5	27-5	.977	5	*110*	*94*	C-212,1-144/O-6(0-1-5),3-2	1.1
WILLIAMS, ART Arthur Franklin B 8.26.1877 Somerville, MA D 5.16.1941 Arlington, VA TR d5.7																								
1902	Chi N	49	167	20	38	3	0	0	14	17	3		.228	.310	.246	74	-4	9	.921	-2	33	0	O-26(4-0-22),1-19	-0.8
WILLIAMS, GUS August Joseph "Gloomy Gus" B 5.7.1888 Omaha, NE D 4.16.1964 Sterling, IL BL/TL 6/185# d4.12 b-Harry																								
1911	StL A	9	26	1	7	3	0	0	4	0	1		.269	.296	.385	93	0	0	.867	-1	106	0	/O-7(LF)	-0.1
1912	StL A	64	216	32	63	13	7	2	32	27	0		.292	.370	.444	138	11	18	.930	2	101	136	O-62(RF)	0.9
1913	StL A	148	538	72	147	21	16	5	53	57	3	87	.273	.346	.400	121	13	31	.951	4	102	118	*O-143(RF)	1.0
1914	StL A	144	499	51	126	19	6	4	47	36	4	120	.253	.308	.339	98	-3	35-20	.933	1	97	131	*O-142(1-0-141)	-0.9
1915	StL A	45	119	15	24	2	2	1	11	6	1	16	.202	.246	.277	59	-7	11-1	.949	-2	92	66	O-35(RF)	-0.8
Total	5	410	1398	171	367	58	31	12	147	126	9	223	.263	.327	.374	110	14	95-21	.939	5	99	120	O-389(8-0-381)	0.1
WILLIAMS, BERNIE Bernabe (Figueroa) B 9.13.1968 San Juan, P.R. BB/TR 6-2/205# d7.7																								
1991	NY A	85	320	43	76	19	4	3	34	48-0	1	57	.237	.336	.350	91	-3	10-5	.979	-1	104	68	O-85(CF)	-0.4
1992	NY A	62	261	39	73	14	2	5	26	29-1	1	36	.280	.354	.406	113	5	7-6	.995	5	109	135	O-62(4-55-4)	0.8
1993	NY A	139	567	67	152	31	4	12	68	53-4	4	106	.268	.333	.400	100	0	9-9	.989	-4	98	64	*O-139(CF)	-0.4
1994	NY A	108	408	80	118	29	1	12	57	61-2	3	54	.289	.384	.453	120	15	16-9	.990	-2	95	119	*O-107(CF)	1.3
1995	†NY A	144	563	93	173	29	9	18	82	75-1	5	98	.307	.392	.487	129	25	8-6	.982	5	117	14	*O-144(CF)	2.9
1996	†NY A	143	551	108	168	26	7	29	102	82-8	0	72	.305	.391	.535	132	28	17-4	.986	-4	96	121	*O-140(CF)/D-2	2.5
1997	†NY A★	129	509	107	167	35	6	21	100	73-7	1	80	.328	.408	.544	148	39	15-8	.993	-15	85	31	*O-128(CF)	2.4
1998	†NY A✱	128	499	101	169	30	5	26	97	74-9	1	81	**.339**	.422	.575	163	49	15-9	.990	-8	93	51	*O-123(CF)/D-5	3.9
1999	†NY A★	158	591	116	202	28	6	25	115	100-**17**	1	95	.342	.435	.536	149	48	9-10	.987	-2	100	96	*O-155(CF)/D-2	4.2
2000	†NY A★	141	537	108	165	37	6	30	121	71-11	5	84	.307	.391	.566	140	34	13-5	**1.000**	-2	104	30	*O-137(CF)/D-4	3.1
2001	†NY A✱	146	540	102	166	38	0	26	94	78-11	6	67	.307	.395	.522	139	34	11-5	.994	-5	101	39	*O-144(CF)/D	3.0
2002	†NY A	154	612	102	204	37	2	19	102	83-7	3	97	.333	.415	.493	141	40	8-4	.986	-12	91	26	*O-147(CF)/D-7	2.9
2003	†NY A	119	445	77	117	19	1	15	64	71-8	3	61	.263	.367	.411	107	7	5-0	.997	-3	99	59	*O-115(CF)/D-4	0.6
Total	13	1656	6403	1143	1950	372	53	241	1062	898-86	34	988	.305	.390	.492	131	321	143-80	.990	-47	99	62	*O-1626(4-1619-4)/D-25	26.8

Year	Tm Lg	G	AB	R	H	2B	3B	HR	RBI	BB-IB	HP	SO	AVG	OBP	SLG	AOPS	ABR	SB-CS	FA	FR	Rng	Thr	G at Pos	BFW
WILLIAMS, BERNIE Bernard B 10.8.1948 Alameda, CA BR/TR 6-1/175# d9.7																								
1970	SF N	7	16	2	5	2	0	0	1	2-0	0	1	.313	.389	.438	122	1	1-1	1.000	1	122	326	/O-6(LF)	0.1
1971	SF N	35	73	8	13	1	0	1	5	12-2	0	24	.178	.294	.233	52	-4	1-1	.933	-3	75	0	O-27(22-0-5)	-0.9
1972	SF N	46	68	12	13	3	1	3	9	7-0	0	22	.191	.267	.397	85	-2	0-0	1.000	2	121	100	O-15(14-1-0)	-0.1
1974	SD N	14	15	1	2	0	0	0	0	0-0	0	6	.133	.133	.133	-26	-3	0-0	1.000	-1	48	0	/O-3(1-2-0)	-0.3
Total	4	102	172	23	33	6	1	4	15	21-2	0	53	.192	.280	.308	66	-8	2-2	.974	-1	95	70	/O-51(43-3-5)	-1.2
WILLIAMS, BILLY Billy Leo B 6.15.1938 Whistler, AL BL/TR 6-1/175# d8.6 C18 HF1987																								
1959	Chi N	18	33	0	5	0	1	0	2	1-0	0	7	.152	.176	.212	3	-5	0-0	1.000	0	123	0	O-10(LF)	-0.5
1960	Chi N	12	47	4	13	0	2	2	7	5-0	0	12	.277	.346	.489	127	1	0-0	.962	-1	100	0	O-12(LF)	0.0
1961	Chi N	146	529	75	147	20	7	25	86	45-11	5	70	.278	.338	.484	114	9	6-0	.954	-6	90	81	*O-135(110-0-27)	-0.4
1962	Chi N★	159	618	94	184	22	8	22	91	70-3	4	72	.298	.369	.466	119	17	9-9	.967	2	92	154	*O-159(158-0-1)	0.9
1963	Chi N	161	612	87	175	36	9	25	95	68-9	2	78	.286	.358	.497	136	30	7-6	.987	5	101	120	*O-160(LF)	2.7
1964	Chi N★	**162**	645	100	201	39	2	33	98	59-8	2	84	.312	.370	.532	145	39	10-7	.950	-7	80	130	*O-162(162-2-0)	2.3
1965	Chi N★	**164**	645	115	203	39	6	34	108	65-7	3	76	.315	.377	.552	155	48	10-1	.968	-7	91	89	*O-164(34-28-106)	3.4
1966	Chi N	**162**	648	100	179	23	5	29	91	69-16	4	61	.276	.347	.461	122	19	6-3	.976	-1	104	75	*O-162(11-0-152)	0.8
1967	Chi N	**162**	634	92	176	21	12	28	84	68-8	2	67	.278	.346	.481	129	23	6-3	.989	-8	96	29	*O-162(161-0-6)	0.7
1968	Chi N★	**163**	642	91	185	30	8	30	98	48-10	2	53	.288	.336	.500	140	30	4-1	.967	-10	94	35	*O-163(137-0-47)	1.2
1969	Chi N	**163**	642	103	188	33	10	21	95	59-15	4	70	.293	.355	.474	116	13	3-2	.957	1	92	163	*O-159(153-0-28)	0.6
1970	Chi N	161	636	**137**	**205**	34	4	42	129	72-9	2	65	.322	.391	.586	142	37	7-1	.989	2	98	118	*O-160(155-0-9)	3.1
1971	Chi N	157	594	86	179	27	5	28	93	77-18	3	44	.301	.383	.505	131	26	7-5	.977	1	101	81	*O-154(151-0-4)	1.9
1972	Chi N★	150	574	95	191	34	6	37	122	62-20	6	59	**.333**	.398	**.606**	166	50	3-1	.984	-6	83	91	*O-144(LF)/1-5	3.8
1973	Chi N★	156	576	72	166	22	2	20	86	76-14	1	72	.288	.369	.438	115	14	4-3	.985	9	94	158	*O-138(LF),1-19	1.4
1974	Chi N	117	404	55	113	22	0	16	68	67-12	1	44	.280	.382	.453	128	17	4-5	.986	3	116	84	1-65,O-43(41-0-4)	1.2
1975	†Oak A	155	520	68	127	20	1	23	81	76-7	2	68	.244	.341	.419	117	13	0-0	.971	0	115	158	*D-145/1-7	0.9
1976	Oak A	120	351	36	74	12	0	11	41	58-15	0	44	.211	.320	.339	98	1	4-2	—	-0	0	0	*D-106/O(LF)	-0.2
Total	18	2488	9350	1410	2711	434	88	426	1475	1045-182	43	1046	.290	.361	.492	131	382	90-49	.973	-21	94	101	*O-2088(1738-30-384),D-251/1-96	23.8
WILLIAMS, DALLAS Dallas McKinley B 2.28.1958 Brooklyn, NY BL/TL 5-11/165# d9.19 C4																								
1981	Bal A	2	2	0	1	0	0	0	0	0-0	0	0	.500	.500	.500	189	0	0-0	1.000	0	399	0	/O(LF)	0.0
1983	Cin N	18	36	2	2	0	0	0	1	3-0	0	6	.056	.128	.056	-46	-7	0-0	1.000	0	111	0	O-12(6-3-3)	-0.8
Total	2	20	38	2	3	0	0	0	1	3-0	0	6	.079	.146	.079	-35	-7	0-0	1.000	0	115	0	/O-13(7-3-3)	-0.8
WILLIAMS, DANA Dana Lamont B 3.20.1963 Weirton, WV BR/TR 5-10/170# d6.21 C1																								
1989	Bos A	8	5	1	1	1	0	0	0	0-0	1	1	.200	.333	.400	100	0	0-0	1.000	1	0	7581	/O(LF)D	0.1
WILLIAMS, DAVEY David Carlous B 11.2.1927 Dallas, TX BR/TR 5-10/160# d9.16 C2																								
1949	NY N	13	50	7	12	1	1	1	5	7	0	4	.240	.333	.360	86	-1	0	.953	-5	76	73	2-13	-0.6
1951	†NY N	30	64	17	17	1	0	2	8	5	0	8	.266	.319	.375	85	-2	1-1	1.000	1	104	71	2-22	0.0
1952	NY N	138	540	70	137	26	3	13	55	48	8	63	.254	.324	.385	95	-4	2-3	.973	-10	98	114	*2-138	-0.7
1953	NY N★	112	340	51	101	11	2	3	34	44	3	19	.297	.382	.368	95	0	2-5	.982	-2	100	87	2-95	0.2
1954	†NY N	142	544	65	121	18	3	9	46	43	5	33	.222	.284	.316	56	-36	1-1	**.982**	-4	97	109	*2-142	-3.0
1955	NY N	82	247	25	62	4	1	4	15	17-2	2	17	.251	.303	.324	67	-12	0-2	.968	-3	99	94	2-71	-1.2
Total	6	517	1785	235	450	61	10	32	163	164-2	18	144	.252	.320	.351	79	-55	6-12	.978	-24	98	102	2-481	-5.3
WILLIAMS, KEITH David Keith B 4.21.1972 Bedford, PA BR/TR 6/190# d6.7																								
1996	SF N	9	20	0	5	0	0	0	0	0-0	0	6	.250	.250	.250	34	-2	0-0	1.000	-0	107	0	/O-4(1-0-3)	-0.2
WILLIAMS, DEWEY Dewey Edgar "Dee" B 2.5.1916 Durham, NC D 3.19.2000 Williston, ND BR/TR 6/160# d6.28																								
1944	Chi N	79	262	23	63	7	2	0	27	23	0	18	.240	.302	.282	65	-12	2	.981	2	*95*	***136***	C-77	-0.6
1945	†Chi N	59	100	16	28	2	2	2	5	13	0	13	.280	.363	.400	114	2	0	.978	3	*147*	*116*	C-54	0.7
1946	Chi N	4	5	0	1	0	0	0	0	0	0	2	.200	.200	.200	14	-1	0	1.000	0	*0*	*0*	/C-2	0.0
1947	Chi N	3	2	0	0	0	0	0	0	0	0	1	.000	.000	.000	-99	-1	0	—	0	*0*	*0*	/C	-0.1
1948	Cin N	48	95	9	16	2	0	1	5	10	0	18	.168	.248	.221	29	-10	0	.961	-4	*71*	*56*	C-47	-1.2
Total	5	193	464	48	108	11	4	3	37	46	0	52	.233	.302	.293	67	-22	2	.976	1	*100*	*114*	C-181	-1.2
WILLIAMS, EARL Earl Baxter B 1.27.1903 Cumberland Gap, TN D 3.10.1958 Knoxville, TN BR/TR 6-0.5/185# d5.27																								
1928	Bos N	3	2	0	0	0	0	0	0	0	0	1	.000	.000	.000	-99	-1	0	1.000	0	*0*	*0*	/C	0.0
WILLIAMS, EARL Earl Craig B 7.14.1948 Newark, NJ BR/TR 6-3/220# d9.13																								
1970	Atl N	10	19	4	7	4	0	0	5	3-0	0	4	.368	.417	.579	165	2	0-0	1.000	2	56	51	/1-4,3-3	0.3
1971	Atl N	145	497	64	129	14	1	33	87	42-5	7	80	.260	.324	.491	121	12	0-1	.981	-10	68	107	C-72,3-42,1-31	0.4
1972	Atl N	151	565	72	146	24	2	28	87	62-6	6	118	.258	.336	.457	113	10	0-0	.980	-19	74	77	*C-116,3-21,1-20	-0.6
1973	†Bal A	132	459	58	109	18	1	22	83	66-8	3	107	.237	.333	.425	114	9	0-2	.987	-1	116	115	C-95,1-42/D-2	0.9
1974	†Bal A	118	413	47	105	16	0	14	52	40-3	7	79	.254	.327	.395	111	6	0-2	.983	-9	96	104	C-75,1-47/D	-0.3
1975	Atl N	111	383	42	92	13	0	11	50	34-2	3	63	.240	.305	.360	82	-10	0-0	.989	-5	83	98	1-90,C-11	-2.3
1976	Atl N	61	184	18	39	3	0	9	26	19-2	1	33	.212	.286	.375	82	-5	0-0	.995	-7	95	25	C-38,1-17	-1.3
	Mon N	61	190	17	45	10	2	8	29	14-2	0	32	.237	.285	.437	100	-1	0-0	.981	4	150	100	1-47,C-13	0.0
	Year	122	374	35	84	13	2	17	55	33-4	1	65	.225	.286	.406	91	-6	0-0	.986	-4	133	94	1-64,C-51	-1.3
1977	Oak A	100	348	39	84	13	0	13	38	18-3	5	58	.241	.288	.391	84	-9	2-0	.989	-2	71	165	D-45,C-36,1-29	-1.1
Total	8	889	3058	361	756	115	6	138	457	298-31	32	574	.247	.318	.424	105	14	2-5	.984	-47	86	98	C-456,1-327/3-66,D-48	-4.0
WILLIAMS, EDDIE Edward Laquan B 11.1.1964 Shreveport, LA BR/TR 6/185# d4.18																								
1986	Cle A	5	7	2	1	0	0	0	1	0-0	0	3	.143	.143	.143	-22	-1	0-0	—	-0	0	0	/O-4(LF)	-0.2
1987	Cle A	22	64	9	11	4	0	1	4	9-0	1	19	.172	.280	.281	50	-4	0-0	.982	2	103	155	3-22	-0.3
1988	Cle A	10	21	3	4	0	0	0	1	0-0	1	3	.190	.227	.190	18	-2	0-0	1.000	1	123	0	3-10	-0.2
1989	Chi A	66	201	25	55	8	0	3	10	18-3	4	31	.274	.341	.358	101	1	1-2	.909	-0	103	193	3-65	0.0
1990	SD N	14	42	5	12	3	0	3	4	5-2	0	6	.286	.362	.571	151	3	0-1	.897	-2	92	118	3-13	0.1
1994	SD N	49	175	32	58	11	1	11	42	15-1	3	26	.331	.392	.594	158	15	0-1	.988	-2	89	83	1-46/3	0.8
1995	SD N	97	296	35	77	11	1	12	47	23-0	4	47	.260	.320	.426	99	-2	0-0	.989	-1	94	97	1-81	-0.9
1996	Det A	77	215	22	43	5	0	6	26	18-0	2	50	.200	.267	.307	45	-19	0-2	1.000	-1	49	228	D-52/1-7,3-3,O-2(RF)	-2.2
1997	LA N	8	7	0	1	0	0	0	1	1-1	0	1	.143	.250	.143	7	-1	0-0	—	0			/H	-0.2
	Pit N	30	89	12	22	5	0	3	11	10-1	2	24	.247	.333	.404	91	-1	1-0	.991	-3	57	101	1-26	-0.6
	Year	38	96	12	23	5	0	3	12	11-2	2	25	.240	.327	.385	87	-2	1-0	.991	-3	57	101	1-26	-0.8
1998	SD N	17	28	1	4	0	0	0	3	2-0	0	6	.143	.194	.143	-9	-5	0-0	1.000	-0	81	80	/1-7	-0.5
Total	10	395	1145	146	288	47	2	39	150	101-8	17	216	.252	.319	.398	91	-16	2-6	.989	-7	85	96	1-167,3-114/D-52,O-6(4-0-2)	-4.2
WILLIAMS, DIB Edwin Dibrell B 1.19.1910 Greenbrier, AR D 4.2.1992 Searcy, AR BR/TR 5-11.5/175# d4.27																								
1930	Phi A	67	191	24	50	10	3	3	22	15	2	19	.262	.322	.393	77	-7	2-1	.951	0	103	77	2-39,S-19/3	-0.4
1931	†Phi A	86	294	41	79	12	2	6	40	19	0	21	.269	.313	.384	78	-11	2-0	.931	2	93	158	S-72,2-10/O(LF)	-0.2
1932	Phi A	62	215	30	54	10	1	4	24	22	3	23	.251	.329	.363	76	-8	0-1	.952	1	105	96	2-53/S-3	-0.3
1933	Phi A	115	408	52	118	20	5	11	73	32	1	35	.289	.342	.444	106	2	1-0	.921	-11	90	64	S-84,2-29/1-2	-0.2
1934	Phi A	66	205	25	56	10	1	2	17	21	0	18	.273	.341	.361	84	-5	0-1	.956	1	109	88	2-53/S-2	-0.1
1935	Phi A	4	10	0	1	0	0	0	0	0	0	1	.100	.100	.100	-49	-2	0-0	1.000	-1	111	0	/2-2	-0.3
	Bos A	75	251	26	63	12	0	3	25	24	1	23	.251	.319	.335	65	-13	2-0	.952	-3	115	126	3-30,2-29,S-15/1	-1.1
	Year	79	261	26	64	12	0	3	25	24	1	24	.245	.311	.326	61	-15	2-0	.973	-3	91	62	2-31,3-30,S-15/1	-1.4
Total	6	475	1574	198	421	74	12	29	201	133	7	140	.267	.327	.385	82	-44	7-3	.955	-11	105	89	2-215,S-195/3-31,1-3,O(LF)	-2.6
WILLIAMS, DENNY Evon Daniel B 12.13.1899 Portland, OR D 3.23.1929 San Clemente, CA BL/TR 5-8.5/150# d4.15																								
1921	Cin N	10	7	0	0	0	0	0	0	0	0	2	.000	.000	.000	-99	-2	0-1	1.000	0	138	0	/O(LF)	-0.2
1924	Bos A	25	85	17	31	3	0	0	4	10	1	5	.365	.438	.400	117	3	3-3	.972	-1	89	54	O-19(LF)	0.0
1925	Bos A	69	218	28	50	1	3	0	13	17	0	11	.229	.285	.261	39	-21	2-6	.953	-2	99	69	O-52(42-11-0)	-2.7
1928	Bos A	16	18	1	4	0	0	0	1	1	0	1	.222	.263	.222	29	-2	0-0	1.000	-0	97	0	/O-6(0-5-1)	-0.2
Total	4	120	328	46	85	4	3	0	18	28	1	19	.259	.319	.290	56	-22	5-10	.959	-3	97	63	/O-78(62-16-1)	-3.1
WILLIAMS, CY Fred B 12.21.1887 Wadena, IN D 4.23.1974 Eagle River, WI BL/TL 6-2/180# d7.18																								
1912	Chi N	28	62	3	15	1	1	0	1	6	0	14	.242	.309	.290	65	-3	2	1.000	1	101	126	O-22(5-17-0)	-0.3

Year	Tm Lg	G	AB	R	H	2B	3B	HR	RBI	BB-IB	HP	SO	AVG	OBP	SLG	AOPS	ABR	SB-CS	FA	FR	Rng	Thr	G at Pos	BFW
1913	Chi N	49	156	17	35	3	3	4	32	5	3	26	.224	.262	.359	76	-6	5-10	.976	-2	95	77	O-44(36-9-0)	-1.2
1914	Chi N	55	94	12	19	2	2	0	5	13	2	13	.202	.312	.266	73	-3	2	.941	-0	105	74	O-27(22-7-0)	-0.5
1915	Chi N	151	518	59	133	22	6	13	64	26	10	49	.257	.305	.398	112	5	15-10	.968	2	106	83	*O-149(CF)	-0.4
1916	Chi N	118	405	55	113	19	9	**12**	66	51	9	64	.279	.372	.459	140	21	6	.989	-8	95	49	*O-116(0-115-1)	0.5
1917	Chi N	138	468	53	113	22	4	5	42	38	7	78	.241	.308	.338	91	-4	8	.960	11	113	135	*O-136(CF)	-0.3
1918	Phi N	94	351	49	97	14	1	6	39	27	5	30	.276	.337	.373	109	4	10	.968	2	106	88	O-91(CF)	0.1
1919	Phi N	109	435	54	121	21	1	9	39	30	7	43	.278	.335	.393	111	6	9	.970	-2	99	89	*O-108(CF)	-0.4
1920	Phi N	148	590	88	192	36	10	**15**	72	32	4	45	.325	.364	.497	139	28	18-12	.972	10	110	110	*O-147(CF)	3.0
1921	Phi N	146	562	67	180	28	6	18	75	30	2	32	.320	.357	.488	112	9	5-15	.979	9	102	137	*O-146(CF)	0.8
1922	Phi N	151	584	98	180	30	6	26	92	74	6	49	.308	.392	.514	120	18	11-14	.973	-5	93	102	*O-150(CF)	0.5
1923	Phi N	136	535	98	157	22	3	**41**	114	59	7	57	.293	.371	.576	131	22	11-10	.981	-5	100	53	*O-135(CF)	1.0
1924	Phi N	148	558	101	183	31	11	24	93	67	3	49	.328	.403	.552	137	30	7-12	.962	-6	95	85	*O-145(CF)	1.5
1925	Phi N	107	314	78	104	11	5	13	60	53	5	34	.331	.435	.522	132	17	4-9	.989	3	104	104	O-96(RF)	1.1
1926	Phi N	107	336	63	116	13	4	18	53	38	4	35	.345	.418	**.568**	155	26	2	.963	-2	85	125	O-93(RF)	1.7
1927	Phi N	131	492	86	135	18	2	**30**	98	61	**9**	57	.274	.365	.502	128	19	0	.970	1	90	141	*O-130(RF)	1.0
1928	Phi N	99	238	31	61	9	0	12	37	54	3	34	.256	.400	.445	117	8	0	1.000	2	92	165	O-69(20-9-40)	0.5
1929	Phi N	66	65	11	19	2	0	5	21	22	0	9	.292	.471	.554	144	6	0	.966	1	119	122	O-11(1-9-1)	0.6
1930	Phi N	21	17	1	8	2	0	0	2	4	0	3	.471	.571	.588	169	2	0	1.000	0	376	0	/O-3(1-1-1)	0.2
Total	19	2002	6780	1024	1981	306	74	251	1005	690	86	721	.292	.365	.470	123	205	115-92	.973	11	100	102	*O-1818(85-1374-362)	9.4
WILLIAMS, PAPA Fred B 7.17.1913 Meridian, MS D 11.2.1993 Meridian, MS BR/TR 6-1/200# d4.19																								
1945	Cle A	16	19	0	4	0	0	0	0	1	0	2	.211	.250	.211	36	-2	0-0	1.000	0	164	149	/1-3	-0.1
WILLIAMS, GEORGE George B 10.23.1939 Detroit, MI BR/TR 5-11/165# d7.16																								
1961	Phi N	17	36	4	9	0	0	0	1	4-0	0	4	.250	.325	.250	56	-2	0-0	.967	1	115	114	2-15	0.0
1962	Hou N	5	8	1	3	1	0	0	2	0-0	0	1	.375	.375	.500	143	0	0-0	1.000	0	127	114	/2-3	0.1
1964	KC A	37	91	10	19	6	0	0	2	6-2	1	12	.209	.265	.275	49	-6	0-0	.970	-1	103	126	2-20/S-2,3-2,O-2(LF)	-0.5
Total	3	59	135	15	31	7	0	0	5	10-2	1	17	.230	.288	.281	56	-8	0-0	.970	1	108	122	/2-38,O-2(LF),3-2,S-2	-0.4
WILLIAMS, GEORGE George Erik B 4.22.1969 LaCrosse, WI BB/TR 5-10/190# d7.14																								
1995	Oak A	29	79	13	23	5	1	3	14	11-2	2	21	.291	.383	.494	136	5	0-0	.956	-2	59	139	C-13,D-10	0.2
1996	Oak A	56	132	17	20	5	0	3	10	28-1	3	32	.152	.311	.258	47	-10	0-0	.982	-6	78	84	C-43,D-11	-1.4
1997	Oak A	76	201	30	58	9	1	3	22	35-0	2	46	.289	.397	.388	108	4	0-1	.984	-8	95	80	C-67/D	0.0
2000	SD N	11	16	2	3	0	0	1	2	0-0	1	4	.188	.235	.375	54	-1	0-0	1.000	-1	58	0	/C-6	-0.2
Total	4	172	428	62	104	19	2	10	48	74-3	8	103	.243	.362	.367	92	-2	0-1	.981	-17	85	85	C-129/D-22	-1.4
WILLIAMS, GERALD Gerald Floyd B 8.10.1966 New Orleans, LA BR/TR 6-2/190# d9.15																								
1992	NY A	15	27	7	8	2	0	3	6	0-0	0	3	.296	.296	.704	174	2	2-0	.913	1	125	190	O-12(RF)	0.3
1993	NY A	42	67	11	10	2	3	0	6	1-0	2	14	.149	.183	.269	21	-8	2-0	.956	-1	87	162	O-37(10-17-12)/D	-0.9
1994	NY A	57	86	19	25	8	0	4	13	4-0	0	17	.291	.319	.523	118	2	1-3	.957	-2	82	112	O-43(26-8-12)/D-2	-0.2
1995	†NY A	100	182	33	45	18	2	6	28	22-1	1	34	.247	.327	.467	106	2	4-2	.993	8	124	162	O-92(70-2-26)/D-2	0.7
1996	NY A	99	233	37	63	15	4	5	30	15-2	4	39	.270	.319	.433	90	-4	7-8	.978	-3	99	23	O-92(70-14-10)/D-2	-1.0
	Mil A	26	92	6	19	4	0	0	4	4-1	1	18	.207	.247	.250	25	-11	3-1	.987	2	111	184	O-26(0-25-1)	-0.7
	Year	125	325	43	82	19	4	5	34	19-3	5	57	.252	.299	.382	71	-15	10-9	.981	-1	102	67	*O-118(70-39-11)/D-2	-1.7
1997	Mil A	155	566	73	143	32	2	10	41	19-1	6	90	.253	.282	.369	68	-28	23-9	.992	1	98	137	*O-154(39-129-0)/D	-2.4
1998	†Atl N	129	266	46	81	19	2	10	44	17-1	3	48	.305	.352	.504	122	8	11-5	.970	5	**125**	47	*O-120(56-11-61)	1.0
1999	†Atl N	143	422	76	116	24	1	17	68	33-1	6	67	.275	.335	.457	98	-2	19-11	.985	0	93	136	*O-139(120-1-32)	-0.6
2000	TB A	146	632	87	173	30	2	21	89	34-0	3	103	.274	.312	.427	86	-16	12-12	.983	-6	96	85	*O-138(CF)/D-7	-2.0
2001	TB A	62	232	30	48	17	0	4	17	13-0	4	42	.207	.261	.332	56	-15	10-4	.989	9	127	159	O-59(CF)	-0.5
	NY A	38	47	12	8	1	0	0	2	5-0	1	13	.170	.264	.191	23	-5	3-1	.967	0	116	0	O-26(6-11-12)/D-7	-0.5
	Year	100	279	42	56	18	0	4	19	18-0	5	55	.201	.262	.308	50	-21	13-5	.986	9	125	131	O-85(6-70-12)/D-7	-1.0
2002	NY A	33	17	6	0	0	0	0	0	2-0	0	4	.000	.105	.000	-69	-4	2-0	1.000	-0	66	211	O-30(7-6-17)	-0.4
2003	Fla N	27	31	5	4	1	0	0	3	2-0	0	5	.129	.182	.161	-10	-5	3-0	.941	-0	110	0	O-16(11-2-3)	-0.5
Total	12	1072	2900	448	743	173	16	80	351	171-7	31	497	.256	.302	.410	82	-84	102-56	.982	13	104	112	O-984(415-423-198)/D-22	-7.7
WILLIAMS, HARRY Harry Peter B 6.23.1890 Omaha, NE D 12.21.1963 Huntington Park, CA BR/TR 6-1.5/200# d8.7 b-Gus																								
1913	NY A	27	82	18	21	3	1	1	12	15	1	10	.256	.378	.354	114	2	6	.981	-2	79	51	1-27	0.0
1914	NY A	59	178	9	29	5	2	1	17	26	5	26	.163	.287	.230	56	-9	3-6	.976	-6	69	74	1-58	-2.0
Total	2	86	260	27	50	8	3	2	29	41	6	36	.192	.316	.269	75	-7	9-6	.977	-8	72	67	/1-85	-2.0
WILLIAMS, JIM James Alfred B 4.29.1947 Zachary, LA BR/TR 6-2/190# d9.8																								
1969	SD N	13	25	4	7	1	0	0	2	3-0	0	11	.280	.345	.320	95	0	0-0	.900	-1	91	0	/O-6(LF)	-0.1
1970	SD N	11	14	4	4	0	0	0	0	1-0	0	3	.286	.333	.286	70	-1	1-0	1.000	-0	88	0	/O-6(1-0-5)	-0.1
Total	2	24	39	8	11	1	0	0	2	4-0	0	14	.282	.341	.308	86	-1	1-0	.938	-1	90	0	/O-12(7-0-5)	-0.2
WILLIAMS, JIMY James Francis B 10.4.1943 Santa Maria, CA BR/TR 5-10/170# d4.26 Mil 1966 M11 C13																								
1966	StL N	13	11	1	3	0	0	0	1	1-0	0	5	.273	.333	.273	71	0	0-0	1.000	-1	81	91	/S-7,2-3	-0.1
1967	StL N	1	2	0	0	0	0	0	0	0-0	0	1	.000	.000	.000	-99	-1	0-0	1.000	-0	30	0	/S	-0.1
Total	2	14	13	1	3	0	0	0	1	1-0	0	6	.231	.286	.231	46	-1	0-0	1.000	-1	63	60	/S-8,2-3	-0.2
WILLIAMS, JIMMY James Thomas B 12.20.1876 St.Louis, MO D 1.16.1965 St.Petersburg, FL BR/TR 5-9/175# d4.15																								
1899	Pit N	153	621	126	220	28	**27**	9	116	60	6		.354	.416	.530	159	49	26	.900	1	101	62	*3-153	4.7
1900	†Pit N	106	416	73	110	15	11	5	68	32	4		.264	.323	.389	95	-4	18	.889	5	101	**164**	*3-103/S-4	0.2
1901	Bal A	130	501	113	159	26	**21**	7	96	56	2		.317	.388	.495	138	25	21	.935	-1	101	81	*2-130	2.2
1902	Bal A	125	498	83	156	27	**21**	8	83	36	1		.313	.361	.500	131	18	14	.945	1	107	93	*2-104,3-19/1	2.0
1903	NY A	132	502	60	134	30	12	3	82	39	5		.267	.326	.392	108	5	9	**.957**	16	**112**	130	*2-132	2.3
1904	NY A	146	559	62	147	31	7	2	74	38	4		.263	.314	.354	106	5	14	.951	15	106	**131**	*2-146	2.3
1905	NY A	129	470	54	107	20	8	6	62	50	3		.228	.306	.343	95	-3	14	**.964**	3	92	**149**	*2-129	0.2
1906	NY A	139	501	61	139	25	7	3	77	44	5		.277	.342	.373	112	8	8	.958	14	107	78	*2-139	2.5
1907	NY A	139	504	53	136	17	11	2	63	35	1		.270	.319	.359	107	3	14	.966	-3	94	90	*2-139	0.2
1908	StL A	148	539	63	127	20	7	4	53	55	3		.236	.310	.321	104	4	7	.963	3	99	114	*2-148	0.9
1909	StL A	110	374	32	73	3	6	0	22	29	2		.195	.257	.235	60	-18	6	.962	-1	94	112	*2-109	-2.1
Total	11	1457	5485	780	1508	242	138	49	796	474	36		.275	.337	.396	114	92	151	.955	52	101	109	*2-1176,3-275/S-4,1	15.4
WILLIAMS, KEN Kenneth Roy B 6.28.1890 Grants Pass, OR D 1.22.1959 Grants Pass, OR BL/TR 6/170# d7.14 Mil 1918																								
1915	Cin N	71	219	22	53	10	4	0	16	15	2	20	.242	.297	.324	86	-4	4-3	.948	3	97	156	O-62(54-8-0)	-0.4
1916	Cin N	10	27	1	3	0	0	0	1	2	0	5	.111	.172	.111	-12	-4	1	.955	1	108	210	O-10(8-1-0)	-0.3
1918	StL A	2	1	0	0	0	0	0	1	1	0	0	.000	.500	.000	53	0	0	—	0			H	0.0
1919	StL A	65	227	32	68	10	5	6	35	26	2	25	.300	.376	.467	133	10	7	.937	2	106	110	O-63(CF)	0.7
1920	StL A	141	521	90	160	34	13	10	72	41	4	26	.307	.362	.480	118	12	18-8	.961	4	107	92	*O-138(104-34-0)	1.0
1921	StL A	146	547	115	190	31	7	24	117	74	4	42	.347	.429	.561	142	36	20-17	.932	4	103	129	*O-145(LF)	2.5
1922	StL A	153	585	128	194	34	11	**39**	**155**	74	7	31	.332	.413	.627	162	52	37-20	.970	2	105	80	*O-153(137-17-0)	4.1
1923	StL A	147	555	106	198	37	12	29	91	79	2	32	.357	.439	.623	168	55	18-17	.967	8	106	128	*O-145(LF)	4.7
1924	StL A	114	398	78	129	21	4	18	84	69	1	17	.324	.425	.533	138	24	20-11	.968	6	109	113	*O-109(LF)	2.0
1925	StL A	102	411	83	136	31	5	25	105	37	3	14	.331	.390	**.613**	144	25	10-5	.955	2	105	92	*O-102(LF)	1.8
1926	StL A	108	347	55	97	15	7	17	74	39	1	23	.280	.354	.510	118	7	5-4	.948	2	101	136	O-92(91-1-0)/2	0.2
1927	StL A	131	423	70	136	23	6	17	74	57	1	30	.322	.403	.525	135	22	9-7	.965	6	105	128	*O-113(110-4-0)	1.7
1928	Bos A	133	462	59	140	25	1	8	67	37	1	15	.303	.356	.413	104	2	4-9	.971	-3	95	85	*O-127(LF)	-1.2
1929	Bos A	74	139	21	48	14	2	3	21	15	0	7	.345	.409	.540	146	10	1-5	.963	0	103	99	O-39(0-30-10)/1-2	0.7
Total	14	1397	4862	860	1552	285	77	196	913	566	28	287	.319	.393	.530	136	247	154-106	.958	38	104	111	*O-1298(1132-158-10)/1-2,2	17.5
WILLIAMS, KENNY Kenneth Royal B 4.6.1964 Berkeley, CA BR/TR 6-2/187# d9.2																								
1986	Chi A	15	31	2	4	0	0	1	1	1-0	1	11	.129	.182	.226	10	-4	1-1	1.000	0	93	189	O-10(1-4-5)/D	-0.4
1987	Chi A	116	391	48	110	18	2	11	50	10-0	9	83	.281	.314	.422	91	-6	21-10	.981	1	102	95	*O-115(0-111-4)	-0.5
1988	Chi A	73	220	18	35	4	2	8	28	10-0	8	64	.159	.221	.305	46	-17	6-5	.959	0	92	108	O-38(0-12-29),3-32/D-3	-1.9
1989	Det A	94	258	29	53	5	1	6	23	18-0	5	63	.205	.269	.302	63	-14	9-4	.979	9	110	257	O-87(28-35-27)/1D	-0.5

Year	Tm Lg	G	AB	R	H	2B	3B	HR	RBI	BB-IB	HP	SO	AVG	OBP	SLG	AOPS	ABR	SB-CS	FA	FR	Rng	Thr	G at Pos	BFW
1990	Det A	57	83	10	11	2	0	0	5	3-0	1	24	.133	.170	.157	-7	-12	2-2	1.000	5	109	299	O-47(17-13-19)/D-6	-0.9
	Tor A	49	72	13	14	6	1	0	8	7-0	1	18	.194	.272	.306	61	-4	7-2	1.000	-1	95	0	O-30(15-9-8)/D-9	-0.4
	Year	106	155	23	25	8	1	0	13	10-0	2	42	.161	.219	.226	25	-16	9-4	1.000	4	104	183	O-77(32-22-27),D-15	-1.3
1991	Tor A	13	29	5	6	2	0	1	3	4-0	1	5	.207	.314	.379	90	0	1-0	1.000	0	95	175	/O-9(1-1-8),D-2	0.0
	Mon N	34	70	11	19	5	2	0	1	3-0	1	22	.271	.311	.400	100	0	2-1	.957	2	116	257	O-24(9-4-11)	0.2
Total	6	451	1154	136	252	42	8	27	119	56-0	27	290	.218	.269	.339	66	-57	49-25	.981	17	103	164	0-360(71-189-111)/3-32,D-22,1	-4.4
WILLIAMS, MARK Mark Westley B 7.28.1953 Elmira, NY BL/TL 6/180# d5.20																								
1977	Oak A	3	2	0	0	0	0	0	1	1-0	0	1	.000	.333	.000	0	0	0-0	1.000	0	220	0	/O(RF)	0.0
WILLIAMS, MATT Matthew Derrick B 11.28.1965 Bishop, CA BR/TR 6-2/210# d4.11 gs-Bert Griffith																								
1987	SF N	84	245	28	46	9	2	8	21	16-4	1	68	.188	.240	.339	54	-18	4-3	.975	15	114	141	S-70,3-17	0.3
1988	SF N	52	156	17	32	6	1	8	19	8-0	2	41	.205	.251	.410	91	-3	0-1	.967	4	121	94	3-43,S-14	0.2
1989	†SF N	84	292	31	59	18	1	18	50	14-1	2	72	.202	.242	.455	98	-3	1-2	.961	4	114	112	3-73,S-30	0.3
1990	SF N★	159	617	87	171	27	2	33	**122**	33-9	7	138	.277	.319	.488	124	16	7-4	.959	9	107	**139**	*3-159	2.6
1991	SF N	157	589	72	158	24	5	34	98	33-6	6	128	.268	.310	.499	129	19	5-5	.964	3	99	122	*3-155/S-4	2.2
1992	SF N	146	529	58	120	13	5	20	66	39-11	6	109	.227	.286	.384	94	-8	7-7	.945	7	105	**144**	*3-144	-0.2
1993	SF N	145	579	105	170	33	4	38	110	27-4	4	80	.294	.325	.561	137	26	1-3	.970	1	95	**160**	*3-144	2.8
1994	SF N★	112	445	74	119	16	3	**43**	96	33-7	2	87	.267	.319	.607	141	22	1-0	.963	12	**115**	130	*3-110	3.4
1995	SF N✳	76	283	53	95	17	1	23	65	30-8	2	58	.336	.399	.647	177	31	2-0	.958	7	119	80	3-74	3.8
1996	SF N✳	105	404	69	122	16	1	22	85	39-9	6	91	.302	.367	.510	135	20	1-2	.951	2	99	117	3-92,1-13/S	2.1
1997	†Cle A	151	596	86	157	32	3	32	105	34-4	4	108	.263	.307	.488	100	-3	12-4	.970	13	114	82	*3-151	1.2
1998	Ari N	135	510	72	136	26	1	20	71	43-8	3	102	.267	.327	.439	100	-1	5-1	.972	7	110	82	*3-134	0.8
1999	†Ari N★	154	627	98	190	37	2	35	142	41-9	2	93	.303	.344	.536	118	15	2-0	.977	3	95	128	*3-153	1.9
2000	Ari N	96	371	43	102	18	2	12	47	20-1	3	51	.275	.315	.431	84	-10	1-2	.964	1	92	123	3-94/D	-0.8
2001	†Ari N	106	408	58	112	30	0	16	65	22-3	3	70	.275	.314	.466	93	-5	1-0	.963	-0	94	115	*3-102/S-2	-0.3
2002	†Ari N	60	215	29	56	7	2	12	40	21-1	0	41	.260	.324	.479	103	-1	3-1	.969	-4	87	75	3-56	-0.4
2003	Ari N	44	134	17	33	9	0	4	16	16-1	2	26	.246	.327	.403	83	-3	0-0	.959	1	100	76	3-42	-0.2
Total	17	1866	7000	997	1878	338	35	378	1218	469-86	55	1363	.268	.317	.489	113	94	53-35	.963	86	104	118	*3-1743,S-121/1-13,D	19.7
WILLIAMS, OTTO Otto George B 11.2.1877 Newark, NJ D 3.19.1937 Omaha, NE BR/TR 5-8/165# d10.5 C4																								
1902	StL N	2	5	0	2	0	0	0	2	1	0		.400	.500	.400	186	1	1	.813	0	119	0	/S-2	0.1
1903	StL N	53	187	10	38	4	2	0	9	9	0		.203	.240	.246	40	-15	6	.885	-4	103	86	S-52/2	-1.7
	Chi N	38	130	14	29	5	0	0	13	4	0		.223	.246	.262	46	-9	8	.937	3	111	111	S-26/2-7,1-3,3	-0.6
	Year	91	317	24	67	9	2	0	22	13	0		.211	.242	.252	42	-25	14	.904	-1	106	94	S-78/2-8,1-3,3	-2.3
1904	Chi N	57	185	21	37	4	1	0	8	13	1		.200	.256	.232	51	-11	9	.973	0	110	139	O-21(0-8-13),1-11,S-10/2-6,3-6	-1.2
1906	Was A	20	51	3	7	0	0	0	2	2	1		.137	.185	.137	1	-6	0	.897	-0	100	42	/S-8,2-6,1-2,3	-0.7
Total	4	170	558	48	113	13	3	0	34	29	2		.203	.244	.237	43	-40	24	.905	-1	106	80	/S-98,O-21(0-8-13),2-20,1-16,3-8	-4.1
WILLIAMS, REGGIE Reginald Bernard B 5.5.1966 Laurens, SC BB/TR 6-1/180# d9.8																								
1992	Cal A	14	26	5	6	1	1	0	2	1-0	0	10	.231	.259	.346	68	-1	0-2	1.000	0	110	0	O-12(CF)/D-2	-0.2
1995	LA N	15	11	2	1	0	0	0	1	2-0	0	3	.091	.231	.091	-12	-2	0-0	1.000	-1	79	0	O-14(10-1-4)	-0.2
1998	Ana A	29	36	7	13	1	0	1	5	7-0	1	11	.361	.477	.472	147	3	3-3	1.000	-0	106	0	O-24(19-5-2)/D-2	0.2
1999	Ana A	30	63	8	14	1	2	1	6	5-0	1	21	.222	.286	.349	62	-4	2-1	.974	2	94	251	O-24(4-3-18)/D-3	-0.3
Total	4	88	136	22	34	3	3	2	14	15-0	2	45	.250	.331	.360	82	-4	5-6	.989	1	99	104	/O-74(33-21-24),D-7	-0.5
WILLIAMS, REGGIE Reginald Dewayne B 8.29.1960 Memphis, TN BR/TR 5-11/185# d9.2																								
1985	LA N	22	9	4	3	0	0	0	0	0-0	0	4	.333	.333	.333	90	0	1-0	.900	1	115	383	O-15(12-2-1)	0.1
1986	LA N	128	303	35	84	14	2	4	32	23-9	2	57	.277	.331	.376	102	0	9-3	.984	-4	90	87	*O-124(26-79-35)	-0.5
1987	LA N	39	36	6	4	0	0	0	4	5-0	0	9	.111	.214	.111	-9	-6	1-1	.913	-1	95	0	O-30(16-6-9)	-0.7
1988	Cle A	11	31	7	7	2	0	1	3	0-0	0	6	.226	.226	.387	66	-2	0-0	1.000	-0	78	212	O-11(10-0-3)	-0.2
Total	4	200	379	52	98	16	2	5	39	28-9	2	76	.259	.311	.351	87	-8	11-4	.974	-5	90	97	O-180(64-87-48)	-1.3
WILLIAMS, DICK Richard Hirschfeld B 5.7.1929 St.Louis, MO BR/TR 6/190# d6.10 M21 C1 OF Total (283-LF 156-CF 64-RF)																								
1951	Bro N	23	60	5	12	3	1	1	5	4	0	10	.200	.250	.333	54	-4	0-0	1.000	-1	84	97	O-15(LF)	-0.6
1952	Bro N	36	68	13	21	4	1	0	11	2	0	10	.309	.329	.397	99	0	0-0	1.000	1	117	76	O-25(19-6-0)/13	0.0
1953	†Bro N	30	55	4	12	2	0	2	5	3	1	10	.218	.271	.364	62	-3	0-0	.923	-1	96	0	O-24(17-2-9)	-0.5
1954	Bro N	16	34	5	5	0	0	1	2	2	0	7	.147	.189	.235	11	-5	0-0	1.000	-1	80	0	O-14(13-2-0)	-0.6
1956	Bro N	7	7	0	2	0	0	0	0	0-0	0	1	.286	.286	.286	50	0	0-0	—	0			H	-0.1
	Bal A	87	353	45	101	18	4	11	37	30-1	0	40	.286	.342	.453	117	7	5-5	.990	-1	104	35	O-81(9-66-19),1-10,2-10/3-4	0.1
1957	Bal A	47	167	16	39	10	2	1	17	14-3	0	21	.234	.293	.335	76	-6	0-1	1.000	3	102	237	O-26(15-14-2),3-15,1-12	-0.6
	Cle A	67	205	33	58	7	0	6	17	12-0	1	19	.283	.324	.405	99	-1	3-4	.973	-2	103	53	O-37(18-20-0),3-19	-0.5
	Year	114	372	49	97	17	2	7	34	26-3	1	40	.261	.310	.374	89	-7	3-5	.984	1	103	125	O-63(33-34-2),3-34,1-12	-1.1
1958	Bal A	128	409	36	113	17	0	4	32	37-4	2	47	.276	.336	.347	94	-2	0-6	1.000	-3	103	144	0-70(34-41-15),3-45,1-26/2-7	-1.2
1959	KC A	130	488	72	130	33	1	16	75	28-1	5	60	.266	.309	.436	102	0	4-1	.957	-2	98	65	3-80,1-32,0-23(13-2-8)/2-3	-0.4
1960	KC A	127	420	47	121	31	0	12	65	39-3	1	68	.288	.346	.448	113	8	0-0	.951	3	99	107	3-57,1-34,O-25(LF)	0.8
1961	Bal A	103	310	37	64	15	2	8	24	20-0	0	38	.206	.251	.345	61	-19	0-4	.968	-5	76	93	O-75(73-2-2),1-20/3-2	-2.9
1962	Bal A	82	178	20	44	7	1	1	18	14-0	1	26	.247	.303	.315	72	-7	0-0	1.000	1	109	0	O-29(21-0-9),1-21/3-4	-0.9
1963	Bos A	79	136	15	35	8	0	2	12	15-0	0	25	.257	.329	.360	91	-1	0-0	.976	-2	94	38	3-17,1-11/O-7(LF)	-0.4
1964	Bos A	61	69	10	11	2	0	5	11	7-0	1	10	.159	.247	.406	74	-3	0-0	1.000	3	163	65	1-21,3-13/O-5(4-1-0)	0.0
Total	13	1023	2959	358	768	157	12	70	331	227-12	12	392	.260	.312	.392	92	-36	12-21	.989	-7	99	81	O-456L,3-257,1-188/2-20	-7.8
WILLIAMS, RINALDO Rinaldo Lewis B 12.18.1893 Santa Cruz, CA D 4.24.1966 Cottonwood, AZ BL/TR d10.8																								
1914	Bro F	4	15	1	4	2	0	0	0	0	0	0	.267	.267	.400	81	-1	0	.923	0	111	0	/3-4	-0.1
WILLIAMS, BOB Robert Elias B 4.27.1884 Monday, OH D 8.6.1962 Nelsonville, OH BR/TR 6/190# d7.3																								
1911	NY A	20	47	3	9	2	0	0	8	5	0		.191	.269	.234	38	-4	1	.942	-1	*95*	*123*	C-20	-0.4
1912	NY A	20	44	7	6	1	0	0	3	9	0		.136	.283	.159	26	-4	0	.930	-2	*90*	*69*	C-20	-0.5
1913	NY A	6	19	0	3	0	0	0	0	1	0	3	.158	.200	.158	5	-2	0	.971	-1	*72*	*120*	/C-6	-0.3
Total	3	46	110	10	18	3	0	0	11	15	0	3	.164	.264	.191	28	-10	1	.941	-4	*89*	*99*	/C-46	-1.2
WILLIAMS, TED Theodore Samuel "The Kid", "The Thumper" or "The Splendid Splinter" B8.30.1918 San Diego, CA D7.5.2002 Inverness, FL BL/TR 6-3/205# d4.20 Mil 1943-45, 1952-53 M4 HF1966																								
1939	Bos A	149	565	131	185	44	11	31	**145**	107	2	64	.327	.436	.609	158	53	2-1	.945	1	106	94	*O-149(RF)	4.1
1940	Bos A★	144	561	**134**	193	43	14	23	113	96	3	54	.344	**.442**	.594	159	53	4-4	.960	-1	96	119	*O-143(128-0-16)/P	4.0
1941	Bos A★	143	456	**135**	185	33	3	**37**	120	**147**	3	27	**.406**	**.553**	**.735**	**232**	**102**	2-4	.961	-3	95	100	*O-133(130-0-4)	**8.5**
1942	Bos A★	150	522	**141**	186	34	5	**36**	**137**	**145**	4	51	**.356**	**.499**	**.648**	**214**	**90**	3-2	.988	4	100	130	*O-150(LF)	**8.5**
1946	†Bos A★	150	514	**142**	176	37	8	38	123	**156**	2	44	.342	**.497**	**.667**	**211**	**88**	0-0	.971	2	106	73	*O-150(LF)	**8.1**
1947	Bos A★	156	528	**125**	181	40	9	**32**	**114**	**162**	2	47	**.343**	**.499**	**.634**	**199**	**83**	0-1	.975	1	100	94	*O-156(LF)	**7.2**
1948	Bos A★	137	509	124	188	**44**	3	25	127	**126**	3	41	**.369**	**.497**	**.615**	**185**	**71**	4-0	.983	-0	99	92	*O-134(LF)	5.9
1949	Bos A★	**155**	566	**150**	194	**39**	3	**43**	**159**	**162**	2	48	.343	**.490**	**.650**	**187**	**80**	1-1	.983	-0	98	103	*O-155(LF)	**6.4**
1950	Bos A★	89	334	82	106	24	1	28	97	82	0	21	.317	.452	.647	163	34	3-0	.956	-5	87	106	O-86(LF)	2.2
1951	Bos A★	148	531	109	169	28	4	30	126	**144**	0	45	.318	**.464**	**.556**	159	**52**	1-1	.988	2	97	105	*O-147(LF)	4.1
1952	Bos A	6	10	2	4	0	1	1	3	2	0	2	.400	.500	.900	264	2	0-0	1.000	0	103	0	/O-2(LF)	0.2
1953	Bos A✳	37	91	17	37	6	0	13	34	19	0	10	.407	.509	.901	261	21	0-1	.970	-2	77	69	O-26(LF)	1.7
1954	Bos A★	117	386	93	133	23	1	29	89	**136**	1	32	.345	**.513**	.635	**193**	**61**	0-0	.982	-4	93	71	*O-115(LF)	**5.1**
1955	Bos A★	98	320	77	114	21	3	28	83	91-**17**	2	24	.356	.496	.703	203	52	2-0	.989	-4	92	68	O-93(LF)	4.3
1956	Bos A★	136	400	71	138	28	2	24	82	102-**11**	1	39	.345	**.479**	.605	164	44	0-0	.973	-7	82	89	*O-110(LF)	2.9
1957	Bos A★	132	420	96	163	28	1	38	87	119-**33**	5	43	**.388**	**.526**	**.731**	**227**	84	0-1	.995	-6	90	32	*O-125(LF)	7.1
1958	Bos A★	129	411	81	135	23	2	26	85	98-12	4	49	**.328**	**.458**	.584	174	48	1-0	.957	-11	78	49	*O-114(LF)	3.2
1959	Bos A★	103	272	32	69	15	0	10	43	52-6	2	27	.254	.372	.419	113	7	0-0	.970	-5	77	103	O-76(LF)	-0.1
1960	Bos A★	113	310	56	98	15	0	29	72	75-7	3	41	.316	.451	.645	187	42	1-1	.993	-1	87	120	O-87(LF)	3.6
Total	19	2292	7706	1798	2654	525	71	521	1839	2021-86	39	709	.344	.482	.634	186	1067	24-17	.974	-38	95	92	*O-2151(1984-0-169)/P	87.0
WILLIAMS, WALT Walter Allen "No-Neck" B 12.19.1943 Brownwood, TX BR/TR 5-6/185# d4.21 C1																								
1964	Hou N	10	9	1	0	0	0	0	0	0-0	0	2	.000	.000	.000	-99	-2	1-0	1.000	0	126	0	/O-5(LF)	-0.2
1967	Chi A	104	275	35	66	16	3	3	15	17-0	2	20	.240	.289	.353	92	-3	3-2	.983	2	97	136	O-73(59-0-21)	-0.5

Year	Tm Lg	G	AB	R	H	2B	3B	HR	RBI	BB-IB	HP	SO	AVG	OBP	SLG	AOPS	ABR	SB-CS	FA	FR	Rng	Thr	G at Pos	BFW
1968	Chi A	63	133	6	32	6	0	1	8	4-1	2	17	.241	.271	.308	75	-4	0-1	1.000	-0	94	119	O-34(9-0-28)	-0.7
1969	Chi A	135	471	59	143	22	1	3	32	26-1	3	33	.304	.343	.374	96	-2	6-2	.985	3	94	156	*O-111(34-0-83)	-0.5
1970	Chi A	110	315	43	79	18	1	3	15	19-0	2	30	.251	.296	.343	73	-11	3-3	.949	3	92	260	O-79(13-3-64)	-1.3
1971	Chi A	114	361	43	106	17	3	8	35	24-1	5	27	.294	.344	.424	114	6	5-5	1.000	1	102	76	O-90(35-0-62)/3	0.1
1972	Chi A	77	221	22	55	7	1	2	11	13-1	0	20	.249	.289	.317	79	-6	6-1	.990	3	102	175	O-57(5-0-53)/3	-0.6
1973	Cle A	104	350	43	101	15	1	8	38	14-2	1	29	.289	.316	.406	101	-1	9-4	.970	4	102	167	O-61(LF),D-26	-0.1
1974	NY A	43	53	5	6	0	0	0	3	1-0	0	10	.113	.127	.113	-30	-9	1-0	.955	-1	88	119	O-24(13-0-13)/D-3	-1.1
1975	NY A	82	185	27	52	5	1	5	16	8-1	3	23	.281	.320	.400	105	0	0-1	.982	-2	102	53	O-31(8-10-14),D-17/2-6	-0.3
Total	10	842	2373	284	640	106	11	33	173	126-7	18	211	.270	.310	.365	91	-32	34-19	.981	13	98	149	0-565(242-13-338)/D-46,2-6,3-2	-5.2
WILLIAMS, WASH Washington J. B Philadelphia, PA D 1.1890 Philadelphia, PA 5-11/180# d8.5																								
1884	Ric AA	2	8	0	2	0	0	0		0	0		.250	.250	.250	64	0		.500	-1	0	0	/O-2(RF)	-0.1
1885	Chi N	1	4	0	1	0	0	0	0	0		0	.250	.250	.250	54	0		.500	-0	0	0	/O(RF)P	-0.1
Total	2	3	12	0	3	0	0	0	0	0		0	.250	.250	.250	61	0		.500	-1	0	0	/O-3(RF),P	-0.2
WILLIAMS, BILLY William B 6.13.1933 Newberry, SC BL/TR 6-3/195# d8.15																								
1969	Sea A	4	10	1	0	0	0	0	0	1-0	1	3	.000	.167	.000	-51	-2	0-0	1.000	1	19	884	/O-3(RF)	-0.2
WILLIAMS, WOODY Woodrow Wilson B 8.21.1912 Pamplin, VA D 2.24.1995 Appomattox, VA BR/TR 5-11/175# d9.5																								
1938	Bro N	20	51	6	17	1	1	0	6	4	0	1	.333	.382	.392	111	1	1	.931	-5	74	52	S-18/3	-0.3
1943	Cin N	30	69	8	26	2	1	0	11	1	0	3	.377	.386	.435	139	3	0	.986	-0	110	71	2-12/3-7,S-5	0.4
1944	Cin N	**155**	653	73	157	23	3	1	35	44	2	24	.240	.290	.289	66	-30	7	**.971**	16	**116**	119	*2-155	-0.6
1945	Cin N	133	482	46	114	14	0	0	27	39	2	24	.237	.296	.266	58	-27	6	.969	-8	102	85	*2-133	-2.8
Total	4	338	1255	133	314	40	5	1	79	88	4	52	.250	.301	.292	69	-53	14	.971	3	110	103	2-300/S-23,3-8	-3.3
WILLIAMSON, ANTONE Anthony Joseph B 7.18.1973 Harbor City, CA BL/TR 6-1/195# d5.31																								
1997	Mil A	24	54	2	11	3	0	0	6	4-0	0	8	.204	.254	.259	35	-5	0-1	.977	-2	56	69	1-14/D-4	-0.8
WILLIAMSON, ED Edward Nagle B 10.24.1857 Philadelphia, PA D 3.3.1894 Mountain Valley Springs, AR BR/TR 5-11/210# d5.1 ▲																								
1878	Ind N	**63**	250	31	58	10	2	1	19	5		15	.232	.247	.300	91	-1		.867	-5	93	77	*3-63	-0.4
1879	Chi N	80	320	66	94	20	13	1	36	24		31	.294	.343	.447	149	17		**.871**	18	**131**	**158**	*3-70/1-6,C-4	3.3
1880	Chi N	75	311	65	78	20	2	0	31	15		26	.251	.285	.328	101	1		**.893**	11	113	88	*3-63,C-11/2-3	1.3
1881	Chi N	82	343	56	92	12	6	1	48	19		19	.268	.307	.347	100	0		**.909**	21	**128**	94	*3-76/2-4,P-3,S-2,C	2.1
1882	Chi N	83	348	66	98	27	4	3	60	27		21	.282	.333	.408	130	13		**.881**	15	**120**	**171**	*3-83/P	2.6
1883	Chi N	**98**	402	83	111	**49**	5	2	59	22		48	.276	.314	.438	116	8		.807	18	**133**	**155**	*3-97/C-3,P	2.4
1884	Chi N	107	417	84	116	18	8	**27**	84	42		56	.278	.344	.554	164	29		.861	22	**131**	**202**	*3-99,C-10/P-2	4.7
1885	†Chi N	**113**	407	87	97	16	5	3	65	**75**		60	.238	.357	.324	107	5		**.892**	9	**115**	140	*3-113/P-2,C	1.5
1886	†Chi N	121	430	69	93	17	8	6	58	80		71	.216	.339	.335	92	-3	13	.869	-5	94	117	*S-121/C-4,P-2	-0.4
1887	Chi N	**127**	439	77	117	20	14	9	78	73	5	57	.267	.377	.437	111	6	45	.890	-33	84	78	*S-127/P	-2.0
1888	Chi N	132	452	75	113	9	14	8	73	65	6	71	.250	.352	.385	126	14	25	.884	-13	96	126	*S-132	0.6
1889	Chi N	47	173	16	41	3	1	1	30	23	4	22	.237	.340	.283	71	-6	2	.844	-22	86	44	S-47	-2.4
1890	Chi P	73	261	34	51	7	3	2	26	36	8	35	.195	.311	.268	53	-17	3	.809	-17	85	77	3-52,S-21	-2.7
Total	13	1201	4553	809	1159	228	85	64	667	506	23	532	.255	.332	.384	112	66	88	.866	20	119	137	3-716,S-450/C-34,P-12,2-7,1-6	10.6
WILLIAMSON, HOWIE Nathaniel Howard B 12.23.1904 Little Rock, AR D 8.15.1969 Texarkana, AR BL/TL 6/170# d7.7																								
1928	StL N	10	9	0	2	0	0	0	0	1	0	4	.222	.300	.222	38	-1	0	—	0			H	-0.1
WILLIGROD, JULIUS Julius B 1857 Marshalltown, IA D 11.27.1906 San Francisco, CA BL d7.15																								
1882	Det N	1	3	0	1	0	0	0	0	0		1	.333	.333	.333	115	0		1.000	-0	80	0	/S	0.0
	Cle N	9	36	5	5	1	1	0	2	3		7	.139	.205	.222	38	-2		.813	-2	0	0	/O-9(0-9-1)	-0.4
	Year	10	39	5	6	1	1	0	2	3		8	.154	.214	.231	44	-2		.813	-2	0	0	/O-9(0-9-1),S	-0.4
WILLINGHAM, HUGH Thomas Hugh B 5.30.1906 Dalhart, TX D 6.15.1988 ElReno, OK BR/TR 6/180# d9.13																								
1930	Chi A	3	4	2	1	0	0	0	0	2	0	1	.250	.500	.250	100	0	0-0	1.000	-0	112	0	/2	0.0
1931	Phi N	23	35	5	9	2	1	1	3	2	0	9	.257	.297	.457	93	-1	0	.875	-1	77	94	/S-8,3-2,O(LF)	-0.1
1932	Phi N	4	2	0	0	0	0	0	0	0	0	0	.000	.000	.000	-89	-1	0	—	0			H	-0.1
1933	Phi N	1	1	0	0	0	0	0	0	0	0	0	.000	.000	.000	-89	0	0	—	0			H	0.0
Total	4	31	42	7	10	2	1	1	3	4	0	10	.238	.304	.405	82	-2	0-0	.875	-2	77	94	/S-8,3-2,O(LF)2	-0.2
WILLS d5.14																								
1884	Was AA	4	15	1	2	2	0	0		0	0		.133	.133	.267	31	-1		.889	2	401	0	/O-4(1-3-0)	0.1
	KC U	5	21	2	3	1	0	0		0			.143	.143	.190	0	-3		1.000	1	208	0	/O-5(CF)	-0.2
Total	1	9	36	3	5	3	0	0		0			.139	.139	.222	13	-4		.938	3	305	0	/O-9(1-8-0)	-0.1
WILLS, DAVE Davis Bowles B 1.26.1877 Charlottesville, VA D 10.12.1959 Washington, DC BL/TL d6.8																								
1899	Lou N	24	94	15	21	3	1	0	12	2	0		.223	.240	.277	41	-8	1	.957	-3	67	65	1-24	-1.0
WILLS, BUMP Elliott Taylor B 7.27.1952 Washington, DC BB/TR 5-9/177# d4.7 f-Maury																								
1977	Tex A	152	541	87	155	28	6	9	62	65-7	0	96	.287	.361	.410	109	9	28-12	.982	6	104	98	*2-150/S-2,1D	2.5
1978	Tex A	157	539	78	135	17	4	9	57	63-3	4	91	.250	.331	.347	91	-5	52-14	.981	22	111	88	*2-156	3.2
1979	Tex A	146	543	90	148	21	3	5	46	53-4	4	58	.273	.340	.350	88	-8	35-11	.976	12	104	96	*2-146	1.5
1980	Tex A	146	578	102	152	31	5	5	58	51-1	3	71	.263	.322	.360	90	-7	34-9	.984	20	102	100	*2-144	2.5
1981	Tex A	102	410	51	103	13	2	2	41	32-2	1	49	.251	.304	.307	82	-10	12-9	.983	11	101	103	*2-101/D	0.6
1982	Chi N	128	419	64	114	18	4	6	38	46-3	5	76	.272	.347	.377	101	2	35-10	.963	-11	97	77	*2-103	0.0
Total	6	831	3030	472	807	128	24	36	302	310-20	17	441	.266	.335	.360	94	-19	196-65	.979	60	104	94	2-800/D-2,S-2,1	10.3
WILLS, MAURY Maurice Morning B 10.2.1932 Washington, DC BB/TR 5-11/170# d6.6 M2 s-Bump																								
1959	†LA N	83	242	27	63	5	2	0	7	13-5	0	27	.260	.298	.298	55	-15	7-3	.966	0	97	88	S-82	-0.9
1960	LA N	148	516	75	152	15	2	0	27	35-8	3	47	.295	.342	.331	80	-13	**50**-12	.945	20	103	100	*S-145	2.6
1961	LA N★	148	613	105	173	12	10	1	31	59-2	1	50	.282	.346	.339	76	-20	**35**-15	.959	10	95	108	*S-148	0.5
1962	LA N★	**165**	695	130	208	13	**10**	6	48	51-1	2	57	.299	.347	.373	100	-2	**104**-13	.956	-8	94	82	*S-165	2.3
1963	†LA N☆	134	527	83	159	19	3	0	34	44-0	1	48	.302	.355	.349	112	9	**40**-19	.959	-3	98	79	*S-109,3-33	1.8
1964	LA N	158	630	81	173	15	5	2	34	41-0	0	73	.275	.318	.324	88	-11	**53**-17	.963	-9	92	96	*S-149/3-6	-0.2
1965	†LA N★	158	650	92	186	14	7	0	33	40-2	4	64	.286	.330	.329	93	-7	**94**-31	.970	15	104	106	*S-155	3.3
1966	†LA N★	143	594	60	162	14	2	1	39	34-0	2	60	.273	.314	.308	80	-17	38-24	.967	7	99	104	*S-139/3-4	0.2
1967	Pit N	149	616	92	186	12	9	3	45	31-1	1	44	.302	.334	.365	100	-2	29-10	.948	9	115	120	*3-144/S-2	1.1
1968	Pit N	153	627	76	174	12	6	0	31	45-1	1	57	.278	.326	.316	95	-4	52-21	.957	-9	98	102	*3-141,S-10	-1.0
1969	Mon N	47	189	23	42	3	0	0	8	20-0	0	21	.222	.295	.238	51	-12	15-6	.950	-2	98	100	S-46/2	-0.7
	LA N	104	434	57	129	7	8	4	39	39-2	1	40	.297	.356	.378	114	7	25-15	.969	11	109	109	*S-104	3.1
	Year	151	623	80	171	10	8	4	47	59-2	1	61	.274	.337	.335	94	-6	40-21	.963	9	106	106	*S-150/2	2.4
1970	LA N	132	522	77	141	19	3	0	34	50-2	0	34	.270	.333	.318	79	-15	28-13	.959	-17	101	83	*S-126/3-4	-1.6
1971	LA N	149	601	73	169	14	3	3	44	40-2	0	44	.281	.323	.329	92	-8	15-8	.978	6	104	105	*S-144/3-4	1.6
1972	LA N	71	132	16	17	3	1	0	4	10-0	0	18	.129	.190	.167	2	-17	1-1	.984	-6	94	115	S-31,3-26	-2.2
Total	14	1942	7588	1067	2134	177	71	20	458	552-26	16	684	.281	.330	.331	88	-127	586-208	.963	25	99	97	*S-1555,3-362/2	9.9
WILLSON, KID Frank Hoxie B 11.3.1895 Bloomington, NE D 4.17.1964 Union Gap, WA BL/TL 6-1/190# d7.2																								
1918	Chi A	4	1	2	0	0	0	0	0	1	0	1	.000	.500	.000	50	0	0	—	0			H	0.0
1927	Chi A	7	10	1	1	0	0	0	1	0	0	2	.100	.100	.100	-49	-2	0-0	1.000	0	143	0	/O-2(1-1-0)	-0.2
Total	2	11	11	3	1	0	0	0	1	1	0	3	.091	.167	.091	-31	-2	0-0	1.000	0	143	0	/O-2(1-1-0)	-0.2
WILMOT, WALT Walter Robert B 10.18.1863 Plover, WI D 2.1.1929 Chicago, IL BB/TR 5-9/165# d4.20																								
1888	Was N	119	473	61	106	16	9	4	43	23	2	55	.224	.263	.321	92	-5	46	.872	12	96	96	*O-119(LF)	0.4
1889	Was N	108	432	88	125	19	**19**	9	57	51	2	32	.289	.367	.484	146	25	40	.927	14	106	92	*O-108(107-1-0)	3.1
1890	Chi N	**139**	571	114	159	15	13	**13**	99	64	2	44	.278	.353	.419	120	12	76	.938	11	110	90	*O-139(27-112-0)	1.6
1891	Chi N	121	498	102	137	14	10	11	71	55	5	21	.275	.353	.410	122	13	42	.922	-4	83	0	*O-121(62-60-0)	0.6
1892	Chi N	92	380	47	82	7	7	2	35	40	4	20	.216	.297	.287	76	-11	31	.903	-2	50	0	O-92(LF)	-2.0
1893	Chi N	94	392	69	118	14	14	3	61	40	1	8	.301	.367	.431	114	6	39	.873	-1	97	27	*O-93(84-10-0)	-0.3
1894	Chi N	135	604	136	199	45	12	5	130	36	1	27	.329	.368	.469	95	-7	76	.870	-7	71	84	*O-135(LF)	-2.0

Year	Tm Lg	G	AB	R	H	2B	3B	HR	RBI	BB-IB	HP	SO	AVG	OBP	SLG	AOPS	ABR	SB-CS	FA	FR	Rng	Thr	G at Pos	BFW
1895	Chi N	108	466	86	132	16	6	8	72	30	0	19	.283	.327	.395	80	-17	28	.914	3	114	130	*O-108(LF)	-1.9
1897	NY N	11	34	8	9	2	0	1	4	2	0		.265	.306	.412	91	-1	1	.938	0	159	0	/O-9(5-1-3)	-0.1
1898	NY N	35	138	16	33	4	2	2	22	9	0		.239	.286	.341	82	-4	4	.886	-4	89	0	O-34(6-0-29)	-0.9
Total	10	962	3988	727	1100	152	92	58	594	350	17	226	.276	.337	.404	105	11	383	.903	23	92	64	O-958(745-184-32)	-1.5
WILSON, ARCHIE Archie Clifton B 11.25.1923 Los Angeles, CA BR/TR 6/175# d9.18																								
1951	NY A	4	4	0	0	0	0	0	0	0	1	0	.000	.200	.000	-44	-1	0-0	1.000	0	139	0	/O-2(RF)	-0.1
1952	NY A	3	2	0	1	0	0	0	1	0	0	0	.500	.500	.500	190	0	0-0	—	0			H	0.0
	Was A	26	96	8	20	2	3	0	14	5	1	11	.208	.255	.292	54	-7	0-0	.971	-0	110	0	O-24(14-10-0)	-0.9
	Bos A	18	38	1	10	3	0	0	2	2	0	3	.263	.300	.342	73	-1	0-0	.944	0	95	152	O-13(2-2-9)	-0.2
	Year	47	136	9	31	5	3	0	17	7	1	14	.228	.271	.309	61	-8	0-0	.966	-0	106	39	O-37(16-12-9)	-1.1
Total	2	51	140	9	31	5	3	0	17	7	2	14	.221	.268	.300	58	-9	0-0	.967	0	107	38	/O-39(16-12-11)	-1.2
WILSON, ART Arthur Earl "Dutch" B 12.11.1885 Macon, IL D 6.12.1960 Chicago, IL BR/TR 5-8/170# d9.29																								
1908	NY N	1	0	0	0	0	0	0	0	0	0		—	—	—	—	0	0	—	0			R	0.0
1909	NY N	19	42	4	10	2	1	0	5	4	0		.238	.304	.333	96	0	0	.985	-2	*97*	*86*	C-19	-0.1
1910	NY N	26	52	10	14	4	1	0	5	9	1	6	.269	.387	.385	125	2	2	.975	-0	*96*	*93*	C-25/1	0.4
1911	†NY N	66	109	17	33	9	1	1	17	19	1	12	.303	.411	.431	132	6	6	.963	-1	*125*	*82*	C-64	0.8
1912	†NY N	65	121	17	35	6	0	3	19	13	0	14	.289	.358	.413	107	1	2	.960	3	*132*	*68*	C-61	0.8
1913	†NY N	54	79	5	15	0	1	0	8	11	0	11	.190	.289	.215	45	-5	1-5	.965	6	127	79	C-49	0.1
1914	Chi F	137	440	78	128	31	8	10	64	70	5	80	.291	.394	.466	142	21	13	.974	21	***143***	*94*	*C-132	**5.4**
1915	Chi F	96	269	44	82	11	2	7	31	65	1	38	.305	.442	.439	157	22	8	.980	-5	*116*	*79*	C-87	2.6
1916	Pit N	53	128	11	33	5	2	1	12	13	1	27	.258	.331	.352	109	2	4	.981	-7	81	92	C-39	-0.2
	Chi N	36	114	5	22	3	1	0	5	6	0	14	.193	.233	.237	40	-8	1	.953	-4	96	107	C-34	-1.1
	Year	89	242	16	55	8	3	1	17	19	1	41	.227	.286	.298	76	-7	5	.967	-11	88	99	C-73	-1.3
1917	Chi N	81	211	17	45	9	2	2	25	32	2	36	.213	.322	.303	85	-2	6	.968	6	*101*	*105*	C-75	1.1
1918	Bos N	89	280	15	69	8	2	0	19	24	2	31	.246	.310	.289	87	-4	5	.977	-11	*89*	*100*	C-85	-0.9
1919	Bos N	71	191	14	49	8	1	0	16	25	1	19	.257	.346	.309	102	2	2	.977	-2	*99*	*98*	C-64/1	0.6
1920	Bos N	16	19	0	1	0	0	0	0	1	1	1	.053	.143	.053	-44	-4	0-0	1.000	-1	81	0	/3-6,C-2	-0.5
1921	Cle A	2	1	0	0	0	0	0	0	0	0	0	.000	.000	.000	-99	0	0-0	1.000	0	*0*	*0*	/C-2	0.0
Total	14	812	2056	237	536	96	22	24	226	292	15	289	.261	.357	.364	110	33	50-5	.972	4	*113*	92	C-738/3-6,1-2	9.0
WILSON, ARTIE Arthur Lee B 10.28.1920 Springville, AL BL/TR 5-10/162# d4.18																								
1951	NY N	19	22	2	4	0	0	0	1	2	0	1	.182	.250	.182	18	-3	2-0	1.000	1	94	235	/2-3,S-3,1-2	-0.1
WILSON, CHARLIE Charles Woodrow "Swamp Baby" B 1.13.1905 Clinton, SC D 12.19.1970 Rochester, NY BB/TR 5-10.5/178# d4.14																								
1931	Bos N	16	58	7	11	4	0	1	11	3	0	5	.190	.230	.310	45	-5	0	.917	-1	100	0	3-14	-0.6
1932	StL N	24	96	7	19	3	3	1	2	3	0	8	.198	.222	.323	43	-8	0	.935	-3	97	98	S-24	-0.9
1933	StL N	1	1	0	0	0	0	0	0	0	0	1	.000	.000	.000	-95	0	0	—	-0	0	0	/S	0.0
1935	StL N	16	31	1	10	0	0	0	1	2	0	2	.323	.364	.323	83	-1	0	.933	-1	81	129	/3-8	-0.1
Total	4	57	186	15	40	7	3	2	14	8	0	16	.215	.247	.317	50	-14	0	.935	-5	97	98	/S-25,3-22	-1.6
WILSON, CRAIG Craig B 11.28.1964 Annapolis, MD BR/TR 5-11/175# d9.6																								
1989	StL N	6	4	1	1	0	0	0	1	1-0	0	2	.250	.400	.250	87	0	0-0	.500	-0	0	0	/3-2	0.0
1990	StL N	55	121	13	30	2	0	0	7	8-0	0	14	.248	.290	.264	55	-8	0-2	.971	0	92	61	3-13,O-13(7-0-7)/2-9,1	-0.8
1991	StL N	60	82	5	14	2	0	0	13	6-2	0	10	.171	.222	.195	20	-9	0-0	.905	-0	77	242	3-12/O-5(LF),1-4,2-3	-1.0
1992	StL N	61	106	6	33	6	0	0	13	10-2	0	18	.311	.368	.368	113	2	1-2	.970	-3	75	82	3-18,2-11/O-3(RF)	-0.1
1993	KC A	21	49	6	13	1	0	1	3	7-0	0	6	.265	.357	.347	85	-1	1-1	1.000	-0	91	204	3-15/2O(LF)	-0.1
Total	5	203	362	31	91	11	0	1	37	32-4	0	50	.251	.308	.290	68	-16	2-5	.957	-3	83	133	/3-60,2-24,O-22(13-0-10),1-5	-2.0
WILSON, CRAIG Craig Alan B 11.30.1976 Fountain Valley, CA BR/TR 6-2/217# d4.22																								
2001	Pit N	88	158	27	49	3	1	13	32	15-1	7	53	.310	.390	.589	146	11	3-1	.994	-3	123	114	1-26,O-14(1-0-13),C-10/D-2	0.7
2002	Pit N	131	368	48	97	16	1	16	57	32-0	**21**	116	.264	.355	.443	112	5	2-3	.982	-1	85	142	O-75(1-0-74),1-42/C-5,D-3	-0.3
2003	Pit N	116	309	49	81	15	4	18	48	35-4	13	89	.262	.360	.511	122	10	3-1	.978	3	124	126	O-46(7-0-40),1-36,C-21/D-3	1.0
Total	3	335	835	124	227	34	6	47	137	82-5	41	258	.272	.363	.496	122	26	8-5	.978	-0	98	138	O-135(9-0-127),1-104/C-36,D-8	1.4
WILSON, CRAIG Craig Franklin B 9.3.1970 Chicago, IL BR/TR 6/185# d9.5																								
1998	Chi A	13	47	14	22	5	0	3	10	3-0	0	6	.468	.490	.766	229	9	1-0	1.000	-3	67	72	/S-8,2-4,3-2	0.6
1999	Chi A	98	252	28	60	8	1	4	26	23-0	0	22	.238	.301	.325	60	-16	1-1	.969	-0	110	112	3-72,S-22/2-7,1D	-1.3
2000	Chi A	28	73	12	19	3	0	0	4	5-0	1	11	.260	.316	.301	57	-5	1-0	.938	6	137	124	3-15,S-10/2-4	0.2
Total	3	139	372	54	101	16	1	7	40	31-0	1	39	.272	.328	.376	80	-12	3-1	.964	2	114	112	/3-89,S-40,2-15,D1	-0.5
WILSON, DAN Daniel Allen B 3.25.1969 Arlington Heights, IL BR/TR 6-3/190# d9.7																								
1992	Cin N	12	25	2	9	1	0	0	3	3-0	0	8	.360	.429	.400	132	1	0-0	1.000	1	127	125	/C-9	0.2
1993	Cin N	36	76	6	17	3	0	0	8	9-4	0	16	.224	.302	.263	54	-5	0-0	.994	-4	68	38	C-35	-0.8
1994	Sea A	91	282	24	61	14	2	3	27	10-0	1	57	.216	.244	.312	42	-25	1-2	.986	12	124	110	C-91	-0.8
1995	†Sea A	119	399	40	111	22	3	9	51	33-1	2	63	.278	.336	.416	94	-4	2-1	.995	14	111	117	*C-119	1.6
1996	Sea A★	138	491	51	140	24	0	18	83	32-2	3	88	.285	.330	.444	94	-6	1-2	.996	10	134	109	*C-135	1.1
1997	†Sea A	146	508	66	137	31	1	15	74	39-1	5	72	.270	.326	.423	95	-4	7-2	.995	12	125	**125**	*C-144	1.7
1998	Sea A	96	325	39	82	17	1	9	44	24-0	5	56	.252	.308	.394	82	-9	2-1	.994	-3	90	93	C-94	-0.5
1999	Sea A	123	414	46	110	23	2	7	38	29-4	2	83	.266	.315	.382	79	-14	5-0	.995	-2	91	70	*C-121/1-5	-0.7
2000	†Sea A	90	268	31	63	12	0	5	27	22-0	0	51	.235	.291	.336	61	-17	1-2	.990	2	142	105	C-88/13	-0.9
2001	†Sea A	123	377	44	100	20	1	10	42	20-0	2	69	.265	.305	.403	90	-7	3-2	**.999**	4	161	56	*C-122/1-2	0.4
2002	Sea A	115	359	35	106	16	1	6	44	18-1	2	81	.295	.326	.396	96	-3	1-0	.997	-2	124	67	*C-113/1-4	0.2
2003	Sea A	96	316	32	76	15	2	4	43	15-0	0	52	.241	.272	.339	63	-18	0-0	**.998**	1	**180**	54	C-96	-1.0
Total	12	1185	3840	416	1012	198	13	86	484	254-13	22	696	.264	.310	.389	82	-111	23-12	.995	43	126	91	*C-1167/1-12,3	0.5
WILSON, DESI Desi Bernard B 5.9.1969 Glen Cove, NY BL/TL 6-7/230# d8.7																								
1996	SF N	41	118	10	32	2	0	2	12	12-2	0	27	.271	.338	.339	83	-3	0-2	.984	-2	89	84	1-33	-0.8
WILSON, EDDIE Edward Francis B 9.7.1909 Hamden, CT D 4.11.1979 Hamden, CT BL/TL 5-11/165# d6.21																								
1936	Bro N	52	173	28	60	8	1	3	25	14	2	25	.347	.402	.457	129	8	3	.926	-3	92	68	O-47(RF)	0.2
1937	Bro N	36	54	11	12	4	1	1	8	17	0	14	.222	.408	.389	116	2	1	.966	-0	102	71	O-21(0-1-20)	0.1
Total	2	88	227	39	72	12	2	4	33	31	2	39	.317	.404	.441	126	10	4	.936	-4	95	69	/O-68(0-1-67)	0.3
WILSON, ENRIQUE Enrique (Martes) B 7.27.1973 Santo Domingo, D.R. BB/TR 5-11/160# d9.24																								
1997	Cle A	5	15	2	5	0	0	0	1	0-0	0	2	.333	.333	.333	72	-1	0-0	.941	1	120	205	/S-4,2	0.0
1998	†Cle A	32	90	13	29	6	0	2	12	4-0	1	8	.322	.354	.456	106	1	2-4	.989	1	107	58	2-22,S-10/3-2	0.2
1999	†Cle A	113	332	41	87	22	1	2	24	25-1	1	41	.262	.310	.352	67	-16	5-4	.965	-12	98	25	3-61,S-35,2-21/D	-2.4
2000	Cle A	40	117	16	38	9	0	2	12	7-0	0	11	.325	.360	.453	103	1	2-1	.950	-3	107	0	3-12/2-7,S-7,D-8	-0.2
	Pit N	40	122	11	32	6	1	3	15	11-2	0	13	.262	.321	.402	82	-4	0-1	.925	-0	110	34	3-16,2-11/S-8	-0.3
2001	Pit N	46	129	7	24	3	0	1	8	3-0	0	23	.186	.203	.233	12	-17	0-3	.974	4	110	102	S-28,2-10/3-2	-1.2
	†NY A	48	99	10	24	5	1	1	12	6-0	0	14	.242	.283	.343	64	-5	0-2	.952	4	99	71	S-20,3-19/2-7,D	-0.1
2002	†NY A	60	105	17	19	2	2	2	11	8-0	0	22	.181	.239	.295	41	-9	1-1	.932	1	99	47	3-26,S-14/2-7,O(RF)D	-0.7
2003	†NY A	63	135	18	31	9	0	3	15	7-0	2	14	.230	.276	.363	68	-6	3-1	.987	-4	78	65	S-33,3-17,2-10/D	-0.8
Total	7	447	1144	135	289	62	5	16	110	71-3	4	148	.253	.296	.358	67	-56	13-17	.966	-9	95	104	S-159,3-155/2-96,D-13,O(RF)	-5.5
WILSON, FRANK Francis Edward "Squash" B 4.20.1901 Malden, MA D 11.25.1974 Leicester, MA BL/TR 6/185# d6.20																								
1924	Bos N	61	215	20	51	7	0	1	15	23	0	22	.237	.311	.284	63	-11	3-4	.973	2	108	86	O-55(35-20-0)	-1.3
1925	Bos N	12	31	3	13	1	1	0	0	4	0	1	.419	.486	.516	171	4	2-1	1.000	1	121	114	O-10(9-0-1)	0.4
1926	Bos N	87	236	22	56	11	3	0	23	20	1	21	.237	.300	.309	70	-10	3	.934	1	107	109	O-56(50-1-6)	-1.3
1928	Cle A	2	1	0	0	0	0	0	0	1	0	0	.000	.500	.000	41	0	0-0	—	0			H	0.0
	StL A	6	5	1	0	0	0	0	0	0	0	0	.000	.000	.000	-97	-1	0-0	—	-0	0	0	/O(RF)	-0.1
	Year	8	6	1	0	0	0	0	0	1	0	0	.000	.143	.000	-58	-1	0-0	—	-0	0	0	/O(RF)	-0.1
Total	4	168	488	46	120	19	4	1	38	48	1	44	.246	.315	.307	72	-18	8-5	.958	4	108	99	O-122(94-21-8)	-2.3
WILSON, TUG George Archer B 1860 Brooklyn, NY D 11.28.1914 New York, NY 5-8/175# d5.9																								
1884	Bro AA	24	82	13	19	4	0	0		5	0		.232	.276	.280	81	-1		.826	-3	93	284	O-12(5-6-1),C-10/1-3,2	-0.4

Year	Tm Lg	G	AB	R	H	2B	3B	HR	RBI	BB-IB	HP	SO	AVG	OBP	SLG	AOPS	ABR	SB-CS	FA	FR	Rng	Thr	G at Pos	BFW
WILSON, SQUANTO George Francis B 3.29.1889 Old Town, ME D 3.26.1967 Winthrop, ME BB/TR 5-9.5/170# d10.2																								
1911	Det A	5	16	2	3	0	0	0	0	2	0		.188	.278	.188	29	-1	0	.900	-1	106	97	/C-5	-0.2
1914	Bos A	1	0	0	0	0	0	0	0	0	0	0	—	—	—	—	0	0	—	0	0	0	/1	0.0
Total	2	6	16	2	3	0	0	0	0	2	0	0	.188	.278	.188	29	-1	0	.900	-1	106	97	/C-5,1	-0.2
WILSON, ICEHOUSE George Peacock B 9.14.1912 Maricopa, CA D 10.13.1973 Moraga, CA BR/TR 6/186# d5.31																								
1934	Det A	1	1	0	0	0	0	0	0	0	0	0	.000	.000	.000	-99	0	0-0	—	0			H	0.0
WILSON, GEORGE George Washington "Teddy" B 8.30.1925 Cherryville, NC D 10.29.1974 Gastonia, NC BL/TR 6-1.5/185# d4.15																								
1952	Chi A	8	9	0	1	0	0	0	1	1	0	2	.111	.200	.111	-12	-1	0-0	1.000	0	109	0	/O(RF)	-0.2
	NY N	62	112	9	27	7	0	2	16	3	0	14	.241	.261	.357	69	-5	0-0	.923	-2	100	0	O-21(16-1-4)/1-2	-0.9
1953	NY N	11	8	0	1	0	0	0	0	2	1	2	.125	.364	.125	34	-1	0-0	—	0			H	-0.1
1956	NY N	53	68	5	9	1	0	1	2	5-1	0	14	.132	.192	.191	3	-9	0-0	1.000	0	91	159	/O-8(2-0-6)	-1.0
	†NY A	11	12	1	2	0	0	0	0	3-0	0	0	.167	.333	.167	37	-1	0-0	.750	-1	68	0	/O-6(1-0-5)	-0.2
Total	3	145	209	15	40	8	0	3	19	14-1	1	32	.191	.246	.273	41	-17	0-0	.932	-3	96	42	/O-36(19-1-16),1-2	-2.4
WILSON, GLENN Glenn Dwight B 12.22.1958 Baytown, TX BR/TR 6-1/190# d4.15 OF Total (118-LF 90-CF 941-RF)																								
1982	Det A	84	322	39	94	15	1	12	34	15-0	0	51	.292	.322	.457	111	4	2-3	.987	3	102	150	O-80(2-71-8)/D-4	0.5
1983	Det A	144	503	55	135	25	6	11	65	25-1	3	79	.268	.306	.408	97	-4	1-1	.988	-7	86	122	*O-143(0-8-140)	-1.8
1984	Phi N	132	341	28	82	21	3	6	31	17-1	1	56	.240	.276	.372	80	-10	7-1	.968	-5	91	60	*O-109(92-3-18)/3-4	-1.9
1985	Phi N★	161	608	73	167	39	5	14	102	35-1	0	117	.275	.311	.424	102	0	7-4	.968	16	117	170	*O-158(2-0-157)	0.8
1986	Phi N	155	584	70	158	30	4	15	84	42-1	4	91	.271	.319	.413	98	-2	5-1	.989	15	112	156	*O-154(1-0-153)	0.5
1987	Phi N	154	569	55	150	21	2	14	54	38-2	1	82	.264	.308	.381	80	-18	3-6	.968	10	106	169	*O-154(RF)/P	-1.7
1988	Sea A	78	284	28	71	10	1	3	17	15-0	0	52	.250	.286	.324	68	-13	1-1	.980	-2	93	92	O-75(RF)/D-2	-1.7
	Pit N	37	126	11	34	8	0	2	15	3-1	1	18	.270	.288	.381	93	-1	0-0	.985	-1	96	59	O-35(0-4-32)	-0.4
1989	Pit N	100	330	42	93	20	4	9	49	32-5	1	39	.282	.342	.448	130	13	1-4	.977	-2	97	86	O-85(0-1-85),1-10	0.8
	Hou N	28	102	8	22	6	0	2	15	5-0	0	14	.216	.250	.333	68	-5	0-1	.966	4	99	426	O-25(RF)	-0.2
	Year	128	432	50	115	26	4	11	64	37-5	1	53	.266	.321	.421	116	8	1-5	.974	2	97	167	*O-110(0-1-110),1-10	0.6
1990	Hou N	118	368	42	90	14	0	10	55	26-1	1	64	.245	.293	.364	83	-10	0-3	.975	10	112	172	*O-108(21-0-92)/1	-0.4
1993	Pit N	10	14	0	2	0	0	0	0	0-0	0	9	.143	.143	.143	-23	-2	0-0	.875	1	76	1203	/O-5(0-3-2)	-0.2
Total	10	1201	4151	451	1098	209	26	98	521	253-13	12	672	.265	.306	.398	93	-48	27-25	.977	42	103	145	*O-1131R/1-11,D-6,3-4,P	-5.7
WILSON, GRADY Grady Herbert B 11.23.1922 Columbus, GA BR/TR 6-0.5/170# d5.15																								
1948	Pit N	12	10	1	1	1	0	0	1	0	0	3	.100	.100	.200	-20	-2	0	.846	-0	68	185	/S-7	-0.2
WILSON, HENRY Henry C. B 4.8.1877 Baltimore, MD d10.12																								
1898	Bal N	1	2	0	0	0	0	0	0	1	0		.000	.333	.000	-2	0	0	1.000	0	87	287	/C	0.0
WILSON, JACK Jack Eugene B 12.29.1977 Westlake Village, CA BR/TR 6/175# d4.3																								
2001	Pit N	108	390	44	87	17	1	3	25	16-2	1	70	.223	.255	.295	41	-35	1-3	.968	9	115	101	*S-107	-1.9
2002	Pit N	147	527	77	133	22	4	4	47	37-2	4	74	.252	.306	.332	71	-25	5-2	.977	20	**118**	100	*S-143	0.5
2003	Pit N	150	558	58	143	21	3	9	62	36-3	4	74	.256	.303	.353	70	-26	5-5	.975	4	**108**	109	*S-149	-1.0
Total	3	405	1475	179	363	60	8	16	134	89-7	9	218	.246	.292	.330	62	-86	11-10	.974	33	113	104	S-399	-2.4
WILSON, JIMMIE James "Ace" B 7.23.1900 Philadelphia, PA D 5.31.1947 Bradenton, FL BR/TR 6-1.5/200# d4.17 M9 C5																								
1923	Phi N	85	252	27	66	9	0	1	25	4	1	17	.262	.276	.310	49	-19	4-2	.960	-9	83	91	C-69/O-2(1-1-0)	-2.2
1924	Phi N	95	280	32	78	16	3	6	39	17	1	12	.279	.322	.421	87	-5	5-4	.968	1	92	**131**	C-82/1-2,O(RF)	0.1
1925	Phi N	108	335	42	110	19	3	3	54	32	2	25	.328	.390	.430	100	2	5-3	.982	-7	97	71	C-89/O	0.0
1926	Phi N	90	279	40	85	10	2	4	32	25	0	20	.305	.362	.398	99	0	3	.950	-4	83	132	C-79	0.1
1927	Phi N	128	443	50	122	15	2	2	45	34	2	15	.275	.330	.332	77	-14	13	.975	-21	82	80	*C-124	-2.7
1928	Phi N	21	70	11	21	4	1	0	13	9	0	8	.300	.380	.386	97	0	3	.990	-0	74	142	C-20	0.1
	†StL N	120	411	45	106	26	2	2	50	45	1	24	.258	.333	.345	76	-13	9	.983	4	130	102	*C-120	-0.1
	Year	141	481	56	127	30	3	2	63	54	1	32	.264	.340	.351	79	-13	12	.985	4	122	108	*C-140	0.0
1929	StL N	120	394	59	128	27	8	4	71	43	2	19	.325	.394	.464	111	8	4	.972	6	115	106	*C-119	1.9
1930	†StL N	107	362	54	115	25	7	1	58	28	1	17	.318	.368	.434	90	-5	8	.987	10	113	**121**	C-99	1.0
1931	†StL N	115	383	45	105	20	2	0	51	28	5	15	.274	.332	.337	77	-11	5	.985	10	100	**128**	*C-110	0.5
1932	StL N	92	274	36	68	16	2	2	28	15	1	18	.248	.290	.343	67	-13	9	.982	2	76	164	C-75/1-3,2	-0.6
1933	StL N★	113	369	34	94	17	0	1	45	23	1	33	.255	.300	.309	71	-13	6	.982	0	87	122	*C-107	-0.7
1934	Phi N	91	277	25	81	11	0	3	35	14	0	10	.292	.326	.365	75	-10	1	.987	4	118	117	C-77/12M	-0.1
1935	Phi N★	93	290	38	81	20	0	1	37	19	1	19	.279	.326	.359	76	-9	4	.982	4	99	92	C-78/2M	0.0
1936	Phi N	85	230	25	64	12	0	1	27	12	0	21	.278	.314	.343	70	-9	5	.960	-5	96	84	C-63/1M	-1.1
1937	Phi N	39	87	15	24	3	0	1	8	6	0	4	.276	.323	.345	75	-3	1	.978	-1	127	91	C-22/1-2,M	-0.3
1938	Phi N	3	2	0	0	0	0	0	0	0	0	1	.000	.000	.000	-99	-1	0	1.000	0	0	0	/CM	0.0
1939	Cin N	4	3	0	1	0	0	0	0	0	0	1	.333	.333	.333	79	0	0	—	-0	0	0	/C	0.0
1940	†Cin N	16	37	2	9	2	0	0	3	2	0	1	.243	.282	.297	59	-2	1	.982	1	101	122	C-16	0.0
Total	18	1525	4778	580	1358	252	32	32	621	356	18	280	.284	.336	.370	82	-117	86-9	.977	-4	99	110	*C-1351/1-9,O-4(1-1-1),2-3	-4.1
WILSON, GARY James Garrett B 1.12.1877 Baltimore, MD D 5.1.1969 Randallstown, MD BR/TR 5-7/168# d9.27																								
1902	Bos A	2	8	0	1	0	0	0	1	0	0		.125	.125	.125	-30	-1	0	.800	-0	88	233	/2-2	-0.2
WILSON, JIM James George B 12.29.1960 Corvallis, OR BR/TR 6-3/230# d9.13																								
1985	Cle A	4	14	2	5	0	0	0	4	1-0	0	3	.357	.400	.357	110	0	0-0	1.000	-0	0	67	/1-2,D-2	0.0
1989	Sea A	5	8	0	0	0	0	0	0	0-0	0	3	.000	.000	.000	-97	-2	0-0	—	0			/D-5	-0.2
Total	2	9	22	2	5	0	0	0	4	1-0	0	6	.227	.261	.227	36	-2	0-0	1.000	-0	0	67	/D-7,1-2	-0.2
WILSON, CHIEF John Owen B 8.21.1883 Austin, TX D 2.22.1954 Bertram, TX BL/TR 6-2/185# d4.15																								
1908	Pit N	144	529	47	120	8	7	3	43	22	2		.227	.260	.285	74	-18	12	.955	-1	108	72	*O-144(1-34-109)	-3.0
1909	†Pit N	**154**	569	64	155	22	12	4	59	19	6		.272	.303	.374	102	-2	17	.957	4	86	161	*O-154(RF)	-0.6
1910	Pit N	146	536	59	148	14	13	4	50	21	7	68	.276	.312	.373	94	-8	8	.972	4	103	112	*O-146(1-7-138)	-1.1
1911	Pit N	148	544	72	163	34	12	12	**107**	41	4	55	.300	.353	.472	125	16	10	.977	5	110	98	*O-146(0-2-145)	1.3
1912	Pit N	**152**	583	80	175	19	**36**	11	95	35	2	67	.300	.342	.513	134	20	16	.961	-0	104	87	*O-152(0-87-69)	1.0
1913	Pit N	**155**	580	71	154	12	14	10	73	32	3	62	.266	.307	.386	102	-3	9-10	.969	2	115	69	*O-155(0-3-153)	-1.1
1914	StL N	154	580	64	150	27	12	9	73	32	4	66	.259	.302	.393	107	2	14	**.983**	12	107	126	*O-154(0-9-148)	0.6
1915	StL N	107	348	33	96	13	6	3	39	19	4	43	.276	.321	.374	110	3	8-15	**.984**	11	107	164	*O-105(3-70-33)	0.4
1916	StL N	120	355	30	85	8	2	3	32	20	5	46	.239	.289	.299	81	-8	4	.955	-4	93	91	*O-113(0-58-61)	-2.1
Total	9	1280	4624	520	1246	157	114	59	571	241	37	407	.269	.311	.391	105	2	98-25	.968	32	104	108	*O-1269(5-270-1010)	-4.6
WILSON, LES Lester Wilbur "Tug" B 7.17.1885 St.Louis, MI D 4.4.1969 Edmonds, WA BL/TR 5-11/170# d7.15																								
1911	Bos A	5	7	0	0	0	0	0	0	2	0		.000	.222	.000	-36	-1	0	1.000	-0	122	0	/O-3(2-0-1)	-0.1
WILSON, HACK Lewis Robert B 4.26.1900 Ellwood City, PA D 11.23.1948 Baltimore, MD BR/TR 5-6/190# d9.29 HF1979																								
1923	NY N	3	10	0	2	0	0	0	0	0	0	1	.200	.200	.200	6	-1	0-0	.857	-1	88	0	/O-3(1-2-0)	-0.2
1924	†NY N	107	383	62	113	19	12	10	57	44	1	46	.295	.369	.486	131	16	4-3	.967	-6	92	78	*O-103(14-90-1)	0.6
1925	NY N	62	180	28	43	7	4	6	30	21	1	33	.239	.322	.422	92	-3	5-2	.975	-5	77	76	O-50(27-23-4)	-0.9
1926	Chi N	142	529	97	170	36	8	**21**	109	**69**	6	61	.321	.406	.539	**150**	**39**	10	.973	-5	95	85	*O-140(CF)	2.8
1927	Chi N	146	551	119	175	30	12	**30**	129	71	6	70	.318	.401	.579	160	46	13	.967	-7	95	80	*O-146(CF)	3.2
1928	Chi N	145	520	89	163	32	9	**31**	120	77	2	94	.313	.404	.588	159	45	4	.960	-13	87	90	*O-143(CF)	2.5
1929	†Chi N	150	574	135	198	30	5	39	**159**	78	2	83	.345	.425	.618	155	49	3	.970	-3	97	101	*O-150(CF)	3.6
1930	Chi N	155	585	146	208	35	6	**56**	**191**	**105**	1	84	.356	.454	**.723**	**177**	**76**	3	.951	-15	87	72	*O-155(CF)	4.7
1931	Chi N	112	395	66	103	22	4	13	61	63	0	69	.261	.362	.435	112	8	1	.978	-4	88	129	*O-103(40-60-3)	0.0
1932	Bro N	135	481	77	143	37	5	23	123	51	1	85	.297	.366	.538	142	29	2	.955	-6	86	120	*O-125(1-8-116)	1.6
1933	Bro N	117	360	41	96	13	2	9	54	52	0	50	.267	.359	.389	119	10	7	.963	-5	99	46	O-90(75-8-7)/2-5	0.2
1934	Bro N	67	172	24	45	5	0	6	27	40	0	33	.262	.401	.395	120	7	0	.974	-1	89	101	O-43(27-0-16)	0.4
	Phi N	7	20	0	2	0	0	0	3	3	0	4	.100	.217	.100	-11	-3	0	1.000	0	109	0	/O-6(5-0-1)	-0.3
	Year	74	192	24	47	5	0	6	30	43	0	37	.245	.383	.365	105	4	0	.977	-1	91	90	O-49(32-0-17)	0.1
Total	12	1348	4760	884	1461	266	67	244	1063	674	20	713	.307	.395	.545	145	318	52-5	.965	-70	91	88	*O-1257(190-925-148)/2-5	18.2

Year	Tm Lg	G	AB	R	H	2B	3B	HR	RBI	BB-IB	HP	SO	AVG	OBP	SLG	AOPS	ABR	SB-CS	FA	FR	Rng	Thr	G at Pos	BFW
WILSON, TACK Michael B 5.16.1955 Shreveport, LA BR/TR 5-10/185# d4.9																								
1983	Min A	5	4	4	1	1	0	0	1	0-0	0	0	.250	.250	.500	97	0	0-0	1.000	-0	39	0	/O(CF)D	0.0
1987	Cal A	7	2	5	1	0	0	0	0	1-0	0	0	.500	.667	.500	224	1	0-0	1.000	-0	47	0	/O-4(LF),D-2	0.0
Total	2	12	6	9	2	1	0	0	1	1-0	0	0	.333	.429	.500	150	1	0-0	1.000	-1	43	0	/O-5(4-1-0),D-4	0.0
WILSON, NIGEL Nigel Edward B 1.12.1970 Oshawa, ON, CAN BL/TL 6-1/185# d9.8																								
1993	Fla N	7	16	0	0	0	0	0	0	0-0	0	11	.000	.000	.000	-95	-4	0-0	1.000	-0	75	0	/O-3(LF)	-0.5
1995	Cin N	5	7	0	0	0	0	0	0	0-0	0	4	.000	.000	.000	-99	-2	0-0	1.000	-0	91	0	/O-2(LF)	-0.2
1996	†Cle A	10	12	2	3	0	0	2	5	1-0	0	6	.250	.308	.750	157	1	0-0	—	-1	0	0	/O(LF)D	0.0
Total	3	22	35	2	3	0	0	2	5	1-0	0	21	.086	.111	.257	-7	-5	0-0	1.000	-1	63	0	/O-6(LF),D-3	-0.7
WILSON, PARKE Parke Asel B 10.26.1867 Keithsburg, IL D 12.20.1934 Hermosa Beach, CA BR/TR 5-11/166# d7.19 OF Total (4-LF 4-CF 4-RF)																								
1893	NY N	31	114	16	28	4	1	2	21	7	0	9	.246	.289	.351	69	-6	5	.969	-3	*99*	*74*	C-31	-0.5
1894	NY N	51	181	35	59	5	5	1	34	15	2	6	.326	.384	.425	95	-2	9	.841	-5	*108*	*64*	C-35,1-16	-0.3
1895	NY N	67	238	32	56	9	0	0	30	14	1	16	.235	.281	.273	44	-20	11	.938	-1	*96*	*117*	C-53,1-11/3-3	-1.3
1896	NY N	75	253	33	60	2	0	0	23	13	1	14	.237	.277	.245	39	-22	9	.936	-6	*94*	*95*	C-71/1-2	-1.9
1897	NY N	47	158	29	47	9	3	0	23	15	1		.297	.362	.392	102	1	6	.929	2	*171*	*75*	C-30,1-11/O-4(CF),2	0.4
1898	NY N	1	4	0	0	0	0	0	0	0	0		.000	.000	.000	-99	-1	0	—	-0	0	0	/O(LF)	-0.1
1899	NY N	98	332	49	89	8	6	0	42	43	4		.268	.359	.328	92	-2	16	.925	-6	*87*	*85*	C-31,1-29,S-19,3-15/O-7(3-0-4)	-0.4
Total	7	370	1280	194	339	37	15	3	173	107	9	45	.265	.326	.324	72	-52	56	.925	-19	*105*	*90*	C-251/1-69,S-19,3-18,O-12L,2	-4.1
WILSON, PRESTON Preston James Richard B 7.19.1974 Bamberg, SC BR/TR 6-2/193# d5.7 f-Mookie																								
1998	NY N	8	20	3	6	2	0	0	2	2-0	0	8	.300	.364	.400	102	0	1-1	.909	-1	93	0	/O-7(4-2-1)	-0.1
	Fla N	14	31	4	2	0	0	1	1	4-0	1	13	.065	.194	.161	-5	-5	0-0	1.000	-1	79	0	O-11(3-7-1)	-0.6
	Year	22	51	7	8	2	0	1	3	6-0	1	21	.157	.259	.255	37	-5	1-1	.958	-2	85	0	O-18(7-9-2)	-0.7
1999	Fla N	149	482	67	135	21	4	26	71	46-3	9	156	.280	.350	.502	120	13	11-4	.973	3	103	136	*O-136(23-111-15)	1.5
2000	Fla N	**161**	605	94	160	35	3	31	121	55-1	8	187	.264	.331	.486	108	6	36-14	.988	-3	101	94	*O-158(CF)	0.7
2001	Fla N	123	468	70	128	30	2	23	71	36-2	6	107	.274	.331	.494	114	8	20-8	.993	3	100	183	*O-121(CF)	1.3
2002	Fla N	141	510	80	124	22	2	23	65	58-3	9	140	.243	.329	.429	106	1	20-11	.981	-6	93	107	*O-138(CF)	-0.4
2003	Col N★	155	600	94	169	43	1	36	**141**	54-1	4	139	.282	.343	.537	110	9	14-7	.980	-10	90	94	*O-155(CF)	0.1
Total	6	751	2716	412	724	153	12	140	472	255-10	37	750	.267	.335	.486	110	32	102-45	.983	-16	97	118	O-726(30-692-17)	2.5
WILSON, BOB Robert B 2.22.1925 Dallas, TX D 4.23.1985 Dallas, TX BR/TR 5-11/197# d5.17																								
1958	LA N	3	5	0	1	0	0	0	0	0-0	0	1	.200	.200	.200	6	-1	0-0	1.000	-0	81	0	/O(RF)	-0.1
WILSON, RED Robert James B 3.7.1929 Milwaukee, WI BR/TR 6/200# d9.22																								
1951	Chi A	4	11	1	3	1	0	0	0	1	0	2	.273	.333	.364	90	0	0-0	1.000	-0	*78*	*167*	/C-4	0.0
1952	Chi A	2	3	0	0	0	0	0	0	0	0	1	.000	.000	.000	-99	-1	0-0	1.000	1	*0*	*0*	/C-2	0.0
1953	Chi A	71	164	21	41	6	1	0	10	26	0	12	.250	.353	.299	75	-5	2-3	.981	5	*98*	*95*	C-63	0.3
1954	Chi A	8	20	2	4	0	0	1	1	1	0	2	.200	.238	.350	58	-1	0-0	1.000	3	*158*	*72*	/C-8	0.2
	Det A	54	170	22	48	11	1	2	22	27	0	12	.282	.379	.394	115	5	3-1	.996	3	*134*	*104*	C-53	1.0
	Year	62	190	24	52	11	1	3	23	28	0	14	.274	.365	.389	108	3	3-1	.997	5	*137*	*100*	C-61	1.2
1955	Det A	78	241	26	53	9	0	2	17	26-3	0	23	.220	.296	.282	57	-14	1-2	.984	-5	*94*	*113*	C-72	-1.7
1956	Det A	78	228	32	66	12	2	7	38	42-7	0	18	.289	.393	.452	124	10	2-1	.991	2	*136*	***127***	C-78	1.5
1957	Det A	60	180	21	43	8	1	3	13	25-2	3	19	.239	.341	.344	86	-3	2-3	1.000	2	*144*	*82*	C-60	0.2
1958	Det A	103	298	31	89	13	1	3	29	35-5	2	30	.299	.373	.379	101	2	10-0	.992	7	*109*	*80*	*C-101	1.7
1959	Det A	67	228	28	60	17	2	4	35	10-1	2	23	.263	.295	.408	88	-4	2-2	.988	0	*125*	*98*	C-64	-0.1
1960	Det A	45	134	17	29	4	0	1	14	16-1	0	14	.216	.298	.269	54	-8	3-0	.980	-1	*100*	*94*	C-45	-0.7
	Cle A	32	88	5	19	3	0	1	10	6-1	1	7	.216	.268	.284	53	-6	0-0	.989	3	*101*	*154*	C-30	-0.1
	Year	77	222	22	48	7	0	2	24	22-2	1	21	.216	.286	.275	53	-14	3-0	.984	2	*100*	*118*	C-75	-0.8
Total	10	602	1765	206	455	84	8	24	189	215-20	8	163	.258	.338	.355	87	-25	25-12	.990	21	*117*	*102*	C-580	2.3
WILSON, MIKE Samuel Marshall B 12.2.1896 Edge Hill, PA D 5.16.1978 Boynton Beach, FL BR/TR 5-10.5/160# d6.4																								
1921	Pit N	5	4	0	0	0	0	0	0	0	0	0	.000	.000	.000	-97	-1	0-0	.833	-0	*0*	*141*	/C-5	-0.1
WILSON, NEIL Samuel O'Neil B 6.14.1935 Lexington, TN BL/TR 6-1/175# d4.17																								
1960	SF N	6	10	0	0	0	0	0	0	1-1	0	2	.000	.091	.000	-77	-3	0-0	.958	-0	*124*	*0*	/C-6	-0.3
WILSON, TOM Thomas G. "Slats" B 6.3.1890 Fleming, KS D 3.7.1953 San Pedro, CA BB/TR 6-1.5/160# d9.8																								
1914	Was A	1	1	0	0	0	0	0	0	0	0	0	.000	.000	.000	-96	0	0	—	-0	*0*	*0*	/C	-0.1
WILSON, TOM Thomas Leroy B 12.19.1970 Fullerton, CA BR/TR 6-3/220# d5.19																								
2001	Oak A	9	21	4	4	0	0	2	4	1-0	1	5	.190	.250	.476	88	-1	0-0	.974	-3	74	0	/C-9	-0.3
2002	Tor A	96	265	33	68	10	0	8	37	28-0	5	79	.257	.334	.385	89	-4	0-0	.988	-10	66	93	C-65,D-12,1-11	-1.1
2003	Tor A	96	256	37	66	19	0	5	35	28-0	1	80	.258	.331	.391	89	-3	0-0	.991	-3	63	93	C-76,1-14/O-2(1-0-1),D	-0.2
Total	3	201	542	74	138	29	0	15	76	57-0	7	164	.255	.330	.391	89	-8	0-0	.989	-16	65	88	C-150/1-25,D-13,O-2(1-0-1)	-1.6
WILSON, VANCE Vance Allen B 3.17.1973 Mesa, AZ BR/TR 5-11/190# d4.24																								
1999	NY N	1	0	0	0	0	0	0	0	0-0	0	0	—	—	—	—	0	0-0	—	-0	0	0	/C	0.0
2000	NY N	4	4	0	0	0	0	0	0	0-0	0	2	.000	.000	.000	-99	-1	0-0	1.000	1	85	0	/C-3	-0.1
2001	NY N	32	57	3	17	3	0	0	6	2-0	2	16	.298	.339	.351	85	-1	0-1	.993	2	187	132	C-27	0.2
2002	NY N	74	163	19	40	7	0	5	26	5-0	8	32	.245	.301	.380	84	-5	0-1	.983	6	101	206	C-66/1	0.4
2003	NY N	96	268	28	65	9	1	8	39	15-1	5	56	.243	.293	.373	75	-11	1-2	.990	6	119	150	C-89	0.0
Total	5	207	492	50	122	19	1	13	71	22-1	15	106	.248	.299	.370	78	-18	1-4	.988	15	121	165	C-186/1	0.5
WILSON, BILL William Donald B 11.6.1928 Central City, NE BR/TR 6-2/200# d9.24 Mil 1951																								
1950	Chi A	3	6	0	0	0	0	0	0	2	0	2	.000	.250	.000	-33	-1	0-0	1.000	-0	80	0	/O-2(CF)	-0.1
1953	Chi A	9	17	1	1	0	0	0	1	0	1	7	.059	.111	.059	-51	-4	0-0	1.000	-0	103	0	/O-3(CF)	-0.4
1954	Chi A	20	35	4	6	1	0	2	5	7	0	5	.171	.310	.371	83	-1	0-1	.943	1	127	0	O-19(15-0-4)	-0.1
	Phi A	94	323	43	77	10	1	15	33	39	8	59	.238	.334	.415	104	1	1-2	.989	4	110	82	O-91(CF)	0.1
	Year	114	358	47	83	11	1	17	38	46	8	64	.232	.332	.411	102	1	1-3	.984	5	112	72	*O-110(15-91-4)	0.0
1955	KC A	98	273	39	61	12	0	15	38	24-0	1	63	.223	.288	.432	91	-5	1-1	.969	-1	101	80	O-82(23-57-4)/P	-1.0
Total	4	224	654	87	145	23	1	32	77	72-0	10	136	.222	.308	.407	92	-10	2-4	.979	3	107	73	O-197(38-153-8)/P	-1.5
WILSON, BILL William G. B 10.28.1867 Hannibal, MO D 5.9.1924 St.Paul, MN TR d4.30																								
1890	Pit N	83	304	30	65	11	3	0	21	22	2	50	.214	.271	.270	65	-13	5	.875	-16	*65*	*137*	C-38,O-25(4-8-13),1-18/S	-2.5
1897	Lou N	107	389	44	83	12	4	1	41	18	5		.213	.257	.272	41	-34	9	.940	-4	*92*	*111*	*C-105/3	-2.5
1898	Lou N	29	102	5	17	1	2	1	13	5	1		.167	.213	.245	32	-10	3	.895	-7	*83*	*119*	C-28/1	-1.3
Total	3	219	795	79	165	24	9	2	75	45	8	50	.208	.257	.268	48	-57	17	.913	-27	*84*	*119*	C-171/O-25(4-8-13),1-19,3S	-6.3
WILSON, MOOKIE William Hayward B 2.9.1956 Bamberg, SC BB/TR 5-10/170# d9.2 C6 s-Preston																								
1980	NY N	27	105	16	26	5	3	0	4	12-0	0	19	.248	.325	.352	91	-1	7-7	.973	-0	106	57	O-26(1-26-0)	-0.3
1981	NY N	92	328	49	89	8	8	3	14	20-3	2	59	.271	.317	.372	96	-3	24-12	.983	5	118	56	O-80(6-68-10)	0.2
1982	NY N	159	639	90	178	25	9	5	55	32-4	2	102	.279	.314	.369	91	-9	58-16	.988	8	110	131	*O-156(CF)	0.4
1983	NY N	152	638	91	176	25	6	7	51	18-3	4	103	.276	.300	.367	85	-16	54-16	.984	1	106	66	*O-148(CF)	-1.1
1984	NY N	154	587	88	162	28	10	10	54	26-2	2	90	.276	.308	.409	102	-2	46-9	.990	10	114	104	*O-146(CF)	1.4
1985	NY N	93	337	56	93	16	8	6	26	28-6	0	52	.276	.331	.424	113	4	24-9	.964	-1	112	0	O-83(4-83-0)	0.5
1986	†NY N	123	381	61	110	17	5	9	45	32-5	1	72	.289	.345	.430	116	7	25-7	.979	9	**119**	126	*O-114(78-65-3)	1.7
1987	NY N	124	385	58	115	19	7	9	34	35-8	2	85	.299	.359	.455	120	11	21-6	.963	0	108	61	*O-109(20-88-14)	1.1
1988	†NY N	112	378	61	112	17	5	8	41	27-2	2	63	.296	.345	.431	128	13	15-4	.976	0	102	102	*O-104(16-83-18)	1.4
1989	NY N	80	249	22	51	10	1	3	18	10-3	1	47	.205	.237	.289	53	-16	7-4	.975	5	124	70	O-71(13-44-25)	-1.4
	†Tor A	54	238	32	71	9	1	2	17	3-0	2	37	.298	.311	.370	93	-3	12-1	.991	-6	83	54	O-54(16-22-20)	-0.8
1990	Tor A	147	588	81	156	36	4	3	51	31-0	0	102	.265	.300	.355	82	-15	23-4	.992	-2	100	67	*O-141(8-133-0)/D-6	-1.6
1991	†Tor A	86	241	26	58	12	4	2	28	8-0	5	35	.241	.277	.349	70	-11	11-3	.973	-2	88	95	O-41(36-5-0),D-34	-1.4
Total	12	1403	5094	731	1397	227	71	67	438	282-36	23	866	.274	.314	.386	96	-41	327-98	.982	25	108	81	*O-1273(198-1067-90)/D-40	0.1
WILSON, WILLIE Willie James B 7.9.1955 Montgomery, AL BB/TR (BR 1976) 6-3/195# d9.4																								
1976	KC A	12	6	0	1	0	0	0	0	0-0	0	2	.167	.167	.167	-2	-1	2-1	.875	1	103	637	/O-6(CF)	0.0

Year	Tm Lg	G	AB	R	H	2B	3B	HR	RBI	BB-IB	HP	SO	AVG	OBP	SLG	AOPS	ABR	SB-CS	FA	FR	Rng	Thr	G at Pos	BFW
1977	KC A	13	34	10	11	2	0	0	1	1-0	0	8	.324	.343	.382	97	0	6-3	.960	-0	109	0	/O-9(CF),D-2	0.0
1978	†KC A	127	198	43	43	8	2	0	16	16-0	2	33	.217	.280	.278	57	-11	46-12	.978	7	**119**	143	*O-112(82-35-0)/D-6	0.0
1979	KC A	154	588	113	185	18	13	6	49	28-3	7	92	.315	.351	.420	106	3	**83**-12	.985	13	**120**	109	*O-152(130-23-5)/D-2	2.4
1980	†KC A	161	705	**133**	**230**	28	**15**	3	49	28-3	6	81	.326	.357	.421	112	9	79-10	.988	14	**121**	73	*O-159(102-62-0)	3.2
1981	†KC A	102	439	54	133	10	7	1	32	18-3	4	42	.303	.335	.364	103	0	34-8	.987	18	127	190	*O-101(83-19-0)	1.9
1982	KC A★	136	585	87	194	19	**15**	3	46	26-2	6	81	**.332**	.365	.431	118	12	37-11	.987	11	**127**	47	*O-135(119-19-0)	2.2
1983	KC A★	137	576	90	159	22	8	2	33	33-2	1	75	.276	.316	.352	84	-14	59-8	.975	-4	104	31	*O-136(63-75-0)	-1.1
1984	†KC A	128	541	81	163	24	9	2	44	39-2	3	56	.301	.350	.390	104	3	47-5	.990	-2	102	67	*O-128(CF)	0.8
1985	†KC A	141	605	87	168	25	**21**	4	43	29-3	5	94	.278	.316	.408	96	-6	43-11	.995	-9	96	43	*O-140(CF)	-1.0
1986	KC A	156	631	77	170	20	7	9	44	31-1	9	97	.269	.313	.366	82	-17	34-8	.993	-3	101	49	*O-155(CF)	-1.6
1987	KC A	146	610	97	170	18	**15**	4	30	32-2	6	88	.279	.320	.377	82	-17	59-11	**.997**	-5	95	48	*O-143(CF)/D-2	-1.4
1988	KC A	147	591	81	155	17	**11**	1	37	22-1	2	106	.262	.289	.333	74	-23	35-7	.989	-8	97	16	*O-142(CF)	-2.7
1989	KC A	112	383	58	97	17	7	3	43	27-0	1	78	.253	.300	.358	86	-8	24-6	.977	-3	102	40	*O-108(CF)/D	-0.9
1990	KC A	115	307	49	89	13	3	2	42	30-1	2	57	.290	.354	.371	106	3	24-6	1.000	-1	99	43	*O-106(54-48-4)/D	0.3
1991	Oak A	113	294	38	70	14	4	0	28	18-1	4	43	.238	.290	.313	71	-12	20-5	.983	3	114	50	O-87(40-33-19)/D-9	-0.8
1992	†Oak A	132	396	38	107	15	5	0	37	35-2	1	65	.270	.329	.333	91	-5	28-8	.981	8	**121**	33	*O-120(0-118-3)/D-5	0.6
1993	Chi N	105	221	29	57	11	3	1	11	11-1	3	40	.258	.301	.348	75	-8	7-2	.991	-5	88	40	O-82(CF)	-1.2
1994	Chi N	17	21	4	5	0	2	0	0	1-0	0	6	.238	.273	.429	80	-1	1-0	1.000	-1	78	0	O-10(CF)	-0.1
Total	19	2154	7731	1169	2207	281	147	41	585	425-27	62	1144	.285	.326	.376	93	-93	668-134	.987	34	109	62	*O-2031(673-1356-31)/D-28	0.6

WINCENIAK, ED Edward Joseph B 4.16.1929 Chicago, IL BR/TR 5-9/165# d4.25

Year	Tm Lg	G	AB	R	H	2B	3B	HR	RBI	BB-IB	HP	SO	AVG	OBP	SLG	AOPS	ABR	SB-CS	FA	FR	Rng	Thr	G at Pos	BFW
1956	Chi N	15	17	1	2	0	0	0	0	1-0	0	3	.118	.167	.118	-22	-3	0-0	.889	-1	64	0	/3-4,2	-0.4
1957	Chi N	17	50	5	12	3	0	1	8	2-0	0	9	.240	.269	.360	68	-2	0-0	1.000	-2	68	73	/S-5,3-4,2-3	-0.4
Total	2	32	67	6	14	3	0	1	8	3-0	0	12	.209	.243	.299	45	-5	0-0	.955	-3	93	221	/3-8,S-5,2-4	-0.8

WINDHORN, GORDIE Gordon Ray B 12.19.1933 Watseka, IL BR/TR 6-1/185# d9.10

Year	Tm Lg	G	AB	R	H	2B	3B	HR	RBI	BB-IB	HP	SO	AVG	OBP	SLG	AOPS	ABR	SB-CS	FA	FR	Rng	Thr	G at Pos	BFW
1959	NY A	7	11	0	0	0	0	0	0	0-0	0	3	.000	.000	.000	-99	-3	0-0	1.000	-0	98	0	/O-4(LF)	-0.3
1961	LA N	34	33	10	8	2	1	2	6	4-1	0	3	.242	.324	.545	115	1	0-1	.944	1	126	177	O-17(5-3-9)	0.1
1962	KC A	14	19	1	3	1	0	0	1	0-0	0	3	.158	.158	.211	-2	-3	0-0	1.000	-0	89	0	/O-7(LF)	-0.3
	LA A	40	45	9	8	6	0	0	1	7-1	0	10	.178	.288	.311	63	-2	1-1	1.000	0	110	0	O-27(22-3-5)	-0.3
	Year	54	64	10	11	7	0	0	2	7-1	0	13	.172	.254	.281	44	-5	1-1	1.000	0	105	0	O-34(29-3-5)	-0.6
Total	3	95	108	20	19	9	1	2	8	11-2	0	19	.176	.252	.333	55	-7	1-2	.981	1	111	55	/O-55(38-6-14)	-0.8

WINDLE, BILL Willis Brewer B 12.13.1904 Galena, KS D 12.8.1981 Corpus Christi, TX BL/TL 5-11.5/170# d9.27

Year	Tm Lg	G	AB	R	H	2B	3B	HR	RBI	BB-IB	HP	SO	AVG	OBP	SLG	AOPS	ABR	SB-CS	FA	FR	Rng	Thr	G at Pos	BFW
1928	Pit N	1	1	1	1	1	0	0	0	0	0	0	1.000	1.000	2.000	641	1	0	1.000	-0	0	0	/1	0.1
1929	Pit N	2	1	0	0	0	0	0	0	0	0	1	.000	.000	.000	-98	0	0	1.000	-0	0	383	/1-2	0.0
Total	2	3	2	1	1	1	0	0	0	0	0	1	.500	.500	1.000	264	1	0	1.000	-0	0	230	/1-3	0.1

WINE, ROBBIE Robert Paul Jr. B 7.13.1962 Norristown, PA BR/TR 6-2/190# d9.2 f-Bobby

Year	Tm Lg	G	AB	R	H	2B	3B	HR	RBI	BB-IB	HP	SO	AVG	OBP	SLG	AOPS	ABR	SB-CS	FA	FR	Rng	Thr	G at Pos	BFW
1986	Hou N	9	12	2	3	1	0	0	0	1-0	0	4	.250	.308	.333	79	0	0-0	1.000	1	69	62	/C-8	0.1
1987	Hou N	14	29	1	3	1	0	0	0	1-0	0	10	.103	.133	.138	-29	-5	0-0	.979	-4	64	92	C-12	-0.9
Total	2	23	41	3	6	2	0	0	0	2-0	0	14	.146	.186	.195	2	-5	0-0	.988	-3	66	83	/C-20	-0.8

WINE, BOBBY Robert Paul Sr. B 9.17.1938 New York, NY BR/TR 6-1/187# d9.20 M1 C20 s-Robbie

Year	Tm Lg	G	AB	R	H	2B	3B	HR	RBI	BB-IB	HP	SO	AVG	OBP	SLG	AOPS	ABR	SB-CS	FA	FR	Rng	Thr	G at Pos	BFW
1960	Phi N	4	14	1	2	0	0	0	0	0-0	0	2	.143	.143	.143	-22	-2	0-0	1.000	0	88	170	/S-4	-0.2
1962	Phi N	112	311	30	76	15	0	4	25	11-3	0	49	.244	.268	.331	62	-17	2-0	.979	8	104	104	S-89,3-20	-0.3
1963	Phi N	142	418	29	90	14	3	6	44	14-5	1	83	.215	.241	.306	58	-24	1-3	.971	13	103	106	*S-132/3-8	-0.1
1964	Phi N	126	283	28	60	8	3	4	34	25-6	0	37	.212	.274	.304	64	-14	1-0	.965	3	99	112	*S-108,3-16	-0.4
1965	Phi N	139	394	31	90	8	1	5	33	31-9	0	69	.228	.284	.292	64	-19	0-0	.967	17	105	113	*S-135/1-4	0.9
1966	Phi N	46	89	8	21	5	0	0	5	6-3	1	13	.236	.292	.292	63	-4	0-1	.974	8	116	128	S-40/O-2(LF)	0.6
1967	Phi N	135	363	27	69	12	5	2	28	29-10	0	77	.190	.249	.267	48	-25	3-2	**.980**	23	108	**138**	*S-134/1-2	0.8
1968	Phi N	27	71	5	12	3	0	2	7	6-1	0	17	.169	.234	.296	58	-4	0-0	.972	2	102	94	S-25/3	0.0
1969	Mon N	121	370	23	74	8	1	3	25	28-6	0	49	.200	.256	.251	43	-29	0-0	.949	20	107	**128**	*S-118/13	0.4
1970	Mon N	159	501	40	116	21	3	3	51	39-5	1	94	.232	.287	.303	59	-30	0-1	.976	19	103	**138**	*S-159	0.6
1971	Mon N	119	340	25	68	9	0	1	16	25-5	0	46	.200	.253	.235	39	-27	0-0	.982	5	96	103	*S-119	-1.0
1972	Mon N	34	18	2	4	1	0	0	0	0-0	0	2	.222	.222	.278	41	-1	0-0	1.000	2	88	0	3-21/S-4,2	0.1
Total	12	1164	3172	249	682	104	16	30	268	214-53	3	538	.215	.264	.286	54	-196	7-7	.971	120	104	119	*S-1067/3-67,1-7,O-2(LF),2	1.4

WINFIELD, DAVE David Mark B 10.3.1951 St.Paul, MN BR/TR 6-6/220# d6.19 HF2001 OF Total (466-LF 219-CF 1879-RF)

Year	Tm Lg	G	AB	R	H	2B	3B	HR	RBI	BB-IB	HP	SO	AVG	OBP	SLG	AOPS	ABR	SB-CS	FA	FR	Rng	Thr	G at Pos	BFW
1973	SD N	56	141	9	39	4	1	3	12	12-1	0	19	.277	.331	.383	107	1	0-0	.956	-2	92	42	O-36(34-2-1)/1	-0.3
1974	SD N	145	498	57	132	18	4	20	75	40-2	1	96	.265	.318	.438	116	7	9-7	.960	6	108	129	*O-131(81-25-34)	0.7
1975	SD N	143	509	74	136	20	2	15	76	69-14	3	82	.267	.354	.403	118	13	23-4	.972	3	106	90	*O-138(RF)	1.3
1976	SD N	137	492	81	139	26	4	13	69	65-8	3	78	.283	.366	.431	138	26	26-7	.982	8	106	132	*O-134(0-10-127)	3.1
1977	SD N★	157	615	104	169	29	7	25	92	58-10	0	75	.275	.335	.467	126	20	16-7	.972	12	115	120	*O-156(RF)	2.4
1978	SD N★	158	587	88	181	30	5	24	97	55-20	2	81	.308	.367	.499	153	39	21-9	.979	-9	92	64	*O-154(1-84-112)/1-2	2.8
1979	SD N★	159	597	97	184	27	10	34	**118**	85-**24**	2	71	.308	.395	.558	**167**	**56**	15-9	.986	4	105	103	*O-157(RF)	5.2
1980	SD N★	162	558	89	154	25	6	20	87	79-14	2	83	.276	.365	.450	135	27	23-7	.987	-1	89	153	*O-159(0-20-154)	2.3
1981	†NY A★	105	388	52	114	25	1	13	68	43-3	1	41	.294	.360	.464	140	21	11-1	.985	-10	92	15	*O-102(80-23-0)/D	1.0
1982	NY A★	140	539	84	151	24	8	37	106	45-7	0	64	.280	.331	.560	143	29	5-3	.974	6	102	**208**	*O-135(LF)/D-4	2.8
1983	NY A★	152	598	99	169	26	8	32	116	58-2	2	77	.283	.345	.513	139	30	15-6	.978	-10	94	44	*O-151(122-39-9)	1.5
1984	NY A★	141	567	106	193	34	4	19	100	53-9	0	71	.340	.393	.515	156	44	6-4	.994	-2	102	35	*O-140(1-16-127)	3.4
1985	NY A★	155	633	105	174	34	6	26	114	52-8	0	96	.275	.328	.471	119	15	19-7	.991	4	101	126	*O-152(RF)/D-2	1.2
1986	NY A★	154	565	90	148	31	5	24	104	77-9	2	106	.262	.349	.462	121	17	6-5	.984	-1	98	88	*O-145(RF)/3-2,D-6	0.9
1987	NY A★	156	575	83	158	22	1	27	97	76-5	0	96	.275	.358	.457	116	14	5-6	.989	-11	85	57	*O-145(RF)/D-8	-0.6
1988	NY A★	149	559	96	180	37	2	25	107	69-10	2	88	.322	.398	.530	159	46	9-4	.989	-11	87	33	*O-141(RF)/D-4	3.1
1990	NY A	20	61	7	13	3	0	2	6	4-0	1	13	.213	.269	.361	75	-2	0-0	1.000	-2	62	0	O-12(LF)/D-7	-0.4
	Cal A	112	414	63	114	18	2	19	72	48-3	1	68	.275	.348	.466	130	16	0-1	.989	-11	74	91	*O-108(RF)/D-3	0.1
	Year	132	475	70	127	21	2	21	78	52-3	2	81	.267	.338	.453	122	14	0-1	.989	-13	73	84	*O-120(12-0-108),D-10	-0.3
1991	Cal A	150	568	75	149	27	4	28	86	56-4	1	109	.262	.326	.472	119	13	7-2	.990	-6	86	87	*O-115(RF),D-34	0.4
1992	†Tor A	156	583	92	169	33	3	26	108	82-10	1	89	.290	.377	.491	136	29	2-3	1.000	-0	103	60	*D-130,O-26(RF)	2.4
1993	Min A	143	547	72	148	27	2	21	76	45-2	0	106	.271	.325	.442	104	1	2-3	1.000	-0	102	91	*D-105,O-31(RF)/1-5	-0.8
1994	Min A	77	294	35	74	15	3	10	43	31-5	0	51	.252	.321	.425	91	-5	2-1	1.000	0	139	0	D-76/O(RF)	-0.9
1995	Cle A	46	115	11	22	5	0	2	4	14-2	1	26	.191	.285	.287	49	-9	1-0	—	0	0	0	D-39	-1.1
Total	22	2973	11003	1669	3110	540	88	465	1833	1216-172	25	1686	.283	.353	.475	130	448	223-96	.982	-33	97	92	*O-2469R,D-419/1-8,3-2	30.5

WINGO, AL Absalom Holbrook "Red" B 5.6.1898 Norcross, GA D 10.9.1964 Detroit, MI BL/TR 5-11/180# d9.9 b-Ivey

Year	Tm Lg	G	AB	R	H	2B	3B	HR	RBI	BB-IB	HP	SO	AVG	OBP	SLG	AOPS	ABR	SB-CS	FA	FR	Rng	Thr	G at Pos	BFW
1919	Phi A	15	59	9	18	1	3	0	2	4	0	12	.305	.349	.424	115	1	0	.815	-2	77	72	O-15(LF)	-0.2
1924	Det A	78	150	21	43	12	2	1	26	21	0	13	.287	.374	.413	105	2	2-5	.925	-2	87	90	O-43(30-7-6)	-0.4
1925	Det A	130	440	104	163	34	10	5	68	69	0	31	.370	.456	.527	151	38	14-13	.971	9	110	120	*O-122(120-2-0)	3.3
1926	Det A	108	298	45	84	19	0	1	45	52	0	32	.282	.389	.356	94	0	4-2	.923	2	97	166	O-74(61-0-14)/3-2	-0.4
1927	Det A	75	137	15	32	8	2	0	20	25	0	14	.234	.352	.321	74	-4	1-0	.891	-1	75	201	O-34(9-4-21)	-0.7
1928	Det A	87	242	30	69	13	2	2	30	40	1	17	.285	.389	.380	101	2	2-2	.968	-2	97	77	O-71(35-28-6)	-0.4
Total	6	493	1326	224	409	87	19	9	191	211	1	119	.308	.404	.423	114	39	23-22	.944	3	98	125	O-359(270-41-47)/3-2	1.2

WINGO, ED Edmond Armand (born Edmond Armand La Riviere) B 10.8.1895 St.Anne De Bellevue, PQ, CAN D 12.5.1964 Lachine, PQ, CAN BR/TR 5-6/145# d10.2

Year	Tm Lg	G	AB	R	H	2B	3B	HR	RBI	BB-IB	HP	SO	AVG	OBP	SLG	AOPS	ABR	SB-CS	FA	FR	Rng	Thr	G at Pos	BFW
1920	Phi A	1	4	0	1	0	0	0	1	0	0	0	.250	.250	.250	32	0	0-0	1.000	0	*87*	*125*	/C	0.0

WINGO, IVEY Ivey Brown B 7.8.1890 Gainesville, GA D 3.1.1941 Waycross, GA BL/TR 5-10/160# d4.20 M1 C3 b-Al

Year	Tm Lg	G	AB	R	H	2B	3B	HR	RBI	BB-IB	HP	SO	AVG	OBP	SLG	AOPS	ABR	SB-CS	FA	FR	Rng	Thr	G at Pos	BFW
1911	StL N	25	57	4	12	2	0	0	3	3	0	7	.211	.250	.246	40	-5	0	.916	-2	*82*	*114*	C-18	-0.6
1912	StL N	100	310	38	82	18	8	2	44	23	1	45	.265	.317	.394	96	-3	8	.957	-7	*74*	***127***	C-92	-0.2
1913	StL N	112	307	25	78	5	8	2	35	17	1	41	.254	.295	.342	83	-9	18-11	.945	-10	79	**117**	C-98/1-5,O(1-1-0)	-1.1
1914	StL N	80	237	24	71	8	5	4	26	18	1	17	.300	.352	.426	132	8	15	.958	-2	*102*	*99*	C-70/O-4(RF)	1.3
1915	Cin N	119	339	26	75	11	6	3	29	13	0	33	.221	.250	.316	69	-14	10-11	.966	-0	*96*	***110***	C-98/O(LF)	-0.9
1916	Cin N	119	347	30	85	8	11	2	40	25	1	27	.245	.298	.349	100	-1	4	.958	-7	82	**138**	*C-107,M	0.1
1917	Cin N	121	399	37	106	16	11	2	39	25	1	13	.266	.311	.376	115	5	9	.967	-7	*88*	*109*	*C-120	1.0
1918	Cin N	100	323	35	82	15	6	0	31	19	1	18	.254	.297	.337	95	-3	6	.973	0	*106*	*101*	C-93/O-5(3-0-1)	0.6

Year	Tm Lg	G	AB	R	H	2B	3B	HR	RBI	BB-IB	HP	SO	AVG	OBP	SLG	AOPS	ABR	SB-CS	FA	FR	Rng	Thr	G at Pos	BFW
1919	†Cin N	76	245	30	67	12	6	0	27	23	0	19	.273	.336	.371	115	5	4	.969	5	*110*	*113*	C-75	1.8
1920	Cin N	108	364	32	96	11	5	2	38	19	0	13	.264	.300	.338	84	-8	6-4	.958	-5	*105*	*101*	*C-107/2-2	-0.5
1921	Cin N	97	295	20	79	7	6	3	38	21	1	14	.268	.319	.363	84	-8	3-2	.959	7	*114*	*100*	C-92/O(LF)	0.5
1922	Cin N	80	260	24	74	13	3	3	45	23	0	11	.285	.343	.392	91	-4	1-4	.964	5	*119*	*120*	C-78	0.5
1923	Cin N	61	171	10	45	9	2	1	24	9	1	11	.263	.304	.357	75	-6	1-1	.969	2	*110*	*124*	C-57	-0.1
1924	Cin N	66	192	21	55	5	4	1	23	14	1	8	.286	.338	.370	91	-3	1-1	.989	3	*99*	*100*	C-65/1	0.4
1925	Cin N	55	146	6	30	7	0	0	12	11	0	8	.205	.261	.253	33	-15	1-2	.965	1	*79*	*116*	C-55	-1.1
1926	Cin N	7	10	0	2	0	0	0	1	1	1	0	.200	.333	.200	48	-1	0	1.000	0	*156*	*0*	/C-7	0.0
1929	Cin N	1	1	0	0	0	0	0	0	0	0	0	.000	.000	.000	-99	0	0	—	0	*0*	*0*	/C	0.0
Total	17	1327	4003	362	1039	147	81	25	455	264	10	285	.260	.307	.355	91	-62	87-36	.962	-17	*97*	*112*	*C-1233/O-12(7-1-5),1-6,2-2	1.7

WINKELMAN, GEORGE George Edward B 2.18.1865 Washington, DC D 5.19.1960 Washington, DC BL/TL 5-9/140# d8.4

Year	Tm Lg	G	AB	R	H	2B	3B	HR	RBI	BB-IB	HP	SO	AVG	OBP	SLG	AOPS	ABR	SB-CS	FA	FR	Rng	Thr	G at Pos	BFW
1883	Lou AA	4	13	2	0	0	0	0		1			.000	.071	.000	-81	-3		.625	-0	185	0	/O-4(3-1-0)	-0.3
1886	Was N	1	5	0	1	0	0	0	0	0		1	.200	.200	.200	24	0	0	—	-0	0	0	/O(RF)P	0.0
Total	2	5	18	2	1	0	0	0	0	1		1	.056	.105	.056	-51	-3	0	.625	-1	178	0	/O-5(3-1-1),P	-0.3

WINN, RANDY Dwight Randolph B 6.9.1974 Los Angeles, CA BB/TR (BR 2000 (part)) 6-2/175# d5.11

Year	Tm Lg	G	AB	R	H	2B	3B	HR	RBI	BB-IB	HP	SO	AVG	OBP	SLG	AOPS	ABR	SB-CS	FA	FR	Rng	Thr	G at Pos	BFW
1998	TB A	109	338	51	94	9	9	1	17	29-0	1	69	.278	.337	.367	82	-10	26-12	.980	-1	95	134	O-96(16-70-12)/D-4	-0.9
1999	TB A	79	303	44	81	16	4	2	24	17-0	1	63	.267	.307	.366	70	-14	9-9	.995	-0	101	92	O-77(CF)	-1.4
2000	TB A	51	159	28	40	5	0	1	16	26-0	2	25	.252	.362	.302	72	-6	6-7	.990	0	93	166	O-47(29-18-0)/D	-0.7
2001	TB A	128	429	54	117	25	6	6	50	38-0	6	81	.273	.339	.401	96	-2	12-10	.981	5	103	**180**	*O-117(9-48-62)/D-3	-0.1
2002	TB A★	152	607	87	181	39	9	14	75	55-3	6	109	.298	.360	.461	119	17	27-8	.993	5	102	162	*O-146(0-138-8)/D-4	2.5
2003	Sea A	157	600	103	177	37	4	11	75	41-0	8	108	.295	.346	.425	106	5	23-5	.992	3	110	33	*O-157(139-20-4)	0.7
Total	6	676	2436	367	690	131	32	35	257	206-3	24	455	.283	.343	.406	97	-10	103-51	.989	13	103	120	O-640(193-371-86)/D-12	0.1

WINNINGHAM, HERM Herman Son B 12.1.1961 Orangeburg, SC BL/TR 5-11/185# d9.1

Year	Tm Lg	G	AB	R	H	2B	3B	HR	RBI	BB-IB	HP	SO	AVG	OBP	SLG	AOPS	ABR	SB-CS	FA	FR	Rng	Thr	G at Pos	BFW
1984	NY N	14	27	5	11	1	1	0	5	1-0	0	7	.407	.429	.519	167	2	2-1	1.000	-1	55	0	O-10(1-9-1)	0.1
1985	Mon N	125	312	30	74	6	5	3	21	28-3	0	72	.237	.297	.317	77	-11	20-9	.983	0	102	108	*O-116(1-115-0)	-1.1
1986	Mon N	90	185	23	40	6	3	4	11	18-3	0	51	.216	.286	.346	74	-7	12-7	.980	-4	92	72	O-66(3-56-7)/S	-1.2
1987	Mon N	137	347	34	83	20	3	4	41	34-7	0	68	.239	.304	.349	71	-14	29-10	.975	-3	98	92	*O-131(CF)	-1.6
1988	Mon N	47	90	10	21	2	1	0	6	12-1	0	18	.233	.320	.278	71	-3	4-5	.982	-1	98	0	O-30(0-29-1)	-0.6
	Cin N	53	113	6	26	1	3	0	15	5-0	0	27	.230	.261	.292	57	-7	8-3	1.000	1	110	68	O-42(14-21-8)	-0.6
	Year	100	203	16	47	3	4	0	21	17-1	0	45	.232	.288	.286	63	-10	12-8	.992	-0	105	38	O-72(14-50-9)	-1.2
1989	Cin N	115	251	40	63	11	3	3	13	24-1	0	50	.251	.316	.355	88	-4	14-5	.980	1	106	92	O-85(34-41-13)	-0.3
1990	†Cin N	84	160	20	41	8	5	3	17	14-1	0	31	.256	.314	.425	98	-1	6-4	1.000	-2	90	139	O-64(5-58-1)	-0.3
1991	Cin N	98	169	17	38	6	1	1	4	11-1	0	40	.225	.272	.290	56	-10	4-4	.953	0	109	94	O-66(12-55-1)	-1.1
1992	Bos A	105	234	27	55	8	1	1	14	10-0	0	53	.235	.266	.291	52	-15	6-5	.975	1	91	220	O-67(36-32-0)/D-6	-1.7
Total	9	868	1888	212	452	69	26	19	147	157-17	0	417	.239	.296	.334	74	-70	105-53	.980	-8	99	104	O-677(106-547-32)/D-6,S	-8.4

WINSETT, TOM John Thomas "Long Tom" B 11.24.1909 McKenzie, TN D 7.20.1987 Memphis, TN BL/TR 6-2/190# d4.20

Year	Tm Lg	G	AB	R	H	2B	3B	HR	RBI	BB-IB	HP	SO	AVG	OBP	SLG	AOPS	ABR	SB-CS	FA	FR	Rng	Thr	G at Pos	BFW
1930	Bos A	1	1	0	0	0	0	0	0	0	0	1	.000	.000	.000	-99	0	0-0	—	0			H	0.0
1931	Bos A	64	76	6	15	1	0	1	7	4	1	21	.197	.247	.250	33	-8	0-0	1.000	0	96	214	/O-8(LF)	-0.7
1933	Bos A	6	12	1	1	0	0	0	0	1	0	6	.083	.154	.083	-36	-2	0-0	1.000	-1	28	0	/O-4(2-0-2)	-0.3
1935	StL N	7	12	2	6	1	0	0	2	2	0	3	.500	.571	.583	203	2	0	—	-0	0	0	/O-2(RF)	0.2
1936	Bro N	22	85	13	20	7	0	1	18	11	1	14	.235	.330	.353	83	-2	0	1.000	1	97	193	O-21(LF)	-0.2
1937	Bro N	118	350	32	83	15	5	5	42	45	3	64	.237	.329	.351	84	-7	3	.960	2	109	88	*O-101(100-1-0)/P	-1.1
1938	Bro N	12	30	6	9	1	0	1	7	6	0	4	.300	.417	.433	131	2	0	.882	-1	96	0	/O-9(5-0-4)	0.0
Total	7	230	566	60	134	25	5	8	76	69	5	113	.237	.325	.341	79	-15	3-0	.963	2	105	104	O-145(136-1-8)/P	-2.1

WINTERS, MATT Matthew Littleton B 3.18.1960 Buffalo, NY BL/TR 6-3/215# d5.30

Year	Tm Lg	G	AB	R	H	2B	3B	HR	RBI	BB-IB	HP	SO	AVG	OBP	SLG	AOPS	ABR	SB-CS	FA	FR	Rng	Thr	G at Pos	BFW
1989	KC A	42	107	14	25	6	0	2	9	14-1	0	23	.234	.320	.346	89	-1	0-0	.939	-2	89	54	O-31(RF)/D-3	-0.4

WIRTS, KETTLE Elwood Vernon B 10.31.1897 Consumne, CA D 7.12.1968 Sacramento, CA BR/TR 5-11/170# d7.20

Year	Tm Lg	G	AB	R	H	2B	3B	HR	RBI	BB-IB	HP	SO	AVG	OBP	SLG	AOPS	ABR	SB-CS	FA	FR	Rng	Thr	G at Pos	BFW
1921	Chi N	7	11	0	2	0	0	0	1	0	0	3	.182	.182	.182	-3	-2	0-0	1.000	1	*92*	*119*	/C-5	-0.1
1922	Chi N	31	58	7	10	2	0	1	6	12	0	15	.172	.314	.259	48	-4	0-0	.968	-3	*112*	*56*	C-27	-0.5
1923	Chi N	5	5	2	1	0	0	0	1	2	0	0	.200	.429	.200	71	0	0-0	1.000	0	*100*	*0*	/C-3	0.1
1924	Chi A	6	12	0	1	0	0	0	0	2	0	2	.083	.214	.083	-22	-2	1-0	1.000	0	*96*	*255*	/C-5	-0.1
Total	4	49	86	9	14	2	0	1	8	16	0	20	.163	.294	.221	35	-8	1-0	.981	-1	*106*	*89*	/C-40	-0.6

WISE, HUGHIE Hugh Edward B 3.9.1906 Campbellsville, KY D 7.21.1987 Plantation, FL BB/TR 6/178# d9.26

Year	Tm Lg	G	AB	R	H	2B	3B	HR	RBI	BB-IB	HP	SO	AVG	OBP	SLG	AOPS	ABR	SB-CS	FA	FR	Rng	Thr	G at Pos	BFW
1930	Det A	2	6	0	2	0	0	0	0	0	0	0	.333	.333	.333	68	0	0-0	1.000	0	*89*	*159*	/C-2	0.0

WISE, CASEY Kendall Cole B 9.8.1932 Lafayette, IN BB/TR 6/170# d4.16

Year	Tm Lg	G	AB	R	H	2B	3B	HR	RBI	BB-IB	HP	SO	AVG	OBP	SLG	AOPS	ABR	SB-CS	FA	FR	Rng	Thr	G at Pos	BFW
1957	Chi N	43	106	12	19	3	1	0	7	11-0	0	14	.179	.256	.226	32	-10	0-0	.940	1	103	100	2-31/S-5	-0.8
1958	†Mil N	31	71	8	14	1	0	0	0	4-0	0	8	.197	.240	.211	23	-8	1-1	1.000	1	122	72	2-10/S-7,3	-0.6
1959	Mil N	22	76	11	13	2	0	1	5	10-0	0	5	.171	.267	.237	39	-7	0-0	.989	-5	79	114	2-20/S-5	-1.0
1960	Det A	30	68	6	10	0	2	2	5	4-0	0	9	.147	.194	.294	29	-7	1-0	.983	2	122	102	2-17,S-10/3	-0.4
Total	4	126	321	37	56	6	3	3	17	29-0	0	36	.174	.243	.240	31	-32	2-1	.968	-1	102	101	/2-78,S-27,3-2	-2.8

WISE, DEWAYNE Larry Dewayne B 2.24.1978 Columbia, SC BL/TL 6-1/180# d4.6

Year	Tm Lg	G	AB	R	H	2B	3B	HR	RBI	BB-IB	HP	SO	AVG	OBP	SLG	AOPS	ABR	SB-CS	FA	FR	Rng	Thr	G at Pos	BFW
2000	Tor A	28	22	3	3	0	0	0	0	1-0	1	5	.136	.208	.136	-10	-4	1-0	1.000	1	144	0	O-18(14-1-3)	-0.3
2002	Tor A	42	112	14	20	4	1	3	13	4-0	0	15	.179	.207	.313	34	-11	5-0	1.000	7	132	276	O-33(6-3-26)/D-3	-0.4
Total	2	70	134	17	23	4	1	3	13	5-0	1	20	.172	.207	.284	27	-15	6-0	1.000	8	134	225	/O-51(20-4-29),D-3	-0.7

WISE, NICK Nicholas Joseph B 6.15.1866 Boston, MA D 1.15.1923 Boston, MA BR/TR 5-11/194# d6.20

Year	Tm Lg	G	AB	R	H	2B	3B	HR	RBI	BB-IB	HP	SO	AVG	OBP	SLG	AOPS	ABR	SB-CS	FA	FR	Rng	Thr	G at Pos	BFW
1888	Bos N	1	3	0	0	0	0	0	0	0	0	0	.000	.000	.000	-97	-1	0	—	-0	0	0	/O(RF)C	-0.1

WISE, SAM Samuel Washington "Modoc" B 8.18.1857 Akron, OH D 1.22.1910 Akron, OH BL/TR 5-10.5/170# d7.30 OF Total (12-LF 36-RF)

Year	Tm Lg	G	AB	R	H	2B	3B	HR	RBI	BB-IB	HP	SO	AVG	OBP	SLG	AOPS	ABR	SB-CS	FA	FR	Rng	Thr	G at Pos	BFW
1881	Det N	1	4	0	2	0	0	0	0	0		2	.500	.500	.500	207	0		.571	-1	111	0	/3	0.0
1882	Bos N	78	298	44	66	11	4	4	34	5		45	.221	.234	.326	77	-8		.852	-13	86	70	*S-72/3-6	-1.7
1883	Bos N	96	406	73	110	25	7	4	58	13		74	.271	.294	.397	105	2		.823	-1	93	92	*S-96	0.3
1884	Bos N	114	426	60	91	15	9	4	41	25		104	.214	.257	.319	81	-10		.884	2	92	81	*S-107/2-7	-0.4
1885	Bos N	107	424	71	120	20	10	4	46	25		61	.283	.323	.406	139	18		.858	6	101	112	*S-79,2-22/O-6(4-0-2)	2.5
1886	Bos N	96	387	71	112	19	12	4	72	33		61	.289	.345	.432	139	18	31	.956	-21	78	75	1-57,2-20,S-18/O(RF)	-0.6
1887	Bos N	113	467	103	156	27	17	9	92	36	7	44	.334	.390	.522	150	31	43	.869	-1	105	98	S-72,O-27(4-0-23),2-16	2.7
1888	Bos N	105	417	66	100	19	12	4	40	34	6	66	.240	.306	.372	112	6	33	.888	3	98	131	S-89/3-6,1-5,O-4(LF),2-2	1.1
1889	Was N	121	472	79	118	15	8	4	62	61	4	62	.250	.341	.341	97	-1	24	.916	-16	98	71	2-72,S-26,3-13,O-10(RF)	-1.2
1890	Buf P	119	505	95	148	29	11	5	102	46	6	45	.293	.359	.424	119	14	19	.906	8	104	87	*2-119	2.1
1891	Bal AA	103	388	70	96	14	5	1	48	62	9	52	.247	.364	.317	94	0	33	.888	-9	**103**	76	*2-99/S-4	-0.5
1893	Was N	122	521	102	162	27	17	5	77	49	4	27	.311	.375	.457	124	16	20	.924	16	104	91	*2-91,3-31	2.9
Total	12	1175	4715	834	1281	221	112	48	672	389	36	643	.272	.332	.397	114	86	203	.859	-26	95	96	S-563,2-448/1-62,3-57,O-48R	7.2

WISNER, PHIL Philip N. B 7.1869 Washington, DC D 7.5.1936 Washington, DC TR d8.30

Year	Tm Lg	G	AB	R	H	2B	3B	HR	RBI	BB-IB	HP	SO	AVG	OBP	SLG	AOPS	ABR	SB-CS	FA	FR	Rng	Thr	G at Pos	BFW
1895	Was N	1	0	0	0	0	0	0	0	0	0	0	—	—	—	—	0	0	.250	-1	63	0	/S	-0.1

WISSMAN, DAVE David Alvin B 2.17.1941 Greenfield, MA BL/TR 6-2/178# d9.15

Year	Tm Lg	G	AB	R	H	2B	3B	HR	RBI	BB-IB	HP	SO	AVG	OBP	SLG	AOPS	ABR	SB-CS	FA	FR	Rng	Thr	G at Pos	BFW
1964	Pit N	16	27	2	4	0	0	0	0	1-0	0	9	.148	.179	.148	-7	-4	0-0	1.000	-0	99	0	O-10(7-3-0)	-0.5

WISTERZIL, TEX George John B 3.7.1888 Detroit, MI D 6.27.1964 San Antonio, TX BR/TR 5-9.5/150# d4.14

Year	Tm Lg	G	AB	R	H	2B	3B	HR	RBI	BB-IB	HP	SO	AVG	OBP	SLG	AOPS	ABR	SB-CS	FA	FR	Rng	Thr	G at Pos	BFW
1914	Bro F	149	534	54	137	18	10	0	66	34	**11**	47	.257	.314	.328	76	-27	17	**.956**	16	107	101	*3-149	-0.8
1915	Bro F	36	106	13	33	3	3	0	21	21	3	7	.311	.438	.396	137	5	8	.949	4	112	148	3-31	1.1
	Chi F	7	20	3	4	1	0	0	0	3	0	2	.200	.304	.250	60	-1	0	.955	0	106	0	/3-6	-0.1
	StL F	8	24	1	5	1	0	0	4	2	1	2	.208	.296	.250	52	-2	2	.939	2	116	0	/3-8	0.0
	Chi F	42	144	12	36	3	1	0	14	5	1	10	.250	.280	.285	63	-10	2	.968	5	106	0	3-42	-0.4
	Year	93	294	29	78	8	4	0	39	31	5	21	.265	.345	.320	90	-7	12	.958	10	112	103	3-87	0.6
Total	2	242	828	83	215	26	14	0	105	65	16	68	.260	.326	.325	81	-35	29	.957	26	109	102	3-236	-0.2

Year	Tm Lg	G	AB	R	H	2B	3B	HR	RBI	BB-IB	HP	SO	AVG	OBP	SLG	AOPS	ABR	SB-CS	FA	FR	Rng	Thr	G at Pos	BFW
WITEK, MICKEY Nicholas Joseph B 12.19.1915 Luzerne, PA D 8.24.1990 Kingston, PA BR/TR 5-10/170# d4.16 Mil 1944-45																								
1940	NY N	119	433	34	111	7	0	3	31	24	0	17	.256	.295	.293	62	-23	2	.958	16	105	86	S-89,2-32	0.2
1941	NY N	26	94	11	34	5	0	1	16	4	0	2	.362	.388	.447	132	4	0	.933	0	98	113	2-23	0.6
1942	NY N	148	553	72	144	19	6	5	48	36	0	20	.260	.306	.344	89	-9	2	**.978**	8	105	86	*2-147	0.8
1943	NY N	153	622	68	195	17	0	6	55	41	0	23	.314	.356	.370	109	6	1	.967	15	**106**	83	*2-153	3.2
1946	NY N	82	284	32	75	13	2	4	29	28	0	10	.264	.330	.366	97	-1	1	.962	-8	91	81	2-42,3-35	-0.8
1947	NY N	51	160	22	35	4	1	3	17	15	0	12	.219	.286	.313	58	-10	1	.983	9	120	108	2-40/3-3	0.1
1949	NY A	2	1	0	1	0	0	0	0	0	0	0	1.000	1.000	1.000	430	0	0-0	—	0			H	0.0
Total	7	581	2147	239	595	65	9	22	196	148	0	84	.277	.324	.347	90	-33	7-0	.969	40	106	88	2-437/S-89,3-38	4.1
WITHROW, FRANK Frank Blaine "Kid" B 6.14.1891 Greenwood, MO D 9.5.1966 Omaha, NE BR/TR 5-11.5/187# d4.15																								
1920	Phi N	48	132	8	24	4	1	0	12	8	2	26	.182	.239	.227	33	-11	0-0	.973	1	*85*	*94*	C-48	-0.7
1922	Phi N	10	21	3	7	2	0	0	3	3	0	5	.333	.417	.429	108	0	0-0	.909	0	*102*	*90*	/C-8	0.1
Total	2	58	153	11	31	6	1	0	15	11	2	31	.203	.265	.255	45	-11	0-0	.965	1	*87*	*93*	/C-56	-0.6
WITHROW, CORKY Raymond Wallace B 11.28.1937 High Coal, WV BR/TR 6-3.5/197# d9.6																								
1963	StL N	6	9	0	0	0	0	0	1	0-0	0	2	.000	.000	.000	-91	-2	0-0	1.000	-0	103	0	/O-2(1-0-1)	-0.3
WITMEYER, RON Ronald Herman B 6.28.1967 West Islip, NY BL/TL 6-3/215# d8.25																								
1991	Oak A	11	19	0	1	0	0	0	0	0-0	0	5	.053	.053	.053	-75	-5	0-0	1.000	0	103	58	/1-8	-0.5
WITT, KEVIN Kevin Joseph B 1.5.1976 High Point, NC BL/TR 6-4/195# d9.15																								
1998	Tor A	5	7	0	1	0	0	0	0	0-0	0	3	.143	.143	.143	-25	-1	0-0	1.000	0	150	0	/1	-0.1
1999	Tor A	15	34	3	7	1	0	1	5	2-0	0	9	.206	.250	.324	44	-3	0-0	—	0	0	0	D-11	-0.4
2001	SD N	14	27	5	5	0	0	2	5	2-0	0	7	.185	.233	.407	69	-2	0-0	1.000	-1	66	76	/1-9	-0.3
2003	Det A	93	270	25	71	9	0	10	26	15-0	1	68	.263	.301	.407	92	-4	1-1	1.000	1	118	135	D-36,1-27,O-13(LF)/3-5	-0.8
Total	4	127	338	33	84	10	0	13	36	19-0	1	87	.249	.287	.393	83	-10	1-1	1.000	1	108	119	/D-47,1-37,O-13(LF),3-5	-1.6
WITT, WHITEY Lawton Walter (born Ladislaw Waldemar Wittkowski) B 9.28.1895 Orange, MA D 7.14.1988 Salem Co., NJ BL/TR 5-7/150# d4.12 Mil 1918																								
1916	Phi A	143	563	64	138	16	15	2	36	55	2	71	.245	.315	.337	101	-2	19	.902	5	99	96	*S-142	1.4
1917	Phi A	128	452	62	114	13	4	0	28	65	0	45	.252	.346	.299	98	2	12	.935	8	108	80	*S-111/O-7(LF),3-6	1.9
1919	Phi A	122	460	56	123	15	6	0	33	46	0	26	.267	.334	.326	85	-9	11	.972	-4	103	43	O-59(40-19-0),2-56/3-2	-1.6
1920	Phi A	65	218	29	70	11	3	1	25	27	0	16	.321	.396	.413	113	5	2-3	.960	-5	88	34	O-50(0-5-45),2-10/S-2	-0.3
1921	Phi A	154	629	100	198	31	11	4	45	77	1	52	.315	.390	.418	106	8	16-15	.959	-3	105	72	*O-154(RF)	-0.8
1922	†NY A	140	528	98	157	11	6	4	40	**89**	1	29	.297	.400	.364	98	3	5-8	.976	-7	96	62	*O-139(0-109-30)	-1.3
1923	†NY A	146	596	113	187	18	10	6	56	67	3	42	.314	.386	.408	107	7	2-7	**.979**	-4	96	85	*O-144(CF)	-0.5
1924	NY A	147	600	88	178	26	5	1	36	45	0	20	.297	.346	.362	83	-16	9-7	.976	-4	97	83	*O-144(CF)	-2.6
1925	NY A	31	40	9	8	2	1	0	0	6	0	2	.200	.304	.300	55	-3	1-1	1.000	1	111	144	O-10(0-9-1)	-0.2
1926	Bro N	63	85	13	22	1	1	0	3	12	0	6	.259	.351	.294	76	-2	1	.920	1	108	126	O-22(3-17-2)	-0.3
Total	10	1139	4171	632	1195	144	62	18	302	489	7	309	.287	.362	.364	97	-7	78-41	.971	-13	99	73	O-729(50-447-232),S-255/2-66,3-8	-4.3
WITTE, JERRY Jerome Charles B 7.30.1915 St.Louis, MO D 4.27.2002 Houston, TX BR/TR 6-1/190# d9.10																								
1946	StL A	18	73	7	14	2	0	2	4	0	0	18	.192	.192	.301	35	-7	0-0	.967	-2	70	95	1-18	-1.0
1947	StL A	34	99	4	14	2	1	2	12	11	0	22	.141	.227	.242	30	-10	0-0	.983	-1	86	86	1-27	-1.3
Total	2	52	172	11	28	4	1	4	16	11	0	40	.163	.213	.267	32	-17	0-0	.977	-4	80	90	/1-45	-2.3
WOCKENFUSS, JOHN Johnny Bilton B 2.27.1949 Welch, WV BR/TR 6/190# d8.11 OF Total (42-LF 69-RF)																								
1974	Det A	13	29	1	4	1	0	0	2	3-0	0	2	.138	.212	.172	13	-3	0-0	.932	-2	112	145	C-13	-0.5
1975	Det A	35	118	15	27	6	3	4	13	10-0	0	15	.229	.287	.432	97	-1	0-0	.982	3	91	107	C-34	0.4
1976	Det A	60	144	18	32	7	2	3	10	17-0	1	14	.222	.309	.361	92	-1	0-3	.941	-6	102	93	C-59	-0.7
1977	Det A	53	164	26	45	8	1	9	25	14-0	0	18	.274	.331	.500	117	3	0-0	.985	-1	111	85	C-37/O-9(6-0-3),D-3	0.3
1978	Det A	71	187	23	53	5	0	7	22	21-4	1	14	.283	.357	.422	116	4	0-1	.978	-6	82	52	O-60(6-0-55)/D-2	-0.5
1979	Det A	87	231	27	61	9	1	15	46	18-0	2	40	.264	.320	.506	116	4	2-2	.996	1	111	112	1-31,C-20,D-18/O-6(5-0-1)	0.4
1980	Det A	126	372	56	102	13	2	16	65	68-4	3	64	.274	.390	.449	126	16	1-4	.983	0	112	95	1-52,D-28,C-25,O-23(21-0-2)	1.2
1981	Det A	70	172	20	37	4	0	9	25	28-1	0	22	.215	.322	.395	103	1	0-0	.984	-3	37	172	D-39,1-25/C-5,O(LF)	-0.5
1982	Det A	70	193	28	58	9	0	8	32	29-2	0	21	.301	.388	.472	135	10	0-0	.981	-4	66	105	C-24,1-17,D-17,O-10(2-0-8)/3	0.6
1983	Det A	92	245	32	66	8	1	9	44	31-1	0	37	.269	.349	.420	114	5	1-1	1.000	5	112	114	D-39,C-29,1-13/3O(LF)	0.9
1984	Phi N	86	180	20	52	3	1	6	24	30-1	0	24	.289	.390	.417	125	7	1-0	.996	-7	79	98	1-39,C-21/3-2	-0.1
1985	Phi N	32	37	1	6	0	0	0	2	8-1	0	7	.162	.311	.162	35	-3	0-0	1.000	-0	33	126	/1-7,C-2	-0.4
Total	12	795	2072	267	543	73	11	86	310	277-14	7	278	.262	.349	.432	114	42	5-11	.972	-20	90	93	C-269,1-184,D-146,O-110R/3-4	1.1
WOEHR, ANDY Andrew Emil B 2.4.1896 Fort Wayne, IN D 7.24.1990 Fort Wayne, IN BR/TR 5-11/165# d9.15																								
1923	Phi N	13	41	3	14	2	0	0	3	1	0	1	.341	.357	.390	87	-1	0-0	.975	2	112	173	3-13	0.2
1924	Phi N	50	152	11	33	4	5	0	17	5	2	8	.217	.252	.309	44	-13	2-2	.920	-5	85	113	3-44/2	-1.6
Total	2	63	193	14	47	6	5	0	20	6	2	9	.244	.274	.326	53	-14	2-2	.935	-3	91	127	/3-57,2	-1.4
WOERLIN, JOE Joseph B 10.9.1864 , France D 6.22.1919 St.Louis, MO d7.21																								
1895	Was N	1	3	1	1	0	0	0	0	0	0	0	.333	.333	.333	73	0	0	1.000	0	125	0	/S	0.0
WOHLFORD, JIM James Eugene B 2.28.1951 Visalia, CA BR/TR 5-11/175# d9.1																								
1972	KC A	15	25	3	6	1	0	0	0	2-0	1	6	.240	.321	.280	80	0	0-0	.950	-3	79	28	/2-8	-0.4
1973	KC A	45	109	21	29	1	3	2	10	11-0	0	12	.266	.333	.385	95	-1	1-1	1.000	3	132	241	D-19,O-13(12-0-1)	0.0
1974	KC A	143	501	55	136	16	7	2	44	39-3	3	74	.271	.327	.343	88	-8	16-13	.982	-1	97	71	*O-138(126-0-16)/D	-1.8
1975	KC A	116	353	45	90	10	5	0	30	34-2	1	37	.255	.317	.312	78	-10	12-7	.953	-1	96	123	*O-102(43-0-66)/D-4	-1.6
1976	†KC A	107	293	47	73	10	2	1	24	29-0	1	24	.249	.314	.307	83	-6	22-16	.975	6	118	107	O-93(84-2-8)/2D	-0.5
1977	Mil A	129	391	41	97	16	3	2	36	21-1	1	49	.248	.285	.320	65	-19	17-16	.981	4	112	74	*O-125(97-4-33)/2D	-2.2
1978	Mil A	46	118	16	35	7	2	1	19	6-0	0	10	.297	.325	.415	108	1	3-2	.982	-2	85	101	O-35(21-4-12)/D-4	-0.2
1979	Mil A	63	175	19	46	13	1	1	17	8-0	0	28	.263	.290	.366	77	-6	6-2	.969	-1	112	0	O-55(35-14-8)/D-5	-0.8
1980	SF N	91	193	17	54	6	4	1	24	13-0	1	23	.280	.324	.368	96	-2	1-4	.989	2	119	69	O-49(40-4-8)/3	-0.3
1981	SF N	50	68	4	11	3	0	1	7	4-0	0	9	.162	.205	.250	30	-6	0-0	1.000	-2	21	152	O-10(LF)	-0.9
1982	SF N	97	250	37	64	12	1	2	25	30-4	0	36	.256	.331	.336	89	-3	8-3	.992	1	103	82	O-72(68-0-6)	-0.4
1983	Mon N	83	141	7	39	8	0	1	14	5-0	0	14	.277	.297	.355	82	-4	0-0	.988	2	125	85	O-61(8-6-48)	-0.3
1984	Mon N	95	213	20	64	13	2	5	29	14-0	0	19	.300	.342	.451	127	7	3-0	.989	-0	94	84	O-59(44-1-14)/3-2	0.6
1985	Mon N	70	125	7	24	5	1	1	15	16-5	0	18	.192	.284	.272	60	-7	0-2	1.000	-1	98	46	O-43(8-0-36)	-1.1
1986	Mon N	70	94	10	25	4	2	1	11	9-3	0	17	.266	.327	.383	97	-1	0-2	1.000	-1	98	121	O-22(10-0-12)/3-6	-0.3
Total	15	1220	3049	349	793	125	33	21	305	241-18	8	376	.260	.313	.343	85	-65	89-68	.980	6	105	84	O-877(606-35-268)/D-37,2-10,3-9	-10.2
WOJCIK, JOHN John Joseph B 4.6.1942 Olean, NY BL/TR 6- /175# d9.9																								
1962	KC A	16	43	8	13	4	0	0	9	13-0	1	4	.302	.474	.395	131	3	3-0	1.000	-0	87	141	O-12(10-0-5)	0.3
1963	KC A	19	59	7	11	0	0	0	2	8-2	0	8	.186	.284	.186	33	-5	2-0	1.000	1	105	89	O-17(10-2-6)	-0.6
1964	KC A	6	22	1	3	0	0	0	0	2-0	0	8	.136	.208	.136	-2	-3	0-0	1.000	-0	102	0	/O-6(LF)	-0.4
Total	3	41	124	16	27	4	0	0	11	23-2	1	20	.218	.345	.250	64	-5	5-0	1.000	0	98	93	/O-35(26-2-11)	-0.7
WOLF, RAY Raymond Bernard "Grandpa" B 7.15.1904 Chicago, IL D 10.6.1979 Fort Worth, TX BR/TR 5-11/175# d7.27																								
1927	Cin N	1	1	0	0	0	0	0	0	0	0	0	.000	.000	.000	-99	0	0	1.000	-0	0	0	/1	0.0
WOLF, JIMMY William Van Winkle "Chicken" B 5.12.1862 Louisville, KY D 5.16.1903 Louisville, KY BR/TR 5-9/190# d5.2 M1 ▲ OF Total (17-LF 3-CF 1024-RF)																								
1882	Lou AA	78	318	46	95	11	8	0		9			.299	.318	.384	144	14		.902	-2	**132**	134	*O-70(3-0-67)/S-9,1P	1.1
1883	Lou AA	**98**	389	59	102	17	9	1		5			.262	.272	.360	110	5		.890	14	**186**	**325**	*O-78(0-1-77),C-20/S-5,2	1.7
1884	Lou AA	**110**	486	79	146	24	11	3	73	4	3		.300	.310	.414	140	20		.884	-2	131	157	*O-101(0-1-101),C-11/S31	1.7
1885	Lou AA	**112**	483	79	141	23	17	1	52	11	3		.292	.309	.416	128	13		.917	-1	100	117	*O-111(RF)/C-2,3P	1.0
1886	Lou AA	130	545	93	148	17	12	3	61	27	3		.272	.310	.363	105	-1	23	.934	7	132	130	*O-122(5-0-119)/1-8,C-3,2P	0.5
1887	Lou AA	**137**	569	103	160	27	13	2	102	34	8		.281	.331	.385	97	-4	45	.940	8	128	116	*O-128(8-1-120),1-11	0.1
1888	Lou AA	128	538	80	154	28	11	0	67	25	2		.286	.320	.379	126	15	41	.886	3	135	124	O-85(1-0-84),S-39/3-4,C-3,1	1.7
1889	Lou AA	130	546	72	159	20	9	3	57	29	5	34	.291	.333	.377	104	1	18	.946	1	94	46	O-88(RF),1-16,2-13,S-10/3-7,M	0.1
1890	†Lou AA	**134**	543	100	**197**	29	11	4	98	43	12		**.363**	.421	.479	169	47	46	.939	-4	72	123	*O-123(RF),3-12	3.6
1891	Lou AA	136	528	67	135	16	8	1	81	42	8	36	.256	.320	.322	85	-11	13	.922	3	117	101	*O-131(RF)/1-5,3	-0.9

Year	Tm Lg	G	AB	R	H	2B	3B	HR	RBI	BB-IB	HP	SO	AVG	OBP	SLG	AOPS	ABR	SB-CS	FA	FR	Rng	Thr	G at Pos	BFW
1892	StL N	3	14	1	2	0	0	0	1	0	0	1	.143	.143	.143	-14	-2	0	1.000	-1	0	0	/O-3(RF)	-0.3
Total	11	1196	4959	779	1439	212	109	18	592	229	42	71	.290	.327	.388	118	97	186	.918	26	120	133	*O-1040R/S-64,1-43,C-39,3-26,2P	10.3

WOLFE, HARRY Harold "Whitey" B 11.24.1890 , MA D 7.28.1971 Fort Wayne, IN BR/TR 5-8/160# d4.15

1917	Chi N	9	5	1	2	0	0	0	1	1	0	1	.400	.500	.400	164	0	0	1.000	0	115	0	/O-2(LF),S	0.1
	Pit N	3	5	0	0	0	0	0	0	1	0	4	.000	.167	.000	-45	-1	0	.875	0	81	343	/2S	-0.1
	Year	12	10	1	2	0	0	0	1	2	0	5	.200	.333	.200	61	0	0	1.000	0	115	0	/O-2(LF),S-2,2	0.0

WOLFE, LARRY Laurence Marcy B 3.2.1953 Melbourne, FL BR/TR 5-11/170# d9.16

1977	Min A	8	25	3	6	1	0	0	6	1-1	0	0	.240	.269	.280	51	-2	0-0	1.000	1	110	88	/3-8	-0.1
1978	Min A	88	235	25	55	10	1	3	25	36-0	0	27	.234	.332	.323	85	-4	0-1	.953	1	104	69	3-81/S-7	-0.4
1979	Bos A	47	78	12	19	4	0	3	15	17-0	1	21	.244	.378	.410	109	2	0-0	.963	3	104	104	2-27/3-9,S-2,C1D	0.5
1980	Bos A	18	23	3	3	1	0	1	4	0-0	0	5	.130	.125	.304	15	-3	0-0	1.000	-2	69	161	3-14/D-4	-0.4
Total	4	161	361	43	83	16	1	7	50	54-1	1	53	.230	.327	.338	84	-7	0-1	.957	3	105	90	3-112/2-27,S-9,D-5,1C	-0.4

WOLFE, POLLY Roy Chamberlain B 9.1.1888 Knoxville, IL D 11.21.1938 Morris, IL BL/TR 5-10/170# d9.22

1912	Chi A	1	1	0	0	0	0	0	0	0	0		.000	.000	.000	-99	0	0	—	0			H	0.0
1914	Chi A	8	28	0	6	0	0	0	0	3	0	6	.214	.290	.214	53	-2	1-1	.875	-1	81	0	/O-7(RF)	-0.4
Total	2	9	29	0	6	0	0	0	0	3	0	6	.207	.281	.207	47	-2	1-1	.875	-1	81	0	/O-7(RF)	-0.4

WOLSTENHOLME, ABE Abraham Lincoln B 3.4.1861 Philadelphia, PA D 3.4.1916 Philadelphia, PA d6.4

1883	Phi N	3	11	0	1	1	0	0	0	0		0	.091	.091	.182	-22	-1		.727	-2			/C-2,O(LF)	-0.3

WOLTER, HARRY Harry Meigs B 7.11.1884 Monterey, CA D 7.6.1970 Palo Alto, CA BL/TL 5-10/175# d5.14 ▲

1907	Cin N	4	15	1	2	0	0	0	1	0	0		.133	.133	.133	-16	-2	0	1.000	-0	0	0	/O-4(RF)	-0.3
	Pit N	1	1	0	0	0	0	0	0	0	0		.000	.000	.000	-99	0	0	—	-0	0	0	/P	0.0
	StL N	16	47	4	16	0	0	0	6	3	0		.340	.380	.340	130	2	1	.962	1	304	236	O-9(1-6-2)/P-3	0.3
	Year	21	63	5	18	0	0	0	7	3	0		.286	.318	.286	91	-1	1	.969	1	241	187	O-13(1-6-6)/P-4	0.0
1909	Bos A	54	121	14	29	2	4	2	10	9	0		.240	.292	.372	107	0	2	.978	-2	120	63	1-17,P-11/O-9(RF)	-0.2
1910	NY A	135	479	84	128	15	9	4	42	66	7		.267	.364	.361	120	14	39	.940	-2	112	65	*O-129(1-0-128)/1-2	0.7
1911	NY A	122	434	78	132	17	15	4	36	62	4		.304	.396	.440	125	15	28	.951	5	114	100	*O-113(0-7-106)/1-2	1.4
1912	NY A	12	32	8	11	2	1	0	1	10	1		.344	.512	.469	171	4	5	.923	-1	76	91	/O-9(0-5-4)	0.3
1913	NY A	127	425	53	108	18	6	2	43	80	4	50	.254	.377	.339	109	10	13	.946	-7	92	82	*O-121(0-106-15)	-0.6
1917	Chi N	117	353	44	88	15	7	0	28	38	1	40	.249	.324	.331	94	-2	7	.942	1	93	132	O-97(3-2-94)/1	-0.6
Total	7	588	1907	286	514	69	42	12	167	268	17	90	.270	.365	.369	114	41	95	.941	-5	106	92	O-491(5-126-362)/1-22,P-15	1.0

WOLVERTON, HARRY Harry Sterling "Fighting Harry" B 12.6.1873 Mt.Vernon, OH D 2.4.1937 Oakland, CA BL/TR 5-11/205# d9.25 M1

1898	Chi N	13	49	4	16	1	0	0	2	1	1		.327	.353	.347	101	0	1	.848	0	113	51	3-13	0.0
1899	Chi N	99	389	50	111	14	11	1	49	30	9		.285	.350	.386	105	2	14	.860	-7	102	85	3-98/S	-0.3
1900	Chi N	3	11	2	2	0	0	0	0	2	0		.182	.308	.182	38	-1	1	.875	-1	82	0	/3-3	-0.1
	Phi N	101	383	42	108	10	8	3	58	20	3		.282	.323	.373	92	-6	4	.881	-10	98	109	*3-101	-1.3
	Year	104	394	44	110	10	8	3	58	22	3		.279	.322	.368	91	-6	5	.881	-11	98	106	*3-104	-1.4
1901	Phi N	93	379	42	117	15	4	0	43	22	6		.309	.356	.369	108	4	13	**.921**	3	**104**	100	3-93	1.0
1902	Was A	59	249	35	62	8	3	1	23	13	2		.249	.292	.317	68	-11	8	.904	3	106	90	3-59	-0.6
	Phi N	34	136	12	40	3	2	0	16	9	2		.294	.347	.346	114	2	3	.931	7	118	214	3-34	1.0
1903	Phi N	123	494	72	152	13	12	0	53	18	8		.308	.342	.383	110	4	10	**.941**	1	99	59	*3-123	0.8
1904	Phi N	102	398	43	106	15	5	0	49	26	6		.266	.321	.329	105	2	18	.925	-1	93	117	*3-102	0.5
1905	Bos N	122	463	38	104	15	7	2	55	23	10		.225	.276	.300	73	-16	10	.934	4	109	81	*3-122	-0.9
1912	NY A	34	50	6	15	1	1	0	4	2	1		.300	.340	.360	94	-1	1	.821	-2	69	95	/3-8,M	-0.2
Total	9	783	3001	346	833	95	53	7	352	166	48		.278	.326	.352	96	-21	83	.909	-2	102	95	3-756/S	-0.1

WOMACK, TONY Anthony Darrell B 9.25.1969 Chatham, VA BL/TR 5-9/160# d9.10

1993	Pit N	15	24	5	2	0	0	0	0	3-0	0	3	.083	.185	.083	-25	-4	2-0	.971	3	134	183	/S-6	0.0
1994	Pit N	5	12	4	4	0	0	0	1	2-0	0	3	.333	.429	.333	101	0	0-0	.750	-2	44	62	/2-3,S-2	-0.2
1996	Pit N	17	30	11	10	3	1	0	7	6-0	1	1	.333	.459	.500	149	3	2-0	1.000	-1	71	0	/O-6(0-5-1),2-4	0.2
1997	Pit N★	155	641	85	178	26	9	6	50	43-2	3	109	.278	.326	.374	81	-19	**60**-7	.974	4	101	86	*2-152/S-4	0.4
1998	Pit N	159	655	85	185	26	7	3	45	38-1	0	94	.282	.319	.357	77	-23	**58**-8	.978	9	105	109	*2-152/O-5(CF),S-2	0.4
1999	†Ari N	144	614	111	170	25	10	4	41	52-0	2	68	.277	.332	.370	78	-22	**72**-13	.992	-3	109	123	*O-123(0-6-122),2-19,S-19	-1.6
2000	Ari N	146	617	95	167	21	**14**	7	57	30-0	5	74	.271	.307	.384	72	-29	45-11	.970	-12	88	89	*S-143/O-2(RF)	-2.3
2001	†Ari N	125	481	66	128	19	5	3	30	23-2	6	54	.266	.307	.345	65	-26	28-7	.955	-7	92	**118**	*S-118/O(CF)	-1.9
2002	†Ari N	153	590	90	160	23	5	5	57	46-2	4	80	.271	.325	.353	76	-23	29-12	.964	-22	85	80	*S-149/O(RF)	-3.2
2003	Ari N	61	219	30	52	10	3	2	15	8-0	2	27	.237	.270	.338	52	-16	8-3	.966	-5	87	89	S-58	-1.6
	Col N	21	79	9	15	2	0	0	5	0-0	1	9	.190	.200	.215	7	-11	3-1	.959	-4	90	60	S-14/2-7,O(CF)	-1.3
	Chi N	21	51	4	12	2	1	0	2	1-0	0	11	.235	.250	.314	47	-4	2-1	1.000	-1	81	58	2-14/S	-0.5
	Year	103	349	43	79	14	4	2	22	9-0	3	47	.226	.251	.307	41	-31	13-5	.965	-10	88	84	S-73,2-21/O(CF)	-3.4
Total	10	1022	4013	595	1083	157	55	30	310	252-7	24	533	.270	.315	.359	72	-174	309-63	.964	-41	89	93	S-516,2-351,O-139(0-18-126)	-11.6

WOMACK, SID Sidney Kirk "Tex" B 10.2.1896 Greensburg, LA D 8.28.1958 Jackson, MS BR/TR 5-10.5/185# d8.15

1926	Bos N	1	3	0	0	0	0	0	1	0	0	0	.000	.000	.000	-99	-1	0	1.000	-0	*44*	*0*	/C	-0.1

WOOD d9.30

1874	Bal NA	1	5	0	0	0	0	0	0	0		1	.000	.000	.000	-99	-1	0-0	.000	-1	0	0	/2	-0.2

WOOD, DOC Charles Spencer B 2.28.1900 Batesville, MS D 11.3.1974 New Orleans, LA BR/TR 5-10/150# d7.21

1923	Phi A	3	3	0	1	0	0	0	0	0	0	0	.333	.333	.333	75	0	0-0	.833	0	161	191	/S-3	0.0

WOOD, TED Edward Robert B 1.4.1967 Mansfield, OH BL/TL 6-2/178# d9.4

1991	SF N	10	25	0	3	0	0	0	1	2-0	0	11	.120	.185	.120	-13	-4	0-0	.909	-1	80	0	/O-8(RF)	-0.5
1992	SF N	24	58	5	12	2	0	1	3	6-0	1	15	.207	.292	.293	70	-2	0-0	.972	1	126	0	O-16(6-0-10)	-0.2
1993	Mon N	13	26	4	5	1	0	0	3	3-1	0	3	.192	.276	.231	36	-2	0-0	1.000	0	117	0	/O-8(8-0-1)	-0.3
Total	3	47	109	9	20	3	0	1	7	11-1	1	29	.183	.264	.239	42	-8	0-0	.968	-0	113	0	/O-32(14-0-19)	-1.0

WOOD, FRED Frederick Llewellyn B 7.21.1863 Hamilton, ON, CAN 5-5/150# d5.14 b-Pete

1884	Det N	12	42	4	2	0	0	0	1	3		18	.048	.111	.048	-51	-7		.889	-2			/C-7,O-6(RF),S	-0.8
1885	Buf N	1	4	0	1	0	0	0	0	0		0	.250	.250	.250	60	0		.833	-0			/C	0.0
Total	2	13	46	4	3	0	0	0	1	3		18	.065	.122	.065	-41	-7		.883	-2			/C-8,O-6(RF),S	-0.8

WOOD, GEORGE George A. "Dandy" B 11.9.1858 Boston, MA D 4.4.1924 Harrisburg, PA BL/TR 5-10.5/175# d5.1 M1 U1 ▲ OF Total (1192-LF 5-CF 36-RF)

1880	Wor N	81	327	37	80	16	5	0	28	10		37	.245	.267	.324	91	-4		.887	-7	53	0	*O-80(LF)/3-2,1	-1.5
1881	Det N	80	337	54	100	18	9	2	32	19		32	.297	.334	.421	131	11		.862	-2	85	124	*O-80(LF)	0.4
1882	Det N	84	375	69	101	12	12	**7**	29	14		30	.269	.296	.421	127	10		.884	2	73	199	*O-84(LF)	0.9
1883	Det N	99	441	81	133	26	11	5	47	25		37	.302	.339	.444	142	23		.876	7	65	76	*O-99(96-3-0)/P	2.3
1884	Det N	**114**	473	79	119	16	10	8	29	39		75	.252	.309	.378	122	14		.896	4	75	25	*O-114(114-0-1)/3	1.3
1885	Det N	82	362	62	105	19	8	5	28	13		19	.290	.315	.428	138	14		.885	2	79	51	O-70(LF),3-12/SP	1.3
1886	Phi N	106	450	81	123	18	15	4	50	23		75	.273	.309	.407	115	6	9	.904	-4	67	77	*O-97(96-1-0)/S-6,3-3	0.0
1887	Phi N	113	491	118	142	22	19	14	66	40	6	51	.289	.350	.497	125	14	19	.873	-10	54	63	*O-104(LF)/S-3,3-3,2-3	0.2
1888	Phi N	106	433	67	99	19	6	6	51	39	7	44	.229	.303	.342	100	1	20	.905	-1	84	90	*O-104(LF)/3-2,P-2	-0.3
1889	Phi N	97	422	77	106	21	4	5	53	53	1	33	.251	.336	.355	86	-9	17	.915	-2	52	31	O-92(LF)/S-6,P	-1.1
	Bal AA	3	10	1	2	0	0	0	1	0	0	2	.200	.200	.200	14	-1	1	1.000	-0	0	0	/O-3(RF)	-0.1
1890	Phi P	**132**	539	115	156	20	14	9	102	51	8	35	.289	.360	.429	108	3	20	.895	14	142	180	*O-132(128-0-4)/3	1.2
1891	Phi AA	132	528	105	163	18	14	3	61	72	7	52	.309	.399	.413	132	23	22	.939	7	115	**222**	*O-122(LF)/3-6,S-5,M	2.3
1892	Bal N	21	76	9	17	1	1	0	10	10	2	8	.224	.330	.263	78	-2	1	.911	2	172	114	O-21(LF)	-0.1
	Cin N	30	107	10	21	2	4	0	14	10	1	17	.196	.271	.290	71	-4	4	.863	-1	111	108	O-30(1-1-28)	-0.6
	Year	51	183	19	38	3	5	0	24	20	3	25	.208	.296	.279	74	-6	5	.885	1	138	111	O-51(22-1-28)	-0.7
Total	13	1280	5371	965	1467	228	132	68	601	418	32	547	.273	.329	.403	116	99	113	.895	11	84	100	*O-1232L/3-30,S-21,P-5,2-3,1	6.2

WOOD, HARRY Harold Austin B 2.10.1881 Waterville, ME D 5.18.1955 Bethesda, MD BL/TR 5-10/155# d4.19

1903	Cin N	2	3	0	0	0	0	0	0	1	0		.000	.250	.000	-24	0	0	—	-0	0	0	/O-2(1-0-1)	-0.1

Year	Tm Lg	G	AB	R	H	2B	3B	HR	RBI	BB-IB	HP	SO	AVG	OBP	SLG	AOPS	ABR	SB-CS	FA	FR	Rng	Thr	G at Pos	BFW
WOOD, JAKE Jacob B 6.22.1937 Elizabeth, NJ BR/TR 6-1/170# d4.11																								
1961	Det A	162	663	96	171	17	**14**	11	69	58-2	4	141	.258	.320	.376	83	-18	30-9	.969	-26	91	81	*2-162	-2.7
1962	Det A	111	367	68	83	10	5	8	30	33-0	1	59	.226	.291	.346	68	-17	24-3	.950	-25	85	59	2-90	-3.1
1963	Det A	85	351	50	95	11	2	11	27	24-0	7	61	.271	.330	.407	102	1	18-5	.958	-8	93	97	2-81/3	0.2
1964	Det A	64	125	11	29	2	2	1	7	4-0	0	24	.232	.254	.304	54	-8	0-0	.989	-2	113	80	1-11,2-10/3-6,O(LF)	-1.1
1965	Det A	58	104	12	30	3	0	2	7	10-0	1	19	.288	.357	.375	107	1	3-3	.977	-3	80	100	2-20/1S3	-0.1
1966	Det A	98	230	39	58	9	3	2	27	28-0	1	48	.252	.336	.343	94	-1	4-3	.968	-10	81	87	2-52/3-4,1-2	-0.8
1967	Det A	14	20	2	1	1	0	0	0	1-0	0	7	.050	.095	.100	-41	-4	0-0	1.000	0	0	261	/1-2,2-2	-0.3
	Cin N	16	17	1	2	0	0	0	1	1-0	0	3	.118	.167	.118	-15	-3	0-0	1.000	0	135	0	/O-2(RF)	-0.3
Total	7	608	1877	279	469	53	26	35	168	159-2	14	362	.250	.312	.362	82	-49	79-23	.963	-73	88	82	2-417/1-16,3-12,O-3(1-0-2),S	-8.2
WOOD, JIMMY James Leon B 12.1.1844 Brooklyn, NY D 11.30.1886 TR 5-8.5/150# d5.8 M4																								
1871	Chi NA	**28**	135	45	51	10	6	1	29	11		3	.378	.425	.563	163	10	18-2	**.887**	8	107	**131**	*2-28,M	1.2
1872	Tro NA	**25**	113	40	38	11	4	2	26	2		1	.336	.348	.558	172	9	0-0	.886	-1	82	54	2-25,M	0.5
	Eck NA	7	31	10	6	1	1	0	0	4		1	.194	.286	.290	91	1	1-0	.840	-0	95	30	/2-7,M	0.0
	Year	32	144	50	44	12	5	2	26	6		2	.306	.333	.500	156	10	1-0	.875	-1	85	49	2-32	0.5
1873	Phi NA	42	209	67	67	11	1	0	27	8		1	.321	.346	.383	112	3	9-3	.856	2	93	**151**	*2-42	0.2
Total	3 NA	102	488	162	162	33	12	3	82	25		6	.332	.365	.467	140	23	28-5	.000	9	94	114	2-102	1.9
WOOD, JASON Jason William B 12.16.1969 San Bernardino, CA BR/TR 6-1/170# d4.1																								
1998	Oak A	3	1	1	0	0	0	0	0	0-0	0	1	.000	.000	.000	-99	0	0-0	1.000	1	198	446	/S-2,3	0.1
	Det A	10	23	5	8	2	0	1	1	3-0	0	4	.348	.423	.565	153	2	0-1	1.000	-1	74	120	/1-6,SD	0.0
	Year	13	24	6	8	2	0	1	1	3-0	0	5	.333	.407	.542	144	2	0-1	1.000	-0	74	120	/1-6,S-3,D-3,3	0.1
1999	Det A	27	44	5	7	1	0	1	8	2-0	0	13	.159	.196	.250	13	-6	0-0	.909	-4	59	0	/3-9,S-9,1-5,2D	-1.0
Total	2	40	68	11	15	3	0	2	9	5-0	0	18	.221	.274	.353	59	-4	0-1	.875	-5	69	66	/S-12,1-11,3-10,D-4,2	-0.9
WOOD, JOE Joe "Smokey Joe" (born Howard Ellsworth Wood) B 10.25.1889 Kansas City, MO D 7.27.1985 West Haven, CT BR/TR 5-11/180# d8.24 s-Joe ▲																								
1908	Bos A	6	7	1	0	0	0	0	0	0	0		.000	.000	.000	-97	-1	0	.889	-0	71	531	/P-6	0.0
1909	Bos A	24	55	4	9	0	1	0	3	2	1		.164	.207	.200	28	0	0	.971	-4	55	0	P-24	0.0
1910	Bos A	35	69	9	18	2	1	1	5	5	0		.261	.311	.362	108	5	0	.975	2	98	188	P-35	0.0
1911	Bos A	44	88	15	23	4	2	2	11	10	1		.261	.343	.420	114	8	1	.947	2	88	143	P-44	0.0
1912	†Bos A	43	124	16	36	13	1	1	13	11	0		.290	.348	.435	118	11	0	.974	8	110	79	P-43	0.0
1913	Bos A	25	56	10	15	5	0	0	10	4	0	7	.268	.317	.357	95	4	1	.955	4	128	73	P-23	0.0
1914	Bos A	21	43	2	6	1	0	0	1	3	1	14	.140	.213	.163	13	0	1	1.000	0	86	0	P-18	0.0
1915	Bos A	29	54	6	14	1	1	1	7	5	0	10	.259	.322	.370	111	4	1-1	.982	1	103	**411**	P-25	0.0
1917	Cle A	10	6	1	0	0	0	0	0	0	0	3	.000	.000	.000	-93	-1	0	1.000	0	108	0	/P-5	0.0
1918	Cle A	119	422	41	125	22	4	5	66	36	3	38	.296	.356	.403	118	9	8	.962	-2	101	79	O-95(84-1-10),2-19/1-4	0.3
1919	Cle A	72	192	30	49	10	6	0	27	32	2	21	.255	.367	.370	101	1	3	.932	-4	88	85	O-64(15-6-43)/P	-0.6
1920	†Cle A	61	137	25	37	11	2	1	30	25	2	16	.270	.390	.401	107	3	1-1	.987	0	99	95	O-55(5-2-48)/P	0.1
1921	Cle A	66	194	32	71	16	5	4	60	25	0	17	.366	.438	.562	151	16	2-0	.973	-3	102	43	O-64(0-21-56)	0.9
1922	Cle A	142	505	74	150	33	8	8	92	50	6	63	.297	.367	.442	109	7	5-1	.960	3	102	119	*O-141(2-1-138)	0.0
Total	14	697	1952	266	553	118	31	23	325	208	16	189	.283	.357	.411	110	66	23-3	.962	8	99	91	O-419(106-31-295),P-225/2-19,1-4	0.7
WOOD, JOE Joseph Perry "J.P." or "Little Joe" B 10.3.1919 Houston, TX D 3.25.1985 Houston, TX BR/TR 5-9.5/160# d5.2 Mil 1944-45																								
1943	Det A	60	164	22	53	4	4	1	17	6	0	13	.323	.347	.415	114	2	2-2	.896	-11	70	45	2-22,3-18	-0.9
WOOD, KEN Kenneth Lanier B 7.1.1924 Lincolnton, NC BR/TR 6/200# d4.28																								
1948	StL A	10	24	2	2	0	1	0	2	1	0	4	.083	.120	.167	-24	-5	0-0	1.000	1	97	275	/O-5(RF)	-0.4
1949	StL A	7	6	0	0	0	0	0	0	1	0	2	.000	.143	.000	-58	-1	0-0	—	-0	0	0	/O-3(2-0-1)	-0.1
1950	StL A	128	369	42	83	24	0	13	62	38	1	58	.225	.299	.396	74	-16	0-4	.952	4	95	223	O-94(7-0-88)	-1.6
1951	StL A	109	333	40	79	19	0	15	44	27	1	49	.237	.296	.429	92	-6	1-2	.959	0	101	111	*O-100(29-4-69)	-1.0
1952	Bos A	15	20	0	2	0	0	0	0	3	0	4	.100	.217	.100	-9	-3	0-0	.889	-1	93	0	O-13(1-0-12)	-0.4
	Was A	61	210	26	50	8	6	6	32	30	0	21	.238	.333	.419	112	3	0-1	.954	4	111	144	O-56(54-3-1)	0.2
	Year	76	230	26	52	8	6	6	32	33	0	25	.226	.323	.391	99	-1	0-1	.951	4	110	134	O-69(55-3-13)	-0.2
1953	Was A	12	33	0	7	1	0	0	3	2	0	3	.212	.257	.242	36	-3	0-0	1.000	1	94	204	/O-7(LF)	-0.3
Total	6	342	995	110	223	52	7	34	143	102	2	141	.224	.298	.393	81	-31	1-7	.956	8	101	160	O-278(100-7-176)	-3.6
WOOD, BOB Robert Lynn B 7.28.1865 Thorn Hill, OH D 5.22.1943 Churchill, OH BR/TR 5-8.5/153# d5.2																								
1898	Cin N	39	109	14	30	6	0	0	16	9	0		.275	.331	.330	84	-2	1	.943	3	*168*	*78*	C-29/O(LF)1	0.4
1899	Cin N	63	195	34	61	11	7	0	24	25	5		.313	.404	.441	129	9	3	.937	-3	*129*	*83*	C-53/O-2(1-1-0),3-2,1	0.9
1900	Cin N	45	139	17	37	8	1	0	22	10	1		.266	.320	.338	84	-3	3	.967	-3	*118*	*106*	C-18,3-15/O(CF)	-0.4
1901	Cle A	98	346	45	101	23	3	1	49	12	6		.292	.327	.384	101	1	6	.952	-3	*93*	*97*	C-84/3-4,O-3(1-0-2),12S	0.5
1902	Cle A	81	258	23	76	18	2	0	40	27	6		.295	.375	.380	114	7	1	.941	-6	*87*	*91*	C-52,1-16/O-2(RF),23	0.5
1904	Det A	49	175	15	43	6	2	1	17	5	1		.246	.271	.320	89	-3	1	.974	4	*90*	*119*	C-47	0.7
1905	Det A	8	24	1	2	1	0	0	0	1	0		.083	.120	.125	-22	-3	0	.886	-2	*75*	*165*	/C-7	-0.5
Total	7	383	1246	149	350	73	15	2	168	89	19		.281	.338	.368	101	6	15	.951	-9	*107*	*98*	C-290/3-22,1-19,O-9(3-2-4),2-2,S	2.1
WOOD, ROY Roy Winton "Woody" B 8.29.1892 Monticello, AR D 4.6.1974 Fayetteville, AR BR/TR 6/175# d6.16																								
1913	Pit N	14	35	4	10	4	0	0	2	1	0	8	.286	.306	.400	105	0	0	.895	2	85	401	/O-8(LF),1	0.2
1914	Cle A	72	220	24	52	6	3	1	15	13	7	26	.236	.300	.305	79	-6	6-9	.946	1	102	128	O-40(5-13-23),1-20	-1.1
1915	Cle A	33	78	5	15	2	1	0	3	2	2	13	.192	.232	.244	41	-6	1-2	.990	-1	77	77	1-21/O-2(1-0-1)	-0.9
Total	3	119	333	33	77	12	4	1	20	16	9	47	.231	.285	.300	73	-12	7-11	.936	1	98	169	/O-50(14-13-24),1-42	-1.8
WOODALL, LARRY Charles Lawrence B 7.26.1894 Staunton, VA D 5.16.1963 Cambridge, MA BR/TR 5-9/165# d5.20 C7																								
1920	Det A	18	49	4	12	1	0	0	5	2	0	6	.245	.275	.265	45	-4	0-0	.988	1	*99*	*130*	C-15	-0.2
1921	Det A	46	80	10	29	4	1	0	14	6	0	7	.363	.407	.438	117	2	1-0	.966	-5	*72*	*63*	C-25	-0.1
1922	Det A	50	125	19	43	2	2	0	18	8	1	11	.344	.388	.392	107	1	0-1	.977	-8	*75*	*39*	C-40	-0.5
1923	Det A	71	148	20	41	12	2	1	19	22	0	9	.277	.371	.405	106	2	2-1	.983	-2	*103*	*106*	C-60	0.3
1924	Det A	67	165	23	51	9	2	0	25	21	0	5	.309	.387	.388	102	1	0-0	.986	-1	*96*	*100*	C-62	0.3
1925	Det A	75	171	20	35	4	1	0	13	24	0	8	.205	.303	.240	39	-16	1-0	.967	-7	*86*	*85*	C-75	-1.8
1926	Det A	67	146	18	34	5	0	0	15	15	0	2	.233	.304	.267	49	-11	0-0	.979	-4	*83*	*112*	C-59	-1.1
1927	Det A	88	246	28	69	8	6	0	39	37	0	9	.280	.375	.362	90	-3	9-1	**.997**	3	*93*	*106*	C-86	0.7
1928	Det A	65	186	19	39	7	1	0	13	24	0	10	.210	.300	.258	47	-14	3-1	.992	2	*101*	*142*	C-62	-0.8
1929	Det A	1	1	0	0	0	0	0	0	0	0	0	.000	.000	.000	-99	0	0-0	—	0			H	0.0
Total	10	548	1317	161	353	52	15	1	161	159	1	67	.268	.347	.333	77	-42	16-4	.984	-21	*91*	*102*	C-484	-3.2
WOODARD, DARRELL Darrell Lee B 12.10.1956 Wilmar, AR BR/TR 5-11/160# d8.6																								
1978	Oak A	33	9	10	0	0	0	0	0	1-0	0	1	.000	.100	.000	-73	-2	3-4	.964	2	114	112	2-14/3D	-0.1
WOODARD, MIKE Michael Cary B 3.2.1960 Melrose Park, IL BL/TR 5-9/155# d9.11																								
1985	SF N	24	82	12	20	1	0	0	9	5-0	0	3	.244	.287	.256	56	-5	6-1	.990	-2	81	107	2-23	-0.6
1986	SF N	48	79	14	20	2	1	1	5	10-0	0	9	.253	.337	.342	92	-1	7-2	.986	-3	89	147	2-23/S-2,3-2	-0.2
1987	SF N	10	19	0	4	1	0	0	1	0-0	0	1	.211	.211	.263	26	-2	0-0	1.000	2	123	158	/2-8	0.1
1988	Chi A	18	45	3	6	0	1	0	4	1-0	1	5	.133	.170	.178	-2	-6	1-1	.975	4	111	99	2-14/D-2	-0.2
Total	4	100	225	29	50	4	2	1	19	16-0	1	18	.222	.277	.271	55	-14	14-4	.985	1	94	121	/2-68,D-2,3-2,S-2	-0.9
WOODHEAD, RED James B 7.9.1851 Chelsea, MA D 9.7.1881 Boston, MA 5-6/160# d4.15																								
1873	Mar NA	1	5	1	0	0	0	0	0	0		0	.000	.000	.000	-99	-1	0-0	.900	1	179	0	/S	0.0
1879	Syr N	34	131	4	21	1	0	0	2	0		23	.160	.160	.168	9	-12		.792	-9	72	86	3-34	-1.9
WOODLING, GENE Eugene Richard B 8.16.1922 Akron, OH D 6.2.2001 Barberton, OH BL/TR 5-9.5/195# d9.23 Mil 1943-45 C4																								
1943	Cle A	8	25	5	8	2	1	1	5	1	0	3	.320	.346	.600	186	2	0-0	1.000	-0	72	267	/O-6(0-1-5)	0.2
1946	Cle A	61	133	8	25	1	4	0	9	16	1	13	.188	.280	.256	54	-9	1-2	1.000	-1	105	0	O-37(6-31-0)	-1.2
1947	Pit N	22	79	7	21	2	2	0	10	7	0	5	.266	.326	.342	75	-3	0	.968	1	111	70	O-21(1-20-0)	-0.3
1949	†NY A	112	296	60	80	13	7	5	44	52	1	21	.270	.381	.412	110	5	2-2	.982	-2	95	89	O-98(82-12-5)	-0.3
1950	†NY A	122	449	81	127	20	10	6	60	70	1	31	.283	.381	.412	106	5	5-3	.993	12	109	**190**	*O-118(117-2-0)	0.8
1951	†NY A	120	420	65	118	15	8	15	71	62	0	37	.281	.373	.462	130	17	0-4	.993	0	104	56	*O-116(101-17-0)	0.7

Year	Tm Lg	G	AB	R	H	2B	3B	HR	RBI	BB-IB	HP	SO	AVG	OBP	SLG	AOPS	ABR	SB-CS	FA	FR	Rng	Thr	G at Pos	BFW
1952	†NY A	122	408	58	126	19	6	12	63	59	1	31	.309	.397	.473	151	29	1-4	**.996**	6	99	**169**	*O-118(112-6-0)	2.6
1953	†NY A	125	395	64	121	26	4	10	58	82	3	29	.306	**.429**	.468	147	32	2-7	**.996**	1	102	71	*O-119(LF)	2.4
1954	NY A	97	304	33	76	12	5	3	40	53	0	35	.250	.358	.352	99	1	3-4	.983	-1	95	94	O-89(LF)	-0.6
1955	Bal A	47	145	22	32	6	2	3	18	24-4	1	18	.221	.329	.352	91	-2	1-1	1.000	-2	96	33	O-44(26-4-25)	-0.5
	Cle A	79	259	33	72	15	1	5	35	36-2	3	15	.278	.368	.402	104	3	2-4	.993	-2	97	74	O-70(64-0-16)	-0.3
	Year	126	404	55	104	21	3	8	53	60-6	4	33	.257	.354	.384	100	2	3-5	.995	-3	97	59	*O-114(90-4-41)	-0.8
1956	Cle A	100	317	56	83	17	0	8	38	69-2	3	29	.262	.395	.391	107	7	2-6	.981	-3	97	50	O-85(85-0-2)	-0.3
1957	Cle A	133	430	74	138	25	2	19	78	64-2	3	35	.321	.408	.521	155	35	0-5	.992	7	103	171	*O-113(LF)	3.4
1958	Bal A	133	413	57	114	16	1	15	65	66-3	2	49	.276	.378	.429	128	18	4-2	.974	-2	95	96	*O-116(61-0-68)	1.2
1959	Bal A★	140	440	63	132	22	2	14	77	78-4	0	35	.300	.402	.455	139	27	1-1	.981	-5	96	29	*O-124(85-0-57)	1.6
1960	Bal A	140	435	68	123	18	3	11	62	84-7	4	40	.283	.401	.414	123	19	3-0	.995	-0	93	96	*O-124(124-0-1)	1.3
1961	Was A	110	342	39	107	16	4	10	57	50-3	2	24	.313	.403	.471	135	19	1-0	.988	-0	94	125	O-90(15-0-77)	1.3
1962	Was A	44	107	19	30	4	0	5	16	24-4	2	5	.280	.421	.458	138	7	1-0	.953	-3	85	0	O-30(3-0-27)	0.3
	NY N	81	190	18	52	8	1	5	24	24-3	1	22	.274	.353	.405	103	1	0-0	.986	-3	97	0	O-48(27-0-21)	-0.4
Total	17	1796	5587	830	1585	257	63	147	830	921-34	28	477	.284	.386	.431	123	213	29-45	.989	4	99	94	*O-1566(1230-93-304)	11.9

WOODRUFF, SAM Orville Francis B 12.27.1876 Chilo, OH D 7.22.1937 Cincinnati, OH BR/TR 5-9/160# d4.14

Year	Tm Lg	G	AB	R	H	2B	3B	HR	RBI	BB-IB	HP	SO	AVG	OBP	SLG	AOPS	ABR	SB-CS	FA	FR	Rng	Thr	G at Pos	BFW
1904	Cin N	87	306	20	58	14	3	0	20	19	3		.190	.244	.255	50	-18	9	.932	-3	100	67	3-61,2-17/S-8,O(RF)	-2.1
1910	Cin N	21	61	6	9	1	0	0	2	7	0	8	.148	.235	.164	18	-6	2	.933	-1	92	127	3-17/2-4	-0.8
Total	2	108	367	26	67	15	3	0	22	26	3	8	.183	.242	.240	45	-24	11	.932	-5	98	80	/3-78,2-21,S-8,O(RF)	-2.9

WOODRUFF, PETE Franklin B 6.1873 , NY BR/TR d9.19

Year	Tm Lg	G	AB	R	H	2B	3B	HR	RBI	BB-IB	HP	SO	AVG	OBP	SLG	AOPS	ABR	SB-CS	FA	FR	Rng	Thr	G at Pos	BFW
1899	NY N	20	61	11	15	1	1	2	7	9	0		.246	.343	.393	105	0	3	1.000	-1	111	0	O-19(RF)/1	-0.1

WOODS, AL Alvis B 8.8.1953 Oakland, CA BL/TL 6-3/195# d4.7

Year	Tm Lg	G	AB	R	H	2B	3B	HR	RBI	BB-IB	HP	SO	AVG	OBP	SLG	AOPS	ABR	SB-CS	FA	FR	Rng	Thr	G at Pos	BFW
1977	Tor A	122	440	58	125	17	4	6	35	36-3	0	38	.284	.336	.382	94	-3	8-7	.969	-1	100	75	*O-115(106-0-15)/D-4	-1.0
1978	Tor A	62	220	19	53	12	3	3	25	11-1	1	23	.241	.278	.364	78	-7	1-2	.978	0	107	50	O-60(LF)	-1.1
1979	Tor A	132	436	57	121	24	4	5	36	40-0	1	28	.278	.337	.385	94	-3	6-4	.967	-1	97	107	*O-127(LF)/D-2	-0.9
1980	Tor A	109	373	54	112	18	2	15	47	37-3	1	35	.300	.364	.480	124	12	4-4	.991	2	104	74	O-88(LF),D-13	0.9
1981	Tor A	85	288	20	71	15	0	1	21	19-5	0	31	.247	.291	.309	69	-11	3-4	.973	-0	101	71	O-77(LF)/D-2	-1.6
1982	Tor A	85	201	20	47	11	1	3	24	21-4	0	20	.234	.302	.343	71	-8	1-3	.970	-2	90	68	O-64(LF),D-10	-1.3
1986	Min A	23	28	5	9	1	0	2	8	3-0	0	5	.321	.375	.571	153	2	0-0	—	0			/D-7	0.2
Total	7	618	1986	233	538	98	14	35	196	167-16	3	180	.271	.326	.387	93	-18	23-24	.974	-2	100	78	O-531(522-0-15)/D-38	-4.8

WOODS, GARY Gary Lee B 7.20.1954 Santa Barbara, CA BR/TR 6-2/190# d9.14

Year	Tm Lg	G	AB	R	H	2B	3B	HR	RBI	BB-IB	HP	SO	AVG	OBP	SLG	AOPS	ABR	SB-CS	FA	FR	Rng	Thr	G at Pos	BFW
1976	Oak A	6	8	0	1	0	0	0	0	0-0	0	3	.125	.125	.125	-28	-1	0-0	1.000	0	162	0	/O-4(1-2-1),D	-0.1
1977	Tor A	60	227	21	49	9	1	0	17	7-0	2	38	.216	.246	.264	38	-20	5-4	.994	0	102	97	O-60(CF)	-2.1
1978	Tor A	8	19	1	3	1	0	0	0	1-0	0	1	.158	.200	.211	15	-2	1-0	1.000	0	111	0	/O-6(0-1-5)	-0.2
1980	†Hou N	19	53	8	20	5	0	2	15	2-0	0	9	.377	.400	.585	186	6	1-0	1.000	-1	80	93	O-14(4-0-12)	0.5
1981	†Hou N	54	110	10	23	4	1	0	12	11-4	0	22	.209	.276	.264	58	-6	2-1	.984	0	112	45	O-40(2-3-35)	-0.8
1982	Chi N	117	245	28	66	15	1	4	30	21-2	0	48	.269	.327	.388	97	-1	3-3	1.000	4	104	141	*O-103(37-67-12)	0.1
1983	Chi N	93	190	25	46	9	0	4	22	15-2	0	27	.242	.296	.353	76	-6	5-3	.971	2	103	141	O-73(40-27-13)/2	-0.6
1984	†Chi N	87	98	13	23	4	1	3	10	15-0	0	21	.235	.333	.388	94	0	2-1	1.000	1	110	124	O-62(36-11-18)/2-3	0.0
1985	Chi N	81	82	11	20	3	0	0	4	14-0	0	18	.244	.354	.280	72	-2	0-1	1.000	0	105	68	O-56(44-4-11)	-0.3
Total	9	525	1032	117	251	50	4	13	110	86-8	2	187	.243	.302	.337	76	-32	19-13	.992	7	104	107	O-418(164-175-107)/2-4,D	-3.5

WOODS, JIM James Jerome "Woody" B 9.17.1939 Chicago, IL BR/TR 6/175# d9.27

Year	Tm Lg	G	AB	R	H	2B	3B	HR	RBI	BB-IB	HP	SO	AVG	OBP	SLG	AOPS	ABR	SB-CS	FA	FR	Rng	Thr	G at Pos	BFW
1957	Chi N	2	0	1	0	0	0	0	0	0-0	0	0	—	—	—	—	0	0-0	—	0			R	0.0
1960	Phi N	11	34	4	6	0	0	1	3	3-1	0	13	.176	.243	.265	39	-3	0-0	.939	1	120	57	3-11	-0.2
1961	Phi N	23	48	6	11	3	0	2	9	4-2	1	15	.229	.296	.417	89	-1	0-0	.968	-0	91	143	3-15	-0.1
Total	3	36	82	11	17	3	0	3	12	7-3	1	28	.207	.275	.354	69	-4	0-0	.953	1	105	101	/3-26	-0.3

WOODS, RON Ronald Lawrence B 2.1.1943 Hamilton, OH BR/TR 5-10/173# d4.22

Year	Tm Lg	G	AB	R	H	2B	3B	HR	RBI	BB-IB	HP	SO	AVG	OBP	SLG	AOPS	ABR	SB-CS	FA	FR	Rng	Thr	G at Pos	BFW
1969	Det A	17	15	3	4	0	0	1	3	2-0	0	3	.267	.353	.467	122	0	0-0	1.000	-0	103	0	/O-7(7-1-0)	0.0
	NY A	72	171	18	30	5	2	1	7	22-1	1	29	.175	.273	.246	48	-12	2-0	1.000	0	108	62	O-67(1-66-0)	-1.3
	Year	89	186	21	34	5	2	2	10	24-1	1	32	.183	.280	.263	54	-12	2-0	1.000	0	108	59	O-74(8-67-0)	-1.3
1970	NY A	95	225	30	51	5	3	8	27	33-3	0	35	.227	.324	.382	100	0	4-2	.974	-3	86	136	O-78(2-9-70)	-0.6
1971	NY A	25	32	4	8	1	0	1	2	4-0	0	2	.250	.333	.375	107	0	0-0	.929	0	136	0	/O-9(3-0-6)	0.0
	Mon N	51	138	26	41	7	3	1	17	19-0	0	18	.297	.382	.413	125	5	0-2	.989	6	114	239	O-45(32-23-0)	1.0
1972	Mon N	97	221	21	57	5	1	10	31	22-2	0	33	.258	.321	.425	110	2	3-3	.991	-4	84	57	O-73(8-58-10)	-0.4
1973	Mon N	135	318	45	73	11	3	3	31	56-3	0	34	.230	.344	.311	80	-7	12-6	.977	3	101	126	*O-114(29-91-4)	-0.7
1974	Mon N	90	127	15	26	0	0	1	12	17-1	1	17	.205	.299	.228	48	-9	6-5	.987	0	108	0	O-61(40-20-5)	-1.1
Total	6	582	1247	162	290	34	12	26	130	175-10	2	171	.233	.326	.342	87	-21	27-18	.984	3	99	103	O-454(122-268-95)	-3.1

WOODSON, TRACY Tracy Michael B 10.5.1962 Richmond, VA BR/TR 6-3/215# d4.7

Year	Tm Lg	G	AB	R	H	2B	3B	HR	RBI	BB-IB	HP	SO	AVG	OBP	SLG	AOPS	ABR	SB-CS	FA	FR	Rng	Thr	G at Pos	BFW
1987	LA N	53	136	14	31	8	1	1	11	9-2	2	21	.228	.284	.324	63	-7	1-1	.958	-3	79	67	3-45/1-7	-1.1
1988	†LA N	65	173	15	43	4	1	3	15	7-1	1	32	.249	.279	.335	79	-6	1-2	.938	-5	86	59	3-41,1-25	-1.3
1989	LA N	4	6	0	0	0	0	0	0	0-0	0	1	.000	.000	.000	-99	-2	0-0	1.000	-0	68	0	/3	-0.2
1992	StL N	31	114	9	35	8	0	1	22	3-0	1	10	.307	.331	.404	110	1	0-0	.945	-6	71	103	3-26/1-3	-0.6
1993	StL N	62	77	4	16	2	0	0	2	1-0	0	14	.208	.215	.234	21	-9	0-0	.909	-0	117	195	3-28,1-11	-0.9
Total	5	215	506	42	125	22	2	5	50	20-3	4	78	.247	.279	.328	70	-23	2-3	.943	-14	83	85	3-141/1-46	-4.1

WOODWARD, CHRIS Christopher Michael B 6.27.1976 Covina, CA BR/TR 6/160# d6.7

Year	Tm Lg	G	AB	R	H	2B	3B	HR	RBI	BB-IB	HP	SO	AVG	OBP	SLG	AOPS	ABR	SB-CS	FA	FR	Rng	Thr	G at Pos	BFW
1999	Tor A	14	26	1	6	1	0	0	2	2-0	0	6	.231	.276	.269	42	-2	0-0	.939	0	111	41	S-10/3-2	-0.1
2000	Tor A	37	104	16	19	7	0	3	14	10-3	0	28	.183	.254	.337	46	-9	1-0	.955	1	103	68	S-22/3-9,1-3,2-3	-0.6
2001	Tor A	37	63	9	12	3	2	2	5	1-0	0	14	.190	.203	.397	52	-5	0-1	.959	10	153	142	2-17,3-10/S-4,1-2,D	0.5
2002	Tor A	90	312	48	86	13	4	13	45	26-0	3	72	.276	.330	.468	107	2	3-0	.965	11	107	120	S-79/2-6,1-3,3-2,D-2	1.9
2003	Tor A	104	349	49	91	22	2	7	45	28-0	3	72	.261	.316	.395	86	-7	1-2	.964	10	108	104	*S-103	1.0
Total	5	282	854	123	214	46	8	25	111	67-3	6	192	.251	.305	.411	85	-21	5-3	.963	32	108	105	S-218/2-26,3-23,1-8,D-3	2.7

WOODWARD, WOODY William Frederick B 9.23.1942 Miami, FL BR/TR 6-2/185# d9.9

Year	Tm Lg	G	AB	R	H	2B	3B	HR	RBI	BB-IB	HP	SO	AVG	OBP	SLG	AOPS	ABR	SB-CS	FA	FR	Rng	Thr	G at Pos	BFW
1963	Mil N	10	2	1	0	0	0	0	0	0-0	0	0	.000	.000	.000	-99	-1	0-0	1.000	1	250	0	/S-5	0.1
1964	Mil N	77	115	18	24	2	1	0	11	6-1	2	28	.209	.260	.243	43	-9	0-1	.958	7	100	148	2-40,S-18/3-7,1	0.1
1965	Mil N	112	265	17	55	7	4	0	11	10-3	0	50	.208	.235	.264	41	-22	2-2	.977	7	99	127	*S-107/2-8	-0.9
1966	Atl N	144	455	46	120	23	3	0	43	37-9	4	54	.264	.323	.327	81	-10	2-2	.973	-12	101	98	2-79,S-73	-1.1
1967	Atl N	136	429	30	97	15	2	0	25	37-5	1	51	.226	.287	.270	62	-21	0-6	**.982**	7	105	113	*2-120,S-16	-0.6
1968	Atl N	12	24	2	4	1	0	0	1	1-0	0	6	.167	.200	.208	23	-2	1-0	.973	1	112	88	/S-6,3-2,2	-0.1
	Cin N	56	119	13	29	2	0	0	10	7-3	2	23	.244	.297	.261	64	-5	1-0	.968	-5	90	80	S-41/2-9,1	-0.8
	Year	68	143	15	33	3	0	0	11	8-3	2	29	.231	.281	.252	58	-7	2-0	.969	-4	94	81	S-47,2-10/3-2,1	-0.9
1969	Cin N	97	241	36	63	12	0	0	15	24-3	2	40	.261	.333	.311	77	-6	3-2	.966	-7	101	71	S-93/2-2	-0.4
1970	†Cin N	100	264	23	59	8	3	1	14	20-6	2	21	.223	.280	.288	53	-18	1-2	.973	4	109	120	S-77,3-20,2-10/1-2	-0.7
1971	Cin N	136	273	22	66	9	1	0	18	27-4	0	28	.242	.309	.282	70	-10	4-0	.987	-9	91	109	S-85,3-63/2-9	-1.2
Total	9	880	2187	208	517	79	14	1	148	169-34	13	301	.236	.294	.287	64	-104	14-15	.974	-7	100	99	S-521,2-278/3-92,1-4	-5.6

WOOTEN, JUNIOR Earl Hazwell B 1.16.1924 Pelzer, SC BR/TL 5-11/160# d9.16

Year	Tm Lg	G	AB	R	H	2B	3B	HR	RBI	BB-IB	HP	SO	AVG	OBP	SLG	AOPS	ABR	SB-CS	FA	FR	Rng	Thr	G at Pos	BFW
1947	Was A	6	24	0	2	0	0	0	1	0	0	4	.083	.083	.083	-55	-5	1-0	.905	-0	113	0	/O-6(1-6-0)	-0.6
1948	Was A	88	258	34	66	8	3	1	23	24	2	21	.256	.324	.322	74	-10	2-1	.979	6	102	168	O-73(0-55-22)/1-6,P	-0.6
Total	2	94	282	34	68	8	3	1	24	24	2	25	.241	.305	.301	64	-15	3-1	.972	5	103	154	/O-79(1-61-22),1-6,P	-1.2

WOOTEN, SHAWN William Shawn B 7.24.1972 Glendora, CA BR/TR 5-10/205# d8.18

Year	Tm Lg	G	AB	R	H	2B	3B	HR	RBI	BB-IB	HP	SO	AVG	OBP	SLG	AOPS	ABR	SB-CS	FA	FR	Rng	Thr	G at Pos	BFW
2000	Ana A	7	9	2	5	1	0	0	1	0-0	0	0	.556	.556	.667	202	1	0-0	1.000	-1	93	0	/C-4,1-3	0.1
2001	Ana A	79	221	24	69	8	1	8	32	5-0	3	42	.312	.332	.466	106	1	2-0	1.000	-1	174	140	D-27,C-25,1-21/3	-0.1
2002	†Ana A	49	113	13	33	8	0	3	19	6-1	1	24	.292	.331	.442	104	1	2-0	1.000	-2	80	52	D-26,1-16/C-2,3	-0.3
2003	Ana A	98	272	25	66	8	0	7	32	24-5	1	45	.243	.303	.349	75	-10	0-4	.995	-3	82	107	1-32,D-28,C-19,3-17	-1.7
Total	4	233	615	64	173	25	1	18	84	35-6	5	111	.281	.322	.413	94	-7	4-4	.993	-7	95	118	/D-81,1-72,C-50,3-19	-2.0

Year	Tm Lg	G	AB	R	H	2B	3B	HR	RBI	BB-IB	HP	SO	AVG	OBP	SLG	AOPS	ABR	SB-CS	FA	FR	Rng	Thr	G at Pos	BFW
WORDSWORTH, FAVEL Favel Perry B 11.22.1850 New York, NY D 8.12.1888 New York, NY d4.28																								
1873	Res NA	12	40	5	10	0	0	0	3	2		1	.250	.286	.250	66	-1	1-0	.662	-4	97	35	S-11/O(RF)	-0.4
WORKMAN, CHUCK Charles Thomas B 1.6.1915 Leeton, MO D 1.3.1953 Kansas City, MO BL/TR 6/175# d9.18																								
1938	Cle A	2	5	1	2	0	0	0	0	0	0	0	.400	.400	.400	103	0	0-0	.500	-0	57	0	/O(RF)	0.0
1941	Cle A	9	4	2	0	0	0	0	0	1	0	1	.000	.200	.000	-45	-1	0-0	—	0			H	-0.1
1943	Bos N	**153**	615	71	153	17	1	10	67	53	3	72	.249	.311	.328	86	-12	12	.988	2	95	130	*O-149(16-0-133)/1-3,3	-2.1
1944	Bos N	140	418	46	87	18	3	11	53	42	4	41	.208	.287	.344	74	-15	1	.983	4	91	167	*O-103(RF),3-19	-1.7
1945	Bos N	139	514	77	141	16	2	25	87	51	6	58	.274	.347	.459	122	13	9	.910	-15	97	91	*3-107,O-24(5-0-19)	-0.2
1946	Bos N	25	48	5	8	2	0	2	7	3	1	11	.167	.231	.333	58	-3	0	.920	-1	94	114	O-12(3-8-1)	-0.4
	Pit N	58	145	11	32	4	1	2	16	11	1	19	.221	.280	.303	64	-7	2	1.000	5	131	94	O-40(3-0-38)/3	-0.4
	Year	83	193	16	40	6	1	4	23	14	2	30	.207	.268	.311	63	-10	2	.986	5	124	98	O-52(6-8-39)/3	-0.8
Total	6	526	1749	213	423	57	7	50	230	161	15	202	.242	.311	.368	91	-25	24-0	.985	-4	99	125	O-329(27-8-295),3-128/1-3	-4.9
WORKMAN, HANK Henry Kilgariff B 2.5.1926 Los Angeles, CA BL/TR 6-1/185# d9.4																								
1950	NY A	2	5	1	1	0	0	0	0	0	0	1	.200	.200	.200	3	-1	0-0	1.000	-0	0	126	/1	-0.1
WORTH, HERB Herbert B 5.2.1847 Brooklyn, NY D 4.27.1914 Brooklyn, NY d7.29																								
1872	Atl NA	1	5	1	1	1	0	0	1	0		0	.200	.200	.400	68	0	0-0	1.000	0	0	0	/O(RF)	0.0
WORTHINGTON, CRAIG Craig Richard B 4.17.1965 Los Angeles, CA BR/TR 6/200# d4.26																								
1988	Bal A	26	81	5	15	2	0	2	4	9-0	0	24	.185	.267	.284	56	-5	1-0	.961	2	116	89	3-26	-0.2
1989	Bal A	145	497	57	123	23	0	15	70	61-2	4	114	.247	.334	.384	105	5	1-2	.951	-6	101	89	*3-145	-0.2
1990	Bal A	133	425	46	96	17	0	8	44	63-2	3	96	.226	.328	.322	86	-6	1-2	.945	-7	96	128	*3-131/D-2	-1.4
1991	Bal A	31	102	11	23	3	0	4	12	12-0	1	14	.225	.313	.373	93	-1	0-1	.975	-2	89	54	3-30	-0.4
1992	Cle A	9	24	0	4	0	0	0	2	2-0	0	4	.167	.231	.167	13	-3	0-1	.857	1	123	155	/3-9	-0.2
1995	Cin N	10	18	1	5	1	0	1	2	2-0	0	1	.278	.350	.500	122	1	0-0	1.000	1	92	126	/1-4,3-2	0.1
	Tex A	26	68	4	15	4	0	2	6	7-0	0	8	.221	.293	.368	69	-3	0-0	.980	-2	90	79	3-26	-0.5
1996	Tex A	13	19	2	3	0	0	1	4	6-0	0	3	.158	.333	.316	69	-1	0-0	.917	0	89	96	/3-7,1-6	-0.1
Total	7	393	1234	126	284	50	0	33	144	162-4	8	264	.230	.322	.351	90	-13	3-6	.950	-13	99	100	3-376/1-10,D-2	-2.9
WORTHINGTON, RED Robert Lee B 4.24.1906 Alhambra, CA D 12.8.1963 Sepulveda, CA BR/TR 5-11/170# d4.14																								
1931	Bos N	128	491	47	143	25	10	4	44	26	1	38	.291	.328	.407	100	-2	1	**.988**	-2	95	113	*O-124(114-0-10)	-1.0
1932	Bos N	105	435	62	132	35	8	8	61	15	2	24	.303	.330	.476	118	10	1	.987	-2	92	120	*O-104(LF)	0.2
1933	Bos N	17	45	3	7	4	0	0	0	1	0	3	.156	.174	.244	20	-5	0	.900	-1	86	119	O-10(3-0-7)	-0.6
1934	Bos N	41	65	6	16	5	0	0	6	6	1	5	.246	.319	.323	78	-2	0	.920	-1	110	0	O-11(RF)	-0.3
	StL N	1	1	0	0	0	0	0	0	0	0	1	.000	.000	.000	-94	0	0	—	0			H	0.0
	Year	42	66	6	16	5	0	0	6	6	1	6	.242	.315	.318	75	-2	0	.920	-1	110	0	O-11(RF)	-0.3
Total	4	292	1037	118	298	69	18	12	111	48	4	71	.287	.321	.423	103	1	2	.981	-5	94	112	O-249(221-0-28)	-1.7
WORTMAN, CHUCK William Lewis B 1.5.1892 Baltimore, MD D 8.19.1977 Las Vegas, NV BR/TR 5-7/150# d7.20																								
1916	Chi N	69	234	17	47	4	2	2	16	18	0	22	.201	.258	.261	54	-13	4	.908	-15	90	88	S-69	-2.7
1917	Chi N	75	190	24	33	4	1	0	9	18	0	23	.174	.245	.205	36	-14	6	.918	-11	88	104	S-65/23	-2.4
1918	†Chi N	17	17	4	2	0	0	1	3	1	0	2	.118	.167	.294	39	-1	3	.864	-0	107	76	/2-8,S-4	-0.2
Total	3	161	441	45	82	8	3	3	28	37	0	47	.186	.249	.238	46	-28	13	.913	-25	89	95	S-138/2-9,3	-5.3
WOTUS, RON Ronald Allan B 3.3.1961 Colchester, CT BR/TR 6-1/164# d9.3 C6																								
1983	Pit N	5	3	0	0	0	0	0	0	0-0	0	1	.000	.000	.000	-98	-1	0-0	1.000	0	71	0	/S-2,2	0.0
1984	Pit N	27	55	4	12	6	0	0	2	6-2	0	8	.218	.290	.327	75	-2	0-0	.976	8	138	153	S-17/2-7	0.8
Total	2	32	58	4	12	6	0	0	2	6-2	0	9	.207	.277	.310	66	-3	0-0	.976	8	136	148	/S-19,2-8	0.8
WOULFE, JIMMY James Joseph B 11.25.1859 New Orleans, LA D 12.20.1924 New Orleans, LA TR 5-11/?# d5.16																								
1884	Cin AA	8	34	3	5	0	1	0	2	1	0		.147	.171	.206	22	-3		.625	-3	0	0	/O-7(1-0-6),3	-0.6
	Pit AA	15	53	7	6	1	0	0	1	0	0		.113	.113	.132	-20	-7		.893	1	119	439	O-15(0-14-1)	-0.6
	Year	23	87	10	11	1	1	0	3	1	0		.126	.136	.161	-3	-10		.795	-2	76	279	O-22(1-14-7)/3	-1.2
WRIGHT, AL Albert Edgar "A-1" B 11.11.1912 San Francisco, CA D 11.13.1998 Oakland, CA BR/TR 6-1.5/170# d4.25																								
1933	Bos N	4	1	0	1	0	0	0	0	0	0	0	1.000	1.000	1.000	515	1	0	.500	-1	0	0	/2-3	0.0
WRIGHT, AB Albert Owen B 11.16.1906 Terlton, OK D 5.23.1995 Muskogee, OK BR/TR 6-3/200# d4.20																								
1935	Cle A	67	160	17	38	11	1	2	18	10	2	17	.237	.291	.356	65	-9	2-1	.984	-2	80	141	O-47(5-5-38)	-1.2
1944	Bos N	71	195	20	50	9	0	7	35	18	2	31	.256	.326	.410	102	0	0	.968	-3	91	53	O-47(35-0-12)	-0.6
Total	2	138	355	37	88	20	1	9	53	28	4	48	.248	.310	.386	85	-9	2-1	.974	-5	86	91	/O-94(40-5-50)	-1.8
WRIGHT, CY Ceylon B 8.16.1893 Minneapolis, MN D 11.7.1947 Hines, IL BL/TR 5-9/150# d6.30																								
1916	Chi A	8	18	0	0	0	0	0	0	1	0	7	.000	.053	.000	-83	-4	0	.844	-1	103	102	/S-8	-0.6
WRIGHT, GLENN Forest Glenn "Buckshot" B 2.6.1901 Archie, MO D 4.6.1984 Olathe, KS BR/TR 5-11/170# d4.15																								
1924	Pit N	**153**	616	80	177	28	18	7	111	27	1	52	.287	.318	.425	96	-6	14-6	.946	9	**110**	**112**	*S-153	2.0
1925	†Pit N	**153**	614	97	189	32	10	18	121	31	0	32	.308	.341	.480	100	-2	3-7	.939	2	102	116	*S-153/3	1.4
1926	Pit N	119	458	73	141	15	15	8	77	19	0	26	.308	.335	.459	106	1	6	.927	-8	99	116	*S-116	0.6
1927	†Pit N	143	570	78	160	26	4	9	105	39	1	46	.281	.328	.388	85	-12	4	.942	-14	94	103	*S-143	-1.1
1928	Pit N	108	407	63	126	20	8	8	66	21	0	53	.310	.343	.457	103	0	3	.927	-20	92	93	*S-101/1O(RF)	-0.9
1929	Bro N	24	25	4	5	0	0	1	6	3	0	6	.200	.286	.320	51	-2	0	.667	-2	37	0	/S-3	-0.4
1930	Bro N	135	532	83	171	28	12	22	126	32	0	70	.321	.360	.543	116	11	2	.964	5	99	113	*S-134	2.6
1931	Bro N	77	268	36	76	9	4	9	32	14	2	35	.284	.324	.448	106	1	1	.942	8	107	109	S-75	1.4
1932	Bro N	127	446	50	122	31	5	11	60	12	0	57	.274	.293	.439	96	-4	4	.939	8	103	**119**	*S-122/1-2	1.1
1933	Bro N	71	192	19	49	13	0	1	18	11	1	24	.255	.299	.339	85	-3	1	.936	-4	92	107	S-51/1-9,3-2	-0.5
1935	Chi A	9	25	1	3	1	0	0	1	0	0	6	.120	.120	.160	-27	-5	0-0	.943	-0	105	82	/2-7	-0.5
Total	11	1119	4153	584	1219	203	76	94	723	209	5	407	.294	.328	.447	99	-21	38-13	.941	-17	100	110	*S-1051/1-12,2-7,3-3,O(RF)	5.7
WRIGHT, GEORGE George B 1.28.1847 Yonkers, NY D 8.21.1937 Boston, MA BR/TR 5-9.5/150# d5.5 M1 HF1937 b-Sam b-Harry																								
1871	Bos NA	16	80	33	33	7	5	0	11	6		1	.412	.453	.625	200	10	9-1	.816	6	111	243	S-15/1	1.1
1872	Bos NA	**48**	255	87	86	16	6	2	35	3		1	.337	.345	.471	141	10	14-4	.836	22	**119**	**324**	*S-48	2.2
1873	Bos NA	59	323	99	125	17	7	3	43	9		2	.387	.404	.511	157	20	9-9	**.826**	20	116	133	*S-59	2.6
1874	Bos NA	60	313	76	103	10	**15**	2	44	5		6	.329	.340	.476	150	15	2-0	.821	6	97	**218**	*S-60/3	1.5
1875	Bos NA	79	408	106	136	20	7	2	61	2		6	.333	.337	.431	159	22	13-6	.861	4	96	153	*S-79/P-2	2.1
1876	Bos N	**70**	335	72	100	18	6	1	34	8		9	.299	.315	.397	134	12		.888	14	114	109	*S-68/2-2,P	2.5
1877	Bos N	**61**	290	58	80	15	1	0	35	9		15	.276	.298	.334	95	-1		.878	10	105	147	*2-58/S-3	1.0
1878	Bos N	59	267	35	60	5	1	0	12	6		22	.225	.242	.251	58	-13		**.947**	10	103	**188**	*S-59	0.0
1879	Pro N	**85**	388	79	107	15	10	1	42	13		20	.276	.299	.374	122	9		.924	20	**112**	95	*S-85,M	2.9
1880	Bos N	1	4	2	1	0	0	0	0	0		0	.250	.250	.250	72	0		1.000	0	118	0	/S	0.0
1881	Bos N	7	25	4	5	0	0	0	0	3		1	.200	.286	.200	58	-1		.963	-1	88	144	/S-7	-0.1
1882	Pro N	46	185	14	30	1	2	0	9	4		36	.162	.180	.189	19	-17		.873	-6	92	140	S-46	-2.0
Total	5 NA	262	1379	401	483	70	40	9	194	25		16	.350	.362	.479	156	77	47-20	.000	57	106	200	S-261/P-2,31	9.5
Total	7	329	1494	264	383	54	20	2	132	43		103	.256	.277	.323	93	-11		.911	48	106	128	S-269/2-60,P	4.3
WRIGHT, GEORGE George De Witt B 12.22.1958 Oklahoma City, OK BB/TR 5-11/180# d4.10																								
1982	Tex A	150	557	69	147	20	5	11	50	30-4	3	78	.264	.305	.377	91	-9	3-7	.981	6	104	147	*O-149(0-147-3)	-0.6
1983	Tex A	162	634	79	175	28	6	18	80	41-9	2	82	.276	.321	.424	106	3	8-7	.985	-4	100	58	*O-161(CF)	-0.3
1984	Tex A	101	383	40	93	19	4	9	48	15-2	2	54	.243	.273	.384	78	-13	0-2	.983	-8	86	58	O-80(0-54-26),D-18	-2.5
1985	Tex A	109	363	21	69	13	0	2	18	25-5	0	49	.190	.241	.242	33	-34	4-7	.991	0	98	131	*O-102(0-53-55)/D-4	-3.8
1986	Tex A	49	106	10	23	3	1	2	7	4-1	1	23	.217	.250	.321	53	-7	3-5	.969	1	104	113	O-42(10-8-27)	-0.9
	Mon N	56	117	12	22	5	2	0	5	11-0	1	28	.188	.258	.265	47	-9	1-1	1.000	-2	84	124	O-32(10-21-3)	-1.1
Total	5	627	2160	231	529	88	18	42	208	126-21	9	314	.245	.288	.361	78	-69	19-29	.984	-7	98	100	O-566(20-444-114)/D-22	-9.2
WRIGHT, JOE Joseph S. B 1873 Pittsburgh, PA BL/TL 5-8/175# d7.14																								
1895	Lou N	60	228	30	63	10	4	1	30	12	1	28	.276	.315	.368	81	-7	7	.963	-1	49	47	O-60(0-43-17)	-0.9

Year	Tm Lg	G	AB	R	H	2B	3B	HR	RBI	BB-IB	HP	SO	AVG	OBP	SLG	AOPS	ABR	SB-CS	FA	FR	Rng	Thr	G at Pos	BFW
1896	Lou N	2	7	0	2	0	0	0	0	0	0	1	.286	.286	.286	53	-1	0	1.000	-0	0	0	/O-2(RF)	-0.1
	Pit N	15	52	5	16	2	1	0	6	1	0	2	.308	.321	.385	89	-1	1	.958	-2	0	0	O-12(CF)/3	-0.3
	Year	17	59	5	18	2	1	0	6	1	0	3	.305	.317	.373	85	-2	1	.962	-2	0	0	O-14(0-12-2)/3	-0.4
Total	2	77	287	35	81	12	5	1	36	13	1	31	.282	.316	.369	82	-9	8	.963	-3	40	38	/O-74(0-55-19),3	-1.3
WRIGHT, PAT Patrick Francis B 7.5.1865 Pottsville, PA D 5.29.1943 Springfield, IL BB/TR 6-2/190# d7.11																								
1890	Chi N	1	2	0	0	0	0	0	0	1	0	0	.000	.333	.000	-1	0	0	1.000	0	122	0	/2	0.0
WRIGHT, RON Ronald Wade B 1.21.1976 Delta, UT BR/TR 6-1/230# d4.14																								
2002	Sea A	1	3	0	0	0	0	0	0	0-0	0	1	.000	.000	.000	-99	-1	0-0	—	0			/D	-0.1
WRIGHT, SAM Samuel B 11.25.1848 New York, NY D 5.6.1928 Boston, MA BR/TR 5-7.5/146# d4.21 b-George b-Harry																								
1875	NH NA	33	127	10	24	4	0	0	5	1		1	.189	.195	.220	51	-5	1-0	.807	11	138	76	S-33	0.5
1876	Bos N	2	8	0	1	0	0	0	0	0		0	.125	.125	.125	-16	-1		.778	-0	111	0	/S-2	-0.1
1880	Cin N	9	34	0	3	0	0	0	0	0		5	.088	.088	.088	-40	-5		.889	-1	105	0	/S-9	-0.5
1881	Bos N	1	4	0	1	0	0	0	0	0		0	.250	.250	.250	60	0		.667	-1	80	0	/S	-0.1
Total	3	12	46	0	5	0	0	0	0	0		5	.109	.109	.109	-27	-6		.843	-2	103	0	/S-12	-0.7
WRIGHT, TAFFY Taft Shedron B 8.10.1911 Tabor City, NC D 10.22.1981 Orlando, FL BL/TR 5-10/180# d4.18 Mil 1943-45																								
1938	Was A	100	263	37	92	18	10	2	36	13	4	17	.350	.389	.517	134	12	1-2	.982	-2	97	63	O-60(14-1-45)	0.7
1939	Was A	129	499	77	154	29	11	4	93	38	1	19	.309	.359	.435	110	6	1-2	.950	-0	98	115	*O-123(39-0-84)	-0.1
1940	Chi A	147	581	79	196	31	9	5	88	43	2	25	.337	.385	.448	114	12	4-7	.963	-6	92	90	*O-144(RF)	-0.4
1941	Chi A	136	513	71	165	35	5	10	97	60	6	27	.322	.399	.468	130	24	5-4	.973	-6	97	59	*O-134(RF)	0.9
1942	Chi A	85	300	43	100	13	5	0	47	48	4	9	.333	.432	.410	141	19	1-8	.968	-2	98	89	O-81(81-0-1)	1.1
1946	Chi A	115	422	46	116	19	4	7	52	42	1	17	.275	.342	.389	108	4	10-3	.991	-5	98	51	*O-107(8-0-99)	-0.4
1947	Chi A	124	401	48	130	13	0	4	54	48	1	17	.324	.398	.387	123	14	8-6	.971	-5	92	81	*O-100(35-0-66)	0.4
1948	Chi A	134	455	50	127	15	6	4	61	38	5	18	.279	.341	.365	91	-7	2-1	.987	-1	95	107	*O-114(6-0-108)	-1.2
1949	Phi A	59	149	14	35	2	5	2	25	16	3	6	.235	.321	.356	82	-5	0-0	.970	-0	90	157	O-35(RF)	-0.6
Total	9	1029	3583	465	1115	175	55	38	553	346	27	155	.311	.376	.423	116	79	32-33	.972	-27	95	86	O-898(183-1-716)	0.4
WRIGHT, TOM Thomas Everette B 9.22.1923 Shelby, NC BL/TR 5-11.5/180# d9.15																								
1948	Bos A	3	2	1	1	0	1	0	0	0	0	0	.500	.500	1.500	400	1	0-0	—	0			H	0.1
1949	Bos A	5	4	1	1	1	0	0	1	1	0	1	.250	.400	.500	128	0	0-0	—	0			H	0.0
1950	Bos A	54	107	17	34	7	0	0	20	6	1	18	.318	.360	.383	82	-3	0-0	.953	-1	97	60	O-24(5-0-19)	-0.4
1951	Bos A	28	63	8	14	1	1	1	9	11	1	8	.222	.347	.317	73	-2	0-0	.950	-2	74	0	O-18(1-0-17)	-0.5
1952	StL A	29	66	6	16	0	0	1	6	12	0	20	.242	.359	.288	79	-1	1-1	.976	1	106	188	O-18(LF)	-0.2
	Chi A	60	132	15	34	10	2	1	21	16	1	16	.258	.342	.386	102	1	1-0	.969	-0	99	95	O-34(22-0-13)	-0.1
	Year	89	198	21	50	10	2	2	27	28	1	36	.253	.348	.354	94	-1	2-1	.971	1	101	128	O-52(40-0-13)	-0.3
1953	Chi A	77	132	14	33	5	3	2	25	12	2	21	.250	.322	.379	86	-3	0-0	.978	-2	90	46	O-33(10-0-24)	-0.6
1954	Was A	76	171	13	42	4	4	1	17	18	2	38	.246	.323	.333	85	-4	0-0	1.000	-1	104	0	O-43(15-0-28)	-0.7
1955	Was A	7	7	0	0	0	0	0	0	0-0	0	1	.000	.000	.000	-99	-2	0-0	—	0			H	-0.2
1956	Was A	2	1	0	0	0	0	0	0	0-0	0	0	.000	.000	.000	-99	0	0-0	—	0			H	0.0
Total	9	341	685	75	175	28	11	6	99	76-0	7	123	.255	.336	.355	85	-13	2-1	.977	-6	97	58	O-170(71-0-101)	-2.6
WRIGHT, DICK Willard James B 5.5.1890 Worcester, NY D 1.24.1952 Bethlehem, PA BR/TR 5-10/170# d6.30																								
1915	Bro F	4	5	0	0	0	0	0	0	0	0	0	.000	.000	.000	-99	-1	0	.833	-1	*113*	*0*	/C-3	-0.2
WRIGHT, HARRY William Henry B 1.10.1835 Sheffield, England D 10.3.1895 Atlantic City, NJ BR/TR 5-9.5/157# d5.5 M23 HF1953 b-George b-Sam ▲																								
1871	Bos NA	**31**	147	42	44	5	2	0	26	13		2	.299	.356	.361	103	1	7-1	.855	-1	146	166	*O-30(CF)/P-9,SM	0.0
1872	Bos NA	**48**	208	39	53	5	1	0	24	9		2	.255	.286	.288	73	-7	0-0	.866	-5	78	121	*O-48(CF)/P-7,M	-0.8
1873	Bos NA	58	263	57	68	7	3	2	36	11		4	.259	.288	.331	77	-9	3-2	.819	-6	104	71	*O-58(CF),P-14,M	-1.1
1874	Bos NA	40	184	44	58	4	2	2	27	4		3	.315	.330	.391	123	4	1-0	.827	-1	103	**367**	*O-40(CF)/P-6,M	0.2
1875	Bos NA	1	4	1	1	0	0	0	0	0		1	.250	.250	.250	72	0	0-0	1.000	-0	0	0	/O(RF)M	0.0
1876	Bos N	1	3	0	0	0	0	0	0	0		1	.000	.000	.000	-98	-1		—	0	0	0	/O(RF)M	-0.1
1877	Bos N	1	4	0	0	0	0	0	0	0		1	.000	.000	.000	-97	-1		.667	0	398	2718	/O(CF)M	0.0
Total	5 NA	178	806	183	224	21	8	4	113	37		12	.278	.310	.339	91	-11	11-3	.000	-13	103	162	O-177(0-176-1)/P-36,S	-1.7
Total	2	2	7	0	0	0	0	0	0	0		2	.000	.000	.000	-97	-2		.667	0	367	2509	/O-2(0-1-1)	-0.1
WRIGHT, BILL William Hiram d9.16																								
1887	Was N	1	3	0	2	0	0	0	0	0	0	0	.667	.667	.667	290	1	0	.778	-1			/C	0.0
WRIGHT, RASTY William Smith B 1.31.1863 Birmingham, MI D 10.14.1922 Duluth, MN BL 6-1/185# d4.17																								
1890	Syr AA	88	348	82	106	10	6	0	27	69	6		.305	.428	.368	150	30	30	.907	2	102	187	O-88(0-70-18)	2.5
	Cle N	13	45	7	5	1	0	0	2	12	0	4	.111	.298	.133	27	-3	3	.917	-1	46	0	O-13(RF)	-0.4
Total	1	101	393	89	111	11	6	0	29	81	6	4	.282	.412	.341	135	27	33	.908	1	95	164	O-101(0-70-31)	2.1
WRIGHTSTONE, RUSS Russell Guy B 3.18.1893 Bowmansdale, PA D 2.25.1969 Harrisburg, PA BL/TR 5-10.5/176# d4.19 OF Total (85-LF 33-RF)																								
1920	Phi N	76	206	23	54	6	1	3	17	10	2	25	.262	.303	.345	82	-5	3-2	.934	3	106	71	3-56/S-2,2	0.0
1921	Phi N	109	372	59	110	13	4	9	51	18	2	20	.296	.332	.425	92	-5	4-4	.922	5	111	60	3-54,O-37(34-0-3)/2-4	0.0
1922	Phi N	99	331	56	101	18	6	5	33	28	3	17	.305	.365	.441	98	-1	4-5	.973	10	120	66	3-40,S-35/1-2	1.3
1923	Phi N	119	392	59	107	21	7	7	57	21	3	19	.273	.315	.416	82	-11	5-2	.942	-0	96	81	3-72,S-21/2-9	-0.4
1924	Phi N	118	388	55	119	24	4	7	58	27	7	15	.307	.363	.443	102	2	5-4	.944	-9	91	108	3-97/2-9,S-5,O(RF)	0.0
1925	Phi N	92	286	48	99	18	5	14	61	19	1	18	.346	.389	.591	135	14	0-3	.937	-10	94	53	O-45(37-0-10),S-12,3-11,2-10/1-6	0.1
1926	Phi N	112	368	55	113	23	1	7	57	27	1	11	.307	.356	.432	106	3	5	.977	2	104	103	1-53,3-37,2-13/O-5(LF)	0.4
1927	Phi N	141	533	62	163	24	5	6	75	48	2	20	.306	.365	.403	104	4	9	.989	2	107	94	*1-136/23	-0.3
1928	Phi N	33	91	7	19	5	1	1	11	14	1	5	.209	.321	.319	65	-4	0	.936	-2	91	48	O-26(9-0-19)/1-4	-0.8
	NY N	30	25	3	4	0	0	1	5	3	0	2	.160	.250	.280	38	-2	0	1.000	-0	0	0	/1-2	-0.2
	Year	63	116	10	23	5	1	2	16	17	1	7	.198	.306	.310	60	-7	0	.936	-2	91	48	O-26(9-0-19)/1-6	-1.0
Total	9	929	2992	427	889	152	34	60	425	215	22	152	.297	.349	.431	99	-5	35-20	.942	3	103	87	3-368,1-203,O-114L/S-75,2-47	0.1
WRIGLEY, ZEKE George Watson B 1.18.1874 Philadelphia, PA D 9.28.1952 Philadelphia, PA 5-8.5/150# d8.31																								
1896	Was N	5	9	1	1	0	0	0	2	1	0	1	.111	.200	.111	-17	-2	0	.909	2	172	0	/2-3,S	0.1
1897	Was N	104	388	65	110	14	8	3	64	21	0		.284	.320	.384	86	-10	5	.885	4	231	455	O-36(4-13-19),S-33,3-30/2-9	-0.5
1898	Was N	111	400	50	98	9	10	2	39	20	1		.245	.283	.333	76	-15	10	.895	11	102	94	S-97,2-11/O-3(0-2-1),3	0.1
1899	NY N	4	15	1	3	0	0	0	1	1	0		.200	.250	.200	25	-2	1	.818	-1	103	0	/3-4	-0.2
	Bro N	15	49	4	10	2	2	0	11	3	0		.204	.250	.327	56	-3	2	.870	-4	78	84	S-14/3	-0.6
	Year	19	64	5	13	2	2	0	12	4	0		.203	.250	.297	49	-5	3	.870	-5	78	84	S-14/3-5	-0.8
Total	4	239	861	121	222	25	20	5	117	46	1	1	.258	.296	.351	78	-32	18	.892	12	101	85	S-145/O-39(4-15-20),3-36,2-23	-1.1
WRONA, RICK Richard James B 12.10.1963 Tulsa, OK BR/TR 6-1/185# d9.3																								
1988	Chi N	4	6	0	0	0	0	0	0	0-0	0	1	.000	.000	.000	-96	-2	0-0	1.000	1	135	181	/C-2	-0.1
1989	†Chi N	38	92	11	26	2	1	2	14	2-1	1	21	.283	.299	.391	91	-1	0-0	.983	1	163	60	C-37	0.2
1990	Chi N	16	29	3	5	0	0	0	0	2-1	0	11	.172	.226	.172	10	-4	1-0	.970	2	221	109	C-16	-0.1
1992	Cin N	11	23	0	4	0	0	0	0	0-0	0	3	.174	.174	.174	-1	-3	0-0	.965	2	259	82	C-10/1	-0.1
1993	Chi A	4	8	0	1	0	0	0	1	0-0	0	4	.125	.125	.125	-33	-2	0-0	1.000	-2	48	0	/C-4	-0.3
1994	Mil A	6	10	2	5	4	0	1	3	1-0	0	1	.500	.545	1.200	319	3	0-0	.923	-1	216	0	/C-5,1	0.2
Total	6	79	168	16	41	6	1	3	18	5-2	1	41	.244	.267	.345	68	-9	1-0	.976	3	182	69	/C-74,1-2	-0.2
WUESTLING, YATS George B 10.18.1903 St.Louis, MO D 4.26.1970 St.Louis, MO BR/TR 5-11/167# d6.15																								
1929	Det A	54	150	13	30	4	1	0	16	9	1	24	.200	.250	.240	27	-17	1-3	.943	-4	104	62	S-52/23	-1.6
1930	Det A	4	9	0	0	0	0	0	0	2	0	3	.000	.182	.000	-48	-2	0-0	.842	-0	105	101	/S-4	-0.2
	NY A	25	58	5	11	0	1	0	3	4	0	14	.190	.242	.224	20	-7	0-1	.918	1	104	100	S-21/3-3	-0.4
	Year	29	67	5	11	0	1	0	3	6	0	17	.164	.233	.194	10	-10	0-1	.904	1	104	100	S-25/3-3	-0.6
Total	2	83	217	18	41	4	2	0	19	15	1	41	.189	.245	.226	21	-26	1-4	.931	-3	104	73	/S-77,3-4,2	-2.2
WYATT, JOE Loral John B 4.6.1900 Petersburg, IN D 12.5.1970 Oblong, IL BR/TR 6-1/175# d9.11																								
1924	Cle A	4	12	1	2	0	0	0	1	2	0	1	.167	.286	.167	18	-1	0-0	.833	-1	83	0	/O-4(RF)	-0.2

Year	Tm Lg	G	AB	R	H	2B	3B	HR	RBI	BB-IB	HP	SO	AVG	OBP	SLG	AOPS	ABR	SB-CS	FA	FR	Rng	Thr	G at Pos	BFW
WYLIE, REN James Renwick B 12.14.1861 Elizabeth, PA D 8.17.1951 Wilkinsburg, PA BR/TR 5-11/155# d8.11																								
1882	Pit AA	1	3	0	0	0	0	0		0			.000	.000	.000	-99	-1		1.000	1	745	0	/O(CF)	0.0
WYMAN, FRANK Frank H. B 5.10.1862 Haverhill, MA D 2.4.1916 Everett, MA d6.10 ▲																								
1884	KC U	30	124	16	27	4	0	0		3			.218	.236	.250	55	-10		.743	2	157	230	O-25(13-11-0)/P-3,1-3,3-3	-0.7
	CP U	2	8	1	3	0	0	0		0			.375	.375	.375	129	0		.846	-0	155	0	/1-2	-0.1
	Year	32	132	17	30	4	0	0		3			.227	.244	.258	60	-10		.743	2	157	230	O-25(13-11-0)/1-5,P-3,3-3	-0.8
WYNEGAR, BUTCH Harold Delano B 3.14.1956 York, PA BB/TR 6/194# d4.9 C1																								
1976	Min A★	149	534	58	139	21	2	10	69	79-7	2	63	.260	.356	.363	109	9	0-0	.978	-7	101	106	*C-137,D-15	0.8
1977	Min A★	144	532	76	139	22	3	10	79	68-5	2	61	.261	.344	.370	97	0	2-3	.993	-6	111	104	*C-142/3	-0.1
1978	Min A	135	454	36	104	22	1	4	45	47-2	6	42	.229	.307	.308	73	-15	1-0	.988	2	114	115	*C-131/3	-0.7
1979	Min A	149	504	74	136	20	0	7	57	74-5	2	36	.270	.363	.351	91	-3	2-2	.992	6	167	122	*C-146/D-2	0.8
1980	Min A	146	486	61	124	18	3	5	57	63-6	2	36	.255	.339	.335	81	-11	3-1	.988	14	146	105	*C-142/D	0.9
1981	Min A	47	150	11	37	5	0	0	10	17-2	1	9	.247	.322	.280	72	-5	0-1	.995	-0	75	145	C-37/D-9	-0.4
1982	Min A	24	86	9	18	4	0	1	8	10-1	0	12	.209	.292	.291	59	-5	0-0	.986	-2	75	71	C-24	-0.6
	NY A	63	191	27	56	8	1	3	20	40-1	1	21	.293	.413	.393	126	10	0-1	.993	1	105	89	C-62	1.3
	Year	87	277	36	74	12	1	4	28	50-2	1	33	.267	.378	.361	106	5	0-1	.991	-1	97	84	C-86	0.7
1983	NY A	94	301	40	89	18	2	6	42	52-1	1	29	.296	.399	.429	133	17	1-1	.985	-9	102	128	C-93	1.2
1984	NY A	129	442	48	118	13	1	6	45	65-6	0	35	.267	.360	.342	99	2	1-4	.993	-1	101	103	*C-126	0.5
1985	NY A	102	309	27	69	15	0	5	32	64-2	0	43	.223	.356	.320	89	-1	0-0	.990	2	109	111	C-96	0.5
1986	NY A	61	194	19	40	4	1	7	29	30-2	0	21	.206	.310	.345	80	-5	0-0	.994	2	98	84	C-57	-0.1
1987	Cal A	31	92	4	19	2	0	0	5	9-0	0	13	.207	.277	.228	37	-8	0-0	.994	4	107	110	C-28/D	-0.3
1988	Cal A	27	55	8	14	4	1	1	8	8-1	0	7	.255	.338	.418	117	1	0-0	.981	2	123	162	C-26	0.4
Total	13	1301	4330	498	1102	176	15	65	506	626-41	17	428	.255	.348	.347	93	-14	10-13	.989	7	116	110	*C-1247/D-28,3-2	4.2
WYNN, JIMMY James Sherman "The Toy Cannon" B 3.12.1942 Hamilton, OH BR/TR 5-9/170# d7.10 OF Total (298-LF 1181-CF 355-RF)																								
1963	Hou N	70	250	31	61	10	5	4	27	30-4	0	53	.244	.319	.372	107	2	4-2	.963	-3	100	146	O-53(43-10-0),S-21/3-2	-0.3
1964	Hou N	67	219	19	49	7	0	5	18	24-2	1	58	.224	.301	.324	81	-5	5-5	.958	2	100	205	O-64(13-51-0)	-0.6
1965	Hou N	157	564	90	155	30	7	22	73	84-3	5	126	.275	.371	.470	146	37	43-4	.978	10	**112**	148	*O-155(CF)	5.2
1966	Hou N	105	418	62	107	21	1	18	62	41-4	1	81	.256	.321	.440	118	10	13-10	.978	4	110	84	*O-104(CF)	1.0
1967	Hou N★	158	594	102	148	29	3	37	107	74-7	2	137	.249	.331	.495	139	29	16-4	.968	0	107	47	*O-157(CF)	2.9
1968	Hou N	156	542	85	146	23	5	26	67	90-9	5	131	.269	.376	.474	158	42	11-17	.988	9	98	**208**	*O-153(56-93-7)	4.6
1969	Hou N	149	495	113	133	17	1	33	87	**148**-14	3	142	.269	.436	.507	168	55	23-7	.985	3	106	109	*O-149(CF)	5.9
1970	Hou N	157	554	82	156	32	2	27	88	106-12	1	96	.282	.394	.493	143	38	24-5	.987	3	98	149	*O-151(66-87-0)	3.8
1971	Hou N	123	404	38	82	16	0	7	45	56-6	2	63	.203	.302	.295	72	-14	10-5	.988	2	96	118	*O-116(1-48-72)	-1.7
1972	Hou N	145	542	117	148	29	3	24	90	103-6	2	99	.273	.389	.470	147	38	17-7	.983	-1	102	75	*O-144(0-12-132)	3.3
1973	Hou N	139	481	90	106	14	5	20	55	91-9	4	102	.220	.347	.395	106	6	14-11	.986	2	108	79	*O-133(2-10-125)	0.1
1974	†LA N★	150	535	104	145	17	4	32	108	108-4	0	104	.271	.387	.497	154	42	18-15	.992	0	101	113	*O-148(CF)	3.8
1975	LA N★	130	412	80	102	16	0	18	58	110-2	1	77	.248	.403	.417	135	26	7-3	.983	-3	99	79	*O-120(21-107-0)	2.1
1976	Atl N	148	449	75	93	19	1	17	66	**127**-1	0	111	.207	.377	.367	107	11	16-6	.971	7	99	**196**	*O-138(90-50-0)	1.4
1977	NY A	30	77	7	11	2	1	1	3	15-1	0	16	.143	.283	.234	43	-6	1-0	1.000	1	121	157	D-15/O-8(5-0-3)	-0.5
	Mil A	36	117	10	23	3	1	0	10	17-0	0	31	.197	.294	.239	49	-8	3-0	.967	-2	91	0	O-17(1-0-16),D-15	-1.0
	Year	66	194	17	34	5	2	1	13	32-1	0	47	.175	.289	.237	46	-14	4-0	.981	-0	102	55	D-30,O-25(6-0-19)	-1.5
Total	15	1920	6653	1105	1665	285	39	291	964	1224-84	27	1427	.250	.366	.436	129	303	225-101	.981	36	103	121	*O-1810C/D-30,S-21,3-2	30.0
WYNNE, MARVELL Marvell B 12.17.1959 Chicago, IL BL/TL 5-11/185# d6.15																								
1983	Pit N	103	366	66	89	16	2	7	26	38-0	3	52	.243	.319	.355	85	-7	12-10	.983	-5	93	66	*O-102(CF)	-1.5
1984	Pit N	154	653	77	174	24	11	0	39	42-0	0	81	.266	.310	.337	82	-17	24-19	.990	-7	93	91	*O-154(CF)	-2.9
1985	Pit N	103	337	21	69	6	3	2	18	18-2	1	48	.205	.247	.258	42	-27	10-5	.987	3	107	132	O-99(CF)	-2.7
1986	SD N	137	288	34	76	19	2	7	37	15-2	1	45	.264	.300	.417	98	-2	11-11	.986	2	113	67	*O-125(CF)	-0.2
1987	SD N	98	188	17	47	8	2	2	24	20-1	0	37	.250	.321	.346	80	-5	11-6	.981	-1	100	71	O-71(33-40-5)	-0.7
1988	SD N	128	333	37	88	13	4	11	42	31-2	0	62	.264	.325	.426	117	6	3-4	.987	4	105	124	*O-113(37-84-10)	0.9
1989	SD N	105	294	19	74	11	1	6	35	12-1	1	41	.252	.282	.357	82	-8	4-1	.971	0	92	169	O-96(39-41-25)	-1.0
	†Chi N	20	48	8	9	2	1	1	4	1-1	1	7	.188	.220	.333	52	-3	2-0	.944	-3	64	0	O-13(4-6-3)	-0.6
	Year	125	342	27	83	13	2	7	39	13-2	2	48	.243	.274	.354	77	-11	6-1	.968	-3	88	147	O-109(43-47-28)	-1.6
1990	Chi N	92	186	21	38	8	2	4	19	14-3	1	25	.204	.264	.333	59	-11	3-2	.991	-0	97	116	O-66(13-54-4)	-1.2
Total	8	940	2693	300	664	107	28	40	244	191-12	8	398	.247	.297	.352	81	-74	80-58	.985	-7	99	102	O-839(126-706-47)	-9.9
WYROSTEK, JOHNNY John Barney B 7.12.1919 Fairmont City, IL D 12.12.1986 St.Louis, MO BL/TR 6-2/180# d9.10 Mil 1944-45																								
1942	Pit N	9	35	0	4	0	1	0	3	3	0	2	.114	.184	.171	4	-4	0	1.000	1	100	177	/O-8(LF)	-0.5
1943	Pit N	51	79	7	12	3	0	0	1	3	0	15	.152	.183	.190	7	-10	0	.919	-2	112	0	O-20(5-6-9)/3-2,12	-1.3
1946	Phi N	145	545	73	153	30	4	6	45	70	3	42	.281	.366	.383	116	13	7	.981	5	102	135	*O-142(6-138-0)	1.5
1947	Phi N	128	454	68	124	24	7	5	51	61	4	45	.273	.364	.390	104	4	7	.971	0	100	109	*O-126(0-27-100)	0.0
1948	Cin N	136	512	74	140	24	9	17	76	52	3	63	.273	.344	.455	119	12	7	.977	-5	96	85	*O-130(CF)	0.3
1949	Cin N	134	474	54	118	20	4	9	46	58	2	63	.249	.333	.365	86	-9	7	.971	-2	99	95	*O-129(2-60-67)	-1.5
1950	Cin N★	131	509	70	145	34	5	8	76	52	5	38	.285	.357	.418	103	3	1	.980	1	106	89	*O-129(11-9-115)/1-4	0.0
1951	Cin N★	142	537	52	167	31	3	2	61	54	2	54	.311	.376	.391	105	6	2-1	.970	-9	93	62	*O-139(1-0-139)	-0.7
1952	Cin N	30	106	12	25	1	3	1	10	18	0	7	.236	.347	.330	89	-1	1-2	1.000	1	93	203	O-29(0-25-6)/1	-0.2
	Phi N	98	321	45	88	16	3	1	37	44	1	26	.274	.363	.352	100	2	1-7	.972	5	115	116	O-88(2-1-87)	0.2
	Year	128	427	57	113	17	6	2	47	62	1	33	.265	.359	.347	97	1	2-9	.980	7	**110**	138	*O-117(2-26-93)/1	0.0
1953	Phi N	125	409	42	111	14	2	6	47	38	4	43	.271	.339	.359	83	-10	0-3	.962	1	97	141	*O-110(8-0-102)	-1.3
1954	Phi N	92	259	28	62	12	4	3	28	29	1	39	.239	.314	.351	74	-10	0-0	.990	-1	105	129	O-55(6-0-49),1-22	-1.4
Total	11	1221	4240	525	1149	209	45	58	481	482	25	437	.271	.349	.383	98	-4	33-13	.975	-5	101	106	*O-1105(49-396-674)/1-28,3-2,2	-4.9
YAIK, HENRY Henry B 3.1.1864 Detroit, MI D 9.21.1935 Detroit, MI BL 5-11/185# d10.3																								
1888	Pit N	2	6	0	2	0	0	0	1	1	0	0	.333	.429	.333	159	1	0	.625	0	436	1104	/O(LF)C	0.1
YALE, AD William M. B 4.17.1870 Bristol, CT D 4.27.1948 Bridgeport, CT BR d9.18																								
1905	Bro N	4	13	1	1	0	0	0	1	1	0		.077	.143	.077	-37	-2	0	1.000	-0	43	190	/1-4	-0.3
YANCY, HUGH Hugh B 10.16.1949 Sarasota, FL BR/TR 5-11/170# d7.5																								
1972	Chi A	3	9	0	1	0	0	0	0	0-0	0	0	.111	.111	.111	-33	-1	0-1	1.000	1	122	0	/3-3	-0.2
1974	Chi A	1	0	0	0	0	0	0	0	0-0	0	0	—	—	—	—	0	0-0	—	0			/D	0.0
1976	Chi A	3	10	0	1	1	0	0	0	0-0	0	3	.100	.100	.200	-14	-1	0-0	1.000	-1	50	157	/2-3	-0.2
Total	3	7	19	0	2	1	0	0	0	0-0	0	3	.105	.105	.158	-23	-2	0-1	1.000	-0	50	157	/2-3,3-3,D	-0.4
YANKOWSKI, GEORGE George Edward B 11.19.1922 Cambridge, MA BR/TR 6/180# d8.17 Mil 1943-46																								
1942	Phi A	6	13	0	2	1	0	0	2	0	0	2	.154	.154	.231	7	-2	0-0	1.000	0	*75*	*191*	/C-6	-0.1
1949	Chi A	12	18	0	3	1	0	0	2	0	0	2	.167	.167	.222	3	-3	0-0	1.000	1	*96*	*131*	/C-6	-0.2
Total	2	18	31	0	5	2	0	0	4	0	0	4	.161	.161	.226	5	-5	0-0	1.000	1	*86*	*160*	/C-12	-0.3
YANTZ, GEORGE George Webb B 7.27.1886 Louisville, KY D 2.26.1967 Louisville, KY BR/TR 5-6.5/168# d9.30																								
1912	Chi N	1	1	0	1	0	0	0	0	0	0	0	1.000	1.000	1.000	450	0	0	—	0	*0*	*0*	/C	0.0
YARYAN, YAM Clarence Everett B 11.5.1892 Knowlton, IA D 11.16.1964 Birmingham, AL BR/TR 5-10.5/180# d4.23																								
1921	Chi A	45	102	11	31	8	2	0	15	9	1	16	.304	.366	.422	102	0	0-0	.933	-5	*77*	*125*	C-34	-0.2
1922	Chi A	36	71	9	14	2	0	2	9	6	1	10	.197	.269	.310	51	-5	1-0	.966	0	*115*	*84*	C-26	-0.4
Total	2	81	173	20	45	10	2	2	24	15	2	26	.260	.326	.376	81	-5	1-0	.948	-5	*93*	*108*	/C-60	-0.6
YASTRZEMSKI, CARL Carl Michael "Yaz" B 8.22.1939 Southampton, NY BL/TR 5-11/182# d4.11 HF1989 OF Total (1917-LF 159-CF 7-RF)																								
1961	Bos A	148	583	71	155	31	6	11	80	50-3	3	96	.266	.324	.396	90	-9	6-5	.963	-5	89	113	*O-147(LF)	-2.2
1962	Bos A	**160**	646	99	191	43	6	19	94	66-7	3	82	.296	.363	.469	118	18	7-4	.969	8	101	162	*O-160(LF)	1.7
1963	Bos A★	151	570	91	**183**	**40**	3	14	68	**95**-6	1	72	**.321**	**.418**	.475	145	**41**	8-5	.980	9	98	**173**	*O-151(151-1-0)	**4.2**
1964	Bos A	151	567	77	164	29	9	15	67	75-6	2	90	.289	.374	.451	122	19	6-5	.973	17	116	196	*O-148(18-131-0)/3-2	3.2
1965	Bos A★	133	494	78	154	**45**	3	20	72	70-8	1	58	.312	**.395**	**.536**	**154**	**38**	7-6	.987	3	95	147	*O-130(125-7-1)	3.5
1966	Bos A☆	160	594	81	165	**39**	2	16	80	84-10	1	60	.278	.368	.431	117	17	8-9	.985	9	105	149	*O-158(157-1-0)	1.7

Year	Tm Lg	G	AB	R	H	2B	3B	HR	RBI	BB-IB	HP	SO	AVG	OBP	SLG	AOPS	ABR	SB-CS	FA	FR	Rng	Thr	G at Pos	BFW
1967	†Bos A★	161	579	**112**	**189**	31	4	**44**	**121**	91-11	4	69	**.326**	**.418**	**.622**	**189**	**67**	10-8	.978	6	102	120	*O-161(161-1-0)	**6.9**
1968	Bos A★	157	539	90	162	32	2	23	74	**119**-13	2	90	**.301**	**.426**	.495	168	**53**	13-6	.991	11	112	124	*O-155(154-1-0)/1-3	**6.2**
1969	Bos A★	**162**	603	96	154	28	2	40	111	101-9	1	91	.255	.362	.507	134	28	15-7	.985	6	90	154	*O-143(140-3-0),1-22	2.7
1970	Bos A★	161	566	**125**	186	29	0	40	102	128-12	1	66	.329	**.452**	**.592**	**174**	**64**	23-13	.990	1	104	83	1-94,O-69(67-3-0)	5.5
1971	Bos A★	148	508	75	129	21	2	15	70	106-12	1	60	.254	.381	.392	112	13	8-7	.993	11	106	**181**	*O-146(LF)	1.6
1972	Bos A★	125	455	70	120	18	2	12	68	67-3	4	44	.264	.357	.391	118	13	5-4	.974	6	95	163	O-83(LF),1-42	1.1
1973	Bos A✳	152	540	82	160	25	4	19	95	105-13	0	58	.296	.407	.463	138	32	9-7	.994	-4	94	100	*1-107,3-31,O-14(LF)	1.8
1974	Bos A★	148	515	**93**	155	25	2	15	79	104-16	3	48	.301	.414	.445	139	33	12-7	.997	-8	90	96	1-84,O-63(LF)/D-4	1.5
1975	†Bos A★	149	543	91	146	30	1	14	60	87-12	2	67	.269	.371	.405	110	11	8-4	.996	-1	94	93	*1-140/O-8(LF),D-2	-0.1
1976	Bos A★	155	546	71	146	23	2	21	102	80-6	1	67	.267	.357	.432	118	14	5-6	.998	-9	76	105	1-94,O-51(LF),D-10	-0.7
1977	Bos A★	150	558	99	165	27	3	28	102	73-6	1	40	.296	.372	.505	124	20	11-1	**1.000**	11	103	**159**	*O-140(138-0-2)/1-7,D-6	2.5
1978	Bos A✳	144	523	70	145	21	2	17	81	76-8	3	44	.277	.367	.423	111	10	4-5	.986	2	86	166	O-71(63-8-0),1-50,D-27	0.5
1979	Bos A★	147	518	69	140	28	1	21	87	62-8	2	46	.270	.346	.450	108	7	3-3	.996	4	142	94	D-56,1-51,O-36(LF)	0.3
1980	Bos A	105	364	49	100	21	1	15	50	44-5	0	38	.275	.350	.462	115	8	0-2	1.000	-2	83	111	D-49,O-39(34-1-4),1-16	0.1
1981	Bos A	91	338	36	83	14	1	7	53	49-4	0	28	.246	.338	.355	95	-1	0-1	.992	3	136	77	D-48,1-39	-0.1
1982	Bos A★	131	459	53	126	22	1	16	72	59-1	2	50	.275	.358	.431	110	8	0-1	1.000	1	130	116	*D-102,1-14/O-2(CF)	0.4
1983	Bos A★	119	380	38	101	24	0	10	56	54-11	2	29	.266	.359	.408	103	4	0-0	1.000	-1	80	56	*D-107/1-2,O(LF)	0.0
Total	23	3308	11988	1816	3419	646	59	452	1844	1845-190	40	1393	.285	.379	.462	128	508	168-116	.981	78	99	142	*O-2076L,1-765,D-411/3-33	42.3
YATES, AL Albert Arthur B 5.26.1945 Jersey City, NJ BR/TR 6-2/210# d5.13																								
1971	Mil A	24	47	5	13	2	0	1	4	3-0	0	7	.277	.308	.383	100	0	1-0	1.000	1	104	317	O-12(3-0-9)	0.1
YEABSLEY, BERT Robert Watkins B 12.17.1893 Philadelphia, PA D 2.8.1961 Philadelphia, PA BR/TR 5-9.5/175# d5.28																								
1919	Phi N	3	0	0	0	0	0	0	0	1	0	0	—	1.000	—	200	0	0	—	0			H	0.0
YEAGER, GEORGE George J. "Doc" B 6.5.1874 Cincinnati, OH D 7.5.1940 Cincinnati, OH BR/TR 5-10/190# d9.25 OF Total (8-LF 5-CF 13-RF)																								
1896	Bos N	2	5	1	1	0	0	0	0	0	0	1	.200	.200	.200	5	-1	0	1.000	-0	0	411	/1-2	-0.1
1897	†Bos N	30	95	20	23	2	3	2	15	7	0		.242	.294	.389	75	-4	2	.970	1	*153*	*78*	C-13,O-10(2-1-7)/2-4,3	-0.2
1898	Bos N	68	221	37	59	13	1	3	24	16	4		.267	.328	.376	96	-1	1	.951	-2	*117*	*86*	C-37,1-17/O-9(6-3-1),S-2	-0.1
1899	Bos N	3	8	1	1	0	0	0	0	1	0		.125	.222	.125	-3	-1	0	1.000	0	0	0	/O-2(0-1-1),C	-0.1
1901	Cle A	39	139	13	31	5	0	0	14	4	1		.223	.250	.259	43	-11	2	.964	0	*97*	*130*	C-25/1-5,O-3(RF),2-2	-0.7
	Pit N	26	91	9	24	2	1	0	10	4	1		.264	.302	.308	75	-3	1	.971	0	*128*	*92*	C-20/3-4,1	-0.1
1902	NY N	39	108	6	22	2	1	0	9	11	0		.204	.277	.241	61	-5	1	.946	-1	*96*	*100*	C-27/1-3,O(RF)	-0.3
	Bal A	11	38	3	7	1	0	0	1	2	0		.184	.225	.211	20	-4	0	.930	-1	*94*	*124*	C-11	-0.3
Total	6	218	705	90	168	25	6	5	73	45	6	1	.238	.290	.312	69	-30	7	.953	-2	*112*	*100*	C-134/1-28,O-25R,2-6,3-5,S-2	-1.9
YEAGER, JOE Joseph F. "Little Joe" B 8.28.1875 Philadelphia, PA D 7.2.1937 Detroit, MI BR/TR 5-10/160# d4.22 ▲ OF Total (10-LF 1-CF 7-RF)																								
1898	Bro N	43	134	12	23	5	1	0	15	7	1		.172	.218	.224	27	-13	1	.908	5	137	125	P-36/O-4(2-1-1),S-2,2	0.1
1899	Bro N	23	47	12	9	0	1	0	4	6	4		.191	.333	.234	55	-3	0	.914	3	117	232	S-11,P-10/O(LF)3	0.1
1900	Bro N	3	9	0	3	0	0	0	0	0	0		.333	.333	.333	79	0	0	1.000	-1	70	0	/P-2,3	0.0
1901	Det A	41	125	18	37	7	1	2	17	4	5		.296	.343	.416	105	1	3	.919	5	115	**209**	P-26,S-12/2	0.4
1902	Det A	50	161	17	39	6	5	1	23	5	4		.242	.282	.360	76	-6	0	.957	1	127	67	P-19,O-13(7-0-6),2-12/S-3,3	-0.4
1903	Det A	109	402	36	103	15	6	0	43	18	9		.256	.303	.323	91	-5	9	.921	-9	86	78	*3-107/PS	-1.1
1905	NY A	115	401	54	107	16	7	0	42	25	13		.267	.330	.342	102	1	8	.923	1	99	78	3-91,S-21	0.6
1906	NY A	57	123	20	37	6	1	0	12	13	9		.301	.407	.366	129	6	3	.905	0	93	133	S-22,2-13/3-3	0.7
1907	StL A	123	436	32	104	21	7	1	44	31	3		.239	.294	.326	98	-1	11	.938	5	104	129	3-91,2-17,S-10	0.7
1908	StL A	10	15	3	5	1	0	0	1	1	3		.333	.474	.400	183	2	2	1.000	0	114	0	/2-4,S	0.2
Total	10	574	1853	204	467	77	29	4	201	110	51		.252	.312	.331	92	-18	37	.927	10	96	93	3-295/P-94,S-83,2-48,O-18L	1.3
YEAGER, STEVE Stephen Wayne B 11.24.1948 Huntington, WV BR/TR 6/190# d8.2																								
1972	LA N	35	106	18	29	0	1	4	15	16-2	1	26	.274	.374	.406	124	4	0-0	.984	5	86	77	C-35	1.1
1973	LA N	54	134	18	34	5	0	2	10	15-1	3	33	.254	.340	.336	93	-1	1-0	.981	-2	97	71	C-50	-0.1
1974	†LA N	94	316	41	84	16	1	12	41	32-5	2	77	.266	.334	.437	120	8	2-2	.992	9	139	87	C-93	2.1
1975	LA N	135	452	34	103	16	1	12	54	40-7	8	75	.228	.298	.347	83	-11	2-5	.992	13	151	56	*C-135	0.7
1976	LA N	117	359	42	77	11	3	11	35	30-3	7	84	.214	.286	.354	83	-9	3-1	.985	13	**137**	98	*C-115	0.9
1977	†LA N	125	387	53	99	21	2	16	55	43-11	4	84	.256	.334	.444	108	4	1-3	.977	18	**163**	73	*C-123	2.7
1978	†LA N	94	228	19	44	7	0	4	23	36-11	0	41	.193	.301	.276	63	-11	0-0	.988	11	138	132	C-91	0.4
1979	LA N	105	310	33	67	9	2	13	41	29-8	0	68	.216	.282	.384	81	-9	1-0	.984	7	126	105	*C-103	0.2
1980	LA N	96	227	20	48	8	0	2	20	20-6	0	54	.211	.274	.273	55	-14	2-3	.984	1	119	62	C-95	-1.1
1981	†LA N	42	86	5	18	2	0	3	7	6-0	0	14	.209	.261	.337	71	-4	0-0	.994	-0	149	84	C-40	-0.3
1982	LA N	82	196	13	48	5	2	2	18	13-3	1	28	.245	.294	.321	74	-7	0-0	.990	5	144	112	C-76	0.0
1983	†LA N	113	335	31	68	8	3	15	41	23-4	1	57	.203	.256	.379	74	-14	1-1	.985	1	139	114	*C-112	-0.9
1984	LA N	74	197	16	45	4	0	4	29	20-1	0	38	.228	.295	.310	72	-7	1-2	.994	-5	106	87	C-65	-1.1
1985	†LA N	53	121	4	25	4	1	0	9	7-2	0	24	.207	.246	.256	43	-10	0-1	.992	7	135	185	C-48	-0.1
1986	Sea A	50	130	10	27	2	0	2	12	12-0	0	23	.208	.273	.269	48	-10	0-0	1.000	-3	113	104	C-49	-1.0
Total	15	1269	3584	357	816	118	16	102	410	342-64	27	726	.228	.298	.355	83	-91	14-18	.987	79	135	92	*C-1230	3.5
YEATMAN, BILL William Suter B 3.1839 Alexandria, VA D 4.20.1901 York, PA d4.20																								
1872	Nat NA	1	4	0	0	0	0	0	0	0		1	.000	.000	.000	-86	-1	0-0	.000	-0	0	0	/O(RF)	-0.1
YELDING, ERIC Eric Girard B 2.22.1965 Montrose, AL BR/TR 5-11/165# d4.9																								
1989	Hou N	70	90	19	21	2	0	0	9	7-0	1	19	.233	.290	.256	61	-5	11-5	1.000	2	102	87	S-15,2-13/O-8(1-4-3)	-0.1
1990	Hou N	142	511	69	130	9	5	1	28	39-1	0	87	.254	.305	.297	69	-23	64-25	.971	-4	109	106	O-94(11-83-6),S-40,2-10/3-3	-2.0
1991	Hou N	78	276	19	67	11	1	1	20	13-3	0	46	.243	.276	.301	66	-13	11-9	.939	-10	87	88	S-72/O-4(0-3-1)	-2.0
1992	Hou N	9	8	1	2	0	0	0	0	0-0	0	3	.250	.250	.250	44	-1	0-0	—	-1	0	0	/S-2,O-2(2-1-0)	-0.1
1993	Chi N	69	108	14	22	5	1	1	10	11-2	0	22	.204	.277	.296	54	-7	3-2	.984	5	120	106	2-32/3-7,SO(CF)	-0.1
Total	5	368	993	122	242	27	7	3	67	70-6	1	177	.244	.292	.294	66	-49	89-41	.948	-8	89	85	S-130,O-109(14-92-10)/2-55,3-10	-4.3
YELLE, ARCHIE Archie Joseph B 6.11.1892 Saginaw, MI D 5.2.1983 Woodland, CA BR/TR 5-10.5/170# d5.12																								
1917	Det A	25	51	4	7	1	0	0	0	5	0	4	.137	.214	.157	13	-5	2	.975	-2	*85*	*94*	C-24	-0.6
1918	Det A	56	144	7	25	3	0	0	7	9	1	15	.174	.227	.194	28	-13	0	.948	-1	*85*	*142*	C-52	-1.2
1919	Det A	6	4	1	0	0	0	0	0	1	0	0	.000	.200	.000	-42	-1	0	.833	-1	*99*	*125*	/C-6	-0.1
Total	3	87	199	12	32	4	0	0	7	15	1	19	.161	.223	.181	23	-19	2	.952	-4	*85*	*130*	/C-82	-1.9
YERKES, STEVE Stephen Douglas B 5.15.1888 Hatboro, PA D 1.31.1971 Lansdale, PA BR/TR 5-9/165# d9.29																								
1909	Bos A	5	7	0	2	0	0	0	0	0	0		.286	.286	.286	79	0	0	1.000	-0	77	0	/S-2	-0.1
1911	Bos A	142	502	70	140	24	3	1	57	52	6		.279	.354	.345	96	-1	14	.927	-14	91	92	*S-116,2-14,3-11	-0.6
1912	†Bos A	131	523	73	132	22	6	0	42	41	4		.252	.312	.317	76	-17	4	.943	-15	92	101	*2-131	-3.0
1913	Bos A	137	483	67	129	29	6	1	48	50	2	32	.267	.338	.358	101	1	11	.957	-21	91	67	*2-129	-1.8
1914	Bos A	92	293	23	64	17	2	1	23	14	2	23	.218	.259	.300	68	-12	5-6	.972	-1	98	154	2-91	-1.4
	Pit F	39	142	18	48	9	5	1	25	11	0	13	.338	.386	.493	139	5	2	.974	7	115	86	S-39	1.5
1915	Pit F	121	434	44	125	17	8	1	49	30	2	27	.288	.337	.371	100	-7	17	**.967**	-1	**101**	92	*2-114/S-8	-0.6
1916	Chi N	44	137	12	36	6	2	1	10	9	0	7	.263	.308	.358	94	-1	1	.919	-1	102	95	2-41	-0.2
Total	7	711	2521	307	676	124	32	6	254	207	16	102	.268	.328	.350	93	-32	54-6	.956	-46	95	97	2-520,S-165/3-11	-6.2
YEWCIC, TOM Thomas "Kibby" B 5.9.1932 Conemaugh, PA BR/TR 5-11/180# d6.27																								
1957	Det A	1	1	0	0	0	0	0	0	0-0	0	0	.000	.000	.000	-97	0	0-0	.833	0	*0*	*0*	/C	0.0
YEWELL, ED Edwin Leonard B 8.22.1862 Washington, DC D 9.15.1940 Washington, DC d5.12																								
1884	Was AA	27	93	14	23	3	1	0		1	1		.247	.263	.301	95	0		.885	0	112	103	2-11/O-8(1-2-5),3-7,S-2	0.0
	Was U	1	4	0	0	0	0	0		0			.000	.000	.000	-99	-1		.571	-1	76	0	/3	-0.2
Total	1	28	97	14	23	3	1	0		1			.237	.253	.289	85	-1		.885	-1	112	103	/2-11,3-8,O-8(1-2-5),S-2	-0.2
YOHE, BILL William Clyde B 9.2.1878 Mt.Erie, IL D 12.24.1938 Bremerton, WA TR 5-8/180# d8.30																								
1909	Was A	21	72	6	15	2	0	0	4	3	0		.208	.240	.236	53	-4	2	.921	2	115	39	3-19	-0.2
YORK, RUDY Preston Rudolph B 8.17.1913 Ragland, AL D 2.5.1970 Rome, GA BR/TR 6-1/209# d8.22 M1 C4																								
1934	Det A	3	6	0	1	0	0	0	0	1	0	3	.167	.286	.167	19	-1	0-0	1.000	0	*0*	*332*	/C-2	-0.1

Year	Tm Lg	G	AB	R	H	2B	3B	HR	RBI	BB-IB	HP	SO	AVG	OBP	SLG	AOPS	ABR	SB-CS	FA	FR	Rng	Thr	G at Pos	BFW
1937	Det A	104	375	72	115	18	3	35	103	41	0	52	.307	.375	.651	150	25	3-2	.960	-16	*86*	*79*	C-54,3-41/1-2	1.3
1938	Det A★	135	463	85	138	27	2	33	127	92	2	74	.298	.417	.579	139	29	1-2	.990	4	***141***	*89*	*C-116,O-14(LF)/1	3.5
1939	Det A	102	329	66	101	16	1	20	68	41	2	50	.307	.387	.544	126	12	5-0	.985	-3	*104*	*111*	C-67,1-19	1.2
1940	†Det A	**155**	588	105	186	46	6	33	134	89	4	88	.316	.410	.583	141	37	3-2	.990	4	105	76	*1-155	2.5
1941	Det A★	**155**	590	91	153	29	3	27	111	92	1	88	.259	.360	.456	104	4	3-1	.986	-2	95	81	*1-155	-1.2
1942	Det A★	153	577	81	150	26	4	21	90	73	0	71	.260	.343	.428	107	5	3-3	.988	15	**133**	90	*1-152	0.6
1943	Det A★	**155**	571	90	155	22	11	**34**	**118**	84	1	88	.271	.366	**.527**	148	33	5-5	.990	19	**141**	81	*1-155	4.6
1944	Det A☆	151	583	77	161	27	7	18	98	68	1	73	.276	.353	.439	119	14	5-3	.989	7	120	**124**	*1-151	1.4
1945	†Det A	**155**	595	71	157	25	5	18	87	60	0	85	.264	.331	.413	109	5	6-6	.988	-1	98	109	*1-155	-0.5
1946	†Bos A★	154	579	78	160	30	6	17	119	86	1	93	.276	.371	.437	118	16	3-2	.994	6	**111**	**118**	*1-154	1.7
1947	Bos A	48	184	16	39	7	0	6	27	22	0	32	.212	.296	.348	73	-7	0-0	.995	2	108	106	1-48	-0.7
	Chi A☆	102	400	40	97	18	4	15	64	36	0	55	.243	.305	.420	104	-1	1-0	.995	1	103	111	*1-102	-0.3
	Year	150	584	56	136	25	4	21	91	58	0	87	.233	.302	.397	94	-8	1-0	**.995**	3	105	109	*1-150	-1.0
1948	Phi A	31	51	4	8	0	0	0	6	7	0	15	.157	.259	.157	12	-6	0-0	.988	-1	83	116	1-14	-0.7
Total	13	1603	5891	876	1621	291	52	277	1152	792	12	867	.275	.362	.483	121	165	38-26	.990	35	112	99	*1-1263,C-239/3-41,O-14(LF)	13.3

YORK, TOM Thomas Jefferson B 7.13.1851 Brooklyn, NY D 2.17.1936 New York, NY BL 5-9/165# d5.9 M2 U2

Year	Tm Lg	G	AB	R	H	2B	3B	HR	RBI	BB-IB	HP	SO	AVG	OBP	SLG	AOPS	ABR	SB-CS	FA	FR	Rng	Thr	G at Pos	BFW
1871	Tro NA	**29**	145	36	37	5	7	2	23	9		1	.255	.299	.428	104	0	2-2	.855	3	152	278	*O-29(CF)	0.2
1872	Bal NA	51	250	66	66	10	4	0	40	3		1	.264	.273	.336	82	-6	6-1	.916	10	120	185	*O-51(51-0-1)	0.4
1873	Bal NA	**57**	278	70	84	11	7	2	50	3		4	.302	.310	.414	114	4	4-1	**.872**	11	123	71	*O-57(56-1-0)	1.2
1874	Phi NA	50	224	36	56	4	7	0	37	5		4	.250	.266	.330	87	-4	1-0	.861	8	80	0	*O-50(49-1-0)	0.4
1875	Har NA	**86**	375	68	111	14	7	0	37	3		6	.296	.302	.371	126	8	7-3	.868	4	50	48	*O-86(LF)	1.3
1876	Har N	67	263	47	68	12	7	1	39	10		4	.259	.286	.369	108	1		.899	3	71	52	*O-67(66-1-0)	0.0
1877	Har N	56	237	43	67	16	7	1	37	3		11	.283	.292	.422	137	11		.865	0	46	58	*O-56(LF)	0.6
1878	Pro N	**62**	269	56	83	19	**10**	1	26	8		19	.309	.329	.465	159	16		.873	4	87	118	*O-62(LF),M	1.5
1879	Pro N	81	342	69	106	25	5	1	50	19		28	.310	.346	.421	154	21		.898	-4	49	106	*O-81(LF)	1.1
1880	Pro N	53	203	21	43	9	2	0	18	8		29	.212	.242	.276	78	-4		.934	-2	41	55	O-53(50-1-2)	-0.9
1881	Pro N	**85**	316	57	96	23	5	2	47	29		26	.304	.362	.427	150	20		.859	-2	75	29	*O-85(LF),M	1.2
1882	Pro N	81	321	48	86	23	7	1	40	19		14	.268	.309	.393	124	9		.876	-2	59	88	*O-81(LF)	0.5
1883	Cle N	**100**	381	56	99	29	5	2	46	**37**		55	.260	.325	.378	114	9		.864	-1	66	89	*O-100(LF)	0.5
1884	Bal AA	83	314	64	70	14	7	1		34	10		.223	.318	.322	105	3		.843	-5	44	42	*O-83(68-0-15)	-0.3
1885	Bal AA	22	87	6	23	4	2	0	12	8	0		.264	.326	.356	117	2		.938	1	103	128	O-22(2-1-19)	0.2
Total	5 NA	273	1272	276	354	44	32	4	187	23	0	16	.278	.291	.373	105	2	20-7	.000	35	95	93	O-273(242-31-1)	3.5
Total	10	690	2733	467	741	174	57	10	315	175	10	186	.271	.317	.387	126	88		.879	-8	62	73	O-690(651-3-36)	4.4

YORK, TONY Tony Batton B 11.27.1912 Irene, TX D 4.18.1970 Hillsboro, TX BR/TR 5-10/165# d4.18 Mil 1945

Year	Tm Lg	G	AB	R	H	2B	3B	HR	RBI	BB-IB	HP	SO	AVG	OBP	SLG	AOPS	ABR	SB-CS	FA	FR	Rng	Thr	G at Pos	BFW
1944	Chi N	28	85	4	20	1	0	0	7	4	0	11	.235	.270	.247	46	-6	0	.940	7	121	64	S-15,3-12	0.2

YOST, NED Edgar Frederick B 8.19.1954 Eureka, CA BR/TR 6-1/190# d4.12 M1 C12

Year	Tm Lg	G	AB	R	H	2B	3B	HR	RBI	BB-IB	HP	SO	AVG	OBP	SLG	AOPS	ABR	SB-CS	FA	FR	Rng	Thr	G at Pos	BFW
1980	Mil A	15	31	0	5	0	0	0	0	0-0	0	6	.161	.161	.161	-12	-5	0-0	1.000	1	108	86	C-15	-0.4
1981	Mil A	18	27	4	6	0	0	3	3	3-0	0	6	.222	.300	.556	150	1	0-0	.956	-1	112	120	C-16	0.1
1982	†Mil A	40	98	13	27	6	3	1	8	7-0	0	20	.276	.324	.429	111	1	3-1	.977	-8	96	19	C-39/D	-0.5
1983	Mil A	61	196	21	44	5	1	6	28	5-0	0	36	.224	.243	.352	67	-10	1-0	.971	-13	68	43	C-61	-2.1
1984	Tex A	80	242	15	44	4	0	6	25	6-0	0	47	.182	.201	.273	29	-24	1-2	.995	-12	61	59	C-78	-3.5
1985	Mon N	5	11	1	2	0	0	0	0	0-0	0	2	.182	.182	.182	2	-1	0-0	.962	-2	27	0	/C-5	-0.4
Total	6	219	605	54	128	15	4	16	64	21-0	0	117	.212	.237	.329	56	-38	5-3	.982	-36	74	51	C-214/D	-6.8

YOST, EDDIE Edward Frederick Joseph "The Walking Man" B 10.13.1926 Brooklyn, NY BR/TR 5-10/170# d8.16 Mil 1945-46 M1 C23

Year	Tm Lg	G	AB	R	H	2B	3B	HR	RBI	BB-IB	HP	SO	AVG	OBP	SLG	AOPS	ABR	SB-CS	FA	FR	Rng	Thr	G at Pos	BFW
1944	Was A	7	14	3	2	0	0	0	0	1	0	2	.143	.200	.143	-1	-2	0-0	.917	-1	74	0	/3-3,S-2	-0.3
1946	Was A	8	25	2	2	1	0	0	1	5	0	5	.080	.233	.120	1	-3	2-1	1.000	1	115	60	/3-7	-0.3
1947	Was A	115	428	52	102	17	3	0	14	45	2	57	.238	.314	.292	71	-16	3-5	.958	-8	91	52	*3-114	-2.7
1948	Was A	145	555	74	138	32	11	2	50	82	4	51	.249	.349	.357	91	-6	4-3	.966	-11	88	71	*3-145	-1.7
1949	Was A	124	435	57	110	19	7	9	45	91	1	41	.253	.383	.391	107	7	3-3	.954	1	100	75	*3-122	0.7
1950	Was A	**155**	573	114	169	26	2	11	58	**141**	8	63	.295	.440	.405	123	32	6-6	.945	-2	96	131	*3-155	2.7
1951	Was A	**154**	568	109	161	**36**	4	12	65	126	11	55	.283	.423	.424	132	34	6-4	.954	-21	80	67	*3-152/O-3(LF)	1.2
1952	Was A☆	**157**	587	92	137	32	3	12	49	**129**	8	73	.233	.378	.359	110	15	4-3	.962	-30	78	68	*3-157	-1.6
1953	Was A	**152**	577	107	157	30	7	9	45	**123**	4	59	.272	.403	.395	119	23	7-4	.965	-11	91	90	*3-152	1.2
1954	Was A	**155**	539	101	138	26	4	11	47	131	5	71	.256	.405	.380	123	26	7-3	.968	-4	98	95	*3-155	2.2
1955	Was A	122	375	64	91	17	5	7	48	95-0	11	54	.243	.407	.371	117	16	4-3	.943	-4	96	95	*3-107	1.1
1956	Was A	152	515	94	119	17	2	11	53	**151**-9	8	82	.231	.412	.336	100	10	8-5	.963	8	104	96	*3-135/O-8(RF)	1.7
1957	Was A	110	414	47	104	13	5	9	38	73-2	5	49	.251	.370	.372	104	5	1-11	.952	-8	93	79	*3-107	-0.7
1958	Was A	134	406	55	91	16	0	8	37	81-2	9	43	.224	.361	.323	93	1	3-6	**.964**	-12	85	83	*3-114/O-4(LF),1-2	-1.4
1959	Det A	148	521	**115**	145	19	0	21	61	**135**-1	12	77	.278	**.435**	.436	133	34	9-2	**.962**	-8	85	85	*3-146/2	2.6
1960	Det A	143	497	78	129	23	2	14	47	**125**-1	8	69	.260	**.414**	.398	118	21	5-4	.933	-27	75	67	*3-142	-0.6
1961	LA A	76	213	29	43	4	0	3	15	50-0	2	48	.202	.358	.263	62	-10	0-1	.964	-5	87	32	3-67	-1.5
1962	LA A	52	104	22	25	9	1	0	10	30-0	1	21	.240	.412	.346	111	4	0-2	.950	-3	92	41	3-28/1-7	0.0
Total	18	2109	7346	1215	1863	337	56	139	683	1614-15	99	920	.254	.394	.371	109	191	72-66	.957	-145	90	81	*3-2008/O-15(7-0-8),1-9,S-2,2	2.6

YOTER, ELMER Elmer Elsworth B 6.26.1900 Plainfield, PA D 7.26.1966 Camp Hill, PA BR/TR 5-7/155# d9.9

Year	Tm Lg	G	AB	R	H	2B	3B	HR	RBI	BB-IB	HP	SO	AVG	OBP	SLG	AOPS	ABR	SB-CS	FA	FR	Rng	Thr	G at Pos	BFW
1921	Phi A	3	3	0	0	0	0	0	0	0	0	0	.000	.000	.000	-99	-1	0-0	—	0			H	-0.1
1924	Cle A	19	66	3	18	1	1	0	7	5	0	8	.273	.324	.318	65	-4	0-0	.905	-1	108	33	3-19	-0.3
1927	Chi N	13	27	2	6	1	1	0	5	4	0	4	.222	.323	.333	76	-1	0	.947	0	118	0	3-11	0.0
1928	Chi N	1	0	0	0	0	0	0	0	0	0	0	—	—	—	—	0	0	—	-0	0	0	/3	0.0
Total	4	36	96	5	24	2	2	0	12	9	0	12	.250	.314	.313	63	-6	0-0	.915	-1	110	24	/3-31	-0.4

YOUNG, DEL Delmer Edward B 5.11.1912 Cleveland, OH D 12.8.1979 San Francisco, CA BB/TR 5-11/168# d4.19 f-Del

Year	Tm Lg	G	AB	R	H	2B	3B	HR	RBI	BB-IB	HP	SO	AVG	OBP	SLG	AOPS	ABR	SB-CS	FA	FR	Rng	Thr	G at Pos	BFW
1937	Phi N	109	360	36	70	9	2	0	24	18	1	55	.194	.235	.231	25	-38	6	.950	7	**111**	103	*2-108	-2.5
1938	Phi N	108	340	27	78	13	2	0	31	20	2	35	.229	.276	.279	55	-21	0	.933	-1	104	78	S-87,2-17	-1.6
1939	Phi N	77	217	22	57	9	2	3	20	8	0	24	.263	.289	.364	77	-8	1	.946	-12	88	59	S-55,2-17	-1.7
1940	Phi N	15	33	2	8	0	1	0	1	2	0	1	.242	.286	.303	65	-2	0	.962	-1	84	107	/S-6,2-5	-0.2
Total	4	309	950	87	213	31	7	3	76	48	3	115	.224	.264	.281	48	-69	7	.938	-7	98	73	S-148,2-147	-6.0

YOUNG, DEL Delmer John B 10.24.1885 Macon, MO D 12.17.1959 Cleveland, OH BL/TR 5-11/195# d9.24 s-Del

Year	Tm Lg	G	AB	R	H	2B	3B	HR	RBI	BB-IB	HP	SO	AVG	OBP	SLG	AOPS	ABR	SB-CS	FA	FR	Rng	Thr	G at Pos	BFW
1909	Cin N	2	7	0	2	0	0	0	1	1	0		.286	.375	.286	106	0	0	1.000	0	371	0	/O-2(1-0-1)	0.0
1914	Buf F	80	174	17	48	5	5	4	22	3	0	13	.276	.288	.431	92	-6	0	.944	-3	98	39	O-41(7-2-32)	-1.1
1915	Buf F	12	15	0	2	0	0	0	0	1	0	0	.133	.188	.133	-9	-2	1	.667	-1	70	0	/O-3(0-1-2)	-0.3
Total	3	94	196	17	52	5	5	4	23	5	0	13	.265	.284	.403	85	-8	1	.933	-3	112	35	/O-46(8-3-35)	-1.4

YOUNG, DMITRI Dmitri Dell B 10.11.1973 Vicksburg, MS BB/TR 6-2/215# d8.29 OF Total (382-LF 101-RF)

Year	Tm Lg	G	AB	R	H	2B	3B	HR	RBI	BB-IB	HP	SO	AVG	OBP	SLG	AOPS	ABR	SB-CS	FA	FR	Rng	Thr	G at Pos	BFW
1996	†StL N	16	29	3	7	0	0	0	2	4-0	1	5	.241	.353	.241	61	-1	0-1	.976	-2	22	103	1-10	-0.4
1997	StL N	110	333	38	86	14	3	5	34	38-3	2	63	.258	.335	.363	85	-7	6-5	.985	-2	88	95	1-74,O-17(9-0-10)/D	-1.6
1998	Cin N	144	536	81	166	48	1	14	83	47-4	2	94	.310	.364	.481	120	17	2-4	.940	-8	89	49	*O-105(91-0-14),1-44	0.0
1999	Cin N	127	373	63	112	30	2	14	56	30-1	2	71	.300	.352	.504	111	6	3-1	.976	0	107	81	O-91(23-0-75)/1-9,D	0.2
2000	Cin N	152	548	68	166	37	6	18	88	36-6	3	80	.303	.346	.491	107	4	0-3	.978	-5	91	65	*O-111(111-0-1),1-36/D-4	-0.8
2001	Cin N	142	540	68	163	28	3	21	69	37-10	5	77	.302	.350	.481	108	6	8-5	.957	-0	96	147	O-87(86-0-1),1-38,3-36	0.1
2002	Det A	54	201	25	57	14	0	7	27	12-5	2	39	.284	.329	.458	113	3	2-0	.971	2	179	40	D-35,1-15/3O(LF)	0.2
2003	Det A☆	155	562	78	167	34	7	29	85	58-16	11	130	.297	.372	.537	148	39	2-1	.985	3	99	131	D-75,O-61(LF),3-16/1	3.3
Total	8	900	3122	424	929	205	22	108	444	262-45	28	559	.296	.353	.480	114	67	23-20	.965	-11	97	93	O-473L,1-227,D-116/3-53	1.0

YOUNG, DON Donald Wayne B 10.18.1945 Houston, TX BR/TR 6-2/185# d9.9

Year	Tm Lg	G	AB	R	H	2B	3B	HR	RBI	BB-IB	HP	SO	AVG	OBP	SLG	AOPS	ABR	SB-CS	FA	FR	Rng	Thr	G at Pos	BFW
1965	Chi N	11	35	1	2	0	0	1	2	0-0	0	11	.057	.056	.143	-45	-7	0-0	.933	-1	83	0	O-11(CF)	-0.9
1969	Chi N	101	272	36	65	12	3	6	27	38-5	5	74	.239	.343	.371	89	-3	1-5	.975	-2	100	75	*O-100(3-94-8)	-1.0
Total	2	112	307	37	67	12	3	7	29	38-5	5	85	.218	.313	.345	76	-10	1-5	.972	-3	99	69	O-111(3-105-8)	-1.9

YOUNG, ERIC Eric Orlando B 5.18.1967 New Brunswick, NJ BR/TR 5-9/180# d7.30

Year	Tm Lg	G	AB	R	H	2B	3B	HR	RBI	BB-IB	HP	SO	AVG	OBP	SLG	AOPS	ABR	SB-CS	FA	FR	Rng	Thr	G at Pos	BFW
1992	LA N	49	132	9	34	1	0	1	11	8-0	0	9	.258	.300	.288	68	-6	6-1	.957	4	104	84	2-43	0.1

Year	Tm Lg	G	AB	R	H	2B	3B	HR	RBI	BB-IB	HP	SO	AVG	OBP	SLG	AOPS	ABR	SB-CS	FA	FR	Rng	Thr	G at Pos	BFW
1993	Col N	144	490	82	132	16	8	3	42	63-3	4	41	.269	.355	.353	78	-13	42-19	.962	-1	104	82	2-79,O-52(46-10-0)	-0.9
1994	Col N	90	228	37	62	13	1	7	30	38-1	2	17	.272	.378	.430	95	0	18-7	.981	-0	95	123	O-60(LF)/2	-0.1
1995	†Col N	120	366	68	116	21	**9**	6	36	49-3	5	29	.317	.404	.473	101	3	35-12	.973	8	107	112	2-77,O-19(LF)	1.6
1996	Col N★	141	568	113	184	23	4	8	74	47-1	21	31	.324	.393	.421	94	-3	**53**-19	.985	27	111	**114**	*2-139	3.5
1997	Col N	118	468	78	132	29	6	6	45	57-0	5	37	.282	.363	.408	83	-10	32-12	.978	**26**	120	117	*2-117	2.4
	LA N	37	154	28	42	4	2	2	16	14-1	4	17	.273	.347	.364	94	-1	13-2	.979	-16	70	82	2-37	-1.3
	Year	155	622	106	174	33	8	8	61	71-1	9	54	.280	.359	.397	85	-11	45-14	.978	10	107	108	*2-154	1.1
1998	LA N	117	452	78	129	24	1	8	43	45-0	5	32	.285	.355	.396	104	3	42-13	.976	-3	96	96	*2-113/D	1.1
1999	LA N	119	456	73	128	24	2	2	41	63-0	5	26	.281	.371	.355	91	-3	51-22	.984	-5	101	88	*2-116	0.1
2000	Chi N	153	607	98	180	40	2	6	47	63-1	8	39	.297	.367	.399	97	-1	54-7	.979	-1	98	90	*2-150	1.4
2001	Chi N	149	603	98	168	43	4	6	42	42-1	9	45	.279	.333	.393	92	-7	31-14	.981	-3	91	80	*2-147	-0.1
2002	Mil N	138	496	57	139	29	3	3	28	39-0	6	38	.280	.338	.369	91	-8	31-11	.979	-2	99	95	*2-123/O-2(1-0-1),D-2	-0.2
2003	Mil N	109	404	71	105	18	1	15	31	48-2	4	34	.260	.344	.421	100	0	25-7	.968	-14	94	81	2-99	-0.6
	SF N	26	71	9	14	2	0	0	3	9-0	1	10	.197	.293	.225	40	-6	3-5	.989	2	112	109	2-18/O-2(CF),D	-0.4
	Year	135	475	80	119	20	1	15	34	57-2	5	44	.251	.336	.392	91	-6	28-12	.971	-12	97	85	*2-117/O-2(CF),D	-1.0
Total	12	1510	5495	899	1565	287	43	73	489	585-13	79	405	.285	.360	.393	91	-52	436-151	.977	23	101	95	*2-1259,O-135(126-12-1)/D-4	6.6
YOUNG, ERNIE Ernest Wesley B 7.8.1969 Chicago, IL BR/TR 6-1/190# d5.17																								
1994	Oak A	11	30	2	2	1	0	0	3	1-0	0	8	.067	.097	.100	-54	-7	0-0	.958	1	123	179	O-10(7-3-1)/D	-0.6
1995	Oak A	26	50	9	10	3	0	2	5	8-0	0	12	.200	.310	.380	83	-1	0-0	.946	-1	103	0	O-24(7-7-10)	-0.2
1996	Oak A	141	462	72	112	19	4	19	64	52-1	7	118	.242	.326	.424	90	-8	7-5	.997	3	104	97	*O-140(8-133-17)	-0.5
1997	Oak A	71	175	22	39	7	0	5	15	19-0	2	57	.223	.303	.349	72	-7	1-3	.980	2	102	169	O-66(2-59-12)/D	-0.6
1998	KC A	25	53	2	10	3	0	1	3	2-0	1	9	.189	.232	.302	36	-5	2-1	1.000	3	130	183	O-24(1-5-19)	-0.3
1999	Ari N	6	11	1	2	0	0	0	0	3-0	1	2	.182	.400	.182	54	-1	0-0	1.000	2	158	480	/O-4(1-0-3)	0.1
2003	Det A	5	11	0	2	0	0	0	0	4-0	0	5	.182	.400	.182	66	0	0-2	—	0			/D-4	-0.1
Total	7	285	792	108	177	33	4	27	90	89-1	11	211	.223	.308	.378	77	-29	10-11	.989	9	107	122	O-268(26-207-62)/D-6	-2.2
YOUNG, GEORGE George Joseph B 4.1.1890 Brooklyn, NY D 3.13.1950 Brightwaters, NY BL/TR 6/185# d8.10																								
1913	Cle A	2	2	0	0	0	0	0	0	0	0	0	.000	.000	.000	-97	-1	0	—	0			H	-0.1
YOUNG, GERALD Gerald Anthony B 10.22.1964 Tela, Honduras BB/TR 6-2/185# d7.8																								
1987	Hou N	71	274	44	88	9	2	1	15	26-0	1	27	.321	.380	.380	107	3	26-9	.980	-1	98	144	O-67(CF)	0.5
1988	Hou N	149	576	79	148	21	9	0	37	66-1	3	66	.257	.334	.325	94	-3	65-27	.992	1	99	156	*O-145(CF)	0.2
1989	Hou N	146	533	71	124	17	3	0	38	74-4	2	60	.233	.326	.276	77	-13	34-25	**.998**	14	111	**197**	*O-143(CF)	-0.2
1990	Hou N	57	154	15	27	4	1	1	4	20-0	0	23	.175	.269	.234	41	-12	6-3	.990	-1	94	177	O-50(CF)	-1.4
1991	Hou N	108	142	26	31	3	1	1	11	24-0	0	17	.218	.327	.275	77	-4	16-5	1.000	2	107	188	O-84(6-76-5)	0.0
1992	Hou N	74	76	14	14	1	1	0	4	10-0	0	11	.184	.279	.224	46	-5	6-2	.964	1	114	0	O-57(6-14-43)	-0.5
1993	Col N	19	19	5	1	0	0	0	1	4-0	0	1	.053	.217	.053	-20	-3	0-1	.882	0	137	0	O-11(4-3-5)	-0.4
1994	StL N	16	41	5	13	3	2	0	3	3-0	0	8	.317	.364	.488	122	1	2-1	1.000	-1	94	0	O-11(3-6-2)	0.1
Total	8	640	1815	259	446	58	19	3	113	227-5	6	213	.246	.329	.304	82	-36	155-73	.990	17	104	160	O-568(19-504-55)	-1.7
YOUNG, HERMAN Herman John B 4.14.1886 Boston, MA D 12.13.1966 Ipswich, MA BR/TR 5-8/155# d6.11																								
1911	Bos N	9	25	2	6	0	0	0	0	0	1	3	.240	.269	.240	40	-2	0	.905	2	122	111	/3-5,S-3	0.0
YOUNG, JOHN John Thomas B 2.9.1949 Los Angeles, CA BL/TL 6-3/210# d9.9																								
1971	Det A	2	4	1	2	1	0	0	1	0-0	0	0	.500	.500	.750	241	1	0-0	1.000	-0	0	0	/1	0.1
YOUNG, KEVIN Kevin Stacey B 6.16.1969 Alpena, MI BR/TR 6-2/219# d7.12																								
1992	Pit N	10	7	2	4	0	0	0	4	2-0	0	0	.571	.667	.571	256	2	1-0	.750	-2	22	0	/3-7,1	0.0
1993	Pit N	141	449	38	106	24	3	6	47	36-3	9	82	.236	.300	.343	73	-17	2-2	**.998**	10	**124**	112	*1-135/3-6	-1.8
1994	Pit N	59	122	15	25	7	2	1	11	8-2	1	34	.205	.258	.320	49	-9	0-2	1.000	-0	66	138	1-37,3-17/O(1-0-1)	-1.2
1995	Pit N	56	181	13	42	9	0	6	22	8-0	2	53	.232	.268	.381	69	-9	1-3	.919	5	120	89	3-48/1-6	-0.5
1996	KC A	55	132	20	32	6	0	8	23	11-0	0	32	.242	.301	.470	91	-3	3-3	1.000	-1	114	142	1-27,O-17(2-0-15)/3-7,D-3	-0.6
1997	Pit N	97	333	59	100	18	3	18	74	16-1	4	89	.300	.332	.535	123	9	11-2	.997	3	106	86	1-77,3-12,O-11(10-0-1)	0.7
1998	Pit N	159	592	88	160	40	2	27	108	44-1	11	127	.270	.328	.481	109	7	15-7	.994	-13	70	112	*1-157	-2.0
1999	Pit N	156	584	103	174	41	6	26	106	75-5	12	124	.298	.387	.522	128	27	22-10	.985	-4	96	**116**	*1-155	0.9
2000	Pit N	132	496	77	128	27	0	20	88	32-1	8	96	.258	.311	.433	87	-12	8-3	.986	-11	73	110	*1-129/D	-3.2
2001	Pit N	142	449	53	104	33	0	14	65	42-3	11	119	.232	.310	.399	81	-13	15-11	.994	-2	96	113	*1-137	-2.6
2002	Pit N	146	468	60	115	26	1	16	51	50-2	4	101	.246	.322	.408	94	-7	4-6	.991	2	110	106	*1-144	-1.9
2003	Pit N	52	84	8	17	4	0	2	7	12-0	0	25	.202	.302	.321	62	-5	1-0	.995	0	113	128	1-44/O(RF)	-0.6
Total	12	1205	3897	536	1007	235	17	144	606	336-18	62	882	.258	.324	.438	96	-30	83-49	.992	-13	95	111	*1-1049/3-97,O-30(13-0-18),D-4	-12.8
YOUNG, PEP Lemuel Floyd B 8.29.1907 Jamestown, NC D 1.14.1962 Jamestown, NC BR/TR 5-9/162# d4.25																								
1933	Pit N	25	20	3	6	1	1	0	0	0	0	5	.300	.300	.450	112	0	0	1.000	-0	93	0	/2S	0.0
1934	Pit N	19	17	3	4	0	0	0	2	0	0	6	.235	.235	.235	26	-2	0	1.000	1	203	189	/2-2,S-2	0.0
1935	Pit N	128	494	60	131	25	10	7	82	21	2	59	.265	.298	.399	83	-14	2	.952	-16	89	86	*2-107/3-6,O-6(1-0-5),S-4	-2.2
1936	Pit N	125	475	47	118	23	10	6	77	29	1	52	.248	.293	.377	77	-17	3	.966	-22	88	57	*2-123	-3.1
1937	Pit N	113	408	43	106	20	3	9	54	26	1	63	.260	.306	.390	88	-8	4	.942	13	116	133	S-45,3-39,2-30	1.1
1938	Pit N	149	562	58	156	36	5	4	79	40	3	64	.278	.329	.381	94	-4	7	.973	25	**110**	**130**	*2-149	3.0
1939	Pit N	84	293	34	81	14	3	3	29	23	2	29	.276	.333	.375	92	-4	1	.967	3	103	108	2-84	0.4
1940	Pit N	54	136	19	34	8	2	2	20	12	2	23	.250	.320	.382	94	-1	1	.909	-4	100	51	2-33/S-7,3-5	-0.4
1941	Cin N	4	12	2	2	0	0	0	0	0	1	1	.167	.231	.167	13	-1	0	.923	0	97	164	/3-3	-0.1
	StL N	2	2	0	0	0	0	0	0	0	0	2	.000	.000	.000	-94	-1	0	—	0			H	-0.1
	Year	6	14	2	2	0	0	0	0	0	1	3	.143	.200	.143	-2	-2	0	.923	0	97	164	/3-3	-0.2
1945	StL N	27	47	5	7	1	0	1	4	1	0	8	.149	.167	.234	10	-6	0	.978	-1	80	72	S-11/3-9,2-3	-0.7
Total	10	730	2466	274	645	128	34	32	347	152	12	312	.262	.308	.380	85	-58	18	.964	-1	98	94	2-532/S-70,3-62,O-6(1-0-5)	-2.1
YOUNG, MIKE Michael B. B 10.19.1976 Covina, CA BR/TR 6/175# d9.29																								
2000	Tex A	2	2	0	0	0	0	0	0	0-0	0	1	.000	.000	.000	-99	-1	0-0	—	-1	0	0	/2	-0.1
2001	Tex A	106	386	57	96	18	4	11	49	26-0	3	91	.249	.298	.402	80	-12	3-1	.984	-1	99	107	*2-104	-0.7
2002	Tex A	156	573	77	150	26	8	9	62	41-1	0	112	.262	.308	.382	79	-18	6-7	.988	14	**104**	95	*2-152,S-11/3-4	0.2
2003	Tex A	160	666	106	204	33	9	14	72	36-1	1	103	.306	.339	.446	97	-4	13-2	.987	8	100	102	*2-159/S-7	1.4
Total	4	424	1627	240	450	77	21	34	183	103-2	4	307	.277	.318	.412	87	-35	22-10	.987	20	101	101	2-416/S-18,3-4	0.8
YOUNG, MIKE Michael Darren B 3.20.1960 Oakland, CA BB/TR 6-2/195# d9.14																								
1982	Bal A	6	2	2	0	0	0	0	0	0-0	0	1	.000	.000	.000	-99	-1	0-0	1.000	0	399	0	/O(LF)D	0.0
1983	Bal A	25	36	5	6	2	1	0	2	2-0	1	8	.167	.231	.278	40	-3	1-0	.929	-0	100	108	O-22(14-0-8)/D-3	-0.4
1984	Bal A	123	401	59	101	17	2	17	52	58-2	7	110	.252	.355	.431	119	12	6-2	.982	-7	92	55	*O-115(40-1-85)/D	0.1
1985	Bal A	139	450	72	123	22	1	28	81	48-5	4	104	.273	.348	.513	136	22	1-5	.975	2	104	106	O-90(83-0-20),D-37	1.7
1986	Bal A	117	369	43	93	15	1	9	42	49-2	3	90	.252	.342	.371	96	-1	3-1	.962	0	113	24	O-69(LF),D-38	-0.4
1987	Bal A	110	363	46	87	10	1	16	39	46-2	2	91	.240	.328	.405	96	-2	10-7	.975	-3	102	0	O-60(54-7-0),D-47	-0.9
1988	Phi N	75	146	13	33	14	0	1	14	26-1	1	43	.226	.343	.342	96	1	0-0	.938	1	126	0	O-42(3-0-39)	0.1
	Mil A	8	14	2	0	0	0	0	0	2-1	1	5	.000	.176	.000	-46	-3	0-0	—	-0	0	0	/O-2(1-0-1),D-5	-0.3
1989	Cle A	32	59	2	11	0	0	1	5	6-1	1	13	.186	.273	.237	44	-4	1-2	1.000	-0	61	0	D-15/O(LF)	-0.6
Total	8	635	1840	244	454	80	6	72	235	237-14	20	465	.247	.338	.414	107	21	22-17	.969	-6	103	50	O-402(266-8-153),D-148	-0.7
YOUNG, BABE Norman Robert B 7.1.1915 Astoria, NY D 12.25.1983 Everett, MA BL/TL 6-2.5/185# d9.26 Mil 1943-45																								
1936	NY N	1	1	0	0	0	0	0	0	0	0	0	.000	.000	.000	-99	0	0	—	0			H	0.0
1939	NY N	22	75	8	23	4	0	3	14	5	3	6	.307	.373	.480	127	3	0	.982	-2	70	101	1-22	-0.1
1940	NY N	149	556	75	159	27	4	17	101	69	2	28	.286	.367	.441	121	17	4	.992	-1	93	96	*1-147	0.2
1941	NY N	152	574	90	152	28	5	25	104	66	5	39	.265	.346	.462	124	17	1	.986	-3	94	98	*1-150	0.0
1942	NY N	101	287	37	80	17	1	11	59	34	5	22	.279	.365	.460	140	15	1	.972	-2	90	93	O-54(CF),1-18	1.0
1946	NY N	104	291	30	81	11	0	7	33	30	0	21	.278	.346	.388	107	3	3	.988	-5	74	64	1-49,O-24(0-17-7)	-0.5
1947	NY N	14	14	0	1	1	0	0	0	0	0	1	.071	.071	.143	-44	-3	0	—	0			H	-0.3
	Cin N	95	364	55	103	21	3	14	79	35	2	26	.283	.349	.473	117	8	0	.990	-1	96	86	1-93	0.4
	Year	109	378	55	104	22	3	14	79	35	2	27	.275	.340	.460	111	5	0	.990	-1	96	86	1-93	0.1

Year	Tm Lg	G	AB	R	H	2B	3B	HR	RBI	BB-IB	HP	SO	AVG	OBP	SLG	AOPS	ABR	SB-CS	FA	FR	Rng	Thr	G at Pos	BFW
1948	Cin N	49	130	11	30	7	2	1	12	19	0	12	.231	.329	.338	84	-3	0	.993	1	106	128	1-31/O(RF)	-0.3
	StL N	41	111	14	27	5	2	1	13	16	0	6	.243	.339	.351	82	-2	0	.996	-4	43	110	1-35	-0.7
	Year	90	241	25	57	12	4	2	25	35	0	18	.237	.333	.344	83	-5	0	.995	-3	75	119	1-66/O(RF)	-1.0
Total	8	728	2403	320	656	121	17	79	415	274	17	161	.273	.352	.436	117	55	9	.989	-18	90	94	1-545/O-79(0-71-8)	-0.3

YOUNG, RALPH Ralph Stuart B 9.19.1889 Philadelphia, PA D 1.24.1965 Philadelphia, PA BB/TR 5-5/165# d4.10

Year	Tm Lg	G	AB	R	H	2B	3B	HR	RBI	BB-IB	HP	SO	AVG	OBP	SLG	AOPS	ABR	SB-CS	FA	FR	Rng	Thr	G at Pos	BFW
1913	NY A	7	15	2	1	0	0	0	0	3	0	3	.067	.222	.067	-15	-2	2	.857	0	110	134	/S-7	-0.2
1915	Det A	123	378	44	92	6	5	0	31	53	2	31	.243	.339	.286	83	-7	12-11	.950	-1	107	101	*2-119	-0.8
1916	Det A	153	528	60	139	16	6	1	45	62	1	43	.263	.342	.322	96	-2	20-20	.966	-6	97	87	*2-146/S-6,3	-0.8
1917	Det A	141	503	64	116	18	2	1	35	61	3	35	.231	.317	.280	83	-8	8	.958	5	107	77	*2-141	-0.1
1918	Det A	91	298	31	56	7	1	0	21	54	0	17	.188	.313	.218	63	-11	15	.939	-12	96	67	2-91	-2.4
1919	Det A	125	456	63	96	13	5	1	25	53	1	32	.211	.294	.268	60	-24	8	.970	11	108	78	*2-120/S-5	-1.1
1920	Det A	150	594	84	173	21	6	0	33	85	2	30	.291	.382	.347	96	1	8-13	.969	-11	93	64	*2-150	-1.0
1921	Det A	107	401	70	120	8	3	0	29	69	3	23	.299	.406	.334	91	-1	11-9	.947	-21	84	78	*2-106	-1.9
1922	Phi A	125	470	62	105	19	2	1	35	55	3	21	.223	.309	.279	53	-32	8-6	.960	-7	97	81	*2-120	-3.6
Total	9	1022	3643	480	898	108	30	4	254	495	15	235	.247	.339	.296	79	-86	92-59	.959	-42	99	79	2-993/S-18,3	-11.9

YOUNG, DICK Richard Ennis B 6.3.1928 Seattle, WA BL/TR (BB 1952) 5-11/175# d9.11

Year	Tm Lg	G	AB	R	H	2B	3B	HR	RBI	BB-IB	HP	SO	AVG	OBP	SLG	AOPS	ABR	SB-CS	FA	FR	Rng	Thr	G at Pos	BFW
1951	Phi N	15	68	7	16	5	0	0	2	3	0	6	.235	.268	.309	55	-4	0-1	.922	-6	83	77	2-15	-1.1
1952	Phi N	5	9	3	2	1	0	0	0	1	0	3	.222	.300	.333	76	0	1-0	.900	-1	80	96	/2-2	0.0
Total	2	20	77	10	18	6	0	0	2	4	0	9	.234	.272	.312	58	-4	1-1	.919	-7	83	79	/2-17	-1.1

YOUNG, BOBBY Robert George B 1.22.1925 Granite, MD D 1.28.1985 Baltimore, MD BL/TR 6-1/175# d7.28

Year	Tm Lg	G	AB	R	H	2B	3B	HR	RBI	BB-IB	HP	SO	AVG	OBP	SLG	AOPS	ABR	SB-CS	FA	FR	Rng	Thr	G at Pos	BFW
1948	StL N	3	1	0	0	0	0	0	0	0	0	1	.000	.000	.000	-95	0	0	1.000	-0	0	0	/3	0.0
1951	StL A	147	611	75	159	13	9	1	31	44	0	51	.260	.310	.316	67	-30	8-7	.980	-4	102	88	*2-147	-2.6
1952	StL A	149	575	59	142	15	9	4	39	56	0	48	.247	.314	.325	76	-20	3-3	.984	-7	97	112	*2-149	-2.0
1953	StL A	148	537	48	137	22	2	4	25	41	1	40	.255	.309	.326	70	-23	2-1	.977	-19	87	97	*2-148	-3.2
1954	Bal A	130	432	43	106	13	6	4	24	54	1	42	.245	.329	.331	88	-7	4-4	.976	-14	92	82	*2-127	-1.3
1955	Bal A	59	186	5	37	3	0	1	8	11-1	0	23	.199	.244	.231	30	-19	1-4	.985	-1	104	100	2-58	-1.8
	Cle A	18	45	7	14	1	1	0	6	1-0	0	2	.311	.326	.378	86	-1	0-0	.983	4	121	192	2-11/3	0.4
	Year	77	231	12	51	4	1	1	14	12-1	0	25	.221	.259	.260	42	-20	1-4	.985	3	107	115	2-69/3	-1.4
1956	Cle A	1	0	0	0	0	0	0	0	0-0	0	0	—	—	—	—	0	0-0	—	0			R	0.0
1958	Phi N	32	60	7	14	1	1	1	4	1-0	0	5	.233	.246	.333	52	-4	0-0	.968	-3	90	65	2-21	-0.7
Total	8	687	2447	244	609	68	28	15	137	208-1	2	212	.249	.308	.318	71	-104	18-19	.980	-44	96	97	2-661/3-2	-11.2

YOUNG, RUSS Russell Charles B 9.15.1902 Bryan, OH D 5.13.1984 Roseville, CA BB/TR 6/175# d4.16

Year	Tm Lg	G	AB	R	H	2B	3B	HR	RBI	BB-IB	HP	SO	AVG	OBP	SLG	AOPS	ABR	SB-CS	FA	FR	Rng	Thr	G at Pos	BFW
1931	StL A	16	34	2	4	0	0	1	2	2	0	4	.118	.167	.206	-3	-5	0-0	1.000	2	*124*	*90*	C-16	-0.3

YOUNGBLOOD, JOEL Joel Randolph B 8.28.1951 Houston, TX BR/TR 6/180# d4.13 C5 OF Total (233-LF 107-CF 454-RF)

Year	Tm Lg	G	AB	R	H	2B	3B	HR	RBI	BB-IB	HP	SO	AVG	OBP	SLG	AOPS	ABR	SB-CS	FA	FR	Rng	Thr	G at Pos	BFW
1976	Cin N	55	57	8	11	1	1	0	1	2-0	1	8	.193	.233	.246	35	-5	1-0	.938	-0	112	241	/O-9(3-3-3),3-6,C2	-0.6
1977	StL N	25	27	1	5	2	0	0	1	3-0	0	5	.185	.267	.259	43	-2	0-2	1.000	-0	76	0	O-11(10-0-1)/3-6	-0.4
	NY N	70	182	16	46	11	1	0	11	13-1	0	40	.253	.301	.324	72	-7	1-3	.954	7	107	140	2-33,O-22(4-7-13),3-10	-0.1
	Year	95	209	17	51	13	1	0	12	16-1	0	45	.244	.296	.316	67	-10	1-5	1.000	7	110	224	O-33(14-7-14),2-33,3-16	-0.5
1978	NY N	113	266	40	67	12	8	7	30	16-1	1	39	.252	.294	.436	106	0	4-0	.989	6	116	303	O-50(7-14-33),2-39/3-9,S	0.7
1979	NY N	158	590	90	162	37	5	16	60	60-7	7	84	.275	.346	.436	117	14	18-13	.985	9	107	155	*O-147(70-5-87),2-13,3-12	1.7
1980	NY N	146	514	58	142	26	2	8	69	52-10	2	69	.276	.340	.381	105	5	14-11	.984	21	**126**	**200**	*O-121(0-39-96),3-21/2-6	2.1
1981	NY N★	43	143	16	50	10	2	4	25	12-1	2	19	.350	.398	.531	167	13	2-5	.962	2	101	202	O-41(4-2-36)	1.2
1982	NY N	80	202	21	52	12	0	3	21	8-1	5	37	.257	.302	.361	85	-4	0-4	.969	-1	99	156	O-63(15-8-43)/2-8,S3	-0.9
	Mon N	40	90	16	18	2	0	0	8	9-1	3	21	.200	.291	.222	45	-6	2-1	1.000	-0	106	57	O-35(0-2-33)	-0.8
	Year	120	292	37	70	14	0	3	29	17-2	8	58	.240	.299	.318	73	-10	2-5	.979	-1	102	120	O-98(15-10-76)/2-8,S3	-1.7
1983	SF N	124	373	59	109	20	3	17	53	33-4	5	59	.292	.356	.499	139	19	7-4	.948	-14	94	79	2-64,3-28,O-22(14-0-8)	0.7
1984	SF N	134	469	50	119	17	1	10	51	48-1	4	86	.254	.328	.358	96	-2	5-6	.887	-22	85	52	*3-117,O-11(4-0-8)/2-5	-2.9
1985	SF N	95	230	24	62	6	0	4	24	30-1	1	37	.270	.355	.348	103	2	3-2	.955	-0	100	121	O-56(7-17-34)/3	-0.1
1986	SF N	97	184	20	47	12	0	5	28	18-0	1	34	.255	.320	.402	105	1	1-1	1.000	-0	87	94	O-45(29-0-17)/1-7,3-5,2-4,S	-0.1
1987	SF N	69	91	9	23	3	0	3	11	5-0	1	13	.253	.296	.385	83	-3	1-1	1.000	1	96	220	O-22(9-1-14)/3-2	-0.3
1988	SF N	83	123	12	31	4	0	0	16	10-0	1	17	.252	.307	.285	76	-4	1-1	.980	-1	101	0	O-45(22-9-18)	-0.6
1989	Cin N	76	118	13	25	5	0	3	13	13-2	2	21	.212	.299	.331	78	-3	0-1	.970	-3	65	75	O-45(35-0-10)	-0.8
Total	14	1408	3659	453	969	180	23	80	422	332-30	36	589	.265	.329	.392	103	18	60-55	.981	3	106	159	O-745R,3-218,2-173/1-7,S-3,C	-1.2

YOUNGMAN, HENRY Henry B 1865 Indiana, PA D 1.24.1936 Pittsburgh, PA TR 5-9/175# d4.19

Year	Tm Lg	G	AB	R	H	2B	3B	HR	RBI	BB-IB	HP	SO	AVG	OBP	SLG	AOPS	ABR	SB-CS	FA	FR	Rng	Thr	G at Pos	BFW
1890	Pit N	13	47	6	6	1	1	0	4	6	0	9	.128	.226	.191	25	-4	1	.750	-3	101	198	/3-7,2-6	-0.6

YOUNGS, ROSS Ross Middlebrook "Pep" (born Royce Middlebrook Youngs) B 4.10.1897 Shiner, TX D 10.22.1927 San Antonio, TX BL/TR 5-8/162# d9.25 HF1972

Year	Tm Lg	G	AB	R	H	2B	3B	HR	RBI	BB-IB	HP	SO	AVG	OBP	SLG	AOPS	ABR	SB-CS	FA	FR	Rng	Thr	G at Pos	BFW
1917	NY N	7	26	5	9	2	3	0	1	1	0	5	.346	.370	.654	218	3	1	1.000	1	93	202	/O-7(1-6-0)	0.4
1918	NY N	121	474	70	143	16	8	1	25	44	6	49	.302	.368	.376	129	18	10	.950	-4	99	89	*O-120(RF)/2-7	0.8
1919	NY N	130	489	73	152	**31**	7	2	43	51	7	47	.311	.384	.415	142	28	24	.942	1	96	117	*O-130(RF)	2.3
1920	NY N	153	581	92	204	27	14	6	78	75	2	55	.351	.427	.477	161	49	18-18	.935	0	96	129	*O-153(RF)	4.1
1921	†NY N	141	504	90	165	24	16	3	102	71	1	47	.327	.411	.456	129	24	21-17	.978	-3	96	87	*O-137(RF)	0.9
1922	†NY N	149	559	105	185	34	10	7	86	55	7	50	.331	.398	.465	121	19	17-9	.942	3	94	144	*O-147(RF)	1.0
1923	†NY N	152	596	**121**	200	33	12	3	87	73	5	36	.336	.412	.446	128	28	13-19	.959	-2	90	123	*O-152(RF)	0.9
1924	†NY N	133	526	112	187	33	12	10	74	77	3	31	.356	.441	.521	161	50	11-9	.955	-3	93	110	*O-132(RF)/2-2	3.5
1925	NY N	130	500	82	132	24	6	6	53	66	4	51	.264	.354	.372	89	-6	17-11	.952	-10	80	123	*O-127(RF)/2-3	-2.5
1926	NY N	95	372	62	114	12	5	4	43	37	2	19	.306	.372	.398	109	5	21	.974	0	87	138	O-94(RF)	-0.2
Total	10	1211	4627	812	1491	236	93	42	592	550	37	390	.322	.399	.441	131	218	153-83	.953	-17	92	119	*O-1199(1-6-1192)/2-12	11.2

YOUNT, EDDIE Floyd Edwin B 12.19.1915 Newton, NC D 10.26.1973 Newton, NC BR/TR 6-1/185# d9.9

Year	Tm Lg	G	AB	R	H	2B	3B	HR	RBI	BB-IB	HP	SO	AVG	OBP	SLG	AOPS	ABR	SB-CS	FA	FR	Rng	Thr	G at Pos	BFW
1937	Phi A	4	7	1	2	0	0	0	1	0	0	1	.286	.286	.286	45	-1	0-0	1.000	-0	91	0	/O-2(1-1-0)	-0.1
1939	Pit N	2	2	0	0	0	0	0	0	0	0	2	.000	.000	.000	-99	-1	0	—	0			H	-0.1
Total	2	6	9	1	2	0	0	0	1	0	0	3	.222	.222	.222	14	-2	0-0	1.000	-0	91	0	/O-2(1-1-0)	-0.2

YOUNT, ROBIN Robin R B 9.16.1955 Danville, IL BR/TR 6/170# d4.5 C2 HF1999 b-Larry OF Total (69-LF 1150-CF)

Year	Tm Lg	G	AB	R	H	2B	3B	HR	RBI	BB-IB	HP	SO	AVG	OBP	SLG	AOPS	ABR	SB-CS	FA	FR	Rng	Thr	G at Pos	BFW
1974	Mil A	107	344	48	86	14	5	3	26	12-0	1	46	.250	.276	.346	79	-11	7-7	.962	-9	103	91	*S-107	-0.9
1975	Mil A	147	558	67	149	28	2	8	52	33-3	1	69	.267	.307	.367	90	-8	12-4	.939	-13	96	86	*S-145	-0.3
1976	Mil A	**161**	638	59	161	19	3	2	54	38-3	0	69	.252	.292	.301	76	-20	16-11	.963	-3	99	102	*S-161/O(CF)	-0.4
1977	Mil A	154	605	66	174	34	4	4	49	41-1	2	80	.288	.333	.377	94	-5	16-7	.964	-3	99	102	*S-153	0.9
1978	Mil A	127	502	66	147	23	9	9	71	24-1	1	43	.293	.323	.428	110	5	16-5	.959	21	114	106	*S-125	4.1
1979	Mil A	149	577	72	154	26	5	8	51	35-3	1	52	.267	.308	.371	83	-15	11-8	.969	4	107	100	*S-149	0.5
1980	Mil A★	143	611	121	179	**49**	10	23	87	26-1	1	67	.293	.321	.519	131	22	20-5	.961	3	106	101	*S-133/D-9	4.1
1981	†Mil A	96	377	50	103	15	5	10	49	22-1	2	37	.273	.312	.419	116	6	4-1	**.985**	30	**124**	**132**	S-93/D-3	4.7
1982	†Mil A★	156	635	129	**210**	**46**	12	29	114	54-2	1	63	.331	.379	**.578**	**171**	**60**	14-3	.969	-4	101	102	*S-154/D	**7.3**
1983	Mil A★	149	578	102	178	42	**10**	17	80	72-6	3	58	.308	.383	.503	155	45	12-5	.973	-3	98	100	*S-139/D-8	5.7
1984	Mil A	160	624	105	186	27	7	16	80	67-7	1	67	.298	.362	.441	127	24	14-4	.971	17	111	104	*S-120,D-39	5.3
1985	Mil A	122	466	76	129	26	3	15	68	49-3	2	56	.277	.342	.442	115	10	10-4	.970	-3	100	56	*O-108(69-40-0),D-12/1-2	0.5
1986	Mil A	140	522	82	163	31	7	9	46	62-7	4	73	.312	.388	.450	124	19	14-5	**.997**	3	103	130	*O-131(CF)/1-3,D-6	2.2
1987	Mil A	158	635	99	198	25	9	21	103	76-10	1	94	.312	.384	.479	124	23	19-9	.987	-2	99	75	*O-150(CF)/D-8	2.0
1988	Mil A	**162**	621	92	190	38	**11**	13	91	63-10	3	63	.306	.369	.465	132	27	22-4	.996	3	99	157	*O-158(CF)/D-4	3.2
1989	Mil A	160	614	101	195	38	9	21	103	63-9	6	71	.318	.384	.511	153	43	19-3	.981	-4	96	104	*O-143(CF),D-17	4.0
1990	Mil A	158	587	98	145	17	5	17	77	78-6	6	89	.247	.337	.380	102	3	15-8	.991	-6	100	36	*O-157(CF)/D	-0.4
1991	Mil A	130	503	66	131	20	4	10	77	54-8	4	79	.260	.332	.376	99	0	6-4	.994	-5	101	16	*O-117(CF),D-13	-0.6
1992	Mil A	150	557	71	147	40	3	8	77	53-9	3	81	.264	.325	.390	103	3	15-6	.995	-6	95	75	*O-139(CF),D-11	-0.3
1993	Mil A	127	454	62	117	25	3	8	51	44-5	5	93	.258	.326	.379	91	-5	9-2	.997	-1	100	96	*O-114(CF)/1-7,D-6	-0.4
Total	20	2856	11008	1632	3142	583	126	251	1406	966-95	48	1350	.285	.342	.430	115	226	271-105	.964	20	104	102	*S-1479,*O-1218C,D-138/1-12	41.2

YURAK, JEFF Jeffrey Lynn B 2.26.1954 Pasadena, CA BB/TR 6-3/195# d9.15

Year	Tm Lg	G	AB	R	H	2B	3B	HR	RBI	BB-IB	HP	SO	AVG	OBP	SLG	AOPS	ABR	SB-CS	FA	FR	Rng	Thr	G at Pos	BFW
1978	Mil A	5	5	0	0	0	0	0	0	1-0	0	0	.000	.167	.000	-49	-1	0-0	1.000	1	332	0	/O(LF)	-0.1

Year	Tm Lg	G	AB	R	H	2B	3B	HR	RBI	BB-IB	HP	SO	AVG	OBP	SLG	AOPS	ABR	SB-CS	FA	FR	Rng	Thr	G at Pos	BFW
YVARS, SAL Salvador Anthony B 2.20.1924 New York, NY BR/TR 5-10/187# d9.27																								
1947	NY N	1	5	0	1	0	0	0	0	0	0	2	.200	.200	.200	6	-1	0	1.000	-0	*0*	*0*	/C	-0.1
1948	NY N	15	38	4	8	1	0	1	6	3	1	1	.211	.286	.316	62	-2	0	1.000	2	*104*	*109*	C-15	0.0
1949	NY N	3	8	0	0	0	0	0	0	1	0	1	.000	.111	.000	-68	-2	0	1.000	0	*69*	*0*	/C-2	-0.2
1950	NY N	9	14	0	2	0	0	0	0	1	0	2	.143	.200	.143	-8	-2	0	.963	1	*137*	*185*	/C-9	-0.1
1951	†NY N	25	41	9	13	2	0	2	3	5	2	7	.317	.417	.512	147	3	0-0	.942	-2	*131*	*78*	C-23	0.2
1952	NY N	66	151	15	37	3	0	4	18	10	1	16	.245	.296	.344	77	-5	0-0	.988	6	*205*	*138*	C-59	0.3
1953	NY N	23	47	1	13	0	0	0	1	7	0	1	.277	.370	.277	71	-2	0-0	1.000	1	*134*	*118*	C-20	0.0
	StL N	30	57	4	14	2	0	1	6	4	1	6	.246	.306	.333	67	-3	0-1	.989	1	*91*	*146*	C-26	-0.1
	Year	53	104	5	27	2	0	1	7	11	1	7	.260	.336	.308	69	-4	0-1	.994	3	*112*	*133*	C-46	-0.1
1954	StL N	38	57	8	14	4	0	2	8	6	1	5	.246	.328	.421	93	-1	1-0	1.000	-1	*140*	*154*	C-21	-0.1
Total	8	210	418	41	102	12	0	10	42	37	6	41	.244	.315	.344	76	-15	1-1	.987	9	*150*	*127*	C-176	-0.1
ZACHER, ELMER Elmer Henry "Silver" B 9.17.1883 Buffalo, NY D 12.20.1944 Buffalo, NY BR/TR 5-9/190# d4.30																								
1910	NY N	1	0	0	0	0	0	0	0	0	0	0	—	—	—	—	0	0	1.000	0	132	0	/O(CF)	0.0
	StL N	47	132	7	28	5	1	0	10	10	2	19	.212	.278	.265	61	-7	3	.966	2	107	143	O-36(11-12-13)/2	-0.6
	Year	48	132	7	28	5	1	0	10	10	2	19	.212	.278	.265	61	-7	3	.966	2	107	142	O-37(11-13-13)/2	-0.6
ZAHNER, FRED Frederick Joseph B 6.5.1870 Louisville, KY D 7.24.1900 Louisville, KY d7.23																								
1894	Lou N	14	49	7	10	0	1	0	4	3	0	6	.204	.250	.245	21	-7	2	.778	-3	*102*	*60*	C-10/O-2(RF),1S	-0.7
1895	Lou N	21	49	7	11	1	1	0	6	6	1	4	.224	.321	.286	61	-3	0	.824	-5	*90*	*114*	C-21	-0.6
Total	2	35	98	14	21	1	2	0	10	9	1	10	.214	.287	.265	41	-10	2	.805	-8	*94*	*94*	/C-31,O-2(RF),S1	-1.3
ZAK, FRANKIE Frank Thomas B 2.22.1922 Passaic, NJ D 2.6.1972 Passaic, NJ BR/TR 5-10/150# d4.21																								
1944	Pit N☆	87	160	33	48	3	1	0	11	22	0	18	.300	.385	.331	99	1	6	.948	-1	104	88	S-67	0.3
1945	Pit N	15	28	2	4	2	0	0	3	3	0	5	.143	.226	.214	22	-3	0	.971	1	117	83	S-10/2	-0.2
1946	Pit N	21	20	8	4	0	0	0	0	1	0	0	.200	.238	.200	24	-2	0	.929	4	159	148	S-10	0.3
Total	3	123	208	43	56	5	1	0	14	26	0	23	.269	.350	.303	82	-4	6	.948	4	110	93	/S-87,2	0.4
ZALUSKY, JACK John Francis B 6.22.1879 Minneapolis, MN D 8.11.1935 Minneapolis, MN BR/TR 5-11.5/172# d9.4																								
1903	NY A	7	16	2	5	0	0	0	1	1	0		.313	.353	.313	95	0	0	1.000	-1	*100*	*63*	/C-6,1	-0.1
ZAMBRANO, EDDIE Eduardo Jose (Guerra) B 2.1.1966 Maracaibo, Venezuela BR/TR 6-2/175# d9.19																								
1993	Chi N	8	17	1	5	0	0	0	2	1-0	0	3	.294	.333	.294	71	-1	0-0	1.000	-1	24	0	/O-4(1-0-3),1-2	-0.2
1994	Chi N	67	116	17	30	7	0	6	18	16-0	1	29	.259	.353	.474	115	3	2-1	.944	-3	85	71	O-27(9-0-18)/1-9,3-4	-0.1
Total	2	75	133	18	35	7	0	6	20	17-0	1	32	.263	.351	.451	109	2	2-1	.946	-4	79	64	/O-31(10-0-21),1-11,3-4	-0.3
ZAPUSTAS, JOE Joseph John B 7.25.1907 Boston, MA D 1.14.2001 Randolph, MA BR/TR 6-1/185# d9.28																								
1933	Phi A	2	5	0	1	0	0	0	0	0	0	0	.200	.200	.200	6	-1	0-0	1.000	-0	83	0	/O-2(1-1-0)	-0.1
ZARDON, JOSE Jose Antonio (Sanchez) "Guineo" B 5.20.1923 Havana, Cuba BR/TR 6/150# d4.18																								
1945	Was A	54	131	13	38	5	3	0	13	7	0	11	.290	.326	.374	112	1	3-1	.972	2	121	64	O-43(16-25-3)	0.2
ZARILLA, AL Allen Lee "Zeke" B 5.1.1919 Los Angeles, CA D 8. 28 1996 Honolulu, HI BL/TR 5-11/180# d6.30 Mil 1945 C1																								
1943	StL A	70	228	27	58	7	1	2	17	17	1	20	.254	.309	.320	82	-5	1-1	.962	1	104	123	O-60(0-6-56)	-0.8
1944	†StL A	100	288	43	86	13	6	6	45	29	6	33	.299	.375	.448	127	10	1-1	.977	-0	104	65	O-79(74-2-4)	0.6
1946	StL A	125	371	46	96	14	9	4	43	27	1	37	.259	.311	.377	87	-8	3-5	.973	10	**111**	169	*O-107(46-17-51)	-0.4
1947	StL A	127	380	34	85	15	6	3	38	40	3	45	.224	.303	.318	71	-15	3-6	.986	-2	97	86	*O-110(23-22-72)	-2.4
1948	StL A★	144	529	77	174	39	3	12	74	48	4	48	.329	.389	.482	128	21	11-6	.962	-9	96	47	*O-136(26-58-61)	0.7
1949	StL A	15	56	10	14	1	0	1	6	8	1	2	.250	.354	.321	76	-2	1-1	1.000	-2	74	0	O-15(10-1-8)	-0.5
	Bos A	124	474	68	133	32	4	9	71	48	4	51	.281	.352	.422	97	-3	4-4	.984	-5	98	52	*O-122(2-2-119)	-1.2
	Year	139	530	78	147	33	4	10	77	56	5	53	.277	.352	.411	95	-4	5-5	.985	-7	96	47	*O-137(12-3-127)	-1.7
1950	Bos A	130	471	92	153	32	10	9	74	76	4	47	.325	.423	.493	122	18	2-3	.976	-4	92	114	*O-128(RF)	0.9
1951	Chi A	120	382	56	98	21	2	10	60	60	4	57	.257	.363	.401	109	6	2-4	.983	-9	80	94	*O-117(7-0-112)	-0.7
1952	Chi A	39	99	14	23	4	1	2	7	14	1	6	.232	.333	.354	90	-1	1-0	.974	-2	80	123	O-32(17-0-18)	-0.4
	StL A	48	130	20	31	6	0	1	9	27	1	15	.238	.373	.308	88	0	2-1	.976	2	101	205	O-35(21-10-8)	0.0
	Bos A	21	60	9	11	0	1	2	8	7	0	8	.183	.269	.317	58	-4	2-0	.941	1	92	247	O-19(0-6-14)	-0.3
	Year	108	289	43	65	10	2	5	24	48	2	29	.225	.339	.325	83	-5	5-1	.968	1	92	188	O-86(38-16-40)	-0.7
1953	Bos A	57	67	11	13	2	0	0	4	14	0	13	.194	.333	.224	50	-4	0-1	.947	-1	85	130	O-18(3-7-9)	-0.5
Total	10	1120	3535	507	975	186	43	61	456	415	30	382	.276	.357	.405	102	13	33-33	.974	-19	96	97	O-978(229-131-660)	-5.0
ZAUCHIN, NORM Norbert Henry B 11.17.1929 Royal Oak, MI D 1.31.1999 Birmingham, AL BR/TR 6-4.5/220# d9.23 Mil 1952																								
1951	Bos A	5	12	0	2	1	0	0	0	0	0	4	.167	.167	.250	11	-2	0-1	.957	0	121	327	/1-4	-0.2
1955	Bos A	130	477	65	114	10	0	27	93	69-1	3	105	.239	.335	.430	97	-3	3-0	**.995**	0	98	95	*1-126	-1.0
1956	Bos A	44	84	12	18	2	0	2	11	14-0	1	22	.214	.333	.310	63	-4	0-0	.990	-1	75	95	1-31	-0.7
1957	Bos A	52	91	11	24	3	0	3	14	9-0	2	13	.264	.343	.396	96	0	0-0	.972	-0	113	147	1-36	-0.2
1958	Was A	96	303	35	69	8	2	15	37	38-1	1	68	.228	.310	.416	101	0	0-0	.995	1	101	86	1-91	-0.4
1959	Was A	19	71	11	15	4	0	3	4	7-0	1	14	.211	.291	.394	87	-1	2-0	.995	-2	48	104	1-19	-0.5
Total	6	346	1038	134	242	28	2	50	159	137-2	8	226	.233	.324	.408	93	-10	5-1	.993	-3	95	99	1-307	-3.0
ZAUN, GREGG Gregory Owen B 4.14.1971 Glendale, CA BB/TR 5-10/170# d6.24																								
1995	Bal A	40	104	18	27	5	0	3	14	16-0	0	14	.260	.358	.394	94	-1	1-1	.987	3	117	98	C-39/D	0.4
1996	Bal A	50	108	16	25	8	1	1	13	11-2	2	15	.231	.309	.352	68	-5	0-0	.987	-5	72	65	C-49	-0.8
	Fla N	10	31	4	9	1	0	1	2	3-1	0	5	.290	.353	.419	106	0	1-0	1.000	2	336	38	C-10	0.3
1997	†Fla N	58	143	21	43	10	2	2	20	26-4	2	18	.301	.415	.441	130	8	1-0	.978	5	95	97	C-50/1	1.5
1998	Fla N	106	298	19	56	12	2	5	29	35-2	1	52	.188	.274	.292	52	-22	5-2	.986	-3	96	114	C-88/2	-1.8
1999	Tex A	43	93	12	23	2	1	1	12	10-0	0	7	.247	.314	.323	62	-5	1-0	.984	2	127	136	C-37/D-2	-0.2
2000	KC A	83	234	36	64	11	0	7	33	43-3	3	34	.274	.390	.410	100	2	7-3	.988	-9	66	76	C-76/12	-0.2
2001	KC A	39	125	15	40	9	0	6	18	12-0	0	16	.320	.377	.536	127	5	1-2	.975	-2	104	84	C-35/D-2	0.4
2002	Hou N	76	185	18	41	7	1	3	24	12-1	2	36	.222	.275	.319	56	-13	1-0	.985	-4	60	46	C-44	-1.4
2003	Hou N	59	120	9	26	7	0	1	13	14-0	1	14	.217	.299	.300	56	-8	1-0	.976	-6	76	145	C-31	-1.1
	Col N	15	46	6	12	1	0	3	8	5-0	0	7	.261	.333	.478	95	0	0-1	.973	-2	87	112	C-14	-0.1
	Year	74	166	15	38	8	0	4	21	19-0	1	21	.229	.309	.349	68	-8	1-1	.975	-7	80	134	C-45	-1.2
Total	9	579	1487	174	366	73	7	33	186	187-13	11	218	.246	.332	.371	82	-39	19-9	.984	-19	93	93	C-473/D-5,2-2,1-2	-3.0
ZDEB, JOE Joseph Edmund B 6.27.1953 Compton, IL BR/TR 5-11/185# d4.7																								
1977	†KC A	105	195	26	58	5	2	2	23	16-3	0	23	.297	.346	.374	97	-1	6-5	.970	-2	93	106	O-93(88-1-8)/3D	-0.5
1978	KC A	60	127	18	32	2	3	0	11	7-0	0	18	.252	.287	.315	69	-6	3-0	.957	-1	95	88	O-52(43-0-12)/23D	-0.8
1979	KC A	15	23	3	4	1	1	0	0	2-0	0	4	.174	.240	.304	45	-2	1-0	1.000	-0	108	0	/O-9(6-0-3)	-0.2
Total	3	180	345	47	94	8	6	2	34	25-3	0	45	.272	.317	.348	83	-9	10-5	.967	-3	95	93	O-154(137-1-23)/D-5,3-2,2	-1.5
ZEARFOSS, DAVE David William Tilden B 1.1.1868 Schenectady, NY D 9.12.1945 Wilmington, DE TR 5-9/174# d4.17																								
1896	NY N	19	60	5	13	1	1	0	6	5	1	5	.217	.288	.267	48	-5	2	.893	-3	*93*	*91*	C-19	-0.6
1897	NY N	5	10	1	3	0	1	0	0	0	0		.300	.300	.500	112	0	0	.880	2	*173*	*198*	/C-5	0.2
1898	NY N	1	1	0	1	0	0	0	0	0	0		1.000	1.000	1.000	489	0	0	1.000	0	*0*	*327*	/C	0.1
1904	StL N	27	80	7	17	2	0	0	9	10	0		.213	.300	.237	70	-2	0	.966	-3	*85*	*86*	C-25	-0.3
1905	StL N	20	51	2	8	0	1	0	2	4	0		.157	.218	.196	24	-5	0	.966	-1	*88*	*109*	C-19	-0.5
Total	5	72	202	15	42	3	3	0	17	19	1	5	.208	.279	.252	56	-12	2	.943	-6	*92*	*101*	/C-69	-1.1
ZEBER, GEORGE George William B 8.29.1950 Ellwood City, PA BB/TR 5-11/170# d5.7																								
1977	†NY A	25	65	8	21	3	0	3	10	9-1	0	11	.323	.405	.508	149	5	0-0	.961	-0	107	102	2-21/S-2,3-2,D	0.5
1978	NY A	3	6	0	0	0	0	0	0	0-0	0	0	.000	.000	.000	-99	-2	0-0	.750	-1	57	0	/2	-0.3
Total	2	28	71	8	21	3	0	3	10	9-1	0	11	.296	.375	.465	129	3	0-0	.953	-1	104	96	/2-22,3-2,S-2,D	0.2
ZEIDER, ROLLIE Rollie Hubert "Bunions" B 11.16.1883 Auburn, IN D 9.12.1967 Garrett, IN BR/TR 5-10/162# d4.14 OF Total (6-LF 1-CF 1-RF)																								
1910	Chi A	136	498	57	108	9	2	0	31	62	1		.217	.305	.243	75	-12	49	.931	-6	96	108	2-87,S-45/3-4	-1.8
1911	Chi A	73	217	39	55	3	0	2	21	29	2		.253	.347	.295	82	-4	28	.997	-4	115	80	1-29,S-17,3-10/2-9	-0.7
1912	Chi A	130	420	57	103	12	10	1	42	50	3		.245	.330	.329	91	-4	48	.979	4	136	91	1-66,3-56/S	-0.1

Year	Tm Lg	G	AB	R	H	2B	3B	HR	RBI	BB-IB	HP	SO	AVG	OBP	SLG	AOPS	ABR	SB-CS	FA	FR	Rng	Thr	G at Pos	BFW
1913	Chi A	16	20	4	7	0	0	0	2	4	0	1	.350	.458	.350	139	1	3	1.000	1	95	0	/3-6,1-3,2	0.3
	NY A	50	159	15	37	2	0	0	12	25	1	9	.233	.341	.245	72	-4	3	.901	-9	78	104	S-24,2-19/1-4,3-2	-1.2
	Year	66	179	19	44	2	0	0	14	29	1	10	.246	.354	.257	79	-3	6	.901	-8	78	104	S-24,2-20/3-8,1-7	-0.9
1914	Chi F	119	452	60	124	13	2	1	36	44	4	28	.274	.344	.319	86	-15	35	.936	-5	94	**170**	*3-117/S	-1.7
1915	Chi F	129	494	65	112	22	2	0	34	43	6	24	.227	.297	.279	66	-30	16	.941	-3	97	125	2-83,3-30,S-21	-3.1
1916	Chi N	98	345	29	81	11	2	1	22	26	3	26	.235	.294	.287	71	-11	9	.928	-2	105	138	3-55,2-33/O-7(6-0-1),S-5,1-2	-1.3
1917	Chi N	108	354	36	86	14	2	0	27	28	2	30	.243	.302	.294	77	-9	17	.901	-14	66	82	S-48,3-26,2-24/1O(CF)	-2.2
1918	†Chi N	82	251	31	56	3	2	0	26	23	0	20	.223	.288	.251	63	-11	16	.956	-7	95	80	2-79/13	-1.9
Total	9	941	3210	393	769	89	22	5	253	334	22	138	.240	.315	.286	77	-99	224	.945	-45	95	97	2-335,3-307,S-162,1-106/O-8L	-13.7
ZEILE, TODD Todd Edward B 9.9.1965 Van Nuys, CA BR/TR 6-1/190# d8.18 OF Total (LF)																								
1989	StL N	28	82	7	21	3	1	1	8	9-1	0	14	.256	.326	.354	92	-1	0-0	.971	1	94	26	C-23	0.2
1990	StL N	144	495	62	121	25	3	15	57	67-3	2	77	.244	.333	.398	101	2	2-4	.988	-5	93	119	*C-105,3-24,1-11/O(LF)	0.1
1991	StL N	155	565	76	158	36	3	11	81	62-3	5	94	.280	.353	.412	115	13	17-11	.943	3	106	76	*3-154	1.6
1992	StL N	126	439	51	113	18	4	7	48	68-4	0	70	.257	.352	.364	108	7	7-10	.960	-5	100	102	*3-124	0.0
1993	StL N	157	571	82	158	36	1	17	103	70-5	0	76	.277	.352	.433	112	11	5-4	.923	-10	103	110	*3-153	0.2
1994	StL N	113	415	62	111	25	1	19	75	52-3	3	56	.267	.348	.470	114	9	1-3	.960	1	104	141	*3-112	1.0
1995	StL N	34	127	16	37	6	0	5	22	18-1	1	23	.291	.378	.457	121	4	1-0	.980	2	129	118	1-34	0.3
	Chi N	79	299	34	68	16	0	9	30	16-0	3	53	.227	.271	.371	69	-14	0-0	.939	-8	95	107	3-75/O-2(LF),1	-2.2
	Year	113	426	50	105	22	0	14	52	34-1	4	76	.246	.305	.397	85	-10	1-0	.939	-7	95	107	3-75,1-35/O-2(LF)	-1.9
1996	Phi N	134	500	61	134	24	0	20	80	67-4	1	88	.268	.353	.436	106	6	1-1	.962	-14	84	77	*3-106,1-28	-1.0
	†Bal A	29	117	17	28	8	0	5	19	15-0	0	16	.239	.326	.436	91	-2	0-0	.964	2	102	170	3-29	0.0
1997	LA N	160	575	89	154	17	0	31	90	85-7	6	112	.268	.365	.459	124	21	8-7	.931	-18	83	105	*3-160	0.4
1998	LA N	40	158	22	40	6	1	7	27	10-0	1	24	.253	.300	.437	97	-2	1-1	.929	-11	68	28	3-40/1	-1.2
	Fla N	66	234	37	68	12	1	6	39	31-2	2	34	.291	.374	.427	117	7	2-3	.971	-4	96	83	3-65	0.3
	Year	106	392	59	108	18	2	13	66	41-2	3	58	.276	.345	.431	110	5	3-4	.957	-15	85	62	*3-105/1	-0.9
	†Tex A	52	180	26	47	14	1	6	28	28-0	1	32	.261	.358	.450	106	2	1-0	.915	0	103	86	3-52	0.3
1999	†Tex A	156	588	80	172	41	1	24	98	56-3	4	94	.293	.354	.488	108	7	1-2	.941	6	108	90	*3-155/1D	1.3
2000	†NY N	153	544	67	146	36	3	22	79	74-4	2	85	.268	.356	.467	111	9	3-4	.992	4	111	78	*1-151	-0.1
2001	NY N	151	531	66	141	25	1	10	62	73-3	6	102	.266	.359	.373	95	-2	1-0	.992	10	129	100	*1-149	-0.5
2002	Col N	144	506	61	138	23	0	18	87	66-3	1	92	.273	.353	.425	94	-5	1-1	.942	-11	96	82	*3-139/P	-1.5
2003	NY A	66	186	29	39	8	0	6	23	24-0	0	36	.210	.294	.349	72	-8	0-0	.917	2	101	199	3-30,1-23/D-8	-0.7
	Mon N	34	113	11	29	2	2	5	19	10-0	3	18	.257	.331	.442	91	-2	1-0	.947	3	115	72	3-34	0.2
Total	15	2021	7225	956	1923	381	23	244	1075	901-46	41	1196	.266	.347	.427	105	62	53-51	.942	-53	98	97	*3-1452,1-399,C-128/D-9,O-3L,P	-1.3
ZELLER, BART Barton Wallace B 7.22.1941 Chicago Heights, IL BR/TR 6-1/185# d5.21 C1																								
1970	StL N	1	0	0	0	0	0	0	0	0-0	0	0	—	—	—	—	0	0-0	1.000	0	0	0	/C	0.0
ZERNIAL, GUS Gus Edward "Ozark Ike" B 6.27.1923 Beaumont, TX BR/TR 6-2.5/210# d4.19																								
1949	Chi A	73	198	29	63	17	2	5	38	15	0	26	.318	.366	.500	132	8	0-1	1.000	-1	88	142	O-46(LF)	0.4
1950	Chi A	143	543	75	152	16	4	29	93	38	3	110	.280	.330	.484	110	2	0-2	.969	1	103	86	*O-137(LF)	-0.7
1951	Chi A	4	19	2	2	0	0	0	4	2	0	2	.105	.190	.105	-19	-3	0-0	.933	1	107	241	/O-4(LF)	-0.3
	Phi A	139	552	90	151	30	5	33	125	61	4	99	.274	.350	.525	132	21	2-2	.974	8	103	155	*O-138(LF)	1.8
	Year	143	571	92	153	30	5	**33**	**129**	63	4	101	.268	.345	.511	127	18	2-2	.972	8	103	158	*O-142(LF)	1.5
1952	Phi A	145	549	76	144	15	1	29	100	70	1	87	.262	.347	.452	114	9	5-1	.972	-3	98	65	*O-141(LF)	-0.4
1953	Phi A★	147	556	85	158	21	3	42	108	57	4	79	.284	.355	.559	138	27	4-0	.972	5	99	**156**	*O-141(LF)	2.4
1954	Phi A	97	336	42	84	8	2	14	62	30	4	60	.250	.316	.411	98	-2	0-0	.953	-1	102	74	O-90(LF)/1-2	-0.9
1955	KC A	120	413	62	105	9	3	30	84	30-1	3	90	.254	.304	.508	116	5	1-0	.964	5	**110**	106	*O-103(LF)	0.4
1956	KC A	109	272	36	61	12	0	16	44	33-2	4	66	.224	.315	.445	99	-2	2-0	.984	3	93	201	O-69(LF)	-0.2
1957	KC A	131	437	56	103	20	1	27	69	34-0	1	84	.236	.290	.471	104	0	1-1	.952	-1	99	70	*O-113(LF)/1	-0.8
1958	Det A	66	124	8	40	7	1	5	23	6-0	0	25	.323	.351	.516	127	4	0-0	.939	-2	82	89	O-24(LF)	0.2
1959	Det A	60	132	11	30	4	0	7	26	7-0	0	27	.227	.262	.417	80	-4	0-0	.972	-3	65	103	1-32/O(RF)	-0.9
Total	11	1234	4131	572	1093	159	22	237	776	383-3	24	755	.265	.329	.486	115	65	15-7	.968	12	100	112	*O-1007(1006-0-1)/1-35	1.0
ZIEGLER, CHARLIE Charles Wallace B 1.13.1875 Canton, OH D 4.18.1904 Canton, OH d9.23																								
1899	Cle N	2	8	2	2	0	0	0	0	0	0		.250	.250	.250	40	-1	0	.750	-1	72	0	/S2	-0.1
1900	Phi N	3	11	0	3	0	0	0	1	0	0		.273	.273	.273	51	-1	0	.889	-1	69	0	/3-3	-0.1
Total	2	5	19	2	5	0	0	0	1	0	0		.263	.263	.263	47	-2	0	.889	-1	69	0	/3-3,2S	-0.2
ZIENTARA, BENNY Benedict Joseph B 2.14.1918 Chicago, IL D 4.16.1985 Lake Elsinore, CA BR/TR 5-9/165# d9.11 Mil 1942-45																								
1941	Cin N	9	21	3	6	0	0	0	2	1	0	3	.286	.318	.286	71	-1	0	.914	-0	105	91	/2-6	-0.1
1946	Cin N	78	280	26	81	10	2	0	16	14	0	11	.289	.323	.339	91	-4	3	.970	18	136	151	2-39,3-36	1.6
1947	Cin N	117	418	60	108	18	1	2	24	23	0	23	.258	.297	.321	64	-22	2	.976	-10	92	81	*2-100,3-13	-2.7
1948	Cin N	74	187	17	35	1	2	0	7	12	0	11	.187	.236	.214	23	-21	0	.990	7	103	103	2-60/3-3,S-2	-1.1
Total	4	278	906	106	230	29	5	2	49	50	0	48	.254	.293	.304	64	-48	5	.976	15	103	100	2-205/3-52,S-2	-2.3
ZIES, BILL William B 6.16.1867 Rock Island, IL D 4.16.1907 Beardstown, IL BL d8.9																								
1891	StL AA	2	3	0	1	0	0	0	0	0	0	0	.333	.333	.333	79	0	0	1.000	0	*155*	*106*	/C-2	0.0
ZIMMER, CHIEF Charles Louis B 11.23.1860 Marietta, OH D 8.22.1949 Cleveland, OH BR/TR 6/190# d7.18 M1 U1																								
1884	Det N	8	29	0	2	1	0	0	0	1		14	.069	.100	.103	-38	-4		.830	-1			/C-6,O-2(RF)	-0.5
1886	NY AA	6	19	1	3	0	0	0	1	1	1		.158	.238	.158	27	-1	0	.893	2			/C-6	0.1
1887	Cle AA	14	52	9	12	5	0	0	4	4	1		.231	.298	.327	77	-1	1	.923	-2			C-12/1-2	-0.2
1888	Cle AA	65	212	27	51	11	4	0	22	18	4		.241	.312	.330	109	3	15	.917	9			C-59/O-3(0-1-2),1-3,S	1.5
1889	Cle N	84	259	47	67	9	9	1	21	44	1	35	.259	.368	.375	110	4	14	.931	11			C-81/1-3	1.8
1890	Cle N	125	444	54	95	16	6	2	57	46	11	54	.214	.303	.291	75	-13	15	.937	21	*117*	***114***	*C-125	1.6
1891	Cle N	116	440	55	112	21	4	3	69	33	4	49	.255	.312	.341	87	-8	15	.936	14	*92*	***138***	*C-116/3	1.4
1892	†Cle N	111	413	63	109	29	13	1	64	32	7	47	.264	.327	.404	116	7	18	.938	21	*130*	*82*	*C-111	3.4
1893	Cle N	57	227	27	70	13	7	2	41	16	1	15	.308	.357	.454	108	1	4	.968	11	*113*	*129*	C-56/3	1.3
1894	Cle N	90	341	55	97	20	5	4	65	17	5	31	.284	.328	.408	73	-17	14	**.963**	27	***161***	*110*	*C-89	1.4
1895	†Cle N	88	315	60	107	21	2	5	56	33	9	30	.340	.417	.467	121	11	14	.975	10	*120*	*88*	C-84/1-3	2.3
1896	†Cle N	91	336	46	93	18	3	3	46	31	9	48	.277	.354	.375	87	-6	4	**.972**	17	***150***	*83*	*C-91/3	1.6
1897	Cle N	80	294	50	93	22	3	0	40	25	4		.316	.378	.412	103	2	8	.976	11	*113*	*96*	C-80	1.7
1898	Cle N	20	63	5	15	2	0	0	4	5	1		.238	.304	.270	66	-3	2	.970	4	*113*	*87*	C-19	0.3
1899	Cle N	20	73	9	25	2	1	2	14	5	3		.342	.407	.479	154	6	1	.957	-5	*59*	*120*	C-20	0.2
	Lou N	75	262	43	78	11	3	2	29	22	8		.298	.370	.385	107	3	9	.985	5	*115*	*102*	C-62,1-11	1.2
	Year	95	335	52	103	13	4	4	43	27	11		.307	.378	.406	117	9	10	**.978**	-0	*102*	*106*	C-82,1-11	1.4
1900	†Pit N	82	271	27	80	7	10	0	35	17	11		.295	.361	.395	108	2	4	.961	6	***129***	*93*	C-78/1-2	1.4
1901	Pit N	69	236	17	52	7	3	0	21	20	4		.220	.292	.275	63	-11	6	.975	-0	*126*	*91*	C-68	-0.4
1902	Pit N	42	142	13	38	4	2	0	17	11	4		.268	.338	.324	101	0	4	.969	2	*144*	*91*	C-41/1	0.7
1903	Phi N	37	118	9	26	3	1	1	19	9	3		.220	.292	.288	68	-5	3	.968	1	*90*	*94*	C-35,M	-0.1
Total	19	1280	4546	617	1225	222	76	26	625	390	91	323	.269	.339	.369	95	-30	151	.952	161	*107*	*89*	*C-1239/1-25,O-5(0-1-4),3-3,S	20.7
ZIMMER, DON Donald William B 1.17.1931 Cincinnati, OH BR/TR 5-9/177# d7.2 M14 C22 OF Total (5-LF 4-RF)																								
1954	Bro N	24	33	3	6	0	1	0	0	3	1	8	.182	.270	.242	34	-3	2-0	.939	2	120	107	S-13	-0.1
1955	†Bro N	88	280	38	67	10	1	15	50	19-5	2	66	.239	.289	.443	89	-6	5-3	.976	3	97	138	2-62,S-21/3-8	0.3
1956	Bro N	17	20	4	6	1	0	0	2	0-0	1	7	.300	.333	.350	78	-1	0-1	.944	1	94	160	/S-8,3-3,2	0.0
1957	Bro N	84	269	23	59	9	1	6	19	16-5	0	63	.219	.262	.327	52	-18	1-3	.957	4	99	51	3-39,S-37/2-5	-1.2
1958	LA N	127	455	52	119	15	2	17	60	28-1	1	92	.262	.305	.415	86	-11	14-2	.965	24	104	118	*S-114,3-12/2O(LF)	2.6
1959	†LA N	97	249	21	41	7	1	4	28	37-7	1	56	.165	.274	.249	38	-22	3-1	.972	2	98	96	S-88/3-5,2	-1.4
1960	Chi N	132	368	37	95	16	7	6	35	27-4	0	56	.258	.307	.389	90	-6	8-6	.980	1	113	57	2-75,3-45/S-5,O-2(LF)	-0.1
1961	Chi N★	128	477	57	120	25	4	13	40	25-1	2	70	.252	.291	.403	81	-14	5-1	.973	4	101	120	*2-116/3-5,O(RF)	-0.1
1962	NY N	14	52	3	4	1	0	0	1	3-0	0	10	.077	.127	.096	-38	-10	0-1	.961	3	134	103	3-14	-0.8
	Cin N	63	192	16	48	11	2	2	16	14-1	1	30	.250	.304	.359	75	-7	1-2	.949	-3	88	85	3-43,2-17/S	-1.0
	Year	77	244	19	52	12	2	2	17	17-1	1	40	.213	.267	.303	51	-17	1-3	.952	-0	100	90	3-57,2-17/S	-1.8
1963	LA N	22	23	4	5	1	0	1	2	3-0	0	10	.217	.308	.391	107	0	0-0	.933	1	125	0	3-10/2S	0.1

Year	Tm Lg	G	AB	R	H	2B	3B	HR	RBI	BB-IB	HP	SO	AVG	OBP	SLG	AOPS	ABR	SB-CS	FA	FR	Rng	Thr	G at Pos	BFW
	Was A	83	298	37	74	12	1	13	44	18-2	2	57	.248	.296	.426	100	-1	3-2	.935	5	111	110	3-78/2-2	0.3
1964	Was A	121	341	38	84	16	2	12	38	27-0	0	94	.246	.302	.411	96	-2	1-3	.955	-6	99	46	3-87/O-4(2-0-3),C-2,2	-1.0
1965	Was A	95	226	20	45	6	0	2	17	26-1	2	59	.199	.284	.252	56	-13	2-0	.966	-4	*93*	*154*	C-33,3-26,2-12	-1.6
Total	12	1095	3283	353	773	130	22	91	352	246-27	13	678	.235	.290	.372	76	-114	45-25	.941	35	101	75	3-375,2-294,S-288/C-35,O-8L	-4.0
ZIMMERMAN, EDDIE Edward Desmond B 1.4.1883 Oceanic, NJ D 5.6.1945 Emmaus, PA BR/TR 5-9/160# d9.29																								
1906	StL N	5	14	0	3	0	0	0	1	0	0		.214	.214	.214	35	-1	0	.929	-0	78	0	/3-5	-0.2
1911	Bro N	122	417	31	77	10	7	3	36	34	2	37	.185	.249	.264	46	-33	9	**.961**	3	99	136	*3-122	-2.7
Total	2	127	431	31	80	10	7	3	37	34	2	37	.186	.248	.262	45	-34	9	.960	2	98	132	3-127	-2.9
ZIMMERMAN, JERRY Gerald Robert B 9.21.1934 Omaha, NE D 9.9.1998 Neskowin, OR BR/TR 6-2/185# d4.14 C13																								
1961	†Cin N	76	204	8	42	5	0	0	10	11-0	2	21	.206	.252	.230	29	-21	1-1	.975	0	*83*	*90*	C-76	-1.8
1962	Min A	34	62	8	17	4	0	0	7	3-0	1	5	.274	.318	.339	74	-2	0-0	.992	2	*154*	*94*	C-34	0.1
1963	Min A	39	56	3	13	1	0	0	3	2-0	0	8	.232	.259	.250	43	-4	0-0	1.000	1	165	62	C-39	-0.3
1964	Min A	63	120	6	24	3	0	0	12	10-0	3	15	.200	.278	.225	42	-9	0-0	.993	3	*111*	*131*	C-63	-0.5
1965	†Min A	83	154	8	33	1	1	1	11	12-3	1	23	.214	.275	.253	49	-10	0-0	**.997**	9	***142***	*86*	C-82	0.1
1966	Min A	60	119	11	30	4	1	1	15	15-4	1	23	.252	.338	.328	88	-1	0-0	.996	7	*107*	*104*	C-59	0.8
1967	Min A	104	234	13	39	3	0	1	12	22-5	2	49	.167	.243	.192	28	-21	0-1	.992	9	113	114	*C-104	-0.9
1968	Min A	24	45	3	5	1	0	0	2	3-0	1	10	.111	.180	.133	-3	-6	0-0	.991	1	131	108	C-24	-0.5
Total	8	483	994	60	203	22	2	3	72	78-12	11	154	.204	.269	.239	43	-74	1-2	.991	31	*117*	*101*	C-481	-3.0
ZIMMERMAN, HEINIE Henry B 2.9.1887 New York, NY D 3.14.1969 New York, NY BR/TR 5-11.5/176# d9.8 OF Total (3-LF 8-CF 2-RF)																								
1907	†Chi N	5	9	0	2	1	0	0	1	0	0		.222	.222	.333	70	0	0	.789	0	114	274	/2-4,SO(LF)	0.0
1908	Chi N	46	113	17	33	4	1	0	9	1	0		.292	.298	.345	101	0	2	.923	-7	76	40	2-20/O-8(2-4-2),S3	-0.8
1909	Chi N	65	183	23	50	9	2	0	21	3	0		.273	.285	.344	93	-3	7	.945	-7	77	94	2-31,S-12/3-4	-0.9
1910	†Chi N	99	335	35	95	16	6	3	38	20	1	36	.284	.326	.394	111	3	7	.948	-8	89	128	2-32,S-26,3-23/O-4(CF),1	-0.4
1911	Chi N	143	535	80	164	22	17	9	85	25	5	50	.307	.343	.462	124	13	23	.946	-5	98	96	*2-108,3-20,1-11	1.0
1912	Chi N	145	557	95	**207**	**41**	14	**14**	99	38	6	60	**.372**	.418	**.571**	**170**	**51**	23	.916	1	106	103	*3-121,1-22	5.3
1913	Chi N	127	447	69	140	28	12	9	95	41	6	40	.313	.379	.490	147	27	18-19	.912	5	107	115	*3-125	3.3
1914	Chi N	146	564	75	167	36	12	4	87	20	5	46	.296	.326	.424	123	13	17	.897	-19	85	83	*3-118,S-15,2-12	-0.2
1915	Chi N	139	520	65	138	28	11	3	62	21	5	33	.265	.300	.379	105	1	19-13	.943	-6	97	75	*2-100,3-36/S-4	-0.2
1916	Chi N	107	398	54	116	25	5	6	64	16	3	33	.291	.324	.425	116	7	15-12	.932	8	116	92	3-85,2-14/S-4	2.0
	NY N	40	151	22	41	4	0	0	19	7	0	10	.272	.304	.298	90	-2	9-8	.943	-1	98	94	3-40/2	-0.3
	Year	147	549	76	157	29	5	6	**83**	23	3	43	.286	.318	.390	110	6	24-20	**.935**	7	**110**	93	*3-125,2-15/S-4	1.7
1917	†NY N	150	585	61	174	22	9	5	**102**	16	1	43	.297	.317	.391	121	11	13	.947	14	**115**	101	*3-149/2-5	3.2
1918	NY N	121	463	43	126	19	10	1	56	13	1	23	.272	.294	.363	102	-2	14	.955	-4	95	53	*3-100,1-19	-0.4
1919	NY N	123	444	56	113	20	6	4	58	21	5	30	.255	.296	.354	96	-3	8	.940	-0	107	93	*3-123	0.0
Total	13	1456	5304	695	1566	275	105	58	796	242	38	404	.295	.331	.419	121	116	175-52	.928	-29	103	92	3-945,2-327/S-63,1-53,O-13C	11.6
ZIMMERMAN, ROY Roy Franklin B 9.13.1916 Pine Grove, PA D 11.22.1991 Pine Grove, PA BL/TL 6-2/187# d8.27																								
1945	NY N	27	98	14	27	1	0	5	15	5	3	16	.276	.330	.439	111	1	1	.988	-2	76	73	1-25/O(RF)	-0.2
ZIMMERMAN, BILL William H. B 1.20.1889 Kengen, Germany D 10.4.1952 Newark, NJ BR/TR 5-8.5/172# d4.14																								
1915	Bro N	22	57	3	16	2	0	0	7	4	0	8	.281	.328	.316	93	0	1	.864	-2	86	0	O-18(RF)	-0.4
ZINN, FRANK Frank Patrick B 12.21.1865 Phoenixville, PA D 5.12.1936 Philadelphia, PA 5-8/150# d4.18																								
1888	Phi AA	2	7	0	0	0	0	0	0	1	0		.000	.125	.000	-59	-1	0	.938	-0			/C-2	-0.1
ZINN, GUY Guy B 2.13.1887 Holbrook, WV D 10.6.1949 Clarksburg, WV BL/TR 5-10.5/170# d9.11																								
1911	NY A	9	27	5	4	0	2	0	1	4	1		.148	.281	.296	57	-2	0	.923	0	77	180	/O-8(2-4-2)	-0.2
1912	NY A	106	401	56	105	15	10	6	55	50	1		.262	.345	.394	105	2	17	.893	-9	92	65	*O-106(13-31-61)	-1.3
1913	Bos N	36	138	15	41	8	2	1	15	4	1	23	.297	.322	.406	105	0	3-4	.948	2	99	161	O-35(1-34-0)	-0.1
1914	Bal F	61	225	30	63	10	6	3	25	16	3	26	.280	.336	.418	101	-4	6	.935	-4	92	65	O-57(31-12-14)	-1.1
1915	Bal F	102	312	30	84	18	3	5	43	35	0	28	.269	.343	.394	104	-2	2	.949	-1	94	107	O-88(63-17-8)	-0.8
Total	5	314	1103	136	297	51	23	15	139	109	6	77	.269	.338	.398	103	-6	28-4	.927	-12	93	93	O-294(110-98-85)	-3.5
ZINTER, ALAN Alan Michael B 5.19.1968 ElPaso, TX BB/TR 6-2/200# d6.18																								
2002	Hou N	39	44	5	6	2	0	2	3	0-0	0	19	.136	.136	.318	16	-6	0-0	1.000	0	98	117	/1-8,C	-0.6
ZIPFEL, BUD Marion Sylvester B 11.18.1938 Belleville, IL BL/TR 6-3/200# d7.26																								
1961	Was A	50	170	17	34	7	5	4	18	15-0	0	49	.200	.262	.371	69	-9	1-1	.983	-5	74	101	1-44	-1.7
1962	Was A	68	184	21	44	4	1	6	21	17-1	1	43	.239	.307	.370	82	-5	1-2	.976	-2	113	71	1-26,O-23(LF)	-1.0
Total	2	118	354	38	78	11	6	10	39	32-1	1	92	.220	.285	.370	76	-14	2-3	.981	-7	87	91	/1-70,O-23(LF)	-2.7
ZISK, RICHIE Richard Walter B 2.6.1949 Brooklyn, NY BR/TR 6-1/208# d9.8																								
1971	Pit N	7	15	2	3	1	0	1	2	4-0	0	7	.200	.368	.467	136	1	0-0	1.000	-0	91	0	/O-6(3-0-3)	0.0
1972	Pit N	17	37	4	7	3	0	0	4	7-0	0	10	.189	.318	.270	70	-1	0-0	.938	-1	73	148	O-12(12-0-1)	-0.2
1973	Pit N	103	333	44	108	23	7	10	54	21-0	0	63	.324	.364	.526	148	20	0-0	.987	2	90	175	O-84(22-0-65)	1.8
1974	†Pit N	149	536	75	168	30	3	17	100	65-7	0	91	.313	.386	.476	146	34	1-1	.985	7	113	90	*O-141(9-0-135)	3.4
1975	†Pit N	147	504	69	146	27	3	20	75	68-9	2	109	.290	.374	.474	136	25	0-1	.975	-5	99	64	*O-140(LF)	1.3
1976	Pit N	155	581	91	168	35	2	21	89	52-3	0	96	.289	.343	.465	128	20	1-0	.987	2	100	102	*O-152(LF)	1.4
1977	Chi A★	141	531	78	154	17	6	30	101	55-7	3	98	.290	.355	.514	135	25	0-4	.982	3	101	120	*O-109(10-0-100),D-28	1.9
1978	Tex A★	140	511	68	134	19	1	22	85	58-7	3	76	.262	.338	.432	116	11	3-3	.988	-6	83	94	O-90(48-0-42),D-49	-0.2
1979	Tex A	144	503	69	132	21	1	18	64	57-4	0	75	.262	.336	.416	103	2	1-1	.972	-6	88	103	*O-134(15-0-126)/D-3	-1.1
1980	Tex A	135	448	48	130	17	1	19	77	39-5	0	72	.290	.344	.460	123	13	0-2	.980	-3	73	129	D-86,O-37(2-0-35)	0.5
1981	Sea A	94	357	42	111	12	1	16	43	28-3	3	63	.311	.366	.485	138	17	0-2	—	0	0	0	D-93	1.4
1982	Sea A	131	503	61	147	28	1	21	62	49-4	1	89	.292	.354	.477	123	16	2-1	—	0	0	0	*D-130	1.2
1983	Sea A	90	285	30	69	12	0	12	36	30-3	0	61	.242	.311	.411	94	-2	0-0	—	0	0	0	D-84	-0.5
Total	13	1453	5144	681	1477	245	26	207	792	533-52	12	910	.287	.353	.466	126	181	8-15	.981	-7	96	103	O-905(413-0-507),D-473	10.9
ZITZMANN, BILLY William Arthur B 11.19.1895 Long Island City, NY D 5.29.1985 Passaic, NJ BR/TR 5-10.5/175# d4.17																								
1919	Pit N	11	26	5	5	1	0	0	2	0	0	6	.192	.192	.231	26	-2	2	.917	-1	103	0	/O-8(LF)	-0.4
	Cin N	2	1	0	0	0	0	0	0	0	0	0	.000	.000	.000	-99	0	0	—	-0	0	0	/O(LF)	0.0
	Year	13	27	5	5	1	0	0	2	0	0	6	.185	.185	.222	22	-3	2	.917	-1	101	0	/O-9(LF)	-0.4
1925	Cin N	104	301	53	76	13	3	0	21	35	6	22	.252	.342	.316	71	-12	11-11	.959	-6	88	72	O-89(80-4-7)/S	-2.3
1926	Cin N	53	94	21	23	2	1	0	3	6	2	7	.245	.304	.287	61	-5	3	.965	-1	111	0	O-31(22-5-2)	-0.8
1927	Cin N	88	232	47	66	10	4	0	24	20	4	18	.284	.352	.362	94	-1	9	.958	-7	98	35	O-60(17-36-7)/S-8,3-3	-1.1
1928	Cin N	101	266	53	79	9	3	3	33	13	3	22	.297	.337	.387	90	-5	13	.958	-1	104	68	O-78(46-12-23)/3	-1.0
1929	Cin N	47	84	18	19	3	0	0	6	9	1	10	.226	.309	.262	45	-7	4	.940	-1	119	0	O-22(15-0-7)/1-5	-0.9
Total	6	406	1004	197	268	38	11	3	89	83	16	85	.267	.333	.336	77	-32	42-11	.956	-16	100	48	O-289(189-57-46)/S-9,1-5,3-4	-6.5
ZOCCOLILLO, PETE Peter J. B 2.6.1977 Bronx, NY BL/TR 6-2/200# d9.5																								
2003	Mil N	20	37	0	4	1	0	0	3	2-0	0	13	.108	.154	.135	-24	-7	0-0	1.000	0	128	0	/O-7(3-0-4)	-0.7
ZOSKY, EDDIE Edward James B 2.10.1968 Whittier, CA BR/TR 6/175# d9.2																								
1991	Tor A	18	27	2	4	1	1	0	2	0-0	0	8	.148	.148	.259	10	-3	0-0	1.000	-2	89	89	S-18	-0.4
1992	Tor A	8	7	1	2	0	1	0	1	0-0	0	2	.286	.250	.571	129	0	0-0	.923	1	126	124	/S-8	0.1
1995	Fla N	6	5	0	1	0	0	0	0	0-0	0	0	.200	.200	.200	6	-1	0-0	.667	-2	23	0	/S-4,2	-0.2
1999	Mil N	8	7	1	1	0	0	0	0	1-0	0	2	.143	.250	.143	3	-1	0-0	1.000	0	90	0	/3-4,2-2	-0.1
2000	Hou N	4	4	0	0	0	0	0	0	0-0	0	1	.000	.000	.000	-95	-1	0-0	—	0			/H	-0.1
Total	5	44	50	4	8	1	2	0	3	1-0	0	13	.160	.173	.260	16	-6	0-0	.963	-3	89	86	/S-30,3-4,2-3	-0.7
ZUBER, JON Jon Edward B 12.10.1969 Encino, CA BL/TL 6/190# d4.19																								
1996	Phi N	30	91	7	23	4	0	1	10	6-1	0	11	.253	.296	.330	65	-5	1-0	.987	-1	77	61	1-22	-0.8
1998	Phi N	38	45	6	11	3	1	2	6	6-0	1	9	.244	.346	.489	115	1	0-0	1.000	-0	84	0	/O-5(LF),1-4	0.0
Total	2	68	136	13	34	7	1	3	16	12-1	1	20	.250	.313	.382	82	-4	1-0	.989	-2	77	62	/1-26,O-5(LF)	-0.8

Year	Tm Lg	G	AB	R	H	2B	3B	HR	RBI	BB-IB	HP	SO	AVG	OBP	SLG	AOPS	ABR	SB-CS	FA	FR	Rng	Thr	G at Pos	BFW
ZULETA, JULIO Julio Ernesto (Tapia) B 3.28.1975 Panama City, Panama BR/TR 6-6/230# d4.6																								
2000	Chi N	30	68	13	20	8	0	3	12	2-0	3	19	.294	.342	.544	122	2	0-1	.966	-0	113	106	1-14/O-6(LF)	0.0
2001	Chi N	49	106	11	23	3	0	6	24	8-1	3	32	.217	.288	.415	84	-3	0-1	.991	-4	42	58	1-35	-0.9
Total	2	79	174	24	43	11	0	9	36	10-1	6	51	.247	.309	.466	99	-1	0-2	.984	-4	63	72	/1-49,O-6(LF)	-0.9
ZUPCIC, BOB Robert B 8.18.1966 Pittsburgh, PA BR/TR 6-4/220# d9.7																								
1991	Bos A	18	25	3	4	0	0	1	3	1-0	0	6	.160	.192	.280	28	-3	0-0	.875	-2	76	0	O-16(3-7-6)	-0.4
1992	Bos A	124	392	46	108	19	1	3	43	25-1	4	60	.276	.322	.352	84	-8	2-2	.977	1	94	176	*O-114(32-68-22)/D-5	-1.0
1993	Bos A	141	286	40	69	24	2	2	26	27-2	2	54	.241	.308	.360	75	-10	5-2	.979	-0	95	129	*O-122(48-37-54)/D-5	-1.2
1994	Bos A	4	4	0	0	0	0	0	0	0-0	0	1	.000	.000	.000	-96	-1	0-1	1.000	-0	72	0	/O-2(LF),D	-0.2
	Chi A	32	88	10	18	4	1	1	8	4-0	0	16	.205	.237	.307	40	-8	0-0	1.000	1	107	128	O-28(15-0-14)/3-2,1	-0.8
	Year	36	92	10	18	4	1	1	8	4-0	0	17	.196	.227	.293	34	-10	0-1	1.000	0	105	121	O-30(17-0-14)/3-2,D1	-1.0
Total	4	319	795	99	199	47	4	7	80	57-3	6	137	.250	.303	.346	73	-30	7-5	.977	-1	95	146	O-282(100-112-96)/D-11,3-2,1	-3.6
ZUPO, FRANK Frank Joseph "Noodles" B 8.29.1939 San Francisco, CA BL/TR 5-11/182# d7.1																								
1957	Bal A	10	12	2	1	0	0	0	0	1-0	0	4	.083	.154	.083	-36	-2	0-0	.913	-0	*93*	*126*	/C-8	-0.3
1958	Bal A	1	2	0	0	0	0	0	0	0-0	0	1	.000	.000	.000	-99	-1	0-0	1.000	0	*0*	*0*	/C	0.0
1961	Bal A	5	4	1	2	1	0	0	0	1-0	0	1	.500	.600	.750	268	1	0-0	1.000	0	*0*	*0*	/C-4	0.1
Total	3	16	18	3	3	1	0	0	0	2-0	0	6	.167	.250	.222	31	-2	0-0	.941	-0	*63*	*85*	/C-13	-0.2
ZUVELLA, PAUL Paul B 10.31.1958 San Mateo, CA BR/TR 6/178# d9.4 C1																								
1982	Atl N	2	1	0	0	0	0	0	0	0-0	0	0	.000	.000	.000	-96	0	0-0	.800	0	225	0	/S	0.0
1983	Atl N	3	5	0	0	0	0	0	0	2-0	1	1	.000	.375	.000	11	0	0-0	.750	-2	39	0	/S-2	-0.2
1984	Atl N	11	25	2	5	1	0	0	1	2-0	0	3	.200	.259	.240	38	-2	0-0	1.000	-0	114	143	/2-6,S-6	-0.2
1985	Atl N	81	190	16	48	8	1	0	4	16-1	0	14	.253	.311	.305	69	-8	2-0	.986	1	110	79	2-42,S-33/3-5	-0.2
1986	NY A	21	48	2	4	1	0	0	2	5-0	0	4	.083	.170	.104	-24	-8	0-0	.966	2	109	115	S-21	-0.4
1987	NY A	14	34	2	6	0	0	0	0	0-0	0	4	.176	.176	.176	-6	-5	0-0	1.000	-0	102	120	/2-7,S-6,3	-0.5
1988	Cle A	51	130	9	30	5	1	0	7	8-0	0	13	.231	.275	.285	56	-8	0-0	.959	-8	87	74	S-49	-1.3
1989	Cle A	24	58	10	16	2	0	2	6	1-0	1	11	.276	.300	.414	98	0	0-0	.963	-4	79	25	S-15/3-5,D-3	-0.4
1991	KC A	2	0	0	0	0	0	0	0	0-0	0	0	—	—	—	—	0	0-0	—	-0	0	0	/3-2	0.0
Total	9	209	491	41	109	17	2	2	20	34-1	2	50	.222	.275	.277	52	-31	2-0	.959	-11	93	91	S-133/2-55,3-13,D-3	-3.2
ZWILLING, DUTCH Edward Harrison B 11.2.1888 St.Louis, MO D 3.27.1978 LaCrescenta, CA BL/TL 5-6.5/160# d8.14 C1																								
1910	Chi A	27	87	7	16	5	0	0	5	11	1		.184	.283	.241	67	-3	1	.940	-2	90	56	O-27(CF)	-0.7
1914	Chi F	154	592	91	185	38	8	**16**	95	46	1	68	.313	.363	.485	138	19	21	.962	-6	99	66	*O-154(0-153-1)	0.2
1915	Chi F	150	548	65	157	32	7	13	**94**	67	2	65	.286	.366	.442	135	17	24	.979	3	105	91	*O-148(CF)/1-3	1.0
1916	Chi N	35	53	4	6	1	0	1	8	4	0	6	.113	.175	.189	11	-6	0	1.000	-1	79	0	O-10(0-5-4)	-0.8
Total	4	366	1280	167	364	76	15	30	202	128	4	139	.284	.351	.438	127	27	46	.969	-7	101	75	O-339(0-333-5)/1-3	-0.3

THE ART OF PITCHING: THE PITCHER REGISTER

Pitching has always been thought of as an *art,* in contrast to hitting, which has generally been considered a *science.* Perhaps this is because the pitcher starts the action and controls the tempo of the game. Perhaps this is because good pitching is seen as aggressive, while hitting seems reactive. "Going after a hitter" is a sign of strength, and giving in to a hitter is a sign of weakness.

Good pitchers are creative, adjusting to the situation while inventing new ways to confound enemy batters. Pitchers who simply rock back and hurl the ball as hard as they can are derided as "throwers" and not "pitchers"—most throwers don't last long unless they can master the art of pitching. Pitchers of modest talent can fashion successful careers if they learn the art. Pitchers blessed with *a lot* of talent can achieve greatness if they combine their physical gifts with the art.

Two of the greatest books ever written on the subject of pitching show how similar the approach of the great pitchers has been over time, even under very different playing conditions. Christy Mathewson's *Pitching in a Pinch* and Tom Seaver's *The Art of Pitching* are both classics of baseball literature. Matty's book (with ghostwriter John Wheeler) was first published in 1912; it was reprinted by the University of Nebraska Press in 1993. Tom Terrific's book, co-authored with Lee Lowenfish, was first published in 1984 and remains in-print today.

During Mathewson's day, each at bat was a game of cat-and-mouse between and the man on the mound and the man at the plate. It was mostly a contest of deception, especially from the pitcher's end. It was not a power game—pitchers didn't have to throw that hard, but they were expected to start 35–40 games and complete almost all of them. If he remained healthy, a star pitcher could expect to log 350 or more innings, and pitch in relief 5–10 times in key games since the failed starters in the bullpen were relegated to mop-up and emergency duty.

What is now called "little ball" was the way of the day in the early twentieth century. Mathewson knew that the secret to being a successful pitcher was letting hitters get themselves out. "All batters who are good waiters, and will not hit at bad balls, are hard to deceive, because it means a twirler has to lay the ball over, and then the hitter always has the better chance," he said. "A pitcher will try to get a man to hit at a bad ball before he will put it near the plate."

What the "Big Six" didn't say—but what he understood and what he presumed the reader would understand as well—was that a *good* pitcher tries to get the batter to swing at *bad* pitches.

Mathewson also understood the critical nature of pacing himself. In his day, a batted ball wouldn't travel nearly as far as it would today, and the fences were usually farther away. Therefore, he could save his very best stuff, especially his devastating screwball (then called a "fadeaway") for when he needed it most: The term *pinches* refers to what would be called *clutch* situations today.

"Many persons have asked me why I do not use my 'fade-away' oftener when it is so effective," he wrote, "and the only answer is that every time I throw the 'fade-away' it takes so much out of my arm. It is a very hard ball to deliver. Pitching it ten or twelve times a game kills my arm, so I save it for the pinches."

Decades later, another dominant NL right-hander named Tom Seaver also talked about a pitcher pacing himself. Seaver wrote about pacing himself *during the at bat* as well as during the game in order to get the job done. In the 1970s Seaver knew that batters could connect for a long ball at almost any time, so he had to be able to reach back and strike a hitter out if necessary.

"If he is thinking ahead," Seaver wrote, "[a pitcher] will select pitches in sequence—for instance, throwing a sinking fastball in spot A in order to get the batter out with a slider in Spot B."

Seaver was the archetype of the modern power pitcher. He made his big league debut immediately after Sandy Koufax retired, and within three years he had joined the corps of great power pitchers of the 1960s like Don Drysdale, Bob Gibson, Jim Maloney, Jim Bunning, Juan Marichal, Bob Veale, and Sam McDowell. Seaver had better control than all of them except Marichal, and he clearly thought about the art of pitching in a very rigorous way.

The game in which Mathewson and Seaver pitched was fundamentally different. Scoring was much higher in Seaver's era, and the bullpens of the 1970s and 1980s were certainly more important than before World War II, so Seaver might expect to finish only about half the games he started.

As Seaver said, "You always have to throw more pitches when you walk batters. Even if they don't score, you are making pitches that you could save for key situations late in the ballgame."

While the game of 1970 was very different than the game of 1910, there is very little difference between Mathewson's description of "pitching in a pinch" and the following quote from Seaver:

"A game may ride on just three or four pitches that the pitcher must choose carefully and throw with accuracy ... [Y]ou can train yourself to identify the outs that you *must* get, and within the bounds of sportsmanship, go about getting them." Sage advice, indeed.

This Pitcher Register chronicles the changes in pitching throughout baseball history, as shown by the records of the practitioners of the art. It allows for meaningful comparisons between Mathewson and Seaver, between Walter Johnson and Roger Clemens—the kind of reflection and analysis that adds so much to our understanding of the National Pastime.

BIOGRAPHICAL INFORMATION

There have been 16,003 major league players through 2003. There are 9,061 players shown in the batter register and 7,254 in the pitcher register, therefore 312 are shown in both registers. In order for a pitcher to be included in the batter register, he must have one season of 10 or more games where pitcher was not his prime position, or he must have 150 more career games played than games pitched. In order for a batter to be shown in the pitcher register, he must have at least 9 career innings pitched (as well as more games at another position than pitcher).

Every pitcher has (at least) a last name and a debut date. If an Hispanic pitcher has a matronymic name, it is placed in parentheses—for example, Marichal, Juan Antonio (Sanchez). Commonly used nicknames are also included on the biographical line; if a player was primarily known by his nickname during his career, it will be part of his listed name—such as Waddell, Rube. Other features and abbreviations for biographical information follow.

B (mm.dd.yyyy) is the place and date of birth.

D (mm.dd.yyyy) is the date and place of death, if death has occurred.

The primary arm a pitcher threw with is expressed *TR* (throws right) or *TL* (throws left). The side of the plate a pitcher bats from is expressed *BR* (bats right), *BL* (bats left), or *BB* (bats both sides). In rare cases when a pitcher throws with both hands during a season, *TB* (throws both) is used and the season is included in parentheses. Likewise, if a pitcher changes from switch-hitting

to hitting from one side during his career, the side of the plate he bats from exclusively and the length of that change are presented in parentheses.

Height is shown by feet followed by inches. Weight is expressed in pounds using **#**.

Debuts are marked *d*, followed by the date the pitcher made his first major league appearance. The debut year is the first year listed in the register, so it is not included in the biographical line.

Besides these basic pieces of information available in the biographical line, there are several other designations for players whose career, family, or duty took them beyond the norm.

If a pitcher on a major league roster missed significant parts of any season serving the United States during wartime, the following abbreviations are used to identify how the player served:

Mil indicates military service in the army, navy, air force, or marines;

Mer indicates the merchant marine;

Def indicates defense plant work.

The seasons the pitcher missed at least a part of are listed after the abbreviation for duty. At least one major leaguer missed time during the seasons below as a result of the following wars (dates include post-war service by some veterans):

Spanish-American War, 1898;

World War I, 1917–19;

World War II, 1941–46;

Korean War 1951–59;

Vietnam War 1962–72.

If the pitcher spent time as a coach, manager, or umpire, that is indicated by the following symbols, which are followed by the number of seasons during which he performed those jobs. Abbreviations are:

C: Coach;

M: Manager;

U: Umpire.

HF indicates that the player is an inductee of the Hall of Fame; the year of election follows *HF*.

If the player had a close family member in the major leagues, the relative's relationship is identified by the codes listed below followed by the relative's first name (and, if it is different, the last name):

b: brother;

twb: twin brother;

f: father;

s: son;

gf: grandfather;

gs: grandson;

ggf: great grandfather;

ggs: great grandson.

▲ at the end of the biographical information indicates that the pitcher is also listed in the player register.

STATISTICAL INFORMATION

Symbols for the first two columns:

† before the team name means the pitcher participated in postseason play that season;

★ after team name means that the pitcher participated in the All-Star Game;

☆ after team name means that the pitcher was selected to the All-Star team that season but did not play;

✳ after team name means that the pitcher was selected to the All-Star team but replaced due to injury.

Boldface statistics in any category indicates a league-leading total or average.

The columns that appear in the pitcher register after **Year**:

TM: Team. Each team is identified by a three-letter code that is usually the first three letters of the city, state, or area where the team is located.

L: League. The leagues in this book include the National League (N), the American League (A), the Federal League (F), the Players League (P), the Union Association (U), the National Association (NA) and the American Association (AA).

W: Wins

L: Losses

Pct.: Winning Percentage. This is calculated by dividing wins by (wins plus losses).

G: Games

GS: Games Started

CG: Complete Games

SHO: Shutouts

SV: Saves. This became an official statistic in 1969. Saves are calculated based on the official definition of saves at the time. Saves before 1969 are based on how many winning games a relief pitcher finished for his team without getting a win.

BS: Blown Saves. These are counted as of 1969 and represent the total number of save opportunities not converted into saves.

IP: Innings Pitched. Exact innings pitched, including thirds of an inning, are available for all of baseball history, but thirds were not included in official innings pitched totals until 1982.

H: Hits Allowed

R: Runs Allowed. This includes unearned runs.

HR: Home Runs Allowed

HB: Hit Batsmen. The rule awarding first base to batters hit by pitches was instituted in 1884 by the American Association. It was adopted in 1887 by the National League.

BB: Bases On Balls Allowed. Generally referred to today as walks.

IB: Intentional Walks Allowed. Walking an opponent on purpose was first counted as a distinct category in 1955.

SO: Strikeouts. Unlike batter strikeouts, these are available for all pitchers in all seasons.

ERA: Earned Run Average. ERA is calculated by dividing earned runs by innings pitched and multiplying by 9.

AERA: Adjusted Earned Run Average. AERA is calculated by normalizing ERA for the context of the offensive level of the league and the player's home park(s) and converting to a scale in which 100 is average.

OAV: Opponents Batting Average. Hits allowed divided by opponent at bats.

OOB: Opponents On-Base Percentage

AB: At Bats. The number of times the pitcher had official at bats as a batter.

SH: Sacrifice Hits. Sacrifice hits by the pitcher. (Sacrifice flies were counted as sacrifice hits from 1908–30 and in 1939.)

AVG: Average. The pitcher's batting average (hits divided by at bats). No average is listed if he did not have an official at bat for a season or a career.

PB: Pitcher Batting Runs. Pitcher batting runs are calculated exactly the same way as adjusted batting runs except that the pitcher's offense is compared to the average offensive level of a pitcher, not an everyday player. The symbol * appears after pitcher batting if the pitcher played in games in addition to the ones in which he pitched.

Sup: Run Support. This is calculated by dividing the total number of runs scored for the pitcher's team(s) in his starts by the pitcher's total Games Started, normalizing the product for the context of the offensive level of the league and the player's home park(s), and converting to a scale in which 100 is average.

APR: Adjusted Pitching Runs. Adjusted Pitcher Runs indicates how many runs the pitcher allowed to score compared to the average pitcher.

PW: Pitcher Wins. This adds the pitcher's adjusted pitching wins, batting wins, and fielding wins to calculate how many wins the pitcher added to or subtracted from his team compared to what the average pitcher would have done.

More details on many of the statistics and formulas shown in this register can be found in the glossary at the end of the encyclopedia.

Year	Tm Lg	W	L	Pct	G	GS	CG-Sho	SV-BS	IP	H	R	HR	HB	BB-IB	SO	ERA	AERA	OAV	OOB	AB-SH	AVG	PB	Sup	APR	PW
AASE, DON Donald William B 9.8.1954 Orange, CA BR/TR 6-3/210# d7.26																									
1977	Bos A	6	2	.750	13	13	4-2	0-0	92.1	85	36	6	1	19-1	49	3.12	144	.244	.283	0-0	—	0	80	12	1.0
1978	Cal A	11	8	.579	29	29	6-1	0-0	178.2	185	88	14	2	80-4	93	4.03	90	.270	.348	0-0	—	0	125	-8	-0.7
1979	†Cal A	9	10	.474	37	28	7-1	2-1	185.1	200	104	19	1	77-7	96	4.81	85	.277	.344	0-0	—	0	121	-13	-1.3
1980	Cal A	8	13	.381	40	21	5-1	2-2	175	193	83	13	1	66-3	74	4.06	97	.287	.347	0-0	—	0	69	0	-0.1
1981	Cal A	4	4	.500	39	0	0	11-0	65.1	56	17	4	0	24-2	38	2.34	156	.234	.303	0-0	—	0		11	1.7
1982	Cal A	3	3	.500	24	0	0	4-4	52	45	20	5	0	23-2	40	3.46	117	.243	.327	0-0	—	0		4	0.5
1984	Cal A	4	1	.800	23	0	0	8-5	39	30	7	1	0	19-5	28	1.62	246	.221	.312	0-0	—	0		11	1.7
1985	Bal A	10	6	.625	54	0	0	14-5	88	83	44	6	1	35-7	67	3.78	107	.258	.330	0-0	—	0		1	0.2
1986	Bal A★	6	7	.462	66	0	0	34-9	81.2	71	29	6	0	28-2	67	2.98	139	.234	.296	0-0	—	0		11	2.2
1987	Bal A	1	0	1.000	7	0	0	2-0	8	8	2	1	0	4-0	3	2.25	196	.276	.364	0-0	—	0		2	0.3
1988	Bal A	0	0	—	35	0	0	0-1	46.2	40	22	4	0	37-5	28	4.05	97	.240	.374	0-0	—	0		0	0.0
1989	NY N	1	5	.167	49	0	0	2-1	59.1	56	27	5	1	26-3	34	3.94	83	.245	.320	5-0	.000	-1		-4	-0.4
1990	LA N	3	1	.750	32	0	0	3-1	38	33	24	5	0	19-4	24	4.97	74	.232	.323	0-0	—	0		-6	-0.7
Total	13	66	60	.524	448	91	22-5	82-29	1109.1	1085	503	89	7	457-45	641	3.80	103	.259	.331	5-0	.000	-1	105	21	4.4
ABBEY, BERT Bert Wood B 11.29.1869 Essex, VT D 6.11.1962 Essex Junction, VT BR/TR 5-11/175# d6.14																									
1892	Was N	5	18	.217	27	22	19	1	195.2	207	139	7	6	76	77	3.45	94	.261	.330	75	.120	-3	88	-7	-0.9
1893	Chi N	2	4	.333	7	7	5	0	56	74	52	1	4	20	6	5.46	85	.308	.371	26	.231	-0	97	-6	-0.5
1894	Chi N	2	7	.222	11	11	10	0	92	119	74	3	3	37	24	5.18	109	.310	.375	39-2	.128	-5	75	5	-0.1
1895	Chi N	0	1	.000	1	1	1	0	8	10	8	0	1	2	3	4.50	113	.303	.361	3-0	.333	-0	42	0	0.0
	Bro N	5	2	.714	8	6	5	0	52	66	34	0	3	9	14	4.33	102	.304	.341	19-0	.263	1	111	0	0.1
	Year	5	3	.625	9	7	6	0	60	76	41	0	4	11	17	4.35	103	.304	.343	22-0	.273	1	100	1	0.1
1896	Bro N	8	8	.500	25	18	12	0	164.1	210	135	7	9	48	37	5.15	80	.308	.361	63-4	.190	-1	109	-21	-1.6
Total	5	22	40	.355	79	65	52	1	568	686	442	18	26	192	161	4.52	92	.292	.352	225-6	.169	-8	94	-29	-3.0
ABBOTT, JIM James Anthony B 9.19.1967 Flint, MI BL/TL 6-3/210# d4.8																									
1989	Cal A	12	12	.500	29	29	4-2	0-0	181.1	190	95	13	4	74-3	115	3.92	97	.274	.345	0-0	—	0	98	-6	-0.8
1990	Cal A	10	14	.417	33	33	4-1	0-0	211.2	246	116	16	5	72-6	105	4.51	85	.295	.353	0-0	—	0	94	-14	-1.3
1991	Cal A	18	11	.621	34	34	5-1	0-0	243	222	85	14	5	73-6	158	2.89	142	.244	.302	0-0	—	0	94	33	4.0
1992	Cal A	7	15	.318	29	29	7	0-0	211	208	73	12	4	68-3	130	2.77	144	.263	.323	0-0	—	0	58	27	2.9
1993	NY A	11	14	.440	32	32	4-1	0-0	214	221	115	22	3	73-4	95	4.37	95	.271	.332	0-0	—	0	104	-6	-0.5
1994	NY A	9	8	.529	24	24	2	0-0	160.1	167	88	24	2	64-1	90	4.55	101	.273	.341	0-0	—	0	101	1	0.1
1995	Chi A	6	4	.600	17	17	3	0-0	112.1	116	50	10	1	35-1	45	3.36	133	.269	.324	0-0	—	0	117	13	1.0
	Cal A	5	4	.556	13	13	1-1	0-0	84.2	93	43	4	1	29-0	41	4.15	113	.280	.337	0-0	—	0	84	5	0.5
	Year	11	8	.579	30	30	4-1	0-0	197	209	47	14	2	64-1	86	3.70	123	.274	.330	0-0	—	0	102	16	1.5
1996	Cal A	2	18	.100	27	23	1	0-0	142	171	128	23	4	78-3	58	7.48	67	.306	.389	0-0	—	0	65	-38	-4.0
1998	Chi A	5	0	1.000	5	5	0	0-0	31.2	35	16	2	1	12-0	14	4.55	100	.292	.358	0-0	—	0	167	1	0.2
1999	Mil N	2	8	.200	20	15	0	0-0	82	110	71	14	2	42-3	37	6.91	66	.317	.393	21-3	.095	-1	96	-23	-2.3
Total	10	87	108	.446	263	254	31-6	0-0	1674	1779	880	154	32	620-30	888	4.25	100	.276	.340	21-3	.095	-1	92	-7	-0.2
ABBOTT, KYLE Lawrence Kyle B 2.18.1968 Newburyport, MA BL/TL 6-4/200# d9.10																									
1991	Cal A	1	2	.333	5	3	0	0-0	19.2	22	11	2	1	13-0	12	4.58	90	.301	.414	0-0	—	0	52	-1	-0.1
1992	Phi N	1	14	.067	31	19	0	0-0	133.1	147	80	20	1	45-0	88	5.13	68	.283	.338	29-6	.069	-1	83	-23	-2.5
1995	Phi N	2	0	1.000	18	0	0	0-0	28.1	28	12	3	0	16-0	21	3.81	111	.267	.361	2-0	.500	0		2	0.2
1996	Cal A	0	1	.000	3	0	0	0-1	4	10	9	1	0	5-0	3	20.25	25	.500	.600	0-0	—	0		-6	-1.0
Total	4	4	17	.190	57	22	0	0-1	185.1	207	112	26	2	79-0	124	5.20	71	.288	.358	31-6	.097	-1	76	-28	-3.4
ABBOTT, DAN Leander Franklin "Big Dan" B 3.16.1862 Portage, OH D 2.13.1930 Ottawa Lake, MI BR/TR 5-11/190# d4.19																									
1890	Tol AA	0	2	.000	3	1	1	1	13	19	14	0	1	8	1	6.23	63	.328	.418	7	.143	0	102	-3	-0.4
ABBOTT, PAUL Paul David B 9.15.1967 Van Nuys, CA BR/TR 6-3/185# d8.21																									
1990	Min A	0	5	.000	7	7	0	0-0	34.2	37	24	0	1	28-0	25	5.97	70	.282	.410	0-0	—	0	75	-6	-0.8
1991	Min A	3	1	.750	15	3	0	0-0	47.1	38	27	5	0	36-1	43	4.75	90	.232	.365	0-0	—	0	86	-2	-0.2
1992	Min A	0	0	—	6	0	0	0-0	11	12	4	1	1	5-0	13	3.27	124	.279	.360	0-0	—	0		1	0.1
1993	Cle A	0	1	.000	5	5	0	0-0	18.1	19	15	5	0	11-1	7	6.38	68	.260	.357	0-0	—	0	93	-4	-0.2
1998	Sea A	3	1	.750	4	4	0	0-0	24.2	24	11	2	0	10-0	22	4.01	116	.255	.324	0-0	—	0	165	2	0.3
1999	Sea A	6	2	.750	25	7	0	0-2	72.2	50	31	9	0	32-3	68	3.10	153	.193	.278	0-0	—	0	101	12	1.1
2000	†Sea A	9	7	.563	35	27	0	0-0	179	164	89	23	5	80-4	100	4.22	112	.243	.325	5-1	.400	1	97	11	0.9
2001	†Sea A	17	4	.810	28	27	1	0-0	163	145	79	21	7	87-5	118	4.25	98	.238	.338	4-1	.250	0	159	0	0.0
2002	Sea A	1	3	.250	7	5	0	0-0	26.1	40	36	5	1	20-0	22	11.96	35	.351	.449	0-0	—	0	119	-23	-2.5
2003	KC A	1	2	.333	10	8	0	0-0	47.2	47	29	8	2	26-2	32	5.29	98	.257	.354	0-0	—	0	98	0	0.0
Total	10	40	26	.606	142	93	1	0-2	624.2	576	345	79	17	335-16	450	4.68	96	.246	.341	9-2	.333	1	116	-9	-1.3
ABBOTT, GLENN William Glenn B 2.16.1951 Little Rock, AR BR/TR 6-6/200# d7.29																									
1973	Oak A	1	0	1.000	5	3	1	0-0	18.2	16	8	3	0	7-0	6	3.86	92	.225	.291	0-0	—	0	159	0	0.0
1974	Oak A	5	7	.417	19	17	3	0-0	96	89	38	4	3	34-3	38	3.00	111	.247	.316	0-0	—	0	91	3	0.4
1975	†Oak A	5	5	.500	30	15	3-1	0-0	114.1	109	61	12	2	50-7	51	4.25	86	.253	.330	0-0	—	0	129	-8	-0.6
1976	Oak A	2	4	.333	19	10	0	0-0	62.1	87	41	6	1	16-0	27	5.49	61	.333	.371	0-0	—	0	113	-15	-1.3
1977	Sea A	12	13	.480	36	34	7	0-0	204.1	212	111	32	12	56-2	100	4.45	93	.270	.327	0-0	—	0	94	-7	-0.8
1978	Sea A	7	15	.318	29	28	8-1	0-0	155.1	191	99	22	2	44-5	67	5.27	72	.303	.349	0-0	—	0	84	-23	-2.9
1979	Sea A	4	10	.286	23	19	3	0-0	116.2	138	78	19	3	38-2	25	5.17	85	.301	.351	0-0	—	0	91	-11	-1.2
1980	Sea A	12	12	.500	31	31	7-2	0-0	215	228	110	27	3	49-4	78	4.10	101	.272	.314	0-0	—	0	96	1	0.2
1981	Sea A	4	9	.308	22	20	1	0-0	130.1	127	64	14	0	28-1	35	3.94	98	.258	.296	0-0	—	0	88	-1	-0.2
1983	Sea A	5	3	.625	14	14	2	0-0	82.1	103	46	9	4	15-2	38	4.59	93	.311	.347	0-0	—	0	103	-2	-0.2
	Det A	2	1	.667	7	7	1-1	0-0	46.2	43	12	5	0	7-1	11	1.93	203	.244	.272	0-0	—	0	70	10	0.6
	Year	7	4	.636	21	21	3-1	0-0	129	146	15	14	4	22-3	49	3.63	114	.288	.321	0-0	—	0	93	7	0.4
1984	Det A	3	4	.429	13	8	1	0-0	44	62	39	9	2	8-1	8	5.93	66	.326	.356	0-0	—	0	112	-13	-1.7
Total	11	62	83	.428	248	206	37-5	0-0	1286	1405	707	162	32	352-28	484	4.39	90	.280	.328	0-0	—	0	96	-66	-7.7
ABER, AL Albert Julius "Lefty" B 7.31.1927 Cleveland, OH D 5.20.1993 Garfield Heights, OH BL/TL 6-2/195# d9.15 Mil 1951																									
1950	Cle A	1	0	1.000	1	1	1	0	9	5	2	0	0	4	4	2.00	217	.167	.265	2-0	.000	0	83	3	0.3
1953	Cle A	1	1	.500	6	0	0	0	6	6	6	0	0	9	4	7.50	50	.240	.441	0-0	—	1		-3	-0.5
	Det A	4	3	.571	17	10	2	0	66.2	63	35	3	0	41	34	4.45	91	.260	.367	23-1	.130	-1	122	-2	-0.3
	Year	5	4	.556	23	10	2	0	72.2	69	41	3	0	50	38	4.71	86	.258	.375	23-1	.130	-1	123	-5	-0.8
1954	Det A	5	11	.313	32	18	4	3	124.2	121	63	8	3	40	54	3.97	93	.257	.318	39-3	.128	-1	86	-4	-0.6
1955	Det A	6	3	.667	39	1	0	3	80	86	32	9	0	28-1	37	3.37	114	.275	.334	17-2	.059	-2	116	5	0.4
1956	Det A	4	4	.500	42	0	0	7	63	65	30	1	2	25-6	21	3.43	120	.270	.341	10-2	.300	1		4	0.5
1957	Det A	3	3	.500	28	0	0	1	37	46	33	6	1	11-3	15	6.81	57	.315	.363	8-0	.125	-0		-13	-1.9
	KC A	0	0	—	3	0	0	0	3	6	4	2	0	2-0	0	12.00	33	.400	.471	1-0	1.000	0		-2	-0.1
	Year	3	3	.500	31	0	0	1	40	52	42	8	1	13-3	15	7.20	54	.323	.373	9-0	.222	0		-16	-2.0
Total	6	24	25	.490	168	30	7	14	389.1	398	205	29	6	160-10	169	4.18	93	.269	.341	100-8	.140	-3	99	-12	-2.2
ABERNATHIE, BILL William Edward B 1.30.1929 Torrance, CA BR/TR 5-10/190# d9.27																									
1952	Cle A	0	0	—	1	0	0	1	2	4	3	1	0	1	0	13.50	25	.444	.500	1-0	.000	-0		-2	-0.2
ABERNATHY, TED Talmadge Lafayette B 10.30.1921 Mebane, NC D 11.16.2001 Charlotte, NC BR/TL 6-2/210# d9.19																									
1942	Phi A	0	0	—	1	0	0	0	2.2	2	3	0	0	3	1	10.13	37	.222	.417	0-0	—	0		-2	0.0
1943	Phi A	0	3	.000	5	2	1	0	14.2	24	22	0	0	13	10	12.89	26	.353	.457	4-0	.250	0	62	-14	-2.2
1944	Phi A	0	0	—	1	0	0	0	3	5	1	0	0	1	2	3.00	116	.417	.462	1-0	.000	-0		0	0.0
Total	3	0	3	.000	7	2	1	0	20.1	31	26	0	0	17	13	11.07	31	.348	.453	5-0	.200	0	62	-16	-2.2
ABERNATHY, TED Theodore Wade B 3.6.1933 Stanley, NC BR/TR 6-4/215# d4.13																									
1955	Was A	5	9	.357	40	14	3-2	0	119.1	136	87	9	7	67-1	79	5.96	64	.294	.386	26-4	.154	-1	78	-28	-2.9
1956	Was A	1	3	.250	5	4	2	0	30.1	35	16	2	1	10-0	18	4.15	104	.292	.348	11-0	.182	-0	57	1	0.1
1957	Was A	2	10	.167	26	16	2	0	85	100	65	9	4	65-1	50	6.78	57	.314	.433	24-2	.167	0	69	-24	-2.9

Year	Tm Lg	W	L	Pct	G	GS	CG-Sho	SV-BS	IP	H	R	HR	HB	BB-IB	SO	ERA	AERA	OAV	OOB	AB-SH	AVG	PB	Sup	APR	PW
1960	Was A	0	0	—	2	0	0	0	3	4	4	0	0	4-0	1	12.00	32	.308	.471	1-0	1.000	0		-2	-0.1
1963	Cle A	7	2	.778	43	0	0	12	59.1	54	25	3	0	29-6	47	2.88	126	.251	.339	5-1	.400	1		3	0.9
1964	Cle A	2	6	.250	53	0	0	11	72.2	66	40	5	2	46-5	57	4.33	83	.247	.360	6-1	.000	-1		-6	-0.8
1965	Chi N	4	6	.400	**84**	0	0	**31**	136.1	113	49	7	5	56-13	104	2.57	143	.227	.309	18-3	.167	0		15	2.1
1966	Chi N	1	3	.250	20	0	0	4	27.2	26	19	4	2	17-1	18	6.18	60	.255	.372	4-0	.000	-0		-6	-1.0
	Atl N	4	4	.500	38	0	0	4	65.1	58	34	5	0	36-10	42	3.86	94	.247	.343	8-0	.250	1		-3	-0.2
	Year	5	7	.417	58	0	0	8	93	84	56	9	2	53-11	60	4.55	80	.249	.352	12-0	.167	0		-10	-1.2
1967	Cin N	6	3	.667	**70**	0	0	**28**	106.1	63	19	1	5	41-5	88	1.27	295	.170	.261	17-0	.059	-1		**26**	3.8
1968	Cin N	10	7	.588	**78**	0	0	13	134.2	111	43	9	4	55-15	64	2.47	128	.228	.307	17-0	.000	-1		9	1.6
1969	Chi N	4	3	.571	56	0	0	3-3	85.1	75	38	8	1	42-11	55	3.16	127	.234	.322	8-0	.250	0		6	0.7
1970	Chi N	0	0	—	11	0	0	1-0	9	9	2	0	1	5-1	2	2.00	225	.281	.395	0-0	—	0		2	0.1
	StL N	1	0	1.000	11	0	0	1-2	18.1	15	6	0	3	12-4	8	2.95	140	.246	.385	3-0	.000	-0		3	0.2
	Year	1	0	1.000	22	0	0	2-2	27.1	24	8	0	4	17-5	10	2.63	161	.258	.388	3-0	.000	-0		5	0.3
	KC A	9	3	.750	36	0	0	12-3	55.2	41	23	3	1	38-0	49	2.59	145	.209	.340	14-3	.214	0		5	1.1
1971	KC A	4	6	.400	63	0	0	23-4	81	60	28	3	6	50-4	55	2.56	134	.210	.336	13-1	.077	-1		7	1.3
1972	KC A	3	4	.429	45	0	0	5-5	58.1	44	15	2	3	19-3	28	1.70	179	.210	.282	6-0	.000	-1		7	1.1
Total	14	63	69	.477	681	34	7-2	148-17	1147.2	1010	513	70	45	592-80	765	3.46	106	.241	.338	181-15	.138	-4	75	15	5.1
ABERNATHY, WOODY Virgil Woodrow B 2.1.1915 Forest City, NC D 12.5.1994 Louisville, KY BL/TL 6/170# d7.28																									
1946	NY N	1	1	.500	15	1	0	1	40	32	16	5	0	10	6	3.37	102	.232	.284	8-0	.000	-1	100	1	-0.1
1947	NY N	0	0	—	1	0	0	0	2	4	3	0	0	1	0	9.00	45	.400	.455	0-0	—	0		-1	-0.1
Total	2	1	1	.500	16	1	0	1	42	36	19	5	0	11	6	3.64	95	.243	.296	8-0	.000	-1	100	0	-0.2
ABLES, HARRY Harry Terrell "Hans" B 10.4.1884 Terrell, TX D 2.8.1951 San Antonio, TX BR/TL 6-2.5/200# d9.4																									
1905	StL A	0	3	.000	6	3	1	0	30.2	37	22	0	0	13	11	3.82	67	.301	.368	10-0	.000	-1	37	-6	-0.7
1909	Cle A	1	1	.500	5	3	3	0	29.2	26	14	1	1	10	24	2.12	120	.226	.294	12-0	.000	-1	119	0	-0.2
1911	NY A	0	1	.000	3	2	0	0	11	16	15	1	0	7	6	9.82	37	.333	.418	4-0	.000	-1	140	-7	-0.6
Total	3	1	5	.167	14	8	4	0	71.1	79	51	2	1	30	41	4.04	67	.276	.347	26-0	.000	-4	102	-13	-1.5
ABRAMS, GEORGE George Allen B 11.9.1899 Seattle, WA D 12.5.1986 Clearwater, FL BR/TR 5-9/170# d4.19																									
1923	Cin N	0	0	—	3	0	0	0	4.2	10	5	0	1	3	1	9.64	40	.500	.583	1-0	1.000	0		-3	-0.1
ABREGO, JOHNNY Johnny Ray B 7.4.1962 Corpus Christi, TX BR/TR 6/185# d9.4																									
1985	Chi N	1	1	.500	6	5	0	0-0	24	32	18	3	0	12-1	13	6.38	63	.352	.423	9-0	.000	-1	133	-5	-0.5
ACEVEDO, JOSE Jose Omar B 12.18.1977 Santo Domingo, D.R. BR/TR 6/185# d6.19																									
2001	Cin N	5	7	.417	18	18	0	0-0	96	101	61	17	3	34-2	68	5.44	84	.272	.336	34-2	.118	-1	114	-8	-1.0
2002	Cin N	4	2	.667	6	5	0	0-0	23.2	28	21	8	2	12-0	14	7.23	59	.292	.382	7-2	.143	0	83	-7	-1.3
2003	Cin N	2	0	1.000	5	4	1	0-0	27	17	8	3	1	6-1	23	2.67	160	.183	.235	9-2	.000	-1	137	5	0.2
Total	3	11	9	.550	29	27	1	0-0	146.2	146	90	28	6	52-3	105	5.22	85	.261	.327	50-6	.100	-2	112	-10	-2.1
ACEVEDO, JUAN Juan Carlos (Lara) B 5.5.1970 Juarez, Mexico BR/TR 6-2/195# d4.30																									
1995	Col N	4	6	.400	17	11	0	0-0	65.2	82	53	15	6	20-2	40	6.44	84	.317	.376	18-0	.056	-2	84	-6	-1.0
1997	NY N	3	1	.750	25	2	0	0-4	47.2	52	24	6	4	22-2	33	3.59	113	.286	.366	6-1	.000	-1	183	1	0.0
1998	StL N	8	3	.727	50	9	0	15-1	98.1	83	30	7	4	29-2	56	2.56	164	.236	.301	17-2	.176	0	90	19	2.5
1999	StL N	6	8	.429	50	12	0	4-2	102.1	115	71	17	4	48-3	52	5.89	78	.291	.369	20-2	.050	-2	116	-14	-1.9
2000	Mil N	3	7	.300	62	0	0	0-2	82.2	77	38	11	1	31-9	51	3.81	120	.246	.315	1-0	.000	0		7	0.7
2001	Col N	0	2	.000	39	0	0	0-5	32	37	24	4	1	19-6	26	5.63	95	.285	.377	0-0	—	0		-2	-0.1
	Fla N	2	3	.400	20	0	0	0-0	28.1	31	11	2	1	16-3	21	2.54	166	.284	.375	3-1	.333	1		4	0.7
	Year	2	5	.286	59	0	0	0-5	60.1	68	41	6	2	35-9	47	4.18	115	.285	.376	3-1	.333	1		2	0.6
2002	Det A	1	5	.167	65	0	0	28-7	74.2	68	33	4	5	23-3	43	2.65	163	.246	.311	0-0	—	0		10	1.4
2003	NY A	0	3	.000	25	0	0	6-1	25.2	34	24	5	2	10-3	19	7.71	57	.315	.374	0-0	—	0		-10	-1.4
	Tor A	1	2	.333	14	0	0	0-1	12.2	18	8	1	0	8-1	9	4.26	108	.327	.413	0-0	—	0		0	0.0
	Year	1	5	.167	39	0	0	6-2	38.1	52	32	6	2	18-4	28	6.57	68	.319	.387	0-0	—	0		-10	-1.4
Total	8	28	40	.412	367	34	0	53-23	570	597	316	72	28	226-34	350	4.33	105	.274	.346	65-6	.092	-3	105	9	0.9
ACKER, JIM James Justin B 9.24.1958 Freer, TX BR/TR 6-2/212# d4.7																									
1983	Tor A	5	1	.833	38	5	0	1-1	97.2	103	52	7	8	38-1	44	4.33	100	.273	.351	0-0	—	0	206	0	0.0
1984	Tor A	3	5	.375	32	3	0	1-2	72	79	39	3	6	25-3	33	4.38	94	.286	.357	0-0	—	0	73	-2	-0.3
1985	†Tor A	7	2	.778	61	0	0	10-3	86.1	86	35	7	3	43-1	42	3.23	130	.268	.358	0-0	—	0		9	1.1
1986	Tor A	2	4	.333	23	5	0	0-2	60	63	34	6	2	22-3	32	4.35	97	.281	.344	0-0	—	0	69	-2	-0.1
	Atl N	3	8	.273	21	14	0	0-1	95	100	47	7	1	26-3	37	3.79	105	.274	.321	28-0	.107	-1	58	1	0.1
1987	Atl N	4	9	.308	68	0	0	14-2	114.2	109	57	11	4	51-4	68	4.16	105	.253	.336	14-0	.214	0		3	0.5
1988	Atl N	0	4	.000	21	1	0	0-0	42	45	26	6	1	14-3	25	4.71	78	.280	.335	5-0	.400	1	0	-5	-0.4
1989	Atl N	0	6	.000	59	0	0	2-3	97.2	84	29	5	1	20-8	68	2.67	137	.237	.278	7-0	.143	-0		12	0.8
	†Tor A	2	1	.667	14	0	0	0-0	28.1	24	7	1	1	12-3	24	1.59	238	.235	.322	0-0	—	0		6	0.7
1990	Tor A	4	4	.500	59	0	0	1-1	91.2	103	49	9	3	30-5	54	3.83	103	.281	.340	0-0	—	0		-2	-0.1
1991	†Tor A	3	5	.375	54	4	0	1-2	88.1	77	53	16	2	36-5	44	5.20	81	.238	.313	0-0	—	0	114	-8	-0.7
1992	Sea A	0	0	—	17	0	0	0-0	30.2	45	19	4	0	12-1	11	5.28	75	.338	.388	0-0	—	0		-4	-0.2
Total	10	33	49	.402	467	32	0	30-17	904.1	918	447	82	32	329-40	482	3.97	103	.267	.334	54-0	.167	0	91	8	1.4
ACKER, TOM Thomas James B 3.7.1930 Paterson, NJ BR/TR 6-4/215# d4.20																									
1956	Cin N	4	3	.571	29	7	1-1	1	83.2	60	23	7	2	29-1	54	2.37	168	.201	.272	19-0	.053	-1	139	15	1.1
1957	Cin N	10	5	.667	49	6	1	4	108.2	122	63	16	8	41-8	67	4.97	83	.293	.361	19-2	.053	-1	111	-9	-1.2
1958	Cin N	4	3	.571	38	10	3	1	124.2	126	64	10	3	43-6	90	4.55	91	.266	.328	30-2	.067	-1	139	-3	-0.4
1959	Cin N	1	2	.333	37	0	0	2	63.1	57	31	10	4	37-5	45	4.12	98	.246	.356	9-2	.111	-0		0	-0.1
Total	4	19	13	.594	153	23	5-1	8	380.1	365	181	43	17	150-20	256	4.12	99	.257	.331	77-6	.065	-3	132	3	-0.6
ACKLEY, FRITZ Florian Frederick B 4.10.1937 Hayward, WI D 5.22.2002 Duluth, MN BL/TR 6-1.5/202# d9.21																									
1963	Chi A	1	0	1.000	2	2	0	0	13	7	4	2	0	7-0	11	2.08	169	.167	.280	5-0	.200	0	127	2	0.2
1964	Chi A	0	0	—	3	2	0	0	6.1	10	6	2	0	4-0	6	8.53	41	.345	.424	1-0	1.000	1	154	-3	0.0
Total	2	1	0	1.000	5	4	0	0	19.1	17	10	4	0	11-0	17	4.19	83	.239	.337	6-0	.333	1	140	-1	0.2
ACOSTA, CY Cecilio (Miranda) B 11.22.1946 Sabino, Mexico BR/TR 5-10/165# d6.4 b-Merito																									
1972	Chi A	3	0	1.000	26	0	0	5-0	34.2	25	6	2	0	17-3	28	1.56	201	.210	.309	4-0	.000	-0		6	0.7
1973	Chi A	10	6	.625	48	0	0	18-4	97	66	30	8	7	39-3	60	2.23	178	.193	.287	1-0	.000	-0		17	3.3
1974	Chi A	0	3	.000	27	0	0	3-4	45.2	43	22	3	5	18-2	19	3.74	100	.256	.338	2-0	.000	-0		0	0.0
1975	Phi N	0	0	—	6	0	0	1-0	8.2	9	7	2	0	3-0	2	6.23	60	.273	.333	0-0	—	0		-2	-0.1
Total	4	13	9	.591	107	0	0	27-8	186	143	65	15	12	77-8	109	2.66	141	.216	.306	7-0	.000	-1		21	3.9
ACOSTA, ED Eduardo Elixbet B 3.9.1944 Boquete, Panama BB/TR 6-5/215# d9.7																									
1970	Pit N	0	0	—	3	0	0	1-0	2.2	5	4	1	1	2-0	1	13.50	29	.417	.500	0-0	—	0		-3	-0.2
1971	SD N	3	3	.500	8	6	3-1	0-0	46	43	18	4	0	7-1	16	2.74	121	.246	.272	17-0	.000	-2	81	2	0.0
1972	SD N	3	6	.333	46	2	0	0-1	89	105	49	7	3	30-7	53	4.45	74	.302	.358	12-0	.083	-0	148	-12	-1.2
Total	3	6	9	.400	57	8	3-1	1-1	137.2	153	71	12	4	39-8	70	4.05	82	.286	.334	29-0	.034	-2	97	-13	-1.4
ACOSTA, JOSE Jose "Acostica" B 3.4.1891 Havana, Cuba D 11.16.1977 Havana, Cuba BR/TR 5-6/134# d7.28																									
1920	Was A	5	4	.556	17	5	4-1	1	82.2	92	40	1	0	26	9	4.03	93	.290	.344	25-2	.240	1	89	0	0.0
1921	Was A	5	4	.556	33	7	2	3	115.2	148	65	4	0	36	30	4.36	94	.317	.366	30-1	.067	-2	96	-2	-0.4
1922	Chi A	0	2	.000	5	1	0	0	15	25	14	4	0	6	6	8.40	48	.417	.470	5-0	.200	0	146	-6	-0.7
Total	3	10	10	.500	55	13	6-1	4	213.1	265	119	9	0	68	45	4.51	88	.314	.365	60-3	.150	-1	97	-8	-1.1
ACRE, MARK Mark Robert B 9.16.1968 Concord, CA BR/TR 6-8/235# d5.13																									
1994	Oak A	5	1	.833	34	0	0	0-1	34.1	24	13	4	1	23-3	21	3.41	130	.202	.333	0-0	—	0		5	0.7
1995	Oak A	1	2	.333	43	0	0	0-4	52	52	35	7	2	28-2	47	5.71	78	.256	.349	0-0	—	0		-7	-0.4

Year	Tm Lg	W	L	Pct	G	GS	CG-Sho	SV-BS	IP	H	R	HR	HB	BB-IB	SO	ERA	AERA	OAV	OOB	AB-SH	AVG	PB	Sup	APR	PW
1996	Oak A	1	3	.250	22	0	0	2-1	25	38	17	4	2	9-4	18	6.12	81	.339	.398	0-0	—	0		-3	-0.4
1997	Oak A	2	0	1.000	15	0	0	0-2	15.2	21	10	1	0	8-0	12	5.74	79	.318	.387	0-0	—	0		-2	-0.2
Total	4	9	6	.600	114	0	0	2-8	127	135	75	16	5	68-9	98	5.17	88	.270	.360	0-0	—	0		-7	-0.3
ADAMS, ACE Ace Townsend B 3.2.1912 Willows, CA BR/TR 5-10.5/182# d4.15																									
1941	NY N	4	1	.800	38	0	0	1	71	84	43	3	1	35	18	4.82	77	.304	.385	12-0	.083	-1		-8	-0.7
1942	NY N	7	4	.636	**61**	0	0	11	88	69	23	1	0	31	33	1.84	183	.223	.293	10-0	.100	-1		**14**	2.1
1943	NY N☆	11	7	.611	**70**	3	1	9	140.1	121	50	5	1	55	46	2.82	122	.236	.311	32-2	.125	-1	189	9	1.1
1944	NY N	8	11	.421	**65**	4	1	**13**	137.2	149	71	8	4	58	32	4.25	86	.279	.354	29-4	.103	-2	63	-6	-1.2
1945	NY N	11	9	.550	65	0	0	**15**	113	109	55	7	2	44	39	3.42	114	.252	.324	16-2	.188	0		3	0.7
1946	NY N	0	1	.000	3	0	0	0	2.2	9	5	2	0	1	3	16.88	20	.500	.526	0-0	—	0		-4	-0.7
Total	6	41	33	.554	302	7	2	49	552.2	541	247	26	8	224	171	3.47	104	.260	.334	99-8	.121	-4	114	8	1.3
ADAMS, BABE Charles Benjamin B 5.18.1882 Tipton, IN D 7.27.1968 Silver Spring, MD BL/TR 5-11.5/185# d4.18																									
1906	StL N	0	1	.000	1	1	0	0	4	9	8	0	0	2	0	13.50	19	.474	.524	1-0	.000	-0	28	-5	-0.7
1907	Pit N	0	2	.000	4	3	1	0	22	40	25	1	3	3	11	6.95	35	.408	.442	7-0	.286	0	68	-11	-0.9
1909	†Pit N	12	3	.800	25	12	7-3	2	130	88	25	0	3	23	65	1.11	246	.196	.240	39-5	.051	-3	88	21	2.3
1910	Pit N	18	9	.667	34	30	16-3	0	245	217	95	4	6	60	101	2.24	138	.240	.291	83-5	.193	1	126	18	1.7
1911	Pit N	22	12	.647	40	37	24-6	0	293.1	253	97	5	8	42	133	2.33	147	.237	**.271**	103-1	.252	4	103	35	3.9
1912	Pit N	11	8	.579	28	20	11-2	0	170.1	169	73	4	3	35	63	2.91	112	.262	.303	53-1	.226	4	104	6	0.9
1913	Pit N	21	10	.677	43	37	24-4	0	313.2	271	94	8	0	49	144	2.15	140	.235	.267	114-3	.289	9	113	33	4.1
1914	Pit N	13	16	.448	40	35	19-3	1	283	253	97	5	7	39	91	2.51	105	.244	**.276**	97-2	.165	1	96	6	0.5
1915	Pit N	14	14	.500	40	30	17-2	2	245	229	90	6	2	34	62	2.87	95	.252	.280	85-2	.141	-2	103	1	-0.2
1916	Pit N	2	9	.182	16	10	4-1	0	72.1	91	51	2	3	12	22	5.72	47	.320	.355	22-1	.273	2	64	-20	-2.6
1918	Pit N	1	1	.500	3	3	2	0	22.2	15	4	0	0	4	6	1.19	241	.197	.237	9-0	.333	1	61	4	0.5
1919	Pit N	17	10	.630	34	29	23-6	1	263.1	213	66	1	3	23	92	1.98	152	.220	**.241**	92-3	.185	-0	83	30	3.0
1920	Pit N	17	13	.567	35	33	19-**8**	2	263	240	83	6	1	18	84	2.16	149	.244	**.259**	89-2	.146	-5	74	28	2.5
1921	Pit N	14	5	.737	25	20	11-2	0	160	155	57	4	0	18	55	2.64	**145**	.251	**.272**	63-2	.254	3	122	20	2.5
1922	Pit N	8	11	.421	27	19	12-4	0	171.1	191	77	1	4	15	39	3.57	114	.287	.307	56-5	.286	4	102	12	1.5
1923	Pit N	13	7	.650	26	22	11	1	158.2	196	83	8	1	25	38	4.42	91	.309	.336	55-1	.273	5	112	-4	-0.1
1924	Pit N	3	1	.750	9	3	2	0	39.2	31	9	1	0	3	5	1.13	338	.209	.225	11-1	.182	-0	74	11	0.9
1925	†Pit N	6	5	.545	33	10	3	3	101.1	129	67	7	3	17	18	5.42	82	.306	.338	31-1	.226	0	104	-7	-0.8
1926	Pit N	2	3	.400	19	0	0	3	36.2	51	32	5	0	8	7	6.14	64	.347	.381	9-0	.222	-0		-9	-1.3
Total	19	194	140	.581	482	354	206-44	15	2995.1	2841	1133	68	47	430	1036	2.76	118	.253	.284	1019-35	.212	24	101	169	17.7
ADAMS, RED Charles Dwight B 10.7.1921 Parlier, CA BR/TR 6/185# d5.5 C12																									
1946	Chi N	0	1	.000	8	0	0	0	12	18	12	1	0	7	8	8.25	40	.353	.431	1-0	.000	-0		-6	-0.5
ADAMS, DAN Daniel Leslie "Rube" B 6.19.1887 St.Louis, MO D 10.6.1964 St.Louis, MO BR/TR 5-11.5/165# d5.22																									
1914	KC F	4	9	.308	36	14	6	3	136	141	67	3	7	52	38	3.51	79	.273	.347	46-1	.152	-2	85	-10	-1.2
1915	KC F	0	2	.000	11	2	0	0	35	41	20	2	1	13	16	4.63	57	.301	.367	9-0	.111	-1	27	-7	-0.4
Total	2	4	11	.267	47	16	6	3	171	182	87	5	8	65	54	3.74	74	.279	.351	55-1	.145	-2	78	-17	-1.6
ADAMS, WILLIE James Irvin B 9.27.1890 Clearfield, PA D 6.18.1937 Albany, NY BR/TR 6-4/180# d6.30																									
1912	StL A	2	3	.400	13	5	0	0	46.1	50	32	0	2	19	16	3.88	85	.284	.360	13-0	.000	-2	67	-5	-0.7
1913	StL A	0	0	—	4	0	0	0	9	12	14	1	3	4	5	10.00	29	.293	.396	1-0	.000	0		-7	-0.4
1914	Pit F	1	1	.500	15	2	1	2	55.1	70	29	4	1	22	14	3.74	77	.326	.391	15-0	.067	-1	120	-5	-0.5
1918	Phi A	5	12	.294	32	14	7	0	169	164	95	2	12	97	39	4.42	66	.272	.383	57-1	.140	-3	57	-22	-2.4
1919	Phi A	0	0	—	1	0	0	0	4.2	7	2	1	1	2	0	3.86	89	.389	.476	2-0	.000	-0		0	0.0
Total	5	8	16	.333	65	21	8	2	284.1	303	172	8	19	144	74	4.37	69	.287	.383	88-1	.102	-6	66	-39	-4.0
ADAMS, JOE Joseph Edward B 10.28.1877 Cowden, IL D 10.8.1952 Montgomery City, MO BR/TL 6/190# d4.26																									
1902	StL N	0	0	—	1	0	0	0	4	9	6	0	1	2	0	9.00	30	.450	.522	2-0	.000	-0		-3	-0.1
ADAMS, KARL Karl Tutwiler "Rebel" B 8.11.1891 Columbus, GA D 9.17.1967 Everett, WA BR/TR 6-2/170# d4.19																									
1914	Cin N	0	0	—	4	0	0	0	8	14	10	1	0	5	5	9.00	33	.424	.500	2-0	.500	0		-5	-0.2
1915	Chi N	1	9	.100	26	12	3	0	107	105	62	5	2	43	57	4.71	59	.267	.342	30-1	.000	-4	65	-19	-2.1
Total	2	1	9	.100	30	12	3	0	115	119	72	6	2	48	62	5.01	56	.279	.355	32-1	.031	-4	65	-24	-2.3
ADAMS, RICK Reuben Alexander B 12.23.1878 Paris, TX D 3.10.1955 Paris, TX BL/TL 6/165# d7.13																									
1905	Was A	2	5	.286	11	6	3-1	0	62.2	63	30	1	8	24	25	3.59	74	.264	.351	23-0	.174	0	71	-5	-0.4
ADAMS, BOB Robert Andrew B 1.20.1907 Birmingham, AL D 3.6.1970 Jacksonville, FL BR/TR 6-0.5/165# d9.27																									
1931	Phi N	0	1	.000	1	1	0	0	6	14	10	0	0	1	3	9.00	47	.424	.441	3-0	.000	-0	40	-4	-0.5
1932	Phi N	0	0	—	4	0	0	0	6	7	1	0	0	2	2	1.50	294	.318	.375	0-0	—	0		2	0.1
Total	2	0	1	.000	5	1	0	0	12	21	11	0	0	3	5	5.25	82	.382	.414	3-0	.000	-0	40	-2	-0.4
ADAMS, BOB Robert Burdette B 7.24.1901 Holyoke, MA D 10.17.1996 Lemoyne, PA BR/TR 5-11/168# d9.22																									
1925	Bos A	0	0	—	2	0	0	0	5.2	10	5	1	0	3	1	7.94	57	.417	.481	3-0	.333	0		-2	0.0
ADAMS, TERRY Terry Wayne B 3.6.1973 Mobile, AL BR/TR 6-3/205# d8.10																									
1995	Chi N	1	1	.500	18	0	0	1-0	18	22	15	0	0	10-1	15	6.50	63	.289	.372	0-0	—	0		-5	-0.5
1996	Chi N	3	6	.333	69	0	0	4-4	101	84	36	6	1	49-6	78	2.94	148	.231	.322	6-0	.000	-0		15	1.3
1997	Chi N	2	9	.182	74	0	0	18-4	74	91	43	3	1	40-6	64	4.62	93	.306	.388	2-0	.000	-0		-3	-0.6
1998	Chi N	7	7	.500	63	0	0	1-6	72.2	72	39	7	1	41-3	73	4.33	102	.255	.349	1-0	.000	-0		0	0.0
1999	Chi N	6	3	.667	52	0	0	13-5	65	60	33	9	0	28-2	57	4.02	112	.245	.319	2-0	.000	-0		3	0.5
2000	LA N	6	9	.400	66	0	0	2-5	84.1	80	42	6	0	39-0	56	3.52	123	.245	.325	2-1	.000	-0		6	1.0
2001	LA N	12	8	.600	43	22	0	0-1	166.1	172	84	9	3	54-1	141	4.33	93	.267	.326	39-5	.051	-2	106	-5	-0.6
2002	Phi N	7	9	.438	46	19	0	0-1	136.2	132	76	9	3	58-5	96	4.35	90	.255	.333	25-6	.080	-1	110	-9	-1.0
2003	Phi N	1	4	.200	66	0	0	0-0	68	68	22	1	2	23-4	51	2.65	151	.268	.331	1-0	.000	-0		11	0.7
Total	9	45	56	.446	497	41	0	39-26	786	781	390	50	11	342-28	631	3.97	105	.260	.336	78-12	.051	-3	101	13	0.8
ADAMS, WILLIE William Edward B 10.8.1972 Gallup, NM BR/TR 6-7/215# d6.11																									
1996	Oak A	3	4	.429	12	12	1-1	0-0	76.1	76	39	11	5	23-3	68	4.01	123	.257	.319	0-0	—	0	86	7	0.5
1997	Oak A	3	5	.375	13	12	0	0-0	58.1	73	53	9	4	32-2	37	8.18	55	.307	.391	0-0	—	0	100	-22	-2.3
Total	2	6	9	.400	25	24	1-1	0-0	134.2	149	92	20	9	55-5	105	5.81	82	.279	.352	0-0	—	0	92	-15	-1.8
ADAMSON, JOEL Joel Lee B 7.2.1971 Lakewood, CA BL/TL 6-4/185# d4.10																									
1996	Fla N	0	0	—	9	0	0	0-0	11	18	9	1	1	7-0	7	7.36	55	.400	.481	0-0	—	0		-4	-0.2
1997	Mil A	5	3	.625	30	6	0	0-0	76.1	78	36	13	5	19-0	56	3.54	131	.265	.319	3-0	.000	-0	86	8	0.7
1998	Ari N	0	3	.000	5	5	0	0-0	23	25	21	5	3	11-0	14	8.22	51	.284	.379	7-1	.429	1	122	-9	-0.9
Total	3	5	6	.455	44	11	0	0-0	110.1	121	66	19	9	37-0	77	4.89	92	.283	.350	10-1	.300	1	101	-5	-0.4
ADAMSON, MIKE John Michael B 9.13.1947 San Diego, CA BR/TR 6-2/185# d7.1																									
1967	Bal A	0	1	.000	3	2	0	0	9.2	9	9	1	0	12-0	8	8.38	38	.257	.438	2-0	.500	1	97	-5	-0.4
1968	Bal A	0	2	.000	2	2	0	0	7.2	9	9	2	0	4-0	4	9.39	31	.281	.361	3-0	.333	0	89	-5	-0.9
1969	Bal A	0	1	.000	6	0	0	0-0	8	10	4	0	0	6-2	2	4.50	79	.357	.444	1-1	.000	-0		-1	-0.1
Total	3	0	4	.000	11	4	0	0-0	25.1	28	22	3	0	22-2	14	7.46	43	.295	.417	6-1	.333	1	89	-11	-1.4
ADKINS, GRADY Grady Emmett "Butcher Boy" B 6.29.1897 Jacksonville, AR D 3.31.1966 Little Rock, AR BR/TR 5-11/175# d4.13																									
1928	Chi A	10	16	.385	36	27	14	1	224.2	235	113	12	6	89	54	3.73	109	.278	.351	70-9	.143	-3*	74	7	0.3
1929	Chi A	2	11	.154	31	15	5	0	138.1	168	98	12	1	67	24	5.33	80	.303	.379	46-1	.239	3*	64	-16	-0.9
Total	2	12	27	.308	67	42	19	1	363	403	211	24	7	156	78	4.34	95	.288	.363	116-10	.181	-1	70	-9	-0.6
ADKINS, DEWEY John Dewey B 5.11.1918 Norcatur, KS D 12.26.1998 Santa Monica, CA BR/TR 6-2/195# d9.19																									
1942	Was A	0	0	—	1	1	0	0	6.1	7	8	0	0	6	3	9.95	37	.259	.394	2-1	.500	0	257	-4	-0.2
1943	Was A	0	0	—	7	0	0	0	10.1	9	3	0	0	5	1	2.61	123	.250	.341	0-0	—	0		1	0.0

Year	Tm Lg	W	L	Pct	G	GS	CG-Sho	SV-BS	IP	H	R	HR	HB	BB-IB	SO	ERA	AERA	OAV	OOB	AB-SH	AVG	PB	Sup	APR	PW
1949	Chi N	2	4	.333	30	5	1	0	82.1	98	58	11	0	39	43	5.68	71	.298	.372	20-0	.200	1	96	-15	-0.8
Total	3	2	4	.333	38	6	1	0	99	114	69	11	0	50	47	5.64	70	.291	.371	22-1	.227	1	123	-18	-1.0
ADKINS, JON Jonathan Scott B 8.30.1977 Huntington, WV BL/TR 6/200# d8.14																									
2003	Chi A	0	0	—	4	0	0	0-0	9.1	8	5	1	1	7-0	3	4.82	94	.250	.390	0-0	—	0		0	0.0
ADKINS, DOC Merle Theron B 8.5.1872 Troy, WI D 2.21.1934 Durham, NC BR/TR 5-10.5/220# d6.24																									
1902	Bos A	1	1	.500	4	2	1	0	20	30	20	2	0	7	3	4.05	88	.345	.394	9-0	.222	-0	70	-3	-0.3
1903	NY A	0	0	—	2	1	0	1	7	10	8	0	1	5	0	7.71	40	.333	.444	3-0	.000	-0	183	-3	-0.2
Total	2	1	1	.500	6	3	1	1	27	40	28	2	1	12	3	5.00	69	.342	.408	12-0	.167	-1	104	-6	-0.5
ADKINS, STEVE Steven Thomas B 10.26.1964 Chicago, IL BR/TL 6-6/210# d9.12																									
1990	NY A	1	2	.333	5	5	0	0-0	24	19	18	4	0	29-0	14	6.38	62	.226	.421	0-0	—	0	105	-6	-0.6
AFFELDT, JEREMY Jeremy David B 6.6.1979 Phoenix, AZ BL/TL 6-4/185# d4.6																									
2002	KC A	3	4	.429	34	7	0	0-1	77.2	85	41	8	3	37-4	67	4.64	108	.274	.356	0-0	—	0	40	4	0.3
2003	KC A	7	6	.538	36	18	0	4-0	126	126	58	12	5	38-1	98	3.93	132	.261	.318	6-0	.333	1	102	16	1.6
Total	2	10	10	.500	70	25	0	4-1	203.2	211	99	20	8	75-5	165	4.20	122	.266	.333	6-0	.333	1	85	20	1.9
AGOSTO, JUAN Juan Roberto (Gonzalez) B 2.23.1958 Rio Piedras, P.R. BL/TL 6-2/190# d9.7																									
1981	Chi A	0	0	—	2	0	0	0-0	5.2	5	3	1	1	0-0	3	4.76	75	.238	.273	0-0	—	0		-1	0.0
1982	Chi A	0	0	—	1	0	0	0-0	2	7	4	0	0	0-0	1	18.00	22	.538	.538	0-0	—	0		-3	-0.1
1983	†Chi A	2	2	.500	39	0	0	7-1	41.2	41	20	2	1	11-1	29	4.10	102	.283	.329	0-0	—	0		1	0.1
1984	Chi A	2	1	.667	49	0	0	7-3	55.1	54	20	2	3	34-7	26	3.09	135	.270	.382	0-0	—	0		7	0.6
1985	Chi A	4	3	.571	54	0	0	1-3	60.1	45	27	3	3	23-1	39	3.58	121	.210	.292	0-0	—	0		4	0.6
1986	Chi A	0	2	.000	9	0	0	0-0	4.2	6	5	0	0	4-0	3	7.71	56	.300	.417	0-0	—	0		-2	-0.4
	Min A	1	2	.333	17	1	0	1-1	20.1	43	25	1	2	14-0	9	8.85	49	.443	.522	0-0	—	0	21	-11	-1.5
	Year	1	4	.200	26	1	0	1-1	25	49	26	1	2	18-0	12	8.64	50	.419	.504	0-0	—	0	21	-13	-1.9
1987	Hou N	1	1	.500	27	0	0	2-2	27.1	26	12	1	0	10-1	6	2.63	149	.248	.313	1-0	.000	-0		3	0.3
1988	Hou N	10	2	.833	75	0	0	4-6	91.2	74	27	6	0	30-13	33	2.26	147	.226	.287	5-1	.000	-0		11	1.7
1989	Hou N	4	5	.444	71	0	0	1-4	83	81	32	3	2	32-10	46	2.93	116	.256	.323	5-0	.200	0		4	0.4
1990	Hou N	9	8	.529	**82**	0	0	4-4	92.1	91	46	4	7	39-8	50	4.29	87	.261	.345	2-0	.000	-0		-4	-0.7
1991	StL N	5	3	.625	72	0	0	2-5	86	92	52	4	8	39-4	34	4.81	77	.291	.380	3-0	.333	1		-11	-0.9
1992	StL N	2	4	.333	22	0	0	0-1	31.2	39	24	2	3	9-2	13	6.25	54	.312	.364	4-0	.000	-0		-10	-1.8
	Sea A	0	0	—	17	1	0	0-1	18.1	27	12	0	0	3-0	12	5.89	68	.346	.366	0-0	—	0	115	-3	-0.2
1993	Hou N	0	0	—	6	0	0	0-0	6	8	4	1	0	0-0	3	6.00	65	.308	.308	0-0	—	0		-1	-0.1
Total	13	40	33	.548	543	2	0	29-31	626.1	639	313	30	30	248-47	307	4.01	94	.272	.345	20-1	.100	-1	72	-16	-2.0
AGUILERA, RICK Richard Warren B 12.31.1961 San Gabriel, CA BR/TR 6-5/205# d6.12																									
1985	NY N	10	7	.588	21	19	2	0-0	122.1	118	49	8	2	37-2	74	3.24	107	.258	.314	36-7	.278	3*	89	3	0.7
1986	†NY N	10	7	.588	28	20	2	0-1	141.2	145	70	15	7	36-1	104	3.88	91	.263	.314	51-3	.157	2*	126	-6	-0.4
1987	NY N	11	3	.786	18	17	1	0-0	115	124	53	12	3	33-2	77	3.60	105	.276	.329	40-6	.225	3	132	2	0.6
1988	†NY N	0	4	.000	11	3	0	0-0	24.2	29	20	2	1	10-2	16	6.93	47	.296	.367	4-0	.250	0	138	-10	-1.4
1989	NY N	6	6	.500	36	0	0	7-4	69.1	59	19	3	2	21-3	80	2.34	140	.231	.294	7-0	.000	-0		8	1.5
	Min A	3	5	.375	11	11	3	0-0	75.2	71	32	5	1	17-1	57	3.21	129	.245	.289	0-0	—	0	93	6	0.7
1990	Min A	5	3	.625	56	0	0	32-7	65.1	55	27	5	4	19-6	61	2.76	151	.224	.291	0-0	—	0		8	1.4
1991	†Min A★	4	5	.444	63	0	0	42-9	69	44	20	3	1	30-6	61	2.35	182	.183	.274	0-0	—	0		14	2.9
1992	Min A★	2	6	.250	64	0	0	41-7	66.2	60	28	7	1	17-4	52	2.84	143	.238	.287	0-0	—	0		7	1.3
1993	Min A★	4	3	.571	65	0	0	34-6	72.1	60	25	9	1	14-3	59	3.11	140	.223	.263	0-0	—	0		11	1.9
1994	Min A	1	4	.200	44	0	0	23-6	44.2	57	23	7	0	10-3	46	3.63	134	.306	.340	0-0	—	0		5	0.9
1995	Min A	1	1	.500	22	0	0	12-3	25	20	7	2	1	6-1	29	2.52	190	.222	.273	0-0	—	0		6	1.0
	†Bos A	2	2	.500	30	0	0	20-1	30.1	26	9	4	0	7-0	23	2.67	183	.228	.268	0-0	—	0		8	1.5
	Year	3	3	.500	52	0	0	32-4	55.1	46	20	6	1	13-1	52	2.60	186	.225	.270	0-0	—	0		14	2.5
1996	Min A	8	6	.571	19	19	2	0-0	111.1	124	69	20	3	27-1	83	5.42	94	.276	.319	0-0	—	0	109	-3	-0.3
1997	Min A	5	4	.556	61	0	0	26-7	68.1	65	29	9	2	22-3	68	3.82	122	.257	.318	0-0	—	0		7	1.4
1998	Min A	4	9	.308	68	0	0	38-11	74.1	75	35	8	1	15-1	57	4.24	113	.262	.299	0-0	—	0		5	1.0
1999	Min A	3	1	.750	17	0	0	6-2	21.1	10	3	2	0	2-0	13	1.27	403	.135	.158	0-0	—	0		9	1.7
	Chi N	6	3	.667	44	0	0	8-5	46.1	44	22	6	2	10-1	32	3.69	122	.254	.299	1-0	.000	-0		4	0.7
2000	Chi N	1	2	.333	54	0	0	29-8	47.2	47	28	11	4	18-2	38	4.91	92	.251	.330	0-0	—	0		-2	-0.3
Total	16	86	81	.515	732	89	10	318-77	1291.1	1233	568	138	36	351-42	1030	3.57	117	.251	.303	139-16	.201	8	107	82	16.8
AGUIRRE, HANK Henry John B 1.31.1931 Azusa, CA D 9.5.1994 Bloomfield Hills, MI BR/TL 6-4/205# d9.10 C3																									
1955	Cle A	2	0	1.000	4	1	1-1	0	12.2	6	3	0	0	12-0	6	1.42	281	.143	.333	4-0	.000	-1	156	3	0.4
1956	Cle A	3	5	.375	16	9	2-1	1	65.1	63	35	7	1	27-1	31	3.72	113	.253	.326	18-3	.111	-2	73	2	0.0
1957	Cle A	1	1	.500	10	1	0	0	20.1	26	15	0	0	13-3	9	5.75	65	.317	.394	4-0	.000	-1	96	-5	-0.5
1958	Det A	3	4	.429	44	3	0	5	69.2	67	31	5	1	27-2	38	3.75	108	.255	.322	14-0	.214	0	67	3	0.4
1959	Det A	0	0	—	3	0	0	0	2.2	4	1	0	0	3-0	3	3.38	120	.364	.500	0-0	—	0		0	0.0
1960	Det A	5	3	.625	37	6	1	10	94.2	75	31	7	3	30-1	80	2.85	139	.217	.283	28-2	.036	-3	115	13	0.9
1961	Det A	4	4	.500	45	0	0	8	55.1	44	22	5	2	38-3	32	3.25	126	.224	.354	9-3	.000	-1		6	0.8
1962	Det A★	16	8	.667	42	22	11-2	3	216	162	67	14	5	65-7	156	**2.21**	**184**	**.205**	**.267**	75-4	.027	-8	80	**41**	3.4
1963	Det A	14	15	.483	38	33	14-3	0	225.2	222	96	25	8	68-3	134	3.67	102	.256	.314	76-2	.132	-2	102	5	0.3
1964	Det A	5	10	.333	32	27	3	1	161.2	134	76	15	8	59-4	88	3.79	97	.223	.300	53-4	.057	-4	92	-3	-0.8
1965	Det A	14	10	.583	32	32	10-2	0	208.1	185	89	24	10	60-2	141	3.59	97	.236	.295	70-4	.086	-2	116	-1	-0.4
1966	Det A	3	9	.250	30	14	2	0	103.2	104	50	14	3	26-2	50	3.82	91	.260	.310	25-2	.120	0	89	-4	-0.5
1967	Det A	0	1	.000	31	1	0	0	41.1	34	15	2	0	17-2	33	2.40	136	.219	.295	2-0	.500	1	294	3	0.3
1968	LA N	1	2	.333	25	0	0	3	39.1	32	8	0	3	13-3	25	0.69	403	.227	.298	3-0	.000	-0		8	0.7
1969	Chi N	1	0	1.000	41	0	0	1-1	45	45	13	2	2	12-1	19	2.60	155	.269	.324	5-0	.400	0		7	0.5
1970	Chi N	3	0	1.000	17	0	0	1-1	14	13	10	3	1	9-1	11	4.50	100	.250	.371	2-0	.000	-0		-1	-0.2
Total	16	75	72	.510	447	149	44-9	33-2	1375.2	1216	562	123	47	479-35	856	3.24	116	.236	.305	388-24	.085	-21	97	77	5.3
AHEARNE, PAT Patrick Howard B 12.10.1969 San Francisco, CA BR/TR 6-3/195# d6.14																									
1995	Det A	0	2	.000	4	3	0	0-0	10	20	13	2	0	5-1	4	11.70	41	.400	.455	0-0	—	0	91	-7	-1.0
AINSWORTH, KURT Kurt Harold B 9.9.1978 Baton Rouge, LA BR/TR 6-3/192# d9.5																									
2001	SF N	0	0	—	2	0	0	0-0	2	3	3	1	1	2-0	3	13.50	30	.333	.500	0-0	—	0		-2	-0.1
2002	SF N	1	2	.333	6	4	0	0-0	25.2	22	7	1	1	12-0	15	2.10	185	.237	.330	6-1	.167	0	77	5	0.6
2003	SF N	5	4	.556	11	11	0	0-0	66	66	31	7	1	26-0	48	3.82	108	.262	.331	22-4	.045	-2*	98	2	0.0
	Bal A	0	1	.000	3	0	0	0-0	2.1	6	3	1	0	1-0	4	11.57	38	.429	.467	0-0	—	0		-2	-0.3
Total	3	6	7	.462	22	15	0	0-0	96	97	44	10	3	41-0	70	3.75	108	.264	.341	28-5	.071	-2	92	3	0.2
AITCHISON, RALEIGH Raleigh Leonidas B 12.5.1887 Tyndall, SD D 9.26.1958 Columbus, KS BR/TL 5-11.5/175# d4.19																									
1911	Bro N	0	1	.000	1	0	0	0	1.1	1	2	0	0	1	0	0.00	—	.200	.333	0-0	—	0		0	-0.1
1914	Bro N	12	7	.632	26	17	8-3	0	172.1	156	71	4	3	60	87	2.66	107	.244	.312	51-3	.196	1	112	4	0.5
1915	Bro N	0	4	.000	7	5	2	0	32.2	36	25	3	2	6	14	4.96	56	.267	.308	8-0	.000	-0	80	-8	-0.9
Total	3	12	12	.500	34	22	10-3	0	206.1	193	98	7	5	67	101	3.01	95	.247	.311	59-3	.169	1	104	-4	-0.5
AKER, JACK Jackie Delane B 7.13.1940 Tulare, CA BR/TR 6-2/190# d5.3 C3																									
1964	KC A	0	1	.000	9	0	0	0	16.1	17	18	6	6	10-1	7	8.82	43	.266	.412	3-0	.000	-0*		-9	-0.5
1965	KC A	4	3	.571	34	0	0	3	51.1	45	18	3	3	18-6	26	3.16	111	.242	.317	8-1	.000	-1		3	0.3
1966	KC A	8	4	.667	66	0	0	**32**	113	81	27	6	3	28-10	68	1.99	171	.201	.256	21-1	.095	-1		**19**	3.2
1967	KC A	3	8	.273	57	0	0	12	88	87	44	9	3	32-8	65	4.30	74	.264	.334	8-3	.125	-0		-9	-1.4
1968	Oak A	4	4	.500	54	0	0	11	74.2	72	39	6	6	33-6	44	4.10	69	.258	.344	7-1	.143	-0		-11	-1.6
1969	Sea A	0	2	.000	15	0	0	3-1	16.2	25	15	4	1	13-4	7	7.56	48	.357	.464	1-0	.000	0		-7	-1.0
	NY A	8	4	.667	38	0	0	11-4	65.2	51	17	4	4	22-5	40	2.06	169	.217	.294	9-0	.111	-0		11	2.4

Year	Tm Lg	W	L	Pct	G	GS	CG-Sho	SV-BS	IP	H	R	HR	HB	BB-IB	SO	ERA	AERA	OAV	OOB	AB-SH	AVG	PB	Sup	APR	PW
	Year	8	6	.571	53	0	0	14-5	82.1	76	36	8	5	35-9	47	3.17	111	.249	.335	10-0	.100	-0		4	1.4
1970	NY A	4	2	.667	41	0	0	16-4	70	57	19	3	4	20-5	36	2.06	171	.226	.291	16-1	.063	-1		12	1.3
1971	NY A	4	4	.500	41	0	0	4-8	55.2	48	20	3	0	26-9	24	2.59	125	.238	.320	3-3	.000	-0		4	0.6
1972	NY A	0	0	—	4	0	0	0-0	6	5	2	0	1	3-0	1	3.00	99	.238	.360	0-0	—	0		0	0.0
	Chi N	6	6	.500	48	0	0	17-3	67	65	31	4	5	23-5	36	2.96	129	.259	.330	6-0	.000	-0		3	0.8
1973	Chi N	4	5	.444	47	0	0	12-3	63.2	76	33	8	2	23-6	25	4.10	96	.308	.370	7-0	.000	-1		-1	-0.2
1974	Atl N	0	1	.000	17	0	0	0-1	16.2	17	11	3	0	9-2	7	3.78	100	.298	.382	1-0	.000	-0		-1	-0.1
	NY N	2	1	.667	24	0	0	2-0	41.1	33	18	4	2	14-1	18	3.48	103	.213	.285	2-0	.500	1		1	0.1
	Year	2	2	.500	41	0	0	2-1	58	50	29	7	2	23-3	25	3.57	102	.236	.313	3-0	.333	1		-1	0.0
Total	11	47	45	.511	495	0	0	123-24	746	679	312	63	40	274-68	404	3.28	105	.247	.322	92-10	.076	-5		15	3.9
AKERFELDS, DARREL Darrel Wayne B 6.12.1962 Denver, CO BR/TR 6-2/210# d8.1 C2																									
1986	Oak A	0	0	—	2	0	0	0-0	5.1	7	5	2	0	3-1	5	6.75	57	.304	.385	0-0	—	0		-2	-0.1
1987	Cle A	2	6	.250	16	13	1	0-0	74.2	84	60	18	7	38-1	42	6.75	67	.284	.374	0-0	—	0	91	-16	-1.4
1989	Tex A	0	1	.000	6	0	0	0-1	11	11	6	1	0	5-2	9	3.27	121	.250	.320	0-0	—	0		0	0.0
1990	Phi N	5	2	.714	71	0	0	3-0	93	65	45	10	3	54-8	42	3.77	101	.201	.316	6-0	.167	-0		0	-0.1
1991	Phi N	2	1	.667	30	0	0	0-0	49.2	49	30	5	3	27-4	31	5.26	70	.257	.354	3-0	.000	-0		-8	-0.5
Total	5	9	10	.474	125	13	1	3-1	233.2	216	146	36	13	127-16	129	5.08	79	.246	.346	9-0	.111	-0	91	-26	-2.1
AKERS, JERRY Albert Earl B 11.1.1887 Shelbyville, IN D 5.15.1979 Bay Pines, FL BR/TR 5-11/175# d5.4																									
1912	Was A	1	1	.500	5	1	0	0	20.1	24	17	1	2	15	11	4.87	68	.300	.423	6-0	.333	0	22	-4	-0.4
ALBA, GIBSON Gibson Alberto (Rosado) B 1.18.1960 Santiago, D.R. BL/TL 6-2/160# d5.3																									
1988	StL N	0	0	—	3	0	0	0-0	3.1	1	2	0	0	2-0	3	2.70	129	.091	.214	0-0	—	0		0	0.0
ALBANESE, JOE Joseph Peter B 6.26.1933 New York, NY D 6.17.2000 New York, NY BR/TR 6-3/215# d7.18																									
1958	Was A	0	0	—	6	0	0	0	6	8	3	1	0	2-0	3	4.50	85	.348	.370	0-0	—	0		0	0.0
ALBERRO, JOSE José Edgardo B 6.29.1969 San Juan, P.R. BR/TR 6-2/190# d4.27																									
1995	Tex A	0	0	—	12	0	0	0-0	20.2	26	18	2	1	12-1	10	7.40	65	.299	.386	0-0	—	0		-6	-0.2
1996	Tex A	0	1	.000	5	1	0	0-0	9.1	14	6	1	0	7-1	2	5.79	91	.368	.457	0-0	—	0	35	0	0.0
1997	Tex A	0	3	.000	10	4	0	0-0	28.1	37	33	4	1	17-1	11	7.94	60	.303	.390	0-0	—	0	86	-12	-1.0
Total	3	0	4	.000	27	5	0	0-0	58.1	77	57	7	2	36-3	23	7.41	66	.312	.399	0-0	—	0	76	-18	-1.2
ALBERTS, CY Frederick Joseph B 1.14.1882 Grand Rapids, MI D 8.27.1917 Fort Wayne, IN BR/TR 6/230# d9.17																									
1910	StL N	1	2	.333	4	3	2	0	27.2	35	22	1	0	20	10	6.18	48	.330	.437	7-1	.000	-0	83	-9	-0.9
ALBOSTA, ED Edward John "Rube" B 10.27.1918 Saginaw, MI D 1.7.2003 Saginaw, MI BR/TR 6-1/175# d9.3 Mil 1943-45																									
1941	Bro N	0	2	.000	2	2	0	0	13	11	9	1	0	8	5	6.23	59	.239	.352	4-0	.000	-1	46	-3	-0.4
1946	Pit N	0	6	.000	17	6	0	0	39.2	41	34	3	1	35	19	6.13	58	.266	.405	8-0	.125	-0	40	-12	-1.7
Total	2	0	8	.000	19	8	0	0	52.2	52	43	4	1	43	24	6.15	58	.260	.393	12-0	.083	-1	42	-15	-2.1
ALBRECHT, ED Edward Arthur B 2.28.1929 Affton, MO D 12.29.1979 Cahokia, IL BR/TR 5-10.5/165# d10.2																									
1949	StL A	1	0	1.000	1	1	1	0	5	1	3	0	0	4	1	5.40	84	.063	.250	2-0	.000	-0	99	0	0.0
1950	StL A	0	1	.000	2	1	0	0	6.2	6	7	0	0	7	1	5.40	92	.250	.419	1-0	.000	-0	109	-1	-0.2
Total	2	1	1	.500	3	2	1	0	11.2	7	10	0	0	11	2	5.40	88	.175	.353	3-0	.000	-0	104	-1	-0.2
ALBURY, VIC Victor B 5.12.1947 Key West, FL BL/TL 6/190# d8.7																									
1973	Min A	1	0	1.000	14	0	0	0-0	23.1	13	7	1	0	19-2	13	2.70	147	.169	.333	0-0	—	0		4	0.1
1974	Min A	8	9	.471	32	22	4-1	0-0	164	159	83	19	6	80-1	85	4.12	91	.259	.348	0-0	—	0	102	-6	-0.6
1975	Min A	6	7	.462	32	15	2	1-0	135	115	82	16	4	97-1	72	4.53	85	.237	.364	1-0	.000	-0*	98	-12	-1.1
1976	Min A	3	1	.750	23	0	0	0-0	50.1	51	22	0	2	24-3	23	3.58	100	.271	.352	0-0	—	0		1	0.0
Total	4	18	17	.514	101	37	6-1	1-0	372.2	338	194	36	12	220-7	193	4.11	92	.247	.353	1-0	.000	-0	101	-13	-1.6
ALCALA, SANTO Santo (b: Santo Anibal (Alcala)) B 12.23.1952 San Pedro De Macoris, D.R. BR/TR 6-5/195# d4.10																									
1976	Cin N	11	4	.733	30	21	3-1	0-1	132	131	72	12	3	67-3	67	4.70	75	.261	.348	43-5	.140	-0	154	-16	-1.7
1977	Cin N	1	1	.500	7	2	0	0-0	15.2	22	11	1	1	7-1	9	5.74	68	.349	.417	3-0	.000	-0	79	-3	-0.4
	Mon N	2	6	.250	31	10	0	2-1	101.2	104	55	12	2	47-5	64	4.69	81	.263	.343	25-2	.080	-1	65	-8	-0.8
	Year	3	7	.300	38	12	0	2-1	117.1	126	58	13	3	54-6	73	4.83	79	.275	.353	28-2	.071	-1	68	-12	-1.2
Total	2	14	11	.560	68	33	3-1	2-2	249.1	257	138	25	6	121-9	140	4.76	77	.268	.351	71-7	.113	-2	120	-27	-2.9
ALDERSON, DALE Dale Leonard B 3.9.1918 Belden, NE D 2.12.1982 Garden Grove, CA BR/TR 5-10/190# d9.18 Mil 1944-45																									
1943	Chi N	0	1	.000	4	2	0	0	14	21	12	2	0	3	4	6.43	52	.356	.387	3-0	.000	-0	127	-5	-0.4
1944	Chi N	0	0	—	12	1	0	0	21.2	31	18	2	0	9	7	6.65	53	.344	.404	4-0	.000	-1	166	-7	-0.4
Total	2	0	1	.000	16	3	0	0	35.2	52	30	4	0	12	11	6.56	53	.349	.398	7-0	.000	-1	138	-12	-0.8
ALDRED, SCOTT Scott Phillip B 6.12.1968 Flint, MI BL/TL 6-4/195# d9.9																									
1990	Det A	1	2	.333	4	3	0	0-0	14.1	13	6	0	1	10-1	7	3.77	105	.265	.393	0-0	—	0	54	1	0.1
1991	Det A	2	4	.333	11	11	1	0-0	57.1	58	37	9	0	30-2	35	5.18	80	.266	.352	0-0	—	0	116	-7	-0.6
1992	Det A	3	8	.273	16	13	0	0-0	65	80	51	12	3	33-4	34	6.78	58	.307	.387	0-0	—	0	98	-19	-2.7
1993	Col N	0	0	—	5	0	0	0-0	6.2	10	10	1	1	9-1	5	10.80	44	.357	.526	0-0	—	0		-4	-0.2
	Mon N	1	0	1.000	3	0	0	0-1	5.1	9	4	1	0	1-0	4	6.75	62	.375	.400	0-0	—	0		-1	-0.2
	Year	1	0	1.000	8	0	0	0-1	12	19	18	2	1	10-1	9	9.00	50	.365	.476	0-0	—	0		-6	-0.4
1996	Det A	0	4	.000	11	8	0	0-0	43.1	60	52	9	3	26-3	36	9.35	54	.328	.416	0-0	—	0	89	-22	-1.6
	Min A	6	5	.545	25	17	0	0-0	122	134	73	20	3	42-1	75	5.09	101	.281	.340	0-0	—	0	128	0	0.0
	Year	6	9	.400	36	25	0	0-0	165.1	194	80	29	6	68-4	111	6.21	82	.294	.362	0-0	—	0	116	-21	-1.6
1997	Min A	2	10	.167	17	15	0	0-0	77.1	102	66	20	3	28-2	33	7.68	61	.323	.382	0-0	—	0	103	-23	-2.8
1998	TB A	0	0	—	48	0	0	0-0	31.1	33	13	1	2	12-3	21	3.73	128	.280	.356	0-0	—	0		4	0.2
1999	TB A	3	2	.600	37	0	0	0-0	24.1	26	15	1	2	14-0	22	5.18	96	.274	.375	0-0	—	0		0	0.0
	Phi N	1	1	.500	29	0	0	1-3	32.1	33	15	1	0	15-3	19	3.90	121	.277	.345	1-0	.000	-0		3	0.2
2000	Phi N	1	3	.250	23	0	0	0-1	20.1	23	14	3	1	10-0	21	5.75	81	.284	.362	0-0	—	0		-2	-0.4
Total	9	20	39	.339	229	67	1	1-5	499.2	581	356	78	19	230-20	312	6.02	77	.295	.371	1-0	.000	-0	105	-70	-8.0
ALDRICH, JAY Jay Robert B 4.14.1961 Alexandria, LA BR/TR 6-3/210# d6.5																									
1987	Mil A	3	1	.750	31	0	0	0-0	58.1	71	33	8	2	13-3	22	4.94	93	.306	.344	0-0	—	0		-1	-0.1
1989	Mil A	1	0	1.000	16	0	0	1-1	26	24	11	3	1	13-2	12	3.81	101	.253	.349	0-0	—	0		1	0.1
	Atl N	1	2	.333	8	0	0	0-1	12.1	7	5	0	0	6-1	7	2.19	167	.167	.265	1-0	.000	-0		1	0.2
1990	Bal A	1	2	.333	7	0	0	1-2	12	17	13	1	0	7-3	5	8.25	46	.327	.407	0-0	—	0		-7	-1.2
Total	3	6	5	.545	62	0	0	2-4	108.2	119	62	12	3	39-9	46	4.72	89	.283	.345	1-0	.000	-0		-6	-1.0
ALDRIDGE, VIC Victor Eddington B 10.25.1893 Indian Springs, IN D 4.17.1973 Terre Haute, IN BR/TR 5-9.5/175# d4.15 Mil 1918																									
1917	Chi N	6	6	.500	30	6	1-1	2	106.2	100	52	1	2	37	44	3.12	93	.252	.319	29-1	.138	-2	69	-3	-0.4
1918	Chi N	0	1	.000	3	0	0	0	12.1	11	3	0	0	6	10	1.46	191	.275	.370	3-1	.333	0		2	0.2
1922	Chi N	16	15	.516	36	34	20-2	0	258.1	287	129	14	12	56	66	3.52	119	.286	.332	100-7	.260	3	96	16	2.0
1923	Chi N	16	9	.640	30	30	15-2	0	217	209	101	17	1	67	64	3.48	115	.251	.307	71-5	.268	3	101	13	1.6
1924	Chi N	15	12	.556	32	32	20	0	244.1	261	110	10	7	80	74	3.50	112	.279	.341	85-7	.176	-3	107	12	0.9
1925	†Pit N	15	7	.682	30	26	14-1	0	213.1	218	99	15	5	74	88	3.63	123	.269	.334	86-2	.233	-1	119	21	1.6
1926	Pit N	10	13	.435	30	26	12-1	1	190	204	100	7	4	73	61	4.07	97	.279	.348	71-4	.225	-1	98	-1	-0.3
1927	†Pit N	15	10	.600	35	34	17-1	1	239.1	248	123	16	5	74	86	4.25	97	.270	.328	96-3	.219	-0	112	0	-0.2
1928	NY N	4	7	.364	22	16	3	2	119.1	133	68	7	3	45	33	4.83	81	.285	.352	40-2	.275	2	112	-10	-0.7
Total	9	97	80	.548	248	204	102-8	6	1600.2	1671	785	87	39	512	526	3.76	107	.273	.333	581-32	.229	2	106	50	4.7
ALEXANDER, DOYLE Doyle Lafayette B 9.4.1950 Cordova, AL BR/TR 6-3/205# d6.26																									
1971	LA N	6	6	.500	17	12	4	0-0	92.1	105	45	6	1	18-0	30	3.80	85	.282	.316	33-1	.273	3	107	-7	-0.6
1972	Bal A	6	8	.429	35	9	2-2	2-1	106.1	78	36	5	1	30-8	49	2.45	126	.203	.261	25-3	.080	-1	93	6	0.8
1973	†Bal A	12	8	.600	29	26	10	0-0	174.2	169	85	19	7	52-5	63	3.86	97	.258	.317	0-0	—	0	148	-3	-0.2

Year	Tm Lg	W	L	Pct	G	GS	CG-Sho	SV-BS	IP	H	R	HR	HB	BB-IB	SO	ERA	AERA	OAV	OOB	AB-SH	AVG	PB	Sup	APR	PW
1974	Bal A	6	9	.400	30	12	2	0-2	114.1	127	65	7	4	43-4	40	4.01	86	.290	.356	0-0	—	0	98	-11	-1.1
1975	Bal A	8	8	.500	32	11	3-1	1-3	133.1	127	47	7	1	47-7	46	3.04	116	.251	.316	0-0	—	0	112	9	1.1
1976	Bal A	3	4	.429	11	6	2-1	0-0	64.1	58	27	3	0	24-2	17	3.50	94	.247	.312	0-0	—	0	98	-1	-0.1
	†NY A	10	5	.667	19	19	5-2	0-0	136.2	114	54	9	3	39-0	41	3.29	104	.229	.287	0-0	—	0	110	3	0.2
	Year	13	9	.591	30	25	7-3	0-0	201	172	58	12	3	63-2	58	3.36	100	.235	.295	0-0	—	0	107	2	0.1
1977	Tex A	17	11	.607	34	34	12-1	0-0	237	221	103	24	2	82-2	82	3.65	112	.246	.309	0-0	—	0	98	14	1.6
1978	Tex A	9	10	.474	31	28	7-1	0-0	191	198	84	18	1	71-1	81	3.86	97	.270	.333	0-0	—	0	96	2	0.2
1979	Tex A	5	7	.417	23	18	0	0-0	113.1	114	65	3	1	69-3	50	4.45	94	.268	.366	0-0	—	0	88	-4	-0.3
1980	Atl N	14	11	.560	35	35	7-1	0-0	231.2	227	120	20	4	74-5	114	4.20	89	.256	.315	83-3	.181	0	116	-11	-1.0
1981	SF N	11	7	.611	24	24	1-1	0-0	152.1	156	51	11	2	44-2	77	2.89	119	.263	.315	51-4	.176	1	114	11	1.4
1982	NY A	1	7	.125	16	11	0	0-0	66.2	81	52	14	0	14-2	26	6.08	66	.298	.329	0-0	—	0	71	-17	-1.7
1983	NY A	0	2	.000	8	5	0	0-0	28.1	31	21	6	0	7-0	17	6.35	61	.277	.317	0-0	—	0	112	-7	-0.5
	Tor A	7	6	.538	17	15	5	0-0	116.2	126	55	14	1	26-1	46	3.93	110	.279	.317	0-0	—	0	86	5	0.5
	Year	7	8	.467	25	20	5	0-0	145	157	59	20	1	33-1	63	4.41	96	.278	.317	0-0	—	0	91	-1	0.0
1984	Tor A	17	6	**.739**	36	35	11-2	0-0	261.2	238	99	21	3	59-1	139	3.13	131	.242	.284	0-0	—	0	103	28	2.3
1985	†Tor A	17	10	.630	36	36	6-1	0-0	260.2	268	105	28	6	67-0	142	3.45	122	.266	.315	0-0	—	0	92	24	2.3
1986	Tor A	5	4	.556	17	17	3	0-0	111	120	56	18	4	20-1	65	4.46	95	.273	.308	0-0	—	0	123	-1	-0.1
	Atl N	6	6	.500	17	17	2	0-0	117.1	135	58	9	0	17-1	74	3.84	104	.287	.311	38-6	.211	1*	95	1	0.2
1987	Atl N	5	10	.333	16	16	3	0-0	117.2	115	57	21	2	27-5	64	4.13	105	.257	.300	35-6	.029	-3	74	4	0.1
	†Det A	9	0	1.000	11	11	3-3	0-0	88.1	63	16	3	0	26-0	44	1.53	277	.201	.263	0-0	—	0	125	28	2.9
1988	Det A☆	14	11	.560	34	34	5-1	0-0	229	260	122	30	5	46-7	126	4.32	88	.282	.317	0-0	—	0	113	-14	-1.5
1989	Det A	6	18	.250	33	33	5-1	0-0	223	245	118	28	5	76-3	95	4.44	86	.280	.337	0-0	—	0	78	-12	-1.2
Total	19	194	174	.527	561	464	98-18	3-6	3367.2	3376	1541	324	53	978-60	1528	3.76	103	.261	.314	265-23	.166	1	103	47	5.3

ALEXANDER, GERALD Gerald Paul B 3.26.1968 Baton Rouge, LA BR/TR 5-11/190# d9.9

Year	Tm Lg	W	L	Pct	G	GS	CG-Sho	SV-BS	IP	H	R	HR	HB	BB-IB	SO	ERA	AERA	OAV	OOB	AB-SH	AVG	PB	Sup	APR	PW
1990	Tex A	0	0	—	3	2	0	0-0	7	14	6	0	1	5-0	8	7.71	51	.438	.513	0-0	—	0	139	-3	-0.1
1991	Tex A	5	3	.625	30	9	0	0-0	89.1	93	56	11	3	48-7	50	5.24	77	.272	.364	0-0	—	0	131	-11	-0.9
1992	Tex A	1	0	1.000	3	0	0	0-0	1.2	5	5	1	0	1-0	1	27.00	14	.500	.500	0-0	—	0		-4	-0.7
Total	3	6	3	.667	36	11	0	0-0	98	112	67	12	4	54-7	59	5.79	70	.292	.380	0-0	—	0	132	-18	-1.7

ALEXANDER, GROVER Grover Cleveland "Pete" B 2.26.1887 Elba, NE D 11.4.1950 St.Paul, NE BR/TR 6-1/185# d4.15 Mil 1918 HF1938

Year	Tm Lg	W	L	Pct	G	GS	CG-Sho	SV-BS	IP	H	R	HR	HB	BB-IB	SO	ERA	AERA	OAV	OOB	AB-SH	AVG	PB	Sup	APR	PW
1911	Phi N	**28**	13	.683	48	37	**31-7**	3	**367**	285	133	5	8	129	227	2.57	134	**.219**	.293	138-0	.174	-2*	101	37	3.7
1912	Phi N	19	17	.528	46	34	25-3	3	**310.1**	289	133	11	6	105	**195**	2.81	129	.251	.317	102-9	.186	0	90	27	3.0
1913	Phi N	22	8	.733	47	36	23-**9**	2	306.1	288	106	9	3	75	159	2.79	120	.254	.302	103-3	.126	-4	95	22	1.8
1914	Phi N	**27**	15	.643	46	39	**32**-6	1	**355**	327	133	8	11	76	**214**	2.38	123	.244	.290	137-2	.234	2*	105	22	3.1
1915	†Phi N	**31**	10	**.756**	49	42	**36-12**	3	**376.1**	253	86	3	10	64	**241**	**1.22**	**225**	**.191**	**.234**	130-5	.169	0	116	**58**	**7.5**
1916	Phi N	**33**	12	.733	48	**45**	**38-16**	3	**389**	323	90	6	10	50	**167**	**1.55**	**171**	.230	.262	138-3	.239	8*	96	**47**	**7.2**
1917	Phi N	**30**	13	.698	45	**44**	**34-8**	0	**388**	336	107	4	6	56	**200**	**1.83**	153	.234	.266	139-7	.216	4*	101	**39**	**5.4**
1918	Chi N	2	1	.667	3	3	3	0	26	19	7	0	1	3	15	1.73	161	.207	.240	10-0	.100	-1	127	3	0.3
1919	Chi N	16	11	.593	30	27	20-**9**	1	235	180	51	3	0	38	121	**1.72**	**167**	**.211**	.245	70-4	.171	1	92	34	**4.6**
1920	Chi N	**27**	14	.659	46	**40**	**33**-7	5	**363.1**	335	96	8	1	69	**173**	**1.91**	**168**	.248	.285	118-6	.229	4	83	**52**	**6.9**
1921	Chi N	15	13	.536	31	30	21-**3**	1	252	286	110	10	1	33	77	3.39	113	.296	.320	95-5	.305	6	100	12	1.8
1922	Chi N	16	13	.552	33	31	20-1	1	245.2	283	111	8	3	34	48	3.63	116	.295	.321	85-4	.176	-2	84	18	1.9
1923	Chi N	22	12	.647	39	36	26-3	2	305	308	128	17	0	30	72	3.19	126	.259	**.277**	111-7	.216	0	112	29	3.1
1924	Chi N	12	5	.706	21	20	12	0	169.1	183	82	9	1	25	33	3.03	129	.272	.299	65-4	.231	1	115	10	1.1
1925	Chi N	15	11	.577	32	30	20-1	0	236	270	106	14	3	29	63	3.39	127	.288	.312	79-9	.241	3	94	23	2.3
1926	Chi N	3	3	.500	7	7	4	0	52	55	26	0	0	7	12	3.46	111	.270	.294	15-3	.467	3	87	1	0.5
	†StL N	9	7	.563	23	16	11-2	2	148.1	136	57	8	2	24	35	2.91	134	.242	.276	50-3	.120	-4	79	16	1.3
	Year	12	10	.545	30	23	15-2	2	200.1	191	61	8	2	31	47	3.05	127	.250	**.281**	65-6	.200	-1	81	18	1.8
1927	StL N	21	10	.677	37	30	22-2	3	268	261	94	11	1	38	48	2.52	157	.258	**.286**	94-3	.245	3	109	**41**	**5.0**
1928	†StL N	16	9	.640	34	31	18-1	2	243.2	262	107	15	2	37	59	3.36	119	.277	.306	86-8	.291	6	122	18	2.2
1929	StL N	9	8	.529	22	19	8	2	132	149	65	10	1	23	33	3.89	120	.285	.317	41-3	.049	-4	103	12	1.0
1930	Phi N	0	3	.000	9	3	0	0	21.2	40	24	5	0	6	6	9.14	60	.396	.430	4-0	.000	-0	64	-7	-0.8
Total	20	373	208	.642	696	600	437-90	32	5190	4868	1852	164	70	951	2198	2.56	135	.250	.288	1810-88	.209	24	100	514	62.9

ALEXANDER, BOB Robert Somerville B 8.7.1922 Vancouver, BC, CAN D 4.7.1993 Oceanside, CA BR/TR 6-2.5/205# d4.11

Year	Tm Lg	W	L	Pct	G	GS	CG-Sho	SV-BS	IP	H	R	HR	HB	BB-IB	SO	ERA	AERA	OAV	OOB	AB-SH	AVG	PB	Sup	APR	PW
1955	Bal A	1	0	1.000	4	0	0	0	4	8	6	0	1	2-0	1	13.50	28	.444	.500	0-0	—	0		-4	-0.7
1957	Cle A	0	1	.000	5	0	0	0	7	10	7	0	1	5-2	1	9.00	41	.357	.457	1-0	.000	-0		-4	-0.5
Total	2	1	1	.500	9	0	0	0	11	18	13	0	2	7-2	2	10.64	35	.391	.474	1-0	.000	-0		-8	-1.2

ALFONSECA, ANTONIO Antonio B 4.16.1972 LaRomana, D.R. BR/TR 6-5/235# d6.17

Year	Tm Lg	W	L	Pct	G	GS	CG-Sho	SV-BS	IP	H	R	HR	HB	BB-IB	SO	ERA	AERA	OAV	OOB	AB-SH	AVG	PB	Sup	APR	PW
1997	†Fla N	1	3	.250	17	0	0	0-2	25.2	36	16	3	1	10-3	19	4.91	82	.324	.385	3-0	.000	-0		-3	-0.4
1998	Fla N	4	6	.400	58	0	0	8-6	70.2	75	36	10	3	33-9	46	4.08	100	.281	.359	4-0	.000	-0		0	-0.2
1999	Fla N	4	5	.444	73	0	0	21-4	77.2	79	28	4	4	29-6	46	3.24	134	.274	.348	2-0	.000	-0		11	1.7
2000	Fla N	5	6	.455	68	0	0	**45-4**	70	82	35	7	1	24-3	47	4.24	105	.291	.347	0-0	—	0		2	0.4
2001	Fla N	4	4	.500	58	0	0	28-6	61.2	68	24	6	5	15-3	40	3.06	138	.281	.335	0-0	—	0		8	1.5
2002	Chi N	2	5	.286	66	0	0	19-9	74.1	73	34	5	3	36-3	61	4.00	101	.257	.344	3-0	.667	1		1	0.3
2003	†Chi N	3	1	.750	60	0	0	0-4	66.1	76	43	7	2	27-3	51	5.83	72	.290	.360	0-1	—	0		-10	-0.6
Total	7	23	30	.434	400	0	0	121-35	446.1	489	216	42	19	174-30	310	4.11	102	.282	.351	12-1	.167	-0		9	2.7

ALLARD, BRIAN Brian Marshall B 1.3.1958 Spring Valley, IL BR/TR 6-1/175# d8.8

Year	Tm Lg	W	L	Pct	G	GS	CG-Sho	SV-BS	IP	H	R	HR	HB	BB-IB	SO	ERA	AERA	OAV	OOB	AB-SH	AVG	PB	Sup	APR	PW
1979	Tex A	1	3	.250	7	4	2	0-0	33.1	36	17	4	0	13-2	14	4.32	96	.283	.348	0-0	—	0	44	0	0.0
1980	Tex A	0	1	.000	5	2	0	0-0	14.1	13	13	0	1	10-1	10	5.65	69	.236	.358	0-0	—	0	115	-4	-0.3
1981	Sea A	3	2	.600	7	7	1	0-0	48	48	22	5	0	8-0	20	3.75	103	.265	.296	0-0	—	0	103	1	0.0
Total	3	4	6	.400	19	13	3	0-0	95.2	97	52	9	1	31-3	44	4.23	94	.267	.325	0-0	—	0	85	-3	-0.3

ALLEN, FRANK Frank Leon B 8.26.1889 Newbern, AL D 7.30.1933 Gainesville, AL BR/TL 5-9/175# d4.24

Year	Tm Lg	W	L	Pct	G	GS	CG-Sho	SV-BS	IP	H	R	HR	HB	BB-IB	SO	ERA	AERA	OAV	OOB	AB-SH	AVG	PB	Sup	APR	PW
1912	Bro N	3	9	.250	20	15	5-1	0	109	119	70	1	1	57	58	3.63	92	.285	.373	36-2	.167	2	83	-8	-0.5
1913	Bro N	4	18	.182	34	25	11	2	174.2	144	75	6	10	81	82	2.83	116	.231	.329	51-2	.137	-1	74	7	0.6
1914	Bro N	8	14	.364	36	21	10-1	0	171.1	165	79	6	3	57	68	3.10	92	.265	.330	47-3	.128	0*	85	-2	-0.3
	Pit F	1	0	1.000	1	1	1	0	7	9	4	0	0	0	3	5.14	56	.321	.321	2-0	.500	1	191	-1	-0.1
1915	Pit F	23	13	.639	41	37	24-6	0	283.1	230	90	9	11	100	127	2.51	108	.227	.304	89-4	.079	-6	87	9	0.4
1916	Bos N	8	2	.800	19	14	7-2	1	113	102	32	1	4	31	63	2.07	120	.244	.302	34-3	.206	3	122	6	0.9
1917	Bos N	3	10	.231	29	14	2	0	112	124	61	3	6	47	56	3.94	65	.297	.376	29-0	.172	2	89	-18	-2.0
Total	6	50	66	.431	180	127	60-10	3	970.1	893	411	26	35	373	457	2.93	98	.252	.330	288-14	.135	1	88	-7	-1.0

ALLEN, JOHN John Marshall B 10.27.1890 Berkeley Springs, WV D 9.24.1967 Hagerstown, MD BR/TR 6-1/170# d6.2

Year	Tm Lg	W	L	Pct	G	GS	CG-Sho	SV-BS	IP	H	R	HR	HB	BB-IB	SO	ERA	AERA	OAV	OOB	AB-SH	AVG	PB	Sup	APR	PW
1914	Bal F	0	0	—	1	0	0	0	2	2	4	0	1	2	2	18.00	17	.286	.500	0-0	—	0		-3	-0.1

ALLEN, JOHNNY John Thomas B 9.30.1905 Lenoir, NC D 3.29.1959 St.Petersburg, FL BR/TR 6/180# d4.19

Year	Tm Lg	W	L	Pct	G	GS	CG-Sho	SV-BS	IP	H	R	HR	HB	BB-IB	SO	ERA	AERA	OAV	OOB	AB-SH	AVG	PB	Sup	APR	PW
1932	†NY A	17	4	**.810**	33	21	13-3	4	192	162	86	10	5	76	109	3.70	110	.228	.306	73-3	.123	-2	119	11	0.9
1933	NY A	15	7	.682	25	24	10-1	1	184.2	171	96	9	4	87	119	4.39	89	.242	.328	72-2	.181	0	131	-7	-0.8
1934	NY A	5	2	.714	13	10	4	0	71.2	62	30	3	2	32	54	2.89	141	.227	.313	26-2	.192	1	120	9	0.8
1935	NY A	13	6	.684	23	23	12-2	0	167	149	76	11	4	58	113	3.61	112	**.238**	.307	67-3	.224	1	133	11	1.2
1936	Cle A	20	10	.667	36	31	19-4	1	243	234	108	5	1	97	165	3.44	146	.256	.328	87-8	.161	-3*	116	43	4.3
1937	Cle A	15	1	**.938**	24	20	14	0	173	157	55	4	5	60	87	2.55	181	.244	.313	67-4	.090	-7	139	40	2.7
1938	Cle A★	14	8	.636	30	27	13	0	200	189	107	15	3	81	112	4.18	111	.246	.321	79-3	.253	4	122	10	1.4
1939	Cle A	9	7	.563	28	26	9-2	0	175	199	96	9	3	56	79	4.58	96	.291	.347	71-2	.225	1*	118	-1	0.1
1940	Cle A	9	8	.529	32	17	5-3	5	138.2	126	61	3	3	48	62	3.44	123	.243	.311	48-0	.208	0	66	12	1.4
1941	StL A	2	5	.286	20	9	2	1	67	89	53	4	2	29	27	6.58	65	.319	.387	22-1	.136	0	119	-15	-1.4
	†Bro N	3	0	1.000	11	4	1	0	57.1	38	18	6	0	12	21	2.51	146	.188	.234	20-1	.050	-2	145	8	0.2
1942	Bro N	10	6	.625	27	15	5-1	3	118	106	53	11	2	39	50	3.20	102	.238	.302	39-4	.179	-0	105	-1	-0.2
1943	Bro N	5	1	.833	17	1	0	1	38	42	21	3	2	25	15	4.26	79	.280	.390	7-2	.429	2	227	-4	-0.4

Year	Tm Lg	W	L	Pct	G	GS	CG-Sho	SV-BS	IP	H	R	HR	HB	BB-IB	SO	ERA	AERA	OAV	OOB	AB-SH	AVG	PB	Sup	APR	PW
	NY N	1	3	.250	15	0	0	2	41	37	16	4	0	14	24	3.07	112	.245	.309	14-1	.000	-2		2	0.0
	Year	6	4	.600	32	1	0	3	79	79	46	7	2	39	39	3.65	93	.262	.351	21-3	.143	-0	224	-2	-0.4
1944	NY N	4	7	.364	18	13	2-1	0	84	88	48	7	2	24	33	4.07	90	.260	.313	24-0	.083	-2*	86	-5	-0.9
Total	13	142	75	.654	352	241	109-17	18	1950.1	1849	924	104	38	738	1070	3.75	113	.249	.321	716-36	.173	-8	119	113	9.3
ALLEN, LLOYD Lloyd Cecil B 5.8.1950 Merced, CA BR/TR 6-1/185# d9.1																									
1969	Cal A	0	1	.000	4	1	0	0-0	10	5	7	1	0	10-0	5	5.40	65	.147	.341	2-0	.500	1	0	-2	-0.1
1970	Cal A	1	1	.500	8	2	0	0-0	24	23	7	0	1	11-2	12	2.63	138	.261	.347	4-0	.000	-0	74	3	0.2
1971	Cal A	4	6	.400	54	1	0	15-3	94	75	29	4	0	40-8	72	2.49	130	.221	.302	17-0	.294	2	55	9	1.5
1972	Cal A	3	7	.300	42	6	0	5-3	85.1	76	38	7	3	55-5	53	3.48	84	.240	.356	17-3	.118	-1	51	-6	-0.9
1973	Cal A	0	0	—	5	0	0	1-0	8.2	15	10	0	0	5-0	4	10.38	34	.417	.465	0-0	—	0		-6	-0.3
	Tex A	0	6	.000	23	5	0	1-0	41	58	59	3	5	39-2	25	9.22	40	.326	.453	0-0	—	0	120	-31	-3.9
	Year	0	6	.000	28	5	0	2-0	49.2	73	64	3	5	44-2	29	9.42	39	.341	.455	0-0	—	0	121	-38	-4.2
1974	Tex A	0	1	.000	14	0	0	0-0	22	24	17	2	1	18-0	18	6.55	55	.276	.398	0-0	—	0		-7	-0.4
	Chi A	0	1	.000	6	2	0	0-0	7	7	9	0	1	12-1	3	10.29	36	.259	.500	0-0	—	0	177	-5	-0.6
	Year	0	2	.000	20	2	0	0-0	29	31	17	2	2	30-1	21	7.45	48	.272	.426	0-0	—	0	183	-12	-1.0
1975	Chi A	0	2	.000	3	2	0	0-0	5.1	8	7	2	0	6-0	2	11.81	33	.348	.467	0-0	—	0	11	-4	-0.7
Total	7	8	25	.242	159	19	0	22-6	297.1	291	183	19	11	196-18	194	4.69	71	.258	.369	40-3	.200	2	84	-49	-5.2
ALLEN, MYRON Myron Smith "Zeke" B 3.22.1854 Kingston, NY D 3.8.1924 Kingston, NY BR/TR 5-8/150# d7.19 ▲																									
1883	NY N	0	1	.000	1	1	1	0	8	8	5	0		3	0	1.13	275	.276	.344	4	.000	-1	69	1	0.0
1887	Cle AA	1	0	1.000	2	0	0	0	9.2	9	4	0	1	3	1	0.93	466	.243	.317	463	.276	0*		3	0.2
1888	KC AA	0	2	.000	2	2	2	0	18	17	7	0	2	1	2	2.50	137	.239	.270	136	.213	0*	34	2	0.2
Total	3	1	3	.250	5	3	3	0	35.2	34	16	0	3	7	3	1.77	205	.248	.299	603	.260	-0	43	6	0.4
ALLEN, NEIL Neil Patrick B 1.24.1958 Kansas City, KS BR/TR 6-2/190# d4.15																									
1979	NY N	6	10	.375	50	5	0	8-1	99	100	46	4	0	47-13	65	3.55	103	.268	.345	14-0	.000	-2	53	0	-0.2
1980	NY N	7	10	.412	59	0	0	22-5	97.1	87	43	7	0	40-9	79	3.70	96	.244	.317	14-1	.143	-0		-1	-0.2
1981	NY N	7	6	.538	43	0	0	18-9	66.2	64	26	4	0	26-8	50	2.97	117	.259	.326	5-2	.200	1		4	0.9
1982	NY N	3	7	.300	50	0	0	19-5	64.2	65	22	5	1	30-5	59	3.06	119	.266	.348	6-1	.167	1		6	1.2
1983	NY N	2	7	.222	21	4	1-1	2-2	54	57	29	6	0	36-5	32	4.50	81	.278	.384	10-1	.000	-1	97	-4	-0.8
	StL N	10	6	.625	25	18	4-2	0-1	121.2	122	55	6	1	48-4	74	3.70	98	.265	.335	39-6	.128	-1	106	0	-0.1
	Year	12	13	.480	46	22	5-3	2-3	175.2	179	59	12	1	84-9	106	3.94	92	.269	.351	49-7	.102	-2	104	-6	-0.9
1984	StL N	9	6	.600	57	1	0	3-1	119	105	54	6	0	49-9	66	3.55	98	.239	.314	25-0	.240	2	51	-2	-0.1
1985	StL N	1	4	.200	23	1	0	2-1	29	32	22	3	1	17-6	10	5.59	63	.283	.373	2-0	.000	-0	50	-7	-1.3
	NY A	1	0	1.000	17	0	0	1-0	29.1	26	9	1	0	13-0	16	2.76	145	.234	.315	0-0	—	0		5	0.2
1986	Chi A	7	2	.778	22	17	2-2	0-0	113	101	50	8	2	38-1	57	3.82	113	.244	.306	0-0	—	0	115	7	0.5
1987	Chi A	0	7	.000	15	10	0	0-0	49.2	74	40	6	2	26-0	26	7.07	65	.365	.438	0-0	—	0	56	-12	-1.4
	NY A	0	1	.000	8	1	0	0-0	24.2	23	12	2	0	10-1	16	3.65	121	.242	.314	0-0	—	0	62	1	0.1
	Year	0	8	.000	23	11	0	0-0	74.1	97	15	8	2	36-1	42	5.93	76	.326	.399	0-0	—	0	57	-11	-1.3
1988	NY A	5	3	.625	41	2	0-1	0-2	117.1	121	51	14	2	37-7	61	3.84	103	.268	.322	0-0	—	0	58	3	0.1
1989	Cle A	0	1	.000	3	0	0	0-0	3	8	5	1	0	0-0	0	15.00	26	.500	.471	0-0	—	0		-3	-0.6
Total	11	58	70	.453	434	59	7-6	75-27	988.1	985	464	73	9	417-68	611	3.88	98	.264	.336	115-11	.130	-1	95	-3	-1.7
ALLEN, BOB Robert Earl "Thin Man" B 7.2.1914 Smithville, TN BR/TR 6-1/165# d9.19																									
1937	Phi N	0	1	.000	3	1	0	0	12	18	12	2	0	8	8	6.75	64	.321	.406	3-0	.333	0	20	-4	-0.3
ALLEN, BOB Robert Gray B 10.23.1937 Tatum, TX BL/TL 6-2/185# d4.14																									
1961	Cle A	3	2	.600	48	0	0	3	81.2	96	42	7	1	40-5	42	3.75	105	.294	.373	12-1	.167	0		0	0.0
1962	Cle A	1	1	.500	30	0	0	4	30.2	29	24	5	0	25-3	23	5.87	66	.250	.378	5-0	.000	-1		-8	-0.7
1963	Cle A	1	2	.333	43	0	0	2	56	58	37	5	1	29-6	51	4.66	78	.266	.352	5-0	.200	-0		-8	-0.5
1966	Cle A	2	2	.500	36	0	0	5	51.1	56	27	2	2	13-6	33	4.21	82	.273	.318	9-1	.111	-0		-4	-0.4
1967	Cle A	0	5	.000	47	0	0	5	54.1	49	22	4	1	25-7	50	2.98	110	.243	.329	0-0	—	0		1	0.2
Total	5	7	12	.368	204	0	0	19	274	288	152	23	5	132-27	199	4.11	89	.270	.351	31-2	.129	-1		-19	-1.4
ALLISON, DANA Dana Eric B 8.14.1966 Front Royal, VA BR/TL 6-3/215# d4.9																									
1991	Oak A	1	1	.500	11	0	0	0-0	11	16	9	0	0	5-1	4	7.36	52	.381	.438	0-0	—	0		-4	-0.7
ALLISON, MACK Mack Pendleton B 1.23.1887 Owensboro, KY D 3.13.1964 Mount Vernon, MO BR/TR 6-1/185# d9.13																									
1911	StL A	2	1	.667	3	3	3	0	26.1	24	9	0	2	5	2	2.05	165	.253	.304	10-0	.200	-0	93	4	0.3
1912	StL A	6	17	.261	31	20	11-1	1	169	171	102	4	6	49	43	3.62	92	.269	.327	52-1	.135	-3	58	-9	-1.5
1913	StL A	1	3	.250	11	4	3	0	51.1	52	24	0	3	13	12	2.28	129	.291	.349	14-0	.000	-2	19	1	-0.2
Total	3	9	21	.300	45	27	17-1	1	246.2	247	135	4	11	67	57	3.17	102	.271	.329	76-1	.118	-6	57	-4	-1.4
ALMANZA, ARMANDO Armando N. B 10.26.1972 ElPaso, TX BL/TL 6-3/205# d7.29																									
1999	Fla N	0	1	.000	14	0	0	0-0	15.2	8	4	1	1	9-1	20	1.72	253	.154	.286	3-0	.000	-0		4	0.2
2000	Fla N	4	2	.667	67	0	0	0-4	46.1	38	27	3	2	43-6	46	4.86	91	.228	.388	1-1	.000	-0		-2	-0.3
2001	Fla N	2	2	.500	52	0	0	0-2	41	34	24	8	0	26-1	45	4.83	87	.230	.339	0-0	—	0		-3	-0.3
2002	Fla N	3	2	.600	51	0	0	2-2	45.2	36	22	8	0	23-1	57	4.34	91	.224	.316	0-0	—	0		-1	-0.1
2003	Fla N	4	5	.444	51	0	0	0-2	50.1	59	37	10	2	25-2	49	6.08	67	.296	.376	0-0	—	0		-12	-1.9
Total	5	13	12	.520	235	0	0	2-10	199	175	114	30	5	126-11	217	4.79	87	.241	.352	4-1	.000	-0		-14	-2.4
ALMANZAR, CARLOS Carlos Manuel (Giron) B 11.6.1973 Santiago, D.R. BR/TR 6-2/166# d9.4																									
1997	Tor A	0	1	.000	4	0	0	0-0	3.1	1	1	1	0	1-0	4	2.70	170	.091	.167	0-0	—	0		1	0.1
1998	Tor A	2	2	.500	25	0	0	0-3	28.2	34	18	4	1	8-2	20	5.34	87	.286	.336	0-0	—	0		-2	-0.2
1999	SD N	0	0	—	28	0	0	0-0	37.1	48	32	6	3	15-2	30	7.47	56	.316	.386	1-0	.000	-0		-14	-0.7
2000	SD N	4	5	.444	62	0	0	0-3	69.2	73	35	12	4	25-2	56	4.39	98	.266	.333	3-0	.000	-0		1	0.1
2001	NY A	0	1	.000	10	0	0	0-2	10.2	14	4	2	0	2-1	6	3.38	133	.333	.356	0-0	—	0		1	0.1
2002	Cin N	0	1	.000	8	1	0	0-0	11.2	6	4	0	0	5-1	7	2.31	184	.158	.244	0-0	—	0	43	2	0.2
Total	6	6	10	.375	137	1	0	0-8	161.1	176	94	25	8	56-8	123	5.02	87	.277	.339	4-0	.000	-0	43	-11	-0.4
ALMONTE, ED Edwin B 12.17.1976 Santiago, D.R. BR/TR 6-3/200# d7.7																									
2003	NY N	0	0	—	12	0	0	0-0	11.1	21	15	3	0	5-1	7	11.12	37	.412	.464	1-0	.000	-0		-9	-0.4
ALMONTE, HECTOR Hector Radhames (Moreta) B 10.17.1975 Santo Domingo, D.R. BR/TR 6-2/190# d7.26																									
1999	Fla N	0	2	.000	15	0	0	0-0	15	20	7	1	0	6-2	8	4.20	104	.339	.394	0-0	—	0		1	0.1
2003	Bos A	0	1	.000	7	0	0	0-0	7.2	9	7	1	0	7-1	6	8.22	56	.310	.421	0-0	—	0		-3	-0.3
	Mon N	1	1	.500	28	0	0	0-1	29	34	22	4	2	17-2	26	6.83	69	.291	.390	1-0	.000	-0		-5	-0.3
Total	2	1	4	.200	50	0	0	0-1	51.2	63	36	6	2	30-5	40	6.27	73	.307	.396	1-0	.000	-0		-7	-0.5
ALOMA, LUIS Luis (Barba) "Witto" B 6.19.1923 Havana, Cuba D 4.7.1997 Park Ridge, IL BR/TR 6-2/195# d4.19																									
1950	Chi A	7	2	.778	42	0	0	4	87.2	77	44	6	1	53	49	3.80	118	.234	.342	15-1	.067	-2		6	0.4
1951	Chi A	6	0	1.000	25	1	1-1	3	69.1	52	14	3	2	24	25	1.82	222	.215	.291	20-1	.350	2	198	18	1.8
1952	Chi A	3	1	.750	25	0	0	6	40	42	20	5	1	11	18	4.27	85	.278	.331	7-0	.000	-1		-2	-0.4
1953	Chi A	2	0	1.000	24	0	0	2	38.1	41	20	7	0	23	23	4.70	86	.283	.381	6-0	.000	-1		-2	-0.2
Total	4	18	3	.857	116	1	1-1	15	235.1	212	98	21	4	111	115	3.44	120	.245	.333	48-2	.167	-2	198	20	1.6
ALSTON, GARVIN Garvin James B 12.8.1971 Mt.Vernon, NY BR/TR 6-2/185# d6.6																									
1996	Col N	1	0	1.000	6	0	0	0-0	6	9	6	1	1	3-0	5	9.00	58	.375	.433	1-0	.000	-0		-2	-0.3
ALTAMIRANO, PORFI Porfirio (Ramirez) B 5.17.1952 Darillo, Nicaragua BR/TR 6/175# d5.9																									
1982	Phi N	5	1	.833	29	0	0	2-1	39	41	19	2	1	14-3	26	4.15	88	.281	.339	4-0	.250	0		-2	-0.2
1983	Phi N	2	3	.400	31	0	0	0-0	41.1	38	18	9	2	15-3	24	3.70	97	.255	.329	2-0	.000	-0		0	0.0
1984	Chi N	0	0	—	5	0	0	0-0	11.1	8	6	2	0	1-0	7	4.76	82	.195	.209	2-0	.000	-0		-1	0.0
Total	3	7	4	.636	65	0	0	2-1	91.2	87	43	13	3	30-6	57	4.03	91	.259	.320	8-0	.125	-0		-3	-0.2

Year	Tm Lg	W	L	Pct	G	GS	CG-Sho	SV-BS	IP	H	R	HR	HB	BB-IB	SO	ERA	AERA	OAV	OOB	AB-SH	AVG	PB	Sup	APR	PW
ALTEN, ERNIE Ernest Matthias "Lefty" B 12.1.1894 Avon, OH D 9.9.1981 Napa, CA BR/TL 6/175# d4.17																									
1920	Det A	0	1	.000	14	1	0	0	23	40	27	2	1	9	4	9.00	41	.392	.446	3-0	.000	-1	213	-12	-0.6
ALTROCK, NICK Nicholas B 9.15.1876 Cincinnati, OH D 1.20.1965 Washington, DC BB/TL 5-10/197# d7.14 C42																									
1898	Lou N	3	3	.500	11	7	6	0	70	89	54	2	3	21	13	4.50	80	.307	.360	29-0	.241	0	127	-10	-0.6
1902	Bos A	0	2	.000	3	2	1	1	18	19	13	0	1	7	5	2.00	179	.271	.346	8-0	.000	-1	70	1	0.0
1903	Bos A	0	1	.000	1	1	1	0	8	13	10	0	0	4	3	9.00	34	.361	.425	3-0	.667	1	71	-5	-0.3
	Chi A	4	3	.571	12	8	6-1	0	71	59	35	3	3	19	19	2.15	130	.226	.286	30-0	.300	2*	130	2	0.6
	Year	4	4	.500	13	9	7-1	0	79	72	40	3	3	23	22	2.85	99	.242	.303	33-0	.333	4	123	-4	0.3
1904	Chi A	19	14	.576	38	36	31-6	1	307	274	117	2	3	48	87	2.96	83	.240	.272	111-6	.198	1*	126	-10	-0.8
1905	Chi A	23	12	.657	38	34	31-3	0	315.2	274	89	3	2	63	97	1.88	131	.236	.276	112-5	.125	-3*	122	24	2.7
1906	†Chi A	20	13	.606	38	30	25-4	0	287.2	269	95	0	3	42	99	2.06	123	.250	.281	100-2	.160	-1	105	15	1.9
1907	Chi A	7	13	.350	30	21	15-1	2	213.2	210	76	3	2	31	61	2.57	93	.259	.288	72-0	.181	1	67	-2	0.2
1908	Chi A	5	7	.417	23	13	8-1	2	136	127	55	2	2	18	21	2.71	85	.248	.276	49-1	.204	1	111	-6	-0.2
1909	Chi A	0	1	.000	1	1	1	0	9	16	6	0	0	1	2	5.00	47	.485	.500	3-0	.000	-0	60	-2	-0.3
	Was A	1	3	.250	9	5	2	0	38	55	23	0	1	5	9	5.45	45	.333	.357	19-0	.053	-1*	70	-10	-1.0
	Year	1	4	.200	10	6	3	0	47	71	25	0	1	6	11	5.36	45	.359	.380	22-0	.045	-1	68	-12	-1.3
1912	Was A	0	1	.000	1	0	0	0	1	1	2	0	0	2	0	18.00	19	.200	.429	1-0	.000	-0		-1	-0.2
1913	Was A	0	0	—	4	0	0	0	9	7	5	0	1	4	2	5.00	59	.194	.293	1-0	.000	-0		-1	-0.1
1914	Was A	0	0	—	1	0	0	0	1	3	0	0	0	0	0	0.00	—	.750	.750	0-0	—	0		0	0.0
1915	Was A	0	0	—	1	0	0	1	3	7	4	0	0	1	2	9.00	33	.438	.471	1-0	.000	-0		-2	-0.2
1918	Was A	1	2	.333	5	3	1	0	24	24	11	1	1	6	5	3.00	91	.279	.333	8-1	.125	0	55	-1	0.0
1919	Was A	0	0	—	1	0	0	0	0	4	4	0	0	0	0	∞	—	1.000	1.000	0-0	—	0		-4	-0.3
1924	Was A	0	0	—	1	0	0	0	2	4	1	0	0	0	0	0.00	—	.500	.500	1-0	1.000	1		1	0.1
Total	16	83	75	.525	218	161	128-16	7	1514	1455	600	16	22	272	425	2.67	95	.255	.291	548-15	.175	1	108	-11	1.5
ALVAREZ, TAVO Cesar Octavio B 11.25.1971 Ciudad Obregon, Mexico BR/TR 6-3/245# d8.21																									
1995	Mon N	1	5	.167	8	8	0	0-0	37.1	46	30	2	3	14-0	17	6.75	64	.297	.366	12-2	.000	-1	95	-10	-1.4
1996	Mon N	2	1	.667	11	5	0	0-0	21	19	10	0	1	12-1	9	3.00	144	.235	.340	4-1	.500	1	100	2	0.3
Total	2	3	6	.333	19	13	0	0-0	58.1	65	40	2	4	26-1	26	5.40	80	.275	.357	16-3	.125	-1	97	-8	-1.1
ALVAREZ, JOSE Jose Lino B 4.12.1956 Tampa, FL BR/TR 5-10/170# d10.1																									
1981	Atl N	0	0	—	1	0	0	0-0	2	0	0	0	0	0-0	2	0.00	—	.000	.000	0-0	—	0		1	0.0
1982	Atl N	0	0	—	7	0	0	0-0	7.2	8	4	1	0	2-1	6	4.70	80	.308	.357	0-0	—	0		-1	0.0
1988	Atl N	5	6	.455	60	0	0	3-1	102.1	88	34	7	6	53-12	81	2.99	123	.240	.343	8-1	.375	1*		9	1.2
1989	Atl N	3	3	.500	30	0	0	2-3	50.1	44	18	4	1	24-2	45	2.86	128	.237	.325	3-2	.000	-0		4	0.5
Total	4	8	9	.471	98	0	0	5-4	162.1	140	56	12	7	79-15	134	2.99	123	.240	.335	11-3	.273	1		13	1.7
ALVAREZ, JUAN Juan M. B 8.9.1973 Coral Gables, FL BL/TL 6-1/175# d9.1																									
1999	Ana A	0	1	.000	8	0	0	0-0	3	1	1	0	0	4-0	4	3.00	162	.111	.385	0-0	—	0		1	0.1
2000	Ana A	0	0	—	11	0	0	0-0	6	14	9	3	0	7-1	2	13.50	38	.467	.553	0-0	—	0		-5	-0.2
2002	Tex A	0	4	.000	52	0	0	0-3	39.2	35	22	7	3	21-0	30	4.76	99	.241	.345	0-0	—	0		0	0.0
2003	Fla N	0	0	—	9	0	0	0-0	11.2	8	4	2	1	8-1	6	3.09	133	.216	.370	0-0	—	0		2	0.1
Total	4	0	5	.000	80	0	0	0-3	60.1	58	36	12	4	40-2	42	5.22	89	.262	.381	0-0	—	0		-2	0.0
ALVAREZ, VICTOR Victor Aurelio B 11.8.1976 Culiacan, Mexico BL/TL 5-10/150# d7.30																									
2002	LA N	0	1	.000	4	1	0	0-0	10.1	9	5	1	0	2-0	7	4.35	88	.237	.275	2-0	.000	-0	0	0	-0.1
2003	LA N	0	1	.000	5	0	0	0-0	5.2	9	8	1	1	6-0	3	12.71	32	.391	.533	0-0	—	0		-5	-0.8
Total	2	0	2	.000	9	1	0	0-0	16	18	13	2	1	8-0	10	7.31	53	.295	.386	2-0	.000	-0	0	-5	-0.9
ALVAREZ, WILSON Wilson Eduardo (Fuenmayor) B 3.24.1970 Maracaibo, Venezuela BL/TL 6-1/235# d7.24																									
1989	Tex A	0	1	.000	1	1	0	0-0	0	3	3	2	0	2-0	0	∞	—	1.000	1.000	0-0	—	0	68	-3	-0.2
1991	Chi A	3	2	.600	10	9	2-1	0-0	56.1	47	26	9	0	29-0	32	3.51	113	.230	.325	0-0	—	0	128	2	0.2
1992	Chi A	5	3	.625	34	9	0	1-0	100.1	103	64	12	4	65-2	66	5.20	74	.272	.381	0-0	—	0	150	-15	-1.1
1993	†Chi A	15	8	.652	31	31	1-1	0-0	207.2	168	78	14	7	122-8	155	2.95	142	.230	.344	0-0	—	0	101	28	2.9
1994	Chi A★	12	8	.600	24	24	2-1	0-0	161.2	147	72	16	0	62-1	108	3.45	135	.241	.309	0-0	—	0	103	21	2.2
1995	Chi A	8	11	.421	29	29	3	0-0	175	171	96	21	2	93-4	118	4.32	103	.258	.349	0-0	—	0	102	1	0.2
1996	Chi A	15	10	.600	35	35	0	0-0	217.1	216	106	21	4	97-3	181	4.22	112	.258	.337	0-0	—	0	119	15	1.5
1997	Chi A	9	8	.529	22	22	2-1	0-0	145.2	126	61	9	3	55-1	110	3.03	145	.232	.303	3-0	.000	-0	81	20	2.0
	†SF N	4	3	.571	11	11	0	0-0	66.1	54	36	9	1	36-3	69	4.48	91	.224	.326	23-1	.130	-0	131	-3	-0.3
1998	TB A	6	14	.300	25	25	0	0-0	142.2	130	78	18	9	68-0	107	4.73	101	.239	.332	0-0	—	0	65	2	0.1
1999	TB A	9	9	.500	28	28	1	0-0	160	159	92	22	6	79-1	128	4.22	118	.260	.349	3-0	.000	-0	100	10	1.0
2002	TB A	2	3	.400	23	10	0	1-0	75	80	47	13	4	36-3	56	5.28	85	.272	.356	4-0	.000	-0	112	-6	-0.5
2003	LA N	6	2	.750	21	12	1-1	1-0	95	80	27	5	5	23-1	82	2.37	170	.231	.288	29-1	.172	0	105	19	1.5
Total	12	94	82	.534	294	246	12-5	3-0	1603	1484	786	171	45	767-27	1212	3.93	114	.247	.335	62-2	.129	-1	103	91	9.5
AMES, RED Leon Kessling B 8.2.1882 Warren, OH D 10.8.1936 Warren, OH BB/TR 5-10.5/185# d9.14																									
1903	NY N	2	0	1.000	2	2	2-1	0	14	5	2	0	0	8	14	1.29	260	.114	.250	6-0	.000	-1	121	3	0.3
1904	NY N	4	6	.400	16	13	11-1	3	115	94	44	2	3	38	93	2.27	120	.222	.291	40-0	.125	-1	76	5	0.2
1905	†NY N	22	8	.733	34	31	21-2	0	262.2	220	113	2	3	105	198	2.74	107	.230	.308	97-6	.144	-1	140	5	0.4
1906	NY N	12	10	.545	31	25	15-1	1	203.1	166	79	1	3	93	156	2.66	98	.223	.312	61-1	.066	-3	109	0	-0.2
1907	NY N	10	12	.455	39	26	17-2	1	233.1	184	93	4	10	108	146	2.16	115	.219	.315	69-4	.174	2	113	2	0.5
1908	NY N	7	4	.636	18	15	5	1	114.1	96	35	0	1	27	81	1.81	133	.232	.281	36-4	.194	-0	132	6	0.7
1909	NY N	15	10	.600	34	27	20-2	1	244	217	109	2	4	81	156	2.69	95	.241	.306	81-3	.074	-5	118	-4	-0.5
1910	NY N	12	11	.522	33	23	13-3	0	190.1	161	78	3	6	63	94	2.22	133	.237	.308	62-2	.177	-1	96	11	1.4
1911	†NY N	11	10	.524	34	23	13-1	2	205	170	80	0	4	54	118	2.68	126	.223	.277	64-3	.094	-3	87	16	1.3
1912	†NY N	11	5	.688	33	22	9-2	2	179	194	82	3	4	35	83	2.46	137	.281	.320	58-1	.224	1	109	14	1.4
1913	NY N	2	1	.667	8	5	2	1	41.2	35	11	0	1	8	30	2.16	144	.241	.286	13-1	.154	-1	121	5	0.5
	Cin N	11	13	.458	31	24	12-1	2	187.1	185	82	7	5	70	80	2.88	113	.265	.336	59-4	.102	-4	86	7	0.4
	Year	13	14	.481	39	29	14-1	3	229	220	86	7	6	78	110	2.75	117	.261	.328	72-5	.111	-5	92	14	0.9
1914	Cin N	15	23	.395	47	37	18-4	**6**	297	274	125	7	6	94	128	2.64	111	.248	.311	94-5	.128	-4	78	9	1.0
1915	Cin N	2	4	.333	17	7	4-1	1	68	82	39	2	0	24	26	4.50	64	.311	.368	20-0	.050	-1	82	-10	-1.0
	StL N	9	3	.750	15	14	8-2	1	113.1	93	35	1	0	32	48	2.46	113	.226	.282	35-3	.114	-2	116	6	0.6
	Year	11	7	.611	32	21	12-3	2	181.1	175	39	3	0	56	74	3.23	87	.259	.316	55-3	.091	-3	104	-3	-0.4
1916	StL N	11	16	.407	45	25	10-2	**8**	228	225	100	3	5	57	98	2.64	100	.263	.313	68-2	.176	-0	90	-4	-0.6
1917	StL N	15	10	.600	43	19	10-2	3	209	189	75	2	3	57	62	2.71	99	.249	.304	64-3	.188	2	93	0	0.5
1918	StL N	9	14	.391	27	25	17	1	206.2	192	75	1	5	52	68	2.31	117	.252	.304	64-4	.156	-1	81	8	0.8
1919	StL N	3	5	.375	23	6	1	1	70	88	44	1	1	25	19	4.89	57	.314	.373	18-1	.222	-0	123	-15	-1.8
	Phi N	0	2	.000	3	2	1	1	16	26	12	0	0	3	4	6.19	52	.400	.426	5-0	.400	1	37	-4	-0.4
	Year	3	7	.300	26	8	2	2	86	114	14	1	1	28	23	5.13	56	.330	.382	23-1	.261	1	100	-19	-2.2
Total	17	183	167	.523	533	371	209-27	36	3198	2896	1313	41	64	1034	1702	2.63	108	.245	.310	1014-47	.141	-21	101	60	5.5
AMOLE, DOC Morris George B 7.5.1878 Coatesville, PA D 3.7.1912 Wilmington, DE BR/TL 5-9/165# d8.19																									
1897	Bal N	4	4	.500	11	7	6	0	70	67	34	0	6	17	19	2.57	162	.250	.309	28-0	.107	-3	73	11	0.8
1898	Was N	0	6	.000	7	5	4	0	49.1	83	57	0	6	22	11	7.84	47	.369	.439	20-0	.100	-2	93	-21	-2.0
Total	2	4	10	.286	18	12	10	0	119.1	150	91	0	12	39	30	4.75	83	.304	.369	48-0	.104	-4	81	-10	-1.2
AMOR, VICENTE Vicente (Alvarez) B 8.8.1932 Havana, Cuba BR/TR 6-3/182# d4.16																									
1955	Chi N	0	1	.000	4	0	0	0	6	11	3	0	0	3-1	3	4.50	91	.407	.467	0-0	—	0		0	0.0
1957	Cin N	1	2	.333	9	4	1	0	27.1	39	19	2	2	10-1	9	5.93	69	.345	.402	6-0	.167	-0	112	-5	-0.5
Total	2	1	3	.250	13	4	1	0	33.1	50	22	2	2	13-2	12	5.67	72	.357	.414	6-0	.167	-0	112	-5	-0.5
ANCKER, WALTER Walter B 4.10.1894 New York, NY D 2.13.1954 Englewood, NJ BR/TR 6-1/190# d9.3																									
1915	Phi A	0	0	—	4	1	0	0	17.2	19	10	1	3	17	4	3.57	82	.279	.443	6-0	.000	-1	150	-1	-0.2

Year	Tm Lg	W	L	Pct	G	GS	CG-Sho	SV-BS	IP	H	R	HR	HB	BB-IB	SO	ERA	AERA	OAV	OOB	AB-SH	AVG	PB	Sup	APR	PW
ANDERSEN, LARRY Larry Eugene B 5.6.1953 Portland, OR BR/TR 6-3/205# d9.5																									
1975	Cle A	0	0	—	3	0	0	0-0	5.2	4	3	0	0	2-0	4	4.76	80	.200	.261	0-0	—	0		0	0.0
1977	Cle A	0	1	.000	11	0	0	0-0	14.1	10	7	1	0	9-3	8	3.14	126	.200	.322	0-0	—	0		1	0.1
1979	Cle A	0	0	—	8	0	0	0-0	16.2	25	14	3	0	4-0	7	7.56	56	.357	.382	0-0	—	0		-5	-0.2
1981	Sea A	3	3	.500	41	0	0	5-3	67.2	57	27	4	2	18-2	40	2.66	145	.228	.282	0-0	—	0		6	0.6
1982	Sea A	0	0	—	40	1	0	1-0	79.2	100	56	16	4	23-1	32	5.99	71	.311	.361	0-0	—	0	107	-13	-0.6
1983	†Phi N	1	0	1.000	17	0	0	0-1	26.1	19	7	0	0	9-1	14	2.39	149	.200	.267	2-0	.000	-0		4	0.2
1984	Phi N	3	7	.300	64	0	0	4-6	90.2	85	32	5	0	25-6	54	2.38	153	.248	.296	4-0	.000	-0		11	1.2
1985	Phi N	3	3	.500	57	0	0	3-6	73	78	41	5	3	26-4	50	4.32	86	.274	.340	4-1	.000	-0		-5	-0.4
1986	Phi N	0	0	—	10	0	0	0-0	12.2	19	8	0	0	3-0	9	4.26	91	.388	.415	0-1	—	0		-1	0.0
	†Hou N	2	1	.667	38	0	0	1-3	64.2	64	22	2	1	23-10	33	2.78	130	.276	.338	6-0	.000	-1		6	0.3
	Year	2	1	.667	48	0	0	1-3	77.1	83	35	2	1	26-10	42	3.03	121	.295	.351	6-1	.000	-1		5	0.3
1987	Hou N	9	5	.643	67	0	0	5-4	101.2	95	46	7	2	41-10	94	3.45	114	.246	.319	6-0	.167	0		4	0.5
1988	Hou N	2	4	.333	53	0	0	5-4	82.2	82	29	3	1	20-8	66	2.94	113	.254	.297	6-0	.333	1		4	0.4
1989	Hou N	4	4	.500	60	0	0	3-3	87.2	63	19	2	0	24-4	85	1.54	220	.198	.251	3-1	.333	0		18	1.7
1990	Hou N	5	2	.714	50	0	0	6-1	73.2	61	19	2	1	24-5	68	1.95	190	.229	.291	3-1	.000	-0		14	1.5
	†Bos A	0	0	—	15	0	0	1-3	22	18	3	0	1	3-0	25	1.23	333	.220	.256	0-0	—	0		7	0.3
1991	SD N	3	4	.429	38	0	0	13-3	47	39	13	0	0	13-3	40	2.30	165	.231	.283	2-0	.000	-0		8	1.5
1992	SD N	1	1	.500	34	0	0	2-0	35	26	14	2	1	8-2	35	3.34	107	.202	.252	1-0	.000	0		1	0.1
1993	†Phi N	3	2	.600	64	0	0	0-4	61.2	54	22	4	1	21-2	67	2.92	136	.233	.299	1-0	1.000	0		8	0.6
1994	Phi N	1	2	.333	29	0	0	0-0	32.2	33	20	2	0	15-3	27	4.41	97	.256	.333	0-0	—	0		-1	-0.1
Total	17	40	39	.506	699	1	0	49-41	995.1	932	402	58	17	311-64	758	3.15	120	.249	.306	38-4	.132	-0	107	67	7.7
ANDERSON, ALLAN Allan Lee B 1.7.1964 Lancaster, OH BL/TL 6/186# d6.11																									
1986	Min A	3	6	.333	21	10	1	0-0	84.1	106	54	11	1	30-3	51	5.55	78	.316	.371	0-0	—	0*	78	-10	-0.9
1987	Min A	1	0	1.000	4	2	0	0-0	12.1	20	15	3	0	10-2	3	10.95	42	.392	.492	0-0	—	0	177	-8	-0.5
1988	Min A	16	9	.640	30	30	3-1	0-0	202.1	199	70	14	7	37-1	83	**2.45**	**167**	.261	.299	0-0	—	0	87	31	3.8
1989	Min A	17	10	.630	33	33	4-1	0-0	196.2	214	97	15	7	53-1	69	3.80	109	.275	.325	1-0	.000	-0*	125	4	0.5
1990	Min A	7	18	.280	31	31	5-1	0-0	188.2	214	106	20	5	39-1	82	4.53	92	.289	.325	0-0	—	0	70	-8	-0.8
1991	Min A	5	11	.313	29	22	2	0-0	134.1	148	82	24	5	42-4	51	4.96	86	.281	.336	0-0	—	0	79	-10	-1.1
Total	6	49	54	.476	148	128	15-3	0-0	818.2	901	424	87	25	211-12	339	4.11	102	.282	.329	1-0	.000	-0	92	-1	1.0
ANDERSON, RED Arnold Revola B 6.19.1912 Lawton, IA D 8.7.1972 Sioux City, IA BR/TR 6-3/210# d9.19 Mil 1942																									
1937	Was A	0	1	.000	2	1	0	0	10.2	11	9	0	1	11	3	6.75	66	.282	.451	3-0	.000	-0	20	-3	-0.2
1940	Was A	1	1	.500	2	2	2	0	14	12	6	0	0	5	3	3.86	108	.245	.315	5-0	.600	1	74	1	0.3
1941	Was A	4	6	.400	32	6	1	0	112	127	69	7	3	53	34	4.18	97	.296	.377	31-2	.258	2	100	-5	-0.2
Total	3	5	8	.385	36	9	3	0	136.2	150	84	7	4	69	40	4.35	94	.290	.378	39-2	.282	3	85	-7	-0.1
ANDERSON, BRIAN Brian James B 4.26.1972 Portsmouth, VA BL/TL 6-1/190# d9.10																									
1993	Cal A	0	0	—	4	1	0	0-0	11.1	11	5	1	0	2-0	4	3.97	114	.256	.289	0-0	—	0	61	1	0.0
1994	Cal A	7	5	.583	18	18	0	0-0	101.2	120	63	13	5	27-0	47	5.22	94	.300	.347	0-0	—	0	116	-4	-0.4
1995	Cal A	6	8	.429	18	17	1	0-0	99.2	110	66	24	3	30-2	45	5.87	80	.282	.334	0-0	—	0	108	-11	-1.3
1996	Cle A	3	1	.750	10	9	0	0-0	51.1	58	29	9	0	14-1	21	4.91	100	.296	.338	0-0	—	0	137	1	0.1
1997	†Cle A	4	2	.667	8	8	0	0-0	48	55	28	7	0	11-0	22	4.69	100	.301	.332	0-0	—	0	113	0	0.0
1998	Ari N	12	13	.480	32	32	2-1	0-0	208	221	109	39	4	24-2	95	4.33	97	.274	.297	66-6	.106	-2*	97	-2	-0.3
1999	†Ari N	8	2	.800	31	19	2-1	1-1	130	144	69	18	1	28-3	75	4.57	100	.279	.317	38-1	.132	1*	119	2	0.4
2000	Ari N	11	7	.611	33	32	2	0-0	213.1	226	101	38	3	39-7	104	4.05	116	.275	.308	69-9	.188	1*	99	16	1.4
2001	†Ari N	4	9	.308	29	22	1	0-1	133.1	156	93	25	1	30-2	55	5.20	88	.295	.332	37-0	.135	-0*	104	-13	-1.0
2002	Ari N	6	11	.353	35	24	0	0-0	156	174	86	23	1	32-3	81	4.79	93	.284	.317	43-5	.116	-1*	88	-4	-0.4
2003	Cle A	9	10	.474	25	24	0	0-0	148	162	88	21	4	32-3	72	3.71	119	.282	.319	1-0	.000	0*	101	4	0.5
	KC A	5	1	.833	7	7	2-1	0-0	49.2	50	22	6	0	11-0	15	3.99	130	.272	.310	0-0	—	0	130	6	0.7
	Year	14	11	.560	32	31	2-1	0-0	197.2	212	29	27	4	43-3	87	3.78	122	.279	.317	1-0	.000	0	108	10	1.2
Total	11	75	69	.521	250	213	10-3	1-2	1350.1	1487	759	224	22	280-23	636	4.58	100	.283	.319	254-21	.138	-2	106	-4	-0.3
ANDERSON, DAVE David S. B 10.10.1868 Chester, PA D 3.22.1897 Chester, PA TL d8.24																									
1889	Phi N	0	1	.000	5	2	1	0	23	30	21	2	0	14	8	7.43	59	.306	.393	11	.182	-0	93	-5	-0.2
1890	Phi N	1	1	.500	3	2	1	0	19.1	31	25	0	1	11	7	7.45	49	.352	.430	9	.111	-1	112	-8	-0.6
	Pit N	2	11	.154	13	13	13	0	108	116	84	2	7	49	41	4.67	71	.265	.349	42	.071	-5	65	-16	-1.7
	Year	3	12	.200	16	15	14	0	127.1	147	87	2	8	60	48	5.09	66	.280	.363	51	.078	-6	72	-26	-2.3
Total	2	3	13	.188	21	17	15	0	150.1	177	130	4	8	74	56	5.45	64	.284	.367	62	.097	-6	74	-29	-2.5
ANDERSON, JIMMY James Drew B 1.22.1976 Portsmouth, VA BL/TL 6-1/195# d7.4																									
1999	Pit N	2	1	.667	13	4	0	0-0	29.1	25	15	2	1	16-2	13	3.99	115	.234	.336	9-0	.333	1	121	2	0.3
2000	Pit N	5	11	.313	27	26	1	0-0	144	169	94	13	7	58-2	73	5.25	88	.294	.364	50-4	.140	-1	94	-11	-1.0
2001	Pit N	9	17	.346	34	34	1	0-0	206.1	232	123	15	11	83-14	89	5.10	88	.287	.358	59-6	.119	-1	77	-12	-1.4
2002	Pit N	8	13	.381	28	25	1	0-0	140.2	167	91	20	5	63-5	47	5.44	77	.299	.372	42-3	.119	-1	96	-18	-2.4
2003	Cin N	1	5	.167	8	7	0	0-0	38.2	60	39	8	0	14-1	13	8.84	48	.359	.402	9-2	.111	0	116	-19	-2.2
Total	5	25	47	.347	110	96	3	0-0	559	653	362	58	24	234-24	235	5.43	82	.295	.365	169-15	.136	-2	91	-58	-6.7
ANDERSON, JASON Jason R. B 6.9.1979 Danville, IL BL/TR 6/170# d3.31																									
2003	NY A	1	0	1.000	22	0	0	0-0	20.2	23	13	3	2	14-4	9	4.79	92	.280	.390	0-0	—	0		-1	-0.1
	NY N	0	0	—	6	0	0	0-0	10.2	10	6	2	1	5-1	7	5.06	82	.256	.340	0-0	—	0		-1	0.0
Total	1	1	0	1.000	28	0	0	0-0	31.1	33	19	5	3	19-5	16	4.88	88	.273	.374	0-0	—	0		-2	-0.1
ANDERSON, JOHN John Charles B 11.23.1929 St.Paul, MN D 12.20.1998 Houston, TX BR/TR 6-1/190# d8.17																									
1958	Phi N	0	0	—	5	1	0	0	16	26	17	5	1	4-0	9	7.88	50	.361	.403	3-0	.000	-0	113	-7	-0.4
1960	Bal A	0	0	—	4	0	0	0	4.2	8	7	0	0	4-0	1	13.50	28	.444	.522	0-0	—	0		-5	-0.2
1962	StL N	0	0	—	5	0	0	1	6.1	4	1	0	0	3-2	3	1.42	300	.182	.269	0-0	—	0		2	0.1
	Hou N	0	0	—	10	0	0	0	17.2	26	12	1	0	3-1	6	5.09	73	.338	.363	2-0	.000	-0		-3	-0.1
	Year	0	0	—	15	0	0	1	24	30	18	1	0	6-3	9	4.13	94	.303	.340	2-0	.000	-0		-1	0.0
Total	3	0	0	—	24	1	0	1	44.2	64	37	6	1	14-3	19	6.45	60	.339	.383	5-0	.000	-0	113	-13	-0.6
ANDERSON, FRED John Frederick B 12.11.1885 Calahaln, NC D 11.8.1957 Winston-Salem, NC BR/TR 6-2/180# d9.25 Mil 1918																									
1909	Bos A	0	0	—	1	1	0	0	8	3	3	0	0	1	5	1.13	222	.115	.148	3-0	.000	-0	113	1	0.0
1913	Bos A	0	6	.000	10	8	4	0	57.1	84	51	0	1	21	32	5.97	49	.353	.408	20-0	.050	-2	104	-19	-1.9
1914	Buf F	13	15	.464	37	28	21-2	0	260.1	243	115	8	2	64	144	3.08	96	.249	.297	90-0	.189	-3*	79	-5	-0.9
1915	Buf F	19	13	.594	36	28	14-5	0	240	192	80	5	3	72	142	2.51	111	.222	.285	80-1	.150	-5	88	9	0.5
1916	NY N	9	13	.409	38	27	13-2	2	188	206	99	7	5	38	98	3.40	72	.277	.316	58-4	.138	-0	130	-26	-3.3
1917	†NY N	8	8	.500	38	18	8-1	3	162	122	40	1	2	34	69	1.44	**177**	.209	**.255**	42-5	.071	-3	100	18	1.6
1918	NY N	4	2	.667	18	4	2-1	**3**	70.2	62	27	1	2	17	24	2.67	98	.246	.299	19-3	.000	-3	151	0	-0.2
Total	7	53	57	.482	178	114	62-11	8	986.1	912	415	22	15	247	514	2.86	95	.248	.298	312-13	.131	-16	99	-22	-4.2
ANDERSON, BUD Karl Adam B 5.27.1956 Westbury, NY BR/TR 6-3/210# d6.11																									
1982	Cle A	3	4	.429	25	5	1	0-1	80.2	84	37	4	1	30-2	44	3.35	122	.268	.330	0-0	—	0	58	5	0.4
1983	Cle A	1	6	.143	39	1	0	7-3	68.1	64	34	8	0	32-6	32	4.08	104	.255	.337	0-0	—	0	21	1	0.1
Total	2	4	10	.286	64	6	1	7-4	149	148	71	12	1	62-8	76	3.68	113	.262	.333	0-0	—	0	51	6	0.5
ANDERSON, LARRY Lawrence Dennis B 12.3.1952 Maywood, CA BR/TR 6-3/190# d9.25																									
1974	Mil A	0	0	—	2	0	0	0-0	2.1	2	0	0	0	1-0	3	0.00	—	.250	.333	0-0	—	0		1	0.1
1975	Mil A	1	0	1.000	8	1	1-1	0-0	30.1	36	18	3	0	6-0	13	5.04	76	.298	.328	0-0	—	0	161	-3	-0.2
1977	Chi A	1	3	.250	6	0	0	0-1	8.2	10	10	1	0	15-4	7	9.35	44	.286	.490	0-0	—	0		-5	-0.9
Total	3	2	3	.400	16	1	1-1	0-1	41.1	48	28	4	0	22-4	23	5.66	69	.293	.372	0-0	—	0	161	-7	-1.0
ANDERSON, MATT Matthew Jason B 8.17.1976 Louisville, KY BR/TR 6-4/200# d6.25																									
1998	Det A	5	1	.833	42	0	0	0-4	44	38	16	3	2	31-4	44	3.27	144	.250	.378	0-0	—	0		8	0.9

Year	Tm Lg	W	L	Pct	G	GS	CG-Sho	SV-BS	IP	H	R	HR	HB	BB-IB	SO	ERA	AERA	OAV	OOB	AB-SH	AVG	PB	Sup	APR	PW
1999	Det A	2	1	.667	37	0	0	0-2	38	33	27	8	1	35-1	32	5.68	87	.232	.383	0-0	—	0		-4	-0.3
2000	Det A	3	2	.600	69	0	0	1-0	74.1	61	44	8	3	45-4	71	4.72	102	.228	.339	0-0	—	0		0	0.0
2001	Det A	3	1	.750	62	0	0	22-2	56	56	33	2	0	18-4	52	4.82	90	.257	.311	0-0	—	0		-3	-0.4
2002	Det A	2	1	.667	12	0	0	0-2	11	17	13	1	2	8-1	8	9.00	48	.378	.474	0-0	—	0		-6	-1.1
2003	Det A	0	1	.000	23	0	0	3-1	23.1	25	17	5	1	9-1	13	5.40	80	.272	.340	0-0	—	0		-4	-0.2
Total	6	15	7	.682	245	0	0	26-11	246.2	230	150	27	9	146-15	220	4.89	95	.251	.354	0-0	—	0		-9	-1.1
ANDERSON, MIKE Michael James B 7.30.1966 Austin, TX BR/TR 6-3/200# d9.7																									
1993	Cin N	0	0	—	3	0	0	0-0	5.1	12	11	3	0	3-0	4	18.56	22	.444	.500	1-0	.000	-0		-8	-0.4
ANDERSON, CRAIG Norman Craig B 7.1.1938 Washington, DC BR/TR 6-2/205# d6.23																									
1961	StL N	4	3	.571	25	0	0	1	38.2	38	15	3	1	12-0	21	3.26	135	.255	.313	9-0	.333	1		5	0.9
1962	NY N	3	17	.150	50	14	2	4	131.1	150	108	18	5	63-2	62	5.35	78	.278	.357	32-3	.094	-2	79	-22	-3.1
1963	NY N	0	2	.000	3	2	0	0	9.1	17	15	0	0	3-0	6	8.68	40	.362	.400	3-0	.333	0	25	-7	-1.1
1964	NY N	0	1	.000	4	1	0	0	13	21	9	0	0	3-0	5	5.54	65	.382	.407	3-0	.000	-0	0	-3	-0.2
Total	4	7	23	.233	82	17	2	5	192.1	226	147	21	6	81-2	94	5.10	81	.286	.355	47-3	.149	-1	69	-27	-3.5
ANDERSON, RICK Richard Arlen B 11.29.1956 Everett, WA BR/TR 6/175# d6.9 C2																									
1986	NY N	2	1	.667	15	5	0	1-0	49.2	45	17	3	0	11-3	21	2.72	130	.245	.281	11-1	.091	-1	81	5	0.2
1987	KC A	0	2	.000	6	2	0	0-0	13	26	22	3	2	9-1	12	13.85	33	.394	.481	0-0	—	0	10	-13	-1.5
1988	KC A	2	1	.667	7	3	0	0-0	34	41	17	3	1	9-2	9	4.24	94	.308	.349	0-0	—	0	61	-1	-0.1
Total	3	4	4	.500	28	10	0	1-0	96.2	112	56	9	3	29-6	42	4.75	81	.292	.341	11-1	.091	-1	59	-9	-1.4
ANDERSON, RICK Richard Lee B 12.25.1953 Inglewood, CA D 6.23.1989 Wilmington, CA BR/TR 6-2/210# d9.18																									
1979	NY A	0	0	—	1	0	0	0-0	2.1	1	1	0	0	4-0	0	3.86	106	.167	.500	0-0	—	0		0	0.0
1980	Sea A	0	0	—	5	2	0	0-0	9.2	8	5	1	0	10-2	7	3.72	111	.229	.400	0-0	—	0	151	0	0.0
Total	2	0	0	—	6	2	0	0-0	12	9	6	1	0	14-2	7	3.75	110	.220	.418	0-0	—	0	151	0	0.0
ANDERSON, BOB Robert Carl B 9.29.1935 E.Chicago, IN BR/TR 6-4.5/210# d7.31																									
1957	Chi N	0	1	.000	8	0	0	0	16.1	20	16	2	1	8-1	7	7.71	50	.317	.397	4-0	.000	-1		-7	-0.4
1958	Chi N	3	3	.500	17	8	2	0	65.2	61	29	3	1	29-1	51	3.97	99	.255	.335	17-0	.118	-1	109	1	0.0
1959	Chi N	12	13	.480	37	36	7-1	0	235.1	245	117	21	5	77-3	113	4.13	96	.272	.329	80-6	.075	-4	96	-4	-0.7
1960	Chi N	9	11	.450	38	30	5	1	203.2	201	105	26	7	68-8	115	4.11	92	.255	.320	71-5	.169	0*	90	-7	-0.6
1961	Chi N	7	10	.412	57	12	1	8	152	162	85	14	2	56-11	96	4.26	98	.275	.338	42-2	.143	0	81	-2	-0.1
1962	Chi N	2	7	.222	57	4	0	4	107.2	111	70	9	5	60-5	82	5.02	83	.266	.361	23-2	.130	0	79	-11	-0.9
1963	Det A	3	1	.750	32	3	0	0	60	58	28	5	6	21-2	38	3.30	113	.258	.335	9-0	.444	2	87	1	0.2
Total	7	36	46	.439	246	93	15-1	13	840.2	858	450	80	27	319-31	502	4.26	93	.266	.335	246-15	.134	-4	91	-29	-2.5
ANDERSON, SCOTT Scott Richard B 8.1.1962 Corvallis, OR BR/TR 6-6/190# d4.8																									
1987	Tex A	0	1	.000	8	0	0	0-1	11.1	17	12	0	1	8-2	6	9.53	47	.347	.448	0-0	—	0		-6	-0.4
1990	Mon N	0	1	.000	4	3	0	0-0	18	12	6	1	0	5-0	16	3.00	122	.188	.243	4-1	.000	-0	124	2	0.0
1995	KC A	1	0	1.000	6	4	0	0-0	25.1	29	15	3	1	8-0	6	5.33	90	.290	.349	0-0	—	0	117	-1	-0.1
Total	3	1	2	.333	18	7	0	0-1	54.2	58	33	4	2	21-2	28	5.43	80	.272	.342	4-1	.000	-0	118	-5	-0.5
ANDERSON, VARNEY Varney Samuel "Varn" B 6.18.1866 Geneva, IL D 11.5.1941 Rockford, IL BR/TR 5-10/165# d8.1																									
1889	Ind N	0	1	.000	2	1	1	0	12	13	10	0	3	9	3	4.50	93	.265	.410	5	.000	-1	161	-1	-0.1
1894	Was N	0	2	.000	2	2	2	0	14	15	12	0	1	6	3	7.07	75	.273	.355	7-0	.429	0	60	-1	-0.1
1895	Was N	9	16	.360	29	25	18	0	204.2	288	199	13	10	97	35	5.89	82	.327	.400	97-2	.289	3*	104	-19	-1.3
1896	Was N	0	1	.000	2	2	1	0	9	23	16	0	0	3	0	13.00	34	.469	.500	5-0	.600	1	129	-7	-0.5
Total	4	9	20	.310	35	30	22	0	239.2	339	237	13	14	115	41	6.16	78	.328	.402	114-2	.298	4	104	-28	-2.0
ANDERSON, WALTER Walter Carl "Lefty" B 9.25.1897 Grand Rapids, MI D 1.6.1990 Battle Creek, MI BL/TL 6-2/160# d5.14 Mil 1918																									
1917	Phi A	0	0	—	14	2	0	0	38.2	32	16	0	1	21	10	3.03	91	.246	.355	7-0	.429	1	78	0	0.1
1919	Phi A	1	0	1.000	3	0	0	0	14	13	8	0	1	8	10	3.86	89	.245	.355	4-1	.000	-1		-1	-0.1
Total	2	1	0	1.000	17	2	0	0	52.2	45	24	0	2	29	20	3.25	90	.246	.355	11-1	.273	0	78	-1	0.0
ANDERSON, BILL William Edward "Lefty" B 11.28.1895 Boston, MA D 3.13.1983 Medford, MA BR/TL 6-1/165# d9.10																									
1925	Bos N	0	0	—	2	0	0	0	2.2	5	3	0	0	2	1	10.13	40	.500	.583	1-0	.000	-0		-2	-0.1
ANDERSON, WINGO Wingo Charlie B 8.13.1886 Alvarado, TX D 12.19.1950 Fort Worth, TX BL/TL 5-10.5/150# d4.16																									
1910	Cin N	0	0	—	7	2	0	0	17.1	16	15	0	1	17	11	4.67	62	.258	.425	5-0	.200	-0	153	-4	-0.3
ANDRE, JOHN John Edward B 1.3.1923 Brockton, MA D 11.25.1976 Barnstable, MA BL/TR 6-4/200# d4.16																									
1955	Chi N	0	1	.000	22	3	0	1	45	45	34	7	1	28-4	19	5.80	70	.259	.361	9-0	.111	-1	153	-9	-0.5
ANDREWS, CLAYTON Clayton John B 5.15.1978 Dunedin, FL BR/TL 6/175# d4.16																									
2000	Tor A	1	2	.333	8	2	0	0-0	20.2	34	23	6	0	9-0	12	10.02	51	.374	.426	3-0	.000	-0	138	-10	-1.2
ANDREWS, ELBERT Elbert De Vore B 12.11.1901 Greenwood, SC D 11.25.1979 Greenwood, SC BL/TR 6/175# d5.1																									
1925	Phi A	0	0	—	6	0	0	0	8	12	12	0	0	11	0	10.13	46	.375	.535	0-0	—	0		-5	-0.2
ANDREWS, HUB Herbert Carl B 8.31.1922 Burbank, OK BR/TR 6/170# d4.20																									
1947	NY N	0	0	—	7	0	0	0	8.2	14	7	1	0	4	2	6.23	65	.368	.429	0-0	—	0		-2	-0.1
1948	NY N	0	0	—	1	0	0	0	3	3	1	0	0	0	0	0.00	—	.300	.300	0-0	—	0		1	0.1
Total	2	0	0	—	8	0	0	0	11.2	17	8	1	0	4	2	4.63	87	.354	.404	0-0	—	0		-1	0.0
ANDREWS, IVY Ivy Paul "Poison" B 5.6.1907 Dora, AL D 11.24.1970 Birmingham, AL BR/TR 6-1/200# d8.15																									
1931	NY A	2	0	1.000	7	3	1	0	34.1	36	17	3	0	8	10	4.19	95	.273	.314	11-0	.182	0	248	0	0.0
1932	NY A	2	1	.667	4	1	1	0	24.2	20	8	0	0	9	7	1.82	223	.215	.284	9-1	.222	1	167	6	0.8
	Bos A	8	6	.571	25	19	8	0	141.2	144	76	4	2	53	30	3.81	118	.262	.329	51-2	.137	-3*	96	9	0.4
	Year	10	7	.588	29	20	9	0	166.1	164	81	4	2	62	37	3.52	126	.255	.322	60-3	.150	-2	100	15	1.2
1933	Bos A	7	13	.350	34	17	5	1	140	157	96	8	1	61	37	4.95	88	.279	.350	42-4	.214	-0*	87	-11	-1.4
1934	StL A	4	11	.267	43	13	2	3	139	166	84	7	0	65	51	4.66	107	.301	.375	40-1	.350	3	102	5	0.7
1935	StL A	13	7	.650	50	20	10	1	213.1	231	95	10	1	53	43	3.54	135	.273	.317	68-4	.132	-5	81	28	1.7
1936	StL A	7	12	.368	36	25	11	1	191.1	221	109	19	0	50	33	4.84	111	.286	.330	59-2	.169	-1	74	14	1.0
1937	Cle A	3	4	.429	20	4	1-1	0	59.2	76	33	3	0	9	16	4.37	105	.311	.336	12-1	.250	1	66	2	0.2
	†NY A	3	2	.600	11	5	3-1	1	49	49	19	2	0	17	17	3.12	142	.259	.320	15-2	.067	-1	67	8	0.6
	Year	6	6	.500	31	9	4-2	1	108.2	125	22	5	0	26	33	3.81	119	.289	.329	27-3	.148	-1	66	10	0.8
1938	NY A	1	3	.250	19	1	1	1	48	51	25	3	0	17	13	3.00	151	.268	.329	12-0	.167	-0	19	6	0.4
Total	8	50	59	.459	249	108	43-2	8	1041	1151	562	59	4	342	257	4.14	115	.279	.335	319-17	.185	-6	89	67	4.4
ANDREWS, JOHN John Richard B 2.9.1949 Monterey Park, CA BL/TL 5-10/175# d4.8																									
1973	StL N	1	1	.500	16	0	0	0-0	18.1	16	10	3	0	11-1	5	4.42	83	.235	.342	2-0	.500	0		-1	-0.1
ANDREWS, NATE Nathan Hardy B 9.30.1913 Pembroke, NC D 4.26.1991 Winston-Salem, NC BR/TR 6/195# d5.1																									
1937	StL N	0	0	—	4	0	0	0	9	12	4	1	0	3	6	4.00	100	.324	.375	0-0	—	0		0	0.1
1939	StL N	1	2	.333	11	1	0	0	16	24	14	0	0	12	6	6.75	61	.343	.439	2-0	.000	-0	106	-5	-0.8
1940	Cle A	0	1	.000	6	0	0	0	12	16	9	1	0	6	3	6.00	70	.327	.400	0-0	—	0		-2	-0.1
1941	Cle A	0	0	—	2	0	0	0	2.1	3	4	0	0	2	1	11.57	34	.300	.417	1-0	.000	-0		-2	-0.1
1943	Bos N	14	20	.412	36	34	23-3	0	283.2	253	100	11	6	75	80	2.57	133	.238	.291	90-6	.156	-0	72	26	3.2
1944	Bos N☆	16	15	.516	37	34	16-2	2	257.1	263	106	14	2	74	76	3.22	119	.261	.312	88-3	.114	-4	85	18	1.7
1945	Bos N	7	12	.368	21	19	8	0	137.2	160	75	9	0	52	26	4.58	84	.295	.356	43-7	.209	0*	78	-8	-1.0
1946	Cin N	2	4	.333	7	7	3	0	43.1	50	29	2	1	8	13	3.95	85	.281	.316	14-3	.071	-1	113	-6	-0.8
	NY N	1	0	1.000	3	2	0	0	12	17	9	2	0	4	5	6.00	57	.362	.412	2-0	.500	1	236	-3	-0.2
	Year	3	4	.429	10	9	3	0	55.1	67	19	4	1	12	18	4.39	77	.298	.336	16-3	.125	-0	141	-9	-1.0
Total	8	41	54	.432	127	97	50-5	2	773.1	798	350	40	9	236	216	3.46	106	.265	.321	240-19	.146	-4	84	18	2.0

Year	Tm Lg	W	L	Pct	G	GS	CG-Sho	SV-BS	IP	H	R	HR	HB	BB-IB	SO	ERA	AERA	OAV	OOB	AB-SH	AVG	PB	Sup	APR	PW
ANDRUS, FRED Frederick Hotham B 8.23.1850 Washington, MI D 11.10.1937 Detroit, MI BR/TR 6-2/185# d7.25.1876 ▲																									
1884	Chi N	1	0	1.000	1	1	1	0	9	11	3	1		2	2	2.00	157	.297	.333	5	.200	0	372	1	0.1
ANDUJAR, JOAQUIN Joaquin B 12.21.1952 San Pedro De Macoris, D.R. BB/TR 6/180# d4.8																									
1976	Hou N	9	10	.474	28	25	9-4	0-0	172.1	163	74	8	1	75-2	59	3.60	89	.255	.332	57-2	.140	-0	85	-6	-0.7
1977	Hou N☆	11	8	.579	26	25	4-1	0-0	158.2	149	80	11	4	64-3	69	3.69	97	.251	.325	53-4	.189	2	110	-6	-0.3
1978	Hou N	5	7	.417	35	13	2	1-0	110.2	88	45	3	4	58-6	55	3.42	97	.224	.327	23-4	.130	-0*	90	-1	0.0
1979	Hou N★	12	12	.500	46	23	8	4-3	194	168	86	7	2	88-6	77	3.43	103	.233	.316	57-5	.088	-0	82	1	0.3
1980	†Hou N	3	8	.273	35	14	0	2-2	122	132	59	8	0	43-2	75	3.91	84	.277	.335	29-5	.172	2	95	-8	-0.4
1981	Hou N	2	3	.400	9	3	0	0-1	23.2	29	17	2	0	12-0	18	4.94	67	.296	.366	4-1	.000	-0	108	-6	-1.1
	StL N	6	1	.857	11	8	1	0-1	55.1	56	24	4	0	11-1	19	3.74	95	.265	.302	19-1	.000	-2*	112	-1	-0.3
	Year	8	4	.667	20	11	1	0-2	79	85	29	6	0	23-1	37	4.10	85	.275	.323	23-2	.000	-2	111	-5	-1.4
1982	†StL N	15	10	.600	38	37	9-5	0-0	265.2	237	85	11	7	50-7	137	2.47	147	.240	.281	95-9	.158	-1	97	32	2.9
1983	StL N	6	16	.273	39	34	5-2	1-0	225	215	112	23	3	75-7	125	4.16	87	.253	.315	73-5	.082	-3	97	-10	-1.0
1984	StL N❖	**20**	14	.588	36	36	12-**4**	0-0	**261.1**	218	104	20	7	70-13	147	3.34	104	.229	.284	84-7	.131	3	112	6	1.2
1985	†StL N❖	21	12	.636	38	38	10-2	0-0	269.2	265	113	15	11	82-12	112	3.40	104	.260	.321	94-7	.106	-2	122	5	0.4
1986	Oak A	12	7	.632	28	26	7-1	1-0	155.1	139	70	23	4	56-1	72	3.82	101	.239	.308	0-0	—	0	100	2	0.3
1987	Oak A	3	5	.375	13	13	1	0-0	60.2	63	43	11	3	26-0	32	6.08	68	.269	.348	0-0	—	0	120	-13	-1.4
1988	Hou N	2	5	.286	23	10	0	0-1	78.2	94	43	9	5	21-5	35	4.00	83	.297	.346	19-1	.211	2	128	-8	-0.4
Total	13	127	118	.518	405	305	68-19	9-8	2153	2016	955	155	51	731-65	1032	3.58	99	.250	.314	607-51	.127	-1	104	-13	-0.5
ANDUJAR, LUIS Luis (Sanchez) B 11.22.1972 Bani, D.R. BR/TR 6-2/175# d9.8																									
1995	Chi A	2	1	.667	5	5	0	0-0	30.1	26	12	4	1	14-2	9	3.26	137	.230	.320	0-0	—	0	92	4	0.3
1996	Chi A	0	2	.000	5	5	0	0-0	23	32	22	4	0	15-0	6	8.22	58	.337	.420	0-0	—	0	117	-9	-0.6
	Tor A	1	1	.500	3	2	0	0-0	14.1	14	8	4	1	1-0	5	5.02	100	.264	.281	0-0	—	0	74	0	0.0
	Year	1	3	.250	8	7	0	0-0	37.1	46	12	8	1	16-0	11	6.99	69	.311	.373	0-0	—	0	104	-9	-0.6
1997	Tor A	0	6	.000	17	8	0	0-0	50	76	45	9	0	21-1	28	6.48	71	.352	.402	0-0	—	0	95	-13	-1.3
1998	Tor A	0	0	—	5	0	0	0-0	5.2	12	6	0	0	2-0	1	9.53	49	.429	.467	0-0	—	0		-3	-0.1
Total	4	3	10	.231	35	20	0	0-0	123.1	160	93	21	2	53-3	49	5.98	78	.317	.379	0-0	—	0	98	-21	-1.7
ANGELINI, NORM Norman Stanley B 9.24.1947 San Francisco, CA BL/TL 5-11/175# d7.22																									
1972	KC A	2	1	.667	21	0	0	2-1	16	13	4	1	1	12-1	16	2.25	135	.228	.371	2-0	.000	-0		2	0.3
1973	KC A	0	0	—	7	0	0	1-0	3.2	2	2	0	0	7-0	3	4.91	84	.200	.500	0-0	—	0		0	0.0
Total	2	2	1	.667	28	0	0	3-1	19.2	15	6	1	1	19-1	19	2.75	118	.224	.398	2-0	.000	-0		2	0.3
ANKIEL, RICK Richard Alexander B 7.19.1979 Fort Pierce, FL BL/TL 6-1/210# d8.23																									
1999	StL N	0	1	.000	9	5	0	1-0	33	26	12	2	1	14-0	39	3.27	140	.215	.301	10-1	.100	-1	76	5	0.2
2000	†StL N	11	7	.611	31	30	0	0-0	175	137	80	21	6	90-2	194	3.50	132	.219	.320	68-1	.250	6*	105	19	2.3
2001	StL N	1	2	.333	6	6	0	0-0	24	25	21	7	3	25-0	27	7.13	60	.275	.434	8-1	.000	-1	119	-8	-0.9
Total	3	12	10	.545	46	41	0	1-0	232	188	113	30	10	129-2	260	3.84	119	.225	.332	86-3	.209	5	103	16	1.6
ANTONELLI, JOHNNY John August B 4.12.1930 Rochester, NY BL/TL 6/190# d7.4 Mil 1951																									
1948	Bos N	0	0	—	4	0	0	1	4	2	1	0	0	3	0	2.25	170	.143	.294	0-0	—	0		1	0.1
1949	Bos N	3	7	.300	22	10	3-1	0	96	99	49	6	2	42	48	3.56	106	.273	.351	25-5	.120	-1	51	0	-0.1
1950	Bos N	2	3	.400	20	6	2-1	0	57.2	81	46	3	4	22	33	5.93	65	.335	.399	16-0	.125	-1	84	-15	-1.2
1953	Mil N	12	12	.500	31	26	11-2	1	175.1	167	83	15	1	71	131	3.18	123	.242	.314	62-4	.177	0	118	11	1.4
1954	†NY N★	21	7	**.750**	39	37	18-**6**	2	258.2	209	78	22	5	94	152	**2.30**	**176**	**.219**	.292	98-4	.163	0	109	**50**	**5.3**
1955	NY N	14	16	.467	38	34	14-2	1	235.1	206	105	24	11	82-5	143	3.33	121	.234	.306	82-3	.207	3	94	16	2.3
1956	NY N★	20	13	.606	41	36	15-5	1	258.1	225	93	20	3	75-10	145	2.86	132	.234	.291	89-6	.157	1*	76	26	3.5
1957	NY N☆	12	18	.400	40	30	8-3	0	212.1	228	98	19	3	67-7	114	3.77	104	.276	.330	72-1	.153	3*	66	5	0.9
1958	SF N☆	16	13	.552	41	34	13	3	241.2	216	101	31	3	87-7	143	3.28	116	.239	.306	84-5	.226	4*	110	14	1.9
1959	SF N★	19	10	.655	40	38	17-**4**	1	282	247	107	29	3	76-6	165	3.10	123	.233	.285	101-5	.158	1*	110	25	2.6
1960	SF N	6	7	.462	41	10	1-1	11	112.1	106	51	7	2	47-10	57	3.77	92	.253	.326	34-1	.235	2*	71	-2	0.0
1961	Cle A	0	4	.000	11	7	0	0	48	68	39	8	1	18-0	23	6.56	60	.338	.390	15-1	.267	1*	83	-14	-0.9
	Mil N	1	0	1.000	9	0	0	0	10.2	16	9	2	0	3-0	8	7.59	49	.340	.373	1-0	.000	-0		-5	-0.4
Total	12	126	110	.534	377	268	102-25	21	1992.1	1870	860	186	38	687-45	1162	3.34	116	.247	.312	679-35	.178	15	95	112	15.4
APODACA, BOB Robert John B 1.31.1950 Los Angeles, CA BR/TR 5-11/170# d9.18 C7																									
1973	NY N	0	0	—	1	0	0	0-0	0	0	1	0	0	2-0	0	∞	—	—	1.000	0-0	—	0		-1	-0.1
1974	NY N	6	6	.500	35	8	1	3-2	103	92	47	7	2	42-9	54	3.50	102	.241	.318	25-1	.120	0	113	1	0.1
1975	NY N	3	4	.429	46	0	0	13-1	84.2	66	18	4	0	28-9	45	1.49	233	.222	.286	11-0	.364	2		18	2.4
1976	NY N	3	7	.300	43	3	0	5-2	89.2	71	34	4	3	29-12	45	2.81	117	.223	.291	16-1	.125	0	89	4	0.6
1977	NY N	4	8	.333	59	0	0	5-5	84	83	38	7	1	30-11	53	3.43	109	.255	.318	6-1	.167	-0		2	0.3
Total	5	16	25	.390	184	11	1	26-10	361.1	312	138	22	6	131-41	197	2.86	123	.236	.305	58-3	.172	2	107	24	3.3
APONTE, LUIS Luis Eduardo (Yuripe) B 6.14.1953 ElTigre, Venezuela BR/TR 6/185# d9.4																									
1980	Bos A	0	0	—	4	0	0	0-0	7	6	1	0	0	2-1	1	1.29	329	.250	.308	0-0	—	0		2	0.1
1981	Bos A	1	0	1.000	7	0	0	1-0	15.2	11	1	0	0	3-0	11	0.57	675	.208	.250	0-0	—	0		5	0.5
1982	†Bos A	2	2	.500	40	0	0	3-0	85	78	31	5	0	25-3	44	3.18	136	.246	.299	0-0	—	0		11	0.6
1983	Bos A	5	4	.556	34	0	0	3-1	62	74	28	7	2	23-3	32	3.63	120	.301	.364	0-0	—	0		5	0.7
1984	Cle A	1	0	1.000	25	0	0	0-0	50.1	53	25	5	1	15-0	25	4.11	100	.269	.322	0-0	—	0		0	0.0
Total	5	9	6	.600	110	0	0	7-1	220	222	86	17	3	68-7	113	3.27	130	.265	.321	0-0	—	0		23	1.9
APPIER, KEVIN Robert Kevin B 12.6.1967 Lancaster, CA BR/TR 6-2/195# d6.14																									
1989	KC A	1	4	.200	6	5	0	0-0	21.2	34	22	3	0	12-1	10	9.14	42	.374	.434	0-0	—	0	70	-12	-2.0
1990	KC A	12	8	.600	32	24	3-3	0-0	185.2	179	67	13	6	54-2	127	2.76	139	.252	.307	0-0	—	0	100	22	2.2
1991	KC A	13	10	.565	34	31	6-3	0-0	207.2	205	97	13	2	61-3	158	3.42	120	.255	.307	0-0	—	0	104	13	1.3
1992	KC A	15	8	.652	30	30	3	0-0	208.1	167	59	10	2	68-5	150	2.46	165	.217	.281	0-0	—	0	78	37	4.1
1993	KC A	18	8	.692	34	34	5-1	0-0	238.2	183	74	8	1	81-3	186	**2.56**	**179**	.212	.279	0-0	—	0	89	**50**	**5.1**
1994	KC A	7	6	.538	23	23	1	0-0	155	137	68	11	4	63-7	145	3.83	131	.240	.317	0-0	—	0	96	21	1.5
1995	KC A★	15	10	.600	31	31	4-1	0-0	201.1	163	90	14	8	80-1	185	3.89	123	.221	.303	0-0	—	0	95	22	2.3
1996	KC A	14	11	.560	32	32	5-1	0-0	211.1	192	87	17	5	75-2	207	3.62	138	.245	.314	0-0	—	0	87	35	3.5
1997	KC A	9	13	.409	34	34	4-1	0-0	235.2	215	96	24	4	74-2	196	3.40	139	.243	.303	6-0	.000	-1	76	34	2.7
1998	KC A	1	2	.333	3	3	0	0-0	15	21	13	3	1	5-1	9	7.80	62	.339	.391	0-0	—	0	64	-4	-0.7
1999	KC A	9	9	.500	22	22	1	0-0	140.1	153	81	18	6	51-3	78	4.87	103	.279	.345	2-0	.000	-0	98	3	0.3
	Oak A	7	5	.583	12	12	0	0-0	68.2	77	50	9	1	33-1	53	5.77	81	.280	.357	0-0	—	0	112	-9	-1.3
	Year	16	14	.533	34	34	1	0-0	209	230	56	27	7	84-4	131	5.17	95	.279	.349	2-0	.000	-0	102	-7	-1.0
2000	†Oak A	15	11	.577	31	31	1-1	0-0	195.1	200	109	23	9	102-10	129	4.52	105	.262	.354	6-0	.167	-0	123	5	0.5
2001	NY N	11	10	.524	33	33	1-1	0-0	206.2	181	89	22	15	64-4	172	3.57	116	.237	.306	62-3	.113	-2	89	14	1.0
2002	†Ana A	14	12	.538	32	32	0	0-0	188.1	191	89	23	7	64-2	132	3.92	113	.267	.330	2-2	.000	-0	94	11	1.2
2003	Ana A	7	7	.500	19	19	0	0-0	92.2	105	60	17	8	36-4	50	5.63	77	.279	.353	5-0	.000	-0	102	-13	-1.7
	KC A	1	2	.333	4	4	0	0-0	19	15	9	4	0	7-0	5	4.26	121	.217	.289	0-0	—	0	67	2	0.2
	Year	8	9	.471	23	23	0	0-0	111.2	120	13	21	8	43-4	55	5.40	83	.269	.343	5-0	.000	-0	95	-10	-1.5
Total	15	169	136	.554	412	400	34-12	0-0	2591.1	2418	1160	232	79	930-51	1992	3.72	122	.247	.315	83-5	.096	-3	94	231	20.2
APPLEGATE, FRED Frederick Romaine B 5.9.1879 Williamsport, PA D 4.21.1968 Williamsport, PA BR/TR 6-2/180# d9.30																									
1904	Phi A	1	2	.333	3	3	3	0	21	29	18	0	1	8	12	6.43	42	.330	.392	7-1	.286	0	115	-7	-0.9
APPLETON, ED Edward Samuel "Whitey" B 2.29.1892 Arlington, TX D 1.27.1932 Arlington, TX BR/TR 6-0.5/173# d4.16																									
1915	Bro N	4	10	.286	34	10	5	0	138.1	133	71	3	8	66	50	3.32	84	.263	.357	44-0	.159	-0	86	-9	-1.0
1916	Bro N	1	2	.333	14	3	1	1	47	49	25	1	1	18	14	3.06	88	.278	.349	12-0	.167	-0	102	-3	-0.3
Total	2	5	12	.294	48	13	6	1	185.1	182	96	4	9	84	64	3.25	85	.267	.355	56-0	.161	-1	89	-12	-1.3

Year	Tm Lg	W	L	Pct	G	GS	CG-Sho	SV-BS	IP	H	R	HR	HB	BB-IB	SO	ERA	AERA	OAV	OOB	AB-SH	AVG	PB	Sup	APR	PW
APPLETON, PETE Peter William "Jake" (a.k.a. Jablonowski In 1927-33) B 5.20.1904 Terryville, CT D 1.18.1974 Trenton, NJ BR/TR 5-11/180# d9.14 Mil 1943-45																									
1927	Cin N	2	1	.667	6	2	2-1	0	29.2	29	7	0	0	17	3	1.82	208	.261	.359	11-0	.545	2	45	7	0.9
1928	Cin N	3	4	.429	31	3	0	0	82.2	101	50	7	2	22	20	4.68	85	.311	.358	31-2	.323	3*	128	-7	-0.1
1930	Cle A	8	7	.533	39	7	2	1	118.2	122	71	8	5	53	45	4.02	120	.274	.357	40-1	.200	-1	84	8	0.8
1931	Cle A	4	4	.500	29	4	3	0	79.2	100	51	2	1	29	25	4.63	100	.293	.350	24-1	.208	0*	87	-1	-0.1
1932	Cle A	0	0	—	4	0	0	0	5	11	11	1	0	3	1	16.20	29	.407	.467	0-0	—	0		-6	-0.3
	Bos A	0	3	.000	11	3	0	0	46	49	35	2	2	26	15	4.11	109	.265	.362	17-0	.176	-0	51	-2	0.0
	Year	0	3	.000	15	3	0	0	51	60	38	3	2	29	16	5.29	85	.283	.374	17-0	.176	-0	50	-8	-0.3
1933	NY A	0	0	—	1	0	0	0	2	3	0	0	0	1	0	0.00	—	.375	.444	0-0	—	0		1	0.1
1936	Was A	14	9	.609	38	20	12-1	3	201.2	199	94	7	3	77	77	3.53	135	.254	.324	76-1	.250	2	88	29	3.0
1937	Was A	8	15	.348	35	18	7-4	2	168	167	103	16	5	72	62	4.39	101	.260	.339	59-1	.186	-2	66	-2	-0.3
1938	Was A	7	9	.438	43	10	5	5	164.1	175	99	12	1	61	62	4.60	98	.270	.333	59-2	.254	3	103	-2	0.1
1939	Was A	5	10	.333	40	4	2	6	102.2	104	62	7	4	48	50	4.56	95	.265	.351	25-3	.160	-1	71	-4	-0.5
1940	Chi A	4	0	1.000	25	0	0	5	57.2	54	39	8	1	28	21	5.62	79	.248	.336	17-1	.176	-0		-6	-0.5
1941	Chi A	0	3	.000	13	0	0	1	27.1	27	21	4	2	17	12	5.27	78	.257	.371	4-0	.250	0		-5	-0.5
1942	Chi A	0	0	—	4	0	0	0	4.2	2	2	0	0	3	2	3.86	93	.133	.278	0-0	—	0		0	0.0
	StL A	1	1	.500	14	0	0	2	27.1	25	9	1	0	11	12	2.96	125	.243	.316	6-0	.167	1		3	0.4
	Year	1	1	.500	18	0	0	2	32	27	15	1	0	14	14	3.09	119	.229	.311	6-0	.167	1		3	0.4
1945	StL A	0	0	—	2	0	0	0	2.1	3	5	0	0	7	1	15.43	23	.273	.556	0-0	—	0		-3	-0.1
	Was A	1	0	1.000	6	2	1	1	21.1	16	8	1	0	11	12	3.38	92	.211	.310	5-0	.200	-0	137	0	0.0
	Year	1	0	1.000	8	2	1	1	23.2	19	13	1	0	18	13	4.56	69	.218	.352	5-0	.200	-0	135	-4	-0.1
Total	14	57	66	.463	341	73	34-6	26	1141	1187	667	76	26	486	420	4.30	104	.268	.343	374-12	.233	7	84	10	2.9
AQUINO, LUIS Luis Antonio (Colon) B 5.19.1964 Santurce, P.R. BR/TR 6-1/195# d8.8																									
1986	Tor A	1	1	.500	7	0	0	0-1	11.1	14	8	2	0	3-1	5	6.35	67	.304	.340	0-0	—	0		-2	-0.4
1988	KC A	1	0	1.000	7	5	1-1	0-0	29	33	15	1	1	17-0	11	2.79	143	.282	.375	0-0	—	0	169	2	0.1
1989	KC A	6	8	.429	34	16	2-1	0-0	141.1	148	62	6	4	35-4	68	3.50	110	.271	.317	0-0	—	0	100	5	0.5
1990	KC A	4	1	.800	20	3	1	0-0	68.1	59	25	6	4	27-6	28	3.16	122	.237	.319	0-0	—	0	142	6	0.4
1991	KC A	8	4	.667	38	18	1-1	3-1	157	152	67	10	4	47-5	80	3.44	120	.253	.308	0-0	—	0	105	12	0.9
1992	KC A	3	6	.333	15	13	0	0-1	67.2	81	35	5	1	20-1	11	4.52	90	.303	.351	0-0	—	0	61	-2	-0.2
1993	Fla N	6	8	.429	38	13	0	0-1	110.2	115	43	6	5	40-1	67	3.42	127	.276	.345	25-4	.080	-2	69	12	1.3
1994	Fla N	2	1	.667	29	1	0	0-0	50.2	39	22	3	3	22-4	22	3.73	117	.210	.300	6-1	.167	-0	63	4	0.2
1995	Mon N	0	2	.000	29	0	0	2-2	37.1	47	24	4	3	11-1	22	3.86	111	.301	.357	3-0	.333	1		-1	0.0
	SF N	0	1	.000	5	0	0	0-0	5	10	10	2	0	2-1	4	14.40	28	.400	.444	1-0	.000	-0		-6	-1.0
	Year	0	3	.000	34	0	0	2-2	42.1	57	37	6	3	13-2	26	5.10	84	.315	.369	4-0	.250	0		-7	-1.0
Total	9	31	32	.492	222	69	5-3	5-6	678.1	698	311	45	25	224-24	318	3.68	111	.267	.329	35-5	.114	-1	93	30	1.8
ARCHER, FRED Frederick Marvin "Lefty" B 3.7.1910 Johnson City, TN D 10.31.1981 Charlotte, NC BL/TL 6/193# d9.5																									
1936	Phi A	2	3	.400	6	5	2	0	36.2	41	28	3	3	15	9	6.38	80	.289	.369	15-0	.267	0	86	-4	-0.4
1937	Phi A	0	0	—	1	0	0	0	3	4	2	0	0	0	2	6.00	79	.333	.333	0-0	—	0		0	0.0
Total	2	2	3	.400	7	5	2	0	39.2	45	30	3	3	15	11	6.35	80	.292	.366	15-0	.267	1	86	-4	-0.4
ARCHER, JIM James William B 5.25.1932 Max Meadows, VA BR/TL 6/190# d4.30																									
1961	KC A	9	15	.375	39	27	9-2	5	205.1	204	99	11	5	60-6	110	3.20	131	.257	.309	63-6	.063	-5	80	16	1.3
1962	KC A	0	1	.000	18	1	0	0	27.2	40	30	8	0	10-0	12	9.43	45	.342	.394	1-0	1.000	0	106	-14	-0.7
Total	2	9	16	.360	57	28	9-2	5	233	244	129	19	5	70-6	122	3.94	106	.268	.320	64-6	.078	-4	81	2	0.6
ARDIZOIA, RUGGER Rinaldo Joseph B 11.20.1919 Oleggio, Italy BR/TR 5-11/180# d4.30																									
1947	NY A	0	0	—	1	0	0	0	2	4	2	1	0	1	0	9.00	39	.500	.556	0-0	—	0		-1	-0.1
ARELLANES, FRANK Frank Julian B 1.28.1882 Santa Cruz, CA D 12.13.1918 San Jose, CA BR/TR 6/180# d7.28																									
1908	Bos A	4	3	.571	11	8	6-1	0	79	60	26	1	3	18	33	1.82	135	.205	.259	30-0	.167	0*	97	5	0.3
1909	Bos A	16	12	.571	45	28	17-1	**8**	230.2	192	80	3	5	43	82	2.18	114	.229	.270	78-6	.167	-1*	114	7	0.8
1910	Bos A	4	7	.364	18	13	2	0	100	106	41	1	3	24	33	2.88	89	.283	.332	34-1	.176	0	93	-2	-0.2
Total	3	24	22	.522	74	49	25-2	8	409.2	358	147	5	11	85	148	2.28	110	.238	.283	142-7	.169	-1	105	10	0.9
ARIAS, RUDY Rodolfo (Martinez) B 6.6.1931 Las Villas, Cuba BL/TL 5-10/165# d4.10																									
1959	Chi A	2	0	1.000	34	0	0	2	44	49	23	7	1	20-7	28	4.09	92	.277	.354	4-0	.000	-1		-2	-0.1
ARLICH, DON Donald Louis B 2.15.1943 Wayne, MI BL/TL 6-2/185# d10.2																									
1965	Hou N	0	0	—	1	1	0	0	6	5	2	0	0	1-0	0	3.00	112	.227	.261	2-0	.000	-0	78	0	0.0
1966	Hou N	0	1	.000	7	0	0	0	4	11	9	0	1	4-0	1	15.75	22	.478	.571	1-0	.000	-0		-6	-1.2
Total	2	0	1	.000	8	1	0	0	10	16	11	0	1	5-0	1	8.10	42	.356	.431	3-0	.000	-0	78	-6	-1.2
ARLIN, STEVE Stephen Ralph B 9.25.1945 Seattle, WA BR/TR 6-3.5/195# d6.17																									
1969	SD N	0	1	.000	4	1	0	0-0	10.2	13	11	2	0	9-1	9	9.28	38	.289	.407	2-0	.000	-0	0	-6	-0.5
1970	SD N	1	0	1.000	2	2	1-1	0-0	12.2	11	4	0	0	8-0	3	2.84	140	.244	.352	5-0	.000	-1	101	2	0.1
1971	SD N	9	19	.321	36	34	10-4	0-0	227.2	211	114	8	6	103-10	156	3.48	95	.244	.327	73-6	.123	-1	92	-9	-1.3
1972	SD N	10	21	.323	38	37	12-3	0-0	250	217	115	19	9	122-15	159	3.60	91	.237	.329	72-4	.153	3	75	-10	-0.9
1973	SD N	11	14	.440	34	27	7-3	0-1	180	196	107	26	1	72-7	98	5.10	68	.278	.343	60-2	.167	1	81	-29	-3.4
1974	SD N	1	7	.125	16	12	1	1-0	64	85	46	5	2	37-4	18	5.91	60	.326	.408	18-1	.111	-1	82	-16	-1.9
	Cle A	2	5	.286	11	10	1	0-0	43.2	59	34	1	0	22-4	20	6.60	55	.333	.405	0-0	—	0	95	-13	-1.9
Total	6	34	67	.337	141	123	32-11	1-1	788.2	792	431	61	18	373-41	463	4.33	78	.263	.345	230-13	.139	1	83	-81	-9.8
ARMAS, TONY Antonio Jose B 4.29.1978 Puerto Piritu, Venezuela BR/TR 6-4/205# d8.16 f-Tony																									
1999	Mon N	0	1	.000	1	1	0	0-0	6	8	4	0	0	2-1	2	1.50	299	.320	.357	2-0	.000	-0	82	1	0.1
2000	Mon N	7	9	.438	17	17	0	0-0	95	74	49	10	3	50-2	59	4.36	110	.218	.321	26-3	.038	-2	87	5	0.6
2001	Mon N	9	14	.391	34	34	0	0-0	196.2	180	101	18	10	91-6	176	4.03	111	.247	.336	53-6	.151	-1	82	7	0.6
2002	Mon N	12	12	.500	29	29	0	0-0	164.1	149	87	22	7	78-12	131	4.44	101	.243	.335	50-5	.100	-2	88	2	0.1
2003	Mon N	2	1	.667	5	5	0	0-0	31	25	9	4	1	8-0	23	2.61	179	.225	.279	10-0	.200	-0	96	7	0.6
Total	5	30	37	.448	86	86	0	0-0	493	436	250	54	21	229-21	391	4.11	111	.240	.330	141-14	.113	-6	86	22	2.0
ARMBRUST, ORVILLE Orville Martin B 3.2.1910 Beirne, AR D 10.2.1967 Mobile, AL BR/TR 5-10/195# d9.18																									
1934	Was A	1	0	1.000	3	2	0	0	12.2	10	3	1	0	3	3	2.13	203	.208	.255	4-0	.000	-1	50	3	0.2
ARMSTRONG, HOWARD Howard Elmer B 12.2.1889 E.Claridon, OH D 3.8.1926 Canisteo, NY BR/TR 5-9/165# d9.30																									
1911	Phi A	0	1	.000	1	0	0	0	3	3	2	0	0	1	0	0.00	—	.273	.333	1-0	.000	-0		0	0.1
ARMSTRONG, JACK Jack William B 3.7.1965 Englewood, NJ BR/TR 6-5/215# d6.21																									
1988	Cin N	4	7	.364	14	13	0	0-0	65.1	63	44	8	0	38-2	45	5.79	62	.256	.349	21-1	.095	-1	76	-14	-2.2
1989	Cin N	2	3	.400	9	8	0	0-0	42.2	40	24	5	0	21-4	23	4.64	78	.245	.330	8-3	.000	-1*	92	-4	-0.5
1990	†Cin N★	12	9	.571	29	27	2-1	0-0	166	151	72	9	6	59-7	110	3.42	116	.241	.310	47-13	.106	-2	97	8	0.8
1991	Cin N	7	13	.350	27	24	1	0-0	139.2	158	90	25	2	54-2	93	5.48	69	.293	.354	43-5	.093	-2	92	-23	-3.0
1992	Cle A	6	15	.286	35	23	1	0-0	166.2	176	100	23	3	67-0	114	4.64	84	.269	.337	0-0	—	0	89	-16	-1.7
1993	Fla N	9	17	.346	36	33	0	0-0	196.1	210	105	29	7	78-6	118	4.49	96	.271	.339	66-4	.152	-2	66	-3	-0.5
1994	Tex A	0	1	.000	2	2	0	0-0	10	9	4	3	0	2-0	7	3.60	134	.231	.268	0-0	—	0	114	2	0.1
Total	7	40	65	.381	152	130	4-1	0-0	786.2	807	439	102	18	319-21	510	4.58	87	.265	.335	185-26	.114	-6	84	-50	-7.0
ARMSTRONG, MIKE Michael Dennis B 3.7.1954 Glen Cove, NY BR/TR 6-3/206# d8.12																									
1980	SD N	0	0	—	11	0	0	0-0	14.1	16	10	3	0	13-5	14	5.65	61	.296	.433	3-0	.000	-0		-4	-0.3
1981	SD N	0	2	.000	10	0	0	0-0	12	14	9	1	0	11-3	9	6.00	54	.311	.446	0-0	—	0		-4	-0.6
1982	KC A	5	5	.500	52	0	0	6-2	112.2	88	45	9	3	43-4	75	3.20	128	.215	.290	0-0	—	0		11	0.9
1983	KC A	10	7	.588	58	0	0	3-3	102.2	86	53	11	3	45-3	52	3.86	106	.228	.312	0-0	—	0*		1	0.2
1984	NY A	3	2	.600	36	0	0	1-3	54.1	47	21	6	0	26-4	43	3.48	109	.239	.322	0-0	—	0		3	0.3
1985	NY A	0	0	—	9	0	0	0-0	14.2	9	5	4	0	2-0	11	3.07	130	.173	.204	0-0	—	0		2	0.1

Year	Tm Lg	W	L	Pct	G	GS	CG-Sho	SV-BS	IP	H	R	HR	HB	BB-IB	SO	ERA	AERA	OAV	OOB	AB-SH	AVG	PB	Sup	APR	PW
1986	NY A	0	1	.000	7	1	0	0-0	8.2	13	9	4	0	5-1	8	9.35	44	.351	.429	0-0	—	0	177	-5	-0.5
1987	Cle A	1	0	1.000	14	0	0	1-0	18.2	27	18	4	0	10-0	9	8.68	52	.333	.407	0-0	—	0		-7	-0.4
Total	8	19	17	.528	197	1	0	11-8	338	300	170	42	6	155-20	221	4.10	98	.240	.323	3-0	.000	-0	177	-3	-0.3
ARNOLD, JAMIE James Lee B 3.24.1974 Dearborn, MI BR/TR 6-2/190# d4.20																									
1999	LA N	2	4	.333	36	3	0	1-2	69	81	50	6	6	34-2	26	5.48	78	.300	.390	10-1	.200	0	186	-12	-0.8
2000	Chi N	0	3	.000	12	4	0	1-0	32.2	34	28	1	3	19-0	13	6.61	69	.274	.376	9-0	.111	0	71	-9	-0.7
	LA N	0	0	—	2	0	0	0-0	6.2	4	3	0	1	5-0	3	4.05	107	.174	.333	0-0	—	0		0	0.0
	Year	0	3	.000	14	4	0	1-0	39.1	38	35	1	4	24-0	16	6.18	73	.259	.369	9-0	.111	0	71	-9	-0.7
Total	2	2	7	.222	50	7	0	2-2	108.1	119	81	7	10	58-2	42	5.73	76	.285	.382	19-1	.158	0	120	-21	-1.5
ARNOLD, SCOTT Scott Gentry B 8.18.1962 Lexington, KY BR/TR 6-2/210# d4.7																									
1988	StL N	0	0	—	6	0	0	0-0	6.2	9	4	0	0	4-1	8	5.40	64	.321	.406	0-0	—	0		-1	-0.1
ARNOLD, TONY Tony Dale B 5.3.1959 ElPaso, TX BR/TR 5-11/170# d8.9																									
1986	Bal A	0	2	.000	11	0	0	0-0	25.1	25	15	0	0	11-3	7	3.55	117	.278	.356	0-0	—	0		0	0.1
1987	Bal A	0	0	—	27	0	0	0-0	53	71	35	8	2	17-5	18	5.77	76	.330	.383	0-0	—	0		-7	-0.2
Total	2	0	2	.000	38	0	0	0-0	78.1	96	50	8	2	28-8	25	5.06	86	.315	.375	0-0	—	0		-7	-0.1
ARNSBERG, BRAD Bradley James B 8.20.1963 Seattle, WA BR/TR 6-4/215# d9.6 C4																									
1986	NY A	0	0	—	2	1	0	0-0	8	13	3	1	0	1-0	3	3.38	121	.342	.359	0-0	—	0	111	1	0.0
1987	NY A	1	3	.250	6	2	0	0-0	19.1	22	12	5	0	13-3	14	5.59	79	.289	.385	0-0	—	0	62	-2	-0.4
1989	Tex A	2	1	.667	16	1	0	1-0	48	45	27	6	3	22-0	26	4.13	96	.247	.337	0-0	—	0	68	-2	0.0
1990	Tex A	6	1	.857	53	0	0	5-1	62.2	56	20	4	2	33-1	44	2.15	182	.235	.331	0-0	—	0		11	1.3
1991	Tex A	0	1	.000	9	0	0	0-0	9.2	10	9	5	0	5-0	8	8.38	48	.256	.341	0-0	—	0		-4	-0.4
1992	Cle A	0	0	—	8	0	0	0-0	10.2	13	14	6	2	11-0	5	11.81	33	.317	.481	0-0	—	0		-9	-0.4
Total	6	9	6	.600	94	4	0	6-1	158.1	159	85	27	7	85-4	100	4.26	94	.259	.353	0-0	—	0	79	-5	0.1
ARNTZEN, ORIE Orie Edgar "Old Folks" B 10.18.1909 Beverly, IL D 1.28.1970 Cedar Rapids, IA BR/TR 6-1/200# d4.20																									
1943	Phi A	4	13	.235	32	20	9	0	164.1	172	85	5	5	69	66	4.22	81	.277	.354	50-2	.160	-1	66	-13	-1.6
AROCHA, RENE Rene (Magaly) B 2.24.1966 Havana, Cuba BR/TR 6/180# d4.9																									
1993	StL N	11	8	.579	32	29	1	0-0	188	197	89	20	3	31-2	96	3.78	105	.271	.302	58-7	.103	-2	103	4	0.1
1994	StL N	4	4	.500	45	7	1-1	11-1	83	94	42	9	4	21-4	62	4.01	104	.286	.335	9-3	.111	0	103	0	0.0
1995	StL N	3	5	.375	41	0	0	0-7	49.2	55	24	6	3	18-4	25	3.99	105	.297	.365	1-0	.000	-0		2	0.2
1997	SF N	0	0	—	6	0	0	0-1	10.1	17	14	2	1	5-2	7	11.32	36	.370	.434	1-0	.000	-0		-8	-0.4
Total	4	18	17	.514	124	36	2-1	11-9	331	363	169	37	11	75-12	190	4.11	99	.282	.325	69-10	.101	-2	102	-2	-0.1
ARRIGO, GERRY Gerald William B 6.12.1941 Chicago, IL BL/TL 6-1/195# d6.12																									
1961	Min A	0	1	.000	7	2	0	0	9.2	9	12	0	2	10-0	6	10.24	41	.265	.429	2-0	.500	0	198	-6	-0.5
1962	Min A	0	0	—	1	0	0	0	1	3	3	0	0	1-0	1	18.00	23	.600	.667	0-0	—	0		-2	-0.1
1963	Min A	1	2	.333	5	1	0	0	15.2	12	5	2	0	4-0	13	2.87	127	.211	.262	4-0	.000	-0	24	2	0.3
1964	Min A	7	4	.636	41	12	2-1	1	105.1	97	48	11	2	45-3	96	3.84	93	.244	.323	29-1	.172	1	122	-1	-0.1
1965	Cin N	2	4	.333	27	5	0	2	54	75	38	4	2	30-5	43	6.17	61	.342	.420	12-0	.167	1*	103	-12	-1.4
1966	Cin N	0	0	—	3	0	0	0	7.1	7	4	2	0	3-0	3	4.91	79	.250	.323	1-0	.000	-0		-1	-0.1
	NY N	3	3	.500	17	5	0	0	43.1	47	20	5	0	16-2	28	3.74	97	.276	.337	10-0	.500	3	73	0	0.4
	Year	3	3	.500	20	5	0	0	50.2	54	23	7	0	19-2	31	3.91	94	.273	.335	11-0	.455	3	72	-1	0.3
1967	Cin N	6	6	.500	32	5	1-1	1	74	61	31	6	4	35-5	56	3.16	119	.232	.326	19-2	.211	1	61	4	0.6
1968	Cin N	12	10	.545	36	31	5-1	0	205.1	181	84	13	4	77-7	140	3.33	95	.237	.309	67-3	.075	-2	107	-3	-0.4
1969	Cin N	4	7	.364	20	16	1	0-0	91	89	50	9	8	61-3	35	4.15	91	.256	.376	31-1	.161	-0	79	-5	-0.6
1970	Chi A	0	3	.000	5	3	0	0-0	13.1	24	20	4	0	9-1	12	12.83	30	.393	.465	4-1	.000	-0	38	-12	-2.0
Total	10	35	40	.467	194	80	9-3	4-0	620	605	315	56	22	291-26	433	4.14	85	.258	.342	179-8	.151	2	96	-36	-3.9
ARROJO, ROLANDO Luis Rolando B 7.18.1968 Santa Clara, Cuba BR/TR 6-4/215# d4.1																									
1998	TB A★	14	12	.538	32	32	2-2	0-0	202	195	84	21	19	65-2	152	3.56	135	.256	.329	3-0	.000	-0	84	28	3.3
1999	TB A	7	12	.368	24	24	2	0-0	140.2	162	84	23	14	60-2	107	5.18	96	.296	.378	0-0	—	0	83	0	0.1
2000	Col N	5	9	.357	19	19	0	0-0	101.1	120	77	14	12	46-6	80	6.04	96	.299	.381	28-3	.107	-2	86	-4	-0.5
	Bos A	5	2	.714	13	13	0	0-0	71.1	67	41	10	4	22-0	44	5.05	100	.245	.310	0-0	—	0	107	1	0.1
2001	Bos A	5	4	.556	41	9	0	5-2	103.1	88	44	8	12	35-4	78	3.48	129	.230	.313	4-0	.000	-0	103	12	1.0
2002	Bos A	4	3	.571	29	8	0	1-3	81.1	83	47	7	6	27-1	51	4.98	90	.269	.337	2-1	.000	-0	77	-3	-0.3
Total	5	40	42	.488	158	105	4-2	6-5	700	715	377	83	67	255-15	512	4.55	108	.267	.344	37-4	.081	-3	89	34	3.7
ARROYO, BRONSON Bronson Anthony B 2.24.1977 Key West, FL BR/TR 6-5/180# d6.12																									
2000	Pit N	2	6	.250	20	12	0	0-0	71.2	88	61	10	4	36-6	50	6.40	72	.302	.384	21-2	.143	-0*	110	-16	-1.5
2001	Pit N	5	7	.417	24	13	1	0-0	88.1	99	54	12	4	34-6	39	5.09	88	.289	.355	21-0	.048	-1	96	-6	-0.8
2002	Pit N	2	1	.667	9	4	0	0-0	27	30	14	1	0	15-3	22	4.00	105	.283	.369	6-0	.000	-1	94	0	0.0
2003	†Bos A	0	0	—	6	0	0	1-0	17.1	10	5	0	1	4-2	14	2.08	220	.164	.227	0-0	—	0		4	0.2
Total	4	9	14	.391	59	29	1	1-0	204.1	227	134	23	9	89-17	125	5.15	87	.284	.358	48-2	.083	-2	102	-18	-2.1
ARROYO, FERNANDO Fernando B 3.21.1952 Sacramento, CA BR/TR 6-3/195# d6.28																									
1975	Det A	2	1	.667	14	2	1	0-0	53.1	56	28	5	1	22-2	25	4.56	88	.272	.343	0-0	—	0	77	-1	0.0
1977	Det A	8	18	.308	38	28	8-1	0-0	209.1	227	102	23	1	52-5	60	4.17	103	.278	.319	0-0	—	0	75	6	0.9
1978	Det A	0	0	—	2	0	0	0-0	4.1	8	4	1	1	0-0	1	8.31	47	.400	.429	0-0	—	0		-2	-0.1
1979	Det A	1	1	.500	6	0	0	0-0	12	17	11	3	0	4-2	7	8.25	53	.340	.382	0-0	—	0		-5	-0.6
1980	Min A	6	6	.500	21	11	1-1	0-0	92.1	97	55	7	2	32-2	27	4.68	93	.273	.332	0-0	—	0	89	-3	-0.4
1981	Min A	7	10	.412	23	19	2	0-0	128.1	144	66	11	5	34-1	39	3.93	101	.290	.341	0-0	—	0	86	-1	-0.1
1982	Min A	0	1	.000	6	0	0	0-0	13.2	17	8	2	0	6-1	4	5.27	81	.321	.383	0-0	—	0*		-1	0.0
	Oak A	0	0	—	10	0	0	0-1	22.1	23	14	4	1	7-0	9	5.24	75	.271	.330	0-0	—	0		-3	-0.2
	Year	0	1	.000	16	0	0	0-1	36	40	26	6	1	13-1	13	5.25	77	.290	.351	0-0	—	0		-4	-0.2
1986	Oak A	0	0	—	1	0	0	0-0	0	0	0	0	0	3-0	0	—	—	—	1.000	0-0	—	0		0	0.0
Total	8	24	37	.393	121	60	12-2	0-1	535.2	589	288	56	11	160-13	172	4.44	94	.283	.335	0-0	—	0	81	-10	-0.5
ARROYO, LUIS Luis Enrique B 2.18.1927 Penuelas, P.R. BL/TL 5-8/190# d4.20																									
1955	StL N☆	11	8	.579	35	24	9-1	0	159	162	80	22	2	63-6	68	4.19	97	.261	.329	56-4	.232	1	99	-2	-0.3
1956	Pit N	3	3	.500	18	2	1	0	28.2	36	17	5	0	12-1	17	4.71	80	.298	.361	4-2	.500	1	163	-3	-0.5
1957	Pit N	3	11	.214	54	10	0	1	130.2	151	76	19	7	31-9	101	4.68	81	.282	.329	32-1	.156	-1*	67	-12	-1.3
1959	Cin N	1	0	1.000	10	0	0	0	13.2	17	11	0	0	11-3	8	3.95	103	.321	.418	2-0	.000	-0		-2	-0.1
1960	†NY A	5	1	.833	29	0	0	7	40.2	30	14	2	0	22-3	29	2.88	125	.207	.311	5-0	.000	-0		4	0.7
1961	†NY A☆	15	5	.750	**65**	0	0	**29**	119	83	34	5	3	49-8	87	2.19	169	.199	.284	25-3	.280	2		**21**	**4.4**
1962	NY A	1	3	.250	27	0	0	7	33.2	33	20	5	1	17-2	21	4.81	78	.262	.352	4-0	.500	1		-4	-0.6
1963	NY A	1	1	.500	6	0	0	0	6	12	9	0	0	3-1	5	13.50	26	.444	.484	0-1	—	0		-6	-1.2
Total	8	40	32	.556	244	36	10-1	44	531.1	524	261	58	13	208-33	336	3.93	98	.256	.326	128-11	.227	3	97	-4	1.1
ARROYO, RUDY Rudolph B 6.19.1950 New York, NY BL/TL 6-2/195# d6.1																									
1971	StL N	0	1	.000	9	0	0	0-0	11.2	18	8	2	0	5-1	5	5.40	67	.375	.426	1-0	.000	-0		-2	-0.2
ARUNDEL, HARRY Harry B 2.1855 Philadelphia, PA D 3.25.1904 Cleveland, OH TR 5-6/145# d7.19																									
1875	Atl NA	0	1	.000	1	1	0	0	2.1	6	6	0		0	0	7.71	27	.400	.400	4	.000	-1	51	-2	-0.3
1882	Pit AA	4	10	.286	14	14	13	0	120	155	112	3		23	47	4.65	56	.294	.323	53	.189	0	105	-26	-2.1
1884	Pro N	1	0	1.000	1	1	1	0	9	8	2	0		4	4	1.00	285	.250	.333	3	.333	0	205	2	0.2
Total	2	5	10	.333	15	15	14	0	129	163	114	3		27	51	4.40	60	.291	.324	56	.196	0	112	-24	-1.9
ASENCIO, MIGUEL Miguel (Depaula) B 9.29.1980 Villa Mella, D.R. BR/TR 6-2/190# d4.6																									
2002	KC A	4	7	.364	31	21	0	0-0	123.1	136	73	17	3	64-2	58	5.11	98	.282	.366	2-0	.000	-0	91	0	-0.1
2003	KC A	2	1	.667	8	8	1	0-0	48.1	54	29	4	3	21-0	27	5.21	99	.295	.368	0-0	—	0	124	0	0.0
Total	2	6	8	.429	39	29	1	0-0	171.2	190	102	21	6	85-2	85	5.14	99	.286	.366	2-0	.000	-0	100	0	-0.1

Year	Tm Lg	W	L	Pct	G	GS	CG-Sho	SV-BS	IP	H	R	HR	HB	BB-IB	SO	ERA	AERA	OAV	OOB	AB-SH	AVG	PB	Sup	APR	PW
ASH, KEN Kenneth Lowther B 9.16.1901 Anmoore, WV D 11.15.1979 Clarksburg, WV BR/TR 5-11/165# d4.17																									
1925	Chi A	0	0	—	2	0	0	0	4	7	4	2	0	0	0	9.00	46	.389	.389	0-0	—	0		-2	-0.1
1928	Cin N	3	3	.500	8	5	2	0	36	43	26	1	1	13	6	6.50	61	.314	.377	14-1	.071	-1*	98	-9	-1.3
1929	Cin N	1	5	.167	29	7	2	2	82	91	57	2	5	30	26	4.83	95	.292	.363	21-0	.143	-1*	79	-6	-0.5
1930	Cin N	2	0	1.000	16	1	1	0	39.1	37	22	1	0	16	15	3.43	141	.268	.344	11-0	.182	-1*	90	4	0.2
Total	4	6	8	.429	55	13	5	2	161.1	178	109	6	6	59	47	4.96	90	.294	.363	46-1	.130	-3	85	-13	-1.7
ASHBY, ANDY Andrew Jason B 7.11.1967 Kansas City, MO BR/TR 6-1/190# d6.10																									
1991	Phi N	1	5	.167	8	8	0	0-0	42	41	28	5	3	19-0	26	6.00	61	.256	.341	12-1	.083	-1	74	-10	-1.3
1992	Phi N	1	3	.250	10	8	0	0-0	37	42	31	6	1	21-0	24	7.54	46	.290	.379	11-2	.091	-0	113	-15	-1.5
1993	Col N	0	4	.000	20	9	0	1-0	54	89	54	5	3	32-4	33	8.50	56	.377	.453	15-0	.267	0	117	-18	-1.1
	SD N	3	6	.333	12	12	0	0-0	69	79	46	14	1	24-1	44	5.48	76	.295	.350	21-2	.048	-1	105	-9	-1.1
	Year	3	10	.231	32	21	0	1-0	123	168	51	19	4	56-5	77	6.80	65	.333	.399	36-2	.139	-1	111	-28	-2.2
1994	SD N	6	11	.353	24	24	4	0-0	164.1	145	75	16	3	43-12	121	3.40	121	.233	.285	49-9	.163	-0	70	11	1.0
1995	SD N	12	10	.545	31	**31**	2-2	0-0	192.2	180	79	17	11	62-3	150	2.94	137	.252	.320	49-17	.163	-0	106	21	2.1
1996	†SD N	9	5	.643	24	24	1	0-0	150.2	147	60	17	3	34-1	85	3.23	123	.259	.304	45-9	.244	3*	105	13	1.5
1997	SD N	9	11	.450	30	30	2	0-0	200.2	207	108	17	5	49-2	144	4.13	94	.266	.311	60-7	.067	-3*	121	-9	-1.0
1998	†SD N★	17	9	.654	33	33	5-1	0-0	226.2	223	90	23	7	58-8	151	3.34	117	.259	.309	72-9	.111	-2	115	16	1.6
1999	SD N★	14	10	.583	31	31	4-**3**	0-0	206	204	95	26	7	54-4	132	3.80	111	.258	.311	62-7	.129	-0	94	11	1.1
2000	Phi N	4	7	.364	16	16	1	0-0	101.1	113	75	17	5	38-5	51	5.68	82	.288	.351	28-5	.179	0	89	-14	-1.2
	†Atl N	8	6	.571	15	15	2-1	0-0	98	103	49	12	1	23-4	55	4.13	111	.271	.314	33-4	.121	-1*	93	5	0.5
	Year	12	13	.480	31	31	3-1	0-0	199.1	216	54	29	6	61-9	106	4.92	94	.280	.333	61-9	.148	-1	91	-10	-0.7
2001	LA N	2	0	1.000	2	2	0	0-0	11.2	14	5	2	0	1-0	7	3.86	104	.292	.306	2-2	.500	1*	138	0	0.1
2002	LA N	9	13	.409	30	30	0	0-0	181.2	179	85	20	8	65-3	107	3.91	98	.261	.330	48-6	.125	0	93	-2	-0.3
2003	LA N	3	10	.231	21	12	0	0-0	73	90	42	8	3	17-2	41	5.18	78	.311	.354	14-3	.000	-2	55	-8	-1.4
Total	13	98	110	.471	307	285	21-7	1-0	1808.2	1856	922	205	61	540-49	1171	4.13	99	.268	.324	521-83	.134	-5	99	-8	-1.0
ASSENMACHER, PAUL Paul Andre B 12.10.1960 Detroit, MI BL/TL 6-3/200# d4.12																									
1986	Atl N	7	3	.700	61	0	0	7-4	68.1	61	23	5	0	26-4	56	2.50	159	.241	.311	6-0	.000	-0		10	1.7
1987	Atl N	1	1	.500	52	0	0	2-4	54.2	58	41	8	1	24-4	39	5.10	85	.260	.333	4-2	.000	-0		-7	-0.4
1988	Atl N	8	7	.533	64	0	0	5-6	79.1	72	28	4	1	32-11	71	3.06	120	.251	.327	3-1	.333	1		6	1.3
1989	Atl N	1	3	.250	49	0	0	0-2	57.2	55	26	2	1	16-7	64	3.59	102	.249	.300	2-0	.000	-0		0	0.0
	†Chi N	2	1	.667	14	0	0	0-1	19	19	11	1	0	12-1	15	5.21	72	.275	.378	3-0	.000	-0		-2	-0.4
	Year	3	4	.429	63	0	0	0-3	76.2	74	41	3	1	28-8	79	3.99	92	.255	.320	5-0	.000	-1		-2	-0.4
1990	Chi N	7	2	.778	74	1	0	10-10	103	90	33	10	1	36-8	95	2.80	146	.239	.305	8-2	.000	-1	111	15	1.4
1991	Chi N	7	8	.467	75	0	0	15-9	102.2	85	41	10	3	31-6	117	3.24	120	.223	.284	4-0	.250	0		7	1.2
1992	Chi N	4	4	.500	70	0	0	8-5	68	72	32	6	3	26-5	67	4.10	88	.271	.340	4-2	.000	-0		-2	-0.4
1993	Chi N	2	1	.667	46	0	0	0-4	38.2	44	15	5	0	13-3	34	3.49	114	.288	.343	2-0	.500	0		3	0.2
	NY A	2	2	.500	26	0	0	0-1	17.1	10	6	0	1	9-3	11	3.12	134	.175	.299	0-0	—	0		2	0.4
1994	Chi A	1	2	.333	44	0	0	1-2	33	26	13	2	1	13-2	29	3.55	132	.224	.301	0-0	—	0		5	0.4
1995	†Cle A	6	2	.750	47	0	0	0-1	38.1	32	13	3	3	12-3	40	2.82	167	.225	.296	0-0	—	0		8	1.5
1996	†Cle A	4	2	.667	63	0	0	1-2	46.2	46	18	1	4	14-5	44	3.09	159	.260	.325	0-0	—	0		9	1.0
1997	†Cle A	5	0	1.000	75	0	0	4-1	49	43	17	5	1	15-5	53	2.94	160	.231	.289	0-0	—	0		9	1.0
1998	†Cle A	2	5	.286	69	0	0	3-5	47	54	22	5	1	19-6	43	3.26	147	.286	.351	0-0	—	0		6	0.8
1999	†Cle A	2	1	.667	55	0	0	0-2	33	50	32	6	1	17-5	29	8.18	62	.347	.415	0-0	—	0		-11	-0.8
Total	14	61	44	.581	884	1	0	56-59	855.2	817	371	73	22	315-78	807	3.53	118	.252	.320	36-7	.083	-0	111	58	8.9
ASTACIO, PEDRO Pedro Julio (Pura) B 11.28.1969 Hato Mayor, D.R. BR/TR 6-2/190# d7.3																									
1992	LA N	5	5	.500	11	11	4-4	0-0	82	80	23	1	2	20-4	43	1.98	175	.255	.302	24-5	.125	-1	88	13	1.5
1993	LA N	14	9	.609	31	31	3-2	0-0	186.1	165	80	14	5	68-5	122	3.57	107	.239	.309	62-7	.161	-1	100	8	0.7
1994	LA N	6	8	.429	23	23	3-1	0-0	149	142	77	18	4	47-4	108	4.29	92	.252	.312	47-4	.064	-3	104	-6	-0.9
1995	†LA N	7	8	.467	48	11	1-1	0-1	104	103	53	12	4	29-5	80	4.24	90	.261	.316	24-2	.125	-0	102	-4	-0.5
1996	†LA N	9	8	.529	35	32	0	0-0	211.2	207	86	18	9	67-9	130	3.44	112	.261	.324	68-8	.088	-4	94	14	0.7
1997	LA N	7	9	.438	26	24	2-1	0-0	153.2	151	75	15	4	47-0	115	4.10	94	.256	.313	41-10	.146	-0	95	-4	-0.3
	Col N	5	1	.833	7	7	0	0-0	48.2	49	23	9	5	14-0	51	4.25	122	.262	.327	13-1	.077	-1	112	5	0.5
	Year	12	10	.545	33	31	2-1	0-0	202.1	200	29	24	9	61-0	166	4.14	101	.258	.317	54-11	.130	-1	99	3	0.2
1998	Col N	13	14	.481	35	34	0	0-0	209.1	245	160	39	17	74-0	170	6.23	83	.294	.363	62-11	.129	-3	97	-22	-2.6
1999	Col N	17	11	.607	34	34	7	0-0	232	258	140	38	11	75-6	210	5.04	115	.285	.343	86-7	.233	-0*	95	15	1.6
2000	Col N	12	9	.571	32	32	3	0-0	196.1	217	119	32	15	77-5	193	5.27	110	.281	.356	82-1	.098	-6	95	11	0.4
2001	Col N	6	13	.316	22	22	4-1	0-0	141	151	91	21	10	50-3	125	5.49	97	.276	.345	42-10	.095	-3	94	-1	-0.5
	Hou N	2	1	.667	4	4	0	0-0	28.2	30	10	1	3	4-0	19	3.14	146	.280	.322	11-1	.091	-1	101	5	0.4
	Year	8	14	.364	26	26	4-1	0-0	169.2	181	15	22	13	54-3	144	5.09	102	.276	.341	53-11	.094	-4	95	3	-0.1
2002	NY N	12	11	.522	31	31	3-1	0-0	191.2	192	106	32	16	63-5	152	4.79	83	.262	.330	62-6	.161	0	106	-14	-1.5
2003	NY N	3	2	.600	7	7	0	0-0	36.2	47	30	8	3	18-1	20	7.36	57	.311	.393	11-3	.091	-1	100	-12	-1.4
Total	12	118	109	.520	346	303	30-11	0-1	1971	2037	1073	258	108	653-47	1538	4.58	99	.269	.333	635-76	.132	-23	99	8	-1.9
ATCHLEY, JUSTIN Justin Scott B 9.5.1973 Sedro-Woolley, WA BL/TL 6-3/215# d4.7																									
2001	Cin N	0	0	—	15	0	0	0-2	10.1	12	7	4	1	5-2	8	6.10	75	.286	.375	1-0	.000	-0		-1	-0.1
ATHERTON, KEITH Keith Rowe B 2.19.1959 Newport News, VA BR/TR 6-4/200# d7.14																									
1983	Oak A	2	5	.286	29	0	0	4-4	68.1	53	22	7	1	23-4	40	2.77	140	.215	.280	1-0	.000	-0		9	0.9
1984	Oak A	7	6	.538	57	0	0	2-3	104	110	51	13	2	39-8	58	4.33	87	.274	.336	0-0	—	0		-5	-0.7
1985	Oak A	4	7	.364	56	0	0	3-2	104.2	89	51	17	0	42-8	77	4.30	90	.231	.303	0-0	—	0		-3	-0.4
1986	Oak A	1	2	.333	13	0	0	0-0	15.1	18	10	2	0	11-1	8	5.87	66	.295	.392	0-0	—	0		-3	-0.5
	Min A	5	8	.385	47	0	0	10-4	81.2	82	37	9	1	35-3	59	3.75	115	.264	.336	0-0	—	0		5	0.9
	Year	6	10	.375	60	0	0	10-4	97	100	52	11	1	46-4	67	4.08	104	.269	.346	0-0	—	0		3	0.4
1987	†Min A	7	5	.583	59	0	0	2-4	79.1	81	46	10	4	30-4	51	4.54	102	.262	.332	0-0	—	0		0	0.0
1988	Min A	7	5	.583	49	0	0	3-4	74	65	29	10	2	22-4	43	3.41	120	.235	.293	0-0	—	0		6	0.9
1989	Cle A	0	3	.000	32	0	0	2-0	39	48	22	7	0	13-4	13	4.15	96	.293	.345	0-0	—	0		-2	-0.2
Total	7	33	41	.446	342	0	0	26-21	566.1	546	268	75	10	215-36	349	3.99	102	.253	.320	1-0	.000	-0		7	0.9
ATKINS, TOMMY Francis Montgomery B 12.9.1887 Ponca, NE D 5.7.1956 Cleveland, OH BL/TL 5-10.5/165# d10.2																									
1909	Phi A	0	0	—	1	1	0	0	6	6	4	0	0	5	4	4.50	53	.261	.393	2-0	.000	-0	176	-1	-0.1
1910	Phi A	3	2	.600	15	3	2	2	57	53	33	0	1	23	29	2.68	88	.254	.330	17-0	.118	-1	113	-4	-0.5
Total	2	3	2	.600	16	4	2	2	63	59	37	0	1	28	33	2.86	83	.254	.337	19-0	.105	-1	128	-5	-0.6
ATKINS, JAMES James Curtis B 3.10.1921 Birmingham, AL BL/TR 6-3/205# d9.29																									
1950	Bos A	0	0	—	1	0	0	0	4.2	4	2	1	1	4	0	3.86	127	.235	.409	2-0	.000	-0		1	0.0
1952	Bos A	0	1	.000	3	1	0	0	10.1	11	6	0	0	7	2	3.48	113	.275	.383	3-0	.667	1	44	0	0.1
Total	2	0	1	.000	4	1	0	0	15	15	8	1	1	11	2	3.60	118	.263	.391	5-0	.400	0	44	1	0.1
ATKINSON, AL Albert Wright B 3.9.1861 Clinton, IL D 6.17.1952 Elkhorn Township, MO BR/TR 5-11.5/165# d5.1																									
1884	Phi AA	11	11	.500	22	22	20-1	0	184.1	186	130	3	10	21	93	4.20	81	.244	.274	83	.193	-1	104	-16	-1.6
	CP U	6	10	.375	16	16	16-1	0	140	127	83	1		21	104	2.76	88	.226	.253	68	.206	-5*	66	-5	-0.9
	Bal U	3	5	.375	8	8	8	0	69.1	60	34	4		12	50	2.34	115	.217	.250	29	.138	-4	66	3	-0.1
	Year	9	15	.375	24	24	24-1	0	209.1	187	38	5		33	154	2.62	96	.223	.252	97	.186	-9	66	-3	-1.0
1886	Phi AA	25	17	.595	45	45	44-1	0	396.2	414	288	11	22	101	154	3.95	89	.256	.308	148	.122	-6	114	-15	-1.9
1887	Phi AA	6	8	.429	15	15	11	0	124.2	156	121	2	6	54	34	5.92	72	.292	.364	59	.203	-1*	120	-23	-1.8
Total	3	51	51	.500	106	106	99-3	0	915	943	656	21	38	209	435	3.96	85	.251	.297	387	.165	-16	102	-56	-6.3
ATKINSON, BILL William Cecil Glenn B 10.4.1954 Chatham, ON, CAN BL/TR 5-7/165# d9.18																									
1976	Mon N	0	0	—	4	0	0	0-0	5	3	0	0	0	1-1	4	0.00	—	.176	.222	0-0	—	0		2	0.1
1977	Mon N	7	2	.778	55	0	0	7-1	83.1	72	33	12	0	29-11	56	3.35	114	.234	.296	5-1	.200	-0*		5	0.7

Year	Tm Lg	W	L	Pct	G	GS	CG-Sho	SV-BS	IP	H	R	HR	HB	BB-IB	SO	ERA	AERA	OAV	OOB	AB-SH	AVG	PB	Sup	APR	PW
1978	Mon N	2	2	.500	29	0	0	3-1	45.1	45	23	5	1	28-4	32	4.37	81	.268	.370	4-0	.500	1		-4	-0.3
1979	Mon N	2	0	1.000	10	0	0	1-0	13.2	9	4	0	0	4-1	7	1.98	186	.170	.228	1-0	.000	-0		2	0.3
Total	4	11	4	.733	98	0	0	11-2	147.1	129	60	17	1	62-17	99	3.42	108	.236	.312	10-1	.300	1		5	0.8
AUCOIN, DEREK Derek Alfred B 3.27.1970 Lachine, PQ, CAN BR/TR 6-7/235# d5.21																									
1996	Mon N	0	1	.000	2	0	0	0-0	2.2	3	1	0	0	1-0	1	3.38	128	.300	.364	0-0	—	0		0	0.1
AUGUST, DON Donald Glenn B 7.3.1963 Inglewood, CA BR/TR 6-3/190# d6.2																									
1988	Mil A	13	7	.650	24	22	6-1	0-0	148.1	137	55	12	0	48-6	66	3.09	129	.245	.303	0-0	—	0	99	15	2.1
1989	Mil A	12	12	.500	31	25	2-1	0-0	142.1	175	93	17	2	58-2	51	5.31	72	.302	.364	0-0	—	0	91	-23	-3.3
1990	Mil A	0	3	.000	5	0	0	0-1	11	13	10	0	0	5-0	2	6.55	59	.295	.367	0-0	—	0		-4	-0.7
1991	Mil A	9	8	.529	28	23	1-1	0-0	138.1	166	87	18	3	47-2	62	5.47	73	.301	.358	0-0	—	0	122	-21	-2.2
Total	4	34	30	.531	88	70	9-3	0-1	440	491	245	47	5	158-10	181	4.64	85	.283	.343	0-0	—	0	104	-33	-4.1
AUGUSTINE, JERRY Gerald Lee B 7.24.1952 Kewaunee, WI BL/TL 6/185# d9.9																									
1975	Mil A	2	0	1.000	5	3	1	0-0	26.2	26	9	2	1	12-1	8	3.04	126	.274	.355	0-0	—	0	122	3	0.2
1976	Mil A	9	12	.429	39	24	5-3	0-3	171.2	167	69	9	4	56-4	59	3.30	106	.261	.321	0-0	—	0	94	5	0.5
1977	Mil A	12	18	.400	33	33	10-1	0-0	209	222	119	23	3	72-3	68	4.48	91	.277	.334	0-0	—	0	88	-11	-1.3
1978	Mil A	13	12	.520	35	30	9-2	0-0	188.1	204	100	14	4	61-2	59	4.54	83	.280	.335	0-0	—	0	128	-13	-1.5
1979	Mil A	9	6	.600	43	2	0	5-2	85.2	95	38	6	1	30-4	41	3.47	121	.284	.341	0-0	—	0	130	6	1.0
1980	Mil A	4	3	.571	39	1	0	2-1	69.2	83	37	5	2	36-5	22	4.52	86	.301	.382	0-0	—	0	46	-4	-0.4
1981	Mil A	2	2	.500	27	2	0	2-1	61.1	75	30	4	1	18-3	26	4.26	81	.300	.348	0-0	—	0	196	-5	-0.4
1982	Mil A	1	3	.250	20	2	1	0-0	62	63	43	13	2	26-2	22	5.08	75	.267	.340	0-0	—	0	84	-12	-0.7
1983	Mil A	3	3	.500	34	7	1	2-0	64.1	89	45	11	1	25-4	40	5.74	65	.328	.383	0-0	—	0	135	-16	-1.4
1984	Mil A	0	0	—	4	0	0	0-0	5.1	4	1	0	1	4-0	3	0.00	—	.211	.375	0-0	—	0		2	0.1
Total	10	55	59	.482	279	104	27-6	11-7	944	1028	491	87	20	340-28	348	4.23	90	.281	.342	0-0	—	0	107	-45	-3.9
AUKER, ELDEN Elden Le Roy "Submarine" B 9.21.1910 Norcatur, KS BR/TR 6-2/194# d8.10																									
1933	Det A	3	3	.500	15	6	2-1	0	55	63	34	3	2	25	17	5.24	82	.285	.363	17-1	.118	-1	109	-4	-0.5
1934	†Det A	15	7	.682	43	18	10-2	1	205	234	103	9	3	56	86	3.42	128	.288	.336	74-7	.149	-2	113	16	1.4
1935	†Det A	18	7	**.720**	36	25	13-2	0	195	213	86	13	9	61	63	3.83	109	.279	.340	74-4	.216	1	122	12	1.5
1936	Det A	13	16	.448	35	31	14-2	0	215.1	263	140	11	3	83	66	4.89	101	.302	.365	78-7	.308	7	100	-1	0.7
1937	Det A	17	9	.654	39	32	19-1	1	252.2	250	127	13	6	97	73	3.88	120	.260	.331	91-6	.198	4*	107	20	2.4
1938	Det A	11	10	.524	27	24	12-1	0	160.2	184	97	14	5	56	46	5.27	95	.284	.346	57-3	.088	-4	114	-1	-0.4
1939	Bos A	9	10	.474	31	25	6-1	0	151	183	108	13	1	61	43	5.36	88	.294	.358	53-3	.226	2	114	-12	-1.0
1940	StL A	16	11	.593	38	35	20-2	0	263.2	299	129	17	3	96	78	3.96	116	.281	.342	89-1	.213	3	105	18	2.0
1941	StL A	14	15	.483	34	31	13	0	216	268	150	20	1	85	60	5.50	78	.303	.365	80-3	.125	-3*	110	-28	-3.3
1942	StL A	14	13	.519	35	34	17-2	0	249	273	132	16	3	86	62	4.08	91	.277	.337	87-6	.161	-1*	111	-10	-1.1
Total	10	130	101	.563	333	261	126-14	2	1963.1	2230	1106	129	36	706	594	4.42	101	.285	.347	700-41	.187	6	110	10	1.7
AUSANIO, JOE Joseph John B 12.9.1965 Kingston, NY BR/TR 6-1/205# d7.14																									
1994	NY A	2	1	.667	13	0	0	0-0	15.2	16	9	3	0	6-0	15	5.17	89	.254	.319	0-0	—	0		-1	-0.1
1995	NY A	2	0	1.000	28	0	0	1-2	37.2	42	24	9	0	23-0	36	5.73	81	.286	.378	0-0	—	0		-4	-0.2
Total	2	4	1	.800	41	0	0	1-2	53.1	58	33	12	0	29-0	51	5.57	83	.276	.361	0-0	—	0		-5	-0.3
AUST, DENNIS Dennis Kay B 11.25.1940 Tecumseh, NE BR/TR 5-11/180# d9.6																									
1965	StL N	0	0	—	6	0	0	1	7.1	6	4	0	0	2-1	7	4.91	78	.214	.267	1-0	.000	-0		-1	0.0
1966	StL N	0	1	.000	9	0	0	1	9.2	12	7	1	0	6-2	7	6.52	55	.308	.391	1-0	.000	-0		-3	-0.3
Total	2	0	1	.000	15	0	0	2	17	18	11	1	0	8-3	14	5.82	64	.269	.342	2-0	.000	-0		-4	-0.3
AUSTIN, JIM James Parker B 12.7.1963 Farmville, VA BR/TR 6-2/200# d7.4																									
1991	Mil A	0	0	—	5	0	0	0-0	8.2	8	8	1	3	11-1	3	8.31	48	.276	.500	0-0	—	0		-4	-0.2
1992	Mil A	5	2	.714	47	0	0	0-1	58.1	38	13	2	2	32-6	30	1.85	208	.191	.308	0-0	—	0		13	1.4
1993	Mil A	1	2	.333	31	0	0	0-2	33	28	15	3	1	13-1	15	3.82	112	.230	.309	0-0	—	0		2	0.1
Total	3	6	4	.600	83	0	0	0-3	100	74	36	6	6	56-8	48	3.06	131	.211	.329	0-0	—	0		11	1.3
AUSTIN, JEFF Jeffrey Wellington B 10.19.1976 San Bernardino, CA BR/TR 6/185# d6.26																									
2001	KC A	0	0	—	21	0	0	0-0	26	27	17	4	1	14-2	27	5.54	89	.273	.362	0-0	—	0		-1	-0.1
2002	KC A	0	0	—	10	0	0	0-0	11	14	6	0	0	6-1	6	4.91	102	.318	.385	0-0	—	0		0	0.0
2003	Cin N	2	3	.400	7	7	0	0-0	28.1	28	27	9	0	21-0	22	8.58	50	.255	.374	8-2	.125	-0	113	-13	-1.7
Total	3	2	3	.400	38	7	0	0-0	65.1	69	50	13	1	41-3	55	6.75	69	.273	.371	8-2	.125	-0	113	-14	-1.8
AUSTIN, RICK Rick Gerald B 10.27.1946 Seattle, WA BR/TL 6-4/190# d6.21																									
1970	Cle A	2	5	.286	31	8	1-1	3-0	67.2	74	36	10	3	26-6	53	4.79	83	.281	.352	18-0	.111	0	84	-5	-0.4
1971	Cle A	0	0	—	23	0	0	1-1	23	25	15	3	3	20-4	20	5.09	75	.291	.429	1-0	.000	-0		-3	-0.2
1975	Mil A	2	3	.400	32	0	0	2-2	40	32	19	3	1	32-5	30	4.05	95	.222	.367	0-0	—	0		0	-0.1
1976	Mil A	0	0	—	3	0	0	0-0	5.1	10	3	1	1	0-0	3	5.06	69	.435	.423	0-0	—	0		-1	0.0
Total	4	4	8	.333	89	8	1-1	6-3	136	141	73	17	8	78-15	106	4.63	84	.273	.373	19-0	.105	0	84	-9	-0.7
AUTRY, AL Albert B 2.29.1952 Modesto, CA BR/TR 6-5/225# d9.14																									
1976	Atl N	1	0	1.000	1	1	0	0-0	5	4	3	2	0	3-0	3	5.40	70	.222	.333	2-0	.000	-0	93	-1	-0.1
AVERY, STEVE Steven Thomas B 4.14.1970 Trenton, MI BL/TL 6-4/190# d6.13																									
1990	Atl N	3	11	.214	21	20	1-1	0-0	99	121	79	7	2	45-2	75	5.64	72	.302	.372	30-2	.133	-1	92	-20	-2.5
1991	†Atl N	18	8	.692	35	35	3-1	0-0	210.1	189	89	21	3	65-0	137	3.38	115	.240	.299	79-5	.215	3*	122	12	1.8
1992	†Atl N	11	11	.500	35	**35**	2-2	0-0	233.2	216	95	14	0	71-3	129	3.20	115	.246	.300	76-9	.171	2	98	11	1.1
1993	†Atl N★	18	6	.750	35	35	3-1	0-0	223.1	216	81	14	0	43-5	125	2.94	137	.261	.295	75-8	.160	1	106	27	2.9
1994	Atl N	8	3	.727	24	24	1	0-0	151.2	127	71	15	4	55-4	122	4.04	105	.227	.298	49-6	.102	-2	124	5	0.2
1995	†Atl N	7	13	.350	29	29	3-1	0-0	173.1	165	92	22	6	52-4	141	4.67	91	.252	.311	53-8	.208	3	90	-5	-0.1
1996	†Atl N	7	10	.412	24	23	1	0-0	131	146	70	10	4	40-8	86	4.47	99	.285	.339	46-1	.239	5	103	0	0.6
1997	Bos A	6	7	.462	22	18	0	0-0	96.2	127	76	15	2	49-0	51	6.42	72	.320	.394	1-0	.000	-0*	124	-19	-2.1
1998	Bos A	10	7	.588	34	23	0	0-1	123.2	128	74	14	4	64-0	57	5.02	94	.269	.361	1-0	.000	-0*	116	-4	-0.2
1999	Cin N	6	7	.462	19	19	0	0-0	96	75	62	11	1	78-0	51	5.16	90	.222	.364	26-2	.077	-2	92	-6	-0.8
2003	Det A	2	0	1.000	19	0	0	0-1	16	19	11	5	0	7-1	6	5.63	77	.302	.371	1-0	1.000	0		-2	-0.2
Total	11	96	83	.536	297	261	14-6	0-2	1554.2	1529	800	148	26	569-27	980	4.19	100	.259	.325	437-41	.174	9	107	-1	0.7
AVREA, JAY James Epherium B 7.6.1920 Cleburne, TX D 6.26.1987 Dallas, TX BR/TR 6-1.5/175# d4.22																									
1950	Cin N	0	0	—	2	0	0	0	5.1	6	2	0	0	3	2	3.38	125	.273	.360	2-0	.000	-0		1	0.0
AYALA, LUIS Luis Ignacio B 1.12.1978 Los Mochis, Mexico BR/TR 6-2/170# d3.31																									
2003	Mon N	10	3	.769	65	0	0	5-3	71	65	27	8	5	13-3	46	2.92	161	.244	.291	1-0	.000	-0		12	2.3
AYALA, BOBBY Robert Joseph B 7.8.1969 Ventura, CA BR/TR 6-3/200# d9.5																									
1992	Cin N	2	1	.667	5	5	0	0-0	29	33	15	1	1	13-2	23	4.34	83	.297	.376	9-1	.000	-1	131	-2	-0.3
1993	Cin N	7	10	.412	43	9	0	3-2	98	106	72	16	7	45-4	65	5.60	72	.274	.358	21-2	.095	-1	82	-20	-3.2
1994	Sea A	4	3	.571	46	0	0	18-6	56.2	42	25	2	0	26-0	76	2.86	171	.203	.289	0-0	—	0		11	1.7
1995	†Sea A	6	5	.545	63	0	0	19-8	71	73	42	9	6	30-4	77	4.44	107	.262	.343	0-0	—	0		1	0.1
1996	Sea A	6	3	.667	50	0	0	3-3	67.1	65	45	10	2	25-3	61	5.88	84	.256	.325	0-0	—	0		-6	-0.7
1997	†Sea A	10	5	.667	71	0	0	8-4	96.2	91	45	14	3	41-3	92	3.82	118	.260	.338	0-0	—	0		7	1.0
1998	Sea A	1	10	.091	62	0	0	8-9	75.1	100	66	9	1	26-4	68	7.29	64	.323	.370	0-0	—	0		-22	-3.0
1999	Mon N	1	6	.143	53	0	0	0-1	66	60	36	6	4	34-1	64	3.68	122	.235	.331	1-0	.000	-0		4	0.3
	Chi N	0	1	.000	13	0	0	0-0	16	11	7	4	2	5-1	15	2.81	161	.193	.281	0-0	—	0		2	0.1
	Year	1	7	.125	66	0	0	0-1	82	71	47	10	6	39-2	79	3.51	128	.228	.322	1-0	.000	-0		5	0.4
Total	8	37	44	.457	406	14	0	59-33	576	581	353	71	26	245-22	541	4.78	94	.263	.340	31-3	.065	-2	86	-25	-4.0

Year	Tm Lg	W	L	Pct	G	GS	CG-Sho	SV-BS	IP	H	R	HR	HB	BB-IB	SO	ERA	AERA	OAV	OOB	AB-SH	AVG	PB	Sup	APR	PW
AYBAR, MANNY Manuel Antonio B 5.4.1972 Bani, D.R. BR/TR 6-1/165# d8.4																									
1997	StL N	2	4	.333	12	12	0	0-0	68	66	33	8	4	29-0	41	4.24	98	.263	.344	21-0	.143	-0	93	1	0.0
1998	StL N	6	6	.500	20	14	0	0-0	81.1	90	58	6	2	42-1	57	5.98	70	.281	.367	27-1	.222	1	118	-15	-1.8
1999	StL N	4	5	.444	65	1	0	3-2	97	104	67	13	4	36-3	74	5.47	84	.272	.338	12-1	.083	-1*	181	-11	-1.0
2000	Col N	0	1	.000	1	0	0	0-0	1.2	5	3	1	0	0-0	0	16.20	36	.500	.500	0-0	—	0		-1	-0.2
	Cin N	1	1	.500	32	0	0	0-0	50.1	51	31	7	2	22-2	31	4.83	98	.262	.338	6-1	.000	-0		-1	-0.1
	Fla N	1	0	1.000	21	0	0	0-1	27.1	18	8	3	0	13-1	14	2.63	169	.184	.277	0-0	—	0		6	0.3
	Year	2	2	.500	54	0	0	0-1	79.1	74	51	11	2	35-3	45	4.31	108	.244	.323	6-1	.000	-0		2	0.0
2001	Chi N	2	1	.667	17	1	0	0-0	22.2	28	19	5	2	17-0	16	6.35	65	.304	.420	3-1	1.000	2	245	-7	-0.6
2002	†SF N	1	0	1.000	15	0	0	0-0	14.1	16	6	1	1	3-2	11	2.51	155	.271	.317	1-0	.000	-0		2	0.1
2003	SF N	0	0	—	3	0	0	0-0	3	4	2	1	0	3-0	2	6.00	69	.333	.438	0-0	—	0		-1	0.0
Total	7	17	18	.486	186	28	0	3-3	365.2	382	227	45	15	165-9	246	5.05	87	.269	.348	70-4	.186	1	109	-27	-3.3
AYDELOTT, JAKE Jacob Stuart B 7.6.1861 N.Manchester, IN D 10.22.1926 Detroit, MI BL/TR 6/180# d5.15																									
1884	Ind AA	5	7	.417	12	12	11	0	106	129	100	0	0	29	30	4.92	67	.282	.324	44	.114	-3	93	-19	-1.9
1886	Phi AA	0	2	.000	2	2	2	0	18	21	11	0	0	12	5	4.00	88	.304	.407	6	.000	-1	34	0	-0.1
Total	2	5	9	.357	14	14	13	0	124	150	111	0	0	41	35	4.79	69	.285	.336	50	.100	-4	84	-19	-2.0
AYERS, BILL William Oscar B 9.27.1919 Newnan, GA D 9.24.1980 Newnan, GA BR/TR 6-3/185# d4.17																									
1947	NY N	0	3	.000	13	4	0	1	35.1	46	35	7	1	14	22	8.15	50	.322	.386	8-2	.250	0	87	-15	-1.1
AYERS, DOC Yancy Wyatt B 5.20.1890 Fancy Gap, VA D 5.26.1968 Pulaski, VA BR/TR 6-1/185# d9.9																									
1913	Was A	1	1	.500	4	2	1-1	1	17.2	12	7	0	1	4	17	1.53	193	.188	.246	7-0	.000	-1	100	2	0.1
1914	Was A	11	15	.423	49	32	8-3	3	265.1	221	106	5	8	54	148	2.54	111	.238	.286	83-2	.169	-0	91	4	0.3
1915	Was A	14	9	.609	40	16	8-2	3	211.1	178	66	1	7	38	96	2.21	134	.234	.276	63-1	.190	-1	95	19	1.7
1916	Was A	5	8	.385	43	17	7	2	157	173	89	4	4	52	69	3.78	74	.285	.346	43-2	.140	-2	86	-19	-2.0
1917	Was A	11	10	.524	40	15	12-3	1	207.2	192	67	3	8	59	78	2.17	121	.256	.317	63-3	.206	-0	89	10	1.0
1918	Was A	10	12	.455	40	24	11-4	3	219.2	215	91	2	7	63	67	2.83	96	.261	.319	66-5	.152	-2	102	0	-0.2
1919	Was A	0	6	.000	11	5	0	1	43.2	52	27	0	4	17	12	2.89	111	.317	.395	12-0	.417	2	49	-2	0.0
	Det A	5	3	.625	24	5	3-1	0	93.2	88	34	2	3	31	32	2.69	119	.254	.320	24-2	.125	-1	113	6	0.3
	Year	5	9	.357	35	10	3-1	1	137.1	140	39	2	7	48	44	2.75	116	.274	.345	36-2	.222	0	81	4	0.3
1920	Det A	7	14	.333	46	23	8-3	1	208.2	217	115	6	8	62	103	3.88	96	.280	.340	59-2	.153	-2	86	-2	-0.4
1921	Det A	0	0	—	2	1	0	0	4	9	6	0	0	2	0	9.00	47	.450	.500	0-0	—	0	117	-2	-0.1
Total	9	64	78	.451	299	140	58-17	15	1428.2	1357	608	23	50	382	622	2.84	105	.259	.315	420-17	.171	-8	91	16	0.7
AYRAULT, BOB Robert Cunningham B 4.27.1966 South Lake Tahoe, CA BR/TR 6-4/230# d6.7																									
1992	Phi N	2	2	.500	30	0	0	0-0	43.1	32	16	0	1	17-1	27	3.12	112	.209	.287	0-0	—	0		2	0.2
1993	Phi N	2	0	1.000	10	0	0	0-1	10.1	18	11	1	1	10-1	8	9.58	41	.375	.492	2-0	.000	-0		-6	-1.0
	Sea A	1	1	.500	14	0	0	0-1	19.2	18	8	1	0	6-1	7	3.20	138	.254	.304	0-0	—	0		2	0.2
Total	2	5	3	.625	54	0	0	0-2	73.1	68	35	2	2	33-3	42	4.05	94	.250	.330	2-0	.000	-0		-2	-0.6
BABCOCK, BOB Robert Ernest B 8.25.1949 New Castle, PA BR/TR 6-5/210# d7.22																									
1979	Tex A	0	0	—	4	0	0	0-0	5.1	7	7	1	0	7-0	6	10.13	41	.318	.452	0-0	—	0		-4	-0.2
1980	Tex A	1	2	.333	19	0	0	0-1	23.1	20	13	3	2	8-1	15	4.63	84	.238	.309	0-0	—	0		-2	-0.2
1981	Tex A	1	1	.500	16	0	0	0-2	28.2	21	7	2	1	16-1	18	2.20	158	.219	.333	0-0	—	0		5	0.3
Total	3	2	3	.400	39	0	0	0-3	57.1	48	27	6	3	31-2	39	3.92	95	.238	.339	0-0	—	0		-1	-0.1
BABICH, JOHNNY John Charles B 5.14.1913 Albion, CA D 1.19.2001 Richmond, CA BR/TR 6-1.5/185# d6.19																									
1934	Bro N	7	11	.389	25	18	7	1	135	148	76	5	2	51	62	4.20	93	.281	.347	50-1	.140	-3	98	-5	-0.8
1935	Bro N	7	14	.333	37	24	7-2	0	143.1	191	124	7	2	52	55	6.66	60	.317	.373	49-2	.184	-0	102	-42	-5.0
1936	Bos N	0	0	—	3	0	0	0	6	11	8	1	1	6	1	10.50	37	.440	.563	1-0	.000	-0		-5	-0.2
1940	Phi A	14	13	.519	31	30	16-1	0	229.1	222	111	16	1	80	94	3.73	119	.248	.310	86-2	.116	-6	98	19	1.4
1941	Phi A	2	7	.222	16	14	4	0	78.1	85	57	9	3	31	19	6.09	69	.281	.353	25-2	.400	4	106	-15	-1.0
Total	5	30	45	.400	112	86	34-3	1	592	657	376	38	9	220	231	4.93	85	.279	.343	211-7	.171	-5	100	-48	-5.6
BACKE, BRANDON Brandon Allen B 4.5.1978 Galveston, TX BR/TR 6/182# d7.19																									
2002	TB A	0	0	—	9	0	0	0-0	13	15	10	3	2	7-0	6	6.92	65	.288	.393	0-0	—	0		-3	-0.2
2003	TB A	1	1	.500	28	0	0	0-0	44.2	40	28	6	2	25-1	36	5.44	83	.247	.353	0-0	—	0*		-4	-0.2
Total	2	1	1	.500	37	0	0	0-0	57.2	55	38	9	4	32-1	42	5.77	78	.257	.363	0-0	—	0		-7	-0.4
BACKMAN, LES Lester John B 3.20.1888 Cleves, OH D 11.8.1975 Cincinnati, OH BR/TR 6-0.5/195# d7.3																									
1909	StL N	3	11	.214	21	15	8	0	128.1	146	69	1	3	39	35	4.14	61	.302	.357	39-1	.103	-1	81	-19	-2.1
1910	StL N	6	7	.462	26	11	4	2	116	117	55	4	2	53	41	3.03	98	.265	.346	35-0	.114	0	89	-3	-0.3
Total	2	9	18	.333	47	26	12	2	244.1	263	124	5	5	92	76	3.61	76	.284	.352	74-1	.108	-1	84	-22	-2.4
BACSIK, MIKE Michael Joseph B 11.11.1977 Dallas, TX BL/TL 6-3/190# d8.5 f-Mike																									
2001	Cle A	0	0	—	3	0	0	0-0	9	13	10	0	1	3-1	4	9.00	50	.325	.378	0-0	—	0		-4	-0.2
2002	NY N	3	2	.600	11	9	1	0-0	55.2	63	29	8	4	19-3	30	4.37	91	.289	.355	18-3	.111	-0	124	-2	-0.1
2003	NY N	1	2	.333	5	3	0	0-0	17.2	28	21	5	0	8-0	12	10.19	41	.368	.424	3-0	.000	-0	60	-12	-1.6
Total	3	4	4	.500	19	12	1	0-0	82.1	104	60	13	5	30-4	46	6.12	66	.311	.374	21-3	.095	-1	106	-18	-1.9
BACSIK, MIKE Michael James B 4.1.1952 Dallas, TX BR/TR 6-1/185# d6.15 s-Mike																									
1975	Tex A	1	2	.333	7	3	0	0-0	26.2	28	17	1	1	9-1	13	3.71	101	.275	.336	0-0	—	0	86	-2	-0.2
1976	Tex A	3	2	.600	23	0	0	0-2	55	66	31	3	2	26-4	21	4.25	84	.308	.385	0-0	—	0		-4	-0.4
1977	Tex A	0	0	—	2	0	0	0-0	2.1	9	5	1	0	0-0	1	19.29	21	.563	.563	0-0	—	0		-4	-0.2
1979	Min A	4	2	.667	31	0	0	0-1	65.2	61	39	6	0	29-4	33	4.39	100	.249	.325	0-0	—	0		-2	-0.2
1980	Min A	0	0	—	10	0	0	0-0	23	26	12	1	0	11-0	9	4.30	101	.286	.359	0-0	—	0		0	0.0
Total	5	8	6	.571	73	3	0	0-3	172.2	190	104	12	3	75-9	77	4.43	91	.284	.356	0-0	—	0	86	-12	-1.0
BACZEWSKI, FRED Frederic John "Lefty" B 5.15.1926 St.Paul, MN D 11.14.1976 Culver City, CA BL/TL 6-2.5/185# d4.26																									
1953	Chi N	0	0	—	9	0	0	0	10	20	9	1	1	6	3	6.30	71	.435	.509	2-1	.500	0		-2	-0.1
	Cin N	11	4	.733	24	18	10-1	1	138.1	125	56	13	1	52	58	3.45	126	.244	.315	45-3	.178	-0	96	15	1.3
	Year	11	4	.733	33	18	10-1	1	148.1	145	61	14	2	58	61	3.64	120	.260	.332	47-4	.191	0	96	12	1.2
1954	Cin N	6	6	.500	29	22	4-1	0	130	159	82	22	1	53	43	5.26	80	.305	.368	42-6	.071	-3	107	-14	-1.5
1955	Cin N	0	0	—	1	0	0	0	1	2	2	2	0	0-0	0	18.00	24	.400	.400	0-0	—	0		-1	-0.1
Total	3	17	10	.630	63	40	14-2	1	279.1	306	149	38	3	111-0	104	4.45	96	.282	.349	89-10	.135	-3	102	-2	-0.4
BADER, LORE Lore Verne "King" B 4.27.1888 Bader, IL D 6.2.1973 LeRoy, KS BL/TR 6/175# d9.30 C1																									
1912	NY N	2	0	1.000	2	1	1	0	10	9	2	0	1	6	3	0.90	376	.250	.372	3-0	.000	-0	87	3	0.5
1917	Bos A	2	0	1.000	15	1	0	1	38.1	48	15	1	1	18	14	2.35	110	.306	.381	10-1	.300	1	84	0	0.1
1918	Bos A	1	3	.250	5	4	2-1	0	27	26	13	1	3	12	10	3.33	81	.271	.369	9-0	.111	-1	42	-2	-0.4
Total	3	5	3	.625	22	6	3-1	1	75.1	83	30	2	5	36	27	2.51	109	.287	.376	22-1	.182	-0	58	1	0.2
BAECHT, ED Edward Joseph B 5.15.1907 Paden, OK D 8.15.1957 Grafton, IL BR/TR 6-3/195# d4.24																									
1926	Phi N	2	0	1.000	28	1	1	0	56	73	43	4	1	28	14	6.11	68	.324	.402	14-0	.143	-1	101	-10	-0.5
1927	Phi N	0	1	.000	1	1	0	0	6	12	8	0	0	2	0	12.00	34	.429	.467	2-0	.000	-0	185	-5	-0.5
1928	Phi N	1	1	.500	9	1	0	0	24	37	16	1	0	9	10	6.00	71	.385	.438	7-0	.143	-0	59	-3	-0.3
1931	Chi N	2	4	.333	22	6	2	0	67	64	34	1	8	32	34	3.76	103	.250	.351	18-3	.278	1	119	0	0.1
1932	Chi N	0	0	—	1	0	0	0	1	1	0	0	0	1	0	0.00	—	.333	.500	0-0	—	0		0	0.0
1937	StL A	0	0	—	3	0	0	0	6.1	13	15	3	2	6	3	12.79	38	.419	.538	1-0	.000	-0		-7	-0.3
Total	6	5	6	.455	64	9	3	0	160.1	200	116	9	11	78	61	5.56	73	.313	.397	42-3	.190	-1	113	-25	-1.5
BAEZ, BENITO Benito (Ceri) B 5.6.1977 Bonao, D.R. BL/TL 6/160# d8.25																									
2001	Fla N	0	0	—	8	0	0	0-0	9.1	22	14	3	0	6-0	14	13.50	31	.449	.509	1-0	.000	-0		-9	-0.5

Year	Tm Lg	W	L	Pct	G	GS	CG-Sho	SV-BS	IP	H	R	HR	HB	BB-IB	SO	ERA	AERA	OAV	OOB	AB-SH	AVG	PB	Sup	APR	PW
BAEZ, DANYS Danys B 9.10.1977 Pinar Del Rio, Cuba BR/TR 6-3/225# d5.13																									
2001	†Cle A	5	3	.625	43	0	0	0-1	50.1	34	22	5	3	20-4	52	2.50	181	.191	.282	0-0	—	0		8	1.1
2002	Cle A	10	11	.476	39	26	1	6-2	165.1	160	84	14	9	82-5	130	4.41	100	.256	.347	2-0	.000	-0	90	1	0.1
2003	Cle A	2	9	.182	73	0	0	25-10	75.2	65	36	9	4	23-0	66	3.81	116	.229	.295	1-0	.000	-0		6	1.0
Total	3	17	23	.425	155	26	1	31-13	291.1	259	142	28	16	125-9	248	3.92	113	.238	.323	3-0	.000	-0	90	15	2.2
BAGBY, JIM James Charles Jacob Jr. B 9.8.1916 Cleveland, OH D 9.2.1988 Marietta, GA BR/TR 6-2/170# d4.18 Mer 1944 f-Jim																									
1938	Bos A	15	11	.577	43	25	10-1	2	198.2	218	110	9	3	90	73	4.21	117	.283	.360	68-8	.191	-1*	119	14	1.6
1939	Bos A	5	5	.500	21	11	3	0	80	119	66	7	2	36	35	7.09	67	.347	.412	34-2	.294	3	117	-17	-1.5
1940	Bos A	10	16	.385	36	21	6-1	2	182.2	217	104	15	1	83	57	4.73	95	.296	.368	74-6	.203	-0*	93	-4	-0.5
1941	Cle A	9	15	.375	33	27	12	2	200.2	214	104	10	6	76	53	4.04	98	.273	.341	74-4	.243	2*	90	-4	-0.1
1942	Cle A☆	17	9	.654	38	**35**	16-4	1	270.2	267	105	19	1	64	54	2.96	117	.258	.302	95-7	.189	1*	109	15	1.5
1943	Cle A☆	17	14	.548	36	**33**	16-3	1	**273**	248	112	15	3	80	70	3.10	100	.240	.296	112-1	.268	4*	102	-1	0.6
1944	Cle A	4	5	.444	13	10	2	0	79	101	48	2	4	34	12	4.33	76	.312	.384	31-0	.226	1*	104	-11	-1.0
1945	Cle A	8	11	.421	25	19	11-3	1	159.1	171	70	3	2	59	38	3.73	87	.279	.344	58-1	.293	3	101	-6	-0.2
1946	†Bos A	7	6	.538	21	11	6-1	0	106.2	117	55	4	1	49	16	3.71	99	.279	.356	42-0	.119	-2	87	-3	-0.5
1947	Pit N	5	4	.556	37	6	2	0	115.2	143	75	14	5	37	23	4.67	90	.304	.361	32-3	.219	1	136	-8	-0.4
Total	10	97	96	.503	303	198	84-13	9	1666.1	1815	849	98	28	608	431	3.96	97	.278	.342	620-32	.226	12	104	-25	-0.5
BAGBY, JIM James Charles Jacob Sr. "Sarge" B 10.5.1889 Barnett, GA D 7.28.1954 Marietta, GA BB/TR 6/170# d4.22 s-Jim																									
1912	Cin N	2	1	.667	5	1	0	0	17.1	17	6	2	0	9	10	3.12	108	.270	.361	5-0	.000	-1	87	1	0.1
1916	Cle A	16	17	.485	48	27	14-3	5	272.2	253	109	2	8	67	88	2.61	115	.251	.303	90-9	.167	-1*	116	10	1.0
1917	Cle A	23	13	.639	49	37	26-8	7	320.2	277	91	6	6	73	83	1.99	142	.235	.283	108-3	.231	2	102	30	3.9
1918	Cle A	17	16	.515	**45**	31	23-2	6	271.1	274	107	0	2	78	57	2.69	112	.276	.330	99-3	.212	-0*	92	8	1.0
1919	Cle A	17	11	.607	35	32	21	3	241.1	258	96	3	4	44	61	2.80	120	.275	.310	89-4	.258	5*	121	15	2.2
1920	†Cle A	**31**	12	**.721**	**48**	38	**30**-3	0	**339.2**	338	122	9	5	79	73	2.89	132	.266	.311	131-7	.252	6*	133	39	4.7
1921	Cle A	14	12	.538	40	26	13	4	191.2	238	112	14	4	44	37	4.70	91	.308	.348	76-2	.197	-1*	108	-6	-0.9
1922	Cle A	4	5	.444	25	10	4	1	98.1	134	77	5	3	39	25	6.32	63	.340	.404	42-0	.262	3	136	-24	-1.6
1923	Pit N	3	2	.600	21	6	2	3	68.2	95	49	6	1	25	16	5.24	76	.336	.392	20-2	.050	-2	126	-10	-0.9
Total	9	127	89	.588	316	208	133-16	29	1821.2	1884	769	47	33	458	450	3.11	110	.273	.321	660-30	.218	11	114	63	9.5
BAHNSEN, STAN Stanley Raymond B 12.15.1944 Council Bluffs, IA BR/TR 6-2/203# d9.9																									
1966	NY A	1	1	.500	4	3	1	1	23	15	9	3	0	7-0	16	3.52	94	.181	.244	7-0	.143	-0	141	0	0.0
1968	NY A	17	12	.586	37	34	10-1	0	267.1	216	72	14	2	68-6	162	2.05	141	.221	.271	81-10	.049	-4	97	26	2.4
1969	NY A	9	16	.360	40	33	5-2	1-0	220.2	222	102	28	0	90-9	130	3.83	91	.260	.330	60-9	.083	-3	88	-7	-1.0
1970	NY A	14	11	.560	36	35	6-2	0-0	232.2	227	100	23	2	75-4	116	3.33	106	.256	.312	74-8	.149	-0	104	5	0.5
1971	NY A	14	12	.538	36	34	14-3	0-0	242	221	99	20	5	72-8	110	3.35	97	.248	.304	79-8	.152	0	123	-1	0.1
1972	Chi A	21	16	.568	43	41	5-1	0-0	252.1	263	107	22	6	73-1	157	3.60	87	.268	.321	92-3	.152	-1*	103	-10	-1.5
1973	Chi A	18	21	.462	42	42	14-4	0-0	282.1	290	128	20	5	117-2	120	3.57	111	.269	.341	0-0	—	0	93	11	1.5
1974	Chi A	12	15	.444	38	35	10-1	0-0	216.1	230	128	17	4	110-6	102	4.70	79	.277	.362	0-0	—	0	96	-23	-2.6
1975	Chi A	4	6	.400	12	12	2	0-0	67.1	78	49	9	3	40-0	31	6.01	65	.291	.389	0-0	—	0	106	-15	-1.9
	Oak A	6	7	.462	21	16	2	0-1	100	88	42	2	3	37-1	49	3.24	112	.238	.310	1-0	.000	-0	101	4	0.5
	Year	10	13	.435	33	28	4	0-1	167.1	166	46	11	6	77-1	80	4.36	86	.261	.344	1-0	.000	-0	104	-11	-1.4
1976	Oak A	8	7	.533	35	14	1-1	0-2	143	124	55	13	2	43-3	82	3.34	101	.232	.290	0-0	—	0	110	3	0.3
1977	Oak A	1	2	.333	11	2	0	1-1	22	24	16	5	1	13-5	21	6.14	66	.286	.380	0-0	—	0	89	-5	-0.6
	Mon N	8	9	.471	23	22	3-1	0-0	127.1	142	76	14	0	38-2	58	4.81	79	.283	.332	42-4	.119	-1	104	-15	-1.8
1978	Mon N	1	5	.167	44	1	0	7-2	75	74	35	9	0	31-2	44	3.84	92	.261	.333	11-1	.091	-1	153	-2	-0.3
1979	Mon N	3	1	.750	55	0	0	5-2	94.1	80	34	10	0	42-4	71	3.15	117	.236	.319	14-0	.071	-0		7	0.4
1980	Mon N	7	6	.538	57	0	0	4-3	91.1	80	40	7	0	33-4	48	3.05	117	.235	.300	9-0	.111	1		3	0.5
1981	†Mon N	2	1	.667	25	3	0	1-1	49	45	27	7	1	24-0	28	4.96	70	.247	.338	9-0	.111	-0	59	-7	-0.5
1982	Cal A	0	1	.000	7	0	0	0-0	9.2	13	6	0	0	8-1	5	4.66	87	.310	.420	0-0	—	0		-1	-0.1
	Phi N	0	0	—	8	0	0	0-0	13.1	8	2	0	0	3-1	9	1.35	272	.182	.229	0-0	—	0		3	0.2
Total	16	146	149	.495	574	327	73-16	20-12	2529	2440	1127	223	34	924-59	1359	3.60	97	.255	.321	479-43	.117	-9	101	-24	-3.9
BAHR, ED Edson Garfield B 10.16.1919 Rouleau, SK, CAN BR/TR 6-1.5/172# d5.1																									
1946	Pit N	8	6	.571	27	14	7	0	136.2	128	57	8	5	52	44	2.63	134	.254	.330	45-1	.178	-1*	116	9	0.8
1947	Pit N	3	5	.375	19	11	1	0	82.1	82	45	5	3	43	25	4.59	92	.263	.358	23-3	.087	-2*	74	-2	-0.4
Total	2	11	11	.500	46	25	8	0	219	210	102	13	8	95	69	3.37	112	.257	.341	68-4	.147	-3	97	7	0.4
BAICHLEY, GROVER Grover Cleveland B 12.10.1889 Toledo, IL D 6.28.1956 San Jose, CA BR/TR 5-8/165# d8.24																									
1914	StL A	0	0	—	4	0	0	0	7	9	5	0	0	3	3	5.14	53	.346	.414	1-0	.000	-0		-2	-0.1
BAILES, SCOTT Scott Alan B 12.18.1961 Chillicothe, OH BL/TL 6-2/184# d4.9																									
1986	Cle A	10	10	.500	62	10	0	7-6	112.2	123	70	12	1	43-5	60	4.95	84	.276	.339	0-0	—	0	116	-10	-1.7
1987	Cle A	7	8	.467	39	17	0	6-2	120.1	145	75	21	4	47-1	65	4.64	98	.296	.358	0-0	—	0	101	-3	-0.3
1988	Cle A	9	14	.391	37	21	5-2	0-2	145	149	89	22	2	46-0	53	4.90	84	.266	.322	0-0	—	0	91	-13	-1.8
1989	Cle A	5	9	.357	34	11	0	0-1	113.2	116	57	7	3	29-4	47	4.28	93	.269	.316	0-0	—	0	66	-3	-0.3
1990	Cal A	2	0	1.000	27	0	0	0-0	35.1	46	30	8	1	20-0	16	6.37	60	.315	.390	0-0	—	0		-11	-0.5
1991	Cal A	1	2	.333	42	0	0	0-1	51.2	41	26	5	4	22-5	41	4.18	98	.218	.310	0-0	—	0		0	0.0
1992	Cal A	3	1	.750	32	0	0	0-0	38.2	59	34	7	1	28-4	25	7.45	54	.351	.442	0-0	—	0		-14	-1.3
1997	Tex A	1	0	1.000	24	0	0	0-0	22	18	9	2	0	10-2	14	2.86	167	.231	.315	0-0	—	0		4	0.2
1998	Tex A	1	0	1.000	46	0	0	0-0	40.1	61	33	5	0	11-0	30	6.47	75	.351	.385	0-0	—	0		-8	-0.4
Total	9	39	44	.470	343	59	5-2	13-12	679.2	758	423	89	16	256-21	351	4.95	85	.283	.345	0-0	—	0	94	-58	-6.1
BAILEY, SWEETBREADS Abraham Lincoln B 2.12.1895 Joliet, IL D 9.27.1939 Joliet, IL BR/TR 6/184# d5.23																									
1919	Chi N	3	5	.375	21	5	0	0	71.1	75	30	2	3	20	19	3.15	91	.288	.346	18-0	.389	3	77	-1	0.3
1920	Chi N	1	2	.333	21	1	0	0	36.2	55	38	1	2	11	8	7.12	45	.359	.410	7-1	.143	-0	25	-16	-1.3
1921	Chi N	0	0	—	3	0	0	0	5	6	2	0	1	2	2	3.60	106	.300	.391	0-0	—	0		0	0.0
	Bro N	0	0	—	7	0	0	0	24.1	35	15	1	1	7	6	5.18	75	.368	.417	5-0	.000	-0		-3	-0.2
	Year	0	0	—	10	0	0	0	29.1	41	18	1	2	9	8	4.91	79	.357	.413	5-0	.000	-0		-2	-0.2
Total	3	4	7	.364	52	6	0	0	137.1	171	85	4	7	40	35	4.59	69	.324	.379	30-1	.267	2	63	-20	-1.2
BAILEY, ROGER Charles Roger B 10.3.1970 Chattahoochee, FL BR/TR 6-1/180# d4.27																									
1995	Col N	7	6	.538	39	6	0	0-0	81.1	88	49	9	1	39-3	33	4.98	108	.283	.363	16-3	.125	-1	140	3	0.3
1996	Col N	2	3	.400	24	11	0	1-0	83.2	94	64	7	1	52-0	45	6.24	84	.288	.384	19-3	.263	2	91	-8	-0.1
1997	Col N	9	10	.474	29	29	5-2	0-0	191	210	103	27	13	70-2	84	4.29	121	.283	.354	62-5	.210	-0*	111	14	1.5
Total	3	18	19	.486	92	46	5-2	1-0	356	392	216	43	15	161-5	162	4.90	107	.284	.363	97-11	.206	1	109	9	1.7
BAILEY, HARVEY Harvey Francis B 11.24.1876 Adrian, MI D 7.10.1922 Toledo, OH TL 6/160# d6.30																									
1899	Bos N	6	4	.600	12	11	8	0	86.2	83	42	7	6	35	26	3.95	105	.252	.334	34-0	.235	0	85	5	0.4
1900	Bos N	0	0	—	4	1	0	0	20	24	16	0	2	11	9	4.95	83	.296	.394	9-0	.222	0	167	-2	0.0
Total	2	6	4	.600	16	12	8	0	106.2	107	58	7	8	46	35	4.13	100	.260	.346	43-0	.233	0	92	3	0.4
BAILEY, HOWARD Howard L B 7.31.1957 Grand Haven, MI BR/TL 6/195# d4.12																									
1981	Det A	1	4	.200	9	5	0	0-0	36.2	45	31	4	3	13-2	17	7.36	51	.308	.372	0-0	—	0	67	-14	-1.6
1982	Det A	0	0	—	8	0	0	1-0	10	6	0	0	0	2-1	3	0.00	—	.182	.222	0-0	—	0		5	0.2
1983	Det A	5	5	.500	33	3	0	0-1	72	69	45	11	2	25-3	21	4.88	80	.255	.321	0-0	—	0	100	-9	-1.1
Total	3	6	9	.400	50	8	0	1-1	118.2	120	76	15	5	40-6	41	5.23	74	.267	.331	0-0	—	0	78	-18	-2.5
BAILEY, JIM James Hopkins B 12.16.1934 Strawberry Plains, TN BB/TL 6-2.5/210# d9.10 b-Ed																									
1959	Cin N	0	1	.000	3	1	0	0	11.2	17	8	1	1	6-1	7	6.17	66	.333	.414	3-0	.000	-0	66	-2	-0.2
BAILEY, KING Linwood C. B 11.1870 , VA D 11.19.1917 Macon, GA BL/TL 6- /185# d9.21																									
1895	Cin N	1	0	1.000	1	1	1	0	8	13	8	0	1	0	0	5.63	88	.361	.378	4-0	.500	1	273	-1	0.0

Year	Tm Lg	W	L	Pct	G	GS	CG-Sho	SV-BS	IP	H	R	HR	HB	BB-IB	SO	ERA	AERA	OAV	OOB	AB-SH	AVG	PB	Sup	APR	PW
BAILEY, CORY Phillip Cory B 1.24.1971 Marion, IL BR/TR 6-1/202# d9.1																									
1993	Bos A	0	1	.000	11	0	0	0-0	15.2	12	7	0	0	12-3	11	3.45	134	.231	.369	0-0	—	0		2	0.1
1994	Bos A	0	1	.000	5	0	0	0-1	4.1	10	6	2	0	3-1	4	12.46	40	.476	.542	0-0	—	0		-3	-0.6
1995	StL N	0	0	—	3	0	0	0-0	3.2	2	3	0	0	2-1	5	7.36	57	.154	.267	0-0	—	0		-1	0.0
1996	StL N	5	2	.714	51	0	0	0-1	57	57	21	1	1	30-3	38	3.00	140	.263	.353	1-1	.000	1		8	0.9
1997	SF N	0	1	.000	7	0	0	0-0	9.2	15	9	1	0	4-0	5	8.38	49	.375	.422	1-0	1.000	0		-4	-0.4
1998	SF N	0	0	—	5	0	0	0-0	3.1	2	1	1	0	1-0	2	2.70	147	.167	.231	0-0	—	0		1	0.0
2001	KC A	1	1	.500	53	0	0	0-1	67.1	57	28	3	0	33-2	61	3.48	141	.234	.321	0-0	—	0		10	0.5
2002	KC A	3	4	.429	37	0	0	1-6	46	53	24	5	2	31-7	24	4.11	122	.306	.413	0-0	—	0		3	0.5
Total	8	9	10	.474	172	0	0	1-9	207	208	99	13	3	116-17	150	3.96	117	.269	.364	2-1	.500	1		16	1.0
BAILEY, STEVE Steven John B 2.12.1942 Bronx, NY BR/TR 6-1/194# d4.14																									
1967	Cle A	2	5	.286	32	1	0	2	64.2	62	31	5	3	42-4	46	3.90	84	.259	.372	10-0	.000	-1	53	-4	-0.5
1968	Cle A	0	1	.000	2	1	0	0	5	4	3	1	0	2-0	1	3.60	82	.235	.300	0-0	—	0	88	-1	-0.1
Total	2	2	6	.250	34	2	0	2	69.2	66	34	6	3	44-4	47	3.88	84	.258	.367	10-0	.000	-1	67	-5	-0.6
BAILEY, BILL William F. B 4.12.1889 Ft.Smith, AR D 11.2.1926 Houston, TX BL/TL 5-11/165# d9.17																									
1907	StL A	4	1	.800	6	5	3	0	48.1	39	16	0	4	15	17	2.42	104	.223	.299	20-1	.150	-1	102	1	0.0
1908	StL A	3	5	.375	22	12	7	0	106.2	85	53	2	3	50	42	3.04	79	.220	.314	34-2	.088	-2	109	-8	-1.0
1909	StL A	9	10	.474	32	20	17-1	0	199	174	71	2	6	75	114	2.44	99	.248	.325	77-2	.286	5*	79	0	0.6
1910	StL A	3	18	.143	34	20	13	0	192.1	186	133	2	10	97	90	3.32	74	.262	.359	63-1	.206	0	64	-26	-2.7
1911	StL A	0	3	.000	7	2	2	0	31.2	42	26	1	2	16	8	4.55	74	.339	.423	11-0	.000	-2	43	-5	-0.6
1912	StL A	0	1	.000	3	2	0	0	10.2	15	12	0	0	10	2	9.28	36	.341	.463	2-0	.500	1	78	-6	-0.4
1914	Bal F	7	9	.438	19	18	10-1	0	128.2	106	58	2	7	68	131	3.08	99	.230	.338	43-1	.163	-1	78	-1	-0.1
1915	Bal F	6	19	.240	36	23	11-2	0	190.1	179	118	8	9	115	98	4.63	62	.255	.366	65-7	.231	-0	103	-33	-4.0
	Chi F	3	1	.750	5	5	3-3	0	33.1	23	9	1	0	10	24	2.16	116	.202	.266	9-0	.222	0	117	2	0.3
	Year	9	20	.310	41	28	14-5	0	223.2	202	13	9	9	125	122	4.27	66	.247	.353	74-7	.230	-0	105	-30	-3.7
1918	Det A	1	2	.333	8	4	1	0	37.2	53	34	0	1	26	13	5.97	45	.368	.468	13-0	.077	-1	85	-15	-1.2
1921	StL N	2	5	.286	19	6	3-1	0	74	95	41	1	2	22	20	4.26	86	.330	.381	22-0	.091	-2	60	-4	-0.5
1922	StL N	0	2	.000	12	0	0	0	31.2	38	22	1	0	23	11	5.40	72	.325	.436	7-0	.286	0		-5	-0.2
Total	11	38	76	.333	203	117	70-8	0	1084.1	1035	593	20	44	527	570	3.57	77	.261	.354	366-14	.194	-3	84	-100	-9.8
BAIN, LOREN Herbert Loren B 7.4.1922 Staples, MN D 11.24.1996 Chetek, WI BR/TR 6/190# d6.23																									
1945	NY N	0	0	—	3	0	0	0	8	10	7	1	1	4	1	7.88	50	.323	.417	3-0	.333	0		-3	-0.1
BAIR, DOUG Charles Douglas B 8.22.1949 Defiance, OH BR/TR 6/180# d9.13																									
1976	Pit N	0	0	—	4	0	0	0-0	6.1	4	4	0	0	5-1	4	5.68	61	.174	.321	0-0	—	0		-1	-0.1
1977	Oak A	4	6	.400	45	0	0	8-6	83.1	78	39	11	0	57-9	68	3.46	117	.253	.364	0-0	—	0		5	0.6
1978	Cin N	7	6	.538	70	0	0	28-5	100.1	87	23	6	0	38-3	91	1.97	180	.236	.305	14-1	.143	-0		18	3.4
1979	†Cin N	11	7	.611	65	0	0	16-7	94.1	93	47	7	3	51-12	86	4.29	87	.256	.350	8-0	.000	-1		-4	-1.0
1980	Cin N	3	6	.333	61	0	0	6-0	85	91	42	7	1	39-10	62	4.24	85	.277	.351	2-0	.000	-0		-6	-0.6
1981	Cin N	2	2	.500	24	0	0	0-2	39	42	28	5	0	17-4	16	5.77	62	.271	.343	3-0	.333	1		-10	-0.9
	StL N	2	0	1.000	11	0	0	1-0	15.2	13	6	0	0	2-0	14	3.45	103	.224	.250	3-0	.000	-0		0	0.0
	Year	4	2	.667	35	0	0	1-2	54.2	55	37	5	0	19-4	30	5.10	70	.258	.319	6-0	.167	1		-8	-0.9
1982	†StL N	5	3	.625	63	0	0	8-1	91.2	69	27	7	1	36-13	68	2.55	142	.211	.288	13-2	.077	-1		12	1.1
1983	StL N	1	1	.500	26	0	0	1-2	29.2	24	11	4	0	13-3	21	3.03	120	.224	.306	2-0	.000	-0		2	0.1
	Det A	7	3	.700	27	1	0	4-4	55.2	51	27	8	1	19-4	39	3.88	101	.242	.307	0-0	—	0	46	0	0.0
1984	†Det A	5	3	.625	47	1	0	4-3	93.2	82	42	10	0	36-2	57	3.75	105	.238	.306	0-0	—	0	161	3	0.3
1985	Det A	2	0	1.000	21	3	0	0-0	49	54	38	3	1	25-5	30	6.24	65	.281	.360	0-0	—	0	171	-12	-0.6
	StL N	0	0	—	2	0	0	0-0	2	1	0	0	0	2-0	0	0.00	—	.167	.375	0-0	—	0		1	0.0
1986	Oak A	2	3	.400	31	0	0	4-4	45	37	15	5	0	18-0	40	3.00	129	.224	.296	0-0	—	0		6	0.7
1987	Phi N	2	0	1.000	11	0	0	0-1	13.2	17	9	4	0	5-0	10	5.93	72	.309	.361	1-1	.000	-0		-2	-0.3
1988	Tor A	0	0	—	10	0	0	0-0	13.1	14	6	2	0	3-0	8	4.05	97	.280	.321	0-0	—	0		0	0.0
1989	Pit N	2	3	.400	44	0	0	1-1	67.1	52	19	4	0	28-10	56	2.27	148	.211	.291	5-0	.200	0		9	0.7
1990	Pit N	0	0	—	22	0	0	0-0	24.1	30	15	3	0	11-1	19	4.81	75	.306	.376	1-0	.000	-0		-3	-0.2
Total	15	55	43	.561	584	5	0	81-36	909.1	839	398	86	7	405-77	689	3.63	103	.246	.325	52-4	.096	-2	153	18	3.2
BAIRD, BOB Robert Allen B 1.16.1940 Knoxville, TN D 4.11.1974 Chattanooga, TN BL/TL 6-4/195# d9.3																									
1962	Was A	0	1	.000	3	3	0	0	10.2	13	8	0	0	8-0	3	6.75	60	.310	.412	3-0	.000	-0	66	-3	-0.3
1963	Was A	0	3	.000	5	3	0	0	11.2	12	15	1	1	7-0	7	7.71	48	.261	.364	3-0	.333	0	112	-7	-1.2
Total	2	0	4	.000	8	6	0	0	22.1	25	23	1	1	15-0	10	7.25	53	.284	.387	6-0	.167	-0	88	-10	-1.5
BAKELY, JERSEY Edward Enoch (b: Edward Enoch Bakley) B 4.17.1864 Blackwood, NJ D 2.17.1915 Philadelphia, PA BR/TR 5-8/170# d5.11																									
1883	Phi AA	5	3	.625	8	8	7	0	61.1	65	47	0		12	14	3.23	110	.255	.288	26	.192	1	112	1	0.2
1884	Phi U	14	25	.359	39	38	38-1	0	344.2	390	305	0		76	204	4.47	52	.267	.303	167	.132	-16*	99	-86	-8.4
	Wil U	0	2	.000	2	2	2	0	17	24	17	0		1	9	4.24	63	.312	.321	5	.000	-1	32	-2	-0.3
	KC U	2	3	.400	5	5	3	0	33	29	16	0		4	13	2.45	91	.220	.243	20	.150	-2*	76	0	-0.2
	Year	16	30	.348	46	45	43-1	0	394.2	443	20	0		81	226	4.29	54	.265	.299	192	.130	-18	93	-86	-8.9
1888	Cle AA	25	33	.431	61	61	60-4	0	532.2	518	321	14	15	128	212	2.97	104	.246	.294	194	.134	-6	86	2	-0.3
1889	Cle N	12	22	.353	36	34	33-2	0	304.1	296	169	9	8	106	105	2.96	136	.247	.313	111	.135	-1	65	29	2.6
1890	Cle P	12	25	.324	43	38	32	0	326.1	412	307	13	7	147	67	4.47	89	.295	.365	138	.203	-2	95	-18	-1.7
1891	Was AA	2	10	.167	13	12	11	0	104.1	127	107	6	6	60	32	5.35	70	.291	.384	45	.222	-0	76	-19	-1.7
	Bal AA	4	2	.667	8	6	5	0	59	48	32	1	1	30	13	2.29	163	.214	.310	21	.095	0	103	8	0.6
	Year	6	12	.333	21	18	16	0	163.1	175	38	7	7	90	45	4.24	88	.265	.359	66	.182	-0	85	-12	-1.1
Total	6	76	125	.378	215	204	191-7	0	1782.2	1909	1321	43	37	564	669	3.66	91	.262	.318	727	.153	-26	87	-85	-9.2
BAKENHASTER, DAVE David Lee B 3.5.1945 Columbus, OH BR/TR 5-10/168# d6.20																									
1964	StL N	0	0	—	2	0	0	0	3	9	6	1	0	1-0	0	6.00	63	.474	.500	0-0	—	0		-2	-0.1
BAKER, AL Albert Jones B 2.28.1906 Batesville, MS D 11.6.1982 Kenedy, TX BR/TR 5-11/170# d8.20																									
1938	Bos A	0	0	—	3	0	0	0	7.2	13	8	2	1	2	2	9.39	53	.371	.421	4-0	.000	-1		-3	-0.2
BAKER, BOCK Charles "Smiling Bock" B 7.17.1878 Troy, NY D 8.17.1940 New York, NY TL 5-9/181# d4.28																									
1901	Cle A	0	1	.000	1	1	1	0	8	23	13	0	1	6	0	5.63	63	.500	.566	4-0	.000	-1	19	-4	-0.4
	Phi A	0	1	.000	1	1	0	0	6	6	11	0	0	6	1	10.50	36	.261	.414	3-0	.333	0	90	-5	-0.5
	Year	0	2	.000	2	2	1	0	14	29	16	0	1	12	1	7.71	47	.420	.512	7-0	.143	-1	56	-8	-0.9
BAKER, ERNIE Earnest Gould B 8.8.1875 Concord, MI D 10.25.1945 Homer, MI BR/TR 5-10/160# d8.18																									
1905	Cin N	0	0	—	1	0	0	0	4	7	4	1	1	0	1	4.50	73	.412	.444	2-0	.000	-0		-1	-0.1
BAKER, JESSE Jesse Ormond B 6.3.1888 Anderson Island, WA D 9.26.1972 Tacoma, WA BL/TL 5-11/188# d4.23																									
1911	Chi A	2	7	.222	22	8	3	1	94	101	52	3	4	30	51	3.93	82	.288	.351	29-0	.103	-2	70	-6	-0.6
BAKER, KIRTLEY Kirtley "Whitey" B 6.24.1869 Aurora, IN D 4.15.1927 Covington, KY BR/TR 5-9/160# d5.7																									
1890	Pit N	3	19	.136	25	21	19-2	0	178.1	209	176	11	20	86	76	5.60	59	.283	.373	68	.147	-1*	63	-50	-4.6
1893	Bal N	3	8	.273	15	12	8	0	91.2	138	111	5	5	58	26	8.44	56	.337	.426	57	.298	2*	114	-33	-2.4
1894	Bal N	0	1	.000	1	0	0	0	0	1	5	0	0	2	0	∞	—	1.000	1.000	4-0	.000	-0*		-4	-0.3
1898	Was N	2	3	.400	6	5	4	0	47	56	31	1	0	18	7	3.06	120	.293	.354	18-0	.278	2	101	0	0.1
1899	Was N	1	7	.125	11	6	3	0	54	79	65	3	6	22	6	6.83	57	.339	.410	19-0	.158	-1*	89	-20	-2.2
Total	5	9	38	.191	58	44	34-2	0	371	483	388	20	31	186	115	6.28	60	.307	.391	166-0	.211	1	88	-107	-9.4
BAKER, NEAL Neal Vernon B 4.30.1904 Harlingen, TX D 1.5.1982 Houston, TX BR/TR 6-1/175# d6.26																									
1927	Phi A	0	0	—	5	2	0	0	17.1	27	17	2	0	7	3	5.71	75	.365	.420	6-0	.167	-0	98	-4	-0.2
BAKER, NORM Norman Leslie B 10.14.1863 Philadelphia, PA D 2.20.1949 Hurffville, NJ d5.21																									
1883	Pit AA	0	2	.000	3	3	2	0	19	24	16	0		11	5	3.32	98	.289	.372	12	.000	-2*	106	-2	-0.3

Year	Tm Lg	W	L	Pct	G	GS	CG-Sho	SV-BS	IP	H	R	HR	HB	BB-IB	SO	ERA	AERA	OAV	OOB	AB-SH	AVG	PB	Sup	APR	PW
1885	Lou AA	13	12	.520	25	24	24-1	0	217	210	142	3	10	69	79	3.40	95	.241	.304	87	.207	-1	88	1	0.0
1890	Bal AA	1	1	.500	2	2	2	0	17	16	9	0	0	6	10	3.71	109	.242	.306	7	.000	-1	83	1	0.0
Total	3	14	15	.483	30	29	28-1	0	253	250	167	3	10	86	94	3.42	96	.245	.309	106	.170	-3	90	0	-0.3
BAKER, SCOTT Scott B 5.18.1970 San Jose, CA BL/TL 6-2/175# d7.17																									
1995	Oak A	0	0	—	1	0	0	0-0	3.2	5	4	0	1	5-0	3	9.82	46	.333	.500	0-0	—	0		-2	-0.1
BAKER, STEVE Steven Byrne B 8.30.1956 Eugene, OR BR/TR 6/185# d5.25																									
1978	Det A	2	4	.333	15	10	0	0-1	63.1	66	37	6	0	42-0	39	4.55	85	.276	.379	0-0	—	0	76	-5	-0.5
1979	Det A	1	7	.125	21	12	0	1-1	84	97	63	13	6	51-2	54	6.64	65	.296	.396	0-0	—	0	106	-19	-1.6
1982	Oak A	1	1	.500	5	3	0	0-0	25.2	30	14	3	0	4-0	14	4.56	86	.288	.312	0-0	—	0	85	-2	-0.1
1983	Oak A	3	3	.500	35	1	0	5-6	54	59	32	4	2	26-4	23	4.33	89	.282	.363	0-0	—	0	141	-4	-0.6
	StL N	0	1	.000	8	0	0	0-0	10	10	4	0	1	4-1	1	1.80	202	.286	.366	0-0	—	0		1	0.1
Total	4	7	16	.304	84	26	0	6-8	237	262	150	26	9	127-7	131	5.13	79	.286	.374	0-0	—	0	96	-29	-2.7
BAKER, TOM Thomas Calvin "Rattlesnake" B 6.11.1913 Nursery, TX D 1.3.1991 Fort Worth, TX BR/TR 6-1.5/180# d8.15																									
1935	Bro N	1	0	1.000	11	1	1	0	42	48	25	2	0	20	10	4.29	93	.277	.352	19-0	.474	4	85	-2	0.2
1936	Bro N	1	8	.111	35	8	2	2	87.2	98	56	3	2	48	35	4.72	88	.288	.379	30-0	.233	1*	85	-6	-0.4
1937	Bro N	0	1	.000	7	0	0	0	8.1	14	10	1	1	5	2	8.64	47	.378	.465	0-0	—	0		-4	-0.4
	NY N	1	0	1.000	13	0	0	0	31	30	15	0	0	16	11	4.06	96	.268	.359	9-0	.222	-0		0	0.0
	Year	1	1	.500	20	0	0	0	39.1	44	29	1	1	21	13	5.03	78	.295	.386	9-0	.222	-0		-4	-0.4
1938	NY N	0	0	—	2	0	0	0	4	5	3	0	0	3	0	6.75	56	.313	.421	0-0	—	0		-1	0.0
Total	4	3	9	.250	68	9	3	2	173	195	109	6	3	92	58	4.73	85	.288	.375	58-0	.310	5	87	-13	-0.6
BAKER, TOM Thomas Henry B 5.6.1934 Port Townsend, WA D 3.9.1980 Port Townsend, WA BL/TL 6/195# d8.2																									
1963	Chi N	0	1	.000	10	1	0	0	18	20	12	2	1	7-0	14	3.00	117	.282	.346	3-0	.000	-0	25	-1	-0.1
BALAS, MIKE Mitchell Francis (b: Mitchell Francis Balaski) B 5.17.1910 Lowell, MA BR/TR 6/195# d4.27																									
1938	Bos N	0	0	—	1	0	0	0	1.1	3	3	0	0	0	0	6.75	51	.375	.375	0-0	—	0		-1	-0.1
BALDSCHUN, JACK Jack Edward B 10.16.1936 Greenville, OH BR/TR 6/190# d4.28																									
1961	Phi N	5	3	.625	**65**	0	0	3	99.2	90	53	7	5	49-11	59	3.88	105	.243	.337	11-1	.000	-1		0	-0.1
1962	Phi N	12	7	.632	67	0	0	13	112.2	95	41	6	2	58-9	95	2.96	131	.231	.326	16-2	.063	-1		12	2.1
1963	Phi N	11	7	.611	65	0	0	16	113.2	99	37	7	3	42-10	89	2.30	141	.232	.304	20-1	.000	-2		10	1.9
1964	Phi N	6	9	.400	71	0	0	21	118.1	111	50	8	3	40-7	96	3.12	111	.246	.310	16-2	.250	1		4	0.8
1965	Phi N	5	8	.385	65	0	0	6	99	102	53	4	4	42-12	81	3.82	91	.273	.347	7-2	.000	-1		-6	-0.9
1966	Cin N	1	5	.167	42	0	0	0	57.1	71	35	4	4	25-8	44	5.49	71	.318	.395	3-0	.333	0		-8	-0.8
1967	Cin N	0	0	—	9	0	0	0	13	15	6	0	0	9-3	12	4.15	90	.283	.387	1-0	.000	-0		0	0.0
1969	SD N	7	2	.778	61	0	0	1-1	77	80	45	7	2	29-6	67	4.79	74	.264	.331	4-0	.250	0		-11	-1.1
1970	SD N	1	0	1.000	12	0	0	0-1	13.1	24	15	2	0	4-1	12	10.13	39	.375	.406	0-0	—	0		-8	-0.6
Total	9	48	41	.539	457	0	0	60-2	704	687	335	45	23	298-67	555	3.69	98	.257	.334	78-8	.090	-3		-7	1.3
BALDWIN, LADY Charles Busted B 4.8.1859 Oramel, NY D 3.7.1937 Hastings, MI BR/TL 5-11/160# d9.30																									
1884	Mil U	1	1	.500	2	2	2	0	17	7	5	0		1	21	2.65	50	.117	.131	27	.222	-0*	129	-4	-0.3
1885	Det N	11	9	.550	21	20	19-1	1	179.1	137	84	2		28	135	1.86	153	**.197**	**.228**	124	.242	3*	112	16	1.9
1886	Det N	**42**	13	.764	56	56	55-**7**	0	487	371	194	11		100	**323**	2.24	149	**.202**	**.243**	204	.201	3*	124	55	5.7
1887	†Det N	13	10	.565	24	24	24-1	0	211	225	136	8	5	61	60	3.84	106	.269	.323	85	.271	3	102	3	0.5
1888	Det N	3	3	.500	6	6	5	0	53	76	50	5	1	15	26	5.43	51	.322	.365	23	.261	2	172	-14	-1.2
1890	Bro N	1	0	1.000	2	1	0	0	7.2	15	6	0	0	4	4	7.04	49	.395	.452	3	.000	-0	312	-2	-0.2
	Buf P	2	5	.286	7	7	7	0	62	90	72	5	3	24	13	4.50	91	.325	.385	28	.286	1	85	-11	-0.7
Total	6	73	41	.640	118	116	112-9	1	1017	921	547	31	9	233	582	2.85	119	.232	.276	494	.231	11	117	43	5.7
BALDWIN, DAVE David George B 3.30.1938 Tucson, AZ BR/TR 6-2/200# d9.6																									
1966	Was A	0	0	—	4	0	0	0	7	8	3	0	0	1-0	4	3.86	90	.267	.290	0-0	—	0		0	0.0
1967	Was A	2	4	.333	58	0	0	12	68.2	53	19	2	4	20-4	52	1.70	186	.215	.282	4-0	.000	-0		10	1.2
1968	Was A	0	2	.000	40	0	0	5	42	40	19	7	0	12-0	30	4.07	72	.260	.310	2-0	.000	0		-4	-0.3
1969	Was A	2	4	.333	43	0	0	4-0	66.2	57	31	4	5	34-2	51	4.05	86	.236	.337	7-0	.000	-1		-3	-0.4
1970	Mil A	2	1	.667	28	0	0	1-2	35.1	25	11	4	0	18-6	26	2.55	149	.205	.307	2-0	.500	0		5	0.6
1973	Chi A	0	0	—	3	0	0	0-0	5	7	2	0	0	4-1	1	3.60	110	.368	.478	0-0	—	0		0	0.0
Total	6	6	11	.353	176	0	0	22-2	224.2	190	85	17	9	89-13	164	3.08	108	.234	.313	15-0	.067	-1		8	1.1
BALDWIN, HARRY Howard Edward B 6.3.1900 Baltimore, MD D 1.23.1958 Baltimore, MD BR/TR 5-11/160# d5.4																									
1924	†NY N	3	1	.750	10	2	1	0	33.2	42	18	5	0	11	5	4.28	86	.309	.361	11-1	.364	1*	104	-2	-0.2
1925	NY N	0	0	—	1	0	0	0	1	3	2	0	0	1	0	9.00	45	.500	.571	0-0	—	0		-1	0.0
Total	2	3	1	.750	11	2	1	0	34.2	45	20	5	0	12	5	4.41	83	.317	.370	11-1	.364	1	104	-3	-0.2
BALDWIN, JAMES James J. B 7.15.1971 Southern Pines, NC BR/TR 6-3/210# d4.30																									
1995	Chi A	0	1	.000	6	4	0	0-0	14.2	32	22	6	0	9-1	10	12.89	35	.444	.506	0-0	—	0	214	-14	-0.8
1996	Chi A	11	6	.647	28	28	0	0-0	169	168	88	24	4	57-3	127	4.42	107	.257	.319	0-0	—	0	100	7	0.5
1997	Chi A	12	15	.444	32	32	1	0-0	200	205	128	19	5	83-3	140	5.27	83	.262	.334	3-1	.000	-0	116	-19	-2.2
1998	Chi A	13	6	.684	37	24	1	0-1	159	176	103	18	10	60-2	108	5.32	86	.278	.347	2-0	.000	-0	103	-13	-1.4
1999	Chi A	12	13	.480	35	33	1	0-0	199.1	219	119	34	7	81-1	123	5.10	96	.278	.348	2-0	.500	1	90	-2	-0.2
2000	†Chi A★	14	7	.667	29	28	2-1	0-0	178	185	96	34	8	59-3	116	4.65	107	.272	.335	4-1	.000	-0	105	10	1.0
2001	Chi A	7	5	.583	17	16	2-1	0-0	95.2	109	56	15	4	38-0	42	4.61	100	.286	.353	2-0	.000	-0	98	-1	-0.1
	LA N	3	6	.333	12	12	0	0-0	79.1	82	39	10	3	25-1	53	4.20	96	.274	.334	26-1	.077	-1	79	-1	-0.3
2002	Sea A	7	10	.412	30	23	0	0-0	150	179	95	26	7	49-2	88	5.28	80	.298	.357	2-0	.500	0	113	-19	-1.7
2003	Min A	0	1	.000	10	0	0	1-1	15	21	10	6	0	4-1	7	5.40	84	.333	.362	0-0	—	0		-2	-0.1
Total	9	79	70	.530	236	200	7-2	1-2	1260	1376	756	192	48	465-17	814	5.02	92	.278	.343	41-3	.098	-1	104	-54	-5.3
BALDWIN, MARK Marcus Elmore "Fido" B 10.29.1863 Pittsburgh, PA D 11.10.1929 Pittsburgh, PA BR/TR 6/190# d5.2																									
1887	Chi N	18	17	.514	40	39	35-1	1	334	329	218	22	17	122	164	3.40	132	.248	.319	139	.187	-4*	83	33	2.2
1888	Chi N	13	15	.464	30	30	27-2	0	251	241	137	13	13	99	157	2.76	110	.249	.327	106	.151	-1	100	5	0.4
1889	Col AA	27	34	.443	**63**	**59**	54-6	1	**513.2**	458	358	9	20	274	**368**	3.61	100	.231	.331	208	.188	1*	92	-10	-0.9
1890	Chi P	**33**	24	.579	**58**	**56**	**53**-1	0	**492**	494	321	10	16	249	**206**	3.35	130	.250	.339	212	.212	-1	95	49	4.1
1891	Pit N	21	28	.429	53	51	48-2	1	437.2	385	278	10	23	227	197	2.76	119	.227	.327	177	.153	-3	94	21	1.6
1892	Pit N	26	27	.491	56	53	45	0	440.1	447	272	11	22	194	157	3.47	95	.253	.334	178	.101	-12	91	-3	-1.5
1893	Pit N	0	0	—	1	1	0	0	2.1	6	4	0	0	1	0	11.57	39	.462	.500	1	.000	-0	61	-2	-0.1
	NY N	16	20	.444	45	39	33-2	2	331.1	335	228	6	12	141	100	4.10	114	.255	.332	134	.127	-11	87	18	0.4
	Year	16	20	.444	46	40	33-2	**2**	333.2	341	234	6	12	142	100	4.15	112	.257	.334	135	.126	-11	87	22	0.3
Total	7	154	165	.483	346	328	295-14	5	2802.1	2695	1816	81	123	1307	1349	3.37	113	.244	.331	1155	.163	-31	91	111	6.2
BALDWIN, O. F. Orson F. B 11.3.1881 Carson City, MI D 2.16.1942 Los Angeles, CA TR ?/185# d9.6																									
1908	StL N	1	3	.250	4	4	0	0	14.2	16	10	0	3	11	5	6.14	38	.302	.448	6-0	.000	-1	52	-4	-1.0
BALDWIN, RICK Rickey Alan B 6.1.1953 Fresno, CA BL/TR 6-3/180# d4.10																									
1975	NY N	3	5	.375	54	0	0	6-5	97.1	97	39	4	4	34-4	54	3.33	104	.263	.329	15-2	.200	0		2	0.2
1976	NY N	0	0	—	11	0	0	0-0	22.2	14	6	0	2	10-1	9	2.38	139	.189	.292	3-0	.333	0		3	0.2
1977	NY N	1	2	.333	40	0	0	1-1	62.2	62	32	6	5	31-9	23	4.45	84	.265	.360	4-0	.500	1		-4	-0.1
Total	3	4	7	.364	105	0	0	7-6	182.2	173	77	10	11	75-14	86	3.60	98	.256	.336	22-2	.273	1		1	0.3
BALE, JOHN John Robert B 5.22.1974 Cheverly, MD BL/TL 6-4/195# d9.30																									
1999	Tor A	0	0	—	1	0	0	0-0	2	2	3	1	0	2-0	4	13.50	37	.250	.400	0-0	—	0		-2	-0.1
2000	Tor A	0	0	—	2	0	0	0-0	3.2	5	7	1	2	3-0	6	14.73	35	.313	.455	0-0	—	0		-4	-0.2
2001	Bal A	1	0	1.000	14	0	0	0-0	26.2	18	14	2	1	17-0	21	3.04	141	.194	.319	0-0	—	0		2	0.1
2003	Cin N	1	2	.333	10	9	0	0-0	46.1	50	24	7	2	12-2	37	4.47	96	.281	.330	17-0	.118	-1	64	-1	-0.1
Total	4	2	2	.500	27	9	0	0-0	78.2	75	48	11	5	34-2	68	4.69	92	.254	.336	17-0	.118	-1	64	-5	-0.3

Year	Tm Lg	W	L	Pct	G	GS	CG-Sho	SV-BS	IP	H	R	HR	HB	BB-IB	SO	ERA	AERA	OAV	OOB	AB-SH	AVG	PB	Sup	APR	PW
BALFOUR, GRANT Grant Robert B 12.30.1977 Sydney, Australia BR/TR 6-2/170# d7.22																									
2001	Min A	0	0	—	2	0	0	0-0	2.2	3	4	2	0	3-0	2	13.50	34	.333	.462	0-0	—	0		-2	-0.1
2003	Min A	1	0	1.000	17	1	0	0-1	26	23	12	4	0	14-2	30	4.15	109	.235	.327	0-0	—	0	121	1	0.1
Total	2	1	0	1.000	19	1	0	0-1	28.2	26	16	6	0	17-2	32	5.02	91	.243	.341	0-0	—	0	121	-1	0.0
BALLARD, JEFF Jeffrey Scott B 8.13.1963 Billings, MT BL/TL 6-2/198# d5.9																									
1987	Bal A	2	8	.200	14	14	0	0-0	69.2	100	60	15	0	35-1	27	6.59	67	.344	.413	0-0	—	0	118	-19	-2.1
1988	Bal A	8	12	.400	25	25	6-1	0-0	153.1	167	83	15	6	42-2	41	4.40	89	.278	.330	0-0	—	0	96	-9	-1.1
1989	Bal A	18	8	.692	35	35	4-1	0-0	215.1	240	95	16	4	57-5	62	3.43	111	.287	.334	0-0	—	0	135	6	0.9
1990	Bal A	2	11	.154	44	17	0	0-0	133.1	152	79	22	3	42-6	50	4.93	77	.289	.344	0-0	—	0	94	-17	-1.5
1991	Bal A	6	12	.333	26	22	0	0-0	123.2	153	91	16	2	28-2	37	5.60	71	.302	.340	0-0	—	0	88	-28	-3.4
1993	Pit N	4	1	.800	25	5	0	0-0	53.2	70	31	3	2	15-3	16	4.86	83	.332	.380	11-1	.364	1	129	-5	-0.2
1994	Pit N	1	1	.500	28	0	0	2-3	24.1	32	19	5	1	10-3	11	6.66	65	.323	.387	2-0	.500	0		-6	-0.5
Total	7	41	53	.436	197	118	10-2	2-3	773.1	914	458	92	18	229-22	244	4.71	84	.298	.348	13-1	.385	2	110	-78	-7.9
BALLER, JAY Jay Scot B 10.6.1960 Stayton, OR BR/TR 6-7/225# d9.19																									
1982	Phi N	0	0	—	4	1	0	0-0	8	7	4	1	1	2-0	7	3.38	109	.226	.294	0-0	—	0	120	0	0.0
1985	Chi N	2	3	.400	20	4	0	1-0	52	52	21	8	1	17-7	31	3.46	116	.260	.320	8-1	.000	-1	50	3	0.2
1986	Chi N	2	4	.333	36	0	0	5-5	53.2	58	37	7	2	28-4	42	5.37	75	.275	.361	5-1	.000	-1		-8	-1.1
1987	Chi N	0	1	.000	23	0	0	0-1	29.1	38	22	4	0	20-2	27	6.75	63	.325	.423	1-0	1.000	0		-7	-0.3
1990	KC A	0	1	.000	3	0	0	0-1	2.1	4	4	1	1	2-1	1	15.43	25	.364	.500	0-0	—	0		-3	-0.5
1992	Phi N	0	0	—	8	0	0	0-0	11	10	10	5	0	10-0	9	8.18	43	.250	.392	0-0	—	0		-5	-0.3
Total	6	4	9	.308	94	5	0	6-7	156.1	169	98	26	5	79-14	117	5.24	77	.277	.362	14-2	.071	-1	62	-20	-2.0
BALLINGER, MARK Mark Alan B 1.31.1949 Glendale, CA BR/TR 6-6/205# d8.6																									
1971	Cle A	1	2	.333	18	0	0	0-0	34.2	30	21	3	1	13-1	25	4.67	82	.233	.303	5-0	.200	-0		-3	-0.3
BALLOU, WIN Noble Winfield B 11.30.1897 Mount Morgan, KY D 1.29.1963 San Francisco, CA BR/TL 5-10.5/170# d8.24																									
1925	†Was A	1	1	.500	10	1	1	0	27.2	38	17	1	0	13	13	4.55	93	.342	.411	7-0	.143	-0	80	-1	-0.1
1926	StL A	11	10	.524	43	14	5	2	154	186	99	12	4	71	59	4.79	90	.311	.387	42-4	.048	-3	83	-9	-1.2
1927	StL A	5	6	.455	21	11	4	0	90.1	105	56	4	1	46	17	4.78	91	.309	.393	28-1	.036	-4	66	-3	-0.7
1929	Bro N	2	3	.400	25	2	0	0	57.2	69	52	5	0	38	20	6.71	69	.304	.404	16-0	.063	-2	76	-14	-1.1
Total	4	19	20	.487	99	28	10	2	329.2	398	224	22	5	168	109	5.11	86	.312	.394	93-5	.054	-9	75	-27	-3.1
BALSAMO, TONY Anthony Fred B 11.21.1937 Brooklyn, NY BR/TR 6-2/185# d4.14																									
1962	Chi N	0	1	.000	18	0	0	0	29.1	34	22	1	1	20-2	27	6.44	64	.293	.396	5-0	.200	0		-6	-0.2
BAMBERGER, GEORGE George Irvin B 8.1.1925 Staten Island, NY BR/TR 6/175# d4.19 M7 C10																									
1951	NY N	0	0	—	2	0	0	0	2	4	4	2	0	2	1	18.00	22	.444	.545	0-0	—	0		-3	-0.1
1952	NY N	0	0	—	5	0	0	0	4	6	4	1	0	6	0	9.00	41	.353	.522	0-0	—	0*		-2	-0.1
1959	Bal A	0	0	—	3	1	0	1	8.1	15	7	1	0	2-0	2	7.56	50	.405	.436	2-0	.000	-0	163	-3	-0.2
Total	3	0	0	—	10	1	0	1	14.1	25	15	4	0	10-0	3	9.42	40	.397	.479	2-0	.000	-0	163	-8	-0.4
BANE, EDDIE Edward Norman B 3.22.1952 Chicago, IL BR/TL 5-9/160# d7.4																									
1973	Min A	0	5	.000	23	6	0	2-2	60.1	62	40	5	2	30-0	42	4.92	81	.270	.353	0-0	—	0	79	-7	-0.5
1975	Min A	3	1	.750	4	4	0	0-0	28.1	28	11	2	1	15-0	14	2.86	134	.262	.355	0-0	—	0	80	3	0.3
1976	Min A	4	7	.364	17	15	1	0-0	79.1	92	52	6	0	39-2	24	5.11	70	.290	.367	0-0	—	0*	134	-13	-1.7
Total	3	7	13	.350	44	25	1	2-2	168	182	103	13	3	84-2	80	4.66	81	.278	.360	0-0	—	0	110	-17	-1.9
BANEY, DICK Richard Lee B 11.1.1946 Fullerton, CA BR/TR 6/185# d7.11																									
1969	Sea A	1	0	1.000	9	1	0	0-0	18.2	21	8	2	0	7-1	9	3.86	94	.292	.346	2-1	.000	-0	97	0	0.0
1973	Cin N	2	1	.667	11	1	0	2-0	30.2	26	10	1	4	6-1	17	2.93	116	.234	.298	9-1	.222	1	52	2	0.2
1974	Cin N	1	0	1.000	22	1	0	1-0	41	51	27	4	0	17-2	12	5.49	64	.305	.366	5-1	.000	-1	175	-9	-0.6
Total	3	4	1	.800	42	3	0	3-0	90.1	98	45	7	4	30-4	38	4.28	82	.280	.340	16-3	.125	-0	109	-7	-0.4
BANKHEAD, DAN Daniel Robert B 5.3.1920 Empire, AL D 5.2.1976 Houston, TX BR/TR 6-1/184# d8.26																									
1947	†Bro N	0	0	—	4	0	0	1	10	15	8	1	1	8	6	7.20	57	.341	.453	4-0	.250	1*		-3	0.0
1950	Bro N	9	4	.692	41	12	2-1	3	129.1	119	84	16	2	88	96	5.50	75	.252	.371	39-0	.231	1	128	-19	-1.7
1951	Bro N	0	1	.000	7	1	0	0	14	27	24	5	0	14	9	15.43	25	.422	.526	2-0	.000	-0*	157	-17	-1.0
Total	3	9	5	.643	52	13	2-1	4	153.1	161	116	22	3	110	111	6.52	63	.277	.395	45-0	.222	2	130	-39	-2.7
BANKHEAD, SCOTT Michael Scott B 7.31.1963 Raleigh, NC BR/TR 5-10/185# d5.25																									
1986	KC A	8	9	.471	24	17	0	0-0	121	121	66	14	3	37-7	94	4.61	92	.259	.314	0-0	—	0	96	-4	-0.5
1987	Sea A	9	8	.529	27	25	2	0-0	149.1	168	96	35	3	37-0	95	5.42	87	.283	.326	0-0	—	0	98	-9	-1.0
1988	Sea A	7	9	.438	21	21	2-1	0-0	135	115	53	8	1	38-5	102	3.07	136	.224	.278	0-0	—	0	67	15	1.6
1989	Sea A	14	6	.700	33	33	3-2	0-0	210.1	187	84	19	3	63-1	140	3.34	121	.239	.295	0-0	—	0	101	18	1.5
1990	Sea A	0	2	.000	4	4	0	0-0	13	18	16	2	0	7-0	10	11.08	36	.333	.397	0-0	—	0	132	-9	-1.1
1991	Sea A	3	6	.333	17	9	0	0-0	60.2	73	35	8	2	21-2	28	4.90	84	.297	.354	0-0	—	0	74	-5	-0.6
1992	Cin N	10	4	.714	54	0	0	1-4	70.2	57	26	4	3	29-5	53	2.93	123	.218	.301	9-2	.222	0		5	0.9
1993	Bos A	2	1	.667	40	0	0	0-2	64.1	59	28	7	0	29-3	47	3.50	132	.250	.327	0-0	—	0		8	0.3
1994	Bos A	3	2	.600	27	0	0	0-0	37.2	34	21	5	0	12-3	25	4.54	111	.239	.295	0-0	—	0		2	0.2
1995	NY A	1	1	.500	20	1	0	0-0	39	44	26	9	0	16-0	20	6.00	77	.278	.343	0-0	—	0	141	-5	-0.3
Total	10	57	48	.543	267	110	7-3	1-6	901	876	451	111	15	289-26	614	4.18	103	.254	.311	9-2	.222	0	92	16	1.0
BANKS, BILL William John (b: William John Yerrick) B 2.26.1874 Danville, PA D 9.8.1936 Danville, PA BR/TR 5-11/150# d9.27																									
1895	Bos N	1	0	1.000	1	1	1	0	7	7	2	0	0	4	4	0.00	—	.259	.355	3-0	.000	-1	196	3	0.3
1896	Bos N	0	3	.000	4	3	2	0	23	42	31	2	2	13	6	10.57	43	.389	.463	11-0	.273	0	73	-11	-1.0
Total	2	1	3	.250	5	4	3	0	30	49	33	2	2	17	10	8.10	58	.363	.442	14-0	.214	-1	107	-8	-0.7
BANKS, WILLIE Willie Anthony B 2.27.1969 Jersey City, NJ BR/TR 6-1/202# d7.31																									
1991	Min A	1	1	.500	5	3	0	0-0	17.1	21	15	1	0	12-0	16	5.71	75	.288	.388	0-0	—	0	114	-4	-0.4
1992	Min A	4	4	.500	16	12	0	0-0	71	80	46	6	2	37-0	37	5.70	71	.288	.370	0-0	—	0	86	-11	-1.1
1993	Min A	11	12	.478	31	30	0	0-0	171.1	186	91	17	3	78-2	138	4.04	108	.280	.356	0-0	—	0	98	3	0.3
1994	Chi N	8	12	.400	23	23	1-1	0-0	138.1	139	88	16	2	56-3	91	5.40	77	.261	.332	41-7	.122	-1	80	-19	-2.4
1995	Chi N	0	1	.000	10	0	0	0-1	11.2	27	23	5	0	12-4	9	15.43	27	.458	.542	1-0	.000	-0		-15	-1.1
	LA N	0	2	.000	6	6	0	0-0	29	36	21	2	1	16-2	23	4.03	94	.303	.387	8-1	.125	0	139	-4	-0.2
	Fla N	2	3	.400	9	9	0	0-0	50	43	27	7	1	30-1	30	4.32	98	.235	.344	17-0	.353	2*	67	-1	0.1
	Year	2	6	.250	25	15	0	0-1	90.2	106	30	14	2	58-7	62	5.66	72	.294	.392	26-1	.269	2	93	-20	-1.2
1997	NY A	3	0	1.000	5	1	0	0-1	14	9	3	0	1	6-0	8	1.93	231	.188	.291	0-0	—	0	83	4	0.9
1998	NY A	1	1	.500	9	0	0	0-0	14.1	20	16	4	1	12-2	8	10.05	44	.323	.440	0-0	—	0		-9	-1.0
	Ari N	1	2	.333	33	0	0	1-1	43.2	34	21	2	1	25-2	32	3.09	136	.217	.326	1-0	.000	-0		3	0.2
2001	Bos A	0	0	—	5	0	0	0-0	10.2	5	4	0	0	4-0	10	0.84	532	.132	.214	0-0	—	0		3	0.1
2002	Bos A	2	1	.667	29	0	0	1-0	39	32	15	5	3	14-0	26	3.23	139	.222	.302	0-0	—	0		6	0.4
Total	9	33	39	.458	181	84	1-1	2-3	610.1	632	370	65	15	302-16	428	4.75	89	.268	.353	68-8	.176	1	90	-44	-4.2
BANNISTER, FLOYD Floyd Franklin B 6.10.1955 Pierre, SD BL/TL 6-1/195# d4.19																									
1977	Hou N	8	9	.471	24	23	4-1	0-0	142.2	138	70	11	4	68-1	112	4.04	88	.254	.339	48-6	.188	0	145	-7	-0.8
1978	Hou N	3	9	.250	28	16	2-2	0-0	110.1	120	59	13	1	63-4	94	4.81	69	.280	.372	31-5	.161	0	80	-17	-1.8
1979	Sea A	10	15	.400	30	30	6-2	0-0	182.1	185	92	25	4	68-4	115	4.05	108	.260	.327	0-0	—	0	81	6	0.7
1980	Sea A	9	13	.409	32	32	8	0-0	217.2	200	96	24	2	66-6	155	3.47	119	.239	.295	0-0	—	0	72	15	1.4
1981	Sea A	9	9	.500	21	20	5-2	0-0	121.1	128	62	14	3	39-0	85	4.45	87	.268	.327	0-0	—	0	80	-6	-0.8
1982	Sea A★	12	13	.480	35	35	5-3	0-0	247	225	112	32	3	77-0	**209**	3.43	124	.243	.301	0-0	—	0	99	19	1.7
1983	†Chi A	16	10	.615	34	34	5-2	0-0	217.1	191	88	19	2	71-3	193	3.35	125	.233	.294	0-0	—	0	103	20	2.2
1984	Chi A	14	11	.560	34	33	4	0-0	218	211	127	30	6	80-2	152	4.83	86	.252	.318	1-0	.000	-0	100	-15	-1.6
1985	Chi A	10	14	.417	34	34	4-1	0-0	210.2	211	121	30	4	100-5	198	4.87	89	.261	.343	0-0	—	0	96	-11	-1.1

Year	Tm Lg	W	L	Pct	G	GS	CG-Sho	SV-BS	IP	H	R	HR	HB	BB-IB	SO	ERA	AERA	OAV	OOB	AB-SH	AVG	PB	Sup	APR	PW
1986	Chi A	10	14	.417	28	27	6-1	0-0	165.1	162	81	17	2	48-0	92	3.54	122	.259	.311	0-0	—	0	69	10	1.3
1987	Chi A	16	11	.593	34	34	11-2	0-0	228.2	216	100	38	0	49-0	124	3.58	128	.246	.285	0-0	—	0	90	24	2.4
1988	KC A	12	13	.480	31	31	2	0-0	189.1	182	102	22	5	68-6	113	4.33	92	.248	.316	0-0	—	0	93	-7	-0.8
1989	KC A	4	1	.800	14	14	0	0-0	75.1	87	40	8	1	18-1	35	4.66	83	.290	.330	0-0	—	0	112	-5	-0.3
1991	Cal A	0	0	—	16	0	0	0-0	25	25	12	5	0	10-1	16	3.96	104	.266	.337	0-0	—	0		0	0.0
1992	Tex A	1	1	.500	36	0	0	0-1	37	39	27	3	3	21-6	30	6.32	60	.281	.371	0-0	—	0		-10	-0.5
Total	15	134	143	.484	431	363	62-16	0-1	2388	2320	1189	291	40	846-39	1723	4.06	102	.253	.317	80-11	.175	0	93	16	2.0
BANNON, JIMMY James Henry "Foxy Grandpa" B 5.5.1871 Amesbury, MA D 3.24.1948 Glen Rock, NJ BR/TR 5-5/160# d6.15 b-Tom ▲																									
1893	StL N	0	1	.000	1	1	0	0	4	10	18	1	2	5	1	22.50	21	.455	.586	107	.336	0*	370	-9	-0.9
1894	Bos N	0	0	—	1	0	0	0	2	4	3	1	0	1	0	0.00	—	.400	.455	494-6	.336	0*		0	0.0
1895	Bos N	0	0	—	1	0	0	0	3	4	2	0	0	2	1	6.00	85	.308	.400	493-12	.347	0*		0	0.0
Total	3	0	1	.000	3	1	0	0	9	18	23	2	2	8	2	12.00	42	.400	.509	1094-18	.341	1	370	-9	-0.9
BANTA, JACK Jackie Kay B 6.24.1925 Hutchinson, KS BL/TR 6-2.5/175# d9.18																									
1947	Bro N	0	1	.000	3	1	0	0	7.2	7	6	1	1	4	3	7.04	59	.226	.333	2-0	.000	-0	149	-2	-0.2
1948	Bro N	0	1	.000	2	1	0	0	3.1	5	6	0	0	5	1	8.10	49	.385	.556	1-0	.000	-0	0	-3	-0.5
1949	†Bro N	10	6	.625	48	12	2-1	3	152.1	125	63	12	6	68	97	3.37	122	.223	.314	46-1	.109	-2	102	12	1.0
1950	Bro N	4	4	.500	16	5	1	2	41.1	39	22	2	3	36	15	4.35	94	.252	.402	12-0	.167	-0	134	-1	-0.3
Total	4	14	12	.538	69	19	3-1	5	204.2	176	97	15	10	113	116	3.78	108	.232	.339	61-1	.115	-2	108	6	0.0
BAPTIST, TRAVIS Travis Steven B 12.30.1971 Forest Grove, OR BL/TL 6/195# d8.1																									
1998	Min A	0	1	.000	13	0	0	0-0	27	34	18	5	0	11-1	11	5.67	84	.321	.366	0-0	—	0		-3	-0.1
BARBER, BRIAN Brian Scott B 3.4.1973 Hamilton, OH BR/TR 6-1/170# d8.12																									
1995	StL N	2	1	.667	9	4	0	0-0	29.1	31	17	4	0	16-0	27	5.22	80	.279	.362	8-0	.125	-0	140	-2	-0.2
1996	StL N	0	0	—	1	1	0	0-0	3	4	5	0	1	6-0	1	15.00	28	.364	.550	0-0	—	0	129	-3	-0.2
1998	KC A	2	4	.333	8	8	0	0-0	42	45	28	5	1	13-1	24	6.00	80	.276	.328	0-0	—	0	67	-4	-0.5
1999	KC A	1	3	.250	8	3	0	1-0	18.2	31	20	6	2	10-2	7	9.64	52	.383	.457	0-1	—	0	124	-9	-1.4
Total	4	5	8	.385	26	16	0	1-0	93	111	70	15	4	45-3	59	6.77	69	.303	.377	8-1	.125	-0	99	-18	-2.3
BARBER, STEVE Stephen David B 2.22.1938 Takoma Park, MD BL/TL 6/200# d4.21																									
1960	Bal A	10	7	.588	36	27	6-1	2	181.2	148	78	10	3	113-1	112	3.22	118	.226	.340	54-4	.056	-4	90	10	0.5
1961	Bal A	18	12	.600	37	34	14-**8**	1	248.1	194	102	13	2	130-4	150	3.33	115	.218	.317	80-9	.162	2	95	15	2.2
1962	Bal A	9	6	.600	28	19	5-2	0	140.1	145	66	9	1	61-2	89	3.46	107	.262	.335	42-5	.071	-2	107	2	0.0
1963	Bal A❖	20	13	.606	39	36	11-2	0	258.2	253	99	12	4	92-10	180	2.75	126	.258	.323	87-5	.138	-0	92	17	2.2
1964	Bal A	9	13	.409	36	26	4	1	157	144	72	15	7	81-5	118	3.84	93	.248	.345	47-1	.149	1	80	-4	-0.3
1965	Bal A	15	10	.600	37	32	7-2	0	220.2	177	79	16	2	81-5	130	2.69	129	.224	.294	65-6	.077	-2	83	19	2.0
1966	Bal A☆	10	5	.667	25	22	5-3	0	133.1	104	38	6	3	49-1	91	2.30	145	.218	.294	44-7	.068	-3	124	16	1.5
1967	Bal A	4	9	.308	15	15	1-1	0	74.2	47	39	5	5	61-2	48	4.10	77	.185	.351	22-1	.091	-1	83	-9	-1.5
	NY A	6	9	.400	17	17	3-1	0	97.2	103	47	4	3	54-3	70	4.05	77	.278	.371	29-2	.172	1	75	-9	-1.2
	Year	10	18	.357	32	32	4-2	0	172.1	150	50	9	8	115-5	118	4.07	77	.240	.363	51-3	.137	1	79	-16	-2.7
1968	NY A	6	5	.545	20	19	3-1	0	128.1	127	63	7	3	64-4	87	3.23	90	.256	.342	39-2	.051	-1	117	-9	-0.8
1969	Sea A	4	7	.364	25	16	0	0-0	86.1	99	51	9	1	48-2	69	4.80	76	.292	.379	25-1	.200	1	100	-11	-1.1
1970	Chi N	0	1	.000	5	0	0	0-0	5.2	10	6	0	0	6-3	3	9.53	47	.417	.533	0-0	—	0		-3	-0.4
	Atl N	0	1	.000	5	2	0	0-0	14.2	17	10	3	1	5-0	11	4.91	88	.288	.354	4-0	.250	0	115	-1	-0.1
	Year	0	2	.000	10	2	0	0-0	20.1	27	16	3	1	11-3	14	6.20	70	.325	.411	4-0	.250	0	113	-4	-0.5
1971	Atl N	3	1	.750	39	3	0	2-0	75	92	42	6	2	25-2	40	4.80	77	.301	.356	13-0	.154	-0	127	-7	-0.4
1972	Atl N	0	0	—	5	0	0	0-0	15.2	18	10	1	1	6-0	6	5.74	66	.290	.357	5-0	.200	-0		-3	-0.1
	Cal A	4	4	.500	34	3	0	2-2	58	37	16	4	1	30-11	34	2.02	145	.188	.297	7-2	.143	1	61	6	0.9
1973	Cal A	3	2	.600	50	1	0	4-2	89.1	90	40	5	3	32-3	58	3.53	101	.265	.332	0-0	—	0	76	0	0.0
1974	SF N	0	1	.000	13	0	0	1-0	13.2	13	12	0	0	12-1	13	5.27	72	.255	.391	0-0	—	0		-3	-0.3
Total	15	121	106	.533	466	272	59-21	13-4	1999	1818	870	125	42	950-59	1309	3.36	105	.245	.332	563-45	.115	-6	94	26	3.1
BARBER, STEVE Steven Lee B 3.13.1948 Grand Rapids, MI BR/TR 6-1/190# d4.9																									
1970	Min A	0	0	—	18	0	0	2-0	27.1	26	14	1	2	18-2	14	4.61	81	.263	.377	2-1	.000	-0*		-2	-0.1
1971	Min A	1	0	1.000	4	2	0	0-0	11.2	8	9	2	0	13-1	4	6.17	58	.190	.382	5-0	.000	-1*	139	-3	-0.3
Total	2	1	0	1.000	22	2	0	2-0	39	34	23	3	2	31-3	18	5.08	72	.241	.379	7-1	.000	-1	139	-5	-0.4
BARBERICH, FRANK Frank Frederick B 2.3.1882 Newtown, NY D 5.1.1965 Ocala, FL BB/TR 5-10.5/175# d9.17																									
1907	Bos N	1	1	.500	2	2	1	0	12.1	19	10	0	0	5	1	5.84	44	.358	.414	4-1	.000	-0	167	-4	-0.6
1910	Bos A	0	0	—	2	0	0	0	5	7	6	0	0	2	0	7.20	35	.350	.409	1-0	.000	-0		-3	-0.1
Total	2	1	1	.500	4	2	1	0	17.1	26	16	0	0	7	1	6.23	41	.356	.412	5-1	.000	-1	167	-7	-0.7
BARCELO, LORENZO Lorenzo Antonio B 8.10.1977 San Pedro De Macoris, D.R. BR/TR 6-4/220# d7.22																									
2000	†Chi A	4	2	.667	22	1	0	0-1	39	34	17	5	0	9-1	26	3.69	135	.231	.274	0-0	—	0	94	6	0.7
2001	Chi A	1	0	1.000	17	0	0	0-0	21	24	13	1	1	8-2	15	4.71	98	.282	.347	0-0	—	0		-1	0.0
2002	Chi A	0	1	.000	4	0	0	0-0	6	9	6	1	0	1-0	1	9.00	50	.333	.357	0-0	—	0		-3	-0.3
Total	3	5	3	.625	43	1	0	0-1	66	67	36	7	1	18-3	42	4.50	107	.259	.307	0-0	—	0	94	2	0.4
BARCLAY, CURT Curtis Cordell B 8.22.1931 Chicago, IL D 3.25.1985 Missoula, MT BR/TR 6-3/210# d4.21																									
1957	NY N	9	9	.500	37	28	5-2	0	183	196	85	21	2	48-4	67	3.44	114	.274	.319	58-1	.190	0	94	7	0.8
1958	SF N	1	0	1.000	6	1	0	0	16	16	5	3	3	5-3	6	2.81	136	.258	.343	6-0	.667	2	188	2	0.4
1959	SF N	0	0	—	1	0	0	0	0.1	2	5	0	0	2-0	0	54.00	7	.500	.667	0-0	—	0		-3	-0.1
Total	3	10	9	.526	44	29	5-2	0	199.1	214	95	24	5	55-7	73	3.48	113	.274	.323	64-1	.234	2	97	6	1.1
BARE, RAY Raymond Douglas B 4.15.1949 Miami, FL D 3.29.1994 Miami, FL BR/TR 6-2/195# d7.30																									
1972	StL N	0	1	.000	14	0	0	1-1	16.2	18	2	0	0	6-2	5	0.54	630	.281	.343	0-0	—	0		5	0.3
1974	StL N	1	2	.333	10	3	0	0-0	24.1	25	17	2	0	9-0	6	5.92	61	.281	.343	5-0	.200	-0	81	-6	-0.6
1975	Det A	8	13	.381	29	21	6-1	0-0	150.2	174	81	10	1	47-5	71	4.48	90	.293	.343	0-0	—	0	76	-4	-0.5
1976	Det A	7	8	.467	30	21	3-2	0-0	134	157	85	13	0	51-6	59	4.63	80	.293	.353	0-0	—	0	106	-15	-1.5
1977	Det A	0	2	.000	5	4	0	0-0	14.1	24	21	3	0	7-1	4	12.56	34	.381	.443	0-0	—	0	94	-12	-1.2
Total	5	16	26	.381	88	49	9-3	1-1	340	398	206	28	1	120-14	145	4.79	80	.296	.351	5-0	.200	-0	91	-32	-3.5
BARFIELD, JOHN John David B 10.15.1964 Pine Bluff, AR BL/TL 6-1/185# d9.7																									
1989	Tex A	0	1	.000	4	2	0	0-0	11.2	15	10	0	0	4-0	9	6.17	64	.319	.373	0-0	—	0	103	-3	-0.2
1990	Tex A	4	3	.571	33	0	0	1-0	44.1	42	25	2	1	13-3	17	4.67	84	.268	.320	0-0	—	0		-3	-0.5
1991	Tex A	4	4	.500	28	9	0	1-0	83.1	96	51	11	0	22-3	27	4.54	89	.289	.330	0-0	—	0	133	-7	-0.6
Total	3	8	8	.500	65	11	0	2-0	139.1	153	86	13	1	39-6	53	4.72	85	.285	.330	0-0	—	0	129	-13	-1.3
BARFOOT, CLYDE Clyde Raymond "Foots" B 7.8.1891 Richmond, VA D 3.11.1971 Highland Park, CA BR/TR 6/170# d4.13																									
1922	StL N	4	5	.444	42	2	1	2	117.2	139	75	2	10	30	19	4.21	92	.307	.363	34-0	.353	5	148	-8	-0.1
1923	StL N	3	3	.500	33	2	1-1	1	101.1	112	49	7	1	27	23	3.73	105	.289	.337	37-1	.189	-1*	168	3	0.1
1926	Det A	1	2	.333	11	1	0	2	31.1	42	27	4	0	9	7	4.88	83	.318	.362	5-0	.200	0	104	-5	-0.5
Total	3	8	10	.444	86	5	2-1	5	250.1	293	151	13	11	66	49	4.10	95	.301	.353	76-1	.263	4	147	-10	-0.5
BARGAR, GREG Greg Robert B 1.27.1959 Inglewood, CA BR/TR 6-2/185# d7.17																									
1983	Mon N	2	0	1.000	8	3	0	0-0	20	23	15	6	1	8-0	9	6.75	53	.271	.340	6-0	.167	-0	139	-6	-0.6
1984	Mon N	0	1	.000	3	1	0	0-0	8	8	7	1	0	7-1	2	7.88	44	.286	.417	1-0	.000	-0	26	-4	-0.4
1986	StL N	0	2	.000	22	0	0	0-0	27.1	36	19	3	3	10-1	12	5.60	65	.330	.395	2-0	.000	-0		-6	-0.4
Total	3	2	3	.400	33	4	0	0-0	55.1	67	41	10	4	25-2	23	6.34	57	.302	.378	9-0	.111	-0	111	-16	-1.4
BARGER, CY Eros Bolivar B 5.18.1885 Jamestown, KY D 9.23.1964 Columbia, KY BL/TR 6/160# d8.30																									
1906	NY A	0	0	—	2	1	0	1	5.1	7	8	0	0	3	3	10.13	29	.318	.400	3-0	.333	0	218	-4	-0.2
1907	NY A	0	0	—	1	0	0	0	6	10	2	0	1	1	0	3.00	93	.370	.414	2-0	.000	-0		0	-0.1
1910	Bro N	15	15	.500	35	30	25-2	1	271.2	267	105	2	6	107	87	2.88	105	.275	.351	104-3	.231	3*	78	7	1.2

Year	Tm Lg	W	L	Pct	G	GS	CG-Sho	SV-BS	IP	H	R	HR	HB	BB-IB	SO	ERA	AERA	OAV	OOB	AB-SH	AVG	PB	Sup	APR	PW
1911	Bro N	11	15	.423	30	30	21-1	0	217.1	224	112	4	7	71	60	3.52	95	.279	.342	145-5	.228	1*	82	-6	-0.4
1912	Bro N	1	9	.100	16	11	6	0	94	120	78	4	4	42	30	5.46	61	.326	.401	37-0	.189	-0*	76	-23	-2.0
1914	Pit F	10	16	.385	33	26	18-1	1	228.1	252	125	7	6	63	70	4.34	66	.290	.342	83-1	.205	-1*	78	-31	-3.4
1915	Pit F	9	8	.529	34	13	8-1	6	153	130	49	1	4	47	47	2.29	118	.238	.303	54-0	.278	2*	83	7	0.9
Total	7	46	63	.422	151	111	78-5	9	975.2	1010	479	18	28	334	297	3.56	85	.280	.346	428-9	.227	5	81	-50	-4.0
BARK, BRIAN Brian Stuart B 8.26.1968 Baltimore, MD BL/TL 5-9/170# d7.6																									
1995	Bos A	0	0	—	3	0	0	0-0	2.1	2	0	0	0	1-0	0	0.00	—	.286	.375	0-0	—	0		1	0.1
BARKER, LEN Leonard Harold B 7.7.1955 Fort Knox, KY BR/TR 6-5/225# d9.14																									
1976	Tex A	1	0	1.000	2	2	1-1	0-0	15	7	4	0	2	6-0	7	2.40	150	.149	.273	0-0	—	0	86	2	0.1
1977	Tex A	4	1	.800	15	3	0	1-1	47.1	36	15	1	1	24-3	51	2.66	154	.217	.318	0-0	—	0	168	8	0.8
1978	Tex A	1	5	.167	29	0	0	4-2	52.1	63	31	6	2	29-2	33	4.82	78	.304	.395	0-0	—	0		-6	-0.7
1979	Cle A	6	6	.500	29	19	2	0-0	137.1	146	79	6	2	70-1	93	4.92	87	.277	.360	0-0	—	0	96	-8	-0.7
1980	Cle A	19	12	.613	36	36	8-1	0-0	246.1	237	127	17	3	92-3	**187**	4.17	98	.252	.318	0-0	—	0	101	-4	-0.5
1981	Cle A★	8	7	.533	22	22	9-3	0-0	154.1	150	72	7	1	46-0	**127**	3.91	93	.249	.301	0-0	—	0	132	-4	-0.4
1982	Cle A	15	11	.577	33	33	10-1	0-0	244.2	211	117	17	3	88-2	187	3.90	105	.232	.299	0-0	—	0	103	6	0.5
1983	Cle A	8	13	.381	24	24	4-1	0-0	149.2	150	92	16	2	52-3	105	5.11	83	.266	.327	0-0	—	0	94	-13	-1.6
	Atl N	1	3	.250	6	6	0	0-0	33	31	17	0	0	14-2	21	3.82	102	.248	.321	8-2	.125	-0	80	-1	-0.1
1984	Atl N	7	8	.467	21	20	1	0-0	126.1	120	59	10	2	38-2	95	3.85	100	.254	.309	38-4	.053	-1	102	1	0.2
1985	Atl N	2	9	.182	20	18	0	0-0	73.2	84	55	10	1	37-1	47	6.35	61	.288	.369	17-0	.000	-2	66	-17	-2.5
1987	Mil A	2	1	.667	11	11	0	0-0	43.2	54	27	6	2	17-1	22	5.36	86	.303	.371	0-0	—	0	98	-3	-0.2
Total	11	74	76	.493	248	194	35-7	5-3	1323.2	1289	695	96	21	513-20	975	4.34	93	.256	.325	63-6	.048	-3	100	-39	-5.1
BARKER, RICHIE Richard Frank B 10.29.1972 Revere, MA BR/TR 6-2/210# d4.25																									
1999	Chi N	0	0	—	5	0	0	0-0	5	6	4	0	0	4-1	3	7.20	63	.300	.400	0-0	—	0		-1	-0.1
BARKLEY, BRIAN Brian Edward B 12.8.1975 Conroe, TX BL/TL 6-2/180# d5.28 gf-Red																									
1998	Bos A	0	0	—	6	0	0	0-0	11	16	13	2	1	9-1	2	9.82	48	.340	.441	0-0	—	0		-6	-0.3
BARKLEY, JEFF Jeffrey Carver B 11.21.1959 Hickory, NC BB/TR 6-3/185# d9.16																									
1984	Cle A	0	0	—	3	0	0	0-0	4	6	3	0	0	1-0	4	6.75	61	.353	.368	0-0	—	0		-1	0.0
1985	Cle A	0	3	.000	21	0	0	1-3	41	37	26	5	0	15-3	30	5.27	79	.243	.308	0-0	—	0		-5	-0.3
Total	2	0	3	.000	24	0	0	1-3	45	43	29	5	0	16-3	34	5.40	77	.254	.314	0-0	—	0		-6	-0.3
BARLOW, MIKE Michael Roswell B 4.30.1948 Stamford, NY BL/TR 6-6/215# d6.18																									
1975	StL N	0	0	—	9	0	0	0-0	7.2	11	6	0	1	3-1	2	4.70	80	.355	.405	0-0	—	0		-1	-0.1
1976	Hou N	2	2	.500	16	0	0	0-1	22	27	13	0	0	17-1	11	4.50	71	.318	.431	3-0	.000	-0		-4	-0.6
1977	Cal A	4	2	.667	20	1	0	1-0	59	53	33	3	4	27-6	25	4.58	86	.249	.343	0-0	—	0	92	-4	-0.3
1978	Cal A	0	0	—	1	0	0	0-0	2	3	1	0	0	0-0	1	4.50	80	.375	.375	0-0	—	0		0	0.0
1979	†Cal A	1	1	.500	35	0	0	0-0	86	106	54	8	4	30-2	33	5.13	80	.314	.373	0-0	—	0		-10	-0.5
1980	Tor A	3	1	.750	40	1	0	5-2	55	57	29	4	2	21-4	19	4.09	105	.273	.343	0-0	—	0	83	1	0.1
1981	Tor A	0	0	—	12	0	0	0-1	15	22	11	1	4	6-1	5	4.20	94	.338	.416	0-0	—	0		-2	-0.1
Total	7	10	6	.625	133	2	0	6-4	246.2	279	147	16	15	104-15	96	4.63	86	.294	.370	3-0	.000	-0	90	-20	-1.5
BARNABE, CHUCK Charles Edward B 6.12.1900 Russell Gulch, CO D 8.16.1977 Waco, TX BL/TL 5-11.5/164# d4.14																									
1927	Chi A	0	5	.000	17	4	1	0	61	86	46	2	5	20	5	5.31	76	.351	.411	19-1	.158	1*	72	-10	-0.6
1928	Chi A	0	2	.000	7	2	0	0	9.2	17	9	0	1	0	3	6.52	62	.395	.409	8-0	.500	2*	52	-3	-0.2
Total	2	0	7	.000	24	6	1	0	70.2	103	55	2	6	20	8	5.48	74	.358	.411	27-1	.259	3	65	-13	-0.8
BARNES, BRIAN Brian Keith B 3.25.1967 Roanoke Rapids, NC BL/TL 5-9/170# d9.14																									
1990	Mon N	1	1	.500	4	4	1	0-0	28	25	10	2	0	7-0	23	2.89	126	.236	.283	9-0	.000	-1	93	2	0.1
1991	Mon N	5	8	.385	28	27	1	0-0	160	135	82	16	6	84-2	117	4.22	86	.233	.333	49-3	.082	-1	86	-10	-0.7
1992	Mon N	6	6	.500	21	17	0	0-0	100	77	34	9	3	46-1	65	2.97	117	.213	.306	29-6	.276	2	107	7	1.1
1993	Mon N	2	6	.250	52	8	0	3-2	100	105	53	9	0	48-2	60	4.41	95	.274	.353	20-2	.150	-0	84	0	-0.1
1994	Cle A	0	1	.000	6	0	0	0-0	13.1	12	10	2	0	15-2	5	5.40	87	.235	.403	0-0	—	0		-1	-0.1
	LA N	0	0	—	5	0	0	0-0	5	10	4	1	0	4-1	5	7.20	55	.400	.483	0-0	—	0		-2	-0.1
Total	5	14	22	.389	116	56	2	3-2	406.1	364	193	39	9	204-8	275	3.94	95	.242	.334	107-11	.140	1	90	-4	0.2
BARNES, FRANK Frank B 8.26.1926 Longwood, MS BR/TR 6/170# d9.22																									
1957	StL N	0	1	.000	3	1	0	0	10	13	5	0	0	9-1	5	4.50	88	.317	.440	2-0	.000	-0*	67	0	-0.1
1958	StL N	1	1	.500	8	1	0	0	19	19	16	3	2	16-0	17	7.58	54	.260	.402	6-0	.167	-0*	131	-6	-0.6
1960	StL N	0	1	.000	4	1	0	1	7.2	8	5	1	1	9-0	8	3.52	116	.267	.450	2-0	.000	-0	0	0	-0.1
Total	3	1	3	.250	15	3	0	1	36.2	40	26	4	3	34-1	30	5.89	69	.278	.423	10-0	.100	-1	65	-6	-0.8
BARNES, FRANK Frank Samuel "Lefty" B 1.9.1900 Dallas, TX D 9.27.1967 Houston, TX BL/TL 6-2.5/195# d4.18																									
1929	Det A	0	1	.000	4	1	0	0	5	10	8	0	1	3	0	7.20	60	.400	.483	1-0	.000	-0	59	-3	-0.5
1930	NY A	0	1	.000	2	2	0	0	12.1	13	11	0	1	13	2	8.03	54	.283	.450	6-0	.333	1*	130	-4	-0.1
Total	2	0	2	.000	6	3	0	0	17.1	23	19	0	2	16	2	7.79	55	.324	.461	7-0	.286	1	106	-7	-0.6
BARNES, JESSE Jesse Lawrence "Nubby" B 8.26.1892 Perkins, OK D 9.9.1961 Santa Rosa, NM BL/TR 6/170# d7.30 Mil 1918 b-Virgil																									
1915	Bos N	3	0	1.000	9	3	2	0	45.1	41	14	1	4	10	16	1.39	186	.244	.302	17-1	.176	0	124	5	0.3
1916	Bos N	6	15	.286	33	18	9-3	1	163	154	63	3	5	37	55	2.37	105	.254	.302	48-2	.188	0	97	-1	0.2
1917	Bos N	13	21	.382	50	33	26-2	1	295	261	115	3	3	50	107	2.68	95	.241	.277	101-1	.238	4*	83	-7	-0.1
1918	NY N	6	1	.857	9	9	4-2	0	54.2	53	15	0	0	13	12	1.81	145	.255	.299	18-3	.222	-0	141	5	0.7
1919	NY N	**25**	9	.735	38	34	23-4	1	295.2	263	98	8	2	35	92	2.40	117	.236	.260	120-7	.267	5*	127	14	2.4
1920	NY N	20	15	.571	43	34	23-2	0	292.2	271	108	9	2	56	63	2.64	113	.250	.288	108-4	.204	-2*	109	11	1.2
1921	†NY N	15	9	.625	42	31	15-1	6	258.2	298	108	13	3	44	56	3.10	118	.299	.331	92-4	.207	-1	125	15	1.3
1922	†NY N	13	8	.619	37	29	14-2	1	212.2	236	108	10	3	38	52	3.51	114	.278	.311	77-4	.182	-1	127	9	0.8
1923	NY N	3	1	.750	12	4	1	1	36	48	25	1	0	13	12	6.25	61	.329	.384	11-0	.273	0	161	-9	-0.8
	Bos N	10	14	.417	31	23	12-5	2	195.1	204	86	8	0	43	41	2.76	144	.270	.310	68-1	.147	-4	81	21	2.2
	Year	13	15	.464	43	27	13-5	3	231.1	252	90	9	0	56	53	3.31	120	.280	.322	79-1	.165	-4	92	10	1.4
1924	Bos N	15	20	.429	37	32	21-**4**	0	267.2	292	115	7	0	53	49	3.23	118	.284	.319	90-9	.222	-1	76	16	1.9
1925	Bos N	11	16	.407	32	28	17	0	216.1	255	127	14	1	63	55	4.53	88	.297	.346	81-3	.198	-1	95	-12	-1.3
1926	Bro N	10	11	.476	31	24	10-1	1	158	204	104	6	2	35	29	5.24	73	.321	.358	59-1	.237	-0	108	-22	-2.5
1927	Bro N	2	10	.167	18	10	2	0	78.2	106	64	5	0	25	14	5.72	69	.331	.380	23-1	.217	-0	67	-17	-2.2
Total	13	152	150	.503	422	312	179-26	13	2569.2	2686	1150	88	25	515	653	3.22	104	.273	.310	913-41	.214	1	105	28	4.1
BARNES, JUNIE Junie Shoaf "Lefty" B 12.1.1911 Linwood, NC D 12.31.1963 Jacksonville, NC BL/TL 5-11.5/170# d9.12																									
1934	Cin N	0	0	—	2	0	0	0	0.1	0	0	0	0	1	0	0.00	—	.000	.500	0-0	—	0		0	0.0
BARNES, RICH Richard Monroe B 7.21.1959 Palm Beach, FL BR/TL 6-4/186# d7.18																									
1982	Chi A	0	2	.000	6	2	0	1-0	17	21	15	1	2	4-0	6	4.76	85	.292	.342	0-0	—	0	45	-3	-0.4
1983	Cle A	1	1	.500	4	2	0	0-0	11.2	18	10	0	0	10-2	2	6.94	61	.375	.475	0-0	—	0	128	-3	-0.5
Total	2	1	3	.250	10	4	0	1-0	28.2	39	25	1	2	14-2	8	5.65	73	.325	.399	0-0	—	0	88	-6	-0.9
BARNES, BOB Robert Avery "Lefty" B 1.6.1902 Washburn, IL D 12.8.1993 Peoria, IL BL/TL 5-11.5/150# d7.8																									
1924	Chi A	0	0	—	2	0	0	0	4.2	14	11	1	0	0	1	19.29	21	.519	.519	2-0	.000	-0		-8	-0.4
BARNES, VIRGIL Virgil Jennings "Zeke" B 3.5.1897 Ontario, KS D 7.24.1958 Wichita, KS BR/TR 6/165# d9.25 b-Jesse																									
1919	NY N	0	0	—	1	0	0	0	2	6	4	0	0	1	1	18.00	16	.545	.583	0-0	—	0		-3	-0.2
1920	NY N	0	1	.000	1	1	0	0	7	9	3	0	0	1	2	3.86	78	.310	.333	1-1	.000	-0	52	0	-0.1
1922	NY N	1	0	1.000	22	2	1	2	51.2	46	27	1	0	11	16	3.48	115	.243	.285	12-1	.167	-1	214	2	0.1
1923	†NY N	2	3	.400	22	2	0	1	53	59	31	2	0	19	6	3.91	98	.285	.345	14-0	.000	-2	86	-3	-0.4
1924	†NY N	16	10	.615	35	29	15-1	3	229.1	239	87	10	0	57	59	3.06	120	.270	.314	77-4	.182	-2	139	18	1.8
1925	NY N	15	11	.577	32	27	17-1	2	221.2	242	110	9	1	53	53	3.53	114	.281	.323	89-2	.101	-9	114	10	0.1

Year	Tm Lg	W	L	Pct	G	GS	CG-Sho	SV-BS	IP	H	R	HR	HB	BB-IB	SO	ERA	AERA	OAV	OOB	AB-SH	AVG	PB	Sup	APR	PW
1926	NY N	8	13	.381	31	25	9-2	1	185	183	73	4	3	56	54	2.87	131	.261	.318	56-1	.054	-7	78	17	1.0
1927	NY N	14	11	.560	35	29	12-2	2	228.2	251	116	14	4	51	66	3.98	97	.283	.325	83-4	.108	-7	110	-2	-0.9
1928	NY N	3	3	.500	10	9	3-1	0	55.1	71	32	3	0	18	11	5.04	78	.330	.382	22-0	.091	-2	127	-5	-0.7
	Bos N	2	7	.222	16	10	1	0	60.1	86	42	3	0	26	7	5.82	67	.344	.406	17-2	.059	-2	87	-11	-1.5
	Year	5	10	.333	26	19	4-1	0	115.2	157	46	6	0	44	18	5.45	72	.338	.395	39-2	.077	-3	106	-17	-2.2
Total	9	61	59	.508	205	134	58-7	11	1094	1192	525	46	8	293	275	3.66	105	.282	.329	371-15	.108	-31	111	23	-0.8
BARNEY, REX Rex Edward B 12.19.1924 Omaha, NE D 8.12.1997 Baltimore, MD BR/TR 6-3/185# d8.18 Mil 1944-45																									
1943	Bro N	2	2	.500	9	8	1	0	45.1	36	32	4	2	41	23	6.35	53	.217	.378	18-0	.056	-2	139	-13	-1.2
1946	Bro N	2	5	.286	16	9	1	0	53.2	46	42	2	0	51	36	5.87	58	.240	.399	17-0	.235	1	93	-15	-1.7
1947	†Bro N	5	2	.714	28	9	0	0	77.2	66	52	4	2	59	36	4.75	87	.240	.378	27-0	.111	-1	159	-7	-0.8
1948	Bro N	15	13	.536	44	34	12-4	0	246.2	193	101	17	6	122	138	3.10	129	.217	.315	84-4	.167	-2	102	23	1.9
1949	†Bro N	9	8	.529	38	20	6-2	1	140.2	108	75	15	3	89	80	4.41	93	.216	.338	47-3	.213	0	128	-5	-0.6
1950	Bro N	2	1	.667	20	1	0	0	33.2	25	26	6	2	48	23	6.42	64	.214	.449	8-0	.125	0	151	-9	-0.7
Total	6	35	31	.530	155	81	20-6	1	597.2	474	328	48	15	410	336	4.31	91	.221	.350	201-7	.164	-4	117	-26	-3.1
BARNHART, EDGAR Edgar Vernon B 9.16.1904 Providence, MO D 9.14.1984 Columbia, MO BL/TR 5-10/160# d9.23																									
1924	StL A	0	0	—	1	0	0	0	1	0	0	0	0	2	0	0.00	—	.000	.400	0-0	—	0		0	0.0
BARNHART, LES Leslie Earl "Barney" B 2.23.1905 Hoxie, KS D 10.7.1971 Scottsdale, AZ BR/TR 6/180# d9.22																									
1928	Cle A	0	1	.000	2	1	0	0	9	13	7	1	0	4	1	7.00	59	.325	.386	2-0	.500	0	41	-2	-0.2
1930	Cle A	1	0	1.000	1	1	0	0	8.1	12	7	0	0	4	1	6.48	74	.364	.432	3-1	.000	-1	160	-1	-0.2
Total	2	1	1	.500	3	2	0	0	17.1	25	14	1	0	8	2	6.75	66	.342	.407	5-1	.200	-0	105	-3	-0.4
BARNICLE, GEORGE George Bernard "Barney" B 8.26.1917 Fitchburg, MA D 10.10.1990 Largo, FL BR/TR 6-2/175# d9.6																									
1939	Bos N	2	2	.500	6	1	0	0	18.1	16	11	1	0	8	15	4.91	75	.235	.316	5-0	.000	-1	0	-2	-0.5
1940	Bos N	1	0	1.000	13	2	1	0	32.2	28	28	1	6	31	11	7.44	50	.233	.414	11-0	.000	-1	152	-13	-0.7
1941	Bos N	0	1	.000	1	1	0	0	6.2	5	5	0	1	4	2	6.75	53	.238	.385	2-0	.000	-0	0	-2	-0.3
Total	3	3	3	.500	20	4	1	0	57.2	49	44	2	7	43	28	6.55	56	.234	.382	18-0	.000	-2	76	-17	-1.5
BARNOWSKI, ED Edward Anthony B 8.23.1943 Scranton, PA BR/TR 6-2/195# d9.8																									
1965	Bal A	0	0	—	4	0	0	0	4.1	3	1	0	0	7-0	6	2.08	167	.200	.455	0-0	—	0		1	0.0
1966	Bal A	0	0	—	2	0	0	0	3	4	1	0	0	1-0	2	3.00	111	.364	.417	0-0	—	0		0	0.0
Total	2	0	0	—	6	0	0	0	7.1	7	2	0	0	8-0	8	2.45	139	.269	.441	0-0	—	0		1	0.0
BAROJAS, SALOME Salome (Romero) B 6.16.1957 Cordoba, Mexico BR/TR 5-9/188# d4.11																									
1982	Chi A	6	6	.500	61	0	0	21-6	106.2	96	43	9	1	46-6	56	3.54	114	.244	.322	0-0	—	0		8	1.4
1983	†Chi A	3	3	.500	52	0	0	12-4	87.1	70	24	2	5	32-2	38	2.47	170	.224	.304	0-0	—	0		17	1.6
1984	Chi A	3	2	.600	24	0	0	1-4	39.1	48	24	3	0	19-1	18	4.58	91	.310	.385	0-0	—	0		-3	-0.3
	Sea A	6	5	.545	19	14	0	1-0	95.1	88	46	12	3	41-1	37	3.97	101	.249	.331	0-0	—	0	126	1	0.1
	Year	9	7	.563	43	14	0	2-4	134.2	136	52	15	3	60-2	55	4.14	98	.268	.347	0-0	—	0	124	-3	-0.2
1985	Sea A	0	5	.000	17	4	0	0-0	52.2	65	40	6	0	33-5	27	5.98	70	.305	.395	0-0	—	0	38	-11	-0.9
1988	Phi N	0	0	—	6	0	0	0-0	8.2	7	9	1	0	8-0	1	8.31	43	.250	.395	0-0	—	0		-4	-0.2
Total	5	18	21	.462	179	18	0	35-14	390	374	186	33	9	179-15	177	3.95	104	.257	.340	0-0	—	0	105	8	1.7
BARR, JIM James Leland B 2.10.1948 Lynwood, CA BR/TR 6-3/205# d7.31																									
1971	†SF N	1	1	.500	17	0	0	0-0	35.1	33	15	3	1	5-1	16	3.57	95	.254	.281	4-1	.000	-0		0	0.0
1972	SF N	8	10	.444	44	18	8-2	2-1	179	166	66	16	3	41-8	86	2.87	122	.246	.290	49-4	.184	1	89	12	1.3
1973	SF N	11	17	.393	41	33	8-3	2-0	231.1	240	105	24	5	49-7	88	3.81	100	.268	.307	66-12	.152	-1	96	3	0.3
1974	SF N	13	9	.591	44	27	11-5	2-1	239.2	223	81	17	2	47-10	84	2.74	139	.251	.288	71-6	.254	4*	82	29	3.2
1975	SF N	13	14	.481	35	33	12-2	0-0	244	244	94	17	3	58-10	77	3.06	124	.265	.309	76-12	.118	-3*	93	19	1.9
1976	SF N	15	12	.556	37	37	8-3	0-0	252.1	260	104	9	2	60-7	75	2.89	126	.266	.308	74-12	.162	2*	102	17	2.2
1977	SF N	12	16	.429	38	38	6-2	0-0	234.1	286	130	18	3	56-4	97	4.76	82	.306	.345	76-13	.132	-2*	92	-16	-1.7
1978	SF N	8	11	.421	32	25	5-2	1-0	163	180	69	7	0	35-6	44	3.53	98	.281	.315	50-5	.100	-3*	87	-1	-0.3
1979	Cal A	10	12	.455	36	25	5	0-1	197	217	100	22	3	55-5	69	4.20	97	.287	.335	0-0	—	0	100	-2	-0.1
1980	Cal A	1	4	.200	24	7	0	1-0	68	90	43	12	3	23-2	22	5.56	71	.323	.373	0-0	—	0	104	-11	-0.8
1982	SF N	4	3	.571	53	9	1-1	2-2	128.2	125	54	9	4	20-5	36	3.29	110	.262	.291	32-2	.250	1	120	5	0.4
1983	SF N	5	3	.625	53	0	0	2-3	92.2	106	47	7	1	20-9	47	3.98	89	.294	.325	15-1	.133	-0		-4	-0.4
Total	12	101	112	.474	454	252	64-20	12-8	2065.1	2170	908	161	30	469-74	741	3.56	105	.273	.313	513-68	.162	-0	95	51	6.0
BARR, BOB Robert Alexander B 3.12.1908 Newton, MA D 7.25.2002 Dover, NH BR/TR 6/175# d9.11																									
1935	Bro N	0	0	—	2	0	0	0	2.1	5	3	0	0	2	0	3.86	103	.385	.467	0-0	—	0		-1	0.0
BARR, BOB Robert McClelland B 12.1856 Washington, DC D 3.11.1930 Washington, DC BR/TR 6-1/192# d6.23																									
1883	Pit AA	6	18	.250	26	23	19	**1**	203.1	263	166	5		28	81	4.38	74	.294	.316	142	.246	3*	86	-27	-2.2
1884	Was AA	9	23	.281	32	32	32-2	0	281.1	312	210	9	13	31	138	3.45	88	.259	.285	135	.148	-2*	67	-13	-1.4
	Ind AA	3	11	.214	16	16	15	0	131.2	159	117	2	5	19	69	4.99	66	.274	.302	65	.185	0*	92	-22	-1.8
	Year	12	34	.261	48	48	47-2	0	413	471	122	11	18	50	207	3.94	79	.264	.291	200	.160	-2	76	-41	-3.2
1886	Was N	3	18	.143	23	23	21-1	0	191.2	221	153	7		54	80	4.41	73	.280	.326	79	.165	-2	72	-27	-2.5
1890	Roc AA	28	24	.538	57	54	52-3	0	493.1	458	267	7	14	219	209	3.25	110	.239	.321	201	.179	-1	107	21	1.8
1891	NY N	0	4	.000	5	4	2	0	27	47	25	1	3	12	11	5.33	60	.367	.434	11	.091	-0	103	-6	-0.7
Total	5	49	98	.333	159	152	141-6	1	1328.1	1460	938	31	35	363	588	3.85	86	.265	.314	633	.185	-3	89	-74	-6.8
BARR, STEVE Steven Charles B 9.8.1951 St.Louis, MO BL/TL 6-4/200# d10.1																									
1974	Bos A	1	0	1.000	1	1	1	0-0	9	7	4	0	0	6-0	3	4.00	96	.212	.333	0-0	—	0	160	0	0.0
1975	Bos A	0	1	.000	3	2	0	0-0	7	11	9	1	0	7-0	2	2.57	159	.367	.474	0-0	—	0	108	-2	-0.2
1976	Tex A	2	6	.250	20	10	3	0-0	67.2	70	51	10	0	44-1	27	5.59	64	.269	.373	0-0	—	0	113	-16	-1.7
Total	3	3	7	.300	24	13	4	0-0	83.2	88	64	11	0	57-1	32	5.16	71	.272	.379	0-0	—	0	116	-18	-1.9
BARRETT, RED Charles Henry B 2.14.1915 Santa Barbara, CA D 7.28.1990 Wilson, NC BR/TR 5-11/183# d9.15																									
1937	Cin N	0	0	—	1	0	0	0	6.1	5	1	0	0	2	1	1.42	263	.227	.292	3-0	.000	-0		2	0.0
1938	Cin N	2	0	1.000	6	2	2	0	28.2	28	13	2	0	15	5	3.14	116	.257	.347	7-4	.143	-0	151	1	0.0
1939	Cin N	0	0	—	2	0	0	0	5.1	5	1	0	0	1	1	1.69	227	.263	.300	1-0	.000	-0		1	0.1
1940	Cin N	1	0	1.000	3	0	0	0	2.2	5	2	0	0	1	0	6.75	56	.455	.500	0-0	—	0		-1	-0.1
1943	Bos N	12	18	.400	38	31	14-3	0	255	240	107	11	2	63	64	3.18	107	.250	.298	81-8	.136	-4	71	8	0.5
1944	Bos N	9	16	.360	42	30	11-1	2	230.1	257	124	13	2	63	54	4.06	94	.279	.327	75-12	.173	-1	97	-6	-0.6
1945	Bos N	2	3	.400	9	5	2	2	38	43	22	6	1	16	13	4.74	81	.281	.353	9-4	.222	-0	137	-3	-0.4
	StL N❖	21	9	.700	36	29	22-3	0	246.2	244	84	12	1	38	63	2.74	137	.256	.285	89-11	.112	-5	129	29	2.7
	Year	**23**	12	.657	45	34	**24**-3	2	**284.2**	287	90	18	2	54	76	3.00	125	.259	.295	98-15	.122	-5	130	25	2.3
1946	StL N	3	2	.600	23	9	1-1	2	67	75	35	5	2	24	22	4.03	86	.282	.346	17-2	.059	-1	152	-4	-0.4
1947	Bos N	11	12	.478	36	30	12-3	1	210.2	200	102	16	2	53	53	3.55	110	.244	.292	72-7	.111	-2	94	5	0.3
1948	†Bos N	7	8	.467	34	13	3	0	128.1	132	56	9	0	26	40	3.65	105	.268	.305	39-4	.179	-1	84	4	0.3
1949	Bos N	1	1	.500	23	0	0	0	44.1	58	32	4	2	10	17	5.68	66	.326	.368	5-0	.200	-0		-10	-0.4
Total	11	69	69	.500	253	149	67-11	7	1263.1	1292	579	78	12	312	333	3.53	105	.264	.309	398-52	.136	-16	102	26	2.0
BARRETT, FRANK Francis Joseph "Red" B 7.1.1913 Ft.Lauderdale, FL D 3.6.1998 Leesburg, FL BR/TR 6-2/173# d10.1																									
1939	StL N	0	1	.000	1	0	0	0	1.2	1	1	0	0	1	3	5.40	76	.167	.286	0-0	—	0		0	0.0
1944	Bos A	8	7	.533	38	2	0	8	90.1	93	45	5	1	42	40	3.69	92	.271	.352	28-1	.143	-1	160	-4	-0.8
1945	Bos A	4	3	.571	37	0	0	3	86	77	30	0	0	29	35	2.62	130	.249	.314	20-0	.250	1		7	0.6
1946	Bos N	2	4	.333	23	0	0	1	35.1	35	21	2	1	17	12	5.09	67	.252	.338	6-0	.000	-1		-6	-0.9
1950	Pit N	1	2	.333	5	0	0	0	4.1	5	3	1	0	1	0	4.15	106	.357	.400	0-0	—	0		0	0.0
Total	5	15	17	.469	104	2	0	12	217.2	211	100	8	2	90	90	3.51	98	.260	.336	54-1	.167	-1	160	-3	-1.1
BARRETT, TIM Timothy Wayne B 1.24.1961 Huntingburg, IN BL/TR 6-1/185# d7.18																									
1988	Mon N	0	0	—	4	0	0	1-0	9.1	10	6	2	0	2-0	5	5.79	62	.270	.308	2-0	.000	-0		-2	-0.1

Year	Tm Lg	W	L	Pct	G	GS	CG-Sho	SV-BS	IP	H	R	HR	HB	BB-IB	SO	ERA	AERA	OAV	OOB	AB-SH	AVG	PB	Sup	APR	PW
BARRETT, DICK Tracy Souter "Kewpie Dick" (a.k.a. Richard Oliver 1933; Richard Oliver Barrett 1934-43) B9.28.1906 Montoursville, PA D10.30.1966 Seattle, WA BR/TR 5-9/175# d6.27																									
1933	Phi A	4	4	.500	15	7	3	0	70.1	74	51	2	1	49	26	5.76	74	.272	.385	21-2	.286	2	113	-10	-0.8
1934	Bos N	1	3	.250	15	3	0	0	32.1	50	27	2	0	12	14	6.68	57	.365	.416	7-0	.143	-0	83	-11	-1.1
1943	Chi N	0	4	.000	15	4	0	0	45	52	28	2	1	28	20	4.80	70	.291	.389	9-1	.111	-1	51	-7	-0.7
	Phi N	10	9	.526	23	20	10-2	1	169.1	137	53	5	2	51	65	2.39	141	.221	.282	49-6	.143	-0	80	18	2.1
	Year	10	13	.435	38	24	10-2	1	214.1	189	56	7	3	79	85	2.90	116	.237	.308	58-7	.138	-1	76	11	1.4
1944	Phi N	12	18	.400	37	28	11-1	0	221.1	223	110	7	3	88	74	3.86	94	.262	.333	74-6	.216	2	89	-6	-0.4
1945	Phi N	8	20	.286	36	30	8	1	190.2	217	129	11	7	92	72	5.38	71	.281	.363	62-2	.145	-1	83	-28	-3.6
Total	5	35	58	.376	141	92	32-3	2	729	753	398	29	14	320	271	4.28	86	.266	.343	222-17	.180	1	86	-44	-4.5
BARRIOS, FRANCISCO Francisco Javier (Jimenez) B 6.10.1953 Hermosillo, Mexico D 4.9.1982 Hermosillo, Mexico BR/TR 6-3/195# d8.18																									
1974	Chi A	0	0	—	2	0	0	0-0	2	7	6	0	0	2-0	2	27.00	14	.538	.600	0-0	—	0		-5	-0.2
1976	Chi A	5	9	.357	35	14	6	3-1	141.2	136	72	13	4	46-3	81	4.32	83	.255	.314	0-0	—	0	127	-11	-1.1
1977	Chi A	14	7	.667	33	31	9	0-0	231.1	241	117	22	5	58-1	119	4.12	99	.267	.313	0-0	—	0	122	0	0.0
1978	Chi A	9	15	.375	33	32	9-2	0-0	195.2	180	93	13	7	85-2	79	4.05	94	.246	.327	0-0	—	0	82	-3	-0.3
1979	Chi A	8	3	.727	15	15	2	0-0	94.2	88	49	9	5	33-1	28	3.61	118	.242	.311	0-0	—	0	113	5	0.4
1980	Chi A	1	1	.500	3	3	0	0-0	16.1	21	9	4	1	8-0	2	4.96	81	.323	.400	0-0	—	0	111	-1	-0.1
1981	Chi A	1	3	.250	8	7	1	0-0	36.1	45	23	3	1	14-1	12	3.96	90	.292	.355	0-0	—	0	100	-4	-0.4
Total	7	38	38	.500	129	102	27-2	3-1	718	718	369	64	23	246-8	323	4.15	94	.260	.323	0-0	—	0	108	-19	-1.7
BARRIOS, MANUEL Manuel Antonio B 9.21.1974 Cabecera, Panama BR/TR 6/170# d9.16																									
1997	Hou N	0	0	—	2	0	0	0-0	3	6	4	0	0	3-0	3	12.00	33	.400	.500	0-0	—	0		-3	-0.1
1998	Fla N	0	0	—	2	0	0	0-0	2.2	4	1	1	0	2-0	1	3.38	120	.364	.462	0-0	—	0		0	0.0
	LA N	0	0	—	1	0	0	0-0	1	0	0	0	0	2-0	0	0.00	—	.000	.500	0-0	—	0		0	0.0
	Year	0	0	—	3	0	0	0-0	3.2	4	6	1	0	4-0	1	2.45	164	.308	.471	0-0	—	0		1	0.0
Total	2	0	0	—	5	0	0	0-0	6.2	10	5	1	0	7-0	4	6.75	60	.357	.486	0-0	—	0		-3	-0.1
BARRON, FRANK Frank John B 8.6.1890 St.Marys, WV D 9.18.1964 St.Marys, WV BL/TL 6-1/175# d8.19																									
1914	Was A	0	0	—	1	0	0	0	1	1	0	0	0	0	1	0.00	—	.333	.333	0-0	—	0		0	0.0
BARRY, ED Edward "Jumbo" B 10.2.1882 Madison, WI D 6.19.1920 Montague, MA BR/TL 6-3/185# d8.21																									
1905	Bos A	1	2	.333	7	5	2	0	40.2	38	19	2	4	15	18	2.88	94	.248	.331	11-1	.091	-0	131	-2	-0.2
1906	Bos A	0	3	.000	3	3	3	0	21	23	22	2	3	5	10	6.00	46	.280	.344	9-0	.111	-0	44	-9	-1.0
1907	Bos A	0	1	.000	2	2	1	0	17.1	13	6	1	1	5	6	2.08	124	.210	.279	3-1	.000	-0	52	1	0.0
Total	3	1	6	.143	12	10	6	0	79	74	47	5	8	25	34	3.53	76	.249	.324	23-2	.087	-1	89	-10	-1.2
BARRY, HARDIN Hardin "Finn" B 3.26.1891 Susanville, CA D 11.5.1969 Carson City, NV BR/TR 6/185# d6.21																									
1912	Phi A	0	0	—	3	0	0	0	13	18	11	0	1	4	3	7.62	40	.360	.418	4-0	.000	-0		-6	-0.3
BARRY, TOM Thomas Arthur B 4.10.1879 St.Louis, MO D 6.4.1946 St.Louis, MO TR 5-9/155# d4.15																									
1904	Phi N	0	1	.000	1	1	0	0	0.2	6	5	0	0	1	1	40.50	7	.667	.700	0-0	—	0	0	-3	-0.5
BARTHELSON, BOB Robert Edward B 7.15.1924 New Haven, CT D 4.14.2000 Branford, CT BR/TR 6/185# d7.4																									
1944	NY N	1	1	.500	7	1	0	0	9.2	13	9	2	0	5	4	4.66	79	.310	.383	0-0	—	0	0	-2	-0.4
BARTHOLD, JOHN John Francis "Hans" B 4.14.1882 Philadelphia, PA D 11.4.1946 Fairview Village, PA BB/TR 5-11/180# d5.17																									
1904	Phi A	0	0	—	4	0	0	0	10.2	12	9	0	1	8	5	5.06	53	.286	.412	3-0	.333	1		-3	-0.1
BARTHOLOMEW, LES Lester Justin B 4.4.1903 Madison, WI D 9.19.1972 Barrington, IL BR/TL 5-11.5/195# d4.11																									
1928	Pit N	0	0	—	6	0	0	0	22.2	31	18	2	0	9	6	7.15	57	.356	.417	7-0	.143	-0		-6	-0.3
1932	Chi A	0	0	—	3	0	0	0	5.1	5	3	0	0	6	1	5.06	85	.250	.423	1-0	.000	-0		0	0.0
Total	2	0	0	—	9	0	0	0	28	36	21	2	0	15	7	6.75	61	.336	.418	8-0	.125	-0		-6	-0.3
BARTLEY, BILL William Jackson B 1.8.1885 Cincinnati, OH D 5.17.1965 Cincinnati, OH BR/TR 5-11.5/190# d9.15																									
1903	NY N	0	0	—	1	0	0	0	3	3	4	0	0	4	2	0.00	—	.273	.467	1-0	.000	-0		0	0.0
1906	Phi A	0	0	—	3	0	0	1	8.2	10	9	0	0	6	6	9.35	29	.294	.400	3-0	.333	1		-5	-0.2
1907	Phi A	0	1	.000	15	3	2	0	56.1	44	22	0	0	19	16	2.24	116	.218	.285	21-0	.095	-2	130	2	-0.1
Total	3	0	1	.000	19	3	2	1	68	57	35	0	0	29	24	3.04	87	.231	.312	25-0	.120	-1	130	-3	-0.3
BARTON, SHAWN Shawn Edward B 5.14.1963 Los Angeles, CA BR/TL 6-3/195# d8.6																									
1992	Sea A	0	1	.000	14	0	0	0-1	12.1	10	5	1	0	7-2	4	2.92	136	.238	.347	0-0	—	0		1	0.1
1995	SF N	4	1	.800	52	0	0	1-3	44.1	37	22	3	2	19-1	22	4.26	96	.237	.322	0-1	—	0		0	0.0
1996	SF N	0	0	—	7	0	0	0-0	8.1	19	12	2	0	1-0	3	9.72	42	.442	.455	0-0	—	0		-6	-0.3
Total	3	4	2	.667	73	0	0	1-4	65	66	39	6	2	27-3	29	4.71	86	.274	.348	0-1	—	0		-5	-0.2
BARTSON, CHARLIE Charles Franklin B 3.13.1865 Peoria, IL D 6.9.1936 Peoria, IL 6/170# d5.14																									
1890	Chi P	9	10	.474	26	20	17	1	197	226	145	8	13	66	52	4.11	106	.276	.339	78	.167	-3	92	7	0.5
BASKETTE, JIM James Blaine "Big Jim" B 12.10.1887 Athens, TN D 7.30.1942 Athens, TN BR/TR 6-2/185# d9.22																									
1911	Cle A	1	2	.333	4	2	2	0	21.1	21	8	0	1	9	8	3.38	101	.273	.356	6-0	.333	1	74	1	0.2
1912	Cle A	8	4	.667	29	11	7-1	1	116	109	50	2	7	46	51	3.18	107	.252	.334	40-1	.125	-1	114	5	0.3
1913	Cle A	0	0	—	2	1	0	0	4.2	8	3	1	0	2	0	5.79	52	.400	.455	1-0	1.000	1	268	-1	0.1
Total	3	9	6	.600	35	14	9-1	1	142	138	61	3	8	57	59	3.30	103	.261	.342	47-1	.170	1	118	5	0.6
BASS, NORM Norman Delaney B 1.21.1939 Laurel, MS BR/TR 6-3/205# d4.23																									
1961	KC A	11	11	.500	40	23	6-2	0	170.2	164	98	17	4	82-0	74	4.69	89	.255	.340	59-3	.119	-2*	116	-7	-1.2
1962	KC A	2	6	.250	22	10	0	0	75.1	96	55	7	0	46-2	33	6.09	69	.317	.402	22-1	.045	-2	97	-14	-1.4
1963	KC A	0	0	—	3	1	0	0	7.2	11	11	2	0	9-0	4	11.74	33	.333	.465	1-0	.000	-0	137	-6	-0.3
Total	3	13	17	.433	65	34	6-2	0	253.2	271	164	26	4	137-2	111	5.32	79	.277	.364	82-4	.098	-4	111	-27	-2.9
BASS, DICK Richard William B 7.7.1906 Rogersville, TN D 2.3.1989 Graceville, FL BR/TR 6-2/175# d9.21																									
1939	Was A	0	1	.000	1	1	0	0	8	7	6	0	1	6	1	6.75	64	.241	.389	2-0	.000	-0	61	-2	-0.2
BATCHELDER, JOE Joseph Edmund "Win" B 7.11.1898 Wenham, MA D 5.5.1989 Beverly, MA BR/TL 5-7/165# d9.29																									
1923	Bos N	1	0	1.000	4	1	1	0	9	12	7	2	1	1	2	7.00	57	.353	.389	1-0	.000	0	83	-2	-0.2
1924	Bos N	0	0	—	3	0	0	0	4.2	4	2	0	0	2	2	3.86	99	.235	.316	1-0	.000	-0		0	0.0
1925	Bos N	0	0	—	4	0	0	0	7	10	5	0	0	1	2	5.14	78	.357	.379	1-0	.000	-0		-1	0.0
Total	3	1	0	1.000	11	1	1	0	20.2	26	14	2	1	4	6	5.66	70	.329	.369	3-0	.000	-0	83	-3	-0.2
BATCHELOR, RICHARD Richard Anthony B 4.8.1967 Florence, SC BR/TR 6-1/195# d9.3																									
1993	StL N	0	0	—	9	0	0	0-0	10	14	12	1	0	3-1	4	8.10	49	.359	.386	1-0	.000	-0		-6	-0.3
1996	StL N	2	0	1.000	11	0	0	0-0	15	9	2	0	0	1-0	11	1.20	349	.173	.189	1-0	.000	-0		5	0.6
1997	StL N	1	1	.500	10	0	0	0-1	16	21	12	0	2	7-1	8	4.50	92	.323	.405	0-0	—	0		-2	-0.2
	SD N	2	0	1.000	13	0	0	0-1	12.2	19	11	2	1	7-1	10	7.82	50	.358	.443	0-0	—	0		-5	-0.7
	Year	3	1	.750	23	0	0	0-2	28.2	40	27	2	3	14-2	18	5.97	68	.339	.422	0-0	—	0		-7	-0.9
Total	3	5	1	.833	43	0	0	0-2	53.2	63	37	3	3	18-3	33	5.03	81	.301	.362	2-0	.000	-0		-8	-0.6
BATES, DICK Charles Richard B 10.7.1945 McArthur, OH BL/TR 6/190# d4.27																									
1969	Sea A	0	0	—	1	0	0	0-0	1.2	3	5	1	0	3-0	3	27.00	13	.375	.545	0-0	—	0		-4	-0.2
BATES, FRANK Creed Frank B Chattanooga, TN d10.7																									
1898	Cle N	2	1	.667	4	4	4	0	29	30	15	0	1	11	5	3.10	117	.265	.336	9-1	.111	0	73	1	0.1
1899	StL N	0	0	—	2	0	0	0	8.2	7	2	0	0	5	0	1.04	383	.219	.324	3-0	.333	1		3	0.2
	Cle N	1	18	.053	20	19	17	0	153	239	181	6	23	105	13	7.24	51	.355	.458	65-0	.215	1*	58	-67	-5.7
	Year	1	18	.053	22	19	17	0	161.2	246	184	6	23	110	13	6.90	54	.348	.452	68-0	.221	2	57	-59	-5.5
Total	2	3	19	.136	26	23	21	0	190.2	276	198	6	24	121	18	6.33	58	.337	.437	77-1	.208	2	60	-63	-5.4

Year	Tm Lg	W	L	Pct	G	GS	CG-Sho	SV-BS	IP	H	R	HR	HB	BB-IB	SO	ERA	AERA	OAV	OOB	AB-SH	AVG	PB	Sup	APR	PW
BATES, JOHN John William B 5.28.1868 , OH D 3.24.1919 Oakland, CA d8.25																									
1889	KC AA	0	1	.000	1	1	1	0	8	15	14	0	0	5	3	13.50	31	.385	.455	4	.000	-1	44	-6	-0.5
BATISTA, MIGUEL Miguel Jerez (Decartes) B 2.19.1971 Santo Domingo, D.R. BR/TR 6/160# d4.11																									
1992	Pit N	0	0	—	1	0	0	0-0	2	4	2	1	0	3-0	1	9.00	38	.400	.538	0-0	—	0		-1	-0.1
1996	Fla N	0	0	—	9	0	0	0-0	11.1	9	8	0	0	7-2	6	5.56	73	.231	.348	0-0	—	0		-2	-0.1
1997	Chi N	0	5	.000	11	6	0	0-0	36.1	36	24	4	1	24-2	27	5.70	76	.267	.372	8-0	.000	-1	82	-5	-0.7
1998	Mon N	3	5	.375	56	13	0	0-0	135	141	66	12	6	65-7	92	3.80	111	.274	.359	32-2	.000	-4	82	5	-0.1
1999	Mon N	8	7	.533	39	17	2-1	1-0	134.2	146	88	10	7	58-2	95	4.88	92	.280	.353	35-4	.200	2	119	-8	-0.6
2000	Mon N	0	1	.000	4	0	0	0-2	8.1	19	14	2	2	3-0	7	14.04	34	.452	.500	1-0	.000	0		-8	-0.7
	KC A	2	6	.250	14	9	0	0-0	57	66	54	17	0	34-2	30	7.74	66	.292	.383	3-0	.000	-0	85	-17	-1.9
2001	†Ari N	11	8	.579	48	18	0	0-0	139.1	113	57	13	10	60-2	90	3.36	136	.226	.320	32-2	.063	-2	84	18	1.9
2002	†Ari N	8	9	.471	36	29	1	0-0	184.2	172	99	12	6	70-3	112	4.29	104	.245	.316	51-2	.157	1	98	1	0.2
2003	Ari N	10	9	.526	36	29	2-1	0-0	193.1	197	85	13	8	60-3	142	3.54	132	.267	.326	57-4	.070	-4	98	22	1.6
Total	9	42	50	.457	254	121	5-2	1-2	902	903	497	84	40	384-23	602	4.39	103	.263	.341	219-14	.096	-7	96	5	-0.5
BATTON, CHRIS Christopher Sean B 8.24.1954 Los Angeles, CA BR/TR 6-4/195# d9.19																									
1976	Oak A	0	0	—	2	1	0	0-0	4	5	4	1	0	3-0	4	9.00	37	.313	.421	0-0	—	0	236	-2	-0.1
BAUER, ALBERT Albert B 8.7.1859 Columbus, OH D 2.23.1944 Columbus, OH TL d9.22 U1																									
1884	Col AA	1	2	.333	3	3	3	0	25	22	21	1	0	14	13	4.68	65	.224	.321	11	.273	0	47	-5	-0.4
1886	StL N	0	4	.000	4	4	3	0	28.2	31	27	1		27	13	5.97	54	.267	.406	12	.167	-1	86	-7	-0.8
Total	2	1	6	.143	7	7	6	0	53.2	53	48	2		41	26	5.37	58	.248	.369	23	.217	-0	69	-12	-1.2
BAUER, LOU Louis Walter B 11.30.1898 Egg Harbor City, NJ D 2.4.1979 Pomona, NJ BR/TR 6/175# d8.13																									
1918	Phi A	0	0	—	1	0	0	0	0	0	2	0	0	2	0	∞	—	—	1.000	0-0	—	0		-1	-0.1
BAUER, RICK Richard Edward B 1.10.1977 Garden Grove, CA BR/TR 6-6/212# d9.2																									
2001	Bal A	0	5	.000	6	6	0	0-0	33	35	22	7	1	9-0	16	4.64	93	.265	.315	0-0	—	0	54	-3	-0.4
2002	Bal A	6	7	.462	56	1	0	1-4	83.2	84	41	12	4	36-4	45	3.98	108	.268	.348	0-0	—	0	65	2	0.3
2003	Bal A	0	0	—	35	0	0	0-1	61.1	58	36	5	4	24-3	43	4.55	97	.256	.333	0-0	—	0		-2	-0.1
Total	3	6	12	.333	97	7	0	1-5	178	177	99	24	9	69-7	104	4.30	101	.263	.337	0-0	—	0	55	-3	-0.2
BAUERS, RUSS Russell Lee B 5.10.1914 Townsend, WI D 1.1.1995 Hines, IL BL/TR 6-3/195# d8.20 Mil 1944-45																									
1936	Pit N	0	0	—	1	1	0	0	1.1	2	5	0	1	4	0	33.75	12	.500	.778	0-0	—	0	167	-4	-0.2
1937	Pit N	13	6	.684	34	19	11-2	1	187.2	174	70	2	4	80	118	2.88	134	.245	.325	69-1	.217	1	115	21	2.2
1938	Pit N	13	14	.481	40	34	12-2	3	243	207	102	7	6	99	117	3.07	124	.233	.314	88-3	.239	4	89	18	2.1
1939	Pit N	2	4	.333	15	8	1	1	53.2	46	27	4	1	25	12	3.35	114	.240	.330	19-1	.211	-0	94	1	0.1
1940	Pit N	0	2	.000	15	2	0	0	30.2	42	29	2	2	18	11	7.63	50	.323	.413	7-0	.286	0	80	-13	-0.7
1941	Pit N	1	3	.250	8	5	1	0	37.1	40	28	1	0	25	20	5.54	65	.267	.371	14-0	.357	1	136	-8	-0.7
1946	Chi N	2	1	.667	15	2	2	1	43.1	45	17	1	1	19	22	3.53	94	.273	.351	10-0	.300	1	90	0	0.2
1950	StL A	0	0	—	1	0	0	0	2	6	4	0	0	1	0	4.50	110	.600	.636	0-0	—	0		-1	0.0
Total	8	31	30	.508	129	71	27-4	6	599	562	282	17	15	271	300	3.53	107	.250	.334	207-5	.242	7	101	14	3.0
BAUMANN, FRANK Frank Matt "The Beau" B 7.1.1933 St.Louis, MO BL/TL 6-1/210# d7.31																									
1955	Bos A	2	1	.667	7	5	0	0	34	38	28	2	1	17-0	27	5.82	74	.281	.361	13-0	.231	-0	108	-7	-0.5
1956	Bos A	2	1	.667	7	1	0	0	24.2	22	11	3	0	14-0	18	3.28	141	.234	.333	9-1	.333	1	231	3	0.4
1957	Bos A	1	0	1.000	4	1	0	0	12	13	5	1	1	3-0	7	3.75	106	.277	.333	2-1	.500	0	67	1	0.1
1958	Bos A	2	2	.500	10	7	2	0	52.1	56	27	4	4	27-2	31	4.47	90	.276	.370	14-1	.214	1	77	-1	0.0
1959	Bos A	6	4	.600	26	10	2	1	95.2	96	47	11	1	55-3	48	4.05	100	.259	.356	29-1	.207	1	104	0	0.1
1960	Chi A	13	6	.684	47	20	7-2	3	185.1	169	67	11	1	53-8	71	**2.67**	142	.247	.300	52-0	.154	1	122	21	2.1
1961	Chi A	10	13	.435	53	23	5-1	3	187.2	249	128	22	2	59-4	75	5.61	70	.318	.366	61-1	.262	6*	124	-35	-3.2
1962	Chi A	7	6	.538	40	10	3-1	4	119.2	117	46	10	2	36-5	55	3.38	115	.258	.314	30-1	.267	4	101	9	1.4
1963	Chi A	2	1	.667	24	1	0	1	50.1	52	22	2	0	17-2	31	3.04	115	.265	.322	11-0	.091	-0	25	1	0.1
1964	Chi A	0	3	.000	22	0	0	1	32	40	22	4	0	16-8	19	6.19	56	.320	.392	4-1	.000	-0		-9	-0.9
1965	Chi N	0	1	.000	4	0	0	0	3.2	4	3	0	0	3-0	2	7.36	50	.286	.412	0-0	—	0		-1	-0.2
Total	11	45	38	.542	244	78	19-4	13	797.1	856	406	70	12	300-32	384	4.11	95	.276	.340	225-7	.218	14	113	-18	-0.6
BAUMGARDNER, GEORGE George Washington B 7.22.1891 Barboursville, WV D 12.13.1970 Barboursville, WV BL/TR 5-11/178# d4.14																									
1912	StL A	11	13	.458	30	27	18-2	0	218.1	222	101	1	11	79	102	3.38	98	.274	.346	76-1	.145	-0	91	3	0.3
1913	StL A	10	20	.333	38	31	23-2	1	253.1	267	119	6	10	84	78	3.13	94	.286	.351	78-0	.167	2	86	-5	-0.4
1914	StL A	16	14	.533	45	18	9-3	1	183.2	152	72	3	8	84	93	2.79	97	.229	.323	53-4	.132	-1	109	0	-0.1
1915	StL A	0	2	.000	7	1	1	0	22.1	29	15	0	0	11	6	4.43	65	.358	.435	6-0	.000	-1	0	-4	-0.4
1916	StL A	1	0	1.000	4	2	0	0	8	12	8	0	0	5	4	7.88	35	.364	.447	2-0	.000	0	96	-4	-0.5
Total	5	38	49	.437	124	79	51-7	2	685.2	682	315	10	29	263	283	3.22	93	.270	.346	215-5	.144	-0	93	-10	-1.1
BAUMGARTEN, ROSS Ross B 5.27.1955 Highland Park, IL BL/TL 6-1/180# d8.16																									
1978	Chi A	2	2	.500	7	4	1-1	0-0	23	29	15	3	1	9-0	15	5.87	65	.315	.375	0-0	—	0	106	-5	-0.7
1979	Chi A	13	8	.619	28	28	4-3	0-0	190.2	175	82	18	1	83-1	72	3.54	120	.243	.319	0-0	—	0	104	17	1.7
1980	Chi A	2	12	.143	24	23	3-1	0-0	136	127	60	10	1	52-0	66	3.44	117	.256	.324	0-0	—	0	45	9	1.0
1981	Chi A	5	9	.357	19	19	2-1	0-0	101.2	101	56	9	1	40-3	52	4.07	88	.260	.329	0-0	—	0*	119	-7	-0.9
1982	Pit N	0	5	.000	12	10	0	0-0	44	60	33	3	0	27-1	17	6.55	57	.347	.429	12-0	.083	-1	100	-12	-1.3
Total	5	22	36	.379	90	84	10-6	0-0	495.1	492	246	43	4	211-5	222	4.00	100	.263	.336	12-0	.083	-1	90	2	-0.2
BAUMGARTNER, HARRY Harry E. B 10.8.1892 S.Pittsburg, TN D 12.3.1930 Augusta, GA BR/TR 5-11/175# d9.6																									
1920	Det A	0	1	.000	9	0	0	0	18	18	10	1	0	6	7	4.00	93	.273	.333	4-0	.250	0		0	0.0
BAUMGARTNER, STAN Stanwood Fulton B 12.14.1894 Houston, TX D 10.4.1955 Philadelphia, PA BL/TL 6/175# d6.26																									
1914	Phi N	2	2	.500	15	4	2-1	0	60.1	60	29	0	2	16	24	3.28	90	.270	.325	19-0	.053	-1	105	-1	-0.3
1915	Phi N	0	2	.000	16	1	0	0	48.1	38	22	2	1	23	27	2.42	113	.226	.323	12-0	.083	-1*	81	0	0.0
1916	Phi N	0	0	—	1	0	0	0	4	5	2	0	0	1	0	2.25	118	.333	.375	1-0	.000	-0		0	0.0
1921	Phi N	3	6	.333	22	7	2	0	66.2	103	72	8	2	22	13	7.02	60	.355	.404	30-0	.200	0*	72	-19	-2.1
1922	Phi N	1	1	.500	6	1	0	0	9.2	18	9	1	0	5	2	6.52	72	.409	.469	3-0	.333	0	105	-2	-0.2
1924	Phi A	13	6	.684	36	16	12-1	4	181	181	72	6	4	73	45	2.88	**149**	.271	.347	60-5	.217	-0	91	26	2.4
1925	Phi A	6	3	.667	37	12	2-1	3	113.1	120	55	2	7	35	18	3.57	130	.275	.338	30-1	.233	-0	101	12	0.9
1926	Phi A	1	1	.500	10	1	0	0	22.1	28	10	0	0	10	0	4.03	103	.326	.396	3-1	.333	0	182	1	0.2
Total	8	26	21	.553	143	42	18-3	7	505.2	553	271	19	16	185	129	3.70	109	.287	.354	158-7	.190	-2	98	17	0.9
BAUSEWINE, GEORGE George W. B 3.22.1869 Philadelphia, PA D 7.29.1947 Norristown, PA 6-2/207# d9.14 U1																									
1889	Phi AA	1	4	.200	7	6	6	0	55.1	64	46	1	9	33	18	3.90	97	.281	.393	21	.048	-2	85	-3	-0.3
BAUTA, ED Eduardo (Galvez) B 1.6.1935 Florida, Cuba BR/TR 6-3/200# d7.6																									
1960	StL N	0	0	—	9	0	0	1	15.2	14	11	4	1	11-1	6	6.32	65	.237	.366	1-0	.000	-0		-3	-0.2
1961	StL N	2	0	1.000	13	0	0	5	19.1	12	5	2	0	5-1	12	1.40	315	.171	.224	4-0	.500	1		5	0.9
1962	StL N	1	0	1.000	20	0	0	1	32.1	28	18	5	1	21-1	25	5.01	85	.239	.357	4-0	.250	0		-1	-0.1
1963	StL N	3	4	.429	38	0	0	3	52.2	55	26	2	2	21-4	30	3.93	90	.279	.351	5-1	.000	-1		-2	-0.4
	NY N	0	0	—	9	0	0	0	19	22	11	0	0	9-0	13	5.21	67	.289	.360	3-0	.000	-0		-3	-0.2
	Year	3	4	.429	47	0	0	3	71.2	77	42	2	2	30-4	43	4.27	83	.282	.354	8-1	.000	-1		-4	-0.6
1964	NY N	0	2	.000	8	0	0	1	10	17	6	1	0	3-1	3	5.40	66	.395	.435	0-0	—	0		-2	-0.3
Total	5	6	6	.500	97	0	0	11	149	148	77	14	4	70-8	89	4.35	89	.263	.346	17-1	.176	-0		-6	-0.3
BAUTISTA, JOSE Jose Joaquin (Arias) B 7.25.1964 Bani, D.R. BR/TR 6-2/205# d4.9																									
1988	Bal A	6	15	.286	33	25	3	0-0	171.2	171	86	21	7	45-3	76	4.30	91	.258	.310	0-0	—	0	63	-5	-0.7
1989	Bal A	3	4	.429	15	10	0	0-0	78	84	46	17	1	15-0	30	5.31	72	.274	.309	0-0	—	0	83	-12	-1.0
1990	Bal A	1	0	1.000	22	0	0	0-0	26.2	28	15	4	0	7-3	15	4.05	94	.272	.315	0-0	—	0		-2	-0.1
1991	Bal A	0	1	.000	5	0	0	0-0	5.1	13	10	1	1	5-0	3	16.88	23	.464	.559	0-0	—	0		-8	-1.1

Year	Tm Lg	W	L	Pct	G	GS	CG-Sho	SV-BS	IP	H	R	HR	HB	BB-IB	SO	ERA	AERA	OAV	OOB	AB-SH	AVG	PB	Sup	APR	PW
1993	Chi N	10	3	.769	58	7	1	2-0	111.2	105	38	11	5	27-3	63	2.82	142	.250	.301	21-2	.190	0*	155	15	1.7
1994	Chi N	4	5	.444	58	0	0	1-3	69.1	75	30	10	3	17-7	45	3.89	107	.284	.330	2-0	.000	-0		3	0.3
1995	SF N	3	8	.273	52	6	0	0-0	100.2	120	77	24	5	26-3	45	6.44	64	.295	.341	18-1	.000	-2	77	-26	-2.6
1996	SF N	3	4	.429	37	1	0	0-1	69.2	66	32	10	2	15-5	28	3.36	122	.249	.291	9-1	.111	-0	44	5	0.4
1997	Det A	2	2	.500	21	0	0	0-0	40.1	55	32	6	2	12-3	19	6.69	69	.324	.375	0-0	—	0		-9	-0.8
	StL N	0	0	—	11	0	0	0-0	12.1	15	10	2	1	2-1	4	6.57	63	.300	.340	0-0	—	0		-3	-0.2
Total	9	32	42	.432	312	49	4	3-4	685.2	732	376	106	27	171-28	328	4.62	87	.273	.321	50-4	.100	-2	80	-42	-4.1
BAYNE, BILL William Lear "Beverly" B 4.18.1899 Pittsburgh, PA D 5.22.1981 St.Louis, MO BL/TL 5-9/160# d9.20																									
1919	StL A	1	1	.500	2	2	1	0	12	16	8	0	0	6	0	5.25	63	.320	.393	5-0	.400	0	118	-2	-0.3
1920	StL A	5	6	.455	18	13	6-1	0	99.2	102	51	3	7	41	38	3.70	106	.279	.363	35-1	.171	-2	89	2	-0.1
1921	StL A	11	5	.688	47	14	6-1	3	164	167	103	8	5	80	82	4.72	95	.270	.358	60-0	.300	5	121	-4	0.0
1922	StL A	4	5	.444	26	9	3	2	92.2	86	49	5	9	37	38	4.56	91	.249	.338	30-0	.233	-1	87	-1	-0.2
1923	StL A	2	2	.500	19	2	0	0	46	49	25	4	3	31	15	4.50	93	.287	.405	13-2	.231	-0	79	-1	-0.1
1924	StL A	1	3	.250	22	3	0	0	50.2	47	31	4	8	29	20	4.44	102	.250	.373	14-0	.429	2	118	0	0.2
1928	Cle A	2	5	.286	37	6	3	3	108.2	128	68	3	10	43	39	5.13	81	.309	.388	30-0	.367	3	119	-9	-0.2
1929	Bos A	5	5	.500	27	6	2	0	84.1	111	72	9	8	29	26	6.72	64	.326	.392	25-1	.320	2	63	-21	-1.8
1930	Bos A	0	0	—	1	0	0	0	4	5	2	1	0	1	1	4.50	102	.294	.333	2-0	.500	0		0	0.0
Total	9	31	32	.492	199	55	21-2	8	662	711	409	37	50	297	259	4.84	87	.283	.370	214-4	.290	10	99	-36	-2.5
BEALL, WALTER Walter Esau B 7.29.1899 Washington, DC D 1.28.1959 Suitland, MD BR/TR 5-10/178# d9.3																									
1924	NY A	2	0	1.000	4	2	0	0	23	19	11	2	0	17	18	3.52	118	.237	.371	7-0	.143	-1	152	1	0.0
1925	NY A	0	1	.000	8	1	0	0	11.1	11	17	0	3	19	8	12.71	34	.282	.541	3-0	.000	-1	39	-10	-0.8
1926	NY A	2	4	.333	20	9	1	1	81.2	71	46	2	6	68	56	3.53	109	.240	.392	22-1	.136	0	124	0	0.0
1927	NY A	0	0	—	1	0	0	0	1	1	1	0	0	0	0	9.00	43	.333	.333	0-0	—	0		-1	0.0
1929	Was A	1	0	1.000	3	0	0	0	7	8	4	0	0	7	3	3.86	110	.348	.500	3-0	.000	-1		0	0.0
Total	5	5	5	.500	36	12	1	1	124	110	79	4	9	111	85	4.43	90	.249	.410	35-1	.114	-1	120	-10	-0.8
BEAM, ALEX Alexander Rodger B 11.21.1870 Johnstown, PA D 4.17.1938 Nogales, AZ d5.25																									
1889	Pit N	1	1	.500	2	2	2	0	18	11	16	0	0	15	1	6.50	58	.172	.329	6	.167	0	63	-5	-0.4
BEAM, ERNIE Ernest Joseph B 3.17.1867 Mansfield, OH D 9.12.1918 Mansfield, OH TR 6-0.5/185# d5.2																									
1895	Phi N	0	2	.000	9	1	1	**3**	24.2	33	33	1	1	25	3	11.31	42	.317	.454	11-0	.182	-1*	179	-15	-1.2
BEAMON, CHARLIE Charles Alfonzo Sr. B 12.25.1934 Oakland, CA BR/TR 5-11/195# d9.26 s-Charlie																									
1956	Bal A	2	0	1.000	2	1	1-1	0	13	9	2	0	0	8-0	14	1.38	283	.191	.309	5-0	.000	-1	23	4	0.6
1957	Bal A	0	0	—	4	1	0	0	8.2	8	6	1	1	7-0	5	5.19	69	.229	.372	2-0	.000	-0	273	-2	-0.1
1958	Bal A	1	3	.250	21	3	0	0	49.2	47	27	3	6	21-1	26	4.35	83	.266	.361	10-1	.000	-1*	108	-5	-0.3
Total	3	3	3	.500	27	5	1-1	0	71.1	64	35	4	7	36-1	45	3.91	93	.247	.353	17-1	.000	-2	123	-3	0.2
BEAN, BELVE Beveric Benton "Bill" B 4.23.1905 Mullin, TX D 6.1.1988 Comanche, TX BR/TR 6-1.5/197# d5.30																									
1930	Cle A	3	3	.500	23	3	1	2	74.1	99	58	7	0	32	19	5.45	89	.331	.396	26-0	.346	2	107	-6	-0.2
1931	Cle A	0	1	.000	4	0	0	0	7	11	5	0	1	4	3	6.43	72	.379	.471	1-0	.000	-0		-1	-0.1
1933	Cle A	1	2	.333	27	2	0	0	70.1	80	43	6	1	20	41	5.25	85	.300	.351	22-0	.182	-1	105	-4	-0.2
1934	Cle A	5	1	.833	21	1	0	0	51.1	53	25	2	3	21	20	3.86	118	.265	.344	15-1	.200	0	96	4	0.5
1935	Cle A	0	0	—	1	0	0	0	1	2	1	1	0	0	0	9.00	50	.400	.400	0-0	—	0		0	0.0
	Was A	2	0	1.000	10	2	0	0	31	43	28	5	0	19	6	7.26	60	.339	.425	8-0	.375	3	181	-10	-0.3
	Year	2	0	1.000	11	2	0	0	32	45	37	6	0	19	6	7.31	59	.341	.424	8-0	.375	3	181	-11	-0.3
Total	5	11	7	.611	86	8	1	2	235	288	160	21	5	96	89	5.32	86	.311	.378	72-1	.264	4	122	-17	-0.3
BEARD, DAVE Charles David B 10.2.1959 Atlanta, GA BL/TR 6-5/215# d7.16																									
1980	Oak A	0	1	.000	13	0	0	1-0	16	12	6	0	1	7-1	12	3.38	112	.218	.313	0-0	—	0		1	0.1
1981	†Oak A	1	1	.500	8	0	0	3-1	13	9	5	1	1	4-1	15	2.77	126	.191	.264	0-0	—	0		1	0.2
1982	Oak A	10	9	.526	54	2	0	11-8	91.2	85	41	9	1	35-6	73	3.44	114	.244	.308	0-0	—	0	58	4	0.8
1983	Oak A	5	5	.500	43	0	0	10-3	61	55	39	8	2	36-4	40	5.61	69	.246	.351	0-0	—	0		-11	-2.0
1984	Sea A	3	2	.600	43	0	0	5-3	76	88	56	15	4	33-5	40	5.80	69	.291	.362	0-0	—	0		-16	-1.1
1985	Chi N	0	0	—	9	0	0	0-0	12.2	16	9	2	0	7-2	4	6.39	63	.314	.397	0-0	—	0		-3	-0.1
1989	Det A	0	2	.000	2	1	0	0-0	5.1	9	7	2	1	2-0	1	5.06	76	.375	.444	0-0	—	0	47	-2	-0.4
Total	7	19	20	.487	172	3	0	30-15	275.2	274	163	37	10	124-19	185	4.70	83	.261	.339	0-0	—	0	54	-26	-2.5
BEARD, MIKE Michael Richard B 6.21.1950 Little Rock, AR BL/TL 6-1/185# d9.7																									
1974	Atl N	0	0	—	6	0	0	0-0	9.1	5	3	1	1	1-0	7	2.89	131	.156	.206	0-0	—	0		1	0.1
1975	Atl N	4	0	1.000	34	2	0	0-3	70.1	71	31	4	2	28-5	27	3.20	118	.265	.333	9-1	.111	-0	105	4	0.2
1976	Atl N	0	2	.000	30	0	0	1-2	33.2	38	18	1	0	14-3	8	4.28	89	.299	.364	1-0	.000	-0		-2	-0.1
1977	Atl N	0	0	—	4	0	0	0-0	4.2	14	11	3	0	2-0	1	9.64	46	.452	.485	0-0	—	0		-4	-0.2
Total	4	4	2	.667	74	2	0	1-5	118	128	63	9	3	45-8	43	3.74	102	.279	.343	10-1	.100	-0	105	-1	0.0
BEARD, RALPH Ralph William B 2.11.1929 Cincinnati, OH D 2.10.2003 West Palm Beach, FL BR/TR 6-5/200# d6.29																									
1954	StL N	0	4	.000	13	10	0	0	58	62	32	2	2	28	17	3.72	110	.278	.357	17-0	.059	-1	69	0	-0.2
BEARDEN, GENE Henry Eugene B 9.5.1920 Lexa, AR BL/TL 6-3/204# d5.10																									
1947	Cle A	0	0	—	1	0	0	0	0.1	2	3	0	0	1	0	81.00	4	.667	.750	0-0	—	0		-3	-0.1
1948	†Cle A	20	7	.741	37	29	15-6	1	229.2	187	72	9	3	106	80	**2.43**	**167**	.229	.320	90-2	.256	5	145	**43**	5.5
1949	Cle A	8	8	.500	32	19	5	0	127	140	77	6	2	92	41	5.10	78	.286	.401	45-2	.111	-3	99	-15	-1.7
1950	Cle A	1	3	.250	14	3	0	0	45.1	57	32	5	0	32	10	6.15	70	.328	.432	13-0	.154	1	111	-8	-0.6
	Was A	3	5	.375	12	9	4	0	68.1	81	35	1	2	33	20	4.21	107	.297	.377	22-1	.227	1*	74	3	0.4
	Year	4	8	.333	26	12	4	0	113.2	138	39	6	2	65	30	4.99	89	.309	.399	35-1	.200	2	83	-5	-0.2
1951	Was A	0	0	—	1	1	0	0	2.2	6	5	0	0	2	1	16.88	24	.429	.500	0-0	—	0	152	-4	-0.2
	Det A	3	4	.429	37	4	2-1	0	106	112	58	6	1	58	38	4.33	96	.275	.366	32-1	.188	1	101	-2	0.0
	Year	3	4	.429	38	5	2-1	0	108.2	118	63	6	1	60	39	4.64	90	.280	.371	32-1	.188	1	111	-5	-0.2
1952	StL A	7	8	.467	34	16	3	0	150.2	158	89	13	1	78	45	4.30	91	.270	.357	65-1	.354	6*	81	-9	-0.1
1953	Chi A	3	3	.500	25	3	0	0	58.1	48	27	8	0	33	24	2.93	137	.223	.327	21-2	.190	-1*	169	4	0.3
Total	7	45	38	.542	193	84	29-7	1	788.1	791	398	48	9	435	259	3.96	103	.266	.361	288-9	.236	10	111	9	3.5
BEARE, GARY Gary Ray B 8.22.1952 San Diego, CA BR/TR 6-4/205# d9.7																									
1976	Mil A	2	3	.400	6	5	2	0-0	41	43	16	4	0	15-0	32	3.29	106	.274	.335	0-0	—	0	126	1	0.1
1977	Mil A	3	3	.500	17	6	0	0-0	58.2	63	46	6	1	38-3	32	6.44	63	.276	.378	0-0	—	0	125	-15	-1.3
Total	2	5	6	.455	23	11	2	0-0	99.2	106	62	10	1	53-3	64	5.15	75	.275	.361	0-0	—	0	124	-14	-1.2
BEARNARTH, LARRY Lawrence Donald B 9.11.1941 New York, NY D 12.31.1999 Seminole, FL BR/TR 6-2/203# d4.16 C11																									
1963	NY N	3	8	.273	58	2	0	4	126.1	127	61	7	5	47-9	48	3.42	102	.268	.338	30-0	.200	1	111	-1	0.2
1964	NY N	5	5	.500	44	1	0	3	78	79	38	6	2	38-1	31	4.15	86	.271	.358	14-0	.143	-0	123	-4	-0.4
1965	NY N	3	5	.375	40	3	0	1	60.2	75	43	6	4	28-2	16	4.60	77	.304	.381	9-0	.111	0	49	-11	-1.3
1966	NY N	2	3	.400	29	1	0	0	54.2	59	31	11	1	20-6	27	4.45	82	.281	.342	9-0	.111	-0	0	-5	-0.4
1971	Mil A	0	0	—	2	0	0	0-0	3	10	6	1	0	2-0	2	18.00	19	.556	.600	0-0	—	0		-4	-0.2
Total	5	13	21	.382	173	7	0	8-0	322.2	350	179	31	12	135-18	124	4.13	86	.282	.356	62-0	.161	1	70	-25	-2.1
BEARSE, KEVIN Kevin Gerard B 11.7.1965 Jersey City, NJ BL/TL 6-2/195# d4.15																									
1990	Cle A	0	2	.000	3	3	0	0-0	7.2	16	11	2	2	5-0	2	12.91	30	.421	.511	0-0	—	0	62	-7	-1.2
BEASLEY, CHRIS Christopher Charles B 6.23.1962 Jackson, TN BR/TR 6-2/190# d7.20																									
1991	Cal A	0	1	.000	22	0	0	0-0	26.2	26	14	2	1	10-1	14	3.38	122	.257	.327	0-0	—	0		1	0.1
BEATIN, ED Ebenezer Ambrose B 8.10.1866 Baltimore, MD D 5.9.1925 Baltimore, MD BR/TL 5-9/162# d8.2																									
1887	Det N	1	1	.500	2	2	2	0	18	13	11	2	1	8	6	4.00	102	.203	.301	7	.000	-1	103	0	-0.1
1888	Det N	5	7	.417	12	12	12-1	0	107	111	60	6	2	16	44	2.86	98	.251	.280	56	.250	5*	84	-1	0.3

Year	Tm Lg	W	L	Pct	G	GS	CG-Sho	SV-BS	IP	H	R	HR	HB	BB-IB	SO	ERA	AERA	OAV	OOB	AB-SH	AVG	PB	Sup	APR	PW
1889	Cle N	20	15	.571	36	36	35-3	0	317.2	316	179	12	6	141	126	3.57	113	.251	.330	121	.116	-5*	86	19	1.1
1890	Cle N	22	30	.423	54	54	53-1	0	474.1	518	300	11	15	186	155	3.83	94	.269	.338	191	.141	-9	80	-11	-1.6
1891	Cle N	0	3	.000	5	4	2	0	29	39	44	1	6	21	4	5.28	66	.310	.431	13	.077	-1	86	-9	-0.8
Total	5	48	56	.462	109	108	104-5	0	946	997	594	32	30	372	335	3.68	99	.261	.332	388	.144	-13	83	-2	-1.1
BEATTIE, JIM James Louis B 7.4.1954 Hampton, VA BR/TR 6-6/220# d4.25																									
1978	†NY A	6	9	.400	25	22	0	0-0	128	123	60	8	8	51-2	65	3.73	98	.255	.335	0-0	—	0	102	-1	-0.1
1979	NY A	3	6	.333	15	13	1-1	0-0	76	85	45	5	0	41-0	32	5.21	78	.294	.375	0-0	—	0	90	-8	-0.8
1980	Sea A	5	15	.250	33	29	3	0-0	187.1	205	115	19	4	98-9	67	4.85	85	.286	.372	0-0	—	0	93	-15	-1.4
1981	Sea A	3	2	.600	13	9	0	1-0	66.2	59	24	2	2	18-0	36	2.97	130	.232	.288	0-0	—	0	80	6	0.5
1982	Sea A	8	12	.400	28	26	6-1	0-0	172.1	149	73	13	1	65-0	140	3.34	127	.233	.303	0-0	—	0	82	16	1.7
1983	Sea A	10	15	.400	30	29	8-2	0-0	196.2	197	89	12	3	66-6	132	3.84	111	.259	.320	0-0	—	0	73	11	1.5
1984	Sea A	12	16	.429	32	32	12-2	0-0	211	206	86	13	5	75-6	119	3.41	117	.260	.326	0-0	—	0	91	15	1.9
1985	Sea A	5	6	.455	18	15	1-1	0-0	70.1	93	61	9	3	33-0	45	7.29	58	.316	.385	0-0	—	0	131	-23	-3.0
1986	Sea A	0	6	.000	9	7	0	0-0	40.1	57	28	7	3	14-2	24	6.02	71	.341	.398	0-0	—	0	73	-7	-0.8
Total	9	52	87	.374	203	182	31-7	1-0	1148.2	1174	581	88	29	461-25	660	4.17	98	.267	.338	0-0	—	0	90	-6	-0.5
BEATTY, BLAINE Gordon Blaine B 4.25.1964 Victoria, TX BL/TL 6-2/185# d9.16																									
1989	NY N	0	0	—	2	1	0	0-0	6	5	1	1	0	2-0	3	1.50	218	.217	.280	2-0	.500	0	189	1	0.1
1991	NY N	0	0	—	5	0	0	0-0	9.2	9	3	0	0	4-1	7	2.79	130	.250	.317	0-0	—	0		1	0.1
Total	2	0	0	—	7	1	0	0-0	15.2	14	4	1	0	6-1	10	2.30	152	.237	.303	2-0	.500	0	189	2	0.2
BEAZLEY, JOHNNY John Andrew "Nig" B 5.25.1918 Nashville, TN D 4.21.1990 Nashville, TN BR/TR 6-1.5/190# d9.28 Mil 1943-45																									
1941	StL N	1	0	1.000	1	1	1	0	9	10	1	0	0	3	4	1.00	376	.294	.351	3-0	.000	-0	68	3	0.3
1942	†StL N	21	6	.778	43	23	13-3	3	215.1	181	67	4	3	73	91	2.13	161	.226	.293	73-9	.137	-1	120	28	3.5
1946	†StL N	7	5	.583	19	18	5	0	103	109	55	6	4	55	36	4.46	77	.275	.368	33-3	.242	1	114	-9	-0.9
1947	Bos N	2	0	1.000	9	2	2	0	28.2	30	15	1	0	19	12	4.40	89	.273	.380	7-2	.000	-1	193	-1	-0.2
1948	Bos N	0	1	.000	3	2	0	0	16	19	13	2	0	7	4	4.50	85	.284	.351	4-1	.000	-1	127	-3	-0.2
1949	Bos N	0	0	—	1	0	0	0	2	0	0	0	0	0	0	0.00	—	.000	.000	0-0	—	0		1	0.0
Total	6	31	12	.721	76	46	21-3	3	374	349	151	13	7	157	147	3.01	116	.247	.325	120-15	.150	-1	120	19	2.5
BECANNON, BUCK James Melvin B 8.22.1859 New York, NY D 11.5.1923 New York, NY 5-10/165# d10.15																									
1884	†NY AA	1	0	1.000	1	1	1	0	6	2	2	0	0	2	2	1.50	208	.091	.167	3	.000	-0	251	1	0.1
1885	NY AA	2	8	.200	10	10	10	0	85	108	84	5	5	24	13	6.25	50	.296	.348	33	.303	2	108	-28	-2.2
Total	2	3	8	.273	11	11	11	0	91	110	86	5	5	26	15	5.93	53	.284	.337	36	.278	1	121	-27	-2.1
BECHLER, STEVE Steven Scott B 11.18.1979 Medford, OR D 2.17.2003 Ft.Lauderdale, FL BR/TR 6-2/207# d9.6																									
2002	Bal A	0	0	—	3	0	0	0-0	4.2	6	7	3	1	4-0	3	13.50	32	.300	.440	0-0	—	0		-5	-0.2
BECHTEL, GEORGE George A. B 1848 Philadelphia, PA 5-11/165# d5.20 ▲																									
1871	Ath NA	1	2	.333	3	3	2	0	26	43	42	0		11	1	7.96	51	.319	.370	94	.351	1*	99	-11	-0.6
1873	Phi NA	0	2	.000	3	2	1	0	16	27	24	0		2	0	4.50	73	.318	.333	258	.244	0*	103	-3	-0.2
1874	Phi NA	1	3	.250	6	4	4	0	39	57	42	0		1	0	1.62	137	.297	.301	151	.278	1*	85	1	0.1
1875	Cen NA	2	12	.143	14	14	14	0	126	169	138	0		5	6	2.71	80	.274	.280	61	.279	3	81	-8	-0.3
	Ath NA	3	1	.750	4	4	4	0	36	41	19	0		3	3	2.50	96	.279	.293	164	.280	0*	158	0	0.0
	Year	5	13	.278	18	18	18	0	162	210	30	0		8	9	2.67	83	.275	.283	225	.280	4	99	-15	-0.3
Total	4 NA	7	20	.259	30	27	25	0	243	337	265	0		22	10	3.19	78	.287	.300	728	.276	6	98	-21	-1.0
BECK, GEORGE Ernest George B. B 2.21.1890 South Bend, IN D 10.29.1973 South Bend, IN BR/TR 5-11/165# d5.15																									
1914	Cle A	0	0	—	1	0	0	0	1	1	0	0	1	0	0	0.00	—	.250	.400	0-0	—	0		0	0.0
BECK, FRANK Frank J. (b: Frank J. Hengstebeck) B 11.1857 TR 5-9/141# d5.2																									
1884	Pit AA	0	3	.000	3	3	3	0	25	33	29	0	5	6	11	6.12	54	.306	.370	12	.333	1	79	-8	-0.7
	Bal U	0	2	.000	2	2	1	0	9	17	13	0		4	7	8.00	33	.378	.429	20	.100	-1*	112	-4	-0.7
Total	1	0	5	.000	5	5	4	0	34	50	42	0	5	10	18	6.62	48	.327	.387	32	.188	-0	95	-12	-1.4
BECK, RICH Richard Henry B 1.21.1941 Pasco, WA BB/TR 6-3/190# d9.14 Mil 1966-67																									
1965	NY A	2	1	.667	3	3	1-1	0	21	22	6	1	0	7-1	10	2.14	159	.275	.333	7-0	.000	-0	77	3	0.4
BECK, ROD Rodney Roy B 8.3.1968 Burbank, CA BR/TR 6-1/236# d5.6																									
1991	SF N	1	1	.500	31	0	0	1-0	52.1	53	22	4	1	13-2	38	3.78	95	.273	.319	2-0	.500	0		0	0.0
1992	SF N	3	3	.500	65	0	0	17-6	92	62	20	4	2	15-2	87	1.76	188	.190	.228	2-0	.500	0		17	1.7
1993	SF N★	3	1	.750	76	0	0	48-4	79.1	57	20	11	3	13-4	86	2.16	182	.201	.241	4-1	.000	-0		16	2.4
1994	SF N★	2	4	.333	48	0	0	28-0	48.2	49	17	10	0	13-2	39	2.77	145	.261	.304	3-0	.000	-0		7	1.3
1995	SF N	5	6	.455	60	0	0	33-10	58.2	60	31	7	2	21-3	42	4.45	92	.267	.331	3-0	.333	0		-2	-0.3
1996	SF N	0	9	.000	63	0	0	35-7	62	56	23	9	1	10-2	48	3.34	123	.238	.270	3-0	.333	0		7	1.3
1997	†SF N☆	7	4	.636	73	0	0	37-8	70	67	31	7	2	8-2	53	3.47	118	.248	.275	0-0	—	0		5	0.9
1998	†Chi N	3	4	.429	**81**	0	0	51-7	80.1	86	33	11	2	20-4	81	3.02	146	.269	.311	1-0	.000	-0		10	1.9
1999	Chi N	2	4	.333	31	0	0	7-4	30	41	26	5	0	13-3	13	7.80	58	.331	.388	0-0	—	0		-10	-1.8
	†Bos A	0	1	.000	12	0	0	3-1	14	9	3	0	1	5-0	12	1.93	258	.184	.273	0-0	—	0		5	0.5
2000	Bos A	3	0	1.000	34	0	0	0-3	40.2	34	15	2	2	12-1	35	3.10	163	.222	.287	0-0	—	0		9	0.5
2001	Bos A	6	4	.600	68	0	0	6-5	80.2	77	42	15	3	28-6	63	3.90	115	.252	.319	1-0	.000	-0		4	0.5
2003	SD N	3	2	.600	36	0	0	20-0	35.1	25	7	4	1	11-2	32	1.78	221	.197	.266	0-0	—	0		9	1.9
Total	12	38	43	.469	678	0	0	286-55	744	676	290	89	20	182-33	629	3.21	127	.241	.290	19-1	.211	0		77	10.8
BECK, BOOM-BOOM Walter William B 10.16.1904 Decatur, IL D 5.7.1987 Champaign, IL BR/TR 6-2/200# d9.22 C3																									
1924	StL A	0	0	—	1	0	0	0	1	2	0	0	0	1	0	0.00	—	.667	.750	0-0	—	0		0	0.0
1927	StL A	1	0	1.000	3	1	1	0	11.1	15	8	0	1	5	6	5.56	78	.333	.412	4-0	.250	-0	153	-1	-0.1
1928	StL A	2	3	.400	16	4	2	0	49	52	29	4	4	20	17	4.41	95	.289	.373	14-0	.429	1	96	-2	0.0
1933	Bro N	12	20	.375	43	**35**	15-3	1	257	270	128	9	11	69	89	3.54	91	.267	.321	95-2	.189	0	111	-12	-1.4
1934	Bro N	2	6	.250	22	9	2	0	57	72	50	6	5	32	24	7.42	53	.301	.395	17-1	.235	1	118	-21	-2.3
1939	Phi N	7	14	.333	34	16	12	3	182.2	203	104	11	3	64	77	4.73	85	.284	.345	68-4	.132	-3	68	-13	-1.6
1940	Phi N	4	9	.308	29	15	4	0	129.1	147	69	13	9	41	38	4.31	90	.286	.349	36-3	.056	-3	58	-5	-0.7
1941	Phi N	1	9	.100	34	7	2	0	95.1	104	52	8	2	35	34	4.63	80	.276	.341	25-1	.120	-2	62	-8	-1.0
1942	Phi N	0	1	.000	26	1	0	0	53	69	30	4	1	17	10	4.75	70	.325	.378	12-0	.333	1*	102	-8	-0.3
1943	Phi N	0	0	—	4	0	0	0	13.2	24	15	1	2	5	3	9.88	34	.393	.456	4-0	.500	1		-9	-0.4
1944	Det A	1	2	.333	28	2	0	1	74	67	36	5	3	27	25	3.89	92	.243	.317	22-1	.318	2	105	-1	0.0
1945	Cin N	2	4	.333	11	6	2	1	47.2	42	21	0	1	12	9	3.40	111	.236	.288	14-2	.214	-0	68	2	0.2
	Pit N	6	1	.857	14	5	4	0	63	54	19	2	0	14	20	2.14	184	.234	.278	16-5	.125	-1	94	12	1.1
	Year	8	5	.615	25	11	6	1	110.2	96	23	2	1	26	29	2.68	144	.235	.282	30-7	.167	-1	81	13	1.3
Total	12	38	69	.355	265	101	44-3	6	1034	1121	561	63	42	342	352	4.30	86	.277	.340	327-19	.187	-2	89	-66	-6.5
BECKER, CHARLIE Charles S. "Buck" B 10.14.1888 Washington, DC D 7.30.1928 Washington, DC BL/TL 6-2/180# d8.2																									
1911	Was A	3	5	.375	11	5	5-1	0	71.1	80	44	2	7	23	31	4.04	81	.268	.335	22-1	.227	-0	48	-5	-0.5
1912	Was A	0	0	—	4	0	0	0	9	8	6	0	0	6	5	3.00	111	.258	.378	2-0	.500	0		0	0.0
Total	2	3	5	.375	15	5	5-1	0	80.1	88	50	2	7	29	36	3.92	84	.267	.340	24-1	.250	0	48	-5	-0.5
BECKER, BOB Robert Charles B 8.15.1875 Syracuse, NY D 10.11.1951 Syracuse, NY TL d9.6																									
1897	Phi N	0	2	.000	5	2	2	0	24	32	18	0	1	7	10	5.63	75	.317	.367	9-0	.111	-0	85	-3	-0.3
1898	Phi N	0	0	—	1	0	0	0	5	6	6	0	0	5	0	10.80	32	.300	.440	1-0	.000	0		-3	-0.1
Total	2	0	2	.000	6	2	2	0	29	38	24	0	1	12	10	6.52	62	.314	.381	10-0	.100	-0	85	-6	-0.4
BECKETT, JOSH Joshua Patrick B 5.15.1980 Spring, TX BR/TR 6-4/190# d9.4																									
2001	Fla N	2	2	.500	4	4	0	0-0	24	14	9	3	1	11-0	24	1.50	281	.161	.263	7-2	.286	1	115	5	1.0
2002	Fla N	6	7	.462	23	21	0	0-0	107.2	93	56	13	1	44-2	113	4.10	96	.232	.307	31-5	.032	-3	108	-3	-0.6
2003	†Fla N	9	8	.529	24	23	0	0-0	142	132	54	9	2	56-4	152	3.04	135	.246	.319	46-5	.152	0	121	16	1.8

Year	Tm Lg	W	L	Pct	G	GS	CG-Sho	SV-BS	IP	H	R	HR	HB	BB-IB	SO	ERA	AERA	OAV	OOB	AB-SH	AVG	PB	Sup	APR	PW
Total	3	17	17	.500	51	48	0	0-0	273.2	239	119	25	4	111-6	289	3.32	122	.233	.309	84-12	.119	-2	115	18	2.2
BECKETT, ROBBIE Robert Joseph B 7.16.1972 Austin, TX BR/TL 6-5/235# d9.12																									
1996	Col N	0	0	—	5	0	0	0-1	5.1	6	8	3	0	9-0	6	13.50	39	.286	.484	0-0	—	0		-4	-0.2
1997	Col N	0	0	—	2	0	0	0-0	1.2	1	1	0	0	1-1	2	5.40	96	.167	.286	0-0	—	0		0	0.0
Total	2	0	0	—	7	0	0	0-1	7	7	9	3	0	10-1	8	11.57	45	.259	.447	0-0	—	0		-4	-0.2
BECKMAN, JIM James Joseph (b: Reinhardt Boeckman) B 3.1.1905 Cincinnati, OH D 12.5.1974 Montgomery, OH BR/TR 5-10/172# d7.27																									
1927	Cin N	0	1	.000	4	1	0	0	12.1	18	10	2	1	6	0	5.84	65	.340	.417	1-0	.000	0	67	-3	-0.2
1928	Cin N	0	1	.000	6	0	0	0	15.1	19	12	1	0	9	4	5.87	67	.306	.394	3-0	.000	-0		-4	-0.3
Total	2	0	2	.000	10	1	0	0	27.2	37	22	3	1	15	4	5.86	66	.322	.405	4-0	.000	-0	67	-7	-0.5
BECKMANN, BILL William Aloysius B 12.8.1907 Clayton, MO D 1.2.1990 Florissant, MO BR/TR 6/175# d5.2																									
1939	Phi A	7	11	.389	27	19	7-2	0	155.1	198	104	15	1	41	20	5.39	87	.312	.355	52-6	.250	0	98	-9	-0.9
1940	Phi A	8	4	.667	34	9	6-2	1	127.1	132	68	11	1	35	47	4.17	107	.265	.314	39-3	.205	-1	81	5	0.2
1941	Phi A	5	9	.357	22	15	4	1	130	141	76	11	2	33	28	4.57	92	.270	.315	47-4	.191	0	92	-6	-0.6
1942	Phi A	0	1	.000	5	1	0	0	20.1	24	17	1	0	9	10	7.08	53	.289	.359	4-1	.500	1	113	-6	-0.2
	StL N	1	0	1.000	2	0	0	0	7	4	0	0	0	1	3	0.00	—	.200	.238	1-0	.000	-0		3	0.4
Total	4	21	25	.457	90	44	17-4	2	440	499	265	38	4	119	108	4.79	92	.284	.330	143-14	.224	1	94	-13	-1.1
BECKWITH, JOE Thomas Joseph B 1.28.1955 Opelika, AL BL/TR 6-3/200# d7.21																									
1979	LA N	1	2	.333	17	0	0	2-0	37.1	42	18	4	0	15-1	28	4.34	84	.284	.350	5-1	.000	-1		-2	-0.2
1980	LA N	3	3	.500	38	0	0	0-0	59.2	60	17	1	1	23-4	40	1.96	179	.263	.331	2-0	.000	0		9	0.9
1982	LA N	2	1	.667	19	1	0	1-0	40	38	14	2	0	14-5	33	2.70	129	.252	.311	7-1	.000	-1	229	3	0.1
1983	†LA N	3	4	.429	42	3	0	1-0	71	73	40	5	1	35-11	50	3.55	101	.264	.347	5-0	.200	0	49	-2	-0.2
1984	KC A	8	4	.667	49	1	0	2-1	100.2	92	39	13	2	25-1	75	3.40	119	.247	.293	0-0	—	0	0	8	0.9
1985	†KC A	1	5	.167	49	0	0	1-2	95	99	45	9	3	32-8	80	4.07	102	.269	.330	0-0	—	0		2	0.1
1986	LA N	0	0	—	15	0	0	0-1	18.1	28	16	5	0	6-0	13	6.87	50	.350	.395	0-0	—	0		-8	-0.4
Total	7	18	19	.486	229	5	0	7-4	422	432	189	39	7	150-30	319	3.54	107	.266	.328	19-2	.053	-1	71	10	1.2
BEDARD, ERIK Erik Joseph B 3.5.1979 Navan, ON, CAN BL/TL 6-1/180# d4.17																									
2002	Bal A	0	0	—	2	0	0	0-0	0.2	2	1	0	0	0-0	1	13.50	32	.500	.500	0-0	—	0		-1	0.0
BEDGOOD, PHIL Phillip Burlette B 3.8.1898 Harrison, GA D 11.8.1927 Fort Pierce, FL BR/TR 6-3/218# d9.20																									
1922	Cle A	1	0	1.000	1	1	1	0	9	7	4	0	3	4	5	4.00	100	.233	.378	2-1	.000	-0	106	0	0.0
1923	Cle A	0	2	.000	9	2	0	0	18.2	16	13	0	2	14	7	5.30	75	.246	.395	4-0	.250	0	167	-3	-0.2
Total	2	1	2	.333	10	3	1	0	27.2	23	17	0	5	18	12	4.88	82	.242	.390	6-1	.167	0	147	-3	-0.2
BEDIENT, HUGH Hugh Carpenter B 10.23.1889 Gerry, NY D 7.21.1965 Jamestown, NY BR/TR 6/185# d4.26																									
1912	†Bos A	20	9	.690	41	28	19	2	231	206	93	6	3	55	122	2.92	116	.240	.288	73-6	.192	1	102	14	1.7
1913	Bos A	15	14	.517	43	28	15-1	5	259	255	104	0	6	67	122	2.78	106	.263	.314	80-5	.125	-3	80	7	0.2
1914	Bos A	8	12	.400	42	16	7-1	2	177.1	187	97	4	5	45	70	3.60	75	.281	.331	50-1	.100	-2	129	-19	-2.3
1915	Buf F	16	18	.471	53	30	16-2	**10**	269.1	284	131	5	3	69	106	3.17	88	.274	.321	83-5	.108	-5	92	-16	-2.7
Total	4	59	53	.527	179	102	57-4	19	936.2	932	425	15	17	236	420	3.08	96	.264	.313	286-17	.133	-9	98	-14	-3.1
BEDNAR, ANDY Andrew Jackson B 8.16.1908 Streator, IL D 11.26.1937 Graham, TX BR/TR 5-10.5/180# d9.6																									
1930	Pit N	0	0	—	2	0	0	0	1.1	4	4	0	0	1	1	27.00	18	.500	.556	0-0	—	0		-3	-0.1
1931	Pit N	0	0	—	3	0	0	0	4	10	5	1	0	0	2	11.25	34	.476	.476	0-0	—	0		-3	-0.1
Total	2	0	0	—	5	0	0	0	5.1	14	9	1	0	1	3	15.19	27	.483	.500	0-0	—	0		-6	-0.2
BEDROSIAN, STEVE Stephen Wayne B 12.6.1957 Methuen, MA BR/TR 6-3/200# d8.14																									
1981	Atl N	1	2	.333	15	1	0	0-1	24.1	15	14	2	1	15-2	9	4.44	81	.169	.292	2-0	.000	-0	99	-2	-0.3
1982	†Atl N	8	6	.571	64	3	0	11-6	137.2	102	39	7	4	57-5	123	2.42	155	.206	.292	26-4	.038	-2	79	21	2.1
1983	Atl N	9	10	.474	70	1	0	19-7	120	100	50	11	4	51-8	114	3.60	108	.229	.313	19-1	.105	-1	68	5	0.7
1984	Atl N	9	6	.600	40	4	0	11-2	83.2	65	23	5	1	33-5	81	2.37	163	.210	.288	17-1	.118	-1	109	14	2.6
1985	Atl N	7	15	.318	37	37	0	0-0	206.2	198	101	17	5	111-6	134	3.83	101	.254	.349	64-6	.078	-4	86	0	-0.5
1986	Phi N	8	6	.571	68	0	0	29-9	90.1	79	39	12	0	34-10	82	3.39	114	.232	.299	5-0	.200	0		5	0.9
1987	Phi N★	5	3	.625	65	0	0	**40-8**	89	79	31	11	1	28-5	74	2.83	150	.237	.297	4-0	.000	-0		14	2.1
1988	Phi N	6	6	.500	57	0	0	28-6	74.1	75	34	6	0	27-5	61	3.75	95	.257	.317	2-0	.000	-0		-1	-0.3
1989	Phi N	2	3	.400	28	0	0	6-3	33.2	21	13	7	1	17-1	24	3.21	111	.183	.289	0-0	—	0		2	0.3
	†SF N	1	4	.200	40	0	0	17-5	51	35	18	5	0	22-4	34	2.65	128	.192	.277	6-0	.167	-0		4	0.5
	Year	3	7	.300	68	0	0	23-8	84.2	56	35	12	1	39-5	58	2.87	120	.189	.282	6-0	.167	-0		5	0.8
1990	SF N	9	9	.500	68	0	0	17-5	79.1	72	40	6	2	44-9	43	4.20	87	.241	.341	4-0	.500	1		-5	-0.9
1991	†Min A	5	3	.625	56	0	0	6-1	77.1	70	42	11	3	35-6	44	4.42	97	.243	.327	0-0	—	0		-1	-0.2
1993	Atl N	5	2	.714	49	0	0	0-0	49.2	34	11	4	2	14-2	33	1.63	246	.194	.256	2-0	.000	-0		13	1.6
1994	Atl N	0	2	.000	46	0	0	0-2	46	41	20	4	2	18-5	43	3.33	128	.243	.319	2-0	.500	0		4	0.2
1995	Atl N	1	2	.333	29	0	0	0-2	28	40	21	6	1	12-2	22	6.11	70	.354	.414	0-0	—	0		-6	-0.6
Total	14	76	79	.490	732	46	0	184-57	1191	1026	496	114	27	518-75	921	3.38	115	.232	.314	153-12	.098	-7	87	67	8.2
BEEBE, FRED Frederick Leonard B 12.31.1880 Lincoln, NE D 10.30.1957 Elgin, IL BR/TR 6-1/190# d4.17																									
1906	Chi N	6	1	.857	14	6	4	1	70	56	27	1	5	32	55	2.70	98	.210	.306	29-0	.103	-1	170	0	-0.2
	StL N	9	9	.500	20	19	16-1	0	160.2	115	65	1	9	68	116	3.02	87	.208	.305	58-3	.172	0	88	-5	-0.5
	Year	15	10	.600	34	25	20-1	1	230.2	171	68	2	14	100	**171**	2.93	90	.209	.305	87-3	.149	-1	107	-5	-0.7
1907	StL N	7	19	.269	31	29	24-4	0	238.1	192	95	1	10	109	141	2.72	92	.230	.326	86-3	.128	-3	62	-2	-0.5
1908	StL N	5	13	.278	29	19	12	0	174.1	134	88	3	4	66	72	2.63	90	**.193**	.267	56-3	.125	-2	83	-8	-1.0
1909	StL N	15	21	.417	44	34	18-1	1	287.2	256	142	5	7	104	105	2.82	90	.229	.299	108-3	.167	-2	114	-16	-2.1
1910	Cin N	12	14	.462	35	26	11-2	0	214.1	193	101	3	7	94	93	3.07	95	.246	.333	73-1	.164	-2	89	-2	-0.4
1911	Phi N	3	3	.500	9	8	3	0	48.1	52	26	2	3	24	20	4.47	77	.297	.391	19-0	.263	2*	104	-3	-0.1
1916	Cle A	5	3	.625	20	12	5-1	2	100.2	92	43	1	1	37	32	2.41	125	.251	.321	28-3	.214	1	88	4	0.3
Total	7	62	83	.428	202	153	93-9	4	1294.1	1090	587	17	46	534	634	2.86	93	.227	.311	457-16	.158	-8	93	-32	-4.5
BEECH, MATT Lucas Matthew B 1.20.1972 Oakland, CA BL/TL 6-2/190# d8.8																									
1996	Phi N	1	4	.200	8	8	0	0-0	41.1	49	32	8	3	11-0	33	6.97	62	.306	.350	14-0	.071	-1	94	-10	-1.1
1997	Phi N	4	9	.308	24	24	0	0-0	136.2	147	81	25	5	57-9	120	5.07	84	.279	.351	30-11	.167	-0	93	-11	-0.9
1998	Phi N	3	9	.250	21	21	0	0-0	117	126	78	19	4	63-2	113	5.15	84	.275	.366	33-6	.152	-1	83	-13	-1.3
Total	3	8	22	.267	53	53	0	0-0	295	322	191	52	12	131-11	266	5.37	80	.281	.357	77-17	.143	-2	89	-34	-3.3
BEECHER, ROY Leroy "Colonel" B 5.10.1884 Swanton, OH D 10.11.1952 Toledo, OH BL/TR 6-2/180# d9.29																									
1907	NY N	0	2	.000	2	2	2	0	14	17	8	0	0	6	5	2.57	96	.293	.359	5-0	.000	-1	43	-1	-0.2
1908	NY N	0	0	—	2	0	0	1	5.2	11	5	0	0	3	0	7.94	30	.440	.500	3-0	.333	1*		-3	-0.1
Total	2	0	2	.000	4	2	2	1	19.2	28	13	0	0	9	5	4.12	60	.337	.402	8-0	.125	-0	43	-4	-0.3
BEENE, FRED Freddy Ray B 11.24.1942 Angleton, TX BB/TR 5-9/160# d9.18																									
1968	Bal A	0	0	—	1	0	0	0	1	2	1	0	0	1-0	1	9.00	33	.500	.500	0-0	—	0		-1	0.0
1969	Bal A	0	0	—	2	0	0	0-0	2.2	2	0	0	0	1-0	0	0.00	—	.200	.273	0-0	—	0		1	0.1
1970	Bal A	0	0	—	4	0	0	0-0	6	8	5	1	0	5-4	4	6.00	61	.320	.433	0-0	—	0		-2	-0.1
1972	NY A	1	3	.250	29	1	0	3-0	57.2	55	21	3	1	24-5	37	2.34	126	.256	.332	9-0	.000	-1*	539	2	0.1
1973	NY A	6	0	1.000	19	4	0	1-0	91	67	21	5	1	27-5	49	1.68	218	.209	.271	0-0	—	0	110	20	1.4
1974	NY A	0	0	—	6	0	0	1-0	10	9	4	1	1	2-0	10	2.70	131	.231	.286	0-0	—	0		1	0.1
	Cle A	4	4	.500	32	0	0	2-3	73	68	44	7	1	26-2	35	4.93	73	.246	.310	0-0	—	0*		-10	-1.0
	Year	4	4	.500	38	0	0	3-3	83	77	53	8	2	28-2	45	4.66	77	.244	.307	0-0	—	0		-10	-0.9
1975	Cle A	1	0	1.000	19	1	0	1-1	46.2	63	42	4	3	25-3	20	6.94	55	.323	.406	0-0	—	0*	256	-17	-0.8
Total	7	12	7	.632	112	6	0	8-4	288	274	138	21	7	111-19	156	3.63	97	.253	.324	9-0	.000	-1	197	-6	-0.2
BEENE, ANDY Ramon Andrew B 10.13.1956 Freeport, TX BR/TR 6-3/205# d9.22																									
1983	Mil A	0	0	—	1	0	0	0-0	2	3	3	0	0	1-1	0	4.50	83	.333	.400	0-0	—	0		-1	-0.1

Year	Tm Lg	W	L	Pct	G	GS	CG-Sho	SV-BS	IP	H	R	HR	HB	BB-IB	SO	ERA	AERA	OAV	OOB	AB-SH	AVG	PB	Sup	APR	PW
1984	Mil A	0	2	.000	5	3	0	0-0	18.2	28	23	1	2	9-0	11	11.09	35	.350	.424	0-0	—	0	102	-14	-1.2
Total	2	0	2	.000	6	3	0	0-0	20.2	31	26	1	2	10-1	11	10.45	37	.348	.422	0-0	—	0	102	-15	-1.3
BEERS, CLARENCE Clarence Scott B 12.9.1918 ElDorado, KS BR/TR 6/175# d5.2																									
1948	StL N	0	0	—	1	0	0	0	0.2	3	4	0	0	1	0	13.50	30	.500	.571	0-0	—	0		-2	-0.1
BEGGS, JOE Joseph Stanley "Fireman" B 11.4.1910 Rankin, PA D 7.19.1983 Indianapolis, IN BR/TR 6-1/182# d4.19 Mil 1944-45																									
1938	NY A	3	2	.600	14	9	4	0	58.1	69	41	7	0	20	8	5.40	84	.299	.355	20-0	.250	1	95	-6	-0.3
1940	†Cin N	12	3	.800	37	1	0	**7**	76.2	68	19	1	1	21	25	2.00	190	.243	.298	21-1	.190	-0	275	**15**	3.2
1941	Cin N	4	3	.571	37	0	0	5	57	57	29	2	0	27	19	3.79	95	.313	.402	10-0	.300	1		-2	-0.2
1942	Cin N	6	5	.545	38	0	0	8	88.2	65	28	4	1	33	24	2.13	154	.206	.283	21-1	.000	-3		11	1.4
1943	Cin N	7	6	.538	39	4	4-2	6	115.1	121	38	0	0	25	28	2.34	142	.276	.315	35-2	.143	-1	58	**11**	1.2
1944	Cin N	1	0	1.000	1	1	1	0	9	8	2	0	0	0	2	2.00	174	.222	.222	4-0	.000	-1	96	2	0.1
1946	Cin N	12	10	.545	28	22	14-2	1	190	175	63	15	1	39	38	2.32	144	.247	.287	63-7	.222	2	97	20	2.6
1947	Cin N	0	3	.000	11	4	0	0	32.1	42	26	4	0	6	11	5.29	78	.316	.345	11-1	.091	-1	118	-6	-0.6
	NY N	3	3	.500	32	0	0	2	66	81	38	6	1	18	23	4.23	96	.300	.346	13-2	.077	-1		-2	-0.3
	Year	3	6	.333	43	4	0	2	98.1	123	70	10	1	24	34	4.58	89	.305	.346	24-3	.083	-2	119	-9	-0.9
1948	NY N	0	0	—	1	0	0	0	0.1	2	0	0	0	0	0	0.00	—	.667	.667	0-0	—	0		0	0.0
Total	9	48	35	.578	238	41	23-4	29	693.2	688	284	39	4	189	178	2.96	122	.265	.316	198-14	.167	-3	101	43	7.1
BEGLEY, ED Edward N. (b: Edward N. Bagley) B 1863 New York, NY D 7.24.1919 Waterbury, CT d5.3																									
1884	NY N	12	18	.400	31	30	30	0	266	296	209	9		99	104	4.16	72	.263	.323	121	.182	-3*	93	-33	-3.2
1885	NY AA	4	9	.308	15	14	10	0	115	131	102	5	8	48	44	4.93	63	.278	.355	52	.173	-1	91	-25	-2.1
Total	2	16	27	.372	46	44	40	0	381	427	311	14	8	147	148	4.39	69	.268	.333	173	.179	-3	92	-58	-5.3
BEHAN, PETIE Charles Frederick B 12.11.1887 Dallas City, PA D 1.22.1957 Bradford, PA BR/TR 5-10/160# d9.16																									
1921	Phi N	0	1	.000	2	2	1	0	10.2	17	8	0	0	1	3	5.91	72	.354	.367	4-0	.000	-1	68	-1	-0.2
1922	Phi N	4	2	.667	7	5	3-1	0	47.1	49	27	3	1	14	13	2.47	189	.259	.314	20-0	.250	-0	112	7	0.7
1923	Phi N	3	12	.200	31	17	5	2	131	182	102	11	1	57	27	5.50	84	.336	.401	43-4	.186	-2*	88	-13	-1.5
Total	3	7	15	.318	40	24	9-1	2	189	248	137	14	2	72	43	4.76	97	.319	.378	67-4	.194	-3	91	-7	-1.0
BEHENNA, RICK Richard Kipp B 3.6.1960 Miami, FL BR/TR 6-2/170# d4.12																									
1983	Atl N	3	3	.500	14	6	0	0-0	37.1	37	20	7	1	12-2	17	4.58	85	.255	.314	12-0	.333	2	91	-2	-0.2
	Cle A	0	2	.000	5	4	0	0-0	26	22	13	0	1	14-1	9	4.15	102	.232	.336	0-0	—	0	69	0	0.0
1984	Cle A	0	3	.000	3	3	0	0-0	9.2	17	15	5	1	8-0	6	13.97	29	.386	.491	0-0	—	0	37	-10	-1.5
1985	Cle A	0	2	.000	4	4	0	0-0	19.2	29	17	3	0	8-0	4	7.78	53	.354	.407	0-0	—	0	93	-7	-0.6
Total	3	3	10	.231	26	17	0	0-0	92.2	105	65	15	3	42-3	36	6.12	67	.287	.363	12-0	.333	2	77	-19	-2.3
BEHNEY, MEL Melvin Brian B 9.2.1947 Newark, NJ BL/TL 6-2/180# d8.14 Mil 1970																									
1970	Cin N	0	2	.000	5	1	0	0-0	10	15	11	1	0	8-2	2	4.50	90	.341	.442	1-0	.000	-0	89	-3	-0.5
BEHRMAN, HANK Henry Bernard B 6.27.1921 Brooklyn, NY D 1.20.1987 New York, NY BR/TR 5-11/174# d4.17																									
1946	Bro N	11	5	.688	47	11	2	4	150.2	138	63	3	2	69	78	2.93	115	.241	.325	42-4	.095	-3	134	6	0.2
1947	†Bro N	0	0	—	2	0	0	0	3.2	3	4	1	0	4	2	9.82	42	.231	.412	0-0	—	0		-2	-0.1
	Pit N	0	2	.000	10	2	0	0	24.2	33	26	6	2	17	11	9.12	46	.347	.456	6-1	.000	-1	125	-12	-0.9
	†Bro N	5	3	.625	38	6	0	8	88.1	94	60	9	0	44	31	5.30	78	.274	.357	26-4	.231	1	164	-11	-1.1
	Year	5	5	.500	50	8	0	8	116.2	130	68	16	2	65	44	6.25	66	.288	.380	32-5	.188	-0	154	-26	-2.1
1948	Bro N	5	4	.556	34	4	2-1	7	91	95	51	7	3	42	42	4.05	99	.268	.350	28-4	.107	-2	128	-2	-0.4
1949	NY N	3	3	.500	43	4	1-1	0	71.1	64	46	5	0	52	25	4.92	81	.239	.363	13-0	.077	-1	100	-7	-0.6
Total	4	24	17	.585	174	27	5-2	19	429.2	427	250	31	7	228	189	4.40	87	.259	.352	115-13	.122	-5	133	-28	-2.9
BEIMEL, JOE Joseph Ronald B 4.19.1977 St.Marys, PA BL/TL 6-3/205# d4.8																									
2001	Pit N	7	11	.389	42	15	0	0-0	115.1	131	72	12	6	49-4	58	5.23	86	.290	.366	26-4	.269	1	88	-9	-1.1
2002	Pit N	2	5	.286	53	8	0	0-1	85.1	88	49	9	4	45-12	53	4.64	90	.267	.359	10-2	.300	1	110	-5	-0.2
2003	Pit N	1	3	.250	69	0	0	0-5	62.1	69	35	7	4	33-6	42	5.05	87	.299	.388	5-0	.000	-1*		-3	-0.2
Total	3	10	19	.345	164	23	0	0-6	263	288	156	28	14	127-22	153	5.00	87	.284	.369	41-6	.244	2	96	-17	-1.5
BEIRNE, KEVIN Kevin Patrick B 1.1.1974 Houston, TX BL/TR 6-4/210# d5.17																									
2000	Chi A	1	3	.250	29	1	0	0-1	49.2	50	41	9	4	20-1	41	6.70	75	.263	.338	0-0	—	0	56	-9	-0.6
2001	Tor A	0	0	—	5	0	0	0-0	7	13	10	1	0	6-1	5	12.86	36	.394	.487	0-0	—	0		-6	-0.3
2002	LA N	2	0	1.000	12	3	0	0-1	29	26	11	4	2	17-2	17	3.41	112	.245	.357	5-1	.400	1	177	2	0.2
Total	3	3	3	.500	46	4	0	0-2	85.2	89	62	14	6	43-4	63	6.09	75	.271	.359	5-1	.400	1	128	-13	-0.7
BELCHER, TIM Timothy Wayne B 10.19.1961 Mount Gilead, OH BR/TR 6-3/220# d9.6																									
1987	LA N	4	2	.667	6	5	0	0-0	34	30	11	2	0	7-0	23	2.38	167	.240	.278	10-0	.200	0	64	6	1.0
1988	†LA N	12	6	.667	36	27	4-1	4-1	179.2	143	65	8	2	51-7	152	2.91	115	.217	.275	56-5	.071	-2	110	9	0.7
1989	LA N	15	12	.556	39	30	**10-8**	1-0	230	182	81	20	7	80-5	200	2.82	121	.217	.289	70-10	.100	-2	92	16	1.5
1990	LA N	9	9	.500	24	24	5-2	0-0	153	136	76	17	2	48-0	102	4.00	92	.240	.299	43-9	.163	1	93	-5	-0.6
1991	LA N	10	9	.526	33	33	2-1	0-0	209.1	189	76	10	2	75-3	156	2.62	137	.240	.306	67-7	.119	-2	93	20	1.5
1992	Cin N	15	14	.517	35	34	2-1	0-0	227.2	201	104	17	3	80-2	149	3.91	92	.238	.303	76-7	.105	-2	109	-6	-1.0
1993	Cin N	9	6	.600	22	22	4-2	0-0	137	134	72	11	7	47-4	101	4.47	90	.254	.322	50-3	.200	1	118	-6	-0.6
	†Chi A	3	5	.375	12	11	1-1	0-0	71.2	64	36	8	1	27-0	34	4.40	95	.242	.313	0-0	—	0	78	0	-0.1
1994	Det A	7	15	.318	25	25	3	0-0	162	192	124	21	4	78-10	76	5.89	82	.290	.367	0-0	—	0	105	-22	-2.3
1995	†Sea A	10	12	.455	28	28	1	0-0	179.1	188	101	19	5	88-5	96	4.52	105	.269	.352	0-0	—	0	93	3	0.3
1996	KC A	15	11	.577	35	35	4-1	0-0	238.2	262	117	28	6	68-4	113	3.92	128	.281	.331	0-0	—	0	92	26	2.4
1997	KC A	13	12	.520	32	32	3-1	0-0	213.1	242	128	31	5	70-2	113	5.02	94	.288	.345	6-0	.000	-1	110	-6	-0.7
1998	KC A	14	14	.500	34	34	2	0-0	234	247	127	37	7	73-0	130	4.27	113	.272	.328	5-1	.200	0	92	11	1.0
1999	Ana A	6	8	.429	24	24	0	0-0	132.1	168	104	27	5	46-0	52	6.73	72	.315	.369	5-0	.200	0	95	-26	-2.2
2000	Ana A	4	5	.444	9	9	1	0-0	40.2	45	31	8	2	22-1	22	6.86	74	.281	.373	0-0	—	0	88	-7	-1.2
Total	14	146	140	.510	394	373	42-18	5-1	2442.2	2423	1253	264	58	860-43	1519	4.16	101	.259	.323	388-42	.124	-6	99	13	-0.3
BELINDA, STAN Stanley Peter B 8.6.1966 Huntingdon, PA BR/TR 6-3/187# d9.8																									
1989	Pit N	0	1	.000	8	0	0	0-0	10.1	13	8	0	0	2-0	10	6.10	55	.295	.326	0-0	—	0		-3	-0.3
1990	†Pit N	3	4	.429	55	0	0	8-5	58.1	48	23	4	1	29-3	55	3.55	102	.227	.321	5-1	.000	-1		2	0.2
1991	†Pit N	7	5	.583	60	0	0	16-4	78.1	50	30	10	4	35-4	71	3.45	104	.184	.283	7-2	.000	-0		3	0.5
1992	†Pit N	6	4	.600	59	0	0	18-6	71.1	58	26	8	0	29-5	57	3.15	109	.223	.295	3-0	.667	1		3	0.6
1993	Pit N	3	1	.750	40	0	0	19-3	42.1	35	18	4	1	11-4	30	3.61	112	.224	.276	1-0	.000	-0		2	0.3
	KC A	1	1	.500	23	0	0	0-1	27.1	30	13	2	1	6-0	25	4.28	107	.280	.325	0-0	—	0		1	0.1
1994	KC A	2	2	.500	37	0	0	1-1	49	47	36	6	5	24-3	37	5.14	97	.250	.345	0-0	—	0		-3	-0.3
1995	†Bos A	8	1	.889	63	0	0	10-4	69.2	51	25	5	4	28-3	57	3.10	157	.205	.291	0-0	—	0		14	1.8
1996	Bos A	2	1	.667	31	0	0	2-2	28.2	31	22	3	4	20-1	18	6.59	77	.272	.399	0-0	—	0		-4	-0.4
1997	Cin N	1	5	.167	84	0	0	1-4	99.1	84	42	11	9	33-6	114	3.71	115	.229	.304	3-0	.333	0		7	0.3
1998	Cin N	4	8	.333	40	0	0	1-1	61.1	46	23	7	1	28-6	57	3.23	133	.212	.304	1-0	.000	-0		7	1.3
1999	Cin N	3	1	.750	29	0	0	2-0	42.2	42	26	11	1	18-3	40	5.27	88	.258	.333	4-0	.250	0		-2	-0.2
2000	Col N	1	3	.250	46	0	0	1-6	35.2	39	32	10	2	17-4	40	7.07	82	.277	.358	1-0	.000	-0*		-5	-0.5
	Atl N	0	0	—	10	0	0	0-0	11	16	12	4	1	5-1	11	9.82	47	.348	.407	0-0	—	0		-6	-0.3
	Year	1	3	.250	56	0	0	1-6	46.2	55	49	14	3	22-5	51	7.71	71	.294	.370	1-0	.000	-0		-10	-0.8
Total	12	41	37	.526	585	0	0	79-37	685.1	590	336	85	34	285-43	622	4.15	103	.233	.315	25-3	.160	1		16	3.1
BELINSKY, BO Robert B 12.7.1936 New York, NY D 11.23.2001 Las Vegas, NV BL/TL 6-2/191# d4.18																									
1962	LA A	10	11	.476	33	31	5-3	1	187.1	149	86	12	13	122-3	145	3.56	109	.216	.343	60-2	.167	1*	81	7	0.8
1963	LA A	2	9	.182	13	13	2	0	76.2	78	54	12	4	35-2	60	5.75	60	.262	.345	27-0	.074	-2	88	-20	-2.5
1964	LA A	9	8	.529	23	22	4-1	0	135.1	120	45	8	6	49-5	91	2.86	115	.240	.314	42-5	.095	-1	95	10	1.0
1965	Phi N	4	9	.308	30	14	3	1	109.2	103	72	13	6	48-5	71	4.84	71	.248	.331	32-1	.188	1*	105	-19	-2.1
1966	Phi N	0	2	.000	9	1	0	0	15.1	14	5	3	3	5-1	8	2.93	123	.250	.344	3-0	.333	0	147	1	0.2

Year	Tm Lg	W	L	Pct	G	GS	CG-Sho	SV-BS	IP	H	R	HR	HB	BB-IB	SO	ERA	AERA	OAV	OOB	AB-SH	AVG	PB	Sup	APR	PW
1967	Hou N	3	9	.250	27	18	0	0	115.1	112	74	12	8	54-0	80	4.68	71	.255	.345	39-1	.077	-2	103	-20	-2.2
1969	Pit N	0	3	.000	8	3	0	0-0	17.2	17	10	1	2	14-2	15	4.58	76	.266	.412	2-0	.000	-0	42	-2	-0.4
1970	Cin N	0	0	—	3	0	0	0-0	8	10	6	0	0	6-0	6	4.50	90	.294	.400	1-0	1.000	1		-1	0.0
Total	8	28	51	.354	146	102	14-4	2-0	665.1	603	352	61	42	333-18	476	4.10	86	.241	.339	206-9	.131	-2	91	-44	-5.2
BELISLE, MATT Matthew Thomas B 6.6.1980 McCallum, TX BB/TR 6-3/190# d9.7																									
2003	Cin N	1	1	.500	6	0	0	0-1	8.2	10	5	1	1	2-0	6	5.19	82	.303	.351	1-0	.000	-0		-1	-0.1
BELITZ, TODD Todd Stephen B 10.23.1975 Des Moines, IA BL/TL 6-1/220# d9.4																									
2000	Oak A	0	0	—	5	0	0	0-0	3.1	4	2	0	0	4-0	3	2.70	176	.267	.421	0-0	—	0		0	0.0
2001	Col N	1	1	.500	8	0	0	0-0	9.1	9	8	2	0	3-0	5	7.71	69	.250	.308	1-0	.000	-0		-2	-0.3
Total	2	1	1	.500	13	0	0	0-0	12.2	13	10	2	0	7-0	8	6.39	82	.255	.345	1-0	.000	-0		-2	-0.3
BELL, CHARLIE Charles C. B 8.12.1868 Cincinnati, OH D 2.7.1937 Cincinnati, OH TR d10.13 b-Frank																									
1889	KC AA	1	0	1.000	1	1	1	0	9	4	5	0	1	3	3	1.00	418	.129	.229	6	.167	0*	89	2	0.3
1891	Lou AA	2	6	.250	10	9	8	0	77	93	65	4	8	20	16	4.68	78	.289	.346	28	.036	-2	64	-10	-1.0
	Cin AA	1	0	1.000	1	1	1	0	9	2	2	0	1	3	1	0.00	—	.069	.182	4	.500	0	121	3	0.4
	Year	3	6	.333	11	10	9	0	86	95	10	4	9	23	17	4.19	88	.271	.332	32	.094	-2	70	-4	-0.6
Total	2	4	6	.400	12	11	10	0	95	99	72	4	10	26	20	3.88	96	.259	.323	38	.105	-2	72	-5	-0.3
BELL, ERIC Eric Alvin B 10.27.1963 Modesto, CA BL/TL 6-3/195# d9.24																									
1985	Bal A	0	0	—	4	0	0	0-0	5.2	4	3	1	0	4-0	4	4.76	85	.200	.333	0-0	—	0		0	0.0
1986	Bal A	1	2	.333	4	4	0	0-0	23.1	23	14	4	0	14-0	18	5.01	83	.258	.356	0-0	—	0	93	-2	-0.3
1987	Bal A	10	13	.435	33	29	2	0-0	165	174	113	32	2	78-0	111	5.45	81	.271	.350	0-0	—	0	86	-21	-2.4
1991	Cle A	4	0	1.000	10	0	0	0-0	18	5	2	0	1	5-0	7	0.50	832	.091	.180	0-0	—	0		7	1.5
1992	Cle A	0	2	.000	7	1	0	0-0	15.1	22	13	1	1	9-0	10	7.63	51	.349	.432	0-0	—	0	23	-6	-0.6
1993	Hou N	0	1	.000	10	0	0	0-0	7.1	10	5	0	0	2-0	2	6.14	63	.313	.353	0-0	—	0		-2	-0.2
Total	6	15	18	.455	68	34	2	0-0	234.2	238	150	38	4	112-0	152	5.18	83	.264	.346	0-0	—	0	87	-24	-2.0
BELL, GARY Gary B 11.17.1936 San Antonio, TX BR/TR 6-1/198# d6.1																									
1958	Cle A	12	10	.545	33	23	10	1	182	141	70	18	5	73-0	110	3.31	110	.213	.294	56-5	.196	2	112	9	1.1
1959	Cle A	16	11	.593	44	28	12-1	5	234	208	107	28	5	105-4	136	4.04	91	.238	.321	75-8	.240	3	113	-5	-0.3
1960	Cle A★	9	10	.474	28	23	6-2	1	154.2	139	78	15	7	82-2	109	4.13	90	.242	.340	47-8	.149	-0*	94	-6	-0.6
1961	Cle A	12	16	.429	34	34	11-2	0	228.1	214	125	32	6	100-2	163	4.10	96	.245	.324	81-9	.198	1	116	-8	-0.8
1962	Cle A	10	9	.526	57	6	1	12	107.2	104	56	14	3	52-8	80	4.26	91	.264	.349	24-0	.208	1	100	-4	-0.7
1963	Cle A	8	5	.615	58	7	0	5	119	91	48	13	4	52-10	98	2.95	123	.208	.298	26-2	.115	-1	67	7	0.7
1964	Cle A	8	6	.571	56	2	0	4	106	106	56	15	4	53-5	89	4.33	83	.260	.349	16-3	.375	2	136	-8	-0.9
1965	Cle A	6	5	.545	60	0	0	17	103.2	86	43	7	2	50-10	86	3.04	115	.226	.318	16-1	.063	-0		4	0.4
1966	Cle A☆	14	15	.483	40	37	12	0	254.1	211	102	19	4	79-3	194	3.22	107	.228	.289	76-8	.132	-1	77	6	0.7
1967	Cle A	1	5	.167	9	9	1	0	60.2	50	28	7	1	24-1	39	3.71	88	.234	.311	15-5	.000	-2	89	-3	-0.4
	†Bos A	12	8	.600	29	24	8	3	165.1	143	70	16	4	47-3	115	3.16	110	.231	.288	59-2	.203	1	115	4	0.6
	Year	13	13	.500	38	33	9	3	226	193	75	23	5	71-4	154	3.31	104	.232	.294	74-7	.162	-1	108	2	0.2
1968	Bos A☆	11	11	.500	35	27	9-3	1	199.1	177	82	7	5	68-6	103	3.12	101	.239	.306	59-5	.220	2	101	0	0.2
1969	Sea A	2	6	.250	13	11	1-1	2-0	61.1	76	40	8	2	34-8	30	4.70	77	.305	.389	14-5	.214	1	80	-9	-0.9
	Chi A	0	0	—	23	2	0	0-0	38.2	48	27	8	2	23-2	26	6.28	61	.308	.403	5-0	.000	-0	160	-9	-0.5
	Year	2	6	.250	36	13	1-1	2-0	100	124	34	16	4	57-10	56	5.31	70	.306	.394	19-5	.158	1	91	-17	-1.4
Total	12	121	117	.508	519	233	71-9	51-0	2015	1794	932	207	54	842-64	1378	3.68	98	.239	.318	569-61	.185	9	101	-22	-1.4
BELL, GEORGE George Glenn "Farmer" B 11.2.1874 Greenwood, NY D 12.25.1941 New York, NY BR/TR 6/195# d4.17																									
1907	Bro N	8	16	.333	35	27	20-3	1	263.2	222	102	1	6	77	88	2.25	104	.238	.300	84-2	.095	-2	99	0	-0.1
1908	Bro N	4	15	.211	29	19	12-2	1	155.1	162	80	3	2	45	63	3.59	65	.270	.324	47-5	.170	1	70	-20	-2.3
1909	Bro N	16	15	.516	33	30	29-6	1	256	236	103	5	4	73	95	2.71	96	.251	.307	90-2	.167	1	85	-4	-0.3
1910	Bro N	10	27	.270	44	36	25-4	1	310	267	127	4	4	82	102	2.64	115	.241	.296	97-2	.134	-4	69	9	0.5
1911	Bro N	5	6	.455	19	12	6-2	0	101	123	59	2	2	28	28	4.28	78	.315	.364	33-1	.121	-1	88	-10	-1.0
Total	5	43	79	.352	160	124	92-17	4	1086	1010	471	15	18	305	376	2.85	94	.254	.310	351-12	.137	-6	81	-25	-3.2
BELL, HI Herman S B 7.16.1897 Mt.Sherman, KY D 6.7.1949 Glendale, CA BR/TR 6/185# d4.16																									
1924	StL N	3	8	.273	28	10	5	1	113.1	124	68	5	5	29	29	4.92	77	.292	.344	31-0	.065	-2	83	-12	-1.3
1926	†StL N	6	6	.500	27	8	3	2	85	82	41	1	2	17	27	3.18	123	.255	.296	25-1	.120	-1	67	5	0.4
1927	StL N	1	3	.250	25	1	0	0	57.1	71	37	5	1	22	31	3.92	101	.317	.381	11-0	.091	-1	172	-2	-0.3
1929	StL N	0	2	.000	7	0	0	0	13	19	15	1	0	4	4	6.92	67	.339	.383	3-0	.000	-0		-5	-0.6
1930	†StL N	4	3	.571	39	9	2	**8**	115.1	143	65	4	2	23	42	3.90	129	.299	.334	26-3	.077	-3	108	**11**	0.5
1932	NY N	8	4	.667	35	10	3	2	120	132	58	12	2	16	25	3.68	101	.280	.307	34-1	.088	-2	129	1	-0.2
1933	†NY N	6	5	.545	38	7	1-1	5	105.1	100	31	4	2	20	24	2.05	157	.246	.285	29-1	.138	-1	104	**13**	1.4
1934	NY N	4	3	.571	22	2	0	6	54	72	25	2	2	12	9	3.67	105	.319	.358	19-1	.105	-1	268	2	0.1
Total	8	32	34	.485	221	47	14-1	24	663.1	743	340	34	16	143	191	3.69	107	.285	.326	178-7	.096	-12	108	13	-0.0
BELL, JERRY Jerry Houston B 10.6.1947 Madison, TN BB/TR 6-4/190# d9.6																									
1971	Mil A	2	1	.667	8	0	0	0-0	14.2	10	5	0	0	6-1	8	3.07	113	.200	.281	0-0	—	0		1	0.2
1972	Mil A	5	1	.833	25	3	0	0-0	70.2	50	15	1	3	33-4	20	1.66	184	.209	.310	14-1	.071	-1	136	11	0.9
1973	Mil A	9	9	.500	31	25	8	1-3	183.2	185	95	14	5	70-5	57	3.97	95	.263	.332	0-0	—	0	127	-6	-0.5
1974	Mil A	1	0	1.000	5	0	0	0-0	14	17	6	2	0	5-0	4	2.57	141	.315	.373	0-0	—	0		1	0.1
Total	4	17	11	.607	69	28	8	1-3	283	262	121	17	8	114-10	89	3.28	109	.250	.327	14-1	.071	-1	132	7	0.7
BELL, RALPH Ralph Albert "Lefty" B 11.6.1890 Kahoka, MO D 10.18.1959 Burlington, IA BL/TL 5-11.5/170# d7.16																									
1912	Chi A	0	0	—	3	0	0	0	6	8	7	1	0	8	5	9.00	36	.333	.500	2-0	.000	-0		-4	-0.2
BELL, ROB Robert Allen B 1.17.1977 Newburgh, NY BR/TR 6-5/225# d4.8																									
2000	Cin N	7	8	.467	26	26	1	0-0	140.1	130	84	32	1	73-6	112	5.00	94	.243	.334	45-3	.067	-3	107	-4	-0.7
2001	Cin N	0	5	.000	9	9	0	0-0	44.1	46	28	9	3	17-1	33	5.48	83	.275	.351	7-2	.143	0	65	-4	-0.3
	Tex A	5	5	.500	18	18	0	0-0	105.1	130	87	23	4	47-0	64	7.18	65	.310	.378	0-0	—	0	128	-27	-2.1
2002	Tex A	4	3	.571	17	15	0	0-0	94	113	69	16	1	35-0	70	6.22	76	.296	.351	1-0	.000	0	126	-15	-0.8
2003	TB A	5	4	.556	19	18	0	0-0	101	103	64	15	5	39-1	44	5.52	82	.263	.336	2-0	.000	-0	107	-10	-0.8
Total	4	21	25	.457	89	86	1	0-0	485	522	332	95	14	211-8	323	5.86	79	.275	.349	55-5	.073	-3	110	-60	-4.7
BELL, BILL William Samuel "Ding Dong" B 10.24.1933 Goldsboro, NC D 10.11.1962 Durham, NC BR/TR 6-3/200# d9.5 Mil 1953																									
1952	Pit N	0	1	.000	4	1	0	0	15.2	16	11	3	0	13	4	4.60	87	.254	.382	4-0	.000	-0	0	-2	-0.1
1955	Pit N	0	0	—	1	0	0	0	1	0	0	0	0	1-0	0	0.00	—	.000	.250	0-0	—	0		0	0.0
Total	2	0	1	.000	5	1	0	0	16.2	16	11	3	0	14-0	4	4.32	93	.242	.375	4-0	.000	-0	0	-2	-0.1
BELTRAN, FRANCIS Francis Lebron B 7.25.1979 Santo Domingo, D.R. BR/TR 6-5/220# d6.28																									
2002	Chi N	0	0	—	11	0	0	0-0	12	14	11	2	0	16-1	11	7.50	54	.311	.484	1-0	.000	-0		-5	-0.2
BELTRAN, RIGO Rigoberto B 11.13.1969 Tijuana, Mexico BL/TL 5-11/185# d6.2																									
1997	StL N	1	2	.333	35	4	0	1-0	54.1	47	25	3	0	17-0	50	3.48	119	.237	.294	7-0	.143	0	89	4	0.2
1998	NY N	0	0	—	7	0	0	0-0	8	6	3	1	0	4-0	5	3.38	123	.214	.303	1-0	.000	-0		1	0.0
1999	NY N	1	1	.500	21	0	0	0-0	31	30	15	5	0	12-2	35	3.48	126	.250	.318	1-0	.000	-0		2	0.1
	Col N	0	0	—	12	0	0	0-0	11	20	9	2	1	7-1	15	7.36	79	.385	.467	2-0	.500	0		-1	0.0
	Year	1	1	.500	33	0	0	0-0	42	50	28	7	1	19-3	50	4.50	106	.291	.365	3-0	.333	0		1	0.1
2000	Col N	0	0	—	1	1	0	0-0	1.1	6	6	2	0	3-0	1	40.50	14	.600	.692	0-0	—	0	158	-4	-0.2
Total	4	2	3	.400	76	5	0	1-0	105.2	109	58	13	1	43-3	106	4.34	101	.267	.336	11-0	.182	0	109	2	0.1
BENDER, CHIEF Charles Albert B 5.5.1884 Crow Wing Co., MN D 5.22.1954 Philadelphia, PA BR/TR 6-2/185# d4.20 C6 HF1953																									
1903	Phi A	17	14	.548	36	33	29-2	0	270	239	115	6	25	65	127	3.07	100	.237	.299	120-4	.183	-1*	114	1	0.0
1904	Phi A	10	11	.476	29	20	18-4	0	203.2	167	90	1	4	59	149	2.87	93	.225	.285	79-2	.228	3*	78	-4	-0.2
1905	†Phi A	18	11	.621	35	23	18-4	0	229	193	103	5	11	90	142	2.83	94	.230	.313	92-2	.217	2*	111	-4	-0.2

Year	Tm Lg	W	L	Pct	G	GS	CG-Sho	SV-BS	IP	H	R	HR	HB	BB-IB	SO	ERA	AERA	OAV	OOB	AB-SH	AVG	PB	Sup	APR	PW
1906	Phi A	15	10	.600	36	27	24	**3**	238.1	208	98	5	8	48	159	2.53	108	.238	.284	99-2	.253	7*	116	4	1.2
1907	Phi A	16	8	.667	33	24	20-4	3	219.1	185	67	1	3	34	112	2.05	127	.231	.265	100-4	.230	3*	112	15	2.0
1908	Phi A	8	9	.471	18	17	14-2	1	138.2	121	48	1	3	21	85	1.75	146	.236	.270	50-1	.220	2*	85	8	1.3
1909	Phi A	18	8	.692	34	29	24-5	1	250	196	68	1	5	45	161	1.66	145	.214	.254	93-5	.215	4*	130	20	2.7
1910	†Phi A	23	5	**.821**	30	28	25-3	0	250	182	63	1	10	47	155	1.58	150	.207	.255	93-4	.269	8*	130	25	4.1
1911	†Phi A	17	5	**.773**	31	24	16-2	3	216.1	198	66	2	4	58	114	2.16	146	.252	.307	79-5	.165	-3*	117	26	2.2
1912	Phi A	13	8	.619	27	19	12-1	2	171	169	63	1	1	33	90	2.74	113	.277	.315	60-3	.150	-1	115	10	0.9
1913	†Phi A	21	10	.677	48	21	14-2	**13**	236.2	208	78	2	3	59	135	2.21	125	.236	.287	78-5	.154	0	154	13	1.7
1914	†Phi A	17	3	**.850**	28	23	14-7	2	179	159	49	4	1	55	107	2.26	115	.240	.299	62-4	.145	0	152	10	1.2
1915	Bal F	4	16	.200	26	23	15	1	178.1	198	103	5	7	37	89	3.99	72	.298	.342	60-0	.267	3	81	-22	-2.0
1916	Phi N	7	7	.500	27	13	4	3	122.2	137	71	3	10	34	43	3.74	71	.287	.347	43-1	.279	4*	143	-16	-1.4
1917	Phi N	8	2	.800	20	10	8-4	2	113	84	24	1	7	26	43	1.67	168	.215	.277	39-0	.205	1	113	15	1.5
1925	Chi A	0	0	—	1	0	0	0	1	1	2	1	0	1	0	18.00	23	.333	.500	0-0	—	0		-1	-0.1
Total	16	212	127	.625	459	334	255-40	34	3017	2645	1108	40	102	712	1711	2.46	111	.239	.292	1147-42	.212	33	117	100	14.9
BENES, ALAN Alan Paul B 1.21.1972 Evansville, IN BR/TR 6-5/215# d9.19 b-Andy																									
1995	StL N	1	2	.333	3	3	0	0-0	16	24	15	2	1	4-0	20	8.44	50	.343	.387	6-0	.000	-1	43	-7	-1.0
1996	†StL N	13	10	.565	34	32	3-1	0-0	191	192	120	27	7	87-3	131	4.90	86	.266	.347	61-7	.148	-0	110	-18	-1.9
1997	StL N	9	9	.500	23	23	2	0-0	161.2	128	60	13	4	68-3	160	2.89	143	.219	.303	52-2	.173	0	74	22	2.3
1999	StL N	0	0	—	2	0	0	0-0	2	2	0	0	0	0-0	2	0.00	—	.286	.286	0-0	—	0		1	0.1
2000	StL N	2	2	.500	30	0	0	0-1	46	54	33	7	2	23-2	26	5.67	81	.290	.373	4-0	.500	1		-6	-0.4
2001	StL N	2	0	1.000	9	1	0	0-0	14.2	14	12	5	0	12-0	10	7.36	58	.250	.382	2-0	.500	0	130	-5	-0.5
2002	Chi N	2	2	.500	7	7	0	0-0	39.1	42	22	3	0	12-1	32	4.35	93	.276	.325	13-0	.077	-1	95	-2	-0.2
2003	Chi N	0	0	—	3	0	0	1-0	8.1	8	2	0	0	6-0	9	2.16	195	.267	.389	1-0	.000	-0		2	0.1
	Tex A	0	3	.000	4	4	0	0-0	15	29	20	2	0	8-0	11	11.40	44	.414	.468	0-0	—	0	88	-10	-1.4
Total	8	29	28	.509	115	70	5-1	1-1	494	493	284	59	14	220-9	401	4.59	92	.263	.341	139-9	.158	0	93	-23	-2.9
BENES, ANDY Andrew Charles B 8.20.1967 Evansville, IN BR/TR 6-6/240# d8.11 b-Alan																									
1989	SD N	6	3	.667	10	10	0	0-0	66.2	51	28	7	1	31-0	66	3.51	100	.213	.303	24-1	.250	2	111	1	0.3
1990	SD N	10	11	.476	32	31	2	0-0	192.1	177	87	18	1	69-5	140	3.60	106	.242	.306	60-5	.100	-2	92	5	0.1
1991	SD N	15	11	.577	33	33	4-1	0-0	223	194	76	23	4	59-7	167	3.03	126	.232	.285	62-7	.032	-2	77	22	2.2
1992	SD N	13	14	.481	34	34	2-2	0-0	231.1	230	90	14	5	61-6	169	3.35	107	.264	.314	67-5	.149	2	71	8	1.1
1993	SD N★	15	15	.500	34	34	4-2	0-0	230.2	200	111	23	4	86-7	179	3.78	109	.232	.303	72-14	.125	-0	84	9	0.9
1994	SD N	6	14	.300	25	25	2-2	0-0	172.1	155	82	20	1	51-2	**189**	3.86	106	.237	.293	49-13	.163	-0	89	5	0.6
1995	SD N	4	7	.364	19	19	1-1	0-0	118.2	121	65	10	4	45-3	126	4.17	97	.262	.330	40-3	.150	-0	103	-3	-0.4
	†Sea A	7	2	.778	12	12	0	0-0	63	72	42	8	2	33-2	45	5.86	81	.287	.369	0-0	—	0	139	-6	-0.8
1996	†StL N	18	10	.643	36	34	3-1	1-0	230.1	215	107	28	6	77-7	160	3.83	109	.247	.310	73-9	.151	-0	109	10	0.9
1997	StL N	10	7	.588	26	26	0	0-0	177	149	64	9	5	61-4	175	3.10	134	.230	.298	55-8	.218	2	97	23	2.2
1998	Ari N	14	13	.519	34	34	1	0-0	231.1	221	111	25	6	74-3	164	3.97	106	.251	.311	65-10	.169	3*	99	7	1.0
1999	Ari N	13	12	.520	33	32	0	0-0	198.1	216	117	34	4	82-3	141	4.81	95	.273	.343	58-10	.155	1	111	-5	-0.6
2000	†StL N	12	9	.571	30	27	1	0-0	166	174	95	30	1	68-0	137	4.88	95	.275	.342	50-6	.080	-1	115	-3	-0.5
2001	StL N	7	7	.500	27	19	0	0-1	107.1	122	92	30	6	61-0	78	7.38	58	.286	.380	32-2	.156	1	125	-36	-3.8
2002	†StL N	5	4	.556	18	17	1	0-0	97	80	39	10	5	51-3	64	2.78	142	.228	.330	34-2	.206	2*	118	10	1.0
Total	14	155	139	.527	403	387	21-9	1-1	2505.1	2377	1206	289	55	909-52	2000	3.97	103	.250	.317	741-95	.143	7	100	47	4.2
BENGE, RAY Raymond Adelphia B 4.22.1902 Jacksonville, TX D 6.27.1997 Centerville, TX BR/TR 5-9.5/160# d9.26																									
1925	Cle A	1	0	1.000	2	2	1-1	0	11.2	9	2	0	0	3	3	1.54	286	.205	.255	5-0	.400	0	133	4	0.3
1926	Cle A	1	0	1.000	8	0	0	0	11.2	15	11	0	0	4	3	3.86	105	.313	.365	3-0	.333	0		-2	-0.1
1928	Phi N	8	18	.308	40	28	12-1	1	201.2	219	117	15	5	88	68	4.55	94	.286	.363	58-7	.207	-0*	80	-6	-0.8
1929	Phi N	11	15	.423	38	26	9-2	4	199	255	147	24	4	77	78	6.29	83	.322	.385	74-3	.203	-3*	91	-18	-2.3
1930	Phi N	11	15	.423	38	29	14	1	225.2	305	178	22	1	81	70	5.70	96	.328	.382	88-3	.205	-3	108	-10	-1.2
1931	Phi N	14	18	.438	38	31	16-2	2	247	251	107	12	5	61	117	3.17	134	.262	.310	88-6	.205	-2	81	26	2.9
1932	Phi N	13	12	.520	41	28	13-2	6	222.1	247	119	15	4	58	89	4.05	109	.281	.329	75-2	.173	-3	102	7	0.4
1933	Bro N	10	17	.370	37	30	16-2	1	228.2	238	104	11	6	55	74	3.42	94	.268	.315	76-6	.184	0	103	-5	-0.7
1934	Bro N	14	12	.538	36	32	14-1	0	227	252	124	11	3	61	64	4.32	90	.272	.319	89-2	.169	-2	117	-9	-1.1
1935	Bro N	9	9	.500	23	17	5-1	1	124.2	142	77	12	1	47	39	4.48	89	.289	.353	47-1	.191	-1	93	-8	-1.2
1936	Bos N	7	9	.438	21	19	2	0	115	161	79	6	1	38	32	5.79	66	.333	.382	43-4	.140	-3	91	-23	-3.0
	Phi N	1	4	.200	15	6	0	1	45.2	70	35	3	0	19	13	4.73	96	.350	.406	10-0	.000	-1	56	-3	-0.5
	Year	8	13	.381	36	25	2	1	160.2	231	38	9	1	57	45	5.49	73	.338	.389	53-4	.113	-4	81	-23	-3.5
1938	Cin N	1	1	.500	9	0	0	2	15.1	13	8	1	0	6	5	4.11	89	.228	.302	3-0	.333	0		-1	-0.1
Total	12	101	130	.437	346	248	102-12	19	1875.1	2177	1108	132	30	598	655	4.52	95	.292	.347	659-34	.188	-17	96	-48	-7.4
BENITEZ, ARMANDO Armando German B 11.3.1972 Ramon Santana, D.R. BR/TR 6-4/180# d7.28																									
1994	Bal A	0	0	—	3	0	0	0-0	10	8	1	0	1	4-0	14	0.90	557	.216	.310	0-0	—	0		4	0.2
1995	Bal A	1	5	.167	44	0	0	2-3	47.2	37	33	8	5	37-2	56	5.66	84	.213	.361	0-0	—	0		-5	-0.7
1996	†Bal A	1	0	1.000	18	0	0	4-1	14.1	7	6	2	0	6-0	20	3.77	131	.143	.232	0-0	—	0		2	0.2
1997	†Bal A	4	5	.444	71	0	0	9-1	73.1	49	22	7	1	43-5	106	2.45	180	.191	.305	0-0	—	0		16	2.0
1998	Bal A	5	6	.455	71	0	0	22-4	68.1	48	29	10	4	39-2	87	3.82	119	.199	.318	0-0	—	0		6	1.2
1999	†NY N	4	3	.571	77	0	0	22-6	78	40	17	4	0	41-4	128	1.85	237	.148	.260	5-0	.000	-1		23	2.8
2000	†NY N	4	4	.500	76	0	0	41-5	76	39	24	10	0	38-2	106	2.61	169	.148	.255	0-0	—	0		16	3.0
2001	NY N	6	4	.600	73	0	0	43-3	76.1	59	32	12	1	40-6	93	3.77	110	.214	.314	1-0	.000	-0		5	0.9
2002	NY N	1	0	1.000	62	0	0	33-4	67.1	46	20	8	3	25-0	79	2.27	175	.190	.272	0-0	—	0		13	1.3
2003	NY N☆	3	3	.500	45	0	0	21-7	49.1	41	18	5	0	24-1	50	3.10	134	.223	.311	1-0	.000	-0		6	1.1
	NY A	1	1	.500	9	0	0	0-0	9.1	8	4	0	0	6-1	10	1.93	227	.235	.350	0-0	—	0		2	0.3
	Sea A	0	0	—	15	0	0	0-1	14.1	10	5	1	0	11-1	15	3.14	138	.189	.328	0-0	—	0		2	0.1
	Year	1	1	.500	24	0	0	0-1	23.2	18	14	1	0	17-2	25	2.66	163	.207	.337	0-0	—	0		4	0.4
Total	10	30	31	.492	564	0	0	197-35	584.1	392	211	67	15	314-24	764	3.03	144	.188	.297	7-0	.000	-1		90	12.4
BENN, HENRY Henry Omer B 1.25.1890 Viola, WI D 6.4.1967 Madison, WI BR/TR 6/190# d9.24																									
1914	Cle A	0	0	—	1	0	0	0	1	0	0	0	0	0	1	0.00	—	.000	.000	0-0	—	0		0	0.0
BENNETT, DAVE David Hans B 11.7.1945 Berkeley, CA BR/TR 6-5/195# d6.12 b-Dennis																									
1964	Phi N	0	0	—	1	0	0	0	1	2	1	0	0	0-0	1	9.00	39	.400	.400	0-0	—	0		-1	0.0
BENNETT, DENNIS Dennis John B 10.5.1939 Oakland, CA BL/TL 6-5/205# d5.12 b-Dave																									
1962	Phi N	9	9	.500	31	24	7-2	3	174.2	144	78	17	6	68-3	149	3.81	102	.224	.302	63-3	.127	-1	98	3	0.2
1963	Phi N	9	5	.643	23	16	6-1	1	119.1	102	44	12	4	33-5	82	2.64	122	.231	.287	40-1	.225	3	123	6	1.1
1964	Phi N	12	14	.462	41	32	7-2	1	208	222	92	23	5	58-8	125	3.68	94	.280	.331	66-2	.197	3	84	-2	0.0
1965	Bos A	5	7	.417	34	18	3	0	141.2	152	76	15	6	53-6	85	4.38	85	.279	.346	39-2	.179	2	98	-8	-0.5
1966	Bos A	3	3	.500	16	13	0	0	75	75	30	9	1	23-2	47	3.24	117	.261	.316	23-2	.130	1	82	5	0.4
1967	Bos A	4	3	.571	13	11	4-1	0	69.2	72	32	12	2	22-2	34	3.88	90	.268	.327	25-1	.120	-0	141	-2	-0.2
	NY N	1	1	.500	8	6	0	0	26.1	37	15	4	1	7-1	14	5.13	66	.336	.378	8-0	.250	0	91	-4	-0.3
1968	Cal A	0	5	.000	16	7	1	1	48.1	46	22	6	4	17-0	36	3.54	82	.250	.324	13-2	.077	-1	47	-4	-0.5
Total	7	43	47	.478	182	127	28-6	6	863	850	389	98	29	281-27	572	3.69	96	.260	.322	277-13	.166	7	97	-6	0.2
BENNETT, ERIK Erik Hans B 9.13.1968 Yreka, CA BR/TR 6-2/205# d5.15																									
1995	Cal A	0	0	—	1	0	0	0-0	0.1	0	0	0	0	0-0	0	0.00	—	.000	.000	0-0	—	0		0	0.0
1996	Min A	2	0	1.000	24	0	0	1-0	27.1	33	24	7	2	16-1	13	7.90	65	.306	.402	0-0	—	0		-8	-0.5
Total	2	2	0	1.000	25	0	0	1-0	27.2	33	24	7	2	16-1	13	7.81	65	.303	.398	0-0	—	0		-8	-0.5
BENNETT, FRANK Francis Allen "Chip" B 10.27.1904 Mardela Springs, MD D 3.18.1966 Wilmington, DE BR/TR 5-10.5/163# d9.17																									
1927	Bos A	0	1	.000	4	1	0	0	12.1	15	4	0	0	6	1	2.92	145	.333	.412	3-0	.000	-1	40	2	0.1
1928	Bos A	0	0	—	1	0	0	0	1	1	0	0	0	0	0	0.00	—	.250	.250	0-0	—	0		0	0.0
Total	2	0	1	.000	5	1	0	0	13.1	16	4	0	0	6	1	2.70	156	.327	.400	3-0	.000	-1	40	2	0.1

Year	Tm Lg	W	L	Pct	G	GS	CG-Sho	SV-BS	IP	H	R	HR	HB	BB-IB	SO	ERA	AERA	OAV	OOB	AB-SH	AVG	PB	Sup	APR	PW
BENNETT, JOEL Joel Todd B 1.31.1970 Binghamton, NY BR/TR 6-1/160# d7.15																									
1998	Bal A	0	0	—	2	0	0	0-0	2	2	1	0	0	3-0	0	4.50	101	.250	.455	0-0	—	0		0	0.0
1999	Phi N	2	1	.667	5	3	0	0-1	17	26	17	10	0	7-0	13	9.00	52	.351	.407	4-1	.000	-0	104	-7	-1.0
Total	2	2	1	.667	7	3	0	0-1	19	28	18	10	0	10-0	13	8.53	55	.341	.413	4-1	.000	-0	104	-7	-1.0
BENNETT, SHAYNE Shayne Anthony B 4.10.1972 Adelaide, South Australia BR/TR 6-5/200# d8.22																									
1997	Mon N	0	1	.000	16	0	0	0-0	22.2	21	9	2	0	9-3	8	3.18	132	.247	.309	1-0	.000	0		3	0.1
1998	Mon N	5	5	.500	62	0	0	1-1	91.2	97	61	8	6	45-3	59	5.50	77	.276	.363	6-1	.000	-0		-12	-1.2
1999	Mon N	0	1	.000	5	1	0	0-0	11.1	24	18	4	1	3-0	4	14.29	31	.444	.475	2-0	.000	-0	82	-11	-0.8
Total	3	5	7	.417	83	1	0	1-1	125.2	142	88	14	7	57-6	71	5.87	72	.290	.365	9-1	.000	-0	82	-20	-1.9
BENOIT, JOAQUIN Joaquin Antonio (Pena) B 7.26.1977 Santiago, D.R. BR/TR 6-3/205# d8.8																									
2001	Tex A	0	0	—	1	1	0	0-0	5	8	6	3	0	3-0	4	10.80	43	.364	.423	0-0	—	0	119	-3	-0.1
2002	Tex A	4	5	.444	17	13	0	1-0	84.2	91	51	6	5	58-2	59	5.31	89	.272	.384	0-0	—	0	91	-4	-0.5
2003	Tex A	8	5	.615	25	17	0	0-0	105	99	67	23	3	51-0	87	5.49	91	.246	.332	2-0	.000	-0	91	-5	-0.5
Total	3	12	10	.545	43	31	0	1-0	194.2	198	124	32	8	112-2	150	5.55	88	.261	.358	2-0	.000	-0	92	-12	-1.1
BENSON, ALLEN Allen Wilbert "Bullet Ben" B 7.12.1908 Hurley, SD D 11.16.1999 Viborg, SD BR/TR 6-1/185# d8.19																									
1934	Was A	0	1	.000	2	2	0	0	9.2	19	14	0	2	5	4	12.10	36	.413	.491	3-2	.000	-0	131	-8	-0.7
BENSON, KRIS Kristen James B 11.7.1974 Kennesaw, GA BR/TR 6-4/190# d4.9																									
1999	Pit N	11	14	.440	31	31	2	0-0	196.2	184	105	16	6	83-5	139	4.07	112	.249	.327	65-6	.154	0	90	9	1.1
2000	Pit N	10	12	.455	32	32	2-1	0-0	217.2	206	104	24	10	86-5	184	3.85	120	.249	.325	65-9	.092	-2	89	18	1.4
2002	Pit N	9	6	.600	25	25	0	0-0	130.1	152	76	18	3	50-8	79	4.70	89	.295	.359	40-4	.175	-0*	108	-8	-0.9
2003	Pit N	5	9	.357	18	18	0	0-0	105	127	67	14	1	36-4	68	4.97	88	.295	.347	30-6	.000	-3	88	-9	-1.3
Total	4	35	41	.461	106	106	4-1	0-0	649.2	669	352	72	20	255-22	470	4.27	105	.266	.336	200-25	.115	-5	93	10	0.3
BENTLEY, CY Clytus G. B 11.23.1850 East Haven, CT D 2.26.1873 Middletown, CT d4.26																									
1872	Man NA	2	15	.118	18	17	14	0	144	259	253	4		12	5	6.06	59	.331	.341	114	.219	-0*	74	-39	-2.6
BENTLEY, JACK John Needles B 3.8.1895 Sandy Spring, MD D 10.24.1969 Olney, MD BL/TL 5-11.5/200# d9.6 ▲																									
1913	Was A	1	0	1.000	3	1	0	1	11	5	0	0	0	2	5	0.00	—	.152	.200	3-0	.000	-0	25	4	0.4
1914	Was A	5	7	.417	30	11	3-2	**4**	125.1	110	49	3	3	53	55	2.37	119	.249	.334	40-0	.275	2	89	4	0.6
1915	Was A	0	2	.000	4	2	0	0	11.1	8	4	0	0	3	0	0.79	374	.200	.256	2-0	.000	-0	12	2	0.3
1916	Was A	0	0	—	2	0	0	0	1.1	0	0	0	0	1	1	0.00	—	.000	.250	0-0	—	0		0	0.0
1923	†NY N	13	8	.619	31	26	12-1	3	183	198	102	10	5	67	80	4.48	85	.277	.343	89-2	.427	16*	118	-13	0.1
1924	†NY N	16	5	.762	28	24	13-1	1	188	196	85	11	4	56	60	3.78	97	.273	.329	98-1	.265	4*	134	0	0.4
1925	NY N	11	9	.550	28	22	11	0	157	200	90	10	1	59	47	5.04	80	.323	.383	99-1	.303	6*	111	-12	-0.3
1926	Phi N	0	2	.000	7	3	0	0	25.1	37	28	2	0	10	7	8.17	51	.327	.382	240-7	.258	1*	107	-11	-0.7
	NY N	0	0	—	1	0	0	0	2	0	0	0	0	2	1	0.00	—	.000	.250	4-0	.250	-0*		1	0.0
	Year	0	2	.000	8	3	0	0	27.1	37	33	2	0	12	8	7.57	54	.311	.374	244-7	.258	1	108	-10	-0.7
1927	NY N	0	0	—	4	0	0	0	9.2	7	7	1	1	10	3	2.79	138	.206	.400	9-0	.222	1*		0	0.0
Total	9	46	33	.582	138	89	39-4	9	714	761	365	37	14	263	259	4.01	91	.280	.346	584-11	.291	28	115	-25	0.8
BENTON, AL John Alton B 3.18.1911 Noble, OK D 4.14.1968 Lynwood, CA BR/TR 6-4/215# d4.18 Mil 1943-44																									
1934	Phi A	7	9	.438	32	21	7	1	155	145	98	7	2	88	58	4.88	90	.249	.349	55-2	.109	-4	109	-10	-1.3
1935	Phi A	3	4	.429	27	9	0	0	78.1	110	81	7	1	47	42	7.70	59	.328	.413	25-1	.040	-3	127	-29	-2.4
1938	Det A	5	3	.625	19	10	6	0	95.1	93	40	10	1	39	33	3.30	151	.259	.333	33-2	.121	-3	95	17	1.0
1939	Det A	6	8	.429	37	16	3	5	150	182	94	11	1	58	67	4.56	107	.294	.355	44-7	.091	-4	101	3	-0.1
1940	Det A	6	10	.375	42	0	0	**17**	79.1	93	44	5	0	36	50	4.42	107	.294	.366	17-4	.000	-3		3	0.4
1941	Det A☆	15	6	.714	38	14	7-1	7	157.2	130	63	11	3	65	63	2.97	153	**.221**	.302	50-9	.060	-5	103	24	2.6
1942	Det A★	7	13	.350	35	30	9-1	2	226.2	210	87	9	0	84	110	2.90	136	.246	.314	67-9	.075	-5	65	25	1.5
1945	†Det A	13	8	.619	31	27	12-5	3	191.2	175	68	7	2	63	76	2.02	174	.241	.303	63-8	.063	-6	91	24	2.2
1946	Det A	11	7	.611	28	15	6-1	1	140.2	132	69	9	1	58	60	3.65	100	.245	.319	49-5	.184	-1	116	-2	-0.3
1947	Det A	6	7	.462	36	14	4	7	133	147	77	11	1	61	33	4.40	86	.288	.365	39-3	.154	-2	101	-10	-1.2
1948	Det A	2	2	.500	30	0	0	3	44.1	45	34	4	1	36	18	5.68	77	.273	.406	11-2	.182	-0		-7	-0.7
1949	Cle A	9	6	.600	40	11	4-2	10	135.2	116	33	7	1	51	41	2.12	188	.238	.312	38-3	.132	-2	65	31	3.3
1950	Cle A	4	2	.667	36	0	0	4	63	57	32	7	1	30	26	3.57	121	.243	.331	12-2	.083	-1		4	0.3
1952	Bos A	4	3	.571	24	0	0	6	37.2	37	11	1	0	17	20	2.39	165	.268	.348	9-2	.000	-1		6	1.2
Total	14	98	88	.527	455	167	58-10	66	1688.1	1672	831	106	15	733	697	3.66	115	.259	.336	512-59	.098	-39	94	79	6.5
BENTON, RUBE John Clebon B 6.27.1887 Clinton, NC D 12.12.1937 Dothan, AL BL/TL 6-1/190# d6.28 Mil 1918																									
1910	Cin N	0	1	.000	12	2	0	0	38	44	34	1	1	23	15	4.74	62	.282	.378	11-0	.091	-1	64	-10	-0.6
1911	Cin N	3	3	.500	6	6	5	0	44.2	44	18	0	3	23	28	2.01	164	.270	.370	14-2	.143	-0	57	5	0.5
1912	Cin N	18	20	.474	**50**	**39**	22-2	2	302	316	143	2	18	118	162	3.10	108	.278	.356	104-3	.135	-6	88	9	0.5
1913	Cin N	11	7	.611	23	22	9-1	0	144.1	140	76	4	9	60	68	3.49	93	.265	.350	48-2	.208	1	108	-4	-0.4
1914	Cin N	16	18	.471	41	35	16-4	2	271	223	124	3	11	95	121	2.96	99	.228	.303	91-3	.143	-3	75	0	-0.3
1915	Cin N	6	13	.316	35	21	6-2	4	176.1	165	79	2	14	67	83	3.32	86	.257	.340	53-2	.208	-0	73	-7	-0.7
	NY N	3	5	.375	10	6	3	1	60.2	57	26	0	5	9	26	2.82	91	.253	.297	23-1	.217	1	131	-2	-0.2
	Year	9	18	.333	45	27	9-2	5	237	222	31	2	19	76	109	3.19	87	.256	.329	76-3	.211	1	85	-7	-0.9
1916	NY N	16	8	.667	38	29	15-3	2	238.2	210	84	5	10	58	115	2.87	85	.241	.296	78-4	.090	-4	109	-8	-1.4
1917	†NY N	15	9	.625	35	25	14-3	3	215	190	78	5	7	41	70	2.72	94	.238	.281	72-5	.167	-1	115	-3	-0.5
1918	NY N	1	2	.333	3	3	2	0	24	17	8	0	0	3	9	1.88	140	.202	.230	7-0	.143	1	86	1	0.3
1919	NY N	17	11	.607	35	28	11-1	2	209	181	71	5	4	52	53	2.63	107	.237	.289	67-3	.194	-1	120	6	0.7
1920	NY N	9	16	.360	33	25	12-4	2	193.1	222	82	8	3	31	52	3.03	99	.291	.321	65-4	.092	-7	96	-1	-0.6
1921	NY N	5	2	.714	18	9	3-1	0	72	72	28	2	0	17	11	2.88	128	.266	.309	21-2	.143	-1	139	6	0.4
1923	Cin N	14	10	.583	33	26	15	1	219	243	106	10	5	57	59	3.66	106	.284	.333	80-3	.287	4	123	8	1.2
1924	Cin N	7	9	.438	32	19	6-1	1	162.2	166	70	2	4	24	42	2.77	136	.266	.297	46-0	.261	2	85	15	1.6
1925	Cin N	9	10	.474	33	16	6-1	1	146.2	182	88	3	1	34	36	4.05	102	.301	.340	45-4	.200	1	94	-1	-0.2
Total	15	150	144	.510	437	311	145-23	21	2517.1	2472	1115	52	95	712	950	3.09	102	.261	.319	825-38	.172	-14	99	14	0.3
BENTON, LARRY Lawrence James B 11.20.1897 St.Louis, MO D 4.3.1953 Amberley, OH BR/TR 5-11/165# d4.25																									
1923	Bos N	5	9	.357	35	9	2	0	128	141	78	4	4	57	42	4.99	80	.293	.373	31-4	.161	-1	53	-11	-1.0
1924	Bos N	5	7	.417	30	13	4	1	128	129	63	4	3	64	41	4.15	92	.274	.365	33-2	.091	-3	77	-2	-0.5
1925	Bos N	14	7	.667	31	21	16-2	1	183.1	170	72	6	2	70	49	3.09	130	.249	.320	58-8	.241	2*	96	21	2.3
1926	Bos N	14	14	.500	43	27	12-1	1	231.2	244	113	10	7	81	103	3.85	92	.280	.346	78-6	.154	-4*	81	-7	-1.2
1927	Bos N	4	2	.667	11	10	3	0	60.1	72	33	3	2	27	25	4.48	83	.310	.387	18-3	.222	1	142	-4	-0.3
	NY N	13	5	.722	29	23	8-1	2	173	183	83	9	2	54	65	3.95	98	.275	.331	50-8	.160	-2*	106	1	-0.1
	Year	17	7	**.708**	40	33	11-1	2	233.1	255	88	12	4	81	90	4.09	93	.284	.346	68-11	.176	-1	116	-2	-0.4
1928	NY N	**25**	9	**.735**	42	36	**28**-2	4	310.1	299	106	14	0	71	90	2.73	144	.258	.300	112-6	.143	-3	124	43	4.1
1929	NY N	11	17	.393	39	31	14-3	4	237	276	129	16	0	61	63	4.14	111	.297	.340	86-1	.105	-6*	82	11	0.6
1930	NY N	1	3	.250	8	4	1	1	30	42	31	8	0	14	16	7.80	61	.323	.389	10-1	.300	2	166	-11	-1.1
	Cin N	7	12	.368	35	22	9	1	177.2	246	124	7	0	45	47	5.12	94	.337	.375	62-2	.177	-2	78	-10	-1.1
	Year	8	15	.348	43	26	10	2	207.2	288	128	15	0	59	63	5.50	87	.334	.377	72-3	.194	-0	91	-22	-2.2
1931	Cin N	10	15	.400	38	23	12-2	2	204.1	240	98	6	1	53	35	3.35	112	.299	.343	66-2	.167	-1	80	5	0.6
1932	Cin N	6	13	.316	35	22	7	2	179.2	201	104	10	0	27	35	4.31	90	.285	.311	54-5	.204	0	89	-9	-0.8
1933	Cin N	10	11	.476	34	19	7-2	2	152.2	160	70	5	3	36	33	3.71	91	.271	.316	53-2	.170	-1	92	-2	-0.5
1934	Cin N	0	1	.000	16	1	0	2	29	53	25	1	0	7	5	6.52	63	.393	.423	7-0	.286	0	85	-8	-0.3
1935	Bos N	2	3	.400	29	0	0	0	72	103	61	6	1	24	21	6.88	55	.338	.388	20-2	.200	0		-25	-1.4
Total	13	127	128	.498	455	261	123-13	22	2297	2559	1190	109	25	691	670	4.03	98	.288	.341	738-52	.165	-17	94	-8	-0.7
BENTON, SID Sidney Wright B 8.4.1895 Buckner, AR D 3.8.1977 Fayetteville, AR BR/TR 6-1/170# d4.18																									
1922	StL N	0	0	—	1	0	0	0	0	0	0	0	0	2	0	—	—	—	1.000	0-0	—	0		0	0.0

Year	Tm Lg	W	L	Pct	G	GS	CG-Sho	SV-BS	IP	H	R	HR	HB	BB-IB	SO	ERA	AERA	OAV	OOB	AB-SH	AVG	PB	Sup	APR	PW
BENZ, JOE Joseph Louis "Blitzen" or "Butcher Boy" B 1.21.1886 New Alsace, IN D 4.22.1957 Chicago, IL BR/TR 6-1.5/196# d8.16																									
1911	Chi A	3	2	.600	12	6	1	0	55.2	52	23	0	2	13	28	2.26	142	.251	.302	17-0	.059	-2	101	5	0.2
1912	Chi A	13	17	.433	42	31	12-3	0	238.2	231	107	5	8	70	97	2.90	110	.259	.319	76-8	.132	-5	89	7	0.3
1913	Chi A	7	10	.412	33	17	6-1	1	151	146	64	1	2	59	79	2.74	107	.257	.329	50-2	.180	-1	106	3	0.5
1914	Chi A	15	19	.441	48	35	16-4	2	283.1	245	103	4	2	66	142	2.26	119	.236	.282	92-4	.130	-3	78	14	1.7
1915	Chi A	15	11	.577	39	28	17-2	0	238.1	209	78	4	3	43	81	2.11	141	.238	.276	79-4	.127	-5	113	21	1.9
1916	Chi A	9	5	.643	28	16	6-4	0	142	108	40	0	3	32	57	2.03	136	.214	.265	46-2	.065	-4	103	13	0.9
1917	Chi A	7	3	.700	19	13	7-2	0	94.2	76	36	1	2	23	25	2.47	108	.220	.272	30-3	.167	-1	150	2	0.1
1918	Chi A	8	8	.500	29	17	10-1	0	154	156	57	1	2	28	30	2.63	104	.269	.304	51-4	.216	-1	110	2	0.4
1919	Chi A	0	0	—	1	0	0	0	2	2	1	0	0	0	0	0.00	—	.250	.250	0-0	—	0		0	0.0
Total	9	77	75	.507	251	163	75-17	3	1359.2	1225	509	16	24	334	539	2.43	119	.244	.294	441-27	.138	-21	101	67	6.0
BERE, JASON Jason Phillip B 5.26.1971 Cambridge, MA BR/TR 6-3/185# d5.27																									
1993	†Chi A	12	5	.706	24	24	1	0-0	142.2	109	60	12	5	81-0	129	3.47	121	.210	.322	0-0	—	0	126	12	1.3
1994	Chi A★	12	2	**.857**	24	24	0	0-0	141.2	119	65	17	1	80-0	127	3.81	123	.229	.331	0-0	—	0	121	15	1.2
1995	Chi A	8	15	.348	27	27	1	0-0	137.2	151	120	21	6	106-6	110	7.19	62	.277	.396	0-0	—	0	100	-44	-5.6
1996	Chi A	0	1	.000	5	5	0	0-0	16.2	26	19	3	0	18-1	19	10.26	46	.356	.478	0-0	—	0	117	-10	-0.5
1997	Chi A	4	2	.667	6	6	0	0-0	28.2	20	15	4	3	17-0	21	4.71	93	.198	.328	0-0	—	0	84	0	-0.1
1998	Chi A	3	7	.300	18	15	0	0-0	83.2	98	71	14	2	58-0	53	6.45	71	.293	.395	0-0	—	0	97	-20	-2.0
	Cin N	3	2	.600	9	7	0	0-0	43.2	39	20	3	1	20-0	31	4.12	104	.242	.326	14-0	.000	-1	123	1	0.0
1999	Cin N	3	0	1.000	12	10	0	0-0	43.1	56	37	6	2	40-3	28	6.85	68	.326	.456	14-2	.286	1	126	-11	-0.5
	Mil N	2	0	1.000	5	4	0	0-0	23.1	23	15	3	0	10-0	19	4.63	98	.256	.327	8-0	.375	1	177	-1	0.0
	Year	5	0	1.000	17	14	0	0-0	66.2	79	24	9	2	50-3	47	6.08	76	.302	.415	22-2	.318	2	141	-12	-0.5
2000	Mil N	6	7	.462	20	20	0	0-0	115	115	66	19	1	63-7	98	4.93	92	.264	.356	39-1	.205	1	96	-3	-0.2
	Cle A	6	3	.667	11	11	0	0-0	54.1	65	41	6	4	26-0	44	6.63	75	.297	.377	0-0	—	0	127	-9	-1.2
2001	Chi N	11	11	.500	32	32	2	0-0	188	171	99	24	1	77-7	175	4.31	96	.241	.314	62-7	.194	2	104	-4	-0.3
2002	Chi N	1	10	.091	16	16	0	0-0	85.2	98	63	13	3	28-1	65	5.67	71	.290	.343	24-7	.125	-0	90	-18	-2.0
2003	Cle A	0	0	—	2	2	0	0-0	6.2	5	3	0	0	2-0	1	4.05	109	.208	.259	0-0	—	0	73	0	0.0
Total	11	71	65	.522	211	203	4	0-0	1111	1095	694	145	29	626-25	920	5.14	86	.258	.354	161-17	.186	4	110	-92	-9.9
BERENGUER, JUAN Juan Bautista B 11.30.1954 Aguadulce, Panama BR/TR 5-11/215# d8.17																									
1978	NY N	0	2	.000	5	3	0	0-0	13	17	12	1	1	11-0	8	8.31	42	.327	.446	3-0	.000	-0	60	-7	-0.9
1979	NY N	1	1	.500	5	5	0	0-0	30.2	28	13	2	1	12-0	25	2.93	124	.252	.328	7-1	.143	0	83	2	0.1
1980	NY N	0	1	.000	6	0	0	0-0	9.1	9	9	1	0	10-2	7	5.79	62	.250	.413	0-0	—	0		-3	-0.3
1981	KC A	0	4	.000	8	3	0	0-0	19.2	22	21	4	2	16-0	20	8.69	42	.289	.412	0-0	—	0	83	-11	-1.9
	Tor A	2	9	.182	12	11	1	0-0	71	62	41	7	3	35-1	29	4.31	92	.235	.327	0-0	—	0	56	-3	-0.5
	Year	2	13	.133	20	14	1	0-0	90.2	84	43	11	5	51-1	49	5.26	74	.247	.347	0-0	—	0	61	-15	-2.4
1982	Det A	0	0	—	2	1	0	0-0	6.2	5	5	0	0	9-1	8	6.75	60	.200	.412	0-0	—	0	134	-2	-0.1
1983	Det A	9	5	.643	37	19	2-1	1-1	157.2	110	58	19	6	71-3	129	3.14	125	.193	.288	0-0	—	0	119	15	1.2
1984	Det A	11	10	.524	31	27	2-1	0-0	168.1	146	75	14	5	79-2	118	3.48	113	.232	.320	0-0	—	0	109	8	0.8
1985	Det A	5	6	.455	31	13	0	0-0	95	96	67	12	1	48-3	82	5.59	73	.259	.343	0-0	—	0	112	-17	-1.7
1986	SF N	2	3	.400	46	4	0	4-4	73.1	64	23	4	2	44-3	72	2.70	131	.242	.353	7-3	.143	-0	114	8	0.5
1987	†Min A	8	1	.889	47	6	0	4-5	112	100	51	10	0	47-7	110	3.94	118	.238	.312	0-0	—	0	125	9	0.6
1988	Min A	8	4	.667	57	1	0	2-3	100	74	44	7	1	61-7	99	3.96	103	.207	.322	0-0	—	0	179	3	0.3
1989	Min A	9	3	.750	56	0	0	3-4	106	96	44	11	2	47-0	93	3.48	119	.246	.326	0-0	—	0		8	0.8
1990	Min A	8	5	.615	51	0	0	0-2	100.1	85	43	9	2	58-4	77	3.41	122	.232	.338	0-0	—	0		7	0.8
1991	Atl N	0	3	.000	49	0	0	17-1	64.1	43	18	5	3	20-2	53	2.24	174	.189	.261	5-0	.000	-1		11	1.0
1992	Atl N	3	1	.750	28	0	0	1-2	33.1	35	22	7	1	16-4	19	5.13	71	.269	.354	2-0	.000	-0		-6	-0.7
	KC A	1	4	.200	19	2	0	0-1	44.2	42	30	3	1	20-3	26	5.64	72	.247	.325	0-0	—	0	22	-7	-0.8
Total	15	67	62	.519	490	95	5-2	32-23	1205.1	1034	576	116	31	604-42	975	3.90	103	.232	.325	24-4	.083	-1	101	15	-0.8
BERENYI, BRUCE Bruce Michael B 8.21.1954 Bryan, OH BR/TR 6-3/215# d7.5																									
1980	Cin N	2	2	.500	6	6	0	0-0	27.2	34	26	1	0	23-0	19	7.81	46	.318	.438	7-4	.000	-1	133	-13	-1.6
1981	Cin N	9	6	.600	21	20	5-3	0-0	126	97	55	3	0	77-0	106	3.50	102	.211	.322	42-3	.190	1	110	0	0.1
1982	Cin N	9	18	.333	34	34	4-1	0-0	222.1	208	90	8	2	96-5	157	3.36	110	.255	.332	62-12	.242	3	62	9	1.5
1983	Cin N	9	14	.391	32	31	4-1	0-0	186.1	173	92	9	2	102-3	151	3.86	99	.247	.343	55-10	.218	2	99	-2	0.0
1984	Cin N	3	7	.300	13	11	0	0-0	51	63	35	0	0	42-2	53	6.00	63	.306	.422	16-2	.063	-1	79	-11	-1.9
	NY N	9	6	.600	19	19	0	0-0	115	100	58	6	1	53-2	81	3.76	94	.238	.324	37-5	.243	2	110	-4	-0.4
	Year	12	13	.480	32	30	0	0-0	166	163	62	6	1	95-4	134	4.45	81	.260	.357	53-7	.189	0	99	-15	-2.3
1985	NY N	1	0	1.000	3	3	0	0-0	13.2	8	6	0	1	10-0	10	2.63	131	.170	.328	4-2	.250	0	119	1	0.1
1986	NY N	2	2	.500	14	7	0	0-0	39.2	47	30	5	1	22-0	30	6.35	56	.299	.383	11-1	.000	-1	115	-12	-1.2
Total	7	44	55	.444	142	131	13-5	0-0	781.2	730	392	32	7	425-12	607	4.03	91	.251	.345	234-39	.197	4	93	-32	-3.4
BERGER, HEINIE Charles B 1.7.1882 LaSalle, IL D 2.10.1954 Lakewood, OH TR 5-9/?# d5.6																									
1907	Cle A	3	3	.500	14	7	5-1	0	87.1	74	35	0	1	20	50	2.99	84	.232	.279	28-3	.179	0	81	-2	-0.2
1908	Cle A	13	8	.619	29	24	16	0	199.1	152	60	1	4	66	101	2.12	113	.219	.290	74-5	.108	-4	134	8	0.4
1909	Cle A	13	14	.481	34	29	19-4	1	247	221	95	2	12	58	162	2.73	94	.256	.312	83-2	.133	-1	78	0	-0.1
1910	Cle A	3	4	.429	13	8	2	0	65.1	57	25	0	3	32	24	3.03	85	.243	.341	21-3	.143	-1	88	-1	-0.3
Total	4	32	29	.525	90	68	42-5	1	599	504	215	3	20	176	337	2.60	96	.239	.303	206-13	.131	-6	98	5	-0.2
BERGMAN, SEAN Sean Frederick B 4.11.1970 Joliet, IL BR/TR 6-4/205# d7.7																									
1993	Det A	1	4	.200	9	6	1	0-0	39.2	47	29	6	1	23-3	19	5.67	76	.294	.382	0-0	—	0	111	-7	-0.7
1994	Det A	2	1	.667	3	3	0	0-0	17.2	22	11	2	1	7-0	12	5.60	87	.301	.366	0-0	—	0	152	-1	-0.1
1995	Det A	7	10	.412	28	28	1-1	0-0	135.1	169	95	19	4	67-8	86	5.12	93	.307	.384	0-0	—	0	92	-11	-1.2
1996	SD N	6	8	.429	41	14	0	0-0	113.1	119	63	14	2	33-3	85	4.37	91	.274	.325	30-0	.100	-1*	117	-6	-0.7
1997	SD N	2	4	.333	44	9	0	0-2	99	126	72	11	3	38-4	74	6.09	64	.316	.376	13-3	.231	1	142	-25	-1.2
1998	Hou N	12	9	.571	31	27	1	0-0	172	183	81	20	5	42-3	100	3.72	109	.268	.315	60-8	.083	-3	134	5	0.1
1999	Hou N	4	6	.400	19	16	2-1	0-0	99	130	60	9	3	26-1	38	5.36	82	.332	.374	28-1	.107	1	90	-9	-0.8
	Atl N	1	0	1.000	6	0	0	0-1	6.1	5	2	0	0	3-0	6	2.84	158	.217	.308	0-0	—	0		1	0.2
	Year	5	6	.455	25	16	2-1	0-1	105.1	135	66	9	3	29-1	44	5.21	85	.325	.370	28-1	.107	1	90	-8	-0.6
2000	Min A	4	5	.444	15	14	0	0-0	68	111	76	18	2	33-1	35	9.66	53	.374	.436	2-0	.500	1	110	-31	-3.0
Total	8	39	47	.453	196	117	5-2	0-3	750.1	912	489	99	21	272-23	455	5.28	82	.303	.362	133-12	.113	-2	114	-84	-7.4
BERLY, JACK John Chambers B 5.24.1903 Natchitoches, LA D 6.26.1977 Houston, TX BR/TR 5-11.5/190# d4.22																									
1924	StL N	0	0	—	4	0	0	0	8	8	5	2	0	4	2	5.63	67	.267	.353	2-0	.000	-0		-1	-0.1
1931	NY N	7	8	.467	27	11	4-1	0	111.1	114	55	6	4	51	45	3.88	95	.270	.354	35-0	.171	-1	122	-1	-0.2
1932	Phi N	1	2	.333	21	1	1	2	46	61	42	4	1	21	15	7.63	58	.333	.405	10-0	.000	-1	76	-13	-1.0
1933	Phi N	2	3	.400	13	6	1-1	0	50	62	30	5	2	22	4	5.04	76	.307	.381	13-1	.308	0	87	-5	-0.4
Total	4	10	13	.435	65	18	6-2	2	215.1	245	132	17	7	98	66	5.02	78	.292	.371	60-1	.167	-2	104	-20	-1.7
BERNAL, VICTOR Victor Hugo B 10.6.1953 Los Angeles, CA BR/TR 6-1/175# d4.6																									
1977	SD N	1	1	.500	15	0	0	0-0	20.1	23	13	4	0	9-2	6	5.31	67	.287	.360	1-0	.000	-0		-4	-0.4
BERNARD, DWIGHT Dwight Vern B 5.31.1952 Mt.Vernon, IL BR/TR 6-2/170# d6.29																									
1978	NY N	1	4	.200	30	1	0	0-2	48	54	25	4	0	27-3	26	4.31	81	.297	.386	5-0	.200	0	129	-4	-0.4
1979	NY N	0	3	.000	32	1	0	0-0	44	59	26	2	0	26-4	20	4.70	78	.331	.411	0-2	—	0	121	-5	-0.3
1981	†Mil A	0	0	—	6	0	0	0-0	5	5	3	0	0	6-1	1	3.60	95	.263	.407	0-0	—	0		-1	0.0
1982	†Mil A	3	1	.750	47	0	0	6-3	79	78	39	4	1	27-0	45	3.76	101	.263	.321	0-0	—	0		-1	-0.1
Total	4	4	8	.333	115	2	0	6-5	176	196	93	10	1	86-8	92	4.14	89	.290	.366	5-2	.200	1	123	-11	-0.8
BERNARD, JOE Joseph Carl "J.C." B 3.24.1882 Brighton, IL D 9.22.1960 Springfield, IL BR/TR 6-1/175# d9.23																									
1909	StL N	0	0	—	1	0	0	0	1	1	0	0	0	2	2	0.00	—	.250	.500	0-0	—	0		0	0.0

Year	Tm Lg	W	L	Pct	G	GS	CG-Sho	SV-BS	IP	H	R	HR	HB	BB-IB	SO	ERA	AERA	OAV	OOB	AB-SH	AVG	PB	Sup	APR	PW
BERNERO, ADAM Adam Gino B 11.28.1976 San Jose, CA BR/TR 6-4/205# d8.1																									
2000	Det A	0	1	.000	12	4	0	0-0	34.1	33	18	3	1	13-1	20	4.19	115	.270	.338	0-0	—	0	97	2	0.1
2001	Det A	0	0	—	5	0	0	0-0	12.1	13	13	4	1	4-0	8	7.30	60	.260	.321	0-0	—	0		-5	-0.2
2002	Det A	4	7	.364	28	11	0	0-0	101.2	128	74	17	6	31-1	69	6.20	70	.309	.362	4-1	.000	-0	100	-20	-1.9
2003	Det A	1	12	.077	18	17	0	0-0	100.2	104	68	14	7	41-0	54	6.08	71	.267	.342	4-0	.000	-0*	56	-18	-1.9
	Col N	0	2	.000	31	0	0	0-2	32.2	33	22	5	1	13-1	26	5.23	94	.266	.336	2-0	.000	-0		-2	-0.1
Total	4	5	22	.185	94	32	0	0-2	281.2	311	195	43	16	102-3	177	5.85	76	.283	.347	10-1	.000	-1	76	-43	-4.0
BERNHARD, BILL William Henry "Strawberry Bill" B 3.16.1871 Clarence, NY D 3.30.1949 San Diego, CA BB/TR 6-1/205# d4.24																									
1899	Phi N	6	6	.500	21	12	10-1	0	132.1	120	66	3	6	36	23	2.65	139	.242	.301	54-0	.241	0	109	12	0.9
1900	Phi N	15	10	.600	32	27	20	2	218.2	284	151	3	5	74	49	4.77	76	.313	.368	91-0	.154	-5	131	-25	-2.8
1901	Phi A	17	10	.630	31	27	26-1	0	257	328	169	6	2	50	58	4.52	84	.307	.339	107-3	.187	-1*	97	-16	-1.3
1902	Phi A	1	0	1.000	1	1	1	0	9	7	1	0	0	3	1	1.00	367	.212	.278	4-0	.000	-1	157	3	0.2
	Cle A	17	5	.773	27	24	22-3	1	217	169	78	4	5	34	57	2.20	157	.216	.253	90-0	.200	-1	120	32	2.9
	Year	18	5	**.783**	28	25	23-3	1	226	176	84	4	5	37	58	2.15	161	**.215**	**.254**	94-0	.191	-2	122	33	3.1
1903	Cle A	14	5	.737	20	19	18-3	0	165.2	151	62	1	0	21	60	2.12	135	.242	.267	65-0	.185	-1	121	13	1.5
1904	Cle A	23	13	.639	38	37	35-4	0	320.2	323	107	3	4	55	137	2.13	119	.263	.296	124-3	.177	-1	127	15	1.6
1905	Cle A	7	13	.350	22	19	17	0	174.1	185	93	5	1	34	56	3.36	78	.274	.309	69-0	.087	-6	72	-16	-2.3
1906	Cle A	16	15	.516	31	30	23-2	0	255.1	235	99	1	5	47	85	2.54	103	.248	.287	99-2	.212	2	123	5	0.9
1907	Cle A	0	4	.000	8	4	3	0	42	58	32	0	0	11	19	3.21	78	.330	.369	15-0	.200	0	74	-7	-0.6
Total	9	116	81	.589	231	200	175-14	3	1792	1860	858	26	28	365	545	3.04	102	.268	.307	718-8	.180	-13	114	16	1.0
BERNHARDT, WALTER Walter Jacob B 5.20.1893 Pleasant Valley, PA D 7.26.1958 Watertown, NY BR/TR 6-2/175# d7.16																									
1918	NY A	0	0	—	1	0	0	0	0.2	0	0	0	0	0	1	0.00	—	.000	.000	0-0	—	0		0	0.0
BERRY, JOE Jonas Arthur "Jittery Joe" B 12.16.1904 Huntsville, AR D 9.27.1958 Anaheim, CA BL/TR 5-10.5/145# d9.6																									
1942	Chi N	0	0	—	2	0	0	0	2	7	4	0	0	2	1	18.00	18	.538	.600	0-0	—	0		-3	-0.2
1944	Phi A	10	8	.556	53	0	0	**12**	111.1	78	32	4	2	23	44	1.94	179	.192	.238	25-3	.120	-1		**17**	3.2
1945	Phi A	8	7	.533	**52**	0	0	5	130.1	114	40	5	0	38	51	2.35	146	.232	.287	35-2	.143	-1		**15**	1.8
1946	Phi A	0	1	.000	5	0	0	0	13	15	5	1	1	3	5	2.77	128	.288	.339	3-1	.333	0		1	0.1
	Cle A	3	6	.333	21	0	0	1	37.1	32	18	4	0	21	16	3.38	98	.235	.338	7-1	.286	0		-1	-0.3
	Year	3	7	.300	26	0	0	1	50.1	47	28	5	1	24	21	3.22	105	.250	.338	10-2	.300	1		0	-0.2
Total	4	21	22	.488	133	0	0	18	294	246	99	14	3	87	117	2.45	140	.224	.282	70-7	.157	-2		29	4.6
BERTAINA, FRANK Frank Louis B 4.14.1944 San Francisco, CA BL/TL 5-11/180# d8.1																									
1964	Bal A	1	0	1.000	6	4	1-1	0	26	18	8	3	0	13-1	18	2.77	129	.198	.298	5-2	.000	-1	93	3	0.1
1965	Bal A	0	0	—	2	1	0	0	6	9	4	0	0	4-0	5	6.00	58	.360	.433	1-0	.000	-0	152	-1	-0.1
1966	Bal A	2	5	.286	16	9	0	0	63.1	52	29	3	4	36-2	46	3.13	107	.226	.338	19-0	.105	-1	120	-1	-0.2
1967	Bal A	1	1	.500	5	2	0	0	21.2	17	9	4	0	14-0	19	3.32	95	.224	.341	9-0	.111	-0	14	-1	-0.1
	Was A	6	5	.545	18	17	4-4	0	95.2	90	36	8	0	37-1	67	2.92	108	.251	.320	35-2	.057	-3*	102	3	0.0
	Year	7	6	.538	23	19	4-4	0	117.1	107	40	12	0	51-1	86	2.99	106	.247	.324	44-2	.068	-3	93	2	-0.1
1968	Was A	7	13	.350	27	23	1	0	127.1	133	76	15	6	69-1	81	4.66	63	.273	.366	38-1	.132	-0	101	-26	-3.8
1969	Was A	1	3	.250	14	5	0	0-0	35.2	43	30	8	0	23-0	25	6.56	53	.291	.384	11-1	.364	2	133	-13	-1.0
	Bal A	0	0	—	3	0	0	0-0	6	1	0	0	0	3-0	5	0.00	—	.063	.200	1-0	1.000	1		2	0.2
	Year	1	3	.250	17	5	0	0-0	41.2	44	35	8	0	26-0	30	5.62	62	.268	.365	12-1	.417	3	132	-10	-0.8
1970	StL N	1	2	.333	8	5	0	0-1	31.1	36	16	1	0	15-3	14	3.16	130	.293	.367	7-0	.143	0	87	2	0.2
Total	7	19	29	.396	99	66	6-5	0-1	413	399	208	42	10	214-8	280	3.84	85	.257	.347	126-6	.127	-1	102	-32	-4.7
BERTOTTI, MIKE Michael David B 1.18.1970 Jersey City, NJ BL/TL 6-1/185# d7.29																									
1995	Chi A	1	1	.500	4	4	0	0-0	14.1	23	20	6	3	11-0	15	12.56	36	.365	.463	0-0	—	0	136	-13	-1.3
1996	Chi A	2	0	1.000	15	2	0	0-1	28	28	18	5	0	20-3	19	5.14	92	.257	.369	0-0	—	0	117	-2	-0.1
1997	Chi A	0	0	—	9	0	0	0-0	3.2	9	3	0	0	2-0	4	7.36	60	.450	.478	0-0	—	0		-1	-0.1
Total	3	3	1	.750	28	6	0	0-1	46	60	41	11	3	33-3	38	7.63	61	.313	.412	0-0	—	0	127	-16	-1.5
BERTRAND, LEFTY Roman Mathias B 2.28.1909 Cobden, MN D 3.17.2002 The Dalles, OR BR/TL 6/180# d4.15																									
1936	Phi N	0	0	—	1	0	0	0	2	3	2	1	0	2	1	9.00	50	.333	.455	0-0	—	0		-1	0.0
BERUMEN, ANDRES Andres B 4.5.1971 Tijuana, Mexico BR/TR 6-2/210# d4.27																									
1995	SD N	2	3	.400	37	0	0	1-3	44.1	37	29	3	3	36-3	42	5.68	71	.226	.369	1-0	.000	-0		-7	-0.8
1996	SD N	0	0	—	3	0	0	0-0	3.1	3	2	1	1	2-1	4	5.40	74	.231	.375	0-0	—	0		0	0.0
Total	2	2	3	.400	40	0	0	1-3	47.2	40	31	4	4	38-4	46	5.66	71	.226	.369	1-0	.000	-0		-7	-0.8
BESANA, FRED Frederick Cyril B 4.5.1931 Lincoln, CA BR/TL 6-3.5/200# d4.18																									
1956	Bal A	1	0	1.000	7	2	0	0	17.2	22	12	0	2	14-0	7	5.60	70	.310	.427	4-0	.000	-0	136	-3	-0.2
BESSE, HERMAN Herman A. B 8.16.1911 St.Louis, MO D 8.13.1972 Los Angeles, CA BL/TL 6-2/190# d4.19 Mil 1944-45																									
1940	Phi A	0	3	.000	17	5	0	0	53	70	56	10	3	34	19	8.83	50	.315	.413	19-0	.263	2	130	-23	-0.9
1941	Phi A	2	0	1.000	6	2	1	0	19.2	28	22	4	0	12	8	10.07	42	.329	.412	5-0	.200	-0	103	-11	-0.9
1942	Phi A	2	9	.182	30	14	4	1	133	163	99	7	4	69	78	6.16	61	.300	.383	53-0	.226	2*	110	-31	-2.2
1943	Phi A	1	1	.500	5	1	0	0	16.1	18	6	2	1	4	3	3.31	103	.295	.348	8-0	.000	-1*	199	1	-0.1
1946	Phi A	0	2	.000	7	3	0	1	20.2	19	12	1	0	9	10	5.23	68	.247	.326	5-0	.000	-0	81	-3	-0.3
Total	5	5	15	.250	65	25	5	2	242.2	298	195	24	8	128	118	6.79	58	.302	.386	90-0	.200	2	114	-67	-4.4
BESSENT, DON Fred Donald B 3.13.1931 Jacksonville, FL D 7.7.1990 Jacksonville, FL BR/TR 6/175# d7.17																									
1955	†Bro N	8	1	.889	24	2	1	3	63.1	51	19	7	0	21-2	29	2.70	150	.220	.283	20-3	.100	-2	132	11	1.3
1956	†Bro N	4	3	.571	38	0	0	9	79.1	63	23	5	0	31-6	52	2.50	159	.221	.295	18-1	.111	-1		13	1.2
1957	Bro N	1	3	.250	27	0	0	0	44	58	28	5	0	19-3	24	5.73	73	.328	.387	4-0	.250	0		-6	-0.5
1958	LA N	1	0	1.000	19	0	0	0	24.1	24	14	3	1	17-0	13	3.33	123	.270	.393	2-1	.000	-0		0	0.0
Total	4	14	7	.667	108	2	1	12	211	196	84	20	1	88-11	118	3.33	122	.250	.324	44-5	.114	-3	132	18	2.0
BEST, KARL Karl Jon B 3.6.1959 Aberdeen, WA BR/TR 6-4/210# d8.19																									
1983	Sea A	0	1	.000	4	0	0	0-0	5.1	14	9	2	2	5-0	3	13.50	32	.483	.583	0-0	—	0		-5	-0.8
1984	Sea A	1	1	.500	5	0	0	0-0	6	7	2	0	0	0-0	6	3.00	133	.292	.280	0-0	—	0		1	0.1
1985	Sea A	2	1	.667	15	0	0	4-0	32.1	25	9	1	1	6-0	32	1.95	216	.207	.250	0-0	—	0		7	0.8
1986	Sea A	2	3	.400	26	0	0	1-2	35.2	35	19	3	1	21-2	23	4.04	105	.255	.354	0-0	—	0		0	0.0
1988	Min A	0	0	—	11	0	0	0-0	12	15	9	1	0	7-1	9	6.00	68	.306	.379	0-0	—	0		-3	-0.1
Total	5	5	6	.455	61	0	0	5-2	91.1	96	48	7	4	39-3	73	4.04	104	.267	.341	0-0	—	0		0	0.0
BETANCOURT, RAFAEL Rafael Jose B 4.29.1975 Cumana, Venezuela BR/TR 6-2/170# d7.13																									
2003	Cle A	2	2	.500	33	0	0	1-2	38	27	11	5	1	13-2	36	2.13	207	.196	.268	0-0	—	0		10	0.9
BETHKE, JIM James Charles B 11.5.1946 Falls City, NE BR/TR 6-3/185# d4.12																									
1965	NY N	2	0	1.000	25	0	0	0	40	41	24	3	6	22-2	19	4.27	83	.266	.377	4-0	.000	-0		-4	-0.2
BETTENDORF, JEFF Jeffrey Allen B 12.10.1960 Lompoc, CA BR/TR 6-3/180# d4.8																									
1984	Oak A	0	0	—	3	0	0	1-0	9.2	9	5	3	0	5-0	5	4.66	81	.243	.333	0-0	—	0		-1	-0.1
BETTS, HARRY Harold Matthew "Chubby" or "Ginger" B 6.19.1881 Alliance, OH D 5.22.1946 San Antonio, TX BR/TR 5-10/200# d9.22																									
1903	StL N	0	1	.000	1	1	1	0	9	11	10	0	2	5	2	10.00	33	.297	.409	3-0	.000	-0	21	-5	-0.4
1913	Cin N	0	0	—	1	0	0	0	3.1	1	1	0	1	3	0	2.70	120	.143	.455	1-0	.000	-0		0	0.0
Total	2	0	1	.000	2	1	1	0	12.1	12	11	0	3	8	2	8.03	41	.273	.418	4-0	.000	-1	21	-5	-0.4
BETTS, HUCK Walter Martin B 2.18.1897 Millsboro, DE D 6.13.1987 Millsboro, DE BR/TR 5-11/170# d4.26																									
1920	Phi N	1	1	.500	27	4	1	0	88.1	86	48	3	2	33	18	3.57	96	.261	.332	25-0	.080	-2	115	-2	-0.4
1921	Phi N	3	7	.300	32	2	1	4	100.2	141	65	8	4	14	28	4.47	95	.337	.365	30-0	.267	0	10	-1	-0.1
1922	Phi N	1	0	1.000	7	0	0	0	15	23	17	3	0	8	4	9.60	49	.348	.419	4-0	.000	-0		-6	-0.4
1923	Phi N	2	4	.333	19	4	3	1	84.1	100	38	7	4	14	18	3.09	149	.314	.351	31-1	.097	-3*	45	11	0.4

Year	Tm Lg	W	L	Pct	G	GS	CG-Sho	SV-BS	IP	H	R	HR	HB	BB-IB	SO	ERA	AERA	OAV	OOB	AB-SH	AVG	PB	Sup	APR	PW
1924	Phi N	7	10	.412	37	9	2	2	144.1	160	76	8	5	42	46	4.30	104	.286	.341	45-6	.156	-2*	93	4	0.1
1925	Phi N	4	5	.444	35	7	1	1	97.1	146	86	10	3	38	28	5.55	86	.342	.400	34-0	.294	2*	121	-12	-0.7
1932	Bos N	13	11	.542	31	27	16-3	1	221.2	229	84	9	0	35	32	2.80	134	.267	.295	79-1	.241	2	94	23	2.4
1933	Bos N	11	11	.500	35	26	17-2	4	242	225	79	9	0	55	40	2.79	110	.248	.290	76-9	.224	2	93	11	1.5
1934	Bos N	17	10	.630	40	27	10-2	3	213	258	105	17	3	42	69	4.06	94	.296	.330	69-6	.188	1	107	-3	-0.4
1935	Bos N	2	9	.182	44	19	2-1	0	159.2	213	118	9	2	40	40	5.47	69	.321	.362	44-2	.159	-0	85	-34	-2.0
Total	10	61	68	.473	307	125	53-8	16	1366.1	1581	716	83	23	321	323	3.93	98	.292	.334	437-25	.197	-2	91	-9	0.4
BEVENS, BILL Floyd Clifford B 10.21.1916 Hubbard, OR D 10.26.1991 Salem, OR BR/TR 6-3.5/210# d5.12																									
1944	NY A	4	1	.800	8	5	3	0	43.2	44	18	4	1	13	16	2.68	130	.273	.331	16-1	.063	-2	163	3	0.1
1945	NY A	13	9	.591	29	25	14-2	0	184	174	83	12	1	68	76	3.67	94	.254	.322	63-4	.111	-4	118	-2	-0.7
1946	NY A	16	13	.552	31	31	18-3	0	249.2	213	73	11	1	78	120	2.23	154	.232	.293	84-8	.083	-4	88	34	3.2
1947	†NY A	7	13	.350	28	23	11-1	0	165	167	79	13	1	77	77	3.82	93	.264	.345	58-3	.121	-3	104	-7	-1.0
Total	4	40	36	.526	96	84	46-6	0	642.1	598	253	40	4	236	289	3.08	113	.250	.318	221-16	.100	-13	106	28	1.6
BEVERLIN, JASON Jason Robert B 11.27.1973 Ashtabula, OH BL/TR 6-5/220# d7.29																									
2002	Cle A	0	0	—	4	0	0	0-0	7.1	9	7	1	0	4-0	9	7.36	60	.290	.371	0-0	—	0		-3	-0.1
	Det A	0	3	.000	3	3	0	0-0	12.1	18	15	2	0	5-0	7	9.49	45	.327	.383	0-0	—	0	50	-8	-1.2
	Year	0	3	.000	7	3	0	0-0	19.2	27	17	3	0	9-0	16	8.69	50	.314	.379	0-0	—	0	50	-10	-1.3
BEVIL, BRIAN Brian Scott B 9.5.1971 Houston, TX BR/TR 6-3/190# d6.17																									
1996	KC A	1	0	1.000	3	1	0	0-0	11	9	7	2	0	5-0	7	5.73	88	.237	.318	0-0	—	0	111	-1	0.0
1997	KC A	1	2	.333	18	0	0	1-4	16.1	16	13	1	1	9-2	13	6.61	71	.267	.361	0-0	—	0		-3	-0.6
1998	KC A	3	1	.750	39	0	0	0-2	40	47	29	4	3	22-1	47	6.30	77	.283	.373	0-0	—	0		-6	-0.5
Total	3	5	3	.625	60	1	0	1-6	67.1	72	49	7	4	36-3	67	6.28	77	.273	.362	0-0	—	0	111	-10	-1.1
BEVIL, LOU Louis Eugene (b: Louis Eugene Bevilacqua) B 11.27.1922 Nelson, IL D 2.1.1973 Dixon, IL BB/TR 5-11.5/190# d9.2 Mil 1943-45																									
1942	Was A	0	1	.000	4	1	0	0	9.2	9	7	0	1	11	2	6.52	56	.265	.457	3-0	.000	-0	140	-3	-0.3
BEVILLE, BEN Clarence Benjamin B 8.28.1877 Colusa, CA D 1.5.1937 Yountville, CA BR/TR 5-9/190# d5.24																									
1901	Bos A	0	2	.000	2	2	1	0	9	8	7	0	1	9	1	4.00	88	.235	.409	7-0	.286	0*	29	-1	-0.1
BIBBY, JIM James Blair B 10.29.1944 Franklinton, NC BR/TR 6-5/235# d9.4																									
1972	StL N	1	3	.250	6	6	0	0-0	40.1	29	18	4	1	19-4	28	3.35	102	.206	.302	8-2	.125	0	104	0	0.0
1973	StL N	0	2	.000	6	3	0	0-0	16	19	17	2	2	17-2	12	9.56	38	.306	.463	2-0	.000	0	81	-9	-1.0
	Tex A	9	10	.474	26	23	11-2	1-0	180.1	121	73	14	6	106-4	155	3.24	115	**.192**	.312	0-0	—	0*	81	11	1.0
1974	Tex A	19	19	.500	41	41	11-5	0-0	264	255	146	25	9	113-4	149	4.74	75	.255	.334	0-0	—	0	119	-29	-3.7
1975	Tex A	2	6	.250	12	12	4-1	0-0	68.1	73	41	2	2	28-0	31	5.00	75	.274	.342	0-0	—	0	115	-8	-0.9
	Cle A	5	9	.357	24	12	2	1-2	112.2	99	48	7	0	50-3	62	3.20	119	.235	.313	0-0	—	0	85	7	0.8
	Year	7	15	.318	36	24	6-1	1-2	181	172	52	9	2	78-3	93	3.88	98	.250	.324	0-0	—	0	100	-2	-0.1
1976	Cle A	13	7	.650	34	21	4-3	1-0	163.1	162	61	6	1	56-1	84	3.20	109	.266	.325	0-0	—	0	97	7	0.8
1977	Cle A	12	13	.480	37	30	9-2	2-0	206.2	197	100	17	4	73-2	141	3.57	111	.250	.315	0-0	—	0	97	5	0.5
1978	Pit N	8	7	.533	34	14	3-2	1-2	107	100	52	10	2	39-7	72	3.53	105	.246	.314	31-0	.129	1	95	1	0.2
1979	†Pit N	12	4	.750	34	17	4-1	0-1	137.2	110	51	9	4	47-6	103	2.81	138	.218	.289	45-6	.178	2	118	15	1.7
1980	Pit N★	19	6	**.760**	35	34	6-1	0-0	238.1	210	95	20	6	88-3	144	3.32	110	.238	.311	77-10	.156	2	127	10	1.1
1981	Pit N	6	3	.667	14	14	2-2	0-0	93.2	79	30	4	2	26-1	48	2.50	144	.225	.279	28-4	.143	1	104	11	1.1
1983	Pit N	5	12	.294	29	12	0	2-1	78	92	60	10	1	51-0	44	6.69	55	.297	.393	18-2	.111	-1	89	-23	-4.5
1984	Tex A	0	0	—	8	0	0	0-0	16.1	19	8	1	0	10-1	6	4.41	94	.297	.392	0-0	—	0		0	0.0
Total	12	111	101	.524	340	239	56-19	8-6	1722.2	1565	800	131	40	723-38	1079	3.76	99	.243	.321	209-24	.148	5	105	-2	-2.9
BICKFORD, VERN Vernon Edgell B 8.17.1920 Hellier, KY D 5.6.1960 Concord, VA BR/TR 6/185# d4.24																									
1948	†Bos N	11	5	.688	33	22	10-1	1	146	125	59	9	3	63	60	3.27	117	.226	.309	49-6	.204	1	131	10	1.0
1949	Bos N★	16	11	.593	37	36	15-2	0	230.2	246	125	20	6	106	101	4.25	89	.273	.354	81-10	.185	-1	123	-12	-1.3
1950	Bos N	19	14	.576	40	**39**	**27-2**	0	**311.2**	293	135	25	6	122	126	3.47	111	.248	.321	116-9	.138	-4	122	16	1.0
1951	Bos N	11	9	.550	25	20	12-3	0	164.2	146	68	7	6	76	76	3.12	118	.240	.330	52-6	.115	-2	125	10	1.0
1952	Bos N	7	12	.368	26	22	7-1	0	161.1	165	73	7	2	64	62	3.74	97	.269	.340	51-5	.176	-0	58	-2	-0.2
1953	Mil N	2	5	.286	20	9	2	1	58	60	35	8	2	35	25	5.28	74	.279	.385	15-1	.067	-1	114	-7	-0.8
1954	Bal A	0	1	.000	1	1	0	0	4	5	5	0	0	1	0	9.00	40	.333	.316	1-0	.000	-0	98	-3	-0.4
Total	7	66	57	.537	182	149	73-9	2	1076.1	1040	500	76	25	467	450	3.71	102	.254	.334	365-37	.156	-7	114	12	0.3
BICKHAM, DAN Daniel Denison B 10.31.1864 Dayton, OH D 3.3.1951 Dayton, OH BR/TR 5-10/160# d8.13																									
1886	Cin AA	1	0	1.000	1	1	1	0	9	13	11	0	0	3	6	3.00	117	.351	.400	3	.333	0	202	-2	-0.1
BICKNELL, CHARLIE Charles Stephen "Bud" B 7.27.1928 Plainfield, NJ BR/TR 5-11/170# d4.22																									
1948	Phi N	0	1	.000	17	1	0	0	25.2	29	20	5	0	17	5	5.96	66	.287	.390	5-0	.000	-1	67	-6	-0.4
1949	Phi N	0	0	—	13	0	0	0	28.1	32	24	3	2	17	4	7.62	52	.291	.395	1-0	.000	1		-11	-0.5
Total	2	0	1	.000	30	1	0	0	54	61	44	8	2	34	9	6.83	58	.289	.393	6-0	.000	-0	67	-17	-0.9
BIDDLE, ROCKY Lee Francis B 5.21.1976 Las Vegas, NV BR/TR 6-3/230# d8.10																									
2000	Chi A	1	2	.333	4	4	0	0-0	22.2	31	25	5	0	8-0	7	8.34	60	.326	.371	0-0	—	0	155	-9	-0.9
2001	Chi A	7	8	.467	30	21	0	0-3	128.2	137	87	16	8	52-3	85	5.39	86	.272	.347	1-1	.000	-0	105	-12	-1.2
2002	Chi A	3	4	.429	44	7	0	1-2	77.2	72	42	13	5	39-4	64	4.06	111	.245	.342	0-0	—	0	112	2	0.2
2003	Mon N	5	8	.385	73	0	0	34-7	71.2	71	43	10	6	40-5	54	4.65	101	.254	.359	1-0	.000	-0		0	-0.2
Total	4	16	22	.421	151	32	0	35-12	300.2	311	197	44	19	139-12	210	5.09	91	.265	.351	2-1	.000	-0	113	-19	-2.1
BIELECKI, MIKE Michael Joseph B 7.31.1959 Baltimore, MD BR/TR 6-3/195# d9.14																									
1984	Pit N	0	0	—	4	0	0	0-0	4.1	4	0	0	0	0-0	1	0.00	—	.250	.250	0-0	—	0		2	0.1
1985	Pit N	2	3	.400	12	7	0	0-0	45.2	45	26	5	1	31-1	22	4.53	79	.257	.372	10-1	.000	-1*	63	-5	-0.5
1986	Pit N	6	11	.353	31	27	0	0-0	148.2	149	87	10	2	83-3	83	4.66	82	.262	.355	48-4	.063	-3	103	-14	-1.8
1987	Pit N	2	3	.400	8	8	2	0-0	45.2	43	25	6	1	12-0	25	4.73	87	.250	.299	16-2	.063	-1	104	-2	-0.4
1988	Chi N	2	2	.500	19	5	0	0-0	48.1	55	22	4	0	16-1	33	3.35	108	.284	.332	10-0	.100	-0	98	0	0.0
1989	†Chi N	18	7	**.720**	33	33	4-3	0-0	212.1	187	82	16	0	81-8	147	3.14	120	.237	.307	70-9	.043	-5	105	14	1.0
1990	Chi N	8	11	.421	36	29	0	1-0	168	188	101	13	5	70-11	103	4.93	83	.287	.359	43-10	.163	-0	95	-14	-1.4
1991	Chi N	13	11	.542	39	25	0	0-1	172	169	91	18	2	54-6	72	4.50	86	.262	.318	46-4	.065	-2	110	-9	-1.4
	Atl N	0	0	—	2	0	0	0-0	1.2	2	0	0	0	2-0	3	0.00	—	.286	.444	0-0	—	0		1	0.0
	Year	13	11	.542	41	25	0	0-1	173.2	171	96	18	2	56-6	75	4.46	87	.262	.319	46-4	.065	-2	110	-9	-1.4
1992	Atl N	2	4	.333	19	14	1-1	0-0	80.2	77	27	2	1	27-1	62	2.57	143	.254	.315	24-4	.125	-1	90	9	0.6
1993	Cle A	4	5	.444	13	13	0	0-0	68.2	90	47	8	2	23-3	38	5.90	74	.310	.363	0-0	—	0	111	-11	-1.1
1994	Atl N	2	0	1.000	19	1	0	0-0	27	28	12	2	1	12-1	18	4.00	106	.277	.360	3-1	.000	-0	150	1	0.1
1995	Cal A	4	6	.400	22	11	0	0-0	75.1	80	56	15	3	31-1	45	5.97	79	.273	.343	0-0	—	0	106	-12	-1.3
1996	†Atl N	4	3	.571	40	5	0	2-0	75.1	63	24	8	0	33-6	71	2.63	168	.224	.303	10-0	.100	0	102	15	1.3
1997	Atl N	3	7	.300	50	0	0	2-4	57.1	56	33	9	1	21-3	60	4.08	103	.250	.316	2-0	.000	0		-1	-0.1
Total	14	70	73	.490	347	178	7-4	5-5	1231	1236	633	116	19	496-45	783	4.18	96	.262	.332	282-35	.078	-14	101	-26	-4.9
BIEMILLER, HARRY Harry Lee B 10.9.1897 Baltimore, MD D 5.25.1965 Orlando, FL BR/TR 6-1/171# d8.26																									
1920	Was A	1	0	1.000	5	2	1	0	17	21	13	1	0	13	10	4.76	78	.318	.430	4-1	.000	-1	128	-3	-0.2
1925	Cin N	0	1	.000	23	1	0	2	47	45	28	2	7	21	9	4.02	102	.280	.386	9-0	.000	-0	103	0	0.0
Total	2	1	1	.500	28	3	1	2	64	66	41	3	7	34	19	4.22	95	.291	.399	13-1	.000	-1	117	-3	-0.2
BIERBAUER, LOU Louis W. B 9.28.1865 Erie, PA D 1.31.1926 Erie, PA BL/TR 5-8/140# d4.17 ▲																									
1886	Phi AA	0	0	—	2	0	0	0	10.2	8	9	0	0	5	1	4.22	83	.178	.260	522	.226	-0*		-1	-0.1
1887	Phi AA	0	0	—	1	0	0	1	1	0	0	0	0	0	1	0.00	—	.000	.000	530	.272	0*		0	0.1
1888	Phi AA	0	0	—	1	0	0	0	3	5	1	0	0	0	3	0.00	—	.357	.357	535	.267	0*		1	0.0
Total	3	0	0	—	4	0	0	1	14.2	13	10	0	0	5	5	3.07	112	.210	.269	1587	.255	0		0	0.0

Year	Tm Lg	W	L	Pct	G	GS	CG-Sho	SV-BS	IP	H	R	HR	HB	BB-IB	SO	ERA	AERA	OAV	OOB	AB-SH	AVG	PB	Sup	APR	PW
BIERBRODT, NICK Nicholas Raymond B 5.16.1978 Tarzana, CA BL/TL 6-5/190# d6.7																									
2001	Ari N	2	2	.500	5	5	0	0-0	23	29	21	6	0	12-0	17	8.22	56	.305	.380	6-2	.667	2*	198	-8	-0.9
	TB A	3	4	.429	11	11	0	0-0	61.1	71	38	11	4	27-1	56	4.55	99	.285	.363	0-0	—	0	92	-2	-0.2
2003	TB A	0	2	.000	13	5	0	0-0	35.1	59	41	9	5	23-3	20	9.68	47	.376	.463	0-0	—	0	118	-20	-1.0
	Cle A	0	0	—	5	0	0	0-0	8	5	6	0	0	4-0	9	6.75	66	.185	.273	0-0	—	0		-2	-0.1
	Year	0	2	.000	18	5	0	0-0	43.1	64	53	9	5	27-3	29	9.14	49	.348	.434	0-0	—	0	118	-22	-1.1
Total	2	5	8	.385	34	21	0	0-0	127.2	164	106	26	9	66-4	102	6.77	67	.311	.392	6-2	.667	2	124	-32	-2.2
BIGBEE, LYLE Lyle Randolph "Al" B 8.22.1893 Sweet Home, OR D 8.5.1942 Portland, OR BL/TR 6/180# d4.15 b-Carson ▲																									
1920	Phi A	0	3	.000	12	2	0	0	45	66	42	5	0	25	12	8.00	50	.369	.446	75-1	.187	0*	128	-14	-0.8
1921	Pit N	0	0	—	5	0	0	0	8	4	1	0	0	4	1	1.13	341	.154	.267	2-0	.000	-0		2	0.1
Total	2	0	3	.000	17	2	0	0	53	70	43	5	0	29	13	6.96	57	.341	.423	77-1	.182	-0	128	-12	-0.7
BIGGS, CHARLIE Charles Orval B 9.15.1906 French Lick, IN D 5.24.1954 French Lick, IN BR/TR 6-1/185# d9.3																									
1932	Chi A	1	1	.500	6	4	0	0	24.2	32	22	2	3	12	1	6.93	62	.314	.402	9-0	.111	-0	138	-7	-0.5
BILBREY, JIM James Melvin B 4.20.1924 Rickman, TN D 12.26.1985 Toledo, OH BR/TR 6-2.5/205# d5.17																									
1949	StL A	0	0	—	1	0	0	0	1	1	2	0	0	3	0	18.00	25	.250	.571	0-0	—	0		-1	-0.1
BILDILLI, EMIL Emil "Hill Billy" B 9.16.1912 Diamond, IN D 9.16.1946 Hartford City, IN BR/TL 5-10/170# d8.24																									
1937	StL A	0	1	.000	4	1	0	0	8	12	9	1	0	3	2	10.13	48	.353	.405	2-0	.000	-0	108	-4	-0.4
1938	StL A	1	2	.333	5	3	2	0	21.2	33	18	3	0	11	11	7.06	70	.359	.427	8-0	.250	-0	53	-4	-0.5
1939	StL A	1	1	.500	2	2	2	0	19	21	8	0	0	6	8	3.32	147	.266	.318	5-1	.000	-0	72	3	0.2
1940	StL A	2	4	.333	28	11	3	1	97	113	68	12	2	52	32	5.57	82	.298	.386	30-1	.200	-1*	105	-10	-0.5
1941	StL A	0	0	—	2	0	0	0	2.1	5	3	0	0	3	2	11.57	37	.417	.533	0-0	—	0		-2	-0.1
Total	5	4	8	.333	41	17	7	1	148	184	106	16	2	75	55	5.84	80	.309	.388	45-2	.178	-2	92	-17	-1.3
BILLIARD, HARRY Harry Pree "Pree" B 11.11.1883 Monroe, IN D 6.3.1923 Wooster, OH BR/TR 6/190# d7.31																									
1908	NY A	0	0	—	6	0	0	0	17	15	15	1	5	14	10	2.65	94	.234	.410	6-0	.167	-0		-3	-0.2
1914	Ind F	8	7	.533	32	16	5	2	125.2	117	71	4	7	63	45	3.72	84	.257	.356	38-0	.184	-1	111	-9	-1.2
1915	New F	0	1	.000	14	2	0	1	28.1	32	23	0	3	28	7	5.72	45	.291	.447	6-1	.333	0	82	-10	-0.5
Total	3	8	8	.500	52	18	5	3	171	164	109	5	15	105	62	3.95	75	.260	.379	50-1	.200	-1	112	-22	-1.9
BILLINGHAM, JACK John Eugene B 2.21.1943 Orlando, FL BR/TR 6-4/215# d4.11																									
1968	LA N	3	0	1.000	50	1	0	8	70.2	54	18	0	2	30-9	46	2.17	128	.215	.304	3-2	.000	0	31	6	0.5
1969	Hou N	6	7	.462	52	4	1	2-3	82.2	92	45	12	5	29-11	71	4.25	83	.290	.357	14-1	.071	0	81	-6	-1.0
1970	Hou N	13	9	.591	46	24	8-2	0-2	187.2	190	102	10	10	63-2	134	3.98	98	.259	.325	58-7	.103	-2	104	-7	-0.8
1971	Hou N	10	16	.385	33	33	8-3	0-0	228.1	205	98	9	16	68-8	139	3.39	99	.243	.310	73-6	.123	-3	85	-2	-0.5
1972	†Cin N	12	12	.500	36	31	8-4	1-0	217.2	197	83	18	7	64-8	137	3.18	101	.241	.300	71-5	.070	-4	121	2	-0.3
1973	†Cin N☆	19	10	.655	40	**40**	16-**7**	0-0	**293.1**	257	112	20	10	95-10	155	3.04	112	.236	.303	93-13	.065	-5	116	12	0.7
1974	Cin N	19	11	.633	36	35	8-3	0-0	212.1	233	105	16	6	64-9	103	3.94	89	.288	.343	67-11	.075	-5	117	-11	-1.9
1975	†Cin N	15	10	.600	33	32	5	0-0	208	222	100	22	9	76-12	79	4.11	88	.279	.347	65-10	.108	-1	133	-11	-1.4
1976	†Cin N	12	10	.545	34	29	5-2	1-1	177	190	96	17	4	62-5	76	4.32	81	.279	.340	59-8	.237	3	146	-17	-1.7
1977	Cin N	10	10	.500	36	23	3-2	0-2	161.2	195	105	16	10	56-9	76	5.23	75	.306	.368	56-6	.161	-1	146	-25	-2.7
1978	Det A	15	8	.652	30	30	10-4	0-0	201.2	218	95	16	8	65-2	59	3.88	100	.284	.341	0-0	—	0	115	0	0.0
1979	Det A	10	7	.588	35	19	2	3-0	158	163	74	13	7	60-11	59	3.30	131	.275	.347	0-0	—	0	97	13	1.2
1980	Det A	0	0	—	8	0	0	0-1	7.1	11	6	1	0	6-1	3	7.36	56	.355	.447	0-0	—	0		-2	-0.1
	Bos A	1	3	.250	7	4	0	0-0	24.1	45	30	6	4	12-0	4	11.10	38	.413	.484	0-0	—	0	74	-17	-2.1
	Year	1	3	.250	15	4	0	0-1	31.2	56	34	7	4	18-1	7	10.23	41	.400	.476	0-0	—	0	75	-18	-2.2
Total	13	145	113	.562	476	305	74-27	15-9	2230.2	2272	1069	176	98	750-97	1141	3.83	94	.268	.333	559-69	.111	-17	117	-65	-10.1
BILLINGS, JOSH Haskell Clark B 9.27.1907 New York, NY D 12.26.1983 Greenbrae, CA BR/TR 5-11/180# d8.17																									
1927	Det A	5	4	.556	10	9	5	0	67	64	36	3	6	39	18	4.84	87	.259	.373	27-0	.259	0	123	-1	-0.1
1928	Det A	5	10	.333	21	16	3-1	0	110.2	118	83	4	5	59	48	5.12	80	.276	.371	35-4	.286	3	109	-15	-1.4
1929	Det A	0	1	.000	8	0	0	0	19.1	27	14	0	1	9	1	5.12	84	.365	.440	6-0	.000	-1		-2	-0.1
Total	3	10	15	.400	39	25	8-1	0	197	209	133	7	12	107	67	5.03	83	.279	.378	68-4	.250	2	114	-18	-1.6
BILLINGSLEY, BRENT Brent Aaron B 4.19.1975 Downey, CA BL/TL 6-2/200# d5.20																									
1999	Fla N	0	0	—	8	0	0	0-0	7.2	11	14	3	2	10-0	3	16.43	27	.379	.548	0-0	—	0		-10	-0.5
BIRD, DOUG James Douglas B 3.5.1950 Corona, CA BR/TR 6-4/180# d4.29																									
1973	KC A	4	4	.500	54	0	0	20-4	102.1	81	37	10	2	30-7	83	2.99	138	.217	.276	0-0	—	0		12	1.3
1974	KC A	7	6	.538	55	1	1	10-7	92.1	100	31	6	1	27-9	62	2.73	140	.286	.333	0-0	—	0	23	11	1.8
1975	KC A	9	6	.600	51	4	0	11-7	105.1	100	42	7	2	40-10	81	3.25	119	.258	.326	0-0	—	0	80	8	1.2
1976	†KC A	12	10	.545	39	27	2-1	2-1	197.2	191	90	17	3	31-3	107	3.37	104	.251	.279	0-0	—	0	104	1	0.1
1977	†KC A	11	4	.733	53	5	0	14-4	118.1	120	52	14	3	29-4	83	3.88	104	.270	.314	0-0	—	0	151	5	0.6
1978	†KC A	6	6	.500	40	6	0	1-4	98.2	110	63	8	2	31-5	48	5.29	73	.284	.336	0-0	—	0	117	-14	-1.6
1979	Phi N	2	0	1.000	32	1	1	0-0	61	73	35	7	2	16-4	33	5.16	74	.305	.349	6-0	.167	0	139	-8	-0.4
1980	NY A	3	0	1.000	22	1	0	1-1	50.2	47	16	3	1	14-1	17	2.66	148	.257	.307	0-0	—	0	296	8	0.5
1981	NY A	5	1	.833	17	4	0	0-1	53.1	58	19	5	0	16-3	28	2.70	133	.280	.326	0-0	—	0	69	5	0.5
	Chi N	4	5	.444	12	12	2-1	0-0	75.1	72	34	5	1	16-3	34	3.58	103	.254	.293	20-2	.100	-1	76	1	0.0
1982	Chi N	9	14	.391	35	33	2-1	0-0	191	230	119	26	3	30-3	71	5.14	73	.297	.324	56-4	.143	-2	104	-27	-3.2
1983	Bos A	1	4	.200	22	6	0	1-0	67.2	91	52	14	2	16-4	33	6.65	66	.324	.360	0-0	—	0	76	-15	-1.0
Total	11	73	60	.549	432	100	8-3	60-29	1213.2	1273	590	122	22	296-56	680	3.99	96	.272	.315	82-6	.134	-2	99	-13	-0.2
BIRD, RED James Edward B 4.25.1890 Stephenville, TX D 3.23.1972 Murfreesboro, AR BL/TL 5-11/170# d9.17																									
1921	Was A	0	0	—	1	0	0	0	5	5	3	0	1	1	2	5.40	76	.294	.368	1-0	.000	-0		0	0.0
BIRKBECK, MIKE Michael Lawrence B 3.10.1961 Orrville, OH BR/TR 6-1/190# d8.17																									
1986	Mil A	1	1	.500	7	4	0	0-0	22	24	12	0	0	12-0	13	4.50	96	.282	.371	0-0	—	0	99	0	0.0
1987	Mil A	1	4	.200	10	10	1	0-0	45	63	33	8	0	19-0	25	6.20	74	.335	.392	0-0	—	0	103	-8	-0.6
1988	Mil A	10	8	.556	23	23	0	0-0	124	141	69	10	1	37-1	64	4.72	85	.285	.335	0-0	—	0	110	-9	-1.0
1989	Mil A	0	4	.000	9	9	1	0-0	44.2	57	32	4	3	22-2	31	5.44	71	.310	.387	0-0	—	0	94	-9	-0.7
1992	NY N	0	1	.000	1	1	0	0-0	7	12	7	3	0	1-1	2	9.00	39	.387	.406	2-0	.000	-0	130	-4	-0.4
1995	NY N	0	1	.000	4	4	0	0-0	27.2	22	5	2	0	2-0	14	1.63	249	.220	.235	6-1	.333	1	33	8	0.5
Total	6	12	19	.387	54	51	2	0-0	270.1	319	158	27	4	93-4	149	4.86	84	.295	.351	8-1	.250	1	100	-22	-2.2
BIRKOFER, RALPH Ralph Joseph "Lefty" B 11.5.1908 Cincinnati, OH D 3.16.1971 Cincinnati, OH BL/TL 5-11/213# d4.25																									
1933	Pit N	4	2	.667	9	8	3-1	0	50.2	43	22	1	1	17	20	2.31	144	.229	.296	22-0	.318	1	135	3	0.5
1934	Pit N	11	12	.478	41	23	11	1	204	227	106	11	5	66	71	4.10	100	.277	.335	75-2	.227	1	90	1	0.0
1935	Pit N	9	7	.563	37	18	8-1	1	150.1	173	87	5	6	42	80	4.07	101	.283	.335	58-0	.241	2*	94	0	0.0
1936	Pit N	7	5	.583	34	13	2	0	109.1	130	73	4	5	41	44	4.69	86	.295	.362	41-0	.220	-0	166	-10	-1.1
1937	Bro N	0	2	.000	11	1	0	0	29.2	45	28	3	0	9	9	6.67	60	.341	.383	11-0	.273	1*	43	-9	-0.5
Total	5	31	28	.525	132	63	24-2	2	544	618	316	24	17	175	224	4.19	96	.282	.340	207-2	.242	5	111	-15	-1.1
BIRRER, BABE Werner Joseph B 7.4.1929 Buffalo, NY BR/TR 6/195# d6.5																									
1955	Det A	4	3	.571	36	3	1	3	80.1	77	39	9	0	29-4	28	4.15	93	.248	.311	19-0	.158	2	85	-1	0.1
1956	Bal A	0	0	—	4	0	0	0	5.1	9	5	0	0	1-0	1	6.75	58	.360	.385	1-0	.000	-0		-2	-0.1
1958	LA N	0	0	—	16	0	0	1	34	43	20	4	1	7-3	16	4.50	91	.309	.342	7-0	.571	2		-2	0.1
Total	3	4	3	.571	56	3	1	4	119.2	129	64	13	1	37-7	45	4.36	90	.272	.324	27-0	.259	4	85	-5	0.1
BIRTSAS, TIM Timothy Dean B 9.5.1960 Pontiac, MI BL/TL 6-7/240# d5.3																									
1985	Oak A	10	6	.625	29	25	2	0-0	141.1	124	72	18	3	91-0	94	4.01	96	.238	.352	0-0	—	0	111	-4	-0.5
1986	Oak A	0	0	—	2	0	0	0-0	2	2	5	1	0	4-1	1	22.50	17	.286	.545	0-0	—	0		-4	-0.2
1988	Cin N	1	3	.250	36	4	0	0-0	64.1	61	34	6	3	24-5	38	4.20	85	.250	.321	10-0	.000	-1	56	-5	-0.4
1989	Cin N	2	2	.500	42	1	0	1-0	69.2	68	33	5	3	27-8	57	3.75	96	.261	.330	4-0	.250	1	74	-1	0.0

Year	Tm Lg	W	L	Pct	G	GS	CG-Sho	SV-BS	IP	H	R	HR	HB	BB-IB	SO	ERA	AERA	OAV	OOB	AB-SH	AVG	PB	Sup	APR	PW
1990	Cin N	1	3	.250	29	0	0	0-0	51.1	69	24	7	1	24-6	41	3.86	102	.325	.395	4-3	.000	-0		0	0.0
Total	5	14	14	.500	138	30	2	1-0	328.2	324	168	37	10	170-20	231	4.08	93	.260	.350	18-3	.056	-0	103	-14	-1.1
BISCAN, FRANK Frank Stephen "Porky" B 3.13.1920 Mt.Olive, IL D 5.22.1959 St.Louis, MO BL/TL 5-11/190# d5.3 Mil 1942-45																									
1942	StL A	0	1	.000	11	0	0	1	27	13	8	1	0	11	10	2.33	159	.143	.235	6-0	.000	-0		4	0.2
1946	StL A	1	1	.500	16	0	0	1	22.2	28	13	0	0	22	9	5.16	72	.318	.455	3-0	.000	-0		-2	-0.3
1948	StL A	6	7	.462	47	4	1	2	98.2	129	78	3	9	71	45	6.11	75	.322	.435	26-0	.192	1	79	-18	-2.0
Total	3	7	9	.438	74	4	1	4	148.1	170	99	4	9	104	64	5.28	81	.294	.409	35-0	.143	-0	79	-16	-2.1
BISHOP, CHARLIE Charles Tuller B 1.1.1924 Atlanta, GA D 7.5.1993 Lawrenceville, GA BR/TR 6-2/195# d8.22																									
1952	Phi A	2	2	.500	6	5	1	0	30.2	29	24	2	0	24	17	6.46	61	.238	.363	9-1	.111	-0	110	-8	-0.9
1953	Phi A	3	14	.176	39	20	1-1	2	160.2	174	106	15	5	86	66	5.66	76	.282	.375	56-0	.089	-4*	81	-21	-2.3
1954	Phi A	4	6	.400	20	12	4	1	96	98	49	10	5	50	34	4.41	89	.275	.369	33-1	.121	-2*	88	-4	-0.6
1955	KC A	1	0	1.000	4	0	0	0	6.2	6	7	1	3	8-2	4	5.40	77	.261	.486	2-0	.500	0		-2	-0.2
Total	4	10	22	.313	69	37	6-1	3	294	307	186	28	13	168-2	121	5.33	77	.275	.375	100-2	.110	-6	87	-35	-4.0
BISHOP, JIM James Morton B 1.28.1898 Montgomery City, MO D 9.20.1973 Montgomery City, MO BR/TR 6/195# d4.26																									
1923	Phi N	0	3	.000	15	0	0	1	32.2	48	31	2	3	11	5	6.34	73	.353	.413	10-0	.000	-2		-6	-0.7
1924	Phi N	0	1	.000	7	1	0	0	16.2	24	14	3	0	7	3	6.48	69	.348	.408	5-0	.200	-0	76	-3	-0.2
Total	2	0	4	.000	22	1	0	1	49.1	72	45	5	3	18	8	6.39	71	.351	.412	15-0	.067	-2	76	-9	-0.9
BISHOP, LLOYD Lloyd Clifton B 4.25.1890 Conway Springs, KS D 6.18.1968 Wichita, KS BR/TR 6/180# d9.5																									
1914	Cle A	0	1	.000	3	1	0	0	8	14	5	0	0	3	1	5.63	51	.389	.436	2-0	.000	-0	101	-2	-0.2
BISHOP, BILL William Henry "Lefty" B 10.22.1900 Houtzdale, PA D 2.14.1956 St.Joseph, MO BR/TR 5-8/170# d9.15																									
1921	Phi A	0	0	—	2	0	0	0	7	8	9	0	0	10	4	9.00	50	.267	.450	3-0	.000	-1		-4	-0.2
BISHOP, BILL William Robinson B 12.27.1869 Adamsburg, PA D 12.15.1932 Pittsburgh, PA 5-8/187# d9.13																									
1886	Pit AA	0	1	.000	2	2	2	0	17	17	14	0	1	11	4	3.18	107	.221	.326	7	.143	-1	105	-1	-0.1
1887	Pit N	0	3	.000	3	3	3	0	27	45	46	2	2	22	4	13.33	29	.354	.457	9	.000	-1	34	-26	-1.8
1889	Chi N	0	0	—	2	0	0	2	3	6	13	0	0	6	1	18.00	23	.400	.571	1	.000	0		-6	-0.6
Total	3	0	4	.000	7	5	5	2	47	68	73	2	3	39	9	9.96	37	.311	.421	17	.059	-2	61	-33	-2.5
BITHORN, HI Hiram Gabriel (Sosa) B 3.18.1916 Santurce, P.R. D 1.1.1952 ElMante, Mexico BR/TR 6-1/200# d4.15 Mil 1944-45																									
1942	Chi N	9	14	.391	38	16	9	2	171.1	191	93	8	0	81	65	3.68	87	.296	.374	57-1	.123	-1	95	-14	-1.9
1943	Chi N	18	12	.600	39	30	19-**7**	2	249.2	227	79	8	2	65	86	2.60	129	.244	.294	92-5	.174	-0	110	23	2.9
1946	Chi N	6	5	.545	26	7	2-1	1	86.2	97	42	5	0	25	34	3.84	86	.283	.332	28-2	.179	-0	111	-5	-0.7
1947	Chi A	1	0	1.000	2	0	0	0	2	2	0	0	0	0	0	0.00	—	.286	.286	0-0	—	0		1	0.2
Total	4	34	31	.523	105	53	30-8	5	509.2	517	214	21	2	171	185	3.16	104	.268	.328	177-8	.158	-2	106	5	0.5
BITKER, JOE Joseph Anthony B 2.12.1964 Glendale, CA BR/TR 6-1/175# d7.31																									
1990	Oak A	0	0	—	1	0	0	0-0	3	1	0	0	0	1-0	2	0.00	—	.111	.200	0-0	—	0		1	0.1
	Tex A	0	0	—	5	0	0	0-0	9	7	3	0	1	3-0	6	3.00	131	.212	.289	0-0	—	0		1	0.1
	Year	0	0	—	6	0	0	0-0	12	8	7	0	1	4-0	8	2.25	172	.190	.271	0-0	—	0		2	0.2
1991	Tex A	1	0	1.000	9	0	0	0-0	14.2	17	11	4	0	8-3	16	6.75	60	.274	.357	0-0	—	0		-4	-0.3
Total	2	1	0	1.000	15	0	0	0-0	26.2	25	14	4	1	12-3	24	4.73	84	.240	.322	0-0	—	0		-2	-0.1
BITTIGER, JEFF Jeffrey Scott B 4.13.1962 Jersey City, NJ BR/TR 5-10/175# d9.2																									
1986	Phi N	1	1	.500	3	3	0	0-0	14.2	16	10	2	1	7-1	8	5.52	70	.271	.358	3-1	.333	1	116	-2	-0.2
1987	Min A	1	0	1.000	3	1	0	0-0	8.1	11	5	2	1	0-0	5	5.40	86	.314	.333	0-0	—	0	158	0	0.0
1988	Chi A	2	4	.333	25	7	0	0-0	61.2	59	31	11	0	29-2	33	4.23	94	.255	.333	0-0	—	0	49	-1	-0.1
1989	Chi A	0	1	.000	2	1	0	0-0	9.2	9	7	2	0	6-0	7	6.52	59	.257	.366	0-0	—	0	71	-3	-0.2
Total	4	4	6	.400	33	12	0	0-0	94.1	95	53	17	2	42-3	53	4.77	84	.264	.341	3-1	.333	1	78	-6	-0.5
BIVIN, JIM James Nathaniel B 12.11.1909 Jackson, MS D 11.7.1982 Pueblo, CO BR/TR 6/155# d4.16																									
1935	Phi N	2	9	.182	47	14	0	1	161.2	220	129	20	3	65	54	5.79	78	.316	.377	48-0	.146	-1	72	-22	-1.4
BLACK, DAVE David B 4.19.1892 Chicago, IL D 10.27.1936 Pittsburgh, PA BL/TR 6-2/175# d5.2																									
1914	Chi F	1	0	1.000	8	1	1	0	25	28	19	1	0	4	19	6.12	43	.311	.340	6-0	.333	1	207	-9	-0.4
1915	Chi F	6	7	.462	25	10	2	0	121.1	104	46	4	6	33	43	2.45	103	.241	.304	37-4	.108	-3	123	0	-0.3
	Bal F	1	3	.250	8	4	1	0	34	32	18	2	2	15	10	3.71	77	.260	.350	12-2	.250	0	110	-3	-0.3
	Year	7	10	.412	33	14	3	0	155.1	136	23	6	8	48	53	2.72	95	.245	.315	49-6	.143	-3	120	-3	-0.6
1923	Bos A	0	0	—	2	0	0	0	1	2	0	0	0	0	0	0.00	—	.500	.500	0-0	—	0		0	0.0
Total	3	8	10	.444	43	15	4	0	181.1	166	83	7	8	52	72	3.18	82	.256	.319	55-6	.164	-2	125	-12	-1.0
BLACK, DON Donald Paul B 7.20.1916 Salix, IA D 4.21.1959 Cuyahoga Falls, OH BR/TR 6/185# d4.24																									
1943	Phi A	6	16	.273	33	26	12-1	1	208	193	105	8	6	110	65	4.20	81	.247	.344	69-2	.188	-1	75	-15	-1.6
1944	Phi A	10	12	.455	29	27	8	0	177.1	177	94	6	4	75	78	4.06	86	.259	.336	59-3	.186	-1	100	-11	-1.3
1945	Phi A	5	11	.313	26	18	8	0	125.1	154	77	5	0	69	47	5.17	66	.307	.391	37-1	.162	-2	81	-21	-2.7
1946	Cle A	1	2	.333	18	4	0	0	43.2	45	26	5	1	21	15	4.53	73	.273	.358	10-1	.200	0	123	-7	-0.4
1947	Cle A	10	12	.455	30	28	8-3	0	190.2	177	90	17	1	85	72	3.92	89	.249	.330	66-3	.182	-1	110	-9	-1.1
1948	Cle A	2	2	.500	18	10	1	0	52	57	33	5	1	40	16	5.37	76	.282	.403	15-1	.200	-0	107	-7	-0.5
Total	6	34	55	.382	154	113	37-4	1	797	803	425	46	13	400	293	4.35	80	.264	.352	256-11	.184	-4	95	-70	-7.6
BLACK, BUD Harry Ralston B 6.30.1957 San Mateo, CA BL/TL 6-2/180# d9.5																									
1981	Sea A	0	0	—	2	0	0	0-0	1	2	0	0	0	3-1	0	0.00	—	.500	.714	0-0	—	0		0	0.0
1982	KC A	4	6	.400	22	14	0	0-0	88.1	92	48	10	3	34-6	40	4.58	89	.269	.338	0-0	—	0*	78	-4	-0.4
1983	KC A	10	7	.588	24	24	3	0-0	161.1	159	75	19	2	43-1	58	3.79	108	.257	.305	0-0	—	0	120	6	0.7
1984	†KC A	17	12	.586	35	35	8-1	0-0	257	226	99	22	4	64-2	140	3.12	129	.233	**.283**	0-0	—	0	86	25	2.9
1985	†KC A	10	15	.400	33	33	5-2	0-0	205.2	216	111	17	8	59-4	122	4.33	96	.268	.323	0-0	—	0	84	-4	-0.4
1986	KC A	5	10	.333	56	4	0	9-2	121	100	49	14	7	43-5	68	3.20	133	.225	.301	0-0	—	0	80	13	1.7
1987	KC A	8	6	.571	29	18	0	1-1	122.1	126	63	16	5	35-2	61	3.60	127	.265	.320	0-0	—	0	109	10	1.0
1988	KC A	2	1	.667	17	0	0	0-1	22	23	12	2	0	11-2	19	4.91	81	.267	.351	0-0	—	0		-2	-0.2
	Cle A	2	3	.400	16	7	0	1-0	59	59	35	6	4	23-1	44	5.03	82	.262	.337	0-0	—	0	92	-5	-0.4
	Year	4	4	.500	33	7	0	1-1	81	82	39	8	4	34-3	63	5.00	82	.264	.341	0-0	—	0	92	-7	-0.6
1989	Cle A	12	11	.522	33	32	6-3	0-0	222.1	213	95	14	1	52-0	88	3.36	118	.252	.295	0-0	—	0	87	13	1.3
1990	Cle A	11	10	.524	29	29	5-2	0-0	191	171	79	17	4	58-1	103	3.53	111	.236	.294	0-0	—	0	104	10	1.0
	Tor A	2	1	.667	3	2	0	0-1	15.2	10	7	2	1	3-0	3	4.02	98	.189	.237	0-0	—	0	69	0	0.0
	Year	13	11	.542	32	31	5-2	0-1	206.2	181	10	19	5	61-1	106	3.57	110	.233	.290	0-0	—	0	102	12	1.0
1991	SF N	12	16	.429	34	34	3-3	0-0	214.1	201	104	25	4	71-8	104	3.99	90	.251	.313	71-9	.183	1*	93	-11	-1.0
1992	SF N	10	12	.455	28	28	2-1	0-0	177	178	88	23	1	59-11	82	3.97	83	.263	.321	54-10	.056	-3	85	-15	-1.9
1993	SF N	8	2	.800	16	16	0	0-0	93.2	89	44	13	2	33-2	45	3.56	110	.256	.321	37-3	.243	2	140	2	0.5
1994	SF N	4	2	.667	10	10	0	0-0	54.1	50	31	9	3	16-1	28	4.47	90	.245	.307	17-5	.059	-1	120	-4	-0.5
1995	Cle A	4	2	.667	11	10	0	0-0	47.1	63	42	8	0	16-2	34	6.85	69	.317	.362	0-0	—	0	123	-12	-1.3
Total	15	121	116	.511	398	296	32-12	11-5	2053.1	1978	982	217	49	623-49	1039	3.84	104	.253	.310	179-27	.145	-1	97	22	3.0
BLACK, JOE Joseph B 2.8.1924 Plainfield, NJ D 5.17.2002 Scottsdale, AZ BR/TR 6-2/220# d5.1																									
1952	†Bro N	15	4	.789	56	2	1	15	142.1	102	40	9	1	41	85	2.15	169	.201	.262	36-6	.139	-1*	135	**23**	3.3
1953	†Bro N	6	3	.667	34	3	0	5	72.2	74	46	12	1	27	42	5.33	80	.259	.325	17-0	.235	0	56	-8	-1.0
1954	Bro N	0	0	—	5	0	0	0	7	11	9	3	0	5	3	11.57	35	.355	.432	0-0	—	0		-5	-0.3
1955	Bro N	1	0	1.000	6	0	0	0	15.1	15	5	1	0	5-1	9	2.93	138	.273	.328	3-0	.333	0		2	0.1
	Cin N	5	2	.714	32	11	1	3	102.1	106	58	13	0	25-3	54	4.22	100	.263	.303	30-3	.100	-2	134	-1	-0.3
	Year	6	2	.750	38	11	1	3	117.2	121	64	14	0	30-4	63	4.05	104	.264	.306	33-3	.121	-2	134	1	-0.2
1956	Cin N	3	2	.600	32	0	0	2	61.2	61	31	11	0	25-3	27	4.52	88	.256	.326	10-0	.000	-1*		-2	-0.2
1957	Was A	0	1	.000	7	0	0	0	12.2	22	11	4	0	1-0	2	7.11	55	.393	.397	0-0	—	0		-4	-0.3
Total	6	30	12	.714	172	16	2	25	414	391	200	53	2	129-7	222	3.91	102	.248	.304	96-9	.135	-5	124	5	1.2

Year	Tm Lg	W	L	Pct	G	GS	CG-Sho	SV-BS	IP	H	R	HR	HB	BB-IB	SO	ERA	AERA	OAV	OOB	AB-SH	AVG	PB	Sup	APR	PW
BLACK, BOB Robert Benjamin B 12.10.1862 Cincinnati, OH D 3.21.1933 Sioux City, IA 5-5.5/155# d8.19 ▲																									
1884	KC U	4	9	.308	16	15	13	0	123	127	79	1		17	93	3.22	69	.249	.273	146	.247	1*	64	-13	-0.8
BLACK, BUD William Carroll B 7.9.1932 St.Louis, MO BR/TR 6-3/197# d9.13 Mil 1953 C4																									
1952	Det A	0	1	.000	2	2	0	0	8	14	11	0	0	5	0	10.13	38	.389	.463	3-0	.000	-0	103	-6	-0.6
1955	Det A	1	1	.500	3	2	1-1	0	14	12	5	0	2	8-0	7	1.29	299	.231	.355	4-1	.250	0	81	3	0.4
1956	Det A	1	1	.500	5	1	0	0	10	10	4	2	0	5-0	7	3.60	114	.256	.333	2-0	.000	-0	86	1	0.1
Total	3	2	3	.400	10	5	1-1	0	32	36	20	2	2	18-0	14	4.22	93	.283	.378	9-1	.111	-1	90	-2	-0.1
BLACKBURN, CHARLIE Foster Edwin B 1.6.1895 Chicago, IL D 3.9.1984 New Port Richey, FL BR/TR 6-1/165# d4.17																									
1915	KC F	0	1	.000	7	2	0	0	15.2	19	15	2	0	13	7	8.62	31	.306	.427	4-0	.000	-1	160	-9	-0.6
1921	Chi A	0	0	—	1	0	0	0	1	0	0	0	0	1	0	0.00	—	.000	.333	0-0	—	0		0	0.0
Total	2	0	1	.000	8	2	0	0	16.2	19	15	2	0	14	7	8.10	34	.297	.423	4-0	.000	-1	160	-9	-0.6
BLACKBURN, GEORGE George W. "Smiling George" B 9.21.1871 Ozark, MO TR 5-11/184# d7.6																									
1897	Bal N	2	2	.500	5	4	3	0	33	34	30	2	1	12	1	6.82	61	.264	.331	13-0	.077	-2	115	-8	-0.9
BLACKBURN, JIM James Ray "Bones" B 6.19.1924 Warsaw, KY D 10.26.1969 Cincinnati, OH BR/TR 6-4/175# d7.24																									
1948	Cin N	0	2	.000	16	0	0	0	32.1	38	18	1	0	14	10	4.18	94	.302	.371	6-0	.000	-0		-1	-0.1
1951	Cin N	0	0	—	2	0	0	0	3.2	8	7	3	2	2	1	17.18	24	.444	.545	0-0	—	0		-5	-0.2
Total	2	0	2	.000	18	0	0	0	36	46	25	4	2	16	11	5.50	71	.319	.395	6-0	.000	-0		-6	-0.3
BLACKBURN, RON Ronald Hamilton B 4.23.1935 Mt.Airy, NC D 4.29.1998 Morganton, NC BR/TR 6-0.5/160# d4.15 Mil 1959																									
1958	Pit N	2	1	.667	38	2	0	3	63.2	61	33	7	3	27-5	31	3.39	114	.261	.338	7-1	.286	1	58	1	0.2
1959	Pit N	1	1	.500	26	0	0	1	44.1	50	21	5	2	15-4	19	3.65	106	.286	.345	5-0	.200	1		1	0.1
Total	2	3	2	.600	64	2	0	4	108	111	54	12	5	42-9	50	3.50	110	.271	.341	12-1	.250	2	58	2	0.3
BLACKWELL, EWELL Ewell "The Whip" B 10.23.1922 Fresno, CA D 10.29.1996 Hendersonville, NC BR/TR 6-6/195# d4.21 Mil 1943-45																									
1942	Cin N	0	0	—	2	0	0	0	3	3	4	0	0	3	1	6.00	55	.231	.375	1-0	.000	-0		-2	-0.1
1946	Cin N★	9	13	.409	33	25	10-**5**	0	194.1	160	62	1	4	79	100	2.45	136	.226	.307	56-6	.107	-3	69	20	2.1
1947	Cin N★	**22**	8	.733	33	33	**23**-6	0	273	227	91	10	4	95	**193**	2.47	166	.234	.304	106-7	.123	-5	94	46	4.5
1948	Cin N★	7	9	.438	22	20	4-1	1	138.2	134	73	12	4	52	114	4.54	86	.251	.323	48-3	.229	1	96	-7	-0.4
1949	Cin N★	5	5	.500	30	4	0	1	76.2	80	36	7	3	34	55	4.23	99	.271	.352	19-1	.211	-0	42	2	0.3
1950	Cin N★	17	15	.531	40	32	18-1	4	261	203	105	12	13	112	188	2.97	143	**.210**	.301	89-7	.146	-2	81	32	3.6
1951	Cin N★	16	15	.516	38	32	11-2	2	232.2	204	110	16	9	97	120	3.44	118	.233	.315	82-2	.293	7*	81	13	2.5
1952	Cin N	3	12	.200	23	17	3	0	102	107	66	6	5	60	48	5.38	70	.275	.379	32-1	.156	-0	71	-18	-2.4
	†NY A	1	0	1.000	5	2	0	1	16	12	2	0	0	12	7	0.56	591	.203	.338	5-0	.200	-0	105	5	0.4
1953	NY A	2	0	1.000	8	4	0	1	19.2	17	10	2	1	13	11	3.66	101	.233	.356	5-0	.000	-1	144	0	-0.1
1955	KC A	0	1	.000	2	0	0	1	4	3	3	1	1	5-0	2	6.75	62	.250	.500	0-1	—	0		-1	-0.2
Total	10	82	78	.512	236	169	69-15	11	1321	1150	562	67	44	562-0	839	3.30	120	.235	.319	443-28	.174	-3	83	90	10.2
BLAEHOLDER, GEORGE George Franklin B 1.26.1904 Orange, CA D 12.29.1947 Garden Grove, CA BR/TR 5-11/175# d4.20																									
1925	StL A	0	0	—	2	0	0	0	2	6	7	3	1	1	1	31.50	15	.600	.667	0-0	—	0		-5	-0.2
1927	StL A	0	1	.000	1	1	1	0	9	8	5	1	1	4	2	5.00	87	.258	.361	3-0	.333	0	77	0	0.0
1928	StL A	10	15	.400	38	26	9-1	3	214.1	235	123	23	2	52	87	4.37	96	.280	.324	71-1	.211	2	95	-5	-0.1
1929	StL A	14	15	.483	42	24	13-**4**	2	222	237	113	18	0	61	72	4.18	106	.275	.323	74-2	.122	-4	74	8	0.8
1930	StL A	11	13	.458	37	23	10-1	4	191.1	235	119	20	2	46	70	4.61	106	.303	.343	65-4	.185	-1	99	3	0.1
1931	StL A	11	15	.423	35	32	13-1	0	226.1	280	137	15	1	56	79	4.53	102	.295	.335	77-3	.143	-3	84	3	0.2
1932	StL A	14	14	.500	42	36	16-1	0	258.1	304	163	19	3	76	80	4.70	103	.290	.340	88-2	.136	-4	91	2	-0.1
1933	StL A	15	19	.441	38	36	14-3	0	255.2	283	146	24	0	69	63	4.72	99	.280	.326	77-7	.182	-1	71	0	0.1
1934	StL A	14	18	.438	39	33	14-1	3	234.1	276	130	16	0	68	66	4.22	118	.296	.343	75-10	.093	-5	75	18	1.7
1935	StL A	1	1	.500	6	2	0	0	17.2	25	15	3	0	6	0	7.13	67	.342	.392	3-1	.000	-1	109	-4	-0.4
	Phi A	6	10	.375	23	22	10-1	0	149	173	78	10	0	49	22	3.99	114	.289	.343	47-6	.043	-6	88	8	0.2
	Year	7	11	.389	29	24	10-1	0	166.2	198	83	13	0	55	22	4.32	106	.295	.348	50-7	.040	-7	89	4	-0.2
1936	Cle A	8	4	.667	35	16	6-1	0	134.1	158	83	21	3	47	30	5.09	99	.295	.356	46-3	.130	-3	126	1	-0.1
Total	11	104	125	.454	338	251	106-14	12	1914.1	2220	1119	173	13	535	572	4.54	103	.290	.337	626-39	.142	-25	87	29	2.2
BLAIR, DENNIS Dennis Herman B 6.5.1954 Middletown, OH BR/TR 6-5/182# d5.26																									
1974	Mon N	11	7	.611	22	22	4-1	0-0	146	113	61	7	5	72-4	76	3.27	118	.210	.307	51-6	.118	-2	127	9	1.0
1975	Mon N	8	15	.348	30	27	1	0-0	163.1	150	77	14	3	106-3	82	3.80	101	.251	.362	49-2	.143	-1	65	1	-0.1
1976	Mon N	0	2	.000	5	4	1	0-0	15.2	21	11	1	2	11-0	9	4.02	93	.300	.405	4-0	.000	-0	77	-2	-0.3
1980	SD N	0	1	.000	5	1	0	0-0	14	18	10	3	0	3-0	11	6.43	54	.310	.344	5-0	.200	0	78	-4	-0.3
Total	4	19	25	.432	62	54	6-1	0-0	339	302	159	25	10	192-7	178	3.69	104	.239	.341	109-8	.128	-4	91	4	0.3
BLAIR, WILLIE William Allen B 12.18.1965 Paintsville, KY BR/TR 6-1/185# d4.11																									
1990	Tor A	3	5	.375	27	6	0	0-0	68.2	66	33	4	1	28-4	43	4.06	97	.250	.320	0-0	—	0	81	-1	-0.1
1991	Cle A	2	3	.400	11	5	0	0-1	36	58	27	7	1	10-0	13	6.75	62	.377	.413	0-0	—	0	75	-9	-1.0
1992	Hou N	5	7	.417	29	8	0	0-0	78.2	74	47	5	2	25-2	48	4.00	84	.249	.309	17-1	.059	-1	84	-10	-1.6
1993	Col N	6	10	.375	46	18	1	0-0	146	184	90	20	3	42-4	84	4.75	101	.306	.350	36-3	.111	-2	60	-1	-0.3
1994	Col N	0	5	.000	47	1	0	3-3	77.2	98	57	9	4	39-3	68	5.79	86	.308	.390	6-0	.000	-1	37	-7	-0.6
1995	SD N	7	5	.583	40	12	0	0-0	114	112	60	11	2	45-3	83	4.34	93	.262	.333	24-4	.000	-2	82	-3	-0.6
1996	†SD N	2	6	.250	60	0	0	1-4	88	80	52	13	7	29-5	67	4.60	86	.240	.311	3-0	.000	-0		-8	-0.7
1997	Det A	16	8	.667	29	27	2	0-0	175	186	85	18	3	46-2	90	4.17	110	.273	.319	4-0	.000	-0	102	9	1.0
1998	Ari N	4	15	.211	23	23	0	0-0	146.2	165	91	27	3	51-2	71	5.34	79	.292	.352	48-4	.083	-3	68	-16	-2.0
	NY N	1	1	.500	11	2	0	0-0	28.2	23	10	4	1	10-0	21	3.14	132	.228	.301	4-0	.250	1	11	4	0.3
	Year	5	16	.238	34	25	0	0-0	175.1	188	11	31	4	61-2	92	4.98	84	.282	.344	52-4	.096	-2	64	-14	-1.7
1999	Det A	3	11	.214	39	16	0	0-0	134	169	107	29	4	44-0	82	6.85	72	.308	.361	1-0	.000	-0	85	-27	-2.3
2000	Det A	10	6	.625	47	17	0	0-2	156.2	185	89	20	2	35-0	74	4.88	99	.296	.331	3-0	.333	0	126	1	0.0
2001	Det A	1	4	.200	9	4	0	0-0	24	38	30	3	3	11-3	15	10.50	41	.369	.437	2-0	.000	-0	80	-17	-2.6
Total	12	60	86	.411	418	139	3	4-10	1274	1438	778	170	36	415-28	759	5.04	88	.286	.342	148-12	.074	-8	85	-85	-10.5
BLAIR, BILL William Ellsworth B 9.17.1863 Pittsburgh, PA D 2.22.1890 Pittsburgh, PA BL/TL 5-8.5/172# d7.19																									
1888	Phi AA	1	3	.250	4	4	3	0	31	29	21	0	1	8	16	2.61	114	.238	.290	13	.308	1	44	0	0.2
BLAISDELL, DICK Howard Carleton B 6.18.1862 Bradford, MA D 8.20.1886 Malden, MA d7.9																									
1884	KC U	0	3	.000	3	3	3	0	26	49	39	0		4	8	8.65	26	.377	.396	16	.313	0*	70	-18	-1.3
BLAKE, ED Edward James B 12.23.1925 E.St.Louis, IL BR/TR 5-11/175# d5.1																									
1951	Cin N	0	0	—	3	0	0	0	4	10	5	3	0	1	1	11.25	36	.476	.500	0-0	—	0		-3	-0.1
1952	Cin N	0	0	—	2	0	0	0	3	3	0	0	0	0	0	0.00	—	.250	.250	0-0	—	0		1	0.1
1953	Cin N	0	0	—	1	0	0	0	0	1	2	0	0	1	0	∞	—	1.000	1.000	0-0	—	0		-2	-0.2
1957	KC A	0	0	—	2	0	0	0	1.2	1	1	1	0	2-1	0	5.40	73	.167	.375	0-0	—	0		0	0.0
Total	4	0	0	—	8	0	0	0	8.2	15	8	4	0	4-1	1	8.31	48	.375	.432	0-0	—	0		-4	-0.2
BLAKE, SHERIFF John Frederick B 9.17.1899 Ansted, WV D 10.31.1982 Beckley, WV BB/TR 6/180# d6.29																									
1920	Pit N	0	0	—	6	0	0	0	13.1	21	14	0	1	6	7	8.10	40	.368	.438	4-0	.250	-0		-7	-0.3
1924	Chi N	6	6	.500	29	11	4	1	106.1	123	58	3	2	44	42	4.57	85	.299	.370	31-1	.290	1	99	-5	-0.4
1925	Chi N	10	18	.357	36	31	14	2	231.1	260	144	17	5	114	93	4.86	89	.287	.370	79-3	.152	-4	78	-14	-1.8
1926	Chi N	11	12	.478	39	27	11-4	1	197.2	204	91	7	6	92	95	3.60	107	.280	.366	65-3	.215	-1	80	7	0.7
1927	Chi N	13	14	.481	32	27	13-2	0	224.1	238	101	3	4	82	64	3.29	117	.282	.348	83-4	.193	-2	104	12	1.3
1928	Chi N	17	11	.607	34	29	16-**4**	1	240.2	209	80	4	3	101	78	2.47	156	.240	.321	88-7	.216	0*	98	37	4.0
1929	†Chi N	14	13	.519	35	29	13-1	1	218.1	244	122	8	2	103	70	4.29	108	.291	.370	81-5	.173	-2*	123	8	0.6
1930	Chi N	10	14	.417	34	24	7	0	186.2	213	127	14	3	99	80	4.82	101	.291	.378	66-3	.227	-1*	95	-3	-0.4
1931	Chi N	0	4	.000	16	5	0	0	50	64	34	4	1	26	29	5.22	74	.312	.392	16-0	.500	3	124	-8	-0.2
	Phi N	4	5	.444	14	9	1	1	71	90	49	2	3	35	31	5.58	76	.305	.384	25-0	.240	0	97	-8	-0.8

Year	Tm Lg	W	L	Pct	G	GS	CG-Sho	SV-BS	IP	H	R	HR	HB	BB-IB	SO	ERA	AERA	OAV	OOB	AB-SH	AVG	PB	Sup	APR	PW
	Year	4	9	.308	30	14	1	1	121	154	54	6	4	61	60	5.43	75	.308	.388	41-0	.341	3	106	-17	-1.0
1937	StL A	2	2	.500	15	1	0	1	36.2	55	33	5	0	20	12	7.61	63	.350	.424	10-1	.100	-1	144	-10	-1.0
	StL N	0	3	.000	14	2	2	0	43.2	45	23	1	0	18	20	3.71	107	.271	.342	10-1	.300	0	65	1	0.1
Total	10	87	102	.460	304	195	81-11	8	1620	1766	876	68	30	740	621	4.13	101	.284	.363	558-28	.211	-6	97	10	1.8
BLANCHE, AL Prosper Albert (b: Prosper Bilangio) B 9.21.1909 Somerville, MA D 4.2.1997 Melrose, MA BR/TR 6/178# d8.23																									
1935	Bos N	0	0	—	6	0	0	0	17.1	14	3	0	0	5	4	1.56	243	.230	.288	6-0	.167	-0		5	0.2
1936	Bos N	0	1	.000	11	0	0	1	16	20	15	1	1	8	4	6.19	62	.303	.387	4-0	.250	0		-5	-0.3
Total	2	0	1	.000	17	0	0	1	33.1	34	18	1	1	13	8	3.78	101	.268	.340	10-0	.200	-0		0	-0.1
BLANCO, GIL Gilbert Henry B 12.15.1945 Phoenix, AZ BL/TL 6-5/205# d4.24																									
1965	NY A	1	1	.500	17	1	0	0	20.1	16	10	1	1	12-0	14	3.98	85	.232	.341	0-0	—	0	26	-1	-0.1
1966	KC A	2	4	.333	11	8	0	0	38.1	31	26	3	4	36-1	21	4.70	72	.237	.415	12-1	.167	-0	84	-7	-1.0
Total	2	3	5	.375	28	9	0	0	58.2	47	36	4	5	48-1	35	4.45	76	.235	.391	12-1	.167	-0	78	-8	-1.1
BLAND, NATE Nathan Garrett B 12.27.1974 Birmingham, AL BL/TL 6-5/190# d5.5																									
2003	Hou N	1	2	.333	22	0	0	0-1	20.1	22	13	3	2	12-2	18	5.75	77	.286	.391	0-0	—	0		-2	-0.3
BLANDING, FRED Frederick James "Fritz" B 2.8.1886 Redlands, CA D 7.16.1950 Salem, VA BR/TR 5-11/185# d9.15																									
1910	Cle A	2	2	.500	6	5	4-1	0	45.1	43	19	0	4	12	25	2.78	93	.254	.319	18-0	.111	-1	99	-1	-0.2
1911	Cle A	7	11	.389	29	16	11	2	176	190	95	5	6	60	80	3.68	93	.283	.347	65-1	.262	2*	70	-4	-0.2
1912	Cle A	18	14	.563	39	31	23-1	1	262	259	117	4	3	79	75	2.92	117	.267	.324	93-9	.226	1	106	14	1.7
1913	Cle A	15	10	.600	41	22	14-3	0	215	234	79	6	3	72	63	2.55	119	.284	.344	86-2	.244	4	101	13	1.7
1914	Cle A	4	9	.308	29	12	5	0	116	133	82	0	1	54	35	3.96	73	.301	.378	39-0	.103	-2*	69	-16	-1.9
Total	5	46	46	.500	144	86	57-5	3	814.1	859	392	15	17	277	278	3.13	102	.279	.342	301-12	.216	4	92	6	1.1
BLANK, MATT Clarence Matthew B 4.5.1976 Texarkana, TX BL/TL 6-2/200# d4.3																									
2000	Mon N	0	1	.000	13	0	0	0-1	14	12	8	1	1	5-1	4	5.14	93	.222	.295	1-0	.000	-0		0	0.0
2001	Mon N	2	2	.500	5	4	0	0-0	22.2	23	14	5	2	13-1	11	5.16	87	.267	.369	8-0	.500	2	109	-2	0.0
Total	2	2	3	.400	18	4	0	0-1	36.2	35	22	6	3	18-2	15	5.15	89	.250	.341	9-0	.444	2	109	-2	0.0
BLANK, FRED Frederick August B 6.18.1874 DeSoto, MO D 2.5.1936 St.Louis, MO BL/TL 6-0.5/175# d6.20																									
1894	Cin N	0	1	.000	1	1	1	0	8	5	4	0	0	9	1	4.50	123	.179	.378	3-0	.000	-1	26	1	0.1
BLANKENSHIP, HOMER Homer "Si" B 8.4.1902 Bonham, TX D 6.22.1974 Longview, TX BR/TR 6/185# d9.6 b-Ted																									
1922	Chi A	0	0	—	4	0	0	0	13	21	7	1	0	5	3	4.85	84	.389	.441	4-0	.000	-1		-1	-0.1
1923	Chi A	1	1	.500	4	0	0	1	5	9	5	0	0	1	1	3.60	110	.429	.455	0-0	—	0		-1	-0.2
1928	Pit N	0	2	.000	5	2	1	0	21.2	27	15	1	0	9	6	5.82	70	.321	.387	8-0	.375	1	31	-3	-0.2
Total	3	1	3	.250	13	2	1	1	39.2	57	27	2	0	15	10	5.22	78	.358	.414	12-0	.250	0	31	-5	-0.5
BLANKENSHIP, KEVIN Kevin De Wayne B 1.26.1963 Anaheim, CA BR/TR 6/180# d9.20																									
1988	Atl N	0	1	.000	2	2	0	0-0	10.2	7	4	0	1	7-0	5	3.38	109	.194	.341	3-0	.000	-0	60	1	0.0
	Chi N	1	0	1.000	1	1	0	0-0	5	7	4	2	0	1-0	4	7.20	50	.318	.348	3-0	.000	-0	221	-2	-0.3
	Year	1	1	.500	3	3	0	0-0	15.2	14	13	2	1	8-0	9	4.60	80	.241	.343	6-0	.000	-1	113	-1	-0.3
1989	Chi N	0	0	—	2	0	0	0-0	5.1	4	1	0	0	2-0	2	1.69	223	.200	.273	1-0	.000	-0		1	0.0
1990	Chi N	0	2	.000	3	2	0	0-0	12.1	13	10	1	0	6-0	5	5.84	70	.265	.333	4-0	.000	-0	66	-3	-0.4
Total	3	1	3	.250	8	5	0	0-0	33.1	31	19	3	1	16-0	16	4.59	83	.244	.329	11-0	.000	-1	93	-3	-0.7
BLANKENSHIP, TED Theodore B 5.10.1901 Bonham, TX D 1.14.1945 Atoka, OK BR/TR 6-1/170# d7.2 b-Homer																									
1922	Chi A	8	10	.444	24	15	7	1	127.2	124	58	4	2	47	42	3.81	107	.266	.335	41-3	.171	-1	78	5	0.5
1923	Chi A	9	14	.391	44	23	9-1	0	204.2	219	115	8	4	100	57	4.35	91	.287	.372	76-2	.211	2	88	-8	-0.7
1924	Chi A	7	6	.538	25	11	7	1	129.1	167	79	1	1	38	36	5.01	82	.317	.364	46-3	.326	6	140	-10	-0.5
1925	Chi A	17	8	.680	40	23	16-3	1	232	218	90	11	0	69	81	3.03	137	.253	.308	88-4	.205	2	110	31	2.9
1926	Chi A	13	10	.565	29	26	15-1	1	209.1	217	96	13	1	65	66	3.61	107	.273	.328	76-6	.132	-2	114	7	0.4
1927	Chi A	12	17	.414	37	34	11-3	0	236.2	280	156	14	2	74	51	5.06	80	.299	.352	80-1	.188	3*	93	-26	-2.5
1928	Chi A	9	11	.450	27	22	8	0	158	186	92	9	2	80	36	4.61	88	.306	.388	59-3	.169	-2	91	-8	-1.1
1929	Chi A	0	2	.000	8	1	0	0	18.1	28	18	3	0	9	7	8.84	48	.359	.425	4-0	.250	-0	20	-8	-0.7
1930	Chi A	2	1	.667	7	1	0	0	14.2	23	15	0	1	7	2	9.20	50	.371	.443	5-0	.200	-0	74	-6	-1.0
Total	9	77	79	.494	241	156	73-8	4	1330.2	1462	719	63	13	489	378	4.29	94	.287	.351	475-22	.196	7	99	-23	-2.7
BLANTON, CY Darrell Elijah B 7.6.1908 Waurika, OK D 9.13.1945 Norman, OK BL/TR 5-11.5/180# d9.23																									
1934	Pit N	0	1	.000	1	1	0	0	8	5	3	1	1	4	5	3.38	122	.161	.278	1-0	.000	0	42	1	0.1
1935	Pit N	18	13	.581	35	30	23-**4**	1	254.1	220	93	3	2	55	142	**2.58**	**159**	**.229**	**.272**	97-3	.134	-4	91	**41**	4.4
1936	Pit N	13	15	.464	44	32	15-**4**	3	235.2	235	114	9	3	55	127	3.51	115	.257	.301	84-5	.155	-3	94	12	1.0
1937	Pit N★	14	12	.538	36	**34**	14-4	0	242.2	250	115	13	5	76	143	3.30	117	.266	.324	85-4	.165	-0	102	12	1.1
1938	Pit N	11	7	.611	29	26	10-1	0	172.2	190	84	13	2	46	80	3.70	103	.281	.329	64-4	.203	-1	132	2	0.2
1939	Pit N	2	3	.400	10	6	1	0	42	45	23	4	0	10	11	4.29	90	.266	.307	14-0	.286	1	102	-2	-0.1
1940	Phi N	4	3	.571	13	10	5	0	77	82	43	7	1	21	24	4.32	90	.272	.322	24-2	.083	-1	85	-4	-0.5
1941	Phi N☆	6	13	.316	28	25	7-1	0	163.2	186	98	11	3	57	64	4.51	82	.284	.344	51-4	.118	-2	82	-16	-2.0
1942	Phi N	0	4	.000	6	3	0	0	22.1	30	15	3	1	13	15	5.64	59	.345	.436	8-0	.125	-0	59	-5	-0.9
Total	9	68	71	.489	202	167	75-14	4	1218.1	1243	588	64	18	337	611	3.55	110	.262	.314	428-22	.154	-11	98	41	3.3
BLASINGAME, WADE Wade Allen B 11.22.1943 Deming, NM BL/TL 6-1/185# d9.17																									
1963	Mil N	0	0	—	2	0	0	0	3	7	4	0	0	2-0	6	12.00	27	.467	.529	0-0	—	0		-3	-0.1
1964	Mil N	9	5	.643	28	13	3-1	2	116.2	113	58	15	0	51-2	70	4.24	83	.257	.333	40-0	.175	3*	142	-7	-0.5
1965	Mil N	16	10	.615	38	36	10-1	1	224.2	200	103	17	5	116-10	117	3.77	94	.244	.339	81-3	.185	3	119	-5	-0.1
1966	Atl N	3	7	.300	16	12	0	0	67.2	71	42	5	2	25-2	34	5.32	68	.272	.340	23-0	.217	1*	75	-11	-1.4
1967	Atl N	1	0	1.000	10	4	0	0	25.1	27	13	1	1	21-1	20	4.62	72	.287	.422	7-0	.143	0	165	-3	-0.1
	Hou N	4	7	.364	15	14	0	0	77	91	57	9	2	27-2	46	5.96	56	.298	.357	22-2	.182	2*	133	-22	-2.6
	Year	5	7	.417	25	18	0	0	102.1	118	62	10	3	48-3	66	5.63	59	.296	.374	29-2	.172	2	140	-25	-2.7
1968	Hou N	1	2	.333	22	2	0	1	36	45	21	3	0	10-1	22	4.75	62	.308	.348	5-0	.000	0	147	-7	-0.5
1969	Hou N	0	5	.000	26	5	0	1-1	52	66	47	4	2	33-7	33	5.37	66	.306	.396	12-0	.000	-1*	50	-15	-1.6
1970	Hou N	3	3	.500	13	13	1	0-0	77.2	76	34	4	2	23-3	55	3.48	112	.261	.318	24-0	.083	-0	96	3	0.2
1971	Hou N	9	11	.450	30	28	2	0-0	158.1	177	90	11	13	45-3	93	4.60	73	.285	.344	49-2	.204	4	119	-23	-2.1
1972	Hou N	0	0	—	10	0	0	0-0	8.1	4	9	1	2	8-0	9	8.64	39	.148	.368	0-0	—	0		-5	-0.3
	NY A	0	1	.000	12	1	0	0-0	17	14	8	5	1	11-1	7	4.24	70	.250	.382	2-1	.000	0	60	-2	-0.1
Total	10	46	51	.474	222	128	16-2	5-1	863.2	891	486	75	30	372-32	512	4.52	77	.271	.348	265-8	.166	14	115	-100	-9.2
BLASS, STEVE Stephen Robert B 4.18.1942 Canaan, CT BR/TR 6/165# d5.10																									
1964	Pit N	5	8	.385	24	13	3-1	0	104.2	107	52	9	1	45-5	67	4.04	87	.266	.339	30-2	.067	-1	91	-6	-0.8
1966	Pit N	11	7	.611	34	25	1	0	155.2	173	80	12	2	46-1	76	3.87	92	.284	.336	52-2	.231	1	109	-8	-0.8
1967	Pit N	6	8	.429	32	16	2	0	126.2	126	65	12	2	47-7	72	3.55	95	.261	.328	39-2	.128	-1	104	-6	-0.7
1968	Pit N	18	6	**.750**	33	31	12-7	0	220.1	191	64	13	4	57-5	132	2.12	138	.234	.287	80-4	.138	-1*	141	19	2.0
1969	Pit N	16	10	.615	38	32	9	2-0	210	207	119	21	6	86-3	147	4.46	78	.258	.333	84-2	.250	6*	146	-24	-2.1
1970	Pit N	10	12	.455	31	31	6-1	0-0	196.2	187	92	14	5	73-8	120	3.52	111	.254	.324	70-3	.114	-2*	107	6	0.3
1971	†Pit N	15	8	.652	33	33	12-**5**	0-0	240	226	81	16	2	68-8	136	2.85	119	.249	.302	83-8	.120	-3*	132	16	1.3
1972	†Pit N★	19	8	.704	33	32	11-2	0-0	249.2	227	80	18	4	84-8	117	2.49	134	.246	.311	82-12	.183	1*	115	24	2.9
1973	Pit N	3	9	.250	23	18	1	0-0	88.2	109	98	11	12	84-4	27	9.85	36	.313	.454	24-5	.417	4*	129	-59	-6.0
1974	Pit N	0	0	—	1	0	0	0-0	5	5	8	2	0	7-0	2	9.00	38	.238	.429	2-0	.000	-0		-4	-0.2
Total	10	103	76	.575	282	231	57-16	2-0	1597.1	1558	739	128	38	597-49	896	3.63	94	.258	.327	546-40	.172	4	123	-42	-4.1
BLATERIC, STEVE Stephen Lawrence B 3.20.1944 Denver, CO BR/TR 6-3/200# d9.17																									
1971	Cin N	0	0	—	2	0	0	0-0	2.2	5	4	2	1	0-0	4	13.50	25	.385	.429	0-0	—	0		-3	-0.1
1972	NY A	0	0	—	1	0	0	0-0	4	2	0	0	0	0-0	4	0.00	—	.143	.143	1-0	.000	-0		1	0.1
1975	Cal A	0	0	—	2	0	0	0-0	4.1	9	5	0	0	1-0	5	6.23	57	.429	.435	0-0	—	0		-2	-0.1

Year	Tm Lg	W	L	Pct	G	GS	CG-Sho	SV-BS	IP	H	R	HR	HB	BB-IB	SO	ERA	AERA	OAV	OOB	AB-SH	AVG	PB	Sup	APR	PW
Total	3	0	0	—	5	0	0	0-0	11	16	9	2	1	1-0	13	5.73	58	.333	.353	1-0	.000	-0		-4	-0.1
BLAUVELT, HENRY Henry Russell B 4.8.1873 Nyack, NY D 12.28.1926 Portland, OR d6.22																									
1890	Roc AA	0	0	—	2	0	0	0	12.1	19	23	0	0	8	5	10.22	35	.339	.422	6	.500	1		-10	-0.3
BLAYLOCK, GARY Gary Nelson B 10.11.1931 Clarkton, MO BR/TR 6/196# d4.10 C4																									
1959	StL N	4	5	.444	26	12	3	0	100	117	61	14	2	43-3	61	5.13	83	.298	.366	34-1	.118	0*	81	-8	-0.7
	NY A	0	1	.000	15	1	0	0	25.2	30	13	0	1	15-0	20	3.51	104	.306	.400	2-0	.500	1	48	0	0.0
Total	1	4	6	.400	41	13	3	0	125.2	147	74	14	3	58-3	81	4.80	86	.300	.373	36-1	.139	1	80	-8	-0.7
BLAYLOCK, BOB Robert Edward B 6.28.1935 Chattanooga, OK BR/TR 6-1/185# d7.22																									
1956	StL N	1	6	.143	14	6	0	0	41	45	32	7	0	24-1	39	6.37	59	.276	.369	11-0	.091	-1	101	-11	-1.7
1959	StL N	0	1	.000	3	1	0	0	9	8	5	1	0	3-0	3	4.00	106	.229	.289	1-0	.000	-0	232	0	0.0
Total	2	1	7	.125	17	7	0	0	50	53	37	8	0	27-1	42	5.94	65	.268	.356	12-0	.083	-1	121	-11	-1.7
BLAZIER, RON Ronald Patrick B 7.30.1971 Altoona, PA BR/TR 6-6/215# d5.31																									
1996	Phi N	3	1	.750	27	0	0	0-0	38.1	49	30	6	0	10-3	25	5.87	74	.310	.347	1-0	1.000	0		-7	-0.7
1997	Phi N	1	1	.500	36	0	0	0-0	53.2	62	31	8	0	21-3	42	5.03	84	.290	.347	5-1	.400	1		-4	-0.2
Total	2	4	2	.667	63	0	0	0-0	92	111	61	14	0	31-6	67	5.38	79	.298	.347	6-1	.500	1		-11	-0.9
BLEMKER, RAY Raymond B 8.9.1937 Huntingburg, IN D 2.15.1994 Evansville, IN BR/TL 5-11/190# d7.3																									
1960	KC A	0	0	—	1	0	0	0	1.2	3	5	1	1	2-0	0	27.00	15	.375	.545	0-0	—	0		-4	-0.2
BLETHEN, CLARENCE Clarence Waldo "Climax" B 7.11.1893 Dover-Foxcroft, ME D 4.11.1973 Frederick, MD BL/TR 5-11/165# d9.17																									
1923	Bos A	0	0	—	5	0	0	0	17.2	29	15	0	0	7	2	7.13	58	.382	.434	6-0	.000	-1		-5	-0.4
1929	Bro N	0	0	—	2	0	0	0	2	4	2	0	0	3	0	9.00	51	.444	.583	0-0	—	0		-1	0.0
Total	2	0	0	—	7	0	0	0	19.2	33	17	0	0	10	2	7.32	57	.388	.453	6-0	.000	-1		-6	-0.4
BLEWETT, BOB Robert Lawrence B 6.28.1877 Fond Du Lac, WI D 3.17.1958 Sedro Woolley, WA BL/TL 5-11/170# d6.17																									
1902	NY N	0	2	.000	5	3	2	0	28	39	26	0	1	7	8	4.82	58	.328	.370	10-0	.000	-1	81	-7	-0.6
BLISS, ELMER Elmer Ward B 3.9.1875 Penfield, PA D 3.18.1962 Bradford, PA BL/TR 6/180# d9.28																									
1903	NY A	1	0	1.000	1	0	0	0	7	4	1	0	0	0	3	0.00	—	.167	.167	3-0	.000	-0		2	0.2
BLOMDAHL, BEN Benjamin Earl B 12.30.1970 Long Beach, CA BR/TR 6-2/185# d4.28																									
1995	Det A	0	0	—	14	0	0	1-0	24.1	36	21	5	0	13-0	15	7.77	61	.356	.430	0-0	—	0		-7	-0.3
BLONG, JOE Joseph Myles B 9.17.1853 St.Louis, MO D 9.17.1892 St.Louis, MO BR/TR d5.4 ▲																									
1875	RS NA	3	12	.200	15	15	12-1	0	129	169	121	0		2	14	3.07	71	.284	.286	68	.147	-4*	47	-10	-0.9
1876	StL N	0	0	—	1	0	0	0	4	2	0	0		1	0	0.00	—	.154	.214	264	.235	-0*		1	0.1
1877	StL N	10	9	.526	25	21	17	0	187.1	203	121	0		38	51	2.74	95	.262	.296	218	.216	0*	106	-5	-0.5
Total	2	10	9	.526	26	21	17	0	191.1	205	121	0		39	51	2.68	97	.260	.295	482	.226	0	106	-4	-0.4
BLUE, VIDA Vida Rochelle B 7.28.1949 Mansfield, LA BB/TL 6/189# d7.20																									
1969	Oak A	1	1	.500	12	4	0	1-0	42	49	34	13	0	18-1	24	6.64	52	.290	.358	10-0	.000	-0	154	-16	-0.9
1970	Oak A	2	0	1.000	6	6	2-2	0-0	38.2	20	12	0	1	12-0	35	2.09	169	.152	.228	15-1	.200	2	130	6	0.5
1971	†Oak A★	24	8	.750	39	39	24-**8**	0-0	312	209	73	19	4	88-3	301	**1.82**	184	**.189**	**.251**	102-13	.118	-2	107	54	5.3
1972	†Oak A	6	10	.375	25	23	5-4	0-0	151	117	55	11	1	48-3	111	2.80	102	.215	.277	45-2	.044	-2*	92	0	-0.4
1973	†Oak A	20	9	.690	37	37	13-4	0-0	263.2	214	108	26	4	105-2	158	3.28	108	.224	.300	1-0	.000	-0*	125	10	0.9
1974	†Oak A	17	15	.531	40	40	12-1	0-0	282.1	246	118	17	1	98-7	174	3.25	102	.236	.299	0-0	—	0	123	3	0.0
1975	†Oak A★	22	11	.667	39	38	13-2	1-0	278	243	103	21	5	99-4	189	3.01	121	.236	.305	0-0	—	0	136	22	2.4
1976	Oak A	18	13	.581	37	37	20-6	0-0	298.1	268	90	9	1	63-3	166	2.35	143	.239	.279	0-0	—	0	93	34	3.4
1977	Oak A❖	14	19	.424	38	38	16-1	0-0	279.2	284	138	23	1	86-5	157	3.83	105	.264	.317	1-0	.000	-0	70	6	0.6
1978	SF N★	18	10	.643	35	35	9-4	0-0	258	233	87	12	0	70-4	171	2.79	124	.246	.295	79-5	.076	2	102	21	2.3
1979	SF N	14	14	.500	34	34	10	0-0	237	246	143	23	1	111-11	138	5.01	70	.272	.348	83-8	.120	0*	124	-40	-3.9
1980	SF N❖	14	10	.583	31	31	10-3	0-0	224	202	79	14	0	61-8	129	2.97	119	.242	.292	68-7	.074	-4	82	17	1.5
1981	SF N★	8	6	.571	18	18	1	0-0	124.2	97	40	7	1	54-3	63	2.45	140	.217	.302	35-5	.200	2	79	13	1.8
1982	KC A	13	12	.520	31	31	6-2	0-0	181	163	80	20	0	80-3	103	3.78	108	.238	.316	0-0	—	0	97	8	1.0
1983	KC A	0	5	.000	19	14	1	0-0	85.1	96	62	12	2	35-0	53	6.01	68	.286	.352	0-0	—	0	102	-17	-0.9
1985	SF N	8	8	.500	33	20	1	0-0	131	115	70	17	1	80-1	103	4.47	77	.240	.348	30-8	.133	1	123	-13	-1.4
1986	SF N	10	10	.500	28	28	0	0-0	156.2	137	65	19	0	77-3	100	3.27	108	.239	.326	43-4	.093	1	100	4	0.6
Total	17	209	161	.565	502	473	143-37	2-0	3343.1	2939	1357	263	23	1185-61	2175	3.27	108	.237	.303	512-53	.104	-2	106	112	12.8
BLUEJACKET, JIM James (b: James Smith) B 7.8.1887 Adair, OK D 3.26.1947 Pekin, IL BR/TR 6-2.5/200# d8.6 ggs-Bill Wilkinson																									
1914	Bro F	4	5	.444	17	7	3-1	1	67	77	34	2	0	19	29	3.76	76	.302	.350	22-0	.136	-1	89	-6	-0.7
1915	Bro F	10	11	.476	24	21	10-2	0	162.2	155	74	2	0	75	48	3.15	86	.258	.340	61-1	.131	-5	98	-7	-1.5
1916	Cin N	0	1	.000	3	2	0	0	7	12	6	0	0	3	1	7.71	34	.400	.455	2-0	.000	-0	144	-3	-0.5
Total	3	14	17	.452	44	30	13-3	1	236.2	244	114	4	0	97	78	3.46	80	.275	.347	85-1	.129	-6	98	-16	-2.7
BLUMA, JAIME James Andrew B 5.18.1972 Beaufort, SC BR/TR 5-11/195# d8.9																									
1996	KC A	0	0	—	17	0	0	5-0	20	18	9	2	2	4-1	14	3.60	139	.247	.300	0-0	—	0		3	0.2
BLUME, CLINT Clinton Willis B 10.17.1898 Brooklyn, NY D 6.12.1973 Islip, NY BR/TR 5-11/175# d9.30																									
1922	NY N	1	0	1.000	1	1	1	0	9	7	3	0	0	1	2	1.00	400	.212	.235	1-0	1.000	1	102	2	0.4
1923	NY N	2	0	1.000	12	1	0	0	24	22	11	0	2	20	2	3.75	102	.265	.419	5-0	.000	-0	129	0	0.0
Total	2	3	0	1.000	13	2	1	0	33	29	14	0	2	21	4	3.00	129	.250	.374	6-0	.167	1	117	2	0.4
BLYLEVEN, BERT Rik Aalbert B 4.6.1951 Zeist, Netherlands BR/TR 6-3/207# d6.5																									
1970	†Min A	10	9	.526	27	25	5-1	0-0	164	143	66	17	2	47-6	135	3.18	117	.232	.288	50-7	.140	-1	94	11	0.9
1971	Min A	16	15	.516	38	38	17-5	0-0	278.1	267	95	21	5	59-1	224	2.81	126	.255	.297	91-7	.132	-3	86	23	2.3
1972	Min A	17	17	.500	39	38	11-3	0-0	287.1	247	93	22	10	69-7	228	2.73	118	.233	.285	94-11	.160	-1	105	20	2.4
1973	Min A★	20	17	.541	40	40	25-**9**	0-0	325	296	109	16	9	67-4	258	2.52	**157**	.242	.284	0-0	—	0	93	**48**	5.3
1974	Min A	17	17	.500	37	37	19-3	0-0	281	244	99	14	9	77-3	249	2.66	140	.233	.290	0-0	—	0	96	31	3.7
1975	Min A	15	10	.600	35	35	20-3	0-0	275.2	219	104	24	4	84-2	233	3.00	128	.219	.281	0-0	—	0	110	26	2.3
1976	Min A	4	5	.444	12	12	4	0-0	95.1	101	39	3	4	35-5	75	3.12	115	.283	.351	0-0	—	0	74	5	0.4
	Tex A	9	11	.450	24	24	14-6	0-0	202.1	182	67	11	8	46-1	144	2.76	130	.242	.292	0-0	—	0	64	20	2.1
	Year	13	16	.448	36	36	18-6	0-0	297.2	283	70	14	12	81-6	219	2.87	125	.255	.312	0-0	—	0	67	24	2.5
1977	Tex A	14	12	.538	30	30	15-5	0-0	234.2	181	81	20	7	69-1	182	2.72	150	.214	.278	0-0	—	0	107	35	3.7
1978	Pit N	14	10	.583	34	34	11-4	0-0	243.2	217	94	17	6	66-5	182	3.03	122	.235	.290	85-7	.129	-2*	103	18	1.5
1979	†Pit N	12	5	.706	37	37	4	0-0	237.1	238	102	21	6	92-8	172	3.60	108	.265	.335	70-15	.129	-3*	106	10	0.2
1980	Pit N	8	13	.381	34	32	5-2	0-2	216.2	219	102	20	0	59-5	168	3.82	95	.262	.310	61-9	.082	-4*	83	-4	-0.8
1981	Cle A	11	7	.611	20	20	9-1	0-0	159.1	145	52	9	5	40-1	107	2.88	126	.245	.296	0-0	—	0	100	15	1.6
1982	Cle A	2	2	.500	4	4	0	0-0	20.1	16	14	2	0	11-0	19	4.87	84	.211	.303	0-0	—	0	123	-3	-0.4
1983	Cle A	7	10	.412	24	24	5	0-0	156.1	160	74	8	10	44-4	123	3.91	109	.267	.325	0-0	—	0	81	6	0.7
1984	Cle A	19	7	.731	33	32	12-4	0-0	245	204	86	19	6	74-4	170	2.87	143	.224	.285	0-0	—	0	117	33	3.3
1985	Cle A★	9	11	.450	23	23	15-4	0-0	179.2	163	76	14	7	49-1	129	3.26	127	.240	.296	0-0	—	0	93	16	1.6
	Min A	8	5	.615	14	14	9-1	0-0	114	101	45	9	2	26-0	77	3.00	147	.237	.281	0-0	—	0	78	15	1.7
	Year	17	16	.515	37	**37**	**24-5**	0-0	**293.2**	264	49	23	9	75-1	**206**	3.16	134	.239	.290	0-0	—	0	87	32	3.3
1986	Min A	17	14	.548	36	36	16-3	0-0	**271.2**	262	134	50	10	58-4	215	4.01	108	.250	.294	0-0	—	0	96	9	0.8
1987	†Min A	15	12	.556	37	37	8-1	0-0	267	249	132	46	9	101-4	196	4.01	116	.249	.321	0-0	—	0	99	17	1.5
1988	Min A	10	17	.370	33	33	7	0-0	207.1	240	128	21	16	51-1	145	5.43	75	.294	.345	0-0	—	0	94	-27	-3.1
1989	Cal A	17	5	.773	33	33	8-**5**	0-0	241	225	76	14	8	44-2	131	2.73	140	.248	.287	0-0	—	0	114	32	2.8
1990	Cal A	8	7	.533	23	23	2	0-0	134	163	85	15	7	25-0	69	5.24	73	.303	.339	0-0	—	0	110	-20	-1.9
1992	Cal A	8	12	.400	25	24	1	0-0	133	150	76	17	5	29-2	70	4.74	84	.285	.326	0-0	—	0	72	-11	-1.5
Total	22	287	250	.534	692	685	242-60	0-2	4970	4632	2029	430	155	1322-71	3701	3.31	118	.247	.301	451-56	.131	-13	97	325	31.1

Year	Tm Lg	W	L	Pct	G	GS	CG-Sho	SV-BS	IP	H	R	HR	HB	BB-IB	SO	ERA	AERA	OAV	OOB	AB-SH	AVG	PB	Sup	APR	PW
BLYZKA, MIKE Michael John (b: Michael John Bliska) B 12.25.1928 Hamtramck, MI BR/TR 5-11.5/190# d4.21																									
1953	StL A	2	6	.250	33	9	2	0	94.1	110	78	6	0	56	23	6.39	66	.292	.383	23-2	.000	-3	73	-23	-2.0
1954	Bal A	1	5	.167	37	0	0	1	86.1	83	48	2	0	51	35	4.69	76	.254	.351	15-1	.133	-1		-10	-0.7
Total	2	3	11	.214	70	9	2	1	180.2	193	126	8	0	107	58	5.58	70	.274	.368	38-3	.053	-4	73	-33	-2.7
BOARDMAN, CHARLIE Charles Louis B 3.27.1893 Seneca Falls, NY D 8.10.1968 Sacramento, CA BL/TR 6-2.5/194# d9.26																									
1913	Phi A	0	2	.000	2	2	1	0	9	10	5	0	0	6	4	2.00	138	.323	.432	3-0	.000	-0	54	0	-0.1
1914	Phi A	0	0	—	2	0	0	0	7.1	10	5	0	0	4	2	4.91	53	.357	.438	2-0	.000	-0		-2	-0.1
1915	StL N	1	0	1.000	3	1	1	0	19	12	12	0	0	15	7	2.84	98	.188	.342	7-0	.286	0	160	-2	-0.1
Total	3	1	2	.333	7	3	2	0	35.1	32	22	0	0	25	13	3.06	90	.260	.385	12-0	.167	-0	90	-4	-0.3
BOCHTLER, DOUG Douglas Eugene B 7.5.1970 W.Palm Beach, FL BR/TR 6-3/205# d5.5																									
1995	SD N	4	4	.500	34	0	0	1-3	45.1	38	18	5	0	19-0	45	3.57	113	.239	.318	2-0	.000	-0		4	0.6
1996	†SD N	2	4	.333	63	0	0	3-4	65.2	45	25	6	1	39-8	68	3.02	132	.195	.311	0-0	—	0		7	0.6
1997	SD N	3	6	.333	54	0	0	2-1	60.1	51	35	3	1	50-4	46	4.77	81	.229	.368	0-0	—	0		-6	-0.9
1998	Det A	0	2	.000	51	0	0	0-2	67.1	73	48	17	3	42-6	45	6.15	77	.279	.381	0-0	—	0		-10	-0.5
1999	LA N	0	0	—	12	0	0	0-0	13	11	8	3	1	6-1	7	5.54	77	.224	.316	0-0	—	0		-2	-0.1
2000	KC A	0	2	.000	6	0	0	0-0	8.1	13	6	2	0	10-4	4	6.48	79	.371	.511	0-0	—	0		-1	-0.2
Total	6	9	18	.333	220	0	0	6-10	260	231	140	36	6	166-23	215	4.57	92	.241	.353	2-0	.000	-0		-8	-0.5
BOCKUS, RANDY Randy Walter B 10.5.1960 Canton, OH BL/TR 6-2/190# d9.10																									
1986	SF N	0	0	—	5	0	0	0-0	7	7	5	1	0	6-1	4	2.57	137	.241	.371	1-0	.000	-0*		0	0.0
1987	SF N	1	0	1.000	12	0	0	0-1	17.1	17	8	2	0	4-1	9	3.63	106	.266	.309	1-0	.000	-0		0	0.0
1988	SF N	1	1	.500	20	0	0	0-1	32	35	19	2	1	13-2	18	4.78	68	.297	.368	6-0	.167	0		-6	-0.3
1989	Det A	0	0	—	2	0	0	0-0	5.1	7	3	0	0	2-1	2	5.06	76	.333	.391	0-0	—	0		-1	0.0
Total	4	2	1	.667	39	0	0	0-2	61.2	66	35	5	1	25-5	33	4.23	83	.284	.355	8-0	.125	-0		-7	-0.3
BODDICKER, MIKE Michael James B 8.23.1957 Cedar Rapids, IA BR/TR 5-11/172# d10.4																									
1980	Bal A	0	1	.000	1	1	0	0-0	7.1	6	6	1	0	5-0	4	6.14	65	.207	.324	0-0	—	0	90	-2	-0.2
1981	Bal A	0	0	—	2	0	0	0-0	5.2	6	4	1	0	2-0	2	4.76	76	.261	.320	0-0	—	0		-1	-0.1
1982	Bal A	1	0	1.000	7	0	0	0-0	25.2	25	10	2	0	12-2	20	3.51	115	.258	.339	0-0	—	0		2	0.1
1983	†Bal A	16	8	.667	27	26	10-**5**	0-0	179	141	65	13	0	52-1	120	2.77	143	**.216**	.273	0-0	—	0	105	23	3.1
1984	Bal A☆	**20**	11	.645	34	34	16-4	0-0	261.1	218	95	23	5	81-1	128	**2.79**	139	.228	.290	0-0	—	0*	101	31	3.8
1985	Bal A	12	17	.414	32	32	9-2	0-0	203.1	227	104	13	5	89-7	135	4.07	99	.286	.361	0-0	—	0*	100	-2	0.0
1986	Bal A	14	12	.538	33	33	7	0-0	218.1	214	125	30	11	74-4	175	4.70	88	.255	.321	0-0	—	0	111	-13	-1.2
1987	Bal A	10	12	.455	33	33	7-2	0-0	226	212	114	29	7	78-4	152	4.18	106	.248	.315	0-0	—	0*	88	6	0.7
1988	Bal A	6	12	.333	21	21	4	0-0	147	149	72	14	11	51-5	100	3.86	101	.265	.333	0-0	—	0	71	0	-0.1
	†Bos A	7	3	.700	15	14	1-1	0-0	89	85	30	3	3	26-1	56	2.63	157	.257	.313	0-0	—	0	122	14	1.6
	Year	13	15	.464	36	35	5-1	0-0	236	234	36	17	14	77-6	156	3.39	118	.262	.326	0-0	—	0	92	14	1.5
1989	Bos A	15	11	.577	34	34	3-2	0-0	211.2	217	101	19	10	71-4	145	4.00	103	.267	.330	0-0	—	0	104	5	0.6
1990	†Bos A	17	8	.680	34	34	4	0-0	228	225	92	16	10	69-6	143	3.36	122	.258	.319	0-0	—	0	111	19	2.0
1991	KC A	12	12	.500	30	29	1	0-0	180.2	188	89	13	13	59-0	79	4.08	101	.272	.340	0-0	—	0	94	2	0.4
1992	KC A	1	4	.200	29	8	0	3-0	86.2	92	50	5	8	37-3	47	4.98	82	.269	.351	0-0	—	0	62	-8	-0.4
1993	Mil A	3	5	.375	10	10	1	0-0	54	77	35	6	4	15-1	24	5.67	75	.338	.387	0-0	—	0	97	-7	-0.9
Total	14	134	116	.536	342	309	63-16	3-0	2123.2	2082	992	188	87	721-39	1330	3.80	107	.257	.323	0-0	—	0	100	69	9.4
BOEHLER, GEORGE George Henry B 1.2.1892 Lawrenceburg, IN D 6.23.1958 Lawrenceburg, IN BR/TR 6-2/180# d9.13																									
1912	Det A	0	2	.000	5	4	2	0	32	50	31	0	2	14	15	6.47	50	.365	.431	10-0	.100	-1	108	-11	-0.6
1913	Det A	0	1	.000	1	1	1	0	8	11	9	0	2	6	2	6.75	43	.367	.500	3-0	.333	1	0	-4	-0.3
1914	Det A	2	3	.400	18	6	2	0	63	54	39	1	8	48	37	3.57	79	.242	.394	17-0	.176	1	121	-7	-0.5
1915	Det A	1	1	.500	8	0	0	0	15	19	10	0	1	4	7	1.80	168	.328	.381	4-0	.750	2*		0	0.1
1916	Det A	1	1	.500	5	2	1	0	13.1	12	8	0	2	9	8	4.73	61	.261	.404	3-0	.000	0	158	-2	-0.3
1920	StL A	0	1	.000	3	1	0	0	7	10	10	1	0	4	2	7.71	51	.303	.378	1-0	.000	0	162	-4	-0.4
1921	StL A	0	0	—	1	0	0	0	1	1	0	0	0	0	0	0.00	—	.500	.500	0-0	—	0		0	0.0
1923	Pit N	1	3	.250	10	3	1	0	28.1	33	26	1	1	26	12	6.04	66	.314	.455	10-0	.300	1	103	-8	-0.9
1926	Bro N	1	0	1.000	10	1	0	0	34.2	42	23	1	3	23	10	4.41	87	.302	.412	12-0	.250	0*	65	-3	-0.2
Total	9	6	12	.333	61	18	7	0	202.1	232	156	4	19	134	93	4.71	70	.300	.416	60-0	.233	3	110	-39	-3.1
BOEHLING, JOE John Joseph B 3.20.1891 Richmond, VA D 9.8.1941 Richmond, VA BL/TL 5-11/168# d6.20																									
1912	Was A	0	0	—	3	0	0	0	5	4	4	0	2	6	2	7.20	46	.235	.480	0-0	—	0		-2	-0.1
1913	Was A	17	7	.708	38	25	18-3	4	235.1	197	82	3	9	82	110	2.14	138	.236	.312	86-1	.221	1	106	18	2.2
1914	Was A	13	8	.619	27	24	14-2	0	196	180	76	3	9	76	91	3.03	93	.258	.339	71-2	.239	4	107	-1	0.4
1915	Was A	14	13	.519	40	32	14-2	0	229.1	217	105	5	9	119	108	3.22	92	.255	.352	75-4	.173	0*	97	-4	-0.2
1916	Was A	9	11	.450	27	19	7-2	0	139.2	134	62	1	3	54	52	3.09	90	.260	.333	41-1	.171	1	66	-5	-0.5
	Cle A	2	4	.333	12	9	3	0	60.2	63	23	0	2	23	18	2.67	113	.281	.353	19-0	.263	1*	67	2	0.4
	Year	11	15	.423	39	28	10-2	0	200.1	197	26	1	5	77	70	2.97	96	.266	.339	60-1	.200	1	66	-3	-0.1
1917	Cle A	1	6	.143	12	7	1	0	46.1	50	27	1	3	16	11	4.66	61	.291	.361	16-1	.188	-0*	54	-7	-1.0
1920	Cle A	0	1	.000	3	2	0	0	13	16	10	0	0	10	4	4.85	78	.333	.448	4-0	.500	1	115	-2	0.0
Total	7	56	50	.528	162	118	57-9	4	925.1	861	389	13	37	386	396	2.97	98	.256	.340	312-9	.212	7	92	-1	1.2
BOEHRINGER, BRIAN Brian Edward B 1.8.1969 St.Louis, MO BB/TR 6-2/180# d4.30																									
1995	NY A	0	3	.000	7	3	0	0-1	17.2	24	27	5	1	22-1	10	13.75	34	.320	.475	0-0	—	0	74	-18	-2.2
1996	†NY A	2	4	.333	15	3	0	0-1	46.1	46	28	6	1	21-2	37	5.44	91	.260	.337	0-0	—	0	75	-2	-0.2
1997	†NY A	3	2	.600	34	0	0	0-3	48	39	16	4	0	32-6	53	2.63	170	.225	.343	0-0	—	0		10	0.9
1998	†SD N	5	2	.714	56	1	0	0-1	76.1	75	38	10	4	45-4	67	4.36	90	.257	.363	7-0	.000	-0	23	-3	-0.3
1999	SD N	6	5	.545	33	11	0	0-2	94.1	97	38	10	1	35-4	64	3.24	129	.267	.330	16-2	.063	-1	93	11	1.0
2000	SD N	0	3	.000	7	3	0	0-1	15.2	18	15	4	0	10-0	9	5.74	75	.286	.378	4-1	.250	0	43	-5	-0.7
2001	NY A	0	1	.000	22	0	0	1-0	34.2	35	15	3	3	12-0	33	3.12	144	.255	.325	0-0	—	0		4	0.2
	SF N	0	3	.000	29	0	0	1-0	34.1	32	20	4	2	17-5	27	4.19	95	.239	.329	3-0	.000	-0		-2	-0.3
2002	Pit N	4	4	.500	70	0	0	1-5	79.2	65	30	5	2	33-6	65	3.39	123	.229	.311	0-0	—	0		8	0.7
2003	Pit N	5	4	.556	62	0	0	0-3	62.1	64	39	11	3	30-3	47	5.49	80	.267	.353	0-0	—	0		-7	-0.9
Total	9	25	31	.446	335	21	0	3-17	509.1	495	266	62	17	257-31	412	4.35	99	.255	.344	30-3	.067	-1	79	-4	-1.8
BOERNER, LARRY Lawrence Hyer B 1.21.1905 Staunton, VA D 10.16.1969 Staunton, VA BR/TR 6-4.5/175# d6.30																									
1932	Bos A	0	4	.000	21	5	0	0	61	71	41	2	3	37	19	5.02	90	.302	.404	17-1	.000	-3	61	-4	-0.4
BOEVER, JOE Joseph Martin B 10.4.1960 Kirkwood, MO BR/TR 6-1/200# d7.19																									
1985	StL N	0	0	—	13	0	0	0-1	16.1	17	8	3	0	4-1	20	4.41	80	.270	.309	0-0	—	0		-1	-0.1
1986	StL N	0	1	.000	11	0	0	0-0	21.2	19	5	2	0	11-0	8	1.66	220	.232	.323	2-0	.500	0		5	0.3
1987	Atl N	1	0	1.000	14	0	0	0-0	18.1	29	15	4	0	12-1	18	7.36	59	.367	.446	0-0	—	0		-5	-0.3
1988	Atl N	0	2	.000	16	0	0	1-0	20.1	12	4	1	1	1-0	7	1.77	208	.182	.206	0-0	—	0		4	0.5
1989	Atl N	4	11	.267	66	0	0	21-9	82.1	78	37	6	1	34-5	68	3.94	93	.252	.328	1-0	.000	-0		-1	-0.1
1990	Atl N	1	3	.250	33	0	0	8-4	42.1	40	23	6	0	35-10	35	4.68	86	.252	.333	2-0	.000	-0		-2	-0.3
	Phi N	2	3	.400	34	0	0	6-1	46	37	12	0	0	16-2	40	2.15	178	.215	.282	1-0	.000	-0		9	1.1
	Year	3	6	.333	67	0	0	14-5	88.1	77	38	6	0	51-12	75	3.36	117	.233	.333	3-0	.000	-0		6	0.8
1991	Phi N	3	5	.375	68	0	0	0-2	98.1	90	45	10	0	54-11	89	3.84	95	.245	.336	3-0	.333	-0		-2	-0.2
1992	Hou N	3	6	.333	**81**	0	0	2-4	111.1	103	38	3	4	45-9	67	2.51	134	.248	.324	7-0	.000	-1		9	0.7
1993	Oak A	4	2	.667	42	0	0	0-1	79.1	87	40	8	4	33-4	49	3.86	106	.280	.353	0-0	—	0		0	0.0
	Det A	2	1	.667	19	0	0	3-1	23	14	10	1	0	11-3	14	2.74	157	.179	.269	0-0	—	0		3	0.4
	Year	6	3	.667	61	0	0	3-2	102.1	101	50	9	4	44-7	63	3.61	115	.260	.336	0-0	—	0		5	0.4
1994	Det A	9	2	.818	46	0	0	3-3	81.1	80	40	12	2	37-12	49	3.98	122	.263	.345	0-0	—	0		8	1.0
1995	Det A	5	7	.417	60	0	0	3-3	98.2	128	74	17	3	44-12	71	6.39	75	.319	.384	0-0	—	0		-17	-1.8
1996	Pit N	0	2	.000	13	0	0	2-1	15	17	11	2	1	6-0	6	5.40	81	.288	.364	1-0	.000	-0		-2	-0.3
Total	12	34	45	.430	516	0	0	49-30	754.1	751	362	75	16	343-70	541	3.93	102	.262	.341	17-0	.118	-1		8	0.9

Year	Tm Lg	W	L	Pct	G	GS	CG-Sho	SV-BS	IP	H	R	HR	HB	BB-IB	SO	ERA	AERA	OAV	OOB	AB-SH	AVG	PB	Sup	APR	PW
BOGART, JOHN John Renzie "Big John" B 9.21.1900 Bloomsburg, PA D 12.7.1986 Clarence, NY BR/TR 6-2/195# d9.17																									
1920	Det A	2	1	.667	4	2	0	0	23.2	16	12	0	0	18	5	3.04	122	.195	.340	8-0	.250	-0	149	1	0.1
BOGGS, RAY Raymond Joseph "Lefty" B 12.12.1904 Reamsville, KS D 11.27.1989 Grand Junction, CO BL/TL 6-0.5/170# d9.1																									
1928	Bos N	0	0	—	4	0	0	0	5	2	3	0	3	7	0	5.40	72	.167	.545	0-0	—	0		-1	0.0
BOGGS, TOMMY Thomas Winton B 10.25.1955 Poughkeepsie, NY BR/TR 6-2/200# d7.19																									
1976	Tex A	1	7	.125	13	13	3	0-0	90.1	87	42	7	1	34-1	36	3.49	103	.257	.322	0-0	—	0	64	0	0.0
1977	Tex A	0	3	.000	6	6	0	0-0	27.1	40	18	1	1	12-0	15	5.93	69	.351	.417	0-0	—	0	106	-5	-0.4
1978	Atl N	2	8	.200	16	12	1-1	0-0	59	80	46	8	1	26-3	21	6.71	60	.323	.386	18-1	.167	0	48	-14	-2.1
1979	Atl N	0	2	.000	3	3	0	0-0	12.2	21	11	0	1	4-0	1	6.39	63	.362	.413	4-0	.250	0	80	-3	-0.4
1980	Atl N	12	9	.571	32	26	4-3	0-0	192.1	180	80	14	4	46-0	84	3.42	110	.249	.295	63-6	.159	-2	95	7	0.4
1981	Atl N	3	13	.188	25	24	2	0-0	142.2	140	72	11	3	54-4	81	4.10	87	.265	.332	46-1	.152	-1	75	-8	-0.9
1982	Atl N	2	2	.500	10	10	0	0-0	46.1	43	22	2	2	22-1	29	3.30	113	.253	.345	17-1	.235	0	109	1	0.1
1983	Atl N	0	0	—	5	0	0	0-0	6.1	8	4	1	0	1-0	5	5.68	68	.320	.346	0-0	—	0		-1	0.0
1985	Tex A	0	0	—	4	0	0	0-1	7	13	9	3	0	2-0	6	11.57	37	.382	.417	0-0	—	0		-5	-0.2
Total	9	20	44	.313	114	94	10-4	0-1	584	612	304	47	13	201-9	278	4.22	89	.273	.334	148-9	.169	-2	82	-28	-3.5
BOGLE, WARREN Warren Frederick B 10.19.1946 Passaic, NJ BL/TL 6-4/220# d7.31																									
1968	Oak A	0	0	—	16	1	0	0	23	26	12	3	0	8-1	26	4.30	65	.283	.337	5-0	.000	-1	186	-4	-0.2
BOHANON, BRIAN Brian Edward B 8.1.1968 Denton, TX BL/TL 6-2/220# d4.10																									
1990	Tex A	0	3	.000	11	6	0	0-0	34	40	30	6	2	18-0	15	6.62	59	.296	.380	0-0	—	0	77	-11	-0.8
1991	Tex A	4	3	.571	11	11	1	0-0	61.1	66	35	4	2	23-0	34	4.84	83	.274	.336	0-0	—	0	152	-5	-0.5
1992	Tex A	1	1	.500	18	7	0	0-0	45.2	57	38	7	1	25-0	29	6.31	60	.297	.377	0-0	—	0	130	-14	-0.7
1993	Tex A	4	4	.500	36	8	0	0-1	92.2	107	54	8	4	46-3	45	4.76	87	.296	.377	0-0	—	0	105	-6	-0.4
1994	Tex A	2	2	.500	11	5	0	0-0	37.1	51	31	7	1	8-1	26	7.23	67	.321	.357	0-0	—	0	91	-9	-0.7
1995	Det A	1	1	.500	52	10	0	1-0	105.2	121	68	10	4	41-5	63	5.54	86	.285	.350	0-0	—	0	141	-8	-0.4
1996	Tor A	0	1	.000	20	0	0	1-0	22	27	19	4	2	19-4	17	7.77	64	.303	.429	0-0	—	0		-6	-0.3
1997	NY N	6	4	.600	19	14	0	0-0	94.1	95	49	9	4	34-2	66	3.82	106	.258	.328	33-1	.182	0*	121	0	0.0
1998	NY N	2	4	.333	25	4	0	0-1	54.1	47	21	4	6	21-2	39	3.15	131	.234	.325	14-0	.429	2	83	6	0.9
	LA N	5	7	.417	14	14	2	0-0	97.1	74	35	9	5	36-0	72	2.40	165	.213	.294	29-4	.207	2	75	15	2.1
	Year	7	11	.389	39	18	2	0-1	151.2	121	38	13	11	57-2	111	2.67	151	.220	.305	43-4	.279	4	76	20	3.0
1999	Col N	12	12	.500	33	33	3-1	0-0	197.1	236	146	30	14	92-1	120	6.20	94	.304	.386	71-5	.197	-0*	92	-7	-0.6
2000	Col N	12	10	.545	34	26	2-1	0-0	177	181	101	24	6	79-4	98	4.68	124	.266	.346	53-11	.208	1*	104	17	1.9
2001	Col N	5	8	.385	20	19	0	0-0	97	127	79	20	7	47-3	47	7.14	75	.323	.404	31-1	.323	2*	104	-14	-1.4
Total	12	54	60	.474	304	157	8-2	2-2	1116	1229	706	142	58	489-25	671	5.19	93	.281	.359	231-22	.229	8	106	-42	-0.9
BOHEN, PAT Leo Ignatius B 9.30.1890 Oakland, IA D 4.8.1942 Napa, CA BR/TR 5-10.5/155# d10.1																									
1913	Phi A	0	1	.000	1	1	1	0	8	3	1	0	0	2	5	1.13	246	.120	.185	3-0	.000	-0	0	2	0.2
1914	Pit N	0	0	—	1	0	0	0	1	2	2	0	1	2	0	18.00	15	.500	.714	1-0	.000	-0		-2	-0.1
Total	2	0	1	.000	2	1	1	0	9	5	3	0	1	4	5	3.00	92	.172	.294	4-0	.000	-1	0	0	0.1
BOHN, CHARLIE Charles B 1857 Cleveland, OH D 8.1.1903 Cleveland, OH BR/TR 5-9/165# d6.20																									
1882	Lou AA	1	1	.500	2	2	2	0	18	21	8	0		3	1	3.00	83	.273	.300	13	.154	-0*	52	0	0.0
BOHNET, JOHN John Kelly B 1.18.1961 Pasadena, CA BB/TL 6/175# d5.10																									
1982	Cle A	0	0	—	3	3	0	0-0	11.2	11	9	4	1	7-0	4	6.94	59	.250	.365	0-0	—	0	89	-3	-0.2
BOITANO, DAN Danny Jon B 3.22.1953 Sacramento, CA BR/TR 6/185# d10.1																									
1978	Phi N	0	0	—	1	0	0	0-0	1	0	0	0	0	1-0	0	0.00	—	.000	.250	0-0	—	0		0	0.0
1979	Mil A	0	0	—	5	0	0	0-0	6	6	1	1	0	3-0	5	1.50	279	.273	.360	0-0	—	0		2	0.1
1980	Mil A	0	1	.000	11	0	0	0-0	17.2	26	17	7	1	6-0	11	8.15	48	.342	.393	0-0	—	0		-8	-0.4
1981	NY N	2	1	.667	15	0	0	0-1	16.1	21	10	2	2	5-0	8	5.51	63	.309	.368	0-0	—	0*		-3	-0.5
1982	Tex A	0	0	—	19	0	0	0-1	30.1	33	19	5	2	13-2	28	5.34	73	.280	.356	0-0	—	0		-5	-0.2
Total	5	2	2	.500	51	0	0	0-2	71.1	86	47	15	5	28-2	52	5.68	67	.300	.367	0-0	—	0		-14	-1.0
BOKELMANN, DICK Richard Werner B 10.26.1926 Arlington Heights, IL BR/TR 6-0.5/180# d8.3																									
1951	StL N	3	3	.500	20	1	0	3	52.1	49	30	2	1	31	22	3.78	105	.245	.349	14-2	.000	-2	67	-2	-0.4
1952	StL N	0	1	.000	11	0	0	0	12.2	20	17	0	0	7	5	9.24	40	.357	.429	0-0	—	0		-9	-0.6
1953	StL N	0	0	—	3	0	0	0	3	4	2	0	0	0	0	6.00	71	.308	.308	0-0	—	0		0	0.0
Total	3	3	4	.429	34	1	0	3	68	73	49	2	1	38	27	4.90	80	.271	.364	14-2	.000	-2	67	-11	-1.0
BOKINA, JOE Joseph B 4.4.1910 Northampton, MA D 10.25.1991 Chattanooga, TN BR/TR 6/184# d4.16																									
1936	Was A	0	2	.000	5	1	0	0	8.1	15	8	0	0	6	5	8.64	55	.395	.477	1-0	.000	-0	18	-3	-0.5
BOLAND, BERNIE Bernard Anthony B 1.21.1892 Rochester, NY D 9.12.1973 Detroit, MI BR/TR 5-8.5/168# d4.14																									
1915	Det A	13	7	.650	45	18	8-1	3	202.2	167	86	2	6	75	72	3.11	98	.230	.307	63-1	.175	-1*	124	1	0.0
1916	Det A	10	3	.769	46	9	5-1	3	130.1	111	69	1	4	73	59	3.94	73	.240	.349	32-2	.250	2*	173	-14	-1.4
1917	Det A	16	11	.593	43	28	13-3	6	238	192	89	0	6	95	89	2.68	99	.226	.308	72-5	.056	-5*	111	4	-0.2
1918	Det A	14	10	.583	29	25	14-4	0	204	176	69	1	6	67	63	2.65	101	.236	.304	69-0	.174	0	103	3	0.3
1919	Det A	14	16	.467	35	30	18-1	1	242.2	222	93	7	3	80	71	3.04	105	.253	.318	74-3	.108	-3	76	8	0.6
1920	Det A	0	2	.000	4	3	1	0	17.1	23	18	0	2	14	4	7.79	48	.348	.476	7-0	.143	-0	114	-7	-0.7
1921	StL A	1	4	.200	7	6	0	0	27	34	36	2	1	28	6	9.33	48	.309	.453	10-0	.100	-1	109	-15	-2.1
Total	7	68	53	.562	209	119	59-10	13	1062	925	460	13	28	432	364	3.25	91	.241	.322	327-11	.138	-8	108	-20	-3.5
BOLDEN, BILL William Horace "Big Bill" B 5.9.1893 Dandridge, TN D 12.8.1966 Jefferson City, TN BR/TR 6-4/200# d6.27																									
1919	StL N	0	1	.000	3	1	0	0	12	17	7	0	1	4	4	5.25	53	.340	.400	3-0	.333	0	57	-3	-0.2
BOLEN, STEW Stewart O'Neal B 10.12.1902 Jackson, AL D 8.30.1969 Mobile, AL BL/TL 5-11/180# d4.15																									
1926	StL A	0	0	—	5	0	0	0	14.2	21	10	2	0	6	7	6.14	70	.356	.415	4-0	.500	1		-2	-0.1
1927	StL A	0	1	.000	3	1	1	0	9.2	14	9	0	0	5	7	8.38	52	.351	.442	3-0	.333	0	96	-3	-0.2
1931	Phi N	3	12	.200	28	16	2	0	98.2	117	75	5	4	63	55	6.39	66	.297	.399	32-0	.156	-1	82	-18	-2.4
1932	Phi N	0	0	—	5	0	0	0	16	18	8	0	2	10	3	2.81	157	.281	.395	7-0	.143	-0		2	0.0
Total	4	3	13	.188	41	17	3	0	139	170	102	7	6	84	72	6.09	70	.306	.403	46-0	.196	-0	82	-21	-2.7
BOLIN, BOBBY Bobby Donald B 1.29.1939 Hickory Grove, SC BR/TR 6-4/200# d4.18																									
1961	SF N	2	2	.500	37	1	0	5	48	37	20	6	3	37-8	48	3.19	120	.210	.352	7-0	.286	0	186	3	0.3
1962	†SF N	7	3	.700	41	5	2	5	92	84	41	10	5	35-5	74	3.62	105	.243	.320	23-0	.261	2	162	2	0.4
1963	SF N	10	6	.625	47	12	2	7	137.1	128	73	13	7	57-4	134	3.28	98	.242	.322	35-4	.143	2	110	-7	-0.9
1964	SF N	6	9	.400	38	23	5-3	1	174.2	143	71	16	10	77-3	146	3.25	110	.220	.312	50-4	.100	0*	102	6	0.5
1965	SF N	14	6	.700	45	13	2	2	163	125	51	17	4	56-4	135	2.76	130	.214	.285	54-1	.167	1	106	17	2.2
1966	SF N	11	10	.524	36	34	10-4	1	224.1	174	85	25	10	70-10	143	2.89	127	.211	.280	76-1	.171	3	82	19	2.0
1967	SF N	6	8	.429	37	15	0	0	120	120	71	16	3	50-9	69	4.88	67	.258	.331	33-2	.242	2	116	-20	-2.0
1968	SF N	10	5	.667	34	19	6-3	0	176.2	128	44	9	4	46-9	126	1.99	148	.200	.258	55-1	.091	-1	101	20	1.7
1969	SF N	7	7	.500	30	22	2	0-0	146.1	149	86	17	7	49-3	102	4.43	79	.260	.323	39-2	.154	3	126	-16	-1.1
1970	Mil A	5	11	.313	32	20	3	1-0	132	131	84	20	4	67-7	81	4.91	77	.256	.343	36-6	.194	2	86	-18	-1.8
	Bos A	2	0	1.000	6	0	0	2-0	8	2	0	0	1	5-2	8	0.00	—	.080	.250	1-0	.000	-0		3	0.7
	Year	7	11	.389	38	20	3	3-0	140	133	88	20	5	72-9	89	4.63	82	.248	.338	37-6	.189	2	86	-13	-1.1
1971	Bos A	5	3	.625	52	0	0	6-3	69.2	74	34	7	0	24-4	51	4.26	87	.273	.329	12-0	.250	0		-3	-0.5
1972	Bos A	1	0	1.000	21	0	0	5-1	30.2	24	11	3	1	11-1	27	2.93	110	.209	.283	2-0	.000	-0		1	0.0
1973	Bos A	3	4	.429	39	0	0	15-5	53.1	45	16	5	1	13-2	31	2.70	149	.232	.282	0-0	—	0		8	1.6
Total	13	88	75	.540	495	164	32-10	50-9	1576	1364	687	164	60	597-71	1175	3.40	103	.231	.306	423-21	.163	15	103	15	3.1
BOLLO, GREG Gregory Gene B 11.16.1943 Detroit, MI BR/TR 6-4/183# d5.9																									
1965	Chi A	0	0	—	15	0	0	0	22.2	12	11	5	2	9-1	16	3.57	89	.152	.256	0-0	—	0		-1	-0.1

Year	Tm Lg	W	L	Pct	G	GS	CG-Sho	SV-BS	IP	H	R	HR	HB	BB-IB	SO	ERA	AERA	OAV	OOB	AB-SH	AVG	PB	Sup	APR	PW
1966	Chi A	0	1	.000	3	1	0	0	7	7	2	0	1	3-0	4	2.57	123	.269	.367	1-0	.000	-0	0	1	0.1
Total	2	0	1	.000	18	1	0	0	29.2	19	13	5	3	12-1	20	3.34	96	.181	.283	1-0	.000	-0	0	0	0.0
BOLTON, ROD Rodney Earl B 9.23.1968 Chattanooga, TN BR/TR 6-2/190# d4.10																									
1993	Chi A	2	6	.250	9	8	0	0-0	42.1	55	40	4	1	16-0	17	7.44	56	.314	.367	0-0	—	0	77	-16	-2.3
1995	Chi A	0	2	.000	8	3	0	0-0	22	33	23	4	0	14-1	10	8.18	55	.351	.431	0-0	—	0	118	-10	-0.7
Total	2	2	8	.200	17	11	0	0-0	64.1	88	63	8	1	30-1	27	7.69	56	.327	.390	0-0	—	0	88	-26	-3.0
BOLTON, TOM Thomas Edward B 5.6.1962 Nashville, TN BL/TL 6-3/175# d5.17																									
1987	Bos A	1	0	1.000	29	0	0	0-0	61.2	83	33	5	2	27-2	49	4.38	104	.329	.394	0-0	—	0		1	0.1
1988	Bos A	1	3	.250	28	0	0	1-0	30.1	35	17	1	0	14-1	21	4.75	87	.285	.355	0-0	—	0		-2	-0.2
1989	Bos A	0	4	.000	4	4	0	0-0	17.1	21	18	1	0	10-1	9	8.31	49	.292	.373	0-0	—	0	33	-8	-1.3
1990	†Bos A	10	5	.667	21	16	3	0-0	119.2	111	46	6	3	47-3	65	3.38	121	.251	.323	0-0	—	0	98	11	1.3
1991	Bos A	8	9	.471	25	19	0	0-0	110	136	72	16	1	51-2	64	5.24	82	.308	.378	0-0	—	0	87	-11	-1.5
1992	Bos A	1	2	.333	21	1	0	0-0	29	34	11	0	2	14-1	23	3.41	124	.286	.370	0-0	—	0	22	3	0.3
	Cin N	3	3	.500	16	8	0	0-0	46.1	52	28	9	2	23-2	27	5.24	69	.284	.368	14-1	.000	-1	113	-8	-1.0
1993	Det A	6	6	.500	43	8	0	0-0	102.2	113	57	5	7	45-10	66	4.47	96	.282	.363	0-0	—	0	129	-2	-0.2
1994	Bal A	1	2	.333	22	0	0	0-0	23.1	29	15	3	0	13-1	12	5.40	93	.309	.389	0-0	—	0		-1	-0.1
Total	8	31	34	.477	209	56	3	1-0	540.1	614	297	46	17	244-23	336	4.56	93	.289	.364	14-1	.000	-1	92	-17	-2.6
BOMBACK, MARK Mark Vincent B 4.14.1953 Portsmouth, VA BR/TR 5-11/170# d9.12																									
1978	Mil A	0	0	—	2	1	0	0-0	1.2	5	3	1	0	1-0	1	16.20	23	.500	.545	0-0	—	0	119	-2	-0.1
1980	NY N	10	8	.556	36	25	2-1	0-0	162.2	191	80	17	4	49-3	68	4.09	87	.297	.347	43-5	.233	3	85	-8	-0.4
1981	Tor A	5	5	.500	20	11	0	0-1	90.1	84	42	6	1	35-2	33	3.89	102	.251	.321	0-0	—	0*	85	2	0.2
1982	Tor A	1	5	.167	16	8	0	0-0	59.2	87	44	10	3	25-0	22	6.03	74	.343	.405	0-0	—	0	74	-9	-0.8
Total	4	16	18	.471	74	45	2-1	0-1	314.1	367	169	34	8	110-5	124	4.47	86	.295	.353	43-5	.233	3	83	-17	-1.1
BOND, TOMMY Thomas Henry B 4.2.1856 Granard, Ireland D 1.24.1941 Boston, MA BR/TR 5-7.5/160# d5.5 M1 U2																									
1874	Atl NA	22	32	.407	55	55	55-1	0	497	606	440	15		8	42	2.03	102	.266	.268	245	.220	-0	76	1	0.6
1875	Har NA	19	16	.543	40	39	37-6	0	352	302	152	3		7	70	1.41	167	.216	.219	289	.266	3*	81	33	3.1
1876	Har N	31	13	.705	45	45	45-6	0	408	355	164	2		13	88	1.68	141	.220	.227	182	.275	1	97	32	3.1
1877	Bos N	**40**	17	**.702**	58	58	58-**6**	0	521	530	248	5		36	**170**	**2.11**	133	.249	**.261**	259	.228	-4*	115	40	3.3
1878	Bos N	**40**	19	**.678**	**59**	**59**	**57-9**	0	**532.2**	571	222	5		33	**182**	2.06	115	.269	.280	236	.212	-4	91	14	0.9
1879	Bos N	43	19	.694	64	64	59-**11**	0	555.1	543	206	8		24	155	**1.96**	**126**	.251	.259	257	.241	2*	136	**39**	**4.1**
1880	Bos N	26	29	.473	63	57	49-3	0	493	559	298	1		45	118	2.67	85	.274	.290	282	.220	-2*	106	-33	-2.9
1881	Bos N	0	3	.000	3	3	2	0	25.1	40	17	3		2	2	4.26	62	.360	.372	10	.200	-0	27	-3	-0.3
1882	Wor N	0	1	.000	2	2	0	0	12.1	12	13	0		7	2	4.38	71	.218	.306	30	.133	-1*	60	-2	-0.2
1884	Bos U	13	9	.591	23	21	19	0	189	185	120	3		14	128	3.00	79	.239	.253	162	.296	-0*	117	-13	-1.1
	Ind AA	0	5	.000	5	5	5	0	43	62	51	5	2	4	15	5.65	58	.310	.330	23	.130	-1*	48	-12	-1.2
Total	2 NA	41	48	.461	95	94	92-7	0	849	908	592	18	0	15	112	1.77	123	.247	.250	534	.245	2	77	34	3.7
Total	8	193	115	.627	322	314	294-35	0	2779.2	2857	1339	32	2	178	860	2.25	110	.255	.267	1441	.236	-9	109	62	5.7
BONDERMAN, JEREMY Jeremy Allen B 10.28.1982 Kennewick, WA BR/TR 6-2/210# d4.2																									
2003	Det A	6	19	.240	33	28	0	0-0	162	193	118	23	4	58-2	108	5.56	78	.294	.352	2-0	.000	-0	77	-28	-3.4
BONES, RICKY Ricardo Ricky B 4.7.1969 Salinas, P.R. BR/TR 6/190# d8.11																									
1991	SD N	4	6	.400	11	11	0	0-0	54	57	33	3	0	18-0	31	4.83	79	.269	.321	13-4	.077	-0	140	-6	-1.1
1992	Mil A	9	10	.474	31	28	0	0-0	163.1	169	90	27	9	48-0	65	4.57	84	.264	.321	0-0	—	0	100	-13	-1.5
1993	Mil A	11	11	.500	32	31	3	0-0	203.2	222	122	28	8	63-3	63	4.86	88	.278	.334	0-0	—	0*	114	-14	-1.3
1994	Mil A☆	10	9	.526	24	24	4-1	0-0	170.2	166	76	17	3	45-1	57	3.43	147	.255	.304	0-0	—	0	85	27	2.5
1995	Mil A	10	12	.455	32	31	3	0-0	200.1	218	108	26	4	83-2	77	4.63	108	.281	.349	0-0	—	0	105	9	0.9
1996	Mil A	7	14	.333	32	23	0	0-0	145	170	104	28	9	62-2	59	5.83	89	.294	.369	0-0	—	0	101	-11	-1.3
	NY A	0	0	—	4	1	0	0-0	7	14	11	2	1	6-0	4	14.14	35	.438	.525	0-0	—	0	94	-7	-0.3
	Year	7	14	.333	36	24	0	0-0	152	184	16	30	10	68-2	63	6.22	83	.301	.378	0-0	—	0	101	-18	-1.6
1997	Cin N	0	1	.000	9	2	0	0-0	17.2	31	22	2	2	11-2	8	10.19	42	.378	.454	2-0	.000	-0	140	-12	-0.6
	KC A	4	7	.364	21	11	1	0-1	78.1	102	59	10	5	25-2	36	5.97	79	.325	.377	0-0	—	0*	108	-12	-1.4
1998	KC A	2	2	.500	32	0	0	1-1	53.1	49	18	4	1	24-5	38	3.04	159	.244	.327	1-0	.000	-0		11	0.8
1999	Bal A	0	3	.000	30	2	0	0-3	43.2	59	29	7	2	19-0	26	5.98	79	.322	.390	0-0	—	0*	40	-5	-0.4
2000	Fla N	2	3	.400	56	0	0	0-3	77.1	94	43	6	3	27-8	59	4.54	98	.303	.358	2-0	.000	0		-1	-0.1
2001	Fla N	4	4	.500	61	0	0	0-0	64	71	39	7	3	33-9	41	5.06	83	.286	.374	2-0	.500	0		-6	-0.6
Total	11	63	82	.434	375	164	11-1	1-8	1278.1	1422	754	167	50	464-34	564	4.85	94	.283	.346	20-4	.100	-0	104	-40	-4.4
BONETTI, JULIO Julio Giacomo B 7.14.1911 Genoa, Italy D 6.17.1952 Belmont, CA BR/TR 6/180# d4.22																									
1937	StL A	4	11	.267	28	16	7	1	143.1	190	103	13	2	60	43	5.84	83	.321	.385	47-2	.149	-2	77	-15	-1.3
1938	StL A	2	3	.400	17	0	0	0	28.1	41	21	1	0	13	7	6.35	78	.350	.415	8-0	.000	-1		-4	-0.6
1940	Chi N	0	0	—	1	0	0	0	1.1	3	3	0	0	4	0	20.25	19	.429	.636	0-0	—	0		-2	-0.1
Total	3	6	14	.300	46	16	7	1	173	234	127	14	2	77	50	6.03	80	.327	.394	55-2	.127	-3	77	-21	-2.0
BONEY, HANK Henry Tate "Haney" B 10.28.1903 Wallace, NC D 6.12.2002 Lake Worth, FL BL/TR 5-11/176# d6.28																									
1927	NY N	0	0	—	3	0	0	0	4	4	1	0	0	2	0	2.25	171	.267	.353	0-0	—	0		1	0.0
BONG, JUNG Jung Keun B 7.15.1980 Seoul, South Korea BL/TL 6-3/175# d4.23																									
2002	Atl N	0	1	.000	1	1	0	0-0	6	8	5	0	0	2-0	4	7.50	55	.320	.370	2-0	.000	-0*	45	-2	-0.3
2003	Atl N	6	2	.750	44	0	0	1-2	57	56	32	8	2	31-6	47	5.05	84	.267	.365	5-1	.000	-0		-4	-0.4
Total	2	6	3	.667	45	1	0	1-2	63	64	37	8	2	33-6	51	5.29	80	.272	.365	7-1	.000	-0	45	-6	-0.7
BONHAM, TINY Ernest Edward B 8.16.1913 Ione, CA D 9.15.1949 Pittsburgh, PA BR/TR 6-2/215# d8.5																									
1940	NY A	9	3	.750	12	12	10-3	0	99.1	83	24	4	0	13	37	1.90	212	.224	.250	37-0	.189	0	76	25	2.8
1941	†NY A	9	6	.600	23	14	7-1	2	126.2	118	44	12	1	31	43	2.98	132	.246	.294	50-1	.160	-1	116	16	1.5
1942	†NY A☆	21	5	**.808**	28	27	**22-6**	0	226	199	65	11	1	24	71	2.27	152	.237	**.259**	74-10	.122	-2	112	31	3.0
1943	†NY A☆	15	8	.652	28	26	17-4	1	225.2	197	63	13	1	52	71	2.27	142	.236	.282	76-5	.197	0	102	26	2.5
1944	NY A	12	9	.571	26	25	17-1	0	213.2	228	84	14	0	41	54	2.99	116	.273	.307	75-5	.133	-3	98	11	0.6
1945	NY A	8	11	.421	23	23	12	0	180.2	186	72	11	1	22	42	3.29	105	.265	.288	63-3	.238	3	79	5	0.7
1946	NY A	5	8	.385	18	14	6-2	3	104.2	97	47	6	0	23	30	3.70	93	.243	.284	31-1	.129	-0	85	-2	-0.3
1947	Pit N	11	8	.579	33	18	7-3	3	149.2	167	67	17	2	35	63	3.85	110	.277	.319	45-6	.156	-0	116	9	0.8
1948	Pit N	6	10	.375	22	20	7	0	135.2	145	71	18	3	23	42	4.31	94	.276	.310	49-1	.163	-2	94	-3	-0.7
1949	Pit N	7	4	.636	18	14	5-1	0	89	81	43	11	0	23	25	4.25	99	.246	.295	22-5	.045	-1	90	1	-0.1
Total	10	103	72	.589	231	193	110-21	9	1551	1501	580	117	9	287	478	3.06	120	.254	.289	522-37	.161	-7	98	119	10.8
BONHAM, BILL William Gordon B 10.1.1948 Glendale, CA BR/TR 6-3/195# d4.7																									
1971	Chi N	2	1	.667	33	2	0	0-1	60	63	38	6	5	36-5	41	4.65	85	.281	.390	12-0	.167	-0	56	-5	-0.3
1972	Chi N	1	1	.500	19	4	0	4-1	57.2	56	22	4	1	25-2	49	3.12	122	.260	.340	14-3	.286	1	116	4	0.4
1973	Chi N	7	5	.583	44	15	3	6-0	152	126	55	10	4	64-7	121	3.02	131	.230	.313	43-6	.093	-3	88	16	1.2
1974	Chi N	11	22	.333	44	36	10-2	1-0	242.2	246	133	13	6	109-8	191	3.86	99	.263	.342	84-5	.143	-3*	75	-5	-0.7
1975	Chi N	13	15	.464	38	36	7-2	0-0	229.1	254	133	15	5	109-6	165	4.71	82	.281	.359	82-8	.183	-0*	114	-19	-2.1
1976	Chi N	9	13	.409	32	31	3	0-0	196	215	102	11	2	96-2	110	4.27	90	.283	.361	65-7	.200	1	101	-7	-0.6
1977	Chi N	10	13	.435	34	34	1	0-0	214.2	207	111	15	3	82-16	134	4.36	101	.254	.324	65-11	.231	1*	92	3	0.6
1978	Cin N	11	5	.688	23	23	1	0-0	140.1	151	59	9	1	50-8	83	3.53	101	.276	.336	43-8	.186	2	132	2	0.6
1979	Cin N	9	7	.563	29	29	2	0-0	175.2	173	80	14	8	60-3	78	3.79	99	.261	.329	57-6	.140	-1	113	0	-0.1
1980	Cin N	2	1	.667	4	4	0	0-0	19	21	10	1	0	5-0	13	4.74	76	.276	.321	6-0	.000	-0	106	-2	-0.3
Total	10	75	83	.475	300	214	27-4	11-2	1487.1	1512	743	98	35	636-57	985	4.01	97	.266	.342	471-54	.172	-2	101	-13	-1.3
BONIKOWSKI, JOE Joseph Peter B 1.16.1941 Philadelphia, PA BR/TR 6/175# d4.12																									
1962	Min A	5	7	.417	30	13	3	2	99.2	95	47	6	1	38-2	45	3.88	105	.255	.323	27-2	.148	-1	106	3	0.3

Year	Tm Lg	W	L	Pct	G	GS	CG-Sho	SV-BS	IP	H	R	HR	HB	BB-IB	SO	ERA	AERA	OAV	OOB	AB-SH	AVG	PB	Sup	APR	PW
BONNESS, BILL William John "Lefty" B 12.15.1923 Cleveland, OH D 12.3.1977 Detroit, MI BR/TL 6-4/200# d9.26																									
1944	Cle A	0	1	.000	2	1	0	0	7	11	6	0	2	5	1	7.71	43	.367	.486	3-0	.000	-0	51	-3	-0.4
BONO, GUS Adlai Wendell B 8.29.1894 Doe Run, MO D 12.3.1948 Dearborn, MI BR/TR 5-11/175# d9.13																									
1920	Was A	0	2	.000	4	1	0	0	12.1	17	13	0	0	6	4	8.76	43	.315	.383	3-0	.000	-0	149	-6	-0.8
BOOKER, GREG Gregory Scott B 6.22.1960 Lynchburg, VA BR/TR 6-6/233# d9.11 C7																									
1983	SD N	0	1	.000	6	1	0	0-0	11.2	18	10	2	0	9-0	5	7.71	45	.375	.474	1-0	.000	-0	76	-5	-0.4
1984	†SD N	1	1	.500	32	1	0	0-1	57.1	67	27	4	0	27-4	28	3.30	108	.295	.367	7-0	.286	1	74	0	0.1
1985	SD N	0	1	.000	17	0	0	0-0	22.1	20	17	3	1	17-2	7	6.85	52	.247	.376	1-0	.000	-0		-7	-0.4
1986	SD N	1	0	1.000	9	0	0	0-0	11	10	5	0	0	4-2	7	1.64	224	.233	.298	0-0	—	0		1	0.1
1987	SD N	1	1	.500	44	0	0	1-0	68.1	62	29	5	3	30-1	17	3.16	125	.246	.332	6-0	.000	-1		5	0.2
1988	SD N	2	2	.500	34	2	0	0-0	63.2	68	31	5	1	19-2	43	3.39	100	.278	.327	8-0	.250	1	144	-2	0.0
1989	SD N	0	1	.000	11	0	0	0-0	19	15	10	2	0	10-1	8	4.26	82	.224	.325	0-0	—	0		-1	-0.1
	Min A	0	0	—	6	0	0	0-0	8.2	11	4	1	0	2-0	3	4.15	100	.306	.342	0-0	—	0		0	0.0
1990	SF N	0	0	—	2	0	0	0-0	2	7	3	0	0	0-0	1	13.50	27	.538	.538	0-0	—	0		-2	-0.1
Total	8	5	7	.417	161	4	0	1-1	264	278	136	22	5	118-12	119	3.89	94	.275	.351	23-0	.174	1	104	-11	-0.6
BOOLES, RED Seabron Jesse B 7.14.1880 Bernice, LA D 3.16.1955 Monroe, LA BL/TR 5-10/150# d7.30																									
1909	Cle A	0	1	.000	4	1	0	0	22.2	20	12	0	1	8	6	1.99	129	.235	.309	6-0	.167	0	55	0	0.0
BOONE, DANNY Daniel Hugh B 1.14.1954 Long Beach, CA BL/TL 5-8/150# d4.11																									
1981	SD N	1	0	1.000	37	0	0	2-0	63.1	63	23	2	1	21-7	43	2.84	115	.267	.327	4-1	.500	1		3	0.3
1982	SD N	1	0	1.000	10	0	0	1-2	16	21	10	2	0	3-0	8	5.63	61	.323	.353	5-0	.200	0		-3	-0.2
	Hou N	0	1	.000	10	0	0	1-1	12.2	7	6	1	0	4-1	4	3.55	94	.171	.239	1-0	.000	-0		-1	-0.1
	Year	1	1	.500	20	0	0	2-3	28.2	28	18	3	0	7-1	12	4.71	72	.264	.307	6-0	.167	0		-4	-0.3
1990	Bal A	0	0	—	4	1	0	0-0	9.2	12	3	1	1	3-0	2	2.79	136	.308	.372	0-0	—	0	72	1	0.1
Total	3	2	1	.667	61	1	0	4-3	101.2	103	42	6	2	31-8	57	3.36	99	.270	.326	10-1	.300	1	72	0	0.1
BOONE, GEORGE George Morris B 3.1.1871 Louisville, KY D 9.24.1910 Louisville, KY d4.23																									
1891	Lou AA	0	0	—	4	1	0	1	15	15	15	0	0	9	4	7.80	47	.250	.348	6	.333	0	68	-5	-0.2
BOONE, DAN James Albert B 1.19.1895 Samantha, AL D 5.11.1968 Tuscaloosa, AL BR/TR 6-2/190# d9.10																									
1919	Phi A	0	1	.000	3	2	0	0	14.2	24	14	0	0	10	1	6.75	51	.375	.459	4-0	.000	-1	91	-5	-0.3
1921	Det A	0	0	—	1	0	0	1	2	1	1	0	0	2	0	0.00	—	.200	.429	1-0	.000	-0		1	0.0
1922	Cle A	4	6	.400	11	10	4-2	0	75.1	87	39	3	1	19	9	4.06	99	.298	.343	26-1	.192	-1	72	0	-0.1
1923	Cle A	4	6	.400	27	4	2	0	70.1	93	56	3	3	31	15	6.01	66	.322	.393	19-0	.211	0	78	-15	-1.6
Total	4	8	13	.381	42	16	6-2	1	162.1	205	110	6	4	62	25	5.10	77	.315	.378	50-1	.180	-1	75	-19	-2.0
BOOTCHECK, CHRIS Christopher Brandon B 10.24.1978 Laporte, IN BR/TR 6-5/200# d9.9																									
2003	Ana A	0	1	.000	4	1	0	0-0	10.1	16	13	5	0	6-0	7	9.58	45	.340	.415	0-0	—	0	21	-7	-0.5
BOOTH, AMOS Amos Smith "Darling" B 9.14.1853 Cincinnati, OH D 7.1.1921 Miamisburg, OH BR/TR 5-9/159# d4.25 ▲																									
1876	Cin N	0	1	.000	3	1	0	0	9.2	22	18	0		0	0	9.31	24	.431	.431	272	.261	0*	264	-7	-0.5
1877	Cin N	1	7	.125	12	8	6	0	86	114	75	1		13	18	3.56	74	.296	.319	157	.172	-1*	74	-11	-0.9
Total	2	1	8	.111	15	9	6	0	95.2	136	93	1		13	18	4.14	63	.312	.332	429	.228	-1	96	-18	-1.4
BOOZER, JOHN John Morgan B 7.6.1938 Columbia, SC D 1.24.1986 Lexington, SC BR/TR 6-3/205# d7.22																									
1962	Phi N	0	0	—	9	0	0	0	20.1	22	13	3	0	10-1	13	5.75	67	.282	.364	1-0	.000	-0		-4	-0.2
1963	Phi N	3	4	.429	26	8	2	1	83	67	31	11	1	33-5	69	2.93	110	.227	.303	21-0	.143	-0	70	3	0.1
1964	Phi N	3	4	.429	22	3	0	2	60.1	64	37	6	2	18-2	51	5.07	68	.271	.327	13-0	.077	-1*	51	-10	-1.2
1966	Phi N	0	0	—	2	2	0	0	5.1	8	5	1	0	3-0	5	6.75	53	.348	.423	2-0	.000	-0	135	-2	-0.1
1967	Phi N	5	4	.556	28	7	1	1	74.2	86	39	6	1	24-5	48	4.10	83	.292	.347	19-0	.211	1	129	-5	-0.6
1968	Phi N	2	2	.500	38	0	0	5	68.2	76	32	3	2	15-3	49	3.67	82	.279	.320	9-2	.111	-0		-5	-0.4
1969	Phi N	1	2	.333	46	2	0	6-3	82	91	46	12	0	36-5	47	4.28	83	.283	.354	9-2	.333	1	50	-8	-0.3
Total	7	14	16	.467	171	22	3	15-3	394.1	414	203	42	6	139-21	282	4.09	82	.272	.334	74-4	.162	-0	91	-31	-2.7
BORBON, PEDRO Pedro (Rodriguez) B 12.2.1946 Valverde, D.R. BR/TR 6-2/185# d4.9 s-Pedro																									
1969	Cal A	2	3	.400	22	0	0	0-0	41	55	31	5	4	11-2	20	6.15	57	.324	.376	3-0	.000	-0		-12	-1.4
1970	Cin N	0	2	.000	12	1	0	0-0	17.1	21	15	2	3	6-1	6	6.75	60	.309	.390	3-0	.000	-0	22	-5	-0.5
1971	Cin N	0	0	—	3	0	0	0-0	4.1	3	3	1	0	1-0	4	4.15	81	.200	.250	0-0	—	0		-1	0.0
1972	†Cin N	8	3	.727	62	2	0	11-1	122	115	45	5	3	32-11	48	3.17	101	.254	.304	21-0	.048	-1	69	2	0.0
1973	†Cin N	11	4	.733	80	0	0	14-5	121	137	33	4	1	35-15	60	2.16	158	.298	.345	15-0	.333	1		18	2.7
1974	Cin N	10	7	.588	73	0	0	14-6	139	133	54	11	4	32-16	53	3.24	108	.255	.300	26-1	.192	-0		5	0.7
1975	†Cin N	9	5	.643	67	0	0	5-1	125	145	47	6	3	21-6	29	2.95	122	.301	.333	24-3	.292	2		8	1.0
1976	†Cin N	4	3	.571	69	1	0	8-3	121	135	49	4	4	31-11	53	3.35	105	.292	.338	18-2	.222	0	251	2	0.2
1977	Cin N	10	5	.667	73	0	0	18-5	127	131	48	7	3	24-4	48	3.19	123	.268	.304	22-2	.182	-0		11	1.4
1978	Cin N	8	2	.800	62	0	0	4-1	99.1	102	56	6	3	27-8	35	4.98	71	.274	.324	11-1	.182	-0		-13	-1.4
1979	Cin N	2	2	.500	30	0	0	2-2	44.2	48	17	2	0	8-4	23	3.43	109	.277	.303	6-0	.333	0		2	0.3
	SF N	4	3	.571	30	0	0	3-1	46	56	28	7	0	13-3	26	4.89	72	.303	.347	3-0	.333	0		-7	-1.1
	Year	6	5	.545	60	0	0	5-3	90.2	104	55	9	0	21-7	49	4.17	87	.291	.326	9-0	.333	1		-5	-0.8
1980	StL N	1	0	1.000	10	0	0	1-0	19	17	10	3	0	10-2	4	3.79	98	.250	.329	4-0	.250	0		-1	0.0
Total	12	69	39	.639	593	4	0	80-25	1026.2	1098	436	63	28	251-83	409	3.52	101	.280	.325	156-9	.205	2	100	9	1.9
BORBON, PEDRO Pedro Felix (Marte) B 11.15.1967 Mao, D.R. BR/TL 6-1/205# d10.2 f-Pedro																									
1992	Atl N	0	1	.000	2	0	0	0-0	1.1	2	1	0	0	1-1	1	6.75	54	.333	.429	0-0	—	0		0	-0.1
1993	Atl N	0	0	—	3	0	0	0-0	1.2	3	4	0	0	3-0	2	21.60	19	.429	.600	0-0	—	0		-3	-0.2
1995	†Atl N	2	2	.500	41	0	0	2-2	32	29	12	2	1	17-4	33	3.09	138	.240	.336	1-0	.000	-0		4	0.5
1996	Atl N	3	0	1.000	43	0	0	1-0	36	26	12	1	1	7-0	31	2.75	160	.203	.250	1-0	1.000	-0		7	0.6
1999	LA N	4	3	.571	70	0	0	1-1	50.2	39	23	5	1	29-1	33	4.09	105	.209	.314	2-1	.000	-0		2	0.2
2000	Tor A	1	1	.500	59	0	0	1-0	41.2	45	37	5	5	38-5	29	6.48	78	.280	.417	0-0	—	0		-8	-0.3
2001	Tor A	2	4	.333	71	0	0	0-5	53.1	48	24	8	4	12-3	45	3.71	124	.244	.298	0-0	—	0		5	0.5
2002	Tor A	1	2	.333	16	0	0	0-2	12.2	12	8	3	1	6-3	11	4.97	93	.231	.317	0-0	—	0		-1	-0.1
	Hou N	3	2	.600	56	0	0	1-2	37.2	41	24	7	2	19-5	39	5.50	78	.287	.367	3-0	.000	-0		-5	-0.6
2003	StL N	0	1	.000	7	0	0	0-0	4	14	9	2	1	2-2	0	20.25	20	.560	.607	0-0	—	0		-7	-1.3
Total	9	16	16	.500	368	0	0	6-12	271	259	154	33	16	134-24	224	4.68	96	.252	.342	7-1	.143	-0		-6	-0.8
BORCHERS, GEORGE George Benard "Chief" B 4.18.1869 Sacramento, CA D 10.24.1938 Sacramento, CA BB/TR 5-10/180# d5.18																									
1888	Chi N	4	4	.500	10	10	7-1	0	67	67	45	2	6	29	26	3.49	87	.251	.338	33	.061	-2	124	-4	-0.5
1895	Lou N	0	1	.000	1	1	0	0	0.2	1	2	0	0	3	0	27.00	17	.333	.667	0-0	—	0	0	-1	-0.2
Total	2	4	5	.444	11	11	7-1	0	67.2	68	47	2	6	32	26	3.72	82	.252	.344	33-0	.061	-2	112	-5	-0.7
BORDEN, JOE Joseph Emley (a.k.a. Joseph Emley Josephs In 1875) B 5.9.1854 Jacobstown, NJ D 10.14.1929 Yeadon, PA BR/TR 5-9/140# d7.24																									
1875	Phi NA	2	4	.333	7	7	7-2	0	66	47	30	0		7	9	1.50	152	**.181**	**.203**	28	.107	-3	80	5	0.1
1876	Bos N	11	12	.478	29	24	16-2	1	218.1	257	155	4		51	34	2.89	78	.276	.313	121	.207	-3*	105	-11	-1.3
BORDI, RICH Richard Albert B 4.18.1959 San Francisco, CA BR/TR 6-7/220# d7.16																									
1980	Oak A	0	0	—	1	0	0	0-0	2	4	1	0	0	0-0	0	4.50	84	.400	.400	0-0	—	0		0	0.0
1981	Oak A	0	0	—	2	0	0	0-0	2	1	0	0	0	1-0	0	0.00	—	.143	.250	0-0	—	0		1	0.0
1982	Sea A	0	2	.000	7	2	0	0-0	13	18	12	4	1	1-0	10	8.31	51	.310	.333	0-0	—	0	75	-5	-0.7
1983	Chi N	0	2	.000	11	1	0	1-0	25.1	34	15	2	0	12-1	20	4.97	76	.321	.390	4-0	.000	-0	23	-3	-0.3
1984	Chi N	5	2	.714	31	7	0	4-0	83.1	78	37	11	0	20-4	41	3.46	113	.242	.284	19-0	.053	-1	136	3	0.1
1985	NY A	6	8	.429	51	3	0	2-0	98	95	41	5	1	29-4	64	3.21	125	.253	.306	0-0	—	0	114	8	1.0
1986	Bal A	6	4	.600	52	1	0	3-2	107	105	56	13	4	41-5	83	4.46	93	.254	.325	0-0	—	0	0	-3	-0.2
1987	NY A	3	1	.750	16	1	0	0-1	33	42	28	7	0	12-0	23	7.64	58	.309	.365	0-0	—	0	83	-11	-1.1
1988	Oak A	0	1	.000	2	2	0	0-0	7.2	6	6	0	0	5-0	6	4.70	81	.214	.324	0-0	—	0	132	-2	-0.2

Year	Tm Lg	W	L	Pct	G	GS	CG-Sho	SV-BS	IP	H	R	HR	HB	BB-IB	SO	ERA	AERA	OAV	OOB	AB-SH	AVG	PB	Sup	APR	PW
Total	9	20	20	.500	173	17	0	10-3	371.1	383	196	42	6	121-14	247	4.34	94	.263	.320	23-0	.043	-2	105	-12	-1.4
BORDLEY, BILL William Clarke B 1.9.1958 Los Angeles, CA BR/TL 6-3/185# d6.30																									
1980	SF N	2	3	.400	8	6	0	0-0	30.2	34	19	3	0	21-1	11	4.70	75	.288	.396	6-2	.167	0	118	-4	-0.6
BORIS, PAUL Paul Stanley B 12.13.1955 Irvington, NJ BR/TR 6-2/200# d5.21																									
1982	Min A	1	2	.333	23	0	0	0-0	49.2	46	24	8	2	19-3	30	3.99	107	.246	.318	0-0	—	0		1	0.0
BORK, FRANK Frank Bernard B 7.13.1940 Buffalo, NY BR/TL 6-2/175# d4.15																									
1964	Pit N	2	2	.500	33	2	0	2	42	51	22	6	1	11-3	31	4.07	86	.295	.341	5-1	.200	0	138	-3	-0.2
BORKOWSKI, DAVE David Richard B 2.7.1977 Detroit, MI BR/TR 6-1/200# d7.17																									
1999	Det A	2	6	.250	17	12	0	0-0	76.2	86	58	10	4	40-0	50	6.10	81	.283	.371	3-0	.000	-0	100	-11	-0.9
2000	Det A	0	1	.000	2	1	0	0-0	5.1	11	13	2	0	7-1	1	21.94	22	.423	.529	0-0	—	0	78	-10	-1.1
2001	Det A	0	2	.000	15	0	0	0-0	29.2	30	21	5	3	15-3	30	6.37	68	.261	.356	0-0	—	0		-6	-0.3
Total	3	2	9	.182	34	13	0	0-0	111.2	127	92	17	7	62-4	81	6.93	69	.285	.378	3-0	.000	-0	102	-27	-2.3
BORLAND, TOM Thomas Bruce "Spike" B 2.14.1933 ElDorado, KS BL/TL 6-3/172# d5.15																									
1960	Bos A	0	4	.000	26	4	0	3	51	67	40	4	0	23-4	32	6.53	62	.322	.388	13-0	.000	-2	125	-13	-1.2
1961	Bos A	0	0	—	1	0	0	0	1	3	2	0	0	0-0	0	18.00	23	.500	.500	0-0	—	0		-1	-0.1
Total	2	0	4	.000	27	4	0	3	52	70	42	4	0	23-4	32	6.75	60	.327	.391	13-0	.000	-2	125	-14	-1.3
BORLAND, TOBY Toby Shawn B 5.29.1969 Ruston, LA BR/TR 6-6/186# d5.27																									
1994	Phi N	1	0	1.000	24	0	0	1-0	34.1	31	10	1	4	14-3	26	2.36	182	.248	.343	3-0	.000	-0		7	0.3
1995	Phi N	1	3	.250	50	0	0	6-3	74	81	37	3	5	37-7	59	3.77	112	.277	.366	5-0	.200	0		2	0.1
1996	Phi N	7	3	.700	69	0	0	0-2	90.2	83	51	9	3	43-3	76	4.07	106	.239	.327	4-0	.000	-0		0	-0.1
1997	NY N	0	1	.000	13	0	0	1-1	13.1	11	9	1	1	14-0	7	6.08	66	.220	.400	0-1	—	0		-3	-0.2
	Bos A	0	0	—	3	0	0	0-0	3.1	6	5	1	2	7-0	1	13.50	34	.400	.625	0-0	—	0		-3	-0.1
1998	Phi N	0	0	—	6	0	0	0-0	9	8	5	1	0	5-0	9	5.00	87	.242	.342	0-0	—	0		0	0.0
2001	Ana A	0	1	.000	2	0	0	0-1	3.1	8	5	1	0	1-0	0	10.80	42	.471	.500	0-0	—	0		-3	-0.4
2002	Fla N	1	0	1.000	15	0	0	0-0	13.2	14	8	3	3	5-0	11	5.27	75	.269	.355	0-0	—	0		-2	-0.1
2003	Fla N	0	0	—	7	0	0	0-0	9.2	3	3	0	0	8-1	4	1.86	220	.097	.275	0-0	—	0		2	0.1
Total	8	10	8	.556	189	0	0	8-7	251.1	245	133	20	18	134-14	193	4.08	104	.254	.354	12-1	.083	-1		0	-0.4
BOROWSKI, JOE Joseph Thomas B 5.4.1971 Bayonne, NJ BR/TR 6-2/225# d7.9																									
1995	Bal A	0	0	—	6	0	0	0-0	7.1	5	1	0	0	4-0	3	1.23	388	.192	.300	0-0	—	0		3	0.1
1996	Atl N	2	4	.333	22	0	0	0-0	26	33	15	4	1	13-4	15	4.85	91	.324	.405	2-1	.000	-0		-1	-0.1
1997	Atl N	2	2	.500	20	0	0	0-0	24	27	11	2	0	16-4	6	3.75	112	.287	.391	0-0	—	0		1	0.2
	NY A	0	1	.000	1	0	0	0-0	2	2	2	0	0	4-1	2	9.00	49	.250	.500	0-0	—	0		-1	-0.2
1998	NY A	1	0	1.000	8	0	0	0-0	9.2	11	7	0	0	4-0	7	6.52	67	.289	.357	0-0	—	0		-2	-0.2
2001	Chi N	0	1	.000	1	1	0	0-0	1.2	6	6	1	0	3-0	1	32.40	13	.667	.750	0-0	—	0	89	-5	-0.7
2002	Chi N	4	4	.500	73	0	0	2-4	95.2	84	31	10	1	29-6	97	2.73	148	.238	.295	7-0	.286	0		14	1.2
2003	†Chi N	2	2	.500	68	0	0	33-4	68.1	53	23	5	1	19-1	66	2.63	160	.207	.264	0-0	—	0		12	1.7
Total	7	11	14	.440	199	1	0	35-8	234.2	221	96	22	3	92-16	197	3.41	123	.249	.321	9-1	.222	0	89	21	2.0
BOROWY, HANK Henry Ludwig B 5.12.1916 Bloomfield, NJ BR/TR 6/175# d4.18																									
1942	†NY A	15	4	.789	25	21	13-4	1	178.1	157	56	6	0	66	85	2.52	136	.233	.301	70-4	.157	-1	132	20	2.0
1943	†NY A	14	9	.609	29	27	14-3	0	217.1	195	75	11	2	72	113	2.82	114	.241	.305	74-8	.203	3	106	12	1.6
1944	NY A★	17	12	.586	35	30	19-3	2	252.2	224	93	15	0	88	107	2.64	132	.236	.301	90-7	.133	-3	97	21	2.1
1945	NY A❖	10	5	.667	18	18	7-1	0	132.1	107	61	6	1	58	35	3.13	111	.221	.305	50-3	.220	1	134	2	0.3
	†Chi N	11	2	.846	15	14	11-1	1	122.1	105	33	2	0	47	47	**2.13**	171	.231	.303	41-7	.171	0	137	22	2.3
1946	Chi N	12	10	.545	32	28	8-1	0	201	220	96	9	1	61	95	3.76	88	.274	.326	72-7	.181	1*	123	-10	-0.9
1947	Chi N	8	12	.400	40	25	7-1	2	183	190	99	19	1	63	75	4.38	90	.267	.328	56-0	.125	-1*	90	-6	-0.7
1948	Chi N	5	10	.333	39	17	2-1	1	127	156	80	9	0	49	50	4.89	80	.308	.369	36-0	.222	2	75	-14	-1.2
1949	Phi N	12	12	.500	28	28	12-1	0	193.1	188	99	19	0	63	43	4.19	94	.259	.319	61-5	.213	3	101	-5	-0.3
1950	Phi N	0	0	—	3	0	0	0	6.1	5	4	0	0	4	3	5.68	71	.250	.375	0-1	—	0		-1	-0.1
	Pit N	1	3	.250	11	3	0	0	25.1	32	19	6	1	9	9	6.39	69	.311	.372	6-2	.167	-0	94	-5	-0.7
	Year	1	3	.250	14	3	0	0	31.2	37	24	6	1	13	12	6.25	69	.301	.372	6-3	.167	-0	95	-6	-0.8
	Det A	1	1	.500	13	2	1	0	32.2	23	15	3	0	16	12	3.31	142	.205	.305	7-2	.143	-0	106	4	0.2
1951	Det A	2	2	.500	26	1	0	0	45.1	58	39	3	1	27	16	6.95	60	.314	.404	8-0	.000	-1	85	-14	-1.1
Total	10	108	82	.568	314	214	94-16	7	1717	1660	769	108	7	623	690	3.50	104	.254	.320	571-46	.173	3	108	26	3.5
BOSIO, CHRIS Christopher Louis B 4.3.1963 Carmichael, CA BR/TR 6-3/225# d8.3 C1																									
1986	Mil A	0	4	.000	10	4	0	0-0	34.2	41	27	9	0	13-0	29	7.01	62	.293	.353	0-0	—	0	79	-8	-0.8
1987	Mil A	11	8	.579	46	19	2-1	2-2	170	187	102	18	1	50-3	150	5.24	88	.276	.326	0-0	—	0	104	-10	-0.9
1988	Mil A	7	15	.318	38	22	9-1	6-0	182	190	80	13	2	38-6	84	3.36	119	.268	.303	0-0	—	0	70	11	1.4
1989	Mil A	15	10	.600	33	33	8-2	0-0	234.2	225	90	16	6	48-1	173	2.95	130	.249	.289	0-0	—	0	124	22	2.3
1990	Mil A	4	9	.308	20	20	4-1	0-0	132.2	131	67	15	3	38-1	76	4.00	97	.258	.311	0-0	—	0	89	-1	0.0
1991	Mil A	14	10	.583	32	32	5-1	0-0	204.2	187	80	15	8	58-0	117	3.25	122	.244	.302	0-0	—	0	114	18	1.9
1992	Mil A	16	6	.727	33	33	4-2	0-0	231.1	223	100	21	4	44-1	120	3.62	106	.254	.291	0-0	—	0	122	7	0.6
1993	Sea A	9	9	.500	29	24	3-1	1-1	164.1	138	75	14	6	59-3	119	3.45	128	.229	.303	0-0	—	0*	80	14	1.4
1994	Sea A	4	10	.286	19	19	4	0-0	125	137	72	15	2	40-3	67	4.32	113	.277	.330	0-0	—	0	82	6	0.6
1995	†Sea A	10	8	.556	31	31	0	0-0	170	211	98	18	5	69-3	85	4.92	96	.312	.375	0-0	—	0	110	-2	-0.2
1996	Sea A	4	4	.500	18	9	0	0-0	60.2	72	44	8	4	24-1	39	5.93	83	.299	.364	0-0	—	0	152	-7	-0.7
Total	11	94	93	.503	309	246	39-9	9-3	1710	1742	835	162	41	481-22	1059	3.96	106	.264	.315	0-0	—	0	104	50	5.6
BOSKIE, SHAWN Shawn Kealoha B 3.28.1967 Hawthorne, NV BR/TR 6-3/200# d5.20																									
1990	Chi N	5	6	.455	15	15	1	0-0	97.2	99	42	8	1	31-3	49	3.69	111	.265	.322	36-2	.222	1	83	5	0.7
1991	Chi N	4	9	.308	28	20	0	0-0	129	150	78	14	5	52-4	62	5.23	74	.294	.361	41-3	.171	2*	95	-16	-1.3
1992	Chi N	5	11	.313	23	18	0	0-0	91.2	96	55	14	4	36-3	39	5.01	72	.284	.354	27-3	.185	1	77	-13	-1.9
1993	Chi N	5	3	.625	39	2	0	0-3	65.2	63	30	7	7	21-2	39	3.43	117	.258	.333	11-0	.273	1	135	3	0.3
1994	Chi N	0	0	—	2	0	0	0-0	3.2	3	0	0	0	0-0	2	0.00	—	.214	.214	0-0	—	0		2	0.1
	Phi N	4	6	.400	18	14	1	0-1	84.1	85	56	14	3	29-2	59	5.23	82	.258	.321	26-1	.115	1*	93	-9	-0.8
	Year	4	6	.400	20	14	1	0-1	88	88	60	14	3	29-2	61	5.01	86	.256	.317	26-1	.115	1	93	-9	-0.7
	Sea A	0	1	.000	2	1	0	0-0	2.2	4	2	1	0	1-1	0	6.75	72	.333	.385	0-0	—	0	38	0	-0.1
1995	Cal A	7	7	.500	20	20	1	0-0	111.2	127	73	16	7	25-0	51	5.64	83	.281	.324	0-0	—	0	109	-11	-1.1
1996	Cal A	12	11	.522	37	28	1	0-0	189.1	226	126	40	13	67-7	133	5.32	94	.294	.358	0-0	—	0	96	-7	-0.7
1997	Bal A	6	6	.500	28	9	0	1-0	77	95	57	14	2	26-1	50	6.43	69	.304	.354	0-0	—	0*	97	-17	-2.2
1998	Mon N	1	3	.250	5	5	0	0-0	17.2	34	21	5	2	4-1	10	9.17	46	.415	.449	4-0	.000	-0	136	-10	-1.7
Total	9	49	63	.438	217	132	4	1-4	870.1	982	540	133	44	292-24	494	5.14	85	.286	.346	145-9	.179	5	95	-73	-8.7
BOSMAN, DICK Richard Allen B 2.17.1944 Kenosha, WI BR/TR 6-3/208# d6.1 C11																									
1966	Was A	2	6	.250	13	7	0	0	39	60	36	4	0	12-4	20	7.62	45	.361	.402	12-2	.250	0	98	-17	-3.0
1967	Was A	3	1	.750	7	7	2-1	0	51.1	38	12	3	0	10-2	25	1.75	180	.204	.242	15-2	.200	0*	98	8	0.7
1968	Was A	2	9	.182	46	10	0	1	139	139	63	9	4	35-5	63	3.69	79	.262	.310	30-1	.200	1	81	-11	-0.8
1969	Was A	14	5	.737	31	26	5-2	1-0	193	156	59	11	2	39-0	99	**2.19**	**158**	.220	.260	64-5	.094	-1*	120	26	2.5
1970	Was A	16	12	.571	36	34	7-3	0-0	230.2	212	81	16	2	71-8	134	3.00	118	.245	.302	80-6	.138	-2	85	17	1.8
1971	Was A	12	16	.429	35	35	7-1	0-0	236.2	245	110	29	5	71-9	113	3.73	89	.272	.327	75-5	.093	-1	104	-11	-1.5
1972	Tex A	8	10	.444	29	29	1-1	0-0	173.1	183	87	11	6	48-6	105	3.63	83	.273	.326	53-13	.094	-2	123	-15	-1.7
1973	Tex A	2	5	.286	7	7	1-1	0-0	40.1	42	24	6	1	17-1	14	4.24	88	.268	.341	0-0	—	0	69	-3	-0.5
	Cle A	1	8	.111	22	17	2	0-0	97	130	74	19	6	29-5	41	6.22	63	.320	.373	0-0	—	0	96	-24	-2.0
	Year	3	13	.188	29	24	3-1	0-0	137.1	172	78	25	7	46-6	55	5.64	69	.306	.364	0-0	—	0	89	-28	-2.5
1974	Cle A	7	5	.583	25	18	2-1	0-0	127.1	126	69	13	1	29-3	56	4.10	88	.255	.297	0-0	—	0	112	-8	-0.9
1975	Cle A	0	2	.000	6	3	0	0-0	28.2	33	17	3	3	8-1	11	4.08	93	.292	.349	0-0	—	0	54	-2	-0.1
	†Oak A	11	4	.733	22	21	2	0-0	122.2	112	50	12	3	24-3	42	3.52	103	.240	.280	0-0	—	0	115	4	0.4

Year	Tm Lg	W	L	Pct	G	GS	CG-Sho	SV-BS	IP	H	R	HR	HB	BB-IB	SO	ERA	AERA	OAV	OOB	AB-SH	AVG	PB	Sup	APR	PW
	Year	11	6	.647	28	24	2	0-0	151.1	145	55	15	6	32-4	53	3.63	101	.250	.294	0-0	—	0	107	2	0.3
1976	Oak A	4	2	.667	27	15	0	0-0	112	118	54	13	1	19-1	34	4.10	82	.274	.305	0-0	—	0	136	-8	-0.4
Total	11	82	85	.491	306	229	29-10	2-0	1591	1594	736	149	34	412-48	757	3.67	93	.261	.310	329-34	.125	-5	106	-44	-5.5

BOSSER, MEL Melvin Edward B 2.8.1914 Johnstown, PA D 3.26.1986 Crossville, TN BR/TR 6/173# d4.29

Year	Tm Lg	W	L	Pct	G	GS	CG-Sho	SV-BS	IP	H	R	HR	HB	BB-IB	SO	ERA	AERA	OAV	OOB	AB-SH	AVG	PB	Sup	APR	PW
1945	Cin N	2	0	1.000	7	1	0	0	16	9	6	0	0	17	3	3.38	111	.158	.351	4-0	.000	-1	68	1	0.0

BOSWELL, ANDY Andrew Cottrell B 9.5.1874 New Gretna, NJ D 2.3.1936 Ocean City, NJ TR 6-1/165# d5.10

Year	Tm Lg	W	L	Pct	G	GS	CG-Sho	SV-BS	IP	H	R	HR	HB	BB-IB	SO	ERA	AERA	OAV	OOB	AB-SH	AVG	PB	Sup	APR	PW
1895	NY N	2	2	.500	5	4	3	0	34	41	35	1	3	22	18	5.82	80	.293	.400	16-0	.188	-1	115	-6	-0.6
	Was N	1	2	.333	6	3	3	0	30	44	32	1	2	19	12	6.00	80	.336	.428	14-0	.286	0*	114	-4	-0.3
	Year	3	4	.429	11	7	6	0	64	85	40	2	5	41	30	5.91	80	.314	.413	30-0	.233	-1	114	-11	-0.9

BOSWELL, DAVE David Wilson B 1.20.1945 Baltimore, MD BR/TR 6-3/185# d9.18

Year	Tm Lg	W	L	Pct	G	GS	CG-Sho	SV-BS	IP	H	R	HR	HB	BB-IB	SO	ERA	AERA	OAV	OOB	AB-SH	AVG	PB	Sup	APR	PW
1964	Min A	2	0	1.000	4	4	0	0	23.1	21	11	4	0	12-1	25	4.24	84	.236	.327	9-1	.222	0	118	-1	0.0
1965	†Min A	6	5	.545	27	12	1	0	106	77	43	20	5	46-0	85	3.40	105	.204	.298	38-0	.316	4*	117	4	0.7
1966	Min A	12	5	.706	28	21	8-1	0	169.1	120	66	19	5	65-2	173	3.14	115	.197	.279	63-2	.143	-1*	117	9	0.8
1967	Min A	14	12	.538	37	32	11-3	0	222.2	162	84	14	7	107-5	204	3.27	106	.202	.301	73-3	.219	4*	100	8	1.3
1968	Min A	10	13	.435	34	28	7-2	0	190	148	79	19	7	87-2	143	3.32	93	.213	.305	60-5	.233	5*	98	-3	0.0
1969	†Min A	20	12	.625	39	38	10	0-0	256.1	215	105	18	8	99-2	190	3.23	113	.226	.303	94-6	.170	3*	116	12	1.6
1970	Min A	3	7	.300	18	15	0	0-0	68.2	80	55	12	2	44-3	45	6.42	58	.292	.390	25-0	.160	-0*	128	-20	-2.5
1971	Det A	0	0	—	3	0	0	0-0	4.1	3	3	0	0	6-0	3	6.23	58	.200	.409	0-0	—	0		-1	0.0
	Bal A	1	2	.333	15	1	0	0-0	24.2	32	16	4	0	15-1	14	4.38	77	.305	.388	5-0	.200	0	53	-4	-0.4
	Year	1	2	.333	18	1	0	0-0	29	35	18	4	0	21-1	17	4.66	73	.292	.392	5-0	.200	0	53	-5	-0.4
Total	8	68	56	.548	205	151	37-6	0-0	1065.1	858	462	110	34	481-16	882	3.52	99	.219	.309	367-17	.202	13	111	4	1.5

BOTELHO, DEREK Derek Wayne B 8.2.1956 Long Beach, CA BR/TR 6-2/180# d7.18

Year	Tm Lg	W	L	Pct	G	GS	CG-Sho	SV-BS	IP	H	R	HR	HB	BB-IB	SO	ERA	AERA	OAV	OOB	AB-SH	AVG	PB	Sup	APR	PW
1982	KC A	2	1	.667	8	4	0	0-0	24	25	11	4	0	8-0	12	4.13	99	.275	.330	0-0	—	0	145	0	0.0
1985	Chi N	1	3	.250	11	7	1	0-0	44	52	27	8	2	23-1	23	5.32	75	.299	.387	14-0	.143	-0	117	-5	-0.5
Total	2	3	4	.429	19	11	1	0-0	68	77	38	12	2	31-1	35	4.90	83	.291	.368	14-0	.143	-0	127	-5	-0.5

BOTTALICO, RICKY Ricky Paul B 8.26.1969 New Britain, CT BL/TR 6-1/200# d7.29

Year	Tm Lg	W	L	Pct	G	GS	CG-Sho	SV-BS	IP	H	R	HR	HB	BB-IB	SO	ERA	AERA	OAV	OOB	AB-SH	AVG	PB	Sup	APR	PW
1994	Phi N	0	0	—	3	0	0	0-0	3	3	0	0	0	1-0	3	0.00	—	.250	.308	0-0	—	0		1	0.1
1995	Phi N	5	3	.625	62	0	0	1-4	87.2	50	25	7	4	42-3	87	2.46	172	.167	.277	5-1	.000	-1		18	1.4
1996	Phi N★	4	5	.444	61	0	0	34-4	67.2	47	24	6	2	23-2	74	3.19	135	.197	.272	3-0	.333	1		9	1.9
1997	Phi N	2	5	.286	69	0	0	34-7	74	68	31	7	2	42-4	89	3.65	116	.245	.347	1-0	.000	-0		6	0.9
1998	Phi N	1	5	.167	39	0	0	6-1	43.1	54	31	7	1	25-5	27	6.44	67	.305	.390	0-0	—	0		-9	-1.3
1999	StL N	3	7	.300	68	0	0	20-8	73.1	83	45	8	3	49-1	66	4.91	93	.284	.392	3-0	.000	-0		-3	-0.5
2000	KC A	9	6	.600	62	0	0	16-7	72.2	65	40	12	2	41-3	56	4.83	106	.239	.342	0-0	—	0		3	0.5
2001	Phi N	3	4	.429	66	0	0	3-4	67	58	31	11	4	25-2	57	3.90	109	.241	.318	3-0	.333	1		3	0.3
2002	Phi N	0	3	.000	30	0	0	0-1	27.1	33	16	3	2	13-2	24	4.61	85	.300	.381	0-0	—	0		-3	-0.3
2003	Ari N	1	0	1.000	2	0	0	0-0	1.2	3	1	0	0	2-1	2	5.40	87	.375	.500	0-0	—	0		0	0.0
Total	10	28	38	.424	462	0	0	114-36	517.2	464	244	61	20	263-23	485	4.03	109	.241	.336	15-1	.133	0		25	3.0

BOTTENFIELD, KENT Kent Dennis B 11.14.1968 Portland, OR BR/TR 6-3/237# d7.6

Year	Tm Lg	W	L	Pct	G	GS	CG-Sho	SV-BS	IP	H	R	HR	HB	BB-IB	SO	ERA	AERA	OAV	OOB	AB-SH	AVG	PB	Sup	APR	PW
1992	Mon N	1	2	.333	10	4	0	1-0	32.1	26	9	1	1	11-1	14	2.23	156	.217	.284	8-1	.375	1	59	4	0.5
1993	Mon N	2	5	.286	23	11	0	0-0	83	93	49	11	5	33-2	33	4.12	101	.288	.362	24-1	.167	-0	76	-1	-0.1
	Col N	3	5	.375	14	14	1	0-0	76.2	86	53	13	1	38-1	30	6.10	78	.302	.382	26-2	.269	1	89	-8	-0.5
	Year	5	10	.333	37	25	1	0-0	159.2	179	58	24	6	71-3	63	5.07	88	.294	.372	50-3	.220	1	85	-10	-0.6
1994	Col N	3	1	.750	15	1	0	1-0	24.2	28	16	1	2	10-0	15	5.84	85	.283	.360	1-0	.000	-0	55	-2	-0.3
	SF N	0	0	—	1	0	0	0-0	1.2	5	2	1	0	0-0	0	10.80	37	.556	.556	0-0	—	0		-1	-0.1
	Year	3	1	.750	16	1	0	1-0	26.1	33	21	2	2	10-0	15	6.15	80	.306	.375	1-0	.000	-0	56	-3	-0.4
1996	Chi N	3	5	.375	48	0	0	1-2	61.2	59	25	3	3	19-4	33	2.63	165	.255	.320	2-1	.500	0		9	1.1
1997	Chi N	2	3	.400	64	0	0	2-2	84	82	39	13	2	35-7	74	3.86	112	.259	.333	4-4	.000	-0		4	0.1
1998	StL N	4	6	.400	44	17	0	4-1	133.2	128	72	13	4	57-3	98	4.44	94	.254	.333	34-5	.088	-2	122	-3	-0.4
1999	StL N★	18	7	.720	31	31	0	0-0	190.1	197	91	21	5	89-5	124	3.97	115	.270	.350	61-8	.148	-1	106	13	1.5
2000	Ana A	7	8	.467	21	21	0	0-0	127.2	144	82	25	3	56-4	75	5.71	89	.285	.357	3-0	.667	1	101	-6	-0.5
	Phi N	1	2	.333	8	8	1-1	0-0	44	41	24	5	0	21-0	31	4.50	104	.240	.320	14-3	.000	-2	74	1	-0.1
2001	Hou N	2	5	.286	13	9	0	1-0	52	61	44	16	2	16-0	39	6.40	71	.288	.338	14-1	.143	-0	83	-12	-1.4
Total	9	46	49	.484	292	116	2-1	10-5	911.2	950	506	123	28	385-27	566	4.54	99	.271	.345	191-26	.162	-3	98	-2	-0.2

BOTTING, RALPH Ralph Wayne B 5.12.1955 Houlton, ME BL/TL 6/195# d6.28

Year	Tm Lg	W	L	Pct	G	GS	CG-Sho	SV-BS	IP	H	R	HR	HB	BB-IB	SO	ERA	AERA	OAV	OOB	AB-SH	AVG	PB	Sup	APR	PW
1979	Cal A	2	0	1.000	12	1	0	0-0	29.2	46	30	6	1	15-1	22	8.80	46	.362	.428	0-0	—	0	111	-15	-0.9
1980	Cal A	0	3	.000	6	6	0	0-0	26.1	40	20	1	0	13-0	12	5.81	68	.348	.411	0-0	—	0	98	-6	-0.6
Total	2	2	3	.400	18	7	0	0-0	56	86	50	7	1	28-1	34	7.39	54	.355	.420	0-0	—	0	99	-21	-1.5

BOTZ, BOB Robert Allen B 4.28.1935 Milwaukee, WI BR/TR 5-11/170# d5.8

Year	Tm Lg	W	L	Pct	G	GS	CG-Sho	SV-BS	IP	H	R	HR	HB	BB-IB	SO	ERA	AERA	OAV	OOB	AB-SH	AVG	PB	Sup	APR	PW
1962	LA A	2	1	.667	35	0	0	2	63	71	30	7	2	11-0	24	3.43	113	.285	.319	9-1	.000	-1		2	-0.1

BOUCHER, DENIS Denis B 3.7.1968 Montreal, PQ, CAN BR/TL 6-1/195# d4.12

Year	Tm Lg	W	L	Pct	G	GS	CG-Sho	SV-BS	IP	H	R	HR	HB	BB-IB	SO	ERA	AERA	OAV	OOB	AB-SH	AVG	PB	Sup	APR	PW
1991	Tor A	0	3	.000	7	7	0	0-0	35.1	39	20	6	2	16-1	16	4.58	92	.279	.358	0-0	—	0	93	-2	-0.1
	Cle A	1	4	.200	5	5	0	0-0	22.2	35	21	6	0	8-0	13	8.34	50	.350	.398	0-0	—	0	53	-9	-1.5
	Year	1	7	.125	12	12	0	0-0	58	74	23	12	2	24-1	29	6.05	69	.308	.375	0-0	—	0	76	-10	-1.6
1992	Cle A	2	2	.500	8	7	0	0-0	41	48	29	9	1	20-0	17	6.37	61	.302	.377	0-0	—	0	130	-10	-0.8
1993	Mon N	3	1	.750	5	5	0	0-0	28.1	24	7	1	0	3-1	14	1.91	219	.229	.243	6-2	.167	0	82	7	1.0
1994	Mon N	0	1	.000	10	2	0	0-1	18.2	24	16	6	0	7-0	17	6.75	63	.324	.378	3-1	.333	1	54	-5	-0.2
Total	4	6	11	.353	35	26	0	0-1	146	170	93	28	3	54-2	77	5.42	76	.294	.353	9-3	.222	1	89	-19	-1.6

BOULDIN, CARL Carl Edward B 9.17.1939 Germantown, KY BB/TR 6-2/180# d9.2

Year	Tm Lg	W	L	Pct	G	GS	CG-Sho	SV-BS	IP	H	R	HR	HB	BB-IB	SO	ERA	AERA	OAV	OOB	AB-SH	AVG	PB	Sup	APR	PW
1961	Was A	0	1	.000	2	1	0	0	3.1	9	6	0	0	2-0	2	16.20	25	.500	.550	1-0	.000	-0	66	-4	-0.7
1962	Was A	1	2	.333	6	3	1	0	20	26	13	0	1	9-0	12	5.85	69	.321	.387	7-0	.000	-1*	81	-3	-0.5
1963	Was A	2	2	.500	10	3	0	0	23.1	31	18	3	0	8-1	10	5.79	64	.307	.355	7-0	.000	-1	88	-6	-0.9
1964	Was A	0	3	.000	9	3	0	0	25	30	20	2	2	11-2	12	5.40	69	.294	.368	6-0	.000	-0*	64	-6	-0.7
Total	4	3	8	.273	27	10	1	0	71.2	96	57	5	3	30-3	36	6.15	62	.318	.379	21-0	.000	-2	77	-19	-2.8

BOULTES, JAKE Jacob John B 8.6.1884 St.Louis, MO D 12.24.1955 St.Louis, MO BR/TR 6-3/?# d4.18

Year	Tm Lg	W	L	Pct	G	GS	CG-Sho	SV-BS	IP	H	R	HR	HB	BB-IB	SO	ERA	AERA	OAV	OOB	AB-SH	AVG	PB	Sup	APR	PW
1907	Bos N	5	9	.357	24	12	11	0	139.2	140	75	1	8	50	49	2.71	94	.266	.338	68-0	.132	-2*	86	-10	-0.9
1908	Bos N	3	5	.375	17	5	1	0	74.2	80	40	7	1	8	28	3.01	80	.274	.296	21-4	.143	-0*	134	-7	-0.8
1909	Bos N	0	0	—	1	0	0	0	8	9	7	2	1	0	1	6.75	42	.290	.313	3-0	.333	0		-3	-0.1
Total	3	8	14	.364	42	17	12	0	222.1	229	122	10	10	58	78	2.96	85	.269	.324	92-4	.141	-2	100	-20	-1.8

BOURGEOIS, STEVE Steven James B 8.4.1972 Lutcher, LA BR/TR 6-1/220# d4.3

Year	Tm Lg	W	L	Pct	G	GS	CG-Sho	SV-BS	IP	H	R	HR	HB	BB-IB	SO	ERA	AERA	OAV	OOB	AB-SH	AVG	PB	Sup	APR	PW
1996	SF N	1	3	.250	15	5	0	0-0	40	60	35	4	4	21-4	17	6.30	65	.355	.434	11-1	.273	2	106	-12	-0.8

BOUTON, JIM James Alan B 3.8.1939 Newark, NJ BR/TR 6/185# d4.22

Year	Tm Lg	W	L	Pct	G	GS	CG-Sho	SV-BS	IP	H	R	HR	HB	BB-IB	SO	ERA	AERA	OAV	OOB	AB-SH	AVG	PB	Sup	APR	PW
1962	NY A	7	7	.500	36	16	3-1	2	133	124	63	9	0	59-1	71	3.99	94	.254	.330	32-4	.063	-2*	122	-2	-0.4
1963	†NY A★	21	7	.750	40	30	12-6	1	249.1	191	79	18	3	87-2	148	2.53	139	.212	.282	83-11	.072	-6	111	27	2.3
1964	†NY A	18	13	.581	38	**37**	11-4	0	271.1	227	100	32	6	60-4	125	3.02	120	.225	.272	100-7	.130	-3	110	18	1.4
1965	NY A	4	15	.211	30	25	2	0	151.1	158	89	23	5	60-1	97	4.82	71	.269	.339	43-2	.093	-0*	97	-23	-2.7
1966	NY A	3	8	.273	24	19	3	1	120.1	117	49	13	1	38-5	65	2.69	123	.257	.313	38-3	.105	-2	91	5	0.3
1967	NY A	1	0	1.000	17	1	0	0	44.1	47	31	5	1	18-5	31	4.67	67	.275	.344	7-1	.000	-0	195	-10	-0.6
1968	NY A	1	1	.500	12	3	1	0	44	49	20	5	2	9-0	24	3.68	79	.287	.326	7-0	.000	-0	90	-3	-0.2
1969	Sea A	2	1	.667	57	1	0	1-0	92	77	48	12	2	38-4	68	3.91	93	.219	.298	9-0	.000	-1	170	-4	-0.3
	Hou N	0	2	.000	16	1	1	1-0	30.2	32	16	1	2	12-1	32	4.11	86	.267	.343	4-0	.000	-0	50	-2	-0.2
1970	Hou N	4	6	.400	29	6	1	0-0	73.1	84	53	5	1	33-3	49	5.40	72	.285	.358	17-1	.353	2	154	-15	-1.5
1978	Atl N	1	3	.250	5	5	0	0-0	29	25	18	4	0	21-1	10	4.97	82	.234	.357	7-0	.000	-1	66	-2	-0.4

Year	Tm Lg	W	L	Pct	G	GS	CG-Sho	SV-BS	IP	H	R	HR	HB	BB-IB	SO	ERA	AERA	OAV	OOB	AB-SH	AVG	PB	Sup	APR	PW
Total	10	62	63	.496	304	144	34-11	6-0	1238.2	1131	566	127	23	435-27	720	3.57	99	.243	.309	347-29	.101	-13	108	-11	-2.3
BOVEE, MIKE Michael Craig B 8.21.1973 San Diego, CA BR/TR 5-10/200# d9.13																									
1997	Ana A	0	0	—	3	0	0	0-0	3.1	3	2	1	0	1-0	5	5.40	85	.231	.286	0-0	—	0		0	0.0
BOWEN, RYAN Ryan Eugene B 2.10.1968 Hanford, CA BR/TR 6/185# d7.22																									
1991	Hou N	6	4	.600	14	13	0	0-0	71.2	73	43	4	3	36-1	49	5.15	68	.268	.353	22-1	.182	1*	114	-13	-1.5
1992	Hou N	0	7	.000	11	9	0	0-0	33.2	48	43	8	2	30-3	22	10.96	31	.333	.455	9-0	.111	-0*	81	-29	-4.6
1993	Fla N	8	12	.400	27	27	2-1	0-0	156.2	156	83	11	3	87-7	98	4.42	98	.263	.358	51-3	.118	-1	87	-1	-0.3
1994	Fla N	1	5	.167	8	8	1	0-0	47.1	50	28	9	2	19-0	32	4.94	88	.273	.345	14-1	.357	2	78	-2	-0.1
1995	Fla N	2	0	1.000	4	3	0	0-0	16.2	23	11	3	0	12-2	15	3.78	112	.329	.417	6-0	.333	0	121	-1	0.0
Total	5	17	28	.378	64	60	3-1	0-0	326	350	208	35	10	184-13	216	5.30	76	.277	.370	102-5	.176	2	91	-46	-6.5
BOWEN, CY Sutherland McCoy B 2.17.1871 Kingston, IN D 1.25.1925 Greensburg, IN BR/TR 6/175# d4.28																									
1896	NY N	0	1	.000	2	1	1	0	12	12	13	0	3	9	3	6.00	70	.261	.414	3-2	.333	0	51	-3	-0.1
BOWERS, SHANE Shane Patrick B 7.27.1971 Glendora, CA BR/TR 6-4/215# d7.26																									
1997	Min A	0	3	.000	5	5	0	0-0	19	27	20	2	1	8-0	7	8.05	58	.329	.391	0-0	—	0	67	-8	-1.0
BOWERS, STEW Stewart Cole "Doc" B 2.26.1915 New Freedom, PA BB/TR 6/170# d8.5																									
1935	Bos A	2	1	.667	10	2	1	0	23.2	26	14	1	0	17	5	3.42	139	.283	.394	5-0	.200	0*	46	2	0.2
1936	Bos A	0	0	—	5	0	0	0	5.2	10	7	1	0	2	0	9.53	56	.370	.414	0-0	—	0*		-3	-0.1
Total	2	2	1	.667	15	2	1	0	29.1	36	21	2	0	19	5	4.60	106	.303	.399	5-0	.200	0	46	-1	0.1
BOWIE, MICAH Micah Andrew B 11.10.1974 Humble, TX BL/TL 6-4/185# d7.24																									
1999	Atl N	0	1	.000	3	0	0	0-0	4	8	6	1	0	4-0	2	13.50	33	.421	.522	0-0	—	0		-4	-0.6
	Chi N	2	6	.250	11	11	0	0-0	47	73	54	8	2	30-2	39	9.96	45	.358	.439	14-0	.214	0	102	-27	-3.3
	Year	2	7	.222	14	11	0	0-0	51	81	59	9	2	34-2	41	10.24	44	.363	.447	14-0	.214	0	102	-31	-3.9
2002	†Oak A	2	0	1.000	13	0	0	0-0	12	12	2	1	1	8-1	8	1.50	293	.261	.382	0-0	—	0		4	0.6
2003	Oak A	0	1	.000	6	0	0	0-0	8.1	13	7	1	0	2-0	4	7.56	60	.361	.395	0-0	—	0		-2	-0.2
Total	3	4	8	.333	33	11	0	0-0	71.1	106	69	11	3	44-3	53	8.45	53	.348	.431	14-0	.214	0	102	-29	-3.5
BOWLER, GRANT Grant Tierney "Moose" B 10.24.1907 Denver, CO D 6.25.1968 Denver, CO BR/TR 6/190# d8.21																									
1931	Chi A	0	1	.000	13	3	1	0	35.1	40	26	1	0	24	15	5.35	80	.288	.393	10-0	.100	-0	106	-5	-0.3
1932	Chi A	0	0	—	4	0	0	0	6.1	15	12	1	0	3	2	15.63	28	.484	.529	2-0	.000	-0		-8	-0.4
Total	2	0	1	.000	17	3	1	0	41.2	55	38	2	0	27	17	6.91	62	.324	.416	12-0	.083	-1	106	-13	-0.7
BOWLES, BRIAN Brian Christopher B 8.18.1976 Harbor City, CA BR/TR 6-5/220# d6.27																									
2001	Tor A	0	0	—	2	0	0	0-0	3.2	4	0	0	0	1-0	4	0.00	—	.286	.333	0-0	—	0		2	0.1
2002	Tor A	2	1	.667	17	0	0	0-1	20	13	11	0	3	14-1	19	4.05	114	.183	.337	0-0	—	0		1	0.1
2003	Tor A	0	0	—	5	0	0	0-0	7	8	4	1	2	2-0	2	2.57	179	.267	.353	0-0	—	0		1	0.0
Total	3	2	1	.667	24	0	0	0-1	30.2	25	15	1	5	17-1	25	3.23	143	.217	.341	0-0	—	0		4	0.2
BOWLES, CHARLIE Charles James B 3.15.1917 Norwood, MA BR/TR 6-3/180# d9.25 Mil 1943-45																									
1943	Phi A	1	1	.500	2	2	2	0	18	17	10	0	0	4	6	3.00	113	.258	.300	8-0	.125	-1*	136	-1	-0.1
1945	Phi A	0	3	.000	8	4	1	0	33.1	35	19	3	0	23	11	5.13	67	.273	.384	21-0	.238	0*	93	-5	-0.4
Total	2	1	4	.200	10	6	3	0	51.1	52	29	3	0	27	17	4.38	78	.268	.357	29-0	.207	-0	108	-6	-0.5
BOWLES, EMMETT Emmett Jerome "Chief" B 8.2.1898 Wanette, OK D 9.3.1959 Flagstaff, AZ BR/TR 6/180# d9.12																									
1922	Chi A	0	0	—	1	0	0	0	1	2	3	0	0	1	0	27.00	15	.500	.600	0-0	—	0		-2	-0.1
BOWMAN, ABE Alvah Edson B 1.25.1893 Greenup, IL D 10.11.1979 Longview, TX BR/TR 6-1/190# d5.19																									
1914	Cle A	2	7	.222	22	10	2-1	0	72.2	74	45	0	4	45	27	4.46	65	.277	.389	21-0	.048	-2	78	-10	-1.4
1915	Cle A	0	1	.000	2	1	0	0	1.1	1	4	0	0	3	0	20.25	15	.250	.571	0-0	—	0	72	-2	-0.4
Total	2	2	8	.200	24	11	2-1	0	74	75	49	0	4	48	27	4.74	61	.277	.393	21-0	.048	-2	78	-12	-1.8
BOWMAN, JOE Joseph Emil B 6.17.1910 Kansas City, KS D 11.22.1990 Kansas City, MO BL/TR 6-2/190# d4.18																									
1932	Phi A	0	1	.000	7	0	0	0	11	14	10	2	3	6	4	8.18	55	.318	.434	1-0	1.000	0		-4	-0.2
1934	NY N	5	4	.556	30	10	3	3	107.1	119	52	9	2	36	36	3.61	107	.279	.338	29-1	.172	0*	125	3	0.2
1935	Phi N	7	10	.412	33	17	6-1	1	148.1	157	86	13	4	56	58	4.25	107	.269	.337	67-1	.194	0*	85	3	0.4
1936	Phi N	9	20	.310	40	28	12	1	203.2	243	140	14	7	53	80	5.04	90	.289	.336	77-1	.195	-1*	90	-10	-1.4
1937	Pit N	8	8	.500	30	19	7	1	128	161	78	11	1	35	38	4.57	85	.306	.351	47-3	.213	2*	110	-10	-1.0
1938	Pit N	3	4	.429	17	1	0	1	60	68	33	2	0	20	25	4.65	82	.285	.340	21-2	.333	2*	134	-4	-0.3
1939	Pit N	10	14	.417	37	27	10-1	1	184.2	217	105	15	7	43	58	4.48	86	.292	.336	96-4	.344	12*	109	-13	-0.3
1940	Pit N	9	10	.474	32	24	10	2	187.2	209	113	10	7	66	57	4.46	85	.274	.337	90-0	.244	9*	132	-16	-0.5
1941	Pit N	3	2	.600	18	7	1-1	1	69.1	77	24	3	1	28	22	2.99	121	.278	.346	31-0	.258	1*	121	6	0.6
1944	Bos A	12	8	.600	26	24	10-1	0	168.1	175	95	14	2	64	53	4.81	71	.269	.336	100-0	.200	3*	138	-23	-2.3
1945	Bos A	0	2	.000	3	3	0	0	11.2	18	12	1	0	9	0	9.26	37	.360	.458	9-0	.222	0*	92	-7	-0.9
	Cin N	11	13	.458	25	24	15-1	0	185.2	198	89	8	7	68	71	3.59	105	.270	.338	71-2	.070	-5*	88	2	-0.4
Total	11	77	96	.445	298	184	74-5	11	1465.2	1656	837	102	41	484	502	4.40	89	.282	.341	639-14	.221	24	108	-73	-6.1
BOWMAN, BOB Robert James B 10.3.1910 Keystone, WV D 9.4.1972 Bluefield, WV BR/TR 5-10.5/160# d4.21																									
1939	StL N	13	5	.722	51	15	4-2	**9**	169.1	141	54	8	1	60	78	2.60	158	.232	.302	47-5	.085	-3	108	28	2.7
1940	StL N	7	5	.583	28	17	7	0	114.1	118	66	9	4	43	43	4.33	92	.267	.337	33-2	.061	-2	121	-5	-0.7
1941	NY N	6	7	.462	29	6	2	1	80.1	100	55	10	1	36	25	5.71	65	.302	.372	21-3	.048	-1	119	-16	-2.4
1942	Chi N	0	0	—	1	0	0	0	1	1	0	0	0	0	0	0.00	—	.250	.250	0-0	—	0		0	0.0
Total	4	26	17	.605	109	38	13-2	10	365	360	175	27	6	139	146	3.82	104	.260	.330	101-10	.069	-5	115	7	-0.4
BOWMAN, ROGER Roger Clinton B 8.18.1927 Amsterdam, NY D 7.21.1997 Los Angeles, CA BR/TL 6/175# d9.22																									
1949	NY N	0	0	—	2	2	0	0	6.1	6	3	1	0	7	4	4.26	93	.261	.433	2-0	.000	-0	100	0	0.0
1951	NY N	2	4	.333	9	5	0	0	26.1	35	18	2	1	22	24	6.15	64	.297	.411	6-1	.000	-0	86	-5	-1.1
1952	NY N	0	0	—	2	1	0	0	3	6	4	0	1	3	3	12.00	31	.429	.556	1-0	.000	-0	216	-2	-0.1
1953	Pit N	0	4	.000	30	2	0	0	65.1	65	42	9	1	29	36	4.82	93	.261	.341	7-0	.286	0	20	-4	-0.1
1955	Pit N	0	3	.000	7	2	0	0	16.2	25	18	2	1	10-2	8	8.64	48	.347	.434	2-1	.500	0	54	-8	-1.1
Total	5	2	11	.154	50	12	0	0	117.2	137	85	14	4	71-2	75	5.81	73	.288	.385	18-2	.167	-0	77	-19	-2.4
BOWMAN, SUMNER Sumner Sallade B 2.9.1867 Millersburg, PA D 1.11.1954 Millersburg, PA BL/TL 6/160# d6.11																									
1890	Phi N	0	0	—	1	1	0	0	8	11	7	0	1	2	2	7.88	46	.314	.368	4	.500	1	138	-2	-0.1
	Pit N	2	5	.286	9	7	6	0	70.2	100	90	1	11	50	22	6.62	50	.323	.434	36	.278	2*	134	-31	-2.0
	Year	2	5	.286	10	8	6	0	78.2	111	97	1	12	52	24	6.75	49	.322	.428	40	.300	2	135	-34	-2.1
1891	Phi AA	2	5	.286	8	8	8	0	68	73	54	0	5	37	22	3.44	110	.265	.363	54	.241	0*	82	-3	-0.2
Total	2	4	10	.286	18	16	14	0	146.2	184	151	1	17	89	46	5.22	68	.297	.399	94	.266	3	107	-36	-2.3
BOWSFIELD, TED Edward Oliver B 1.10.1935 Vernon, BC, CAN BR/TL 6-1/190# d7.20																									
1958	Bos A	4	2	.667	16	10	2	0	65.2	58	32	3	1	36-1	38	3.84	104	.233	.331	26-0	.154	-1*	121	1	0.0
1959	Bos A	0	1	.000	5	2	0	0	9	16	15	2	0	9-0	4	15.00	27	.390	.500	1-0	.000	-0	152	-10	-0.9
1960	Bos A	1	2	.333	17	2	0	2	21	20	12	1	1	13-0	18	5.14	79	.260	.366	4-2	.250	0	163	-2	-0.2
	Cle A	3	4	.429	11	6	1-1	0	40.2	47	30	1	0	20-1	14	5.09	73	.296	.372	10-1	.100	-0	67	-8	-1.2
	Year	4	6	.400	28	8	1-1	2	61.2	67	33	2	1	33-1	32	5.11	75	.284	.370	14-3	.143	-0	92	-10	-1.4
1961	LA A	11	8	.579	41	21	4-1	0	157	154	75	18	1	63-3	88	3.73	121	.255	.323	51-2	.137	-1*	95	12	1.1
1962	LA A	9	8	.529	34	25	1	1	139	154	82	12	2	40-0	52	4.40	88	.277	.325	37-4	.162	1*	104	-10	-1.0
1963	KC A	5	7	.417	41	11	2-1	3	111.1	115	60	14	3	47-5	67	4.45	88	.269	.343	23-2	.043	-1*	83	-6	-0.6
1964	KC A	4	7	.364	50	9	2-1	0	118.2	135	63	12	4	31-4	45	4.10	93	.285	.331	21-2	.095	-1*	78	-5	-0.5
Total	7	37	39	.487	215	86	12-4	6	662.1	699	369	63	12	259-14	326	4.35	93	.270	.336	173-13	.127	-3	99	-28	-3.3
BOYD, OIL CAN Dennis Ray B 10.6.1959 Meridian, MS BR/TR 6-1/155# d9.13																									
1982	Bos A	0	1	.000	3	1	0	0-1	8.1	11	5	2	0	2-0	2	5.40	80	.314	.351	0-0	—	0	21	-1	-0.1

Year	Tm Lg	W	L	Pct	G	GS	CG-Sho	SV-BS	IP	H	R	HR	HB	BB-IB	SO	ERA	AERA	OAV	OOB	AB-SH	AVG	PB	Sup	APR	PW
1983	Bos A	4	8	.333	15	13	5	0-0	98.2	103	46	9	1	23-0	43	3.28	133	.269	.308	0-0	—	0	82	9	0.9
1984	Bos A	12	12	.500	29	26	10-3	0-0	197.2	207	109	18	1	53-5	134	4.37	95	.269	.314	0-0	—	0	109	-4	-0.4
1985	Bos A	15	13	.536	35	35	13-3	0-0	272.1	273	117	26	4	67-3	154	3.70	116	.261	.306	0-0	—	0	108	20	2.0
1986	†Bos A	16	10	.615	30	30	10	0-0	214.1	222	99	32	2	45-1	129	3.78	110	.265	.302	0-0	—	0	120	10	1.1
1987	Bos A	1	3	.250	7	7	0	0-0	36.2	47	31	6	2	9-1	12	5.89	77	.315	.356	0-0	—	0	109	-8	-0.6
1988	Bos A	9	7	.563	23	23	1	0-0	129.2	147	82	25	2	41-2	71	5.34	77	.289	.341	0-0	—	0	113	-16	-1.8
1989	Bos A	3	2	.600	10	10	0	0-0	59	57	31	8	0	19-0	26	4.42	93	.253	.309	0-0	—	0	128	-1	-0.1
1990	Mon N	10	6	.625	31	31	3-3	0-0	190.2	164	64	19	3	52-10	113	2.93	125	.233	.287	59-12	.051	-4	111	18	0.9
1991	Mon N	6	8	.429	19	19	1-1	0-0	120.1	115	49	9	0	40-2	82	3.52	103	.256	.314	36-3	.083	-1	94	3	0.2
	Tex A	2	7	.222	12	12	0	0-0	62	81	47	12	0	17-1	33	6.68	60	.314	.356	0-0	—	0	68	-17	-2.0
Total	10	78	77	.503	214	207	43-10	0-1	1389.2	1427	680	166	15	368-25	799	4.04	101	.266	.313	95-15	.063	-5	106	13	0.1
BOYD, GARY Gary Lee B 8.22.1946 Pasadena, CA BR/TR 6-4/200# d8.1																									
1969	Cle A	0	2	.000	8	3	0	0-0	11	8	11	1	0	14-1	9	9.00	42	.205	.407	1-0	.000	-0	55	-5	-0.9
BOYD, JAKE Jacob Henry B 1.19.1874 Martinsburg, WV D 8.12.1932 Gettysburg, PA TL ?/160# d9.20 ▲																									
1894	Was N	0	3	.000	3	3	3	0	19	37	35	1	1	14	3	8.53	62	.402	.486	21-0	.143	-1*	76	-9	-0.9
1895	Was N	2	11	.154	15	13	8	0	92.2	132	95	1	11	40	18	6.80	71	.329	.405	159-0	.270	2*	73	-15	-1.3
1896	Was N	1	2	.333	4	2	2	0	32	45	34	0	6	15	6	6.75	65	.328	.418	13-0	.077	-1	56	-7	-0.6
Total	3	3	16	.158	22	18	13	0	143.2	214	164	2	18	69	27	7.02	68	.340	.420	193-0	.244	-1	73	-31	-2.8
BOYD, JASON Jason Pernell B 2.23.1973 St.Clair, IL BR/TR 6-3/170# d9.10																									
1999	Pit N	0	0	—	4	0	0	0-0	5.1	5	2	0	1	2-0	4	3.38	135	.250	.333	1-0	.000	-0		1	0.0
2000	Phi N	0	1	.000	30	0	0	0-1	34.1	39	28	2	1	24-4	32	6.55	71	.293	.405	0-0	—	0		-8	-0.3
2002	SD N	1	0	1.000	23	0	0	0-3	28.1	33	29	6	0	15-1	18	7.94	48	.300	.375	0-0	—	0		-15	-0.7
2003	Cle A	3	1	.750	44	0	0	0-1	52.1	38	25	4	3	26-1	31	4.30	103	.200	.303	0-0	—	0		2	0.2
Total	4	4	2	.667	101	0	0	0-5	120.1	115	84	12	5	67-6	85	5.76	75	.254	.352	1-0	.000	-0		-20	-0.8
BOYD, RAY Raymond C. B 2.11.1887 Hortonville, IN D 2.11.1920 Hortonville, IN BR/TR 5-10/160# d9.24																									
1910	StL A	0	2	.000	3	2	1	1	14.1	16	10	0	1	5	6	4.40	56	.286	.355	5-0	.200	-0	41	-3	-0.4
1911	Cin N	2	2	.500	7	4	3	1	44	34	22	0	2	19	20	2.66	124	.206	.296	12-1	.083	-0	62	2	0.1
Total	2	2	4	.333	10	6	4	1	58.1	50	32	0	3	24	26	3.09	101	.226	.310	17-1	.118	-0	55	-1	-0.3
BOYER, CLOYD Cloyd Victor "Junior" B 9.1.1927 Alba, MO BR/TR 6-1/188# d4.23 C8 b-Clete b-Ken																									
1949	StL N	0	0	—	4	1	0	0	3.1	5	4	0	0	7	0	10.80	39	.357	.571	0-0	—	0	85	-2	-0.1
1950	StL N	7	7	.500	36	14	6-1	1	120.1	105	52	15	3	49	82	3.52	122	.233	.312	33-3	.182	0	123	10	1.1
1951	StL N	2	5	.286	19	8	1	1	63.1	68	42	9	3	46	40	5.26	75	.286	.408	20-1	.200	0	123	-10	-1.0
1952	StL N	6	6	.500	23	14	4-2	1	110.1	108	56	11	4	47	44	4.24	88	.258	.338	38-0	.211	2*	101	-5	-0.4
1955	KC A	5	5	.500	30	11	2	0	98.1	107	81	21	7	69-3	32	6.22	67	.282	.398	29-1	.069	-2	97	-24	-2.3
Total	5	20	23	.465	112	48	13-3	2	395.2	393	235	56	17	218-3	198	4.73	86	.262	.361	120-5	.167	1	110	-31	-2.7
BOYLE, HENRY Henry J. "Handsome Henry" B 9.20.1860 Philadelphia, PA D 5.25.1932 Philadelphia, PA BR/TR d7.9 ▲																									
1884	StL U	15	3	.833	19	16	16-2	1	150	118	63	3		10	88	1.74	138	.202	.215	262	.260	-1*	127	10	0.8
1885	StL N	16	24	.400	42	39	39-1	0	366.2	346	207	2		100	133	2.75	100	.239	.288	258	.202	1*	80	-7	-0.6
1886	StL N	9	15	.375	25	24	23-2	0	210	183	106	5		46	101	**1.76**	**183**	.220	.261	108	.250	4*	85	26	3.0
1887	Ind N	13	24	.351	38	38	37	0	328	356	204	11	12	69	85	3.65	114	.265	.307	141	.191	-1*	73	17	1.3
1888	Ind N	15	22	.405	37	37	36-3	0	323	315	179	11	10	58	98	3.26	91	.245	.283	125	.144	-3	108	-14	-1.5
1889	Ind N	21	23	.477	46	45	38-2	0	378.2	422	224	14	14	95	97	3.92	106	.273	.321	155	.245	5	84	14	1.6
Total	6	89	111	.445	207	199	189-10	1	1756.1	1740	983	46	36	378	602	3.06	110	.247	.289	1049	.219	5	89	46	4.6
BOYLES, HARRY Harry "Stretch" B 11.29.1913 Granite City, IL BR/TR 6-5/185# d8.3																									
1938	Chi A	0	4	.000	9	2	1	1	29.1	31	27	2	2	25	18	5.22	94	.263	.400	8-0	.125	-1	36	-4	-0.5
1939	Chi A	0	0	—	2	0	0	0	3.1	4	4	0	0	6	1	10.80	44	.308	.526	1-0	.000	-0		-2	-0.1
Total	2	0	4	.000	11	2	1	1	32.2	35	31	2	2	31	19	5.79	84	.267	.415	9-0	.111	-1	36	-6	-0.6
BOZE, MARSHALL Marshall Wayne B 5.23.1971 San Manuel, AZ BR/TR 6-1/214# d4.28																									
1996	Mil A	0	2	.000	25	0	0	1-1	32.1	47	29	5	6	25-4	19	7.79	67	.362	.481	0-0	—	0		-8	-0.4
BRABENDER, GENE Eugene Mathew B 8.16.1941 Madison, WI D 12.27.1996 Madison, WI BR/TR 6-5.5/225# d5.11																									
1966	Bal A	4	3	.571	31	1	0	2	71	57	30	4	1	29-0	62	3.55	94	.229	.310	13-0	.077	-1	159	-1	-0.2
1967	Bal A	6	4	.600	14	14	3-1	0	94	77	38	6	1	23-1	71	3.35	94	.220	.269	28-1	.071	-1	109	-2	-0.3
1968	Bal A	6	7	.462	37	15	3-2	3	124.2	116	52	9	3	48-4	92	3.32	88	.248	.320	35-3	.086	-0	105	-5	-0.7
1969	Sea A	13	14	.481	40	29	7-1	0-1	202.1	193	111	26	13	103-7	139	4.36	83	.254	.350	70-2	.129	-1*	100	-16	-2.2
1970	Mil A	6	15	.286	29	21	2	1-0	128.2	127	94	9	2	79-7	76	6.02	63	.255	.357	41-3	.098	-2	82	-30	-4.5
Total	5	35	43	.449	151	80	15-4	6-1	620.2	570	325	54	20	282-19	440	4.25	80	.245	.330	187-9	.102	-5	99	-54	-7.9
BRACKEN, JACK John James B 4.14.1881 Cleveland, OH D 7.16.1954 Highland Park, MI BR/TR 5-11/175# d8.7																									
1901	Cle A	4	8	.333	12	12	12	0	100	137	94	4	10	31	18	6.21	57	.322	.381	44-0	.227	0	87	-26	-2.4
BRACKENRIDGE, JOHN John Givler B 12.24.1880 Harrisburg, PA D 3.20.1953 Harrisburg, PA BR/TR 6/?# d4.15																									
1904	Phi N	0	1	.000	7	1	0	0	34	37	32	4	4	16	11	5.56	48	.298	.396	13-0	.154	-0	77	-11	-0.5
BRADEY, DON Donald Eugene B 10.4.1934 Charlotte, NC BR/TR 5-9/180# d9.25																									
1964	Hou N	0	2	.000	3	1	0	0	2.1	6	7	0	0	3-1	2	19.29	18	.429	.500	0-0	—	0	26	-5	-0.9
BRADFORD, CHAD Chadwick Lee B 9.14.1974 Jackson, MS BR/TR 6-5/205# d8.1																									
1998	Chi A	2	1	.667	29	0	0	1-2	30.2	27	16	0	0	7-0	11	3.23	141	.229	.272	0-0	—	0		3	0.3
1999	Chi A	0	0	—	3	0	0	0-0	3.2	9	8	1	0	5-0	0	19.64	25	.474	.583	0-0	—	0		-6	-0.2
2000	†Chi A	1	0	1.000	12	0	0	0-0	13.2	13	4	0	0	1-1	9	1.98	253	.255	.269	0-0	—	0		4	0.3
2001	†Oak A	2	1	.667	35	0	0	1-3	36.2	41	12	6	1	6-0	34	2.70	164	.281	.314	0-0	—	0		7	0.6
2002	†Oak A	4	2	.667	75	0	0	2-3	75.1	73	29	2	5	14-5	56	3.11	142	.253	.298	0-0	—	0		11	0.8
2003	†Oak A	7	4	.636	72	0	0	2-3	77	67	28	7	7	30-9	62	3.04	149	.236	.324	0-0	—	0		13	1.8
Total	6	16	8	.667	226	0	0	6-11	237	230	97	16	13	63-15	172	3.23	140	.254	.311	0-0	—	0		32	3.6
BRADFORD, LARRY Larry B 12.21.1949 Chicago, IL D 9.11.1998 Atlanta, GA BR/TL 6-1/200# d9.24																									
1977	Atl N	0	0	—	2	0	0	0-0	2.2	3	1	1	0	0-0	1	3.38	132	.273	.273	0-0	—	0		0	0.0
1979	Atl N	1	0	1.000	21	0	0	2-1	19	11	5	0	1	10-1	11	0.95	428	.172	.286	1-0	.000	-0		5	0.4
1980	Atl N	3	4	.429	56	0	0	4-3	55.1	49	20	3	1	22-8	32	2.44	154	.243	.317	3-0	.000	-0		6	0.8
1981	Atl N	2	0	1.000	25	0	0	1-0	26.2	26	13	1	0	12-0	14	3.71	97	.268	.342	1-0	1.000	0		-1	0.0
Total	4	6	4	.600	104	0	0	7-4	103.2	89	39	5	2	44-9	58	2.52	150	.238	.317	5-0	.200	-0		10	1.2
BRADFORD, BILL William D B 8.28.1921 Choctaw, AR D 8.22.2000 Fairfield, AR BR/TR 6-2/180# d4.24																									
1956	KC A	0	0	—	1	0	0	0	2	2	2	2	0	1-0	0	9.00	48	.250	.333	0-0	—	0		-1	0.0
BRADLEY, FRED Fred Langdon B 7.31.1920 Parsons, KS BR/TR 6-1/180# d5.1																									
1948	Chi A	0	0	—	8	0	0	0	15.2	11	12	2	1	4	2	4.60	93	.190	.254	1-0	.000	-0		-2	-0.1
1949	Chi A	0	0	—	1	1	0	0	2	4	3	0	0	3	0	13.50	31	.444	.583	1-0	.000	-0	300	-2	-0.1
Total	2	0	0	—	9	1	0	0	17.2	15	15	2	1	7	2	5.60	76	.224	.307	2-0	.000	-0	300	-4	-0.2
BRADLEY, FOGHORN George H. B 7.1.1855 Milford, MA D 3.31.1900 Philadelphia, PA BR/TR d8.23 U6																									
1876	Bos N	9	10	.474	22	21	16-1	1	173.1	201	116	1		16	16	2.49	91	.263	.279	82	.232	-1	103	-3	-0.4
BRADLEY, GEORGE George Washington "Grin" B 7.13.1852 Reading, PA D 10.2.1931 Philadelphia, PA BR/TR 5-10.5/175# d5.4 ▲																									
1875	StL NA	33	26	.559	60	60	57-5	0	535.2	540	304	3		17	60	2.13	94	.241	.247	254	.244	7	93	-5	0.3
1876	StL N	45	19	.703	64	64	63-**16**	0	573	470	229	3		38	103	**1.23**	**174**	**.211**	**.224**	265	.249	4	109	63	6.2
1877	Chi N	18	23	.439	50	44	35-2	0	394	452	266	4		39	59	3.31	90	.269	.286	214	.243	0*	100	-13	-1.1
1879	Tro N	13	40	.245	54	54	53-3	0	487	590	361	12		26	133	2.85	88	.275	.284	251	.247	4*	82	-14	-0.4

Year	Tm Lg	W	L	Pct	G	GS	CG-Sho	SV-BS	IP	H	R	HR	HB	BB-IB	SO	ERA	AERA	OAV	OOB	AB-SH	AVG	PB	Sup	APR	PW
1880	Pro N	13	8	.619	28	20	16-4	2	196	158	66	2		6	54	1.38	160	.210	.217	309	.227	1*	106	18	1.9
1881	Cle N	2	4	.333	6	6	5	0	51	70	36	2		3	6	3.88	67	.320	.329	241	.249	0*	69	-6	-0.6
1882	Cle N	6	9	.400	18	16	15	0	147	164	102	5		22	32	3.73	75	.264	.289	115	.183	-3*	84	-14	-1.2
1883	Phi AA	16	7	.696	26	23	22	0	214.1	215	129	7		22	56	3.15	112	.244	.263	312	.234	-0*	114	13	1.0
1884	Cin U	25	15	.625	41	38	36-3	0	342	350	203	7		23	168	2.71	94	.248	.260	226	.190	-12*	98	-7	-1.6
Total	8	138	125	.525	287	265	245-28	2	2404.1	2469	1392	42		179	611	2.50	103	.248	.262	1933	.231	-5	99	40	4.2
BRADLEY, HERB Herbert Theodore B 1.3.1903 Agenda, KS D 10.16.1959 Clay Center, KS BR/TR 6/170# d5.9																									
1927	Bos A	1	1	.500	6	2	2	0	23	16	9	0	2	7	6	3.13	135	.198	.278	7-0	.429	1	69	3	0.3
1928	Bos A	0	3	.000	15	5	1-1	0	47.1	64	41	2	2	16	14	7.23	57	.339	.396	13-2	.154	-1	74	-15	-0.8
1929	Bos A	0	0	—	3	0	0	0	4	7	3	1	0	2	0	6.75	63	.438	.500	1-0	.000	-0		-1	0.0
Total	3	1	4	.200	24	7	3-1	0	74.1	87	53	3	4	25	20	5.93	70	.304	.368	21-2	.238	-0	72	-13	-0.5
BRADLEY, RYAN Ryan J. B 10.26.1975 Covina, CA BR/TR 6-4/220# d8.22																									
1998	NY A	2	1	.667	5	1	0	0-0	12.2	12	9	2	1	9-0	13	5.68	77	.250	.373	0-0	—	0	85	-2	-0.4
BRADLEY, BERT Steven Bert B 12.23.1956 Athens, GA BB/TR 6-1/190# d9.3																									
1983	Oak A	0	0	—	6	0	0	0-0	8.1	14	7	1	0	4-1	3	6.48	60	.400	.450	0-0	—	0		-3	-0.1
BRADLEY, TOM Thomas William B 3.16.1947 Asheville, NC BR/TR 6-3/185# d9.9																									
1969	Cal A	0	1	.000	3	0	0	0-0	2	9	9	1	0	0-0	2	27.00	13	.600	.600	0-0	—	0		-6	-1.1
1970	Cal A	2	5	.286	17	11	1-1	0-0	69.2	71	38	3	1	33-6	53	4.13	87	.270	.350	18-3	.167	0	94	-5	-0.4
1971	Chi A	15	15	.500	45	39	7-6	2-2	285.2	273	111	16	2	74-5	206	2.96	121	.248	.295	96-7	.156	-1*	87	20	1.8
1972	Chi A	15	14	.517	40	40	11-2	0-0	260	225	94	19	2	65-4	209	2.98	105	.231	.280	91-9	.132	-2*	109	6	0.3
1973	SF N	13	12	.520	35	34	6-1	0-0	224	212	109	26	3	69-10	136	3.90	98	.246	.302	77-6	.195	1	113	-1	-0.1
1974	SF N	8	11	.421	30	21	2	0-0	134.1	152	90	15	1	52-4	72	5.16	74	.282	.342	40-6	.075	-2	105	-19	-2.6
1975	SF N	2	3	.400	13	6	0	0-0	42	57	33	6	1	18-4	13	6.21	61	.326	.390	10-1	.000	-1	108	-11	-1.2
Total	7	55	61	.474	183	151	27-10	2-2	1017.2	999	484	86	10	311-33	691	3.72	96	.254	.309	332-32	.145	-5	103	-16	-3.3
BRADSHAW, JOE Joe Siah B 8.17.1897 RoEllen, TN D 1.30.1985 Tavares, FL BR/TR 6-2.5/200# d5.9																									
1929	Bro N	0	0	—	2	0	0	0	4	3	3	0	2	4	1	4.50	103	.231	.474	0-0	—	0		0	0.0
BRADY, NEAL Cornelius Joseph B 3.4.1897 Covington, KY D 6.19.1947 Fort Mitchell, KY BR/TR 6-0.5/197# d9.25 Mil 1918																									
1915	NY A	0	0	—	2	1	0	0	8.2	9	3	0	0	7	6	3.12	94	.281	.410	4-0	.000	-1	99	0	-0.1
1917	NY A	1	0	1.000	2	1	0	0	9	6	2	0	0	5	4	2.00	134	.188	.297	2-0	.500	0	80	1	0.2
1925	Cin N	1	3	.250	20	3	2	1	63.2	73	44	4	4	20	12	4.66	88	.289	.350	25-0	.240	1	103	-5	-0.2
Total	3	2	3	.400	24	5	2	1	81.1	88	49	4	4	32	22	4.20	91	.278	.351	31-0	.226	1	94	-4	-0.1
BRADY, JIM James Joseph "Diamond Jim" B 3.2.1936 Jersey City, NJ BL/TL 6-2/185# d5.12																									
1956	Det A	0	0	—	6	0	0	0	6.1	15	21	3	0	11-1	3	28.42	14	.484	.619	0-0	—	0		-17	-0.7
BRADY, KING James Ward B 5.28.1881 Elmer, NJ D 8.21.1947 Albany, NY BR/TR 6/190# d9.21																									
1905	Phi N	1	1	.500	2	2	2	0	13	19	7	0	0	2	3	3.46	84	.333	.356	5-0	.200	-0	86	-1	-0.1
1906	Pit N	1	1	.500	3	2	1	0	23	30	7	0	0	4	14	2.35	114	.313	.340	10-0	.100	-1	123	1	0.0
1907	Pit N	0	0	—	1	0	0	0	2	2	1	0	0	1	0	0.00	—	.286	.375	0-0	—	0		0	0.0
1908	Bos A	1	0	1.000	1	1	1-1	0	9	8	0	0	0	0	3	0.00	—	.242	.242	2-0	.000	-0	111	2	0.3
1912	Bos N	0	0	—	1	0	0	0	2.2	5	6	0	0	3	0	20.25	18	.313	.421	1-0	.000	-0		-4	-0.2
Total	5	3	2	.600	8	5	4-1	0	49.2	64	21	0	0	10	20	3.08	89	.306	.338	18-0	.111	-1	105	-2	0.0
BRADY, BILL William Aloysius "King" B 8.18.1889 New York, NY TR 6-2/?# d7.9																									
1912	Bos N	0	0	—	1	0	0	0	1	2	0	0	0	0	0	0.00	—	.500	.500	0-0	—	0		0	0.0
BRAGGINS, DICK Richard Realf B 12.25.1879 Mercer, PA D 8.16.1963 Lake Wales, FL BR/TR 5-11/170# d5.16																									
1901	Cle A	1	2	.333	4	3	2	0	32	44	28	1	1	15	1	4.78	74	.324	.395	13-1	.154	-1	82	-5	-0.5
BRAINARD, ASA Asa "Count" B 1841 Albany, NY D 12.29.1888 Denver, CO TR 5-8.5/150# d5.5																									
1871	Oly NA	12	15	.444	30	30	30	0	264	361	292	4		37	13	4.50	93	.288	.308	134	.224	-6	89	-10	-0.9
1872	Oly NA	2	7	.222	9	9	9	0	79	148	140	0		5	1	6.38	56	.333	.341	43	.372	4	64	-25	-1.4
	Man NA	0	2	.000	2	2	1	0	8	13	17	1		0	0	5.63	64	.260	.260	25	.200	-0*	69	-2	-0.3
	Year	2	9	.182	11	11	10	0	87	161	24	1		5	1	6.31	57	.326	.333	68	.309	3	65	-26	-1.7
1873	Bal NA	5	7	.417	14	14	12	0	108.2	182	139	0		9	3	4.14	79	.326	.336	69	.261	0*	126	-11	-0.8
1874	Bal NA	5	22	.185	30	27	25	0	240	405	329	1		27	8	3.71	60	.327	.341	196	.240	-1*	73	-37	-3.0
Total	4 NA	24	53	.312	85	82	77	0	699.2	1109	917	6		78	25	4.40	75	.313	.327	467	.248	-4	88	-85	-6.4
BRAITHWOOD, AL Alfred B 2.15.1892 Braceville, IL D 11.24.1960 Rowlesburg, WV BR/TL 6-1.5/145# d9.1																									
1915	Pit F	0	0	—	2	0	0	0	3	0	0	0	0	0	2	0.00	—	.000	.000	0-0	—	0		1	0.0
BRAME, ERV Ervin Beckham B 10.12.1901 Big Rock, TN D 11.22.1949 Hopkinsville, KY BL/TR 6-2/190# d4.14																									
1928	Pit N	7	4	.636	24	11	6	0	95.2	110	62	5	1	44	22	5.08	80	.291	.366	49-1	.265	4*	138	-10	-0.6
1929	Pit N	16	11	.593	37	28	19-1	0	229.2	250	123	17	0	71	68	4.55	105	.278	.331	116-2	.310	12*	106	11	2.0
1930	Pit N	17	8	.680	32	28	**22**	1	235.2	291	153	21	5	56	55	4.70	106	.305	.346	116-5	.353	11*	113	4	1.1
1931	Pit N	9	13	.409	26	21	15-2	0	179.2	211	102	14	0	45	33	4.21	91	.295	.336	95-0	.274	6*	103	-7	-0.3
1932	Pit N	3	1	.750	23	3	0	0	51	84	52	6	0	16	10	7.41	51	.365	.407	20-0	.250	1*	154	-21	-1.4
Total	5	52	37	.584	142	91	62-3	1	791.2	946	492	63	6	232	188	4.76	94	.298	.347	396-8	.306	33	113	-23	0.8
BRANCA, RALPH Ralph Theodore Joseph "Hawk" B 1.6.1926 Mt.Vernon, NY BR/TR 6-3/220# d6.12																									
1944	Bro N	0	2	.000	21	1	0	1	44.2	46	36	2	5	32	16	7.05	50	.274	.405	6-0	.000	-1	94	-15	-0.9
1945	Bro N	5	6	.455	16	15	7	1	109.2	73	44	4	0	79	69	3.04	124	.189	.327	40-2	.100	-3	81	10	0.7
1946	Bro N	3	1	.750	24	10	2-2	3	67.1	62	34	4	0	41	42	3.88	87	.246	.352	18-0	.111	0	177	-4	-0.3
1947	†Bro N☆	21	12	.636	43	**36**	15-4	1	280	251	100	22	6	98	148	2.67	155	.240	.309	97-9	.124	-3	94	43	4.2
1948	Bro N★	14	9	.609	36	28	11-1	1	215.2	189	93	24	4	80	122	3.51	114	.232	.304	74-3	.203	1	101	13	1.2
1949	†Bro N☆	13	5	.722	34	27	9-2	1	186.2	181	100	21	2	91	109	4.39	93	.253	.339	62-8	.081	-2	147	-6	-0.9
1950	Bro N	7	9	.438	43	15	5	7	142	152	80	24	0	55	100	4.69	87	.271	.336	34-7	.118	1	132	-9	-0.9
1951	Bro N	13	12	.520	42	27	13-3	3	204	180	81	19	3	85	118	3.26	120	.237	.316	63-6	.175	-1	87	15	1.5
1952	Bro N	4	2	.667	16	7	2	0	61	52	29	8	4	21	26	3.84	95	.232	.309	19-1	.158	-0	136	-2	-0.2
1953	Bro N	0	0	—	7	0	0	0	11	15	12	4	2	5	5	9.82	43	.341	.431	0-0	—	0		-6	-0.3
	Det A	4	7	.364	17	14	7	1	102	98	55	7	2	31	50	4.15	98	.253	.311	34-1	.118	-1	108	-2	-0.4
1954	Det A	3	3	.500	17	5	0	0	45.1	63	33	10	2	30	15	5.76	64	.330	.424	13-0	.308	2	115	-11	-1.1
	NY A	1	0	1.000	5	3	0	0	12.2	9	5	0	1	13	7	2.84	121	.209	.390	4-0	.500	1	77	1	0.1
	Year	4	3	.571	22	8	0	0	58	72	8	10	3	43	22	5.12	71	.308	.417	17-0	.353	2	100	-10	-1.0
1956	Bro N	0	0	—	1	0	0	0	2	1	0	0	0	2-0	2	0.00	—	.143	.333	0-0	—	0		1	0.1
Total	12	88	68	.564	322	188	71-12	19	1484	1372	702	149	31	663-0	829	3.79	104	.245	.328	464-37	.142	-6	111	28	2.8
BRANCH, HARVEY Harvey Alfred B 2.8.1939 Memphis, TN BR/TL 6/175# d9.18																									
1962	StL N	0	1	.000	1	1	0	0	5	5	3	1	0	5-0	2	5.40	79	.263	.417	1-0	.000	-0	62	0	-0.1
BRANCH, NORM Norman Downs "Red" B 3.22.1915 Spokane, WA D 11.21.1971 Navasota, TX BR/TR 6-3/200# d5.5 Mil 1942-45																									
1941	NY A	5	1	.833	27	0	0	2	47	37	16	2	0	26	28	2.87	137	.224	.330	10-0	.000	-1		6	0.7
1942	NY A	0	1	.000	10	0	0	2	15.2	18	15	3	0	16	13	6.32	54	.290	.436	3-0	.333	0		-6	-0.5
Total	2	5	2	.714	37	0	0	4	62.2	55	31	5	0	42	41	3.73	102	.242	.361	13-0	.077	-1		0	0.2
BRANCH, ROY Roy B 7.12.1953 St.Louis, MO BR/TR 6/175# d9.11																									
1979	Sea A	0	1	.000	2	2	0	0-0	11.1	12	11	2	0	7-1	6	7.94	55	.273	.365	0-0	—	0	83	-4	-0.3
BRANDENBURG, MARK Mark Clay B 7.14.1970 Houston, TX BR/TR 6/180# d7.20																									
1995	Tex A	0	1	.000	11	0	0	0-0	27.1	36	18	5	1	7-1	21	5.93	82	.316	.358	0-0	—	0		-3	-0.1
1996	Tex A	1	3	.250	26	0	0	0-1	47.2	48	22	3	2	25-1	37	3.21	163	.262	.354	0-0	—	0		9	0.5

Year	Tm Lg	W	L	Pct	G	GS	CG-Sho	SV-BS	IP	H	R	HR	HB	BB-IB	SO	ERA	AERA	OAV	OOB	AB-SH	AVG	PB	Sup	APR	PW
	Bos A	4	2	.667	29	0	0	0-1	28.1	28	13	5	1	8-1	29	3.81	133	.250	.301	0-0	—	0		4	0.8
	Year	5	5	.500	55	0	0	0-2	76	76	39	8	3	33-2	66	3.43	151	.258	.334	0-0	—	0		13	1.3
1997	Bos A	0	2	.000	31	0	0	0-0	41	49	25	3	2	16-3	34	5.49	85	.299	.364	0-0	—	0		-3	-0.1
Total	3	5	8	.385	97	0	0	0-2	144.1	161	78	16	6	56-6	121	4.49	110	.281	.347	0-0	—	0		7	1.1
BRANDOM, CHICK Chester Milton B 3.31.1887 Coldwater, KS D 10.7.1958 Santa Ana, CA BR/TR 5-8/161# d9.3																									
1908	Pit N	1	0	1.000	3	1	1	1	17	13	5	0	1	4	8	0.53	435	.228	.290	7-0	.143	-0	92	2	0.2
1909	Pit N	1	0	1.000	13	2	0	2	40.2	33	12	0	1	10	21	1.11	246	.239	.295	10-0	.100	-1	77	5	0.3
1915	New F	1	1	.500	16	1	1	0	50.1	55	36	0	1	15	15	3.40	75	.293	.348	10-0	.200	1	137	-9	-0.4
Total	3	3	1	.750	32	4	2	3	108	101	53	0	3	29	44	2.08	124	.264	.320	27-0	.148	-0	95	-2	0.1
BRANDON, BUCKY Darrell G B 7.8.1940 Nacogdoches, TX BR/TR 6-2/200# d4.19																									
1966	Bos A	8	8	.500	40	17	5-2	2	157.2	129	70	13	4	70-3	101	3.31	115	.222	.309	44-6	.182	1*	98	6	0.8
1967	Bos A	5	11	.313	39	19	2	3	157.2	147	86	21	7	59-7	96	4.17	84	.245	.318	43-5	.186	1	96	-13	-1.2
1968	Bos A	0	0	—	8	0	0	0	12.2	19	11	1	1	9-0	10	6.39	49	.333	.433	1-0	.000	-0		-5	-0.3
1969	Sea A	0	1	.000	8	1	0	0-0	15	15	15	4	2	16-1	10	8.40	43	.250	.423	0-0	—	0	170	-8	-0.5
	Min A	0	0	—	3	0	0	0-0	3.1	5	3	1	0	3-2	1	2.70	135	.357	.471	1-0	.000	0		0	0.0
	Year	0	1	.000	11	1	0	0-0	18.1	20	25	5	2	19-3	11	7.36	49	.270	.432	1-0	.000	0	170	-8	-0.5
1971	Phi N	6	6	.500	52	0	0	4-4	83	81	42	5	0	47-9	44	3.90	90	.264	.357	13-2	.154	-0		-4	-0.7
1972	Phi N	7	7	.500	42	6	0	2-2	104.1	106	49	9	6	46-8	67	3.45	104	.268	.352	15-4	.067	-1	98	0	-0.3
1973	Phi N	2	4	.333	36	0	0	2-0	56.1	54	35	5	3	25-7	25	5.43	70	.261	.343	5-0	.200	0		-9	-0.9
Total	7	28	37	.431	228	43	7-2	13-6	590	556	311	59	23	275-37	354	4.04	90	.250	.337	122-17	.164	1	99	-33	-3.1
BRANDT, ED Edward Arthur "Big Ed" B 2.17.1905 Spokane, WA D 11.1.1944 Spokane, WA BL/TL 6-1/190# d4.26																									
1928	Bos N	9	21	.300	38	32	12-1	0	225.1	234	141	22	7	109	84	5.07	77	.273	.359	70-3	.243	5*	80	-25	-2.2
1929	Bos N	8	13	.381	26	21	13	0	167.2	196	111	12	5	83	50	5.53	85	.302	.385	64-3	.234	2*	82	-13	-1.0
1930	Bos N	4	11	.267	41	13	4-1	1	147.1	168	88	15	0	59	65	5.01	99	.291	.356	50-1	.240	1	68	1	0.2
1931	Bos N	18	11	.621	33	29	23-3	2	250	228	94	11	4	77	112	2.92	130	.244	.304	82-7	.256	5*	90	24	3.4
1932	Bos N	16	16	.500	35	31	19-2	1	254	271	122	11	5	57	79	3.97	95	.275	.318	92-5	.207	-0	87	-2	-0.1
1933	Bos N	18	14	.563	41	32	23-4	4	287.2	256	85	10	3	77	104	2.60	118	.245	.298	97-4	.309	9*	93	21	3.5
1934	Bos N	16	14	.533	40	29	20-3	5	255	249	111	13	4	83	106	3.53	108	.254	.315	96-2	.240	4*	114	11	1.5
1935	Bos N	5	19	.208	29	25	12	0	174.2	224	110	12	1	66	61	5.00	76	.319	.378	62-0	.210	-0*	81	-23	-2.6
1936	Bro N	11	13	.458	38	29	12-1	2	234	246	105	14	4	65	104	3.50	118	.268	.319	84-2	.190	0*	93	18	1.6
1937	Pit N	11	10	.524	33	25	7-2	2	176.1	177	73	11	2	67	74	3.11	124	.263	.332	59-1	.169	1	96	15	1.8
1938	Pit N	5	4	.556	24	13	5-1	0	96.1	93	44	3	0	35	38	3.46	110	.250	.314	37-2	.297	2	91	4	0.5
Total	11	121	146	.453	378	279	150-18	17	2268.1	2342	1084	134	35	778	877	3.86	101	.269	.332	793-30	.236	30	89	31	6.6
BRANDT, BILL William George B 3.21.1915 Aurora, IN D 5.16.1968 Fort Wayne, IN BR/TR 5-8.5/170# d9.20 Mil 1944-45																									
1941	Pit N	0	1	.000	2	1	0	0	7	5	3	0	0	3	0	3.86	94	.200	.286	1-0	.000	-0	71	0	0.0
1942	Pit N	1	1	.500	3	3	1	0	16.1	23	10	1	0	5	4	4.96	68	.343	.389	7-0	.143	-0	108	-3	-0.3
1943	Pit N	4	1	.800	29	3	0	0	57.1	57	25	3	1	19	17	3.14	111	.248	.308	7-1	.143	-0	65	2	0.1
Total	3	5	3	.625	34	7	1	0	80.2	85	38	4	1	27	21	3.57	97	.264	.323	15-1	.133	-1	84	-1	-0.2
BRANTLEY, CLIFF Clifford B 4.12.1968 Staten Island, NY BR/TR 6-1/190# d9.3																									
1991	Phi N	2	2	.500	6	5	0	0-0	31.2	26	12	0	2	19-0	25	3.41	108	.228	.341	8-2	.000	-1	103	1	0.1
1992	Phi N	2	6	.250	28	9	0	0-0	76.1	71	45	6	4	58-4	32	4.60	76	.251	.382	14-7	.214	1	138	-10	-0.9
Total	2	4	8	.333	34	14	0	0-0	108	97	57	6	6	77-4	57	4.25	83	.244	.370	22-9	.136	0	126	-9	-0.8
BRANTLEY, JEFF Jeffrey Hoke B 9.5.1963 Florence, AL BR/TR 5-11/190# d8.5																									
1988	SF N	0	1	.000	9	1	0	1-0	20.2	22	13	2	1	6-1	11	5.66	58	.275	.333	2-0	.500	0	27	-5	-0.2
1989	†SF N	7	1	.875	59	1	0	0-1	97.1	101	50	10	2	37-8	69	4.07	83	.271	.337	12-3	.083	-1	52	-8	-0.7
1990	SF N★	5	3	.625	55	0	0	19-5	86.2	77	18	3	3	33-6	61	1.56	234	.240	.315	7-4	.286	1		20	2.7
1991	SF N	5	2	.714	67	0	0	15-4	95.1	78	27	8	5	52-10	81	2.45	146	.225	.332	3-1	.000	-0		13	1.2
1992	SF N	7	7	.500	56	4	0	7-2	91.2	67	32	8	3	45-5	86	2.95	112	.207	.307	9-0	.111	0	103	4	0.7
1993	SF N	5	6	.455	53	12	0	0-3	113.2	112	60	19	7	46-2	76	4.28	92	.259	.336	28-1	.107	-1	115	-5	-0.7
1994	Cin N	6	6	.500	50	0	0	15-6	65.1	46	20	6	0	28-5	63	2.48	167	.202	.288	3-0	.000	-0		12	2.5
1995	†Cin N	3	2	.600	56	0	0	28-4	70.1	53	22	11	1	20-3	62	2.82	146	.206	.263	3-0	.000	-0		11	1.4
1996	Cin N	1	2	.333	66	0	0	**44-5**	71	54	21	7	0	28-6	76	2.41	176	.215	.289	1-1	.000	-0		14	2.1
1997	Cin N	1	1	.500	13	0	0	1-2	11.2	9	5	2	2	7-1	16	3.86	111	.205	.340	0-0	—	0		1	0.1
1998	StL N	0	5	.000	48	0	0	14-8	50.2	40	26	12	1	18-3	48	4.44	95	.220	.289	0-1	—	0		-1	-0.1
1999	Phi N	1	2	.333	10	0	0	5-1	8.2	5	6	0	0	8-0	11	5.19	91	.161	.325	0-0	—	0		-1	-0.1
2000	Phi N	2	7	.222	55	0	0	23-5	55.1	64	36	12	2	29-0	57	5.86	80	.288	.373	0-0	—	0		-6	-1.1
2001	Tex A	0	1	.000	18	0	0	0-0	21	26	12	5	0	9-1	11	5.14	91	.310	.372	0-0	—	0		-1	-0.1
Total	14	43	46	.483	615	18	0	172-46	859.1	754	348	105	27	366-51	728	3.39	114	.237	.319	68-11	.118	-2	101	48	7.7
BRASHEAR, KITTY Norman C. B 8.27.1877 Mansfield, OH D 12.22.1934 Los Angeles, CA BR/TR d6.25 b-Roy																									
1899	Lou N	1	0	1.000	3	0	0	0	8	8	7	0	1	2	5	4.50	86	.258	.324	2-0	.500	0		-1	-0.1
BRAUN, JOHN John Paul B 12.26.1939 Madison, WI BR/TR 6-5/218# d10.2																									
1964	Mil N	0	0	—	1	0	0	0	2	2	0	0	0	1-0	1	0.00	—	.286	.375	0-0	—	0		1	0.0
BRAXTON, GARLAND Edgar Garland B 6.10.1900 Snow Camp, NC D 2.25.1966 Norfolk, VA BB/TL 5-11/152# d5.27																									
1921	Bos N	1	3	.250	17	2	0	0	37.1	44	26	0	2	17	16	4.82	76	.310	.391	7-0	.000	-1	0	-6	-0.7
1922	Bos N	1	2	.333	25	5	2	0	66.2	75	37	3	4	24	15	3.38	118	.286	.355	16-3	.063	-2	102	2	-0.1
1925	NY A	1	1	.500	3	2	0	0	19.1	26	14	1	1	5	11	6.52	65	.338	.386	6-0	.333	0	69	-4	-0.3
1926	NY A	5	1	.833	37	1	0	2	67.1	71	28	1	0	19	30	2.67	144	.275	.325	20-0	.300	1	153	8	0.7
1927	Was A	10	9	.526	**58**	2	0	**13**	155.1	144	62	5	2	33	96	2.95	138	.246	.289	39-3	.231	0	41	**19**	2.3
1928	Was A	13	11	.542	38	24	15-2	6	218.1	177	78	7	5	44	94	**2.51**	**160**	**.222**	**.267**	72-5	.125	-4	88	34	3.2
1929	Was A	12	10	.545	37	20	9	4	182	219	116	6	2	51	59	4.85	88	.299	.346	54-5	.148	-1	97	-12	-1.4
1930	Was A	3	2	.600	15	0	0	5	27.1	22	11	3	0	9	7	3.29	140	.222	.287	5-1	.000	-1		4	0.7
	Chi A	4	10	.286	19	10	2	1	90.2	127	80	9	1	33	44	6.45	72	.333	.388	23-1	.087	-2	69	-18	-2.4
	Year	7	12	.368	34	10	2	6	118	149	84	12	1	42	51	5.72	81	.310	.367	28-2	.071	-2	69	-15	-1.7
1931	Chi A	0	3	.000	17	3	0	1	47.1	71	43	1	2	23	28	6.85	62	.338	.409	11-0	.091	-1	99	-14	-0.8
	StL A	0	0	—	11	1	0	0	18	27	24	2	1	10	7	10.50	44	.370	.452	3-0	.667	1	109	-11	-0.4
	Year	0	3	.000	28	4	0	1	65.1	98	30	3	3	33	35	7.85	56	.346	.420	14-0	.214	0	102	-25	-1.2
1933	StL A	0	1	.000	5	1	0	0	8.1	11	10	0	1	8	5	9.72	48	.289	.426	1-0	.000	-0	146	-4	-0.4
Total	10	50	53	.485	282	71	28-2	32	938	1014	529	38	21	276	412	4.13	101	.278	.332	257-18	.156	-8	88	-2	0.4
BRAZELTON, DEWON Dewon B 6.16.1980 Tullahoma, TN BR/TR 6-4/215# d9.13																									
2002	TB A	0	1	.000	2	2	0	0-0	13	12	7	3	2	6-0	5	4.85	92	.279	.392	0-0	—	0	52	0	0.0
2003	TB A	1	6	.143	10	10	0	0-0	48.1	57	49	9	3	23-1	24	6.89	66	.292	.372	1-0	.000	-0	87	-17	-1.9
Total	2	1	7	.125	12	12	0	0-0	61.1	69	56	12	5	29-1	29	6.46	70	.290	.376	1-0	.000	-0	82	-17	-1.9
BRAZLE, AL Alpha Eugene "Cotton" B 10.19.1913 Loyal, OK D 10.24.1973 Grand Junction, CO BL/TL 6-2/185# d7.25 Mil 1944-45																									
1943	†StL N	8	2	.800	13	9	8-1	0	88	74	18	0	0	29	26	1.53	219	.231	.295	32-0	.281	2	106	18	2.4
1946	†StL N	11	10	.524	37	15	6-2	0	153.1	152	69	1	2	55	58	3.29	105	.261	.327	52-2	.212	-0	119	1	0.1
1947	StL N	14	8	.636	44	19	7	4	168	186	65	7	2	48	85	2.84	146	.284	.335	64-3	.219	1	113	22	3.0
1948	StL N	10	6	.625	42	23	6-2	1	156.1	171	77	8	0	50	55	3.80	108	.281	.335	55-0	.145	-2*	96	3	0.2
1949	StL N	14	8	.636	39	25	9-1	0	206.1	208	85	18	6	61	75	3.18	131	.263	.321	82-1	.134	-4	119	21	1.6
1950	StL N	11	9	.550	46	12	3	6	164.2	188	81	12	4	80	47	4.10	105	.296	.378	61-0	.213	-1*	91	5	0.5
1951	StL N	6	5	.545	56	8	5	7	154.1	139	61	13	5	60	66	3.09	128	.245	.322	46-0	.109	-3	81	14	0.6
1952	StL N	12	5	.706	46	6	3-1	**16**	109.1	75	38	6	1	42	55	2.72	137	.198	.280	32-1	.125	-1	88	12	2.0
1953	StL N	6	7	.462	60	0	0	**18**	92	101	47	8	2	43	57	4.21	101	.280	.360	15-2	.333	1		1	0.3
1954	StL N	5	4	.556	58	0	0	8	84.1	93	48	10	3	24	30	4.16	99	.288	.339	14-0	.000	-2		-2	-0.4
Total	10	97	64	.602	441	117	47-7	60	1376.2	1387	589	83	25	492	554	3.31	120	.266	.332	453-9	.177	-9	105	95	10.3

Year	Tm Lg	W	L	Pct	G	GS	CG-Sho	SV-BS	IP	H	R	HR	HB	BB-IB	SO	ERA	AERA	OAV	OOB	AB-SH	AVG	PB	Sup	APR	PW
BREA, LESLI Lesli Guillermo B 10.12.1973 San Pedro De Macoris, D.R. BR/TR 5-10/170# d8.13																									
2000	Bal A	0	1	.000	6	1	0	0-0	9	12	11	1	1	10-0	5	11.00	43	.324	.469	0-0	—	0	99	-6	-0.6
2001	Bal A	0	0	—	2	0	0	0-0	2	6	4	2	0	3-0	0	18.00	24	.545	.643	0-0	—	0		-3	-0.1
Total	2	0	1	.000	8	1	0	0-0	11	18	15	3	1	13-0	5	12.27	38	.375	.508	0-0	—	0	99	-9	-0.7
BRECHEEN, HARRY Harry David "Harry The Cat" B 10.14.1914 Broken Bow, OK BL/TL 5-10/160# d4.22 C14																									
1940	StL N	0	0	—	3	0	0	0	3.1	2	1	0	0	2	4	0.00	—	.167	.286	0-0	—	0		1	0.1
1943	†StL N	9	6	.600	29	13	8-1	4	135.1	98	41	4	3	39	68	2.26	149	.206	.270	42-4	.190	1	97	16	2.0
1944	†StL N	16	5	.762	30	22	13-3	0	189.1	174	67	8	3	46	88	2.85	124	.242	.290	68-4	.162	1*	125	16	1.7
1945	StL N	15	4	**.789**	24	18	13-3	2	157.1	136	48	5	5	44	63	2.52	149	.238	.298	57-2	.123	-1	97	23	2.5
1946	†StL N	15	15	.500	36	30	14-**5**	3	231.1	212	73	8	4	67	117	2.49	139	.244	.301	83-1	.133	-3*	78	25	3.1
1947	StL N★	16	11	.593	29	28	18-1	1	223.1	220	92	20	3	66	89	3.30	125	.260	.316	83-4	.241	5	109	21	2.9
1948	StL N☆	20	7	**.741**	33	30	21-**7**	1	233.1	193	62	6	2	49	**149**	**2.24**	**183**	.222	**.265**	82-2	.146	-1	98	**47**	5.3
1949	StL N	14	11	.560	32	31	14-2	1	214.2	207	96	18	7	65	88	3.35	124	.252	.312	77-3	.273	5	94	17	2.3
1950	StL N	8	11	.421	27	23	12-2	1	163.1	151	77	18	3	45	80	3.80	113	.244	.298	58-0	.241	3	95	9	1.2
1951	StL N	8	4	.667	24	16	5	2	138.2	134	54	11	1	54	57	3.25	122	.256	.327	55-1	.218	2	97	12	1.1
1952	StL N	7	5	.583	25	13	4-1	2	100.1	82	39	12	3	28	54	3.32	112	.223	.283	29-1	.207	1	109	6	1.0
1953	StL A	5	13	.278	26	16	3	1	117.1	122	51	7	3	31	44	3.07	137	.269	.320	39-2	.179	-1*	41	12	1.7
Total	12	133	92	.591	318	240	125-25	18	1907.2	1731	701	117	37	536	901	2.92	133	.242	.298	673-24	.192	11	95	205	24.9
BRECKINRIDGE, BILL William Robertson B 10.16.1907 Tulsa, OK D 8.23.1958 Tulsa, OK BR/TR 5-11/175# d6.30																									
1929	Phi A	0	0	—	3	1	0	0	10	10	10	0	0	16	2	8.10	52	.270	.491	4-0	.000	-1	199	-4	-0.3
BREINING, FRED Fred Lawrence B 11.15.1955 San Francisco, CA BR/TR 6-4/185# d9.4																									
1980	SF N	0	0	—	5	0	0	0-0	6.2	8	4	0	1	4-1	3	5.40	66	.333	.448	0-0	—	0		-1	-0.1
1981	SF N	5	2	.714	45	1	0	1-0	77.2	66	28	4	2	38-8	37	2.55	135	.243	.334	11-1	.000	-1	103	6	0.4
1982	SF N	11	6	.647	54	9	2	0-1	143.1	146	61	6	1	52-10	98	3.08	117	.269	.333	29-5	.207	1	109	6	0.9
1983	SF N	11	12	.478	32	32	6	0-0	202.2	202	97	15	5	60-11	117	3.82	93	.259	.312	67-5	.149	1	108	-5	-0.5
1984	Mon N	0	0	—	4	0	0	0-0	6.2	4	1	0	0	5-0	5	1.35	254	.190	.346	1-0	.000	-0		2	0.1
Total	5	27	20	.574	140	42	8	1-1	437	426	191	25	9	159-30	260	3.34	106	.260	.325	108-11	.148	1	109	8	0.8
BREITENSTEIN, ALONZO Alonzo B 11.9.1857 Utica, NY D 6.19.1932 Utica, NY d7.7																									
1883	Phi N	0	1	.000	1	1	0	0	5	8	9	0		2	0	9.00	34	.320	.370	2	.000	-0	69	-3	-0.5
BREITENSTEIN, TED Theodore P. "Theo" B 6.1.1869 St.Louis, MO D 5.3.1935 St.Louis, MO BL/TL 5-9/167# d4.28																									
1891	StL AA	2	0	1.000	6	1	1-1	1	28.2	15	14	2	0	14	13	2.20	191	.150	.254	12	.000	-2	118	5	0.2
1892	StL N	9	19	.321	39	32	28-1	0	282.1	280	192	8	6	148	126	4.69	68	.248	.339	131	.122	-3*	88	-40	-3.3
1893	StL N	19	24	.442	48	42	38-1	1	382.2	359	197	8	8	156	102	**3.18**	**149**	.241	.316	160	.181	-5*	78	68	5.6
1894	StL N	27	23	.540	**56**	**50**	**46**-1	0	**447.1**	497	320	21	11	191	140	4.79	113	.278	.352	182-9	.220	-1*	82	35	2.8
1895	StL N	19	30	.388	55	**51**	**47**-1	1	438.2	468	299	16	14	182	131	4.37	111	.269	.343	221-2	.190	-7*	92	22	1.3
1896	StL N	18	26	.409	44	43	37-1	0	339.2	376	236	12	5	138	114	4.48	97	.278	.347	162-7	.259	3*	81	-6	-0.1
1897	Cin N	23	12	.657	40	39	32-2	0	320.1	345	172	3	9	91	98	3.62	126	.273	.326	124-4	.266	3*	96	31	2.9
1898	Cin N	20	14	.588	39	37	32-3	0	315.2	313	170	2	11	123	68	3.42	112	.257	.330	121-5	.215	1*	98	12	1.3
1899	Cin N	13	9	.591	26	24	21	0	210.2	219	111	2	9	71	59	3.59	109	.268	.333	105-4	.352	9*	98	9	1.6
1900	Cin N	10	10	.500	24	20	18-1	0	192.1	205	111	4	14	79	39	3.65	101	.272	.352	126-1	.190	-0*	106	-1	0.0
1901	StL N	0	3	.000	3	3	1	0	15	24	26	1	0	14	3	6.60	48	.358	.469	6-0	.333	0	149	-10	-1.4
Total	11	160	170	.485	380	342	301-12	3	2973.1	3101	1848	79	87	1207	893	4.03	109	.265	.338	1350-32	.216	-4	89	125	10.9
BRENNAN, AD Addison Foster B 7.18.1881 LaHarpe, KS D 1.7.1962 Kansas City, MO BL/TL 5-11/170# d5.19																									
1910	Phi N	2	0	1.000	19	5	2	0	73.1	72	36	2	3	28	28	2.33	134	.264	.339	25-0	.280	1*	162	2	0.2
1911	Phi N	2	1	.667	5	3	1	0	22.2	22	12	0	1	12	12	3.57	96	.259	.357	9-1	.222	-0	124	0	0.0
1912	Phi N	11	9	.550	27	19	13-1	2	174	185	88	4	3	49	78	3.57	102	.274	.326	59-2	.254	4	106	4	0.9
1913	Phi N	14	12	.538	40	24	12-1	1	207	204	76	5	6	46	94	2.39	139	.268	.314	67-3	.164	-2	97	18	1.9
1914	Chi F	5	5	.500	16	11	5-1	0	85.2	84	44	7	2	21	31	3.57	74	.256	.305	32-2	.250	1	96	-9	-0.9
1915	Chi F	3	9	.250	19	13	7-2	0	106	117	55	4	7	30	40	3.74	67	.287	.346	27-3	.185	0*	86	-15	-1.6
1918	Was A	0	0	—	2	1	0	0	5.1	7	4	0	1	5	0	5.06	54	.241	.371	1-0	.000	-0	110	-1	-0.1
	Cle A	0	0	—	1	0	0	0	3	3	1	0	0	3	0	3.00	100	.333	.500	0-0	—	0		0	0.0
	Year	0	0	—	3	1	0	0	8.1	10	9	0	1	8	0	4.32	65	.263	.404	1-0	.000	-0	107	-1	-0.1
Total	7	37	36	.507	129	76	40-5	3	677	694	316	22	23	194	283	3.11	102	.270	.327	220-11	.218	4	103	-1	0.4
BRENNAN, DON James Donald B 12.2.1903 Augusta, ME D 4.26.1953 Boston, MA BR/TR 6/210# d4.16																									
1933	NY A	5	1	.833	18	10	3	3	85	92	56	4	0	47	46	4.98	78	.275	.365	27-3	.259	2	193	-12	-0.6
1934	Cin N	4	3	.571	28	7	2	2	78	89	51	3	1	35	31	3.81	107	.290	.364	22-1	.227	0	109	-2	-0.1
1935	Cin N	5	5	.500	38	5	2-1	5	114.1	101	43	4	4	44	48	3.15	126	.242	.320	30-0	.100	-1	115	13	0.9
1936	Cin N	5	2	.714	41	4	0	9	94.1	117	60	2	1	35	40	4.39	87	.305	.364	25-2	.080	-3	105	-9	-1.0
1937	Cin N	1	1	.500	10	0	0	0	16	25	14	1	0	10	6	6.75	55	.347	.427	5-0	.000	-1		-6	-0.7
	†NY N	1	0	1.000	6	0	0	0	9.1	12	8	0	1	9	1	6.75	58	.316	.458	1-0	.000	0		-3	-0.3
	Year	2	1	.667	16	0	0	0	25.1	37	27	1	1	19	7	6.75	56	.336	.438	6-0	.000	-1		-8	-1.0
Total	5	21	12	.636	141	26	7-1	19	397	436	232	14	7	180	172	4.19	94	.281	.358	110-6	.155	-2	142	-19	-1.8
BRENNAN, TOM Thomas Martin B 10.30.1952 Chicago, IL BR/TR 6-1/180# d9.5																									
1981	Cle A	2	2	.500	7	6	1	0-0	48.1	49	20	5	0	14-1	15	3.17	115	.259	.310	0-0	—	0	91	2	0.2
1982	Cle A	4	2	.667	30	4	0	2-2	92.2	112	51	9	2	10-1	46	4.27	96	.300	.317	0-0	—	0	67	-3	-0.2
1983	Cle A	2	2	.500	11	5	1-1	0-0	39.2	45	22	3	1	8-1	21	3.86	110	.288	.323	0-0	—	0	98	0	0.0
1984	Chi A	0	1	.000	4	1	0	0-0	6.2	8	5	1	0	3-0	3	4.05	103	.308	.379	0-0	—	0	22	-1	-0.1
1985	LA N	1	3	.250	12	4	0	0-0	31.2	41	26	2	0	11-4	17	7.39	47	.333	.374	8-1	.125	-0	70	-12	-1.3
Total	5	9	10	.474	64	20	2-1	2-2	219	255	124	20	3	46-7	102	4.40	89	.294	.327	8-1	.125	-0	79	-14	-1.4
BRENNAN, WILLIAM William Raymond B 1.15.1963 Tampa, FL BR/TR 6-3/200# d7.19																									
1988	LA N	0	1	.000	4	2	0	0-0	9.1	13	7	0	0	6-1	7	6.75	49	.342	.432	2-0	.000	-0	106	-3	-0.3
1993	Chi N	2	1	.667	8	1	0	0-0	15	16	8	2	1	8-1	11	4.20	95	.291	.385	1-1	.000	0	0	0	-0.1
Total	2	2	2	.500	12	3	0	0-0	24.1	29	15	2	1	14-2	18	5.18	72	.312	.404	3-1	.000	0	64	-3	-0.4
BRENNEMAN, JIM James Leroy B 2.13.1941 San Diego, CA D 3.10.1994 Pearl, MS BR/TR 6-2/180# d7.9																									
1965	NY A	0	0	—	3	0	0	0	2	5	5	1	0	3-0	2	18.00	19	.455	.571	0-0	—	0		-4	-0.2
BRENNER, BERT Delbert Henry "Dutch" B 7.18.1887 Minneapolis, MN D 4.11.1971 St.Louis Park, MN BR/TR 6/175# d9.21																									
1912	Cle A	1	0	1.000	2	1	1	0	13	14	8	0	0	4	3	2.77	123	.286	.340	5-0	.000	-1	108	0	-0.1
BRENTON, LYNN Lynn Davis "Buck" or "Herb" B 10.7.1890 Peoria, IL D 10.14.1968 Los Angeles, CA BR/TR 5-10/165# d8.10																									
1913	Cle A	0	0	—	1	0	0	0	2	4	2	0	0	0	2	9.00	34	.400	.400	0-0	—	0		-1	-0.1
1915	Cle A	2	3	.400	11	5	1-1	0	51	60	31	1	2	20	18	3.35	91	.308	.378	17-0	.118	-1	62	-3	-0.5
1920	Cin N	2	1	.667	5	1	1	1	18.1	17	14	0	0	4	13	4.91	62	.236	.276	8-0	.250	0	181	-4	-0.6
1921	Cin N	1	8	.111	17	8	2	1	60	80	35	0	1	17	19	4.05	88	.342	.389	15-3	.133	-0	60	-4	-0.4
Total	4	5	12	.294	34	14	4-1	2	131.1	161	82	1	3	41	52	3.97	83	.315	.369	40-3	.150	-1	69	-12	-1.6
BRESNAHAN, ROGER Roger Philip "The Duke Of Tralee" B 6.11.1879 Toledo, OH D 12.4.1944 Toledo, OH BR/TR 5-9/200# d8.27 M5 C6 HF1945 ▲																									
1897	Was N	4	0	1.000	6	5	3-1	0	41	52	21	1	3	10	12	3.95	110	.306	.355	16-0	.375	1	112	4	0.4
1901	Bal A	0	1	.000	2	1	0	0	6	10	8	0	0	4	3	6.00	64	.370	.452	295-4	.268	0*	105	-2	-0.2
1910	StL N	0	0	—	1	0	0	0	3.1	6	1	0	0	1	0	0.00	—	.400	.438	234-8	.278	0*		1	0.1
Total	3	4	1	.800	9	6	3-1	0	50.1	68	30	1	3	15	15	3.93	107	.321	.374	545-12	.275	2	113	3	0.3
BRESSLER, RUBE Raymond Bloom B 10.23.1894 Coder, PA D 11.7.1966 Cincinnati, OH BR/TL 6/187# d4.24 Mil 1918 ▲																									
1914	Phi A	10	4	.714	29	10	8-1	2	147.2	112	37	1	4	56	96	1.77	148	.220	.302	51-2	.216	4	165	14	1.7
1915	Phi A	4	17	.190	32	20	7-1	0	178.1	183	133	3	7	118	69	5.20	56	.283	.399	55-3	.145	1*	87	-42	-4.2
1916	Phi A	0	2	.000	4	2	0	0	15	16	11	0	2	14	8	6.60	43	.296	.457	5-1	.200	1	79	-5	-0.6

Year	Tm Lg	W	L	Pct	G	GS	CG-Sho	SV-BS	IP	H	R	HR	HB	BB-IB	SO	ERA	AERA	OAV	OOB	AB-SH	AVG	PB	Sup	APR	PW
1917	Cin N	0	0	—	2	1	0	0	9	15	11	0	0	5	2	6.00	44	.429	.500	5-0	.200	-0*	259	-4	-0.2
1918	Cin N	8	5	.615	17	13	10	0	128	124	48	3	1	39	37	2.46	108	.261	.318	62-1	.274	4*	129	2	0.9
1919	Cin N	2	4	.333	13	4	1	0	41.2	37	19	1	0	8	13	3.46	80	.248	.287	165-7	.206	2*	65	-3	-0.3
1920	Cin N	2	0	1.000	10	2	1-1	0	20.1	24	8	0	0	2	4	1.77	172	.300	.317	30-1	.267	0*	142	2	0.2
Total	7	26	32	.448	107	52	27-3	2	540	511	267	8	14	242	229	3.40	81	.262	.348	373-15	.214	12	115	-36	-2.5
BRETT, HERB Herbert James "Duke" B 5.23.1900 Lawrenceville, VA D 11.25.1974 St.Petersburg, FL BR/TR 6/175# d8.8																									
1924	Chi N	0	0	—	1	1	0	0	5.1	6	4	0	0	7	1	5.06	77	.300	.481	2-0	.000	-0	217	-1	-0.1
1925	Chi N	1	1	.500	10	1	0	0	17.1	12	7	0	1	3	6	3.63	119	.194	.242	1-0	.000	-0	20	2	0.2
Total	2	1	1	.500	11	2	0	0	22.2	18	11	0	1	10	7	3.97	106	.220	.312	3-0	.000	-0	110	1	0.1
BRETT, KEN Kenneth Alven B 9.18.1948 Brooklyn, NY D 11.18.2003 Spokane, WA BL/TL 5-11/195# d9.27 b-George																									
1967	†Bos A	0	0	—	1	0	0	0	2	3	1	0	0	0-0	2	4.50	77	.375	.375	0-0	—	0		0	0.0
1969	Bos A	2	3	.400	8	8	0	0-0	39.1	41	24	6	3	22-1	23	5.26	72	.275	.377	10-2	.300	2	102	-5	-0.4
1970	Bos A	8	9	.471	41	14	1	2-0	139.1	118	71	17	3	79-6	155	4.07	97	.223	.327	41-1	.317	6	101	-1	0.6
1971	Bos A	0	3	.000	29	2	0	1-0	59	57	38	7	1	35-6	57	5.34	69	.253	.356	10-1	.200	-0	36	-10	-0.6
1972	Mil A	7	12	.368	26	22	2-1	0-0	133	121	76	13	1	49-9	74	4.53	67	.242	.310	44-1	.227	2*	94	-23	-3.0
1973	Phi N	13	9	.591	31	25	10-1	0-0	211.2	206	91	19	0	74-12	111	3.44	110	.259	.320	80-0	.250	8*	120	8	1.9
1974	†Pit N★	13	9	.591	27	27	10-3	0-0	191	192	81	9	2	52-9	96	3.30	105	.257	.306	87-3	.310	11*	143	3	1.5
1975	†Pit N	9	5	.643	23	16	4-1	0-0	118	110	47	10	2	43-5	47	3.36	106	.250	.318	52-1	.231	4*	102	5	1.0
1976	NY A	0	0	—	2	0	0	1-0	2.1	2	0	0	0	0-0	1	0.00	—	.222	.222	0-0	—	0		1	0.1
	Chi A	10	12	.455	27	26	16-1	1-0	200.2	171	82	5	3	76-3	91	3.32	107	.234	.305	12-0	.083	-1*	85	5	0.5
	Year	10	12	.455	29	26	16-1	2-0	203	173	85	5	3	76-3	92	3.28	109	.233	.304	12-0	.083	-1	85	7	0.6
1977	Chi A	6	4	.600	13	13	2	0-0	82.2	101	47	10	1	15-0	39	5.01	82	.305	.334	0-0	—	0	150	-6	-0.6
	Cal A	7	10	.412	21	21	5	0-0	142	157	73	15	3	38-0	41	4.25	92	.287	.334	0-0	—	0*	88	-3	-0.2
	Year	13	14	.481	34	34	7	0-0	224.2	258	77	25	4	53-0	80	4.53	88	.294	.334	0-0	—	0	113	-10	-0.8
1978	Cal A	3	5	.375	31	10	1-1	1-1	100	100	60	12	1	42-5	43	4.95	73	.262	.335	0-0	—	0	94	-15	-1.0
1979	Min A	0	0	—	9	0	0	0-1	12.2	16	7	1	0	6-0	3	4.97	88	.320	.393	0-0	—	0		-1	0.0
	LA N	4	3	.571	30	0	0	2-1	47	52	20	1	1	12-2	13	3.45	106	.277	.322	11-0	.273	1		1	0.4
1980	KC A	0	0	—	8	0	0	1-0	13.1	8	0	0	1	5-0	4	0.00	—	.174	.269	0-0	—	0		6	0.3
1981	KC A	1	1	.500	22	0	0	2-0	32.1	35	16	2	1	14-4	7	4.18	87	.282	.355	0-0	—	0		-2	-0.1
Total	14	83	85	.494	349	184	51-8	11-3	1526.1	1490	734	127	23	562-62	807	3.93	93	.257	.323	347-9	.262	33	107	-37	0.4
BREUER, MARV Marvin Howard "Baby Face" B 4.29.1914 Rolla, MO D 1.17.1991 Rolla, MO BR/TR 6-2/185# d5.4																									
1939	NY A	0	0	—	1	0	0	0	1	2	1	0	0	1	0	9.00	48	.667	.750	0-0	—	0		0	0.0
1940	NY A	8	9	.471	27	22	10	0	164	175	89	20	0	61	71	4.55	89	.267	.329	54-6	.037	-5	123	-8	-1.2
1941	†NY A	9	7	.563	26	18	7-1	2	141	131	73	10	2	49	77	4.09	96	.243	.308	46-4	.087	-3	99	-2	-0.6
1942	†NY A	8	9	.471	27	19	6	1	164.1	157	67	11	1	37	72	3.07	112	.252	.295	54-5	.056	-3	89	6	0.1
1943	NY A	0	1	.000	5	1	0	0	14	22	16	0	0	6	6	8.36	39	.349	.406	3-0	.333	0	79	-8	-0.5
Total	5	25	26	.490	86	60	23-1	3	484.1	487	246	41	3	154	226	4.03	94	.258	.315	157-15	.064	-11	105	-12	-2.2
BREWER, JIM James Thomas B 11.17.1937 Merced, CA D 11.16.1987 Tyler, TX BL/TL 6-2/195# d7.17 C3																									
1960	Chi N	0	3	.000	5	4	0	0	21.2	25	14	2	1	6-2	7	5.82	65	.272	.323	6-0	.167	0*	47	-4	-0.5
1961	Chi N	1	7	.125	36	11	0	0	86.2	116	65	17	1	21-2	57	5.82	72	.321	.358	22-1	.182	0	114	-15	-1.3
1962	Chi N	0	1	.000	6	1	0	0	5.2	10	6	2	0	3-0	1	9.53	44	.435	.500	0-0	—	0	169	-3	-0.4
1963	Chi N	3	2	.600	29	1	0	0	49.2	59	32	10	0	15-0	35	4.89	72	.294	.339	6-1	.000	0	49	-7	-0.8
1964	LA N	4	3	.571	34	5	1-1	1	93	79	33	5	0	25-5	63	3.00	108	.232	.282	22-0	.273	2	130	4	0.4
1965	†LA N	3	2	.600	19	2	0	2	49.1	33	13	1	0	28-4	31	1.82	179	.196	.311	10-0	.000	-1*	80	8	0.8
1966	†LA N	0	2	.000	13	0	0	2	22	17	9	0	0	11-0	8	3.68	90	.221	.315	0-0	—	0		0	0.0
1967	LA N	5	4	.556	30	11	0	1	100.2	78	32	8	1	31-7	74	2.68	116	.218	.281	22-1	.045	-1	85	6	0.4
1968	LA N	8	3	.727	54	0	0	14	76.1	59	22	5	0	33-13	75	2.48	112	.219	.303	9-1	.222	0		4	0.8
1969	LA N	7	6	.538	59	0	0	20-10	88.1	71	30	5	4	41-6	92	2.55	131	.221	.316	11-0	.091	0		7	1.5
1970	LA N	7	6	.538	58	0	0	24-5	89	66	36	10	0	33-9	91	3.13	122	.207	.280	12-1	.083	-0		6	1.2
1971	LA N	6	5	.545	55	0	0	22-5	81.1	55	17	4	0	24-5	66	1.88	172	.194	.254	9-0	.333	1		14	3.0
1972	LA N	8	7	.533	51	0	0	17-7	78.1	41	16	6	2	25-11	69	1.26	264	.157	.233	1-0	.000	0		18	4.0
1973	LA N★	6	8	.429	56	0	0	20-8	71.2	58	26	8	0	25-9	56	3.01	114	.229	.293	5-2	.400	1		4	1.0
1974	†LA N	4	4	.500	24	0	0	0-2	39.1	29	14	5	0	10-1	26	2.52	136	.207	.258	2-0	.000	-0		4	0.6
1975	LA N	3	1	.750	21	0	0	2-2	33	44	20	2	1	12-2	21	5.18	66	.333	.380	3-0	.000	-0		-6	-0.8
	Cal A	1	0	1.000	21	0	0	5-1	34.2	38	9	2	0	11-1	22	1.82	196	.279	.325	0-0	—	0		7	0.4
1976	Cal A	3	1	.750	13	0	0	2-3	20	20	7	0	0	6-0	16	2.70	123	.256	.306	0-0	—	0		1	0.3
Total	17	69	65	.515	584	35	1-1	132-43	1040.2	898	401	92	10	360-77	810	3.07	111	.236	.300	140-7	.150	1	104	48	10.6
BREWER, JACK John Herndon "Buddy" B 7.21.1919 Los Angeles, CA BR/TR 6-2/170# d7.15																									
1944	NY N	1	4	.200	14	7	2	0	55	66	40	8	3	16	21	5.56	66	.288	.343	19-0	.211	0	85	-11	-0.9
1945	NY N	8	6	.571	28	21	8	0	159.2	162	77	14	3	58	49	3.83	102	.260	.326	56-7	.179	-1	97	1	-0.1
1946	NY N	0	0	—	1	0	0	0	2	3	3	0	0	2	3	13.50	25	.333	.455	0-0	—	0		-2	-0.1
Total	3	9	10	.474	43	28	10	0	216.2	231	120	22	6	76	73	4.36	88	.268	.332	75-7	.187	-1	94	-12	-1.1
BREWER, TOM Thomas Austin B 9.3.1931 Wadesboro, NC BR/TR 6-1/175# d4.18																									
1954	Bos A	10	9	.526	33	23	7	0	162.2	152	90	15	7	95	69	4.65	88	.249	.355	60-2	.267	3*	123	-6	-0.5
1955	Bos A	11	10	.524	31	28	9-2	0	192.2	198	101	21	8	87-3	91	4.20	102	.263	.344	73-3	.151	-2*	121	2	0.2
1956	Bos A★	19	9	.679	32	32	15-4	0	244.1	200	103	14	5	112-6	127	3.50	132	.220	.307	94-1	.298	4*	98	30	3.9
1957	Bos A	16	13	.552	32	32	15-2	0	238.1	225	113	24	7	93-9	128	3.85	103	.250	.324	94-4	.202	-1*	119	4	0.6
1958	Bos A	12	12	.500	33	32	10-1	0	227.1	227	122	21	8	93-2	124	3.72	108	.259	.333	82-3	.195	-0*	111	1	0.3
1959	Bos A	10	12	.455	36	32	11-3	2	215.1	219	96	14	2	88-5	121	3.76	108	.265	.336	72-7	.111	-4*	103	8	0.6
1960	Bos A	10	15	.400	34	29	8-1	1	186.2	220	115	13	6	72-5	60	4.82	84	.301	.364	62-3	.194	0*	92	-17	-1.9
1961	Bos A	3	2	.600	10	9	0	0	42	37	21	4	0	29-0	13	3.43	122	.242	.357	14-0	.286	1*	85	2	0.4
Total	8	91	82	.526	241	217	75-13	3	1509.1	1478	761	126	43	669-30	733	4.00	104	.257	.337	551-23	.207	1	108	24	3.6
BREWER, BILLY William Robert B 4.15.1968 Fort Worth, TX BL/TL 6-1/175# d4.8																									
1993	KC A	2	2	.500	46	0	0	0-2	39	31	16	6	0	20-4	28	3.46	133	.230	.327	0-0	—	0		5	0.4
1994	KC A	4	1	.800	50	0	0	3-4	38.2	28	11	4	2	16-1	25	2.56	196	.207	.297	0-0	—	0		11	1.3
1995	KC A	2	4	.333	48	0	0	0-4	45.1	54	28	9	2	20-1	31	5.56	86	.290	.365	0-0	—	0		-3	-0.3
1996	NY A	1	0	1.000	4	0	0	0-0	5.2	7	6	0	0	8-0	8	9.53	52	.292	.469	0-0	—	0		-3	-0.4
1997	Oak A	0	0	—	3	0	0	0-0	2	4	3	1	0	2-0	1	13.50	34	.444	.500	0-0	—	0		-2	-0.1
	Phi N	1	2	.333	25	0	0	0-2	22	15	8	2	0	11-0	16	3.27	130	.188	.280	1-0	.000	-0		3	0.3
1998	Phi N	0	1	.000	2	0	0	0-0	0.1	3	4	0	0	2-0	0	108.00	4	.750	.833	0-0	—	0		-4	-0.6
1999	Phi N	1	1	.500	25	0	0	2-0	25.2	30	20	4	0	14-1	28	7.01	67	.294	.376	0-0	—	0		-6	-0.5
Total	7	11	11	.500	203	0	0	5-12	178.2	172	96	26	4	93-7	137	4.79	99	.255	.345	1-0	.000	-0		1	0.1
BREWINGTON, JAMIE Jamie Chancellor B 9.28.1971 Greenville, NC BR/TR 6-4/180# d7.24																									
1995	SF N	6	4	.600	13	13	0	0-0	75.1	68	38	8	4	45-6	45	4.54	90	.245	.355	23-4	.217	0*	102	-2	-0.2
2000	Cle A	3	0	1.000	26	0	0	0-0	45.1	56	28	3	2	19-0	34	5.36	93	.311	.379	1-0	.000	0		-2	-0.1
Total	2	9	4	.692	39	13	0	0-0	120.2	124	66	11	6	64-6	79	4.85	91	.271	.364	24-4	.208	1	102	-4	-0.3
BRICE, ALAN Alan Healey B 10.1.1937 New York, NY BR/TR 6-5/215# d9.22																									
1961	Chi A	0	1	.000	3	0	0	0	3.1	4	2	0	0	3-0	3	0.00	—	.308	.438	0-0	—	0		1	0.1
BRICKNER, RALPH Ralph Harold "Brick" B 5.2.1925 Cincinnati, OH D 5.9.1994 Port Jefferson, NY BR/TR 6-3.5/215# d5.4																									
1952	Bos A	3	1	.750	14	1	0	1	33	32	8	1	0	11	9	2.18	181	.264	.326	8-0	.250	0	44	6	0.8
BRIDGES, MARSHALL Marshall "Sheriff" B 6.2.1931 Jackson, MS D 9.3.1990 Jackson, MS BB/TL 6-1/180# d6.17																									
1959	StL N	6	3	.667	27	4	1	1	76	67	38	10	0	37-8	76	4.26	99	.240	.324	23-2	.217	2	95	1	0.1
1960	StL N	2	2	.500	20	1	0	1	31.1	33	15	2	1	16-1	27	3.45	119	.266	.350	6-0	.000	-0	65	1	0.1

Year	Tm Lg	W	L	Pct	G	GS	CG-Sho	SV-BS	IP	H	R	HR	HB	BB-IB	SO	ERA	AERA	OAV	OOB	AB-SH	AVG	PB	Sup	APR	PW
	Cin N	4	0	1.000	14	0	0	2	25.1	14	3	1	0	7-0	26	1.07	359	.161	.223	4-1	.250	0		8	1.4
	Year	6	2	.750	34	1	0	3	56.2	47	21	3	1	23-1	53	2.38	167	.223	.300	10-1	.100	-0	67	9	1.5
1961	Cin N	0	1	.000	13	0	0	0	20.2	26	19	4	1	11-0	17	7.84	52	.317	.400	2-0	.000	-0		-8	-0.4
1962	†NY A	8	4	.667	52	0	0	18	71.2	49	30	4	0	48-6	66	3.14	119	.194	.321	14-1	.000	-2		4	0.8
1963	NY A	2	0	1.000	23	0	0	1	33	27	18	2	1	30-2	35	3.82	92	.237	.392	0-0	—	0		-2	-0.1
1964	Was A	0	3	.000	17	0	0	2	30	37	22	3	0	17-2	16	5.70	65	.303	.383	3-0	.000	-0		-7	-0.7
1965	Was A	1	2	.333	40	0	0	0	57.1	62	26	3	0	25-4	39	2.67	130	.268	.340	7-1	.143	0		2	0.2
Total	7	23	15	.605	206	5	1	25	345.1	315	171	29	3	191-23	302	3.75	102	.244	.339	59-5	.119	-0	97	-1	1.4
BRIDGES, TOMMY Thomas Jefferson Davis B 12.28.1906 Gordonsville, TN D 4.19.1968 Nashville, TN BR/TR 5-10.5/155# d8.13 Mil 1944-45 C2																									
1930	Det A	3	2	.600	8	5	2	0	37.2	28	18	4	0	23	17	4.06	118	.215	.333	10-2	.300	1	104	4	0.5
1931	Det A	8	16	.333	35	23	8-2	0	173	182	120	13	0	108	105	4.99	92	.263	.363	54-5	.148	-2	67	-10	-1.4
1932	Det A	14	12	.538	34	26	10-**4**	1	201	174	95	14	1	119	108	3.36	140	.233	.339	67-5	.164	-1	93	27	2.9
1933	Det A	14	12	.538	33	28	17-2	2	233	192	102	8	6	110	120	3.09	140	**.226**	.319	78-7	.205	2	71	29	3.2
1934	†Det A☆	22	11	.667	36	**35**	23-3	1	275	249	117	16	3	104	151	3.67	120	.241	.312	98-8	.122	-4	117	28	2.4
1935	†Det A☆	21	10	.677	36	34	23-4	1	274.1	277	129	22	3	113	**163**	3.51	119	.259	.332	109-4	.239	3	126	19	2.1
1936	Det A✥	**23**	11	.676	39	**38**	26-5	0	294.2	289	141	21	5	115	**175**	3.60	137	.255	.326	118-6	.212	0	115	43	4.2
1937	Det A★	15	12	.556	34	31	18-3	0	245.1	267	129	15	3	91	138	4.07	115	.274	.338	96-3	.240	2	108	15	1.6
1938	Det A	13	9	.591	25	20	13	1	151	171	83	14	2	58	101	4.59	109	.287	.353	54-4	.130	-1	113	8	0.7
1939	Det A★	17	7	.708	29	26	16-2	2	198	186	87	11	6	61	129	3.50	140	.243	.304	71-8	.197	0	114	30	3.2
1940	†Det A☆	12	9	.571	29	28	12-2	0	197.2	171	89	11	0	88	133	3.37	141	.229	.311	68-4	.176	-2	104	27	2.3
1941	Det A	9	12	.429	25	22	10-1	0	147.2	128	66	10	1	70	90	3.41	133	.233	.320	47-4	.085	-3	65	17	1.9
1942	Det A	9	7	.563	23	22	11-2	1	174	164	66	6	4	61	97	2.74	144	.246	.313	63-1	.095	-2	84	21	1.6
1943	Det A	12	7	.632	25	22	11-3	0	191.2	159	57	9	0	61	124	2.39	147	.226	.287	64-4	.219	2	102	24	2.6
1945	†Det A	1	0	1.000	4	1	0	0	11	14	6	2	0	2	6	3.27	107	.311	.340	3-0	.000	-0	145	0	0.0
1946	Det A	1	1	.500	9	1	0	1	21.1	24	16	5	1	8	17	5.91	62	.279	.347	3-0	.000	0	117	-5	-0.5
Total	16	194	138	.584	424	362	200-33	10	2826.1	2675	1321	181	35	1192	1674	3.57	126	.248	.325	1003-65	.180	-5	101	277	27.3
BRIGGS, BUTTONS Herbert Theodore B 7.8.1875 Poughkeepsie, NY D 2.18.1911 Cleveland, OH BR/TR 6-1/180# d4.23																									
1896	Chi N	12	8	.600	26	21	19	1	194	202	129	6	15	108	84	4.31	105	.266	.368	78-0	.128	-6	97	5	-0.3
1897	Chi N	4	17	.190	22	22	21	0	186.2	246	166	6	9	85	60	5.26	85	.315	.388	81-2	.160	-6	90	-18	-2.0
1898	Chi N	1	3	.250	4	4	3	0	30	38	22	0	1	10	14	5.70	63	.306	.363	14-0	.429	2	119	-4	-0.3
1904	Chi N	19	11	.633	34	30	28-3	3	277	252	102	3	8	77	112	2.05	130	.246	.304	94-2	.170	-0	95	16	1.4
1905	Chi N	8	8	.500	20	20	13-5	0	168	141	58	1	6	52	68	2.14	139	.237	.304	57-3	.053	-4	91	15	0.7
Total	5	44	47	.484	106	97	84-8	4	855.2	879	477	16	39	332	338	3.41	104	.268	.342	324-7	.148	-15	95	14	-0.5
BRIGGS, JOHN Jonathan Tift B 1.24.1934 Natoma, CA BR/TR 5-10/175# d4.17																									
1956	Chi N	0	0	—	3	0	0	0	5.1	5	1	1	3	4-1	1	1.69	223	.238	.429	0-0	—	0		1	0.1
1957	Chi N	0	1	.000	3	0	0	0	4.1	7	6	2	0	3-0	1	12.46	31	.368	.435	0-0	—	0		-4	-0.7
1958	Chi N	5	5	.500	20	17	3-1	0	95.2	99	52	12	1	45-1	46	4.52	87	.270	.351	35-1	.257	2	107	-5	-0.4
1959	Cle A	0	1	.000	4	1	0	0	12.2	12	5	1	0	3-0	5	2.13	173	.245	.283	2-0	.000	-0	96	2	0.1
1960	Cle A	4	2	.667	21	2	0	1	36.1	32	20	4	1	15-0	19	4.46	84	.250	.329	8-1	.125	-0	165	-3	-0.5
	KC A	0	2	.000	8	1	0	0	11.1	19	17	3	0	12-0	8	12.71	31	.380	.500	3-0	.000	-0	66	-10	-1.5
	Year	4	4	.500	29	3	0	1	47.2	51	20	7	1	27-0	27	6.42	59	.287	.380	11-1	.091	-1	132	-13	-2.0
Total	5	9	11	.450	59	21	3-1	1	165.2	174	101	23	5	82-2	80	5.00	77	.275	.360	48-2	.208	1	110	-19	-2.9
BRILES, NELSON Nelson Kelley B 8.5.1943 Dorris, CA BR/TR 5-11/200# d4.19																									
1965	StL N	3	3	.500	37	2	0	4	82.1	79	33	4	6	26-6	52	3.50	110	.258	.327	15-0	.133	-0	216	4	0.2
1966	StL N	4	15	.211	49	17	0	6	154	162	65	14	7	54-11	100	3.21	112	.279	.345	38-1	.079	-2	91	5	0.5
1967	†StL N	14	5	.737	49	14	4-2	6	155.1	139	45	8	5	40-8	94	2.43	135	.236	.289	40-5	.150	0	109	16	2.1
1968	†StL N	19	11	.633	33	33	13-4	0	243.2	251	90	18	7	55-12	141	2.81	103	.266	.310	80-9	.138	1	128	1	0.1
1969	StL N	15	13	.536	36	33	10-3	0-0	227.2	218	104	17	2	63-7	126	3.52	102	.251	.301	76-5	.105	-1	103	0	-0.2
1970	StL N	6	7	.462	30	19	1-1	0-0	106.2	129	84	14	2	36-7	59	6.24	66	.297	.349	39-3	.179	1	155	-25	-2.6
1971	†Pit N	8	4	.667	37	14	4-2	1-1	136	131	51	12	3	35-12	76	3.04	111	.250	.301	39-3	.256	4	151	5	0.9
1972	†Pit N	14	11	.560	28	27	9-2	0-0	195.2	185	83	14	1	43-8	120	3.08	108	.249	.288	70-5	.157	-0	119	3	0.3
1973	Pit N	14	13	.519	33	33	7-1	0-0	218.2	201	87	19	1	51-3	94	2.84	124	.244	.287	72-6	.194	3	105	14	2.0
1974	KC A	5	7	.417	18	17	3	0-0	103	118	48	9	2	21-1	41	4.02	95	.293	.329	0-0	—	0	85	0	0.0
1975	KC A	6	6	.500	24	16	3	2-0	112	127	60	19	5	25-1	73	4.26	91	.285	.329	0-0	—	0	94	-4	-0.4
1976	Tex A	11	9	.550	32	31	7-1	1-0	210	224	87	17	2	47-0	98	3.26	110	.273	.312	0-0	—	0	103	8	0.6
1977	Tex A	6	4	.600	28	15	2-1	1-0	108.1	114	58	13	6	30-1	57	4.24	97	.275	.332	0-0	—	0	108	-2	-0.2
	Bal A	0	0	—	2	0	0	1-0	4	5	3	2	0	0-0	2	6.75	56	.294	.294	0-0	—	0		-1	-0.1
	Year	6	4	.600	30	15	2-1	2-0	112.1	119	66	15	6	30-1	59	4.33	94	.276	.330	0-0	—	0	109	-3	-0.3
1978	Bal A	4	4	.500	16	8	1	0-0	54.1	58	31	6	2	21-2	30	4.64	76	.279	.345	0-0	—	0	125	-7	-1.0
Total	14	129	112	.535	452	279	64-17	22-1	2111.2	2141	929	186	51	547-79	1163	3.44	103	.264	.312	469-37	.154	5	114	17	2.2
BRILL, FRANK Francis Hasbrouck (b: Francis Hasbrouck Briell) B 3.30.1864 Astoria, NY D 11.19.1944 Flushing, NY BR/TR 5-8/155# d6.23																									
1884	Det N	2	10	.167	12	12	12-1	0	103	148	98	7		26	18	5.50	53	.312	.348	44	.136	-3*	79	-24	-2.3
BRILLHEART, JIM James Benson B 9.28.1903 Dublin, VA D 9.2.1972 Radford, VA BR/TL 5-11/170# d4.17																									
1922	Was A	4	6	.400	31	10	3	1	119.2	120	58	3	8	72	47	3.61	107	.275	.388	36-1	.083	-4	114	4	-0.2
1923	Was A	0	1	.000	12	0	0	0	18	27	15	1	1	12	8	7.00	54	.360	.455	2-0	.000	-0		-6	-0.3
1927	Chi N	4	2	.667	32	12	4	0	128.2	140	67	4	4	38	36	4.13	94	.286	.343	44-6	.023	-5	123	-3	-0.7
1931	Bos A	0	0	—	11	1	0	0	19.2	27	16	2	0	15	7	5.49	78	.325	.429	4-0	.500	2	79	-4	0.0
Total	4	8	9	.471	86	23	7	1	286	314	156	10	13	137	98	4.19	93	.290	.376	86-7	.070	-8	117	-9	-1.2
BRINK, BRAD Bradford Albert B 1.20.1965 Roseville, CA BR/TR 6-2/195# d5.17																									
1992	Phi N	0	4	.000	8	7	0	0-0	41.1	53	27	2	1	13-2	16	4.14	85	.308	.360	12-1	.083	-0	63	-6	-0.6
1993	Phi N	0	0	—	2	0	0	0-0	6	3	2	1	0	3-0	8	3.00	132	.143	.250	1-0	.000	-0		1	0.0
1994	SF N	0	0	—	4	0	0	0-0	8.1	4	1	1	0	4-1	3	1.08	371	.143	.250	1-0	.000	-0		3	0.1
Total	3	0	4	.000	14	7	0	0-0	55.2	60	30	4	1	20-3	27	3.56	102	.271	.335	14-1	.071	-1	63	-2	-0.5
BRISCOE, JOHN John Eric B 9.22.1967 LaGrange, IL BR/TR 6-3/185# d4.18																									
1991	Oak A	0	0	—	11	0	0	0-0	14	12	11	3	0	10-0	9	7.07	54	.235	.355	0-0	—	0		-5	-0.3
1992	Oak A	0	1	.000	2	2	0	0-0	7	12	6	0	0	9-0	4	6.43	58	.400	.538	0-0	—	0	110	-2	-0.3
1993	Oak A	1	0	1.000	17	0	0	0-0	24.2	26	25	2	0	26-3	24	8.03	51	.277	.426	0-0	—	0		-12	-0.6
1994	Oak A	4	2	.667	37	0	0	1-1	49.1	31	24	7	1	39-2	45	4.01	110	.185	.340	0-0	—	0*		3	0.2
1995	Oak A	0	1	.000	16	0	0	0-0	18.1	25	17	4	2	21-1	19	8.35	54	.347	.495	0-0	—	0		-8	-0.3
1996	Oak A	0	1	.000	17	0	0	1-1	26.1	18	11	2	0	24-2	14	3.76	131	.205	.368	0-0	—	0*		4	0.2
Total	6	5	5	.500	100	2	0	2-2	139.2	124	94	18	3	129-8	115	5.67	77	.247	.398	0-0	—	0	110	-20	-1.1
BRISSIE, LOU Leland Victor B 6.5.1924 Anderson, SC BL/TL 6-4/215# d9.28																									
1947	Phi A	0	1	.000	1	1	0	0	7	9	5	1	0	5	4	6.43	59	.310	.412	2-0	.000	-0	70	-2	-0.2
1948	Phi A	14	10	.583	39	25	11	5	194	202	100	6	2	95	127	4.13	104	.269	.352	76-5	.237	0	101	2	0.2
1949	Phi A★	16	11	.593	34	29	18	3	229.1	220	113	20	5	118	118	4.28	96	.251	.344	90-6	.267	3	107	0	0.1
1950	Phi A	7	19	.269	46	31	15-2	8	246	237	127	22	4	117	101	4.02	113	.253	.338	87-1	.172	-3	81	12	0.9
1951	Phi A	0	2	.000	2	2	0	0	13.1	20	10	0	0	8	3	6.75	63	.357	.438	5-1	.200	-0	83	-3	-0.4
	Cle A	4	3	.571	54	4	1	9	112.1	90	44	5	3	61	50	3.20	118	.223	.329	23-1	.261	0	135	9	0.6
	Year	4	5	.444	56	6	1	9	125.2	110	50	5	3	69	53	3.58	107	.239	.342	28-2	.250	0	120	5	0.2
1952	Cle A	3	2	.600	42	1	0	2	82.2	68	41	5	0	34	28	3.48	96	.221	.299	12-3	.250	1	52	-3	-0.1
1953	Cle A	0	0	—	16	0	0	2	13	21	11	2	0	13	5	7.62	49	.389	.507	0-0	—	0		-5	-0.3
Total	7	44	48	.478	234	93	45-2	29	897.2	867	451	61	14	451	436	4.07	102	.254	.343	295-17	.227	1	98	10	0.8
BRITT, JIM James Edward B 2.25.1856 Brooklyn, NY D 2.28.1923 San Francisco, CA d5.2																									
1872	Atl NA	9	28	.243	37	37	37	0	336	568	473	6		21	13	4.53	100	.326	.334	155	.265	-7	54	0	-0.3

Year	Tm Lg	W	L	Pct	G	GS	CG-Sho	SV-BS	IP	H	R	HR	HB	BB-IB	SO	ERA	AERA	OAV	OOB	AB-SH	AVG	PB	Sup	APR	PW
1873	Atl NA	17	36	.321	54	**54**	**51**-1	0	480.2	696	519	6		41	16	4.08	74	.301	.313	240	.196	-3	79	-52	-3.7
Total	2 NA	26	64	.289	91	91	88-1	0	816.2	1264	992	12		62	29	4.26	85	.312	.322	395	.223	-10	67	-52	-4.0
BRITTIN, JACK John Albert B 3.4.1924 Athens, IL D 1.5.1994 Springfield, IL BR/TR 5-11/175# d9.15																									
1950	Phi N	0	0	—	3	0	0	0	4	2	2	0	0	3	3	4.50	90	.143	.294	0-0	—	0		0	0.0
1951	Phi N	0	0	—	3	0	0	0	4	5	5	0	0	6	3	9.00	43	.294	.478	0-0	—	0		-3	-0.1
Total	2	0	0	—	6	0	0	0	8	7	7	0	0	9	6	6.75	58	.226	.400	0-0	—	0		-3	-0.1
BRITTON, JIM James Allan B 3.25.1944 N.Tonawanda, NY BR/TR 6-5/225# d9.20																									
1967	Atl N	0	2	.000	2	2	0	0	13.1	15	9	2	0	2-0	4	6.08	55	.278	.304	4-0	.000	-0	66	-4	-0.5
1968	Atl N	4	6	.400	34	9	2-2	3	90	81	35	1	2	34-5	61	3.10	97	.245	.318	21-2	.143	-0	106	-1	-0.1
1969	†Atl N	7	5	.583	24	13	2-1	1-0	88	69	38	10	0	49-1	60	3.78	95	.218	.322	21-4	.190	0	87	0	0.0
1971	Mon N	2	3	.400	16	6	0	0-0	45.2	49	33	10	2	27-1	23	5.72	62	.274	.375	9-1	.000	-1	54	-11	-1.3
Total	4	13	16	.448	76	30	4-3	4-0	237	214	115	23	4	112-7	148	4.03	83	.243	.331	55-7	.127	-2	85	-16	-1.9
BRIZZOLARA, TONY Anthony John B 1.14.1957 Santa Monica, CA BR/TR 6-5/215# d5.19																									
1979	Atl N	6	9	.400	20	19	2	0-0	107.1	133	70	6	3	33-1	64	5.28	77	.303	.352	35-1	.029	-3	87	-12	-1.8
1983	Atl N	1	0	1.000	14	0	0	1-0	20.1	22	8	2	0	6-0	17	3.54	110	.278	.329	0-0	—	0		1	0.0
1984	Atl N	1	2	.333	10	4	0	0-0	29	33	22	4	0	13-1	17	5.28	73	.284	.351	7-2	.000	-1	115	-5	-0.6
Total	3	8	11	.421	44	23	2	1-0	156.2	188	100	12	3	52-2	98	5.06	79	.297	.349	42-3	.024	-4	92	-16	-2.4
BROACA, JOHNNY John Joseph B 10.3.1909 Lawrence, MA D 5.16.1985 Lawrence, MA BR/TR 5-11/190# d6.2																									
1934	NY A	12	9	.571	26	24	13-1	0	177.1	203	94	9	1	65	74	4.16	98	.284	.344	66-4	.030	-7	120	-2	-0.9
1935	NY A	15	7	.682	29	27	14-2	0	201	199	96	16	0	79	78	3.58	113	.254	.323	80-5	.150	-4	133	11	0.5
1936	NY A	12	7	.632	37	27	12-1	3	206	235	110	16	0	66	84	4.24	110	.284	.337	82-3	.110	-6	115	10	0.0
1937	NY A	1	4	.200	7	6	3	0	44	58	27	5	0	17	9	4.70	94	.324	.383	14-1	.000	-2	72	-1	-0.4
1939	Cle A	4	2	.667	22	2	0	0	46	53	39	5	0	28	13	4.70	94	.288	.382	12-0	.000	-2	100	-7	-0.9
Total	5	44	29	.603	121	86	42-4	3	674.1	748	366	51	1	255	258	4.08	105	.278	.341	254-13	.091	-21	118	11	-1.7
BROBERG, PETE Peter Sven B 3.2.1950 W.Palm Beach, FL BR/TR 6-3/205# d6.20																									
1971	Was A	5	9	.357	18	18	7-1	0-0	124.2	104	57	10	10	53-2	89	3.47	96	.228	.319	44-3	.114	0	102	-3	-0.4
1972	Tex A	5	12	.294	39	25	3-2	1-0	176.1	153	93	14	13	85-3	133	4.29	70	.237	.332	51-5	.078	-2	94	-23	-2.4
1973	Tex A	5	9	.357	22	20	6-1	0-0	118.2	130	77	8	5	66-3	57	5.61	66	.283	.375	0-0	—	0*	80	-22	-2.3
1974	Tex A	0	4	.000	12	2	0	0-0	29	29	29	7	1	13-0	15	8.07	44	.264	.344	0-0	—	0	74	-14	-1.7
1975	Mil A	14	16	.467	38	32	7-2	0-0	220.1	219	114	18	16	106-2	100	4.13	93	.263	.356	0-0	—	0	106	-6	-0.8
1976	Mil A	1	7	.125	20	11	1	0-0	92.1	99	59	5	4	72-6	28	4.97	70	.281	.403	0-0	—	0	87	-16	-1.3
1977	Chi N	1	2	.333	22	0	0	0-0	36	34	22	8	0	18-4	20	4.75	92	.256	.340	6-0	.000	-1		-2	-0.2
1978	Oak A	10	12	.455	35	26	2	0-0	165.2	174	101	16	3	65-5	94	4.62	79	.269	.336	0-0	—	0	90	-18	-2.1
Total	8	41	71	.366	206	134	26-6	1-0	963	942	552	86	52	478-25	536	4.56	78	.259	.350	101-8	.089	-3	94	-104	-11.2
BROCAIL, DOUG Douglas Keith B 5.16.1967 Clearfield, PA BL/TR 6-5/235# d9.8																									
1992	SD N	0	0	—	3	3	0	0-0	14	17	10	2	0	5-0	15	6.43	56	.298	.355	5-0	.200	0	118	-4	-0.2
1993	SD N	4	13	.235	24	24	0	0-0	128.1	143	75	16	4	42-4	70	4.56	91	.282	.337	33-11	.182	-0*	87	-6	-0.7
1994	SD N	0	0	—	12	0	0	0-1	17	21	13	1	2	5-3	11	5.82	71	.304	.364	2-0	.000	-0*		-4	-0.2
1995	Hou N	6	4	.600	36	7	0	1-0	77.1	87	40	10	4	22-2	39	4.19	92	.280	.334	16-4	.250	1*	127	-3	-0.2
1996	Hou N	1	5	.167	23	4	0	0-0	53	58	31	7	2	23-1	34	4.58	84	.289	.364	11-0	.000	-1*	23	-5	-0.6
1997	Det A	3	4	.429	61	4	0	2-7	78	74	31	10	3	36-4	60	3.23	142	.256	.341	0-0	—	0	105	11	1.0
1998	Det A	5	2	.714	60	0	0	0-1	62.2	47	23	2	1	18-3	55	2.73	173	.211	.269	0-0	—	0		13	1.2
1999	Det A	4	4	.500	70	0	0	2-2	82	60	23	7	4	25-1	78	2.52	196	.206	.276	0-0	—	0		23	1.9
2000	Det A	5	4	.556	49	0	0	0-5	50.2	57	25	5	1	14-2	41	4.09	118	.285	.330	0-0	—	0		4	0.7
Total	9	28	36	.438	338	42	0	5-16	563	564	271	60	21	190-20	403	3.87	113	.263	.325	67-15	.164	-0	86	29	2.9
BROCK, CHRIS Terrence Christopher B 2.5.1970 Orlando, FL BR/TR 6/175# d6.11																									
1997	Atl N	0	0	—	7	6	0	0-0	30.2	34	23	2	0	19-2	16	5.58	75	.288	.376	10-0	.100	-0	146	-5	-0.3
1998	SF N	0	0	—	13	0	0	0-0	27.2	31	13	3	0	7-1	19	3.90	102	.279	.322	4-0	.250	0		0	0.0
1999	SF N	6	8	.429	19	19	0	0-0	106.2	124	69	18	4	41-2	76	5.48	77	.291	.357	35-4	.200	1	120	-16	-1.6
2000	Phi N	7	8	.467	63	5	0	1-2	93.1	85	48	21	3	41-0	69	4.34	108	.239	.321	9-2	.222	1	51	4	0.6
2001	Phi N	3	0	1.000	24	0	0	0-1	32.2	35	16	6	2	15-2	26	4.13	103	.276	.359	3-0	.333	0		1	0.1
2002	Bal A	2	1	.667	22	0	0	0-0	44	52	24	6	1	14-1	21	4.70	91	.297	.349	2-0	.000	-0		-2	-0.1
Total	6	18	17	.514	148	30	0	1-3	335	361	193	56	10	137-8	227	4.81	90	.275	.345	63-6	.190	3	111	-18	-1.3
BROCKETT, LEW Lewis Albert "King" B 7.23.1880 Brownsville, IL D 9.19.1960 Norris City, IL BR/TR 5-10.5/168# d4.25																									
1907	NY A	1	2	.333	8	4	1	0	46.1	58	36	1	2	26	13	6.22	45	.309	.398	22-0	.182	-0*	73	-13	-0.9
1909	NY A	10	8	.556	26	18	10-3	1	170	148	68	3	6	59	70	2.12	119	.245	.318	60-3	.283	3	94	5	1.1
1911	NY A	2	4	.333	16	8	2	0	75.1	73	45	2	5	39	25	4.66	77	.256	.356	39-0	.308	2*	93	-6	-0.2
Total	3	13	14	.481	50	30	13-3	1	291.2	279	149	6	13	124	108	3.43	83	.259	.343	121-3	.273	5	91	-14	0.0
BRODOWSKI, DICK Richard Stanley B 7.26.1932 Bayonne, NJ BR/TR 6-2/190# d6.15 Mil 1953																									
1952	Bos A	5	5	.500	20	12	4	0	114.2	111	66	12	3	50	42	4.40	90	.252	.333	39-1	.205	1	124	-6	-0.4
1955	Bos A	1	0	1.000	16	0	0	0	32	36	25	5	1	25-2	10	5.63	76	.295	.416	10-0	.500	3		-5	0.0
1956	Was A	0	3	.000	7	3	1	0	17.2	31	18	5	0	12-0	8	9.17	47	.397	.473	5-0	.000	-1	48	-8	-1.2
1957	Was A	0	1	.000	6	0	0	0	11.1	12	15	2	1	10-0	4	11.12	35	.261	.404	1-0	.000	-0		-9	-0.7
1958	Cle A	1	0	1.000	5	0	0	0	10	3	0	0	0	6-0	12	0.00	—	.100	.250	1-0	.000	-0		4	0.4
1959	Cle A	2	2	.500	18	0	0	5	30	19	13	3	3	21-1	9	1.80	205	.181	.328	6-2	.333	0		4	0.6
Total	6	9	11	.450	72	15	5	5	215.2	212	137	27	8	124-3	85	4.76	84	.258	.359	62-3	.242	3	109	-20	-1.3
BROGLIO, ERNIE Ernest Gilbert B 8.27.1935 Berkeley, CA BR/TR 6-2/200# d4.11																									
1959	StL N	7	12	.368	35	25	6-3	0	181.1	174	104	20	0	89-10	133	4.72	90	.250	.334	61-3	.098	-3	80	-9	-1.0
1960	StL N	**21**	9	**.700**	52	24	9-3	0	226.1	172	76	18	2	100-5	188	2.74	**149**	.213	.299	68-4	.206	2	87	32	4.4
1961	StL N	9	12	.429	29	26	7-2	0	174.2	166	97	19	1	75-5	113	4.12	107	.248	.322	62-4	.145	-2	88	4	0.1
1962	StL N	12	9	.571	34	30	11-4	0	222.1	193	80	22	2	93-5	132	3.00	143	.237	.316	72-6	.139	-2	83	31	2.5
1963	StL N	18	8	.692	39	35	11-5	0	250	202	97	24	4	90-4	145	2.99	119	.216	.286	89-10	.112	-3	128	14	1.2
1964	StL N	3	5	.375	11	11	3-1	0	69.1	65	33	7	1	26-2	36	3.50	109	.247	.317	21-2	.095	-0	86	2	0.1
	Chi N	4	7	.364	18	16	3	1	100.1	111	51	12	0	30-4	46	4.04	92	.281	.331	35-2	.286	3	81	-4	-0.2
	Year	7	12	.368	29	27	6-1	1	169.2	176	54	19	1	56-6	82	3.82	98	.267	.325	56-4	.214	2	83	-1	-0.1
1965	Chi N	1	6	.143	26	6	0	0	50.2	63	44	7	0	46-8	22	6.93	53	.313	.440	4-1	.000	-0	111	-17	-2.2
1966	Chi N	2	6	.250	15	11	2	1	62.1	70	46	14	0	38-6	34	6.35	58	.290	.384	19-1	.368	3	104	-16	-1.5
Total	8	77	74	.510	259	184	52-18	2	1337.1	1216	628	143	10	587-49	849	3.74	107	.242	.321	431-33	.158	-2	94	37	3.4
BROHAWN, TROY Michael Troy B 1.14.1973 Cambridge, MD BL/TL 6-1/190# d4.14																									
2001	†Ari N	2	3	.400	59	0	0	1-2	49.1	55	27	5	1	23-2	30	4.93	93	.289	.362	1-0	.000	-0		-1	-0.1
2002	SF N	0	1	.000	11	0	0	0-0	5.2	5	4	1	2	1-0	3	6.35	61	.227	.320	0-0	—	0		-1	-0.2
2003	LA N	2	0	1.000	12	0	0	0-0	11.2	10	6	2	0	4-0	13	3.86	104	.227	.292	1-0	1.000	1		0	0.0
Total	3	4	4	.500	82	0	0	1-2	66.2	70	37	8	3	28-2	46	4.86	91	.273	.347	2-0	.500	0		-2	-0.3
BRONDELL, KEN Kenneth Leroy B 10.17.1921 Bradshaw, NE BR/TR 6-1/195# d5.3																									
1944	NY N	0	1	.000	7	2	1	0	19.1	27	18	3	0	8	1	8.38	44	.329	.389	4-0	.000	-1*	114	-9	-0.5
BRONKEY, JEFF Jacob Jeffrey B 9.18.1965 Kabul, Afghanistan BR/TR 6-3/215# d5.2																									
1993	Tex A	1	1	.500	21	0	0	1-2	36	39	20	4	1	11-4	18	4.00	104	.285	.338	1-0	.000	-0		0	0.0
1994	Mil A	1	1	.500	16	0	0	1-1	20.2	20	10	3	0	12-4	13	4.35	116	.247	.344	0-0	—	0		2	0.2
1995	Mil A	0	0	—	8	0	0	0-0	12.1	15	6	0	0	6-0	5	3.65	137	.313	.389	0-0	—	0		1	0.1
Total	3	2	2	.500	45	0	0	2-3	69	74	36	7	1	29-8	36	4.04	113	.278	.349	1-0	.000	-0		3	0.3
BRONSTAD, JIM James Warren B 6.22.1936 Ft.Worth, TX BR/TR 6-3/196# d6.7																									
1959	NY A	0	3	.000	16	3	0	2	29.1	34	19	2	1	13-0	14	5.22	70	.288	.361	5-0	.000	-0	73	-5	-0.6

Year	Tm Lg	W	L	Pct	G	GS	CG-Sho	SV-BS	IP	H	R	HR	HB	BB-IB	SO	ERA	AERA	OAV	OOB	AB-SH	AVG	PB	Sup	APR	PW
1963	Was A	1	3	.250	25	0	0	1	57.1	66	38	9	1	22-2	22	5.65	66	.297	.359	12-0	.000	-1*		-11	-0.8
1964	Was A	0	1	.000	4	0	0	0	7	10	4	0	0	2-0	9	5.14	72	.345	.387	0-0	—	0		-1	-0.1
Total	3	1	7	.125	45	3	0	3	93.2	110	61	11	2	37-2	45	5.48	67	.298	.362	17-0	.000	-2	73	-17	-1.5
BROOKENS, IKE Edward Dwain B 1.3.1949 Chambersburg, PA BR/TR 6-5/170# d6.17																									
1975	Det A	0	0	—	3	0	0	0-0	10.1	11	6	3	1	5-0	8	5.23	77	.282	.378	0-0	—	0		-1	0.0
BROOKS, HARRY Harry Frank B 11.30.1865 Philadelphia, PA D 12.5.1945 Philadelphia, PA d7.24																									
1886	NY AA	0	1	.000	1	1	0	0	2	9	13	0	0	2	0	36.00	9	.429	.478	1	.000	-0	55	-8	-0.9
BROSNAN, JIM James Patrick B 10.24.1929 Cincinnati, OH BR/TR 6-4/210# d4.15																									
1954	Chi N	1	0	1.000	18	0	0	0	33.1	44	35	9	1	18	17	9.45	44	.331	.409	8-0	.125	-0		-17	-0.8
1956	Chi N	5	9	.357	30	10	1-1	1	95	95	44	9	0	45-8	51	3.79	100	.270	.349	22-2	.182	-0	98	1	0.1
1957	Chi N	5	5	.500	41	5	1	0	98.2	79	38	11	1	46-4	73	3.38	115	.219	.308	20-2	.250	2	96	7	0.9
1958	Chi N	3	4	.429	8	8	2	0	51.2	41	20	3	0	29-3	24	3.14	125	.225	.327	19-0	.105	-1	83	5	0.6
	StL N	8	4	.667	33	12	2	7	115	107	46	10	1	50-3	65	3.44	120	.250	.328	31-3	.097	-1	111	10	1.0
	Year	11	8	.579	41	20	4	7	166.2	148	51	13	1	79-6	89	3.35	121	.243	.328	50-3	.100	-2	99	14	1.6
1959	StL N	1	3	.250	20	1	0	2	33	34	18	5	1	15-5	18	4.91	86	.276	.357	7-0	.286	1	190	-2	-0.1
	Cin N	8	3	.727	26	9	1-1	2	83.1	79	35	7	5	26-2	56	3.35	121	.248	.313	23-1	.043	-2	98	6	0.7
	Year	9	6	.600	46	10	1-1	4	116.1	113	39	12	6	41-7	74	3.79	108	.256	.325	30-1	.100	-1	107	5	0.6
1960	Cin N	7	2	.778	57	2	0	12	99	79	31	5	0	22-5	62	2.36	162	.225	.269	15-1	.200	2	219	15	1.9
1961	†Cin N	10	4	.714	53	0	0	16	80	77	34	7	0	18-3	40	3.04	134	.249	.288	13-1	.154	-0		8	1.5
1962	Cin N	4	4	.500	48	0	0	13	64.2	76	27	6	0	18-5	51	3.34	120	.292	.335	6-2	.000	-1		5	0.7
1963	Cin N	0	1	.000	6	0	0	0	4.2	8	4	2	0	3-1	4	7.71	43	.421	.500	0-0	—	0		-2	-0.4
	Chi A	3	8	.273	45	0	0	14	73	71	24	7	0	22-5	46	2.84	124	.263	.315	13-0	.308	1		6	1.3
Total	9	55	47	.539	385	47	7-2	67	831.1	790	356	81	9	312-44	507	3.54	111	.254	.322	177-12	.153	1	106	42	7.4
BROSS, TERRY Terrence Paul B 3.30.1966 ElPaso, TX BR/TR 6-9/234# d9.4																									
1991	NY N	0	0	—	8	0	0	0-0	10	7	2	1	0	3-0	5	1.80	202	.200	.263	0-0	—	0		2	0.1
1993	SF N	0	0	—	2	0	0	0-0	2	3	2	1	0	1-0	1	9.00	43	.333	.400	0-0	—	0		-1	-0.1
Total	2	0	0	—	10	0	0	0-0	12	10	4	2	0	4-0	6	3.00	123	.227	.292	0-0	—	0		1	0.0
BROSSEAU, FRANK Franklin Lee B 7.31.1944 Drayton, ND BR/TR 6-1/180# d9.10																									
1969	Pit N	0	0	—	2	0	0	0-0	1.2	2	2	0	0	2-1	2	10.80	32	.286	.444	0-0	—	0		-1	-0.1
1971	Pit N	0	0	—	1	0	0	0-0	2	1	0	0	0	0-0	0	0.00	—	.200	.200	0-0	—	0		1	0.1
Total	2	0	0	—	3	0	0	0-0	3.2	3	2	0	0	2-1	2	4.91	70	.250	.357	0-0	—	0		0	0.0
BROUTHERS, DAN Dennis Joseph "Big Dan" B 5.8.1858 Sylvan Lake, NY D 8.2.1932 E.Orange, NJ BL/TL 6-2/207# d6.23 HF1945 ▲																									
1879	Tro N	0	2	.000	3	2	2	0	21	35	30	0		8	6	5.57	45	.343	.391	168	.274	1*	0	-7	-0.5
1883	Buf N	0	0	—	1	0	0	0	2	9	7	0		3	2	31.50	10	.643	.706	425	.374	1*		-5	-0.2
Total	2	0	2	.000	4	2	2	0	23	44	37	0		11	8	7.83	33	.379	.433	593	.346	1	0	-12	-0.7
BROW, SCOTT Scott John B 3.17.1969 Butte, MT BR/TR 6-3/200# d4.28																									
1993	Tor A	1	1	.500	6	3	0	0-0	18	19	15	2	1	10-1	7	6.00	72	.275	.366	0-0	—	0	170	-4	-0.3
1994	Tor A	0	3	.000	18	0	0	2-0	29	34	27	4	1	19-2	15	5.90	82	.288	.386	0-0	—	0		-6	-0.6
1996	Tor A	1	0	1.000	18	1	0	0-1	38.2	45	25	5	0	25-1	23	5.59	90	.294	.391	0-0	—	0	111	-2	-0.1
1998	Ari N	1	0	1.000	17	0	0	0-0	21.1	22	17	2	0	14-2	13	7.17	59	.272	.375	1-0	.000	-0		-6	-0.3
Total	4	3	4	.429	59	4	0	2-1	107	120	84	13	2	68-6	58	6.06	77	.285	.382	1-0	.000	-0	148	-18	-1.3
BROWER, FRANK Frank Willard "Turkeyfoot" B 3.26.1893 Gainesville, VA D 11.20.1960 Baltimore, MD BL/TR 6-2/180# d8.14.1920 ▲																									
1924	Cle A	0	0	—	4	0	0	0	9.2	7	2	0	1	4	0	0.93	459	.212	.316	107-0	.280	1*		3	0.2
BROWER, JIM James Robert B 12.29.1972 Edina, MN BR/TR 6-2/205# d9.5																									
1999	Cle A	3	1	.750	9	2	0	0-0	25.2	27	13	8	1	10-1	18	4.56	111	.270	.339	0-0	—	0	231	2	0.2
2000	Cle A	2	3	.400	17	11	0	0-0	62	80	45	11	2	31-1	32	6.24	80	.309	.387	3-0	.000	-0	91	-8	-0.5
2001	Cin N	7	10	.412	46	10	0	1-1	129.1	119	65	17	5	60-5	94	3.97	115	.247	.335	26-2	.308	2*	126	7	1.2
2002	Cin N	2	0	1.000	22	0	0	0-0	39.1	38	18	2	0	10-1	24	3.89	109	.260	.306	4-1	.000	-0		2	0.1
	Mon N	1	2	.333	30	0	0	0-1	41	39	22	5	4	22-1	33	4.83	93	.245	.351	5-0	.000	-1		0	-0.1
	Year	3	2	.600	52	0	0	0-1	80.1	77	46	7	4	32-2	57	4.37	100	.252	.330	9-1	.000	-1		1	0.0
2003	†SF N	8	5	.615	51	5	0	2-1	100	90	48	8	1	39-2	65	3.96	104	.249	.320	17-1	.176	0	123	1	0.2
Total	5	23	21	.523	175	28	0	3-3	397.1	393	211	51	13	172-11	266	4.44	101	.261	.340	55-4	.200	1	123	4	1.1
BROWN, ALTON Alton Leo "Deacon" B 4.16.1925 Norfolk, VA BR/TR 6-2/195# d4.21																									
1951	Was A	0	0	—	7	0	0	0	11.2	14	12	1	1	12	7	9.26	44	.298	.450	1-0	.000	-0		-6	-0.3
BROWN, BOARDWALK Carroll William B 2.20.1887 Woodbury, NJ D 2.8.1977 Burlington, NJ BR/TR 6-1.5/178# d9.27																									
1911	Phi A	0	1	.000	2	1	1	0	12	12	7	0	0	2	6	4.50	70	.267	.298	4-0	.000	-1	91	-2	-0.2
1912	Phi A	13	11	.542	34	24	15-3	0	199	204	115	2	9	87	64	3.66	84	.283	.367	76-4	.145	-3	142	-17	-2.0
1913	Phi A	17	11	.607	43	35	11-3	1	235.1	200	94	6	10	87	70	2.94	94	.233	.310	82-2	.159	-1	145	-5	-0.8
1914	Phi A	1	5	.167	15	7	2	0	66	64	34	1	0	26	20	4.09	64	.268	.340	20-1	.000	-2	96	-10	-1.1
	NY A	6	5	.545	20	14	8	0	122.1	123	57	2	1	42	57	3.24	85	.271	.334	44-2	.182	1	123	-7	-0.3
	Year	7	10	.412	35	21	10	0	188.1	187	62	3	1	68	77	3.54	77	.270	.336	64-3	.125	-0	114	-14	-1.4
1915	NY A	3	6	.333	19	11	5	0	96.2	95	49	4	5	47	34	4.10	72	.275	.370	32-0	.188	-1*	66	-10	-1.0
Total	5	40	39	.506	133	92	42-6	1	731.1	698	356	15	25	291	251	3.47	83	.262	.340	258-9	.147	-6	126	-51	-5.4
BROWN, CHARLIE Charles E. B 1878 New Haven, IN TL 6/180# d8.4																									
1897	Cle N	1	2	.333	4	4	2	0	24.1	30	25	2	5	17	8	7.77	58	.300	.426	11-0	.273	0	91	-7	-0.6
BROWN, BUSTER Charles Edward "Yank" B 8.31.1881 Boone, IA D 2.9.1914 Sioux City, IA BR/TR 6/180# d6.22																									
1905	StL N	8	11	.421	23	21	17-3	0	178.2	172	80	5	10	62	57	2.97	100	.260	.332	65-0	.092	-3	73	0	-0.2
1906	StL N	8	16	.333	32	27	21	0	238.1	208	98	2	11	112	109	2.64	99	.234	.327	85-6	.165	0	88	-3	-0.1
1907	StL N	1	6	.143	9	8	6	0	63.2	57	38	2	5	45	17	3.39	74	.263	.401	26-1	.269	2	107	-7	-0.4
	Phi N	9	6	.600	21	16	13-4	0	130	118	47	3	6	56	38	2.42	100	.246	.333	53-0	.189	2	120	0	0.1
	Year	10	12	.455	30	24	19-4	0	193.2	175	51	5	11	101	55	2.74	89	.251	.355	79-1	.215	3	115	-6	-0.3
1908	Phi N	0	0	—	3	0	0	0	7	9	6	0	1	5	3	2.57	94	.346	.469	5-0	.200	-0*		-1	0.0
1909	Phi N	0	0	—	7	1	0	0	25	22	10	1	1	16	10	3.24	80	.259	.382	9-0	.000	-1	81	-1	-0.2
	Bos N	4	8	.333	18	17	8-2	0	123.1	108	45	1	7	56	32	3.14	90	.244	.339	48-0	.146	-2	64	1	-0.1
	Year	4	8	.333	25	18	8-2	0	148.1	130	48	2	8	72	42	3.16	88	.247	.346	57-0	.123	-3	66	0	-0.3
1910	Bos N	9	23	.281	46	29	16-1	2	263	251	113	4	4	94	88	2.67	125	.268	.337	81-5	.198	0	63	16	2.1
1911	Bos N	8	18	.308	42	25	13	2	241	258	161	11	10	116	76	4.29	89	.284	.371	84-3	.250	3	80	-15	-1.0
1912	Bos N	4	15	.211	31	21	12	0	168.1	146	107	7	2	66	68	4.01	89	.239	.315	61-1	.213	1	98	-10	-0.8
1913	Bos N	0	0	—	2	0	0	0	13.1	19	10	0	2	3	3	4.73	70	.396	.453	5-0	.000	-0		-2	-0.1
Total	9	51	103	.331	234	165	106-10	4	1451.2	1368	715	36	59	631	501	3.21	96	.258	.343	522-16	.182	3	82	-22	-0.7
BROWN, CURLY Charles Roy "Lefty" B 12.9.1888 Spring Hill, KS D 6.10.1968 Spring Hill, KS BL/TL 5-10.5/165# d9.8																									
1911	StL A	1	2	.333	3	2	2	0	23	22	9	0	1	5	8	2.74	123	.247	.295	9-0	.000	-1	53	2	0.1
1912	StL A	1	3	.250	16	4	2-1	0	64.2	69	56	0	3	35	28	4.87	68	.277	.373	24-0	.208	-0*	78	-14	-0.9
1913	StL A	1	1	.500	2	2	2	0	14	12	5	0	0	4	3	2.57	114	.245	.302	5-0	.400	1	76	1	0.2
1915	Cin N	0	2	.000	7	3	0	0	27	26	20	2	2	6	13	4.67	61	.245	.298	11-0	.364	1*	147	-6	-0.4
Total	4	3	8	.273	28	11	6-1	0	128.2	129	90	2	6	50	52	4.20	76	.262	.337	49-0	.224	0	88	-17	-1.0
BROWN, CLINT Clinton Harold B 7.8.1903 Blackash, PA D 12.31.1955 Rocky River, OH BL/TR 6-1/190# d9.27																									
1928	Cle A	0	1	.000	2	1	1	0	11	14	6	0	0	2	2	4.91	84	.304	.333	5-0	.200	-0	102	0	0.0
1929	Cle A	0	2	.000	3	1	1	0	16.1	18	8	0	0	6	1	3.31	134	.286	.348	7-0	.000	-1	38	2	0.1
1930	Cle A	11	13	.458	35	31	16-**3**	1	213.2	271	138	14	4	51	54	4.97	97	.314	.356	73-3	.247	2	86	0	0.3
1931	Cle A	11	15	.423	39	33	12-2	0	233.1	284	143	10	1	55	50	4.71	98	.295	.333	87-3	.172	-2	104	-1	-0.1

Year	Tm Lg	W	L	Pct	G	GS	CG-Sho	SV-BS	IP	H	R	HR	HB	BB-IB	SO	ERA	AERA	OAV	OOB	AB-SH	AVG	PB	Sup	APR	PW
1932	Cle A	15	12	.556	37	32	21-1	1	262.2	298	143	14	4	50	59	4.08	116	.279	.314	100-5	.250	6*	100	18	2.2
1933	Cle A	11	12	.478	33	23	10-2	1	185	202	83	10	2	34	47	3.41	130	.276	.310	62-3	.145	-3*	81	21	2.2
1934	Cle A	4	3	.571	17	2	0	1	50.1	83	42	3	0	14	15	5.90	77	.359	.396	17-0	.294	1	105	-9	-0.9
1935	Cle A	4	3	.571	23	5	1	2	49	61	34	3	1	14	20	5.14	88	.300	.349	10-0	.200	0	77	-4	-0.5
1936	Chi A	6	2	.750	38	2	0	5	83	106	50	5	3	24	19	4.99	104	.315	.366	25-2	.160	-0	127	**3**	0.2
1937	Chi A	7	7	.500	**53**	0	0	**18**	100	92	47	7	1	36	51	3.42	135	.242	.309	18-1	.222	1		**12**	2.1
1938	Chi A	1	3	.250	8	0	0	2	13.2	16	8	0	0	9	2	4.61	106	.333	.439	2-0	.500	1		1	0.2
1939	Chi A	11	10	.524	**61**	0	0	18	118.1	127	58	8	0	27	41	3.88	122	.281	.322	19-4	.211	1		**11**	2.1
1940	Chi A	4	6	.400	37	0	0	10	66	75	30	5	2	16	23	3.68	120	.284	.330	14-3	.071	-1		6	0.9
1941	Cle A	3	3	.500	41	0	0	5	74.1	77	30	3	1	28	22	3.27	120	.279	.348	17-0	.118	0		6	0.7
1942	Cle A	1	1	.500	7	0	0	0	9	16	10	2	1	2	4	6.00	57	.356	.396	1-0	.000	-0		-4	-0.8
Total	15	89	93	.489	434	130	62-8	64	1485.2	1740	830	84	20	368	410	4.26	109	.291	.335	457-24	.199	5	95	62	8.7

BROWN, CURT Curtis Steven B 1.15.1960 Ft.Lauderdale, FL BR/TR 6-5/200# d6.10

Year	Tm Lg	W	L	Pct	G	GS	CG-Sho	SV-BS	IP	H	R	HR	HB	BB-IB	SO	ERA	AERA	OAV	OOB	AB-SH	AVG	PB	Sup	APR	PW
1983	Cal A	1	1	.500	10	0	0	0-0	16	25	13	1	0	4-1	7	7.31	55	.368	.397	0-0	—	0		-5	-0.6
1984	NY A	1	1	.500	13	0	0	0-1	16.2	18	5	1	0	4-0	10	2.70	141	.281	.319	0-0	—	0		2	0.3
1986	Mon N	0	1	.000	6	0	0	0-0	12	15	6	0	0	2-2	4	3.00	123	.319	.340	1-0	.000	-0		0	0.0
1987	Mon N	0	1	.000	5	0	0	0-0	7	10	7	2	0	4-1	6	7.71	55	.333	.412	0-0	—	0		-3	-0.3
Total	4	2	4	.333	34	0	0	0-1	51.2	68	31	4	0	14-4	27	4.88	80	.325	.363	1-0	.000	-0		-6	-0.6

BROWN, ED Edward P. B Chicago, IL TR ?/178# d8.19 ▲

Year	Tm Lg	W	L	Pct	G	GS	CG-Sho	SV-BS	IP	H	R	HR	HB	BB-IB	SO	ERA	AERA	OAV	OOB	AB-SH	AVG	PB	Sup	APR	PW
1882	StL AA	0	0	—	1	0	0	0	2	2	1	0		0	1	0.00	—	.250	.250	60	.183	-0*		0	0.0
1884	Tol AA	0	1	.000	1	1	1	0	9	19	16	0	1	4	1	9.00	38	.396	.453	153	.176	-0*	0	-5	-0.4
Total	2	0	1	.000	2	1	1	0	11	21	17	0	1	4	2	7.36	45	.375	.426	213	.178	-0	0	-5	-0.4

BROWN, ELMER Elmer Young "Shook" B 3.25.1883 Southport, IN D 1.23.1955 Indianapolis, IN BL/TR 5-11.5/172# d9.16

Year	Tm Lg	W	L	Pct	G	GS	CG-Sho	SV-BS	IP	H	R	HR	HB	BB-IB	SO	ERA	AERA	OAV	OOB	AB-SH	AVG	PB	Sup	APR	PW
1911	StL A	1	1	.500	5	3	1-1	0	16.2	16	17	0	0	14	5	6.48	52	.242	.375	8-0	.125	-1	135	-6	-0.6
1912	StL A	5	8	.385	23	13	2-1	0	120.1	122	56	2	12	42	45	2.99	111	.280	.359	36-2	.167	-1	96	4	0.2
1913	Bro N	0	0	—	3	1	0	0	13	6	3	0	1	10	6	2.08	159	.158	.347	4-0	.000	-1	91	2	0.0
1914	Bro N	1	2	.333	11	5	1	0	36.2	33	28	2	7	23	22	3.93	73	.402	.563	12-1	.083	-1	175	-6	-0.5
1915	Bro N	0	0	—	1	0	0	0	2	4	4	0	0	3	1	9.00	31	.500	.636	0-0	—	0		-2	-0.1
Total	5	7	11	.389	43	22	4-2	0	188.2	181	108	4	20	92	79	3.48	93	.287	.395	60-3	.133	-3	116	-8	-1.0

BROWN, HAL Hector Harold "Skinny" B 12.11.1924 Greensboro, NC BR/TR 6-2/182# d4.19 C1

Year	Tm Lg	W	L	Pct	G	GS	CG-Sho	SV-BS	IP	H	R	HR	HB	BB-IB	SO	ERA	AERA	OAV	OOB	AB-SH	AVG	PB	Sup	APR	PW
1951	Chi A	0	0	—	3	0	0	1	8.2	15	9	3	0	4	4	9.35	43	.385	.442	2-0	1.000	1*		-5	-0.1
1952	Chi A	2	3	.400	24	8	1	0	72.1	82	39	8	0	21	31	4.23	86	.284	.332	19-1	.158	1*	108	-5	-0.3
1953	Bos A	11	6	.647	30	25	6-1	0	166.1	177	94	16	0	57	62	4.65	90	.269	.327	58-4	.293	5	89	-6	-0.1
1954	Bos A	1	8	.111	40	5	1	0	118	126	64	6	3	41	66	4.12	100	.269	.329	24-1	.125	-0	82	-1	-0.1
1955	Bos A	1	0	1.000	2	0	0	0	4	2	1	0	0	2-0	2	2.25	191	.143	.250	1-0	1.000	0		1	0.2
	Bal A	0	4	.000	15	5	1	0	57	51	30	5	0	26-1	26	4.11	93	.241	.322	16-0	.000	-1*	84	-2	-0.3
	Year	1	4	.200	17	5	1	0	61	53	34	5	0	28-1	28	3.98	97	.235	.318	17-0	.059	-1	83	-1	-0.1
1956	Bal A	9	7	.563	35	14	4-1	2	151.2	142	72	18	1	37-3	57	4.04	97	.247	.292	42-3	.190	1*	101	0	0.1
1957	Bal A	7	8	.467	25	20	7-2	1	150	132	68	17	2	37-3	62	3.90	92	.236	.283	48-6	.208	2*	86	-4	-0.2
1958	Bal A	7	5	.583	19	17	4-2	1	96.2	96	35	9	0	20-0	44	3.07	117	.259	.296	27-1	.148	-0*	88	7	0.8
1959	Bal A	11	9	.550	31	21	2	3	164	158	73	16	1	32-5	81	3.79	100	.252	.289	42-9	.048	-3	77	2	-0.1
1960	Bal A	12	5	.706	30	20	6-1	0	159	155	61	14	1	22-3	66	3.06	125	.258	**.283**	44-5	.182	3	135	13	1.6
1961	Bal A	10	6	.625	27	23	6-3	1	166.2	153	62	14	1	33-0	61	3.19	121	.247	.284	50-3	.140	-0	91	15	1.3
1962	Bal A	6	4	.600	22	11	0	1	85.2	88	41	12	3	21-2	25	4.10	90	.268	.317	28-2	.286	2	112	-3	-0.2
	NY A	0	1	.000	2	1	0	0	6.2	9	10	3	0	2-0	2	6.75	56	.333	.367	1-0	.000	-0	71	-4	-0.5
	Year	6	5	.545	24	12	0	1	92.1	97	13	15	3	23-2	27	4.29	86	.273	.321	29-2	.276	1	109	-8	-0.7
1963	Hou N	5	11	.313	26	20	6-3	0	141.1	137	54	14	0	8-0	68	3.31	95	.255	.264	43-3	.093	-2	66	0	-0.3
1964	Hou N	3	15	.167	27	21	3	1	132	154	68	18	2	26-10	53	3.95	86	.292	.326	39-2	.128	-1	45	-8	-1.2
Total	14	85	92	.480	358	211	47-13	11	1680	1677	781	173	14	389-27	710	3.81	98	.260	.302	484-40	.169	8	88	0	0.6

BROWN, JACKIE Jackie Gene B 5.31.1943 Holdenville, OK BR/TR 6-1/195# d7.2 C9 b-Paul

Year	Tm Lg	W	L	Pct	G	GS	CG-Sho	SV-BS	IP	H	R	HR	HB	BB-IB	SO	ERA	AERA	OAV	OOB	AB-SH	AVG	PB	Sup	APR	PW
1970	Was A	2	2	.500	24	5	1	0-0	57	49	28	8	0	37-1	47	3.95	90	.231	.344	13-0	.154	-0	95	-3	-0.3
1971	Was A	3	4	.429	14	9	0	0-0	47	60	34	9	1	27-2	21	5.94	56	.316	.404	15-0	.133	-0	93	-14	-1.9
1973	Tex A	5	5	.500	25	3	2-1	2-4	66.2	82	31	7	2	25-0	45	3.92	95	.309	.372	0-0	—	0	144	0	-0.1
1974	Tex A	13	12	.520	35	26	9-2	0-0	216.2	219	97	13	4	74-4	134	3.57	100	.265	.327	0-0	—	0	108	0	0.0
1975	Tex A	5	5	.500	17	7	2-1	0-0	70.1	70	37	7	2	35-2	35	4.22	89	.266	.355	0-0	—	0	97	-3	-0.5
	Cle A	1	2	.333	25	3	1	1-2	69.1	72	40	9	0	29-6	41	4.28	89	.276	.342	0-0	—	0	178	-5	-0.3
	Year	6	7	.462	42	10	3-1	1-2	139.2	142	48	16	2	64-8	76	4.25	89	.271	.349	0-0	—	0	121	-8	-0.8
1976	Cle A	9	11	.450	32	27	5-2	0-0	180	193	94	14	7	55-4	104	4.25	82	.276	.332	0-0	—	0	108	-15	-1.6
1977	Mon N	9	12	.429	42	25	6-2	0-0	185.2	189	99	15	4	71-5	89	4.51	85	.264	.332	56-4	.125	-2	100	-13	-1.6
Total	7	47	53	.470	214	105	26-8	3-6	892.2	934	460	82	20	353-24	516	4.18	87	.272	.341	84-4	.131	-3	106	-53	-6.3

BROWN, KEVIN James Kevin B 3.14.1965 Milledgeville, GA BR/TR 6-4/195# d9.30

Year	Tm Lg	W	L	Pct	G	GS	CG-Sho	SV-BS	IP	H	R	HR	HB	BB-IB	SO	ERA	AERA	OAV	OOB	AB-SH	AVG	PB	Sup	APR	PW
1986	Tex A	1	0	1.000	1	1	0	0-0	5	6	2	0	0	0-0	4	3.60	120	.316	.316	0-0	—	0	190	0	0.1
1988	Tex A	1	1	.500	4	4	1	0-0	23.1	33	15	2	1	8-0	12	4.24	96	.330	.385	0-0	—	0	156	-1	-0.1
1989	Tex A	12	9	.571	28	28	7	0-0	191	167	81	10	4	70-2	104	3.35	119	.234	.303	0-0	—	0	96	13	1.5
1990	Tex A	12	10	.545	26	26	6-2	0-0	180	175	84	13	3	60-3	88	3.60	109	.255	.315	1-0	.000	-0*	108	5	0.6
1991	Tex A	9	12	.429	33	33	0	0-0	210.2	233	116	17	13	90-5	96	4.40	92	.284	.362	0-0	—	0	111	-10	-0.8
1992	Tex A★	**21**	11	.656	35	35	11-1	0-0	**265.2**	262	117	11	10	76-2	173	3.32	115	.260	.316	0-0	—	0	111	12	1.5
1993	Tex A	15	12	.556	34	34	12-3	0-0	233	228	105	14	15	74-5	142	3.59	116	.252	.318	0-0	—	0*	108	14	1.6
1994	Tex A	7	9	.438	26	25	3	0-0	170	218	109	18	6	50-3	123	4.82	100	.314	.361	0-0	—	0	94	-3	-0.1
1995	Bal A	10	9	.526	26	26	3-1	0-0	172.1	155	73	10	9	48-1	117	3.60	132	.241	.302	0-0	—	0	86	22	2.5
1996	Fla N★	17	11	.607	32	32	5-**3**	0-0	233	187	60	8	16	33-2	159	**1.89**	**215**	.220	.262	75-4	.120	-1*	66	**56**	**6.9**
1997	†Fla N★	16	8	.667	33	33	6-2	0-0	237.1	214	77	10	14	66-7	205	2.69	150	.240	.303	72-6	.125	-0	96	37	3.8
1998	†SD N★	18	7	.720	36	**35**	7-3	0-0	257	225	77	8	10	49-4	257	2.38	164	.235	.279	82-7	.207	4	103	46	4.8
1999	LA N	18	9	.667	35	**35**	5-1	0-0	252.1	210	99	19	7	59-1	221	3.00	143	.222	.273	78-13	.064	-5	94	35	3.1
2000	LA N★	13	6	.684	33	33	5-1	0-0	230	181	76	21	9	47-1	216	**2.58**	168	**.213**	**.261**	66-14	.076	-3	97	46	3.3
2001	LA N	10	4	.714	20	19	1	0-0	115.2	94	41	8	2	38-2	104	2.65	152	.224	.291	36-2	.083	0	102	17	2.0
2002	LA N	3	4	.429	17	10	0	0-0	63.2	68	36	9	5	23-1	58	4.81	80	.274	.348	20-2	.250	2	89	-7	-0.5
2003	LA N✤	14	9	.609	32	32	0	0-0	211	184	67	11	5	56-2	185	2.39	168	.236	.290	63-6	.159	0	87	38	4.1
Total	17	197	131	.601	451	441	72-17	0-0	3051	2840	1235	189	129	847-41	2264	3.16	131	.246	.304	493-54	.128	-3	97	320	34.3

BROWN, JIM James W. H. B 12.12.1860 Clinton Co., PA D 4.6.1908 Williamsport, PA d4.17 ▲

Year	Tm Lg	W	L	Pct	G	GS	CG-Sho	SV-BS	IP	H	R	HR	HB	BB-IB	SO	ERA	AERA	OAV	OOB	AB-SH	AVG	PB	Sup	APR	PW
1884	Alt U	1	9	.100	11	11	7	0	74	99	80	0		36	39	5.35	50	.301	.370	88	.250	-2*	58	-20	-2.0
	NY N	0	1	.000	1	1	1	0	9	10	9	0		8	2	5.00	60	.263	.391	3	.000	-1	0	-2	-0.2
	StP U	1	4	.200	6	6	4-1	0	36	43	34	1		14	20	3.75	35	.277	.337	16	.313	4	97	-18	-1.4
1886	Phi AA	0	1	.000	1	1	1	0	8.1	9	5	0	0	3	4	3.24	108	.265	.324	3	.000	-1	68	0	0.0
Total	2	2	15	.118	19	19	13-1	0	127.1	161	128	1	0	61	65	4.74	50	.290	.360	110	.245	1	62	-40	-3.6

BROWN, JOHN John J. "Ad" B Trenton, NJ d8.11

Year	Tm Lg	W	L	Pct	G	GS	CG-Sho	SV-BS	IP	H	R	HR	HB	BB-IB	SO	ERA	AERA	OAV	OOB	AB-SH	AVG	PB	Sup	APR	PW
1897	Bro N	0	1	.000	1	1	0	0	5	7	8	0	3	4	0	7.20	57	.333	.500	2-0	.500	0	52	-3	-0.3

BROWN, JOPHERY Jophery Clifford B 1.22.1945 Grambling, LA BL/TR 6-2/190# d9.21

Year	Tm Lg	W	L	Pct	G	GS	CG-Sho	SV-BS	IP	H	R	HR	HB	BB-IB	SO	ERA	AERA	OAV	OOB	AB-SH	AVG	PB	Sup	APR	PW
1968	Chi N	0	0	—	1	0	0	0	2	2	1	0	0	1-1	0	4.50	70	.286	.375	0-0	—	0		0	0.0

BROWN, JOE Joseph E. B 4.4.1859 Warren, PA D 6.28.1888 Warren, PA 5-10/162# d8.16 ▲

Year	Tm Lg	W	L	Pct	G	GS	CG-Sho	SV-BS	IP	H	R	HR	HB	BB-IB	SO	ERA	AERA	OAV	OOB	AB-SH	AVG	PB	Sup	APR	PW
1884	Chi N	4	2	.667	7	6	5	0	50	56	36	4		7	27	4.68	67	.258	.281	61	.213	-1*	155	-5	-0.5
1885	Bal AA	0	4	.000	4	4	4	0	38	52	33	0	0	4	9	5.68	57	.306	.322	19	.158	-1*	113	-8	-0.7
Total	2	4	6	.400	11	10	9	0	88	108	69	4	0	11	36	5.11	62	.279	.299	80	.200	-2	139	-13	-1.2

Year	Tm Lg	W	L	Pct	G	GS	CG-Sho	SV-BS	IP	H	R	HR	HB	BB-IB	SO	ERA	AERA	OAV	OOB	AB-SH	AVG	PB	Sup	APR	PW
BROWN, JOE Joseph Henry B 7.3.1900 Little Rock, AR D 3.7.1950 Los Angeles, CA BR/TR 6/176# d5.17																									
1927	Chi A	0	0	—	1	1	0	0	0	2	3	0	0	1	0	∞	—	1.000	1.000	0-0	—	0	62	-3	-0.2
BROWN, KEITH Keith Edward B 2.14.1964 Flagstaff, AZ BB/TR 6-4/215# d8.25																									
1988	Cin N	2	1	.667	4	3	0	0-0	16.1	14	5	1	0	4-0	6	2.76	130	.237	.286	4-1	.000	-0	49	2	0.3
1990	Cin N	0	0	—	8	0	0	0-0	11.1	12	6	2	0	3-0	8	4.76	83	.286	.333	0-0	—	0		-1	0.0
1991	Cin N	0	0	—	11	0	0	0-0	12	15	4	0	0	6-1	4	2.25	169	.306	.382	0-0	—	0		2	0.1
1992	Cin N	0	1	.000	2	2	0	0-0	8	10	5	2	0	5-0	5	4.50	80	.313	.405	2-1	.000	-0	113	-1	-0.2
Total	4	2	2	.500	25	5	0	0-0	47.2	51	20	5	0	18-1	23	3.40	110	.280	.345	6-2	.000	-1	72	2	0.2
BROWN, KEVIN Kevin Dewayne B 3.5.1966 Oroville, CA BL/TL 6-1/185# d7.27																									
1990	NY N	0	0	—	2	0	0	0-0	2	2	0	0	0	1-0	0	0.00	—	.250	.333	0-0	—	0		1	0.1
	Mil A	1	1	.500	5	3	0	0-0	21	14	7	1	1	7-1	12	2.57	151	.182	.256	0-0	—	0	55	3	0.3
1991	Mil A	2	4	.333	15	10	0	0-1	63.2	66	39	6	1	34-2	30	5.51	72	.270	.361	0-0	—	0	120	-9	-0.8
1992	Sea A	0	0	—	2	0	0	0-0	3	4	3	1	0	3-0	2	9.00	44	.333	.467	0-0	—	0		-2	-0.1
Total	3	3	5	.375	24	13	0	0-1	89.2	86	49	8	2	45-3	44	4.82	82	.252	.341	0-0	—	0	105	-7	-0.5
BROWN, LLOYD Lloyd Andrew "Gimpy" B 12.25.1904 Beeville, TX D 1.14.1974 Opa-Locka, FL BL/TL 5-9/170# d7.17																									
1925	Bro N	0	3	.000	17	5	1	0	63.1	79	39	1	2	25	23	4.12	101	.319	.385	23-1	.087	-2	113	-1	-0.3
1928	Was A	4	4	.500	27	10	2	1	107	112	62	7	2	40	38	4.04	99	.273	.341	31-0	.161	0	99	-3	0.0
1929	Was A	8	7	.533	40	15	7-1	0	168	186	92	7	1	69	48	4.18	101	.297	.368	50-2	.220	3	101	1	0.5
1930	Was A	16	12	.571	38	22	10-1	0	197	220	99	6	5	65	59	4.25	108	.293	.354	65-2	.215	2	79	11	1.7
1931	Was A	15	14	.517	42	32	15-1	0	258.2	256	120	13	0	79	79	3.20	134	.257	.311	96-3	.229	3	100	27	3.0
1932	Was A	15	12	.556	46	24	10-2	5	202.2	239	115	11	1	55	53	4.44	97	.296	.342	70-6	.100	-5	99	-4	-0.9
1933	StL A	1	6	.143	8	6	0	0	39	57	35	1	0	17	7	7.15	65	.350	.411	11-0	.273	1	82	-10	-1.3
	Bos A	8	11	.421	33	21	9-2	1	163.1	180	93	4	0	64	37	4.02	109	.281	.347	57-4	.281	6	85	4	1.2
	Year	9	17	.346	41	27	9-2	1	202.1	237	97	5	0	81	44	4.63	96	.295	.360	68-4	.279	7	85	-6	-0.1
1934	Cle A	5	10	.333	38	15	5	6	117	116	67	7	2	51	39	3.85	118	.263	.342	30-1	.233	1	61	6	0.7
1935	Cle A	8	7	.533	42	8	4-2	4	122	123	52	6	3	37	45	3.61	125	.265	.323	37-2	.108	-2	75	**14**	1.4
1936	Cle A	8	10	.444	24	16	12-1	1	140.1	166	78	13	3	45	34	4.17	121	.294	.349	45-4	.222	2	76	12	1.5
1937	Cle A	2	6	.250	31	5	2	0	77	107	59	4	3	27	32	6.55	70	.329	.386	24-0	.167	-1	49	-14	-1.3
1940	Phi N	1	3	.250	18	2	0	3	37.2	58	26	3	0	16	16	6.21	63	.354	.411	13-1	.077	-1	123	-8	-1.0
Total	12	91	105	.464	404	181	77-10	21	1693	1899	937	83	22	590	510	4.20	105	.288	.348	552-26	.192	6	88	35	5.2
BROWN, MACE Mace Stanley B 5.21.1909 North English, IA D 3.24.2002 Greensboro, NC BR/TR 6-1/190# d5.21 Mil 1944-45 C1																									
1935	Pit N	4	1	.800	18	5	2	0	72.2	84	41	5	0	22	28	3.59	114	.287	.337	24-2	.167	-0	141	2	0.2
1936	Pit N	10	11	.476	47	10	3	3	165	178	89	8	1	55	56	3.87	105	.275	.332	60-3	.167	-2	98	1	0.0
1937	Pit N	7	2	.778	50	2	0	**7**	107.2	109	59	2	1	45	60	4.18	92	.261	.334	30-0	.300	2	134	-4	-0.2
1938	Pit N★	15	9	.625	**51**	2	0	5	132.2	155	68	5	0	44	55	3.80	100	.294	.349	38-5	.132	-2	123	-1	-0.3
1939	Pit N	9	13	.409	47	19	8-1	7	200.1	232	90	8	2	52	71	3.37	114	.293	.338	64-4	.109	-4	83	9	0.6
1940	Pit N	10	9	.526	48	17	5-1	**7**	173	181	78	5	2	49	73	3.49	109	.267	.318	52-5	.115	-1	129	6	0.6
1941	Pit N	0	0	—	1	0	0	0	1.1	2	0	0	0	0	0	0.00	—	.333	.333	0-0	—	0		1	0.0
	Bro N	3	2	.600	24	0	0	3	42.2	31	17	3	1	26	22	3.16	116	.208	.330	8-0	.000	-1		3	0.3
	Year	3	2	.600	25	0	0	3	44	33	23	3	1	26	22	3.07	119	.213	.330	8-0	.000	-1		3	0.3
1942	Bos A	9	3	.750	34	0	0	6	60.1	56	27	4	0	28	20	3.43	109	.255	.339	15-3	.067	-1		2	0.3
1943	Bos A	6	6	.500	**49**	0	0	9	93.1	71	26	2	0	51	40	2.12	156	.222	.329	17-1	.059	-1		**12**	1.6
1946	†Bos A	3	1	.750	18	0	0	1	26.1	26	7	2	0	16	10	2.05	179	.268	.372	5-1	.000	-1		4	0.7
Total	10	76	57	.571	387	55	18-2	48	1075.1	1125	502	44	7	388	435	3.46	110	.271	.335	313-24	.137	-11	110	35	3.8
BROWN, MARK Mark Anthony B 7.13.1959 Bellows Falls, VT BB/TR 6-2/190# d8.9																									
1984	Bal A	1	2	.333	9	0	0	0-0	23	22	11	2	1	7-0	10	3.91	99	.256	.319	0-0	—	0		0	0.0
1985	Min A	0	0	—	6	0	0	0-0	15.2	21	13	1	0	7-0	5	6.89	64	.333	.384	0-0	—	0		-4	-0.2
Total	2	1	2	.333	15	0	0	0-0	38.2	43	24	3	1	14-0	15	5.12	80	.289	.347	0-0	—	0		-4	-0.2
BROWN, MIKE Michael Gary B 3.4.1959 Camden County, NJ BR/TR 6-2/195# d9.16 C1																									
1982	Bos A	1	0	1.000	3	0	0	0-0	6	7	0	0	0	1-0	4	0.00	—	.304	.333	0-0	—	0		3	0.4
1983	Bos A	6	6	.500	19	18	3-1	0-0	104	110	62	12	2	43-1	35	4.67	93	.276	.345	0-0	—	0	135	-4	-0.5
1984	Bos A	1	8	.111	15	11	0	0-0	67	104	63	9	3	19-1	32	6.85	61	.347	.388	0-0	—	0	77	-21	-2.4
1985	Bos A	0	0	—	2	1	0	0-0	3.1	9	8	0	0	3-0	3	21.60	20	.500	.545	0-0	—	0	127	-6	-0.3
1986	Bos A	4	4	.500	15	10	0	0-0	57.1	72	35	10	1	25-1	32	5.34	78	.316	.381	0-0	—	0	85	-6	-0.7
	Sea A	0	2	.000	6	2	0	0-0	15.2	19	14	4	0	11-0	9	7.47	57	.302	.405	0-0	—	0	0	-5	-0.6
	Year	4	6	.400	21	12	0	0-0	73	91	14	14	1	36-1	41	5.79	72	.313	.387	0-0	—	0	70	-11	-1.3
1987	Sea A	0	0	—	1	0	0	0-0	0.1	3	2	0	0	0-0	0	54.00	9	.750	.750	0-0	—	0		-2	-0.1
Total	6	12	20	.375	61	42	3-1	0-0	253.2	324	184	35	6	102-3	115	5.75	74	.313	.374	0-0	—	0	102	-41	-4.2
BROWN, MORDECAI Mordecai Peter Centennial "Three Finger" or "Miner" B 10.19.1876 Nyesville, IN D 2.14.1948 Terre Haute, IN BB/TR 5-10/175# d4.19 M1 HF1949																									
1903	StL N	9	13	.409	26	24	19-1	0	201	231	105	7	6	59	83	2.60	126	.293	.347	77-2	.195	-0	77	11	1.1
1904	Chi N	15	10	.600	26	23	21-4	1	212.1	155	74	1	6	50	81	1.86	143	**.199**	**.253**	89-1	.213	1*	100	16	1.9
1905	Chi N	18	12	.600	30	24	24-4	0	249	219	89	3	1	44	89	2.17	138	.235	.271	93-7	.140	-1*	111	20	2.2
1906	†Chi N	26	6	.813	36	32	27-**9**	3	277.1	198	56	1	4	61	144	**1.04**	**254**	.202	**.252**	98-5	.204	1	141	**45**	**6.1**
1907	†Chi N	20	6	.769	34	27	20-6	3	233	180	51	2	6	40	107	1.39	179	.221	.262	85-5	.153	-0*	123	29	3.7
1908	†Chi N	29	9	.763	44	31	27-9	**5**	312.1	214	64	1	5	49	123	1.47	160	.195	.232	121-5	.207	1*	105	32	4.4
1909	Chi N	**27**	9	.750	**50**	34	**32**-8	**7**	**342.2**	246	78	1	7	53	172	1.31	193	.202	.239	125-5	.176	1	125	**45**	5.3
1910	†Chi N	25	14	.641	46	31	**27-6**	**7**	295.1	256	95	3	4	64	143	1.86	155	.232	**.277**	103-6	.175	-0	132	29	4.0
1911	Chi N	21	11	.656	**53**	27	21	**13**	270	267	110	5	6	55	129	2.80	118	.262	.303	91-3	.253	5	113	16	2.3
1912	Chi N	5	6	.455	15	8	5-2	0	88.2	92	35	2	1	20	34	2.64	126	.274	.317	31-1	.290	2*	113	6	0.8
1913	Cin N	11	12	.478	39	16	11-1	6	173.1	174	79	7	1	44	41	2.91	112	.277	.325	54-3	.204	-0	80	5	0.6
1914	StL F	12	6	.667	26	18	13-2	0	175	172	73	7	3	43	81	3.29	92	.254	.302	59-2	.254	1	101	-1	-0.1
	Bro F	2	5	.286	9	8	5	0	57.2	63	33	1	0	18	32	4.21	68	.276	.329	19-0	.211	-1	128	-8	-0.9
	Year	14	11	.560	35	26	18-2	0	232.2	235	38	8	3	61	113	3.52	85	.260	.309	78-2	.244	0	109	-7	-1.0
1915	Chi F	17	8	.680	35	25	17-3	4	236.1	189	75	2	7	64	95	2.09	120	.220	.279	82-4	.293	5*	125	11	1.8
1916	Chi N	2	3	.400	12	4	2	0	48.1	52	27	0	4	9	21	3.91	74	.289	.337	16-0	.250	0	167	-5	-0.5
Total	14	239	130	.648	481	332	271-55	49	3172.1	2708	1044	43	61	673	1375	2.06	137	.233	.278	1143-49	.206	15	114	251	32.7
BROWN, MYRL Myrl Lincoln B 10.10.1894 Waynesboro, PA D 2.23.1981 Harrisburg, PA BR/TR 5-11/172# d8.19																									
1922	Pit N	3	1	.750	7	5	2	0	34.2	42	25	2	0	13	9	5.97	68	.296	.355	11-2	.273	1	164	-6	-0.5
BROWN, NORM Norman Ladelle B 2.1.1919 Evergreen, NC D 5.31.1995 Bennettsville, SC BB/TR 6-3/180# d10.3 Mil 1944-45																									
1943	Phi A	0	0	—	1	1	0	0	7	5	4	0	0	0	1	0.00	—	.185	.185	3-0	.000	-0	99	1	0.0
1946	Phi A	0	1	.000	4	0	0	0	7.1	8	8	2	0	6	3	6.14	58	.267	.389	0-0	—	0		-3	-0.4
Total	2	0	1	.000	5	1	0	0	14.1	13	12	2	0	6	4	3.14	111	.228	.302	3-0	.000	-0	99	-2	-0.4
BROWN, PAUL Paul Dwayne B 6.18.1941 Ft.Smith, AR BR/TR 6-1/190# d7.23 b-Jackie																									
1961	Phi N	0	1	.000	5	1	0	0	10	13	9	3	1	8-0	1	8.10	50	.325	.440	2-0	.500	0	0	-4	-0.3
1962	Phi N	0	6	.000	23	9	0	1	63.2	74	45	9	3	33-0	29	5.94	65	.298	.385	13-1	.154	0	93	-14	-1.2
1963	Phi N	0	1	.000	6	2	0	0	15.1	15	10	2	2	5-0	11	4.11	79	.238	.314	2-0	.500	0	173	-2	-0.1
1968	Phi N	0	0	—	2	0	0	0	4	6	4	0	0	1-0	4	9.00	33	.353	.389	0-0	—	0		-2	-0.1
Total	4	0	8	.000	36	12	0	1	93	108	68	14	6	47-0	45	6.00	63	.293	.380	17-1	.235	1	97	-22	-1.7
BROWN, RAY Paul Percival B 1.31.1889 Chicago, IL D 5.29.1955 Los Angeles, CA BR/TR 6-1/172# d9.29																									
1909	Chi N	1	0	1.000	1	1	1	0	9	5	3	0	0	4	2	2.00	127	.172	.273	3-0	.000	-0	165	0	0.0
BROWN, STUB Richard P. B 8.3.1870 Baltimore, MD D 3.10.1948 Baltimore, MD TL 6-2/220# d8.15																									
1893	Bal N	0	0	—	2	0	0	0	9	13	8	0	1	5	0	6.00	79	.325	.413	5	.200	-0		-1	-0.1
1894	Bal N	4	0	1.000	9	6	3	0	49.2	59	39	3	1	24	8	4.89	112	.292	.370	23-1	.087	-4	104	2	-0.2

Year	Tm Lg	W	L	Pct	G	GS	CG-Sho	SV-BS	IP	H	R	HR	HB	BB-IB	SO	ERA	AERA	OAV	OOB	AB-SH	AVG	PB	Sup	APR	PW
1897	Cin N	0	1	.000	2	1	1	0	13	17	8	1	0	8	2	4.15	110	.315	.403	5-0	.000	-1	0	1	-0.1
Total	3	4	1	.800	13	7	4	0	71.2	89	55	4	2	37	10	4.90	106	.301	.382	33-1	.091	-5	93	2	-0.4
BROWN, BOB Robert Murray B 4.1.1911 Dorchester, MA D 8.3.1990 Pembroke, MA BR/TR 6-0.5/190# d4.21																									
1930	Bos N	0	0	—	3	0	0	0	6	10	7	0	0	8	1	10.50	47	.417	.563	2-0	.000	-0		-3	-0.2
1931	Bos N	0	1	.000	3	1	0	0	6.1	9	7	0	0	3	2	8.53	44	.375	.444	2-0	.500	0	45	-3	-0.4
1932	Bos N	14	7	.667	35	28	9	1	213	187	89	6	2	104	110	3.30	114	.238	.329	67-5	.194	-0	104	13	1.1
1933	Bos N	0	0	—	5	0	0	0	6.2	6	4	0	0	3	3	2.70	114	.250	.333	2-0	.000	-0*		-1	-0.1
1934	Bos N	1	3	.250	16	8	2-1	0	58.1	59	40	2	3	36	21	5.71	67	.262	.371	21-0	.238	0	141	-12	-0.7
1935	Bos N	1	8	.111	15	10	2-1	0	65	79	55	2	0	36	17	6.37	59	.302	.386	19-1	.105	-1*	87	-20	-2.4
1936	Bos N	0	2	.000	2	2	0	0	8.1	10	6	1	0	3	5	5.40	71	.278	.333	2-0	.000	-0	55	-2	-0.3
Total	7	16	21	.432	79	49	13-2	1	363.2	360	208	11	5	193	159	4.48	84	.261	.354	115-6	.183	-2	103	-28	-3.0
BROWN, SCOTT Scott Edward B 8.30.1956 DeQuincy, LA BR/TR 6-2/220# d8.11																									
1981	Cin N	1	0	1.000	10	0	0	0-2	13	16	4	0	0	1-1	7	2.77	128	.314	.321	1-0	.000	-0		1	0.1
BROWN, STEVE Steven Elbert B 2.12.1957 San Francisco, CA BR/TR 6-5/200# d8.1																									
1983	Cal A	2	3	.400	12	4	2-1	0-0	46	45	19	4	0	16-1	23	3.52	114	.256	.314	0-0	—	0	34	3	0.3
1984	Cal A	0	1	.000	3	3	0	0-0	11	16	13	0	0	9-1	5	9.00	44	.340	.439	0-0	—	0	121	-7	-0.5
Total	2	2	4	.333	15	7	2-1	0-0	57	61	32	4	0	25-2	28	4.58	88	.274	.343	0-0	—	0	71	-4	-0.2
BROWN, TOM Thomas Dale B 8.10.1949 Lafayette, LA BR/TR 6-1/170# d9.14																									
1978	Sea A	0	0	—	6	0	0	0-0	13	14	6	2	0	4-0	8	4.15	92	.286	.340	0-0	—	0		0	0.0
BROWN, TOM Thomas Tarlton B 9.21.1860 Liverpool, England D 10.25.1927 Washington, DC BL/TR 5-10/168# d7.6 M2 U4 ▲																									
1882	Bal AA	0	0	—	2	0	0	0	8.1	13	7	0		6	2	1.08	255	.333	.422	181	.304	1*		0	0.0
1883	Col AA	0	1	.000	3	1	1	0	14	14	17	0		10	6	5.79	53	.246	.358	420	.274	1*	93	-5	-0.2
1884	Col AA	2	1	.667	4	0	0	0	19	27	24	0	0	7	5	7.11	43	.281	.330	451	.273	1*		-9	-1.0
1885	Pit AA	0	0	—	2	0	0	0	6	0	3	0	3	3	2	3.00	107	.000	.207	437	.307	1*		0	0.0
1886	Pit AA	0	0	—	1	0	0	0	2	2	4	0	0	5	1	9.00	38	.125	.333	460	.285	0*		-1	0.0
Total	5	2	2	.500	12	1	1	0	49.1	56	55	0	3	31	16	5.29	57	.242	.340	1949	.286	4	93	-15	-1.2
BROWN, JUMBO Walter George B 4.30.1907 Greene, RI D 10.2.1966 Freeport, NY BR/TR 6-4/295# d8.26																									
1925	Chi N	0	0	—	2	0	0	0	6	5	5	0	0	4	0	3.00	144	.217	.333	1-0	.000	-0		0	0.0
1927	Cle A	0	2	.000	8	0	0	0	18.2	19	14	3	1	26	8	6.27	67	.284	.489	3-0	.667	1		-4	-0.2
1928	Cle A	0	1	.000	5	0	0	0	14.2	19	15	0	0	15	12	6.75	61	.365	.507	3-0	.667	1		-5	-0.2
1932	NY A	5	2	.714	19	3	3-1	1	55.2	58	30	1	2	30	31	4.53	90	.270	.364	23-1	.174	-1	70	-2	-0.2
1933	NY A	7	5	.583	21	8	1	0	74	78	48	3	0	52	55	5.23	74	.269	.380	28-1	.179	-1	145	-11	-1.5
1935	NY A	6	5	.545	20	8	3-1	0	87.1	94	41	2	0	37	41	3.61	112	.279	.350	32-0	.313	3	102	5	0.8
1936	NY A	1	4	.200	20	3	0	1	64	93	47	4	0	29	19	5.91	79	.352	.416	19-0	.000	-3	107	-9	-0.8
1937	Cin N	1	0	1.000	4	1	0	0	9.2	16	10	0	0	3	4	8.38	45	.390	.432	2-0	.000	0	139	-5	-0.4
	NY N	1	0	1.000	4	0	0	0	8.2	5	2	0	0	5	4	1.04	374	.172	.294	0-0	—	0		2	0.3
	Year	2	0	1.000	8	1	0	0	18.1	21	18	0	0	8	8	4.91	78	.300	.372	2-0	.000	0	136	-2	-0.1
1938	NY N	5	3	.625	43	0	0	5	90	65	26	5	1	28	42	1.80	209	.204	.271	16-0	.188	1		**18**	1.7
1939	NY N	4	0	1.000	31	0	0	7	56.1	69	30	1	1	25	24	4.15	95	.304	.375	11-0	.364	1		-1	0.0
1940	NY N	2	4	.333	41	0	0	**7**	55.1	49	25	5	0	25	31	3.42	114	.232	.314	10-0	.100	-1		2	0.2
1941	NY N	1	5	.167	31	0	0	**8**	57	49	23	2	0	21	30	3.32	111	.238	.308	9-0	.111	-1		3	0.3
Total	12	33	31	.516	249	23	7-2	29	597.1	619	316	26	5	300	301	4.07	99	.271	.357	157-2	.204	2	116	-7	0.0
BROWN, WALTER Walter Irving B 4.23.1915 Jamestown, NY D 2.3.1991 Westfield, NY BR/TR 5-11/175# d5.16																									
1947	StL A	1	0	1.000	19	0	0	0	46	50	27	3	0	28	10	4.89	79	.294	.394	11-0	.000	-1		-4	-0.3
BROWNING, CAL Calvin Duane B 3.16.1938 Burns Flat, OK BL/TL 5-11/190# d6.12																									
1960	StL N	0	0	—	1	0	0	0	0.2	5	3	1	0	1-0	0	40.50	10	.714	.750	0-0	—	0		-2	-0.1
BROWNING, FRANK Frank "Dutch" B 10.29.1882 Falmouth, KY D 5.20.1948 San Antonio, TX BR/TR 5-6/155# d4.16																									
1910	Det A	2	2	.500	11	6	2	3	49	51	22	0	0	10	16	2.57	102	.262	.298	14-2	.000	-2	119	-1	-0.2
BROWNING, TOM Thomas Leo B 4.28.1960 Casper, WY BL/TL 6-1/190# d9.9																									
1984	Cin N	1	0	1.000	3	3	0	0-0	23.1	27	4	0	0	5-0	14	1.54	245	.303	.340	7-0	.143	-0	70	6	0.3
1985	Cin N	20	9	.690	38	38	6-4	0-0	261.1	242	111	29	3	73-8	155	3.55	107	.245	.297	88-9	.193	2*	112	8	1.1
1986	Cin N	14	13	.519	39	**39**	4-2	0-0	243.1	225	123	26	1	70-6	147	3.81	102	.245	.295	86-7	.163	-1*	108	-1	-0.4
1987	Cin N	10	13	.435	32	31	2	0-0	183	201	107	27	5	61-7	117	5.02	85	.284	.342	52-6	.154	0*	91	-13	-1.4
1988	Cin N	18	5	.783	36	**36**	5-2	0-0	250.2	205	98	36	7	64-3	124	3.41	105	.224	.277	83-9	.145	0*	122	8	0.7
1989	Cin N	15	12	.556	37	**37**	9-2	0-0	249.2	241	109	31	3	64-10	118	3.39	106	.255	.302	78-14	.090	-3*	105	5	0.1
1990	†Cin N	15	9	.625	35	**35**	2-1	0-0	227.2	235	98	24	5	52-13	99	3.80	104	.266	.309	75-9	.093	-3*	93	7	0.3
1991	Cin N☆	14	14	.500	36	36	1	0-0	230.1	241	124	32	4	56-4	115	4.18	91	.266	.309	70-10	.171	2	114	-11	-1.2
1992	Cin N	6	5	.545	16	16	0	0-0	87	108	49	6	2	28-7	33	5.07	71	.311	.362	31-2	.226	1	99	-12	-1.2
1993	Cin N	7	7	.500	21	20	0	0-0	114	159	61	15	1	20-2	53	4.74	85	.333	.359	37-4	.216	2	102	-7	-0.4
1994	Cin N	3	1	.750	7	7	2-1	0-0	40.2	34	20	8	1	13-1	22	4.20	98	.222	.284	14-2	.143	-0	132	0	0.0
1995	KC A	0	2	.000	2	2	0	0-0	10	13	9	2	0	5-0	3	8.10	59	.302	.375	0-0	—	0	39	-3	-0.5
Total	12	123	90	.577	302	300	31-12	0-0	1921	1931	913	236	32	511-61	1000	3.94	97	.262	.310	621-72	.153	2	106	-13	-2.6
BROWNSON, MARK Mark Phillip B 6.17.1975 Lake Worth, FL BL/TR 6-2/185# d7.21																									
1998	Col N	1	0	1.000	2	2	1-1	0-0	13.1	16	7	2	1	2-0	8	4.73	109	.296	.333	5-0	.000	-1	116	1	0.0
1999	Col N	0	2	.000	7	7	0	0-0	29.2	42	26	8	1	8-0	21	7.89	74	.333	.378	9-2	.111	-1	77	-5	-0.3
2000	Phi N	1	0	1.000	2	0	0	0-1	5	7	4	1	0	3-0	3	7.20	65	.333	.417	0-0	—	0		-1	-0.2
Total	3	2	2	.500	11	9	1-1	0-1	48	65	37	11	2	13-0	32	6.94	80	.323	.370	14-2	.071	-1	87	-5	-0.5
BRUBAKER, BRUCE Bruce Ellsworth B 12.29.1941 Harrisburg, PA BR/TR 6-1/198# d4.15																									
1967	LA N	0	0	—	1	0	0	0	1.1	3	3	1	0	0-0	2	20.25	15	.429	.429	0-0	—	0		-3	-0.1
1970	Mil A	0	0	—	1	0	0	0-0	2	2	2	1	0	1-0	0	9.00	42	.250	.333	0-0	—	0		-1	-0.1
Total	2	0	0	—	2	0	0	0-0	3.1	5	5	2	0	1-0	2	13.50	26	.333	.375	0-0	—	0		-4	-0.2
BRUCE, LOU Louis R. B 1.16.1877 St.Regis, NY D 2.9.1968 Ilion, NY BL/TR 5-5/145# d6.22 ▲																									
1904	Phi A	0	0	—	2	0	0	0	11	11	7	1	0	2	2	4.91	55	.262	.295	101-6	.267	0*		-2	-0.1
BRUCE, BOB Robert James B 5.16.1933 Detroit, MI BR/TR 6-3/210# d9.14																									
1959	Det A	0	1	.000	2	1	0	0	2	2	5	1	0	3-0	1	9.00	45	.250	.455	0-0	—	0	87	-2	-0.4
1960	Det A	4	7	.364	34	15	1	0	130	127	68	16	5	56-1	76	3.74	106	.250	.331	39-2	.179	0	89	0	0.1
1961	Det A	1	2	.333	14	6	0	0	44.2	57	28	6	2	24-2	25	4.43	92	.320	.403	9-1	.111	0	129	-3	-0.2
1962	Hou N	10	9	.526	32	27	6	0	175	164	92	16	12	82-3	135	4.06	92	.248	.339	55-1	.200	5	112	-7	-0.1
1963	Hou N	5	9	.357	30	25	1-1	0	170.1	162	73	7	8	60-3	123	3.59	88	.250	.318	55-3	.127	2*	87	-6	-0.3
1964	Hou N	15	9	.625	35	29	9-4	0	202.1	191	70	8	3	33-4	135	2.76	124	.246	.277	63-5	.190	2*	82	16	2.2
1965	Hou N	9	18	.333	35	34	7-1	0	229.2	241	107	22	9	38-4	145	3.72	90	.270	.305	74-4	.122	-1	83	-9	-1.1
1966	Hou N	3	13	.188	25	23	1	0	129.2	160	83	16	8	29-4	71	5.34	64	.301	.344	39-7	.077	-2	91	-27	-3.1
1967	Atl N	2	3	.400	12	7	1	1	38.2	42	25	3	1	15-4	22	4.89	68	.269	.337	12-0	.167	0	132	-7	-0.9
Total	9	49	71	.408	219	167	26-6	1	1122.1	1146	551	95	48	340-25	733	3.85	91	.263	.321	346-23	.150	6	94	-45	-3.8
BRUCKBAUER, FRED Frederick John B 5.27.1938 New Ulm, MN BR/TR 6-1/185# d4.25																									
1961	Min A	0	0	—	1	0	0	0	0	3	3	0	0	1-0	0	∞	—	1.000	1.000	0-0	—	0		-3	-0.2
BRUCKMILLER, ANDY Andrew B 1.1.1882 McKeesport, PA D 1.12.1970 McKeesport, PA BR/TR 5-11/175# d6.26																									
1905	Det A	0	0	—	1	0	0	0	1	4	3	0	0	1	1	27.00	10	.571	.625	1-0	.000	-0		-2	-0.1
BRUHERT, MIKE Michael Edwin B 6.24.1951 Jamaica, NY BR/TR 6-6/220# d4.9																									
1978	NY N	4	11	.267	27	22	1-1	0-0	133.2	171	83	6	1	34-5	56	4.78	73	.317	.357	40-1	.075	-3	102	-22	-2.5

Year	Tm Lg	W	L	Pct	G	GS	CG-Sho	SV-BS	IP	H	R	HR	HB	BB-IB	SO	ERA	AERA	OAV	OOB	AB-SH	AVG	PB	Sup	APR	PW
BRUMLEY, DUFF Duff Lechaun B 8.25.1970 Cleveland, TN BR/TR 6-4/195# d6.1																									
1994	Tex A	0	0	—	2	0	0	0-0	3.1	6	6	1	0	5-0	4	16.20	30	.400	.500	0-0	—	0		-4	-0.2
BRUMMETT, GREG Gregory Scott B 4.20.1967 Wichita, KS BR/TR 6/180# d5.29																									
1993	SF N	2	3	.400	8	8	0	0-0	46	53	25	9	0	13-1	20	4.70	83	.294	.338	15-2	.000	-1	127	-4	-0.5
	Min A	2	1	.667	5	5	0	0-0	26.2	29	17	3	0	15-1	10	5.74	76	.299	.383	0-0	—	0	148	-3	-0.3
Total	1	4	4	.500	13	13	0	0-0	72.2	82	42	12	0	28-2	30	5.08	80	.296	.355	15-2	.000	-1	135	-7	-0.8
BRUNER, JACK Jack Raymond B 7.1.1924 Waterloo, IA D 6.24.2003 Lincoln, NE BL/TL 6-1/185# d9.16																									
1949	Chi A	1	2	.333	4	2	0	0	7.2	10	7	0	0	8	4	8.22	51	.357	.500	1-0	.000	-0	43	-3	-0.6
1950	Chi A	0	0	—	9	0	0	0	12.1	7	6	0	1	14	8	3.65	123	.184	.415	0-0	—	0		1	0.0
	StL A	1	2	.333	13	1	0	1	35	36	21	4	2	23	16	4.63	107	.267	.381	10-0	.000	-1	55	1	0.0
	Year	1	2	.333	22	1	0	1	47.1	43	24	4	3	37	24	4.37	110	.249	.390	10-0	.000	-1	56	2	0.0
Total	2	2	4	.333	26	3	0	1	55	53	34	4	3	45	28	4.91	96	.264	.406	11-0	.000	-1	44	-1	-0.6
BRUNER, ROY Walter Roy B 2.10.1917 Cecilia, KY D 11.30.1986 St.Matthews, KY BR/TR 6/165# d9.14 Mil 1941-45																									
1939	Phi N	0	4	.000	4	4	2	0	27	38	22	3	0	13	11	6.67	60	.339	.408	9-1	.111	-1	65	-8	-1.0
1940	Phi N	0	0	—	2	0	0	0	6.1	5	4	2	0	6	4	5.68	69	.227	.393	2-0	.500	0		-1	0.0
1941	Phi N	0	3	.000	13	1	0	0	29.1	37	17	1	0	25	13	4.91	75	.336	.459	6-0	.000	-0	23	-3	-0.4
Total	3	0	7	.000	19	5	2	0	62.2	80	43	6	0	44	28	5.74	67	.328	.431	17-1	.118	-1	58	-12	-1.4
BRUNET, GEORGE George Stuart "Lefty" B 6.8.1935 Houghton, MI D 10.25.1991 Poza Rica, Mexico BR/TL 6-1/210# d9.14																									
1956	KC A	0	0	—	6	1	0	0	9	10	8	1	0	11-0	5	7.00	62	.286	.457	2-0	.000	-0	144	-3	-0.1
1957	KC A	0	1	.000	4	2	0	0	11.1	13	7	2	0	4-0	3	5.56	71	.277	.333	2-0	.000	-0	68	-2	-0.2
1959	KC A	0	0	—	2	0	0	0	4.2	10	9	2	1	7-1	7	11.57	35	.435	.581	0-0	—	0		-5	-0.2
1960	KC A	0	2	.000	3	2	0	0	10.1	12	6	0	1	10-2	4	4.35	91	.308	.460	3-0	.000	-0	22	-1	-0.1
	Mil N	2	0	1.000	17	6	0	0	49.2	53	31	6	1	22-5	39	5.07	68	.275	.345	11-0	.091	-1	150	-10	-0.6
1961	Mil N	0	0	—	5	0	0	0	5	7	3	1	0	2-0	0	5.40	69	.412	.450	0-0	—	0		-1	0.0
1962	Hou N	2	4	.333	17	11	2	0	54	62	31	2	0	21-1	36	4.50	83	.291	.353	17-1	.059	-1	92	-5	-0.5
1963	Hou N	0	3	.000	5	2	0	0	12.2	24	11	2	0	6-1	11	7.11	44	.393	.448	3-0	.000	-0	55	-6	-1.1
	Bal A	0	1	.000	16	0	0	1	20	25	15	3	1	9-0	13	5.40	64	.301	.372	1-0	.000	-0		-5	-0.3
1964	LA A	2	2	.500	10	7	0	0	42.1	38	17	2	0	25-1	36	3.61	91	.237	.337	11-1	.182	0	77	0	0.0
1965	Cal A	9	11	.450	41	26	8-3	2	197	149	64	9	3	69-8	141	2.56	133	.209	.280	56-6	.054	-2	78	18	1.5
1966	Cal A	13	13	.500	41	32	8-2	0	212	183	88	21	5	106-8	148	3.31	101	.234	.327	68-1	.103	-2	98	1	-0.1
1967	Cal A	11	19	.367	40	37	7-2	1	250	203	99	19	4	90-9	165	3.31	95	.223	.293	78-4	.077	-4	91	-2	-0.7
1968	Cal A	13	17	.433	39	36	8-5	0	245.1	191	83	23	2	68-3	132	2.86	102	.215	.270	74-4	.081	-3	78	3	-0.1
1969	Cal A	6	7	.462	23	19	2-2	0-1	100.2	98	51	15	1	39-4	56	3.84	91	.255	.324	27-2	.037	-1	87	-5	-0.7
	Sea A	2	5	.286	12	11	2	0-0	63.2	70	41	11	0	28-5	37	5.37	68	.280	.353	20-0	.150	1	97	-11	-1.0
	Year	8	12	.400	35	30	4-2	0-1	164.1	168	45	26	1	67-9	93	4.44	80	.265	.335	47-2	.085	-0	91	-16	-1.7
1970	Was A	8	6	.571	24	20	2-1	0-0	118	124	64	10	1	48-4	67	4.42	80	.275	.345	38-4	.158	1	119	-11	-1.1
	Pit N	1	1	.500	12	1	0	0-0	16.2	19	5	1	1	9-1	17	2.70	145	.311	.408	4-0	.000	-0	46	3	0.2
1971	StL N	0	1	.000	7	0	0	0-1	9.1	12	6	3	0	7-0	4	5.79	62	.316	.422	3-0	.333	0		-2	-0.2
Total	15	69	93	.426	324	213	39-15	4-<u>2</u>	1431.2	1303	639	133	21	581-53	921	3.62	92	.244	.318	418-23	.089	-14	91	-44	-5.3
BRUNETTE, JUSTIN Justin Thomas B 10.7.1975 Los Alamitos, CA BL/TL 6-1/200# d4.13																									
2000	StL N	0	0	—	4	0	0	0-0	4.2	8	3	0	0	5-0	2	5.79	80	.364	.481	1-0	1.000	0		0	0.0
BRUNO, TOM Thomas Michael B 1.26.1953 Chicago, IL BR/TR 6-5/210# d8.1																									
1976	KC A	1	0	1.000	12	0	0	0-0	17.1	20	13	3	0	9-1	11	6.75	52	.290	.367	0-0	—	0		-5	-0.3
1977	Tor A	0	1	.000	12	0	0	0-0	18.1	30	18	4	1	13-1	9	7.85	54	.366	.444	0-0	—	0		-7	-0.3
1978	StL N	4	3	.571	18	3	0	1-2	49.2	38	12	3	0	17-1	33	1.99	177	.209	.275	12-2	.083	-1	94	9	1.1
1979	StL N	2	3	.400	27	1	0	0-1	38.1	37	18	1	2	22-5	27	4.23	89	.253	.355	5-1	.200	0	47	-1	-0.1
Total	4	7	7	.500	69	4	0	1-3	123.2	125	61	11	3	61-8	80	4.22	88	.261	.344	17-3	.118	-1	78	-4	0.4
BRUNSON, WILL William Donald B 3.20.1970 Irving, TX BL/TL 6-4/185# d6.21																									
1998	LA N	0	1	.000	2	0	0	0-0	2.1	3	3	0	0	2-0	1	11.57	34	.333	.455	0-0	—	0		-2	-0.4
	Det A	0	0	—	8	0	0	0-0	3	2	0	0	0	1-0	1	0.00	—	.200	.273	0-0	—	0		2	0.1
1999	Det A	1	0	1.000	17	0	0	0-0	12	18	9	3	0	6-1	9	6.00	83	.367	.421	0-0	—	0		-2	-0.1
Total	2	1	1	.500	27	0	0	0-0	17.1	23	12	3	0	9-1	11	5.71	84	.338	.405	0-0	—	0		-2	-0.4
BRUSKE, JIM James Scott B 10.7.1964 E.St.Louis, IL BR/TR 6-1/185# d8.25																									
1995	LA N	0	0	—	9	0	0	1-0	10	12	7	0	1	4-0	5	4.50	84	.300	.378	0-0	—	0		-1	-0.1
1996	LA N	0	0	—	11	0	0	0-0	12.2	17	8	2	1	3-1	12	5.68	68	.315	.362	0-0	—	0		-2	-0.1
1997	SD N	4	1	.800	28	0	0	0-1	44.2	37	22	4	1	25-1	32	3.63	107	.228	.330	6-0	.167	0*		0	0.1
1998	LA N	3	0	1.000	35	0	0	1-1	44	47	18	2	3	19-1	31	3.48	114	.272	.354	3-0	.000	-0		3	0.1
	SD N	0	0	—	4	0	0	0-0	7	10	4	1	0	4-2	4	3.86	101	.333	.412	0-0	—	0		0	0.0
	Year	3	0	1.000	39	0	0	1-1	51	57	25	3	3	23-3	35	3.53	112	.281	.362	3-0	.000	-0		2	0.1
	NY A	1	0	1.000	3	1	0	0-0	9	9	3	2	0	1-0	3	3.00	146	.257	.278	0-0	—	0	170	2	0.2
2000	Mil N	1	0	1.000	15	0	0	0-0	16.2	22	15	5	2	12-1	8	6.48	70	.314	.424	1-0	.000	-0		-4	-0.3
Total	5	9	1	.900	105	1	0	2-2	144	154	77	16	8	68-6	95	4.13	97	.273	.357	10-0	.100	-0	170	-2	-0.1
BRUSSTAR, WARREN Warren Scott B 2.2.1952 Oakland, CA BR/TR 6-3/200# d5.6																									
1977	†Phi N	7	2	.778	46	0	0	3-1	71.1	64	26	7	1	24-3	46	2.65	151	.250	.316	6-1	.000	-1		9	1.1
1978	†Phi N	6	3	.667	58	0	0	0-3	88.2	74	25	0	3	30-7	60	2.33	153	.239	.310	7-0	.143	0		12	1.3
1979	Phi N	1	0	1.000	13	0	0	1-1	14.1	23	12	1	0	4-2	3	6.91	56	.383	.415	0-0	—	0		-5	-0.4
1980	†Phi N	2	2	.500	26	0	0	0-1	38.2	42	16	3	0	13-2	21	3.72	102	.286	.344	1-0	.000	-0		1	0.1
1981	†Phi N	0	1	.000	14	0	0	0-1	12.1	12	6	0	1	10-4	8	4.38	83	.250	.383	0-0	—	0		-1	-0.1
1982	Phi N	2	3	.400	22	0	0	2-1	22.2	31	12	2	1	5-3	11	4.76	77	.348	.381	2-0	.000	-0		-2	-0.4
	Chi A	2	0	1.000	10	0	0	0-0	18.1	19	7	2	1	3-0	8	3.44	118	.257	.295	0-0	—	0		2	0.2
1983	Chi N	3	1	.750	59	0	0	1-3	80.1	67	21	1	2	37-10	46	2.35	162	.234	.321	4-1	.000	-0		13	0.7
1984	†Chi N	1	1	.500	41	0	0	3-2	63.2	57	23	4	1	21-7	36	3.11	126	.247	.307	5-1	.200	1		6	0.4
1985	Chi N	4	3	.571	51	0	0	4-1	74.1	87	55	8	3	36-11	34	6.05	66	.292	.368	7-0	.143	0		-15	-1.6
Total	9	28	16	.636	340	0	0	14-14	484.2	476	203	28	13	183-49	273	3.51	109	.265	.333	32-3	.094	-1		20	1.3
BRYANT, CLAY Claiborne Henry B 11.16.1911 Madison Heights, VA D 4.9.1999 Boca Raton, FL BR/TR 6-2.5/195# d4.19 C3																									
1935	Chi N	1	2	.333	9	1	0	2	22.2	34	15	1	0	7	13	5.16	76	.358	.402	6-1	.333	2*	173	-3	-0.2
1936	Chi N	1	2	.333	26	0	0	0	57.1	57	25	0	2	24	35	3.30	121	.259	.337	12-1	.417	1*		4	0.3
1937	Chi N	9	3	.750	38	9	4-1	3	135.1	117	69	1	1	78	75	4.26	94	.232	.336	45-2	.311	5*	99	-3	0.1
1938	†Chi N	19	11	.633	44	30	17-3	2	270.1	235	105	6	1	125	**135**	3.10	124	.235	.321	106-1	.226	4*	97	22	2.6
1939	Chi N	2	1	.667	4	4	2	0	31.1	42	23	3	1	14	9	5.74	69	.307	.375	14-0	.214	0*	116	-6	-0.5
1940	Chi N	0	1	.000	8	0	0	0	26.1	26	17	2	0	14	5	4.78	78	.265	.357	9-0	.333	1*		-3	-0.1
Total	6	32	20	.615	129	44	23-4	7	543.1	511	254	13	5	262	272	3.73	104	.249	.335	192-5	.266	13	101	11	2.2
BRYANT, RON Ronald Raymond B 11.12.1947 Redlands, CA BB/TL 6/190# d9.29																									
1967	SF N	0	0	—	1	0	0	0	4	3	2	0	1	0-0	2	4.50	73	.200	.250	1-0	.000	-0		0	0.0
1969	SF N	4	3	.571	16	8	0	1-0	57.2	60	29	8	2	25-1	30	4.37	80	.271	.349	16-3	.188	1	123	-4	-0.4
1970	SF N	5	8	.385	34	11	1	0-1	96	103	58	7	2	38-0	66	4.78	83	.274	.342	27-2	.111	-1	76	-9	-1.1
1971	†SF N	7	10	.412	27	22	3-2	0-0	140	146	69	9	3	49-3	79	3.79	90	.272	.333	50-1	.200	1	96	-6	-0.5
1972	SF N	14	7	.667	35	28	11-4	0-0	214	176	81	20	2	77-5	107	2.90	120	.224	.293	70-6	.171	1	126	13	1.1
1973	SF N	**24**	12	.667	41	39	8	0-0	270	240	125	23	9	115-12	143	3.53	108	.234	.315	95-3	.168	1*	104	7	1.0
1974	SF N	3	15	.167	41	23	0	0-1	126.2	142	92	11	4	68-4	75	5.61	68	.286	.372	31-4	.129	-1	76	-23	-3.1
1975	StL N	0	1	.000	10	1	0	0-0	8.2	20	17	2	0	7-1	7	16.62	23	.444	.519	1-0	.000	-0	93	-11	-1.1
Total	8	57	56	.504	205	132	23-6	1-<u>2</u>	917	890	473	80	23	379-26	509	4.02	91	.254	.329	291-19	.165	0	100	-33	-4.1

Year	Tm Lg	W	L	Pct	G	GS	CG-Sho	SV-BS	IP	H	R	HR	HB	BB-IB	SO	ERA	AERA	OAV	OOB	AB-SH	AVG	PB	Sup	APR	PW
BRYDEN, T.R. Thomas Ray B 1.17.1959 Moses Lake, WA BR/TR 6-4/190# d4.10																									
1986	Cal A	2	1	.667	16	0	0	0-1	34.1	38	25	4	2	21-0	25	6.55	63	.290	.386	0-0	—	0		-8	-0.6
BRYNAN, TOD Charles Ruley B 7.1863 Philadelphia, PA D 5.10.1925 Philadelphia, PA BR/TR 5-10/?# d6.22																									
1888	Chi N	2	1	.667	3	3	2	0	25	29	26	2	2	7	11	6.48	47	.271	.328	11	.182	0	128	-8	-0.7
1891	Bos N	0	1	.000	1	1	0	0	1	4	6	0	0	3	0	54.00	7	.571	.700	0	—	0	163	-4	-0.5
Total	2	2	2	.500	4	4	2	0	26	33	32	2	2	10	11	8.31	37	.289	.357	11	.182	0	146	-12	-1.2
BUCHANAN, JIM James Forrest B 7.1.1876 Chatham Hill, VA D 6.15.1949 Norfolk, NE BL/TR 5-10/165# d4.16																									
1905	StL A	5	9	.357	22	15	12-1	**2**	141.1	149	76	2	2	27	54	3.50	73	.272	.309	46-1	.152	-0	96	-15	-1.4
BUCHANAN, BOB Robert Gordon B 5.3.1961 Ridley Park, PA BL/TL 6-1/185# d7.13																									
1985	Cin N	1	0	1.000	14	0	0	0-0	16	25	15	4	0	9-1	3	8.44	45	.368	.442	1-0	.000	-0		-7	-0.4
1989	KC A	0	0	—	2	0	0	0-0	3.1	5	6	1	0	3-2	3	16.20	24	.333	.444	0-0	—	0		-4	-0.2
Total	2	1	0	1.000	16	0	0	0-0	19.1	30	21	5	0	12-3	6	9.78	39	.361	.442	1-0	.000	-0		-11	-0.6
BUCKELS, GARY Gary Scott B 7.22.1965 LaMirada, CA BR/TR 6/185# d7.23																									
1994	StL N	0	1	.000	10	0	0	0-0	12	8	5	2	0	7-1	9	2.25	185	.186	.300	1-0	.000	-0		2	0.1
BUCKEYE, GARLAND Garland Maiers "Gob" B 10.16.1897 Heron Lake, MN D 11.14.1975 Stone Lake, WI BB/TL 6/260# d6.19																									
1918	Was A	0	0	—	1	0	0	0	2	3	4	0	0	6	2	18.00	15	.333	.600	0-0	—	0		-3	-0.1
1925	Cle A	13	8	.619	30	18	11-1	0	153	161	74	3	6	58	49	3.65	121	.267	.338	62-3	.226	2	104	13	1.7
1926	Cle A	6	9	.400	32	18	5-1	0	165.2	160	79	3	6	69	36	3.10	131	.264	.345	60-2	.200	2	103	12	1.1
1927	Cle A	10	17	.370	35	25	13-2	1	204.2	231	106	6	5	74	38	3.96	106	.296	.360	71-2	.268	3	69	6	0.9
1928	Cle A	1	5	.167	9	6	0	0	35	58	32	2	2	5	6	6.69	62	.389	.417	9-0	.111	-1	95	-10	-1.4
	NY N	0	0	—	1	0	0	0	3.2	9	6	1	0	2	3	14.73	27	.409	.458	2-0	.500	1		-4	-0.1
Total	5	30	39	.435	108	67	29-4	1	564	622	301	15	19	214	134	3.91	108	.287	.356	204-7	.230	7	90	14	2.1
BUCKINGHAM, ED Edward Taylor B 5.12.1874 Metuchen, NJ D 7.30.1942 Bridgeport, CT d8.30																									
1895	Was N	0	0	—	1	1	0	0	3	6	5	0	0	2	1	6.00	80	.400	.471	1-0	.000	-0	74	-1	-0.1
BUCKLES, JESS Jesse Robert "Jim" B 5.20.1890 LaVerne, CA D 8.2.1975 Westminster, CA BL/TL 6-2.5/205# d9.17																									
1916	NY A	0	0	—	2	0	0	0	4	3	2	0	0	1	2	2.25	128	.188	.235	1-0	.000	-0		0	0.0
BUCKLEY, JOHN John Edward B 3.20.1869 Marlborough, MA D 5.3.1942 Westborough, MA BL/TR 6-1/200# d7.15																									
1890	Buf P	1	3	.250	4	4	4	0	34	49	32	5	0	16	4	7.68	53	.325	.389	15	.000	-2	82	-10	-0.9
BUDDIE, MIKE Michael Joseph B 12.12.1970 Berea, OH BR/TR 6-3/210# d4.6																									
1998	NY A	4	1	.800	24	2	0	0-0	41.2	46	29	5	3	13-1	20	5.62	78	.284	.346	0-0	—	0	148	-7	-0.7
1999	NY A	0	0	—	2	0	0	0-0	2	3	1	1	0	0-0	1	4.50	105	.333	.333	0-0	—	0		0	0.0
2000	Mil N	0	0	—	5	0	0	0-0	6	8	3	0	0	1-1	5	4.50	101	.320	.346	0-0	—	0		0	0.0
2001	Mil N	0	1	.000	31	0	0	2-0	41.2	34	20	2	4	17-2	22	3.89	111	.225	.316	4-0	.250	0		2	0.2
2002	Mil N	1	2	.333	25	0	0	0-2	39.2	46	23	5	1	21-7	28	4.54	90	.293	.378	2-0	.000	-0		-3	-0.2
Total	5	5	4	.556	87	2	0	2-2	131	137	76	13	8	52-11	76	4.67	92	.272	.347	6-0	.167	-0	148	-8	-0.7
BUDNICK, MIKE Michael Joe B 9.15.1919 Astoria, OR D 12.2.1999 Seattle, WA BR/TR 6-1/200# d4.18																									
1946	NY N	2	3	.400	35	7	1-1	3	88.1	75	40	13	0	48	36	3.16	109	.231	.330	20-0	.300	3	107	1	0.4
1947	NY N	0	0	—	7	1	0	0	12	16	16	0	0	10	6	10.50	39	.314	.426	4-0	.250	0	217	-9	-0.4
Total	2	2	3	.400	42	8	1-1	3	100.1	91	56	13	0	58	42	4.04	87	.242	.343	24-0	.292	3	122	-8	0.0
BUEHRLE, MARK Mark Anthony B 3.23.1979 St.Charles, MO BL/TL 6-2/200# d7.16																									
2000	†Chi A	4	1	.800	28	3	0	0-2	51.1	55	27	5	3	19-1	37	4.21	119	.272	.344	0-0	—	0	94	4	0.4
2001	Chi A	16	8	.667	32	32	4-2	0-0	221.1	188	89	24	8	48-2	126	3.29	140	.230	.279	3-0	.000	-0	105	31	3.3
2002	Chi A★	19	12	.613	34	34	5-2	0-0	239	236	102	25	3	61-7	134	3.58	126	.260	.308	6-0	.167	-0	126	26	3.2
2003	Chi A	14	14	.500	35	35	2	0-0	230.1	250	124	22	5	61-2	119	4.14	110	.278	.325	6-0	.167	-0	96	6	0.7
Total	4	53	35	.602	129	104	11-4	0-2	742	729	342	76	19	189-12	416	3.71	124	.258	.308	15-0	.133	-0	108	67	7.6
BUFFINTON, CHARLIE Charles G. B 6.14.1861 Fall River, MA D 9.23.1907 Fall River, MA BR/TR 6-1/180# d5.17 M1 ▲																									
1882	Bos N	2	3	.400	5	5	4-1	0	42	53	34	2		14	17	4.07	70	.296	.347	50	.260	0*	111	-6	-0.5
1883	Bos N	25	14	.641	43	41	34-4	1	333	346	187	4		51	188	3.03	102	.254	.281	341	.238	0*	135	9	0.7
1884	Bos N	48	16	.750	67	67	63-8	0	587	506	225	15		76	417	2.15	135	.219	.244	352	.267	12*	116	51	5.8
1885	Bos N	22	27	.449	51	50	49-6	0	434.1	425	238	10		112	242	2.88	93	.246	.292	338	.240	5*	99	-7	0.0
1886	Bos N	7	10	.412	18	17	16	0	151	203	129	4		39	47	4.59	70	.308	.346	176	.290	4*	106	-22	-1.6
1887	Phi N	21	17	.553	40	38	35-1	0	332.1	352	224	16	4	92	160	3.66	116	.264	.313	269	.268	2*	102	18	2.0
1888	Phi N	28	17	.622	46	46	43-6	0	400.1	324	139	6	4	59	199	1.91	156	.213	.244	160	.181	-1	76	45	**5.1**
1889	Phi N	28	16	.636	47	43	37-2	0	380	390	196	10	6	121	153	3.24	134	.257	.315	154	.208	-3	89	45	4.0
1890	Phi P	19	15	.559	36	33	28	1	283.1	312	211	8	7	126	89	3.81	112	.268	.343	150	.273	4*	102	10	1.2
1891	Bos AA	29	9	**.763**	48	43	33-2	1	363.2	303	153	8	7	120	158	2.55	137	.219	**.284**	181	.188	-0*	112	45	4.0
1892	Bal N	4	8	.333	13	13	9	0	97	130	88	4	3	46	30	4.92	70	.309	.381	43	.349	4	115	-16	-1.1
Total	11	233	152	.605	414	396	351-30	3	3404	3344	1824	87	31	856	1700	2.96	114	.246	.292	2214	.245	27	105	172	19.6
BUHL, BOB Robert Ray B 8.12.1928 Saginaw, MI D 2.16.2001 Titusville, FL BR/TR 6-2/190# d4.17																									
1953	Mil N	13	8	.619	30	18	8-3	0	154.1	133	59	9	3	73	83	2.97	132	.235	.326	53-5	.113	-3	101	18	1.9
1954	Mil N	2	7	.222	31	14	2-1	3	110.1	117	54	5	2	65	57	4.00	93	.277	.374	31-0	.032	-3	97	-3	-0.5
1955	Mil N	13	11	.542	38	27	11-1	1	201.2	168	85	13	1	109-5	117	3.21	117	.227	.324	57-7	.105	-4	105	11	0.8
1956	Mil N	18	8	.692	38	33	13-2	0	216.2	190	96	18	2	105-7	86	3.32	104	.236	.325	73-6	.096	-4	116	3	-0.1
1957	†Mil N	18	7	**.720**	34	31	14-2	0	216.2	191	77	15	0	121-4	117	2.74	128	.241	.338	73-3	.082	-3	123	19	1.6
1958	Mil N	5	2	.714	11	10	3	1	73	74	33	5	1	30-0	27	3.45	102	.260	.330	25-1	.200	0	115	0	0.0
1959	Mil N	15	9	.625	31	25	12-**4**	0	198	181	76	19	2	74-3	105	2.86	124	.243	.312	70-2	.057	-5	124	15	1.3
1960	Mil N★	16	9	.640	36	33	11-2	0	238.2	202	89	23	3	103-7	121	3.09	111	.229	.310	89-3	.157	-2	115	12	1.1
1961	Mil N	9	10	.474	32	28	9-1	0	188.1	180	99	23	5	98-4	77	4.11	91	.256	.350	60-2	.067	-4	123	-11	-1.3
1962	Mil N	0	1	.000	1	1	0	0	2	6	5	0	0	4-1	1	22.50	17	.545	.625	1-0	.000	-0	92	-4	-0.6
	Chi N	12	13	.480	34	30	8-1	0	212	204	108	23	6	94-6	109	3.69	112	.255	.334	69-7	.000	-6	91	6	0.0
	Year	12	14	.462	35	31	8-1	0	214	210	112	23	6	98-7	110	3.87	107	.259	.339	70-7	.000	-6	91	2	-0.6
1963	Chi N	11	14	.440	37	34	6	0	226	219	96	24	3	62-1	108	3.38	104	.259	.310	74-7	.108	-3	94	4	0.1
1964	Chi N	15	14	.517	36	35	11-3	0	227.2	208	103	22	5	68-4	107	3.83	97	.244	.301	73-5	.096	-2	101	-1	-0.2
1965	Chi N	13	11	.542	32	31	2	0	184.1	207	100	26	0	57-4	92	4.39	84	.284	.333	67-2	.060	-4	101	-12	-1.8
1966	Chi N	0	0	—	1	1	0	0	2.1	4	4	1	0	1-0	1	15.43	24	.400	.417	1-0	.000	-0	215	-3	-0.1
	Phi N	6	8	.429	32	18	1	1	132	156	74	10	4	39-6	59	4.77	75	.298	.349	41-3	.098	-2	111	-16	-1.7
	Year	6	8	.429	33	19	1	1	134.1	160	79	11	4	40-6	60	4.96	73	.300	.351	42-3	.095	-2	117	-20	-1.8
1967	Phi N	0	0	—	3	0	0	0	3	6	4	2	0	2-0	1	12.00	28	.462	.533	0-0	—	0		-3	-0.1
Total	15	166	132	.557	457	369	111-20	6	2587	2446	1162	238	37	1105-**52**	1268	3.55	103	.251	.328	857-53	.089	-43	108	35	0.4
BUICE, DE WAYNE De Wayne Allison B 8.20.1957 Lynwood, CA BR/TR 6/170# d4.25																									
1987	Cal A	6	7	.462	57	0	0	17-4	114	87	45	12	2	40-3	109	3.39	127	.213	.285	0-0	—	0		14	1.8
1988	Cal A	2	4	.333	32	0	0	3-4	41.1	45	29	5	0	19-3	38	5.88	66	.287	.360	0-0	—	0		-9	-1.3
1989	Tor A	1	0	1.000	7	0	0	0-0	17	13	12	2	0	13-1	10	5.82	65	.220	.351	0-0	—	0		-4	-0.2
Total	3	9	11	.450	96	0	0	20-8	172.1	145	86	19	2	72-7	157	4.23	98	.232	.311	0-0	—	0		1	0.3
BUKER, CY Cyril Owen B 2.5.1919 Greenwood, WI BL/TR 5-11/190# d5.17																									
1945	Bro N	7	2	.778	42	4	0	5	87.1	90	41	2	1	45	48	3.30	114	.268	.356	16-3	.188	-0	147	4	0.4
BUKVICH, RYAN Ryan Adrien B 5.13.1978 Naperville, IL BR/TR 6-3/250# d7.12																									
2002	KC A	1	0	1.000	26	0	0	0-1	25	26	19	2	1	19-3	20	6.12	82	.277	.393	0-0	—	0		-3	-0.1
2003	KC A	1	0	1.000	9	0	0	0-0	10.1	12	11	2	0	9-0	8	9.58	54	.293	.412	0-0	—	0		-4	-0.3
Total	2	2	0	1.000	35	0	0	0-1	35.1	38	30	4	1	28-3	28	7.13	71	.281	.399	0-0	—	0		-7	-0.4

Year	Tm Lg	W	L	Pct	G	GS	CG-Sho	SV-BS	IP	H	R	HR	HB	BB-IB	SO	ERA	AERA	OAV	OOB	AB-SH	AVG	PB	Sup	APR	PW
BULLINGER, JIM James Eric B 8.21.1965 New Orleans, LA BR/TR 6-2/185# d5.27 b-Kirk																									
1992	Chi N	2	8	.200	39	9	1	7-0	85	72	49	9	4	54-6	36	4.66	77	.233	.350	20-1	.250	2	78	-9	-0.9
1993	Chi N	1	0	1.000	15	0	0	1-0	16.2	18	9	1	0	9-0	10	4.32	92	.277	.360	1-0	.000	-0		-1	-0.1
1994	Chi N	6	2	.750	33	10	1	2-0	100	87	43	6	1	34-2	72	3.60	116	.235	.298	22-5	.136	1	99	6	0.5
1995	Chi N	12	8	.600	24	24	1-1	0-0	150	152	80	14	9	65-7	93	4.14	99	.265	.346	47-8	.128	1*	120	-2	-0.1
1996	Chi N	6	10	.375	37	20	1-1	1-0	129.1	144	101	15	8	68-5	90	6.54	66	.283	.373	32-3	.250	5*	106	-30	-2.6
1997	Mon N	7	12	.368	36	25	2-2	0-1	155.1	165	106	17	12	74-5	87	5.56	75	.276	.364	43-3	.209	2	90	-23	-2.2
1998	Sea A	0	1	.000	2	1	0	0-0	5.2	13	10	3	0	2-0	4	15.88	29	.433	.455	0-0	—	0	140	-7	-0.8
Total	7	34	41	.453	186	89	6-4	11-1	642	651	398	65	34	306-25	392	5.06	81	.265	.351	165-20	.188	10	103	-66	-6.2
BULLINGER, KIRK Kirk Matthew B 10.28.1969 New Orleans, LA BR/TR 6-2/170# d8.30 b-Jim																									
1998	Mon N	1	0	1.000	8	0	0	0-1	7	14	8	1	0	0-0	2	9.00	47	.400	.400	1-0	.000	-0		-4	-0.5
1999	Bos A	0	0	—	4	0	0	0-0	2	2	1	0	0	2-0	0	4.50	111	.286	.444	0-0	—	0		0	0.0
2000	Phi N	0	0	—	3	0	0	0-0	3.1	4	2	0	0	0-0	4	5.40	86	.308	.286	0-0	—	0		0	0.0
2003	Hou N	0	0	—	7	0	0	0-0	8	7	6	2	0	1-0	5	6.75	66	.219	.242	0-0	—	0		-2	-0.1
Total	4	1	0	1.000	22	0	0	0-1	20.1	27	17	3	0	3-0	11	7.08	63	.310	.330	1-0	.000	-0		-6	-0.6
BULLOCK, RED Malton Joseph B 10.12.1911 Biloxi, MS D 6.27.1988 Pascagoula, MS BL/TL 6-1/192# d5.19																									
1936	Phi A	0	2	.000	12	2	0	0	16.2	19	32	0	0	37	7	14.04	36	.271	.523	4-0	.000	-1	52	-17	-1.6
BUMP, NATE Nathan Louis B 1.24.1976 Towanda, PA BL/TR 6-2/180# d6.28																									
2003	†Fla N	4	0	1.000	32	0	0	0-0	36.1	34	21	3	7	20-0	17	4.71	87	.246	.367	0-1	—	0		-3	-0.3
BUNCH, MELVIN Melvin Lynn B 11.4.1971 Texarkana, TX BR/TR 6-1/165# d5.6																									
1995	KC A	1	3	.250	13	5	0	0-0	40	42	25	11	0	14-1	19	5.62	85	.261	.320	0-0	—	0	89	-3	-0.3
1999	Sea A	0	0	—	5	1	0	0-0	10	20	13	3	0	7-0	4	11.70	41	.426	.491	0-0	—	0	118	-7	-0.3
Total	2	1	3	.250	18	6	0	0-0	50	62	38	14	0	21-1	23	6.84	70	.298	.361	0-0	—	0	94	-10	-0.6
BUNKER, WALLY Wallace Edward B 1.25.1945 Seattle, WA BR/TR 6-2/197# d9.29																									
1963	Bal A	0	1	.000	1	1	0	0	4	10	6	1	0	3-0	1	13.50	26	.476	.542	2-0	.500	0	77	-4	-0.6
1964	Bal A	19	5	**.792**	29	29	12-1	0	214	161	72	17	3	62-5	96	2.69	133	.207	.267	72-2	.069	-2	122	21	2.1
1965	Bal A	10	8	.556	34	27	4-1	2	189	170	79	16	4	58-2	84	3.38	103	.242	.301	55-3	.073	-1	133	4	0.1
1966	†Bal A	10	6	.625	29	24	3	0	142.2	151	74	16	2	48-2	89	4.29	78	.269	.327	48-3	.104	-0*	143	-15	-1.6
1967	Bal A	3	7	.300	29	9	1	1	88	83	46	7	2	31-1	51	4.09	77	.254	.322	26-1	.077	-2	132	-10	-1.3
1968	Bal A	2	0	1.000	18	10	2-1	0	71	59	25	4	1	14-1	44	2.41	121	.225	.265	18-2	.111	-0	158	3	0.1
1969	KC A	12	11	.522	35	31	10-1	2-0	222.2	198	89	29	4	62-3	130	3.23	114	.238	.293	70-7	.143	0	90	12	1.4
1970	KC A	2	11	.154	24	15	2-1	0-0	121.2	109	63	16	0	50-2	59	4.22	89	.238	.312	31-1	.065	-0	59	-5	-0.6
1971	KC A	2	3	.400	7	6	0	0-0	32.1	35	19	7	0	6-0	15	5.01	69	.271	.301	9-0	.000	-1	87	-5	-0.8
Total	9	60	52	.536	206	152	34-5	5-0	1085.1	976	473	113	16	334-16	569	3.51	99	.240	.299	331-19	.094	-5	114	1	-1.2
BUNNING, JIM James Paul David B 10.23.1931 Southgate, KY BR/TR 6-3/195# d7.20 HF1996																									
1955	Det A	3	5	.375	15	8	0	1	51	59	38	8	3	32-2	37	6.35	60	.291	.395	15-2	.200	-0	84	-13	-1.8
1956	Det A	5	1	.833	15	3	0	1	53.1	55	24	6	0	28-4	34	3.71	111	.257	.339	18-2	.333	2	137	3	0.4
1957	Det A★	**20**	8	.714	45	30	14-1	1	**267.1**	214	91	33	11	72-5	182	2.69	143	.218	.277	94-5	.213	3	95	32	3.4
1958	Det A	14	12	.538	35	34	10-3	0	219.2	188	96	28	10	79-4	177	3.52	115	.228	.302	75-6	.187	-1*	105	12	1.1
1959	Det A★	17	13	.567	40	35	14-1	0	249.2	220	111	37	11	75-0	**201**	3.89	104	.234	.297	89-8	.191	1	106	10	0.9
1960	Det A	11	14	.440	36	34	10-3	0	252	217	92	20	11	64-7	**201**	2.79	**142**	.236	.292	81-8	.160	-2*	72	**31**	2.5
1961	Det A★	17	11	.607	38	37	12-4	1	268	232	113	25	9	71-3	194	3.19	128	.229	.284	100-2	.130	-4	103	26	2.0
1962	Det A★	19	10	.655	41	35	12-2	6	258	262	112	28	13	74-3	184	3.59	113	.261	.319	95-4	.242	4*	111	15	1.8
1963	Det A★	12	13	.480	39	35	6-2	1	248.1	245	119	38	5	69-3	196	3.88	97	.254	.306	84-6	.155	-1*	91	-4	-0.5
1964	Phi N★	19	8	.704	41	39	13-5	2	284.1	248	99	23	14	46-3	219	2.63	132	.233	.274	99-9	.121	-2	133	26	1.9
1965	Phi N	19	9	.679	39	39	15-7	0	291	253	92	23	12	62-10	268	2.60	133	.232	.279	103-4	.214	4	102	31	3.4
1966	Phi N★	19	14	.576	43	**41**	16-**5**	1	314	260	91	26	19	55-8	252	2.41	149	.223	.268	106-4	.179	1	97	42	4.4
1967	Phi N	17	15	.531	40	**40**	16-**6**	0	**302.1**	241	94	18	13	73-20	**253**	2.29	149	.217	.271	104-7	.163	2	100	**35**	**3.9**
1968	Pit N	4	14	.222	27	26	3-1	0	160	168	75	14	8	48-6	95	3.88	75	.272	.332	51-2	.098	-2	96	-15	-2.0
1969	Pit N	10	9	.526	25	25	4	0-0	156	147	74	10	6	49-4	124	3.81	92	.249	.311	47-7	.043	-3	103	-6	-1.1
	LA N	3	1	.750	9	9	1	0-0	56.1	65	23	5	1	10-0	33	3.36	99	.288	.321	18-3	.111	-1	107	0	-0.1
	Year	13	10	.565	34	34	5	0-0	212.1	212	27	15	7	59-4	157	3.69	93	.259	.314	65-10	.062	-4	104	-5	-1.2
1970	Phi N	10	15	.400	34	33	4	0-0	219	233	111	19	8	56-9	147	4.11	97	.274	.321	71-3	.127	-2*	86	-4	-0.7
1971	Phi N	5	12	.294	29	16	1	1-1	110	126	72	11	6	37-7	58	5.48	64	.297	.358	25-3	.120	0*	91	-22	-3.1
Total	17	224	184	.549	591	519	151-40	16-1	3760.1	3433	1527	372	160	1000-98	2855	3.27	114	.242	.297	1275-85	.167	-1	100	199	16.4
BURBA, DAVE David Allen B 7.7.1966 Dayton, OH BR/TR 6-4/240# d9.8																									
1990	Sea A	0	0	—	6	0	0	0-0	8	8	6	0	1	2-0	4	4.50	88	.267	.333	0-0	—	0		-1	0.0
1991	Sea A	2	2	.500	22	2	0	1-0	36.2	34	16	6	0	14-3	16	3.68	112	.245	.314	0-0	—	0	89	2	0.2
1992	SF N	2	7	.222	23	11	0	0-0	70.2	80	43	4	2	31-2	47	4.97	67	.287	.358	15-3	.067	-1	77	-14	-1.7
1993	SF N	10	3	.769	54	5	0	0-0	95.1	95	49	14	3	37-5	88	4.25	92	.265	.336	17-3	.294	2	129	-4	-0.3
1994	SF N	3	6	.333	57	0	0	0-3	74	59	39	5	6	45-3	84	4.38	92	.221	.345	3-0	.000	-0		-3	-0.4
1995	SF N	4	2	.667	37	0	0	0-1	43.1	38	26	5	0	25-2	46	4.98	82	.235	.335	0-0	—	0		-4	-0.5
	†Cin N	6	2	.750	15	9	1-1	0-0	63.1	52	24	4	0	26-1	50	3.27	126	.223	.301	15-4	.067	-0	102	6	0.7
	Year	10	4	.714	52	9	1-1	0-1	106.2	90	29	9	0	51-3	96	3.97	104	.228	.315	15-4	.067	-0	103	3	0.2
1996	Cin N	11	13	.458	34	33	0	0-0	195	179	96	18	2	97-9	148	3.83	111	.244	.329	67-3	.104	-1	93	7	0.6
1997	Cin N	11	10	.524	30	27	2	0-0	160	157	88	22	9	73-10	131	4.72	90	.255	.341	46-4	.196	1	91	-7	-0.7
1998	†Cle A	15	10	.600	32	31	0	0-0	203.2	210	100	30	7	69-4	132	4.11	116	.269	.330	6-0	.167	1	104	15	1.6
1999	†Cle A	15	9	.625	34	34	1	0-0	220	211	113	30	8	96-3	174	4.25	119	.254	.336	3-0	.333	1	103	19	1.9
2000	Cle A	16	6	.727	32	32	0	0-0	191.1	199	99	19	2	91-2	180	4.47	111	.267	.346	1-2	.000	-0	110	11	1.1
2001	†Cle A	10	10	.500	32	27	1	0-0	150.2	188	112	16	3	54-2	118	6.21	73	.306	.361	2-2	.000	-0	131	-27	-2.9
2002	Tex A	4	5	.444	23	18	1	0-1	111.1	125	71	13	7	40-3	70	5.42	87	.279	.346	5-0	.200	0	109	-8	-0.6
	Cle A	1	0	1.000	12	3	0	0-1	34	30	20	3	2	17-0	25	4.50	98	.236	.333	0-0	—	0	141	-1	-0.1
	Year	5	5	.500	35	21	1	0-2	145.1	155	27	16	9	57-3	95	5.20	89	.270	.343	5-0	.200	0	114	-8	-0.7
2003	Mil N	1	1	.500	17	2	0	0-0	43.1	42	19	5	4	19-2	35	3.53	120	.250	.340	10-1	.000	-1	88	3	0.1
Total	14	111	86	.563	460	234	6-1	1-6	1700.2	1707	921	194	56	736-51	1348	4.50	99	.261	.339	190-22	.137	1	107	-6	-1.0
BURBACH, BILL William David B 8.22.1947 Dickeyville, WI BR/TR 6-4/215# d4.11																									
1969	NY A	6	8	.429	31	24	2-1	0-0	140.2	112	68	15	2	102-1	82	3.65	95	.219	.349	40-6	.100	-1	98	-4	-0.5
1970	NY A	0	2	.000	4	4	0	0-0	16.2	23	19	2	1	9-0	10	10.26	34	.324	.402	5-0	.000	-1	152	-12	-1.2
1971	NY A	0	1	.000	2	0	0	0-0	3.1	6	6	0	0	5-2	3	10.80	30	.400	.524	2-0	.000	-0		-4	-0.7
Total	3	6	11	.353	37	28	2-1	0-0	160.2	141	93	17	3	116-3	95	4.48	78	.236	.360	47-6	.085	-2	106	-20	-2.4
BURCHART, LARRY Larry Wayne B 2.8.1946 Tulsa, OK BR/TR 6-3/205# d4.10																									
1969	Cle A	0	2	.000	29	0	0	1	42.1	42	28	2	1	24-2	26	4.25	89	.266	.358	0-0	—	0		-4	-0.3
BURCHELL, FRED Frederick Duff B 7.14.1879 Perth Amboy, NJ D 11.20.1951 Jordan, NY BL/TL 5-11/175# d4.17																									
1903	Phi N	0	3	.000	6	3	2	0	44	48	28	0	2	14	12	2.86	114	.293	.356	16-0	.188	-1	7	-1	-0.1
1907	Bos A	0	1	.000	2	1	0	0	10	8	5	0	1	2	6	2.70	95	.222	.282	5-0	.200	-0	131	0	-0.1
1908	Bos A	10	8	.556	31	19	9	0	179.2	161	84	2	11	65	94	2.96	83	.247	.326	69-3	.246	1*	133	-9	-0.9
1909	Bos A	3	3	.500	10	5	1	0	52	51	22	1	2	11	12	2.94	85	.271	.318	19-0	.158	-0	102	-2	-0.2
Total	4	13	15	.464	49	28	12	0	285.2	268	139	3	16	92	124	2.93	89	.258	.328	109-3	.220	-0	108	-12	-1.3
BURDETTE, FREDDIE Freddie Thomason B 9.15.1936 Moultrie, GA BR/TR 6-1/170# d9.5																									
1962	Chi N	0	0	—	8	0	0	1	9.2	5	4	2	0	8-3	5	3.72	111	.161	.325	1-0	.000	-0		1	0.0
1963	Chi N	0	0	—	4	0	0	0	4.2	5	2	1	0	2-0	1	3.86	91	.313	.389	0-0	—	0		0	0.0
1964	Chi N	1	0	1.000	18	0	0	0	20	17	7	2	1	10-2	4	3.15	118	.243	.333	1-0	1.000	0		2	0.1
Total	3	1	0	1.000	30	0	0	1	34.1	27	13	5	1	20-5	10	3.41	112	.231	.338	2-0	.500	0		3	0.1

Year	Tm Lg	W	L	Pct	G	GS	CG-Sho	SV-BS	IP	H	R	HR	HB	BB-IB	SO	ERA	AERA	OAV	OOB	AB-SH	AVG	PB	Sup	APR	PW
BURDETTE, LEW Selva Lewis B 11.22.1926 Nitro, WV BR/TR 6-2/190# d9.26 C2																									
1950	NY A	0	0	—	2	0	0	0	1.1	3	1	0	0	0	0	6.75	64	.500	.500	0-0	—	0		0	0.0
1951	Bos N	0	0	—	3	0	0	0	4.1	6	4	0	1	5	1	6.23	59	.375	.545	1-0	.000	-0		-2	-0.1
1952	Bos N	6	11	.353	45	9	5	7	137	138	58	8	2	47	47	3.61	100	.265	.328	35-6	.114	-0	77	1	0.2
1953	Mil N	15	5	.750	46	13	6-1	8	175	177	73	7	5	56	58	3.24	121	.264	.326	53-5	.170	-1	100	15	1.5
1954	Mil N	15	14	.517	38	32	13-4	0	238	224	87	17	4	62	79	2.76	135	.251	.300	79-5	.089	-5*	84	26	2.5
1955	Mil N	13	8	.619	42	33	11-2	0	230	253	114	25	6	73-9	70	4.03	93	.280	.336	86-3	.233	3*	124	-6	-0.2
1956	Mil N	19	10	.655	39	35	16-**6**	1	256.1	234	92	22	3	52-7	110	**2.70**	128	.241	.281	86-11	.186	1*	125	23	2.6
1957	†Mil N★	17	9	.654	37	33	14-1	0	256.2	260	117	25	2	59-8	78	3.72	94	.264	.304	88-4	.148	1*	137	-6	-0.3
1958	†Mil N	20	10	**.667**	40	36	19-3	0	275.1	279	102	18	5	50-7	113	2.91	121	.264	.300	99-5	.242	9*	123	19	2.9
1959	Mil N★	**21**	15	.583	41	**39**	20-**4**	1	289.2	312	144	38	1	38-3	105	4.07	87	.273	.295	104-5	.202	6*	126	-16	-1.2
1960	Mil N	19	13	.594	45	32	**18**-4	4	275.2	277	116	19	5	35-7	83	3.36	102	.260	.287	91-2	.176	5*	126	3	1.1
1961	Mil N	18	11	.621	40	36	14-3	0	**272.1**	295	131	31	3	33-3	92	4.00	94	.273	.295	103-3	.204	5*	114	-8	-0.2
1962	Mil N	10	9	.526	37	19	6-1	2	143.2	172	85	26	2	23-6	59	4.89	78	.298	.325	51-2	.176	0*	114	-16	-1.9
1963	Mil N	6	5	.545	15	13	4-1	0	84	71	40	15	1	24-4	28	3.64	88	.228	.284	26-4	.038	-0*	109	-5	-0.7
	StL N	3	8	.273	21	14	3	2	98	106	50	6	7	16-2	45	3.77	94	.278	.314	31-3	.097	-1	88	-3	-0.6
	Year	9	13	.409	36	27	7-1	2	182	177	54	21	8	40-6	73	3.71	92	.255	.300	57-7	.070	-2	98	-7	-1.3
1964	StL N	1	0	1.000	8	0	0	0	10	10	3	1	0	3-0	3	1.80	211	.256	.302	1-0	.000	-0		2	0.2
	Chi N	9	9	.500	28	17	8-2	0	131	152	74	15	1	19-2	40	4.88	76	.292	.317	43-3	.279	6	103	-14	-1.1
	Year	10	9	.526	36	17	8-2	0	141	162	78	16	1	22-2	43	4.66	80	.290	.316	44-3	.273	6	103	-11	-0.9
1965	Chi N	0	2	.000	7	3	0	0	20.1	26	17	3	1	4-1	5	5.31	69	.299	.337	6-0	.333	1*	95	-5	-0.3
	Phi N	3	3	.500	19	9	1-1	0	70.2	95	50	5	5	17-2	23	5.48	63	.329	.374	20-2	.300	1	107	-16	-1.1
	Year	3	5	.375	26	12	1-1	0	91	121	54	8	6	21-3	28	5.44	65	.322	.365	26-2	.308	2	104	-22	-1.4
1966	Cal A	7	2	.778	54	0	0	5	79.2	80	32	4	1	12-2	27	3.39	99	.268	.297	8-0	.125	-0		0	0.0
1967	Cal A	1	0	1.000	19	0	0	1	18.1	16	10	4	1	0-0	8	4.91	64	.232	.243	0-0	—	0		-3	-0.2
Total	18	203	144	.585	626	373	158-33	31	3067.1	3186	1400	289	56	628-63	1074	3.66	99	.268	.306	1011-63	.183	30	115	-11	3.1
BURDICK, BILL William Byron B 10.11.1859 Austin, MN D 10.23.1949 Spokane, WA BR/TR d7.23																									
1888	Ind N	10	10	.500	20	20	20	0	176	168	88	12	6	43	55	2.81	105	.242	.292	68	.147	-2*	82	0	-0.3
1889	Ind N	2	4	.333	10	4	2	1	45.2	58	42	7	0	13	16	4.53	92	.301	.345	17	.118	-0	141	-5	-0.5
Total	2	12	14	.462	30	24	22	1	221.2	226	130	19	6	56	71	3.17	101	.255	.304	85	.141	-3	93	-5	-0.8
BURGMEIER, TOM Thomas Henry B 8.2.1943 St.Paul, MN BL/TL 5-11/185# d4.10 C4																									
1968	Cal A	1	4	.200	56	2	0	5	72.2	65	41	5	0	24-3	33	4.33	67	.250	.310	2-0	.000	0*	75	-13	-0.9
1969	KC A	3	1	.750	31	0	0	0-3	54	67	31	5	1	21-3	23	4.17	89	.316	.374	18-0	.167	-0*		-4	-0.2
1970	KC A	6	6	.500	41	0	0	1-1	68.1	59	31	6	0	23-1	43	3.16	118	.236	.297	14-1	.143	-0*		3	0.6
1971	KC A	9	7	.563	67	0	0	17-4	88.1	71	23	3	7	30-4	44	1.73	198	.223	.303	20-0	.250	2*		15	3.7
1972	KC A	6	2	.750	51	0	0	9-3	55.1	67	32	0	1	33-6	18	4.23	72	.313	.401	12-0	.333	1		-9	-1.5
1973	KC A	0	0	—	6	0	0	1-0	10	13	6	2	1	4-0	4	5.40	76	.310	.383	0-0	—	0		-1	-0.1
1974	Min A	5	3	.625	50	0	0	4-1	91.2	92	46	7	2	26-2	34	4.52	83	.270	.319	0-0	—	0*		-5	-0.3
1975	Min A	5	8	.385	46	0	0	11-4	75.2	76	32	7	1	23-2	41	3.09	124	.264	.318	0-0	—	0*		5	1.0
1976	Min A	8	1	.889	57	0	0	1-2	115.1	95	36	11	2	29-3	45	2.50	143	.226	.279	0-0	—	0		14	1.2
1977	Min A	6	4	.600	61	0	0	7-4	97.1	113	56	15	2	33-0	35	5.09	79	.299	.354	0-0	—	0		-10	-1.0
1978	Bos A	2	1	.667	35	1	0	4-2	61.1	74	33	7	3	23-1	24	4.40	94	.302	.368	0-0	—	0	87	-1	0.0
1979	Bos A	3	2	.600	44	0	0	4-3	88.2	89	32	8	4	16-4	60	2.74	162	.263	.302	0-0	—	0		15	0.9
1980	Bos A☆	5	4	.556	62	0	0	24-2	99	87	30	3	2	20-3	54	2.00	211	.241	.283	0-0	—	0		21	3.1
1981	Bos A	4	5	.444	32	0	0	6-1	59.2	61	23	5	4	17-4	35	2.87	135	.268	.329	0-0	—	0		6	1.1
1982	Bos A	7	0	1.000	40	0	0	2-2	102.1	98	30	6	2	22-7	44	2.29	189	.259	.300	0-0	—	0		21	1.6
1983	Oak A	6	7	.462	49	0	0	4-2	96	89	33	2	0	32-8	39	2.81	138	.244	.303	0-0	—	0*		12	1.7
1984	Oak A	3	0	1.000	17	0	0	2-0	23	15	6	2	0	8-4	8	2.35	160	.190	.261	0-0	—	0		4	0.6
Total	17	79	55	.590	745	3	0	102-34	1258.2	1231	521	94	32	384-55	584	3.23	118	.261	.318	66-1	.212	2	70	73	11.5
BURGOS, ENRIQUE Enrique (Calles) B 10.7.1965 Chorrera, Panama BL/TL 6-4/195# d7.15																									
1993	KC A	0	1	.000	5	0	0	0-0	5	5	5	0	1	6-1	6	9.00	51	.238	.429	0-0	—	0		-2	-0.4
1995	SF N	0	0	—	5	0	0	0-0	8.1	14	8	1	1	6-0	12	8.64	47	.378	.477	0-0	—	0		-4	-0.2
Total	2	0	1	.000	10	0	0	0-0	13.1	19	13	1	2	12-1	18	8.78	49	.328	.458	0-0	—	0		-6	-0.6
BURK, SANDY Charles Sanford B 4.22.1887 Columbus, OH D 10.11.1934 Brooklyn, NY BR/TR 5-8/155# d9.12																									
1910	Bro N	0	3	.000	4	3	1	0	19.1	17	16	0	2	27	14	6.05	50	.258	.484	5-0	.000	-1	49	-6	-0.9
1911	Bro N	1	3	.250	13	7	1	0	58	54	36	1	3	47	15	5.12	65	.261	.405	19-1	.105	-1	103	-9	-0.7
1912	Bro N	0	0	—	2	0	0	0	8.1	9	3	0	0	3	2	3.24	103	.273	.333	4-0	.250	0		0	0.1
	StL N	1	3	.250	12	4	2	1	44.2	37	19	0	1	12	17	2.42	142	.236	.294	11-0	.000	-2	43	4	0.1
	Year	1	3	.250	14	4	2	1	53	46	21	0	1	15	19	2.55	134	.242	.301	15-0	.067	-1	43	4	0.2
1913	StL N	0	2	.000	19	7	0	1	70	81	45	1	6	33	29	5.14	63	.290	.377	22-0	.091	-2	113	-14	-0.9
1915	Pit F	2	0	1.000	2	2	1	0	18	8	3	0	0	11	9	1.00	271	.140	.279	6-0	.167	-0	77	3	0.3
Total	5	4	11	.267	52	23	5	2	218.1	206	122	2	12	133	86	4.25	76	.258	.372	67-1	.090	-6	86	-22	-2.0
BURKART, ELMER Elmer Robert "Swede" B 2.1.1917 Philadelphia, PA D 2.6.1995 Baltimore, MD BR/TR 6-2/190# d9.14																									
1936	Phi N	0	0	—	2	2	0	0	7.2	4	3	0	0	12	2	3.52	129	.160	.432	2-0	.000	-0	65	1	0.0
1937	Phi N	0	0	—	7	0	0	0	16	20	11	0	0	9	4	6.19	70	.323	.408	6-0	.000	-1		-2	-0.2
1938	Phi N	0	1	.000	2	1	1	0	10	12	5	0	1	3	1	4.50	86	.286	.348	3-0	.000	-0	22	0	-0.1
1939	Phi N	1	0	1.000	5	0	0	0	8.1	11	4	0	0	2	2	4.32	93	.344	.382	1-0	1.000	1		0	0.1
Total	4	1	1	.500	16	3	1	0	42	47	23	0	1	26	9	4.93	85	.292	.394	12-0	.083	-1	55	-1	-0.2
BURKE, JAMES James B Attleboro, MA d6.10																									
1882	Buf N	0	1	.000	1	1	0	0	4	10	9	0		0	0	11.25	26	.435	.435	4	.000	-1	72	-4	-0.5
1883	Buf N	0	0	—	1	1	0	0	8	9	8	0		3	1	5.63	56	.243	.300	5	.200	-0	152	-2	-0.1
1884	Bos U	19	15	.559	38	36	34	0	322	326	201	10		31	255	2.85	83	.245	.263	184	.223	-7*	109	-18	-2.2
Total	3	19	16	.543	40	38	34	0	334	345	218	10		34	256	3.02	80	.249	.267	193	.218	-8	109	-24	-2.8
BURKE, JOHN John C. B 2.9.1970 Durango, CO BB/TR 6-4/220# d8.13																									
1996	Col N	2	1	.667	11	0	0	0-0	15.2	21	13	3	1	7-0	19	7.47	70	.318	.387	2-0	.500	0		-3	-0.4
1997	Col N	2	5	.286	17	9	0	0-0	59	83	46	13	6	26-0	39	6.56	79	.329	.401	19-2	.158	-1*	57	-7	-0.8
Total	2	4	6	.400	28	9	0	0-0	74.2	104	59	16	7	33-0	58	6.75	77	.327	.398	21-2	.190	-1	57	-10	-1.2
BURKE, JOHN John Patrick B 1.27.1877 Hazleton, PA D 8.4.1950 Jersey City, NJ BR/TR d6.27																									
1902	NY N	0	1	.000	2	1	1	0	14	21	11	0	0	3	3	5.79	49	.344	.375	13-0	.154	-0*	24	-4	-0.3
BURKE, BOBBY Robert James "Lefty" B 1.23.1907 Joliet, IL D 2.8.1971 Joliet, IL BL/TL 6-0.5/150# d4.16																									
1927	Was A	3	2	.600	36	6	1	0	100	91	48	6	7	32	20	3.96	103	.245	.316	24-3	.125	-2	109	3	-0.1
1928	Was A	2	4	.333	26	7	2-1	0	85.1	87	44	1	2	18	27	3.90	103	.277	.320	20-1	.250	1	69	1	0.1
1929	Was A	6	8	.429	37	17	4	0	141	154	91	6	4	55	51	4.79	89	.279	.349	43-7	.140	-3	81	-9	-1.1
1930	Was A	3	4	.429	24	4	2	3	74.1	62	41	2	3	29	35	3.63	127	.229	.310	23-1	.174	-1	168	5	0.3
1931	Was A	8	3	.727	30	13	3-1	2	128.2	124	67	6	2	50	38	4.27	101	.255	.327	47-2	.213	-0	148	3	0.2
1932	Was A	3	6	.333	22	10	2	0	91	98	55	4	1	44	32	5.14	84	.272	.353	25-1	.200	0*	97	-7	-0.6
1933	Was A	4	3	.571	25	6	4-1	0	64	64	29	1	2	31	28	3.23	129	.256	.343	17-2	.235	0	88	6	0.6
1934	Was A	8	8	.500	37	15	7-1	0	168	155	67	2	1	72	52	3.21	134	.245	.323	57-3	.228	2*	75	22	2.0
1935	Was A	1	8	.111	15	10	2	0	66.1	90	63	7	2	27	16	7.46	58	.327	.391	22-1	.182	-0*	72	-24	-2.6
1937	Phi N	0	0	—	2	0	0	0	0	1	1	0	0	2	0	∞	—	.500	.750	0-0	—	0		-1	-0.1
Total	10	38	46	.452	254	88	27-4	5	918.2	926	506	35	24	360	299	4.29	99	.263	.336	278-21	.194	-3	97	-1	-1.3
BURKE, STEVE Steven Michael B 3.5.1955 Stockton, CA BB/TR 6-2/200# d9.10																									
1977	Sea A	0	1	.000	6	0	0	0-0	15.2	12	6	0	0	7-1	6	2.87	144	.226	.311	0-0	—	0		2	0.1
1978	Sea A	0	1	.000	18	0	0	0-0	49	46	22	2	1	24-0	16	3.49	110	.258	.346	0-0	—	0		1	0.1

Year	Tm Lg	W	L	Pct	G	GS	CG-Sho	SV-BS	IP	H	R	HR	HB	BB-IB	SO	ERA	AERA	OAV	OOB	AB-SH	AVG	PB	Sup	APR	PW
Total	2	0	2	.000	24	0	0	0-0	64.2	58	28	2	1	31-1	22	3.34	117	.251	.338	0-0	—	0		3	0.2
BURKE, TIM Timothy Philip B 2.19.1959 Omaha, NE BR/TR 6-3/205# d4.8																									
1985	Mon N	9	4	.692	**78**	0	0	8-1	120.1	86	32	9	7	44-14	87	2.39	142	.204	.288	10-0	.100	-0		16	1.9
1986	Mon N	9	7	.563	68	2	0	4-6	101.1	103	37	7	4	46-13	82	2.93	126	.262	.344	7-1	.000	-0	84	9	1.4
1987	Mon N	7	0	1.000	55	0	0	18-4	91	64	18	3	0	17-6	58	1.19	355	.196	.234	10-2	.000	-1		**28**	2.9
1988	Mon N	3	5	.375	61	0	0	18-6	82	84	36	7	3	25-13	42	3.40	106	.272	.327	2-0	.000	-0		2	0.2
1989	Mon N★	9	3	.750	68	0	0	28-11	84.2	68	24	6	0	22-7	54	2.55	139	.225	.274	3-0	.000	-0		10	2.1
1990	Mon N	3	3	.500	58	0	0	20-5	75	71	29	6	2	21-6	47	2.52	145	.247	.300	6-0	.167	0		7	1.0
1991	Mon N	3	4	.429	37	0	0	5-7	46	41	24	3	4	14-6	25	4.11	88	.243	.314	1-0	.000	-0		-3	-0.4
	NY N	3	3	.500	35	0	0	1-3	55.2	55	22	5	0	12-2	34	2.75	133	.255	.291	5-0	.000	-1		4	0.4
	Year	6	7	.462	72	0	0	6-10	101.2	96	50	8	4	26-8	59	3.36	108	.249	.301	6-0	.000	-1		1	0.0
1992	NY N	1	2	.333	15	0	0	0-2	15.2	26	15	1	0	3-0	7	5.74	61	.366	.387	0-0	—	0		-6	-1.0
	NY A	2	2	.500	23	0	0	0-0	27.2	26	14	2	1	15-4	8	3.25	121	.250	.350	0-0	—	0		1	0.1
Total	8	49	33	.598	498	2	0	102-45	699.1	624	251	49	21	219-71	444	2.72	135	.240	.302	44-3	.045	-2	84	68	8.6
BURKE, BILLY William Ignatius B 7.11.1889 Clinton, MA D 2.9.1967 Worcester, MA BL/TL 5-10/165# d4.30																									
1910	Bos N	1	0	1.000	19	1	1	0	64	68	32	1	2	29	22	4.08	82	.302	.387	21-1	.190	-1*	179	-2	-0.2
1911	Bos N	0	1	.000	2	1	0	0	3.1	6	7	0	0	5	1	18.90	20	.429	.579	1-0	1.000	0	39	-4	-0.7
Total	2	1	1	.500	21	2	1	0	67.1	74	39	1	2	34	23	4.81	70	.310	.400	22-1	.227	-0	111	-6	-0.9
BURKE, TURK William R. B 11.1865 Cincinnati, OH D 3.17.1939 Atchison, KS 6/200# d7.20																									
1887	Det N	0	1	.000	2	2	1	0	15	21	14	0	2	5	3	6.00	68	.318	.384	8	.250	-0	151	-3	-0.2
BURKETT, JESSE Jesse Cail "Crab" B 12.4.1868 Wheeling, WV D 5.27.1953 Worcester, MA BL/TL 5-8/155# d4.22 C1 HF1946 ▲																									
1890	NY N	3	10	.231	21	14	6	0	118	134	123	3	14	92	82	5.57	63	.277	.407	401	.309	8*	80	-26	-1.7
1894	Cle N	0	0	—	1	0	0	0	4	6	2	0	0	1	0	4.50	122	.333	.368	523-10	.358	0*		1	0.0
1902	StL A	0	1	.000	1	0	0	0	1	4	4	0	0	1	2	9.00	39	.571	.625	553-7	.306	0*		-2	-0.3
Total	3	3	11	.214	23	14	6	0	123	144	129	3	14	94	84	5.56	64	.283	.408	1477-17	.325	9	80	-27	-2.0
BURKETT, JOHN John David B 11.28.1964 New Brighton, PA BR/TR 6-2/211# d9.15																									
1987	SF N	0	0	—	3	0	0	0-0	6	7	4	2	1	3-0	5	4.50	86	.304	.407	1-0	.000	-0		-1	0.0
1990	SF N	14	7	.667	33	32	2	1-0	204	201	92	18	4	61-7	118	3.79	96	.257	.313	63-8	.048	-3	128	-3	-0.6
1991	SF N	12	11	.522	36	34	3-1	0-0	206.2	223	103	19	10	60-2	131	4.18	86	.277	.332	55-9	.091	-1	93	-14	-1.6
1992	SF N	13	9	.591	32	32	3-1	0-0	189.2	194	96	13	4	45-6	107	3.84	86	.264	.308	55-8	.018	-3	128	-15	-2.1
1993	SF N★	**22**	7	.759	34	34	2-1	0-0	231.2	224	100	18	11	40-4	145	3.65	107	.255	.294	76-12	.118	-1	125	8	0.8
1994	SF N	6	8	.429	25	25	0	0-0	159.1	176	72	14	7	36-7	85	3.62	111	.286	.330	51-3	.059	-4	88	7	0.2
1995	Fla N	14	14	.500	30	30	4	0-0	188.1	208	95	22	6	57-5	126	4.30	98	.282	.339	66-4	.106	-2*	91	0	-0.2
1996	Fla N	6	10	.375	24	24	1	0-0	154	154	84	15	3	42-2	108	4.32	94	.263	.314	52-3	.173	0	89	-5	-0.5
	†Tex A	5	2	.714	10	10	1-1	0-0	68.2	75	33	4	2	16-2	47	4.06	129	.280	.323	0-0	—	0	87	9	0.7
1997	Tex A	9	12	.429	30	30	2	0-0	189.1	240	106	20	4	30-1	139	4.56	105	.307	.333	5-0	.200	0	103	5	0.5
1998	Tex A	9	13	.409	32	32	0	0-0	195	230	131	19	8	46-1	131	5.68	85	.292	.335	3-0	.000	-0	83	-16	-1.6
1999	Tex A	9	8	.529	30	25	0	0-0	147.1	184	95	18	3	46-1	96	5.62	91	.307	.358	2-0	.000	-0	98	-7	-0.7
2000	†Atl N	10	6	.625	31	22	0	0-1	134.1	162	79	13	4	51-2	110	4.89	94	.303	.365	42-6	.143	-0	117	-4	-0.4
2001	†Atl N★	12	12	.500	34	34	1-1	0-0	219.1	187	83	17	6	70-13	187	3.04	145	.230	.294	65-7	.092	-3	95	33	3.0
2002	Bos A	13	8	.619	29	29	1-1	0-0	173	199	93	25	8	50-5	124	4.53	99	.287	.340	3-1	.000	-0	121	1	-0.1
2003	†Bos A	12	9	.571	32	30	1	0-0	181.2	202	108	20	9	47-1	107	5.15	89	.281	.330	1-1	.000	-0	111	-9	-0.9
Total	15	166	136	.550	445	423	21-6	1-1	2648.1	2866	1374	257	90	700-59	1766	4.31	98	.277	.326	540-62	.093	-18	104	-11	-3.5
BURKHART, KEN Kenneth William (b: Kenneth William Burkhardt) B 11.18.1916 Knoxville, TN BR/TR 6-1/190# d4.21 U17																									
1945	StL N	18	8	.692	42	22	12-4	2	217.1	206	76	9	3	66	67	2.90	129	.251	.309	72-4	.181	1	98	23	2.5
1946	StL N	6	3	.667	25	13	5-2	2	100	111	34	4	2	36	32	2.88	120	.282	.346	34-0	.147	-0	143	8	0.6
1947	StL N	3	6	.333	34	6	1	1	95	108	55	13	4	23	44	5.21	79	.292	.340	24-2	.125	-1	103	-8	-0.8
1948	StL N	0	0	—	20	0	0	1	37.1	50	24	4	2	14	16	5.54	74	.331	.395	4-0	.250	0*		-5	-0.2
	Cin N	0	3	.000	16	0	0	0	41.2	42	34	3	1	16	14	6.91	57	.255	.324	9-0	.333	2		-13	-0.7
	Year	0	3	.000	36	0	0	1	79	92	63	7	3	30	30	6.27	64	.291	.358	13-0	.308	2		-18	-0.9
1949	Cin N	0	0	—	11	0	0	1	28.1	29	10	2	0	10	8	3.18	132	.282	.345	7-0	.286	0		4	0.2
Total	5	27	20	.574	148	41	18-6	7	519.2	546	233	35	12	165	181	3.84	99	.273	.332	150-6	.180	2	110	9	1.6
BURNETT, A.J. Allan James B 1.3.1977 North Little Rock, AR BR/TR 6-5/205# d8.17																									
1999	Fla N	4	2	.667	7	7	0	0-0	41.1	37	23	3	0	25-2	33	3.48	125	.242	.343	17-0	.118	-1	102	2	0.1
2000	Fla N	3	7	.300	13	13	0	0-0	82.2	80	46	8	2	44-3	57	4.79	93	.259	.352	25-2	.280	4	84	-2	0.1
2001	Fla N	11	12	.478	27	27	2-1	0-0	173.1	145	82	20	7	83-3	128	4.05	104	.231	.323	50-7	.080	-2	79	4	0.3
2002	Fla N	12	9	.571	31	29	7-**5**	0-1	204.1	153	84	12	9	90-5	203	3.30	119	.209	.302	57-7	.105	0	90	14	1.3
2003	Fla N	0	2	.000	4	4	0	0-0	23	18	13	2	2	18-2	21	4.70	87	.217	.365	7-0	.143	0	74	-2	-0.1
Total	5	30	32	.484	82	80	9-6	0-1	524.2	433	248	45	20	260-15	442	3.86	108	.227	.323	156-16	.128	3	86	16	1.7
BURNETTE, WALLY Wallace Harper B 6.20.1929 Blairs, VA D 2.12.2003 Danville, VA BR/TR 6-0.5/178# d7.15																									
1956	KC A	6	8	.429	18	14	4-1	0	121.1	115	48	13	2	39-3	54	2.89	150	.252	.312	39-5	.051	-4	79	17	1.3
1957	KC A	7	12	.368	38	9	1	1	113	115	62	8	1	44-3	57	4.30	92	.268	.333	32-3	.250	1	78	-5	-0.6
1958	KC A	1	1	.500	12	4	0	0	28.1	29	14	2	0	14-0	11	3.49	112	.264	.344	6-1	.167	0	132	0	0.0
Total	3	14	21	.400	68	27	5-1	1	262.2	259	124	23	3	97-6	122	3.56	116	.260	.325	77-9	.143	-4	87	12	0.7
BURNS, DENNIS Dennis B 5.24.1898 Tiff City, MO D 5.21.1969 Tulsa, OK BR/TR 5-10/180# d9.22																									
1923	Phi A	2	1	.667	4	3	2	0	27	21	9	1	0	7	8	2.00	205	.210	.262	9-0	.111	-1	81	5	0.5
1924	Phi A	6	8	.429	37	17	7	1	154	191	101	3	1	68	26	5.08	84	.314	.384	42-2	.143	-2	96	-13	-1.2
Total	2	8	9	.471	41	20	9	1	181	212	110	4	1	75	34	4.62	92	.299	.367	51-2	.137	-3	94	-8	-0.7
BURNS, FARMER James "Slab" B Ashtabula, OH TR 5-7/168# d7.6																									
1901	StL N	0	0	—	1	0	0	0	1	2	1	0	1	1	0	9.00	35	.400	.571	0-0	—	0		-1	0.0
BURNS, DICK Richard Simon B 12.26.1863 Holyoke, MA D 11.16.1937 Holyoke, MA BL/TL 5-7/140# d5.3 ▲																									
1883	Det N	2	12	.143	17	13	13	0	127.2	172	122	8		33	30	4.51	69	.301	.339	140	.186	-2*	78	-21	-1.9
1884	Cin U	23	15	.605	40	40	34-1	0	329.2	298	179	7		47	167	2.46	104	.225	.252	350	.306	3*	113	2	0.4
1885	StL N	0	0	—	1	0	0	0	3	3	3	0		0	2	9.00	31	.250	.250	54	.222	0*		-2	0.0
Total	3	25	27	.481	58	53	47-1	0	460.1	473	304	15		80	199	3.07	89	.248	.278	544	.267	2	105	-21	-1.5
BURNS, BRITT Robert Britt B 6.8.1959 Houston, TX BL/TL 6-5/218# d8.5																									
1978	Chi A	0	2	.000	2	2	0	0-0	7.2	14	12	2	0	3-0	3	12.91	30	.378	.425	0-0	—	0	35	-8	-1.1
1979	Chi A	0	0	—	6	0	0	0-1	5	10	5	1	0	1-0	2	5.40	79	.435	.423	0-0	—	0		-1	-0.1
1980	Chi A	15	13	.536	34	32	11-1	0-0	238	213	83	17	4	63-2	133	2.84	142	.241	.293	0-0	—	0	67	33	3.7
1981	Chi A☆	10	6	.625	24	23	5-1	0-0	156.2	139	52	14	6	49-1	108	2.64	136	.238	.300	0-0	—	0	104	17	1.5
1982	Chi A	13	5	.722	28	28	5-1	0-0	169.1	168	89	12	3	67-1	116	4.04	100	.257	.328	0-0	—	0	116	-1	-0.2
1983	†Chi A	10	11	.476	29	26	8-4	0-0	173.2	165	79	14	5	55-2	115	3.58	118	.249	.310	0-0	—	0	77	10	1.0
1984	Chi A	4	12	.250	34	16	2	3-2	117	130	74	7	4	45-1	85	5.00	83	.280	.347	0-0	—	0	79	-11	-1.4
1985	Chi A	18	11	.621	36	34	8-4	0-0	227	206	105	26	2	79-1	172	3.96	109	.242	.306	0-0	—	0	108	11	1.2
Total	8	70	60	.538	193	161	39-11	3-3	1094.1	1045	499	93	24	362-8	734	3.66	111	.251	.313	0-0	—	0	92	50	4.6
BURNS, TOMMY Thomas P. "Oyster" B 9.6.1864 Philadelphia, PA D 11.11.1928 Brooklyn, NY BL/TR 5-8/183# d8.18 ▲																									
1884	Bal AA	0	0	—	2	0	0	**1**	9	12	5	0	0	2	6	3.00	116	.343	.378	131	.298	1*		1	0.1
1885	Bal AA	7	4	.636	15	11	10-1	**3**	105.2	112	76	2	13	21	30	3.58	91	.266	.321	321	.231	3*	101	-6	-0.4
1887	Bal AA	1	0	1.000	3	0	0	0	11.1	16	16	0	3	4	2	9.53	43	.291	.371	551	.341	2*		-6	-0.3
1888	Bal AA	0	1	.000	5	0	0	0	12.2	12	8	0	0	3	2	4.26	70	.240	.283	325	.298	2*		-1	0.0
Total	4	8	5	.615	25	11	10-1	4	138.2	152	105	2	16	30	40	4.09	81	.271	.326	1328	.300	7	101	-12	-0.6

Year	Tm Lg	W	L	Pct	G	GS	CG-Sho	SV-BS	IP	H	R	HR	HB	BB-IB	SO	ERA	AERA	OAV	OOB	AB-SH	AVG	PB	Sup	APR	PW
BURNS, TODD Todd Edward B 7.6.1963 Maywood, CA BR/TR 6-2/190# d5.31																									
1988	†Oak A	8	2	.800	17	14	2	1-0	102.2	93	38	8	1	34-1	57	3.16	120	.241	.303	0-0	—	0	126	8	0.7
1989	†Oak A	6	5	.545	50	2	0	8-3	96.1	66	27	3	1	28-5	49	2.24	165	.196	.259	0-0	—	0	86	17	2.0
1990	†Oak A	3	3	.500	43	2	0	3-1	78.2	78	28	8	0	32-4	43	2.97	125	.263	.331	0-0	—	0	98	7	0.5
1991	Oak A	1	0	1.000	9	0	0	0-0	13.1	10	5	2	0	8-1	3	3.38	114	.217	.321	0-0	—	0		1	0.1
1992	Tex A	3	5	.375	35	10	0	1-1	103	97	54	8	4	32-1	55	3.84	99	.248	.309	0-0	—	0	67	-2	-0.2
1993	Tex A	0	4	.000	25	5	0	0-3	65	63	36	6	2	32-3	35	4.57	91	.253	.339	0-0	—	0	58	-3	-0.2
	StL N	0	4	.000	24	0	0	0-2	30.2	32	21	8	0	9-6	10	6.16	64	.274	.320	3-1	.000	-0		-6	-0.8
Total	6	21	23	.477	203	33	2	13-10	489.2	439	209	43	8	175-21	252	3.47	110	.241	.307	3-1	.000	-0	93	22	2.1
BURNS, BILL William Thomas "Sleepy Bill" B 1.29.1880 San Saba, TX D 6.6.1953 Ramona, CA BB/TL 6-2/195# d4.18																									
1908	Was A	6	11	.353	23	19	11-2	0	164	135	58	3	4	18	55	1.70	134	.229	.257	54-0	.148	-1	71	7	0.8
1909	Was A	1	1	.500	6	4	1	0	29.1	25	7	0	3	7	13	1.23	198	.229	.294	11-0	.273	0	51	3	0.3
	Chi A	7	13	.350	23	19	10-3	0	168	161	64	2	8	34	50	2.04	115	.264	.312	59-1	.153	1	70	2	0.4
	Year	8	14	.364	29	23	11-3	0	197.1	186	66	2	11	41	63	1.92	123	.259	.309	70-1	.171	1	66	7	0.7
1910	Chi A	0	0	—	1	0	0	0	0.1	0	0	0	0	1	0	0.00	—	.000	.500	0-0	—	0		0	0.0
	Cin N	8	13	.381	31	21	13-2	0	178.2	183	103	3	12	49	57	3.48	84	.273	.333	61-1	.262	2*	100	-13	-1.1
1911	Cin N	1	0	1.000	6	3	0	1	17.2	17	11	1	3	3	5	3.06	108	.254	.315	7-0	.429	2	151	-1	0.2
	Phi N	6	10	.375	21	14	8-3	1	121	132	59	5	6	26	47	3.42	101	.287	.333	40-0	.150	-1	59	1	0.0
	Year	7	10	.412	27	17	8-3	2	138.2	149	62	6	9	29	52	3.38	102	.283	.331	47-0	.191	0	75	0	0.2
1912	Det A	1	4	.200	6	5	2	0	38.2	52	29	0	2	9	6	5.35	61	.338	.382	13-0	.231	1	104	-8	-0.8
Total	5	30	52	.366	117	85	45-10	2	717.2	705	331	14	38	147	233	2.72	100	.265	.313	245-2	.196	4	81	-9	-0.2
BURNSIDE, PETE Peter Willits B 7.2.1930 Evanston, IL BR/TL 6-2/190# d9.20																									
1955	NY N	1	0	1.000	2	2	1	0	12.2	10	9	1	0	9-0	2	2.84	142	.204	.328	5-0	.200	0	210	0	0.0
1957	NY N	1	4	.200	10	9	1-1	0	30.2	47	30	5	1	13-0	18	8.80	45	.356	.415	9-2	.000	-1	114	-15	-2.1
1958	SF N	0	0	—	6	1	0	0	10.2	20	10	3	0	5-0	4	6.75	56	.400	.455	0-0	—	0	141	-4	-0.2
1959	Det A	1	3	.250	30	0	0	1	62	55	31	7	2	25-1	49	3.77	108	.237	.315	10-1	.000	-1		1	0.0
1960	Det A	7	7	.500	31	15	2	2	113.2	122	56	14	4	50-1	71	4.28	93	.277	.355	27-5	.148	-1	96	-2	-0.3
1961	Was A	4	9	.308	33	16	4-2	2	113.1	106	66	11	3	51-2	56	4.53	89	.251	.330	34-3	.059	-3	74	-6	-1.0
1962	Was A	5	11	.313	40	20	6	2	149.2	152	82	20	2	51-3	74	4.45	91	.263	.322	35-5	.057	-3	83	-7	-1.0
1963	Bal A	0	1	.000	6	0	0	0	7.1	11	4	0	1	2-0	6	4.91	71	.344	.400	1-0	.000	-0		-1	-0.2
	Was A	0	1	.000	38	1	0	0	67.1	84	49	12	0	24-1	23	6.15	60	.308	.359	11-0	.091	-0	48	-16	-0.9
	Year	0	2	.000	44	1	0	0	74.2	95	51	12	1	26-1	29	6.03	61	.311	.363	12-0	.083	-1	48	-17	-1.1
Total	8	19	36	.345	196	64	14-3	7	567.1	607	337	73	13	230-8	303	4.81	82	.275	.344	132-16	.076	-8	93	-50	-5.7
BURNSIDE, SHELDON Sheldon John B 12.22.1954 South Bend, IN BR/TL 6-5/200# d9.4																									
1978	Det A	0	0	—	2	0	0	0-0	4	4	4	0	0	2-0	3	9.00	43	.250	.333	0-0	—	0		-2	-0.1
1979	Det A	1	1	.500	10	0	0	0-0	21.1	28	16	2	1	8-2	13	6.33	69	.333	.394	0-0	—	0		-4	-0.3
1980	Cin N	1	0	1.000	7	0	0	0-0	4.2	6	1	1	0	1-0	2	1.93	186	.333	.368	1-0	.000	-0		1	0.2
Total	3	2	1	.667	19	0	0	0-0	30	38	21	3	1	11-2	18	6.00	69	.322	.382	1-0	.000	-0		-5	-0.2
BURPO, GEORGE George Harvie B 6.19.1922 Jenkins, KY BR/TL 6/195# d6.9																									
1946	Cin N	0	0	—	2	0	0	0	2.1	4	4	0	0	5	1	15.43	22	.400	.600	0-0	—	0		-3	-0.2
BURRELL, HARRY Harry J. B 5.26.1869 Bethel, VT D 12.11.1914 Omaha, NE BR/TL d9.13																									
1891	StL AA	4	2	.667	7	4	3	1	43	51	36	4	2	21	19	4.81	87	.285	.366	20	.200	-1*	52	-2	-0.3
BURRIS, AL Alva Burton B 1.28.1874 Warwick, MD D 3.25.1938 Salisbury, MD BR/TR d6.22																									
1894	Phi N	0	0	—	1	0	0	0	5	14	10	0	0	2	0	18.00	29	.500	.533	4-0	.500	1		-6	-0.2
BURRIS, RAY Bertram Ray B 8.22.1950 Idabel, OK BR/TR 6-5/200# d4.8 C3																									
1973	Chi N	1	1	.500	31	1	0	0-0	64.2	65	22	2	0	27-7	57	2.92	135	.261	.331	7-1	.143	0	22	8	0.4
1974	Chi N	3	5	.375	40	5	0	1-1	75	91	61	8	4	26-6	40	6.60	58	.300	.359	13-1	.077	-1*	50	-20	-2.2
1975	Chi N	15	10	.600	36	35	8-2	0-0	238.1	259	121	25	4	73-6	108	4.12	94	.281	.334	82-7	.183	1*	111	-6	-0.6
1976	Chi N	15	13	.536	37	36	10-4	0-0	249	251	102	22	5	70-5	112	3.11	124	.263	.315	81-8	.111	-4*	81	17	1.4
1977	Chi N	14	16	.467	39	39	5-1	0-0	221	270	132	29	3	67-9	105	4.72	93	.305	.355	69-9	.174	1*	99	-8	-0.7
1978	Chi N	7	13	.350	40	32	4-1	1-1	199	210	112	15	10	79-11	94	4.75	85	.274	.346	61-7	.115	-1*	97	-13	-1.2
1979	Chi N	0	0	—	14	0	0	0-0	21.2	23	17	0	1	15-1	14	6.23	66	.284	.398	1-0	.000	0		-5	-0.2
	NY A	1	3	.250	15	0	0	0-2	27.2	40	22	5	0	10-1	19	6.18	66	.342	.388	0-0	—	0		-7	-0.9
	NY N	0	2	.000	4	4	0	0-0	21.2	21	10	2	1	6-3	10	3.32	110	.247	.304	6-1	.167	-0	67	0	0.0
1980	NY N	7	13	.350	29	29	1	0-0	170.1	181	86	20	4	54-5	83	4.02	89	.277	.333	51-3	.098	-2	87	-9	-1.3
1981	†Mon N	9	7	.563	22	21	4	0-0	135.2	117	56	9	3	41-3	52	3.05	115	.235	.294	37-7	.189	1	120	4	0.5
1982	Mon N	4	14	.222	37	15	2	2-3	123.2	143	77	14	2	53-7	55	4.73	77	.297	.365	28-4	.179	1	77	-16	-2.1
1983	Mon N	4	7	.364	40	17	2-1	0-0	154	139	68	13	2	56-4	100	3.68	98	.244	.312	39-2	.231	3	84	-1	0.3
1984	Oak A	13	10	.565	34	28	5-1	0-0	211.2	193	84	15	8	90-1	93	3.15	119	.244	.325	0-0	—	0*	107	15	1.3
1985	Mil A	9	13	.409	29	28	6	0-0	170.1	182	95	25	3	53-0	81	4.81	87	.272	.325	0-0	—	0	99	-8	-1.0
1986	StL N	4	5	.444	23	10	0	0-0	82	92	52	13	4	32-4	34	5.60	65	.287	.359	27-0	.148	0	103	-16	-1.6
1987	Mil A	2	2	.500	10	2	0	0-0	23	33	16	4	0	12-3	8	5.87	78	.351	.417	0-0	—	0	80	-3	-0.4
Total	15	108	134	.446	480	302	47-10	4-7	2188.2	2310	1133	221	54	764-76	1065	4.17	93	.274	.335	502-50	.151	-1	96	-68	-8.3
BURROWS, JOHN John B 10.30.1913 Winnfield, LA D 4.27.1987 Coal Run, OH BR/TL 5-10/200# d4.25																									
1943	Phi A	0	1	.000	4	1	0	0	7.2	8	7	0	1	9	3	8.22	41	.276	.462	1-0	.000	-0	0	-4	-0.4
	Chi N	0	2	.000	23	1	0	2	32.2	25	17	0	2	16	18	3.86	87	.205	.307	3-0	.667	1	51	-2	0.0
1944	Chi N	0	0	—	3	0	0	0	3	7	7	0	0	3	1	18.00	20	.467	.556	0-0	—	0		-5	-0.2
Total	2	0	3	.000	30	2	0	2	43.1	40	31	0	3	28	22	5.61	60	.241	.360	4-0	.500	1	25	-11	-0.6
BURROWS, TERRY Terry Dale B 11.28.1968 Lake Charles, LA BL/TL 6-1/185# d6.12																									
1994	Tex A	0	0	—	1	0	0	0-0	1	1	1	1	0	1-0	0	9.00	54	.250	.400	0-0	—	0		0	0.0
1995	Tex A	2	2	.500	28	3	0	1-2	44.2	60	37	11	2	19-0	22	6.45	75	.323	.391	0-0	—	0	96	-9	-0.7
1996	Mil A	2	0	1.000	8	0	0	0-0	12.2	12	4	2	1	10-0	5	2.84	183	.261	.404	0-0	—	0		3	0.4
1997	SD N	0	2	.000	13	0	0	0-0	10.1	12	13	1	1	8-1	8	10.45	37	.286	.412	0-0	—	0		-8	-1.3
Total	4	4	4	.500	50	3	0	1-2	68.2	85	55	15	4	38-1	35	6.42	74	.306	.397	0-0	—	0	96	-14	-1.6
BURTON, JIM Jim Scott B 10.27.1949 Royal Oak, MI BR/TL 6-3/195# d6.10																									
1975	†Bos A	1	2	.333	29	4	0	1-1	53	58	30	6	0	19-2	39	2.89	141	.276	.333	0-0	—	0	86	2	0.1
1977	Bos A	0	0	—	1	0	0	0-0	2.2	2	0	0	0	1-0	3	0.00	—	.200	.273	0-0	—	0		1	0.1
Total	2	1	2	.333	30	4	0	1-1	55.2	60	30	6	0	20-2	42	2.75	149	.273	.331	0-0	—	0	86	3	0.2
BURTSCHY, MOE Edward Frank B 4.18.1922 Cincinnati, OH BR/TR 6-3/208# d6.17																									
1950	Phi A	0	1	.000	9	1	0	0	19	22	16	2	1	21	12	7.11	64	.289	.449	5-0	.000	-0	20	-5	-0.2
1951	Phi A	0	0	—	7	0	0	0	17	18	11	0	1	12	4	5.29	81	.277	.397	3-0	.333	0		-2	-0.1
1954	Phi A	5	4	.556	46	0	0	4	94.2	80	45	7	8	53	54	3.80	103	.234	.346	17-0	.118	-1		1	0.0
1955	KC A	2	0	1.000	7	0	0	0	11.1	17	13	0	1	10-1	9	10.32	40	.354	.467	3-0	.333	0		-7	-1.0
1956	KC A	3	1	.750	21	0	0	0	43.1	41	22	6	3	30-4	18	3.95	110	.263	.389	8-0	.125	-1		1	0.1
Total	5	10	6	.625	90	1	0	4	185.1	178	107	15	14	126-5	97	4.71	88	.259	.381	36-0	.139	-1	20	-12	-1.2
BURTT, DENNIS Dennis Allen B 11.29.1957 San Diego, CA BB/TR 6/180# d9.4																									
1985	Min A	2	2	.500	5	2	0	0-0	28.1	20	13	2	0	7-0	9	3.81	116	.200	.250	0-0	—	0	103	2	0.2
1986	Min A	0	0	—	3	0	0	0-0	2	7	7	1	0	3-1	1	31.50	14	.538	.625	0-0	—	0		-6	-0.3
Total	2	2	2	.500	8	2	0	0-0	30.1	27	20	3	0	10-1	10	5.64	78	.239	.298	0-0	—	0	103	-4	-0.1
BURWELL, DICK Richard Matthew B 1.23.1940 Alton, IL BR/TR 6-1/190# d9.13																									
1960	Chi N	0	0	—	3	1	0	0	9.2	11	6	2	1	7-0	1	5.59	68	.306	.432	3-0	.333	0	140	-2	-0.1
1961	Chi N	0	0	—	2	0	0	0	4	6	4	0	0	4-0	0	9.00	46	.375	.476	1-0	.000	-0		-2	-0.1

Year	Tm Lg	W	L	Pct	G	GS	CG-Sho	SV-BS	IP	H	R	HR	HB	BB-IB	SO	ERA	AERA	OAV	OOB	AB-SH	AVG	PB	Sup	APR	PW
Total	2	0	0	—	5	1	0	0	13.2	17	10	2	1	11-0	1	6.59	59	.327	.446	4-0	.250	0	140	-4	-0.2
BURWELL, BILL William Edwin B 3.27.1895 Jarbalo, KS D 6.11.1973 Ormond Beach, FL BL/TR 5-11/175# d5.1 M1 C8																									
1920	StL A	6	4	.600	33	2	0	4	113.1	133	55	5	4	42	30	3.65	107	.303	.369	42-2	.167	-2*	91	4	0.1
1921	StL A	2	4	.333	33	3	1	2	84.1	102	62	2	2	29	17	5.12	87	.309	.368	25-0	.240	-0	130	-8	-0.5
1928	Pit N	1	0	1.000	4	1	0	0	20.2	18	12	2	0	8	2	5.23	78	.234	.306	9-1	.222	-0	125	-2	-0.1
Total	3	9	8	.529	70	6	1	6	218.1	253	129	9	6	79	49	4.37	95	.299	.363	76-3	.197	-2	118	-6	-0.5
BUSBY, MIKE Michael James B 12.27.1972 Lomita, CA BR/TR 6-4/210# d4.7																									
1996	StL N	0	1	.000	1	1	0	0-0	4	9	13	4	1	4-0	4	18.00	23	.409	.519	2-0	.500	0	65	-8	-0.9
1997	StL N	0	2	.000	3	3	0	0-0	14.1	24	14	2	0	4-0	6	8.79	47	.393	.424	4-0	.500	1	74	-7	-0.7
1998	StL N	5	2	.714	26	2	0	0-2	46	45	23	3	5	15-0	33	4.50	93	.254	.327	3-0	.000	-0	99	0	-0.1
1999	StL N	0	1	.000	15	0	0	0-0	17.2	21	15	2	2	14-0	7	7.13	64	.300	.430	0-0	—	0		-5	-0.2
Total	4	5	6	.455	45	6	0	0-2	82	99	65	11	8	37-0	50	6.48	66	.300	.381	9-0	.333	1	79	-20	-1.9
BUSBY, STEVE Steven Lee B 9.29.1949 Burbank, CA BR/TR 6-2/205# d9.8																									
1972	KC A	3	1	.750	5	5	3	0-0	40	28	9	1	0	8-0	31	1.57	193	.200	.238	15-0	.200	0	117	6	0.7
1973	KC A	16	15	.516	37	37	7-1	0-0	238.1	246	125	18	6	105-7	174	4.23	97	.271	.347	0-0	—	0	94	-3	-0.3
1974	KC A☆	22	14	.611	38	38	20-3	0-0	292.1	284	118	14	9	92-6	198	3.39	113	.258	.319	0-0	—	0	119	17	2.2
1975	KC A★	18	12	.600	34	34	18-3	0-0	260.1	233	96	18	3	81-4	160	3.08	125	.242	.302	0-0	—	0	93	25	2.9
1976	KC A	3	3	.500	13	13	1	0-0	71.2	58	42	7	3	49-1	29	4.40	80	.218	.344	0-0	—	0	154	-8	-0.6
1978	KC A	1	0	1.000	7	5	0	0-0	21.1	24	18	2	2	15-1	10	7.59	51	.282	.402	0-0	—	0	126	-8	-0.4
1979	KC A	6	6	.500	22	12	4	0-0	94.1	71	45	10	0	64-3	45	3.63	118	.220	.343	0-0	—	0	87	6	0.8
1980	KC A	1	3	.250	11	6	0	0-0	42.1	59	30	3	2	19-0	12	6.17	66	.335	.402	0-0	—	0	77	-9	-0.7
Total	8	70	54	.565	167	150	53-7	0-0	1060.2	1003	483	73	25	433-22	659	3.72	105	.253	.328	15-0	.200	0	105	26	4.6
BUSCHHORN, DON Donald Lee B 4.29.1946 Independence, MO BR/TR 6/170# d5.15																									
1965	KC A	0	1	.000	12	3	0	0	31	36	17	7	1	8-0	9	4.35	80	.295	.341	4-0	.500	1*	101	-3	-0.1
BUSH, GUY Guy Terrell "The Mississippi Mudcat" B 8.23.1901 Aberdeen, MS D 7.2.1985 Shannon, MS BR/TR 6/175# d9.17																									
1923	Chi N	0	0	—	1	0	0	0	1	1	0	0	0	0	2	0.00	—	.250	.250	0-0	—	0		0	0.0
1924	Chi N	2	5	.286	16	8	4	0	80.2	91	51	7	2	24	36	4.02	97	.285	.339	26-0	.154	-1	82	-4	-0.6
1925	Chi N	6	13	.316	42	15	5	**4**	182	213	102	15	3	52	76	4.30	101	.300	.350	57-3	.193	-2	83	0	0.0
1926	Chi N	13	9	.591	35	15	7-2	2	157.1	149	58	3	3	42	32	2.86	134	.258	.311	48-3	.167	-2	94	18	2.1
1927	Chi N	10	10	.500	36	22	9-1	2	193.1	177	76	3	6	79	62	3.03	128	.250	.330	65-5	.123	-4	86	18	1.3
1928	Chi N	15	6	.714	42	24	9-2	2	204.1	229	104	10	5	86	61	3.83	100	.293	.367	73-4	.082	-6	112	0	-0.7
1929	†Chi N	18	7	.720	**50**	30	18-2	**8**	270.2	277	135	16	4	107	82	3.66	126	.265	.335	91-10	.165	-4	115	27	1.8
1930	Chi N	15	10	.600	46	25	11	3	225	291	174	22	2	86	75	6.20	79	.316	.376	78-3	.282	3	121	-31	-2.4
1931	Chi N	16	8	.667	39	24	14-1	2	180.1	190	104	9	2	66	54	4.49	86	.268	.332	57-5	.123	-2	132	-13	-1.5
1932	†Chi N	19	11	.633	40	30	15-1	0	238.2	262	106	13	7	70	73	3.21	118	.278	.332	84-6	.179	0	108	13	1.5
1933	Chi N	20	12	.625	41	32	20-4	2	259	261	95	9	1	68	84	2.75	119	.257	.304	88-5	.125	-1	117	16	2.0
1934	Chi N	18	10	.643	40	27	15-1	2	209.1	213	96	15	1	54	75	3.83	101	.262	.309	70-6	.229	1*	110	3	0.5
1935	Pit N	11	11	.500	41	25	8-1	2	204.1	237	115	16	5	40	42	4.32	95	.285	.321	63-3	.127	-1	102	-2	-0.3
1936	Pit N	1	3	.250	16	0	0	2	34.2	49	28	3	0	11	10	5.97	68	.336	.382	9-0	.333	0		-8	-0.8
	Bos N	4	5	.444	15	11	5	0	90.1	98	38	2	0	20	28	3.39	113	.281	.320	25-6	.120	-1	86	5	0.4
	Year	5	8	.385	31	11	5	2	125	147	42	5	0	31	38	4.10	95	.297	.338	34-6	.176	-0	85	-1	-0.4
1937	Bos N	8	15	.348	32	20	11-1	1	180.2	201	77	8	0	48	56	3.54	101	.282	.328	54-2	.111	-2*	71	3	0.2
1938	StL N	0	1	.000	6	0	0	1	6	6	3	1	0	3	1	4.50	88	.286	.375	0-0	—	0		0	0.0
1945	Cin N	0	0	—	4	0	0	1	4.1	5	4	0	0	3	1	8.31	45	.278	.381	0-0	—	0		-2	-0.1
Total	17	176	136	.564	542	308	151-16	34	2722	2950	1366	152	41	859	850	3.86	103	.277	.334	888-61	.161	-22	105	43	3.4
BUSH, JOE Leslie Ambrose "Bullet Joe" B 11.27.1892 Brainerd, MN D 11.1.1974 Ft.Lauderdale, FL BR/TR 5-9/173# d9.30																									
1912	Phi A	0	0	—	1	1	0	0	8	14	10	0	0	4	3	7.88	39	.368	.429	4-0	.500	1	264	-5	-0.1
1913	†Phi A	15	6	.714	39	16	6-1	3	200.1	199	95	3	5	66	81	3.82	72	.261	.324	70-2	.157	-0	126	-21	-1.9
1914	†Phi A	17	13	.567	38	23	14-2	2	206	184	84	2	8	81	109	3.06	85	.242	.322	74-4	.189	2	113	-10	-1.2
1915	Phi A	5	15	.250	25	18	8	0	145.2	137	86	3	4	89	89	4.14	71	.263	.375	49-2	.143	-3	78	-17	-2.4
1916	Phi A	15	24	.385	40	33	25-8	0	286.2	222	109	3	3	130	157	2.57	111	.219	.310	100-2	.140	-4*	69	9	1.1
1917	Phi A	11	17	.393	37	31	17-4	2	233.1	207	101	3	1	111	121	2.47	111	.241	.328	80-0	.200	1	75	3	0.5
1918	†Bos A	15	15	.500	36	31	26-7	2	272.2	241	88	3	3	91	125	2.11	127	.242	.307	98-1	.276	6	80	16	2.8
1919	Bos A	0	0	—	3	2	0	0	9	11	5	0	0	4	3	5.00	60	.324	.395	5-0	.400	1*	195	-2	0.0
1920	Bos A	15	15	.500	35	32	18	1	243.2	287	138	3	10	94	88	4.25	86	.300	.369	102-3	.245	2*	95	-18	-1.6
1921	Bos A	16	9	.640	37	32	21-3	1	254.1	244	111	10	6	93	96	3.50	121	.260	.330	120-3	.325	6*	107	22	2.8
1922	†NY A	26	7	**.788**	39	30	20	3	255.1	240	109	16	1	85	92	3.31	121	.252	.314	95-5	.326	8	118	20	3.2
1923	†NY A	19	15	.559	37	30	22-3	0	275.2	263	115	7	5	117	125	3.43	115	.260	.340	113-0	.274	7*	103	17	2.6
1924	NY A	17	16	.515	39	31	19-3	1	252	262	117	9	7	109	80	3.57	116	.273	.352	124-1	.339	14*	102	16	3.2
1925	StL A	14	14	.500	33	30	15-2	0	208.2	230	129	18	2	91	63	5.09	92	.284	.357	102-1	.255	3*	103	-4	0.2
1926	Was A	1	8	.111	12	11	3	0	71.1	83	54	6	5	35	27	6.69	58	.292	.380	30-0	.233	1*	87	-20	-1.9
	Pit N	6	6	.500	19	12	9-2	3	110.2	97	45	7	2	35	38	3.01	131	.236	.299	49-0	.265	2*	85	11	1.4
1927	Pit N	1	2	.333	5	3	0	0	6.2	14	14	1	0	5	1	13.50	30	.412	.487	5-0	.600	1*	76	-8	-1.2
	NY N	1	1	.500	3	2	1	0	12	18	10	1	0	5	6	7.50	51	.340	.397	4-0	.500	1	99	-4	-0.5
	Year	2	3	.400	8	5	1	0	18.2	32	15	2	0	10	7	9.64	41	.368	.433	9-0	.556	2	86	-12	-1.7
1928	Phi A	2	1	.667	11	2	1	1	35.1	39	21	1	1	18	15	5.09	79	.300	.389	15-0	.067	-1*	106	-3	-0.3
Total	17	196	184	.516	489	370	225-35	19	3087.1	2992	1441	96	63	1263	1319	3.51	99	.260	.336	1239-24	.253	49	98	2	6.7
BUSHELMAN, JACK John Francis B 8.29.1885 Cincinnati, OH D 10.26.1955 Roanoke, VA BR/TR 6-2/175# d10.5																									
1909	Cin N	0	1	.000	1	1	1	0	7	7	7	1	0	4	3	2.57	101	.241	.333	1-0	.000	-0	108	-1	-0.2
1911	Bos A	0	1	.000	3	1	1	0	12	8	9	0	1	10	5	3.00	109	.186	.352	3-0	.000	-0	22	-1	-0.1
1912	Bos A	1	0	1.000	3	0	0	0	7.2	9	4	0	0	5	5	4.70	72	.310	.412	3-0	.000	-0		-1	-0.1
Total	3	1	2	.333	7	2	2	0	26.2	24	20	1	1	19	13	3.38	93	.238	.364	7-0	.000	-1	57	-3	-0.4
BUSHEY, FRANK Francis Clyde B 8.1.1906 Wheaton, KS D 3.18.1972 Topeka, KS BR/TR 6/180# d9.17																									
1927	Bos A	0	0	—	1	0	0	0	1.1	2	1	0	0	2	0	6.75	63	.500	.667	0-0	—	0		0	0.0
1930	Bos A	0	1	.000	11	0	0	0	30	34	22	1	2	15	4	6.30	73	.306	.398	9-0	.111	-1		-5	-0.3
Total	2	0	1	.000	12	0	0	0	31.1	36	23	1	2	17	4	6.32	73	.313	.410	9-0	.111	-1		-5	-0.3
BUSHING, CHRIS Christopher Shaun B 11.4.1967 Rockville Centre, NY BR/TR 6/190# d9.3																									
1993	Cin N	0	0	—	6	0	0	0-0	4.1	9	7	1	0	4-0	3	12.46	32	.450	.520	0-0	—	0		-4	-0.2
BUSKEY, TOM Thomas William B 2.20.1947 Harrisburg, PA D 6.7.1998 Harrisburg, PA BR/TR 6-3/220# d8.5																									
1973	NY A	0	1	.000	8	0	0	1-1	16.2	18	12	2	1	4-0	8	5.40	68	.286	.324	0-0	—	0		-4	-0.2
1974	NY A	0	1	.000	4	0	0	1-0	5.2	10	4	1	1	3-1	3	6.35	56	.400	.483	0-0	—	0		-2	-0.3
	Cle A	2	6	.250	51	0	0	17-7	93	93	36	10	1	33-8	40	3.19	113	.263	.322	0-0	—	0		5	0.7
	Year	2	7	.222	55	0	0	18-7	98.2	103	43	11	2	36-9	43	3.38	107	.272	.333	0-0	—	0		3	0.4
1975	Cle A	5	3	.625	50	0	0	7-3	77	69	27	7	1	29-10	29	2.57	147	.252	.324	0-0	—	0		10	1.2
1976	Cle A	5	4	.556	39	0	0	1-2	94.1	88	42	9	3	34-8	32	3.63	96	.256	.326	0-0	—	0		-1	-0.1
1977	Cle A	0	0	—	21	0	0	0-0	34	45	24	6	1	8-1	15	5.29	75	.313	.348	0-0	—	0		-6	-0.3
1978	Tor A	0	1	.000	8	0	0	0-0	13.1	14	5	1	0	5-4	7	3.38	117	.275	.339	0-0	—	0		1	0.1
1979	Tor A	6	10	.375	44	0	0	7-4	78.2	74	33	10	1	25-7	44	3.43	127	.249	.310	0-0	—	0		8	1.7
1980	Tor A	3	1	.750	33	0	0	0-1	66.2	68	35	11	0	26-6	34	4.45	97	.278	.341	0-0	—	0		0	0.0
Total	8	21	27	.438	258	0	0	34-18	479.1	479	218	57	9	167-45	212	3.66	106	.267	.328	0-0	—	0		11	2.8
BUTCHER, MAX Albert Maxwell B 9.21.1910 Holden, WV D 9.15.1957 Man, WV BR/TR 6-2/220# d4.20																									
1936	Bro N	6	6	.500	38	15	5	2	147.2	154	85	11	1	59	55	3.96	104	.268	.337	48-0	.125	-3*	89	0	-0.3
1937	Bro N	11	15	.423	39	24	8-1	0	191.2	203	106	12	7	75	57	4.27	94	.280	.354	62-1	.161	-1*	69	-2	-0.3
1938	Bro N	5	4	.556	24	8	3	2	72.2	104	66	9	1	39	21	6.56	59	.334	.410	25-2	.160	0*	141	-22	-2.4

Year	Tm Lg	W	L	Pct	G	GS	CG-Sho	SV-BS	IP	H	R	HR	HB	BB-IB	SO	ERA	AERA	OAV	OOB	AB-SH	AVG	PB	Sup	APR	PW
	Phi N	4	8	.333	12	12	11	0	98.1	94	40	6	2	31	29	2.93	133	.253	.314	35-0	.257	1	42	9	1.1
	Year	9	12	.429	36	20	14	2	171	198	42	15	3	70	50	4.47	87	.290	.359	60-2	.217	1	82	-13	-1.3
1939	Phi N	2	13	.133	19	16	3	0	104.1	131	72	10	1	51	27	5.61	71	.308	.383	38-3	.184	-1	75	-18	-2.3
	Pit N	4	4	.500	14	12	5-2	0	86.2	104	37	2	0	23	21	3.43	112	.297	.340	31-3	.097	-2	70	5	0.3
	Year	6	17	.261	33	28	8-2	0	191	235	40	12	1	74	48	4.62	85	.303	.364	69-6	.145	-3	73	-13	-2.0
1940	Pit N	8	9	.471	35	24	6-2	2	136.1	161	99	13	1	46	40	6.01	63	.290	.346	50-1	.300	4*	120	-31	-3.0
1941	Pit N	17	12	.586	33	32	19	0	236	249	98	11	1	66	61	3.05	118	.265	.314	82-5	.183	-1	101	14	1.6
1942	Pit N	5	8	.385	24	18	9	1	150.2	144	59	7	2	44	49	2.93	116	.247	.303	49-2	.143	-2	90	7	0.4
1943	Pit N	10	8	.556	33	21	10-2	1	193.2	191	65	4	2	57	45	2.60	134	.262	.317	61-7	.164	-1	100	20	1.8
1944	Pit N	13	11	.542	35	27	13-5	1	199	216	83	8	1	46	43	3.12	119	.273	.314	63-5	.190	-0*	104	13	1.6
1945	Pit N	10	8	.556	28	20	12-2	0	169.1	184	76	7	4	46	37	3.03	130	.277	.328	54-6	.222	0	105	13	1.3
Total	10	95	106	.473	334	229	104-14	9	1786.1	1935	886	100	23	583	485	3.73	101	.276	.333	598-35	.184	-6	93	8	-0.2
BUTCHER, JOHN John Daniel B 3.8.1957 Glendale, CA BR/TR 6-4/190# d9.8																									
1980	Tex A	3	3	.500	6	6	1	0-0	35.1	34	19	2	0	13-0	27	4.08	96	.248	.313	0-0	—	0	99	-1	-0.1
1981	Tex A	1	2	.333	5	3	1-1	0-0	27.2	18	6	0	0	8-1	19	1.63	213	.186	.248	0-0	—	0	43	6	0.6
1982	Tex A	1	5	.167	18	13	2	1-0	94.1	102	53	10	2	34-4	39	4.87	80	.280	.342	0-0	—	0	94	-10	-0.5
1983	Tex A	6	6	.500	38	6	1-1	5-3	123	128	50	8	1	41-4	58	3.51	114	.270	.328	0-0	—	0	87	9	0.9
1984	Min A	13	11	.542	34	34	8-1	0-0	225	242	98	18	4	53-5	83	3.44	122	.276	.317	0-0	—	0	93	17	1.6
1985	Min A	11	14	.440	34	33	8-2	0-0	207.2	239	125	24	6	43-4	92	4.98	88	.289	.325	0-0	—	0	98	-12	-1.2
1986	Min A	0	3	.000	16	10	1	0-1	70	82	50	11	1	24-1	29	6.30	68	.294	.349	0-0	—	0	105	-13	-0.6
	Cle A	1	5	.167	13	8	1-1	0-0	50.2	86	43	6	3	13-0	16	6.93	60	.381	.416	0-0	—	0	104	-15	-1.5
	Year	1	8	.111	29	18	2-1	0-1	120.2	168	48	17	4	37-1	45	6.56	65	.333	.379	0-0	—	0	104	-28	-2.1
Total	7	36	49	.424	164	113	23-6	6-4	833.2	931	444	79	17	229-19	363	4.42	94	.284	.331	0-0	—	0	96	-19	-0.8
BUTCHER, MIKE Michael Dana B 5.10.1965 Davenport, IA BR/TR 6-1/200# d7.6																									
1992	Cal A	2	2	.500	19	0	0	0-1	27.2	29	11	3	2	13-1	24	3.25	123	.264	.352	0-0	—	0		2	0.3
1993	Cal A	1	0	1.000	23	0	0	8-2	28.1	21	12	2	2	15-1	24	2.86	158	.204	.309	0-0	—	0		4	0.3
1994	Cal A	2	1	.667	33	0	0	1-2	29.2	31	24	2	2	23-5	19	6.67	73	.274	.406	0-0	—	0		-6	-0.5
1995	Cal A	6	1	.857	40	0	0	0-2	51.1	49	28	7	1	31-2	29	4.73	99	.257	.358	0-0	—	0		0	0.0
Total	4	11	4	.733	115	0	0	9-7	137	130	75	14	7	82-9	96	4.47	102	.251	.358	0-0	—	0		0	0.1
BUTLAND, BILL Wilburn Rue B 3.22.1918 Terre Haute, IN D 9.19.1997 Terre Haute, IN BR/TR 6-5/185# d5.29 Mil 1943-45																									
1940	Bos A	1	2	.333	3	3	1	0	21	27	13	0	0	10	5	5.57	81	.307	.378	7-1	.000	-1	59	-2	-0.3
1942	Bos A	7	1	.875	23	10	6-2	1	111.1	85	35	8	3	33	46	2.51	149	.206	.270	28-2	.036	-1	126	15	1.0
1946	Bos A	1	0	1.000	5	2	0	0	16.1	23	20	3	0	13	10	11.02	33	.343	.450	4-0	.250	0	164	-12	-0.6
1947	Bos A	0	0	—	1	0	0	0	2	3	1	0	0	0	1	4.50	86	.333	.333	0-0	—	0		0	0.0
Total	4	9	3	.750	32	15	7-2	1	150.2	138	69	11	3	56	62	3.88	99	.240	.310	39-3	.051	-2	117	1	0.1
BUTLER, ADAM Adam Christopher B 8.17.1973 Fairfax, VA BL/TL 6-2/225# d3.31																									
1998	Atl N	0	1	.000	8	0	0	0-0	5	5	7	1	1	6-1	7	10.80	39	.278	.462	0-0	—	0		-4	-0.7
BUTLER, CECIL Cecil Dean "Slewfoot" B 10.23.1937 Dallas, GA BR/TR 6-4/195# d4.23																									
1962	Mil N	2	0	1.000	9	2	1	0	31	26	13	4	0	9-1	22	2.61	145	.217	.271	8-0	.000	-1	92	3	0.1
1964	Mil N	0	0	—	2	0	0	0	4.1	7	4	2	0	0-0	2	8.31	42	.368	.368	0-0	—	0		-2	-0.1
Total	2	2	0	1.000	11	2	1	0	35.1	33	17	6	0	9-1	24	3.31	114	.237	.284	8-0	.000	-1	92	1	0.0
BUTLER, CHARLIE Charles Thomas B 5.12.1906 Green Cove Springs, FL D 5.10.1964 Brunswick, GA BR/TL 6-1.5/210# d5.1																									
1933	Phi N	0	0	—	1	0	0	0	1	1	1	0	0	2	0	9.00	42	.250	.500	0-0	—	0		0	0.0
BUTLER, IKE Isaac Burr B 8.22.1873 Langston, MI D 3.17.1948 Oakland, CA TR 6/175# d8.5																									
1902	Bal A	1	10	.091	16	14	12	0	116.1	168	103	1	2	45	13	5.34	71	.337	.394	53-2	.113	-3*	90	-20	-1.8
BUTLER, BILL William Franklin B 3.12.1947 Hyattsville, MD BL/TL 6-2/210# d4.9																									
1969	KC A	9	10	.474	34	29	5-4	0-0	193.2	174	91	15	3	91-5	156	3.90	95	.240	.326	60-5	.050	-4	97	-3	-0.7
1970	KC A	4	12	.250	25	25	2-1	0-0	140.2	117	66	17	1	87-1	75	3.77	99	.229	.340	44-1	.045	-3	77	0	-0.4
1971	KC A	1	2	.333	14	6	0	0-0	44.1	45	19	6	0	18-0	32	3.45	100	.268	.339	12-0	.083	-1	122	0	-0.1
1972	Cle A	0	0	—	6	2	0	0-0	11.2	9	3	1	0	10-0	6	1.54	209	.220	.373	1-0	.000	-0	123	2	0.1
1974	Min A	4	6	.400	26	12	2	1-0	98.2	91	47	9	1	56-2	79	4.10	91	.251	.350	0-0	—	0	91	-2	-0.3
1975	Min A	5	4	.556	23	8	1	0-0	81.2	100	61	12	0	35-0	55	5.95	64	.301	.363	0-0	—	0	152	-19	-1.8
1977	Min A	0	1	.000	6	4	0	0-0	21	19	17	5	1	15-0	5	6.86	58	.244	.372	0-0	—	0	203	-6	-0.3
Total	7	23	35	.397	134	86	10-5	1-0	591.2	555	304	65	6	312-8	408	4.21	88	.250	.342	117-6	.051	-7	103	-28	-3.5
BUTTERS, TOM Thomas Arden B 4.8.1938 Delaware, OH BR/TR 6-2/195# d9.8																									
1962	Pit N	0	0	—	4	0	0	0	6	5	1	0	1	6-1	10	1.50	262	.238	.429	0-0	—	0		2	0.1
1963	Pit N	0	0	—	6	1	0	0	16.1	15	8	1	2	8-0	11	4.41	75	.259	.352	3-0	.333	0	105	-1	-0.1
1964	Pit N	2	2	.500	28	4	0	0	64.1	52	21	3	0	37-1	58	2.38	148	.221	.324	11-2	.182	0	69	7	0.4
1965	Pit N	0	1	.000	5	0	0	0	9	9	8	2	0	5-0	6	7.00	50	.250	.341	1-0	.000	-0		-3	-0.4
Total	4	2	3	.400	43	5	0	0	95.2	81	38	6	3	56-2	85	3.10	113	.231	.337	15-2	.200	0	75	5	0.0
BUTTERY, FRANK Frank B 5.13.1851 Silvermine, CT D 12.16.1902 Silvermine, CT d4.26 ▲																									
1872	Man NA	3	2	.600	8	5	5	0	59	94	78	1		3	5	4.27	84	.322	.329	93	.215	-2*	187	-5	-0.3
BUXTON, RALPH Ralph Stanley "Buck" B 6.7.1914 Rainton, SK, CAN D 1.6.1988 San Leandro, CA BR/TR 5-11.5/163# d9.11																									
1938	Phi A	0	1	.000	5	0	0	0	9.1	12	7	1	0	5	9	4.82	100	.324	.405	1-0	.000	-0		0	-0.1
1949	NY A	0	1	.000	14	0	0	2	26.2	22	13	3	0	16	14	4.05	100	.229	.339	3-0	.000	-0		0	0.0
Total	2	0	2	.000	19	0	0	2	36	34	20	4	0	21	23	4.25	100	.256	.357	4-0	.000	-1		0	-0.1
BUZHARDT, JOHN John William B 8.17.1936 Prosperity, SC BR/TR 6-2/198# d9.10																									
1958	Chi N	3	0	1.000	6	2	1	0	24.1	16	5	2	0	7-1	9	1.85	212	.184	.245	8-0	.125	-0	57	6	0.7
1959	Chi N	4	5	.444	31	10	1-1	0	101.1	107	64	12	1	29-4	33	4.97	79	.271	.318	29-2	.069	-1	109	-12	-1.1
1960	Phi N	5	16	.238	30	29	5	0	200.1	198	101	14	2	68-12	73	3.86	100	.259	.319	62-2	.161	-1*	69	-1	-0.3
1961	Phi N	6	18	.250	41	27	6-1	0	202.1	200	107	28	6	65-6	92	4.49	91	.263	.324	57-7	.105	-2	92	-6	-0.9
1962	Chi A	8	12	.400	28	25	8-2	0	152.1	156	75	16	4	59-3	64	4.19	93	.264	.332	51-4	.118	-2	91	-4	-0.5
1963	Chi A	9	4	.692	19	18	6-3	0	126.1	100	35	8	5	31-5	59	2.42	145	.216	.272	48-1	.083	-3*	101	17	1.5
1964	Chi A	10	8	.556	31	25	8-3	0	160	150	60	13	4	35-4	97	2.98	116	.250	.291	54-4	.204	2	119	9	1.2
1965	Chi A	13	8	.619	32	30	4-1	1	188.2	167	69	12	7	56-9	108	3.01	106	.242	.304	56-9	.125	0*	114	5	0.5
1966	Chi A	6	11	.353	33	22	5-4	1	150.1	144	74	13	4	30-4	66	3.83	83	.248	.288	43-1	.116	-1*	104	-11	-1.2
1967	Chi A	3	9	.250	28	7	0	0	88.2	100	44	11	6	37-5	33	3.96	78	.294	.370	20-2	.200	0	104	-7	-0.9
	Bal A	0	1	.000	7	1	0	0	11.2	14	6	1	0	5-1	7	4.63	68	.298	.365	1-0	.000	-0	111	-2	-0.1
	Year	3	10	.231	35	8	0	0	100.1	114	10	12	6	42-6	40	4.04	77	.295	.370	21-2	.190	0	105	-10	-1.0
	Hou N	0	0	—	1	0	0	0	0.2	0	0	0	0	0-0	0	0.00	—	.000	.000	0-0	—	0		0	0.0
1968	Hou N	4	4	.500	39	4	0	5	83.2	73	35	0	4	35-13	37	3.12	95	.239	.319	16-1	.250	1	198	-3	-0.1
Total	11	71	96	.425	326	200	44-15	7	1490.2	1425	675	130	43	457-67	678	3.66	97	.253	.312	445-33	.135	-7	100	-9	-1.2
BYERLY, BUD Eldred William B 10.26.1920 Webster Groves, MO BR/TR 6-2.5/185# d9.26																									
1943	StL N	1	0	1.000	2	2	0	0	13	14	6	0	0	5	6	3.46	97	.280	.345	3-0	.000	-0	88	0	-0.1
1944	†StL N	2	2	.500	9	4	2	0	42.1	37	18	2	0	20	13	3.40	104	.228	.313	12-0	.167	-0	107	1	0.0
1945	StL N	4	5	.444	33	8	2	0	95	111	61	3	1	41	39	4.74	79	.288	.358	23-5	.217	1	158	-12	-0.9
1950	Cin N	0	1	.000	4	1	0	0	14.2	12	4	1	0	4	5	2.45	173	.218	.271	3-0	.000	-0	21	3	0.1
1951	Cin N	2	1	.667	40	0	0	0	66	69	33	6	2	25	28	3.27	125	.267	.337	6-0	.000	-0*		4	0.2
1952	Cin N	0	1	.000	12	2	0	1	24.2	29	15	0	0	7	14	5.11	74	.309	.356	5-0	.200	0	24	-4	-0.2
1956	Was A	2	4	.333	25	0	0	4	51.2	45	19	6	2	14-3	19	2.96	146	.243	.303	11-0	.091	-1		8	0.8
1957	Was A	6	6	.500	47	0	0	6	95	94	38	6	1	22-5	39	3.13	125	.264	.305	15-0	.067	-1		7	0.9
1958	Was A	2	0	1.000	17	0	0	1	24	34	20	4	1	11-2	13	6.75	56	.347	.411	2-0	.000	-0		-8	-0.7

Year	Tm Lg	W	L	Pct	G	GS	CG-Sho	SV-BS	IP	H	R	HR	HB	BB-IB	SO	ERA	AERA	OAV	OOB	AB-SH	AVG	PB	Sup	APR	PW
	Bos A	1	2	.333	18	0	0	0	30.1	31	12	1	1	7-3	16	1.78	225	.272	.312	4-0	.000	-1		5	0.4
	Year	3	2	.600	35	0	0	1	54.1	65	33	5	2	18-5	29	3.98	99	.307	.359	6-0	.000	-1		-3	-0.3
1959	SF N	1	0	1.000	11	0	0	0	13	11	2	2	0	5-1	4	1.38	275	.234	.308	0-0	—	0		4	0.3
1960	SF N	1	0	1.000	19	0	0	2	22	32	14	3	1	6-0	13	5.32	65	.340	.379	1-1	.000	-0		-4	-0.3
Total 11		22	22	.500	237	17	4	14	491.2	519	242	34	9	167-14	209	3.70	105	.273	.333	85-6	.118	-4	112	4	0.5
BYNUM, MIKE Michael Alan B 3.20.1978 Tampa, FL BL/TL 6-4/200# d8.17																									
2002	SD N	1	0	1.000	14	3	0	0-0	27.1	33	16	3	3	15-2	17	5.27	72	.308	.402	8-0	.000	-1	212	-4	-0.3
2003	SD N	1	4	.200	13	5	0	0-0	36	44	35	14	1	15-0	35	8.75	45	.297	.366	10-1	.300	1	105	-20	-2.1
Total 2		2	4	.333	27	8	0	0-0	63.1	77	51	17	4	30-2	52	7.25	53	.302	.381	18-1	.167	-0	145	-24	-2.4
BYRD, HARRY Harry Gladwin B 2.3.1925 Darlington, SC D 5.14.1985 Darlington, SC BR/TR 6-1/188# d4.21																									
1950	Phi A	0	0	—	6	0	0	0	10.2	25	20	3	2	9	2	16.88	27	.481	.571	2-0	.000	-0		-14	-0.6
1952	Phi A	15	15	.500	37	28	15-3	2	228.1	244	100	12	7	98	116	3.31	120	.274	.351	75-6	.133	-3	83	13	1.4
1953	Phi A	11	20	.355	40	**37**	11-2	0	236.2	279	155	23	14	115	122	5.51	78	.294	.379	81-3	.222	-1	82	-29	-3.4
1954	NY A	9	7	.563	25	21	5-1	0	132.1	131	56	10	7	43	52	2.99	115	.258	.321	46-3	.196	1	136	4	0.5
1955	Bal A	3	2	.600	14	8	1-1	1	65.1	64	33	7	7	28-1	25	4.55	84	.261	.350	19-3	.158	-0	125	-3	-0.3
	Chi A	4	6	.400	25	12	1-1	1	91	85	49	10	2	30-4	44	4.65	85	.251	.313	30-3	.067	-3	96	-6	-0.9
	Year	7	8	.467	39	20	2-2	2	156.1	149	53	17	9	58-5	69	4.61	85	.255	.329	49-6	.102	-3	107	-8	-1.2
1956	Chi A	0	1	.000	3	1	0	0	4.1	9	6	0	0	4-0	0	10.38	39	.474	.542	1-0	.000	-0	0	-3	-0.6
1957	Det A	4	3	.571	37	1	0	5	59	53	23	6	2	28-4	20	3.36	115	.249	.339	8-2	.000	-1	208	4	0.3
Total 7		46	54	.460	187	108	33-8	9	827.2	890	442	71	41	355-9	381	4.35	91	.277	.355	262-20	.160	-8	96	-34	-3.6
BYRD, JEFF Jeffrey Alan B 11.11.1956 LaMesa, CA BR/TR 6-3/195# d6.20																									
1977	Tor A	2	13	.133	17	17	1	0-0	87.1	98	68	5	0	68-1	40	6.18	68	.286	.399	0-0	—	0	77	-19	-2.6
BYRD, PAUL Paul Gregory B 12.3.1970 Louisville, KY BR/TR 6-1/185# d7.28																									
1995	NY N	2	0	1.000	17	0	0	0-0	22	18	6	1	1	7-1	26	2.05	198	.222	.286	1-0	1.000	0		5	0.4
1996	NY N	1	2	.333	38	0	0	0-2	46.2	48	22	7	0	21-4	31	4.24	95	.265	.340	2-0	.000	-0		0	0.0
1997	Atl N	4	4	.500	31	4	0	0-0	53	47	34	6	4	28-4	37	5.26	80	.235	.338	7-2	.143	-0	88	-6	-0.8
1998	Atl N	0	0	—	1	0	0	0-0	2	4	3	0	0	1-0	1	13.50	31	.400	.455	0-0	—	0		-2	-0.1
	Phi N	5	2	.714	8	8	2-1	0-0	55	41	16	6	0	17-1	38	2.29	189	.203	.264	18-0	.167	0	103	12	1.5
	Year	5	2	.714	9	8	2-1	0-0	57	45	21	6	0	18-1	39	2.68	161	.212	.273	18-0	.167	0	104	10	1.4
1999	Phi N☆	15	11	.577	32	32	1	0-0	199.2	205	119	34	17	70-2	106	4.60	103	.265	.337	55-11	.127	-1	116	-2	-0.3
2000	Phi N	2	9	.182	17	15	0	0-0	83	89	67	17	3	35-2	53	6.51	72	.271	.345	20-2	.150	0	75	-18	-1.9
2001	Phi N	0	1	.000	3	1	0	0-0	10	10	9	1	1	4-0	3	8.10	53	.278	.349	2-1	.500	0*	65	-4	-0.3
	KC A	6	6	.500	16	15	1	0-0	93.1	110	45	11	1	22-1	49	4.05	121	.297	.335	4-1	.000	-0	87	9	1.0
2002	KC A	17	11	.607	33	33	**7-2**	0-0	228.1	224	111	36	7	38-1	129	3.90	129	.256	.288	2-0	.000	-0	91	23	2.4
Total 8		52	46	.531	196	108	11-3	0-2	793	796	432	119	34	243-16	473	4.39	107	.260	.319	111-17	.144	-1	98	17	1.9
BYRDAK, TIM Timothy Christopher B 10.31.1973 Oak Lawn, IL BL/TL 5-11/170# d8.7																									
1998	KC A	0	0	—	3	0	0	0-0	1.2	5	1	1	0	0-0	1	5.40	89	.556	.556	0-0	—	0		0	0.0
1999	KC A	0	3	.000	33	0	0	1-3	24.2	32	24	5	1	20-2	17	7.66	65	.308	.424	2-0	.500	1		-8	-0.7
2000	KC A	0	1	.000	12	0	0	0-2	6.1	11	8	3	0	4-0	8	11.37	45	.367	.441	0-0	—	0		-4	-0.5
Total 3		0	4	.000	48	0	0	1-5	32.2	48	33	9	1	24-2	26	8.27	61	.336	.435	2-0	.500	1		-12	-1.2
BYRNE, JERRY Gerald Wilfred B 2.2.1907 Parnell, MI D 8.11.1955 Lansing, MI BR/TR 6/170# d8.31																									
1929	Chi A	0	1	.000	3	1	0	0	7.1	11	6	0	0	6	1	7.36	58	.379	.486	2-0	.000	-0	59	-2	-0.3
BYRNE, TOMMY Thomas Joseph B 12.31.1919 Baltimore, MD BL/TL 6-1/182# d4.27 Mil 1944-45																									
1943	NY A	2	1	.667	11	2	0	0	31.2	28	26	1	3	35	22	6.54	49	.248	.437	11-1	.091	-0*	105	-11	-1.0
1946	NY A	0	1	.000	4	1	0	0	9.1	7	8	1	1	8	5	5.79	60	.194	.356	9-0	.222	0*	75	-3	-0.2
1947	NY A	0	0	—	4	1	0	0	4.1	5	2	0	0	6	2	4.15	85	.294	.478	0-0	—	0	225	0	0.0
1948	NY A	8	5	.615	31	11	5-1	2	133.2	79	55	8	9	101	93	3.30	124	.172	.332	46-4	.326	6	123	12	1.6
1949	†NY A	15	7	.682	32	30	12-3	0	196	125	84	11	13	179	129	3.72	109	**.183**	.362	83-1	.193	1*	140	11	1.0
1950	NY A☆	15	9	.625	31	31	10-2	0	203.1	188	115	23	17	160	118	4.74	91	.245	.387	81-0	.272	7*	140	-10	-0.4
1951	NY A	2	1	.667	9	3	0	0	21	16	17	0	3	36	14	6.86	56	.213	.482	9-0	.222	1	124	-7	-0.8
	StL A	4	10	.286	19	17	7-2	0	122.2	104	56	5	12	114	57	3.82	115	.235	.404	57-2	.281	3*	64	8	1.2
	Year	6	11	.353	28	20	7-2	0	143.2	120	59	5	15	150	71	4.26	101	.232	.417	66-2	.273	4	72	3	0.4
1952	StL A	7	14	.333	29	24	14	0	196	182	117	16	10	112	91	4.68	84	.247	.354	84-0	.250	5*	90	-16	-1.2
1953	Chi A	2	0	1.000	6	6	0	0	16	18	18	0	0	26	4	10.13	40	.295	.506	18-0	.167	1*	158	-10	-0.9
	Was A	0	5	.000	6	5	2	0	33.2	35	17	3	1	22	22	4.28	91	.276	.387	17-0	.059	-1*	55	-1	-0.2
	Year	2	5	.286	12	11	2	0	49.2	53	19	3	1	48	26	6.16	64	.282	.430	35-0	.114	-0	113	-11	-1.1
1954	NY A	3	2	.600	5	5	4-1	0	40	36	13	1	0	19	24	2.70	127	.240	.325	19-0	.368	4*	149	4	1.0
1955	†NY A	16	5	**.762**	27	22	9-3	2	160	137	69	12	7	87-3	76	3.15	119	.237	.340	78-1	.205	4*	117	9	1.5
1956	†NY A	7	3	.700	37	8	1	6	109.2	108	50	9	2	72-5	52	3.36	115	.262	.372	52-2	.269	6*	129	5	1.0
1957	†NY A	4	6	.400	30	4	1	2	84.2	70	41	8	7	60-2	57	4.36	82	.227	.363	37-0	.189	4*	87	-5	-0.2
Total 13		85	69	.552	281	170	65-12	12	1362	1138	688	98	85	1037-**10**	766	4.11	97	.229	.370	601-11	.238	41	118	-14	2.4
BYSTROM, MARTY Martin Eugene B 7.26.1958 Coral Gables, FL BR/TR 6-5/200# d9.7																									
1980	†Phi N	5	0	1.000	6	5	1-1	0-0	36	26	6	1	0	9-0	21	1.50	253	.195	.246	14-0	.071	-1	169	9	1.3
1981	Phi N	4	3	.571	9	9	1	0-0	53.2	55	21	3	1	16-1	24	3.35	108	.264	.319	17-1	.118	-1	106	2	0.1
1982	Phi N	5	6	.455	19	16	1	0-0	89	93	53	2	5	35-4	50	4.85	76	.277	.350	24-3	.125	-0	99	-11	-1.3
1983	†Phi N	6	9	.400	24	23	1-1	0-0	119.1	136	75	6	7	44-2	87	4.60	78	.285	.348	38-1	.237	2	108	-15	-1.6
1984	Phi N	4	4	.500	11	11	0	0-0	56.2	66	36	5	0	22-1	36	5.08	72	.283	.341	19-3	.158	-0	110	-8	-1.1
	NY A	2	2	.500	7	7	0	0-0	39.1	34	16	3	1	13-1	24	2.97	128	.230	.296	0-0	—	0	78	3	0.3
1985	NY A	3	2	.600	8	8	0	0-0	41	44	29	8	1	19-0	16	5.71	70	.280	.360	0-0	—	0	108	-8	-0.8
Total 6		29	26	.527	84	79	4-2	0-0	435	454	236	28	15	158-9	258	4.26	87	.268	.333	112-8	.161	0	107	-28	-3.1
CABRERA, JOSE Jose Alberto B 3.24.1972 Santiago, D.R. BR/TR 6/200# d7.15																									
1997	Hou N	0	0	—	12	0	0	0-1	15.1	6	2	1	0	6-0	18	1.17	341	.125	.211	2-0	.000	-0		5	0.2
1998	Hou N	0	0	—	3	0	0	0-0	4.1	7	4	0	0	1-1	1	8.31	49	.389	.421	0-0	—	0		-2	-0.1
1999	†Hou N	4	0	1.000	26	0	0	0-1	29.1	21	7	3	0	9-2	28	2.15	206	.196	.252	0-0	—	0		8	0.9
2000	Hou N	2	3	.400	52	0	0	2-1	59.1	74	40	10	3	17-2	41	5.92	82	.308	.357	1-0	.000	-0		-5	-0.5
2001	Atl N	7	4	.636	55	0	0	2-6	59.1	52	24	5	2	25-4	43	2.88	153	.239	.315	1-0	.000	-0		9	1.5
2002	Mil N	6	10	.375	50	11	0	0-1	103.1	131	84	23	9	36-9	61	6.79	60	.314	.378	19-1	.105	-1	107	-31	-4.2
Total 6		19	17	.528	198	11	0	4-10	271	291	161	42	14	94-18	192	4.95	88	.278	.340	23-1	.087	-1	107	-16	-2.2
CADARET, GREG Gregory James B 2.27.1962 Detroit, MI BL/TL 6-3/214# d7.5																									
1987	Oak A	6	2	.750	29	0	0	0-1	39.2	37	22	6	1	24-1	30	4.54	91	.252	.356	0-0	—	0		-2	-0.3
1988	†Oak A	5	2	.714	58	0	0	3-1	71.2	60	26	2	1	36-1	64	2.89	131	.226	.317	0-0	—	0		7	0.7
1989	Oak A	0	0	—	26	0	0	0-1	27.2	21	9	0	0	19-3	14	2.28	162	.214	.336	0-0	—	0		4	0.2
	NY A	5	5	.500	20	13	3-1	0-1	92.1	109	53	7	2	38-1	66	4.58	85	.298	.364	0-0	—	0	95	-8	-0.7
	Year	5	5	.500	46	13	3-1	0-2	120	130	57	7	2	57-4	80	4.05	95	.280	.358	0-0	—	0	96	-4	-0.5
1990	NY A	5	4	.556	54	6	0	3-1	121.1	120	62	8	1	64-5	80	4.15	96	.268	.359	0-0	—	0	84	-2	-0.1
1991	NY A	8	6	.571	68	5	0	3-4	121.2	110	52	8	2	59-6	105	3.62	114	.246	.335	0-0	—	0	168	8	0.9
1992	NY A	4	8	.333	46	11	1-1	1-2	103.2	104	53	12	2	74-7	73	4.25	92	.267	.385	0-0	—	0	108	-3	-0.3
1993	Cin N	2	1	.667	34	0	0	1-0	32.2	40	19	3	1	23-5	23	4.96	81	.305	.413	2-0	.000	-0		-3	-0.3
	KC A	1	1	.500	13	0	0	0-0	15.1	14	5	0	1	7-0	2	2.93	157	.264	.361	0-0	—	0		3	0.3
1994	Tor A	0	1	.000	21	0	0	0-0	20	24	15	4	0	17-2	15	5.85	82	.289	.410	0-0	—	0		-3	-0.1
	Det A	1	0	1.000	17	0	0	2-0	20	17	9	0	0	16-3	14	3.60	135	.227	.363	0-0	—	0		3	0.2
	Year	1	1	.500	38	0	0	2-0	40	41	29	4	0	33-5	29	4.72	102	.259	.387	0-0	—	0		0	0.1
1997	Ana A	0	0	—	15	0	0	0-0	13.2	11	5	1	2	8-2	11	3.29	139	.220	.350	0-0	—	0		2	0.1
1998	Ana A	1	2	.333	39	0	0	1-1	37	38	17	6	3	15-0	37	4.14	113	.257	.337	0-0	—	0		3	0.2

Year	Tm Lg	W	L	Pct	G	GS	CG-Sho	SV-BS	IP	H	R	HR	HB	BB-IB	SO	ERA	AERA	OAV	OOB	AB-SH	AVG	PB	Sup	APR	PW
	Tex A	0	0	—	11	0	0	0-0	7.2	11	4	1	0	3-0	5	4.70	103	.355	.400	0-0	—	0		0	0.0
	Year	1	2	.333	50	0	0	1-1	44.2	49	21	7	3	18-0	42	4.23	111	.274	.348	0-0	—	0		3	0.2
Total	10	38	32	.543	451	35	4-2	14-12	724.1	716	351	58	16	403-36	539	3.99	102	.262	.358	2-0	.000	-0	105	9	0.8
CADORE, LEON Leon Joseph "Caddy" B 11.20.1890 Chicago, IL D 3.16.1958 Spokane, WA BR/TR 6-1/190# d4.28 Mil 1918																									
1915	Bro N	0	2	.000	7	2	1	0	21	28	15	0	2	8	12	5.57	50	.337	.409	6-0	.000	-1	40	-5	-0.6
1916	Bro N	0	0	—	1	0	0	0	6	10	4	0	0	0	2	4.50	60	.370	.370	3-0	.000	-0		-1	-0.1
1917	Bro N	13	13	.500	37	30	21-1	3	264	231	86	3	7	63	115	2.45	114	.241	.292	92-5	.261	5	92	12	1.7
1918	Bro N	1	0	1.000	2	2	1-1	0	17	6	1	0	1	2	5	0.53	526	.115	.164	4-0	.000	-0	54	4	0.2
1919	Bro N	14	12	.538	35	27	16-3	0	250.2	228	80	5	6	39	94	2.37	125	.245	.280	87-0	.161	-3	94	19	1.5
1920	†Bro N	15	14	.517	35	30	16-4	0	254.1	256	91	4	3	56	79	2.62	122	.270	.313	91-4	.220	2	106	17	2.3
1921	Bro N	13	14	.481	35	30	12-1	0	211.2	243	112	17	6	46	79	4.17	93	.292	.334	75-3	.187	-1	101	-4	-0.6
1922	Bro N	8	15	.348	29	21	13	0	190.1	224	115	13	1	57	49	4.35	94	.299	.349	71-3	.268	4	88	-8	-0.5
1923	Bro N	4	1	.800	8	4	3	0	36	39	14	2	0	13	5	3.25	119	.291	.354	13-0	.077	-1*	106	4	0.3
	Chi A	0	1	.000	1	1	0	0	2.1	6	7	0	0	2	3	23.14	17	.500	.571	0-0	—	0	42	-5	-0.7
1924	NY N	0	0	—	2	0	0	0	4	2	0	0	0	3	2	0.00	—	.154	.313	0-0	—	0		2	0.1
Total	10	68	72	.486	192	147	83-10	3	1257.1	1273	525	44	26	289	445	3.14	106	.269	.314	442-15	.208	5	96	35	3.6
CADY, CHARLIE Charles B. B 12.1865 Chicago, IL D 6.7.1909 Kankakee, IL 5-11/180# d9.5 ▲																									
1883	Cle N	0	1	.000	1	1	1	0	8	13	13	0		4	5	7.88	40	.361	.425	11	.000	-1*	17	-4	-0.4
1884	CP U	3	1	.750	4	4	4	0	35	37	25	0		13	15	2.83	86	.253	.314	20	.100	-1*	157	-2	-0.3
Total	2	3	2	.600	5	5	5	0	43	50	38	0		17	20	3.77	68	.275	.337	31	.065	-2	129	-6	-0.7
CAHILL, JOHN John Patrick Parnell "Patsy" B 4.30.1865 San Francisco, CA D 10.31.1901 Pleasanton, CA BR/TR 5-7.5/168# d5.31 ▲																									
1884	Col AA	1	0	1.000	2	1	1	0	16	15	15	0	3	4	1	5.06	60	.211	.282	210	.219	0*	299	-4	-0.2
1886	StL N	1	0	1.000	2	0	0	0	12	11	5	0		3	2	3.00	107	.268	.318	463	.199	-0*		1	0.1
1887	Ind N	0	2	.000	6	1	1	0	22	40	38	3	2	19	5	14.32	29	.430	.535	263	.205	-1*	47	-19	-1.3
Total	3	2	2	.500	10	2	2	0	50	66	58	3	5	26	8	8.64	41	.322	.411	936	.205	-1	159	-22	-1.4
CAIN, LES Leslie B 1.13.1948 San Luis Obispo, CA BL/TL 6-1/200# d4.28																									
1968	Det A	1	0	1.000	8	4	0	0	24	25	9	1	0	20-1	13	3.00	100	.269	.398	7-0	.143	0	138	0	0.0
1970	Det A	12	7	.632	29	29	5	0-0	180.2	167	92	15	7	98-1	156	3.84	97	.247	.346	68-3	.162	0	116	-5	-0.5
1971	Det A	10	9	.526	26	26	3-1	0-0	144.2	121	77	14	6	91-1	118	4.35	83	.228	.346	55-2	.145	-0*	117	-12	-1.5
1972	Det A	0	3	.000	5	5	0	0-0	23.2	18	12	2	0	16-0	16	3.80	83	.209	.330	7-1	.143	-0	73	-2	-0.3
Total	4	23	19	.548	68	64	8-1	0-0	373	331	190	32	13	225-3	303	3.98	90	.239	.349	137-6	.153	-0	114	-19	-2.3
CAIN, SUGAR Merritt Patrick B 4.5.1907 Macon, GA D 4.3.1975 Atlanta, GA BL/TR 5-11/190# d4.15																									
1932	Phi A	3	4	.429	10	6	3	0	45	42	27	1	0	28	24	5.00	90	.256	.365	12-0	.250	1	75	-2	-0.2
1933	Phi A	13	12	.520	38	32	16-1	1	218	244	132	18	3	137	43	4.25	101	.280	.379	80-4	.200	-1*	109	-3	-0.4
1934	Phi A	9	17	.346	36	32	15	0	230.2	235	128	15	3	128	66	4.41	99	.266	.360	82-5	.159	-3	97	-1	-0.4
1935	Phi A	0	5	.000	6	5	0	0	26	39	22	1	0	19	5	6.58	69	.382	.479	8-0	.000	-1	53	-6	-1.0
	StL A	9	8	.529	31	24	8	0	167.2	197	112	7	4	104	68	5.26	91	.290	.388	57-3	.193	-2	107	-8	-1.0
	Year	9	13	.409	37	29	8	0	193.2	236	118	8	4	123	73	5.44	88	.302	.400	65-3	.169	-4	98	-14	-2.0
1936	StL A	1	1	.500	4	3	1	0	16.1	20	13	0	0	9	8	6.61	81	.286	.367	7-0	.286	0	147	-2	-0.2
	Chi A	14	10	.583	30	26	14-1	0	195.1	228	112	18	5	75	42	4.75	110	.293	.359	68-4	.103	-4*	97	12	0.6
	Year	15	11	.577	34	29	15-1	0	211.2	248	118	18	5	84	50	4.89	107	.292	.360	75-4	.120	-4	102	11	0.4
1937	Chi A	4	2	.667	18	6	1	0	68.2	88	48	7	0	51	17	6.16	75	.325	.432	22-2	.182	-1	133	-9	-0.7
1938	Chi A	0	1	.000	5	3	0	0	19.2	26	17	0	0	18	6	4.58	107	.321	.444	8-0	.000	-1	78	-1	-0.2
Total	7	53	60	.469	178	137	58-2	1	987.1	1119	611	67	15	569	279	4.83	96	.287	.380	344-18	.163	-13	101	-20	-3.5
CAIN, BOB Robert Max "Sugar" B 10.16.1924 Longford, KS D 4.8.1997 Cleveland, OH BL/TL 6/165# d9.18																									
1949	Chi A	0	0	—	6	0	0	1	11	7	3	0	0	5	5	2.45	170	.179	.273	3-0	.000	-0		2	0.0
1950	Chi A	9	12	.429	34	23	11-1	2	171.2	153	80	12	5	109	77	3.93	114	.244	.361	61-3	.197	-0*	93	13	1.3
1951	Chi A	1	2	.333	4	4	1	0	26.1	25	14	3	3	13	3	3.76	107	.248	.350	9-0	.333	1	88	0	0.1
	Det A	11	10	.524	35	22	6-1	2	149.1	135	88	13	11	82	58	4.70	89	.239	.347	53-2	.245	2	120	-9	-0.9
	Year	12	12	.500	39	26	7-1	2	175.2	160	94	16	14	95	61	4.56	91	.241	.348	62-2	.258	3	115	-8	-0.8
1952	StL A	12	10	.545	29	27	8-1	2	170	169	79	15	2	62	70	4.13	95	.264	.331	58-5	.138	-1*	97	0	-0.2
1953	StL A	4	10	.286	32	13	1	1	99.2	129	74	8	1	45	36	6.23	67	.310	.379	30-0	.200	0*	106	-20	-2.5
Total	5	37	44	.457	140	89	27-3	8	628	618	338	51	22	316	249	4.50	93	.259	.351	214-10	.196	0	102	-14	-2.2
CAIRNCROSS, CAMERON Cameron B 5.11.1972 Cairns, Australia BL/TL 6/195# d7.20																									
2000	Cle A	1	0	1.000	15	0	0	0-0	9.1	11	4	1	0	3-1	8	3.86	129	.306	.350	0-0	—	0		1	0.1
CALDWELL, CHARLIE Charles William "Chuck" B 8.2.1901 Bristol, VA D 11.1.1957 Princeton, NJ BR/TR 5-10/180# d7.7																									
1925	NY A	0	0	—	3	0	0	0	2.2	7	6	0	0	3	1	16.88	25	.467	.556	1-0	.000	-0		-4	-0.2
CALDWELL, EARL Earl Welton "Teach" B 4.9.1905 Sparks, TX D 9.15.1981 Mission, TX BR/TR 6-1/178# d9.8																									
1928	Phi N	1	4	.200	5	5	1-1	0	34.2	46	23	5	0	17	6	5.71	75	.348	.423	9-1	.111	-0	44	-4	-0.5
1935	StL A	3	2	.600	6	5	2-1	0	36.2	34	16	2	0	17	5	3.68	130	.245	.327	11-1	.182	-0	65	5	0.6
1936	StL A	7	16	.304	41	25	10-2	2	189	252	146	15	15	83	59	6.00	90	.319	.394	58-4	.190	-1	79	-13	-1.4
1937	StL A	0	0	—	9	2	0	0	29	39	22	3	2	13	8	6.83	71	.317	.391	9-1	.222	0	99	-5	-0.2
1945	Chi A	6	7	.462	27	11	5-1	4	105.1	108	50	8	3	37	45	3.59	92	.265	.331	37-3	.216	-0	110	-4	-0.3
1946	Chi A	13	4	.765	39	0	0	8	90.2	60	28	2	1	29	42	2.08	164	.186	.255	18-2	.167	1		**13**	2.8
1947	Chi A	1	4	.200	40	0	0	8	54.1	53	23	4	1	30	22	3.64	100	.261	.359	7-1	.000	-1		1	0.0
1948	Chi A	1	5	.167	25	1	0	3	39	53	25	3	2	22	10	5.31	80	.335	.423	5-0	.000	-0	42	-4	-0.7
	Bos A	1	1	.500	8	0	0	0	9	11	14	2	1	11	5	13.00	34	.333	.511	3-0	.333	0		-8	-1.5
	Year	2	6	.250	33	1	0	3	48	64	41	5	3	33	15	6.75	63	.335	.441	8-0	.125	-0	42	-12	-2.2
Total	8	33	43	.434	200	49	18-5	25	587.2	656	347	44	25	259	202	4.69	92	.284	.363	157-13	.178	-2	87	-19	-1.2
CALDWELL, RALPH Ralph Grant "Lefty" B 1.18.1884 Philadelphia, PA D 8.5.1969 W.Trenton, NJ BL/TL 5-9/155# d9.10																									
1904	Phi N	2	2	.500	6	5	5	0	41	40	29	1	2	15	30	4.17	64	.242	.313	18-0	.444	3	154	-7	-0.3
1905	Phi N	1	3	.250	7	2	1	1	34	44	25	1	3	7	29	4.24	69	.321	.367	15-0	.000	-2	136	-6	-0.9
Total	2	3	5	.375	13	7	6	1	75	84	54	2	5	22	59	4.20	66	.278	.337	33-0	.242	1	148	-13	-1.2
CALDWELL, MIKE Ralph Michael B 1.22.1949 Tarboro, NC BR/TL 6/185# d9.4																									
1971	SD N	1	0	1.000	6	0	0	0-0	6.2	4	0	0	0	3-3	5	0.00	—	.174	.269	1-0	1.000	1		3	0.5
1972	SD N	7	11	.389	42	20	4-2	2-3	163.2	183	92	10	4	49-14	102	4.01	82	.282	.335	50-4	.140	-1	109	-18	-1.8
1973	SD N	5	14	.263	55	13	3-1	10-2	149	146	77	8	2	53-10	86	3.74	93	.260	.325	35-3	.143	-1*	76	-7	-0.9
1974	SF N	14	5	.737	31	27	6-2	0-1	189.1	176	80	17	4	63-1	83	2.95	129	.249	.312	63-7	.143	-2	120	15	1.4
1975	SF N	7	13	.350	38	21	4	1-0	163.1	194	102	16	5	48-7	57	4.79	79	.296	.346	44-7	.159	-0	109	-19	-2.0
1976	SF N	1	7	.125	50	9	0	2-0	107.1	145	74	5	2	20-2	55	4.86	75	.324	.354	19-1	.158	-0	102	-16	-1.1
1977	Cin N	0	0	—	14	0	0	1-0	24.2	25	11	1	0	8-1	11	4.01	98	.260	.317	4-0	.500	2		0	0.2
	Mil A	5	8	.385	21	12	2	0-0	94.1	101	58	6	2	36-7	38	4.58	89	.271	.337	0-0	—	0	88	-7	-0.7
1978	Mil A	22	9	.710	37	34	**23**-6	1-0	293.1	258	90	14	7	54-3	131	2.36	160	.234	.273	0-0	—	0	102	44	4.8
1979	Mil A	16	6	**.727**	30	30	16-4	0-0	235	252	96	18	4	39-2	89	3.29	127	.278	.309	0-0	—	0	116	23	2.3
1980	Mil A	13	11	.542	34	33	11-2	1-0	225.1	248	112	29	2	56-2	74	4.03	96	.285	.328	0-0	—	0	134	-3	-0.3
1981	†Mil A	11	9	.550	24	23	3	0-0	144.1	151	70	18	1	38-4	41	3.93	87	.272	.317	0-0	—	0	122	-10	-1.2
1982	†Mil A	17	13	.567	35	34	12-3	0-1	258	269	119	30	0	58-3	75	3.91	97	.271	.310	0-0	—	0	116	-1	0.0
1983	Mil A	12	11	.522	32	32	10-2	0-0	228.1	269	125	35	1	51-1	58	4.53	83	.296	.332	0-0	—	0	120	-21	-1.9
1984	Mil A	6	13	.316	26	19	4-1	0-0	126	160	76	11	1	21-2	34	4.64	83	.314	.338	0-0	—	0	86	-12	-1.6
Total	14	137	130	.513	475	307	98-23	18-7	2408.2	2581	1182	218	35	597-62	939	3.81	99	.276	.320	216-22	.157	-2	112	-29	-2.3
CALDWELL, RAY Raymond Benjamin "Rube" or "Sum" B 4.26.1888 Corydon, PA D 8.17.1967 Salamanca, NY BL/TR 6-2/190# d9.9 ▲																									
1910	NY A	1	0	1.000	6	2	1	1	19.1	19	8	1	0	9	17	3.72	71	.260	.341	6-0	.000	-1	126	-1	-0.2
1911	NY A	14	14	.500	41	26	19-1	1	255	240	115	7	13	79	145	3.35	107	.260	.327	147-1	.272	3*	83	11	1.3

Year	Tm Lg	W	L	Pct	G	GS	CG-Sho	SV-BS	IP	H	R	HR	HB	BB-IB	SO	ERA	AERA	OAV	OOB	AB-SH	AVG	PB	Sup	APR	PW
1912	NY A	8	16	.333	30	26	13-3	0	183.1	196	111	1	6	67	95	4.47	80	.277	.344	76-1	.237	1*	92	-11	-1.1
1913	NY A	9	8	.529	27	16	15-2	1	164.1	131	59	5	9	60	87	2.41	124	.221	.303	97-2	.289	3*	113	11	1.7
1914	NY A	18	9	.667	31	23	22-5	0	213	153	53	5	4	51	92	1.94	142	.205	.260	113-5	.195	1*	99	21	3.0
1915	NY A	19	16	.543	36	35	31-3	0	305	266	115	6	5	107	130	2.89	101	.244	.315	144-2	.243	8*	108	4	1.2
1916	NY A	5	12	.294	21	18	14-1	0	165.2	142	62	6	8	65	76	2.99	97	.243	.327	93-0	.204	-0*	61	1	0.1
1917	NY A	13	16	.448	32	29	21-1	0	236	199	92	8	6	76	102	2.86	94	.234	.302	124-0	.258	6*	93	-2	0.8
1918	NY A	9	8	.529	24	21	14-1	1	176.2	173	69	2	1	62	59	3.06	93	.261	.325	151-4	.291	4*	114	-3	0.3
1919	Bos A	7	4	.636	18	12	6-1	0	86.1	92	49	1	3	31	23	3.96	76	.279	.346	48-3	.271	1*	115	-11	-1.1
	Cle A	5	1	.833	6	6	4-1	0	52.2	33	13	1	2	19	24	1.71	196	.181	.266	23-0	.348	2	105	9	1.4
	Year	12	5	.706	24	18	10-2	0	139	125	18	2	5	50	47	3.11	101	.244	.317	71-3	.296	4	111	0	0.3
1920	†Cle A	20	10	.667	34	33	20-1	0	237.2	286	135	9	4	63	80	3.86	98	.303	.350	89-5	.213	1*	137	-6	-0.7
1921	Cle A	6	6	.500	37	12	4-1	4	147	159	91	7	2	49	76	4.90	87	.275	.333	53-1	.208	0*	144	-9	-0.6
Total	12	134	120	.528	343	259	184-21	8	2242	2089	972	59	63	738	1006	3.22	99	.253	.319	1164-24	.248	31	105	14	6.1
CALERO, KIKO Enrique Nomar B 1.9.1975 Santurce, P.R. BR/TR 6-1/180# d4.2																									
2003	StL N	1	1	.500	26	1	0	1-3	38.1	29	12	5	1	20-2	51	2.82	144	.212	.311	4-0	.250	0	92	6	0.3
CALHOUN, JEFF Jeffrey Wilton B 4.11.1958 LaGrange, GA BL/TL 6-2/190# d9.2																									
1984	Hou N	0	1	.000	9	0	0	0-0	15.1	5	3	0	0	2-2	11	1.17	283	.100	.135	0-0	—	0		4	0.2
1985	Hou N	2	5	.286	44	0	0	4-3	63.2	56	21	2	0	24-4	47	2.54	136	.243	.313	5-0	.000	-0		7	0.8
1986	†Hou N	1	0	1.000	20	0	0	0-0	26.2	28	16	3	0	12-1	14	3.71	97	.264	.339	0-0	—	0		-2	-0.1
1987	Phi N	3	1	.750	42	0	0	1-0	42.2	25	13	1	1	26-8	31	1.48	288	.168	.292	1-0	.000	-0		10	0.9
1988	Phi N	0	0	—	3	0	0	0-1	2.1	6	4	2	0	1-0	1	15.43	23	.462	.500	0-0	—	0		-3	-0.1
Total	5	6	7	.462	118	0	0	5-4	150.2	120	57	8	1	65-15	104	2.51	147	.219	.301	6-0	.000	-0		16	1.7
CALIGIURI, FRED Frederick John B 10.22.1918 W.Hickory, PA BR/TR 6/190# d9.3 Mil 1943-46																									
1941	Phi A	2	2	.500	5	5	4	0	43	45	22	2	0	14	7	2.93	143	.257	.312	20-1	.200	1	107	3	0.3
1942	Phi A	0	3	.000	13	2	0	1	36.2	45	27	2	2	18	20	6.38	59	.300	.382	12-0	.083	-0	79	-9	-0.7
Total	2	2	5	.286	18	7	4	1	79.2	90	49	4	2	32	27	4.52	89	.277	.345	32-1	.156	1	101	-6	-0.4
CALIHAN, WILL William T. (b: William T. Callahan) B 1869 Oswego, NY D 12.20.1917 Rochester, NY 5-8/150# d4.17																									
1890	Roc AA	18	15	.545	37	36	31	0	296.1	276	170	4	16	125	127	3.28	109	.239	.322	159	.145	-3*	97	9	0.6
1891	Phi AA	6	6	.500	13	11	11	0	112	151	103	7	12	47	28	6.43	59	.312	.387	56	.196	-1*	97	-28	-2.2
Total	2	24	21	.533	50	47	42	0	408.1	427	273	11	28	172	155	4.14	88	.261	.341	215	.158	-4	96	-19	-1.6
CALLAHAN, BEN Benjamin Franklin B 5.19.1957 Mt.Airy, NC BR/TR 6-7/230# d6.22																									
1983	Oak A	1	2	.333	4	2	0	0-0	9.1	18	16	0	0	5-1	2	12.54	31	.400	.451	0-0	—	0	141	-10	-1.6
CALLAHAN, NIXEY James Joseph B 3.18.1874 Fitchburg, MA D 10.4.1934 Boston, MA BR/TR 5-10.5/180# d5.12 M7 ▲																									
1894	Phi N	1	2	.333	9	2	1	2	33.2	64	52	3	5	17	9	9.89	52	.398	.470	21-0	.238	-1	76	-19	-1.3
1897	Chi N	12	9	.571	23	22	21-1	0	189.2	221	111	6	8	55	52	4.03	111	.289	.343	360-8	.292	3*	108	13	1.5
1898	Chi N	20	10	.667	31	31	30-2	0	274.1	267	137	2	10	71	73	2.46	146	.253	.307	164-4	.262	4*	119	29	3.3
1899	Chi N	21	12	.636	35	34	33-3	0	294.1	327	155	5	24	76	77	3.06	123	.281	.338	150-5	.260	4*	92	22	2.8
1900	Chi N	13	16	.448	32	32	32-2	0	285.1	347	195	5	22	74	77	3.82	94	.299	.353	115-5	.235	2	104	-6	0.0
1901	Chi A	15	8	.652	27	22	20-1	0	215.1	195	94	4	9	50	70	2.42	144	.239	.290	118-4	.331	8*	100	25	3.7
1902	Chi A	16	14	.533	35	31	29-2	0	282.1	287	150	8	11	89	75	3.60	94	.264	.326	218-13	.234	3*	114	-9	-0.2
1903	Chi A	1	2	.333	3	3	3	0	28	40	24	0	1	5	12	4.50	62	.333	.365	439-11	.292	1*	161	-7	-0.5
Total	8	99	73	.576	195	177	169-11	2	1603	1748	918	33	90	437	445	3.39	109	.276	.332	1585-50	.276	25	106	48	9.3
CALLAHAN, JOHN John W. B Moberly, MO d9.3																									
1898	StL N	0	2	.000	2	2	1	0	8.1	18	20	2	2	7	2	16.20	23	.429	.529	4-0	.000	-1	56	-11	-1.4
CALLAHAN, JOE Joseph Thomas B 10.8.1916 E.Boston, MA D 5.24.1949 S.Boston, MA BR/TR 6-2/170# d9.13																									
1939	Bos N	1	0	1.000	4	1	1	0	17.1	17	6	0	1	3	8	3.12	119	.250	.292	4-0	.000	-0	71	2	0.1
1940	Bos N	0	2	.000	6	2	0	0	15	20	17	1	0	13	3	10.20	36	.351	.471	5-0	.000	-1	35	-10	-1.1
Total	2	1	2	.333	10	3	1	0	32.1	37	23	1	1	16	11	6.40	58	.296	.380	9-0	.000	-1	47	-8	-1.0
CALLAHAN, RAY Raymond James "Pat" B 8.29.1891 Ashland, WI D 1.23.1973 Olympia, WA BL/TL 5-10.5/170# d9.12																									
1915	Cin N	0	0	—	3	0	0	0	6.1	12	7	1	0	1	4	8.53	34	.364	.382	3-0	.333	0		-4	-0.2
CALLAWAY, MICKEY Michael Christopher B 5.13.1975 Memphis, TN BR/TR 6-2/190# d6.12																									
1999	TB A	1	2	.333	5	4	0	0-0	19.1	30	20	2	0	14-1	11	7.45	67	.357	.444	3-0	.667	1*	70	-6	-0.6
2001	TB A	0	0	—	2	0	0	0-0	5	3	4	2	0	2-0	2	7.20	62	.167	.250	0-0	—	0		-1	-0.1
2002	Ana A	2	1	.667	6	6	0	0-0	34.1	31	20	4	3	11-0	23	4.19	106	.235	.308	0-0	—	0	129	0	0.0
2003	Ana A	1	4	.200	17	4	0	0-0	38.1	57	32	7	1	16-1	22	6.81	63	.345	.402	0-0	—	0	149	-11	-1.2
	Tex A	0	3	.000	6	3	0	0-0	22.1	27	18	0	1	8-0	19	6.45	77	.314	.367	0-0	—	0	56	-4	-0.4
	Year	1	7	.125	23	7	0	0-0	60.2	84	21	7	2	24-1	41	6.68	68	.335	.390	0-0	—	0	107	-14	-1.6
Total	4	4	10	.286	36	17	0	0-0	119.1	148	94	15	5	51-2	77	6.11	75	.305	.373	3-0	.667	1	106	-22	-2.3
CALMUS, DICK Richard Lee B 1.7.1944 Los Angeles, CA BR/TR 6-4/187# d4.22																									
1963	LA N	3	1	.750	21	1	0	0	44	32	14	3	0	16-1	25	2.66	114	.204	.277	6-0	.000	-1	29	3	0.1
1967	Chi N	0	0	—	1	1	0	0	4.1	5	4	2	0	0-0	1	8.31	43	.278	.278	2-0	.500	0	99	-2	-0.1
Total	2	3	1	.750	22	2	0	0	48.1	37	18	5	0	16-1	26	3.17	97	.211	.277	8-0	.125	-0	70	1	0.0
CALVERT, MARK Mark B 9.29.1956 Tulsa, OK BR/TR 6-1/195# d4.17																									
1983	SF N	1	4	.200	18	4	0	0-0	37.1	46	33	2	3	34-4	14	6.27	57	.307	.441	8-1	.000	-1	150	-13	-1.6
1984	SF N	2	4	.333	10	5	1	0-0	32	40	21	4	1	9-1	5	5.06	69	.303	.350	8-0	.000	-1	116	-6	-1.1
Total	2	3	8	.273	28	9	1	0-0	69.1	86	54	6	4	43-5	19	5.71	62	.305	.402	16-1	.000	-1	131	-19	-2.7
CALVERT, PAUL Paul Leo Emile B 10.6.1917 Montreal, PQ, CAN D 2.1.1999 Sherbrooke, PQ, CAN BR/TR 6/185# d9.24																									
1942	Cle A	0	0	—	1	0	0	0	2	0	0	0	0	2	2	0.00	—	.000	.286	0-0	—	0		1	0.0
1943	Cle A	0	0	—	5	0	0	0	8.1	6	4	0	1	6	2	4.32	72	.200	.351	1-0	.000	-0		-1	-0.1
1944	Cle A	1	3	.250	35	4	0	0	77	89	48	4	0	38	31	4.56	72	.289	.367	15-1	.267	1	120	-12	-0.4
1945	Cle A	0	0	—	1	0	0	0	1.1	3	2	0	0	1	1	13.50	24	.429	.500	0-0	—	0		-1	-0.1
1949	Was A	6	17	.261	34	23	5	1	160.2	175	111	11	2	86	52	5.43	78	.279	.368	51-4	.137	-2*	91	-21	-2.6
1950	Det A	2	2	.500	32	0	0	4	51.1	71	42	7	2	25	14	6.31	74	.324	.398	7-0	.000	-1		-10	-0.8
1951	Det A	0	0	—	1	0	0	0	1	1	0	0	0	0	0	0.00	—	.250	.250	0-0	—	0		0	0.0
Total	7	9	22	.290	109	27	5	5	301.2	345	207	22	5	158	102	5.31	76	.287	.373	74-5	.149	-2	95	-44	-4.0
CAMACHO, ERNIE Ernest Carlos B 2.1.1955 Salinas, CA BR/TR 6-1/180# d5.22																									
1980	Oak A	0	0	—	5	0	0	0-0	11.2	20	9	2	1	5-0	9	6.94	54	.364	.426	0-0	—	0		-4	-0.2
1981	Pit N	0	1	.000	7	3	0	0-0	21.2	23	13	0	0	15-1	11	4.98	72	.295	.400	4-1	.000	-0	90	-3	-0.2
1983	Cle A	0	1	.000	4	0	0	0-0	5.1	5	3	1	1	2-0	2	5.06	84	.250	.348	0-0	—	0		0	-0.1
1984	Cle A	5	9	.357	69	0	0	23-10	100	83	31	6	1	37-5	48	2.43	169	.229	.300	0-0	—	0		18	3.1
1985	Cle A	0	1	.000	2	0	0	0-2	3.1	4	3	0	0	1-0	2	8.10	51	.333	.333	0-0	—	0		-1	-0.2
1986	Cle A	2	4	.333	51	0	0	20-10	57.1	60	26	1	2	31-6	36	4.08	102	.269	.355	0-0	—	0		2	0.3
1987	Cle A	0	1	.000	15	0	0	1-3	13.2	21	14	1	3	5-1	9	9.22	49	.350	.426	0-0	—	0		-6	-0.4
1988	Hou N	0	3	.000	13	0	0	1-0	17.2	25	15	1	0	12-2	13	7.64	44	.352	.446	1-0	.000	-0		-8	-1.3
1989	SF N	3	0	1.000	13	0	0	0-0	16.1	10	5	1	0	11-2	14	2.76	123	.175	.309	1-0	.000	-0		1	0.3
1990	SF N	0	0	—	8	0	0	0-0	10	10	4	1	0	3-0	8	3.60	101	.256	.310	0-0	—	0		0	0.0
	StL N	0	0	—	6	0	0	0-1	5.2	7	6	2	0	6-1	7	7.94	48	.318	.433	0-0	—	0		-3	-0.1
	Year	0	0	—	14	0	0	0-1	15.2	17	14	3	0	9-1	15	5.17	72	.279	.361	0-0	—	0		-3	-0.1
Total	10	10	20	.333	193	3	0	45-26	262.2	268	129	16	8	128-18	159	4.21	94	.268	.351	6-1	.000	-1	90	-4	1.2
CAMBRIA, FRED Frederick Dennis B 1.22.1948 Cambria Heights, NY BR/TR 6-2/195# d8.26																									
1970	Pit N	1	2	.333	6	5	0	0-0	33.1	37	15	2	1	12-0	14	3.51	111	.272	.336	10-2	.200	1	96	1	0.2

Year	Tm Lg	W	L	Pct	G	GS	CG-Sho	SV-BS	IP	H	R	HR	HB	BB-IB	SO	ERA	AERA	OAV	OOB	AB-SH	AVG	PB	Sup	APR	PW
CAMMACK, ERIC Eric Wade B 8.14.1975 Nederland, TX BR/TR 6-1/175# d4.28																									
2000	NY N	0	0	—	8	0	0	0-0	10	7	7	1	1	10-1	9	6.30	70	.194	.375	1-0	1.000	1		-2	0.0
CAMNITZ, HARRY Henry Richardson B 10.26.1884 McKinney, KY D 1.6.1951 Louisville, KY BR/TR 6-1/168# d9.29 b-Howie																									
1909	Pit N	0	0	—	1	0	0	0	4	6	2	0	0	1	1	4.50	60	.353	.389	2-0	.000	-0		0	-0.1
1911	StL N	1	0	1.000	2	0	0	0	2	0	0	0	0	1	2	0.00	—	.000	.143	0-0	—	0		1	0.2
Total	2	1	0	1.000	3	0	0	0	6	6	2	0	0	2	3	3.00	98	.261	.320	2-0	.000	-0		1	0.1
CAMNITZ, HOWIE Samuel Howard "Red" B 8.22.1881 Covington, KY D 3.2.1960 Louisville, KY BR/TR 5-9/169# d4.22 b-Harry																									
1904	Pit N	1	4	.200	10	2	2	0	49	48	39	0	3	20	21	4.22	65	.259	.341	16-0	.063	-1	50	-11	-1.2
1906	Pit N	1	0	1.000	2	1	1-1	0	9	6	2	0	0	5	5	2.00	134	.188	.297	3-0	.000	-0	27	1	0.0
1907	Pit N	13	8	.619	31	19	15-4	1	180	135	65	0	3	59	85	2.15	113	.211	.281	60-3	.050	-5	103	5	0.0
1908	Pit N	16	9	.640	38	26	17-3	2	236.2	182	76	6	5	69	118	1.56	148	.210	.272	72-6	.083	-3	98	13	1.1
1909	†Pit N	25	6	**.806**	41	30	20-6	3	283	207	75	1	7	68	133	1.62	168	.211	.267	87-9	.138	-0	120	31	3.5
1910	Pit N	12	13	.480	38	31	16-1	2	260	246	110	1	12	61	120	3.22	96	.256	.308	88-7	.125	-3	97	1	-0.4
1911	Pit N	20	15	.571	40	33	18-1	1	267.2	245	112	8	4	84	139	3.13	110	.248	.309	84-12	.143	-3	107	12	0.9
1912	Pit N	22	12	.647	41	32	22-2	2	276.2	256	104	8	13	82	121	2.83	115	.251	.315	98-8	.235	1	119	17	1.8
1913	Pit N	6	17	.261	36	22	5-1	2	192.1	203	106	7	8	84	64	3.74	81	.282	.363	59-0	.153	-1	80	-18	-2.1
	Phi N	3	3	.500	9	5	1	1	49	49	25	1	2	23	21	3.67	91	.268	.356	16-0	.063	-1	81	-2	-0.4
	Year	9	20	.310	45	27	6-1	3	241.1	252	29	8	10	107	85	3.73	83	.279	.362	75-0	.133	-3	81	-14	-2.5
1914	Pit F	14	19	.424	36	34	20-1	1	262	256	132	8	8	90	82	3.23	89	.258	.324	87-8	.161	-5	101	-15	-2.4
1915	Pit F	0	0	—	4	2	0	0	20	19	11	1	0	11	6	4.50	60	.257	.353	7-0	.000	-1	77	-4	-0.3
Total	11	133	106	.556	326	237	137-20	15	2085.1	1852	857	41	65	656	915	2.75	106	.242	.307	677-53	.136	-24	103	30	0.5
CAMP, RICK Rick Lamar B 6.10.1953 Trion, GA BR/TR 6/198# d9.15																									
1976	Atl N	0	1	.000	5	1	0	0-0	11.1	13	9	0	0	2-0	6	6.35	60	.302	.326	2-0	.000	-0	70	-3	-0.2
1977	Atl N	6	3	.667	54	0	0	10-4	78.2	89	47	6	1	47-13	51	4.00	111	.283	.373	6-0	.000	-1		1	0.0
1978	Atl N	2	4	.333	42	4	0	0-4	74.1	99	42	5	3	32-10	23	3.75	108	.329	.396	8-1	.000	-1	72	0	-0.1
1980	Atl N	6	4	.600	77	0	0	22-2	108.1	92	26	3	4	29-8	33	1.91	196	.235	.291	9-0	.111	-0		21	3.0
1981	Atl N	9	3	.750	48	0	0	17-5	76	68	17	5	1	12-3	47	1.78	202	.239	.271	12-1	.000	-1		**15**	2.9
1982	†Atl N	11	13	.458	51	21	3	5-2	177.1	199	84	18	1	52-8	68	3.65	102	.291	.339	41-5	.024	-3	72	0	-0.2
1983	Atl N	10	9	.526	40	16	1	0-0	140	146	64	16	4	38-2	61	3.79	102	.270	.321	39-3	.077	-2	101	1	0.0
1984	Atl N	8	6	.571	31	21	1	0-0	148.2	134	59	11	2	63-3	69	3.27	118	.245	.324	45-3	.111	-2	86	10	0.7
1985	Atl N	4	6	.400	66	2	0	3-0	127.2	130	72	8	5	61-11	49	3.95	98	.263	.347	13-1	.231	1	92	-4	-0.3
Total	9	56	49	.533	414	65	5	57-17	942.1	970	420	72	21	336-58	407	3.37	115	.269	.333	175-14	.074	-8	84	41	5.8
CAMP, KID Winfield Scott B 12.8.1869 New Albany, OH D 3.2.1895 Omaha, NE BB/TR 6/160# d5.3 b-Lew																									
1892	Pit N	0	1	.000	4	1	1	0	23	31	23	4	1	9	6	6.26	53	.310	.373	11	.091	-1	77	-6	-0.4
1894	Chi N	0	1	.000	3	2	2	0	22	34	24	0	1	12	6	6.55	86	.351	.427	11-1	.000	-3	57	-2	-0.3
Total	2	0	2	.000	7	3	3	0	45	65	47	4	2	21	12	6.40	69	.330	.400	22-1	.045	-4	66	-8	-0.7
CAMPBELL, ARCHIE Archibald Stewart "Iron Man" B 10.20.1903 Maplewood, NJ D 12.22.1989 Sparks, NV BR/TR 6/180# d4.21																									
1928	NY A	0	1	.000	13	1	0	2	24	30	22	0	0	11	9	5.25	72	.288	.357	4-2	.250	0	90	-7	-0.4
1929	Was A	0	1	.000	4	0	0	0	4	10	7	1	0	5	1	15.75	27	.500	.600	0-0	—	0		-5	-0.8
1930	Cin N	2	4	.333	23	3	1	4	58	71	38	2	1	31	19	5.43	89	.311	.396	15-0	.267	0	42	-3	-0.2
Total	3	2	6	.250	40	4	1	6	86	111	67	3	1	47	29	5.86	77	.315	.398	19-2	.263	0	53	-15	-1.4
CAMPBELL, DAVE David Alan B 9.3.1951 Princeton, IN BR/TR 6-3/210# d5.6																									
1977	Atl N	0	6	.000	65	0	0	13-0	88.2	78	32	7	3	33-6	42	3.05	146	.239	.311	12-2	.083	-1		13	1.0
1978	Atl N	4	4	.500	53	0	0	1-1	69.1	67	39	10	5	49-12	45	4.80	84	.258	.383	0-0	—	0		-4	-0.4
Total	2	4	10	.286	118	0	0	14-1	158	145	71	17	8	82-18	87	3.82	112	.247	.345	12-2	.083	-1		9	0.6
CAMPBELL, HUGH Hugh F. B 1846 , Ireland D 3.1.1881 Newark, NJ d4.28 b-Mat																									
1873	Res NA	2	16	.111	19	18	18	0	165	251	213	6		8	7	2.95	114	.297	.304	86	.151	-5*	42	10	0.5
CAMPBELL, JIM James Marcus B 5.19.1966 Santa Maria, CA BL/TL 5-11/175# d8.21																									
1990	KC A	1	0	1.000	2	2	0	0-0	9.2	15	9	1	0	1-0	2	8.38	46	.349	.364	0-0	—	0	190	-4	-0.4
CAMPBELL, JOHN John Millard B 9.13.1907 Washington, DC D 4.24.1995 Daytona Beach, FL BR/TR 6-1.5/184# d7.23																									
1933	Was A	0	0	—	1	0	0	0	1	1	1	0	0	1	0	0.00	—	.200	.333	0-0	—	0		0	0.0
CAMPBELL, KEVIN Kevin Wade B 12.6.1964 Marianna, AR BR/TR 6-2/225# d7.19																									
1991	Oak A	1	0	1.000	14	0	0	0-1	23	13	7	4	1	14-0	16	2.74	140	.167	.301	0-0	—	0		3	0.2
1992	Oak A	2	3	.400	32	5	0	1-0	65	66	39	4	0	45-3	38	5.12	73	.267	.378	0-0	—	0	88	-9	-0.7
1993	Oak A	0	0	—	11	0	0	0-0	16	20	13	1	1	11-1	9	7.31	56	.313	.416	0-0	—	0		-6	-0.3
1994	Min A	1	0	1.000	14	0	0	0-0	24.2	20	8	2	1	5-0	15	2.92	167	.233	.274	0-0	—	0		6	0.3
1995	Min A	0	0	—	6	0	0	0-0	9.2	8	5	0	0	5-0	5	4.66	103	.235	.333	0-0	—	0		0	0.0
Total	5	4	3	.571	77	5	0	1-1	138.1	127	72	11	3	80-4	83	4.55	89	.250	.351	0-0	—	0	88	-6	-0.5
CAMPBELL, MIKE Michael Thomas B 2.17.1964 Seattle, WA BR/TR 6-3/210# d7.4																									
1987	Sea A	1	4	.200	9	9	1	0-0	49.1	41	29	9	2	25-2	35	4.74	100	.224	.319	0-0	—	0	77	0	0.0
1988	Sea A	6	10	.375	20	20	2	0-0	114.2	128	81	18	0	43-1	63	5.89	71	.280	.339	0-0	—	0	113	-20	-2.4
1989	Sea A	1	2	.333	5	5	0	0-0	21	28	22	4	0	10-0	6	7.29	55	.301	.369	0-0	—	0	121	-8	-1.0
1992	Tex A	0	1	.000	1	0	0	0-0	3.2	3	4	1	0	2-0	2	9.82	39	.231	.333	0-0	—	0		-2	-0.4
1994	SD N	1	1	.500	3	2	0	0-1	8.1	13	12	5	0	5-0	10	12.96	32	.351	.429	3-0	.333	0	111	-8	-1.2
1996	Chi N	3	1	.750	13	5	0	0-0	36.1	29	19	7	0	10-0	19	4.46	97	.216	.269	11-1	.364	2	166	0	0.1
Total	6	12	19	.387	51	41	3	0-1	233.1	242	167	44	2	95-3	135	5.86	73	.264	.331	14-1	.357	2	112	-38	-4.9
CAMPBELL, BILLY William James B 11.5.1873 Pittsburgh, PA D 10.6.1957 Cincinnati, OH BL/TL 5-10/165# d4.17																									
1905	StL N	1	1	.500	2	2	2	0	17	27	17	0	0	7	2	7.41	40	.365	.420	7-1	.143	-0	133	-8	-0.7
1907	Cin N	3	0	1.000	3	3	3	0	21	19	5	0	0	3	4	2.14	121	.244	.272	8-0	.250	0	174	2	0.3
1908	Cin N	12	13	.480	35	24	19-2	2	221.1	203	99	3	10	44	73	2.60	89	.252	.299	72-6	.083	-3	93	-9	-1.2
1909	Cin N	7	11	.389	30	15	7	2	148.1	162	65	0	9	39	37	2.67	97	.288	.344	43-6	.140	-1	104	-1	0.0
Total	4	23	25	.479	70	44	31-2	4	407.2	411	186	3	19	93	116	2.80	88	.270	.320	130-13	.115	-4	105	-16	-1.6
CAMPBELL, BILL William Richard B 8.9.1948 Highland Park, MI BR/TR 6-3/190# d7.14 C1																									
1973	Min A	3	3	.500	28	2	0	7-2	51.2	44	20	5	1	20-1	42	3.14	126	.226	.301	0-0	—	0	45	5	0.7
1974	Min A	8	7	.533	63	0	0	19-8	120.1	109	37	4	2	55-4	89	2.62	143	.242	.326	0-0	—	0		16	2.5
1975	Min A	4	6	.400	47	7	2-1	5-6	121	119	58	13	2	46-2	76	3.79	101	.262	.330	1-0	.000	-0	161	1	0.1
1976	Min A	17	5	**.773**	**78**	0	0	20-10	167.2	145	63	9	5	62-11	115	3.01	119	.234	.305	0-0	—	0		12	1.8
1977	Bos A★	13	9	.591	69	0	0	**31-11**	140	112	48	13	5	60-10	114	2.96	152	.224	.311	0-0	—	0		22	**4.5**
1978	Bos A	7	5	.583	29	0	0	4-11	50.2	62	25	3	0	17-3	47	3.91	106	.308	.362	0-0	—	0		1	0.3
1979	Bos A	3	4	.429	41	0	0	9-8	54.2	55	28	5	1	23-6	25	4.28	103	.262	.338	0-0	—	0		1	0.2
1980	Bos A	4	0	1.000	23	0	0	0-0	41.1	44	26	1	0	22-0	17	4.79	88	.284	.367	0-0	—	0		-3	-0.3
1981	Bos A	1	1	.500	30	0	0	7-0	48.1	45	23	5	0	20-4	37	3.17	122	.245	.316	0-0	—	0		2	0.2
1982	Chi N	3	6	.333	62	0	0	8-5	100	89	44	6	0	40-13	71	3.69	101	.245	.314	7-0	.143	-0		1	0.2
1983	Chi N	6	8	.429	**82**	0	0	8-5	122.1	128	65	4	1	49-18	97	4.49	85	.275	.342	10-0	.100	-1		-8	-0.9
1984	Phi N	6	5	.545	57	0	0	1-4	81.1	68	43	2	0	35-13	52	3.43	106	.222	.301	1-0	.000	-0		-1	-0.2
1985	†StL N	5	3	.625	50	0	0	4-1	64.1	55	32	5	2	21-9	41	3.50	101	.230	.294	6-0	.333	1		-1	-0.1
1986	Det A	3	6	.333	34	0	0	3-1	55.2	46	26	5	1	21-5	37	3.88	106	.230	.302	0-0	—	0		2	0.3
1987	Mon N	0	0	—	7	0	0	0-0	10	18	12	2	0	4-1	4	8.10	52	.360	.400	1-0	.000	0		-5	-0.2
Total	15	83	68	.550	700	9	2-1	126-72	1229.1	1139	550	82	20	495-100	864	3.54	110	.248	.321	26-0	.154	1	134	45	9.1
CAMPER, CARDELL Cardell B 7.6.1952 Boley, OK BR/TR 6-3/208# d9.11																									
1977	Cle A	1	0	1.000	3	1	0	0-0	9.1	7	4	0	0	4-1	9	3.86	103	.200	.282	0-0	—	0	114	0	0.0

Year	Tm Lg	W	L	Pct	G	GS	CG-Sho	SV-BS	IP	H	R	HR	HB	BB-IB	SO	ERA	AERA	OAV	OOB	AB-SH	AVG	PB	Sup	APR	PW
CAMPFIELD, SAL William Holton B 2.19.1868 Meadville, PA D 5.16.1952 Meadville, PA BR/TR 6-0.5/?# d5.15																									
1896	NY N	1	1	.500	6	2	2	0	27	31	15	1	2	6	6	4.00	105	.284	.333	12-0	.167	-0	127	1	0.0
CAMPISI, SAL Salvatore John B 8.11.1942 Brooklyn, NY BR/TR 6-2/210# d8.15																									
1969	StL N	1	0	1.000	7	0	0	0-0	9.2	4	1	0	0	6-2	7	0.93	384	.121	.256	0-0	—	0		3	0.3
1970	StL N	2	2	.500	37	0	0	4-0	49.1	53	19	2	3	37-11	26	2.92	141	.282	.406	1-0	.000	-0		6	0.5
1971	Min A	0	0	—	6	0	0	0-1	4.1	5	2	1	0	4-0	2	4.15	86	.294	.429	0-0	—	0		0	0.0
Total	3	3	2	.600	50	0	0	4-1	63.1	62	22	3	3	47-13	35	2.70	148	.261	.388	1-0	.000	-0		9	0.8
CANAVAN, HUGH Hugh Edward "Hugo" B 5.13.1897 Worcester, MA D 9.4.1967 Boston, MA BL/TL 5-8/160# d4.23 Mil 1918																									
1918	Bos N	0	4	.000	11	3	3	0	46.2	70	42	0	5	15	18	6.36	42	.366	.427	21-0	.095	-0*	94	-19	-1.5
CANDELARIA, JOHN John Robert "Candy Man" B 11.6.1953 New York, NY BL/TL 6-7/232# d6.8																									
1975	†Pit N	8	6	.571	18	18	4-1	0-0	120.2	95	47	8	2	36-9	95	2.76	129	.212	.271	43-0	.140	-0	143	9	0.9
1976	Pit N	16	7	.696	32	31	11-4	1-0	220	173	87	22	2	60-5	138	3.15	111	.216	.271	76-5	.184	3	124	9	1.2
1977	Pit N☆	20	5	**.800**	33	33	6-1	0-0	230.2	197	64	29	2	50-2	133	**2.34**	**170**	.232	.274	80-4	.225	4	94	**43**	4.9
1978	Pit N	12	11	.522	30	29	3-1	1-0	189	191	73	15	5	49-6	94	3.24	114	.261	.311	52-7	.173	3*	93	12	1.8
1979	†Pit N	14	9	.609	33	30	8	0-0	207	201	83	25	3	41-6	101	3.22	121	.253	.290	68-8	.132	-1	105	15	1.5
1980	Pit N	11	14	.440	35	34	7	1-0	233.1	246	114	14	3	50-4	97	4.01	91	.276	.313	77-3	.195	2	101	-8	-0.7
1981	Pit N	2	2	.500	6	6	0	0-0	40.2	42	17	3	0	11-1	14	3.54	102	.271	.317	13-2	.231	0	128	1	0.1
1982	Pit N	12	7	.632	31	30	1-1	1-0	174.2	166	62	13	4	37-3	133	2.94	126	.255	.296	54-3	.222	3*	95	15	2.0
1983	Pit N	15	8	.652	33	32	2	0-0	197.2	191	73	15	2	45-3	157	3.23	115	.257	.300	65-5	.138	-0	95	13	1.4
1984	Pit N	12	11	.522	33	28	3-1	2-1	185.1	179	69	19	1	34-3	133	2.72	133	.256	.289	62-4	.129	1	105	15	1.8
1985	Pit N	2	4	.333	37	0	0	9-6	54.1	57	23	7	1	14-2	47	3.64	98	.275	.319	1-2	.000	-0		0	0.0
	Cal A	7	3	.700	13	13	1-1	0-0	71	70	33	7	3	24-1	53	3.80	108	.262	.327	0-0	—	0	119	3	0.3
1986	†Cal A	10	2	.833	16	16	1-1	0-0	91.2	68	30	4	3	26-2	81	2.55	161	.206	.268	0-0	—	0	132	16	1.9
1987	Cal A	8	6	.571	20	20	0	0-0	116.2	127	70	17	1	20-0	74	4.71	92	.279	.308	0-0	—	0	111	-6	-0.5
	NY N	2	0	1.000	3	3	0	0-0	12.1	17	8	1	0	3-0	10	5.84	65	.333	.364	5-0	.200	0	112	-3	-0.3
1988	NY A	13	7	.650	25	24	6-2	1-0	157	150	69	18	2	23-2	121	3.38	117	.248	.275	0-0	—	0	113	8	0.9
1989	NY A	3	3	.500	10	6	1	0-0	49	49	28	8	0	12-1	37	5.14	75	.258	.299	0-0	—	0	101	-6	-0.6
	Mon N	0	2	.000	12	0	0	0-0	16.1	17	8	3	0	4-2	14	3.31	107	.283	.313	0-0	—	0		0	0.0
1990	Min A	7	3	.700	34	1	0	4-3	58.1	55	23	9	0	9-2	44	3.39	123	.244	.270	0-0	—	0	66	5	0.9
	Tor A	0	3	.000	13	2	0	1-0	21.1	32	13	2	2	11-3	19	5.48	72	.356	.425	0-0	—	0	58	-3	-0.4
	Year	7	6	.538	47	3	0	5-3	79.2	87	16	11	2	20-5	63	3.95	104	.276	.318	0-0	—	0	59	3	0.5
1991	LA N	1	1	.500	59	0	0	2-3	33.2	31	16	3	0	11-2	38	3.74	96	.252	.307	0-0	—	0		-1	-0.1
1992	LA N	2	5	.286	50	0	0	5-2	25.1	20	9	1	0	13-3	23	2.84	121	.220	.311	0-0	—	0		2	0.5
1993	Pit N	0	3	.000	24	0	0	1-2	19.2	25	19	2	1	9-1	17	8.24	49	.313	.385	0-0	—	0		-9	-1.3
Total	19	177	122	.592	600	356	54-13	29-17	2525.2	2399	1038	245	37	592-63	1673	3.33	114	.251	.295	596-43	.174	15	107	130	16.2
CANDINI, MILO Mario Cain B 8.3.1917 Manteca, CA D 3.17.1998 Manteca, CA BR/TR 6/187# d5.1 Mil 1945																									
1943	Was A	11	7	.611	28	21	8-3	1	166	144	55	3	1	65	67	2.49	128	.238	.313	56-6	.161	-1	109	14	1.5
1944	Was A	6	7	.462	28	10	4-2	1	103	110	53	3	1	49	31	4.11	79	.276	.357	32-6	.313	3	118	-8	-0.6
1946	Was A	2	0	1.000	9	0	0	1	21.2	15	5	1	0	4	6	2.08	161	.192	.232	6-0	.333	1		4	0.4
1947	Was A	3	4	.429	38	2	0	1	87	96	53	5	0	35	31	5.17	72	.273	.339	18-2	.167	-0	83	-13	-0.9
1948	Was A	2	3	.400	35	4	1	3	94.1	96	56	1	1	63	23	5.15	84	.267	.378	22-0	.364	3	73	-6	0.0
1949	Was A	0	0	—	3	0	0	1	5.2	4	3	0	0	1	1	4.76	89	.200	.238	1-0	1.000	0		0	0.0
1950	Phi N	1	0	1.000	18	0	0	0	30	32	11	2	0	15	10	2.70	150	.281	.364	6-0	.167	-0		4	0.2
1951	Phi N	1	0	1.000	15	0	0	0	30	33	22	3	0	18	14	6.00	64	.275	.370	3-0	.333	1		-7	-0.3
Total	8	26	21	.553	174	37	13-5	8	537.2	530	258	18	3	250	183	3.92	92	.259	.341	144-14	.243	7	100	-12	0.3
CANDIOTTI, TOM Thomas Caesar B 8.31.1957 Walnut Creek, CA BR/TR 6-2/200# d8.8																									
1983	Mil A	4	4	.500	10	8	2-1	0-0	55.2	62	21	4	2	16-0	21	3.23	116	.291	.343	0-0	—	0	79	4	0.5
1984	Mil A	2	2	.500	8	6	0	0-0	32.1	38	21	5	0	10-0	23	5.29	73	.277	.327	0-0	—	0	82	-5	-0.6
1986	Cle A	16	12	.571	36	34	**17**-3	0-0	252.1	234	112	18	8	106-0	167	3.57	116	.246	.324	0-0	—	0	114	17	1.9
1987	Cle A	7	18	.280	32	32	7-2	0-0	201.2	193	132	28	4	93-2	111	4.78	95	.250	.330	0-0	—	0	74	-9	-1.0
1988	Cle A	14	8	.636	31	31	11-1	0-0	216.2	225	86	15	6	53-3	137	3.28	126	.272	.319	0-0	—	0	99	20	2.0
1989	Cle A	13	10	.565	31	31	4	0-0	206	188	80	10	4	55-5	124	3.10	128	.242	.294	0-0	—	0	75	19	2.2
1990	Cle A	15	11	.577	31	29	3-1	0-0	202	207	92	23	6	55-1	128	3.65	108	.263	.315	0-0	—	0	108	5	0.7
1991	Cle A	7	6	.538	15	15	3	0-0	108.1	88	35	6	2	28-0	86	2.24	185	.218	.268	0-0	—	0	78	21	2.4
	†Tor A	6	7	.462	19	19	3	0-0	129.2	114	47	6	4	45-1	81	2.98	141	.236	.304	0-0	—	0	79	17	1.6
	Year	13	13	.500	34	34	6	0-0	238	202	51	12	6	73-1	167	2.65	158	.228	.288	0-0	—	0	78	39	4.0
1992	LA N	11	15	.423	32	30	6-2	0-0	203.2	177	78	13	3	63-5	152	3.00	115	.237	.297	56-12	.107	-1	82	11	1.3
1993	LA N	8	10	.444	33	32	2	0-0	213.2	192	86	12	6	71-1	155	3.12	123	.241	.305	60-9	.133	-1	69	17	1.3
1994	LA N	7	7	.500	23	22	5	0-0	153	149	77	9	5	54-2	102	4.12	95	.259	.323	50-7	.140	-1	114	-4	-0.4
1995	LA N	7	14	.333	30	30	1-1	0-0	190.1	187	93	18	9	58-2	141	3.50	108	.255	.316	55-5	.109	-1	80	3	0.2
1996	†LA N	9	11	.450	28	27	1	0-0	152.1	172	91	18	3	43-3	79	4.49	86	.288	.336	45-9	.089	-2	98	-13	-1.6
1997	LA N	10	7	.588	41	18	0	0-0	135	128	60	21	11	40-4	89	3.60	107	.248	.314	32-9	.094	-1*	121	4	0.3
1998	Oak A	11	16	.407	33	33	3	0-0	201	222	124	30	9	63-2	98	4.84	95	.281	.338	1-1	1.000	1	93	-7	-0.6
1999	Oak A	3	5	.375	11	11	0	0-0	56.2	67	46	11	2	23-0	30	6.35	73	.298	.362	0-0	—	0	100	-12	-1.3
	Cle A	1	1	.500	7	2	0	0-0	14.2	19	18	3	1	7-0	11	11.05	46	.306	.386	0-0	—	0	176	-9	-0.9
	Year	4	6	.400	18	13	0	0-0	71.1	86	28	14	3	30-0	41	7.32	65	.300	.367	0-0	—	0	112	-22	-2.2
Total	16	151	164	.479	451	410	68-11	0-0	2725	2662	1299	250	85	883-31	1735	3.73	108	.256	.317	299-52	.117	-7	92	79	8.0
CANEIRA, JOHN John Cascaes B 10.7.1952 Waterbury, CT BR/TR 6-3/180# d9.10																									
1977	Cal A	2	2	.500	6	4	0	0-0	28.2	27	15	5	0	16-2	17	4.08	96	.252	.347	0-0	—	0	86	0	-0.1
1978	Cal A	0	0	—	2	2	0	0-0	7.2	8	6	2	0	3-0	0	7.04	51	.286	.344	0-0	—	0	74	-3	-0.2
Total	2	2	2	.500	8	6	0	0-0	36.1	35	21	7	0	19-2	17	4.71	82	.259	.346	0-0	—	0	81	-3	-0.3
CANO, JOSE Joselito (Soriano) B 3.7.1962 Boca Del Soco, D.R. BR/TR 6-3/175# d8.28																									
1989	Hou N	1	1	.500	6	3	1	0-0	23	24	13	2	0	7-2	8	5.09	67	.267	.316	6-0	.000	-1	113	-4	-0.4
CANTRELL, GUY Guy Dewey "Gunner" B 4.9.1904 Clarita, OK D 1.31.1961 McAlester, OK BR/TR 6/190# d8.18																									
1925	Bro N	1	0	1.000	14	3	1	0	36	42	27	0	1	14	13	3.00	139	.294	.361	9-0	.000	-1	121	0	-0.1
1927	Bro N	0	0	—	6	0	0	0	10	10	3	0	0	6	5	2.70	147	.250	.348	3-0	.333	0		2	0.1
	Phi A	0	2	.000	2	2	2	0	18	25	10	0	0	7	7	5.00	85	.338	.395	6-0	.167	-0	39	-1	-0.1
1930	Det A	1	5	.167	16	2	1	0	35	38	30	5	1	20	20	5.66	85	.271	.366	9-0	.000	-2	81	-5	-0.8
Total	3	2	7	.222	38	7	4	0	99	115	70	5	2	47	45	4.27	103	.290	.368	27-0	.074	-3	86	-4	-0.9
CANTWELL, BEN Benjamin Caldwell B 4.13.1902 Milan, TN D 12.4.1962 Salem, MO BR/TR 6-1/168# d8.19																									
1927	NY N	1	1	.500	5	2	1	0	19.2	26	9	1	1	2	6	4.12	94	.313	.337	8-0	.250	0	99	0	0.0
1928	NY N	1	0	1.000	7	1	0	1	18.1	20	10	1	1	4	0	4.42	89	.282	.329	4-0	.500	1	173	-1	0.0
	Bos N	3	3	.500	22	10	3	0	90	112	63	7	2	36	18	5.10	77	.304	.369	29-0	.172	-1	115	-13	-0.8
	Year	4	3	.571	29	11	3	1	108.1	132	68	8	3	40	18	4.98	79	.301	.363	33-0	.212	-0	120	-15	-0.8
1929	Bos N	4	13	.235	27	20	8	2	157	171	98	11	2	52	25	4.47	105	.280	.338	50-3	.180	0	74	-1	0.2
1930	Bos N	9	15	.375	31	21	10	2	173.1	213	99	15	1	45	43	4.88	101	.312	.355	63-2	.302	2*	62	4	0.9
1931	Bos N	7	9	.438	33	16	9-2	2	156.1	160	73	4	0	34	32	3.63	104	.262	.301	57-2	.228	0*	83	2	0.4
1932	Bos N	13	11	.542	37	9	3-1	5	146	133	56	6	5	33	33	2.96	127	.247	.296	50-0	.280	2	99	14	2.6
1933	Bos N	20	10	**.667**	40	29	18-2	2	254.2	242	89	12	3	54	57	2.62	117	.249	.291	85-3	.141	-1*	97	12	1.5
1934	Bos N	5	11	.313	27	19	6-1	5	143.1	163	88	8	2	34	45	4.33	88	.285	.327	43-5	.279	1*	86	-13	-1.1
1935	Bos N	4	25	.138	39	24	13	0	210.2	235	117	15	2	44	34	4.61	82	.282	.320	67-5	.284	4*	54	-16	-1.5
1936	Bos N	9	9	.500	34	12	4	2	133.1	127	55	8	4	35	42	3.04	126	.252	.306	41-3	.195	-1*	82	11	1.4
1937	NY N	0	1	.000	1	1	0	0	4	6	4	1	0	1	1	9.00	43	.375	.412	0-0	—	0	44	-2	-0.3
	Bro N	0	0	—	13	0	0	0	27.1	32	17	1	0	8	12	4.61	88	.288	.336	6-0	.167	-0		-2	0.0
	Year	0	1	.000	14	1	0	0	31.1	38	23	2	0	9	13	5.17	78	.299	.346	6-0	.167	0	43	-4	-0.3

Year	Tm Lg	W	L	Pct	G	GS	CG-Sho	SV-BS	IP	H	R	HR	HB	BB-IB	SO	ERA	AERA	OAV	OOB	AB-SH	AVG	PB	Sup	APR	PW
Total	11	76	108	.413	316	164	75-6	21	1534	1640	778	90	23	382	348	3.91	100	.275	.321	503-23	.231	8	81	-5	3.3
CANTWELL, MIKE Michael Joseph B 1.15.1896 Washington, DC D 1.5.1953 Oteen, NC BL/TL 5-10/155# d8.17 b-Tom																									
1916	NY A	0	0	—	1	0	0	0	2	0	2	0	0	2	0	0.00	—	.000	.333	0-0	—	0		0	0.0
1919	Phi N	1	3	.250	5	3	2	0	27.1	36	19	1	2	9	6	5.60	58	.343	.405	9-0	.222	-0	107	-6	-0.8
1920	Phi N	0	3	.000	5	1	0	0	23.1	25	18	1	3	15	8	3.86	89	.284	.406	7-1	.143	-1	138	-3	-0.4
Total	3	1	6	.143	11	4	2	0	52.2	61	39	2	5	26	14	4.61	71	.310	.404	16-1	.188	-1	114	-9	-1.2
CANTWELL, TOM Thomas Aloysius B 12.23.1888 Washington, DC D 4.1.1968 Washington, DC BR/TR 6/170# d5.19 b-Mike																									
1909	Cin N	1	0	1.000	6	1	1	0	21.2	16	10	0	1	7	7	1.66	156	.205	.279	5-0	.600	1	81	1	0.2
1910	Cin N	0	0	—	2	0	0	0	1.1	2	2	0	0	3	0	13.50	22	.400	.625	0-0	—	0		-1	-0.1
Total	2	1	0	1.000	8	1	1	0	23	18	12	0	1	10	7	2.35	111	.217	.309	5-0	.600	1	81	0	0.1
CAPEL, MIKE Michael Lee B 10.13.1961 Marshall, TX BR/TR 6-1/175# d5.7																									
1988	Chi N	2	1	.667	22	0	0	0-3	29.1	34	19	5	3	13-2	19	4.91	74	.293	.379	2-0	.000	-0		-5	-0.5
1990	Mil A	0	0	—	2	0	0	0-0	0.1	6	6	0	1	1-0	1	135.00	3	.857	.889	0-0	—	0		-5	-0.2
1991	Hou N	1	3	.250	25	0	0	3-1	32.2	33	14	3	0	15-1	23	3.03	116	.266	.343	0-0	—	0		1	0.1
Total	3	3	4	.429	49	0	0	3-4	62.1	73	39	8	4	29-3	43	4.62	77	.296	.377	2-0	.000	-0		-9	-0.6
CAPILLA, DOUG Douglas Edmund B 1.7.1952 Honolulu, HI BL/TL 5-8/175# d9.12																									
1976	StL N	1	0	1.000	7	0	0	0-1	8.1	8	5	0	0	4-0	5	5.40	66	.242	.324	0-0	—	0		-1	-0.2
1977	StL N	0	0	—	2	0	0	0-0	2.1	2	4	0	0	2-0	1	15.43	25	.222	.364	0-0	—	0		-3	-0.1
	Cin N	7	8	.467	22	16	1	0-0	106.1	94	53	10	2	59-1	74	4.23	93	.237	.338	34-3	.059	-3	100	-3	-0.7
	Year	7	8	.467	24	16	1	0-0	108.2	96	57	10	2	61-1	75	4.47	88	.236	.339	34-3	.059	-3	100	-5	-0.8
1978	Cin N	0	1	.000	6	3	0	0-0	11	14	12	1	0	11-0	9	9.82	36	.318	.439	2-0	.000	-0*	169	-7	-0.6
1979	Cin N	1	0	1.000	5	0	0	0-0	6.1	7	6	1	1	5-0	0	8.53	44	.269	.406	1-0	1.000	0		-3	-0.4
	Chi N	0	1	.000	13	1	0	0-0	17.1	14	6	1	0	7-0	10	2.60	159	.206	.280	0-0	—	0	64	3	0.2
	Year	1	1	.500	18	1	0	0-0	23.2	21	9	2	1	12-0	10	4.18	96	.223	.318	1-0	1.000	0	66	0	-0.2
1980	Chi N	2	8	.200	39	11	0	0-1	89.2	82	46	7	3	51-5	51	4.12	95	.253	.355	21-1	.190	0*	39	-1	-0.1
1981	Chi N	1	0	1.000	42	0	0	0-3	51	52	20	1	2	34-3	28	3.18	116	.284	.396	3-0	.000	-0		3	0.1
Total	6	12	18	.400	136	31	1	0-5	292.1	273	152	21	8	173-9	178	4.34	89	.252	.356	61-4	.115	-3	84	-12	-1.8
CAPPUZZELLO, GEORGE George Angelo B 1.15.1954 Youngstown, OH BR/TL 6/175# d5.31																									
1981	Det A	1	1	.500	18	3	0	1-0	33.2	28	14	2	2	18-2	19	3.48	109	.222	.329	0-0	—	0	111	1	0.1
1982	Hou N	0	1	.000	17	0	0	0-2	19.1	16	6	2	3	7-1	13	2.79	119	.232	.321	1-0	.000	-0		2	0.1
Total	2	1	2	.333	35	3	0	1-2	53	44	20	4	5	25-3	32	3.23	112	.226	.326	1-0	.000	-0	111	3	0.2
CAPRA, BUZZ Lee William B 10.1.1947 Chicago, IL BR/TR 5-10/168# d9.15																									
1971	NY N	0	1	.000	3	0	0	0-0	5.1	3	6	0	0	5-1	6	8.44	40	.167	.348	1-0	.000	-0		-3	-0.5
1972	NY N	3	2	.600	14	6	0	0-0	53	50	27	7	0	27-1	45	4.58	73	.253	.341	12-0	.250	1	83	-6	-0.3
1973	NY N	2	7	.222	24	0	0	4-3	42	35	18	4	2	28-9	35	3.86	94	.233	.357	2-1	.000	0		0	0.0
1974	Atl N☆	16	8	.667	39	27	11-5	1-0	217	163	67	13	3	84-6	137	**2.28**	**166**	**.208**	.286	67-7	.164	0	96	33	3.5
1975	Atl N	4	7	.364	12	12	5	0-0	78.1	77	41	8	1	28-1	35	4.25	89	.257	.320	23-5	.043	-2	85	-3	-0.5
1976	Atl N	0	1	.000	5	0	0	0-0	9.1	9	9	0	0	6-2	4	8.68	44	.265	.366	0-0	—	0		-4	-0.4
1977	Atl N	6	11	.353	45	16	0	0-0	139.1	142	88	28	4	80-12	100	5.36	83	.263	.360	36-3	.111	-2	66	-10	-1.2
Total	7	31	37	.456	142	61	16-5	5-3	544.1	479	256	60	10	258-32	362	3.87	101	.237	.324	141-16	.135	-2	85	7	0.6
CAPUANO, CHRIS Christopher Frank B 8.19.1978 Springfield, MA BL/TL 6-3/210# d5.4																									
2003	Ari N	2	4	.333	9	5	0	0-0	33	27	19	3	6	11-1	23	4.64	101	.231	.326	8-0	.000	-1	80	0	-0.1
CARAWAY, PAT Cecil Bradford Patrick B 9.26.1905 Erath Co., TX D 6.9.1974 ElPaso, TX BL/TL 6-4/175# d4.19																									
1930	Chi A	10	10	.500	38	21	9-1	1	193.1	194	96	11	3	57	83	3.86	120	.267	.323	64-3	.172	-1	93	19	1.7
1931	Chi A	10	24	.294	51	32	11-1	2	220	268	177	17	7	101	55	6.22	68	.295	.370	72-8	.194	-1*	79	-47	-5.9
1932	Chi A	2	6	.250	19	9	1	0	64.2	80	55	6	3	37	13	6.82	63	.304	.396	21-1	.143	-1	68	-16	-1.7
Total	3	22	40	.355	108	62	21-2	3	478	542	328	34	13	195	151	5.35	83	.286	.356	157-12	.178	-3	82	-44	-5.9
CARDEN, JOHN John Bruton B 5.19.1921 Killeen, TX D 2.8.1949 Mexia, TX BR/TR 6-5/210# d5.18																									
1946	NY N	0	0	—	1	0	0	0	2	4	7	0	1	4	1	22.50	15	.400	.600	0-0	—	0		-5	-0.2
CARDINAL, CONRAD Conrad Seth B 3.30.1942 Brooklyn, NY BR/TR 6-1/190# d4.11																									
1963	Hou N	0	1	.000	6	1	0	0	13.1	15	14	0	0	7-0	7	6.08	52	.283	.355	2-0	.000	-0	82	-6	-0.4
CARDONI, BEN Armand Joseph "Big Ben" B 8.21.1920 Jessup, PA D 4.2.1969 Jessup, PA BR/TR 6-3/195# d8.22																									
1943	Bos N	0	0	—	11	0	0	1	28	38	20	1	1	14	5	6.43	53	.336	.414	7-0	.000	-1		-8	-0.5
1944	Bos N	0	6	.000	22	5	1	0	75.2	83	40	5	1	37	24	3.93	97	.284	.367	17-4	.235	-0*	48	-1	-0.1
1945	Bos N	0	0	—	3	0	0	0	4	6	5	0	1	3	5	9.00	43	.300	.417	0-0	—	0		-2	-0.1
Total	3	0	6	.000	36	5	1	1	107.2	127	65	6	3	54	34	4.76	78	.299	.382	24-4	.167	-1	48	-11	-0.7
CARDWELL, DON Donald Eugene B 12.7.1935 Winston-Salem, NC BR/TR 6-4/210# d4.21																									
1957	Phi N	4	8	.333	30	19	5-1	1	128.1	122	71	17	4	42-1	92	4.91	78	.251	.313	35-3	.200	1	86	-13	-1.0
1958	Phi N	3	6	.333	16	14	3	0	107.2	99	55	16	2	37-4	77	4.51	88	.241	.306	38-1	.211	1	84	-4	-0.2
1959	Phi N	9	10	.474	25	22	5-1	0	153	135	77	22	4	65-5	106	4.06	101	.238	.317	55-1	.055	-3*	84	1	-0.3
1960	Phi N	1	2	.333	5	4	0	0	28.1	28	14	4	1	11-1	21	4.45	87	.262	.336	8-2	.250	2	119	-1	0.1
	Chi N	8	14	.364	31	26	6-1	0	177	166	101	19	5	68-10	129	4.37	86	.249	.320	69-0	.203	3*	97	-13	-1.2
	Year	9	16	.360	36	30	6-1	0	205.1	194	105	23	6	79-11	150	4.38	87	.251	.322	77-2	.208	5	100	-14	-1.1
1961	Chi N	15	14	.517	39	**38**	13-3	0	259.1	243	121	22	10	88-0	156	3.82	110	.246	.312	95-4	.105	-1*	97	13	1.3
1962	Chi N	7	16	.304	41	29	6-1	4	195.2	205	116	27	9	60-7	104	4.92	84	.267	.326	61-4	.148	-0	74	-14	-1.5
1963	Pit N	13	15	.464	33	32	7-2	0	213.2	195	92	21	16	52-10	112	3.07	107	.245	.303	71-3	.085	-2	91	3	0.2
1964	Pit N	1	2	.333	4	4	1-1	0	19.1	15	9	1	3	7-1	10	2.79	126	.217	.313	7-0	.143	-0	88	1	0.1
1965	Pit N	13	10	.565	37	34	12-2	0	240.1	214	101	21	12	59-1	107	3.18	110	.239	.294	74-10	.162	3	117	8	1.2
1966	Pit N	6	6	.500	32	14	1	1	101.2	112	58	15	6	27-8	60	4.60	78	.282	.335	29-1	.103	-1	106	-12	-1.3
1967	NY N	5	9	.357	26	16	3-3	0	118.1	112	55	8	7	39-8	71	3.57	95	.249	.319	38-0	.158	2*	84	-3	0.0
1968	NY N	7	13	.350	29	25	5-1	1	179.2	156	69	9	10	50-11	82	2.96	102	.233	.293	61-3	.049	-3*	75	0	-0.3
1969	†NY N	8	10	.444	30	21	4	0-0	152.1	145	63	15	5	47-10	60	3.01	121	.252	.313	47-2	.170	1	92	8	1.1
1970	NY N	0	2	.000	16	1	0	0-0	25	31	19	3	3	6-1	8	6.48	62	.316	.364	5-0	.000	-1	45	-6	-0.5
	Atl N	2	1	.667	16	2	1-1	0-1	23	31	23	5	1	13-2	16	9.00	48	.326	.409	5-0	.400	1	115	-10	-1.1
	Year	2	3	.400	32	3	1-1	0-1	48	62	29	8	4	19-3	24	7.69	54	.321	.386	10-0	.200	-0	94	-17	-1.6
Total	14	102	138	.425	410	301	72-17	7-1	2122.2	2009	1044	225	98	671-80	1211	3.92	95	.250	.313	698-34	.135	2	92	-42	-3.4
CARLETON, TEX James Otto B 8.19.1906 Comanche, TX D 1.11.1977 Fort Worth, TX BB/TR 6-1.5/180# d4.17																									
1932	StL N	10	13	.435	44	22	9-3	0	196.1	198	94	12	3	70	113	4.08	96	.261	.326	60-0	.150	-2	88	1	0.0
1933	StL N	17	11	.607	44	33	15-4	3	277	263	117	15	4	97	147	3.38	103	.249	.315	91-8	.187	1*	130	5	0.5
1934	†StL N	16	11	.593	40	31	16	2	240.2	260	126	14	7	52	103	4.26	99	.271	.314	88-3	.193	1*	109	1	0.2
1935	†Chi N	11	8	.579	31	22	8	1	171	169	82	17	3	60	84	3.89	101	.257	.322	62-1	.129	-3	116	3	0.1
1936	Chi N	14	10	.583	35	26	12-**4**	1	197.1	204	85	14	6	67	88	3.65	109	.268	.332	60-4	.233	6	115	9	1.7
1937	Chi N	16	8	.667	32	27	18-4	0	208.1	183	80	10	4	94	105	3.15	126	.236	.321	71-6	.169	1*	117	19	2.2
1938	†Chi N	10	9	.526	33	24	9	0	167.2	213	118	11	8	74	80	5.42	71	.307	.381	65-0	.231	3	125	-31	-2.7
1940	Bro N	6	6	.500	34	17	4-1	2	149	140	68	12	3	47	88	3.81	105	.245	.305	43-5	.186	-0	100	4	0.2
Total	8	100	76	.568	293	202	91-16	9	1607.1	1630	770	105	38	561	808	3.91	100	.261	.326	540-27	.185	6	114	11	2.2
CARLOS, CISCO Francisco Manuel B 9.17.1940 Monrovia, CA BR/TR 6-3/205# d8.25																									
1967	Chi A	2	0	1.000	8	7	1-1	0	41.2	23	5	0	1	9-0	27	0.86	359	.161	.216	16-0	.063	-1	88	11	0.5
1968	Chi A	4	14	.222	29	21	0	0	122.1	121	64	13	10	37-5	57	3.90	78	.258	.324	31-4	.065	-1	67	-12	-1.9
1969	Chi A	4	3	.571	25	4	0	0-1	49.1	52	33	4	5	23-3	28	5.66	68	.274	.367	10-2	.000	-1	132	-9	-1.2
	Was A	1	1	.500	6	4	0	0-0	17.2	23	9	2	0	6-0	5	4.58	76	.348	.403	5-0	.200	1	115	-2	-0.1
	Year	5	4	.556	31	8	0	0-1	67	75	14	6	5	29-3	33	5.37	70	.293	.376	15-2	.067	-0	121	-10	-1.3

Year	Tm Lg	W	L	Pct	G	GS	CG-Sho	SV-BS	IP	H	R	HR	HB	BB-IB	SO	ERA	AERA	OAV	OOB	AB-SH	AVG	PB	Sup	APR	PW
1970	Was A	0	0	—	5	0	0	0-0	6	3	1	0	0	4-0	2	1.50	237	.150	.292	0-0	—	0		1	0.1
Total	4	11	18	.379	73	36	1-1	0-1	237	222	112	19	16	79-8	119	3.72	88	.250	.322	62-6	.065	-3	84	-11	-2.6
CARLSEN, DON Donald Herbert B 10.15.1926 Chicago, IL D 9.22.2002 Denver, CO BR/TR 6-1/175# d4.28																									
1948	Chi N	0	0	—	1	0	0	0	1	5	4	0	0	2	1	36.00	11	.625	.700	0-0	—	0		-3	-0.2
1951	Pit N	2	3	.400	7	6	2	0	43	50	22	4	1	14	20	4.19	101	.292	.349	16-0	.250	0	66	1	0.1
1952	Pit N	0	1	.000	5	1	0	0	10	20	13	1	0	5	2	10.80	37	.417	.472	3-0	.333	0	0	-7	-0.5
Total	3	2	4	.333	13	7	2	0	54	75	39	5	1	21	23	6.00	70	.330	.390	19-0	.263	0	57	-9	-0.6
CARLSON, DAN Daniel Steven B 1.26.1970 Portland, OR BR/TR 6-1/185# d9.13																									
1996	SF N	1	0	1.000	5	0	0	0-0	10	13	6	2	0	2-0	4	2.70	152	.310	.326	1-0	.000	-0		0	0.0
1997	SF N	0	0	—	6	0	0	0-0	15.1	20	14	5	0	8-1	14	7.63	54	.317	.389	3-0	.000	-0		-6	-0.3
1998	TB A	0	0	—	10	0	0	0-0	17.2	25	15	3	3	8-0	16	7.64	63	.347	.429	0-0	—	0		-5	-0.2
1999	Ari N	0	0	—	2	0	0	0-0	4	5	4	0	0	0-0	3	9.00	51	.278	.278	0-0	—	0		-2	-0.1
Total	4	1	0	1.000	23	0	0	0-0	47	63	39	10	3	18-1	37	6.70	66	.323	.382	4-0	.000	-0		-13	-0.6
CARLSON, HAL Harold Gust B 5.17.1892 Rockford, IL D 5.28.1930 Chicago, IL BR/TR 6/180# d4.13 Mil 1918																									
1917	Pit N	7	11	.389	34	17	9-1	1	161.1	140	64	0	4	49	68	2.90	98	.241	.304	49-3	.122	-2	70	-1	-0.2
1918	Pit N	0	1	.000	3	2	0	0	12	12	5	1	0	5	5	3.75	77	.286	.362	5-0	.200	-0	53	-1	-0.1
1919	Pit N	8	10	.444	22	14	7-1	0	141	114	41	0	2	39	49	2.23	135	.243	.303	43-1	.163	-1	58	12	1.5
1920	Pit N	14	13	.519	39	31	16-3	3	246.2	262	102	4	8	63	62	3.36	96	.281	.331	85-2	.271	3	94	0	0.1
1921	Pit N	4	8	.333	31	10	3	4	109.2	121	59	6	2	23	37	4.27	90	.290	.330	34-0	.294	1	79	-4	-0.2
1922	Pit N	9	12	.429	39	18	6	2	145.1	193	106	10	4	58	64	5.70	72	.323	.386	56-4	.268	3	131	-25	-2.6
1923	Pit N	0	0	—	4	0	0	0	13.1	19	9	2	1	2	4	4.73	85	.358	.393	5-0	.000	-0		-1	-0.1
1924	Phi N	8	17	.320	38	23	12-1	2	203.2	267	122	9	3	55	66	4.86	92	.329	.374	76-2	.276	2*	78	-6	-0.4
1925	Phi N	13	14	.481	35	32	18-**4**	0	234	281	131	19	6	52	80	4.23	113	.298	.338	93-2	.183	-2*	101	14	1.2
1926	Phi N	17	12	.586	35	34	20-3	0	267.1	293	116	9	2	47	55	3.23	128	.281	.313	96-3	.240	2*	85	25	2.6
1927	Phi N	4	5	.444	11	9	4	1	63.2	80	41	7	0	18	13	5.23	79	.316	.362	25-1	.240	0*	149	-7	-0.9
	Chi N	12	8	.600	27	22	15-2	0	184.1	201	73	9	2	27	27	3.17	122	.280	.307	67-3	.164	-3	104	16	1.2
	Year	16	13	.552	38	31	19-2	1	248	281	78	16	2	45	40	3.70	106	.289	.322	92-4	.185	-3	118	10	0.3
1928	Chi N	3	2	.600	20	4	2	4	56.1	74	42	4	0	15	11	5.91	65	.329	.371	19-0	.263	0	77	-13	-1.1
1929	†Chi N	11	5	.688	31	13	6-2	2	111.2	131	71	8	1	31	35	5.16	90	.292	.340	39-3	.231	1	144	-5	-0.5
1930	Chi N	4	2	.667	8	6	3	0	51.2	68	31	5	1	14	14	5.05	97	.313	.358	20-0	.250	0	119	0	0.1
Total	14	114	120	.487	377	235	121-17	19	2002	2256	1013	93	36	498	590	3.97	99	.291	.337	712-24	.223	4	98	4	0.6
CARLSON, LEON Leon Alton "Swede" B 2.17.1895 Jamestown, NY D 9.15.1961 Jamestown, NY BR/TR 6-3/195# d5.31																									
1920	Was A	0	0	—	3	0	0	0	12.1	14	7	1	0	2	3	3.65	102	.292	.320	6-0	.167	-0		0	-0.1
CARLTON, STEVE Steven Norman "Lefty" B 12.22.1944 Miami, FL BL/TL 6-4/210# d4.12 HF1994																									
1965	StL N	0	0	—	15	2	0	0	25	27	7	3	1	8-1	21	2.52	153	.287	.350	2-0	.000	-0	148	4	0.2
1966	StL N	3	3	.500	9	9	2-1	0	52	56	22	2	0	18-1	25	3.12	115	.280	.335	15-2	.267	1	82	2	0.4
1967	†StL N	14	9	.609	30	28	11-2	1	193	173	71	10	2	62-1	168	2.98	110	.238	.299	72-1	.153	1	114	7	0.9
1968	†StL N★	13	11	.542	34	33	10-5	0	231.2	214	87	11	3	61-4	162	2.99	97	.246	.295	73-6	.164	2*	107	-2	0.0
1969	StL N★	17	11	.607	31	31	12-2	0-0	236.1	185	66	15	4	93-6	210	2.17	165	.216	.294	80-4	.213	5*	81	36	5.0
1970	StL N	10	19	.345	34	33	13-2	0-0	253.2	239	123	25	2	109-16	193	3.73	111	.251	.326	80-3	.200	2	75	9	1.1
1971	StL N☆	20	9	.690	37	36	18-4	0-0	273.1	275	120	23	5	98-11	172	3.56	101	.262	.326	96-7	.177	1	123	1	0.3
1972	Phi N★	**27**	10	.730	41	**41**	**30**-8	0-0	**346.1**	257	84	17	1	87-8	**310**	**1.97**	**182**	.206	.257	117-7	.197	4	92	**60**	**7.3**
1973	Phi N	13	20	.394	40	**40**	**18**-3	0-0	**293.1**	293	146	29	3	113-12	223	3.90	98	.260	.329	100-4	.160	0	83	-5	-0.5
1974	Phi N☆	16	13	.552	39	39	17-1	0-0	291	249	118	21	5	136-8	**240**	3.22	118	.234	.321	102-7	.245	2	114	17	1.8
1975	Phi N	15	14	.517	37	37	14-3	0-0	255.1	217	116	24	2	104-5	192	3.56	105	.233	.308	90-7	.156	-0	107	4	0.4
1976	†Phi N	20	7	**.741**	35	35	13-2	0-0	252.2	224	94	19	1	72-4	195	3.13	113	.237	.290	92-7	.217	2	151	13	1.4
1977	†Phi N☆	**23**	10	.697	36	36	17-2	0-0	283	229	99	25	4	89-5	198	2.64	152	.223	.286	97-7	.268	8	108	39	5.5
1978	†Phi N	16	13	.552	34	34	12-3	0-0	247.1	228	91	30	3	63-7	161	2.84	126	.246	.295	86-3	.291	7	119	18	3.0
1979	Phi N★	18	11	.621	35	35	13-4	0-0	251	202	112	25	5	89-11	213	3.62	106	.219	.290	94-2	.223	3*	112	4	0.8
1980	†Phi N☆	**24**	9	.727	38	**38**	13-3	0-0	**304**	243	87	15	2	90-12	**286**	2.34	**162**	.218	.276	101-6	.188	-1	103	**48**	**5.2**
1981	†Phi N☆	13	4	.765	24	24	10-1	0-0	190	152	59	9	1	62-3	179	2.42	150	.222	.286	67-2	.134	-0	108	23	2.0
1982	Phi N★	**23**	11	.676	38	**38**	**19-6**	0-0	**295.2**	253	114	17	1	86-5	**286**	3.10	118	.232	.288	101-8	.218	4	104	18	2.5
1983	†Phi N	15	16	.484	37	37	8-3	0-0	**283.2**	277	117	20	3	84-10	**275**	3.11	115	.258	.313	97-6	.196	3	92	14	1.7
1984	Phi N	13	7	.650	33	33	1	0-0	229	214	104	14	0	79-7	163	3.58	102	.246	.306	84-3	.190	2*	127	3	0.3
1985	Phi N	1	8	.111	16	16	0	0-0	92	84	43	6	0	53-4	48	3.33	111	.249	.349	28-1	.179	0	58	2	0.2
1986	Phi N	4	8	.333	16	16	0	0-0	83	102	70	15	0	45-4	62	6.18	62	.297	.376	34-1	.206	1	113	-23	-2.7
	SF N	1	3	.250	6	6	0	0-0	30	36	20	4	1	16-0	18	5.10	69	.303	.390	11-0	.182	1	139	-6	-0.6
	Year	5	11	.313	22	22	0	0-0	113	138	26	19	1	61-4	80	5.89	64	.299	.380	45-1	.200	2	119	-29	-3.3
	Chi A	4	3	.571	10	10	0	0-0	63.1	58	30	6	0	25-0	40	3.69	117	.252	.323	0-0	—	0	84	4	0.4
1987	Cle A	5	9	.357	23	14	3	1-3	109	111	76	17	2	63-3	71	5.37	85	.266	.361	0-0	—	0	108	-11	-1.2
	Min A	1	5	.167	9	7	0	0-0	43	54	35	7	2	23-1	20	6.70	69	.310	.397	0-0	—	0	65	-10	-1.1
	Year	6	14	.300	32	21	3	1-3	152	165	38	24	4	86-4	91	5.74	80	.279	.372	0-0	—	0	93	-23	-2.3
1988	Min A	0	1	.000	4	1	0	0-0	9.2	20	19	5	0	5-1	5	16.76	24	.408	.463	0-0	—	0	45	-13	-1.1
Total	24	329	244	.574	741	709	254-55	2-3	5217.1	4672	2130	414	53	1833-150	4136	3.22	115	.240	.306	1719-94	.201	49	104	256	33.2
CARLYLE, BUDDY Earl L. B 12.21.1977 Omaha, NE BL/TR 6-3/175# d8.29																									
1999	SD N	1	3	.250	7	7	0	0-0	37.2	36	28	7	2	17-0	29	5.97	70	.257	.342	9-0	.222	1	113	-8	-0.6
2000	SD N	0	0	—	4	0	0	0-0	3	6	7	0	0	3-0	2	21.00	21	.400	.500	0-0	—	0		-6	-0.3
Total	2	1	3	.250	11	7	0	0-0	40.2	42	35	7	2	20-0	31	7.08	59	.271	.358	9-0	.222	1	113	-14	-0.9
CARMAN, DON Donald Wayne B 8.14.1959 Oklahoma City, OK BL/TL 6-3/195# d10.1																									
1983	Phi N	0	0	—	1	0	0	1-0	1	0	0	0	0	0-0	0	0.00	—	.000	.000	0-0	—	0		0	0.1
1984	Phi N	0	1	.000	11	0	0	0-0	13.1	14	9	2	0	6-4	16	5.40	67	.255	.328	1-0	.000	-0		-2	-0.2
1985	Phi N	9	4	.692	71	0	0	7-5	86.1	52	25	6	2	38-3	87	2.08	177	.178	.273	3-1	.000	-0		14	2.2
1986	Phi N	10	5	.667	50	14	2-1	1-6	134.1	113	50	11	3	52-11	98	3.22	120	.234	.311	31-2	.000	-3	79	11	1.0
1987	Phi N	13	11	.542	35	35	3-2	0-0	211	194	110	34	5	69-7	125	4.22	101	.244	.306	61-10	.082	-3	97	1	-0.4
1988	Phi N	10	14	.417	36	32	2	0-0	201.1	211	101	20	4	70-6	116	4.29	83	.270	.330	63-8	.048	-5	96	-13	-2.1
1989	Phi N	5	15	.250	49	20	0	0-0	149.1	152	98	21	3	86-6	81	5.24	68	.260	.355	34-7	.029	-3	84	-27	-3.7
1990	Phi N	6	2	.750	59	1	0	1-1	86.2	69	43	13	4	38-7	58	4.15	92	.218	.307	11-0	.273	1	94	-3	-0.2
1991	Cin N	0	2	.000	28	0	0	1-0	36	40	23	8	1	19-1	15	5.25	72	.286	.373	5-0	.000	-1		-5	-0.3
1992	Tex A	0	0	—	2	0	0	0-0	2.1	4	3	0	0	0-0	2	7.71	49	.364	.364	0-0	—	0		-1	-0.1
Total	10	53	54	.495	342	102	7-3	11-12	921.2	849	462	115	22	378-45	598	4.11	93	.245	.321	209-28	.057	-14	92	-25	-3.7
CARMICHAEL, CHET Chester Keller B 1.9.1888 Muncie, IN D 8.22.1960 Rochester, NY BR/TR 5-11.5/200# d9.5																									
1909	Cin N	0	0	—	2	0	0	0	7	9	6	0	2	3	2	0.00	—	.321	.424	2-0	.000	-0		0	0.0
CARMONA, RAFAEL Rafael B 10.2.1972 Rio Piedras, P.R. BL/TR 6-2/185# d5.18																									
1995	Sea A	2	4	.333	15	3	0	1-1	47.2	55	31	9	2	34-1	28	5.66	84	.293	.397	0-0	—	0	124	-4	-0.4
1996	Sea A	8	3	.727	53	1	0	1-4	90.1	95	47	11	3	55-9	62	4.28	116	.273	.375	0-0	—	0	75	7	0.7
1997	Sea A	0	0	—	4	0	0	0-0	5.2	3	3	1	0	2-0	6	3.18	142	.150	.227	0-0	—	0		0	0.0
1999	Sea A	1	0	1.000	9	0	0	0-0	11.1	18	11	3	0	9-1	0	7.94	60	.409	.491	0-0	—	0		-4	-0.3
Total	4	11	7	.611	81	4	0	2-5	155	171	92	24	5	100-11	96	4.94	98	.285	.387	0-0	—	0	110	-1	-0.0
CARNEY, PAT Patrick Joseph "Doc" B 8.7.1876 Holyoke, MA D 1.9.1953 Worcester, MA BL/TL 6/200# d9.20.1901 ▲																									
1902	Bos N	0	1	.000	2	1	0	0	5	6	5	1	1	3	3	9.00	31	.300	.417	522-4	.270	0*	48	-3	-0.4
1903	Bos N	4	5	.444	10	9	9	0	78	93	52	2	2	31	29	4.04	79	.284	.349	392-5	.240	2*	105	-7	-0.5
1904	Bos N	0	4	.000	4	3	1	0	26.1	40	27	1	1	12	5	5.81	47	.364	.431	279-8	.204	0*	62	-10	-1.2
Total	3	4	10	.286	16	13	10	0	109.1	139	84	4	4	46	37	4.69	66	.303	.372	1193-17	.245	2	95	-20	-2.1

Year	Tm Lg	W	L	Pct	G	GS	CG-Sho	SV-BS	IP	H	R	HR	HB	BB-IB	SO	ERA	AERA	OAV	OOB	AB-SH	AVG	PB	Sup	APR	PW
CARPENTER, CHRIS Christopher John B 4.27.1975 Exeter, NH BR/TR 6-6/215# d5.12																									
1997	Tor A	3	7	.300	14	13	1-1	0-0	81.1	108	55	7	2	37-0	55	5.09	90	.325	.394	0-0	—	0	71	-6	-0.7
1998	Tor A	12	7	.632	33	24	1-1	0-0	175	177	97	18	5	61-1	136	4.37	107	.265	.329	1-0	.000	-0	114	4	0.3
1999	Tor A	9	8	.529	24	24	4-1	0-0	150	177	81	16	3	48-1	106	4.38	113	.294	.346	1-0	.000	0	104	9	0.8
2000	Tor A	10	12	.455	34	27	2	0-0	175.1	204	130	30	5	83-1	113	6.26	81	.290	.369	2-0	.000	-0	93	-20	-2.2
2001	Tor A	11	11	.500	34	34	3-2	0-0	215.2	229	112	29	16	75-5	157	4.09	112	.274	.345	6-1	.167	-0	107	9	0.8
2002	Tor A	4	5	.444	13	13	1	0-0	73.1	89	45	11	4	27-0	45	5.28	88	.306	.368	1-1	1.000	0	85	-5	-0.5
Total	6	49	50	.495	152	135	12-5	0-0	870.2	984	520	111	35	331-8	612	4.83	99	.287	.354	11-2	.182	0	99	-9	-1.5
CARPENTER, CRIS Cris Howell B 4.5.1965 St.Augustine, FL BR/TR 6-1/185# d5.14																									
1988	StL N	2	3	.400	8	8	1	0-0	47.2	56	27	3	1	9-2	24	4.72	74	.298	.327	14-3	.143	-0	102	-6	-0.6
1989	StL N	4	4	.500	36	5	0	0-2	68	70	30	4	2	26-9	35	3.18	114	.262	.328	9-2	.444	1	102	2	0.3
1990	StL N	0	0	—	4	0	0	0-0	8	5	4	2	0	2-1	6	4.50	85	.167	.219	1-0	.000	-0		0	0.0
1991	StL N	10	4	.714	59	0	0	0-0	66	53	31	6	0	20-9	47	4.23	88	.220	.278	3-0	.333	0		-2	-0.4
1992	StL N	5	4	.556	73	0	0	1-7	88	69	29	10	4	27-8	46	2.97	114	.220	.288	3-1	.333	0		6	0.6
1993	Fla N	0	1	.000	29	0	0	0-2	37.1	29	15	1	2	13-2	26	2.89	150	.212	.288	0-1	—	0		5	0.3
	Tex A	4	1	.800	27	0	0	1-1	32	35	15	4	2	12-1	27	4.22	99	.289	.355	0-0	—	0		0	0.1
1994	Tex A	2	5	.286	47	0	0	5-6	59	69	35	7	0	20-7	39	5.03	96	.291	.342	0-0	—	0		0	-0.1
1996	Mil A	0	0	—	8	0	0	0-0	8.1	12	8	1	0	2-0	2	7.56	69	.333	.359	0-0	—	0		-2	-0.1
Total	8	27	22	.551	291	13	1	7-18	414.1	398	194	38	11	131-39	252	3.91	99	.254	.312	30-7	.267	1	95	3	0.1
CARPENTER, LEW Lewis Emmett B 8.16.1913 Woodstock, GA D 4.25.1979 Marietta, GA BR/TR 6-2/195# d5.1																									
1943	Was A	0	0	—	4	0	0	0	3.1	1	0	0	1	4	1	0.00	—	.125	.462	0-0	—	0		1	0.1
CARPENTER, PAUL Paul Calvin B 8.12.1894 Granville, OH D 3.14.1968 Newark, OH BR/TR 5-11/165# d7.26																									
1916	Pit N	0	0	—	5	0	0	0	7.2	8	3	0	0	4	5	1.17	229	.258	.343	2-0	.000	-0		1	0.0
CARPENTER, BOB Robert Louis B 12.12.1917 Chicago, IL BR/TR 6-3/195# d9.12 Mil 1943-45																									
1940	NY N	2	0	1.000	5	3	2	0	33	29	11	2	0	14	25	2.73	142	.238	.316	10-0	.100	-0	127	4	0.2
1941	NY N	11	6	.647	29	19	8-1	2	131.2	138	71	15	2	42	42	3.83	97	.265	.323	45-2	.156	-0	128	-5	-0.7
1942	NY N	11	10	.524	28	25	12-2	0	185.2	192	73	13	1	51	53	3.15	107	.263	.312	65-6	.185	-1	117	6	0.4
1946	NY N	1	3	.250	12	6	1-1	0	39	37	22	7	0	18	13	4.85	71	.245	.325	10-2	.100	-0	54	-5	-0.5
1947	NY N	0	0	—	2	0	0	0	3	5	5	0	0	3	0	12.00	34	.385	.500	0-0	—	0		-3	-0.1
	Chi N	0	1	.000	4	1	0	0	7.1	10	5	1	0	4	1	4.91	80	.323	.400	1-0	1.000	0	45	-1	-0.1
	Year	0	1	.000	6	1	0	0	10.1	15	7	1	0	7	1	6.97	57	.341	.431	1-0	1.000	0	44	-4	-0.2
Total	5	25	20	.556	80	54	23-4	2	399.2	411	187	38	3	132	134	3.60	98	.262	.321	131-10	.168	-1	113	-4	-0.8
CARPIN, FRANK Frank Dominic B 9.14.1938 Brooklyn, NY BL/TL 5-10/172# d5.25																									
1965	Pit N	3	1	.750	39	0	0	4	39.2	35	16	0	3	24-3	27	3.18	111	.243	.360	1-0	.000	-0		2	0.3
1966	Hou N	1	0	1.000	10	0	0	0	6	9	7	0	0	6-0	2	7.50	46	.346	.469	0-0	—	0		-3	-0.5
Total	2	4	1	.800	49	0	0	4	45.2	44	23	0	3	30-3	29	3.74	93	.259	.377	1-0	.000	-0		-1	-0.2
CARRARA, GIOVANNI Giovanni (Jimenez) B 3.4.1968 Edo Anzoategui, Venezuela BR/TR 6-2/210# d7.29																									
1995	Tor A	2	4	.333	12	7	1	0-0	48.2	64	46	10	1	25-1	27	7.21	65	.320	.395	0-0	—	0	116	-15	-1.5
1996	Tor A	0	1	.000	11	0	0	0-1	15	23	19	5	0	12-2	10	11.40	44	.359	.461	0-0	—	0		-10	-0.5
	Cin N	1	0	1.000	8	5	0	0-0	23	31	17	6	2	13-1	13	5.87	72	.323	.414	7-0	.000	-1	162	-4	-0.3
1997	Cin N	0	1	.000	2	2	0	0-0	10.1	14	9	4	0	6-1	5	7.84	54	.333	.417	2-2	.000	-0	65	-4	-0.3
2000	Col N	0	1	.000	8	0	0	0-1	13.1	21	19	5	1	11-2	15	12.83	45	.356	.458	1-0	.000	-0		-8	-0.5
2001	LA N	6	1	.857	47	3	0	0-3	85.1	73	30	12	1	24-3	70	3.16	127	.231	.287	12-0	.250	1	138	10	0.8
2002	LA N	6	3	.667	63	1	0	1-5	90.2	83	34	14	6	32-4	56	3.28	117	.243	.318	6-1	.000	-0	73	7	0.6
2003	Sea A	2	0	1.000	23	0	0	0-0	29	40	22	6	2	14-0	13	6.83	63	.333	.412	0-0	—	0		-8	-0.4
Total	7	17	11	.607	174	18	1	1-10	315.1	349	196	62	13	137-14	209	5.31	80	.282	.358	28-3	.107	-1	128	-32	-2.1
CARRASCO, D.J. Daniel B 4.12.1977 Safford, AZ BR/TR 6-1/210# d4.2																									
2003	KC A	6	5	.545	50	2	0	2-3	80.1	82	44	8	7	40-4	57	4.82	107	.271	.364	2-0	.000	-0	116	4	0.4
CARRASCO, HECTOR Hector (Pacheco) B 10.22.1969 San Pedro De Macoris, D.R. BR/TR 6-2/175# d4.4																									
1994	Cin N	5	6	.455	45	0	0	6-2	56.1	42	17	3	2	30-1	41	2.24	185	.210	.319	6-0	.000	-1		12	2.2
1995	†Cin N	2	7	.222	64	0	0	5-4	87.1	86	45	1	2	46-5	64	4.12	100	.257	.344	7-0	.000	-1		-1	-0.2
1996	Cin N	4	3	.571	56	0	0	0-2	74.1	58	37	6	1	45-5	59	3.75	113	.214	.324	5-0	.200	0		3	0.2
1997	Cin N	1	2	.333	38	0	0	0-0	51.1	51	25	3	4	25-2	46	3.68	116	.250	.342	0-0	—	0		2	0.1
	KC A	1	6	.143	28	0	0	0-2	34.2	29	21	4	4	16-3	30	5.45	87	.227	.327	0-0	—	0		-2	-0.3
1998	Min A	4	2	.667	63	0	0	1-1	61.2	75	30	4	1	31-1	46	4.38	109	.304	.373	0-0	—	0		4	0.3
1999	Min A	2	3	.400	39	0	0	1-1	49	48	29	3	1	18-0	35	4.96	103	.261	.328	0-0	—	0		1	0.0
2000	Min A	4	3	.571	61	0	0	1-4	72	75	38	6	3	33-0	57	4.25	122	.270	.349	0-0	—	0		6	0.5
	Bos A	1	1	.500	8	1	0	0-1	6.2	15	8	2	1	5-1	7	9.45	53	.469	.553	0-0	—	0	37	-3	-0.6
	Year	5	4	.556	69	1	0	1-5	78.2	90	10	8	4	38-1	64	4.69	110	.290	.371	0-0	—	0	36	4	-0.1
2001	Min A	4	3	.571	56	0	0	1-1	73.2	77	40	8	0	30-3	70	4.64	99	.277	.344	0-0	—	0		0	-0.1
2003	Bal A	2	6	.250	40	0	0	1-2	38.1	40	22	5	2	20-3	27	4.93	89	.270	.365	0-0	—	0		-2	-0.4
Total	9	30	42	.417	498	1	0	16-20	605.1	596	312	45	21	299-24	482	4.22	107	.259	.345	18-0	.056	-1	41	20	1.7
CARRASQUEL, ALEX Alejandro Eloy (Aparicio) B 7.24.1912 Caracas, Venezuela D 8.19.1969 Caracas, Venezuela BR/TR 6-1/182# d4.23																									
1939	Was A	5	9	.357	40	17	7	2	159.1	165	89	7	1	68	41	4.69	93	.266	.340	42-5	.167	1	91	-3	-0.2
1940	Was A	6	2	.750	28	0	0	0	48	42	26	4	0	29	19	4.88	86	.240	.348	7-0	.000	-1		-2	-0.4
1941	Was A	6	2	.750	35	5	4	2	96.2	103	44	7	1	49	30	3.44	117	.278	.364	21-2	.095	0	133	7	0.7
1942	Was A	7	7	.500	35	15	7-1	4	152.1	161	74	7	1	53	40	3.43	107	.267	.327	44-4	.136	-0	103	2	0.2
1943	Was A	11	7	.611	39	13	4-1	5	144.1	160	76	3	1	54	48	3.68	87	.279	.342	43-4	.186	1	144	-10	-1.1
1944	Was A	8	7	.533	43	7	3	2	134	143	68	8	2	50	35	3.43	95	.273	.339	36-0	.194	1	110	-5	-0.3
1945	Was A	7	5	.583	35	7	5-2	1	122.2	105	43	5	0	40	38	2.71	114	.228	.289	36-1	.083	-2	145	7	0.5
1949	Chi A	0	0	—	3	0	0	0	3.2	8	6	1	0	4	1	14.73	28	.421	.522	0-0	—	0		-4	-0.2
Total	8	50	39	.562	258	64	30-4	16	861	887	426	42	6	347	252	3.73	98	.265	.335	229-16	.144	0	115	-8	-0.8
CARRENO, AMALIO Amalio Rafael (Adrian) B 4.11.1964 Chacachacare, Venezuela BR/TR 6/170# d7.7																									
1991	Phi N	0	0	—	3	0	0	0-0	3.1	5	6	1	2	3-0	2	16.20	23	.333	.500	1-0	.000	-0		-4	-0.2
CARRICK, BILL William Martin "Doughnut Bill" B 9.5.1873 Erie, PA D 3.7.1932 Philadelphia, PA TR 5-10/150# d7.30																									
1898	NY N	3	1	.750	5	4	4	0	39.2	39	23	0	5	21	10	3.40	102	.255	.363	18-0	.167	-1	138	0	0.0
1899	NY N	16	27	.372	44	**43**	**40**-3	0	361.2	485	250	4	18	122	60	4.65	81	.320	.378	130-4	.138	-6	87	-32	-3.4
1900	NY N	19	22	.463	**45**	**41**	32-1	0	341.2	415	224	7	13	92	63	3.53	102	.299	.348	115-4	.174	-3	97	-2	-0.5
1901	Was A	14	22	.389	42	37	34	0	324	367	198	12	20	93	70	3.75	98	.282	.339	126-3	.159	-5	76	-5	-0.8
1902	Was A	11	17	.393	31	30	28	0	257.2	344	194	10	9	72	36	4.86	76	.320	.368	108-4	.185	-2*	100	-34	-3.3
Total	5	63	89	.414	167	155	138-4	0	1324.2	1650	889	33	65	400	239	4.14	89	.304	.359	497-15	.163	-16	90	-73	-8.0
CARRITHERS, DON Donald George B 9.15.1949 Lynwood, CA BR/TR 6-2/180# d8.1																									
1970	SF N	2	1	.667	11	2	0	0-0	22	31	19	5	0	14-1	14	7.36	54	.333	.417	6-0	.000	-0	56	-8	-0.9
1971	†SF N	5	3	.625	22	12	2-1	1-0	80.1	77	48	6	2	37-1	41	4.03	84	.254	.331	17-4	.176	0	137	-8	-0.7
1972	SF N	4	8	.333	25	14	2	1-0	90	108	66	10	5	42-4	42	5.80	60	.296	.375	29-1	.207	1*	129	-23	-2.8
1973	SF N	1	2	.333	25	3	0	0-1	58	64	40	2	4	35-2	36	4.81	80	.278	.381	16-1	.250	0*	85	-8	-0.3
1974	Mon N	5	2	.714	22	3	0	1-1	60	56	22	6	3	17-4	31	3.00	128	.249	.306	14-1	.286	0	121	6	0.8
1975	Mon N	5	3	.625	19	14	5-2	0-0	101	90	39	7	4	38-1	37	3.30	116	.240	.316	34-1	.176	0	105	7	0.7
1976	Mon N	6	12	.333	34	19	2	0-0	140.1	153	84	9	7	78-13	71	4.43	84	.286	.381	37-3	.108	-1*	56	-12	-1.6
1977	Min A	0	1	.000	7	0	0	0-0	14.1	16	13	2	1	6-1	3	6.91	58	.271	.348	0-0	—	0		-5	-0.3
Total	8	28	32	.467	165	67	11-3	3-2	566	595	331	47	26	267-27	275	4.45	83	.272	.355	153-11	.176	0	98	-51	-5.1

Year	Tm Lg	W	L	Pct	G	GS	CG-Sho	SV-BS	IP	H	R	HR	HB	BB-IB	SO	ERA	AERA	OAV	OOB	AB-SH	AVG	PB	Sup	APR	PW
CARROLL, CLAY Clay Palmer "Hawk" B 5.2.1941 Clanton, AL BR/TR 6-1/200# d9.2																									
1964	Mil N	2	0	1.000	11	1	0	1	20.1	15	4	1	0	3-1	17	1.77	199	.200	.231	2-0	.000	-0	200	4	0.5
1965	Mil N	0	1	.000	19	1	0	1	34.2	35	18	3	1	13-2	16	4.41	80	.269	.336	5-1	.000	-1	99	-3	-0.2
1966	Atl N	8	7	.533	**73**	3	0	11	144.1	127	45	8	4	29-4	67	2.37	154	.236	.277	30-8	.100	-2	201	19	2.1
1967	Atl N	6	12	.333	42	7	1	0	93	111	62	6	3	29-10	35	5.52	60	.304	.357	16-2	.063	-1	113	-22	-3.9
1968	Atl N	0	1	.000	10	0	0	0	22.1	26	15	1	0	6-2	10	4.84	62	.310	.348	5-0	.000	-0		-5	-0.3
	Cin N	7	7	.500	58	1	0	17	121.2	102	35	3	6	32-10	61	2.29	138	.230	.289	24-1	.250	1	27	11	2.0
	Year	7	8	.467	68	1	0	17	144	128	36	4	6	38-12	71	2.69	117	.242	.299	29-1	.207	1	28	6	1.7
1969	Cin N	12	6	.667	71	4	0	7-10	150.2	149	70	9	7	78-18	90	3.52	107	.262	.356	29-5	.207	2	182	3	0.7
1970	†Cin N	9	4	.692	65	0	0	16-2	104.1	104	38	4	2	27-9	63	2.59	156	.259	.309	14-0	.071	-1		15	2.2
1971	Cin N☆	10	4	.714	61	0	0	15-3	93.2	78	26	5	2	42-9	64	2.50	134	.234	.323	10-3	.100	-1		10	2.0
1972	†Cin N☆	6	4	.600	**65**	0	0	**37-3**	96	89	27	5	1	32-9	51	2.25	143	.256	.316	11-1	.182	0		11	2.2
1973	†Cin N	8	8	.500	53	5	0	14-4	92.2	111	47	5	5	34-11	41	3.69	92	.307	.372	14-4	.214	0	88	-6	-1.0
1974	Cin N	12	5	.706	57	3	0	6-3	100.2	96	27	3	0	30-9	46	2.15	163	.256	.308	18-0	.167	-0	100	16	2.8
1975	†Cin N	7	5	.583	56	2	0	7-6	96.1	93	30	2	3	32-8	44	2.62	138	.255	.315	19-2	.000	-2	146	11	1.2
1976	Chi A	4	4	.500	29	0	0	6-4	77.1	67	26	1	2	24-2	38	2.56	139	.242	.306	0-0	—	0		8	0.9
1977	StL N	4	2	.667	51	1	0	4-4	90	77	28	8	1	24-8	34	2.50	154	.238	.290	11-3	.091	-1	69	14	0.9
	Chi A	1	3	.250	8	0	0	1-0	11.1	14	7	3	0	4-0	4	4.76	86	.311	.367	0-0	—	0		-1	-0.2
1978	Pit N	0	0	—	2	0	0	0-0	4	2	1	0	0	3-0	0	2.25	165	.143	.294	0-0	—	0		1	0.0
Total	15	96	73	.568	731	28	1	143-39	1353.1	1296	506	67	37	442-112	681	2.94	121	.257	.319	208-30	.130	-5	127	86	11.9
CARROLL, ED Edgar Fleischer B 7.27.1907 Baltimore, MD D 10.13.1984 Rossville, MD BR/TR 6-3/185# d5.1																									
1929	Bos A	1	0	1.000	24	2	0	0	67.1	77	46	6	4	20	13	5.61	76	.291	.349	16-3	.063	-2	99	-8	-0.6
CARROLL, OWNIE Owen Thomas B 11.11.1902 Kearny, NJ D 6.8.1975 Orange, NJ BR/TR 5-10.5/165# d6.20																									
1925	Det A	2	2	.500	10	4	1	0	40.2	46	30	1	2	28	12	3.76	114	.293	.406	16-0	.375	1*	112	-2	-0.1
1927	Det A	10	6	.625	31	15	8	0	172	186	99	5	6	73	41	3.98	106	.281	.358	69-1	.174	-2*	110	3	0.1
1928	Det A	16	12	.571	34	28	19-2	2	231	219	100	6	7	87	51	3.27	126	.262	.337	98-9	.194	-0*	95	22	2.5
1929	Det A	9	17	.346	34	26	12	1	202	249	133	10	8	86	54	4.63	93	.310	.383	74-2	.230	2*	94	-11	-0.9
1930	Det A	0	5	.000	6	3	0	0	20.1	30	24	3	0	9	4	10.62	45	.333	.394	7-0	.143	-1	66	-11	-1.8
	NY A	0	1	.000	10	1	0	0	32.2	49	32	2	4	18	8	6.61	65	.374	.464	10-1	.200	0*	140	-10	-0.4
	Year	0	6	.000	16	4	0	0	53	79	39	5	4	27	12	8.15	55	.357	.437	17-1	.176	-0	86	-21	-2.2
	Cin N	0	1	.000	3	2	1	0	14	17	9	3	0	3	0	4.50	107	.309	.345	5-0	.200	-0	45	0	0.0
1931	Cin N	3	9	.250	29	12	4	0	107.1	135	76	6	4	51	24	5.53	67	.314	.392	34-1	.206	0*	86	-21	-2.0
1932	Cin N	10	19	.345	32	26	15	1	210	245	124	7	9	44	55	4.50	86	.286	.328	77-2	.208	2*	76	-14	-1.5
1933	Bro N	13	15	.464	33	31	11	0	226.1	248	117	9	7	54	45	3.78	85	.281	.327	74-4	.149	-1*	112	-16	-1.7
1934	Bro N	1	3	.250	26	5	0	1	74.1	108	64	9	1	33	17	6.42	61	.342	.406	25-0	.240	1*	115	-22	-0.8
Total	9	64	90	.416	248	153	71-2	5	1330.2	1532	808	61	48	486	311	4.43	89	.294	.359	489-20	.200	2	95	-82	-6.6
CARROLL, DICK Richard Thomas "Shadow" B 7.21.1884 Cleveland, OH D 11.22.1945 Cleveland, OH BR/TR 6-2/?# d9.25																									
1909	NY A	0	0	—	2	1	0	0	5	7	6	1	0	1	1	3.60	70	.292	.320	2-0	.500	0	307	-2	-0.1
CARROLL, TOM Thomas Michael B 11.5.1952 Utica, NY BL/TR 6-3/190# d7.7																									
1974	Cin N	4	3	.571	16	13	0	0-0	78.1	68	44	11	0	44-3	37	3.68	95	.231	.331	26-2	.154	-1	123	-5	-0.5
1975	Cin N	4	1	.800	12	7	0	0-0	47	52	28	1	2	26-0	14	4.98	72	.284	.379	14-0	.000	-2	115	-7	-0.9
Total	2	8	4	.667	28	20	0	0-0	125.1	120	72	12	2	70-3	51	4.16	85	.252	.350	40-2	.100	-2	120	-12	-1.4
CARSEY, KID Wilfred B 10.22.1870 New York, NY D 3.29.1960 Miami, FL BL/TR 5-7/168# d4.8																									
1891	Was AA	14	37	.275	54	53	46-1	0	415	513	358	17	28	161	174	4.99	75	.293	.362	187	.150	-5*	79	-49	-4.7
1892	Phi N	19	16	.543	43	36	30-1	1	317.2	317	160	6	12	104	76	3.12	104	.250	.312	131	.153	-3*	109	7	0.4
1893	Phi N	20	15	.571	39	35	30-1	0	318.1	375	229	7	19	124	50	4.81	95	.285	.355	145	.186	-7	110	-7	-1.2
1894	Phi N	18	12	.600	37	32	26	0	288.1	366	241	22	18	106	43	5.52	93	.306	.371	129-1	.279	4	136	-12	-0.5
1895	Phi N	24	16	.600	44	40	35	1	342.1	460	274	14	21	118	64	4.92	97	.317	.376	141-11	.291	3	124	-13	-0.9
1896	Phi N	11	11	.500	27	21	18-1	1	187.1	273	164	4	9	72	36	5.62	77	.337	.397	81-3	.222	1	130	-29	-2.3
1897	Phi N	2	1	.667	4	4	2	0	28	35	20	0	1	16	1	5.14	82	.304	.394	13-1	.231	-1	153	-2	-0.3
	StL N	3	8	.273	12	11	11	0	99	133	81	5	4	31	14	6.00	73	.319	.372	43-0	.302	2*	74	-13	-0.9
	Year	5	9	.357	16	15	13	0	127	168	86	5	5	47	15	5.81	75	.316	.377	56-1	.286	2	94	-16	-1.2
1898	StL N	2	12	.143	20	13	10	0	123.2	177	112	2	10	37	10	6.33	60	.333	.387	105-4	.200	-0*	72	-30	-2.7
1899	Cle N	1	8	.111	10	9	8	0	77.2	109	66	2	2	24	11	5.68	65	.330	.379	36-0	.278	1*	89	-17	-1.3
	Was N	1	2	.333	4	3	2	0	29	27	14	0	1	4	3	3.72	105	.248	.281	11-1	.000	-2	92	1	0.0
	Year	2	10	.167	14	12	10	0	106.2	136	19	2	3	28	14	5.15	73	.310	.355	47-1	.213	-1	90	-13	-1.3
1901	Bro N	1	0	1.000	2	0	0	0	7	9	9	1	1	3	4	10.29	33	.310	.394	2-0	.000	-0		-5	-0.5
Total	10	116	138	.457	296	257	218-4	3	2233.1	2794	1728	80	126	800	486	4.95	85	.300	.363	1024-21	.212	-8	108	-169	-14.9
CARSON, AL Albert James "Soldier" B 8.22.1882 Chicago, IL D 11.26.1962 San Diego, CA BR/TR 5-10.5/162# d5.6																									
1910	Chi N	0	0	—	2	0	0	0	6.2	6	5	0	0	1	2	4.05	71	.240	.269	1-0	.000	0		-1	-0.1
CARTER, ANDY Andrew Godfrey B 11.9.1968 Philadelphia, PA BL/TL 6-5/200# d5.3																									
1994	Phi N	0	2	.000	20	0	0	0-0	34.1	34	18	5	6	12-2	18	4.46	96	.268	.351	6-0	.000	-1		0	-0.1
1995	Phi N	0	0	—	4	0	0	0-0	7.1	4	5	3	1	2-1	6	6.14	69	.167	.250	1-0	1.000	0		-1	0.0
Total	2	0	2	.000	24	0	0	0-0	41.2	38	23	8	7	14-3	24	4.75	90	.252	.335	7-0	.143	-0		-1	-0.1
CARTER, ARNOLD Arnold Lee "Hook" or "Lefty" B 3.14.1918 Rainelle, WV D 4.12.1989 Louisville, KY BL/TL 5-10/170# d4.29																									
1944	Cin N	11	7	.611	33	18	9-3	3	148.2	143	54	1	3	40	33	2.60	134	.256	.309	48-2	.250	5*	91	13	2.2
1945	Cin N	2	4	.333	13	6	2-1	0	46.2	54	21	2	2	13	4	3.09	122	.286	.338	17-0	.176	0*	38	2	0.3
Total	2	13	11	.542	46	24	11-4	3	195.1	197	75	3	5	53	37	2.72	131	.264	.317	65-2	.231	5	77	15	2.5
CARTER, NICK Conrad Powell B 5.19.1879 Oatlands, VA D 11.23.1961 Grasonville, MD BR/TR 5-8/140# d4.14																									
1908	Phi A	2	5	.286	14	4	2	0	60.2	58	26	1	2	17	17	2.97	86	.270	.329	20-0	.100	-2	40	-2	-0.3
CARTER, JEFF Jeffrey Allen B 12.3.1964 Tampa, FL BR/TR 6-3/195# d7.31																									
1991	Chi A	0	1	.000	5	2	0	0-0	12	8	8	1	0	5-0	2	5.25	76	.182	.265	0-0	—	0	161	-2	-0.2
CARTER, LANCE Lance David B 12.18.1974 Bradenton, FL BR/TR 6-1/190# d9.15																									
1999	KC A	0	1	.000	6	0	0	0-0	5.1	3	3	2	0	3-0	3	5.06	99	.167	.286	0-0	—	0		0	0.0
2002	TB A	2	0	1.000	8	0	0	2-0	20.1	15	3	2	0	5-1	14	1.33	336	.203	.253	0-0	—	0		7	0.8
2003	TB A☆	7	5	.583	62	0	0	26-7	79	72	39	12	4	19-6	47	4.33	105	.242	.291	0-0	—	0		3	0.5
Total	3	9	6	.600	76	0	0	28-7	104.2	90	45	16	4	27-7	64	3.78	120	.231	.283	0-0	—	0		10	1.3
CARTER, LARRY Larry Gene B 5.22.1965 Charleston, WV BR/TR 6-5/195# d9.6																									
1992	SF N	1	5	.167	6	6	0	0-0	33	34	17	6	0	18-0	21	4.64	71	.270	.359	10-1	.200	1	68	-4	-0.7
CARTER, PAUL Paul Warren "Nick" B 5.1.1894 Lake Park, GA D 9.11.1984 Lake Park, GA BL/TR 6-3/175# d9.15																									
1914	Cle A	1	3	.250	5	4	1	0	24.2	35	15	0	0	5	9	2.92	99	.340	.370	7-0	.000	-1	69	-1	-0.3
1915	Cle A	1	1	.500	11	2	2	0	42	44	22	1	0	18	14	3.21	95	.272	.344	14-1	.214	1*	72	-1	0.0
1916	Chi N	2	2	.500	8	5	2	0	36	26	16	1	0	17	14	2.75	106	.203	.297	12-1	.167	-0	98	0	0.0
1917	Chi N	5	8	.385	23	13	6	2	113.1	115	47	2	3	19	34	3.26	89	.276	.313	35-1	.171	-0	76	-1	-0.2
1918	Chi N	3	2	.600	21	4	1	2	73	78	29	2	1	19	13	2.71	103	.290	.339	25-0	.240	0	129	1	0.2
1919	Chi N	5	4	.556	28	7	2	1	85	81	36	1	2	28	17	2.65	109	.252	.316	26-0	.269	1*	110	1	0.1
1920	Chi N	3	6	.333	31	8	2	2	106	131	68	3	5	36	14	4.67	69	.324	.387	35-1	.171	-1	144	-16	-1.5
Total	7	20	26	.435	127	43	16	7	480	510	233	10	11	142	115	3.32	89	.283	.339	154-4	.195	-1	101	-17	-1.7
CARTER, SOL Solomon Mobley "Buck" B 12.23.1908 Picayune, MS BR/TR 6/178# d4.15																									
1931	Phi A	0	0	—	2	0	0	0	2.1	1	5	0	0	4	1	19.29	23	.143	.455	0-0	—	0		-3	-0.1

CARUTHERS, BOB Robert Lee "Parisian Bob" B 1.5.1864 Memphis, TN D 8.5.1911 Peoria, IL BL/TR 5-7/138# d9.7 M1 U2 ▲

Year	Tm Lg	W	L	Pct	G	GS	CG-Sho	SV-BS	IP	H	R	HR	HB	BB-IB	SO	ERA	AERA	OAV	OOB	AB-SH	AVG	PB	Sup	APR	PW
1884	StL AA	7	2	.778	13	7	7	0	82.2	61	34	1	3	15	58	2.61	125	.189	.232	82	.268	2*	122	9	0.9
1885	†StL AA	**40**	13	**.755**	53	53	53-6	0	482.1	430	196	3	19	57	190	**2.07**	**158**	.230	.260	222	.225	6*	103	**61**	**6.3**
1886	†StL AA	30	14	.682	44	43	42-2	0	387.1	323	164	3	7	86	166	2.32	148	.217	.263	317	.334	26*	113	51	7.2
1887	†StL AA	29	9	**.763**	39	39	39-2	0	341	337	185	6	16	61	74	3.30	138	.247	.287	364	.357	20*	122	45	5.9
1888	Bro AA	29	15	.659	44	43	42-4	0	391.2	337	176	4	10	53	140	2.39	125	.224	.255	335	.230	10*	112	28	3.7
1889	†Bro AA	**40**	11	**.784**	56	50	46-**7**	1	445	444	215	16	13	104	118	3.13	119	.252	.298	172	.250	17*	123	33	4.6
1890	†Bro N	23	11	.676	37	33	30-1	0	300	292	163	9	12	87	64	3.09	112	.247	.305	238	.265	11*	100	12	2.2
1891	Bro N	18	14	.563	38	32	29-2	1	297	323	185	7	13	107	69	3.12	106	.267	.333	171	.281	11*	111	-1	1.0
1892	StL N	2	10	.167	16	10	10	1	101.2	131	75	10	6	27	21	5.84	55	.300	.350	513	.277	6*	55	-23	-1.8
Total	9	218	99	.688	340	310	298-24	3	2828.2	2678	1393	59	99	597	900	2.83	123	.240	.285	2414	.282	111	112	215	30.0

CARY, CHUCK Charles Douglas B 3.3.1960 Whittier, CA BL/TL 6-4/210# d8.22

Year	Tm Lg	W	L	Pct	G	GS	CG-Sho	SV-BS	IP	H	R	HR	HB	BB-IB	SO	ERA	AERA	OAV	OOB	AB-SH	AVG	PB	Sup	APR	PW
1985	Det A	0	1	.000	16	0	0	2-1	23.2	16	9	2	2	8-1	22	3.42	119	.190	.274	0-0	—	0		2	0.1
1986	Det A	1	2	.333	22	0	0	0-1	31.2	33	18	3	0	15-4	21	3.41	121	.273	.348	0-0	—	0		0	0.0
1987	Atl N	1	1	.500	13	0	0	1-1	16.2	17	7	3	1	4-3	15	3.78	115	.266	.319	1-0	.000	-0		1	0.2
1988	Atl N	0	0	—	7	0	0	0-0	8.1	8	6	1	1	4-0	7	6.48	57	.250	.351	0-0	—	0		-2	-0.1
1989	NY A	4	4	.500	22	11	2	0-0	99.1	78	42	13	0	29-6	79	3.26	119	.209	.266	0-0	—	0	100	6	0.3
1990	NY A	6	12	.333	28	27	2	0-0	156.2	155	77	21	1	55-1	134	4.19	95	.260	.321	0-0	—	0	76	-2	-0.3
1991	NY A	1	6	.143	10	9	0	0-0	53.1	61	35	6	0	32-2	34	5.91	70	.285	.378	0-0	—	0	76	-9	-1.0
1993	Chi A	1	0	1.000	16	0	0	0-0	20.2	22	12	1	3	11-0	10	5.23	80	.286	.379	0-0	—	0		-2	-0.1
Total	8	14	26	.350	134	47	4	3-3	410.1	390	206	50	8	158-17	322	4.17	96	.250	.319	1-0	.000	-0	81	-6	-0.9

CARY, SCOTT Scott Russell "Red" B 4.11.1923 Kendallville, IN BL/TL 5-11.5/168# d5.1

Year	Tm Lg	W	L	Pct	G	GS	CG-Sho	SV-BS	IP	H	R	HR	HB	BB-IB	SO	ERA	AERA	OAV	OOB	AB-SH	AVG	PB	Sup	APR	PW
1947	Was A	3	1	.750	23	3	1	0	54.2	73	38	5	1	20	25	5.93	63	.312	.369	13-1	.077	-1	119	-12	-0.9

CASALE, JERRY Jerry Joseph B 9.27.1933 Brooklyn, NY BR/TR 6-2/200# d9.14

Year	Tm Lg	W	L	Pct	G	GS	CG-Sho	SV-BS	IP	H	R	HR	HB	BB-IB	SO	ERA	AERA	OAV	OOB	AB-SH	AVG	PB	Sup	APR	PW
1958	Bos A	0	0	—	2	0	0	0	3	1	0	0	0	2-0	3	0.00	—	.111	.273	0-0	—	0		1	0.1
1959	Bos A	13	8	.619	31	26	9-3	0	179.2	162	89	20	5	89-3	93	4.31	94	.238	.329	59-4	.169	3	110	-2	-0.2
1960	Bos A	2	9	.182	29	14	1	0	96.1	113	78	14	1	67-5	54	6.17	66	.294	.394	33-0	.273	3	87	-24	-2.1
1961	LA A	1	5	.167	13	7	0	1	42.2	52	34	9	1	25-0	35	6.54	69	.297	.386	13-0	.462	3	56	-8	-0.7
	Det A	0	0	—	3	1	0	0	12	15	8	3	0	3-0	6	5.25	78	.313	.353	3-0	.000	-0	108	-1	-0.1
	Year	1	5	.167	16	8	0	1	54.2	67	13	12	1	28-0	41	6.26	71	.300	.379	16-0	.375	3	63	-10	-0.8
1962	Det A	1	2	.333	18	1	0	0	36.2	33	19	5	0	18-1	16	4.66	87	.236	.321	8-0	.000	-1	88	-1	-0.2
Total	5	17	24	.415	96	49	10-3	1	370.1	376	228	51	7	204-9	207	5.08	81	.262	.354	116-4	.216	7	95	-35	-3.2

CASCARELLA, JOE Joseph Thomas "Crooning Joe" B 6.28.1907 Philadelphia, PA D 5.22.2002 Baltimore, MD BR/TR 5-10.5/175# d4.17

Year	Tm Lg	W	L	Pct	G	GS	CG-Sho	SV-BS	IP	H	R	HR	HB	BB-IB	SO	ERA	AERA	OAV	OOB	AB-SH	AVG	PB	Sup	APR	PW
1934	Phi A	12	15	.444	42	22	9-2	1	194.1	214	111	8	3	104	71	4.68	94	.288	.377	64-3	.094	-4	86	-5	-0.9
1935	Phi A	1	6	.143	9	3	1	0	32.1	29	21	1	0	22	15	5.29	86	.252	.372	8-2	.125	-1	32	-2	-0.4
	Bos A	0	3	.000	6	4	0	0	17	25	17	3	0	11	9	6.88	69	.329	.414	2-1	.000	-0	78	-4	-0.7
	Year	1	9	.100	15	7	1	0	49.1	54	21	4	0	33	24	5.84	79	.283	.388	10-3	.100	-1	59	-7	-1.1
1936	Bos A	0	2	.000	10	1	0	0	20.2	27	16	0	0	9	7	6.97	76	.329	.396	4-0	.000	-1	265	-3	-0.3
	Was A	9	8	.529	22	16	7-1	1	139.1	147	66	7	6	54	34	4.07	117	.276	.349	49-4	.143	-2	113	15	1.2
	Year	9	10	.474	32	17	7-1	1	160	174	72	7	6	63	41	4.44	109	.283	.355	53-4	.132	-3	122	12	0.9
1937	Was A	0	5	.000	10	4	1	1	32.1	50	41	3	1	23	10	8.07	55	.347	.440	9-0	.222	-0	59	-17	-2.0
	Cin N	1	2	.333	11	3	2	1	43.2	44	24	1	0	22	16	3.92	95	.263	.349	11-0	.091	-1	54	-2	-0.2
1938	Cin N	4	7	.364	33	1	0	4	61	66	33	2	0	22	30	4.57	80	.275	.336	18-0	.167	-1	116	-5	-1.0
Total	5	27	48	.360	143	54	20-3	8	540.2	602	329	25	10	267	192	4.84	91	.287	.370	165-10	.121	-9	93	-23	-4.3

CASE, CHARLIE Charles Emmett B 9.7.1879 Smith Landing, OH D 4.16.1964 Batavia, OH BR/TR 6/170# d7.5

Year	Tm Lg	W	L	Pct	G	GS	CG-Sho	SV-BS	IP	H	R	HR	HB	BB-IB	SO	ERA	AERA	OAV	OOB	AB-SH	AVG	PB	Sup	APR	PW
1901	Cin N	1	2	.333	3	3	3	0	27	34	21	0	0	6	5	4.67	69	.306	.342	10-0	.100	-1	66	-5	-0.5
1904	Pit N	10	5	.667	18	17	14-3	0	141	129	56	0	4	31	49	2.94	93	.243	.290	53-0	.170	1	118	-1	0.0
1905	Pit N	11	11	.500	31	24	18-3	1	217	202	81	2	15	66	57	2.57	117	.251	.319	68-1	.103	-2	79	10	0.6
1906	Pit N	1	1	.500	2	2	1	0	11	8	9	0	1	5	3	5.73	47	.190	.292	2-0	.500	1	150	-3	-0.5
Total	4	23	19	.548	54	46	36-6	1	396	373	167	2	20	108	114	2.93	99	.251	.310	133-1	.135	-1	95	1	-0.4

CASEY, DAN Daniel Maurice B 11.20.1862 Binghamton, NY D 2.8.1943 Washington, DC BR/TL 6/180# d8.18 b-Dennis

Year	Tm Lg	W	L	Pct	G	GS	CG-Sho	SV-BS	IP	H	R	HR	HB	BB-IB	SO	ERA	AERA	OAV	OOB	AB-SH	AVG	PB	Sup	APR	PW
1884	Wil U	1	1	.500	2	2	2	0	18	23	17	0		4	10	1.00	266	.291	.325	6	.167	-1	32	1	0.0
1885	Det N	4	8	.333	12	12	12-1	0	104	105	61	1		35	79	3.29	86	.256	.315	43	.116	-3	90	-2	-0.4
1886	Phi N	24	18	.571	44	44	39-4	0	369	326	169	9		104	193	2.41	136	.223	.275	151	.152	-5	95	37	3.0
1887	Phi N	28	13	.683	45	45	43-**4**	0	390.1	377	199	15	14	115	119	**2.86**	**148**	.246	.305	164	.165	-11	91	57	3.6
1888	Phi N	14	18	.438	33	33	31-2	0	285.2	298	156	6	5	48	108	3.15	94	.259	.291	118	.153	-4	76	-3	-0.7
1889	Phi N	6	10	.375	20	20	15-1	0	152.2	170	92	4	8	72	65	3.77	115	.273	.356	68	.221	-2	74	10	0.7
1890	Syr AA	19	22	.463	45	42	40-2	0	360.2	365	249	8	14	165	169	4.14	85	.255	.337	160	.162	-4*	98	-35	-3.3
Total	7	96	90	.516	201	198	182-14	0	1680.1	1664	943	43	41	543	743	3.18	113	.249	.309	710	.162	-28	88	65	2.9

CASEY, HUGH Hugh Thomas B 10.14.1913 Atlanta, GA D 7.3.1951 Atlanta, GA BR/TR 6-1/207# d4.29 Mil 1943-45

Year	Tm Lg	W	L	Pct	G	GS	CG-Sho	SV-BS	IP	H	R	HR	HB	BB-IB	SO	ERA	AERA	OAV	OOB	AB-SH	AVG	PB	Sup	APR	PW
1935	Chi N	0	0	—	13	0	0	0	25.2	29	13	2	0	14	10	3.86	102	.279	.364	6-0	.167	-0		0	0.0
1939	Bro N	15	10	.600	40	25	15	1	227.1	228	88	13	11	54	79	2.93	137	.260	.311	74-10	.203	0	101	25	2.7
1940	Bro N	11	8	.579	44	10	5-2	2	154	136	63	13	6	51	53	3.62	110	.237	.306	36-8	.250	2*	130	9	1.3
1941	†Bro N	14	11	.560	45	18	4-1	7	162	155	81	8	1	57	61	3.89	94	.251	.316	50-5	.120	-1	96	-4	-0.6
1942	Bro N	6	3	.667	50	2	0	**13**	112	91	32	3	2	44	54	2.25	145	.221	.300	27-4	.148	-0	51	13	1.3
1946	Bro N	11	5	.688	46	1	0	5	99.2	101	31	2	2	33	31	1.99	170	.267	.329	22-5	.136	-1	101	**14**	2.4
1947	†Bro N	10	4	.714	46	0	0	**18**	76.2	75	36	7	2	29	40	3.99	104	.260	.331	18-2	.056	-1		2	0.3
1948	Bro N	3	0	1.000	22	0	0	4	36	59	36	6	2	17	7	8.00	50	.391	.459	7-1	.000	-1		-16	-1.6
1949	Pit N	4	1	.800	33	0	0	5	38.2	50	24	4	1	14	9	4.66	90	.314	.374	3-1	.333	0		-3	-0.4
	NY A	1	0	1.000	4	0	0	0	7.2	11	10	0	0	8	5	8.22	49	.324	.452	1-0	.000	-0		-5	-0.5
Total	9	75	42	.641	343	56	24-3	55	939.2	935	414	58	27	321	349	3.45	110	.260	.325	244-36	.164	-2	105	35	4.9

CASEY, BILL William B. B St.Louis, MO d8.17

Year	Tm Lg	W	L	Pct	G	GS	CG-Sho	SV-BS	IP	H	R	HR	HB	BB-IB	SO	ERA	AERA	OAV	OOB	AB-SH	AVG	PB	Sup	APR	PW
1887	Phi AA	0	0	—	1	0	0	0	1	4	3	0	0	1	0	18.00	24	.667	.714	0	—	0		-2	-0.1

CASHION, CARL Jay Carl B 6.6.1891 Mecklenburg Co, NC D 11.17.1935 Lake Millicent, WI BL/TR 6-2/200# d8.4

Year	Tm Lg	W	L	Pct	G	GS	CG-Sho	SV-BS	IP	H	R	HR	HB	BB-IB	SO	ERA	AERA	OAV	OOB	AB-SH	AVG	PB	Sup	APR	PW
1911	Was A	1	5	.167	11	9	5	0	71.1	67	45	4	7	47	26	4.16	79	.220	.338	37-1	.324	2*	51	-6	-0.2
1912	Was A	10	6	.625	26	17	13-1	1	170.1	150	84	4	5	103	84	3.17	105	.250	.365	103-1	.214	2*	109	4	0.5
1913	Was A	1	1	.500	4	3	0	0	9	7	11	0	3	14	3	6.00	49	.333	.632	12-0	.250	0*	134	-4	-0.8
1914	Was A	0	1	.000	2	1	0	0	5	4	7	0	1	6	1	10.80	26	.250	.478	1-0	.000	-0	52	-4	-0.7
Total	4	12	13	.480	43	30	18-1	1	255.2	228	147	8	16	170	114	3.70	89	.243	.368	153-2	.242	5	91	-10	-1.2

CASIAN, LARRY Lawrence Paul B 10.28.1965 Lynwood, CA BR/TL 6/170# d9.9

Year	Tm Lg	W	L	Pct	G	GS	CG-Sho	SV-BS	IP	H	R	HR	HB	BB-IB	SO	ERA	AERA	OAV	OOB	AB-SH	AVG	PB	Sup	APR	PW
1990	Min A	2	1	.667	5	3	0	0-0	22.1	26	9	2	0	4-0	11	3.22	129	.306	.333	0-0	—	0	95	2	0.3
1991	Min A	0	0	—	15	0	0	0-0	18.1	28	16	4	1	7-2	6	7.36	58	.354	.414	0-0	—	0		-6	-0.3
1992	Min A	1	0	1.000	6	0	0	0-0	6.2	7	2	0	0	1-0	2	2.70	150	.259	.286	0-0	—	0		1	0.2
1993	Min A	5	3	.625	54	0	0	1-2	56.2	59	23	1	1	14-2	31	3.02	145	.268	.311	0-0	—	0		7	0.9
1994	Min A	1	3	.250	33	0	0	1-0	40.2	57	34	11	2	12-2	18	7.08	69	.343	.390	0-0	—	0		-10	-0.8
	Cle A	0	2	.000	7	0	0	0-0	8.1	16	9	1	0	4-1	2	8.64	55	.421	.476	0-0	—	0		-4	-0.6
	Year	1	5	.167	40	0	0	1-0	49	73	47	12	2	16-3	20	7.35	66	.358	.406	0-0	—	0		-13	-1.4
1995	Chi N	1	0	1.000	42	0	0	0-3	23.1	23	6	1	0	15-6	11	1.93	213	.258	.358	2-0	.000	-0		6	0.3
1996	Chi N	1	1	.500	35	0	0	0-1	24	14	5	2	1	11-3	15	1.88	231	.187	.295	0-0	—	0		7	0.5
1997	Chi N	0	1	.000	12	0	0	0-0	9.2	16	9	3	1	2-1	7	7.45	58	.364	.388	1-0	.000	-0		-3	-0.3
	KC A	0	2	.000	32	0	0	0-2	26.2	32	15	5	0	6-1	16	5.06	93	.299	.333	0-0	—	0		0	0.0
1998	Chi A	0	0	—	4	0	0	0-0	4	8	5	0	2	1-0	6	11.25	40	.400	.478	0-0	—	0		-3	-0.1
Total	9	11	13	.458	245	3	0	2-8	240.2	286	133	30	8	77-18	125	4.56	97	.301	.354	3-0	.000	-0	95	-3	0.1

Year	Tm Lg	W	L	Pct	G	GS	CG-Sho	SV-BS	IP	H	R	HR	HB	BB-IB	SO	ERA	AERA	OAV	OOB	AB-SH	AVG	PB	Sup	APR	PW
CASKEY, CRAIG Craig Douglas B 12.11.1949 Visalia, CA BB/TL 5-11/185# d7.19																									
1973	Mon N	0	0	—	9	1	0	0-1	14.1	15	11	3	1	4-0	6	5.65	68	.278	.339	1-1	.000	-0	139	-3	-0.2
CASSIAN, ED Edward T. B 11.8.1867 Wilbraham, MA D 9.10.1918 Meriden, CT TR 5-8/160# d6.26																									
1891	Phi N	1	3	.250	6	4	3	0	38	40	20	0	3	16	10	2.84	120	.260	.341	17	.118	-1	57	2	0.0
	Was AA	2	4	.333	7	5	5	0	53	73	63	4	5	35	14	5.60	67	.316	.417	26	.346	2	133	-13	-0.9
Total	1	3	7	.300	13	9	8	0	91	113	83	4	8	51	24	4.45	81	.294	.387	43	.256	1	100	-11	-0.9
CASSIDY, JOHN John P. B 1857 Brooklyn, NY D 7.2.1891 Brooklyn, NY BR/TL 5-8/168# d4.24 ▲																									
1875	Atl NA	1	21	.045	30	22	18	0	213.2	284	242	3		11	9	3.03	69	.277	.285	166	.175	-3*	47	-27	-2.2
1877	Har N	1	1	.500	2	2	2	0	18	24	11	0		1	2	5.00	49	.320	.329	251	.378	1*	170	-3	-0.2
CASSIDY, SCOTT Scott Robert B 10.3.1975 Syracuse, NY BR/TR 6-2/175# d4.1																									
2002	Tor A	1	4	.200	58	0	0	0-7	66	52	42	12	7	32-3	48	5.73	81	.222	.327	0-0	—	0		-6	-0.4
CASTER, GEORGE George Jasper "Ug" B 8.4.1907 Colton, CA D 12.18.1955 Lakewood, CA BR/TR 6-1.5/180# d9.10																									
1934	Phi A	3	2	.600	5	3	2	0	37	32	16	3	3	14	15	3.41	129	.235	.320	15-0	.267	0	106	4	0.5
1935	Phi A	1	4	.200	25	1	0	1	63.1	86	59	8	2	37	24	6.25	73	.322	.408	22-0	.227	0*	0	-15	-1.0
1937	Phi A	12	19	.387	34	33	19-3	0	231.2	227	141	23	2	107	100	4.43	106	.258	.339	90-1	.211	-1*	85	5	0.5
1938	Phi A	16	20	.444	42	**40**	20-2	1	281.1	310	156	25	3	117	112	4.35	111	.277	.347	101-2	.198	1	84	17	2.0
1939	Phi A	9	9	.500	28	17	7-1	0	136	144	82	16	3	45	59	4.90	96	.276	.337	43-2	.209	-1	78	-1	-0.1
1940	Phi A	4	19	.174	36	24	11	2	178.1	234	160	18	3	69	75	6.56	68	.312	.372	62-2	.129	-3	82	-43	-4.8
1941	StL A	3	7	.300	32	9	3	3	104.1	105	66	12	2	37	36	5.00	86	.259	.324	29-1	.103	-2	74	-8	-0.9
1942	StL A	8	2	.800	39	0	0	5	80	62	30	3	3	39	34	2.81	132	.217	.317	15-0	.067	-1		8	0.9
1943	StL A	6	8	.429	35	0	0	8	76.1	69	22	4	1	41	43	2.12	157	.246	.345	22-0	.136	-1		10	2.0
1944	StL A	6	6	.500	42	0	0	**12**	81	91	37	5	0	33	46	2.44	147	.284	.351	20-0	.250	0		6	1.0
1945	StL A	1	2	.333	10	0	0	1	15.2	20	13	0	0	7	9	6.89	51	.308	.375	3-0	.333	0		-5	-1.0
	†Det A	5	1	.833	22	0	0	2	51.1	47	25	3	2	27	23	3.86	91	.250	.350	11-2	.182	0		-1	-0.1
	Year	6	3	.667	32	0	0	3	67	67	42	3	2	34	32	4.57	77	.265	.356	14-2	.214	0		-7	-1.1
1946	Det A	2	1	.667	26	0	0	4	41.1	42	26	1	1	24	19	5.66	65	.264	.364	7-1	.143	-0		-7	-0.7
Total	12	76	100	.432	376	127	62-6	39	1377.2	1469	833	121	25	597	595	4.54	96	.273	.349	440-11	.184	-7	87	-30	-1.7
CASTILLO, TONY Antonio Jose (Jimenez) B 3.1.1963 Quibor, Venezuela BL/TL 5-10/188# d8.14																									
1988	Tor A	1	0	1.000	14	0	0	0-0	15	10	5	2	0	2-0	14	3.00	131	.200	.222	0-0	—	0		2	0.1
1989	Tor A	1	1	.500	17	0	0	1-0	17.2	23	14	0	1	10-5	10	6.11	62	.333	.405	0-0	—	0		-5	-0.6
	Atl N	0	1	.000	12	0	0	0-0	9.1	8	5	0	0	4-1	5	4.82	76	.222	.300	1-0	.000	-0		-1	-0.1
1990	Atl N	5	1	.833	52	3	0	1-1	76.2	93	41	5	1	20-3	64	4.23	96	.302	.342	7-2	.143	0	142	-2	-0.1
1991	Atl N	1	1	.500	7	0	0	0-0	8.2	13	9	3	0	5-0	8	7.27	54	.342	.419	0-0	—	0		-4	-0.7
	NY N	1	0	1.000	10	3	0	0-0	23.2	27	7	1	0	6-1	10	1.90	192	.281	.320	4-2	.000	-0	74	4	0.2
	Year	2	1	.667	17	3	0	0-0	32.1	40	10	4	0	11-1	18	3.34	111	.299	.349	4-2	.000	-0	73	0	-0.5
1993	†Tor A	3	2	.600	51	0	0	0-1	50.2	44	19	4	0	22-5	28	3.38	128	.242	.320	0-0	—	0		6	0.6
1994	Tor A	5	2	.714	41	0	0	1-3	68	66	22	7	3	28-1	43	2.51	192	.260	.337	0-0	—	0		17	1.6
1995	Tor A	1	5	.167	55	0	0	13-8	72.2	64	27	7	3	24-1	38	3.22	146	.243	.308	0-0	—	0		13	1.3
1996	Tor A	2	3	.400	40	0	0	1-1	72.1	72	38	9	2	20-1	48	4.23	118	.260	.312	0-0	—	0		6	0.4
	Chi A	3	1	.750	15	0	0	1-3	22.2	23	7	1	1	4-1	9	1.59	299	.267	.298	0-0	—	0		7	1.1
	Year	5	4	.556	55	0	0	2-4	95	95	45	10	3	24-2	57	3.60	137	.262	.309	0-0	—	0		12	1.5
1997	Chi A	4	4	.500	64	0	0	4-5	62.1	74	48	6	1	23-7	42	4.91	89	.296	.358	1-0	.000	-0		-9	-0.9
1998	Chi A	1	2	.333	25	0	0	0-0	27	38	25	7	2	11-0	14	8.00	57	.328	.395	0-0	—	0		-10	-0.9
Total	10	28	23	.549	403	6	0	22-22	526.2	555	267	52	14	179-26	333	3.93	114	.274	.333	13-4	.077	-1	96	24	2.0
CASTILLO, CARLOS Carlos B 4.21.1975 Boston, MA BR/TR 6-2/240# d4.2																									
1997	Chi A	2	1	.667	37	2	0	1-0	66.1	68	35	9	1	33-3	43	4.48	98	.265	.346	1-0	1.000	0	136	0	0.0
1998	Chi A	6	4	.600	54	2	0	0-2	100.1	94	61	17	5	35-1	64	5.11	89	.246	.312	1-0	.000	-0	82	-5	-0.4
1999	Chi A	2	2	.500	18	2	0	0-0	41	45	26	10	0	14-1	23	5.71	86	.274	.331	0-0	—	0	114	-2	-0.2
2001	Bos A	0	0	—	2	0	0	0-0	3	3	2	1	0	0-0	0	6.00	75	.273	.250	0-0	—	0		0	0.0
Total	4	10	7	.588	111	6	0	1-2	210.2	210	124	37	6	82-5	130	5.04	91	.258	.326	2-0	.500	0	112	-7	-0.6
CASTILLO, FRANK Frank Anthony B 4.1.1969 ElPaso, TX BR/TR 6-1/190# d6.27																									
1991	Chi N	6	7	.462	18	18	4	0-0	111.2	107	56	5	0	33-2	73	4.35	89	.252	.304	35-6	.143	-0	89	-4	-0.5
1992	Chi N	10	11	.476	33	33	0	0-0	205.1	179	91	19	6	63-6	135	3.46	104	.232	.293	65-5	.092	-2	87	2	-0.1
1993	Chi N	5	8	.385	29	25	2	0-0	141.1	162	83	20	9	39-4	84	4.84	83	.293	.348	43-8	.163	-0	97	-13	-1.0
1994	Chi N	2	1	.667	4	4	1	0-0	23	25	13	3	0	5-0	19	4.30	97	.278	.316	9-0	.000	-1	153	-1	-0.2
1995	Chi N	11	10	.524	29	29	2-2	0-0	188	179	75	22	6	52-4	135	3.21	128	.248	.302	59-7	.102	-2	84	19	1.7
1996	Chi N	7	16	.304	33	33	1-1	0-0	182.1	209	112	28	8	46-4	139	5.28	82	.288	.335	57-4	.088	-3	88	-16	-2.1
1997	Chi N	6	9	.400	20	19	0	0-0	98	113	64	9	4	44-1	67	5.42	79	.292	.370	33-4	.152	-1	92	-12	-1.7
	Col N	6	3	.667	14	14	0	0-0	86.1	107	57	16	4	25-3	59	5.42	96	.308	.360	25-6	.080	-2	121	-2	-0.4
	Year	12	12	.500	34	33	0	0-0	184.1	220	64	25	8	69-4	126	5.42	87	.300	.365	58-10	.121	-2	105	-13	-2.1
1998	Det A	3	9	.250	27	19	0	1-0	116	150	91	17	5	44-0	81	6.83	69	.316	.376	1-0	.000	-0	100	-25	-2.1
2000	Tor A	10	5	.667	25	24	0	0-0	138	112	58	18	5	56-0	104	3.59	142	.220	.303	7-0	.143	-0	105	23	2.2
2001	Bos A	10	9	.526	26	26	0	0-0	136.2	138	72	14	5	35-2	89	4.21	107	.260	.308	2-1	.000	-0	94	4	0.4
2002	Bos A	6	15	.286	36	23	0	1-1	163.1	174	101	19	7	58-6	112	5.07	89	.274	.337	1-1	.000	-0	82	-10	-1.1
Total	11	82	103	.443	294	267	10-3	2-1	1590	1655	873	190	59	500-32	1097	4.55	95	.268	.327	337-42	.110	-12	94	-35	-4.9
CASTILLO, JUAN Juan Francisco (Azdura) B 6.23.1970 Caracas, Venezuela BR/TR 6-5/205# d7.26																									
1994	NY N	0	0	—	2	2	0	0-0	11.2	17	9	2	0	5-0	1	6.94	60	.362	.423	5-0	.200	0	174	-3	-0.1
CASTILLO, BOBBY Robert Ernie B 4.18.1955 Los Angeles, CA BR/TR 5-10/170# d9.10																									
1977	LA N	1	0	1.000	6	1	0	0-0	11.1	12	5	2	0	2-0	7	3.97	96	.279	.304	1-0	.000	-0	70	0	0.0
1978	LA N	0	4	.000	18	0	0	1-1	34	28	19	2	0	33-7	30	3.97	88	.239	.399	7-0	.000	-1		-3	-0.4
1979	LA N	2	0	1.000	19	0	0	7-1	24.1	26	5	0	1	13-1	25	1.11	328	.277	.364	3-0	.000	-0		6	0.9
1980	LA N	8	6	.571	61	0	0	5-1	98.1	70	31	4	1	45-5	60	2.75	128	.206	.297	9-1	.111	-0*		10	1.4
1981	†LA N	2	4	.333	34	1	0	5-2	50.2	50	31	5	0	24-4	35	5.33	62	.262	.341	9-0	.444	2	80	-11	-1.3
1982	Min A	13	11	.542	40	25	6-1	0-0	218.2	194	96	26	0	85-7	123	3.66	116	.241	.310	0-0	—	0	89	14	1.3
1983	Min A	8	12	.400	27	25	3	0-0	158.1	170	91	17	1	65-4	90	4.77	89	.278	.347	0-0	—	0	84	-8	-0.9
1984	Min A	2	1	.667	10	2	0	0-0	25.1	14	7	2	0	19-2	7	1.78	237	.177	.327	0-0	—	0	32	6	0.6
1985	†LA N	2	2	.500	35	5	0	0-0	68	59	42	9	1	41-6	57	5.43	64	.230	.337	10-2	.100	-0*	132	-12	-0.7
Total	9	38	40	.487	250	59	9-1	18-5	689	623	327	67	4	327-36	434	3.94	100	.246	.329	39-3	.154	0	92	2	0.9
CASTLEMAN, SLICK Clydell B 9.8.1913 Donelson, TN D 3.2.1998 Nashville, TN BR/TR 6/185# d5.9																									
1934	NY N	1	0	1.000	7	0	0	0	16.2	18	11	1	0	10	5	5.40	72	.277	.373	4-0	.250	1		-3	0.0
1935	NY N	15	6	.714	29	25	9-1	0	173.2	186	93	14	1	64	64	4.09	94	.268	.330	67-0	.179	-0	110	-6	-0.6
1936	†NY N	4	7	.364	29	12	2-1	1	111.2	148	80	6	5	56	54	5.64	69	.323	.403	39-0	.128	-1*	94	-22	-1.9
1937	NY N	11	6	.647	23	23	10-2	0	160.1	148	66	19	0	33	78	3.31	117	.247	.287	57-3	.070	-5	109	11	0.5
1938	NY N	4	5	.444	21	14	4	0	90.2	108	55	4	3	37	18	4.17	90	.296	.365	31-3	.097	-2*	130	-7	-0.8
1939	NY N	1	2	.333	12	4	0	0	33.2	36	18	1	0	23	6	4.54	86	.286	.396	9-1	.333	1	106	-2	-0.1
Total	6	36	26	.581	121	78	25-4	1	586.2	644	323	45	9	223	225	4.25	91	.279	.345	207-7	.135	-6	110	-29	-2.9
CASTLETON, ROY Royal Eugene B 7.26.1885 Salt Lake City, UT D 6.24.1967 Los Angeles, CA BR/TL 5-11/167# d4.16																									
1907	NY A	1	1	.500	3	2	1	0	16	11	6	1	0	3	3	2.81	99	.196	.237	5-0	.000	-1	60	0	0.0
1909	Cin N	1	1	.500	4	1	1	0	14	14	6	0	2	6	5	1.93	135	.275	.373	3-0	.667	1	350	1	0.2
1910	Cin N	1	2	.333	4	2	1	0	13.2	15	5	0	1	6	5	3.29	89	.288	.373	5-0	.000	-1	128	0	0.0
Total	3	3	4	.429	11	5	3	0	43.2	40	17	1	3	15	13	2.68	104	.252	.328	13-0	.154	-0	142	1	0.2
CASTNER, PAUL Paul Henry "Lefty" B 2.16.1897 St.Paul, MN D 3.3.1986 St.Paul, MN BL/TL 5-11/187# d8.6																									
1923	Chi A	0	0	—	6	0	0	0	10	14	9	0	0	5	0	6.30	63	.326	.396	3-2	.000	-0		-3	-0.2

Year	Tm Lg	W	L	Pct	G	GS	CG-Sho	SV-BS	IP	H	R	HR	HB	BB-IB	SO	ERA	AERA	OAV	OOB	AB-SH	AVG	PB	Sup	APR	PW
CASTRO, BILL William Radhames (Checo) B 12.13.1953 Santiago, D.R. BR/TR 5-11/170# d8.20 C12																									
1974	Mil A	0	0	—	8	0	0	0-0	18	19	10	2	0	5-0	10	4.50	81	.264	.308	0-0	—	0		-2	-0.1
1975	Mil A	3	2	.600	18	5	0	1-0	75	78	28	3	2	17-5	25	2.52	152	.271	.313	0-0	—	0	119	9	0.6
1976	Mil A	4	6	.400	39	0	0	8-2	70.1	70	29	4	3	19-5	23	3.45	101	.265	.322	0-0	—	0		1	0.1
1977	Mil A	8	6	.571	51	0	0	13-6	69.1	76	34	7	2	23-10	28	4.15	98	.293	.347	0-0	—	0		0	0.1
1978	Mil A	5	4	.556	42	0	0	8-5	49.2	43	14	2	6	14-5	17	1.81	208	.234	.306	0-0	—	0		10	2.0
1979	Mil A	3	1	.750	39	0	0	6-6	44.1	40	14	2	0	13-5	10	2.03	206	.244	.296	0-0	—	0		9	1.0
1980	Mil A	2	4	.333	56	0	0	8-4	84.1	89	35	2	2	17-6	32	2.77	140	.274	.311	0-0	—	0		8	0.7
1981	NY A	1	1	.500	11	0	0	0-0	19	26	13	2	0	5-1	4	3.79	94	.329	.369	0-0	—	0		-2	-0.2
1982	KC A	3	2	.600	21	4	0	1-0	75.2	72	34	8	2	20-4	37	3.45	119	.243	.292	0-0	—	0	139	4	0.2
1983	KC A	2	0	1.000	18	0	0	0-0	40.2	51	34	4	5	12-1	17	6.64	62	.300	.358	0-0	—	0		-12	-0.6
Total	10	31	26	.544	303	9	0	45-23	546.1	564	245	36	22	145-42	203	3.33	117	.268	.319	0-0	—	0	130	25	3.8
CATES, ELI Eli Eldo B 1.26.1877 Greens Fork, IN D 5.29.1964 Anderson, IN BR/TR 5-9.5/175# d4.20 ▲																									
1908	Was A	4	8	.333	19	10	7	0	113.2	112	46	3	1	32	33	2.53	90	.261	.314	59-5	.186	1*	90	-3	0.0
CATHER, MIKE Michael Peter B 12.17.1970 San Diego, CA BR/TR 6-2/195# d7.13																									
1997	†Atl N	2	4	.333	35	0	0	0-3	37.2	23	12	1	2	19-4	29	2.39	176	.174	.288	1-0	.000	-0		7	1.0
1998	Atl N	2	2	.500	36	0	0	0-3	41.1	39	21	7	2	12-1	33	3.92	106	.255	.314	0-0	—	0		1	0.1
1999	Atl N	1	0	1.000	4	0	0	0-1	2.2	5	3	2	0	1-0	0	10.13	44	.417	.462	0-0	—	0		-2	-0.3
Total	3	5	6	.455	75	0	0	0-7	81.2	67	36	10	4	32-5	62	3.42	123	.226	.307	1-0	.000	-0		6	0.8
CATHEY, HARDIN Hardin Abner "Lil Abner" B 7.6.1919 Burns, TN D 7.27.1997 Nashville, TN BR/TR 6-4/190# d4.16																									
1942	Was A	1	1	.500	12	2	0	0	30.1	44	26	1	0	16	8	7.42	49	.341	.414	8-1	.375	1	187	-11	-0.6
CATO, KEEFE John Keefe B 5.6.1958 Yonkers, NY BR/TR 6-1/185# d6.13																									
1983	Cin N	1	0	1.000	4	0	0	0-0	3.2	2	1	0	0	1-0	3	2.45	155	.154	.214	0-1	—	0		1	0.1
1984	Cin N	0	1	.000	8	0	0	1-0	15.2	22	14	5	0	4-0	12	8.04	47	.344	.371	4-0	.500	1		-6	-0.4
Total	2	1	1	.500	12	0	0	1-0	19.1	24	15	5	0	5-0	15	6.98	54	.312	.345	4-1	.500	1		-5	-0.3
CATTANACH, JOHN John Leckie B 5.10.1863 Providence, RI D 11.10.1926 Providence, RI 5-10/190# d6.5																									
1884	Pro N	0	0	—	1	1	0	0	5	2	7	0		4	2	9.00	32	.100	.250	4	.000	-1	149	-3	-0.2
	StL U	1	1	.500	2	2	2	0	17	12	10	0		4	13	2.12	113	.185	.232	7	.000	-2	80	0	-0.1
Total	1	1	1	.500	3	3	2	0	22	14	17	0		8	15	3.68	68	.165	.237	11	.000	-2	102	-3	-0.3
CAUDILL, BILL William Holland B 7.13.1956 Santa Monica, CA BR/TR 6-1/210# d5.12																									
1979	Chi N	1	7	.125	29	12	0	0-0	90	89	57	16	4	41-5	104	4.80	86	.255	.337	17-4	.059	-1	77	-7	-0.7
1980	Chi N	4	6	.400	72	2	0	1-3	127.2	100	37	10	1	59-12	112	2.19	180	.223	.309	9-1	.222	0	68	22	1.7
1981	Chi N	1	5	.167	30	10	0	0-2	71	87	50	9	2	31-2	45	5.83	63	.301	.368	14-1	.143	0	98	-15	-1.2
1982	Sea A	12	9	.571	70	0	0	26-6	95.2	65	25	9	1	35-4	111	2.35	181	.192	.269	0-0	—	0		21	**4.2**
1983	Sea A	2	8	.200	63	0	0	26-3	72.2	70	39	10	2	38-6	73	4.71	91	.257	.348	0-0	—	0		-2	-0.4
1984	Oak A★	9	7	.563	68	0	0	36-8	96.1	77	30	9	0	31-4	89	2.71	138	.218	.278	1-0	.000	-0		13	2.6
1985	Tor A	4	6	.400	67	0	0	14-5	69.1	53	26	9	2	35-6	46	2.99	141	.209	.306	0-0	—	0		9	1.5
1986	Tor A	2	4	.333	40	0	0	2-2	36.1	36	25	6	2	17-1	32	6.19	68	.254	.342	0-0	—	0		-7	-1.1
1987	Oak A	0	0	—	6	0	0	1-0	8	10	8	3	0	1-0	8	9.00	46	.294	.314	0-0	—	0		-4	-0.2
Total	9	35	52	.402	445	24	0	106-29	667	587	297	81	14	288-40	620	3.68	110	.237	.316	41-6	.122	-1	84	30	6.4
CAUSEY, RED Cecil Algernon B 8.11.1893 Georgetown, FL D 11.11.1960 Avon Park, FL BR/TR 6-1/160# d4.26																									
1918	NY N	11	6	.647	29	18	10-2	2	158.1	143	58	2	7	42	48	2.79	94	.245	.304	48-1	.125	-3	126	-1	-0.5
1919	NY N	9	3	.750	19	16	6	0	105	99	52	5	2	38	25	3.69	76	.251	.320	38-1	.132	-1*	160	-10	-1.3
	Bos N	4	5	.444	10	10	3	0	69	81	38	1	1	20	14	4.57	63	.308	.359	21-2	.095	-2	86	-11	-1.5
	Year	13	8	.619	29	26	9	0	174	180	41	6	3	58	39	4.03	70	.274	.336	59-3	.119	-3	131	-21	-2.8
1920	Phi N	7	14	.333	35	26	11-1	3	181.1	203	109	4	5	79	30	4.32	79	.299	.376	59-2	.186	-2*	104	-16	-2.1
1921	Phi N	3	3	.500	7	7	4	0	50.2	58	22	4	1	11	8	2.84	149	.294	.335	20-0	.150	-1*	83	7	0.7
	NY N	1	1	.500	7	1	0	0	14.2	13	8	0	0	6	1	2.45	149	.228	.302	3-0	.333	0*	67	1	0.1
	Year	4	4	.500	14	8	4	0	65.1	71	11	4	1	17	9	2.76	149	.280	.327	23-0	.174	-1	83	7	0.8
1922	NY N	4	3	.571	24	2	1	1	70.2	69	34	2	0	34	13	3.18	126	.262	.347	21-1	.238	-0*	214	5	0.5
Total	5	39	35	.527	131	80	35-3	6	649.2	666	321	18	16	230	139	3.59	89	.273	.340	210-7	.157	-9	115	-25	-4.1
CAVET, PUG Tillar H. B 12.26.1889 McGregor, TX D 8.4.1966 San Luis Obispo, CA BL/TL 6-3/176# d4.25																									
1911	Det A	0	0	—	1	1	0	0	4	6	5	0	0	1	1	4.50	77	.316	.350	1-0	.000	-0	229	-1	-0.1
1914	Det A	7	7	.500	31	14	6-1	2	151.1	129	61	2	9	44	51	2.44	115	.238	.306	47-2	.106	-2	102	4	0.3
1915	Det A	4	2	.667	17	7	2	1	71	83	39	2	2	22	26	4.06	75	.300	.355	24-1	.250	1	131	-7	-0.4
Total	3	11	9	.550	49	22	8-1	3	226.1	218	105	4	11	67	78	2.98	97	.260	.323	72-3	.153	-0	119	-4	-0.2
CECCARELLI, ART Arthur Edward "Chic" B 4.2.1930 New Haven, CT BR/TL 6/190# d5.3																									
1955	KC A	4	7	.364	31	16	3-1	0	123.2	123	81	20	0	71-2	68	5.31	79	.258	.351	38-3	.079	-3	84	-15	-1.5
1956	KC A	0	1	.000	3	2	0	0	10	13	13	3	1	4-1	2	7.20	60	.317	.391	3-0	.000	-0	123	-5	-0.4
1957	Bal A	0	5	.000	20	8	1	0	58	62	34	3	2	31-3	30	4.50	80	.278	.371	14-0	.000	-2	62	-7	-0.8
1959	Chi N	5	5	.500	18	15	4-2	0	102	95	58	19	1	37-6	56	4.76	83	.245	.309	33-2	.091	-1	110	-8	-0.9
1960	Chi N	0	0	—	7	1	0	0	13	16	12	1	0	4-0	10	5.54	68	.296	.339	0-1	—	0	210	-4	-0.2
Total	5	9	18	.333	79	42	8-3	0	306.2	309	198	46	4	147-12	166	5.05	79	.261	.342	88-6	.068	-6	94	-39	-3.8
CECENA, JOSE Jose Isabel (Lugo) B 8.20.1963 Ciudad Obregon, Mexico BR/TR 5-11/180# d4.6																									
1988	Tex A	0	0	—	22	0	0	1-1	26.1	20	16	2	2	23-1	27	4.78	85	.213	.372	0-0	—	0		-2	-0.1
CECIL, REX Rex Rolston B 10.8.1916 Lindsay, OK D 10.30.1966 Long Beach, CA BL/TR 6-3/195# d8.13																									
1944	Bos A	4	5	.444	11	9	4	0	61	72	44	5	1	33	33	5.16	66	.286	.371	18-2	.278	2	112	-14	-1.6
1945	Bos A	2	5	.286	7	7	1	0	45	46	37	4	0	27	30	5.20	66	.261	.360	20-0	.300	1	114	-12	-1.5
Total	2	6	10	.375	18	16	5	0	106	118	81	9	1	60	63	5.18	66	.276	.366	38-2	.289	2	113	-26	-3.1
CENTER, PETE Marvin Earl B 4.22.1912 Hazel Green, KY BR/TR 6-4/190# d9.11 Mil 1943-44																									
1942	Cle A	0	0	—	1	0	0	0	3.1	7	6	0	1	4	0	16.20	21	.438	.571	1-0	.000	-0		-5	-0.2
1943	Cle A	1	2	.333	24	1	0	1	42.1	29	18	3	0	18	10	2.76	112	.201	.290	5-0	.000	-1	108	0	-0.1
1945	Cle A	6	3	.667	31	8	2	1	85.2	89	42	2	1	28	34	3.99	81	.270	.329	22-0	.091	-2	141	-7	-1.0
1946	Cle A	0	2	.000	21	0	0	1	29	29	16	2	1	20	6	4.97	67	.269	.388	3-0	.000	-0		-5	-0.4
Total	4	7	7	.500	77	9	2	3	160.1	154	82	7	3	70	50	4.10	79	.258	.338	31-0	.065	-3	138	-17	-1.7
CERDA, JAIME Jaime M. B 10.26.1978 Fresno, CA BL/TL 6/175# d6.28																									
2002	NY N	0	0	—	32	0	0	0-0	25.2	22	7	0	1	14-0	21	2.45	162	.232	.327	1-0	.000	-0		5	0.2
2003	NY N	1	1	.500	27	0	0	0-1	32.1	32	21	4	0	20-1	19	5.85	71	.267	.366	1-0	.000	-0		-6	-0.3
Total	2	1	1	.500	59	0	0	0-1	58	54	28	4	1	34-1	40	4.34	94	.251	.349	2-0	.000	-0		-1	-0.1
CERROS, JUAN R.Juan B 9.25.1976 Monterrey, Mexico BR/TR 6-1/200# d9.8																									
2003	Cin N	0	0	—	11	0	0	0-0	13	11	7	1	2	5-2	9	4.85	88	.224	.316	0-0	—	0		-1	0.0
CERUTTI, JOHN John Joseph B 4.28.1960 Albany, NY BL/TL 6-2/200# d9.1																									
1985	Tor A	0	2	.000	4	1	0	0-0	6.2	10	7	1	1	4-0	5	5.40	78	.323	.417	0-0	—	0	0	-2	-0.4
1986	Tor A	9	4	.692	34	20	2-1	1-0	145.1	150	73	25	1	47-2	89	4.15	102	.268	.324	0-0	—	0	122	1	0.1
1987	Tor A	11	4	.733	44	21	2	0-0	151.1	144	75	30	1	59-5	92	4.40	102	.251	.321	0-0	—	0	120	4	0.3
1988	Tor A	6	7	.462	46	12	0	1-1	123.2	120	56	12	3	42-6	65	3.13	126	.256	.320	0-0	—	0	104	7	0.9
1989	†Tor A	11	11	.500	33	31	3-1	0-0	205.1	214	90	19	6	53-2	69	3.07	123	.273	.322	0-0	—	0	109	11	1.3
1990	Tor A	9	9	.500	30	23	0	0-0	140	162	77	23	4	49-3	49	4.76	83	.297	.356	0-0	—	0	112	-12	-1.3
1991	Det A	3	6	.333	38	8	1	2-3	88.2	94	49	9	2	37-9	29	4.57	91	.276	.348	0-0	—	0	93	-4	-0.3
Total	7	49	43	.533	229	116	8-2	4-4	861	894	427	119	18	291-27	398	3.94	103	.271	.331	0-0	—	0	111	5	0.6

Year	Tm Lg	W	L	Pct	G	GS	CG-Sho	SV-BS	IP	H	R	HR	HB	BB-IB	SO	ERA	AERA	OAV	OOB	AB-SH	AVG	PB	Sup	APR	PW
CHACON, SHAWN Shawn Anthony B 12.23.1977 Anchorage, AK BR/TR 6-3/212# d4.29																									
2001	Col N	6	10	.375	27	27	0	0-0	160	157	96	26	10	87-10	134	5.06	105	.260	.360	47-7	.043	-4	86	4	-0.1
2002	Col N	5	11	.313	21	21	0	0-0	119.1	122	84	25	7	60-3	67	5.73	83	.263	.355	35-2	.257	1	67	-11	-1.2
2003	Col N❖	11	8	.579	23	23	0	0-0	137	124	73	12	12	58-4	93	4.60	107	.243	.331	46-2	.196	1	98	5	0.7
Total	3	22	29	.431	71	71	0	0-0	416.1	403	253	63	29	205-17	294	5.10	99	.255	.349	128-11	.156	-3	84	-2	-0.6
CHADWICK, RAY Ray Charles B 11.17.1962 Durham, NC BB/TR 6-2/180# d7.29																									
1986	Cal A	0	5	.000	7	7	0	0-0	27.1	39	26	5	1	15-0	9	7.24	57	.336	.417	0-0	—	0	76	-10	-1.5
CHAGNON, LEON Leon Wilbur "Shag" B 9.28.1902 Pittsfield, NH D 7.30.1953 Amesbury, MA BR/TR 6/182# d10.5																									
1929	Pit N	0	0	—	1	1	0	0	7	11	7	1	0	1	4	9.00	53	.333	.353	2-0	.000	-0	146	-3	-0.1
1930	Pit N	0	3	.000	18	4	3	0	62	92	52	9	5	23	27	6.82	73	.355	.418	20-0	.200	-1	118	-11	-0.5
1932	Pit N	9	6	.600	30	10	4-1	0	128	140	62	10	2	34	52	3.94	97	.276	.324	40-1	.225	2	88	1	0.2
1933	Pit N	6	4	.600	39	5	1	1	100	100	48	2	3	17	35	3.69	90	.259	.296	21-2	.048	-2	156	-3	-0.5
1934	Pit N	4	1	.800	33	0	0	1	58	68	32	5	1	24	19	4.81	86	.288	.356	13-0	.231	0		-3	-0.1
1935	NY N	0	2	.000	14	1	0	1	38.1	32	17	7	0	5	16	3.52	109	.232	.259	9-0	.000	-1	0	2	0.0
Total	6	19	16	.543	135	21	8-1	3	393.1	443	218	34	11	104	153	4.51	87	.284	.333	105-3	.162	-2	109	-17	-1.0
CHAKALES, BOB Robert Edward "Chick" B 8.10.1927 Asheville, NC BR/TR 6-1/185# d4.21																									
1951	Cle A	3	4	.429	17	10	2-1	0	68.1	80	40	3	0	43	32	4.74	80	.292	.388	20-1	.350	2	82	-7	-0.5
1952	Cle A	1	2	.333	5	1	0	0	12	19	13	2	0	8	7	9.75	34	.388	.474	4-0	.500	1	287	-8	-1.4
1953	Cle A	0	2	.000	7	3	1	0	27	28	13	2	1	10	6	2.67	141	.283	.355	7-0	.286	0	32	2	0.1
1954	Cle A	2	0	1.000	3	0	0	0	10.1	4	1	0	0	12	3	0.87	422	.114	.340	3-1	.333	1		3	0.7
	Bal A	3	7	.300	38	6	0	3	89.1	81	43	8	1	43	44	3.73	96	.245	.331	22-2	.364	2	131	-2	0.0
	Year	5	7	.417	41	6	0	3	99.2	85	48	8	1	55	47	3.43	105	.232	.332	25-3	.360	3	131	1	0.7
1955	Chi A	0	0	—	7	0	0	0	12.1	11	2	2	0	6-1	6	1.46	271	.256	.347	2-0	.000	-0		3	0.2
	Was A	2	3	.400	29	0	0	0	54.2	55	38	4	1	25-3	28	5.27	73	.263	.342	8-0	.000	-1		-10	-0.9
	Year	2	3	.400	36	0	0	0	67	66	40	6	1	31-4	34	4.57	84	.262	.343	10-0	.000	-1		-6	-0.7
1956	Was A	4	4	.500	43	1	0	4	96	94	53	3	3	57-7	33	4.03	107	.268	.369	20-3	.150	-1	123	1	0.1
1957	Was A	0	1	.000	4	2	0	0	18.1	20	13	2	0	10-1	12	5.40	72	.274	.357	7-0	.143	0	172	-3	-0.1
	Bos A	0	2	.000	18	0	0	3	32	53	30	5	1	11-0	16	8.16	49	.379	.425	3-1	.667	1		-13	-1.0
	Year	0	3	.000	22	2	0	3	50.1	73	51	7	1	21-1	28	7.15	55	.343	.401	10-1	.300	1	169	-17	-1.1
Total	7	15	25	.375	171	23	3-1	10	420.1	445	246	31	7	225-12	187	4.54	85	.277	.366	96-8	.271	5	102	-34	-2.8
CHALMERS, GEORGE George W. "Dut" B 6.7.1888 Edinburgh, Scotland D 8.5.1960 Bronx, NY BR/TR 6-1/189# d9.21																									
1910	Phi N	1	1	.500	4	3	2	0	22	21	17	0	1	11	12	5.32	59	.280	.379	7-0	.143	-0	151	-5	-0.4
1911	Phi N	13	10	.565	38	22	11-3	4	208.2	196	107	5	4	101	101	3.11	111	.256	.346	73-2	.178	-1	96	3	0.2
1912	Phi N	3	4	.429	12	8	3	0	57.2	64	34	4	2	37	22	3.28	111	.296	.404	16-1	.188	-0	111	1	0.0
1913	Phi N	3	10	.231	26	15	4	1	116	133	75	3	5	51	46	4.81	69	.296	.374	33-1	.212	-1	83	-17	-1.8
1914	Phi N	0	3	.000	3	2	1	0	18	23	17	0	1	15	6	5.50	53	.324	.448	6-0	.000	-1	73	-5	-0.8
1915	†Phi N	8	9	.471	26	20	13-1	1	170.1	159	58	3	0	45	82	2.48	110	.255	.305	59-2	.169	-0	89	8	0.7
1916	Phi N	1	4	.200	12	8	2	0	53.2	49	31	2	2	19	21	3.19	83	.244	.315	15-3	.000	-2	106	-5	-0.7
Total	7	29	41	.414	121	78	36-4	6	646.1	645	339	17	15	279	290	3.41	93	.269	.348	209-9	.163	-5	96	-20	-2.8
CHAMBERLAIN, CRAIG Craig Philip B 2.2.1957 Hollywood, CA BR/TR 6-1/190# d8.12																									
1979	KC A	4	4	.500	10	10	4	0-0	69.2	68	31	7	1	18-0	30	3.75	114	.261	.306	0-0	—	0	102	5	0.4
1980	KC A	0	1	.000	5	0	0	0-1	9.1	10	8	3	0	5-2	3	6.75	60	.270	.349	0-0	—	0		-3	-0.3
Total	2	4	5	.444	15	10	4	0-1	79	78	39	10	1	23-2	33	4.10	104	.262	.312	0-0	—	0	102	2	0.1
CHAMBERLAIN, ELTON Elton P. "Icebox" B 11.5.1867 Buffalo, NY D 9.22.1929 Baltimore, MD BR/TR 5-9/168# d9.13																									
1886	Lou AA	0	3	.000	4	4	4	0	31.1	39	43	0	0	17	18	6.61	55	.287	.366	19	.158	-0*	57	-9	-0.7
1887	Lou AA	18	16	.529	36	36	35-1	0	309	340	226	8	14	117	118	3.79	116	.274	.343	131	.198	-3*	97	17	1.2
1888	Lou AA	14	9	.609	24	24	21-1	0	196	178	123	2	11	59	119	2.53	122	.233	.298	94	.191	0*	131	8	0.9
	†StL AA	11	2	.846	14	14	13-1	0	112	61	34	1	6	27	57	1.61	203	.154	.220	50	.100	-3	128	20	1.7
	Year	25	11	.694	38	38	34-2	0	308	239	41	3	17	86	176	2.19	143	.206	.271	144	.160	-3	130	26	2.6
1889	StL AA	32	15	.681	53	51	44-3	1	421.2	376	220	18	17	165	202	2.97	142	.231	.309	171	.199	-2	94	**56**	4.6
1890	StL AA	3	1	.750	5	5	3	0	35	47	37	1	0	26	14	5.91	73	.311	.412	15	.133	-1	125	-6	-0.7
	Col AA	12	6	.667	25	21	19-6	0	175	128	69	2	8	70	114	2.21	162	.198	.285	65	.231	3	87	28	2.6
	Year	15	7	.682	30	26	22-**6**	0	210	175	74	3	8	96	128	2.83	131	.220	.310	80	.213	1	96	16	1.9
1891	Phi AA	22	23	.489	49	46	44	0	405.2	397	263	10	12	206	204	4.22	90	.248	.338	176	.188	2*	86	-15	-1.1
1892	Cin N	19	23	.452	52	49	43-2	0	406.1	391	230	8	17	170	169	3.39	96	.243	.322	160	.225	2*	88	-5	-0.5
1893	Cin N	16	12	.571	34	27	19-1	0	241	248	148	3	15	112	59	3.73	128	.258	.345	97	.196	-3	95	24	1.7
1894	Cin N	10	9	.526	23	22	18-1	0	177.2	220	155	10	12	91	57	5.77	96	.301	.387	70-3	.314	4	91	-2	0.2
1896	Cle N	0	1	.000	2	2	1	0	11	21	12	0	1	5	2	7.36	62	.396	.458	3-0	.000	-0	180	-3	-0.2
Total	10	157	120	.567	321	301	264-16	1	2521.2	2446	1560	63	113	1065	1133	3.57	112	.247	.327	1051-3	.203	-2	97	113	9.7
CHAMBERLAIN, BILL William Vincent B 4.21.1909 Stoughton, MA D 2.6.1994 Brockton, MA BR/TL 5-10.5/173# d8.2																									
1932	Chi A	0	5	.000	12	5	0	0	41.1	39	30	3	0	25	11	4.57	95	.250	.354	10-0	.100	-1	32	-3	-0.4
CHAMBERS, CLIFF Clifford Day "Lefty" B 1.10.1922 Portland, OR BL/TL 6-3/208# d4.24																									
1948	Chi N	2	9	.182	29	12	3-1	0	103.2	100	57	4	3	48	51	4.43	88	.254	.339	30-3	.133	-1	74	-5	-0.6
1949	Pit N	13	7	.650	34	21	10-1	0	177.1	186	89	15	5	58	93	3.96	106	.268	.329	55-6	.236	3	99	3	0.7
1950	Pit N	12	15	.444	37	33	11-2	0	249.1	262	138	18	6	92	93	4.30	102	.265	.332	90-2	.289	7	92	1	0.7
1951	Pit N	3	6	.333	10	10	2-1	0	59.2	64	38	5	4	31	19	5.58	76	.276	.371	21-1	.333	2	67	-7	-0.7
	StL N	11	6	.647	21	16	9-1	0	129.1	120	59	13	0	56	45	3.83	104	.251	.329	49-1	.163	0	129	3	0.3
	Year	14	12	.538	31	26	11-2	0	189	184	65	18	4	87	64	4.38	92	.259	.343	70-2	.214	2	105	-2	-0.4
1952	StL N	4	4	.500	26	13	2-1	1	98.1	110	51	8	2	33	47	4.12	90	.285	.344	32-1	.281	3	105	-4	0.1
1953	StL N	3	6	.333	32	8	0	0	79.2	82	50	7	1	43	26	4.86	88	.266	.358	17-0	.118	-1	76	-7	-0.7
Total	6	48	53	.475	189	113	37-7	1	897.1	924	482	70	21	361	374	4.29	96	.266	.338	294-14	.235	13	95	-16	-0.2
CHAMBERS, JOHNNIE Johnnie Monroe B 9.10.1911 Copperhill, TN D 5.11.1977 Palatka, FL BL/TR 6/185# d5.4																									
1937	StL N	0	0	—	2	0	0	0	2	5	4	0	0	2	1	18.00	22	.455	.538	0-0	—	0		-3	-0.1
CHAMBERS, ROME Richard Jerome B 8.31.1875 Weaverville, NC D 8.30.1902 Weaverville, NC BL/TL 6-2/173# d5.7																									
1900	Bos N	0	0	—	1	0	0	1	4	5	6	0	0	5	2	11.25	37	.313	.476	1-0	.000	-0		-2	-0.1
CHAMBERS, BILL William Christopher B 9.13.1889 Cameron, WV D 3.27.1962 Fort Wayne, IN BR/TR 5-9/185# d7.11																									
1910	StL N	0	0	—	1	0	0	0	1	1	1	0	0	0	0	0.00	—	.250	.250	0-0	—	0		0	0.0
CHAMPION, BILL Buford Billy B 9.18.1947 Shelby, NC BR/TR 6-4/188# d6.4																									
1969	Phi N	5	10	.333	23	20	4-2	1-0	116.2	130	68	7	3	63-4	70	5.01	71	.286	.373	35-3	.171	0	115	-17	-1.9
1970	Phi N	0	2	.000	7	1	0	0-0	14	21	14	3	1	10-2	12	9.00	44	.375	.471	3-0	.000	-0	67	-7	-0.9
1971	Phi N	3	5	.375	37	9	0	0-0	108.2	100	61	10	3	48-4	49	4.39	80	.249	.329	27-0	.111	-1	61	-11	-0.8
1972	Phi N	4	14	.222	30	22	2	0-0	132.2	155	80	11	1	54-8	54	5.09	71	.301	.366	34-5	.147	0*	74	-20	-2.4
1973	Mil A	5	8	.385	37	11	2	1-1	136.1	139	58	11	4	62-4	67	3.70	102	.267	.349	0-0	—	0	91	4	0.4
1974	Mil A	11	4	.733	31	23	2	0-0	161.2	168	72	12	0	49-3	60	3.62	100	.270	.321	0-0	—	0	99	-1	-0.1
1975	Mil A	6	6	.500	27	13	3-1	0-0	110	125	77	11	0	55-8	40	5.89	65	.290	.367	0-0	—	0	97	-22	-2.1
1976	Mil A	0	1	.000	10	3	0	0-0	24.1	35	20	0	1	13-2	8	7.03	50	.361	.430	0-0	—	0	100	-9	-0.4
Total	8	34	50	.405	202	102	13-3	2-1	804.1	873	450	64	13	354-35	360	4.69	78	.282	.355	99-8	.141	-1	92	-83	-8.2
CHANCE, DEAN Wilmer Dean B 6.1.1941 Plain Twsp., OH BR/TR 6-3/200# d9.11																									
1961	LA A	0	2	.000	5	4	0	0	18.1	33	15	0	1	5-1	11	6.87	66	.412	.443	5-0	.000	-1	69	-4	-0.4
1962	LA A	14	10	.583	50	24	6-2	8	206.2	195	83	14	5	66-5	127	2.96	130	.250	.311	65-7	.062	-5	109	20	1.8
1963	LA A	13	18	.419	45	35	6-2	3	248	229	109	10	10	90-7	168	3.19	107	.243	.315	80-7	.150	-1	89	4	0.4
1964	LA A★	**20**	9	.690	46	35	**15-11**	4	**278.1**	194	56	7	2	86-9	207	**1.65**	**199**	.195	.260	89-8	.079	-5	80	**58**	**5.6**

Year	Tm Lg	W	L	Pct	G	GS	CG-Sho	SV-BS	IP	H	R	HR	HB	BB-IB	SO	ERA	AERA	OAV	OOB	AB-SH	AVG	PB	Sup	APR	PW
1965	Cal A	15	10	.600	36	33	10-4	0	225.2	197	86	12	9	101-10	164	3.15	108	.238	.327	75-5	.093	-2	104	7	0.8
1966	Cal A	12	17	.414	41	37	11-2	1	259.2	206	113	18	7	114-9	180	3.08	109	.222	.310	76-8	.026	-6	103	2	-0.4
1967	Min A★	20	14	.588	41	**39**	**18**-5	1	**283.2**	244	109	17	7	68-7	220	2.73	127	.229	.278	92-7	.033	-6	107	18	1.6
1968	Min A	16	16	.500	43	39	15-6	1	292	224	96	15	10	63-8	234	2.53	122	.211	.260	93-9	.054	-6	94	18	1.6
1969	†Min A	5	4	.556	20	15	1	0-0	88.1	76	39	6	4	35-3	50	2.95	124	.233	.314	24-5	.042	-1	118	4	0.2
1970	Cle A	9	8	.529	45	19	1-1	4-0	155	172	80	18	6	59-11	109	4.24	93	.287	.355	42-4	.071	-3	94	-5	-0.9
	NY N	0	1	.000	3	0	0	1-0	2	3	3	0	0	2-1	0	13.50	30	.500	.625	0-0	—	0		-2	-0.4
1971	Det A	4	6	.400	31	14	0	0-0	89.2	91	43	5	4	50-4	64	3.51	102	.265	.363	21-1	.000	-2	77	-1	-0.4
Total	11	128	115	.527	406	294	83-33	23-0	2147.1	1864	832	122	65	739-75	1534	2.92	119	.234	.303	662-61	.066	-37	97	119	9.5
CHANDLER, ED Edward Oliver B 2.17.1922 Pinson, AL D 7.6.2003 Las Vegas, NV BR/TR 6-2/190# d4.18																									
1947	Bro N	0	1	.000	15	1	0	1	29.2	31	23	7	0	12	8	6.37	65	.263	.331	2-1	.000	0	85	-7	-0.3
CHANDLER, SPUD Spurgeon Ferdinand B 9.12.1907 Commerce, GA D 1.9.1990 S.Pasadena, FL BR/TR 6/181# d5.6 Mil 1944-45 C2																									
1937	NY A	7	4	.636	12	10	6-2	0	82.1	79	31	8	1	20	31	2.84	156	.253	.300	30-5	.133	-2	129	15	1.7
1938	NY A	14	5	.737	23	23	14-2	0	172	183	86	7	2	47	36	4.03	113	.271	.320	69-3	.203	2	128	12	1.5
1939	NY A	3	0	1.000	11	0	0	0	19	26	7	0	0	9	4	2.84	153	.329	.398	5-0	.400	1		3	0.6
1940	NY A	8	7	.533	27	24	6-1	0	172	184	100	12	6	60	56	4.60	88	.275	.341	60-4	.150	1	141	-12	-0.7
1941	†NY A	10	4	.714	28	20	11-4	4	163.2	146	68	5	0	60	60	3.19	123	.239	.307	60-3	.183	-1	120	14	1.2
1942	†NY A★	16	5	.762	24	24	17-3	0	200.2	176	64	13	4	74	74	2.38	145	.237	.309	71-6	.211	4	138	24	3.0
1943	†NY A☆	**20**	4	**.833**	30	30	**20-5**	0	253	197	62	5	4	54	134	**1.64**	**197**	.215	**.261**	97-3	.258	7	110	**42**	**5.3**
1944	NY A	0	0	—	1	1	0	0	6	6	3	1	1	1	1	4.50	77	.300	.364	1-1	.000	-0	144	0	0.0
1945	NY A	2	1	.667	4	4	2-1	0	31	30	16	2	0	7	12	4.65	75	.250	.291	12-0	.333	1	111	-3	-0.2
1946	NY A☆	20	8	.714	34	32	20-6	2	257.1	200	71	7	1	90	138	2.10	164	.218	.288	94-5	.149	-0	119	38	4.5
1947	†NY A☆	9	5	.643	17	16	13-2	0	128	100	41	4	0	41	68	2.46	144	.214	.277	49-3	.245	4	106	15	2.2
Total	11	109	43	.717	211	184	109-26	6	1485	1327	549	64	19	463	614	2.84	132	.240	.301	548-33	.201	17	124	148	19.1
CHANEY, ESTY Esty Clyon B 1.29.1891 Hadley, PA D 2.5.1952 Cleveland, OH BR/TR 5-11/170# d8.2																									
1913	Bos A	0	0	—	1	0	0	0	1	1	1	0	0	2	0	9.00	33	.200	.429	0-0	—	0		-1	0.0
1914	Bro F	0	0	—	1	0	0	0	4	7	3	0	0	2	1	6.75	43	.389	.450	1-0	.000	-0		-1	-0.1
Total	2	0	0	—	2	0	0	0	5	8	4	0	0	4	1	7.20	40	.348	.444	1-0	.000	-0		-2	-0.1
CHAPIN, DARRIN Darrin John B 2.1.1966 Warren, OH BR/TR 6/170# d9.21																									
1991	NY A	0	1	.000	3	0	0	0-0	5.1	3	3	0	0	6-0	5	5.06	82	.158	.360	0-0	—	0		0	-0.1
1992	Phi N	0	0	—	1	0	0	0-0	2	2	2	1	0	0-0	1	9.00	39	.250	.250	0-0	—	0		-1	-0.1
Total	2	0	1	.000	4	0	0	0-0	7.1	5	5	1	0	6-0	6	6.14	65	.185	.333	0-0	—	0		-1	-0.2
CHAPLIN, TINY James Bailey B 7.13.1905 Los Angeles, CA D 3.25.1939 National City, CA BR/TR 6-1/195# d4.13																									
1928	NY N	0	2	.000	12	1	0	0	24	27	15	0	0	8	5	4.50	87	.284	.340	5-0	.000	-1	152	-2	-0.2
1930	NY N	2	6	.250	19	8	3	1	73	89	45	8	4	16	20	5.18	91	.305	.349	19-1	.105	-0	62	-2	-0.2
1931	NY N	3	0	1.000	16	3	1	1	42.1	39	17	2	2	16	7	3.19	116	.242	.318	11-1	.182	0	155	3	0.2
1936	Bos N	10	15	.400	40	31	14	2	231.2	273	131	21	3	62	86	4.12	93	.294	.340	84-5	.202	-0	113	-12	-1.1
Total	4	15	23	.395	87	43	18	4	371	428	208	31	9	102	118	4.25	94	.290	.340	119-7	.176	-1	105	-13	-1.3
CHAPMAN, ED Edwin Volney B 11.28.1905 Courtland, MS D 5.3.2000 Clarksdale, MS BB/TR 6-1/185# d8.6																									
1933	Was A	0	0	—	6	1	0	0	9	10	9	2	0	2	4	8.00	52	.270	.308	3-0	.000	-0	163	-4	-0.2
CHAPMAN, FRED Frederick Joseph B 11.24.1872 Little Cooley, PA D 12.14.1957 Union City, PA BR/TR 5-8/165# d7.22																									
1887	Phi AA	0	0	—	1	1	1	0	5	8	6	0	0	2	4	7.20	60	.364	.417	2	.000	-0	59	-2	-0.1
CHAPMAN, BEN William Benjamin B 12.25.1908 Nashville, TN D 7.7.1993 Hoover, AL BR/TR 6/190# d4.15.1930 M4 C1 ▲																									
1944	Bro N	5	3	.625	11	9	6	0	79.1	75	36	4	3	33	37	3.40	104	.242	.321	38-1	.368	6*	157	1	0.7
1945	Bro N	3	3	.500	10	7	2	0	53.2	64	33	3	3	32	23	5.53	68	.296	.394	22-0	.136	-1*	110	-7	-0.7
	Phi N	0	0	—	3	0	0	0	7	7	8	0	0	6	4	7.71	50	.259	.394	51-0	.314	0*		-3	-0.1
	Year	3	3	.500	13	7	2	0	60.2	71	46	3	3	38	27	5.79	65	.292	.394	73-0	.260	-0	109	-12	-0.8
1946	Phi N	0	0	—	1	0	0	0	1	1	0	0	0	0	1	0.00	—	.200	.200	1-0	.000	-0		0	0.0
Total	3	8	6	.571	25	16	8	0	141	147	77	7	6	71	65	4.40	83	.263	.353	112-1	.295	6	136	-9	-0.1
CHAPPELLE, BILL William Hogan "Big Bill" B 3.22.1884 Waterloo, NY D 12.31.1944 Mineola, NY BR/TR 6-2/206# d8.20																									
1908	Bos N	2	4	.333	13	6	3-1	0	70.1	60	28	0	4	17	23	1.79	135	.233	.290	21-2	.048	-1	54	2	0.1
1909	Bos N	1	1	.500	5	3	2	0	29	31	13	0	1	11	8	1.86	151	.279	.350	11-0	.364	2	107	1	0.4
	Cin N	0	0	—	1	0	0	1	4	5	2	0	1	2	0	2.25	115	.278	.381	1-0	.000	-0		0	0.0
	Year	1	1	.500	6	3	2	1	33	36	19	0	2	13	8	1.91	146	.279	.354	12-0	.333	2	108	1	0.4
1914	Bro F	4	2	.667	16	6	4	0	74.1	71	43	1	3	29	31	3.15	91	.255	.332	23-1	.000	-4	119	-6	-0.9
Total	3	7	7	.500	35	15	9-1	1	177.2	167	86	1	9	59	62	2.38	113	.251	.321	56-3	.089	-3	91	-3	-0.4
CHARLTON, NORM Norman Wood B 1.6.1963 Fort Polk, LA BB/TL 6-3/205# d8.19																									
1988	Cin N	4	5	.444	10	10	0	0-0	61.1	60	27	6	2	20-2	39	3.96	91	.256	.318	15-4	.000	-1	72	-1	-0.3
1989	Cin N	8	3	.727	69	0	0	0-1	95.1	67	38	5	2	40-7	98	2.93	123	.197	.284	5-0	.000	-1		6	0.6
1990	†Cin N	12	9	.571	56	16	1-1	2-1	154.1	131	53	10	4	70-4	117	2.74	144	.231	.319	37-0	.135	0*	77	19	2.6
1991	Cin N	3	5	.375	39	11	0	1-3	108.1	92	37	6	6	34-4	77	2.91	131	.236	.306	23-4	.043	-2*	64	12	0.7
1992	Cin N★	4	2	.667	64	0	0	26-8	81.1	79	39	7	3	26-4	90	2.99	121	.262	.323	5-2	.200	0		1	0.1
1993	Sea A	1	3	.250	34	0	0	18-3	34.2	22	12	4	0	17-0	48	2.34	189	.179	.277	0-0	—	0		7	1.3
1995	Phi N	2	5	.286	25	0	0	0-1	22	23	19	2	3	15-3	12	7.36	57	.280	.406	1-0	1.000	1		-7	-1.3
	†Sea A	2	1	.667	30	0	0	14-1	47.2	23	12	2	1	16-0	58	1.51	314	.143	.223	0-0	—	0		16	1.7
1996	Sea A	4	7	.364	70	0	0	20-7	75.2	68	37	7	1	38-1	73	4.04	122	.244	.334	0-0	—	0		8	1.3
1997	†Sea A	3	8	.273	71	0	0	14-11	69.1	89	59	7	4	47-2	55	7.27	62	.312	.417	0-0	—	0		-21	-3.4
1998	Bal A	2	1	.667	36	0	0	0-1	35	46	27	5	0	25-0	41	6.94	66	.305	.401	0-0	—	0		-9	-0.6
	Atl N	0	0	—	13	0	0	1-0	13	7	2	0	1	8-0	6	1.38	300	.167	.308	1-0	.000	-0		4	0.2
1999	TB A	2	3	.400	42	0	0	0-1	50.2	49	29	4	1	36-0	45	4.44	112	.257	.372	0-0	—	0		3	0.2
2000	Cin N	0	0	—	2	0	0	0-0	3	6	9	1	0	6-0	1	27.00	17	.429	.600	0-0	—	0		-7	-0.3
2001	†Sea A	4	2	.667	44	0	0	1-1	47.2	36	19	4	4	11-0	48	3.02	138	.212	.274	0-0	—	0		6	0.7
Total	13	51	54	.486	605	37	1-1	97-39	899.1	798	419	70	32	409-27	808	3.71	112	.240	.327	87-10	.092	-2	67	37	3.5
CHARTON, PETE Frank Lane B 12.21.1942 Jackson, TN BL/TR 6-2/190# d4.19																									
1964	Bos A	0	2	.000	25	5	0	0	65	67	39	12	1	24-1	37	5.26	73	.275	.342	10-0	.100	-0	55	-8	-0.4
CHASE, KEN Kendall Fay "Lefty" B 10.6.1913 Oneonta, NY D 1.16.1985 Oneonta, NY BL/TL 6-2/210# d4.23																									
1936	Was A	0	0	—	1	0	0	0	2.1	2	3	0	0	4	1	11.57	41	.250	.500	1-0	1.000	1		-2	0.0
1937	Was A	4	3	.571	14	9	4	0	76.1	74	41	4	0	60	43	4.13	107	.257	.385	29-1	.034	-4	79	3	-0.2
1938	Was A	9	10	.474	32	21	7	1	150	151	99	4	4	113	64	5.58	81	.268	.394	48-4	.208	1	91	-14	-1.4
1939	Was A	10	19	.345	32	31	15-1	0	232	215	116	10	1	114	118	3.80	114	.243	.330	89-0	.169	-3	78	13	1.2
1940	Was A	15	17	.469	35	34	20-1	0	261.2	260	120	14	5	143	129	3.23	129	.261	.357	92-5	.163	-1	81	24	2.6
1941	Was A	6	18	.250	33	30	8-1	0	205.2	228	136	11	3	115	98	5.08	80	.280	.371	74-1	.149	-2	90	-23	-2.4
1942	Bos A	5	1	.833	13	10	4	0	80.1	82	37	5	0	41	34	3.81	98	.263	.348	33-3	.182	1	154	0	0.0
1943	Bos A	0	4	.000	7	5	0	0	27.1	36	25	0	0	30	9	6.91	48	.316	.458	11-0	.091	-1	66	-12	-1.5
	NY N	4	12	.250	21	20	4-1	0	129.1	140	70	7	2	74	86	4.11	84	.275	.369	42-3	.214	0*	76	-11	-1.3
Total	8	53	84	.387	188	160	62-4	1	1165	1188	647	55	15	694	582	4.27	97	.265	.365	419-17	.165	-8	86	-22	-3.0
CHAVEZ, ANTHONY Anthony Francisco B 10.22.1970 Turlock, CA BR/TR 5-11/180# d9.2																									
1997	Ana A	0	0	—	7	0	0	0-0	9.2	7	1	1	0	5-1	10	0.93	492	.206	.300	0-0	—	0		4	0.2
CHAVEZ, NESTOR Nestor Isais (Silva) B 7.6.1947 Chacao, Venezuela D 3.16.1969 Maracaibo, Venezuela BR/TR 6/170# d9.9																									
1967	SF N	1	0	1.000	2	0	0	0	5	4	2	0	0	3-1	3	0.00	—	.211	.318	1-0	.000	-0		1	0.2

Year	Tm Lg	W	L	Pct	G	GS	CG-Sho	SV-BS	IP	H	R	HR	HB	BB-IB	SO	ERA	AERA	OAV	OOB	AB-SH	AVG	PB	Sup	APR	PW
CHEADLE, DAVE David Baird B 2.19.1952 Greensboro, NC BL/TL 6-2/203# d9.16																									
1973	Atl N	0	1	.000	2	0	0	0-0	2	2	4	1	0	3-2	2	18.00	22	.250	.455	0-0	—	0		-3	-0.5
CHECH, CHARLIE Charles William B 4.27.1878 Madison, WI D 1.31.1938 Los Angeles, CA BR/TR 5-11.5/190# d4.14																									
1905	Cin N	14	14	.500	39	25	20-1	0	267.2	300	139	4	11	77	79	2.89	114	.288	.344	89-8	.191	1	113	9	0.9
1906	Cin N	1	4	.200	11	5	5	3	66	59	32	1	6	24	17	2.32	119	.243	.326	25-0	.200	1	74	0	0.1
1908	Cle A	11	7	.611	27	20	14-4	0	165.2	136	51	2	7	34	51	1.74	137	.229	.279	48-3	.104	-1	92	10	1.2
1909	Bos A	7	5	.583	17	13	6-1	0	106.2	107	51	3	5	27	40	2.95	85	.260	.314	36-0	.083	-2	115	-6	-1.0
Total	4	33	30	.524	94	63	45-6	3	606	602	273	10	29	162	187	2.52	113	.263	.320	198-11	.152	-1	103	13	1.2
CHECO, ROBINSON Robinson (Perez) B 9.9.1971 Santo Domingo, D.R. BR/TR 6-1/185# d9.16																									
1997	Bos A	1	1	.500	5	2	0	0-0	13.1	12	5	0	0	3-0	14	3.38	137	.235	.278	0-0	—	0	50	2	0.3
1998	Bos A	0	2	.000	2	2	0	0-0	7.2	11	8	3	0	5-0	5	9.39	50	.379	.471	0-0	—	0	89	-4	-0.6
1999	LA N	2	2	.500	9	2	0	0-0	15.2	24	20	5	0	13-1	11	10.34	41	.333	.435	3-1	.333	0	139	-11	-1.9
Total	3	3	5	.375	16	6	0	0-0	36.2	47	33	8	0	21-1	30	7.61	59	.309	.393	3-1	.333	0	92	-13	-2.2
CHEEVES, VIRGIL Virgil Earl "Chief" B 2.12.1901 Oklahoma City, OK D 5.5.1979 Dallas, TX BR/TR 6/195# d9.7																									
1920	Chi N	0	0	—	5	2	0	0	18	16	7	0	0	7	3	3.50	92	.250	.324	4-0	.000	-0	61	0	-0.1
1921	Chi N	11	12	.478	37	22	9-1	0	163	192	97	8	9	47	39	4.64	82	.309	.366	48-4	.167	-2	85	-14	-2.1
1922	Chi N	12	11	.522	39	22	9-1	2	182.2	195	99	9	10	76	40	4.09	103	.281	.360	62-2	.210	1	88	2	0.3
1923	Chi N	3	4	.429	19	8	0	0	71.1	89	54	8	3	37	13	6.18	65	.314	.399	23-0	.174	-1	121	-15	-1.3
1924	Cle A	0	0	—	8	1	0	0	17.1	26	17	2	1	17	2	7.79	55	.388	.518	4-0	.250	0	138	-6	-0.3
1927	NY N	0	0	—	3	0	0	0	6.1	8	3	1	0	4	1	4.26	90	.333	.429	0-1	—	0		0	0.0
Total	6	26	27	.491	111	55	18-2	2	458.2	526	277	28	23	188	98	4.73	84	.300	.375	141-7	.184	-1	92	-33	-3.5
CHELINI, ITALO Italo Vincent "Chilly" or "Lefty" B 10.10.1914 San Francisco, CA D 8.25.1972 San Francisco, CA BL/TL 5-10.5/175# d9.12																									
1935	Chi A	0	0	—	2	0	0	0	5	7	7	1	1	4	1	12.60	37	.350	.480	2-0	.500	0		-4	-0.2
1936	Chi A	4	3	.571	18	6	5	0	83.2	100	51	8	0	30	16	4.95	105	.291	.348	32-0	.156	-1	110	3	0.0
1937	Chi A	0	1	.000	4	0	0	0	8.2	15	10	2	1	0	3	10.38	44	.405	.421	1-0	.000	0		-5	-0.4
Total	3	4	4	.500	24	6	5	0	97.1	122	68	11	2	34	20	5.83	88	.304	.362	35-0	.171	-1	110	-6	-0.6
CHEN, BRUCE Bruce Kastulo B 6.19.1977 Panama City, Panama BL/TL 6-1/150# d9.7																									
1998	Atl N	2	0	1.000	4	4	0	0-0	20.1	23	9	3	1	9-1	17	3.98	104	.287	.367	7-2	.143	-0	149	1	0.0
1999	Atl N	2	2	.500	16	7	0	0-0	51	38	32	11	2	27-3	45	5.47	82	.208	.315	11-1	.000	-1	73	-5	-0.5
2000	Atl N	4	0	1.000	22	0	0	0-0	39.2	35	15	4	1	19-2	32	2.50	184	.232	.318	5-2	.000	-1		8	0.6
	Phi N	3	4	.429	15	15	0	0-0	94.1	81	39	14	1	27-2	80	3.63	129	.232	.288	25-5	.040	-2	89	12	0.5
	Year	7	4	.636	37	15	0	0-0	134	116	44	18	2	46-4	112	3.29	141	.232	.298	30-7	.033	-3	90	19	1.1
2001	Phi N	4	5	.444	16	16	0	0-0	86.1	90	53	19	1	31-4	79	5.00	85	.262	.322	28-3	.107	-1	118	-8	-0.8
	NY N	3	2	.600	11	11	0	0-0	59.2	56	37	10	0	28-0	47	4.68	88	.255	.335	19-2	.158	-0	128	-5	-0.4
	Year	7	7	.500	27	27	0	0-0	146	146	43	29	1	59-4	126	4.87	86	.259	.327	47-5	.128	-1	122	-13	-1.2
2002	NY N	0	0	—	1	0	0	0-0	0.2	1	0	0	0	0-0	0	0.00	—	.333	.333	0-0	—	0		0	0.0
	Mon N	2	3	.400	15	5	0	0-0	37.1	47	29	9	1	23-3	43	6.99	64	.303	.397	12-1	.417	2	58	-8	-0.8
	Cin N	0	2	.000	39	1	0	0-0	39.2	37	24	7	1	20-2	37	4.31	99	.243	.330	3-1	.000	-0	65	-1	-0.1
	Year	2	5	.286	55	6	0	0-0	77.2	85	27	16	2	43-5	80	5.56	78	.274	.363	15-2	.333	1	60	-10	-0.9
2003	Hou N	0	0	—	11	0	0	0-0	12	14	8	2	2	8-1	8	6.00	74	.311	.421	1-0	.000	-0		-2	-0.1
	Bos A	0	1	.000	5	2	0	0-0	12.1	12	8	4	0	2-0	12	5.11	89	.255	.280	0-0	—	0	131	-1	-0.1
Total	6	20	19	.513	155	61	0	0-0	453.1	434	254	83	10	194-18	400	4.59	96	.251	.327	111-17	.117	-4	103	-9	-1.7
CHENEY, LARRY Laurance Russell B 5.2.1886 Belleville, KS D 1.6.1969 Daytona Beach, FL BR/TR 6-1.5/185# d9.9																									
1911	Chi N	1	0	1.000	3	1	0	0	10	8	0	0	0	3	11	0.00	—	.229	.289	4-0	.250	0	113	4	0.4
1912	Chi N	**26**	10	.722	42	37	**28**-4	0	303.1	262	122	5	7	111	140	2.85	117	.234	.307	106-10	.226	5	119	17	2.2
1913	Chi N	21	14	.600	**54**	36	25-2	**11**	305	271	117	7	8	98	136	2.57	124	.241	.306	104-6	.192	2*	108	20	2.6
1914	Chi N	20	18	.526	**50**	40	21-6	5	311.1	239	136	9	10	140	157	2.54	109	.215	.308	100-5	.180	3	100	8	1.3
1915	Chi N	8	9	.471	25	18	6-2	0	131.1	120	69	1	4	55	68	3.56	78	.246	.327	40-2	.150	-1	107	-12	-1.6
	Bro N	0	2	.000	5	4	1	0	27	16	10	0	2	17	11	1.67	167	.174	.315	7-0	.143	0	94	2	0.2
	Year	8	11	.421	30	22	7-2	0	158.1	136	14	1	6	72	79	3.24	86	.234	.325	47-2	.149	-1	105	-9	-1.4
1916	†Bro N	18	12	.600	41	32	15-5	0	253	178	91	5	10	105	166	1.92	140	**.198**	.289	79-4	.114	-3	105	15	1.6
1917	Bro N	8	12	.400	35	24	14-1	2	210.1	185	80	4	5	73	102	2.35	119	.239	.309	68-1	.206	2	88	6	0.8
1918	Bro N	11	13	.458	32	21	15	1	200.2	177	84	2	10	74	83	3.00	93	.241	.319	66-3	.242	2*	71	-3	-0.1
1919	Bro N	1	3	.250	9	4	2	0	39	45	21	1	2	14	14	4.15	72	.300	.367	11-0	.182	-0	80	-4	-0.5
	Bos N	0	2	.000	8	2	0	0	33	35	20	0	0	15	13	3.55	81	.294	.373	11-0	.182	0	125	-4	-0.2
	Phi N	2	5	.286	9	6	5	0	57.1	69	34	2	1	28	25	4.55	71	.315	.395	21-0	.095	-2	82	-7	-1.1
	Year	3	10	.231	26	12	7	0	129.1	149	37	3	3	57	52	4.18	73	.305	.381	43-0	.140	-2	89	-15	-1.8
Total	9	116	100	.537	313	225	132-20	19	1881.1	1605	784	36	59	733	926	2.70	109	.234	.313	617-31	.186	9	102	42	5.6
CHENEY, TOM Thomas Edgar B 10.14.1934 Morgan, GA D 11.1.2001 Rome, GA BR/TR 6/180# d4.21																									
1957	StL N	0	1	.000	4	3	0	0	9	6	6	0	0	15-0	10	5.00	79	.207	.477	2-1	.000	-0	126	-1	-0.1
1959	StL N	0	1	.000	11	2	0	0	11.2	17	9	2	2	11-2	8	6.94	61	.354	.484	0-0	—	0	105	-3	-0.2
1960	†Pit N	2	2	.500	11	8	1-1	0	52	44	25	5	0	33-0	35	3.98	94	.238	.352	17-1	.176	0	103	-1	-0.1
1961	Pit N	0	0	—	1	0	0	0	0	1	5	1	0	4-0	0	∞	—	.500	.833	0-0	—	0		-4	-0.3
	Was A	1	3	.250	10	7	0	0	29.2	32	30	8	0	26-0	20	8.80	46	.283	.408	8-1	.500	2*	91	-14	-1.4
1962	Was A	7	9	.438	37	23	4-3	1	173.1	134	68	12	2	97-0	147	3.17	127	.213	.318	48-6	.063	-3	79	16	1.1
1963	Was A	8	9	.471	23	21	7-4	0	136.1	99	51	14	1	40-3	97	2.71	137	.202	.262	46-2	.109	-3*	75	13	1.2
1964	Was A	1	3	.250	15	6	1	1	48.2	45	26	10	0	13-1	25	3.70	100	.245	.293	12-4	.250	0	84	-1	-0.1
1966	Was A	0	1	.000	3	1	0	0	5.1	4	4	1	1	6-0	3	5.06	68	.222	.440	0-0	—	0	178	-1	-0.2
Total	8	19	29	.396	115	71	13-8	2	466	382	224	53	6	245-6	345	3.77	103	.225	.322	133-15	.135	-3	86	4	-0.1
CHESBRO, JACK John Dwight "Happy Jack" B 6.5.1874 N.Adams, MA D 11.6.1931 Conway, MA BR/TR 5-9/180# d7.12 C1 HF1946																									
1899	Pit N	6	9	.400	19	17	15	0	149	165	99	3	11	59	28	4.11	93	.280	.357	58-2	.155	-3	88	-6	-0.9
1900	Pit N	15	13	.536	32	26	20-3	1	215.2	220	123	4	12	79	56	3.67	99	.264	.336	85-0	.176	-1	112	1	-0.1
1901	Pit N	21	10	**.677**	36	28	26-**6**	1	287.2	261	104	4	14	52	129	2.38	137	.240	.284	116-4	.216	3	108	32	3.3
1902	Pit N	**28**	6	**.824**	35	33	31-**8**	1	286.1	242	81	1	21	62	136	2.17	126	.229	.285	112-4	.179	-2	147	23	2.3
1903	NY A	21	15	.583	40	36	33-1	0	324.2	300	140	7	9	74	147	2.77	113	.245	.293	124-3	.185	-1	93	12	1.2
1904	NY A	**41**	12	**.774**	**55**	**51**	**48**-6	0	**454.2**	338	128	4	7	88	239	1.82	149	**.208**	.252	174-3	.236	6*	113	**41**	**6.1**
1905	NY A	19	15	.559	41	38	24-3	0	303.1	262	125	5	6	71	156	2.20	134	.235	.284	112-2	.188	0	98	16	1.8
1906	NY A	23	17	.575	**49**	**42**	24-4	1	325	314	138	2	10	75	152	2.96	100	.257	.305	125-0	.208	-1	103	0	-0.1
1907	NY A	10	10	.500	30	25	17-1	0	206	192	83	0	6	46	78	2.53	110	.249	.297	76-0	.197	-1	82	6	0.6
1908	NY A	14	20	.412	45	31	20-3	1	288.2	276	134	6	14	67	124	2.93	85	.256	.307	102-3	.176	-2	80	-12	-1.6
1909	NY A	0	4	.000	9	4	2	0	49.2	70	47	2	3	13	17	6.34	40	.347	.394	17-0	.176	-0	77	-19	-1.4
	Bos A	0	1	.000	1	1	0	0	6	7	4	1	0	4	3	4.50	56	.318	.423	2-0	.500	0	141	-1	-0.2
	Year	0	5	.000	10	5	2	0	55.2	77	9	3	3	17	20	6.14	41	.344	.398	19-0	.211	0	89	-20	-1.6
Total	11	198	132	.600	392	332	260-35	5	2896.2	2647	1206	39	113	690	1265	2.68	111	.244	.297	1103-21	.197	-2	103	93	11.0
CHESNES, BOB Robert Vincent B 5.6.1921 Oakland, CA D 5.23.1979 Everett, WA BB/TR 6/180# d5.6																									
1948	Pit N	14	6	.700	25	23	15	0	194.1	180	92	13	4	90	69	3.57	114	.247	.333	91-0	.275	7*	134	8	1.6
1949	Pit N	7	13	.350	27	25	8-1	1	145.1	153	104	16	5	82	49	5.88	71	.276	.374	68-0	.250	6*	98	-26	-2.3
1950	Pit N	3	3	.500	9	7	2	0	39	44	26	7	3	17	12	5.54	79	.293	.376	13-0	.154	-0	118	-4	-0.5
Total	3	24	22	.522	61	55	25-1	1	378.2	377	222	36	12	189	130	4.66	89	.263	.354	172-0	.256	12	116	-22	-1.2
CHETKOVICH, MITCH Mitchell B 7.21.1917 Fairpoint, OH D 8.24.1971 Grass Valley, CA BR/TR 6-3.5/208# d4.19																									
1945	Phi N	0	0	—	4	0	0	0	3	2	2	0	0	3	0	0.00	—	.182	.357	0-0	—	0		0	0.0
CHEVEZ, TONY Silvio Antonio (b: Silvio Antonio Aguilera (Chevez)) B 6.20.1954 Telica, Nicaragua BR/TR 5-11/177# d5.31																									
1977	Bal A	0	0	—	4	0	0	0-0	8	10	13	3	2	8-1	7	12.38	31	.294	.435	0-0	—	0		-9	-0.4

Year	Tm Lg	W	L	Pct	G	GS	CG-Sho	SV-BS	IP	H	R	HR	HB	BB-IB	SO	ERA	AERA	OAV	OOB	AB-SH	AVG	PB	Sup	APR	PW
CHIAMPARINO, SCOTT Scott Michael B 8.22.1966 San Mateo, CA BR/TR 6-2/190# d9.5																									
1990	Tex A	1	2	.333	6	6	0	0-0	37.2	36	14	1	2	12-0	19	2.63	150	.250	.314	0-0	—	0	70	5	0.3
1991	Tex A	1	0	1.000	5	5	0	0-0	22.1	26	11	1	0	12-0	8	4.03	100	.295	.380	0-0	—	0	122	0	0.0
1992	Tex A	0	4	.000	4	4	0	0-0	25.1	25	11	2	0	5-0	13	3.55	107	.260	.294	0-0	—	0	48	1	0.1
Total	3	2	6	.250	15	15	0	0-0	85.1	87	36	4	2	29-0	40	3.27	120	.265	.327	0-0	—	0	82	6	0.4
CHIASSON, SCOTT Scott Christopher B 8.14.1977 Norwich, CT BR/TR 6-3/200# d9.19																									
2001	Chi N	1	1	.500	6	0	0	0-0	6.2	5	2	2	1	2-0	6	2.70	153	.200	.286	0-0	—	0		1	0.3
2002	Chi N	0	0	—	4	0	0	0-0	4.2	11	12	2	0	6-1	3	23.14	17	.440	.548	0-0	—	0		-10	-0.5
Total	2	1	1	.500	10	0	0	0-0	11.1	16	14	4	1	8-1	9	11.12	37	.320	.424	0-0	—	0		-9	-0.2
CHIFFER, FLOYD Floyd John B 4.20.1956 Glen Cove, NY BR/TR 6-2/185# d4.7																									
1982	SD N	4	3	.571	51	0	0	4-7	79.1	73	33	9	4	34-1	48	2.95	116	.247	.330	8-0	.000	-1		3	0.1
1983	SD N	0	2	.000	15	0	0	1-0	22.2	17	10	0	0	10-1	15	3.18	110	.210	.297	1-0	.000	-0		0	0.0
1984	SD N	1	0	1.000	15	1	0	0-0	28	42	24	1	0	16-2	20	7.71	46	.347	.417	3-0	.000	-0	198	-12	-0.7
Total	3	5	5	.500	81	1	0	5-7	130	132	67	10	4	60-4	83	4.02	86	.266	.346	12-0	.000	-1	198	-9	-0.6
CHILD, HARRY Harry Stephen Patrick (b: Harry Stephen Patrick Chesley) B 5.23.1905 Baltimore, MD D 11.8.1972 Alexandria, VA BB/TR 5-11/187# d7.16																									
1930	Was A	0	0	—	5	0	0	0	10	10	7	1	0	5	5	6.30	73	.263	.349	4-0	.250	-0		-1	-0.1
CHILDERS, MATT Matthew Wilkie B 12.3.1978 Douglas, GA BR/TR 6-5/215# d8.3																									
2002	Mil N	0	0	—	8	0	0	0-0	9	13	12	2	1	8-1	6	12.00	34	.342	.468	1-0	.000	-0		-7	-0.4
CHILDERS, BILL William B St.Louis, MO d7.27																									
1895	Lou N	0	0	—	1	0	0	0	0	2	6	0	0	5	0	∞	—	1.000	1.000	0-0	—	0		-5	-0.4
CHILDRESS, ROCKY Rodney Osborne B 2.18.1962 Santa Rosa, CA BR/TR 6-2/195# d5.17																									
1985	Phi N	0	1	.000	16	1	0	0-0	33.1	45	23	3	0	9-3	14	6.21	59	.326	.362	6-2	.167	-0	0	-8	-0.4
1986	Phi N	0	0	—	2	0	0	0-0	2.2	4	3	0	0	1-0	1	6.75	57	.364	.417	0-0	—	0		-1	-0.1
1987	Hou N	1	2	.333	32	0	0	0-4	48.1	46	17	4	0	18-6	26	2.98	132	.260	.323	2-0	.000	-0		6	0.3
1988	Hou N	1	0	1.000	11	0	0	0-0	23.1	26	17	3	1	9-2	24	6.17	54	.280	.350	4-0	.250	0		-7	-0.4
Total	4	2	3	.400	61	1	0	0-4	107.2	121	60	10	1	37-11	65	4.76	78	.289	.344	12-2	.167	-0	0	-10	-0.6
CHIPMAN, BOB Robert Howard "Mr. Chips" B 10.11.1918 Brooklyn, NY D 11.8.1973 Huntington, NY BL/TL 6-2/190# d9.28																									
1941	Bro N	1	0	1.000	1	0	0	0	5	3	0	0	0	1	3	0.00	—	.150	.190	3-0	.000	-0		2	0.4
1942	Bro N	0	0	—	2	0	0	0	1.1	1	0	0	0	2	1	0.00	—	.250	.500	0-0	—	0		0	0.0
1943	Bro N	0	0	—	1	0	0	0	1.2	2	0	0	0	2	0	0.00	—	.400	.571	0-0	—	0		1	0.0
1944	Bro N	3	1	.750	11	3	1	0	36.1	38	19	1	0	24	20	4.21	84	.270	.376	11-2	.182	-0	197	-2	-0.2
	Chi N	9	9	.500	26	21	8-1	2	129	147	62	9	0	40	41	3.49	101	.288	.340	48-0	.104	-3	122	0	-0.3
	Year	12	10	.545	37	24	9-1	2	165.1	185	67	10	0	64	61	3.65	97	.284	.348	59-2	.119	-3	131	-2	-0.5
1945	†Chi N	4	5	.444	25	10	3-1	0	72	63	37	4	1	34	29	3.50	104	.230	.317	17-3	.176	1	100	-1	0.0
1946	Chi N	6	5	.545	34	10	5-3	2	109.1	103	44	8	1	54	42	3.13	106	.255	.344	33-1	.061	-3	80	2	-0.1
1947	Chi N	7	6	.538	32	17	5-1	0	134.2	135	58	6	0	66	51	3.68	107	.264	.348	44-3	.091	-3*	80	7	0.4
1948	Chi N	2	1	.667	34	3	0	4	60.1	73	34	5	0	24	16	3.58	109	.293	.355	16-0	.250	1	129	0	0.1
1949	Chi N	7	8	.467	38	11	3-1	1	113.1	110	65	8	2	63	46	3.97	102	.248	.344	24-3	.125	-0	83	-3	-0.4
1950	Bos N	7	7	.500	27	12	4	1	124	127	75	10	4	37	40	4.43	87	.262	.319	39-1	.154	-1	94	-11	-1.2
1951	Bos N	4	3	.571	33	0	0	4	52	59	29	5	2	19	17	4.85	76	.284	.349	10-0	.100	-1		-6	-0.9
1952	Bos N	1	1	.500	29	0	0	0	41.2	28	15	5	0	20	16	2.81	129	.188	.284	5-0	.400	1		4	0.3
Total	12	51	46	.526	293	87	29-7	14	880.2	889	438	61	10	386	322	3.72	100	.261	.338	250-13	.128	-8	101	-7	-1.9
CHITREN, STEVE Stephen Vincent B 6.8.1967 Tokyo, Japan BR/TR 6/180# d9.15																									
1990	Oak A	1	0	1.000	8	0	0	0-0	17.2	7	2	0	0	4-0	19	1.02	366	.117	.172	0-0	—	0		6	0.3
1991	Oak A	1	4	.200	56	0	0	4-3	60.1	59	31	8	4	32-4	47	4.33	89	.258	.356	0-0	—	0		-4	-0.3
Total	2	2	4	.333	64	0	0	4-3	78	66	33	8	4	36-4	66	3.58	107	.228	.320	0-0	—	0		2	0.0
CHITTUM, NELSON Nelson Boyd B 3.25.1933 Harrisonburg, VA BR/TR 6-1/180# d8.17																									
1958	StL N	0	1	.000	13	2	0	0	29.1	31	21	5	1	7-0	13	6.44	64	.265	.310	4-0	.250	0	141	-6	-0.3
1959	Bos A	3	0	1.000	21	0	0	0	30.1	29	9	0	0	11-2	12	1.19	342	.266	.333	5-1	.200	0		7	0.7
1960	Bos A	0	0	—	6	0	0	0	8.1	8	4	0	0	6-1	5	4.32	94	.242	.359	1-0	.000	-0		0	0.0
Total	3	3	1	.750	40	2	0	0	68	68	34	5	1	24-3	30	3.84	106	.263	.326	10-1	.200	0	141	1	0.4
CHLUPSA, BOB Robert Joseph B 9.16.1945 New York, NY BR/TR 6-7/215# d7.16																									
1970	StL N	0	2	.000	14	0	0	0-0	16.1	26	16	2	0	9-3	10	8.82	47	.366	.432	0-0	—	0		-8	-0.8
1971	StL N	0	0	—	1	0	0	0-0	2	3	2	0	0	0-0	1	9.00	40	.333	.333	0-0	—	0		-1	0.0
Total	2	0	2	.000	15	0	0	0-0	18.1	29	18	2	0	9-3	11	8.84	46	.363	.422	0-0	—	0		-9	-0.8
CHO, JIN HO Jin Ho B 8.16.1975 Jun Ju City, South Korea BR/TR 6/175# d7.4																									
1998	Bos A	0	3	.000	4	4	0	0-0	18.2	28	17	4	1	3-0	15	8.20	58	.341	.368	0-0	—	0	94	-6	-0.8
1999	Bos A	2	3	.400	9	7	0	0-0	39.1	45	26	7	2	8-0	16	5.72	87	.287	.324	1-0	.000	-0	72	-2	-0.3
Total	2	2	6	.250	13	11	0	0-0	58	73	43	11	3	11-0	31	6.52	75	.305	.339	1-0	.000	-0	80	-8	-1.1
CHOATE, DON Donald Leon B 7.2.1938 Potosi, MO BR/TR 6/185# d9.12																									
1960	SF N	0	0	—	4	0	0	0	8	7	4	0	0	4-0	7	2.25	155	.233	.324	0-0	—	0		0	0.0
CHOATE, RANDY Randol Doyle B 9.5.1975 San Antonio, TX BL/TL 6-3/180# d7.1																									
2000	†NY A	0	1	.000	22	0	0	0-0	17	14	10	3	1	8-0	12	4.76	102	.215	.307	0-0	—	0		0	0.0
2001	†NY A	3	1	.750	37	0	0	0-0	48.1	34	21	0	9	27-2	35	3.35	134	.202	.341	3-0	.000	-0		6	0.4
2002	NY A	0	0	—	18	0	0	0-0	22.1	18	18	1	3	15-0	17	6.04	72	.217	.356	1-0	.000	-0		-5	-0.2
2003	NY A	0	0	—	5	0	0	0-0	3.2	7	3	0	0	1-0	0	7.36	60	.467	.500	0-0	—	0		-1	-0.1
Total	4	3	2	.600	82	0	0	0-0	91.1	73	52	4	13	51-2	64	4.43	102	.221	.345	4-0	.000	-0		0	0.1
CHOUINARD, BOBBY Robert William B 5.1.1972 Manila, Philippines BR/TR 6-1/188# d5.26																									
1996	Oak A	4	2	.667	13	11	0	0-0	59	75	41	10	3	32-3	32	6.10	81	.316	.400	0-0	—	0	128	-7	-0.5
1998	Mil N	0	0	—	1	0	0	0-0	3	5	1	0	0	0-0	1	3.00	142	.455	.417	0-0	—	0		0	0.0
	Ari N	0	2	.000	26	2	0	0-1	38.1	41	23	5	0	11-2	26	4.23	100	.268	.315	2-0	.000	-0	175	-2	-0.1
	Year	0	2	.000	27	2	0	0-1	41.1	46	31	5	0	11-2	27	4.14	102	.280	.322	2-0	.000	-0	174	-1	-0.1
1999	†Ari N	5	2	.714	32	0	0	1-1	40.1	31	16	3	0	12-2	23	2.68	171	.220	.274	3-1	.000	-0		7	1.1
2000	Col N	2	2	.500	31	0	0	0-2	32.2	35	17	4	1	9-2	23	3.86	150	.273	.324	3-0	.333	-0		5	0.5
2001	Col N	0	0	—	8	0	0	0-0	7.2	10	7	4	0	1-1	5	8.22	65	.303	.324	0-0	—	0		-2	-0.1
Total	5	11	8	.579	111	13	0	1-4	181	197	105	26	4	65-10	110	4.57	106	.280	.340	8-1	.125	-0	133	1	0.9
CHOUNEAU, CHIEF William (b: William Cadreau) B 9.2.1888 Cloquet, MN D 9.17.1946 Cloquet, MN BR/TR 5-9/150# d10.9																									
1910	Chi A	0	1	.000	1	1	0	0	5.1	7	2	0	0	0	1	3.38	71	.292	.292	1-0	.000	1	28	0	0.0
CHRIS, MIKE Michael B 10.8.1957 Santa Monica, CA BL/TL 6-3/180# d7.31																									
1979	Det A	3	3	.500	13	8	0	0-0	39	46	30	3	0	21-0	31	6.92	63	.297	.376	0-0	—	0	68	-10	-1.2
1982	SF N	0	2	.000	9	6	0	0-0	26	23	16	2	1	26-2	10	4.85	74	.245	.410	7-0	.143	-0	106	-4	-0.2
1983	SF N	0	0	—	7	0	0	0-0	13.1	16	14	1	2	16-2	5	8.10	44	.308	.479	2-0	.000	-0		-7	-0.4
Total	3	3	5	.375	29	14	0	0-0	78.1	85	60	6	3	63-4	46	6.43	61	.282	.407	9-0	.111	-0	84	-21	-1.8
CHRISTENSON, GARY Gary Richard B 5.5.1953 Mineola, NY BL/TL 6-5/200# d9.1																									
1979	KC A	0	0	—	6	0	0	0-1	10.2	10	5	1	0	2-0	4	3.38	127	.250	.279	0-0	—	0		1	0.0
1980	KC A	3	0	1.000	24	0	0	1-2	31.1	35	23	4	2	18-1	16	5.17	79	.278	.372	0-0	—	0		-5	-0.4
Total	2	3	0	1.000	30	0	0	1-3	42	45	28	5	2	20-1	20	4.71	87	.271	.351	0-0	—	0		-4	-0.4
CHRISTENSON, LARRY Larry Richard B 11.10.1953 Everett, WA BR/TR 6-4/215# d4.13																									
1973	Phi N	1	4	.200	10	9	1	0-0	34.1	53	25	3	1	20-1	11	6.55	58	.366	.443	10-0	.000	-1	72	-9	-1.2

Year	Tm Lg	W	L	Pct	G	GS	CG-Sho	SV-BS	IP	H	R	HR	HB	BB-IB	SO	ERA	AERA	OAV	OOB	AB-SH	AVG	PB	Sup	APR	PW
1974	Phi N	1	1	.500	10	1	0	2-0	23	20	11	2	0	15-3	18	4.30	88	.241	.357	4-1	.000	-1	46	-1	-0.1
1975	Phi N	11	6	.647	29	26	5-2	1-0	171.2	149	73	12	1	45-2	88	3.67	102	.236	.286	57-8	.246	5	108	4	0.8
1976	Phi N	13	8	.619	32	29	2	0-0	168.2	199	77	8	1	42-4	54	3.68	96	.297	.338	51-6	.196	4	123	-3	-0.1
1977	†Phi N	19	6	.760	34	34	5-1	0-0	219.1	229	113	21	7	69-1	118	4.06	99	.268	.324	74-10	.135	1	141	-3	-0.3
1978	†Phi N	13	14	.481	33	33	9-3	0-0	228	209	90	16	1	47-7	131	3.24	110	.244	.282	67-7	.075	-2	86	9	0.7
1979	Phi N	5	10	.333	19	17	2	0-0	106	118	56	9	2	30-3	53	4.50	85	.291	.339	31-3	.290	5	68	-7	-0.4
1980	†Phi N	5	1	.833	14	14	0	0-0	73.2	62	35	4	3	27-4	49	4.03	94	.227	.303	19-3	.368	3	118	-1	0.3
1981	†Phi N	4	7	.364	20	15	0	1-0	106.2	108	48	8	1	30-3	70	3.54	102	.267	.313	30-3	.100	-1	96	0	-0.2
1982	Phi N	9	10	.474	33	33	3	0-0	223	212	95	15	3	53-5	145	3.47	106	.253	.297	67-12	.075	-3	98	6	0.1
1983	Phi N	2	4	.333	9	9	0	0-0	48.1	42	25	2	1	17-1	44	3.91	91	.233	.297	17-1	.059	-1	88	-2	-0.3
Total	11	83	71	.539	243	220	27-6	4-0	1402.2	1401	648	100	21	395-34	781	3.79	98	.262	.313	427-54	.150	10	105	-7	-0.7
CHRISTIANSEN, CLAY Clay C. B 6.28.1958 Wichita, KS BR/TR 6-5/205# d5.10																									
1984	NY A	2	4	.333	24	1	0	2-2	38.2	50	28	4	1	12-0	27	6.05	63	.309	.356	0-0	—	0	0	-10	-1.5
CHRISTIANSEN, JASON Jason Samuel B 9.21.1969 Omaha, NE BR/TL 6-5/230# d4.26																									
1995	Pit N	1	3	.250	63	0	0	0-4	56.1	49	28	5	3	34-9	53	4.15	104	.234	.345	1-0	.000	-0		1	0.1
1996	Pit N	3	3	.500	33	0	0	0-2	44.1	56	34	7	1	19-2	38	6.70	65	.311	.374	4-1	.000	-0		-10	-1.2
1997	Pit N	3	0	1.000	39	0	0	0-2	33.2	37	11	2	2	17-3	37	2.94	146	.274	.364	0-0	—	0		5	0.4
1998	Pit N	3	3	.500	60	0	0	6-4	64.2	51	22	2	0	27-7	71	2.51	172	.216	.295	4-0	.250	0		12	1.2
1999	Pit N	2	3	.400	39	0	0	3-2	37.2	26	17	2	2	22-4	35	4.06	113	.198	.321	1-0	.000	-0*		3	0.4
2000	Pit N	2	8	.200	44	0	0	1-2	38	28	22	2	0	25-4	41	4.97	93	.207	.329	0-0	—	0		-1	-0.1
	†StL N	1	0	1.000	21	0	0	0-1	10	13	7	1	2	2-1	12	5.40	85	.317	.378	0-0	—	0		-1	-0.1
	Year	3	8	.273	65	0	0	1-3	48	41	29	3	2	27-5	53	5.06	91	.233	.340	0-0	—	0		-3	-0.2
2001	StL N	1	1	.500	30	0	0	3-0	19.1	15	10	4	1	10-1	19	4.66	92	.211	.313	0-0	—	0		0	-0.1
	SF N	1	0	1.000	25	0	0	0-1	17	14	3	1	0	5-0	12	1.59	251	.241	.292	0-0	—	0		5	0.3
	Year	2	1	.667	55	0	0	3-1	36.1	29	13	5	1	15-1	31	3.22	128	.225	.304	0-0	—	0		4	0.2
2002	SF N	0	1	.000	6	0	0	0-0	5	6	3	1	0	2-0	1	5.40	72	.316	.381	0-0	—	0		-1	-0.1
2003	†SF N	0	0	—	40	0	0	0-1	26	25	15	3	1	11-0	22	5.19	79	.243	.322	0-0	—	0		-3	-0.1
Total	9	17	22	.436	400	0	0	13-19	352	320	172	30	12	174-31	341	4.17	104	.243	.334	10-1	.100	-1		10	0.7
CHRISTMAN, TIM Timothy Arthur B 3.31.1975 Oneonta, NY BL/TL 6/195# d4.21																									
2001	Col N	0	0	—	1	0	0	0-0	2	1	1	1	0	0-0	2	4.50	119	.143	.143	0-0	—	0		0	0.0
CHRISTOPHER, MIKE Michael Wayne B 11.3.1963 Petersburg, VA BR/TR 6-5/206# d9.10																									
1991	LA N	0	0	—	3	0	0	0-0	4	2	0	0	0	3-0	2	0.00	—	.167	.333	0-0	—	0		2	0.1
1992	Cle A	0	0	—	10	0	0	0-0	18	17	8	2	0	10-1	13	3.00	130	.254	.346	0-0	—	0		1	0.1
1993	Cle A	0	0	—	9	0	0	0-0	11.2	14	6	3	0	2-1	8	3.86	113	.286	.314	0-0	—	0		0	0.0
1995	Det A	4	0	1.000	36	0	0	1-1	61.1	71	28	8	2	14-2	34	3.82	125	.292	.333	0-0	—	0		6	0.4
1996	Det A	1	1	.500	13	0	0	0-0	30	47	36	12	0	11-2	19	9.30	54	.351	.389	0-0	—	0		-15	-0.8
Total	5	5	1	.833	71	0	0	1-1	125	151	78	25	2	40-6	76	4.90	95	.299	.348	0-0	—	0		-6	-0.2
CHRISTOPHER, RUSS Russell Ormand B 9.12.1917 Richmond, CA D 12.5.1954 Richmond, CA BR/TR 6-3/180# d4.14 b-Loyd																									
1942	Phi A	4	13	.235	30	18	10	1	165	154	78	8	3	99	58	3.82	99	.254	.362	56-3	.089	-3	78	1	0.1
1943	Phi A	5	8	.385	24	15	5	2	133	120	58	3	3	58	56	3.45	98	.242	.325	45-1	.156	-1	93	-1	0.2
1944	Phi A	14	14	.500	35	24	13-1	1	215.1	200	91	6	9	63	84	2.97	117	.245	.306	81-1	.222	3	68	9	1.8
1945	Phi A❖	13	13	.500	33	27	17-2	2	227.1	213	92	9	9	75	100	3.17	108	.251	.319	76-6	.171	-1*	80	6	1.1
1946	Phi A	5	7	.417	30	13	1	0	119.1	119	71	5	3	44	79	4.30	82	.254	.322	36-1	.139	-0	112	-12	-0.9
1947	Phi A	10	7	.588	44	0	0	12	80.2	70	30	4	0	33	33	2.90	131	.236	.313	16-2	.125	-0		8	1.6
1948	†Cle A	3	2	.600	45	0	0	**17**	59	55	21	3	0	27	14	2.90	140	.247	.328	6-2	.000	-0		8	1.1
Total	7	54	64	.458	241	97	46-3	35	999.2	931	441	38	27	399	424	3.37	106	.248	.325	316-16	.158	-3	82	19	5.0
CHULK, VINNIE Charles Vincent B 12.19.1978 Miami, FL BR/TR 6-2/180# d9.8																									
2003	Tor A	0	0	—	3	0	0	0-1	5.1	6	3	0	0	3-0	2	5.06	91	.273	.360	0-0	—	0		0	0.0
CHURCH, BUBBA Emory Nicholas B 9.12.1924 Birmingham, AL D 9.17.2001 Birmingham, AL BR/TR 6/180# d4.30																									
1950	Phi N	8	6	.571	31	18	8-2	1	142	113	50	12	0	56	50	2.73	149	.225	.303	44-3	.182	0*	84	21	1.9
1951	Phi N	15	11	.577	38	33	15-4	1	247	246	107	17	1	90	104	3.53	109	.261	.326	86-7	.256	5*	99	9	1.2
1952	Phi N	0	0	—	2	1	0	0	5	11	6	0	1	1	3	10.80	34	.440	.481	1-0	.000	-0	195	-4	-0.2
	Cin N	5	9	.357	29	22	5-1	0	153.1	173	85	21	3	48	47	4.34	87	.301	.358	50-1	.240	3*	98	-12	-0.7
	Year	5	9	.357	31	23	5-1	0	158.1	184	89	21	4	49	50	4.55	83	.307	.363	51-1	.235	3	102	-13	-0.9
1953	Cin N	3	3	.500	11	7	2	0	43.2	55	32	9	2	19	12	5.98	73	.318	.392	15-0	.267	1*	129	-8	-0.8
	Chi N	4	5	.444	27	11	1	1	104.1	115	67	16	2	49	47	5.00	89	.276	.355	33-1	.212	1	97	-6	-0.4
	Year	7	8	.467	38	18	3	1	148	170	72	25	4	68	59	5.29	84	.289	.366	48-1	.229	2	108	-16	-1.2
1954	Chi N	1	3	.250	7	3	1	0	14.2	21	18	8	0	13	8	9.82	43	.350	.459	5-0	.000	-1*	156	-9	-1.6
1955	Chi N	0	0	—	2	0	0	1	3.1	4	2	1	0	1-0	3	5.40	76	.286	.333	1-0	.000	-0*		0	0.0
Total	6	36	37	.493	147	95	32-7	4	713.1	738	367	84	9	277-0	274	4.10	97	.272	.342	235-12	.226	9	100	-9	-0.6
CHURCH, LEN Leonard B 3.21.1942 Chicago, IL D 4.22.1988 Richardson, TX BB/TR 6/190# d8.27																									
1966	Chi N	0	1	.000	4	0	0	0	6	10	6	1	0	7-2	3	7.50	49	.400	.515	1-0	.000	-0		-3	-0.4
CHURN, CHUCK Clarence Nottingham B 2.1.1930 Bridgetown, VA BR/TR 6-3/205# d4.18																									
1957	Pit N	0	0	—	5	0	0	0	8.1	9	4	1	0	4-1	4	4.32	88	.333	.406	1-0	.000	-0		0	0.0
1958	Cle A	0	0	—	6	0	0	0	8.2	12	7	1	0	5-0	4	6.23	59	.343	.425	0-0	—	0		-3	-0.1
1959	†LA N	3	2	.600	14	0	0	1	30.2	28	17	2	1	10-4	24	4.99	85	.255	.315	6-0	.167	0		-2	-0.2
Total	3	3	2	.600	25	0	0	1	47.2	49	28	4	1	19-5	32	5.10	79	.285	.352	7-0	.143	0		-5	-0.3
CIARDI, MARK Mark Thomas B 8.19.1961 New Brunswick, NJ BR/TR 6- /180# d4.9																									
1987	Mil A	1	1	.500	4	3	0	0-0	16.1	26	17	5	0	9-0	8	9.37	49	.361	.432	0-0	—	0	86	-8	-0.7
CICOTTE, AL Alva Warren "Bozo" B 12.23.1929 Melvindale, MI D 11.29.1982 Westland, MI BR/TR 6-3/185# d4.22																									
1957	NY A	2	2	.500	20	2	0	2	65.1	57	25	5	1	30-1	36	3.03	118	.237	.324	20-0	.150	-0	50	4	0.2
1958	Was A	0	3	.000	8	4	0	0	28	36	18	3	0	14-0	14	4.82	79	.316	.388	10-0	.200	-0*	59	-4	-0.4
	Det A	3	1	.750	14	2	0	0	43	50	19	1	0	15-1	21	3.56	113	.307	.359	17-0	.176	-1*	134	2	0.2
	Year	3	4	.429	22	6	0	0	71	86	25	4	0	29-1	35	4.06	97	.310	.371	27-0	.185	-1	83	-1	-0.2
1959	Cle A	3	1	.750	26	1	0	1	44	46	29	4	2	25-3	23	5.32	69	.299	.395	3-1	.333	1	192	-8	-0.7
1961	StL N	2	6	.250	29	7	0	1	75	83	47	16	2	34-2	51	5.28	83	.283	.362	21-0	.286	1	72	-5	-0.4
1962	Hou N	0	0	—	5	0	0	0	4.2	8	4	1	0	1-0	4	3.86	97	.381	.409	0-0	—	0		-1	0.0
Total	5	10	13	.435	102	16	0	4	260	280	142	30	5	119-7	149	4.36	90	.284	.361	71-1	.211	0	83	-12	-1.1
CICOTTE, EDDIE Edward Victor "Knuckles" B 6.19.1884 Springwells, MI D 5.5.1969 Detroit, MI BB/TR 5-9/175# d9.3																									
1905	Det A	1	1	.500	3	1	1	0	18	25	8	0	0	5	6	3.50	78	.329	.370	7-0	.429	1	78	-1	0.0
1908	Bos A	11	12	.478	39	24	17-2	2	207.1	198	77	0	11	59	95	2.43	101	.256	.318	72-0	.236	2*	109	2	0.5
1909	Bos A	14	5	.737	27	17	10-1	3	162.1	117	63	3	1	56	82	1.94	129	.207	.280	51-3	.235	3	134	5	0.9
1910	Bos A	15	11	.577	36	30	20-3	0	250	213	94	4	13	86	104	2.74	93	.233	.308	85-4	.141	-1	116	0	0.1
1911	Bos A	11	15	.423	35	25	16-1	0	220	236	121	2	4	73	106	2.82	116	.282	.342	71-5	.141	-2	99	7	0.5
1912	Bos A	1	3	.250	9	6	2	0	46	58	34	0	1	15	20	5.67	60	.319	.374	13-0	.154	0	137	-10	-0.7
	Chi A	9	7	.563	20	18	13-1	0	152	159	63	3	0	37	70	2.84	113	.277	.320	53-3	.245	1	97	7	0.9
	Year	10	10	.500	29	24	15-1	0	198	217	67	3	1	52	90	3.50	93	.287	.333	66-3	.227	1	108	-2	0.2
1913	Chi A	18	11	.621	41	30	18-3	1	268	224	77	2	3	73	121	1.58	185	.227	.283	91-4	.143	-3	93	36	4.1
1914	Chi A	11	16	.407	45	30	15-4	3	269.1	220	96	0	3	72	122	2.04	132	.232	.288	86-6	.163	-1	79	17	2.1
1915	Chi A	13	12	.520	39	26	15-1	3	223.1	216	89	2	6	48	106	3.02	99	.261	.306	67-10	.209	1*	121	3	0.4
1916	Chi A	15	7	**.682**	44	19	11-2	5	187	138	56	1	1	70	91	1.78	155	.218	.296	57-8	.211	2	143	18	2.6
1917	†Chi A	**28**	12	.700	49	35	29-7	4	**346.2**	246	76	2	3	70	150	**1.53**	**174**	.203	**.248**	112-8	.179	1	105	**45**	**5.7**
1918	Chi A	12	19	.387	38	30	24-1	2	266	275	102	2	2	40	104	2.77	99	.271	.300	86-1	.163	2	84	1	0.2

Year	Tm Lg	W	L	Pct	G	GS	CG-Sho	SV-BS	IP	H	R	HR	HB	BB-IB	SO	ERA	AERA	OAV	OOB	AB-SH	AVG	PB	Sup	APR	PW
1919	†Chi A	**29**	7	**.806**	40	35	**30**-5	1	**306.2**	256	77	5	2	49	110	1.82	175	.228	.261	99-11	.202	1	108	47	5.5
1920	Chi A	21	10	.677	37	35	28-4	2	303.1	316	128	6	2	74	87	3.26	115	.275	.320	112-4	.196	-3	121	19	1.5
Total	14	209	148	.585	502	361	249-35	24	3226	2897	1161	32	52	827	1374	2.38	123	.245	.297	1062-67	.186	4	108	196	24.3
CIMINO, PETE Peter William B 10.17.1942 Philadelphia, PA BR/TR 6-2/195# d9.22																									
1965	Min A	0	0	—	1	0	0	0	1	0	0	0	0	0-0	0	0.00	—	.000	.000	0-0	—	0		0	0.0
1966	Min A	2	5	.286	35	0	0	4	64.2	53	27	4	1	30-3	57	2.92	123	.222	.310	6-1	.000	-0		4	0.3
1967	Cal A	3	3	.500	46	1	0	1	88.1	73	38	12	2	31-4	80	3.26	96	.229	.297	12-0	.417	2	111	-2	0.0
1968	Cal A	0	0	—	4	0	0	0	7	7	5	0	0	4-0	2	2.57	113	.259	.355	0-0	—	0		-1	-0.1
Total	4	5	8	.385	86	1	0	5	161	133	70	16	3	65-7	139	3.07	108	.226	.304	18-1	.278	1	111	1	0.2
CIMORELLI, FRANK Frank Thomas B 8.2.1968 Poughkeepsie, NY BR/TR 6/175# d4.30																									
1994	StL N	0	0	—	11	0	0	1-0	13.1	20	14	0	2	10-2	1	8.78	47	.345	.444	2-0	.000	-0		-7	-0.4
CIOLA, LOU Louis Alexander B 9.6.1922 Norfolk, VA D 10.18.1981 Austin, MN BR/TR 5-9/165# d7.25 Mil 1944-46																									
1943	Phi A	1	3	.250	12	3	2	0	43.2	48	33	2	1	22	7	5.56	61	.273	.357	18-0	.167	-1	157	-11	-1.0
CISCO, GALEN Galen Bernard B 3.7.1936 St.Marys, OH BR/TR 5-11/215# d6.11 C28																									
1961	Bos A	2	4	.333	17	8	0	0	52.1	67	40	5	0	28-0	26	6.71	62	.325	.397	10-3	.100	-0*	72	-12	-1.2
1962	Bos A	4	7	.364	23	9	1	0	83	95	66	11	3	50-1	43	6.72	61	.292	.387	25-0	.080	-1	77	-21	-2.4
	NY N	1	1	.500	4	2	1	0	19.1	15	7	0	3	11-2	13	3.26	128	.208	.337	7-0	.000	-1	63	2	0.1
1963	NY N	7	15	.318	51	17	1	0	155.2	165	88	15	7	64-1	81	4.34	80	.273	.348	38-2	.132	0	62	-14	-1.8
1964	NY N	6	19	.240	36	25	5-2	0	191.2	182	85	17	6	54-4	78	3.62	99	.256	.311	54-6	.111	-0	83	0	0.1
1965	NY N	4	8	.333	35	17	1-1	0	112.1	119	63	12	1	51-2	58	4.49	79	.272	.348	27-4	.259	2	102	-11	-1.0
1967	Bos A	0	1	.000	11	0	0	1	22.1	21	10	4	0	8-0	8	3.63	96	.266	.326	3-0	.000	-0		0	-0.1
1969	KC A	1	1	.500	15	0	0	1-0	22.1	17	11	4	0	15-0	18	3.63	102	.215	.340	0-0	—	0		0	0.0
Total	7	25	56	.309	192	78	9-3	2-0	659	681	370	68	20	281-10	325	4.56	81	.271	.346	164-15	.128	0	80	-56	-6.3
CITARELLA, RALPH Ralph Alexander B 2.7.1958 East Orange, NJ BR/TR 6/180# d9.13																									
1983	StL N	0	0	—	6	0	0	0-0	11	8	2	0	0	3-1	4	1.64	222	.205	.262	1-0	.000	-0		3	0.1
1984	StL N	0	1	.000	10	2	0	0-0	22.1	20	9	0	3	7-2	15	3.63	96	.238	.319	4-0	.250	0	165	0	0.0
1987	Chi A	0	0	—	5	0	0	0-0	11	13	9	4	2	4-0	9	7.36	62	.302	.388	0-0	—	0		-3	-0.1
Total	3	0	1	.000	21	2	0	0-0	44.1	41	20	4	5	14-3	28	4.06	93	.247	.324	5-0	.200	0	165	0	0.0
CLANCY, JIM James B 12.18.1955 Chicago, IL BR/TR 6-4/220# d7.26																									
1977	Tor A	4	9	.308	13	13	4-1	0-0	76.2	80	47	7	0	47-1	44	5.05	83	.280	.374	0-0	—	0	82	-6	-0.9
1978	Tor A	10	12	.455	31	30	7	0-0	193.2	199	96	10	1	91-1	106	4.09	96	.270	.347	0-0	—	0	76	-4	-0.4
1979	Tor A	2	7	.222	12	11	2	0-0	63.2	65	44	8	0	31-0	33	5.51	79	.272	.349	0-0	—	0	72	-8	-0.9
1980	Tor A	13	16	.448	34	34	15-2	0-0	250.2	217	108	19	2	128-4	152	3.30	131	.233	.326	0-0	—	0	68	24	2.6
1981	Tor A	6	12	.333	22	22	2	0-0	125	126	77	12	5	64-0	56	4.90	81	.262	.352	0-0	—	0	83	-12	-1.7
1982	Tor A★	16	14	.533	40	**40**	11-3	0-0	266.2	251	122	26	2	77-1	139	3.71	121	.248	.301	0-0	—	0	87	21	2.0
1983	Tor A	15	11	.577	34	34	11-1	0-0	223	238	115	23	1	61-0	99	3.91	110	.271	.315	0-0	—	0	102	6	0.5
1984	Tor A	13	15	.464	36	**36**	5	0-0	219.2	249	132	25	3	88-2	118	5.12	80	.287	.353	0-0	—	0	93	-22	-2.4
1985	†Tor A	9	6	.600	23	23	1	0-0	128.2	117	54	15	0	37-0	66	3.78	111	.241	.292	0-0	—	0	113	9	0.9
1986	Tor A	14	14	.500	34	34	6-3	0-0	219.1	202	100	24	4	63-0	126	3.94	107	.243	.296	0-0	—	0	100	9	1.1
1987	Tor A	15	11	.577	37	37	5-1	0-0	241.1	234	103	24	1	80-5	180	3.54	127	.255	.314	0-0	—	0	105	26	2.5
1988	Tor A	11	13	.458	36	31	4	1-0	196.1	207	106	26	9	47-3	118	4.49	88	.272	.321	0-0	—	0	102	-11	-1.2
1989	Hou N	7	14	.333	33	26	1	0-0	147	155	100	13	0	66-15	91	5.08	67	.269	.342	41-7	.146	-0	84	-32	-4.2
1990	Hou N	2	8	.200	33	10	0	1-1	76	100	58	4	3	33-9	44	6.51	57	.322	.387	14-2	.214	0	63	-22	-2.6
1991	Hou N	0	3	.000	30	0	0	5-1	55	37	19	5	0	20-3	33	2.78	126	.193	.266	3-1	.000	-0		5	0.2
	†Atl N	3	2	.600	24	0	0	3-2	34.2	36	23	3	1	14-1	17	5.71	68	.267	.336	3-0	.000	-0		-6	-0.9
	Year	3	5	.375	54	0	0	8-3	89.2	73	45	8	1	34-4	50	3.91	93	.223	.295	6-1	.000	-1		-2	-0.7
Total	15	140	167	.456	472	381	74-11	10-4	2517.1	2513	1304	244	32	947-45	1422	4.23	98	.261	.326	61-10	.148	-0	91	-23	-5.4
CLARK, BRYAN Bryan Donald B 7.12.1956 Madera, CA BL/TL 6-2/185# d4.11																									
1981	Sea A	2	5	.286	29	9	1	2-3	93.1	92	54	3	1	55-4	52	4.34	89	.261	.359	0-0	—	0*	88	-7	-0.4
1982	Sea A	5	2	.714	37	5	1-1	0-0	114.2	104	44	6	0	58-2	70	2.75	155	.241	.330	0-0	—	0	99	16	1.0
1983	Sea A	7	10	.412	41	17	2	0-0	162.1	160	82	14	3	72-6	76	3.94	109	.261	.340	0-0	—	0	78	5	0.6
1984	Tor A	1	2	.333	20	3	0	0-0	45.2	66	33	6	1	22-2	21	5.91	69	.342	.410	0-0	—	0	110	-9	-0.5
1985	Cle A	3	4	.429	31	3	0	2-2	62.2	78	47	8	0	34-2	24	6.32	65	.311	.390	0-0	—	0	81	-14	-1.4
1986	Chi A	0	0	—	5	0	0	0-0	8	8	4	0	0	2-0	5	4.50	96	.276	.323	0-0	—	0		0	0.0
1987	Chi A	0	0	—	11	0	0	0-0	18.2	19	5	1	0	8-0	8	2.41	191	.297	.365	0-0	—	0		5	0.2
1990	Sea A	2	0	1.000	12	0	0	0-0	11	9	4	0	0	10-0	3	3.27	121	.237	.396	0-0	—	0		1	0.2
Total	8	20	23	.465	186	37	4-1	4-5	516.1	536	273	38	5	261-16	259	4.15	100	.272	.356	0-0	—	0	85	-3	-0.3
CLARK, ED Edward C. B Cincinnati, OH d7.4																									
1886	Phi AA	0	1	.000	1	1	1	0	8	10	8	2	2	2	2	6.75	52	.294	.368	2	.000	-0	0	-2	-0.2
1891	Col AA	0	0	—	1	0	0	0	2	2	0	0	0	0	1	0.00	—	.250	.250	1	.000	-0		1	0.0
Total	2	0	1	.000	2	1	1	0	10	12	8	2	2	2	3	5.40	65	.286	.348	3	.000	-0	0	-1	-0.2
CLARK, GEORGE George Myron B 5.19.1891 Smithland, IA D 11.14.1940 Sioux City, IA BR/TL 6/190# d5.16																									
1913	NY A	0	1	.000	11	1	0	0	19	22	23	1	3	19	5	9.00	33	.278	.436	4-0	.500	1	50	-11	-0.5
CLARK, GINGER Harvey Daniel B 3.7.1879 Wooster, OH D 5.10.1943 Lake Charles, LA BR/TR 5-11/165# d8.11																									
1902	Cle A	1	0	1.000	1	0	0	0	6	10	6	0	1	3	1	6.00	57	.370	.452	4-0	.500	1		-2	-0.2
CLARK, MARK Mark Willard B 5.12.1968 Bath, IL BR/TR 6-5/225# d9.6																									
1991	StL N	1	1	.500	7	2	0	0-0	22.1	17	10	3	0	11-0	13	4.03	92	.215	.301	7-1	.000	-1	85	0	-0.1
1992	StL N	3	10	.231	20	20	1-1	0-0	113.1	117	59	12	0	36-2	44	4.45	76	.265	.318	36-4	.139	-1	96	-13	-1.5
1993	Cle A	7	5	.583	26	15	1	0-0	109.1	119	55	18	1	25-1	57	4.28	101	.279	.320	0-0	—	0	96	2	0.1
1994	Cle A	11	3	.786	20	20	4-1	0-0	127.1	133	61	14	4	40-0	60	3.82	124	.273	.329	0-0	—	0	127	13	1.3
1995	Cle A	9	7	.563	22	21	2	0-0	124.2	143	77	13	4	42-0	68	5.27	89	.288	.344	0-0	—	0	101	-7	-0.7
1996	NY N	14	11	.560	32	32	2	0-0	212.1	217	98	20	3	48-8	142	3.43	117	.265	.306	69-10	.043	-5	110	12	0.7
1997	NY N	8	7	.533	23	22	1	0-0	142	158	74	18	3	47-2	72	4.25	95	.289	.347	43-4	.047	-2	99	-3	-0.5
	Chi N	6	1	.857	9	9	2	0-0	63	55	22	6	1	12-1	51	2.86	151	.226	.264	23-2	.000	-2	112	10	0.8
	Year	14	8	.636	32	31	3	0-0	205	213	27	24	4	59-3	123	3.82	108	.270	.322	66-6	.030	-4	102	7	0.3
1998	†Chi N	9	14	.391	33	33	2-1	0-0	213.2	236	116	23	4	48-4	161	4.84	91	.278	.318	62-8	.065	-3	87	-7	-1.0
1999	Tex A	3	7	.300	15	15	0	0-0	74.1	103	73	17	1	34-1	44	8.60	59	.329	.392	2-0	.000	-0	103	-27	-2.8
2000	Tex A	3	5	.375	12	8	0	0-0	44	66	42	10	3	24-2	16	7.98	63	.347	.425	0-0	—	0	108	-14	-1.9
Total	10	74	71	.510	219	197	15-3	0-0	1246.1	1364	687	154	24	367-21	728	4.61	93	.279	.330	242-29	.058	-14	103	-34	-5.6
CLARK, MIKE Michael John B 2.12.1922 Camden, NJ D 1.25.1996 Camden, NJ BR/TR 6-4/190# d7.27																									
1952	StL N	2	0	1.000	12	4	0	0	25.1	32	18	2	0	14	10	6.04	61	.311	.393	5-0	.000	-1	150	-6	-0.5
1953	StL N	1	0	1.000	23	2	0	1	35.2	46	21	2	2	21	17	4.79	89	.315	.408	6-0	.000	-1	115	-2	-0.2
Total	2	3	0	1.000	35	6	0	1	61	78	39	4	2	35	27	5.31	76	.313	.402	11-0	.000	-1	133	-8	-0.7
CLARK, PHIL Philip James B 10.3.1932 Albany, GA BR/TR 6-3/210# d4.15																									
1958	StL N	0	1	.000	7	0	0	1	7.2	11	5	2	0	3-0	1	3.52	117	.355	.412	1-0	.000	-0*		0	-0.1
1959	StL N	0	1	.000	7	0	0	0	7	8	11	0	0	8-1	5	12.86	33	.286	.444	0-0	—	0		-6	-0.7
Total	2	0	2	.000	14	0	0	1	14.2	19	16	2	0	11-1	6	7.98	52	.322	.429	1-0	.000	-0		-6	-0.8
CLARK, RICKEY Rickey Charles B 3.21.1946 Mt.Clemens, MI BR/TR 6-2/170# d4.22																									
1967	Cal A	12	11	.522	32	30	1-1	0	174	144	69	15	6	69-0	81	2.59	121	.224	.303	50-9	.040	-4	100	6	0.4
1968	Cal A	1	11	.083	21	17	0	0	94.1	74	51	4	1	54-1	60	3.53	82	.217	.323	28-3	.107	-1	92	-11	-1.5
1969	Cal A	0	0	—	6	1	0	0-0	9.2	12	6	2	0	7-1	6	5.59	62	.300	.404	2-0	.500	0	25	-2	-0.1
1971	Cal A	2	1	.667	11	7	1-1	1-0	44	36	15	6	2	28-2	28	2.86	113	.220	.340	15-1	.267	1	122	2	0.2

Year	Tm Lg	W	L	Pct	G	GS	CG-Sho	SV-BS	IP	H	R	HR	HB	BB-IB	SO	ERA	AERA	OAV	OOB	AB-SH	AVG	PB	Sup	APR	PW
1972	Cal A	4	9	.308	26	15	2	1-1	109.2	105	59	10	2	55-2	61	4.51	65	.261	.345	31-1	.097	-1*	73	-19	-2.3
Total	5	19	32	.373	96	70	4-2	2-1	431.2	371	200	37	11	213-6	236	3.38	90	.233	.325	126-14	.103	-5	94	-24	-3.3

CLARK, BOB Robert William B 8.22.1897 Newport, PA D 5.18.1944 Carlsbad, NM BR/TR 6-3/188# d5.26

Year	Tm Lg	W	L	Pct	G	GS	CG-Sho	SV-BS	IP	H	R	HR	HB	BB-IB	SO	ERA	AERA	OAV	OOB	AB-SH	AVG	PB	Sup	APR	PW
1920	Cle A	1	2	.333	11	2	2-1	0	42	59	19	0	1	13	8	3.43	111	.383	.435	10-0	.200	-0	73	2	0.1
1921	Cle A	0	0	—	5	0	0	0	9.1	23	17	2	1	6	2	14.46	29	.511	.577	3-0	.000	-1		-10	-0.5
Total	2	1	2	.333	16	2	2-1	0	51.1	82	36	2	2	19	10	5.44	71	.412	.468	13-0	.154	-1	73	-8	-0.4

CLARK, TERRY Terry Lee B 10.18.1960 Los Angeles, CA BR/TR 6-2/196# d7.7

Year	Tm Lg	W	L	Pct	G	GS	CG-Sho	SV-BS	IP	H	R	HR	HB	BB-IB	SO	ERA	AERA	OAV	OOB	AB-SH	AVG	PB	Sup	APR	PW
1988	Cal A	6	6	.500	15	15	2-1	0-0	94	120	54	8	0	31-6	39	5.07	76	.323	.370	0-0	—	0	123	-11	-1.2
1989	Cal A	0	2	.000	4	2	0	0-0	11	13	8	0	0	3-0	7	4.91	78	.310	.348	0-0	—	0	83	-2	-0.3
1990	Hou N	0	0	—	1	1	0	0-0	4	9	7	0	0	3-0	2	13.50	28	.429	.500	2-0	.500	0	194	-5	-0.2
1995	Atl N	0	0	—	3	0	0	0-0	3.2	3	2	0	0	5-0	2	4.91	87	.231	.444	0-0	—	0		0	0.0
	Bal A	2	5	.286	38	0	0	1-0	39	40	15	3	1	15-5	18	3.46	137	.276	.346	0-0	—	0		6	0.9
1996	KC A	1	1	.500	12	0	0	0-0	17.1	28	15	3	0	7-1	12	7.79	64	.350	.402	0-0	—	0		-5	-0.5
	Hou N	0	2	.000	5	0	0	0-0	6.1	16	10	1	1	2-1	5	11.37	34	.471	.514	0-0	—	0		-6	-1.1
1997	Cle A	0	3	.000	4	4	0	0-0	26.1	29	21	3	0	13-1	13	6.15	76	.284	.359	0-0	—	0	44	-5	-0.4
	Tex A	1	4	.200	9	5	0	0-0	30.2	41	20	3	2	10-0	11	5.87	82	.325	.384	1-0	1.000	0	42	-3	-0.3
	Year	1	7	.125	13	9	0	0-0	57	70	22	6	2	23-1	24	6.00	79	.307	.373	1-0	1.000	0	43	-8	-0.7
Total	6	10	23	.303	91	27	2-1	1-0	232.1	299	152	21	4	89-14	109	5.54	78	.320	.378	3-0	.667	1	89	-31	-3.1

CLARK, OTEY William Otis B 5.22.1915 Boscobel, WI BR/TR 6-1.5/190# d4.17

Year	Tm Lg	W	L	Pct	G	GS	CG-Sho	SV-BS	IP	H	R	HR	HB	BB-IB	SO	ERA	AERA	OAV	OOB	AB-SH	AVG	PB	Sup	APR	PW
1945	Bos A	4	4	.500	12	9	4-1	0	82	86	33	6	1	19	20	3.07	111	.268	.311	24-3	.208	0	75	3	0.1

CLARK, WATTY William Watson "Lefty" B 5.16.1902 St.Joseph, LA D 3.4.1972 Clearwater, FL BL/TL 6-0.5/175# d5.28

Year	Tm Lg	W	L	Pct	G	GS	CG-Sho	SV-BS	IP	H	R	HR	HB	BB-IB	SO	ERA	AERA	OAV	OOB	AB-SH	AVG	PB	Sup	APR	PW
1924	Cle A	1	3	.250	12	1	0	0	25.2	38	27	0	2	14	6	7.01	61	.345	.429	9-0	.222	1	20	-9	-1.0
1927	Bro N	7	2	.778	27	3	1	2	73.2	74	23	2	0	19	32	2.32	171	.265	.312	21-1	.143	-1	86	**13**	1.5
1928	Bro N	12	9	.571	40	19	10-2	3	194.2	193	75	4	1	50	85	2.68	148	.259	.306	66-6	.152	-2	105	28	2.6
1929	Bro N	16	19	.457	41	**39**	19-3	1	**279**	295	136	14	3	71	140	3.74	123	.270	.316	97-4	.165	-3*	96	29	2.7
1930	Bro N	13	13	.500	44	24	9-1	6	200	209	110	20	0	38	81	4.18	117	.271	.306	68-1	.206	0	87	17	2.0
1931	Bro N	14	10	.583	34	28	16-3	1	233.1	243	86	4	1	52	96	3.20	119	.267	.308	84-3	.250	4	93	21	2.3
1932	Bro N	20	12	.625	40	**36**	19-2	0	273	282	122	10	4	49	99	3.49	109	.264	.299	97-4	.216	1	105	9	1.2
1933	Bro N	2	4	.333	11	8	4-1	1	50.2	61	29	2	3	6	14	4.80	67	.303	.333	13-2	.154	-0	68	-8	-0.9
	NY N	3	4	.429	16	5	0	0	44	58	25	3	1	11	11	4.70	68	.317	.359	11-0	.273	1	161	-6	-0.8
	Year	5	8	.385	27	13	4-1	1	94.2	119	31	5	4	17	25	4.75	68	.310	.346	24-2	.208	1	104	-15	-1.7
1934	NY N	1	2	.333	5	4	1	0	18.2	23	15	5	0	5	6	6.75	57	.295	.337	6-1	.167	0	78	-5	-0.7
	Bro N	2	0	1.000	17	1	0	0	25.1	40	19	0	1	9	10	5.33	73	.345	.397	8-0	.125	-1	111	-5	-0.4
	Year	3	2	.600	22	5	1	0	44	63	24	5	1	14	16	5.93	66	.325	.373	14-1	.143	-0	84	-10	-1.1
1935	Bro N	13	8	.619	33	25	11-1	0	207	215	93	11	1	28	35	3.30	120	.264	.289	79-3	.177	-0*	97	15	1.4
1936	Bro N	7	11	.389	33	16	1-1	2	120	162	73	11	0	28	28	4.43	93	.316	.351	39-0	.231	0	63	-4	-0.6
1937	Bro N	0	0	—	2	0	0	0	2.1	4	3	0	0	3	0	7.71	52	.308	.438	0-0	—	0		-1	0.0
Total	12	111	97	.534	355	209	91-14	16	1747.1	1897	836	86	17	383	643	3.66	112	.275	.315	598-25	.196	1	94	94	9.3

CLARKE, LEFTY Alan Thomas B 3.8.1896 Clarksville, MD D 3.11.1975 Cheverly, MD BB/TL 5-11/180# d10.2

Year	Tm Lg	W	L	Pct	G	GS	CG-Sho	SV-BS	IP	H	R	HR	HB	BB-IB	SO	ERA	AERA	OAV	OOB	AB-SH	AVG	PB	Sup	APR	PW
1921	Cin N	0	1	.000	1	1	1	0	5	7	7	0	0	2	1	5.40	66	.304	.360	1-0	.000	-0	0	-2	-0.4

CLARKE, HENRY Henry Tefft B 8.28.1875 Bellevue, NE D 3.28.1950 Colorado Springs, CO BR/TR d6.26

Year	Tm Lg	W	L	Pct	G	GS	CG-Sho	SV-BS	IP	H	R	HR	HB	BB-IB	SO	ERA	AERA	OAV	OOB	AB-SH	AVG	PB	Sup	APR	PW
1897	Cle N	0	4	.000	5	4	3	0	30.2	32	29	4	3	12	3	5.87	76	.267	.348	25-0	.280	0*	83	-5	-0.5
1898	Chi N	1	0	1.000	1	1	1	0	9	8	4	0	1	5	1	2.00	179	.235	.350	4-0	.250	0*	99	1	0.1
Total	2	1	4	.200	6	5	4	0	39.2	40	33	4	4	17	4	4.99	86	.260	.349	29-0	.276	0	86	-4	-0.4

CLARKE, RUFE Rufus Rivers B 4.13.1900 Estill, SC D 2.8.1983 Columbia, SC BR/TR 6-1/203# d9.3 b-Sumpter

Year	Tm Lg	W	L	Pct	G	GS	CG-Sho	SV-BS	IP	H	R	HR	HB	BB-IB	SO	ERA	AERA	OAV	OOB	AB-SH	AVG	PB	Sup	APR	PW
1923	Det A	1	1	.500	5	0	0	0	6	6	3	0	1	6	2	4.50	86	.300	.481	0-0	—	0		0	0.0
1924	Det A	0	0	—	2	0	0	0	5.1	3	2	0	1	5	1	3.38	122	.158	.360	1-0	.000	-0		1	0.0
Total	2	1	1	.500	7	0	0	0	11.1	9	5	0	2	11	3	3.97	100	.231	.423	1-0	.000	-0		1	0.0

CLARKE, STAN Stanley Martin B 8.9.1960 Toledo, OH BL/TL 6-1/180# d6.7

Year	Tm Lg	W	L	Pct	G	GS	CG-Sho	SV-BS	IP	H	R	HR	HB	BB-IB	SO	ERA	AERA	OAV	OOB	AB-SH	AVG	PB	Sup	APR	PW
1983	Tor A	1	1	.500	10	0	0	0-1	11	10	4	2	0	5-0	7	3.27	132	.256	.333	0-0	—	0		1	0.2
1985	Tor A	0	0	—	4	0	0	0-1	4	3	2	1	0	2-0	2	4.50	94	.214	.313	0-0	—	0		0	0.0
1986	Tor A	0	1	.000	10	0	0	0-0	12.2	18	13	4	0	10-1	9	9.24	46	.375	.475	0-0	—	0		-6	-0.4
1987	Sea A	2	2	.500	22	0	0	0-0	23	31	14	7	0	10-1	13	5.48	86	.333	.387	0-0	—	0		-1	-0.2
1989	KC A	0	2	.000	2	2	0	0-0	7	14	12	2	0	4-0	2	15.43	25	.438	.500	0-0	—	0	35	-8	-1.2
1990	StL N	0	0	—	2	0	0	0-0	3.1	2	1	0	0	0-0	3	2.70	142	.167	.167	0-0	—	0		0	0.0
Total	6	3	6	.333	50	2	0	0-2	61	78	46	16	0	31-2	36	6.79	64	.328	.398	0-0	—	0	35	-14	-1.6

CLARKE, WEBBO Vibert Ernesto B 6.8.1928 Colon, Panama D 6.14.1970 Cristobal, Canal Zone BL/TL 6/165# d9.4

Year	Tm Lg	W	L	Pct	G	GS	CG-Sho	SV-BS	IP	H	R	HR	HB	BB-IB	SO	ERA	AERA	OAV	OOB	AB-SH	AVG	PB	Sup	APR	PW
1955	Was A	0	0	—	7	2	0	0	21.1	17	11	2	0	14-0	9	4.64	83	.221	.341	6-0	.167	-0	151	-1	-0.1

CLARKE, DAD William H. B 1.7.1865 Oswego, NY D 6.3.1911 Lorain, OH BB/TR 5-7/160# d4.23

Year	Tm Lg	W	L	Pct	G	GS	CG-Sho	SV-BS	IP	H	R	HR	HB	BB-IB	SO	ERA	AERA	OAV	OOB	AB-SH	AVG	PB	Sup	APR	PW
1888	Chi N	1	0	1.000	2	2	1	0	16	23	17	2	2	6	6	5.06	60	.315	.383	7	.286	2	223	-4	0.0
1891	Col AA	1	2	.333	4	3	2	0	21	30	21	0	1	16	2	6.86	50	.326	.431	9	.111	0	150	-7	-0.7
1894	NY N	3	4	.429	15	6	5	1	84	114	76	3	3	26	15	4.93	107	.320	.371	37-0	.216	-0*	108	1	0.0
1895	NY N	18	15	.545	37	30	27-1	1	281.2	336	174	5	11	60	67	3.39	137	.292	.333	121-0	.240	-2	105	33	2.6
1896	NY N	17	24	.415	48	40	33-1	1	351	431	246	9	11	60	66	4.26	99	.300	.332	147-1	.204	-4*	89	-5	-1.0
1897	NY N	2	1	.667	6	4	2	0	31	43	34	1	2	11	10	6.10	68	.326	.386	18-0	.167	-1*	137	-8	-0.6
	Lou N	2	4	.333	7	6	6	0	54.2	74	33	3	2	10	7	3.95	108	.320	.354	22-0	.227	-1	56	3	0.2
	Year	4	5	.444	13	10	8	0	85.2	117	36	4	4	21	17	4.73	89	.322	.366	40-0	.200	-2	88	-7	-0.4
1898	Lou N	0	1	.000	1	1	1	0	9	10	7	1	2	2	1	5.00	72	.278	.350	3-0	.000	-1	139	-2	-0.2
Total	7	44	51	.463	120	92	77-2	3	848.1	1061	608	24	34	191	174	4.17	106	.302	.344	364-1	.214	-6	100	11	0.3

CLARKSON, DAD Arthur Hamilton B 8.31.1866 Cambridge, MA D 2.5.1911 Somerville, MA BR/TR 5-10/165# d8.20 b-John b-Walter

Year	Tm Lg	W	L	Pct	G	GS	CG-Sho	SV-BS	IP	H	R	HR	HB	BB-IB	SO	ERA	AERA	OAV	OOB	AB-SH	AVG	PB	Sup	APR	PW
1891	NY N	1	2	.333	5	2	1	0	28	24	23	0	3	18	11	2.89	111	.222	.349	9	.444	2	121	-1	0.1
1892	Bos N	1	0	1.000	1	1	1	0	7	5	1	0	0	3	0	1.29	273	.192	.276	3	.000	-0	54	2	0.2
1893	StL N	12	9	.571	24	21	17-1	0	186.1	194	116	4	14	79	37	3.48	136	.260	.342	75	.133	-5*	82	23	1.6
1894	StL N	8	17	.320	32	32	24-1	0	233.1	318	236	9	11	117	46	6.36	85	.321	.399	88-0	.182	-4*	74	-26	-2.1
1895	StL N	1	6	.143	7	7	7	0	61	91	66	7	2	26	9	7.38	65	.340	.402	23-0	.043	-3	53	-16	-1.5
	Bal N	12	3	.800	20	14	10	0	142	169	84	5	4	64	23	3.87	123	.291	.365	57-3	.140	-4	119	13	0.8
	Year	13	9	.591	27	21	17	0	203	260	92	12	6	90	32	4.92	97	.306	.377	80-3	.112	-7	96	0	-0.7
1896	Bal N	4	2	.667	7	4	3	0	47	72	40	1	2	18	7	4.98	86	.348	.405	18-1	.278	0	116	-5	-0.5
Total	6	39	39	.500	96	81	63-2	0	704.2	873	566	26	36	325	133	4.90	99	.298	.376	273-4	.161	-14	85	-10	-1.4

CLARKSON, JOHN John Gibson B 7.1.1861 Cambridge, MA D 2.4.1909 Belmont, MA BR/TR 5-10/155# d5.2 HF1963 b-Dad b-Walter

Year	Tm Lg	W	L	Pct	G	GS	CG-Sho	SV-BS	IP	H	R	HR	HB	BB-IB	SO	ERA	AERA	OAV	OOB	AB-SH	AVG	PB	Sup	APR	PW
1882	Wor N	1	2	.333	3	3	2	0	24	49	31	0		2	3	4.50	69	.392	.402	11	.364	1	74	-5	-0.4
1884	Chi N	10	3	.769	14	13	12	0	118	94	64	10		25	102	2.14	147	.208	.249	84	.262	4*	168	10	1.4
1885	†Chi N	**53**	16	.768	**70**	**70**	**68-10**	0	**623**	497	255	21		97	**308**	1.85	163	.208	.239	283	.216	2*	131	**71**	**7.3**
1886	†Chi N	36	17	.679	55	55	50-3	0	466.2	419	248	19		86	313	2.41	150	.229	.264	210	.233	1	110	50	5.0
1887	Chi N	**38**	21	.644	**60**	**59**	**56**-2	0	**523**	513	283	19	8	92	**237**	3.08	146	.246	.281	215	.242	2*	101	**76**	**7.5**
1888	Bos N	33	20	.623	54	54	53-3	0	**483.1**	448	247	17	10	119	223	2.76	104	.236	.284	205	.195	2*	129	9	1.2
1889	Bos N	**49**	19	**.721**	**73**	**72**	**68-8**	1	**620**	589	280	16	17	203	**284**	**2.73**	**153**	.243	**.306**	262	.206	0	85	**93**	**8.9**
1890	Bos N	26	18	.591	44	44	43-2	0	383	370	186	14	16	140	138	3.27	115	.246	.316	173	.249	3*	91	28	2.8
1891	Bos N	33	19	.635	55	51	47-3	**3**	460.2	435	244	18	15	154	141	2.79	131	.240	.305	187	.225	3	84	41	4.4
1892	Bos N	8	6	.571	16	16	15-4	0	145.2	115	65	4	5	60	48	2.35	150	.208	.292	57	.228	1	107	15	1.4
	†Cle N	17	10	.630	29	28	27-1	1	243.1	235	132	4	4	72	91	2.55	133	.244	.299	101	.139	-5	118	18	1.1
	Year	25	16	.610	45	44	42-5	1	389	350	138	8	9	132	139	2.48	139	.231	.296	158	.171	-4	114	36	2.5
1893	Cle N	16	17	.485	36	35	31	0	295	358	240	11	5	95	62	4.45	110	.291	.344	131	.206	-4*	110	10	0.7

Year	Tm Lg	W	L	Pct	G	GS	CG-Sho	SV-BS	IP	H	R	HR	HB	BB-IB	SO	ERA	AERA	OAV	OOB	AB-SH	AVG	PB	Sup	APR	PW
1894	Cle N	8	10	.444	22	18	13-1	0	150.2	173	109	6	0	46	28	4.42	124	.285	.335	55-4	.200	-3	93	16	1.2
Total	12	328	178	.648	531	518	485-37	5	4536.1	4295	2384	159	80	1191	1978	2.81	134	.240	.291	1974-4	.219	9	106	432	42.5
CLARKSON, WALTER Walter Hamilton B 11.3.1878 Cambridge, MA D 10.10.1946 Cambridge, MA BR/TR 5-10/150# d7.2 b-Dad b-John																									
1904	NY A	1	2	.333	13	4	2	1	66.1	63	42	3	10	25	43	5.02	54	.251	.343	26-0	.269	2	105	-14	-0.6
1905	NY A	3	3	.500	9	4	3	0	46	40	26	1	2	13	35	3.91	75	.235	.297	19-0	.053	-2	72	-4	-0.7
1906	NY A	9	4	.692	32	16	9-3	0	151	135	59	6	5	55	64	2.32	128	.242	.316	51-3	.157	-1	106	7	0.4
1907	NY A	1	1	.500	5	2	0	1	17.1	19	12	1	2	8	3	6.23	45	.279	.372	7-0	.286	0	145	-4	-0.5
	Cle A	4	6	.400	17	10	9-1	0	90.2	77	40	1	3	29	32	1.99	126	.232	.299	28-1	.036	-3	75	2	-0.2
	Year	5	7	.417	22	12	9-1	1	108	96	43	2	5	37	35	2.67	96	.240	.312	35-1	.086	-3	88	-3	-0.7
1908	Cle A	0	0	—	2	1	0	0	3.1	6	4	0	2	2	1	10.80	22	.400	.526	1-0	1.000	0	315	-3	-0.1
Total	5	18	16	.529	78	37	23-4	2	374.2	340	183	12	24	132	178	3.17	88	.244	.320	132-4	.152	-4	102	-16	-1.7
CLARKSON, BILL William Henry "Blackie" B 9.27.1898 Portsmouth, VA D 8.27.1971 Raleigh, NC BR/TR 5-11/160# d5.2																									
1927	NY N	3	9	.250	26	7	2	2	86.2	92	50	3	1	52	28	4.36	88	.280	.380	20-0	.050	-1*	44	-5	-0.8
1928	NY N	0	0	—	4	0	0	0	5.2	10	6	0	0	1	3	7.94	49	.455	.478	0-0	—	0		-3	-0.1
	Bos N	0	2	.000	19	2	0	0	34.2	53	29	2	1	22	8	6.75	58	.349	.434	3-0	.000	-0	0	-10	-0.5
	Year	0	2	.000	23	2	0	0	40.1	63	29	2	1	23	11	6.92	57	.362	.439	3-0	.000	-0	0	-14	-0.6
1929	Bos N	0	1	.000	2	1	0	0	7	16	10	0	0	4	0	10.29	45	.485	.541	2-0	.500	0	112	-5	-0.5
Total	3	3	12	.200	51	10	2	2	134	171	95	5	2	79	39	5.44	72	.319	.408	25-0	.080	-1	48	-23	-1.9
CLARY, MARTY Martin Keith B 4.3.1962 Detroit, MI BR/TR 6-4/190# d9.5																									
1987	Atl N	0	1	.000	7	1	0	0-0	14.2	20	13	2	1	4-0	7	6.14	71	.328	.373	1-0	.000	-0	62	-3	-0.2
1989	Atl N	4	3	.571	18	17	2-1	0-0	108.2	103	47	6	1	31-3	30	3.15	116	.249	.301	31-5	.161	0	88	4	0.3
1990	Atl N	1	10	.091	33	14	0	0-0	101.2	128	72	9	1	39-4	44	5.67	71	.308	.364	28-2	.000	-3	81	-17	-1.9
Total	3	5	14	.263	58	32	2-1	0-0	225	251	132	17	3	74-7	81	4.48	86	.282	.336	60-7	.083	-2	84	-16	-1.8
CLASET, GOWELL Gowell Sylvester "Lefty" B 11.26.1907 Battle Creek, MI D 3.8.1981 St.Petersburg, FL BB/TL 6-3.5/210# d4.12																									
1933	Phi A	2	0	1.000	8	1	0	0	11.1	23	15	1	0	11	1	9.53	45	.426	.523	2-0	.500	1	258	-7	-0.9
CLAUSEN, FRITZ Frederick William B 4.26.1869 New York, NY D 2.11.1960 Memphis, TN BR/TL 5-11/190# d7.23																									
1892	Lou N	9	13	.409	24	24	24-2	0	200	181	120	3	3	87	94	3.06	100	.232	.311	84	.155	-3	87	-3	-0.6
1893	Lou N	1	4	.200	5	5	3	0	33	41	25	2	1	22	4	6.00	73	.295	.395	14	.214	-1	89	-5	-0.5
	Chi N	6	2	.750	10	9	8	1	76	71	46	1	5	39	31	3.08	150	.240	.338	33	.121	-3	96	10	0.6
	Year	7	6	.538	15	14	11	1	109	112	52	3	6	61	35	3.96	115	.257	.357	47	.149	-4	93	9	0.1
1894	Chi N	0	1	.000	2	2	0	0	4.1	5	7	0	0	5	1	14.54	39	.294	.455	1-0	.000	-0	75	-3	-0.4
1896	Lou N	0	2	.000	2	2	1	0	11	17	13	1	3	6	4	6.55	66	.347	.448	4-0	.000	-1	123	-3	-0.4
Total	4	16	22	.421	43	42	36-2	1	324.1	315	211	7	12	159	134	3.64	100	.246	.334	136-0	.147	-8	93	-4	-1.3
CLAUSS, AL Albert Stanley "Lefty" B 6.24.1891 New Haven, CT D 9.13.1952 New Haven, CT BR/TL 5-10.5/178# d4.22																									
1913	Det A	0	1	.000	5	1	0	0	13.1	11	9	0	2	12	1	4.73	62	.224	.397	4-0	.000	-1	0	-2	-0.2
CLAUSSEN, BRANDON Brandon Allen B 5.1.1979 Rapid City, SD BR/TL 6-2/200# d6.28																									
2003	NY A	1	0	1.000	1	1	0	0-0	6.1	8	2	1	0	1-0	5	1.42	309	.296	.321	4-0	.250	0	189	2	0.3
CLAY, DANNY Danny Bruce B 10.24.1961 Sun Valley, CA BR/TR 6-1/190# d5.1																									
1988	Phi N	0	1	.000	17	0	0	0-0	24	27	17	5	0	21-2	12	6.00	59	.303	.432	2-1	.000	-0		-6	-0.4
CLAY, KEN Kenneth Earl B 4.6.1954 Lynchburg, VA BR/TR 6-3/195# d6.7																									
1977	†NY A	2	3	.400	21	3	0	1-1	55.2	53	32	6	1	24-3	20	4.37	91	.251	.329	0-0	—	0	129	-3	-0.3
1978	†NY A	3	4	.429	28	6	0	0-0	75.2	89	41	3	2	21-3	32	4.28	85	.291	.338	0-0	—	0	132	-6	-0.5
1979	NY A	1	7	.125	32	5	0	2-2	78.1	88	49	12	2	25-1	28	5.40	76	.291	.346	0-0	—	0	58	-11	-1.0
1980	Tex A	2	3	.400	8	8	0	0-0	43	43	24	4	3	29-2	17	4.60	85	.256	.373	0-0	—	0	109	-3	-0.3
1981	Sea A	2	7	.222	22	14	0	0-0	101	116	62	10	3	42-3	32	4.63	83	.294	.363	0-0	—	0	70	-10	-0.9
Total	5	10	24	.294	111	36	0	3-3	353.2	389	208	35	11	141-12	129	4.68	83	.281	.350	0-0	—	0	91	-33	-3.0
CLEAR, MARK Mark Alan B 5.27.1956 Los Angeles, CA BR/TR 6-4/215# d4.4																									
1979	†Cal A★	11	5	.688	52	0	0	14-7	109	87	48	6	3	68-5	98	3.63	112	.219	.333	0-0	—	0		6	0.9
1980	Cal A	11	11	.500	58	0	0	9-6	106.1	82	51	2	5	65-9	105	3.30	119	.216	.336	0-0	—	0		4	0.8
1981	Bos A	8	3	.727	34	0	0	9-5	76.2	69	36	11	2	51-2	82	4.11	94	.239	.357	0-0	—	0		0	-0.1
1982	Bos A☆	14	9	.609	55	0	0	14-9	105	92	39	11	7	61-6	109	3.00	144	.238	.348	0-0	—	0		14	2.9
1983	Bos A	4	5	.444	48	0	0	4-1	96	101	71	10	3	68-5	81	6.28	70	.273	.385	0-0	—	0		-18	-1.7
1984	Bos A	8	3	.727	47	0	0	8-2	67	47	38	2	2	70-3	76	4.03	104	.198	.378	0-0	—	0		-1	-0.1
1985	Bos A	1	3	.250	41	0	0	3-3	55.2	45	26	1	5	50-10	55	3.72	115	.225	.389	0-0	—	0		3	0.3
1986	Mil A	5	5	.500	59	0	0	16-3	73.2	53	23	4	1	36-2	85	2.20	197	.201	.295	0-0	—	0		16	2.6
1987	Mil A	8	5	.615	58	1	0	6-3	78.1	70	46	9	5	55-3	81	4.48	102	.239	.363	0-0	—	0	99	-1	-0.1
1988	Mil A	1	0	1.000	25	0	0	0-0	29	23	12	4	0	21-0	26	2.79	143	.215	.338	0-0	—	0		3	0.1
1990	Cal A	0	0	—	4	0	0	0-0	7.2	5	7	0	2	9-0	6	5.87	65	.200	.421	0-0	—	0		-2	-0.1
Total	11	71	49	.592	481	1	0	83-39	804.1	674	397	60	35	554-45	804	3.85	109	.228	.353	0-0	—	0	99	24	5.5
CLEARY, JOE Joseph Christopher "Fire" B 12.3.1918 Cork, Ireland BR/TR 5-9/150# d8.4																									
1945	Was A	0	0	—	1	0	0	0	0.1	5	7	0	0	3	1	189.00	2	.833	.889	0-0	—	0		-7	-0.3
CLEMENS, ROGER William Roger "Rocket" B 8.4.1962 Dayton, OH BR/TR 6-4/220# d5.15																									
1984	Bos A	9	4	.692	21	20	5-1	0-0	133.1	146	67	13	2	29-3	126	4.32	97	.271	.309	0-0	—	0	133	0	0.0
1985	Bos A	7	5	.583	15	15	3-1	0-0	98.1	83	38	5	3	37-0	74	3.29	130	.228	.303	0-0	—	0	86	11	1.3
1986	†Bos A★	**24**	4	**.857**	33	33	10-1	0-0	254	179	77	21	4	67-0	238	**2.48**	**168**	**.195**	**.252**	0-0	—	0	132	**48**	5.1
1987	Bos A	**20**	9	**.690**	36	36	**18-7**	0-0	281.2	248	100	19	9	83-4	256	2.97	153	.235	.295	0-0	—	0	111	**49**	**4.5**
1988	†Bos A★	18	12	.600	35	35	**14-8**	0-0	264	217	93	17	6	62-4	**291**	2.93	141	.220	.270	0-0	—	0	97	34	3.6
1989	Bos A	17	11	.607	35	35	8-3	0-0	253.1	215	101	20	8	93-5	230	3.13	131	.231	.305	0-0	—	0	100	26	2.7
1990	†Bos A☆	21	6	.778	31	31	7-**4**	0-0	228.1	193	59	7	7	54-3	209	**1.93**	**212**	.228	.278	0-0	—	0	94	**50**	**6.2**
1991	Bos A★	18	10	.643	35	**35**	13-**4**	0-0	**271.1**	219	93	15	5	65-12	**241**	**2.62**	**164**	.221	.270	0-0	—	0	95	**46**	**4.7**
1992	Bos A★	18	11	.621	32	32	11-**5**	0-0	246.2	203	80	11	9	62-5	208	**2.41**	**175**	.224	.278	0-0	—	0	87	**45**	**5.3**
1993	Bos A	11	14	.440	29	29	2-1	0-0	191.2	175	99	17	11	67-4	160	4.46	104	.244	.315	0-0	—	0	64	7	0.8
1994	Bos A	9	7	.563	24	24	3-1	0-0	170.2	124	62	15	4	71-1	168	2.85	**177**	**.203**	.288	0-0	—	0	71	38	3.2
1995	†Bos A	10	5	.667	23	23	0	0-0	140	141	70	15	14	60-0	132	4.18	117	.259	.346	0-0	—	0	108	11	1.1
1996	Bos A	10	13	.435	34	34	6-2	0-0	242.2	216	106	19	4	106-2	**257**	3.63	140	.237	.317	1-0	1.000	0	81	41	3.3
1997	Tor A★	**21**	7	.750	34	34	**9-3**	0-0	**264**	204	65	9	12	68-1	**292**	**2.05**	**225**	.213	**.273**	2-0	.500	1	91	**75**	**7.9**
1998	Tor A★	**20**	6	.769	33	33	5-3	0-0	234.2	169	78	11	7	88-0	**271**	**2.65**	**176**	**.197**	.277	4-1	.000	-0	91	**52**	**5.2**
1999	†NY A	14	10	.583	30	30	1-1	0-0	187.2	185	101	20	9	90-0	163	4.60	103	.261	.350	4-1	.000	-0	88	5	0.6
2000	†NY A	13	8	.619	32	32	1	0-0	204.1	184	96	26	10	84-0	188	3.70	131	.236	.317	3-0	.000	-0	93	24	2.2
2001	†NY A★	20	3	**.870**	33	33	0	0-0	220.1	205	94	19	5	72-1	213	3.51	128	.246	.309	2-0	.000	-0	121	24	2.3
2002	†NY A	13	6	.684	29	29	0	0-0	180	172	94	18	7	63-6	192	4.35	101	.250	.317	3-0	.667	1	115	2	0.3
2003	†NY A★	17	9	.654	33	33	1-1	0-0	211.2	199	99	24	5	58-1	190	3.91	112	.247	.299	1-1	.000	-0	107	12	1.4
Total	20	310	160	.660	607	606	117-46	0-0	4278.2	3677	1672	321	141	1379-52	4099	3.19	140	.231	.296	20-3	.200	2	98	600	61.7
CLEMENSEN, BILL William Melville B 6.20.1919 New Brunswick, NJ D 2.18.1994 Alta, CA BR/TR 6-1/193# d5.22 Mil 1942-45																									
1939	Pit N	0	1	.000	12	1	0	0	27	32	26	0	3	20	13	7.33	52	.311	.437	6-0	.333	1	23	-11	-0.4
1941	Pit N	1	0	1.000	2	1	1	0	13	7	5	0	0	7	4	2.77	130	.159	.275	4-0	.000	-1	71	1	0.0
1946	Pit N	0	0	—	1	0	0	0	2	0	0	0	0	0	2	0.00	—	.000	.000	0-0	—	0		1	0.0
Total	3	1	1	.500	15	2	1	0	42	39	31	0	3	27	19	5.57	67	.255	.377	10-0	.200	0	46	-9	-0.4
CLEMENT, MATT Matthew Paul B 8.12.1974 McCandless Twsp., PA BR/TR 6-3/190# d9.6																									
1998	SD N	2	0	1.000	4	2	0	0-0	13.2	15	8	0	0	7-1	13	4.61	85	.283	.367	2-2	.000	-0	94	-1	-0.2
1999	SD N	10	12	.455	31	31	0	0-0	180.2	190	106	18	9	86-2	135	4.48	94	.273	.358	52-6	.077	-2	103	-9	-1.2

Year	Tm Lg	W	L	Pct	G	GS	CG-Sho	SV-BS	IP	H	R	HR	HB	BB-IB	SO	ERA	AERA	OAV	OOB	AB-SH	AVG	PB	Sup	APR	PW
2000	SD N	13	17	.433	34	34	0	0-0	205	194	131	22	16	125-4	170	5.14	84	.248	.361	60-5	.067	-2	97	-20	-2.6
2001	Fla N	9	10	.474	31	31	0	0-0	169.1	172	102	15	15	85-2	134	5.05	84	.267	.365	50-8	.080	-2*	113	-16	-1.7
2002	Chi N	12	11	.522	32	32	3-2	0-0	205	162	84	18	6	85-7	215	3.60	112	.215	.299	61-10	.049	-3	110	13	0.9
2003	†Chi N	14	12	.538	32	32	2-1	0-0	201.2	169	100	22	14	79-2	171	4.11	103	.227	.312	62-8	.145	-1	91	3	0.3
Total	6	60	62	.492	164	162	5-3	0-0	975.1	902	531	95	60	467-18	838	4.46	94	.246	.339	287-39	.084	-10	102	-30	-4.5
CLEMENTS, PAT Patrick Brian B 2.2.1962 McCloud, CA BR/TL 6/180# d4.9																									
1985	Cal A	5	0	1.000	41	0	0	1-1	62	47	23	4	2	25-2	19	3.34	123	.218	.305	0-0	—	0		7	0.5
	Pit N	0	2	.000	27	0	0	2-4	34.1	39	14	2	0	15-3	17	3.67	98	.289	.358	3-1	.333	0		0	0.0
1986	Pit N	0	4	.000	65	0	0	2-3	61	53	20	1	2	32-6	31	2.80	137	.251	.349	6-0	.000	-1		7	0.5
1987	NY A	3	3	.500	55	0	0	7-3	80	91	45	4	3	30-2	36	4.95	89	.299	.364	0-0	—	0		-4	-0.3
1988	NY A	0	0	—	6	1	0	0-1	8.1	12	8	1	0	4-0	3	6.48	61	.343	.390	0-0	—	0	69	-3	-0.2
1989	SD N	4	1	.800	23	1	0	0-1	39	39	17	4	0	15-5	18	3.92	89	.267	.333	6-0	.000	-1	76	-1	-0.1
1990	SD N	0	0	—	9	0	0	0-0	13	20	9	1	0	7-1	6	4.15	92	.357	.429	0-0	—	0		-1	-0.1
1991	SD N	1	0	1.000	12	0	0	0-0	14.1	13	8	0	0	9-4	8	3.77	101	.255	.349	1-0	.000	-0		-1	0.0
1992	SD N	2	1	.667	27	0	0	0-1	23.2	25	9	0	2	12-4	11	2.66	135	.281	.379	1-0	.000	-0		2	0.2
	Bal A	2	0	1.000	23	0	0	0-0	24.2	23	10	0	2	11-0	9	3.28	123	.258	.350	0-0	—	0		2	0.2
Total	8	17	11	.607	288	2	0	12-14	360.1	362	163	17	11	160-27	158	3.77	105	.272	.351	17-1	.059	-1	69	8	0.7
CLEMONS, CHRIS Christopher Hale B 10.31.1972 Baytown, TX BR/TR 6-4/220# d7.23																									
1997	Chi A	0	2	.000	5	2	0	0-0	12.2	19	13	4	1	11-0	8	8.53	51	.345	.463	0-0	—	0	21	-6	-0.7
CLEMONS, LANCE Lance Levis B 7.6.1947 Philadelphia, PA BL/TL 6-2/205# d8.12																									
1971	KC A	1	0	1.000	10	3	0	0-0	24	26	16	2	1	12-0	20	4.13	83	.263	.345	7-1	.286	2	122	-4	0.0
1972	StL N	0	1	.000	3	1	0	0-0	5.1	8	7	1	1	5-0	2	10.13	34	.364	.500	1-0	.000	-0	52	-4	-0.7
1974	Bos A	1	0	1.000	6	0	0	0-0	6.1	8	8	1	1	4-3	1	9.95	39	.296	.406	0-0	—	0		-4	-0.6
Total	3	2	1	.667	19	4	0	0-0	35.2	42	31	4	3	21-3	23	6.06	58	.284	.382	8-1	.250	2	102	-12	-1.3
CLEVELAND, REGGIE Reginald Leslie B 5.23.1948 Swift Current, SK, CAN BR/TR 6-1/195# d10.1																									
1969	StL N	0	0	—	1	1	0	0-0	4	7	4	0	0	1-0	3	9.00	40	.368	.400	1-1	.000	-0	149	-2	-0.1
1970	StL N	0	4	.000	16	1	0	0-0	26	31	27	3	0	18-6	22	7.62	54	.298	.392	4-0	.250	0	152	-11	-1.5
1971	StL N	12	12	.500	34	34	10-2	0-0	222	238	107	20	6	53-12	148	4.01	90	.271	.315	82-4	.171	-1	101	-8	-1.0
1972	StL N	14	15	.483	33	33	11-3	0-0	230.2	229	120	21	5	60-12	153	3.94	86	.258	.306	71-11	.239	3	103	-17	-1.8
1973	StL N	14	10	.583	32	32	6-3	0-0	224	211	88	13	4	61-12	122	3.01	121	.246	.298	74-9	.230	4	101	15	1.9
1974	Bos A	12	14	.462	41	27	10	0-0	221.1	234	121	25	9	69-5	103	4.31	89	.271	.329	0-0	—	0	115	-13	-1.3
1975	†Bos A	13	9	.591	31	20	3-1	0-1	170.2	173	90	19	3	52-1	78	4.43	92	.263	.317	0-0	—	0	104	-5	-0.6
1976	Bos A	10	9	.526	41	14	3	2-2	170	159	73	3	4	61-4	76	3.07	127	.246	.314	0-0	—	0	82	12	1.3
1977	Bos A	11	8	.579	36	27	9-1	2-1	190.1	211	97	20	4	43-2	85	4.26	106	.281	.320	0-0	—	0	107	5	0.4
1978	Bos A	0	1	.000	1	0	0	0-0	0.1	1	1	0	0	0-0	0	0.00	—	.333	.333	0-0	—	0		0	-0.1
	Tex A	5	7	.417	53	0	0	12-7	75.2	65	33	5	3	23-6	46	3.09	122	.236	.295	0-0	—	0		4	0.8
	Year	5	8	.385	54	0	0	12-7	76	66	39	5	3	23-6	46	3.08	122	.237	.296	0-0	—	0		4	0.7
1979	Mil A	1	5	.167	29	1	0	4-2	55	77	44	9	0	23-4	22	6.71	62	.344	.394	0-0	—	0	130	-15	-1.7
1980	Mil A	11	9	.550	45	13	5-2	4-2	154.1	150	73	9	5	49-2	54	3.73	104	.254	.312	0-0	—	0	110	2	0.3
1981	Mil A	2	3	.400	35	0	0	1-0	64.2	57	41	5	1	30-2	18	5.15	67	.239	.326	0-0	—	0		-14	-1.1
Total	13	105	106	.498	428	203	57-12	25-15	1809	1843	919	152	44	543-68	930	4.01	95	.264	.318	232-25	.211	6	104	-47	-4.5
CLEVENGER, TEX Truman Eugene B 7.9.1932 Visalia, CA BR/TR 6-1/180# d4.18																									
1954	Bos A	2	4	.333	23	8	1	0	67.2	67	42	9	2	29	43	4.79	86	.262	.337	14-0	.214	0*	70	-5	-0.4
1956	Was A	0	0	—	20	1	0	0	31.2	33	22	4	0	21-0	17	5.40	80	.264	.365	2-0	.000	-0	144	-4	-0.2
1957	Was A	7	6	.538	52	9	2	8	139.2	139	69	11	4	47-4	75	4.19	93	.261	.322	33-4	.212	1	87	-4	-0.1
1958	Was A	9	9	.500	**55**	4	0	6	124	119	65	12	1	50-6	70	4.35	88	.251	.321	22-2	.136	0	59	-8	-1.0
1959	Was A	8	5	.615	50	7	2-2	8	117.1	114	56	8	2	51-3	71	3.91	100	.256	.332	23-4	.174	1	84	1	0.5
1960	Was A	5	11	.313	53	11	1	7	128.2	150	77	10	3	49-10	49	4.20	93	.298	.358	22-4	.091	-1	70	-7	-1.0
1961	LA A	2	1	.667	12	0	0	1	16	13	5	1	0	13-1	11	1.69	267	.220	.361	3-0	.000	-0		4	0.7
	NY A	1	1	.500	21	0	0	0	31.2	35	20	3	1	21-1	14	4.83	77	.287	.396	4-0	.250	0		-5	-0.2
	Year	3	2	.600	33	0	0	1	47.2	48	28	4	1	34-2	25	3.78	105	.265	.384	7-0	.143	0		0	0.5
1962	NY A	2	0	1.000	21	0	0	0	38	36	14	3	1	17-5	11	2.84	132	.248	.329	4-0	.000	-0*		4	0.1
Total	8	36	37	.493	307	40	6-2	30	694.2	706	370	61	14	298-30	361	4.18	94	.265	.339	127-14	.157	1	78	-24	-1.6
CLIBURN, STEW Stewart Walker B 12.19.1956 Jackson, MS BR/TR 6/195# d9.17 twb-Stan																									
1984	Cal A	0	0	—	1	0	0	0-0	2	3	3	0	0	1-1	1	13.50	29	.333	.400	0-0	—	0		-2	-0.1
1985	Cal A	9	3	.750	44	0	0	6-1	99	87	25	5	1	26-6	48	2.09	197	.241	.292	0-0	—	0		23	2.9
1988	Cal A	4	2	.667	40	1	0	0-4	84	83	45	11	6	32-6	42	4.07	95	.266	.342	0-0	—	0*	47	-3	-0.2
Total	3	13	5	.722	85	1	0	6-5	185	173	73	16	7	59-13	91	3.11	128	.254	.317	0-0	—	0	47	18	2.6
CLINTON, JIM James Lawrence "Big Jim" B 8.10.1850 New York, NY D 9.3.1921 Brooklyn, NY BR/TR 5-8.5/174# d5.18 U1 ▲																									
1872	Eck NA	0	1	.000	1	1	1	0	9	25	36	1		1	1	7.00	48	.373	.382	98	.245	0*	0	-8	-0.4
1875	Atl NA	1	13	.071	17	14	9	0	123	141	104	0		5	7	2.41	86	.262	.268	81	.123	-5*	40	-5	-0.7
1876	Lou N	0	1	.000	1	1	1	0	9	12	11	0		0	1	6.00	45	.279	.279	65	.338	0*	28	-2	-0.1
Total	2 NA	1	14	.067	18	15	10	0	132	166	140	1		6	8	2.73	80	.274	.281	179	.190	-5	36	-13	-1.1
CLONINGER, TONY Tony Lee B 8.13.1940 Lincoln Co., NC BR/TR 6/210# d6.15 C12																									
1961	Mil N	7	2	.778	19	10	3	0	84	84	49	16	1	33-1	51	5.25	71	.258	.326	30-2	.167	-0	154	-13	-1.2
1962	Mil N	8	3	.727	24	15	4-1	0	111	113	61	10	1	46-1	69	4.30	88	.264	.335	39-2	.103	-2	123	-7	-0.8
1963	Mil N	9	11	.450	41	18	4-2	1	145.1	131	68	17	2	63-12	100	3.78	85	.239	.318	37-5	.135	-0	125	-9	-1.3
1964	Mil N	19	14	.576	38	34	15-3	2	242.2	206	112	20	3	82-9	163	3.56	99	.231	.294	87-11	.241	3	112	-2	0.0
1965	Mil N	24	11	.686	40	38	16-1	1	279	247	115	20	3	119-5	211	3.29	107	.236	.315	105-7	.162	2*	133	7	0.9
1966	Atl N	14	11	.560	39	38	11-1	1	257.2	253	134	29	6	116-9	178	4.12	88	.258	.336	111-2	.234	10*	129	-14	-0.3
1967	Atl N	4	7	.364	16	16	1	0	76.2	85	50	13	0	31-4	55	5.17	64	.285	.348	25-0	.200	1	111	-16	-2.0
1968	Atl N	1	3	.250	8	1	0	0	19	15	9	0	0	11-2	7	4.26	70	.227	.329	4-0	.000	-0	58	-2	-0.5
	Cin N	4	3	.571	17	17	2-2	0	91.1	81	49	7	3	48-6	65	4.04	78	.233	.330	34-3	.206	3*	156	-9	-0.4
	Year	5	6	.455	25	18	2-2	0	110.1	96	55	7	3	59-8	72	4.08	77	.232	.330	38-3	.184	3	152	-12	-0.9
1969	Cin N	11	17	.393	35	34	6-2	0-0	189.2	184	123	24	5	103-4	103	5.03	75	.250	.344	72-3	.167	1*	118	-26	-3.5
1970	†Cin N	9	7	.563	30	18	0	1-1	148	136	69	10	4	78-6	56	3.83	105	.249	.346	47-2	.213	3	97	5	0.9
1971	Cin N	3	6	.333	28	8	1-1	0-0	97.1	79	42	12	4	49-3	51	3.88	87	.230	.328	27-2	.259	-1	129	-4	-0.2
1972	StL N	0	2	.000	17	0	0	0-1	26	29	17	2	1	19-3	11	5.19	66	.293	.405	3-0	.000	-0		-5	-0.4
Total	12	113	97	.538	352	247	63-13	6-2	1767.2	1643	898	180	33	798-65	1120	4.07	88	.247	.328	621-39	.192	21	124	-95	-8.8
CLONTZ, BRAD John Bradley B 4.25.1971 Stuart, VA BR/TR 6-1/180# d4.26																									
1995	†Atl N	8	1	.889	59	0	0	4-2	69	71	29	5	4	22-4	55	3.65	117	.269	.332	2-0	.000	-0		5	0.7
1996	†Atl N	6	3	.667	**81**	0	0	1-5	80.2	78	53	11	2	33-8	49	5.69	78	.255	.328	2-1	.000	-0		-9	-0.9
1997	Atl N	5	1	.833	51	0	0	1-1	48	52	24	3	1	18-3	42	3.75	112	.286	.350	1-0	.000	-0		2	0.1
1998	LA N	2	0	1.000	18	0	0	0-1	20.2	15	13	3	2	10-4	14	5.66	70	.200	.310	2-0	.000	-0		-3	-0.4
	NY N	0	0	—	2	0	0	0-0	3	4	3	1	0	2-0	2	9.00	46	.333	.429	0-0	—	0		-2	-0.1
	Year	2	0	1.000	20	0	0	0-1	23.2	19	21	4	2	12-4	16	6.08	66	.218	.327	2-0	.000	-0		-5	-0.5
1999	Pit N	1	3	.250	56	0	0	2-1	49.1	49	21	6	3	24-5	40	2.74	167	.254	.344	3-0	.000	-0		8	0.6
2000	Pit N	0	0	—	5	0	0	0-0	7	7	4	1	0	11-2	8	5.14	89	.269	.486	0-0	—	0		0	0.0
Total	6	22	8	.733	272	0	0	8-10	277.2	276	147	30	12	120-26	210	4.34	100	.261	.340	10-1	.000	-0		1	0.0
CLOSTER, AL Alan Edward B 6.15.1943 Creighton, NE BL/TL 6-2/190# d4.19																									
1966	Was A	0	0	—	1	0	0	0	0.1	1	0	0	0	2-0	0	0.00	—	.500	.750	0-0	—	0		0	0.0
1971	NY A	2	2	.500	14	1	0	0-0	28.1	33	22	4	2	13-7	22	5.08	64	.289	.364	6-1	.000	-1	28	-8	-1.1
1972	NY A	0	0	—	2	0	0	0-0	2.1	2	3	1	0	4-0	2	11.57	26	.250	.500	1-0	.000	-0		-2	-0.1
1973	Atl N	0	0	—	4	0	0	0-1	4.1	7	7	1	0	4-1	2	14.54	27	.389	.500	0-0	—	0		-4	-0.2

Year	Tm Lg	W	L	Pct	G	GS	CG-Sho	SV-BS	IP	H	R	HR	HB	BB-IB	SO	ERA	AERA	OAV	OOB	AB-SH	AVG	PB	Sup	APR	PW
Total	4	2	2	.500	21	1	0	0-1	35.1	43	32	6	2	23-8	26	6.62	50	.303	.400	7-1	.000	-1	28	-14	-1.4
CLOUDE, KEN Kenneth Brian B 1.9.1975 Baltimore, MD BR/TR 6-1/200# d8.9																									
1997	Sea A	4	2	.667	10	9	0	0-0	51	41	32	8	3	26-0	46	5.12	88	.218	.321	2-0	.000	-0	122	-4	-0.4
1998	Sea A	8	10	.444	30	30	0	0-0	155.1	187	116	29	3	80-4	114	6.37	73	.296	.376	3-0	.000	-0	110	-28	-2.7
1999	Sea A	4	4	.500	31	6	0	1-2	72.1	106	67	10	5	46-5	35	7.96	60	.346	.435	2-0	.000	-0	157	-26	-2.4
Total	3	16	16	.500	71	45	0	1-2	278.2	334	215	47	11	152-9	195	6.56	71	.297	.383	7-0	.000	-1	118	-58	-5.5
CLOUGH, ED Edgar George "Big Ed" or "Spec" B 10.28.1906 Wiconisco, PA D 1.30.1944 Harrisburg, PA BL/TL 6/188# d8.28.1924 ▲																									
1925	StL N	0	1	.000	3	1	0	0	10	11	9	1	1	5	3	8.10	53	.289	.386	4-0	.250	-0	59	-3	-0.3
1926	StL N	0	0	—	1	0	0	0	2	5	6	0	1	3	0	22.50	17	.556	.692	1-0	.000	-0		-4	-0.2
Total	2	0	1	.000	4	1	0	0	12	16	15	1	2	8	3	10.50	40	.340	.456	5-0	.200	-0	59	-7	-0.5
CLOWERS, BILL William Perry B 8.14.1898 San Marcos, TX D 1.13.1978 Sweeny, TX BL/TL 5-11/175# d7.20																									
1926	Bos A	0	0	—	2	0	0	0	1.2	2	1	0	0	0	0	0.00	—	.333	.333	0-0	—	0		0	0.0
CLUTTERBUCK, BRYAN Bryan Richard B 12.17.1959 Detroit, MI BR/TR 6-4/223# d7.18																									
1986	Mil A	0	1	.000	20	0	0	0-0	56.2	68	32	8	2	16-2	38	4.29	101	.296	.345	0-0	—	0		0	0.0
1989	Mil A	2	5	.286	14	11	1	0-0	67.1	73	39	11	0	16-1	29	4.14	93	.269	.306	0-0	—	0	94	-4	-0.5
Total	2	2	6	.250	34	11	1	0-0	124	141	71	19	2	32-3	67	4.21	97	.281	.324	0-0	—	0	94	-4	-0.5
CLYDE, DAVID David Eugene B 4.22.1955 Kansas City, KS BL/TL 6-1/185# d6.27																									
1973	Tex A	4	8	.333	18	18	0	0-0	93.1	106	63	8	4	54-1	74	5.01	74	.293	.388	0-0	—	0	103	-15	-1.7
1974	Tex A	3	9	.250	28	21	4	0-0	117	129	64	14	4	47-0	52	4.38	81	.286	.355	0-0	—	0	96	-10	-1.0
1975	Tex A	0	1	.000	1	1	0	0-0	7	6	3	0	0	6-0	2	2.57	146	.273	.429	0-0	—	0	47	1	0.1
1978	Cle A	8	11	.421	28	25	5	0-0	153.1	166	80	4	3	60-3	83	4.28	88	.280	.345	0-0	—	0*	93	-9	-1.0
1979	Cle A	3	4	.429	9	8	1	0-0	45.2	50	33	7	1	13-0	17	5.91	72	.279	.330	0-0	—	0	96	-8	-1.1
Total	5	18	33	.353	84	73	10	0-0	416.1	457	243	33	12	180-4	228	4.63	81	.285	.358	0-0	—	0	96	-41	-4.7
CLYDE, TOM Thomas Knox B 8.17.1923 Wachapreague, VA BR/TR 6-3/195# d5.31 Mil 1944-46																									
1943	Phi A	0	0	—	4	0	0	0	6	7	8	1	1	4	0	9.00	38	.304	.429	2-0	.000	-0		-4	-0.3
COAKLEY, ANDY Andrew James (a.k.a. Jack McAllister In 1902) B 11.20.1882 Providence, RI D 9.27.1963 New York, NY BL/TR 6/165# d9.17																									
1902	Phi A	2	1	.667	3	3	3	0	27	25	15	0	2	9	9	2.67	138	.245	.319	8-0	.375	1	92	2	0.3
1903	Phi A	0	3	.000	6	3	2	0	37.2	48	31	2	2	11	20	5.50	56	.310	.363	15-0	.200	-0	70	-10	-0.8
1904	Phi A	4	3	.571	8	8	7-2	0	62	48	19	1	2	23	33	1.89	142	.215	.294	23-1	.087	-2	63	5	0.3
1905	†Phi A	18	8	.692	35	31	21-3	0	255	227	93	2	6	73	145	1.84	145	.240	.299	94-4	.138	-3	123	17	1.3
1906	Phi A	7	8	.467	22	16	10	0	149	144	78	0	3	44	59	3.14	87	.257	.314	49-2	.143	-2	115	-8	-1.1
1907	Cin N	17	16	.515	37	30	21-1	1	265.1	269	97	1	7	79	89	2.34	111	.274	.332	84-6	.071	-6	91	8	0.2
1908	Cin N	8	18	.308	32	28	20-4	2	242.1	219	79	3	4	64	61	1.86	124	.249	.303	76-5	.092	-4	66	10	0.4
	Chi N	2	0	1.000	4	3	2-1	0	20.1	14	4	0	0	6	7	0.89	266	.192	.253	6-0	.000	-1	140	3	0.2
	Year	10	18	.357	36	31	22-5	2	262.2	233	9	3	4	70	68	1.78	130	.245	.299	82-5	.085	-5	74	10	0.6
1909	Chi N	0	1	.000	1	1	0	0	2	7	7	0	0	3	1	18.00	14	.583	.667	0-0	—	0	55	-4	-0.6
1911	NY A	0	1	.000	2	1	1	0	11.2	20	13	0	0	2	4	5.40	67	.377	.400	4-0	.250	-0	60	-3	-0.2
Total	9	58	59	.496	150	124	87-11	3	1072.1	1021	436	9	26	314	428	2.35	111	.256	.315	359-18	.117	-16	95	20	-0.0
COATES, JIM James Alton B 8.4.1932 Farnham, VA BR/TR 6-4/192# d9.21																									
1956	NY A	0	0	—	2	0	0	0	2	1	3	0	1	4-0	0	13.50	29	.167	.545	0-0	—	0		-2	-0.1
1959	NY A	6	1	.857	37	4	2	3	100.1	89	39	10	3	36-4	64	2.87	127	.234	.305	21-0	.095	-1	133	8	0.4
1960	†NY A★	13	3	.813	35	18	6-2	1	149.1	139	78	16	2	66-4	73	4.28	84	.248	.327	48-8	.250	4	189	-11	-0.8
1961	†NY A	11	5	.688	43	11	4-1	5	141.1	128	60	15	7	53-0	80	3.44	108	.243	.318	35-8	.029	-3	104	4	0.1
1962	†NY A	7	6	.538	50	6	0	6	117.2	119	62	9	5	50-5	67	4.44	84	.263	.339	32-3	.125	-1	107	-8	-1.1
1963	Was A	2	4	.333	20	2	0	0	44.1	51	29	4	3	21-4	31	5.28	70	.297	.377	6-0	.000	-1	144	-7	-1.0
	Cin N	0	0	—	9	0	0	0	16.1	21	10	2	0	7-1	11	5.51	61	.313	.378	3-0	.000	-0		-3	-0.2
1965	Cal A	2	0	1.000	17	0	0	3	28	23	13	1	0	16-2	15	3.54	96	.228	.325	1-0	.000	-0		-1	-0.1
1966	Cal A	1	1	.500	9	4	1-1	0	31.2	32	16	3	0	10-0	16	3.98	84	.258	.311	11-0	.091	-1	118	-2	-0.2
1967	Cal A	1	2	.333	25	1	0	0	52.1	47	26	5	4	23-5	39	4.30	73	.244	.336	3-0	.333	1	28	-6	-0.2
Total	9	43	22	.662	247	46	13-4	18	683.1	650	336	65	25	286-25	396	4.00	90	.252	.330	160-19	.131	-3	142	-28	-3.2
COBB, GEORGE George Woodworth B 9.25.1865 Independence, IA D 8.19.1926 Pomona, CA 6/168# d4.15																									
1892	Bal N	10	37	.213	53	47	42	0	394.1	495	333	21	19	140	159	4.86	71	.295	.356	172	.209	5*	93	-55	-4.6
COBB, HERB Herbert Edward B 8.6.1904 Pinetops, NC D 1.8.1980 Tarboro, NC BR/TR 5-11/150# d4.21																									
1929	StL A	0	0	—	1	0	0	0	1	3	4	1	0	1	0	36.00	12	.600	.667	0-0	—	0		-3	-0.1
COCANOWER, JAIME James Stanley B 2.14.1957 San Juan, P.R. BR/TR 6-4/200# d9.7																									
1983	Mil A	2	0	1.000	5	3	1	0-0	30	21	8	1	1	12-0	8	1.80	208	.200	.288	0-0	—	0	194	6	0.4
1984	Mil A	8	16	.333	33	27	1	0-1	174.2	188	99	13	9	78-3	65	4.02	96	.279	.359	0-0	—	0	84	-8	-1.0
1985	Mil A	6	8	.429	24	15	3-1	0-0	116.1	122	72	6	8	73-2	44	4.33	96	.274	.383	0-0	—	0	98	-6	-0.6
1986	Mil A	0	1	.000	17	2	0	0-0	44.2	40	29	1	2	38-0	22	4.43	98	.248	.396	0-0	—	0	94	-2	0.0
Total	4	16	25	.390	79	47	5-1	0-1	365.2	371	208	21	20	201-5	139	3.99	100	.268	.366	0-0	—	0	95	-10	-1.2
COCHRAN, GOAT Alvah Jackson "Al" or "Goat" B 1.31.1891 Concord, GA D 5.23.1947 Atlanta, GA BR/TR 5-10/175# d8.25																									
1915	Cin N	0	0	—	1	0	0	0	2	5	3	0	0	0	1	9.00	32	.455	.455	0-0	—	0		-1	-0.1
COCO, PASQUAL Pasqual (Reynoso) B 9.8.1977 Santo Domingo, D.R. BR/TR 6-1/185# d7.17																									
2000	Tor A	0	0	—	1	1	0	0-0	4	5	4	1	1	5-0	2	9.00	57	.294	.478	0-0	—	0	92	-2	-0.1
2001	Tor A	1	0	1.000	7	1	0	0-0	14.1	12	8	0	2	6-0	9	4.40	105	.226	.323	0-0	—	0	141	0	0.0
2002	Tor A	0	1	.000	2	0	0	0-0	1	4	2	0	0	3-1	0	18.00	26	.571	.700	0-0	—	0		-1	-0.2
Total	3	1	1	.500	10	2	0	0-0	19.1	21	14	1	3	14-1	11	6.05	78	.273	.400	0-0	—	0	119	-3	-0.3
COCREHAM, GENE Eugene B 11.14.1884 Luling, TX D 12.27.1945 Luling, TX BR/TR 6-3.5/192# d9.25																									
1913	Bos N	0	1	.000	1	1	0	0	8.1	13	7	0	1	4	3	7.56	43	.371	.450	4-0	.000	-1	138	-3	-0.3
1914	Bos N	3	4	.429	15	3	1	0	44.2	48	30	2	0	27	15	4.84	57	.296	.397	10-1	.100	-0	112	-10	-1.6
1915	Bos N	0	0	—	1	0	0	0	1.2	3	2	0	0	0	0	5.40	48	.429	.429	0-0	—	0		-1	-0.1
Total	3	3	5	.375	17	4	1	0	54.2	64	39	2	1	31	18	5.27	54	.314	.407	14-1	.071	-1	121	-14	-2.0
CODIROLI, CHRIS Christopher Allen B 3.26.1958 Oxnard, CA BR/TR 6-1/160# d9.11																									
1982	Oak A	1	2	.333	3	3	0	0-0	16.2	16	8	1	0	4-0	5	4.32	91	.246	.290	0-0	—	0	47	0	0.0
1983	Oak A	12	12	.500	37	31	7-2	1-0	205.2	208	115	17	7	72-4	85	4.46	87	.264	.328	0-0	—	0	109	-15	-1.7
1984	Oak A	6	4	.600	28	14	1	1-1	89.1	111	67	16	3	34-4	44	5.84	64	.304	.366	0-0	—	0	114	-23	-2.3
1985	Oak A	14	14	.500	37	**37**	4	0-0	226	228	125	23	3	78-2	111	4.46	87	.259	.318	0-0	—	0	113	-17	-1.9
1986	Oak A	5	8	.385	16	16	1	0-0	91.2	91	54	15	2	38-2	43	4.03	96	.250	.323	0-0	—	0	113	-6	-0.7
1987	Oak A	0	2	.000	3	3	0	0-0	11.1	12	11	1	1	8-0	4	8.74	47	.273	.396	0-0	—	0	96	-6	-0.8
1988	Cle A	0	4	.000	14	2	0	1-1	19.1	32	22	2	3	10-2	12	9.31	44	.372	.455	0-0	—	0	55	-11	-2.0
1990	KC A	0	1	.000	6	2	0	0-0	10.1	13	11	1	4	17-1	8	9.58	40	.325	.557	0-0	—	0	12	-6	-0.5
Total	8	38	47	.447	144	108	13-2	3-2	670.1	711	413	76	23	261-15	312	4.87	79	.270	.339	0-0	—	0	106	-84	-9.9
COFFMAN, SLICK George David B 12.11.1910 Veto, AL D 5.8.2003 Birmingham, AL BR/TR 6/155# d5.21 b-Dick																									
1937	Det A	7	5	.583	28	5	1	0	101	121	61	8	3	39	22	4.37	107	.295	.361	29-4	.172	0	116	1	0.1
1938	Det A	4	4	.500	39	6	1	2	95.2	120	70	6	0	48	31	6.02	83	.310	.386	24-1	.167	-0	103	-10	-0.8
1939	Det A	2	1	.667	23	1	0	0	42.1	51	36	4	1	22	10	6.38	77	.295	.378	5-0	.000	-0	126	-7	-0.5
1940	StL A	2	2	.500	31	4	1	1	74.2	108	62	5	0	23	26	6.27	73	.334	.379	15-2	.200	-0*	101	-15	-0.7
Total	4	15	12	.556	121	16	3	3	313.2	400	229	23	4	132	89	5.60	85	.309	.375	73-7	.164	-0	108	-31	-1.9
COFFMAN, KEVIN Kevin Reese B 1.19.1965 Austin, TX BR/TR 6-2/175# d9.5																									
1987	Atl N	2	3	.400	5	5	0	0-0	25.1	31	14	2	3	22-0	14	4.62	94	.313	.448	10-0	.100	-0	62	0	0.0

Year	Tm Lg	W	L	Pct	G	GS	CG-Sho	SV-BS	IP	H	R	HR	HB	BB-IB	SO	ERA	AERA	OAV	OOB	AB-SH	AVG	PB	Sup	APR	PW
1988	Atl N	2	6	.250	18	11	0	0-0	67	62	52	3	4	54-2	24	5.78	64	.251	.390	22-1	.227	2*	90	-16	-1.6
1990	Chi N	0	2	.000	8	2	0	0-0	18.1	26	24	0	0	19-0	9	11.29	36	.333	.459	5-0	.200	0	100	-13	-1.2
Total	3	4	11	.267	31	18	0	0-0	110.2	119	90	5	7	95-2	47	6.42	61	.281	.416	37-1	.189	1	83	-29	-2.8
COFFMAN, DICK Samuel Richard B 12.18.1906 Veto, AL D 3.24.1972 Athens, AL BR/TR 6-2/195# d4.28 b-Slick																									
1927	Was A	0	1	.000	5	2	0	0	16	20	9	0	2	2	5	3.38	120	.313	.353	3-1	.333	0	62	0	0.1
1928	StL A	4	5	.444	29	7	3	1	85.2	122	68	7	1	37	25	6.09	69	.359	.423	23-2	.043	-3	95	-18	-1.9
1929	StL A	1	1	.500	27	3	1-1	1	52.2	61	40	3	3	14	11	5.98	74	.295	.348	7-0	.000	-1	70	-9	-0.5
1930	StL A	8	18	.308	38	30	12-1	1	196	250	134	14	5	69	54	5.14	95	.311	.369	66-2	.136	-5	78	-8	-1.3
1931	StL A	9	13	.409	32	17	11-2	1	169.1	159	81	10	2	51	39	3.88	119	.241	.298	51-6	.078	-5	72	16	1.3
1932	StL A	5	3	.625	9	6	3-1	0	61	66	24	3	2	21	14	3.10	157	.277	.341	22-0	.045	-2	85	11	1.1
	Was A	1	6	.143	22	9	2	0	76.1	92	45	2	1	31	17	4.83	89	.307	.373	22-0	.091	-1	88	-4	-0.4
	Year	6	9	.400	31	15	5-1	0	137.1	158	49	5	3	52	31	4.06	112	.294	.359	44-0	.068	-3	86	10	0.7
1933	StL A	3	7	.300	21	13	3-1	1	81	114	57	9	2	39	19	5.89	79	.329	.399	27-0	.037	-3	86	-9	-1.2
1934	StL A	9	10	.474	40	21	6-1	3	173	212	112	11	1	59	55	4.53	110	.303	.358	51-5	.216	-1	71	5	0.4
1935	StL A	5	11	.313	41	18	5	2	143.2	206	116	14	2	46	34	6.14	78	.335	.383	41-4	.146	-1	87	-21	-2.1
1936	†NY N	7	5	.583	42	2	0	7	101.2	119	53	7	2	23	26	3.90	100	.296	.337	20-1	.200	-0	0	-1	-0.1
1937	†NY N	8	3	.727	42	1	0	3	80	93	36	4	4	31	30	3.04	128	.289	.359	19-0	.368	2	222	**6**	1.0
1938	NY N	8	4	.667	**51**	3	1-1	**12**	111.1	116	50	3	3	21	21	3.48	108	.268	.306	28-0	.071	-3	67	4	0.1
1939	NY N	1	2	.333	28	0	0	3	38	50	18	1	3	6	9	3.08	128	.316	.353	4-0	.000	-1		2	0.1
1940	Bos N	1	5	.167	31	0	0	3	48.1	63	33	4	2	11	11	5.40	69	.323	.365	12-0	.083	-1		-9	-1.3
1945	Phi N	2	1	.667	14	0	0	0	26.1	39	18	0	0	2	2	5.13	75	.351	.363	4-0	.250	0		-4	-0.3
Total	15	72	95	.431	472	132	47-8	38	1460.1	1782	894	92	35	463	372	4.65	96	.302	.357	400-21	.127	-22	83	-39	-5.0
COGAN, TONY Anthony Michael B 12.21.1976 Chicago, IL BL/TL 6-2/205# d4.2																									
2001	KC A	0	4	.000	39	0	0	0-2	24.2	32	17	7	5	13-0	17	5.84	84	.320	.420	0-0	—	0		-2	-0.3
COGAN, DICK Richard Henry B 12.5.1871 Paterson, NJ D 5.2.1948 Paterson, NJ BR/TR 5-7/150# d5.10																									
1897	Bal N	0	0	—	1	0	0	0	2	4	3	0	1	2	0	13.50	31	.400	.538	1-0	.000	-0		-2	-0.1
1899	Chi N	2	3	.400	5	5	5	0	44	54	32	1	4	24	9	4.30	87	.302	.396	25-1	.200	1*	92	-3	-0.2
1900	NY N	0	0	—	2	0	0	0	8	10	6	0	0	6	1	6.75	54	.303	.410	8-0	.125	-0*		-2	-0.1
Total	3	2	3	.400	8	5	5	0	54	68	41	1	5	32	10	5.00	75	.306	.405	34-1	.176	0	92	-7	-0.4
COGGIN, DAVID David Raymond B 10.30.1976 Covina, CA BR/TR 6-4/195# d6.23																									
2000	Phi N	2	0	1.000	5	5	0	0-0	27	35	20	2	1	12-0	17	5.33	87	.315	.387	7-1	.000	-1	158	-3	-0.3
2001	Phi N	6	7	.462	17	17	0	0-0	95	99	46	7	5	39-6	62	4.17	102	.272	.348	33-1	.061	-1	75	2	0.0
2002	Phi N	2	5	.286	38	7	0	0-0	77	65	42	4	4	51-3	64	4.68	84	.231	.355	8-2	.000	-1	84	-6	-0.6
Total	3	10	12	.455	60	29	0	0-0	199	199	108	13	10	102-9	143	4.52	92	.263	.356	48-4	.042	-3	95	-7	-0.9
COHEN, HY Hyman B 1.29.1931 Brooklyn, NY BR/TR 6-5/220# d4.17																									
1955	Chi N	0	0	—	7	1	0	0	17	28	17	2	1	10-0	4	7.94	51	.378	.459	3-0	.000	-0	174	-7	-0.4
COHEN, SYD Sydney Harry B 5.7.1906 Baltimore, MD D 4.9.1988 ElPaso, TX BB/TL 5-11/180# d9.18 b-Andy																									
1934	Was A	1	1	.500	3	2	2	0	18	25	15	2	0	6	6	7.50	58	.333	.383	11-0	.273	0*	91	-6	-0.4
1936	Was A	0	2	.000	19	1	0	1	36	44	27	4	3	14	21	5.25	91	.303	.377	8-0	.000	-1	111	-3	-0.2
1937	Was A	2	4	.333	33	0	0	4	55	64	30	1	0	17	22	3.11	142	.299	.351	14-0	.143	-1		5	0.6
Total	3	3	7	.300	55	3	2	5	109	133	72	7	3	37	49	4.54	100	.306	.365	33-0	.152	-2	97	-4	0.0
COLBERT, VINCE Vincent Norman B 12.20.1945 Washington, DC BR/TR 6-4/200# d5.19																									
1970	Cle A	1	1	.500	23	0	0	2-1	31	37	25	4	1	16-2	17	7.26	55	.298	.380	2-0	.000	-0		-10	-0.7
1971	Cle A	7	6	.538	50	10	2	2-1	142.2	140	71	11	6	71-9	74	3.97	96	.265	.355	29-2	.138	-0*	63	-3	-0.3
1972	Cle A	1	7	.125	22	11	1-1	0-0	74.2	74	42	8	7	38-5	36	4.58	70	.267	.365	20-1	.200	1*	77	-11	-1.0
Total	3	9	14	.391	95	21	3-1	4-2	248.1	251	138	23	14	125-16	127	4.57	80	.270	.361	51-3	.157	0	67	-24	-2.0
COLBORN, JIM James William B 5.22.1946 Santa Paula, CA BR/TR 6/191# d7.13 C3																									
1969	Chi N	1	0	1.000	6	2	0	0-0	14.2	15	6	2	1	9-1	4	3.07	131	.283	.397	3-0	.000	-0	88	1	0.1
1970	Chi N	3	1	.750	34	5	0	4-3	72.2	88	37	3	1	23-6	50	3.59	125	.298	.347	15-1	.067	-1	147	5	0.2
1971	Chi N	0	1	.000	14	0	0	0-0	10.1	18	8	1	0	3-0	2	6.97	57	.383	.420	0-0	—	0		-3	-0.2
1972	Mil A	7	7	.500	39	12	4-1	0-0	147.2	135	53	14	2	43-7	97	3.11	98	.245	.300	37-2	.081	-1	100	1	-0.2
1973	Mil A☆	20	12	.625	43	36	22-4	1-0	314.1	297	133	21	3	87-5	135	3.18	118	.251	.302	0-0	—	0	110	18	1.8
1974	Mil A	10	13	.435	33	31	10-1	0-0	224	230	104	27	6	60-4	83	4.06	89	.268	.319	0-0	—	0	93	-8	-0.8
1975	Mil A	11	13	.458	36	29	8-1	2-0	206.1	215	111	18	5	65-5	79	4.27	90	.270	.327	0-0	—	0	110	-9	-0.9
1976	Mil A	9	15	.375	32	32	7	0-0	225.2	232	97	20	2	54-9	101	3.71	94	.268	.310	0-0	—	0	88	-2	-0.2
1977	KC A	18	14	.563	36	35	6-1	0-0	239	233	106	22	13	81-2	103	3.62	112	.255	.323	0-0	—	0*	109	13	1.6
1978	KC A	1	2	.333	8	3	0	0-0	28.1	31	18	4	2	12-1	8	4.76	81	.282	.363	0-0	—	0	86	-3	-0.3
	Sea A	3	10	.231	20	19	3	0-0	114.1	125	77	21	6	38-1	26	5.35	71	.279	.341	0-0	—	0	85	-20	-1.8
	Year	4	12	.250	28	22	3	0-0	142.2	156	81	25	8	50-2	34	5.24	73	.280	.345	0-0	—	0	85	-22	-2.1
Total	10	83	88	.485	301	204	60-8	7-3	1597.1	1619	750	153	41	475-41	688	3.80	98	.265	.320	55-3	.073	-3	102	-7	-0.7
COLCOLOUGH, TOM Thomas Bernard B 10.8.1870 Charleston, SC D 12.10.1919 Charleston, SC BR/TR 5-10.5/180# d8.1																									
1893	Pit N	1	0	1.000	8	3	1	2	43.2	45	30	1	0	32	7	4.12	110	.259	.374	14	.143	0	113	2	0.1
1894	Pit N	8	5	.615	23	14	11	0	150.2	213	147	5	5	72	29	7.23	73	.329	.401	70-1	.200	-3	129	-28	-1.8
1895	Pit N	1	1	.500	7	6	3	0	43.1	54	49	3	5	21	16	6.65	68	.300	.388	17-1	.294	3*	140	-11	-0.3
1899	NY N	4	5	.444	11	8	7	0	81.2	85	49	1	3	41	14	3.97	95	.268	.357	37-0	.270	1*	101	-1	0.0
Total	4	14	11	.560	49	31	22	2	319.1	397	275	10	13	166	66	5.89	79	.301	.385	138-2	.225	1	123	-38	-2.0
COLE, BERT Albert George B 7.1.1896 San Francisco, CA D 5.30.1975 San Mateo, CA BL/TL 6-1/180# d4.19																									
1921	Det A	7	4	.636	20	11	7-1	1	109.2	134	66	3	4	36	22	4.27	100	.305	.363	46-3	.283	3*	115	0	0.2
1922	Det A	1	6	.143	23	5	2-1	0	79.1	105	60	4	1	39	21	4.88	80	.313	.387	25-0	.160	-1*	92	-13	-1.0
1923	Det A	13	5	.722	52	13	6-1	5	163	183	95	9	5	61	32	4.14	93	.284	.351	55-1	.255	2*	161	-8	-0.6
1924	Det A	3	9	.250	28	12	2-1	2	109.1	135	69	4	4	35	16	4.69	88	.314	.371	37-2	.270	1*	82	-7	-0.5
1925	Det A	2	3	.400	14	2	1	1	33.2	44	27	2	1	15	7	5.88	73	.336	.408	11-0	.273	0	146	-7	-0.8
	Cle A	1	1	.500	13	2	0	1	44	55	33	1	1	25	9	6.14	72	.322	.411	13-0	.154	-0	95	-7	-0.3
	Year	3	4	.429	27	4	1	2	77.2	99	38	3	2	40	16	6.03	73	.328	.410	24-0	.208	0	120	-12	-1.1
1927	Chi A	1	4	.200	27	2	0	0	66.2	79	43	3	3	19	12	4.72	86	.309	.363	18-2	.167	-1	93	-6	-0.4
Total	6	28	32	.467	177	47	18-4	10	605.2	735	393	26	19	230	119	4.67	87	.305	.370	205-8	.239	5	116	-48	-3.4
COLE, DAVE David Bruce B 8.29.1930 Williamsport, MD BR/TR 6-2/175# d9.9																									
1950	Bos N	0	1	.000	4	0	0	0	8	7	2	0	1	3	8	1.13	342	.259	.355	1-0	.000	-0		2	0.2
1951	Bos N	2	4	.333	23	7	1	0	67.2	64	43	3	2	64	33	4.26	86	.254	.409	17-0	.353	4	117	-8	-0.2
1952	Bos N	1	1	.500	22	3	0	0	44.2	38	21	2	3	42	22	4.03	90	.241	.409	8-0	.000	-1	132	-2	-0.2
1953	Mil N	0	1	.000	10	0	0	0	14.2	17	14	1	0	14	13	8.59	46	.279	.413	2-0	.500	1		-7	-0.3
1954	Chi N	3	8	.273	18	14	2-1	0	84	74	56	7	1	62	37	5.36	78	.241	.365	28-1	.214	1*	85	-11	-1.1
1955	Phi N	0	3	.000	7	3	0	0	18.1	21	15	3	0	14-0	6	6.38	62	.304	.412	5-0	.200	-0	82	-5	-0.7
Total	6	6	18	.250	84	27	3-1	0	237.1	221	151	16	7	199-0	119	4.93	79	.253	.393	61-1	.230	5	99	-31	-2.3
COLE, ED Edward William (b: Edward William Kisleauskas) B 3.22.1909 Wilkes-Barre, PA D 7.28.1999 Nashville, TN BR/TR 5-11/170# d4.22																									
1938	StL A	1	5	.167	36	6	1	3	88.2	116	69	8	5	48	26	5.18	96	.313	.399	21-0	.143	-1	97	-7	-0.6
1939	StL A	0	2	.000	6	0	0	0	6.1	8	7	1	0	6	5	7.11	68	.308	.438	1-0	.000	-0		-2	-0.4
Total	2	1	7	.125	42	6	1	3	95	124	76	9	5	54	31	5.31	94	.312	.401	22-0	.136	-2	97	-9	-1.0
COLE, KING Leonard Leslie B 4.15.1886 Toledo, IA D 1.6.1916 Bay City, MI BR/TR 6-1/170# d10.6																									
1909	Chi N	1	0	1.000	1	1	1-1	0	9	6	0	0	0	3	1	0.00	—	.194	.265	4-0	.750	2	220	3	0.7
1910	†Chi N	20	4	**.833**	33	29	21-4	1	239.2	174	64	2	9	130	114	1.80	**160**	**.211**	.325	91-5	.231	2*	138	29	3.1
1911	Chi N	18	7	.720	32	27	13-2	0	221.1	188	87	3	9	99	101	3.13	106	.236	.328	79-3	.152	-2	120	10	0.8

Year	Tm Lg	W	L	Pct	G	GS	CG-Sho	SV-BS	IP	H	R	HR	HB	BB-IB	SO	ERA	AERA	OAV	OOB	AB-SH	AVG	PB	Sup	APR	PW
1912	Chi N	1	2	.333	8	3	0	0	19	36	26	2	2	8	9	10.89	31	.409	.469	5-0	.400	1	147	-15	-1.8
	Pit N	2	2	.500	12	5	2	0	49	61	42	1	2	18	11	6.43	51	.330	.395	15-1	.133	-1	180	-17	-1.2
	Year	3	4	.429	20	8	2	0	68	97	50	3	4	26	20	7.68	43	.355	.419	20-1	.200	0	168	-32	-3.0
1914	NY A	10	9	.526	33	15	8-2	0	141.2	151	63	3	1	51	43	3.30	84	.288	.352	42-2	.048	-3	90	-8	-1.5
1915	NY A	2	3	.400	10	6	2	1	51	41	27	2	3	22	19	3.18	92	.224	.317	13-2	.077	-1	87	-3	-0.4
Total	6	54	27	.667	129	86	47-9	2	730.2	657	309	13	26	331	298	3.12	97	.250	.340	249-13	.173	-2	125	-1	-0.3

COLE, VICTOR Victor Alexander B 1.23.1968 Leningrad, USSR BB/TR 5-10/160# d6.6

Year	Tm Lg	W	L	Pct	G	GS	CG-Sho	SV-BS	IP	H	R	HR	HB	BB-IB	SO	ERA	AERA	OAV	OOB	AB-SH	AVG	PB	Sup	APR	PW
1992	Pit N	0	2	.000	8	4	0	0-0	23	23	14	1	0	14-0	12	5.48	63	.261	.359	4-1	.000	-0	72	-5	-0.4

COLEMAN, JOHN John B Bristol, PA TR d6.23

Year	Tm Lg	W	L	Pct	G	GS	CG-Sho	SV-BS	IP	H	R	HR	HB	BB-IB	SO	ERA	AERA	OAV	OOB	AB-SH	AVG	PB	Sup	APR	PW
1890	Phi N	0	1	.000	1	1	0	0	1.2	4	8	0	0	3	2	21.60	17	.444	.583	0	—	0	207	-4	-0.5

COLEMAN, JOHN John Francis B 3.6.1863 Saratoga Springs, NY D 5.31.1922 Detroit, MI BL/TR 5-9.5/170# d5.1 ▲

Year	Tm Lg	W	L	Pct	G	GS	CG-Sho	SV-BS	IP	H	R	HR	HB	BB-IB	SO	ERA	AERA	OAV	OOB	AB-SH	AVG	PB	Sup	APR	PW
1883	Phi N	12	48	.200	65	61	59-3	0	538.1	772	510	17		48	159	4.87	63	.309	.322	354	.234	4*	82	-110	-8.5
1884	Phi N	5	15	.250	21	19	14-1	0	154.1	216	147	9		22	37	4.90	61	.308	.329	171	.246	2*	78	-29	-2.6
	Phi AA	0	2	.000	3	2	2	0	21	28	14	0	4	2	5	3.43	99	.304	.347	107	.206	0*	36	-1	0.0
1885	Phi AA	2	2	.500	8	3	3	0	60.1	82	46	0	0	5	12	3.43	100	.366	.380	398	.299	2*	92	0	0.2
1886	Phi AA	1	1	.500	3	1	1	0	20.2	18	9	1	1	5	2	2.61	134	.225	.279	492	.246	0*	85	2	0.2
1889	Phi AA	3	2	.600	5	5	4	0	34	38	23	2	1	14	6	2.91	130	.273	.344	19	.053	-2*	144	2	0.0
1890	Pit N	0	2	.000	2	2	1	0	14	28	23	1	0	6	3	9.64	34	.400	.447	11	.182	0*	105	-10	-0.9
Total	6	23	72	.242	107	93	84-4	0	842.2	1182	772	30	6	102	224	4.68	67	.311	.330	1552	.251	7	84	-146	-11.6

COLEMAN, JOE Joseph Howard B 2.3.1947 Boston, MA BR/TR 6-3/195# d9.28 C11 s-Joe

Year	Tm Lg	W	L	Pct	G	GS	CG-Sho	SV-BS	IP	H	R	HR	HB	BB-IB	SO	ERA	AERA	OAV	OOB	AB-SH	AVG	PB	Sup	APR	PW
1965	Was A	2	0	1.000	2	2	2	0	18	9	3	0	0	8-0	7	1.50	232	.153	.254	6-1	.000	-1	114	4	0.5
1966	Was A	1	0	1.000	1	1	1	0	9	6	2	0	0	2-0	4	2.00	173	.188	.235	3-0	.000	-0	76	2	0.2
1967	Was A	8	9	.471	28	22	3	0	134	154	78	6	9	47-4	77	4.63	68	.291	.355	36-5	.056	-1	120	-22	-2.8
1968	Was A	12	16	.429	33	33	12-2	0	223	212	98	18	12	51-3	139	3.27	89	.250	.299	70-6	.129	-1*	92	-11	-1.6
1969	Was A	12	13	.480	40	36	12-4	1-2	247.2	222	102	26	6	100-7	182	3.27	106	.243	.320	84-4	.107	-2	101	6	0.4
1970	Was A	8	12	.400	39	29	6-1	0-1	218.2	190	98	25	4	89-6	152	3.58	99	.233	.309	67-4	.119	2	96	-1	0.1
1971	Det A	20	9	.690	39	38	16-3	0-0	286	241	106	17	7	96-3	236	3.15	114	.229	.296	96-9	.094	-3	109	15	1.0
1972	†Det A❖	19	14	.576	40	39	9-3	0-0	280	216	99	23	9	110-7	222	2.80	113	.214	.296	82-15	.110	-2	106	10	0.9
1973	Det A	23	15	.605	40	40	13-2	0-0	288.1	283	125	32	10	93-2	202	3.53	116	.258	.321	0-0	—	0	87	15	1.9
1974	Det A	14	12	.538	41	41	11-2	0-0	285.2	272	160	30	12	158-13	177	4.32	88	.254	.355	0-0	—	0	101	-17	-1.3
1975	Det A	10	18	.357	31	31	6-1	0-0	201	234	137	27	9	85-6	125	5.55	73	.291	.363	0-0	—	0	88	-28	-3.4
1976	Det A	2	5	.286	12	12	1	0-0	66.2	80	44	1	5	34-0	38	4.86	76	.308	.395	0-0	—	0	101	-9	-0.8
	Chi N	2	8	.200	39	4	0	4-4	79	72	43	9	2	35-8	66	4.10	94	.246	.327	13-0	.154	-0	51	-3	-0.4
1977	Oak A	4	4	.500	43	12	2	2-2	127.2	114	51	11	2	49-2	55	2.96	136	.241	.313	0-0	—	0	124	14	0.8
1978	Oak A	3	0	1.000	10	0	0	0-0	19.2	12	3	1	0	5-0	4	1.37	266	.185	.239	0-0	—	0		5	0.8
	Tor A	2	0	1.000	31	0	0	0-1	60.2	67	34	6	1	30-3	28	4.60	86	.286	.364	0-0	—	0		-5	-0.3
	Year	5	0	1.000	41	0	0	0-1	80.1	79	43	7	1	35-3	32	3.81	102	.264	.338	0-0	—	0		1	0.5
1979	SF N	0	0	—	5	0	0	0-0	3.2	3	2	0	1	2-0	0	0.00	—	.231	.353	0-0	—	0		1	0.0
	Pit N	0	0	—	10	0	0	0-0	20.2	29	17	1	1	9-1	14	6.10	64	.326	.390	5-0	.200	0		-5	-0.3
	Year	0	0	—	15	0	0	0-0	24.1	32	19	1	2	11-1	14	5.18	74	.314	.385	5-0	.200	0		-5	-0.3
Total	15	142	135	.513	484	340	94-18	7-10	2569.1	2416	1202	233	90	1003-65	1728	3.70	98	.250	.324	462-44	.106	-10	99	-29	-4.3

COLEMAN, JOE Joseph Patrick B 7.30.1922 Medford, MA D 4.9.1997 Ft.Myers, FL BR/TR 6-2.5/200# d9.19 Mil 1943-45 f-Joe

Year	Tm Lg	W	L	Pct	G	GS	CG-Sho	SV-BS	IP	H	R	HR	HB	BB-IB	SO	ERA	AERA	OAV	OOB	AB-SH	AVG	PB	Sup	APR	PW
1942	Phi A	0	1	.000	1	0	0	0	6	8	5	0	0	1	0	3.00	126	.308	.333	4-0	.000	-1		-1	-0.1
1946	Phi A	0	2	.000	4	2	0	0	13	19	8	1	0	8	8	5.54	64	.345	.429	5-0	.400	1	97	-2	-0.3
1947	Phi A	6	12	.333	32	21	9-2	1	160.1	171	84	17	0	62	65	4.32	88	.275	.341	48-3	.146	-1	65	-8	-1.0
1948	Phi A★	14	13	.519	33	29	13-3	0	215.2	224	105	11	1	90	86	4.09	105	.269	.341	74-6	.122	-4	95	6	0.2
1949	Phi A	13	14	.481	33	30	18-1	1	240.1	249	119	12	3	127	109	3.86	107	.271	.361	79-7	.177	0	80	6	0.4
1950	Phi A	0	5	.000	15	6	2	0	54	74	54	9	0	50	12	8.50	54	.332	.454	17-0	.059	-1	83	-23	-1.8
1951	Phi A	1	6	.143	28	9	1	1	96.1	117	69	12	3	59	34	5.98	72	.305	.402	27-1	.259	1	108	-17	-1.0
1953	Phi A	3	4	.429	21	9	2-1	0	90	85	46	8	1	49	18	4.00	107	.254	.352	28-0	.286	1	78	2	0.2
1954	Bal A	13	17	.433	33	32	15-4	0	221.1	184	102	16	3	96	103	3.50	102	.232	.315	74-4	.176	2	75	0	0.3
1955	Bal A	0	1	.000	6	2	0	0	11.2	19	15	5	1	10-0	4	10.80	35	.373	.469	3-0	.667	1	116	-9	-0.5
	Det A	2	1	.667	17	0	0	3	25.1	22	9	1	1	14-0	5	3.20	120	.239	.346	4-1	.750	1		2	0.5
	Year	2	2	.500	23	2	0	3	37	41	29	6	2	24-0	9	5.59	69	.287	.392	7-1	.714	3	116	-6	0.0
Total	10	52	76	.406	223	140	60-11	6	1134	1172	616	92	13	566-0	444	4.38	92	.271	.356	363-22	.182	2	82	-44	-3.1

COLEMAN, PERCY Pierce D. B 10.15.1876 Mason, OH D 2.16.1948 Van Nuys, CA TR d7.2

Year	Tm Lg	W	L	Pct	G	GS	CG-Sho	SV-BS	IP	H	R	HR	HB	BB-IB	SO	ERA	AERA	OAV	OOB	AB-SH	AVG	PB	Sup	APR	PW
1897	StL N	1	2	.333	13	5	3	0	66.1	108	76	0	8	33	10	7.19	61	.362	.440	31-0	.226	-1	133	-21	-0.9
1898	Cin N	0	1	.000	1	1	1	0	9	13	7	0	1	3	2	3.00	128	.333	.395	3-0	.000	-1	56	0	-0.1
Total	2	1	3	.250	14	6	4	0	75.1	121	83	0	9	36	12	6.69	65	.359	.435	34-0	.206	-1	120	-21	-1.0

COLEMAN, RIP Walter Gary B 7.31.1931 Troy, NY BL/TL 6-2/185# d8.15

Year	Tm Lg	W	L	Pct	G	GS	CG-Sho	SV-BS	IP	H	R	HR	HB	BB-IB	SO	ERA	AERA	OAV	OOB	AB-SH	AVG	PB	Sup	APR	PW
1955	†NY A	2	1	.667	10	6	0	1	29	40	19	2	1	16-0	15	5.28	71	.331	.413	10-1	.200	1	135	-5	-0.4
1956	NY A	3	5	.375	29	9	0	2	88.1	97	42	6	1	42-1	42	3.67	105	.285	.363	24-2	.042	-3	153	2	-0.1
1957	KC A	0	7	.000	19	6	1-1	0	41	53	32	5	0	25-0	15	5.93	67	.325	.408	9-1	.000	-1	64	-9	-1.5
1959	KC A	2	10	.167	29	11	2	2	81	85	46	8	1	34-0	54	4.56	88	.273	.345	25-1	.080	-2	78	-4	-0.8
	Bal A	0	0	—	3	0	0	0	4	4	0	0	0	2-0	4	0.00	—	.267	.353	0-0	—	0		2	0.1
	Year	2	10	.167	32	11	2	2	85	89	50	8	1	36-0	58	4.34	92	.273	.345	25-1	.080	-2	78	-3	-0.7
1960	Bal A	0	2	.000	5	1	0	0	4	8	5	0	1	5-1	0	11.25	34	.444	.583	1-0	.000	-0	46	-3	-0.6
Total	5	7	25	.219	95	33	3-1	5	247.1	287	144	21	4	124-2	130	4.58	85	.296	.376	69-5	.072	-5	104	-17	-3.3

COLEMAN, WALTER Walter L. B 6.13.1873 Lees Summit, MO D 11.20.1925 Bunceton, MO TL 5-10/174# d9.25

Year	Tm Lg	W	L	Pct	G	GS	CG-Sho	SV-BS	IP	H	R	HR	HB	BB-IB	SO	ERA	AERA	OAV	OOB	AB-SH	AVG	PB	Sup	APR	PW
1895	StL N	0	1	.000	1	1	1	0	8	12	15	1	1	8	5	13.50	36	.343	.477	5-0	.200	-0	118	-7	-0.5

COLLAMORE, ALLAN Allan Edward B 6.5.1887 Worcester, MA D 8.8.1980 Battle Creek, MI BR/TR 6/170# d4.15

Year	Tm Lg	W	L	Pct	G	GS	CG-Sho	SV-BS	IP	H	R	HR	HB	BB-IB	SO	ERA	AERA	OAV	OOB	AB-SH	AVG	PB	Sup	APR	PW
1911	Phi A	0	1	.000	2	0	0	0	2	6	9	0	2	3	1	36.00	9	.600	.733	0-0	—	0		-7	-1.1
1914	Cle A	3	7	.300	27	8	3	0	105.1	100	52	3	6	49	32	3.25	89	.264	.357	32-1	.094	-2	73	-3	-0.6
1915	Cle A	2	5	.286	11	6	5-2	0	64.1	52	22	1	0	22	15	2.38	128	.235	.305	23-0	.174	0*	72	5	0.6
Total	3	5	13	.278	40	14	8-2	0	171.2	158	83	4	8	74	48	3.30	89	.259	.347	55-1	.127	-2	72	-5	-1.1

COLLARD, HAP Earl Clinton B 8.29.1898 Williams, AZ D 7.9.1968 Jamestown, CA BR/TR 6/170# d4.23

Year	Tm Lg	W	L	Pct	G	GS	CG-Sho	SV-BS	IP	H	R	HR	HB	BB-IB	SO	ERA	AERA	OAV	OOB	AB-SH	AVG	PB	Sup	APR	PW
1927	Cle A	0	0	—	4	0	0	0	5.1	8	7	0	0	3	2	5.06	83	.333	.407	0-0	—	0		-2	-0.1
1928	Cle A	0	0	—	1	0	0	0	4	4	3	0	0	4	1	2.25	184	.250	.400	1-0	1.000	0		0	0.0
1930	Phi N	6	12	.333	30	15	4	0	127	188	106	15	3	39	25	6.80	80	.350	.397	44-0	.205	-2*	88	-15	-1.7
Total	3	6	12	.333	35	15	4	0	136.1	200	116	15	3	46	28	6.60	81	.347	.398	45-0	.222	-1	88	-17	-1.8

COLLIER, ORLIN Orlin Edward B 2.17.1907 E.Prairie, MO D 9.9.1944 Memphis, TN BR/TR 5-11.5/180# d9.11

Year	Tm Lg	W	L	Pct	G	GS	CG-Sho	SV-BS	IP	H	R	HR	HB	BB-IB	SO	ERA	AERA	OAV	OOB	AB-SH	AVG	PB	Sup	APR	PW
1931	Det A	0	1	.000	2	2	0	0	10.1	17	12	0	0	7	3	7.84	59	.362	.444	3-0	.000	-0	83	-4	-0.4

COLLIFLOWER, HARRY James Harry "Collie" B 3.11.1869 Petersville, MD D 8.12.1961 Washington, DC BL/TL 5-11.5/175# d7.21 U1

Year	Tm Lg	W	L	Pct	G	GS	CG-Sho	SV-BS	IP	H	R	HR	HB	BB-IB	SO	ERA	AERA	OAV	OOB	AB-SH	AVG	PB	Sup	APR	PW
1899	Cle N	1	11	.083	14	12	11	0	98	152	122	6	11	41	8	8.17	45	.353	.422	76-0	.303	2*	85	-50	-4.1

COLLINS, DAN Daniel Thomas B 7.12.1854 St.Louis, MO D 9.21.1883 New Orleans, LA d6.8 ▲

Year	Tm Lg	W	L	Pct	G	GS	CG-Sho	SV-BS	IP	H	R	HR	HB	BB-IB	SO	ERA	AERA	OAV	OOB	AB-SH	AVG	PB	Sup	APR	PW
1874	Chi NA	1	1	.500	2	2	1	0	11	22	17	0		2	0	4.91	45	.386	.407	12	.083	-1*	59	-3	-0.4

COLLINS, DON Donald Edward B 9.15.1952 Lyons, GA BR/TL 6-2/195# d5.4

Year	Tm Lg	W	L	Pct	G	GS	CG-Sho	SV-BS	IP	H	R	HR	HB	BB-IB	SO	ERA	AERA	OAV	OOB	AB-SH	AVG	PB	Sup	APR	PW
1977	Atl N	3	9	.250	40	6	0	2-1	70.2	82	43	8	1	41-8	27	5.09	87	.299	.389	11-1	.000	-1	47	-3	-0.7
1980	Cle A	0	0	—	4	0	0	0-0	6	9	5	0	0	7-1	0	7.50	54	.346	.485	0-0	—	0		-2	-0.1
Total	2	3	9	.250	44	6	0	2-1	76.2	91	48	8	1	48-9	27	5.28	84	.303	.398	11-1	.000	-1	47	-5	-0.8

Year	Tm Lg	W	L	Pct	G	GS	CG-Sho	SV-BS	IP	H	R	HR	HB	BB-IB	SO	ERA	AERA	OAV	OOB	AB-SH	AVG	PB	Sup	APR	PW
COLLINS, RIP Harry Warren B 2.26.1896 Weatherford, TX D 5.27.1968 Bryan, TX BR/TR 6-1/205# d4.19																									
1920	NY A	14	8	.636	36	18	10-2	1	187.1	171	83	6	14	79	66	3.22	119	.247	.337	62-8	.129	-4	109	12	0.9
1921	†NY A	11	5	.688	28	16	7-2	0	137.1	158	103	6	10	78	64	5.44	78	.293	.392	56-2	.196	-1	128	-19	-2.0
1922	Bos A	14	11	.560	32	29	15-3	0	210.2	219	101	4	10	103	69	3.76	109	.274	.364	76-1	.158	-3*	86	9	0.6
1923	Det A	3	7	.300	17	14	3-1	0	92.1	104	61	3	10	22	25	4.87	79	.284	.342	27-2	.111	-2	99	-11	-1.2
1924	Det A	14	7	.667	34	30	11-1	0	216	199	99	6	4	63	75	3.21	128	.249	.307	76-5	.145	-5*	117	20	1.2
1925	Det A	6	11	.353	26	20	5	0	140	149	86	7	6	52	33	4.56	94	.281	.352	42-2	.119	-4	88	-5	-0.7
1926	Det A	8	8	.500	30	13	5-3	1	122	128	53	4	7	44	44	2.73	149	.278	.350	39-1	.154	-1*	105	15	1.7
1927	Det A	13	7	.650	30	25	10-1	0	172.2	207	116	5	8	59	37	4.69	90	.312	.375	54-7	.204	0	126	-10	-0.8
1929	StL A	11	6	.647	26	20	10-1	1	155.1	162	79	16	6	73	47	4.00	111	.270	.355	62-1	.274	4	120	7	1.1
1930	StL A	9	7	.563	35	20	6-1	2	171.2	168	90	11	5	63	75	4.35	112	.259	.330	54-4	.130	-2	89	12	0.7
1931	StL A	5	5	.500	17	14	2	0	107	130	55	5	1	38	34	3.79	122	.307	.366	34-2	.147	-1	82	9	0.8
Total	11	108	82	.568	311	219	84-15	5	1712.1	1795	926	73	81	674	569	3.99	106	.275	.351	582-35	.165	-18	105	39	2.3
COLLINS, PHIL Philip Eugene "Fidgety Phil" B 8.27.1901 Chicago, IL D 8.14.1948 Chicago, IL BR/TR 5-11/175# d10.7																									
1923	Chi N	1	0	1.000	1	1	0	0	5	8	2	0	0	1	2	3.60	111	.400	.429	2-0	.000	-0	205	0	0.1
1929	Phi N	9	7	.563	43	11	3	5	153.1	172	106	18	4	83	61	5.75	90	.284	.374	58-0	.190	-0*	125	-7	-0.7
1930	Phi N	16	11	.593	47	25	17-1	3	239	287	148	22	10	86	87	4.78	114	.299	.363	87-2	.253	3*	101	17	1.8
1931	Phi N	12	16	.429	42	27	16-2	4	240.1	268	126	14	5	83	73	3.86	110	.283	.344	95-0	.168	-4*	92	8	0.6
1932	Phi N	14	12	.538	43	21	6	3	184.1	231	117	21	6	65	66	5.27	84	.314	.375	68-0	.265	2	123	-12	-1.4
1933	Phi N	8	13	.381	42	13	5-1	**6**	151	178	79	9	6	57	40	4.11	93	.293	.360	53-1	.132	-2*	57	-4	-0.8
1934	Phi N	13	18	.419	45	32	15	1	254	277	138	30	3	87	72	4.18	113	.273	.333	88-7	.170	-5*	83	13	0.8
1935	Phi N	0	2	.000	3	3	0	0	14.2	24	20	5	0	9	4	11.66	39	.348	.423	6-0	.000	-1	94	-9	-1.0
	StL N	7	6	.538	26	9	2	2	82.2	96	48	6	3	26	18	4.57	90	.290	.347	25-4	.160	-1	129	-4	-0.7
	Year	7	8	.467	29	12	2	2	97.1	120	54	11	3	35	22	5.64	74	.300	.361	31-4	.129	-2	120	-13	-1.7
Total	8	80	85	.485	292	142	64-4	24	1324.1	1541	784	125	37	497	423	4.66	100	.291	.356	482-14	.193	-8	99	2	-1.3
COLLINS, RAY Ray Williston B 2.11.1887 Colchester, VT D 1.9.1970 Burlington, VT BL/TL 6-1/185# d7.19																									
1909	Bos A	4	3	.571	12	8	4-2	0	73.2	70	29	2	0	18	31	2.81	89	.269	.317	23-1	.130	-0	120	-1	-0.1
1910	Bos A	13	11	.542	35	26	18-4	1	244.2	205	73	1	1	41	109	1.62	158	.229	.264	84-4	.179	-1	90	22	1.9
1911	Bos A	11	12	.478	31	24	14	1	194.2	184	81	1	4	44	86	2.40	136	.256	.302	60-3	.150	0	76	19	2.0
1912	†Bos A	13	8	.619	27	24	17-4	0	199.1	192	65	4	2	42	82	2.53	135	.256	.297	65-3	.169	0	118	22	2.1
1913	Bos A	19	8	.704	30	30	19-3	0	246.2	242	88	3	2	37	88	2.63	112	.264	.294	80-7	.150	2	108	12	1.3
1914	Bos A	20	13	.606	39	30	16-6	0	272.1	252	95	3	0	56	72	2.51	107	.258	.298	79-9	.139	-0	91	8	0.7
1915	Bos A	4	7	.364	25	9	2	2	104.2	101	62	1	1	31	43	4.30	65	.261	.317	28-1	.286	5	122	-17	-1.4
Total	7	84	62	.575	199	151	90-19	4	1336	1246	493	15	10	269	511	2.51	115	.254	.294	419-28	.165	6	100	65	6.5
COLLUM, JACKIE Jack Dean B 6.21.1927 Victor, IA BL/TL 5-7/163# d9.21																									
1951	StL N	2	1	.667	3	2	1-1	0	17	11	3	0	0	10	5	1.59	250	.204	.328	7-0	.429	1	111	5	1.0
1952	StL N	0	0	—	2	0	0	0	3	2	1	0	0	1	0	0.00	—	.200	.273	0-0	—	0		1	0.1
1953	StL N	0	0	—	7	0	0	0	11.1	15	10	1	0	4	5	6.35	67	.326	.380	3-0	.000	-0		-3	-0.1
	Cin N	7	11	.389	30	12	4-1	3	124.2	123	57	8	6	39	51	3.75	116	.263	.328	36-3	.278	3	92	9	1.5
	Year	7	11	.389	37	12	4-1	3	136	138	62	9	6	43	56	3.97	109	.269	.333	39-3	.256	2	92	5	1.4
1954	Cin N	7	3	.700	36	2	1	0	79	86	43	8	5	32	28	3.76	112	.283	.359	13-2	.231	2	106	1	0.4
1955	Cin N	9	8	.529	32	17	5	1	134	128	65	17	2	37-4	49	3.63	117	.254	.306	40-5	.250	2	131	7	1.1
1956	StL N	6	2	.750	38	1	0	7	60	63	29	6	2	27-6	17	4.20	90	.281	.358	14-0	.214	1	140	-1	-0.1
1957	Chi N	1	1	.500	9	0	0	1	10.2	8	8	0	1	9-1	7	6.75	57	.211	.367	0-0	—	0		-3	-0.6
	Bro N	0	0	—	3	0	0	0	4.1	7	4	1	0	1-0	3	8.31	50	.368	.381	0-0	—	0		-2	-0.1
	Year	1	1	.500	12	0	0	1	15	15	18	1	1	10-1	10	7.20	55	.263	.371	0-0	—	0		-5	-0.7
1958	LA N	0	0	—	2	0	0	0	3.1	4	3	2	0	2-0	0	8.10	51	.308	.400	1-0	.000	-0		-1	-0.1
1962	Min A	0	2	.000	8	3	0	0	15.1	29	22	1	0	11-0	5	11.15	37	.414	.482	4-0	.000	-0	95	-12	-1.3
	Cle A	0	0	—	1	0	0	0	1.1	4	2	0	0	0-0	1	13.50	29	.571	.571	0-0	—	0		-1	-0.1
	Year	0	2	.000	9	3	0	0	16.2	33	28	1	0	11-0	6	11.34	36	.429	.489	4-0	.000	-0	95	-13	-1.4
Total	9	32	28	.533	171	37	11-2	12	464	480	247	44	16	173-11	171	4.15	101	.273	.342	118-10	.246	8	115	0	1.7
COLOME, JESUS Jesus (De La Cruz) B 12.23.1977 San Pedro De Macoris, D.R. BR/TR 6-2/170# d6.21																									
2001	TB A	2	3	.400	30	0	0	0-0	48.2	37	22	8	2	25-4	31	3.33	135	.208	.309	0-0	—	0		6	0.4
2002	TB A	2	7	.222	32	0	0	0-5	41.1	56	41	6	2	33-5	33	8.27	54	.341	.455	0-0	—	0		-17	-3.1
2003	TB A	3	7	.300	54	0	0	2-6	74	69	37	9	3	46-5	69	4.50	101	.247	.355	0-0	—	0		2	0.2
Total	3	7	17	.292	116	0	0	2-11	164	162	100	23	7	104-14	133	5.10	88	.261	.369	0-0	—	0		-9	-2.5
COLON, BARTOLO Bartolo B 5.24.1973 Altamira, D.R. BR/TR 6/185# d4.4																									
1997	Cle A	4	7	.364	19	17	1	0-0	94	107	66	12	3	45-1	66	5.65	83	.286	.366	1-0	.000	-0	104	-11	-1.0
1998	†Cle A★	14	9	.609	31	31	6-2	0-0	204	205	91	15	3	79-5	158	3.71	129	.260	.329	2-0	.500	0	101	23	2.4
1999	†Cle A	18	5	.783	32	32	1-1	0-0	205	185	97	24	7	76-5	161	3.95	128	.242	.314	7-1	.143	-0	121	24	2.5
2000	Cle A	15	8	.652	30	30	2-1	0-0	188	163	86	21	4	98-4	212	3.88	128	.233	.329	5-0	.000	-1	101	22	2.3
2001	Cle A	14	12	.538	34	34	1	0-0	222.1	220	106	26	2	90-2	201	4.09	111	.261	.332	7-0	.143	-0	102	13	1.3
2002	Cle A	10	4	.714	16	16	4-2	0-0	116.1	104	37	11	2	31-1	75	2.55	172	.245	.297	6-0	.167	-0	82	24	2.7
	Mon N	10	4	.714	17	17	4-1	0-0	117	115	48	9	0	39-4	74	3.31	135	.259	.317	39-2	.128	-1	108	14	1.4
2003	Chi A	15	13	.536	34	34	**9**	0-0	242	223	107	30	5	67-3	173	3.87	118	.248	.301	6-1	.000	-1	104	21	1.9
Total	7	100	62	.617	213	211	28-7	0-0	1388.2	1322	638	148	26	525-25	1120	3.86	122	.252	.322	73-4	.123	-3	104	130	13.5
COLPAERT, DICK Richard Charles B 1.3.1944 Fraser, MI BR/TR 5-10/182# d7.21																									
1970	Pit N	1	0	1.000	8	0	0	0-0	10.2	9	7	3	0	8-2	6	5.91	66	.237	.370	0-0	—	0		-2	-0.2
COLSON, LOYD Loyd Albert B 11.4.1947 Wellington, TX BR/TR 6-1/190# d9.25																									
1970	NY A	0	0	—	1	0	0	0-0	2	3	1	0	0	0-0	3	4.50	78	.333	.333	0-0	—	0		0	0.0
COLTON, LARRY Lawrence Robert B 6.8.1942 Los Angeles, CA BL/TR 6-3/200# d5.6																									
1968	Phi N	0	0	—	1	0	0	0	2	3	1	0	0	0-0	2	4.50	67	.333	.333	0-0	—	0		0	0.0
COLYER, STEVE Stephen Edward B 2.22.1979 St.Louis, MO BL/TL 6-4/200# d4.3																									
2003	LA N	0	0	—	13	0	0	0-0	19.2	22	6	0	0	9-0	16	2.75	146	.297	.373	0-0	—	0		3	0.2
COMBE, GEOFF Geoffrey Wade B 2.1.1956 Melrose, MA BR/TR 6-2/185# d9.2																									
1980	Cin N	0	0	—	4	0	0	0-0	6.2	9	8	0	0	4-1	10	10.80	33	.346	.433	0-0	—	0		-5	-0.3
1981	Cin N	1	0	1.000	14	0	0	0-0	17.2	27	15	3	0	10-1	9	7.64	47	.370	.440	0-0	—	0		-7	-0.4
Total	2	1	0	1.000	18	0	0	0-0	24.1	36	23	3	0	14-2	19	8.51	42	.364	.439	0-0	—	0		-12	-0.7
COMBS, PAT Patrick Dennis B 10.29.1966 Newport, RI BL/TL 6-3/200# d9.5																									
1989	Phi N	4	0	1.000	6	6	1-1	0-0	38.2	36	10	2	0	6-1	30	2.09	169	.248	.278	12-1	.167	0	104	6	0.7
1990	Phi N	10	10	.500	32	31	3-2	0-0	183.1	179	90	12	4	86-7	108	4.07	94	.257	.339	60-4	.150	0	92	-4	-0.3
1991	Phi N	2	6	.250	14	13	1	0-0	64.1	64	41	7	2	43-1	41	4.90	75	.254	.365	15-2	.133	1	102	-10	-1.1
1992	Phi N	1	1	.500	4	4	0	0-0	18.2	20	16	0	0	12-0	11	7.71	45	.278	.376	8-1	.125	0	136	-8	-0.7
Total	4	17	17	.500	56	54	5-3	0-0	305	299	157	21	6	147-9	190	4.22	89	.257	.340	95-8	.147	2	99	-16	-1.4
COMELLAS, JORGE Jorge (Pous) "Pancho" B 12.7.1916 Havana, Cuba D 9.13.2001 Miami, FL BR/TR 6/190# d4.19																									
1945	Chi N	0	2	.000	7	1	0	0	12	11	7	1	0	6	6	4.50	81	.244	.333	3-0	.000	-0	93	-1	-0.1
COMER, STEVE Steven Michael B 1.13.1954 Minneapolis, MN BB/TR 6-3/205# d4.15 C1																									
1978	Tex A	11	5	.688	30	11	3-2	1-2	117.1	107	36	5	1	37-3	65	2.30	163	.249	.309	0-0	—	0	137	18	2.5
1979	Tex A	17	12	.586	36	36	6-1	0-0	242.1	230	114	24	8	84-4	86	3.68	113	.252	.319	0-0	—	0	94	12	1.3
1980	Tex A	2	4	.333	12	11	0	0-0	41.2	65	41	5	2	22-0	9	7.99	49	.367	.441	0-0	—	0	150	-19	-2.2
1981	Tex A	8	2	.800	36	1	0	6-3	77.1	70	25	1	1	31-8	22	2.56	136	.241	.313	0-0	—	0	0	8	1.2
1982	Tex A	1	6	.143	37	3	1	6-2	97	133	64	11	2	36-9	23	5.10	76	.342	.395	0-0	—	0	78	-16	-1.2

Year	Tm Lg	W	L	Pct	G	GS	CG-Sho	SV-BS	IP	H	R	HR	HB	BB-IB	SO	ERA	AERA	OAV	OOB	AB-SH	AVG	PB	Sup	APR	PW
1983	Phi N	1	0	1.000	3	1	0	0-0	8.2	11	6	0	0	3-0	1	5.19	69	.314	.368	1-1	.000	-0	198	-2	-0.2
1984	Cle A	4	8	.333	22	20	1	0-0	117.1	146	80	11	4	39-2	39	5.68	72	.309	.360	0-0	—	0	84	-19	-1.7
Total	7	44	37	.543	176	83	11-3	13-7	701.2	762	366	57	18	252-26	245	4.13	96	.281	.344	1-1	.000	-0	106	-18	-0.3
COMISKEY, CHARLIE Charles Albert "Commy" or "The Old Roman" B 8.15.1859 Chicago, IL D 10.26.1931 Eagle River, WI BR/TR 6/180# d5.2 M12 HF1939 ▲																									
1882	StL AA	0	1	.000	2	1	1	0	8	12	8	0		3	2	0.00	—	.324	.375	329	.243	0*	55	1	0.1
1884	StL AA	0	0	—	1	0	0	0	4	1	1	0	0	0	4	2.25	145	.059	.059	460	.237	0*		1	0.0
1889	StL AA	0	0	—	1	0	0	0	0.1	0	0	0	0	0	0	0.00	—	.000	.000	587	.286	0*		0	0.0
Total	3	0	1	.000	4	1	1	0	12.1	13	9	0	0	3	6	0.73	410	.236	.276	1376	.259	0	55	2	0.1
COMPTON, JACK Harry Leroy B 3.9.1882 Lancaster, OH D 7.4.1974 Lancaster, OH BR/TR 5-9/157# d9.7																									
1911	Cin N	0	1	.000	8	3	0	1	25.1	19	11	0	1	15	6	3.91	85	.204	.321	6-0	.333	0	129	0	0.0
COMPTON, CLINT Robert Clinton B 11.1.1950 Montgomery, AL BL/TL 5-11/185# d10.3																									
1972	Chi N	0	0	—	1	0	0	0-0	2	2	2	0	0	2-0	0	9.00	42	.286	.444	0-0	—	0		-1	-0.1
COMSTOCK, KEITH Keith Martin B 12.23.1955 San Francisco, CA BL/TL 6/175# d4.3																									
1984	Min A	0	0	—	4	0	0	0-0	6.1	6	6	2	0	4-0	2	8.53	49	.261	.370	0-0	—	0		-3	-0.1
1987	SF N	2	0	1.000	15	0	0	1-1	20.2	19	8	1	0	10-2	21	3.05	126	.253	.337	1-0	.000	-0		2	0.2
	SD N	0	1	.000	26	0	0	0-0	36	33	22	4	0	21-3	38	5.50	72	.252	.348	1-0	.000	-0		-5	-0.3
	Year	2	1	.667	41	0	0	1-1	56.2	52	36	5	0	31-5	59	4.61	85	.252	.344	2-0	.000	-0		-3	-0.1
1988	SD N	0	0	—	7	0	0	0-1	8	8	6	1	0	3-1	9	6.75	50	.250	.314	0-0	—	0		-3	-0.1
1989	Sea A	1	2	.333	31	0	0	0-1	25.2	26	8	2	0	10-2	22	2.81	144	.268	.330	0-0	—	0		4	0.4
1990	Sea A	7	4	.636	60	0	0	2-5	56	40	22	4	0	26-5	50	2.89	137	.206	.296	0-0	—	0		6	1.2
1991	Sea A	0	0	—	1	0	0	0-0	0.1	2	2	0	0	1-0	0	54.00	8	.667	.750	0-0	—	0		-2	-0.1
Total	6	10	7	.588	144	0	0	3-8	153	134	74	14	0	75-13	142	4.06	97	.241	.327	2-0	.000	-0		-1	1.2
COMSTOCK, RALPH Ralph Remick "Commy" B 11.24.1890 Sylvania, OH D 9.13.1966 Toledo, OH BR/TR 5-10/168# d8.26																									
1913	Det A	2	5	.286	10	7	1	1	60.1	90	55	0	1	16	37	5.37	54	.346	.386	22-0	.227	1	112	-18	-1.8
1915	Bos A	1	0	1.000	3	0	0	0	9	10	3	2	0	2	1	2.00	139	.294	.333	2-0	.000	0		1	0.1
	Pit F	3	3	.500	12	7	3	2	52.2	44	25	2	1	7	18	3.25	83	.237	.268	16-1	.000	-2	103	-4	-0.7
1918	Pit N	5	6	.455	15	8	6	1	81	78	33	0	2	14	44	3.00	96	.259	.297	26-0	.192	-0	69	0	-0.1
Total	3	11	14	.440	40	22	10	4	203	222	116	4	4	39	100	3.72	76	.284	.322	66-1	.152	-2	94	-21	-2.5
CONDREY, CLAY Clayton Lee B 11.19.1975 Beaumont, TX BR/TR 6-3/195# d8.28																									
2002	SD N	1	2	.333	9	3	0	0-0	26.2	20	7	1	2	8-1	16	1.69	224	.217	.288	6-0	.000	-1	33	6	0.5
2003	SD N	1	2	.333	9	6	0	0-0	34	43	32	7	3	21-4	25	8.47	47	.305	.406	10-0	.200	0	135	-17	-1.2
Total	2	2	4	.333	18	9	0	0-0	60.2	63	39	8	5	29-5	41	5.49	70	.270	.361	16-0	.125	-1	102	-11	-0.7
CONE, DAVID David Brian B 1.2.1963 Kansas City, MO BL/TR 6-1/190# d6.8																									
1986	KC A	0	0	—	11	0	0	0-0	22.2	29	14	2	1	13-1	21	5.56	77	.309	.398	0-0	—	0		-3	-0.1
1987	NY N	5	6	.455	21	13	1	1-0	99.1	87	46	11	5	44-1	68	3.71	102	.239	.327	31-3	.065	-1	90	1	-0.1
1988	†NY N★	20	3	**.870**	35	28	8-4	0-0	231.1	178	67	10	4	80-7	213	2.22	145	.213	.283	80-5	.150	1	128	27	2.8
1989	NY N	14	8	.636	34	33	7-2	0-0	219.2	183	92	20	4	74-6	190	3.52	93	.223	.289	77-6	.234	4	123	-5	-0.1
1990	NY N	14	10	.583	31	30	6-2	0-0	211.2	177	84	21	1	65-1	**233**	3.23	116	.226	.284	70-9	.200	3*	119	13	1.7
1991	NY N	14	14	.500	34	34	5-2	0-0	232.2	204	95	13	5	73-2	**241**	3.29	111	.235	.296	72-6	.125	-1	95	10	1.1
1992	NY N★	13	7	.650	27	27	7-**5**	0-0	196.2	162	75	12	9	82-5	214	2.88	121	.223	.307	65-7	.092	-2	112	11	0.9
	†Tor A	4	3	.571	8	7	0	0-0	53	39	16	3	3	29-2	47	2.55	161	.206	.317	0-0	—	0	77	9	1.1
1993	KC A	11	14	.440	34	34	6-1	0-0	254	205	102	20	10	114-2	191	3.33	138	.223	.312	0-0	—	0	60	33	2.9
1994	KC A★	16	5	.762	23	23	4-3	0-0	171.2	130	60	15	7	54-0	132	2.94	171	.209	.277	0-0	—	0	90	**39**	**4.3**
1995	Tor A	9	6	.600	17	17	5-2	0-0	130.1	113	53	12	5	41-2	102	3.38	139	.232	.297	0-0	—	0	103	20	2.0
	†NY A	9	2	.818	13	13	1	0-0	99	82	42	12	1	47-0	89	3.82	121	.223	.312	0-0	—	0	129	10	1.0
	Year	18	8	.692	30	30	6-2	0-0	**229.1**	195	48	24	6	88-2	191	3.57	131	.228	.304	0-0	—	0	114	29	3.0
1996	†NY A	7	2	.778	11	11	1	0-0	72	50	25	3	2	34-0	71	2.88	172	.198	.293	0-0	—	0	126	16	1.8
1997	†NY A★	12	6	.667	29	29	1	0-0	195	155	67	17	4	86-2	222	2.82	158	.218	.305	3-0	.000	-0	97	36	2.9
1998	†NY A	**20**	7	.741	31	31	3	0-0	207.2	186	89	20	15	59-1	209	3.55	123	.237	.302	3-1	.000	-0	134	19	2.2
1999	†NY A★	12	9	.571	31	31	1-1	0-0	193.1	164	84	21	11	90-2	177	3.44	138	.229	.322	3-0	.333	1	109	27	2.5
2000	†NY A	4	14	.222	30	29	0	0-0	155	192	124	25	9	82-3	120	6.91	70	.306	.389	3-0	.333	0	92	-34	-3.1
2001	Bos A	9	7	.563	25	25	0	0-0	135.2	148	74	17	10	57-4	115	4.31	104	.275	.351	1-1	.000	-0	95	2	0.1
2003	NY N	1	3	.250	5	4	0	0-0	18	20	13	4	0	13-1	13	6.50	64	.282	.393	4-0	.250	0	51	-4	-0.8
Total	17	194	126	.606	450	419	56-22	1-0	2898.2	2504	1222	258	106	1137-42	2668	3.46	120	.232	.309	412-38	.155	5	104	227	23.1
CONE, BOB Robert Earl B 2.27.1894 Galveston, TX D 5.24.1955 Galveston, TX BR/TR 6-2/172# d7.25																									
1915	Phi A	0	0	—	1	1	0	0	0.2	5	3	0	0	0	0	40.50	7	.714	.714	0-0	—	0	100	-2	-0.1
CONGER, DICK Richard B 4.3.1921 Los Angeles, CA D 2.16.1970 Los Angeles, CA BR/TR 6/185# d4.22 Mil 1944-46																									
1940	Det A	1	0	1.000	2	0	0	0	3	2	1	0	0	3	1	3.00	159	.200	.385	0-0	—	0		1	0.1
1941	Pit N	0	0	—	2	1	0	0	4	3	0	0	0	3	2	0.00	—	.214	.353	0-0	—	0	24	2	0.1
1942	Pit N	0	0	—	2	1	0	0	8.1	9	3	0	0	5	3	2.16	157	.290	.389	3-0	.000	-0*	74	1	0.0
1943	Phi N	2	7	.222	13	10	2	0	54.2	72	46	3	5	24	18	6.09	55	.327	.406	16-0	.063	-1	91	-18	-2.6
Total	4	3	7	.300	19	12	2	0	70	86	50	3	5	35	24	5.14	67	.313	.400	19-0	.053	-1	82	-14	-2.4
CONKWRIGHT, ALLEN Allen Howard "Red" B 12.4.1896 Sedalia, MO D 7.30.1991 LaMesa, CA BR/TR 5-10/170# d9.16																									
1920	Det A	2	1	.667	5	3	0	1	19.1	29	16	0	0	16	4	6.98	53	.397	.506	5-0	.200	1	164	-6	-0.7
CONLEY, GENE Donald Eugene B 11.10.1930 Muskogee, OK BR/TR 6-8/225# d4.17																									
1952	Bos N	0	3	.000	4	3	0	0	12.2	23	16	4	2	9	6	7.82	46	.397	.493	5-0	.400	1	66	-8	-1.3
1954	Mil N★	14	9	.609	28	27	12-2	0	194.1	171	73	17	7	79	113	2.96	126	.240	.320	77-3	.156	-2	100	18	1.6
1955	Mil N★	11	7	.611	22	21	10	0	158	152	81	23	1	52-9	107	4.16	90	.254	.313	54-8	.204	-1	122	-7	-0.8
1956	Mil N	8	9	.471	31	19	5-1	3	158.1	169	74	13	2	52-10	68	3.13	111	.276	.333	45-8	.156	-1	106	2	0.1
1957	†Mil N	9	9	.500	35	18	6-1	1	148	133	63	9	2	64-5	61	3.16	111	.244	.323	46-2	.196	1	94	4	0.6
1958	Mil N	0	6	.000	26	7	0	2	72	89	44	8	4	17-1	53	4.88	72	.309	.353	16-0	.188	1	106	-13	-0.9
1959	Phi N★	12	7	.632	25	22	12-3	1	180	159	68	13	2	42-6	102	3.00	**137**	.235	.280	67-4	.239	2	119	21	2.4
1960	Phi N	8	14	.364	29	25	9-2	0	183.1	192	85	10	2	42-4	117	3.68	105	.272	.311	63-2	.127	-1	77	4	0.2
1961	Bos A	11	14	.440	33	30	6-2	1	199.2	229	116	33	3	65-2	113	4.91	85	.287	.343	73-2	.219	4	94	-12	-1.0
1962	Bos A	15	14	.517	34	33	9-2	1	241.2	238	116	28	5	68-5	134	3.95	105	.256	.308	87-1	.207	3	98	6	1.0
1963	Bos A	3	4	.429	9	9	0	0	40.2	51	31	4	1	21-0	14	6.64	57	.305	.386	15-1	.200	0	128	-11	-1.7
Total	11	91	96	.487	276	214	69-13	9	1588.2	1606	767	162	31	511-42	888	3.82	101	.264	.322	548-31	.192	8	101	4	0.2
CONLEY, ED Edward J. B 7.10.1864 Sandwich, MA D 10.16.1894 Cumberland, RI 5-8/142# d7.20																									
1884	Pro N	4	4	.500	8	8	8-1	0	71	63	47	4		22	33	2.15	132	.223	.280	28	.143	-2	88	3	0.0
CONLEY, SNIPE James Patrick B 4.25.1894 Cressona, PA D 1.7.1978 DeSoto, TX BR/TR 5-11.5/179# d5.20																									
1914	Bal F	4	6	.400	35	11	4-2	1	125	112	49	2	6	47	86	2.52	120	.259	.340	35-0	.114	-3	84	5	0.0
1915	Bal F	1	4	.200	25	6	4	0	86	97	48	5	4	32	40	4.29	67	.314	.386	24-0	.250	1	69	-11	-0.5
1918	Cin N	2	0	1.000	5	0	0	1	13.2	17	10	2	0	5	2	5.27	51	.321	.379	4-1	.250	0		-4	-0.6
Total	3	7	10	.412	65	17	8-2	2	224.2	226	107	9	10	84	128	3.36	88	.284	.360	63-1	.175	-1	80	-10	-1.1
CONLEY, BOB Robert Burns B 2.1.1934 Mousie, KY BR/TR 6-1/188# d9.11																									
1958	Phi N	0	0	—	2	2	0	0	8.1	9	7	0	0	1-0	0	7.56	52	.273	.278	1-1	.000	-0	136	-3	-0.2
CONN, BERT Albert Thomas B 9.22.1879 Philadelphia, PA D 11.2.1944 Philadelphia, PA TR 6/178# d9.16 ▲																									
1898	Phi N	0	1	.000	1	1	0	0	7	13	9	1	0	2	3	6.43	53	.394	.429	3-0	.333	1	103	-3	-0.3
1900	Phi N	0	2	.000	4	1	1	0	17.1	29	29	0	6	16	2	8.31	44	.372	.510	9-0	.333	1*	76	-12	-1.0
Total	2	0	3	.000	5	2	1	0	24.1	42	38	1	6	18	5	7.77	46	.378	.489	12-0	.333	2	88	-15	-1.3

Year	Tm Lg	W	L	Pct	G	GS	CG-Sho	SV-BS	IP	H	R	HR	HB	BB-IB	SO	ERA	AERA	OAV	OOB	AB-SH	AVG	PB	Sup	APR	PW
CONNALLY, SARGE George Walter B 8.31.1898 McGregor, TX D 1.27.1978 Temple, TX BR/TR 5-11/170# d9.10																									
1921	Chi A	0	1	.000	5	2	0	0	22.1	29	16	0	1	10	6	6.45	66	.330	.404	8-0	.500	2	59	-5	-0.1
1923	Chi A	0	0	—	3	0	0	0	8.2	7	6	0	1	12	3	6.23	64	.241	.476	3-1	.333	0		-2	-0.1
1924	Chi A	7	13	.350	44	13	6	6	160	177	95	4	9	68	55	4.05	102	.290	.369	50-1	.220	-1	82	-3	-0.3
1925	Chi A	6	7	.462	40	2	0	8	104.2	122	66	2	2	58	45	4.64	89	.310	.402	28-4	.250	1	91	-7	-0.6
1926	Chi A	6	5	.545	31	8	5	3	108.1	128	51	0	2	35	47	3.16	122	.300	.356	32-4	.156	-1	117	6	0.5
1927	Chi A	10	15	.400	43	18	11-1	5	198.1	217	108	8	9	83	58	4.08	99	.292	.370	67-7	.328	4	77	-1	0.3
1928	Chi A	2	5	.286	28	5	1	2	74.1	89	52	1	4	29	28	4.84	84	.313	.385	19-1	.105	-1	67	-8	-0.9
1929	Chi A	0	0	—	11	0	0	1	11.1	13	6	0	0	8	3	4.76	90	.317	.429	0-0	—	0		0	0.0
1931	Cle A	5	5	.500	17	9	5	1	85.2	87	56	7	6	50	37	4.20	110	.256	.361	27-4	.185	0	73	1	0.1
1932	Cle A	8	6	.571	35	7	4-1	3	112.1	119	59	6	3	42	32	4.33	110	.266	.333	40-2	.175	-0	126	7	0.7
1933	Cle A	5	3	.625	41	3	1	1	103	112	60	4	3	49	30	4.89	91	.271	.353	26-3	.231	1	83	-2	-0.2
1934	Cle A	0	0	—	5	0	0	1	5.1	4	3	0	0	5	1	5.06	90	.222	.391	1-0	.000	-0		0	0.0
Total	12	49	60	.450	303	67	33-2	31	994.1	1104	578	32	40	449	345	4.30	98	.288	.368	301-27	.233	5	87	-14	-0.6
CONNELLY, STEVE Steven Lee B 4.27.1974 Long Beach, CA BR/TR 6-4/210# d6.28																									
1998	Oak A	0	0	—	3	0	0	0-0	4.2	10	1	0	1	4-0	1	1.93	237	.435	.536	0-0	—	0		1	0.1
CONNELLY, BILL William Wirt "Wild Bill" B 6.29.1925 Alberta, VA D 11.27.1980 Richmond, VA BL/TR 6/175# d8.22																									
1945	Phi A	1	1	.500	2	1	0	0	8	7	4	0	0	8	0	4.50	76	.259	.429	1-0	.000	0	25	-1	-0.1
1950	Chi A	0	0	—	2	0	0	0	2.1	5	3	1	0	1	0	11.57	39	.455	.500	0-0	—	0		-2	-0.1
	Det A	0	0	—	2	0	0	0	4	4	3	1	0	2	1	6.75	69	.250	.333	1-0	.000	0		-1	0.0
	Year	0	0	—	4	0	0	0	6.1	9	7	2	0	3	1	8.53	54	.333	.400	1-0	.000	0		-2	-0.1
1952	NY N	5	0	1.000	11	4	0	0	31.2	22	18	4	0	25	22	4.55	81	.208	.359	11-0	.364	3	150	-3	-0.1
1953	NY N	0	1	.000	8	2	0	0	20.1	33	26	4	0	17	11	11.07	39	.371	.472	6-0	.000	-1	73	-14	-0.7
Total	4	6	2	.750	25	7	0	0	66.1	71	54	10	0	53	34	6.92	57	.285	.411	19-0	.211	3	106	-21	-1.0
CONNOLLY, ED Edward Joseph Jr. B 12.3.1939 Brooklyn, NY D 7.1.1998 New Canaan, CT BL/TL 6-1/190# d4.19 f-Ed																									
1964	Bos A	4	11	.267	27	15	1-1	0	80.2	80	50	3	6	64-2	73	4.91	79	.261	.395	18-2	.167	0	57	-9	-1.6
1967	Cle A	2	1	.667	15	4	0	0	49.1	63	46	6	1	34-2	45	7.48	44	.315	.414	11-1	.182	0	133	-22	-1.3
Total	2	6	12	.333	42	19	1-1	0	130	143	96	9	7	98-4	118	5.88	62	.282	.402	29-3	.172	0	73	-31	-2.9
CONNOR, JOHN John B 7.1861 Nashua, NH D 11.14.1905 Nashua, NH d7.26																									
1884	Bos N	1	4	.200	7	7	7	0	60	70	44	1		18	29	3.15	92	.275	.322	25	.080	-3	79	-5	-0.5
1885	Buf N	0	1	.000	1	1	1	0	9	14	9	0		2	0	4.00	75	.378	.410	3	.000	-0	76	-2	-0.2
	Lou AA	1	3	.250	4	4	4	0	35	43	27	0	2	12	19	4.89	66	.295	.356	14	.143	-1	69	-4	-0.5
Total	2	2	8	.200	12	12	12	0	104	127	80	1	2	32	48	3.81	79	.290	.341	42	.095	-4	75	-11	-1.2
CONNORS, JOE Joseph C. (b: Joseph C. O'Connor) B 1862 Paterson, NJ D 1.13.1891 Denver, CO d5.3																									
1884	Alt U	0	1	.000	1	1	1	0	9	18	14	0		5	0	7.00	38	.391	.451	11	.091	-1*	80	-4	-0.3
	KC U	0	1	.000	2	1	1	0	12	24	14	1		0	1	4.50	50	.393	.393	11	.091	-1*	57	-4	-0.3
	Year	0	2	.000	3	2	2	0	21	42	17	1		5	1	5.57	43	.393	.420	22	.091	-2	71	-8	-0.6
CONNORS, BILL William Joseph B 11.2.1941 Schenectady, NY BR/TR 6-1/180# d5.3 C17																									
1966	Chi N	0	1	.000	11	0	0	0	16	20	13	4	0	7-1	3	7.31	50	.308	.370	0-0	—	0		-5	-0.3
1967	NY N	0	0	—	6	1	0	0	13	8	9	3	1	5-0	13	6.23	54	.170	.264	1-0	.000	-0	130	-4	-0.2
1968	NY N	0	1	.000	9	0	0	0	14	21	14	0	1	7-1	8	9.00	34	.339	.414	1-1	1.000	1		-8	-0.5
Total	3	0	2	.000	26	1	0	0	43	49	36	7	2	19-2	24	7.53	45	.282	.357	2-1	.500	1	130	-17	-1.0
CONOVAR, TED Theodore "Huck" B 3.10.1868 Lexington, KY D 7.27.1910 Paris, KY BR/TR 5-10.5/165# d5.26																									
1889	Cin AA	0	0	—	1	0	0	1	2	4	4	0	0	2	1	13.50	29	.400	.500	0	—	0		-2	-0.2
CONROY, TIM Timothy James B 4.3.1960 McKeesport, PA BL/TL 5-11/185# d6.23																									
1978	Oak A	0	0	—	2	2	0	0-0	4.2	3	6	0	1	9-0	0	7.71	47	.188	.481	0-0	—	0	160	-3	-0.1
1982	Oak A	2	2	.500	5	5	1	0-0	25.1	20	13	1	0	18-0	17	3.55	110	.222	.349	0-0	—	0	112	0	0.0
1983	Oak A	7	10	.412	39	18	3-1	0-0	162.1	141	89	17	2	98-2	112	3.94	98	.232	.338	0-0	—	0	83	-6	-0.7
1984	Oak A	1	6	.143	38	14	0	0-1	93	82	58	11	2	63-0	69	5.23	72	.236	.353	0-0	—	0	84	-15	-1.1
1985	Oak A	0	1	.000	16	2	0	0-1	25.1	22	15	3	1	15-1	8	4.26	91	.237	.345	0-0	—	0	71	-2	-0.1
1986	StL N	5	11	.313	25	21	1	0-0	115.1	122	72	15	3	56-7	79	5.23	70	.275	.353	29-8	.138	1*	91	-20	-2.4
1987	StL N	3	2	.600	10	9	0	0-0	40.2	48	26	0	1	25-3	22	5.53	75	.306	.400	15-2	.000	-2	150	-6	-0.8
Total	7	18	32	.360	135	71	5-1	0-2	466.2	438	279	47	10	284-13	307	4.69	81	.249	.353	44-10	.091	-1	99	-52	-5.2
CONSTABLE, JIM Jimmy Lee "Sheriff" B 6.14.1933 Jonesborough, TN BB/TL 6-1/185# d6.24																									
1956	NY N	0	0	—	3	0	0	0	4.1	9	7	0	1	7-0	1	14.54	26	.429	.586	0-0	—	0		-5	-0.2
1957	NY N	1	1	.500	16	0	0	0	28.1	27	10	2	4	7-0	13	2.86	138	.262	.333	5-0	.000	-0		3	0.2
1958	SF N	1	0	1.000	9	0	0	1	8	10	6	1	0	3-0	4	5.63	68	.323	.382	1-0	1.000	1		-2	-0.1
	Cle A	0	1	.000	6	2	0	0	9.1	17	13	2	1	4-0	3	11.57	32	.415	.478	2-0	1.000	1	74	-8	-0.7
	Was A	0	1	.000	15	2	0	0	27.2	29	15	3	1	15-0	25	4.88	78	.271	.360	4-0	.250	0	71	-3	-0.1
	Year	0	2	.000	21	4	0	0	37	46	18	5	2	19-0	28	6.57	57	.311	.392	6-0	.500	1	71	-11	-0.8
1962	Mil N	1	1	.500	3	2	1-1	1	18	14	4	1	0	4-0	12	2.00	190	.222	.265	5-1	.000	-0	46	4	0.4
1963	SF N	0	0	—	4	0	0	0	2.1	3	1	0	0	1-0	1	3.86	83	.333	.400	0-0	—	0		0	0.0
Total	5	3	4	.429	56	6	1-1	2	98	109	56	9	7	41-0	59	4.87	78	.291	.369	17-1	.235	2	62	-11	-0.5
CONSUEGRA, SANDY Sandalio Simeon (Castello) B 9.3.1920 Potrerillos, Cuba BR/TR 5-10/165# d6.10																									
1950	Was A	7	8	.467	21	18	8-2	2	124.2	132	71	6	1	57	38	4.40	102	.270	.347	40-4	.175	-1*	102	1	0.0
1951	Was A	7	8	.467	40	12	5	3	146	140	71	10	0	63	31	4.01	102	.251	.327	43-3	.233	-0	112	2	0.2
1952	Was A	6	0	1.000	30	2	0	5	73.2	80	30	2	0	27	19	3.05	116	.276	.338	17-2	.176	-0	368	4	0.3
1953	Was A	0	0	—	4	0	0	0	5	9	6	0	0	4	0	10.80	36	.391	.481	0-0	—	0		-4	-0.2
	Chi A	7	5	.583	29	13	5-1	3	124	122	39	9	2	28	30	2.54	158	.258	.302	35-6	.057	-4	65	20	1.7
	Year	7	5	.583	33	13	5-1	3	129	131	42	9	2	32	30	2.86	141	.264	.311	35-6	.057	-4	65	16	1.5
1954	Chi A★	16	3	**.842**	39	17	3-2	3	154	142	52	9	0	35	31	2.69	139	.248	.289	48-4	.229	1	107	17	2.3
1955	Chi A	6	5	.545	44	7	3	7	126.1	120	42	4	2	18-7	35	2.64	150	.256	.283	29-3	.103	-2	125	**18**	1.4
1956	Chi A	1	2	.333	28	1	0	3	38.1	45	25	0	1	11-3	7	5.17	79	.296	.345	4-0	.000	-1	22	-5	-0.5
	Bal A	1	1	.500	4	1	0	0	8.2	10	4	2	0	2-0	1	4.15	94	.294	.324	2-0	.500	0	91	0	0.0
	Year	2	3	.400	32	2	0	3	47	55	8	2	1	13-3	8	4.98	82	.296	.342	6-0	.167	-0	55	-5	-0.5
1957	Bal A	0	0	—	5	0	0	0	5	4	1	0	0	0-0	0	1.80	200	.211	.200	0-0	—	0		1	0.1
	NY N	0	0	—	4	0	0	0	3.2	7	5	1	0	1-1	1	2.45	160	.389	.400	0-0	—	0		-1	0.0
Total	8	51	32	.614	248	71	24-5	26	809.1	811	346	43	6	246-11	193	3.37	119	.262	.316	218-22	.170	-5	107	53	5.3
CONTRERAS, NARDI Arnaldo Juan B 9.19.1951 Tampa, FL BB/TR 6-2/193# d5.23 C7																									
1980	Chi A	0	0	—	8	0	0	0-0	13.2	18	10	1	2	7-2	8	5.93	68	.333	.422	0-0	—	0		-3	-0.1
CONTRERAS, JOSE Jose Ariel B 12.12.1971 Las Martinas, Cuba BR/TR 6-4/230# d3.31																									
2003	†NY A	7	2	.778	18	9	0	0-1	71	52	27	4	5	30-1	72	3.30	133	.202	.297	3-0	.000	-0	107	10	1.0
CONVERSE, JIM James Daniel B 8.17.1971 San Francisco, CA BL/TR 5-9/180# d5.22																									
1993	Sea A	1	3	.250	4	4	0	0-0	20.1	23	12	0	0	14-2	10	5.31	83	.295	.398	0-0	—	0	52	-2	-0.2
1994	Sea A	0	5	.000	13	8	0	0-0	48.2	73	49	5	1	40-4	39	8.69	56	.353	.454	0-0	—	0	56	-19	-1.5
1995	Sea A	0	3	.000	6	1	0	1-0	11	16	9	2	0	8-0	9	7.36	64	.348	.444	0-0	—	0	39	-3	-0.5
	KC A	1	0	1.000	9	0	0	0-0	12.1	12	8	0	0	8-2	5	5.84	82	.267	.377	0-0	—	0		-1	-0.1
	Year	1	3	.250	15	1	0	1-0	23.1	28	19	2	0	16-2	14	6.56	73	.308	.411	0-0	—	0	39	-4	-0.6
1997	KC A	0	0	—	3	0	0	0-0	5	4	2	2	0	5-0	3	3.60	131	.222	.391	0-0	—	0		1	0.0
Total	4	2	11	.154	35	13	0	1-0	97.1	128	80	9	1	75-8	66	7.21	66	.325	.430	0-0	—	0	54	-24	-2.3
CONWAY, JIM James P. B 10.8.1858 Clifton, PA TR d5.5 b-Pete																									
1884	Bro AA	3	9	.250	13	13	10	0	105.1	132	84	4	3	15	25	4.44	75	.289	.316	47	.128	-4*	110	-13	-1.5

Year	Tm Lg	W	L	Pct	G	GS	CG-Sho	SV-BS	IP	H	R	HR	HB	BB-IB	SO	ERA	AERA	OAV	OOB	AB-SH	AVG	PB	Sup	APR	PW
1885	Phi AA	0	1	.000	2	2	1	0	12.1	19	16	0	0	2	0	7.30	47	.358	.382	6	.000	-0	154	-4	-0.3
1889	KC AA	19	19	.500	41	37	33	0	335	334	232	12	14	90	115	3.25	129	.252	.306	149	.208	-6	92	27	1.9
Total	3	22	29	.431	56	52	44	0	452.2	485	332	16	17	107	140	3.64	109	.264	.311	202	.183	-10	98	10	0.1
CONWAY, JERRY Jerome Patrick B 6.7.1901 Holyoke, MA D 4.16.1980 Holyoke, MA BL/TL 6-2/190# d8.31																									
1920	Was A	0	0	—	1	0	0	0	2	1	0	0	0	1	0	0.00	—	.167	.286	0-0	—	0		1	0.0
CONWAY, PETE Peter J. B 10.30.1866 Burmont, PA D 1.13.1903 Clifton Heights, PA BR/TR 5-10.5/162# d8.10 b-Jim ▲																									
1885	Buf N	10	17	.370	27	27	26-1	0	210	256	173	10		44	94	4.67	64	.287	.320	90	.111	-4*	71	-35	-3.8
1886	KC N	5	15	.250	23	20	19	0	180	236	185	6		61	81	5.75	65	.294	.343	194	.242	0*	76	-38	-3.2
	Det N	6	5	.545	11	11	11	0	91	93	55	1		25	35	3.36	99	.255	.303	43	.186	1*	127	-1	-0.1
	Year	11	20	.355	34	31	30	0	271	329	62	7		86	116	4.95	73	.282	.331	237	.232	1	93	-38	-3.3
1887	†Det N	8	9	.471	17	17	16	0	146	132	95	3	5	47	40	2.90	141	.235	.300	95	.232	0*	95	9	0.9
1888	Det N	30	14	.682	45	45	43-4	0	391	315	170	11	13	57	176	2.26	124	.208	**.243**	167	.275	14	131	23	3.9
1889	Pit N	2	1	.667	3	3	2	0	22	26	16	1	0	16	2	4.91	76	.286	.393	10	.100	0	113	-3	-0.2
Total	5	61	61	.500	126	123	117-5	0	1040	1058	694	32	18	250	428	3.59	90	.250	.295	599	.224	12	101	-45	-2.5
CONWAY, DICK Richard Butler B 4.25.1865 Lowell, MA D 9.9.1926 Lowell, MA BL/TR 5-7.5/140# d7.22 b-Bill																									
1886	Bal AA	2	7	.222	9	9	8	0	76.2	106	91	6	3	43	64	6.81	50	.312	.394	34	.206	0	121	-28	-2.3
1887	Bos N	9	15	.375	26	26	25	0	222.1	249	161	10	7	86	45	4.66	88	.276	.343	145	.248	2*	81	-12	-0.8
1888	Bos N	4	2	.667	6	6	6	0	53	49	31	2	4	8	12	2.38	121	.240	.282	25	.160	-1*	117	1	0.0
Total	3	15	24	.385	41	41	39	0	352	404	283	18	14	137	121	4.78	79	.279	.347	204	.230	1	94	-39	-3.1
CONZELMAN, JOE Joseph Harrison B 7.14.1885 Bristol, CT D 4.17.1979 Mountain Brook, AL BR/TR 6/170# d5.1																									
1913	Pit N	0	1	.000	3	2	1	0	15	13	4	0	1	5	9	1.20	252	.245	.322	4-0	.000	-1	37	3	0.1
1914	Pit N	5	6	.455	33	9	4-1	2	101	88	39	2	3	40	39	2.94	90	.254	.337	27-0	.111	-2	66	-2	-0.3
1915	Pit N	1	1	.500	18	1	0	0	47.1	41	18	0	3	20	22	3.42	80	.248	.340	11-0	.091	-1	82	-2	-0.2
Total	3	6	8	.429	54	12	5-1	2	163.1	142	61	2	7	65	70	2.92	93	.252	.336	42-0	.095	-3	63	-1	-0.4
COOK, AARON Aaron Lane B 2.8.1979 Fort Campbell, KY BR/TR 6-3/175# d8.10																									
2002	Col N	2	1	.667	9	5	0	0-0	35.2	41	18	4	2	13-0	14	4.54	105	.295	.364	11-1	.091	-1	85	1	0.1
2003	Col N	4	6	.400	43	16	1	0-0	124	160	89	8	8	57-7	43	6.02	82	.317	.391	29-6	.172	-0	105	-13	-0.9
Total	2	6	7	.462	52	21	1	0-0	159.2	201	107	12	10	70-7	57	5.69	86	.313	.385	40-7	.150	-1	100	-12	-0.8
COOK, ANDY Andrew Bernard B 8.30.1967 Memphis, TN BR/TR 6-5/215# d5.9																									
1993	NY A	0	1	.000	4	0	0	0-0	5.1	4	3	1	0	7-0	4	5.06	82	.200	.407	0-0	—	0		0	-0.1
COOK, DENNIS Dennis Bryan B 10.4.1962 LaMarque, TX BL/TL 6-3/185# d9.12																									
1988	SF N	2	1	.667	4	4	1-1	0-0	22	9	8	1	0	11-1	13	2.86	114	.125	.233	4-1	.000	1	116	1	0.2
1989	SF N	1	0	1.000	2	2	1	0-0	15	13	3	1	0	5-0	9	1.80	188	.245	.310	6-0	.167	1	131	3	0.3
	Phi N	6	8	.429	21	16	1-1	0-0	106	97	56	17	2	33-6	58	3.99	89	.243	.303	36-2	.222	1*	98	-6	-0.7
	Year	7	8	.467	23	18	2-1	0-0	121	110	60	18	2	38-6	67	3.72	95	.243	.304	42-2	.214	2	102	-4	-0.4
1990	Phi N	8	3	.727	42	13	2-1	1-1	141.2	132	61	13	2	54-9	58	3.56	108	.250	.319	42-4	.310	4*	127	5	0.8
	LA N	1	1	.500	5	3	0	0-0	14.1	23	13	7	0	2-0	6	7.53	49	.365	.373	7-0	.286	1	123	-6	-0.6
	Year	9	4	.692	47	16	2-1	1-1	156	155	18	20	2	56-9	64	3.92	97	.262	.325	49-4	.306	5	126	-1	0.2
1991	LA N	1	0	1.000	20	1	0	0-1	17.2	12	3	0	0	7-1	8	0.51	706	.203	.279	1-1	.000	-0	50	5	0.3
1992	Cle A	5	7	.417	32	25	1	0-0	158	156	79	29	2	50-2	96	3.82	103	.255	.312	0-0	—	0	106	0	-0.1
1993	Cle A	5	5	.500	25	6	0	0-2	54	62	36	9	2	16-1	34	5.67	77	.295	.348	0-0	—	0	88	-7	-1.2
1994	Chi A	3	1	.750	38	0	0	0-1	33	29	17	4	0	14-3	26	3.55	132	.230	.307	0-0	—	0		3	0.3
1995	Cle A	0	0	—	11	0	0	0-0	12.2	16	9	3	1	10-2	13	6.39	73	.320	.443	0-0	—	0		-2	-0.1
	Tex A	0	2	.000	35	1	0	2-0	45	47	23	6	1	16-1	40	4.00	121	.280	.337	0-0	—	0	116	3	0.1
	Year	0	2	.000	46	1	0	2-0	57.2	63	29	9	2	26-3	53	4.53	106	.289	.363	0-0	—	0	116	1	0.0
1996	†Tex A	5	2	.714	60	0	0	0-2	70.1	53	34	2	7	35-7	64	4.09	128	.214	.322	0-0	—	0		9	0.7
1997	†Fla N	1	2	.333	59	0	0	0-2	62.1	64	28	4	2	28-4	63	3.90	103	.267	.347	9-0	.556	3*		2	0.4
1998	NY N	8	4	.667	73	0	0	1-4	68	60	21	5	3	27-4	79	2.38	174	.240	.318	3-0	.000	-0		13	2.0
1999	†NY N	10	5	.667	71	0	0	3-3	63	50	27	11	1	27-1	68	3.86	114	.216	.299	1-0	.000	-0		4	0.8
2000	†NY N	6	3	.667	68	0	0	2-6	59	63	35	8	5	31-4	53	5.34	83	.270	.368	0-1	—	0		-5	-0.6
2001	NY N	1	1	.500	43	0	0	0-2	36	28	18	6	1	10-1	34	4.25	97	.207	.265	1-0	.000	-0		0	0.0
	Phi N	0	0	—	19	0	0	0-1	9.2	15	6	2	1	4-2	4	5.59	76	.385	.455	0-0	—	0		-1	-0.1
	Year	1	1	.500	62	0	0	0-3	45.2	43	24	8	2	14-3	38	4.53	92	.247	.309	1-0	.000	-0		-1	-0.1
2002	Ana A	1	1	.500	37	0	0	0-1	24	21	9	2	1	10-0	13	3.38	131	.241	.320	0-0	—	0		3	0.2
Total	15	64	46	.582	665	71	6-3	9-26	1011.2	950	486	130	31	390-49	739	3.91	105	.250	.322	110-9	.264	9	100	24	2.7
COOK, EARL Earl Davis B 12.10.1908 Stouffville, ON, CAN D 11.21.1996 Markham, ON, CAN BR/TR 6/195# d9.12																									
1941	Det A	0	0	—	1	0	0	0	2	4	1	0	0	0	1	4.50	101	.400	.400	0-0	—	0		0	0.0
COOK, GLEN Glen Patrick B 9.8.1959 Buffalo, NY BR/TR 5-11/180# d6.23																									
1985	Tex A	2	3	.400	9	7	0	0-0	40	53	42	12	3	18-1	19	9.45	45	.327	.396	0-0	—	0	107	-21	-2.1
COOK, MIKE Michael Horace B 8.14.1963 Charleston, SC BR/TR 6-3/200# d7.1																									
1986	Cal A	0	2	.000	5	1	0	0-1	9	13	12	3	0	7-1	6	9.00	46	.333	.435	0-0	—	0	66	-6	-1.0
1987	Cal A	1	2	.333	16	1	0	0-1	34.1	34	21	7	0	18-0	27	5.50	78	.264	.354	0-0	—	0	0	-3	-0.2
1988	Cal A	0	1	.000	3	0	0	0-0	3.2	4	2	0	1	1-0	2	4.91	79	.308	.400	0-0	—	0		0	-0.1
1989	Min A	0	1	.000	15	0	0	0-0	21.1	22	12	1	1	17-1	15	5.06	82	.268	.392	0-0	—	0		-2	-0.1
1993	Bal A	0	0	—	2	0	0	0-0	3	1	0	0	0	2-1	3	0.00	—	.091	.231	0-0	—	0		1	0.1
Total	5	1	6	.143	41	2	0	0-2	71.1	74	47	11	2	45-3	53	5.55	76	.270	.375	0-0	—	0	32	-10	-1.3
COOK, ROLLIN Rollin Edward B 10.5.1890 Toledo, OH D 8.11.1975 Toledo, OH BR/TR 5-9/152# d7.6																									
1915	StL A	0	0	—	5	0	0	0	13.2	16	14	0	1	9	7	7.24	40	.276	.382	4-0	.250	0		-6	-0.3
COOK, RON Ronald Wayne B 7.11.1947 Jefferson, TX BL/TL 6-1/175# d4.10																									
1970	Hou N	4	4	.500	41	7	0	2-0	82.1	80	37	4	3	42-4	50	3.72	104	.274	.367	17-1	.235	2*	102	2	0.4
1971	Hou N	0	4	.000	5	4	0	0-0	25.2	23	14	2	1	8-1	10	4.91	69	.237	.299	8-0	.250	0*	26	-4	-0.5
Total	2	4	8	.333	46	11	0	2-0	108	103	51	6	4	50-5	60	4.00	94	.265	.350	25-1	.240	2	76	-2	-0.1
COOKE, STEVE Steven Montague B 1.14.1970 Lihue, HI BR/TL 6-6/229# d7.28																									
1992	Pit N	2	0	1.000	11	0	0	1-0	23	22	9	2	0	4-1	10	3.52	98	.253	.286	3-2	.333	0		0	0.0
1993	Pit N	10	10	.500	32	32	3-1	0-0	210.2	207	101	22	3	59-4	132	3.89	104	.258	.310	71-6	.155	-1	104	1	0.0
1994	Pit N	4	11	.267	25	23	2	0-0	134.1	157	79	21	5	46-7	74	5.02	86	.298	.358	42-5	.190	0	84	-8	-0.8
1996	Pit N	0	0	—	3	0	0	0-0	8.1	11	7	1	0	5-0	7	7.56	58	.314	.390	1-0	.000	-0		-3	-0.1
1997	Pit N	9	15	.375	32	32	0	0-0	167.1	184	95	15	9	77-11	109	4.30	100	.284	.366	52-7	.058	-4	76	-3	-0.7
1998	Cin N	1	0	1.000	1	1	0	0-0	6	4	1	0	1	0-0	3	1.50	286	.182	.217	2-0	.500	0	107	2	0.4
Total	6	26	36	.419	104	88	5-1	1-0	549.2	585	292	61	18	191-23	335	4.31	97	.276	.339	171-20	.140	-3	89	-11	-1.2
COOMBS, DANNY Daniel Bernard B 3.23.1942 Lincoln, ME BR/TL 6-5/210# d9.27 Mil 1964																									
1963	Hou N	0	0	—	1	0	0	0	0.1	3	1	0	0	0-0	0	27.00	12	.750	.750	0-0	—	0		-1	0.0
1964	Hou N	1	1	.500	7	1	0	0	18	21	10	1	1	10-0	14	5.00	68	.300	.395	4-0	.000	-0	154	-3	-0.3
1965	Hou N	0	2	.000	26	3	0	0	47	54	26	3	3	23-1	35	4.79	70	.292	.374	9-0	.111	0	35	-7	-0.3
1966	Hou N	0	0	—	2	0	0	0	2.2	4	1	0	0	0-0	3	3.38	101	.333	.333	1-0	.000	-0		0	0.0
1967	Hou N	3	0	1.000	6	2	0	0	24.1	21	9	0	0	9-4	23	3.33	99	.233	.300	8-0	.125	0	80	1	0.1
1968	Hou N	4	3	.571	40	2	0	2	46.2	52	21	0	1	17-4	29	3.28	90	.286	.345	10-0	.400	1	88	-3	-0.2
1969	Hou N	0	1	.000	8	0	0	0-0	8	12	6	0	1	2-1	3	6.75	52	.364	.417	2-0	.000	-0		-2	-0.3
1970	SD N	10	14	.417	35	27	5-1	0-0	188.1	185	83	12	2	76-14	105	3.30	121	.256	.326	52-7	.096	-2	81	12	1.2
1971	SD N	1	6	.143	19	7	0	0-1	57.2	81	52	10	0	25-5	37	6.24	53	.327	.387	14-2	.214	1	130	-22	-2.2
Total	9	19	27	.413	144	42	5-1	2-1	393	433	209	26	8	162-29	249	4.08	88	.280	.349	100-9	.140	-0	90	-25	-2.0

COOMBS, JACK John Wesley "Colby Jack" B 11.18.1882 LeGrand, IA D 4.15.1957 Palestine, TX BB/TR 6/185# d7.5 M1 C1 ▲

Year	Tm Lg	W	L	Pct	G	GS	CG-Sho	SV-BS	IP	H	R	HR	HB	BB-IB	SO	ERA	AERA	OAV	OOB	AB-SH	AVG	PB	Sup	APR	PW
1906	Phi A	10	10	.500	23	18	13-1	0	173	144	65	0	7	68	90	2.50	109	.229	.312	67-1	.239	1*	81	5	0.7
1907	Phi A	6	9	.400	23	17	10-2	2	132.2	109	58	2	9	64	73	3.12	83	.227	.329	48-2	.167	-1*	93	-5	-0.7
1908	Phi A	7	5	.583	26	18	10-4	0	153	130	63	1	3	64	80	2.00	128	.233	.316	220-9	.255	4*	104	4	0.7
1909	Phi A	12	11	.522	30	24	18-6	1	205.2	156	63	1	6	73	97	2.32	104	.213	.289	83-2	.169	1*	104	6	0.8
1910	†Phi A	**31**	9	.775	**45**	38	35-**13**	1	353	248	74	0	7	115	224	1.30	183	.201	.273	132-1	.220	4*	110	**47**	5.8
1911	†Phi A	**28**	12	.700	47	**40**	26-1	2	336.2	360	166	8	16	119	185	3.53	89	.280	.348	141-3	.319	14*	150	-12	-0.2
1912	Phi A	21	10	.677	40	32	23-1	2	262.1	227	120	5	10	94	120	3.29	93	.241	.316	110-2	.255	6*	121	-4	0.2
1913	Phi A	0	0	—	2	2	0	0	5.1	5	9	0	1	6	0	10.13	27	.313	.522	3-0	.333	1	201	-5	-0.2
1914	Phi A	0	1	.000	2	2	0	0	8	8	4	0	1	3	1	4.50	58	.267	.353	11-0	.273	0*	56	-1	-0.1
1915	Bro N	15	10	.600	29	24	17-2	0	195.2	166	71	1	16	91	56	2.58	108	.236	.337	75-1	.280	4	88	6	1.0
1916	†Bro N	13	8	.619	27	19	10-3	0	159	136	54	3	2	44	47	2.66	101	.239	.296	61-0	.180	-0	94	4	0.3
1917	Bro N	7	11	.389	31	14	9	0	141	147	76	7	8	49	34	3.96	71	.284	.355	44-1	.227	2*	79	-17	-2.1
1918	Bro N	8	14	.364	27	20	16-2	0	189	191	97	10	2	49	44	3.81	73	.266	.315	113-1	.168	-0*	74	-18	-2.2
1920	Det A	0	0	—	2	0	0	0	5.2	7	5	0	0	2	1	3.18	117	.318	.375	2-0	.000	-0		-1	-0.1
Total	14	158	110	.590	354	268	187-35	8	2320	2034	925	38	88	841	1052	2.78	99	.241	.316	1110-23	.235	36	107	9	3.9

COOMBS, BOBBY Raymond Franklin B 2.2.1908 Goodwins Mills, ME D 10.21.1991 Ogunquit, ME BR/TR 5-9.5/160# d6.8

Year	Tm Lg	W	L	Pct	G	GS	CG-Sho	SV-BS	IP	H	R	HR	HB	BB-IB	SO	ERA	AERA	OAV	OOB	AB-SH	AVG	PB	Sup	APR	PW
1933	Phi A	0	1	.000	21	0	0	2	31.1	47	30	4	0	20	8	7.47	57	.348	.432	5-0	.400	1		-11	-0.4
1943	NY N	0	1	.000	9	0	0	0	16	33	26	1	0	8	5	12.94	27	.423	.477	2-0	.000	0		-17	-0.9
Total	2	0	2	.000	30	0	0	2	47.1	80	56	5	0	28	13	9.32	43	.376	.448	7-0	.286	1		-28	-1.3

COONEY, JOHNNY John Walter B 3.18.1901 Cranston, RI D 7.8.1986 Sarasota, FL BR/TL 5-10/165# d4.19 M1 C21 f-Jimmy b-Jimmy ▲

Year	Tm Lg	W	L	Pct	G	GS	CG-Sho	SV-BS	IP	H	R	HR	HB	BB-IB	SO	ERA	AERA	OAV	OOB	AB-SH	AVG	PB	Sup	APR	PW
1921	Bos N	0	1	.000	8	1	0	0	20.2	19	12	3	0	10	9	3.92	93	.241	.326	5-0	.200	-0	113	-1	-0.1
1922	Bos N	1	2	.333	4	3	1	0	25	19	10	0	1	6	7	2.16	185	.224	.283	8-0	.000	-1	41	4	0.3
1923	Bos N	3	5	.375	23	8	5-2	0	98	92	43	3	3	22	23	3.31	121	.246	.293	66-3	.379	4*	64	8	0.9
1924	Bos N	8	9	.471	34	19	12-2	2	181	176	79	4	4	50	67	3.18	120	.260	.314	130-5	.254	2*	64	11	1.1
1925	Bos N	14	14	.500	31	29	20-2	0	245.2	267	123	18	3	50	65	3.48	115	.274	.312	103-5	.320	5*	95	11	2.1
1926	Bos N	3	3	.500	19	8	3-1	0	83.1	106	52	0	7	29	23	4.00	89	.320	.387	126-8	.302	3*	132	-8	-0.2
1928	Bos N	3	7	.300	24	5	2	1	89.2	106	47	7	0	31	18	4.32	91	.303	.360	41-1	.171	-0*	105	-2	-0.1
1929	Bos N	2	3	.400	14	2	1	3	45	57	29	4	0	22	11	5.00	94	.315	.389	72-0	.319	2*	56	-2	0.0
1930	Bos N	0	0	—	2	0	0	0	7	16	14	2	1	3	1	18.00	27	.471	.526	3-0	.000	-1*		-9	-0.4
Total	9	34	44	.436	159	75	44-7	6	795.1	858	409	41	19	223	224	3.72	106	.278	.331	554-22	.289	15	85	12	3.6

COONEY, BOB Robert Daniel B 7.12.1907 Glens Falls, NY D 5.4.1976 Glens Falls, NY BR/TR 5-11/160# d9.6

Year	Tm Lg	W	L	Pct	G	GS	CG-Sho	SV-BS	IP	H	R	HR	HB	BB-IB	SO	ERA	AERA	OAV	OOB	AB-SH	AVG	PB	Sup	APR	PW
1931	StL A	0	3	.000	5	4	1	0	39.1	46	21	1	1	20	13	4.12	113	.291	.374	13-0	.385	1	64	2	0.3
1932	StL A	1	2	.333	23	3	1	1	71	94	61	8	2	36	23	6.97	70	.324	.402	22-0	.000	-3*	82	-14	-1.0
Total	2	1	5	.167	28	7	2	1	110.1	140	82	9	3	56	36	5.95	80	.313	.393	35-0	.143	-2	71	-12	-0.7

COOPER, WILBUR Arley Wilbur B 2.24.1892 Bearsville, WV D 8.7.1973 Encino, CA BR/TL 5-11/175# d8.29

Year	Tm Lg	W	L	Pct	G	GS	CG-Sho	SV-BS	IP	H	R	HR	HB	BB-IB	SO	ERA	AERA	OAV	OOB	AB-SH	AVG	PB	Sup	APR	PW
1912	Pit N	3	0	1.000	6	4	3-2	0	38	32	7	1	0	15	30	1.66	197	.227	.301	13-2	.154	-0	129	8	0.5
1913	Pit N	5	3	.625	30	9	3-1	0	93	98	52	0	2	45	39	3.29	92	.276	.361	26-1	.077	-1	166	-6	-0.7
1914	Pit N	16	15	.516	40	34	19	0	266.2	246	99	4	5	79	102	2.13	125	.254	.313	92-3	.207	1	100	9	1.1
1915	Pit N	5	16	.238	38	20	11-1	4	185.2	180	92	4	9	52	71	3.30	83	.262	.323	60-2	.117	-3	101	-13	-1.8
1916	Pit N	12	11	.522	42	23	16-2	2	246	189	72	4	4	74	111	1.87	144	.215	.279	79-7	.215	0*	73	20	2.1
1917	Pit N	17	11	.607	40	34	23-7	1	297.2	276	96	4	4	54	99	2.36	120	.258	.297	103-2	.204	2*	100	16	1.7
1918	Pit N	19	14	.576	38	29	26-2	**3**	273.1	219	86	2	10	65	117	2.11	136	.223	.279	95-5	.242	3	84	22	3.0
1919	Pit N	19	13	.594	35	32	**27**-4	1	286.2	229	97	10	15	74	106	2.67	113	.225	.287	101-1	.287	6*	90	11	1.7
1920	Pit N	24	15	.615	44	37	28-3	2	327	307	113	4	11	52	114	2.39	134	.253	.290	113-2	.221	1	85	26	3.0
1921	Pit N	**22**	14	.611	38	**38**	29-2	0	**327**	341	145	9	10	80	134	3.25	118	.272	.320	122-4	.254	4	95	19	2.2
1922	Pit N	23	14	.622	41	36	**27**-4	0	294.2	330	130	13	7	61	129	3.18	128	.286	.326	108-3	.269	9	110	**27**	**3.9**
1923	Pit N	17	19	.472	39	**38**	26-1	0	294.2	331	136	11	11	71	77	3.57	112	.288	.335	107-3	.262	4	90	15	1.8
1924	Pit N	20	14	.588	38	35	25-**4**	1	268.2	296	116	13	5	40	62	3.28	117	.283	.313	104-1	.346	10	122	16	2.7
1925	Chi N	12	14	.462	32	26	13	0	212.1	249	115	18	4	61	41	4.28	101	.291	.341	82-1	.207	1	100	2	0.1
1926	Chi N	2	1	.667	8	8	3-2	0	55	65	32	6	0	21	18	4.42	87	.311	.374	18-0	.389	3	168	-3	0.1
	Det A	0	4	.000	8	3	0	0	13.2	27	18	0	3	9	2	11.20	36	.443	.534	4-1	.000	-1	83	-10	-1.7
Total	15	216	178	.548	517	406	279-35	14	3480	3415	1406	103	100	853	1252	2.89	116	.262	.312	1227-38	.239	39	101	159	19.7

COOPER, BRIAN Brian John B 8.19.1974 Hollywood, CA BR/TR 6-1/175# d9.7

Year	Tm Lg	W	L	Pct	G	GS	CG-Sho	SV-BS	IP	H	R	HR	HB	BB-IB	SO	ERA	AERA	OAV	OOB	AB-SH	AVG	PB	Sup	APR	PW
1999	Ana A	1	1	.500	5	5	0	0-0	27.2	23	15	3	4	18-0	15	4.88	100	.228	.363	0-0	—	0	127	1	0.1
2000	Ana A	4	8	.333	15	15	1-1	0-0	87	105	66	18	2	35-1	36	5.90	86	.299	.362	4-0	.000	-0	76	-10	-1.1
2001	Ana A	0	1	.000	7	1	0	0-0	13.2	10	5	2	0	4-0	7	2.63	173	.200	.255	0-0	—	0	41	3	0.1
2002	Tor A	0	1	.000	2	2	0	0-0	8.1	14	13	5	0	4-0	3	14.04	33	.400	.450	0-0	—	0	201	-8	-0.7
Total	4	5	11	.313	29	23	1-1	0-0	136.2	152	99	28	6	61-1	61	5.86	85	.283	.358	4-0	.000	-0	96	-14	-1.6

COOPER, CAL Calvin Asa B 8.11.1922 Great Falls, SC D 7.4.1994 Clinton, SC BR/TR 6-2.5/180# d9.14

Year	Tm Lg	W	L	Pct	G	GS	CG-Sho	SV-BS	IP	H	R	HR	HB	BB-IB	SO	ERA	AERA	OAV	OOB	AB-SH	AVG	PB	Sup	APR	PW
1948	Was A	0	0	—	1	0	0	0	1	5	5	1	0	1	0	45.00	10	.625	.667	0-0	—	0		-4	-0.2

COOPER, DON Donald James B 1.15.1957 New York, NY BR/TR 6-1/185# d4.9 C2

Year	Tm Lg	W	L	Pct	G	GS	CG-Sho	SV-BS	IP	H	R	HR	HB	BB-IB	SO	ERA	AERA	OAV	OOB	AB-SH	AVG	PB	Sup	APR	PW
1981	Min A	1	5	.167	27	2	0	0-0	58.2	61	33	9	1	32-4	33	4.30	92	.274	.364	0-0	—	0	91	-3	-0.3
1982	Min A	0	1	.000	6	1	0	0-0	11.1	14	12	0	0	11-2	5	9.53	45	.311	.439	0-0	—	0	150	-6	-0.5
1983	Tor A	0	0	—	4	0	0	0-0	5.1	8	4	3	0	0-0	5	6.75	64	.348	.348	0-0	—	0		-1	-0.1
1985	NY A	0	0	—	7	0	0	0-0	10	12	6	2	0	3-0	4	5.40	74	.300	.341	0-0	—	0		-1	-0.1
Total	4	1	6	.143	44	3	0	0-0	85.1	95	55	14	1	46-6	47	5.27	76	.287	.372	0-0	—	0	112	-11	-1.0

COOPER, GUY Guy Evans "Rebel" B 1.28.1893 Rome, GA D 8.2.1951 Santa Monica, CA BB/TR 6-1/185# d5.2

Year	Tm Lg	W	L	Pct	G	GS	CG-Sho	SV-BS	IP	H	R	HR	HB	BB-IB	SO	ERA	AERA	OAV	OOB	AB-SH	AVG	PB	Sup	APR	PW
1914	NY A	0	0	—	1	0	0	0	3	3	3	0	0	2	3	9.00	31	.273	.385	1-0	.000	-0		-2	-0.1
	Bos A	1	0	1.000	9	1	0	0	22	23	15	1	3	9	5	5.32	51	.299	.393	7-0	.000	-1*	244	-6	-0.4
	Year	1	0	1.000	10	1	0	0	25	26	24	1	3	11	8	5.76	47	.295	.392	8-0	.000	-1	243	-7	-0.5
1915	Bos A	0	0	—	1	0	0	0	2	0	0	0	0	2	0	0.00	—	.000	.286	0-0	—	0		1	0.0
Total	2	1	0	1.000	11	1	0	0	27	26	18	1	3	13	8	5.33	51	.280	.385	8-0	.000	-1	242	-7	-0.5

COOPER, MORT Morton Cecil B 3.2.1913 Atherton, MO D 11.17.1958 Little Rock, AR BR/TR 6-2/210# d9.14 b-Walker

Year	Tm Lg	W	L	Pct	G	GS	CG-Sho	SV-BS	IP	H	R	HR	HB	BB-IB	SO	ERA	AERA	OAV	OOB	AB-SH	AVG	PB	Sup	APR	PW
1938	StL N	2	1	.667	4	3	1	1	23.2	17	11	1	1	12	11	3.04	130	.195	.300	9-1	.222	0	86	2	0.3
1939	StL N	12	6	.667	45	26	7-2	4	210.2	208	94	6	2	97	130	3.25	127	.260	.342	69-6	.232	3*	96	16	1.5
1940	StL N	11	12	.478	38	29	16-3	3	230.2	225	103	12	3	86	95	3.63	110	.253	.321	83-7	.157	-2	97	11	0.7
1941	StL N	13	9	.591	29	25	12	0	186.2	175	88	15	3	69	118	3.91	96	.244	.313	70-1	.186	-0	92	0	-0.1
1942	†StL N★	**22**	7	.759	37	35	22-**10**	0	278.2	207	73	9	5	68	152	**1.78**	**193**	**.204**	**.258**	103-7	.184	-1	106	**47**	**4.7**
1943	†StL N★	**21**	8	**.724**	37	32	24-6	3	274	228	81	5	5	79	141	2.30	146	.226	.286	100-5	.170	-1	117	**33**	3.3
1944	†StL N	22	7	.759	34	33	22-**7**	1	252.1	227	74	6	5	60	97	2.46	143	.239	.288	94-4	.202	2	146	33	3.7
1945	StL N	2	0	1.000	4	3	1	0	23.2	20	7	1	1	7	14	1.52	246	.227	.292	6-1	.333	1	143	5	0.5
	Bos N❖	7	4	.636	20	11	4-1	1	78	77	35	4	1	27	45	3.35	115	.257	.320	26-0	.231	1	135	4	0.6
	Year	9	4	.692	24	14	5-1	1	101.2	97	41	5	2	34	59	2.92	130	.250	.314	32-1	.250	2	136	8	1.1
1946	Bos N☆	13	11	.542	28	27	15-4	1	199	181	76	16	0	39	83	3.12	110	.239	**.276**	67-8	.209	1	107	9	1.0
1947	Bos N	2	5	.286	10	7	2	0	46.2	48	26	2	2	13	15	4.05	96	.271	.328	13-1	.000	-1	71	-2	-0.4
	NY N	1	5	.167	8	8	2	0	36.2	51	32	7	0	13	12	7.12	57	.323	.374	14-2	.429	4	89	-12	-1.3
	Year	3	10	.231	18	15	4	0	83.1	99	36	9	2	26	27	5.40	74	.296	.350	27-3	.222	2	81	-14	-1.7
1949	Chi N	0	0	—	1	0	0	0	0	2	3	1	0	1	0	∞	—	1.000	1.000	0-0	—	0		-3	-0.2
Total	11	128	75	.631	295	239	128-33	14	1840.2	1666	703	85	28	571	913	2.97	123	.240	.300	654-43	.194	6	109	143	14.3

COPELAND, MAYS Mays B 8.31.1913 Mountain View, AR D 11.29.1982 Indio, CA BR/TR 6/180# d4.27

Year	Tm Lg	W	L	Pct	G	GS	CG-Sho	SV-BS	IP	H	R	HR	HB	BB-IB	SO	ERA	AERA	OAV	OOB	AB-SH	AVG	PB	Sup	APR	PW
1935	StL N	0	0	—	1	0	0	0	0.2	2	1	0	0	0	0	13.50	30	.667	.667	0-0	—	0		-1	0.0

Year	Tm Lg	W	L	Pct	G	GS	CG-Sho	SV-BS	IP	H	R	HR	HB	BB-IB	SO	ERA	AERA	OAV	OOB	AB-SH	AVG	PB	Sup	APR	PW
COPPINGER, ROCKY John Thomas B 3.19.1974 ElPaso, TX BR/TR 6-5/245# d6.11																									
1996	†Bal A✧	10	6	.625	23	22	0	0-0	125	126	76	25	2	60-1	104	5.18	95	.263	.344	0-0	—	0	124	-3	-0.4
1997	Bal A	1	1	.500	5	4	0	0-0	20	21	14	2	1	16-1	22	6.30	70	.273	.400	0-0	—	0	146	-4	-0.3
1998	Bal A	0	0	—	6	1	0	0-0	15.2	16	9	3	0	7-1	13	5.17	88	.246	.319	0-0	—	0	245	-1	-0.1
1999	Bal A	0	1	.000	11	2	0	0-0	21.2	25	21	8	0	19-0	17	8.31	57	.294	.419	1-0	1.000	0	119	-9	-0.4
	Mil N	5	3	.625	29	0	0	0-2	36.2	35	16	5	0	23-3	39	3.68	123	.250	.354	2-0	.000	-0		4	0.6
2001	Mil N	1	0	1.000	8	3	0	0-0	22.2	24	17	5	1	15-0	15	6.75	64	.282	.392	5-1	.000	-1	143	-6	-0.3
Total	5	17	11	.607	82	32	0	0-2	241.2	247	153	48	4	140-6	210	5.47	86	.265	.361	8-1	.125	-0	133	-19	-0.9
COPPOLA, HENRY Henry Peter B 8.4.1912 E.Douglas, MA D 7.10.1990 Norfolk, MA BR/TR 5-11/175# d4.19																									
1935	Was A	3	4	.429	19	5	2-1	0	59.1	72	40	6	1	29	19	5.92	73	.300	.378	14-0	.071	-0	88	-9	-0.9
1936	Was A	0	0	—	6	0	0	1	14	17	9	1	0	12	2	4.50	106	.315	.439	3-0	.333	1		0	0.1
Total	2	3	4	.429	25	5	2-1	1	73.1	89	49	7	1	41	21	5.65	78	.303	.390	17-0	.118	0	88	-9	-0.8
CORBETT, DOUG Douglas Mitchell B 11.4.1952 Sarasota, FL BR/TR 6-1/185# d4.10																									
1980	Min A	8	6	.571	73	0	0	23-7	136.1	102	31	7	1	42-8	89	1.98	221	.213	.277	0-0	—	0		**35**	**4.8**
1981	Min A☆	2	6	.250	**54**	0	0	17-8	87.2	80	29	5	0	34-13	60	2.57	154	.239	.305	0-0	—	0		12	1.7
1982	Min A	0	2	.000	10	0	0	3-3	22	27	13	3	0	10-1	15	5.32	80	.300	.370	0-0	—	0		-2	-0.2
	Cal A	1	7	.125	33	0	0	8-4	57	46	32	8	0	25-5	37	5.05	80	.223	.307	0-0	—	0		-5	-0.8
	Year	1	9	.100	43	0	0	11-7	79	73	49	11	0	35-6	52	5.13	80	.247	.326	0-0	—	0		-7	-1.0
1983	Cal A	1	1	.500	11	0	0	0-1	17.1	26	10	1	1	4-2	18	3.63	111	.351	.392	0-0	—	0		0	0.0
1984	Cal A	5	1	.833	45	1	0	4-3	85	76	22	2	2	30-12	48	2.12	188	.244	.310	0-0	—	0	136	18	1.3
1985	Cal A	3	3	.500	30	0	0	0-1	46	49	33	7	1	20-3	24	4.89	84	.274	.348	0-0	—	0		-6	-0.7
1986	†Cal A	4	2	.667	46	0	0	10-0	78.2	66	36	11	1	22-2	36	3.66	112	.231	.286	0-0	—	0		4	0.4
1987	Bal A	0	2	.000	11	0	0	1-1	23	25	20	5	0	13-3	16	7.83	56	.281	.369	0-0	—	0		-8	-0.6
Total	8	24	30	.444	313	1	0	66-28	553	497	226	49	6	200-49	343	3.32	125	.242	.310	0-0	—	0	136	48	5.9
CORBETT, JOE Joseph A. B 12.4.1875 San Francisco, CA D 5.2.1945 San Francisco, CA BR/TR 5-10/?# d8.23																									
1895	Was N	0	2	.000	3	3	3	0	19	26	22	3	2	9	3	5.68	84	.321	.402	15-0	.133	-1*	69	-3	-0.3
1896	†Bal N	3	0	1.000	8	3	3	1	41	31	17	0	5	17	28	2.20	195	.208	.310	22-0	.273	1*	116	9	0.5
1897	†Bal N	24	8	.750	37	37	34-1	0	313	330	173	2	21	115	149	3.11	134	.269	.341	150-1	.247	-0*	147	31	2.5
1904	StL N	5	8	.385	14	14	12	0	108.2	110	75	2	8	51	68	4.39	61	.240	.327	43-0	.209	1	118	-20	-1.9
Total	4	32	18	.640	62	57	52-1	1	481.2	497	287	7	36	192	248	3.42	113	.259	.338	230-1	.235	1	134	17	0.8
CORBETT, SHERMAN Sherman Stanley B 11.3.1962 New Braunfels, TX BL/TL 6-4/205# d5.29																									
1988	Cal A	2	1	.667	34	0	0	1-1	45.2	47	23	2	0	23-3	28	4.14	93	.273	.350	0-0	—	0		-1	-0.1
1989	Cal A	0	0	—	4	0	0	0-0	5.1	3	2	1	0	1-0	3	3.38	113	.158	.200	0-0	—	0		0	0.0
1990	Cal A	0	0	—	4	0	0	0-0	5	8	5	0	0	3-0	2	9.00	43	.364	.423	0-0	—	0		-3	-0.1
Total	3	2	1	.667	42	0	0	1-1	56	58	30	3	0	27-3	33	4.50	86	.272	.346	0-0	—	0		-4	-0.2
CORBIN, RAY Alton Ray B 2.12.1949 Live Oak, FL BR/TR 6-2/200# d4.6																									
1971	Min A	8	11	.421	52	11	2	3-1	140.1	141	74	19	3	70-11	83	4.10	87	.265	.351	34-4	.206	1	87	-9	-1.1
1972	Min A	8	9	.471	31	19	5-3	0-0	161.2	135	56	12	6	53-3	83	2.62	123	.230	.299	49-2	.082	-2*	97	11	0.8
1973	Min A	8	5	.615	51	7	1	14-2	148.1	124	58	7	5	60-4	83	3.03	131	.229	.308	0-0	—	0	129	14	1.4
1974	Min A	7	6	.538	29	15	1	0-1	112.1	133	78	8	3	40-4	50	5.29	71	.294	.352	0-0	—	0	110	-20	-2.1
1975	Min A	5	7	.417	18	11	3	0-0	89.2	105	59	13	2	38-5	49	5.12	75	.295	.363	0-0	—	0	86	-13	-1.5
Total	5	36	38	.486	181	63	12-3	17-4	652.1	638	325	59	19	261-27	348	3.84	95	.258	.331	83-6	.133	-2	99	-17	-2.5
CORBIN, ARCHIE Archie Ray B 12.30.1967 Beaumont, TX BR/TR 6-4/190# d9.10																									
1991	KC A	0	0	—	2	0	0	0-0	2.1	3	1	0	0	2-0	1	3.86	107	.300	.417	0-0	—	0		0	0.0
1996	Bal A	2	0	1.000	18	0	0	0-0	27.1	22	7	2	1	22-0	20	2.30	214	.222	.366	0-0	—	0		8	0.5
1999	Fla N	0	1	.000	17	0	0	0-0	21	25	20	2	1	15-0	30	7.29	60	.291	.398	1-0	.000	-0		-8	-0.4
Total	3	2	1	.667	37	0	0	0-0	50.2	50	28	4	2	39-0	51	4.44	105	.256	.382	1-0	.000	-0		0	0.1
CORCORAN, LARRY Lawrence J. B 8.10.1859 Brooklyn, NY D 10.14.1891 Newark, NJ BL/TR ?/120# d5.1 b-Mike ▲																									
1880	Chi N	43	14	.754	63	60	57-4	2	536.1	404	218	6		99	**268**	1.95	124	.199	.236	286	.231	-0*	128	29	2.9
1881	Chi N	**31**	14	.689	45	44	43-4	0	396.2	380	205	10		78	150	2.31	118	.242	.278	189	.222	-1*	128	16	1.2
1882	Chi N	27	12	**.692**	39	39	38-3	0	355.2	281	153	5		63	170	**1.95**	**148**	**.200**	**.234**	169	.207	-2*	136	34	2.9
1883	Chi N	34	20	.630	56	53	51-3	0	473.2	483	281	7		82	216	2.49	132	.247	.277	263	.209	-2*	116	37	3.2
1884	Chi N	35	23	.603	60	59	57-7	0	516.2	473	286	35		116	272	2.40	130	.229	.270	251	.243	2*	118	35	3.5
1885	Chi N	5	2	.714	7	7	6-1	0	59.1	63	38	2		24	10	3.64	83	.259	.326	22	.273	2	156	-2	-0.1
	NY N	2	1	.667	3	3	2	0	25	24	12	1		11	10	2.88	93	.245	.321	14	.357	1	191	0	0.2
	Year	7	3	.700	10	10	8-1	0	84.1	87	21	3		35	20	3.42	85	.255	.324	36	.306	3	165	-4	0.1
1886	Was N	0	1	.000	2	1	1	0	14	16	11	0		4	3	5.79	56	.271	.317	81	.185	0*	76	-3	-0.2
1887	Ind N	0	2	.000	2	2	1	0	15	23	31	2	2	19	4	12.60	33	.338	.494	10	.200	-0*	94	-14	-1.1
Total	8	177	89	.665	277	268	256-22	2	2392.1	2147	1235	68	2	496	1103	2.36	123	.226	.264	1285	.223	-1	125	132	12.5
CORCORAN, MIKE Michael B Brooklyn, NY d7.15 b-Larry																									
1884	Chi N	0	1	.000	1	1	1	0	9	16	14	1		7	2	4.00	78	.372	.460	3	.000	-0	0	-2	-0.2
CORCORAN, ROY Roy Elliot B 5.11.1980 Baton Rogue, LA BR/TR 5-10/170# d7.30																									
2003	Mon N	0	0	—	5	0	0	0-0	7.1	7	2	0	0	3-0	2	1.23	382	.250	.323	1-0	.000	-0		2	0.1
CORDERO, CHAD Chad B 4.18.1982 Upland, CA BR/TR 6/190# d8.30																									
2003	Mon N	1	0	1.000	12	0	0	1-0	11	4	2	1	0	3-1	12	1.64	287	.111	.179	0-1	—	0		4	0.3
CORDERO, FRANCISCO Francisco Javier B 5.11.1975 Santo Domingo, D.R. BR/TR 6-2/200# d8.2																									
1999	Det A	2	2	.500	20	0	0	0-0	19	19	7	2	0	18-2	19	3.32	149	.284	.416	0-0	—	0		4	0.7
2000	Tex A	1	2	.333	56	0	0	0-3	77.1	87	51	11	4	48-3	49	5.35	94	.285	.383	0-0	—	0		-3	-0.2
2001	Tex A	0	1	.000	3	0	0	0-0	2.1	3	1	0	0	2-1	1	3.86	121	.300	.417	0-0	—	0		0	0.0
2002	Tex A	2	0	1.000	39	0	0	10-2	45.1	33	12	2	2	13-1	41	1.79	265	.204	.271	1-0	.000	-0		13	1.0
2003	Tex A	5	8	.385	73	0	0	15-10	82.2	70	33	4	2	38-6	90	2.94	169	.230	.315	0-0	—	0		15	2.6
Total	5	10	13	.435	191	0	0	25-15	226.2	212	104	19	8	119-13	200	3.57	138	.250	.342	1-0	.000	-0		29	4.1
CORDOVA, FRANCISCO Francisco B 4.26.1972 Veracruz, Mexico BR/TR 5-11/165# d4.2																									
1996	Pit N	4	7	.364	59	6	0	12-6	99	103	49	11	2	20-6	95	4.09	107	.263	.303	16-2	.125	-1	127	3	0.4
1997	Pit N	11	8	.579	29	29	2-2	0-0	178.2	175	80	14	9	49-4	121	3.63	118	.259	.314	56-8	.089	-2	110	13	1.1
1998	Pit N	13	14	.481	33	33	3-2	0-0	220.1	204	91	22	3	69-5	157	3.31	130	.245	.303	75-2	.120	-2	86	25	2.6
1999	Pit N	8	10	.444	27	27	2	0-0	160.2	166	83	16	4	59-6	98	4.43	103	.273	.339	49-5	.163	-0	95	5	0.5
2000	Pit N	6	8	.429	18	17	0	0-0	95	107	63	12	2	38-4	66	5.21	88	.285	.352	35-0	.114	-1	96	-7	-0.9
Total	5	42	47	.472	166	112	7-4	12-6	753.2	755	366	75	20	235-25	537	3.96	111	.262	.320	231-17	.121	-6	98	39	3.7
COREY, BRYAN Bryan Scott B 10.21.1973 Thousand Oaks, CA BR/TR 6-1/170# d5.13																									
1998	Ari N	0	0	—	3	0	0	0-0	4	6	4	1	1	2-0	1	9.00	47	.375	.474	0-0	—	0		-2	-0.1
2002	LA N	0	0	—	1	0	0	0-0	1	0	0	0	0	0-0	0	0.00	—	.000	.000	0-0	—	0		0	0.0
Total	2	0	0	—	4	0	0	0-0	5	6	4	1	1	2-0	1	7.20	57	.316	.409	0-0	—	0		-2	-0.1
COREY, ED Edward Norman "Ike" (b: Abraham Simon Cohen) B 7.13.1899 Chicago, IL D 9.17.1970 Kenosha, WI BR/TR 6/170# d7.2																									
1918	Chi A	0	0	—	1	0	0	0	2	2	1	0	0	1	0	4.50	61	.333	.429	1-0	.000	-0		0	0.0
COREY, FRED Frederick Harrison B 1857 S.Kingston, RI D 11.27.1912 Providence, RI BR/TR 5-7/160# d5.1 ▲																									
1878	Pro N	1	2	.333	5	5	2	0	23	22	10	0		7	7	2.35	94	.250	.305	21	.143	-1*	146	0	0.0
1880	Wor N	8	9	.471	25	17	9-2	2	148.1	131	72	6		16	47	2.43	107	.219	.239	138	.174	-3*	77	4	0.0
1881	Wor N	6	15	.286	23	21	20-1	0	188.2	231	127	3		31	33	3.72	81	.299	.326	203	.222	-1*	79	-12	-1.2
1882	Wor N	1	13	.071	21	14	12	0	139	180	132	5		19	36	3.56	87	.286	.307	255	.247	0*	83	-10	-0.7
1883	Phi AA	10	7	.588	18	16	15	0	148.1	182	106	3		24	42	3.40	104	.283	.309	298	.258	2*	123	3	0.4

Year	Tm Lg	W	L	Pct	G	GS	CG-Sho	SV-BS	IP	H	R	HR	HB	BB-IB	SO	ERA	AERA	OAV	OOB	AB-SH	AVG	PB	Sup	APR	PW
1885	Phi AA	1	0	1.000	1	1	1	0	9	18	9	2	0	1	3	7.00	49	.419	.432	384	.245	0*	257	-2	-0.2
Total	6	27	46	.370	93	74	59-3	2	656.1	764	456	19	0	98	168	3.32	92	.276	.300	1299	.236	-3	96	-17	-1.7
COREY, MARK Mark Franklin B 11.16.1974 Coudersport, PA BR/TR 6-2/220# d10.2																									
2001	NY N	0	0	—	2	0	0	0-0	1.2	5	3	0	0	3-1	3	16.20	26	.500	.615	0-0	—	0		-2	-0.1
2002	NY N	0	3	.000	12	0	0	0-0	10	10	7	2	1	8-1	9	4.50	88	.250	.388	1-0	.000	-0*		-1	-0.3
	Col N	0	0	—	14	0	0	0-0	12	22	16	7	2	8-1	12	12.00	40	.400	.492	1-0	.000	-0		-8	-0.4
	Year	0	3	.000	26	0	0	0-0	22	32	28	9	3	16-2	21	8.59	51	.337	.447	2-0	.000	-0		-10	-0.7
2003	Pit N	1	2	.333	22	0	0	0-0	30.1	29	19	2	1	11-1	27	5.34	82	.252	.315	0-0	—	0		-3	-0.3
Total	3	1	5	.167	50	0	0	0-0	54	66	45	11	4	30-4	51	7.00	63	.300	.389	2-0	.000	-0		-14	-1.1
CORKHILL, POP John Stewart B 4.11.1858 Parkesburg, PA D 4.3.1921 Pennsauken, NJ BL/TR 5-10/180# d5.1.1883 ▲																									
1884	Cin AA	1	0	1.000	1	0	0	0	5	1	1	0	0	2	4	1.80	185	.063	.167	452	.274	0*		1	0.2
1885	Cin AA	1	4	.200	8	1	0	1	37	36	25	2	1	10	12	3.65	89	.243	.296	440	.252	1*	18	-2	-0.2
1886	Cin AA	0	0	—	1	0	0	0	0.2	1	1	0	0	0	1	13.50	26	.333	.333	540	.265	0*		-1	0.0
1887	Cin AA	1	0	1.000	5	0	0	0	14.2	22	15	0	0	5	3	5.52	79	.324	.370	541	.311	1*		-2	-0.1
1888	Cin AA	0	0	—	2	0	0	1	5	8	6	1	0	0	1	10.80	29	.348	.348	490	.271	0*		-3	-0.1
Total	5	3	4	.429	17	1	0	2	62.1	68	48	3	1	17	21	4.62	76	.264	.312	2463	.276	3	18	-7	-0.2
CORKINS, MIKE Michael Patrick B 5.25.1946 Riverside, CA BR/TR 6-1/200# d9.8																									
1969	SD N	1	3	.250	6	4	0	0-0	17	27	17	3	0	8-1	13	8.47	42	.370	.427	3-0	.000	0	75	-9	-1.6
1970	SD N	5	6	.455	24	18	1	0-1	111	109	62	11	4	79-10	75	4.62	86	.258	.377	37-5	.216	2*	114	-7	-0.4
1971	SD N	0	0	—	8	0	0	0-0	13	14	6	1	0	6-0	16	3.46	95	.280	.357	0-0	—	0		0	0.0
1972	SD N	6	9	.400	47	9	2-1	6-4	140	125	61	14	4	62-9	108	3.54	93	.240	.322	38-4	.237	3	66	-3	-0.1
1973	SD N	5	8	.385	47	11	2	3-2	122	130	79	12	11	61-10	82	4.50	77	.274	.367	33-1	.212	4*	115	-18	-1.5
1974	SD N	2	2	.500	25	2	0	0-0	56.1	53	32	5	1	32-4	41	4.79	74	.255	.354	8-1	.000	-0*	122	-7	-0.5
Total	6	19	28	.404	157	44	5-1	9-7	459.1	458	257	46	20	248-34	335	4.39	81	.262	.357	119-11	.202	10	105	-44	-4.1
CORMIER, RHEAL Rheal Paul B 4.23.1967 Moncton, NB, CAN BL/TL 5-10/185# d8.15																									
1991	StL N	4	5	.444	11	10	2	0-0	67.2	74	35	5	2	8-1	38	4.12	90	.277	.300	21-1	.238	1	77	-3	-0.4
1992	StL N	10	10	.500	31	30	3	0-0	186	194	83	15	5	33-2	117	3.68	92	.269	.305	59-10	.102	-2	106	-6	-0.8
1993	StL N	7	6	.538	38	21	1	0-0	145.1	163	80	18	4	27-3	75	4.33	92	.284	.319	47-6	.234	2	115	-7	-0.3
1994	StL N	3	2	.600	7	7	0	0-0	39.2	40	24	6	3	7-0	26	5.45	76	.256	.298	14-0	.286	1*	106	-5	-0.4
1995	†Bos A	7	5	.583	48	12	0	0-2	115	131	60	12	3	31-2	69	4.07	120	.294	.342	0-0	—	0	97	9	0.8
1996	Mon N	7	10	.412	33	27	1-1	0-0	159.2	165	80	16	9	41-3	100	4.17	104	.270	.321	43-11	.186	1	79	3	0.5
1997	Mon N	0	1	.000	1	1	0	0-0	1.1	4	5	1	0	1-0	0	33.75	12	.500	.556	0-0	—	0	66	-4	-0.6
1999	†Bos A	2	0	1.000	60	0	0	0-3	63.1	61	34	4	5	18-2	39	3.69	135	.246	.307	0-0	—	0		7	0.3
2000	Bos A	3	3	.500	64	0	0	0-2	68.1	74	40	7	0	17-2	43	4.61	110	.275	.316	0-0	—	0		2	0.2
2001	Phi N	5	6	.455	60	0	0	1-5	51.1	49	26	5	4	17-4	37	4.21	101	.247	.320	1-0	.000	-0		0	0.1
2002	Phi N	5	6	.455	54	0	0	0-3	60	61	38	6	4	32-6	49	5.25	74	.265	.362	3-0	.333	1		-10	-1.4
2003	Phi N	8	0	1.000	65	0	0	1-3	84.2	54	18	4	1	25-2	67	1.70	235	.182	.248	2-0	.500	1		23	2.2
Total	12	61	54	.530	472	108	7-1	2-18	1042.1	1070	523	99	40	257-27	660	4.04	103	.266	.314	190-28	.189	4	93	9	0.2
CORNEJO, NATE Nathan J. B 9.24.1979 Wellington, KS BR/TR 6-5/200# d8.8 f-Mardie																									
2001	Det A	4	4	.500	10	10	0	0-0	42.2	63	38	10	3	28-4	22	7.38	59	.342	.437	0-0	—	0	126	-15	-2.1
2002	Det A	1	5	.167	9	9	1	0-0	50	63	33	6	2	18-0	23	5.04	86	.303	.362	0-0	—	0	74	-5	-0.5
2003	Det A	6	17	.261	32	32	2	0-0	194.2	236	111	18	3	58-8	46	4.67	92	.307	.356	4-1	.000	-0	67	-8	-0.8
Total	3	11	26	.297	51	51	3	0-0	287.1	362	182	34	8	104-12	91	5.14	84	.312	.371	4-1	.000	-0	80	-28	-3.4
CORNEJO, MARDIE Nieves Mardie B 8.5.1951 Wellington, KS BR/TR 6-3/200# d4.8 s-Nate																									
1978	NY N	4	2	.667	25	0	0	3-0	36.2	37	12	1	3	14-5	17	2.45	142	.285	.358	0-0	—	0		4	0.7
CORNELIUS, REID Jonathan Reid B 6.2.1970 Thomasville, AL BR/TR 6/200# d4.29																									
1995	Mon N	0	0	—	8	0	0	0-0	9	11	8	3	2	5-0	4	8.00	54	.306	.419	0-0	—	0		-3	-0.2
	NY N	3	7	.300	10	10	0	0-0	57.2	64	36	8	1	25-5	35	5.15	79	.284	.354	20-0	.100	-1	100	-7	-1.1
	Year	3	7	.300	18	10	0	0-0	66.2	75	41	11	3	30-5	39	5.54	74	.287	.364	20-0	.100	-1	100	-10	-1.3
1999	Fla N	1	0	1.000	5	2	0	0-0	19.1	16	7	0	0	5-1	12	3.26	134	.229	.280	5-1	.200	0	84	3	0.2
2000	Fla N	4	10	.286	22	21	0	0-0	125	135	74	19	4	50-4	50	4.82	92	.282	.351	37-4	.135	-1*	75	-6	-0.5
Total	3	8	17	.320	45	33	0	0-0	211	226	125	30	7	85-10	101	4.91	88	.279	.349	62-5	.129	-2	83	-13	-1.6
CORNELL, JEFF Jeffery Ray B 2.10.1957 Kansas City, MO BB/TR 5-11/170# d6.2																									
1984	SF N	1	3	.250	23	0	0	0-1	38.1	51	30	4	1	22-6	19	6.10	58	.340	.423	4-0	.000	-0		-12	-1.2
CORNETT, BRAD Brad Byron B 2.4.1969 Lamesa, TX BR/TR 6-3/190# d6.8																									
1994	Tor A	1	3	.250	9	4	0	0-0	31	40	25	1	3	11-2	22	6.68	72	.331	.394	0-0	—	0	52	-6	-0.7
1995	Tor A	0	0	—	5	0	0	0-0	5	9	6	1	1	3-0	4	9.00	52	.429	.520	0-0	—	0		-3	-0.1
Total	2	1	3	.250	14	4	0	0-0	36	49	31	2	4	14-2	26	7.00	69	.345	.414	0-0	—	0	52	-9	-0.8
CORNUTT, TERRY Terry Stanton B 10.2.1952 Roseburg, OR BR/TR 6-2/195# d4.9																									
1977	SF N	1	2	.333	28	1	0	0-0	44.1	38	24	4	0	22-5	23	3.86	102	.229	.316	1-1	.000	-0	0	0	-0.1
1978	SF N	0	0	—	1	0	0	0-0	3	1	0	0	0	0-0	0	0.00	—	.100	.100	0-0	—	0		1	0.1
Total	2	1	2	.333	29	1	0	0-0	47.1	39	24	4	0	22-5	23	3.61	108	.222	.305	1-1	.000	-0	0	1	0.0
CORREA, ED Edwin Josue (Andino) B 4.29.1966 Hato Rey, P.R. BR/TR 6-2/192# d9.18																									
1985	Chi A	1	0	1.000	5	1	0	0-0	10.1	11	9	2	0	11-0	10	6.97	62	.275	.431	0-0	—	0	63	-3	-0.3
1986	Tex A	12	14	.462	32	32	4-2	0-0	202.1	167	102	15	3	126-2	189	4.23	102	.223	.336	0-0	—	0	82	4	0.6
1987	Tex A	3	5	.375	15	15	0	0-0	70	83	63	17	4	52-2	61	7.59	59	.296	.411	0-0	—	0	111	-22	-2.0
Total	3	16	19	.457	52	48	4-2	0-0	282.2	261	174	34	7	189-4	260	5.16	84	.244	.360	0-0	—	0	91	-21	-1.7
CORREIA, KEVIN Kevin John B 8.24.1980 San Diego, CA BR/TR 6-3/200# d7.10																									
2003	SF N	3	1	.750	10	7	0	0-0	39.1	41	16	6	4	18-1	28	3.66	112	.275	.366	13-1	.154	-0	124	3	0.2
CORRIDON, FRANK Frank J. "Fiddler" B 11.25.1880 Newport, RI D 2.21.1941 Syracuse, NY BR/TR 6/170# d4.15																									
1904	Chi N	5	5	.500	12	10	9	0	100.1	88	43	2	7	37	34	3.05	87	.240	.321	58-1	.224	0*	72	-2	0.0
	Phi N	6	5	.545	12	11	11-1	0	94.1	88	33	2	8	28	44	2.19	122	.250	.320	35-0	.171	-0	65	6	0.8
	Year	11	10	.524	24	21	20-1	0	194.2	176	36	4	15	65	78	2.64	101	.245	.320	93-1	.204	0	69	4	0.8
1905	Phi N	10	12	.455	35	26	18-1	1	212	203	109	2	16	57	79	3.48	84	.257	.319	72-2	.208	4	101	-12	-0.6
1907	Phi N	18	14	.563	37	32	23-3	2	274	228	107	0	9	89	131	2.46	98	.230	.299	97-0	.165	0*	112	-4	-0.2
1908	Phi N	14	10	.583	27	24	18-2	1	208.1	178	69	0	6	48	50	2.51	97	.239	.290	73-3	.123	-2	109	1	0.2
1909	Phi N	11	7	.611	27	19	11-3	0	171	147	61	0	6	61	69	2.11	123	.242	.318	59-3	.186	0	119	7	1.0
1910	StL N	6	14	.300	30	18	9	3	156	168	88	1	9	55	51	3.81	78	.283	.353	51-1	.196	-0	83	-16	-1.8
Total	6	70	67	.511	180	140	99-10	7	1216	1100	510	7	61	375	458	2.80	95	.247	.315	445-10	.180	3	99	-20	-0.6
CORSI, JIM James Bernard B 9.9.1961 Newton, MA BR/TR 6-1/220# d6.28																									
1988	Oak A	0	1	.000	11	1	0	0-0	21.1	20	10	1	0	6-1	10	3.80	100	.260	.302	0-0	—	0	169	0	0.0
1989	Oak A	1	2	.333	22	0	0	0-0	38.1	26	8	2	1	10-0	21	1.88	196	.194	.252	0-0	—	0		9	0.6
1991	Hou N	0	5	.000	47	0	0	0-3	77.2	76	37	6	0	23-5	53	3.71	95	.259	.310	1-0	.000	-0		-2	-0.1
1992	†Oak A	4	2	.667	32	0	0	0-0	44	44	12	2	0	18-2	19	1.43	262	.273	.343	0-0	—	0		10	1.3
1993	Fla N	0	2	.000	15	0	0	0-0	20.1	28	15	1	0	10-3	7	6.64	65	.337	.404	0-0	—	0		-4	-0.4
1995	Oak A	2	4	.333	38	0	0	2-2	45	31	14	2	2	26-1	26	2.20	203	.203	.324	0-0	—	0		11	1.4
1996	Oak A	6	0	1.000	56	0	0	3-3	73.2	71	33	6	3	34-4	43	4.03	122	.269	.356	0-0	—	0		9	0.7
1997	Bos A	5	3	.625	52	0	0	2-7	57.2	56	26	1	4	21-7	40	3.43	135	.255	.327	0-0	—	0		7	0.9
1998	†Bos A	3	2	.600	59	0	0	0-3	66	58	23	6	1	23-2	49	2.59	182	.235	.301	1-0	.000	-0		14	1.0
1999	Bos A	1	2	.333	23	0	0	0-3	24	25	15	4	2	19-3	14	5.25	95	.284	.418	0-0	—	0		0	0.0
	Bal A	0	1	.000	13	0	0	0-1	13.1	15	4	2	0	1-0	8	2.70	174	.294	.308	0-0	—	0		3	0.2
	Year	1	3	.250	36	0	0	0-4	37.1	40	26	6	2	20-3	22	4.34	112	.288	.383	0-0	—	0		2	0.2

Year	Tm Lg	W	L	Pct	G	GS	CG-Sho	SV-BS	IP	H	R	HR	HB	BB-IB	SO	ERA	AERA	OAV	OOB	AB-SH	AVG	PB	Sup	APR	PW
Total	10	22	24	.478	368	1	0	7-22	481.1	450	197	33	13	191-28	290	3.25	132	.254	.328	2-0	.000	-0	169	57	5.6
CORT, BARRY Barry Lee B 4.15.1956 Toronto, ON, CAN BR/TR 6-5/210# d4.22																									
1977	Mil A	1	1	.500	7	3	1	0-0	24.1	25	9	1	1	9-1	17	3.33	123	.281	.350	0-0	—	0	81	2	0.2
CORTES, DAVID David C. B 10.15.1973 Mexicali, Mexico BR/TR 5-11/195# d8.30																									
1999	Atl N	0	0	—	4	0	0	0-0	3.2	3	3	0	0	4-0	2	4.91	92	.214	.389	0-0	—	0		-1	0.0
2003	Cle A	0	0	—	2	0	0	0-0	3	8	5	1	0	0-0	1	12.00	37	.471	.444	0-0	—	0		-3	-0.1
Total	2	0	0	—	6	0	0	0-0	6.2	11	8	1	0	4-0	3	8.10	55	.355	.417	0-0	—	0		-4	-0.1
CORWIN, AL Elmer Nathan B 12.3.1926 Newburgh, NY D 10.23.2003 Geneva, IL BR/TR 6-1/170# d7.25																									
1951	†NY N	5	1	.833	15	8	3-1	1	59	49	27	7	0	21	30	3.66	107	.222	.289	20-2	.050	-2	110	2	-0.1
1952	NY N	6	1	.857	21	7	1	2	67.2	58	23	5	0	36	36	2.66	139	.237	.335	21-1	.095	-1*	117	8	0.7
1953	NY N	6	4	.600	48	7	2-1	2	106.2	122	65	17	3	68	49	4.98	86	.290	.393	32-2	.281	4*	110	-7	-0.3
1954	NY N	1	3	.250	20	0	0	0	31.1	35	19	4	0	14	14	4.02	100	.297	.363	3-0	.000	-0*		-1	-0.2
1955	NY N	0	1	.000	13	0	0	0	24.2	25	11	3	0	17-2	13	4.01	100	.263	.372	3-0	.000	-0		1	0.0
Total	5	18	10	.643	117	22	6-2	5	289.1	289	145	36	3	156-2	142	3.98	101	.263	.355	79-5	.152	0	111	3	0.1
COSGROVE, MIKE Michael John B 2.17.1951 Phoenix, AZ BL/TL 6-1/180# d9.10																									
1972	Hou N	0	1	.000	7	1	0	1-0	13.2	16	8	2	0	3-0	7	4.61	73	.286	.317	2-1	.000	-0	53	-2	-0.2
1973	Hou N	1	1	.500	13	0	0	0-1	10	11	2	1	0	8-2	2	1.80	202	.282	.396	0-0	—	0		2	0.4
1974	Hou N	7	3	.700	45	0	0	2-3	90	76	35	2	1	39-3	47	3.50	99	.232	.313	18-2	.056	-1		2	0.1
1975	Hou N	1	2	.333	32	3	1	5-3	71.1	62	24	2	0	37-1	32	3.03	112	.245	.338	13-2	.154	0	95	4	0.2
1976	Hou N	3	4	.429	22	16	1-1	0-0	89.2	106	63	6	2	58-2	34	5.52	58	.303	.399	23-5	.087	-1	127	-25	-1.9
Total	5	12	11	.522	119	20	2-1	8-7	274.2	271	132	13	3	145-8	122	4.03	83	.264	.353	56-10	.089	-2	114	-19	-1.4
COSMAN, JIM James Henry B 2.19.1943 Brockport, NY BR/TR 6-4.5/211# d10.2																									
1966	StL N	1	0	1.000	1	1	1-1	0	9	2	0	0	1	2-0	5	0.00	—	.074	.167	3-0	.000	-0	49	4	0.4
1967	StL N	1	0	1.000	10	5	0	0	31.1	21	12	2	5	24-2	11	3.16	104	.198	.368	8-1	.125	-0	112	1	0.0
1970	Chi N	0	0	—	1	0	0	0-0	1	3	3	1	0	1-1	0	27.00	17	.600	.667	0-0	—	0		-2	-0.1
Total	3	2	0	1.000	12	6	1-1	0-0	41.1	26	15	3	6	27-3	16	3.05	111	.188	.343	11-1	.091	-1	100	3	0.3
COSTELLO, JOHN John Reilly B 12.24.1960 Bronx, NY BR/TR 6-1/190# d6.2																									
1988	StL N	5	2	.714	36	0	0	1-1	49.2	44	15	3	0	25-4	38	1.81	192	.235	.324	5-0	.000	-0		7	1.0
1989	StL N	5	4	.556	48	0	0	3-3	62.1	48	24	5	2	20-7	40	3.32	109	.213	.278	6-2	.000	-1		3	0.3
1990	StL N	0	0	—	4	0	0	0-0	4.1	7	3	1	1	1-1	1	6.23	61	.368	.429	0-0	—	0		-1	-0.1
	Mon N	0	0	—	4	0	0	0-1	6.1	5	5	2	0	1-0	1	5.68	64	.208	.231	0-0	—	0		-2	-0.1
	Year	0	0	—	8	0	0	0-1	10.2	12	12	3	1	2-1	2	5.91	63	.279	.319	0-0	—	0		-3	-0.2
1991	SD N	1	0	1.000	27	0	0	0-1	35	37	15	2	0	17-3	24	3.09	123	.276	.353	1-1	.000	-0		2	0.1
Total	4	11	6	.647	119	0	0	4-6	157.2	141	62	13	3	64-15	104	2.97	122	.239	.313	12-3	.000	-1		9	1.2
COTTER, DAN Daniel Joseph B 4.14.1867 Boston, MA D 9.4.1935 Boston, MA BR/TR d7.16																									
1890	Buf P	0	1	.000	1	1	1	0	9	18	19	1	0	7	0	14.00	29	.400	.481	4	.000	-1	0	-9	-0.6
COTTRELL, ENSIGN Ensign Stover B 8.29.1888 Hoosick Falls, NY D 2.27.1947 Syracuse, NY BL/TL 5-9.5/173# d6.21																									
1911	Pit N	0	0	—	1	0	0	0	1	4	4	0	0	1	0	9.00	38	.667	.714	0-0	—	0		-2	-0.1
1912	Chi N	0	0	—	1	0	0	0	4	8	4	0	0	1	1	9.00	37	.444	.474	1-0	.000	-0		-2	-0.1
1913	Phi A	1	0	1.000	2	1	1	0	10	15	7	0	0	2	3	5.40	51	.333	.362	4-0	.250	1	268	-3	-0.2
1914	Bos N	0	1	.000	1	1	0	0	1	2	2	0	0	3	1	9.00	31	.333	.556	0-0	—	0	26	-1	-0.2
1915	NY A	0	1	.000	7	0	0	0	21.1	29	12	2	1	7	7	3.38	87	.330	.385	7-0	.000	-1		-2	-0.2
Total	5	1	2	.333	12	2	1	0	37.1	58	29	2	1	14	12	4.82	61	.356	.410	12-0	.083	-0	137	-10	-0.8
COTTS, NEAL Neal James B 3.25.1980 Belleville, IL BL/TL 6-2/200# d8.12																									
2003	Chi A	1	1	.500	4	4	0	0-0	13.1	15	12	1	0	17-0	10	8.10	56	.294	.471	0-0	—	0	131	-5	-0.6
COUCH, JOHNNY John Daniel B 3.31.1891 Vaughn, MT D 12.8.1975 San Mateo, CA BL/TR 6/180# d4.11 Mil 1918																									
1917	Det A	0	0	—	3	0	0	0	13.1	13	6	0	0	1	1	2.70	98	.255	.269	4-0	.000	-0		0	0.0
1922	Cin N	16	9	.640	43	33	18-2	1	264	301	132	13	5	56	45	3.89	103	.289	.328	91-3	.132	-3	105	7	0.3
1923	Cin N	2	7	.222	19	8	1	0	69.1	98	60	2	0	15	14	5.97	65	.344	.377	23-1	.174	-1	85	-18	-2.0
	Phi N	2	4	.333	11	7	2	0	65	91	45	4	3	21	18	5.26	87	.335	.389	24-0	.250	0*	105	-4	-0.3
	Year	4	11	.267	30	15	3	0	134.1	189	51	6	3	36	32	5.63	75	.339	.383	47-1	.213	-1	95	-24	-2.3
1924	Phi N	4	8	.333	37	7	3	3	137	170	97	13	1	39	23	4.73	94	.306	.352	49-2	.204	-1	65	-9	-0.7
1925	Phi N	5	6	.455	34	7	2-1	2	94.1	112	71	9	1	39	11	5.44	88	.298	.365	31-1	.161	-1	76	-7	-0.7
Total	5	29	34	.460	147	62	26-3	6	643	785	411	41	10	171	112	4.63	91	.304	.350	222-7	.167	-6	93	-31	-3.4
COUCHEE, MIKE Michael Eugene B 12.4.1957 San Jose, CA BR/TR 6/190# d4.5 C1																									
1983	SD N	0	1	.000	8	0	0	0-0	14	12	8	1	0	6-1	5	5.14	68	.214	.286	2-0	.500	0		-2	-0.1
COUGHLIN, ROSCOE William Edward B 3.15.1868 Walpole, MA D 3.20.1951 Chelsea, MA TR 5-10/160# d4.22																									
1890	Chi N	4	6	.400	11	10	10	0	95	102	60	3	4	40	29	4.26	86	.266	.341	39	.256	1	84	-3	-0.2
1891	NY N	3	4	.429	8	7	6	0	61	74	50	5	3	23	22	3.84	83	.289	.355	23	.130	1	115	-6	-0.4
Total	2	7	10	.412	19	17	16	0	156	176	110	8	7	63	51	4.10	85	.275	.346	62	.210	2	96	-9	-0.6
COUMBE, FRITZ Frederick Nicholas B 12.13.1889 Antrim, PA D 3.21.1978 Paradise, CA BL/TL 6/152# d4.22																									
1914	Bos A	1	2	.333	17	5	1	1	62.1	49	20	0	0	16	17	1.44	186	.222	.274	18-0	.111	-1	97	6	0.3
	Cle A	1	5	.167	14	5	2	0	55.1	59	31	0	4	16	22	3.25	89	.288	.351	23-0	.261	1	71	-3	-0.2
	Year	2	7	.222	31	10	3	1	117.2	108	34	0	4	32	39	2.29	121	.254	.312	41-0	.195	0	84	3	0.1
1915	Cle A	4	7	.364	30	12	4-1	2	114	123	63	1	3	37	37	3.47	88	.294	.355	37-3	.270	1*	74	-6	-0.3
1916	Cle A	7	5	.583	29	13	7-2	0	120.1	121	36	1	1	27	39	2.02	149	.279	.323	35-2	.057	-3*	87	12	1.2
1917	Cle A	8	6	.571	34	10	4-1	5	134.1	119	54	0	3	35	30	2.14	132	.251	.307	39-2	.154	-1*	109	6	0.7
1918	Cle A	13	7	.650	30	17	9	3	150	164	61	4	1	52	41	3.06	98	.286	.347	56-5	.214	-1*	131	1	0.3
1919	Cle A	1	1	.500	8	2	0	1	23.2	32	15	2	0	9	7	5.32	63	.348	.406	6-1	.500	1	129	-4	-0.2
1920	Cin N	0	1	.000	3	0	0	0	14.2	17	13	0	0	4	7	4.91	62	.304	.350	13-0	.231	1*		-4	-0.2
1921	Cin N	3	4	.429	28	6	3	1	86.2	89	42	2	1	21	12	3.22	111	.280	.326	25-1	.320	1*	80	2	0.4
Total	8	38	38	.500	193	70	30-4	13	761.1	773	335	10	13	217	212	2.80	108	.277	.332	252-14	.206	-1	98	10	2.0
COURTNEY, HARRY Henry Seymour B 11.19.1898 Asheville, NC D 12.11.1954 Lyme, CT BL/TL 6-4/185# d9.13																									
1919	Was A	3	0	1.000	4	3	2-1	0	26.1	25	9	0	0	19	6	2.73	117	.269	.393	10-1	.200	-0	163	2	0.1
1920	Was A	8	11	.421	37	24	10-1	0	188	223	128	6	9	77	48	4.74	79	.298	.371	69-3	.232	4	99	-23	-1.7
1921	Was A	6	9	.400	30	15	3	1	132.2	159	103	7	8	71	26	5.63	73	.305	.397	47-1	.298	2*	95	-24	-2.1
1922	Was A	0	1	.000	5	0	0	0	10	11	4	0	0	9	4	3.60	107	.306	.444	4-0	.000	-1		1	0.0
	Chi A	5	6	.455	18	11	5	0	86.2	100	52	5	1	37	28	4.98	82	.299	.371	33-0	.273	3	82	-8	-0.6
	Year	5	7	.417	23	11	5	0	96.2	111	56	5	1	46	32	4.84	84	.300	.379	37-0	.243	2	82	-5	-0.6
Total	4	22	27	.449	94	53	20-2	1	443.2	518	296	18	18	213	112	4.91	79	.299	.382	163-5	.252	7	97	-52	-4.3
COURTRIGHT, JOHN John Charles B 5.30.1970 Marion, OH BL/TL 6-2/185# d5.6																									
1995	Cin N	0	0	—	1	0	0	0-0	1	2	1	0	0	0-0	0	9.00	46	.500	.500	0-0	—	0		-1	0.0
COVELESKI, HARRY Harry Frank "The Giant Killer" (b: Harry Frank Kowalewski) B 4.23.1886 Shamokin, PA D 8.4.1950 Shamokin, PA BB/TL 6/180# d9.10 b-Stan																									
1907	Phi N	1	0	1.000	4	0	0	0	20	10	2	0	1	3	6	0.00	—	.147	.194	8-0	.000	-0		5	0.2
1908	Phi N	4	1	.800	6	5	5-2	0	43.2	29	7	0	2	12	22	1.24	196	.196	.265	15-2	.133	-0	99	6	0.8
1909	Phi N	6	10	.375	24	17	8-2	1	121.2	109	51	0	5	49	56	2.74	95	.247	.329	37-3	.108	-2	63	-2	-0.5
1910	Cin N	1	1	.500	7	4	2	0	39.1	35	41	1	4	42	27	5.26	55	.246	.431	16-1	.063	-1	172	-14	-0.8
1914	Det A	22	12	.647	44	36	23-5	2	303.1	251	109	4	12	100	124	2.49	113	.227	.298	95-6	.242	5	97	13	2.3
1915	Det A	22	13	.629	**50**	38	20-1	4	312.2	271	123	2	20	87	150	2.45	124	.233	.298	103-8	.175	-2	114	16	1.7
1916	Det A	21	11	.656	44	39	22-3	2	324.1	278	105	6	11	63	108	1.97	145	.237	.282	118-1	.212	1	100	26	3.1
1917	Det A	4	6	.400	16	11	2	0	69	70	39	0	2	14	15	2.61	101	.265	.307	22-1	.227	-0	146	-3	-0.4

Year	Tm Lg	W	L	Pct	G	GS	CG-Sho	SV-BS	IP	H	R	HR	HB	BB-IB	SO	ERA	AERA	OAV	OOB	AB-SH	AVG	PB	Sup	APR	PW
1918	Det A	0	1	.000	3	1	1	0	14	17	9	0	0	6	3	3.86	69	.315	.383	4-0	.250	0	57	-3	-0.1
Total	9	81	55	.596	198	151	83-13	9	1248	1070	486	13	57	376	511	2.39	118	.235	.301	418-22	.189	-0	104	44	6.3
COVELESKI, STAN Stanley Anthony (b: Stanislaus Kowalewski) B 7.13.1889 Shamokin, PA D 3.20.1984 South Bend, IN BR/TR 5-11/166# d9.10 HF1969 b-Harry																									
1912	Phi A	2	1	.667	5	2	2-1	0	21	18	9	0	1	4	9	3.43	90	.231	.277	7-0	.143	-0	48	0	-0.1
1916	Cle A	15	13	.536	45	27	11-1	3	232	247	100	6	1	58	76	3.41	88	.278	.323	75-4	.173	-0	115	-4	-0.4
1917	Cle A	19	14	.576	45	36	24-**9**	4	298.1	202	78	3	1	94	133	1.81	157	**.194**	.261	97-7	.134	-4*	77	33	3.2
1918	Cle A	22	13	.629	38	33	25-2	1	311	261	90	2	4	76	87	1.82	165	.229	.279	110-5	.191	-3	87	35	3.9
1919	Cle A	24	12	.667	43	34	24-4	4	286	286	99	2	5	60	118	2.61	128	.267	.308	94-3	.213	4	98	26	3.9
1920	†Cle A	24	14	.632	41	38	26-3	2	315	284	110	6	4	65	**133**	2.49	153	**.243**	**.285**	111-9	.225	3	105	**44**	**5.5**
1921	Cle A	23	13	.639	43	**40**	28-2	2	315	341	137	6	4	84	99	3.37	126	.280	.325	116-11	.155	-6	116	33	3.0
1922	Cle A	17	14	.548	35	33	21-3	2	276.2	292	120	14	2	64	98	3.32	121	.274	.316	99-2	.101	-7	96	20	1.4
1923	Cle A	13	14	.481	33	31	17-**5**	2	228	251	98	8	2	42	54	**2.76**	**143**	.282	.316	79-9	.089	-8	98	26	2.2
1924	Cle A	15	16	.484	37	33	18-2	0	240.1	286	140	6	4	73	58	4.04	106	.294	.346	82-4	.134	-5	96	3	-0.1
1925	†Was A	20	5	**.800**	32	32	15-3	0	241	230	86	7	2	73	58	**2.84**	**149**	.255	.312	81-11	.111	-8	107	**41**	2.9
1926	Was A	14	11	.560	36	34	11-3	1	245.1	272	112	1	0	81	50	3.12	124	.286	.342	82-3	.207	1	108	16	1.6
1927	Was A	2	1	.667	5	4	0	0	14.1	13	7	0	0	8	3	3.14	129	.250	.350	6-0	.333	0	113	1	0.2
1928	NY A	5	1	.833	12	8	2	0	58	72	41	5	0	20	5	5.74	66	.323	.379	19-4	.053	-2	158	-12	-1.2
Total	14	215	142	.602	450	385	224-38	21	3082	3055	1227	66	30	802	981	2.89	128	.262	.311	1058-72	.159	-34	102	262	26.0
COVINGTON, CHET Chester Rogers "Chesty" B 11.6.1910 Cairo, IL D 6.11.1976 Pembroke Park, FL BB/TL 6-2/195# d4.23																									
1944	Phi N	1	1	.500	19	0	0	0	38.2	46	22	2	0	8	13	4.66	78	.297	.331	6-0	.000	-1		-4	-0.3
COVINGTON, TEX William Wilkes B 3.19.1887 Henryville, TN D 12.10.1931 Denison, TX BL/TR 6-1/175# d4.25 b-Sam																									
1911	Det A	7	1	.875	17	6	5	0	83.2	94	43	2	10	33	29	4.09	85	.297	.381	32-0	.188	-1	160	-3	-0.4
1912	Det A	3	4	.429	14	9	2-1	0	63.1	58	33	0	3	30	19	4.12	79	.253	.347	15-0	.133	0	75	-4	-0.4
Total	2	10	5	.667	31	15	7-1	0	147	152	76	2	13	63	48	4.10	82	.278	.367	47-0	.170	-1	109	-7	-0.8
COWLEY, JOE Joseph Alan B 8.15.1958 Lexington, KY BR/TR 6-5/210# d4.13																									
1982	Atl N	1	2	.333	17	8	0	0-0	52.1	53	27	6	1	16-2	27	4.47	84	.265	.321	15-1	.200	-0	94	-3	-0.2
1984	NY A	9	2	.818	16	11	3-1	0-0	83.1	75	34	12	2	31-1	71	3.56	107	.234	.303	0-0	—	0	164	3	0.4
1985	NY A	12	6	.667	30	26	1	0-0	159.2	132	75	29	6	85-2	97	3.95	101	.224	.327	0-0	—	0	117	3	0.2
1986	Chi A	11	11	.500	27	27	4	0-0	162.1	133	81	20	3	83-1	132	3.88	111	.223	.319	0-0	—	0*	97	6	0.7
1987	Phi N	0	4	.000	5	4	0	0-0	11.2	21	26	2	2	17-1	5	15.43	28	.389	.548	3-0	.333	1	43	-16	-2.4
Total	5	33	25	.569	95	76	8-1	0-0	469.1	414	243	69	14	232-7	332	4.20	97	.235	.327	18-1	.222	1	110	-7	-1.3
COX, DANNY Danny Bradford B 9.21.1959 Northampton, England BR/TR 6-4/235# d8.6																									
1983	StL N	3	6	.333	12	12	0	0-0	83	92	38	6	0	23-2	36	3.25	112	.286	.332	27-3	.074	-2	69	2	0.0
1984	StL N	9	11	.450	29	27	1-1	0-0	156.1	171	81	9	7	54-6	70	4.03	86	.289	.353	53-1	.132	0*	97	-11	-1.3
1985	†StL N	18	9	.667	35	35	10-4	0-0	241	226	91	19	3	64-5	131	2.88	123	.251	.300	79-8	.152	1	107	16	1.8
1986	StL N	12	13	.480	32	32	8	0-0	220	189	85	14	2	60-6	108	2.90	126	.234	.288	65-16	.077	-3	84	16	1.1
1987	†StL N	11	9	.550	31	31	2	0-0	199.1	224	99	17	3	71-6	101	3.88	107	.290	.351	69-4	.116	-2*	106	3	0.1
1988	StL N	3	8	.273	13	13	0	0-0	86	89	40	6	1	25-7	47	3.98	88	.272	.323	23-5	.043	-2	71	-4	-0.6
1991	Phi N	4	6	.400	23	17	0	0-0	102.1	98	57	14	1	39-2	46	4.57	80	.258	.323	29-4	.103	-1	120	-11	-1.1
1992	Phi N	2	2	.500	9	7	0	0-0	38.1	46	28	3	0	19-1	30	5.40	65	.299	.371	11-0	.091	-1	115	-9	-0.9
	†Pit N	3	1	.750	16	0	0	3-2	24.1	20	9	2	0	8-1	18	3.33	104	.225	.286	3-0	.000	-0		1	0.1
	Year	5	3	.625	25	7	0	3-2	62.2	66	41	5	0	27-2	48	4.60	76	.272	.341	14-0	.071	-1	115	-9	-0.8
1993	†Tor A	7	6	.538	44	0	0	2-4	83.2	73	31	8	0	29-5	84	3.12	139	.230	.293	0-0	—	0		12	1.6
1994	Tor A	1	1	.500	10	0	0	3-0	18.2	7	3	0	1	7-1	14	1.45	334	.113	.211	0-0	—	0		7	0.9
1995	Tor A	1	3	.250	24	0	0	0-2	45	57	40	4	1	33-4	38	7.40	64	.317	.419	0-0	—	0		-13	-1.0
Total	11	74	75	.497	278	174	21-5	8-8	1298	1292	602	102	19	432-46	723	3.64	103	.263	.323	359-41	.109	-9	96	9	0.7
COX, ERNIE Ernest Thompson B 2.19.1894 Birmingham, AL D 4.29.1974 Birmingham, AL BL/TR 6-1/180# d5.5																									
1922	Chi A	0	0	—	1	0	0	0	1	1	2	0	0	2	0	18.00	23	.250	.500	0-0	—	0		-1	-0.1
COX, GEORGE George Melvin B 11.15.1904 Sherman, TX D 12.17.1995 Bedford, TX BR/TR 6-1/170# d4.12																									
1928	Chi A	1	2	.333	26	2	0	0	89	110	58	6	2	39	22	5.26	77	.313	.385	26-1	.077	-2	94	-10	-0.6
COX, GLENN Glenn Melvin B 2.3.1931 Montebello, CA BR/TR 6-2/210# d9.20																									
1955	KC A	0	2	.000	2	2	0	0	2.1	11	8	0	0	1-0	2	30.86	14	.611	.632	1-0	.000	-0	32	-6	-1.0
1956	KC A	0	2	.000	3	3	1	0	23.1	15	11	2	0	22-0	6	4.24	102	.203	.381	7-0	.000	-1	34	1	-0.1
1957	KC A	1	0	1.000	10	0	0	0	14.1	18	9	1	0	9-1	8	5.02	79	.321	.415	2-0	.000	0		-2	-0.1
1958	KC A	0	0	—	2	0	0	0	3.2	6	4	1	0	3-0	1	9.82	40	.400	.500	0-0	—	0		-2	-0.1
Total	4	1	4	.200	17	5	1	0	43.2	50	32	4	0	35-1	17	6.39	65	.307	.427	10-0	.000	-1	34	-9	-1.3
COX, CASEY Joseph Casey B 7.3.1941 Long Beach, CA BR/TR 6-5/200# d4.15																									
1966	Was A	4	5	.444	66	0	0	7	113	104	53	6	4	35-15	46	3.50	99	.250	.310	8-1	.000	-1		-2	-0.3
1967	Was A	7	4	.636	54	0	0	1	73	67	33	2	4	21-7	32	2.96	107	.250	.311	3-0	.000	-0		-1	-0.1
1968	Was A	0	1	.000	4	0	0	0	7.2	7	2	0	0	0-0	4	2.35	124	.250	.241	0-0	—	0		1	0.1
1969	Was A	12	7	.632	52	13	4	0-2	171.2	161	62	15	1	64-7	73	2.78	125	.251	.318	47-6	.106	-2	122	13	1.2
1970	Was A	8	12	.400	37	30	1	1-1	192.1	211	108	27	4	44-4	68	4.45	80	.285	.324	58-7	.121	-2	99	-21	-2.3
1971	Was A	5	7	.417	54	11	0	7-3	124.1	131	69	9	7	40-8	43	3.98	83	.273	.335	26-1	.077	-1	101	-13	-1.5
1972	Tex A	3	5	.375	35	4	0	4-3	65.1	73	41	7	1	26-7	27	4.41	69	.277	.341	9-0	.111	1	37	-12	-1.6
	NY A	0	1	.000	5	1	0	0-0	11.2	13	6	0	2	3-1	4	4.63	64	.289	.353	0-1	—	0	0	-2	-0.2
	Year	3	6	.333	40	5	0	4-3	77	86	6	7	3	29-8	31	4.44	68	.278	.343	9-1	.111	1	29	-14	-1.8
1973	NY A	0	0	—	1	0	0	0-0	3	5	3	0	2	1-0	0	6.00	61	.357	.444	0-0	—	0		-1	-0.1
Total	8	39	42	.481	308	59	5	20-9	762	772	377	66	25	234-49	297	3.70	92	.266	.323	151-16	.099	-6	100	-38	-4.8
COX, LES Leslie Warren B 8.14.1905 Junction, TX D 10.14.1934 San Angelo, TX BR/TR 6/164# d9.11																									
1926	Chi A	0	1	.000	2	0	0	0	5	6	10	2	0	5	3	5.40	72	.261	.393	2-0	.500	0		-4	-0.6
COX, RED Plateau Rex B 2.16.1895 Laurel Springs, NC D 10.15.1984 Roanoke, VA BL/TR 6-2/190# d4.17																									
1920	Det A	0	0	—	3	0	0	0	5	9	4	0	0	3	1	5.40	69	.375	.444	1-0	.000	-0		-1	-0.1
COX, TERRY Terry Lee B 3.30.1949 Odessa, TX BR/TR 6-5/215# d9.7																									
1970	Cal A	0	0	—	3	0	0	0-0	2.1	4	1	0	0	0-0	3	3.86	94	.400	.400	0-0	—	0		0	0.0
COX, BILL William Donald B 6.23.1913 Ashmore, IL D 2.16.1988 Charleston, IL BR/TR 6-1/185# d6.6																									
1936	StL N	0	0	—	2	0	0	0	2.2	4	5	0	0	1	1	6.75	58	.333	.385	0-0	—	0		-2	-0.1
1937	Chi A	1	0	1.000	3	2	1-1	0	12.2	9	1	0	0	5	8	0.71	648	.200	.280	4-0	.250	0	47	6	0.4
1938	Chi A	0	2	.000	7	1	0	0	11.2	11	14	0	0	13	5	6.94	70	.244	.414	2-0	.000	-0	18	-4	-0.6
	StL A	1	4	.200	22	7	1	0	63	81	53	8	0	35	16	7.00	71	.315	.397	17-0	.059	-1*	81	-13	-0.9
	Year	1	6	.143	29	8	1	0	74.2	92	58	8	0	48	21	6.99	71	.305	.400	19-0	.053	-2	73	-17	-1.5
1939	StL A	0	2	.000	4	2	1	0	9.1	10	10	0	0	8	8	9.64	50	.256	.383	1-0	.000	-0	63	-4	-0.7
1940	StL A	0	1	.000	12	0	0	0	17.1	23	17	3	0	12	7	7.27	63	.333	.432	1-0	.000	-0*		-5	-0.3
Total	5	2	9	.182	50	12	3-1	0	116.2	138	100	11	0	74	45	6.56	74	.296	.392	25-0	.080	-2	68	-22	-2.2
COYLE, BILL William Claude B 9.20.1871 , KY D 6.4.1941 San Francisco, CA TR d7.7																									
1893	Bos N	0	1	.000	2	1	0	0	8	14	10	1	0	3	2	9.00	55	.368	.415	4	.000	-1	184	-3	-0.3
COZART, CHARLIE Charles Rhubin B 10.17.1919 Lenoir, NC BR/TL 6/190# d4.17																									
1945	Bos N	1	0	1.000	5	0	0	0	8	10	11	2	0	15	4	10.13	38	.303	.521	2-0	.000	-0		-6	-0.6
CRABB, ROY James Roy B 8.23.1890 Monticello, IA D 3.30.1940 Lewistown, MT BR/TR 5-11/160# d8.10																									
1912	Chi A	0	1	.000	2	1	0	0	8.2	6	2	0	0	4	3	1.04	308	.214	.313	3-0	.000	-0	23	2	0.2
	Phi A	2	4	.333	7	7	3	0	43.1	48	22	0	4	17	12	3.74	82	.287	.367	16-1	.000	-3	103	-3	-0.6
	Year	2	5	.286	9	8	3	0	52	54	26	0	4	21	15	3.29	94	.277	.359	19-1	.000	-3	92	0	-0.4

Year	Tm Lg	W	L	Pct	G	GS	CG-Sho	SV-BS	IP	H	R	HR	HB	BB-IB	SO	ERA	AERA	OAV	OOB	AB-SH	AVG	PB	Sup	APR	PW
CRABLE, GEORGE George E. B 12.1885 , NE BL/TL 6-1/190# d8.3																									
1910	Bro N	0	0	—	2	1	1	0	7.1	5	4	0	2	5	3	4.91	62	.217	.400	2-0	.000	0	123	-1	-0.1
CRABTREE, TIM Timothy Lyle B 10.13.1969 Jackson, MI BR/TR 6-4/205# d6.23																									
1995	Tor A	0	2	.000	31	0	0	0-2	32	30	16	1	2	13-0	21	3.09	152	.240	.319	0-0	—	0		4	0.3
1996	Tor A	5	3	.625	53	0	0	1-4	67.1	59	26	4	3	22-4	57	2.54	197	.231	.298	0-0	—	0		16	1.7
1997	Tor A	3	3	.500	37	0	0	2-3	40.2	65	32	7	2	17-3	26	7.08	65	.374	.431	0-0	—	0		-10	-1.3
1998	†Tex A	6	1	.857	64	0	0	0-1	85.1	86	40	3	3	35-2	60	3.59	135	.264	.335	1-0	.000	-0		10	0.7
1999	†Tex A	5	1	.833	68	0	0	0-3	65	71	26	4	1	18-1	54	3.46	147	.280	.328	0-0	—	0		11	0.9
2000	Tex A	2	7	.222	68	0	0	2-7	80.1	86	52	7	2	31-6	54	5.15	97	.274	.339	0-0	—	0		-2	-0.1
2001	Tex A	0	5	.000	21	0	0	4-2	23.1	37	18	3	1	14-2	16	6.56	71	.385	.456	0-0	—	0		-5	-0.9
Total	7	21	22	.488	342	0	0	9-22	394	434	210	29	14	150-18	288	4.20	117	.281	.346	1-0	.000	-0		24	1.3
CRADDOCK, WALT Walter Anderson B 3.25.1932 Pax, WV D 7.6.1980 Parma Heights, OH BR/TL 5-11.5/176# d9.3																									
1955	KC A	0	2	.000	4	2	0	0	15	18	14	3	0	10-0	9	7.80	54	.300	.400	5-0	.000	-1	43	-6	-0.7
1956	KC A	0	2	.000	2	2	0	0	9.1	9	7	1	0	10-0	8	6.75	64	.265	.432	2-0	.000	-0	21	-2	-0.4
1958	KC A	0	3	.000	23	1	0	0	36.2	41	25	4	1	20-0	22	5.89	66	.289	.376	2-0	.000	-0	69	-7	-0.5
Total	3	0	7	.000	29	5	0	0	61	68	46	8	1	40-0	39	6.49	62	.288	.391	9-0	.000	-1	40	-15	-1.6
CRAFT, MOLLY Maurice Montague B 11.28.1895 Portsmouth, VA D 10.25.1978 Los Angeles, CA BR/TR 6-2/165# d8.8 Mil 1918																									
1916	Was A	0	1	.000	2	1	1	0	11	12	5	0	0	6	9	3.27	85	.316	.409	4-0	.000	-0*	27	-1	0.0
1917	Was A	0	0	—	8	0	0	1	14	17	10	0	0	8	2	3.86	68	.315	.403	2-0	.500	0		-3	-0.1
1918	Was A	0	0	—	3	0	0	0	7	5	1	0	0	1	5	1.29	212	.208	.240	2-0	.000	-0		1	0.0
1919	Was A	0	3	.000	16	2	0	1	48.2	59	28	2	2	18	17	3.88	83	.309	.374	18-1	.111	-2	98	-4	-0.4
Total	4	0	4	.000	29	3	1	2	80.2	93	44	2	2	33	33	3.57	84	.303	.374	26-1	.115	-2	77	-7	-0.5
CRAGHEAD, HOWARD Howard Oliver "Judge" B 5.25.1908 Selma, CA D 7.15.1962 San Diego, CA BR/TR 6-2/200# d4.30																									
1931	Cle A	0	0	—	4	0	0	0	5.2	8	4	0	0	2	2	6.35	73	.320	.370	0-0	—	0		-1	0.0
1933	Cle A	0	0	—	11	0	0	0	17.1	19	13	1	1	10	2	6.23	71	.292	.395	3-0	.000	-0		-3	-0.2
Total	2	0	0	—	15	0	0	0	23	27	17	1	1	12	4	6.26	72	.300	.388	3-0	.000	-0		-4	-0.2
CRAIG, GEORGE George McCarthy "Lefty" B 11.15.1887 Philadelphia, PA D 4.23.1911 Indianapolis, IN TL d7.19																									
1907	Phi A	0	0	—	2	0	0	0	1.2	2	3	0	2	3	0	10.80	24	.286	.583	1-0	.000	-0		-2	-0.1
CRAIG, PETE Peter Joel B 7.10.1940 LaSalle, ON, CAN BL/TR 6-5/220# d9.6																									
1964	Was A	0	0	—	2	1	0	0	1.2	8	9	1	0	4-1	0	48.60	8	.667	.750	0-0	—	0	192	-8	-0.4
1965	Was A	0	3	.000	3	3	0	0	14.1	18	15	1	0	8-1	2	8.16	43	.321	.394	3-0	.667	1	101	-7	-1.1
1966	Was A	0	0	—	1	0	0	0	2	2	2	0	0	1-1	1	4.50	77	.250	.333	0-0	—	0		-1	0.0
Total	3	0	3	.000	6	4	0	0	18	28	26	2	0	13-3	3	11.50	30	.368	.451	3-0	.667	1	126	-16	-1.5
CRAIG, ROGER Roger Lee B 2.17.1930 Durham, NC BR/TR 6-4/191# d7.17 M10 C13																									
1955	†Bro N	5	3	.625	21	10	3	2	90.2	81	37	8	1	43-6	48	2.78	146	.238	.323	26-1	.077	-2	132	11	0.6
1956	†Bro N	12	11	.522	35	32	8-2	1	199	169	90	25	4	87-5	109	3.71	107	.231	.313	61-5	.016	-5	104	6	-0.1
1957	Bro N	6	9	.400	32	13	1	0	111.1	102	58	18	2	47-5	69	4.61	90	.249	.328	29-2	.138	-1	67	-2	-0.4
1958	LA N	2	1	.667	9	2	1	0	32	30	20	3	0	12-1	16	4.50	91	.242	.309	9-0	.000	-1	121	-2	-0.3
1959	†LA N	11	5	.688	29	17	7-**4**	0	152.2	122	49	13	1	45-3	76	2.06	205	.217	.275	52-4	.058	-4	88	30	2.6
1960	LA N	8	3	.727	21	15	6-1	0	115.2	99	48	8	3	43-4	69	3.27	121	.230	.304	36-3	.056	-2	117	8	0.5
1961	LA N	5	6	.455	40	14	2	2	112.2	130	87	22	4	52-7	63	6.15	71	.288	.365	27-3	.148	-0	104	-21	-2.0
1962	NY N	10	24	.294	42	33	13	3	233.1	261	133	35	7	70-3	118	4.51	93	.288	.341	76-4	.053	-5	79	-6	-1.1
1963	NY N	5	22	.185	46	31	14	2	236	249	117	28	6	58-2	108	3.78	92	.267	.312	69-3	.087	-2	57	-7	-0.9
1964	†StL N	7	9	.438	39	19	3	5	166	180	76	16	4	35-4	84	3.25	117	.276	.316	48-1	.208	2	80	7	1.1
1965	Cin N	1	4	.200	40	0	0	3	64.1	74	33	6	3	25-7	30	3.64	103	.289	.355	11-2	.182	-0		-1	-0.1
1966	Phi N	2	1	.667	14	0	0	1	22.2	31	15	4	0	5-1	13	5.56	65	.326	.353	4-0	.000	-0		-5	-0.6
Total	12	74	98	.430	368	186	58-7	19	1536.1	1528	763	186	35	522-48	803	3.83	104	.259	.321	448-28	.085	-22	89	18	-0.7
CRAM, JERRY Gerald Allen B 12.9.1947 Los Angeles, CA BR/TR 6/180# d9.3																									
1969	KC A	0	1	.000	5	2	0	0-0	16.2	15	8	0	0	6-1	10	3.24	114	.231	.296	3-0	.000	-0	108	0	0.0
1974	NY N	0	1	.000	10	0	0	0-0	22.1	22	4	1	0	4-3	8	1.61	222	.275	.310	3-0	.333	0		5	0.3
1975	NY N	0	1	.000	4	0	0	0-0	5	7	3	2	0	2-0	2	5.40	64	.333	.391	0-0	—	0		-1	-0.2
1976	KC A	0	0	—	4	0	0	0-0	4.1	8	3	0	0	1-0	2	6.23	56	.421	.450	0-0	—	0		-1	-0.1
Total	4	0	3	.000	23	2	0	0-0	48.1	52	18	3	0	13-4	22	2.98	121	.281	.328	6-0	.167	-0	108	3	0.0
CRAMER, BILL William Wendell B 5.21.1891 Bedford, IN D 9.11.1966 Fort Wayne, IN BR/TR 6/175# d6.25																									
1912	Cin N	0	0	—	1	0	0	0	2.1	6	6	0	0	0	2	0.00	—	.500	.500	1-0	.000	-0		-1	-0.1
CRANDALL, DOC James Otis B 10.8.1887 Wadena, IN D 8.17.1951 Bell, CA BR/TR 5-10.5/180# d4.24 C4 ▲																									
1908	NY N	12	12	.500	32	24	13	0	214.2	198	83	3	9	59	77	2.93	82	.248	.307	72-6	.222	5*	125	-8	-0.5
1909	NY N	6	4	.600	30	8	4	6	122	117	58	5	3	33	55	2.88	89	.252	.305	41-2	.244	3	150	-4	0.0
1910	NY N	17	4	.810	42	18	13-2	5	207.2	194	86	10	4	43	73	2.56	116	.246	.289	73-3	.342	10*	157	8	1.8
1911	†NY N	15	5	.750	41	15	9-2	5	198.2	199	82	10	6	51	94	2.63	128	.256	.307	113-5	.239	5*	138	14	2.1
1912	†NY N	13	7	.650	37	10	7	2	162	181	85	7	2	35	60	3.61	94	.286	.326	80-3	.313	6*	167	-1	0.6
1913	†NY N	2	4	.333	24	1	1	5	55.1	61	28	2	1	13	28	3.09	101	.293	.338	25-0	.280	2*	0	-1	0.1
	†NY N	2	0	1.000	11	1	1	1	42.1	41	17	1	0	11	14	2.55	122	.248	.295	22-0	.364	3*	289	2	0.5
	Year	4	4	.500	35	2	2	6	97.2	102	29	3	1	24	42	2.86	109	.273	.319	47-0	.319	5	145	**2**	0.6
1914	StL F	13	9	.591	27	21	18-1	0	196	194	94	8	2	52	84	3.54	86	.256	.305	278-5	.309	7*	104	-9	0.0
1915	StL F	21	15	.583	51	33	22-4	1	312.2	307	116	5	10	77	117	2.59	111	.263	.314	141-0	.284	12*	102	7	2.2
1916	StL A	0	0	—	2	0	0	0	1.1	7	9	0	1	1	0	27.00	10	.636	.692	12-0	.083	-0*		-5	-0.3
1918	Bos N	1	2	.333	5	3	3	0	34	39	11	1	1	4	4	2.38	113	.307	.333	28-0	.286	1*	56	1	0.3
Total	10	102	62	.622	302	134	91-9	25	1546.2	1538	669	52	39	379	606	2.92	101	.261	.310	885-24	.286	54	124	4	6.8
CRANE, ED Edward Nicholas "Cannon-Ball" B 5.27.1862 Boston, MA D 9.20.1896 Rochester, NY BR/TR 5-10.5/204# d4.17 ▲																									
1884	Bos U	0	2	.000	4	2	1	0	18	17	14	1		6	13	4.00	59	.233	.291	428	.285	0*	36	-3	-0.2
1886	Was N	1	7	.125	10	8	7-1	0	70	91	85	4		53	39	7.20	45	.313	.419	292	.171	-1*	38	-30	-2.5
1888	†NY N	5	6	.455	12	11	11-2	1	92.2	70	51	3	2	40	58	2.43	113	.193	.277	37	.162	1	75	2	0.3
1889	†NY N	14	11	.560	29	25	23	0	230.2	221	159	10	10	136	130	3.63	109	.244	.350	103	.204	3	112	5	0.5
1890	NY P	16	19	.457	43	35	28	0	330.1	323	280	12	10	208	116	4.63	98	.245	.352	146	.315	7	108	-5	0.0
1891	Cin AA	14	14	.500	32	31	25-1	0	250	216	151	3	14	139	122	**2.45**	**167**	.225	.332	110	.155	-6*	76	35	2.6
	Cin N	4	8	.333	15	13	11-1	0	116.2	134	91	3	3	64	51	4.09	83	.277	.365	46	.109	-3	90	-10	-1.1
1892	NY N	16	24	.400	47	42	35-2	1	364.1	350	276	10	12	189	174	3.80	85	.243	.335	163	.245	4*	112	-28	-2.3
1893	NY N	2	4	.333	10	7	4	0	68.1	84	62	2	6	41	11	5.93	79	.294	.393	26	.462	4*	144	-8	-0.1
	Bro N	0	2	.000	2	2	1	0	10	19	19	2	1	9	5	13.50	33	.388	.492	5	.400	0*	79	-10	-1.1
	Year	2	6	.250	12	9	5	0	78.1	103	24	4	7	50	16	6.89	67	.307	.408	31	.452	5	129	-16	-1.2
Total	8	72	97	.426	204	176	146-7	2	1551	1525	1188	50	58	885	719	3.99	95	.247	.347	1356	.237	11	98	-52	-3.9
CRAWFORD, CARLOS Carlos Lamonte B 10.4.1971 Charlotte, NC BR/TR 6-1/185# d6.7																									
1996	Phi N	0	1	.000	1	1	0	0-0	3.2	7	10	1	1	2-0	4	4.91	88	.389	.476	1-0	.000	-0	104	-4	-0.5
CRAWFORD, LARRY Charles Lowrie B 4.27.1914 Swissvale, PA D 12.20.1994 Hanover, PA BL/TL 6-1/165# d7.21																									
1937	Phi N	0	0	—	6	0	0	0	6	12	10	2	0	1	2	15.00	29	.387	.406	0-0	—	0		-6	-0.3
CRAWFORD, JIM James Frederick "Catfish" B 9.29.1950 Chicago, IL BL/TL 6-3/200# d4.6																									
1973	Hou N	2	4	.333	48	0	0	6-4	70	69	41	7	2	33-8	56	4.50	81	.256	.338	13-0	.231	1		-8	-0.6
1975	Hou N	3	5	.375	44	2	0	4-3	86.2	92	40	0	2	37-4	37	3.63	93	.280	.354	17-1	.294	2	91	-4	-0.1
1976	Det A	1	8	.111	32	5	1	2-1	109.1	115	65	4	0	43-4	68	4.53	82	.275	.335	0-0	—	0	57	-10	-0.6
1977	Det A	7	8	.467	37	7	0	1-2	126	156	82	13	1	50-5	91	4.79	90	.310	.369	0-0	—	0	78	-9	-1.0
1978	Det A	2	3	.400	20	0	0	0-0	39.1	45	24	3	2	19-3	24	4.35	89	.292	.371	0-0	—	0		-3	-0.4

Year	Tm Lg	W	L	Pct	G	GS	CG-Sho	SV-BS	IP	H	R	HR	HB	BB-IB	SO	ERA	AERA	OAV	OOB	AB-SH	AVG	PB	Sup	APR	PW
Total	5	15	28	.349	181	14	1	13-10	431.1	477	252	27	7	182-24	276	4.40	87	.285	.353	30-1	.267	3	75	-34	-2.7
CRAWFORD, JOE Joseph Randal B 5.2.1970 Gainesville, FL BL/TL 6-3/225# d4.7																									
1997	NY N	4	3	.571	19	2	0	0-0	46.1	36	18	7	0	13-1	25	3.30	122	.216	.272	11-0	.000	-1	46	4	0.5
CRAWFORD, PAXTON Paxton Keith B 8.4.1977 Little Rock, AR BR/TR 6-3/205# d7.1																									
2000	Bos A	2	1	.667	7	4	0	0-0	29	25	15	0	2	13-2	17	3.41	148	.240	.325	0-0	—	0	74	4	0.3
2001	Bos A	3	0	1.000	8	7	0	0-0	36	40	19	3	2	13-0	25	4.75	95	.276	.342	0-0	—	0	141	0	0.0
Total	2	5	1	.833	15	11	0	0-0	65	65	34	3	4	26-2	42	4.15	114	.261	.335	0-0	—	0	114	4	0.3
CRAWFORD, STEVE Steven Ray B 4.29.1958 Pryor, OK BR/TR 6-5/225# d9.2																									
1980	Bos A	2	0	1.000	6	4	2	0-0	32.1	41	14	3	0	8-2	10	3.62	117	.306	.345	0-0	—	0	143	2	0.1
1981	Bos A	0	5	.000	14	11	0	0-0	57.2	69	38	10	3	18-0	29	4.99	78	.301	.354	0-0	—	0	107	-7	-0.6
1982	Bos A	1	0	1.000	5	0	0	0-0	9	14	3	0	0	0-0	2	2.00	216	.341	.341	0-0	—	0		2	0.2
1984	Bos A	5	0	1.000	35	0	0	1-3	62	69	31	6	1	21-5	21	3.34	125	.286	.341	0-0	—	0		3	0.3
1985	Bos A	6	5	.545	44	1	0	12-4	91	103	47	5	0	28-8	58	3.76	114	.289	.338	0-0	—	0	106	3	0.4
1986	†Bos A	0	2	.000	40	0	0	4-4	57.1	69	29	5	0	19-7	32	3.92	106	.308	.359	0-0	—	0		1	0.0
1987	Bos A	5	4	.556	29	0	0	0-0	72.2	91	48	13	2	32-2	43	5.33	86	.314	.386	0-0	—	0		-7	-0.7
1989	KC A	3	1	.750	25	0	0	0-1	54	48	19	2	3	19-3	33	2.83	136	.242	.317	0-0	—	0		6	0.5
1990	KC A	5	4	.556	46	0	0	1-1	80	79	38	7	3	23-3	54	4.16	92	.254	.310	0-0	—	0		-1	-0.1
1991	KC A	3	2	.600	33	0	0	1-0	46.2	60	31	3	1	18-5	38	5.98	69	.311	.367	0-0	—	0		-8	-0.8
Total	10	30	23	.566	277	16	2	19-13	562.2	643	298	54	13	186-35	320	4.17	99	.290	.346	0-0	—	0	114	-6	-0.7
CREEK, DOUG Paul Douglas B 3.1.1969 Winchester, VA BL/TL 5-10/205# d9.17																									
1995	StL N	0	0	—	6	0	0	0-0	6.2	2	0	0	0	3-0	10	0.00	—	.095	.208	0-0	—	0		3	0.1
1996	SF N	0	2	.000	63	0	0	0-1	48.1	45	41	11	2	32-2	38	6.52	63	.243	.361	1-1	.000	-0		-14	-0.7
1997	SF N	1	2	.333	3	3	0	0-0	13.1	12	12	1	0	14-0	14	6.75	61	.240	.406	3-2	.333	0	90	-4	-0.7
1999	Chi N	0	0	—	3	0	0	0-0	6	6	7	1	0	8-1	6	10.50	43	.261	.438	0-0	—	0		-4	-0.2
2000	TB A	1	3	.250	45	0	0	1-2	60.2	49	33	10	2	39-3	73	4.60	108	.224	.342	0-0	—	0		3	0.2
2001	TB A	2	5	.286	66	0	0	0-3	62.2	51	34	7	4	49-5	66	4.31	104	.230	.374	0-0	—	0		1	0.1
2002	TB A	2	1	.667	29	0	0	0-2	37.1	39	27	8	3	21-1	37	6.27	71	.264	.366	1-0	.000	-0		-7	-0.5
	Sea A	1	1	.500	23	0	0	0-0	18.1	18	10	2	4	14-1	19	4.91	86	.257	.404	0-0	—	0		-1	-0.1
	Year	3	2	.600	52	0	0	0-2	55.2	57	41	10	7	35-2	56	5.82	75	.261	.379	1-0	.000	-0		-8	-0.6
2003	Tor A	0	0	—	21	0	0	0-1	13.2	14	6	2	2	12-3	11	3.29	140	.264	.406	0-0	—	0		2	0.1
Total	8	7	14	.333	259	3	0	1-9	267	236	170	42	17	192-16	274	5.19	86	.238	.368	5-3	.200	0	90	-21	-1.7
CREEL, JACK Jack Dalton "Tex" B 4.23.1916 Kyle, TX D 8.13.2002 Houston, TX BR/TR 6/165# d4.22																									
1945	StL N	5	4	.556	26	8	2	2	87	78	41	5	6	45	34	4.14	90	.245	.349	26-4	.077	-2*	116	-2	-0.3
CREEL, KEITH Steven Keith B 2.4.1959 Dallas, TX BR/TR 6-2/180# d5.25																									
1982	KC A	1	4	.200	9	6	0	0-0	41.2	43	28	8	0	25-0	13	5.40	76	.267	.362	0-0	—	0	74	-6	-0.6
1983	KC A	2	5	.286	25	10	1	0-0	89.1	116	66	17	2	35-0	31	6.35	64	.320	.380	0-0	—	0	87	-20	-1.4
1985	Cle A	2	5	.286	15	8	0	0-0	62	73	35	7	2	23-2	31	4.79	86	.296	.354	0-0	—	0	110	-4	-0.4
1987	Tex A	0	0	—	6	0	0	0-0	9.2	12	5	2	0	5-0	5	4.66	96	.293	.370	0-0	—	0		0	0.0
Total	4	5	14	.263	55	24	1	0-0	202.2	244	134	34	4	88-2	80	5.60	74	.300	.368	0-0	—	0	91	-30	-2.4
CREMINS, BOB Robert Anthony "Lefty" or "Crooked Arm" B 2.15.1906 Pelham Manor, NY BL/TL 5-11/178# d8.17																									
1927	Bos A	0	0	—	4	0	0	0	5.1	5	4	0	0	3	0	5.06	83	.250	.348	0-0	—	0		-1	0.0
CRESS, WALKER Walker James "Foots" B 3.6.1917 Ben Hur, VA D 4.21.1996 Baton Rouge, LA BR/TR 6-5/205# d4.27																									
1948	Cin N	0	1	.000	30	2	1	0	60	60	32	2	1	42	33	4.50	87	.271	.390	8-1	.500	2*	79	-3	0.0
1949	Cin N	0	0	—	3	0	0	0	2	2	0	0	0	3	0	0.00	—	.286	.500	0-0	—	0		1	0.0
Total	2	0	1	.000	33	2	1	0	62	62	32	2	1	45	33	4.35	90	.272	.394	8-1	.500	2	79	-2	0.0
CRESSEND, JACK John Baptiste B 5.13.1975 New Orleans, LA BR/TR 6-1/185# d8.26																									
2000	Min A	0	0	—	11	0	0	0-0	13.2	20	8	0	0	6-0	6	5.27	98	.364	.426	0-0	—	0		0	0.0
2001	Min A	3	2	.600	44	0	0	0-2	56.1	50	24	6	1	16-0	40	3.67	125	.237	.291	0-0	—	0		6	0.5
2002	Min A	0	1	.000	23	0	0	0-0	32	40	25	6	1	19-4	22	5.91	76	.305	.392	0-0	—	0		-6	-0.3
2003	Cle A	2	1	.667	33	0	0	0-1	43	40	12	1	2	9-1	28	2.51	176	.252	.300	0-0	—	0		10	0.5
Total	4	5	4	.556	111	0	0	0-3	145	150	69	13	4	50-5	96	3.97	115	.270	.332	0-0	—	0		10	0.7
CREWS, TIM Stanley Timothy B 4.3.1961 Tampa, FL D 3.23.1993 Orlando, FL BR/TR 6/192# d7.27																									
1987	LA N	1	1	.500	20	0	0	3-3	29	30	9	2	2	8-1	20	2.48	160	.268	.325	2-0	.000	-0		5	0.4
1988	LA N	4	0	1.000	42	0	0	0-1	71.2	77	29	3	0	16-7	45	3.14	106	.278	.312	5-1	.200	0		1	0.0
1989	LA N	0	1	.000	44	0	0	1-2	61.2	69	27	7	2	23-9	56	3.21	107	.284	.351	0-0	—	0		0	0.0
1990	LA N	4	5	.444	66	2	0	5-4	107.1	98	40	9	1	24-6	76	2.77	132	.238	.280	7-0	.000	-1	99	10	0.7
1991	LA N	2	3	.400	60	0	0	6-2	76	75	30	7	0	19-11	53	3.43	105	.256	.299	1-0	.000	0		3	0.2
1992	LA N	0	3	.000	49	2	0	0-1	78	95	46	6	2	20-9	43	5.19	66	.310	.351	7-0	.286	0	66	-13	-0.7
Total	6	11	13	.458	281	4	0	15-13	423.2	444	181	34	7	110-43	293	3.44	103	.270	.316	22-1	.136	-0	82	6	0.6
CRIDER, JERRY Jerry Stephen B 9.2.1941 Sioux Falls, SD BR/TR 6-2/200# d5.21																									
1969	Min A	1	0	1.000	21	1	0	1-1	28.2	31	15	3	2	15-6	16	4.71	78	.284	.378	9-0	.444	2	266	-2	0.1
1970	Chi A	4	7	.364	32	8	0	4-0	91	101	49	13	2	34-2	40	4.45	88	.288	.350	24-2	.083	-1	83	-4	-0.8
Total	2	5	7	.417	53	9	0	5-1	119.2	132	64	16	4	49-8	56	4.51	85	.287	.357	33-2	.182	1	103	-6	-0.7
CRIM, CHUCK Charles Robert B 7.23.1961 Van Nuys, CA BR/TR 6/185# d4.8																									
1987	Mil A	6	8	.429	53	5	0	12-5	130	133	60	15	3	39-5	56	3.67	125	.266	.322	0-0	—	0	115	12	1.3
1988	Mil A	7	6	.538	**70**	0	0	9-2	105	95	38	11	2	28-3	58	2.91	137	.247	.298	0-0	—	0		12	1.6
1989	Mil A	9	7	.563	**76**	0	0	7-7	117.2	114	42	7	2	36-9	59	2.83	136	.259	.314	0-0	—	0		13	1.8
1990	Mil A	3	5	.375	67	0	0	11-5	85.2	88	39	7	2	23-4	39	3.47	112	.261	.309	0-0	—	0		4	0.4
1991	Mil A	8	5	.615	66	0	0	3-2	91.1	115	52	9	2	25-9	39	4.63	86	.305	.351	0-0	—	0		-7	-0.9
1992	Cal A	7	6	.538	57	0	0	1-2	87	100	56	11	6	29-6	30	5.17	77	.293	.355	0-0	—	0		-12	-1.6
1993	Cal A	2	2	.500	11	0	0	0-0	15.1	17	11	2	2	5-1	10	5.87	77	.298	.369	0-0	—	0		-2	-0.4
1994	Chi N	5	4	.556	49	1	0	2-3	64.1	69	36	9	1	24-6	43	4.48	93	.271	.336	2-0	.000	-0	175	-3	-0.4
Total	8	47	43	.522	449	6	0	45-26	696.1	731	334	71	20	209-43	334	3.83	107	.272	.326	2-0	.000	-0	138	17	1.8
CRIMIAN, JACK John Melvin B 2.17.1926 Philadelphia, PA BR/TR 5-10/180# d7.3																									
1951	StL N	1	0	1.000	11	0	0	1	17	24	17	3	0	8	5	9.00	44	.338	.405	3-0	.333	0		-9	-0.6
1952	StL N	0	0	—	5	0	0	0	8.1	15	9	4	0	4	4	9.72	38	.417	.475	1-0	.000	0		-5	-0.2
1956	KC A	4	8	.333	54	7	0	3	129	129	87	19	5	49-2	59	5.51	79	.265	.334	22-5	.227	1*	94	-16	-1.3
1957	Det A	0	1	.000	4	0	0	0	5.2	9	8	1	0	4-2	1	12.71	30	.375	.448	0-0	—	0		-5	-0.8
Total	4	5	9	.357	74	7	0	4	160	177	121	27	5	65-4	69	6.36	67	.287	.355	26-5	.231	1	94	-35	-2.9
CRISS, DODE Dode B 3.12.1885 Sherman, MS D 9.8.1955 Sherman, MS BL/TR 6-2/200# d4.20 ▲																									
1908	StL A	0	1	.000	9	1	0	0	18	15	14	1	3	13	9	6.50	37	.250	.408	82-0	.341	1*	343	-7	-0.2
1909	StL A	1	5	.167	11	6	3	0	55.1	53	33	0	2	32	43	3.42	71	.262	.369	48-0	.292	5*	78	-8	-0.3
1910	StL A	2	1	.667	6	0	0	0	19.1	12	7	0	4	9	9	1.40	177	.176	.309	91-0	.231	1*		2	0.4
1911	StL A	0	2	.000	4	2	0	0	18.1	24	21	0	2	10	9	8.35	40	.333	.429	83-1	.253	0*	43	-9	-0.7
Total	4	3	9	.250	30	9	3	0	111	104	75	1	11	64	70	4.38	59	.259	.375	304-1	.276	8	96	-22	-0.8
CRISTALL, BILL William Arthur "Lefty" B 9.12.1878 Odessa, Russia D 1.28.1939 Buffalo, NY BL/TL 5-7/145# d9.3																									
1901	Cle A	1	5	.167	6	6	5-1	0	48.1	54	42	1	4	30	12	4.84	73	.280	.388	20-1	.350	2	111	-8	-0.5
CRISTANTE, LEO Dante Leo B 12.10.1926 Detroit, MI D 8.24.1977 Dearborn, MI BR/TR 6-1/195# d4.21																									
1951	Phi N	1	1	.500	10	1	0	0	22	28	13	3	1	9	6	4.91	78	.318	.388	6-1	.167	-0	206	-3	-0.2
1955	Det A	0	1	.000	20	1	0	0	36.2	37	15	1	0	14-2	9	3.19	120	.261	.325	7-0	.000	-1	162	3	0.0
Total	2	1	2	.333	30	2	0	0	58.2	65	28	4	1	23-2	15	3.84	100	.283	.349	13-1	.077	-1	184	0	-0.2

Year	Tm Lg	W	L	Pct	G	GS	CG-Sho	SV-BS	IP	H	R	HR	HB	BB-IB	SO	ERA	AERA	OAV	OOB	AB-SH	AVG	PB	Sup	APR	PW
CRITCHLEY, MORRIE Morris Arthur B 3.26.1850 New London, CT D 3.6.1910 Pittsburgh, PA 6-1/190# d5.8																									
1882	Pit AA	1	0	1.000	1	1	1-1	0	9	7	0	0		1	3	0.00	—	.200	.222	5	.000	-1	39	3	0.2
	StL AA	0	4	.000	4	4	4	0	34	43	31	3		7	2	4.24	66	.289	.321	14	.214	-0	87	-4	-0.5
	Year	1	4	.200	5	5	5-1	0	43	50	36	3		8	5	3.35	83	.272	.302	19	.158	-1	78	-3	-0.3
CROCKER, CLAUDE Claude Arthur B 7.20.1924 Caroleen, NC D 12.19.2002 Clinton, SC BR/TR 6-2/185# d8.1																									
1944	Bro N	0	0	—	2	0	0	0	3.1	6	4	0	0	5	1	10.80	33	.400	.550	1-0	1.000	0		-2	-0.1
1945	Bro N	0	0	—	1	0	0	1	2	2	0	0	0	1	1	0.00	—	.286	.375	0-0	—	0		1	0.1
Total	2	0	0	—	3	0	0	1	5.1	8	4	0	0	6	2	6.75	54	.364	.500	1-0	1.000	0		-1	0.0
CRONE, RAY Raymond Hayes B 8.7.1931 Memphis, TN BR/TR 6-2/185# d4.13																									
1954	Mil N	1	0	1.000	19	2	1	1	49	44	11	6	1	19	33	2.02	184	.247	.322	10-0	.200	-0	48	11	0.5
1955	Mil N	10	9	.526	33	15	6-1	0	140.1	117	63	11	0	42-7	76	3.46	108	.227	.285	44-3	.159	-1	90	4	0.4
1956	Mil N	11	10	.524	35	21	6	2	169.2	173	92	19	1	44-3	73	3.87	89	.263	.307	49-5	.122	1	122	-11	-1.2
1957	Mil N	3	1	.750	11	5	2	0	42.1	54	23	8	0	15-2	15	4.46	78	.312	.365	11-1	.182	1	161	-5	-0.3
	NY N	4	8	.333	25	17	2	1	120.2	131	68	11	3	40-1	56	4.33	91	.272	.330	40-1	.025	-4	113	-6	-0.8
	Year	7	9	.438	36	22	4	1	163	185	73	19	3	55-3	71	4.36	88	.282	.339	51-2	.059	-3	124	-11	-1.1
1958	SF N	1	2	.333	14	1	0	0	24	35	18	5	0	13-0	7	6.75	56	.354	.421	2-0	.000	-0	94	-7	-0.8
Total	5	30	30	.500	137	61	17-1	4	546	554	275	60	5	173-13	260	3.87	95	.263	.319	156-10	.115	-3	112	-14	-2.2
CRONIN, JACK John J. B 5.26.1874 Staten Island, NY D 7.12.1929 Middletown, NY BR/TR 6- /200# d8.24																									
1895	Bro N	0	0	—	2	0	0	2	5	10	8	0	0	3	1	10.80	41	.417	.481	2-0	.500	1		-4	-0.2
1898	Pit N	2	2	.500	4	4	2-1	0	28	35	14	0	0	8	9	3.54	101	.304	.350	10-0	.100	-0	140	1	0.1
1899	Cin N	2	2	.500	5	5	5	0	41	56	35	2	5	16	9	5.49	71	.324	.397	17-0	.118	-1	136	-7	-0.7
1901	Det A	13	16	.448	30	28	21-1	0	219.2	261	145	6	11	42	62	3.89	99	.292	.331	85-4	.247	2*	83	1	0.1
1902	Det A	0	0	—	4	0	0	0	17.1	26	23	1	3	8	5	9.35	39	.347	.430	7-0	.000	-1		-10	-0.5
	Bal A	3	5	.375	10	8	8	0	75.2	66	29	1	0	24	20	2.62	144	.236	.296	27-2	.148	-1	69	10	1.0
	Year	3	5	.375	14	8	8	0	93	92	33	2	3	32	25	3.87	97	.259	.326	34-2	.118	-2	70	1	0.5
	NY N	5	6	.455	13	12	11	0	114	105	49	3	0	18	52	2.45	115	.245	.275	65-2	.169	-1*	73	4	0.3
1903	NY N	6	4	.600	20	11	8	1	115.2	130	67	5	6	37	50	3.81	88	.284	.345	46-2	.196	0	114	-6	-0.5
1904	Bro N	12	23	.343	40	34	33-4	0	307	284	132	10	12	79	110	2.70	102	.245	.300	108-3	.157	-3	80	4	0.2
Total	7	43	58	.426	128	102	88-6	3	923.1	973	502	28	37	235	318	3.40	96	.270	.321	367-13	.180	-5	89	-7	-0.2
CROSBY, GEORGE George Washington B 1860 , IA D 1.9.1913 San Francisco, CA d5.22																									
1884	Chi N	1	2	.333	3	3	3	0	28	27	21	3		12	11	3.54	89	.227	.298	13	.308	1	85	-1	0.0
CROSBY, KEN Kenneth Stewart B 12.15.1947 New Denver, BC, CAN BR/TR 6-2/179# d8.5																									
1975	Chi N	1	0	1.000	9	0	0	0-0	8.1	10	3	0	0	7-0	6	3.24	119	.294	.415	0-0	—	0		1	0.1
1976	Chi N	0	0	—	7	1	0	0-0	12	20	16	3	0	8-0	5	12.00	32	.377	.459	2-0	.500	0	114	-9	-0.4
Total	2	1	0	1.000	16	1	0	0-0	20.1	30	19	3	0	15-0	11	8.41	46	.345	.441	2-0	.500	1	114	-8	-0.3
CROSS, LEM George Lewis B 1.9.1872 Sanbornton, NH D 10.9.1930 Manchester, NH TR 5-9/155# d8.6																									
1893	Cin N	0	2	.000	3	3	2	0	21	24	16	3	0	9	7	5.57	86	.279	.347	6	.333	1	54	-1	0.0
1894	Cin N	3	4	.429	8	7	3	0	53	94	73	9	5	21	11	8.49	65	.381	.440	26-0	.231	-1*	111	-17	-1.5
Total	2	3	6	.333	11	10	5	0	74	118	89	12	5	30	18	7.66	69	.354	.416	32-0	.250	-0	95	-18	-1.5
CROTHERS, DOUG Douglas B 11.16.1859 Natchez, MS D 3.29.1907 St.Louis, MO BR/TR d8.3																									
1884	KC U	1	2	.333	3	3	3	0	25	26	15	0		6	11	1.80	124	.250	.291	15	.133	-2*	115	0	-0.2
1885	NY AA	7	11	.389	18	18	18-1	0	154	192	135	4	2	49	40	5.08	61	.293	.344	51	.157	0	117	-34	-2.9
Total	2	8	13	.381	21	21	21-1	0	179	218	150	4	2	55	51	4.63	65	.287	.337	66	.152	-2	116	-34	-3.1
CROUCH, BILL William Henry "Skip" B 12.3.1886 Marshallton, DE D 12.22.1945 Highland Park, MI BL/TL 6-1/210# d7.12 s-Bill																									
1910	StL A	0	0	—	1	1	1	0	8	6	4	0	0	7	2	3.38	73	.231	.394	3-0	.000	-0	108	-1	-0.1
CROUCH, BILL Wilmer Elmer B 8.20.1910 Wilmington, DE D 12.26.1980 Howell, MI BB/TR 6-1/180# d5.9 f-Bill																									
1939	Bro N	4	0	1.000	6	3	3	0	38.1	37	14	3	0	14	10	2.58	156	.255	.321	15-1	.133	-1	224	5	0.4
1941	Phi N	2	3	.400	20	5	1	1	59	65	31	4	0	17	26	4.42	84	.286	.336	11-3	.091	-0	83	-4	-0.2
	StL N	1	2	.333	18	4	0	6	45	45	16	2	0	14	15	3.00	125	.271	.328	13-1	.000	-1	39	4	0.2
	Year	3	5	.375	38	9	1	7	104	110	18	6	0	31	41	3.81	98	.280	.333	24-4	.042	-2	63	1	0.0
1945	StL N	1	0	1.000	6	0	0	0	13.1	12	5	1	1	7	4	3.38	111	.255	.364	2-0	.000	-0		1	0.0
Total	3	8	5	.615	50	12	4	7	155.2	159	66	10	1	52	55	3.47	110	.272	.332	41-5	.073	-3	105	6	0.4
CROUCH, ZACH Zachary Quinn B 10.26.1965 Folsom, CA BL/TL 6-3/180# d6.4																									
1988	Bos A	0	0	—	3	0	0	0-0	1.1	4	1	0	0	2-0	0	6.75	61	.571	.667	0-0	—	0		0	0.0
CROUSHORE, RICH Richard Steven B 8.7.1970 Lakehurst, NJ BR/TR 6-4/210# d5.18																									
1998	StL N	0	3	.000	41	0	0	8-3	54.1	44	31	6	4	29-2	47	4.97	84	.213	.320	0-2	—	0		-4	-0.2
1999	StL N	3	7	.300	59	0	0	3-7	71.2	68	42	9	3	43-4	88	4.14	110	.247	.354	3-0	.333	1		1	0.1
2000	Col N	2	0	1.000	6	0	0	0-0	11.1	15	11	1	1	6-1	11	8.74	66	.313	.393	1-1	1.000	0		-3	-0.4
	Bos A	0	1	.000	5	0	0	0-0	4.2	4	3	0	1	5-1	3	5.79	87	.250	.435	0-0	—	0		0	0.0
Total	3	5	11	.313	111	0	0	11-10	142	131	87	16	9	83-8	149	4.88	93	.240	.347	4-3	.500	1		-6	-0.5
CROW, DEAN Paul Dean B 8.21.1972 Garland, TX BL/TR 6-4/215# d5.29																									
1998	Det A	2	2	.500	32	0	0	0-0	45.2	55	22	6	2	16-6	18	3.94	120	.313	.374	0-0	—	0		4	0.3
CROWDER, ALVIN Alvin Floyd "General" B 1.11.1899 Winston-Salem, NC D 4.3.1972 Winston-Salem, NC BL/TR 5-10/170# d7.24																									
1926	Was A	7	4	.636	19	12	6	1	100	97	52	3	2	60	26	3.96	98	.261	.367	38-2	.237	1	122	-1	0.0
1927	Was A	4	7	.364	15	11	4-2	0	67.1	58	44	3	2	42	22	4.54	89	.232	.347	22-1	.136	-1	95	-5	-0.9
	StL A	3	5	.375	21	8	2-1	3	73.2	71	44	3	1	42	30	5.01	87	.260	.361	23-1	.261	0	103	-3	-0.3
	Year	7	12	.368	36	19	6-3	3	141	129	49	6	3	84	52	4.79	88	.247	.354	45-2	.200	-1	98	-9	-1.2
1928	StL A	21	5	**.808**	41	31	19-1	2	244	238	113	11	1	91	99	3.69	114	.258	.325	80-9	.188	-2	114	15	1.0
1929	StL A	17	15	.531	40	34	19-**4**	4	266.2	272	133	22	0	93	79	3.92	113	.271	.332	96-1	.188	-3	89	14	1.1
1930	StL A	3	7	.300	13	10	5-1	1	77.1	85	43	11	1	27	42	4.66	105	.283	.345	25-0	.160	-2	78	3	0.2
	Was A	15	9	.625	27	25	20	1	202.1	191	90	6	1	69	65	3.60	128	.249	.312	76-6	.171	-2	111	24	2.0
	Year	18	16	.529	40	35	25-1	2	279.2	276	96	17	2	96	107	3.89	120	.259	.321	101-6	.168	-4	101	30	2.2
1931	Was A	18	11	.621	44	26	13-1	2	234.1	255	117	13	1	72	85	3.88	111	.275	.328	88-3	.216	-1	99	12	1.0
1932	Was A	**26**	13	.667	50	**39**	21-3	1	**327**	319	136	17	0	77	103	3.33	130	.252	.295	122-5	.221	2*	98	37	3.8
1933	†Was A	★**24**	15	.615	**52**	35	17	4	299.1	311	140	14	3	81	110	3.97	105	.267	.316	102-8	.186	1	110	11	1.2
1934	Was A	4	10	.286	29	13	4	3	100.2	142	88	9	0	38	39	6.79	64	.326	.380	32-2	.219	1	116	-30	-3.4
	†Det A	5	1	.833	9	9	3-1	0	66.2	81	35	3	0	20	30	4.18	105	.295	.342	30-0	.133	-2	117	2	-0.1
	Year	9	11	.450	38	22	7-1	3	167.1	223	41	12	0	58	69	5.75	76	.314	.365	62-2	.177	-1	116	-27	-3.5
1935	†Det A	16	10	.615	33	32	16-2	0	241	269	127	16	4	67	59	4.26	98	.285	.335	93-5	.183	-2	118	-1	-0.5
1936	Det A	4	3	.571	9	7	1	0	44	64	42	5	0	21	10	8.39	59	.342	.409	20-1	.150	-1	135	-15	-1.8
Total	11	167	115	.592	402	292	150-16	22	2344.1	2453	1204	136	16	800	799	4.12	105	.270	.330	847-44	.194	-12	106	63	3.3
CROWELL, JIM James Everette B 5.14.1974 Minneapolis, MN BL/TL 6-4/220# d9.12																									
1997	Cin N	0	1	.000	2	1	0	0-0	6.1	12	7	2	0	5-0	3	9.95	43	.414	.500	2-0	.000	-0	108	-4	-0.5
CROWELL, CAP Minot Joy B 9.5.1892 Roxbury, MA D 9.30.1962 Central Falls, RI BR/TR 6-1/178# d6.23																									
1915	Phi A	2	6	.250	10	8	4	0	54.1	56	53	1	5	47	15	5.47	54	.292	.443	22-0	.227	-0	78	-18	-2.3
1916	Phi A	0	5	.000	9	6	1	0	39.2	43	33	0	2	34	15	4.99	57	.289	.427	12-0	.000	-2	57	-11	-1.4
Total	2	2	11	.154	19	14	5	0	94	99	86	1	7	81	30	5.27	55	.290	.436	34-0	.147	-2	69	-29	-3.7
CROWELL, BILLY William Theodore B 11.6.1865 Cincinnati, OH D 7.24.1935 Ft.Worth, TX BR/TR 5-8.5/160# d4.20																									
1887	Cle AA	14	31	.311	45	45	45-1	0	389.1	541	350	9	20	138	72	4.88	89	.327	.386	156	.141	-13	71	-17	-2.5
1888	Cle AA	5	13	.278	18	18	16	0	150.2	212	148	8	9	61	61	5.79	53	.320	.385	58	.086	-5	93	-39	-3.9

Year	Tm Lg	W	L	Pct	G	GS	CG-Sho	SV-BS	IP	H	R	HR	HB	BB-IB	SO	ERA	AERA	OAV	OOB	AB-SH	AVG	PB	Sup	APR	PW
	Lou AA	0	1	.000	1	1	1	0	9	12	14	1	1	6	5	6.00	51	.308	.413	3	.000	-0	57	-3	-0.3
	Year	5	14	.263	19	19	17	0	159.2	224	17	9	10	67	66	5.81	53	.320	.387	61	.082	-5	91	-41	-4.2
Total	2	19	45	.297	64	64	62-1	0	549	765	512	18	30	205	138	5.15	77	.325	.386	217	.124	-18	76	-59	-6.7
CROWSON, WOODY Thomas Woodrow B 9.9.1918 Fuquay Sprgs., NC D 8.14.1947 Mayodan, NC BR/TR 6-2/185# d4.17																									
1945	Phi A	0	0	—	1	0	0	0	3	2	2	0	0	3	2	6.00	57	.200	.385	1-0	.000	-0		-1	0.0
CRUDALE, MIKE Michael Christopher B 1.3.1977 San Diego, CA BR/TR 6/205# d4.10																									
2002	†StL N	3	0	1.000	49	1	0	0-1	52.2	43	11	3	1	14-2	47	1.88	211	.228	.276	2-0	.000	-0	117	13	0.6
2003	StL N	0	1	.000	13	0	0	0-1	11.1	11	5	1	1	12-1	6	2.38	171	.250	.414	0-0	—	0		1	0.1
	Mil N	0	0	—	9	0	0	0-0	9.1	1	3	0	0	6-0	7	2.89	147	.036	.206	0-0	—	0		2	0.1
	Year	0	1	.000	22	0	0	0-1	20.2	12	13	1	1	18-1	13	2.61	159	.167	.337	0-0	—	0		3	0.2
Total	2	3	1	.750	71	1	0	0-2	73.1	55	19	4	2	32-3	60	2.09	193	.211	.295	2-0	.000	-0	117	16	0.8
CRUM, CAL Calvin N. B 7.27.1890 Cooks Mills, IL D 12.7.1945 Tulsa, OK BR/TR 6-1/175# d4.17																									
1917	Bos N	0	0	—	1	0	0	0	1	1	0	0	0	1	0	0.00	—	.250	.400	0-0	—	0		0	0.0
1918	Bos N	0	1	.000	1	1	0	0	2.1	6	4	0	1	3	0	15.43	17	.600	.714	1-0	.000	-0	56	-3	-0.5
Total	2	0	1	.000	2	1	0	0	3.1	7	4	0	1	4	0	10.80	24	.500	.632	1-0	.000	-0	56	-3	-0.5
CRUMPLER, ROY Roy Maxton B 7.8.1896 Clinton, NC D 10.6.1969 Fayetteville, NC BL/TL 6-1/195# d9.16																									
1920	Det A	1	0	1.000	2	2	1	0	13	17	13	2	1	11	2	5.54	67	.315	.439	9-0	.333	1*	245	-4	-0.1
1925	Phi N	0	0	—	3	1	0	0	4.2	8	4	0	0	2	1	7.71	62	.381	.435	2-0	.000	-0	124	-1	-0.1
Total	2	1	0	1.000	5	3	1	0	17.2	25	17	2	1	13	3	6.11	65	.333	.438	11-0	.273	1	203	-5	-0.2
CRUTCHER, DICK Richard Louis B 11.25.1889 Frankfort, KY D 6.19.1952 Frankfort, KY BR/TR 5-9/148# d4.14																									
1914	Bos N	5	7	.417	33	15	5-1	0	158.2	169	73	4	6	66	48	3.46	80	.293	.371	54-1	.148	-1	100	-11	-0.8
1915	Bos N	2	2	.500	14	4	1	2	43.2	50	28	1	2	16	17	4.33	60	.309	.378	13-1	.231	1	115	-9	-0.8
Total	2	7	9	.438	47	19	6-1	2	202.1	219	101	5	8	82	65	3.65	75	.296	.373	67-2	.164	-0	103	-20	-1.6
CRUZ, JUAN Juan Carlos B 10.15.1978 Bonao, D.R. BR/TR 6-2/155# d8.21																									
2001	Chi N	3	1	.750	8	8	0	0-0	44.2	40	16	4	2	17-1	39	3.22	129	.244	.322	16-2	.125	-1*	134	6	0.4
2002	Chi N	3	11	.214	45	9	0	1-3	97.1	84	56	11	8	59-4	81	3.98	101	.241	.356	14-2	.143	-0	77	-4	-0.5
2003	†Chi N	2	7	.222	25	6	0	0-1	61	66	44	7	7	28-0	65	6.05	70	.275	.365	12-1	.250	1	89	-12	-1.4
Total	3	8	19	.296	78	23	0	1-4	203	190	116	22	17	104-5	185	4.43	93	.252	.352	42-5	.167	0	100	-10	-1.5
CRUZ, NELSON Nelson B 9.13.1972 Puerto Plata, D.R. BR/TR 6-1/160# d8.1																									
1997	Chi A	0	2	.000	19	0	0	0-0	26.1	29	19	6	0	9-1	23	6.49	68	.274	.330	0-0	—	0		-5	-0.4
1999	Det A	2	5	.286	29	6	0	0-0	66.2	74	44	11	3	23-1	46	5.67	87	.281	.341	0-0	—	0	91	-5	-0.3
2000	Det A	5	2	.714	27	0	0	0-1	41	39	14	4	3	13-3	34	3.07	157	.253	.320	1-0	.000	-0		9	1.3
2001	†Hou N	3	3	.500	66	0	0	2-2	82.1	72	41	11	9	24-4	75	4.15	110	.237	.310	6-0	.167	-0		4	0.3
2002	Hou N	2	6	.250	43	5	0	0-2	78.1	90	44	12	6	29-4	61	4.48	95	.284	.352	13-2	.000	-1	125	-3	-0.3
2003	Col N	3	5	.375	20	7	0	0-1	53.2	65	43	15	3	11-2	38	7.21	68	.301	.341	13-2	.154	-0	134	-11	-1.4
Total	6	15	23	.395	204	18	0	2-6	348.1	369	205	59	24	109-15	277	5.04	92	.271	.333	33-4	.091	-2	119	-11	-0.8
CRUZ, VICTOR Victor Manuel (b: Victor Manuel De La Cruz (Gil)) B 12.24.1957 Rancho Viejo, D.R. BR/TR 5-9/200# d6.24																									
1978	Tor A	7	3	.700	32	0	0	9-3	47.1	28	10	0	1	35-4	51	1.71	230	.179	.330	0-0	—	0		11	2.4
1979	Cle A	3	9	.250	61	0	0	10-5	78.2	70	41	10	1	44-4	63	4.23	101	.244	.341	0-0	—	0		0	-0.1
1980	Cle A	6	7	.462	55	0	0	12-8	86	71	36	10	3	27-8	88	3.45	118	.229	.289	0-0	—	0		6	0.9
1981	Pit N	1	1	.500	22	0	0	1-3	34	33	10	6	1	15-4	28	2.65	136	.264	.348	4-1	.000	-0		4	0.2
1983	Tex A	1	3	.250	17	0	0	5-2	25	16	7	2	1	10-3	18	1.44	279	.184	.270	0-0	—	0		6	1.2
Total	5	18	23	.439	187	0	0	37-21	271	218	104	28	7	131-23	248	3.09	131	.226	.317	4-1	.000	-0		27	4.6
CUBILLAN, DARWIN Darwin Harrikson (Salom) B 11.15.1972 Bobures, Venezuela BR/TR 6-2/170# d5.20																									
2000	Tor A	1	0	1.000	7	0	0	0-0	15.2	20	14	5	1	11-0	14	8.04	63	.317	.427	1-0	.000	-0		-4	-0.2
	Tex A	0	0	—	13	0	0	0-0	17.2	32	22	4	0	14-0	13	10.70	47	.400	.474	0-0	—	0		-10	-0.5
	Year	1	0	1.000	20	0	0	0-0	33.1	52	42	9	1	25-0	27	9.45	53	.364	.453	1-0	.000	-0		-15	-0.7
2001	Mon N	0	0	—	29	0	0	0-0	26.1	31	13	1	0	12-1	19	4.10	109	.295	.358	0-0	—	0		1	0.0
Total	2	1	0	1.000	49	0	0	0-0	59.2	83	49	10	1	37-1	46	7.09	68	.335	.414	1-0	.000	-0		-13	-0.7
CUCCURULLO, COOKIE Arthur Joseph B 2.8.1918 Asbury Park, NJ D 1.23.1983 W.Orange, NJ BL/TL 5-10/168# d10.3																									
1943	Pit N	0	1	.000	1	1	0	0	7	10	7	0	0	3	3	6.43	54	.357	.419	0-0	—	1	73	-3	-0.2
1944	Pit N	2	1	.667	32	4	0	4	106.1	110	65	5	3	44	31	4.06	91	.270	.346	38-0	.368	5*	152	-6	0.2
1945	Pit N	1	3	.250	29	4	0	1	56.2	68	41	2	1	34	17	5.24	75	.305	.399	14-0	.214	-0	70	-9	-0.6
Total	3	3	5	.375	62	9	0	5	170	188	113	7	4	81	51	4.55	83	.286	.367	52-0	.327	5	106	-18	-0.6
CUDWORTH, JIM James Alaric "Cuddy" B 8.22.1858 Fairhaven, MA D 12.21.1943 Middleboro, MA BR/TR 6/165# d7.27 ▲																									
1884	KC U	0	0	—	2	1	1	0	17	19	16	1		3	6	4.24	53	.264	.293	116	.147	-1*	153	-4	-0.3
CUELLAR, CHARLIE Jesus Patracis B 8.23.1917 Ybor City, FL D 10.11.1994 Tampa, FL BR/TR 5-11/183# d7.2																									
1950	Chi A	0	0	—	2	0	0	0	1.1	6	6	0	0	3	1	33.75	13	.600	.692	0-0	—	0		-5	-0.2
CUELLAR, MIKE Miguel Angel (Santana) B 5.8.1937 Santa Clara, Cuba BL/TL 5-11/175# d4.18																									
1959	Cin N	0	0	—	2	0	0	0	4	7	8	1	0	4-1	5	15.75	26	.368	.458	1-0	.000	-0		-5	-0.3
1964	StL N	5	5	.500	32	7	1	4	72	80	43	8	1	33-4	56	4.50	85	.288	.362	18-0	.000	-2	102	-5	-0.9
1965	Hou N	1	4	.200	25	4	0	2	56	55	24	3	1	21-4	46	3.54	95	.262	.330	12-1	.000	-1	52	-1	-0.1
1966	Hou N	12	10	.545	38	28	11-1	2	227.1	193	79	10	0	52-8	175	2.22	154	.229	.273	71-4	.113	-1	106	25	2.4
1967	Hou N★	16	11	.593	36	32	16-3	1	246.1	233	99	16	1	63-3	203	3.03	109	.248	.295	93-3	.140	1*	97	6	0.8
1968	Hou N	8	11	.421	28	24	11-2	1	170.2	152	60	8	1	45-7	133	2.74	108	.237	.286	57-3	.193	2	97	3	0.7
1969	†Bal A	23	11	.676	39	39	18-5	0-0	290.2	213	94	18	1	79-7	182	2.38	150	.204	**.260**	103-8	.117	-3	106	35	3.7
1970	†Bal A☆	**24**	8	**.750**	40	**40**	**21**-4	0-0	297.2	273	126	34	1	69-5	190	3.48	105	.242	.284	112-9	.089	-4*	128	7	0.1
1971	†Bal A★	20	9	.690	38	38	21-4	0-0	292.1	250	111	30	1	78-1	124	3.08	109	.234	.285	107-8	.103	-4	111	10	0.6
1972	Bal A	18	12	.600	35	35	17-4	0-0	248.1	197	78	21	0	71-4	132	2.57	120	.220	.276	87-7	.126	-1	106	14	1.7
1973	†Bal A	18	13	.581	38	38	17-2	0-0	267	265	120	29	0	84-2	140	3.27	114	.258	.313	0-0	—	0	112	9	1.0
1974	†Bal A☆	22	10	**.688**	38	38	20-5	0-0	269.1	253	106	17	2	86-4	106	3.11	111	.252	.310	0-0	—	0	112	11	1.1
1975	Bal A	14	12	.538	36	36	17-5	0-0	256	229	112	17	1	84-5	105	3.66	96	.249	.310	0-0	—	0	99	-4	-0.2
1976	Bal A	4	13	.235	26	19	2-1	1-0	107	129	63	8	2	50-5	32	4.96	66	.307	.379	0-0	—	0	85	-20	-3.0
1977	Cal A	0	1	.000	2	1	0	0-1	3.1	9	7	2	0	3-1	3	18.90	21	.500	.571	0-0	—	0	23	-5	-0.8
Total	15	185	130	.587	453	379	172-36	11-1	2808	2538	1130	222	12	822-61	1632	3.14	110	.243	.297	661-43	.115	-13	106	80	6.8
CUELLAR, BOBBY Robert B 8.20.1952 Alice, TX BR/TR 5-11/188# d9.9 C7																									
1977	Tex A	0	0	—	4	0	0	0-0	6.2	4	1	1	0	2-0	3	1.35	303	.182	.250	0-0	—	0		2	0.1
CUETO, BERT Dagoberto (Concepcion) B 8.14.1937 San Luis, Cuba BR/TR 6-4/170# d6.18																									
1961	Min A	1	3	.250	7	5	0	0	21.1	27	24	7	1	10-0	5	7.17	59	.300	.376	5-2	.000	-0	138	-8	-1.3
CULLEN, JACK John Patrick B 10.6.1939 Newark, NJ BR/TR 5-11/170# d9.9																									
1962	NY A	0	0	—	2	0	0	1	3	2	0	0	0	2-0	2	0.00	—	.182	.308	0-0	—	0		1	0.1
1965	NY A	3	4	.429	12	9	2-1	0	59	59	22	2	0	21-2	25	3.05	112	.262	.324	20-0	.150	-0	72	3	0.3
1966	NY A	1	0	1.000	5	0	0	0	11.1	11	5	0	0	5-2	7	3.97	84	.256	.327	3-0	.000	-0		-1	-0.1
Total	3	4	4	.500	19	9	2-1	1	73.1	72	27	2	0	28-4	34	3.07	111	.258	.324	23-0	.130	-1	72	3	0.3
CULLOP, NICK Norman Andrew B 9.17.1887 Chilhowie, VA D 4.15.1961 Tazewell, VA BL/TL 5-11.5/172# d5.20																									
1913	Cle A	3	6	.333	23	8	4	0	97.2	105	58	3	3	35	30	4.42	69	.294	.362	31-3	.129	-1	98	-12	-1.1
1914	Cle A	0	1	.000	1	0	0	0	3.1	4	3	0	0	1	3	2.70	107	.364	.417	1-0	.000	-0		0	-0.1
	KC F	14	19	.424	44	36	22-4	1	295.2	256	116	6	12	87	149	2.34	119	.235	.299	99-4	.141	-5	84	9	0.5
1915	KC F	22	11	.667	44	36	22-3	2	302.1	278	105	8	9	67	111	2.44	108	.249	.297	96-9	.188	-1	108	7	1.0
1916	NY A	13	6	.684	28	22	9	1	167	151	60	4	3	32	77	2.05	141	.243	.284	55-1	.109	-3	113	11	0.7

Year	Tm Lg	W	L	Pct	G	GS	CG-Sho	SV-BS	IP	H	R	HR	HB	BB-IB	SO	ERA	AERA	OAV	OOB	AB-SH	AVG	PB	Sup	APR	PW
1917	NY A	5	9	.357	30	18	5-2	1	146.1	161	70	2	2	31	27	3.32	81	.307	.348	44-2	.159	-1	88	-9	-1.0
1921	StL A	0	2	.000	4	1	0	0	11.2	18	12	1	0	6	3	8.49	53	.340	.407	3-0	.000	-1	93	-5	-0.6
Total	6	57	54	.514	174	121	62-9	5	1024	973	424	24	29	259	400	2.73	102	.258	.311	329-19	.149	-12	97	1	-0.6
CULLOTON, BUD Bernard Aloysius B 5.19.1897 Kingston, NY D 11.9.1976 Kingston, NY BR/TR 5-11/180# d4.16																									
1925	Pit N	0	1	.000	9	1	0	0	21	19	8	1	0	1	3	2.57	173	.241	.250	3-1	.000	-0	19	4	0.1
1926	Pit N	0	0	—	4	0	0	0	3.2	3	4	0	0	6	1	7.36	53	.214	.450	0-0	—	0		-1	-0.1
Total	2	0	1	.000	13	1	0	0	24.2	22	12	1	0	7	4	3.28	133	.237	.290	3-1	.000	-0	19	3	0.0
CULP, RAY Raymond Leonard B 8.6.1941 Elgin, TX BR/TR 6/200# d4.10																									
1963	Phi N★	14	11	.560	34	30	10-5	0	203.1	148	76	15	6	102-8	176	2.97	109	.206	.308	66-7	.136	-0	106	7	0.8
1964	Phi N	8	7	.533	30	19	3-1	0	135	139	77	15	5	56-4	96	4.13	84	.263	.337	44-0	.114	-1	112	-12	-1.4
1965	Phi N	14	10	.583	33	30	11-2	0	204.1	188	89	14	12	78-9	134	3.22	108	.243	.321	68-8	.088	-2	114	4	0.1
1966	Phi N	7	4	.636	34	12	1	1	110.2	106	66	19	7	53-4	100	5.04	71	.246	.337	26-5	.077	-2	100	-17	-1.8
1967	Chi N	8	11	.421	30	22	4-1	0	152.2	138	69	22	2	59-4	111	3.89	91	.239	.309	51-8	.098	-1	115	-4	-0.7
1968	Bos A	16	6	.727	35	30	11-6	0	216.1	166	79	18	9	82-8	190	2.91	108	.210	.291	70-7	.114	-1	109	6	0.4
1969	Bos A★	17	8	.680	32	32	9-2	0-0	227	195	103	25	6	79-6	172	3.81	100	.231	.299	79-6	.152	1	125	3	0.4
1970	Bos A	17	14	.548	33	33	15-1	0-0	251.1	211	104	22	11	91-8	197	3.04	130	.224	.299	97-5	.124	-3	104	22	2.1
1971	Bos A	14	16	.467	35	35	12-3	0-0	242.1	236	108	21	5	67-4	151	3.60	103	.253	.305	68-17	.118	-2	85	1	-0.1
1972	Bos A	5	8	.385	16	16	4-1	0-0	105	104	60	8	3	53-3	52	4.46	72	.260	.347	33-4	.212	1	129	-14	-1.6
1973	Bos A	2	6	.250	10	9	0	0-0	50.1	46	32	9	4	32-0	32	4.47	90	.247	.366	0-0	—	0	76	-4	-0.6
Total	11	122	101	.547	322	268	80-22	1-0	1898.1	1677	863	188	70	752-58	1411	3.58	99	.235	.313	602-67	.123	-11	107	-8	-2.4
CULP, BILL William Edward B 6.11.1887 Bellaire, OH D 9.3.1969 Arnold, PA BB/TR 6-1.5/165# d9.8																									
1910	Phi N	0	0	—	4	0	0	1	6.2	8	6	0	0	4	4	8.10	39	.333	.429	2-0	.000	-0		-3	-0.1
CULVER, GEORGE George Raymond B 7.8.1943 Salinas, CA BR/TR 6-2/185# d9.7																									
1966	Cle A	0	2	.000	5	1	0	0	9.2	15	9	1	1	7-0	6	8.38	41	.357	.460	2-0	.000	-0	103	-5	-0.9
1967	Cle A	7	3	.700	53	1	0	3	75	71	40	2	6	31-9	41	3.96	82	.258	.344	4-0	.250	0	80	-7	-0.9
1968	Cin N	11	16	.407	42	35	5-2	2	226.1	229	95	8	14	84-7	114	3.22	98	.264	.336	66-11	.121	-1*	101	-2	-0.3
1969	Cin N	5	7	.417	32	13	0	4-0	101.1	117	55	8	9	52-6	58	4.26	88	.291	.383	31-2	.097	-2	91	-5	-0.8
1970	StL N	3	3	.500	11	7	2	0-0	56.2	64	31	6	1	24-4	23	4.61	89	.284	.355	17-1	.176	0	112	-2	-0.1
	Hou N	3	3	.500	32	0	0	3-0	45	44	17	1	3	21-2	31	3.20	121	.254	.343	4-1	.250	0		4	0.5
	Year	6	6	.500	43	7	2	3-0	101.2	108	53	7	4	45-6	54	3.98	101	.271	.350	21-2	.190	0	115	2	0.4
1971	Hou N	5	8	.385	59	0	0	7-2	95.1	89	33	4	2	38-10	57	2.64	128	.257	.331	11-3	.091	-1		7	1.0
1972	Hou N	6	2	.750	45	0	0	2-1	97.1	73	33	7	5	43-3	82	3.05	110	.212	.306	19-2	.158	0		5	0.5
1973	LA N	4	4	.500	28	0	0	2-2	42	45	15	4	1	21-6	23	3.00	115	.292	.376	4-0	.000	-0		3	0.5
	Phi N	3	1	.750	14	0	0	0-1	18.2	26	10	0	0	15-6	7	4.82	79	.342	.451	0-0	—	0		-2	-0.3
	Year	7	5	.583	42	0	0	2-3	60.2	71	25	4	1	36-12	30	3.56	100	.309	.401	4-0	.000	-0		1	0.2
1974	Phi N	1	0	1.000	14	0	0	0-0	21.2	20	16	1	1	16-1	9	6.65	57	.267	.394	3-0	.000	-0		-6	-0.4
Total	9	48	49	.495	335	57	7-2	23-6	789	793	354	42	43	352-54	451	3.62	96	.266	.350	161-20	.124	-4	99	-10	-1.2
CUMBERLAND, JOHN John Sheldon B 5.10.1947 Westbrook, ME BR/TL 6/190# d9.27 C5																									
1968	NY A	0	0	—	1	0	0	0	2	3	4	1	0	1-0	1	9.00	32	.333	.400	0-0	—	0		-2	-0.1
1969	NY A	0	0	—	2	0	0	0-0	4	3	2	0	0	4-1	0	4.50	77	.231	.389	0-0	—	0		0	0.0
1970	NY A	3	4	.429	15	8	1	0-0	64	62	31	9	0	15-3	38	3.94	89	.252	.292	17-3	.059	-1	79	-3	-0.4
	SF N	2	0	1.000	7	0	0	0-0	11	6	3	0	0	4-0	6	0.82	486	.158	.233	1-0	.000	-0		3	0.5
1971	†SF N	9	6	.600	45	21	5-2	2-1	185	153	66	22	0	55-6	65	2.92	117	.223	.280	59-1	.119	-2	103	13	0.6
1972	SF N	0	4	.000	9	6	0	0-0	25	38	29	6	0	7-0	8	8.64	40	.336	.372	9-0	.111	-0	114	-15	-2.1
	StL N	1	1	.500	14	1	0	0-0	21.2	23	17	6	0	7-0	7	6.65	51	.291	.341	5-1	.000	-1	78	-7	-0.7
	Year	1	5	.167	23	7	0	0-0	46.2	61	20	12	0	14-0	15	7.71	45	.318	.359	14-1	.071	-1	110	-22	-2.8
1974	Cal A	0	1	.000	17	0	0	0-1	21.2	24	9	2	0	10-2	12	3.74	92	.289	.362	0-0	—	0		0	0.0
Total	6	15	16	.484	110	36	6-2	2-2	334.1	312	161	46	0	103-12	137	3.82	90	.246	.301	91-5	.099	-5	99	-11	-2.2
CUMMINGS, JOHN John Russell B 5.10.1969 Torrance, CA BL/TL 6-3/200# d4.10																									
1993	Sea A	0	6	.000	10	8	1	0-0	46.1	59	34	6	2	16-2	19	6.02	73	.316	.372	0-0	—	0	63	-8	-0.9
1994	Sea A	2	4	.333	17	8	0	0-0	64	66	43	7	0	37-2	33	5.63	87	.270	.363	0-0	—	0	85	-4	-0.4
1995	Sea A	0	0	—	4	0	0	0-0	5.1	8	8	0	0	7-2	4	11.81	40	.400	.517	0-0	—	0		-4	-0.2
	†LA N	3	1	.750	35	0	0	0-0	39	38	16	3	0	10-4	21	3.00	127	.250	.294	3-0	.000	-0		3	0.3
1996	LA N	0	1	.000	4	0	0	0-0	5.1	12	7	1	0	2-1	5	6.75	57	.462	.483	0-0	—	0		-3	-0.5
	Det A	3	3	.500	21	0	0	0-1	31.2	36	20	3	2	20-3	24	5.12	99	.283	.387	0-0	—	0		0	-0.1
1997	Det A	2	0	1.000	19	0	0	0-0	24.2	32	22	3	0	14-1	8	5.47	84	.311	.393	0-0	—	0		-5	-0.3
Total	5	10	15	.400	110	16	1	0-1	216.1	251	150	23	4	106-15	114	5.33	85	.292	.369	3-0	.000	-0	76	-21	-2.1
CUMMINGS, STEVE Steven Brent B 7.15.1964 Houston, TX BB/TR 6-2/200# d6.24																									
1989	Tor A	2	0	1.000	5	2	0	0-0	21	18	9	1	1	11-0	8	3.00	126	.231	.333	0-0	—	0	192	1	0.1
1990	Tor A	0	0	—	6	2	0	0-0	12.1	22	7	4	1	5-0	4	5.11	77	.431	.491	0-0	—	0	81	-1	-0.1
Total	2	2	0	1.000	11	4	0	0-0	33.1	40	16	5	2	16-0	12	3.78	102	.310	.395	0-0	—	0	136	0	0.0
CUMMINGS, CANDY William Arthur B 10.18.1848 Ware, MA D 5.16.1924 Toledo, OH BR/TR 5-9/120# d4.22 HF1939																									
1872	Mut NA	33	20	.623	**55**	**55**	**53-3**	0	**497**	604	347	2		31	45	3.01	112	.272	.282	249	.209	-3	106	23	1.1
1873	Bal NA	28	14	.667	42	42	42-1	0	382	475	292	4		33	34	2.80	116	.274	.287	192	.250	2	123	28	2.1
1874	Phi NA	28	26	.519	54	54	52-3	0	483	616	386	4		18	61	1.96	113	.276	.282	231	.225	-4	110	16	0.7
1875	Har NA	35	12	.745	48	47	46-**7**	0	416	397	184	0		4	**82**	1.60	146	.235	.236	221	.199	-5*	111	**34**	2.7
1876	Har N	16	8	.667	24	24	24-5	0	216	215	97	0		14	26	1.67	142	.239	.251	105	.162	-8	109	15	0.5
1877	Cin N	5	14	.263	19	19	16	0	155.2	219	144	2		13	11	4.34	61	.315	.327	70	.200	0	106	-29	-2.6
Total	4 NA	124	72	.633	199	198	193-14	0	1778	2092	1209	10		86	222	2.35	120	.266	.274	893	.219	-10	111	101	6.6
Total	2	21	22	.488	43	43	40-5	0	371.2	434	241	2		27	37	2.78	90	.272	.284	175	.177	-7	107	-14	-2.1
CUNNANE, WILL William Joseph B 4.24.1974 Suffern, NY BR/TR 6-2/175# d4.3																									
1997	SD N	6	3	.667	54	8	0	0-2	91.1	114	69	11	5	49-3	79	5.81	67	.305	.392	14-1	.357	3*	160	-23	-1.7
1998	SD N	0	0	—	3	0	0	0-0	3	4	2	1	0	1-1	1	6.00	65	.308	.357	0-0	—	0		-1	0.0
1999	SD N	2	1	.667	24	0	0	0-0	31	34	19	8	0	12-3	22	5.23	80	.293	.359	3-0	.000	-0		-3	-0.3
2000	SD N	1	1	.500	27	3	0	0-0	38.1	35	21	2	1	21-0	34	4.23	102	.241	.339	7-0	.143	0	142	0	0.0
2001	Mil N	0	3	.000	31	1	0	0-0	51.2	66	34	6	2	22-6	37	5.40	80	.320	.390	7-0	.000	-1*	64	-7	-0.4
2002	Chi N	1	1	.500	16	0	0	0-1	26.1	27	16	5	1	13-1	30	5.47	74	.270	.360	4-0	.250	0		-4	-0.2
2003	†Atl N	2	2	.500	20	0	0	3-0	20	14	6	2	0	6-2	20	2.70	157	.189	.250	0-0	—	0		4	0.7
Total	7	12	11	.522	175	12	0	3-3	261.2	294	167	35	9	124-16	223	5.16	80	.286	.367	35-1	.200	3	144	-34	-1.9
CUNNINGHAM, BRUCE Bruce Lee B 9.29.1905 San Francisco, CA D 3.8.1984 Hayward, CA BR/TR 5-10.5/165# d5.7																									
1929	Bos N	4	6	.400	17	8	4	1	91.2	100	52	7	2	32	22	4.52	104	.282	.344	27-2	.148	-0*	58	2	0.2
1930	Bos N	5	6	.455	36	6	2	0	106.2	121	73	7	0	41	28	5.48	90	.289	.352	31-0	.194	0*	53	-7	-0.4
1931	Bos N	3	12	.200	33	16	6-1	1	136.2	157	74	7	2	54	32	4.48	85	.296	.363	42-0	.071	-4*	74	-9	-1.1
1932	Bos N	1	0	1.000	18	3	0	0	47	50	21	1	4	19	21	3.45	109	.281	.363	9-0	.222	2	157	2	0.3
Total	4	13	24	.351	104	33	12-1	2	382	428	220	22	8	146	103	4.64	93	.289	.356	109-2	.138	-2	70	-12	-1.0
CUNNINGHAM, BERT Ellsworth Elmer B 11.25.1865 Wilmington, DE D 5.14.1952 Cragmere, DE BR/TR 5-6/187# d9.15 U1																									
1887	Bro AA	0	2	.000	3	3	3	0	23	26	22	0	4	13	8	5.09	85	.263	.371	8	.000	-1	44	-3	-0.2
1888	Bal AA	22	29	.431	51	51	50	0	453.1	412	275	8	30	157	186	3.39	88	.233	.307	177	.186	-2	88	-25	-2.5
1889	Bal AA	16	19	.457	39	33	29	1	279.1	306	245	11	15	141	140	4.87	81	.270	.358	131	.206	-3*	96	-25	-2.6
1890	Phi P	3	9	.250	14	11	11	0	108.2	133	103	0	7	67	33	5.22	82	.289	.387	52	.115	-4*	82	-11	-1.1
	Buf P	9	15	.375	25	25	24-2	0	211	251	190	8	6	134	78	5.84	70	.283	.381	101	.228	1*	79	-35	-2.6
	Year	12	24	.333	39	36	35-2	0	319.2	384	195	8	13	201	111	5.63	74	.285	.383	153	.190	-4	80	-42	-3.7
1891	Bal AA	11	14	.440	30	25	21	0	237.2	241	181	8	11	138	59	4.01	93	.254	.356	100	.150	-2*	115	-7	-0.7

Year	Tm Lg	W	L	Pct	G	GS	CG-Sho	SV-BS	IP	H	R	HR	HB	BB-IB	SO	ERA	AERA	OAV	OOB	AB-SH	AVG	PB	Sup	APR	PW
1895	Lou N	11	16	.407	31	28	24-1	0	231	299	185	6	5	104	49	4.75	97	.309	.378	100-0	.300	6*	79	-5	0.2
1896	Lou N	7	14	.333	27	20	17	1	189.1	242	168	6	17	74	37	5.09	85	.308	.380	88-1	.250	3*	89	-18	-1.2
1897	Lou N	14	13	.519	30	28	26	0	242.2	294	152	3	14	72	49	4.15	103	.297	.353	97-5	.227	-1*	83	9	0.8
1898	Lou N	28	15	.651	44	42	41	0	362	387	174	8	20	65	34	3.16	114	.272	.313	140-0	.229	2	109	15	1.6
1899	Lou N	17	17	.500	39	37	33-1	0	323.2	385	188	4	15	75	36	3.84	100	.295	.340	154-4	.260	3*	108	7	1.1
1900	Chi N	4	3	.571	8	7	7	0	64	84	53	0	4	21	7	4.36	83	.316	.375	27-0	.148	-1	131	-6	-0.7
1901	Chi N	0	1	.000	1	1	1	0	9	11	6	0	0	3	2	5.00	65	.297	.350	1-2	.000	0	88	-1	-0.1
Total	12	142	167	.460	342	311	287-4	2	2734.2	3071	1942	62	148	1064	718	4.22	91	.277	.349	1176-12	.216	1	94	-105	-8.0

CUNNINGHAM, GEORGE George Harold B 7.13.1894 Sturgeon Lake, MN D 3.10.1972 Chattanooga, TN BR/TR 5-11/185# d4.14

Year	Tm Lg	W	L	Pct	G	GS	CG-Sho	SV-BS	IP	H	R	HR	HB	BB-IB	SO	ERA	AERA	OAV	OOB	AB-SH	AVG	PB	Sup	APR	PW
1916	Det A	7	10	.412	35	14	5	2	150.1	146	71	0	3	74	68	2.75	104	.269	.360	41-1	.268	5	126	-3	0.3
1917	Det A	2	7	.222	44	8	4	4	139	113	72	2	4	51	49	2.91	91	.227	.304	34-2	.176	1	150	-7	-0.4
1918	Det A	6	7	.462	27	14	10	1	140	131	68	0	5	38	39	3.15	84	.255	.312	112-4	.223	3*	97	-10	-0.5
1919	Det A	1	1	.500	17	0	0	1	47.2	54	36	0	5	15	11	4.91	65	.292	.361	23-0	.217	2*		-11	-0.3
Total	4	16	25	.390	123	36	19	8	477	444	247	2	17	178	167	3.13	89	.255	.330	210-7	.224	11	119	-31	-0.9

CUNNINGHAM, MIKE Mody B 6.14.1882 Lancaster, SC D 12.10.1969 Lancaster, SC BR/TR 5-10.5/175# d8.31

Year	Tm Lg	W	L	Pct	G	GS	CG-Sho	SV-BS	IP	H	R	HR	HB	BB-IB	SO	ERA	AERA	OAV	OOB	AB-SH	AVG	PB	Sup	APR	PW
1906	Phi A	1	0	1.000	5	1	1	0	28	29	15	1	1	9	15	3.21	85	.271	.333	12-0	.333	1*	132	-2	0.0

CUPPY, NIG George Joseph (b: George Koppe) B 7.3.1869 Logansport, IN D 7.27.1922 Elkhart, IN BR/TR 5-7/160# d4.16

Year	Tm Lg	W	L	Pct	G	GS	CG-Sho	SV-BS	IP	H	R	HR	HB	BB-IB	SO	ERA	AERA	OAV	OOB	AB-SH	AVG	PB	Sup	APR	PW
1892	†Cle N	28	13	.683	47	42	38-1	1	376	333	175	9	10	121	103	2.51	135	.228	.292	168	.214	0*	113	37	3.7
1893	Cle N	17	10	.630	31	30	24	0	243.2	316	200	6	10	75	39	4.47	109	.305	.357	109	.248	1*	106	8	0.6
1894	Cle N	24	15	.615	43	33	29-**3**	0	316	381	246	11	10	128	65	4.56	120	.295	.363	135-1	.259	1*	91	26	2.4
1895	†Cle N	26	14	.650	47	40	36-1	2	353	384	210	9	8	95	91	3.54	141	.273	.323	140-4	.286	7	101	51	5.2
1896	†Cle N	25	14	.641	46	40	35-1	1	358	388	173	8	7	75	86	3.12	146	.274	.314	141-4	.270	6*	90	55	5.5
1897	Cle N	10	6	.625	19	17	13-1	0	138	150	69	3	5	26	23	3.20	140	.275	.314	55-1	.145	-4*	77	19	1.3
1898	Cle N	9	8	.529	18	15	13-1	0	128	147	62	4	6	25	27	3.30	110	.286	.327	48-2	.104	-4	76	6	0.2
1899	StL N	11	8	.579	21	21	18-1	0	171.2	203	89	3	5	26	25	3.15	127	.294	.324	70-2	.186	-3	104	15	1.2
1900	Bos N	8	4	.667	17	13	9	1	105.1	107	64	8	6	24	23	3.08	134	.263	.314	42-0	.262	1	117	7	0.8
1901	Bos A	4	6	.400	13	11	9	0	93.1	111	58	1	2	14	22	4.15	85	.292	.321	49-1	.204	0*	106	-5	-0.5
Total	10	162	98	.623	302	262	224-9	5	2283	2520	1346	62	69	609	504	3.48	127	.275	.325	957-15	.233	6	98	219	20.4

CURRAN, SAMMY Simon Francis B 10.30.1874 Dorchester, MA D 5.19.1936 Dorchester, MA TL d8.1

Year	Tm Lg	W	L	Pct	G	GS	CG-Sho	SV-BS	IP	H	R	HR	HB	BB-IB	SO	ERA	AERA	OAV	OOB	AB-SH	AVG	PB	Sup	APR	PW
1902	Bos N	0	0	—	1	0	0	0	6.2	6	1	0	0	0	3	1.35	209	.240	.240	2-0	.000	-0		1	0.0

CURRENCE, LAFAYETTE Delancy Lafayette B 12.3.1951 Rock Hill, SC BB/TL 5-11/175# d7.24

Year	Tm Lg	W	L	Pct	G	GS	CG-Sho	SV-BS	IP	H	R	HR	HB	BB-IB	SO	ERA	AERA	OAV	OOB	AB-SH	AVG	PB	Sup	APR	PW
1975	Mil A	0	2	.000	8	1	0	0-0	18.2	25	17	5	0	14-1	7	7.71	50	.316	.415	0-0	—	0	115	-7	-0.7

CURRIE, MURPHY Archibald Murphy B 8.31.1893 Fayetteville, NC D 6.22.1939 Asheboro, NC BR/TR 5-11.5/185# d8.31

Year	Tm Lg	W	L	Pct	G	GS	CG-Sho	SV-BS	IP	H	R	HR	HB	BB-IB	SO	ERA	AERA	OAV	OOB	AB-SH	AVG	PB	Sup	APR	PW
1916	StL N	0	0	—	6	0	0	0	14.1	7	4	1	0	9	8	1.88	140	.149	.286	3-0	.000	-0		1	0.0

CURRIE, CLARENCE Clarence Franklin B 12.30.1878 Glencoe, ON, CAN D 7.15.1941 Little Chute, WI BR/TR d4.25

Year	Tm Lg	W	L	Pct	G	GS	CG-Sho	SV-BS	IP	H	R	HR	HB	BB-IB	SO	ERA	AERA	OAV	OOB	AB-SH	AVG	PB	Sup	APR	PW
1902	Cin N	3	4	.429	10	7	6-1	0	65.1	70	37	1	2	17	20	3.72	81	.273	.324	24-1	.083	-2	68	-4	-0.5
	StL N	7	5	.583	15	12	10-2	0	124.2	125	54	0	6	35	30	2.60	106	.261	.319	46-1	.196	-0*	81	2	0.3
	Year	10	9	.526	25	19	16-3	0	190	195	57	1	8	52	50	2.98	95	.265	.321	70-2	.157	-2	76	-5	-0.2
1903	StL N	4	12	.250	22	16	13-1	1	148	155	93	7	10	60	52	4.01	81	.281	.362	47-2	.085	-3	63	-8	-0.9
	Chi N	1	2	.333	6	3	2	1	33.1	35	25	1	3	9	9	2.97	106	.254	.313	12-0	.417	2	79	-2	0.0
	Year	5	14	.263	28	19	15-1	2	181.1	190	29	8	13	69	61	3.82	85	.275	.352	59-2	.153	-1	66	-16	-0.9
Total	2	15	23	.395	53	38	31-4	2	371.1	385	209	9	21	121	111	3.39	89	.270	.336	129-4	.155	-4	70	-12	-1.1

CURRIE, BILL William Cleveland B 11.29.1928 Leary, GA BR/TR 6/175# d4.13

Year	Tm Lg	W	L	Pct	G	GS	CG-Sho	SV-BS	IP	H	R	HR	HB	BB-IB	SO	ERA	AERA	OAV	OOB	AB-SH	AVG	PB	Sup	APR	PW
1955	Was A	0	0	—	3	0	0	0	4.1	7	7	3	1	2-0	2	12.46	31	.350	.435	0-0	—	0		-4	-0.2

CURRY, GEORGE George James "Soldier Boy" B 12.21.1888 Bridgeport, CT D 10.5.1963 West Haven, CT BR/TR 6/185# d7.16

Year	Tm Lg	W	L	Pct	G	GS	CG-Sho	SV-BS	IP	H	R	HR	HB	BB-IB	SO	ERA	AERA	OAV	OOB	AB-SH	AVG	PB	Sup	APR	PW
1911	StL A	0	3	.000	3	3	0	0	15.2	19	15	0	0	24	2	7.47	45	.339	.538	5-0	.000	-1	78	-6	-0.9

CURRY, STEVE Stephen Thomas B 9.13.1965 Winter Park, FL BR/TR 6-6/217# d7.10

Year	Tm Lg	W	L	Pct	G	GS	CG-Sho	SV-BS	IP	H	R	HR	HB	BB-IB	SO	ERA	AERA	OAV	OOB	AB-SH	AVG	PB	Sup	APR	PW
1988	Bos A	0	1	.000	3	3	0	0-0	11	15	10	0	0	14-2	4	8.18	50	.357	.500	0-0	—	0	133	-4	-0.3

CURRY, WES Wesley B 4.1.1860 Wilmington, DE D 5.19.1933 Philadelphia, PA d8.6 U6

Year	Tm Lg	W	L	Pct	G	GS	CG-Sho	SV-BS	IP	H	R	HR	HB	BB-IB	SO	ERA	AERA	OAV	OOB	AB-SH	AVG	PB	Sup	APR	PW
1884	Ric AA	0	2	.000	2	2	2	0	16	15	14	2	1	3	1	5.06	66	.221	.264	8	.250	-0	55	-3	-0.3

CURTIS, CLIFF Clifton Garfield B 7.3.1881 Delaware, OH D 4.23.1943 Utica, OH BR/TR 6-2/180# d8.23

Year	Tm Lg	W	L	Pct	G	GS	CG-Sho	SV-BS	IP	H	R	HR	HB	BB-IB	SO	ERA	AERA	OAV	OOB	AB-SH	AVG	PB	Sup	APR	PW
1909	Bos N	4	5	.444	10	9	8-2	0	83	53	17	1	2	30	22	1.41	200	.191	.275	29-0	.034	-3	47	12	1.2
1910	Bos N	6	24	.200	43	37	12-2	2	251	251	154	9	12	124	75	3.55	94	.277	.371	82-2	.146	-4	68	-11	-1.3
1911	Bos N	1	8	.111	12	9	5	1	77	79	50	4	2	34	23	4.44	86	.265	.344	28-1	.250	-0	72	-5	-0.5
	Chi N	1	2	.333	4	1	0	0	7	7	4	0	3	5	4	3.86	86	.241	.405	2-0	.500	0	0	0	-0.1
	Phi N	2	1	.667	8	5	3-1	0	45	45	19	0	1	15	13	2.60	132	.260	.323	15-1	.267	0	87	3	0.2
	Year	4	11	.267	24	15	8-1	1	129	131	23	4	6	54	40	3.77	97	.262	.341	45-2	.267	0	72	-3	-0.4
1912	Phi N	2	5	.286	10	8	2	0	50	55	30	3	4	17	20	3.24	112	.286	.357	15-0	.000	-2	78	0	-0.1
	Bro N	4	7	.364	19	9	3	1	80	72	44	4	6	37	22	3.94	85	.250	.347	26-2	.308	1	102	-4	-0.4
	Year	6	12	.333	29	17	5	1	130	127	49	7	10	54	42	3.67	94	.265	.351	41-2	.195	-1	91	-5	-0.5
1913	Bro N	8	9	.471	30	16	6	2	151.2	145	75	1	7	55	57	3.26	101	.255	.328	49-5	.122	-3	93	-1	-0.4
Total	5	28	61	.315	136	94	39-5	6	744.2	707	393	22	37	317	236	3.31	101	.259	.344	246-11	.159	-10	76	-6	-1.4

CURTIS, JACK Jack Patrick B 1.11.1937 Rhodhiss, NC BL/TL 5-10/175# d4.22

Year	Tm Lg	W	L	Pct	G	GS	CG-Sho	SV-BS	IP	H	R	HR	HB	BB-IB	SO	ERA	AERA	OAV	OOB	AB-SH	AVG	PB	Sup	APR	PW
1961	Chi N	10	13	.435	31	27	6	0	180.1	220	117	23	1	51-6	57	4.89	85	.303	.346	60-2	.167	3	90	-15	-1.3
1962	Chi N	0	2	.000	4	3	0	0	18	18	8	2	0	6-1	8	3.50	118	.277	.333	4-0	.250	0	42	1	0.1
	Mil N	4	4	.500	30	5	0	1	75.2	82	39	8	2	27-3	40	4.16	91	.282	.345	18-0	.222	2	120	-3	-0.1
	Year	4	6	.400	34	8	0	1	93.2	100	44	10	2	33-4	48	4.04	96	.281	.343	22-0	.227	2	91	-2	0.0
1963	Cle A	0	0	—	4	0	0	0	5	8	10	0	1	5-1	3	18.00	20	.348	.483	0-0	—	0		-7	-0.4
Total	3	14	19	.424	69	35	6	1	279	328	174	33	4	89-11	108	4.84	84	.297	.349	82-2	.183	5	91	-24	-1.7

CURTIS, JOHN John Duffield B 3.9.1948 Newton, MA BL/TL 6-2/185# d8.13

Year	Tm Lg	W	L	Pct	G	GS	CG-Sho	SV-BS	IP	H	R	HR	HB	BB-IB	SO	ERA	AERA	OAV	OOB	AB-SH	AVG	PB	Sup	APR	PW
1970	Bos A	0	0	—	1	0	0	0-0	2.1	4	4	1	0	1-0	1	11.57	34	.333	.385	0-0	—	0		-2	-0.1
1971	Bos A	2	2	.500	5	3	1	0-1	26	30	9	3	0	6-1	19	3.12	119	.291	.330	9-0	.111	-0	65	2	0.2
1972	Bos A	11	8	.579	26	21	8-3	0-0	154.1	161	69	8	0	50-6	106	3.73	86	.271	.327	53-3	.094	-2*	101	-6	-1.1
1973	Bos A	13	13	.500	35	30	10-4	0-0	221.1	225	103	24	2	83-10	101	3.58	112	.264	.330	0-0	—	0	91	8	0.9
1974	StL N	10	14	.417	33	29	5-2	1-0	195	199	91	15	2	83-6	89	3.78	95	.267	.340	63-6	.159	-0*	104	-4	-0.5
1975	StL N	8	9	.471	39	18	4	1-0	146.2	151	70	13	2	65-6	67	3.44	110	.268	.342	38-5	.211	2	91	4	0.7
1976	StL N	6	11	.353	37	15	3-1	1-0	134	139	68	11	0	65-10	52	4.50	79	.276	.357	35-5	.200	2*	75	-10	-1.1
1977	SF N	3	3	.500	43	9	1-1	1-2	77	95	48	5	1	48-9	47	5.49	71	.314	.406	13-3	.231	1*	121	-11	-0.6
1978	SF N	4	3	.571	46	0	0	1-2	63	60	31	1	0	29-8	38	3.71	93	.262	.336	2-1	.000	-0		-3	-0.3
1979	SF N	10	9	.526	27	18	3-2	0-0	120.2	121	62	15	0	42-7	85	4.18	84	.257	.316	34-6	.147	1*	89	-9	-1.3
1980	SD N	10	8	.556	30	27	6	0-0	187	184	84	9	2	67-13	71	3.51	98	.262	.328	62-5	.194	1*	97	-3	-0.1
1981	SD N	2	6	.250	28	8	0	0-1	66.2	70	41	11	1	30-2	31	5.13	64	.275	.349	13-1	.077	-1	126	-15	-1.7
1982	SD N	8	6	.571	26	18	1-1	0-0	116.1	121	62	15	1	46-0	54	4.10	84	.271	.340	37-4	.297	3	123	-10	-0.8
	Cal A	0	1	.000	8	0	0	1-1	12	16	8	0	0	3-2	10	6.00	68	.320	.358	0-0	—	0		-2	-0.2
1983	Cal A	1	2	.333	37	3	0	5-3	90	89	44	5	2	40-11	36	3.80	106	.258	.334	0-0	—	0	75	1	0.0
1984	Cal A	1	2	.333	17	0	0	0-0	28.2	30	16	4	0	11-1	18	4.40	90	.263	.325	0-0	—	0		-2	-0.2
Total	15	89	97	.478	438	199	42-14	11-10	1641	1695	810	140	13	669-92	825	3.96	92	.270	.339	359-39	.175	5	97	-62	-6.2

CURTIS, VERN Vernon Eugene "Turk" B 5.24.1920 Cairo, IL D 6.24.1992 Cairo, IL BR/TR 6/170# d9.6 Mil 1944-45

Year	Tm Lg	W	L	Pct	G	GS	CG-Sho	SV-BS	IP	H	R	HR	HB	BB-IB	SO	ERA	AERA	OAV	OOB	AB-SH	AVG	PB	Sup	APR	PW
1943	Was A	0	0	—	2	0	0	0	4	3	3	0	0	6	1	6.75	47	.200	.429	0-0	—	0		-1	-0.1
1944	Was A	0	1	.000	3	1	0	0	9.2	8	3	0	0	3	2	2.79	117	.235	.297	2-0	.000	-0	0	1	0.0
1946	Was A	0	0	—	11	0	0	0	16.1	19	13	1	0	10	7	7.16	47	.297	.392	2-0	.000	-0		-6	-0.3

Year	Tm Lg	W	L	Pct	G	GS	CG-Sho	SV-BS	IP	H	R	HR	HB	BB-IB	SO	ERA	AERA	OAV	OOB	AB-SH	AVG	PB	Sup	APR	PW
Total	3	0	1	.000	16	1	0	0	30	30	19	1	0	19	10	5.70	58	.265	.371	4-0	.000	-1	0	-6	-0.4
CUSHMAN, ED Edgar Leander B 3.27.1852 Eagleville, OH D 9.26.1915 Erie, PA BR/TL 6/177# d7.6																									
1883	Buf N	3	3	.500	7	7	5	0	50.1	61	41	0		17	34	3.93	81	.285	.338	23	.217	-0	130	-4	-0.4
1884	Mil U	4	0	1.000	4	4	4-2	0	36	10	4	0		3	47	1.00	132	.082	.104	11	.091	-2	145	3	0.2
1885	Phi AA	3	7	.300	10	10	10	0	87	101	77	1	3	17	37	3.52	98	.269	.306	37	.189	-1	127	-4	-0.5
	NY AA	8	14	.364	22	22	22	0	191	158	105	2	3	33	133	2.78	112	.210	.246	69	.145	-1	72	4	0.2
	Year	11	21	.344	32	32	32	0	278	259	109	3	6	50	170	3.01	107	.229	.266	106	.160	-2	91	-3	-0.3
1886	NY AA	17	21	.447	38	38	37-2	0	325.2	278	180	6	1	99	167	3.12	105	.220	.277	126	.151	-6	82	7	0.1
1887	NY AA	10	15	.400	26	26	25	0	220	310	232	9	9	83	64	5.97	71	.325	.384	93	.247	3	97	-43	-3.1
1890	Tol AA	17	21	.447	40	38	34	1	315.2	346	208	5	10	107	125	4.19	94	.270	.331	130	.100	-9	101	-4	-1.5
Total	6	62	81	.434	147	145	137-4	1	1225.2	1264	847	23	26	359	607	3.86	92	.254	.308	489	.160	-16	96	-41	-5.0
CUSHMAN, HARVEY Harvey Barnes B 7.10.1877 Rockland, ME D 12.27.1920 Emsworth, PA d8.24																									
1902	Pit N	0	4	.000	4	4	3	0	25.2	30	31	0	2	31	12	7.36	37	.291	.463	10-0	.200	-0	50	-14	-1.7
CVENGROS, MIKE Michael John B 12.1.1901 Pana, IL D 8.2.1970 Hot Springs, AR BL/TL 5-8/159# d9.30																									
1922	NY N	0	1	.000	1	1	1	0	9	6	5	1	1	3	3	4.00	100	.194	.286	3-0	.000	-0	20	0	0.0
1923	Chi A	12	13	.480	40	26	14	3	214.1	216	110	6	13	107	86	4.41	90	.269	.364	74-4	.203	-1*	98	-5	-0.6
1924	Chi A	3	12	.200	26	15	2	0	105.2	119	80	5	3	67	36	5.88	70	.300	.405	30-1	.200	2	93	-20	-2.2
1925	Chi A	3	9	.250	22	11	4	0	104.2	109	56	7	3	55	32	4.30	97	.278	.371	33-3	.152	-1	105	-1	-0.2
1927	†Pit N	2	1	.667	23	4	0	1	53.2	55	25	3	1	24	21	3.35	123	.271	.351	19-1	.158	-0	114	4	0.2
1929	Chi N	5	4	.556	32	4	0	2	64	82	39	2	1	29	23	4.64	99	.319	.390	15-0	.400	2*	109	0	0.2
Total	6	25	40	.385	144	61	21	6	551.1	587	315	24	22	285	201	4.59	90	.282	.374	174-9	.201	1	98	-22	-2.6
CYR, ERIC Eric B 2.11.1979 Montreal, PQ, CAN BR/TL 6-4/200# d6.23																									
2002	SD N	0	1	.000	5	0	0	0-0	6	6	7	0	0	6-1	4	10.50	36	.286	.429	1-0	.000	-0		-5	-0.7
CZAJKOWSKI, JIM James Mark B 12.18.1963 Parma, OH BB/TR 6-4/215# d7.29																									
1994	Col N	0	0	—	5	0	0	0-0	8.2	9	4	2	3	6-1	2	4.15	120	.281	.439	0-0	—	0		1	0.1
DAAL, OMAR Omar Jesus (Cordero) B 3.1.1972 Maracaibo, Venezuela BL/TL 6-3/175# d4.24																									
1993	LA N	2	3	.400	47	0	0	0-1	35.1	36	20	5	0	21-3	19	5.09	75	.277	.373	0-0	—	0		-4	-0.4
1994	LA N	0	0	—	24	0	0	0-0	13.2	12	5	1	0	5-0	9	3.29	119	.245	.315	0-0	—	0		1	0.1
1995	LA N	4	0	1.000	28	0	0	0-1	20	29	16	1	1	15-4	11	7.20	53	.354	.455	0-0	—	0		-7	-1.3
1996	Mon N	4	5	.444	64	6	0	0-4	87.1	74	40	10	1	37-3	82	4.02	108	.228	.308	11-0	.000	-1	87	4	0.3
1997	Mon N	1	2	.333	33	0	0	1-2	30.1	48	35	4	2	15-3	16	9.79	43	.378	.448	5-0	.200	0		-18	-1.6
	Tor A	1	1	.500	9	3	0	0-0	27	34	13	3	0	6-0	28	4.00	115	.304	.339	0-0	—	0	80	2	0.1
1998	Ari N	8	12	.400	33	23	3-1	0-0	162.2	146	60	12	3	51-3	132	2.88	146	.245	.305	46-5	.109	-1	69	23	2.7
1999	†Ari N	16	9	.640	32	32	2-1	0-0	214.2	188	92	21	7	79-3	148	3.65	125	.236	.308	69-6	.232	3	107	24	2.8
2000	Ari N	2	10	.167	20	16	0	0-0	96	127	88	17	7	42-11	45	7.22	65	.315	.385	27-3	.259	2	90	-29	-2.6
	Phi N	2	9	.182	12	12	0	0-0	71	81	40	9	2	30-0	51	4.69	99	.290	.362	18-2	.278	2	72	0	0.3
	Year	4	19	.174	32	28	0	0-0	167	208	44	26	9	72-11	96	6.14	76	.305	.376	45-5	.267	5	83	-30	-2.3
2001	Phi N	13	7	.650	32	32	0	0-0	185.2	199	100	26	5	56-3	107	4.46	95	.273	.327	55-7	.236	2	113	-5	-0.2
2002	LA N	11	9	.550	39	23	0	0-0	161.1	142	73	20	4	54-3	105	3.90	98	.239	.304	39-8	.154	1	97	0	0.2
2003	Bal A	4	11	.267	19	17	0	0-0	93.2	134	69	11	2	30-1	53	6.34	69	.343	.390	0-0	—	0	87	-20	-2.5
Total	11	68	78	.466	392	164	5-2	1-8	1198.2	1250	651	140	34	441-37	806	4.55	95	.271	.337	270-31	.196	10	95	-29	-2.1
D'ACQUISTO, JOHN John Francis B 12.24.1951 San Diego, CA BR/TR 6-2/205# d9.2																									
1973	SF N	1	1	.500	7	3	1	0-0	27.2	23	14	4	0	19-0	29	3.58	107	.219	.336	9-0	.000	-1	146	0	-0.1
1974	SF N	12	14	.462	38	36	5-1	0-0	215	182	101	13	6	124-7	167	3.77	101	.227	.334	71-2	.113	-1*	81	3	0.1
1975	SF N	2	4	.333	10	6	0	0-0	28	29	35	5	2	34-0	22	10.29	37	.264	.445	7-0	.000	-0	115	-19	-3.2
1976	SF N	3	8	.273	28	19	0	0-0	106	93	69	5	3	102-1	53	5.35	68	.243	.401	26-4	.269	2	94	-17	-1.5
1977	StL N	0	0	—	3	2	0	0-0	8.1	5	4	0	1	10-0	9	4.32	89	.185	.410	2-0	.000	-0	139	0	0.0
	SD N	1	2	.333	17	12	0	0-0	44	49	41	3	1	47-0	45	6.95	51	.297	.451	6-2	.000	-0	117	-19	-1.2
	Year	1	2	.333	20	14	0	0-0	52.1	54	46	3	2	57-0	54	6.54	55	.281	.445	8-2	.000	-1	120	-20	-1.2
1978	SD N	4	3	.571	45	3	0	10-0	93	60	24	2	1	56-2	104	2.13	156	.185	.305	21-0	.190	1	54	14	1.4
1979	SD N	9	13	.409	51	11	1-1	2-4	133.2	140	83	15	3	86-6	97	4.92	72	.275	.380	31-3	.129	1	96	-22	-3.3
1980	SD N	2	3	.400	39	0	0	1-1	67	67	29	2	1	36-9	44	3.76	91	.270	.359	8-2	.000	-1		-2	-0.2
	Mon N	0	2	.000	11	0	0	2-1	20.2	14	7	0	0	9-0	15	2.18	164	.206	.295	0-0	—	0		3	0.3
	Year	2	5	.286	50	0	0	3-2	87.2	81	40	2	1	45-9	59	3.39	102	.256	.345	8-2	.000	-1		1	0.1
1981	Cal A	0	0	—	6	0	0	0-0	19.1	26	24	2	1	12-0	8	10.71	34	.338	.415	0-0	—	0		-14	-0.7
1982	Oak A	0	1	.000	11	0	0	0-0	17	20	11	1	0	9-0	7	5.29	74	.290	.372	0-0	—	0		-3	-0.1
Total	10	34	51	.400	266	92	7-2	15-6	779.2	708	442	52	19	544-25	600	4.56	80	.245	.365	181-13	.127	0	97	-76	-8.5
DAGENHARD, JOHN John Douglas B 4.25.1917 Magnolia, OH D 7.16.2001 Bolivar, OH BR/TR 6-2/195# d9.28																									
1943	Bos N	1	0	1.000	2	1	1	0	11	9	2	0	2	4	2	0.00	—	.225	.326	3-1	.000	-0	124	3	0.3
DAGLIA, PETE Peter George B 2.28.1907 Napa, CA D 3.11.1952 Willits, CA BR/TR 6-3/210# d6.8																									
1932	Chi A	2	4	.333	12	5	2	0	50	67	35	4	4	20	16	5.76	75	.324	.394	13-2	.077	-1	83	-6	-0.7
DAHL, JAY Jay Steven B 12.6.1945 San Bernardino, CA D 6.20.1965 Salisbury, NC BB/TL 5-10/183# d9.27																									
1963	Hou N	0	1	.000	1	1	0	0	2.2	7	7	0	0	0-0	0	16.88	19	.438	.438	0-0	—	0	82	-5	-0.7
DAHLKE, JERRY Jerome Alexander "Joe" B 6.8.1930 Marathon, WI BR/TR 6/180# d5.6																									
1956	Chi A	0	0	—	5	0	0	0	2.1	5	5	0	0	6-0	1	19.29	21	.455	.647	0-0	—	0		-4	-0.2
DAILEY, SAM Samuel Laurence B 3.31.1904 Oakford, IL D 12.2.1979 Columbia, MO BL/TR 5-11/168# d7.4																									
1929	Phi N	2	2	.500	20	4	0	0	51.1	74	48	5	1	23	18	7.54	69	.349	.415	17-0	.059	-2	80	-12	-1.0
DAILEY, BILL William Garland B 5.13.1935 Arlington, VA BR/TR 6-3/185# d8.17																									
1961	Cle A	1	0	1.000	12	0	0	0	19	16	4	0	0	6-1	7	0.95	415	.232	.289	2-0	.000	-0		6	0.3
1962	Cle A	2	2	.500	27	0	0	1	42.2	43	18	0	2	17-4	24	3.59	108	.270	.341	3-0	.000	-0		2	0.1
1963	Min A	6	3	.667	66	0	0	21	108.2	80	26	9	0	19-5	72	1.99	183	.208	.244	21-1	.238	2		21	2.9
1964	Min A	1	2	.333	14	0	0	0	15.1	23	16	3	4	17-2	6	8.22	44	.377	.537	0-0	—	0		-8	-1.4
Total	4	10	7	.588	119	0	0	22	185.2	162	64	12	6	59-12	109	2.76	135	.241	.304	26-1	.192	1		21	1.9
DAILY, ED Edward M. B 9.7.1862 Providence, RI D 10.21.1891 Washington, DC BR/TR 5-10.5/174# d5.4 b-Con ▲																									
1885	Phi N	26	23	.531	50	50	49-4	0	440	370	212	12		90	140	2.21	126	.217	.256	184	.207	-0	82	29	2.6
1886	Phi N	16	9	.640	27	23	22-1	0	218	211	123	7		59	95	3.06	108	.242	.290	309	.227	3*	104	7	0.9
1887	Phi N	0	4	.000	6	5	4	0	41.1	52	52	2	0	25	7	7.19	59	.289	.376	106	.283	1*	101	-13	-0.8
	Was N	0	1	.000	1	1	1	0	7	5	6	0	0	6	3	7.71	52	.208	.367	311	.251	0*	48	-2	-0.2
	Year	0	5	.000	7	6	5	0	48.1	57	9	2	0	31	10	7.26	58	.279	.374	417	.259	1	92	-14	-1.0
1888	Was N	2	7	.222	9	8	8	0	73.2	88	69	7	3	19	20	4.89	57	.278	.325	453	.225	1*	77	-20	-1.8
1889	Col AA	0	0	—	2	0	0	1	1.2	1	7	0	0	4	2	21.60	17	.167	.500	578	.256	0*		-4	-0.4
1890	Bro AA	10	15	.400	27	27	27	0	235.2	252	161	3	18	93	82	4.05	96	.265	.342	394	.239	3*	95	-2	0.3
	NY N	2	0	1.000	2	1	1	0	16	6	6	0	4	6	0	2.25	156	.113	.254	15	.133	-1*	72	3	0.2
	†Lou AA	6	3	.667	12	10	9-1	0	93	83	35	2	4	30	31	1.94	199	.232	.298	80	.250	2*	107	20	2.0
1891	Lou AA	4	8	.333	15	14	11	0	111.1	149	109	6	8	48	27	5.74	64	.310	.382	64	.250	2*	101	-26	-1.9
Total	7	66	70	.485	151	139	132-6	1	1237.2	1217	780	39	37	380	407	3.39	98	.246	.305	2494	.240	12	93	-8	0.9
DAILY, HUGH Hugh Ignatius "One Arm" (b: Harry Criss) B 1848 , Ireland BR/TR 6-2/180# d5.1																									
1882	Buf N	15	14	.517	29	29	29	0	255.2	246	165	7		70	116	2.99	98	.234	.282	110	.164	-6	103	-7	-1.4
1883	Cle N	23	19	.548	45	43	40-4	1	378.2	360	193	5		99	171	2.42	130	.243	.291	142	.127	-10	72	34	2.1
1884	CP U	27	27	.500	56	56	54-5	0	484.2	430	257	11		71	469	2.43	100	.222	.249	196	.219	-11*	78	1	-0.9
	Was U	1	1	.500	2	2	2	0	16	16	11	0		1	14	2.25	107	.242	.254	5	.000	-1	89	-1	-0.2

Year	Tm Lg	W	L	Pct	G	GS	CG-Sho	SV-BS	IP	H	R	HR	HB	BB-IB	SO	ERA	AERA	OAV	OOB	AB-SH	AVG	PB	Sup	APR	PW
	Year	28	28	.500	58	58	56-5	0	500.2	446	16	11		72	**483**	2.43	100	.223	.250	201	.214	-12	78	-4	-1.1
1885	StL N	3	8	.273	11	11	10-1	0	91.1	92	72	5		44	31	3.94	70	.252	.333	35	.086	-3	71	-14	-1.6
1886	Was N	0	6	.000	6	6	6	0	49	69	60	2		40	15	7.35	44	.332	.440	16	.125	-1	69	-22	-1.9
1887	Cle AA	4	12	.250	16	16	16	0	139.2	181	108	1	3	44	30	3.67	118	.311	.362	58	.069	-8	77	8	0.0
Total	6	73	87	.456	165	163	157-10	1	1415	1394	866	31	3	369	846	2.92	101	.245	.291	562	.157	-39	80	-1	-3.9
DalCANTON, BRUCE John Bruce B 6.15.1942 California, PA BR/TR 6-2/205# d9.3 C5																									
1967	Pit N	2	1	.667	8	2	1	0	24	19	5	1	1	10-3	13	1.88	179	.211	.297	6-0	.333	1	65	4	0.6
1968	Pit N	1	1	.500	7	0	0	2	17	7	4	0	2	6-2	8	2.12	138	.127	.234	3-1	.000	-0		2	0.2
1969	Pit N	8	2	.800	57	0	0	5-1	86.1	79	34	3	0	49-12	56	3.34	105	.252	.351	10-0	.300	2		2	0.5
1970	Pit N	9	4	.692	41	6	1	1-3	84.2	94	48	7	1	39-8	53	4.57	85	.282	.356	16-1	.000	-1	180	-7	-1.0
1971	KC A	8	6	.571	25	22	2	0-0	141.1	144	63	8	0	44-0	58	3.44	100	.262	.315	46-6	.087	-3	106	-2	-0.5
1972	KC A	6	6	.500	35	16	1	2-0	132.1	135	54	7	1	29-6	75	3.40	89	.265	.304	41-5	.098	-2	124	-5	-0.7
1973	KC A	4	3	.571	32	3	1	3-3	97.1	108	60	8	4	46-12	38	4.81	86	.284	.367	0-0	—	0	43	-8	-0.6
1974	KC A	8	10	.444	31	22	9-2	0-0	175.1	135	71	5	5	82-3	96	3.13	122	.211	.304	0-0	—	0	110	13	1.3
1975	KC A	0	2	.000	4	2	0	0-0	8.2	23	18	0	1	7-0	5	15.58	25	.479	.554	0-0	—	0	103	-11	-1.8
	Atl N	2	7	.222	26	9	0	3-3	67	63	33	2	6	24-1	38	3.36	113	.248	.321	19-0	.105	-1	77	2	0.1
1976	Atl N	3	5	.375	42	1	0	1-0	73.1	67	41	6	2	42-8	36	3.56	107	.244	.344	9-1	.222	0	70	-2	-0.1
1977	Chi A	0	2	.000	8	0	0	2-0	24	20	11	1	0	13-0	9	3.75	109	.230	.330	0-0	—	0		1	0.1
Total	11	51	49	.510	316	83	15-2	19-10	931.1	894	442	48	23	391-55	485	3.67	99	.253	.329	150-14	.113	-3	107	-11	-1.9
DALE, GENE Emmett Eugene B 6.16.1889 St.Louis, MO D 3.20.1958 St.Louis, MO BR/TR 6-3/179# d9.19																									
1911	StL N	0	2	.000	5	2	0	0	14.2	13	12	0	2	16	13	6.75	50	.250	.443	5-0	.400	1	100	-5	-0.5
1912	StL N	0	5	.000	19	3	1	0	61.2	76	58	4	3	51	37	6.57	52	.311	.436	22-0	.273	1*	43	-19	-1.3
1915	Cin N	18	17	.514	49	35	20-4	3	296.2	256	115	6	6	107	104	2.46	116	.243	.316	91-8	.220	2	90	9	1.2
1916	Cin N	3	4	.429	17	5	2	0	69.2	80	44	3	2	33	23	5.17	50	.304	.386	21-0	.143	-0	98	-17	-1.7
Total	4	21	28	.429	90	45	23-4	3	442.2	425	229	13	13	207	177	3.60	81	.263	.352	139-8	.223	3	87	-32	-2.3
DALE, CARL James Carl B 12.7.1972 Indianapolis, IN BR/TR 6-2/215# d9.7																									
1999	Mil N	0	1	.000	4	0	0	0-0	4	8	9	2	1	6-0	4	20.25	22	.400	.556	0-0	—	0		-7	-1.1
DALEY, BUD Leavitt Leo B 10.7.1932 Orange, CA BL/TL 6-1/185# d9.10																									
1955	Cle A	0	1	.000	2	1	0	0	7	10	5	1	0	1-0	2	6.43	62	.333	.355	2-0	.000	-0	45	-2	-0.2
1956	Cle A	1	0	1.000	14	0	0	0	20.1	21	15	2	5	14-1	13	6.20	68	.273	.408	2-1	.000	-0		-4	-0.2
1957	Cle A	2	8	.200	34	10	1	2	87.1	99	59	6	10	40-4	54	4.43	84	.279	.367	20-2	.200	0	79	-11	-1.1
1958	KC A	3	2	.600	26	5	1	0	70.2	67	29	5	6	19-1	39	3.31	118	.249	.312	16-1	.125	-1	78	4	0.3
1959	KC A★	16	13	.552	39	29	12-2	1	216.1	212	90	24	11	62-2	125	3.16	127	.257	.317	78-5	.295	4	100	19	2.9
1960	KC A★	16	16	.500	37	35	13-1	0	231	234	129	27	10	96-3	126	4.56	87	.263	.339	75-6	.160	1	114	-13	-1.4
1961	KC A	4	8	.333	16	10	2	1	63.2	84	46	6	5	22-2	36	4.95	84	.319	.378	18-1	.111	-1	87	-8	-1.3
	†NY A	8	9	.471	23	17	7	0	129.2	127	63	17	4	51-6	83	3.96	94	.257	.330	45-2	.133	-1	119	-4	-0.6
	Year	12	17	.414	39	27	9	1	193.1	211	68	23	9	73-8	119	4.28	90	.278	.347	63-3	.127	-2	107	-12	-1.9
1962	†NY A	7	5	.583	43	6	0	4	105.1	105	47	8	5	21-0	55	3.59	104	.258	.301	27-1	.185	-0	147	2	0.2
1963	NY A	0	0	—	1	0	0	1	1	2	0	0	0	0-0	0	0.00	—	.667	.500	0-0	—	0		0	0.1
1964	NY A	3	2	.600	13	3	0	1	35	37	19	3	4	25-1	16	4.63	78	.274	.400	8-1	.250	1	147	-4	-0.4
Total	10	60	64	.484	248	116	36-3	10	967.1	998	502	99	60	351-20	549	4.03	97	.266	.337	291-20	.192	3	107	-21	-1.7
DALEY, BILL William B 6.27.1868 Poughkeepsie, NY D 5.4.1922 Poughkeepsie, NY TL 5-7/140# d7.17																									
1889	Bos N	3	3	.500	9	7	4	0	48	34	29	1	2	43	40	4.31	97	.193	.357	20	.150	-1	94	1	0.1
1890	Bos P	18	7	**.720**	34	25	19-2	2	235	246	178	7	9	167	110	3.60	122	.258	.373	110	.155	-5*	113	12	0.5
1891	Bos AA	8	6	.571	19	11	10	2	126.2	119	76	6	7	81	68	2.98	117	.240	.354	59	.169	-3*	169	5	0.2
Total	3	29	16	.644	62	43	33-2	4	409.2	399	283	14	18	291	218	3.49	117	.245	.366	189	.159	-8	123	18	0.8
DALTON, MIKE Michael Edward B 3.27.1963 Palo Alto, CA BR/TL 6/215# d5.31																									
1991	Det A	0	0	—	4	0	0	0-0	8	12	3	2	0	2-0	4	3.38	123	.333	.368	0-0	—	0		1	0.0
DALY, GEORGE George Josephs "Pecks" B 7.28.1887 Buffalo, NY D 12.12.1957 Buffalo, NY BR/TR 5-10.5/175# d9.26																									
1909	NY N	0	3	.000	3	3	3	0	21	31	19	0	1	8	8	6.00	43	.341	.400	9-0	.111	-1	55	-7	-1.0
D'AMICO, JEFF Jeffrey Charles B 12.27.1975 St.Petersburg, FL BR/TR 6-7/250# d6.28																									
1996	Mil A	6	6	.500	17	17	0	0-0	86	88	53	21	0	31-0	53	5.44	95	.267	.327	0-0	—	0	101	-1	-0.1
1997	Mil A	9	7	.563	23	23	1-1	0-0	135.2	139	81	25	8	43-2	94	4.71	98	.264	.327	4-1	.000	-0	92	-2	-0.3
1999	Mil N	0	0	—	1	0	0	0-0	1	1	0	0	0	0-0	1	0.00	—	.250	.250	0-0	—	0		1	0.0
2000	Mil N	12	7	.632	23	23	1-1	0-0	162.1	143	55	14	6	46-5	101	2.66	171	.238	.297	44-6	.091	-0	77	34	3.5
2001	Mil N	2	4	.333	10	10	0	0-0	47.1	60	42	11	1	16-4	32	6.08	71	.306	.360	15-0	.067	0	110	-13	-1.3
2002	NY N	6	10	.375	29	22	1-1	0-0	145.2	152	84	20	3	37-8	101	4.94	80	.267	.313	37-5	.108	-1	105	-14	-1.5
2003	Pit N	9	16	.360	29	29	2-1	0-0	175.1	204	104	23	7	42-6	100	4.77	92	.291	.336	48-9	.125	1	93	-9	-1.2
Total	7	44	50	.468	132	124	5-4	0-0	753.1	787	419	114	25	215-25	482	4.49	99	.269	.322	148-21	.101	-1	95	-4	-0.9
D'AMICO, JEFF Jeffrey Michael B 11.9.1974 Inglewood, CA BR/TR 6-3/200# d6.3																									
2000	KC A	0	1	.000	7	1	0	0-0	13.2	19	14	2	0	15-1	9	9.22	56	.345	.486	0-0	—	0	55	-6	-0.3
DAMMANN, BILL William Henry "Wee Willie" B 8.9.1872 Chicago, IL D 12.6.1948 Lynnhaven, VA BL/TL 5-7/155# d4.24																									
1897	Cin N	6	4	.600	16	11	7-1	0	95	122	65	2	5	37	21	4.74	96	.309	.375	31-0	.161	-1	100	-1	-0.1
1898	Cin N	16	10	.615	35	22	16-2	2	224.2	277	132	3	7	67	51	3.61	106	.301	.353	82-1	.195	1	101	2	0.1
1899	Cin N	2	1	.667	9	5	3-1	1	48	74	30	0	1	11	2	4.88	80	.351	.386	18-0	.056	-2	143	-3	-0.3
Total	3	24	15	.615	60	38	26-4	3	367.2	473	227	5	13	115	74	4.06	99	.310	.363	131-1	.168	-1	106	-2	-0.3
DANEKER, PAT Patrick Rees B 1.14.1976 Williamsport, PA BR/TR 6-3/195# d7.2																									
1999	Chi A	0	0	—	3	2	0	0-0	15	14	8	1	0	6-0	5	4.20	116	.255	.323	2-0	.000	-0	153	1	0.0
DANEY, ART Arthur Lee B 7.9.1904 Talihina, OK D 3.11.1988 Phoenix, AZ BR/TR 5-11/165# d5.25																									
1928	Phi A	0	0	—	1	0	0	0	1	1	0	0	0	0	0	0.00	—	.250	.250	0-0	—	0		0	0.0
DANFORTH, DAVE David Charles "Dauntless Dave" B 3.7.1890 Granger, TX D 9.19.1970 Baltimore, MD BL/TL 6/167# d8.1																									
1911	Phi A	4	1	.800	14	2	1	1	33.2	29	18	1	3	17	21	3.74	84	.240	.348	6-1	.167	0	126	-2	-0.3
1912	Phi A	0	0	—	3	0	0	0	20.1	26	14	0	0	12	8	3.98	77	.338	.427	8-0	.250	0		-3	-0.1
1916	Chi A	6	5	.545	28	8	1	2	93.2	87	43	1	3	37	49	3.27	85	.259	.338	23-2	.087	-1	82	-4	-0.6
1917	†Chi A	11	6	.647	**50**	9	1-1	**9**	173	155	56	1	3	74	79	2.65	100	.244	.325	46-5	.130	0	96	5	0.4
1918	Chi A	6	15	.286	39	11	5	2	139	148	73	1	5	40	48	3.43	80	.288	.345	42-2	.143	-2	68	-13	-2.1
1919	Chi A	1	2	.333	15	1	0	1	41.2	58	44	1	1	20	17	7.78	41	.333	.405	9-1	.111	0	49	-21	-1.5
1922	StL A	5	2	.714	20	10	3	1	79.2	93	37	1	1	38	48	3.28	127	.304	.383	23-0	.087	-2	113	7	0.3
1923	StL A	16	14	.533	38	29	16	1	226.1	221	111	4	12	87	96	3.94	106	.262	.340	71-8	.211	2	100	9	1.3
1924	StL A	15	12	.556	41	27	12-1	4	219.2	246	126	16	3	69	65	4.51	100	.292	.348	76-6	.171	-2	91	1	-0.2
1925	StL A	7	9	.438	38	15	5	2	159	172	96	19	3	61	53	4.36	107	.284	.353	46-5	.174	-2	115	4	0.0
Total	10	71	66	.518	286	112	44-2	23	1186	1235	618	45	34	455	484	3.89	95	.277	.349	350-30	.160	-6	102	-17	-2.8
DANIEL, CHUCK Charles Edward B 9.17.1933 Bluffton, AR BR/TR 6-2/195# d9.21																									
1957	Det A	0	0	—	1	0	0	0	2.1	3	2	1	0	0-0	2	7.71	50	.333	.333	0-0	—	0		-1	0.0
DANIELS, BENNIE Bennie B 6.17.1932 Tuscaloosa, AL BL/TR 6-1.5/193# d9.24																									
1957	Pit N	0	1	.000	1	1	0	0	7	5	2	0	0	3-0	2	1.29	295	.208	.296	2-0	.000	-0	0	2	0.2
1958	Pit N	0	3	.000	8	5	1	0	27.2	31	19	3	1	15-1	7	5.53	70	.290	.379	8-0	.125	-0	56	-5	-0.5
1959	Pit N	7	9	.438	34	12	0	1	100.2	115	69	9	2	39-6	67	5.45	71	.287	.351	29-0	.310	6*	83	-18	-2.0
1960	Pit N	1	3	.250	10	6	0	0	40.1	52	35	4	0	17-1	16	7.81	48	.311	.371	16-0	.188	-0	122	-17	-1.4
1961	Was A	12	11	.522	32	28	12-1	0	212	184	90	14	3	80-8	110	3.44	117	.237	.309	76-3	.197	3	96	15	1.9
1962	Was A	7	16	.304	44	21	3-1	2	161.1	172	98	14	2	68-5	66	4.85	83	.280	.351	46-4	.130	-1	78	-15	-1.8

Year	Tm Lg	W	L	Pct	G	GS	CG-Sho	SV-BS	IP	H	R	HR	HB	BB-IB	SO	ERA	AERA	OAV	OOB	AB-SH	AVG	PB	Sup	APR	PW
1963	Was A	5	10	.333	35	24	6-1	1	168.2	163	90	19	1	58-9	88	4.38	85	.250	.310	46-6	.152	1*	93	-11	-0.6
1964	Was A	8	10	.444	33	24	3-2	0	163	147	75	20	0	64-8	73	3.70	100	.245	.314	47-4	.128	0	82	1	0.2
1965	Was A	5	13	.278	33	18	1	1	116.1	135	75	16	0	39-7	42	4.72	74	.290	.343	30-3	.133	0	70	-18	-2.6
Total	9	45	76	.372	230	139	26-5	5	997	1004	553	99	9	383-45	471	4.44	86	.264	.330	300-20	.170	9	85	-66	-6.6

DANIELS, CHARLIE Charles L. B 7.1.1861 Roxbury, MA D 2.9.1938 Boston, MA d4.18

Year	Tm Lg	W	L	Pct	G	GS	CG-Sho	SV-BS	IP	H	R	HR	HB	BB-IB	SO	ERA	AERA	OAV	OOB	AB-SH	AVG	PB	Sup	APR	PW
1884	Bos U	0	2	.000	2	2	2	0	16.2	20	14	0		2	12	4.32	55	.278	.297	11	.273	0*	108	-3	-0.3

DANIELS, PETE Peter J. "Smiling Pete" B 4.8.1864 County Cavan, Ireland D 2.13.1928 Indianapolis, IN BL/TL d4.19

Year	Tm Lg	W	L	Pct	G	GS	CG-Sho	SV-BS	IP	H	R	HR	HB	BB-IB	SO	ERA	AERA	OAV	OOB	AB-SH	AVG	PB	Sup	APR	PW
1890	Pit N	1	2	.333	4	4	3	0	28	40	29	1	3	12	8	7.07	47	.325	.399	12	.333	1	153	-11	-0.7
1898	StL N	1	6	.143	10	6	3	0	54.2	62	41	0	3	14	13	3.62	105	.283	.335	17-0	.176	0	62	-3	-0.3
Total	2	2	8	.200	14	10	6	0	82.2	102	70	1	6	26	21	4.79	76	.298	.358	29-0	.241	1	98	-14	-1.0

DARBY, GEORGE George William "Deacon" B 2.6.1869 Kansas City, MO D 2.25.1937 Sacramento, CA BR/TR 5-10.5/160# d4.28

Year	Tm Lg	W	L	Pct	G	GS	CG-Sho	SV-BS	IP	H	R	HR	HB	BB-IB	SO	ERA	AERA	OAV	OOB	AB-SH	AVG	PB	Sup	APR	PW
1893	Cin N	1	1	.500	4	3	2	0	29	41	32	2	3	18	6	7.76	62	.323	.419	10	.300	0	83	-9	-0.4

DARCY, PAT Patrick Leonard B 5.12.1950 Troy, OH BL/TR 6-3/175# d9.12

Year	Tm Lg	W	L	Pct	G	GS	CG-Sho	SV-BS	IP	H	R	HR	HB	BB-IB	SO	ERA	AERA	OAV	OOB	AB-SH	AVG	PB	Sup	APR	PW
1974	Cin N	1	0	1.000	6	2	0	0-0	17	17	7	2	0	8-1	14	3.71	94	.262	.342	3-1	.333	0	125	0	0.0
1975	†Cin N	11	5	.688	27	22	1	1-1	130.2	134	54	4	0	59-9	46	3.58	101	.269	.344	47-2	.085	-3	113	1	-0.2
1976	Cin N	2	3	.400	11	4	0	2-0	39	41	27	2	0	22-2	15	6.23	56	.279	.368	11-1	.182	1	163	-11	-1.3
Total	3	14	8	.636	44	28	1	3-1	186.2	192	88	8	0	89-12	75	4.15	86	.270	.349	61-4	.115	-2	121	-10	-1.5

DARENSBOURG, VIC Victor Anthony B 11.13.1970 Los Angeles, CA BL/TL 5-10/165# d4.1

Year	Tm Lg	W	L	Pct	G	GS	CG-Sho	SV-BS	IP	H	R	HR	HB	BB-IB	SO	ERA	AERA	OAV	OOB	AB-SH	AVG	PB	Sup	APR	PW
1998	Fla N	0	7	.000	59	0	0	1-1	71	52	29	5	0	30-6	74	3.68	110	.207	.289	8-0	.000	-1*		5	0.3
1999	Fla N	0	1	.000	56	0	0	0-1	34.2	50	36	3	5	21-1	16	8.83	49	.340	.434	0-0	—	0		-17	-0.8
2000	Fla N	5	3	.625	56	0	0	0-1	62	61	32	7	2	28-1	59	4.06	109	.260	.336	8-0	.250	0		2	0.3
2001	Fla N	1	2	.333	58	0	0	1-2	48.2	52	24	4	1	10-6	33	4.25	99	.277	.313	0-0	—	0*		0	0.0
2002	Fla N	1	2	.333	42	0	0	0-0	48.1	61	34	10	2	26-4	33	6.14	64	.305	.385	1-1	.000	-0*		-12	-0.7
2003	Col N	0	0	—	3	0	0	0-0	2.1	4	1	0	0	0-0	0	0.00	—	.333	.333	0-0	—	0		1	0.0
	Mon N	0	0	—	6	0	0	0-0	6.2	13	8	2	0	1-0	4	10.80	43	.406	.424	1-0	.000	-0*		-4	-0.2
	Year	0	0	—	9	0	0	0-0	9	17	14	2	0	1-0	4	8.00	59	.386	.400	1-0	.000	-0		-3	-0.2
Total	6	7	15	.318	280	0	0	2-5	273.2	293	164	31	10	116-18	219	5.10	83	.275	.347	18-1	.111	-0		-25	-1.1

DARLING, RON Ronald Maurice B 8.19.1960 Honolulu, HI BR/TR 6-3/195# d9.6

Year	Tm Lg	W	L	Pct	G	GS	CG-Sho	SV-BS	IP	H	R	HR	HB	BB-IB	SO	ERA	AERA	OAV	OOB	AB-SH	AVG	PB	Sup	APR	PW
1983	NY N	1	3	.250	5	5	1	0-0	35.1	31	11	0	3	17-1	23	2.80	130	.248	.352	10-1	.100	-1	63	4	0.4
1984	NY N	12	9	.571	33	33	2-2	0-0	205.2	179	97	17	5	104-2	136	3.81	93	.235	.328	67-6	.149	-1*	110	-4	-0.4
1985	NY N☆	16	6	.727	36	35	4-2	0-0	248	214	93	21	3	114-1	167	2.90	119	.235	.321	76-13	.171	2*	105	14	1.6
1986	†NY N	15	6	.714	34	34	4-2	0-0	237	203	84	21	3	81-2	184	2.81	126	.234	.300	81-10	.099	-2	124	20	1.6
1987	NY N	12	8	.600	32	32	2	0-0	207.2	183	111	24	3	96-3	167	4.29	88	.233	.318	65-10	.123	1	120	-12	-0.8
1988	†NY N	17	9	.654	34	34	7-4	0-0	240.2	218	97	24	5	60-2	161	3.25	99	.245	.294	82-9	.220	6	117	0	0.7
1989	NY N	14	14	.500	33	33	4	0-0	217.1	214	100	19	3	70-7	153	3.52	93	.258	.314	73-5	.123	1*	106	-9	-0.9
1990	NY N	7	9	.438	33	18	1	0-0	126	135	73	20	5	44-4	99	4.50	83	.273	.336	31-5	.129	0*	106	-12	-1.3
1991	NY N	5	6	.455	17	17	0	0-0	102.1	96	50	9	6	28-1	58	3.87	94	.251	.310	34-5	.118	-0	97	-3	-0.3
	Mon N	0	2	.000	3	3	0	0-0	17	25	16	6	1	5-0	11	7.41	49	.333	.383	6-1	.167	0	91	-7	-0.7
	Year	5	8	.385	20	20	0	0-0	119.1	121	20	15	7	33-1	69	4.37	83	.265	.321	40-6	.125	-0	96	-11	-1.0
	Oak A	3	7	.300	12	12	0	0-0	75	64	34	7	2	38-2	60	4.08	94	.237	.331	0-0	—	—	62	-1	-0.1
1992	†Oak A	15	10	.600	33	33	4-3	0-0	206.1	198	98	15	4	72-5	99	3.66	102	.253	.318	0-0	—	0*	103	0	0.0
1993	Oak A	5	9	.357	31	29	3	0-0	178	198	107	22	5	72-5	95	5.16	79	.281	.349	0-0	—	0*	117	-21	-1.5
1994	Oak A	10	11	.476	25	**25**	4	0-0	160	162	89	18	7	59-3	108	4.50	98	.267	.337	1-0	.000	-0*	90	-2	-0.2
1995	Oak A	4	7	.364	21	21	1	0-0	104	124	79	16	4	46-2	69	6.23	72	.296	.365	0-0	—	0*	121	-22	-1.8
Total	13	136	116	.540	382	364	37-13	0-0	2360.1	2244	1139	239	59	906-40	1590	3.87	95	.252	.323	526-65	.144	6	108	-55	-3.7

DARNELL, BOB Robert Jack B 11.6.1930 Wewoka, OK D 1.1.1995 Fredericksburg, TX BR/TR 5-10/175# d8.10

Year	Tm Lg	W	L	Pct	G	GS	CG-Sho	SV-BS	IP	H	R	HR	HB	BB-IB	SO	ERA	AERA	OAV	OOB	AB-SH	AVG	PB	Sup	APR	PW
1954	Bro N	0	0	—	6	1	0	0	14.1	15	7	2	0	7	5	3.14	130	.278	.361	2-1	.000	-0	131	1	0.0
1956	Bro N	0	0	—	1	0	0	0	1.1	1	0	0	0	0-0	0	0.00	—	.200	.200	0-0	—	0		1	0.0
Total	2	0	0	—	7	1	0	0	15.2	16	7	2	0	7-0	5	2.87	142	.271	.348	2-1	.000	-0	131	2	0.0

DARR, MIKE Michael Edward B 3.23.1956 Pomona, CA BR/TR 6-4/190# d9.6

Year	Tm Lg	W	L	Pct	G	GS	CG-Sho	SV-BS	IP	H	R	HR	HB	BB-IB	SO	ERA	AERA	OAV	OOB	AB-SH	AVG	PB	Sup	APR	PW
1977	Tor A	0	1	.000	1	1	0	0-0	1.1	3	5	1	1	4-0	1	33.75	12	.429	.667	0-0	—	0	43	-4	-0.6

DARROW, GEORGE George Oliver B 7.12.1903 Beloit, KS D 3.24.1983 Sun City, AZ BL/TL 6/180# d4.22

Year	Tm Lg	W	L	Pct	G	GS	CG-Sho	SV-BS	IP	H	R	HR	HB	BB-IB	SO	ERA	AERA	OAV	OOB	AB-SH	AVG	PB	Sup	APR	PW
1934	Phi N	2	6	.250	17	8	2	1	49	57	37	4	4	28	14	5.51	86	.302	.403	15-0	.133	0	103	-5	-0.6

DARWIN, DANNY Daniel Wayne B 10.25.1955 Bonham, TX BR/TR 6-3/190# d9.8 b-Jeff

Year	Tm Lg	W	L	Pct	G	GS	CG-Sho	SV-BS	IP	H	R	HR	HB	BB-IB	SO	ERA	AERA	OAV	OOB	AB-SH	AVG	PB	Sup	APR	PW
1978	Tex A	1	0	1.000	3	1	0	0-0	8.2	11	4	0	0	1-0	8	4.15	90	.324	.333	0-0	—	0	96	0	0.0
1979	Tex A	4	4	.500	20	6	1	0-0	78	50	36	5	5	30-2	58	4.04	103	.186	.274	0-0	—	0	138	3	0.2
1980	Tex A	13	4	.765	53	2	0	8-6	109.2	98	37	4	2	50-7	104	2.63	149	.243	.324	0-0	—	0	149	16	2.6
1981	Tex A	9	9	.500	22	22	6-2	0-0	146	115	67	12	6	57-5	98	3.64	95	.218	.300	0-0	—	0	121	-4	-0.5
1982	Tex A	10	8	.556	56	1	0	7-7	89	95	38	6	2	37-8	61	3.44	113	.279	.349	0-0	—	0	47	4	0.9
1983	Tex A	8	13	.381	28	26	9-2	0-0	183	175	86	9	3	62-3	92	3.49	115	.250	.310	0-0	—	0	89	8	0.8
1984	Tex A	8	12	.400	35	32	5-1	0-0	223.2	249	110	19	4	54-2	123	3.94	105	.279	.322	0-0	—	0	90	6	0.4
1985	Mil A	8	18	.308	39	29	11-1	2-0	217.2	212	112	34	4	65-4	125	3.80	110	.254	.308	0-0	—	0	74	6	0.5
1986	Mil A	6	8	.429	27	14	5-1	0-1	130.1	120	62	13	3	35-1	80	3.52	123	.246	.297	0-0	—	0	70	10	1.0
	Hou N	5	2	.714	12	8	1	0-0	54.1	50	19	3	0	9-0	40	2.32	156	.239	.267	16-2	.063	-1	114	6	0.7
1987	Hou N	9	10	.474	33	30	3-1	0-0	195.2	184	87	17	5	69-12	134	3.59	109	.246	.313	66-1	.182	2*	102	7	0.8
1988	Hou N	8	13	.381	44	20	3	3-0	192	189	86	20	7	48-9	129	3.84	87	.259	.307	56-2	.071	-1	99	-8	-0.9
1989	Hou N	11	4	.733	68	0	0	7-4	122	92	34	8	2	33-9	104	2.36	144	.212	.268	17-0	.118	-1		15	1.8
1990	Hou N	11	4	.733	48	17	3	2-2	162.2	136	42	11	4	31-4	109	**2.21**	**168**	.225	**.266**	38-3	.132	1*	97	29	2.6
1991	Bos A	3	6	.333	12	12	0	0-0	68	71	39	15	4	15-1	42	5.16	83	.263	.309	0-0	—	0	74	-4	-0.5
1992	Bos A	9	9	.500	51	15	2	3-3	161.1	159	76	11	5	53-9	124	3.96	107	.257	.319	0-0	—	0	79	7	0.6
1993	Bos A	15	11	.577	34	34	2-1	0-0	229.1	196	93	31	3	49-8	130	3.26	142	.230	**.272**	0-0	—	0	87	33	3.5
1994	Bos A	7	5	.583	13	13	0	0-0	75.2	101	54	13	1	24-6	54	6.30	80	.317	.361	0-0	—	0	119	-8	-1.1
1995	Tor A	1	8	.111	13	11	1	0-0	65	91	60	13	3	24-2	36	7.62	62	.340	.393	0-0	—	0	65	-21	-2.3
	Tex A	2	2	.500	7	4	0	0-0	34	40	27	12	1	7-1	22	7.15	68	.292	.331	0-0	—	0	135	-8	-0.7
	Year	3	10	.231	20	15	1	0-0	99	131	34	25	4	31-3	58	7.45	64	.323	.373	0-0	—	0	84	-30	-3.0
1996	Pit N	7	9	.438	19	19	0	0-0	122.1	117	48	9	6	16-0	69	3.02	145	.253	.285	39-5	.205	2	80	17	2.4
	Hou N	3	2	.600	15	6	0	0-2	42.1	43	31	7	6	11-3	27	5.95	65	.267	.331	10-2	.100	-0	105	-10	-1.1
	Year	10	11	.476	34	25	0	0-2	164.2	160	36	16	12	27-3	96	3.77	112	.257	.297	49-7	.184	2	86	8	1.3
1997	Chi A	4	8	.333	21	17	1	0-0	113.1	130	60	21	1	31-1	62	4.13	106	.286	.329	3-1	.000	-0	92	2	0.2
	SF N	1	3	.250	10	7	0	0-0	44	51	26	5	1	14-0	30	4.91	83	.288	.342	15-0	.133	-0	119	-4	-0.3
1998	SF N	8	10	.444	33	25	0	0-0	148.2	176	97	23	3	49-4	81	5.51	72	.297	.352	45-4	.089	-2	117	-27	-2.9
Total	21	171	182	.484	716	371	53-9	32-25	3016.2	2951	1431	321	81	874-101	1942	3.84	106	.256	.310	305-20	.128	0	96	75	8.7

DARWIN, JEFF Jeffrey Scott B 7.6.1969 Sherman, TX BR/TR 6-3/180# d6.13 b-Danny

Year	Tm Lg	W	L	Pct	G	GS	CG-Sho	SV-BS	IP	H	R	HR	HB	BB-IB	SO	ERA	AERA	OAV	OOB	AB-SH	AVG	PB	Sup	APR	PW
1994	Sea A	0	0	—	2	0	0	0-0	4	7	6	1	1	3-1	1	13.50	36	.389	.500	0-0	—	0		-3	-0.2
1996	Chi A	0	1	.000	22	0	0	0-1	30.2	26	10	5	2	9-1	15	2.93	162	.232	.301	0-0	—	0		7	0.3
1997	Chi A	0	1	.000	14	0	0	0-0	13.2	17	8	1	0	7-0	9	5.27	83	.298	.369	0-0	—	0		-1	-0.1
Total	3	0	2	.000	38	0	0	0-1	48.1	50	24	7	3	19-2	25	4.47	104	.267	.343	0-0	—	0		3	0.0

DASHNER, LEE Lee Claire "Lefty" B 4.25.1887 Renault, IL D 12.16.1959 ElDorado, KS BB/TL 5-11.5/192# d8.4

Year	Tm Lg	W	L	Pct	G	GS	CG-Sho	SV-BS	IP	H	R	HR	HB	BB-IB	SO	ERA	AERA	OAV	OOB	AB-SH	AVG	PB	Sup	APR	PW
1913	Cle A	0	0	—	1	0	0	0	1.2	0	1	0	0	0	2	5.40	56	.000	.000	0-0	—	0		0	0.0

DASSO, FRANK Francis Joseph Nicholas B 8.31.1917 Chicago, IL BR/TR 5-11.5/185# d4.22

Year	Tm Lg	W	L	Pct	G	GS	CG-Sho	SV-BS	IP	H	R	HR	HB	BB-IB	SO	ERA	AERA	OAV	OOB	AB-SH	AVG	PB	Sup	APR	PW
1945	Cin N	4	5	.444	16	12	6	0	95.2	89	50	9	0	53	39	3.67	102	.253	.351	31-4	.161	-1	99	-1	-0.2
1946	Cin N	0	0	—	2	0	0	0	1	2	3	0	0	2	1	27.00	12	.400	.571	0-0	—	0		-2	-0.1

Year	Tm Lg	W	L	Pct	G	GS	CG-Sho	SV-BS	IP	H	R	HR	HB	BB-IB	SO	ERA	AERA	OAV	OOB	AB-SH	AVG	PB	Sup	APR	PW
Total	2	4	5	.444	18	12	6	0	96.2	91	53	9	0	55	40	3.91	96	.255	.354	31-4	.161	-1	99	-3	-0.3
DAUB, DAN Daniel William "Mickey" B 1.12.1868 Middletown, OH D 3.25.1951 Bradenton, FL BR/TR 5-10/160# d8.31																									
1892	Cin N	1	2	.333	4	3	2	0	25	23	10	0	2	13	7	2.88	113	.235	.336	7	.000	-1	39	2	0.1
1893	Bro N	6	6	.500	12	12	12	0	103	104	64	3	5	61	25	3.84	115	.254	.358	42	.190	-2	91	7	0.6
1894	Bro N	10	12	.455	34	27	15	0	224	291	209	7	18	91	45	6.11	81	.311	.383	95-4	.189	-6	103	-29	-2.4
1895	Bro N	10	10	.500	25	21	16	0	184.2	212	134	5	11	51	36	4.29	103	.284	.339	71-0	.197	-2	100	-5	-0.5
1896	Bro N	12	11	.522	32	24	18	0	225	255	120	4	8	63	53	3.60	115	.283	.335	84-0	.226	2	95	16	1.6
1897	Bro N	6	11	.353	19	16	11	0	137.2	180	117	8	10	48	19	6.08	67	.313	.376	49-2	.224	2	105	-28	-2.3
Total	6	45	52	.464	126	103	74	0	899.1	1065	654	27	54	327	185	4.75	93	.291	.357	348-6	.201	-6	98	-37	-2.9
DAUSS, HOOKS George August (b: George August Daus) B 9.22.1889 Indianapolis, IN D 7.27.1963 St.Louis, MO BR/TR 5-10.5/168# d9.28																									
1912	Det A	1	1	.500	2	2	2	0	17	11	7	0	3	9	7	3.18	103	.186	.324	4-0	.250	1	68	1	0.2
1913	Det A	13	12	.520	33	29	22-2	1	225	188	96	4	13	82	107	2.48	118	.231	.311	79-1	.177	3*	113	8	1.1
1914	Det A	19	15	.559	45	35	22-3	3	302	286	126	3	18	87	150	2.86	98	.257	.321	97-5	.216	6*	102	0	0.7
1915	Det A	24	13	.649	46	35	27-1	2	309.2	261	115	1	11	115	132	2.50	121	.235	.313	103-5	.146	0	125	17	2.6
1916	Det A	19	12	.613	39	29	18-1	4	238.2	220	102	2	16	90	95	3.21	89	.257	.339	72-4	.222	8	117	-6	0.1
1917	Det A	17	14	.548	37	31	22-6	2	270.2	243	105	3	7	87	102	2.43	109	.245	.311	87-3	.126	-1*	105	7	1.0
1918	Det A	12	16	.429	33	26	21-1	3	249.2	243	105	3	9	58	73	2.99	89	.263	.313	77-4	.182	3	103	-10	-0.6
1919	Det A	21	9	.700	34	32	22-2	0	256.1	262	125	9	5	63	73	3.55	90	.267	.315	97-5	.144	-3	146	-9	-1.0
1920	Det A	13	21	.382	38	32	18	0	270.1	308	158	11	8	84	82	3.56	105	.289	.345	83-3	.169	1	88	-1	0.5
1921	Det A	10	15	.400	32	28	16	1	233	275	141	11	13	81	68	4.33	99	.297	.362	88-2	.261	2	106	-2	0.3
1922	Det A	13	13	.500	39	25	12-1	4	218.2	251	123	7	6	59	78	4.20	92	.289	.339	72-3	.208	3	110	-9	-0.6
1923	Det A	21	13	.618	50	39	22-4	3	316	331	140	10	7	78	105	3.62	107	.272	.319	104-6	.231	5	118	14	1.9
1924	Det A	12	11	.522	40	10	5	6	131.1	155	78	6	1	40	44	4.59	90	.302	.354	38-2	.132	-2	109	-6	-1.0
1925	Det A	16	11	.593	35	30	16-1	1	228	238	110	11	4	85	58	3.16	136	.272	.339	81-0	.185	1	114	23	2.4
1926	Det A	12	6	.667	35	5	0	9	124.1	135	63	6	0	49	27	4.20	97	.287	.354	42-2	.238	4	112	1	0.5
Total	15	223	182	.551	538	388	245-22	39	3390.2	3407	1594	87	121	1067	1201	3.30	103	.266	.329	1124-45	.189	32	112	28	8.1
DAVENPORT, CLAUDE Claude Edwin "Big Dave" B 5.28.1898 Runge, TX D 6.13.1976 Corpus Christi, TX BR/TR 6-6/193# d10.2 b-Dave																									
1920	NY N	0	0	—	1	0	0	0	2	2	1	1	0	1	0	4.50	67	.250	.333	1-0	.000	-0		0	0.0
DAVENPORT, DAVE David W. B 2.20.1890 DeRidder, LA D 10.16.1954 ElDorado, AR BR/TR 6-6/220# d4.17 b-Claude																									
1914	Cin N	2	2	.500	10	6	3-1	2	54	38	18	1	3	30	22	2.50	117	.202	.321	18-1	.111	-1	106	4	0.2
	StL F	8	13	.381	33	26	13-2	4	215.2	204	100	3	7	80	142	3.46	88	.251	.324	68-3	.088	-6	79	-7	-1.3
1915	StL F	22	18	.550	**55**	**46**	**30-10**	1	**392.2**	300	116	5	5	96	**229**	2.20	131	**.215**	.268	130-7	.092	-11	101	**28**	1.2
1916	StL A	12	11	.522	**59**	31	13-1	2	290.2	267	112	4	8	100	129	2.85	96	.256	.326	73-5	.137	3	105	0	0.2
1917	StL A	17	17	.500	47	**39**	20-2	2	280.2	273	137	5	8	105	100	3.08	84	.260	.331	92-4	.098	-6	107	-17	-2.7
1918	StL A	10	11	.476	31	22	12-2	1	180	182	84	0	7	69	60	3.25	84	.273	.347	52-5	.135	1	96	-10	-0.9
1919	StL A	2	11	.154	24	16	5	0	123.1	135	74	4	2	41	37	3.94	84	.280	.339	39-3	.077	-4	78	-10	-1.3
Total	6	73	83	.468	259	186	96-18	12	1537	1399	641	22	40	521	719	2.93	97	.248	.316	472-28	.104	-24	97	-12	-4.6
DAVENPORT, JOE Joseph Jonathan B 3.24.1976 Chicago, IL BR/TR 6-5/225# d7.20																									
1999	Chi A	0	0	—	3	0	0	0-0	1.2	1	0	0	0	2-0	0	0.00	—	.200	.429	0-0	—	0		1	0.0
2001	Col N	0	0	—	7	0	0	0-0	10.1	8	7	1	0	7-0	8	3.48	153	.222	.349	1-0	1.000	0		1	0.1
Total	2	0	0	—	10	0	0	0-0	12	9	7	1	0	9-0	8	3.00	176	.220	.360	1-0	1.000	0		2	0.1
DAVENPORT, LUM Joubert Lum B 6.27.1900 Tucson, AZ D 4.21.1961 Dallas, TX BL/TL 6-1/165# d5.2																									
1921	Chi A	0	3	.000	13	2	0	0	35.1	41	35	1	1	32	9	6.88	62	.318	.457	17-0	.412	2*	158	-12	-0.7
1922	Chi A	1	1	.500	9	1	0	0	16.2	14	21	2	0	13	9	10.80	38	.233	.370	3-0	.000	-0*	188	-12	-1.2
1923	Chi A	0	0	—	2	0	0	0	4.1	7	4	0	0	4	1	6.23	64	.438	.550	1-1	1.000	0		-1	0.0
1924	Chi A	0	0	—	1	0	0	0	2	1	1	0	0	2	1	0.00	—	.125	.300	0-0	—	0		1	0.0
Total	4	1	4	.200	25	3	0	0	58.1	63	61	3	1	51	20	7.71	54	.296	.434	21-1	.381	2	168	-24	-1.9
DAVEY, MIKE Michael Gerard B 6.2.1952 Spokane, WA BR/TL 6-2/190# d8.13																									
1977	Atl N	0	0	—	16	0	0	2-0	16	19	9	1	0	9-4	7	5.06	88	.302	.389	1-0	.000	-0		0	0.0
1978	Atl N	0	0	—	3	0	0	0-0	2.2	1	0	0	0	1-0	0	0.00	—	.125	.222	0-0	—	0		1	0.0
Total	2	0	0	—	19	0	0	2-0	18.2	20	9	1	0	10-4	7	4.34	101	.282	.370	1-0	.000	-0		1	0.0
DAVEY, TOM Thomas Joseph B 9.11.1973 Garden City, MI BR/TR 6-7/215# d4.6																									
1999	Tor A	1	1	.500	29	0	0	1-0	44	40	28	5	3	26-0	42	4.70	105	.241	.350	0-0	—	0		0	0.0
	Sea A	1	0	1.000	16	0	0	0-0	21	22	13	0	4	14-1	17	4.71	101	.268	.400	0-0	—	0		0	0.0
	Year	2	1	.667	45	0	0	1-0	65	62	49	5	7	40-1	59	4.71	104	.250	.367	0-0	—	0		-1	0.0
2000	SD N	2	1	.667	11	0	0	0-1	12.2	12	1	0	0	2-0	6	0.71	608	.250	.280	0-0	—	0		6	1.1
2001	SD N	2	4	.333	39	0	0	0-4	38	41	22	3	1	17-3	37	4.50	89	.272	.349	0-0	—	0		-3	-0.3
2002	SD N	1	0	1.000	19	0	0	0-1	21	23	14	2	3	11-1	21	5.57	68	.287	.381	0-0	—	0		-4	-0.2
Total	4	7	6	.538	114	0	0	1-6	136.2	138	78	10	11	70-5	123	4.41	100	.262	.357	0-0	—	0		-1	0.6
DAVIAULT, RAY Raymond Joseph Robert B 5.27.1934 Montreal, PQ, CAN BR/TR 6-1/170# d4.13																									
1962	NY N	1	5	.167	36	3	0	0	81	92	64	14	4	48-1	51	6.22	67	.288	.384	15-0	.067	-1	91	-16	-1.2
DAVIDSON, BOB Robert Banks B 1.6.1963 Bad Kurznach, W.Germany BR/TR 6/185# d7.15																									
1989	NY A	0	0	—	1	0	0	0-0	1	1	2	1	0	1-0	0	18.00	22	.250	.400	0-0	—	0		-1	-0.1
DAVIDSON, TED Thomas Eugene B 10.4.1939 Las Vegas, NV BR/TL 6/192# d7.24																									
1965	Cin N	4	3	.571	24	1	0	1	68.2	57	21	5	2	17-4	54	2.23	168	.233	.285	17-2	.000	-2	140	10	0.9
1966	Cin N	5	4	.556	54	0	0	4	85.1	82	41	11	1	23-2	54	3.90	100	.253	.302	12-0	.000	-1		0	-0.2
1967	Cin N	1	0	1.000	9	0	0	0	13	13	6	0	0	3-1	6	4.15	90	.250	.291	0-0	—	0		0	0.0
1968	Cin N	1	0	1.000	23	0	0	0	21.2	27	15	3	0	7-0	7	6.23	51	.307	.358	2-0	.000	-0		-6	-0.4
	Atl N	0	0	—	4	0	0	0	6.2	10	5	2	0	4-1	3	6.75	44	.345	.424	0-0	—	0		-2	-0.1
	Year	1	0	1.000	27	0	0	0	28.1	37	26	5	0	11-1	10	6.35	49	.316	.375	2-0	.000	0		-9	-0.5
Total	4	11	7	.611	114	1	0	5	195.1	189	88	21	3	54-8	124	3.69	101	.256	.307	31-2	.000	-3	140	2	0.2
DAVIE, JERRY Gerald Lee B 2.10.1933 Detroit, MI BR/TR 6/180# d4.14																									
1959	Det A	2	2	.500	11	5	1	0	36.2	40	25	8	4	17-1	20	4.17	97	.265	.351	10-0	.400	2	100	-3	-0.1
DAVIES, GEORGE George Washington B 2.22.1868 Portage, WI D 9.22.1906 Waterloo, WI ?/180# d8.18																									
1891	Mil AA	7	5	.583	12	12	12-1	0	102	94	48	2	3	35	61	2.65	166	.237	.303	37	.243	1	67	18	1.8
1892	Cle N	10	16	.385	26	26	23	0	215.2	201	112	4	6	69	95	2.59	131	.237	.299	87	.138	-5	69	17	1.3
1893	Cle N	0	2	.000	3	3	1	0	15	28	25	1	0	10	3	11.40	43	.389	.463	6	.333	0	110	-9	-0.8
	NY N	1	1	.500	5	1	1	0	36.1	41	31	1	0	13	7	6.19	75	.275	.333	12	.333	2	120	-4	0.0
	Year	1	3	.250	8	4	2	0	51.1	69	39	2	0	23	10	7.71	61	.312	.377	18	.333	2	115	-13	-0.8
Total	3	18	24	.429	46	42	37-1	0	369	364	216	8	9	127	166	3.32	116	.248	.312	142	.190	-3	73	22	2.3
DAVIES, CHICK Lloyd Garrison B 3.6.1892 Peabody, MA D 9.5.1973 Middletown, CT BL/TL 5-8/145# d7.11 ▲																									
1914	Phi A	1	0	1.000	1	1	1	0	9	8	4	0	0	3	4	1.00	261	.258	.324	46-3	.239	0*	167	0	0.1
1915	Phi A	1	2	.333	4	2	0	0	15.1	20	16	0	1	12	2	8.80	33	.339	.458	132-5	.182	0*	125	-8	-1.3
1925	NY N	0	0	—	2	1	0	0	7.1	13	8	0	0	4	5	6.14	66	.361	.425	6-0	.000	-0*	188	-3	-0.1
1926	NY N	2	4	.333	38	1	0	**6**	89	96	60	3	0	35	27	3.94	95	.277	.344	18-0	.222	1	44	-8	-0.5
Total	4	4	6	.400	45	5	1	6	120.2	137	88	3	1	54	38	4.48	80	.290	.364	202-8	.193	1	123	-19	-1.8
DAVIS, CURT Curtis Benton "Coonskin" B 9.7.1903 Greenfield, MO D 10.13.1965 Covina, CA BR/TR 6-2/185# d4.21																									
1934	Phi N	19	17	.528	**51**	31	18-3	5	274.1	283	114	14	7	60	99	2.95	160	.269	.313	95-7	.211	-2	71	43	5.7
1935	Phi N	16	14	.533	44	27	19-3	2	231	264	103	14	7	47	74	3.66	124	.285	.324	75-4	.173	-1*	70	23	2.8
1936	Phi N	2	4	.333	10	8	3	0	60.1	71	37	6	1	19	18	4.62	98	.291	.345	26-0	.154	-1*	94	0	-0.1
	Chi N★	11	9	.550	24	20	10	1	153	146	60	11	1	31	52	3.00	133	.251	.290	53-6	.151	-2	102	15	1.8

Year	Tm Lg	W	L	Pct	G	GS	CG-Sho	SV-BS	IP	H	R	HR	HB	BB-IB	SO	ERA	AERA	OAV	OOB	AB-SH	AVG	PB	Sup	APR	PW
	Year	13	13	.500	34	28	13	1	213.1	217	65	17	2	50	70	3.46	120	.263	.307	79-6	.152	-3	99	17	1.7
1937	Chi N	10	5	.667	28	14	8	1	123.2	138	64	7	5	30	32	4.08	98	.286	.334	40-5	.300	4	122	-2	0.2
1938	StL N	12	8	.600	40	21	8-2	3	173.1	187	80	9	1	27	36	3.63	109	.272	.301	57-4	.228	2	99	8	1.1
1939	StL N☆	22	16	.579	49	31	13-3	7	248	279	121	18	3	48	70	3.63	113	.280	.315	105-7	.381	12*	108	10	2.8
1940	StL N	0	4	.000	14	7	0	1	54	73	34	4	1	19	12	5.17	77	.327	.383	19-1	.000	-2	65	-6	-0.6
	Bro N	8	7	.533	22	18	9	2	137	135	62	13	1	19	46	3.81	105	.256	.283	47-4	.128	-1	110	4	0.4
	Year	8	11	.421	36	25	9	3	191	208	67	17	2	38	58	4.19	95	.277	.314	66-5	.091	-3	97	-1	-0.2
1941	†Bro N	13	7	.650	28	16	10-5	2	154.1	141	58	6	2	27	50	2.97	123	.244	.280	59-5	.186	2*	137	12	1.9
1942	Bro N	15	6	.714	32	26	13-5	2	206	179	62	10	7	51	60	2.36	138	.233	.287	68-8	.176	-0	129	21	2.3
1943	Bro N	10	13	.435	31	21	8-2	3	164.1	182	85	8	2	39	47	3.78	89	.281	.324	55-4	.164	-1	123	-11	-1.4
1944	Bro N	10	11	.476	31	23	12-1	4	194	207	84	12	5	39	49	3.34	106	.270	.310	63-6	.159	-2	90	5	0.4
1945	Bro N	10	10	.500	24	18	10	0	149.2	171	66	9	3	21	39	3.25	116	.280	.308	51-2	.137	-1	101	9	1.0
1946	Bro N	0	0	—	1	0	0	0	2	3	3	1	1	2	0	13.50	25	.375	.545	0-0	—	0		-2	-0.1
Total	13	158	131	.547	429	281	141-24	33	2325	2459	1033	142	47	479	684	3.42	116	.270	.310	813-63	.203	7	100	129	18.2
DAVIS, DOUG Douglas P. B 9.21.1975 Sacramento, CA BR/TL 6-3/185# d8.9																									
1999	Tex A	0	0	—	2	0	0	0-0	2.2	12	10	3	0	0-0	3	33.75	15	.600	.600	0-0	—	0		-8	-0.3
2000	Tex A	7	6	.538	30	13	1	0-3	98.2	109	61	14	3	58-3	66	5.38	93	.288	.383	0-0	—	0	109	-2	-0.2
2001	Tex A	11	10	.524	30	30	1	0-0	186	220	103	14	3	69-1	115	4.45	105	.295	.354	3-1	.000	-0	101	2	0.1
2002	Tex A	3	5	.375	10	10	1-1	0-0	59.2	67	36	7	3	22-0	28	4.98	95	.290	.355	0-0	—	0	90	-2	-0.2
2003	Tex A	0	0	—	1	1	0	0-0	3	4	4	2	0	4-0	2	12.00	41	.308	.471	0-0	—	0	93	-2	-0.1
	Tor A	4	6	.400	12	11	0	0-0	54	70	33	6	1	26-1	25	5.00	92	.318	.393	1-0	.000	-0	113	-2	-0.4
	Year	4	6	.400	13	12	0	0-0	57	74	39	8	1	30-1	27	5.37	86	.318	.398	1-0	.000	-0	111	-4	-0.5
	Mil N	3	2	.600	8	8	1	0-0	52.1	49	18	8	0	21-0	35	2.58	165	.247	.317	20-1	.100	-1	83	9	0.6
Total	5	28	29	.491	93	73	4-1	0-3	456.1	531	265	54	10	200-5	274	4.79	98	.294	.365	24-2	.083	-1	101	-5	-0.5
DAVIS, DIXIE Frank Talmadge B 10.12.1890 Wilsons Mills, NC D 2.4.1944 Raleigh, NC BR/TR 5-11/155# d7.12 Mil 1918																									
1912	Cin N	0	1	.000	7	0	0	0	26.2	25	17	0	1	16	12	2.70	124	.258	.368	10-0	.200	-0		0	-0.1
1915	Chi A	0	0	—	2	0	0	0	3	2	0	0	1	2	2	0.00	—	.250	.455	0-0	—	0		1	0.1
1918	Phi N	0	2	.000	17	2	1	0	47	43	25	1	0	30	18	3.06	98	.247	.358	9-0	.000	-0*	101	-2	-0.2
1920	StL A	18	12	.600	38	31	22	0	269.1	250	117	10	7	149	85	3.17	123	.256	.359	94-7	.266	3	110	22	2.2
1921	StL A	16	16	.500	40	36	20-2	0	265.1	279	150	12	10	123	100	4.44	101	.281	.366	95-4	.211	-3	99	4	0.0
1922	StL A	11	6	.647	25	25	7-2	0	174.1	162	91	10	8	87	65	4.08	102	**.250**	.345	59-6	.136	-3	111	3	0.0
1923	StL A	4	6	.400	19	17	5-1	0	109.1	106	61	4	5	63	36	3.62	115	.259	.365	40-1	.250	0	77	3	0.2
1924	StL A	11	13	.458	29	24	11-5	0	160.1	159	84	9	6	72	45	4.10	110	.263	.347	46-7	.152	-2	85	8	0.7
1925	StL A	12	7	.632	35	22	9	1	180.1	192	121	10	6	106	58	4.59	102	.279	.380	64-5	.172	-4	108	-3	-0.6
1926	StL A	3	8	.273	27	7	2	1	83	93	56	7	1	40	39	4.66	92	.292	.372	24-0	.167	-0	76	-5	-0.6
Total	10	75	71	.514	239	164	77-10	2	1318.2	1311	722	63	45	688	460	3.97	107	.267	.362	441-30	.197	-10	99	31	1.7
DAVIS, GEORGE George Allen "Iron" B 3.9.1890 Lancaster, NY D 6.4.1961 Buffalo, NY BB/TR 5-10.5/175# d7.16																									
1912	NY A	1	4	.200	10	7	5	0	54	61	43	3	3	28	22	6.50	55	.293	.385	18-0	.111	-1	111	-12	-1.1
1913	Bos N	0	0	—	2	0	0	0	8	7	5	1	0	5	3	4.50	73	.241	.353	2-0	.000	-0		-1	-0.1
1914	Bos N	3	3	.500	9	6	4-1	0	55.2	42	25	1	3	26	26	3.40	81	.215	.317	18-0	.167	0	117	-3	-0.4
1915	Bos N	3	3	.500	15	9	4	0	73.1	85	45	2	4	19	26	3.80	68	.304	.356	23-1	.261	1	134	-12	-0.8
Total	4	7	10	.412	36	22	13-1	0	191	195	118	7	10	78	77	4.48	66	.274	.354	61-1	.180	-0	122	-28	-2.4
DAVIS, STORM George Earl B 12.26.1961 Dallas, TX BR/TR 6-4/207# d4.29																									
1982	Bal A	8	4	.667	29	8	1	0-1	100.2	96	40	8	0	28-4	67	3.49	116	.257	.304	0-0	—	0	121	7	0.7
1983	†Bal A	13	7	.650	34	29	6-1	0-0	200.1	180	90	14	2	64-4	125	3.59	110	.238	.298	0-0	—	0	122	8	0.6
1984	Bal A	14	9	.609	35	31	10-2	1-1	225	205	86	7	5	71-6	105	3.12	124	.247	.307	0-0	—	0	99	20	1.8
1985	Bal A	10	8	.556	31	28	8-1	0-0	175	172	92	11	1	70-5	93	4.53	89	.256	.325	0-0	—	0	122	-8	-0.7
1986	Bal A	9	12	.429	25	25	2	0-0	154	166	70	16	0	49-2	96	3.62	114	.275	.329	0-0	—	0	87	8	1.1
1987	SD N	2	7	.222	21	10	0	0-0	62.2	70	48	5	2	36-6	37	6.18	64	.280	.372	16-1	.063	-1	71	-16	-2.0
	Oak A	1	1	.500	5	5	0	0-0	30.1	28	13	3	0	11-0	28	3.26	127	.241	.305	0-0	—	0	141	3	0.1
1988	†Oak A	16	7	.696	33	33	1	0-0	201.2	211	86	16	1	91-2	127	3.70	102	.274	.349	0-0	—	0	128	4	0.3
1989	†Oak A	19	7	.731	31	31	1	0-0	169.1	187	91	19	3	68-1	91	4.36	85	.288	.354	0-0	—	0	138	-12	-1.7
1990	KC A	7	10	.412	21	20	0	0-0	112	129	66	9	0	35-1	62	4.74	81	.281	.330	0-0	—	0	110	-11	-1.5
1991	KC A	3	9	.250	51	9	1-1	2-1	114.1	140	69	11	1	46-9	53	4.96	83	.306	.367	0-0	—	0	81	-10	-1.0
1992	Bal A	7	3	.700	48	2	0	4-3	89.1	79	35	5	2	36-6	53	3.43	118	.244	.320	0-0	—	0	57	6	0.7
1993	Oak A	2	6	.250	19	8	0	0-0	62.2	68	45	5	2	33-2	37	6.18	66	.276	.364	0-0	—	0	93	-15	-1.6
	Det A	0	2	.000	24	0	0	4-1	35.1	25	12	4	1	15-4	36	3.06	141	.198	.287	0-0	—	0		6	0.4
	Year	2	8	.200	43	8	0	4-1	98	93	61	9	3	48-6	73	5.05	82	.250	.338	0-0	—	0	91	-8	-1.2
1994	Det A	2	4	.333	35	0	0	0-1	48	36	23	3	0	34-7	38	3.56	136	.207	.335	0-0	—	0		6	0.7
Total	13	113	96	.541	442	239	30-5	11-8	1780.2	1792	866	136	20	687-59	1048	4.02	99	.263	.330	16-1	.063	-1	111	-4	-2.1
DAVIS, JIM James Bennett B 9.15.1924 Red Bluff, CA D 11.30.1995 San Mateo, CA BB/TL 6/180# d4.18																									
1954	Chi N	11	7	.611	46	12	2	4	127.2	114	57	12	3	51	58	3.52	119	.247	.321	32-0	.063	-1	99	9	1.1
1955	Chi N	7	11	.389	42	16	0	3	133.2	122	79	16	2	58-5	62	4.44	92	.246	.323	37-3	.027	-4	63	-8	-1.4
1956	Chi N	5	7	.417	46	11	2-1	2	120.1	116	56	11	6	59-4	66	3.66	103	.256	.347	28-3	.179	-0	68	2	0.2
1957	StL N	0	1	.000	10	0	0	1	13.2	18	8	1	0	6-0	5	5.27	75	.340	.400	1-0	.000	-0		-2	-0.1
	NY N	1	0	1.000	10	0	0	0	11	13	9	2	0	5-1	6	6.55	60	.283	.353	1-0	1.000	0		-3	-0.2
	Year	1	1	.500	20	0	0	1	24.2	31	20	3	0	11-1	11	5.84	68	.313	.378	2-0	.500	0		-5	-0.3
Total	4	24	26	.480	154	39	4-1	10	406.1	383	209	42	11	179-10	197	4.01	100	.253	.333	99-6	.091	-5	76	-2	-0.4
DAVIS, JASON Jason Thomas B 5.8.1980 Chattanooga, TN BR/TR 6-6/195# d9.9																									
2002	Cle A	1	0	1.000	3	2	0	0-0	14.2	12	3	1	0	4-0	11	1.84	239	.218	.271	0-0	—	0	84	4	0.3
2003	Cle A	8	11	.421	27	27	1	0-0	165.1	172	101	25	8	47-4	85	4.68	94	.273	.329	2-1	.000	-0*	89	-6	-0.6
Total	2	9	11	.450	30	29	1	0-0	180	184	104	26	8	51-4	96	4.45	99	.268	.325	2-1	.000	-0	89	-2	-0.3
DAVIS, JOEL Joel Clark B 1.30.1965 Jacksonville, FL BL/TR 6-5/205# d8.11																									
1985	Chi A	3	3	.500	12	11	1	0-0	71.1	71	34	6	1	26-0	37	4.16	104	.256	.320	0-0	—	0	103	2	0.1
1986	Chi A	4	5	.444	19	19	1	0-0	105.1	115	64	9	1	51-0	54	4.70	92	.280	.359	0-0	—	0	87	-6	-0.4
1987	Chi A	1	5	.167	13	9	1	0-1	55	56	35	7	0	29-1	25	5.73	80	.264	.351	0-0	—	0	73	-5	-0.6
1988	Chi A	0	1	.000	5	2	0	0-0	16	21	12	4	0	5-0	10	6.75	59	.328	.371	0-0	—	0	69	-4	-0.2
Total	4	8	14	.364	49	41	3	0-1	247.2	263	145	26	2	111-1	126	4.91	89	.273	.347	0-0	—	0	88	-13	-1.1
DAVIS, DAISY John Henry Albert B 11.28.1858 Boston, MA D 11.5.1902 Lynn, MA TR 5-6.5/150# d5.6																									
1884	StL AA	10	12	.455	25	24	20-1	0	198.1	196	113	1	14	35	143	2.90	112	.249	.293	87	.172	-2	85	9	0.5
	Bos N	1	3	.250	4	4	3	0	31	50	36	2		8	13	7.84	37	.355	.389	16	.000	-3	87	-15	-1.5
1885	Bos N	5	6	.455	11	11	10-1	0	94.1	110	58	2		28	30	4.29	63	.280	.328	37	.189	-0	90	-11	-1.1
Total	2	16	21	.432	40	39	33-2	0	323.2	356	207	5	14	71	186	3.78	81	.269	.313	140	.157	-5	87	-17	-2.1
DAVIS, JOHN John Kirk B 1.5.1963 Chicago, IL BR/TR 6-7/215# d7.24																									
1987	KC A	5	2	.714	27	0	0	2-1	43.2	29	13	0	2	26-4	24	2.27	202	.195	.315	0-0	—	0		11	1.6
1988	Chi A	2	5	.286	34	1	0	1-3	63.2	77	58	5	4	50-10	37	6.64	60	.297	.413	0-0	—	0	46	-21	-2.1
1989	Chi A	0	1	.000	4	0	0	1-0	6	5	4	2	0	2-0	5	4.50	85	.217	.280	0-0	—	0		-1	-0.1
1990	SD N	0	1	.000	6	0	0	0-0	9.1	9	7	1	0	4-0	7	5.79	66	.257	.333	1-0	.000	-0		-2	-0.2
Total	4	7	9	.438	71	1	0	4-4	122.2	120	82	8	6	82-14	73	4.92	85	.258	.370	1-0	.000	-0	46	-13	-0.8
DAVIS, BUD John Wilbur "Country" B 12.7.1896 Merry Point, VA D 5.26.1967 Williamsburg, VA BL/TR 6/207# d4.19																									
1915	Phi A	0	2	.000	18	2	2	0	66.2	65	53	1	6	59	18	4.05	72	.273	.429	26-0	.308	2*	62	-13	-0.4
DAVIS, LANCE Johnny Lance B 9.1.1976 Winter Haven, FL BR/TL 6/170# d6.16																									
2001	Cin N	8	4	.667	20	20	1	0-0	106.1	124	60	12	1	34-0	53	4.74	96	.294	.348	33-4	.121	-1*	106	-1	-0.1

Year	Tm Lg	W	L	Pct	G	GS	CG-Sho	SV-BS	IP	H	R	HR	HB	BB-IB	SO	ERA	AERA	OAV	OOB	AB-SH	AVG	PB	Sup	APR	PW
DAVIS, KANE Kane Thomas B 6.25.1975 Ripley, WV BR/TR 6-3/194# d6.12																									
2000	Cle A	0	3	.000	5	2	0	0-0	11	20	21	3	1	8-0	2	14.73	34	.385	.475	1-0	.000	-0	57	-13	-1.9
	Mil N	0	0	—	3	0	0	0-0	4	7	3	1	1	5-0	2	6.75	68	.389	.542	0-0	—	0		-1	0.0
2001	Col N	2	4	.333	57	0	0	0-5	68.1	66	36	11	1	32-4	47	4.35	123	.252	.331	5-0	.000	-1		6	0.4
2002	NY N	1	1	.500	16	0	0	0-0	14	15	11	2	1	11-2	24	7.07	56	.273	.397	0-0	—	0		-4	-0.6
Total	3	3	8	.273	81	2	0	0-5	97.1	108	71	17	4	56-6	75	6.01	84	.279	.372	6-0	.000	-1	57	-12	-2.1
DAVIS, MARK Mark William B 10.19.1960 Livermore, CA BL/TL 6-4/205# d9.12 C1																									
1980	Phi N	0	0	—	2	1	0	0-0	7	4	2	0	0	5-0	5	2.57	148	.160	.300	2-0	.500	0	165	1	0.1
1981	Phi N	1	4	.200	9	9	0	0-0	43	49	37	7	0	24-0	29	7.74	47	.299	.380	11-1	.091	-0	92	-17	-1.8
1983	SF N	6	4	.600	20	20	2-2	0-0	111	93	51	14	3	50-4	83	3.49	102	.227	.313	30-9	.133	0	125	0	0.1
1984	SF N	5	17	.227	46	27	1	0-2	174.2	201	113	25	5	54-12	124	5.36	66	.293	.344	46-6	.130	0	101	-34	-3.9
1985	SF N	5	12	.294	77	1	0	7-9	114.1	89	49	13	3	41-7	131	3.54	97	.219	.294	12-4	.250	1	51	0	0.1
1986	SF N	5	7	.417	67	2	0	4-3	84.1	63	33	6	1	34-7	90	2.99	118	.212	.291	8-0	.125	0	51	5	0.7
1987	SF N	4	5	.444	20	11	1	0-1	70.2	72	38	9	4	28-1	51	4.71	82	.273	.349	23-2	.217	2*	120	-6	-0.5
	SD N	5	3	.625	43	0	0	2-1	62.1	51	26	5	2	31-7	47	3.18	125	.224	.322	7-0	.286	0		5	0.7
	Year	9	8	.529	63	11	1	2-2	133	123	69	14	6	59-8	98	3.99	98	.250	.336	30-2	.233	2	118	0	0.2
1988	SD N★	5	10	.333	62	0	0	28-6	98.1	70	24	2	0	42-11	102	2.01	169	.199	.284	10-1	.200	1		16	3.6
1989	SD N★	4	3	.571	70	0	0	**44-4**	92.2	66	21	6	2	31-1	92	1.85	190	.200	.270	13-0	.000	-1		17	2.7
1990	KC A	2	7	.222	53	3	0	6-4	68.2	71	43	9	4	52-3	73	5.11	75	.259	.383	0-0	—	0	119	-9	-1.2
1991	KC A	6	3	.667	29	5	0	1-1	62.2	55	36	6	1	39-0	47	4.45	93	.240	.347	0-0	—	0	93	-3	-0.4
1992	KC A	1	3	.250	13	6	0	0-0	36.1	42	31	6	0	28-0	19	7.18	57	.294	.400	0-0	—	0	112	-12	-1.1
	Atl N	1	0	1.000	14	0	0	0-0	16.2	22	13	3	1	13-2	15	7.02	52	.314	.424	1-0	.000	-0		-5	-0.3
1993	Phi N	1	2	.333	25	0	0	0-1	31.1	35	22	4	1	24-1	28	5.17	77	.273	.392	3-0	.333	0		-5	-0.4
	SD N	0	3	.000	35	0	0	4-2	38.1	44	15	6	0	20-6	42	3.52	118	.295	.376	1-1	.000	-0		3	0.3
	Year	1	5	.167	60	0	0	4-3	69.2	79	42	10	1	44-7	70	4.26	95	.285	.384	4-1	.250	0		-2	-0.1
1994	SD N	0	1	.000	20	0	0	0-0	16.1	20	18	4	0	13-1	15	8.82	47	.299	.412	0-0	—	0		-9	-0.5
1997	Mil A	0	0	—	19	0	0	0-1	16.1	21	10	4	1	5-0	14	5.51	84	.323	.380	0-0	—	0		-1	0.0
Total	15	51	84	.378	624	85	4-2	96-35	1145	1068	582	129	28	534-63	1007	4.17	88	.249	.333	167-24	.156	5	108	-54	-1.8
DAVIS, BOB Robert Edward B 9.11.1933 New York, NY D 12.22.2001 New York, NY BR/TR 6/170# d7.26																									
1958	KC A	0	4	.000	8	4	0	0	31	45	28	5	2	12-0	22	7.84	50	.346	.410	6-1	.167	-0	75	-12	-1.3
1960	KC A	0	0	—	21	0	0	1	32	31	15	1	1	22-1	28	3.66	109	.263	.383	4-0	.250	0		1	0.1
Total	2	0	4	.000	29	4	0	1	63	76	43	6	3	34-1	50	5.71	69	.306	.396	10-1	.200	-0	75	-11	-1.2
DAVIS, RON Ronald Gene B 8.6.1955 Houston, TX BR/TR 6-4/207# d7.29																									
1978	NY A	0	0	—	4	0	0	0-0	2.1	3	4	0	0	3-0	0	11.57	31	.333	.500	0-0	—	0		-2	-0.1
1979	NY A	14	2	.875	44	0	0	9-10	85.1	84	29	5	1	28-9	43	2.85	143	.262	.320	1-0	.000	-0		12	2.4
1980	†NY A	9	3	.750	53	0	0	7-2	131	121	50	9	5	32-3	65	2.95	133	.246	.296	1-0	.000	-0		14	1.3
1981	†NY A★	4	5	.444	43	0	0	6-2	73	47	22	6	0	25-3	83	2.71	132	.186	.256	0-0	—	0		8	1.1
1982	Min A	3	9	.250	63	0	0	22-5	106	106	53	16	1	47-12	89	4.42	96	.261	.338	0-0	—	0		0	-0.1
1983	Min A	5	8	.385	66	0	0	30-3	89	89	34	6	3	33-3	84	3.34	128	.266	.332	0-0	—	0		10	1.9
1984	Min A	7	11	.389	64	0	0	29-14	83	79	44	11	2	41-9	74	4.55	92	.253	.338	0-0	—	0		-2	-0.5
1985	Min A	2	6	.250	57	0	0	25-3	64.2	55	28	7	4	35-6	72	3.48	127	.230	.333	0-0	—	0		6	1.1
1986	Min A	2	6	.250	36	0	0	2-4	38.2	55	42	7	4	29-8	30	9.08	48	.340	.449	0-0	—	0		-19	-3.5
	Chi N	0	2	.000	17	0	0	0-0	20	31	18	3	0	3-0	10	7.65	53	.356	.374	2-0	.000	-0		-7	-0.7
1987	Chi N	0	0	—	21	0	0	0-0	32.1	43	23	8	0	12-1	31	5.85	73	.328	.382	0-0	—	0		-5	-0.3
	LA N	0	0	—	4	0	0	0-0	4	7	4	0	1	6-2	1	6.75	59	.412	.560	0-0	—	0		-2	-0.1
	Year	0	0	—	25	0	0	0-0	36.1	50	30	8	1	18-3	32	5.94	71	.338	.408	0-0	—	0		-7	-0.4
1988	SF N	1	1	.500	9	0	0	0-0	17.1	15	10	4	1	6-0	15	4.67	70	.234	.310	2-0	.000	-0		-3	-0.3
Total	11	47	53	.470	481	0	0	130-43	746.2	735	361	82	22	300-56	597	4.05	101	.260	.332	6-0	.000	-1		10	2.2
DAVIS, PEACHES Roy Thomas B 5.31.1905 Glen Rose, TX D 4.28.1995 Duncan, OK BL/TR 6-3.5/190# d7.11																									
1936	Cin N	8	8	.500	26	15	5	5	125.2	139	62	7	2	36	32	3.58	107	.280	.331	43-1	.163	-1	101	2	0.2
1937	Cin N	11	13	.458	42	24	11-1	3	218	252	105	5	2	51	59	3.59	104	.295	.337	78-3	.128	-4	105	3	-0.3
1938	Cin N	7	12	.368	29	19	11-1	1	167.2	193	86	9	1	40	28	3.97	92	.290	.331	61-3	.246	1	98	-7	-0.7
1939	Cin N	1	0	1.000	20	0	0	2	30.2	43	24	5	1	11	4	6.46	59	.341	.399	3-0	.333	0		-8	-0.4
Total	4	27	33	.450	117	58	27-2	11	542	627	277	26	6	138	123	3.87	96	.293	.337	185-7	.178	-4	101	-10	-1.2
DAVIS, STEVE Steven Kennon B 8.4.1960 San Antonio, TX BL/TL 6-1/195# d8.25																									
1985	Tor A	2	1	.667	10	5	0	0-0	28	23	14	5	0	13-0	22	3.54	119	.223	.308	0-0	—	0	134	1	0.1
1986	Tor A	0	0	—	3	0	0	0-0	3.2	8	7	2	0	5-1	5	17.18	25	.471	.591	0-0	—	0		-5	-0.2
1989	Cle A	1	1	.500	12	2	0	0-0	25.2	34	24	2	0	14-1	12	8.06	49	.318	.397	0-0	—	0	103	-11	-0.8
Total	3	3	2	.600	25	7	0	0-0	57.1	65	45	9	0	32-2	39	6.44	64	.286	.373	0-0	—	0	126	-15	-0.9
DAVIS, TIM Timothy Howard B 7.14.1970 Marianna, FL BL/TL 5-11/165# d4.4																									
1994	Sea A	2	2	.500	42	1	0	2-2	49.1	57	25	4	1	25-5	28	4.01	122	.295	.374	0-0	—	0	207	5	0.4
1995	Sea A	2	1	.667	5	5	0	0-0	24	30	21	2	0	18-2	19	6.38	74	.306	.410	0-0	—	0	141	-5	-0.5
1996	Sea A	2	2	.500	40	0	0	0-0	42.2	43	21	4	2	17-1	34	4.01	124	.259	.333	0-0	—	0		4	0.3
1997	Sea A	0	0	—	2	0	0	0-0	6.2	6	5	1	1	4-0	10	6.75	67	.231	.355	0-0	—	0		-2	-0.1
Total	4	6	5	.545	89	6	0	2-2	122.2	136	72	11	4	64-8	91	4.62	105	.282	.367	0-0	—	0	149	2	0.1
DAVIS, WILEY Wiley Anderson B 8.1.1875 Seymour, TN D 9.22.1942 Detroit, MI BR/TR 5-10/165# d4.18																									
1896	Cin N	1	1	.500	2	0	0	0	4.1	8	4	0	0	2	1	8.31	56	.400	.455	1-0	.000	0		-1	-0.2
DAVIS, WOODY Woodrow Wilson "Babe" B 4.25.1913 Nicholls, GA BL/TR 6-1/200# d5.2																									
1938	Det A	0	0	—	2	0	0	0	6	3	1	0	0	4	1	1.50	333	.158	.304	1-0	.000	-0		2	0.1
DAVISON, MIKE Michael Lynn B 8.4.1945 Galesburg, IL BL/TL 6-1/170# d10.1																									
1969	SF N	0	0	—	1	0	0	0-0	2	2	1	0	0	0-0	2	4.50	78	.250	.250	0-0	—	0		0	0.0
1970	SF N	3	5	.375	31	0	0	1-2	36	46	29	4	0	22-4	21	6.50	61	.324	.410	1-0	.000	0		-10	-1.9
Total	2	3	5	.375	32	0	0	1-2	38	48	30	4	0	22-4	23	6.39	62	.320	.402	1-0	.000	0		-10	-1.9
DAVISON, SCOTT Scotty Ray B 10.16.1970 Inglewood, CA BR/TR 6/190# d9.4																									
1995	Sea A	0	0	—	3	0	0	0-0	4.1	7	3	1	0	1-0	3	6.23	76	.350	.381	0-0	—	0		-1	0.0
1996	Sea A	0	0	—	5	0	0	0-0	9	11	9	6	0	3-0	9	9.00	55	.297	.350	0-0	—	0		-4	-0.2
Total	2	0	0	—	8	0	0	0-0	13.1	18	12	7	0	4-0	12	8.10	60	.316	.361	0-0	—	0		-5	-0.2
DAWLEY, JOEY Joseph Thomas B 9.19.1971 Riverside, CA BR/TR 6-4/205# d9.29																									
2002	Atl N	0	0	—	1	0	0	0-0	0.1	0	0	0	0	0-0	1	0.00	—	.000	.000	0-0	—	0		0	0.0
2003	Atl N	0	0	—	5	0	0	0-0	7	15	14	3	1	3-0	8	18.00	23	.405	.463	1-0	.000	-0		-10	-0.5
Total	2	0	0	—	6	0	0	0-0	7.1	15	14	3	1	3-0	9	17.18	25	.395	.452	1-0	.000	-0		-10	-0.5
DAWLEY, BILL William Chester B 2.6.1958 Norwich, CT BR/TR 6-4/240# d4.15																									
1983	Hou N★	6	6	.500	48	0	0	14-2	79.2	51	26	9	1	22-4	60	2.82	121	.185	.247	9-0	.222	0		7	1.2
1984	Hou N	11	4	.733	60	0	0	5-5	98	82	24	5	0	35-9	47	1.93	172	.234	.298	9-2	.333	2		17	2.8
1985	Hou N	5	3	.625	49	0	0	2-1	81	76	35	7	0	37-7	48	3.56	98	.259	.337	10-0	.200	0		0	0.1
1986	Chi A	0	7	.000	46	0	0	2-2	97.2	91	38	10	1	28-3	66	3.32	130	.247	.300	2-0	.000	-0		11	0.7
1987	StL N	5	8	.385	60	0	0	2-5	96.2	93	51	15	1	38-11	65	4.47	93	.259	.330	12-1	.167	0		-3	-0.3
1988	Phi N	0	2	.000	8	0	0	0-0	8.2	16	13	3	0	4-1	3	13.50	26	.381	.426	0-0	—	0		-9	-1.7
1989	Oak A	0	0	—	4	0	0	0-0	9	11	5	0	1	2-0	3	4.00	92	.297	.341	0-0	—	0		-1	0.0
Total	7	27	30	.474	275	0	0	25-15	470.2	420	192	49	4	166-35	292	3.42	109	.243	.308	42-3	.214	3		22	2.8
DAWSON, JOE Ralph Fenton B 3.9.1897 Bow, WA D 1.4.1978 Longview, TX BR/TR 5-11/182# d7.4																									
1924	Cle A	1	2	.333	4	4	0	0	20.1	24	17	0	1	21	7	6.64	64	.300	.451	7-1	.286	0	64	-5	-0.5

Year	Tm Lg	W	L	Pct	G	GS	CG-Sho	SV-BS	IP	H	R	HR	HB	BB-IB	SO	ERA	AERA	OAV	OOB	AB-SH	AVG	PB	Sup	APR	PW
1927	†Pit N	3	7	.300	20	7	4	0	80.2	80	47	2	0	32	17	4.46	92	.268	.338	25-1	.200	-1	80	-3	-0.5
1928	Pit N	7	7	.500	31	7	1	3	128.2	116	54	6	1	56	36	3.29	124	.242	.322	43-1	.279	3	51	12	1.4
1929	Pit N	0	1	.000	4	0	0	0	8.2	13	9	2	0	3	2	8.31	57	.342	.390	2-0	.500	1		-3	-0.2
Total	4	11	17	.393	59	18	5	3	238.1	233	127	10	2	112	62	4.15	99	.260	.343	77-3	.260	3	65	1	0.2
DAWSON, REX Rexford Paul B 2.10.1889 Skagit Co., WA D 10.20.1958 Indianapolis, IN BL/TR 6/185# d10.3																									
1913	Was A	0	0	—	1	0	0	0	1	1	0	0	0	0	1	0.00	—	.250	.250	0-0	—	0		0	0.0
DAY, PEA RIDGE Clyde Henry B 8.26.1899 Pea Ridge, AR D 3.21.1934 Kansas City, MO BR/TR 6/190# d9.19																									
1924	StL N	1	1	.500	3	3	1	0	17.2	22	11	0	0	6	3	4.58	82	.306	.359	8-0	.125	-1	105	-2	-0.3
1925	StL N	2	4	.333	17	4	1	1	40	53	31	5	3	7	13	6.30	69	.325	.364	13-0	.154	-1	142	-8	-1.1
1926	Cin N	0	0	—	4	0	0	0	7.1	13	13	1	0	2	2	7.36	50	.406	.441	2-0	.000	-0		-6	-0.3
1931	Bro N	2	2	.500	22	2	1	1	57.1	75	38	5	0	13	30	4.55	84	.315	.351	18-0	.222	0	56	-7	-0.5
Total	4	5	7	.417	46	9	3	2	122.1	163	93	11	3	28	48	5.30	75	.323	.362	41-0	.171	-2	114	-23	-2.2
DAY, ZACH Stephen Zachary B 6.15.1978 Cincinnati, OH BR/TR 6-4/185# d6.15																									
2002	Mon N	4	1	.800	19	2	0	1-1	37.1	28	18	3	1	15-2	25	3.62	124	.207	.289	6-2	.167	0	114	3	0.4
2003	Mon N	9	8	.529	23	23	1-1	0-0	131.1	132	64	8	10	59-3	61	4.18	112	.262	.348	47-1	.043	-4	91	8	0.6
Total	2	13	9	.591	42	25	1-1	1-1	168.2	160	82	11	11	74-5	86	4.06	114	.250	.336	53-3	.057	-4	94	11	1.0
DAY, BILL William M. B 7.28.1867 Wilmington, DE D 8.16.1923 Wilmington, DE TR 5-8/150# d8.20																									
1889	Phi N	0	3	.000	4	3	2	0	19	16	24	0	0	23	20	5.21	83	.222	.411	10	.000	-2	77	-4	-0.6
1890	Phi N	1	1	.500	4	2	2	0	23.2	26	16	0	0	12	9	3.04	120	.271	.352	10	.100	-1	78	1	-0.1
	Pit N	0	6	.000	6	6	6	0	50	66	50	1	1	24	10	5.22	63	.308	.381	23	.043	-4	73	-13	-1.4
	Year	1	7	.125	10	8	8	0	73.2	92	54	1	1	36	19	4.52	76	.297	.372	33	.061	-5	74	-13	-1.5
Total	2	1	10	.091	14	11	10	0	92.2	108	90	1	1	59	39	4.66	77	.283	.380	43	.047	-6	76	-16	-2.1
DAYLEY, KEN Kenneth Grant B 2.25.1959 Jerome, ID BL/TL 6/175# d5.13																									
1982	Atl N	5	6	.455	20	11	0	0-0	71.1	79	39	9	0	25-2	34	4.54	82	.286	.340	20-1	.250	1	114	-5	-0.8
1983	Atl N	5	8	.385	24	16	0	0-0	104.2	100	59	12	2	39-2	70	4.30	90	.257	.326	32-5	.219	1*	115	-6	-0.7
1984	Atl N	0	3	.000	4	4	0	0-0	18.2	28	18	5	1	6-1	10	5.30	73	.341	.393	4-0	.500	1*	97	-5	-0.6
	StL N	0	2	.000	3	2	0	0-0	5	16	10	1	0	5-0	0	18.00	19	.615	.677	0-1	—	0	76	-8	-1.3
	Year	0	5	.000	7	6	0	0-0	23.2	44	13	6	1	11-1	10	7.99	47	.407	.467	4-1	.500	1	90	-12	-1.9
1985	†StL N	4	4	.500	57	0	0	11-5	65.1	65	24	2	0	18-9	62	2.76	129	.263	.311	5-0	.400	1		5	0.9
1986	StL N	0	3	.000	31	0	0	5-2	38.2	42	19	1	1	11-3	33	3.26	112	.275	.325	5-0	.200	0*		0	0.1
1987	†StL N	9	5	.643	53	0	0	4-6	61	52	21	2	2	33-8	63	2.66	157	.234	.337	0-0	—	0		9	1.9
1988	StL N	2	7	.222	54	0	0	5-3	55.1	48	20	2	1	19-7	38	2.77	126	.239	.306	4-0	.000	-0		4	0.6
1989	StL N	4	3	.571	71	0	0	12-5	75.1	63	26	3	0	30-10	40	2.87	127	.228	.303	5-0	.000	-1		6	0.6
1990	StL N	4	4	.500	58	0	0	2-5	73.1	63	32	5	0	30-7	51	3.56	107	.233	.305	6-0	.000	-1		2	0.2
1991	Tor A	0	0	—	8	0	0	0-0	4.1	7	3	0	1	5-0	3	6.23	68	.368	.500	0-0	—	0		-1	0.0
1993	Tor A	0	0	—	2	0	0	0-0	0.2	1	2	0	0	4-0	2	0.00	—	.333	.714	0-0	—	0		-1	0.0
Total	11	33	45	.423	385	33	0	39-26	573.2	564	273	42	8	225-49	406	3.64	103	.261	.330	81-7	.210	3	113	0	0.9
DEAGLE, REN Lorenzo Burroughs B 6.26.1858 New York, NY D 12.24.1936 Kansas City, MO BR/TR 5-9/190# d5.17																									
1883	Cin AA	10	8	.556	18	18	17-1	0	148	136	78	0		34	48	2.31	141	.229	.270	70	.129	-5*	91	14	0.9
1884	Cin AA	3	1	.750	4	4	4-1	0	34	38	26	0	1	9	12	5.03	66	.314	.366	13	.000	-2	86	-6	-0.7
	Lou AA	4	6	.400	12	12	8	0	87.1	81	43	0	7	13	23	2.58	120	.241	.284	45	.133	-3	83	6	0.3
	Year	7	7	.500	16	16	12-1	0	121.1	119	47	0	8	22	35	3.26	97	.260	.306	58	.103	-5	84	1	-0.4
Total	2	17	15	.531	34	34	29-2	0	269.1	255	147	0	8	56	83	2.74	117	.242	.286	128	.117	-9	87	14	0.5
DEAGO, ROGER Roger I. (Villarreal) B 6.21.1977 Monagrillo, Panama BR/TL 5-10/180# d5.10																									
2003	SD N	0	1	.000	2	2	0	0-0	10.1	11	9	0	0	8-0	10	7.84	50	.282	.396	4-0	.000	-0	95	-5	-0.4
DEAL, COT Ellis Fergason B 1.23.1923 Arapaho, OK BB/TR 5-10.5/185# d9.11 C15																									
1947	Bos A	0	1	.000	5	2	0	0	12.2	20	13	0	0	7	6	9.24	42	.364	.435	4-0	.500	1*	125	-6	-0.4
1948	Bos A	1	0	1.000	4	0	0	0	4	3	0	0	0	3	2	0.00	—	.200	.333	0-0	—	0		2	0.4
1950	StL N	0	0	—	3	0	0	0	1	3	5	0	0	2	1	18.00	24	.500	.625	0-0	—	0		-3	-0.1
1954	StL N	2	3	.400	33	0	0	1	71.2	85	56	14	4	36	25	6.28	65	.297	.379	20-0	.100	0		-17	-1.0
Total	4	3	4	.429	45	2	0	1	89.1	111	74	14	4	48	34	6.55	63	.307	.390	24-0	.167	1	125	-24	-1.1
DEAN, CHUBBY Alfred Lovell B 8.24.1915 Mt.Airy, NC D 12.21.1970 Riverside, NJ BL/TL 5-11/181# d4.14.1936 Mil 1943-46 ▲																									
1937	Phi A	1	0	1.000	2	1	0	0	9	7	4	0	0	6	4	4.00	118	.219	.342	309-7	.262	0*	148	1	0.1
1938	Phi A	2	1	.667	6	1	0	0	23	22	10	3	0	15	3	3.52	137	.250	.359	20-0	.300	2*	91	4	0.6
1939	Phi A	5	8	.385	54	1	0	7	116.2	132	93	8	0	80	39	5.25	90	.289	.395	77-3	.351	8*	37	-12	-0.4
1940	Phi A	6	13	.316	30	19	8-1	1	159.1	220	136	21	0	63	38	6.61	67	.324	.381	90-2	.289	4*	88	-36	-2.7
1941	Phi A	2	4	.333	18	7	2	0	75.2	90	53	9	0	35	22	6.19	68	.294	.367	37-1	.243	2*	71	-14	-0.7
	Cle A	1	4	.200	8	8	2	0	53.1	57	31	3	0	24	14	4.39	90	.282	.358	25-1	.160	0*	77	-4	-0.2
	Year	3	8	.273	26	15	4	0	129	147	35	12	0	59	36	5.44	75	.289	.363	62-2	.210	2	73	-16	-0.9
1942	Cle A	8	11	.421	27	22	8	1	172.2	170	83	7	0	66	46	3.81	91	.261	.329	101-0	.267	8*	87	-6	0.1
1943	Cle A	5	5	.500	17	9	3	0	76	83	46	1	1	34	29	4.50	69	.281	.358	46-1	.196	1*	157	-13	-1.5
Total	7	30	46	.395	162	68	23-1	9	685.2	781	456	52	1	323	195	5.08	79	.288	.364	705-15	.268	25	89	-80	-4.7
DEAN, DORY Charles Wilson B 11.6.1852 Cincinnati, OH D 5.4.1935 Nashville, TN BR/TR d6.22																									
1876	Cin N	4	26	.133	30	30	26	0	262.2	397	268	1		24	22	3.73	59	.322	.335	138	.261	1*	70	-48	-3.8
DEAN, HARRY James Harry B 5.12.1915 Rockmart, GA D 6.1.1960 Rockmart, GA BR/TR 6-4/185# d4.16																									
1941	Was A	0	0	—	2	0	0	0	2	2	3	0	1	3	0	4.50	90	.250	.500	0-0	—	0		-1	-0.1
DEAN, DIZZY Jay Hanna B 1.16.1910 Lucas, AR D 7.17.1974 Reno, NV BR/TR 6-2/182# d9.28 C1 HF1953 b-Paul																									
1930	StL N	1	0	1.000	1	1	1	0	9	3	1	0	0	3	5	1.00	502	.103	.188	3-0	.333	0	52	4	0.5
1932	StL N	18	15	.545	46	33	16-**4**	2	**286**	280	122	14	5	102	**191**	3.30	119	.260	.327	97-8	.258	5*	91	20	2.5
1933	StL N	20	18	.526	**48**	34	**26**-3	4	293	279	113	11	5	64	**199**	3.04	114	.250	.293	105-3	.181	1*	107	15	1.7
1934	†StL N★	**30**	7	**.811**	50	33	24-**7**	7	311.2	288	110	14	6	75	**195**	2.66	159	.241	.289	118-7	.246	4*	119	51	**6.1**
1935	StL N★	**28**	12	.700	50	**36**	**29**-3	5	**325.1**	324	126	16	4	77	**190**	3.04	135	.256	.300	128-4	.234	4*	124	38	**4.5**
1936	StL N★	24	13	.649	**51**	34	**28**-2	**11**	**315**	310	128	21	3	53	195	3.17	124	.253	.285	121-3	.223	1	118	27	3.0
1937	StL N★	13	10	.565	27	25	17-4	1	197.1	200	76	9	2	33	120	2.69	148	.259	.291	66-9	.227	2	100	25	2.8
1938	†Chi N	7	1	.875	13	10	3-1	0	74.2	63	20	2	1	8	22	1.81	212	.226	.250	26-1	.192	-0	113	15	1.5
1939	Chi N	6	4	.600	19	13	7-2	0	96.1	98	40	4	1	17	27	3.36	117	.261	.294	34-2	.147	-1	119	7	0.5
1940	Chi N	3	3	.500	10	9	3	0	54	68	35	4	0	20	18	5.17	73	.306	.364	18-2	.222	0	93	-8	-0.8
1941	Chi N	0	0	—	1	1	0	0	1	3	3	0	0	0	1	18.00	19	.429	.429	0-0	—	0	193	-2	-0.1
1947	StL A	0	0	—	1	1	0	0	4	3	0	0	0	1	0	0.00	—	.231	.286	1-0	1.000	0	46	2	0.1
Total	12	150	83	.644	317	230	154-26	30	1967.1	1919	774	95	27	453	1163	3.02	130	.253	.298	717-39	.225	15	110	194	22.3
DEAN, PAUL Paul Dee "Daffy" B 8.14.1913 Lucas, AR D 3.17.1981 Springdale, AR BR/TR 6/175# d4.18 b-Dizzy																									
1934	†StL N	19	11	.633	39	26	16-5	2	233.1	225	96	19	5	52	150	3.43	123	.248	.292	83-3	.241	1	101	23	2.5
1935	StL N	19	12	.613	46	33	19-2	5	269.2	261	109	16	9	55	143	3.37	122	.249	.292	90-4	.133	-5	102	25	1.8
1936	StL N	5	5	.500	17	14	5	1	92	113	57	3	1	20	28	4.60	86	.300	.337	34-3	.059	-4	105	-8	-1.3
1937	StL N	0	0	—	1	0	0	0	0	1	3	0	0	2	0	∞	—	1.000	1.000	0-0	—	0		-3	-0.2
1938	StL N	3	1	.750	5	4	2-1	0	31	37	12	3	0	5	14	2.61	151	.298	.326	11-0	.182	-0	96	4	0.4
1939	StL N	0	1	.000	16	2	0	0	43	54	30	4	1	10	16	6.07	68	.310	.351	9-1	.111	-1	74	-8	-0.5
1940	NY N	4	4	.500	27	7	2	0	99.1	110	50	8	0	29	32	3.90	100	.281	.330	26-5	.115	-2	90	0	-0.3
1941	NY N	0	0	—	5	0	0	0	5.2	8	2	0	0	3	3	3.18	116	.320	.393	0-0	—	0		0	0.0
1943	StL A	0	0	—	3	1	0	0	13.1	16	5	0	1	3	1	3.38	99	.296	.345	3-0	.000	-0	152	0	0.0
Total	9	50	34	.595	159	87	44-8	8	787.1	825	364	53	17	179	387	3.75	109	.266	.309	256-16	.156	-10	101	33	2.4

Year	Tm Lg	W	L	Pct	G	GS	CG-Sho	SV-BS	IP	H	R	HR	HB	BB-IB	SO	ERA	AERA	OAV	OOB	AB-SH	AVG	PB	Sup	APR	PW
DEAN, WAYLAND Wayland Ogden B 6.20.1902 Richwood, WV D 4.10.1930 Huntington, WV BB/TR 6-1/178# d4.17																									
1924	†NY N	6	12	.333	26	20	6	0	125.2	139	80	9	5	45	39	5.01	73	.280	.346	40-1	.200	1	106	-19	-2.2
1925	NY N	10	7	.588	33	14	6-1	1	151.1	169	98	13	4	50	53	4.64	87	.282	.342	51-0	.235	3	85	-13	-1.0
1926	Phi N	8	16	.333	33	26	15-1	0	203.2	245	136	9	3	89	52	4.91	84	.307	.379	102-3	.265	5*	84	-17	-1.3
1927	Phi N	0	1	.000	2	0	0	0	3	6	4	0	0	2	1	12.00	34	.500	.571	3-0	.667	1*		-2	-0.3
	Chi N	0	0	—	2	0	0	0	2	0	0	0	1	2	2	0.00	—	.000	.429	0-0	—	0		1	0.1
	Year	0	1	.000	4	0	0	0	5	6	8	0	1	4	3	7.20	56	.375	.524	3-0	.667	1		-1	-0.2
Total	4	24	36	.400	96	60	27-2	1	485.2	559	318	31	13	188	147	4.87	82	.293	.360	196-4	.250	10	90	-50	-4.7
DeBARR, DENNIS Dennis Lee B 1.16.1953 Cheyenne, WY BL/TL 6-2/190# d5.14																									
1977	Tor A	0	1	.000	14	0	0	0-1	21.1	29	14	1	0	8-0	10	5.91	71	.337	.385	0-0	—	0		-3	-0.2
DeBERRY, JOE Joseph Gaddy B 11.29.1896 Mt.Gilead, NC D 10.9.1944 Southern Pines, NC BL/TR 6-1/175# d8.24																									
1920	StL A	2	4	.333	10	7	3-1	0	54.2	65	35	2	2	20	12	4.94	79	.307	.372	18-2	.167	-1	87	-5	-0.5
1921	StL A	0	1	.000	10	1	0	0	12.1	15	9	0	0	10	1	6.57	68	.300	.417	2-0	.000	-0	75	-2	-0.2
Total	2	2	5	.286	20	8	3-1	0	67	80	44	2	2	30	13	5.24	77	.305	.381	20-2	.150	-1	85	-7	-0.7
DeBUSSCHERE, DAVE David Albert B 10.16.1940 Detroit, MI D 5.14.2003 New York, NY BR/TR 6-6/225# d4.22 Mil 1964																									
1962	Chi A	0	0	—	12	0	0	0	18	5	7	1	1	23-1	8	2.00	195	.089	.358	0-0	—	0		3	0.1
1963	Chi A	3	4	.429	24	10	1-1	0	84.1	80	35	9	4	34-1	53	3.09	113	.249	.327	22-2	.045	-2	89	3	0.1
Total	2	3	4	.429	36	10	1-1	0	102.1	85	42	10	5	57-2	61	2.90	123	.225	.333	22-2	.045	-2	89	6	0.2
DECATUR, ART Arthur Rue B 1.14.1894 Cleveland, OH D 4.25.1966 Talladega, AL BR/TR 6-1/190# d4.15																									
1922	Bro N	3	4	.429	29	3	1	1	87.2	87	31	3	1	29	31	2.77	147	.265	.327	25-1	.080	-2	67	13	0.7
1923	Bro N	3	3	.500	36	5	2	3	97.2	101	44	3	2	32	25	2.58	150	.264	.325	21-1	.000	-3	64	**11**	0.3
1924	Bro N	10	9	.526	31	10	3	1	126.1	156	74	12	4	27	38	4.13	91	.308	.348	44-0	.114	-4	68	-7	-1.4
1925	Bro N	0	0	—	1	0	0	0	1	3	2	0	0	0	0	18.00	23	.600	.600	0-0	—	0		-1	-0.1
	Phi N	4	13	.235	25	15	4	2	128	170	87	13	2	35	31	5.27	91	.316	.360	41-4	.049	-5	71	-4	-1.0
	Year	4	13	.235	26	15	4	2	129	173	91	13	2	35	31	5.37	89	.319	.362	41-4	.049	-5	71	-5	-1.1
1926	Phi N	0	0	—	2	1	0	0	3	6	3	0	0	2	0	6.00	69	.375	.444	1-0	.000	-0	40	-1	-0.1
1927	Phi N	3	5	.375	29	3	0	0	94.2	130	78	11	4	20	27	7.42	56	.334	.373	27-3	.222	0	48	-29	-2.2
Total	6	23	34	.404	153	37	10	7	538.1	653	319	42	13	145	152	4.51	92	.302	.349	159-9	.094	-14	68	-18	-3.8
DECKER, MARTY Dee Martin B 6.7.1957 Upland, CA BR/TR 5-10/168# d9.20																									
1983	SD N	0	0	—	4	0	0	0-0	8.2	5	2	1	1	3-0	9	2.08	168	.167	.265	0-0	—	0		2	0.1
DECKER, JOE George Henry B 6.16.1947 Storm Lake, IA D 3.2.2003 Fraser, MI BR/TR 6/180# d9.18																									
1969	Chi N	1	0	1.000	4	1	0	0-0	12.1	10	4	0	0	6-0	13	2.92	138	.222	.314	2-0	.000	-0	66	2	0.1
1970	Chi N	2	7	.222	24	17	1	0-1	108.2	108	64	12	4	56-3	79	4.64	97	.263	.354	34-2	.176	1	76	-2	-0.1
1971	Chi N	3	2	.600	21	4	0	0-0	45.2	62	24	2	0	25-3	37	4.73	83	.343	.418	8-1	.250	1*	62	-2	-0.1
1972	Chi N	1	0	1.000	5	1	0	0-0	12.2	9	3	1	0	4-0	7	2.13	179	.188	.250	2-3	.000	-0	348	2	0.1
1973	Min A	10	10	.500	29	24	6-3	0-0	170.1	167	87	12	4	88-0	109	4.17	95	.260	.350	0-0	—	0	101	-3	-0.3
1974	Min A	16	14	.533	37	37	11-1	0-0	248.2	234	105	24	2	97-1	158	3.29	113	.252	.321	0-0	—	0	89	11	1.2
1975	Min A	1	3	.250	10	7	1	0-0	26.1	25	25	2	0	36-0	8	8.54	45	.260	.462	0-0	—	0	108	-12	-1.6
1976	Min A	2	7	.222	13	12	0	0-0	58	60	37	3	1	51-0	35	5.28	68	.273	.404	0-0	—	0	104	-10	-1.3
1979	Sea A	0	1	.000	9	2	0	0-0	27.1	27	14	2	0	14-1	12	4.28	102	.255	.339	0-0	—	0	83	0	0.1
Total	9	36	44	.450	152	105	19-4	0-1	710	702	363	58	11	377-8	458	4.17	94	.262	.353	46-6	.174	1	93	-14	-1.9
DEDMON, JEFF Jeffrey Linden B 3.4.1960 Torrance, CA BL/TR 6-2/200# d9.2																									
1983	Atl N	0	0	—	5	0	0	0-2	4	10	6	1	0	0-0	3	13.50	29	.455	.455	0-0	—	0		-4	-0.2
1984	Atl N	4	3	.571	54	0	0	4-2	81	86	39	5	2	35-9	51	3.78	102	.277	.352	6-1	.000	-1		1	0.1
1985	Atl N	6	3	.667	60	0	0	0-4	86	84	52	5	1	49-14	41	4.08	94	.264	.363	9-1	.111	-0		-5	-0.3
1986	Atl N	6	6	.500	57	0	0	3-6	99.2	90	43	8	4	39-5	58	2.98	134	.242	.319	16-1	.125	-1		8	1.0
1987	Atl N	3	4	.429	53	3	0	4-5	89.2	82	46	8	1	42-1	40	3.91	111	.246	.327	16-3	.250	1	152	3	0.4
1988	Cle A	1	0	1.000	21	0	0	1-0	33.2	35	20	3	3	21-1	17	4.54	91	.276	.383	0-0	—	0		-2	0.0
Total	6	20	16	.556	250	3	0	12-19	394	387	206	30	11	186-30	210	3.84	105	.261	.345	47-6	.149	-0	152	1	1.0
DEDRICK, JIM James Michael B 4.4.1968 Los Angeles, CA BB/TR 6/185# d8.12																									
1995	Bal A	0	0	—	6	0	0	0-0	7.2	8	2	1	1	6-0	3	2.35	203	.308	.429	0-0	—	0		2	0.1
DEEGAN, DUMMY William John B 11.16.1874 Bronx, NY D 5.17.1957 Bronx, NY d8.3																									
1901	NY N	0	1	.000	2	1	1	0	17	27	17	0	0	6	8	6.35	52	.355	.402	5-0	.000	-1	43	-6	-0.3
DEERING, JOHN John Thomas B 6.25.1879 Lynn, MA D 2.15.1943 Beverly, MA BR/TR 6/180# d5.12																									
1903	Det A	3	4	.429	10	8	5	0	60.2	77	38	3	1	24	14	3.86	75	.308	.371	24-1	.333	2	83	-6	-0.5
	NY A	4	3	.571	9	7	6-1	0	60	59	33	0	1	18	14	3.75	83	.257	.313	23-0	.043	-3	92	-3	-0.7
	Year	7	7	.500	19	15	11-1	0	120.2	136	37	3	2	42	28	3.80	79	.283	.344	47-1	.191	-0	87	-10	-1.2
DEGERICK, MIKE Michael Arthur B 4.1.1943 New York, NY BR/TR 6-2/178# d9.4																									
1961	Chi A	0	0	—	1	0	0	0	1.2	2	1	0	0	1-0	0	5.40	72	.400	.429	0-0	—	0		0	0.0
1962	Chi A	0	0	—	1	0	0	0	1	1	0	0	0	1-0	0	0.00	—	.250	.400	0-0	—	0		0	0.0
Total	2	0	0	—	2	0	0	0	2.2	3	1	0	0	2-0	0	3.38	116	.333	.417	0-0	—	0		0	0.0
DeHART, RICK Rick Allen B 3.21.1970 Topeka, KS BL/TL 6-1/180# d7.16																									
1997	Mon N	2	1	.667	23	0	0	0-1	29.1	33	21	7	0	14-4	29	5.52	76	.292	.364	2-0	.000	-0		-5	-0.4
1998	Mon N	0	0	—	26	0	0	1-1	28	34	22	3	0	13-1	14	4.82	87	.291	.359	0-0	—	0		-4	-0.2
1999	Mon N	0	0	—	3	0	0	0-0	1.2	6	4	2	0	3-1	1	21.60	21	.545	.643	0-0	—	0		-3	-0.1
2003	KC A	0	2	.000	4	0	0	0-0	4	8	6	1	0	2-0	1	13.50	38	.421	.476	1-0	.000	-0		-3	-0.5
Total	4	2	3	.400	56	0	0	1-2	63	81	53	13	0	32-6	45	6.14	69	.312	.383	3-0	.000	-0		-15	-1.2
DEININGER, PEP Otto Charles B 10.10.1877 Wasseralfingen, Germany D 9.25.1950 Boston, MA BL/TL 5-8.5/180# d4.26 ▲																									
1902	Bos A	0	0	—	2	1	0	0	12	19	16	3	2	9	2	9.75	37	.358	.469	6-0	.333	1	101	-7	-0.2
DeJEAN, MIKE Michel Dwain B 9.28.1970 Baton Rouge, LA BR/TR 6-2/205# d5.2																									
1997	Col N	5	0	1.000	55	0	0	2-2	67.2	74	34	4	3	24-2	38	3.99	130	.280	.346	3-1	.333	0*		7	0.5
1998	Col N	3	1	.750	59	1	0	2-1	74.1	78	29	4	1	24-1	27	3.03	171	.285	.340	5-0	.000	-1	124	14	0.6
1999	Col N	2	4	.333	56	0	0	0-4	61	83	61	13	2	32-8	31	8.41	69	.335	.411	2-0	.000	-0*		-14	-1.1
2000	Col N	4	4	.500	54	0	0	0-4	53.1	54	31	9	0	30-6	34	4.89	119	.269	.362	2-0	.000	-0		4	0.5
2001	Mil N	4	2	.667	75	0	0	2-2	84.1	75	31	4	9	39-7	68	2.77	155	.236	.332	3-0	.000	-0		13	0.9
2002	Mil N	1	5	.167	68	0	0	27-3	75	66	28	7	2	39-8	65	3.12	131	.237	.332	1-0	.000	-0		8	1.1
2003	Mil N	4	7	.364	58	0	0	18-8	64.2	69	38	12	1	27-7	58	4.87	87	.271	.339	0-0	—	0		-5	-0.8
	StL N	1	1	.500	18	0	0	1-0	18	17	8	1	1	12-0	13	4.00	102	.262	.385	0-0	—	0		0	0.0
	Year	5	8	.385	76	0	0	19-8	82.2	86	53	13	2	39-7	71	4.68	90	.269	.349	0-0	—	0		-4	-0.8
Total	7	24	24	.500	443	1	0	52-24	498.1	516	260	54	19	227-39	334	4.26	114	.271	.351	16-1	.063	-1	124	27	1.7
DeJESUS, JOSE Jose Luis B 1.6.1965 Brooklyn, NY BR/TR 6-5/195# d9.9																									
1988	KC A	0	1	.000	2	1	0	0-0	2.2	6	10	0	0	5-1	2	27.00	15	.429	.579	0-0	—	0	137	-7	-1.1
1989	KC A	0	0	—	3	1	0	0-0	8	7	4	1	0	8-0	2	4.50	86	.241	.405	0-0	—	0	70	0	0.0
1990	Phi N	7	8	.467	22	22	3-1	0-0	130	97	63	10	2	73-3	87	3.74	102	.210	.321	38-4	.079	-1	88	0	-0.1
1991	Phi N	10	9	.526	31	29	3	1-0	181.2	147	74	7	4	128-4	118	3.42	107	.224	.353	62-4	.129	-1	91	5	0.3
1994	KC A	3	1	.750	5	4	0	0-0	26.2	27	14	2	0	13-0	12	4.73	106	.276	.360	0-0	—	0	96	1	0.1
Total	5	20	19	.513	63	57	6-1	1-0	349	284	165	20	6	227-8	221	3.84	100	.226	.346	100-8	.110	-2	91	-1	-0.8
DeLA CRUZ, TOMMY Tomas (Rivero) B 9.18.1911 Marianao, Cuba D 9.6.1958 Havana, Cuba BR/TR 6-2/168# d4.20																									
1944	Cin N	9	9	.500	34	20	9	1	191.1	170	73	9	1	45	65	3.25	108	.238	.284	58-4	.155	-0*	89	9	0.7

Year	Tm Lg	W	L	Pct	G	GS	CG-Sho	SV-BS	IP	H	R	HR	HB	BB-IB	SO	ERA	AERA	OAV	OOB	AB-SH	AVG	PB	Sup	APR	PW
DeLa MAZA, ROLAND Roland Robert B 11.11.1971 Granada Hills, CA BR/TR 6-2/195# d9.26																									
1997	KC A	0	0	—	1	0	0	0-0	2	1	1	1	0	1-0	1	4.50	105	.125	.222	0-0	—	0		0	0.0
DELANEY, ART Arthur Dewey "Swede" (b: Arthur Dewey Helenius) B 1.5.1895 Chicago, IL D 5.2.1970 Hayward, CA BR/TR 5-10.5/178# d4.16																									
1924	StL N	1	0	1.000	8	1	1	0	20	19	4	0	0	6	2	1.80	210	.250	.305	7-0	.286	0	157	5	0.3
1928	Bos N	9	17	.346	39	22	8	2	192.1	197	100	11	1	56	45	3.79	103	.267	.319	63-1	.143	-3	80	2	0.0
1929	Bos N	3	5	.375	20	8	3-1	0	75	103	59	6	1	35	17	6.12	76	.336	.405	21-2	.143	0	86	-13	-1.1
Total	3	13	22	.371	67	31	12-1	2	287.1	319	163	17	2	97	64	4.26	96	.285	.343	91-3	.154	-2	84	-6	-0.8
DeLa ROSA, FRANCISCO Francisco (Jimenez) B 3.3.1966 LaRomana, D.R. BB/TR 5-11/185# d9.7																									
1991	Bal A	0	0	—	2	0	0	0-0	4	6	3	0	0	2-0	1	4.50	88	.353	.400	0-0	—	0		-1	0.0
DeLEON, JOSE Jose (Chestaro) B 12.20.1960 Rancho Viejo, D.R. BR/TR 6-3/215# d7.23																									
1983	Pit N	7	3	.700	15	15	3-2	0-0	108	75	36	5	1	47-2	118	2.83	131	.196	.283	34-3	.059	-1	103	11	0.9
1984	Pit N	7	13	.350	30	28	5-1	0-1	192.1	147	86	10	3	92-5	153	3.74	96	.214	.307	59-4	.085	-4	79	-2	-0.7
1985	Pit N	2	19	.095	31	25	1	3-0	162.2	138	93	15	3	89-3	149	4.70	76	.231	.332	36-7	.056	-2	57	-20	-2.6
1986	Pit N	1	3	.250	9	1	0	1-0	16.1	17	16	2	1	17-3	11	8.27	46	.266	.427	1-0	.000	0	93	-7	-1.4
	Chi A	4	5	.444	13	13	1	0-0	79	49	30	7	4	42-0	68	2.96	146	.179	.296	0-0	—	0	73	11	1.2
1987	Chi A	11	12	.478	33	31	2	0-0	206	177	106	24	10	97-4	153	4.02	114	.230	.322	0-0	—	0	90	10	0.8
1988	StL N	13	10	.565	34	34	3-1	0-0	225.1	198	95	13	2	86-7	208	3.67	95	.237	.308	72-12	.139	-0*	97	-1	-0.3
1989	StL N	16	12	.571	36	36	5-3	0-0	244.2	173	96	16	6	80-5	**201**	3.05	119	**.197**	.268	83-9	.096	-4	81	14	0.8
1990	StL N	7	19	.269	32	32	0	0-0	182.2	168	96	15	5	86-9	164	4.43	86	.246	.331	56-5	.107	-1	74	-10	-1.6
1991	StL N	5	9	.357	28	28	1	0-0	162.2	144	57	15	6	61-1	118	2.71	137	.239	.313	46-5	.043	-4	97	17	0.9
1992	StL N	2	7	.222	29	15	0	0-0	102.1	95	56	7	2	43-1	72	4.57	74	.245	.320	21-4	.048	-1	96	-14	-1.3
	Phi N	0	1	.000	3	3	0	0-0	15	16	7	0	0	5-0	7	3.00	117	.281	.339	5-1	.400	1	104	0	0.1
	Year	2	8	.200	32	18	0	0-0	117.1	111	11	7	2	48-1	79	4.37	78	.250	.322	26-5	.115	-0	97	-13	-1.2
1993	Phi N	3	0	1.000	24	3	0	0-1	47	39	25	5	5	27-3	34	3.26	122	.229	.348	6-1	.000	-1	91	1	0.0
	†Chi A	0	0	—	11	0	0	0-1	10.1	5	2	2	1	3-0	6	1.74	241	.152	.243	0-0	—	0		3	0.1
1994	Chi A	3	2	.600	42	0	0	2-2	67	48	28	5	6	31-5	67	3.36	139	.200	.301	0-0	—	0		10	0.7
1995	Chi A	5	3	.625	38	0	0	0-5	67.2	60	41	10	6	28-2	53	5.19	86	.238	.323	0-0	—	0		-5	-0.6
	Mon N	0	1	.000	7	0	0	0-0	8.1	7	7	2	1	7-0	12	7.56	57	.233	.375	0-1	—	0		-3	-0.3
Total	13	86	119	.420	415	264	21-7	6-10	1897.1	1556	877	153	62	841-50	1594	3.76	102	.224	.311	419-52	.091	-16	83	15	-3.3
DeLEON, LUIS Luis Antonio (Tricoche) B 8.19.1958 Ponce, P.R. BR/TR 6-1/153# d9.6																									
1981	StL N	0	1	.000	10	0	0	0-0	15.1	11	4	1	0	3-2	8	2.35	152	.200	.241	1-0	.000	-0		2	0.1
1982	SD N	9	5	.643	61	0	0	15-8	102	77	25	10	1	16-9	60	2.03	169	.212	.246	11-1	.091	0		17	2.9
1983	SD N	6	6	.500	63	0	0	13-6	111	89	34	8	1	27-7	90	2.68	131	.224	.269	14-3	.143	0*		12	1.4
1984	SD N	2	2	.500	32	0	0	0-3	42.2	44	34	12	4	12-2	44	5.48	65	.256	.317	4-1	.000	-0		-11	-1.0
1985	SD N	0	3	.000	29	0	0	3-2	38.2	39	18	6	3	10-4	31	4.19	85	.267	.325	5-0	.200	0		-2	-0.2
1987	Bal A	0	2	.000	11	0	0	1-1	20.2	19	15	1	2	8-2	13	4.79	92	.253	.326	0-0	—	0		-2	-0.2
1989	Sea A	0	0	—	1	1	0	0-0	4	5	1	1	1	1-0	2	2.25	179	.313	.389	0-0	—	0	157	1	0.0
Total	7	17	19	.472	207	1	0	32-20	334.1	284	131	39	12	77-26	248	3.12	114	.232	.280	35-5	.114	-0	157	17	3.0
DELHI, FLAME Lee William B 11.5.1892 Harqua Hala, AZ D 5.9.1966 Greenbrae, CA BR/TR 6-2.5/198# d4.16																									
1912	Chi A	0	0	—	1	0	0	0	3	7	6	0	0	3	2	9.00	36	.412	.500	0-0	—	0		-3	-0.1
DELL, WHEEZER William George B 6.11.1886 Tuscarora, NV D 8.24.1966 Independence, CA BR/TR 6-4/210# d4.22																									
1912	StL N	0	0	—	3	0	0	0	2.1	3	3	0	0	3	0	11.57	30	.188	.316	0-0	—	0		-2	-0.1
1915	Bro N	11	10	.524	40	24	12-4	1	215	166	80	5	8	100	94	2.34	119	.218	.315	66-2	.152	-1	91	9	0.8
1916	†Bro N	8	9	.471	32	16	9-2	1	155	143	52	2	4	43	76	2.26	118	.256	.314	44-2	.091	-2	77	8	0.5
1917	Bro N	0	4	.000	17	4	0	1	58	55	35	3	2	25	28	3.72	75	.263	.347	16-0	.063	-2	108	-8	-0.8
Total	4	19	23	.452	92	44	21-6	3	430.1	367	170	10	14	171	198	2.55	108	.237	.319	126-4	.119	-5	88	7	0.4
DELOCK, IKE Ivan Martin B 11.11.1929 Highland Park, MI BR/TR 5-11/175# d4.17																									
1952	Bos A	4	9	.308	39	7	1-1	5	95	88	50	9	2	50	46	4.26	92	.245	.341	22-1	.045	-1	89	-3	-0.5
1953	Bos A	3	1	.750	23	1	0	1	48.2	60	27	2	2	20	22	4.44	95	.308	.378	10-0	.100	-1	42	-1	-0.2
1955	Bos A	9	7	.563	29	18	6	3	143.2	136	67	17	4	61-2	88	3.76	114	.247	.325	49-2	.143	-1	91	8	0.8
1956	Bos A	13	7	.650	48	8	1	9	128.1	122	65	12	5	80-3	105	4.21	110	.252	.359	29-7	.103	-2	67	7	0.9
1957	Bos A	9	8	.529	49	2	0	11	94	80	40	11	3	45-7	62	3.83	104	.230	.322	21-0	.048	-1	34	4	0.6
1958	Bos A	14	8	.636	31	19	9-1	2	160	155	66	13	0	56-6	82	3.37	119	.252	.314	48-5	.063	-4	90	12	1.1
1959	Bos A	11	6	.647	28	17	4	0	134.1	120	53	12	2	62-1	55	2.95	138	.236	.318	47-5	.064	-3	116	14	1.2
1960	Bos A	9	10	.474	24	23	3-1	0	129.1	145	77	21	4	52-3	49	4.73	85	.283	.353	43-6	.116	-3	104	-10	-1.6
1961	Bos A	6	9	.400	28	28	3-1	0	156	185	110	24	2	52-2	80	4.90	85	.293	.346	48-5	.104	-2	111	-17	-1.7
1962	Bos A	4	5	.444	17	13	4-2	0	86.1	89	39	10	0	24-2	49	3.75	110	.268	.315	23-4	.087	-1	73	4	0.2
1963	Bos A	1	2	.333	6	6	1	0	32	31	18	4	0	12-0	23	4.50	84	.246	.309	12-0	.000	-1	98	-3	-0.4
	Bal A	1	3	.250	7	5	0	0	30.1	25	17	7	0	16-1	11	5.04	69	.236	.336	9-0	.000	-1	56	-5	-0.7
	Year	2	5	.286	13	11	1	0	62.1	56	19	11	0	28-1	34	4.76	76	.241	.322	21-0	.000	-3	80	-7	-1.1
Total	11	84	75	.528	329	147	32-6	31	1238	1236	629	142	24	530-27	672	4.03	102	.259	.335	361-35	.086	-20	94	10	-0.3
DeLOS SANTOS, LUIS Luis B 11.1.1977 Santo Domingo, D.R. BR/TR 6-2/216# d7.20																									
2002	TB A	0	3	.000	3	3	0	0-0	14	24	19	5	3	4-0	7	11.57	39	.387	.437	0-0	—	0	83	-11	-1.5
DeLOS SANTOS, RAMON Ramon (Genero) B 1.19.1949 Santo Domingo, D.R. BL/TL 6-1/175# d8.21																									
1974	Hou N	1	1	.500	12	0	0	0-0	12.1	11	6	0	0	9-4	7	2.19	159	.234	.351	0-0	—	0		1	0.1
DeLOS SANTOS, VALERIO Valerio Lorenzo B 10.6.1972 Las Matas De Farfan, D.R. BL/TL 6-4/185# d7.31																									
1998	Mil N	0	0	—	13	0	0	0-0	21.2	11	7	4	0	2-0	18	2.91	147	.151	.173	0-0	—	0		4	0.2
1999	Mil N	0	1	.000	7	0	0	0-0	8.1	12	6	1	1	7-0	5	6.48	70	.343	.465	0-0	—	0		-2	-0.2
2000	Mil N	2	3	.400	66	2	0	0-1	73.2	72	43	15	1	33-7	70	5.13	89	.254	.333	6-0	.000	-1	71	-3	-0.3
2001	Mil N	0	0	—	1	0	0	0-0	1	1	1	0	0	1-0	1	9.00	48	.250	.400	0-0	—	0		0	0.0
2002	Mil N	2	3	.400	51	0	0	0-0	57.2	42	21	4	2	26-3	38	3.12	131	.211	.299	2-2	.000	0		7	0.5
2003	Mil N	3	3	.500	45	0	0	1-3	48	38	24	8	4	22-0	35	4.13	103	.225	.322	1-0	.000	-0		1	0.1
	Phi N	1	0	1.000	6	0	0	0-0	4	7	7	0	1	3-0	4	9.00	44	.389	.500	0-0	—	0		-4	-0.7
	Year	4	3	.571	51	0	0	1-3	52	45	35	8	5	25-0	39	4.50	94	.241	.339	1-0	.000	-0		-3	-0.6
Total	6	8	10	.444	189	2	0	1-4	214.1	183	109	32	9	94-10	171	4.28	101	.234	.319	9-2	.000	-1	71	3	-0.4
DelTORO, MIGUEL Miguel B 6.22.1972 Obregon, Mexico D 10.6.2001 Obregon, Mexico BR/TR 6-1/160# d4.6																									
1999	SF N	0	0	—	14	0	0	0-0	23.2	24	11	5	0	11-0	20	4.18	101	.264	.343	4-1	.000	-0		1	0.0
2000	†SF N	2	0	1.000	9	1	0	0-0	17.1	17	10	3	2	6-2	16	5.19	82	.250	.329	2-0	.500	0	195	-2	-0.1
Total	2	2	0	1.000	23	1	0	0-0	41	41	21	8	2	17-2	36	4.61	91	.258	.337	6-1	.167	-0	195	-1	-0.1
DeLUCIA, RICH Richard Anthony B 10.7.1964 Reading, PA BR/TR 6/185# d9.8																									
1990	Sea A	1	2	.333	5	5	1	0-0	36	30	9	2	0	9-0	20	2.00	198	.226	.275	0-0	—	0	55	8	0.6
1991	Sea A	12	13	.480	32	31	0	0-0	182	176	107	31	4	78-4	98	5.09	81	.260	.333	0-0	—	0	111	-17	-2.1
1992	Sea A	3	6	.333	30	11	0	1-2	83.2	100	55	13	2	35-1	66	5.49	73	.293	.361	0-0	—	0	115	-14	-1.4
1993	Sea A	3	6	.333	30	1	0	0-4	42.2	46	24	5	1	23-3	48	4.64	95	.272	.361	0-0	—	0	83	-1	-0.2
1994	Cin N	0	0	—	8	0	0	0-0	10.2	9	6	4	0	5-0	15	4.22	98	.214	.298	0-0	—	0		0	0.0
1995	StL N	8	7	.533	56	1	0	0-1	82.1	63	38	9	3	36-2	76	3.39	124	.213	.303	10-1	.200	0	86	6	1.1
1996	SF N	3	6	.333	56	0	0	0-2	61.2	62	44	8	3	31-6	55	5.84	70	.259	.349	4-0	.250	0		-12	-1.4
1997	SF N	0	0	—	3	0	0	0-0	1.2	6	3	0	0	0-0	2	10.80	38	.500	.500	0-0	—	0		-2	-0.1
	Ana A	6	4	.600	33	0	0	3-4	42.1	29	18	5	1	27-2	42	3.61	127	.204	.331	0-0	—	0		5	0.9
1998	Ana A	2	6	.250	61	0	0	3-3	71.2	56	36	10	3	46-5	73	4.27	110	.221	.340	0-0	—	0		4	0.3
1999	Cle A	0	1	.000	6	0	0	0-0	9.1	13	7	4	0	9-2	7	6.75	75	.317	.440	0-0	—	0		-1	-0.1
Total	10	38	51	.427	320	49	1	7-16	624	590	347	91	17	299-25	502	4.62	92	.251	.337	14-1	.214	1	101	-24	-2.4

Year	Tm Lg	W	L	Pct	G	GS	CG-Sho	SV-BS	IP	H	R	HR	HB	BB-IB	SO	ERA	AERA	OAV	OOB	AB-SH	AVG	PB	Sup	APR	PW
DEMARAIS, FRED Frederick B 11.1.1866 , , CAN D 3.6.1919 Stamford, CT TR 5-9/168# d7.26																									
1890	Chi N	0	0	—	1	0	0	0	2	1	0	0	0	1	1	0.00	—	.143	.250	2	.000	-0		1	0.0
DEMAREE, AL Albert Wentworth B 9.8.1884 Quincy, IL D 4.30.1962 Los Angeles, CA BL/TR 6/170# d9.26																									
1912	NY N	1	0	1.000	2	2	1-1	0	16	17	3	0	0	2	11	1.69	200	.288	.311	5-0	.000	-1	87	3	0.1
1913	†NY N	13	4	.765	31	25	11-2	2	199.2	176	65	4	5	38	76	2.21	141	.243	.286	66-1	.106	-3	106	21	1.2
1914	NY N	10	17	.370	38	29	13-2	0	224	219	97	3	8	77	89	3.09	86	.263	.331	68-2	.132	-2	116	-11	-1.6
1915	Phi N	14	11	.560	32	26	13-3	1	209.2	201	84	4	3	58	69	3.05	90	.260	.314	68-3	.176	0	112	-2	-0.5
1916	Phi N	19	14	.576	39	35	25-4	1	285	252	99	4	8	48	130	2.62	101	.242	.281	101-1	.109	-4	105	6	-0.2
1917	Chi N	5	9	.357	24	18	6-1	1	141.1	125	53	5	2	37	43	2.55	114	.244	.297	41-1	.122	-1	84	6	0.5
	NY N	4	5	.444	15	11	1	0	78.1	70	33	1	1	17	23	2.64	97	.239	.283	18-3	.111	-1	67	-3	-0.4
	Year	9	14	.391	39	29	7-1	1	219.2	195	35	6	3	54	66	2.58	108	.242	.292	59-4	.119	-2	78	2	0.1
1918	NY N	8	6	.571	26	14	8-2	1	142	143	56	5	2	25	39	2.47	106	.262	.297	47-4	.128	-3	152	0	-0.3
1919	Bos N	6	6	.500	25	13	6	3	128	147	66	8	1	35	34	3.80	75	.300	.348	42-0	.048	-5	111	-13	-1.8
Total	8	80	72	.526	232	173	84-15	9	1424	1350	556	34	30	337	514	2.77	100	.256	.304	456-15	.118	-20	107	7	-3.0
DEMERY, LARRY Lawrence Calvin B 6.4.1953 Bakersfield, CA BR/TR 6/170# d6.2																									
1974	†Pit N	6	6	.500	19	15	2	0-0	95.1	95	47	12	0	51-5	51	4.25	81	.262	.351	33-3	.152	1*	133	-7	-0.8
1975	†Pit N	7	5	.583	45	8	1	4-1	114.2	95	40	7	3	43-6	59	2.90	122	.230	.305	24-2	.125	1*	167	10	1.1
1976	Pit N	10	7	.588	36	15	4-1	2-1	145	123	56	8	2	58-8	72	3.17	110	.234	.309	40-4	.125	-1*	93	6	0.6
1977	Pit N	6	5	.545	39	8	0	1-1	90.1	100	59	13	0	47-3	35	5.08	79	.279	.360	20-0	.150	-0*	95	-12	-1.3
Total	4	29	23	.558	139	46	7-1	7-3	445.1	413	202	40	5	199-22	217	3.72	97	.249	.328	117-9	.137	0	118	-3	-0.4
DeMILLER, HARRY Harry B 11.12.1867 Wooster, OH D 10.19.1928 Santa Ana, CA BR/TL d8.20																									
1892	Chi N	1	1	.500	4	2	2	0	24	29	22	1	1	16	15	6.38	52	.287	.390	10	.300	1	105	-6	-0.3
DeMOLA, DON Donald John B 7.5.1952 Glen Cove, NY BR/TR 6-2/185# d4.13																									
1974	Mon N	1	0	1.000	25	1	0	0-0	57.2	46	21	7	0	21-1	47	3.12	123	.223	.295	4-0	.000	-1	23	5	0.2
1975	Mon N	4	7	.364	60	0	0	1-1	97.2	92	47	8	4	42-4	63	4.15	93	.251	.333	8-0	.000	-1		-2	-0.4
Total	2	5	7	.417	85	1	0	1-1	155.1	138	68	15	4	63-5	110	3.77	102	.241	.320	12-0	.000	-1	23	3	-0.2
DeMOTT, BEN Benyew Harrison B 4.2.1889 Green Village, NJ D 7.5.1963 Somerville, NJ BR/TR 6/192# d8.12																									
1910	Cle A	0	3	.000	6	4	1	0	28.1	45	25	0	1	8	13	5.40	48	.388	.432	18-0	.167	-0*	58	-9	-0.9
1911	Cle A	0	1	.000	1	1	0	0	3.2	10	5	0	0	2	2	12.27	28	.588	.632	4-0	.000	-0*	21	-3	-0.4
Total	2	0	4	.000	7	5	1	0	32	55	30	0	1	10	15	6.19	43	.414	.458	22-0	.136	-0	51	-12	-1.3
DEMPSEY, CON Cornelius Francis B 9.16.1923 San Francisco, CA BR/TR 6-4/190# d4.28																									
1951	Pit N	0	2	.000	3	2	0	0	7	11	7	2	0	4	3	9.00	47	.393	.469	1-0	.000	-0	31	-3	-0.6
DEMPSEY, MARK Mark Steven B 12.17.1957 Dayton, OH BR/TR 6-6/220# d9.4																									
1982	SF N	0	0	—	3	1	0	0-0	5.2	11	5	1	0	2-0	4	7.94	45	.440	.464	1-0	.000	-0	123	-2	-0.1
DEMPSTER, RYAN Ryan Scott B 5.3.1977 Sechelt, BC, CAN BR/TR 6-2/195# d5.23																									
1998	Fla N	1	5	.167	14	11	0	0-1	54.2	72	47	6	9	38-1	35	7.08	57	.336	.446	13-1	.000	-1	78	-19	-1.8
1999	Fla N	7	8	.467	25	25	0	0-0	147	146	77	21	6	93-2	126	4.71	92	.262	.370	49-1	.102	-2*	96	-3	-0.4
2000	Fla N☆	14	10	.583	33	33	2-1	0-0	226.1	210	102	30	5	97-7	209	3.66	121	.243	.322	77-4	.078	-4	89	20	1.4
2001	Fla N	15	12	.556	34	34	2-1	0-0	211.1	218	123	21	10	112-5	171	4.94	85	.269	.362	61-16	.049	-4	115	-17	-2.1
2002	Fla N	5	8	.385	18	18	3	0-0	120.1	126	66	12	7	55-1	87	4.79	82	.281	.366	34-4	.059	-2	121	-10	-1.1
	Cin N	5	5	.500	15	15	1	0-0	88.2	102	61	16	3	38-1	66	6.19	69	.293	.365	29-5	.207	1*	125	-15	-1.4
	Year	10	13	.435	33	33	4	0-0	209	228	67	28	10	93-2	153	5.38	76	.286	.365	63-9	.127	-1	123	-27	-2.5
2003	Cin N	3	7	.300	22	20	0	0-0	115.2	134	89	14	5	70-4	84	6.54	65	.293	.390	33-1	.030	-3*	98	-28	-2.4
Total	6	50	55	.476	161	156	8-2	0-1	964	1008	565	120	45	503-21	778	5.01	85	.273	.363	296-32	.078	-15	103	-72	-7.8
DENEHY, BILL William Francis B 3.31.1946 Middletown, CT BB/TR 6-3/200# d4.16																									
1967	NY N	1	7	.125	15	8	0	0	53.2	51	38	8	0	29-2	35	4.70	72	.248	.338	9-2	.000	-1	26	-11	-1.5
1968	Was A	0	0	—	3	0	0	0	2	4	3	0	0	4-1	1	9.00	32	.444	.615	0-0	—	0		-2	-0.1
1971	Det A	0	3	.000	31	1	0	1-0	49	47	25	4	4	28-0	27	4.22	85	.250	.357	2-1	.000	1	25	-3	-0.2
Total	3	1	10	.091	49	9	0	1-0	104.2	102	66	12	4	61-3	63	4.56	76	.253	.355	11-3	.000	0	26	-16	-1.8
DENMAN, BRIAN Brian John B 2.12.1956 Minneapolis, MN BR/TR 6-4/205# d8.22																									
1982	Bos A	3	4	.429	9	9	2-1	0-0	49	55	32	6	0	9-3	9	4.78	90	.282	.312	0-0	—	0	96	-4	-0.5
DENNIS, DON Donald Ray B 3.3.1942 Uniontown, KS BR/TR 6-2/190# d6.18																									
1965	StL N	2	3	.400	41	0	0	6	55	47	17	3	1	16-11	29	2.29	168	.236	.294	5-0	.400	1		8	1.1
1966	StL N	4	2	.667	38	1	0	2	59.2	73	36	8	1	17-10	25	4.98	72	.302	.346	12-0	.083	-1	221	-9	-0.8
Total	2	6	5	.545	79	1	0	8	114.2	120	53	11	2	33-21	54	3.69	101	.272	.322	17-0	.176	-0	221	-1	0.3
DENNY, JOHN John Allen B 11.8.1952 Prescott, AZ BR/TR 6-3/190# d9.12																									
1974	StL N	0	0	—	2	0	0	0-0	2	3	2	0	0	0-0	1	0.00	—	.273	.273	0-0	—	0		0	0.0
1975	StL N	10	7	.588	25	24	3-2	0-0	136	149	73	5	3	51-6	72	3.97	95	.280	.344	44-6	.227	1*	96	-4	-0.3
1976	StL N	11	9	.550	30	30	8-3	0-0	207	189	71	11	8	74-3	74	**2.52**	**140**	.246	.318	67-7	.224	2	104	21	2.4
1977	StL N	8	8	.500	26	26	3-1	0-0	149.2	165	85	9	5	62-0	60	4.51	85	.281	.353	51-5	.098	-3	139	-11	-1.2
1978	StL N	14	11	.560	33	33	11-2	0-0	234	200	81	13	6	74-4	103	2.96	119	.238	.302	73-7	.178	2	106	18	2.6
1979	StL N	8	11	.421	31	31	5-2	0-0	206	206	116	24	3	100-7	99	4.85	78	.264	.349	70-8	.129	-1	105	-21	-1.8
1980	Cle A	8	6	.571	16	16	4-1	0-0	108.2	116	54	4	5	47-2	59	4.39	93	.284	.363	0-0	—	0	90	-2	-0.2
1981	Cle A	10	6	.625	19	19	6-3	0-0	145.2	139	62	9	3	66-3	94	3.15	115	.254	.335	0-0	—	0	104	5	0.8
1982	Cle A	6	11	.353	21	21	5	0-0	138.1	126	80	11	6	73-2	94	5.01	82	.240	.338	0-0	—	0	97	-12	-1.2
	Phi N	0	2	.000	4	4	0	0-0	22.1	18	12	1	0	10-1	19	4.03	91	.217	.301	6-0	.167	0	30	-1	0.0
1983	†Phi N	**19**	6	**.760**	36	36	7-1	0-0	242.2	229	77	9	4	53-5	139	2.37	151	.250	.293	77-17	.169	0	113	**32**	3.4
1984	Phi N	7	7	.500	22	22	2	0-0	154.1	122	53	11	4	29-2	94	2.45	149	.214	.256	47-5	.191	0	104	19	1.9
1985	Phi N	11	14	.440	33	33	6-2	0-0	230.2	252	112	15	3	83-5	123	3.82	97	.282	.342	81-3	.123	-2	104	-4	-0.4
1986	Cin N	11	10	.524	27	27	2-1	0-0	171.1	179	89	15	4	56-9	115	4.20	92	.272	.331	54-5	.222	2	93	-6	-0.4
Total	13	123	108	.532	325	322	62-18	0-0	2148.2	2093	967	137	54	778-49	1146	3.59	104	.258	.325	570-63	.170	2	105	34	5.6
DENT, EDDIE Elliott Estill B 12.8.1887 Baltimore, MD D 11.25.1974 Birmingham, AL BR/TR 6-1/190# d8.31																									
1909	Bro N	2	4	.333	6	5	4	0	42	47	23	2	0	15	17	4.29	60	.307	.369	15-0	.067	-1	119	-7	-1.0
1911	Bro N	2	1	.667	5	3	1	0	31.2	30	15	0	2	10	3	3.69	90	.256	.326	10-0	.100	-0	158	-1	-0.1
1912	Bro N	0	0	—	1	0	0	0	1	4	4	0	0	1	1	36.00	9	.571	.625	1-0	.000	-0		-3	-0.2
Total	3	4	5	.444	12	8	5	0	74.2	81	42	2	2	26	21	4.46	65	.292	.357	26-0	.077	-2	133	-11	-1.3
DENZER, ROGER Roger "Peaceful Valley" B 10.5.1871 LeSueur, MN D 9.18.1949 LeSueur, MN BL/TR 6/180# d4.24																									
1897	Chi N	2	8	.200	12	10	8	0	94.2	125	91	4	2	34	17	5.13	87	.315	.372	39-0	.154	-3	85	-10	-1.1
1901	NY N	2	6	.250	11	9	3-1	0	61.2	69	30	2	2	5	22	3.36	98	.280	.300	22-0	.091	-1	52	1	-0.1
Total	2	4	14	.222	23	19	11-1	0	156.1	194	121	6	4	39	39	4.43	90	.302	.345	61-0	.131	-4	70	-9	-1.2
DePAULA, JORGE Jorge B 11.10.1978 Sabana Grande, D.R. BR/TR 6-1/160# d9.5																									
2003	NY A	0	0	—	4	1	0	0-0	11.1	3	1	1	1	1-0	7	0.79	552	.083	.132	0-0	—	0	42	5	0.2
DePAULA, SEAN Sean Michael B 11.7.1973 Newton, MA BR/TR 6-4/215# d8.31																									
1999	†Cle A	0	0	—	11	0	0	0-0	11.2	8	6	0	0	3-0	18	4.63	109	.200	.256	0-0	—	0		1	0.0
2000	Cle A	0	0	—	13	0	0	0-2	16.2	20	11	3	0	14-2	16	5.94	84	.294	.410	0-0	—	0		-1	-0.1
2002	Cle A	1	1	.500	5	0	0	0-2	6.1	11	9	3	0	3-0	8	12.79	34	.367	.424	0-0	—	0		-6	-1.0
Total	3	1	1	.500	29	0	0	0-4	34.2	39	26	6	0	20-2	42	6.75	72	.283	.371	0-0	—	0		-6	-1.1
DERBY, GEORGE George H. "Jonah" B 7.6.1857 Webster, MA D 7.4.1925 Philadelphia, PA BL/TR 6/175# d5.2																									
1881	Det N	29	26	.527	56	55	55-**9**	0	494.2	505	252	3		86	**212**	2.20	132	.251	.281	236	.186	-10*	99	**34**	**2.3**
1882	Det N	17	20	.459	40	39	38-3	0	362	386	267	8		81	182	3.26	90	.256	.294	149	.195	-6	84	-20	-2.1

Year	Tm Lg	W	L	Pct	G	GS	CG-Sho	SV-BS	IP	H	R	HR	HB	BB-IB	SO	ERA	AERA	OAV	OOB	AB-SH	AVG	PB	Sup	APR	PW
1883	Buf N	2	10	.167	14	13	12	1	107.2	173	120	3		15	34	5.85	54	.334	.353	59	.237	-1*	92	-30	-2.5
Total	3	48	56	.462	110	107	105-12	1	964.1	1064	639	14		182	428	3.01	98	.263	.295	444	.196	-17	92	-16	-2.3
DERRINGER, PAUL Samuel Paul "Duke" B 10.17.1906 Springfield, KY D 11.17.1987 Sarasota, FL BR/TR 6-3.5/205# d4.16																									
1931	†StL N	18	8	**.692**	35	23	15-4	2	211.2	225	88	9	4	65	134	3.36	117	.274	.330	72-6	.097	-6	99	15	1.1
1932	StL N	11	14	.440	39	30	14-1	0	233.1	296	133	6	2	67	78	4.05	97	.310	.356	73-3	.178	-0	92	-8	-0.8
1933	StL N	0	2	.000	3	2	1	0	17	24	11	0	1	9	3	4.24	82	.353	.436	5-0	.000	-1	12	-2	-0.3
	Cin N	7	25	.219	33	31	16-2	1	231	240	106	4	5	51	86	3.23	105	.271	.315	76-2	.184	-1	55	3	0.4
	Year	7	27	.206	36	33	17-2	1	248	264	108	4	6	60	89	3.30	103	.277	.324	81-2	.173	-2	53	-3	0.1
1934	Cin N	15	21	.417	47	31	18-1	4	261	297	129	8	4	59	122	3.59	114	.283	.323	92-3	.196	0	79	14	1.7
1935	Cin N★	22	13	.629	45	33	20-3	2	276.2	295	132	13	4	49	120	3.51	113	.271	.305	93-6	.140	-5	90	13	1.1
1936	Cin N	19	19	.500	**51**	**37**	13-2	5	282.1	331	147	11	4	42	121	4.02	95	.289	.316	90-7	.200	-1	110	-5	-0.7
1937	Cin N	10	14	.417	43	26	12-1	1	222.2	240	112	7	0	55	94	4.04	92	.271	.313	80-2	.200	1	116	-5	-0.4
1938	Cin N☆	21	14	.600	41	**37**	**26**-4	3	**307**	315	110	20	0	49	132	2.93	124	.262	.291	119-4	.176	-0	114	28	2.9
1939	†Cin N★	25	7	**.781**	38	35	28-5	0	301	321	115	15	3	35	128	2.93	131	.272	.295	110-17	.209	0	134	30	2.9
1940	†Cin N★	20	12	.625	37	**37**	26-3	0	296.2	280	110	17	0	48	115	3.06	124	.246	**.276**	108-4	.167	-2	97	25	2.1
1941	Cin N★	12	14	.462	29	28	17-2	1	228.1	233	91	16	0	54	76	3.31	109	.266	.309	84-2	.155	-3	78	10	0.7
1942	Cin N✥	10	11	.476	29	27	13-1	0	208.2	203	83	4	4	49	68	3.06	107	.250	.296	68-6	.132	-2	81	7	0.3
1943	Chi N	10	14	.417	32	22	10-2	3	174	184	90	7	0	39	75	3.57	93	.264	.303	58-4	.224	1	99	-8	-1.2
1944	Chi N	7	13	.350	42	16	7	3	180	205	96	13	0	39	69	4.15	85	.284	.321	57-2	.158	-2	104	-11	-1.4
1945	†Chi N	16	11	.593	35	30	15-1	4	213.2	223	99	8	1	51	86	3.45	106	.265	.308	75-9	.200	0	97	4	0.4
Total	15	223	212	.513	579	445	251-32	29	3645	3912	1652	158	32	761	1507	3.46	108	.272	.310	1260-77	.175	-20	96	110	8.8
DERRINGTON, JIM Charles James "Blackie" B 11.29.1939 Compton, CA BL/TL 6-3/190# d9.30																									
1956	Chi A	0	1	.000	1	1	0	0	6	9	6	2	0	6-0	3	7.50	55	.375	.500	2-0	.500	0	130	-3	-0.3
1957	Chi A	0	1	.000	20	5	0	0	37	29	21	4	1	29-0	14	4.86	77	.216	.358	4-2	.000	-0	158	-4	-0.3
Total	2	0	2	.000	21	6	0	0	43	38	27	6	1	35-0	17	5.23	72	.241	.379	6-2	.167	0	153	-7	-0.6
DESHAIES, JIM James Joseph B 6.23.1960 Massena, NY BL/TL 6-4/220# d8.7																									
1984	NY A	0	1	.000	2	2	0	0-0	7	14	9	1	0	7-0	5	11.57	33	.438	.525	0-0	—	0	95	-6	-0.6
1985	Hou N	0	0	—	2	0	0	0-0	3	1	0	0	0	0-0	2	0.00	—	.100	.100	0-0	—	0		1	0.1
1986	Hou N	12	5	.706	26	26	1-1	0-0	144	124	58	16	2	59-2	128	3.25	111	.234	.311	43-4	.047	-1	105	6	0.4
1987	Hou N	11	6	.647	26	25	1	0-0	152	149	81	22	0	57-7	104	4.62	85	.257	.322	53-4	.094	-0	107	-10	-1.0
1988	Hou N	11	14	.440	31	31	3-2	0-0	207	164	77	20	2	72-5	127	3.00	111	.218	.284	63-6	.048	-4	78	8	0.4
1989	Hou N	15	10	.600	34	34	6-3	0-0	225.2	180	80	15	4	79-8	153	2.91	117	.217	.287	75-9	.120	-2*	108	13	1.1
1990	Hou N	7	12	.368	34	34	2	0-0	209.1	186	93	21	8	84-9	119	3.78	98	.245	.322	63-7	.063	-3	95	1	-0.3
1991	Hou N	5	12	.294	28	28	1	0-0	161	156	90	19	1	72-5	98	4.98	71	.259	.336	41-8	.098	-1	87	-23	-2.3
1992	SD N	4	7	.364	15	15	0	0-0	96	92	40	6	1	33-2	46	3.28	109	.258	.321	29-5	.207	1	72	2	0.4
1993	Min A	11	13	.458	27	27	1	0-0	167.1	159	85	24	6	51-1	80	4.41	99	.254	.313	0-0	—	0	85	1	0.1
	SF N	2	2	.500	5	4	0	0-0	17	24	9	2	1	6-0	5	4.24	92	.348	.408	5-1	.000	-1	104	-1	-0.2
1994	Min A	6	12	.333	25	**25**	0	0-0	130.1	170	109	30	2	54-0	78	7.39	66	.321	.382	0-0	—	0	104	-33	-3.5
1995	Phi N	0	1	.000	2	2	0	0-0	5.1	15	12	3	0	1-0	6	20.25	21	.484	.500	1-0	.000	-0	75	-9	-1.1
Total	12	84	95	.469	257	253	15-6	0-0	1525	1434	743	179	27	575-39	951	4.14	91	.251	.320	373-44	.088	-12	95	-50	-6.5
DeSHONG, JIMMIE James Brooklyn B 11.30.1909 Harrisburg, PA D 10.16.1993 Lower Paxton Township, PA BR/TR 5-11/165# d4.12																									
1932	Phi A	0	0	—	6	0	0	0	10	17	14	3	1	9	5	11.70	39	.378	.491	3-0	.000	-0		-8	-0.4
1934	NY A	6	7	.462	31	12	6	3	133.2	126	71	6	2	56	40	4.11	99	.243	.319	42-4	.190	2	103	-1	0.1
1935	NY A	4	1	.800	29	3	0	3	69	64	30	6	2	33	30	3.26	124	.242	.331	14-2	.071	-1	121	6	0.4
1936	Was A	18	10	.643	34	31	16-2	2	223.2	255	135	11	3	96	59	4.63	103	.285	.356	79-8	.190	2*	128	4	0.5
1937	Was A	14	15	.483	37	34	20	1	264.1	290	161	15	3	124	86	4.90	90	.280	.359	94-4	.202	2	111	-10	-0.8
1938	Was A	5	8	.385	31	14	1	0	131.1	160	104	11	1	83	41	6.58	69	.310	.407	46-1	.261	3	106	-28	-2.0
1939	Was A	0	3	.000	7	6	1	0	40.2	56	45	7	0	31	12	8.63	50	.337	.442	15-0	.200	0	128	-21	-1.1
Total	7	47	44	.516	175	100	44-2	9	872.2	968	560	59	12	432	273	5.08	87	.281	.363	293-19	.198	7	117	-58	-3.3
DeSILVA, JOHN John Reed B 9.30.1967 Fort Bragg, CA BR/TR 6/193# d8.15																									
1993	Det A	0	0	—	1	0	0	0-0	1	2	1	0	0	0-0	0	9.00	48	.667	.500	0-0	—	0		0	0.0
	LA N	0	0	—	3	0	0	0-0	5.1	6	4	0	0	1-0	6	6.75	57	.273	.304	0-0	—	0		-2	-0.1
1995	Bal A	1	0	1.000	2	2	0	0-0	8.2	8	7	3	1	7-0	1	7.27	65	.258	.400	0-0	—	0	196	-2	-0.2
Total	2	1	0	1.000	6	2	0	0-0	15	16	12	3	1	8-0	7	7.20	61	.286	.373	0-0	—	0	196	-4	-0.3
DesJARDIEN, SHORTY Paul Raymond B 8.24.1893 Coffeyville, KS D 3.7.1956 Monrovia, CA BR/TR 6-4.5/205# d5.20																									
1916	Cle A	0	0	—	1	0	0	0	1	1	2	0	0	1	0	18.00	17	.200	.333	0-0	—	0		-1	-0.1
DESSAU, RUBE Frank Rolland B 3.29.1883 New Galilee, PA D 5.6.1952 York, PA BB/TR 5-11/175# d9.22																									
1907	Bos N	0	1	.000	2	2	1	0	9.1	13	11	0	1	10	1	10.61	24	.394	.545	4-0	.000	-0	167	-7	-0.6
1910	Bro N	2	3	.400	19	0	0	1	51.1	67	48	0	5	29	24	5.79	52	.328	.424	15-1	.067	-1		-18	-1.8
Total	2	2	4	.333	21	2	1	1	60.2	80	59	0	6	39	25	6.53	45	.338	.443	19-1	.053	-1	167	-25	-2.4
DESSENS, ELMER Elmer B 1.13.1971 Hermosillo, Mexico BR/TR 6/190# d6.24																									
1996	Pit N	0	2	.000	15	3	0	0-0	25	40	23	2	0	4-0	13	8.28	53	.385	.404	5-0	.400	1	62	-9	-0.6
1997	Pit N	0	0	—	3	0	0	0-0	3.1	2	0	0	1	0-0	2	0.00	—	.167	.231	0-0	—	0		2	0.1
1998	Pit N	2	6	.250	43	5	0	0-1	74.2	90	50	10	0	25-2	43	5.67	76	.300	.351	8-3	.000	-1	51	-10	-1.0
2000	Cin N	11	5	.688	40	16	1	1-0	147.1	170	73	10	3	43-7	85	4.28	110	.296	.344	40-1	.100	-0	120	9	0.8
2001	Cin N	10	14	.417	34	34	1-1	0-0	205	221	103	32	1	56-1	128	4.48	102	.279	.325	57-10	.193	1*	86	6	0.7
2002	Cin N	7	8	.467	30	30	0	0-0	178	173	70	24	7	49-8	93	3.03	140	.257	.314	45-9	.200	1*	85	22	1.8
2003	Ari N	8	8	.500	34	30	0	0-0	175.2	212	107	22	4	57-6	113	5.07	92	.299	.354	46-10	.196	1*	103	-6	-0.5
Total	7	38	43	.469	199	118	2-1	1-1	809	908	426	100	16	234-24	477	4.46	101	.287	.337	201-33	.174	3	93	14	1.3
DETTMER, JOHN John Franklin B 3.4.1970 Centreville, IL BR/TR 6/185# d6.16																									
1994	Tex A	0	6	.000	11	9	0	0-0	54	63	42	10	3	20-3	27	4.33	111	.286	.347	0-0	—	0	95	-3	-0.3
1995	Tex A	0	0	—	1	0	0	0-0	0.1	2	1	0	0	0-0	0	27.00	18	.667	.500	0-0	—	0		-1	0.0
Total	2	0	6	.000	12	9	0	0-0	54.1	65	43	10	3	20-3	27	4.47	108	.291	.349	0-0	—	0	95	-4	-0.3
DETTORE, TOM Thomas Anthony B 11.17.1947 Canonsburg, PA BL/TR 6-4/200# d6.11																									
1973	Pit N	0	1	.000	12	1	0	0-0	22.2	33	19	1	3	14-4	13	5.96	59	.340	.435	4-1	.000	-0	25	-7	-0.4
1974	Chi N	3	5	.375	16	9	0	0-1	64.2	64	39	4	6	31-3	43	4.18	92	.255	.348	20-1	.250	1	152	-4	-0.3
1975	Chi N	5	4	.556	36	5	0	0-2	85.1	88	57	8	9	31-4	46	5.38	72	.270	.348	24-0	.250	1	68	-13	-1.2
1976	Chi N	0	1	.000	4	0	0	0-1	7	11	8	3	0	2-0	4	10.29	38	.355	.394	0-0	—	0		-4	-0.5
Total	4	8	11	.421	68	15	0	0-4	179.2	196	123	16	18	78-11	106	5.21	73	.278	.362	48-2	.229	2	117	-28	-2.4
DEUTSCH, MEL Melvin Elliott B 7.26.1915 Caldwell, TX D 11.18.2001 Austin, TX BR/TR 6-4/215# d4.21																									
1946	Bos A	0	0	—	3	0	0	0	6.1	7	5	1	0	3	2	5.68	64	.280	.357	2-0	.000	-0		-2	-0.1
DEVENS, CHARLIE Charles B 1.1.1910 Milton, MA D 8.13.2003 Milton, MA BR/TR 6-1/180# d9.24																									
1932	NY A	1	0	1.000	1	1	1	0	9	6	2	0	0	7	4	2.00	204	.200	.351	2-1	.000	0	167	2	0.2
1933	NY A	3	3	.500	14	8	2	0	62	59	39	1	0	50	23	4.35	89	.250	.381	21-1	.095	-1	148	-5	-0.6
1934	NY A	1	0	1.000	1	1	1	0	11	9	3	0	0	5	4	1.64	248	.225	.311	2-0	.500	1	86	3	0.5
Total	3	5	3	.625	16	10	4	0	82	74	44	1	0	62	31	3.73	105	.242	.370	25-2	.120	0	143	0	0.1
DEVINE, ADRIAN Paul Adrian B 12.2.1951 Galveston, TX BR/TR 6-4/205# d6.27																									
1973	Atl N	2	3	.400	24	1	0	4-1	32.1	45	24	6	2	12-3	15	6.40	62	.338	.399	4-0	.250	0	112	-7	-1.2
1975	Atl N	1	0	1.000	5	2	0	0-0	16.1	19	8	2	1	7-1	8	4.41	86	.284	.360	5-0	.000	-1	151	0	-0.1
1976	Atl N	5	6	.455	48	1	0	9-2	73	72	30	3	1	26-7	48	3.21	118	.255	.316	14-2	.000	-2	139	4	0.5
1977	Tex A	11	6	.647	56	2	0	15-4	105.2	102	43	8	4	31-11	67	3.58	114	.259	.316	0-0	—	0	121	8	1.5
1978	Atl N	5	4	.556	31	6	0	3-1	65.1	84	45	3	0	25-5	26	5.92	68	.323	.380	11-1	.091	-1	107	-10	-1.5

Year	Tm Lg	W	L	Pct	G	GS	CG-Sho	SV-BS	IP	H	R	HR	HB	BB-IB	SO	ERA	AERA	OAV	OOB	AB-SH	AVG	PB	Sup	APR	PW
1979	Atl N	1	2	.333	40	0	0	0-2	66.2	84	28	8	2	25-5	22	3.24	125	.311	.372	7-0	.000	-1		6	0.2
1980	Tex A	1	1	.500	13	0	0	0-0	28	49	22	4	1	9-1	8	4.82	81	.377	.415	0-0	—	0		-5	-0.3
Total	7	26	22	.542	217	12	0	31-10	387.1	455	200	34	11	135-33	194	4.21	95	.296	.354	41-3	.049	-3	119	-4	-0.9
DEVINEY, HAL Harold John B 4.11.1893 Newton, MA D 1.4.1933 Westwood, MA BR/TR d7.30																									
1920	Bos A	0	0	—	1	0	0	0	3	7	5	0	0	2	0	15.00	24	.500	.563	2-0	1.000	2		-4	0.0
DEVLIN, JIM James Alexander B 1849 Philadelphia, PA D 10.10.1883 Philadelphia, PA BR/TR 5-11/175# d4.21.1873 ▲																									
1875	Chi NA	7	16	.304	28	24	24	0	224	254	179	0		12	23	1.93	118	.256	.265	318	.289	7*	81	8	1.2
1876	Lou N	30	35	.462	**68**	**68**	**66**-5	0	**622**	566	309	3		37	**122**	1.56	174	.224	.235	298	.315	2	58	**67**	**6.2**
1877	Lou N	35	25	.583	**61**	**61**	**61**-4	0	**559**	617	288	4		41	141	2.25	**147**	.270	.283	268	.269	-2	82	**56**	**5.0**
Total	2	65	60	.520	129	129	127-9	0	1181	1183	597	7		78	263	1.89	159	.246	.258	566	.293	1	69	123	11.2
DEVLIN, JIM James H. B 4.16.1866 Troy, NY D 12.14.1900 Troy, NY TL 5-7/135# d6.28																									
1886	NY N	0	0	—	1	0	0	1	2	3	5	0		4	2	18.00	18	.250	.438	1	.000	-0		-3	-0.3
1887	Phi N	0	2	.000	2	2	2	0	18	20	19	0	3	10	6	6.00	71	.267	.375	6	.333	0	122	-3	-0.2
1888	†StL AA	6	5	.545	11	11	10	0	90.1	82	54	3	8	20	45	3.19	102	.233	.289	37	.297	2	103	1	0.3
1889	StL AA	5	3	.625	9	8	5	0	60	56	38	0	7	24	37	2.40	176	.239	.328	26	.192	-2	101	8	0.7
Total	4	11	10	.524	23	21	17	1	170.1	161	116	3	18	58	90	3.38	109	.239	.316	70	.257	1	105	3	0.5
DEWALD, CHARLIE Charles H. B 9.1867 Newark, NJ D 8.22.1904 Cleveland, OH TL d9.2																									
1890	Cle P	2	0	1.000	2	2	2	0	14	13	7	0	0	5	6	0.64	618	.236	.300	8	.375	1	108	4	0.5
DEWEY, MARK Mark Alan B 1.3.1965 Grand Rapids, MI BR/TR 6/207# d8.24																									
1990	SF N	1	1	.500	14	0	0	0-1	22.2	22	7	1	0	5-1	11	2.78	131	.259	.300	1-0	.000	0		3	0.2
1992	NY N	1	0	1.000	20	0	0	0-0	33.1	37	16	2	0	10-2	24	4.32	81	.280	.331	1-0	.000	-0		-2	-0.1
1993	Pit N	1	2	.333	21	0	0	7-5	26.2	14	8	0	3	10-1	14	2.36	172	.157	.257	0-0	—	0		5	0.8
1994	Pit N	2	1	.667	45	0	0	1-1	51.1	61	22	4	3	19-3	30	3.68	117	.303	.371	1-0	1.000	0		4	0.2
1995	SF N	1	0	1.000	27	0	0	0-0	31.2	30	12	2	0	17-6	32	3.13	131	.254	.346	1-0	.000	-0		4	0.1
1996	SF N	6	3	.667	78	0	0	0-5	83.1	79	40	9	5	41-9	57	4.21	97	.257	.350	7-0	.000	-0		1	0.1
Total	6	12	7	.632	205	0	0	8-12	249	243	105	18	11	102-22	168	3.65	110	.261	.338	11-0	.091	0		15	1.3
DeWITT, MATT Matthew Brian B 9.4.1977 San Bernardino, CA BR/TR 6-4/220# d6.20																									
2000	Tor A	1	0	1.000	8	0	0	0-0	13.2	20	13	4	2	9-0	6	8.56	59	.351	.456	0-0	—	0		-5	-0.3
2001	Tor A	0	2	.000	16	0	0	0-0	19	22	8	2	1	10-5	13	3.79	121	.293	.384	0-0	—	0		2	0.2
2002	SD N	0	1	.000	5	0	0	0-0	7.1	6	2	1	0	3-0	5	1.23	308	.231	.300	0-0	—	0		2	0.2
Total	3	1	3	.250	29	0	0	0-0	40	48	23	7	3	22-5	24	4.95	93	.304	.397	0-0	—	0		-1	0.1
DIAZ, CARLOS Carlos Antonio B 1.7.1958 Kaneohe, HI BR/TL 6/170# d6.30																									
1982	Atl N	3	2	.600	19	0	0	1-0	25.1	31	15	3	0	9-2	16	4.62	81	.307	.360	3-0	.000	-0		-3	-0.5
	NY N	0	0	—	4	0	0	0-0	3.2	6	2	0	0	4-1	0	0.00	—	.353	.476	0-0	—	0		1	0.0
	Year	3	2	.600	23	0	0	1-0	29	37	24	3	0	13-3	16	4.03	92	.314	.379	3-0	.000	-0		-2	-0.5
1983	NY N	3	1	.750	54	0	0	2-1	83.1	62	22	1	1	35-13	64	2.05	177	.211	.294	5-1	.000	-0		15	0.8
1984	LA N	1	0	1.000	37	0	0	1-1	41	47	26	4	0	24-5	36	5.49	64	.285	.374	1-1	.000	-0		-8	-0.4
1985	†LA N	6	3	.667	46	0	0	0-1	79.1	70	28	7	0	18-6	73	2.61	134	.230	.272	4-0	.000	-0		8	0.7
1986	LA N	0	0	—	19	0	0	0-1	25.1	33	14	2	0	7-2	18	4.26	81	.317	.357	1-0	.000	-0		-3	-0.1
Total	5	13	6	.684	179	0	0	4-4	258	249	107	17	1	97-29	207	3.21	111	.253	.318	14-2	.000	-1		10	0.5
DIBBLE, ROB Robert Keith B 1.24.1964 Bridgeport, CT BL/TR 6-4/230# d6.29																									
1988	Cin N	1	1	.500	37	0	0	0-1	59.1	43	12	2	1	21-5	59	1.82	197	.207	.279	2-2	.000	-0		12	0.6
1989	Cin N	10	5	.667	74	0	0	2-6	99	62	23	4	3	39-11	141	2.09	172	.176	.261	8-0	.000	-1		18	2.5
1990	†Cin N★	8	3	.727	68	0	0	11-6	98	62	22	3	1	34-3	136	1.74	226	.183	.255	7-3	.000	-1		**22**	2.8
1991	Cin N★	3	5	.375	67	0	0	31-5	82.1	67	32	5	0	25-2	124	3.17	120	.223	.280	2-1	.000	-0		6	0.9
1992	Cin N	3	5	.375	63	0	0	25-5	70.1	48	26	3	2	31-2	110	3.07	117	.193	.285	5-0	.400	1		4	0.8
1993	Cin N	1	4	.200	45	0	0	19-9	41.2	34	33	8	2	42-0	49	6.48	62	.225	.400	1-0	1.000	0		-12	-2.0
1995	Chi A	0	1	.000	16	0	0	1-0	14.1	7	10	1	3	27-2	16	6.28	71	.156	.481	0-0	—	0		-3	-0.2
	Mil A	1	1	.500	15	0	0	0-1	12	9	11	1	0	19-0	10	8.25	60	.225	.444	0-0	—	0		-4	-0.5
	Year	1	2	.333	31	0	0	1-1	26.1	16	21	2	3	46-2	26	7.18	65	.188	.464	0-0	—	0		-7	-0.7
Total	7	27	25	.519	385	0	0	89-33	477	332	169	27	12	238-25	645	2.98	128	.197	.297	25-6	.120	-1		43	4.9
DIBUT, PEDRO Pedro (Villafana) B 11.18.1892 Cienfuegos, Cuba D 12.4.1979 Hialeah, FL BR/TR 5-8/190# d5.1																									
1924	Cin N	3	0	1.000	7	2	2	0	36.2	24	9	1	0	12	15	2.21	170	.188	.257	11-1	.273	1	203	7	0.7
1925	Cin N	0	0	—	1	0	0	0	0	3	2	0	0	0	0	∞	—	1.000	1.000	0-0	—	0		-2	-0.2
Total	2	3	0	1.000	8	2	2	0	36.2	27	11	1	0	12	15	2.70	139	.206	.273	11-1	.273	1	203	5	0.5
DICKERMAN, LEO Leo Louis B 10.31.1896 DeSoto, MO D 4.30.1982 Atkins, AR BR/TR 6-4/192# d4.21																									
1923	Bro N	8	12	.400	35	20	7-1	0	159.2	180	95	4	2	72	58	3.72	104	.283	.357	52-4	.250	3	112	-2	0.2
1924	Bro N	0	0	—	7	2	0	0	19.2	20	16	0	2	16	9	5.49	68	.263	.404	6-0	.167	-0	181	-5	-0.2
	StL N	7	4	.636	18	13	8-1	0	119.2	108	43	6	0	51	28	2.41	157	.249	.328	39-3	.231	1	128	17	1.5
	Year	7	4	.636	25	15	8-1	0	139.1	128	49	6	2	67	37	2.84	133	.251	.340	45-3	.222	1	135	11	1.3
1925	StL N	4	11	.267	29	18	7-2	1	130.2	135	95	10	2	79	40	5.58	77	.273	.376	44-3	.114	-3	92	-18	-1.8
Total	3	19	27	.413	89	53	22-4	1	429.2	443	249	20	6	218	135	4.00	99	.270	.358	141-10	.199	1	112	-8	-0.3
DICKERSON, GEORGE George Clark B 12.1.1892 Renner, TX D 7.9.1938 Los Angeles, CA BR/TR 6-1/170# d8.2																									
1917	Cle A	0	0	—	1	0	0	0	1	0	0	0	0	0	0	0.00	—	.000	.000	0-0	—	0		0	0.0
DICKEY, R.A. Robert Alan B 10.29.1974 Nashville, TN BR/TR 6-3/205# d4.22																									
2001	Tex A	0	1	.000	4	0	0	0-0	12	13	9	3	0	7-1	4	6.75	69	.283	.377	0-0	—	0		-2	-0.2
2003	Tex A	9	8	.529	38	13	1-1	1-0	116.2	135	68	16	5	38-5	94	5.09	98	.292	.350	1-0	1.000	0	88	0	0.0
Total	2	9	9	.500	42	13	1-1	1-0	128.2	148	77	19	5	45-6	98	5.25	94	.291	.352	1-0	1.000	0	88	-2	-0.2
DICKMAN, EMERSON George Emerson B 11.12.1914 Buffalo, NY D 4.27.1981 New York, NY BR/TR 6-2/175# d6.27 Mil 1941-42																									
1936	Bos A	0	0	—	1	0	0	0	1	2	2	0	0	1	2	9.00	59	.400	.500	0-0	—	0		-1	0.0
1938	Bos A	5	5	.500	32	11	3-1	0	104	117	74	9	4	54	22	5.28	93	.288	.377	35-2	.286	4	104	-5	-0.1
1939	Bos A	8	3	.727	48	1	0	5	113.2	126	70	10	3	43	46	4.43	107	.282	.349	36-0	.056	-4	317	2	-0.1
1940	Bos A	8	6	.571	35	9	2	3	100	121	74	15	4	38	40	6.03	75	.291	.356	28-2	.107	-2	109	-17	-2.1
1941	Bos A	1	1	.500	9	3	1	0	31	37	23	4	0	17	16	6.39	65	.301	.386	11-0	.091	-1	138	-6	-0.5
Total	5	22	15	.595	125	24	6-1	8	349.2	403	243	38	11	153	126	5.33	88	.288	.363	110-4	.145	-2	118	-27	-2.8
DICKSON, JIM James Edward B 4.20.1938 Portland, OR BL/TR 6-1/185# d7.2																									
1963	Hou N	0	1	.000	13	0	0	2	14.2	22	13	0	0	2-0	6	6.14	51	.344	.353	1-0	.000	-0		-6	-0.6
1964	Cin N	1	0	1.000	4	0	0	0	5	8	4	0	0	5-1	6	7.20	50	.444	.542	0-0	—	0		-2	-0.3
1965	KC A	3	2	.600	68	0	0	0	85.2	68	40	6	2	47-7	54	3.47	101	.220	.324	2-0	.000	-0		-1	-0.1
1966	KC A	1	0	1.000	24	1	0	1	37	37	28	4	0	23-2	20	5.35	63	.264	.366	4-0	.250	0	104	-9	-0.5
Total	4	5	3	.625	109	1	0	3	142.1	135	85	10	2	77-10	86	4.36	79	.254	.347	7-0	.143	-0	104	-18	-1.5
DICKSON, JASON Jason Royce B 3.30.1973 London, ON, CAN BL/TR 6/190# d8.21																									
1996	Cal A	1	4	.200	7	7	0	0-0	43.1	52	22	6	1	18-1	20	4.57	110	.306	.374	0-0	—	0	63	3	0.3
1997	Ana A☆	13	9	.591	33	32	2-1	0-0	203.2	236	111	32	7	56-3	115	4.29	107	.289	.338	2-0	.000	-0	105	4	0.2
1998	Ana A	10	10	.500	27	18	0	0-0	122	147	89	17	6	41-1	61	6.05	78	.303	.359	4-0	.000	-0	99	-18	-2.5
2000	Ana A	2	2	.500	6	6	0	0-0	28	39	20	5	1	7-0	18	6.11	83	.336	.379	0-0	—	0	105	-3	-0.3
Total	4	26	25	.510	73	63	2-1	0-0	397	474	242	60	15	122-5	214	4.99	94	.299	.351	6-0	.000	-0	99	-14	-2.3
DICKSON, LANCE Lance Michael B 10.19.1969 Fullerton, CA BR/TL 6/185# d8.9																									
1990	Chi N	0	3	.000	3	3	0	0-0	13.2	20	12	2	0	4-1	4	7.24	56	.370	.407	3-0	.000	-0	66	-4	-0.8

DICKSON, MURRY Murry Monroe B 8.21.1916 Tracy, MO D 9.21.1989 Kansas City, KS BR/TR 5-10.5/157# d9.30 Mil 1944-45

Year	Tm Lg	W	L	Pct	G	GS	CG-Sho	SV-BS	IP	H	R	HR	HB	BB-IB	SO	ERA	AERA	OAV	OOB	AB-SH	AVG	PB	Sup	APR	PW
1939	StL N	0	0	—	1	0	0	0	3.2	1	0	0	0	1	2	0.00	—	.091	.167	1-0	.000	-0		2	0.1
1940	StL N	0	0	—	1	1	0	0	1.2	5	4	0	0	1	0	16.20	25	.500	.545	0-0	—	0	174	-2	-0.1
1942	StL N	6	3	.667	36	7	2	2	120.2	91	41	1	1	61	66	2.91	118	.216	.316	42-1	.190	-0*	137	9	0.7
1943	†StL N	8	2	.800	31	7	2	0	115.2	119	51	4	1	49	44	3.58	94	.269	.343	34-3	.265	1	101	-2	0.0
1946	†StL N	15	6	**.714**	47	19	12-2	1	184.1	160	71	8	4	56	82	2.88	120	.234	.295	65-1	.277	4	129	11	1.9
1947	StL N	13	16	.448	47	25	11-4	3	231.2	211	101	16	2	88	111	3.07	135	.243	.315	80-2	.213	1	87	23	2.8
1948	StL N	12	16	.429	42	29	11-1	1	252.1	257	121	39	0	85	113	4.14	99	.265	.325	96-4	.281	4*	107	1	0.5
1949	Pit N	12	14	.462	44	20	11-2	0	224.1	216	97	17	6	80	89	3.29	128	.255	.324	84-1	.202	0	94	19	2.3
1950	Pit N	10	15	.400	51	22	8	3	225	227	104	20	2	83	76	3.80	115	.260	.326	82-0	.256	3*	75	15	2.0
1951	Pit N	20	16	.556	45	35	19-3	2	288.2	294	151	32	6	101	112	4.02	105	.262	.327	110-4	.273	5*	101	5	1.3
1952	Pit N	14	21	.400	43	34	21-2	2	277.2	278	128	26	1	76	112	3.57	112	.261	.311	107-2	.224	2*	88	11	1.8
1953	Pit N★	10	19	.345	45	26	10-1	4	200.2	240	121	27	3	58	88	4.53	99	.298	.348	61-4	.115	-4	64	-4	-0.9
1954	Phi N	10	20	.333	40	31	12-4	3	226.1	256	107	31	2	73	64	3.78	107	.286	.339	79-4	.190	0	77	7	0.9
1955	Phi N	12	11	.522	36	28	12-4	0	216	190	98	27	4	82-8	92	3.50	113	.238	.309	82-3	.220	1	98	10	1.1
1956	Phi N	0	3	.000	3	3	0	0	23	20	15	1	0	12-1	1	5.09	73	.241	.337	9-0	.333	1	71	-4	-0.3
	StL N	13	8	.619	28	27	12-3	0	196.1	175	75	20	1	57-4	109	3.07	123	.240	.295	77-2	.247	4*	122	16	2.3
	Year	13	11	.542	31	30	12-3	0	219.1	195	80	21	1	69-5	110	3.28	115	.240	.300	86-2	.256	4	117	11	2.0
1957	StL N	5	3	.625	14	13	3-1	0	74	87	41	8	1	25-0	29	4.14	96	.296	.350	27-0	.222	1	135	-3	-0.1
1958	KC A	9	5	.643	27	9	3	1	99	99	42	12	2	31-4	46	3.27	119	.258	.317	35-2	.257	2*	102	6	1.1
	†NY A	1	2	.333	6	2	0	1	20.1	18	17	4	1	12-0	9	5.75	61	.237	.348	7-0	.286	0	127	-6	-0.8
	Year	10	7	.588	33	11	3	2	119.1	117	22	16	3	43-4	55	3.70	104	.255	.322	42-2	.262	2	106	0	0.3
1959	KC A	2	1	.667	38	0	0	0	71	85	46	9	0	27-1	36	4.94	81	.290	.349	17-0	.176	-1		-8	-0.4
Total	18	172	181	.487	625	338	149-27	23	3052.1	3029	1431	302	37	1058-**18**	1281	3.66	110	.260	.323	1095-33	.231	25	97	106	16.2

DICKSON, WALT Walter R. "Hickory" B 12.3.1878 New Summerfield, TX D 12.9.1918 Ardmore, OK BR/TR 5-11.5/175# d4.26

Year	Tm Lg	W	L	Pct	G	GS	CG-Sho	SV-BS	IP	H	R	HR	HB	BB-IB	SO	ERA	AERA	OAV	OOB	AB-SH	AVG	PB	Sup	APR	PW
1910	NY N	1	0	1.000	12	1	0	0	29.2	31	19	1	0	9	9	5.46	54	.272	.325	4-0	.250	0	176	-6	-0.3
1912	Bos N	3	19	.136	36	20	9-1	1	189	233	123	2	3	61	47	3.86	93	.320	.375	60-3	.167	-1	85	-11	-1.1
1913	Bos N	6	7	.462	19	15	8	0	128	118	71	4	1	45	47	3.23	102	.249	.316	45-1	.178	-1	134	-1	-0.3
1914	Pit F	9	19	.321	40	32	19-3	1	256.2	262	117	5	2	74	63	3.16	91	.273	.327	83-5	.084	-9	82	-9	-1.8
1915	Pit F	7	5	.583	27	11	4	0	96.2	115	51	5	2	33	36	4.19	65	.316	.376	31-3	.129	-1	152	-14	-1.7
Total	5	26	50	.342	134	79	40-4	2	700	759	381	17	8	222	202	3.60	86	.288	.345	223-12	.135	-12	103	-41	-5.2

DIEHL, GEORGE George Krause B 2.25.1918 Emmaus, PA D 8.24.1986 Kingsport, TN BR/TR 6-2/196# d4.19

Year	Tm Lg	W	L	Pct	G	GS	CG-Sho	SV-BS	IP	H	R	HR	HB	BB-IB	SO	ERA	AERA	OAV	OOB	AB-SH	AVG	PB	Sup	APR	PW
1942	Bos N	0	0	—	1	0	0	0	3.2	2	2	0	1	2	0	2.45	136	.167	.333	1-0	.000	-0		0	0.0
1943	Bos N	0	0	—	1	0	0	0	4	4	2	0	0	3	1	4.50	76	.267	.389	1-0	.000	-0		0	0.0
Total	2	0	0	—	2	0	0	0	7.2	6	4	0	1	5	1	3.52	96	.222	.364	2-0	.000	-0		0	0.0

DIERKER, LARRY Lawrence Edward B 9.22.1946 Hollywood, CA BR/TR 6-4/215# d9.22 Mil 1967 M5

Year	Tm Lg	W	L	Pct	G	GS	CG-Sho	SV-BS	IP	H	R	HR	HB	BB-IB	SO	ERA	AERA	OAV	OOB	AB-SH	AVG	PB	Sup	APR	PW
1964	Hou N	0	1	.000	3	1	0	0	9	7	4	1	0	3-0	5	2.00	171	.219	.278	3-0	.000	-0	26	1	0.0
1965	Hou N	7	8	.467	26	19	1	0	146.2	135	69	16	3	37-4	109	3.50	96	.240	.288	50-4	.100	-1	88	-4	-0.6
1966	Hou N	10	8	.556	29	28	8-2	0	187	173	73	17	1	45-0	108	3.18	108	.240	.284	67-2	.149	1	95	7	0.7
1967	Hou N	6	5	.545	15	15	4	0	99	95	44	4	1	25-0	68	3.36	98	.252	.300	31-1	.226	2	95	-1	0.1
1968	Hou N	12	15	.444	32	32	10-1	0	233.2	206	95	14	8	89-12	161	3.31	89	.240	.314	73-9	.068	-3*	96	-9	-1.5
1969	Hou N★	20	13	.606	39	37	20-4	0-0	305.1	240	97	18	1	72-6	232	2.33	152	.214	**.261**	118-7	.144	-1	102	40	4.2
1970	Hou N	16	12	.571	37	36	17-2	1-0	269.2	263	124	31	6	82-4	191	3.87	100	.254	.311	92-9	.174	-0	113	3	0.2
1971	Hou N✣	12	6	.667	24	23	6-2	0-1	159	150	50	8	2	33-1	91	2.72	124	.248	.287	54-3	.074	-3	111	13	1.1
1972	Hou N	15	8	.652	31	31	12-5	0-0	214.2	209	87	14	5	51-0	115	3.40	99	.256	.301	78-6	.167	-0	140	0	-0.2
1973	Hou N	1	1	.500	14	3	0	0-1	27	27	14	3	2	13-0	18	4.33	84	.265	.356	4-0	.000	-0	73	-2	-0.2
1974	Hou N	11	10	.524	33	33	7-3	0-0	223.2	189	76	18	6	82-4	150	2.90	120	.232	.306	71-11	.197	1	90	17	1.7
1975	Hou N	14	16	.467	34	34	14-2	0-0	232	225	109	24	7	91-6	127	4.00	85	.260	.331	76-13	.092	-4	105	-16	-2.3
1976	Hou N	13	14	.481	28	28	7-4	0-0	187.2	171	85	9	6	72-6	112	3.69	87	.243	.317	64-3	.141	-1	110	-10	-1.4
1977	StL N	2	6	.250	11	9	0	0-0	39.1	40	21	7	2	16-0	6	4.58	84	.267	.343	8-2	.000	-1	49	-3	-0.6
Total	14	139	123	.531	356	329	106-25	1-2	2333.2	2130	948	184	50	711-43	1493	3.31	104	.243	.302	789-70	.136	-12	103	36	1.2

DIETRICH, BILL William John "Bullfrog" B 3.29.1910 Philadelphia, PA D 6.20.1978 Philadelphia, PA BR/TR 6/185# d4.13

Year	Tm Lg	W	L	Pct	G	GS	CG-Sho	SV-BS	IP	H	R	HR	HB	BB-IB	SO	ERA	AERA	OAV	OOB	AB-SH	AVG	PB	Sup	APR	PW
1933	Phi A	0	1	.000	8	1	0	0	17	13	11	1	0	19	4	5.82	74	.236	.432	3-0	.333	1	20	-2	0.0
1934	Phi A	11	12	.478	39	23	14-4	3	207.2	201	121	12	3	114	88	4.68	94	.255	.351	72-4	.208	3*	81	-7	-0.4
1935	Phi A	7	13	.350	43	15	8-1	3	185.1	203	128	7	1	101	59	5.39	84	.276	.364	60-3	.083	-6*	82	-17	-2.2
1936	Phi A	4	6	.400	21	4	0	3	71.2	91	55	4	0	40	34	6.53	78	.305	.388	27-1	.111	-2	60	-9	-1.2
	Was A	0	1	.000	5	0	0	0	8.1	13	11	0	0	6	4	9.72	49	.351	.442	0-0	—	0		-5	-0.5
	Chi A	4	4	.500	14	11	6-1	0	82.2	93	50	8	1	36	39	4.68	111	.284	.356	30-2	.267	1	97	4	0.3
	Year	8	11	.421	40	15	6-1	3	162.2	197	56	12	1	82	77	5.75	89	.297	.375	57-3	.193	-1	88	-9	-1.4
1937	Chi A	8	10	.444	29	20	7-1	1	143.1	162	93	15	0	72	62	4.90	94	.285	.366	44-3	.182	1	90	-6	-0.5
1938	Chi A	2	4	.333	8	7	1	0	48	49	33	7	0	31	11	5.44	90	.259	.364	16-0	.063	-1	67	-2	-0.4
1939	Chi A	7	8	.467	25	19	2	0	127.2	134	81	14	2	56	43	5.22	91	.272	.349	37-2	.216	2	88	-6	-0.4
1940	Chi A	10	6	.625	23	17	6-1	0	149.2	154	78	10	0	65	43	4.03	110	.266	.340	50-3	.240	3	89	7	0.8
1941	Chi A	5	8	.385	19	15	4-1	0	109.1	114	73	7	4	50	26	5.35	77	.263	.345	34-1	.088	0	92	-14	-1.4
1942	Chi A	6	11	.353	26	23	6	0	160	173	92	16	5	70	39	4.89	74	.277	.355	48-7	.104	-1	93	-19	-1.9
1943	Chi A	12	10	.545	26	26	12-2	0	186.2	180	72	4	2	53	52	2.80	119	.253	.307	56-6	.143	0	82	10	1.3
1944	Chi A	16	17	.485	36	36	15-2	0	246	269	132	15	2	68	70	3.62	95	.279	.328	77-8	.117	-3	90	-11	-1.7
1945	Chi A	7	10	.412	18	16	6-3	0	122.1	136	61	4	0	36	43	4.19	79	.279	.329	36-3	.167	0	109	-10	-1.2
1946	Chi A	3	3	.500	11	9	3	1	62	63	21	4	0	24	20	2.61	131	.267	.335	19-0	.053	-2	84	6	0.5
1947	Phi A	5	2	.714	11	9	2-1	0	60.2	48	24	0	2	40	18	3.12	122	.223	.350	16-4	.063	-2	116	4	0.3
1948	Phi A	1	2	.333	4	2	0	0	15.1	21	10	0	0	9	5	5.87	73	.356	.441	2-0	.000	-0	42	-2	-0.4
Total	16	108	128	.458	366	253	92-17	11	2003.2	2117	1146	128	22	890	660	4.48	92	.271	.348	627-47	.150	-5	87	-79	-9.0

DIETZ, DUTCH Lloyd Arthur B 2.9.1912 Cincinnati, OH D 10.29.1972 Beaumont, TX BR/TR 5-11.5/180# d4.26 Mil 1944-45

Year	Tm Lg	W	L	Pct	G	GS	CG-Sho	SV-BS	IP	H	R	HR	HB	BB-IB	SO	ERA	AERA	OAV	OOB	AB-SH	AVG	PB	Sup	APR	PW
1940	Pit N	0	1	.000	4	2	0	0	15.1	22	11	2	0	4	8	5.87	65	.355	.394	7-0	.143	-0*	148	-3	-0.2
1941	Pit N	7	2	.778	33	6	4-1	1	100.1	88	28	6	2	33	22	2.33	155	.233	.298	25-1	.160	-1	67	16	1.3
1942	Pit N	6	9	.400	40	13	3	3	134.1	139	67	8	1	57	35	3.95	86	.268	.342	35-2	.200	1	84	-7	-0.9
1943	Pit N	0	3	.000	8	0	0	0	9	12	6	0	1	4	4	6.00	58	.324	.405	0-0	—	0*		-2	-0.3
	Phi N	1	1	.500	21	0	0	2	36	42	29	2	0	15	10	6.50	52	.292	.358	6-0	.167	0		-12	-0.8
	Year	1	4	.200	29	0	0	2	45	54	38	2	1	19	14	6.40	53	.298	.368	6-0	.167	0		-14	-1.1
Total	4	14	16	.467	106	21	7-1	6	295	303	141	18	4	113	79	3.87	90	.266	.334	73-3	.178	-0	85	-8	-0.9

DIGGINS, BEN Benjamin Howard B 6.13.1979 Leoti, KS BR/TR 6-7/230# d9.2

Year	Tm Lg	W	L	Pct	G	GS	CG-Sho	SV-BS	IP	H	R	HR	HB	BB-IB	SO	ERA	AERA	OAV	OOB	AB-SH	AVG	PB	Sup	APR	PW
2002	Mil N	0	4	.000	5	5	0	0-0	24	28	24	4	1	18-1	15	8.63	48	.298	.409	7-1	.143	-0	50	-12	-1.5

DIGGS, REESE Reese Wilson "Diggsy" B 9.22.1915 Mathews, VA D 10.30.1978 Baltimore, MD BB/TR 6-2/180# d9.15

Year	Tm Lg	W	L	Pct	G	GS	CG-Sho	SV-BS	IP	H	R	HR	HB	BB-IB	SO	ERA	AERA	OAV	OOB	AB-SH	AVG	PB	Sup	APR	PW
1934	Was A	1	2	.333	4	3	2	0	21.1	26	17	3	0	15	2	6.75	64	.313	.418	8-2	.250	0	155	-6	-0.6

DiLAURO, JACK Jack Edward B 5.3.1943 Akron, OH BB/TL 6-2/185# d5.15

Year	Tm Lg	W	L	Pct	G	GS	CG-Sho	SV-BS	IP	H	R	HR	HB	BB-IB	SO	ERA	AERA	OAV	OOB	AB-SH	AVG	PB	Sup	APR	PW
1969	NY N	1	4	.200	23	4	0	1-1	63.2	50	19	4	0	18-5	27	2.40	152	.216	.269	12-0	.000	-1	67	9	0.5
1970	Hou N	1	3	.250	42	0	0	3-6	33.2	34	23	4	0	17-2	23	4.28	91	.262	.340	2-0	.000	-0*		-4	-0.5
Total	2	2	7	.222	65	4	0	4-7	97.1	84	42	8	0	35-7	50	3.05	123	.232	.295	14-0	.000	-2	67	5	0.0

DILLARD, GORDON Gordon Lee B 5.20.1964 Salinas, CA BL/TL 6-1/190# d8.12

Year	Tm Lg	W	L	Pct	G	GS	CG-Sho	SV-BS	IP	H	R	HR	HB	BB-IB	SO	ERA	AERA	OAV	OOB	AB-SH	AVG	PB	Sup	APR	PW
1988	Bal A	0	0	—	2	1	0	0-0	3	3	2	1	0	4-0	2	6.00	65	.273	.467	0-0	—	0	93	-1	0.0
1989	Phi N	0	0	—	5	0	0	0-0	4	7	3	0	0	0-0	2	6.75	53	.368	.368	0-0	—	0		-1	-0.1
Total	2	0	0	—	7	1	0	0-0	7	10	5	1	0	4-0	4	6.43	58	.333	.412	0-0	—	0	93	-2	-0.1

DILLINGER, HARLEY Harley Hugh "Hoke" or "Lefty" B 10.30.1894 Pomeroy, OH D 1.8.1959 Cleveland, OH BR/TL 5-11/175# d8.16

Year	Tm Lg	W	L	Pct	G	GS	CG-Sho	SV-BS	IP	H	R	HR	HB	BB-IB	SO	ERA	AERA	OAV	OOB	AB-SH	AVG	PB	Sup	APR	PW
1914	Cle A	0	1	.000	11	2	1	0	33.2	41	28	0	1	25	11	4.54	64	.325	.441	10-0	.000	-1	189	-7	-0.6

Year	Tm Lg	W	L	Pct	G	GS	CG-Sho	SV-BS	IP	H	R	HR	HB	BB-IB	SO	ERA	AERA	OAV	OOB	AB-SH	AVG	PB	Sup	APR	PW
DILLMAN, BILL William Howard B 5.25.1945 Trenton, NJ BR/TR 6-2/180# d4.14																									
1967	Bal A	5	9	.357	32	15	2-1	3	124	115	61	13	3	33-2	69	4.35	72	.249	.301	31-4	.161	-0*	87	-15	-1.8
1970	Mon N	2	3	.400	18	0	0	0-0	30.2	28	18	4	1	18-4	17	5.28	78	.255	.356	2-0	.000	-0		-3	-0.4
Total	2	7	12	.368	50	15	2-1	3-0	154.2	143	79	17	4	51-6	86	4.54	74	.250	.313	33-4	.152	-1	87	-18	-2.2
DILLON, STEVE Stephen Edward B 3.20.1943 Yonkers, NY BL/TL 5-10/160# d9.5																									
1963	NY N	0	0	—	1	0	0	0	1.2	3	2	0	0	0-0	1	10.80	32	.429	.429	0-0	—	0		-1	-0.1
1964	NY N	0	0	—	2	0	0	0	3	4	3	1	0	2-0	2	9.00	40	.333	.400	0-0	—	0		-2	-0.1
Total	2	0	0	—	3	0	0	0	4.2	7	5	1	0	2-0	3	9.64	37	.368	.409	0-0	—	0		-3	-0.2
DiMICHELE, FRANK Frank Lawrence B 2.16.1965 Philadelphia, PA BR/TL 6-3/205# d4.8																									
1988	Cal A	0	0	—	4	0	0	0-0	4.2	5	5	2	0	2-0	1	9.64	40	.263	.333	0-0	—	0		-3	-0.1
DINGMAN, CRAIG Craig Allen B 3.12.1974 Wichita, KS BR/TR 6-4/215# d6.30																									
2000	NY A	0	0	—	10	0	0	0-0	11	18	8	1	0	3-0	8	6.55	74	.375	.412	0-0	—	0		-2	-0.1
2001	Col N	0	0	—	7	0	0	1-0	7.1	11	11	4	2	3-2	2	13.50	40	.355	.444	0-0	—	0		-5	-0.2
Total	2	0	0	—	17	0	0	1-0	18.1	29	19	5	2	6-2	10	9.33	54	.367	.425	0-0	—	0		-7	-0.3
DINNEEN, BILL William Henry "Big Bill" (b: William Henry Dineen) B 4.5.1876 Syracuse, NY D 1.13.1955 Syracuse, NY BR/TR 6-1/190# d4.22 U29																									
1898	Was N	9	16	.360	29	27	22	0	218.1	238	140	6	16	88	83	4.00	92	.275	.353	80-1	.100	-4*	89	-9	-1.2
1899	Was N	14	20	.412	37	35	30	0	291	350	191	6	11	106	91	3.93	100	.297	.361	119-2	.303	5	94	-6	0.1
1900	Bos N	20	14	.588	40	37	33-1	0	320.2	304	161	11	9	105	107	3.12	133	.250	.314	125-6	.280	2*	98	**32**	**3.1**
1901	Bos N	15	18	.455	37	34	31	0	309.1	295	136	8	6	77	141	2.94	123	.250	.299	147-4	.211	0*	70	22	2.1
1902	Bos A	21	21	.500	42	42	39-2	0	371.1	348	155	9	8	99	136	2.93	122	.248	.302	141-2	.128	-6*	95	33	2.3
1903	†Bos A	21	13	.618	37	34	32-6	**2**	299	255	98	6	4	66	148	2.26	134	.230	.276	106-5	.160	-1	103	28	2.9
1904	Bos A	23	14	.622	37	37	37-5	0	335.2	283	115	8	2	63	153	2.20	122	.230	.268	120-4	.208	-0	105	17	1.7
1905	Bos A	12	14	.462	31	29	23-2	1	243.2	235	117	7	7	50	97	3.73	72	.255	.299	88-4	.148	-3	100	-22	-2.6
1906	Bos A	8	19	.296	28	27	22-1	0	218.2	209	101	4	1	52	60	2.92	94	.255	.300	63-3	.111	-1	67	-6	-1.0
1907	Bos A	0	4	.000	5	5	3	0	32.2	42	25	5	2	8	8	5.23	49	.313	.361	10-0	.000	-1	63	-9	-1.1
	StL A	7	10	.412	24	16	15-2	4	155.1	153	67	3	5	33	38	2.43	103	.260	.305	49-3	.204	2	97	-2	-0.2
	Year	7	14	.333	29	21	18-2	**4**	188	195	71	8	7	41	46	2.92	86	.270	.315	59-3	.169	1	89	-10	-1.3
1908	StL A	14	7	.667	27	16	11-2	0	167	133	52	2	4	53	39	2.10	114	.231	.300	59-1	.203	0	89	7	0.8
1909	StL A	6	7	.462	17	13	8-3	0	112	112	53	3	1	29	26	3.46	70	.267	.316	36-1	.194	2	90	-12	-1.1
Total	12	170	177	.490	391	352	306-24	7	3074.2	2957	1411	78	76	829	1127	3.01	107	.254	.308	1143-36	.192	-6	92	73	5.8
DIORIO, RON Ronald Michael B 7.15.1946 Waterbury, CT BR/TR 6-6/212# d8.9																									
1973	Phi N	0	0	—	23	0	0	1-0	19.1	18	5	1	0	6-4	11	2.33	163	.257	.312	0-0	—	0		3	0.2
1974	Phi N	0	0	—	2	0	0	0-0	1	2	2	1	0	1-0	0	18.00	21	.400	.500	0-0	—	0		-1	-0.1
Total	2	0	0	—	25	0	0	1-0	20.1	20	7	2	0	7-4	11	3.10	123	.267	.325	0-0	—	0		2	0.1
DiPINO, FRANK Frank Michael B 10.22.1956 Syracuse, NY BL/TL 6/180# d9.14																									
1981	Mil A	0	0	—	2	0	0	0-0	2.1	0	0	0	0	3-0	3	0.00	—	.000	.300	0-0	—	0		1	0.0
1982	Hou N	2	2	.500	6	6	0	0-0	28.1	32	20	1	0	11-1	25	6.04	55	.302	.361	8-1	.000	-1	102	-9	-1.1
1983	Hou N	3	4	.429	53	0	0	20-9	71.1	52	21	2	1	20-5	67	2.65	129	.205	.263	6-0	.167	1		8	1.3
1984	Hou N	4	9	.308	57	0	0	14-4	75.1	74	32	3	1	36-11	65	3.35	99	.260	.343	10-0	.000	-1		0	-0.1
1985	Hou N	3	7	.300	54	0	0	6-2	76	69	44	7	2	43-6	49	4.03	86	.248	.350	12-0	.167	-0		-7	-1.0
1986	Hou N	1	3	.250	31	0	0	3-3	40.1	27	18	5	2	16-1	27	3.57	101	.189	.278	5-0	.200	0		0	0.0
	Chi N	2	4	.333	30	0	0	0-2	40	47	27	6	0	14-5	43	5.17	78	.297	.351	1-0	.000	-0		-6	-0.7
	Year	3	7	.300	61	0	0	3-5	80.1	74	49	11	2	30-6	70	4.37	88	.246	.315	6-0	.167	-0		-5	-0.7
1987	Chi N	3	3	.500	69	0	0	4-1	80	75	31	7	1	34-2	61	3.15	136	.252	.326	2-1	.500	0		10	0.8
1988	Chi N	2	3	.400	63	0	0	6-2	90.1	102	54	6	0	32-7	69	4.98	73	.285	.338	10-1	.100	-0		-13	-0.9
1989	StL N	9	0	1.000	67	0	0	0-3	88.1	73	26	6	0	20-7	44	2.45	149	.227	.269	13-1	.077	-1		12	1.1
1990	StL N	5	2	.714	62	0	0	3-2	81	92	45	8	1	31-12	49	4.56	84	.294	.352	4-1	.250	0		-6	-0.4
1992	StL N	0	0	—	9	0	0	0-0	11	9	2	0	0	3-0	8	1.64	207	.220	.273	1-0	1.000	0		2	0.2
1993	KC A	1	1	.500	11	0	0	0-0	15.2	21	12	2	2	6-0	5	6.89	67	.328	.392	0-0	—	0		-3	-0.4
Total	12	35	38	.479	514	6	0	56-28	700	673	332	53	10	269-57	515	3.83	96	.256	.324	72-5	.125	-1	102	-11	-1.2
DIPOTO, JERRY Gerard Peter B 5.24.1968 Jersey City, NJ BR/TR 6-2/200# d5.11																									
1993	Cle A	4	4	.500	46	0	0	11-6	56.1	57	21	0	1	30-7	41	2.40	181	.270	.361	0-0	—	0		10	1.7
1994	Cle A	0	0	—	7	0	0	0-0	15.2	26	14	1	1	10-0	9	8.04	59	.406	.468	0-0	—	0		-5	-0.2
1995	NY N	4	6	.400	58	0	0	2-4	78.2	77	41	2	4	29-8	49	3.78	107	.267	.340	5-1	.000	-1		0	0.0
1996	NY N	7	2	.778	57	0	0	0-5	77.1	91	44	5	3	45-8	52	4.19	96	.298	.389	1-0	.000	-0		-3	-0.3
1997	Col N	5	3	.625	74	0	0	16-5	95.2	108	56	6	4	33-5	74	4.70	110	.288	.346	9-0	.111	-1		3	0.3
1998	Col N	3	4	.429	68	0	0	19-4	71.1	61	31	8	3	25-3	49	3.53	146	.232	.304	1-0	.000	0		10	1.4
1999	Col N	4	5	.444	63	0	0	1-0	86.2	91	44	10	3	44-4	69	4.26	137	.279	.365	5-0	.000	-0		12	1.0
2000	Col N	0	0	—	17	0	0	0-1	13.2	16	6	1	0	5-2	9	3.95	147	.314	.362	1-0	.000	-0		2	0.1
Total	8	27	24	.529	390	0	0	49-25	495.1	527	257	33	19	221-37	352	4.05	119	.280	.356	22-1	.045	-2		29	4.0
DISCH, GEORGE George Charles B 3.15.1879 Lincoln, MO D 8.25.1950 Rapid City, SD TR 5-11/?# d8.8																									
1905	Det A	0	2	.000	8	3	1	0	47.2	43	19	1	2	8	14	2.64	103	.243	.283	19-0	.105	-1	52	1	-0.1
DISHMAN, GLENN Glenelg Edward B 11.5.1970 Baltimore, MD BR/TL 6-1/195# d6.22																									
1995	SD N	4	8	.333	19	16	0	0-0	97	104	60	11	4	34-1	43	5.01	81	.278	.342	30-2	.200	1	109	-10	-1.1
1996	SD N	0	0	—	3	0	0	0-0	2.1	3	2	0	0	1-0	0	7.71	52	.300	.364	0-0	—	0		-1	0.0
	Phi N	0	0	—	4	1	0	0-0	7	9	6	2	0	2-0	3	7.71	56	.321	.355	0-2	—	0	188	-2	-0.1
	Year	0	0	—	7	1	0	0-0	9.1	12	15	2	0	3-0	3	7.71	55	.316	.357	0-2	—	0	192	-3	-0.1
1997	Det A	1	2	.333	7	4	0	0-0	29	30	18	4	2	8-0	20	5.28	87	.268	.323	0-0	—	0	115	-2	-0.1
Total	3	5	10	.333	33	21	0	0-0	135.1	146	86	17	6	45-1	66	5.25	79	.279	.339	30-4	.200	1	114	-15	-1.3
DISTASO, ALEC Alec John B 12.23.1948 Los Angeles, CA BR/TR 6-2/200# d4.20																									
1969	Chi N	0	0	—	2	0	0	0-0	4.2	6	2	0	0	1-0	1	3.86	104	.316	.350	0-0	—	0		0	0.0
DITMAR, ART Arthur John B 4.3.1929 Winthrop, MA BR/TR 6-2/196# d4.19																									
1954	Phi A	1	4	.200	14	5	0	0	39.1	50	35	4	1	36	14	6.41	61	.314	.442	8-1	.125	0	131	-12	-1.3
1955	KC A	12	12	.500	35	22	7-1	1	175.1	180	109	23	7	86-5	79	5.03	83	.270	.358	62-4	.210	-0	107	-16	-1.9
1956	KC A	12	22	.353	44	34	14-2	1	254.1	254	141	30	7	108-6	126	4.42	98	.262	.338	91-4	.143	-4	90	-3	-0.8
1957	†NY A	8	3	.727	46	11	0	6	127.1	128	55	9	2	35-1	64	3.25	110	.261	.312	35-1	.200	-0	115	4	0.3
1958	†NY A	9	8	.529	38	13	4	4	139.2	124	71	14	5	38-2	52	3.42	103	.237	.292	44-2	.250	2	143	-2	-0.2
1959	NY A	13	9	.591	38	25	7-1	1	202	156	75	17	8	52-2	96	2.90	126	.211	**.268**	76-1	.197	2	118	18	1.9
1960	†NY A	15	9	.625	34	28	8-1	0	200	195	77	25	1	56-1	65	3.06	117	.256	.308	69-3	.159	0*	117	13	1.4
1961	NY A	2	3	.400	12	8	1	0	54.1	59	33	9	2	14-0	24	4.64	80	.285	.329	19-0	.053	-2	128	-7	-0.7
	KC A	0	5	.000	20	5	0	1	54	60	34	6	2	23-1	19	5.67	74	.286	.359	12-1	.167	-0	55	-6	-0.6
	Year	2	8	.200	32	13	1	1	108.1	119	37	15	4	37-1	43	5.15	77	.285	.344	31-1	.097	-2	96	-14	-1.3
1962	KC A	0	2	.000	6	5	0	0	21.2	31	19	1	2	13-1	13	6.65	64	.323	.411	6-0	.167	-0	97	-6	-0.5
Total	9	72	77	.483	287	156	41-5	14	1268	1237	649	138	37	461-19	552	3.98	97	.256	.324	422-17	.178	-3	110	-17	-2.4
DIVEN, FRANK Frank Robert B 8.29.1859 D 5.30.1914 Nutley, NJ TL d5.9																									
1883	Bal AA	1	1	.500	2	2	1	0	11	15	15	0		1	3	7.36	47	.306	.320	9	.222	-0	174	-4	-0.5
DIXON, SONNY John Craig B 11.5.1924 Charlotte, NC BB/TR 6-2.5/205# d4.20																									
1953	Was A	5	8	.385	43	6	3	3	120	123	57	13	2	31	40	3.75	104	.267	.316	26-2	.154	0	99	2	0.3
1954	Was A	1	2	.333	16	0	0	1	29.2	26	15	3	0	12	7	3.03	117	.236	.309	6-0	.000	-1		0	0.0
	Phi A	5	7	.417	38	6	1	4	107.1	136	63	8	3	27	42	4.86	80	.308	.349	28-0	.250	2	75	-10	-0.8
	Year	6	9	.400	**54**	6	1	5	137	162	66	11	3	39	49	4.47	86	.293	.341	34-0	.206	1	77	-10	-0.8
1955	KC A	0	0	—	2	0	0	0	1.2	6	3	1	0	0-0	0	16.20	26	.545	.545	0-0	—	0		-2	-0.1

Year	Tm Lg	W	L	Pct	G	GS	CG-Sho	SV-BS	IP	H	R	HR	HB	BB-IB	SO	ERA	AERA	OAV	OOB	AB-SH	AVG	PB	Sup	APR	PW
1956	NY A	0	1	.000	3	0	0	1	4.1	5	3	0	0	5-1	1	2.08	186	.294	.455	1-0	.000	-0		0	0.0
Total	4	11	18	.379	102	12	4	9	263	296	141	25	5	75-1	90	4.17	93	.284	.334	61-2	.180	1	88	-10	-0.6
DIXON, KEN Kenneth John B 10.17.1960 Monroe, VA BB/TR 5-11/166# d9.22																									
1984	Bal A	0	1	.000	2	2	0	0-0	13	14	6	1	0	4-0	8	4.15	93	.269	.321	0-0	—	0	58	0	0.0
1985	Bal A	8	4	.667	34	18	3-1	1-0	162	144	68	20	2	64-7	108	3.67	110	.237	.311	0-0	—	0*	118	9	0.5
1986	Bal A	11	13	.458	35	33	2	0-0	202.1	194	111	33	1	83-6	170	4.58	90	.249	.320	0-0	—	0	94	-9	-0.9
1987	Bal A	7	10	.412	34	15	0	5-4	105	128	81	31	1	27-4	91	6.43	69	.292	.333	0-0	—	0	109	-23	-3.3
Total	4	26	28	.481	105	68	5-1	6-4	482.1	480	266	85	4	178-17	377	4.66	89	.256	.320	0-0	—	0	103	-23	-3.7
DIXON, STEVE Steven Ross B 8.3.1969 Cincinnati, OH BL/TL 6/190# d9.7																									
1993	StL N	0	0	—	4	0	0	0-0	2.2	7	10	1	0	5-0	2	33.75	12	.538	.667	0-0	—	0		-8	-0.4
1994	StL N	0	0	—	2	0	0	0-0	2.1	3	6	0	0	8-0	1	23.14	18	.333	.611	0-0	—	0		-5	-0.2
Total	2	0	0	—	6	0	0	0-0	5	10	16	1	0	13-0	3	28.80	14	.455	.639	0-0	—	0		-13	-0.6
DIXON, TOM Thomas Earl B 4.23.1955 Orlando, FL BR/TR 5-11/175# d7.30																									
1977	Hou N	1	0	1.000	9	4	1	0-0	30.1	40	12	0	1	7-0	15	3.26	109	.320	.361	7-3	.000	-1	156	1	0.0
1978	Hou N	7	11	.389	30	19	3-2	1-0	140	140	70	8	1	40-3	66	3.99	83	.265	.312	40-3	.100	-2	91	-12	-1.7
1979	Hou N	1	2	.333	19	1	0	0-1	25.2	39	23	2	0	15-1	9	6.66	53	.348	.425	1-0	1.000	1	126	-10	-1.0
1983	Mon N	0	1	.000	4	0	0	0-0	3.2	6	4	1	1	1-0	4	9.82	37	.375	.421	0-0	—	0		-2	-0.5
Total	4	9	14	.391	62	24	4-2	1-1	199.2	225	109	11	3	63-4	94	4.33	78	.288	.338	48-6	.104	-2	104	-23	-3.2
DOAK, BILL William Leopold "Spittin' Bill" B 1.28.1891 Pittsburgh, PA D 11.26.1954 Bradenton, FL BR/TR 6-0.5/165# d9.1																									
1912	Cin N	0	0	—	1	1	0	0	2	4	2	0	0	1	0	4.50	75	.444	.500	0-0	—	0	240	0	0.0
1913	StL N	2	8	.200	15	12	5-1	1	93	79	42	4	5	39	51	3.10	104	.236	.325	31-0	.032	-3	39	0	-0.3
1914	StL N	19	6	.760	36	33	16-7	1	256	193	79	2	7	87	118	**1.72**	**162**	.216	.290	85-3	.118	-3	94	27	2.6
1915	StL N	16	18	.471	38	36	19-3	1	276	263	103	4	8	85	124	2.64	106	.261	.323	86-10	.174	1	102	6	1.3
1916	StL N	12	8	.600	29	26	11-2	0	192	177	76	5	3	55	82	2.63	101	.251	.308	62-4	.129	-2	114	0	-0.1
1917	StL N	16	20	.444	44	37	16-3	2	281.1	257	123	6	9	85	111	3.10	87	.250	.312	95-2	.126	-4	94	-16	-2.2
1918	StL N	9	15	.375	31	23	16-1	1	211	191	76	3	4	60	74	2.43	111	.249	.306	66-7	.182	1	87	7	1.2
1919	StL N	13	14	.481	31	29	13-3	0	202.2	182	87	5	2	55	69	3.11	90	.246	.299	64-5	.109	-4	93	-7	-1.1
1920	StL N	20	12	.625	39	37	20-5	1	270	256	94	7	6	80	90	2.53	118	.253	.312	88-8	.114	-6	105	15	1.1
1921	StL N	15	6	**.714**	32	29	13-1	1	208.2	224	85	3	4	37	83	**2.59**	142	.278	.313	70-10	.143	-3	118	21	1.7
1922	StL N	11	13	.458	37	29	8-2	2	180.1	222	127	12	3	69	73	5.54	70	.311	.374	54-7	.130	-3	125	-32	-3.8
1923	StL N	8	13	.381	30	26	7-2	0	185	199	85	4	3	69	53	3.26	120	.279	.346	67-3	.045	-9	96	12	0.5
1924	StL N	2	1	.667	11	1	0	3	22	25	8	0	0	14	7	3.27	116	.313	.415	5-0	.200	-0	67	2	0.3
	Bro N	11	5	.688	21	16	8-2	0	149.1	130	58	8	3	35	32	3.07	122	.239	.289	56-2	.179	-0	105	13	1.4
	Year	13	6	.684	32	17	8-2	3	171.1	155	63	8	3	49	39	3.10	121	.249	.307	61-2	.180	-1	102	14	1.7
1927	Bro N	11	8	.579	27	20	6-1	0	145	153	73	6	3	40	32	3.48	114	.271	.322	47-8	.128	-3	85	5	0.4
1928	Bro N	3	8	.273	28	12	4-1	3	99.1	104	51	1	5	35	12	3.26	122	.271	.340	27-1	.111	-2	50	6	0.5
1929	StL N	1	2	.333	3	2	0	0	9	17	15	1	0	5	3	12.00	39	.415	.478	2-1	.000	0	103	-8	-1.2
Total	16	169	157	.518	453	369	162-34	16	2782.2	2676	1184	71	65	851	1014	2.98	107	.259	.319	905-71	.127	-42	99	51	2.3
DOANE, WALT Walter Rudolph B 3.12.1887 Bellevue, ID D 10.19.1935 W.Brandywine Township, PA BL/TR 6/165# d9.20																									
1909	Cle A	0	1	.000	1	1	0	0	5	10	7	0	0	1	2	5.40	47	.400	.423	9-0	.111	-0*	110	-2	-0.4
1910	Cle A	0	0	—	6	0	0	0	17.2	31	21	1	1	8	7	5.60	46	.413	.476	7-0	.286	1		-8	-0.4
Total	2	0	1	.000	7	1	0	0	22.2	41	28	1	1	9	9	5.56	46	.410	.464	16-0	.188	1	110	-10	-0.8
DOBB, JOHN John Kenneth "Lefty" B 11.15.1901 Muskegon, MI D 7.31.1991 Muskegon, MI BR/TL 6-2/180# d8.13																									
1924	Chi A	0	0	—	2	0	0	0	2	4	2	0	0	1	2	9.00	46	.400	.455	0-0	—	0		-1	0.0
DOBENS, RAY Raymond Joseph "Lefty" B 7.28.1906 Nashua, NH D 4.21.1980 Stuart, FL BL/TL 5-8/175# d7.7																									
1929	Bos A	0	0	—	11	1	0	0	28.1	32	12	0	1	9	4	3.81	112	.302	.362	8-1	.375	1	197	2	0.1
DOBERNIC, JESS Andrew Joseph B 11.20.1917 Mt.Olive, IL D 7.16.1998 St.Louis, MO BR/TR 5-10/170# d7.2																									
1939	Chi A	0	1	.000	4	0	0	0	3.1	3	6	0	1	6	1	13.50	35	.231	.500	1-0	.000	-0		-3	-0.6
1948	Chi N	7	2	.778	54	0	0	1	85.2	67	33	8	1	40	48	3.15	124	.213	.303	10-0	.200	-0		8	0.7
1949	Chi N	0	0	—	4	0	0	0	4	9	9	2	0	4	0	20.25	20	.450	.542	0-0	—	0		-7	-0.3
	Cin N	0	0	—	14	0	0	0	19.1	28	22	7	0	16	6	9.78	43	.329	.436	2-0	.000	0		-11	-0.5
	Year	0	0	—	18	0	0	0	23.1	37	41	9	0	20	6	11.57	36	.352	.456	2-0	.000	0		-17	-0.8
Total	3	7	3	.700	76	0	0	1	112.1	107	70	17	2	66	55	5.21	76	.247	.349	13-0	.154	-0		-13	-0.7
DOBSON, CHUCK Charles Thomas B 1.10.1944 Kansas City, MO BR/TR 6-4/200# d4.19																									
1966	KC A	4	6	.400	14	14	1	0	83.2	71	41	7	2	50-0	61	4.09	83	.234	.345	26-2	.115	-1	69	-5	-0.7
1967	KC A	10	10	.500	32	29	4-1	0	197.2	172	83	17	3	75-6	110	3.69	86	.233	.305	72-3	.181	0*	102	-7	-0.7
1968	Oak A	12	14	.462	35	34	11-3	0	225.1	197	91	20	4	80-10	168	3.00	94	.234	.302	75-6	.200	2	99	-7	-0.5
1969	Oak A	15	13	.536	35	35	11-1	0-0	235.1	244	111	16	1	80-2	137	3.86	89	.270	.328	79-9	.101	-3	113	-11	-1.7
1970	Oak A	16	15	.516	41	**40**	13-**5**	0-0	267	230	122	32	5	92-7	149	3.74	95	.229	.296	93-5	.118	-3	114	-5	-1.0
1971	Oak A	15	5	.750	30	30	7-1	0-0	189	185	84	24	1	71-6	100	3.81	88	.259	.326	66-5	.197	3	165	-7	-0.4
1973	Oak A	0	1	.000	1	1	0	0-0	2.1	6	4	1	0	2-0	3	7.71	46	.429	.500	0-0	—	0	101	-2	-0.3
1974	Cal A	2	3	.400	5	5	2	0-0	30	39	19	3	0	13-1	16	5.70	60	.315	.380	0-0	—	0	46	-7	-0.9
1975	Cal A	0	2	.000	9	2	0	0-0	28	30	26	5	2	13-1	14	6.75	53	.275	.349	0-0	—	0	74	-11	-0.7
Total	9	74	69	.517	202	190	49-11	0-0	1258.1	1174	581	125	18	476-33	758	3.78	87	.247	.316	411-30	.153	-2	112	-62	-6.9
DOBSON, JOE Joseph Gordon "Burrhead" B 1.20.1917 Durant, OK D 6.23.1994 Jacksonville, FL BR/TR 6-2/197# d4.26 Mil 1944-45																									
1939	Cle A	2	3	.400	35	3	0	1	78	87	56	3	1	51	27	5.88	75	.290	.395	18-1	.056	-2	87	-13	-0.9
1940	Cle A	3	7	.300	40	7	2-1	3	100	101	60	8	0	48	57	4.95	85	.268	.351	24-0	.125	-1	71	-7	-0.7
1941	Bos A	12	5	.706	27	18	7-1	0	134.1	136	70	8	2	67	69	4.49	93	.262	.349	47-3	.149	0	119	-1	-0.2
1942	Bos A	11	9	.550	30	23	10-3	0	182.2	155	73	9	2	68	72	3.30	113	.231	.303	69-5	.145	-1	92	10	1.0
1943	Bos A	7	11	.389	25	20	9-3	0	164.1	144	63	4	0	57	63	3.12	106	.239	.305	52-3	.096	-3	98	4	-0.1
1946	†Bos A	13	7	.650	32	24	9-1	0	166.2	148	72	11	1	68	91	3.24	113	.234	.309	50-6	.100	-2	119	6	0.5
1947	Bos A	18	8	.692	33	31	15-1	1	228.2	203	84	15	1	73	110	2.95	132	.238	**.299**	77-7	.208	1	110	23	2.6
1948	Bos A☆	16	10	.615	38	32	16-5	2	245.1	237	115	14	1	92	116	3.56	123	.253	.320	84-8	.202	1	124	19	1.8
1949	Bos A	14	12	.538	33	27	12-2	2	212.2	219	103	12	2	97	87	3.85	113	.269	.348	68-5	.147	-1	94	10	0.9
1950	Bos A	15	10	.600	39	27	12-1	4	206.2	217	103	15	0	81	81	4.18	117	.275	.343	70-8	.214	1	115	16	1.9
1951	Chi A	7	6	.538	28	21	6	3	146.2	136	68	17	0	51	67	3.62	111	.248	.312	46-7	.065	-6	131	7	0.0
1952	Chi A	14	10	.583	29	25	11-3	1	200.2	164	66	11	0	60	101	2.51	145	.222	.280	63-10	.190	0	90	24	2.7
1953	Chi A	5	5	.500	23	15	3-1	1	100.2	96	46	10	0	37	50	3.67	110	.249	.314	29-1	.069	-2	85	4	0.1
1954	Bos A	0	0	—	2	0	0	0	2.2	5	2	0	0	1	1	6.75	61	.385	.429	0-0	—	0		-1	0.0
Total	14	137	103	.571	414	273	112-22	18	2170	2048	981	137	10	851	992	3.62	112	.250	.322	697-64	.152	-15	107	101	9.6
DOBSON, PAT Patrick Edward B 2.12.1942 Depew, NY BR/TR 6-3/190# d5.31 C8																									
1967	Det A	1	2	.333	28	1	0	0	49.1	38	20	6	2	27-1	34	2.92	112	.216	.324	5-0	.000	-1	80	1	0.0
1968	†Det A	5	8	.385	47	10	2-1	7	125	89	39	13	2	48-6	93	2.66	113	.200	.280	28-2	.143	0	90	5	0.7
1969	Det A	5	10	.333	49	9	1	9-4	105	100	48	10	1	39-5	64	3.60	104	.253	.316	22-2	.091	-1	118	1	0.1
1970	SD N	14	15	.483	40	34	8-1	1-0	251	257	126	28	4	78-13	185	3.76	106	.265	.320	71-19	.141	-0	111	3	0.2
1971	†Bal A	20	8	.714	38	37	18-4	1-0	282.1	248	104	24	2	63-2	187	2.90	116	.235	.278	91-13	.110	-3	134	14	0.9
1972	Bal A☆	16	18	.471	38	36	13-3	0-0	268.1	220	89	13	4	69-7	161	2.65	116	.224	.277	85-8	.141	-2	81	12	1.3
1973	Atl N	3	7	.300	12	10	1-1	0-0	57.2	73	33	1	1	19-5	23	4.99	79	.315	.362	15-3	.067	-1	60	-5	-0.9
	NY A	9	8	.529	22	21	6-1	0-0	142.1	150	72	22	2	34-8	70	4.17	88	.266	.309	0-0	—	0	121	-7	-0.7
1974	NY A	19	15	.559	39	39	12-2	0-0	281	282	111	23	4	75-5	157	3.07	115	.262	.311	0-0	—	0	91	15	1.7
1975	NY A	11	14	.440	33	30	7-1	0-0	207.2	205	105	21	1	83-10	129	4.07	91	.261	.330	0-0	—	0	98	-8	-1.0
1976	Cle A	16	12	.571	35	35	6	0-0	217.1	226	98	13	2	65-7	117	3.48	100	.272	.323	0-0	—	0	88	-2	-0.3
1977	Cle A	3	12	.200	33	17	0	1-0	133.1	155	94	23	1	65-7	81	6.14	64	.299	.376	0-0	—	0	86	-30	-2.9

Year	Tm Lg	W	L	Pct	G	GS	CG-Sho	SV-BS	IP	H	R	HR	HB	BB-IB	SO	ERA	AERA	OAV	OOB	AB-SH	AVG	PB	Sup	APR	PW
Total	11	122	129	.486	414	279	74-14	19-4	2120.1	2043	939	197	26	665-76	1301	3.54	100	.255	.312	317-47	.123	-8	100	-1	-0.9
DOCKINS, GEORGE George Woodrow "Lefty" B 5.5.1917 Clyde, KS D 1.22.1997 Clyde, KS BL/TL 6/175# d5.5																									
1945	StL N	8	6	.571	31	12	5-2	0	126.1	132	53	4	0	38	33	3.21	117	.269	.321	34-4	.176	1	106	7	0.8
1947	Bro N	0	0	—	4	0	0	0	5.1	10	7	2	0	2	1	11.81	35	.400	.444	1-0	.000	-0		-4	-0.2
Total	2	8	6	.571	35	12	5-2	0	131.2	142	60	6	0	40	34	3.55	106	.275	.327	35-4	.171	1	106	3	0.6
DODD, ROBERT Robert Wayne B 3.14.1973 Kansas City, KS BL/TL 6-3/195# d5.28																									
1998	Phi N	1	0	1.000	4	0	0	0-0	5	7	6	1	1	1-0	4	7.20	60	.333	.360	0-0	—	0		-2	-0.4
DODGE, SAM Samuel Edward B 12.9.1889 Neath, PA D 4.5.1966 Utica, NY BR/TR 6-1/170# d9.24																									
1921	Bos A	0	0	—	1	0	0	0	1	1	1	0	0	1	0	9.00	47	.500	.667	0-0	—	0		0	0.0
1922	Bos A	0	0	—	3	0	0	0	6	11	6	0	0	3	3	4.50	91	.379	.438	2-0	.000	-0		-1	-0.1
Total	2	0	0	—	4	0	0	0	7	12	7	0	0	4	3	5.14	80	.387	.457	2-0	.000	-0		-1	-0.1
DOE, FRED Alfred George "Count" B 4.18.1864 Rockport, MA D 10.4.1938 Quincy, MA BR/TR 5-10/165# d8.23																									
1890	Buf P	0	1	.000	1	1	1	0	6	10	10	0	0	7	2	12.00	34	.357	.486	2	.000	-0	0	-5	-0.5
	Pit P	0	0	—	1	0	0	0	4	4	2	0	0	2	2	4.50	87	.250	.333	2	.500	0		0	0.0
	Year	0	1	.000	2	1	1	0	10	14	12	0	0	9	4	9.00	45	.318	.434	4	.250	-0	0	-4	-0.5
DOHENY, ED Edwin Richard B 11.24.1873 Northfield, VT D 12.29.1916 Medfield, MA BL/TL 5-10.5/165# d9.16																									
1895	NY N	0	3	.000	3	3	3	0	25.2	37	29	2	3	19	9	6.66	70	.333	.444	10-0	.100	-1	82	-6	-0.6
1896	NY N	6	7	.462	17	15	9	0	108.1	112	78	3	6	59	39	4.49	94	.265	.363	40-0	.150	-2	119	-4	-0.5
1897	NY N	4	4	.500	10	10	10	0	85	69	45	0	8	45	37	2.12	196	.220	.333	35-0	.200	-1	79	15	1.1
1898	NY N	7	19	.269	28	27	23	0	213	238	164	1	20	101	96	3.68	95	.280	.370	86-0	.163	-1	108	-15	-1.5
1899	NY N	14	17	.452	36	34	31-1	0	277.2	291	207	2	37	158	120	4.41	85	.269	.381	116-0	.233	-1	99	-26	-2.1
1900	NY N	4	14	.222	20	18	12	0	133.2	148	134	2	22	96	44	5.45	66	.280	.411	54-0	.222	-0	103	-31	-3.1
1901	NY N	2	5	.286	10	6	6	0	74	88	53	1	6	17	36	4.50	73	.293	.344	29-1	.345	3*	104	-10	-0.5
	Pit N	6	2	.750	11	10	6-1	0	76.2	68	36	1	5	22	28	2.00	164	.236	.302	26-0	.115	0	135	7	0.7
	Year	8	7	.533	21	16	12-1	0	150.2	156	42	2	11	39	64	3.23	102	.265	.323	55-1	.236	4	123	-2	0.2
1902	Pit N	16	4	.800	22	21	19-2	0	188.1	161	68	0	15	61	88	2.53	108	.231	.307	77-1	.156	-2	141	6	0.3
1903	Pit N	16	8	.667	27	25	22-2	2	222.2	209	122	1	19	89	75	3.19	101	.252	.338	91-1	.209	-0	125	0	0.2
Total	9	75	83	.475	184	169	141-6	2	1405	1421	936	13	141	667	572	3.73	94	.262	.358	564-3	.197	-4	112	-64	-6.0
DOHERTY, JOHN John Harold B 6.11.1967 New York, NY BR/TR 6-4/210# d4.8																									
1992	Det A	7	4	.636	47	11	0	3-1	116	131	61	4	4	25-5	37	3.88	102	.287	.328	0-0	—	0	130	-2	-0.2
1993	Det A	14	11	.560	32	31	3-2	0-0	184.2	205	104	19	5	48-7	63	4.44	97	.286	.333	0-0	—	0	115	-4	-0.6
1994	Det A	6	7	.462	18	17	2	0-0	101.1	139	75	13	3	26-6	28	6.48	75	.337	.374	0-0	—	0	106	-16	-1.5
1995	Det A	5	9	.357	48	2	0	6-3	113	130	66	10	6	37-10	46	5.10	93	.288	.349	0-0	—	0	88	-3	-0.3
1996	Bos A	0	0	—	3	0	0	0-0	6.1	8	10	1	1	4-0	3	5.68	89	.276	.382	0-0	—	0		-3	-0.1
Total	5	32	31	.508	148	61	5-2	9-4	521.1	613	316	47	19	140-28	177	4.87	91	.296	.344	0-0	—	0	113	-28	-2.7
DOLAN, JOHN John B 9.12.1867 Newport, KY D 5.8.1948 Springfield, OH TR 5-10/170# d9.5																									
1890	Cin N	1	1	.500	2	2	2	0	18	17	13	3	1	10	9	4.50	79	.243	.346	8	.125	-1	80	-1	-0.2
1891	Col AA	12	11	.522	27	24	19	0	203.1	216	131	8	0	84	68	4.16	83	.263	.331	78	.090	-4*	92	-13	-1.5
1892	Was N	2	2	.500	5	4	3	0	37	39	26	0	1	15	8	4.38	74	.260	.331	13	.231	0	112	-3	-0.3
1893	StL N	0	1	.000	3	1	1	1	17.1	26	22	2	1	7	1	4.15	114	.338	.400	7	.143	0	74	-2	-0.1
1895	Chi N	0	1	.000	2	2	1	0	11	16	12	0	1	6	1	6.55	78	.333	.418	3-0	.000	-0	77	-2	-0.1
Total	5	15	16	.484	39	33	26	1	286.2	314	204	13	4	122	87	4.30	83	.269	.341	109-0	.110	-5	92	-21	-2.2
DOLAN, COZY Patrick Henry B 12.3.1872 Cambridge, MA D 3.29.1907 Louisville, KY BL/TL 5-10/160# d4.26 ▲																									
1895	Bos N	11	7	.611	25	21	18-3	1	198.1	215	142	11	14	67	47	4.27	119	.272	.340	83-1	.241	-1*	90	16	1.1
1896	Bos N	1	4	.200	6	5	3	0	41	55	44	1	3	27	14	4.83	94	.318	.419	14-2	.143	-1	122	-4	-0.5
1905	Bos N	0	1	.000	2	0	0	0	4	7	5	2	0	1	1	9.00	34	.368	.400	433-9	.275	1*		-2	-0.4
1906	Bos N	0	1	.000	2	0	0	0	12	12	6	1	0	6	7	4.50	60	.300	.391	549-13	.248	0*		-2	-0.1
Total	4	12	13	.480	35	26	21-3	1	255.1	289	197	15	17	101	69	4.44	109	.283	.357	1079-25	.257	-2	98	8	0.1
DOLL, ART Arthur James "Moose" B 5.7.1913 Chicago, IL D 4.28.1978 Calumet City, IL BR/TR 6-1/190# d9.21.1935																									
1936	Bos N	0	1	.000	1	1	0	0	8	11	3	1	1	2	2	3.38	114	.355	.412	2-0	.000	-0	44	1	0.0
1938	Bos N	0	0	—	3	0	0	0	4	4	1	0	0	3	1	2.25	153	.286	.412	1-0	1.000	1		1	0.1
Total	2	0	1	.000	4	1	0	0	12	15	4	1	1	5	3	3.00	123	.333	.412	3-0	.333	0	44	2	0.1
DOMINGUEZ, JUAN Juan A. B 5.18.1980 Sanchez Ramirez, D.R. BR/TR 6-2/180# d8.12																									
2003	Tex A	0	2	.000	6	3	0	0-0	16.1	16	14	5	0	12-0	13	7.16	69	.271	.389	0-0	—	0	68	-4	-0.4
DONAHUE, RED Francis Rostell B 1.23.1873 Waterbury, CT D 8.25.1913 Philadelphia, PA BR/TR 6/187# d5.6																									
1893	NY N	0	0	—	2	0	0	1	5	8	10	1	2	3	1	9.00	52	.348	.464	2	.000	-0		-3	-0.2
1895	StL N	0	1	.000	1	1	1	0	8	9	6	2	1	3	2	6.75	72	.281	.361	3-0	.000	-1	0	-1	-0.1
1896	StL N	7	24	.226	32	32	28	0	267	376	235	6	13	98	70	5.80	75	.329	.389	107-3	.159	-8*	78	-42	-4.2
1897	StL N	10	35	.222	46	42	**38**-1	1	348	485	306	16	22	106	64	6.13	72	.327	.380	155-4	.213	-3*	72	-57	-5.4
1898	Phi N	16	17	.485	35	35	33-1	0	284.1	327	165	7	14	80	57	3.55	97	.286	.340	112-7	.143	-7	105	-4	-0.9
1899	Phi N	21	8	.724	35	31	27-4	0	279	292	147	6	11	63	51	3.39	109	.269	.316	111-5	.180	-5	136	11	0.6
1900	Phi N	15	10	.600	32	24	21-2	0	240	299	144	6	9	50	41	3.60	100	.304	.344	90-5	.222	-1	123	-4	-0.5
1901	Phi N	20	13	.606	34	33	33-1	1	295.1	299	111	2	9	59	88	2.59	131	.261	.302	113-3	.097	-9	88	28	1.8
1902	StL A	22	11	.667	35	34	33-2	0	316.1	322	134	7	8	65	63	2.76	128	.264	.306	118-5	.093	-9	91	25	1.6
1903	StL A	8	7	.533	16	15	14	0	131	145	59	0	0	22	51	2.75	106	.279	.309	51-2	.157	-2	126	1	-0.1
	Cle A	7	9	.438	16	15	14-4	0	136.2	142	61	3	6	12	45	2.44	117	.267	.291	53-1	.151	-1	112	5	0.5
	Year	15	16	.484	32	30	28-4	0	267.2	287	65	3	6	34	96	2.59	111	.273	.300	104-3	.154	-3	119	4	0.4
1904	Cle A	19	14	.576	35	32	30-6	0	277	281	96	2	5	49	127	2.40	105	.264	.299	101-5	.168	-1	118	8	0.9
1905	Cle A	6	12	.333	20	18	14-1	0	137.2	132	68	2	5	25	45	3.40	77	.254	.295	53-3	.075	-5	93	-11	-1.8
1906	Det A	13	14	.481	28	28	26-3	0	241	260	96	1	8	54	82	2.73	101	.278	.323	81-5	.123	-4*	86	1	-0.4
Total	13	164	175	.484	367	340	312-25	3	2966.1	3377	1638	61	113	689	787	3.61	96	.286	.331	1150-48	.152	-56	97	-43	-8.2
DONAHUE, DEACON John Stephen Michael B 6.23.1920 Chicago, IL BR/TR 6/180# d9.16																									
1943	Phi N	0	0	—	2	0	0	0	4	4	3	0	1	1	1	4.50	75	.235	.316	0-0	—	0		-1	0.0
1944	Phi N	0	2	.000	6	0	0	0	9.1	18	8	0	0	2	2	7.71	47	.429	.455	1-0	.000	-0		-4	-0.7
Total	2	0	2	.000	8	0	0	0	13.1	22	11	0	1	3	3	6.75	52	.373	.413	1-0	.000	-0		-5	-0.7
DONALD, ATLEY Richard Atley "Swampy" B 8.19.1910 Morton, MS D 10.19.1992 West Monroe, LA BL/TR 6-1/186# d4.21																									
1938	NY A	0	1	.000	2	2	0	0	12	7	8	0	1	14	6	5.25	86	.175	.400	6-0	.167	-0	78	-1	-0.1
1939	NY A	13	3	.813	24	20	11-2	1	153	144	74	12	0	60	55	3.71	118	.247	.317	60-0	.250	3	138	10	1.0
1940	NY A	8	3	.727	24	11	6-1	0	118.2	113	49	11	2	59	60	3.03	133	.249	.339	41-5	.146	-2	111	13	0.7
1941	†NY A	9	5	.643	22	20	10	0	159	141	69	11	3	69	71	3.57	110	.237	.320	62-0	.081	-4	117	8	0.2
1942	†NY A	11	3	.786	20	19	10-1	0	147.2	133	58	6	0	45	53	3.11	111	.239	.296	61-2	.148	-1	144	6	0.2
1943	NY A	6	4	.600	22	15	2	0	119.1	134	69	10	0	38	57	4.60	70	.276	.329	47-4	.128	-2	159	-18	-1.7
1944	NY A	13	10	.565	30	19	9	0	159	173	77	13	2	59	48	3.34	104	.280	.345	55-1	.182	-0	138	-1	-0.2
1945	NY A	5	4	.556	9	9	6-2	0	63.2	62	29	3	0	25	19	2.97	117	.248	.316	24-2	.208	0	126	2	0.1
Total	8	65	33	.663	153	115	54-6	1	932.1	907	433	66	8	369	369	3.52	107	.253	.325	356-14	.160	-7	132	19	0.2
DONALDS, ED Edward Alexander "Erston" B 6.22.1885 Bidwell, OH D 7.3.1950 Columbus, OH BR/TR 5-11/180# d9.1																									
1912	Cin N	1	0	1.000	1	0	0	0	4	7	2	0	0	0	1	4.50	75	.438	.438	1-0	.000	-0		0	-0.1
DONLIN, MIKE Michael Joseph "Turkey Mike" B 5.30.1878 Peoria, IL D 9.24.1933 Hollywood, CA BL/TL 5-9/170# d7.19 ▲																									
1899	StL N	0	1	.000	3	1	0	0	15.1	15	15	1	1	14	6	7.63	52	.254	.405	266-3	.323	1*	126	-5	-0.1
1902	Cin N	0	0	—	1	0	0	0	1	1	0	0	0	0	0	0.00	—	.250	.250	143-0	.287	0*		0	0.0
Total	2	0	1	.000	4	1	0	0	16.1	16	15	1	1	14	6	7.16	55	.254	.397	409-3	.311	1	126	-5	-0.1

Year	Tm Lg	W	L	Pct	G	GS	CG-Sho	SV-BS	IP	H	R	HR	HB	BB-IB	SO	ERA	AERA	OAV	OOB	AB-SH	AVG	PB	Sup	APR	PW
DONNELLY, BRENDAN Brendan Kevin B 7.4.1971 Washington, DC BR/TR 6-3/205# d4.9																									
2002	†Ana A	1	1	.500	46	0	0	1-2	49.2	32	13	2	2	19-3	54	2.17	204	.184	.270	0-0	—	0		13	0.6
2003	Ana A★	2	2	.500	63	0	0	3-2	74	55	14	2	4	24-1	79	1.58	273	.200	.273	0-0	—	0		24	1.2
Total	2	3	3	.500	109	0	0	4-4	123.2	87	27	4	6	43-4	133	1.82	240	.194	.272	0-0	—	0		37	1.8
DONNELLY, ED Edward "Big Ed" or "Ned" (b: Edward O'Donnell) B 7.29.1880 Hampton, NY D 11.28.1957 Rutland, VT BR/TR 6-1/205# d9.19																									
1911	Bos N	3	2	.600	5	4	4-1	0	36.2	33	15	0	2	9	16	2.45	156	.236	.291	14-0	.071	-1	98	4	0.4
1912	Bos N	5	10	.333	37	18	10	0	184.1	225	127	10	5	72	67	4.35	82	.304	.370	69-4	.275	3*	83	-18	-0.9
Total	2	8	12	.400	42	22	14-1	0	221	258	142	10	7	81	83	4.03	90	.293	.357	83-4	.241	1	86	-14	-0.5
DONNELLY, ED Edward Vincent B 12.10.1932 Allen, MI D 12.25.1997 Houston, TX BR/TR 6/175# d8.1																									
1959	Chi N	1	1	.500	9	0	0	0	14.1	18	7	1	0	9-1	6	3.14	126	.305	.397	0-0	—	0		1	0.1
DONNELLY, FRANK Franklin Marion B 10.7.1869 Tamaroa, IL D 2.3.1953 Canton, IL 5-6/180# d8.15																									
1893	Chi N	3	1	.750	7	5	3	2	42	51	42	1	4	17	6	5.36	86	.291	.367	18	.444	4	124	-5	-0.1
1894	Chi N	0	0	—	1	0	0	0	4.2	6	8	0	0	8	1	15.43	37	.316	.519	1-0	.000	-0		-4	-0.1
Total	2	3	1	.750	8	5	3	2	46.2	57	50	1	4	25	7	6.36	74	.294	.386	19-0	.421	4	124	-9	-0.2
DONNELLY, BLIX Sylvester Urban B 1.21.1914 Olivia, MN D 6.20.1976 Olivia, MN BR/TR 5-10/178# d5.6																									
1944	†StL N	2	1	.667	27	4	2-1	2	76.1	61	26	2	2	34	45	2.12	166	.218	.307	16-2	.063	-1	119	10	0.5
1945	StL N	8	10	.444	31	23	9-4	2	166.1	157	79	10	6	87	76	3.52	106	.250	.346	54-6	.130	-2	101	2	-0.2
1946	StL N	1	2	.333	13	0	0	0	13.2	17	7	1	1	10	11	3.95	87	.347	.467	0-0	—	0		-1	-0.1
	Phi N	3	4	.429	12	8	2	1	76.1	64	31	7	2	24	38	2.95	116	.220	.284	25-0	.280	2	90	3	0.5
	Year	4	6	.400	25	8	2	1	90	81	35	8	3	34	49	3.10	111	.238	.313	25-0	.280	2	90	3	0.4
1947	Phi N	4	6	.400	38	10	5-1	5	120.2	113	44	6	3	46	31	2.98	134	.265	.340	32-5	.063	-2	97	15	1.0
1948	Phi N	5	7	.417	26	19	8-1	2	131.2	125	65	13	0	49	46	3.69	107	.261	.330	45-1	.222	2	102	3	0.3
1949	Phi N	2	1	.667	23	10	1	0	78.1	84	50	7	1	40	36	5.06	78	.294	.382	23-1	.174	-1	123	-10	-0.7
1950	Phi N	2	4	.333	14	1	0	0	21	30	13	5	0	10	10	4.29	94	.330	.396	5-0	.200	-0	65	-1	-0.2
1951	Bos N	0	1	.000	6	0	0	0	7.1	8	6	1	1	6	3	7.36	50	.286	.429	1-0	.000	-0		-3	-0.3
Total	8	27	36	.429	190	75	27-7	12	691.2	659	321	52	16	306	296	3.49	109	.257	.340	201-15	.159	-1	104	18	0.8
DONOHUE, JIM James Thomas B 10.31.1938 St.Louis, MO BR/TR 6-4/190# d4.11																									
1961	Det A	1	1	.500	14	0	0	1	20.1	23	10	2	0	15-2	20	3.54	116	.287	.400	1-0	.000	-0		1	0.1
	LA A	4	6	.400	38	7	0	5	100.1	93	48	16	0	50-4	79	4.31	105	.246	.332	27-0	.148	-1	84	5	0.3
	Year	5	7	.417	52	7	0	6	120.2	116	52	18	0	65-6	99	4.18	106	.253	.344	28-0	.143	-1	85	5	0.4
1962	LA A	1	0	1.000	12	1	0	0	24.1	24	14	4	2	11-0	14	3.70	104	.258	.349	4-1	.250	0	46	-1	0.0
	Min A	0	1	.000	6	1	0	1	10.1	12	8	2	0	6-0	3	6.97	59	.324	.419	2-0	.000	-0	109	-3	-0.3
	Year	1	1	.500	18	2	0	1	34.2	36	13	6	2	17-0	17	4.67	84	.277	.369	6-1	.167	0	80	-4	-0.3
Total	2	6	8	.429	70	9	0	7	155.1	152	80	24	2	82-6	116	4.29	101	.259	.350	34-1	.147	-1	84	2	0.1
DONOHUE, PETE Peter Joseph B 11.5.1900 Athens, TX D 2.23.1988 Ft.Worth, TX BR/TR 6-2/185# d7.1																									
1921	Cin N	7	6	.538	21	11	7	1	118.1	117	48	5	0	26	44	3.35	107	.263	.304	38-4	.211	1	98	6	0.8
1922	Cin N	18	9	**.667**	33	30	18-2	1	242	257	110	7	5	43	66	3.12	128	.276	.312	88-5	.182	-3	117	22	1.9
1923	Cin N	21	15	.583	42	36	19-2	3	274.1	304	138	3	10	68	84	3.38	114	.278	.326	96-4	.250	3	87	12	1.7
1924	Cin N	16	9	.640	35	31	16-3	0	222.1	248	100	9	9	36	72	3.60	105	.285	.321	73-4	.192	-0*	100	8	0.7
1925	Cin N	21	14	.600	42	**38**	**27**-3	2	**301**	310	122	3	2	49	78	3.08	133	.268	.299	109-7	.294	7*	97	38	4.6
1926	Cin N	**20**	14	.588	47	**36**	17-**5**	2	**285.2**	298	133	6	9	39	73	3.37	109	.268	.298	106-5	.311	9	112	9	1.7
1927	Cin N	6	16	.273	33	24	12-1	1	190.2	253	111	3	1	32	48	4.11	92	.328	.356	64-3	.250	1	91	-9	-0.8
1928	Cin N	7	11	.389	23	18	8	0	150	180	84	10	3	32	37	4.74	83	.309	.348	48-3	.146	-0	96	-10	-1.0
1929	Cin N	10	13	.435	32	24	7	0	177.2	243	123	12	4	51	30	5.42	84	.331	.377	60-4	.333	4	93	-18	-1.5
1930	Cin N	1	3	.250	8	5	2	1	34.1	53	24	0	1	13	4	6.29	77	.363	.419	10-1	.100	-1	76	-4	-0.5
	NY N	7	6	.538	18	11	4	1	86.2	135	65	6	2	18	26	6.13	77	.360	.392	33-2	.273	1	129	-12	-1.4
	Year	8	9	.471	26	16	6	2	121	188	72	6	3	31	30	6.17	77	.361	.400	43-3	.233	0	112	-18	-1.9
1931	NY N	0	1	.000	4	1	0	0	11.1	14	7	1	0	4	4	5.56	66	.311	.367	2-0	.000	-0	23	-2	-0.2
	Cle A	0	0	—	2	0	0	0	5.1	9	6	1	0	5	4	8.44	55	.429	.538	2-0	.000	-0		-2	-0.1
1932	Bos A	0	1	.000	4	2	0	0	12.2	18	11	2	0	6	1	7.82	57	.340	.407	3-0	.000	-0	66	-4	-0.3
Total	12	134	118	.532	344	267	137-16	12	2112.1	2439	1082	68	46	422	571	3.87	103	.293	.330	732-42	.246	21	100	34	5.6
DONOSO, LINO Lino (Galeta) B 9.23.1922 Havana, Cuba D 10.13.1990 Veracruz, Mexico BL/TL 5-11/160# d6.18																									
1955	Pit N	4	6	.400	25	9	3	1	95	106	58	16	1	35-3	38	5.31	78	.287	.345	27-3	.185	-1	108	-10	-1.0
1956	Pit N	0	0	—	3	0	0	0	1.2	2	0	0	0	1-0	1	0.00	—	.250	.333	0-0	—	0		1	0.0
Total	2	4	6	.400	28	9	3	1	96.2	108	58	16	1	36-3	39	5.21	79	.286	.345	27-3	.185	-1	108	-9	-1.0
DONOVAN, DICK Richard Edward B 12.7.1927 Boston, MA D 1.6.1997 Weymouth, MA BL/TR 6-3/205# d4.24																									
1950	Bos N	0	2	.000	10	3	0	0	29.2	28	28	4	2	34	9	8.19	47	.255	.438	6-0	.167	1	115	-14	-0.7
1951	Bos N	0	0	—	8	2	0	0	13.2	17	11	0	0	11	4	5.27	70	.298	.412	3-0	.333	1	264	-3	0.0
1952	Bos N	0	2	.000	7	2	0	1	13	18	10	1	2	12	6	5.54	65	.346	.485	3-0	.000	-0	25	-3	-0.5
1954	Det A	0	0	—	2	0	0	0	6	9	7	1	0	5	2	10.50	35	.360	.438	1-0	.000	-0		-4	-0.2
1955	Chi A☆	15	9	.625	29	24	11-5	0	187	186	77	17	3	48-5	88	3.32	119	.261	.310	76-1	.224	5*	94	12	1.9
1956	Chi A	12	10	.545	34	31	14-3	0	234.2	212	99	22	6	59-6	120	3.64	113	.240	**.290**	90-1	.222	8*	117	15	2.1
1957	Chi A	16	6	**.727**	28	28	**16**-2	0	220.2	203	76	17	8	45-8	88	2.77	135	.247	.291	83-1	.145	2*	118	23	2.4
1958	Chi A	15	14	.517	34	34	16-4	0	248	240	92	23	7	53-5	127	3.01	121	.251	.295	80-2	.112	-1	81	18	1.8
1959	†Chi A	9	10	.474	31	29	5-1	0	179.2	171	84	15	5	58-3	71	3.66	103	.247	.308	61-3	.131	1	86	1	0.1
1960	Chi A	6	1	.857	33	8	0	3	78.2	87	49	13	0	25-3	30	5.38	70	.283	.333	23-0	.130	-0	114	-13	-1.1
1961	Was A★	10	10	.500	23	22	11-2	0	168.2	138	60	10	3	35-3	62	**2.40**	**167**	.224	**.267**	56-1	.179	2*	86	27	3.3
1962	Cle A★	20	10	.667	34	34	16-**5**	0	250.2	255	109	23	2	47-5	94	3.59	108	.263	.297	89-2	.180	6	107	10	1.6
1963	Cle A	11	13	.458	30	30	7-3	0	206	211	106	27	5	28-5	84	4.24	85	.265	.292	69-3	.130	-1*	102	-12	-1.5
1964	Cle A	7	9	.438	30	23	5	1	158.1	181	86	19	2	29-6	83	4.55	79	.290	.321	48-4	.146	3*	117	-15	-1.1
1965	Cle A	1	3	.250	12	3	0	0	22.2	32	15	6	0	6-0	12	5.96	58	.333	.373	6-0	.000	-1	76	-5	-0.9
Total	15	122	99	.552	345	273	101-25	5	2017.1	1988	909	198	45	495-49	880	3.67	104	.258	.305	694-18	.163	24	102	37	7.2
DONOVAN, BILL Willard Earl B 7.6.1916 Maywood, IL D 9.25.1997 Maywood, IL BB/TL 6-2/198# d4.19 Mil 1943-45																									
1942	Bos N	3	6	.333	31	10	2	0	89.1	97	43	2	0	32	23	3.43	97	.283	.344	25-2	.240	1	75	-2	0.0
1943	Bos N	1	0	1.000	7	0	0	0	14.2	17	4	0	0	9	1	1.84	185	.304	.400	3-0	.333	0		2	0.2
Total	2	4	6	.400	38	10	2	0	104	114	47	2	0	41	24	3.20	105	.286	.352	28-2	.250	1	75	0	0.2
DONOVAN, BILL William Edward "Wild Bill" B 10.13.1876 Lawrence, MA D 12.9.1923 Forsyth, NY BR/TR 5-11/190# d4.22 M4 C1 ▲																									
1898	Was N	1	6	.143	17	7	6	0	88	88	74	0	7	69	36	4.30	85	.259	.394	103-1	.165	-1*	41	-11	-0.8
1899	Bro N	1	2	.333	5	2	2	1	25	35	22	0	0	13	11	4.32	91	.330	.403	13-0	.231	-0	110	-3	-0.3
1900	Bro N	1	2	.333	5	4	2	0	31	36	23	0	3	18	13	6.68	57	.290	.393	13-0	.000	-2	104	-7	-0.6
1901	Bro N	**25**	15	.625	**45**	38	36-2	**3**	351	324	151	1	8	152	226	2.77	121	.244	.325	135-8	.170	-1*	117	23	2.2
1902	Bro N	17	15	.531	35	33	30-4	1	297.2	250	122	1	7	111	170	2.78	99	.228	.303	161-2	.174	-0*	98	1	0.1
1903	Det A	17	16	.515	35	34	**34**-4	0	307	247	104	3	5	95	187	2.29	127	.220	.284	124-9	.242	4*	106	25	3.0
1904	Det A	16	16	.500	34	34	30-3	0	293	251	111	5	10	94	137	2.46	104	.232	.300	140-5	.271	5*	100	4	1.1
1905	Det A	18	15	.545	34	32	27-5	0	280.2	236	111	2	10	101	135	2.60	105	.230	.305	130-13	.192	1*	100	5	0.7
1906	Det A	9	15	.375	25	25	22	0	211.2	221	92	4	8	72	85	3.15	88	.272	.337	91-4	.121	-5*	76	-7	-1.3
1907	†Det A	25	4	**.862**	32	28	27-3	1	271	222	96	3	8	82	123	2.19	119	.226	.291	109-4	.266	7*	156	13	1.9
1908	†Det A	18	7	.720	29	28	25-6	0	242.2	210	78	2	6	53	141	2.08	116	.231	.278	82-1	.159	0*	122	11	0.8
1909	†Det A	8	7	.533	21	17	13-4	2	140.1	121	50	0	6	60	76	2.31	109	.235	.322	45-5	.200	1*	97	3	0.3
1910	Det A	17	7	.708	26	23	20-3	0	206.2	184	74	4	7	61	107	2.44	108	.243	.305	69-2	.145	-2	101	5	0.0
1911	Det A	10	9	.526	20	19	15-1	0	168.1	160	83	4	3	64	81	3.31	104	.250	.321	60-1	.200	3*	133	3	0.4
1912	Det A	1	0	1.000	3	1	0	0	10	5	2	0	1	2	6	0.90	362	.147	.216	13-0	.077	-1*	226	2	0.1
1915	NY A	0	3	.000	9	1	0	0	33.2	35	18	1	1	10	17	4.81	61	.278	.336	12-0	.083	-1*	99	-5	-0.6
1916	NY A	0	0	—	1	0	0	0	1	1	0	0	0	1	0	0.00	—	.250	.400	0-0	—	0		0	0.0

Year	Tm Lg	W	L	Pct	G	GS	CG-Sho	SV-BS	IP	H	R	HR	HB	BB-IB	SO	ERA	AERA	OAV	OOB	AB-SH	AVG	PB	Sup	APR	PW
1918	Det A	1	0	1.000	2	1	0	0	6	5	1	0	0	1	1	1.50	177	.227	.261	2-0	.500	0	198	1	0.2
Total	18	185	139	.571	378	327	289-35	8	2964.2	2631	1212	30	90	1059	1552	2.69	106	.239	.310	1302-55	.193	8	108	63	7.2

DOPSON, JOHN John Robert B 7.14.1963 Baltimore, MD BL/TR 6-4/225# d9.4

Year	Tm Lg	W	L	Pct	G	GS	CG-Sho	SV-BS	IP	H	R	HR	HB	BB-IB	SO	ERA	AERA	OAV	OOB	AB-SH	AVG	PB	Sup	APR	PW
1985	Mon N	0	2	.000	4	3	0	0-0	13	25	17	4	0	4-0	4	11.08	31	.379	.414	4-0	.000	0	52	-11	-1.3
1988	Mon N	3	11	.214	26	26	1	0-0	168.2	150	69	15	1	58-3	101	3.04	118	.235	.299	51-4	.059	-3	81	9	0.3
1989	Bos A	12	8	.600	29	28	2	0-0	169.1	166	84	14	2	69-0	95	3.99	103	.257	.328	0-0	—	0	102	3	0.4
1990	Bos A	0	0	—	4	4	0	0-0	17.2	13	7	2	0	9-0	9	2.04	201	.200	.293	0-0	—	0	95	3	0.2
1991	Bos A	0	0	—	1	0	0	0-0	1	2	2	0	0	1-0	0	18.00	24	.500	.500	0-0	—	0		-1	-0.1
1992	Bos A	7	11	.389	25	25	0	0-0	141.1	159	78	17	2	38-2	55	4.08	104	.287	.334	0-0	—	0	81	0	0.1
1993	Bos A	7	11	.389	34	28	1-1	0-0	155.2	170	93	16	2	59-12	89	4.97	93	.281	.343	0-0	—	0	98	-4	-0.3
1994	Cal A	1	4	.200	21	5	0	1-1	58.2	67	41	6	3	26-3	33	6.14	80	.288	.365	0-0	—	0	71	-7	-0.5
Total	8	30	47	.390	144	119	4-1	1-1	725.1	752	391	74	10	264-20	386	4.27	98	.268	.331	55-4	.055	-3	89	-8	-1.2

DORAN, JOHN John F. B 1867 Chicago, IL TL 5-11/175# d4.11

Year	Tm Lg	W	L	Pct	G	GS	CG-Sho	SV-BS	IP	H	R	HR	HB	BB-IB	SO	ERA	AERA	OAV	OOB	AB-SH	AVG	PB	Sup	APR	PW
1891	Lou AA	5	10	.333	15	14	12-1	0	126	160	111	3	13	75	55	5.43	67	.299	.398	53	.189	-2	78	-23	-2.2

DORGAN, MIKE Michael Cornelius B 10.2.1853 Middletown, CT D 4.26.1909 Hartford, CT BR/TR 5-9/180# d5.8.1877 M3 b-Jerry ▲

Year	Tm Lg	W	L	Pct	G	GS	CG-Sho	SV-BS	IP	H	R	HR	HB	BB-IB	SO	ERA	AERA	OAV	OOB	AB-SH	AVG	PB	Sup	APR	PW
1879	Syr N	0	0	—	2	0	0	0	12	13	6	0		2	8	2.25	105	.260	.288	270	.267	0*		0	0.0
1880	Pro N	0	0	—	1	0	0	0	8	4	3	0		0	2	1.13	196	.138	.138	321	.246	0*		1	0.1
1883	NY N	0	1	.000	1	1	1	0	7	8	7	0		6	3	3.86	80	.286	.412	261	.234	0*	35	-1	-0.1
1884	NY N	8	6	.571	14	14	12	0	113	98	84	5		51	90	3.50	85	.215	.294	341	.276	2*	130	-8	-0.6
Total	4	8	7	.533	18	15	13	0	140	123	100	5		59	103	3.28	88	.218	.293	1193	.256	3	126	-8	-0.6

DORISH, HARRY Harry "Fritz" B 7.13.1921 Swoyersville, PA D 12.31.2000 Wilkes-Barre, PA BR/TR 5-11/206# d4.15 C5

Year	Tm Lg	W	L	Pct	G	GS	CG-Sho	SV-BS	IP	H	R	HR	HB	BB-IB	SO	ERA	AERA	OAV	OOB	AB-SH	AVG	PB	Sup	APR	PW
1947	Bos A	7	8	.467	41	9	2	2	136	149	80	6	1	54	50	4.70	83	.283	.351	35-4	.143	-1	94	-11	-1.3
1948	Bos A	0	1	.000	9	0	0	0	14.1	18	13	1	0	6	5	5.65	78	.281	.343	4-0	.250	-0		-3	-0.2
1949	Bos A	0	0	—	5	0	0	0	7.2	7	2	1	0	1	5	2.35	186	.241	.267	0-0	—	0		2	0.1
1950	StL A	4	9	.308	29	13	4	0	109	162	90	13	9	36	36	6.44	77	.337	.394	31-1	.161	0*	91	-16	-1.6
1951	Chi A	5	6	.455	32	4	2-1	0	96.2	101	50	6	0	31	29	3.54	114	.272	.328	31-0	.258	0	88	3	0.4
1952	Chi A	8	4	.667	39	1	1	**11**	91	66	28	4	1	42	47	2.47	148	.208	.303	22-2	.091	-1	72	**12**	1.8
1953	Chi A	10	6	.625	55	6	2	18	145.2	140	59	9	6	52	69	3.40	118	.254	.325	41-3	.171	-2	92	11	1.3
1954	Chi A	6	4	.600	37	6	2-1	6	109	88	35	9	1	29	48	2.72	137	.228	.282	27-2	.111	-2	106	13	1.0
1955	Chi A	2	0	1.000	13	0	0	1	17	16	4	0	0	9-1	6	1.59	249	.258	.352	3-0	.333	0		4	0.5
	Bal A	3	3	.500	35	1	0	6	65.2	58	25	5	1	28-2	22	3.15	121	.238	.318	10-1	.000	-1	0	6	0.5
	Year	5	3	.625	48	1	0	7	82.2	74	25	5	1	37-3	28	2.83	136	.242	.325	13-1	.077	-1	0	10	1.0
1956	Bal A	0	0	—	13	0	0	0	19.2	22	10	3	0	3-0	4	4.12	95	.297	.316	0-0	—	0		0	0.0
	Bos A	0	2	.000	15	0	0	0	22.2	23	10	1	0	10-1	11	3.57	129	.277	.351	0-0	—	0		3	0.3
	Year	0	2	.000	28	0	0	0	42.1	45	20	4	0	13-1	15	3.83	112	.287	.335	0-0	—	0		2	0.3
Total	10	45	43	.511	323	40	13-2	44	834.1	850	406	58	19	301-4	332	3.83	106	.267	.333	204-13	.157	-6	95	24	2.8

DORNER, GUS Augustus B 8.18.1876 Chambersburg, PA D 5.4.1956 Chambersburg, PA BR/TR 5-10/176# d9.17

Year	Tm Lg	W	L	Pct	G	GS	CG-Sho	SV-BS	IP	H	R	HR	HB	BB-IB	SO	ERA	AERA	OAV	OOB	AB-SH	AVG	PB	Sup	APR	PW
1902	Cle A	3	1	.750	4	4	4-1	0	36	33	13	1	1	13	5	1.25	275	.244	.315	13-1	.385	2	63	7	1.0
1903	Cle A	3	5	.375	12	8	4-2	0	73.2	83	51	4	1	24	28	4.52	63	.283	.340	25-3	.080	-2	106	-12	-1.3
1906	Cin N	0	1	.000	2	1	1	0	15	16	5	0	1	4	5	1.20	230	.276	.333	5-0	.000	-1	26	2	0.0
	Bos N	8	25	.242	34	32	29	0	273.1	264	152	5	16	103	104	3.65	74	.260	.338	100-5	.140	-4	68	-28	-3.5
	Year	8	26	.235	36	33	30	0	288.1	280	155	5	17	107	109	3.53	76	.261	.338	105-5	.133	-5	66	-29	-3.5
1907	Bos N	12	16	.429	36	31	24-2	0	271.1	253	120	4	15	92	85	3.12	82	.255	.327	92-7	.130	-3	81	-15	-2.1
1908	Bos N	8	19	.296	38	28	14-3	0	216.1	176	120	3	15	77	41	3.54	68	.224	.305	67-5	.179	-1	103	-27	-3.3
1909	Bos N	1	2	.333	5	2	0	1	24.2	17	11	1	2	17	7	2.55	110	.198	.343	6-1	.167	-0	37	0	0.0
Total	6	35	69	.337	131	106	76-8	1	910.1	842	472	18	51	330	275	3.37	78	.250	.326	308-22	.149	-9	82	-73	-9.2

DORR, BERT Charles Albert B 2.2.1862 , NY D 6.16.1914 Dickinson, NY d8.24

Year	Tm Lg	W	L	Pct	G	GS	CG-Sho	SV-BS	IP	H	R	HR	HB	BB-IB	SO	ERA	AERA	OAV	OOB	AB-SH	AVG	PB	Sup	APR	PW
1882	StL AA	2	6	.250	8	8	8	0	66	53	39	0		1	34	2.59	108	.205	.208	26	.154	-2	64	2	0.1

DORSETT, CAL Calvin Leavelle "Preacher" B 6.10.1913 Lone Oak, TX D 10.22.1970 Elk City, OK BR/TR 6/180# d8.19 Mil 1942-45

Year	Tm Lg	W	L	Pct	G	GS	CG-Sho	SV-BS	IP	H	R	HR	HB	BB-IB	SO	ERA	AERA	OAV	OOB	AB-SH	AVG	PB	Sup	APR	PW
1940	Cle A	0	0	—	1	0	0	0	1	1	1	1	0	0	0	9.00	47	.250	.250	0-0	—	0		0	0.0
1941	Cle A	0	1	.000	5	2	0	0	11.1	21	15	0	0	10	5	10.32	38	.382	.477	2-0	.000	-0	88	-9	-0.6
1947	Cle A	0	0	—	2	0	0	0	1.1	3	4	1	0	3	1	27.00	13	.500	.667	0-1	—	0		-4	-0.2
Total	3	0	1	.000	8	2	0	0	13.2	25	20	2	0	13	6	11.85	33	.385	.487	2-1	.000	-0	88	-13	-0.8

DORSEY, JIM James Edward B 8.2.1955 Oak Park, IL BR/TR 6-7/190# d9.2

Year	Tm Lg	W	L	Pct	G	GS	CG-Sho	SV-BS	IP	H	R	HR	HB	BB-IB	SO	ERA	AERA	OAV	OOB	AB-SH	AVG	PB	Sup	APR	PW
1980	Cal A	1	2	.333	4	4	0	0-0	15.2	25	16	2	1	8-0	8	9.19	43	.368	.436	0-0	—	0	97	-9	-1.2
1984	Bos A	0	0	—	2	0	0	0-0	2.2	6	3	0	0	2-0	4	10.13	41	.462	.533	0-0	—	0		-2	-0.1
1985	Bos A	0	1	.000	2	1	0	0-0	5.1	12	12	2	0	10-1	2	20.25	21	.444	.595	0-0	—	0	64	-9	-1.1
Total	3	1	3	.250	8	5	0	0-0	23.2	43	31	4	1	20-1	14	11.79	34	.398	.492	0-0	—	0	89	-20	-2.4

DORSEY, JERRY Michael Jeremiah B 1854 , , CAN D 11.3.1938 Auburn, NY BL d7.9

Year	Tm Lg	W	L	Pct	G	GS	CG-Sho	SV-BS	IP	H	R	HR	HB	BB-IB	SO	ERA	AERA	OAV	OOB	AB-SH	AVG	PB	Sup	APR	PW
1884	Bal U	0	1	.000	1	1	0	0	4	7	8	1		0	3	9.00	30	.368	.368	3	.000	-1	32	-3	-0.4

DOSCHER, JACK John Henry Jr. B 7.27.1880 Troy, NY D 5.27.1971 Park Ridge, NJ BL/TL 6-1/205# d7.2 f-Herm

Year	Tm Lg	W	L	Pct	G	GS	CG-Sho	SV-BS	IP	H	R	HR	HB	BB-IB	SO	ERA	AERA	OAV	OOB	AB-SH	AVG	PB	Sup	APR	PW
1903	Chi N	0	1	.000	1	1	0	0	3	6	5	0	1	2	5	12.00	26	.429	.529	1-0	.000	-0	43	-3	-0.4
	Bro N	0	0	—	3	0	0	0	7	8	8	1	1	9	4	7.71	41	.296	.486	3-0	.000	-0		-3	-0.2
	Year	0	1	.000	4	1	0	0	10	14	15	1	2	11	9	9.00	35	.341	.500	4-0	.000	-1	42	-6	-0.6
1904	Bro N	0	0	—	2	0	0	0	6.1	1	1	0	0	1	2	0.00	—	.053	.100	2-0	.500	0		2	0.1
1905	Bro N	1	5	.167	12	7	6	0	71	60	34	1	3	30	33	3.17	91	.232	.318	24-1	.083	-2	78	-2	-0.4
1906	Bro N	0	1	.000	2	1	1	0	14	12	3	0	0	4	10	1.29	196	.250	.308	5-0	.000	-1	0	2	0.0
1908	Cin N	1	3	.250	7	4	3	0	44.1	31	19	1	3	22	7	1.83	126	.196	.306	15-0	.133	0	53	0	0.0
Total	5	2	10	.167	27	13	10	0	145.2	118	70	3	8	68	61	2.84	95	.225	.323	50-1	.100	-3	63	-4	-0.9

DOTEL, OCTAVIO Octavio Eduardo (Diaz) B 11.25.1973 Santo Domingo, D.R. BR/TR 6/175# d6.26

Year	Tm Lg	W	L	Pct	G	GS	CG-Sho	SV-BS	IP	H	R	HR	HB	BB-IB	SO	ERA	AERA	OAV	OOB	AB-SH	AVG	PB	Sup	APR	PW
1999	†NY N	8	3	.727	19	14	0	0-0	85.1	69	52	12	6	49-1	85	5.38	81	.226	.340	24-1	.125	1	121	-10	-1.0
2000	Hou N	3	7	.300	50	16	0	16-7	125	127	80	26	7	61-3	142	5.40	90	.265	.351	32-7	.031	-3	93	-6	-0.9
2001	†Hou N	7	5	.583	61	4	0	2-2	105	79	35	5	2	47-2	145	2.66	172	.205	.294	11-1	.091	-1	101	21	2.2
2002	Hou N	6	4	.600	83	0	0	6-4	97.1	58	21	7	4	27-2	118	1.85	231	.173	.239	1-0	.000	-0		**26**	2.6
2003	Hou N	6	4	.600	76	0	0	4-2	87	53	25	9	3	31-2	97	2.48	179	.172	.253	6-0	.000	-1		19	1.9
Total	5	30	23	.566	289	34	0	28-15	499.2	386	213	59	22	215-10	587	3.62	125	.213	.300	74-9	.068	-4	108	50	4.8

DOTSON, RICHARD Richard Elliott B 1.10.1959 Cincinnati, OH BR/TR 6/204# d9.4

Year	Tm Lg	W	L	Pct	G	GS	CG-Sho	SV-BS	IP	H	R	HR	HB	BB-IB	SO	ERA	AERA	OAV	OOB	AB-SH	AVG	PB	Sup	APR	PW
1979	Chi A	2	0	1.000	5	5	1-1	0-0	24.1	28	13	0	0	6-0	13	3.70	115	.286	.321	0-0	—	0	128	1	0.1
1980	Chi A	12	10	.545	33	32	8	0-0	198	185	105	20	6	87-2	109	4.27	94	.247	.328	0-0	—	0*	99	-4	-0.3
1981	Chi A	9	8	.529	24	24	5-**4**	0-0	141	145	67	13	4	49-0	73	3.77	95	.270	.333	0-0	—	0*	140	-2	-0.3
1982	Chi A	11	15	.423	34	31	3-1	0-0	196.2	219	97	19	5	73-4	109	3.84	105	.282	.345	0-0	—	0	93	4	0.5
1983	†Chi A	22	7	**.759**	35	35	8-1	0-0	240	209	92	19	8	106-1	137	3.23	130	.240	.325	0-0	—	0	127	26	3.2
1984	Chi A★	14	15	.483	32	32	14-1	0-0	245.2	216	110	24	7	103-5	120	3.59	116	.238	.317	0-0	—	0*	93	14	1.5
1985	Chi A	3	4	.429	9	9	0	0-0	52.1	53	30	5	3	17-1	33	4.47	97	.261	.324	0-0	—	0	66	-1	-0.2
1986	Chi A	10	17	.370	34	34	3-1	0-0	197	226	125	24	2	69-2	110	5.48	79	.289	.347	0-0	—	0	81	-21	-2.5
1987	Chi A	11	12	.478	31	31	7-2	0-0	211.1	201	109	24	0	86-2	114	4.17	110	.249	.320	0-0	—	0	79	8	0.8
1988	NY A	12	9	.571	32	29	4	0-0	171	178	103	27	4	72-3	77	5.00	79	.266	.338	0-0	—	0	131	-20	-2.2
1989	NY A	2	5	.286	11	9	1	0-0	51.2	69	33	8	1	17-0	14	5.57	70	.317	.366	0-0	—	0	101	-9	-1.1
	Chi A	3	7	.300	17	17	1	0-0	99.2	112	51	8	0	41-3	55	3.88	98	.282	.348	0-0	—	0	99	-2	-0.2
	Year	5	12	.294	28	26	2	0-0	151.1	181	55	16	1	58-3	69	4.46	86	.294	.354	0-0	—	0	100	-11	-1.3
1990	KC A	0	4	.000	8	7	0	0-0	28.2	43	29	3	0	14-1	9	8.48	45	.355	.410	0-0	—	0	95	-14	-1.6
Total	12	111	113	.496	305	295	55-11	0-0	1857.1	1884	964	194	40	740-24	973	4.23	97	.264	.334	0-0	—	0	102	-20	-2.3

Year	Tm Lg	W	L	Pct	G	GS	CG-Sho	SV-BS	IP	H	R	HR	HB	BB-IB	SO	ERA	AERA	OAV	OOB	AB-SH	AVG	PB	Sup	APR	PW
DOTTER, GARY Gary Richard B 8.7.1942 St.Louis, MO BL/TL 6-1/180# d9.10																									
1961	Min A	0	0	—	2	0	0	0	6	6	6	0	0	4-1	2	9.00	47	.273	.357	1-0	.000	-0		-3	-0.1
1963	Min A	0	0	—	2	0	0	0	2	0	0	0	0	0-0	2	0.00	—	.000	.000	0-0	—	0		1	0.1
1964	Min A	0	0	—	3	0	0	0	4.1	3	2	1	0	3-0	6	2.08	172	.188	.316	0-0	—	0		0	0.0
Total	3	0	0	—	7	0	0	0	12.1	9	8	1	0	7-1	10	5.11	76	.205	.302	1-0	.000	-0		-2	0.0
DOTY, BABE Elmer L. B 12.17.1867 Lyons, NY D 11.20.1929 Toledo, OH BL/TR 6/160# d8.18																									
1890	Tol AA	1	0	1.000	1	1	1	0	9	9	1	0	0	1	4	1.00	395	.250	.270	3	.000	-0	85	3	0.3
DOUGHERTY, JIM James E. B 3.8.1968 Brentwood, NY BR/TR 6/210# d4.27																									
1995	Hou N	8	4	.667	56	0	0	0-2	67.2	76	37	7	3	25-1	49	4.92	79	.292	.357	8-1	.125	-0		-6	-0.9
1996	Hou N	0	2	.000	12	0	0	0-1	13	14	14	2	1	11-1	6	9.00	43	.280	.413	0-0	—	0		-8	-1.0
1998	Oak A	0	2	.000	9	0	0	0-1	12	17	11	2	1	7-0	3	8.25	55	.340	.431	0-0	—	0		-4	-0.6
1999	Pit N	0	0	—	2	0	0	0-0	2	3	3	0	0	3-0	1	9.00	51	.333	.500	0-0	—	0		-1	0.0
Total	4	8	8	.500	79	0	0	0-4	94.2	110	65	11	5	46-2	59	5.99	66	.298	.380	8-1	.125	0		-19	-2.5
DOUGHERTY, TOM Thomas James "Sugar Boy" B 5.30.1881 Chicago, IL D 11.6.1953 Milwaukee, WI BL/TR ?/195# d4.24																									
1904	Chi A	1	0	1.000	1	0	0	0	2	0	0	0	0	0	0	0.00	—	.000	.000	1-0	.000	-0		1	0.1
DOUGLAS, WHAMMY Charles William B 2.17.1935 Carrboro, NC BR/TR 6-2/185# d7.29																									
1957	Pit N	3	3	.500	11	8	0	0	47	48	23	5	3	30-2	28	3.26	116	.270	.384	16-0	.063	-1	93	1	0.0
DOUGLAS, LARRY Lawrence Howard B 6.5.1890 Jellico, TN D 11.4.1949 Jellico, TN 6-3/175# d6.17																									
1915	Bal F	1	0	1.000	2	1	0	0	3	3	1	0	0	2	1	3.00	96	.273	.385	0-0	—	0		0	0.0
DOUGLAS, PHIL Phillip Brooks "Shufflin' Phil" B 6.17.1890 Cedartown, GA D 8.1.1952 Sequatchie, TN BR/TR 6-3/190# d8.30																									
1912	Chi A	0	1	.000	3	1	0	0	12.1	21	17	0	0	6	7	7.30	44	.382	.443	2-1	.000	-0	46	-7	-0.5
1914	Cin N	11	18	.379	45	25	13	1	239.1	186	111	7	11	92	121	2.56	115	.223	.308	73-4	.137	-2	91	5	0.2
1915	Cin N	1	5	.167	8	7	0	0	46.2	53	35	0	0	23	29	5.40	53	.299	.380	17-0	.118	-1	97	-12	-1.5
	Bro N	5	5	.500	20	13	5-1	0	116.2	104	45	1	5	17	63	2.62	106	.241	.278	39-0	.154	-1	101	2	0.1
	Chi N	1	1	.500	4	4	2-1	0	25	17	9	0	1	7	18	2.16	129	.187	.253	8-0	.000	-1	100	1	0.0
	Year	7	11	.389	32	24	7-2	0	188.1	174	13	1	6	47	110	3.25	86	.249	.301	64-0	.125	-3	100	-8	-1.4
1917	Chi N	14	20	.412	**51**	37	20-5	1	293.1	269	123	13	6	50	151	2.55	114	.250	.287	87-7	.126	-4	80	8	0.7
1918	†Chi N	10	9	.526	25	19	11-2	2	156.2	145	57	2	1	31	51	2.13	131	.246	.285	55-2	.255	1	90	9	1.4
1919	Chi N	10	6	.625	25	19	8-4	0	161.2	133	52	0	2	34	63	2.00	144	.230	.275	51-3	.157	-2	93	14	1.5
	NY N	2	4	.333	8	6	4	0	51.1	53	22	0	1	6	21	2.10	133	.264	.288	15-1	.000	-2	90	1	-0.1
	Year	12	10	.545	33	25	12-4	0	213	186	25	0	3	40	84	2.03	141	.238	.278	66-4	.121	-4	92	15	1.4
1920	NY N	14	10	.583	46	21	10-3	2	226	225	84	6	2	55	71	2.71	111	.263	.309	73-2	.151	-4	125	8	0.4
1921	†NY N	15	10	.600	40	27	13-**3**	2	221.2	266	119	17	2	55	55	4.22	87	.308	.351	81-5	.198	0	147	-13	-1.2
1922	NY N	11	4	.733	24	21	9-1	0	157.2	154	56	6	4	35	33	**2.63**	**152**	**.257**	**.302**	58-1	.207	1	115	25	2.1
Total	9	94	93	.503	299	200	95-20	8	1708.1	1626	730	52	35	411	683	2.80	111	.256	.305	559-26	.161	-16	105	41	3.1
DOUGLASS, SEAN Sean R. B 4.28.1979 Lancaster, CA BR/TR 6-6/198# d7.18																									
2001	Bal A	2	1	.667	4	4	0	0-0	20.1	21	12	3	1	11-0	17	5.31	81	.259	.351	0-0	—	0	124	-2	-0.2
2002	Bal A	0	5	.000	15	8	0	0-0	53.1	58	41	10	2	35-2	44	6.08	70	.283	.391	0-0	—	0	90	-12	-0.9
2003	Bal A	0	0	—	3	0	0	0-0	8	14	12	2	1	6-0	3	13.50	33	.378	.477	0-0	—	0		-8	-0.4
Total	3	2	6	.250	22	12	0	0-0	81.2	93	65	15	4	52-2	64	6.61	65	.288	.391	0-0	—	0	101	-22	-1.5
DOWD, SKIP James Joseph B 2.16.1889 Holyoke, MA D 12.20.1960 Holyoke, MA BR/TR 5-10.5/160# d7.5																									
1910	Pit N	0	0	—	1	0	0	0	2	4	4	0	1	2	1	0.00	—	.400	.538	0-0	—	0		-1	0.0
DOWLING, DAVE David Barclay B 8.23.1942 Baton Rouge, LA BR/TL 6-2/181# d10.3																									
1964	StL N	0	0	—	1	0	0	0	1	2	0	0	0	0-0	0	0.00	—	.400	.400	0-0	—	0		0	0.0
1966	Chi N	1	0	1.000	1	1	1	0	9	10	2	0	0	0-0	3	2.00	184	.270	.270	2-2	.000	-0	167	2	0.2
Total	2	1	0	1.000	2	1	1	0	10	12	2	0	0	0-0	3	1.80	205	.286	.286	2-2	.000	-0	167	2	0.2
DOWLING, PETE Henry Peter B St.Louis, MO D 6.30.1905 Hot Lake, OR BL/TL 5-11/165# d7.17																									
1897	Lou N	1	2	.333	4	4	2	0	26	39	30	0	6	8	3	5.88	72	.342	.414	10-0	.200	-0	121	-6	-0.5
1898	Lou N	13	20	.394	36	32	30	0	285.2	284	176	7	22	120	84	4.16	86	.257	.342	107-2	.196	1	85	-19	-1.7
1899	Lou N	13	17	.433	35	33	30	0	298.1	329	166	6	17	95	89	3.05	127	.279	.342	119-2	.227	-1	90	22	1.7
1901	Mil A	1	3	.250	10	4	3	1	49.2	71	49	1	4	14	25	5.62	64	.332	.384	19-0	.211	1	103	-12	-0.7
	Cle A	11	22	.333	33	30	28-2	0	256.1	269	160	1	15	104	99	3.86	92	.267	.344	99-1	.162	-4	71	-6	-1.0
	Year	12	25	.324	43	34	31-2	1	306	340	164	2	19	118	124	4.15	86	.278	.351	118-1	.169	-3	75	-21	-1.7
Total	4	39	64	.379	118	103	93-2	1	916	992	581	15	64	341	300	3.84	96	.274	.347	354-5	.198	-3	85	-21	-2.2
DOWNING, AL Alphonso Erwin B 6.28.1941 Trenton, NJ BR/TL 5-11/177# d7.19																									
1961	NY A	0	1	.000	5	1	0	0	9	7	8	0	1	12-0	12	8.00	46	.212	.426	1-0	.000	-0	48	-4	-0.4
1962	NY A	0	0	—	1	0	0	0	1	0	0	0	0	0-0	1	0.00	—	.000	.000	0-0	—	0		0	0.0
1963	†NY A	13	5	.722	24	22	10-4	0	175.2	114	52	7	0	80-1	171	2.56	137	**.184**	.277	58-3	.103	-2	106	21	1.8
1964	†NY A	13	8	.619	37	35	11-1	2	244	201	104	18	0	120-5	**217**	3.47	104	.223	.312	85-4	.176	1*	107	4	0.4
1965	NY A	12	14	.462	35	32	8-2	0	212	185	92	16	2	105-2	179	3.40	100	.237	.326	74-6	.108	-1*	104	0	-0.1
1966	NY A	10	11	.476	30	30	1	0	200	178	90	23	1	79-3	152	3.56	94	.235	.307	70-5	.100	-2	109	-5	-0.9
1967	NY A★	14	10	.583	31	28	10-4	0	201.2	158	65	13	6	61-1	171	2.63	119	.217	.281	66-1	.121	1	88	13	1.7
1968	NY A	3	3	.500	15	12	1	0	61.1	54	24	7	1	20-2	40	3.52	82	.237	.299	17-0	.176	0	65	-3	-0.2
1969	NY A	7	5	.583	30	15	5-1	0-0	130.2	117	57	12	0	49-6	85	3.38	103	.240	.306	44-2	.136	-0	114	1	0.0
1970	Oak A	3	3	.500	10	6	1	0-0	41	39	19	5	1	22-0	26	3.95	90	.252	.346	11-1	.182	-0	122	-1	-0.1
	Mil A	2	10	.167	17	16	1	0-0	94.1	79	47	8	3	59-2	53	3.34	114	.232	.346	24-7	.083	-2	57	1	0.0
	Year	5	13	.278	27	22	2	0-0	135.1	118	49	13	4	81-2	79	3.52	105	.238	.346	35-8	.114	-2	74	1	-0.1
1971	LA N	20	9	.690	37	36	12-**5**	0-0	262.1	245	93	16	3	84-3	136	2.68	121	.247	.307	92-8	.174	2	127	15	1.8
1972	LA N	9	9	.500	31	30	7-4	0-0	202.2	196	81	13	7	67-2	117	2.98	112	.254	.317	66-6	.121	-1	117	9	0.9
1973	LA N	9	9	.500	30	28	5-2	0-0	193	155	87	19	1	68-3	124	3.31	104	.219	.288	57-7	.088	-1	112	0	-0.1
1974	†LA N	5	6	.455	21	16	1-1	0-1	98.1	94	52	7	3	45-0	63	3.66	93	.255	.338	29-3	.172	-0	133	-6	-0.5
1975	LA N	2	1	.667	22	6	0	1-2	74.2	59	31	6	2	28-1	39	2.89	118	.215	.292	16-0	.000	-1	103	3	0.1
1976	LA N	1	2	.333	17	3	0	0-0	46.2	43	21	3	0	18-1	30	3.86	88	.250	.318	6-0	.000	-1	52	-2	-0.2
1977	LA N	0	1	.000	12	1	0	0-0	20	22	15	4	0	16-0	23	6.75	57	.278	.400	1-0	.000	-0	116	-6	-0.3
Total	17	123	107	.535	405	317	73-24	3-3	2268.1	1946	938	177	31	933-32	1639	3.22	106	.232	.309	717-53	.127	-7	106	40	3.9
DOWNS, DAVE David Ralph B 6.21.1952 Logan, UT BR/TR 6-5/220# d9.2 b-Kelly																									
1972	Phi N	1	1	.500	4	4	1-1	0-0	23	25	7	1	1	3-0	5	2.74	131	.294	.326	8-0	.250	0	80	2	0.2
DOWNS, KELLY Kelly Robert B 10.25.1960 Ogden, UT BR/TR 6-4/200# d7.29 b-Dave																									
1986	SF N	4	4	.500	14	14	1	0-0	88.1	78	29	5	3	30-7	64	2.75	128	.236	.302	29-0	.172	0*	81	9	0.8
1987	†SF N	12	9	.571	41	28	4-3	1-0	186	185	83	14	4	67-11	137	3.63	106	.258	.324	56-7	.143	-0	94	5	0.2
1988	SF N	13	9	.591	27	26	6-3	0-0	168	140	67	11	3	47-8	118	3.32	98	.225	.279	54-4	.167	2	147	0	0.3
1989	†SF N	4	8	.333	18	15	0	0-0	82.2	82	47	7	1	26-4	49	4.79	71	.261	.316	22-3	.091	-1	80	-12	-1.8
1990	SF N	3	2	.600	13	9	0	0-0	63	56	26	2	2	20-4	31	3.43	106	.233	.297	13-3	.000	-1	94	2	0.0
1991	SF N	10	4	.714	45	11	0	0-2	111.2	99	59	12	3	53-9	62	4.19	86	.239	.326	23-2	.087	-1	73	-9	-1.1
1992	SF N	1	2	.333	19	7	0	0-0	62.1	65	27	4	3	24-0	33	3.47	96	.275	.347	14-2	.000	-1	98	-1	-0.3
	†Oak A	5	5	.500	18	13	0	0-0	82	72	36	4	4	46-3	38	3.29	114	.237	.341	0-0	—	0	97	3	0.3
1993	Oak A	5	10	.333	42	12	0	0-1	119.2	135	80	14	2	60-8	66	5.64	72	.287	.368	0-0	—	0	94	-22	-2.4
Total	8	57	53	.518	237	135	11-6	1-3	963.2	912	454	73	25	373-54	598	3.86	94	.250	.321	211-21	.123	-2	99	-25	-4.0
DOWNS, SCOTT Scott Jeremy B 3.17.1976 Louisville, KY BL/TL 6-2/180# d4.9																									
2000	Chi N	4	3	.571	18	18	0	0-0	94	117	59	13	5	37-1	63	5.17	88	.310	.375	26-4	.077	-1	117	-7	-0.6
	Mon N	0	0	—	1	1	0	0-0	3	5	3	0	0	3-0	0	9.00	53	.385	.500	2-0	.000	-0	172	-1	-0.1
	Year	4	3	.571	19	19	0	0-0	97	122	12	13	5	40-1	63	5.29	86	.312	.380	28-4	.071	-1	120	-9	-0.7

Year	Tm Lg	W	L	Pct	G	GS	CG-Sho	SV-BS	IP	H	R	HR	HB	BB-IB	SO	ERA	AERA	OAV	OOB	AB-SH	AVG	PB	Sup	APR	PW
2003	Mon N	0	1	.000	1	1	0	0-0	3	5	5	2	0	3-2	4	15.00	31	.357	.471	1-0	.000	-0	40	-3	-0.5
Total	2	4	4	.500	20	20	0	0-0	100	127	67	15	5	43-3	67	5.58	82	.314	.383	29-4	.069	-2	116	-11	-1.2
DOYLE, JESS Jesse Herbert B 4.14.1898 Knoxville, TN D 4.15.1961 Belleville, IL BR/TR 5-11/175# d4.14																									
1925	Det A	4	7	.364	45	3	0	8	118.1	158	83	6	5	50	31	5.93	73	.340	.410	33-0	.242	3	98	-18	-1.4
1926	Det A	0	0	—	2	0	0	1	4.1	6	3	0	0	1	2	4.15	98	.316	.350	1-1	1.000	0		0	0.0
1927	Det A	0	0	—	7	0	0	0	12.1	16	11	0	0	5	5	8.03	52	.314	.375	3-0	.333	0		-4	-0.2
1931	StL A	0	0	—	1	0	0	0	1	3	3	0	0	1	0	27.00	17	.500	.571	0-0	—	0		-2	-0.1
Total	4	4	7	.364	55	3	0	9	136	183	100	6	5	57	38	6.22	69	.338	.406	37-1	.270	4	98	-24	-1.7
DOYLE, JOHN John Aloysius B 1858 Nova Scotia, , CAN D 12.24.1915 Providence, RI d7.26																									
1882	StL AA	0	3	.000	3	3	3	0	24	41	33	0		3	5	2.63	107	.353	.370	11	.182	-0	24	-3	-0.4
DOYLE, SLOW JOE Judd Bruce B 9.15.1881 Clay Center, KS D 11.21.1947 Tannersville, NY BR/TR 5-8/150# d8.25																									
1906	NY A	2	1	.667	9	6	3-2	0	45.1	34	15	1	1	13	28	2.38	124	.211	.274	14-0	.214	-0	81	3	0.2
1907	NY A	11	11	.500	29	23	15-1	1	193.2	169	86	2	6	67	94	2.65	105	.237	.308	58-4	.138	-1	92	2	0.0
1908	NY A	1	1	.500	12	4	2-1	0	48	42	24	1	2	14	20	2.63	94	.235	.297	14-0	.214	0	110	-2	-0.1
1909	NY A	8	6	.571	17	15	8-3	0	125.2	103	49	3	2	37	57	2.58	98	.232	.294	42-2	.167	0	132	1	-0.1
1910	NY A	0	2	.000	3	2	1	0	12.1	19	13	0	1	5	6	8.03	33	.365	.431	4-0	.250	0	38	-6	-0.8
	Cin N	0	0	—	5	0	0	0	11.1	16	19	0	0	11	4	6.35	46	.327	.450	3-0	.000	-0		-7	-0.4
Total	5	22	21	.512	75	50	29-7	1	436.1	383	206	7	12	147	209	2.85	95	.240	.308	135-6	.163	-1	101	-9	-1.2
DOYLE, PAUL Paul Sinnott B 10.2.1939 Philadelphia, PA BL/TL 5-11/172# d5.28																									
1969	†Atl N	2	0	1.000	36	0	0	4-3	39	31	9	4	0	16-3	25	2.08	174	.231	.307	3-0	.000	-0		7	0.5
1970	Cal A	3	1	.750	40	0	0	5-2	42	43	25	7	1	21-3	34	5.14	70	.267	.355	3-0	.000	-0		-7	-0.7
	SD N	0	2	.000	9	0	0	2-0	7	9	5	0	0	6-1	2	6.43	62	.360	.469	1-0	.000	-0		-2	-0.3
1972	Cal A	0	0	—	2	0	0	0-0	2.1	2	0	0	0	3-0	4	0.00	—	.250	.455	0-0	—	0		1	0.1
Total	3	5	3	.625	87	0	0	11-5	90.1	85	39	11	1	46-7	65	3.79	96	.259	.348	7-0	.000	-1		-1	-0.4
DOYLE, CARL William Carl B 7.30.1912 Knoxville, TN D 9.4.1951 Knoxville, TN BR/TR 6-1/185# d8.5																									
1935	Phi A	2	7	.222	14	9	3	0	79.2	86	63	3	2	72	34	5.99	76	.282	.422	30-0	.133	-2	85	-13	-1.4
1936	Phi A	0	3	.000	8	6	1	0	38.2	66	53	4	5	29	12	10.94	47	.369	.469	15-0	.267	1	126	-24	-1.3
1939	Bro N	1	2	.333	5	1	1-1	1	17.2	8	5	1	0	7	7	1.02	395	.136	.227	6-0	.167	0	174	5	0.8
1940	Bro N	0	0	—	3	0	0	1	5.2	18	17	3	4	6	4	27.00	15	.545	.651	1-0	1.000	1		-13	-0.5
	StL N	3	3	.500	21	5	1	0	81	99	57	7	6	41	44	5.89	68	.294	.380	30-0	.200	2	100	-14	-0.8
	Year	3	3	.500	24	5	1	1	86.2	117	62	10	10	47	48	7.27	55	.316	.407	31-0	.226	2	100	-28	-1.3
Total	4	6	15	.286	51	21	6-1	2	222.2	277	195	18	17	155	101	6.95	63	.303	.414	82-0	.195	1	109	-59	-3.2
DOZIER, TOM Thomas Dean B 9.5.1961 San Pablo, CA BR/TR 6-2/190# d5.17																									
1986	Oak A	0	0	—	4	0	0	0-0	6.1	6	6	1	0	5-1	4	5.68	68	.261	.367	0-0	—	0		-2	-0.1
DOZIER, BUZZ William Joseph B 8.31.1927 Waco, TX BR/TR 6-3/185# d9.12																									
1947	Was A	0	0	—	2	0	0	0	4.2	2	0	0	0	1	2	0.00	—	.133	.188	1-0	.000	-0		2	0.1
1949	Was A	0	0	—	2	0	0	0	6.1	12	8	0	0	6	1	11.37	37	.429	.529	2-0	.000	-0		-4	-0.2
Total	2	0	0	—	4	0	0	0	11	14	8	0	0	7	3	6.55	62	.326	.420	3-0	.000	-0		-2	-0.1
DRABEK, DOUG Douglas Dean B 7.25.1962 Victoria, TX BR/TR 6-1/185# d5.30																									
1986	NY A	7	8	.467	27	21	0	0-0	131.2	126	64	13	3	50-1	76	4.10	100	.251	.322	0-0	—	0	96	1	0.1
1987	Pit N	11	12	.478	29	28	1-1	0-0	176.1	165	86	22	0	46-2	120	3.88	106	.247	.294	59-7	.119	-1*	97	4	0.4
1988	Pit N	15	7	.682	33	32	3-1	0-0	219.1	194	83	21	6	50-4	127	3.08	111	.239	.286	76-5	.171	3	117	8	1.1
1989	Pit N	14	12	.538	35	34	8-5	0-0	244.1	215	83	21	3	69-3	123	2.80	120	.238	.293	77-6	.104	-2*	77	17	1.6
1990	†Pit N	**22**	6	**.786**	33	33	9-3	0-0	231.1	190	78	15	3	56-2	131	2.76	131	.225	.274	84-7	.214	5	134	24	3.6
1991	†Pit N	15	14	.517	35	35	5-2	0-0	234.2	245	92	16	3	62-6	142	3.07	116	.274	.321	84-4	.179	1*	110	13	1.7
1992	†Pit N	15	11	.577	34	34	10-4	0-0	256.2	218	84	17	6	54-8	177	2.77	124	.231	.274	89-8	.157	1*	103	20	2.2
1993	Hou N	9	18	.333	34	34	7-2	0-0	237.2	242	108	18	3	60-12	157	3.79	102	.267	.312	71-9	.085	-2	74	5	0.3
1994	Hou N★	12	6	.667	23	23	6-2	0-0	164.2	132	58	14	2	45-2	121	2.84	139	.220	.275	58-4	.241	3*	117	22	2.7
1995	Hou N	10	9	.526	31	**31**	2-1	0-0	185	205	104	18	8	54-4	143	4.77	81	.282	.337	60-8	.233	4*	118	-17	-1.1
1996	Hou N	7	9	.438	30	30	1	0-0	175.1	208	102	21	7	60-5	137	4.57	85	.298	.355	56-7	.179	0*	113	-16	-1.2
1997	Chi A	12	11	.522	31	31	0	0-0	169.1	170	109	30	4	69-5	85	5.74	76	.261	.334	1-1	.000	-0*	104	-21	-2.4
1998	Bal A	6	11	.353	23	21	1	0-0	108.2	138	90	20	5	29-2	55	7.29	63	.312	.355	1-0	.000	-0	114	-33	-4.0
Total	13	155	134	.536	398	387	53-21	0-0	2535	2448	1141	246	53	704-56	1594	3.73	101	.255	.308	716-66	.166	13	106	27	5.0
DRABOWSKY, MOE Myron Walter B 7.21.1935 Ozanna, Poland BR/TR 6-2/200# d8.7 C2																									
1956	Chi N	2	4	.333	9	7	3	0	51	37	19	1	2	39-3	36	2.47	153	.207	.353	16-2	.250	0	70	6	0.7
1957	Chi N	13	15	.464	36	33	12-2	0	239.2	214	103	22	10	94-6	170	3.53	110	.242	.319	82-3	.183	2	85	10	1.4
1958	Chi N	9	11	.450	22	20	4-1	0	125.2	118	73	19	5	73-4	77	4.51	87	.245	.349	45-3	.156	-1	110	-9	-1.4
1959	Chi N	5	10	.333	31	23	3-1	0	141.2	138	78	21	3	75-4	70	4.13	96	.251	.343	45-0	.111	-1	91	-6	-0.7
1960	Chi N	3	1	.750	32	7	0	1	50.1	71	44	3	1	23-0	26	6.44	59	.338	.397	6-1	.000	-1*	137	-16	-1.3
1961	Mil N	0	2	.000	16	0	0	2	25.1	26	15	4	1	18-3	5	4.62	81	.277	.391	4-0	.250	0		-3	-0.2
1962	Cin N	2	6	.250	23	10	1	1	83	84	49	13	6	31-0	56	4.99	81	.267	.340	17-1	.000	-2	74	-8	-0.9
	KC A	1	1	.500	10	3	0	0	28	29	20	8	1	10-0	19	5.14	82	.266	.328	6-1	.167	-0	120	-4	-0.3
1963	KC A	7	13	.350	26	22	9-2	0	174.1	135	62	16	8	64-2	109	3.05	128	.214	.294	62-3	.161	1	81	17	1.9
1964	KC A	5	13	.278	53	21	1	1	168.1	176	103	24	8	72-5	119	5.29	72	.273	.350	43-1	.023	-4*	84	-24	-2.8
1965	KC A	1	5	.167	14	5	0	0	38.2	44	22	5	3	18-2	25	4.42	79	.291	.367	11-0	.091	-1	96	-4	-0.7
1966	†Bal A	6	0	1.000	44	3	0	7	96	62	31	10	1	29-5	98	2.81	118	.181	.246	22-1	.364	4	106	7	0.9
1967	Bal A	7	5	.583	43	0	0	12	95.1	66	21	7	2	25-3	96	1.60	196	.194	.252	20-3	.350	2		16	2.8
1968	Bal A	4	4	.500	45	0	0	7	61.1	35	17	3	4	25-5	46	1.91	153	.166	.266	7-0	.286	0		6	1.1
1969	KC A	11	9	.550	52	0	0	11-5	98	68	33	10	2	30-2	76	2.94	126	.190	.255	17-2	.235	1		10	2.2
1970	KC A	1	2	.333	24	0	0	2-4	35.2	28	13	3	2	12-3	38	3.28	114	.217	.288	4-0	.250	0		3	0.2
	†Bal A	4	2	.667	21	0	0	1-1	33.1	30	17	7	1	15-3	21	3.78	97	.233	.317	5-1	.000	-1		-1	-0.3
	Year	5	4	.556	45	0	0	3-5	69	58	34	10	3	27-6	59	3.52	105	.225	.302	9-1	.111	-0		2	-0.1
1971	StL N	6	1	.857	51	0	0	8-2	60.1	45	23	2	2	33-8	49	3.43	105	.207	.315	6-0	.167	-0		2	0.3
1972	StL N	1	1	.500	30	0	0	2-1	27.2	29	13	4	1	14-4	22	2.60	131	.259	.346	1-0	.000	-0		1	0.0
	Chi A	0	0	—	7	0	0	0-0	7.1	6	2	0	0	2-0	4	2.45	128	.240	.296	1-0	.000	-0		1	0.0
Total	17	88	105	.456	589	154	33-6	55-13	1641	1441	758	182	63	702-62	1162	3.71	101	.236	.318	420-22	.162	-0	94	4	2.9
DRAGO, DICK Richard Anthony B 6.25.1945 Toledo, OH BR/TR 6-1/190# d4.11																									
1969	KC A	11	13	.458	41	26	10-2	1-0	200.2	190	95	19	2	65-6	108	3.77	98	.248	.306	52-9	.058	-3	74	-1	-0.4
1970	KC A	9	15	.375	35	34	7-1	0-0	240	239	110	20	7	72-5	127	3.75	100	.266	.322	76-9	.053	-6	88	2	-0.5
1971	KC A	17	11	.607	35	34	15-4	0-0	241.1	251	84	14	9	46-1	109	2.98	115	.276	.315	77-7	.130	1	95	14	1.7
1972	KC A	12	17	.414	34	33	11-2	0-0	239.1	230	88	22	6	51-4	135	3.01	101	.254	.297	68-7	.059	-2*	82	1	-0.3
1973	KC A	12	14	.462	37	33	10-1	0-0	212.2	252	116	16	7	76-10	98	4.23	97	.300	.360	0-0	—	0*	105	-5	-0.5
1974	Bos A	7	10	.412	33	18	8	3-1	175.2	165	71	17	5	56-9	90	3.48	110	.251	.313	0-0	—	0	69	8	0.7
1975	†Bos A	2	2	.500	40	2	0	15-3	72.2	69	31	5	0	31-3	43	3.84	106	.247	.321	0-0	—	0	183	3	0.3
1976	Cal A	7	8	.467	43	0	0	6-3	79.1	80	42	7	5	31-8	43	4.42	75	.264	.338	0-0	—	0		-9	-1.8
1977	Cal A	0	1	.000	13	0	0	2-1	21	22	8	3	0	3-2	15	3.00	131	.272	.291	0-0	—	0		2	0.1
	Bal A	6	3	.667	36	0	0	3-6	39.2	49	19	2	1	15-4	20	3.63	105	.308	.363	0-0	—	0		0	0.0
	Year	6	4	.600	49	0	0	5-7	60.2	71	36	5	1	18-6	35	3.41	113	.296	.340	0-0	—	0		3	0.1
1978	Bos A	4	4	.500	37	1	0	7-3	77.1	71	30	5	4	32-5	42	3.03	136	.246	.327	0-0	—	0	218	8	1.0
1979	Bos A	10	6	.625	53	1	0	13-4	89	85	33	6	3	21-6	67	3.03	146	.254	.300	0-0	—	0	389	13	2.6
1980	Bos A	7	7	.500	43	7	1	3-4	132.2	127	67	17	5	44-7	63	4.14	102	.251	.316	1-0	.000	-0	82	1	0.1
1981	Sea A	4	6	.400	39	0	0	5-3	53.2	71	33	4	0	15-5	27	5.53	70	.324	.361	0-0	—	0		-8	-1.5
Total	13	108	117	.480	519	189	62-10	58-28	1875	1901	827	157	54	558-75	987	3.62	103	.266	.321	274-32	.077	-11	89	29	1.5

Year	Tm Lg	W	L	Pct	G	GS	CG-Sho	SV-BS	IP	H	R	HR	HB	BB-IB	SO	ERA	AERA	OAV	OOB	AB-SH	AVG	PB	Sup	APR	PW
DRAHMAN, BRIAN Brian Stacy B 11.7.1966 Kenton, KY BR/TR 6-3/205# d4.16																									
1991	Chi A	3	2	.600	28	0	0	0-2	30.2	21	12	4	0	13-1	18	3.23	123	.193	.276	0-0	—	0		3	0.4
1992	Chi A	0	0	—	5	0	0	0-0	7	6	3	0	0	2-0	1	2.57	150	.222	.276	0-0	—	0		1	0.0
1993	Chi A	0	0	—	5	0	0	1-0	5.1	7	0	0	0	2-0	3	0.00	—	.333	.391	0-0	—	0		3	0.1
1994	Fla N	0	0	—	9	0	0	0-0	13	15	9	2	0	6-1	7	6.23	70	.300	.362	0-0	—	0		-2	-0.1
Total	4	3	2	.600	47	0	0	1-2	56	49	24	6	0	23-2	29	3.54	115	.237	.309	0-0	—	0		5	0.4
DRAKE, LOGAN Logan Gaffney "L.G." B 12.26.1900 Spartanburg, SC D 6.1.1940 Columbia, SC BR/TR 5-10.5/165# d9.21																									
1922	Cle A	0	0	—	1	0	0	0	3	4	1	0	0	2	1	3.00	134	.364	.462	1-0	.000	-0		0	0.0
1923	Cle A	0	0	—	4	0	0	0	4.1	2	2	0	1	4	2	4.15	95	.133	.350	0-0	—	0		0	0.0
1924	Cle A	0	1	.000	5	1	0	0	11.1	18	15	0	1	10	8	10.32	41	.400	.518	1-0	.000	-0	138	-7	-0.5
Total	3	0	1	.000	10	1	0	0	18.2	24	18	0	2	16	11	7.71	54	.338	.472	2-0	.000	-0	138	-7	-0.5
DRAKE, TOM Thomas Kendall B 8.7.1912 Birmingham, AL D 7.2.1988 Birmingham, AL BR/TR 6-1/185# d4.24																									
1939	Cle A	0	1	.000	8	1	0	0	15	23	18	2	2	19	1	9.00	49	.377	.537	2-1	.000	-0	160	-9	-0.5
1941	Bro N	1	1	.500	10	2	0	0	24.2	26	13	2	0	9	12	4.38	84	.280	.343	5-0	.400	0*	81	-1	-0.1
Total	2	1	2	.333	18	3	0	0	39.2	49	31	4	2	28	13	6.13	65	.318	.429	7-1	.286	0	109	-10	-0.6
DRAPER, MIKE Michael Anthony B 9.14.1966 Hagerstown, MD BR/TR 6-2/180# d4.10																									
1993	NY N	1	1	.500	29	1	0	0-2	42.1	53	22	2	0	14-3	16	4.25	95	.327	.370	3-0	.667	1	224	-1	0.1
DRAVECKY, DAVE David Francis B 2.14.1956 Youngstown, OH BR/TL 6-1/195# d6.15																									
1982	SD N	5	3	.625	31	10	0	2-0	105	86	37	8	1	33-3	59	2.57	133	.225	.288	23-4	.130	-0*	93	9	0.8
1983	SD N★	14	10	.583	28	28	9-1	0-0	183.2	181	78	18	3	44-4	74	3.58	98	.262	.307	61-6	.098	-1	100	0	-0.1
1984	†SD N	9	8	.529	50	14	3-2	8-2	156.2	125	53	12	4	51-0	71	2.93	122	.222	.289	41-5	.098	-1	124	13	1.4
1985	SD N	13	11	.542	34	31	7-2	0-0	214.2	200	79	18	1	57-5	105	2.93	121	.249	.299	69-6	.116	-0	89	15	1.5
1986	SD N	9	11	.450	26	26	3-1	0-0	161.1	149	68	17	1	54-7	87	3.07	119	.246	.307	50-6	.140	0*	84	8	1.0
1987	SD N	3	7	.300	30	10	1	0-0	79	71	39	10	3	31-4	60	3.76	105	.240	.315	18-2	.167	0*	80	1	0.1
	†SF N	7	5	.583	18	18	4-3	0-0	112.1	115	43	8	2	33-3	78	3.20	120	.272	.325	38-2	.132	0	111	9	1.0
	Year	10	12	.455	48	28	5-3	0-0	191.1	186	48	18	5	64-7	138	3.43	113	.259	.321	56-4	.143	1	100	10	1.1
1988	SF N	2	2	.500	7	7	1	0-0	37	33	19	4	0	8-0	19	3.16	103	.243	.279	10-3	.100	-0	101	-2	-0.2
1989	SF N	2	0	1.000	2	2	0	0-0	13	8	5	2	1	4-0	5	3.46	98	.182	.265	3-0	.333	1	92	0	0.1
Total	8	64	57	.529	226	146	28-9	10-2	1062.2	968	421	97	16	315-26	558	3.13	115	.245	.302	313-34	.121	-2	96	53	5.6
DREES, TOM Thomas Kent B 6.17.1963 Des Moines, IA BB/TL 6-6/210# d9.3																									
1991	Chi A	0	0	—	4	0	0	0-0	7.1	10	10	4	0	6-0	2	12.27	32	.345	.444	0-0	—	0		-7	-0.3
DREIFORT, DARREN Darren James B 5.3.1972 Wichita, KS BR/TR 6-2/205# d4.7																									
1994	LA N	0	5	.000	27	0	0	6-3	29	45	21	0	4	15-3	22	6.21	63	.357	.441	1-1	1.000	1*		-8	-1.3
1996	†LA N	1	4	.200	19	0	0	0-2	23.2	23	13	2	0	12-4	24	4.94	78	.256	.340	3-0	.000	-0*		-2	-0.4
1997	LA N	5	2	.714	48	0	0	4-3	63	45	21	3	1	34-2	63	2.86	135	.202	.308	7-0	.143	-0		8	1.0
1998	LA N	8	12	.400	32	26	1-1	0-0	180	171	84	12	10	57-2	168	4.00	99	.256	.321	49-5	.224	3*	93	2	0.7
1999	LA N	13	13	.500	30	29	1-1	0-0	178.2	177	105	20	7	76-2	140	4.79	90	.260	.340	62-4	.210	4	120	-11	-0.8
2000	LA N	12	9	.571	32	32	1-1	0-0	192.2	175	105	31	12	87-1	164	4.16	104	.238	.329	68-1	.162	4	120	1	0.6
2001	LA N	4	7	.364	16	16	0	0-0	94.2	89	62	11	6	47-0	91	5.13	78	.251	.347	33-3	.152	2	109	-14	-1.2
2003	LA N	4	4	.500	10	10	0	0-0	60.1	58	29	6	0	25-0	67	4.03	100	.250	.322	15-3	.133	0	61	0	0.2
Total	8	47	56	.456	214	113	3-3	10-8	822	783	440	85	40	353-14	739	4.36	95	.252	.335	238-17	.185	13	109	-24	-1.2
DREISEWERD, CLEM Clemens Johann "Steamboat" B 1.24.1916 Old Monroe, MO D 9.11.2001 Ocean Springs, MS BL/TL 6-1.5/195# d8.29 Mil 1945																									
1944	Bos A	2	4	.333	7	7	3	0	48.2	52	25	2	0	9	9	4.07	84	.268	.300	16-2	.188	0	95	-4	-0.4
1945	Bos A	0	1	.000	2	2	0	0	9.2	13	5	0	1	2	3	4.66	73	.325	.372	3-0	.000	-0	50	-1	-0.2
1946	†Bos A	4	1	.800	20	1	0	0	47.1	50	22	3	0	15	19	4.18	88	.276	.332	10-2	.000	-1	210	-1	-0.2
1948	StL A	0	2	.000	13	0	0	1	22.1	28	15	6	0	8	6	5.64	81	.318	.375	5-0	.000	-1		-2	-0.3
	NY N	0	0	—	4	0	0	1	12.2	17	8	3	0	5	2	5.68	69	.321	.379	4-0	.250	1		-2	0.0
Total	4	6	8	.429	46	10	3	2	140.2	160	75	14	1	39	39	4.54	82	.288	.336	38-4	.105	-1	93	-10	-1.1
DRESE, RYAN Ryan Thomas B 4.5.1976 San Francisco, CA BR/TR 6-3/220# d7.29																									
2001	Cle A	1	2	.333	9	4	0	0-0	36.2	32	15	2	1	15-2	24	3.44	132	.242	.324	0-0	—	0	92	5	0.3
2002	Cle A	10	9	.526	26	26	1	0-0	137.1	176	104	15	6	62-1	102	6.55	67	.317	.386	3-1	.000	0	114	-32	-3.4
2003	Tex A	2	4	.333	11	8	0	0-0	46	61	42	8	5	24-1	26	6.85	73	.314	.404	0-0	—	0	123	-11	-1.2
Total	3	13	15	.464	46	38	1	0-0	220	269	161	25	12	101-4	152	6.10	74	.305	.381	3-1	.000	0	114	-38	-4.3
DRESSENDORFER, KIRK Kirk Richard B 4.8.1969 Houston, TX BR/TR 5-11/190# d4.13																									
1991	Oak A	3	3	.500	7	7	0	0-0	34.2	33	28	5	0	21-0	17	5.45	70	.244	.344	0-0	—	0	157	-10	-1.4
DRESSER, BOB Robert Nicholson B 10.4.1878 Newton, MA D 7.27.1924 Duxbury, MA BL/TL d8.13																									
1902	Bos N	0	1	.000	1	1	1	0	9	12	6	0	0	0	8	3.00	94	.316	.316	4-0	.250	0	24	-1	-0.1
DRESSLER, ROB Robert Anthony B 2.2.1954 Portland, OR BR/TR 6-3/180# d9.7																									
1975	SF N	1	0	1.000	3	2	1	0-0	16.1	17	3	0	0	4-2	6	1.10	346	.274	.318	4-0	.000	-0	92	4	0.3
1976	SF N	3	10	.231	25	19	0	0-1	107.2	125	68	8	2	35-4	33	4.43	82	.291	.343	31-2	.129	-1	69	-11	-1.3
1978	StL N	0	1	.000	3	2	0	0-0	13	12	3	0	0	4-1	4	2.08	170	.267	.327	3-1	.000	-0	89	2	0.1
1979	Sea A	3	2	.600	21	11	2	0-0	104	134	61	11	0	22-3	36	4.93	89	.312	.344	0-0	—	0	89	-5	-0.3
1980	Sea A	4	10	.286	30	14	3	0-0	149.1	161	75	14	3	33-7	50	3.98	104	.280	.318	0-0	—	0	90	2	0.2
Total	5	11	23	.324	82	48	6	0-1	390.1	449	210	33	5	98-17	129	4.17	97	.291	.333	38-3	.105	-1	80	-8	-1.0
DREW, TIM Timothy Andrew B 8.31.1978 Valdosta, GA BR/TR 6-1/195# d5.24 b-J.D.																									
2000	Cle A	1	0	1.000	3	3	0	0-0	9	17	12	1	1	8-0	5	10.00	50	.425	.510	0-0	—	0	145	-6	-0.5
2001	Cle A	0	2	.000	8	6	0	0-0	35	51	39	9	4	16-0	15	7.97	57	.340	.413	0-0	—	0	143	-15	-0.7
2002	Mon N	1	0	1.000	7	1	0	2-1	16	12	8	1	0	2-0	10	2.81	159	.200	.222	4-0	.000	-0	145	2	0.1
2003	Mon N	0	2	.000	6	1	0	0-0	8.2	12	12	3	0	8-1	3	12.46	38	.343	.444	1-1	.000	-0	100	-6	-1.1
Total	4	2	4	.333	24	11	0	2-1	68.2	92	71	14	5	34-1	33	7.60	61	.323	.396	5-1	.000	-1	141	-25	-2.2
DREWS, KARL Karl August B 2.22.1920 Staten Island, NY D 8.15.1963 Dania, FL BR/TR 6-4/198# d9.8																									
1946	NY A	0	1	.000	3	1	0	0	6.1	6	6	0	1	6	4	8.53	40	.250	.419	1-0	.000	-0	199	-3	-0.5
1947	†NY A	6	6	.500	30	10	0	1	91.2	92	57	6	5	55	45	4.91	72	.264	.373	27-1	.037	-2	105	-16	-2.1
1948	NY A	2	3	.400	19	2	0	1	38	35	17	3	0	31	11	3.79	108	.248	.384	7-2	.000	-1	55	2	0.2
	StL A	3	2	.600	20	2	0	2	38	43	35	3	0	38	11	8.05	57	.289	.433	8-0	.000	-0	59	-13	-1.6
	Year	5	5	.500	39	4	0	3	76	78	38	6	0	69	22	5.92	73	.269	.409	15-2	.000	-1	58	-12	-1.4
1949	StL A	4	12	.250	31	23	3-1	0	139.2	180	113	11	9	66	35	6.64	68	.317	.397	46-1	.000	-5	75	-27	-3.1
1951	Phi N	1	0	1.000	5	3	1	0	23	29	16	2	4	7	13	6.26	61	.296	.367	8-0	.250	1	130	-6	-0.2
1952	Phi N	14	15	.483	33	30	15-5	0	228.2	213	79	13	4	52	96	2.72	135	.252	.298	82-2	.110	-2	76	25	2.9
1953	Phi N	9	10	.474	47	27	6	3	185.1	218	116	26	10	50	72	4.52	93	.293	.346	59-1	.119	-2	101	-10	-1.1
1954	Phi N	1	0	1.000	8	0	0	0	16	18	10	2	0	8	6	5.63	72	.300	.377	4-0	.000	-1		-2	-0.2
	Cin N	4	4	.500	22	9	1-1	0	60	79	44	6	2	19	29	6.00	70	.326	.376	12-1	.167	1	135	-11	-1.2
	Year	5	4	.556	30	9	1-1	0	76	97	50	8	2	27	35	5.92	70	.321	.376	16-1	.125	1	136	-14	-1.4
Total	8	44	53	.454	218	107	26-7	7	826.2	913	493	72	35	332	322	4.76	84	.284	.356	254-8	.083	-12	92	-61	-6.9
DREYER, STEVE Steven William B 11.19.1969 Ames, IA BR/TR 6-3/180# d8.8																									
1993	Tex A	3	3	.500	10	6	0	0-0	41	48	26	7	1	20-1	23	5.71	73	.291	.371	0-0	—	0	144	-6	-0.8
1994	Tex A	1	1	.500	5	3	0	0-0	17.1	19	15	1	1	8-0	11	5.71	84	.271	.350	0-0	—	0	159	-3	-0.3
Total	2	4	4	.500	15	9	0	0-0	58.1	67	41	8	2	28-1	34	5.71	76	.285	.365	0-0	—	0	150	-9	-1.1
DRISCOLL, DENNY John F. B 11.19.1855 Lowell, MA D 7.11.1886 Lowell, MA BL/TL 5-10.5/160# d7.1 ▲																									
1880	Buf N	1	3	.250	6	4	4	0	41.2	48	33	1		9	17	3.89	63	.270	.305	65	.154	-1*	95	-6	-0.6
1882	Pit AA	13	9	.591	23	23	23	0	201	162	73	0		12	59	**1.21**	**216**	.206	.218	80	.138	-2	101	27	2.1

Year	Tm Lg	W	L	Pct	G	GS	CG-Sho	SV-BS	IP	H	R	HR	HB	BB-IB	SO	ERA	AERA	OAV	OOB	AB-SH	AVG	PB	Sup	APR	PW
1883	Pit AA	18	21	.462	41	40	35-1	0	336.1	427	239	3		39	79	3.99	82	.290	.309	148	.182	-5	111	-27	-2.5
1884	Lou AA	6	6	.500	13	13	10	0	102	110	69	3	2	7	16	3.44	90	.252	.267	48	.188	-1	126	-4	-0.4
Total	4	38	39	.494	83	80	72-1	0	681	747	414	7	2	67	171	3.08	97	.260	.277	341	.167	-9	110	-10	-1.4
DRISCOLL, MICHAEL Michael Columbus B 10.19.1892 N.Abington, MA D 3.22.1953 Foxboro, MA BR/TR 5-11/160# d7.6																									
1916	Phi A	0	1	.000	1	0	0	0	5	6	5	0	0	2	0	5.40	53	.273	.333	2-0	.000	-0		-2	-0.3
DRISKILL, TRAVIS Travis Corey B 8.1.1971 Omaha, NE BR/TR 6/185# d4.26																									
2002	Bal A	8	8	.500	29	19	0	0-0	132.2	150	78	21	8	48-1	78	4.95	86	.284	.351	3-0	.000	0	86	-10	-1.1
2003	Bal A	3	5	.375	20	0	0	1-0	48	62	35	8	1	9-2	33	6.00	73	.310	.340	1-0	.000	-0		-9	-1.3
Total	2	11	13	.458	49	19	0	1-0	180.2	212	113	29	9	57-3	111	5.23	82	.291	.348	4-0	.000	-0	86	-19	-2.4
DROHAN, TOM Thomas F B 8.26.1887 Fall River, MA D 9.17.1926 Kewanee, IL BR/TR 5-10/175# d5.1																									
1913	Was A	0	0	—	2	0	0	0	2	5	2	1	0	0	2	9.00	33	.500	.500	0-0	—	0		-1	-0.1
DROTT, DICK Richard Fred "Hummer" B 7.1.1936 Cincinnati, OH D 8.16.1985 Glendale Heights, IL BR/TR 6/185# d4.16																									
1957	Chi N	15	11	.577	38	32	7-3	0	229	200	107	22	7	129-2	170	3.58	108	.234	.337	80-3	.100	-5	107	5	0.0
1958	Chi N	7	11	.389	39	31	4	0	167.1	156	118	23	6	99-6	127	5.43	72	.245	.347	55-1	.273	3	121	-30	-2.5
1959	Chi N	1	2	.333	8	6	1-1	0	27.1	25	19	5	0	26-1	15	5.93	67	.245	.398	8-0	.125	-0	94	-6	-0.6
1960	Chi N	0	6	.000	23	9	0	0	55.1	63	49	7	3	42-0	32	7.16	53	.296	.409	10-0	.100	-1	83	-20	-2.0
1961	Chi N	1	4	.200	35	8	0	0	98	75	54	13	1	51-0	48	4.22	99	.215	.311	22-0	.273	1	69	-1	0.0
1962	Hou N	1	0	1.000	6	1	0	0	13	12	12	1	0	9-0	10	7.62	49	.240	.356	4-0	.000	-0	188	-6	-0.4
1963	Hou N	2	12	.143	27	14	2-1	0	97.2	95	61	13	6	49-2	58	4.98	63	.257	.349	23-1	.130	-1	49	-20	-2.8
Total	7	27	46	.370	176	101	14-5	0	687.2	626	420	84	23	405-11	460	4.78	80	.243	.347	202-5	.168	-2	99	-78	-8.3
DRUCKE, LOUIS Louis Frank B 12.3.1888 Waco, TX D 9.22.1955 Waco, TX BR/TR 6-1/188# d9.25																									
1909	NY N	2	1	.667	3	3	2	0	24	20	9	0	0	13	8	2.25	114	.227	.327	8-2	.125	-0	146	1	0.0
1910	NY N	12	10	.545	34	27	15	0	215.1	174	73	3	11	82	151	2.47	120	.228	.312	70-9	.214	4	115	15	2.0
1911	NY N	4	4	.500	15	10	4	0	75.2	83	39	1	8	41	42	4.04	83	.281	.384	23-1	.087	-1*	121	-4	-0.4
1912	NY N	0	0	—	1	0	0	1	2	5	4	0	0	1	0	13.50	25	.417	.462	0-0	—	0		-2	-0.2
Total	4	18	15	.545	53	40	21	1	317	282	125	4	19	137	201	2.90	105	.243	.333	101-12	.178	2	119	10	1.4
DRUHOT, CARL Carl A. "Collie" B 9.1.1882 , OH D 2.11.1918 Portland, OR BL/TL 5-7/150# d4.18																									
1906	Cin N	2	2	.500	4	3	1	0	25	27	17	0	2	7	14	4.32	64	.270	.330	9-0	.222	0	150	-4	-0.6
	StL N	6	7	.462	15	13	12-1	0	130.1	117	55	1	5	46	45	2.62	100	.238	.310	56-1	.232	1	105	-2	0.0
	Year	8	9	.471	19	16	13-1	0	155.1	144	59	1	7	53	59	2.90	91	.244	.313	65-1	.231	1	113	-7	-0.6
1907	StL N	0	1	.000	1	1	0	0	2.1	3	5	0	1	4	1	15.43	16	.600	.800	0-0	—	0	57	-3	-0.5
Total	2	8	10	.444	20	17	13-1	0	157.2	147	77	1	8	57	60	3.08	86	.247	.321	65-1	.231	1	110	-9	-1.1
DRUMMOND, TIM Timothy Darnell B 12.24.1964 LaPlata, MD BR/TR 6-3/170# d9.12																									
1987	Pit N	0	0	—	6	0	0	0-0	6	5	3	0	0	3-0	5	4.50	91	.227	.320	1-0	.000	-0		0	0.0
1989	Min A	0	0	—	8	0	0	1-0	16.1	16	7	0	2	8-1	9	3.86	108	.246	.347	0-0	—	0		1	0.0
1990	Min A	3	5	.375	35	4	0	1-1	91	104	46	8	1	36-1	49	4.35	96	.295	.357	0-0	—	0	38	-1	-0.1
Total	3	3	5	.375	49	4	0	2-1	113.1	125	56	8	3	47-2	63	4.29	97	.284	.354	1-0	.000	-0	38	0	-0.1
DRYSDALE, DON Donald Scott B 7.23.1936 Van Nuys, CA D 7.3.1993 Montreal, PQ, CAN BR/TR 6-6/216# d4.17 HF1984																									
1956	†Bro N	5	5	.500	25	12	2	0	99	95	35	9	3	31-3	55	2.64	150	.255	.315	26-2	.192	1*	89	13	1.4
1957	Bro N	17	9	.654	34	29	9-4	0	221	197	76	17	7	61-3	148	2.69	155	.236	.293	73-3	.123	-0*	108	**33**	**4.1**
1958	LA N	12	13	.480	44	29	6-1	0	211.2	214	107	21	14	72-6	131	4.17	98	.263	.331	66-3	.227	8*	90	0	0.9
1959	†LA N★	17	13	.567	44	36	15-**4**	2	270.2	237	113	26	18	93-9	**242**	3.46	122	.233	.308	91-8	.165	3*	86	23	2.9
1960	LA N	15	14	.517	41	36	15-5	2	269	214	93	27	10	72-5	**246**	2.84	140	.215	**.274**	83-9	.157	2	88	**33**	4.0
1961	LA N☆	13	10	.565	40	37	10-3	0	244	236	111	29	20	83-15	182	3.69	118	.254	.326	83-5	.193	4	91	17	1.8
1962	LA N★	**25**	9	.735	43	**41**	19-2	1	**314.1**	272	122	21	11	78-12	**232**	2.83	128	.230	.282	111-8	.198	5	137	27	3.3
1963	†LA N★	19	17	.528	42	**42**	17-3	0	315.1	287	114	25	10	57-13	251	2.63	115	.242	.282	96-6	.167	5	98	13	2.1
1964	LA N★	18	16	.529	40	**40**	21-5	0	**321.1**	242	91	15	10	68-9	237	2.18	148	.207	.255	110-14	.173	4	116	**41**	**5.0**
1965	†LA N★	23	12	.657	44	**42**	20-7	1	308.1	270	113	30	12	66-11	210	2.77	118	.232	.279	130-2	.300	22*	114	16	4.2
1966	†LA N	13	16	.448	40	40	11-3	0	273.2	279	114	21	17	45-8	177	3.42	96	.265	.304	106-2	.189	4*	97	-1	0.2
1967	LA N★	13	16	.448	38	38	9-3	0	282	269	101	19	8	60-19	196	2.74	113	.251	.295	93-2	.129	-0	81	10	1.2
1968	LA N★	14	12	.538	31	31	12-8	0	239	201	68	11	12	56-10	155	2.15	129	.231	.284	79-4	.177	1	91	17	2.3
1969	LA N	5	4	.556	12	12	1-1	0-0	62.2	71	34	9	2	13-0	24	4.45	75	.291	.327	22-1	.136	0	122	-8	-1.0
Total	14	209	166	.557	518	465	167-49	6-0	3432	3084	1292	280	154	855-123	2486	2.95	121	.239	.293	1169-69	.186	60	101	234	32.4
DUBIEL, MONK Walter John B 2.12.1918 Hartford, CT D 10.23.1969 Hartford, CT BR/TR 6/190# d4.19																									
1944	NY A	13	13	.500	30	28	19-3	0	232	217	93	12	1	86	79	3.38	103	.248	.316	83-5	.181	-2*	93	7	0.5
1945	NY A	10	9	.526	26	20	9-1	0	151.1	157	88	9	0	62	45	4.64	75	.266	.335	58-4	.276	4	133	-18	-1.8
1948	Phi N	8	10	.444	37	17	6-2	4	150.1	139	84	13	1	58	42	3.89	101	.248	.320	42-4	.167	0*	93	-2	-0.3
1949	Chi N	6	9	.400	32	20	3-1	4	147.2	142	75	16	1	54	52	4.14	97	.250	.317	35-7	.286	3*	101	-1	0.3
1950	Chi N	6	10	.375	39	12	4-2	2	142.2	152	79	12	1	67	51	4.16	101	.270	.348	45-1	.200	1	96	0	0.2
1951	Chi N	2	2	.500	22	0	0	1	54.2	46	17	3	0	22	19	2.30	178	.232	.309	12-0	.000	-1		10	0.6
1952	Chi N	0	0	—	1	0	0	0	0.2	1	0	0	0	0	1	0.00	—	.333	.333	0-0	—	0		0	0.0
Total	7	45	53	.459	187	97	41-9	11	879.1	854	436	65	4	349	289	3.87	98	.254	.325	275-21	.207	5	102	-4	-0.5
DuBOIS, BRIAN Brian Andrew B 4.18.1967 Joliet, IL BL/TL 5-10/195# d8.17																									
1989	Det A	0	4	.000	6	5	0	1-0	36	29	14	2	2	17-3	13	1.75	219	.218	.314	0-0	—	0	38	6	0.6
1990	Det A	3	5	.375	12	11	0	0-0	58.1	70	37	9	1	22-1	34	5.09	78	.310	.368	0-0	—	0	117	-8	-1.0
Total	2	3	9	.250	18	16	0	1-0	94.1	99	51	11	3	39-4	47	3.82	103	.276	.347	0-0	—	0	93	-2	-0.4
DUBOSE, ERIC Eric Ladell B 5.15.1976 Bradenton, FL BL/TL 6-3/230# d9.19																									
2002	Bal A	0	0	—	4	0	0	0-0	6	7	2	1	1	1-0	4	3.00	143	.304	.360	0-0	—	0		1	0.0
2003	Bal A	3	6	.333	17	10	1	0-1	73.2	60	33	6	5	25-2	44	3.79	116	.222	.297	0-0	—	0	50	5	0.6
Total	2	3	6	.333	21	10	1	0-1	79.2	67	35	7	6	26-2	48	3.73	118	.229	.302	0-0	—	0	50	6	0.6
DUBUC, JEAN Jean Joseph Octave Arthur "Chauncey" B 9.15.1888 St.Johnsbury, VT D 8.28.1958 Fort Myers, FL BR/TR 5-10.5/185# d6.25 C2																									
1908	Cin N	5	6	.455	15	9	7-1	0	85.1	62	34	2	5	41	32	2.74	84	.205	.309	29-2	.138	-1	75	-3	-0.4
1909	Cin N	2	5	.286	19	5	2	1	71.1	72	58	0	4	46	19	3.66	71	.269	.384	18-1	.167	0	70	-13	-1.2
1912	Det A	17	10	.630	37	26	23-2	3	250	217	107	2	7	109	97	2.77	118	.235	.321	108-1	.269	6*	128	13	2.2
1913	Det A	15	14	.517	36	28	22-1	2	242.2	228	113	1	8	91	73	2.89	101	.254	.329	135-4	.267	5*	111	-1	1.3
1914	Det A	12	14	.462	36	27	15-2	1	224	216	124	3	6	76	70	3.46	81	.257	.324	124-4	.226	7*	117	-18	-1.0
1915	Det A	17	12	.586	39	33	22-5	2	258	231	116	5	10	88	74	3.21	94	.245	.316	112-3	.205	0*	115	-3	-0.2
1916	Det A	10	10	.500	36	16	8-1	1	170.1	134	66	1	5	84	40	2.96	97	.233	.336	78-2	.256	5*	106	0	0.8
1918	†Bos A	0	1	.000	2	1	1	0	10.2	11	5	1	0	5	1	4.22	64	.268	.348	6-0	.167	0*	84	-1	-0.1
1919	NY N	6	4	.600	36	5	1	3	132	119	49	4	2	37	32	2.66	105	.246	.303	42-0	.143	-1*	85	2	0.1
Total	9	84	76	.525	256	150	101-12	13	1444.1	1290	672	19	47	577	438	3.04	96	.245	.325	652-17	.230	21	113	-24	1.5
DUCHSCHERER, JUSTIN Justin Craig B 11.19.1977 Aberdeen, SD BR/TR 6-3/164# d7.25																									
2001	Tex A	1	1	.500	5	2	0	0-0	14.2	24	20	5	4	4-0	11	12.27	38	.353	.421	0-0	—	0	79	-11	-1.2
2003	Oak A	1	1	.500	4	3	0	0-0	16.1	17	7	1	2	3-0	15	3.31	137	.262	.314	0-0	—	0	115	2	0.2
Total	2	2	2	.500	9	5	0	0-0	31	41	27	6	6	7-0	26	7.55	61	.308	.370	0-0	—	0	100	-9	-1.0
DUCKWORTH, BRANDON Brandon J. B 1.23.1976 Salt Lake City, UT BB/TR 6-2/185# d8.7																									
2001	Phi N	3	2	.600	11	11	0	0-0	69	57	29	2	6	29-5	40	3.52	121	.234	.326	22-2	.227	2	85	6	0.5
2002	Phi N	8	9	.471	30	29	0	0-0	163	167	103	26	7	69-5	167	5.41	72	.261	.338	48-6	.188	2	111	-27	-2.3
2003	Phi N	4	7	.364	24	18	0	0-0	93	98	58	12	10	44-3	68	4.94	81	.272	.366	27-1	.185	1	103	-12	-1.2
Total	3	15	18	.455	65	58	0	0-0	325	322	190	40	23	142-13	275	4.87	82	.259	.344	97-9	.196	4	103	-33	-3.0

Year	Tm Lg	W	L	Pct	G	GS	CG-Sho	SV-BS	IP	H	R	HR	HB	BB-IB	SO	ERA	AERA	OAV	OOB	AB-SH	AVG	PB	Sup	APR	PW
DUCKWORTH, JIM James Raymond B 5.24.1939 National City, CA BR/TR 6-4/194# d4.13																									
1963	Was A	4	12	.250	37	15	2	0	120.2	131	89	13	10	67-3	66	6.04	61	.278	.373	27-3	.000	-3	93	-29	-3.8
1964	Was A	1	6	.143	30	2	0	3	56	52	37	9	3	25-4	56	4.34	85	.244	.332	9-0	.222	0	60	-6	-0.8
1965	Was A	2	2	.500	17	8	0	0	64	45	30	11	2	36-4	74	3.94	88	.202	.314	18-1	.000	-2	88	-2	-0.4
1966	Was A	0	3	.000	5	4	0	0	14.1	14	12	2	1	10-1	14	5.02	69	.259	.379	3-0	.000	-0	76	-4	-0.8
	KC A	0	2	.000	8	0	0	1	12	14	12	2	1	10-0	10	9.00	38	.292	.424	2-0	.000	-0		-7	-1.2
	Year	0	5	.000	13	4	0	1	26.1	28	27	4	2	20-1	24	6.84	50	.275	.400	5-0	.000	-1	77	-10	-2.0
Total	4	7	25	.219	97	29	2	4	267	256	180	37	17	148-12	220	5.26	69	.253	.355	59-4	.034	-5	87	-48	-7.0
DUDLEY, CLISE Elzie Clise B 8.8.1903 Graham, NC D 1.12.1989 Moncks Corner, SC BL/TR 6-1/195# d4.18																									
1929	Bro N	6	14	.300	35	20	8-1	0	156.2	202	130	9	10	64	33	5.69	81	.315	.385	51-3	.098	-1*	75	-24	-2.5
1930	Bro N	2	4	.333	21	7	2	1	66.2	103	62	3	2	27	18	6.35	77	.371	.430	24-0	.208	-0	104	-13	-0.9
1931	Phi N	8	14	.364	30	24	8	0	179	206	95	10	6	56	50	3.52	121	.287	.343	84-1	.214	-0*	82	9	1.1
1932	Phi N	1	1	.500	13	0	0	1	17.2	23	14	3	0	8	5	7.13	62	.329	.397	14-0	.286	3*		-4	-0.2
1933	Pit N	0	0	—	1	0	0	0	0.1	6	5	0	0	1	0	135.00	2	.857	.875	0-0	—	0		-4	-0.2
Total	5	17	33	.340	100	51	18-1	2	420.1	540	306	25	18	156	106	5.03	90	.315	.378	173-4	.185	1	82	-36	-2.7
DUES, HAL Hal Joseph B 9.22.1954 LaMarque, TX BR/TR 6-3/180# d9.9																									
1977	Mon N	1	1	.500	6	4	0	0-0	23	26	14	2	0	9-1	9	4.30	89	.265	.327	5-1	.000	-1	70	-2	-0.2
1978	Mon N	5	6	.455	25	12	1	1-0	99	85	29	5	4	42-4	36	2.36	149	.240	.326	31-0	.194	0	76	13	1.4
1980	Mon N	0	1	.000	6	1	0	0-0	12.1	17	9	1	0	4-1	2	6.57	54	.333	.382	3-0	.000	-0	100	-4	-0.3
Total	3	6	8	.429	37	17	1	1-0	134.1	128	52	8	4	55-6	47	3.08	116	.254	.332	39-1	.154	-1	77	7	0.9
DUFF, LARRY Cecil Elba B 11.30.1897 Radersburg, MT D 11.10.1969 Bend, OR BL/TR 6-1/175# d9.5																									
1922	Chi A	1	1	.500	3	1	0	0	12.2	16	7	1	0	3	7	4.97	82	.340	.380	5-0	.400	0	42	-1	-0.1
DUFF, MATT Matthew Clark B 10.6.1974 Clarksdale, MS BR/TR 6-1/192# d7.30																									
2002	StL N	0	0	—	7	0	0	0-0	5.2	3	3	0	0	8-2	4	4.76	83	.150	.393	0-0	—	0		0	0.0
DUFFALO, JIM James Francis B 11.25.1935 Helvetia, PA BR/TR 6-1/175# d4.12																									
1961	SF N	5	1	.833	24	4	1	1	61.2	59	31	9	2	32-7	37	4.23	90	.257	.347	17-0	.294	3*	140	-2	0.0
1962	SF N	1	2	.333	24	2	0	0	42	42	27	3	0	23-3	29	3.64	104	.256	.344	6-1	.000	-0	104	-3	-0.3
1963	SF N	4	2	.667	34	5	0	2	75.1	56	26	3	2	37-6	55	2.87	112	.209	.307	18-1	.111	-1	81	4	0.3
1964	SF N	5	1	.833	35	3	1	3	74	57	25	9	2	31-4	55	2.92	122	.209	.293	14-0	.071	-1	82	6	0.4
1965	SF N	0	1	.000	2	0	0	0	0.1	1	1	0	0	2-0	0	27.00	13	.500	.750	0-0	—	0		-1	-0.2
	Cin N	0	1	.000	22	0	0	0	44.1	33	21	3	5	30-2	34	3.45	109	.212	.351	8-0	.000	-1		1	0.0
	Year	0	2	.000	24	0	0	0	44.2	34	25	3	5	32-2	34	3.63	103	.215	.359	8-0	.000	-1		0	-0.2
Total	5	15	8	.652	141	14	2	6	297.2	248	131	27	11	155-22	210	3.39	106	.227	.326	63-2	.127	1	101	5	0.2
DUFFIE, JOHN John Brown B 10.4.1945 Greenwood, SC BR/TR 6-7/210# d9.18																									
1967	LA N	0	2	.000	2	2	0	0	9.2	11	6	1	0	4-1	6	2.79	111	.282	.341	2-0	.000	-0	43	-1	-0.2
DUFFY, BERNIE Bernard Allen B 8.18.1893 Vinson, OK D 2.9.1962 Abilene, TX BR/TR 5-11/180# d9.20																									
1913	Pit N	0	0	—	3	2	0	0	11.1	18	8	0	0	3	8	5.56	54	.360	.396	4-0	.250	0	87	-3	-0.1
DUGAN, DAN Daniel Phillip B 2.22.1907 Plainfield, NJ D 6.25.1968 Green Brook, NJ BL/TL 6-1.5/187# d9.5 b-Bill																									
1928	Chi A	0	0	—	1	0	0	0	0.1	0	0	0	0	0	0	0.00	—	.000	.000	0-0	—	0		0	0.0
1929	Chi A	1	4	.200	19	2	0	1	65	77	51	8	2	19	15	6.65	64	.300	.353	20-1	.150	-1	30	-14	-1.1
Total	2	1	4	.200	20	2	0	1	65.1	77	51	8	2	19	15	6.61	65	.298	.351	20-1	.150	-1	30	-14	-1.1
DUGAN, ED Edward John B 1864 Brooklyn, NY TR d8.5																									
1884	Ric AA	5	14	.263	20	20	20	0	166.1	196	137	5	2	15	60	4.49	74	.267	.284	70	.114	-4*	77	-23	-2.5
DUGGLEBY, BILL William James "Frosty Bill" B 3.16.1874 Utica, NY D 8.30.1944 Redfield, NY TR d4.21																									
1898	Phi N	3	3	.500	9	5	4	0	54	70	39	4	6	18	12	5.50	62	.311	.378	21-1	.238	2	149	-10	-0.6
1901	Phi N	20	12	.625	35	29	26-5	0	284.2	302	120	9	10	41	95	2.88	118	.270	.302	115-3	.165	-3	92	18	1.7
1902	Phi A	1	1	.500	2	2	2	0	17	19	9	0	0	4	4	3.18	116	.284	.324	7-0	.000	-1	78	1	0.0
	Phi N	11	17	.393	33	27	25	1	258.2	282	130	2	12	57	60	3.38	83	.277	.323	98-1	.173	-1	93	-15	-1.5
1903	Phi N	13	16	.448	36	30	28-3	2	264.1	318	162	4	12	79	57	3.75	87	.303	.358	104-3	.231	2	98	-18	-1.4
1904	Phi N	12	13	.480	32	27	22-2	1	223.2	265	138	3	11	53	55	3.78	71	.292	.338	82-2	.171	0	124	-26	-2.6
1905	Phi N	18	17	.514	38	36	27-1	0	289.1	270	116	10	13	83	75	2.46	119	.253	.315	101-3	.109	-2	102	12	1.2
1906	Phi N	13	19	.406	42	30	22-5	2	280.1	241	93	5	12	66	83	2.25	116	.227	.280	99-1	.141	-2*	80	14	1.5
1907	Phi N	0	2	.000	5	2	2	0	29	43	27	2	5	11	8	7.45	33	.371	.447	9-0	.111	0	103	-14	-0.8
	Pit N	2	2	.500	9	3	1-1	0	40.1	34	17	0	2	12	4	2.68	91	.239	.308	13-0	.154	-0	88	-1	0.0
	Year	2	4	.333	14	5	3-1	0	69.1	77	20	2	7	23	12	4.67	52	.298	.372	22-0	.136	0	94	-14	-0.8
Total	8	93	102	.477	241	191	159-17	6	1741.1	1844	851	39	83	424	453	3.18	93	.272	.323	649-14	.165	-4	99	-39	-2.5
DUKE, MARTIN Martin F. "Duck" (b: Martin F. Duck) B 1867 Zanesville, OH D 12.31.1898 Minneapolis, MN TL 5-8/157# d8.24																									
1891	Was AA	0	3	.000	4	3	2	0	23	36	33	0	0	19	5	7.43	50	.346	.447	9	.111	-1	44	-10	-0.9
DUKES, JAN Noble Jan B 8.16.1945 Cheyenne, WY BL/TL 5-11/175# d9.6																									
1969	Was A	0	2	.000	8	0	0	0-0	11	8	3	0	0	4-1	3	2.45	141	.216	.293	1-0	.000	0		1	0.3
1970	Was A	0	0	—	5	0	0	0-0	6.2	6	3	0	1	1-0	4	2.70	132	.240	.286	1-0	.000	-0		0	0.0
1972	Tex A	0	0	—	3	0	0	0-0	2.1	1	2	0	0	5-1	0	3.86	78	.167	.500	0-0	—	0		-1	0.0
Total	3	0	2	.000	16	0	0	0-0	20	15	8	0	1	10-2	7	2.70	128	.221	.321	2-0	.000	0		0	0.3
DUKES, TOM Thomas Earl B 8.31.1942 Knoxville, TN BR/TR 6-2/185# d8.15																									
1967	Hou N	0	2	.000	17	0	0	1	23.2	25	14	2	2	11-1	23	5.32	62	.275	.362	2-0	.500	0		-4	-0.4
1968	Hou N	2	2	.500	43	0	0	4	52.2	62	31	3	2	28-12	37	4.27	69	.291	.376	4-0	.000	-0		-9	-0.9
1969	SD N	1	0	1.000	13	0	0	1-0	22.1	26	18	2	0	10-2	15	7.25	49	.295	.360	1-0	.000	-0		-8	-0.4
1970	SD N	1	6	.143	53	0	0	10-6	69	62	39	7	2	25-9	56	4.04	98	.246	.312	7-0	.000	-1		-2	-0.4
1971	†Bal A	1	5	.167	28	0	0	4-1	38.1	40	15	4	1	8-2	30	3.52	95	.263	.299	7-0	.143	0		0	0.0
1972	Cal A	0	1	.000	7	0	0	1-0	11	11	3	1	1	0-0	8	1.64	179	.262	.279	0-0	—	0		1	0.1
Total	6	5	16	.238	161	0	0	21-7	217	226	120	19	8	82-26	169	4.35	79	.270	.335	21-0	.095	-1		-22	-2.0
DULIBA, BOB Robert John B 1.9.1935 Glen Lyon, PA BR/TR 5-10/185# d8.11																									
1959	StL N	0	1	.000	11	0	0	1	22.2	19	7	2	0	12-1	14	2.78	153	.237	.330	4-0	.000	-0		4	0.2
1960	StL N	4	4	.500	27	0	0	0	40.2	49	20	6	0	16-4	23	4.20	97	.310	.367	5-0	.200	-0		0	0.0
1962	StL N	2	0	1.000	28	0	0	2	39.1	33	11	3	0	17-0	22	2.06	207	.239	.321	4-0	.000	-0		9	0.5
1963	LA A	1	1	.500	6	0	0	1	7.2	3	1	0	0	6-0	4	1.17	292	.125	.290	1-0	.000	-0		2	0.4
1964	LA A	6	4	.600	58	0	0	9	72.2	80	35	5	1	22-3	33	3.59	91	.287	.339	5-1	.000	-1		-3	-0.5
1965	Bos A	4	2	.667	39	0	0	1	64.1	60	31	6	0	22-7	27	3.78	99	.248	.308	7-0	.000	-0		0	-0.1
1967	KC A	0	0	—	7	0	0	0	9.2	13	7	3	0	1-0	6	6.52	49	.342	.359	0-0	—	0		-3	-0.2
Total	7	17	12	.586	176	0	0	14	257	257	112	25	1	96-15	129	3.47	108	.268	.332	26-1	.038	-2		9	0.3
DUMONT, GEORGE George Henry "Pea Soup" B 11.13.1895 Minneapolis, MN D 10.13.1956 Minneapolis, MN BR/TR 5-11/163# d9.14																									
1915	Was A	2	1	.667	6	4	3-2	0	40	23	17	0	2	12	18	2.02	147	.169	.247	12-2	.167	-0	80	2	0.1
1916	Was A	2	3	.400	17	5	2	1	53	37	25	0	1	17	21	3.06	91	.194	.263	14-1	.071	-0	125	-2	-0.3
1917	Was A	5	14	.263	37	23	8-2	2	204.2	171	76	3	6	76	65	2.55	103	.227	.303	58-2	.034	-5	67	2	-0.6
1918	Was A	1	1	.500	4	1	1	0	14	18	12	0	0	6	12	5.14	53	.295	.358	3-0	.333	1	0	-4	-0.4
1919	Bos A	0	4	.000	13	2	0	0	35.1	45	21	1	1	19	12	4.33	70	.326	.411	7-0	.000	-0	52	-6	-0.6
Total	5	10	23	.303	77	35	14-4	3	347	294	151	4	10	130	128	2.85	96	.230	.306	94-5	.064	-5	74	-8	-1.8
DUMOULIN, DAN Daniel Lynn B 8.20.1953 Kokomo, IN BR/TR 6/175# d9.5																									
1977	Cin N	0	0	—	5	0	0	0-0	5.1	12	8	0	0	3-1	5	13.50	29	.462	.517	0-0	—	0		-5	-0.3
1978	Cin N	1	0	1.000	3	0	0	0-0	5	7	1	0	1	3-1	2	1.80	197	.368	.478	0-0	—	0		1	0.2
Total	2	1	0	1.000	8	0	0	0-0	10.1	19	9	0	1	6-2	7	7.84	48	.422	.500	0-0	—	0		-4	-0.1

Year	Tm Lg	W	L	Pct	G	GS	CG-Sho	SV-BS	IP	H	R	HR	HB	BB-IB	SO	ERA	AERA	OAV	OOB	AB-SH	AVG	PB	Sup	APR	PW
DUMOVICH, NICK Nicholas B 1.2.1902 Sacramento, CA D 12.12.1978 Laguna Hills, CA BL/TL 6/170# d4.20																									
1923	Chi N	3	5	.375	28	8	1	1	94	118	60	4	3	45	23	4.60	87	.319	.397	29-0	.241	1	98	-7	-0.4
DUNBAR, MATT Matthew Marshall B 10.15.1968 Tallahassee, FL BL/TL 6/170# d4.25																									
1995	Fla N	0	1	.000	8	0	0	0-0	7	12	9	0	1	11-3	5	11.57	36	.387	.558	0-0	—	0		-5	-0.6
DUNCAN, COURTNEY Courtney Demond B 10.9.1974 Mobile, AL BL/TR 6/185# d4.2																									
2001	Chi N	3	3	.500	36	0	0	0-2	42.2	42	24	5	2	25-3	49	5.06	82	.259	.359	3-0	.000	0		-4	-0.4
2002	Chi N	0	0	—	2	0	0	0-0	2.1	2	0	0	0	1-0	1	0.00	—	.222	.300	0-0	—	0		1	0.1
Total	2	3	3	.500	38	0	0	0-2	45	44	24	5	2	26-3	50	4.80	86	.257	.356	3-0	.000	0		-3	-0.3
DUNDON, ED Edward Joseph "Dummy" B 7.10.1859 Columbus, OH D 8.18.1893 Columbus, OH TR 6/170# d6.2 ▲																									
1883	Col AA	3	16	.158	20	19	16	0	166.2	213	153	7		38	31	4.48	69	.292	.327	93	.161	-3*	85	-30	-2.7
1884	Col AA	6	4	.600	11	9	7	0	81	85	55	9	0	15	37	3.78	80	.249	.281	86	.140	-1*	73	-8	-0.8
Total	2	9	20	.310	31	28	23	0	247.2	298	208	16	0	53	68	4.25	72	.278	.312	179	.151	-4	81	-38	-3.5
DUNEGAN, JIM James William B 8.6.1947 Burlington, IA BR/TR 6-1/205# d5.28																									
1970	Chi N	0	2	.000	7	0	0	0-0	13.1	13	7	2	0	12-1	3	4.73	95	.277	.417	4-0	.250	0*		0	0.1
DUNHAM, WILEY Henry Huston B 1.30.1877 Piketon, OH D 1.16.1934 Cleveland, OH 6-1/180# d5.24																									
1902	StL N	2	3	.400	7	5	3	1	38	47	31	1	3	13	15	5.68	48	.303	.368	12-0	.083	-1	55	-11	-1.4
DUNKLE, DAVEY Edward Perks B 8.30.1872 Philipsburg, PA D 11.19.1941 Lock Haven, PA BB/TR 6-2/220# d8.28																									
1897	Phi N	5	2	.714	7	7	7	0	62	72	41	0	1	23	9	3.48	120	.288	.350	23-1	.174	-1	82	2	0.0
1898	Phi N	1	4	.200	12	7	4	0	68.1	83	70	1	9	38	21	6.98	49	.297	.399	28-0	.214	-0	133	-25	-1.5
1899	Was N	0	2	.000	4	2	2	0	26	46	34	3	1	14	9	10.04	39	.383	.452	11-0	.273	-0	18	-15	-0.9
1903	Chi A	4	4	.500	12	7	6	1	82	96	58	1	3	31	26	4.06	69	.291	.357	33-0	.303	2	98	-13	-1.1
	Was A	5	9	.357	14	13	10	0	108.1	111	60	4	4	33	51	4.24	74	.264	.324	41-0	.098	-4	58	-10	-1.6
	Year	9	13	.409	26	20	16	1	190.1	207	63	5	7	64	77	4.16	72	.276	.339	74-0	.189	-2	72	-23	-2.7
1904	Was A	2	9	.182	12	11	7	0	74.1	95	56	1	3	23	23	4.96	54	.311	.366	28-0	.143	-2*	85	-19	-2.6
Total	5	17	30	.362	61	47	36	1	421	503	319	10	21	162	139	5.02	65	.295	.364	164-1	.189	-4	82	-80	-7.7
DUNLEAVY, JACK John Francis B 9.14.1879 Harrison, NJ D 4.11.1944 S.Norwalk, CT BL/TL 5-6/167# d5.30 ▲																									
1903	StL N	6	8	.429	14	13	9	0	102	101	59	2	8	57	51	4.06	80	.264	.371	193-7	.249	2*	91	-4	-0.3
1904	StL N	1	4	.200	7	5	5	0	55	63	32	4	1	23	28	4.42	61	.275	.344	172-1	.233	2*	82	-8	-0.5
Total	2	7	12	.368	21	18	14	0	157	164	91	6	9	80	79	4.18	73	.268	.361	365-8	.241	4	90	-12	-0.8
DUNN, JIM James William "Bill" B 2.25.1931 Valdosta, GA D 1.6.1999 Gadsden, AL BR/TR 6-0.5/185# d8.26																									
1952	Pit N	0	0	—	3	0	0	0	5.1	4	2	0	0	3	2	3.38	118	.190	.292	1-0	.000	-0		0	0.0
DUNN, JACK John Joseph B 10.6.1872 Meadville, PA D 10.22.1928 Towson, MD BR/TR 5-9/?# d5.6 ▲																									
1897	Bro N	14	9	.609	25	21	21	0	216.2	251	147	6	9	66	26	4.57	90	.288	.344	131-4	.221	-2*	116	-10	-1.0
1898	Bro N	16	21	.432	41	37	31	0	322.2	352	180	10	15	82	66	3.60	100	.275	.327	167-1	.246	1*	82	0	-0.1
1899	Bro N	23	13	.639	41	34	29-2	2	299.1	323	161	8	18	86	48	3.70	106	.275	.334	122-2	.246	0*	108	12	1.3
1900	Bro N	3	4	.429	10	7	5	0	63	88	48	1	4	28	6	5.57	69	.330	.401	26-0	.231	-0	93	-10	-0.9
	Phi N	5	5	.500	10	9	9-1	0	80	87	50	2	5	29	12	4.84	75	.276	.347	33-0	.303	1	59	-8	-0.7
	Year	8	9	.471	20	16	14-1	0	143	175	53	3	9	57	18	5.16	72	.301	.372	59-0	.271	1	74	-16	-1.6
1901	Phi N	0	1	.000	2	2	0	0	4.2	11	16	0	2	7	1	21.21	16	.458	.606	1-0	1.000	1	219	-9	-1.2
	Bal A	3	3	.500	9	6	6	0	59.2	74	45	2	1	21	5	3.62	107	.301	.358	362-14	.249	0*	102	-1	0.0
1902	NY N	0	3	.000	3	2	2	0	26.2	28	14	0	0	12	6	3.71	76	.269	.345	342-19	.211	0*	24	-2	-0.1
1904	NY N	0	0	—	1	0	0	1	4	3	3	1	0	3	1	4.50	61	.167	.286	181-5	.309	0*		-1	0.0
Total	7	64	59	.520	142	118	103-3	3	1076.2	1217	664	30	54	334	171	4.11	92	.283	.342	1365-45	.245	1	97	-29	-2.7
DUNNE, MIKE Michael Dennis B 10.27.1962 South Bend, IN BR/TR 6-4/200# d6.5																									
1987	Pit N	13	6	.684	23	23	5-1	0-0	163.1	143	66	10	1	68-8	72	3.03	136	.240	.317	53-7	.094	-1	87	17	1.9
1988	Pit N	7	11	.389	30	28	1	0-0	170	163	88	15	5	88-3	70	3.92	87	.255	.345	46-7	.109	-1*	102	-12	-1.3
1989	Pit N	1	1	.500	3	3	0	0-0	14.1	21	12	1	1	9-1	4	7.53	45	.328	.419	4-0	.250	0	132	-6	-0.7
	Sea A	2	9	.182	15	15	1	0-0	85.1	104	61	7	2	37-1	38	5.27	77	.307	.373	0-0	—	0	84	-13	-1.4
1990	SD N	0	3	.000	10	6	0	0-0	28.2	28	21	4	0	17-0	15	5.65	68	.241	.338	6-0	.000	-1	90	-6	-0.6
1992	Chi A	2	0	1.000	4	1	0	0-1	12.2	12	7	0	1	6-1	6	4.26	91	.255	.352	0-0	—	0	94	-1	-0.1
Total	5	25	30	.455	85	76	7-1	0-1	474.1	471	255	37	10	225-14	205	4.08	93	.261	.344	109-14	.101	-1	93	-21	-2.2
DUNNING, ANDY Andrew Jackson B 8.12.1871 New York, NY D 6.21.1952 New York, NY BR/TR 6/175# d5.23																									
1889	Pit N	0	2	.000	2	2	2	0	18	20	19	1	0	16	4	7.00	54	.274	.404	7	.000	-1	63	-7	-0.6
1891	NY N	0	1	.000	1	1	0	0	2	3	5	1	0	3	1	4.50	71	.333	.500	0	—	0	93	-1	-0.2
Total	2	0	3	.000	3	3	2	0	20	23	24	2	0	19	5	6.75	55	.280	.416	7	.000	-1	72	-8	-0.8
DUNNING, STEVE Steven John B 5.15.1949 Denver, CO BR/TR 6-2/205# d6.14																									
1970	Cle A	4	9	.308	19	17	0	0-1	94.1	93	55	16	4	54-3	77	4.96	80	.261	.362	31-3	.161	-1	87	-9	-1.2
1971	Cle A	8	14	.364	31	29	3-1	1-0	184	173	98	25	5	109-5	132	4.50	85	.254	.359	55-8	.182	1*	79	-11	-1.1
1972	Cle A	6	4	.600	16	16	1	0-0	105	98	39	16	0	43-8	52	3.26	99	.248	.321	33-3	.273	5*	89	1	0.7
1973	Cle A	0	2	.000	4	3	0	0-0	18	17	15	2	0	13-0	10	6.50	60	.250	.370	0-0	—	0	83	-5	-0.5
	Tex A	2	6	.250	23	12	2	0-1	94.1	101	63	11	1	52-2	38	5.34	70	.275	.362	0-0	—	0*	98	-17	-1.3
	Year	2	8	.200	27	15	2	0-1	112.1	118	67	13	1	65-2	48	5.53	68	.271	.364	0-0	—	0	95	-23	-1.8
1974	Tex A	0	0	—	1	0	0	0-0	2.1	3	5	2	0	3-1	1	19.29	19	.333	.500	0-0	—	0		-4	-0.2
1976	Cal A	0	0	—	4	0	0	0-0	6	9	9	2	0	6-1	4	7.50	44	.310	.417	0-0	—	0		-4	-0.2
	Mon N	2	6	.250	32	7	1	0-0	91.1	93	50	6	2	33-4	72	4.14	90	.274	.338	15-3	.133	-0	74	-5	-0.4
1977	Oak A	1	0	1.000	6	0	0	0-0	18.1	17	8	2	0	10-1	4	3.93	103	.254	.351	0-0	—	0		1	0.0
Total	7	23	41	.359	136	84	7-1	1-2	613.2	604	342	82	12	323-25	390	4.56	82	.261	.352	134-17	.194	6	85	-53	-4.2
DUPEE, FRANK Frank Oliver B 4.29.1877 Monkton, VT D 8.14.1956 Portland, ME TR 6-1/200# d8.24																									
1901	Chi A	0	1	.000	1	1	0	0	0	0	3	0	0	3	0	∞	—	—	1.000	0-0	—	0	78	-3	-0.2
DUPREE, MIKE Michael Dennis B 5.29.1953 Kansas City, KS BR/TR 6-1/185# d4.13																									
1976	SD N	0	0	—	12	0	0	0-0	15.2	18	17	4	0	7-0	5	9.19	36	.286	.352	1-0	1.000	1		-10	-0.5
DURAN, ROBERTO Roberto Alejandro B 3.6.1973 Moca, D.R. BL/TL 6/167# d7.6																									
1997	Det A	0	0	—	13	0	0	0-0	10.2	7	9	0	3	15-0	11	7.59	60	.189	.446	0-0	—	0		-3	-0.2
1998	Det A	0	1	.000	18	0	0	0-0	15.1	9	10	0	2	17-0	12	5.87	80	.170	.389	0-0	—	0		-2	-0.1
Total	2	0	1	.000	31	0	0	0-0	26	16	19	0	5	32-0	23	6.58	71	.178	.414	0-0	—	0		-5	-0.3
DURBIN, KID Blaine Alphonsus B 9.10.1886 Lamar, MO D 9.11.1943 Kirkwood, MO BL/TL 5-8/155# d4.24 ▲																									
1907	Chi N	0	1	.000	5	1	1	1	16.2	14	13	0	1	10	5	5.40	46	.233	.352	18-0	.333	1*	57	-5	-0.3
DURBIN, CHAD Chad Griffin B 12.3.1977 Spring Valley, IL BR/TR 6-1/175# d9.26																									
1999	KC A	0	0	—	1	0	0	0-0	2.1	1	0	0	0	1-0	3	0.00	—	.125	.222	0-0	—	0		1	0.1
2000	KC A	2	5	.286	16	16	0	0-0	72.1	91	71	14	0	43-1	37	8.21	62	.301	.385	0-0	—	0	107	-24	-1.8
2001	KC A	9	16	.360	29	29	2	0-0	179	201	109	26	11	58-0	95	4.93	100	.288	.348	1-1	.000	-0	70	-1	-0.1
2002	KC A	0	1	.000	2	2	0	0-0	8.1	13	11	3	1	4-0	5	11.88	42	.342	.419	0-0	—	0	74	-5	-0.5
2003	Cle A	0	1	.000	3	1	0	0-0	8.2	18	12	2	0	3-0	8	7.27	61	.429	.467	0-0	—	0	146	-5	-0.4
Total	5	11	23	.324	51	48	2	0-0	270.2	324	203	45	12	109-1	148	6.05	82	.298	.365	1-1	.000	-0	84	-34	-2.7
DUREN, RYNE Rinold George B 2.22.1929 Cazenovia, WI BR/TR 6-1/195# d9.25																									
1954	Bal A	0	0	—	1	0	0	0	2	3	3	0	0	1	2	9.00	40	.333	.400	0-0	—	0		-2	-0.1
1957	KC A	0	3	.000	14	6	0	1	42.2	37	26	4	2	30-1	37	5.27	75	.236	.359	14-0	.071	-1	53	-5	-0.5
1958	†NY A☆	6	4	.600	44	1	0	**20**	75.2	40	20	4	7	43-1	87	2.02	175	.157	.296	13-4	.077	0	51	14	2.6
1959	NY A★	3	6	.333	41	0	0	14	76.2	49	18	6	3	43-2	96	1.88	194	.181	.300	14-3	.000	-1		16	2.4

Year	Tm Lg	W	L	Pct	G	GS	CG-Sho	SV-BS	IP	H	R	HR	HB	BB-IB	SO	ERA	AERA	OAV	OOB	AB-SH	AVG	PB	Sup	APR	PW
1960	†NY A	3	4	.429	42	1	0	9	49	27	29	3	7	49-1	67	4.96	72	.160	.367	6-1	.000	-1	123	-7	-1.3
1961	NY A	0	1	.000	4	0	0	0	5	2	3	2	0	4-0	7	5.40	69	.125	.300	0-0	—	0		-1	-0.2
	LA A☆	6	12	.333	40	14	1-1	2	99	87	70	13	3	75-1	108	5.18	87	.233	.361	25-1	.040	-2	90	-9	-1.6
	Year	6	13	.316	44	14	1-1	2	104	89	75	15	3	79-1	115	5.19	86	.229	.358	25-1	.040	-2	90	-10	-1.8
1962	LA A	2	9	.182	42	3	0	8	71.1	53	38	1	6	57-2	74	4.42	87	.206	.361	15-1	.067	-1	154	-3	-0.7
1963	Phi N	6	2	.750	33	7	1	2	87.1	65	33	6	5	52-1	84	3.30	98	.210	.332	21-0	.143	1*	118	1	0.1
1964	Phi N	0	0	—	2	0	0	0	3	5	3	0	1	1-0	5	6.00	58	.357	.438	0-0	—	0		-1	-0.1
	Cin N	0	2	.000	26	0	0	1	43.2	41	17	1	3	15-1	39	2.89	125	.248	.319	5-0	.000	-0		3	0.1
	Year	0	2	.000	28	0	0	1	46.2	46	24	1	4	16-1	44	3.09	117	.257	.328	5-0	.000	-0		2	0.0
1965	Phi N	0	0	—	6	0	0	0	11	10	7	0	1	4-1	6	3.27	106	.270	.349	1-0	.000	-0		-1	0.0
	Was A	1	1	.500	16	0	0	0	23	24	17	0	3	18-4	18	6.65	52	.286	.421	0-0	—	0		-7	-0.6
Total	10	27	44	.380	311	32	2-1	57	589.1	443	284	40	41	392-15	630	3.83	98	.209	.341	114-10	.061	-5	100	-2	0.1
DURHAM, DON Donald Gary B 3.21.1949 Yosemite, KY BR/TR 6/170# d7.16																									
1972	StL N	2	7	.222	10	8	1	0-0	47.2	42	28	1	0	22-5	35	4.34	78	.240	.318	14-0	.500	4*	49	-6	-0.6
1973	Tex A	0	4	.000	15	4	0	1-0	40.1	49	35	7	1	23-0	23	7.59	49	.304	.390	0-0	—	0*	78	-16	-1.5
Total	2	2	11	.154	25	12	1	1-0	88	91	63	8	1	45-5	58	5.83	61	.271	.353	14-0	.500	4	58	-22	-2.1
DURHAM, ED Edward Fant "Bull" B 8.17.1908 Chester, SC D 4.27.1976 Chester, SC BL/TR 5-11/170# d4.19																									
1929	Bos A	1	0	1.000	14	1	0	0	22.1	34	24	2	0	14	6	9.27	46	.374	.457	4-0	.000	-0	39	-11	-0.5
1930	Bos A	4	15	.211	33	12	6-1	1	140	144	81	9	2	43	28	4.69	98	.270	.326	41-2	.098	-4	54	0	-0.4
1931	Bos A	8	10	.444	38	15	7-2	0	165.1	175	91	9	4	50	53	4.25	101	.266	.322	54-1	.056	-6*	64	0	-0.6
1932	Bos A	6	13	.316	34	22	4	0	175.1	187	90	13	4	49	52	3.80	118	.274	.327	57-1	.123	-3*	71	13	0.9
1933	Chi A	10	6	.625	24	21	6	0	138.2	137	74	12	5	46	65	4.48	95	.256	.320	46-8	.217	0	118	0	0.0
Total	5	29	44	.397	143	71	23-3	1	641.2	677	360	45	15	202	204	4.45	99	.271	.329	202-12	.119	-14	79	2	-0.6
DURHAM, JOHN John Garfield B 10.7.1881 Douglass, KS D 5.7.1949 Coffeyville, KS BR/TR 6/175# d9.15																									
1902	Chi A	1	1	.500	3	3	3	0	20	21	15	0	0	16	3	5.85	58	.269	.394	15-0	.067	-1*	57	-5	-0.4
DURHAM, BULL Louis Raphael (b: Louis Raphael Staub) B 6.27.1877 New Oxford, PA D 6.28.1960 Bentley, KS BR/TR 5-10/?# d9.15																									
1904	Bro N	2	0	1.000	2	2	1	0	11	10	5	0	0	5	1	3.27	84	.250	.333	4-0	.250	0	213	0	-0.1
1907	Was A	0	0	—	2	0	0	0	5	10	9	0	1	4	1	12.60	19	.417	.517	1-0	.000	-0		-5	-0.3
1908	NY N	0	0	—	1	0	0	0	2	2	2	0	0	1	2	9.00	27	.250	.333	0-0	—	0		-1	-0.1
1909	NY N	0	0	—	4	0	0	1	11	15	8	0	0	2	2	3.27	78	.326	.354	2-0	.000	-0		-2	-0.1
Total	4	2	0	1.000	9	2	1	1	29	37	24	0	1	12	6	5.28	49	.314	.382	7-0	.143	-0	213	-8	-0.6
DURNING, RICH Richard Knott B 10.10.1892 Louisville, KY D 9.23.1948 Castle Point, NY BL/TL 6-2/178# d4.16																									
1917	Bro N	0	0	—	1	0	0	0	1	0	0	0	0	0	0	0.00	—	.000	.000	0-0	—	0		0	0.0
1918	Bro N	0	0	—	1	0	0	0	2	3	5	0	0	4	0	13.50	21	.375	.583	0-0	—	0		-3	-0.1
Total	2	0	0	—	2	0	0	0	3	3	5	0	0	4	0	9.00	31	.273	.467	0-0	—	0		-3	-0.1
DUROCHER, JAYSON Jayson Paul B 8.18.1974 Hartford, CT BR/TR 6-3/195# d6.11																									
2002	Mil N	1	1	.500	39	0	0	0-1	48	27	13	3	2	21-2	44	1.88	219	.164	.265	2-0	.000	-0		11	0.5
2003	Mil N	2	0	1.000	6	0	0	0-0	7.1	9	9	4	1	2-0	7	11.05	39	.300	.364	0-0	—	0		-5	-0.9
Total	2	3	1	.750	45	0	0	0-1	55.1	36	22	7	3	23-2	51	3.09	133	.185	.279	2-0	.000	-0		6	-0.4
DURYEA, JESSE James Newton "Cyclone Jim" B 9.7.1859 Osage, IA D 8.19.1942 Algona, IA BR/TR 5-10/175# d4.20																									
1889	Cin AA	32	19	.627	53	48	38-2	1	401	372	208	9	16	127	183	2.56	153	.238	.302	162	.272	6*	114	51	**5.7**
1890	Cin N	16	12	.571	33	32	29-2	0	274	270	148	11	8	60	108	2.92	122	.249	.294	99	.152	1	93	21	1.8
1891	Cin N	1	9	.100	10	10	8	0	77	101	67	4	7	25	23	5.38	63	.305	.366	32	.031	-5	71	-14	-1.8
	StL AA	1	1	.500	3	3	2	0	24	19	13	0	0	10	13	3.38	124	.211	.290	11	.364	1	99	3	0.2
1892	Cin N	2	5	.286	9	7	5	0	68	55	37	3	3	26	21	3.57	91	.212	.292	27	.111	-1	94	-1	-0.1
	Was N	3	11	.214	18	15	13-1	2	127	102	59	6	9	45	48	2.41	135	.211	.291	50	.120	-2	64	12	1.1
	Year	5	16	.238	27	22	18-1	2	195	157	62	9	12	71	69	2.82	116	.212	.291	77	.117	-3	73	12	1.0
1893	Was N	4	10	.286	17	15	9	0	117	182	137	8	13	56	20	7.54	61	.345	.420	47	.277	2	118	-36	-2.8
Total	5	59	67	.468	143	130	104-5	3	1088	1101	669	41	56	349	416	3.45	109	.254	.318	428	.201	3	100	36	4.1
DUSAK, ERV Ervin Frank "Four Sack" B 7.29.1920 Chicago, IL D 11.6.1994 Glendale Heights, IL BR/TR 6-2/185# d9.18.1941 Mil 1943-45 ▲																									
1948	StL N	0	0	—	1	0	0	0	1	0	0	0	0	1	0	0.00	—	.000	.250	311-5	.209	0*		0	0.0
1950	StL N	0	2	.000	14	2	0	1	36.1	27	17	2	1	27	16	3.72	116	.211	.353	12-0	.083	-0*	72	2	0.1
1951	StL N	0	0	—	5	0	0	0	10	14	8	0	0	7	8	7.20	55	.333	.429	2-0	.500	1		-3	0.0
	Pit N	0	1	.000	3	1	0	0	6.2	10	10	2	1	9	2	12.15	35	.357	.526	39-0	.308	1*	84	-5	-0.6
	Year	0	1	.000	8	1	0	0	16.2	24	14	2	1	16	10	9.18	44	.343	.471	41-0	.317	2	87	-8	-0.6
Total	3	0	3	.000	23	3	0	1	54	51	35	4	2	44	26	5.33	79	.254	.393	364-5	.217	2	77	-6	-0.5
DUSER, CARL Carl Robert B 7.22.1932 Hazleton, PA BL/TL 6-1/175# d9.15																									
1956	KC A	1	1	.500	2	2	0	0	6	14	6	0	0	2-0	5	9.00	48	.452	.485	3-0	.000	-0	134	-3	-0.5
1958	KC A	0	0	—	1	0	0	0	2	5	1	0	0	1-1	0	4.50	87	.500	.545	0-0	—	0		0	0.0
Total	2	1	1	.500	3	2	0	0	8	19	7	0	0	3-1	5	7.88	54	.463	.500	3-0	.000	-0	134	-3	-0.5
DUSTAL, BOB Robert Andrew B 9.28.1935 Sayreville, NJ BR/TR 6/172# d4.9																									
1963	Det A	0	1	.000	7	0	0	0	6	10	9	0	0	5-1	4	9.00	42	.357	.455	0-0	—	0		-4	-0.6
DUVALL, MIKE Michael Alan B 10.11.1974 Warrenton, VA BR/TL 6/185# d9.22																									
1998	TB A	0	0	—	3	0	0	0-0	4	4	3	0	0	2-0	1	6.75	71	.267	.353	0-0	—	0		-1	0.0
1999	TB A	1	1	.500	40	0	0	0-1	40	46	21	5	2	27-1	18	4.05	123	.293	.401	0-0	—	0		4	0.2
2000	TB A	0	0	—	2	0	0	0-0	2.1	5	2	0	0	1-0	0	7.71	64	.455	.500	0-0	—	0		-1	0.0
2001	Min A	0	0	—	8	0	0	0-1	4.2	7	4	1	0	2-0	4	7.71	60	.368	.409	0-0	—	0		-1	-0.1
Total	4	1	1	.500	53	0	0	0-2	51	62	30	6	2	32-1	23	4.76	103	.307	.403	0-0	—	0		1	0.1
DUZEN, BILL William George B 2.21.1870 Buffalo, NY D 3.11.1944 Buffalo, NY BR/TR 5-11/165# d9.21																									
1890	Buf P	0	2	.000	2	2	2	0	13	20	24	2	0	14	5	13.85	30	.339	.466	4	.250	1	89	-12	-1.0
DWYER, FRANK John Francis B 3.25.1868 Lee, MA D 2.4.1943 Pittsfield, MA BR/TR 5-8/145# d9.20 M1																									
1888	Chi N	4	1	.800	5	5	5-1	0	42	32	20	1	0	9	17	1.07	283	.198	.240	21	.190	-0	170	5	0.6
1889	Chi N	16	13	.552	32	30	27	0	276	307	177	14	7	72	63	3.59	116	.273	.321	135	.200	-2*	94	16	1.0
1890	Chi P	3	6	.333	12	6	6	1	69.1	98	71	4	0	25	17	6.23	70	.319	.370	53	.264	-0*	94	-11	-1.1
1891	Cin AA	13	19	.406	35	31	29-1	0	289	332	225	10	10	124	101	4.52	91	.279	.351	141	.284	3*	87	-1	0.2
	Mil AA	6	4	.600	10	10	10	0	86	92	41	2	4	21	27	2.20	199	.264	.314	40	.225	-1*	79	17	1.5
	Year	19	23	.452	45	41	39-1	0	375	424	47	12	14	145	128	3.98	104	.275	.343	181	.271	1	85	11	1.7
1892	StL N	2	8	.200	10	10	6	0	64	90	58	1	2	24	16	5.63	57	.319	.377	25	.080	-1	113	-18	-2.1
	Cin N	20	10	.667	34	28	25-3	1	268.1	262	101	6	5	49	47	2.31	141	.246	.282	132	.159	-4*	106	30	2.2
	Year	22	18	.550	44	38	31-3	1	332.1	352	106	7	7	73	63	2.95	110	.261	.302	157	.146	-6	107	19	0.1
1893	Cin N	18	15	.545	37	30	28-1	**2**	287.1	332	187	17	5	93	53	4.13	116	.281	.336	120	.200	-3*	96	18	1.4
1894	Cin N	19	21	.475	45	39	34-1	1	348	471	282	26	15	106	49	5.07	109	.320	.371	172-0	.267	1*	97	17	1.5
1895	Cin N	18	15	.545	37	31	23-2	0	280.1	355	191	10	14	74	46	4.24	117	.304	.353	113-1	.265	2	90	19	1.7
1896	Cin N	24	11	.686	36	34	30-3	1	288.2	321	144	8	11	60	57	3.15	147	.279	.321	110-3	.264	4	90	42	4.4
1897	Cin N	18	13	.581	37	31	22	0	247.1	315	142	5	11	56	41	3.78	120	.307	.350	94-7	.266	0	88	19	1.7
1898	Cin N	16	10	.615	31	28	24	0	240	257	117	3	16	42	29	3.04	126	.272	.314	85-1	.141	-4	86	18	1.2
1899	Cin N	0	5	.000	5	5	2	0	32.2	48	26	1	1	9	2	5.51	71	.340	.384	11-0	.364	1	48	-5	-0.6
Total	12	177	151	.540	366	318	271-12	6	2819	3312	1782	108	101	764	565	3.84	115	.286	.336	1252-12	.229	-7	93	166	13.6
DYER, EDDIE Edwin Hawley B 10.11.1900 Morgan City, LA D 4.20.1964 Houston, TX BL/TL 5-11.5/168# d7.8 M5 ▲																									
1922	StL N	0	0	—	2	0	0	0	3.2	7	2	0	0	0	3	2.45	157	.412	.412	3-0	.333	1*		0	0.1
1923	StL N	2	1	.667	4	3	2-1	0	22	30	10	0	1	5	7	4.09	95	.333	.375	45-0	.267	0*	70	0	0.2
1924	StL N	8	11	.421	29	15	7-1	0	136.2	174	82	6	4	51	23	4.61	82	.331	.395	76-3	.237	1*	133	-12	-1.2

Year	Tm Lg	W	L	Pct	G	GS	CG-Sho	SV-BS	IP	H	R	HR	HB	BB-IB	SO	ERA	AERA	OAV	OOB	AB-SH	AVG	PB	Sup	APR	PW
1925	StL N	4	3	.571	27	5	1	3	82.1	93	52	4	7	24	25	4.15	104	.278	.340	31-1	.097	-2*	137	-1	-0.3
1926	StL N	1	0	1.000	6	0	0	0	9.1	7	14	0	1	14	4	11.57	34	.219	.468	2-0	.500	0		-8	-0.7
1927	StL N	0	0	—	1	0	0	0	2	5	4	1	0	2	1	18.00	22	.500	.583	0-0	—	0		-3	-0.1
Total	6	15	15	.500	69	23	10-2	3	256	316	164	11	13	96	63	4.75	84	.313	.380	157-4	.223	1	124	-24	-2.0

DYER, MIKE Michael Lawrence B 9.8.1966 Upland, CA BR/TR 6-3/195# d6.29

Year	Tm Lg	W	L	Pct	G	GS	CG-Sho	SV-BS	IP	H	R	HR	HB	BB-IB	SO	ERA	AERA	OAV	OOB	AB-SH	AVG	PB	Sup	APR	PW
1989	Min A	4	7	.364	16	12	1	0-0	71	74	43	2	2	37-0	37	4.82	86	.273	.362	0-0	—	0	80	-6	-0.9
1994	Pit N	1	1	.500	14	0	0	4-2	15.1	15	12	1	3	12-4	13	5.87	74	.268	.411	1-0	.000	-0		-3	-0.5
1995	Pit N	4	5	.444	55	0	0	0-2	74.2	81	40	9	5	30-3	53	4.34	99	.281	.358	7-1	.571	1		0	0.1
1996	Mon N	5	5	.500	70	1	0	2-4	75.2	79	40	7	5	34-4	51	4.40	98	.277	.360	7-0	.000	-1	63	0	-0.1
Total	4	14	18	.438	155	13	1	6-8	236.2	249	135	19	15	113-11	154	4.60	93	.277	.364	15-1	.267	1	77	-9	-1.4

DYGERT, JIMMY James Henry "Sunny Jim" B 7.5.1884 Utica, NY D 2.8.1936 New Orleans, LA BR/TR 5-10/185# d9.8

Year	Tm Lg	W	L	Pct	G	GS	CG-Sho	SV-BS	IP	H	R	HR	HB	BB-IB	SO	ERA	AERA	OAV	OOB	AB-SH	AVG	PB	Sup	APR	PW
1905	Phi A	1	4	.200	6	3	2	0	35.1	41	20	2	2	11	24	4.33	61	.291	.351	15-0	.267	0	89	-5	-0.6
1906	Phi A	11	13	.458	35	25	15-4	0	213.2	175	88	1	10	91	106	2.70	101	.226	.316	74-2	.176	-0	95	2	0.1
1907	Phi A	21	8	.724	42	28	18-5	1	261.2	200	98	2	18	85	151	2.34	111	**.214**	.292	94-6	.128	-4	121	8	0.4
1908	Phi A	11	15	.423	41	28	15-5	1	238.2	184	95	3	11	97	164	2.87	89	.220	.309	75-5	.080	-6	77	-4	-1.0
1909	Phi A	9	5	.643	32	13	6-1	0	137.1	117	60	1	11	50	79	2.42	99	.242	.327	44-3	.205	0	156	-4	-0.4
1910	Phi A	4	4	.500	19	8	6-1	0	99.1	81	44	0	3	49	59	2.54	94	.231	.331	36-0	.083	-2	124	-2	-0.5
Total	6	57	49	.538	175	105	62-16	2	986	798	405	9	55	383	583	2.65	97	.227	.312	338-16	.139	-11	107	-5	-2.0

DYKHOFF, RADHAMES Radhames Alviro B 9.27.1974 Paradera, Aruba BL/TL 6/205# d6.7

Year	Tm Lg	W	L	Pct	G	GS	CG-Sho	SV-BS	IP	H	R	HR	HB	BB-IB	SO	ERA	AERA	OAV	OOB	AB-SH	AVG	PB	Sup	APR	PW
1998	Bal A	0	0	—	1	0	0	0-0	1	2	2	0	0	1-0	1	18.00	25	.400	.500	0-0	—	0		-1	-0.1

EARLEY, ARNOLD Arnold Carl B 6.4.1933 Lincoln Park, MI D 9.29.1999 Flint, MI BL/TL 6-1/200# d9.27

Year	Tm Lg	W	L	Pct	G	GS	CG-Sho	SV-BS	IP	H	R	HR	HB	BB-IB	SO	ERA	AERA	OAV	OOB	AB-SH	AVG	PB	Sup	APR	PW
1960	Bos A	0	1	.000	2	0	0	0	4	9	8	1	0	4-0	5	15.75	26	.429	.520	1-0	.000	0		-5	-0.8
1961	Bos A	2	4	.333	33	0	0	7	49.2	42	31	3	0	34-3	44	3.99	105	.226	.345	6-0	.000	-1		-1	-0.3
1962	Bos A	4	5	.444	38	3	0	5	68.1	76	53	8	1	46-1	59	5.80	71	.281	.384	10-0	.200	0	58	-14	-1.8
1963	Bos A	3	7	.300	53	4	0	1	115.2	124	73	13	8	43-8	97	4.75	80	.270	.342	18-0	.278	1	112	-14	-1.1
1964	Bos A	1	1	.500	25	3	1	1	50.1	51	17	3	1	18-0	45	2.68	144	.266	.332	9-1	.111	0	123	6	0.4
1965	Bos A	0	1	.000	57	0	0	0	74.1	79	42	5	3	29-8	47	3.63	103	.271	.338	6-0	.000	-0		-2	-0.1
1966	Chi N	2	1	.667	13	0	0	0	17.2	14	11	1	0	9-0	12	3.57	103	.226	.319	1-1	.000	-0		-1	-0.2
1967	Hou N	0	0	—	2	0	0	0	1.1	5	5	1	0	1-0	1	27.00	12	.625	.667	0-0	—	0		-4	-0.2
Total	8	12	20	.375	223	10	1	14	381.1	400	240	35	13	184-20	310	4.48	87	.269	.352	51-2	.157	0	98	-35	-4.1

EARLEY, TOM Thomas Francis Aloysius B 2.19.1917 Roxbury, MA D 4.5.1988 Nantucket, MA BR/TR 6/180# d9.27 Mil 1943-44

Year	Tm Lg	W	L	Pct	G	GS	CG-Sho	SV-BS	IP	H	R	HR	HB	BB-IB	SO	ERA	AERA	OAV	OOB	AB-SH	AVG	PB	Sup	APR	PW
1938	Bos N	1	0	1.000	2	1	1	0	11	8	9	2	1	1	4	3.27	105	.186	.222	4-0	.000	-1	99	-2	-0.2
1939	Bos N	1	4	.200	14	2	0	1	40	49	28	1	2	19	9	4.72	78	.304	.385	10-0	.300	1	59	-6	-0.7
1940	Bos N	2	0	1.000	4	1	1-1	0	16.1	16	7	1	2	3	5	3.86	96	.267	.323	5-0	.400	1	187	0	0.1
1941	Bos N	6	8	.429	33	13	6-1	3	138.2	120	52	9	3	46	54	2.53	141	.233	.300	47-2	.234	1*	93	14	1.5
1942	Bos N	6	11	.353	27	18	6	1	112.2	120	65	10	1	55	28	4.71	71	.276	.359	34-3	.118	-1	95	-16	-2.2
1945	Bos N	2	1	.667	11	2	1	0	41	36	22	4	0	19	4	4.61	83	.235	.320	14-1	.214	1*	166	-2	-0.1
Total	6	18	24	.429	91	37	15-2	5	359.2	349	183	27	9	143	104	3.78	94	.256	.330	114-6	.202	2	98	-12	-1.6

EARLEY, BILL William Albert B 1.30.1956 Cincinnati, OH BR/TL 6-4/200# d9.22

Year	Tm Lg	W	L	Pct	G	GS	CG-Sho	SV-BS	IP	H	R	HR	HB	BB-IB	SO	ERA	AERA	OAV	OOB	AB-SH	AVG	PB	Sup	APR	PW
1986	StL N	0	0	—	3	0	0	0-0	3	0	0	0	0	2-0	2	0.00	—	.000	.182	0-0	—	0		1	0.1

EARNSHAW, GEORGE George Livingston "Moose" B 2.15.1900 New York, NY D 12.1.1976 Little Rock, AR BR/TR 6-4/210# d6.3 C2

Year	Tm Lg	W	L	Pct	G	GS	CG-Sho	SV-BS	IP	H	R	HR	HB	BB-IB	SO	ERA	AERA	OAV	OOB	AB-SH	AVG	PB	Sup	APR	PW
1928	Phi A	7	7	.500	26	22	7-3	1	158.1	143	81	7	1	100	117	3.81	105	.240	.351	57-5	.246	1	123	3	0.3
1929	†Phi A	**24**	8	.750	44	33	13-3	1	254.2	233	110	8	5	125	149	3.29	129	**.241**	.331	87-10	.172	-2	118	27	2.6
1930	†Phi A	22	13	.629	49	**39**	20-**3**	2	296	299	162	20	1	139	193	4.44	105	.266	.347	114-7	.228	1	118	10	1.0
1931	†Phi A	21	7	.750	43	30	23-3	6	281.2	255	130	16	3	75	152	3.67	122	.236	.288	114-3	.263	6	118	28	3.1
1932	Phi A	19	13	.594	36	33	21-1	0	245.1	262	147	28	4	94	109	4.77	95	.270	.336	91-11	.286	4	121	-9	-0.6
1933	Phi A	5	10	.333	21	18	4	0	117.2	153	93	8	1	58	37	5.97	72	.311	.385	44-2	.182	-0	133	-22	-2.3
1934	Chi A	14	11	.560	33	30	16-2	0	227	242	128	28	4	104	97	4.52	105	.270	.349	79-3	.203	-0	82	7	0.6
1935	Chi A	1	2	.333	3	3	0	0	18	26	19	2	0	11	8	9.00	51	.342	.425	7-1	.286	0	138	-8	-0.9
	Bro N	8	12	.400	25	22	6-2	0	166	175	87	14	0	53	72	4.12	96	.270	.325	60-1	.217	1	110	-1	0.0
1936	Bro N	4	9	.308	19	13	4-1	1	93	113	63	7	3	30	40	5.32	78	.297	.354	33-1	.242	0	81	-11	-1.2
	StL N	2	1	.667	20	6	1	1	57.2	80	43	4	3	20	28	6.40	62	.333	.392	18-0	.222	-0	122	-14	-0.7
	Year	6	10	.375	39	19	5-1	2	150.2	193	49	11	6	50	68	5.73	71	.311	.368	51-1	.235	0	93	-23	-1.9
Total	9	127	93	.577	319	249	115-18	12	1915.1	1981	1063	142	25	809	1002	4.38	100	.265	.339	704-44	.230	9	113	10	1.9

EASLEY, LOGAN Kenneth Logan B 11.4.1961 Salt Lake City, UT BR/TR 6-1/185# d4.9

Year	Tm Lg	W	L	Pct	G	GS	CG-Sho	SV-BS	IP	H	R	HR	HB	BB-IB	SO	ERA	AERA	OAV	OOB	AB-SH	AVG	PB	Sup	APR	PW
1987	Pit N	1	1	.500	17	0	0	1-0	26.1	23	17	5	1	17-4	21	5.47	75	.242	.357	2-0	.000	-0		-4	-0.2
1989	Pit N	1	0	1.000	10	0	0	1-0	12.1	8	6	1	1	7-1	6	4.38	77	.190	.320	1-0	.000	-0		-1	-0.1
Total	2	2	1	.667	27	0	0	2-0	38.2	31	23	6	2	24-5	27	5.12	76	.226	.345	3-0	.000	-0		-5	-0.3

EASON, MAL Malcolm Wayne "Kid" B 3.13.1879 Brookville, PA D 4.16.1970 Douglas, AZ BR/TR 6/175# d10.1 U8

Year	Tm Lg	W	L	Pct	G	GS	CG-Sho	SV-BS	IP	H	R	HR	HB	BB-IB	SO	ERA	AERA	OAV	OOB	AB-SH	AVG	PB	Sup	APR	PW
1900	Chi N	1	0	1.000	1	1	1	0	9	9	2	0	0	3	2	1.00	361	.257	.316	3-0	.000	-1	77	3	0.2
1901	Chi N	8	17	.320	27	25	23-1	0	220.2	246	136	9	13	60	68	3.59	90	.280	.335	87-1	.138	-5	76	-10	-1.5
1902	Chi N	1	1	.500	2	2	2	0	18	21	7	0	0	2	4	1.00	271	.292	.311	5-1	.200	0	75	2	0.3
	Bos N	9	12	.429	27	27	20-2	0	213.1	249	100	4	12	61	51	2.91	97	.291	.347	72-6	.083	-6	94	-3	-1.0
	Year	10	13	.435	29	29	22-2	0	231.1	270	104	4	12	63	55	2.76	102	.291	.344	77-7	.091	-6	92	-2	-0.7
1903	Det A	2	5	.286	7	6	6-1	0	56.1	60	33	1	3	19	21	3.36	87	.271	.337	20-0	.100	-2	53	-4	-0.5
1905	Bro N	5	21	.192	27	27	20-3	0	207	230	128	5	5	72	64	4.30	67	.292	.355	81-2	.173	-1*	69	-29	-3.2
1906	Bro N	10	17	.370	34	26	18-3	1	227	212	109	1	9	74	64	3.25	78	.256	.323	88-1	.091	-4*	98	-19	-2.6
Total	6	36	73	.330	125	114	90-10	1	951.1	1027	515	20	42	291	274	3.42	84	.279	.339	356-11	.121	-19	82	-60	-8.3

EAST, HUGH Gordon Hugh B 7.7.1919 Birmingham, AL D 11.2.1981 Charleston, SC BR/TR 6-2/185# d9.13 Mil 1943-45

Year	Tm Lg	W	L	Pct	G	GS	CG-Sho	SV-BS	IP	H	R	HR	HB	BB-IB	SO	ERA	AERA	OAV	OOB	AB-SH	AVG	PB	Sup	APR	PW
1941	NY N	1	1	.500	2	2	0	0	15.2	19	12	0	0	9	4	3.45	107	.297	.384	9-0	.222	0	138	-2	-0.2
1942	NY N	0	2	.000	4	1	0	0	7.1	15	16	1	0	7	2	9.82	34	.429	.524	2-0	.500	2	50	-8	-1.2
1943	NY N	1	3	.250	13	5	1	0	40.1	51	27	4	0	25	21	5.36	64	.298	.388	13-0	.077	-1*	64	-8	-0.9
Total	3	2	6	.250	19	8	1	0	63.1	85	55	5	0	41	27	5.40	65	.315	.405	24-0	.167	1	82	-18	-2.3

EASTERLY, JAMIE James Morris B 2.17.1953 Houston, TX BL/TL 5-9/180# d4.6

Year	Tm Lg	W	L	Pct	G	GS	CG-Sho	SV-BS	IP	H	R	HR	HB	BB-IB	SO	ERA	AERA	OAV	OOB	AB-SH	AVG	PB	Sup	APR	PW
1974	Atl N	0	0	—	3	0	0	0-0	2.2	6	7	0	0	4-0	0	16.88	22	.400	.526	0-0	—	0		-4	-0.2
1975	Atl N	2	9	.182	21	13	0	0-0	68.2	73	47	5	2	42-2	34	4.98	76	.275	.375	18-3	.056	-2	91	-10	-1.6
1976	Atl N	1	1	.500	4	4	0	0-0	22	23	12	0	0	13-1	11	4.91	77	.280	.379	9-0	.111	-0	70	-2	-0.2
1977	Atl N	2	4	.333	22	5	0	1-0	58.2	72	46	5	3	30-4	37	6.14	73	.303	.386	15-2	.267	1*	92	-10	-0.9
1978	Atl N	3	6	.333	37	6	0	1-1	78	91	52	9	2	45-6	42	5.65	72	.299	.391	19-1	.211	0	85	-11	-1.1
1979	Atl N	0	0	—	4	0	0	0-0	2.2	7	6	0	0	3-0	3	13.50	30	.467	.556	0-0	—	0		-3	-0.2
1981	†Mil A	3	3	.500	44	0	0	4-3	62	46	23	0	0	34-4	31	3.19	107	.219	.321	0-0	—	0		2	0.2
1982	Mil A	0	2	.000	28	0	0	2-1	30.2	39	19	6	0	15-0	16	4.70	81	.312	.380	0-0	—	0		-4	-0.3
1983	Mil A	0	1	.000	12	0	0	1-1	11.2	14	7	0	2	10-1	6	3.86	97	.350	.491	1-1	.000	-0*		-1	-0.1
	Cle A	4	2	.667	41	0	0	3-4	57	69	25	4	2	22-4	39	3.63	117	.309	.375	0-0	—	0		4	0.4
	Year	4	3	.571	53	0	0	4-5	68.2	83	36	4	4	32-5	45	3.67	114	.316	.395	1-1	.000	-0		3	0.3
1984	Cle A	3	1	.750	26	1	0	2-0	69.1	74	31	3	1	23-3	42	3.38	121	.273	.330	0-0	—	0	88	4	0.3
1985	Cle A	4	1	.800	50	7	0	0-0	98.2	96	52	9	4	53-4	58	3.92	105	.264	.356	0-0	—	0	160	0	0.0
1986	Cle A	0	2	.000	13	0	0	0-0	17.2	27	16	3	0	12-0	9	7.64	54	.365	.443	0-0	—	0		-6	-0.6
1987	Cle A	1	1	.500	16	0	0	0-1	31.2	26	17	4	1	13-1	22	4.55	100	.218	.296	0-0	—	0		1	0.0
Total	13	23	33	.411	321	36	0	14-11	611.1	663	360	48	17	319-30	350	4.62	87	.283	.368	62-7	.161	-1	102	-40	-4.3

EASTON, JACK John S. B 2.28.1867 Bridgeport, OH D 11.28.1903 Steubenville, OH d9.23

Year	Tm Lg	W	L	Pct	G	GS	CG-Sho	SV-BS	IP	H	R	HR	HB	BB-IB	SO	ERA	AERA	OAV	OOB	AB-SH	AVG	PB	Sup	APR	PW
1889	Col AA	1	0	1.000	4	1	1	1	18	13	8	0	3	21	7	3.50	104	.197	.411	7	.000	-1	120	1	0.0
1890	Col AA	15	14	.517	37	29	23	1	255.2	213	148	4	20	125	147	3.52	102	.220	.321	107	.178	0*	109	4	0.4

Year	Tm Lg	W	L	Pct	G	GS	CG-Sho	SV-BS	IP	H	R	HR	HB	BB-IB	SO	ERA	AERA	OAV	OOB	AB-SH	AVG	PB	Sup	APR	PW
1891	Col AA	5	10	.333	18	16	13	0	135.1	145	111	3	15	59	52	4.52	76	.265	.352	63	.238	2*	86	-20	-1.5
	StL AA	3	2	.600	7	6	4	0	47.2	48	38	3	4	23	22	5.10	82	.253	.346	28	.179	-1*	108	-2	-0.3
	Col AA	0	2	.000	2	2	2	0	15	15	8	2	2	4	13	3.60	96	.250	.318	11	.000	-1*	18	0	-0.1
	Year	8	14	.364	27	24	19	0	198	208	9	8	21	86	87	4.59	79	.261	.348	102	.196	-0	88	-17	-1.9
1892	StL N	2	0	1.000	5	2	2	0	31	38	31	2	3	26	4	6.39	50	.290	.419	17	.176	-1	188	-11	-0.6
1894	Pit N	0	1	.000	3	1	1	0	19.2	26	16	0	3	4	1	4.12	127	.313	.367	5-2	.000	-1	54	1	-0.1
Total	5	26	29	.473	76	57	46	2	522.1	498	360	14	50	262	246	4.12	89	.243	.343	238-2	.176	-2	100	-27	-2.2
EASTWICK, RAWLY Rawlins Jackson B 10.24.1950 Camden, NJ BR/TR 6-3/180# d9.12																									
1974	Cin N	0	0	—	8	0	0	2-0	17.2	12	5	1	0	5-0	14	2.04	172	.188	.243	1-0	.000	-0		3	0.1
1975	†Cin N	5	3	.625	58	0	0	**22-3**	90	77	26	6	2	25-4	61	2.60	139	.229	.287	15-1	.067	-1		11	1.4
1976	†Cin N	11	5	.688	71	0	0	**26-9**	107.2	93	30	3	2	27-3	70	2.09	168	.232	.282	17-2	.000	-2		16	2.9
1977	Cin N	2	2	.500	23	0	0	7-2	43.1	40	14	3	0	8-1	17	2.91	135	.244	.279	6-1	.167	-0		5	0.6
	StL N	3	7	.300	41	1	0	4-2	53.2	74	34	6	0	21-3	30	4.70	82	.332	.385	5-0	.400	1	115	-6	-1.1
	Year	5	9	.357	64	1	0	11-4	97	114	39	9	0	29-4	47	3.90	100	.295	.341	11-1	.273	1	114	-1	-0.5
1978	NY A	2	1	.667	8	0	0	0-0	24.2	22	9	2	1	4-0	13	3.28	111	.232	.270	0-0	—	0		2	0.2
	†Phi N	2	1	.667	22	0	0	0-2	40.1	31	21	5	0	18-2	14	4.02	89	.209	.292	3-0	.000	-0		-3	-0.3
1979	Phi N	3	6	.333	51	0	0	6-3	82.2	90	46	8	1	25-3	47	4.90	78	.284	.336	7-0	.000	-1		-8	-1.1
1980	KC A	0	1	.000	14	0	0	0-1	22	37	14	2	2	8-2	5	5.32	76	.363	.416	0-0	—	0		-3	-0.1
1981	Chi N	0	1	.000	30	0	0	1-1	43.1	43	16	2	0	15-3	24	2.28	162	.264	.322	2-0	.000	-0		5	0.3
Total	8	28	27	.509	326	1	0	68-23	525.1	519	215	38	8	156-21	295	3.31	112	.258	.312	56-4	.071	-3	120	22	2.9
EATON, ADAM Adam Thomas B 11.23.1977 Seattle, WA BR/TR 6-2/190# d5.30																									
2000	SD N	7	4	.636	22	22	0	0-0	135	134	63	14	2	61-3	90	4.13	105	.260	.338	38-0	.289	6*	109	6	1.0
2001	SD N	8	5	.615	17	17	2	0-0	116.2	108	61	20	5	40-3	109	4.32	93	.241	.308	38-2	.105	0*	118	-4	-0.2
2002	SD N	1	1	.500	6	6	0	0-0	33.1	28	20	5	2	17-0	25	5.40	70	.235	.336	9-0	.111	-0	94	-6	-0.3
2003	SD N	9	12	.429	31	31	1	0-0	183	173	91	20	7	68-6	146	4.08	97	.246	.316	56-7	.196	5*	101	-4	0.2
Total	4	25	22	.532	76	76	3	0-0	468	443	235	59	16	186-12	370	4.25	95	.248	.322	141-9	.191	11	107	-8	0.7
EATON, CRAIG Craig B 9.7.1954 Glendale, OH BR/TR 5-11/175# d9.5																									
1979	KC A	0	0	—	5	0	0	0-0	10	8	3	0	0	3-2	4	2.70	158	.222	.282	0-0	—	0		2	0.1
EATON, ZEB Zebulon Vance "Red" B 2.2.1920 Cooleemee, NC D 12.17.1989 W.Palm Beach, FL BR/TR 5-10/185# d4.18																									
1944	Det A	0	0	—	6	0	0	0	15.2	19	12	2	0	8	4	5.74	62	.322	.403	10-0	.100	-1*		-4	-0.2
1945	†Det A	4	2	.667	17	3	0	0	53.1	48	28	0	3	40	15	4.05	87	.247	.384	32-0	.250	2*	40	-3	-0.1
Total	2	4	2	.667	23	3	0	0	69	67	40	2	3	48	19	4.43	80	.265	.388	42-0	.214	2	40	-7	-0.3
EAVE, GARY Gary Louis B 7.22.1963 Monroe, LA BR/TR 6-4/200# d4.12																									
1988	Atl N	0	0	—	5	0	0	0-0	5	7	5	0	0	3-0	0	9.00	41	.333	.417	0-0	—	0		-3	-0.1
1989	Atl N	2	0	1.000	3	3	0	0-0	20.2	15	3	0	1	12-0	9	1.31	280	.200	.318	6-1	.000	-1	81	5	0.4
1990	Sea A	0	3	.000	8	5	0	0-0	30	27	16	5	2	20-1	16	4.20	94	.241	.366	0-0	—	0	87	-1	-0.1
Total	3	2	3	.400	16	8	0	0-0	55.2	49	24	5	3	35-1	25	3.56	108	.236	.354	6-1	.000	-1	85	1	0.2
EAVES, VALLIE Vallie Ennis "Chief" B 9.6.1911 Allen, OK D 4.19.1960 Norman, OK BR/TR 6-2.5/180# d9.12																									
1935	Phi A	1	2	.333	3	3	1	0	14	12	9	0	0	15	6	5.14	88	.240	.415	4-0	.000	-1	57	-1	-0.2
1939	Chi A	0	1	.000	2	1	1	0	11.2	11	7	1	1	8	5	4.63	102	.250	.377	6-0	.333	0	56	0	0.0
1940	Chi A	0	2	.000	5	3	0	0	18.2	22	16	2	1	24	11	6.75	66	.301	.480	5-1	.000	-1	73	-5	-0.5
1941	Chi N	3	3	.500	12	7	4	0	58.2	56	27	4	3	21	24	3.53	99	.253	.327	20-1	.100	-1	100	0	-0.2
1942	Chi N	0	0	—	2	0	0	0	3	4	3	0	1	2	0	9.00	36	.308	.438	0-0	—	0		-2	-0.1
Total	5	4	8	.333	24	14	6	0	106	105	62	7	6	70	46	4.58	86	.262	.379	35-2	.114	-3	82	-8	-1.0
EAYRS, EDDIE Edwin B 11.10.1890 Blackstone, MA D 11.30.1969 Warwick, RI BL/TL 5-7/160# d6.30 ▲																									
1913	Pit N	0	0	—	2	0	0	0	8	8	6	0	0	6	5	2.25	134	.267	.389	6-0	.167	-0*		-1	-0.1
1920	Bos N	1	2	.333	7	3	0	0	26.1	36	18	1	2	12	7	5.47	56	.346	.424	244-6	.328	2*	69	-7	-0.5
1921	Bos N	0	0	—	2	0	0	0	4.2	9	10	0	0	9	1	17.36	21	.391	.563	15-0	.067	-2*		-7	-0.5
Total	3	1	2	.333	11	3	0	0	39	53	34	1	2	27	13	6.23	50	.338	.441	265-6	.309	0	69	-15	-1.1
EBERT, DERRIN Derrin Lee B 8.21.1976 Anaheim, CA BR/TL 6-3/200# d4.6																									
1999	Atl N	0	1	.000	5	0	0	1-0	8	9	5	2	0	5-1	4	5.63	80	.300	.400	1-0	.000	-0		-1	-0.1
ECCLES, HARRY Harry Josiah "Bugs" B 7.9.1893 Kennedy, NY D 6.2.1955 Jamestown, NY BL/TL 6-2/170# d9.13																									
1915	Phi A	0	1	.000	5	1	0	1	21	18	16	2	0	6	13	4.71	62	.240	.296	6-0	.167	-0	125	-4	-0.3
ECKENSTAHLER, ERIC Eric Ryan B 12.17.1976 Waukegan, IL BL/TL 6-7/210# d9.9																									
2002	Det A	1	0	1.000	7	0	0	0-0	8	14	5	1	0	2-0	13	5.63	77	.378	.410	0-0	—	0		-1	-0.1
2003	Det A	0	0	—	20	0	0	0-0	15.2	9	6	0	2	15-1	12	2.87	150	.167	.366	0-0	—	0		2	0.1
Total	2	1	0	1.000	27	0	0	0-0	23.2	23	11	1	2	17-1	25	3.80	113	.253	.382	0-0	—	0		1	0.0
ECKERSLEY, DENNIS Dennis Lee B 10.3.1954 Oakland, CA BR/TR 6-2/190# d4.12 HF2004																									
1975	Cle A	13	7	.650	34	24	6-2	2-1	186.2	147	61	16	7	90-8	152	2.60	146	.215	.310	0-0	—	0	110	25	2.5
1976	Cle A	13	12	.520	36	30	9-3	1-0	199.1	155	82	13	5	78-2	200	3.43	102	.214	.293	0-0	—	0	95	2	0.3
1977	Cle A★	14	13	.519	33	33	12-3	0-0	247.1	214	100	31	7	54-11	191	3.53	112	.231	**.276**	0-0	—	0*	92	16	1.4
1978	Bos A	20	8	.714	35	35	16-3	0-0	268.1	258	99	30	7	71-8	162	2.99	138	.251	.302	0-0	—	0	111	32	3.2
1979	Bos A	17	10	.630	33	33	17-2	0-0	246.2	234	89	29	6	59-4	150	2.99	**148**	.250	.297	0-0	—	0	106	**38**	4.0
1980	Bos A	12	14	.462	30	30	8	0-0	197.2	188	101	25	2	44-7	121	4.28	99	.248	.289	0-0	—	0	88	0	-0.1
1981	Bos A	9	8	.529	23	23	8-2	0-0	154	160	82	9	3	35-2	79	4.27	91	.267	.308	0-0	—	0	112	-6	-0.6
1982	Bos A★	13	13	.500	33	33	11-3	0-0	224.1	228	101	31	2	43-3	127	3.73	116	.261	.296	0-0	—	0	79	14	1.4
1983	Bos A	9	13	.409	28	28	2	0-0	176.1	223	119	27	6	39-4	77	5.61	78	.303	.341	0-0	—	0	79	-22	-2.3
1984	Bos A	4	4	.500	9	9	2	0-0	64.2	71	38	10	1	13-2	33	5.01	83	.284	.318	0-0	—	0	120	-5	-0.4
	†Chi N	10	8	.556	24	24	2	0-0	160.1	152	59	11	4	36-7	81	3.03	129	.250	.294	55-1	.109	-3	99	15	1.4
1985	Chi N	11	7	.611	25	25	6-2	0-0	169.1	145	61	15	3	19-4	117	3.08	130	.229	.254	56-2	.125	0*	89	16	1.8
1986	Chi N	6	11	.353	33	32	1	0-0	201	226	109	21	3	43-3	137	4.57	89	.285	.320	69-2	.159	1	89	-10	-0.7
1987	Oak A	6	8	.429	54	2	0	16-4	115.2	99	41	11	3	17-3	113	3.03	136	.228	.260	0-0	—	0	77	17	2.2
1988	†Oak A★	4	2	.667	60	0	0	**45-8**	72.2	52	20	5	1	11-2	70	2.35	161	.198	.230	0-0	—	0		12	2.3
1989	†Oak A	4	0	1.000	51	0	0	33-6	57.2	32	10	5	1	3-0	55	1.56	236	.162	.175	0-0	—	0		15	2.5
1990	†Oak A★	4	2	.667	63	0	0	48-2	73.1	41	9	2	0	4-1	73	0.61	607	.160	.172	0-0	—	0		25	4.7
1991	Oak A★	5	4	.556	67	0	0	43-8	76	60	26	11	1	9-3	87	2.96	130	.208	.235	0-0	—	0		8	1.7
1992	†Oak A★	7	1	.875	69	0	0	**51-3**	80	62	17	5	1	11-6	93	1.91	196	.211	.242	0-0	—	0		18	3.7
1993	Oak A	2	4	.333	64	0	0	36-10	67	67	32	7	2	13-4	80	4.16	98	.261	.299	0-0	—	0		0	0.0
1994	Oak A	5	4	.556	45	0	0	19-6	44.1	49	26	5	1	13-2	47	4.26	104	.275	.328	0-0	—	0		-1	-0.1
1995	Oak A	4	6	.400	52	0	0	29-9	50.1	53	29	5	1	11-0	40	4.83	93	.269	.308	0-0	—	0		-2	-0.4
1996	†StL N	0	6	.000	63	0	0	30-4	60	65	26	8	4	6-2	49	3.30	127	.274	.300	1-0	.000	-0		5	0.9
1997	StL N	1	5	.167	57	0	0	36-7	53	49	24	9	2	8-0	45	3.91	106	.238	.273	0-0	—	0		2	0.4
1998	†Bos A	4	1	.800	50	0	0	1-3	39.2	46	21	6	2	8-3	22	4.76	99	.291	.331	0-0	—	0		1	0.0
Total	24	197	171	.535	1071	361	100-20	390-71	3285.2	3076	1382	347	75	738-91	2401	3.50	116	.246	.290	181-5	.133	-1	96	215	29.8
ECKERT, AL Albert George "Obbie" B 5.17.1906 Milwaukee, WI D 4.20.1974 Milwaukee, WI BL/TL 5-10/174# d4.21																									
1930	Cin N	0	1	.000	2	1	0	0	5	7	6	0	0	4	1	7.20	67	.304	.407	1-0	.000	-0	54	-2	-0.3
1931	Cin N	0	1	.000	14	1	0	0	18.2	26	20	3	0	9	5	9.16	41	.325	.393	3-0	.333	0	92	-11	-0.5
1935	StL N	0	0	—	2	0	0	0	3	7	4	0	0	1	1	12.00	34	.467	.500	0-0	—	0		-2	-0.1
Total	3	0	2	.000	18	2	0	0	26.2	40	30	3	0	14	7	9.11	44	.339	.409	4-0	.250	0	76	-15	-0.9
ECKERT, CHARLIE Charles William "Buzz" B 8.8.1897 Philadelphia, PA D 8.22.1986 Trevose, PA BR/TR 5-10.5/165# d9.18																									
1919	Phi A	0	1	.000	2	1	1	0	16	17	9	1	0	3	6	3.94	87	.270	.303	6-0	.167	-0	23	-1	-0.1
1920	Phi A	0	0	—	2	0	0	0	5.2	8	3	0	1	1	1	4.76	84	.421	.476	1-0	.000	-0		0	0.0

Year	Tm Lg	W	L	Pct	G	GS	CG-Sho	SV-BS	IP	H	R	HR	HB	BB-IB	SO	ERA	AERA	OAV	OOB	AB-SH	AVG	PB	Sup	APR	PW
1922	Phi A	0	2	.000	21	0	0	0	50	61	33	7	1	23	15	4.68	91	.319	.395	11-0	.091	-1		-3	-0.2
Total 3		0	3	.000	25	1	1	0	71.2	86	45	8	2	27	22	4.52	90	.315	.381	18-0	.111	-2	23	-4	-0.3
EDDY, CHRIS Christopher Mark B 11.27.1969 Dallas, TX BL/TL 6-3/200# d4.26																									
1995	Oak A	0	0	—	6	0	0	0-0	3.2	7	3	0	2	2-0	2	7.36	61	.438	.550	0-0	—	0		-1	0.0
EDDY, DON Donald Eugene B 10.25.1946 Mason City, IA BR/TL 5-11/170# d9.7																									
1970	Chi A	0	0	—	7	0	0	0-0	11.2	10	4	0	0	6-0	9	2.31	168	.244	.340	0-0	—	0		2	0.1
1971	Chi A	0	2	.000	22	0	0	0-1	22.2	19	6	3	0	19-2	14	2.38	151	.232	.373	1-0	1.000	1		3	0.4
Total 2		0	2	.000	29	0	0	0-1	34.1	29	10	3	0	25-2	23	2.36	157	.236	.362	1-0	1.000	1		5	0.5
EDDY, STEVE Steven Allen B 8.21.1957 Sterling, IL BR/TR 6-2/185# d6.13																									
1979	Cal A	1	1	.500	7	4	0	0-0	32.1	36	19	1	2	20-0	7	4.73	86	.290	.389	0-0	—	0	128	-2	-0.1
EDELEN, JOE Benny Joe B 9.16.1955 Durant, OK BR/TR 6/165# d4.18																									
1981	StL N	1	0	1.000	13	0	0	0-0	17.1	29	18	2	1	3-1	10	9.35	38	.367	.393	3-0	.333	0		-10	-0.5
	Cin N	1	0	1.000	5	0	0	0-0	12.2	5	1	1	0	0-0	5	0.71	500	.128	.128	2-0	.000	-0		4	0.3
	Year	2	0	1.000	18	0	0	0-0	30	34	25	3	1	3-1	15	5.70	62	.288	.309	5-0	.200	0		-6	-0.2
1982	Cin N	0	0	—	9	0	0	0-0	15.1	22	15	2	0	8-3	11	8.80	42	.344	.411	2-0	.500	0		-8	-0.4
Total 2		2	0	1.000	27	0	0	0-0	45.1	56	34	5	1	11-4	26	6.75	53	.308	.347	7-0	.286	0		-14	-0.6
EDELEN, ED Edward Joseph "Doc" B 3.16.1912 Bryantown, MD D 2.1.1982 LaPlata, MD BR/TR 6/191# d8.20																									
1932	Was A	0	0	—	2	0	0	0	1	0	3	0	0	6	0	27.00	16	.000	.600	0-0	—	0		-2	-0.1
EDELMAN, JOHN John Rogers B 7.27.1935 Philadelphia, PA BR/TR 6-3/185# d6.2																									
1955	Mil N	0	0	—	5	0	0	0	5.2	7	7	0	0	8-0	3	11.12	34	.304	.484	0-0	—	0		-5	-0.2
EDEN, CHARLIE Charles M. B 1.18.1855 Lexington, KY D 9.17.1920 Cincinnati, OH BL/TL ?/168# d8.17.1877 ▲																									
1884	Pit AA	0	1	.000	2	1	1	0	12	12	9	1	1	3	3	6.00	55	.255	.314	122	.270	1*	91	-2	-0.1
1885	Pit AA	1	2	.333	4	1	0	0	15.2	22	13	0	0	3	5	5.17	62	.314	.342	405	.254	1*	92	-3	-0.4
Total 2		1	3	.250	6	2	1	0	27.2	34	22	1	1	6	8	5.53	59	.291	.331	527	.258	1	92	-5	-0.5
EDENFIELD, KEN Kenneth Edward B 3.18.1967 Jesup, GA BR/TR 6-1/165# d5.11																									
1995	Cal A	0	0	—	7	0	0	0-0	12.2	15	7	1	0	5-0	6	4.26	110	.300	.357	0-0	—	0		0	0.0
1996	Cal A	0	0	—	2	0	0	0-0	4.1	10	5	2	1	2-0	4	10.38	48	.435	.500	0-0	—	0		-2	-0.1
Total 2		0	0	—	9	0	0	0-0	17	25	12	3	1	7-0	10	5.82	82	.342	.402	0-0	—	0		-2	-0.1
EDENS, TOM Thomas Patrick B 6.9.1961 Ontario, OR BR/TR 6-2/188# d6.2																									
1987	NY N	0	0	—	2	2	0	0-0	8	15	6	2	0	4-0	4	6.75	56	.417	.475	3-0	.000	-0	143	-2	-0.1
1990	Mil A	4	5	.444	35	6	0	2-0	89	89	52	8	4	33-3	40	4.45	87	.262	.331	0-0	—	0	102	-6	-0.6
1991	Min A	2	2	.500	8	6	0	0-0	33	34	15	2	0	10-1	19	4.09	104	.256	.308	0-0	—	0	107	1	0.2
1992	Min A	6	3	.667	52	0	0	3-2	76.1	65	26	1	2	36-3	57	2.83	144	.236	.329	0-0	—	0		10	1.2
1993	Hou N	1	1	.500	38	0	0	0-1	49	47	17	4	0	19-7	21	3.12	124	.263	.332	1-0	.000	-0		5	0.3
1994	Hou N	4	1	.800	39	0	0	1-2	50	55	25	3	2	17-4	38	4.50	88	.289	.349	2-1	.000	-0		-2	-0.1
	Phi N	1	0	1.000	3	0	0	0-0	4	4	1	0	0	1-0	1	2.25	191	.267	.313	0-0	—	0		1	0.2
	Year	5	1	.833	42	0	0	1-2	54	59	31	3	2	18-4	39	4.33	92	.288	.346	2-1	.000	-0		-1	0.1
1995	Chi N	1	0	1.000	5	0	0	0-0	3	6	3	0	0	3-0	2	6.00	68	.400	.500	0-0	—	0		-1	-0.2
Total 7		19	12	.613	182	14	0	6-5	312.1	315	145	20	8	123-18	182	3.86	103	.266	.337	6-1	.000	-1	111	6	0.9
EDGE, BUTCH Claude Lee B 7.18.1956 Houston, TX BR/TR 6-3/203# d8.13																									
1979	Tor A	3	4	.429	9	9	1	0-0	51.2	60	32	6	1	24-1	19	5.23	83	.283	.357	0-0	—	0	86	-4	-0.5
EDGERTON, BILL William Albert B 8.16.1941 South Bend, IN BL/TL 6-2/185# d9.3																									
1966	KC A	0	1	.000	6	1	0	0	8.1	10	3	0	0	7-2	3	3.24	105	.303	.425	0-1	—	0	26	0	0.1
1967	KC A	1	0	1.000	7	0	0	0	8.1	11	4	1	1	3-0	6	2.16	147	.324	.395	0-0	—	0		0	0.0
1969	Sea A	0	1	.000	4	0	0	0-0	4	10	7	1	1	0-0	2	13.50	27	.455	.478	0-0	—	0		-4	-0.8
Total 3		1	2	.333	17	1	0	0-0	20.2	31	14	2	2	10-2	11	4.79	70	.348	.426	0-1	—	0	26	-4	-0.7
EDMONDSON, BRIAN Brian Christopher B 1.29.1973 Fontana, CA BR/TR 6-2/165# d4.2																									
1998	Atl N	0	1	.000	10	0	0	0-1	16.2	14	10	2	0	8-1	8	4.32	96	.215	.301	2-0	.000	-0		-1	0.0
	Fla N	4	3	.571	43	0	0	0-2	59.1	62	28	8	3	29-4	32	3.79	107	.281	.367	10-1	.000	-1		2	0.0
	Year	4	4	.500	53	0	0	0-3	76	76	39	10	3	37-5	40	3.91	104	.266	.353	12-1	.000	-1		0	0.0
1999	Fla N	5	8	.385	68	0	0	1-5	94	106	65	11	6	44-5	58	5.84	75	.290	.370	11-0	.364	2		-15	-1.6
Total 2		9	12	.429	121	0	0	1-8	170	182	103	21	9	81-10	98	4.98	85	.280	.362	23-1	.174	0		-14	-1.6
EDMONDSON, GEORGE George Henderson "Big Ed" B 5.18.1896 Waxahachie, TX D 7.11.1973 Waco, TX BR/TR 6-1/179# d8.15																									
1922	Cle A	0	0	—	2	0	0	0	2	4	2	0	0	0	0	9.00	45	.444	.444	0-0	—	0		-1	0.0
1923	Cle A	0	0	—	1	0	0	0	4	8	5	0	1	3	0	11.25	35	.444	.545	1-0	.000	-0		-3	-0.1
1924	Cle A	0	0	—	5	1	0	0	8	10	8	1	0	5	3	9.00	47	.294	.385	3-0	.333	0	178	-3	-0.2
Total 3		0	0	—	8	1	0	0	14	22	15	1	1	8	3	9.64	43	.361	.443	4-0	.250	-0	178	-7	-0.3
EDMONDSON, PAUL Paul Michael B 2.12.1943 Kansas City, KS D 2.13.1970 Santa Barbara, CA BR/TR 6-5/195# d6.20																									
1969	Chi A	1	6	.143	14	13	1	0-1	87.2	72	36	5	4	39-4	46	3.70	105	.227	.316	29-1	.172	-1	62	3	0.3
EDMONDSON, BOB Robert E. B 4.30.1879 Paris, KY D 8.14.1931 Lawrence, KS BR/TR 5-11/185# d9.15 ▲																									
1906	Was A	0	1	.000	2	1	1	0	10	10	8	0	0	2	0	4.50	59	.263	.300	3-0	.333	0*	27	-3	-0.2
EDMONSTON, SAM Samuel Sherwood "Big Sam" B 8.30.1883 Washington, DC D 4.12.1979 Corpus Christi, TX BL/TL 5-11.5/185# d6.24																									
1907	Was A	0	0	—	1	0	0	0	3	8	3	0	0	1	0	9.00	27	.500	.529	2-0	.000	-0		-2	-0.1
EDWARDS d9.11																									
1875	Atl NA	0	1	.000	1	1	0	0	2	4	6	0		0	0	4.50	46	.308	.308	5	.200	-0	102	-1	-0.2
EDWARDS, FOSTER Foster Hamilton "Eddie" B 9.1.1903 Holstein, IA D 1.4.1980 Orleans, MA BR/TR 6-3/175# d7.2																									
1925	Bos N	0	0	—	1	0	0	0	2	6	5	0	0	1	1	9.00	45	.545	.583	0-0	—	0		-2	-0.1
1926	Bos N	2	0	1.000	3	3	1	0	25	20	4	0	0	13	4	0.72	492	.230	.330	9-0	.000	-2	55	8	0.4
1927	Bos N	2	8	.200	29	11	1	0	92	95	59	2	3	45	37	4.99	74	.274	.362	22-4	.045	-2*	85	-13	-1.5
1928	Bos N	2	1	.667	21	3	2	0	49.1	67	36	2	2	23	17	5.66	69	.327	.400	11-2	.091	-1	108	-9	-0.6
1930	NY A	0	0	—	2	0	0	0	1.2	5	4	0	0	2	1	21.60	20	.500	.583	0-0	—	0		-3	-0.1
Total 5		6	9	.400	56	17	4	0	170	193	108	4	5	84	60	4.76	79	.292	.377	42-6	.048	-5	84	-19	-1.9
EDWARDS, JIM JOE James Corbette "Little Joe" B 12.14.1894 Banner, MS D 1.19.1965 Sarepta, MS BR/TL 6-2/185# d5.14																									
1922	Cle A	3	8	.273	25	7	0	0	92.2	113	56	1	5	40	44	4.47	90	.313	.389	23-0	.087	-2	58	-6	-0.9
1923	Cle A	10	10	.500	38	21	7-1	1	179.1	200	101	5	5	75	68	3.71	107	.286	.359	59-2	.119	-5	110	1	-0.4
1924	Cle A	4	3	.571	10	7	5-1	0	57	64	29	3	0	34	15	2.84	150	.305	.402	20-2	.150	-1	82	6	0.5
1925	Cle A	0	3	.000	13	3	1	0	36	60	44	0	1	23	12	8.25	54	.382	.464	9-0	.111	-1	101	-17	-1.2
	Chi A	1	2	.333	9	4	1-1	0	45.1	46	25	4	1	23	20	3.97	105	.263	.352	17-0	.176	-1	101	0	0.0
	Year	1	5	.167	22	7	2-1	0	81.1	106	30	4	2	46	32	5.86	73	.319	.405	26-0	.154	-2	101	-16	-1.2
1926	Chi A	6	9	.400	32	16	8-3	1	142	140	76	4	1	63	41	4.18	92	.264	.343	46-3	.109	-3	94	-5	-0.9
1928	Cin N	2	2	.500	18	1	0	2	32	43	29	1	0	20	11	7.59	52	.347	.438	10-0	.300	0	43	-12	-1.4
Total 6		26	37	.413	145	59	22-6	4	584.1	666	360	18	13	278	211	4.37	92	.295	.376	184-7	.130	-13	94	-33	-4.3
EDWARDS, SHERMAN Sherman Stanley B 7.25.1909 Mt.Ida, AR D 3.8.1992 ElDorado, AR BR/TR 6/165# d9.21																									
1934	Cin N	0	0	—	1	0	0	0	3	4	1	0	0	1	1	3.00	136	.333	.385	1-0	.000	-0		0	0.0
EDWARDS, WAYNE Wayne Maurice B 3.7.1964 Burbank, CA BL/TL 6-5/185# d9.11																									
1989	Chi A	0	0	—	7	0	0	0-0	7.1	7	3	1	0	3-0	9	3.68	104	.269	.333	0-0	—	0		0	0.0
1990	Chi A	5	3	.625	42	5	0	2-0	95	81	39	6	3	41-2	63	3.22	119	.234	.319	0-0	—	0	86	6	0.5
1991	Chi A	0	2	.000	13	0	0	0-0	23.1	22	14	2	0	17-3	12	3.86	103	.259	.375	0-0	—	0		-1	-0.1

Year	Tm Lg	W	L	Pct	G	GS	CG-Sho	SV-BS	IP	H	R	HR	HB	BB-IB	SO	ERA	AERA	OAV	OOB	AB-SH	AVG	PB	Sup	APR	PW
Total	3	5	5	.500	62	5	0	2-0	125.2	110	56	9	3	61-5	84	3.37	115	.241	.331	0-0	—	0	86	5	0.4
EELLS, HARRY Harry Archibald "Slippery" B 2.14.1881 Ida Grove, IA D 10.15.1940 Los Angeles, CA BR/TR 6-1/195# d4.22																									
1906	Cle A	4	5	.444	14	8	6-1	0	86.1	77	39	1	3	48	35	2.61	100	.242	.347	32-0	.188	1	124	-1	0.0
EGAN, WISH Aloysius Jerome B 6.16.1881 Evart, MI D 4.13.1951 Detroit, MI BR/TR 6-3/185# d9.3																									
1902	Det A	0	2	.000	3	3	2	0	22	23	12	0	0	6	0	2.86	127	.271	.319	8-0	.250	-0	92	1	0.1
1905	StL N	6	15	.286	23	19	18	0	171.1	189	93	2	9	39	29	3.57	83	.285	.333	59-2	.102	-3	74	-12	-1.4
1906	StL N	2	9	.182	16	12	7	0	86.1	97	45	3	2	27	23	4.59	57	.278	.333	29-1	.069	-2	76	-14	-1.8
Total	3	8	26	.235	42	34	27	0	279.2	309	150	5	11	72	52	3.83	76	.282	.332	96-3	.104	-5	76	-25	-3.1
EGAN, JIM James K. "Troy Terrier" B 1858 Derby, CT D 9.26.1884 New Haven, CT TL d5.15 ▲																									
1882	Tro N	4	6	.400	12	10	10	0	100	133	79	2		24	20	4.14	68	.315	.352	115	.200	-2*	116	-12	-1.1
EGAN, RIP John Joseph B 7.9.1871 Philadelphia, PA D 12.22.1950 Cranston, RI TR 5-11/168# d4.30 U9																									
1894	Was N	0	0	—	1	0	0	0	5	8	6	1	0	2	2	10.80	49	.364	.417	3-0	.000	-0		-2	-0.1
EGAN, DICK Richard Wallis B 3.24.1937 Berkeley, CA BL/TL 6-4/193# d4.9 C2																									
1963	Det A	0	1	.000	20	0	0	0	21	25	12	4	0	3-0	16	5.14	73	.287	.311	0-0	—	0		-3	-0.1
1964	Det A	0	0	—	23	0	0	2	34.1	33	22	4	1	17-1	21	4.46	82	.246	.333	3-0	.000	-0		-5	-0.2
1966	Cal A	0	0	—	11	0	0	0	14.1	17	7	2	0	6-2	11	4.40	76	.309	.365	1-0	.000	-0		-1	-0.1
1967	LA N	1	1	.500	20	0	0	0	31.2	34	25	3	4	15-4	20	6.25	50	.272	.368	1-0	.000	-0		-12	-0.8
Total	4	1	2	.333	74	0	0	2	101.1	109	66	13	5	41-7	68	5.15	67	.272	.344	5-0	.000	-1		-21	-1.2
EGLOFF, BRUCE Bruce Edward B 4.10.1965 Denver, CO BR/TR 6-2/215# d4.13																									
1991	Cle A	0	0	—	6	0	0	0-0	5.2	8	3	0	0	4-1	8	4.76	87	.333	.429	0-0	—	0		0	0.0
EHMKE, HOWARD Howard Jonathan "Bob" B 4.24.1894 Silver Creek, NY D 3.17.1959 Philadelphia, PA BR/TR 6-3/190# d4.12 Mil 1918																									
1915	Buf F	0	2	.000	18	2	0	0	53.2	69	46	2	5	25	18	5.53	51	.325	.409	12-0	.000	-2	100	-18	-1.1
1916	Det A	3	1	.750	5	4	4	0	37.1	34	16	0	0	15	15	3.13	91	.252	.327	14-0	.143	-1	152	-1	-0.1
1917	Det A	10	15	.400	35	25	13-4	2	206	174	84	3	5	88	90	2.97	89	.243	.330	69-1	.246	2	104	-2	0.1
1919	Det A	17	10	.630	33	31	20-2	0	248.2	255	114	5	6	107	79	3.18	100	.274	.353	91-3	.253	3	109	-1	0.4
1920	Det A	15	18	.455	38	33	23-2	3	268.1	250	132	8	13	124	98	3.25	115	.253	.344	105-2	.238	2	83	13	2.0
1921	Det A	13	14	.481	30	22	13-1	0	196.1	220	123	15	13	81	68	4.54	94	.286	.364	74-4	.284	2	114	-5	-0.4
1922	Det A	17	17	.500	45	29	16-1	1	279.2	299	146	12	23	101	108	4.22	92	.281	.356	102-4	.157	-4	95	-6	-1.0
1923	Bos A	20	17	.541	43	39	28-2	3	316.2	318	155	12	20	119	121	3.78	109	.272	.349	112-6	.223	-2	89	16	1.9
1924	Bos A	19	17	.528	45	36	26-4	4	**315**	324	139	9	11	81	119	3.46	126	.265	.316	126-4	.222	-2*	94	33	3.4
1925	Bos A	9	20	.310	34	31	**22**	1	260.2	285	141	8	11	85	95	3.73	122	.285	.348	88-6	.148	-5	61	21	1.7
1926	Bos A	3	10	.231	14	14	7-1	0	97.1	115	69	3	4	45	38	5.46	75	.303	.382	34-1	.147	-1	103	-15	-1.7
	Phi A	12	4	.750	20	18	10-1	0	147.1	125	54	1	4	50	55	2.81	148	.232	.302	46-9	.152	-2*	92	23	2.1
	Year	15	14	.517	34	32	17-2	0	244.2	240	59	4	8	95	93	3.86	107	.261	.336	80-10	.150	-3	97	7	0.4
1927	Phi A	12	10	.545	30	27	10-1	0	189.2	200	103	13	14	60	68	4.22	101	.281	.349	68-3	.206	-1	93	2	0.2
1928	Phi A	9	8	.529	23	18	5-1	0	139.1	135	65	6	4	44	34	3.62	111	.254	.316	46-10	.239	1	109	7	0.9
1929	†Phi A	7	2	.778	11	8	2	0	54.2	48	24	2	1	15	20	3.29	129	.233	.288	19-0	.105	-2	100	6	0.6
1930	Phi A	0	1	.000	3	1	0	0	10	22	13	4	3	2	4	11.70	40	.458	.509	3-0	.333	0	18	-7	-0.5
Total	15	166	166	.500	427	338	199-20	14	2820.2	2873	1424	103	137	1042	1030	3.75	104	.271	.343	1009-53	.208	-11	94	66	8.5
EHRET, RED Philip Sydney B 8.31.1868 Louisville, KY D 7.28.1940 Cincinnati, OH BR/TR 6/175# d7.7 ▲																									
1888	KC AA	3	2	.600	7	6	5	0	52	58	30	1	3	22	12	3.98	86	.272	.349	63	.190	-1*	135	-1	-0.1
1889	Lou AA	10	29	.256	45	38	35-1	0	364	441	287	11	18	115	135	4.80	80	.290	.347	258	.252	2*	73	-28	-2.0
1890	†Lou AA	25	14	.641	43	38	35-4	2	359	351	182	5	17	79	174	2.53	152	.248	.296	146	.212	-3	99	50	4.1
1891	Lou AA	13	13	.500	26	24	23-2	0	220.2	225	150	2	11	70	76	3.47	105	.255	.318	91	.242	1	100	-2	-0.1
1892	Pit N	16	20	.444	39	36	32	0	316	290	183	7	22	83	101	2.65	124	.234	.294	132	.258	3*	94	16	1.6
1893	Pit N	18	18	.500	39	35	32-**4**	0	314.1	322	203	3	23	115	70	3.44	132	.257	.331	136	.176	-6*	95	29	2.1
1894	Pit N	19	21	.475	46	38	31-1	0	346.2	441	269	12	10	128	102	5.14	102	.306	.367	135-10	.170	-11	87	3	-0.7
1895	StL N	6	19	.240	37	32	18	0	231.2	360	223	11	10	88	55	6.02	80	.349	.405	96-3	.219	-3	98	-32	-2.7
1896	Cin N	18	14	.563	34	33	29-2	0	276.2	298	147	5	9	74	60	3.42	135	.273	.324	102-5	.196	-3	91	34	2.8
1897	Cin N	8	10	.444	34	19	11	2	184.1	256	135	3	13	47	43	4.78	95	.326	.374	66-2	.197	-3	84	-6	-0.7
1898	Lou N	3	7	.300	12	10	9	0	89	130	72	3	3	20	20	5.76	62	.338	.375	40-0	.225	1*	89	-20	-1.8
Total	11	139	167	.454	362	309	260-14	4	2754.1	3172	1881	63	139	841	848	4.02	105	.282	.339	1265-20	.217	-22	92	43	2.5
EHRHARDT, RUBE Welton Claude B 11.20.1894 Beecher, IL D 4.27.1980 Chicago Heights, IL BR/TR 6-2/190# d7.18																									
1924	Bro N	5	3	.625	15	9	6-2	0	83.2	71	27	5	1	17	13	2.26	166	.232	.275	29-1	.138	-2	103	14	0.9
1925	Bro N	10	14	.417	36	25	12	1	207.2	239	134	10	3	62	47	5.03	83	.293	.345	71-2	.211	2	113	-17	-1.3
1926	Bro N	2	5	.286	44	1	0	4	97	101	52	5	0	35	25	3.90	98	.275	.338	24-2	.250	0	109	-1	-0.1
1927	Bro N	3	7	.300	46	3	2	2	95.2	90	46	3	3	37	22	3.57	111	.264	.341	24-0	.250	1	86	4	0.6
1928	Bro N	1	3	.250	28	2	1	2	54	74	36	1	1	27	12	4.67	85	.352	.429	14-0	.286	0	64	-4	-0.2
1929	Cin N	1	2	.333	24	1	1-1	1	49.1	58	29	2	1	22	9	4.74	96	.305	.380	11-0	.182	-0	172	-1	-0.1
Total	6	22	34	.393	193	41	22-3	10	587.1	633	324	26	9	200	128	4.15	97	.284	.345	173-5	.214	1	109	-5	-0.2
EIBEL, HACK Henry Hack B 12.6.1893 Brooklyn, NY D 10.16.1945 Macon, GA BL/TL 5-11/220# d6.13.1912 ▲																									
1920	Bos A	0	0	—	3	0	0	0	10.1	10	4	0	0	3	5	3.48	105	.270	.325	43-1	.186	-0*		0	0.0
EICHELBERGER, JUAN Juan Tyrone B 10.21.1953 St.Louis, MO BR/TR 6-3/205# d9.7																									
1978	SD N	0	0	—	3	0	0	0-0	3.1	4	4	0	0	2-0	2	10.80	31	.267	.353	0-0	—	0		-3	-0.1
1979	SD N	1	1	.500	3	3	1	0-0	21	15	10	1	0	11-1	12	3.43	103	.211	.313	5-1	.400	1	75	0	0.1
1980	SD N	4	2	.667	15	13	0	0-0	88.2	73	41	8	1	55-4	43	3.65	94	.233	.348	27-4	.111	-1	132	-3	-0.3
1981	SD N	8	8	.500	25	24	3-1	0-0	141.1	136	60	5	3	74-5	81	3.50	93	.259	.351	46-6	.087	-3	103	-4	-0.7
1982	SD N	7	14	.333	31	24	8	0-0	177.2	171	98	23	2	72-5	74	4.20	82	.251	.321	55-5	.091	-2	103	-18	-2.1
1983	Cle A	4	11	.267	28	15	2	0-1	134	132	80	10	2	59-3	56	4.90	87	.259	.336	0-0	—	0	85	-9	-0.9
1988	Atl N	2	0	1.000	20	0	0	0-0	37.1	44	19	3	0	10-2	13	3.86	95	.297	.333	3-0	.000	-0		-1	0.0
Total	7	26	36	.419	125	79	14-1	0-1	603.1	575	312	50	8	283-20	281	4.10	87	.254	.336	136-16	.103	-4	101	-38	-4.0
EICHHORN, MARK Mark Anthony B 11.21.1960 San Jose, CA BR/TR 6-3/210# d8.30																									
1982	Tor A	0	3	.000	7	7	0	0-0	38	40	28	4	0	14-1	16	5.45	82	.260	.318	0-0	—	0	78	-5	-0.4
1986	Tor A	14	6	.700	69	0	0	10-3	157	105	32	8	7	45-14	166	1.72	246	.191	.260	0-0	—	0		**44**	**5.8**
1987	Tor A	10	6	.625	**89**	0	0	4-2	127.2	110	47	14	6	52-13	96	3.17	142	.234	.315	0-0	—	0		20	2.4
1988	Tor A	0	3	.000	37	0	0	1-0	66.2	79	32	3	6	27-4	28	4.18	94	.304	.381	0-0	—	0		-1	0.0
1989	Atl N	5	5	.500	45	0	0	0-2	68.1	70	36	6	1	19-8	49	4.35	84	.275	.323	2-1	.000	-0		-4	-0.5
1990	Cal A	2	5	.286	60	0	0	13-3	84.2	98	36	2	6	23-0	69	3.08	124	.289	.341	0-0	—	0		6	0.7
1991	Cal A	3	3	.500	70	0	0	1-3	81.2	63	21	2	2	13-1	49	1.98	207	.219	.255	0-0	—	0		19	1.4
1992	Cal A	2	4	.333	42	0	0	2-4	56.2	51	19	2	0	18-8	42	2.38	168	.238	.294	0-0	—	0		9	1.0
	†Tor A	2	0	1.000	23	0	0	0-0	31	35	15	1	2	7-0	19	4.35	94	.285	.328	0-0	—	0		0	0.0
	Year	4	4	.500	65	0	0	2-4	87.2	86	38	3	2	25-8	61	3.08	131	.255	.306	0-0	—	0		9	1.0
1993	†Tor A	3	1	.750	54	0	0	0-2	72.2	76	26	3	3	22-7	47	2.72	159	.272	.330	0-0	—	0		12	0.7
1994	Bal A	6	5	.545	43	0	0	1-4	71	62	19	1	5	19-4	35	2.15	233	.240	.301	0-0	—	0		**21**	2.9
1996	Cal A	1	2	.333	24	0	0	0-2	30.1	36	17	3	2	11-3	24	5.04	99	.308	.371	0-0	—	0		1	0.1
Total	11	48	43	.527	563	7	0	32-25	885.2	825	328	49	40	270-63	640	3.00	142	.249	.311	2-1	.000	-0	78	122	14.1
EILAND, DAVE David William B 7.5.1966 Dade City, FL BR/TR 6-3/205# d8.3																									
1988	NY A	0	0	—	3	3	0	0-0	12.2	15	9	6	2	4-0	7	6.39	62	.294	.368	0-0	—	0	162	-3	-0.1
1989	NY A	1	3	.250	6	6	0	0-0	34.1	44	25	5	2	13-3	11	5.77	67	.328	.391	0-0	—	0	105	-7	-0.8
1990	NY A	2	1	.667	5	5	0	0-0	30.1	31	14	2	0	5-0	16	3.56	112	.254	.283	0-0	—	0	146	1	0.1
1991	NY A	2	5	.286	18	13	0	0-0	72.2	87	51	10	3	23-1	18	5.33	78	.302	.356	0-0	—	0	73	-11	-1.0
1992	SD N	0	2	.000	7	7	0	0-0	27	33	21	1	0	5-0	10	5.67	63	.287	.317	9-1	.111	1	101	-7	-0.4

Year	Tm Lg	W	L	Pct	G	GS	CG-Sho	SV-BS	IP	H	R	HR	HB	BB-IB	SO	ERA	AERA	OAV	OOB	AB-SH	AVG	PB	Sup	APR	PW
1993	SD N	0	3	.000	10	9	0	0-0	48.1	58	33	5	1	17-1	14	5.21	79	.297	.353	12-3	.083	-1	94	-6	-0.4
1995	NY A	1	1	.500	4	1	0	0-0	10	16	10	1	1	3-1	6	6.30	73	.348	.392	0-0	—	0	161	-3	-0.5
1998	TB A	0	1	.000	1	1	0	0-0	2.2	6	6	0	0	3-0	1	20.25	24	.429	.529	0-0	—	0	19	-4	-0.6
1999	TB A	4	8	.333	21	15	0	0-1	80.1	98	59	8	3	27-1	53	5.60	89	.294	.349	1-1	.000	-0	85	-6	-0.8
2000	TB A	2	3	.400	17	10	0	0-0	54.2	77	46	8	4	18-0	17	7.24	68	.326	.381	0-0	—	0	82	-13	-0.9
Total	10	12	27	.308	92	70	0	0-1	373	465	274	46	16	118-7	153	5.74	76	.303	.356	22-5	.091	-0	93	-59	-5.4
EILERS, DAVE David Louis B 12.3.1936 Oldenburg, TX BR/TR 5-11/188# d7.27																									
1964	Mil N	0	0	—	6	0	0	0	7.2	11	5	1	1	1-1	1	4.70	75	.333	.351	0-0	—	0		-1	-0.1
1965	Mil N	0	0	—	6	0	0	0	3.2	8	5	1	0	0-0	1	12.27	29	.421	.421	0-0	—	0		-3	-0.2
	NY N	1	1	.500	11	0	0	2	18	20	11	2	2	4-3	9	4.00	88	.274	.325	1-0	1.000	0		-2	-0.2
	Year	1	1	.500	17	0	0	2	21.2	28	20	3	2	4-3	10	5.40	65	.304	.343	1-0	1.000	0		-5	-0.4
1966	NY N	1	1	.500	23	0	0	0	34.2	39	18	7	1	7-2	14	4.67	78	.287	.326	1-0	.000	-0		-3	-0.1
1967	Hou N	6	4	.600	35	0	0	1	59.1	68	29	3	3	17-7	27	3.94	84	.296	.349	7-2	.000	-1		-4	-0.7
Total	4	8	6	.571	81	0	0	3	123.1	146	68	14	7	29-13	52	4.45	78	.297	.342	9-2	.111	-0		-13	-1.3
EINERTSON, DARRELL Darrell Lee B 9.4.1972 Rhinelander, WI BR/TR 6-2/190# d4.15																									
2000	NY A	0	0	—	11	0	0	0-0	12.2	16	9	1	0	4-0	3	3.55	136	.302	.345	0-0	—	0		0	0.0
EISCHEN, JOEY Joseph Raymond B 5.25.1970 West Covina, CA BL/TL 6-1/190# d6.19																									
1994	Mon N	0	0	—	1	0	0	0-0	0.2	4	4	0	1	0-0	1	54.00	8	.667	.714	0-0	—	0		-3	-0.2
1995	LA N	0	0	—	17	0	0	0-0	20.1	19	9	1	2	11-1	15	3.10	123	.232	.337	1-0	.000	-0		1	0.0
1996	LA N	0	1	.000	28	0	0	0-0	43.1	48	25	4	4	20-4	36	4.78	81	.282	.369	6-0	.000	-1		-4	-0.3
	Det A	1	1	.500	24	0	0	0-2	25	27	11	3	0	14-3	15	3.24	156	.284	.373	0-0	—	0		4	0.3
1997	Cin N	0	0	—	1	0	0	0-0	1.1	2	2	0	0	1-0	2	6.75	63	.333	.429	1-0	.000	-0		-1	0.0
2001	Mon N	0	1	.000	24	0	0	0-2	29.2	29	17	4	1	16-1	19	4.85	92	.257	.354	0-0	—	0		-1	0.0
2002	Mon N	6	1	.857	59	0	0	2-1	53.2	43	11	1	2	18-5	51	1.34	333	.224	.294	8-0	.125	0		16	2.1
2003	Mon N	2	2	.500	70	0	0	1-3	53	57	27	7	3	13-1	40	3.06	153	.282	.335	4-0	.250	0*		6	0.5
Total	7	9	6	.600	224	0	0	3-8	227	229	106	20	13	93-15	179	3.41	129	.264	.343	20-0	.100	-1		18	2.4
EISENHART, JAKE Jacob Henry B 10.3.1922 Perkasie, PA D 12.20.1987 Huntingdon, PA BL/TL 6-3.5/195# d6.10																									
1944	Cin N	0	0	—	1	0	0	0	0.1	0	0	0	0	1	0	0.00	—	.000	.500	0-0	—	0		0	0.0
EISENSTAT, HARRY Harry B 10.10.1915 Brooklyn, NY D 3.21.2003 Beachwood, OH BL/TL 5-11/185# d5.19 Mil 1943-46																									
1935	Bro N	0	1	.000	2	0	0	0	4.2	9	8	0	0	2	2	13.50	29	.429	.478	1-0	.000	-0		-5	-0.7
1936	Bro N	1	2	.333	5	2	1	0	14.1	22	17	1	0	6	5	5.65	73	.344	.400	3-0	.333	0	72	-5	-0.8
1937	Bro N	3	3	.500	13	5	0	0	47.2	61	28	2	1	11	12	3.97	102	.308	.348	11-1	.000	-1	68	0	-0.1
1938	Det A	9	6	.600	32	9	5	4	125.1	131	60	7	1	29	37	3.73	134	.266	.308	36-5	.139	-1	78	16	1.6
1939	Det A	2	2	.500	10	2	1	0	29.2	39	24	3	0	9	6	6.98	70	.315	.361	8-1	.375	1	162	-5	-0.5
	Cle A	6	7	.462	26	11	4-1	2	103.2	109	45	8	0	23	38	3.30	133	.265	.304	32-2	.250	1	80	12	1.4
	Year	8	9	.471	36	13	5-1	2	133.1	148	49	11	0	32	44	4.12	110	.277	.317	40-3	.275	1	93	6	0.9
1940	Cle A	1	4	.200	27	3	0	4	71.2	78	25	6	0	12	27	3.14	134	.282	.311	22-0	.273	1	76	**11**	0.8
1941	Cle A	1	1	.500	21	0	0	2	34	43	16	2	2	16	11	4.24	93	.312	.391	6-0	.333	1		0	0.0
1942	Cle A	2	1	.667	29	1	0	2	47.2	58	19	1	0	6	19	2.45	140	.304	.325	4-0	.250	0	25	4	0.3
Total	8	25	27	.481	165	33	11-1	14	478.2	550	242	30	4	114	157	3.84	114	.287	.328	123-9	.211	1	83	28	2.0
EITELJORGE, ED Edward Henry B 10.14.1871 Berlin, Germany D 12.5.1942 Greencastle, IN BR/TR 6-2/190# d5.2																									
1890	Chi N	0	1	.000	1	1	0	0	2	5	7	0	0	1	1	22.50	16	.455	.500	1	.000	-0	155	-4	-0.5
1891	Was AA	1	5	.167	8	7	6	0	61.1	79	67	3	9	41	23	6.16	61	.303	.415	26	.192	-1	86	-15	-1.1
Total	2	1	6	.143	9	8	6	0	63.1	84	74	3	9	42	24	6.68	56	.309	.418	27	.185	-1	94	-19	-1.6
ELARTON, SCOTT Vincent Scott B 2.23.1976 Lamar, CO BR/TR 6-7/240# d6.20																									
1998	†Hou N	2	1	.667	28	2	0	2-1	57	40	21	5	1	20-0	56	3.32	122	.196	.270	7-3	.000	-1	159	6	0.2
1999	†Hou N	9	5	.643	42	15	0	1-3	124	111	55	8	4	43-0	121	3.48	127	.238	.306	26-7	.192	0*	108	12	1.1
2000	Hou N	17	7	.708	30	30	2	0-0	192.2	198	117	29	6	84-1	131	4.81	101	.263	.339	63-6	.159	-0	127	-1	-0.2
2001	Hou N	4	8	.333	20	20	0	0-0	109.2	126	88	26	6	49-1	76	7.14	64	.290	.368	30-5	.067	-1	124	-27	-2.5
	Col N	0	2	.000	4	4	0	0-0	23	20	17	8	0	10-1	11	6.65	80	.233	.313	8-0	.125	-0	65	-2	-0.2
	Year	4	10	.286	24	24	0	0-0	132.2	146	21	34	6	59-2	87	7.06	67	.280	.359	38-5	.079	-1	113	-28	-2.7
2003	Col N	4	4	.500	11	10	0	0-0	51.2	73	46	13	4	20-3	20	6.27	78	.329	.388	14-1	.071	-1	117	-10	-1.3
Total	5	36	27	.571	135	81	2	3-4	558	568	344	89	21	226-6	415	5.03	92	.262	.335	148-22	.128	-3	121	-22	-2.9
ELDER, DAVE David Matthew B 9.23.1975 Atlanta, GA BR/TR 6/180# d7.24																									
2002	Cle A	0	2	.000	15	0	0	0-0	23	18	10	1	1	14-3	23	3.13	141	.220	.333	0-0	—	0		3	0.2
2003	Cle A	1	1	.500	4	0	0	0-1	2.1	5	5	2	0	4-0	3	19.29	23	.417	.563	0-0	—	0		-4	-0.6
Total	2	1	3	.250	19	0	0	0-1	25.1	23	15	3	1	18-3	26	4.62	95	.245	.365	0-0	—	0		-1	-0.4
ELDER, HEINIE Henry Knox B 8.23.1890 Seattle, WA D 11.13.1958 Long Beach, CA BL/TL 6-2/200# d7.7																									
1913	Det A	0	0	—	1	0	0	0	3.1	4	3	0	0	5	0	8.10	36	.286	.474	1-0	.000	-0		-1	-0.1
ELDRED, CAL Calvin John B 11.24.1967 Cedar Rapids, IA BR/TR 6-4/235# d9.24																									
1991	Mil A	2	0	1.000	3	3	0	0-0	16	20	9	2	0	6-0	10	4.50	88	.299	.356	0-0	—	0	100	-1	-0.1
1992	Mil A	11	2	.846	14	14	2-1	0-0	100.1	76	21	4	2	23-0	62	1.79	214	.207	.257	0-0	—	0	134	24	3.2
1993	Mil A	16	16	.500	36	**36**	8-1	0-0	**258**	232	120	32	10	91-5	180	4.01	106	.239	.308	0-0	—	0	98	10	1.1
1994	Mil A	11	11	.500	25	**25**	6	0-0	179	158	96	23	4	84-0	98	4.68	108	.236	.322	0-0	—	0	85	10	1.0
1995	Mil A	1	1	.500	4	4	0	0-0	23.2	24	10	4	1	10-0	18	3.42	146	.261	.340	0-0	—	0	98	4	0.3
1996	Mil A	4	4	.500	15	15	0	0-0	84.2	82	43	8	4	38-0	50	4.46	116	.259	.342	0-0	—	0	101	8	0.6
1997	Mil A	13	15	.464	34	34	1-1	0-0	202	207	118	31	9	89-0	122	4.99	93	.266	.346	3-1	.000	-0	93	-6	-0.8
1998	Mil N	4	8	.333	23	23	0	0-0	133	157	82	14	4	61-3	86	4.80	89	.297	.372	32-5	.125	-0*	111	-10	-0.9
1999	Mil N	2	8	.200	20	15	0	0-0	82	101	75	19	1	46-0	60	7.79	58	.297	.379	24-4	.083	-1*	109	-29	-2.9
2000	Chi A	10	2	.833	20	20	2-1	0-0	112	103	61	12	5	59-0	97	4.58	109	.243	.342	4-0	.250	1	124	6	0.7
2001	Chi A	0	1	.000	2	2	0	0-0	6	12	9	1	3	3-1	6	13.50	34	.429	.529	0-0	—	0	110	-5	-0.6
2003	StL N	7	4	.636	62	0	0	8-6	67.1	62	32	9	4	31-4	67	3.74	109	.248	.337	2-0	.500	0*		1	0.3
Total	12	81	72	.529	258	191	19-4	8-6	1264	1234	676	159	47	541-13	856	4.52	100	.256	.334	65-10	.123	-0	104	12	1.9
ELLER, HOD Horace Owen B 7.5.1894 Muncie, IN D 7.18.1961 Indianapolis, IN BR/TR 5-11.5/185# d4.16																									
1917	Cin N	10	5	.667	37	11	7-1	1	152.1	131	60	2	3	37	77	2.36	111	.239	.290	45-3	.133	-2	149	4	0.1
1918	Cin N	16	12	.571	37	22	14	1	217.2	205	71	1	6	59	84	2.36	113	.253	.309	70-5	.157	-2	82	9	0.7
1919	†Cin N	19	9	.679	38	30	16-7	2	248.1	216	80	7	4	50	137	2.39	116	.238	.281	93-1	.280	7	137	12	2.1
1920	Cin N	13	12	.520	35	23	15-1	0	210.1	208	79	6	5	52	76	2.95	103	.266	.315	87-2	.253	1*	93	6	0.7
1921	Cin N	2	2	.500	13	3	0	1	34.1	46	23	3	0	15	7	4.98	72	.322	.386	13-0	.231	0	138	-5	-0.6
Total	5	60	40	.600	160	89	52-9	5	863	806	313	19	18	213	381	2.62	108	.253	.303	308-11	.221	5	113	26	3.0
ELLINGSEN, BRUCE Harold Bruce B 4.26.1949 Pocatello, ID BL/TL 6/180# d7.4																									
1974	Cle A	1	1	.500	16	2	0	0-1	42	45	21	5	0	17-4	16	3.21	113	.278	.339	0-0	—	0	97	0	0.0
ELLIOTT, CLAUD Claud Judson "Chaucer" or "Old Pardee" B 11.17.1876 Pardeeville, WI D 6.21.1923 Pardeeville, WI BR/TR 6/190# d4.16																									
1904	Cin N	3	1	.750	9	6	4-1	0	57.2	53	25	1	4	23	19	2.97	99	.247	.331	24-0	.208	1	131	1	0.1
	NY N	0	1	.000	3	1	1	0	15	21	14	2	0	3	8	3.00	91	.328	.358	5-0	.200	0	0	-3	-0.2
	Year	3	2	.600	12	7	5-1	0	72.2	74	14	3	4	26	27	2.97	97	.265	.337	29-0	.207	1	116	-2	-0.1
1905	NY N	0	1	.000	10	2	2	**6**	38	41	20	3	1	12	20	4.03	73	.270	.327	16-0	.188	-0	62	-3	-0.2
Total	2	3	3	.500	22	9	7-1	6	110.2	115	59	6	5	38	47	3.33	87	.267	.333	45-0	.200	1	106	-5	-0.3
ELLIOTT, DONNIE Donald Glenn B 9.20.1968 Pasadena, TX BR/TR 6-4/190# d4.23																									
1994	SD N	0	1	.000	30	1	0	0-1	33	31	12	3	1	21-2	24	3.27	126	.250	.363	1-1	.000	-0	177	4	0.2
1995	SD N	0	0	—	1	0	0	0-0	2	2	0	0	0	1-0	3	0.00	—	.250	.333	0-0	—	0		1	0.0
Total	2	0	1	.000	31	1	0	0-1	35	33	12	3	1	22-2	27	3.09	133	.250	.361	1-1	.000	-0	177	5	0.2

ELLIOTT, HAL Harold William B 5.29.1899 Mt.Clemens, MI D 4.25.1963 Honolulu, HI BR/TR 6-1.5/170# d4.19

Year	Tm Lg	W	L	Pct	G	GS	CG-Sho	SV-BS	IP	H	R	HR	HB	BB-IB	SO	ERA	AERA	OAV	OOB	AB-SH	AVG	PB	Sup	APR	PW
1929	Phi N	3	7	.300	40	8	2	2	114.1	146	94	5	0	59	32	6.06	86	.313	.390	30-0	.167	-1	84	-13	-1.0
1930	Phi N	6	11	.353	**48**	11	2	0	117.1	191	120	7	1	58	37	7.67	71	.382	.447	32-1	.094	-3	77	-27	-3.2
1931	Phi N	0	2	.000	16	4	0	2	33	46	36	5	1	19	8	9.55	44	.338	.423	9-0	.111	-0	136	-15	-1.0
1932	Phi N	2	4	.333	16	7	0	0	57.2	70	45	5	0	38	13	5.77	76	.297	.394	18-0	.167	-0	95	-8	-0.9
Total	4	11	24	.314	120	30	4	4	322.1	453	295	22	2	174	90	6.95	73	.338	.415	89-1	.135	-5	88	-63	-6.1

ELLIOTT, GLENN Herbert Glenn "Lefty" B 11.11.1919 Sapulpa, OK D 7.27.1969 Portland, OR BB/TL 5-10/170# d4.17

Year	Tm Lg	W	L	Pct	G	GS	CG-Sho	SV-BS	IP	H	R	HR	HB	BB-IB	SO	ERA	AERA	OAV	OOB	AB-SH	AVG	PB	Sup	APR	PW
1947	Bos N	0	1	.000	11	0	0	1	19	18	10	4	0	11	8	4.74	82	.269	.372	2-1	.500	0		-1	0.0
1948	Bos N	1	0	1.000	1	1	0	0	3	5	1	0	0	1	2	3.00	128	.357	.400	2-0	.000	-0	254	0	0.0
1949	Bos N	3	4	.429	22	6	1	0	68.1	70	35	7	0	27	15	3.95	96	.269	.338	17-1	.059	-1	74	-2	-0.2
Total	3	4	5	.444	34	7	1	1	90.1	93	46	11	0	39	25	4.08	93	.273	.347	21-2	.095	-1	99	-3	-0.2

ELLIOTT, JUMBO James Thomas B 10.22.1900 St.Louis, MO D 1.7.1970 Terre Haute, IN BR/TL 6-3/235# d4.21

Year	Tm Lg	W	L	Pct	G	GS	CG-Sho	SV-BS	IP	H	R	HR	HB	BB-IB	SO	ERA	AERA	OAV	OOB	AB-SH	AVG	PB	Sup	APR	PW
1923	StL A	0	0	—	1	0	0	0	1	1	3	0	0	3	0	27.00	15	.333	.667	0-0	—	0		-2	-0.1
1925	Bro N	0	2	.000	3	1	0	0	10.2	17	14	0	1	9	3	8.44	50	.362	.474	4-0	.000	-1	61	-6	-0.9
1927	Bro N	6	13	.316	30	21	12-2	3	188.1	188	82	5	1	60	99	3.30	120	.269	.327	64-1	.141	-1	80	14	1.0
1928	Bro N	9	14	.391	41	21	7-2	1	192	194	106	8	6	64	74	3.89	102	.268	.332	68-0	.176	2	117	2	0.3
1929	Bro N	1	2	.333	6	3	0	0	19	21	17	2	1	16	7	6.63	70	.280	.413	4-0	.250	0	69	-4	-0.5
1930	Bro N	10	7	.588	35	21	6-2	1	198.1	204	100	16	5	70	59	3.95	124	.271	.337	68-1	.147	-2	101	23	1.4
1931	Phi N	**19**	14	.576	**52**	30	12-2	5	249	288	138	15	4	83	99	4.27	100	.287	.344	90-2	.122	-6	92	1	-0.8
1932	Phi N	11	10	.524	39	22	8	0	166	210	115	14	2	47	62	5.42	81	.300	.346	61-0	.197	-1	111	-16	-1.9
1933	Phi N	6	10	.375	35	21	6	2	161.2	188	89	8	3	49	43	3.84	99	.295	.348	52-2	.231	0*	95	-3	-0.5
1934	Phi N	0	1	.000	3	1	0	0	5.1	8	7	0	1	4	1	10.13	47	.333	.448	1-0	.000	-0	18	-3	-0.4
	Bos N	1	1	.500	7	3	0	0	15.1	19	16	2	1	9	6	5.87	65	.284	.377	4-0	.250	0	105	-6	-0.6
	Year	1	2	.333	10	4	0	0	20.2	27	21	2	2	13	7	6.97	58	.297	.396	5-0	.200	0	80	-8	-1.0
Total	10	63	74	.460	252	144	51-8	12	1206.2	1338	687	70	25	414	453	4.24	100	.283	.344	416-6	.163	-8	97	0	-3.0

ELLIS, DOCK Dock Phillip B 3.11.1945 Los Angeles, CA BB/TR 6-3/210# d6.18

Year	Tm Lg	W	L	Pct	G	GS	CG-Sho	SV-BS	IP	H	R	HR	HB	BB-IB	SO	ERA	AERA	OAV	OOB	AB-SH	AVG	PB	Sup	APR	PW
1968	Pit N	6	5	.545	26	10	2	0	104	82	35	4	1	38-4	52	2.51	117	.213	.285	29-3	.069	-1*	122	4	0.3
1969	Pit N	11	17	.393	35	33	8-2	0-0	218.2	206	101	14	4	76-7	173	3.58	97	.250	.314	68-7	.088	-3*	84	-4	-0.8
1970	†Pit N	13	10	.565	30	30	9-4	0-0	201.2	194	81	9	10	87-11	128	3.21	122	.257	.340	70-4	.100	-3*	91	16	1.4
1971	†Pit N★	19	9	.679	31	31	11-2	0-0	226.2	207	93	15	2	63-5	137	3.06	111	.239	.290	79-10	.203	2*	150	5	0.9
1972	†Pit N	15	7	.682	25	25	4-1	0-0	163.1	156	60	6	3	33-4	96	2.70	123	.253	.292	59-1	.153	-1*	128	10	1.2
1973	Pit N	12	14	.462	28	28	3-1	0-0	192	176	86	7	6	55-7	122	3.05	116	.240	.297	65-6	.108	-3*	92	6	0.5
1974	Pit N	12	9	.571	26	26	9	0-0	176.2	163	71	13	7	41-5	91	3.16	109	.242	.291	56-5	.214	3*	111	6	1.0
1975	†Pit N	8	9	.471	27	24	5-2	0-0	140	163	69	9	3	43-9	69	3.79	94	.292	.342	36-7	.111	0*	94	-4	-0.5
1976	†NY A	17	8	.680	32	32	8-1	0-0	211.2	195	83	14	4	76-1	65	3.19	107	.247	.312	0-0	—	0	96	6	0.5
1977	NY A	1	1	.500	3	3	1	0-0	19.2	18	9	1	0	8-0	5	1.83	216	.237	.306	0-0	—	0	99	3	0.2
	Oak A	1	5	.167	7	7	0	0-0	26	35	33	5	1	14-0	11	9.69	42	.315	.394	0-0	—	0	83	-17	-2.7
	Tex A	10	6	.625	23	22	7-1	1-0	167.1	158	60	13	0	42-1	90	2.90	141	.254	.297	0-0	—	0	106	22	2.0
	Year	12	12	.500	33	32	8-1	1-0	213	211	65	19	1	64-1	106	3.63	112	.260	.312	0-0	—	0	100	8	-0.5
1978	Tex A	9	7	.563	22	22	3	0-0	141.1	131	81	15	2	46-0	45	4.20	89	.245	.305	0-0	—	0	120	-10	-1.0
1979	Tex A	1	5	.167	10	9	0	0-0	46.2	64	34	5	0	16-2	10	5.98	70	.323	.372	0-0	—	0	109	-9	-1.0
	NY N	3	7	.300	17	14	1	0-0	85	110	60	9	1	34-10	41	6.04	60	.320	.377	26-1	.077	-1	128	-21	-2.3
	Pit N	0	0	—	3	1	0	0-0	7	9	2	1	0	2-0	1	2.57	151	.346	.393	1-0	.000	-0	137	1	0.0
	Year	3	7	.300	20	15	1	0-0	92	119	8	10	1	36-10	42	5.77	64	.322	.378	27-1	.074	-2	129	-20	-2.3
Total	12	138	119	.537	345	317	71-14	1-0	2127.2	2067	958	140	44	674-66	1136	3.46	103	.255	.313	489-44	.133	-7	108	14	-0.3

ELLIS, JIM James Russell B 3.25.1945 Tulare, CA BR/TL 6-2/185# d8.11

Year	Tm Lg	W	L	Pct	G	GS	CG-Sho	SV-BS	IP	H	R	HR	HB	BB-IB	SO	ERA	AERA	OAV	OOB	AB-SH	AVG	PB	Sup	APR	PW
1967	Chi N	1	1	.500	8	1	0	0	16.2	20	7	1	0	9-1	8	3.24	109	.313	.397	5-1	.200	0	74	0	0.1
1969	StL N	0	0	—	2	1	0	0-0	5.1	7	1	0	0	3-1	0	1.69	212	.318	.400	0-1	—	0	149	1	0.1
Total	2	1	1	.500	10	2	0	0-0	22	27	8	1	0	12-2	8	2.86	124	.314	.398	5-2	.200	0	111	1	0.2

ELLIS, ROBERT Robert Randolph B 12.15.1970 Baton Rouge, LA BR/TR 6-5/220# d9.12

Year	Tm Lg	W	L	Pct	G	GS	CG-Sho	SV-BS	IP	H	R	HR	HB	BB-IB	SO	ERA	AERA	OAV	OOB	AB-SH	AVG	PB	Sup	APR	PW
1996	Cal A	0	0	—	3	0	0	0-0	5	0	0	0	0	4-0	5	0.00	—	.000	.211	0-0	—	0		3	0.1
2001	Ari N	6	5	.545	19	17	0	0-0	92	106	61	12	4	34-2	41	5.77	79	.293	.354	26-1	.154	-0	109	-10	-1.1
2002	LA N	0	1	.000	3	0	0	0-0	2.2	6	3	1	0	0-0	0	10.13	38	.462	.462	0-0	—	0		-2	-0.4
2003	Tex A	1	1	.500	4	4	0	0-0	18.1	26	17	7	1	10-0	8	8.35	60	.342	.416	0-0	—	0	134	-6	-0.5
Total	4	7	7	.500	29	21	0	0-0	118	138	81	20	5	48-2	54	6.03	77	.296	.362	26-1	.154	-0	115	-15	-1.9

ELLIS, SAMMY Samuel Joseph B 2.11.1941 Youngstown, OH BL/TR 6-1/180# d4.14 C12

Year	Tm Lg	W	L	Pct	G	GS	CG-Sho	SV-BS	IP	H	R	HR	HB	BB-IB	SO	ERA	AERA	OAV	OOB	AB-SH	AVG	PB	Sup	APR	PW
1962	Cin N	2	2	.500	8	4	0	0	28	29	25	6	1	29-0	27	6.75	60	.269	.424	10-0	.200	-0	125	-9	-1.1
1964	Cin N	10	3	.769	52	5	2	14	122.1	101	38	9	1	28-2	125	2.57	140	.223	.269	24-3	.083	-0	165	14	1.9
1965	Cin N☆	22	10	.688	44	39	15-2	2	263.2	222	119	22	6	104-4	183	3.79	99	.226	.303	96-7	.125	-1	131	1	-0.2
1966	Cin N	12	19	.387	41	36	7	0	221	226	135	35	3	78-8	154	5.29	74	.264	.324	70-9	.114	-2*	98	-29	-4.1
1967	Cin N	8	11	.421	32	27	8-1	0	175.2	197	86	18	4	67-7	80	3.84	98	.286	.351	49-6	.082	-2	101	-2	-0.5
1968	Cal A	9	10	.474	42	24	3	2	164	150	80	22	6	56-4	93	3.95	74	.244	.310	44-7	.045	-3	116	-19	-2.7
1969	Chi A	0	3	.000	10	5	0	0-0	29.1	42	20	6	1	16-2	15	5.83	66	.336	.415	6-1	.167	0	105	-6	-0.5
Total	7	63	58	.521	229	140	35-3	18-0	1004	967	503	118	22	378-27	677	4.15	88	.253	.321	299-33	.104	-8	114	-50	-7.2

ELLISON, GEORGE George Russell B 1.24.1895 , CA D 1.20.1978 San Francisco, CA BR/TR 6-3/185# d8.21

Year	Tm Lg	W	L	Pct	G	GS	CG-Sho	SV-BS	IP	H	R	HR	HB	BB-IB	SO	ERA	AERA	OAV	OOB	AB-SH	AVG	PB	Sup	APR	PW
1920	Cle A	0	0	—	1	0	0	0	1	0	0	0	0	2	1	0.00	—	.000	.400	0-0	—	0		0	0.0

ELLSWORTH, DICK Richard Clark B 3.22.1940 Lusk, WY BL/TL 6-4/195# d6.22 s-Steve

Year	Tm Lg	W	L	Pct	G	GS	CG-Sho	SV-BS	IP	H	R	HR	HB	BB-IB	SO	ERA	AERA	OAV	OOB	AB-SH	AVG	PB	Sup	APR	PW
1958	Chi N	0	1	.000	1	1	0	0	2.1	4	4	0	1	3-0	0	15.43	25	.364	.533	1-0	.000	-0	46	-3	-0.4
1960	Chi N	7	13	.350	31	27	6	0	176.2	170	83	12	2	72-8	94	3.72	102	.257	.329	48-6	.042	-3	86	1	-0.1
1961	Chi N	10	11	.476	37	31	7-1	0	186.2	213	90	23	3	48-3	91	3.86	108	.292	.337	56-5	.036	-5	86	8	0.5
1962	Chi N	9	20	.310	37	33	6	1	208.2	241	131	23	5	77-6	113	5.09	81	.291	.354	62-2	.113	1	80	-19	-2.2
1963	Chi N	22	10	.688	37	37	19-4	0	290.2	223	75	14	2	75-7	185	2.11	**167**	.210	.262	94-8	.096	-2	98	44	**5.0**
1964	Chi N☆	14	18	.438	37	36	16-1	0	256.2	267	129	34	3	71-9	148	3.75	99	.266	.315	87-6	.046	-5	92	-6	-1.1
1965	Chi N	14	15	.483	36	34	8	1	222.1	227	108	22	4	57-7	130	3.81	97	.265	.312	73-6	.096	-2	92	-2	-0.3
1966	Chi N	8	22	.267	38	37	9	0	269.1	321	150	28	5	51-5	144	3.98	92	.294	.326	90-5	.156	-0	92	-14	-1.4
1967	Phi N	6	7	.462	32	21	3-1	0	125.1	152	75	6	5	36-10	45	4.38	78	.306	.357	37-4	.108	-1	126	-15	-1.5
1968	Bos A	16	7	.696	31	28	10-1	0	196	196	74	16	7	37-3	106	3.03	104	.260	.300	72-5	.056	-5	129	3	-0.2
1969	Bos A	0	0	—	2	2	0	0-0	12	16	5	1	0	4-0	4	3.75	102	.320	.370	3-1	.000	-0	81	0	0.0
	Cle A	6	9	.400	34	22	3-1	0-0	135	162	73	10	5	40-10	48	4.13	91	.301	.353	45-1	.133	-1	100	-6	-0.7
	Year	6	9	.400	36	24	3-1	0-0	147	178	77	11	5	44-10	52	4.10	92	.302	.354	48-2	.125	-2	99	-6	-0.7
1970	Cle A	3	3	.500	29	1	0	2-2	43.2	49	23	4	1	14-2	13	4.53	87	.299	.354	4-0	.000	-0	157	-2	-0.3
	Mil A	0	0	—	14	0	0	1-0	15.2	11	3	0	1	3-0	9	1.72	220	.196	.250	0-1	—	0		4	0.2
	Year	3	3	.500	43	1	0	3-2	59.1	60	33	4	2	17-2	22	3.79	103	.273	.328	4-1	.000	-0	159	2	-0.1
1971	Mil A	0	1	.000	11	0	0	0-0	14.2	22	10	1	1	7-1	10	4.91	71	.361	.423	1-0	.000	-0		-3	-0.2
Total	13	115	137	.456	407	310	87-9	5-2	2155.2	2274	1033	194	45	595-71	1140	3.72	100	.272	.322	673-50	.088	-25	96	-10	-2.7

ELLSWORTH, STEVE Steven Clark B 7.30.1960 Chicago, IL BR/TR 6-8/220# d4.7 f-Dick

Year	Tm Lg	W	L	Pct	G	GS	CG-Sho	SV-BS	IP	H	R	HR	HB	BB-IB	SO	ERA	AERA	OAV	OOB	AB-SH	AVG	PB	Sup	APR	PW
1988	Bos A	1	6	.143	8	7	0	0-0	36	47	29	7	1	16-1	16	6.75	61	.315	.383	0-0	—	0	117	-10	-1.6

ELSTON, DON Donald Ray B 4.6.1929 Campbellstown, OH D 1.2.1995 Arlington Heights, IL BR/TR 6/170# d9.17

Year	Tm Lg	W	L	Pct	G	GS	CG-Sho	SV-BS	IP	H	R	HR	HB	BB-IB	SO	ERA	AERA	OAV	OOB	AB-SH	AVG	PB	Sup	APR	PW
1953	Chi N	0	1	.000	2	1	0	0	5	11	8	1	0	0	2	14.40	31	.458	.458	1-0	.000	-0	80	-5	-0.7
1957	Bro N	0	0	—	1	0	0	0	1	1	0	0	0	0-0	1	0.00	—	.250	.250	0-0	—	0		0	0.0
	Chi N	6	7	.462	39	14	2	8	144	139	61	15	5	55-4	102	3.56	109	.259	.332	37-2	.108	-2	76	6	0.4
	Year	6	7	.462	40	14	2	8	145	140	64	15	5	55-4	103	3.54	109	.259	.331	37-2	.108	-2	76	7	0.4
1958	Chi N	9	8	.529	**69**	0	0	10	97	75	35	9	1	39-10	84	2.88	136	.214	.291	14-1	.357	1		**11**	2.3
1959	Chi N★	10	8	.556	**65**	0	0	13	97.2	77	40	11	3	46-7	82	3.32	119	.218	.310	19-3	.211	0		7	1.4

Year	Tm Lg	W	L	Pct	G	GS	CG-Sho	SV-BS	IP	H	R	HR	HB	BB-IB	SO	ERA	AERA	OAV	OOB	AB-SH	AVG	PB	Sup	APR	PW
1960	Chi N	8	9	.471	60	0	0	11	127	109	57	17	4	55-8	85	3.40	111	.231	.312	24-2	.125	-1		4	0.4
1961	Chi N	6	7	.462	58	0	0	8	93.1	108	64	11	6	45-12	59	5.59	75	.297	.381	11-3	.182	-0		-13	-1.8
1962	Chi N	4	8	.333	57	0	0	8	66.1	57	25	6	1	32-7	37	2.44	170	.247	.338	8-0	.000	-1		10	1.9
1963	Chi N	4	1	.800	51	0	0	4	70	57	26	6	2	21-3	41	2.83	124	.226	.290	4-1	.000	-0		5	0.3
1964	Chi N	2	5	.286	48	0	0	1	54.1	68	38	4	3	34-12	26	5.30	70	.330	.422	6-0	.167	-0		-10	-1.2
Total	9	49	54	.476	450	15	2	63	755.2	702	354	80	25	327-63	519	3.69	106	.251	.332	124-12	.153	-3	77	15	3.0
ELVIRA, NARCISO Narciso Chicho (Delgado) B 10.29.1967 Veracruz, Mexico BL/TL 5-10/160# d9.9																									
1990	Mil A	0	0	—	4	0	0	0-0	5	6	3	0	0	5-0	6	5.40	72	.300	.440	0-0	—	0		-1	0.0
ELY, HARRY Harry d9.24																									
1892	Bal N	0	1	.000	1	1	1	0	7	14	9	0	2	7	0	7.71	44	.400	.523	3	.000	-0	0	-3	-0.3
ELY, BONES William Frederick B 6.7.1863 N.Girard, PA D 1.10.1952 Berkeley, CA BR/TR 6-1/155# d6.19 ▲																									
1884	Buf N	0	1	.000	1	1	0	0	5	17	15	1		5	4	14.40	22	.500	.564	4	.000	-1	34	-6	-0.7
1886	Lou AA	0	4	.000	6	4	4	1	44	53	47	0	0	26	28	5.32	68	.280	.367	32	.156	-1*	94	-7	-0.6
1890	Syr AA	0	0	—	1	0	0	0	2	7	5	0	0	0	0	22.50	16	.538	.538	496	.262	0*		-4	-0.1
1894	StL N	0	0	—	1	0	0	0	1	0	0	0	0	3	0	0.00	—	.000	.500	510-13	.306	0*		1	0.0
Total	4	0	5	.000	9	5	4	1	52	77	67	1	0	34	32	6.75	54	.322	.407	1042-13	.279	-1	82	-16	-1.4
EMBREE, ALAN Alan Duane B 1.23.1970 Vancouver, WA BL/TL 6-2/185# d9.15																									
1992	Cle A	0	2	.000	4	4	0	0-0	18	19	14	3	1	8-0	12	7.00	56	.271	.346	0-0	—	0	88	-6	-0.5
1995	†Cle A	3	2	.600	23	0	0	1-0	24.2	23	16	2	0	16-0	23	5.11	92	.253	.358	0-0	—	0		-1	-0.3
1996	†Cle A	1	1	.500	24	0	0	0-0	31	30	26	10	0	21-3	33	6.39	77	.259	.364	0-0	—	0		-6	-0.3
1997	†Atl N	3	1	.750	66	0	0	0-0	46	36	13	1	2	20-2	45	2.54	165	.221	.312	0-0	—	0		9	0.7
1998	Atl N	1	0	1.000	20	0	0	0-1	18.2	23	14	2	0	10-0	19	4.34	96	.307	.384	1-0	.000	-0		-2	-0.1
	Ari N	3	2	.600	35	0	0	1-1	35	33	18	5	1	13-0	24	4.11	102	.248	.320	0-0	—	0		0	0.0
	Year	4	2	.667	55	0	0	1-2	53.2	56	36	7	1	23-0	43	4.19	100	.269	.343	1-0	.000	0		-2	-0.1
1999	SF N	3	2	.600	68	0	0	0-3	58.2	42	22	6	3	26-2	53	3.38	125	.200	.295	0-0	—	0		7	0.5
2000	†SF N	3	5	.375	63	0	0	2-3	60	62	34	4	3	25-2	49	4.95	86	.274	.347	0-0	—	0		-4	-0.5
2001	SF N	0	2	.000	22	0	0	0-1	20	34	26	7	2	10-2	25	11.25	35	.374	.434	1-0	.000	-0		-17	-1.5
	Chi A	1	2	.333	39	0	0	0-2	34	31	21	7	1	7-0	34	5.03	92	.242	.281	0-0	—	0		-2	-0.1
2002	SD N	3	4	.429	36	0	0	0-2	28.2	23	7	2	0	9-2	38	1.26	301	.211	.271	0-0	—	0		7	1.5
	Bos A	1	2	.333	32	0	0	2-3	33.1	24	12	4	1	11-1	43	2.97	152	.203	.273	0-0	—	0		6	0.5
2003	†Bos A	4	1	.800	65	0	0	1-1	55	49	26	5	0	16-3	45	4.25	107	.241	.294	0-0	—	0		3	0.3
Total	10	26	26	.500	497	4	0	7-17	463	429	249	58	14	192-17	443	4.43	98	.248	.323	2-0	.000	0	88	-6	0.2
EMBREE, RED Charles Willard B 8.30.1917 ElMonte, CA D 9.24.1996 Eugene, OR BR/TR 6/165# d9.10 Def 1943, Mil 1945-46																									
1941	Cle A	0	1	.000	1	1	0	0	4	7	3	0	1	3	4	6.75	58	.438	.550	1-0	.000	-0	88	-1	-0.2
1942	Cle A	3	4	.429	19	6	2	0	63	58	31	0	2	31	44	3.86	89	.242	.333	15-1	.133	-0	66	-3	-0.3
1944	Cle A	0	1	.000	3	1	0	0	3.1	2	5	0	0	5	4	13.50	24	.167	.412	0-0	—	0	25	-4	-0.7
1945	Cle A	4	4	.500	8	8	5-1	0	70	56	17	3	0	26	42	1.93	168	.215	.287	21-4	.143	-1	105	11	1.3
1946	Cle A	8	12	.400	28	26	8	0	200	170	86	15	2	79	87	3.47	95	.227	.302	70-7	.186	1	100	-3	-0.2
1947	Cle A	8	10	.444	27	21	6	0	162.2	137	65	13	1	67	56	3.15	110	.233	.313	52-6	.173	-1*	116	5	0.4
1948	NY A	5	3	.625	20	8	4	0	76.2	77	37	6	1	30	25	3.76	109	.261	.331	27-0	.148	-1	133	2	0.0
1949	StL A	3	13	.188	35	19	4	1	127.1	146	90	13	3	89	24	5.37	84	.294	.405	37-3	.162	-1*	89	-11	-1.4
Total	8	31	48	.392	141	90	29-1	1	707	653	334	50	10	330	286	3.72	98	.246	.331	223-21	.166	-4	102	-4	-1.1
EMBREY, SLIM Charles Akin B 8.17.1901 Columbia, TN D 10.10.1947 Nashville, TN BR/TR 6-2/184# d10.1																									
1923	Chi A	0	0	—	1	0	0	0	2.2	7	6	0	0	2	1	10.13	39	.500	.563	0-0	—	0		-3	-0.1
EMIG, CHARLIE Charles Henry B 4.5.1875 Cincinnati, OH D 10.2.1975 Oklahoma City, OK TL d9.4																									
1896	Lou N	0	1	.000	1	1	1	0	8	12	17	1	3	7	1	7.88	55	.343	.489	3-0	.000	-1	49	-5	-0.4
EMMERICH, SLIM William Peter B 9.29.1919 Allentown, PA D 9.17.1998 Allentown, PA BR/TR 6-1/170# d5.14																									
1945	NY N	4	4	.500	31	7	1	0	100	111	55	8	1	33	27	4.86	80	.278	.334	25-4	.120	-2	84	-8	-0.7
1946	NY N	0	0	—	2	0	0	0	4	6	2	1	0	0	1	4.50	76	.400	.400	0-0	—	0		0	0.0
Total	2	4	4	.500	33	7	1	0	104	117	57	9	1	33	28	4.85	80	.282	.336	25-4	.120	-2	84	-8	-0.7
EMSLIE, BOB Robert Daniel B 1.27.1859 Guelph, ON, CAN D 4.26.1943 St.Thomas, ON, CAN BR/TR 5-11/?# d7.25 U35																									
1883	Bal AA	9	13	.409	24	23	21-1	0	201.1	188	149	3		41	62	3.17	110	.231	.268	97	.165	-3*	78	4	0.1
1884	Bal AA	32	17	.653	50	50	50-4	0	455.1	419	241	5	14	88	264	2.75	126	.224	.264	195	.190	-5*	96	36	2.8
1885	Bal AA	3	10	.231	13	13	11	0	107	131	87	0	5	30	27	4.29	76	.298	.350	51	.235	0	112	-14	-1.3
	Phi AA	0	4	.000	4	4	3	0	28.2	37	30	1	0	6	9	6.28	55	.291	.323	12	.083	-1	107	-6	-0.7
	Year	3	14	.176	17	17	14	0	135.2	168	36	1	5	36	36	4.71	70	.297	.344	63	.206	-1	111	-22	-2.0
Total	3	44	44	.500	91	90	85-5	0	792.1	775	507	9	19	165	362	3.19	108	.239	.279	355	.186	-9	94	20	0.9
ENCARNACION, LUIS Luis Martin Lora (b: Luis Martin Lora (Encarcnacion)) B 10.20.1963 Santo Domingo, D.R. BR/TR 5-10/178# d7.27																									
1990	KC A	0	0	—	4	0	0	0-0	10.1	14	10	1	0	4-0	8	7.84	49	.311	.367	0-0	—	0		-5	-0.2
ENDERS, TREVOR Trevor Hale B 12.22.1974 Milwaukee, WI BR/TL 6-1/205# d9.2																									
2000	TB A	0	1	.000	9	0	0	0-1	9.1	14	13	2	0	5-0	5	10.61	47	.359	.432	0-0	—	0		-6	-0.5
ENGEL, JOE Joseph William B 3.12.1893 Washington, DC D 6.12.1969 Chattanooga, TN BR/TL 6-1.5/183# d5.30																									
1912	Was A	2	5	.286	17	10	2	1	75	70	41	2	4	50	29	3.96	84	.253	.375	17-1	.059	-1	102	-3	-0.3
1913	Was A	8	9	.471	36	24	6-2	0	164.2	124	75	2	11	85	70	3.06	97	.218	.331	49-1	.061	-5	93	-2	-0.8
1914	Was A	7	5	.583	35	15	1	3	124.1	108	53	2	5	75	41	2.97	95	.254	.372	28-2	.107	1	123	-2	-0.2
1915	Was A	0	3	.000	11	3	0	0	33.2	30	15	0	3	19	9	3.21	93	.261	.380	6-0	.000	-1	57	0	-0.1
1917	Cin N	0	1	.000	1	1	1	0	8	12	8	0	0	6	2	5.63	47	.353	.450	3-0	.000	-0	0	-3	-0.3
1919	Cle A	0	0	—	1	0	0	0	0	0	3	0	0	3	0	∞	—	—	1.000	0-0	—	0		-2	-0.2
1920	Was A	0	0	—	1	0	0	0	1.2	0	4	0	1	4	0	21.60	17	.000	.556	1-0	.000	-0*		-3	-0.2
Total	7	17	23	.425	102	53	10-2	4	407.1	344	199	6	24	242	151	3.38	88	.242	.361	104-4	.067	-6	99	-15	-2.1
ENGEL, STEVE Steven Michael B 12.31.1961 Cincinnati, OH BR/TL 6-3/216# d7.30																									
1985	Chi N	1	5	.167	11	8	1	1-0	51.2	61	36	10	0	26-1	29	5.57	72	.298	.375	16-0	.188	1	91	-9	-0.8
ENGLE, RICK Richard Douglas B 4.7.1957 Corbin, KY BR/TL 5-11.5/181# d9.2																									
1981	Mon N	0	0	—	1	0	0	0-0	2	6	4	0	0	1-0	2	18.00	19	.500	.538	0-0	—	0		-3	-0.2
ENNIS, JOHN John Wayne B 10.17.1979 Montrose, CO BR/TR 6-5/220# d4.10																									
2002	Atl N	0	0	—	1	1	0	0-0	4	5	2	0	0	3-0	1	4.50	91	.385	.471	1-0	.000	-0	113	0	0.0
ENRIGHT, JACK Jackson Percy B 11.29.1895 Fort Worth, TX D 8.18.1975 Pompano Beach, FL BR/TR 5-11/177# d9.26																									
1917	NY A	0	1	.000	1	1	0	0	5	5	5	0	0	3	1	5.40	50	.294	.400	1-0	.000	-0	27	-2	-0.3
ENYART, TERRY Terry Gene B 10.10.1950 Ironton, OH BR/TL 6-2/190# d6.17																									
1974	Mon N	0	0	—	2	0	0	0-0	1.2	4	6	0	0	4-0	2	16.20	24	.444	.615	0-0	—	0		-3	-0.2
ENZMANN, JOHNNY John "Gentleman John" B 3.4.1890 Brooklyn, NY D 3.14.1984 Riverhead, NY BR/TR 5-10/165# d7.10																									
1914	Bro N	1	0	1.000	7	1	0	0	19	21	16	1	3	8	5	4.74	60	.300	.395	6-0	.000	-1	275	-4	-0.3
1918	Cle A	5	7	.417	30	14	8	2	136.2	130	44	2	5	29	38	2.37	127	.263	.310	47-2	.149	-2	86	10	0.7
1919	Cle A	3	2	.600	14	4	2	0	55.1	67	29	0	2	8	13	2.28	147	.312	.342	15-1	.133	-0	111	2	0.1
1920	Phi N	2	3	.400	16	2	1	0	58.2	79	40	1	5	16	35	3.84	89	.320	.373	24-0	.167	1*	115	-5	-0.4
Total	4	11	12	.478	67	21	11	2	269.2	297	129	4	15	61	91	2.84	111	.289	.338	92-3	.141	-3	102	3	0.1
EPPERLY, AL Albert Paul "Tub" or "Pard" B 5.7.1918 Glidden, IA D 4.14.2003 McFarland, MI BL/TR 6-2/194# d4.25																									
1938	Chi N	2	0	1.000	9	4	1	0	27	28	11	1	0	15	10	3.67	104	.264	.355	8-0	.250	1	243	1	0.2
1950	Bro N	0	0	—	5	0	0	0	9	14	8	1	0	5	3	5.00	82	.378	.452	0-0	—	0		-2	-0.1

Year	Tm Lg	W	L	Pct	G	GS	CG-Sho	SV-BS	IP	H	R	HR	HB	BB-IB	SO	ERA	AERA	OAV	OOB	AB-SH	AVG	PB	Sup	APR	PW
Total	2	2	0	1.000	14	4	1	0	36	42	19	2	0	20	13	4.00	97	.294	.380	8-0	.250	1	243	-1	0.1
ERARDI, GREG Joseph Gregory B 5.31.1954 Syracuse, NY BR/TR 6-1/190# d9.6																									
1977	Sea A	0	1	.000	5	0	0	0-0	9	12	8	3	0	6-1	5	6.00	69	.300	.391	0-0	—	0		-2	-0.2
ERAUTT, EDDIE Edward Lorenz Sebastian B 9.26.1924 Portland, OR BR/TR 6/186# d4.16 b-Joe																									
1947	Cin N	4	9	.308	36	10	2	0	119	146	78	5	2	53	43	5.07	81	.307	.379	29-3	.069	-1	77	-14	-1.4
1948	Cin N	0	0	—	2	0	0	0	3	3	2	0	0	1	0	6.00	65	.250	.308	0-0	—	0		-1	0.0
1949	Cin N	4	11	.267	39	9	1	1	112.2	99	53	9	3	61	43	3.36	125	.247	.351	23-1	.174	0	47	8	1.0
1950	Cin N	4	2	.667	33	2	1	1	65.1	82	48	9	6	22	35	5.65	75	.307	.373	13-1	.154	0	83	-11	-0.9
1951	Cin N	0	0	—	30	0	0	0	39.1	50	31	4	3	23	20	5.72	71	.314	.411	3-0	.000	-0		-8	-0.4
1953	Cin N	0	0	—	4	0	0	0	4.2	11	3	1	0	3	1	5.79	75	.500	.560	1-0	.000	-0		-1	0.0
	StL N	3	1	.750	20	1	0	0	35.2	43	25	6	2	16	15	6.31	67	.299	.377	6-1	.167	-0	84	-7	-0.7
	Year	3	1	.750	24	1	0	0	40.1	54	29	7	2	19	16	6.25	68	.325	.401	7-1	.143	-0	84	-8	-0.7
Total	6	15	23	.395	164	22	4	2	379.2	434	240	34	16	179	157	4.86	86	.293	.376	75-6	.120	-2	66	-34	-2.4
ERDOS, TODD Todd Michael B 11.21.1973 Washington, PA BR/TR 6-1/205# d6.8																									
1997	SD N	2	0	1.000	11	0	0	0-0	13.2	17	9	1	2	4-0	13	5.27	74	.293	.359	1-0	.000	-0		-2	-0.3
1998	NY A	0	0	—	2	0	0	0-0	2	5	2	0	0	1-1	0	9.00	49	.500	.545	0-0	—	0		-1	-0.1
1999	NY A	0	0	—	4	0	0	0-0	7	5	4	2	0	4-0	4	3.86	123	.192	.290	0-0	—	0		0	0.0
2000	NY A	0	0	—	14	0	0	1-0	25	31	14	2	1	11-0	18	5.04	96	.304	.377	1-0	.000	-0		-0	0.0
	SD N	0	0	—	22	0	0	1-1	29.2	32	24	5	6	17-1	16	6.67	65	.271	.379	1-0	.000	-0		-8	-0.4
2001	Bos A	0	0	—	10	0	0	0-0	16.1	15	9	2	3	8-1	7	4.96	91	.263	.366	0-0	—	0		0	0.0
Total	5	2	0	1.000	63	0	0	2-1	93.2	105	62	12	12	45-3	58	5.57	80	.283	.372	3-0	.000	-0		-11	-0.8
ERICKS, JOHN John Edward B 6.16.1967 Tinley Park, IL BR/TR 6-7/220# d6.24																									
1995	Pit N	3	9	.250	19	18	1	0-0	106	108	59	7	2	50-4	80	4.58	94	.263	.343	31-6	.097	-2	72	-3	-0.5
1996	Pit N	4	5	.444	28	4	0	8-2	46.2	56	35	11	0	19-2	46	5.79	75	.292	.354	5-0	.000	-1	72	-8	-1.6
1997	Pit N	1	0	1.000	10	0	0	6-1	9.1	7	3	1	0	4-0	6	1.93	222	.200	.282	0-0	—	0		2	0.4
Total	3	8	14	.364	57	22	1	14-3	162	171	97	19	2	73-6	132	4.78	90	.268	.343	36-6	.083	-2	72	-9	-1.7
ERICKSON, DON Don Lee B 12.13.1931 Springfield, IL BR/TR 6/175# d9.1																									
1958	Phi N	0	1	.000	9	0	0	1	11.2	11	7	3	0	9-1	9	4.63	86	.244	.364	1-0	.000	-0		-1	-0.1
ERICKSON, ERIC Eric George Adolph B 3.13.1895 Goteborg, Sweden D 5.19.1965 Jamestown, NY BR/TR 6-2/190# d10.6 Mil 1918																									
1914	NY N	0	1	.000	1	1	0	0	5	8	7	0	0	3	3	0.00	—	.364	.440	1-0	.000	-0	0	-1	-0.3
1916	Det A	0	0	—	8	0	0	0	16	13	6	0	1	8	7	2.81	102	.220	.324	4-0	.000	-1		0	-0.1
1918	Det A	4	5	.444	12	9	8	1	94.1	81	32	2	3	29	48	2.48	107	.240	.306	33-1	.121	-3	97	2	-0.2
1919	Det A	0	2	.000	3	2	0	0	14.2	17	17	0	1	10	4	6.75	47	.293	.406	5-0	.200	-0	123	-7	-0.8
	Was A	6	11	.353	20	15	7-1	0	132	130	69	7	7	63	86	3.95	81	.254	.344	48-4	.146	-1	111	-8	-1.2
	Year	6	13	.316	23	17	7-1	0	146.2	147	74	7	8	73	90	4.23	76	.258	.351	53-4	.151	-2	112	-16	-2.0
1920	Was A	12	16	.429	39	27	12	1	239.1	231	142	13	11	128	87	3.84	97	.264	.365	83-8	.277	4	107	-8	-0.6
1921	Was A	8	10	.444	32	22	9-3	0	179	181	90	7	9	65	71	3.62	114	.269	.341	60-3	.150	-3	71	9	0.3
1922	Was A	4	12	.250	30	17	6-2	2	141.2	144	95	8	3	73	61	4.96	78	.279	.372	45-1	.133	-2	80	-18	-2.1
Total	7	34	57	.374	145	93	42-6	4	822	805	458	37	35	379	367	3.85	93	.264	.352	279-17	.179	-6	92	-31	-5.0
ERICKSON, HAL Harold James B 7.17.1919 Portland, OR BR/TR 6-5/230# d4.14																									
1953	Det A	0	1	.000	18	0	0	1	32.1	43	23	4	2	10	19	4.73	86	.323	.379	4-0	.000	-1		-4	-0.3
ERICKSON, PAUL Paul Walford "Li'L Abner" B 12.14.1915 Zion, IL D 4.5.2002 Fond Du Lac, WI BR/TR 6-2/200# d6.29																									
1941	Chi N	5	7	.417	32	15	7-1	1	141	126	70	2	2	64	85	3.70	95	.234	.318	46-1	.152	0	100	-4	-0.3
1942	Chi N	1	6	.143	18	7	1	0	63	70	40	4	0	41	26	5.43	59	.288	.391	21-0	.143	-1	60	-14	-1.5
1943	Chi N	1	3	.250	15	4	0	0	42.2	47	32	4	2	22	24	6.12	55	.280	.370	15-0	.200	0	172	-12	-1.1
1944	Chi N	5	9	.357	33	15	5-3	1	124.1	113	59	5	0	67	82	3.55	100	.243	.338	36-0	.056	-1	93	0	-0.1
1945	†Chi N	7	4	.636	28	9	3	3	108.1	94	41	5	7	48	53	3.32	110	.233	.325	32-4	.156	0	147	7	0.7
1946	Chi N	9	7	.563	32	14	5-1	0	137	119	46	2	3	65	70	2.43	137	.232	.321	40-6	.050	-4	105	13	0.9
1947	Chi N	7	12	.368	40	20	6	1	174	179	90	17	5	93	82	4.34	91	.268	.362	60-0	.250	3	85	-4	-0.1
1948	Chi N	0	0	—	3	0	0	0	5.2	7	5	0	0	6	4	6.35	61	.292	.433	1-0	.000	-0		-2	-0.1
	Phi N	2	0	1.000	4	2	0	0	17.1	19	10	2	0	17	5	5.19	76	.292	.439	7-0	.143	-0	112	-2	-0.2
	NY N	0	0	—	2	0	0	0	1	0	0	0	0	2	1	0.00	—	.000	.400	0-0	—	0		0	0.0
	Year	2	0	1.000	9	2	0	0	24	26	15	2	0	25	10	5.25	75	.283	.436	8-0	.125	-0	113	-3	-0.3
Total	8	37	48	.435	207	86	27-5	6	814.1	774	393	41	19	425	432	3.86	93	.250	.345	258-11	.147	-2	101	-18	-1.8
ERICKSON, RALPH Ralph Lief B 6.25.1902 Dubois, ID D 6.27.2002 Chandler, AZ BL/TL 6-1/175# d9.11																									
1929	Pit N	0	0	—	1	0	0	0	1	2	3	0	0	2	0	27.00	18	.500	.667	0-0	—	0		-2	-0.1
1930	Pit N	1	0	1.000	7	0	0	0	14	21	12	1	0	10	2	7.07	70	.375	.470	4-0	.250	-0		-3	-0.2
Total	2	1	0	1.000	8	0	0	0	15	23	15	1	0	12	2	8.40	59	.383	.486	4-0	.250	-0		-5	-0.3
ERICKSON, ROGER Roger Farrell B 8.30.1956 Springfield, IL BR/TR 6-3/190# d4.6																									
1978	Min A	14	13	.519	37	37	14	0-0	265.2	268	129	19	8	79-1	121	3.96	97	.263	.319	0-0	—	0	105	-2	-0.2
1979	Min A	3	10	.231	24	21	0	0-0	123	154	86	17	1	48-1	47	5.63	78	.310	.368	0-0	—	0	91	-17	-1.6
1980	Min A	7	13	.350	32	27	7	0-0	191.1	198	83	13	4	56-0	97	3.25	135	.268	.320	0-0	—	0*	70	20	2.0
1981	Min A	3	8	.273	14	14	1	0-0	91.1	93	48	7	0	31-4	44	3.84	103	.262	.316	0-0	—	0	63	-1	-0.1
1982	Min A	4	3	.571	7	7	2	0-0	40.2	56	29	6	1	12-1	12	4.87	87	.326	.369	0-0	—	0	119	-5	-0.7
	NY A	4	5	.444	16	11	0	1-0	70.2	86	36	5	0	17-1	37	4.46	90	.301	.334	0-0	—	0	79	-2	-0.4
	Year	8	8	.500	23	18	2	1-0	111.1	142	39	11	1	29-2	49	4.61	89	.310	.347	0-0	—	0	95	-7	-1.1
1983	NY A	0	1	.000	5	0	0	0-0	16.2	13	8	1	0	8-1	7	4.32	90	.213	.304	0-0	—	0		0	0.0
Total	6	35	53	.398	135	117	24	1-0	799.1	868	419	68	14	251-9	365	4.13	99	.277	.331	0-0	—	0	88	-7	-1.0
ERICKSON, SCOTT Scott Gavin B 2.2.1968 Long Beach, CA BR/TR 6-4/224# d6.25																									
1990	Min A	8	4	.667	19	17	1	0-0	113	108	49	9	5	51-4	53	2.87	145	.256	.342	0-0	—	0	112	11	1.1
1991	†Min A	**20**	8	**.714**	32	32	5-3	0-0	204	189	80	13	6	71-3	108	3.18	135	.248	.314	0-0	—	0	115	23	3.1
1992	Min A	13	12	.520	32	32	5-3	0-0	212	197	86	18	8	83-3	101	3.40	120	.252	.328	0-0	—	0	88	16	1.8
1993	Min A	8	19	.296	34	34	1	0-0	218.2	266	138	17	10	71-1	116	5.19	84	.305	.359	0-0	—	0	92	-20	-2.0
1994	Min A	8	11	.421	23	23	2-1	0-0	144	173	95	15	9	59-0	104	5.44	90	.299	.370	0-0	—	0	86	-9	-1.0
1995	Min A	4	6	.400	15	15	0	0-0	87.2	102	61	11	4	32-0	45	5.95	80	.291	.356	0-0	—	0	101	-10	-0.9
	Bal A	9	4	.692	17	16	7-2	0-0	108.2	111	47	7	1	35-0	61	3.89	122	.273	.330	0-0	—	0	122	12	1.3
	Year	13	10	.565	32	31	7-2	0-0	196.1	213	53	18	5	67-0	106	4.81	99	.281	.342	0-0	—	0	112	0	0.4
1996	†Bal A	13	12	.520	34	34	6	0-0	222.1	262	137	21	11	66-4	100	5.02	98	.297	.352	0-0	—	0	103	-4	-0.2
1997	†Bal A	16	7	.696	34	33	3-2	0-0	221.2	218	100	16	5	61-5	131	3.69	119	.257	.309	2-2	.000	0	104	17	1.7
1998	Bal A	16	13	.552	36	**36**	**11**-2	0-0	**251.1**	284	125	23	13	69-4	186	4.01	114	.281	.334	2-1	.000	1	108	11	1.4
1999	Bal A	15	12	.556	34	34	6-**3**	0-0	230.1	244	127	27	11	99-4	106	4.81	98	.280	.358	6-1	.000	-1	96	-1	0.0
2000	Bal A	5	8	.385	16	16	1	0-0	92.2	127	81	14	5	48-0	41	7.87	60	.330	.406	5-0	.400	1*	92	-31	-3.2
2002	Bal A	5	12	.294	29	28	3-1	0-0	160.2	192	109	20	8	68-2	74	5.55	77	.303	.374	4-0	.000	-0	96	-25	-2.2
Total	12	140	128	.522	355	350	51-17	0-0	2267	2473	1235	211	96	813-30	1226	4.51	100	.281	.346	19-4	.105	1	101	-10	0.9
ERRICKSON, DICK Richard Merriwell "Lief" B 3.5.1912 Vineland, NJ D 11.28.1999 Vineland, NJ BL/TR 6-1/175# d4.27																									
1938	Bos N	9	7	.563	34	10	6-1	6	122.2	113	53	1	2	56	40	3.15	109	.246	.330	35-5	.114	-1	106	3	0.4
1939	Bos N	6	9	.400	28	11	3	1	128.1	143	63	6	1	54	33	4.00	92	.293	.365	44-2	.227	1	75	-3	-0.2
1940	Bos N	12	13	.480	34	29	17-3	4	236.1	241	91	8	1	90	34	3.16	118	.270	.338	83-5	.157	-2	87	16	1.5
1941	Bos N	6	12	.333	38	23	5-2	1	165.2	192	100	12	4	62	45	4.78	75	.287	.351	45-4	.178	-0	85	-21	-2.1
1942	Bos N	2	5	.286	21	4	0	1	59.1	76	34	8	0	20	15	5.01	67	.309	.361	16-1	.125	-1	82	-9	-1.2
	Chi N	1	1	.500	13	0	0	0	24	39	12	1	1	8	9	4.13	78	.411	.462	5-0	.000	-1		-2	-0.2
	Year	3	6	.333	34	4	0	1	83.1	115	49	9	1	28	24	4.75	69	.337	.389	21-1	.095	-1	83	-11	-1.4
Total	5	36	47	.434	168	77	31-6	13	736.1	804	353	36	9	290	176	3.85	93	.282	.350	228-17	.162	-5	87	-16	-1.8

Year	Tm Lg	W	L	Pct	G	GS	CG-Sho	SV-BS	IP	H	R	HR	HB	BB-IB	SO	ERA	AERA	OAV	OOB	AB-SH	AVG	PB	Sup	APR	PW
ERSKINE, CARL Carl Daniel "Oisk" B 12.13.1926 Anderson, IN BR/TR 5-10/165# d7.25																									
1948	Bro N	6	3	.667	17	9	3	0	64	51	28	5	1	35	29	3.23	124	.231	.339	21-0	.095	-2	109	5	0.4
1949	†Bro N	8	1	.889	22	3	2	0	79.2	68	44	6	2	51	49	4.63	89	.235	.354	26-2	.115	-2	179	-4	-0.6
1950	Bro N	7	6	.538	22	13	3	1	103	109	56	15	1	35	50	4.72	87	.273	.333	37-1	.243	2	121	-6	-0.6
1951	Bro N	16	12	.571	46	19	7	4	189.2	206	105	23	2	78	95	4.46	88	.280	.351	61-3	.131	-2	130	-12	-1.9
1952	†Bro N	14	6	.700	33	26	10-4	2	206.2	167	72	17	2	71	131	2.70	135	.220	.289	66-7	.152	-0*	116	20	2.0
1953	†Bro N	20	6	**.769**	39	33	16-4	3	246.2	213	106	21	3	95	187	3.54	120	.230	.304	93-7	.215	0*	138	20	1.8
1954	Bro N★	18	15	.545	38	37	12-2	1	260.1	239	128	31	4	92	166	4.15	98	.243	.310	88-5	.159	-1*	94	0	-0.1
1955	†Bro N	11	8	.579	31	29	7-2	1	194.2	185	89	29	0	64-3	84	3.79	107	.253	.312	74-0	.203	-0*	98	8	0.6
1956	†Bro N	13	11	.542	31	28	8-1	0	186.1	189	92	25	1	57-5	95	4.25	93	.264	.317	66-5	.121	-3*	95	-3	-0.7
1957	Bro N	5	3	.625	15	7	1	0	66	62	27	8	0	20-1	26	3.55	118	.248	.301	22-0	.091	-2*	88	5	0.4
1958	LA N	4	4	.500	31	9	2-1	0	98.1	115	61	14	0	35-3	54	5.13	80	.297	.353	27-1	.037	-3*	105	-10	-1.0
1959	LA N	0	3	.000	10	3	0	1	23.1	33	22	5	0	13-1	15	7.71	55	.320	.397	7-0	.000	-1	70	-8	-1.1
Total	12	122	78	.610	335	216	71-14	13	1718.2	1637	830	199	16	646-13	981	4.00	101	.252	.320	588-31	.156	-13	111	15	-0.8
ESCARREGA, CHICO Ernesto (Acosta) B 12.27.1949 Los Mochis, Mexico BR/TR 5-11/185# d4.26																									
1982	Chi A	1	3	.250	38	2	0	1-1	73.2	73	33	3	0	16-2	33	3.67	110	.263	.299	0-0	—	0	56	4	0.2
ESCOBAR, KELVIM Kelvim Jose (Bolivar) B 4.11.1976 LaGuaira, Venezuela BR/TR 6-1/205# d6.29																									
1997	Tor A	3	2	.600	27	0	0	14-3	31	28	12	1	0	19-2	36	2.90	158	.237	.343	0-0	—	0		5	1.0
1998	Tor A	7	3	.700	22	10	0	0-1	79.2	72	37	5	0	35-0	72	3.73	125	.237	.313	0-0	—	0	123	8	0.8
1999	Tor A	14	11	.560	33	30	1	0-0	174	203	118	19	10	81-2	129	5.69	87	.293	.371	1-0	.000	-0	109	-13	-1.7
2000	Tor A	10	15	.400	43	24	3-1	2-1	180	186	118	26	3	85-3	142	5.35	95	.267	.347	7-0	.000	-1	77	-5	-0.7
2001	Tor A	6	8	.429	59	11	1-1	0-0	126	93	51	8	3	52-5	121	3.50	131	.204	.287	0-0	—	0	90	16	1.5
2002	Tor A	5	7	.417	76	0	0	38-8	78	75	39	10	5	44-6	85	4.27	108	.246	.350	0-0	—	0		3	0.6
2003	Tor A	13	9	.591	41	26	1-1	4-1	180.1	189	94	15	9	78-3	159	4.29	107	.270	.348	6-0	.167	-0	87	6	0.7
Total	7	58	55	.513	301	101	6-3	58-14	849	846	469	84	30	394-21	744	4.58	104	.258	.341	14-0	.071	-1	96	20	2.2
ESHELMAN, VAUGHN Vaughn Michael B 5.22.1969 Philadelphia, PA BL/TL 6-3/205# d5.2																									
1995	Bos A	6	3	.667	23	14	0	0-0	81.2	86	47	3	1	36-0	41	4.85	101	.272	.346	0-0	—	0	106	1	0.1
1996	Bos A	6	3	.667	39	10	0	0-0	87.2	112	79	13	2	58-4	59	7.08	72	.311	.405	0-0	—	0	128	-19	-1.6
1997	Bos A	3	3	.500	21	6	0	0-1	42.2	58	32	3	2	17-5	18	6.33	73	.330	.391	4-0	.250	0	119	-8	-0.9
Total	3	15	9	.625	83	30	0	0-1	212	256	158	19	5	111-9	118	6.07	81	.300	.380	4-0	.250	0	116	-26	-2.4
ESPER, DUKE Charles H. (b: Charles Esbacher) B 7.28.1868 Salem, NJ D 8.31.1910 Philadelphia, PA TL 5-11.5/185# d4.18																									
1890	Phi AA	8	9	.471	18	16	14-1	0	143.2	176	99	1	5	67	61	4.89	79	.292	.368	61	.295	4	108	-12	-0.7
	Pit N	0	2	.000	2	2	2	0	17	18	16	0	1	10	9	5.29	62	.265	.367	7	.143	-1	10	-4	-0.4
	Phi N	5	0	1.000	5	5	4	0	41	40	22	1	0	16	18	3.07	119	.247	.315	19	.158	-1	131	3	0.2
	Year	5	2	.714	7	7	6	0	58	58	30	1	1	26	27	3.72	95	.252	.331	26	.154	-2	99	-2	-0.2
1891	Phi N	20	15	.571	39	36	25-1	1	296	302	185	8	7	121	108	3.56	96	.254	.327	123	.220	1	102	-8	-0.6
1892	Phi N	11	6	.647	21	18	14	1	160.1	171	84	2	1	60	45	3.42	95	.262	.325	70	.243	2*	112	0	0.1
	Pit N	2	0	1.000	3	3	1	0	18.1	18	13	0	0	12	5	5.40	61	.247	.353	9	.000	-1	179	-3	-0.4
	Year	13	6	.684	24	21	15	1	178.2	189	22	2	1	72	50	3.63	90	.261	.328	79	.215	0	121	0	-0.3
1893	Was N	12	28	.300	42	36	34	0	334.1	442	277	14	12	156	78	4.71	98	.309	.381	143	.287	7	87	-10	-0.2
1894	Was N	5	10	.333	18	14	7	0	116	177	132	8	2	39	24	7.45	71	.346	.395	54-0	.259	1*	98	-20	-1.6
	†Bal N	10	2	.833	16	9	8	2	101	107	56	1	1	36	25	3.92	139	.269	.331	45-0	.222	-1	117	18	1.5
	Year	15	12	.556	34	23	15	2	217	284	65	9	3	75	49	5.81	92	.312	.367	99-0	.242	0	105	-6	-0.1
1895	†Bal N	10	12	.455	34	25	16-1	1	218.1	248	132	2	0	79	39	3.92	122	.281	.341	90-2	.178	-6	98	19	0.8
1896	Bal N	14	5	.737	20	18	14-1	0	155.2	168	80	3	2	39	19	3.58	119	.273	.319	66-1	.197	-2	95	14	1.1
1897	StL N	1	6	.143	8	8	7	0	61.1	95	51	5	1	12	8	5.28	83	.351	.380	25-0	.320	1	63	-6	-0.4
1898	StL N	3	5	.375	10	8	6	0	64.2	86	49	1	0	22	14	5.98	63	.316	.367	27-0	.370	2*	66	-11	-1.0
Total	9	101	100	.502	236	198	152-4	5	1727.2	2048	1196	46	32	669	453	4.39	96	.288	.351	739-3	.241	5	97	-20	-1.6
ESPINOSA, NINO Arnulfo Acevedo (b: Arnulfo Acevedo (Espinosa)) B 8.15.1953 Villa Altagracia, D.R. D 12.24.1987 Villa Altagracia, D.R. BR/TR 6-1/192# d9.13																									
1974	NY N	0	0	—	2	1	0	0-0	9	12	5	1	0	0-0	2	5.00	72	.324	.324	2-0	.500	0	73	-1	0.0
1975	NY N	0	1	.000	2	0	0	0-0	3	8	6	0	0	1-0	2	18.00	19	.471	.500	0-0	—	0		-5	-0.8
1976	NY N	4	4	.500	12	5	0	0-0	41.2	41	21	3	0	13-3	30	3.67	90	.265	.316	9-1	.000	-1	64	-3	-0.6
1977	NY N	10	13	.435	32	29	7-1	0-0	200	188	82	17	5	55-5	105	3.42	109	.249	.304	62-7	.129	-1	88	8	0.7
1978	NY N	11	15	.423	32	32	6-1	0-0	203.2	230	117	24	3	75-10	76	4.73	74	.292	.352	67-7	.209	2	110	-28	-2.9
1979	Phi N	14	12	.538	33	33	8-3	0-0	212	211	94	20	3	65-8	88	3.65	105	.262	.318	72-4	.194	2*	83	4	0.6
1980	Phi N	3	5	.375	12	12	1	0-0	76.1	73	36	9	2	19-2	13	3.77	101	.250	.298	26-3	.115	-1*	82	0	-0.1
1981	Phi N	2	5	.286	14	14	2	0-0	73.2	98	52	11	1	24-2	22	6.11	59	.333	.378	20-3	.200	-0	114	-18	-1.6
	Tor A	0	0	—	1	0	0	0-0	1	4	1	0	0	0-0	0	9.00	44	.667	.667	0-0	—	0		0	0.0
Total	8	44	55	.444	140	126	24-5	0-0	820.1	865	414	85	14	252-30	338	4.17	88	.275	.329	258-25	.171	1	93	-43	-4.7
ESSER, MARK Mark Gerald B 4.1.1956 Erie, PA BR/TL 6-1/190# d4.22																									
1979	Chi A	0	0	—	2	0	0	0-0	1.2	2	3	0	0	4-0	1	16.20	26	.286	.545	0-0	—	0		-2	-0.1
ESSICK, BILL William Earl "Vinegar Bill" B 12.18.1880 Grand Ridge, IL D 10.12.1951 Los Angeles, CA TR 5-10/175# d9.12																									
1906	Cin N	2	2	.500	6	4	3	0	39.1	39	18	1	2	16	16	2.97	93	.273	.354	13-2	.077	-1	106	-1	-0.2
1907	Cin N	0	2	.000	3	2	2	0	21.2	23	15	0	1	8	7	2.91	89	.274	.344	8-0	.000	-1	41	-2	-0.3
Total	2	2	4	.333	9	6	5	0	61	62	33	1	3	24	23	2.95	91	.273	.350	21-2	.048	-2	85	-3	-0.5
ESTELLE, DICK Richard Henry B 1.18.1942 Lakewood, NJ BB/TL 6-2/170# d9.4																									
1964	SF N	1	2	.333	6	6	0	0	41.2	39	15	3	0	23-0	23	3.02	118	.247	.341	15-1	.067	-1	107	3	0.1
1965	SF N	0	0	—	6	1	0	0	11.1	12	6	0	1	8-1	6	3.97	91	.261	.375	1-0	.000	0	146	-1	0.0
Total	2	1	2	.333	12	7	0	0	53	51	21	3	1	31-1	29	3.23	111	.250	.349	16-1	.063	-0	112	2	0.1
ESTES, SHAWN Aaron Shawn B 2.18.1973 San Bernardino, CA BR/TL 6-2/185# d9.16																									
1995	SF N	0	3	.000	3	3	0	0-0	17.1	16	14	2	1	5-0	14	6.75	61	.229	.289	5-0	.000	-1	37	-5	-0.7
1996	SF N	3	5	.375	11	11	0	0-0	70	63	30	3	2	39-3	60	3.60	114	.243	.347	19-6	.158	-0*	92	5	0.5
1997	†SF N★	19	5	.792	32	32	3-2	0-0	201	162	80	12	8	100-2	181	3.18	129	.223	.323	68-7	.147	1*	123	20	2.4
1998	SF N	7	12	.368	25	25	1-1	0-0	149.1	150	89	14	5	80-6	136	5.06	78	.269	.364	42-8	.190	1*	93	-19	-1.9
1999	SF N	11	11	.500	32	32	1-1	0-0	203	209	121	21	5	112-2	159	4.92	85	.268	.362	61-10	.164	2*	119	-17	-1.3
2000	†SF N	15	6	.714	30	30	4-2	0-0	190.1	194	99	11	3	108-1	136	4.26	100	.275	.371	68-11	.206	4*	160	0	0.6
2001	SF N	9	8	.529	27	27	0	0-0	159	151	78	11	5	77-7	109	4.02	99	.253	.339	42-6	.071	-2	99	-1	-0.1
2002	NY N	4	9	.308	23	23	1-1	0-0	132.2	133	70	12	5	66-9	92	4.55	87	.267	.356	35-5	.086	-1*	85	-6	-0.7
	Cin N	1	3	.250	6	6	0	0-0	28	38	24	1	4	17-0	17	7.71	55	.345	.444	8-2	.000	-1	120	-9	-1.1
	Year	5	12	.294	29	29	1-1	0-0	160.2	171	30	13	9	83-9	109	5.10	79	.281	.373	43-7	.070	-2	93	-18	-1.8
2003	Chi N	8	11	.421	29	28	1-1	0-0	152.1	182	113	20	1	83-1	103	5.73	74	.305	.387	39-9	.179	2*	107	-29	-2.8
Total	9	77	73	.513	218	217	11-8	0-0	1303	1298	718	107	39	687-31	1007	4.53	91	.265	.357	387-64	.150	6	112	-61	-5.1
ESTOCK, GEORGE George John B 11.2.1924 Stirling, NJ BR/TR 6/185# d4.21																									
1951	Bos N	0	1	.000	37	1	0	3	60.1	56	33	2	0	37	11	4.33	85	.258	.366	7-1	.286	1	0	-5	-0.1
ESTRADA, CHUCK Charles Leonard B 2.15.1938 San Luis Obispo, CA BR/TR 6-1/185# d4.21 C6																									
1960	Bal A★	**18**	11	.621	36	25	12-1	2	208.2	162	87	18	15	101-3	144	3.58	106	**.218**	.319	64-9	.141	-0	105	8	1.0
1961	Bal A	15	9	.625	33	31	6-1	0	212	159	91	19	10	132-0	160	3.69	104	**.207**	.329	70-9	.114	-3	116	7	0.3
1962	Bal A	9	17	.346	34	33	6	0	223.1	199	112	24	10	121-16	165	3.83	97	.240	.341	66-8	.152	-0*	81	-5	-0.7
1963	Bal A	3	2	.600	8	7	0	0	31.1	26	17	2	1	19-0	16	4.60	76	.226	.336	10-2	.100	-1	121	-4	-0.6
1964	Bal A	3	2	.600	17	6	0	0	54.2	62	34	8	2	21-5	32	5.27	68	.282	.348	14-2	.143	-0*	162	-10	-0.9
1966	Chi N	1	1	.500	9	1	0	0	12.1	16	12	2	1	5-0	3	7.30	50	.314	.379	3-0	.000	-0	167	-5	-0.8
1967	NY N	1	2	.333	9	2	0	0	22	28	24	5	1	17-1	15	9.41	36	.326	.442	5-0	.000	-1	0	-14	-1.7
Total	7	50	44	.532	146	105	24-2	2	764.1	652	377	78	40	416-25	535	4.07	92	.232	.336	232-30	.129	-5	103	-23	-3.4

Year	Tm Lg	W	L	Pct	G	GS	CG-Sho	SV-BS	IP	H	R	HR	HB	BB-IB	SO	ERA	AERA	OAV	OOB	AB-SH	AVG	PB	Sup	APR	PW
ESTRADA, HORACIO Horacio (Jimenez) B 10.19.1975 San Joaquin, Venezuela BL/TL 6-1/185# d5.4																									
1999	Mil N	0	0	—	4	0	0	0-0	7.1	10	6	4	0	4-0	5	7.36	62	.313	.389	2-0	.000	-0		-2	-0.1
2000	Mil N	3	0	1.000	7	4	0	0-0	24.1	30	18	5	2	20-4	13	6.29	73	.300	.423	7-1	.143	-0	181	-4	-0.5
2001	Col N	1	1	.500	4	0	0	0-0	4.1	8	7	1	1	1-0	4	14.54	37	.400	.455	0-0	—	0		-3	-0.6
Total	3	4	1	.800	15	4	0	0-0	36	48	31	10	3	25-4	22	7.50	62	.316	.420	9-1	.111	-0	181	-9	-1.2
ESTRADA, OSCAR Oscar B 2.15.1904 Havana, Cuba D 1.2.1978 Havana, Cuba BL/TL 5-8/160# d4.21																									
1929	StL A	0	0	—	1	0	0	0	1	1	0	0	0	1	0	0.00	—	.250	.400	0-0	—	0		0	0.0
ESTRELLA, LEO Leoncio (Ramirez) B 2.20.1975 Puerto Plata, D.R. BR/TR 6-1/185# d7.18																									
2000	Tor A	0	0	—	2	0	0	0-0	4.2	9	3	1	0	0-0	3	5.79	88	.450	.429	0-0	—	0		0	0.0
2003	Mil N	7	3	.700	58	0	0	3-5	66	75	32	10	3	21-5	25	4.36	97	.290	.346	0-0	—	0		0	0.1
Total	2	7	3	.700	60	0	0	3-5	70.2	84	35	11	3	21-5	28	4.46	97	.301	.352	0-0	—	0		0	0.1
ETHERTON, SETH Seth Michael B 10.17.1976 Laguna Beach, CA BR/TR 6-1/200# d5.26																									
2000	Ana A	5	1	.833	11	11	0	0-0	60.1	68	38	16	1	22-0	32	5.52	92	.278	.338	2-0	.000	0	116	-2	-0.1
2003	Cin N	2	4	.333	7	7	0	0-0	30	39	23	4	3	15-1	17	6.90	62	.322	.401	7-3	.143	-0	75	-8	-1.3
Total	2	7	5	.583	18	18	0	0-0	90.1	107	61	20	4	37-1	49	5.98	80	.292	.360	9-3	.111	-0	101	-10	-1.4
ETTLES, MARK Mark Edward B 10.30.1966 Perth, Australia BR/TR 6/178# d6.5																									
1993	SD N	1	0	1.000	14	0	0	0-0	18	23	16	4	0	4-1	9	6.50	64	.307	.333	2-0	.000	-0		-5	-0.3
EUBANK, JOHN John Franklin "Honest John" B 9.9.1872 Servia, IN D 11.3.1958 Bellevue, MI BR/TR 6-2/215# d9.19																									
1905	Det A	1	0	1.000	3	2	0	0	17.1	13	12	0	1	3	1	2.08	132	.210	.258	14-0	.357	1*	194	-1	0.0
1906	Det A	4	10	.286	24	12	7-1	2	135	147	69	0	8	35	38	3.53	78	.280	.335	63-2	.206	0*	69	-11	-1.1
1907	Det A	3	3	.500	15	8	4-1	0	81	88	40	0	0	20	17	2.67	98	.279	.322	31-0	.129	-1	110	-2	-0.3
Total	3	8	13	.381	42	22	11-2	2	233.1	248	121	0	9	58	56	3.12	87	.275	.325	108-2	.204	-1	96	-14	-1.4
EUBANKS, UEL Uel Melvin "Poss" B 2.14.1903 Quinlan, TX D 11.21.1954 Dallas, TX BR/TR 6-3/175# d7.20																									
1922	Chi N	0	0	—	2	0	0	0	1.2	5	9	0	0	4	1	27.00	16	.556	.692	1-0	1.000	1		-5	-0.2
EUFEMIA, FRANK Frank Anthony B 12.23.1959 Bronx, NY BR/TR 5-11/185# d5.21																									
1985	Min A	4	2	.667	39	0	0	2-0	61.2	56	27	7	0	21-7	30	3.79	116	.250	.310	0-0	—	0		5	0.5
EVANS, BART Bart Steven B 12.30.1970 Springfield, MO BR/TR 6-2/210# d6.16																									
1998	KC A	0	0	—	8	0	0	0-0	9	7	3	1	0	0-0	7	2.00	241	.206	.206	0-0	—	0		2	0.1
EVANS, CHICK Charles Franklin B 10.15.1889 Arlington, VT D 9.2.1916 Schenectady, NY BR/TR d9.19																									
1909	Bos N	0	3	.000	4	3	1	0	21.2	25	16	0	0	14	11	4.57	62	.305	.406	9-0	.000	-1	50	-4	-0.6
1910	Bos N	1	1	.500	13	1	0	2	31	28	20	1	3	27	12	5.23	64	.275	.439	10-0	.100	-1	22	-4	-0.4
Total	2	1	4	.200	17	4	1	2	52.2	53	36	1	3	41	23	4.96	63	.288	.425	19-0	.053	-2	41	-8	-1.0
EVANS, ROY Roy B 3.19.1874 Knoxville, TN D 8.15.1915 Galveston, TX BR/TR 6/180# d5.15																									
1897	StL N	0	0	—	3	0	0	0	13	33	27	1	0	13	4	9.69	45	.471	.554	3-0	.000	0		-10	-0.4
	Lou N	5	4	.556	9	8	6	0	59.1	66	40	4	8	24	20	4.10	104	.280	.366	23-0	.130	-2	94	2	0.0
	Year	5	4	.556	12	8	6	0	72.1	99	46	5	8	37	24	5.10	84	.324	.410	26-0	.115	-2	93	-10	-0.4
1898	Was N	3	3	.500	7	6	4	0	50.2	50	27	0	7	25	11	3.38	109	.256	.361	19-0	.053	-2	94	2	-0.1
1899	Was N	3	4	.429	7	7	6	0	54	60	40	1	0	25	27	5.67	69	.280	.356	20-2	.200	-1	100	-8	-0.8
1902	NY N	8	13	.381	23	17	17	0	176	186	87	2	9	58	48	3.17	89	.271	.336	54-4	.148	-1	54	-5	-0.5
	Bro N	5	6	.455	13	11	11-2	0	97.1	91	42	0	2	33	35	2.68	103	.247	.313	34-0	.265	2	58	0	0.1
	Year	13	19	.406	36	28	28-2	0	273.1	277	44	2	11	91	83	3.00	93	.263	.328	88-4	.193	1	56	-8	-0.4
1903	Bro N	5	9	.357	15	12	9	0	110	121	75	1	7	41	42	3.27	98	.297	.371	29-4	.172	0	58	-7	-0.8
	StL A	0	4	.000	7	7	4	0	54	66	30	1	3	14	24	4.17	70	.300	.350	19-1	.105	-1	60	-6	-0.5
Total	5	29	43	.403	84	68	57-2	0	614.1	673	368	10	36	233	211	3.66	88	.281	.353	201-11	.159	-4	72	-32	-3.0
EVANS, RED Russell Edison B 11.12.1906 Chicago, IL D 6.14.1982 Lakeview, AR BR/TR 5-11/168# d4.24																									
1936	Chi A	0	3	.000	17	0	0	1	47.1	70	46	4	0	22	19	7.61	68	.338	.402	15-0	.133	-1*		-12	-0.7
1939	Bro N	1	8	.111	24	6	0	1	64.1	74	43	4	0	26	28	5.18	78	.284	.348	13-2	.308	1	29	-9	-0.9
Total	2	1	11	.083	41	6	0	2	111.2	144	89	8	0	48	47	6.21	73	.308	.372	28-2	.214	-0	29	-21	-1.6
EVANS, JAKE Uriah L. P. "Bloody Jake" B 9.1856 Baltimore, MD D 1.16.1907 Baltimore, MD TR 5-8/154# d5.1.1879 ▲																									
1880	Tro N	0	0	—	1	0	0	0	4	11	8	0		0	0	13.50	19	.524	.524	180	.256	0*		-4	-0.1
1882	Wor N	0	1	.000	1	1	1	0	8	13	10	1		0	2	5.63	55	.317	.317	334	.213	-0*	119	-2	-0.2
1883	Cle N	0	0	—	1	0	0	0	3	0	0	0		0	1	0.00	—	.000	.000	332	.238	0*		1	0.1
Total	3	0	1	.000	3	1	1	0	15	24	18	1		0	3	6.60	45	.338	.338	846	.232	-0	119	-5	-0.2
EVANS, ART William Arthur B 8.3.1911 Elvins, MO D 1.8.1952 Wichita, KS BB/TL 6-1.5/181# d6.20																									
1932	Chi A	0	0	—	7	0	0	0	18	19	9	1	0	10	6	3.00	144	.257	.345	5-0	.000	-0		2	0.1
EVANS, BILL William James B 2.10.1894 Reidsville, NC D 12.21.1946 Burlington, NC BR/TR 6/175# d8.13 Mil 1918																									
1916	Pit N	2	5	.286	13	7	3	0	63	57	27	2	3	16	21	3.00	89	.249	.306	20-1	.150	-1	56	-2	-0.2
1917	Pit N	0	4	.000	8	2	1	0	26.2	24	14	0	1	14	5	3.38	84	.231	.328	9-0	.111	-0	27	-2	-0.3
1919	Pit N	0	4	.000	7	3	2	0	36.2	41	25	1	0	18	15	5.65	53	.297	.378	11-1	.000	-1	44	-10	-1.1
Total	3	2	13	.133	28	12	6	0	126.1	122	66	3	4	48	41	3.85	73	.259	.333	40-2	.100	-2	47	-14	-1.6
EVANS, BILL William Lawrence B 3.25.1919 Quanah, TX D 11.30.1983 Grand Junction, CO BR/TR 6-2/180# d4.21																									
1949	Chi A	0	1	.000	4	0	0	0	6.1	6	6	0	0	8	1	7.11	59	.261	.452	1-0	.000	-0		-2	-0.3
1951	Bos A	0	0	—	9	0	0	0	15.1	15	8	0	0	8	3	4.11	109	.268	.359	4-0	.000	-1		1	-0.1
Total	2	0	1	.000	13	0	0	0	21.2	21	14	0	0	16	4	4.98	88	.266	.389	5-0	.000	-1		-1	-0.4
EVERITT, LEON Edward Leon B 1.12.1947 Marshall, TX BL/TR 6-1.5/195# d4.21																									
1969	SD N	0	1	.000	5	0	0	0-0	15.2	18	14	4	1	12-1	11	8.04	44	.300	.425	3-0	.000	-0*		-7	-0.4
EVERSGERD, BRYAN Bryan David B 2.11.1969 Centralia, IL BR/TL 6-1/190# d4.30																									
1994	StL N	2	3	.400	40	1	0	0-1	67.2	75	36	8	2	20-1	47	4.52	92	.295	.349	6-2	.000	-1	66	-3	-0.2
1995	Mon N	0	0	—	25	0	0	0-0	21	22	13	2	1	9-2	8	5.14	84	.268	.340	1-0	.000	-0		-2	-0.1
1997	Tex A	0	2	.000	3	0	0	0-0	1.1	5	3	0	0	3-0	2	20.25	24	.556	.667	0-0	—	0		-2	-0.4
1998	StL N	0	0	—	8	0	0	0-0	6	9	7	1	1	2-0	4	9.00	47	.346	.387	0-0	—	0		-3	-0.2
Total	4	2	5	.286	76	1	0	0-1	96	111	59	11	4	34-3	61	5.16	81	.299	.359	7-2	.000	-1	66	-10	-0.9
EWING, BOB George Lemuel "Long Bob" B 4.24.1873 New Hampshire, OH D 6.20.1947 Wapakoneta, OH BR/TR 6-1.5/170# d4.19																									
1902	Cin N	5	6	.455	15	12	10	0	117.2	126	67	1	3	47	44	2.98	101	.274	.345	71-0	.169	-1*	125	-2	-0.4
1903	Cin N	14	13	.519	29	28	27-1	1	246.2	254	127	3	10	64	104	2.77	128	.265	.317	95-1	.253	4*	93	17	2.3
1904	Cin N	11	13	.458	26	24	22	0	212	198	85	3	4	58	99	2.46	119	.253	.308	97-0	.258	5*	92	11	1.7
1905	Cin N	20	11	.645	40	34	30-4	0	311.2	284	125	5	11	79	164	2.51	132	.246	.301	122-5	.262	4*	113	27	2.9
1906	Cin N	13	14	.481	33	32	26-2	0	287.2	248	98	4	2	60	145	2.38	116	.238	.281	101-1	.139	-3	87	15	1.0
1907	Cin N	17	19	.472	41	37	32-2	0	332.2	279	104	2	7	85	147	1.73	150	.231	.286	123-10	.154	-1*	100	26	2.6
1908	Cin N	17	15	.531	37	32	23-4	3	293.2	247	105	5	5	57	95	2.21	105	.241	.284	94-4	.149	-0	100	3	0.2
1909	Cin N	11	12	.478	31	29	14-2	0	218.1	195	94	1	6	63	86	2.43	107	.238	.298	73-5	.110	-4	105	2	-0.4
1910	Phi N	16	14	.533	34	32	20-4	0	255.1	235	110	5	7	86	102	3.00	104	.251	.318	90-4	.222	2	106	5	0.6
1911	Phi N	0	1	.000	4	3	1	0	24	29	25	2	0	14	12	7.88	44	.309	.398	6-1	.333	0	138	-11	-0.5
1912	StL N	0	0	—	1	1	0	0	1.1	2	0	0	0	1	0	0.00	—	.333	.429	0-0	—	0	86	1	0.0
Total	11	124	118	.512	291	264	205-19	4	2301	2097	940	31	55	614	998	2.49	116	.247	.302	872-31	.195	7	102	94	10.0
EWING, JOHN John "Long John" B 6.1.1863 Cincinnati, OH D 4.23.1895 Denver, CO TR 6-1/168# d6.18.1883 b-Buck																									
1888	Lou AA	8	13	.381	21	21	21-2	0	191	175	105	3	8	34	87	2.83	109	.235	.276	79	.203	-2	78	8	0.6
1889	Lou AA	6	30	.167	40	39	37-1	0	331	407	296	6	14	147	155	4.87	79	.293	.367	134	.172	-6*	64	-37	-3.3
1890	NY P	18	12	.600	35	31	27-1	2	267.1	294	196	6	16	104	145	4.24	107	.267	.339	114	.211	-3	92	10	0.6

Year	Tm Lg	W	L	Pct	G	GS	CG-Sho	SV-BS	IP	H	R	HR	HB	BB-IB	SO	ERA	AERA	OAV	OOB	AB-SH	AVG	PB	Sup	APR	PW
1891	NY N	21	8	**.724**	33	30	28-5	0	269.1	237	118	2	11	105	138	**2.27**	141	.227	.305	113	.204	-2	108	30	2.5
Total 4		53	63	.457	129	121	113-9	2	1058.2	1113	715	17	49	390	525	3.68	101	.260	.329	440	.195	-12	85	11	0.4
EWING, BUCK William B 10.17.1859 Hoagland, OH D 10.20.1906 Cincinnati, OH BR/TR 5-10/188# d9.9.1880 M7 HF1939 b-John ▲																									
1882	Tro N	0	0	—	1	0	0	0	1	2	1	0		1	0	9.00	31	.400	.500	328	.271	0*		0	0.0
1884	NY N	0	1	.000	1	1	1	0	8	7	3	0		4	3	1.13	265	.241	.333	382	.277	0*	36	1	0.2
1885	NY N	0	1	.000	1	0	0	0	2	4	4	0		3	0	4.50	59	.444	.583	342	.304	0*		-1	-0.2
1888	†NY N	0	0	—	2	0	0	0	7	8	9	1	1	4	6	2.57	107	.174	.255	415	.306	1*		-1	0.0
1889	†NY N	2	0	1.000	3	2	2	0	20	23	14	0	0	8	12	4.05	97	.280	.344	407	.327	2*	136	0	0.1
1890	NY P	0	1	.000	1	1	1	0	9	11	5	1	0	3	2	4.00	114	.289	.341	352	.338	0*	27	1	0.1
Total 6		2	3	.400	9	4	4	0	47	55	36	2	1	23	23	3.45	105	.263	.339	2226	.305	4	86	0	0.2
EYRE, SCOTT Scott Alan B 5.30.1972 Inglewood, CA BL/TL 6-1/160# d8.1																									
1997	Chi A	4	4	.500	11	11	0	0-0	60.2	62	36	11	1	31-1	36	5.04	87	.267	.353	2-0	.500	0	91	-4	-0.4
1998	Chi A	3	8	.273	33	17	0	0-0	107	114	78	24	2	64-0	73	5.38	85	.271	.368	3-0	.000	-0	101	-13	-1.1
1999	Chi A	1	1	.500	21	0	0	0-0	25	38	22	6	1	15-2	17	7.56	65	.339	.419	0-0	—	0		-7	-0.5
2000	Chi A	1	1	.500	13	1	0	0-0	19	29	15	3	1	12-0	16	6.63	75	.372	.452	0-0	—	0	94	-3	-0.3
2001	Tor A	1	2	.333	17	0	0	2-1	15.2	15	6	1	1	7-2	16	3.45	133	.263	.348	0-0	—	0		2	0.4
2002	Tor A	2	4	.333	49	3	0	0-1	63.1	69	37	4	0	29-7	51	4.97	93	.278	.349	0-0	—	0	127	-2	-0.2
	†SF N	0	0	—	21	0	0	0-0	11.1	11	4	0	0	7-1	7	1.59	245	.256	.360	0-0	—	0		2	0.1
2003	†SF N	2	1	.667	74	0	0	1-2	57	60	23	4	1	26-0	35	3.32	124	.268	.343	2-0	.500	0		5	0.3
Total 7		14	21	.400	239	32	0	3-4	359	398	221	53	7	191-13	251	4.94	91	.281	.366	7-0	.286	0	101	-20	-1.7
EYRICH, GEORGE George Lincoln B 3.3.1925 Reading, PA BR/TR 5-11/175# d6.13 Mil 1943-46																									
1943	Phi N	0	0	—	9	0	0	0	18.2	27	8	1	0	9	5	3.38	100	.342	.409	2-0	.000	-0		0	0.0
FABER, RED Urban Charles B 9.6.1888 Cascade, IA D 9.25.1976 Chicago, IL BB/TR 6-2/180# d4.17 Mil 1918 C3 HF1964																									
1914	Chi A	10	9	.526	40	19	11-2	**4**	181.1	154	77	3	12	64	88	2.68	100	.239	.319	55-2	.145	2	100	0	0.3
1915	Chi A	24	14	.632	**50**	32	21-2	2	299.2	264	118	3	11	99	182	2.55	117	.240	.309	84-12	.131	2	134	12	1.9
1916	Chi A	17	9	.654	35	25	15-3	1	205.1	167	67	1	5	61	87	2.02	137	.228	.292	63-4	.095	-3	102	15	1.7
1917	†Chi A	16	13	.552	41	29	16-3	3	248	224	92	1	10	85	84	1.92	138	.247	.319	69-8	.058	-4	113	13	1.2
1918	Chi A	4	1	.800	11	9	5-1	1	80.2	70	23	3	0	23	26	1.23	223	.245	.301	24-2	.042	-2	98	10	0.5
1919	Chi A	11	9	.550	25	20	9	0	162.1	185	92	7	8	45	45	3.83	83	.287	.341	54-3	.185	-0	112	-14	-1.6
1920	Chi A	23	13	.639	40	**39**	28-2	1	319	332	136	8	4	88	108	2.99	126	.277	.328	104-6	.106	-4	124	24	2.0
1921	Chi A	25	15	.625	43	39	**32**-4	1	330.2	293	107	10	7	87	124	**2.48**	**171**	**.242**	**.297**	108-8	.148	-4	84	**64**	**6.8**
1922	Chi A	21	17	.553	43	38	**31**-4	2	**352**	334	128	10	6	83	148	**2.81**	**145**	.252	**.299**	125-10	.200	-2	89	**47**	4.6
1923	Chi A	14	11	.560	32	31	15-2	0	232.1	233	114	6	6	62	91	3.41	116	.259	.311	69-8	.217	3*	100	10	1.4
1924	Chi A	9	11	.450	21	20	9	0	161.1	173	78	5	2	58	47	3.85	107	.282	.346	54-2	.148	-2	106	7	0.4
1925	Chi A	12	11	.522	34	32	16-1	0	238	266	117	8	2	59	71	3.78	110	.289	.333	77-6	.104	-4	106	10	0.5
1926	Chi A	15	9	.625	27	25	13-1	0	184.2	203	84	3	2	57	65	3.56	109	.281	.335	60-6	.150	-0	110	7	0.6
1927	Chi A	4	7	.364	18	15	6	0	110.2	131	64	2	5	41	39	4.55	89	.312	.380	37-5	.270	2	77	-5	-0.2
1928	Chi A	13	9	.591	27	27	16-2	0	201.1	223	98	11	4	68	43	3.75	108	.286	.347	70-4	.114	-3	94	7	0.4
1929	Chi A	13	13	.500	31	31	15-1	0	234	241	119	10	9	61	68	3.88	110	.273	.327	78-4	.128	-3	87	11	0.8
1930	Chi A	8	13	.381	29	26	10	1	169	188	101	7	5	49	62	4.21	110	.283	.337	49-5	.041	-5	83	7	0.3
1931	Chi A	10	14	.417	44	19	5-1	1	184	210	96	11	3	57	49	3.82	112	.285	.339	53-4	.075	-3	70	8	0.6
1932	Chi A	2	11	.154	42	5	0	6	106	123	61	0	1	38	26	3.74	116	.290	.350	18-4	.222	3	118	5	0.8
1933	Chi A	3	4	.429	36	2	0	5	86.1	92	41	2	1	28	18	3.44	123	.275	.332	18-1	.000	-3	50	7	0.3
Total 20		254	213	.544	669	483	273-29	28	4086.2	4106	1813	111	103	1213	1471	3.15	119	.266	.323	1269-104	.134	-31	100	245	23.3
FACE, ROY Elroy Leon B 2.20.1928 Stephentown, NY BR/TR 5-8/155# d4.16																									
1953	Pit N	6	8	.429	41	13	2	0	119	145	90	19	2	30	56	6.58	68	.297	.340	30-4	.133	-1*	81	-23	-2.5
1955	Pit N	5	7	.417	42	10	4	5	125.2	128	58	10	0	40-4	84	3.58	115	.268	.323	26-3	.115	-1*	58	7	0.5
1956	Pit N	12	13	.480	**68**	3	0	6	135.1	131	57	16	1	42-15	96	3.52	107	.256	.313	26-1	.192	-0*	86	5	1.0
1957	Pit N	4	6	.400	59	1	0	10	93.2	97	41	9	1	24-5	53	3.07	123	.270	.311	16-1	.125	-1	70	6	0.6
1958	Pit N	5	2	.714	57	0	0	**20**	84	77	30	6	0	22-6	47	2.89	134	.244	.293	7-2	.000	-1		9	1.2
1959	Pit N★	18	1	**.947**	57	0	0	10	93.1	91	29	5	1	25-8	69	2.70	143	.266	.315	13-1	.231	0*		14	2.8
1960	†Pit N★	10	8	.556	**68**	0	0	24	114.2	93	39	11	0	29-9	72	2.90	129	.226	.274	17-2	.412	2		11	2.6
1961	Pit N★	6	12	.333	62	0	0	**17**	92	94	44	12	1	10-4	55	3.82	105	.267	.287	11-0	.273	0		2	0.5
1962	Pit N	8	7	.533	63	0	0	**28**	91	74	23	7	1	18-7	45	1.88	209	.231	.270	12-1	.083	-1		**20**	4.1
1963	Pit N	3	9	.250	56	0	0	16	69.2	75	33	6	3	19-11	41	3.23	102	.285	.338	8-0	.250	0		-1	-0.1
1964	Pit N	3	3	.500	55	0	0	4	79.2	82	48	11	1	27-10	63	5.20	68	.269	.324	4-0	.000	-0		-13	-1.1
1965	Pit N	5	2	.714	16	0	0	0	20.1	20	6	1	0	7-5	19	2.66	132	.263	.321	1-0	.000	-0		2	0.5
1966	Pit N	6	6	.500	54	0	0	18	70	68	24	9	1	24-5	67	2.70	132	.262	.325	11-1	.000	-1		7	1.3
1967	Pit N	7	5	.583	61	0	0	17	74.1	62	23	5	0	22-11	41	2.42	139	.230	.286	6-0	.000	-1		8	1.6
1968	Pit N	2	4	.333	43	0	0	13	52	46	17	3	2	7-2	34	2.60	113	.238	.271	4-1	.000	-0		2	0.3
	Det A	0	0	—	2	0	0	0	1	2	0	0	0	1-1	1	0.00	—	.500	.600	0-0	—	0		0	0.0
1969	Mon N	4	2	.667	44	0	0	5-1	59.1	62	29	11	0	15-3	34	3.94	93	.263	.307	2-1	.500	0		-1	-0.1
Total 16		104	95	.523	848	27	6	193-1	1375	1347	591	141	14	362-**106**	877	3.48	109	.260	.308	194-18	.160	-4	81	55	13.2
FAETH, TONY Anthony Joseph B 7.9.1893 Aberdeen, SD D 12.22.1982 St.Paul, MN BR/TR 6/180# d8.10																									
1919	Cle A	0	0	—	6	0	0	0	18.1	13	4	0	0	10	7	0.49	682	.224	.338	4-0	.000	-1		5	0.2
1920	Cle A	0	0	—	13	0	0	0	25	31	19	0	1	20	14	4.32	88	.333	.456	5-0	.000	-1		-3	-0.2
Total 2		0	0	—	19	0	0	0	43.1	44	23	0	1	30	21	2.70	134	.291	.412	9-0	.000	-1		2	0.0
FAGAN, EVERETT Everett Joseph B 1.13.1918 Pottersville, NJ D 2.16.1983 Morristown, NJ BR/TR 6/195# d4.24 Mil 1943-46																									
1943	Phi A	2	6	.250	18	2	0	3	37.1	41	28	4	2	14	9	6.27	54	.283	.354	7-0	.000	-0	124	-11	-2.2
1946	Phi A	0	1	.000	20	0	0	0	45	47	27	2	3	24	12	4.80	74	.264	.361	14-0	.286	1		-6	-0.2
Total 2		2	7	.222	38	2	0	3	82.1	88	55	6	5	38	21	5.47	64	.272	.358	21-0	.190	1	124	-17	-2.4
FAGAN, BILL William A. "Clinkers" B 2.15.1869 Troy, NY D 3.21.1930 Troy, NY TL 5-11/165# d9.15																									
1887	NY AA	1	4	.200	6	6	6	0	45	55	34	1	2	24	12	4.00	106	.306	.393	21	.143	-2	50	0	-0.1
1888	KC AA	5	11	.313	17	17	15	0	142.1	179	148	4	1	75	49	5.69	60	.296	.375	65	.215	-1*	91	-33	-2.8
Total 2		6	15	.286	23	23	21	0	187.1	234	182	5	3	99	61	5.28	69	.298	.379	86	.198	-3	79	-33	-2.9
FAHEY, FRANK Francis Raymond B 1.22.1896 Milford, MA D 3.19.1954 Boston, MA BB/TR 6-1/190# d4.25 ▲																									
1918	Phi A	0	0	—	3	0	0	0	9	5	7	0	1	14	1	6.00	49	.200	.500	17-1	.176	-0*		-3	-0.2
FAHR, JERRY Gerald Warren B 12.9.1924 Marmaduke, AR BR/TR 6-5/185# d4.29																									
1951	Cle A	0	0	—	5	0	0	0	5.2	11	3	0	0	2	0	4.76	80	.500	.542	0-0	—	0		0	0.0
FAHRER, PETE Clarence Willie B 3.10.1890 Holgate, OH D 6.10.1967 Fremont, MI BL/TR 6/190# d8.17																									
1914	Cin N	0	0	—	5	0	0	0	8	8	3	0	0	4	2	1.13	260	.308	.400	1-0	.000	-0		1	0.1
FAIRBANK, JIM James Lee "Lee" or "Smoky" B 3.17.1881 Deansboro, NY D 12.27.1955 Utica, NY BR/TR 5-9.5/175# d9.18																									
1903	Phi A	1	1	.500	4	1	1	0	24	33	14	1	0	12	10	4.88	63	.327	.398	10-0	.100	-1	164	-4	-0.3
1904	Phi A	0	1	.000	3	1	1	0	17	19	14	0	2	13	6	6.35	42	.284	.415	6-0	.000	-1	0	-6	-0.4
Total 2		1	2	.333	7	2	2	0	41	52	28	1	2	25	16	5.49	53	.310	.405	16-0	.063	-1	86	-10	-0.7
FAIRCLOTH, RAGS James Lamar B 8.19.1892 Kenton, TN D 10.5.1953 Tucson, AZ BR/TR 5-11/160# d5.6																									
1919	Phi N	0	0	—	2	0	0	0	2	5	2	0	0	0	0	9.00	36	.625	.625	0-0	—	0		-1	-0.1
FAJARDO, HECTOR Hector (Nabaratte) B 11.16.1970 Sahuayo, Mexico BR/TR 6-4/185# d8.10																									
1991	Pit N	0	0	—	2	2	0	0-0	6.1	10	7	0	0	7-0	8	9.95	36	.357	.486	3-0	.000	-0	189	-4	-0.2
	Tex A	0	2	.000	4	3	0	0-0	19	25	13	2	1	4-0	15	5.68	71	.329	.357	0-0	—	0	113	-3	-0.3
1993	Tex A	0	0	—	1	0	0	0-0	0.2	0	0	0	0	0-0	1	0.00	—	.000	.000	0-0	—	0		0	0.0
1994	Tex A	5	7	.417	18	12	0	0-0	83.1	95	67	15	2	26-0	45	6.91	70	.284	.336	0-0	—	0	76	-17	-1.9

Year	Tm Lg	W	L	Pct	G	GS	CG-Sho	SV-BS	IP	H	R	HR	HB	BB-IB	SO	ERA	AERA	OAV	OOB	AB-SH	AVG	PB	Sup	APR	PW
1995	Tex A	0	0	—	5	0	0	0-0	15	19	13	2	1	5-0	9	7.80	62	.311	.373	0-0	—	0		-4	-0.2
Total	4	5	9	.357	30	17	0	0-0	124.1	149	100	19	4	42-0	78	6.95	67	.297	.352	3-0	.000	-0	91	-28	-2.6
FALCONE, PETE Peter Frank B 10.1.1953 Brooklyn, NY BL/TL 6-2/185# d4.13																									
1975	SF N	12	11	.522	34	32	3-1	0-0	190	171	97	16	4	111-7	131	4.17	91	.244	.348	65-4	.062	-5	92	-6	-1.2
1976	StL N	12	16	.429	32	32	9-2	0-0	212	173	87	12	2	93-1	138	3.23	110	.222	.303	62-12	.129	-1	85	8	0.6
1977	StL N	4	8	.333	27	22	1-1	1-0	124	130	79	19	3	61-3	75	5.44	71	.273	.355	41-4	.244	2	126	-20	-1.6
1978	StL N	2	7	.222	19	14	0	0-0	75	94	52	9	2	48-2	28	5.76	61	.319	.414	21-2	.238	1	87	-18	-1.9
1979	NY N	6	14	.300	33	31	1-1	0-0	184	194	91	24	1	76-10	113	4.16	88	.276	.343	52-5	.173	0	83	-9	-1.0
1980	NY N	7	10	.412	37	23	1	1-0	157.1	163	89	16	2	58-9	109	4.52	79	.269	.332	41-6	.146	-1	117	-17	-1.9
1981	NY N	5	3	.625	35	9	3-1	1-0	95.1	84	32	3	0	36-4	56	2.55	137	.241	.308	22-0	.182	1	119	10	0.8
1982	NY N	8	10	.444	40	23	3	2-1	171	159	82	24	1	71-4	101	3.84	95	.252	.326	53-2	.113	-2	85	-3	-0.6
1983	Atl N	9	4	.692	33	15	2	0-0	106.2	102	47	14	1	60-2	59	3.63	107	.256	.352	26-5	.115	-1	120	3	0.1
1984	Atl N	5	7	.417	35	16	2-1	2-1	120	115	61	15	0	57-3	55	4.13	94	.252	.333	33-3	.212	1	99	-3	-0.2
Total	10	70	90	.438	325	217	25-7	7-2	1435.1	1385	717	152	16	671-45	865	4.07	90	.257	.337	416-43	.149	-6	99	-55	-6.9
FALK, CHET Chester Emanuel "Spot" B 5.15.1905 Austin, TX D 1.7.1982 Austin, TX BL/TL 6-2/170# d4.20 b-Bibb																									
1925	StL A	0	0	—	13	0	0	0	25	38	26	2	0	17	7	8.28	56	.362	.451	8-0	.625	2*		-9	-0.2
1926	StL A	4	4	.500	18	8	3	0	74	95	53	1	6	27	7	5.35	80	.338	.408	31-0	.194	-1*	115	-8	-0.9
1927	StL A	1	0	1.000	9	0	0	0	15.2	25	18	1	0	10	2	5.74	76	.352	.432	5-0	.200	-0		-5	-0.3
Total	3	5	4	.556	40	8	3	0	114.2	158	97	4	6	54	16	6.04	73	.346	.422	44-0	.273	1	115	-22	-1.4
FALKENBERG, CY Frederick Peter B 12.17.1879 Chicago, IL D 4.15.1961 San Francisco, CA BR/TR 6-5/180# d4.21																									
1903	Pit N	1	5	.167	10	6	3	0	56	65	43	0	2	32	24	3.86	84	.295	.390	21-1	.190	-0	90	-6	-0.5
1905	Was A	7	2	.778	12	10	6-2	0	75.1	71	41	1	5	31	35	3.82	69	.251	.335	32-0	.125	-2	209	-8	-1.1
1906	Was A	14	20	.412	40	36	30-2	1	298.2	277	136	1	13	108	178	2.86	92	.249	.323	106-4	.170	1	118	-9	-0.8
1907	Was A	6	17	.261	32	24	17-1	1	233.2	195	105	0	8	77	108	2.35	103	.229	.299	86-0	.140	-3*	99	-3	-0.6
1908	Was A	6	2	.750	17	8	5-1	0	82.2	70	29	2	2	21	34	1.96	117	.236	.291	27-1	.222	0	150	2	0.3
	Cle A	2	4	.333	8	7	2	0	46.1	52	25	1	2	10	17	3.88	62	.284	.328	17-0	.118	-1	135	-6	-0.9
	Year	8	6	.571	25	15	7-1	0	129	122	30	3	4	31	51	2.65	88	.254	.305	44-1	.182	-1	143	-4	-0.6
1909	Cle A	10	9	.526	24	18	13-2	0	165	135	56	0	5	50	82	2.40	107	.231	.297	52-3	.173	-1	69	5	0.7
1910	Cle A	14	13	.519	37	29	18-3	1	256.2	246	114	3	8	75	107	2.95	88	.261	.320	82-3	.183	-0	85	-9	-0.8
1911	Cle A	8	5	.615	15	13	7	1	106.2	117	56	0	3	24	46	3.29	104	.282	.326	40-5	.175	-1*	102	0	-0.1
1913	Cle A	23	10	.697	39	36	23-6	0	276	238	85	2	5	88	166	2.22	137	.237	.302	84-6	.119	-2	97	27	2.9
1914	Ind F	25	16	.610	**49**	**43**	33-**9**	3	**377.1**	332	127	5	5	89	**236**	2.22	141	.236	.284	125-12	.168	-4	109	33	3.2
1915	New F	9	11	.450	25	21	14	1	172	175	78	6	9	47	76	3.24	79	.268	.326	57-5	.053	-7	105	-11	-1.9
	Bro F	3	3	.500	7	7	5-1	0	48	31	15	1	1	12	20	1.50	181	.189	.249	15-1	.067	-2	59	5	0.4
	Year	12	14	.462	32	28	19-1	1	220	206	17	7	10	59	96	2.86	91	.252	.311	72-6	.056	-9	93	-7	-1.5
1917	Phi A	2	6	.250	15	8	4	0	80.2	86	53	1	0	26	35	3.35	82	.293	.350	27-2	.185	0	72	-9	-0.7
Total	12	130	123	.514	330	266	180-27	8	2275	2090	963	23	68	690	1164	2.68	103	.248	.311	771-43	.152	-23	104	11	0.1
FALKENBORG, BRIAN Brian Thomas B 1.18.1978 Newport Beach, CA BR/TR 6-6/187# d10.1																									
1999	Bal A	0	0	—	2	0	0	0-0	3	2	0	0	0	2-0	1	0.00	—	.200	.333	0-0	—	0		2	0.1
FALLENSTEIN, ED Edward Joseph "Jack" (b: Edward Joseph Valestin) B 12.22.1908 Newark, NJ D 11.24.1971 Orange, NJ BR/TR 6-3/180# d4.16																									
1931	Phi N	0	0	—	24	0	0	0	41.2	56	37	2	0	26	15	7.13	60	.333	.423	5-0	.200	0		-11	-0.5
1933	Bos N	2	1	.667	9	4	1-1	0	35	43	23	1	1	13	5	3.60	85	.305	.368	8-1	.375	1*	122	-6	-0.3
Total	2	2	1	.667	33	4	1-1	0	76.2	99	60	3	1	39	20	5.52	67	.320	.398	13-1	.308	1	122	-17	-0.8
FALLON, BOB Robert Joseph B 2.18.1960 Bronx, NY BL/TL 6-3/200# d4.26																									
1984	Chi A	0	0	—	3	3	0	0-0	14.2	12	7	0	0	11-0	10	3.68	113	.235	.371	0-0	—	0	130	1	0.0
1985	Chi A	0	0	—	10	0	0	0-0	16	25	11	5	0	9-2	17	6.19	70	.362	.430	0-0	—	0		-3	-0.1
Total	2	0	0	—	13	3	0	0-0	30.2	37	18	5	0	20-2	27	4.99	85	.308	.404	0-0	—	0	130	-2	-0.1
FALTEISEK, STEVE Steven James B 1.28.1972 Mineola, NY BR/TR 6-2/200# d7.21																									
1997	Mon N	0	0	—	5	0	0	0-0	8	8	4	0	1	3-0	2	3.38	124	.286	.353	2-1	.000	-0		0	0.0
1999	Mil N	0	0	—	10	0	0	0-0	12	18	10	3	0	3-0	5	7.50	61	.375	.404	1-0	.000	-0*		-4	-0.2
Total	2	0	0	—	15	0	0	0-0	20	26	14	3	1	6-0	7	5.85	75	.342	.384	3-1	.000	-0		-4	-0.2
FANNIN, CLIFF Clifford Bryson "Mule" B 5.13.1924 Louisa, KY D 12.11.1966 Sandusky, OH BL/TR 6/170# d9.2																									
1945	StL A	0	0	—	5	0	0	0	10.1	8	3	0	0	5	5	2.61	135	.222	.317	1-0	.000	-0		1	0.0
1946	StL A	5	2	.714	27	7	4-1	2	86.2	76	37	4	1	42	52	3.01	124	.236	.326	31-0	.161	-1	128	5	0.3
1947	StL A	6	8	.429	26	18	6-2	1	145.2	134	70	10	1	77	77	3.58	108	.245	.340	46-4	.196	-0	94	3	0.2
1948	StL A	10	14	.417	34	29	10-3	1	213.2	198	106	14	1	104	102	4.17	109	.245	.332	65-6	.169	-0*	94	10	0.9
1949	StL A	8	14	.364	30	25	5	1	143	177	106	15	0	93	57	6.17	73	.308	.404	55-1	.164	-2*	92	-21	-3.0
1950	StL A	5	9	.357	25	16	3	1	102	116	82	18	0	58	42	6.53	76	.280	.369	34-0	.176	-2*	87	-15	-1.9
1951	StL A	0	2	.000	7	1	0	0	15.1	20	16	7	0	5	11	6.46	68	.317	.368	4-0	.250	-0*	202	-5	-0.5
1952	StL A	0	2	.000	10	2	0	0	16.1	34	25	5	0	9	6	12.67	31	.453	.512	1-0	.000	0*	67	-14	-1.5
Total	8	34	51	.400	164	98	28-6	6	733	763	445	73	3	393	352	4.85	89	.269	.358	237-11	.173	-5	96	-36	-5.5
FANNING, JACK John Jacob B 1863 S.Orange, NJ D 6.10.1917 Aberdeen, WA TR 5-9/163# d9.20																									
1889	Ind N	0	1	.000	1	1	0	0	1	3	3	0	0	2	0	18.00	23	.500	.625	1	.000	-0	161	-2	-0.2
1894	Phi N	1	3	.250	6	4	2	0	34.1	54	52	4	2	22	7	8.91	58	.353	.441	14-0	.143	-1	100	-17	-1.3
Total	2	1	4	.200	7	5	2	0	35.1	57	55	4	2	24	7	9.17	56	.358	.449	15-0	.133	-1	108	-19	-1.5
FANOK, HARRY Harry Michael "The Flame Thrower" B 5.11.1940 Whippany, NJ BB/TR 6/180# d4.16																									
1963	StL N	2	1	.667	12	0	0	1	25.2	24	16	3	1	21-1	25	5.26	67	.255	.387	5-0	.400	1		-4	-0.4
1964	StL N	0	0	—	4	0	0	0	7.2	5	6	0	0	3-0	10	5.87	65	.179	.250	1-0	.000	-0		-2	-0.1
Total	2	2	1	.667	16	0	0	1	33.1	29	22	3	1	24-1	35	5.40	67	.238	.358	6-0	.333	1		-6	-0.5
FANOVICH, FRANK Frank Joseph "Lefty" B 1.11.1922 New York, NY BL/TL 5-11/180# d4.25																									
1949	Cin N	0	2	.000	29	1	0	0	43.1	44	31	2	2	28	27	5.40	77	.257	.368	4-0	.000	-0	42	-6	-0.3
1953	Phi A	0	3	.000	26	3	0	0	61.2	62	41	5	6	37	37	5.55	77	.273	.389	11-0	.182	-0	69	-8	-0.5
Total	2	0	5	.000	55	4	0	0	105	106	72	7	8	65	64	5.49	77	.266	.380	15-0	.133	-1	63	-14	-0.8
FANSLER, STAN Stanley Robert B 2.12.1965 Elkins, WV BR/TR 5-11/180# d9.6																									
1986	Pit N	0	3	.000	5	5	0	0-0	24	20	12	2	0	15-0	13	3.75	102	.247	.361	6-1	.167	-0	56	0	0.0
FANWELL, HARRY Harry Clayton B 10.16.1886 Patapsco, MD D 7.15.1965 Baltimore, MD BR/TR 6/175# d7.23																									
1910	Cle A	2	9	.182	17	11	5-1	0	92	87	52	0	6	38	30	3.62	71	.260	.347	30-1	.033	-3	47	-10	-1.5
FARMER, ED Edward Joseph B 10.18.1949 Evergreen Park, IL BR/TR 6-5/210# d6.9																									
1971	Cle A	5	4	.556	43	4	0	4-1	78.2	77	42	9	3	41-3	48	4.35	88	.263	.356	14-1	.071	-1	64	-4	-0.6
1972	Cle A	2	5	.286	46	1	0	7-2	61.1	51	32	10	1	27-6	33	4.40	73	.231	.316	7-1	.143	-0	137	-7	-1.0
1973	Cle A	0	2	.000	16	0	0	1-1	17.1	25	12	4	0	5-0	10	4.67	84	.325	.361	0-0	—	0		-2	-0.3
	Det A	3	0	1.000	24	0	0	2-0	45	52	26	3	2	27-0	28	5.00	82	.292	.389	0-0	—	0		-4	-0.3
	Year	3	2	.600	40	0	0	3-1	62.1	77	43	7	2	32-0	38	4.91	82	.302	.381	0-0	—	0		-6	-0.6
1974	Phi N	2	1	.667	14	3	0	0-0	31	41	32	5	0	27-0	20	8.42	45	.323	.433	9-0	.111	-1	131	-15	-1.4
1977	Bal A	0	0	—	1	0	0	0-0	0	1	1	0	0	1-0	0	∞	—	1.000	1.000	0-0	—	0		-1	-0.1
1978	Mil A	1	0	1.000	3	0	0	1-0	11	7	1	1	0	4-0	6	0.82	461	.175	.250	0-0	—	0		4	0.4
1979	Tex A	2	0	1.000	11	2	0	0-1	33	30	21	2	2	19-2	25	4.36	95	.252	.359	0-0	—	0	163	-2	-0.1
	Chi A	3	7	.300	42	3	0	14-3	81.1	66	36	2	1	34-8	48	2.43	175	.219	.299	0-0	—	0	57	12	1.8
	Year	5	7	.417	53	5	0	14-4	114.1	96	39	4	3	53-10	73	2.99	142	.229	.317	0-0	—	0	98	10	1.7
1980	Chi A★	7	9	.438	64	0	0	30-11	99.2	92	37	6	1	56-11	54	3.34	121	.244	.343	0-0	—	0		10	2.1
1981	Chi A	3	3	.500	42	0	0	10-5	52.2	53	33	5	1	34-1	42	4.61	78	.262	.368	0-0	—	0		-7	-1.0
1982	Phi N	2	6	.250	47	4	0	6-3	76	66	44	2	0	50-11	58	4.86	76	.234	.347	11-2	.000	-1	108	-9	-1.2

Year	Tm Lg	W	L	Pct	G	GS	CG-Sho	SV-BS	IP	H	R	HR	HB	BB-IB	SO	ERA	AERA	OAV	OOB	AB-SH	AVG	PB	Sup	APR	PW
1983	Phi N	0	6	.000	12	3	0	0-0	26.2	35	22	2	1	20-8	16	6.08	59	.307	.412	6-1	.167	-0	66	-8	-1.5
	Oak A	0	0	—	5	1	0	0-0	10.1	15	4	1	0	0-0	7	3.48	111	.366	.357	0-0	—	0	188	1	0.0
Total	11	30	43	.411	370	21	0	75-27	624	611	343	52	12	345-50	395	4.30	90	.257	.352	47-5	.085	-3	99	-32	-3.2
FARMER, HOWARD Howard Earl B 11.18.1966 Gary, IN BR/TR 6-3/185# d7.2 b-Mike																									
1990	Mon N	0	3	.000	6	4	0	0-0	23	26	18	9	0	10-1	14	7.04	52	.302	.371	5-1	.400	1	136	-8	-0.8
FARMER, MIKE Michael Anthony B 7.3.1968 Gary, IN BB/TL 6-1/193# d5.4 b-Howard																									
1996	Col N	0	1	.000	7	4	0	0-0	28	32	25	8	0	13-0	16	7.71	68	.286	.360	10-0	.400	1	151	-6	-0.2
FARNSWORTH, JEFF Jeffrey Ellis B 10.6.1975 Wichita, KS BR/TR 6-2/190# d4.3																									
2002	Det A	2	3	.400	44	0	0	0-1	70	100	47	6	2	29-8	28	5.79	75	.338	.399	0-0	—	0		-10	-0.7
FARNSWORTH, KYLE Kyle Lynn B 4.14.1976 Wichita, KS BR/TR 6-4/205# d4.29																									
1999	Chi N	5	9	.357	27	21	1-1	0-0	130	140	80	28	3	52-1	70	5.05	89	.271	.340	35-6	.086	-1	112	-8	-0.9
2000	Chi N	2	9	.182	46	5	0	1-5	77	90	58	14	4	50-8	74	6.43	71	.291	.392	14-2	.071	-1	105	-16	-2.1
2001	Chi N	4	6	.400	76	0	0	2-1	82	65	26	8	1	29-2	107	2.74	151	.213	.282	2-0	.000	-0		14	1.5
2002	Chi N	4	6	.400	45	0	0	1-6	46.2	53	47	9	1	24-7	46	7.33	55	.293	.370	1-0	.000	-0		-20	-3.8
2003	†Chi N	3	2	.600	77	0	0	0-3	76.1	53	31	6	0	36-1	92	3.30	128	.196	.289	1-0	.000	-0		8	0.5
Total	5	18	32	.360	271	26	1-1	4-15	412	401	242	65	9	191-19	389	4.78	91	.253	.335	53-8	.075	-2	116	-22	-4.8
FARR, JIM James Alfred B 5.18.1956 Waverly, NY BR/TR 6-1/195# d9.7																									
1982	Tex A	0	0	—	5	0	0	0-0	18	20	8	0	0	7-2	6	2.50	155	.278	.338	0-0	—	0		2	0.1
FARR, STEVE Steven Michael B 12.12.1956 LaPlata, MD BR/TR 5-11/200# d5.16																									
1984	Cle A	3	11	.214	31	16	0	1-1	116	106	61	14	5	46-3	83	4.58	89	.245	.323	0-0	—	0	69	-4	-0.5
1985	†KC A	2	1	.667	16	3	0	1-0	37.2	34	15	2	2	20-4	36	3.11	134	.245	.344	0-0	—	0	95	4	0.3
1986	KC A	8	4	.667	56	0	0	8-1	109.1	90	39	10	4	39-8	83	3.13	136	.228	.302	0-0	—	0		15	1.7
1987	KC A	4	3	.571	47	0	0	1-4	91	97	47	9	2	44-4	88	4.15	110	.270	.350	0-0	—	0		4	0.2
1988	KC A	5	4	.556	62	1	0	20-6	82.2	74	25	5	2	30-6	72	2.50	160	.240	.309	0-0	—	0	46	14	2.0
1989	KC A	2	5	.286	51	2	0	18-4	63.1	75	35	5	1	22-5	56	4.12	94	.296	.351	0-0	—	0	82	-3	-0.5
1990	KC A	13	7	.650	57	6	1-1	1-1	127	99	32	6	5	48-9	94	1.98	194	.220	.301	0-0	—	0	67	**27**	4.1
1991	NY A	5	5	.500	60	0	0	23-6	70	57	19	4	5	20-3	60	2.19	190	.219	.288	0-0	—	0		15	2.8
1992	NY A	2	2	.500	50	0	0	30-6	52	34	10	2	2	19-0	37	1.56	252	.186	.267	0-0	—	0		14	2.3
1993	NY A	2	2	.500	49	0	0	25-6	47	44	22	8	2	28-4	39	4.21	99	.253	.356	0-0	—	0		1	0.2
1994	Cle A	1	1	.500	19	0	0	4-2	15.1	17	12	3	2	15-1	12	5.28	89	.279	.430	0-0	—	0		-2	-0.3
	Bos A	1	0	1.000	11	0	0	0-1	13	24	9	2	0	3-0	8	6.23	81	.407	.435	0-0	—	0		-1	-0.1
	Year	2	1	.667	30	0	0	4-3	28.1	41	24	5	2	18-1	20	5.72	85	.342	.433	0-0	—	0		-3	-0.4
Total	11	48	45	.516	509	28	1-1	132-38	824.1	751	326	70	32	334-47	668	3.25	127	.244	.322	0-0	—	0	70	84	12.2
FARRELL, JOHN John Edward B 8.4.1962 Monmouth Beach, NJ BR/TR 6-4/210# d8.18																									
1987	Cle A	5	1	.833	10	9	1	0-0	69	68	29	7	5	22-1	28	3.39	134	.256	.323	0-0	—	0	132	9	0.7
1988	Cle A	14	10	.583	31	30	4	0-0	210.1	216	106	15	9	67-3	92	4.24	97	.269	.330	0-0	—	0	97	-1	-0.2
1989	Cle A	9	14	.391	31	31	7-2	0-0	208	196	97	14	7	71-4	132	3.63	109	.244	.309	0-0	—	0	84	6	0.5
1990	Cle A	4	5	.444	17	17	1	0-0	96.2	108	49	10	1	33-1	44	4.28	92	.286	.344	0-0	—	0	102	-3	-0.3
1993	Cal A	3	12	.200	21	17	0	0-0	90.2	110	74	22	7	44-3	45	7.35	62	.301	.385	0-0	—	0	78	-24	-3.2
1994	Cal A	1	2	.333	3	3	0	0-0	13	16	14	2	1	8-0	10	9.00	54	.308	.410	0-0	—	0	88	-6	-0.9
1995	Cle A	0	0	—	1	0	0	0-0	4.2	7	4	0	0	0-0	4	3.86	122	.368	.350	0-0	—	0		0	0.0
1996	Det A	0	2	.000	2	2	0	0-0	6.1	11	10	2	1	5-0	0	14.21	36	.407	.515	0-0	—	0	73	-6	-0.9
Total	8	36	46	.439	116	109	13-2	0-0	698.2	732	383	72	31	250-12	355	4.56	91	.270	.336	0-0	—	0	94	-25	-4.3
FARRELL, KERBY Major Kerby B 9.3.1913 Leapwood, TN D 12.17.1975 Nashville, TN BL/TL 5-11/172# d4.24 M1 C6 ▲																									
1943	Bos N	0	1	.000	5	0	0	0	23	24	11	1	0	9	4	4.30	79	.276	.344	280-7	.268	1*		-1	0.0
FARRELL, TURK Richard Joseph B 4.8.1934 Boston, MA D 6.10.1977 Great Yarmouth, England BR/TR 6-4/220# d9.21																									
1956	Phi N	0	1	.000	1	1	0	0	4.1	6	6	0	1	3-0	0	12.46	30	.353	.476	1-1	.000	-0	71	-4	-0.6
1957	Phi N	10	2	.833	52	0	0	10	83.1	74	29	2	2	36-9	54	2.38	160	.242	.323	9-0	.111	0		11	1.9
1958	Phi N★	8	9	.471	54	0	0	11	94	84	41	7	0	40-7	73	3.35	118	.244	.320	24-0	.208	0		6	1.0
1959	Phi N	1	6	.143	38	0	0	6	57	61	30	9	0	25-7	31	4.74	87	.288	.354	6-1	.167	-0		-2	-0.3
1960	Phi N	10	6	.625	59	0	0	11	103.1	88	36	3	4	29-6	70	2.70	144	.239	.298	15-2	.200	1		13	2.2
1961	Phi N	2	1	.667	5	0	0	0	9.2	10	8	3	1	6-1	10	6.52	63	.270	.386	2-0	.500	0		-3	-0.5
	LA N	6	6	.500	50	0	0	10	89	107	56	12	1	43-14	80	5.06	86	.296	.371	18-3	.000	-2		-6	-1.2
	Year	8	7	.533	55	0	0	10	98.2	117	67	15	2	49-15	90	5.20	83	.294	.373	20-3	.050	-2		-9	-1.7
1962	Hou N★	10	20	.333	43	29	11-2	4	241.2	210	91	21	5	55-2	203	3.02	124	.233	.279	78-3	.179	2	64	22	2.7
1963	Hou N	14	13	.519	34	26	12	1	202.1	161	76	12	2	35-2	141	3.02	104	.219	.255	63-3	.143	1	71	4	0.7
1964	Hou N★	11	10	.524	32	27	7	0	198.1	196	80	21	3	52-4	117	3.27	105	.261	.308	69-2	.072	-3	96	5	0.1
1965	Hou N★	11	11	.500	33	29	8-3	1	208.1	202	94	18	3	35-8	122	3.50	96	.252	.284	74-2	.135	-1	99	-4	-0.6
1966	Hou N	6	10	.375	32	21	3	2	152.2	167	84	23	0	28-4	101	4.60	74	.278	.307	48-1	.146	-0	87	-18	-1.9
1967	Hou N	1	0	1.000	7	0	0	0	11.2	11	7	0	1	7-1	10	4.63	72	.244	.358	1-0	.000	-0		-2	-0.2
	Phi N	9	6	.600	50	1	0	12	92	76	26	6	1	15-5	68	2.05	166	.228	.258	19-1	.105	-0	52	13	2.5
	Year	10	6	.625	57	1	0	12	103.2	87	28	6	2	22-6	78	2.34	145	.230	.271	20-1	.100	-0	52	11	2.3
1968	Phi N	4	6	.400	54	0	0	12	83	83	40	7	2	32-6	57	3.47	87	.271	.340	6-0	.167	-0		-6	-1.0
1969	Phi N	3	4	.429	46	0	0	3-3	74.1	92	33	8	1	27-6	40	4.00	89	.307	.364	3-1	.000	-0		-2	-0.3
Total	14	106	111	.488	590	134	41-5	83-3	1705	1628	737	152	27	468-82	1177	3.45	103	.254	.304	436-20	.135	-3	80	27	4.5
FASSERO, JEFF Jeffrey Joseph B 1.5.1963 Springfield, IL BL/TL 6-1/195# d5.4																									
1991	Mon N	2	5	.286	51	0	0	8-3	55.1	39	17	1	1	17-1	42	2.44	148	.196	.263	3-2	.000	0		7	1.1
1992	Mon N	8	7	.533	70	0	0	1-6	85.2	81	35	1	2	34-6	63	2.84	122	.249	.322	7-1	.143	0		4	0.7
1993	Mon N	12	5	.706	56	15	1	1-2	149.2	119	50	7	0	54-0	140	2.29	183	.216	.284	32-5	.063	-2	78	**28**	2.8
1994	Mon N	8	6	.571	21	21	1	0-0	138.2	119	54	13	1	40-4	119	2.99	142	.229	.285	44-9	.068	-2	92	18	1.6
1995	Mon N	13	14	.481	30	30	1	0-0	189	207	102	15	2	74-3	164	4.33	99	.283	.348	57-8	.070	-3	95	-2	-0.5
1996	Mon N	15	11	.577	34	34	5-1	0-0	231.2	217	95	20	3	55-3	222	3.30	131	.244	.289	64-14	.094	-1	90	25	2.6
1997	†Sea A	16	9	.640	35	**35**	2-1	0-0	234.1	226	108	21	3	84-6	189	3.61	125	.249	.312	5-0	.200	0	114	21	2.0
1998	Sea A	13	12	.520	32	32	7	0-0	224.2	223	115	33	10	66-2	176	3.97	117	.259	.316	3-0	.000	-0	104	14	1.3
1999	Sea A	4	14	.222	30	24	0	0-0	139	188	123	34	4	73-3	101	7.38	64	.321	.397	7-0	.000	-1	107	-42	-4.2
	†Tex A	1	0	1.000	7	3	0	0-0	17.1	20	12	1	0	10-0	13	5.71	89	.286	.370	0-0	—	0	128	-1	-0.1
	Year	5	14	.263	37	27	0	0-0	156.1	208	19	35	4	83-3	114	7.20	66	.318	.394	7-0	.000	-1	110	-43	-4.3
2000	Bos A	8	8	.500	38	23	0	0-0	130	153	72	16	1	50-2	97	4.78	106	.296	.358	2-1	.000	-0	94	5	0.6
2001	Chi N	4	4	.500	82	0	0	12-5	73.2	66	31	6	1	23-5	79	3.42	121	.235	.293	2-0	.000	-0		6	0.7
2002	Chi N	5	6	.455	57	0	0	0-1	51	65	37	5	3	22-5	44	6.18	65	.313	.385	3-0	.333	0		-12	-2.2
	†StL N	3	0	1.000	16	0	0	0-2	18	16	6	4	0	5-0	12	3.00	132	.232	.284	0-0	—	0		2	0.4
	Year	8	6	.571	73	0	0	0-3	69	81	48	9	3	27-5	56	5.35	75	.292	.360	3-0	.333	0		-10	-1.8
2003	StL N	1	7	.125	62	6	0	3-3	77.2	93	51	17	2	34-4	55	5.68	72	.296	.368	9-1	.000	-1	131	-14	-1.5
Total	13	113	108	.511	621	223	17-2	25-22	1815.2	1832	908	194	33	641-44	1516	4.00	109	.261	.323	238-41	.076	-10	103	59	5.3
FAST, FRED Frederick Peter B 10.30.1859 Milwaukee, WI D 7.5.1930 Burnt Mill, CO d7.11																									
1887	Ind N	0	1	.000	4	2	1	1	15.2	25	22	1	2	8	0	10.34	40	.347	.427	11	.182	-1	94	-9	-0.5
FAST, DARCY Darcy Rae B 3.10.1947 Dallas, OR BL/TL 6-3/195# d6.15 Mil 1969																									
1968	Chi N	0	1	.000	8	1	0	0	10	8	6	1	0	8-0	10	5.40	59	.216	.348	3-0	.000	-0	110	-2	-0.2
FASZHOLZ, JACK John Edward "Preacher" B 4.11.1927 St.Louis, MO BR/TR 6-3/205# d4.25																									
1953	StL N	0	0	—	4	1	0	0	11.2	16	9	3	1	1	7	6.94	61	.327	.353	3-0	.000	-0	126	-3	-0.2
FAUL, BILL William Alvan B 4.21.1940 Cincinnati, OH D 2.21.2002 Cincinnati, OH BR/TR 5-10/190# d9.19																									
1962	Det A	0	0	—	1	0	0	0	1.2	4	6	1	1	3-0	2	32.40	13	.444	.615	0-0	—	0		-5	-0.2

Year	Tm Lg	W	L	Pct	G	GS	CG-Sho	SV-BS	IP	H	R	HR	HB	BB-IB	SO	ERA	AERA	OAV	OOB	AB-SH	AVG	PB	Sup	APR	PW
1963	Det A	5	6	.455	28	10	2	1	97	93	55	14	4	48-3	64	4.64	81	.251	.340	27-1	.148	0	93	-9	-1.0
1964	Det A	0	0	—	1	1	0	0	5	5	6	2	0	2-0	1	10.80	34	.250	.318	2-0	.000	-0	146	-4	-0.2
1965	Chi N	6	6	.500	17	16	5-3	0	96.2	83	43	12	3	18-0	59	3.54	104	.232	.274	30-0	.100	-1	84	2	0.1
1966	Chi N	1	4	.200	17	6	1	0	51.1	47	31	12	4	18-1	32	5.08	72	.242	.318	13-0	.000	-2	44	-7	-0.8
1970	SF N	0	0	—	7	0	0	1-0	9.2	15	9	1	0	6-2	6	7.45	53	.357	.438	0-0	—	0		-4	-0.2
Total	6	12	16	.429	71	33	8-3	2-0	261.1	247	150	42	12	95-6	164	4.72	79	.249	.320	72-1	.097	-2	81	-27	-2.3
FAULKNER, JIM James Leroy "Lefty" B 7.27.1899 Beatrice, NE D 6.1.1962 W.Palm Beach, FL BB/TL 6-3/190# d9.15																									
1927	NY N	1	0	1.000	3	1	0	0	9.2	13	4	0	1	5	2	3.72	104	.317	.404	2-0	.500	1	243	0	0.1
1928	NY N	9	8	.529	38	8	3	2	117.1	131	61	5	3	41	32	3.53	111	.289	.351	39-2	.231	1	84	2	0.3
1930	Bro N	0	0	—	2	1	0	1	0.1	2	3	1	0	1	0	81.00	6	.667	.750	0-0	—	0	266	-3	-0.4
Total	3	10	8	.556	43	10	3	3	127.1	146	68	6	4	47	34	3.75	104	.293	.359	41-2	.244	2	124	-1	0.0
FAUSETT, BUCK Robert Shaw "Leaky" B 4.8.1908 Sheridan, AR D 5.2.1994 College Station, TX BL/TR 5-10/170# d4.18 ▲																									
1944	Cin N	0	0	—	2	0	0	0	10.2	13	8	0	2	7	3	5.91	59	.295	.415	31-1	.097	-0*		-3	-0.2
FAUST, CHARLIE Charles Victor "Victory" B 10.9.1880 Marion, KS D 6.18.1915 Fort Steilacoom, WA BR/TR 6-2/?# d10.7																									
1911	NY N	0	0	—	2	0	0	0	2	2	1	0	0	0	0	4.50	75	.250	.250	0-0	—	0		0	0.0
FAUVER, CLAY Clayton King "Cayt" B 8.1.1872 N.Eaton, OH D 3.3.1942 Chatsworth, GA BB/TR 5-10/?# d9.7																									
1899	Lou N	1	0	1.000	1	1	1	0	9	11	4	0	0	2	1	0.00	—	.297	.333	4-0	.000	-1	75	3	0.2
FEAR, VERN Luvern Carl B 8.21.1924 Everly, IA D 9.6.1976 Spencer, IA BB/TR 6/170# d8.3																									
1952	Chi N	0	0	—	4	0	0	0	8	9	7	1	1	3	4	7.88	49	.290	.371	1-0	.000	-0		-3	-0.2
FEE, JACK John B 12.23.1867 Carbondale, PA D 3.3.1913 Carbondale, PA d9.14																									
1889	Ind N	2	2	.500	7	3	2	0	40	39	29	2	6	31	10	4.27	98	.248	.392	21	.143	-2	96	-1	-0.2
FELDMAN, HARRY Harry B 11.10.1919 New York, NY D 3.16.1962 Fort Smith, AR BR/TR 6/175# d9.10																									
1941	NY N	1	1	.500	3	3	1-1	0	20.1	21	10	0	0	6	9	3.98	93	.280	.333	6-1	.167	0	115	0	-0.1
1942	NY N	7	1	.875	31	6	2-1	0	114	100	46	5	1	73	49	3.16	106	.236	.350	39-1	.282	3	121	3	0.5
1943	NY N	4	5	.444	31	10	1	0	104.2	114	59	7	4	58	49	4.30	80	.279	.374	30-0	.133	-1*	79	-11	-1.0
1944	NY N	11	13	.458	40	27	8-1	2	205.1	214	120	18	2	91	70	4.16	88	.266	.342	73-3	.205	0*	110	-14	-1.6
1945	NY N	12	13	.480	35	30	10-3	1	217.2	213	92	14	1	69	74	3.27	120	.251	.308	72-0	.097	-3*	77	14	1.1
1946	NY N	0	2	.000	3	2	0	0	4	9	8	1	0	3	3	18.00	19	.474	.545	1-0	.000	-0	25	-6	-1.0
Total	6	35	35	.500	143	78	22-6	3	666	671	335	45	8	300	254	3.80	96	.260	.339	221-5	.172	-1	93	-14	-2.1
FELICIANO, PEDRO Pedro Juan (Molina) B 8.25.1976 Rio Piedras, P.R. BL/TL 5-11/165# d9.4																									
2002	NY N	0	0	—	6	0	0	0-0	6	9	5	0	0	1-0	4	7.50	53	.360	.385	0-0	—	0		-2	-0.1
2003	NY N	0	0	—	23	0	0	0-0	48.1	52	21	5	3	21-3	43	3.35	124	.269	.349	3-1	.000	-0		4	0.2
Total	2	0	0	—	29	0	0	0-0	54.1	61	26	5	3	22-3	47	3.81	109	.280	.352	3-1	.000	-0		2	0.1
FELIX, HARRY Harry B 1870 Brooklyn, NY D 10.17.1961 Miami, FL BR/TR 5-7.5/160# d10.5																									
1901	NY N	0	0	—	1	0	0	0	2	3	0	0	0	0	0	0.00	—	.333	.333	1-0	.000	-0		1	0.0
1902	Phi N	1	3	.250	9	5	3	0	45	61	37	1	0	11	10	5.60	50	.323	.360	37-3	.135	-1*	53	-13	-1.1
Total	2	1	3	.250	10	5	3	0	47	64	37	1	0	11	10	5.36	53	.323	.359	38-3	.132	-1	53	-12	-1.1
FELLER, BOB Robert William Andrew "Rapid Robert" (b: Robert William Feller) B 11.3.1918 Van Meter, IA BR/TR 6/185# d7.19 Mil 1942-45 HF1962																									
1936	Cle A	5	3	.625	14	8	5	1	62	52	29	1	4	47	76	3.34	151	.229	.371	22-1	.136	-2	109	11	1.0
1937	Cle A	9	7	.563	26	19	9	1	148.2	116	68	4	2	106	150	3.39	136	.218	.351	53-0	.170	-1	80	19	1.7
1938	Cle A☆	17	11	.607	39	36	20-2	1	277.2	225	136	13	7	208	**240**	4.08	114	**.220**	.356	94-9	.181	2	104	21	1.8
1939	Cle A★	**24**	9	.727	39	35	**24**-4	1	**296.2**	227	105	13	3	142	**246**	2.85	154	**.210**	.303	99-6	.212	5	114	**54**	**6.0**
1940	Cle A★	**27**	11	.711	**43**	**37**	**31-4**	4	**320.1**	245	102	13	5	118	**261**	**2.61**	161	**.210**	**.285**	115-6	.157	1	99	**61**	**6.8**
1941	Cle A★	**25**	13	.658	**44**	**40**	28-**6**	2	**343**	284	129	15	5	194	**260**	3.15	125	.226	.332	120-10	.150	2	108	34	3.6
1945	Cle A	5	3	.625	9	9	7-1	0	72	50	21	1	2	35	59	2.50	130	.192	.293	25-1	.160	-0	111	7	0.7
1946	Cle A★	**26**	15	.634	**48**	**42**	**36-10**	4	**371.1**	277	101	11	3	153	**348**	2.18	152	.208	.291	124-8	.129	-2	80	50	5.4
1947	Cle A❖	**20**	11	.645	42	**37**	20-**5**	3	**299**	230	97	17	4	127	**196**	2.68	130	.215	.300	98-8	.184	3	105	**29**	3.2
1948	†Cle A❖	19	15	.559	44	**38**	18-2	3	280.1	255	123	20	2	116	**164**	3.56	114	.241	.317	95-9	.095	-8	109	17	1.0
1949	Cle A	15	14	.517	36	28	15	0	211	198	104	18	1	84	108	3.75	106	.248	.320	72-7	.236	4	95	3	0.5
1950	Cle A★	16	11	.593	35	34	16-3	0	247	230	105	20	5	103	119	3.43	126	.247	.325	83-8	.120	-2	99	27	2.1
1951	Cle A	**22**	8	**.733**	33	32	16-4	0	249.2	239	105	22	7	95	111	3.50	108	.253	.325	81-10	.123	-4	125	11	0.6
1952	Cle A	9	13	.409	30	30	11	0	191.2	219	124	13	3	83	81	4.74	71	.288	.360	60-3	.117	1	152	-36	-3.5
1953	Cle A	10	7	.588	25	25	10-1	0	175.2	163	78	16	3	60	60	3.59	105	.251	.317	56-8	.107	-2	124	4	0.2
1954	Cle A	13	3	.813	19	19	9-1	0	140	127	53	13	3	39	59	3.09	119	.239	.292	48-3	.188	1	128	10	1.1
1955	Cle A	4	4	.500	25	11	2-1	0	83	71	43	7	1	31-2	25	3.47	115	.235	.305	21-3	.048	-2	93	2	-0.1
1956	Cle A	0	4	.000	19	4	2	1	58	63	34	7	0	23-4	18	4.97	85	.280	.344	16-0	.000	-2	69	-4	-0.5
Total	18	266	162	.621	570	484	279-44	21	3827	3271	1557	224	60	1764-**6**	2581	3.25	122	.231	.319	1282-100	.151	-7	107	320	31.6
FELTON, TERRY Terry Lane B 10.29.1957 Texarkana, AR BR/TR 6-1/180# d9.28																									
1979	Min A	0	0	—	1	0	0	0-0	2	0	0	0	0	0-0	1	0.00	—	.000	.000	0-0	—	0		1	0.0
1980	Min A	0	3	.000	5	4	0	0-0	17.2	20	18	2	1	9-1	14	7.13	61	.286	.370	0-0	—	0	56	-6	-0.8
1981	Min A	0	0	—	1	0	0	0-0	1.1	4	6	1	0	2-0	1	40.50	10	.500	.600	0-0	—	0		-5	-0.2
1982	Min A	0	13	.000	48	6	0	3-3	117.1	99	71	18	4	76-8	92	4.99	85	.230	.348	0-0	—	0	50	-10	-1.1
Total	4	0	16	.000	55	10	0	3-3	138.1	123	95	21	5	87-9	108	5.53	77	.240	.352	0-0	—	0	53	-20	-2.1
FENNER, HOD Horace Alfred B 7.12.1897 Martin, MI D 11.20.1954 Detroit, MI BR/TR 5-10.5/165# d9.9																									
1921	Chi A	0	0	—	2	1	0	0	7	14	6	0	0	3	1	7.71	55	.452	.500	2-0	.000	-0	394	-2	-0.2
FERENS, STAN Stanley "Lefty" B 3.5.1915 Wendel, PA D 10.7.1994 Hempfield Township, PA BB/TL 5-11/170# d6.10																									
1942	StL A	3	4	.429	19	3	1	0	69	76	31	2	0	21	23	3.78	98	.279	.331	21-1	.143	-1	192	1	0.0
1946	StL A	2	9	.182	34	6	1	0	88	100	60	3	3	38	28	4.50	83	.293	.369	24-2	.167	-1	77	-10	-1.3
Total	2	5	13	.278	53	9	2	0	157	176	91	5	3	59	51	4.18	89	.287	.353	45-3	.156	-1	115	-9	-1.3
FERGUSON, CHARLIE Charles Augustus B 5.10.1875 Okemos, MI D 5.17.1931 Sault Ste.Marie, MI TR 5-11/?# d9.20																									
1901	Chi N	0	0	—	1	0	0	0	2	1	0	0	0	2	0	0.00	—	.143	.333	1-0	.000	-0		1	0.0
FERGUSON, CHARLIE Charles J. B 4.17.1863 Charlottesville, VA D 4.29.1888 Philadelphia, PA BB/TR 6/165# d5.1																									
1884	Phi N	21	25	.457	50	47	46-2	1	416.2	443	297	13		93	194	3.54	84	.253	.291	203	.246	7*	98	-21	-1.2
1885	Phi N	26	20	.565	48	45	45-5	0	405	345	197	5		81	197	2.22	126	.219	.257	235	.306	17*	104	26	4.3
1886	Phi N	30	9	.769	48	45	43-4	**2**	395.2	317	145	11		69	212	1.98	166	.210	.244	261	.253	12*	101	**59**	**6.5**
1887	Phi N	22	10	.688	37	33	31-2	1	297.1	297	154	13	11	47	125	3.00	142	.254	.289	264	.337	14*	106	40	4.7
Total	4	99	64	.607	183	170	165-13	4	1514.2	1402	793	42	11	290	728	2.67	122	.233	.270	963	.288	49	102	104	14.3
FERGUSON, GEORGE George Cecil "Cecil" B 8.19.1886 Ellsworth, IN D 9.5.1943 Orlando, FL BR/TR 5-10/165# d4.19																									
1906	NY N	2	0	1.000	22	1	1-1	**7**	52.1	43	22	1	2	24	32	2.58	101	.229	.322	15-0	.333	2	56	0	0.3
1907	NY N	3	2	.600	15	5	4	1	64	63	32	2	5	20	37	2.11	118	.266	.336	18-1	.056	-1	138	-2	-0.3
1908	Bos N	11	11	.500	37	21	13-3	0	208	168	72	1	8	84	98	2.47	98	.230	.316	65-3	.169	1*	113	2	0.1
1909	Bos N	5	23	.179	36	30	19-3	0	226.2	235	121	2	12	83	87	3.73	76	.282	.355	73-1	.205	1	65	-18	-1.9
1910	Bos N	7	7	.500	26	14	10-1	0	123	110	56	3	7	58	40	3.80	87	.254	.351	40-2	.175	-1	85	0	-0.1
1911	Bos N	1	3	.250	6	3	0	0	24	40	29	3	0	12	4	9.75	39	.388	.452	7-0	.286	1	52	-12	-1.5
Total	6	29	46	.387	142	74	47-8	8	698	659	332	12	34	281	298	3.34	83	.261	.343	218-7	.188	3	86	-30	-3.4
FERGUSON, ALEX James Alexander B 2.16.1897 Montclair, NJ D 4.26.1976 Sepulveda, CA BR/TR 6/180# d8.16 Mil 1918																									
1918	NY A	0	0	—	1	0	0	0	1.2	2	0	0	0	2	1	0.00	—	.333	.500	1-0	.000	-0		1	0.0
1921	NY A	3	1	.750	17	4	1	1	56.1	64	40	4	4	27	9	5.91	72	.296	.385	19-0	.211	-1	118	-8	-0.6
1922	Bos A	9	16	.360	39	27	10-1	2	198.1	201	108	5	6	62	44	4.31	95	.265	.326	65-6	.092	-6	69	-3	-1.0

Year	Tm Lg	W	L	Pct	G	GS	CG-Sho	SV-BS	IP	H	R	HR	HB	BB-IB	SO	ERA	AERA	OAV	OOB	AB-SH	AVG	PB	Sup	APR	PW
1923	Bos A	9	13	.409	34	27	11	0	198.1	229	115	5	9	67	72	4.04	102	.297	.360	62-6	.097	-5	77	1	-0.6
1924	Bos A	14	17	.452	41	32	15	2	237.2	259	115	6	6	108	78	3.79	115	.286	.366	86-8	.140	-6	78	17	1.4
1925	Bos A	0	2	.000	5	4	0	1	15.2	22	22	6	1	5	5	10.91	42	.314	.368	4-0	.000	-0	88	-10	-1.1
	NY A	4	2	.667	21	6	0	1	54.1	83	57	3	2	42	20	7.79	55	.358	.460	15-2	.133	-1	135	-23	-2.1
	†Was A	5	1	.833	7	6	3	0	55.1	52	22	2	2	23	24	3.25	130	.256	.338	20-4	.050	-3	126	7	0.3
	Year	9	5	.643	33	16	3	2	125.1	157	28	11	5	70	49	6.18	69	.311	.400	39-6	.077	-4	120	-24	-2.9
1926	Was A	3	4	.429	19	4	0	1	47.2	69	51	4	3	18	16	7.74	50	.343	.405	11-1	.182	-0	136	-23	-2.8
1927	Phi N	8	16	.333	31	31	16	0	227	280	132	15	6	65	73	4.84	85	.313	.363	70-10	.100	-5	85	-15	-1.8
1928	Phi N	5	10	.333	34	19	5-1	2	134.2	168	91	14	6	52	51	5.88	73	.315	.382	39-2	.026	-4	118	-19	-2.2
1929	Phi N	1	2	.333	5	4	1	0	12.2	19	18	2	0	10	3	12.08	43	.345	.446	4-0	.000	-1	50	-8	-1.4
	Bro N	0	1	.000	3	2	0	0	2	7	7	2	0	1	1	22.50	21	.583	.615	1-0	1.000	0	189	-4	-0.7
	Year	1	3	.250	8	6	1	0	14.2	26	17	4	0	11	4	13.50	38	.388	.474	5-0	.200	-0	91	-13	-2.1
Total	10	61	85	.418	257	166	62-2	10	1241.2	1455	778	68	45	482	397	4.93	85	.299	.368	397-39	.106	-33	90	-87	-12.6

FERGUSON, BOB Robert Lester B 4.18.1919 Birmingham, AL BR/TR 6-1.5/180# d4.29

Year	Tm Lg	W	L	Pct	G	GS	CG-Sho	SV-BS	IP	H	R	HR	HB	BB-IB	SO	ERA	AERA	OAV	OOB	AB-SH	AVG	PB	Sup	APR	PW
1944	Cin N	0	3	.000	9	2	0	1	16	24	17	3	2	10	9	9.00	39	.358	.456	3-0	.333	0	84	-9	-1.6

FERGUSON, BOB Robert Vavasour B 1.31.1845 Brooklyn, NY D 5.3.1894 Brooklyn, NY BB/TR 5-9.5/149# d5.18 M16 U10 ▲

Year	Tm Lg	W	L	Pct	G	GS	CG-Sho	SV-BS	IP	H	R	HR	HB	BB-IB	SO	ERA	AERA	OAV	OOB	AB-SH	AVG	PB	Sup	APR	PW
1871	Mut NA	0	0	—	1	0	0	0	1	8	9	0		0	0	27.00	14	.571	.571	158	.241	-0*		-3	-0.1
1873	Atl NA	0	1	.000	4	1	1	0	19.1	41	30	2		2	0	5.59	54	.383	.394	228	.259	1*	47	-6	-0.2
1874	Atl NA	0	1	.000	1	1	1	0	9	12	10	0		3	0	4.00	51	.273	.319	245	.261	0*	99	-1	-0.1
1875	Har NA	0	0	—	1	0	0	0	2	9	7	1		0	0	22.50	10	.600	.600	366	.240	0*		-3	-0.1
1877	Har N	1	1	.500	3	2	2	0	25	38	15	0		2	1	3.96	61	.352	.364	254	.256	0*	140	-2	-0.1
1883	Phi N	0	0	—	1	0	0	0	1	2	2	0		0	0	9.00	34	.286	.286	329	.258	0*		-1	0.0
Total	4 NA	0	2	.000	7	2	2	0	31.1	70	56	3		5	0	6.89	40	.389	.405	997	.250	1	69	-13	-0.5
Total	2	1	1	.500	4	2	2	0	26	40	17	0		2	1	4.15	59	.348	.359	583	.257	0	139	-3	-0.1

FERMIN, RAMON Ramon Antonio (Ventura) B 11.25.1972 San Francisco De Macoris, D.R. BR/TR 6-3/180# d8.6

Year	Tm Lg	W	L	Pct	G	GS	CG-Sho	SV-BS	IP	H	R	HR	HB	BB-IB	SO	ERA	AERA	OAV	OOB	AB-SH	AVG	PB	Sup	APR	PW
1995	Oak A	0	0	—	1	0	0	0-0	1.1	4	2	0	0	1-0	0	13.50	33	.500	.556	0-0	—	0		-1	-0.1

FERNANDEZ, ALEX Alexander B 8.13.1969 Miami Beach, FL BR/TR 6-1/215# d8.2

Year	Tm Lg	W	L	Pct	G	GS	CG-Sho	SV-BS	IP	H	R	HR	HB	BB-IB	SO	ERA	AERA	OAV	OOB	AB-SH	AVG	PB	Sup	APR	PW
1990	Chi A	5	5	.500	13	13	3	0-0	87.2	89	40	6	3	34-0	61	3.80	101	.265	.338	0-0	—	0	90	0	0.0
1991	Chi A	9	13	.409	34	32	2	0-0	191.2	186	100	16	2	88-2	145	4.51	88	.259	.337	0-0	—	0	83	-9	-0.9
1992	Chi A	8	11	.421	29	29	4-2	0-0	187.2	199	100	21	8	50-3	95	4.27	91	.270	.322	0-0	—	0	113	-9	-0.8
1993	†Chi A	18	9	.667	34	34	3-1	0-0	247.1	221	95	27	6	67-5	169	3.13	134	.240	.295	0-0	—	0	112	30	3.1
1994	Chi A	11	7	.611	24	24	4-3	0-0	170.1	163	83	25	1	50-4	122	3.86	121	.250	.302	0-0	—	0	119	15	1.6
1995	Chi A	12	8	.600	30	30	5-2	0-0	203.2	200	98	19	0	65-7	159	3.80	117	.255	.310	0-0	—	0	115	14	1.2
1996	Chi A	16	10	.615	35	35	6-1	0-0	258	248	110	34	7	72-4	200	3.45	137	.253	.307	0-0	—	0	97	38	3.4
1997	†Fla N	17	12	.586	32	32	5-1	0-0	220.2	193	93	25	4	69-2	183	3.59	112	.238	.299	66-7	.152	3*	103	13	2.0
1999	Fla N	7	8	.467	24	24	1	0-0	141	135	60	10	4	41-1	91	3.38	129	.252	.307	43-3	.233	4*	86	15	1.9
2000	Fla N	4	4	.500	8	8	0	0-0	52.1	59	25	7	0	16-1	27	4.13	108	.292	.342	17-0	.118	1*	85	2	0.4
Total	10	107	87	.552	263	261	33-10	0-0	1760.1	1693	804	190	35	552-29	1252	3.74	114	.254	.312	126-10	.175	8	102	109	11.9

FERNANDEZ, SID Charles Sidney B 10.12.1962 Honolulu, HI BL/TL 6-1/230# d9.20

Year	Tm Lg	W	L	Pct	G	GS	CG-Sho	SV-BS	IP	H	R	HR	HB	BB-IB	SO	ERA	AERA	OAV	OOB	AB-SH	AVG	PB	Sup	APR	PW
1983	LA N	0	1	.000	2	1	0	0-0	6	7	4	0	1	7-0	9	6.00	60	.280	.455	1-0	1.000	0	74	-1	-0.1
1984	NY N	6	6	.500	15	15	0	0-0	90	74	40	8	0	34-3	62	3.50	101	.226	.295	28-3	.179	-0	110	1	0.0
1985	NY N	9	9	.500	26	26	3	0-0	170.1	108	56	14	2	80-3	180	2.80	124	**.181**	.279	52-7	.212	2	103	14	1.6
1986	†NY N★	16	6	.727	32	31	2-1	1-0	204.1	161	82	13	2	91-1	200	3.52	101	.216	.300	68-6	.162	1	130	4	0.5
1987	NY N★	12	8	.600	28	27	3-1	0-0	156	130	75	16	8	67-8	134	3.81	99	.224	.310	43-10	.163	1*	125	-1	-0.1
1988	†NY N	12	10	.545	31	31	1-1	0-0	187	127	69	15	6	70-1	189	3.03	106	**.191**	.271	56-7	.250	6	110	6	1.2
1989	NY N	14	5	.737	35	32	6-2	0-0	219.1	157	73	21	6	75-3	198	2.83	115	.198	.271	71-10	.211	4	127	13	1.4
1990	NY N	9	14	.391	30	30	2-1	0-0	179.1	130	79	18	5	67-4	181	3.46	108	**.200**	.277	58-5	.190	1	101	5	0.6
1991	NY N	1	3	.250	8	8	0	0-0	44	36	18	4	0	9-0	31	2.86	127	.222	.262	13-1	.154	0	93	3	0.3
1992	NY N	14	11	.560	32	32	5-2	0-0	214.2	162	67	12	4	67-4	193	2.73	128	.210	.273	74-7	.203	2	113	20	2.6
1993	NY N	5	6	.455	18	18	1-1	0-0	119.2	82	42	17	3	36-0	81	2.93	137	.192	.260	32-8	.094	-1	83	16	1.1
1994	Bal A	6	6	.500	19	19	2	0-0	115.1	109	66	27	2	46-2	95	5.15	97	.248	.320	0-0	—	0	102	0	-0.1
1995	Bal A	0	4	.000	8	7	0	0-0	28	36	26	9	0	17-2	31	7.39	64	.305	.390	0-0	—	0	101	-9	-1.0
	Phi N	6	1	.857	11	11	0	0-0	64.2	48	25	11	1	21-0	79	3.34	127	.200	.267	23-1	.043	-2	109	7	0.4
1996	Phi N	3	6	.333	11	11	0	0-0	63	50	25	5	1	26-2	77	3.43	126	.215	.294	19-2	.105	0	68	7	0.9
1997	Hou N	1	0	1.000	1	1	0	0-0	5	4	2	1	0	2-0	3	3.60	111	.211	.286	1-0	.000	-0	138	0	0.1
Total	15	114	96	.543	307	300	25-9	1-0	1866.2	1421	749	191	41	715-33	1743	3.36	110	.209	.286	539-67	.182	15	110	85	9.4

FERNANDEZ, JARED Jared Wade B 2.2.1972 Salt Lake City, UT BR/TR 6-2/223# d9.19

Year	Tm Lg	W	L	Pct	G	GS	CG-Sho	SV-BS	IP	H	R	HR	HB	BB-IB	SO	ERA	AERA	OAV	OOB	AB-SH	AVG	PB	Sup	APR	PW
2001	Cin N	0	1	.000	5	2	0	0-0	12.1	13	9	1	2	6-0	5	4.38	104	.265	.368	2-0	.000	-0	71	-1	-0.1
2002	Cin N	1	3	.250	14	8	0	0-0	50.2	59	31	5	3	24-1	36	4.44	96	.294	.374	10-2	.200	0	101	-2	-0.1
2003	Hou N	3	3	.500	12	6	0	0-0	38.1	37	17	2	2	12-2	19	3.99	111	.259	.323	9-1	.000	-1	74	3	0.3
Total	3	4	7	.364	31	16	0	0-0	101.1	109	57	8	7	42-3	60	4.26	102	.277	.355	21-3	.095	-1	87	0	0.1

FERNANDEZ, OSVALDO Osvaldo B 11.4.1968 Holguin, Cuba BR/TR 6-2/190# d4.5

Year	Tm Lg	W	L	Pct	G	GS	CG-Sho	SV-BS	IP	H	R	HR	HB	BB-IB	SO	ERA	AERA	OAV	OOB	AB-SH	AVG	PB	Sup	APR	PW
1996	SF N	7	13	.350	30	28	2	0-0	171.2	193	95	20	10	57-4	106	4.61	89	.286	.348	57-5	.088	-3*	79	-8	-1.1
1997	SF N	3	4	.429	11	11	0	0-0	56.1	74	39	9	0	15-2	31	4.95	83	.314	.353	17-2	.000	-1*	102	-8	-1.0
2000	Cin N	4	3	.571	15	14	1	0-0	79.2	69	33	6	2	31-2	36	3.62	130	.238	.313	22-5	.091	-1	96	10	0.7
2001	Cin N	5	6	.455	20	14	0	0-1	79.1	103	62	8	0	33-3	35	6.92	66	.316	.376	19-3	.053	-1	88	-17	-2.1
Total	4	19	26	.422	76	67	3	0-1	387	439	229	43	12	136-11	208	4.93	87	.287	.348	115-15	.070	-7	89	-23	-3.5

FERRARESE, DON Donald Hugh B 6.19.1929 Oakland, CA BR/TL 5-9/170# d4.11

Year	Tm Lg	W	L	Pct	G	GS	CG-Sho	SV-BS	IP	H	R	HR	HB	BB-IB	SO	ERA	AERA	OAV	OOB	AB-SH	AVG	PB	Sup	APR	PW
1955	Bal A	0	0	—	6	0	0	0	9	8	3	0	0	11-0	5	3.00	127	.276	.463	1-0	.000	-0		1	0.0
1956	Bal A	4	10	.286	36	14	3-1	2	102	86	60	8	3	64-0	81	5.03	78	.229	.342	28-0	.036	-3	81	-12	-1.7
1957	Bal A	1	1	.500	8	2	0	0	19	14	13	1	0	12-1	13	4.74	76	.200	.317	3-0	.000	-0	137	-4	-0.4
1958	Cle A	3	4	.429	28	10	2	1	94.2	91	45	4	1	46-2	62	3.71	98	.254	.340	26-0	.115	-1	91	-1	-0.3
1959	Cle A	5	3	.625	15	10	4	0	76	58	29	6	1	51-2	45	3.20	115	.219	.346	27-1	.259	2	105	5	0.7
1960	Chi A	0	1	.000	5	0	0	0	4	8	8	2	0	9-0	4	18.00	21	.400	.586	2-0	.500	0		-6	-1.1
1961	Phi N	5	12	.294	42	14	3-1	1	138.2	120	64	14	1	68-4	89	3.76	108	.234	.325	35-4	.171	-1*	72	5	0.4
1962	Phi N	0	1	.000	5	0	0	0	6.2	9	8	1	0	3-0	6	8.10	48	.310	.364	1-0	1.000	0		-4	-0.4
	StL N	1	4	.200	38	0	0	1	56.2	55	19	2	1	31-4	45	2.70	158	.270	.367	5-0	.200	1		9	0.9
	Year	1	5	.167	43	0	0	1	63.1	64	30	3	1	34-4	51	3.27	129	.275	.367	6-0	.333	1		6	0.5
Total	8	19	36	.345	183	50	12-2	5	506.2	449	249	38	7	295-13	350	4.00	98	.241	.345	128-5	.156	-2	86	-7	-1.9

FERRARI, ANTHONY Anthony Michael B 6.22.1978 San Francisco, CA BL/TL 5-9/160# d6.7

Year	Tm Lg	W	L	Pct	G	GS	CG-Sho	SV-BS	IP	H	R	HR	HB	BB-IB	SO	ERA	AERA	OAV	OOB	AB-SH	AVG	PB	Sup	APR	PW
2003	Mon N	0	0	—	4	0	0	0-0	4	4	3	1	1	5-1	1	6.75	69	.267	.476	0-0	—	0		-1	0.0

FERRAZZI, BILL William Joseph B 4.19.1907 W.Quincy, MA D 8.10.1993 Gainesville, FL BR/TR 6-2.5/200# d9.7

Year	Tm Lg	W	L	Pct	G	GS	CG-Sho	SV-BS	IP	H	R	HR	HB	BB-IB	SO	ERA	AERA	OAV	OOB	AB-SH	AVG	PB	Sup	APR	PW
1935	Phi A	1	2	.333	3	2	0	0	7	7	5	0	0	5	0	5.14	88	.269	.387	1-0	.000	0	76	-1	-0.1

FERREIRA, TONY Anthony Ross B 10.4.1962 Riverside, CA BL/TL 6-1/160# d9.17

Year	Tm Lg	W	L	Pct	G	GS	CG-Sho	SV-BS	IP	H	R	HR	HB	BB-IB	SO	ERA	AERA	OAV	OOB	AB-SH	AVG	PB	Sup	APR	PW
1985	KC A	0	0	—	2	0	0	0-0	5.2	6	5	0	0	2-0	5	7.94	52	.273	.333	0-0	—	0		-2	-0.1

FERRELL, WES Wesley Cheek B 2.2.1908 Greensboro, NC D 12.9.1976 Sarasota, FL BR/TR 6-2/195# d9.9 b-Rick ▲

Year	Tm Lg	W	L	Pct	G	GS	CG-Sho	SV-BS	IP	H	R	HR	HB	BB-IB	SO	ERA	AERA	OAV	OOB	AB-SH	AVG	PB	Sup	APR	PW
1927	Cle A	0	0	—	1	0	0	0	1	3	3	0	0	2	0	27.00	16	.600	.714	0-0	—	0		-2	-0.1
1928	Cle A	0	2	.000	2	2	1	0	16	15	5	0	0	5	4	2.25	184	.242	.299	4-0	.250	1	0	3	0.5
1929	Cle A	21	10	.677	43	25	18-1	5	242.2	256	112	7	3	109	100	3.60	124	.279	.358	93-3	.237	4*	105	24	3.3
1930	Cle A	25	13	.658	43	35	25-1	3	296.2	299	141	14	0	106	143	3.31	146	.262	.325	118-3	.297	8*	113	46	5.9
1931	Cle A	22	12	.647	40	35	**27**-2	3	276.1	276	134	9	3	130	123	3.75	123	.255	.336	116-2	.319	17*	111	27	5.0
1932	Cle A	23	13	.639	38	34	26-3	1	287.2	299	141	17	0	104	105	3.66	130	.264	.326	128-6	.242	5*	90	32	4.0
1933	Cle A☆	11	12	.478	28	26	16-1	0	201	225	108	8	2	70	41	4.21	106	.282	.341	140-1	.271	7*	97	7	1.8

Year	Tm Lg	W	L	Pct	G	GS	CG-Sho	SV-BS	IP	H	R	HR	HB	BB-IB	SO	ERA	AERA	OAV	OOB	AB-SH	AVG	PB	Sup	APR	PW
1934	Bos A	14	5	.737	26	23	17-3	1	181	205	87	4	0	49	67	3.63	132	.282	.327	78-3	.282	8*	106	22	2.8
1935	Bos A	**25**	14	.641	41	**38**	**31**-3	0	**322.1**	336	149	16	3	108	110	3.52	135	.267	.326	150-8	.347	20*	101	41	**6.8**
1936	Bos A	20	15	.571	39	**38**	**28**-3	0	**301**	330	160	11	6	119	106	4.19	127	.274	.343	135-5	.267	11*	89	36	4.4
1937	Bos A	3	6	.333	12	11	5	0	73.1	111	66	14	1	34	31	7.61	62	.348	.412	33-1	.364	6*	134	-21	-1.4
	Was A☆	11	13	.458	25	24	21	0	207.2	214	111	11	2	88	92	3.94	112	.265	.339	106-2	.255	5*	87	10	1.5
	Year	14	19	.424	37	35	**26**	0	**281**	325	115	25	3	122	123	4.90	92	.289	.360	139-3	.281	11	103	-11	0.1
1938	Was A	13	8	.619	23	22	9	0	149	193	111	12	1	68	36	5.92	76	.311	.380	49-6	.224	7*	119	-23	-1.9
	NY A	2	2	.500	5	4	1	0	30	52	33	6	0	18	7	8.10	56	.388	.461	12-0	.167	0	121	-13	-1.2
	Year	15	10	.600	28	26	10	0	179	245	39	18	1	86	43	6.28	72	.325	.394	61-6	.213	7	119	-39	-3.1
1939	NY A	1	2	.333	3	3	1	0	19.1	14	10	2	0	17	6	4.66	94	.219	.383	8-0	.125	-0	47	0	0.0
1940	Bro N	0	0	—	1	0	0	0	4	4	3	0	1	4	4	6.75	59	.250	.429	2-0	.000	-0*		-1	-0.1
1941	Bos N	2	1	.667	4	3	1	0	14	13	8	1	1	9	10	5.14	69	.241	.359	4-0	.500	2	103	-2	-0.2
Total	15	193	128	.601	374	323	227-17	13	2623	2845	1382	132	23	1040	985	4.04	117	.275	.343	1176-40	.280	100	102	186	31.1
FERRICK, TOM Thomas Jerome B 1.6.1915 New York, NY D 10.15.1996 Lima, PA BR/TR 6-2.5/220# d4.19 Mil 1943-45 C12																									
1941	Phi A	8	10	.444	36	4	2-1	7	119.1	130	61	8	0	33	30	3.77	111	.275	.322	44-0	.205	1	134	4	0.9
1942	Cle A	3	2	.600	31	2	2	3	81.1	56	20	3	0	32	28	1.99	173	.200	.282	19-1	.211	0	186	**14**	1.1
1946	Cle A	0	0	—	9	0	0	1	18	25	12	3	0	4	9	5.00	66	.321	.354	3-0	.667	1		-4	-0.1
	StL A	4	1	.800	25	1	0	5	32.1	26	13	1	0	5	13	2.78	134	.224	.256	4-0	.000	-1	69	3	0.5
	Year	4	1	.800	34	1	0	6	50.1	51	16	4	0	9	22	3.58	100	.263	.296	7-0	.286	1	72	-1	0.4
1947	Was A	1	7	.125	31	0	0	9	60	57	24	1	0	20	23	3.15	118	.256	.317	10-0	.100	-1		4	0.6
1948	Was A	2	5	.286	37	0	0	10	73.2	75	37	3	0	38	34	4.15	105	.261	.348	15-0	.067	-1		2	0.2
1949	StL A	6	4	.600	50	0	0	6	104.1	102	51	9	1	41	34	3.88	117	.258	.329	21-2	.143	-1*		8	0.7
1950	StL A	1	3	.250	16	0	0	2	24	24	15	2	0	7	6	4.13	120	.267	.320	4-0	.250	-0		1	0.2
	†NY A	8	4	.667	30	0	0	9	56.2	49	26	5	0	22	20	3.65	118	.233	.306	14-1	.143	0		4	0.8
	Year	9	7	.563	46	0	0	11	80.2	73	41	7	0	29	26	3.79	118	.243	.310	18-1	.167	0		5	1.0
1951	NY A	1	1	.500	9	0	0	1	12	21	12	4	0	7	3	7.50	51	.389	.459	1-1	1.000	1		-6	-0.8
	Was A	2	0	1.000	22	0	0	2	41.2	36	16	3	0	7	17	2.38	172	.234	.267	7-1	.286	0		6	0.4
	Year	3	1	.750	31	0	0	3	53.2	57	28	7	0	14	20	3.52	115	.274	.320	8-2	.375	1		1	-0.4
1952	Was A	4	3	.571	27	0	0	1	50.2	53	19	2	0	11	28	3.02	118	.273	.312	5-1	.200	1		3	0.6
Total	9	40	40	.500	323	7	4-1	56	674	654	306	44	1	227	245	3.47	117	.256	.317	147-7	.184	1	137	39	5.1
FERRIS, BOB Robert Eugene B 5.7.1955 Arlington, VA BR/TR 6-6/225# d9.12																									
1979	Cal A	0	0	—	2	0	0	0-0	6	5	2	1	0	3-1	2	1.50	272	.217	.308	0-0	—	0		1	0.1
1980	Cal A	0	2	.000	5	3	0	0-0	15.1	23	13	2	0	9-0	4	5.87	67	.354	.432	0-0	—	0	83	-4	-0.5
Total	2	0	2	.000	7	3	0	0-0	21.1	28	15	3	0	12-1	6	4.64	86	.318	.400	0-0	—	0	83	-3	-0.4
FERRISS, DAVE David Meadow "Boo" B 12.5.1921 Shaw, MS BL/TR 6-2/208# d4.29 C5																									
1945	Bos A❖	21	10	.677	35	31	26-5	2	264.2	263	101	6	7	85	94	2.96	115	.264	.327	120-1	.267	11*	118	13	3.0
1946	†Bos A☆	25	6	**.806**	40	35	26-6	3	274	274	109	14	3	71	106	3.25	113	.259	.308	115-2	.209	2*	144	13	1.8
1947	Bos A	12	11	.522	33	28	14-1	0	218.1	241	106	14	7	92	64	4.04	96	.287	.362	99-0	.273	7*	113	-1	0.5
1948	Bos A	7	3	.700	31	9	1	3	115.1	127	71	7	7	61	30	5.23	84	.286	.381	37-2	.243	2	135	-9	-0.6
1949	Bos A	0	0	—	4	0	0	0	6.2	7	3	1	1	4	1	4.05	108	.292	.414	1-0	1.000	1		0	0.1
1950	Bos A	0	0	—	1	0	0	0	1	2	2	0	0	1	1	18.00	27	.500	.600	0-0	—	0		-1	-0.1
Total	6	65	30	.684	144	103	67-12	8	880	914	392	42	25	314	296	3.64	103	.272	.338	372-5	.250	23	126	15	4.7
FERRY, CY Alfred Joseph B 9.27.1878 Hudson, NY D 9.27.1938 Pittsfield, MA BR/TR 6-1/170# d5.12 b-Jack																									
1904	Det A	0	1	.000	3	1	1	0	13	12	9	0	1	11	4	6.23	41	.245	.393	6-0	.333	1	196	-4	-0.2
1905	Cle A	0	0	—	1	1	0	0	2	3	3	1	2	0	2	13.50	19	.333	.455	1-0	.000	-0	135	-2	-0.1
Total	2	0	1	.000	4	2	1	0	15	15	12	1	3	11	6	7.20	36	.259	.403	7-0	.286	1	167	-6	-0.3
FERRY, JACK John Francis B 4.7.1887 Pittsfield, MA D 8.29.1954 Pittsfield, MA BR/TR 5-11/175# d9.4 b-Cy																									
1910	Pit N	1	2	.333	6	3	2	0	31	26	10	0	1	8	12	2.32	133	.230	.287	9-2	.333	1	48	3	0.4
1911	Pit N	6	4	.600	26	8	4-1	3	85.2	83	35	3	2	27	32	3.15	109	.260	.322	29-2	.310	3*	148	4	0.7
1912	Pit N	2	0	1.000	11	3	1-1	1	39	33	21	1	1	23	10	3.00	109	.234	.345	13-0	.077	-1	142	-1	-0.1
1913	Pit N	1	0	1.000	4	0	0	0	5	4	3	0	0	2	2	5.40	56	.286	.375	0-0	—	0		-1	-0.2
Total	4	10	6	.625	47	14	7-2	4	160.2	146	69	4	4	60	56	3.02	110	.249	.323	51-4	.255	3	127	5	0.8
FERSON, ALEX Alexander "Colonel" B 7.14.1866 Philadelphia, PA D 12.5.1957 Boston, MA BR/TR 5-9/165# d5.4																									
1889	Was N	17	17	.500	36	34	28-1	0	288.1	319	199	9	12	105	85	3.90	101	.272	.338	114	.114	-5	83	0	-0.5
1890	Buf P	1	7	.125	10	10	7	0	71	88	66	5	1	40	13	5.45	75	.291	.376	32	.219	1*	104	-11	-0.7
1892	Bal N	0	1	.000	2	1	1	0	9	17	13	1	0	6	8	11.00	31	.386	.460	4	.000	-1	55	-6	-0.5
Total	3	18	25	.419	48	45	36-1	0	368.1	424	278	15	13	151	106	4.37	91	.279	.349	150	.133	-5	88	-17	-1.7
FETTE, LOU Louis Henry William B 3.15.1907 Alma, MO D 1.3.1981 Warrensburg, MO BR/TR 6-1.5/200# d4.26																									
1937	Bos N	20	10	.667	35	33	23-**5**	0	259	243	93	5	4	81	70	2.88	124	.251	.311	92-7	.239	3*	103	23	2.8
1938	Bos N	11	13	.458	33	32	17-3	1	239.2	235	95	11	4	79	83	3.15	109	.258	.320	85-2	.188	0	89	10	1.0
1939	Bos N★	10	10	.500	27	26	11-**6**	0	146	123	62	7	1	61	35	2.96	125	.229	.309	49-4	.061	-4	87	10	0.9
1940	Bos N	0	5	.000	7	5	0	0	32.1	38	23	0	1	18	2	5.57	67	.302	.393	8-1	.375	1	56	-7	-0.8
	Bro N	0	0	—	2	0	0	0	3	3	0	0	0	2	0	0.00	—	.300	.417	0-0	—	0		1	0.1
	Year	0	5	.000	9	5	0	0	35.1	41	25	0	1	20	2	5.09	73	.301	.395	8-1	.375	1	56	-5	-0.7
1945	Bos N	0	2	.000	5	1	0	0	11	16	10	1	1	7	4	5.73	67	.356	.453	2-0	.000	-0	0	-3	-0.5
Total	5	41	40	.506	109	97	51-14	1	691	658	283	24	11	248	194	3.15	113	.253	.321	236-14	.186	-0	91	34	3.5
FETTERS, MIKE Michael Lee B 12.19.1964 Van Nuys, CA BR/TR 6-4/212# d9.1																									
1989	Cal A	0	0	—	1	0	0	0-0	3.1	5	4	1	0	1-0	4	8.10	47	.333	.375	0-0	—	0		-2	-0.1
1990	Cal A	1	1	.500	26	2	0	1-0	67.2	77	33	9	2	20-0	35	4.12	93	.287	.341	0-0	—	0	262	-1	0.0
1991	Cal A	2	5	.286	19	4	0	0-1	44.2	53	29	4	3	28-2	24	4.84	85	.305	.410	0-0	—	0	95	-5	-0.7
1992	Mil A	5	1	.833	50	0	0	2-3	62.2	38	15	3	7	24-2	43	1.87	206	.185	.290	0-0	—	0		14	1.3
1993	Mil A	3	3	.500	45	0	0	0-0	59.1	59	29	4	2	22-4	23	3.34	128	.278	.344	0-0	—	0		4	0.4
1994	Mil A	1	4	.200	42	0	0	17-3	46	41	16	0	1	27-5	31	2.54	198	.243	.345	0-0	—	0		11	1.8
1995	Mil A	0	3	.000	40	0	0	22-5	34.2	40	16	3	0	20-4	33	3.38	148	.286	.373	0-0	—	0		5	0.9
1996	Mil A	3	3	.500	61	0	0	32-6	61.1	65	28	4	1	26-4	53	3.38	154	.274	.343	0-0	—	0		11	1.8
1997	Mil A	1	5	.167	51	0	0	6-5	70.1	62	30	4	1	33-3	62	3.45	134	.244	.329	0-0	—	0		9	0.8
1998	Oak A	1	6	.143	48	0	0	5-3	47.1	48	26	3	1	21-2	34	3.99	115	.258	.333	0-0	—	0		2	0.3
	Ana A	1	2	.333	12	0	0	0-1	11.1	14	8	2	0	4-0	9	5.56	84	.304	.360	0-0	—	0		-1	-0.2
	Year	2	8	.200	60	0	0	5-4	58.2	62	38	5	1	25-2	43	4.30	107	.267	.338	0-0	—	0		0	0.1
1999	Bal A	1	0	1.000	27	0	0	0-3	31	35	23	5	2	22-2	22	5.81	81	.278	.393	0-0	—	0		-5	-0.2
2000	LA N	6	2	.750	51	0	0	5-2	50	35	18	7	2	25-2	40	3.24	134	.205	.313	0-0	—	0		7	1.2
2001	LA N	2	1	.667	34	0	0	1-2	29.2	33	23	6	1	13-0	26	6.07	66	.273	.341	0-0	—	0		-8	-0.8
	Pit N	1	1	.500	20	0	0	8-1	17.2	16	9	1	3	13-1	11	4.58	98	.235	.381	0-0	—	0		0	0.0
	Year	3	2	.600	54	0	0	9-3	47.1	49	32	7	4	26-1	37	5.51	76	.259	.356	0-0	—	0		-7	-0.8
2002	Pit N	1	0	1.000	32	0	0	0-1	30.1	25	13	3	1	18-1	29	3.26	128	.219	.328	0-0	—	0		3	0.1
	†Ari N	2	3	.400	33	0	0	0-1	24.2	28	18	1	2	19-5	24	5.11	87	.292	.415	0-0	—	0		-3	-0.5
	Year	3	3	.500	65	0	0	0-2	55	53	31	4	3	37-6	53	4.09	105	.252	.369	0-0	—	0		-1	-0.4
2003	Min A	0	0	—	5	0	0	0-0	6	2	0	0	1	1-0	1	0.00	—	.100	.182	0-0	—	0		3	0.1
Total	15	31	40	.437	597	6	0	99-37	698	676	338	60	30	337-37	504	3.73	119	.258	.346	0-0	—	0	135	44	6.2
FICK, JOHN John Ralph B 5.18.1921 Baltimore, MD D 6.9.1958 Somers Point, NJ BL/TL 5-10/150# d7.29																									
1944	Phi N	0	0	—	4	0	0	0	5.1	3	2	0	1	3	2	3.38	107	.150	.292	0-0	—	0		0	0.0
FIDRYCH, MARK Mark Steven "The Bird" B 8.14.1954 Worcester, MA BR/TR 6-3/175# d4.20																									
1976	Det A★	19	9	.679	31	29	**24**-4	0-0	250.1	217	76	12	3	53-3	97	**2.34**	**159**	.235	.277	0-0	—	0	85	**36**	**4.4**
1977	Det A❖	6	4	.600	11	11	7-1	0-0	81	82	29	2	1	12-2	42	2.89	149	.269	.295	0-0	—	0	95	12	1.4

Year	Tm Lg	W	L	Pct	G	GS	CG-Sho	SV-BS	IP	H	R	HR	HB	BB-IB	SO	ERA	AERA	OAV	OOB	AB-SH	AVG	PB	Sup	APR	PW
1978	Det A	2	0	1.000	3	3	2	0-0	22	17	6	1	0	5-0	10	2.45	158	.213	.259	0-0	—	0	147	4	0.4
1979	Det A	0	3	.000	4	4	0	0-0	14.2	23	17	3	1	9-2	5	10.43	42	.371	.458	0-0	—	0	99	-9	-1.4
1980	Det A	2	3	.400	9	9	1	0-0	44.1	58	35	5	1	20-2	16	5.68	72	.309	.376	0-0	—	0*	147	-10	-0.9
Total	5	29	19	.604	58	56	34-5	0-0	412.1	397	163	23	6	99-9	170	3.10	126	.255	.300	0-0	—	0	103	33	3.9
FIEBER, CLARENCE Clarence Thomas "Lefty" B 9.4.1913 San Francisco, CA D 8.20.1985 Redwood City, CA BL/TL 6-4/187# d5.18																									
1932	Chi A	1	0	1.000	3	0	0	0	5.1	6	1	0	0	3	1	1.69	256	.273	.360	0-0	—	0		2	0.3
FIELD, JIM James C. B 4.24.1863 Philadelphia, PA D 5.13.1953 Atlantic City, NJ 6-1/170# d6.2.1883 ▲																									
1890	Roc AA	1	0	1.000	2	1	1	1	9.2	7	4	0	1	4	2	2.79	128	.194	.293	188	.202	1*	189	1	0.1
FIELD, NATE Nathan Patrick B 12.11.1975 Denver, CO BR/TR 6-2/185# d4.12																									
2002	KC A	0	0	—	5	0	0	0-0	5	8	5	2	0	3-1	3	9.00	56	.364	.440	0-0	—	0		-2	-0.1
2003	KC A	1	1	.500	19	0	0	0-0	21.2	19	10	3	1	14-1	19	4.15	125	.235	.351	0-0	—	0		2	0.2
Total	2	1	1	.500	24	0	0	0-0	26.2	27	15	5	1	17-2	22	5.06	102	.262	.369	0-0	—	0		0	0.1
FIENE, LOU Louis Henry "Big Finn" B 12.29.1884 Ft.Dodge, IA D 12.22.1964 Chicago, IL BR/TR 6/175# d5.7																									
1906	Chi A	1	1	.500	6	2	1	0	31	35	17	0	4	9	12	2.90	87	.287	.356	10-0	.200	0	57	-2	-0.1
1907	Chi A	0	1	.000	6	1	1	1	26	30	17	0	2	7	15	4.15	58	.291	.348	11-0	.182	-0*	113	-6	-0.3
1908	Chi A	0	1	.000	1	1	1	0	9	9	7	0	0	1	3	4.00	58	.257	.278	3-0	.000	-0	30	-2	-0.3
1909	Chi A	2	5	.286	13	6	4	0	72	75	37	1	5	18	24	4.13	57	.284	.341	29-1	.069	-2*	65	-11	-1.2
Total	4	3	8	.273	26	10	7	1	138	149	78	1	11	35	54	3.85	62	.284	.342	53-1	.113	-2	64	-21	-1.9
FIFE, DANNY Danny Wayne B 10.5.1949 Harrisburg, IL BR/TR 6-3/175# d8.18																									
1973	Min A	3	2	.600	10	7	1	0-0	51.2	54	26	2	3	29-0	18	4.35	91	.270	.369	0-0	—	0	129	-1	-0.1
1974	Min A	0	0	—	4	0	0	0-0	4.2	10	11	0	1	4-0	3	17.36	22	.417	.517	0-0	—	0		-7	-0.4
Total	2	3	2	.600	14	7	1	0-0	56.1	64	37	2	4	33-0	21	5.43	73	.286	.385	0-0	—	0	129	-8	-0.5
FIFIELD, JACK John Proctor B 10.5.1871 Enfield, NH D 11.27.1939 Syracuse, NY BR/TR 5-11/160# d4.28																									
1897	Phi N	5	18	.217	27	26	21	0	210.2	263	163	8	9	80	38	5.51	76	.303	.368	77-2	.234	3	88	-28	-2.0
1898	Phi N	11	9	.550	21	21	18-2	0	171.1	170	91	2	18	60	31	3.31	104	.257	.336	64-3	.109	-4	123	3	-0.2
1899	Phi N	3	8	.273	14	11	9-1	1	92.2	110	64	0	4	36	8	4.08	90	.294	.362	35-0	.257	1	106	-5	-0.4
	Was N	2	4	.333	6	6	6	0	47	73	44	1	2	17	12	6.13	64	.353	.407	20-0	.200	-0*	123	-11	-1.1
	Year	5	12	.294	20	17	15-1	1	139.2	183	51	1	6	53	20	4.77	79	.315	.378	55-0	.236	1	112	-15	-1.5
Total	3	21	39	.350	68	64	54-3	1	521.2	616	362	11	33	193	89	4.59	83	.292	.360	196-5	.194	-0	105	-41	-3.7
FIGGEMEIER, FRANK Frank Y. B 4.22.1873 St.Louis, MO D 4.15.1915 St.Louis, MO d9.25																									
1894	Phi N	0	1	.000	1	1	1	0	8	12	14	1	3	4	2	11.25	46	.343	.452	3-1	.333	0	97	-6	-0.4
FIGUEROA, ED Eduardo (Padilla) B 10.14.1948 Ciales, P.R. BR/TR 6-1/190# d4.9																									
1974	Cal A	2	8	.200	25	12	5-1	0-0	105.1	119	46	3	4	36-2	49	3.67	94	.294	.355	0-0	—	0	81	-1	-0.1
1975	Cal A	16	13	.552	33	32	16-2	0-0	244.2	213	96	14	5	84-6	139	2.91	122	.233	.299	0-0	—	0	101	17	1.9
1976	†NY A	19	10	.655	34	34	14-4	0-0	256.2	237	101	13	3	94-0	119	3.02	113	.246	.312	0-0	—	0	132	10	0.8
1977	†NY A	16	11	.593	32	32	12-2	0-0	239.1	228	102	19	3	75-1	104	3.57	111	.252	.308	0-0	—	0	103	12	1.2
1978	†NY A	20	9	.690	35	35	12-2	0-0	253	233	96	22	3	77-4	92	2.99	122	.248	.305	0-0	—	0	112	18	2.0
1979	NY A	4	6	.400	16	16	4-1	0-0	104.2	109	49	6	0	35-1	42	4.13	99	.275	.333	0-0	—	0	98	1	0.1
1980	NY A	3	3	.500	15	9	0	1-0	58	90	47	3	1	24-2	16	6.98	56	.363	.417	0-0	—	0	104	-18	-1.7
	Tex A	0	7	.000	8	8	0	0-0	39.2	62	29	9	0	12-0	9	5.90	66	.365	.400	0-0	—	0	57	-9	-1.2
	Year	3	10	.231	23	17	0	1-0	97.2	152	32	12	1	36-2	25	6.54	60	.364	.410	0-0	—	0	82	-27	-2.9
1981	Oak A	0	0	—	2	1	0	0-0	8.1	8	5	1	0	6-0	1	5.40	65	.258	.378	0-0	—	0	103	-2	-0.1
Total	8	80	67	.544	200	179	63-12	1-0	1309.2	1299	571	90	19	443-16	571	3.51	105	.261	.322	0-0	—	0	106	28	2.9
FIGUEROA, NELSON Nelson Walter B 5.18.1974 Brooklyn, NY BB/TR 6-1/155# d6.3																									
2000	Ari N	0	1	.000	3	3	0	0-0	15.2	17	13	4	0	5-0	7	7.47	63	.283	.328	3-1	.333	0	117	-4	-0.2
2001	Phi N	4	5	.444	19	13	0	0-0	89	95	40	8	7	37-3	61	3.94	108	.275	.357	24-1	.250	2	105	4	0.4
2002	Mil N	1	7	.125	30	11	0	0-0	93	96	59	18	4	37-6	51	5.03	81	.270	.342	15-4	.133	-0	109	-11	-0.9
2003	Pit N	2	1	.667	12	3	0	0-0	35.1	28	13	8	2	13-2	23	3.31	133	.220	.299	7-0	.000	-1	100	5	0.3
Total	4	7	14	.333	64	30	0	0-0	233	236	125	38	13	92-11	142	4.52	94	.266	.341	49-6	.184	1	108	-6	-0.4
FIKAC, JEREMY Jeremy Joseph B 4.8.1975 Shiner, TX BR/TR 6-2/185# d8.16																									
2001	SD N	2	0	1.000	23	0	0	0-2	26.1	15	6	2	1	5-1	19	1.37	293	.165	.216	0-0	—	0		8	0.5
2002	SD N	4	7	.364	65	0	0	0-6	69	74	50	13	3	34-8	66	5.35	71	.267	.351	2-0	.000	-0		-16	-2.3
2003	Oak A	0	1	.000	14	0	0	0-0	16	14	8	4	3	11-1	9	4.50	100	.246	.394	0-0	—	0		0	0.0
Total	3	6	8	.429	102	0	0	0-8	111.1	103	64	19	7	50-10	94	4.28	92	.242	.331	2-0	.000	-0		-8	-1.8
FILE, BOB Robert Michael B 1.28.1977 Philadelphia, PA BR/TR 6-4/215# d4.14																									
2001	Tor A	5	3	.625	60	0	0	0-2	74.1	57	28	6	7	29-8	38	3.27	141	.220	.314	0-0	—	0		11	1.1
2002	Tor A	0	1	.000	5	0	0	0-0	3.1	8	7	0	0	2-0	2	18.90	24	.471	.526	0-0	—	0		-5	-0.9
Total	2	5	4	.556	65	0	0	0-2	77.2	65	35	6	7	31-8	40	3.94	117	.236	.327	0-0	—	0		6	0.2
FILER, TOM Thomas Carson B 12.1.1956 Philadelphia, PA BR/TR 6-1/198# d6.8																									
1982	Chi N	1	2	.333	8	8	0	0-0	40.2	50	25	5	0	18-2	15	5.53	68	.301	.370	12-1	.083	-0	88	-6	-0.4
1985	Tor A	7	0	1.000	11	9	0	0-0	48.2	38	21	6	0	18-0	24	3.88	108	.222	.295	0-0	—	0	156	3	0.3
1988	Mil A	5	8	.385	19	16	2-1	0-0	101.2	108	54	8	1	33-4	39	4.43	90	.281	.333	0-0	—	0	99	-4	-0.4
1989	Mil A	7	3	.700	13	13	0	0-0	72.1	74	30	6	4	23-1	20	3.61	107	.271	.337	0-0	—	0*	131	3	0.4
1990	Mil A	2	3	.400	7	4	0	0-0	22	26	17	2	0	9-0	8	6.14	63	.289	.354	0-0	—	0	47	-5	-1.0
1992	NY N	0	1	.000	9	1	0	0-0	22	18	8	2	0	6-2	9	2.05	170	.222	.276	3-0	.000	-0	26	2	0.1
Total	6	22	17	.564	67	51	2-1	0-0	307.1	314	155	29	5	107-9	115	4.25	92	.269	.331	15-1	.067	-1	111	-7	-1.0
FILES, EDDIE Charles Edward B 5.19.1883 Portland, ME D 5.10.1954 Cornish, ME BR/TR d10.3																									
1908	Phi A	0	0	—	2	0	0	0	9	8	7	0	2	3	6	6.00	43	.286	.394	3-0	.000	-0		-3	-0.2
FILLEY, MARC Marcus Lucius B 2.28.1912 Lansingburgh, NY D 1.20.1995 Yarmouth, ME BR/TR 5-11/172# d4.19																									
1934	Was A	0	0	—	1	0	0	0	0.1	2	1	0	0	0	0	27.00	16	.667	.667	0-0	—	0		-1	0.0
FILLINGIM, DANA Dana B 11.6.1893 Columbus, GA D 2.3.1961 Tuskegee, AL BL/TR 5-10/175# d8.2 Mil 1918																									
1915	Phi A	0	5	.000	8	4	1	0	39.1	42	25	0	1	32	17	3.43	85	.313	.449	12-1	.167	-0	62	-4	-0.5
1918	Bos N	7	6	.538	14	13	10-4	0	113	99	37	0	5	28	29	2.23	120	.243	.300	42-1	.214	0	104	6	0.7
1919	Bos N	6	13	.316	32	18	9	2	186.1	185	80	2	2	39	50	3.38	85	.270	.312	65-4	.246	1	79	-8	-0.5
1920	Bos N	12	21	.364	37	31	22-2	0	272	292	123	8	3	79	66	3.11	98	.287	.340	92-1	.174	-2*	75	-5	-0.5
1921	Bos N	15	10	.600	44	23	11-**3**	1	239.2	249	108	10	2	56	54	3.45	106	.272	.316	85-1	.247	5*	107	5	0.9
1922	Bos N	5	9	.357	25	12	5-1	2	117	143	74	6	1	37	25	4.54	88	.311	.363	38-1	.158	-2	75	-7	-0.9
1923	Bos N	1	9	.100	35	12	1	0	100.1	141	74	6	1	36	27	5.20	77	.345	.399	31-1	.226	1*	69	-15	-1.2
1925	Phi N	1	0	1.000	5	1	0	0	8.2	19	12	0	0	6	2	10.38	46	.432	.500	3-0	.000	0	230	-5	-0.4
Total	8	47	73	.392	200	114	59-10	5	1076.1	1170	533	32	15	313	270	3.56	93	.287	.340	368-10	.209	4	86	-33	-2.4
FILSON, PETE William Peter B 9.28.1958 Darby, PA BB/TL 6-2/195# d5.15																									
1982	Min A	0	2	.000	5	3	0	0-0	12.1	17	12	2	0	8-1	10	8.76	49	.321	.397	0-0	—	0	71	-6	-0.8
1983	Min A	4	1	.800	26	8	0	1-0	90	87	34	9	1	29-0	49	3.40	125	.252	.310	0-0	—	0	91	10	0.4
1984	Min A	6	5	.545	55	7	0	1-2	118.2	106	56	14	3	54-7	59	4.10	103	.238	.323	0-0	—	0	98	3	0.2
1985	Min A	4	5	.444	40	6	1	2-1	95.2	93	42	13	0	30-4	42	3.67	120	.251	.305	0-0	—	0	93	8	0.7
1986	Min A	0	0	—	4	0	0	0-0	6.1	13	4	1	1	2-0	4	5.68	76	.406	.457	0-0	—	0		-1	0.0
	Chi A	0	1	.000	3	1	0	0-0	11.2	14	9	4	0	5-0	4	6.17	70	.286	.352	0-0	—	0	42	-2	-0.2
	Year	0	1	.000	7	1	0	0-0	18	27	11	5	1	7-0	8	6.00	72	.333	.393	0-0	—	0	42	-3	-0.2
1987	NY A	1	0	1.000	7	2	0	0-0	22	26	10	2	1	9-1	10	3.27	134	.299	.371	0-0	—	0	73	2	0.1
1990	KC A	0	4	.000	8	7	0	0-0	35	42	31	6	2	13-0	9	5.91	65	.282	.345	0-0	—	0	71	-10	-1.0
Total	7	15	18	.455	148	34	1	4-3	391.2	398	198	51	8	150-13	187	4.18	102	.260	.327	0-0	—	0	83	4	-0.6

Year	Tm Lg	W	L	Pct	G	GS	CG-Sho	SV-BS	IP	H	R	HR	HB	BB-IB	SO	ERA	AERA	OAV	OOB	AB-SH	AVG	PB	Sup	APR	PW
FINCH, JOEL Joel D B 8.20.1956 South Bend, IN BR/TR 6-2/175# d6.12																									
1979	Bos A	0	3	.000	15	7	0	0-0	57.1	65	31	5	1	25-3	25	4.87	91	.289	.361	1-0	.000	-0	79	-1	0.0
FINCHER, BILL William Allen B 5.26.1894 Atlanta, GA D 5.7.1946 Shreveport, LA BR/TR 6-1/180# d4.23																									
1916	StL A	0	1	.000	12	1	0	0	21	22	11	0	0	7	5	2.14	128	.282	.341	4-0	.250	0	55	0	0.1
FINE, TOMMY Thomas Morgan B 10.10.1914 Cleburne, TX BB/TR 6/180# d4.26																									
1947	Bos A	1	2	.333	9	7	1	0	36	41	24	0	1	19	10	5.50	71	.285	.372	9-2	.333	1	124	-6	-0.3
1950	StL A	0	1	.000	14	0	0	0	36.2	53	38	6	0	25	6	8.10	61	.342	.433	12-0	.333	1*		-12	-0.4
Total	2	1	3	.250	23	7	1	0	72.2	94	62	6	1	44	16	6.81	65	.314	.404	21-2	.333	2	124	-18	-0.7
FINGERS, ROLLIE Roland Glen B 8.25.1946 Steubenville, OH BR/TR 6-4/195# d9.15 HF1992																									
1968	Oak A	0	0	—	1	0	0	0	1.1	4	4	1	1	1-0	0	27.00	10	.571	.667	0-0	—	0		-4	-0.2
1969	Oak A	6	7	.462	60	8	1-1	12-6	119	116	60	13	4	41-5	61	3.71	93	.257	.323	25-3	.200	0	135	-6	-0.7
1970	Oak A	7	9	.438	45	19	1	2-1	148	137	65	13	2	48-5	79	3.65	97	.250	.310	39-4	.103	-0	89	-1	-0.1
1971	†Oak A	4	6	.400	48	8	2-1	17-3	129.1	94	46	14	8	30-3	98	2.99	112	.207	.266	33-5	.212	1	87	6	0.9
1972	†Oak A	11	9	.550	65	0	0	21-5	111.1	85	35	8	1	32-7	113	2.51	114	.212	.271	19-1	.316	3		5	1.3
1973	†Oak A★	7	8	.467	62	2	0	22-5	126.2	107	41	5	4	39-6	110	1.92	185	.226	.288	1-0	.000	-0	25	20	3.0
1974	†Oak A★	9	5	.643	**76**	0	0	18-7	119	104	41	5	1	29-6	95	2.65	126	.240	.282	0-0	—	0		10	1.5
1975	†Oak A☆	10	6	.625	**75**	0	0	24-8	126.2	95	43	13	6	33-5	115	2.98	122	.213	.274	1-0	.000	-0*		12	1.9
1976	Oak A☆	13	11	.542	70	0	0	20-14	134.2	118	40	3	7	40-10	113	2.47	136	.243	.304	0-0	—	0		15	3.2
1977	SD N	8	9	.471	**78**	0	0	**35-11**	132.1	123	47	12	1	36-12	113	2.99	118	.248	.298	20-1	.050	-2		11	1.6
1978	SD N★	6	13	.316	67	0	0	**37-10**	107.1	84	33	4	1	29-12	72	2.52	132	.212	.265	12-2	.167	-0		11	2.4
1979	SD N	9	9	.500	54	0	0	13-10	83.2	91	47	7	1	37-8	65	4.52	78	.281	.351	12-1	.083	-1		-9	-2.0
1980	SD N	11	9	.550	66	0	0	23-6	103	101	35	3	0	32-13	69	2.80	123	.263	.315	18-1	.278	2		8	1.9
1981	†Mil A★	6	3	.667	47	0	0	**28-6**	78	55	9	3	1	13-5	61	1.04	330	.198	.235	0-0	—	0		**22**	**4.6**
1982	Mil A★	5	6	.455	50	0	0	29-6	79.2	63	23	5	1	20-5	71	2.60	146	.220	.268	0-0	—	0		13	2.6
1984	Mil A	1	2	.333	33	0	0	23-3	46	38	13	5	0	13-2	40	1.96	197	.213	.267	0-0	—	0		9	1.5
1985	Mil A	1	6	.143	47	0	0	17-8	55.1	59	33	9	0	19-5	24	5.04	83	.272	.329	0-0	—	0		-4	-0.7
Total	17	114	118	.491	944	37	4-2	341-**109**	1701.1	1474	615	123	39	492-109	1299	2.90	119	.235	.292	180-18	.172	2	95	118	22.7
FINK, HERMAN Herman Adam B 8.22.1911 Concord, NC D 8.24.1980 Salisbury, NC BR/TR 6-2/198# d9.16																									
1935	Phi A	0	3	.000	5	3	0	0	15.2	18	19	0	1	10	2	9.19	49	.290	.397	5-0	.200	-0	57	-8	-1.2
1936	Phi A	8	16	.333	34	24	9	3	188.2	222	126	18	0	78	53	5.39	95	.294	.360	64-0	.125	-4	65	-5	-0.9
1937	Phi A	2	1	.667	28	3	1	1	80	82	43	6	1	35	18	4.05	116	.263	.339	24-0	.208	-1	99	6	0.2
Total	3	10	20	.333	67	30	10	4	284.1	322	188	24	2	123	73	5.22	95	.285	.356	93-0	.151	-5	68	-7	-1.9
FINLAYSON, PEMBROKE Pembroke B 7.31.1888 Cheraw, SC D 3.6.1912 Brooklyn, NY BR/TR 5-6/140# d6.6																									
1908	Bro N	0	0	—	1	0	0	0	0.1	0	5	0	0	4	0	135.00	2	.000	.800	0-0	—	0		-4	-0.2
1909	Bro N	0	0	—	1	0	0	0	7	7	4	0	0	4	2	5.14	50	.212	.297	3-0	.000	-0		-2	-0.1
Total	2	0	0	—	2	0	0	0	7.1	7	9	0	0	8	2	11.05	23	.206	.357	3-0	.000	-0		-6	-0.3
FINLEY, CHUCK Charles Edward B 11.26.1962 Monroe, LA BL/TL 6-6/214# d5.29																									
1986	†Cal A	3	1	.750	25	0	0	0-0	46.1	40	17	2	1	23-1	37	3.30	125	.235	.330	0-0	—	0		5	0.4
1987	Cal A	2	7	.222	35	3	0	0-2	90.2	102	54	7	3	43-3	63	4.67	93	.287	.367	0-0	—	0	141	-4	-0.3
1988	Cal A	9	15	.375	31	31	2	0-0	194.1	191	95	15	6	82-7	111	4.17	93	.263	.339	0-0	—	0	91	-5	-0.6
1989	Cal A☆	16	9	.640	29	29	9-1	0-0	199.2	171	64	13	2	82-0	156	2.57	149	.233	.311	0-0	—	0	91	27	3.2
1990	Cal A★	18	9	.667	32	32	7-2	0-0	236	210	77	17	2	81-3	177	2.40	159	.243	.308	0-0	—	0	107	36	4.0
1991	Cal A	18	9	.667	34	34	4-2	0-0	227.1	205	102	23	8	101-1	171	3.80	108	.244	.330	0-0	—	0	107	9	0.9
1992	Cal A	7	12	.368	31	31	4-1	0-0	204.1	212	99	24	3	98-2	124	3.96	101	.277	.358	0-0	—	0	93	0	-0.1
1993	Cal A	16	14	.533	35	35	**13**-2	0-0	251.1	243	108	22	6	82-1	187	3.15	143	.253	.314	0-0	—	0	80	32	3.5
1994	Cal A	10	10	.500	25	**25**	7-2	0-0	**183.1**	178	95	21	3	71-0	148	4.32	113	.260	.329	0-0	—	0	80	11	0.9
1995	Cal A☆	15	12	.556	32	32	2-1	0-0	203	192	106	20	7	93-1	195	4.21	112	.249	.333	0-0	—	0	113	9	1.0
1996	†Cal A★	15	16	.484	35	35	4-1	0-0	238	241	124	27	11	94-5	215	4.16	120	.263	.336	0-0	—	0	69	22	2.4
1997	Ana A	13	6	.684	25	25	3-1	0-0	164	152	79	20	5	65-0	155	4.23	108	.248	.323	6-0	.000	-1	107	9	0.8
1998	Ana A	11	9	.550	34	34	1-1	0-0	223.1	210	97	20	6	109-1	212	3.39	139	.246	.334	4-0	.000	-0	84	30	2.3
1999	Ana A	12	11	.522	33	33	1	0-0	213.1	197	117	23	8	94-2	200	4.43	110	.246	.330	4-1	.000	-0	90	9	0.8
2000	Cle A☆	16	11	.593	34	34	3	0-0	218	211	108	23	2	101-3	189	4.17	119	.256	.337	7-0	.000	-1	112	19	1.8
2001	†Cle A	8	7	.533	22	22	1	0-0	113.2	131	78	14	2	35-0	96	5.54	82	.290	.341	0-0	—	0	115	-13	-1.5
2002	Cle A	4	11	.267	18	18	1	0-0	105.1	114	56	6	0	48-3	91	4.44	99	.284	.356	4-0	.000	-0	66	-1	-0.1
	†StL N	7	4	.636	14	14	1-1	0-0	85.1	69	41	7	1	30-3	83	3.80	104	.219	.288	28-5	.107	-1	115	1	-0.1
Total	17	200	173	.536	524	467	63-15	0-2	3197.1	3069	1517	304	76	1332-36	2610	3.85	115	.255	.331	53-6	.057	-4	95	196	19.3
FINNERAN, HAPPY Joseph Ignatius "Smokey Joe" B 10.29.1891 E.Orange, NJ D 2.3.1942 Orange, NJ BR/TR 5-10.5/169# d8.20																									
1912	Phi N	0	2	.000	14	4	0	1	46.1	50	27	2	1	10	10	2.53	144	.282	.324	10-0	.200	0	86	2	0.1
1913	Phi N	0	0	—	3	0	0	0	5	12	7	0	0	2	0	7.20	46	.462	.500	3-0	.667	1		-3	0.0
1914	Bro F	12	11	.522	27	23	13-2	1	175.1	153	77	6	6	60	54	3.18	90	.237	.308	55-4	.127	-5	92	-4	-1.1
1915	Bro F	10	12	.455	37	24	12-1	2	215.1	197	90	2	9	87	68	2.80	97	.249	.331	74-0	.149	-5*	91	-2	-0.7
1918	Det A	0	2	.000	5	2	0	1	13.2	22	17	0	0	8	2	9.88	27	.393	.469	3-0	.000	-0*	170	-11	-1.5
	NY A	3	6	.333	23	13	4	0	114.1	134	52	7	2	35	34	3.78	75	.305	.359	39-1	.231	1	123	-9	-0.7
	Year	3	8	.273	28	15	4	1	128	156	57	7	2	43	36	4.43	63	.315	.372	42-1	.214	0	129	-18	-2.2
Total	5	25	33	.431	109	66	29-3	5	570	568	270	17	18	202	168	3.30	87	.266	.335	184-5	.168	-7	99	-27	-3.9
FINNVOLD, GAR Anders Gar B 3.11.1968 Boynton Beach, FL BR/TR 6-5/195# d5.10																									
1994	Bos A	0	4	.000	8	8	0	0-0	36.1	45	27	4	3	15-0	17	5.94	85	.304	.377	0-0	—	0	78	-4	-0.4
FIORE, TONY Anthony James B 10.12.1971 Oak Park, IL BR/TR 6-4/210# d8.27																									
2000	TB A	1	1	.500	11	0	0	0-1	15	21	16	3	2	9-2	8	8.40	59	.333	.432	0-0	—	0		-6	-0.7
2001	TB A	0	0	—	3	0	0	0-0	3.1	4	2	0	1	1-0	3	5.40	83	.308	.400	0-0	—	0		0	0.0
	Min A	0	1	.000	4	0	0	0-0	6.1	5	4	0	0	2-0	5	5.68	81	.208	.269	0-0	—	0		-1	-0.1
	Year	0	1	.000	7	0	0	0-0	9.2	9	10	0	1	3-0	8	5.59	82	.243	.317	0-0	—	0		-1	-0.1
2002	†Min A	10	3	.769	48	2	0	0-0	91	74	32	10	5	43-4	55	3.16	142	.224	.320	3-0	.000	-0	134	14	1.8
2003	Min A	1	1	.500	21	0	0	0-0	36	32	25	5	3	21-1	23	5.50	83	.242	.352	1-0	.000	-0		-5	-0.2
Total	4	12	6	.667	87	2	0	0-1	151.2	136	79	18	11	76-7	94	4.39	104	.242	.340	4-0	.000	-0	134	2	0.8
FIREOVID, STEVE Stephen John B 6.6.1957 Bryan, OH BB/TR 6-2/195# d9.6																									
1981	SD N	0	1	.000	5	4	0	0-0	26.1	30	8	2	0	7-0	11	2.73	119	.294	.336	7-0	.143	-0	82	2	0.1
1983	SD N	0	0	—	3	0	0	0-0	5	4	2	0	0	2-0	1	1.80	194	.235	.316	0-0	—	0		1	0.0
1984	Phi N	0	0	—	6	0	0	0-0	5.2	4	1	0	0	0-0	3	1.59	229	.200	.200	0-0	—	0		1	0.1
1985	Chi A	0	0	—	4	0	0	0-0	7	17	4	0	0	2-0	2	5.14	84	.472	.500	0-0	—	0		0	0.0
1986	Sea A	2	0	1.000	10	1	0	0-0	21	28	11	1	1	4-0	10	4.29	99	.333	.371	0-0	—	0	43	0	0.0
1992	Tex A	1	0	1.000	3	0	0	0-0	6.2	10	5	0	0	4-2	0	4.05	94	.370	.452	0-0	—	0		-1	-0.1
Total	6	3	1	.750	31	5	0	0-0	71.2	93	31	3	1	19-2	27	3.39	110	.325	.368	7-0	.143	-0	67	3	0.1
FIRTH, TED John E. B 5.6.1855 Lowell, MA D 6.23.1902 Tewksbury, MA d8.15																									
1884	Ric AA	0	1	.000	1	1	1	0	9	14	13	0	0	5	0	8.00	41	.326	.396	3	.333	0	55	-5	-0.4
FISCHER, CARL Charles William B 11.5.1905 Medina, NY D 12.10.1963 Medina, NY BR/TL 6/180# d7.19																									
1930	Was A	1	1	.500	8	4	1	1	33.1	37	22	0	2	18	21	4.86	95	.285	.380	9-0	.000	-1	93	-2	-0.2
1931	Was A	13	9	.591	46	23	7	3	191	207	98	12	2	80	96	4.38	98	.273	.344	66-5	.121	-5	103	3	-0.3
1932	Was A	3	2	.600	12	7	1-1	1	50.2	57	30	4	0	31	23	4.97	87	.282	.378	15-2	.200	1	169	-3	-0.3
	StL A	3	7	.300	24	11	4	0	97	122	65	12	0	45	35	5.57	87	.310	.380	34-3	.265	0	69	-5	-0.4
	Year	6	9	.400	36	18	5-1	1	147.2	179	69	16	0	76	58	5.36	87	.300	.379	49-5	.245	1	104	-6	-0.7
1933	Det A	11	15	.423	35	22	9	3	182.2	176	86	5	3	84	93	3.55	122	.251	.334	62-4	.145	-3	73	15	1.5

Year	Tm Lg	W	L	Pct	G	GS	CG-Sho	SV-BS	IP	H	R	HR	HB	BB-IB	SO	ERA	AERA	OAV	OOB	AB-SH	AVG	PB	Sup	APR	PW
1934	Det A	6	4	.600	20	15	4-1	1	95	107	50	5	1	38	39	4.36	101	.288	.356	31-5	.065	-3	119	2	-0.2
1935	Det A	0	1	.000	3	1	0	0	12	16	8	2	1	5	7	6.00	69	.320	.393	2-0	.000	-0	62	-2	-0.2
	Chi A	5	5	.500	24	11	3-1	0	88.2	102	67	7	2	39	31	6.19	75	.283	.356	21-2	.190	-0	80	-14	-1.4
	Year	5	6	.455	27	12	3-1	0	100.2	118	71	9	3	44	38	6.17	74	.287	.360	23-2	.174	-1	79	-16	-1.6
1937	Cle A	0	1	.000	2	0	0	0	0.2	2	2	0	0	1	1	27.00	17	.667	.750	0-0	—	0		-2	-0.3
	Was A	4	5	.444	17	11	2	2	72	74	43	6	0	31	30	4.38	101	.270	.344	22-2	.136	-1	106	0	-0.2
	Year	4	6	.400	19	11	2	2	72.2	76	48	6	0	32	31	4.58	97	.274	.350	22-2	.136	-1	106	-2	-0.5
Total	7	46	50	.479	191	105	31-3	11	823	900	471	53	11	372	376	4.63	96	.277	.354	262-23	.145	-12	96	-8	-2.0

FISCHER, HANK Henry William "Bulldog" B 1.11.1940 Yonkers, NY BR/TR 6/190# d4.16

Year	Tm Lg	W	L	Pct	G	GS	CG-Sho	SV-BS	IP	H	R	HR	HB	BB-IB	SO	ERA	AERA	OAV	OOB	AB-SH	AVG	PB	Sup	APR	PW
1962	Mil N	2	3	.400	29	0	0	4	37.1	43	27	4	0	20-1	29	5.30	72	.291	.373	4-0	.000	-0		-7	-1.1
1963	Mil N	4	3	.571	31	6	1	0	74.1	74	46	8	5	28-4	72	4.96	65	.262	.333	19-2	.105	-0	219	-15	-1.4
1964	Mil N	11	10	.524	37	28	9-5	2	168.1	177	95	17	3	39-5	99	4.01	88	.265	.308	52-4	.154	1*	117	-14	-1.6
1965	Mil N	8	9	.471	31	19	2	0	122.2	126	61	18	3	39-5	79	3.89	91	.270	.329	37-2	.108	-1*	80	-6	-1.0
1966	Atl N	2	3	.400	14	8	0	0	48.1	55	23	3	1	14-1	22	3.91	93	.296	.343	13-2	.000	-2	73	-1	-0.3
	Cin N	0	6	.000	11	9	0	0	38	53	31	3	3	15-0	24	6.63	59	.331	.394	11-0	.091	-1	100	-11	-1.6
	Year	2	9	.182	25	17	0	0	86.1	108	35	6	4	29-1	46	5.11	73	.312	.367	24-2	.042	-2	88	-13	-1.9
	Bos A	2	3	.400	6	5	1	0	31	35	12	4	1	11-1	26	2.90	131	.287	.351	9-0	.222	0	46	3	0.5
1967	Bos A	1	2	.333	9	2	1	1	26.2	24	15	3	1	8-0	18	2.36	148	.229	.289	7-1	.143	-0	137	0	0.0
Total	6	30	39	.435	168	77	14-5	7	546.2	587	310	60	17	174-17	369	4.23	84	.275	.332	152-11	.118	-3	104	-51	-6.5

FISCHER, JEFF Jeffrey Thomas B 8.17.1963 W.Palm Beach, FL BR/TR 6-3/185# d6.19

Year	Tm Lg	W	L	Pct	G	GS	CG-Sho	SV-BS	IP	H	R	HR	HB	BB-IB	SO	ERA	AERA	OAV	OOB	AB-SH	AVG	PB	Sup	APR	PW
1987	Mon N	0	1	.000	4	2	0	0-0	13.2	21	14	3	0	5-0	6	8.56	49	.362	.400	5-0	.200	0	150	-6	-0.4
1989	LA N	0	0	—	2	0	0	0-0	3.1	7	5	1	0	0-0	2	13.50	25	.438	.438	0-0	—	0		-4	-0.2
Total	2	0	1	.000	6	2	0	0-0	17	28	19	4	0	5-0	8	9.53	42	.378	.407	5-0	.200	0	150	-10	-0.6

FISCHER, RUBE Reuben Walter B 9.19.1916 Carlock, SD D 7.16.1997 Green Bay, WI BR/TR 6-4/190# d9.12

Year	Tm Lg	W	L	Pct	G	GS	CG-Sho	SV-BS	IP	H	R	HR	HB	BB-IB	SO	ERA	AERA	OAV	OOB	AB-SH	AVG	PB	Sup	APR	PW
1941	NY N	1	0	1.000	2	1	1	0	11	10	3	0	0	6	9	2.45	151	.238	.333	3-0	.333	0	161	2	0.2
1943	NY N	5	10	.333	22	17	4	1	130.2	140	69	4	2	59	47	4.61	75	.281	.360	43-1	.256	3	71	-14	-1.2
1944	NY N	6	14	.300	38	18	2-1	2	128.2	128	83	7	6	87	39	5.18	71	.266	.384	40-2	.125	-2	93	-19	-3.0
1945	NY N	3	8	.273	31	4	0	1	76.2	90	55	6	1	49	27	5.63	69	.288	.387	19-0	.211	2	92	-15	-1.7
1946	NY N	1	2	.333	15	1	0	0	35.2	48	32	3	0	21	14	6.31	55	.316	.399	9-0	.111	-1	124	-12	-1.0
Total	5	16	34	.320	108	41	7-1	4	382.2	416	242	20	9	222	136	5.10	71	.280	.377	114-3	.193	2	86	-58	-6.7

FISCHER, TODD Todd Richard B 9.15.1960 Columbus, OH BR/TR 5-10/170# d5.29

Year	Tm Lg	W	L	Pct	G	GS	CG-Sho	SV-BS	IP	H	R	HR	HB	BB-IB	SO	ERA	AERA	OAV	OOB	AB-SH	AVG	PB	Sup	APR	PW
1986	Cal A	0	0	—	9	0	0	0-0	17	18	8	4	0	8-2	7	4.24	97	.286	.361	0-0	—	0		0	0.0

FISCHER, BILL William Charles B 10.11.1930 Wausau, WI BR/TR 6/190# d4.21 C14

Year	Tm Lg	W	L	Pct	G	GS	CG-Sho	SV-BS	IP	H	R	HR	HB	BB-IB	SO	ERA	AERA	OAV	OOB	AB-SH	AVG	PB	Sup	APR	PW
1956	Chi A	0	0	—	3	0	0	0	1.2	6	4	0	0	1-0	2	21.60	19	.545	.583	0-0	—	0		-3	-0.1
1957	Chi A	7	8	.467	33	11	3-1	1	124	139	50	1	3	35-6	48	3.48	107	.291	.342	40-3	.150	-2	91	5	0.3
1958	Chi A	2	3	.400	17	3	0	0	36.1	43	28	6	0	13-1	16	6.69	54	.301	.357	7-1	.143	-0	82	-12	-1.4
	Det A	2	4	.333	22	0	0	2	30.2	46	34	6	0	13-2	16	7.63	53	.362	.415	1-1	.000	0		-13	-2.5
	Was A	0	3	.000	3	3	0	0	21	24	9	1	1	5-1	10	3.86	99	.320	.366	5-0	.200	0	16	0	0.1
	Year	4	10	.286	42	6	0	2	88	113	10	13	1	31-4	42	6.34	60	.328	.381	13-2	.154	0	47	-25	-3.8
1959	Was A	9	11	.450	34	29	6-1	0	187.1	211	98	16	4	43-2	62	4.28	92	.281	.321	54-7	.130	-2	106	-5	-0.5
1960	Was A	3	5	.375	20	7	1	0	77	85	45	7	0	17-2	31	4.91	79	.281	.318	19-2	.158	1	65	-7	-0.5
	Det A	5	3	.625	20	6	1	0	55	50	23	6	0	18-3	24	3.44	115	.244	.301	11-2	.364	2	111	3	0.7
	Year	8	8	.500	40	13	2	0	132	135	28	13	0	35-5	55	4.30	91	.266	.311	30-4	.233	3	87	-4	0.2
1961	Det A	3	2	.600	26	1	0	3	46.2	54	28	10	0	17-2	18	5.01	82	.292	.351	7-0	.000	-1	86	-4	-0.5
	KC A	1	0	1.000	15	0	0	2	21	26	9	1	0	6-0	12	3.86	108	.321	.364	2-1	.000	-0		1	0.1
	Year	4	2	.667	41	1	0	5	67.2	80	41	11	0	23-2	30	4.66	89	.301	.355	9-1	.000	-1	86	-3	-0.4
1962	KC A	4	12	.250	34	16	5	2	127.2	150	61	16	1	8-2	38	3.95	107	.293	.302	38-1	.105	-2	67	4	0.2
1963	KC A	9	6	.600	45	2	0	3	95.2	86	44	13	3	29-5	34	3.57	109	.242	.302	15-3	.067	-0	171	2	0.3
1964	Min A	0	1	.000	9	0	0	0	7.1	16	6	2	0	5-3	2	7.36	49	.471	.525	0-0	—	0		-3	-0.3
Total	9	45	58	.437	281	78	16-2	13	831.1	936	439	85	12	210-29	313	4.34	91	.287	.330	199-21	.136	-4	90	-32	-4.1

FISHEL, LEO Leo B 12.13.1877 Babylon, NY D 5.19.1960 Hempstead, NY BR/TR 6/175# d5.3

Year	Tm Lg	W	L	Pct	G	GS	CG-Sho	SV-BS	IP	H	R	HR	HB	BB-IB	SO	ERA	AERA	OAV	OOB	AB-SH	AVG	PB	Sup	APR	PW
1899	NY N	0	1	.000	1	1	1	0	9	9	7	0	2	6	6	6.00	63	.257	.395	4-0	.250	-0	57	-2	-0.1

FISHER, BRIAN Brian Kevin B 3.18.1962 Honolulu, HI BR/TR 6-4/210# d5.7

Year	Tm Lg	W	L	Pct	G	GS	CG-Sho	SV-BS	IP	H	R	HR	HB	BB-IB	SO	ERA	AERA	OAV	OOB	AB-SH	AVG	PB	Sup	APR	PW
1985	NY A	4	4	.500	55	0	0	14-4	98.1	77	32	4	0	29-3	85	2.38	168	.216	.273	0-0	—	0		17	1.7
1986	NY A	9	5	.643	62	0	0	6-9	96.2	105	61	14	1	37-2	67	4.93	83	.277	.341	0-0	—	0		-10	-1.4
1987	Pit N	11	9	.550	37	26	6-3	0-0	185.1	185	99	27	4	72-7	117	4.52	91	.262	.332	58-5	.190	5	101	-7	-0.3
1988	Pit N	8	10	.444	33	22	1-1	1-1	146.1	157	78	13	5	57-4	66	4.61	74	.277	.345	42-2	.048	-2	116	-17	-2.3
1989	Pit N	0	3	.000	9	3	0	1-0	17	25	17	2	0	10-3	8	7.94	42	.329	.402	5-0	.000	-1	79	-9	-1.5
1990	Hou N	0	0	—	4	0	0	0-0	5	9	5	1	0	0-0	1	7.20	52	.409	.375	0-0	—	0		-2	-0.1
1992	Sea A	4	3	.571	22	14	0	1-0	91.1	80	49	9	1	47-2	26	4.53	88	.234	.326	0-0	—	0	115	-5	-0.4
Total	7	36	34	.514	222	65	7-4	23-14	640	638	341	70	11	252-21	370	4.39	89	.261	.330	105-7	.124	2	106	-33	-4.3

FISHER, CHAUNCEY Chauncey Burr "Peach" or "Whoa Bill" B 1.8.1872 Anderson, IN D 4.27.1939 Los Angeles, CA BR/TR 5-11/175# d9.20 b-Tom

Year	Tm Lg	W	L	Pct	G	GS	CG-Sho	SV-BS	IP	H	R	HR	HB	BB-IB	SO	ERA	AERA	OAV	OOB	AB-SH	AVG	PB	Sup	APR	PW
1893	Cle N	0	2	.000	2	2	2	0	18	26	18	0	0	9	9	5.50	89	.329	.398	8	.250	-0	79	-1	-0.1
1894	Cle N	0	2	.000	3	2	0	0	11	22	17	0	1	5	0	11.45	48	.407	.467	4-0	.000	-1	52	-6	-0.7
	Cin N	2	8	.200	12	12	11	0	100	153	123	4	1	46	17	7.47	74	.347	.410	47-0	.213	-2	67	-22	-1.6
	Year	2	10	.167	15	14	11	0	111	175	128	4	2	51	17	7.86	70	.354	.416	51-0	.196	-3	65	-28	-2.3
1896	Cin N	10	7	.588	27	15	13-2	2	159.2	199	111	9	5	36	25	4.45	104	.303	.344	57-4	.246	0	122	2	0.1
1897	Bro N	9	7	.563	20	13	11-1	1	149	184	96	5	2	43	31	4.23	97	.301	.349	59-1	.203	-1	153	-2	-0.3
1901	NY N	0	0	—	1	1	0	0	4	11	9	0	0	2	1	15.75	21	.500	.542	2-0	.000	-0	279	-5	-0.3
	StL N	0	0	—	1	0	0	0	3	7	5	0	0	1	0	15.00	21	.438	.471	1-0	.000	-0		-3	-0.2
	Year	0	0	—	2	1	0	0	7	18	27	0	0	3	1	15.43	21	.474	.512	3-0	.000	-0	284	-8	-0.5
Total	5	21	26	.447	66	45	37-3	3	444.2	602	379	18	9	142	83	5.44	85	.320	.371	178-5	.213	-4	111	-37	-3.1

FISHER, CLARENCE Clarence Henry B 8.27.1898 Letart, WV D 11.2.1965 Point Pleasant, WV BR/TR 6/174# d9.14

Year	Tm Lg	W	L	Pct	G	GS	CG-Sho	SV-BS	IP	H	R	HR	HB	BB-IB	SO	ERA	AERA	OAV	OOB	AB-SH	AVG	PB	Sup	APR	PW
1919	Was A	0	0	—	2	0	0	0	4	8	6	0	0	3	1	13.50	24	.421	.500	0-0	—	0		-4	-0.2
1920	Was A	0	1	.000	2	0	0	0	3.2	5	4	0	0	5	0	9.82	38	.714	.833	1-0	.000	-0		-2	-0.4
Total	2	0	1	.000	4	0	0	0	7.2	13	10	0	0	8	1	11.74	29	.500	.618	1-0	.000	-0		-6	-0.6

FISHER, DON Donald Raymond B 2.6.1916 Cleveland, OH D 7.29.1973 Mayfield Heights, OH BR/TR 6/210# d8.25

Year	Tm Lg	W	L	Pct	G	GS	CG-Sho	SV-BS	IP	H	R	HR	HB	BB-IB	SO	ERA	AERA	OAV	OOB	AB-SH	AVG	PB	Sup	APR	PW
1945	NY N	1	0	1.000	2	1	1-1	0	18	12	4	0	2	7	4	2.00	196	.190	.292	7-0	.143	-0	22	4	0.2

FISHER, EDDIE Eddie Gene B 7.16.1936 Shreveport, LA BR/TR 6-2.5/200# d6.22

Year	Tm Lg	W	L	Pct	G	GS	CG-Sho	SV-BS	IP	H	R	HR	HB	BB-IB	SO	ERA	AERA	OAV	OOB	AB-SH	AVG	PB	Sup	APR	PW
1959	SF N	2	6	.250	17	5	0	1	40	57	37	8	1	8-0	15	7.87	48	.339	.369	8-0	.000	-1	75	-17	-3.0
1960	SF N	1	0	1.000	3	1	1	0	12.2	11	5	2	0	2-0	7	3.55	98	.244	.260	5-0	.600	1	279	0	0.2
1961	SF N	0	2	.000	15	1	0	1	33.2	36	23	7	0	9-3	16	5.35	71	.267	.313	7-0	.143	0	442	-6	-0.4
1962	Chi A	9	5	.643	57	12	2-1	5	182.2	169	74	17	1	45-1	88	3.10	126	.245	.291	46-8	.130	-0	116	14	1.1
1963	Chi A	9	8	.529	33	15	2-1	0	120.2	114	57	14	2	28-2	67	3.95	89	.244	.286	36-1	.139	-1	110	-5	-0.7
1964	Chi A	6	3	.667	59	2	0	9	125	86	43	13	3	32-3	74	3.02	114	.192	.249	18-1	.167	-0	206	8	0.7
1965	Chi A★	15	7	.682	**82**	0	0	24	165.1	118	51	13	2	43-8	90	2.40	133	.205	.259	29-1	.138	0		15	2.5
1966	Chi A	1	3	.250	23	0	0	6	35.1	27	11	1	1	17-1	18	2.29	138	.214	.310	2-0	.000	-0		4	0.5
	Bal A	5	3	.625	44	0	0	13	71.2	60	26	4	2	19-1	39	2.64	126	.226	.280	13-0	.154	0		4	0.7
	Year	6	6	.500	**67**	0	0	19	107	87	45	5	3	36-2	57	2.52	130	.222	.290	15-0	.133	-0		8	1.2
1967	Bal A	4	3	.571	46	0	0	1	89.2	82	40	7	4	26-3	53	3.61	87	.245	.304	5-2	.200	0		-5	-0.4
1968	Cle A	4	2	.667	54	0	0	4	94.2	87	36	8	2	17-3	42	2.85	104	.248	.283	12-0	.000	-1		1	0.0
1969	Cal A	3	2	.600	52	1	0	2-0	96.2	100	46	9	1	28-3	47	3.63	96	.272	.322	13-2	.000	-1	101	-2	-0.3
1970	Cal A	4	4	.500	67	2	0	8-4	130.1	117	51	15	2	35-1	74	3.04	119	.239	.291	11-3	.091	-1	123	8	0.5
1971	Cal A	10	8	.556	57	3	0	3-2	119	92	46	11	2	50-5	82	2.72	119	.211	.293	16-1	.063	-1	148	5	0.7

Year	Tm Lg	W	L	Pct	G	GS	CG-Sho	SV-BS	IP	H	R	HR	HB	BB-IB	SO	ERA	AERA	OAV	OOB	AB-SH	AVG	PB	Sup	APR	PW
1972	Cal A	4	5	.444	43	1	0	4-2	81.1	73	35	6	0	31-3	32	3.76	78	.247	.314	17-0	.118	-1	30	-6	-0.9
	Chi A	0	1	.000	6	4	0	0-0	22.1	31	13	1	0	9-0	10	4.43	71	.348	.404	7-0	.000	-1	120	-3	-0.3
	Year	4	6	.400	49	5	0	4-2	103.2	104	17	7	0	40-3	42	3.91	76	.271	.335	24-0	.083	-1	107	-10	-1.2
1973	Chi A	6	7	.462	26	16	2	0-0	110.2	135	64	12	3	38-1	57	4.88	81	.301	.358	0-0	—	0	107	-9	-1.0
	StL N	2	1	.667	6	0	0	0-0	7	3	1	1	1	1-0	1	1.29	284	.125	.192	1-0	1.000	0		2	0.5
Total	15	85	70	.548	690	63	7-2	81-8	1538.2	1398	659	149	27	438-38	812	3.41	101	.243	.297	246-19	.122	-5	127	8	0.4
FISHER, ED Edward Fredrick B 10.31.1876 Wayne, MI D 7.24.1951 Spokane, WA BR/TR 6-2/200# d9.5																									
1902	Det A	0	0	—	1	0	0	0	4	4	0	0	0	1	0	0.00	—	.267	.313	2-0	.000	-0		2	0.0
FISHER, FRITZ Frederick Brown B 11.28.1941 Adrian, MI BL/TL 6-1/180# d4.19																									
1964	Det A	0	0	—	1	0	0	0	0.1	2	4	0	0	2-0	1	108.00	3	.667	.800	0-0	—	0		-4	-0.2
FISHER, HARRY Harry Devereux B 1.3.1926 Newbury, ON, CAN D 9.20.1981 Waterloo, ON, CAN BL/TR 6/180# d9.16.1951 ▲																									
1952	Pit N	1	2	.333	8	3	0	0	18.1	17	14	4	2	13	5	6.87	58	.266	.405	15-0	.333	1*	74	-5	-0.6
FISHER B Philadelphia, PA d7.17																									
1884	Phi U	1	7	.125	8	8	8	0	70.2	76	49	0		13	42	3.57	65	.257	.288	36	.222	-1*	69	-10	-1.0
1885	Buf N	0	1	.000	1	1	1	0	9	10	9	0		2	4	5.00	60	.256	.293	4	.000	-1	95	-2	-0.2
Total	2	1	8	.111	9	9	9	0	79.2	86	58	0		15	46	3.73	64	.257	.289	40	.200	-2	72	-12	-1.2
FISHER, JACK John Howard "Fat Jack" B 3.4.1939 Frostburg, MD BR/TR 6-2/215# d4.14																									
1959	Bal A	1	6	.143	27	7	1-1	2	88.2	76	36	7	1	38-1	52	3.05	124	.230	.307	23-0	.130	-1	57	6	0.4
1960	Bal A	12	11	.522	40	20	8-3	2	197.2	174	87	13	2	78-4	99	3.41	111	.241	.315	60-4	.183	2	110	8	1.1
1961	Bal A	10	13	.435	36	25	10-1	1	196	205	104	17	4	75-3	118	3.90	99	.270	.335	56-10	.089	-2	94	-5	-0.9
1962	Bal A	7	9	.438	32	25	4	1	152	173	101	23	2	56-3	81	5.09	73	.284	.345	49-3	.102	-1*	128	-27	-2.6
1963	SF N	6	10	.375	36	12	2	1	116	132	77	12	5	38-3	57	4.58	70	.284	.342	29-2	.103	1	106	-22	-2.8
1964	NY N	10	17	.370	40	34	8-1	0	227.2	256	124	23	10	56-0	115	4.23	85	.283	.330	76-2	.158	1	105	-17	-1.8
1965	NY N	8	24	.250	43	36	10	1	253.2	252	121	22	4	68-6	116	3.94	90	.259	.309	78-4	.154	0	69	-9	-0.9
1966	NY N	11	14	.440	38	33	10-2	0	230	229	108	26	8	54-2	127	3.68	99	.260	.308	67-6	.090	-2	84	-1	-0.1
1967	NY N	9	18	.333	39	30	7-1	0	220.1	251	121	21	4	64-10	117	4.70	72	.287	.336	70-6	.100	-2	77	-28	-3.3
1968	Chi A	8	13	.381	35	28	2	0	180.2	176	68	14	7	48-4	80	2.99	101	.257	.310	53-5	.113	-1	62	2	0.0
1969	Cin N	4	4	.500	34	15	0	1-0	113	137	77	15	5	30-3	55	5.50	69	.295	.344	33-3	.121	-1	129	-20	-1.6
Total	11	86	139	.382	400	265	62-9	9-0	1975.2	2061	1024	193	52	605-39	1017	4.06	88	.269	.325	594-45	.125	-6	92	-113	-12.5
FISHER, MAURICE Maurice Wayne B 2.16.1931 Uniondale, IN BR/TR 6-5/210# d4.16																									
1955	Cin N	0	0	—	1	0	0	0	2.2	5	2	1	0	2-0	1	6.75	63	.385	.467	1-0	.000	-0		-1	0.0
FISHER, RAY Ray Lyle "Pick" B 10.4.1887 Middlebury, VT D 11.3.1982 Ann Arbor, MI BR/TR 5-11.5/180# d7.2 Mil 1918																									
1910	NY A	5	3	.625	17	7	3	1	92.1	95	41	0	3	18	42	2.92	91	.274	.315	29-1	.103	-2	101	-3	-0.3
1911	NY A	10	11	.476	29	22	8-2	0	171.2	178	85	3	5	55	99	3.25	111	.269	.330	59-3	.119	-3	88	6	0.5
1912	NY A	2	8	.200	17	13	5	0	90.1	107	70	2	2	32	47	5.88	61	.312	.374	31-3	.065	-4	74	-17	-1.9
1913	NY A	12	16	.429	43	31	14-1	1	246.1	244	113	3	9	71	92	3.18	94	.263	.321	79-6	.278	3	84	-3	0.1
1914	NY A	10	12	.455	29	26	17-2	1	209	177	65	2	4	61	86	2.28	121	.241	.303	65-5	.138	-2	78	12	1.2
1915	NY A	18	11	.621	30	28	20-4	0	247.2	219	82	7	5	62	97	2.11	139	.243	.295	83-4	.108	-5	100	19	1.7
1916	NY A	11	8	.579	31	21	9-1	2	179	191	81	4	4	51	56	3.17	91	.285	.339	62-1	.177	1	113	-6	-0.6
1917	NY A	8	9	.471	23	18	12-3	0	144	126	49	3	2	43	64	2.19	123	.243	.304	50-2	.180	-0	89	7	0.9
1919	†Cin N	14	5	.737	26	20	12-5	1	174.1	141	55	4	1	38	41	2.17	128	.226	.271	59-2	.271	3	136	12	1.9
1920	Cin N	10	11	.476	33	21	10-1	1	201	189	86	5	8	50	56	2.73	111	.249	.302	70-3	.243	1	113	4	0.6
Total	10	100	94	.515	278	207	110-19	7	1755.2	1667	727	33	43	481	680	2.82	106	.257	.312	587-30	.179	-8	97	31	4.1
FISHER, TOM Thomas Chalmers "Red" B 11.1.1880 Anderson, IN D 9.3.1972 Anderson, IN BR/TR 5-10.5/185# d4.17 b-Chauncey																									
1904	Bos N	6	16	.273	31	21	19-2	0	214	257	165	5	10	82	84	4.25	65	.302	.370	99-0	.212	3*	78	-42	-3.7
FISHER, TOM Thomas Gene B 4.4.1942 Cleveland, OH BR/TR 6/180# d9.20																									
1967	Bal A	0	0	—	2	0	0	0	3.1	2	0	0	0	2-0	1	0.00	—	.182	.308	0-0	—	0		1	0.1
FISHER, CHEROKEE William Charles B 12.1845 Philadelphia, PA D 9.26.1912 New York, NY BR/TR 5-9/164# d5.6 ▲																									
1871	Rok NA	4	16	.200	24	24	22-1	0	213	295	257	3		31	15	4.35	94	.281	.302	123	.228	-3*	89	-3	-0.2
1872	Bal NA	10	1	.909	19	11	9-1	1	110	93	78	0		11	20	**1.80**	**204**	**.197**	**.216**	225	.231	-1*	172	19	1.2
1873	Ath NA	3	4	.429	13	5	5	2	84.1	90	73	1		10	14	**1.81**	**188**	**.231**	**.250**	253	.261	1*	75	10	0.6
1874	Har NA	13	23	.361	39	35	31	0	322.1	416	277	1		13	25	2.32	100	.277	.284	241	.224	-4*	98	1	-0.3
1875	Phi NA	22	19	.537	41	41	36-2	0	358	345	189	6		9	18	1.99	115	.229	.233	177	.232	-1	99	13	0.9
1876	Cin N	4	20	.167	28	24	22	0	229.1	294	206	6		6	29	3.02	73	.285	.289	129	.248	-1*	60	-26	-2.2
1878	Pro N	0	1	.000	1	1	1	0	9	14	12	0		0	2	4.00	55	.304	.304	3	.000	-0	79	-3	-0.2
Total	5 NA	52	63	.452	136	116	103-4	3	1087.2	1239	874	11		74	92	2.52	115	.252	.263	1019	.237	-8	102	40	2.2
Total	2	4	21	.160	29	25	23	0	238.1	308	218	6		6	31	3.06	72	.285	.289	132	.242	-2	61	-29	-2.4
FISKE, MAX Maximilian Patrick "Ski" B 10.12.1888 Chicago, IL D 5.25.1928 Chicago, IL BR/TR 5-11/185# d4.19																									
1914	Chi F	12	12	.500	38	22	7	0	198	161	84	7	7	59	87	3.14	85	.231	.298	68-1	.235	0*	105	-8	-0.9
FITTERY, PAUL Paul Clarence B 10.10.1887 Lebanon, PA D 1.28.1974 Cartersville, GA BR/TL 5-8.5/156# d9.5																									
1914	Cin N	0	2	.000	8	4	2	0	43.2	41	20	0	1	12	21	3.09	95	.246	.300	17-1	.059	-1*	79	0	-0.2
1917	Phi N	1	1	.500	17	2	1	0	55.2	69	36	1	5	27	13	4.53	62	.317	.404	22-1	.091	-1*	188	-10	-0.5
Total	2	1	3	.250	25	6	3	0	99.1	110	56	1	6	39	34	3.90	73	.286	.360	39-2	.077	-2	116	-10	-0.7
FITZGERALD, BRIAN Brian Michael B 12.26.1974 Woodbridge, VA BL/TL 5-11/175# d4.17																									
2002	Sea A	0	0	—	6	0	0	0-0	6.1	11	8	2	1	2-0	3	8.53	50	.344	.389	0-0	—	0		-4	-0.2
FITZGERALD, JOHN John Francis B 9.15.1933 Brooklyn, NY BL/TL 6-3/190# d9.28																									
1958	SF N	0	0	—	1	1	0	0	3	1	1	1	0	1-0	3	3.00	127	.111	.200	1-0	.000	-0	165	0	0.0
FITZGERALD, JOHN John H. B 5.30.1870 Natick, MA D 3.31.1921 Boston, MA d7.18																									
1891	Bos AA	1	1	.500	6	3	2	1	32	49	32	2	2	11	16	5.63	62	.340	.395	14	.071	-2	89	-8	-0.5
FITZGERALD, JOHN John J. B 1866 D 12.20.1892 Waterbury, CT d4.18																									
1890	Roc AA	3	8	.273	11	11	8-1	0	78	77	51	0	6	45	35	4.04	88	.250	.357	31	.194	-0	91	-3	-0.4
FITZGERALD, WARREN Warren B. B 4.1872 , PA D 11.7.1930 Phoenix, AZ TL 5-9/162# d6.4																									
1891	Lou AA	14	17	.452	32	31	28-3	0	267	265	157	5	12	89	110	3.34	110	.250	.316	108	.176	1*	84	8	0.6
1892	Lou N	1	3	.250	4	4	4	0	34	45	27	2	1	11	3	4.24	72	.306	.358	15	.133	-0	98	-5	-0.5
Total	2	15	20	.429	36	35	32-3	0	301	310	184	7	13	100	113	3.44	104	.257	.321	123	.171	0	86	3	0.1
FITZKE, PAUL Robert Paul "Bob" (b: Frederick Herman Fitzke) B 7.30.1900 LaCrosse, WI D 6.30.1950 Sacramento, CA BR/TR 5-11.5/185# d9.1																									
1924	Cle A	0	0	—	1	0	0	0	4	5	2	0	0	3	1	4.50	95	.313	.421	1-0	.000	-0		0	0.0
FITZMORRIS, AL Alan James B 3.21.1946 Buffalo, NY BB/TR 6-2/190# d9.8																									
1969	KC A	1	1	.500	7	0	0	2-0	10.2	9	5	1	0	4-0	3	4.22	88	.237	.310	1-0	.000	-0		0	-0.1
1970	KC A	8	5	.615	43	11	2	1-1	117.2	112	60	14	0	52-6	47	4.44	84	.254	.330	31-0	.290	4*	178	-6	-0.2
1971	KC A	7	5	.583	36	15	2-1	0-1	127.1	112	61	6	1	55-2	53	4.17	82	.245	.324	44-2	.250	2	136	-9	-0.5
1972	KC A	2	5	.286	38	2	0	3-1	101	99	46	10	1	28-5	51	3.74	81	.252	.303	23-0	.174	1*	102	-8	-0.4
1973	KC A	8	3	.727	15	13	3-1	0-0	89	88	29	5	0	25-3	26	2.83	145	.259	.309	0-0	—	0	95	13	1.6
1974	KC A	13	6	.684	34	27	9-4	1-1	190	189	73	8	0	63-10	53	2.79	137	.260	.317	0-0	—	0	98	19	2.0
1975	KC A	16	12	.571	35	35	11-3	0-0	242	239	104	16	5	76-6	78	3.57	108	.262	.320	0-0	—	0	106	10	1.1
1976	KC A	15	11	.577	35	33	8-2	0-0	220.1	227	89	6	2	56-8	80	3.06	114	.273	.316	0-0	—	0*	90	10	1.3
1977	Cle A	6	10	.375	29	21	1	0-0	133	164	87	12	1	53-4	54	5.41	73	.306	.367	0-0	—	0	109	-21	-2.2
1978	Cle A	0	1	.000	7	0	0	0-0	14.1	19	10	3	1	7-2	5	6.28	60	.333	.415	0-0	—	0		-4	-0.2
	Cal A	1	0	1.000	9	2	0	0-0	31.2	26	9	2	0	14-3	8	1.71	212	.236	.317	0-0	—	0	186	6	0.3

Year	Tm Lg	W	L	Pct	G	GS	CG-Sho	SV-BS	IP	H	R	HR	HB	BB-IB	SO	ERA	AERA	OAV	OOB	AB-SH	AVG	PB	Sup	APR	PW
	Year	1	1	.500	16	2	0	0-0	46	45	17	5	1	21-5	13	3.13	117	.269	.351	0-0	—	0	184	2	0.1
Total	10	77	59	.566	288	159	36-11	7-4	1277	1284	573	83	11	433-47	458	3.65	101	.265	.324	99-2	.242	7	111	10	2.7
FITZSIMMONS, FREDDIE Frederick Landis "Fat Freddie" B 7.28.1901 Mishawaka, IN D 11.18.1979 Yucca Valley, CA BR/TR 5-11/185# d8.12 M3 C14																									
1925	NY N	6	3	.667	10	8	6-1	0	74.2	70	25	4	0	18	17	2.65	152	.248	.293	29-1	.310	2	120	13	1.7
1926	NY N	14	10	.583	37	26	12	0	219	224	90	7	4	58	48	2.88	130	.272	.322	86-1	.128	-6	117	19	1.3
1927	NY N	17	10	.630	42	31	14-1	3	244.2	260	127	15	4	67	78	3.72	104	.275	.325	87-8	.207	-0	128	0	0.1
1928	NY N	20	9	.690	40	32	16-1	1	261.1	264	119	13	4	65	67	3.68	106	.268	.316	94-5	.191	1	103	9	1.0
1929	NY N	15	11	.577	37	30	14-4	1	221.2	242	122	14	2	66	55	4.10	112	.285	.338	82-2	.183	-2	135	11	1.1
1930	NY N	19	7	**.731**	41	29	17-1	1	224.1	230	125	26	1	59	76	4.25	111	.266	.314	83-5	.265	5	148	12	1.8
1931	NY N	18	11	.621	35	33	19-4	0	253.2	242	111	16	0	62	78	3.05	121	.251	.296	92-3	.228	9	130	15	2.9
1932	NY N	11	11	.500	35	31	11	0	237.2	287	132	18	3	83	65	4.43	84	.299	.356	86-6	.221	4	139	-16	-0.6
1933	†NY N	16	11	.593	36	**35**	13-1	0	251.2	243	106	14	2	72	65	2.90	111	.251	.305	95-3	.200	3	110	6	1.2
1934	NY N	18	14	.563	38	37	14-3	1	263.1	266	114	12	1	51	73	3.04	127	.261	.297	95-2	.232	5	105	22	3.2
1935	NY N	4	8	.333	18	15	6-**4**	0	94	104	43	7	1	22	23	4.02	96	.281	.323	31-2	.258	1	81	0	0.2
1936	†NY N	10	7	.588	28	17	7-1	2	141	147	58	6	0	39	35	3.32	117	.274	.323	47-5	.149	-2	96	10	1.0
1937	NY N	2	2	.500	6	4	1-1	0	27.1	28	14	3	0	8	13	4.61	84	.272	.324	10-1	.300	2	144	-1	0.0
	Bro N	4	8	.333	13	13	4	0	90.2	91	47	2	1	32	29	4.27	95	.263	.327	30-1	.167	-1	72	0	0.0
	Year	6	10	.375	19	17	5-1	0	118	119	50	5	1	40	42	4.35	92	.265	.327	40-2	.200	1	89	-2	0.0
1938	Bro N	11	8	.579	27	26	12-3	0	202.2	205	83	8	3	43	38	3.02	129	.261	.302	70-4	.171	-1	98	18	1.8
1939	Bro N	7	9	.438	27	20	5	3	151.1	178	79	6	3	28	44	3.87	104	.293	.327	47-3	.234	3	76	0	0.6
1940	Bro N	16	2	**.889**	20	18	11-4	1	134.1	120	43	5	1	25	35	2.81	142	.233	.269	47-4	.106	-2	121	19	2.3
1941	†Bro N	6	1	.857	13	12	3-1	0	82.2	78	33	3	2	26	19	2.07	177	.245	.305	28-1	.143	-0	106	10	0.9
1942	Bro N	0	0	—	1	1	0	0	3	6	5	1	0	1	0	15.00	22	.400	.438	2-0	.500	0	154	-4	-0.1
1943	Bro N	3	4	.429	9	7	1	0	44.2	50	29	6	1	21	12	5.44	62	.281	.360	14-1	.071	-1	97	-10	-1.4
Total	19	217	146	.598	513	425	186-30	13	3223.2	3335	1505	186	33	846	870	3.51	111	.268	.316	1155-58	.200	21	115	133	19.0
FLAHERTY, PATSY Patrick Joseph B 6.29.1876 Mansfield, PA D 1.23.1968 Alexandria, LA BL/TL 5-8/165# d9.8 ▲																									
1899	Lou N	2	3	.400	5	4	4	0	39	41	21	0	1	5	5	2.31	167	.270	.297	24-0	.208	1*	75	5	0.5
1900	Pit N	0	0	—	4	1	0	0	22	30	16	0	5	9	5	6.14	59	.323	.411	9-0	.111	-1	152	-4	-0.2
1903	Chi A	11	25	.306	40	34	29-2	1	293.2	338	173	9	14	50	65	3.74	75	.288	.324	102-3	.137	-3	80	-29	-3.4
1904	Chi A	1	2	.333	5	5	4	0	43	36	19	1	1	10	14	2.09	117	.228	.278	12-0	.333	2	134	0	0.3
	Pit N	19	9	.679	29	28	28-5	0	242	210	81	3	11	59	54	2.05	134	.232	.287	104-4	.212	5*	135	16	2.8
1905	Pit N	10	10	.500	27	20	15	1	187.2	197	87	2	6	49	44	3.50	86	.272	.324	76-1	.197	2*	125	-8	-0.5
1907	Bos N	12	15	.444	27	25	23	0	217	197	90	4	7	59	34	2.70	95	.248	.306	115-0	.191	2*	95	-5	-0.2
1908	Bos N	12	18	.400	31	31	21	0	244	221	109	6	8	81	50	3.25	74	.236	.303	86-5	.140	-0*	94	-17	-2.0
1910	Phi N	0	0	—	1	0	0	0	0.1	1	4	0	0	1	0	0.00	—	.333	.500	2-0	.500	0*		-1	-0.1
1911	Bos N	0	2	.000	4	2	1	0	14	21	15	0	3	8	0	7.07	54	.350	.451	94-1	.287	1*	98	-5	-0.5
Total	9	67	84	.444	173	150	125-7	2	1302.2	1292	615	25	56	331	271	3.10	89	.259	.312	624-14	.197	10	104	-48	-3.3
FLANAGAN, MIKE Michael Kendall B 12.16.1951 Manchester, NH BL/TL 6/195# d9.5 C2																									
1975	Bal A	0	1	.000	2	1	0	0-0	9.2	9	4	0	0	6-1	7	2.79	126	.250	.357	0-0	—	0	50	0	0.0
1976	Bal A	3	5	.375	20	10	4	0-0	85	83	41	7	0	33-0	56	4.13	79	.260	.326	0-0	—	0	102	-8	-0.7
1977	Bal A	15	10	.600	36	33	15-2	1-0	235	235	100	17	2	70-5	149	3.64	105	.266	.318	0-0	—	0	107	6	0.6
1978	Bal A☆	19	15	.559	40	**40**	17-2	0-0	281.1	271	128	22	3	87-2	167	4.03	87	.257	.314	0-0	—	0	109	-11	-1.3
1979	†Bal A	**23**	9	.719	39	38	16-**5**	0-0	265.2	245	107	23	3	70-1	190	3.08	130	.245	.296	0-0	—	0	110	27	2.9
1980	Bal A	16	13	.552	37	37	12-2	0-0	251.1	278	121	27	2	71-3	128	4.12	96	.287	.333	0-0	—	0*	101	-3	-0.3
1981	Bal A	9	6	.600	20	20	3-2	0-0	116	108	55	11	2	37-1	72	4.19	87	.244	.305	0-0	—	0	103	-5	-0.5
1982	Bal A	15	11	.577	36	35	11-1	0-0	236	233	110	24	4	76-5	103	3.97	102	.259	.317	0-0	—	0	106	2	0.2
1983	†Bal A	12	4	.750	20	20	3-1	0-0	125.1	135	53	10	2	31-2	50	3.30	120	.278	.321	0-0	—	0	119	9	1.0
1984	Bal A	13	13	.500	34	34	10-2	0-0	226.2	213	103	24	1	81-5	115	3.53	110	.250	.314	0-0	—	0	100	8	0.8
1985	Bal A	4	5	.444	15	15	1	0-0	86	101	49	14	2	28-0	42	5.13	79	.297	.352	0-0	—	0	90	-8	-0.8
1986	Bal A	7	11	.389	29	28	2	0-1	172	179	95	15	1	66-4	96	4.24	98	.270	.334	0-0	—	0	89	-4	-0.5
1987	Bal A	3	6	.333	16	16	4	0-0	94.2	102	57	9	0	36-1	50	4.94	89	.278	.342	0-0	—	0	103	-6	-0.5
	Tor A	3	2	.600	7	7	0	0-0	49.1	46	15	3	0	15-3	43	2.37	190	.237	.292	0-0	—	0	78	11	1.0
	Year	6	8	.429	23	23	4	0-0	144	148	19	12	0	51-4	93	4.06	109	.264	.325	0-0	—	0	96	5	0.5
1988	Tor A	13	13	.500	34	34	2-1	0-0	211	220	106	23	6	80-1	99	4.18	94	.271	.339	0-0	—	0	116	-4	-0.4
1989	†Tor A	8	10	.444	30	30	1-1	0-0	171.2	186	82	10	5	47-0	47	3.93	96	.283	.331	0-0	—	0	106	-2	-0.2
1990	Tor A	2	2	.500	5	5	0	0-0	20.1	28	14	3	0	8-0	5	5.31	74	.329	.387	0-0	—	0	147	-4	-0.6
1991	Bal A	2	7	.222	64	1	0	3-2	98.1	84	27	6	3	25-6	55	2.38	166	.236	.289	0-0	—	0	69	18	1.7
1992	Bal A	0	0	—	42	0	0	0-0	34.2	50	34	3	5	23-1	17	8.05	50	.338	.438	0-0	—	0		-16	-0.7
Total	18	167	143	.539	526	404	101-19	4-3	2770	2806	1301	251	41	890-41	1491	3.90	100	.266	.323	0-0	—	0	105	10	1.7
FLANIGAN, RAY Raymond Arthur B 1.8.1923 Morgantown, WV D 3.28.1993 Baltimore, MD BR/TR 6/190# d9.20																									
1946	Cle A	0	1	.000	3	1	0	0	9	11	12	1	0	8	2	11.00	30	.289	.413	2-0	.500	1	78	-8	-0.7
FLANIGAN, TOM Thomas Anthony B 9.6.1934 Cincinnati, OH BR/TL 6-3/175# d4.14																									
1954	Chi A	0	0	—	2	0	0	0	1.2	1	0	0	0	1	0	0.00	—	.200	.286	0-0	—	0		1	0.0
1958	StL N	0	0	—	1	0	0	0	1	2	1	1	0	1-0	0	9.00	46	.500	.600	0-0	—	0		0	0.0
Total	2	0	0	—	3	0	0	0	2.2	3	1	1	0	2-0	0	3.38	115	.333	.417	0-0	—	0		1	0.0
FLATER, JACK John William B 9.22.1880 Sandymount, MD D 3.20.1970 Westminster, MD BR/TR 5-10/175# d9.18																									
1908	Phi A	1	3	.250	5	3	3	0	39.1	35	15	0	2	12	8	2.06	124	.252	.320	15-1	.133	-0	62	1	0.2
FLAVIN, JOHN John Thomas B 5.7.1942 Albany, CA BL/TL 6-2/208# d8.25																									
1964	Chi N	0	1	.000	5	1	0	0	4.2	11	7	0	0	3-1	5	13.50	28	.500	.538	1-0	.000	-0	95	-5	-0.9
FLEET, FRANK Frank H. B 1848 New York, NY D 6.13.1900 New York, NY d10.18 ▲																									
1871	Mut NA	0	1	.000	1	1	1	0	9	20	21	0		3	0	10.00	38	.370	.404	6	.333	0	73	-6	-0.3
1873	Res NA	0	3	.000	3	3	2	0	24	57	47	0		0	1	5.25	64	.404	.404	89	.258	0*	53	-3	-0.2
1875	StL NA	2	1	.667	3	3	3	0	27	33	17	0		3	3	3.33	60	.277	.295	16	.063	-1*	140	-3	-0.3
	Atl NA	0	1	.000	2	1	1	0	15.1	26	20	0		0	0	4.70	44	.333	.333	111	.225	-0*	118	-4	-0.2
	Year	2	2	.500	5	4	4	0	42.1	59	27	0		3	3	3.83	53	.299	.310	127	.205	-1	134	-7	-0.5
Total	3 NA	2	6	.250	9	8	7	0	75.1	136	105	0		6	4	5.02	53	.347	.357	222	.230	-1	90	-16	-1.0
FLEMING, DAVE David Anthony B 11.7.1969 Jackson Heights, NY BL/TL 6-3/200# d8.6																									
1991	Sea A	1	0	1.000	9	3	0	0-0	17.2	19	13	3	3	3-0	11	6.62	62	.284	.342	0-0	—	0	133	-4	-0.2
1992	Sea A	17	10	.630	33	33	7-4	0-0	228.1	225	95	13	4	60-3	112	3.39	117	.257	.306	0-0	—	0	98	14	1.6
1993	Sea A	12	5	.706	26	26	1-1	0-0	167.1	189	84	15	6	67-6	75	4.36	101	.290	.357	0-0	—	0	107	3	0.3
1994	Sea A	7	11	.389	23	23	0	0-0	117	152	93	17	1	65-4	65	6.46	76	.311	.391	0-0	—	0	105	-19	-2.4
1995	Sea A	1	5	.167	16	7	1	0-1	48	57	44	15	0	34-3	26	7.50	63	.294	.394	0-0	—	0	101	-15	-1.5
	KC A	0	1	.000	9	5	0	0-0	32	27	17	4	2	19-1	14	3.66	131	.229	.343	0-0	—	0	54	3	0.1
	Year	1	6	.143	25	12	1	0-1	80	84	20	19	2	53-4	40	5.96	80	.269	.375	0-0	—	0	81	-13	-1.4
Total	5	38	32	.543	116	97	9-5	0-1	610.1	669	346	67	16	248-17	303	4.67	94	.279	.349	0-0	—	0	102	-18	-2.1
FLEMING, BILL Leslie Fletchard B 7.31.1913 Rowland, CA BR/TR 6/190# d8.21 Mil 1945																									
1940	Bos A	1	2	.333	10	6	1	0	46.1	53	27	4	2	20	24	4.86	93	.290	.366	13-2	.000	-2	94	-2	-0.3
1941	Bos A	1	1	.500	16	1	0	1	41.1	32	21	4	0	24	20	3.92	106	.212	.320	9-0	.222	1	125	1	0.1
1942	Chi N	5	6	.455	33	14	4-2	2	134.1	117	51	9	3	63	59	3.01	106	.230	.318	39-1	.051	-4	79	4	-0.1
1943	Chi N	0	1	.000	11	0	0	0	32.1	41	24	2	3	12	12	6.40	52	.311	.381	8-0	.000	-1		-10	-0.6
1944	Chi N	9	10	.474	39	18	9-1	0	158.1	163	74	6	1	62	42	3.13	113	.269	.337	53-4	.170	-1*	104	4	0.4
1946	Chi N	0	1	.000	14	1	0	0	29.1	37	23	2	1	12	10	6.14	54	.301	.368	3-0	.000	-0	26	-9	-0.5
Total	6	16	21	.432	123	40	14-3	3	442	443	220	27	10	193	167	3.79	94	.260	.339	125-7	.104	-7	94	-12	-1.0

Year	Tm Lg	W	L	Pct	G	GS	CG-Sho	SV-BS	IP	H	R	HR	HB	BB-IB	SO	ERA	AERA	OAV	OOB	AB-SH	AVG	PB	Sup	APR	PW
FLENER, HUCK Gregory Alan B 2.25.1969 Austin, TX BB/TL 5-11/185# d9.14																									
1993	Tor A	0	0	—	6	0	0	0-0	6.2	7	3	0	0	4-1	2	4.05	107	.269	.367	0-0	—	0		0	0.0
1996	Tor A	3	2	.600	15	11	0	0-0	70.2	68	40	9	1	33-1	44	4.58	109	.251	.330	0-0	—	0	89	3	0.2
1997	Tor A	0	1	.000	8	1	0	0-0	17.1	40	19	3	0	6-0	9	9.87	47	.444	.474	0-0	—	0	60	-9	-0.5
Total 3		3	3	.500	29	12	0	0-0	94.2	115	62	12	1	43-2	55	5.51	89	.297	.365	0-0	—	0	88	-6	-0.3
FLETCHER, VAN Alfred Vanoide B 8.6.1924 East Bend, NC BR/TR 6-2/185# d4.12																									
1955	Det A	0	0	—	9	0	0	0	12	13	10	1	0	2-1	4	3.00	128	.260	.288	0-0	—	0		-1	0.0
FLETCHER, PAUL Edward Paul B 1.14.1967 Gallipolis, OH BR/TR 6-1/185# d7.11																									
1993	Phi N	0	0	—	1	0	0	0-0	0.1	0	0	0	0	0-0	0	0.00	—	.000	.000	0-0	—	0		0	0.0
1995	Phi N	1	0	1.000	10	0	0	0-0	13.1	15	8	2	1	9-2	10	5.40	78	.288	.397	0-0	—	0		-1	-0.1
1996	Oak A	0	0	—	1	0	0	0-0	1.1	6	3	0	0	1-0	0	20.25	24	.667	.700	0-0	—	0		-2	-0.1
Total 3		1	0	1.000	12	0	0	0-0	15	21	11	2	1	10-2	10	6.60	65	.339	.432	0-0	—	0		-3	-0.2
FLETCHER, SAM Samuel S. B Altoona, PA TR 6-2/210# d10.6																									
1909	Bro N	0	1	.000	1	1	1	0	9	13	8	0	0	2	5	8.00	32	.351	.385	3-0	.000	-0	108	-4	-0.4
1912	Cin N	0	0	—	2	0	0	0	9.2	15	15	1	0	11	3	12.10	28	.366	.500	4-0	.500	1		-8	-0.3
Total 2		0	1	.000	3	1	1	0	18.2	28	23	1	0	13	8	10.13	30	.359	.451	7-0	.286	0	108	-12	-0.7
FLETCHER, TOM Thomas Wayne B 6.28.1942 Elmira, NY BB/TL 6/170# d9.12 s-Darrin																									
1962	Det A	0	0	—	1	0	0	0	2	2	0	0	0	2-0	1	0.00	—	.250	.400	0-0	—	0		1	0.0
FLINN, JOHN John Richard B 9.2.1954 Merced, CA BR/TR 6/175# d5.6																									
1978	Bal A	1	1	.500	13	0	0	0-1	15.2	24	18	3	0	13-3	8	8.04	44	.348	.446	0-0	—	0		-10	-1.1
1979	Bal A	0	0	—	4	0	0	0-0	2.2	2	0	0	0	1-0	0	0.00	—	.222	.273	0-0	—	0		1	0.1
1980	Mil A	2	1	.667	20	1	0	2-1	37	31	20	3	0	20-2	15	3.89	100	.220	.313	0-0	—	0	323	-1	-0.1
1982	Bal A	2	0	1.000	5	0	0	0-0	13.2	13	3	1	0	3-1	13	1.32	307	.260	.302	0-0	—	0		4	0.5
Total 4		5	2	.714	42	1	0	2-2	69	70	41	7	0	37-6	36	4.17	92	.260	.345	0-0	—	0	323	-6	-0.6
FLITCRAFT, HILLY Hildreth Milton B 8.21.1923 Woodstown, NJ D 4.2.2003 Boulder, CO BL/TL 6-2/180# d8.31																									
1942	Phi N	0	0	—	3	0	0	0	3.1	6	4	0	0	2	1	8.10	41	.429	.500	0-0	—	0		-2	-0.1
FLOHR, MORT Moritz Herman "Dutch" B 8.15.1911 Canisteo, NY D 6.2.1994 Hornell, NY BL/TL 6/173# d6.8																									
1934	Phi A	0	2	.000	14	3	0	0	30.2	34	21	3	1	33	6	5.87	75	.296	.456	12-0	.333	1*	73	-5	-0.1
FLORENCE, DON Donald Emery B 3.16.1967 Manchester, NH BR/TL 6/195# d8.8																									
1995	NY N	3	0	1.000	14	0	0	0-1	12	17	3	0	0	6-0	5	1.50	270	.340	.411	1-0	.000	-0		3	0.6
FLORES, JESSE Jesse (Sandoval) B 11.2.1914 Guadalajara, Mexico D 12.17.1991 Orange, CA BR/TR 5-10/175# d4.16																									
1942	Chi N	0	1	.000	4	0	0	0	5.1	5	5	1	0	2	6	3.38	95	.227	.292	0-0	—	0		-1	-0.2
1943	Phi A	12	14	.462	31	27	13	0	231.1	208	88	13	5	70	113	3.11	109	.240	.301	80-5	.175	-0	82	9	1.0
1944	Phi A	9	11	.450	27	25	11-2	0	185.2	172	75	8	4	49	65	3.39	103	.245	.298	64-6	.172	-0	92	5	0.4
1945	Phi A	7	10	.412	29	24	9-4	1	191.1	180	79	6	4	63	52	3.43	100	.250	.314	61-7	.148	-2	103	2	-0.2
1946	Phi A	9	7	.563	29	15	8-4	1	155	147	51	8	1	38	48	2.32	153	.249	.295	44-5	.250	3	85	19	2.2
1947	Phi A	4	13	.235	28	20	4	0	151.1	139	72	10	0	59	41	3.39	112	.244	.315	44-2	.227	1	59	4	0.4
1950	Cle A	3	3	.500	28	2	1-1	4	53	53	24	3	1	25	27	3.74	116	.261	.345	11-0	.000	-2	73	4	0.2
Total 7		44	59	.427	176	113	46-11	6	973	904	394	49	15	306	352	3.18	112	.246	.307	304-25	.181	-0	84	42	3.8
FLORES, RANDY Randy Alan B 7.31.1975 Bellflower, CA BL/TL 6/180# d4.23																									
2002	Tex A	0	0	—	20	0	0	1-1	12	11	7	2	0	8-2	7	4.50	105	.268	.373	0-0	—	0		0	0.0
	Col N	0	2	.000	8	2	0	0-0	17	29	19	5	3	8-1	7	9.53	50	.382	.460	4-0	.000	-0	106	-7	-0.8
Total 1		0	2	.000	28	2	0	1-1	29	40	26	7	3	16-3	14	7.45	64	.342	.428	4-0	.000	-0	106	-7	-0.8
FLORIE, BRYCE Bryce Bettencourt B 5.21.1970 Charleston, SC BR/TR 6/185# d7.17																									
1994	SD N	0	0	—	9	0	0	0-0	9.1	8	1	0	0	3-0	8	0.96	426	.242	.297	0-0	—	0		3	0.2
1995	SD N	2	2	.500	47	0	0	1-3	68.2	49	30	8	4	38-3	68	3.01	134	.202	.319	2-0	.000	-0		6	0.3
1996	SD N	2	2	.500	39	0	0	0-1	49.1	45	24	1	6	27-3	51	4.01	99	.239	.351	3-0	.000	-0		0	0.0
	Mil A	0	1	.000	15	0	0	0-2	19	20	16	3	0	13-2	12	6.63	78	.270	.371	0-0	—	0		-3	-0.2
1997	Mil A	4	4	.500	32	8	0	0-1	75	74	43	4	3	42-2	53	4.32	107	.262	.360	0-0	—	0	87	1	0.0
1998	Det A	8	9	.471	42	16	0	0-0	133	141	80	16	4	59-6	97	4.80	98	.275	.354	3-1	.333	1	73	-2	-0.1
1999	Det A	2	1	.667	27	3	0	0-0	51.1	61	31	6	1	20-2	40	4.56	109	.292	.355	1-0	.000	-0	94	1	0.0
	Bos A	2	0	1.000	14	2	0	0-0	30	33	19	2	1	15-3	25	4.80	104	.282	.366	0-0	—	0	140	0	0.0
	Year	4	1	.800	41	5	0	0-0	81.1	94	27	8	2	35-5	65	4.65	107	.288	.359	1-0	.000	-0	113	1	0.0
2000	Bos A	0	4	.000	29	0	0	1-1	49.1	57	30	5	1	19-6	34	4.56	111	.294	.355	0-0	—	0		1	0.2
2001	Bos A	0	1	.000	7	0	0	0-0	8.2	12	11	1	0	7-3	7	11.42	39	.316	.422	0-0	—	0		-6	-0.6
Total 8		20	24	.455	261	29	0	2-8	493.2	500	285	46	20	243-30	395	4.47	103	.265	.352	9-1	.111	0	86	1	-0.2
FLOWERS, BEN Bennett B 6.15.1927 Wilson, NC BR/TR 6-4/195# d9.29																									
1951	Bos A	0	0	—	1	0	0	0	3	2	0	0	0	1	2	0.00	—	.200	.273	1-0	.000	-0		1	0.0
1953	Bos A	1	4	.200	32	6	1-1	3	79.1	87	39	6	1	24	36	3.86	109	.280	.333	19-1	.158	-0	74	3	0.2
1955	Det A	0	0	—	4	0	0	0	6	5	4	1	0	2-0	2	6.00	64	.238	.292	1-0	.000	-0		-1	-0.1
	StL N	1	0	1.000	4	4	0	0	27.1	27	12	1	0	12-0	19	3.62	112	.255	.328	10-0	.100	-1	104	1	0.0
1956	StL N	1	1	.500	3	3	0	0	11.2	15	9	1	0	5-1	5	6.94	54	.341	.392	3-0	.000	-0	147	-4	-0.5
	Phi N	0	2	.000	32	0	0	0	41	54	29	9	1	10-1	22	5.71	65	.331	.369	2-0	.000	0		-9	-0.4
	Year	1	3	.250	35	3	0	0	52.2	69	44	10	1	15-2	27	5.98	62	.333	.374	5-0	.000	-0	149	-13	-0.9
Total 4		3	7	.300	76	13	1-1	3	168.1	190	93	18	2	54-2	86	4.49	90	.290	.343	36-1	.111	-2	100	-9	-0.8
FLOWERS, WES Charles Wesley B 8.13.1913 Vanndale, AR D 12.31.1988 Wynne, AR BL/TL 6-1.5/190# d8.8																									
1940	Bro N	1	1	.500	5	2	0	0	21	23	10	2	3	10	8	3.43	117	.299	.400	5-0	.200	-0	54	1	0.1
1944	Bro N	1	1	.500	9	1	0	0	17.1	26	17	3	1	13	3	7.79	46	.333	.435	5-0	.600	1	212	-8	-0.7
Total 2		2	2	.500	14	3	0	0	38.1	49	27	5	4	23	11	5.40	70	.316	.418	10-0	.400	1	105	-7	-0.6
FLYNN, CARNEY Cornelius Francis Xavier B 1.23.1875 Cincinnati, OH D 2.10.1947 Cincinnati, OH BL/TL 5-11/165# d7.17																									
1894	Cin N	0	2	.000	2	1	0	0	7.2	16	15	4	1	10	4	17.61	31	.421	.551	3-0	.000	-1	115	-8	-1.0
1896	NY N	0	2	.000	3	2	1	0	10.2	18	22	0	5	8	4	11.81	36	.367	.500	4-0	.500	2	177	-10	-1.1
	Was N	0	1	.000	4	1	1	0	20	43	31	0	2	10	3	8.55	52	.430	.491	8-0	.250	-0	97	-9	-0.4
	Year	0	3	.000	7	3	2	0	30.2	61	37	0	7	18	7	9.68	45	.409	.494	12-0	.333	1	147	-21	-1.5
Total 2		0	5	.000	9	4	2	0	38.1	77	68	4	8	28	11	11.27	41	.412	.507	15-0	.267	1	140	-27	-2.5
FLYNN, JOCKO John A. B 6.30.1864 Lawrence, MA D 12.30.1907 Lawrence, MA BR/TR 5-6.5/143# d5.1																									
1886	Chi N	23	6	**.793**	32	29	28-2	1	257	207	127	9		63	146	2.24	161	.210	.257	205	.200	1*	122	32	3.3
FLYTHE, STU Stuart McGuire B 12.5.1911 Conway, NC D 10.18.1963 Durham, NC BR/TR 6-2/175# d5.31																									
1936	Phi A	0	0	—	17	3	0	0	39.1	49	63	4	3	61	14	13.04	39	.302	.500	15-0	.267	0	172	-33	-1.4
FODGE, GENE Gene Arlan "Suds" B 7.9.1931 South Bend, IN BR/TR 6/175# d4.20																									
1958	Chi N	1	1	.500	16	4	1	0	39.2	47	22	5	0	11-3	15	4.76	82	.296	.337	7-1	.000	-1	132	-3	-0.2
FOGARTY, JIM James G. B 2.12.1864 San Francisco, CA D 5.20.1891 Philadelphia, PA BR/TR 5-10.5/180# d5.1 M1 b-Joe ▲																									
1884	Phi N	0	0	—	1	0	0	0	1	2	2	0		0	1	0.00	—	.333	.333	378	.212	0*		0	0.0
1886	Phi N	0	1	.000	1	0	0	0	6	7	6	0		0	4	0.00	—	.250	.250	280	.293	0*		0	0.1
1887	Phi N	0	0	—	1	0	0	0	3	3	4	0	0	1	0	9.00	47	.200	.250	495	.261	0*		-1	-0.1
1889	Phi N	0	0	—	4	0	0	0	4	4	4	0	0	2	0	9.00	48	.250	.333	499	.259	1*		-1	-0.1
Total 4		0	1	.000	7	0	0	0	14	16	16	0	0	3	5	4.50	84	.246	.279	1652	.254	2		-2	-0.1
FOGG, JOSH Joshua Smith B 12.13.1976 Lynn, MA BR/TR 6-2/205# d9.2																									
2001	Chi A	0	0	—	11	0	0	0-0	13.1	10	3	0	1	3-1	17	2.03	228	.208	.264	0-0	—	0		4	0.2

Year	Tm Lg	W	L	Pct	G	GS	CG-Sho	SV-BS	IP	H	R	HR	HB	BB-IB	SO	ERA	AERA	OAV	OOB	AB-SH	AVG	PB	Sup	APR	PW
2002	Pit N	12	12	.500	33	33	0	0-0	194.1	199	102	28	8	69-12	113	4.35	96	.267	.334	58-2	.121	-2*	80	-3	-0.6
2003	Pit N	10	9	.526	26	26	1	0-0	142	166	90	22	9	40-0	71	5.26	83	.293	.347	42-7	.190	0	120	-14	-1.6
Total 3		22	21	.512	70	59	1	0-0	349.2	375	195	50	18	112-13	201	4.63	92	.276	.337	100-9	.150	-1	98	-13	-2.0
FOLEY, CURRY Charles Joseph B 1.14.1856 Milltown, Ireland D 10.20.1898 Boston, MA TL 5-10/160# d5.13 ▲																									
1879	Bos N	9	9	.500	21	16	16-1	0	161.2	175	111	1		15	57	2.51	99	.252	.268	146	.315	5*	77	-7	-0.3
1880	Bos N	14	14	.500	36	28	21-1	0	238	264	150	1		40	68	3.89	58	.274	.303	332	.292	8*	105	-35	-2.8
1881	Buf N	3	4	.429	10	6	2	0	41	70	48	1		5	2	5.27	53	.337	.352	375	.256	1*	107	-12	-1.5
1882	Buf N	0	0	—	1	0	0	0	1	2	2	0		0	0	18.00	16	.333	.333	341	.305	0*		-1	-0.1
1883	Buf N	1	0	1.000	1	0	0	0	1	0	0	0		4	0	0.00	—	.000	.667	111	.270	0*		0	0.1
Total 5		27	27	.500	69	50	39-2	0	442.2	511	311	3		64	127	3.54	68	.273	.297	1305	.286	14	95	-55	-4.6
FOLEY, JOHN John J B 10.25.1857 Brattleboro, VT TL d9.18																									
1885	Pro N	0	1	.000	1	1	1	0	8	6	7	0		5	2	4.50	60	.188	.297	2	.000	0	63	-2	-0.2
FOLKERS, RICH Richard Nevin B 10.17.1946 Waterloo, IA BL/TL 6-2/180# d6.10																									
1970	NY N	0	2	.000	16	1	0	2-2	29.1	36	21	6	0	25-4	15	6.44	63	.313	.433	6-0	.333	0	89	-7	-0.4
1972	StL N	1	0	1.000	9	0	0	0-1	13.1	12	5	0	0	5-0	7	3.38	101	.240	.309	1-0	.000	-0		0	0.0
1973	StL N	4	4	.500	34	9	1	3-0	82.1	74	34	10	3	34-4	44	3.61	101	.239	.319	20-1	.100	-1	94	2	0.1
1974	StL N	6	2	.750	55	0	0	2-2	90	65	31	4	2	38-10	57	3.00	120	.207	.292	10-1	.100	-1		7	0.5
1975	SD N	6	11	.353	45	15	4	0-1	142	155	70	8	1	39-3	87	4.18	83	.278	.323	36-4	.167	1	91	-8	-0.7
1976	SD N	2	3	.400	33	3	0	0-0	59.2	67	39	10	2	25-8	26	5.28	62	.279	.348	4-1	.000	-0	63	-14	-1.1
1977	Mil A	0	1	.000	3	0	0	0-1	6.1	7	7	2	0	4-1	6	4.26	96	.269	.367	0-0	—	0		-2	-0.2
Total 7		19	23	.452	195	28	5	7-7	423	416	207	40	8	170-30	242	4.11	86	.258	.329	77-7	.143	-1	89	-22	-1.8
FONTENOT, JOE Joseph Daniel B 3.20.1977 Scott, LA BR/TR 6-2/185# d5.23																									
1998	Fla N	0	7	.000	8	8	0	0-0	42.2	56	34	5	5	20-1	24	6.33	64	.320	.403	10-1	.000	-1	51	-12	-1.6
FONTENOT, RAY Silton Ray B 8.8.1957 Lake Charles, LA BL/TL 6/175# d6.30																									
1983	NY A	8	2	.800	15	15	3-1	0-0	97.1	101	41	3	1	25-0	27	3.33	117	.266	.313	0-0	—	0	133	6	0.6
1984	NY A	8	9	.471	35	24	0	0-0	169.1	189	77	8	3	58-4	85	3.61	105	.290	.349	0-0	—	0	101	3	0.3
1985	Chi N	6	10	.375	38	23	0	0-1	154.2	177	86	23	0	45-4	70	4.36	92	.294	.342	41-4	.049	-3	92	-7	-1.0
1986	Chi N	3	5	.375	42	0	0	2-1	56	57	30	5	0	21-3	24	3.86	105	.266	.332	6-0	.167	-0		-1	-0.1
	Min A	0	0	—	15	0	0	0-0	16.1	27	19	3	2	4-0	10	9.92	44	.360	.407	1-0	.000	-0		-10	-0.5
Total 4		25	26	.490	145	62	3-1	2-2	493.2	551	253	42	6	153-11	216	4.03	98	.287	.340	48-4	.063	-4	104	-9	-0.7
FOOR, JIM James Emerson B 1.13.1949 St.Louis, MO BL/TL 6-2/170# d4.9																									
1971	Det A	0	0	—	3	0	0	0-0	1	2	2	0	0	4-0	2	18.00	20	.400	.667	0-0	—	0		-1	-0.1
1972	Det A	1	0	1.000	7	0	0	0-0	3.2	6	6	1	0	6-1	2	14.73	21	.353	.522	0-0	—	0		-4	-0.9
1973	Pit N	0	0	—	3	0	0	0-0	1.1	2	0	0	0	1-1	1	0.00	—	.286	.375	0-0	—	0		1	0.0
Total 3		1	0	1.000	13	0	0	0-0	6	10	8	1	0	11-2	5	12.00	28	.345	.525	0-0	—	0		-4	-1.0
FOPPERT, JESSE Jesse William B 7.10.1980 Reading, PA BR/TR 6-6/210# d4.14																									
2003	SF N	8	9	.471	23	21	0	0-0	111	103	69	16	3	69-4	101	5.03	82	.249	.354	37-0	.081	-1	103	-13	-1.8
FORCE, DAVY David W. "Wee Davy" or "Tom Thumb" B 7.27.1849 New York, NY D 6.21.1918 Englewood, NJ BR/TR 5-4/130# d5.5.1871 ▲																									
1873	Bal NA	1	1	.500	3	1	1	0	18	23	20	0		1	0	2.50	130	.258	.267	233	.365	1*	154	0	0.1
1874	Chi NA	0	0	—	1	0	0	0	7	22	24	4		0	0	15.43	14	.431	.431	294	.313	0*		-8	-0.3
Total 2 NA		1	1	.500	4	1	1	0	25	45	44	4		1	0	6.12	49	.321	.326	527	.336	2	161	-8	-0.2
FORD, BEN Benjamin Cooper B 8.15.1975 Cedar Rapids, IA BR/TR 6-7/200# d8.20																									
1998	Ari N	0	0	—	8	0	0	0-0	10	13	12	2	2	3-0	5	9.90	43	.295	.367	0-0	—	0		-6	-0.3
2000	NY A	0	1	.000	4	2	0	0-0	11	14	11	1	3	7-0	5	9.00	54	.333	.462	0-0	—	0	87	-5	-0.3
Total 2		0	1	.000	12	2	0	0-0	21	27	23	3	5	10-0	10	9.43	48	.314	.416	0-0	—	0	87	-11	-0.6
FORD, DAVE David Alan B 12.29.1956 Cleveland, OH BR/TR 6-4/190# d9.2																									
1978	Bal A	1	0	1.000	2	1	0	0-0	15	10	0	0	0	2-0	5	0.00	—	.196	.226	0-0	—	0	26	6	0.4
1979	Bal A	2	1	.667	9	2	0	2-1	30	23	7	2	0	7-0	7	2.10	192	.219	.265	0-0	—	0	124	7	0.8
1980	Bal A	1	3	.250	25	3	1	1-0	69.2	66	34	11	2	13-2	22	4.26	93	.251	.291	0-0	—	0	60	-2	-0.1
1981	Bal A	1	2	.333	15	2	0	0-0	40	61	33	2	0	10-2	12	6.52	56	.359	.390	0-0	—	0	74	-13	-0.9
Total 4		5	6	.455	51	8	1	3-1	154.2	160	74	15	2	32-4	46	4.02	96	.272	.310	0-0	—	0	76	-2	0.2
FORD, WHITEY Edward Charles "Chairman Of The Board" B 10.21.1928 New York, NY BL/TL 5-10/181# d7.1 Mil 1951 C4 HF1974																									
1950	†NY A	9	1	.900	20	12	7-2	1	112	87	39	7	2	52	59	2.81	153	.216	.309	36-4	.194	0	131	19	1.5
1953	†NY A	18	6	.750	32	30	11-3	0	207	187	77	13	4	110	110	3.00	123	.245	.344	75-1	.267	6*	151	18	2.5
1954	NY A★	16	8	.667	34	28	11-3	1	210.2	170	72	10	1	101	125	2.82	122	.227	.317	62-7	.161	2	116	17	2.1
1955	†NY A★	**18**	7	.720	39	33	**18**-5	2	253.2	188	83	20	1	113-7	137	2.63	143	.208	.296	86-3	.163	2	119	34	3.4
1956	†NY A★	19	6	**.760**	31	30	18-2	1	225.2	187	70	13	4	84-3	141	**2.47**	156	.228	.301	78-5	.218	3	110	38	4.6
1957	†NY A	11	5	.688	24	17	5	0	129.1	114	46	10	1	53-3	84	2.57	139	.237	.313	42-5	.143	-1	132	14	1.6
1958	†NY A☆	14	7	.667	30	29	15-**7**	1	219.1	174	62	14	3	62-3	145	**2.01**	**176**	.217	**.276**	73-5	.205	2	114	**37**	**3.9**
1959	NY A★	16	10	.615	35	29	9-2	1	204	194	82	13	1	89-5	114	3.04	120	.250	.327	65-3	.231	7	109	13	2.6
1960	†NY A★	12	9	.571	33	29	8-**4**	0	192.2	168	76	15	1	65-5	85	3.08	116	.235	.297	53-4	.151	2	109	11	1.5
1961	†NY A★	**25**	4	**.862**	39	**39**	11-3	0	**283**	242	108	23	1	92-3	209	3.21	116	.229	.291	96-5	.177	3	135	19	2.1
1962	†NY A	17	8	.680	38	37	7	0	257.2	243	90	22	4	69-1	160	2.90	129	.246	.296	85-3	.118	-1	107	27	2.7
1963	†NY A	**24**	7	**.774**	38	**37**	13-3	1	**269.1**	240	94	26	2	56-3	189	2.74	128	.241	.281	92-5	.141	0	116	22	2.5
1964	†NY A☆	17	6	.739	39	36	12-8	1	244.2	212	67	10	2	57-3	172	2.13	170	.230	.276	67-7	.119	1	101	39	3.9
1965	NY A	16	13	.552	37	36	9-2	1	244.1	241	97	22	1	50-2	162	3.24	105	.258	.296	82-6	.183	2*	100	6	1.0
1966	NY A	2	5	.286	22	9	0	0	73	79	33	8	0	24-6	43	2.47	135	.277	.330	18-0	.000	-2	85	3	0.2
1967	NY A	2	4	.333	7	7	2-1	0	44	40	11	2	0	9-0	21	1.64	191	.247	.285	13-2	.154	-0	92	7	1.1
Total 16		236	106	.690	498	438	156-45	10	3170.1	2766	1107	228	28	1086-**44**	1956	2.75	133	.235	.300	1023-65	.173	27	115	324	37.2
FORD, GENE Eugene Matthew B 6.23.1912 Ft.Dodge, IA D 9.7.1970 Emmetsburg, IA BR/TR 6-2/195# d6.17																									
1936	Bos N	0	0	—	1	0	0	0	2	2	1	0	0	0	0	4.50	85	.250	.250	0-0	—	0		0	0.0
1938	Chi A	0	0	—	4	0	0	0	14	21	16	1	0	12	2	10.29	48	.350	.458	6-0	.167	-0		-7	-0.3
Total 2		0	0	—	5	0	0	0	16	23	17	1	0	12	2	9.56	50	.338	.438	6-0	.167	-0		-7	-0.3
FORD, GENE Eugene Wyman B 4.16.1881 Milton, NS, CAN D 8.23.1973 Dunedin, FL BR/TR 6/170# d5.5 b-Russ																									
1905	Det A	0	1	.000	7	1	1	0	35	51	30	0	2	14	20	5.66	48	.340	.404	10-1	.000	-1	26	-11	-0.6
FORD, MATT Matthew Lee B 4.8.1981 Plantation, FL BB/TL 6-1/170# d4.2																									
2003	Mil N	0	3	.000	25	4	0	0-0	43.2	46	23	5	1	21-0	26	4.33	98	.264	.345	7-0	.143	0	105	-1	0.0
FORD, WENTY Percival Edmund Wentworth B 11.25.1946 Nassau, Bahamas D 7.8.1980 Nassau, Bahamas BR/TR 5-11/165# d9.10																									
1973	Atl N	1	2	.333	4	2	1	0-0	16.1	17	10	3	1	8-0	4	5.51	72	.279	.366	5-0	.400	1	146	-2	-0.3
FORD, RUSS Russell William B 4.25.1883 Brandon, MB, CAN D 1.24.1960 Rockingham, NC BR/TR 5-11/175# d4.28 b-Gene																									
1909	NY A	0	0	—	1	0	0	0	3	4	4	0	3	4	2	9.00	28	.333	.579	1-0	.000	-0		-2	-0.1
1910	NY A	26	6	.813	36	33	29-8	1	299.2	194	69	4	8	70	209	1.65	161	.188	.245	96-6	.208	4	102	34	4.2
1911	NY A	22	11	.667	37	33	26-1	0	281.1	251	119	3	4	76	158	2.27	158	.237	.291	102-4	.196	-2	99	30	3.0
1912	NY A	13	21	.382	36	35	30	0	291.2	317	165	11	5	79	112	3.55	101	.280	.329	112-7	.286	5*	92	0	0.6
1913	NY A	12	18	.400	33	28	15-1	2	237	244	101	9	4	58	72	2.66	113	.277	.324	74-2	.162	0	77	7	0.7
1914	Buf F	21	6	**.778**	35	26	19-5	**6**	247.1	190	63	11	7	41	123	1.82	**163**	.214	.254	78-4	.128	-4	92	30	3.0
1915	Buf F	5	9	.357	21	15	7	0	127.1	140	74	7	3	48	34	4.52	62	.285	.352	43-3	.279	3*	100	-22	-1.9
Total 7		99	71	.582	199	170	126-15	9	1487.1	1340	595	45	34	376	710	2.59	121	.244	.296	506-26	.209	5	94	77	9.5

FORD, TOM Thomas Walter B 1866 Chattanooga, TN D 5.27.1917 Chattanooga, TN 5-10.5/155# d5.6

Year	Tm Lg	W	L	Pct	G	GS	CG-Sho	SV-BS	IP	H	R	HR	HB	BB-IB	SO	ERA	AERA	OAV	OOB	AB-SH	AVG	PB	Sup	APR	PW
1890	Col AA	0	0	—	1	0	0	0	2	0	0	0	0	3	0	0.00	—	.000	.333	1	.000	-0		1	0.0
	Bro AA	0	6	.000	7	6	6	0	49	70	60	2	0	32	12	5.14	76	.326	.413	30	.033	-3*	92	-12	-1.2
	Year	0	6	.000	8	6	6	0	51	70	65	2	0	35	12	4.94	79	.317	.410	31	.032	-3	93	-14	-1.2

FORD, BILL William Brown B 10.14.1915 Buena Vista, PA D 4.6.1994 Jefferson, PA 6-2/200# d9.27

Year	Tm Lg	W	L	Pct	G	GS	CG-Sho	SV-BS	IP	H	R	HR	HB	BB-IB	SO	ERA	AERA	OAV	OOB	AB-SH	AVG	PB	Sup	APR	PW
1936	Bos N	0	0	—	1	1	0	0	0	0	3	0	0	3	0	∞	—	—	1.000	0-0	—	0	155	-3	-0.3

FORDHAM, TOM Thomas James B 2.20.1974 San Diego, CA BL/TL 6-2/210# d8.19

Year	Tm Lg	W	L	Pct	G	GS	CG-Sho	SV-BS	IP	H	R	HR	HB	BB-IB	SO	ERA	AERA	OAV	OOB	AB-SH	AVG	PB	Sup	APR	PW
1997	Chi A	0	1	.000	7	1	0	0-1	17.1	17	13	2	1	10-2	10	6.23	70	.266	.364	0-0	—	0	105	-4	-0.2
1998	Chi A	1	2	.333	29	5	0	0-0	48	51	36	7	1	42-0	23	6.75	67	.279	.414	1-0	.000	-0	90	-10	-0.5
Total	2	1	3	.250	36	6	0	0-1	65.1	68	49	9	2	52-2	33	6.61	68	.275	.401	1-0	.000	-0	93	-14	-0.7

FOREMAN, HAPPY August G. B 7.20.1897 Memphis, TN D 2.13.1953 New York, NY BL/TL 5-7/160# d9.3

Year	Tm Lg	W	L	Pct	G	GS	CG-Sho	SV-BS	IP	H	R	HR	HB	BB-IB	SO	ERA	AERA	OAV	OOB	AB-SH	AVG	PB	Sup	APR	PW
1924	Chi A	0	0	—	3	0	0	0	4	7	3	0	0	4	1	2.25	183	.467	.579	2-0	.000	-0*		0	0.0
1926	Bos A	0	0	—	3	0	0	0	7.1	3	3	0	0	5	3	3.68	111	.130	.286	2-0	.000	-0		1	0.0
Total	2	0	0	—	6	0	0	0	11.1	10	6	0	0	9	4	3.18	129	.263	.404	4-0	.000	-1		1	0.0

FOREMAN, FRANK Francis Isaiah "Monkey" B 5.1.1863 Baltimore, MD D 11.19.1957 Baltimore, MD BL/TL 6/160# d5.15 b-Brownie

Year	Tm Lg	W	L	Pct	G	GS	CG-Sho	SV-BS	IP	H	R	HR	HB	BB-IB	SO	ERA	AERA	OAV	OOB	AB-SH	AVG	PB	Sup	APR	PW
1884	CP U	1	2	.333	3	3	1	0	18	23	17	0		2	10	4.00	61	.291	.309	11	.091	-2	70	-3	-0.5
	KC U	0	1	.000	1	1	1	0	8	17	12	0		2	5	5.63	40	.405	.432	3	.000	-1	57	-4	-0.4
	Year	1	3	.250	4	4	2	0	26	40	15	0		4	15	4.50	53	.331	.352	14	.071	-3	67	-8	-0.9
1885	Bal AA	2	1	.667	3	3	2	0	27	33	32	0	1	9	11	6.00	54	.284	.341	14	.286	1	218	-9	-0.7
1889	Bal AA	23	21	.523	51	48	43-5	0	414	364	257	8	40	137	180	3.52	112	.229	.306	181	.144	-10*	83	24	0.9
1890	Cin N	13	10	.565	25	24	20	0	198.1	201	139	6	20	89	57	3.95	90	.254	.345	75	.133	-0	110	-6	-0.7
1891	Was AA	18	20	.474	43	41	39-1	1	345.1	381	245	9	43	142	170	3.73	100	.271	.355	153	.222	9*	87	-1	0.8
1892	Was N	2	4	.333	11	7	4	0	60	53	39	3	5	37	16	3.30	99	.227	.345	28	.464	8	117	-1	0.6
	Bal N	0	3	.000	4	3	2	0	25	40	29	4	1	11	5	6.84	50	.348	.409	23	.174	0*	80	-8	-0.7
	Year	2	7	.222	15	10	6	0	85	93	33	7	6	48	21	4.34	76	.267	.366	51	.333	8	105	-9	-0.1
1893	NY N	0	1	.000	2	1	0	0	5.2	19	17	1	1	10	0	27.00	17	.528	.638	3	.000	-1	90	-11	-1.2
1895	Cin N	11	14	.440	32	27	19	1	219	253	142	11	15	92	55	4.11	121	.285	.362	94-1	.309	5	85	19	1.9
1896	Cin N	14	7	.667	27	22	17	1	185.2	212	110	2	8	62	33	3.97	116	.285	.346	74-5	.243	-1	115	13	1.0
1901	Bos A	0	1	.000	1	1	1	0	8	8	9	1	2	2	1	9.00	39	.258	.343	4-0	.000	-1	77	-4	-0.4
	Bal A	12	6	.667	24	22	18-1	1	191.1	225	120	2	6	58	41	3.67	105	.290	.344	80-1	.325	5	121	4	0.6
	Year	12	7	.632	25	23	19-1	1	199.1	233	127	3	8	60	42	3.88	99	.288	.344	84-1	.310	4	119	-1	0.2
1902	Bal A	0	2	.000	2	2	2	0	16.1	28	18	0	0	6	2	6.06	62	.378	.425	7-0	.429	1	76	-5	-0.3
Total	11	96	93	.508	229	205	169-7	4	1721.2	1857	1186	47	142	659	586	3.97	100	.268	.344	750-7	.224	12	97	8	0.9

FOREMAN, BROWNIE John Davis B 8.6.1875 Baltimore, MD D 10.10.1926 Baltimore, MD BL/TL 5-8/150# d7.18 b-Frank

Year	Tm Lg	W	L	Pct	G	GS	CG-Sho	SV-BS	IP	H	R	HR	HB	BB-IB	SO	ERA	AERA	OAV	OOB	AB-SH	AVG	PB	Sup	APR	PW
1895	Pit N	8	6	.571	19	16	12	2	139.2	131	83	0	19	64	54	3.22	140	**.244**	.346	46-1	.065	-6	100	18	1.0
1896	Pit N	3	3	.500	9	9	5	0	61.2	73	55	4	8	35	18	6.57	64	.292	.396	20-0	.150	0	120	-15	-1.0
	Cin N	1	3	.250	4	4	3-1	0	23	41	30	2	2	16	9	11.35	41	.383	.472	10-0	.200	-0	69	-13	-1.5
	Year	4	6	.400	13	13	8-1	0	84.2	114	35	6	10	51	27	7.87	55	.319	.419	30-0	.167	-0	104	-27	-2.5
Total	2	12	12	.500	32	29	20-1	2	224.1	245	168	6	29	115	81	4.97	89	.274	.375	76-1	.105	-6	101	-10	-1.5

FORMAN, BILL William Orange B 10.10.1886 Venango, PA D 10.2.1958 Uniontown, PA BB/TR 5-11/180# d9.20

Year	Tm Lg	W	L	Pct	G	GS	CG-Sho	SV-BS	IP	H	R	HR	HB	BB-IB	SO	ERA	AERA	OAV	OOB	AB-SH	AVG	PB	Sup	APR	PW
1909	Was A	0	2	.000	2	2	1	0	11	8	8	0	2	7	2	4.91	50	.211	.362	3-0	.333	0	44	-3	-0.4
1910	Was A	0	0	—	1	0	0	0	0.2	1	1	0	0	0	0	13.50	18	.333	.333	0-0	—	0		-1	0.0
Total	2	0	2	.000	3	2	1	0	11.2	9	9	0	2	7	2	5.40	45	.220	.360	3-0	.333	1	44	-4	-0.4

FORNIELES, MIKE Jose Miguel (Torres) B 1.18.1932 Havana, Cuba D 2.11.1998 St.Petersburg, FL BR/TR 5-11/172# d9.2

Year	Tm Lg	W	L	Pct	G	GS	CG-Sho	SV-BS	IP	H	R	HR	HB	BB-IB	SO	ERA	AERA	OAV	OOB	AB-SH	AVG	PB	Sup	APR	PW
1952	Was A	2	2	.500	4	2	2-1	0	26.1	13	4	1	0	11	12	1.37	260	.143	.235	10-0	.000	-1	86	7	0.9
1953	Chi A	8	7	.533	39	16	5	3	153	160	68	8	2	61	72	3.59	112	.270	.340	41-9	.098	-3	121	7	0.5
1954	Chi A	1	2	.333	15	6	0	1	42	41	24	4	0	14	18	4.29	87	.252	.309	11-1	.273	0*	146	-3	-0.2
1955	Chi A	6	3	.667	26	9	2	2	86.1	84	37	12	2	29-3	23	3.86	102	.255	.317	29-2	.103	-2*	115	2	0.0
1956	Chi A	0	1	.000	6	0	0	0	15.2	22	9	1	0	6-1	6	4.60	89	.306	.354	5-1	.200	0		-1	0.0
	Bal A	4	7	.364	30	11	1-1	1	111	109	59	7	0	25-2	53	3.97	99	.266	.306	30-1	.167	-1*	58	-3	-0.3
	Year	4	8	.333	36	11	1-1	1	126.2	131	62	8	0	31-3	59	4.05	97	.272	.313	35-2	.171	-1	57	-4	-0.3
1957	Bal A	2	6	.250	15	4	1-1	0	57	57	30	4	0	17-2	43	4.26	84	.257	.308	18-1	.278	1*	81	-5	-0.5
	Bos A	8	7	.533	25	18	7-1	2	125.1	136	61	7	3	38-3	64	3.52	113	.271	.324	44-2	.136	-2*	123	4	0.2
	Year	10	13	.435	40	22	8-2	2	182.1	193	67	11	3	55-5	107	3.75	103	.267	.319	62-3	.177	-1	118	-2	-0.3
1958	Bos A	4	6	.400	37	7	1	1	110.2	123	62	10	6	33-0	49	4.96	81	.284	.339	29-0	.207	-0	90	-8	-0.7
1959	Bos A	5	3	.625	46	0	0	11	82	77	29	6	1	29-3	54	3.07	132	.254	.318	19-0	.158	-1		9	1.1
1960	Bos A	10	5	.667	**70**	0	0	**14**	109	86	38	6	6	49-7	64	2.64	153	.219	.312	15-2	.400	2		15	2.6
1961	Bos A★	9	8	.529	57	2	1	15	119.1	121	65	18	2	54-7	70	4.68	89	.265	.341	32-1	.156	0	74	-4	-0.5
1962	Bos A	3	6	.333	42	1	0	5	82.1	96	57	14	8	37-4	36	5.36	77	.303	.385	16-1	.188	-0	0	-12	-1.3
1963	Bos A	0	0	—	9	0	0	0	14	16	10	0	0	5-0	5	6.43	59	.286	.339	3-0	.333	1		-4	-0.1
	Min A	1	1	.500	11	0	0	0	22.2	24	14	0	2	13-0	7	4.76	76	.273	.371	6-0	.167	0		-3	-0.2
	Year	1	1	.500	20	0	0	0	36.2	40	24	0	2	18-0	12	5.40	68	.278	.359	9-0	.222	1		-6	-0.3
Total	12	63	64	.496	432	76	20-4	55	1156.2	1165	567	98	32	421-32	576	3.96	100	.263	.329	308-21	.169	-6	104	1	1.5

FORSCH, KEN Kenneth Roth B 9.8.1946 Sacramento, CA BR/TR 6-4/210# d9.7 b-Bob

Year	Tm Lg	W	L	Pct	G	GS	CG-Sho	SV-BS	IP	H	R	HR	HB	BB-IB	SO	ERA	AERA	OAV	OOB	AB-SH	AVG	PB	Sup	APR	PW
1970	Hou N	1	2	.333	4	4	1	0-0	24	28	15	1	0	5-0	13	5.63	69	.298	.333	6-3	.000	-1	133	-4	-0.5
1971	Hou N	8	8	.500	33	23	7-2	0-0	188.1	162	60	8	4	53-5	131	2.53	133	.230	.287	59-3	.136	-1	88	17	1.2
1972	Hou N	6	8	.429	30	24	1	0-0	156.1	163	75	19	0	62-1	113	3.91	86	.273	.339	41-7	.146	-1	82	-10	-1.1
1973	Hou N	9	12	.429	46	26	5	4-3	201.1	197	101	18	4	74-7	149	4.20	87	.257	.323	62-5	.065	-4	119	-12	-1.7
1974	Hou N	8	7	.533	70	0	0	10-9	103.1	98	38	3	4	37-13	48	2.79	125	.255	.322	7-1	.000	-1		7	1.1
1975	Hou N	4	8	.333	34	9	2	2-2	109	114	42	9	2	30-3	54	3.22	105	.277	.325	22-3	.045	-1	84	2	0.2
1976	Hou N★	4	3	.571	52	0	0	19-7	92	76	23	5	2	26-7	49	2.15	149	.226	.284	11-2	.091	-0		13	1.6
1977	Hou N	5	8	.385	42	5	0	8-2	86	80	32	2	2	28-6	45	2.72	131	.246	.308	13-1	.077	-1	40	8	1.2
1978	Hou N	10	6	.625	52	6	4-2	7-4	133.1	136	44	2	1	37-13	71	2.70	123	.268	.315	27-2	.185	0	81	10	1.3
1979	Hou N	11	6	.647	26	24	10-2	0-0	177.2	155	67	14	0	35-2	58	3.04	116	.236	**.273**	58-6	.138	0	113	11	1.1
1980	†Hou N	12	13	.480	32	32	6-3	0-0	222.1	230	90	15	7	41-1	84	3.20	103	.266	.303	77-6	.234	4	97	3	0.8
1981	Cal A★	11	7	.611	20	20	10-**4**	0-0	153	143	54	7	4	27-2	55	2.88	127	.250	.286	0-0	—	0	118	14	1.6
1982	Cal A	13	11	.542	37	35	12-4	0-0	228	225	108	25	11	57-2	73	3.87	105	.258	.309	0-0	—	0	107	4	0.3
1983	Cal A	11	12	.478	31	31	11-1	0-0	219.1	226	107	21	4	61-6	81	4.06	99	.266	.317	0-0	—	0	113	0	-0.1
1984	Cal A	1	1	.500	2	2	1	0-0	16.1	14	4	2	0	3-0	10	2.20	180	.237	.274	0-0	—	0	34	3	0.5
1986	Cal A	0	1	.000	10	0	0	1-1	17	24	21	4	2	10-0	13	9.53	43	.343	.429	0-0	—	0		-11	-0.7
Total	16	114	113	.502	521	241	70-18	51-28	2127.1	2071	881	155	47	586-68	1047	3.37	106	.257	.309	383-39	.136	-5	104	55	6.8

FORSCH, BOB Robert Herbert B 1.13.1950 Sacramento, CA BR/TR 6-4/200# d7.7 b-Ken

Year	Tm Lg	W	L	Pct	G	GS	CG-Sho	SV-BS	IP	H	R	HR	HB	BB-IB	SO	ERA	AERA	OAV	OOB	AB-SH	AVG	PB	Sup	APR	PW
1974	StL N	7	4	.636	19	14	5-2	0-1	100	84	38	5	1	34-4	39	2.97	121	.230	.295	29-6	.241	1*	125	7	0.9
1975	StL N	15	10	.600	34	34	7-4	0-0	230	213	89	14	3	70-8	108	2.86	132	.244	.300	78-6	.308	9*	98	22	3.4
1976	StL N	8	10	.444	33	32	2	0-1	194	209	112	17	3	71-8	76	3.94	90	.277	.339	62-9	.177	1*	116	-15	-1.1
1977	StL N	20	7	.741	35	35	8-2	0-0	217.1	210	97	20	3	69-2	95	3.48	111	.251	.310	72-12	.167	0	108	8	0.9
1978	StL N	11	17	.393	34	34	7-3	0-0	233.2	205	110	15	5	97-9	114	3.70	95	.238	.316	83-5	.181	3	88	-5	-0.2
1979	StL N	11	11	.500	33	32	7-1	0-0	218.2	215	102	16	3	52-1	92	3.83	99	.262	.304	73-4	.110	-0	100	0	0.0
1980	StL N	11	10	.524	31	31	8	0-0	214.2	225	102	12	4	33-6	87	3.77	98	.273	.301	78-9	.295	9*	131	-2	0.9
1981	StL N	10	5	.667	20	20	1	0-0	124.1	106	47	7	4	29-3	41	3.18	112	.232	.281	41-6	.122	-1	112	6	0.5
1982	†StL N	15	9	.625	36	34	6-2	1-0	233	238	95	16	4	54-7	69	3.48	104	.268	.310	73-14	.205	3	106	6	0.8
1983	StL N	10	12	.455	34	30	6-2	0-0	187	190	104	23	3	54-2	56	4.28	85	.266	.317	54-7	.241	4*	99	-15	-1.2
1984	StL N	2	5	.286	16	11	1	0-0	52.1	64	38	6	0	19-0	21	6.02	58	.303	.358	16-1	.250	1	76	-15	-1.6
1985	†StL N	9	6	.600	34	19	3-1	2-0	136	132	63	11	2	47-4	48	3.90	91	.258	.322	45-2	.244	4	118	-4	-0.1

Year	Tm Lg	W	L	Pct	G	GS	CG-Sho	SV-BS	IP	H	R	HR	HB	BB-IB	SO	ERA	AERA	OAV	OOB	AB-SH	AVG	PB	Sup	APR	PW
1986	StL N	14	10	.583	33	33	3	0-0	230	211	91	19	2	68-11	104	3.25	112	.247	.301	76-11	.171	3*	105	11	1.4
1987	†StL N	11	7	.611	33	30	2-1	0-0	179	189	90	15	4	45-4	89	4.32	96	.273	.318	57-11	.298	8*	123	-2	0.6
1988	StL N	9	4	.692	30	12	1-1	0-0	108.2	111	51	8	1	38-8	40	3.73	93	.270	.330	25-5	.280	2*	98	-3	-0.3
	Hou N	1	4	.200	6	6	0	0-0	27.2	42	22	2	2	6-1	14	6.51	51	.359	.385	7-1	.143	0	62	-10	-1.5
	Year	10	8	.556	36	18	1-1	0-0	136.1	153	24	10	3	44-9	54	4.29	80	.290	.342	32-6	.250	2	86	-12	-1.8
1989	Hou N	4	5	.444	37	15	0	0-0	108.1	133	68	10	1	46-6	40	5.32	64	.303	.367	24-6	.167	-0	108	-22	-1.8
Total	16	168	136	.553	498	422	67-19	3-2	2794.2	2777	1319	216	45	832-84	1133	3.76	97	.261	.315	893-115	.213	48	107	-33	1.6
FORSTER, SCOTT Scott Christian B 10.27.1971 Philadelphia, PA BR/TL 6-1/194# d6.18																									
2000	Mon N	0	1	.000	42	0	0	0-0	32	28	31	5	2	25-1	23	7.88	61	.230	.362	0-0	—	0		-11	-0.5
FORSTER, TERRY Terry Jay B 1.14.1952 Sioux Falls, SD BL/TL 6-3/210# d4.11																									
1971	Chi A	2	3	.400	45	3	0	1-0	49.2	46	23	5	1	23-3	48	3.99	90	.241	.323	5-0	.400	1	75	-1	0.0
1972	Chi A	6	5	.545	62	0	0	29-6	100	75	31	0	3	44-3	104	2.25	139	.208	.296	19-2	.526	4*		8	2.1
1973	Chi A	6	11	.353	51	12	4	16-3	172.2	174	69	7	0	78-6	120	3.23	123	.266	.342	1-0	.000	-0*	68	14	1.8
1974	Chi A	7	8	.467	59	1	0	**24-10**	134.1	120	57	6	8	48-3	105	3.62	103	.245	.319	0-0	—	0	24	3	0.7
1975	Chi A	3	3	.500	17	1	0	4-3	37	30	12	0	0	24-4	32	2.19	177	.236	.358	0-0	—	0	136	6	1.2
1976	Chi A	2	12	.143	29	16	1	1-0	111.1	126	61	7	1	41-4	70	4.37	82	.288	.350	0-0	—	0	82	-11	-1.2
1977	Pit N	6	4	.600	33	6	0	1-2	87.1	90	47	7	2	32-3	58	4.43	90	.269	.332	26-1	.346	3*	78	-4	-0.1
1978	†LA N	5	4	.556	47	0	0	22-4	65.1	56	19	2	0	23-4	46	1.93	182	.233	.300	8-1	.500	2		10	2.4
1979	LA N	1	2	.333	17	0	0	2-0	16.1	18	11	0	0	11-4	8	5.51	66	.295	.397	0-0	—	0		-3	-0.6
1980	LA N	0	0	—	9	0	0	0-0	11.2	10	4	0	0	4-0	2	3.09	114	.222	.286	0-0	—	0		1	0.1
1981	†LA N	0	1	.000	21	0	0	0-1	30.2	37	14	1	0	15-3	17	4.11	81	.308	.385	2-0	.000	-0		-2	-0.1
1982	LA N	5	6	.455	56	0	0	3-2	83	66	38	3	4	31-9	52	3.04	114	.221	.298	2-0	.000	-0		1	0.2
1983	Atl N	3	2	.600	56	0	0	13-3	79.1	60	19	3	2	31-9	54	2.16	180	.217	.301	8-1	.500	2		15	1.6
1984	Atl N	2	0	1.000	25	0	0	5-0	26.2	30	9	1	0	7-3	10	2.70	143	.297	.339	3-0	.667	1		3	0.4
1985	Atl N	2	3	.400	46	0	0	1-2	59.1	49	22	7	0	28-4	37	2.28	169	.222	.307	4-1	.000	-0		8	0.6
1986	Cal A	4	1	.800	41	0	0	5-3	41	47	18	2	3	17-1	28	3.51	117	.297	.374	0-0	—	0		3	0.4
Total	16	54	65	.454	614	39	5	127-39	1105.2	1034	454	51	24	457-63	791	3.23	115	.251	.327	78-6	.397	11	77	51	9.5
FORTUGNO, TIM Timothy Shawn B 4.11.1962 Clinton, MA BL/TL 6-1/195# d7.20																									
1992	Cal A	1	1	.500	14	5	1-1	1-0	41.2	37	24	5	0	19-0	31	5.18	77	.236	.316	0-0	—	0	128	-4	-0.2
1994	Cin N	1	0	1.000	25	0	0	0-0	30	32	14	2	3	14-0	29	4.20	99	.288	.380	3-0	.333	0		1	0.1
1995	Chi A	1	3	.250	37	0	0	0-1	38.2	30	24	7	0	19-2	24	5.59	80	.213	.302	0-0	—	0		-4	-0.3
Total	3	3	4	.429	76	5	1-1	1-1	110.1	99	62	14	3	52-2	84	5.06	83	.242	.329	3-0	.333	0	128	-7	-0.4
FORTUNE, GARY Garrett Reese B 10.11.1894 High Point, NC D 9.23.1955 Washington, DC BB/TR 5-11.5/176# d10.5																									
1916	Phi N	0	1	.000	1	1	0	0	5	2	2	0	0	4	3	3.60	74	.118	.286	2-0	.000	-0	28	0	-0.1
1918	Phi N	0	2	.000	5	2	1	0	31	41	30	2	1	19	10	8.13	37	.333	.427	10-0	.200	0	114	-14	-0.8
1920	Bos A	0	2	.000	14	3	1	0	41.2	46	32	0	0	23	10	5.83	63	.282	.371	12-0	.167	-0	94	-11	-0.6
Total	3	0	5	.000	20	6	2	0	77.2	89	64	2	1	46	23	6.61	51	.294	.389	24-0	.167	-0	89	-25	-1.5
FOSNOW, JERRY Gerald Eugene B 9.21.1940 Deshler, OH BR/TL 6-4/195# d6.29																									
1964	Min A	0	1	.000	7	0	0	0	10.2	13	13	3	0	8-0	9	10.97	33	.302	.404	0-0	—	0		-8	-0.7
1965	Min A	3	3	.500	29	0	0	2	46.2	33	29	7	1	25-2	35	4.44	80	.193	.299	5-0	.000	-1		-5	-0.7
Total	2	3	4	.429	36	0	0	2	57.1	46	42	10	1	33-2	44	5.65	63	.215	.321	5-0	.000	-1		-13	-1.4
FOSS, LARRY Larry Curtis B 4.18.1936 Castleton, KS BR/TR 6-2/187# d9.18																									
1961	Pit N	1	1	.500	3	3	0	0	15.1	15	11	3	2	11-0	9	5.87	68	.273	.406	6-0	.167	-0	96	-3	-0.4
1962	NY N	0	1	.000	5	1	0	0	11.2	17	6	2	1	7-0	3	4.63	90	.362	.446	1-0	.000	-0	126	0	0.0
Total	2	1	2	.333	8	4	0	0	27	32	17	5	3	18-0	12	5.33	76	.314	.424	7-0	.143	-0	103	-3	-0.4
FOSSAS, TONY Emilio Antonio (Morejon) B 9.23.1957 Havana, Cuba BL/TL 6/187# d5.15																									
1988	Tex A	0	0	—	5	0	0	0-0	5.2	11	3	0	0	2-0	0	4.76	86	.423	.464	0-0	—	0		0	0.0
1989	Mil A	2	2	.500	51	0	0	1-2	61	57	27	3	1	22-7	42	3.54	109	.256	.321	0-0	—	0		2	0.1
1990	Mil A	2	3	.400	32	0	0	0-2	29.1	44	23	5	0	10-2	24	6.44	60	.331	.375	0-0	—	0		-8	-1.2
1991	Bos A	3	2	.600	64	0	0	1-1	57	49	27	3	3	28-9	29	3.47	124	.236	.335	0-0	—	0		4	0.4
1992	Bos A	1	2	.333	60	0	0	2-1	29.2	31	9	1	1	14-3	19	2.43	174	.279	.365	0-0	—	0		6	0.6
1993	Bos A	1	1	.500	71	0	0	0-2	40	38	28	4	2	15-4	39	5.17	89	.242	.314	0-0	—	0		-3	-0.1
1994	Bos A	2	0	1.000	44	0	0	1-0	34	35	18	6	1	15-1	31	4.76	106	.263	.342	0-0	—	0		2	0.1
1995	StL N	3	0	1.000	58	0	0	0-0	36.2	28	6	1	1	10-3	40	1.47	285	.214	.273	0-0	—	0		11	0.8
1996	†StL N	0	4	.000	65	0	0	2-5	47	43	19	7	0	21-3	36	2.68	156	.231	.308	1-0	.000	-0		6	0.5
1997	StL N	2	7	.222	71	0	0	0-1	51.2	62	32	7	1	26-3	41	3.83	108	.298	.377	0-0	—	0		-1	-0.1
1998	Sea A	0	3	.000	23	0	0	0-1	11.1	19	11	1	0	6-0	10	8.74	53	.404	.463	0-0	—	0		-5	-0.9
	Chi N	0	0	—	8	0	0	0-0	4	8	4	0	0	6-0	6	9.00	49	.421	.560	0-0	—	0		-2	-0.1
	Tex A	1	0	1.000	10	0	0	0-0	7.1	3	0	0	0	4-0	7	0.00	—	.120	.241	0-0	—	0		4	0.4
1999	NY A	0	0	—	5	0	0	0-0	1	6	4	1	0	1-1	0	36.00	13	.667	.700	0-0	—	0		-3	-0.2
Total	12	17	24	.415	567	0	0	7-15	415.2	434	211	39	10	180-36	324	3.90	109	.269	.344	1-0	.000	-0		13	0.3
FOSSUM, CASEY Casey Paul B 1.6.1978 Cherry Hill, NJ BB/TL 6-1/160# d7.28																									
2001	Bos A	3	2	.600	13	7	0	0-0	44.1	44	26	4	6	20-1	26	4.87	92	.259	.355	0-0	—	0	118	-2	-0.2
2002	Bos A	5	4	.556	43	12	0	1-0	106.2	113	56	12	4	30-0	101	3.46	130	.268	.320	0-0	—	0	96	7	0.5
2003	Bos A	6	5	.545	19	14	0	1-0	79	82	55	9	4	34-0	63	5.47	84	.270	.348	0-0	—	0	140	-9	-1.1
Total	3	14	11	.560	75	33	0	2-0	230	239	137	25	14	84-1	190	4.42	102	.267	.337	0-0	—	0	120	-4	-0.8
FOSTER, ALAN Alan Benton B 12.8.1946 Pasadena, CA BR/TR 6/180# d4.25																									
1967	LA N	0	1	.000	4	2	0	0	16.2	10	4	0	0	3-0	15	2.16	143	.169	.210	4-0	.000	-0	28	2	0.1
1968	LA N	1	1	.500	3	3	0	0	15.2	11	4	1	0	2-0	10	1.72	160	.200	.228	4-1	.250	0	63	2	0.3
1969	LA N	3	9	.250	24	15	2-2	0-0	102.2	119	55	11	4	29-4	59	4.38	76	.290	.341	27-3	.074	-1	94	-12	-1.4
1970	LA N	10	13	.435	33	33	7-1	0-0	198.2	200	104	22	2	81-2	83	4.26	90	.264	.334	64-8	.109	-2	112	-10	-1.2
1971	Cle A	8	12	.400	36	26	3	0-0	181.2	158	93	19	4	82-5	97	4.16	92	.232	.316	51-7	.039	-4*	70	-7	-1.4
1972	Cal A	0	1	.000	8	0	0	0-1	12.2	12	8	3	2	6-0	11	4.97	59	.245	.351	0-0	—	0		-3	-0.2
1973	StL N	13	9	.591	35	29	6-2	0-0	203.2	195	82	17	5	63-3	106	3.14	116	.254	.313	68-5	.191	1	108	11	1.1
1974	StL N	7	10	.412	31	25	5-1	0-0	162.1	167	81	16	3	61-7	78	3.88	92	.268	.335	48-7	.167	-1*	94	-6	-0.8
1975	SD N	3	1	.750	17	4	1	0-0	44.2	41	14	1	0	21-5	20	2.42	144	.244	.326	11-0	.091	-1*	95	6	0.4
1976	SD N	3	6	.333	26	11	2	0-0	86.2	75	36	9	1	35-2	22	3.22	102	.235	.311	18-3	.056	-0*	73	0	0.0
Total	10	48	63	.432	217	148	26-6	0-1	1025.1	988	481	99	21	383-28	501	3.74	97	.254	.322	295-34	.119	-8	94	-17	-3.1
FOSTER, ED Eddy Lee "Slim" B , GA D 3.1.1929 Montgomery, AL BR/TR 6-1/?# d7.31																									
1908	Cle A	1	0	1.000	6	1	1	2	21	16	5	1	2	12	11	2.14	111	.229	.357	6-0	.000	-0	143	1	0.0
FOSTER, RUBE George B 1.5.1888 Lehigh, OK D 3.1.1976 Bokoshe, OK BR/TR 5-7.5/170# d4.10																									
1913	Bos A	3	3	.500	19	8	4-1	0	68.1	64	35	1	4	28	36	3.16	93	.252	.336	21-0	.095	-1*	88	-2	-0.3
1914	Bos A	14	8	.636	32	27	17-5	0	211.2	164	68	2	7	52	89	1.70	158	.218	.274	63-5	.175	0*	89	18	2.0
1915	†Bos A	19	8	.704	37	33	21-5	1	255.1	217	83	3	10	86	82	2.11	131	.237	.310	83-9	.277	7*	105	19	2.9
1916	†Bos A	14	7	.667	33	19	9-3	2	182.1	173	73	0	4	86	53	3.06	90	.263	.352	62-2	.177	0*	98	-5	-0.4
1917	Bos A	8	7	.533	17	16	9-1	0	124.2	108	43	0	4	53	34	2.53	102	.243	.329	41-3	.268	2	110	2	0.5
Total	5	58	33	.637	138	103	60-15	3	842.1	726	302	6	29	305	294	2.36	116	.240	.316	270-19	.215	9	99	32	4.7
FOSTER, KRIS John Kristian B 8.30.1974 Riverdale, NJ BR/TR 6-1/200# d8.3																									
2001	Bal A	0	0	—	7	0	0	0-0	10	9	4	1	0	8-0	8	2.70	159	.231	.362	0-0	—	0		2	0.1
FOSTER, JOHN John Norman B 5.17.1978 Stockton, CA BL/TL 6/180# d4.24																									
2002	Atl N	1	0	1.000	5	0	0	0-0	5	6	6	3	1	6-0	6	10.80	38	.286	.464	0-0	—	0		-3	-0.6
2003	Mil N	2	0	1.000	23	0	0	0-2	21	30	11	5	1	8-2	16	4.71	90	.341	.398	0-0	—	0		-1	-0.1
Total	2	3	0	1.000	28	0	0	0-2	26	36	17	8	2	14-2	22	5.88	72	.330	.413	0-0	—	0		-4	-0.7

Year	Tm Lg	W	L	Pct	G	GS	CG-Sho	SV-BS	IP	H	R	HR	HB	BB-IB	SO	ERA	AERA	OAV	OOB	AB-SH	AVG	PB	Sup	APR	PW
FOSTER, KEVIN Kevin Christopher B 1.13.1969 Evanston, IL BR/TR 6-1/170# d9.12																									
1993	Phi N	0	1	.000	2	1	0	0-0	6.2	13	11	3	0	7-0	6	14.85	27	.394	.500	2-0	.000	-0	23	-8	-0.8
1994	Chi N	3	4	.429	13	13	0	0-0	81	70	31	7	1	35-1	75	2.89	144	.234	.315	27-3	.074	-2	83	10	0.6
1995	Chi N	12	11	.522	30	28	0	0-0	167.2	149	90	32	6	65-4	146	4.51	91	.240	.315	60-5	.250	5*	119	-6	-0.3
1996	Chi N	7	6	.538	17	16	1	0-0	87	98	63	16	2	35-3	53	6.21	70	.288	.354	27-3	.296	5*	104	-16	-1.6
1997	Chi N	10	7	.588	26	25	1	0-0	146.1	141	79	27	2	66-4	118	4.61	93	.255	.333	47-11	.128	-1*	106	-4	-0.6
1998	Chi N	0	0	—	3	0	0	0-0	3.1	8	6	1	0	2-0	3	16.20	27	.500	.500	0-0	—	0		-4	-0.2
2001	Tex A	0	1	.000	9	0	0	0-0	17.2	21	14	2	3	10-0	16	6.62	71	.309	.415	0-0	—	0		-4	-0.2
Total	7	32	30	.516	100	83	2	0-0	509.2	500	294	88	14	220-12	417	4.86	87	.259	.336	163-22	.190	7	105	-32	-3.1
FOSTER, LARRY Larry Lynn B 12.24.1937 Lansing, MI BL/TR 6/185# d9.18																									
1963	Det A	0	0	—	1	0	0	0	2	4	3	0	0	1-0	1	13.50	28	.364	.417	0-0	—	0		-2	-0.1
FOSTER, STEVE Stephen Eugene B 8.16.1966 Dallas, TX BR/TR 6/180# d8.22																									
1991	Cin N	0	0	—	11	0	0	0-0	14	7	5	1	0	4-0	11	1.93	197	.143	.208	0-0	—	0		2	0.1
1992	Cin N	1	1	.500	31	1	0	2-1	50	52	16	4	0	13-1	34	2.88	125	.275	.319	5-0	.200	0	25	5	0.3
1993	Cin N	2	2	.500	17	0	0	0-0	25.2	23	8	1	1	5-2	16	1.75	230	.235	.279	0-1	—	0		5	0.7
Total	3	3	3	.500	59	1	0	2-1	89.2	82	29	6	1	22-3	61	2.41	156	.244	.291	5-1	.200	0	25	12	1.1
FOUCAULT, STEVE Steven Raymond B 10.3.1949 Duluth, MN BL/TR 6/205# d4.7																									
1973	Tex A	2	4	.333	32	0	0	8-6	55.2	54	26	6	3	31-4	28	3.88	96	.262	.364	0-0	—	0		0	0.0
1974	Tex A	8	9	.471	69	0	0	12-8	144.1	123	51	8	5	40-5	106	2.24	159	.234	.291	0-0	—	0		17	2.3
1975	Tex A	8	4	.667	59	0	0	10-9	107	96	57	10	4	55-15	56	4.12	91	.249	.344	0-0	—	0		-4	-0.6
1976	Tex A	8	8	.500	46	0	0	5-5	75.2	68	31	9	4	25-7	41	3.33	108	.249	.318	0-0	—	0		3	0.7
1977	Det A	7	7	.500	44	0	0	13-5	74.1	64	29	7	0	17-4	58	3.15	137	.226	.270	0-0	—	0		9	1.8
1978	Det A	2	4	.333	24	0	0	4-0	37.1	48	18	1	1	21-4	18	3.13	124	.324	.405	0-0	—	0		1	0.2
	KC A	0	0	—	3	0	0	0-0	2.1	5	1	0	0	1-1	0	3.86	99	.417	.462	0-0	—	0		0	0.0
	Year	2	4	.333	27	0	0	4-0	39.2	53	20	1	1	22-5	18	3.18	122	.331	.409	0-0	—	0		2	0.2
Total	6	35	36	.493	277	0	0	52-33	496.2	458	213	41	17	190-40	307	3.21	117	.250	.323	0-0	—	0		26	4.4
FOULKE, KEITH Keith Charles B 10.19.1972 San Diego, CA BR/TR 6/195# d5.21																									
1997	SF N	1	5	.167	11	8	0	0-1	44.2	60	41	9	4	18-1	33	8.26	49	.324	.396	13-2	.154	-0	70	-19	-2.1
	Chi A	3	0	1.000	16	0	0	3-2	28.2	28	11	4	0	5-1	21	3.45	127	.255	.284	0-0	—	0		4	0.4
1998	Chi A	3	2	.600	54	0	0	1-1	65.1	51	31	9	4	20-3	57	4.13	110	.213	.283	0-0	—	0		4	0.3
1999	Chi A	3	3	.500	67	0	0	9-4	105.1	72	28	11	3	21-4	123	2.22	220	.188	.235	2-0	.000	-0		**31**	2.0
2000	†Chi A	3	1	.750	72	0	0	34-5	88	66	31	9	2	22-2	91	2.97	168	.207	.261	0-0	—	0		20	2.1
2001	Chi A	4	9	.308	72	0	0	42-3	81	57	21	3	8	22-1	75	2.33	198	.199	.274	0-0	—	0		**21**	4.1
2002	Chi A	2	4	.333	65	0	0	11-3	77.2	65	26	7	2	13-2	58	2.90	156	.225	.263	1-0	.000	-0		15	1.3
2003	†Oak A★	9	1	.900	72	0	0	**43-5**	86.2	57	21	10	7	20-2	88	2.08	218	.184	.249	0-0	—	0		24	4.7
Total	7	28	25	.528	429	8	0	143-24	577.1	456	210	62	30	141-16	546	3.16	146	.215	.273	16-2	.125	-0	70	100	12.8
FOURNIER, HENRY Julius Henry "Frenchy" B 8.8.1865 Syracuse, NY D 12.8.1945 Detroit, MI TL d8.22																									
1894	Cin N	1	3	.250	6	4	4	0	45	71	51	4	2	20	5	5.40	103	.353	.417	19-0	.105	-3	73	-4	-0.4
FOUTZ, DAVE David Luther "Scissors" B 9.7.1856 Carroll Co., MD D 3.5.1897 Waverly, MD BR/TR 6-2/161# d7.29 M4 b-Frank ▲																									
1884	StL AA	15	6	.714	25	25	19-2	0	206.2	167	100	7	9	36	95	2.18	150	.212	.255	119	.227	1*	100	22	2.2
1885	†StL AA	33	14	.702	47	46	46-2	0	407.2	351	200	8	18	92	147	2.63	125	.227	.278	238	.248	5*	114	29	3.5
1886	†StL AA	**41**	16	**.719**	59	57	55-11	**1**	504	418	216	5	10	144	283	**2.11**	**163**	.216	.274	414	.280	11*	112	71	**7.6**
1887	†StL AA	25	12	.676	40	38	36-1	0	339.1	369	244	7	10	90	94	3.87	117	.258	.306	423	.357	15*	123	16	2.4
1888	Bro AA	12	7	.632	23	19	19	0	176	146	85	3	5	35	73	2.51	119	.218	.262	563	.277	6*	92	10	1.5
1889	†Bro AA	3	0	1.000	12	4	3	0	59.2	70	50	2	0	19	21	4.37	85	.283	.335	553	.275	3*	158	-7	-0.1
1890	†Bro N	2	1	.667	5	2	2	**2**	29	29	10	0	1	6	4	1.86	185	.252	.295	509	.303	2*	46	5	0.6
1891	Bro N	3	2	.600	6	5	5	0	52	51	24	1	1	16	14	3.29	100	.246	.304	521	.257	1*	98	2	0.3
1892	Bro N	13	8	.619	27	20	17	1	203	210	119	3	4	63	56	3.41	93	.256	.313	220	.186	0*	122	-9	-0.6
1893	Bro N	0	0	—	6	0	0	0	18	28	17	2	0	8	3	7.50	59	.346	.404	557	.246	1*		-5	-0.1
1894	Bro N	0	0	—	1	0	0	0	2	4	3	0	0	1	0	13.50	37	.400	.455	297-8	.303	0*		-2	-0.1
Total	11	147	66	.690	251	216	202-16	4	1997.1	1843	1068	38	58	510	790	2.84	124	.235	.286	4414-8	.276	45	113	132	17.2
FOWLER, JESSE Jesse Peter "Pete" B 10.30.1898 Spartanburg, SC D 9.23.1973 Columbia, SC BR/TL 5-10.5/158# d7.29 b-Art																									
1924	StL N	1	1	.500	13	3	0	0	32.2	28	21	0	2	18	5	4.41	86	.226	.333	9-0	.222	0	82	-3	-0.2
FOWLER, ART John Arthur B 7.3.1922 Converse, SC BR/TR 5-11/180# d4.17 C15 b-Jesse																									
1954	Cin N	12	10	.545	40	29	8-1	0	227.2	256	112	20	4	85	93	3.83	109	.286	.348	60-12	.100	-1	90	7	0.4
1955	Cin N	11	10	.524	46	28	8-3	2	207.2	198	96	20	1	63-3	94	3.90	109	.250	.303	60-7	.200	-0	83	10	0.9
1956	Cin N	11	11	.500	45	23	8	1	177.2	191	92	15	0	35-3	86	4.05	98	.278	.311	48-5	.146	-0	92	-3	-0.3
1957	Cin N	3	0	1.000	33	7	1	0	87.2	111	65	11	2	24-2	45	6.47	64	.310	.355	17-3	.176	0	156	-20	-1.0
1959	LA N	3	4	.429	36	0	0	2	61	70	39	8	0	23-7	47	5.31	80	.294	.350	12-1	.083	-1		-6	-0.8
1961	LA A	5	8	.385	53	3	0	11	89	68	42	12	0	29-3	78	3.64	124	.209	.272	13-3	.077	-1	72	7	1.0
1962	LA A	4	3	.571	48	0	0	5	77	67	25	6	1	25-3	38	2.81	138	.234	.296	11-0	.273	1		11	1.1
1963	LA A	5	3	.625	57	0	0	10	89.1	70	26	5	0	19-8	53	2.42	142	.219	.260	9-2	.222	0		11	1.3
1964	LA A	0	2	.000	4	0	0	1	7	8	8	2	1	5-2	5	10.29	32	.296	.424	1-0	.000	-0		-5	-1.0
Total	9	54	51	.514	362	90	25-4	32	1024	1039	505	99	9	308-31	539	4.03	102	.265	.317	231-33	.152	-2	94	12	1.6
FOWLER, DICK Richard John B 3.30.1921 Toronto, ON, CAN D 5.22.1972 Oneonta, NY BR/TR 6-4.5/215# d9.13 Mil 1943-45																									
1941	Phi A	1	2	.333	4	3	1	0	24	26	11	4	0	8	8	3.38	124	.289	.347	9-0	.000	-1	131	2	0.1
1942	Phi A	6	11	.353	31	17	4	1	140	159	90	13	0	45	38	4.95	76	.287	.341	50-1	.160	-1*	65	-17	-2.1
1945	Phi A	1	2	.333	7	3	2-1	0	37.1	41	21	1	0	18	21	4.82	71	.283	.362	18-0	.444	3*	33	-5	0.0
1946	Phi A	9	16	.360	32	28	14-1	0	205.2	213	101	16	2	75	89	3.28	108	.263	.327	71-2	.183	-1	75	0	-0.1
1947	Phi A	12	11	.522	36	31	16-3	0	227.1	210	77	12	3	85	75	2.81	136	.249	.319	82-4	.171	-3	105	26	2.1
1948	Phi A	15	8	.652	29	26	16-2	2	204.2	221	93	15	4	76	50	3.78	113	.281	.348	82-4	.171	-2	113	12	0.9
1949	Phi A	15	11	.577	31	28	15-4	1	213.2	210	108	13	2	115	43	3.75	110	.262	.357	77-2	.234	3	102	5	0.9
1950	Phi A	1	5	.167	11	9	2	0	66.2	75	52	7	3	56	15	6.48	70	.300	.434	26-0	.192	-1	59	-14	-1.1
1951	Phi A	5	11	.313	22	22	4	0	125	141	89	11	1	72	29	5.62	76	.291	.384	42-1	.190	-0	96	-19	-2.1
1952	Phi A	1	2	.333	18	3	1	0	58.2	71	43	4	4	28	14	6.44	61	.302	.386	15-0	.000	-2	44	-13	-0.8
Total	10	66	79	.455	221	170	75-11	4	1303	1367	685	96	19	578	382	4.11	97	.273	.351	472-14	.186	-6	92	-23	-2.2
FOWLKES, ALAN Alan Kim B 8.8.1958 Brawley, CA BR/TR 6-2/190# d4.7																									
1982	SF N	4	2	.667	21	15	1	0-0	85	111	55	12	5	24-3	50	5.19	69	.321	.366	26-2	.115	-1	108	-14	-1.0
1985	Cal A	0	0	—	2	0	0	0-0	7	8	7	4	0	4-0	5	9.00	46	.276	.364	0-0	—	0		-3	-0.2
Total	2	4	2	.667	23	15	1	0-0	92	119	62	16	5	28-3	55	5.48	66	.317	.365	26-2	.115	-1	108	-17	-1.2
FOX, CHAD Chad Douglas B 9.3.1970 Coronado, CA BR/TR 6-3/175# d7.13																									
1997	Atl N	0	1	.000	30	0	0	0-1	27.1	24	12	4	0	16-0	28	3.29	128	.231	.333	0-0	—	0		2	0.1
1998	Mil N	1	4	.200	49	0	0	0-2	57	56	27	4	1	20-0	64	3.95	108	.260	.326	3-1	.000	-0		2	0.1
1999	Mil N	0	0	—	6	0	0	0-0	6.2	11	8	1	1	4-0	12	10.80	42	.355	.444	1-0	.000	-0		-4	-0.2
2001	Mil N	5	2	.714	65	0	0	2-2	66.2	44	16	6	5	36-7	80	1.89	227	.181	.298	3-0	.000	-0		18	1.7
2002	Mil N	1	0	1.000	3	0	0	0-0	4.2	6	3	0	0	5-1	3	5.79	71	.316	.458	0-0	—	0		-1	-0.2
2003	Bos A	1	2	.333	17	0	0	3-2	18	19	10	2	1	17-2	19	4.50	101	.264	.407	0-0	—	0		0	0.0
	†Fla N	2	1	.667	21	0	0	0-0	25.1	16	6	1	0	14-2	27	2.13	192	.190	.294	0-0	—	0		6	0.6
Total	6	10	10	.500	191	0	0	5-7	205.2	176	82	18	8	112-12	233	3.28	130	.229	.331	7-1	.000	-1		23	2.1
FOX, HENRY Henry (b: Henry Fuchs) B 11.18.1874 Scranton, PA D 6.6.1927 Scranton, PA d9.4																									
1902	Phi N	0	0	—	1	0	0	1	1	2	3	0	0	1	1	18.00	16	.400	.500	0-0	—	0		-2	-0.3

Year	Tm Lg	W	L	Pct	G	GS	CG-Sho	SV-BS	IP	H	R	HR	HB	BB-IB	SO	ERA	AERA	OAV	OOB	AB-SH	AVG	PB	Sup	APR	PW
FOX, HOWIE Howard Francis B 3.1.1921 Coburg, OR D 10.9.1955 San Antonio, TX BR/TR 6-3/210# d9.28																									
1944	Cin N	0	0	—	2	0	0	0	2.1	2	0	0	0	0	0	0.00	—	.222	.222	1-0	.000	-0		1	0.0
1945	Cin N	8	13	.381	45	15	7	0	164.1	169	102	6	6	77	54	4.93	76	.268	.353	46-5	.283	3	93	-21	-1.9
1946	Cin N	0	0	—	4	0	0	0	5	12	13	2	0	5	1	18.00	19	.462	.548	0-0	—	0		-9	-0.4
1948	Cin N	6	9	.400	34	24	5	1	171	185	100	11	1	62	63	4.53	86	.280	.343	60-1	.200	1*	93	-13	-0.8
1949	Cin N	6	19	.240	38	30	9	0	215	221	120	13	4	77	60	3.98	105	.265	.330	72-6	.236	2*	79	0	0.4
1950	Cin N	11	8	.579	34	22	10-1	1	187	196	97	14	2	85	64	4.33	98	.269	.347	63-3	.175	-0*	88	0	0.1
1951	Cin N	9	14	.391	40	30	9-4	2	228	239	105	16	2	69	57	3.83	107	.272	.326	70-8	.114	-2	74	10	0.7
1952	Phi N	2	7	.222	13	11	2	0	62	70	41	8	0	26	16	5.08	72	.287	.356	21-3	.048	-2	120	-10	-1.4
1954	Bal A	1	2	.333	38	0	0	2	73.2	80	33	2	2	34	27	3.67	98	.289	.366	16-0	.250	1		0	0.1
Total	9	43	72	.374	248	132	42-5	6	1108.1	1174	611	72	17	435	342	4.33	92	.274	.343	349-26	.189	2	87	-42	-3.2
FOX, JOHN John Joseph B 2.7.1859 Roxbury, MA D 4.18.1893 Boston, MA d6.2																									
1881	Bos N	6	8	.429	17	16	12	0	124.1	144	90	0		39	30	3.33	80	.279	.329	118	.178	-4*	85	-11	-1.3
1883	Bal AA	6	13	.316	20	19	18	0	165.1	209	140	2		32	49	4.03	86	.289	.320	92	.152	-4*	82	-9	-1.1
1884	Pit AA	1	6	.143	7	7	7	0	59	76	59	2	3	16	22	5.64	59	.291	.339	25	.240	0*	60	-15	-1.3
1886	Was N	0	1	.000	1	1	1	0	8	11	13	0		11	3	9.00	36	.314	.478	3	.333	0	57	-5	-0.4
Total	4	13	28	.317	45	43	38	0	356.2	440	302	4	3	98	104	4.16	76	.287	.331	238	.176	-7	79	-40	-4.1
FOX, TERRY Terrence Edward B 7.31.1935 Chicago, IL BR/TR 6/175# d9.4																									
1960	Mil N	0	0	—	5	0	0	0	8.1	6	5	0	0	6-0	5	4.32	79	.200	.333	1-0	.000	-0		-1	-0.1
1961	Det A	5	2	.714	39	0	0	12	57.1	42	12	6	3	16-1	32	1.41	290	.200	.265	12-1	.167	-0		16	2.6
1962	Det A	3	1	.750	44	0	0	16	58	48	13	2	1	16-6	23	1.71	238	.227	.283	8-1	.250	2*		15	2.1
1963	Det A	8	6	.571	46	0	0	11	80.1	81	37	9	2	20-5	35	3.59	104	.263	.310	11-1	.091	-0		1	0.2
1964	Det A	4	3	.571	32	0	0	5	61	77	26	4	1	16-1	28	3.39	108	.316	.357	12-0	.250	1		1	0.3
1965	Det A	6	4	.600	42	0	0	10	77.2	59	26	7	3	31-2	34	2.78	125	.214	.298	15-4	.000	-1		6	0.9
1966	Det A	0	1	.000	4	0	0	1	10	9	8	3	0	2-0	6	6.30	55	.243	.282	3-0	.000	-0		-3	-0.4
	Phi N	3	2	.600	36	0	0	4	44.1	57	22	3	2	17-8	22	4.47	80	.322	.384	3-1	.000	-0*		-3	-0.4
Total	7	29	19	.604	248	0	0	59	397	379	149	34	12	124-23	185	2.99	125	.254	.314	65-8	.123	1		32	5.2
FOXEN, BILL William Aloysius B 5.31.1884 Tenafly, NJ D 4.17.1937 Brooklyn, NY BL/TL 5-11.5/165# d5.5																									
1908	Phi N	7	7	.500	22	16	10-2	0	147.1	126	45	2	8	53	52	1.95	124	.240	.319	53-1	.094	-3	113	7	0.5
1909	Phi N	3	7	.300	18	7	5-1	0	83.1	65	40	0	4	32	37	3.35	78	.219	.303	24-0	.208	3	65	-6	-0.1
1910	Phi N	5	5	.500	16	9	5	0	77.2	73	30	2	3	40	33	2.55	123	.268	.368	23-1	.174	-1	71	5	0.6
	Chi N	0	0	—	2	0	0	0	5	7	5	0	0	3	2	9.00	32	.350	.435	2-0	.000	-0		-3	-0.2
	Year	5	5	.500	18	9	5	0	82.2	80	38	2	3	43	35	2.94	106	.274	.373	25-1	.160	-1	72	1	0.4
1911	Chi N	1	1	.500	3	1	0	0	13	12	6	0	0	12	6	2.08	159	.255	.407	4-0	.250	1	113	1	0.3
Total	4	16	20	.444	61	33	20-3	0	326.1	283	126	4	15	140	130	2.56	104	.244	.333	106-2	.142	0	90	4	1.1
FOXX, JIMMIE James Emory "Beast" or "Double X" B 10.22.1907 Sudlersville, MD D 7.21.1967 Miami, FL BR/TR 6/195# d5.1.1925 C1 HF1951 ▲																									
1939	Bos A☆	0	0	—	1	0	0	0	1	0	0	0	0	0	1	0.00	—	.000	.000	467-5	.360	1*		1	0.0
1945	Phi N	1	0	1.000	9	2	0	0	22.2	13	4	0	1	14	10	1.59	241	.171	.308	224-1	.268	2*	77	6	0.4
Total	2	1	0	1.000	10	2	0	0	23.2	13	4	0	1	14	11	1.52	254	.165	.298	691-6	.330	3	77	7	0.4
FOYTACK, PAUL Paul Eugene B 11.16.1930 Scranton, PA BR/TR 5-11/180# d4.21																									
1953	Det A	0	0	—	6	0	0	0	9.2	15	12	1	1	9	7	11.17	36	.375	.500	1-0	.000	-0		-7	-0.4
1955	Det A	0	1	.000	22	1	0	0	49.2	48	29	4	0	36-3	38	5.26	73	.259	.375	11-0	.091	-1	139	-6	-0.4
1956	Det A	15	13	.536	43	33	16-1	1	256	211	114	24	2	142-4	184	3.59	115	.226	.327	90-6	.122	-6	122	16	0.9
1957	Det A	14	11	.560	38	27	8-1	1	212	175	79	19	4	104-12	118	3.14	123	.226	.318	63-12	.222	1	81	17	1.9
1958	Det A	15	13	.536	39	33	16-2	1	230	198	98	23	3	77-1	135	3.44	117	.233	.298	75-7	.240	2	97	14	1.8
1959	Det A	14	14	.500	39	**37**	11-2	1	240.1	239	137	34	2	64-3	110	4.64	87	.259	.307	81-6	.111	-4	106	-12	-1.7
1960	Det A	2	11	.154	28	13	1	2	96.2	108	70	11	0	49-3	38	6.14	64	.286	.366	25-2	.280	2*	96	-21	-2.4
1961	Det A	11	10	.524	32	20	6	0	169.2	152	81	27	2	56-0	89	3.93	104	.238	.300	54-6	.222	2	112	5	0.6
1962	Det A	10	7	.588	29	21	5-1	0	143.2	145	80	18	1	86-2	63	4.39	93	.259	.358	42-2	.143	-1	105	-5	-0.7
1963	Det A	0	1	.000	9	0	0	1	17.2	18	18	4	0	8-0	7	8.66	43	.265	.338	4-0	.000	-0		-9	-0.6
	LA A	5	5	.500	25	8	0	0	70.1	68	35	9	0	29-6	37	3.71	92	.255	.326	15-2	.267	1*	84	-3	-0.3
	Year	5	6	.455	34	8	0	1	88	86	38	13	0	37-6	44	4.70	74	.257	.328	19-2	.211	1	83	-13	-0.9
1964	LA A	0	1	.000	2	0	0	0	2.1	4	4	2	0	2-1	1	15.43	21	.364	.462	0-0	—	0		-3	-0.6
Total	11	86	87	.497	312	193	63-7	7	1498	1381	757	176	15	662-35	827	4.14	97	.246	.324	461-43	.178	-3	103	-14	-1.9
FRAILING, KEN Kenneth Douglas B 1.19.1948 Marion, WI BL/TL 6/190# d9.1																									
1972	Chi A	1	0	1.000	4	0	0	0-0	3	3	1	1	0	1-0	1	3.00	105	.250	.308	0-0	—	0		0	0.0
1973	Chi A	0	0	—	10	0	0	0-0	18.1	18	6	1	1	7-0	15	1.96	202	.254	.325	0-0	—	0		3	0.2
1974	Chi N	6	9	.400	55	16	1	1-1	125.1	150	65	11	1	43-10	71	3.88	99	.296	.351	31-4	.258	1*	87	-1	0.0
1975	Chi N	2	5	.286	41	0	0	1-1	53	61	37	6	2	26-2	39	5.43	71	.293	.374	7-1	.143	0		-9	-1.0
1976	Chi N	1	2	.333	6	3	0	0-0	18.2	20	7	0	0	5-0	10	2.41	160	.274	.316	3-1	.000	-0	46	2	0.3
Total	5	10	16	.385	116	19	1	2-2	218.1	252	116	19	4	82-12	136	3.96	97	.290	.351	41-6	.220	1	81	-5	-0.5
FRANCE, OSSIE Osman Beverly "O. B." B 10.4.1858 Greensburg, OH D 5.2.1947 Akron, OH BL/TL 5-8/155# d7.14																									
1890	Chi N	0	0	—	1	0	0	0	2	3	3	0	0	2	0	13.50	27	.333	.455	1	.000	-0		-2	-0.1
FRANCIS, EARL Earl Coleman B 7.14.1935 Slab Fork, WV D 7.3.2002 Pittsburgh, PA BR/TR 6-2/215# d6.30																									
1960	Pit N	1	0	1.000	7	0	0	0	18	14	5	0	1	4-0	8	2.00	188	.222	.275	5-0	.000	-1		3	0.1
1961	Pit N	2	8	.200	23	15	0	0	102.2	110	60	4	1	47-7	53	4.21	95	.274	.348	28-0	.107	-1	88	-5	-0.5
1962	Pit N	9	8	.529	36	23	5-1	0	176	153	68	8	2	83-10	121	3.07	128	.235	.322	61-3	.164	1	92	18	1.7
1963	Pit N	4	6	.400	33	13	0	0	97.1	107	59	6	4	43-11	72	4.53	73	.284	.361	26-0	.308	3*	82	-13	-1.0
1964	Pit N	0	1	.000	2	1	0	0	6.1	7	7	2	1	1-0	6	8.53	41	.269	.321	1-0	.000	-0	0	-4	-0.5
1965	StL N	0	0	—	2	0	0	0	5.1	7	4	1	0	3-2	3	5.06	76	.318	.385	1-0	.000	-0		-1	-0.1
Total	6	16	23	.410	103	52	5-1	0	405.2	398	203	21	9	181-30	263	3.77	100	.258	.337	122-3	.172	2	87	-2	-0.3
FRANCIS, RAY Ray James B 3.8.1893 Sherman, TX D 7.6.1934 Atlanta, GA BL/TL 6-1.5/182# d4.18																									
1922	Was A	7	18	.280	39	26	15-2	2	225	265	136	7	6	66	64	4.28	90	.303	.356	78-3	.167	-2	85	-13	-1.5
1923	Det A	5	8	.385	33	6	0	1	79.1	95	51	2	4	28	27	4.42	87	.308	.374	21-0	.143	-2*	96	-7	-1.2
1925	NY A	0	0	—	4	0	0	0	4.2	5	4	0	1	3	1	7.71	55	.278	.409	0-0	—	0		-2	-0.1
	Bos A	0	2	.000	6	4	0	0	28	44	29	3	1	13	4	7.71	59	.373	.439	8-0	.125	-0	79	-9	-0.5
	Year	0	2	.000	10	4	0	0	32.2	49	33	3	2	16	5	7.71	58	.360	.435	8-0	.125	-0	79	-11	-0.6
Total	3	12	28	.300	82	36	15-2	3	337	409	220	12	12	110	96	4.65	84	.310	.368	107-3	.159	-4	86	-31	-3.3
FRANCO, JOHN John Anthony B 9.17.1960 Brooklyn, NY BL/TL 5-10/185# d4.24																									
1984	Cin N	6	2	.750	54	0	0	4-5	79.1	74	28	3	2	36-4	55	2.61	145	.256	.338	3-1	.000	-0		9	0.9
1985	Cin N	12	3	.800	67	0	0	12-3	99	83	27	5	1	40-8	61	2.18	174	.234	.313	6-2	.333	0		**17**	3.0
1986	Cin N☆	6	6	.500	74	0	0	29-9	101	90	40	7	2	44-12	84	2.94	132	.242	.323	4-0	.000	-0		9	1.5
1987	Cin N★	8	5	.615	68	0	0	32-9	82	76	26	6	0	27-6	61	2.52	168	.245	.304	2-0	.000	-0		15	2.9
1988	Cin N	6	6	.500	70	0	0	**39-3**	86	60	18	3	0	27-3	46	1.57	229	.198	.263	1-0	.000	-0		**18**	4.0
1989	Cin N☆	4	8	.333	60	0	0	32-7	80.2	77	35	3	0	36-8	60	3.12	115	.258	.334	3-0	.333	0		3	0.7
1990	NY N★	5	3	.625	55	0	0	**33-6**	67.2	66	22	4	0	21-2	56	2.53	148	.252	.306	5-0	.000	-1		9	1.8
1991	NY N	5	9	.357	52	0	0	30-5	55.1	61	27	2	1	18-4	45	2.93	124	.271	.328	1-0	.000	-0		2	0.3
1992	NY N	6	2	.750	31	0	0	15-2	33	24	6	1	0	11-2	20	1.64	213	.209	.273	1-0	.000	-0		7	1.7
1993	NY N	4	3	.571	35	0	0	10-7	36.1	46	24	6	1	19-3	29	5.20	77	.313	.393	1-0	.000	-0		-5	-0.9
1994	NY N	1	4	.200	47	0	0	**30-6**	50	47	20	2	1	19-0	42	2.70	155	.244	.313	3-0	.000	-0		7	1.3
1995	NY N	5	3	.625	48	0	0	29-7	51.2	48	17	4	0	17-2	41	2.44	166	.251	.311	0-0	—	0		9	1.8
1996	NY N	4	3	.571	51	0	0	28-8	54	54	15	2	0	21-0	48	1.83	219	.260	.328	1-0	.000	-0		13	2.5
1997	NY N	5	3	.625	59	0	0	36-6	60	49	18	3	1	20-2	53	2.55	158	.226	.293	0-0	—	0		11	2.2
1998	NY N	0	8	.000	61	0	0	38-8	64.2	66	28	4	4	29-7	59	3.62	114	.267	.347	2-0	.000	-0		4	0.8

Year	Tm Lg	W	L	Pct	G	GS	CG-Sho	SV-BS	IP	H	R	HR	HB	BB-IB	SO	ERA	AERA	OAV	OOB	AB-SH	AVG	PB	Sup	APR	PW
1999	†NY N	0	2	.000	46	0	0	19-2	40.2	40	14	1	2	19-1	41	2.88	152	.255	.341	0-0	—	0		7	0.8
2000	†NY N	5	4	.556	62	0	0	4-0	55.2	46	24	6	2	26-6	56	3.40	130	.221	.314	1-0	.000	-0		6	0.9
2001	NY N	6	2	.750	58	0	0	2-5	53.1	55	25	8	2	19-2	50	4.05	102	.264	.330	0-0	—	0		1	0.1
2003	NY N	0	3	.000	38	0	0	2-1	34.1	35	11	5	1	13-2	16	2.62	159	.265	.333	0-0	—	0		6	0.6
Total	19	88	79	.527	1036	0	0	424-99	1184.2	1097	425	75	20	462-74	923	2.74	144	.247	.319	34-3	.088	-2		148	26.9
FRANKHOUSE, FRED Frederick Meloy B 4.9.1904 Port Royal, PA D 8.17.1989 Port Royal, PA BR/TR 5-11/175# d9.11																									
1927	StL N	5	1	.833	6	6	5-1	0	50	41	18	2	1	16	20	2.70	146	.218	.283	20-1	.250	0*	133	7	0.8
1928	StL N	3	2	.600	21	10	1	1	84	91	47	6	5	36	29	3.96	101	.277	.358	27-2	.185	1*	133	-1	0.1
1929	StL N	7	2	.778	30	10	6	1	133.1	149	70	9	4	43	37	4.12	113	.289	.349	52-2	.288	4*	140	8	0.9
1930	StL N	2	3	.400	8	1	0	0	19.2	31	16	1	0	11	4	7.32	69	.373	.447	5-0	.000	-1*	17	-4	-0.7
	Bos N	7	6	.538	27	11	3-1	0	110.2	138	72	13	2	43	30	5.61	88	.313	.377	39-1	.359	4	82	-6	-0.2
	Year	9	9	.500	35	12	3-1	0	130.1	169	77	14	2	54	34	5.87	84	.323	.388	44-1	.318	3	76	-10	-0.9
1931	Bos N	8	8	.500	26	15	6	1	127.1	125	64	4	3	43	50	4.03	94	.252	.315	40-1	.150	-0	71	-3	-0.3
1932	Bos N	4	6	.400	37	6	3	0	108.2	113	56	7	3	45	35	3.56	106	.278	.355	30-2	.100	-1*	101	0	0.0
1933	Bos N	16	15	.516	43	30	14-2	2	244.2	249	97	12	3	77	83	3.16	97	.267	.324	80-7	.237	4	102	-2	0.4
1934	Bos N★	17	9	.654	37	30	13-2	1	233.2	239	102	10	4	77	78	3.20	120	.262	.322	85-7	.200	2	114	14	1.6
1935	Bos N	11	15	.423	40	29	10-1	0	230.2	278	147	12	6	81	64	4.76	80	.293	.352	76-1	.263	6	109	-29	-1.9
1936	Bro N	13	10	.565	41	31	9-1	2	234.1	236	112	18	3	89	84	3.65	113	.257	.325	91-1	.143	-4*	93	13	0.8
1937	Bro N	10	13	.435	33	25	9-1	0	179.1	214	104	8	4	78	64	4.27	95	.297	.369	58-7	.190	-0*	105	-4	-0.3
1938	Bro N	3	5	.375	30	8	2-1	0	93.2	92	48	6	4	44	32	4.04	97	.256	.344	26-3	.154	-1*	71	-1	-0.1
1939	Bos N	0	2	.000	23	0	0	4	38	37	16	3	1	18	12	2.61	142	.253	.339	7-0	.000	-1		3	0.1
Total	13	106	97	.522	402	212	81-10	12	1888	2033	969	111	43	701	622	3.92	100	.275	.341	636-35	.208	12	102	-5	1.2
FRANKLIN, WAYNE Gary Wayne B 3.9.1974 Wilmington, DE BL/TL 6-2/195# d7.24																									
2000	Hou N	0	0	—	25	0	0	0-0	21.1	24	14	2	4	12-1	21	5.48	89	.282	.388	2-0	.000	-0		-1	-0.1
2001	Hou N	0	0	—	11	0	0	0-0	12	17	9	4	0	9-0	9	6.75	68	.333	.433	0-0	—	0		-2	-0.1
2002	Mil N	2	1	.667	4	4	0	0-0	24	16	8	1	0	17-1	17	2.63	156	.188	.324	6-0	.000	-0	62	4	0.5
2003	Mil N	10	13	.435	36	34	1-1	0-0	194.2	201	129	36	10	94-2	116	5.50	77	.268	.355	59-12	.169	-0	115	-28	-2.9
Total	4	12	14	.462	76	38	1-1	0-0	252	258	160	43	14	132-4	163	5.29	81	.265	.360	67-12	.149	-1	108	-27	-2.6
FRANKLIN, JACK Jack Wilford B 10.20.1919 Paris, IL D 11.15.1991 Panama City, FL BR/TR 5-11.5/170# d6.12																									
1944	Bro N	0	0	—	1	0	0	0	2	2	3	1	2	4	0	13.50	26	.250	.571	0-0	—	0		-2	-0.1
FRANKLIN, JAY John William B 3.16.1953 Arlington, VA BR/TR 6-2/180# d9.4																									
1971	SD N	0	1	.000	3	1	0	0-0	5.2	5	5	3	0	4-0	4	6.35	52	.250	.375	1-0	.000	-0	54	-2	-0.3
FRANKLIN, RYAN Ryan Ray B 3.5.1973 Fort Smith, AR BR/TR 6-3/165# d5.15																									
1999	Sea A	0	0	—	6	0	0	0-0	11.1	10	6	2	1	8-1	6	4.76	99	.238	.373	0-0	—	0		0	0.0
2001	Sea A	5	1	.833	38	0	0	0-1	78.1	76	32	13	4	24-4	60	3.56	117	.250	.311	0-0	—	0		6	0.4
2002	Sea A	7	5	.583	41	12	0	0-1	118.2	117	62	14	5	22-1	65	4.02	105	.255	.294	0-0	—	0	82	0	0.0
2003	Sea A	11	13	.458	32	32	2-1	0-0	212	199	93	34	9	61-3	99	3.57	121	.251	.310	4-1	.250	0	99	17	1.6
Total	4	23	19	.548	117	44	2-1	0-2	420.1	402	193	63	19	115-9	230	3.73	115	.252	.307	4-1	.250	0	95	23	2.0
FRASCATORE, JOHN John Vincent B 2.4.1970 Ozone Park, NY BR/TR 6-1/200# d7.21																									
1994	StL N	0	1	.000	1	1	0	0-0	3.1	7	6	2	0	2-0	2	16.20	26	.438	.500	1-0	.000	-0	22	-4	-0.6
1995	StL N	1	1	.500	14	4	0	0-0	32.2	39	19	3	2	16-1	21	4.41	95	.298	.380	7-1	.000	-0	97	-1	-0.1
1997	StL N	5	2	.714	59	0	0	0-4	80	74	25	5	6	33-5	58	2.47	168	.247	.329	3-0	.000	-0		15	1.1
1998	StL N	3	4	.429	69	0	0	0-2	95.2	95	48	11	3	36-3	49	4.14	101	.256	.326	6-0	.167	-0		1	0.0
1999	Ari N	1	4	.200	26	0	0	0-1	33	31	16	6	1	12-4	15	4.09	112	.256	.326	0-0	—	0		2	0.2
	Tor A	7	1	.875	33	0	0	1-1	37	42	16	5	1	9-4	22	3.41	145	.292	.333	0-0	—	0		6	1.1
2000	Tor A	2	4	.333	60	0	0	0-5	73	87	51	14	7	33-2	30	5.42	94	.301	.381	0-0	—	0		-4	-0.3
2001	Tor A	1	0	1.000	12	0	0	0-1	16.1	16	4	4	0	4-1	9	2.20	209	.246	.290	0-0	—	0		4	0.3
Total	7	20	17	.541	274	5	0	1-14	371	391	185	50	20	145-20	206	4.00	112	.272	.344	17-1	.059	-1	78	19	1.7
FRASER, CHICK Charles Carrolton B 3.17.1871 Chicago, IL D 5.8.1940 Wendell, ID BR/TR 5-10.5/188# d4.19 C1																									
1896	Lou N	12	27	.308	43	38	36	1	349.1	396	282	9	29	166	91	4.87	89	.283	.371	146-0	.151	-9*	89	-19	-2.2
1897	Lou N	15	19	.441	36	34	32	0	294.1	334	226	11	22	139	70	4.04	106	.283	.369	115-2	.157	-5*	92	0	-0.2
1898	Lou N	7	17	.292	26	26	20-1	0	203	230	157	4	23	100	58	5.32	67	.283	.378	78-3	.167	-2	93	-39	-3.6
	Cle N	2	3	.400	6	6	6	0	42	49	34	2	6	12	19	5.57	65	.290	.358	16-0	.250	0	101	-8	-0.7
	Year	9	20	.310	32	32	26-1	0	245	279	39	6	29	112	77	5.36	67	.284	.374	94-3	.181	-2	94	-42	-4.3
1899	Phi N	21	12	.636	35	33	29-4	0	270.2	278	146	1	22	85	68	3.36	110	.265	.333	117-1	.179	-2*	123	10	0.9
1900	Phi N	15	9	.625	29	26	22-1	0	223.1	250	117	7	11	93	58	3.14	115	.282	.358	85-5	.259	4	106	9	1.2
1901	Phi A	22	16	.579	40	37	35-2	0	331	344	210	6	32	132	110	3.81	99	.265	.347	139-5	.187	-3*	103	-5	-0.7
1902	Phi N	12	13	.480	27	26	24-3	0	224	238	115	2	15	74	97	3.42	82	.272	.339	86-0	.174	0*	81	-14	-1.4
1903	Phi N	12	17	.414	31	29	26-1	1	250	260	160	8	16	97	104	4.50	73	.267	.344	93-2	.204	4*	94	-30	-2.3
1904	Phi N	14	24	.368	42	36	32-2	1	302	287	164	5	11	100	127	3.25	82	.246	.311	110-5	.155	-1*	88	-18	-2.1
1905	Bos N	14	21	.400	39	37	35-2	0	334.1	320	174	8	15	149	130	3.28	94	.254	.340	156-3	.224	3*	83	-10	-0.5
1906	Cin N	10	20	.333	31	28	25-2	0	236	221	92	1	8	80	58	2.67	103	.259	.329	82-4	.171	-1	78	4	0.5
1907	Chi N	8	5	.615	22	15	9-2	1	138.1	112	51	1	3	46	41	2.28	110	.229	.299	45-3	.067	-3	80	3	0.0
1908	Chi N	11	9	.550	26	17	11-2	2	162.2	141	71	4	6	61	66	2.27	104	.244	.323	50-5	.120	-2	130	-5	-0.6
1909	Chi N	0	0	—	1	0	0	0	3	2	1	0	0	4	1	0.00	—	.222	.462	1-0	.000	-0		1	0.0
Total	14	175	212	.452	434	388	342-22	6	3364	3462	2000	69	219	1338	1098	3.67	92	.266	.345	1319-38	.178	-15	95	-121	-11.7
FRASER, WILLIE William Patrick B 5.26.1964 New York, NY BR/TR 6-1/206# d9.10																									
1986	Cal A	0	0	—	1	1	0	0-0	4.1	6	4	0	0	1-0	2	8.31	50	.353	.368	0-0	—	0	154	-2	-0.1
1987	Cal A	10	10	.500	36	23	5-1	1-0	176.2	160	85	26	6	63-3	106	3.92	110	.240	.310	0-0	—	0	99	9	0.7
1988	Cal A	12	13	.480	34	32	2	0-0	194.2	203	129	33	9	80-7	86	5.41	72	.267	.340	0-0	—	0	109	-34	-3.8
1989	Cal A	4	7	.364	44	0	0	2-1	91.2	80	33	6	5	23-4	46	3.24	118	.235	.291	0-0	—	0		7	0.9
1990	Cal A	5	4	.556	45	0	0	2-3	76	69	29	4	0	24-3	32	3.08	124	.241	.297	0-0	—	0		7	0.7
1991	Tor A	0	2	.000	13	1	0	0-0	26.1	33	20	4	3	11-2	12	6.15	68	.303	.382	0-0	—	0	174	-6	-0.4
	StL N	3	3	.500	35	0	0	0-0	49.1	44	28	9	3	21-3	25	4.93	76	.242	.325	2-0	.000	-0		-6	-0.7
1994	Fla N	2	0	1.000	9	0	0	0-0	12.1	20	9	1	0	6-3	7	5.84	75	.370	.426	0-0	—	0		-2	-0.3
1995	Mon N	2	1	.667	22	0	0	2-0	25.2	25	17	6	3	9-1	12	5.61	77	.248	.327	2-0	.000	-0		-3	-0.4
Total	8	38	40	.487	239	57	7-1	7-4	657	640	354	89	29	238-26	328	4.47	90	.254	.323	4-0	.000	-0	108	-30	-3.4
FRASIER, VIC Victor Patrick B 8.5.1904 Ruston, LA D 1.10.1977 Jacksonville, TX BR/TR 6/182# d4.18																									
1931	Chi A	13	15	.464	46	29	13-2	4	254	258	156	11	5	127	87	4.46	95	.259	.345	86-3	.209	1	97	-8	-0.7
1932	Chi A	3	13	.188	29	21	4	0	146	180	121	14	4	70	33	6.23	69	.297	.374	44-5	.091	-3	94	-30	-2.8
1933	Chi A	1	1	.500	10	1	0	0	20.1	32	22	2	0	11	4	8.85	48	.368	.439	4-0	.000	-1	100	-10	-0.8
	Det A	5	5	.500	20	14	4	0	104.1	129	85	9	1	59	26	6.64	65	.312	.399	37-4	.189	-0	116	-24	-1.9
	Year	6	6	.500	30	15	4	0	124.2	161	91	11	1	70	30	7.00	61	.321	.406	41-4	.171	-1	115	-34	-2.7
1934	Det A	1	3	.250	8	2	0	0	22.2	30	19	0	1	12	11	5.96	74	.313	.394	7-0	.286	0	169	-5	-0.6
1937	Bos N	0	0	—	3	0	0	0	8	12	7	1	0	1	2	5.63	64	.364	.382	1-0	.000	-0		-3	-0.1
1939	Chi A	0	1	.000	10	1	0	0	23.2	45	27	0	0	11	7	10.27	46	.405	.459	7-0	.286	0	37	-13	-0.6
Total	6	23	38	.377	126	68	21-2	4	579	686	437	37	11	291	170	5.77	75	.293	.373	186-12	.177	-3	101	-93	-7.5
FRAZIER, GEORGE George Allen B 10.13.1954 Oklahoma City, OK BR/TR 6-5/205# d5.25																									
1978	StL N	0	3	.000	14	0	0	0-0	22	22	14	2	0	6-2	8	4.09	86	.250	.292	3-0	.333	0		-3	-0.3
1979	StL N	2	4	.333	25	0	0	0-2	32.1	35	19	3	1	12-2	14	4.45	85	.278	.343	1-0	.000	-0		-3	-0.5
1980	StL N	1	4	.200	22	0	0	3-4	23	24	10	2	0	7-3	11	2.74	135	.273	.326	0-0	—	0		1	0.3
1981	†NY A	0	1	.000	16	0	0	3-0	27.2	26	7	1	0	11-2	17	1.63	220	.245	.316	0-0	—	0		6	0.3
1982	NY A	4	4	.500	63	0	0	1-1	111.2	103	51	7	5	39-5	69	3.47	115	.252	.321	0-0	—	0		5	0.3
1983	NY A	4	4	.500	61	0	0	8-2	115.1	94	44	5	3	45-4	78	3.43	114	.227	.300	0-0	—	0		9	0.7

Year	Tm Lg	W	L	Pct	G	GS	CG-Sho	SV-BS	IP	H	R	HR	HB	BB-IB	SO	ERA	AERA	OAV	OOB	AB-SH	AVG	PB	Sup	APR	PW
1984	Cle A	3	2	.600	22	0	0	1-2	44.1	45	19	3	0	14-4	24	3.65	112	.259	.314	0-0	—	0		2	0.2
	†Chi N	6	3	.667	37	0	0	3-1	63.2	53	30	4	1	26-8	58	4.10	95	.221	.296	7-0	.286	0		0	-0.1
1985	Chi N	7	8	.467	51	0	0	2-2	76	88	57	11	3	52-9	46	6.39	63	.299	.409	6-0	.000	-1		-17	-3.3
1986	Chi N	2	4	.333	35	0	0	0-0	51.2	63	36	5	1	34-4	41	5.40	75	.310	.407	4-0	.000	-0		-8	-1.0
	Min A	1	1	.500	15	0	0	6-3	26.2	23	13	2	0	16-1	25	4.39	98	.232	.331	0-0	—	0		0	0.1
1987	†Min A	5	5	.500	54	0	0	2-5	81.1	77	49	9	2	51-4	58	4.98	93	.258	.359	0-0	—	0		-3	-0.4
Total	10	35	43	.449	415	0	0	29-22	675.2	653	349	54	16	313-48	449	4.20	96	.257	.338	21-0	.143	-1		-11	-3.7
FREDERICK, KEVIN Kevin Albert Francis B 11.4.1976 Evanston, IL BL/TR 6-1/208# d7.15																									
2002	Min A	0	0	—	8	0	0	0-0	11.2	13	13	3	0	10-0	5	10.03	45	.283	.411	0-0	—	0		-7	-0.3
FREDRICKSON, SCOTT Scott Eric B 8.19.1967 Manchester, NH BR/TR 6-3/215# d4.30																									
1993	Col N	0	1	.000	25	0	0	0-0	29	33	25	3	1	17-2	20	6.21	77	.287	.378	3-0	.000	-0		-5	-0.3
FREEMAN, BUCK Alexander Vernon B 7.5.1893 Mart, TX D 2.21.1953 Fort Sam Houston, TX BB/TR 5-10/167# d4.13																									
1921	Chi N	9	10	.474	38	20	6	3	177.1	189	96	12	8	70	42	4.11	93	.281	.356	53-1	.208	0	102	-7	-0.7
1922	Chi N	0	1	.000	11	1	0	1	25.2	47	28	0	2	10	10	8.77	48	.412	.468	8-0	.125	-0	78	-12	-0.5
Total	2	9	11	.450	49	21	6	4	203	236	124	12	10	80	52	4.70	82	.300	.372	61-1	.197	-0	100	-19	-1.2
FREEMAN, HARVEY Harvey Bayard "Buck" B 12.22.1897 Mottville, MI D 1.10.1970 Kalamazoo, MI BR/TR 5-10/160# d7.10																									
1921	Phi A	1	4	.200	18	4	2	0	48	65	50	2	5	35	5	7.69	58	.346	.461	12-1	.083	-2	70	-16	-1.5
FREEMAN, HERSH Hershell Baskin "Buster" B 7.1.1928 Gadsden, AL BR/TR 6-3/220# d9.10																									
1952	Bos A	1	0	1.000	4	1	1	0	13.2	13	5	1	1	5	5	3.29	120	.260	.339	4-0	.500	1	66	1	0.2
1953	Bos A	1	4	.200	18	2	0	0	39	50	31	2	0	17	15	5.54	76	.316	.383	11-0	.091	-1	21	-7	-0.9
1955	Bos A	0	0	—	2	0	0	0	1.2	1	0	0	0	1-1	1	0.00	—	.200	.333	0-0	—	0		1	0.0
	Cin N	7	4	.636	52	0	0	11	91.2	94	31	3	2	30-6	37	2.16	196	.276	.335	18-0	.167	1*		**18**	2.5
1956	Cin N	14	5	.737	64	0	0	18	108.2	112	44	2	1	34-11	50	3.40	117	.274	.329	18-0	.056	-1		7	1.4
1957	Cin N	7	2	.778	52	0	0	8	83.2	90	49	14	3	14-4	36	4.52	91	.277	.308	10-0	.200	0		-5	-0.6
1958	Cin N	0	0	—	3	0	0	0	7.2	4	3	0	0	5-0	7	3.52	118	.154	.281	1-0	.000	-0		1	0.0
	Chi N	0	1	.000	9	0	0	0	13	23	13	3	0	3-0	7	8.31	47	.354	.382	1-0	.000	-0		-6	-0.4
	Year	0	1	.000	12	0	0	0	20.2	27	17	3	0	8-0	14	6.53	61	.297	.350	2-0	.000	-0		-5	-0.4
Total	6	30	16	.652	204	3	1	37	359	387	176	25	7	109-22	158	3.74	110	.281	.334	63-0	.143	-0	36	10	2.2
FREEMAN, JIMMY Jimmy Lee B 6.29.1951 Carlsbad, NM BL/TL 6-4/180# d9.1																									
1972	Atl N	2	2	.500	6	6	1	0-0	36	40	26	5	0	22-1	18	6.00	63	.278	.373	13-0	.077	-0*	120	-8	-0.8
1973	Atl N	0	2	.000	13	5	0	1-2	37.1	50	33	7	0	25-1	20	7.71	51	.327	.417	13-0	.154	-0*	143	-13	-0.8
Total	2	2	4	.333	19	11	1	1-2	73.1	90	59	12	0	47-2	38	6.87	56	.303	.396	26-0	.115	-1	131	-21	-1.6
FREEMAN, BUCK John Frank B 10.30.1871 Catasauqua, PA D 6.25.1949 Wilkes-Barre, PA BL/TL 5-9/169# d6.27 ▲																									
1891	Was AA	3	2	.600	5	4	4	0	44	35	32	0	4	33	28	3.89	96	.211	.355	18	.222	0	96	-1	0.0
1899	Was N	0	0	—	2	0	0	0	7	15	13	3	3	3	0	7.71	51	.429	.512	588-5	.318	1*		-5	-0.2
Total	2	3	2	.600	7	4	4	0	51	50	45	3	7	36	28	4.41	85	.249	.381	606-5	.315	1	96	-6	-0.2
FREEMAN, JULIE Julius Benjamin B 11.7.1868 , MO D 6.10.1921 St.Louis, MO BR d10.10																									
1888	StL AA	0	1	.000	1	1	0	0	6.1	7	5	0	1	4	1	4.26	77	.269	.387	3	.333	0	71	-1	-0.1
FREEMAN, MARK Mark Price B 12.7.1930 Memphis, TN BR/TR 6-4/220# d4.18																									
1959	KC A	0	0	—	3	0	0	0	3.2	6	6	0	0	3-0	1	9.82	41	.375	.450	0-0	—	0		-3	-0.1
	NY A	0	0	—	1	1	0	0	7	6	2	0	1	2-0	4	2.57	142	.240	.310	2-0	.000	-0	48	1	0.0
	Year	0	0	—	4	1	0	0	10.2	12	4	0	1	5-0	5	5.06	74	.293	.367	2-0	.000	-0	47	-2	-0.1
1960	Chi N	3	3	.500	30	8	1	1	76.2	70	51	10	5	33-3	50	5.63	67	.240	.325	20-1	.150	-0	146	-14	-1.2
Total	2	3	3	.500	34	9	1	1	87.1	82	59	10	6	38-3	55	5.56	68	.246	.331	22-1	.136	-1	135	-16	-1.3
FREEMAN, MARVIN Marvin B 4.10.1963 Chicago, IL BR/TR 6-7/222# d9.16																									
1986	Phi N	2	0	1.000	3	3	0	0-0	16	6	4	0	0	10-0	8	2.25	172	.120	.262	6-1	.000	-1	162	3	0.3
1988	Phi N	2	3	.400	11	11	0	0-0	51.2	55	36	2	1	43-2	37	6.10	59	.276	.406	14-3	.214	0	102	-13	-1.1
1989	Phi N	0	0	—	1	1	0	0-0	3	2	2	0	0	5-0	0	6.00	59	.182	.438	2-0	.000	-0	199	-1	-0.1
1990	Phi N	0	2	.000	16	3	0	1-0	32.1	34	21	5	3	14-2	26	5.57	69	.264	.349	7-0	.000	-1	87	-6	-0.4
	Atl N	1	0	1.000	9	0	0	0-0	15.2	7	3	0	2	3-0	12	1.72	234	.130	.203	0-0	—	0		4	0.2
	Year	1	2	.333	25	3	0	1-0	48	41	28	5	5	17-2	38	4.31	90	.224	.307	7-0	.000	-1	85	-1	-0.2
1991	Atl N	1	0	1.000	34	0	0	1-0	48	37	19	2	2	13-1	34	3.00	130	.214	.275	7-0	.000	-1		4	0.1
1992	†Atl N	7	5	.583	58	0	0	3-3	64.1	61	26	7	1	29-7	41	3.22	114	.251	.332	4-0	.500	1		3	0.6
1993	Atl N	2	0	1.000	21	0	0	0-0	23.2	24	16	1	1	10-2	25	6.08	66	.261	.340	0-2	—	0		-5	-0.4
1994	Col N	10	2	.833	19	18	0	0-0	112.2	113	39	10	5	23-2	67	2.80	178	.262	.306	36-3	.111	-0	97	23	2.3
1995	Col N	3	7	.300	22	18	0	0-1	94.2	122	64	15	2	41-1	61	5.89	92	.318	.384	23-6	.087	-1	87	-3	-0.4
1996	Col N	7	9	.438	26	23	0	0-1	129.2	151	100	21	6	57-1	71	6.04	87	.294	.370	41-4	.122	-2	112	-11	-1.4
	Chi A	0	0	—	1	1	0	0-0	2	4	3	0	0	1-0	1	13.50	35	.364	.417	0-0	—	0	254	-2	-0.1
Total	10	35	28	.556	221	78	0	5-5	593.2	616	333	63	23	249-18	383	4.64	98	.269	.345	140-19	.114	-5	111	-4	-0.4
FREEZE, JAKE Carl Alexander B 4.25.1900 Huntington, AR D 4.9.1983 San Angelo, TX BR/TR 5-8/150# d7.1																									
1925	Chi A	0	0	—	2	0	0	0	3.2	5	7	1	0	3	1	2.45	169	.333	.444	1-0	.000	-0		-2	-0.1
FREISLEBEN, DAVE David James B 10.31.1951 Coraopolis, PA BR/TR 5-11/200# d4.26																									
1974	SD N	9	14	.391	33	31	6-2	0-0	211.2	194	100	13	7	112-9	130	3.66	98	.241	.338	64-9	.172	2	85	-4	-0.2
1975	SD N	5	14	.263	36	27	4-1	0-0	181	206	102	11	7	82-9	77	4.28	81	.289	.366	48-6	.083	-1	77	-16	-1.7
1976	SD N	10	13	.435	34	24	6-3	1-0	172	163	73	10	5	66-7	81	3.51	93	.248	.320	37-9	.189	1	67	-3	-0.1
1977	SD N	7	9	.438	33	23	1	0-0	138.2	140	86	21	2	71-9	72	4.61	77	.266	.353	37-2	.135	0	112	-20	-2.1
1978	SD N	0	3	.000	12	4	0	0-0	26.2	41	22	3	0	15-3	16	6.08	55	.363	.427	6-1	.000	-1	88	-9	-1.0
	Cle A	1	4	.200	12	10	0	0-0	44.1	52	37	4	2	31-1	19	7.11	53	.299	.405	0-0	—	0	103	-16	-1.6
1979	Tor A	2	3	.400	42	2	0	3-2	91	101	57	5	2	53-3	35	4.95	88	.294	.388	0-0	—	0	62	-6	-0.4
Total	6	34	60	.362	202	121	17-6	4-2	865.1	897	477	67	25	430-41	430	4.30	83	.269	.355	192-27	.141	2	85	-74	-7.1
FREITAS, TONY Antonio B 5.5.1908 Mill Valley, CA D 3.14.1994 Orangevale, CA BR/TL 5-8/161# d5.31																									
1932	Phi A	12	5	.706	23	18	10-1	0	150.1	150	68	11	4	48	31	3.83	118	.263	.325	54-8	.148	-1	136	12	1.2
1933	Phi A	2	4	.333	19	9	2	1	64.1	90	56	8	2	24	15	7.27	59	.337	.396	16-2	.063	-1	130	-19	-1.6
1934	Cin N	6	12	.333	30	18	5	1	152.2	194	80	6	3	25	37	4.01	102	.311	.341	47-1	.191	0*	73	3	0.5
1935	Cin N	5	10	.333	31	18	5	2	143.2	174	95	6	2	38	51	4.57	87	.295	.340	46-4	.130	-0	90	-13	-1.2
1936	Cin N	0	2	.000	4	0	0	0	7	6	2	0	0	2	1	1.29	297	.240	.296	2-0	.000	-0		2	0.3
Total	5	25	33	.431	107	63	22-1	4	518	614	301	31	11	137	135	4.48	94	.296	.343	165-15	.145	-2	105	-15	-0.8
FRENCH, LARRY Lawrence Herbert B 11.1.1907 Visalia, CA D 2.9.1987 San Diego, CA BR/TL 6-1/195# d4.18 Mil 1943-45																									
1929	Pit N	7	5	.583	30	13	6	1	123	130	78	10	3	62	49	4.90	97	.276	.364	42-1	.190	-1	107	-2	-0.1
1930	Pit N	17	18	.486	42	35	21-3	1	274.2	325	163	20	6	89	90	4.36	114	.295	.351	91-11	.242	1	88	16	1.6
1931	Pit N	15	13	.536	39	33	20-1	1	275.2	301	127	9	1	70	73	3.26	118	.278	.322	95-6	.179	-1	97	16	1.4
1932	Pit N	18	16	.529	**47**	33	19-3	4	274.1	301	127	17	1	62	72	3.02	126	.276	.316	92-4	.207	1	96	19	2.1
1933	Pit N	18	13	.581	47	**35**	21-5	1	291.1	290	106	9	5	55	88	2.72	122	.257	.294	101-3	.149	-2	92	21	1.8
1934	Pit N	12	18	.400	49	34	16-3	1	263.2	299	135	8	3	59	103	3.58	115	.281	.321	84-10	.190	-0	96	9	0.8
1935	†Chi N	17	10	.630	42	30	16-**4**	2	246.1	279	94	10	2	44	90	2.96	133	.286	.318	85-9	.141	-4	104	28	2.5
1936	Chi N	18	9	.667	43	28	16-**4**	3	252.1	262	103	16	6	54	104	3.39	118	.266	.308	85-10	.212	0	100	18	1.6
1937	Chi N	16	10	.615	42	28	11-4	0	208	229	106	17	1	65	100	3.98	100	.274	.327	71-4	.127	-4	104	-1	-0.5
1938	†Chi N	10	19	.345	43	27	10-3	0	201.1	210	95	17	1	62	83	3.80	101	.271	.326	62-6	.210	2	79	1	0.5
1939	Chi N	15	8	.652	36	21	10-2	1	194	205	80	7	1	50	98	3.29	120	.269	.314	73-4	.192	1	104	15	1.8
1940	Chi N★	14	14	.500	40	33	18-3	2	246	240	93	12	4	64	107	3.29	114	.256	.306	85-4	.165	1	102	18	2.2
1941	Chi N	5	14	.263	26	18	6-1	0	138	161	88	10	2	43	60	4.63	76	.285	.338	47-3	.191	1	78	-19	-2.3
	†Bro N	0	0	—	6	1	0	0	15.2	16	6	1	1	4	8	3.45	106	.267	.323	4-0	.250	0	116	1	0.1

Year	Tm Lg	W	L	Pct	G	GS	CG-Sho	SV-BS	IP	H	R	HR	HB	BB-IB	SO	ERA	AERA	OAV	OOB	AB-SH	AVG	PB	Sup	APR	PW
	Year	5	14	.263	32	19	6-1	0	153.2	177	11	11	3	47	68	4.51	78	.283	.336	51-3	.196	1	80	-20	-2.2
1942	Bro N	15	4	**.789**	38	14	8-4	0	147.2	127	39	1	5	36	62	1.83	178	.233	.287	40-9	.300	4	109	22	3.3
Total	14	197	171	.535	570	383	198-40	17	3152	3375	1440	164	42	819	1187	3.44	114	.272	.320	1057-84	.188	0	96	162	16.8
FRENCH, BILL William B Baltimore, MD d4.14 ▲																									
1873	Mar NA	0	1	.000	1	1	1	0	9	30	27	0		0	0	12.00	27	.462	.462	18	.222	-0*	77	-7	-0.4
FREY, BENNY Benjamin Rudolph B 4.6.1906 Dexter, MI D 11.1.1937 Spring Arbor Township, MI BR/TR 5-10/165# d9.18																									
1929	Cin N	1	2	.333	3	3	2	0	24	29	12	2	0	8	1	4.13	111	.302	.356	8-1	.375	1	83	1	0.3
1930	Cin N	11	18	.379	44	28	14-2	1	245	295	145	15	3	62	43	4.70	103	.305	.349	88-3	.284	4	63	4	1.1
1931	Cin N	8	12	.400	34	17	7-1	2	133.2	166	76	2	2	36	19	4.92	76	.319	.365	44-1	.318	4	80	-14	-1.3
1932	StL N	0	2	.000	2	0	0	0	3	6	5	0	0	2	0	12.00	33	.600	.667	1-0	.000	-0		-3	-0.5
	Cin N	4	10	.286	28	15	5	0	131.1	159	72	10	1	30	27	4.32	89	.299	.338	44-0	.205	-0	93	-5	-0.3
	Year	4	12	.250	30	15	5	0	134.1	165	76	10	1	32	27	4.49	86	.305	.345	45-0	.200	-0	93	-9	-0.8
1933	Cin N	6	4	.600	37	9	1-1	0	132	144	67	4	0	21	12	3.82	89	.281	.309	42-1	.262	3*	79	-5	0.1
1934	Cin N	11	16	.407	39	30	12-2	2	245.1	288	118	10	2	42	33	3.52	116	.289	.319	82-2	.171	-0*	88	15	1.7
1935	Cin N	6	10	.375	38	13	3-1	2	114.1	164	100	6	4	32	24	6.85	58	.335	.381	32-3	.344	4	105	-35	-3.8
1936	Cin N	10	8	.556	31	12	5	0	131.1	164	73	5	0	30	20	4.25	90	.296	.332	44-2	.250	2*	92	-6	-0.6
Total	8	57	82	.410	256	127	49-7	7	1160	1415	668	54	12	263	179	4.50	90	.303	.341	385-13	.255	17	83	-48	-3.3
FREY, STEVE Steven Francis B 7.29.1963 Meadowbrook, PA BR/TL 5-9/170# d5.10																									
1989	Mon N	3	2	.600	20	0	0	0-0	21.1	29	15	4	1	11-1	15	5.48	64	.326	.398	0-0	—	0		-5	-1.0
1990	Mon N	8	2	.800	51	0	0	9-0	55.2	44	15	4	1	29-6	29	2.10	174	.219	.318	1-0	.000	-0		10	1.9
1991	Mon N	0	1	.000	31	0	0	1-1	39.2	43	31	3	1	23-4	21	4.99	73	.281	.374	2-0	.000	0		-9	-0.5
1992	Cal A	4	2	.667	51	0	0	4-1	45.1	39	18	6	2	22-3	24	3.57	112	.238	.330	0-0	—	0		3	0.4
1993	Cal A	2	3	.400	55	0	0	13-3	48.1	41	20	1	3	26-1	22	2.98	152	.230	.337	0-0	—	0		7	0.9
1994	SF N	1	0	1.000	44	0	0	0-3	31	37	17	6	2	15-3	20	4.94	81	.322	.397	0-0	—	0		-3	-0.1
1995	SF N	0	1	.000	9	0	0	0-0	6.1	7	6	1	0	2-0	5	4.26	96	.280	.321	0-0	—	0		-1	-0.2
	Sea A	0	3	.000	13	0	0	0-0	11.1	16	7	0	1	6-1	7	4.76	100	.356	.434	0-0	—	0		0	0.0
	Phi N	0	0	—	9	0	0	1-0	10.2	3	1	1	0	2-1	2	0.84	501	.091	.143	1-0	.000	-0		4	0.2
1996	Phi N	0	1	.000	31	0	0	0-0	34.1	38	19	4	0	18-3	12	4.72	91	.295	.376	0-0	—	0		-1	0.0
Total	8	18	15	.545	314	0	0	28-8	304	297	149	30	11	154-23	157	3.76	107	.262	.351	4-0	.000	-0		5	1.6
FRICANO, MARION Marion John B 7.15.1923 Brant, NY D 5.18.1976 Tijuana, Mexico BR/TR 6/170# d9.6																									
1952	Phi A	1	0	1.000	2	0	0	0	5	5	1	0	0	1	0	1.80	220	.238	.273	0-1	—	0		1	0.2
1953	Phi A	9	12	.429	39	23	10	0	211	206	105	21	6	90	67	3.88	110	.257	.337	69-3	.145	-3*	83	6	0.2
1954	Phi A	5	11	.313	37	20	4	1	151.2	163	98	17	4	64	43	5.16	76	.275	.347	41-6	.098	-3*	89	-21	-2.4
1955	KC A	0	0	—	10	0	0	0	20	19	9	2	0	9-0	5	3.15	133	.253	.333	3-0	.667	1		2	0.2
Total	4	15	23	.395	88	43	14	1	387.2	393	213	40	10	164-0	115	4.32	96	.264	.340	113-10	.142	-5	85	-12	-1.8
FRIDAY, SKIPPER Grier William B 10.26.1897 Gastonia, NC D 8.25.1962 Gastonia, NC BR/TR 5-11/170# d6.17																									
1923	Was A	0	1	.000	7	2	1	0	30	35	27	2	2	22	9	6.90	55	.313	.434	9-0	.222	0	99	-11	-0.4
FRIED, CY Arthur Edwin B 7.23.1897 San Antonio, TX D 10.10.1970 San Antonio, TX BL/TL 5-11.5/150# d9.17																									
1920	Det A	0	0	—	2	0	0	0	1.2	3	4	0	0	4	0	16.20	23	.500	.700	0-0	—	0		-2	-0.1
FRIEDRICHS, BOB Robert George B 8.30.1906 Cincinnati, OH D 4.15.1997 Jasper, IN BR/TR 5-11.5/165# d5.17																									
1932	Was A	0	0	—	2	0	0	0	4	4	5	0	1	7	2	11.25	38	.250	.500	1-0	.000	-0		-3	-0.2
FRIEND, DANNY Daniel Sebastian B 4.18.1873 Cincinnati, OH D 6.1.1942 Chillicothe, OH BL/TL 5-9/175# d9.10																									
1895	Chi N	2	2	.500	5	5	5	0	41	50	27	5	3	14	10	5.27	97	.296	.360	17-1	.235	-1	92	2	0.0
1896	Chi N	18	14	.563	36	33	28-1	0	290.2	298	196	11	39	139	86	4.74	96	.263	.363	126-4	.238	-1*	78	0	-0.2
1897	Chi N	12	11	.522	24	24	23	0	203	244	144	5	17	86	58	4.52	99	.295	.373	88-1	.284	2*	94	1	0.2
1898	Chi N	0	2	.000	2	2	2	0	17	20	15	1	1	10	4	5.29	68	.290	.387	7-0	.286	0	79	-3	-0.1
Total	4	32	29	.525	67	64	58-1	0	551.2	612	382	22	60	249	158	4.71	96	.279	.368	238-6	.256	0	85	0	-0.1
FRIEND, BOB Robert Bartmess "Warrior" B 11.24.1930 Lafayette, IN BR/TR 6/190# d4.28																									
1951	Pit N	6	10	.375	34	22	3-1	0	149.2	173	94	12	0	68	41	4.27	99	.293	.366	44-1	.091	-2	104	-6	-0.7
1952	Pit N	7	17	.292	35	23	6-1	0	185	186	96	15	3	84	75	4.18	95	.258	.338	52-7	.058	-4	74	-3	-0.8
1953	Pit N	8	11	.421	32	24	8	0	170.2	193	103	18	3	57	66	4.90	91	.286	.344	52-3	.135	-2	99	-7	-0.9
1954	Pit N	7	12	.368	35	20	4-2	2	170.1	204	106	16	1	58	73	5.07	83	.302	.355	51-1	.275	5	93	-14	-1.0
1955	Pit N	14	9	.609	44	20	9-2	2	200.1	178	80	18	2	52-4	98	**2.83**	**145**	.242	.291	61-6	.164	-2	88	**25**	2.7
1956	Pit N★	17	17	.500	49	**42**	19-4	3	**314.1**	310	137	25	2	85-18	166	3.46	109	.258	.306	97-11	.165	-1	91	11	1.0
1957	Pit N	14	18	.438	40	**38**	17-3	0	**277**	273	121	28	1	68-8	143	3.38	112	.257	.301	87-6	.184	1	89	13	1.4
1958	Pit N★	**22**	14	.611	38	**38**	16-1	0	274	299	120	25	4	61-11	135	3.68	105	.281	.320	94-10	.106	-4	106	8	0.6
1959	Pit N	8	19	.296	35	35	7-2	0	234.2	267	129	19	7	52-9	104	4.03	96	.283	.324	73-12	.164	0	90	-9	-0.9
1960	†Pit N★	18	12	.600	38	37	16-4	1	275.2	266	97	18	0	45-10	183	3.00	125	.251	.280	88-11	.068	-5	106	25	2.0
1961	Pit N	14	19	.424	41	35	10-1	1	236	271	119	16	3	45-10	108	3.85	104	.289	.322	79-9	.139	-3	80	2	-0.2
1962	Pit N	18	14	.563	39	36	13-**5**	1	261.2	280	99	23	2	53-10	144	3.06	129	.273	.309	91-8	.121	-3	92	27	2.8
1963	Pit N	17	16	.515	39	38	12-4	0	268.2	236	87	13	5	44-9	144	2.34	141	.233	.267	86-10	.105	-3	88	27	2.9
1964	Pit N	13	18	.419	35	35	13-3	0	240.1	253	98	10	4	50-12	128	3.33	105	.271	.309	71-11	.070	-3	81	6	0.4
1965	Pit N	8	12	.400	34	34	8-2	0	222	221	89	17	8	47-7	74	3.24	108	.260	.304	71-6	.042	-5	91	9	0.2
1966	NY A	1	4	.200	12	8	0	0	44.2	61	25	2	0	9-1	22	4.84	69	.330	.359	11-3	.000	-1	70	-7	-0.8
	NY N	5	8	.385	22	12	2-1	1	86	101	52	11	1	16-6	30	4.40	83	.289	.321	29-5	.034	-3	111	-9	-1.6
Total	16	197	230	.461	602	497	163-36	11	3611	3772	1652	286	46	894-**115**	1734	3.58	107	.269	.313	1137-120	.121	-36	92	98	7.1
FRIES, PETE Peter Martin B 10.30.1857 Scranton, PA D 7.30.1937 Chicago, IL BL/TL 5-8/160# d8.10																									
1883	Col AA	0	3	.000	3	3	3	0	25	34	31	1		14	7	6.48	48	.304	.381	10	.300	1	125	-10	-0.7
FRILL, JOHN John Edmond B 4.3.1879 Reading, PA D 9.28.1918 Westerly, RI BR/TL 5-10.5/170# d4.16																									
1910	NY A	2	2	.500	10	5	3-1	1	48.1	55	33	1	1	5	27	4.47	59	.289	.311	18-1	.111	-1	111	-9	-0.9
1912	StL A	0	1	.000	3	3	0	0	4.1	16	11	1	1	1	2	20.77	16	.571	.600	2-0	.500	0	163	-7	-1.2
	Cin N	1	0	1.000	3	2	0	0	15	19	11	0	2	1	4	6.00	56	.345	.379	4-0	.250	0	87	-3	-0.2
Total	2	3	3	.500	16	10	3-1	1	67.2	90	55	2	4	7	33	5.85	49	.330	.356	24-1	.167	-1	125	-19	-2.3
FRISELLA, DANNY Daniel Vincent "Bear" B 3.4.1946 San Francisco, CA D 1.1.1977 Phoenix, AZ BL/TR 6/195# d7.27																									
1967	NY N	1	6	.143	14	11	0	0	74	68	32	6	0	33-1	51	3.41	100	.249	.325	23-0	.087	-1	54	0	-0.1
1968	NY N	2	4	.333	19	4	0	2	50.2	53	23	5	0	17-0	47	3.91	77	.270	.326	12-0	.083	-1	72	-4	-0.6
1969	NY N	0	0	—	3	0	0	0-0	4.2	8	4	1	0	3-0	5	7.71	47	.381	.458	1-0	.000	-0		-2	-0.1
1970	NY N	8	3	.727	30	1	0	1-1	65.2	49	23	4	0	34-11	54	3.02	134	.204	.302	13-1	.308	1	111	8	1.4
1971	NY N	8	5	.615	53	0	0	12-3	90.2	76	28	6	3	30-9	93	1.99	172	.227	.295	13-1	.231	1		12	2.2
1972	NY N	5	8	.385	39	0	0	9-4	67.1	63	31	8	0	20-5	46	3.34	101	.243	.296	7-0	.286	0		-1	-0.1
1973	Atl N	1	2	.333	42	0	0	8-8	45	40	27	5	1	23-2	27	4.20	94	.241	.332	2-0	.500	0		-3	-0.2
1974	Atl N	3	4	.429	36	1	0	6-4	41.2	37	26	4	0	28-8	27	5.18	73	.240	.357	1-0	.000	0	115	-6	-1.1
1975	SD N	1	6	.143	65	0	0	9-2	97.2	86	36	7	2	51-16	67	3.13	111	.242	.335	5-0	.200	0		6	0.5
1976	StL N	0	0	—	18	0	0	1-0	22.2	19	10	3	0	13-1	11	3.97	89	.232	.330	1-0	.000	-0		0	0.0
	Mil A	5	2	.714	32	0	0	9-3	49.1	30	16	4	1	34-5	43	2.74	128	.175	.314	0-0	—	0		5	0.8
Total	10	34	40	.459	351	17	0	57-25	609.1	529	256	53	7	286-58	471	3.32	106	.235	.320	78-2	.179	1	63	15	2.7
FRISK, EMIL John Emil B 10.15.1874 Kalkaska, MI D 1.27.1922 Seattle, WA BL/TR 6-1/190# d9.2 ▲																									
1899	Cin N	3	6	.333	9	9	9	0	68.1	81	52	1	6	17	17	3.95	99	.295	.349	25-0	.280	1	100	-4	-0.3
1901	Det A	5	4	.556	11	7	6	0	74.2	94	60	1	2	26	22	4.34	89	.304	.362	48-0	.313	2*	130	-5	-0.1
Total	2	8	10	.444	20	16	15	0	143	175	112	2	8	43	39	4.15	93	.300	.356	73-0	.301	3	113	-9	-0.4
FRITZ, CHARLIE Charles Cornelius B 6.18.1882 Mobile, AL D 7.30.1943 Mobile, AL TL d10.5																									
1907	Phi A	0	0	—	1	1	0	0	3	0	1	0	1	3	1	3.00	87	.000	.333	1-0	.000	-0	104	0	0.0

Year	Tm Lg	W	L	Pct	G	GS	CG-Sho	SV-BS	IP	H	R	HR	HB	BB-IB	SO	ERA	AERA	OAV	OOB	AB-SH	AVG	PB	Sup	APR	PW
FROATS, BILL William John B 10.20.1930 New York, NY D 2.9.1998 Minneapolis, MN BL/TL 6/180# d4.22																									
1955	Det A	0	0	—	1	0	0	0	2	0	0	0	0	2-0	0	0.00	—	.000	.333	0-0	—	0		1	0.1
FROCK, SAM Samuel William B 12.23.1882 Baltimore, MD D 11.3.1925 Baltimore, MD BR/TR 6/168# d9.21																									
1907	Bos N	1	2	.333	5	3	3-1	0	33.1	28	17	1	2	11	12	2.97	86	.243	.320	14-0	.071	-1	149	-2	-0.4
1909	Pit N	2	1	.667	8	4	3	1	36.1	44	19	0	3	4	11	2.48	110	.299	.331	14-0	.143	-1	161	-1	-0.1
1910	Pit N	0	0	—	1	0	0	0	2	2	4	0	1	2	1	4.50	69	.400	.625	0-0	—	0		-1	-0.1
	Bos N	12	19	.387	45	29	13-2	2	255.1	245	133	8	4	91	170	3.21	104	.262	.330	84-5	.190	-3	75	1	-0.1
	Year	12	19	.387	46	29	13-2	2	257.1	247	136	8	5	93	171	3.22	103	.263	.333	84-5	.190	-3	75	-4	-0.2
1911	Bos N	0	1	.000	4	1	1	0	16	29	18	0	1	5	8	5.63	68	.426	.473	5-0	.200	-0	39	-4	-0.3
Total	4	15	23	.395	63	37	20-3	3	343	348	191	9	11	113	202	3.23	99	.274	.339	117-5	.171	-5	87	-7	-1.0
FROHWIRTH, TODD Todd Gerard B 9.28.1962 Milwaukee, WI BR/TR 6-4/205# d8.10																									
1987	Phi N	1	0	1.000	10	0	0	0-0	11	12	0	0	0	2-0	9	0.00	—	.293	.326	1-1	.000	-0		5	0.4
1988	Phi N	1	2	.333	12	0	0	0-1	12	16	11	2	0	11-6	11	8.25	43	.327	.443	0-0	—	0		-6	-1.1
1989	Phi N	1	0	1.000	45	0	0	0-1	62.2	56	26	4	3	18-0	39	3.59	99	.240	.302	1-1	.000	-0		1	0.0
1990	Phi N	0	1	.000	5	0	0	0-0	1	3	2	0	0	6-2	1	18.00	21	.500	.750	0-0	—	0		-1	-0.3
1991	Bal A	7	3	.700	51	0	0	3-2	96.1	64	24	2	1	29-3	77	1.87	212	.190	.255	0-0	—	0		**22**	2.4
1992	Bal A	4	3	.571	65	0	0	4-3	106	97	33	4	3	41-4	58	2.46	164	.247	.323	0-0	—	0		17	1.3
1993	Bal A	6	7	.462	70	0	0	3-4	96.1	91	47	7	3	44-8	50	3.83	117	.256	.342	0-0	—	0		5	0.8
1994	Bos A	0	3	.000	22	0	0	1-0	26.2	40	36	3	2	17-2	13	10.80	47	.339	.431	0-0	—	0		-17	-1.6
1996	Cal A	0	0	—	4	0	0	0-0	5.2	10	11	1	1	4-0	1	11.12	45	.370	.455	0-0	—	0		-5	-0.2
Total	9	20	19	.513	284	0	0	11-11	417.2	389	190	23	13	172-25	259	3.60	114	.250	.328	2-2	.000	-0		21	1.7
FROMME, ART Arthur Henry B 9.3.1883 Quincy, IL D 8.24.1956 Los Angeles, CA BR/TR 6/178# d9.14																									
1906	StL N	1	2	.333	3	3	3-1	0	25	19	6	0	1	10	11	1.44	183	.221	.309	9-0	.222	0	28	3	0.4
1907	StL N	5	13	.278	23	16	13-2	0	145.2	138	73	3	4	67	67	2.90	86	.256	.343	55-2	.182	1	73	-7	-0.8
1908	StL N	5	13	.278	20	14	9-2	0	116	102	59	1	2	50	62	2.72	87	.218	.296	36-2	.139	-1	72	-6	-1.1
1909	Cin N	19	13	.594	37	34	22-4	2	279.1	195	84	2	3	101	126	1.90	137	.201	.278	94-6	.191	2	97	23	3.2
1910	Cin N	3	4	.429	11	5	1	0	49.1	44	22	2	1	39	10	2.92	100	.260	.402	15-1	.133	-1	77	0	0.0
1911	Cin N	10	11	.476	38	26	11-1	0	208	190	111	8	16	79	107	3.46	96	.248	.331	74-4	.189	-1	93	-4	-0.5
1912	Cin N	16	18	.471	43	37	23-3	0	296	285	126	7	11	88	120	2.74	123	.260	.321	103-5	.087	-9	88	20	1.1
1913	Cin N	1	4	.200	9	7	2	0	56	55	30	1	3	21	24	4.18	78	.274	.351	21-0	.143	-0	63	-4	-0.4
	NY N	11	6	.647	26	12	3	0	112.1	112	58	5	2	29	50	4.01	78	.260	.310	35-3	.171	-0	84	-8	-1.1
	Year	12	10	.545	35	19	5	0	168.1	167	62	6	5	50	74	4.06	78	.264	.323	56-3	.161	-1	76	-10	-1.5
1914	NY N	9	5	.643	38	12	3-1	2	138	142	57	7	7	44	57	3.20	83	.283	.349	31-3	.226	1	124	-7	-0.4
1915	NY N	0	1	.000	4	1	0	0	12.1	15	11	1	0	2	4	5.84	44	.306	.333	3-0	.333	1	87	-5	-0.3
Total	10	80	90	.471	252	167	90-14	4	1438	1297	637	37	50	530	638	2.90	100	.246	.320	476-26	.162	-8	88	5	0.1
FROST, DAVE Carl David B 11.17.1952 Long Beach, CA BR/TR 6-6/235# d9.11																									
1977	Chi A	1	1	.500	4	3	0	0-0	23.2	30	9	0	1	3-0	15	3.04	135	.323	.343	0-0	—	0	95	3	0.2
1978	Cal A	5	4	.556	11	10	2-1	0-0	80.1	71	24	6	2	24-3	30	2.58	141	.240	.298	0-0	—	0	60	11	1.2
1979	†Cal A	16	10	.615	36	33	12-2	1-0	239.1	226	108	17	5	77-4	107	3.57	114	.251	.311	0-0	—	0	128	13	1.2
1980	Cal A	4	8	.333	15	15	2	0-0	78.1	97	53	8	2	21-1	28	5.29	75	.308	.352	0-0	—	0	94	-13	-1.7
1981	Cal A	1	8	.111	12	9	0	0-0	47.1	44	30	3	1	19-0	16	5.51	66	.250	.323	0-0	—	0	68	-9	-1.4
1982	KC A	6	6	.500	21	14	0	0-0	81.2	103	53	7	3	30-0	26	5.51	74	.313	.372	0-0	—	0	105	-12	-1.6
Total	6	33	37	.471	99	84	16-3	1-0	550.2	571	277	41	14	174-8	222	4.10	97	.271	.327	0-0	—	0	103	-7	-2.1
FRY, JOHNSON Johnson "Jay" B 11.21.1901 Huntington, WV D 4.7.1959 Carmi, IL BR/TR 6-1/150# d8.24																									
1923	Cle A	0	0	—	1	0	0	0	3.2	6	5	0	0	4	0	12.27	32	.353	.476	1-0	1.000	1		-3	-0.1
FRYE, CHARLIE Charles Andrew B 7.17.1914 Hickory, NC D 5.25.1945 Hickory, NC BR/TR 6-1/175# d7.28																									
1940	Phi N	0	6	.000	15	5	1	0	50.1	58	32	3	0	26	18	4.65	84	.291	.373	19-0	.263	1*	27	-5	-0.4
FRYMAN, WOODIE Woodrow Thompson B 4.15.1940 Ewing, KY BR/TL 6-2/205# d4.15																									
1966	Pit N	12	9	.571	36	28	9-3	1	181.2	182	86	13	1	47-9	105	3.81	94	.261	.308	63-4	.159	-1	107	-5	-0.7
1967	Pit N	3	8	.273	28	18	3-1	1	113.1	121	67	12	4	44-3	74	4.05	83	.276	.344	34-1	.118	-1	104	-12	-1.2
1968	Phi N☆	12	14	.462	34	32	10-5	0	213.2	198	78	12	6	64-2	151	2.78	108	.246	.305	71-7	.085	-2	105	4	0.2
1969	Phi N	12	15	.444	36	35	10-1	0-0	228.1	243	123	15	11	89-3	150	4.41	80	.270	.343	76-8	.118	-2	110	-21	-2.4
1970	Phi N	8	6	.571	27	20	4-3	0-1	127.2	122	61	11	1	43-2	97	4.09	98	.253	.313	39-3	.128	-2	108	-1	-0.2
1971	Phi N	10	7	.588	37	17	3-2	2-2	149.1	133	61	7	3	46-1	104	3.38	105	.242	.301	37-5	.189	0	102	4	0.6
1972	Phi N	4	10	.286	23	17	3-2	1-0	119.2	131	64	15	2	39-9	69	4.36	82	.279	.335	33-2	.152	1	100	-10	-1.0
	†Det A	10	3	.769	16	14	6-1	0-0	113.2	93	31	6	7	31-3	72	2.06	153	.220	.284	40-4	.125	-2	114	13	1.3
1973	Det A	6	13	.316	34	29	1	0-0	169.2	200	106	23	3	64-5	119	5.36	76	.294	.356	0-0	—	0	83	-21	-2.0
1974	Det A	6	9	.400	27	22	4-1	0-0	141.2	120	73	16	4	67-2	92	4.32	88	.233	.324	0-0	—	0	84	-6	-0.6
1975	Mon N	9	12	.429	38	20	7-3	3-4	157	141	69	10	5	68-7	118	3.32	115	.239	.323	49-5	.204	1	77	7	1.1
1976	Mon N☆	13	13	.500	34	32	4-2	2-0	216.1	218	89	14	9	76-7	123	3.37	111	.263	.328	64-11	.109	-3	89	10	0.8
1977	Cin N	5	5	.500	17	12	0	1-0	75.1	83	45	13	2	45-2	57	5.38	73	.292	.390	22-3	.318	2	109	-10	-1.0
1978	Chi N	2	4	.333	13	9	0	0-1	55.2	64	37	6	0	37-5	28	5.17	78	.309	.407	16-3	.063	-1	74	-7	-0.7
	Mon N	5	7	.417	19	17	4-3	1-0	94.2	93	39	4	3	37-1	53	3.61	98	.260	.334	34-2	.059	-2	109	1	-0.2
	Year	7	11	.389	32	26	4-3	1-1	150.1	157	43	10	3	74-6	81	4.19	89	.278	.362	50-5	.060	-3	96	-8	-0.9
1979	Mon N	3	6	.333	44	0	0	10-1	58	52	25	4	3	22-4	44	2.79	132	.248	.328	7-0	.000	-1		4	0.7
1980	Mon N	7	4	.636	61	0	0	17-6	80	61	23	1	2	30-9	59	2.25	159	.209	.285	12-2	.167	-0		12	2.0
1981	†Mon N	5	3	.625	35	0	0	7-8	43	38	16	1	1	14-1	25	1.88	186	.247	.308	3-2	.667	1		5	1.2
1982	Mon N	9	4	.692	60	0	0	12-6	69.2	66	36	3	1	26-4	46	3.75	97	.259	.326	9-1	.222	0		-2	-0.3
1983	Mon N	0	3	.000	6	0	0	0-1	3	8	7	1	0	1-0	1	21.00	17	.571	.600	0-0	—	0		-6	-1.0
Total	18	141	155	.476	625	322	68-27	58-30	2411.1	2367	1136	187	68	890-79	1587	3.77	96	.259	.327	609-63	.138	-12	98	-41	-3.4
FUCHS, CHARLIE Charles Thomas B 11.18.1912 Union Hill, NJ D 6.10.1969 Weehawken, NJ BB/TR 5-8/168# d4.17																									
1942	Det A	3	3	.500	9	4	1-1	0	36.2	43	27	5	1	19	15	6.63	60	.285	.368	13-0	.077	-1	76	-8	-1.2
1943	Phi N	2	7	.222	17	9	4-1	1	77.2	76	40	4	3	34	12	4.29	79	.266	.350	22-3	.091	-2	87	-7	-1.0
	StL A	0	0	—	13	0	0	0	35.2	42	22	4	1	11	9	4.04	82	.294	.348	7-0	.000	-1		-4	-0.3
1944	Bro N	1	0	1.000	8	0	0	0	15.2	25	16	2	1	9	5	5.74	62	.347	.427	1-0	.000	0		-6	-0.3
Total	3	6	10	.375	47	13	5-2	1	165.2	186	105	15	6	73	41	4.89	72	.285	.363	43-3	.070	-4	84	-25	-2.8
FUENTES, BRIAN Brian Christopher B 8.9.1975 Merced, CA BL/TL 6-4/220# d6.2																									
2001	Sea A	1	1	.500	10	0	0	0-1	11.2	6	6	2	3	8-0	10	4.63	90	.171	.362	0-0	—	0		0	0.0
2002	Col N	2	0	1.000	31	0	0	0-0	26.2	25	14	4	3	13-0	38	4.73	101	.250	.347	0-0	—	0		1	0.0
2003	Col N	3	3	.500	75	0	0	4-2	75.1	64	24	7	6	34-2	82	2.75	179	.231	.325	1-0	.000	-0		16	1.3
Total	3	6	4	.600	116	0	0	4-3	113.2	95	44	13	12	55-2	130	3.40	141	.231	.334	1-0	.000	-0		17	1.3
FUENTES, MIGUEL Miguel (Pinet) B 5.10.1946 Loiza Aldea, P.R. D 1.29.1970 Loiza Aldea, P.R. BR/TR 6/160# d9.1																									
1969	Sea A	1	3	.250	8	4	1	0-0	26	29	15	1	0	16-1	14	5.19	70	.284	.381	6-2	.333	0	79	-4	-0.5
FUHR, OSCAR Oscar Lawrence B 8.22.1893 Defiance, MO D 3.27.1975 Dallas, TX BL/TL 6-0.5/176# d4.19																									
1921	Chi N	0	0	—	1	0	0	0	4	11	9	1	0	0	2	9.00	42	.500	.500	1-0	.000	-0		-4	-0.2
1924	Bos A	3	6	.333	23	10	4-1	0	80.1	100	71	1	5	39	30	5.94	74	.310	.392	22-1	.182	-1	133	-17	-1.6
1925	Bos A	0	6	.000	39	5	0	0	91.1	138	83	7	3	30	27	6.60	69	.364	.415	20-0	.250	0	129	-20	-1.0
Total	3	3	12	.200	63	15	4-1	0	175.2	249	163	9	8	69	59	6.35	70	.344	.407	43-1	.209	-1	131	-41	-2.8
FULGHAM, JOHN John Thomas B 6.9.1956 St.Louis, MO BR/TR 6-2/205# d6.19																									
1979	StL N	10	6	.625	20	19	10-2	0-0	146	123	47	10	3	26-3	75	2.53	149	.227	.266	42-11	.143	1*	91	20	2.1
1980	StL N	4	6	.400	15	14	4-1	0-0	85.1	66	33	7	1	32-1	48	3.38	110	.219	.295	27-3	.000	-3*	83	4	0.1
Total	2	14	12	.538	35	33	14-3	0-0	231.1	189	80	17	4	58-4	123	2.84	132	.224	.276	69-14	.087	-2	88	24	2.2

Year	Tm Lg	W	L	Pct	G	GS	CG-Sho	SV-BS	IP	H	R	HR	HB	BB-IB	SO	ERA	AERA	OAV	OOB	AB-SH	AVG	PB	Sup	APR	PW
FULLER, ED Edward Ashton B 3.22.1868 Washington, DC D 3.16.1935 Hyattsville, MD BR/TR 6/158# d7.17																									
1886	Was N	0	1	.000	2	1	1	0	13	15	12	0		5	3	6.92	47	.375	.444	7	.143	-0	76	-4	-0.3
FULLERTON, CURT Curtis Hooper B 9.13.1898 Ellsworth, ME D 1.2.1975 Winthrop, MA BL/TR 6/162# d4.14																									
1921	Bos A	0	1	.000	4	1	1	0	15.1	22	17	3	1	10	4	8.80	48	.355	.452	4-0	.000	-0	118	-8	-0.5
1922	Bos A	1	4	.200	31	3	0	0	64.1	70	40	4	5	35	17	5.46	75	.290	.391	8-0	.250	1	103	-7	-0.3
1923	Bos A	2	15	.118	37	15	6	1	143.1	167	108	9	6	71	37	5.09	81	.300	.385	37-1	.297	2	51	-17	-1.7
1924	Bos A	7	12	.368	33	20	9	2	152	166	93	1	6	73	33	4.32	101	.283	.368	42-2	.071	-3	77	-1	-0.5
1925	Bos A	0	3	.000	4	2	0	0	22.2	22	11	1	2	9	3	3.18	143	.259	.344	10-1	.200	-0	46	3	0.4
1933	Bos A	0	2	.000	6	2	2	0	25.1	36	24	1	1	13	10	8.53	51	.364	.442	9-0	.222	0	39	-10	-0.6
Total	6	10	37	.213	115	43	18	3	423	483	293	19	21	211	104	5.11	83	.296	.384	110-4	.182	-1	68	-40	-3.2
FULTON, BILL William David B 10.22.1963 Pittsburgh, PA BR/TR 6-3/195# d9.12																									
1987	NY A	1	0	1.000	3	0	0	0-0	4.2	9	6	4	1	1-0	2	11.57	38	.409	.458	0-0	—	0		-4	-0.6
FULTZ, AARON Richard Aaron B 9.4.1973 Memphis, TN BL/TL 6/196# d4.5																									
2000	†SF N	5	2	.714	58	0	0	1-2	69.1	67	38	8	3	28-0	62	4.67	91	.263	.336	6-1	.333	1		-3	-0.1
2001	SF N	3	1	.750	66	0	0	1-1	71	70	40	9	1	21-3	67	4.56	87	.258	.310	5-0	.400	1		-5	-0.1
2002	†SF N	2	2	.500	43	0	0	0-1	41.1	47	22	4	3	19-3	31	4.79	81	.294	.377	1-0	.000	-0*		-3	-0.3
2003	Tex A	1	3	.250	64	0	0	0-0	67.1	75	43	9	2	27-7	53	5.21	95	.287	.356	0-0	—	0		-2	-0.1
Total	4	11	8	.579	231	0	0	2-4	249	259	143	30	9	95-13	213	4.81	89	.273	.341	12-1	.333	1		-13	-0.6
FUNK, FRANK Franklin Ray B 8.30.1935 Washington, DC BR/TR 6/175# d9.3 C11																									
1960	Cle A	4	2	.667	9	0	0	1	31.2	27	8	3	0	9-3	18	1.99	188	.248	.305	9-0	.111	-0		6	1.2
1961	Cle A	11	11	.500	56	0	0	11	92.1	79	35	9	4	31-6	64	3.31	119	.234	.303	17-0	.059	-1		8	1.5
1962	Cle A	2	1	.667	47	0	0	6	80.2	62	35	11	4	32-1	49	3.24	120	.212	.293	15-0	.067	-1		5	0.1
1963	Mil N	3	3	.500	25	0	0	0	43.2	42	14	3	1	13-3	19	2.68	120	.258	.315	4-0	.000	-0*		3	0.3
Total	4	20	17	.541	137	0	0	18	248.1	210	92	26	9	85-13	150	3.01	125	.233	.302	45-0	.067	-3		22	3.1
FUNK, TOM Thomas James B 3.13.1962 Kansas City, MO BL/TL 6-2/210# d7.24																									
1986	Hou N	0	0	—	8	0	0	0-0	8.1	10	6	1	0	6-0	2	6.48	56	.286	.390	1-0	.000	-0		-2	-0.1
FUSSELBACK, EDDIE Edward L. B 7.17.1856 Philadelphia, PA D 4.14.1926 Philadelphia, PA BR 5-6/156# d5.3 ▲																									
1882	StL AA	1	2	.333	4	2	2	**1**	23	34	24	0		2	3	4.70	60	.321	.333	136	.228	0*	119	-4	-0.5
FUSSELL, CHRIS Christopher Wren B 5.19.1976 Oregon, OH BR/TR 6-2/200# d9.15																									
1998	Bal A	0	1	.000	3	2	0	0-0	9.2	11	9	1	0	9-1	8	8.38	54	.306	.435	0-0	—	0	82	-4	-0.3
1999	KC A	0	5	.000	17	8	0	2-0	56	72	51	9	5	36-3	37	7.39	68	.329	.428	0-0	—	0	102	-15	-1.2
2000	KC A	5	3	.625	20	9	0	0-0	70	76	52	18	2	44-2	46	6.30	81	.286	.385	2-0	.000	-0	128	-9	-0.9
Total	3	5	9	.357	40	19	0	2-0	135.2	159	112	28	7	89-6	91	6.90	73	.305	.407	2-0	.000	-0	112	-28	-2.4
FUSSELL, FRED Frederick Morris "Moonlight Ace" B 10.7.1895 Sheridan, MO D 10.23.1966 Syracuse, NY BL/TL 5-10/155# d9.23																									
1922	Chi N	1	1	.500	3	2	1	0	19	24	11	0	0	8	4	4.74	89	.333	.400	6-0	.000	-1	78	-1	-0.1
1923	Chi N	3	5	.375	28	2	1	3	76.1	90	51	2	3	31	38	5.54	72	.298	.369	20-0	.200	-0	62	-11	-1.0
1928	Pit N	8	9	.471	28	20	9-2	1	159.2	183	79	6	1	41	43	3.61	113	.295	.340	58-1	.121	-3	108	7	0.2
1929	Pit N	2	2	.500	21	3	0	1	39.2	68	42	8	1	8	18	8.62	55	.389	.418	16-0	.250	2	171	-16	-1.2
Total	4	14	17	.452	80	27	11-2	5	294.2	365	183	16	5	88	103	4.86	85	.312	.363	100-1	.150	-2	110	-21	-2.1
FYHRIE, MIKE Michael Edwin B 12.9.1969 Long Beach, CA BR/TR 6-2/190# d9.14																									
1996	NY N	0	1	.000	2	0	0	0-0	2.1	4	4	0	0	3-0	0	15.43	26	.364	.500	0-0	—	0		-3	-0.5
1999	Ana A	0	4	.000	16	7	0	0-0	51.2	61	32	8	0	21-1	26	5.05	96	.286	.349	0-0	—	0	71	-1	-0.1
2000	Ana A	0	0	—	32	0	0	0-0	52.2	54	14	4	0	15-4	43	2.39	212	.269	.315	0-0	—	0		16	0.7
2001	Chi N	0	2	.000	15	0	0	0-0	15	16	7	1	0	7-0	6	4.20	99	.281	.359	2-0	.000	-0		0	0.0
	Oak A	0	0	—	3	0	0	0-0	5	2	0	0	0	1-0	5	0.00	—	.125	.176	0-0	—	0		2	0.1
2002	Oak A	2	4	.333	16	4	0	0-0	48.2	46	25	3	4	20-1	29	4.44	99	.246	.332	0-0	—	0	142	0	0.0
Total	5	2	11	.154	84	11	0	0-0	175.1	183	82	16	4	67-6	109	4.00	118	.267	.334	2-0	.000	-0	95	14	0.2
GABLER, FRANK Frank Harold "The Great Gabbo" B 11.6.1911 E.Highlands, CA D 11.1.1967 Long Beach, CA BR/TR 6-1/175# d4.19																									
1935	NY N	2	1	.667	26	1	0	0	60	79	43	6	0	20	24	5.70	68	.315	.365	16-0	.125	-1	154	-13	-0.7
1936	†NY N	9	8	.529	43	14	5	6	161.2	170	62	11	3	34	46	3.12	125	.274	.315	48-6	.208	2	110	16	1.7
1937	NY N	0	0	—	6	0	0	0	9	20	14	1	0	2	3	10.00	39	.455	.478	0-0	—	0		-7	-0.3
	Bos N	4	7	.364	19	9	2-1	2	76	84	45	7	0	16	19	5.09	70	.283	.319	22-0	.182	0	72	-12	-1.5
	Year	4	7	.364	25	9	2-1	2	85	104	48	8	0	18	22	5.61	64	.305	.340	22-0	.182	0	71	-18	-1.8
1938	Bos N	0	0	—	1	0	0	0	0.1	3	3	0	0	1	0	81.00	4	1.000	1.000	0-0	—	0		-3	-0.1
	Chi A	1	7	.125	18	7	3	0	69.1	101	74	12	1	34	17	9.09	54	.348	.418	21-0	.238	0	85	-28	-2.5
Total	4	16	23	.410	113	31	10-1	8	376.1	457	241	37	4	107	109	5.26	76	.303	.351	107-6	.196	1	95	-47	-3.4
GABLER, JOHN John Richard "Gab" B 10.2.1930 Kansas City, MO BB/TR 6-2/165# d9.18																									
1959	NY A	1	1	.500	3	1	0	0	19.1	21	6	1	1	10-0	11	2.79	130	.284	.376	6-0	.000	-1	24	2	0.1
1960	NY A	3	3	.500	21	4	0	1	52	46	27	2	0	32-1	19	4.15	86	.242	.348	11-1	.091	-0	86	-3	-0.4
1961	Was A	3	8	.273	29	9	0	4	92.2	104	61	5	1	37-3	33	4.86	83	.283	.349	25-0	.200	1*	47	-10	-1.0
Total	3	7	12	.368	53	14	0	5	164	171	94	8	2	79-4	63	4.39	87	.271	.352	42-1	.143	-0	56	-11	-1.3
GABLES, KEN Kenneth Harlin "Coral" B 1.31.1919 Walnut Grove, MO D 1.2.1960 Walnut Grove, MO BR/TR 5-11/210# d4.18																									
1945	Pit N	11	7	.611	29	16	6	1	138.2	139	69	5	4	46	49	4.15	95	.256	.319	39-3	.103	-3	117	0	-0.4
1946	Pit N	2	4	.333	32	7	0	1	100.2	113	64	3	1	52	39	5.27	67	.281	.365	24-2	.250	1	80	-17	-0.9
1947	Pit N	0	0	—	1	0	0	0	0.1	3	2	1	0	0	0	54.00	8	.750	.750	0-0	—	0		-2	-0.1
Total	3	13	11	.542	62	23	6	2	239.2	255	135	9	5	98	88	4.69	80	.269	.340	63-5	.159	-1	108	-19	-1.4
GADDY, JOHN John Wilson "Sheriff" B 2.5.1914 Wadesboro, NC D 5.3.1966 Albemarle, NC BR/TR 6-0.5/182# d9.27																									
1938	Bro N	2	0	1.000	2	2	1	0	13	13	3	0	1	4	3	0.69	564	.255	.321	6-0	.000	-1	130	4	0.5
GAFF, BRENT Brent Allen B 10.5.1958 Fort Wayne, IN BR/TR 6-2/200# d7.7																									
1982	NY N	0	3	.000	7	5	0	0-0	31.2	41	22	3	1	10-0	14	4.55	80	.323	.374	8-1	.000	-0	78	-5	-0.4
1983	NY N	1	0	1.000	4	0	0	0-0	10.1	18	9	0	0	1-1	4	6.10	60	.360	.365	3-0	.000	-0		-3	-0.3
1984	NY N	3	2	.600	47	0	0	1-0	84.1	77	39	4	1	36-11	42	3.63	98	.247	.320	6-0	.000	-1		-1	-0.1
Total	3	4	5	.444	58	5	0	1-0	126.1	136	70	7	2	47-12	60	4.06	88	.278	.338	17-1	.000	-1	78	-9	-0.8
GAGNE, ERIC Eric Serge B 1.7.1976 Montreal, PQ, CAN BR/TR 6-2/195# d9.7																									
1999	LA N	1	1	.500	5	5	0	0-0	30	18	8	3	0	15-0	30	2.10	204	.175	.280	10-0	.200	0	73	8	0.4
2000	LA N	4	6	.400	20	19	0	0-0	101.1	106	62	20	3	60-1	79	5.15	84	.270	.368	28-6	.143	-1	105	-9	-0.8
2001	LA N	6	7	.462	33	24	0	0-0	151.2	144	90	24	16	46-1	130	4.75	85	.251	.320	44-6	.136	2	123	-15	-1.1
2002	LA N★	4	1	.800	77	0	0	52-4	82.1	55	18	6	2	16-4	114	1.97	194	.189	.235	1-0	.000	-0		19	3.2
2003	LA N★	2	3	.400	77	0	0	**55-0**	82.1	37	12	2	3	20-2	137	1.20	334	.133	.199	0-0	—	0		**27**	4.9
Total	5	17	18	.486	212	48	0	107-4	447.2	360	190	55	24	157-8	490	3.50	116	.220	.295	83-12	.145	1	113	30	6.6
GAGUS, CHARLIE Charles Frederick (b: Charles Frederick Geggus) B 3.25.1862 San Francisco, CA D 1.16.1917 San Francisco, CA ?/150# d8.7																									
1884	Was U	10	9	.526	23	21	19	0	177.1	143	100	2		38	156	2.54	94	.206	.247	154	.247	-3*	98	-5	-0.6
GAILLARD, EDDIE Julian Edward B 8.13.1970 Camden, NJ BR/TR 6-1/180# d8.11																									
1997	Det A	1	0	1.000	16	0	0	1-1	20.1	16	12	2	0	10-2	12	5.31	86	.211	.295	0-0	—	0		-1	-0.1
1998	TB A	0	0	—	6	0	0	0-0	7.2	4	5	3	0	3-0	5	5.87	82	.148	.233	0-0	—	0		-1	0.0
1999	TB A	1	0	1.000	8	0	0	0-0	8.2	12	9	1	1	4-0	7	2.08	240	.324	.405	0-0	—	0		0	0.0
Total	3	2	0	1.000	30	0	0	1-1	36.2	32	26	6	1	17-2	24	4.66	101	.229	.313	0-0	—	0		-2	-0.1
GAINES, NEMO Willard Roland B 12.23.1897 Alexandria, VA D 1.26.1979 Warrenton, VA BL/TL 6/180# d6.26																									
1921	Was A	0	0	—	4	0	0	0	4.2	5	0	0	0	2	1	0.00	—	.294	.368	1-0	.000	-0		2	0.1

Year	Tm Lg	W	L	Pct	G	GS	CG-Sho	SV-BS	IP	H	R	HR	HB	BB-IB	SO	ERA	AERA	OAV	OOB	AB-SH	AVG	PB	Sup	APR	PW
GAISER, FRED Frederick Jacob B 8.31.1885 Stuttgart, Germany D 10.9.1918 Trenton, NJ d9.3																									
1908	StL N	0	0	—	1	0	0	0	2.1	4	2	0	0	3	2	7.71	31	.444	.583	1-0	.000	-0		-1	-0.1
GAJKOWSKI, STEVE Stephen Robert B 12.30.1969 Seattle, WA BR/TR 6-2/200# d5.25																									
1998	Sea A	0	0	—	9	0	0	0-0	8.2	14	8	3	2	4-0	3	7.27	64	.389	.476	0-0	—	0		-3	-0.1
GAKELER, DAN Daniel Michael B 5.1.1964 Mt.Holly, NJ BR/TR 6-6/215# d6.9																									
1991	Det A	1	4	.200	31	7	0	2-2	73.2	73	52	5	1	39-6	43	5.74	72	.256	.345	0-0	—	0	101	-13	-0.8
GALASSO, BOB Robert Joseph B 1.13.1952 Connellsville, PA BL/TR 6-1/205# d7.24																									
1977	Sea A	0	6	.000	11	7	0	0-0	35	57	36	8	3	8-0	21	9.00	46	.365	.402	0-0	—	0	62	-17	-2.4
1979	Mil A	3	1	.750	31	0	0	3-3	51.1	64	30	5	0	26-3	28	4.38	95	.299	.372	0-0	—	0		-2	-0.2
1981	Sea A	1	1	.500	13	1	0	1-0	31.2	32	19	2	0	13-1	14	4.83	80	.264	.331	0-0	—	0	23	-3	-0.2
Total	3	4	8	.333	55	8	0	4-3	118	153	85	15	3	47-4	63	5.87	70	.312	.371	0-0	—	0	58	-22	-2.8
GALE, RICH Richard Blackwell B 1.19.1954 Littleton, NH BR/TR 6-7/225# d4.30 C2																									
1978	KC A	14	8	.636	31	30	9-3	0-0	192.1	171	78	10	3	100-3	88	3.09	124	.244	.339	0-0	—	0	110	15	1.5
1979	KC A	9	10	.474	34	31	2-1	0-0	181.2	197	131	19	4	99-4	103	5.65	76	.278	.366	0-0	—	0	126	-28	-2.5
1980	†KC A	13	9	.591	32	28	6-1	1-1	190.2	169	90	16	2	78-2	97	3.92	104	.239	.315	0-0	—	0	110	4	0.4
1981	KC A	6	6	.500	19	15	2	0-0	101.2	107	63	14	2	38-0	47	5.40	67	.270	.335	0-0	—	0	86	-18	-2.0
1982	SF N	7	14	.333	33	29	2	0-1	170.1	193	91	9	5	81-11	102	4.23	85	.294	.370	48-1	.125	1	79	-11	-1.2
1983	Cin N	4	6	.400	33	7	0	1-0	89.2	103	64	8	1	43-8	53	5.82	66	.286	.362	20-1	.150	1	96	-19	-1.9
1984	Bos A	2	3	.400	13	4	0	0-0	43.2	57	27	6	1	18-0	28	5.56	75	.315	.380	0-0	—	0	130	-5	-0.5
Total	7	55	56	.495	195	144	21-5	2-2	970	997	544	82	18	457-28	518	4.54	86	.269	.349	68-2	.132	2	105	-62	-6.2
GALEHOUSE, DENNY Dennis Ward B 12.7.1911 Marshallville, OH D 10.12.1998 Doylestown, OH BR/TR 6-1/195# d4.30 Def 1944, Mil 1945																									
1934	Cle A	0	0	—	1	0	0	0	1	2	3	0	0	1	0	18.00	25	.500	.600	0-0	—	0		-2	-0.1
1935	Cle A	1	0	1.000	5	1	1	0	13	16	14	1	1	9	8	9.00	50	.314	.426	4-0	.250	-0	135	-6	-0.4
1936	Cle A	8	7	.533	36	15	5	1	148.1	161	86	5	2	68	71	4.85	104	.280	.358	47-1	.170	-0	95	6	0.4
1937	Cle A	9	14	.391	36	29	7	3	200.2	238	114	11	1	83	78	4.57	101	.302	.369	72-2	.208	-1	80	2	0.1
1938	Cle A	7	8	.467	36	12	5-1	3	114	119	62	12	1	65	66	4.34	107	.275	.371	39-0	.154	-1	104	4	0.3
1939	Bos A	9	10	.474	30	18	6-1	0	146.2	160	84	6	1	52	68	4.54	104	.276	.337	47-4	.064	-3	77	4	0.1
1940	Bos A	6	6	.500	25	20	5	0	120	155	77	10	0	41	53	5.18	87	.313	.366	39-7	.077	-4	109	-9	-1.1
1941	StL A	9	10	.474	30	24	11-2	0	190.1	183	85	10	4	68	61	3.64	118	.253	.320	68-5	.191	-0	86	14	1.3
1942	StL A	12	12	.500	32	28	12-3	1	192.1	193	91	5	4	79	75	3.60	103	.262	.337	72-4	.194	1	115	2	0.3
1943	StL A	11	11	.500	31	28	14-2	1	224	217	80	8	1	74	114	2.77	120	.255	.315	72-8	.125	-3	106	13	0.8
1944	†StL A	9	10	.474	24	19	6-2	0	153	162	64	6	1	44	80	3.12	115	.266	.316	48-4	.063	-4	82	7	0.3
1946	StL A	8	12	.400	30	24	11-2	0	180	194	82	9	0	52	90	3.65	102	.273	.322	55-6	.091	-3	88	3	-0.2
1947	StL A	1	3	.250	9	4	0	1	32.1	42	26	3	0	16	11	6.12	63	.311	.384	8-2	.000	-1	114	-8	-1.0
	Bos A	11	7	.611	21	21	11-3	0	149	150	60	7	0	34	38	3.32	117	.260	.301	52-9	.096	-4	117	10	0.6
	Year	12	10	.545	30	25	11-3	1	181.1	192	65	10	0	50	49	3.82	102	.269	.317	60-11	.083	-5	117	2	-0.4
1948	Bos A	8	8	.500	27	15	6-1	3	137.1	152	68	10	2	46	38	4.00	110	.282	.341	42-3	.167	-0	95	6	0.5
1949	Bos A	0	0	—	2	0	0	0	2	4	3	1	0	3	0	13.50	32	.400	.538	0-0	—	0		-2	-0.1
Total	15	109	118	.480	375	258	100-17	13	2004	2148	999	104	18	735	851	3.97	105	.275	.338	665-55	.138	-25	95	44	1.8
GALLAGHER, DOUG Douglas Eugene B 2.21.1940 Fremont, OH BR/TL 6-3.5/195# d4.9																									
1962	Det A	0	4	.000	9	2	0	1	25	31	18	2	0	15-1	14	4.68	87	.290	.371	6-0	.333	1	132	-3	-0.4
GALLAGHER, ED Edward Michael "Lefty" B 11.28.1910 Dorchester, MA D 12.22.1981 Hyannis, MA BB/TL 6-2/197# d7.8																									
1932	Bos A	0	3	.000	9	3	0	0	23.2	30	36	3	0	28	6	12.55	36	.323	.479	5-0	.000	-1	38	-20	-1.9
GALLAGHER, BILL William John B Philadelphia, PA TL d5.2 ▲																									
1883	Bal AA	0	5	.000	7	5	4	0	51.2	79	57	0		6	19	5.40	64	.331	.347	61	.164	-1*	89	-10	-0.8
1884	Phi U	1	2	.333	3	3	3	0	25	32	29	3		4	12	3.24	72	.291	.316	11	.091	-2	92	-7	-0.7
Total	2	1	7	.125	10	8	7	0	76.2	111	86	3		10	31	4.70	66	.318	.337	72	.153	-3	90	-17	-1.5
GALLIA, BERT Melvin Allys B 10.14.1891 Beeville, TX D 3.19.1976 Devine, TX BR/TR 6/165# d9.4																									
1912	Was A	0	0	—	2	0	0	0	2	0	0	0	0	3	0	0.00	—	.000	.333	0-0	—	0		1	0.0
1913	Was A	1	5	.167	31	4	0	3	96	85	66	2	7	46	46	4.13	72	.232	.329	23-0	.087	-2	69	-15	-1.1
1914	Was A	0	0	—	2	0	0	0	6	3	4	0	0	4	4	4.50	63	.120	.241	2-0	.000	-0		-1	-0.1
1915	Was A	17	11	.607	43	29	14-3	1	259.2	220	90	2	4	64	130	2.29	130	.234	.286	85-3	.165	-2	97	20	1.8
1916	Was A	17	13	.567	49	31	13-1	2	283.2	278	109	3	8	99	120	2.76	101	.266	.334	93-4	.194	1	111	2	0.1
1917	Was A	9	13	.409	42	23	9-1	1	207.2	191	92	1	4	93	84	2.99	88	.258	.344	67-2	.209	2*	100	-9	-0.8
1918	StL A	8	6	.571	19	17	10-1	0	124	126	63	1	6	61	48	3.48	79	.268	.359	46-1	.130	-3	115	-10	-1.5
1919	StL A	12	14	.462	34	25	14-1	1	222.1	220	109	10	8	92	83	3.60	92	.264	.343	72-4	.153	-2	99	-5	-0.6
1920	StL A	0	1	.000	2	1	0	0	3.2	8	7	0	0	3	0	7.36	53	.400	.478	1-0	.000	-0	81	-3	-0.5
	Phi N	2	6	.250	18	5	1	2	72	79	48	2	3	29	35	4.50	76	.287	.362	23-1	.174	-1*	60	-9	-1.1
Total	9	66	69	.489	242	135	61-7	10	1277	1210	588	21	40	494	550	3.14	94	.256	.332	412-15	.167	-7	100	-29	-3.8
GALLIVAN, PHIL Philip Joseph B 5.29.1907 Seattle, WA D 11.24.1969 St.Paul, MN BR/TR 6/170# d4.21																									
1931	Bro N	0	1	.000	6	1	0	0	15.1	23	11	2	0	7	1	5.28	72	.354	.417	3-0	.000	-0	22	-3	-0.1
1932	Chi A	1	3	.250	13	3	1	0	33.1	49	32	4	1	24	12	7.56	57	.338	.435	8-0	.375	1	79	-11	-1.0
1934	Chi A	4	7	.364	35	7	3	1	126.2	155	97	14	1	64	55	5.61	84	.295	.373	40-3	.225	1	110	-14	-1.0
Total	3	5	11	.313	54	11	4	1	175.1	227	140	20	2	95	68	5.95	77	.309	.389	51-3	.235	1	95	-28	-2.1
GALLO, MIKE Michael Dwain B 4.2.1977 Long Beach, CA BL/TL 6/170# d7.2																									
2003	Hou N	1	0	1.000	32	0	0	0-1	30	28	10	3	1	10-2	16	3.00	148	.267	.328	2-0	.000	-0		5	0.3
GALVEZ, BALVINO Balvino (Jerez) B 3.31.1964 San Pedro De Macoris, D.R. BR/TR 6/170# d5.7																									
1986	LA N	0	1	.000	10	0	0	0-2	20.2	19	10	3	0	12-2	11	3.92	88	.241	.341	2-0	.000	-0		-1	-0.1
GALVIN, JIM James Francis "Pud", "Gentle Jeems" or "The Little Steam Engine" B 12.25.1856 St.Louis, MO D 3.7.1902 Pittsburgh, PA BR/TR 5-8/190# d5.22 M1 U1 HF1965																									
1875	StL NA	4	2	.667	8	7	7	1	62	53	37	0		1	8	**1.16**	**173**	.209	.212	46	.130	-1*	105	3	0.2
1879	Buf N	37	27	.578	66	66	65-6	0	593	585	299	3		31	136	2.28	115	.243	.253	265	.249	5*	85	20	2.5
1880	Buf N	20	35	.364	58	54	46-5	0	458.2	528	281	5		32	128	2.71	91	.273	.284	241	.212	-4*	86	-14	-1.7
1881	Buf N	28	24	.538	56	53	48-5	0	474	546	250	4		46	136	2.37	117	.274	.291	236	.212	-1*	103	18	2.0
1882	Buf N	28	23	.549	52	51	48-3	0	445.1	476	255	8		40	162	3.17	93	.256	.272	206	.214	-5*	109	-8	-1.2
1883	Buf N	46	29	.613	**76**	**75**	**72-5**	0	**656.1**	676	367	9		50	279	2.72	117	.251	.265	322	.220	-4*	106	31	2.4
1884	Buf N	46	22	.676	72	72	71-**12**	0	636.1	566	254	23		63	369	1.99	158	.227	.246	274	.179	-14	103	81	6.3
1885	Buf N	13	19	.406	33	32	31-3	1	284	356	204	8		37	93	4.09	73	.292	.313	122	.189	-2	94	-30	-2.7
	Pit AA	3	7	.300	11	11	9	0	88.1	97	64	2	0	7	27	3.67	88	.266	.280	38	.105	-4	82	-6	-0.8
1886	Pit AA	29	21	.580	50	50	49-2	0	434.2	457	229	3	7	75	72	2.67	127	.263	.296	194	.253	2	114	31	3.2
1887	Pit N	28	21	.571	49	48	47-3	0	440.2	490	259	12	11	67	76	3.29	117	.269	.299	193	.212	-2	98	20	1.9
1888	Pit N	23	25	.479	50	50	49-6	0	437.1	446	190	9	8	53	107	2.63	100	.255	.280	175	.143	-6	83	5	0.1
1889	Pit N	23	16	.590	41	40	38-4	0	341	392	230	19	10	78	77	4.17	90	.280	.322	150	.187	-1	109	-19	-1.7
1890	Pit P	12	13	.480	26	25	23-1	0	217	275	192	3	9	49	35	4.35	90	.296	.337	97	.206	-1	102	-16	-1.2
1891	Pit N	15	14	.517	33	30	23-2	0	246.2	256	143	9	13	62	46	2.88	114	.258	.310	109	.165	-4	106	14	0.9
1892	Pit N	5	6	.455	12	12	10	0	96	104	51	0	0	28	29	2.63	126	.265	.314	41	.122	-3	109	6	0.3
	StL N	5	6	.455	12	12	10	0	92	102	47	4	3	26	27	3.23	99	.270	.322	39	.051	-5	89	0	-0.5
	Year	10	12	.455	24	24	20	0	188	206	52	4	3	54	56	2.92	111	.268	.318	80	.087	-7	99	9	-0.2
Total	14	361	308	.540	697	681	639-57	1	5941.1	6352	3315	121	61	744	1799	2.87	108	.261	.284	2702	.202	-47	99	133	9.8
GALVIN, LOU Louis J. B 4.1862 St.Paul, MN D 6.17.1895 d10.1																									
1884	StP U	0	2	.000	3	3	3	0	25	21	18	0		10	17	2.88	46	.212	.284	9	.222	-1	65	-8	-0.5

Year	Tm Lg	W	L	Pct	G	GS	CG-Sho	SV-BS	IP	H	R	HR	HB	BB-IB	SO	ERA	AERA	OAV	OOB	AB-SH	AVG	PB	Sup	APR	PW
GAMBLE, BOB Robert J. B 2.6.1867 Philadelphia, PA TR 5-10/155# d5.2																									
1888	Phi AA	0	1	.000	1	1	1	0	9	10	10	0	0	3	2	8.00	37	.270	.325	3	.333	0	19	-4	-0.3
GANDARILLAS, GUS Gustavo B 7.19.1971 Coral Gables, FL BR/TR 6/190# d7.17																									
2001	Mil N	0	0	—	16	0	0	0-0	19.2	25	13	2	0	10-3	7	5.49	78	.321	.398	0-0	—	0		-3	-0.1
GANNON, GUSSIE James Edward B 11.26.1873 Erie, PA D 4.12.1966 Erie, PA BL/TL 5-11/154# d6.15																									
1895	Pit N	0	0	—	1	0	0	0	5	7	4	0	0	2	0	1.80	250	.333	.391	2-0	.000	-0		1	0.0
GANNON, JOE Michael Joseph B 2.22.1877 St.Louis, MO D 3.19.1931 St.Louis, MO d8.28																									
1898	StL N	0	1	.000	1	1	1	0	9	13	13	0	1	5	2	11.00	34	.333	.422	3-0	.000	-1	37	-6	-0.5
GARAGOZZO, KEITH Keith John B 10.25.1969 Camden, NJ BL/TL 6/170# d4.5																									
1994	Min A	0	0	—	7	0	0	0-0	9.1	9	10	3	0	13-2	3	9.64	51	.273	.468	0-0	—	0		-4	-0.2
GARBER, GENE Henry Eugene B 11.13.1947 Lancaster, PA BR/TR 5-10/175# d6.17																									
1969	Pit N	0	0	—	2	1	0	0-0	5	6	3	3	0	1-0	3	5.40	65	.333	.368	1-0	.000	-0	102	-1	-0.1
1970	Pit N	0	3	.000	14	0	0	0-3	22.1	22	13	4	2	10-1	7	5.24	75	.275	.366	3-0	.667	1		-3	-0.2
1972	Pit N	0	0	—	4	0	0	0-0	6.1	7	5	3	0	3-0	3	7.11	47	.269	.345	1-0	.000	-0		-2	-0.1
1973	KC A	9	9	.500	48	8	4	11-5	152.2	164	78	14	2	49-15	60	4.24	97	.283	.338	0-0	—	0*	71	-1	-0.1
1974	KC A	1	2	.333	17	0	0	1-2	28	35	21	3	1	13-9	14	4.82	79	.313	.389	0-0	—	0		-4	-0.5
	Phi N	4	0	1.000	34	0	0	4-3	48	39	15	1	1	31-15	27	2.06	184	.236	.357	3-0	.000	-0		8	0.7
1975	Phi N	10	12	.455	**71**	0	0	14-6	110	104	48	13	2	27-11	69	3.60	104	.254	.302	12-1	.167	-0		2	0.4
1976	†Phi N	9	3	.750	59	0	0	11-3	92.2	78	33	4	4	30-8	92	2.82	126	.228	.295	7-3	.286	1		7	1.3
1977	†Phi N	8	6	.571	64	0	0	19-6	103.1	82	30	6	2	23-8	78	2.35	170	.220	.268	10-0	.000	-1		19	3.0
1978	Phi N	2	1	.667	22	0	0	3-1	38.2	26	6	1	3	11-3	24	1.40	256	.191	.267	3-0	.000	-0		10	0.9
	Atl N	4	4	.500	43	0	0	22-4	78.1	58	26	11	2	13-3	61	2.53	160	.204	.244	11-0	.091	-0*		11	1.9
	Year	6	5	.545	65	0	0	25-5	117	84	35	12	5	24-6	85	2.15	181	.200	.252	14-0	.071	-1		**20**	2.8
1979	Atl N	6	16	.273	68	0	0	25-8	106	121	66	10	5	24-9	56	4.33	94	.283	.326	10-2	.300	1		-6	-0.9
1980	Atl N	5	5	.500	68	0	0	7-2	82.1	95	42	6	0	24-5	51	3.83	98	.288	.335	2-0	.500	0		-2	-0.2
1981	Atl N	4	6	.400	35	0	0	2-3	58.2	49	23	2	0	20-9	34	2.61	137	.214	.277	5-0	.000	-1		4	0.8
1982	†Atl N	8	10	.444	69	0	0	30-8	119.1	100	40	4	2	32-16	68	2.34	160	.231	.285	15-2	.133	0		16	3.2
1983	Atl N	4	5	.444	43	0	0	9-8	60.2	72	37	8	2	23-7	45	4.60	85	.300	.358	3-0	.000	0		-6	-0.9
1984	Atl N	3	6	.333	62	0	0	11-5	106	103	45	7	2	24-9	55	3.06	126	.254	.294	14-1	.143	-0		7	0.7
1985	Atl N	6	6	.500	59	0	0	1-2	97.1	98	41	8	2	25-8	66	3.61	107	.263	.313	5-1	.200	0		4	0.5
1986	Atl N	5	5	.500	61	0	0	24-5	78	76	23	3	1	20-7	56	2.54	157	.260	.309	6-1	.167	0		13	2.3
1987	Atl N	8	10	.444	49	0	0	10-6	69.1	87	39	7	1	28-10	48	4.41	99	.311	.372	4-0	.000	-0		-1	-0.1
	KC A	0	0	—	13	0	0	8-0	14.1	13	5	1	1	1-0	3	2.51	182	.245	.273	0-0	—	0		3	0.4
1988	KC A	0	4	.000	26	0	0	6-2	32.2	29	15	4	2	13-2	20	3.58	112	.238	.321	0-0	—	0		1	0.2
Total	19	96	113	.459	931	9	4	218-82	1510	1464	654	123	37	445-155	940	3.34	117	.257	.312	115-11	.148	-0	76	79	13.2
GARBER, BOB Robert Mitchell B 9.10.1928 Hunker, PA D 6.7.1999 Redwood City, CA BR/TR 6-1/190# d5.13																									
1956	Pit N	0	0	—	2	0	0	0	4	3	1	1	0	3-1	3	2.25	168	.200	.333	0-0	—	0		1	0.0
GARCES, RICH Richard Aron (Mendoza) B 5.18.1971 Maracay, Venezuela BR/TR 6/250# d9.18																									
1990	Min A	0	0	—	5	0	0	2-0	5.2	4	2	0	0	4-0	1	1.59	262	.200	.333	0-0	—	0		1	0.1
1993	Min A	0	0	—	3	0	0	0-0	4	4	2	0	0	2-0	3	0.00	—	.250	.333	0-0	—	0		1	0.0
1995	Chi N	0	0	—	7	0	0	0-0	11	11	6	0	0	3-0	6	3.27	126	.256	.304	1-0	.000	-0		0	0.0
	Fla N	0	2	.000	11	0	0	0-1	13.1	14	9	1	0	8-2	16	5.40	78	.264	.361	0-0	—	0		-2	-0.3
	Year	0	2	.000	18	0	0	0-1	24.1	25	18	1	0	11-2	22	4.44	94	.260	.336	1-0	.000	-0		-2	-0.3
1996	Bos A	3	2	.600	37	0	0	0-2	44	42	26	5	0	33-5	55	4.91	103	.251	.366	0-0	—	0		1	0.2
1997	Bos A	0	1	.000	12	0	0	0-2	13.2	14	9	2	1	9-0	12	4.61	101	.255	.364	0-0	—	0		-1	0.0
1998	Bos A	1	1	.500	30	0	0	1-2	46	36	19	6	2	27-3	34	3.33	142	.213	.327	0-0	—	0		7	0.3
1999	†Bos A	5	1	.833	30	0	0	2-1	40.2	25	9	1	0	18-1	33	1.55	321	.171	.262	0-0	—	0		15	2.0
2000	Bos A	8	1	.889	64	0	0	1-4	74.2	64	28	7	1	23-5	69	3.25	155	.229	.286	0-0	—	0		15	1.5
2001	Bos A	6	1	.857	62	0	0	1-1	67	55	32	6	4	25-1	51	3.90	115	.219	.299	2-0	.000	-0		4	0.4
2002	Bos A	0	1	.000	26	0	0	0-0	21.1	21	20	4	3	12-2	16	7.59	59	.273	.379	0-0	—	0		-7	-0.3
Total	10	23	10	.697	287	0	0	7-13	341.1	290	162	32	11	164-19	296	3.74	127	.227	.317	3-0	.000	-0		34	3.9
GARCIA, MIKE Edward Miguel "The Big Bear" B 11.17.1923 San Gabriel, CA D 1.13.1986 Fairview Park, OH BR/TR 6-1/200# d10.3																									
1948	Cle A	0	0	—	1	0	0	0	2	3	0	0	0	0	1	0.00	—	.333	.333	0-0	—	0		1	0.1
1949	Cle A	14	5	.737	41	20	8-5	2	175.2	154	51	6	2	60	94	**2.36**	**169**	.241	.308	51-8	.235	3	81	34	3.7
1950	Cle A	11	11	.500	33	29	11	0	184	191	88	15	0	74	76	3.86	112	.266	.334	65-5	.200	-1	111	11	1.1
1951	Cle A	20	13	.606	47	30	15-1	6	254	239	101	10	3	82	118	3.15	120	.246	.307	85-9	.212	2	97	20	2.6
1952	Cle A☆	22	11	.667	46	**36**	19-**6**	4	292.1	284	93	9	7	87	143	2.37	141	.253	.310	95-10	.137	-2	116	33	3.7
1953	Cle A★	18	9	.667	38	35	21-3	0	271.2	260	106	18	3	81	134	3.25	116	.250	.307	96-6	.250	4	107	18	2.1
1954	†Cle A✧	19	8	.704	45	34	13-**5**	5	258.2	220	85	6	2	71	129	**2.64**	**139**	.229	**.282**	81-6	.136	-2	89	**31**	3.0
1955	Cle A	11	13	.458	38	31	6-2	3	210.2	230	101	17	3	56-6	120	4.02	99	.278	.326	69-3	.217	2	101	2	0.4
1956	Cle A	11	12	.478	35	30	8-4	0	197.2	213	93	18	5	74-5	119	3.78	111	.272	.338	61-8	.115	-3	104	10	0.6
1957	Cle A	12	8	.600	38	27	9-1	0	211.1	221	98	14	6	73-6	110	3.75	99	.269	.331	75-3	.160	-1	117	1	-0.2
1958	Cle A	1	0	1.000	6	1	0	0	8	15	10	2	1	7-0	2	9.00	41	.395	.500	1-0	.000	-0	123	-5	-0.6
1959	Cle A	3	6	.333	29	8	1	1	72	72	39	4	0	31-3	49	4.00	92	.265	.340	14-0	.071	-1	138	-4	-0.6
1960	Chi A	0	0	—	15	0	0	2	17.2	23	9	2	0	10-0	8	4.58	82	.338	.423	3-0	.333	0		-1	0.0
1961	Was A	0	1	.000	16	0	0	0	19	23	14	1	1	13-3	14	4.74	85	.287	.385	0-0	—	0		-3	-0.2
Total	14	142	97	.594	428	281	111-27	23	2174.2	2148	888	122	33	719-231	1117	3.27	117	.257	.318	696-58	.182	1	105	148	15.7
GARCIA, FREDDY Freddy Antonio B 6.10.1976 Caracas, Venezuela BR/TR 6-4/235# d4.7																									
1999	Sea A	17	8	.680	33	33	2-1	0-0	201.1	205	96	18	10	90-4	170	4.07	117	.263	.345	4-2	.250	0*	122	17	1.8
2000	†Sea A	9	5	.643	21	20	0	0-0	124.1	112	62	16	2	64-4	79	3.91	121	.241	.335	3-3	.667	1	113	10	1.0
2001	†Sea A★	18	6	.750	34	34	4-3	0-0	**238.2**	199	88	16	5	69-6	163	**3.05**	136	**.225**	.283	7-2	.143	-0	111	32	3.0
2002	Sea A★	16	10	.615	34	34	1	0-0	223.2	227	110	30	6	63-3	181	4.39	96	.260	.311	6-1	.333	1	110	-1	0.0
2003	Sea A	12	14	.462	33	33	1	0-0	201.1	196	109	31	11	71-2	144	4.51	96	.255	.323	5-0	.200	0	93	-5	-0.6
Total	5	72	43	.626	155	154	8-4	0-0	989.1	939	465	111	34	357-19	737	3.97	111	.249	.317	25-8	.280	2	110	53	5.2
GARCIA, MIKE Michael R. B 5.11.1968 Riverside, CA BR/TR 6-2/220# d9.10																									
1999	Pit N	1	0	1.000	7	0	0	0-0	7	2	1	1	0	3-0	9	1.29	355	.091	.200	0-0	—	0		3	0.3
2000	Pit N	0	2	.000	13	0	0	0-1	11.1	21	15	1	0	7-1	9	11.12	41	.429	.475	3-0	.333	0		-8	-1.1
Total	2	1	2	.333	20	0	0	0-1	18.1	23	16	2	0	10-1	18	7.36	62	.324	.393	3-0	.333	0		-5	-0.8
GARCIA, MIGUEL Miguel Angel (Silfontes) B 4.3.1967 Caracas, Venezuela BL/TL 5-11/173# d4.30																									
1987	Cal A	0	0	—	1	0	0	0-0	1.2	3	4	0	0	3-0	0	16.20	27	.375	.545	0-0	—	0		-3	-0.1
	Pit N	0	0	—	1	0	0	0-0	0.2	0	0	0	0	0-0	0	0.00	—	.000	.000	0-0	—	0		0	0.0
1988	Pit N	0	0	—	1	0	0	0-0	2	3	2	1	1	2-0	2	4.50	76	.375	.500	0-0	—	0		-1	0.0
1989	Pit N	0	2	.000	11	0	0	0-0	16	25	15	2	0	7-3	9	8.44	40	.357	.416	1-0	1.000	0		-9	-0.9
Total	3	0	2	.000	14	0	0	0-0	20.1	31	21	3	1	12-3	11	8.41	41	.352	.431	1-0	1.000	0		-13	-1.0
GARCIA, RALPH Ralph B 12.14.1948 Los Angeles, CA BR/TR 6/195# d9.26																									
1972	SD N	0	0	—	3	0	0	0-0	5	4	1	0	0	3-2	3	1.80	183	.211	.318	0-0	—	0		1	0.1
1974	SD N	0	0	—	8	0	0	0-0	10.1	15	8	1	0	7-2	9	6.10	59	.357	.431	0-0	—	0		-3	-0.1
Total	2	0	0	—	11	0	0	0-0	15.1	19	9	1	0	10-4	12	4.70	74	.311	.397	0-0	—	0		-2	0.0
GARCIA, RAMON Ramon (Garcia) B 3.5.1924 LaEsperanza, Cuba BR/TR 5-10/170# d4.19																									
1948	Was A	0	0	—	4	0	0	0	3.2	11	7	0	1	4	2	17.18	25	.524	.615	1-0	1.000	0		-5	-0.2

Year	Tm Lg	W	L	Pct	G	GS	CG-Sho	SV-BS	IP	H	R	HR	HB	BB-IB	SO	ERA	AERA	OAV	OOB	AB-SH	AVG	PB	Sup	APR	PW
GARCIA, RAMON Ramon Antonio (Fortunato) B 12.9.1969 Guanare, Venezuela BR/TR 6-2/200# d5.31																									
1991	Chi A	4	4	.500	16	15	0	0-0	78.1	79	50	13	2	31-2	40	5.40	74	.269	.340	0-0	—	0	130	-12	-1.0
1996	Mil A	4	4	.500	37	2	0	4-3	75.2	84	58	17	6	21-3	40	6.66	78	.287	.342	0-0	—	0	116	-11	-1.0
1997	†Hou N	9	8	.529	42	20	1-1	1-0	158.2	155	71	20	9	52-1	120	3.69	108	.262	.330	36-7	.111	-0	124	6	0.6
Total	3	17	16	.515	95	37	1-1	5-3	312.2	318	179	50	17	104-6	200	4.84	88	.270	.335	36-7	.111	-0	120	-17	-1.4
GARCIA, REYNALDO Reynaldo B 4.15.1974 Nagua, D.R. BR/TR 6-3/170# d7.19																									
2002	Tex A	0	0	—	3	0	0	0-0	2	7	7	3	0	1-0	2	31.50	15	.538	.571	0-0	—	0		-5	-0.3
2003	Tex A	0	0	—	17	0	0	0-0	18	19	18	6	2	14-0	15	9.00	55	.275	.407	0-0	—	0		-7	-0.3
Total	2	0	0	—	20	0	0	0-0	20	26	25	9	2	15-0	17	11.25	44	.317	.430	0-0	—	0		-12	-0.6
GARCIA, ROSMAN Rosman J. B 1.3.1979 Maracay, Venezuela BR/TR 6-2/160# d4.19																									
2003	Tex A	1	2	.333	46	0	0	0-2	46.1	63	33	4	2	23-0	25	6.02	83	.320	.395	0-0	—	0		-5	-0.3
GARDINER, ART Arthur Cecil B 12.26.1899 Brooklyn, NY D 10.21.1954 Copiague, NY BR/TR d9.25																									
1923	Phi N	0	0	—	1	0	0	0	0	1	0	0	0	1	0	—	—	1.000	1.000	0-0	—	0		0	0.0
GARDINER, MIKE Michael James B 10.19.1965 Sarnia, ON, CAN BB/TR 6/200# d9.8																									
1990	Sea A	0	2	.000	5	3	0	0-0	12.2	22	17	1	2	5-0	6	10.66	37	.379	.439	0-0	—	0	92	-9	-1.2
1991	Bos A	9	10	.474	22	22	0	0-0	130	140	79	18	0	47-2	91	4.85	89	.274	.333	0-0	—	0	103	-8	-1.1
1992	Bos A	4	10	.286	28	18	0	0-0	130.2	126	78	12	2	58-2	79	4.75	89	.253	.330	0-0	—	0	71	-7	-0.7
1993	Mon N	2	3	.400	24	2	0	0-1	38	40	28	3	1	19-2	21	5.21	80	.268	.349	4-0	.000	-0	140	-5	-0.6
	Det A	0	0	—	10	0	0	0-1	11.1	12	5	0	0	7-1	4	3.97	108	.279	.380	0-0	—	0		1	0.0
1994	Det A	2	2	.500	38	1	0	5-1	58.2	53	35	10	0	23-5	31	4.14	117	.233	.302	0-0	—	0	171	2	0.1
1995	Det A	0	0	—	9	0	0	0-1	12.1	27	20	5	0	2-1	7	14.59	33	.458	.460	0-0	—	0		-13	-0.6
Total	6	17	27	.386	136	46	0	5-4	393.2	420	262	49	5	161-13	239	5.21	84	.272	.339	4-0	.000	-0	91	-39	-4.1
GARDNER, CHRIS Christopher John B 3.30.1969 Long Beach, CA BR/TR 6/175# d9.10																									
1991	Hou N	1	2	.333	5	4	0	0-0	24.2	19	12	5	0	14-1	12	4.01	87	.218	.327	5-0	.000	-0	77	-1	-0.1
GARDNER, GID Frank Washington B 5.6.1859 Boston, MA D 8.1.1914 Cambridge, MA ?/165# d8.23 ▲																									
1879	Tro N	0	2	.000	2	2	2	0	14	27	21	0		0	3	5.79	43	.365	.365	6	.167	-0	37	-5	-0.5
1880	Cle N	1	8	.111	9	9	9	0	77	80	53	2		20	21	2.57	91	.254	.299	32	.188	-0*	58	-4	-0.4
1883	Bal AA	1	0	1.000	2	0	0	0	7	9	7	1		1	2	5.14	68	.290	.313	161	.273	1*		-1	-0.1
1884	CP U	0	1	.000	1	1	0	0	6	10	8	0		1	4	6.00	41	.345	.367	149	.255	-0*	17	-2	-0.3
1885	Bal AA	0	1	.000	1	1	1	0	9	16	13	2	1	6	3	10.00	33	.372	.460	170	.218	0*	36	-6	-0.4
Total	5	2	12	.143	15	13	12	0	113	142	102	5	1	28	33	3.90	64	.289	.328	518	.243	0	49	-18	-1.7
GARDNER, HARRY Harry Ray B 6.1.1887 Quincy, MI D 8.2.1961 Canby, OR BR/TR 6-2/180# d4.17																									
1911	Pit N	1	1	.500	13	3	2	2	42	39	25	2	2	20	24	4.50	76	.244	.335	14-0	.214	0	95	-4	-0.3
1912	Pit N	0	0	—	1	0	0	0	0.1	3	6	0	0	1	0	0.00	—	.500	.571	0-0	—	0		-2	-0.1
Total	2	1	1	.500	14	3	2	2	42.1	42	31	2	2	21	24	4.46	77	.253	.344	14-0	.214	0	95	-6	-0.4
GARDNER, JIM James Anderson B 10.4.1874 Pittsburgh, PA D 4.24.1905 Pittsburgh, PA TR d6.20																									
1895	Pit N	8	2	.800	11	10	8	0	85.1	99	53	1	6	27	31	2.64	171	.286	.348	34-0	.265	1	120	13	1.2
1897	Pit N	5	5	.500	14	11	8	0	95.1	115	72	4	9	32	35	5.19	80	.296	.363	76-2	.158	-1*	88	-10	-0.8
1898	Pit N	10	13	.435	25	22	19-1	0	185.1	179	96	3	8	48	41	3.21	111	.252	.306	91-2	.154	-2*	71	6	0.3
1899	Pit N	1	0	1.000	6	3	0	0	32.1	52	37	1	0	13	2	7.52	51	.361	.414	13-0	.231	1	163	-13	-0.6
1902	Chi N	1	2	.333	3	3	2	0	25	23	12	0	0	10	6	2.88	94	.245	.317	10-0	.200	0	101	0	0.0
Total	5	25	22	.532	59	49	37-1	0	423.1	468	270	9	23	130	115	3.85	100	.278	.338	224-4	.179	-1	93	-4	0.1
GARDNER, MARK Mark Allan B 3.1.1962 Los Angeles, CA BR/TR 6-1/205# d5.16 C1																									
1989	Mon N	0	3	.000	7	4	0	0-0	26.1	26	16	2	2	11-1	21	5.13	69	.250	.333	6-1	.167	-0	56	-4	-0.5
1990	Mon N	7	9	.438	27	26	3-3	0-0	152.2	129	62	13	9	61-5	135	3.42	107	.230	.312	44-8	.114	-1	93	5	0.5
1991	Mon N	9	11	.450	27	27	0	0-0	168.1	139	78	17	4	75-1	107	3.85	94	.230	.318	55-4	.091	-2	87	-3	-0.7
1992	Mon N	12	10	.545	33	30	0	0-0	179.2	179	91	15	9	60-2	132	4.36	80	.259	.324	50-8	.140	1	108	-16	-1.8
1993	KC A	4	6	.400	17	16	0	0-0	91.2	92	65	17	4	36-0	54	6.19	74	.271	.342	0-0	—	0	81	-14	-1.4
1994	Fla N	4	4	.500	20	14	0	0-0	92.1	97	53	14	1	30-2	57	4.87	90	.276	.331	25-4	.040	-2	98	-3	-0.5
1995	Fla N	5	5	.500	39	11	1-1	1-0	102.1	109	60	14	5	43-5	87	4.49	94	.272	.350	21-4	.190	-0	103	-5	-0.5
1996	SF N	12	7	.632	30	28	4-1	0-0	179.1	200	105	28	8	57-3	145	4.42	93	.283	.341	68-8	.162	0*	133	-9	-0.9
1997	SF N	12	9	.571	30	30	2-1	0-0	180.1	188	92	28	1	57-6	136	4.29	95	.272	.326	61-3	.115	-2*	101	-2	-0.4
1998	SF N	13	6	.684	33	33	4-2	0-0	212	203	106	29	6	65-5	151	4.33	92	.253	.311	73-4	.164	2	133	-7	-0.4
1999	SF N	5	11	.313	29	21	1	0-1	139	142	103	27	8	57-2	86	6.47	65	.267	.341	39-6	.103	0	118	-35	-3.2
2000	†SF N	11	7	.611	30	20	0	0-0	149	155	72	16	5	42-2	92	4.05	105	.270	.322	43-7	.116	-2	85	4	0.2
2001	SF N	5	5	.500	23	15	0	0-0	91.2	93	57	17	3	34-3	53	5.40	74	.263	.330	21-4	.000	-2	97	-14	-1.5
Total	13	99	93	.516	345	275	15-8	1-1	1764.2	1752	960	237	65	628-37	1256	4.56	88	.261	.327	506-61	.123	-8	104	-103	-11.1
GARDNER, GLENN Miles Glenn B 1.25.1916 Burnsville, NC D 7.7.1964 Rochester, NY BR/TR 5-11/180# d7.19																									
1945	StL N	3	1	.750	17	4	2-1	1	54.2	50	21	2	0	27	20	3.29	114	.242	.329	21-1	.333	2	130	4	0.4
GARDNER, ROB Richard Frank B 12.19.1944 Binghamton, NY BR/TL 6-1/176# d9.1																									
1965	NY N	0	2	.000	5	4	0	0	28	23	13	4	0	7-0	19	3.21	110	.217	.265	7-1	.000	-1	62	0	0.0
1966	NY N	4	8	.333	41	17	3	1	133.2	147	82	15	3	64-4	74	5.12	71	.285	.366	41-1	.171	-0*	87	-19	-1.7
1967	Chi N	0	2	.000	18	5	0	0	31.2	33	14	2	0	6-0	16	3.98	89	.260	.289	6-0	.000	-0	89	-1	-0.1
1968	Cle A	0	0	—	5	0	0	0	2.2	5	3	0	0	2-0	6	6.75	44	.417	.467	0-0	—	0		-1	-0.1
1970	NY A	1	0	1.000	1	1	0	0-0	7.1	8	4	2	0	4-0	6	4.91	72	.276	.364	3-0	.333	1	152	-1	0.0
1971	Oak A	0	0	—	4	1	0	0-0	7.2	8	2	1	0	3-0	5	2.35	142	.267	.333	2-0	.500	0	134	1	0.1
	NY A	0	0	—	2	0	0	0-0	3	3	1	0	0	2-0	2	3.00	108	.273	.385	0-0	—	0		0	0.0
	Year	0	0	—	6	1	0	0-0	10.2	11	8	1	0	5-0	7	2.53	131	.268	.348	2-0	.500	0	135	1	0.1
1972	NY A	8	5	.615	20	14	1	0-1	97	91	43	9	0	28-3	58	3.06	97	.243	.295	28-5	.107	-1	111	-4	-0.7
1973	Oak A	0	0	—	3	0	0	0-0	7.1	10	4	2	0	4-0	2	4.91	72	.370	.452	0-0	—	0		-1	-0.1
	Mil A	1	1	.500	10	0	0	1-0	12.2	17	14	0	1	13-1	5	9.95	38	.327	.470	0-0	—	0		-8	-1.2
	Year	1	1	.500	13	0	0	1-0	20	27	22	2	1	17-1	7	8.10	46	.342	.464	0-0	—	0		-9	-1.3
Total	8	14	18	.438	109	42	4	2-1	331	345	180	35	4	133-8	193	4.35	78	.269	.338	87-7	.138	-2	94	-34	-3.8
GARDNER, LEE Terrence Lee B 1.16.1975 Hartland, MI BR/TR 6/219# d5.24																									
2002	TB A	1	1	.500	12	0	0	0-2	13.1	12	11	3	3	8-0	8	4.05	110	.235	.359	0-0	—	0		-1	-0.2
GARDNER, WES Wesley Brian B 4.29.1961 Benton, AR BR/TR 6-4/197# d7.29																									
1984	NY N	1	1	.500	21	0	0	1-2	25.1	34	19	0	0	8-2	19	6.39	55	.321	.365	1-0	.000	-0		-7	-0.6
1985	NY N	0	2	.000	9	0	0	0-0	12	18	14	1	0	8-2	11	5.25	66	.375	.456	0-0	—	0		-5	-0.8
1986	Bos A	0	0	—	1	0	0	0-0	1	1	1	0	0	0-0	1	9.00	46	.333	.250	0-0	—	0		0	0.0
1987	Bos A	3	6	.333	49	1	0	10-2	89.2	98	55	17	2	42-7	70	5.42	84	.279	.358	0-0	—	0	80	-7	-0.8
1988	†Bos A	8	6	.571	36	18	1	2-0	149	119	61	17	3	64-2	106	3.50	118	.220	.302	0-0	—	0	98	11	1.0
1989	Bos A	3	7	.300	22	16	0	0-0	86	97	64	10	1	47-7	81	5.97	69	.287	.372	0-0	—	0	116	-17	-1.7
1990	Bos A	3	7	.300	34	9	0	0-2	77.1	77	43	6	2	35-0	58	4.89	84	.259	.339	0-0	—	0	74	-5	-0.6
1991	SD N	0	1	.000	14	0	0	1-0	20.1	27	16	1	0	12-1	9	7.08	54	.310	.394	2-0	.000	-0		-6	-0.4
	KC A	0	0	—	3	0	0	0-0	5.2	5	4	0	0	2-0	3	1.59	260	.208	.269	0-0	—	0		0	0.0
Total	8	18	30	.375	189	44	1	14-6	466.1	476	277	52	8	218-21	358	4.90	84	.265	.344	3-0	.000	-0	99	-36	-3.9
GARDNER, BILL William A. B 9.1868 Baltimore, MD d8.9																									
1887	Bal AA	0	1	.000	3	2	1	0	13	23	20	0	1	10	3	11.08	37	.426	.523	11	.273	0*	124	-9	-0.5
GARFIELD, BILL William Milton B 10.26.1867 Sheffield, OH D 12.16.1941 Danville, IL BR/TR 5-11.5/160# d7.10																									
1889	Pit N	0	2	.000	4	2	2	0	29	45	35	2	1	17	4	7.76	48	.344	.423	13	.000	-2	81	-14	-0.8
1890	Cle N	1	7	.125	9	8	7	0	70	91	64	3	8	35	16	4.89	73	.304	.392	26	.154	-1	42	-12	-1.1

Year	Tm Lg	W	L	Pct	G	GS	CG-Sho	SV-BS	IP	H	R	HR	HB	BB-IB	SO	ERA	AERA	OAV	OOB	AB-SH	AVG	PB	Sup	APR	PW
Total	2	1	9	.100	13	10	9	0	99	136	99	5	9	52	20	5.73	64	.316	.401	39	.103	-3	50	-26	-1.9
GARIBALDI, BOB Robert Roy B 3.3.1942 Stockton, CA BL/TR 6-4/210# d7.15																									
1962	SF N	0	0	—	9	0	0	1	12.1	13	7	1	0	5-0	9	5.11	74	.265	.327	1-0	.000	-0		-1	-0.1
1963	SF N	0	1	.000	4	0	0	1	8	8	2	0	1	4-2	4	1.13	284	.276	.382	1-0	.000	-0		2	0.2
1966	SF N	0	0	—	1	0	0	0	1	1	0	0	0	0-0	0	0.00	—	.250	.250	0-0	—	0		0	0.0
1969	SF N	0	1	.000	1	1	0	0-0	5	6	4	0	0	2-0	1	1.80	195	.316	.381	2-0	.000	-0	101	0	-0.1
Total	4	0	2	.000	15	1	0	2-0	26.1	28	13	1	1	11-2	14	3.08	116	.277	.351	4-0	.000	-0	101	1	0.0
GARIBAY, DANIEL Daniel (Bravo) B 2.14.1973 Maneadero, Mexico BL/TL 5-8/154# d4.9																									
2000	Chi N	2	8	.200	30	8	0	0-2	74.2	88	54	9	1	39-1	46	6.03	75	.299	.376	15-4	.133	-1	66	-13	-1.4
GARLAND, JON Jon Steven B 9.27.1979 Valencia, CA BR/TR 6-6/205# d7.4																									
2000	Chi A	4	8	.333	15	13	0	0-0	69.2	82	55	10	1	40-0	42	6.46	77	.292	.380	0-0	—	0	103	-11	-1.5
2001	Chi A	6	7	.462	35	16	0	1-0	117	123	59	16	4	55-2	61	3.69	125	.277	.358	2-0	.000	-0	87	9	0.9
2002	Chi A	12	12	.500	33	33	1-1	0-0	192.2	188	109	23	9	83-1	112	4.58	99	.258	.340	2-1	.000	-0	85	-2	-0.2
2003	Chi A	12	13	.480	32	32	0	0-0	191.2	188	103	28	4	74-1	108	4.51	101	.260	.329	2-1	.000	0	101	1	0.2
Total	4	34	40	.459	115	94	1-1	1-0	571	581	326	77	18	252-4	323	4.60	100	.267	.345	6-2	.000	-0	94	-3	-0.6
GARLAND, LOU Louis Lyman B 7.16.1905 Archie, MO D 8.30.1990 Idaho Falls, ID BR/TR 6-2.5/200# d8.31																									
1931	Chi A	0	2	.000	7	2	0	0	16.2	30	24	2	1	14	4	10.26	41	.400	.500	3-0	.000	-0	109	-12	-1.1
GARLAND, WAYNE Marcus Wayne B 10.26.1950 Nashville, TN BR/TR 6/195# d9.13																									
1973	Bal A	0	1	.000	4	1	0	0-0	16	14	8	1	0	7-0	10	3.94	95	.233	.313	0-0	—	0	48	0	0.0
1974	†Bal A	5	5	.500	20	6	0	1-0	91	68	37	5	3	26-3	40	2.97	117	.211	.272	0-0	—	0	98	4	0.4
1975	Bal A	2	5	.286	29	1	0	4-1	87.1	80	37	7	1	31-6	46	3.71	95	.252	.316	0-0	—	0	125	-1	-0.1
1976	Bal A	20	7	.741	38	25	14-4	1-1	232.1	224	81	10	6	64-9	113	2.67	123	.255	.306	0-0	—	0	107	14	1.7
1977	Cle A	13	19	.406	38	38	21-1	0-0	282.2	281	130	23	2	88-8	118	3.60	110	.261	.316	0-0	—	0	95	10	1.0
1978	Cle A	2	3	.400	6	6	0	0-0	29.2	43	27	6	1	16-1	13	7.89	48	.347	.423	0-0	—	0	104	-13	-1.7
1979	Cle A	4	10	.286	18	14	2	0-0	94.2	120	70	11	3	34-2	40	5.23	82	.318	.371	0-0	—	0	76	-14	-1.8
1980	Cle A	6	9	.400	25	20	4-1	0-0	150.1	163	85	18	6	48-2	55	4.61	89	.276	.334	0-0	—	0	120	-9	-0.9
1981	Cle A	3	7	.300	12	10	2-1	0-0	56	89	40	8	0	14-0	15	5.79	63	.374	.399	0-0	—	0	77	-14	-2.1
Total	9	55	66	.455	190	121	43-7	6-2	1040	1082	515	89	22	328-31	450	3.89	96	.272	.327	0-0	—	0	99	-23	-3.5
GARMAN, MIKE Michael Douglas B 9.16.1949 Caldwell, ID BR/TR 6-3/215# d9.22																									
1969	Bos A	1	0	1.000	2	2	0	0-0	12.1	13	6	0	0	10-0	10	4.38	87	.277	.404	5-0	.400	1	116	0	0.0
1971	Bos A	1	1	.500	3	3	0	0-0	18.2	15	8	3	1	9-1	6	3.86	96	.217	.313	6-0	.333	0	105	0	0.0
1972	Bos A	0	1	.000	3	1	0	0-0	3.1	4	4	1	0	2-0	1	10.80	30	.286	.375	0-0	—	0	82	-2	-0.5
1973	Bos A	0	0	—	12	0	0	0-0	22	32	15	1	0	15-3	9	5.32	76	.352	.439	0-0	—	0		-3	-0.2
1974	StL N	7	2	.778	64	0	0	6-3	81.2	66	26	4	2	27-10	45	2.64	136	.227	.297	10-1	.100	-1		9	1.0
1975	StL N	3	8	.273	66	0	0	10-6	79	73	31	3	1	48-23	48	2.39	157	.245	.347	2-0	.000	-0		9	1.4
1976	Chi N	2	4	.333	47	2	0	1-1	76.1	79	48	7	3	35-8	37	4.95	78	.273	.351	7-0	.000	-1	23	-9	-0.7
1977	†LA N	4	4	.500	49	0	0	12-5	62.2	60	20	7	2	22-5	29	2.73	140	.254	.323	7-0	.000	-1		8	1.2
1978	LA N	0	1	.000	10	0	0	0-1	16.1	15	8	3	0	3-0	5	4.41	80	.259	.295	0-0	—	0		-1	-0.1
	Mon N	4	6	.400	47	0	0	13-6	61.1	54	32	5	0	31-8	23	4.40	80	.238	.327	5-0	.000	-1		-5	-1.2
	Year	4	7	.364	57	0	0	13-7	77.2	69	41	8	0	34-8	28	4.40	80	.242	.321	5-0	.000	-1		-7	-1.3
Total	9	22	27	.449	303	8	0	42-22	433.2	411	198	34	9	202-58	213	3.63	103	.254	.337	42-1	.119	-2	83	6	0.9
GARONI, WILLIE William B 7.28.1877 Ft.Lee, NJ D 9.9.1914 Ft.Lee, NJ BR/TR 6-1/165# d9.7																									
1899	NY N	0	1	.000	3	1	1	0	10	12	7	0	0	2	2	4.50	83	.300	.333	4-0	.000	-1	77	-1	-0.1
GARRELTS, SCOTT Scott William B 10.30.1961 Urbana, IL BR/TR 6-4/195# d10.2																									
1982	SF N	0	0	—	1	0	0	0-0	2	3	3	0	0	2-0	4	13.50	27	.333	.455	0-0	—	0		-2	-0.1
1983	SF N	2	2	.500	5	5	1-1	0-0	35.2	33	11	4	2	19-4	16	2.52	140	.254	.358	9-3	.222	0	65	4	0.5
1984	SF N	2	3	.400	21	3	0	0-1	43	45	33	6	1	34-1	32	5.65	62	.274	.398	10-0	.100	-0	218	-12	-1.3
1985	SF N☆	9	6	.600	74	0	0	13-8	105.2	76	37	2	3	58-12	106	2.30	150	.198	.306	9-0	.222	1		11	2.0
1986	SF N	13	9	.591	53	18	2	10-6	173.2	144	65	17	2	74-11	125	3.11	113	.231	.311	45-7	.178	2*	90	10	1.6
1987	†SF N	11	7	.611	64	0	0	12-10	106.1	70	41	10	0	55-4	127	3.22	120	.192	.297	10-0	.200	1*		8	1.5
1988	SF N	5	9	.357	65	0	0	13-6	98	80	42	3	2	46-10	86	3.58	91	.226	.317	13-0	.077	-1		-3	-0.5
1989	†SF N	14	5	.737	30	29	2-1	0-0	193.1	149	58	11	0	46-3	119	**2.28**	**148**	.212	**.258**	66-2	.136	1*	120	23	2.3
1990	SF N	12	11	.522	31	31	4-2	0-0	182	190	91	16	3	70-8	80	4.15	88	.272	.339	66-0	.061	-3*	94	-11	-1.6
1991	SF N	1	1	.500	8	3	0	0-0	19.2	25	14	5	0	9-0	8	6.41	56	.313	.378	4-1	.000	-0*	201	-6	-0.6
Total	10	69	53	.566	352	89	9-4	48-31	959.1	815	395	74	13	413-53	703	3.29	107	.232	.313	232-13	.125	-1	108	22	3.8
GARRETT, CLARENCE Clarence Raymond "Laz" B 3.6.1891 Reader, WV D 2.11.1977 Moundsville, WV BR/TR 6-5.5/185# d9.13																									
1915	Cle A	2	2	.500	4	4	2	0	23.1	19	13	1	1	6	5	2.31	132	.224	.283	8-0	.000	-0	102	0	0.1
GARRETT, GREG Gregory B 3.12.1948 Atascadero, CA D 6.7.2003 Newhall, CA BB/TL 6/200# d4.24																									
1970	Cal A	5	6	.455	32	7	0	0-0	74.2	48	23	6	1	44-9	53	2.65	136	.190	.309	15-1	.067	-1	88	9	1.2
1971	Cin N	0	1	.000	2	1	0	0-0	8.2	7	1	0	0	10-0	2	1.04	324	.250	.447	3-0	.333	0	0	2	0.3
Total	2	5	7	.417	34	8	0	0-0	83.1	55	24	6	1	54-9	55	2.48	145	.196	.324	18-1	.111	-1	78	11	1.5
GARRISON, CLIFF Clifford William B 8.13.1906 Bellemont, OK D 8.25.1994 Woodland, CA BR/TR 6/180# d4.16																									
1928	Bos A	0	0	—	6	0	0	0	16	22	15	2	0	6	0	7.88	52	.361	.418	3-0	.000	-0		-6	-0.3
GARRY, JIM James Thomas B 9.21.1869 Great Barrington, MA D 1.15.1917 Pittsfield, MA BL/TL 5-10/165# d5.2																									
1893	Bos N	0	1	.000	1	0	0	0	1	5	8	0	0	4	2	63.00	8	.625	.750	1	.000	-0		-6	-0.7
GARVER, NED Ned Franklin B 12.25.1925 Ney, OH BR/TR 5-10.5/180# d4.28																									
1948	StL A	7	11	.389	38	24	7	5	198	200	92	14	1	95	75	3.41	134	.268	.352	66-9	.288	4*	78	20	2.2
1949	StL A	12	17	.414	41	32	16-1	3	223.2	245	126	14	3	102	70	3.98	114	.277	.354	75-4	.187	1*	78	9	1.2
1950	StL A	13	18	.419	37	31	**22**-2	0	260	264	120	18	4	108	85	3.39	**146**	.264	.338	91-7	.286	4*	75	**39**	**4.9**
1951	StL A★	20	12	.625	33	30	**24**-1	0	246	237	114	17	5	96	84	3.73	118	.255	.328	95-5	.305	7*	97	17	2.9
1952	StL A	7	10	.412	21	21	7-2	0	148.2	130	67	14	4	55	60	3.69	106	.235	.309	49-1	.184	0*	76	5	0.6
	Det A	1	0	1.000	1	1	1	0	9	9	2	1	0	3	3	2.00	190	.265	.324	2-0	.000	0	92	2	0.3
	Year	8	10	.444	22	22	8-2	0	157.2	139	6	15	4	58	63	3.60	109	.237	.310	51-1	.176	0	77	7	0.9
1953	Det A	11	11	.500	30	26	13	1	198.1	228	107	16	2	66	69	4.45	91	.290	.347	72-4	.153	-1	93	-7	-0.8
1954	Det A	14	11	.560	35	32	16-3	1	246.1	216	93	20	4	62	93	2.81	131	.236	.286	79-5	.165	-0*	106	22	2.2
1955	Det A	12	16	.429	33	32	16-1	0	230.2	251	115	21	5	67-10	83	3.98	97	.279	.330	76-3	.224	5	111	-3	0.1
1956	Det A	0	2	.000	6	3	1	0	17.2	15	10	2	1	13-0	6	4.08	101	.234	.367	5-0	.000	-0	79	0	-0.1
1957	KC A	6	13	.316	24	23	6-1	0	145.1	120	72	13	5	55-5	61	3.84	103	.223	.298	44-2	.182	0	82	1	0.1
1958	KC A	12	11	.522	31	28	10-3	1	201	192	97	24	2	66-8	72	4.03	97	.244	.303	69-4	.174	0	103	-2	0.2
1959	KC A	10	13	.435	32	30	9-2	1	201.1	214	94	22	3	42-0	61	3.71	108	.270	.308	71-4	.282	6	104	7	1.4
1960	KC A	4	9	.308	28	15	5-2	0	122.1	110	57	15	2	35-2	50	3.83	104	.240	.293	27-4	.074	-1	65	3	0.2
1961	LA A	0	3	.000	12	2	0	0	29	40	18	2	0	16-0	9	5.59	81	.348	.427	6-1	.000	-1	29	-2	-0.2
Total	14	129	157	.451	402	330	153-18	12	2477.1	2471	1184	213	41	881-25	881	3.73	112	.260	.325	827-53	.218	24	89	111	15.2
GARVIN, JERRY Theodore Jared B 10.21.1955 Oakland, CA BL/TL 6-3/195# d4.10																									
1977	Tor A	10	18	.357	34	34	12-1	0-0	244.2	247	127	33	4	85-5	127	4.19	100	.264	.326	0-0	—	0	77	1	0.4
1978	Tor A	4	12	.250	26	22	3	0-1	144.2	189	92	20	4	48-4	67	5.54	71	.319	.372	0-0	—	0	88	-23	-2.2
1979	Tor A	0	1	.000	8	1	0	0-1	22.2	15	9	2	2	10-0	14	2.78	157	.197	.300	0-0	—	0	166	3	0.1
1980	Tor A	4	7	.364	61	0	0	8-5	82.2	70	23	6	0	27-7	52	2.29	189	.233	.296	0-0	—	0		18	2.6
1981	Tor A	1	2	.333	35	4	0	0-1	53	46	20	3	0	23-4	25	3.40	116	.240	.318	0-0	—	0	63	4	0.2
1982	Tor A	1	1	.500	32	4	0	0-1	58.1	81	48	10	1	26-2	35	7.25	62	.335	.400	0-0	—	0	107	-15	-0.6
Total	6	20	41	.328	196	65	15-1	8-9	606	648	319	74	11	219-22	320	4.43	94	.277	.340	0-0	—	0	82	-12	0.5

Year	Tm Lg	W	L	Pct	G	GS	CG-Sho	SV-BS	IP	H	R	HR	HB	BB-IB	SO	ERA	AERA	OAV	OOB	AB-SH	AVG	PB	Sup	APR	PW
GARVIN, NED Virgil Lee B 1.1.1874 Navasota, TX D 6.16.1908 Fresno, CA BR/TR 6-3.5/160# d7.13																									
1896	Phi N	0	1	.000	2	1	1	0	13	19	13	0	0	7	4	7.62	57	.339	.413	6-0	.000	-1	132	-4	-0.3
1899	Chi N	9	13	.409	24	23	22-4	0	199	202	101	1	12	42	69	2.85	132	.263	.311	71-5	.155	-5	102	19	1.3
1900	Chi N	10	18	.357	30	28	25-1	0	246.1	225	126	4	18	63	107	2.41	150	.243	.304	91-0	.154	-5	73	28	2.4
1901	Mil A	8	20	.286	37	27	22-1	1	257.1	258	155	4	14	90	122	3.46	104	.258	.328	93-4	.108	-9	63	2	-0.5
1902	Chi A	10	10	.500	23	19	16-2	0	175.1	169	68	3	8	43	55	2.21	153	.254	.307	59-1	.153	-2	76	19	1.8
	Bro N	1	1	.500	2	2	2-1	0	18	15	3	0	0	4	7	1.00	277	.227	.271	7-0	.143	-0	98	3	0.4
1903	Bro N	15	18	.455	38	34	30-2	2	298	277	163	2	13	84	154	3.08	104	.248	.308	106-5	.075	-8	109	-1	-0.6
1904	Bro N	5	15	.250	23	22	16-2	0	181.2	141	81	6	6	78	86	1.68	163	.218	.308	63-3	.127	-4	66	12	1.1
	NY A	0	1	.000	2	2	0	0	12	14	4	0	0	2	8	2.25	121	.292	.320	4-0	.000	-1	53	1	0.0
Total	7	58	97	.374	181	158	134-13	3	1400.2	1320	714	20	71	413	612	2.72	125	.249	.312	500-18	.122	-35	83	79	5.6
GASPAR, HARRY Harry Lambert B 4.28.1883 Kingsley, IA D 5.14.1940 Orange, CA BR/TR 6/180# d4.21																									
1909	Cin N	19	11	.633	44	29	19-4	2	260	228	97	0	9	57	65	2.01	129	.242	.291	82-10	.122	-3	103	14	1.0
1910	Cin N	15	17	.469	48	31	16-4	**7**	275	257	103	6	15	75	74	2.59	113	.255	.317	87-1	.115	-3	100	14	1.2
1911	Cin N	11	17	.393	44	32	11-2	4	253.2	272	112	9	14	69	76	3.30	100	.283	.340	85-1	.153	-2	92	6	0.3
1912	Cin N	1	3	.250	7	6	2-1	0	36.2	38	21	0	1	16	13	4.17	81	.277	.357	12-0	.250	0	127	-3	-0.2
Total	4	46	48	.489	143	98	48-11	13	825.1	795	333	15	39	217	228	2.69	110	.261	.318	266-12	.135	-9	100	31	2.3
GASSAWAY, CHARLIE Charles Cason "Sheriff" B 8.12.1918 Gassaway, TN D 1.15.1992 Miami, FL BL/TL 6-2.5/210# d9.25																									
1944	Chi N	0	1	.000	2	2	0	0	11.2	20	11	3	0	10	7	7.71	46	.385	.484	4-0	.250	0	95	-5	-0.3
1945	Phi A	4	7	.364	24	11	4	0	118	114	59	4	2	55	50	3.74	92	.252	.336	39-0	.154	-2	72	-5	-0.7
1946	Cle A	1	1	.500	13	6	0	0	50.2	54	25	2	4	26	23	3.91	85	.273	.368	15-0	.067	-1	99	-4	-0.3
Total	3	5	9	.357	39	19	4	0	180.1	188	95	9	6	91	80	4.04	84	.268	.357	58-0	.138	-3	83	-14	-1.3
GASTON, MILT Nathaniel Milton B 1.27.1896 Ridgefield Park, NJ D 4.26.1996 Barnstable, MA BR/TR 6-1/185# d4.20 b-Alex																									
1924	NY A	5	3	.625	29	2	0	1	86	92	48	3	6	44	24	4.50	92	.286	.382	27-2	.222	-1	51	-3	-0.4
1925	StL A	15	14	.517	42	29	16	1	238.2	284	146	8	5	101	84	4.41	106	.305	.376	80-6	.262	2	102	4	0.6
1926	StL A	10	18	.357	32	28	14-1	0	214.1	227	116	13	4	101	39	4.33	99	.283	.366	78-2	.167	-2	79	2	0.0
1927	StL A	13	17	.433	37	30	21	1	254	275	177	18	3	100	77	5.00	87	.281	.350	96-5	.260	5	102	-20	-1.4
1928	Was A	6	12	.333	28	22	8-3	0	148.2	179	102	3	0	53	45	5.51	73	.302	.360	49-4	.143	-3	108	-23	-2.5
1929	Bos A	12	19	.387	39	28	20-1	2	243.2	265	121	15	3	81	83	3.73	115	.289	.348	78-4	.192	0	76	14	1.6
1930	Bos A	13	20	.394	38	34	20-2	2	273	272	138	15	0	98	99	3.92	117	.259	.323	98-5	.204	-4	81	20	1.8
1931	Bos A	2	13	.133	23	18	4	0	119	137	76	4	0	41	33	4.46	96	.291	.348	38-1	.158	-2	60	-6	-0.8
1932	Chi A	7	17	.292	28	25	7-1	1	166.2	183	101	10	1	73	44	4.00	108	.279	.352	60-0	.233	2	80	3	0.6
1933	Chi A	8	12	.400	30	25	7-1	0	167	177	106	9	1	60	39	4.85	87	.272	.334	52-2	.154	-0	84	-11	-1.1
1934	Chi A	6	19	.240	29	28	10-1	0	194	247	146	16	1	84	48	5.85	81	.313	.379	68-1	.147	-3	77	-23	-2.5
Total	11	97	164	.372	355	269	127-10	8	2105	2338	1277	114	24	836	615	4.55	97	.287	.355	724-32	.200	-5	85	-43	-4.1
GASTON, WELCOME Welcome Thornburg B 12.19.1872 Guernsey Co., OH D 12.13.1944 Columbus, OH TL d10.6																									
1898	Bro N	1	1	.500	2	2	2	0	16	17	9	0	0	9	0	2.81	127	.270	.361	8-0	.125	-0	178	1	0.0
1899	Bro N	0	0	—	1	0	0	0	3	3	1	0	1	4	0	3.00	130	.250	.471	1-0	1.000	1		0	0.1
Total	2	1	1	.500	3	2	2	0	19	20	10	0	1	13	0	2.84	128	.267	.382	9-0	.222	1	178	1	0.1
GASTRIGHT, HANK Henry Carl (b: Henry Carl Gastreich) B 3.29.1865 Covington, KY D 10.9.1937 Cold Spring, KY BR/TR 6-2/190# d4.19																									
1889	Col AA	10	16	.385	32	26	21	0	222.2	255	175	8	5	104	115	4.57	79	.279	.355	94	.181	-4	76	-24	-2.4
1890	Col AA	30	14	.682	48	45	41-4	0	401.1	312	204	8	18	135	199	2.94	122	.208	.281	169	.213	3	131	30	2.7
1891	Col AA	12	19	.387	35	33	28-1	0	283.2	280	196	7	11	136	109	3.78	91	.249	.336	117	.197	2	105	-16	-1.1
1892	Was N	3	3	.500	11	8	6	0	79.2	94	54	3	3	38	32	5.08	64	.282	.361	29	.138	0*	136	-10	-0.6
1893	Pit N	3	1	.750	9	5	3	0	59	74	54	3	3	39	12	6.25	73	.297	.399	24	.042	-4	120	-10	-0.7
	Bos N	12	4	.750	19	18	16	0	156	179	117	9	9	76	27	5.13	96	.279	.364	68	.191	-3*	105	-1	-0.4
	Year	15	5	**.750**	28	23	19	0	215	253	124	12	12	115	39	5.44	89	.284	.374	92	.152	-6	108	-4	-1.1
1894	Bro N	2	6	.250	16	8	6-1	2	93	135	85	1	6	55	20	6.39	78	.335	.422	41-0	.171	-3	112	-13	-1.0
1896	Cin N	0	0	—	1	0	0	0	6	8	6	0	0	1	0	4.50	103	.320	.346	2-0	.000	-0		-1	-0.1
Total	7	72	63	.533	171	143	121-6	2	1301.1	1337	891	39	55	584	514	4.20	92	.258	.339	544-0	.186	-8	110	-45	-3.6
GATEWOOD, AUBREY Aubrey Lee B 11.17.1938 Little Rock, AR BR/TR 6-1/170# d9.11																									
1963	LA A	1	1	.500	4	3	1	0	24	12	5	0	0	16-0	13	1.50	228	.148	.283	8-0	.000	-1	69	5	0.3
1964	LA A	3	3	.500	15	7	0	0	60.1	59	18	4	1	12-1	25	2.24	147	.258	.295	20-0	.100	-1*	85	8	0.6
1965	Cal A	4	5	.444	46	3	0	0	92	91	41	5	1	37-3	37	3.42	99	.266	.336	14-0	.214	1	43	-1	0.0
1970	Atl N	0	0	—	3	0	0	0-0	2	4	6	0	1	2-1	0	4.50	95	.364	.500	0-0	—	0		-2	-0.1
Total	4	8	9	.471	68	13	1	0-0	178.1	166	70	9	3	67-5	75	2.78	122	.250	.318	42-0	.119	-1	70	10	0.8
GAUDIN, CHAD Chad Edward B 3.24.1983 Metairie, LA BR/TR 5-10/170# d8.1																									
2003	TB A	2	0	1.000	15	3	0	0-0	40	37	18	4	1	16-0	23	3.60	126	.240	.312	0-0	—	0	115	4	0.2
GAW, CHIPPY George Joseph B 3.13.1892 W.Newton, MA D 5.26.1968 Boston, MA BR/TR 5-11/180# d4.20																									
1920	Chi N	1	1	.500	6	1	0	0	13	16	9	1	1	3	4	4.85	66	.320	.370	4-0	.250	-0	74	-2	-0.4
GEAR, DALE Dale Dudley B 2.2.1872 Lone Elm, KS D 9.23.1951 Topeka, KS BR/TR 5-11/165# d8.15 ▲																									
1896	Cle N	0	2	.000	3	2	2	0	23	35	23	1	2	6	6	5.48	83	.347	.394	15-0	.400	2*	102	-3	-0.1
1901	Was A	4	11	.267	24	16	14-1	1	163	199	100	9	4	22	35	4.03	91	.297	.324	199-2	.236	0*	78	-5	-0.3
Total	2	4	13	.235	27	18	16-1	1	186	234	123	10	6	28	41	4.21	90	.304	.333	214-2	.248	2	81	-8	-0.4
GEARIN, DINTY Dennis John B 10.15.1897 Providence, RI D 3.11.1959 Providence, RI BL/TL 5-4/148# d8.6																									
1923	†NY N	1	1	.500	6	2	1	0	24	23	11	1	0	10	9	3.38	113	.264	.340	7-0	.286	0	65	1	0.1
1924	NY N	1	2	.333	6	3	2	0	29	30	9	3	0	16	4	2.48	148	.275	.368	9-0	.333	0*	154	4	0.4
	Bos N	0	1	.000	1	1	0	0	0	3	5	0	0	2	0	∞	—	1.000	1.000	0-0	—	0	178	-5	-0.4
	Year	1	3	.250	7	4	2	0	29	33	13	3	0	18	4	4.03	91	.295	.392	9-0	.333	0	162	-1	0.0
Total	2	2	4	.333	13	6	3	0	53	56	25	4	0	28	13	3.74	100	.281	.370	16-0	.313	1	127	0	0.1
GEARY, GEOFF Geoffrey Michael B 8.26.1976 Buffalo, NY BR/TR 6/170# d8.27																									
2003	Phi N	0	0	—	5	0	0	0-0	6	8	3	0	0	3-0	3	4.50	89	.333	.407	0-0	—	0		0	0.0
GEARY, BOB Robert Norton "Speed" B 5.10.1891 Cincinnati, OH D 1.3.1980 Cincinnati, OH BR/TR 5-11/168# d4.25 Mil 1918																									
1918	Phi A	2	5	.286	16	7	6-2	4	87	94	37	0	3	31	22	2.69	109	.289	.357	27-1	.148	-1	81	1	0.0
1919	Phi A	0	3	.000	9	2	1	0	32.1	32	22	1	0	18	9	4.73	72	.264	.360	10-0	.500	2	69	-5	-0.2
1921	Cin N	1	1	.500	10	1	0	0	29	38	17	1	0	2	10	4.34	82	.333	.345	8-0	.250	0	138	-2	-0.2
Total	3	3	9	.250	35	10	7-2	4	148.1	164	76	2	3	51	41	3.46	92	.293	.355	45-1	.244	1	83	-6	-0.4
GEBHARD, BOB Robert Henry B 1.3.1943 Lamberton, MN BR/TR 6-2/210# d8.2 C1																									
1971	Min A	1	2	.333	17	0	0	0-0	18	17	6	0	1	11-3	13	3.00	119	.243	.354	0-0	—	0		1	0.3
1972	Min A	0	1	.000	13	0	0	1-0	21	36	29	3	2	13-2	13	8.57	38	.371	.447	0-0	—	0		-14	-0.8
1974	Mon N	0	0	—	1	0	0	0-0	2	5	1	1	0	0-0	0	4.50	86	.500	.500	0-0	—	0		0	0.0
Total	3	1	3	.250	31	0	0	1-0	41	58	36	4	3	24-5	26	5.93	57	.328	.413	0-0	—	0		-13	-0.5
GEBRIAN, PETE Peter "Gabe" B 8.10.1923 Bayonne, NJ BR/TR 6/170# d5.6																									
1947	Chi A	2	3	.400	27	4	0	5	66.1	61	40	7	2	33	17	4.48	82	.247	.340	13-1	.000	-2	48	-7	-0.8
GEDDES, JIM James Lee B 3.23.1949 Columbus, OH BR/TR 6-2/200# d4.28																									
1972	Chi A	0	0	—	5	1	0	0-0	10.1	12	9	1	1	10-0	3	6.97	45	.293	.442	1-1	.000	-0*	170	-4	-0.3
1973	Chi A	0	0	—	6	1	0	0-0	15.2	14	6	0	3	14-0	7	2.87	138	.255	.431	0-0	—	0	45	2	0.1
Total	2	0	0	—	11	2	0	0-0	26	26	15	1	4	24-0	10	4.50	81	.271	.435	1-1	.000	-0	98	-2	-0.2
GEDNEY, COUNT Alfred W. B 5.10.1849 Brooklyn, NY D 3.26.1922 Hackensack, NJ 5-9/140# d4.27.1872 ▲																									
1875	Mut NA	1	0	1.000	2	1	1	0	11	7	4	0		1	2	0.82	285	.167	.186	267	.206	-0*	136	1	0.1

Year	Tm Lg	W	L	Pct	G	GS	CG-Sho	SV-BS	IP	H	R	HR	HB	BB-IB	SO	ERA	AERA	OAV	OOB	AB-SH	AVG	PB	Sup	APR	PW
GEE, JOHNNY John Alexander "Whiz" B 12.7.1915 Syracuse, NY D 1.23.1988 Cortland, NY BL/TL 6-9/225# d9.17 Def 1945																									
1939	Pit N	1	2	.333	3	3	1	0	19.2	20	17	0	0	10	16	4.12	93	.253	.337	6-0	.000	-1	83	-4	-0.5
1941	Pit N	0	2	.000	3	2	0	0	7.1	10	10	0	0	5	2	6.14	59	.294	.385	3-0	.333	0	106	-4	-0.7
1943	Pit N	4	4	.500	15	10	2	0	82	89	42	5	0	27	18	4.28	81	.280	.336	26-2	.115	-1	122	-4	-0.6
1944	Pit N	0	0	—	4	0	0	0	11.1	20	10	0	0	5	3	7.15	52	.377	.431	2-0	.500	0		-4	-0.2
	NY N	0	0	—	4	0	0	0	4.2	5	1	0	0	0	3	0.00	—	.263	.263	0-0	—	0		1	0.1
	Year	0	0	—	8	0	0	0	16	25	16	0	0	5	6	5.06	73	.347	.390	2-0	.500	0		-2	-0.1
1945	NY N	0	0	—	2	0	0	1	3	5	3	0	0	2	1	9.00	43	.385	.467	1-0	.000	-0		-1	-0.1
1946	NY N	2	4	.333	13	6	1	0	47.1	60	27	3	2	15	22	3.99	86	.308	.363	13-1	.231	0	46	-4	-0.5
Total	6	7	12	.368	44	21	4	1	175.1	209	110	8	2	64	65	4.41	80	.294	.354	51-3	.157	-1	93	-20	-2.5
GEHRING, HENRY Henry B 1.24.1881 St.Paul, MN D 4.18.1912 Kansas City, MO BR/TR d7.16																									
1907	Was A	3	7	.300	15	9	8-2	0	87	92	44	1	1	14	31	3.31	73	.274	.305	44-0	.205	3*	93	-8	-0.7
1908	Was A	0	1	.000	3	1	0	0	5	9	8	0	2	2	0	14.40	16	.450	.542	5-0	.600	2*	90	-6	-0.7
Total	2	3	8	.273	18	10	8-2	0	92	101	52	1	3	16	31	3.91	62	.284	.320	49-0	.245	5	93	-14	-1.4
GEHRMAN, PAUL Paul Arthur "Dutch" B 5.3.1912 Marquam, OR D 10.23.1986 Bend, OR BR/TR 6/195# d9.15																									
1937	Cin N	0	1	.000	2	1	0	0	9.1	11	8	0	0	5	1	2.89	129	.282	.364	3-0	.000	-0	116	-1	-0.1
GEIS, EMIL Emil Michael B 3.1861 Villmar, Germany BR/TR 5-11/170# d7.19																									
1882	Bal AA	4	9	.308	13	13	10-1	0	95.2	84	73	2		22	10	4.80	57	.220	.263	41	.146	-2	59	-16	-1.9
GEISEL, DAVE John David B 1.18.1955 Windber, PA BL/TL 6-3/210# d6.13																									
1978	Chi N	1	0	1.000	18	1	0	0-0	23.1	27	12	0	0	11-4	15	4.24	95	.278	.352	3-0	.000	-0	89	0	-0.1
1979	Chi N	0	0	—	7	0	0	0-0	15	10	1	0	1	4-1	5	0.60	688	.189	.259	1-0	.000	-0		5	0.3
1981	Chi N	2	0	1.000	11	2	0	0-1	16	11	3	0	0	10-1	7	0.56	657	.204	.318	3-0	.000	-0	120	4	0.5
1982	Tor A	1	1	.500	16	2	0	0-0	31.2	32	15	6	2	17-2	22	3.98	113	.260	.359	0-0	—	0	81	2	0.1
1983	Tor A	0	3	.000	47	0	0	5-3	52.1	47	28	4	2	31-5	50	4.64	93	.240	.349	0-0	—	0		-1	-0.1
1984	Sea A	1	1	.500	20	3	0	3-0	43.1	47	22	2	2	9-3	28	4.15	96	.273	.314	0-0	—	0	98	-1	-0.1
1985	Sea A	0	0	—	12	0	0	0-0	27	35	21	3	0	15-3	17	6.33	67	.310	.391	0-0	—	0		-6	-0.3
Total	7	5	5	.500	131	8	0	8-4	208.2	209	102	15	7	97-19	144	4.01	104	.259	.342	7-0	.000	-1	95	3	0.3
GEISHERT, VERN Vernon William B 1.10.1946 Madison, WI BR/TR 6-1/215# d8.26																									
1969	Cal A	1	1	.500	11	3	0	1-0	31	32	18	4	1	7-3	18	4.65	75	.267	.308	9-0	.000	-1	144	-4	-0.3
GEISS, EMIL Emil August B 3.20.1867 Chicago, IL D 10.4.1911 Chicago, IL BR/TR 5-11/170# d5.18 b-Bill ▲																									
1887	Chi N	0	1	.000	1	1	1	0	9	17	11	0	0	3	4	8.00	56	.395	.435	12	.083	-1*	58	-3	-0.2
GELNAR, JOHN John Richard B 6.25.1943 Granite, OK BR/TR 6-1.5/190# d8.4																									
1964	Pit N	0	0	—	7	0	0	0	9	11	5	2	0	1-0	4	5.00	70	.314	.333	0-0	—	0		-1	-0.1
1967	Pit N	0	1	.000	10	1	0	0	19	30	18	4	2	11-1	5	8.05	42	.375	.453	6-0	.167	0	104	-9	-0.5
1969	Sea A	3	10	.231	39	10	0	3-2	108.2	103	49	7	5	26-5	69	3.31	110	.250	.299	19-3	.053	-2*	61	2	0.1
1970	Mil A	4	3	.571	53	0	0	4-2	92.1	98	46	7	5	23-5	48	4.19	90	.277	.326	12-0	.083	-1		-3	-0.2
1971	Mil A	0	0	—	2	0	0	0-0	1.1	3	2	0	0	1-0	0	13.50	26	.429	.500	0-0	—	0		-1	-0.1
Total	5	7	14	.333	111	11	0	7-4	230.1	245	120	20	12	62-11	126	4.18	88	.276	.328	37-3	.081	-2	64	-12	-0.8
GENEWICH, JOE Joseph Edward B 1.15.1897 Elmira, NY D 12.21.1985 Lockport, NY BR/TR 6/174# d9.3																									
1922	Bos N	0	2	.000	6	2	1	0	23	29	19	2	0	11	4	7.04	57	.319	.392	6-0	.167	-0	102	-7	-0.5
1923	Bos N	13	14	.481	43	24	12-1	1	227.1	272	110	15	7	46	54	3.72	107	.303	.341	77-1	.247	2	83	9	1.2
1924	Bos N	10	19	.345	34	27	11-2	1	200.1	258	136	4	8	65	43	5.21	73	.329	.386	60-5	.167	-2	72	-32	-4.0
1925	Bos N	12	10	.545	34	21	10	0	169	185	87	4	6	41	34	3.99	100	.279	.327	55-4	.273	1	94	2	0.3
1926	Bos N	8	16	.333	37	26	12-2	2	216	239	114	6	6	63	59	3.88	92	.288	.342	67-5	.164	-1	88	-10	-1.1
1927	Bos N	11	8	.579	40	19	7	1	181	199	93	7	2	54	38	3.83	97	.279	.332	57-3	.193	-1	93	-3	-0.4
1928	Bos N	3	7	.300	13	11	4	0	80.2	88	43	14	3	18	15	4.13	95	.280	.325	26-4	.038	-3	77	-1	-0.4
	NY N	11	4	.733	26	18	10-2	3	158.1	136	62	10	1	54	37	3.18	123	.232	.298	64-2	.203	-1	112	14	1.2
	Year	14	11	.560	39	29	14-2	3	239	224	67	24	4	72	52	3.50	112	.249	.307	90-6	.156	-4	99	12	0.8
1929	NY N	3	7	.300	21	9	1	1	85	133	70	9	1	30	19	6.78	68	.359	.409	32-0	.375	3*	104	-19	-1.6
1930	NY N	2	5	.286	18	9	3	3	61	71	44	6	1	20	13	5.61	84	.297	.354	20-1	.150	-1*	92	-6	-0.6
Total	9	73	92	.442	272	166	71-7	12	1401.2	1610	778	77	35	402	316	4.29	91	.293	.345	464-25	.207	-4	89	-53	-5.9
GENTRY, GARY Gary Edward B 10.6.1946 Phoenix, AZ BR/TR 6/183# d4.10																									
1969	†NY N	13	12	.520	35	35	6-3	0-0	233.2	192	94	24	5	81-5	154	3.43	107	.222	.291	74-7	.081	-4	90	8	0.5
1970	NY N	9	9	.500	32	29	5-2	1-1	188.1	155	88	19	9	86-7	134	3.68	109	.224	.316	59-5	.068	-2	101	7	0.2
1971	NY N	12	11	.522	32	31	8-3	0-0	203.1	167	84	16	6	82-8	155	3.23	106	.224	.304	68-6	.074	-5	93	3	-0.2
1972	NY N	7	10	.412	32	26	3	0-0	164	153	82	20	6	75-5	120	4.01	84	.250	.334	48-3	.104	-1	95	-12	-1.2
1973	Atl N	4	6	.400	16	14	3	1-0	86.2	74	37	7	1	35-3	42	3.43	115	.231	.305	30-3	.233	1*	101	5	0.5
1974	Atl N	0	0	—	3	1	0	0-0	6.2	4	1	1	1	2-0	0	1.35	281	.167	.259	1-0	.000	-0	46	2	0.1
1975	Atl N	1	1	.500	7	2	0	0-1	20	25	14	3	0	8-1	10	4.95	76	.313	.371	5-1	.000	-1	46	-3	-0.3
Total	7	46	49	.484	157	138	25-8	2-2	902.2	770	400	90	28	369-29	615	3.56	103	.231	.310	285-25	.095	-12	94	10	-0.4
GENTRY, RUFE James Ruffus B 5.18.1918 Daisy Station, NC D 7.3.1997 Winston-Salem, NC BR/TR 6-1/180# d9.10 b-Harvey																									
1943	Det A	1	3	.250	4	4	2	0	29.1	30	12	2	2	12	8	3.68	96	.268	.349	10-0	.000	-1	60	0	-0.1
1944	Det A	12	14	.462	37	30	10-3	0	203.2	211	104	9	4	108	68	4.24	84	.273	.365	76-2	.197	-1	85	-10	-1.2
1946	Det A	0	0	—	2	0	0	0	3	4	5	0	0	7	1	15.00	24	.333	.579	0-0	—	0		-3	-0.2
1947	Det A	0	0	—	1	0	0	0	0.1	1	3	0	0	2	0	81.00	5	.500	.750	0-0	—	0		-3	-0.1
1948	Det A	0	0	—	4	0	0	0	6.2	5	2	0	1	5	1	2.70	162	.208	.367	1-0	1.000	0		1	0.1
Total	5	13	17	.433	48	34	12-3	0	243	251	126	11	7	134	78	4.37	82	.272	.368	87-2	.184	-1	82	-15	-1.5
GEORGE, CHRIS Christopher Coleman B 9.16.1979 Houston, TX BL/TL 6-2/200# d7.26																									
2001	KC A	4	8	.333	13	13	1	0-0	74	83	48	14	0	18-0	32	5.59	88	.288	.326	0-0	—	0	94	-4	-0.6
2002	KC A	0	4	.000	6	6	0	0-0	27.1	37	17	2	1	8-0	13	5.60	90	.325	.371	0-0	—	0	83	-1	-0.1
2003	KC A	9	6	.600	18	18	0	0-0	93.2	120	75	22	3	44-2	39	7.11	73	.309	.380	1-2	1.000	0	99	-16	-2.0
Total	3	13	18	.419	37	37	1	0-0	195	240	140	38	4	70-2	84	6.32	80	.304	.360	1-2	1.000	0	95	-21	-2.7
GEORGE, CHRIS Christopher Sean B 9.24.1966 Pittsburgh, PA BR/TR 6-2/200# d10.1																									
1991	Mil A	0	0	—	2	1	0	0-0	6	8	2	0	0	0-0	2	3.00	133	.333	.320	0-0	—	0	46	1	0.0
GEORGE, LEFTY Thomas Edward B 8.13.1886 Pittsburgh, PA D 5.13.1955 York, PA BL/TL 6/155# d4.14																									
1911	StL A	4	9	.308	27	13	6-1	0	116.1	136	81	3	9	51	23	4.18	81	.256	.332	44-2	.114	-3	82	-12	-1.5
1912	Cle A	0	5	.000	11	5	2	0	44.1	69	38	1	2	18	18	4.87	70	.373	.434	14-1	.214	1	74	-9	-0.8
1915	Cin N	2	2	.500	5	3	2-1	0	28	24	12	1	5	8	11	3.86	74	.242	.330	12-0	.333	2*	78	-2	0.0
1918	Bos N	1	5	.167	9	5	4	0	54.1	56	23	0	3	21	22	2.32	116	.281	.359	22-0	.091	-2*	90	0	0.0
Total	4	7	21	.250	52	26	14-2	0	243	285	154	5	19	98	74	3.85	82	.281	.355	92-3	.152	-2	82	-23	-2.3
GEORGE, BILL William M. B 1.27.1865 Bellaire, OH D 8.23.1916 Wheeling, WV BR/TL 5-8/165# d5.11																									
1887	NY N	3	9	.250	13	13	10	0	108	126	112	1	14	89	49	5.25	72	.292	.429	53	.170	-4	146	-23	-2.0
1888	†NY N	2	1	.667	4	3	3-1	0	33.2	18	9	0	1	11	26	1.34	205	.149	.226	39	.231	1*	164	5	0.5
1889	Col AA	0	0	—	2	0	0	0	8	11	13	1	0	3	3	7.88	46	.314	.368	17	.235	-0*		-5	-0.2
Total	3	5	10	.333	19	16	13-1	0	149.2	155	134	2	15	103	78	4.51	78	.264	.387	109	.202	-3	149	-23	-1.7
GEORGY, OSCAR Oscar John B 11.25.1916 New Orleans, LA D 1.15.1999 New Orleans, LA BR/TR 6-3.5/180# d6.4																									
1938	NY N	0	0	—	1	0	0	0	1	2	2	0	0	1	0	18.00	21	.400	.500	0-0	—	0		-1	-0.1
GERARD, DAVE David Frederick B 8.6.1936 New York, NY D 10.10.2001 Newtown, PA BR/TR 6-2/205# d4.10																									
1962	Chi N	2	3	.400	39	0	0	3	58.2	67	40	10	1	28-5	30	4.91	84	.289	.365	8-0	.375	1		-6	-0.5

Year	Tm Lg	W	L	Pct	G	GS	CG-Sho	SV-BS	IP	H	R	HR	HB	BB-IB	SO	ERA	AERA	OAV	OOB	AB-SH	AVG	PB	Sup	APR	PW
GERBERMAN, GEORGE George Alois B 3.8.1942 ElCampo, TX BR/TR 6/180# d9.23																									
1962	Chi N	0	0	—	1	1	0	0	5.1	3	1	1	0	5-0	1	1.69	246	.158	.333	1-0	.000	0	21	1	0.1
GERHARDT, RUSTY Allen Russell B 8.13.1950 Baltimore, MD BB/TL 5-9/175# d7.27																									
1974	SD N	2	1	.667	23	1	0	1-0	35.2	44	28	1	2	17-5	22	7.07	51	.308	.384	6-0	.167	-0	73	-13	-1.1
GERHEAUSER, AL Albert "Lefty" B 6.24.1917 St.Louis, MO D 5.28.1972 Springfield, MO BL/TL 6-3/190# d4.24																									
1943	Phi N	10	19	.345	38	31	11-2	0	215	222	108	10	2	70	92	3.60	94	.263	.321	71-1	.113	-3	92	-9	-1.5
1944	Phi N	8	16	.333	30	29	10-2	0	182.2	210	102	8	1	65	66	4.58	79	.285	.344	65-1	.231	3*	77	-17	-1.7
1945	Pit N	5	10	.333	32	14	5	1	140.1	170	72	5	1	54	55	3.91	101	.304	.366	48-0	.250	3	107	1	0.4
1946	Pit N	2	2	.500	35	3	1	0	81.2	92	42	2	1	25	32	3.97	89	.286	.339	21-0	.333	2*	97	-4	0.1
1948	StL A	0	3	.000	14	2	0	0	23.1	32	23	0	1	10	10	7.33	62	.317	.384	6-0	.333	0	50	-8	-0.8
Total	5	25	50	.333	149	79	27-4	1	643	726	347	25	6	224	255	4.13	88	.283	.342	211-2	.209	5	88	-37	-3.5
GERKIN, STEVE Stephen Paul "Splinter" B 11.19.1912 Grafton, WV D 11.9.1978 Bay Pines, FL BR/TR 6-1/162# d5.13																									
1945	Phi A	0	12	.000	21	12	3	0	102	112	49	4	3	27	25	3.62	95	.285	.336	34-1	.059	-4	70	-3	-0.7
GERMAN, FRANKLYN Franklyn Miguel (Made) B 1.20.1980 San Cristobal, D.R. BR/TR 6-6/245# d9.7																									
2002	Det A	1	0	1.000	7	0	0	1-0	6.2	3	0	0	1	2-1	6	0.00	—	.150	.261	0-0	—	0		3	0.5
2003	Det A	2	4	.333	45	0	0	5-2	44.2	47	32	5	2	45-3	41	6.04	71	.273	.427	0-0	—	0		-9	-1.2
Total	2	3	4	.429	52	0	0	6-2	51.1	50	32	5	3	47-4	47	5.26	82	.260	.412	0-0	—	0		-6	-0.7
GERMAN, LES Lester Stanley B 6.1.1869 Baltimore, MD D 6.10.1934 Germantown, MD BR/TR 5-8/165# d8.27																									
1890	Bal AA	5	11	.313	17	16	15	0	132.1	147	95	2	13	54	37	4.83	84	.273	.353	51	.118	-2	75	-10	-1.2
1893	NY N	8	8	.500	20	18	14	0	152	162	109	6	9	70	35	4.14	112	.265	.349	74	.311	2*	98	6	0.6
1894	NY N	9	8	.529	24	16	11	1	143	186	139	7	12	68	21	5.54	95	.311	.392	60-2	.300	0	114	-6	-0.4
1895	NY N	7	11	.389	25	18	16	0	178.1	243	159	7	9	78	36	5.96	78	.320	.390	111-1	.261	3*	99	-23	-1.4
1896	NY N	0	0	—	1	0	0	0	2.2	9	6	0	0	1	0	13.50	31	.529	.556	1-0	.000	-0		-3	-0.1
	Was N	2	20	.091	28	20	14	1	166.2	240	174	6	5	74	20	6.32	70	.334	.400	70-0	.229	0*	84	-32	-3.0
	Year	2	20	.091	29	20	14	1	169.1	249	179	6	5	75	20	6.43	69	.339	.404	71-0	.225	-0	84	-41	-3.1
1897	Was N	3	5	.375	15	5	4	0	83.2	117	74	2	7	33	2	5.59	78	.328	.395	44-1	.341	2*	92	-10	-0.5
Total	6	34	63	.351	130	93	74	2	858.2	1104	756	30	55	378	151	5.45	84	.307	.381	411-4	.260	5	95	-78	-6.0
GERNER, ED Edwin Frederick "Lefty" B 7.22.1897 Philadelphia, PA D 5.15.1970 Philadelphia, PA BL/TL 5-8.5/175# d5.14																									
1919	Cin N	1	0	1.000	5	1	0	0	17	22	10	0	2	3	2	3.18	87	.333	.380	6-0	.167	0*	230	-2	-0.1
GERVAIS, LEFTY Lucien Edward B 7.6.1890 Grover, WI D 10.19.1950 Los Angeles, CA BL/TL 5-10/165# d4.17																									
1913	Bos N	0	1	.000	5	2	1	0	15.2	18	11	0	0	4	1	5.74	57	.383	.431	5-0	.000	-0*	80	-3	-0.2
GESSNER, CHARLIE Charles R. B 12.1863 Philadelphia, PA D 5.25.1922 Washington, DC 5-8/?# d7.19																									
1886	Phi AA	0	1	.000	1	1	1	0	8	13	14	0	2	5	0	9.00	39	.351	.455	4	.250	-0	136	-5	-0.4
GETTEL, AL Allen Jones B 9.17.1917 Norfolk, VA BR/TR 6-3.5/200# d4.20																									
1945	NY A	9	8	.529	27	17	9	3	154.2	141	70	11	7	53	67	3.90	89	.243	.314	57-2	.281	2	93	-4	-0.3
1946	NY A	6	7	.462	26	11	5-2	0	103	89	40	6	2	40	54	2.97	116	.229	.305	32-3	.125	-2	81	5	0.5
1947	Cle A	11	10	.524	31	21	9-2	0	149	122	54	12	3	62	64	3.20	109	.229	.313	51-2	.294	4*	93	7	1.4
1948	Cle A	0	1	.000	5	2	0	0	7.2	15	15	2	1	10	4	17.61	23	.385	.520	3-0	.000	-0	211	-11	-1.2
	Chi A	8	10	.444	22	19	7	1	148	154	76	7	4	60	49	4.01	106	.268	.342	54-3	.241	0*	96	3	0.3
	Year	8	11	.421	27	21	7	1	155.2	169	81	9	5	70	53	4.68	91	.276	.355	57-3	.228	-0	106	-8	-0.9
1949	Chi A	2	5	.286	19	7	1-1	1	63	69	48	12	2	26	22	6.43	65	.283	.357	18-0	.167	-0	95	-15	-1.5
	Was A	0	2	.000	16	1	0	1	34.2	43	24	4	0	24	7	5.45	78	.314	.416	8-0	.000	-1	105	-5	-0.3
	Year	2	7	.222	35	8	1-1	2	97.2	112	29	16	2	50	29	6.08	69	.294	.379	26-0	.115	-1	96	-20	-1.8
1951	NY N	1	2	.333	30	1	0	0	57.1	52	37	12	0	25	36	4.87	80	.240	.318	12-0	.083	-1	158	-6	-0.4
1955	StL N	1	0	1.000	8	0	0	0	17	26	18	6	0	10-0	7	9.00	45	.361	.429	6-0	.500	1		-9	-0.4
Total	7	38	45	.458	184	79	31-5	6	734.1	711	382	72	19	310-0	310	4.28	88	.255	.334	241-10	.228	3	96	-35	-1.9
GETTIG, CHARLIE Charles Henry B 12.1870 Baltimore, MD D 4.11.1935 Baltimore, MD BR 5-10/172# d8.5 ▲																									
1896	NY N	1	0	1.000	4	1	1	1	14	20	17	0	2	8	5	9.64	44	.333	.429	9-0	.333	1*	253	-7	-0.4
1897	NY N	1	1	.500	3	2	2	0	19	23	23	0	2	9	7	5.21	80	.295	.382	75-0	.200	0*	120	-4	-0.3
1898	NY N	6	3	.667	17	8	7	0	115	141	72	1	8	39	14	3.83	91	.299	.363	196-1	.250	2*	186	-4	0.0
1899	NY N	7	8	.467	18	15	12	0	128	161	102	3	4	54	25	4.43	85	.307	.376	97-3	.247	1*	103	-15	-1.2
Total	4	15	12	.556	42	26	22	1	276	345	214	4	16	110	51	4.50	82	.304	.374	377-4	.241	4	136	-30	-1.9
GETZIEN, CHARLIE Charles H. "Pretzels" B 2.14.1864 , Germany D 6.19.1932 Chicago, IL BR/TR 5-10/172# d8.13																									
1884	Det N	5	12	.294	17	17	17-1	0	147.1	118	73	2		25	107	1.95	148	.204	.237	55	.109	-4	61	13	0.9
1885	Det N	12	25	.324	37	37	37-1	0	330	360	222	8		92	110	3.03	94	.264	.311	137	.212	-1*	96	-10	-1.1
1886	Det N	30	11	.732	43	43	42-1	0	386.2	388	203	6		85	172	3.03	110	.250	.288	165	.176	-3	121	11	0.5
1887	†Det N	29	13	**.690**	43	42	41-2	0	366.2	373	217	24	2	106	135	3.73	109	.254	.305	156	.186	-2	109	14	1.0
1888	Det N	19	25	.432	46	46	45-2	0	404	411	225	13	8	54	202	3.05	92	.251	.279	167	.246	9	107	-9	-0.2
1889	Ind N	18	22	.450	45	44	36	1	349	395	256	27	9	100	139	4.54	92	.277	.328	139	.180	2	94	-16	-1.3
1890	Bos N	23	17	.575	40	40	39-4	0	350	342	201	5	3	82	140	3.19	118	.248	.291	147	.231	5*	88	17	1.9
1891	Bos N	4	5	.444	11	9	7	0	89	112	62	4	0	23	29	3.84	95	.296	.337	41	.171	1*	82	-1	0.1
	Cle N	0	1	.000	1	1	1	0	9	12	9	1	0	4	4	8.00	43	.308	.372	4	.000	-1	52	-3	-0.3
	Year	4	6	.400	12	10	8	0	98	124	12	5	0	27	33	4.22	86	.297	.340	45	.156	0	79	-3	-0.2
1892	StL N	5	8	.385	13	13	12	0	108	159	87	5	6	31	32	5.67	56	.329	.377	45	.200	0	81	-26	-2.4
Total	9	145	139	.511	296	292	277-11	1	2539.2	2670	1555	95	28	602	1070	3.46	99	.259	.302	1056	.198	7	99	-10	-0.9
GEYER, RUBE Jacob Bowman B 3.26.1884 Allegheny, PA D 10.12.1962 Ford Township, MN BR/TR 5-10/170# d4.24																									
1910	StL N	0	1	.000	4	0	0	0	4	5	3	0	0	3	5	4.50	66	.294	.400	1-0	.000	-0		-1	-0.2
1911	StL N	9	6	.600	29	11	7-1	0	148.2	141	80	7	6	56	46	3.27	103	.259	.335	57-2	.228	1	103	-2	-0.2
1912	StL N	7	14	.333	41	18	5	0	181	191	110	4	4	84	61	3.28	104	.288	.371	53-1	.208	-0	70	-3	-0.3
1913	StL N	1	5	.167	30	4	2	1	78.2	83	57	6	2	38	21	5.26	61	.282	.368	22-1	.091	-2	76	-19	-1.6
Total	4	17	26	.395	104	33	14-1	1	412.1	420	250	17	12	181	133	3.67	92	.276	.358	133-4	.195	-1	82	-25	-2.3
GHELFI, TONY Anthony Paul B 8.23.1961 LaCrosse, WI BR/TR 6-3/185# d9.1																									
1983	Phi N	1	1	.500	3	3	0	0-0	14.1	15	5	2	0	6-0	14	3.14	114	.268	.339	4-0	.250	0	58	1	0.2
GIALLOMBARDO, BOB Robert Paul B 5.20.1937 Brooklyn, NY BL/TL 6/175# d6.21																									
1958	LA N	1	1	.500	6	5	0	0	26.1	29	14	3	0	15-0	14	3.76	109	.284	.376	6-3	.167	-0*	92	0	0.0
GIARD, JOE Joseph Oscar "Peco" B 10.7.1898 Ware, MA D 7.10.1956 Worcester, MA BL/TL 5-10.5/170# d4.18																									
1925	StL A	10	5	.667	30	21	9-4	0	160.2	179	96	13	5	87	43	5.04	93	.295	.388	53-3	.057	-6	98	-1	-0.6
1926	StL A	3	10	.231	22	15	2	0	90	113	81	7	1	67	18	7.00	61	.318	.428	29-3	.276	0	94	-24	-2.9
1927	NY A	0	0	—	16	0	0	0	27	38	25	1	0	19	10	8.00	48	.352	.449	7-0	.286	0		-12	-0.5
Total	3	13	15	.464	68	36	11-4	0	277.2	330	202	21	6	173	71	5.96	75	.309	.408	89-6	.146	-6	97	-37	-4.0
GIBBON, JOE Joseph Charles B 4.10.1935 Hickory, MS BR/TL 6-4/210# d4.17																									
1960	†Pit N	4	2	.667	27	9	0	0	80.1	87	40	5	0	31-5	60	4.03	93	.277	.341	19-4	.211	1	115	-3	-0.1
1961	Pit N	13	10	.565	30	29	7-3	0	195.1	185	85	16	4	57-4	145	3.32	120	.251	.306	59-10	.136	-2*	107	13	1.2
1962	Pit N	3	4	.429	19	8	0	0	57	53	29	4	0	24-3	26	3.63	108	.250	.324	17-1	.176	-0	112	1	0.1
1963	Pit N	5	12	.294	37	22	5	1	147.1	147	61	7	5	54-15	110	3.30	100	.258	.326	43-3	.093	-2*	87	1	0.0
1964	Pit N	10	7	.588	28	24	3	0	146.2	145	66	10	6	54-10	97	3.68	95	.262	.331	47-5	.255	3*	118	-2	0.2
1965	Pit N	4	9	.308	31	15	1	1	105.2	85	57	7	4	34-6	63	4.51	78	.221	.288	26-2	.115	-0	101	-10	-1.1
1966	SF N	4	6	.400	37	10	1	1	81	86	41	4	2	16-1	48	3.67	100	.275	.310	15-0	.200	0	96	-1	0.0
1967	SF N	6	2	.750	28	10	3-1	1	82	65	31	4	3	33-4	63	3.07	107	.220	.302	24-1	.042	-1	142	3	0.2
1968	SF N	1	2	.333	29	0	0	1	40	33	10	3	2	19-4	22	1.57	187	.234	.331	1-0	.000	-0		5	0.5
1969	SF N	1	3	.250	16	0	0	2-1	20	15	10	1	1	13-4	9	3.60	97	.211	.341	3-0	.000	-0		0	-0.1

Year	Tm Lg	W	L	Pct	G	GS	CG-Sho	SV-BS	IP	H	R	HR	HB	BB-IB	SO	ERA	AERA	OAV	OOB	AB-SH	AVG	PB	Sup	APR	PW
	Pit N	5	1	.833	35	0	0	9-0	51.1	38	14	5	2	17-2	35	1.93	181	.208	.281	5-2	.000	-1		8	1.3
	Year	6	4	.600	51	0	0	11-1	71.1	53	29	6	3	30-6	44	2.40	146	.209	.299	8-2	.000	-1		8	1.2
1970	†Pit N	0	1	.000	41	0	0	5-1	41	44	25	2	2	24-8	26	4.83	81	.280	.380	3-0	.000	-0		-5	-0.3
1971	Cin N	5	6	.455	50	0	0	11-4	64.1	54	25	3	1	32-11	34	2.94	114	.239	.332	1-1	.000	-0		2	0.5
1972	Cin N	0	0	—	2	0	0	0-0	0.1	3	2	1	0	1-1	1	54.00	6	.750	.800	0-0	—	0		-2	-0.1
	Hou N	0	0	—	9	0	0	0-0	7.1	13	9	2	1	5-2	4	9.82	34	.394	.487	0-0	—	0		-6	-0.3
	Year	0	0	—	11	0	0	0-0	7.2	16	11	3	1	6-3	5	11.74	29	.432	.523	0-0	—	0		-7	-0.4
Total	13	61	65	.484	419	127	20-4	32-6	1119.2	1053	505	74	33	414-80	743	3.52	102	.251	.321	263-29	.144	-3	109	4	2.0

GIBSON, NORWOOD Norwood Ringold "Gibby" B 3.11.1877 Peoria, IL D 7.7.1959 Peoria, IL BR/TR 5-10/165# d4.29

1903	Bos A	13	9	.591	24	21	17-2	0	183.1	166	95	2	7	65	76	3.19	95	.241	.313	64-5	.266	5*	96	-4	-0.1
1904	Bos A	17	14	.548	33	32	29-1	0	273	216	111	8	4	81	112	2.21	121	.219	.281	92-5	.065	-6	91	8	0.0
1905	Bos A	4	7	.364	23	17	9	0	134	118	77	9	5	55	67	3.69	73	.238	.321	42-2	.095	-2	97	-16	-1.6
1906	Bos A	0	2	.000	5	2	1	0	18.2	25	21	2	0	7	3	5.30	52	.325	.381	5-0	.200	0	13	-7	-0.7
Total	4	34	32	.515	85	72	56-3	0	609	525	304	21	16	208	258	2.93	95	.233	.303	203-12	.138	-4	92	-19	-2.4

GIBSON, PAUL Paul Marshall B 1.4.1960 Southampton, NY BR/TL 6/185# d4.8

1988	Det A	4	2	.667	40	1	0	0-2	92	83	33	6	2	34-8	50	2.93	130	.240	.307	0-0	—	0	191	9	0.6
1989	Det A	4	8	.333	45	13	0	0-2	132	129	71	11	6	57-12	77	4.64	82	.259	.339	0-0	—	0	77	-9	-0.8
1990	Det A	5	4	.556	61	0	0	3-3	97.1	99	36	10	1	44-12	56	3.05	130	.269	.344	0-0	—	0		10	0.9
1991	Det A	5	7	.417	68	0	0	8-5	96	112	51	10	3	48-8	52	4.59	91	.297	.379	0-0	—	0		-4	-0.4
1992	NY N	0	1	.000	43	1	0	0-0	62	70	37	7	0	25-0	49	5.23	67	.287	.352	6-1	.000	-0	104	-11	-0.6
1993	NY N	1	1	.500	8	0	0	0-1	8.2	14	6	1	0	2-0	12	5.19	77	.350	.381	0-0	—	0		-1	-0.2
	NY A	2	0	1.000	20	0	0	0-0	35.1	31	15	4	0	9-0	25	3.06	136	.238	.282	0-0	—	0		4	0.2
1994	NY A	1	1	.500	30	0	0	0-2	29	26	17	5	1	17-3	21	4.97	92	.236	.338	0-0	—	0		-1	-0.1
1996	NY A	0	0	—	4	0	0	0-0	4.1	6	3	1	0	0-0	3	6.23	79	.316	.316	0-0	—	0		-1	0.0
Total	8	22	24	.478	319	15	0	11-15	556.2	570	269	55	13	236-43	345	4.07	97	.267	.341	6-1	.000	-0	83	-4	-0.4

GIBSON, BOB Robert (b: Pack Robert Gibson) B 11.9.1935 Omaha, NE BR/TR 6-1.5/195# d4.15 C5 HF1981

1959	StL N	3	5	.375	13	9	2-1	0	75.2	77	35	4	1	39-2	48	3.33	127	.273	.360	26-1	.115	-1*	61	5	0.4
1960	StL N	3	6	.333	27	12	2	0	86.2	97	61	7	1	48-6	69	5.61	73	.284	.371	28-1	.179	-0*	92	-14	-1.3
1961	StL N	13	12	.520	35	27	10-2	1	211.1	186	91	13	6	119-7	166	3.24	136	.239	.342	66-3	.197	2*	81	24	2.9
1962	StL N★	15	13	.536	32	30	15-**5**	1	233.2	174	84	15	10	95-9	208	2.85	**150**	.204	.291	76-6	.263	6*	84	34	**4.7**
1963	StL N	18	9	.667	36	33	14-2	0	254.2	224	110	19	13	96-1	204	3.39	105	.233	.309	87-5	.207	7*	116	5	1.2
1964	†StL N	19	12	.613	40	36	17-2	1	287.1	250	106	25	9	86-9	245	3.01	127	.232	.293	96-6	.156	1	94	27	2.9
1965	StL N★	20	12	.625	38	36	20-6	1	299	243	110	34	11	103-6	270	3.07	125	.222	.293	104-8	.240	8*	107	25	3.5
1966	StL N❖	21	12	.636	35	35	20-**5**	0	280.1	210	90	20	5	78-5	225	2.44	147	.207	.265	100-7	.200	3*	81	35	4.4
1967	†StL N★	13	7	.650	24	24	10-2	0	175.1	151	62	10	3	40-3	147	2.98	110	.231	.278	60-6	.133	1*	125	8	1.0
1968	†StL N☆	22	9	.710	34	34	28-**13**	0	304.2	198	49	11	7	62-6	**268**	**1.12**	**258**	**.184**	**.233**	94-7	.170	4*	91	**60**	**7.6**
1969	StL N★	20	13	.606	35	35	**28**-4	0-0	314	251	84	12	10	95-7	269	2.18	164	.219	.283	118-5	.246	8*	89	**50**	**6.3**
1970	StL N★	**23**	7	**.767**	34	34	23-3	0-0	294	262	111	13	4	88-9	274	3.12	132	.237	.293	109-6	.303	12*	108	34	**4.5**
1971	StL N	16	13	.552	31	31	20-**5**	0-0	245.2	215	96	14	7	76-11	185	3.04	119	.232	.294	87-2	.172	2	100	13	1.8
1972	StL N★	19	11	.633	34	34	23-4	0-0	278	226	83	14	3	88-11	208	2.46	138	.224	.286	103-2	.194	7	100	31	4.4
1973	StL N	12	10	.545	25	25	13-1	0-0	195	159	71	12	3	57-6	142	2.77	132	.224	.281	65-2	.185	2	97	18	2.2
1974	StL N	11	13	.458	33	33	9-1	0-0	240	236	111	24	5	104-14	129	3.83	94	.259	.335	81-1	.210	3	109	-5	-0.3
1975	StL N	3	10	.231	22	14	1	2-1	109	120	66	10	4	62-6	60	5.04	75	.287	.382	28-4	.179	0	87	-12	-1.3
Total	17	251	174	.591	528	482	255-56	6-1	3884.1	3279	1420	257	102	1336-118	3117	2.91	127	.228	.297	1328-72	.206	65	97	338	44.9

GIBSON, BOB Robert Louis B 6.19.1957 Philadelphia, PA BR/TR 6/195# d4.13

1983	Mil A	3	4	.429	27	7	0	2-3	80.2	71	40	6	1	46-2	46	3.90	96	.237	.334	0-0	—	0	97	-2	-0.2
1984	Mil A	2	5	.286	18	9	1-1	0-0	69	61	43	10	0	47-2	54	4.96	78	.236	.352	0-0	—	0	102	-9	-0.8
1985	Mil A	6	7	.462	41	1	0	11-3	92.1	86	44	10	1	49-3	53	3.90	107	.260	.353	0-0	—	0	44	3	0.5
1986	Mil A	1	2	.333	11	1	0	0-0	26.2	23	18	3	0	23-1	11	4.73	92	.232	.374	0-0	—	0	126	-2	-0.2
1987	NY N	0	0	—	1	0	0	0-0	1	0	0	0	0	1-0	2	0.00	—	.000	.250	0-0	—	0		0	0.0
Total	5	12	18	.400	98	18	1-1	13-6	269.2	241	145	29	2	166-8	166	4.24	94	.243	.349	0-0	—	0	95	-10	-0.7

GIBSON, ROBERT Robert Murray B 8.20.1869 Duncansville, PA D 12.19.1949 Pittsburgh, PA BR/TR 6-3/185# d6.4

1890	Chi N	1	0	1.000	1	1	1	0	9	6	1	0	0	2	1	0.00	—	.182	.229	4	.000	-0	17	3	0.3
	Pit N	0	3	.000	3	3	2	0	12	24	38	0	3	23	3	17.25	19	.400	.581	13	.231	-0	153	-21	-2.5
	Year	1	3	.250	4	4	3	0	21	30	46	0	3	25	4	9.86	35	.323	.479	17	.176	-1	114	-17	-2.2

GIBSON, SAM Samuel Braxton B 8.5.1899 King, NC D 1.31.1983 High Point, NC BL/TR 6-2/198# d4.19

1926	Det A	12	9	.571	35	24	16-2	2	196.1	199	94	6	6	75	61	3.48	117	.269	.341	72-1	.250	2*	93	12	1.3
1927	Det A	11	12	.478	33	26	11	0	184.2	201	113	9	8	86	76	3.80	111	.285	.369	66-3	.212	-1	126	2	0.1
1928	Det A	5	8	.385	20	18	5-1	0	119.2	155	83	4	7	52	29	5.42	76	.322	.396	42-1	.286	2	102	-15	-1.3
1930	NY A	0	1	.000	2	2	0	0	6	14	11	1	0	6	3	15.00	29	.424	.513	3-0	.333	0	260	-7	-0.8
1932	NY N	4	8	.333	41	5	1-1	3	81.2	107	51	7	2	30	39	4.85	77	.322	.382	19-1	.263	0	82	-10	-1.3
Total	5	32	38	.457	131	75	33-4	5	588.1	676	352	27	23	249	208	4.28	95	.295	.370	202-6	.248	3	112	-18	-2.0

GICK, GEORGE George Edward B 10.18.1915 Dunnington, IN BB/TR 6/190# d10.3

1937	Chi A	0	0	—	1	0	0	1	2	0	0	0	0	0	1	0.00	—	.000	.000	0-0	—	0		1	0.1
1938	Chi A	0	0	—	1	0	0	0	1	0	0	0	1	0	1	0.00	—	.000	.250	0-0	—	0		1	0.0
Total	2	0	0	—	2	0	0	1	3	0	0	0	1	0	2	0.00	—	.000	.100	0-0	—	0		2	0.1

GIDEON, BRETT Byron Brett B 8.8.1963 Ozona, TX BR/TR 6-2/200# d7.5

1987	Pit N	1	5	.167	29	0	0	3-3	36.2	34	22	6	1	10-3	31	4.66	88	.243	.298	1-0	1.000	1		-3	-0.4
1989	Mon N	0	0	—	4	0	0	0-0	4.2	5	1	1	0	5-1	2	1.93	183	.294	.455	0-0	—	0		1	0.0
1990	Mon N	0	0	—	1	0	0	0-0	1	2	1	0	0	4-1	0	9.00	41	.500	.750	0-0	—	0		-1	0.0
Total	3	1	5	.167	34	0	0	3-3	42.1	41	24	7	1	19-5	33	4.46	90	.255	.337	1-0	1.000	1		-3	-0.4

GIDEON, JIM James Leslie B 9.26.1953 Taylor, TX BR/TR 6-3/190# d9.14

1975	Tex A	0	0	—	1	1	0	0-0	5.2	7	6	1	0	5-0	2	7.94	47	.292	.414	0-0	—	0	211	-3	-0.1

GIEBELL, FLOYD Floyd George B 12.10.1909 Pennsboro, WV BL/TR 6-2.5/172# d4.21

1939	Det A	1	1	.500	9	0	0	0	15.1	19	7	1	0	12	9	2.93	167	.317	.431	2-1	.000	-0		3	0.2
1940	Det A	2	0	1.000	2	2	2-1	0	18	14	2	2	0	4	11	1.00	476	.206	.250	6-1	.000	-1	139	7	0.7
1941	Det A	0	0	—	17	2	0	0	34.1	45	29	3	0	26	10	6.03	75	.313	.418	6-1	.333	0	162	-6	-0.3
Total	3	3	1	.750	28	4	2-1	0	67.2	78	38	6	0	42	30	3.99	117	.287	.382	14-3	.143	-1	149	4	0.6

GIEL, PAUL Paul Robert B 2.29.1932 Winona, MN D 5.22.2002 Minneapolis, MN BR/TR 5-11/185# d7.10 Mil 1956

1954	NY N	0	0	—	6	0	0	0	4.1	8	4	0	0	2	4	8.31	49	.421	.455	0-0	—	0		-2	-0.1
1955	NY N	4	4	.500	34	2	0	0	82.1	70	36	8	2	50-5	47	3.39	119	.233	.345	19-1	.053	-2	55	6	0.3
1958	SF N	4	5	.444	29	9	0	0	92	89	56	12	2	55-4	55	4.70	81	.259	.363	27-4	.074	-2	86	-10	-1.0
1959	Pit N	0	0	—	4	0	0	0	7.2	17	12	0	0	6-1	3	14.09	27	.472	.548	0-0	—	0		-8	-0.4
1960	Pit N	2	0	1.000	16	0	0	0	33	35	25	3	0	15-1	21	5.73	65	.276	.350	7-1	.000	-1		-8	-0.6
1961	Min A	1	0	1.000	12	0	0	0	19.1	24	27	6	0	17-1	14	9.78	43	.289	.406	2-0	.500	0*		-13	-0.6
	KC A	0	0	—	1	0	0	0	1.2	6	7	1	0	3-0	1	37.80	11	.600	.692	0-0	—	0		-6	-0.2
	Year	1	0	1.000	13	0	0	0	21	30	38	7	0	20-1	15	12.00	35	.323	.439	2-0	.500	0		-18	-0.8
Total	6	11	9	.550	102	11	0	0	240.1	249	167	30	4	148-12	145	5.39	73	.271	.372	55-6	.073	-4	79	-41	-2.6

GIGGIE, BOB Robert Thomas B 8.13.1933 Dorchester, MA BR/TR 6-1/200# d4.18

1959	Mil N	1	0	1.000	13	0	0	1	20	24	10	2	0	10-0	15	4.05	87	.316	.395	1-0	.000	-0		-1	0.0
1960	Mil N	0	0	—	3	0	0	0	4.1	5	2	0	0	4-1	5	4.15	83	.278	.409	0-0	—	0		0	0.0
	KC A	1	0	1.000	10	0	0	0	18.2	24	12	1	0	15-2	8	5.79	69	.333	.443	2-0	.000	-0		-3	-0.2

Year	Tm Lg	W	L	Pct	G	GS	CG-Sho	SV-BS	IP	H	R	HR	HB	BB-IB	SO	ERA	AERA	OAV	OOB	AB-SH	AVG	PB	Sup	APR	PW
1962	KC A	1	1	.500	4	2	0	0	14.1	17	11	5	1	3-0	4	6.28	67	.293	.339	4-0	.000	-0	74	-3	-0.4
Total	3	3	1	.750	30	2	0	1	57.1	70	35	8	1	32-3	32	5.18	74	.313	.399	7-0	.000	-1	74	-7	-0.6
GILBERT, BILL Alfred Gideon B 3.13.1868 Havre De Grace, MD 6/180# d9.15																									
1892	Bal N	0	1	.000	2	1	1	0	14	14	15	1	0	17	5	5.79	59	.250	.425	6	.333	1	37	-4	-0.2
GILBERT, JOE Joe Dennis B 4.20.1952 Jasper, TX BR/TL 6-1/167# d4.30																									
1972	Mon N	0	1	.000	22	0	0	0-0	33	41	31	3	0	18-3	25	8.45	42	.306	.386	3-0	.000	-0		-16	-0.9
1973	Mon N	1	2	.333	21	0	0	1-0	29	30	18	1	0	19-1	17	4.97	77	.270	.374	2-0	.000	0		-3	-0.3
Total	2	1	3	.250	43	0	0	1-0	62	71	49	4	0	37-4	42	6.82	54	.290	.380	5-0	.000	-0		-19	-1.2
GILBRETH, BILL William Freeman B 9.3.1947 Abilene, TX BL/TL 6/180# d6.25																									
1971	Det A	2	1	.667	9	5	2	0-0	30	28	17	4	2	21-1	14	4.80	75	.264	.395	11-0	.182	-0	120	-4	-0.3
1972	Det A	0	0	—	2	0	0	0-0	5	10	9	1	0	4-0	2	16.20	19	.476	.519	1-0	.000	-0		-7	-0.3
1974	Cal A	0	0	—	3	0	0	0-1	1.1	2	2	0	0	1-0	0	13.50	26	.400	.429	0-0	—	0		-1	-0.1
Total	3	2	1	.667	14	5	2	0-1	36.1	40	28	5	2	26-1	16	6.69	53	.303	.417	12-0	.167	-0	120	-12	-0.7
GILFILLAN, JASON Jason Edward B 8.31.1976 Shelby, NC BR/TR 6-5/220# d5.16																									
2003	KC A	2	0	1.000	13	0	0	0-1	16.1	22	14	3	1	10-1	12	7.71	67	.310	.402	0-0	—	0		-4	-0.4
GILKS, BOB Robert James B 7.2.1864 Cincinnati, OH D 8.21.1944 Brunswick, GA BR/TR 5-8/178# d8.25 ▲																									
1887	Cle AA	7	5	.583	13	13	12-1	0	108	104	66	1	9	42	28	3.08	141	.245	.326	83	.313	2*	98	15	1.5
1888	Cle AA	0	2	.000	4	2	2	**1**	21	26	23	1	1	8	3	8.14	38	.292	.357	484	.229	0*	103	-9	-0.7
1890	Cle N	2	2	.500	4	3	3	0	31.2	34	17	0	4	9	5	4.26	84	.266	.333	544	.213	-0*	70	0	-0.1
Total	3	9	9	.500	21	18	17-1	1	160.2	164	106	2	14	59	36	3.98	101	.256	.332	1111	.228	2	96	6	0.7
GILL, ED Edward James B 8.7.1895 Somerville, MA D 10.10.1995 Brockton, MA BL/TR 5-10/165# d7.5																									
1919	Was A	1	1	.500	16	2	0	0	37.1	38	25	0	2	21	7	4.82	67	.260	.361	7-0	.000	-1	110	-6	-0.4
GILL, GEORGE George Lloyd B 2.13.1909 Catchings, MS D 2.21.1999 Jackson, MS BR/TR 6-1/185# d5.4																									
1937	Det A	11	4	.733	31	10	4-1	1	127.2	146	74	11	1	42	40	4.51	104	.285	.340	50-1	.140	-3	130	2	-0.1
1938	Det A	12	9	.571	24	23	13-1	0	164	195	82	15	2	50	30	4.12	121	.296	.348	57-5	.105	-4	98	16	1.3
1939	Det A	0	1	.000	3	1	0	0	8.2	14	8	1	0	3	1	8.31	59	.368	.415	2-0	.000	-0	72	-3	-0.3
	StL A	1	12	.077	27	11	5	0	95	139	89	10	3	34	24	7.11	68	.343	.398	26-1	.154	-2	86	-24	-2.7
	Year	1	13	.071	30	12	5	0	103.2	153	94	11	3	37	25	7.21	68	.345	.400	28-1	.143	-2	85	-27	-3.0
Total	3	24	26	.480	85	45	22-2	1	395.1	494	253	37	6	129	95	5.05	96	.306	.360	135-7	.126	-9	102	-9	-1.8
GILL, HADDIE Harold Edward B 1.23.1899 Brockton, MA D 8.1.1932 Brockton, MA BL/TL 5-11/165# d8.16																									
1923	Cin N	0	0	—	1	0	0	0	1	1	0	0	0	1	1	0.00	—	.333	.500	0-0	—	0		0	0.0
GILLENWATER, CLARAL Claral Lewis B 5.20.1900 Sims, IN D 2.26.1978 Bradenton, FL BR/TR 6/187# d8.20																									
1923	Chi A	1	3	.250	5	3	1-1	0	21.1	28	15	2	1	6	2	5.48	72	.337	.389	6-1	.000	-1	56	-3	-0.6
GILLES, TOM Thomas Bradford B 7.2.1962 Peoria, IL BR/TR 6-1/185# d6.7																									
1990	Tor A	1	0	1.000	2	0	0	0-0	1.1	2	1	0	0	0-0	1	6.75	59	.333	.333	0-0	—	0		0	-0.1
GILLESPIE, DUKE John Patrick "Silent John" B 2.25.1900 Oakland, CA D 2.15.1954 Vallejo, CA BR/TR 5-11.5/172# d4.12																									
1922	Cin N	3	3	.500	31	4	1	0	77.2	84	43	2	4	29	21	4.52	88	.294	.367	15-1	.133	-1	153	-2	-0.2
GILLESPIE, BOB Robert William "Bunch" B 10.8.1919 Columbus, OH D 11.4.2001 Winston-Salem, NC BR/TR 6-4/187# d5.11																									
1944	Det A	0	1	.000	7	0	0	0	11	7	8	0	0	12	4	6.55	54	.194	.396	2-0	.000	-0		-3	-0.3
1947	Chi A	5	8	.385	25	17	1	0	118	133	71	4	1	53	36	4.73	77	.291	.366	33-0	.061	-3	90	-13	-1.5
1948	Chi A	0	4	.000	25	6	1	0	72	81	45	3	1	33	19	5.13	83	.287	.364	16-1	.000	-2	53	-7	-0.5
1950	Bos A	0	0	—	1	0	0	0	1.1	2	3	1	0	4	0	20.25	24	.333	.600	0-0	—	0		-2	-0.1
Total	4	5	13	.278	58	23	2	0	202.1	223	127	8	2	102	59	5.07	76	.286	.369	51-1	.039	-5	78	-25	-2.4
GILLIFORD, PAUL Paul Gant "Gorilla" B 1.12.1945 Bryn Mawr, PA BR/TL 5-11/210# d9.20																									
1967	Bal A	0	0	—	2	0	0	0	3	6	4	1	0	1-0	2	12.00	26	.429	.467	0-0	—	0		-3	-0.1
GILLIGAN, JACK John Patrick (b: John Peter Gilgen) B 10.18.1885 Chicago, IL D 11.19.1980 Modesto, CA BB/TR 6/190# d9.16																									
1909	StL A	1	2	.333	3	3	3	0	23	28	19	1	2	9	4	5.48	44	.315	.390	9-1	.111	-1	58	-8	-1.0
1910	StL A	0	3	.000	9	5	2	0	39.1	37	21	0	1	28	10	3.66	68	.253	.377	15-0	.200	-0	119	-4	-0.3
Total	2	1	5	.167	12	8	5	0	62.1	65	40	1	3	37	14	4.33	57	.277	.382	24-1	.167	-1	97	-12	-1.3
GILLPATRICK, GEORGE George F. B 2.28.1875 Holden, MO D 12.15.1941 Kansas City, MO BR d5.22																									
1898	StL N	0	2	.000	7	3	1	0	35	42	38	0	2	19	12	6.94	55	.296	.387	16-0	.125	-2	87	-12	-0.7
GILMORE, FRANK Frank T. "Shadow" B 4.27.1864 Webster, MA D 7.21.1929 Hartford, CT BR d9.11																									
1886	Was N	4	4	.500	9	9	9-1	0	75	57	35	3		22	75	2.52	128	.200	.257	29	.000	-4	80	5	0.1
1887	Was N	7	20	.259	28	27	27-1	0	234.2	247	172	7	13	92	114	3.87	104	.262	.336	93	.065	-11	59	1	-1.0
1888	Was N	1	9	.100	12	11	10	0	95.2	131	101	4	7	29	23	6.59	42	.323	.378	41	.024	-5*	115	-39	-3.6
Total	3	12	33	.267	49	47	46-2	0	405.1	435	308	14	20	143	212	4.26	84	.266	.333	163	.043	-20	73	-33	-4.5
GILMORE, LEN Leonard Preston "Meow" B 11.3.1917 Fairview Park, IN BR/TR 6-3/175# d10.1																									
1944	Pit N	0	1	.000	1	1	1	0	8	13	7	2	0	0	0	7.88	47	.361	.361	2-0	.000	-0	23	-3	-0.3
GILROY, JOHN John M. B 10.26.1869 Washington, DC D 8.4.1897 Norfolk, VA d8.30																									
1895	Was N	1	4	.200	8	4	2	0	41.1	63	48	3	4	24	2	6.53	74	.344	.431	29-0	.241	-1*	82	-8	-0.7
1896	Was N	0	0	—	1	0	0	0	2	0	0	0	0	1	0	0.00	—	.000	.143	1-0	.000	-0		1	0.0
Total	2	1	4	.200	9	4	2	0	43.1	63	48	3	4	25	2	6.23	77	.333	.422	30-0	.233	-1	82	-7	-0.7
GILSON, HAL Harold "Lefty" B 2.9.1942 Los Angeles, CA BR/TL 6-5/195# d4.14																									
1968	StL N	0	2	.000	13	0	0	2	21.2	27	11	1	0	11-1	19	4.57	63	.310	.388	4-1	.000	-0		-3	-0.5
	Hou N	0	0	—	2	0	0	0	3.2	7	4	0	1	1-1	1	7.36	40	.412	.474	0-0	—	0*		-2	-0.1
	Year	0	2	.000	15	0	0	2	25.1	34	21	1	1	12-2	20	4.97	58	.327	.402	4-1	.000	-0		-6	-0.6
GING, BILLY William Joseph B 11.7.1872 Elmira, NY D 9.14.1950 Elmira, NY BR/TR 5-10/170# d9.25																									
1899	Bos N	1	0	1.000	1	1	1	0	8	5	1	0	0	5	2	1.13	370	.179	.303	2-1	.000	-0	35	3	0.2
GINGRAS, JOE Joseph Elzead John B 1.10.1894 New York, NY D 9.6.1947 Jersey City, NJ BR/TR 6-2/188# d6.18																									
1915	KC F	0	0	—	2	0	0	0	4	6	3	0	0	1	2	6.75	39	.353	.389	1-0	.000	-0		-2	-0.1
GINTER, MATT Matthew Shane B 12.24.1977 Lexington, KY BR/TR 6-2/220# d9.1																									
2000	Chi A	1	0	1.000	7	0	0	0-1	9.1	18	14	5	0	7-0	6	13.50	37	.409	.481	0-0	—	0		-8	-0.7
2001	Chi A	1	0	1.000	20	0	0	0-0	39.2	34	23	2	7	14-2	24	5.22	88	.238	.329	0-0	—	0		-2	-0.1
2002	Chi A	1	0	1.000	33	0	0	1-0	54.1	59	34	6	1	21-0	37	4.47	101	.278	.343	0-0	—	0		-2	-0.1
2003	Chi A	0	0	—	3	0	0	0-0	3.1	2	5	1	2	1-0	0	13.50	34	.182	.357	0-0	—	0		-3	-0.1
Total	4	3	0	1.000	63	0	0	1-1	106.2	113	76	14	10	43-2	67	5.82	79	.276	.354	0-0	—	0		-15	-1.0
GIRARD, CHARLIE Charles August B 12.16.1884 Brooklyn, NY D 8.6.1936 Brooklyn, NY BR/TR 5-10/175# d9.14																									
1910	Phi N	1	2	.333	7	1	0	1	26.2	33	26	2	2	12	11	6.41	49	.308	.388	8-0	.125	-0	95	-10	-1.1
GIUSTI, DAVE David John B 11.27.1939 Seneca Falls, NY BR/TR 5-11/195# d4.13																									
1962	Hou N	2	3	.400	22	5	0	0	73.2	82	49	7	0	30-1	43	5.62	66	.280	.346	24-1	.292	3*	117	-14	-0.6
1964	Hou N	0	0	—	8	0	0	0	25.2	24	10	1	0	8-1	16	3.16	108	.253	.308	7-0	.286	1		1	0.2
1965	Hou N	8	7	.533	38	13	4-1	3	131.1	132	67	13	1	46-11	92	4.32	78	.259	.319	35-3	.171	2	96	-13	-1.1
1966	Hou N	15	14	.517	34	33	9-4	0	210	215	112	23	5	54-3	131	4.20	81	.260	.309	74-6	.230	5*	117	-19	-1.9
1967	Hou N	11	15	.423	37	33	8-1	1	221.2	231	114	20	3	58-4	157	4.18	79	.265	.311	84-2	.155	3*	119	-20	-2.0
1968	Hou N	11	14	.440	37	34	12-2	1	251	226	95	15	4	67-7	186	3.19	93	.239	.291	82-5	.183	2*	79	-4	-0.1
1969	StL N	3	7	.300	22	12	2-1	0-0	99.2	96	46	7	1	37-2	62	3.61	99	.255	.321	25-1	.200	1	52	-1	0.1

Year	Tm Lg	W	L	Pct	G	GS	CG-Sho	SV-BS	IP	H	R	HR	HB	BB-IB	SO	ERA	AERA	OAV	OOB	AB-SH	AVG	PB	Sup	APR	PW
1970	†Pit N	9	3	.750	66	1	0	26-6	103	98	38	7	0	39-9	85	3.06	128	.259	.325	16-1	.188	2	161	10	1.8
1971	†Pit N	5	6	.455	58	0	0	**30-6**	86	79	31	5	1	31-8	55	2.93	116	.241	.305	17-0	.059	-1		5	0.8
1972	†Pit N	7	4	.636	54	0	0	22-5	74.2	59	18	3	0	20-6	54	1.93	172	.219	.271	10-1	.000	-1		12	2.6
1973	Pit N★	9	2	.818	67	0	0	20-6	98.2	89	31	9	0	37-13	64	2.37	149	.241	.308	13-2	.308	1		13	1.9
1974	†Pit N	7	5	.583	64	2	0	12-6	105.2	101	43	2	0	40-11	53	3.32	104	.258	.323	9-1	.111	-0	63	2	0.4
1975	†Pit N	5	4	.556	61	0	0	17-6	91.2	79	38	3	0	42-17	38	2.95	121	.237	.320	10-4	.300	1		5	0.8
1976	Pit N	5	4	.556	40	0	0	6-2	58.1	59	31	5	0	27-9	24	4.32	81	.267	.345	4-0	.000	-0		-5	-0.8
1977	Oak A	3	3	.500	40	0	0	6-1	60.1	54	22	4	0	20-5	28	2.98	135	.245	.308	0-0	—	0		8	0.9
	Chi N	0	2	.000	20	0	0	1-1	25.1	30	19	2	0	14-2	15	6.04	73	.297	.379	2-0	.000	-0		-4	-0.4
Total	15	100	93	.518	668	133	35-9	145-39	1716.2	1654	764	126	15	570-109	1103	3.60	95	.253	.313	412-27	.187	18	96	-24	2.6
GIVENS, BRIAN Brian Allen B 11.6.1965 Lompoc, CA BR/TL 6-6/220# d6.24																									
1995	Mil A	5	7	.417	19	19	0	0-0	107.1	116	71	11	3	54-0	73	4.95	101	.275	.360	0-0	—	0	99	-3	-0.3
1996	Mil A	1	3	.250	4	4	0	0-0	14	32	22	3	0	7-0	10	12.86	40	.438	.481	0-0	—	0	94	-12	-1.7
Total	2	6	10	.375	23	23	0	0-0	121.1	148	93	14	3	61-0	83	5.86	86	.299	.378	0-0	—	0	99	-15	-2.0
GLADDING, FRED Fred Earl B 6.28.1936 Flat Rock, MI BL/TR 6/225# d7.1 C3																									
1961	Det A	1	0	1.000	8	0	0	0	16.1	18	7	1	2	11-1	11	3.31	124	.286	.397	3-0	.000	-0		1	0.0
1962	Det A	0	0	—	6	0	0	0	5	3	0	0	0	2-0	4	0.00	—	.176	.263	0-0	—	0		2	0.1
1963	Det A	1	1	.500	22	0	0	7	27.1	19	6	1	0	14-1	24	1.98	189	.198	.297	1-0	.000	-0		6	0.7
1964	Det A	7	4	.636	42	0	0	7	67.1	57	23	7	2	27-4	59	3.07	119	.233	.312	9-0	.000	-1		5	0.9
1965	Det A	6	2	.750	46	0	0	5	70	63	22	6	4	29-5	43	2.83	123	.239	.323	7-1	.000	-1		6	0.6
1966	Det A	5	0	1.000	51	0	0	2	74	62	33	6	1	29-6	57	3.28	106	.230	.306	2-0	.000	-0		0	0.0
1967	Det A	6	4	.600	42	1	0	12	77	62	20	6	4	19-0	64	1.99	164	.227	.286	18-1	.000	-2	27	10	1.5
1968	Hou N	0	0	—	7	0	0	2	4.1	8	7	0	1	3-1	2	14.54	20	.421	.500	0-0	—	0		-5	-0.6
1969	Hou N	4	8	.333	57	0	0	**29-6**	72.2	83	39	2	1	27-6	40	4.21	84	.289	.352	10-0	.100	-1		-5	-1.1
1970	Hou N	7	4	.636	63	0	0	18-4	71	84	39	4	3	24-8	46	4.06	96	.293	.352	6-1	.000	-1		-3	-0.6
1971	Hou N	4	5	.444	48	0	0	12-4	51.1	51	17	0	7	22-7	17	2.10	160	.268	.362	2-0	.000	-0		6	1.1
1972	Hou N	5	6	.455	42	0	0	14-2	48.2	38	16	1	2	12-5	18	2.77	121	.222	.278	5-1	.000	-1		4	0.6
1973	Hou N	2	0	1.000	16	0	0	1-2	16	18	8	4	0	4-1	9	4.50	81	.290	.333	0-0	—	0		-1	-0.1
Total	13	48	34	.585	450	1	0	109-18	601	566	237	38	27	223-45	394	3.13	113	.252	.325	63-4	.016	-6	27	26	3.1
GLADE, FRED Frederick Monroe "Lucky" B 1.25.1876 Dubuque, IA D 11.21.1934 Grand Island, NE BR/TR 6/190# d5.27																									
1902	Chi N	0	1	.000	1	1	1	0	8	13	11	0	1	3	3	9.00	30	.361	.425	3-0	.333	1	50	-5	-0.4
1904	StL A	18	15	.545	35	34	30-6	1	289	248	101	2	13	58	156	2.27	109	.233	.281	102-3	.186	1	87	6	1.0
1905	StL A	6	25	.194	32	32	28-2	0	275	257	109	3	11	58	127	2.81	90	.249	.296	98-0	.092	-6	69	-3	-0.8
1906	StL A	15	14	.517	35	32	28-4	1	266.2	215	91	4	10	59	96	2.36	109	.224	.276	95-2	.137	-4	100	11	0.7
1907	StL A	13	9	.591	24	22	18-2	0	202	187	81	2	9	45	71	2.67	94	.248	.298	73-2	.205	2	121	-3	-0.3
1908	NY A	0	4	.000	5	5	2	0	32	30	18	0	4	14	11	4.22	59	.275	.378	10-0	.000	-1	66	-5	-0.7
Total	6	52	68	.433	132	126	107-14	2	1072.2	950	411	11	48	237	464	2.62	97	.240	.291	381-7	.150	-7	91	1	-0.5
GLAISER, JOHN John Burke "Bert" B 7.28.1894 Yoakum, TX D 3.7.1959 Houston, TX BL/TR 5-8/165# d4.20																									
1920	Det A	0	0	—	9	1	0	1	17	23	12	1	1	8	3	6.35	59	.354	.432	3-0	.000	-0	171	-4	-0.1
GLASS, TOM Thomas Joseph B 4.29.1898 Greensboro, NC D 12.15.1981 Greensboro, NC BR/TR 6-3/170# d6.12																									
1925	Phi A	1	0	1.000	2	0	0	0	5	9	4	0	0	0	2	5.40	86	.409	.409	2-1	.000	-0		-1	-0.1
GLAUBER, KEITH Keith Harris B 1.18.1972 Brooklyn, NY BR/TR 6-2/190# d9.8																									
1998	Cin N	0	0	—	3	0	0	0-0	7.2	6	2	0	0	1-0	4	2.35	182	.214	.226	2-0	.000	-0		2	0.0
2000	Cin N	0	0	—	4	0	0	0-0	7.1	5	3	0	1	2-0	4	3.68	128	.185	.267	1-0	.000	-0		1	0.0
Total	2	0	0	—	7	0	0	0-0	15	11	5	0	1	3-0	8	3.00	150	.200	.246	3-0	.000	-0		3	0.0
GLAVENICH, LUKE Luke Frank B 1.17.1893 Jackson, CA D 5.22.1935 Stockton, CA BR/TR 5-9.5/189# d4.12																									
1913	Cle A	0	0	—	1	0	0	0	1	3	5	0	0	3	1	9.00	34	.500	.667	0-0	—	0		-2	-0.1
GLAVINE, TOM Thomas Michael B 3.25.1966 Concord, MA BL/TL 6-1/190# d8.17 b-Mike																									
1987	Atl N	2	4	.333	9	9	0	0-0	50.1	55	34	5	3	33-4	20	5.54	79	.279	.386	16-0	.125	-0	85	-6	-0.6
1988	Atl N	7	17	.292	34	34	1	0-0	195.1	201	111	12	8	63-7	84	4.56	81	.270	.329	60-8	.183	1*	95	-18	-1.8
1989	Atl N	14	8	.636	29	29	6-4	0-0	186	172	88	20	2	40-3	90	3.68	99	.243	.283	67-4	.149	0*	127	-1	0.0
1990	Atl N	10	12	.455	33	33	1	0-0	214.1	232	111	18	1	78-10	129	4.28	94	.281	.343	62-7	.113	0*	93	-4	-0.2
1991	†Atl N★	**20**	11	.645	34	34	**9-1**	0-0	246.2	201	83	17	2	69-6	192	2.55	**152**	.222	.277	74-15	.230	4*	105	**33**	**4.9**
1992	†Atl N★	**20**	8	.714	33	33	7-**5**	0-0	225	197	81	6	2	70-7	129	2.76	133	.235	.293	77-9	.247	4*	114	20	3.0
1993	†Atl N☆	**22**	6	.786	36	**36**	4-2	0-0	239.1	236	91	16	2	90-7	120	3.20	126	.259	.327	81-11	.173	1	123	23	2.6
1994	Atl N	13	9	.591	25	25	2	0-0	165.1	173	76	10	1	70-10	140	3.97	107	.268	.338	56-9	.179	1*	116	7	1.1
1995	†Atl N	16	7	.696	29	29	3-1	0-0	198.2	182	76	9	5	66-0	127	3.08	139	.246	.310	63-8	.222	3	93	25	3.2
1996	†Atl N★	15	10	.600	36	**36**	1	0-0	235.1	222	91	14	0	85-7	181	2.98	148	.249	.314	76-15	.289	6*	90	34	4.3
1997	†Atl N☆	14	7	.667	33	33	5-2	0-0	240	197	86	20	4	79-9	152	2.96	142	.226	.292	63-17	.222	4	104	34	3.2
1998	†Atl N★	**20**	6	.769	33	33	4-3	0-0	229.1	202	67	13	2	74-2	157	2.47	168	.238	.300	71-14	.239	3	114	45	5.6
1999	†Atl N	14	11	.560	35	**35**	2	0-0	234	259	115	18	4	83-14	138	4.12	109	.287	.346	65-7	.138	-0*	105	12	1.3
2000	†Atl N★	**21**	9	.700	35	**35**	4-2	0-0	241	222	101	24	4	65-6	152	3.40	135	.244	.296	68-14	.147	1*	108	32	3.7
2001	†Atl N	16	7	.696	35	**35**	1-1	0-0	219.1	213	92	24	2	97-10	116	3.57	124	.261	.338	57-17	.140	0	105	22	2.2
2002	†Atl N☆	18	11	.621	36	**36**	2-1	0-0	224.2	210	85	21	8	78-8	127	2.96	138	.252	.320	68-13	.103	-2*	98	27	3.3
2003	NY N	9	14	.391	32	32	0	0-0	183.1	205	94	21	2	66-7	82	4.52	92	.288	.348	53-10	.151	1*	77	-5	-0.4
Total	17	251	157	.615	537	537	52-22	0-0	3528	3379	1482	268	52	1206-117	2136	3.43	121	.254	.317	1077-178	.185	27	103	280	35.4
GLAZE, RALPH Daniel Ralph B 3.13.1881 Denver, CO D 10.31.1968 Atascadero, CA BR/TR 5-9/165# d6.1																									
1906	Bos A	4	6	.400	19	10	7	0	123	110	58	4	5	32	56	3.59	77	.242	.299	55-1	.182	0*	107	-8	-0.6
1907	Bos A	9	13	.409	32	21	11-1	0	182.1	150	75	4	4	48	68	2.32	111	.227	.283	61-2	.180	0	97	3	0.1
1908	Bos A	2	2	.500	10	3	2	0	34.2	43	24	1	0	5	13	3.38	73	.253	.274	13-0	.077	-1	111	-5	-0.7
Total	3	15	21	.417	61	34	20-1	0	340	303	157	9	9	85	137	2.89	91	.236	.288	129-3	.171	-1	102	-10	-1.2
GLAZNER, WHITEY Charles Franklin B 9.17.1893 Sycamore, AL D 6.6.1989 Orlando, FL BR/TR 5-9/165# d9.26																									
1920	Pit N	0	0	—	2	0	0	0	8.2	9	3	0	0	2	1	3.12	103	.300	.344	3-0	.000	-0		0	-0.1
1921	Pit N	14	5	.737	36	25	15	1	234	214	88	5	12	58	88	2.77	139	**.250**	.306	76-6	.132	-3	96	26	1.4
1922	Pit N	11	12	.478	34	26	10-1	1	193	238	118	9	2	52	77	4.38	93	.309	.354	65-5	.246	3	86	-9	-0.6
1923	Pit N	2	1	.667	7	4	1-1	1	30	29	18	5	0	11	8	3.30	122	.250	.315	12-0	.333	2	149	0	0.2
	Phi N	7	14	.333	28	23	12-2	1	161.1	195	104	11	6	63	51	4.69	98	.304	.371	53-1	.170	-1	81	-2	-0.2
	Year	9	15	.375	35	27	13-3	2	191.1	224	109	16	6	74	59	4.47	101	.296	.363	65-1	.200	1	90	-5	0.0
1924	Phi N	7	16	.304	35	24	8-2	0	156.2	210	108	14	4	63	41	5.92	75	.339	.403	51-3	.157	-4	69	-18	-2.5
Total	5	41	48	.461	142	102	46-6	4	783.2	895	439	44	24	249	266	4.21	99	.295	.353	260-15	.181	-3	86	-3	-1.8
GLEASON, JOE Joseph Paul B 7.9.1895 Phelps, NY D 9.8.1990 Phelps, NY BR/TR 5-10.5/175# d9.11																									
1920	Was A	0	0	—	3	0	0	0	8	14	13	2	1	6	2	13.50	28	.326	.420	2-0	.000	1		-8	-0.3
1922	Was A	2	2	.500	8	5	3	0	40.2	53	26	3	1	18	12	4.65	83	.319	.389	14-0	.143	-0	141	-4	-0.4
Total	2	2	2	.500	11	5	3	0	48.2	67	39	5	2	24	14	6.10	63	.321	.396	16-0	.125	0	141	-12	-0.7
GLEASON, BILL William B 1868 Cleveland, OH D 12.2.1893 Cleveland, OH d4.24																									
1890	Cle P	0	1	.000	1	1	1	0	4	14	16	1	0	6	0	27.00	15	.538	.625	2	.000	-0	230	-9	-1.0
GLEASON, KID William J. B 10.26.1866 Camden, NJ D 1.2.1933 Philadelphia, PA BB/TR 5-7/158# d4.20 M5 C16 b-Harry ▲																									
1888	Phi N	7	16	.304	24	23	23	0	199.2	199	112	11	12	53	89	2.84	105	.252	.309	83	.205	0	84	0	-0.1
1889	Phi N	9	15	.375	29	21	15	1	205	242	177	8	9	97	64	5.58	78	.285	.364	99	.253	2*	92	-23	-1.9
1890	Phi N	38	17	.691	60	55	54-6	**2**	506	479	253	8	15	167	222	2.63	139	.242	.306	224	.210	-6*	94	51	4.0
1891	Phi N	24	22	.522	53	44	40-1	1	418	431	237	11	13	165	100	3.51	97	.256	.328	214	.248	6*	93	-2	0.2
1892	StL N	20	24	.455	47	45	43-2	0	400	389	244	11	10	151	133	3.33	96	.245	.314	233	.215	8*	112	-16	-0.4

Year	Tm Lg	W	L	Pct	G	GS	CG-Sho	SV-BS	IP	H	R	HR	HB	BB-IB	SO	ERA	AERA	OAV	OOB	AB-SH	AVG	PB	Sup	APR	PW
1893	StL N	21	22	.488	48	45	37-1	1	380.1	436	276	18	10	187	86	4.61	103	.279	.360	199	.256	4*	93	11	1.3
1894	StL N	2	6	.250	8	8	6	0	58	75	50	2	3	21	9	6.05	90	.310	.372	28-0	.250	-0*	60	-2	-0.2
	†Bal N	15	5	.750	21	20	19	0	172	224	111	3	3	44	35	4.45	123	.312	.354	86-4	.349	4*	109	19	1.9
	Year	17	11	.607	29	28	25	0	230	299	119	5	6	65	44	4.85	112	.311	.359	114-4	.325	4	95	21	1.7
1895	†Bal N	2	4	.333	9	5	3	1	50.1	77	51	4	3	21	6	6.97	68	.345	.409	421-6	.309	2*	185	-12	-1.0
Total	8	138	131	.513	299	266	240-10	6	2389.1	2552	1511	76	78	906	744	3.79	103	.265	.333	1587-10	.258	20	98	26	3.8
GLEATON, JERRY DON Jerry Don B 9.14.1957 Brownwood, TX BL/TL 6-3/210# d7.11																									
1979	Tex A	0	1	.000	5	2	0	0-0	9.2	15	7	0	1	2-0	2	6.52	64	.375	.409	0-0	—	0	65	-2	-0.2
1980	Tex A	0	0	—	5	0	0	0-0	7	5	2	0	0	4-0	2	2.57	152	.208	.300	0-0	—	0		1	0.1
1981	Sea A	4	7	.364	20	13	1	0-0	85.1	88	50	10	2	38-2	31	4.75	81	.273	.350	0-0	—	0	125	-8	-1.0
1982	Sea A	0	0	—	3	0	0	0-0	4.2	7	7	3	1	2-0	1	13.50	31	.333	.417	0-0	—	0		-4	-0.2
1984	Chi A	1	2	.333	11	1	0	2-1	18.1	20	12	2	1	6-0	4	3.44	121	.286	.333	0-0	—	0	0	0	-0.1
1985	Chi A	1	0	1.000	31	0	0	1-1	29.2	37	19	3	0	13-3	22	5.76	75	.316	.382	0-0	—	0		-4	-0.2
1987	KC A	4	4	.500	48	0	0	5-2	50.2	38	28	4	0	28-3	44	4.26	107	.216	.319	0-0	—	0		1	0.3
1988	KC A	0	4	.000	42	0	0	3-1	38	33	17	2	3	17-1	29	3.55	112	.232	.327	0-0	—	0		2	0.2
1989	KC A	0	0	—	15	0	0	0-0	14.1	20	10	0	0	6-0	9	5.65	68	.345	.394	0-0	—	0		-3	-0.1
1990	Det A	1	3	.250	57	0	0	13-3	82.2	62	27	5	3	25-2	56	2.94	135	.213	.279	0-0	—	0		10	0.7
1991	Det A	3	2	.600	47	0	0	2-1	75.1	74	37	7	0	39-8	47	4.06	102	.269	.355	0-0	—	0		1	0.1
1992	Pit N	1	0	1.000	23	0	0	0-2	31.2	34	16	4	0	19-3	18	4.26	81	.283	.379	2-1	.000	0		-3	-0.1
Total	12	15	23	.395	307	16	1	26-11	447.1	433	232	40	11	199-22	265	4.25	95	.261	.340	2-1	.000	0	107	-9	-0.5
GLENDON, MARTIN Martin J. B 2.8.1877 Milwaukee, WI D 11.6.1950 Norwood Park, IL BR/TR 5-8/165# d4.18																									
1902	Cin N	0	1	.000	1	1	0	0	3	5	5	0	0	4	0	12.00	25	.357	.500	1-0	.000	-0	45	-2	-0.4
1903	Cle A	1	2	.333	3	3	3	0	27.2	20	9	0	0	7	9	0.98	292	.202	.255	8-1	.000	-1	117	5	0.4
Total	2	1	3	.250	4	4	3	0	30.2	25	14	0	0	11	9	2.05	140	.221	.290	9-1	.000	-1	99	3	0.0
GLENN, BOB Burdette B 6.16.1894 W.Sunbury, PA D 6.3.1977 Richmond, CA BR/TR d7.27																									
1920	StL N	0	0	—	2	0	0	0	2	2	0	0	0	0	0	0.00	—	.222	.222	0-0	—	0		1	0.0
GLIATTO, SAL Salvador Michael B 5.7.1902 Chicago, IL D 11.2.1995 Tyler, TX BB/TR 5-8.5/150# d4.19																									
1930	Cle A	0	0	—	8	0	0	2	15	21	15	1	2	9	7	6.60	73	.328	.427	2-0	.000	-0*		-3	-0.2
GLINATSIS, GEORGE George B 6.29.1969 Youngstown, OH BR/TR 6-4/195# d7.18																									
1994	Sea A	0	1	.000	2	2	0	0-0	5.1	9	8	2	0	6-0	1	13.50	36	.429	.536	0-0	—	0	85	-5	-0.6
GLOVER, GARY John Gary B 12.3.1976 Cleveland, OH BR/TR 6-5/200# d9.30																									
1999	Tor A	0	0	—	1	0	0	0-0	1	0	0	0	0	1-0	0	0.00	—	.000	.333	0-0	—	0		1	0.0
2001	Chi A	5	5	.500	46	11	0	0-1	100.1	98	61	16	4	32-3	63	4.93	94	.252	.314	0-0	—	0	91	-4	-0.3
2002	Chi A	7	8	.467	41	22	0	1-0	138.1	136	86	21	7	52-1	70	5.20	87	.253	.326	1-0	.000	-0	124	-9	-0.9
2003	Chi A	1	0	1.000	24	0	0	0-0	35.2	43	18	3	2	14-2	23	4.54	100	.305	.369	0-0	—	0		1	0.0
	Ana A	1	0	1.000	18	0	0	0-0	27	34	15	3	1	8-1	14	5.00	86	.315	.361	0-0	—	0		-1	-0.1
	Year	2	0	1.000	42	0	0	0-0	62.2	77	39	6	3	22-3	37	4.74	94	.309	.366	0-0	—	0		0	-0.1
Total	4	14	13	.519	130	33	0	1-1	302.1	311	180	43	14	107-7	170	5.00	91	.264	.331	1-0	.000	-0	113	-12	-1.3
GLYNN, ED Edward Paul B 6.3.1953 Flushing, NY BR/TL 6-2/180# d9.19																									
1975	Det A	0	2	.000	3	1	0	0-0	14.2	11	8	1	0	8-0	8	4.30	94	.220	.322	0-0	—	0	0	0	0.0
1976	Det A	1	3	.250	5	4	1	0-0	23.2	22	18	3	0	20-1	17	6.08	61	.265	.396	0-0	—	0	112	-6	-0.9
1977	Det A	2	1	.667	8	3	0	0-0	27.1	36	17	3	0	12-1	13	5.27	82	.316	.372	0-0	—	0	153	-2	-0.2
1978	Det A	0	0	—	10	0	0	0-0	14.2	11	5	3	0	4-0	9	3.07	126	.208	.259	0-0	—	0		2	0.1
1979	NY N	1	4	.200	46	0	0	7-4	60	57	22	3	2	40-10	32	3.00	122	.259	.372	4-0	.000	-0		5	0.4
1980	NY N	3	3	.500	38	0	0	1-1	52.1	49	26	5	0	23-4	32	4.13	86	.246	.321	6-2	.000	-1		-3	-0.4
1981	Cle A	0	0	—	4	0	0	0-0	7.2	5	1	0	0	4-0	4	1.17	309	.192	.300	0-0	—	0		2	0.1
1982	Cle A	5	2	.714	47	0	0	4-4	49.2	43	27	6	0	30-5	54	4.17	98	.232	.336	0-0	—	0		-1	-0.2
1983	Cle A	0	2	.000	11	0	0	0-1	12.1	22	11	2	0	6-0	13	5.84	73	.373	.424	0-0	—	0		-3	-0.4
1985	Mon N	0	0	—	3	0	0	0-0	2.1	5	5	0	0	4-0	2	19.29	18	.455	.600	0-0	—	0		-4	-0.2
Total	10	12	17	.414	175	8	1	12-10	264.2	261	140	26	2	151-21	184	4.25	90	.261	.354	10-2	.000	-1	119	-10	-1.7
GLYNN, RYAN Ryan David B 11.1.1974 Portsmouth, VA BR/TR 6-3/195# d5.16																									
1999	Tex A	2	4	.333	13	10	0	0-0	54.2	71	46	10	1	35-0	39	7.24	70	.316	.408	1-0	.000	-0	136	-12	-1.1
2000	Tex A	5	7	.417	16	16	0	0-0	88.2	107	65	15	3	41-2	33	5.58	90	.293	.369	2-0	.000	-0	83	-7	-0.8
2001	Tex A	1	5	.167	12	9	0	0-0	46	59	38	7	0	26-1	15	7.04	66	.309	.388	0-0	—	0	79	-12	-1.2
Total	3	8	16	.333	41	35	0	0-0	189.1	237	149	32	4	102-3	87	6.42	77	.303	.385	3-0	.000	-0	98	-31	-3.1
GOAR, JOT Joshua Mercer B 1.31.1870 New Lisbon, IN D 4.4.1947 New Castle, IN BR/TR 5-9/160# d4.18																									
1896	Pit N	0	1	.000	3	0	0	0	13.1	36	33	1	1	8	3	16.88	25	.486	.542	6-0	.167	-1		-19	-1.0
1898	Cin N	0	0	—	1	0	0	0	2	4	3	0	0	1	0	9.00	43	.400	.455	0-0	—	0		-1	0.0
Total	2	0	1	.000	4	0	0	0	15.1	40	36	1	1	9	3	15.85	26	.476	.532	6-0	.167	-1		-20	-1.0
GOBBLE, JIMMY Billy James B 7.19.1981 Bristol, TN BL/TL 6-3/190# d8.3																									
2003	KC A	4	5	.444	9	9	0	0-0	52.2	56	32	8	4	15-0	31	4.61	112	.271	.328	0-0	—	0	67	2	0.2
GOETZ, GEORGE George Burt B Greencastle, PA 6-2/180# d6.17																									
1889	Bal AA	1	0	1.000	1	1	0	0	9	12	6	0	0	0	2	4.00	99	.308	.308	4	.000	-1	157	0	0.0
GOETZ, JOHN John Hardy B 10.24.1937 Goetzville, MI BR/TR 6/185# d4.16																									
1960	Chi N	0	0	—	4	0	0	0	6.1	10	9	2	0	4-1	6	12.79	30	.370	.452	1-0	.000	-0		-6	-0.3
GOGOLEWSKI, BILL William Joseph B 10.26.1947 Oshkosh, WI BL/TR 6-4/190# d9.3																									
1970	Was A	2	2	.500	8	5	0	0-0	33.2	33	18	2	1	25-1	19	4.81	74	.260	.386	7-2	.000	-0	65	-4	-0.4
1971	Was A	6	5	.545	27	17	4-1	0-0	124.1	112	39	5	2	39-6	70	2.75	120	.241	.301	32-4	.156	0	100	10	0.9
1972	Tex A	4	11	.267	36	21	2-1	2-0	150.2	136	74	9	6	58-9	95	4.24	71	.239	.315	40-2	.125	-1	84	-17	-1.9
1973	Tex A	3	6	.333	49	1	0	6-2	123.2	139	67	10	1	48-16	77	4.22	88	.286	.348	0-0	—	0	96	-7	-0.5
1974	Cle A	0	0	—	5	0	0	0-0	13.2	15	7	1	1	2-0	3	4.61	79	.283	.321	0-0	—	0		-1	0.0
1975	Chi A	0	0	—	19	0	0	2-1	55	61	35	5	1	28-3	37	5.24	74	.292	.377	0-0	—	0		-8	-0.4
Total	6	15	24	.385	144	44	6-2	10-3	501	496	240	32	12	200-35	301	4.02	85	.260	.332	79-8	.127	-1	83	-27	-2.3
GOHR, GREG Gregory James B 10.29.1967 Santa Clara, CA BR/TR 6-3/205# d4.7																									
1993	Det A	0	0	—	16	0	0	0-1	22.2	26	15	1	2	14-2	23	5.96	72	.289	.393	0-0	—	0		-3	-0.2
1994	Det A	2	2	.500	8	6	0	0-0	34	36	19	3	0	21-1	21	4.50	108	.263	.358	0-0	—	0	70	1	0.1
1995	Det A	1	0	1.000	10	0	0	0-0	10.1	9	1	0	0	3-0	12	0.87	547	.243	.300	0-0	—	0		4	0.4
1996	Det A	4	8	.333	17	16	0	0-0	91.2	129	76	24	3	34-2	60	7.17	71	.328	.383	0-0	—	0	81	-20	-2.1
	Cal A	1	1	.500	15	0	0	1-0	24	34	20	7	0	10-0	15	7.50	67	.337	.393	0-0	—	0		-6	-0.4
	Year	5	9	.357	32	16	0	1-0	115.2	163	100	31	3	44-2	75	7.24	70	.330	.385	0-0	—	0	81	-26	-2.5
Total	4	8	11	.421	66	22	0	1-1	182.2	234	131	35	5	82-5	131	6.21	79	.309	.377	0-0	—	0	80	-24	-2.2
GOLDEN, JIM James Edward B 3.20.1936 Eldon, MO BL/TR 6/175# d9.30																									
1960	LA N	1	0	1.000	1	1	0	0	7	6	5	1	0	4-0	4	6.43	62	.240	.333	3-0	.333	0	156	-2	-0.1
1961	LA N	1	1	.500	28	0	0	0	42	52	30	7	0	20-2	18	5.79	75	.306	.377	3-0	.000	-0		-6	-0.4
1962	Hou N	7	11	.389	37	18	5-2	1	152.2	163	84	13	0	50-4	88	4.07	92	.270	.324	54-3	.222	4*	108	-8	-0.4
1963	Hou N	0	1	.000	3	1	0	0	6.1	12	4	0	0	2-0	5	5.68	55	.429	.467	0-0	—	0	0	-2	-0.2
Total	4	9	13	.409	69	20	5-2	1	208	233	123	21	0	76-6	115	4.54	85	.282	.340	60-3	.217	4	103	-18	-1.1
GOLDEN, MIKE Michael Henry B 9.11.1851 Shirley, MA D 1.11.1929 Rockford, IL BR/TR 5-8/168# d5.5 ▲																									
1875	Wes NA	1	12	.077	13	13	13	0	113	111	88	0		12	20	1.83	133	.225	.243	46	.130	-4	50	7	0.3
	Chi NA	6	7	.462	14	14	12-1	0	119	129	95	0		8	14	1.89	120	.247	.258	155	.258	1*	95	5	0.4
	Year	7	19	.269	27	27	25-1	0	232	240	101	0		20	34	1.86	126	.236	.251	201	.229	-3	73	1	0.7

Year	Tm Lg	W	L	Pct	G	GS	CG-Sho	SV-BS	IP	H	R	HR	HB	BB-IB	SO	ERA	AERA	OAV	OOB	AB-SH	AVG	PB	Sup	APR	PW
1878	Mil N	3	13	.188	22	18	15	0	161	217	171	1		33	52	4.14	63	.295	.325	214	.206	-2*	79	-22	-1.8
GOLDEN, ROY Roy Kramer B 7.12.1888 Madisonville, OH D 10.4.1961 Norwood, OH BR/TR 6-1/195# d9.7																									
1910	StL N	2	3	.400	7	6	3	0	42.2	44	28	3	2	33	31	4.43	67	.286	.418	15-2	.267	1	92	-7	-0.7
1911	StL N	4	9	.308	30	25	6	0	148.2	127	90	6	5	129	81	5.02	67	.240	.394	44-1	.114	-1	125	-21	-1.7
Total	2	6	12	.333	37	31	9	0	191.1	171	118	9	7	162	112	4.89	67	.250	.399	59-3	.153	-1	119	-28	-2.4
GOLDSMITH, FRED Fredrick Ernest B 5.15.1852 New Haven, CT D 3.28.1939 Berkley, MI BR/TR 6-1/195# d10.23.1875 U2																									
1879	Tro N	2	4	.333	8	7	7	0	63	61	38	0		1	31	1.57	159	.237	.240	38	.237	0*	69	4	0.4
1880	Chi N	21	3	**.875**	26	24	22-4	1	210.1	189	80	2		18	90	1.75	138	.231	.247	142	.261	2*	123	15	1.7
1881	Chi N	24	13	.649	39	39	37-5	0	330	328	166	4		44	76	2.59	106	.247	.271	158	.241	3*	131	9	1.2
1882	Chi N	28	17	.622	45	45	45-4	0	405	377	192	7		38	109	2.42	119	.236	.254	183	.230	-2	129	23	1.8
1883	Chi N	25	19	.568	46	45	40-2	0	383.1	456	256	14		39	82	3.15	105	.277	.294	235	.221	-1*	108	10	0.8
1884	Chi N	9	11	.450	21	21	20-1	0	188	245	140	11		29	34	4.26	74	.298	.322	81	.136	-2*	125	-15	-1.6
	Bal AA	3	1	.750	4	4	3	0	30	29	12	0	1	2	11	2.70	128	.238	.256	14	.143	-0	87	3	0.4
Total	6	112	68	.622	189	185	174-16	1	1609.2	1685	884	38	1	171	433	2.73	107	.256	.275	851	.224	-2	120	49	4.7
GOLDSMITH, HAL Harold Eugene B 8.18.1898 Peconic, NY D 10.20.1985 Riverhead, NY BR/TR 6/174# d6.23																									
1926	Bos N	5	7	.417	19	15	5	0	101	135	62	2	1	28	16	4.37	81	.333	.377	38-1	.211	0	119	-12	-1.1
1927	Bos N	1	3	.250	22	5	1	1	71.2	83	34	4	0	26	13	3.52	106	.289	.348	21-1	.238	0	128	1	0.1
1928	Bos N	0	0	—	4	0	0	0	8.1	14	5	2	0	1	1	3.24	121	.359	.375	2-0	.000	-0		0	0.0
1929	StL N	0	0	—	2	0	0	0	4	3	3	1	0	1	0	6.75	69	.214	.267	1-0	.000	-0		-1	-0.1
Total	4	6	10	.375	47	20	6	1	185	235	104	9	1	56	30	4.04	90	.315	.364	62-2	.210	0	120	-12	-1.1
GOLDSTEIN, IZZY Isidore B 6.6.1908 Odessa, Russia D 9.24.1993 Delray Beach, FL BB/TR 6/160# d4.24																									
1932	Det A	3	2	.600	16	6	2	0	56.1	63	42	2	3	41	14	4.47	105	.276	.393	17-0	.294	1	82	-2	-0.1
GOLTZ, DAVE David Allan B 6.23.1949 Pelican Rapids, MN BR/TR 6-4/215# d7.18																									
1972	Min A	3	3	.500	15	11	2	1-0	91	75	30	5	0	26-3	38	2.67	121	.224	.278	29-3	.103	-1	98	6	0.3
1973	Min A	6	4	.600	32	10	1	1-1	106.1	138	68	11	2	32-1	65	5.25	76	.318	.363	0-0	—	0	133	-14	-1.1
1974	Min A	10	10	.500	28	24	5-1	1-0	174.1	192	81	14	7	45-1	89	3.25	115	.282	.330	0-0	—	0	109	5	0.6
1975	Min A	14	14	.500	32	32	15-1	0-0	243	235	112	18	6	72-2	128	3.67	105	.255	.312	0-0	—	0	96	5	0.6
1976	Min A	14	14	.500	36	35	13-4	0-0	249.1	239	113	14	5	91-4	133	3.36	107	.254	.320	0-0	—	0*	97	4	0.4
1977	Min A	**20**	11	.645	39	**39**	19-2	0-0	303	284	129	23	2	91-4	186	3.36	119	.247	.303	0-0	—	0*	124	20	1.8
1978	Min A	15	10	.600	29	29	13-2	0-0	220.1	209	72	12	1	67-1	116	2.49	154	.253	.307	0-0	—	0	91	31	3.5
1979	Min A	14	13	.519	36	35	12-1	0-0	250.2	282	124	22	1	69-3	132	4.16	106	.288	.334	0-0	—	0	96	7	0.6
1980	LA N	7	11	.389	35	27	2-2	1-1	171.1	198	91	12	0	59-3	91	4.31	81	.299	.353	47-7	.128	0	110	-16	-1.6
1981	†LA N	2	7	.222	26	8	0	1-4	77	83	35	4	0	25-3	48	4.09	81	.288	.343	17-2	.059	-1	117	-6	-0.7
1982	LA N	0	1	.000	2	1	0	0-0	3.2	6	4	0	0	0-0	3	4.91	71	.353	.353	1-0	.000	-0	76	-1	-0.3
	†Cal A	8	5	.615	28	7	1	3-0	86	82	43	4	1	32-1	49	4.08	100	.252	.317	0-0	—	0	128	-1	-0.2
1983	Cal A	0	6	.000	15	6	0	0-2	63.2	81	48	10	1	37-2	27	6.22	65	.315	.399	0-0	—	0	98	-16	-1.3
Total	12	113	109	.509	353	264	83-13	8-8	2039.2	2104	950	149	26	646-28	1105	3.69	104	.269	.325	94-12	.106	-1	105	24	2.6
GOMES, WAYNE Wayne Maurice B 1.15.1973 Hampton, VA BR/TR 6/215# d6.13																									
1997	Phi N	5	1	.833	37	0	0	0-1	42.2	45	26	4	1	24-0	24	5.27	81	.274	.370	2-0	.000	0		-4	-0.6
1998	Phi N	9	6	.600	71	0	0	1-7	93.1	94	48	9	3	35-4	86	4.24	102	.258	.328	2-0	.000	-0		1	0.0
1999	Phi N	5	5	.500	73	0	0	19-5	74	70	38	5	2	56-2	58	4.26	111	.255	.381	1-0	.000	-0		4	0.5
2000	Phi N	4	6	.400	65	0	0	7-4	73.2	72	41	6	3	35-3	49	4.40	106	.262	.347	0-0	—	0		1	0.1
2001	Phi N	4	3	.571	42	0	0	1-4	48	51	23	4	1	22-4	35	4.31	99	.276	.351	1-0	1.000	1		1	0.1
	SF N	2	0	1.000	13	0	0	0-0	15	21	14	3	0	7-2	17	8.40	47	.350	.412	0-0	—	0		-7	-0.8
	Year	6	3	.667	55	0	0	1-4	63	72	42	7	1	29-6	52	5.29	79	.294	.366	1-0	1.000	1		-6	-0.7
2002	Bos A	1	2	.333	20	0	0	1-0	21.1	20	11	2	3	12-2	15	4.64	97	.241	.357	0-0	—	0		0	0.0
Total	6	30	23	.566	321	0	0	29-21	368	373	201	33	13	191-17	284	4.60	97	.265	.356	6-0	.167	1		-4	-0.7
GOMEZ, PAT Patrick Alexander B 3.17.1968 Roseville, CA BL/TL 5-11/185# d4.6																									
1993	SD N	1	2	.333	27	1	0	0-0	31.2	35	19	2	0	19-4	26	5.12	81	.292	.378	5-0	.000	-1*	87	-3	-0.3
1994	SF N	0	1	.000	26	0	0	0-0	33.1	23	14	2	0	20-1	14	3.78	106	.211	.328	2-1	.000	-0		2	0.0
1995	SF N	0	0	—	18	0	0	0-0	14	16	8	2	0	12-1	15	5.14	80	.276	.400	1-0	.000	-0		-1	-0.1
Total	3	1	3	.250	71	1	0	0-0	79	74	41	6	0	51-6	55	4.56	90	.258	.363	8-1	.000	-1	87	-2	-0.4
GOMEZ, RUBEN Ruben (Colon) B 7.13.1927 Arroyo, P.R. BR/TR 6/175# d4.17																									
1953	NY N	13	11	.542	29	26	13-3	0	204	166	89	17	4	101	113	3.40	126	.218	.313	72-6	.208	-0*	81	20	2.2
1954	†NY N	17	9	.654	37	32	10-4	0	221.2	202	85	20	7	109	106	2.88	140	.244	.336	81-4	.173	0*	104	27	3.0
1955	NY N	9	10	.474	33	31	9-3	1	185.1	207	103	20	7	63-6	79	4.56	88	.285	.345	60-4	.300	4*	103	-9	-0.3
1956	NY N	7	17	.292	40	31	4-2	0	196.1	191	108	19	9	77-8	76	4.58	83	.259	.334	60-1	.183	-0*	84	-15	-1.6
1957	NY N	15	13	.536	38	36	16-1	0	238.1	233	110	28	5	71-10	92	3.78	104	.254	.309	87-4	.184	1*	103	5	0.9
1958	SF N	10	12	.455	42	30	8-1	1	207.2	204	107	21	8	77-3	112	4.38	87	.261	.330	70-4	.200	1*	126	-10	-0.7
1959	Phi N	3	8	.273	20	12	2-1	1	72.1	90	55	12	0	24-2	37	6.10	67	.300	.350	17-3	.176	0*	82	-15	-2.0
1960	Phi N	0	3	.000	22	1	0	1	52.1	68	37	7	1	9-2	24	5.33	73	.321	.344	12-1	.083	-1	273	-9	-0.6
1962	Cle A	1	2	.333	15	4	0	1	45.1	50	23	5	2	25-3	21	4.37	89	.292	.383	13-0	.231	0*	104	-2	-0.1
	Min A	1	1	.500	6	2	1	0	19.1	17	11	3	0	11-2	8	4.66	88	.254	.354	5-0	.000	-0	87	-1	-0.1
	Year	2	3	.400	21	6	1	1	64.2	67	15	8	2	36-5	29	4.45	88	.282	.375	18-0	.167	-0	98	-3	-0.2
1967	Phi N	0	0	—	7	0	0	0	11.1	8	6	2	0	7-3	9	3.97	86	.211	.333	0-0	—	0		-1	0.0
Total	10	76	86	.469	289	205	63-15	5	1454	1436	734	154	43	574-39	677	4.09	97	.259	.331	477-27	.199	6	100	-10	0.7
GOMEZ, LEFTY Vernon Louis "Goofy" B 11.26.1908 Rodeo, CA D 2.17.1989 Greenbrae, CA BL/TL 6-2/173# d4.29 Def 1943 HF1972																									
1930	NY A	2	5	.286	15	6	2	1	60	66	41	12	1	28	22	5.55	78	.280	.358	20-3	.150	-2	120	-7	-0.8
1931	NY A	21	9	.700	40	26	17-1	3	243	206	88	7	4	85	150	2.67	149	.226	.295	83-4	.133	-3	126	36	3.6
1932	†NY A	24	7	.774	37	31	21-1	1	265.1	266	140	23	2	105	176	4.21	97	.259	.329	104-5	.173	-1	145	-2	-0.5
1933	NY A★	16	10	.615	35	30	14-4	2	234.2	218	108	16	0	106	**163**	3.18	122	.240	.319	80-5	.112	-3	107	15	1.0
1934	NY A★	**26**	5	**.839**	38	33	**25-6**	1	**281.2**	223	86	12	0	96	**158**	**2.33**	174	**.215**	**.282**	99-13	.131	-3	125	**59**	5.5
1935	NY A★	12	15	.444	34	30	15-2	1	246	223	104	18	2	86	138	3.18	127	.242	.309	83-7	.120	-6	96	26	1.8
1936	†NY A☆	13	7	.650	31	30	10	0	188.2	184	104	6	1	122	105	4.39	106	.254	.362	69-8	.145	-3	117	6	0.2
1937	†NY A★	**21**	11	.656	34	34	25-**6**	0	278.1	233	88	10	1	93	**194**	**2.33**	191	**.223**	.287	105-5	.200	-1	106	**67**	**6.8**
1938	†NY A★	18	12	.600	32	32	20-**4**	0	239	239	110	7	1	99	129	3.35	135	.260	.332	86-9	.151	-2	107	31	3.2
1939	†NY A☆	12	8	.600	26	26	14-2	0	198	173	80	11	3	84	102	3.41	128	.235	.316	73-4	.151	-2	100	24	1.9
1940	NY A	3	3	.500	9	5	0	0	27.1	37	20	2	1	18	14	6.59	61	.325	.421	9-0	.000	-1	139	-7	-1.4
1941	NY A	15	5	**.750**	23	23	8-2	0	156.1	151	76	10	1	103	76	3.74	105	.250	.360	59-4	.153	-1	128	3	0.1
1942	NY A	6	4	.600	13	13	2	0	80	67	42	4	2	65	41	4.27	80	.237	.383	33-1	.152	-1	153	-7	-1.0
1943	Was A	0	1	.000	1	1	0	0	4.2	4	4	0	0	5	0	5.79	55	.250	.429	1-0	.000	-0	26	-2	-0.3
Total	14	189	102	.649	368	320	173-28	9	2503	2290	1091	138	19	1095	1468	3.34	125	.242	.321	904-68	.147	-30	117	242	20.1
GONZALES, JOE Joe Madrid "Smokey" B 3.19.1915 San Francisco, CA D 11.16.1996 Torrance, CA BR/TR 5-9/175# d8.25																									
1937	Bos A	1	2	.333	8	2	2	0	31	37	16	1	0	11	11	4.35	109	.291	.348	10-1	.000	-2	73	2	0.0
GONZALES, VINCE Wenceslao (O'Reilly) B 9.28.1925 Quivican, Cuba D 3.11.1981 Ciudad Del Carmen, Mexico BL/TL 6-1/165# d4.13																									
1955	Was A	0	0	—	1	0	0	0	2	6	6	0	0	3-0	1	27.00	14	.500	.600	0-0	—	0		-5	-0.2
GONZALEZ, DICKY Dicky Angel B 12.21.1978 Bayamon, P.R. BR/TR 5-11/170# d5.1																									
2001	NY N	3	2	.600	16	7	0	0-0	59	72	33	4	1	17-3	31	4.88	85	.306	.347	20-1	.100	-1	134	-4	-0.4
GONZALEZ, EDGAR Edgar Gerardo B 2.23.1983 Monterrey, Mexico BR/TR 6/220# d6.1																									
2003	Ari N	2	1	.667	9	2	0	0-1	18.1	28	10	3	0	7-2	14	4.91	95	.368	.417	4-1	.250	0	131	0	0.0

Year	Tm Lg	W	L	Pct	G	GS	CG-Sho	SV-BS	IP	H	R	HR	HB	BB-IB	SO	ERA	AERA	OAV	OOB	AB-SH	AVG	PB	Sup	APR	PW
GONZALEZ, GABE Gabriel B 5.24.1972 Long Beach, CA BB/TL 6-1/160# d4.1																									
1998	Fla N	0	0	—	3	0	0	0-0	1	1	1	0	1	1-0	0	9.00	45	.333	.600	0-0	—	0		-1	0.0
GONZALEZ, JEREMI Geremis Segundo (Acosta) B 1.8.1975 Maracaibo, Venezuela BR/TR 6-2/200# d5.27																									
1997	Chi N	11	9	.550	23	23	1-1	0-0	144	126	73	16	2	69-5	93	4.25	101	.236	.323	40-8	.100	-1	99	1	-0.1
1998	Chi N	7	7	.500	20	20	1-1	0-0	110	124	72	13	3	41-5	70	5.32	83	.281	.344	32-8	.188	0*	111	-12	-1.3
2003	TB A	6	11	.353	25	25	2	0-0	156.1	131	71	18	12	69-1	97	3.91	116	.228	.319	6-0	.000	-1	71	12	1.0
Total	3	24	27	.471	68	68	4-2	0-0	410.1	381	216	47	17	179-11	260	4.41	100	.246	.327	78-16	.128	-2	92	1	-0.4
GONZALEZ, GERMAN German Jose (Caraballo) B 3.7.1962 Rio Caribe, Venezuela BR/TR 6/170# d8.5																									
1988	Min A	0	0	—	16	0	0	1-0	21.1	20	8	4	1	8-1	19	3.38	121	.244	.319	0-0	—	0		2	0.1
1989	Min A	3	2	.600	22	0	0	0-0	29	32	17	2	4	11-1	25	4.66	89	.274	.353	0-0	—	0		-2	-0.3
Total	2	3	2	.600	38	0	0	1-0	50.1	52	25	6	5	19-2	44	4.11	100	.261	.339	0-0	—	0		0	-0.2
GONZALEZ, JULIO Julio Enrique (Herrera) B 12.20.1920 Banes, Cuba D 2.15.1991 Banes, Cuba BR/TR 5-11/150# d8.9																									
1949	Was A	0	0	—	13	0	0	0	34.1	33	20	3	1	27	5	4.72	90	.256	.389	5-0	.200	0		-2	0.0
GONZALEZ, LARIEL Lariel Alfonso B 5.25.1976 San Cristobal, D.R. BR/TR 6-4/228# d9.22																									
1998	Col N	0	0	—	1	0	0	0-0	1	0	0	0	0	0-0	0	0.00	—	.000	.000	0-0	—	0		0	0.0
GONZALEZ, MIKE Michael Vela B 5.23.1978 Corpus Christi, TX BR/TL 6-2/210# d8.11																									
2003	Pit N	0	1	.000	16	0	0	0-0	8.1	7	7	4	0	6-0	6	7.56	58	.233	.351	0-0	—	0		-3	-0.3
GOOD, ANDREW Andrew Richard B 9.19.1979 San Diego, CA BR/TR 6-3/170# d4.18																									
2003	Ari N	4	2	.667	16	10	0	0-0	66.1	74	42	15	3	16-3	42	5.29	88	.281	.325	16-4	.125	-1	88	-4	-0.4
GOOD, RALPH Ralph Nelson "Holy" B 4.25.1886 Monticello, ME D 11.24.1965 Waterville, ME BR/TR 6/165# d7.1																									
1910	Bos N	0	0	—	2	0	0	0	9	6	4	0	2	2	4	2.00	166	.188	.278	3-0	.000	-0		1	0.0
GOOD, WILBUR Wilbur David "Lefty" B 9.28.1885 Punxsutawney, PA D 12.30.1963 Brooksville, FL BL/TL 5-11.5/180# d8.18 ▲																									
1905	NY A	0	2	.000	5	2	0	0	19	18	17	1	0	14	13	4.74	62	.250	.372	8-0	.375	1	24	-4	-0.4
GOODALL, HERB Herbert Frank B 3.10.1870 Mansfield, PA D 1.20.1938 Mansfield, PA BR/TR 5-9/180# d4.29																									
1890	Lou AA	8	5	.615	18	13	8-1	**4**	109	94	73	2	10	51	46	3.39	114	.225	.324	45	.422	6*	104	5	1.1
GOODELL, JOHN John Henry William "Lefty" B 4.5.1907 Muskogee, OK D 9.21.1993 Mesquite, TX BR/TL 5-10/165# d4.19																									
1928	Chi A	0	0	—	2	0	0	0	3	6	6	0	1	2	0	18.00	23	.500	.600	0-0	—	0		-4	-0.2
GOODEN, DWIGHT Dwight Eugene "Doc" B 11.16.1964 Tampa, FL BR/TR 6-3/210# d4.7																									
1984	NY N★	17	9	.654	31	31	7-3	0-0	218	161	72	7	2	73-2	**276**	2.60	136	**.202**	**.269**	70-10	.200	1	93	**24**	2.9
1985	NY N☆	**24**	4	.857	35	35	**16**-8	0-0	**276.2**	198	51	13	2	69-4	**268**	**1.53**	**227**	.201	.254	93-9	.226	6	125	**62**	**7.5**
1986	†NY N★	17	6	.739	33	33	12-2	0-0	250	197	92	17	4	80-3	200	2.84	125	.215	.278	81-13	.086	-3	117	19	1.5
1987	NY N	15	7	**.682**	25	25	7-3	0-0	179.2	162	68	11	2	53-2	148	3.21	118	.244	.299	64-5	.219	2	121	14	1.8
1988	†NY N★	18	9	.667	34	34	10-3	0-0	248.1	242	98	8	6	57-4	175	3.19	101	.256	.301	90-9	.178	3	154	2	0.8
1989	NY N	9	4	.692	19	17	0	1-0	118.1	93	42	9	2	47-2	101	2.89	113	.211	.288	40-3	.200	2	97	6	0.8
1990	NY N	19	7	.731	34	34	2-1	0-0	232.2	229	106	10	7	70-3	223	3.83	98	.258	.314	75-14	.187	4*	142	0	0.4
1991	NY N	13	7	.650	27	27	3-1	0-0	190	185	80	12	3	56-2	150	3.60	101	.257	.311	63-8	.238	4	124	4	0.8
1992	NY N	10	13	.435	31	31	3	0-0	206	197	93	11	3	70-7	145	3.67	95	.255	.317	72-4	.264	7*	85	-5	0.3
1993	NY N	12	15	.444	29	29	7-2	0-0	208.2	188	89	16	9	61-1	149	3.45	116	.242	.302	70-6	.200	4*	91	15	2.2
1994	NY N	3	4	.429	7	7	0	0-0	41.1	46	32	9	1	15-1	40	6.31	66	.282	.346	12-4	.167	-0	112	-10	-1.3
1996	NY A	11	7	.611	29	29	1-1	0-0	170.2	169	101	19	9	88-4	126	5.01	99	.259	.352	0-0	—	0	94	-2	-0.1
1997	†NY A	9	5	.643	20	19	0	0-0	106.1	116	61	14	7	53-1	66	4.91	91	.283	.373	4-0	.000	-0	100	-4	-0.5
1998	†Cle A	8	6	.571	23	23	0	0-0	134	135	59	13	9	51-0	83	3.76	127	.262	.337	2-0	.000	-0	84	15	1.4
1999	Cle A	3	4	.429	26	22	0	0-0	115	127	90	18	9	67-3	88	6.26	81	.282	.382	2-0	.500	2	141	-16	-0.7
2000	Hou N	0	0	—	1	1	0	0-0	4	6	4	1	0	3-0	1	9.00	54	.353	.450	1-0	.000	-0	151	-2	-0.1
	TB A	2	3	.400	8	8	0	0-0	36.2	47	32	14	3	20-0	23	6.63	75	.315	.407	0-0	—	0	85	-8	-0.9
	†NY A	4	2	.667	18	5	0	2-0	64.1	66	28	8	0	21-3	31	3.36	144	.266	.321	2-0	.000	-0	108	10	0.9
	Year	6	5	.545	26	13	0	2-0	101	113	34	22	3	41-3	54	4.54	107	.285	.354	2-0	.000	-0	95	2	0.0
Total	16	194	112	.634	430	410	68-24	3-0	2800.2	2564	1198	210	78	954-42	2293	3.51	110	.244	.309	741-85	.196	30	113	124	17.7
GOODWIN, ART Arthur Ingram B 2.27.1877 Whiteley Twnshp, PA D 6.19.1943 Franklin Township, PA TR 5-8/195# d10.7																									
1905	NY A	0	0	—	1	0	0	0	0.1	2	4	0	0	2	0	81.00	4	.667	.800	0-0	—	0		-3	-0.1
GOODWIN, CLYDE Clyde Samuel B 11.12.1886 Athens, OH D 10.12.1963 Dayton, OH BR/TR 5-11/145# d9.18																									
1906	Was A	0	2	.000	4	3	1	0	22.1	20	16	0	1	13	9	4.43	59	.244	.354	5-1	.200	-0	118	-5	-0.4
GOODWIN, JIM James Patrick B 8.15.1926 St.Louis, MO BL/TL 6-1/170# d4.24																									
1948	Chi A	0	0	—	8	1	0	1	10.1	9	11	0	1	12	3	8.71	49	.237	.431	2-0	.500	0	85	-5	-0.2
GOODWIN, MARV Marvin Mardo B 1.16.1891 Gordonsville, VA D 10.21.1925 Houston, TX BR/TR 5-11/168# d9.7 Mil 1918																									
1916	Was A	0	0	—	3	0	0	0	5.2	5	4	0	0	3	1	3.18	88	.217	.308	1-0	.000	-0		-1	-0.1
1917	StL N	6	4	.600	14	12	6-3	0	85.1	70	33	1	0	19	38	2.21	122	.222	.266	23-5	.174	-0	100	1	0.2
1919	StL N	11	9	.550	33	17	7	0	179	163	66	3	8	33	48	2.51	111	.245	.289	60-1	.200	1*	127	5	0.6
1920	StL N	3	8	.273	32	12	3	1	116.1	153	79	1	5	28	23	4.95	60	.314	.357	35-3	.200	-0	119	-26	-2.5
1921	StL N	1	2	.333	14	4	1	1	36.1	47	21	1	1	9	7	3.72	99	.315	.358	6-3	.000	-1	157	-1	-0.1
1922	StL N	0	0	—	2	0	0	0	4	3	1	0	0	3	0	2.25	172	.250	.400	0-0	—	0		1	0.1
1925	Cin N	0	2	.000	4	3	2	0	20.2	26	14	2	1	5	4	4.79	86	.317	.364	4-1	.250	0	62	-2	-0.1
Total	7	21	25	.457	102	48	19-3	2	447.1	467	218	8	15	100	121	3.30	90	.269	.315	129-13	.186	0	117	-23	-1.9
GORDINIER, RAY Raymond Cornelius "Gordy" B 4.11.1892 Rochester, NY D 11.15.1960 Rochester, NY BB/TR 5-8.5/170# d9.17																									
1921	Bro N	1	0	1.000	3	3	0	0	12	10	8	0	0	8	4	5.25	74	.227	.346	4-0	.250	0	134	-2	-0.1
1922	Bro N	0	0	—	5	0	0	0	11.1	13	11	3	0	8	5	8.74	47	.289	.396	2-0	.000	-0		-5	-0.3
Total	2	1	0	1.000	8	3	0	0	23.1	23	19	3	0	16	9	6.94	57	.258	.371	6-0	.167	-0	134	-7	-0.4
GORDON, DON Donald Thomas B 10.10.1959 New York, NY BR/TR 6-1/175# d4.10																									
1986	Tor A	0	1	.000	14	0	0	1-1	21.2	28	20	1	1	8-1	13	7.06	60	.311	.366	0-0	—	0		-7	-0.4
1987	Tor A	0	0	—	5	0	0	0-0	11	8	5	2	0	3-0	3	4.09	110	.200	.256	0-0	—	0		1	0.0
	Cle A	0	3	.000	21	0	0	1-0	39.2	49	31	3	4	12-3	20	4.08	111	.295	.353	0-0	—	0		-2	-0.1
	Year	0	3	.000	26	0	0	1-0	50.2	57	42	5	4	15-3	23	4.09	111	.277	.335	0-0	—	0		-3	-0.1
1988	Cle A	3	4	.429	38	0	0	1-2	59.1	65	33	5	3	19-3	20	4.40	94	.284	.341	0-0	—	0		-2	-0.2
Total	3	3	8	.273	78	0	0	3-3	131.2	150	89	11	8	42-7	56	4.72	91	.286	.343	0-0	—	0		-10	-0.7
GORDON, TOM Thomas B 11.18.1967 Sebring, FL BR/TR 5-9/180# d9.8																									
1988	KC A	0	2	.000	5	2	0	0-0	15.2	16	9	1	0	7-0	18	5.17	77	.267	.343	0-0	—	0	57	-2	-0.2
1989	KC A	17	9	.654	49	16	1-1	1-6	163	122	67	10	1	86-4	153	3.64	106	.210	.311	0-0	—	0	85	7	1.1
1990	KC A	12	11	.522	32	32	6-1	0-0	195.1	192	99	17	3	99-1	175	3.73	103	.257	.346	0-0	—	0	116	0	0.0
1991	KC A	9	14	.391	45	14	1	1-3	158	129	76	16	4	87-6	167	3.87	107	.221	.324	0-0	—	0*	100	5	0.6
1992	KC A	6	10	.375	40	11	0	0-2	117.2	116	67	9	4	55-4	98	4.59	89	.258	.340	0-0	—	0	88	-7	-0.9
1993	KC A	12	6	.667	48	14	2	1-5	155.2	125	65	11	1	77-5	143	3.58	128	.223	.315	0-0	—	0	103	17	1.8
1994	KC A	11	7	.611	24	24	0	0-0	155.1	136	79	15	3	87-3	126	4.35	115	.237	.336	0-0	—	0	87	12	1.3
1995	KC A	12	12	.500	31	31	2	0-0	189	204	110	12	4	89-4	119	4.43	108	.279	.355	0-0	—	0*	88	3	0.4
1996	Bos A	12	9	.571	34	34	4-1	0-0	215.2	249	143	28	4	105-5	171	5.59	91	.284	.359	0-0	—	0	131	-8	-0.6
1997	Bos A	6	10	.375	42	25	2-1	11-2	182.2	155	85	10	3	78-1	159	3.74	124	.226	.306	0-0	—	0	96	17	1.5
1998	†Bos A★	7	4	.636	73	0	0	**46**-1	79.1	55	24	2	0	25-1	78	2.72	173	.191	.254	0-0	—	0		18	3.5
1999	†Bos A	0	2	.000	21	0	0	11-2	17.2	17	11	2	1	12-2	24	5.60	89	.246	.366	0-0	—	0		-1	-0.1
2001	Chi N	1	2	.333	47	0	0	27-4	45.1	32	18	4	1	16-1	67	3.38	123	.188	.262	0-0	—	0		4	0.7
2002	Chi N	1	1	.500	19	0	0	0-0	23.2	27	12	1	1	10-1	31	3.42	118	.293	.369	0-0	—	0		1	0.1

Year	Tm Lg	W	L	Pct	G	GS	CG-Sho	SV-BS	IP	H	R	HR	HB	BB-IB	SO	ERA	AERA	OAV	OOB	AB-SH	AVG	PB	Sup	APR	PW
	Hou N	0	2	.000	15	0	0	0-0	19	15	7	2	0	6-2	17	3.32	129	.217	.280	1-0	.000	-0		2	0.2
	Year	1	3	.250	34	0	0	0-0	42.2	42	24	3	1	16-3	48	3.38	123	.261	.331	1-0	.000	-0		3	0.3
2003	Chi A	7	6	.538	66	0	0	12-5	74	57	29	4	4	31-3	91	3.16	144	.213	.301	0-0	—	0		11	2.0
Total	15	113	107	.514	591	203	18-4	110-30	1807	1647	901	144	34	870-43	1637	4.07	110	.242	.328	1-0	.000	-0	103	79	11.4

GORECKI, RICK Richard John B 8.27.1973 Evergreen Park, IL BR/TR 6-3/167# d9.10

Year	Tm Lg	W	L	Pct	G	GS	CG-Sho	SV-BS	IP	H	R	HR	HB	BB-IB	SO	ERA	AERA	OAV	OOB	AB-SH	AVG	PB	Sup	APR	PW
1997	LA N	1	0	1.000	4	1	0	0-0	6	9	10	3	0	6-1	6	15.00	26	.346	.469	0-1	—	0	215	-8	-1.0
1998	TB A	1	2	.333	3	3	0	0-0	16.2	15	9	1	0	10-0	7	4.86	99	.259	.357	0-0	—	0	58	0	0.0
Total	2	2	2	.500	7	4	0	0-0	22.2	24	19	4	0	16-1	13	7.54	60	.286	.392	0-1	—	0	92	-8	-1.0

GORIN, CHARLIE Charles Perry B 2.6.1928 Waco, TX BL/TL 5-10/165# d5.29

Year	Tm Lg	W	L	Pct	G	GS	CG-Sho	SV-BS	IP	H	R	HR	HB	BB-IB	SO	ERA	AERA	OAV	OOB	AB-SH	AVG	PB	Sup	APR	PW
1954	Mil N	0	1	.000	5	0	0	0	9.2	5	3	0	0	6	12	1.86	200	.152	.282	3-0	.000	-0		2	0.1
1955	Mil N	0	0	—	2	0	0	0	0.1	1	2	0	0	3-0	0	54.00	7	.500	.800	0-0	—	0		-2	-0.1
Total	2	0	1	.000	7	0	0	0	10	6	5	0	0	9-0	12	3.60	103	.171	.341	3-0	.000	-0		0	0.0

GORMAN, JACK John F. "Stooping Jack" B 1859 St.Louis, MO D 9.9.1889 St.Louis, MO d7.1.1883 ▲

Year	Tm Lg	W	L	Pct	G	GS	CG-Sho	SV-BS	IP	H	R	HR	HB	BB-IB	SO	ERA	AERA	OAV	OOB	AB-SH	AVG	PB	Sup	APR	PW
1884	Pit AA	1	2	.333	3	3	3	0	25	22	20	0	1	5	10	4.68	71	.212	.255	27	.148	-0*	91	-4	-0.4

GORMAN, TOM Thomas Aloysius B 1.4.1925 New York, NY D 12.26.1992 Valley Stream, NY BR/TR 6-1/190# d7.16

Year	Tm Lg	W	L	Pct	G	GS	CG-Sho	SV-BS	IP	H	R	HR	HB	BB-IB	SO	ERA	AERA	OAV	OOB	AB-SH	AVG	PB	Sup	APR	PW
1952	†NY A	6	2	.750	12	6	1-1	1	60.2	63	34	8	2	22	31	4.60	72	.272	.340	23-0	.087	-1	127	-9	-1.2
1953	†NY A	4	5	.444	40	1	0	6	77	65	32	5	6	32	38	3.39	109	.226	.317	15-1	.133	-1	48	3	0.3
1954	NY A	0	0	—	23	0	0	2	36.2	30	14	1	1	14	31	2.21	156	.222	.300	4-0	.000	-1		4	0.1
1955	KC A	7	6	.538	57	0	0	18	109	98	48	11	4	36-5	46	3.55	118	.246	.311	24-1	.083	-1		7	0.8
1956	KC A	9	10	.474	52	13	1	3	171.1	168	83	23	2	68-7	56	3.83	113	.258	.329	39-1	.051	-4	77	9	0.5
1957	KC A	5	9	.357	38	12	3-1	3	124.2	125	59	18	1	33-7	66	3.83	103	.261	.307	33-1	.121	-2	83	2	0.0
1958	KC A	4	4	.500	50	1	0	8	89.2	86	41	8	3	20-0	44	3.51	111	.258	.305	17-0	.118	-1	46	3	0.1
1959	KC A	1	0	1.000	17	0	0	1	20.1	24	21	3	1	14-0	9	7.08	57	.293	.398	0-0	—	0		-8	-0.5
Total	8	36	36	.500	289	33	5-2	42	689.1	659	332	77	20	239-19	321	3.77	105	.254	.320	155-4	.090	-10	86	11	0.1

GORMAN, TOM Thomas David "Big Tom" B 3.16.1916 New York, NY D 8.11.1986 Closter, NJ BR/TL 6-2/200# d9.14 U26

Year	Tm Lg	W	L	Pct	G	GS	CG-Sho	SV-BS	IP	H	R	HR	HB	BB-IB	SO	ERA	AERA	OAV	OOB	AB-SH	AVG	PB	Sup	APR	PW
1939	NY N	0	0	—	4	0	0	0	5	7	4	0	0	1	2	7.20	55	.350	.381	1-0	.000	-0		-2	-0.1

GORMAN, TOM Thomas Patrick B 12.16.1957 Portland, OR BL/TL 6-4/200# d9.2

Year	Tm Lg	W	L	Pct	G	GS	CG-Sho	SV-BS	IP	H	R	HR	HB	BB-IB	SO	ERA	AERA	OAV	OOB	AB-SH	AVG	PB	Sup	APR	PW
1981	Mon N	0	0	—	9	0	0	0-0	15	12	7	0	1	6-2	13	4.20	83	.222	.306	0-0	—	0		-1	0.0
1982	Mon N	1	0	1.000	5	0	0	0-0	7	8	4	0	0	4-0	6	5.14	71	.286	.364	0-0	—	0		-1	-0.1
	NY N	0	1	.000	3	1	0	0-0	9.1	8	1	0	0	0-0	7	0.96	377	.235	.235	1-1	.000	-0	24	3	0.3
	Year	1	1	.500	8	1	0	0-0	16.1	16	2	0	0	4-0	13	2.76	132	.258	.299	1-1	.000	-0	24	2	0.2
1983	NY N	1	4	.200	25	4	0	0-0	49.1	45	29	3	0	15-4	30	4.93	74	.245	.299	4-1	.250	0	49	-6	-0.6
1984	NY N	6	0	1.000	36	0	0	0-2	57.2	51	20	6	1	13-3	40	2.97	119	.238	.284	3-0	.000	-0		5	0.4
1985	NY N	4	4	.500	34	2	0	0-3	52.2	56	32	8	0	18-2	32	5.13	68	.277	.335	5-1	.000	-1	128	-10	-1.3
1986	Phi N	0	1	.000	8	0	0	0-0	11.2	21	10	0	0	5-1	8	7.71	50	.382	.426	1-0	.000	-0		-4	-0.3
1987	SD N	0	0	—	6	0	0	0-0	11	11	5	1	0	5-0	8	4.09	97	.262	.340	0-0	—	0		0	0.0
Total	7	12	10	.545	126	7	0	0-5	213.2	212	108	18	2	66-12	144	4.34	83	.261	.315	14-3	.071	-1	67	-14	-1.6

GORMLEY, JOE Joseph B 12.20.1866 Summit Hill, PA D 7.2.1950 Summit Hill, PA BL/TL d6.16

Year	Tm Lg	W	L	Pct	G	GS	CG-Sho	SV-BS	IP	H	R	HR	HB	BB-IB	SO	ERA	AERA	OAV	OOB	AB-SH	AVG	PB	Sup	APR	PW
1891	Phi N	0	1	.000	1	1	1	0	8	10	8	0	0	5	2	5.63	61	.294	.385	4	.000	-1	53	-2	-0.2

GORNICKI, HANK Henry Frank B 1.14.1911 Niagara Falls, NY D 2.16.1996 Riviera Beach, FL BR/TR 6-1/145# d4.17 Mil 1944-45

Year	Tm Lg	W	L	Pct	G	GS	CG-Sho	SV-BS	IP	H	R	HR	HB	BB-IB	SO	ERA	AERA	OAV	OOB	AB-SH	AVG	PB	Sup	APR	PW
1941	StL N	1	0	1.000	4	1	1-1	0	11.1	6	4	0	1	9	6	3.18	118	.158	.333	4-0	.250	0	135	1	0.1
	Chi N	0	0	—	1	0	0	0	2	3	1	0	0	0	2	4.50	78	.375	.375	0-0	—	0		0	0.0
	Year	1	0	1.000	5	1	1-1	0	13.1	9	11	0	1	9	8	3.38	110	.196	.339	4-0	.250	0	137	1	0.1
1942	Pit N	5	6	.455	25	14	7-2	2	112	89	45	2	1	40	48	2.57	132	.215	.286	35-2	.114	-1	113	7	0.5
1943	Pit N	9	13	.409	42	18	4-1	4	147	165	86	10	2	47	63	3.98	87	.286	.342	40-2	.175	-1	80	-10	-1.5
1946	Pit N	0	0	—	7	0	0	0	12.2	12	10	0	0	11	4	3.55	99	.255	.397	3-0	.000	-0		-2	-0.1
Total	4	15	19	.441	79	33	12-4	6	285	275	146	12	4	107	123	3.38	102	.254	.323	82-4	.146	-2	96	-4	-1.0

GORSICA, JOHNNY John Joseph Perry (b: John Joseph Perry Gorczyca) B 3.29.1915 Bayonne, NJ D 12.16.1998 Charlottesville, VA BR/TR 6-2/180# d4.22 Mil 1945-46

Year	Tm Lg	W	L	Pct	G	GS	CG-Sho	SV-BS	IP	H	R	HR	HB	BB-IB	SO	ERA	AERA	OAV	OOB	AB-SH	AVG	PB	Sup	APR	PW
1940	†Det A	7	7	.500	29	20	5-2	0	160	170	85	10	4	57	68	4.33	110	.272	.337	62-1	.194	0	102	9	0.9
1941	Det A	9	11	.450	33	21	8-1	2	171	193	98	14	2	55	59	4.47	102	.281	.336	57-3	.298	4	75	1	0.7
1942	Det A	3	2	.600	28	0	0	4	53	63	31	2	3	26	19	4.75	83	.310	.397	10-1	.100	-0*		-3	-0.2
1943	Det A	4	5	.444	35	4	1	5	96.1	88	43	3	2	40	45	3.36	105	.247	.327	23-2	.174	0*	84	1	0.3
1944	Det A	6	14	.300	34	19	8-1	4	162	192	88	5	4	32	47	4.11	87	.296	.333	52-0	.135	-1*	88	-9	-1.0
1946	Det A	0	0	—	14	0	0	1	23.2	28	13	5	0	11	14	4.56	80	.301	.375	3-0	.667	1		-2	0.0
1947	Det A	2	0	1.000	31	0	0	1	57.2	44	27	5	2	26	20	3.75	101	.208	.300	10-0	.200	0		0	0.1
Total	7	31	39	.443	204	64	22-4	17	723.2	778	385	44	17	247	272	4.18	98	.276	.338	217-7	.207	4	91	-3	0.8

GOSSAGE, RICH Richard Michael "Goose" B 7.5.1951 Colorado Springs, CO BR/TR 6-3/217# d4.16

Year	Tm Lg	W	L	Pct	G	GS	CG-Sho	SV-BS	IP	H	R	HR	HB	BB-IB	SO	ERA	AERA	OAV	OOB	AB-SH	AVG	PB	Sup	APR	PW
1972	Chi A	7	1	.875	36	1	0	2-0	80	72	44	2	4	44-3	57	4.27	73	.247	.351	16-1	.000	-2	57	-11	-1.3
1973	Chi A	0	4	.000	20	4	1	0-0	49.2	57	44	9	3	37-2	33	7.43	53	.311	.427	0-0	—	0*	23	-17	-1.3
1974	Chi A	4	6	.400	39	3	0	1-1	89.1	92	45	4	2	47-7	64	4.13	90	.272	.361	0-0	—	0	79	-3	-0.4
1975	Chi A★	9	8	.529	62	0	0	**26-5**	141.2	99	32	3	5	70-15	130	1.84	211	.201	.306	0-0	—	0		**31**	5.1
1976	Chi A☆	9	17	.346	31	29	15	1-1	224	214	104	16	9	90-3	135	3.94	91	.254	.330	0-0	—	0	75	-8	-0.9
1977	Pit N★	11	9	.550	72	0	0	26-10	133	78	27	9	2	49-6	151	1.62	246	.170	.250	23-1	.217	1		**34**	**6.4**
1978	†NY A★	10	11	.476	63	0	0	**27-10**	134.1	87	41	9	2	59-8	122	2.01	181	.187	.277	0-0	—	0		**22**	4.3
1979	NY A	5	3	.625	36	0	0	18-3	58.1	48	18	5	0	19-4	41	2.62	156	.227	.291	0-0	—	0		10	1.9
1980	†NY A★	6	2	.750	64	0	0	**33-4**	99	74	29	5	1	37-3	103	2.27	173	.211	.285	0-0	—	0		18	2.7
1981	†NY A❖	3	2	.600	32	0	0	20-3	46.2	22	6	2	1	14-1	48	0.77	464	.141	.215	0-0	—	0		14	3.0
1982	NY A☆	4	5	.444	56	0	0	30-9	93	63	23	5	0	28-5	102	2.23	179	.196	.259	0-0	—	0		20	3.2
1983	NY A	13	5	.722	57	0	0	22-13	87.1	82	27	5	1	25-5	90	2.27	172	.248	.298	0-0	—	0		15	3.1
1984	†SD N★	10	6	.625	62	0	0	25-11	102.1	75	34	6	1	36-4	84	2.90	123	.204	.275	22-2	.182	0		9	1.7
1985	SD N★	5	3	.625	50	0	0	26-6	79	64	21	1	1	17-1	52	1.82	194	.226	.269	11-0	.000	-1		14	2.2
1986	SD N	5	7	.417	45	0	0	21-11	64.2	69	36	8	2	20-0	63	4.45	82	.273	.326	7-0	.000	-1		-6	-1.3
1987	SD N	5	4	.556	40	0	0	11-6	52	47	18	4	0	19-6	44	3.12	127	.244	.307	4-0	.000	-0		6	1.1
1988	Chi N	4	4	.500	46	0	0	13-10	43.2	50	23	3	3	15-5	30	4.33	83	.291	.356	1-0	.000	-0		-3	-0.7
1989	SF N	2	1	.667	31	0	0	4-1	43.2	32	16	2	0	27-3	24	2.68	126	.212	.328	1-0	.000	-0		3	0.2
	NY A	1	0	1.000	11	0	0	1-0	14.1	14	6	0	1	3-1	6	3.77	103	.275	.327	0-0	—	0		0	0.0
1991	Tex A	4	2	.667	44	0	0	1-4	40.1	33	16	4	3	16-1	28	3.57	113	.228	.317	0-0	—	0		3	0.4
1992	Oak A	0	2	.000	30	0	0	0-1	38	32	13	5	2	19-4	26	2.84	132	.230	.327	0-0	—	0		4	0.2
1993	Oak A	4	5	.444	39	0	0	1-3	47.2	49	24	6	1	26-2	40	4.53	90	.266	.357	0-0	—	0		-2	-0.3
1994	Sea A	3	0	1.000	36	0	0	1-0	47.1	44	23	6	3	15-1	29	4.18	117	.251	.318	0-0	—	0		4	0.2
Total	22	124	107	.537	1002	37	16	310-112	1809.1	1497	670	119	47	732-90	1502	3.01	126	.228	.308	85-4	.106	-3	66	157	29.5

GOTT, JIM James William B 8.3.1959 Hollywood, CA BR/TR 6-4/220# d4.9

Year	Tm Lg	W	L	Pct	G	GS	CG-Sho	SV-BS	IP	H	R	HR	HB	BB-IB	SO	ERA	AERA	OAV	OOB	AB-SH	AVG	PB	Sup	APR	PW
1982	Tor A	5	10	.333	30	23	1-1	0-0	136	134	76	15	3	66-0	82	4.43	101	.255	.340	0-0	—	0	64	0	0.0
1983	Tor A	9	14	.391	34	30	6-1	0-1	176.2	195	103	15	5	68-5	121	4.74	91	.280	.347	0-0	—	0	98	-8	-1.0
1984	Tor A	7	6	.538	35	12	1-1	2-3	109.2	93	54	7	3	49-3	73	4.02	102	.233	.317	0-0	—	0	97	1	0.0
1985	SF N	7	10	.412	26	26	2	0-0	148.1	144	73	10	1	51-3	78	3.88	89	.254	.315	51-4	.196	4	98	-7	-0.3
1986	SF N	0	0	—	9	2	0	1-0	13	16	12	0	0	13-2	9	7.62	46	.314	.446	3-0	.000	0	177	-6	-0.3
1987	SF N	1	0	1.000	30	3	0	0-1	56	53	32	4	2	32-5	63	4.50	86	.244	.345	10-0	.100	1	165	-5	-0.2
	Pit N	0	2	.000	25	0	0	13-3	31	28	11	0	0	8-2	27	1.45	283	.233	.281	1-0	.000	-0		7	0.9
	Year	1	2	.333	55	3	0	13-4	87	81	50	4	2	40-7	90	3.41	116	.240	.324	11-0	.091	0	161	3	0.7
1988	Pit N	6	6	.500	67	0	0	34-6	77.1	68	30	9	2	22-5	76	3.49	98	.243	.300	1-0	.000	-0		1	0.1
1989	Pit N	0	0	—	1	0	0	0-0	0.2	1	0	0	0	1-0	1	0.00	—	.333	.500	0-0	—	0		0	0.0
1990	LA N	3	5	.375	50	0	0	3-2	62	59	27	5	0	34-7	44	2.90	126	.257	.347	1-0	.000	-0		4	0.4

Year	Tm Lg	W	L	Pct	G	GS	CG-Sho	SV-BS	IP	H	R	HR	HB	BB-IB	SO	ERA	AERA	OAV	OOB	AB-SH	AVG	PB	Sup	APR	PW
1991	LA N	4	3	.571	55	0	0	2-3	76	63	28	5	1	32-7	73	2.96	121	.223	.304	2-1	.500	0		6	0.6
1992	LA N	3	3	.500	68	0	0	6-1	88	72	27	4	1	41-13	75	2.45	141	.225	.314	2-0	.500	0		10	0.9
1993	LA N	4	8	.333	62	0	0	25-4	77.2	71	23	6	1	17-5	67	2.32	165	.248	.291	1-0	.000	-0		14	2.7
1994	LA N	5	3	.625	37	0	0	2-5	36.1	46	24	3	3	20-4	29	5.94	66	.322	.413	0-0	—	0		-8	-1.5
1995	Pit N	2	4	.333	25	0	0	3-0	31.1	38	26	2	1	12-2	19	6.03	71	.288	.349	1-0	.000	-0		-7	-1.3
Total	14	56	74	.431	554	96	10-3	91-29	1120	1081	546	85	23	466-63	837	3.87	101	.254	.329	73-5	.178	5	97	2	1.0
GOULAIT, TED Theodore Lee B 8.12.1889 St.Clair, MI D 7.15.1936 St.Clair, MI BR/TR 5-9.5/172# d9.28																									
1912	NY N	0	0	—	1	1	1	0	7	11	6	0	0	4	6	6.43	53	.367	.441	2-1	.500	0	130	-2	-0.1
GOULD, AL Albert Frank "Pudgy" B 1.20.1893 Muscatine, IA D 8.8.1982 San Jose, CA BR/TR 5-6.5/160# d7.11																									
1916	Cle A	5	6	.455	30	9	6-1	1	106.2	101	37	0	3	40	41	2.53	119	.256	.329	29-3	.103	-2	112	6	0.4
1917	Cle A	4	4	.500	27	7	1	0	94	95	44	1	3	52	24	3.64	78	.281	.382	24-1	.208	1	109	-5	-0.3
Total	2	9	10	.474	57	16	7-1	1	200.2	196	81	1	6	92	65	3.05	96	.267	.354	53-4	.151	-1	111	1	0.1
GOWELL, LARRY Lawrence Clyde B 5.2.1948 Lewiston, ME BR/TR 6-2/182# d9.21																									
1972	NY A	0	1	.000	2	1	0	0-0	7	3	1	0	0	2-0	7	1.29	230	.143	.208	1-0	1.000	1	0	1	0.3
GOZZO, MAURO Mauro Paul B 3.7.1966 New Britain, CT BR/TR 6-3/212# d8.8																									
1989	Tor A	4	1	.800	9	3	0	0-1	31.2	35	19	1	1	9-1	10	4.83	78	.289	.338	0-0	—	0	160	-4	-0.6
1990	Cle A	0	0	—	2	0	0	0-0	3	2	0	0	0	2-0	2	0.00	—	.182	.308	0-0	—	0		1	0.1
1991	Cle A	0	0	—	2	2	0	0-0	4.2	9	10	0	0	7-0	3	19.29	22	.450	.571	0-0	—	0	165	-7	-0.3
1992	Min A	0	0	—	2	0	0	0-0	1.2	7	5	2	0	0-0	1	27.00	15	.583	.583	0-0	—	0		-4	-0.2
1993	NY N	0	1	.000	10	0	0	1-0	14	11	5	1	0	5-1	6	2.57	156	.212	.281	0-0	—	0		2	0.1
1994	NY N	3	5	.375	23	8	0	0-1	69	86	48	5	1	28-10	33	4.83	87	.304	.363	16-1	.250	1	120	-8	-0.7
Total	6	7	7	.500	48	13	0	1-2	124	150	87	9	2	51-12	55	5.30	76	.301	.363	16-1	.250	1	136	-20	-1.6
GRABOW, JOHN John William B 11.4.1978 Arcadia, CA BL/TL 6-2/190# d9.14																									
2003	Pit N	0	0	—	5	0	0	0-0	5	6	3	0	0	0-0	9	3.60	122	.273	.273	0-0	—	0		0	0.0
GRABOWSKI, AL Alfons Francis B 9.6.1901 Syracuse, NY D 10.29.1966 Memphis, NY BL/TL 5-11.5/175# d9.11 b-Reggie																									
1929	StL N	3	2	.600	6	6	4-2	0	50	44	18	0	0	8	22	2.52	185	.227	.257	16-1	.250	2	97	11	1.2
1930	StL N	6	4	.600	33	8	1	1	107	120	66	7	3	49	43	4.79	105	.290	.369	33-0	.364	3*	122	3	0.4
Total	2	9	6	.600	39	14	5-2	1	157	164	84	7	3	57	65	4.07	120	.270	.335	49-1	.327	4	111	14	1.6
GRABOWSKI, REGGIE Reginald John B 7.16.1907 Syracuse, NY D 4.2.1955 Syracuse, NY BR/TR 6-0.5/185# d4.15 b-Al																									
1932	Phi N	2	2	.500	14	2	0	0	34.1	38	18	2	2	22	15	3.67	120	.273	.380	6-1	.000	-1	95	2	0.1
1933	Phi N	1	3	.250	10	5	4-1	0	48	38	13	4	1	10	9	2.44	157	.220	.266	16-0	.125	-1	52	7	0.5
1934	Phi N	1	3	.250	27	5	0	0	65.1	114	72	13	3	23	13	9.23	51	.384	.433	18-1	.056	-2	88	-26	-1.6
Total	3	4	8	.333	51	12	4-1	0	147.2	190	103	19	6	55	37	5.73	76	.312	.375	40-2	.075	-3	75	-17	-1.0
GRACE, MIKE Michael James B 6.20.1970 Joliet, IL BR/TR 6-4/210# d9.1																									
1995	Phi N	1	1	.500	2	2	0	0-0	11.1	10	4	0	0	4-0	7	3.18	133	.238	.304	2-2	.000	-0	43	1	0.2
1996	Phi N	7	2	.778	12	12	1-1	0-0	80	72	33	9	1	16-1	49	3.49	124	.238	.279	29-1	.138	-0	101	8	0.9
1997	Phi N	3	2	.600	6	6	1-1	0-0	39	32	16	3	1	10-1	26	3.46	123	.230	.285	12-0	.083	-1	94	4	0.3
1998	Phi N	4	7	.364	21	15	0	0-0	90.1	116	61	10	8	30-1	46	5.48	79	.312	.375	23-3	.087	-1	108	-12	-1.4
1999	Phi N	1	4	.200	27	5	0	0-0	55	80	48	5	6	30-0	28	7.69	61	.346	.430	7-3	.000	-1	62	-16	-1.3
Total	5	16	16	.500	68	40	2-2	0-0	275.2	310	162	27	16	90-3	156	4.96	88	.285	.348	73-9	.096	-2	94	-15	-1.3
GRAFF, JOHN John J. B 11.1866 Washington, DC D 4.2.1932 Washington, DC d7.19																									
1893	Was N	0	1	.000	2	1	1	0	12	21	21	2	1	13	4	11.25	41	.368	.493	5	.200	-0	60	-9	-0.5
GRAHAM, SKINNY Kyle B 8.14.1899 Oak Grove, AL D 12.1.1973 Oak Grove, AL BR/TR 6-2/172# d9.3																									
1924	Bos N	0	4	.000	5	4	1	0	33	33	14	0	0	11	15	3.82	100	.287	.349	7-2	.000	-1	17	1	0.0
1925	Bos N	7	12	.368	34	23	5	1	157	177	90	6	3	62	32	4.41	91	.296	.365	44-7	.136	-2	81	-6	-0.9
1926	Bos N	3	3	.500	15	4	1	0	36.1	54	32	3	2	19	7	7.93	45	.370	.449	12-0	.167	-1	153	-16	-2.3
1929	Det A	1	3	.250	13	6	2	1	51.2	70	41	2	3	33	7	5.57	77	.340	.438	19-0	.105	-1	183	-8	-0.7
Total	4	11	22	.333	67	37	9	2	278	334	177	11	8	125	61	5.02	79	.314	.390	82-9	.122	-5	100	-29	-3.9
GRAHAM, OSCAR Oscar M. B 7.20.1878 Plattsmouth, NE D 10.15.1931 Moline, IL BL/TL 6-0.5/?# d4.16																									
1907	Was A	4	9	.308	20	14	6	0	104	116	66	3	10	29	44	3.98	61	.284	.347	48-1	.229	3*	128	-18	-1.8
GRAHAM, BILL William Albert B 1.21.1937 Flemingsburg, KY BR/TR 6-3/217# d10.2																									
1966	Det A	0	0	—	1	0	0	0	2	2	0	0	0	0-0	2	0.00	—	.250	.250	0-0	—	0		1	0.0
1967	NY N	1	2	.333	5	3	1	0	27.1	20	10	3	0	11-0	14	2.63	129	.200	.279	8-0	.125	-0	43	2	0.1
Total	2	1	2	.333	6	3	1	0	29.1	22	10	3	0	11-0	16	2.45	138	.204	.277	8-0	.125	-0	43	3	0.1
GRAHAME, BILL William James B 7.22.1884 Owosso, MI D 2.15.1936 Holt, MI TL 6/?# d4.18																									
1908	StL A	6	7	.462	21	13	7	0	117.1	104	46	0	12	32	47	2.30	104	.240	.310	42-2	.119	-3	83	0	-0.3
1909	StL A	8	14	.364	34	21	13-3	1	187.1	171	78	3	5	60	82	3.12	77	.256	.322	63-0	.159	-0	86	-12	-1.4
1910	StL A	0	8	.000	9	6	1	0	43	46	31	2	4	13	12	3.56	70	.297	.366	13-0	.154	-0	41	-7	-1.3
Total	3	14	29	.326	64	40	21-3	1	347.2	321	155	5	21	105	141	2.90	83	.256	.323	118-2	.144	-3	78	-19	-3.0
GRAHE, JOE Joseph Milton B 8.14.1967 W.Palm Beach, FL BR/TR 6/200# d8.4																									
1990	Cal A	3	4	.429	8	8	0	0-0	43.1	51	30	3	3	23-1	25	4.98	77	.293	.385	0-0	—	0	101	-7	-0.9
1991	Cal A	3	7	.300	18	10	1	0-0	73	84	43	2	3	33-0	40	4.81	85	.288	.365	0-0	—	0	65	-6	-0.7
1992	Cal A	5	6	.455	46	7	0	21-3	94.2	85	37	5	6	39-2	39	3.52	113	.246	.329	0-0	—	0	108	6	0.9
1993	Cal A	4	1	.800	45	0	0	11-2	56.2	54	22	5	2	25-4	31	2.86	158	.251	.331	0-0	—	0		9	1.1
1994	Cal A	2	5	.286	40	0	0	13-6	43.1	68	33	5	6	18-4	26	6.65	74	.362	.428	0-0	—	0		-8	-1.4
1995	Col N	4	3	.571	17	9	0	0-0	56.2	69	42	6	3	27-2	27	5.08	106	.301	.378	12-6	.417	1	99	-1	0.0
1999	Phi N	1	4	.200	13	5	0	0-0	32.2	40	16	1	3	17-0	16	3.86	122	.308	.392	7-0	.143	0	43	3	0.4
Total	7	22	30	.423	187	39	1	45-11	400.1	451	223	27	26	182-13	204	4.41	100	.287	.366	19-6	.316	1	85	-4	-0.6
GRAMLY, TOMMY Bert Thomas B 4.19.1945 Dallas, TX BR/TR 6-3/175# d4.18																									
1968	Cle A	0	1	.000	3	0	0	0	3.1	3	1	0	0	2-2	1	2.70	110	.250	.357	0-0	—	0*		0	0.0
GRAMPP, HANK Henry Erchardt B 9.28.1903 New York, NY D 3.24.1986 New York, NY BR/TR 6-1/185# d8.29																									
1927	Chi N	0	0	—	2	0	0	0	3	4	3	0	0	1	3	9.00	43	.333	.385	0-0	—	0		-2	-0.1
1929	Chi N	0	1	.000	1	1	0	0	2	4	6	0	1	3	0	27.00	17	.500	.667	0-0	—	0	57	-5	-0.6
Total	2	0	1	.000	3	1	0	0	5	8	9	0	1	4	3	16.20	26	.400	.520	0-0	—	0	57	-7	-0.7
GRANGER, JEFF Jeffrey Adam B 12.16.1971 San Pedro, CA BR/TL 6-4/200# d9.16																									
1993	KC A	0	0	—	1	0	0	0-0	1	3	3	0	0	2-0	1	27.00	17	.500	.625	0-0	—	0		-2	-0.1
1994	KC A	0	1	.000	2	2	0	0-0	9.1	13	8	2	0	6-0	3	6.75	74	.325	.404	0-0	—	0	73	-2	-0.2
1996	KC A	0	0	—	15	0	0	0-0	16.1	21	13	3	2	10-0	11	6.61	76	.313	.412	0-0	—	0		-3	-0.1
1997	Pit N	0	0	—	9	0	0	0-0	5	10	10	3	0	8-1	4	18.00	24	.417	.563	0-0	—	0		-7	-0.3
Total	4	0	1	.000	27	2	0	0-0	31.2	47	34	8	2	26-1	19	9.09	54	.343	.449	0-0	—	0	73	-14	-0.7
GRANGER, WAYNE Wayne Allan B 3.15.1944 Springfield, MA BR/TR 6-2/165# d6.5																									
1968	†StL N	4	2	.667	34	0	0	4	44	40	14	2	2	12-3	27	2.25	129	.238	.297	5-0	.200	0		3	0.5
1969	Cin N	9	6	.600	**90**	0	0	27-10	144.2	143	64	10	7	40-14	68	2.80	135	.262	.316	21-3	.095	-0		10	1.4
1970	†Cin N	6	5	.545	67	0	0	**35-4**	84.2	79	33	5	1	27-8	38	2.66	152	.252	.311	10-0	.100	-1		11	2.3
1971	Cin N	7	6	.538	**70**	0	0	11-0	100	94	39	8	1	28-7	51	3.33	101	.251	.303	7-1	.143	1		1	0.4
1972	Min A	4	6	.400	63	0	0	19-6	89.2	83	42	7	2	28-6	45	3.01	107	.243	.303	10-0	.200	0		0	0.0
1973	StL N	2	4	.333	33	0	0	5-4	46.2	50	29	3	2	21-7	14	4.24	86	.284	.363	3-0	.000	-0		-5	-0.7
	NY A	0	1	.000	7	0	0	0-0	15.1	19	7	1	1	3-1	10	1.76	208	.279	.319	0-0	—	0		2	0.1
1974	Chi A	0	0	—	5	0	0	0-0	7.2	16	8	1	0	3-0	4	8.22	45	.432	.475	0-0	—	0		-4	-0.2
1975	Hou N	2	5	.286	55	0	0	5-3	74	76	39	7	4	23-7	30	3.65	93	.264	.324	9-0	.000	-1		-6	-0.6

Year	Tm Lg	W	L	Pct	G	GS	CG-Sho	SV-BS	IP	H	R	HR	HB	BB-IB	SO	ERA	AERA	OAV	OOB	AB-SH	AVG	PB	Sup	APR	PW
1976	Mon N	1	0	1.000	27	0	0	2-2	32	32	15	3	2	16-4	16	3.66	102	.264	.355	3-2	.000	-0		0	0.0
Total	9	35	35	.500	451	0	0	108-29	638.2	632	290	47	22	201-57	303	3.14	113	.260	.319	68-6	.103	-1		12	3.2
GRANT, GEORGE George Addison B 1.6.1903 E.Tallassee, AL D 3.25.1986 Montgomery, AL BR/TR 5-11.5/175# d9.17																									
1923	StL A	0	0	—	4	0	0	0	8.2	15	7	0	0	3	2	5.19	80	.395	.439	2-0	.000	-0		-1	-0.1
1924	StL A	1	2	.333	22	2	0	0	51.1	69	43	4	1	25	11	6.31	72	.325	.399	13-0	.000	-2	75	-10	-0.7
1925	StL A	0	2	.000	12	0	0	0	16.1	26	15	2	0	8	7	6.06	77	.400	.466	4-0	.250	-0		-3	-0.3
1927	Cle A	4	6	.400	25	3	2	1	74.2	85	46	1	0	40	19	4.46	94	.300	.387	21-2	.095	-2	146	-3	-0.5
1928	Cle A	10	8	.556	28	18	6-1	0	155.1	196	102	7	2	76	39	5.04	82	.319	.395	60-2	.183	-2*	91	-14	-1.4
1929	Cle A	0	2	.000	12	0	0	0	24	41	29	2	0	23	5	10.50	42	.414	.525	2-0	.000	-0		-14	-0.9
1931	Pit N	0	0	—	11	0	0	0	17	28	16	0	1	7	6	7.41	52	.364	.424	2-0	.000	-0		-6	-0.3
Total	7	15	20	.429	114	23	8-1	1	347.1	460	258	16	4	182	89	5.65	75	.331	.410	104-4	.135	-8	95	-51	-4.2
GRANT, JIM James Ronald B 8.4.1894 Coalville, IA D 11.30.1985 Des Moines, IA BR/TL 5-11/180# d4.21																									
1923	Phi N	0	0	—	2	0	0	0	4	10	8	0	1	4	0	13.50	34	.588	.682	1-0	.000	-0		-4	-0.2
GRANT, MUDCAT James Timothy "Jim" B 8.13.1935 Lacoochee, FL BR/TR 6-1/186# d4.17																									
1958	Cle A	10	11	.476	44	28	11-1	4	204	173	93	20	1	104-5	111	3.84	95	.228	.317	66-4	.076	-4*	106	-3	-0.8
1959	Cle A	10	7	.588	38	19	6-1	3	165.1	140	80	23	2	81-4	85	4.14	89	.232	.323	55-1	.200	1*	100	-6	-0.5
1960	Cle A	9	8	.529	33	19	5	0	159.2	147	88	26	2	78-4	75	4.40	85	.243	.330	57-1	.281	4*	133	-12	-0.8
1961	Cle A	15	9	.625	35	35	11-3	0	244.2	207	118	32	3	109-3	146	3.86	102	.227	.310	88-5	.170	1*	123	2	0.3
1962	Cle A	7	10	.412	26	23	6-1	0	149.2	128	75	24	0	81-4	90	4.27	91	.233	.330	53-1	.151	-0*	99	-5	-0.5
1963	Cle A☆	13	14	.481	38	32	10-2	1	229.1	213	107	30	4	87-3	157	3.69	98	.243	.312	69-7	.188	3*	100	-2	-0.1
1964	Cle A	3	4	.429	13	9	1	0	62	82	41	11	1	25-2	43	5.95	60	.324	.384	22-1	.273	4*	112	-14	-1.0
	Min A	11	9	.550	26	23	10-1	1	166	162	73	21	0	36-2	75	2.82	127	.248	.286	60-2	.167	0*	139	9	1.0
	Year	14	13	.519	39	32	11-1	1	228	244	79	32	1	61-4	118	3.67	98	.270	.314	82-3	.195	4	132	-5	0.0
1965	†Min A★	**21**	7	**.750**	41	39	14-**6**	0	270.1	252	107	34	0	61-2	142	3.30	108	.247	.287	97-5	.155	2*	135	12	1.4
1966	Min A	13	13	.500	35	35	10-3	0	249	248	104	23	6	49-2	110	3.25	111	.260	.298	78-10	.192	2	96	9	1.3
1967	Min A	5	6	.455	27	14	2	0	95.1	121	56	10	1	17-0	50	4.72	73	.315	.343	28-2	.179	0	131	-12	-1.4
1968	LA N	6	4	.600	37	4	1	3	94.2	77	29	1	6	19-3	35	2.09	132	.226	.275	31-0	.129	0*	94	6	0.8
1969	Mon N	1	6	.143	11	10	1	0-0	50.2	64	33	7	1	14-1	20	4.80	77	.299	.343	16-0	.125	-1	92	-7	-0.9
	StL N	7	5	.583	30	3	1	7-2	63.1	62	31	9	2	22-8	35	4.12	87	.252	.319	17-2	.294	2*	83	-3	-0.5
	Year	8	11	.421	41	13	2	7-2	114	126	34	16	3	36-9	55	4.42	82	.274	.330	33-2	.212	1	90	-10	-1.4
1970	Oak A	6	2	.750	72	0	0	24-1	123.1	104	26	8	3	30-8	54	1.82	194	.235	.287	9-5	.222	2		**26**	2.8
	Pit N	2	1	.667	8	0	0	0-1	12	8	3	2	0	2-0	4	2.25	174	.190	.227	2-0	.000	-0		2	0.5
1971	Pit N	5	3	.625	42	0	0	7-4	75	79	32	8	1	28-8	22	3.60	94	.274	.340	8-0	.250	1		-1	0.0
	†Oak A	1	0	1.000	15	0	0	3-1	27.1	25	9	3	0	6-0	13	1.98	169	.243	.284	3-2	.333	0		3	0.2
Total	14	145	119	.549	571	293	89-18	53-9	2441.2	2292	1105	292	33	849-59	1267	3.63	100	.248	.311	759-48	.178	16	115	4	1.8
GRANT, MARK Mark Andrew B 10.24.1963 Aurora, IL BR/TR 6-2/205# d4.27																									
1984	SF N	1	4	.200	11	10	0	1-0	53.2	56	40	6	1	19-0	32	6.37	55	.272	.332	17-2	.000	-2	111	-16	-1.5
1986	SF N	0	1	.000	4	1	0	0-0	10	6	4	0	0	5-0	5	3.60	98	.176	.282	1-1	.000	-0	25	0	0.0
1987	SF N	1	2	.333	16	8	0	1-0	61	66	29	6	1	21-5	32	3.54	109	.282	.342	12-3	.083	-0	94	1	0.0
	SD N	6	7	.462	17	17	2-1	0-0	102.1	104	59	16	0	52-3	58	4.66	85	.263	.348	32-3	.094	-1*	87	-8	-1.0
	Year	7	9	.438	33	25	2-1	1-0	163.1	170	63	22	1	73-8	90	4.24	92	.270	.346	44-6	.091	-1	90	-7	-1.0
1988	SD N	2	8	.200	33	11	0	0-1	97.2	97	41	14	2	36-6	61	3.69	92	.268	.334	16-4	.000	-1	62	-2	-0.3
1989	SD N	8	2	.800	50	0	0	2-1	116.1	105	45	11	3	32-6	69	3.33	105	.248	.304	20-1	.050	-0		4	0.3
1990	SD N	1	1	.500	26	0	0	0-1	39	47	23	5	0	19-8	29	4.85	79	.305	.375	2-0	.500	0		-4	-0.1
	Atl N	1	2	.333	33	1	0	3-2	52.1	61	30	4	1	18-3	40	4.64	87	.293	.349	4-0	.250	1	89	-3	-0.1
	Year	2	3	.400	59	1	0	3-3	91.1	108	34	9	1	37-11	69	4.73	84	.298	.360	6-0	.333	1	91	-7	-0.2
1992	Sea A	2	4	.333	23	10	0	0-0	81	100	39	6	2	22-2	42	3.89	102	.311	.357	0-0	—	0	103	1	0.0
1993	Hou N	0	0	—	6	0	0	0-0	11	11	4	0	0	5-2	6	0.82	474	.275	.348	0-0	—	0		3	0.2
	Col N	0	1	.000	14	0	0	1-1	14.1	23	20	4	0	6-1	8	12.56	38	.377	.426	0-0	—	0		-10	-0.7
	Year	0	1	.000	20	0	0	1-1	25.1	34	29	4	0	11-3	14	7.46	59	.337	.395	0-0	—	0		-8	-0.5
Total	8	22	32	.407	233	58	2-1	8-6	638.2	676	334	72	10	235-36	382	4.31	87	.277	.341	104-14	.067	-3	89	-34	-3.2
GRAPENTHIN, RICK Richard Ray B 4.16.1958 Linn Grove, IA BR/TR 6-2/205# d5.3																									
1983	Mon N	0	1	.000	1	0	0	0-0	4	4	4	2	0	1-0	3	9.00	40	.267	.313	1-0	.000	-0		-2	-0.4
1984	Mon N	1	2	.333	13	1	0	2-0	23	19	9	3	0	7-0	9	3.52	97	.235	.289	5-0	.200	0	77	0	0.0
1985	Mon N	0	0	—	5	0	0	0-0	7	13	11	0	1	8-2	4	14.14	24	.394	.512	1-0	1.000	1		-8	-0.4
Total	3	1	3	.250	19	1	0	2-0	34	36	24	5	1	16-2	16	6.35	54	.279	.356	7-0	.286	0	77	-10	-0.8
GRASMICK, LOU Louis Junior B 9.11.1924 Baltimore, MD BR/TR 6/195# d4.22																									
1948	Phi N	0	0	—	2	0	0	0	5	3	4	1	0	8	2	7.20	55	.176	.440	1-0	1.000	0		-2	0.0
GRATE, DON Donald "Buckeye" B 8.27.1923 Greenfield, OH BR/TR 6-2.5/180# d7.6																									
1945	Phi N	0	1	.000	4	2	0	0	8.1	18	16	0	0	12	6	17.28	22	.439	.566	3-0	.000	-0*	55	-11	-1.1
1946	Phi N	1	0	1.000	3	0	0	0	8	4	1	0	0	2	2	1.13	305	.160	.222	1-0	.000	0		2	0.3
Total	2	1	1	.500	7	2	0	0	16.1	22	17	0	0	14	8	9.37	39	.333	.450	4-0	.000	-0	55	-9	-0.8
GRATER, MARK Mark Anthony B 1.19.1964 Rochester, PA BR/TR 5-10/205# d6.12																									
1991	StL N	0	0	—	3	0	0	0-0	3	5	0	0	0	2-0	0	0.00	—	.385	.467	0-0	—	0		1	0.1
1993	Det A	0	0	—	6	0	0	0-0	5	6	3	0	0	4-1	4	5.40	80	.286	.400	0-0	—	0		0	0.0
Total	2	0	0	—	9	0	0	0-0	8	11	3	0	0	6-1	4	3.38	121	.324	.425	0-0	—	0		1	0.1
GRATEROL, BEIKER Beiker B 11.9.1974 Lara, Venezuela BR/TR 6-2/165# d4.9																									
1999	Det A	0	1	.000	1	1	0	0-0	4	4	7	3	0	4-1	2	15.75	31	.250	.400	0-0	—	0	56	-4	-0.6
GRAVES, DANNY Daniel Peter B 8.7.1973 Saigon, South Vietnam BR/TR 5-11/200# d7.13																									
1996	Cle A	2	0	1.000	15	0	0	0-1	29.2	29	18	2	0	10-0	22	4.55	108	.246	.302	0-0	—	0		0	0.0
1997	Cle A	0	0	—	5	0	0	0-0	11.1	15	8	2	0	9-0	4	4.76	99	.326	.429	0-0	—	0		-1	-0.1
	Cin N	0	0	—	10	0	0	0-0	14.2	26	14	0	0	11-1	7	6.14	70	.413	.493	1-0	.000	-0		-4	-0.2
1998	Cin N	2	1	.667	62	0	0	8-0	81.1	76	31	6	2	28-4	44	3.32	129	.251	.314	4-0	.000	-0		9	0.4
1999	Cin N	8	7	.533	75	0	0	27-9	111	90	42	10	2	49-4	69	3.08	151	.227	.314	5-0	.000	-1		19	3.0
2000	Cin N★	10	5	.667	66	0	0	30-5	91.1	81	31	8	3	42-7	53	2.56	184	.243	.330	2-0	.500	2		20	4.2
2001	Cin N	6	5	.545	66	0	0	32-7	80.1	83	41	7	4	18-6	49	4.15	110	.268	.314	4-0	.250	1		4	0.9
2002	Cin N	7	3	.700	68	4	0	32-7	98.2	99	37	7	3	25-9	58	3.19	133	.264	.311	6-2	.000	-1*	43	12	1.8
2003	Cin N	4	15	.211	30	26	2-1	2-0	169	204	108	30	7	41-6	60	5.33	80	.298	.343	54-3	.111	-3*	86	-20	-2.1
Total	8	39	36	.520	397	30	2-1	131-29	687.1	703	330	72	21	233-37	366	3.89	115	.268	.329	76-5	.105	-2	76	39	7.9
GRAY, CHARLIE Charles A. B 6.1864 Indianapolis, IN D 6.1.1900 Indianapolis, IN d4.23																									
1890	Pit N	1	4	.200	5	4	3	0	31	48	35	0	1	24	10	7.55	44	.343	.442	15	.200	-0	43	-14	-1.6
GRAY, DAVE David Alexander B 1.7.1943 Ogden, UT BR/TR 6-1/190# d6.14																									
1964	Bos A	0	0	—	9	1	0	0	13	18	20	3	0	20-0	17	9.00	43	.321	.494	1-0	1.000	0	138	-9	-0.4
GRAY, CHUMMY George Edward B 7.17.1873 Rockland, ME D 8.14.1913 Rockland, ME TR 5-11.5/163# d9.14																									
1899	Pit N	3	3	.500	9	7	6	0	70.2	85	35	1	4	24	9	3.44	111	.297	.360	26-0	.038	-3	81	4	0.1
GRAY, JEFF Jeffrey Edward B 4.10.1963 Richmond, VA BR/TR 6-1/175# d6.21																									
1988	Cin N	0	0	—	5	0	0	0-0	9.1	12	4	0	0	4-2	5	3.86	93	.333	.381	1-1	.000	-0		0	0.0
1990	†Bos A	2	4	.333	41	0	0	9-3	50.2	53	27	3	1	15-3	50	4.44	92	.268	.321	0-0	—	0		-2	-0.2
1991	Bos A	2	3	.400	50	0	0	1-3	61.2	39	17	7	1	10-4	41	2.34	184	.181	.219	0-0	—	0		13	1.0
Total	3	4	7	.364	96	0	0	10-6	121.2	104	48	10	2	29-9	96	3.33	125	.231	.278	1-1	.000	-0		11	0.8

Year	Tm Lg	W	L	Pct	G	GS	CG-Sho	SV-BS	IP	H	R	HR	HB	BB-IB	SO	ERA	AERA	OAV	OOB	AB-SH	AVG	PB	Sup	APR	PW
GRAY, JOHNNY John Leonard B 12.11.1926 W.Palm Beach, FL BR/TR 6-4/226# d7.18																									
1954	Phi A	3	12	.200	18	16	5	0	105	111	83	10	0	91	51	6.51	60	.273	.406	34-1	.029	-4*	66	-28	-3.7
1955	KC A	0	3	.000	8	5	0	0	26.2	28	23	2	1	24-0	11	6.41	65	.277	.417	8-0	.125	-0	85	-7	-0.8
1957	Cle A	1	3	.250	7	3	1-1	0	20	21	17	1	0	13-1	3	5.85	64	.288	.395	4-1	.000	-1	72	-6	-1.0
1958	Phi N	0	0	—	15	0	0	0	17.1	12	9	3	0	14-3	10	4.15	95	.222	.377	1-0	.000	-0		0	0.0
Total	4	4	18	.182	48	24	6-1	0	169	172	132	16	1	142-4	75	6.18	64	.271	.404	47-2	.043	-5	71	-41	-5.5
GRAY, DOLLY Samuel David "Sam" B 10.15.1897 Van Alstyne, TX D 4.16.1953 McKinney, TX BR/TR 5-11/175# d4.19																									
1924	Phi A	8	7	.533	34	19	8-2	2	151.2	169	95	5	6	89	54	3.98	108	.284	.383	57-0	.175	-2	98	-1	-0.4
1925	Phi A	16	8	.667	32	28	14-4	3	203.2	199	90	11	3	63	80	3.27	142	.260	.319	67-2	.179	-2	106	29	2.7
1926	Phi A	11	12	.478	38	18	5	0	150.2	164	81	9	4	50	82	3.64	114	.279	.340	51-5	.216	1	97	7	1.0
1927	Phi A	9	6	.600	37	13	3-1	3	133.1	153	79	4	4	51	49	4.59	93	.295	.362	42-3	.190	-1	123	-4	-0.5
1928	StL A	20	12	.625	35	31	21-2	3	262.2	256	119	11	1	86	102	3.19	132	.260	.320	101-4	.188	-2	100	24	2.7
1929	StL A	18	15	.545	43	**37**	23-**4**	1	**305**	336	142	18	1	96	109	3.72	119	.285	.340	103-9	.184	-2	88	24	2.0
1930	StL A	4	15	.211	27	24	7	0	167.2	215	133	17	4	52	51	6.28	78	.316	.368	54-1	.204	-2	73	-25	-2.3
1931	StL A	11	24	.314	43	**37**	13	2	258	323	187	20	4	54	88	5.09	91	.297	.332	79-5	.177	-1	76	-17	-2.0
1932	StL A	7	12	.368	52	18	7-3	4	206.2	250	126	9	1	53	79	4.53	107	.294	.336	62-1	.210	-0	77	5	0.4
1933	StL A	7	4	.636	38	6	0	4	112	131	55	7	1	45	36	4.10	114	.301	.368	32-1	.219	1	94	7	0.8
Total	10	111	115	.491	379	231	101-16	22	1951.1	2196	1107	111	29	639	730	4.18	108	.286	.343	648-31	.191	-10	91	49	4.4
GRAY, TED Ted Glenn B 12.31.1924 Detroit, MI BB/TL 5-11/175# d5.15																									
1946	Det A	0	2	.000	3	2	0	1	11.2	17	12	4	0	5	5	8.49	43	.340	.400	3-0	.000	-0	129	-6	-0.9
1948	Det A	6	2	.750	26	11	3-1	0	85.1	73	43	2	3	72	60	4.22	104	.236	.385	29-2	.241	1	117	3	0.2
1949	Det A	10	10	.500	34	27	8-3	1	195	163	83	11	5	103	96	3.51	119	.227	.328	63-3	.127	-3*	96	15	1.2
1950	Det A★	10	7	.588	27	21	7	1	149.1	139	85	22	2	72	102	4.40	107	.248	.335	50-4	.140	-2	102	3	0.0
1951	Det A	7	14	.333	34	28	9-1	1	197.1	194	103	17	6	95	131	4.06	103	.256	.343	63-4	.143	-3*	77	1	-0.2
1952	Det A	12	17	.414	35	32	13-2	0	224	212	118	21	3	101	138	4.14	92	.249	.331	76-8	.171	-2*	73	-9	-1.2
1953	Det A	10	15	.400	30	28	8	0	176	166	102	25	7	76	115	4.60	88	.252	.336	61-1	.230	2*	83	-11	-1.2
1954	Det A	3	5	.375	19	10	2	0	72	70	48	8	2	56	29	5.38	69	.268	.395	22-0	.045	-2	93	-13	-1.6
1955	Chi A	0	0	—	2	1	0	0	3	9	6	0	0	2-0	1	18.00	22	.500	.550	0-0	—	0	180	-4	-0.2
	Cle A	0	0	—	2	0	0	0	2	5	4	1	0	2-0	1	18.00	22	.455	.538	0-0	—	0		-3	-0.1
	NY A	0	0	—	1	1	0	0	3	3	1	0	0	0-0	1	3.00	125	.300	.273	1-0	.000	-0	190	0	0.0
	Bal A	1	2	.333	9	1	0	0	15.1	21	19	3	0	11-1	8	8.22	46	.344	.438	2-0	.000	-0	93	-9	-1.5
	Year	1	2	.333	14	3	0	0	23.1	38	23	4	0	15-1	11	9.64	40	.380	.453	3-0	.000	-0	154	-16	-1.8
Total	9	59	74	.444	222	162	50-7	4	1134	1072	624	114	28	595-1	687	4.37	94	.251	.346	370-22	.159	-10	90	-33	-5.5
GRAY, DOLLY William Denton B 12.3.1878 Houghton, MI D 4.3.1956 Yuba City, CA BL/TL 6-2/160# d4.13																									
1909	Was A	5	19	.208	36	26	19	0	218	210	123	1	9	77	87	3.59	68	.258	.329	89-1	.146	-1*	81	-29	-3.2
1910	Was A	8	19	.296	34	29	21-3	0	229	216	106	3	10	65	84	2.63	95	.249	.309	85-1	.247	4*	74	-6	-0.2
1911	Was A	2	13	.133	28	15	6	0	121	160	90	4	3	40	42	5.06	65	.331	.385	44-0	.227	1	85	-21	-2.1
Total	3	15	51	.227	98	70	46-3	0	568	586	319	8	22	182	213	3.52	75	.271	.333	218-2	.202	3	79	-56	-5.5
GRBA, ELI Eli B 8.9.1934 Chicago, IL BR/TR 6-2/207# d7.10																									
1959	NY A	2	5	.286	19	6	0	0	50.1	52	44	6	0	39-0	23	6.44	57	.269	.387	14-1	.214	1	109	-18	-2.0
1960	†NY A	6	4	.600	24	9	1	1	80.2	65	45	9	2	46-3	32	3.68	97	.226	.333	21-3	.238	2*	90	-4	-0.3
1961	LA A	11	13	.458	40	30	8	2	211.2	197	119	26	7	114-10	105	4.25	106	.242	.339	64-8	.234	4*	103	3	0.7
1962	LA A	8	9	.471	40	29	1	1	176.1	185	101	19	2	75-5	90	4.54	85	.267	.338	58-3	.207	3*	110	-12	-0.8
1963	LA A	1	2	.333	12	1	0	0	17.1	14	9	2	1	10-1	5	4.67	73	.222	.333	3-0	.000	-0*	130	-2	-0.3
Total	5	28	33	.459	135	75	10	4	536.1	513	318	62	12	284-19	255	4.48	90	.250	.342	160-15	.219	10	106	-33	-2.7
GREASON, JOHN John R. TL d8.27																									
1873	Was NA	1	6	.143	7	7	7	0	63	113	90	3		10	5	5.86	57	.359	.378	27	.148	-2	52	-13	-1.0
GREASON, BILL William Henry "Booster" B 9.3.1924 Atlanta, GA BR/TR 5-10/170# d5.31																									
1954	StL N	0	1	.000	3	2	0	0	4	8	8	4	0	4	2	13.50	30	.421	.522	1-0	.000	-0	130	-5	-0.8
GREEN, CHRIS Christopher De Wayne B 9.5.1960 Los Angeles, CA BL/TL 6-2/214# d4.17																									
1984	Pit N	0	0	—	4	0	0	0-0	3	5	2	0	0	1-0	3	6.00	60	.417	.429	0-0	—	0		-1	0.0
GREEN, JASON David Jason B 6.5.1975 Port Hope, ON, CAN BR/TR 6-1/205# d7.23																									
2000	Hou N	1	1	.500	14	0	0	0-0	17.2	15	16	3	1	20-1	19	6.62	73	.234	.424	1-0	.000	-0		-4	-0.4
GREEN, ED Edward M. B 1850 Philadelphia, PA d4.22																									
1890	Phi AA	7	15	.318	25	22	20-1	1	191	267	184	4	6	94	56	5.80	67	.321	.393	126	.119	-4*	70	-43	-3.9
GREEN, FRED Fred Allen B 9.14.1933 Titusville, NJ D 12.22.1996 Titusville, NJ BR/TL 6-4/190# d4.15 s-Gary																									
1959	Pit N	1	2	.333	17	1	0	1	37.1	37	16	2	0	15-8	20	3.13	123	.259	.327	6-0	.000	-1	0	2	0.1
1960	†Pit N	8	4	.667	45	0	0	3	70	61	26	4	1	33-8	49	3.21	117	.243	.328	8-0	.375	3		5	1.1
1961	Pit N	0	0	—	13	0	0	0	20.2	27	16	2	0	9-2	4	4.79	83	.321	.387	3-0	.000	-0		-3	-0.2
1962	Was A	0	1	.000	5	0	0	0	7	7	6	3	0	6-1	2	6.43	63	.250	.382	0-0	—	0		-2	-0.3
1964	Pit N	0	0	—	8	0	0	0	7.1	10	1	1	0	0-0	2	1.23	286	.323	.313	0-0	—	0		2	0.1
Total	5	9	7	.563	88	1	0	4	142.1	142	65	12	1	63-19	77	3.48	110	.264	.339	17-0	.176	2	0	4	0.8
GREEN, DALLAS George Dallas B 8.4.1934 Newport, DE BL/TR 6-5/210# d6.18 M8																									
1960	Phi N	3	6	.333	23	10	5-1	0	108.2	100	54	10	2	44-4	51	4.06	96	.248	.321	34-2	.206	0*	75	-2	-0.1
1961	Phi N	2	4	.333	42	10	1-1	1	128	160	77	8	2	47-6	51	4.85	84	.315	.372	33-1	.152	0	102	-11	-0.5
1962	Phi N	6	6	.500	37	10	2	1	129.1	145	58	10	5	43-6	58	3.83	101	.289	.350	32-3	.063	-1*	84	2	0.2
1963	Phi N	7	5	.583	40	14	4	2	120	134	53	10	2	38-8	68	3.23	100	.286	.339	35-0	.086	-1*	103	-1	-0.2
1964	Phi N	2	1	.667	25	0	0	0	42	63	31	4	2	14-0	21	5.79	60	.362	.414	3-0	.000	-0*		-11	-0.8
1965	Was A	0	0	—	6	2	0	0	14.1	14	6	0	0	3-0	6	3.14	111	.241	.279	4-0	.000	-0	139	0	0.0
1966	NY N	0	0	—	4	0	0	0	5	6	3	2	0	2-1	1	5.40	67	.333	.400	0-0	—	0		-1	0.0
1967	Phi N	0	0	—	8	0	0	0	15	25	16	2	1	6-2	12	9.00	38	.362	.421	1-0	.000	-0		-9	-0.4
Total	8	20	22	.476	185	46	12-2	4	562.1	647	298	46	14	197-27	268	4.26	88	.294	.353	142-6	.120	-3	93	-33	-1.8
GREEN, HARVEY Harvey George "Buck" B 2.9.1915 Kenosha, WI D 7.24.1970 Franklin, LA BB/TR 6-2.5/185# d9.12																									
1935	Bro N	0	0	—	2	0	0	0	1	2	1	0	1	3	0	9.00	44	.400	.667	0-0	—	0		0	0.0
GREEN, STEVE Steve B 1.26.1978 Greenfield Park, PQ, CAN BR/TR 6-2/195# d4.7																									
2001	Ana A	0	0	—	1	1	0	0-0	6	4	2	0	0	6-0	4	3.00	152	.190	.370	0-0	—	0	41	1	0.1
GREEN, TYLER Tyler Scott B 2.18.1970 Springfield, OH BR/TR 6-5/185# d4.9																									
1993	Phi N	0	0	—	3	2	0	0-0	7.1	16	9	1	0	5-0	7	7.36	54	.444	.512	2-1	.000	-0	147	-4	-0.2
1995	Phi N★	8	9	.471	26	25	4-2	0-0	140.2	157	86	15	4	66-3	85	5.31	80	.290	.367	44-8	.182	2*	113	-15	-1.4
1997	Phi N	4	4	.500	14	14	0	0-0	76.2	72	50	8	1	45-4	58	4.93	86	.247	.347	26-1	.308	3	108	-8	-0.4
1998	Phi N	6	12	.333	27	27	0	0-0	159.1	142	97	23	9	85-1	113	5.03	86	.239	.340	41-6	.146	-0	92	-13	-1.4
Total	4	18	25	.419	70	68	4-2	0-0	384	387	242	47	14	201-8	263	5.16	83	.265	.356	113-16	.195	4	104	-40	-3.4
GREENE, TOMMY Ira Thomas B 4.6.1967 Lumberton, NC BR/TR 6-5/227# d9.10																									
1989	Atl N	1	2	.333	4	4	1-1	0-0	26.1	22	12	5	0	6-1	17	4.10	89	.234	.275	10-0	.100	-1	54	-1	-0.1
1990	Atl N	1	0	1.000	5	2	0	0-0	12.1	14	11	3	1	9-0	4	8.03	50	.286	.407	1-1	.000	-0	123	-5	-0.4
	Phi N	2	3	.400	10	7	0	0-0	39	36	20	5	0	17-1	17	4.15	92	.247	.325	11-2	.182	0	57	-1	-0.1
	Year	3	3	.500	15	9	0	0-0	51.1	50	22	8	1	26-1	21	5.08	76	.256	.347	12-3	.167	0	72	-6	-0.5
1991	Phi N	13	7	.650	36	27	3-2	0-0	207.2	177	85	19	3	66-4	154	3.38	109	.230	.290	71-3	.268	7*	102	6	1.2
1992	Phi N	3	3	.500	13	12	0	0-0	64.1	75	39	5	0	34-2	39	5.32	66	.291	.371	24-0	.125	-1	117	-12	-1.1
1993	†Phi N	16	4	.800	31	30	7-2	0-0	200	175	84	12	3	62-3	167	3.42	116	.233	.291	72-6	.222	6*	136	14	1.8
1994	Phi N	2	0	1.000	7	7	0	0-0	35.2	37	20	5	0	22-0	28	4.54	95	.272	.371	13-1	.385	2	149	-1	0.2

Year	Tm Lg	W	L	Pct	G	GS	CG-Sho	SV-BS	IP	H	R	HR	HB	BB-IB	SO	ERA	AERA	OAV	OOB	AB-SH	AVG	PB	Sup	APR	PW
1995	Phi N	0	5	.000	11	6	0	0-0	33.2	45	32	6	3	20-0	24	8.29	51	.319	.412	8-1	.000	-0	68	-14	-1.8
1997	Hou N	0	1	.000	2	2	0	0-0	9	10	7	2	0	5-0	11	7.00	57	.286	.375	3-1	.333	1	138	-3	-0.2
Total	8	38	25	.603	119	97	11-5	0-0	628	591	310	62	10	241-11	461	4.14	93	.249	.317	213-15	.221	14	112	-17	-0.5
GREENE, JUNE Julius Foust B 6.25.1899 Ramseur, NC D 3.19.1974 Glendora, CA BL/TR 6-2.5/185# d4.20 ▲																									
1928	Phi N	0	0	—	1	0	0	0	2	5	2	0	0	0	0	9.00	47	.556	.556	6-1	.500	2*		-1	0.2
1929	Phi N	0	0	—	5	0	0	0	13.2	33	32	2	3	9	4	19.76	26	.465	.542	19-0	.211	0*		-19	-0.8
Total	2	0	0	—	6	0	0	0	15.2	38	34	2	3	9	4	18.38	28	.475	.543	25-1	.280	2		-20	-0.6
GREENE, NELSON Nelson George "Lefty" B 9.20.1900 Philadelphia, PA D 4.6.1983 Lebanon, PA BL/TL 6/185# d4.28																									
1924	Bro N	0	1	.000	4	1	0	0	9	14	6	1	0	2	3	4.00	94	.350	.381	1-0	.000	-0	45	-1	-0.1
1925	Bro N	2	0	1.000	11	0	0	1	22	45	28	4	0	7	4	10.64	39	.417	.452	7-0	.286	0		-15	-1.2
Total	2	2	1	.667	15	1	0	1	31	59	34	5	0	9	7	8.71	47	.399	.433	8-0	.250	-0	45	-16	-1.3
GREENE, RICK Richard Douglas B 1.2.1971 Fort Knox, KY BR/TR 6-5/200# d6.19																									
1999	Cin N	0	0	—	1	0	0	0-0	5.2	7	4	2	0	1-0	3	4.76	98	.292	.320	2-0	.000	-0		0	0.0
GREENFIELD, KENT Kent B 7.1.1902 Guthrie, KY D 3.14.1978 Guthrie, KY BR/TR 6-1/180# d9.28																									
1924	NY N	0	1	.000	1	1	0	0	3	9	8	1	0	1	1	15.00	24	.500	.526	0-0	—	0	139	-5	-0.7
1925	NY N	12	8	.600	29	20	12	0	171.2	195	86	4	2	64	66	3.88	104	.288	.352	62-3	.081	-6	85	4	-0.2
1926	NY N	13	12	.520	39	28	8-1	1	222.2	206	111	17	5	82	74	3.96	95	.251	.322	65-3	.092	-5	90	-3	-0.9
1927	NY N	2	2	.500	12	1	0	0	20	39	25	3	2	13	4	9.45	41	.411	.491	2-1	.000	-0	110	-13	-2.1
	Bos N	11	14	.440	27	26	11-1	0	190	203	92	3	5	59	59	3.84	97	.282	.341	64-7	.172	-2	82	-1	-0.3
	Year	13	16	.448	39	27	11-1	0	210	242	96	6	7	72	63	4.37	85	.297	.359	66-8	.167	-2	83	-13	-2.4
1928	Bos N	3	11	.214	32	20	5	0	143.2	173	100	6	5	60	30	5.32	73	.307	.378	38-7	.053	-4	88	-22	-2.2
1929	Bos N	0	0	—	6	2	0	0	15.2	33	19	1	2	15	7	10.91	43	.465	.568	5-0	.000	-1	140	-10	-0.5
	Bro N	0	0	—	6	0	0	0	8.2	13	8	1	0	3	1	8.31	56	.382	.432	1-0	.000	-0*		-3	-0.1
	Year	0	0	—	12	2	0	0	24.1	46	35	2	2	18	8	9.99	47	.438	.528	6-0	.000	-1	140	-13	-0.6
Total	6	41	48	.461	152	98	36-2	1	775.1	871	449	36	21	297	242	4.54	85	.290	.358	237-21	.101	-18	88	-53	-7.0
GREENIG, JOHN John A. B 1848 Philadelphia, PA D 7.28.1913 Philadelphia, PA d5.9																									
1888	Was N	0	1	.000	1	1	1	0	9	17	13	2	0	4	2	11.00	25	.405	.457	3	.000	-0	44	-7	-0.6
GREENWOOD, BOB Robert Chandler "Greenie" B 3.13.1928 Cananea, Mexico D 9.1.1994 Hayward, CA BR/TR 6-5/200# d4.21																									
1954	Phi N	1	2	.333	11	4	0	0	36.2	28	16	2	0	18	9	3.19	127	.209	.301	9-1	.000	-1*	99	3	0.2
1955	Phi N	0	0	—	1	0	0	0	2.1	7	4	1	0	0-0	0	15.43	26	.500	.500	1-0	.000	-0		-3	-0.1
Total	2	1	2	.333	12	4	0	0	39	35	20	3	0	18-0	9	3.92	103	.236	.317	10-1	.000	-1	99	0	0.1
GREER, KENNY Kenneth William B 5.12.1967 Boston, MA BR/TR 6-2/210# d9.29																									
1993	NY N	1	0	1.000	1	0	0	0-0	1	0	0	0	0	0-0	2	0.00	—	.000	.000	0-0	—	0		0	0.1
1995	SF N	0	2	.000	8	0	0	0-1	12	15	12	3	1	5-2	7	5.25	78	.288	.356	1-0	.000	-0		-4	-0.5
Total	2	1	2	.333	9	0	0	0-1	13	15	12	3	1	5-2	9	4.85	84	.273	.339	1-0	.000	-0		-4	-0.4
GREGG, DAVE David Charles "Highpockets" B 3.14.1891 Chehalis, WA D 11.12.1965 Clarkston, WA BR/TR 6-1/185# d6.15 b-Vean																									
1913	Cle A	0	0	—	1	0	0	0	1	2	2	0	1	0	0	18.00	17	.400	.500	0-0	—	0		-1	-0.1
GREGG, HAL Harold Dana "Skeets" B 7.11.1921 Anaheim, CA D 5.13.1991 Bishop, CA BR/TR 6-3.5/195# d8.18																									
1943	Bro N	0	3	.000	5	4	0	0	18.2	21	21	2	0	21	7	9.64	35	.304	.467	2-1	.000	0	88	-12	-1.6
1944	Bro N	9	16	.360	39	31	6	2	197.2	201	142	12	9	137	92	5.46	65	.258	.376	68-4	.206	-0*	117	-43	-4.9
1945	Bro N✤	18	13	.581	42	34	13-2	2	254.1	221	116	5	8	120	139	3.47	108	.232	.323	91-8	.220	3	106	11	1.6
1946	Bro N	6	4	.600	26	16	4-1	2	117.1	103	46	3	1	44	54	2.99	113	.236	.308	32-6	.125	-1	95	5	0.2
1947	†Bro N	4	5	.444	37	16	2-1	1	104.1	115	79	6	4	55	59	5.87	70	.272	.361	34-0	.265	2	107	-20	-1.4
1948	Pit N	2	4	.333	22	8	1	1	74.1	72	40	3	3	34	25	4.60	88	.255	.342	22-2	.273	2	131	-3	-0.1
1949	Pit N	1	1	.500	8	1	0	0	18.2	20	10	1	1	8	9	3.38	125	.303	.387	5-2	.000	-0	126	1	0.0
1950	Pit N	0	1	.000	5	1	0	0	5.1	10	10	2	1	7	3	13.50	32	.400	.545	1-0	.000	-0	60	-5	-0.8
1952	NY N	0	1	.000	16	4	1	1	36.1	42	22	7	2	17	13	4.71	79	.286	.367	8-0	.125	-0	138	-4	-0.3
Total	9	40	48	.455	200	115	27-4	9	827	805	486	41	29	443	401	4.54	82	.253	.350	263-23	.205	4	110	-70	-7.3
GREGG, KEVIN Kevin Marschall B 6.20.1978 Corvallis, OR BR/TR 6-6/200# d8.9																									
2003	Ana A	2	0	1.000	5	3	0	0-0	24.2	18	9	3	1	8-0	14	3.28	131	.205	.278	0-0	—	0	50	3	0.2
GREGG, VEAN Sylveanus Augustus B 4.13.1885 Chehalis, WA D 7.29.1964 Aberdeen, WA BR/TL 6-1/185# d4.12 b-Dave																									
1911	Cle A	23	7	.767	34	26	22-5	0	244.2	172	67	2	10	86	125	**1.80**	**189**	**.205**	.286	85-5	.165	-4	93	43	4.6
1912	Cle A	20	13	.606	37	34	26-1	2	271.1	242	99	4	10	90	184	2.59	132	.246	.316	97-8	.175	-3	94	27	2.8
1913	Cle A	20	13	.606	44	34	23-3	3	285.2	258	103	2	13	124	166	2.24	136	.250	.338	99-4	.131	-4	93	22	1.9
1914	Cle A	9	3	.750	17	12	6-1	0	96.2	88	46	0	3	48	56	3.07	94	.251	.347	34-1	.176	1	120	-2	-0.2
	Bos A	3	4	.429	12	9	4	0	68.1	71	39	0	0	37	24	3.95	68	.283	.375	19-2	.211	0	117	-9	-0.9
	Year	12	7	.632	29	21	10-1	0	165	159	43	0	3	85	80	3.44	82	.265	.358	53-3	.189	1	119	-11	-1.1
1915	Bos A	4	2	.667	18	9	3-1	3	75	71	37	2	5	32	43	3.36	83	.260	.348	20-2	.350	2	137	-5	-0.2
1916	Bos A	2	5	.286	21	7	3	0	77.2	71	30	0	3	30	41	3.01	92	.259	.339	18-0	.111	-1	94	-1	-0.2
1918	Phi A	9	14	.391	30	25	17-3	2	199.1	180	85	4	5	67	63	3.12	94	.251	.320	71-1	.169	-3	75	-2	-0.6
1925	Was A	2	2	.500	26	5	1	2	74.1	87	41	3	2	38	18	4.12	103	.318	.404	14-4	.214	0	143	1	0.0
Total	8	92	63	.594	239	161	105-14	12	1393	1240	547	17	51	552	720	2.70	117	.248	.329	457-27	.171	-12	97	74	7.2
GREGORY, FRANK Frank Ernst B 7.25.1888 Spring Valley Township, WI D 11.5.1955 Beloit, WI BR/TR 5-11/185# d9.5																									
1912	Cin N	2	0	1.000	4	2	1	0	15.2	19	12	0	1	7	4	4.60	73	.297	.375	5-0	.200	0	109	-3	-0.3
GREGORY, LEE Grover Leroy B 6.2.1938 Bakersfield, CA BL/TL 6-1/180# d4.17																									
1964	Chi N	0	0	—	11	0	0	0	18	23	8	3	0	5-2	8	3.50	106	.333	.373	13-0	.077	0*		0	0.0
GREGORY, HOWIE Howard Watterson B 11.18.1886 Hannibal, MO D 5.30.1970 Tulsa, OK BL/TR 6/175# d4.16																									
1911	StL A	0	1	.000	3	1	0	0	7	11	5	0	0	4	1	5.14	66	.393	.469	2-0	.000	-0	21	-1	-0.2
GREGORY, PAUL Paul Edwin "Pop" B 6.9.1908 Tomnolen, MS D 9.16.1999 Southaven, MS BR/TR 6-2/180# d4.20																									
1932	Chi A	5	3	.625	33	9	3	0	117.2	125	75	8	2	51	39	4.51	96	.273	.348	38-3	.079	-3	105	-3	-0.3
1933	Chi A	4	11	.267	23	17	5	0	103.2	124	75	10	1	47	18	4.95	86	.296	.368	35-1	.143	-1	93	-11	-1.4
Total	2	9	14	.391	56	26	8	0	221.1	249	150	18	3	98	57	4.72	91	.284	.358	73-4	.110	-4	97	-14	-1.7
GREIF, BILL William Briley B 4.25.1950 Ft.Stockton, TX BR/TR 6-5/205# d7.19																									
1971	Hou N	1	1	.500	7	3	0	0-0	16	18	10	1	2	8-0	14	5.06	67	.290	.384	3-0	.333	0	105	-3	-0.3
1972	SD N	5	16	.238	34	22	2-1	2-1	125.1	143	86	18	8	47-4	91	5.60	59	.287	.353	33-5	.030	-3	70	-33	-5.3
1973	SD N	10	17	.370	36	31	9-3	1-0	199.1	181	88	20	5	62-12	120	3.21	109	.246	.306	61-2	.098	-2	78	4	0.3
1974	SD N	9	19	.321	43	35	7-1	1-1	226	244	126	17	14	95-11	137	4.66	77	.279	.356	56-9	.071	-2*	87	-26	-3.0
1975	SD N	4	6	.400	59	1	0	9-3	72	74	44	7	5	38-17	43	3.88	90	.269	.366	1-1	.000	-0	202	-6	-1.1
1976	SD N	1	3	.250	5	5	0	0-0	22.1	27	20	2	0	11-0	5	8.06	41	.297	.369	8-0	.000	-1	140	-11	-1.7
	StL N	1	5	.167	47	0	0	6-0	54.2	60	28	5	2	26-5	32	4.12	86	.290	.367	4-0	.000	0		-3	-0.4
	Year	2	8	.200	52	5	0	6-0	77	87	53	7	2	37-5	37	5.26	66	.292	.367	12-0	.000	-1	132	-14	-2.1
Total	6	31	67	.316	231	97	18-5	19-5	715.2	747	402	70	36	287-49	442	4.41	79	.272	.345	166-17	.072	-7	84	-78	-11.5
GREISINGER, SETH Seth Adam B 7.29.1975 Kansas City, KS BR/TR 6-4/190# d6.3																									
1998	Det A	6	9	.400	21	21	0	0-0	130	142	79	17	4	48-2	66	5.12	92	.282	.346	4-0	.250	0	75	-5	-0.6
2002	Det A	2	2	.500	8	8	0	0-0	37.2	46	26	4	1	13-2	14	6.21	69	.303	.359	0-0	—	0	86	-7	-0.6
Total	2	8	11	.421	29	29	0	0-0	167.2	188	105	21	5	61-4	80	5.37	86	.287	.349	4-0	.250	0	78	-12	-1.2
GREVELL, BILL William J. B 3.5.1898 Williamstown, NJ D 6.21.1923 Philadelphia, PA BR/TR 5-11/170# d5.14																									
1919	Phi A	0	0	—	5	2	0	0	12	15	20	0	1	18	3	14.25	24	.306	.500	5-0	.000	-1	183	-12	-0.6

Year	Tm Lg	W	L	Pct	G	GS	CG-Sho	SV-BS	IP	H	R	HR	HB	BB-IB	SO	ERA	AERA	OAV	OOB	AB-SH	AVG	PB	Sup	APR	PW
GRIFFETH, LEE Leon Clifford B 5.20.1925 Carmel, NY BB/TL 5-11.5/180# d6.25																									
1946	Phi A	0	0	—	10	0	0	0	15.1	13	7	1	2	6	4	2.93	121	.232	.328	1-0	.000	0		1	0.0
GRIFFIN, HANK James Linton "Pepper" B 7.11.1886 Whitehouse, TX D 2.11.1950 Terrell, TX BR/TR 6/165# d5.5																									
1911	Chi N	0	0	—	1	1	0	0	1	1	2	1	0	3	1	18.00	18	.250	.571	0-0	—	0	45	-1	-0.1
	Bos N	0	6	.000	15	6	1	0	82.2	96	70	3	6	34	30	5.23	73	.305	.383	30-0	.233	-0	92	-14	-0.9
	Year	0	6	.000	16	7	1	0	83.2	97	75	4	6	37	31	5.38	71	.304	.387	30-0	.233	-0	84	-15	-1.0
1912	Bos N	0	0	—	3	0	0	0	1.2	3	5	0	1	3	0	27.00	13	.750	.875	0-0	—	0		-4	-0.2
Total	2	0	6	.000	19	7	1	0	85.1	100	77	4	7	40	31	5.80	66	.310	.397	30-0	.233	-0	84	-19	-1.2
GRIFFIN, MARTY Martin John B 9.2.1901 San Francisco, CA D 11.19.1951 Los Angeles, CA BR/TR 6-2/200# d7.25																									
1928	Bos A	0	3	.000	11	3	0	0	37.2	42	21	0	0	17	9	5.02	82	.300	.376	13-0	.308	1*	27	-2	-0.1
GRIFFIN, MIKE Michael Leroy B 6.26.1957 Colusa, CA BR/TR 6-5/197# d9.17																									
1979	NY A	0	0	—	3	0	0	1-0	4.1	5	2	0	0	2-0	5	4.15	98	.313	.389	0-0	—	0		0	0.0
1980	NY A	2	4	.333	13	9	0	0-0	54	64	36	6	1	23-2	25	4.83	81	.287	.353	0-0	—	0	124	-7	-0.7
1981	NY A	0	0	—	2	0	0	0-0	4.1	5	1	0	0	0-0	4	2.08	172	.278	.278	0-0	—	0		1	0.1
	Chi N	2	5	.286	16	9	0	1-0	52	64	27	4	0	9-0	20	4.50	82	.302	.327	13-2	.154	-0	67	-3	-0.5
1982	SD N	0	1	.000	7	0	0	0-0	10.1	9	4	0	0	3-0	4	3.48	99	.237	.293	1-0	.000	-0		0	0.0
1987	Bal A	3	5	.375	23	6	1	1-1	74.1	78	39	9	3	33-3	42	4.36	101	.269	.347	0-0	—	0	52	1	0.0
1989	Cin N	0	0	—	3	0	0	0-0	4.1	10	6	0	0	3-2	1	12.46	29	.500	.520	1-0	1.000	0		-4	-0.1
Total	6	7	15	.318	67	24	1	3-1	203.2	235	115	19	4	73-7	101	4.60	87	.288	.346	15-2	.200	-0	83	-12	-1.2
GRIFFIN, PAT Patrick Richard B 5.6.1893 Niles, OH D 6.7.1927 Youngstown, OH BR/TR 6-2/180# d7.23																									
1914	Cin N	0	0	—	1	0	0	0	1	3	3	0	0	2	0	9.00	33	.750	.833	0-0	—	0		-1	0.0
GRIFFIN, TOM Thomas James B 2.22.1948 Los Angeles, CA BR/TR 6-3/210# d4.10																									
1969	Hou N	11	10	.524	31	31	6-3	0-0	188.1	156	80	19	7	93-4	200	3.54	100	.220	.317	62-4	.145	2	114	3	0.5
1970	Hou N	3	13	.188	23	20	2-1	0-0	111.1	118	72	9	3	72-1	72	5.74	68	.275	.381	33-4	.061	-2	89	-21	-2.7
1971	Hou N	0	6	.000	10	6	0	0-1	37.2	44	22	4	2	20-1	29	4.78	71	.288	.375	9-0	.111	-0	44	-6	-0.9
1972	Hou N	5	4	.556	39	5	1-1	3-3	94.1	92	39	7	3	38-5	83	3.24	104	.258	.333	25-3	.280	3	110	1	0.4
1973	Hou N	4	6	.400	25	12	4	0-0	99.2	83	51	10	2	46-6	69	4.15	88	.229	.316	28-4	.107	0	91	-6	-0.5
1974	Hou N	14	10	.583	34	34	8-3	0-0	211	202	97	14	5	89-7	110	3.54	98	.250	.326	68-9	.294	8*	129	-3	0.6
1975	Hou N	3	8	.273	17	13	3-1	0-0	79.1	89	52	11	2	46-5	56	5.33	63	.288	.384	22-2	.136	-0	92	-19	-2.3
1976	Hou N	5	3	.625	20	2	0	0-0	41.2	44	29	4	1	37-2	33	6.05	53	.278	.412	5-1	.000	-0	96	-13	-2.2
	SD N	4	3	.571	11	11	2	0-0	70.1	56	27	0	1	42-1	36	2.94	111	.222	.333	26-3	.077	-2*	90	2	0.0
	Year	9	6	.600	31	13	2	0-0	112	100	30	4	2	79-3	69	4.10	79	.244	.365	31-4	.065	-2	92	-10	-2.2
1977	SD N	6	9	.400	38	20	0	0-0	151.1	144	88	17	5	88-8	79	4.46	79	.254	.356	45-3	.133	1*	113	-18	-1.5
1978	Cal A	3	4	.429	24	4	0	0-0	56	63	39	8	1	31-2	35	4.02	90	.279	.364	0-0	—	0	93	-8	-0.8
1979	SF N	5	6	.455	59	3	0	2-2	94.1	83	46	9	4	46-8	82	3.91	90	.237	.331	14-1	.071	-1	42	-4	-0.5
1980	SF N	5	1	.833	42	4	0	0-0	107.2	80	35	8	8	49-6	79	2.76	128	.212	.312	18-2	.111	0*	95	11	0.6
1981	SF N	8	8	.500	22	22	3-1	0-0	129.1	121	62	8	7	57-8	83	3.76	91	.249	.335	41-6	.195	2	98	-5	-0.3
1982	Pit N	1	3	.250	6	4	0	0-0	22.1	32	23	5	1	15-2	8	8.87	42	.330	.425	9-0	.222	0	107	-12	-1.7
Total	14	77	94	.450	401	191	29-10	5-6	1494.2	1407	762	133	52	769-66	1054	4.07	86	.249	.343	405-42	.163	12	103	-98	-11.3
GRIFFITH, CLARK Clark Calvin "The Old Fox" B 11.20.1869 Clear Creek, MO D 10.27.1955 Washington, DC BR/TR 5-6.5/156# d4.11 M20 HF1946																									
1891	StL AA	11	8	.579	27	17	12	2	186.1	195	122	8	15	58	68	3.33	126	.260	.326	77	.156	-3	106	15	0.9
	Bos AA	3	1	.750	7	4	3	0	40	47	33	3	5	15	20	5.62	62	.283	.360	23	.174	2*	161	-8	-0.4
	Year	14	9	.609	34	21	15	2	226.1	242	42	11	20	73	88	3.74	109	.264	.332	100	.160	-1	115	9	0.5
1893	Chi N	1	2	.333	4	2	2	0	19.2	24	14	1	1	5	9	5.03	92	.293	.341	11	.182	-1	113	0	-0.1
1894	Chi N	21	14	.600	36	30	28	0	261.1	328	193	12	14	85	71	4.92	114	.303	.362	142-0	.232	-0*	107	25	2.3
1895	Chi N	26	14	.650	42	41	39	0	353	434	228	11	22	91	79	3.93	130	.298	.348	144-2	.319	5*	93	40	3.9
1896	Chi N	23	11	.676	36	35	35	0	317.2	370	189	3	12	70	81	3.54	128	.289	.331	135-2	.267	3*	86	29	2.7
1897	Chi N	21	18	.538	41	38	**38**-1	1	343.2	410	231	3	17	86	102	3.72	120	.293	.342	162-3	.235	3*	90	20	2.2
1898	Chi N	24	10	.706	38	38	36-4	0	325.2	305	105	1	20	64	97	**1.88**	**191**	.246	.294	122-2	.164	-2	106	**63**	5.9
1899	Chi N	22	14	.611	38	38	35	0	319.2	329	163	5	14	65	73	2.79	134	.266	.310	120-4	.258	6*	113	31	3.9
1900	Chi N	14	13	.519	30	30	27-4	0	248	245	126	6	16	51	61	3.05	118	.258	.306	95-1	.253	5	79	20	2.2
1901	Chi A	24	7	**.774**	35	30	26-**5**	1	266.2	275	114	4	4	50	67	2.67	131	.263	.299	89-3	.303	14	142	29	4.2
1902	Chi A	15	9	.625	28	24	20-3	0	213	247	117	11	16	47	51	4.18	81	.290	.339	92-3	.217	2*	105	-15	-1.3
1903	NY A	14	11	.560	25	24	22-2	0	213	201	92	3	6	33	69	2.70	116	.249	.283	69-2	.159	2	76	8	1.0
1904	NY A	7	5	.583	16	11	8-1	0	100.1	91	40	3	4	16	36	2.87	94	.243	.281	42-1	.143	-1	112	-1	-0.2
1905	NY A	9	6	.600	25	7	4-2	1	101.2	82	30	1	1	15	46	1.68	174	.223	.255	32-2	.219	1*	76	12	1.8
1906	NY A	2	2	.500	17	2	1	2	59.2	58	30	0	4	15	16	3.02	98	.258	.316	18-2	.111	-1	146	-2	-0.1
1907	NY A	0	0	—	4	0	0	0	8.1	15	16	0	0	6	5	8.64	32	.395	.477	2-0	.000	-0*		-6	-0.3
1909	Cin N	0	1	.000	1	1	1	0	6	11	8	0	0	2	3	6.00	43	.379	.419	2-0	.000	-0	27	-3	-0.4
1912	Was A	0	0	—	1	0	0	0	0	1	1	1	0	0	0	∞	—	1.000	1.000	1-0	.000	-0		-1	-0.1
1913	Was A	0	0	—	1	0	0	0	1	1	0	0	0	0	0	0.00	—	.250	.250	1-0	1.000	1		0	0.1
1914	Was A	0	0	—	1	0	0	1	1	1	0	0	0	0	1	0.00	—	.250	.250	1-0	1.000	1		0	0.1
Total	20	237	146	.619	453	372	337-22	8	3385.2	3670	1852	76	171	774	955	3.31	121	.274	.322	1380-27	.233	35	101	256	28.3
GRIFFITH, FRANK Frank Wesley B 11.18.1872 Gilman, IL D 12.8.1908 Waterman, IL BL/TL d8.13																									
1892	Chi N	0	1	.000	1	1	0	0	4	3	5	1	0	6	3	11.25	30	.200	.429	1	.000	-0	38	-3	-0.4
1894	Cle N	1	2	.333	7	6	3	0	42.1	64	62	5	9	37	15	9.99	55	.344	.474	24-1	.333	2	125	-19	-0.8
Total	2	1	3	.250	8	7	3	0	46.1	67	67	6	9	43	18	10.10	52	.333	.470	25-1	.320	2	114	-22	-1.2
GRIFFITHS, JEREMY Jeremy Richard B 3.22.1978 Fairview, OH BR/TR 6-6/240# d6.5																									
2003	NY N	1	4	.200	9	6	0	0-0	41	57	34	5	2	19-2	25	7.02	59	.328	.400	9-1	.000	-1	90	-13	-1.4
GRIGGS, HAL Harold Lloyd B 8.24.1928 Shannon, GA BR/TR 6/170# d4.18																									
1956	Was A	1	6	.143	34	12	1	1	98.2	120	82	14	1	76-2	48	6.02	72	.307	.415	16-2	.000	-1*	72	-21	-1.4
1957	Was A	0	1	.000	2	2	0	0	13.2	11	5	1	0	7-0	12	3.29	118	.229	.327	4-0	.250	0	46	1	0.1
1958	Was A	3	11	.214	32	21	3	0	137	138	91	20	2	74-1	69	5.52	69	.262	.353	41-2	.122	-2	85	-26	-2.6
1959	Was A	2	8	.200	37	10	2-1	2	97.2	103	63	8	1	52-4	43	5.25	75	.270	.356	18-0	.056	-2	59	-13	-1.5
Total	4	6	26	.188	105	45	6-1	3	347	372	241	43	4	209-7	172	5.50	73	.276	.372	79-4	.089	-5	73	-59	-5.4
GRILLI, GUIDO Guido John B 1.9.1939 Memphis, TN BL/TL 6/188# d4.12																									
1966	Bos A	0	1	.000	6	0	0	0	4.2	5	6	1	0	9-0	4	7.71	49	.278	.519	2-0	.500	0		-2	-0.4
	KC A	0	1	.000	16	0	0	1	15.2	19	15	0	3	11-4	8	6.89	49	.302	.429	0-0	—	0		-7	-0.5
	Year	0	2	.000	22	0	0	1	20.1	24	24	1	3	20-4	12	7.08	49	.296	.452	2-0	.500	0		-9	-0.9
GRILLI, JASON Jason Michael B 11.11.1976 Royal Oak, MI BR/TR 6-4/185# d5.11 f-Steve																									
2000	Fla N	1	0	1.000	1	1	0	0-0	6.2	11	4	0	2	2-0	3	5.40	82	.379	.455	2-0	.500	0	103	-1	0.0
2001	Fla N	2	2	.500	6	5	0	0-0	26.2	30	18	6	2	11-0	17	6.08	69	.297	.377	7-2	.286	1	118	-5	-0.5
Total	2	3	2	.600	7	6	0	0-0	33.1	41	22	6	4	13-0	20	5.94	72	.315	.395	9-2	.333	2	115	-6	-0.5
GRILLI, STEVE Stephen Joseph B 5.2.1949 Brooklyn, NY BR/TR 6-2/170# d9.19 s-Jason																									
1975	Det A	0	0	—	3	0	0	0-0	6.2	3	2	0	0	6-1	5	1.35	298	.136	.310	0-0	—	0		2	0.1
1976	Det A	3	1	.750	36	0	0	3-1	66	63	43	5	5	41-5	36	4.64	80	.258	.369	0-0	—	0		-8	-0.5
1977	Det A	1	2	.333	30	2	0	0-0	72.2	71	42	8	3	49-2	49	4.83	89	.265	.383	0-0	—	0	63	-3	-0.2
1979	Tor A	0	0	—	1	0	0	0-0	2.1	1	0	0	0	0-0	1	0.00	—	.143	.143	0-0	—	0		1	0.1
Total	4	4	3	.571	70	2	0	3-1	147.2	138	87	13	8	96-8	91	4.51	89	.255	.371	0-0	—	0	63	-8	-0.5
GRIM, BOB Robert Anton B 3.8.1930 New York, NY D 10.23.1996 Shawnee, KS BR/TR 6-1/185# d4.18																									
1954	NY A	20	6	.769	37	20	8-1	0	199	175	78	9	3	85	108	3.26	106	.244	.322	70-7	.143	-1	141	6	0.5
1955	†NY A	7	5	.583	26	11	1-1	4	92.1	81	49	9	3	42-2	63	4.19	89	.238	.321	25-4	.120	-1	134	-5	-0.7

Year	Tm Lg	W	L	Pct	G	GS	CG-Sho	SV-BS	IP	H	R	HR	HB	BB-IB	SO	ERA	AERA	OAV	OOB	AB-SH	AVG	PB	Sup	APR	PW
1956	NY A	6	1	.857	26	6	1	5	74.2	64	27	3	2	31-0	48	2.77	139	.235	.317	16-1	.063	-0	123	9	0.8
1957	†NY A★	12	8	.600	46	0	0	**19**	72	60	22	5	0	36-5	52	2.63	137	.239	.330	9-3	.111	1		9	2.0
1958	NY A	0	1	.000	11	0	0	0	16.1	12	10	3	1	10-0	11	5.51	64	.211	.338	1-1	.000	-0		-3	-0.2
	KC A	7	6	.538	26	14	5-1	0	113.2	118	54	7	3	41-4	54	3.56	110	.269	.334	32-3	.188	-0	87	2	0.1
	Year	7	7	.500	37	14	5-1	0	130	130	58	10	4	51-4	65	3.81	101	.263	.335	33-4	.182	-1	88	0	-0.1
1959	KC A	6	10	.375	40	9	3-1	4	125.1	124	69	10	3	57-6	65	4.09	98	.260	.341	32-6	.094	-1	125	-3	-0.5
1960	Cle A	0	1	.000	3	0	0	0	2.1	6	3	0	0	1-0	2	11.57	32	.500	.538	0-0	—	0		-2	-0.4
	Cin N	2	2	.500	26	0	0	2	30.1	32	18	3	0	10-2	22	4.45	86	.274	.321	1-0	.000	-0		-3	-0.4
	StL N	1	0	1.000	15	0	0	0	20.2	22	7	1	0	9-1	15	3.05	134	.272	.337	1-0	.000	-0		3	0.1
	Year	3	2	.600	41	0	0	2	51	54	31	4	0	19-3	37	3.88	101	.273	.327	2-0	.000	-0		0	-0.3
1962	KC A	0	1	.000	12	0	0	3	13	14	9	0	0	8-2	3	6.23	68	.292	.393	2-0	.000	-0		-2	-0.3
Total	8	61	41	.598	268	60	18-4	37	759.2	708	346	50	15	330-22	443	3.61	104	.252	.330	189-25	.127	-4	122	11	1.0

GRIMES, BURLEIGH Burleigh Arland "Ol' Stubblebeard" B 8.18.1893 Emerald, WI D 12.6.1985 Clear Lake, WI BR/TR 5-10/175# d9.10 M2 C1 HF1964

Year	Tm Lg	W	L	Pct	G	GS	CG-Sho	SV-BS	IP	H	R	HR	HB	BB-IB	SO	ERA	AERA	OAV	OOB	AB-SH	AVG	PB	Sup	APR	PW
1916	Pit N	2	3	.400	6	5	4	0	45.2	40	19	1	0	10	20	2.36	114	.241	.284	17-1	.176	-0	78	1	0.0
1917	Pit N	3	16	.158	37	17	8-1	0	194	186	101	5	6	70	72	3.53	80	.260	.331	69-4	.232	2*	67	-17	-1.3
1918	Bro N	19	9	.679	**40**	30	19-7	1	269.2	210	94	3	4	76	113	2.14	130	.216	.276	90-6	.200	0*	91	15	1.9
1919	Bro N	10	11	.476	25	21	13-1	0	181.1	179	97	2	7	60	82	3.47	86	.256	.321	69-2	.246	1*	107	-12	-1.1
1920	†Bro N	23	11	**.676**	40	33	25-5	2	303.2	271	101	5	4	67	131	2.22	144	.238	.282	111-6	.306	10*	116	30	4.9
1921	Bro N	**22**	13	.629	37	35	**30**-2	0	302.1	313	120	6	5	76	**136**	2.83	138	.274	.322	114-4	.237	2	92	**33**	**4.0**
1922	Bro N	17	14	.548	36	34	18-1	1	259	324	159	17	7	84	99	4.76	85	.308	.363	93-4	.237	4	104	-17	-1.1
1923	Bro N	21	18	.538	39	**38**	**33**-2	0	**327**	356	165	9	11	100	119	3.58	108	.280	.338	126-7	.238	3*	104	11	1.8
1924	Bro N	22	13	.629	38	**36**	**30**-1	1	**310.2**	351	161	15	6	91	135	3.82	98	.287	.339	124-3	.298	6*	114	-3	0.6
1925	Bro N	12	19	.387	33	31	19	0	246.2	305	164	15	7	102	73	5.04	83	.309	.377	96-2	.250	5*	109	-23	-1.5
1926	Bro N	12	13	.480	30	29	18-1	0	225.1	238	114	4	5	88	64	3.71	103	.276	.346	81-3	.222	1*	95	2	0.5
1927	NY N	19	8	.704	39	34	15-2	2	259.2	274	116	12	4	87	102	3.54	109	.276	.337	96-5	.188	-0	117	11	1.3
1928	Pit N	**25**	14	.641	**48**	**37**	**28-4**	3	**330.2**	311	146	11	9	77	97	2.99	136	.248	.297	131-5	.321	11	138	32	4.9
1929	Pit N	17	7	.708	33	29	18-2	2	232.2	245	108	11	4	70	62	3.13	**152**	.269	.324	91-2	.286	6	118	36	4.0
1930	Bos N	3	5	.375	11	9	1	0	49	72	53	4	3	22	15	7.35	67	.353	.424	16-2	.188	-0	112	-17	-2.0
	†StL N	13	6	.684	22	19	10-1	0	152.1	174	66	5	4	43	58	3.01	166	.293	.345	57-3	.263	2*	122	31	3.6
	Year	16	11	.593	33	28	11-1	0	201.1	246	73	9	7	65	73	4.07	123	.308	.366	73-5	.247	2	118	13	1.6
1931	†StL N	17	9	.654	29	28	17-3	0	212.1	240	97	11	10	59	67	3.65	108	.286	.340	76-9	.184	-2	112	8	0.8
1932	†Chi N	6	11	.353	30	18	5-1	1	141.1	174	89	8	1	50	36	4.78	79	.297	.354	44-5	.250	1	104	-17	-1.6
1933	Chi N	3	6	.333	17	7	3-1	3	69.2	71	29	2	1	29	12	3.49	94	.277	.353	20-2	.150	-1	109	0	-0.1
	StL N	0	1	.000	4	3	0	1	13.2	15	13	1	1	8	4	5.27	66	.263	.364	5-0	.200	0	144	-4	-0.4
	Year	3	7	.300	21	10	3-1	4	83.1	86	19	3	2	37	16	3.78	87	.275	.355	25-2	.160	-0	121	-5	-0.5
1934	StL N	2	1	.667	4	0	0	0	7.2	5	3	1	0	2	1	3.52	120	.179	.233	0-1	—	0		1	0.2
	NY A	1	2	.333	10	0	0	1	18	22	11	0	1	14	5	5.50	74	.319	.440	2-0	.000	-0		-2	-0.3
	Pit N	1	2	.333	8	4	0	0	27.1	36	24	0	1	10	9	7.24	57	.310	.370	7-0	.143	-0	73	-9	-0.8
Total	19	270	212	.560	616	497	314-35	18	4179.2	4412	2050	148	101	1295	1512	3.53	107	.273	.331	1535-76	.248	52	109	90	18.3

GRIMES, JOHN John Thomas B 4.17.1869 Woodstock, MD D 1.17.1964 San Francisco, CA BR/TR 5-11/160# d7.28

Year	Tm Lg	W	L	Pct	G	GS	CG-Sho	SV-BS	IP	H	R	HR	HB	BB-IB	SO	ERA	AERA	OAV	OOB	AB-SH	AVG	PB	Sup	APR	PW
1897	StL N	0	2	.000	3	1	1	0	19.2	24	23	0	6	8	4	5.95	74	.300	.404	7-0	.286	1	81	-5	-0.2

GRIMSLEY, JASON Jason Alan B 8.7.1967 Cleveland, TX BR/TR 6-3/180# d9.8

Year	Tm Lg	W	L	Pct	G	GS	CG-Sho	SV-BS	IP	H	R	HR	HB	BB-IB	SO	ERA	AERA	OAV	OOB	AB-SH	AVG	PB	Sup	APR	PW
1989	Phi N	1	3	.250	4	4	0	0-0	18.1	19	13	2	0	19-1	7	5.89	60	.268	.422	5-2	.000	-1	62	-4	-0.9
1990	Phi N	3	2	.600	11	11	0	0-0	57.1	47	21	1	2	43-0	41	3.30	116	.227	.364	16-3	.188	0*	105	4	0.5
1991	Phi N	1	7	.125	12	12	0	0-0	61	54	34	4	3	41-3	42	4.87	75	.242	.364	17-0	.059	-1	74	-7	-0.9
1993	Cle A	3	4	.429	10	6	0	0-0	42.1	52	26	3	1	20-1	27	5.31	82	.302	.378	0-0	—	0	53	-4	-0.6
1994	Cle A	5	2	.714	14	13	1	0-0	82.2	91	47	7	6	34-1	59	4.57	103	.283	.360	0-0	—	0	123	2	0.1
1995	Cle A	0	0	—	15	2	0	1-0	34	37	24	4	2	32-1	25	6.09	77	.289	.433	0-0	—	0	109	-5	-0.2
1996	Cal A	5	7	.417	35	20	2-1	0-0	130.1	150	110	14	13	74-5	82	6.84	73	.286	.385	0-0	—	0	102	-26	-1.9
1999	†NY A	7	2	.778	55	0	0	1-3	75	66	39	7	4	40-5	49	3.60	132	.231	.330	0-0	—	0		7	0.8
2000	†NY A	3	2	.600	63	4	0	1-3	96.1	100	58	10	5	42-1	53	5.04	96	.268	.345	1-0	.000	1	136	-2	0.0
2001	KC A	1	5	.167	73	0	0	0-7	80.1	71	32	8	2	28-5	61	3.02	162	.241	.311	0-0	—	0		14	0.9
2002	KC A	4	7	.364	70	0	0	1-2	71.1	64	32	4	1	37-8	59	3.91	128	.236	.330	0-0	—	0		8	1.2
2003	KC A	2	6	.250	76	0	0	0-7	75	88	47	6	5	36-5	58	5.16	100	.299	.379	0-0	—	0		0	0.1
Total	12	35	47	.427	438	72	3-1	4-22	824	839	483	70	44	446-36	563	4.81	98	.265	.361	39-5	.103	-0	93	-13	-0.9

GRIMSLEY, ROSS Ross Albert I B 6.4.1922 Americus, KS D 2.6.1994 Memphis, TN BL/TL 6/175# d9.3 s-Ross

Year	Tm Lg	W	L	Pct	G	GS	CG-Sho	SV-BS	IP	H	R	HR	HB	BB-IB	SO	ERA	AERA	OAV	OOB	AB-SH	AVG	PB	Sup	APR	PW
1951	Chi A	0	0	—	7	0	0	0	14	12	8	1	0	10	8	3.86	105	.235	.361	2-1	.000	-0		0	-0.1

GRIMSLEY, ROSS Ross Albert II B 1.7.1950 Topeka, KS BL/TL 6-3/200# d5.16 f-Ross

Year	Tm Lg	W	L	Pct	G	GS	CG-Sho	SV-BS	IP	H	R	HR	HB	BB-IB	SO	ERA	AERA	OAV	OOB	AB-SH	AVG	PB	Sup	APR	PW
1971	Cin N	10	7	.588	26	26	6-3	0-0	161.1	151	67	15	2	43-2	67	3.57	94	.250	.301	51-6	.118	-1	119	-3	-0.5
1972	†Cin N	14	8	.636	30	28	4-1	1-0	197.2	194	73	18	0	50-8	79	3.05	105	.260	.305	66-11	.121	-2	115	4	0.2
1973	†Cin N	13	10	.565	38	36	8-1	1-0	242.1	245	96	24	0	68-11	90	3.23	106	.266	.315	82-8	.061	-6*	103	5	-0.3
1974	†Bal A	18	13	.581	40	39	17-4	1-0	295.2	267	111	26	3	76-9	158	3.07	112	.244	.292	0-0	—	0	101	15	1.6
1975	Bal A	10	13	.435	35	32	8-1	0-0	197	210	95	29	1	47-1	89	4.07	87	.276	.317	0-0	—	0	91	-12	-1.3
1976	Bal A	8	7	.533	28	19	2	0-0	136.2	143	66	8	1	35-2	41	3.95	83	.270	.315	0-0	—	0	130	-11	-1.1
1977	Bal A	14	10	.583	34	34	11-2	0-0	218.1	230	105	24	1	74-2	53	3.96	96	.277	.335	0-0	—	0	99	-5	-0.3
1978	Mon N☆	20	11	.645	36	36	19-3	0-0	263	237	103	17	2	67-6	84	3.05	116	.243	.291	90-11	.144	-1	108	12	1.4
1979	Mon N	10	9	.526	32	27	2	0-1	151.1	199	102	18	3	41-1	42	5.35	69	.322	.363	55-3	.200	1	116	-28	-3.0
1980	Mon N	2	4	.333	11	7	0	0-0	41.1	61	31	5	1	12-1	11	6.31	57	.351	.385	9-0	.222	0	86	-12	-1.5
	Cle A	4	5	.444	14	11	2	0-0	74.2	103	63	11	1	24-1	18	6.75	60	.331	.376	0-0	—	0	116	-23	-2.3
1982	Bal A	1	2	.333	21	0	0	0-2	60	65	35	7	0	22-5	18	5.25	77	.283	.343	0-0	—	0		-7	-0.3
Total	11	124	99	.556	345	295	79-15	3-3	2039.1	2105	947	202	15	559-49	750	3.81	92	.270	.318	353-39	.127	-10	107	-65	-7.4

GRINER, DAN Donald Dexter "Rusty" B 3.7.1888 Centerville, TN D 6.3.1950 Bishopville, SC BL/TR 6-1.5/200# d8.17

Year	Tm Lg	W	L	Pct	G	GS	CG-Sho	SV-BS	IP	H	R	HR	HB	BB-IB	SO	ERA	AERA	OAV	OOB	AB-SH	AVG	PB	Sup	APR	PW
1912	StL N	3	4	.429	12	7	2	0	54	59	35	3	3	15	20	3.17	108	.278	.335	13-0	.077	-0	89	-1	-0.2
1913	StL N	10	22	.313	34	34	18-1	0	225	279	150	12	10	66	79	5.08	64	.312	.366	81-2	.259	5	91	-46	-5.0
1914	StL N	9	13	.409	37	17	11-2	2	179	163	66	3	3	57	74	2.51	111	.254	.318	55-3	.255	4	70	7	1.4
1915	StL N	5	11	.313	37	17	9-3	3	150.1	137	59	4	8	46	46	2.81	99	.259	.328	52-2	.269	4*	78	1	0.5
1916	StL N	0	0	—	4	0	0	1	11	15	5	0	1	3	3	4.09	65	.341	.396	4-0	.250	0		-1	-0.1
1918	Bro N	1	5	.167	11	6	3-1	0	54.1	47	16	0	7	15	22	2.15	129	.267	.348	14-0	.071	-1*	50	4	0.4
Total	6	28	55	.337	135	81	43-7	6	673.2	700	331	22	32	202	244	3.49	86	.280	.342	219-7	.237	12	83	-36	-3.0

GRISSOM, LEE Lee Theo B 10.23.1907 Sherman, TX D 10.4.1998 Corning, CA BB/TL 6-3/200# d9.2 Mil 1942-45 b-Marv

Year	Tm Lg	W	L	Pct	G	GS	CG-Sho	SV-BS	IP	H	R	HR	HB	BB-IB	SO	ERA	AERA	OAV	OOB	AB-SH	AVG	PB	Sup	APR	PW
1934	Cin N	0	1	.000	4	1	0	0	7	13	12	0	0	7	4	15.43	26	.382	.488	1-0	.000	-0	42	-8	-0.9
1935	Cin N	1	1	.500	3	3	1	0	21	31	10	0	0	4	13	3.86	103	.333	.361	7-1	.000	-1	114	1	0.0
1936	Cin N	1	1	.500	6	4	0	0	24.1	33	18	1	0	9	13	6.29	61	.320	.375	9-0	.000	-1	133	-6	-0.5
1937	Cin N★	12	17	.414	50	30	14-**5**	6	223.2	193	89	7	4	93	149	3.26	114	.232	.313	64-6	.109	-3*	74	15	1.5
1938	Cin N	2	3	.400	14	7	0	0	51	60	38	4	2	22	16	5.29	69	.300	.376	16-0	.188	-0	76	-11	-1.0
1939	†Cin N	9	7	.563	33	21	3	0	153.2	145	77	14	1	56	53	4.10	93	.249	.316	47-3	.085	-2	114	-3	-0.6
1940	NY A	0	0	—	5	0	0	0	4.2	4	0	0	0	2	1	0.00	—	.250	.333	0-0	—	0		2	0.1
	Bro N	2	5	.286	14	10	3-1	0	73.2	59	30	3	0	34	56	2.81	142	.215	.302	23-0	.217	0	52	7	0.6
1941	Bro N	0	0	—	4	1	0	1	11.1	10	3	2	0	8	5	2.38	154	.238	.360	2-1	.500	0	232	2	0.1
	Phi N	2	13	.133	29	18	2	0	131.1	120	69	4	2	70	74	3.97	93	.242	.338	36-3	.167	-1	84	-5	-0.6
	Year	2	13	.133	33	19	2	1	142.2	130	73	6	2	78	79	3.85	96	.242	.340	38-4	.184	-0	92	-3	-0.5
Total	8	29	48	.377	162	95	23-6	7	701.2	668	346	35	9	305	384	3.89	97	.250	.329	205-14	.127	-8	88	-6	-1.3

GRISSOM, MARV Marvin Edward B 3.31.1918 Los Molinos, CA BR/TR 6-3/195# d9.10 C15 b-Lee

Year	Tm Lg	W	L	Pct	G	GS	CG-Sho	SV-BS	IP	H	R	HR	HB	BB-IB	SO	ERA	AERA	OAV	OOB	AB-SH	AVG	PB	Sup	APR	PW
1946	NY N	0	2	.000	4	3	0	0	18.2	17	11	1	1	13	9	4.34	79	.254	.383	5-0	.200	-0	75	-2	-0.2
1949	Det A	2	4	.333	27	2	0	0	39.1	56	32	6	1	34	17	6.41	65	.335	.450	9-0	.222	1	140	-10	-1.3

Year	Tm Lg	W	L	Pct	G	GS	CG-Sho	SV-BS	IP	H	R	HR	HB	BB-IB	SO	ERA	AERA	OAV	OOB	AB-SH	AVG	PB	Sup	APR	PW
1952	Chi A	12	10	.545	28	24	7-1	0	166	156	79	6	3	79	97	3.74	98	.250	.337	53-8	.151	-1	101	-3	-0.5
1953	Bos A	2	6	.250	13	11	1-1	0	59.1	61	34	5	1	30	31	4.70	89	.266	.354	18-2	.000	-3	109	-2	-0.6
	NY N	4	2	.667	21	7	3	0	84.1	83	40	6	1	31	46	3.95	109	.255	.321	27-1	.074	-2	140	4	0.2
1954	†NY N★	10	7	.588	56	3	1-1	19	122.1	100	37	13	7	50	64	2.35	171	.226	.312	32-2	.156	-1	74	23	3.7
1955	NY N	5	4	.556	55	0	0	8	89.1	76	35	6	6	41-5	49	2.92	138	.237	.332	13-1	.154	-1		10	1.1
1956	NY N	1	1	.500	43	2	0	7	80.2	71	15	3	1	16-3	49	1.56	242	.241	.279	11-0	.091	-0	70	**20**	1.0
1957	NY N	4	4	.500	55	0	0	14	82.2	74	36	6	2	23-6	51	2.61	151	.243	.300	12-0	.167	0		8	1.1
1958	SF N	7	5	.583	51	0	0	10	65.1	71	34	11	5	26-7	46	3.99	95	.287	.367	9-1	.000	-1		-2	-0.4
1959	StL N	0	0	—	3	0	0	0	2	6	5	2	0	0-0	0	22.50	19	.500	.500	0-0	—	0		-4	-0.2
Total	10	47	45	.511	356	52	12-3	58	810	771	358	65	28	343-21	459	3.41	115	.254	.334	189-15	.122	-7	105	42	3.9
GROB, CONNIE Conrad George B 11.9.1932 Cross Plains, WI D 9.28.1997 Madison, WI BL/TR 6-0.5/180# d4.22																									
1956	Was A	4	5	.444	37	1	0	1	79.1	121	79	14	1	26-1	27	7.83	55	.353	.396	18-1	.333	1	82	-30	-2.7
GRODZICKI, JOHNNY John "Grod" B 2.26.1917 Nanticoke, PA D 5.2.1998 Daytona Beach, FL BR/TR 6-1.5/200# d4.18 Mil 1942-46 C1																									
1941	StL N	2	1	.667	5	1	0	0	13.1	6	7	0	0	11	10	1.35	279	.130	.298	2-1	.000	0	90	2	0.4
1946	StL N	0	0	—	3	0	0	0	4	4	5	1	0	4	2	9.00	38	.250	.400	0-0	—	0		-3	-0.1
1947	StL N	0	1	.000	16	0	0	0	23.1	21	17	5	0	19	8	5.40	77	.253	.392	1-0	.000	-0		-4	-0.2
Total	3	2	2	.500	24	1	0	0	40.2	31	29	6	0	34	20	4.43	89	.214	.363	3-1	.000	0	90	-5	0.1
GROMEK, STEVE Stephen Joseph B 1.15.1920 Hamtramck, MI D 3.12.2002 Clinton Twsp., MI BB/TR 6-2/180# d8.18																									
1941	Cle A	1	1	.500	9	2	1	2	23.1	25	12	0	0	11	19	4.24	93	.266	.343	6-0	.167	-0	143	-1	-0.1
1942	Cle A	2	0	1.000	14	0	0	0	44.1	46	24	2	0	23	14	3.65	94	.267	.354	15-0	.333	3		-2	0.1
1943	Cle A	0	0	—	3	0	0	0	4	6	4	0	0	0	4	9.00	35	.353	.353	2-0	1.000	1		-2	0.0
1944	Cle A	10	9	.526	35	21	12-2	1	203.2	160	74	5	3	70	115	2.56	129	**.219**	.290	73-5	.260	5*	102	15	1.7
1945	Cle A❖	19	9	.679	33	30	21-3	1	251	229	80	6	4	66	101	2.55	128	.243	.295	91-3	.231	3*	101	21	2.6
1946	Cle A	5	15	.250	29	21	5-2	4	153.2	159	79	20	3	47	75	4.33	76	.264	.321	56-0	.196	0*	75	-16	-2.0
1947	Cle A	3	5	.375	29	7	0	4	84.1	77	43	8	1	36	39	3.74	93	.240	.318	22-0	.318	2*	127	-5	-0.3
1948	†Cle A	9	3	.750	38	9	4-1	2	130	109	52	10	6	51	50	2.84	143	.226	.307	41-1	.146	-1	106	16	1.2
1949	Cle A	4	6	.400	27	12	3	0	92	86	41	8	2	40	22	3.33	120	.250	.332	24-2	.167	-0	107	6	0.5
1950	Cle A	10	7	.588	31	13	4-1	0	113.1	94	50	10	3	36	43	3.65	119	.226	.292	38-2	.158	-2	90	10	1.1
1951	Cle A	7	4	.636	27	8	4	1	107.1	98	41	6	4	29	40	2.77	137	.238	.295	27-1	.296	3	123	12	1.4
1952	Cle A	7	7	.500	29	13	3-1	1	122.2	109	55	14	2	28	65	3.67	91	.232	.278	30-3	.100	-0*	108	-3	-0.5
1953	Cle A	1	1	.500	5	1	0	0	11	11	4	0	1	3	8	3.27	115	.268	.333	2-1	.000	-0	24	1	0.1
	Det A	6	8	.429	19	17	6-1	1	125.2	138	70	17	8	36	59	4.51	90	.276	.335	41-5	.073	-4	94	-6	-1.1
	Year	7	9	.438	24	18	6-1	1	136.2	149	74	17	9	39	67	4.41	92	.275	.334	43-6	.070	-4	90	-6	-1.0
1954	Det A	18	16	.529	36	32	17-4	1	252.2	236	85	26	12	57	102	2.74	135	.246	.294	79-10	.190	2	84	28	**3.7**
1955	Det A	13	10	.565	28	25	8-2	0	181	183	89	26	9	37-5	73	3.98	97	.261	.305	54-4	.167	4	138	-2	0.1
1956	Det A	8	6	.571	40	13	4	4	141	142	74	25	9	47-7	64	4.28	96	.263	.329	27-3	.148	2	83	-2	-0.1
1957	Det A	0	1	.000	15	1	0	1	23.2	32	16	3	1	13-3	11	6.08	63	.333	.414	2-0	.000	-0	69	-5	-0.3
Total	17	123	108	.532	447	225	92-17	23	2064.2	1940	893	186	68	630-15	904	3.41	108	.247	.308	630-40	.197	15	101	65	8.1
GROOM, BOB Robert B 9.12.1884 Belleville, IL D 2.19.1948 Belleville, IL BR/TR 6-2/175# d4.13																									
1909	Was A	7	26	.212	44	31	17-1	0	260.2	218	114	2	13	105	131	2.87	85	.229	.314	88-7	.091	-6*	60	-12	-2.0
1910	Was A	12	17	.414	34	30	22-3	0	257.2	244	117	8	9	77	98	2.76	90	.260	.322	92-3	.120	-6	81	-8	-1.6
1911	Was A	13	17	.433	37	32	20-2	2	254.2	280	148	9	8	67	135	3.82	86	.282	.332	82-6	.134	-4	81	-13	-1.7
1912	Was A	24	13	.649	43	40	28-2	1	316	287	133	3	5	94	179	2.62	127	.246	.305	103-12	.117	-7	105	25	1.8
1913	Was A	16	16	.500	37	36	17-4	0	264.1	258	118	8	5	81	156	3.23	91	.261	.320	92-5	.163	1	95	-5	-0.5
1914	StL F	13	20	.394	42	34	23-1	1	280.2	281	141	9	4	75	167	3.24	94	.262	.312	94-1	.160	-4	77	-10	-1.5
1915	StL F	11	11	.500	37	26	11-4	2	209	200	93	6	2	73	111	3.27	88	.261	.327	66-3	.152	-3	86	-9	-1.2
1916	StL A	13	9	.591	41	26	8-1	4	217.1	174	82	1	3	98	92	2.57	107	.226	.315	63-6	.111	-2	121	4	0.3
1917	StL A	8	19	.296	38	28	11-4	3	232.2	193	80	3	5	95	82	2.94	88	.233	.315	72-3	.111	-4	77	0	-0.5
1918	Cle A	2	2	.500	14	5	0	0	43.1	70	42	0	1	18	8	7.06	43	.380	.438	12-1	.083	-1	125	-17	-1.6
Total	10	119	150	.442	367	288	157-22	13	2336.1	2205	1068	49	55	783	1159	3.10	93	.255	.320	764-47	.128	-35	88	-45	-8.5
GROOM, BUDDY Wedsel Gary B 7.10.1965 Dallas, TX BL/TL 6-2/200# d6.20																									
1992	Det A	0	5	.000	12	7	0	1-1	38.2	48	28	4	0	22-4	15	5.82	68	.320	.402	0-0	—	0	76	-8	-1.0
1993	Det A	0	2	.000	19	3	0	0-0	36.2	48	25	4	2	13-5	15	6.14	70	.322	.375	0-0	—	0	114	-6	-0.3
1994	Det A	0	1	.000	40	0	0	1-0	32	31	14	4	2	13-2	27	3.94	123	.256	.331	0-0	—	0		4	0.1
1995	Det A	1	3	.250	23	4	0	1-2	40.2	55	35	6	2	26-4	23	7.52	63	.322	.413	0-0	—	0	103	-12	-1.0
	Fla N	1	2	.333	14	0	0	0-0	15	26	12	2	0	6-0	12	7.20	59	.400	.451	0-0	—	0		-4	-0.7
1996	Oak A	5	0	1.000	72	1	0	2-2	77.1	85	37	8	3	34-3	57	3.84	128	.281	.360	0-0	—	0	56	9	0.5
1997	Oak A	2	2	.500	78	0	0	3-2	64.2	75	38	9	0	24-1	45	5.15	88	.292	.347	0-0	—	0		-4	-0.2
1998	Oak A	3	1	.750	75	0	0	0-6	57.1	62	30	4	1	20-1	36	4.24	108	.274	.332	0-0	—	0		2	0.1
1999	Oak A	3	2	.600	**76**	0	0	0-3	46	48	29	1	1	18-5	32	5.09	91	.274	.345	0-0	—	0		-2	-0.1
2000	Bal A	6	3	.667	70	0	0	4-7	59.1	63	37	5	0	21-2	44	4.85	97	.275	.329	0-0	—	0		-2	-0.3
2001	Bal A	1	4	.200	70	0	0	11-2	66	64	28	4	1	9-0	54	3.55	121	.252	.279	0-0	—	0		6	0.5
2002	Bal A	3	2	.600	70	0	0	2-2	62	44	11	4	2	12-3	48	1.60	268	.196	.243	0-0	—	0		20	1.5
2003	Bal A	1	3	.250	60	0	0	1-2	45.1	58	27	7	3	14-2	34	5.36	82	.309	.364	0-0	—	0		-4	-0.3
Total	12	26	30	.464	679	15	0	26-29	641	707	351	62	17	232-32	442	4.62	98	.282	.343	0-0	—	0	86	-1	-1.2
GROSS, DON Donald John B 6.30.1931 Weidman, MI BL/TL 5-11/186# d7.21																									
1955	Cin N	4	5	.444	17	11	2-1	0	67.1	79	33	11	1	16-0	33	4.14	102	.298	.337	19-3	.158	-1	97	2	0.1
1956	Cin N	3	0	1.000	19	7	2	0	69.1	69	25	4	1	20-2	47	1.95	204	.257	.309	19-0	.105	-1	114	11	0.6
1957	Cin N	7	9	.438	43	16	5	1	148.1	152	75	21	3	33-3	73	4.31	95	.264	.304	46-6	.109	-2	100	-2	-0.5
1958	Pit N	5	7	.417	40	3	0	7	74.2	67	37	5	1	38-7	59	3.98	97	.241	.333	18-1	.056	-1	124	-1	-0.3
1959	Pit N	1	1	.500	21	0	0	2	33	28	16	3	1	10-3	15	3.55	109	.228	.289	2-1	.000	-0		1	0.1
1960	Pit N	0	0	—	5	0	0	0	5.1	5	2	1	0	0-0	3	3.38	111	.238	.238	0-0	—	0		0	0.0
Total	6	20	22	.476	145	37	9-1	10	398	400	188	45	7	117-15	230	3.73	108	.261	.314	104-11	.106	-5	106	11	0.0
GROSS, KEVIN Kevin Frank B 6.8.1961 Downey, CA BR/TR 6-5/215# d6.25																									
1983	Phi N	4	6	.400	17	17	1-1	0-0	96	100	46	13	3	35-3	66	3.56	100	.265	.332	33-1	.091	-1	99	-1	-0.1
1984	Phi N	8	5	.615	44	14	1	1-2	129	140	66	8	5	44-4	84	4.12	88	.277	.339	30-2	.067	-2	92	-5	-0.6
1985	Phi N	15	13	.536	38	31	6-2	0-1	205.2	194	86	11	7	81-6	151	3.41	108	.251	.326	65-8	.138	0*	80	7	1.0
1986	Phi N	12	12	.500	37	36	7-2	0-0	241.2	240	115	28	8	94-2	154	4.02	96	.259	.331	80-9	.188	3	104	-1	0.2
1987	Phi N	9	16	.360	34	33	3-1	0-0	200.2	205	107	26	10	87-7	110	4.35	98	.267	.347	63-8	.190	2	76	-2	-0.1
1988	Phi N★	12	14	.462	33	33	5-1	0-0	231.2	209	101	18	11	89-5	162	3.69	97	.239	.315	75-8	.173	1	90	-1	0.0
1989	Mon N	11	12	.478	31	31	4-3	0-0	201.1	188	105	20	6	88-6	158	4.38	81	.247	.329	64-6	.141	1	90	-17	-1.7
1990	Mon N	9	12	.429	31	26	2-1	0-0	163.1	171	86	9	4	65-7	111	4.57	80	.272	.340	50-7	.200	4*	90	-15	-1.5
1991	LA N	10	11	.476	46	10	0	3-3	115.2	123	55	10	2	50-6	95	3.58	100	.275	.348	25-2	.280	2*	95	-1	0.1
1992	LA N	8	13	.381	34	30	4-3	0-0	204.2	182	82	11	3	77-10	158	3.17	109	.241	.311	63-3	.095	-1	89	7	0.6
1993	LA N	13	13	.500	33	32	3	0-0	202.1	224	110	15	5	74-7	150	4.14	92	.281	.344	64-8	.203	5	120	-9	-0.4
1994	LA N	9	7	.563	25	23	1	1-0	157.1	162	64	11	2	43-2	124	3.60	109	.263	.313	47-4	.149	1	81	8	1.0
1995	Tex A	9	15	.375	31	30	4	0-0	183.2	200	124	27	8	89-8	106	5.54	87	.279	.362	0-0	—	0	92	-15	-1.6
1996	Tex A	11	8	.579	28	19	1	0-0	129.1	151	78	19	4	50-2	78	5.22	100	.293	.355	0-0	—	0	101	1	0.2
1997	Ana A	2	1	.667	12	3	0	0-0	25.1	30	20	4	1	20-1	20	6.75	68	.313	.429	1-0	.000	-0	134	-6	-0.6
Total	15	142	158	.473	474	368	42-14	5-6	2487.2	2519	1245	230	79	986-76	1727	4.11	95	.264	.335	660-66	.161	14	93	-50	-3.5
GROSS, KIP Kip Lee B 8.24.1964 Scottsbluff, NE BR/TR 6-2/195# d4.21																									
1990	Cin N	0	0	—	5	0	0	0-0	6.1	6	3	0	0	2-0	3	4.26	93	.273	.320	0-0	—	0		0	0.0
1991	Cin N	6	4	.600	29	9	1	0-0	85.2	93	43	8	0	40-2	40	3.47	110	.279	.355	22-3	.091	-1	129	1	-0.1
1992	LA N	1	1	.500	16	1	0	0-0	23.2	32	14	1	0	10-1	14	4.18	82	.323	.385	2-1	1.000	1	210	-2	-0.1
1993	LA N	0	0	—	10	0	0	0-0	15	13	1	0	0	4-0	12	0.60	637	.236	.288	0-0	—	0		6	0.3

Year	Tm Lg	W	L	Pct	G	GS	CG-Sho	SV-BS	IP	H	R	HR	HB	BB-IB	SO	ERA	AERA	OAV	OOB	AB-SH	AVG	PB	Sup	APR	PW
1999	Bos A	0	2	.000	11	1	0	0-1	12.2	15	11	3	3	8-2	9	7.82	64	.294	.413	0-0	—	0	169	-3	-0.4
2000	Hou N	0	1	.000	2	1	0	0-0	4.1	9	8	2	0	2-0	3	10.38	47	.429	.478	1-0	.000	-0	19	-4	-0.6
Total	6	7	8	.467	73	12	1	0-1	147.2	168	80	14	3	66-5	81	3.90	100	.289	.362	25-4	.160	-0	130	-2	-0.9
GROSSMAN, HARLEY Harley Joseph B 5.5.1930 Evansville, IN BR/TR 6/170# d4.22																									
1952	Was A	0	0	—	1	0	0	0	0.1	2	2	1	0	0	0	54.00	7	.667	.667	0-0	—	0		-2	-0.1
GROTH, ERNIE Ernest John "Dango" B 12.24.1884 Cedarburg, WI D 5.23.1950 Milwaukee, WI BR/TR 5-11/175# d9.6																									
1904	Chi N	0	2	.000	3	2	2	1	16	22	13	1	1	6	9	5.63	47	.310	.372	6-0	.000	-1	26	-5	-0.7
GROTH, ERNEST Ernest William B 5.3.1922 Beaver Falls, PA BR/TR 5-9/185# d9.11																									
1947	Cle A	0	0	—	2	0	0	0	1.1	0	0	0	0	1	1	0.00	—	.000	.250	0-0	—	0		1	0.0
1948	Cle A	0	0	—	1	0	0	0	1	1	1	0	0	2	0	9.00	45	.250	.500	0-0	—	0*		-1	0.0
1949	Chi A	0	1	.000	3	0	0	0	5	2	3	2	1	3	1	5.40	77	.125	.300	0-0	—	0		-1	-0.1
Total	3	0	1	.000	6	0	0	0	7.1	3	4	2	1	6	2	4.91	82	.130	.333	0-0	—	0		-1	-0.1
GROTT, MATT Matthew Allen B 12.5.1967 LaPorte, IN BL/TL 6-1/210# d5.4																									
1995	Cin N	0	0	—	2	0	0	0-0	1.2	6	4	1	0	0-0	2	21.60	19	.545	.545	0-0	—	0		-3	-0.1
GROVE, ORVAL Orval Leroy B 8.29.1919 Mineral, KS D 4.20.1992 Carmichael, CA BR/TR 6-3/196# d5.28																									
1940	Chi A	0	0	—	3	0	0	0	6	4	2	0	0	4	1	3.00	147	.182	.308	1-0	.000	-0		1	0.0
1941	Chi A	0	0	—	2	0	0	0	7	9	8	2	0	5	5	10.29	40	.321	.424	2-0	.000	-0		-4	-0.2
1942	Chi A	4	6	.400	12	8	4	0	66.1	77	47	1	1	33	21	5.16	70	.283	.363	22-3	.227	1	62	-13	-1.5
1943	Chi A	15	9	.625	32	25	18-3	2	216.1	192	84	9	4	72	76	2.75	122	.239	.304	66-7	.182	2	109	12	1.6
1944	Chi A☆	14	15	.483	34	33	11-2	0	234.2	237	112	11	8	71	105	3.72	92	.263	.322	77-4	.104	-3	81	-6	-0.8
1945	Chi A	14	12	.538	33	30	16-4	1	217	233	100	12	5	68	54	3.44	96	.273	.330	71-2	.099	-4	101	-5	-0.9
1946	Chi A	8	13	.381	33	26	10-1	0	205.1	213	96	10	3	78	60	3.02	113	.272	.340	65-3	.108	-2	102	5	0.3
1947	Chi A	6	8	.429	25	19	6-1	0	135.2	158	78	10	4	70	33	4.44	82	.296	.382	48-1	.146	-0	93	-12	-1.1
1948	Chi A	2	10	.167	32	11	1	1	87.2	110	64	6	3	42	18	6.16	69	.315	.393	21-1	.095	-2	64	-17	-2.1
1949	Chi A	0	0	—	1	0	0	0	0.2	4	4	1	1	1	1	54.00	8	.667	.750	0-0	—	0		-3	-0.2
Total	10	63	73	.463	207	152	66-11	4	1176.2	1237	595	62	29	444	374	3.78	93	.272	.340	373-21	.129	-9	92	-42	-4.9
GROVE, LEFTY Robert Moses B 3.6.1900 Lonaconing, MD D 5.22.1975 Norwalk, OH BL/TL 6-3/190# d4.14 HF1947																									
1925	Phi A	10	12	.455	45	18	5	1	197	207	120	11	5	131	**116**	4.75	98	.278	.390	65-2	.123	-6	91	0	-0.5
1926	Phi A	13	13	.500	45	33	20-1	6	258	227	97	6	6	101	**194**	**2.51**	**166**	.244	.322	81-9	.099	-5	96	44	3.7
1927	Phi A	20	13	.606	51	28	14-1	9	262.1	251	116	6	2	79	**174**	3.19	134	.252	.309	80-9	.125	-3	110	28	3.0
1928	Phi A	**24**	8	.750	39	31	24-4	4	261.2	228	93	10	1	64	**183**	2.58	156	.229	.277	88-5	.170	1	110	**41**	**4.7**
1929	†Phi A	20	6	**.769**	42	**37**	19-2	4	275.1	278	104	8	3	81	**170**	**2.81**	**151**	.262	.316	102-8	.216	1	139	**43**	3.6
1930	†Phi A	**28**	5	**.848**	**50**	32	22-2	**9**	291	273	101	8	5	60	**209**	**2.54**	**184**	**.247**	**.288**	110-4	.200	0	125	**66**	**6.9**
1931	†Phi A	**31**	4	**.886**	41	30	**27-4**	5	288.2	249	84	10	1	62	**175**	**2.06**	**218**	.229	**.271**	115-4	.200	-2	103	**74**	**8.2**
1932	Phi A	25	10	.714	44	30	**27-4**	7	291.2	269	101	13	1	79	188	**2.84**	**159**	.241	**.292**	107-4	.168	0	115	**54**	**5.9**
1933	Phi A★	**24**	8	**.750**	45	28	**21**-2	6	275.1	280	113	12	4	83	114	3.20	134	.261	.316	105-4	.086	-7	109	35	3.1
1934	Bos A	8	8	.500	22	12	5	0	109.1	149	84	5	1	32	43	6.50	74	.320	.365	37-3	.162	-0	88	-15	-1.9
1935	Bos A☆	20	12	.625	35	30	23-2	1	273	269	105	6	3	65	121	**2.70**	**176**	.257	.302	89-6	.079	-5	76	**55**	5.5
1936	Bos A★	17	12	.586	35	30	22-**6**	2	253.1	237	90	14	4	65	130	**2.81**	**189**	.246	**.297**	80-12	.138	-3	78	**67**	**6.6**
1937	Bos A☆	17	9	.654	32	32	21-3	0	262	269	101	9	1	83	153	3.02	157	.261	.317	91-6	.143	-3	92	49	3.9
1938	Bos A★	14	4	.778	24	21	12-1	1	163.2	169	65	8	1	52	99	**3.08**	**160**	.263	.319	54-7	.148	-1	110	33	3.0
1939	Bos A☆	15	4	**.789**	23	23	17-2	0	191	180	63	8	1	58	81	**2.54**	**186**	.249	.305	67-9	.134	-1*	96	45	3.7
1940	Bos A	7	6	.538	22	21	9-1	0	153.1	159	73	20	1	50	62	3.99	113	.269	.328	53-5	.151	-1*	96	9	0.5
1941	Bos A	7	7	.500	21	21	10	0	134	155	84	8	2	42	54	4.37	95	.287	.340	45-6	.111	-1	125	-6	-0.8
Total	17	300	141	.680	616	457	298-35	55	3940.2	3849	1594	162	42	1187	2266	3.06	148	.255	.311	1369-103	.148	-37	104	622	59.1
GROVER, CHARLIE Charles Byrd "Bugs" B 6.20.1890 Gallipolis, OH D 5.24.1971 Emmett Township, MI BL/TR 6-1.5/185# d9.9																									
1913	Det A	0	0	—	2	1	0	0	10.2	9	4	0	0	7	2	3.38	86	.273	.400	3-1	.000	-0	51	0	0.0
GRUBBS, TOM Thomas Dillard "Judge" B 2.22.1894 Mt.Sterling, KY D 1.28.1986 Lexington, KY BR/TR 6-2/165# d10.3																									
1920	NY N	0	1	.000	1	1	0	0	5	9	4	0	0	0	0	7.20	42	.409	.409	1-0	.000	-0	26	-2	-0.3
GRUBER, HENRY Henry John B 12.14.1863 Hamden, CT D 9.26.1932 New Haven, CT BR/TR 5-9/155# d7.28																									
1887	Det N	4	3	.571	7	7	7	0	62.1	63	29	3	0	21	12	2.74	149	.262	.322	24	.167	1	118	9	0.7
1888	Det N	11	14	.440	27	25	25-3	0	240	196	121	8	4	41	71	2.29	122	.213	.249	92	.141	-1	91	9	0.7
1889	Cle N	7	16	.304	25	23	23	1	205	198	125	6	8	94	74	3.64	111	.246	.331	69	.101	-1	75	8	0.6
1890	Cle P	22	23	.489	48	44	39-1	0	383.1	464	352	15	15	204	110	4.27	93	.286	.371	163	.221	6*	99	-15	-0.7
1891	Cle N	17	22	.436	44	40	35-1	0	348.2	407	258	10	7	119	79	4.13	84	.281	.338	141	.163	1*	96	-16	-1.2
Total	5	61	78	.439	151	139	129-5	1	1239.1	1328	885	42	34	479	346	3.67	99	.264	.332	489	.170	5	94	-5	0.1
GRUNDT, KEN Kenneth Allan B 8.26.1969 Melrose Park, IL BL/TL 6-4/195# d8.8																									
1996	Bos A	0	0	—	1	0	0	0-0	0.1	1	1	0	0	0-0	0	27.00	19	.500	.500	0-0	—	0		-1	0.0
1997	Bos A	0	0	—	2	0	0	0-0	3	5	3	0	0	0-0	0	9.00	52	.357	.357	0-0	—	0		-1	-0.1
Total	2	0	0	—	3	0	0	0-0	3.1	6	4	0	0	0-0	0	10.80	43	.375	.375	0-0	—	0		-2	-0.1
GRUNWALD, AL Alfred Henry "Stretch" B 2.13.1930 Los Angeles, CA BL/TL 6-4/210# d4.18																									
1955	Pit N	0	0	—	3	0	0	0	7.2	7	4	1	0	7-0	2	4.70	88	.241	.389	4-0	.500	1		0	0.0
1959	KC A	0	1	.000	6	1	0	1	11.1	18	14	1	0	11-1	9	7.94	50	.360	.475	4-0	.000	-1*	88	-6	-0.6
Total	2	0	1	.000	9	1	0	1	19	25	18	2	0	18-1	11	6.63	61	.316	.443	8-0	.250	0	88	-6	-0.6
GRYBOSKI, KEVIN Kevin John B 11.15.1973 Wilkes-Barre, PA BR/TR 6-5/220# d4.13																									
2002	†Atl N	2	1	.667	57	0	0	0-2	51.2	50	20	6	5	37-5	33	3.48	118	.256	.388	0-0	—	0		4	0.2
2003	†Atl N	6	4	.600	64	0	0	0-4	44.1	44	22	3	2	23-6	32	3.86	110	.272	.369	1-0	.000	-0		1	0.3
Total	2	8	5	.615	121	0	0	0-6	96	94	42	9	7	60-11	65	3.66	114	.263	.380	1-0	.000	-0		5	0.5
GRZANICH, MIKE Michael Edward B 8.24.1972 Canton, IL BR/TR 6-1/180# d5.14																									
1998	Hou N	0	0	—	1	0	0	0-0	1	1	2	0	0	2-0	1	18.00	23	.333	.500	0-0	—	0		-2	-0.1
GRZENDA, JOE Joseph Charles B 6.8.1937 Scranton, PA BR/TL 6-2/180# d4.26																									
1961	Det A	1	0	1.000	4	0	0	0	5.2	9	5	2	0	2-1	0	7.94	52	.375	.423	1-0	1.000	0		-2	-0.3
1964	KC A	0	2	.000	20	0	0	0	25	34	15	2	1	13-2	17	5.40	71	.324	.400	2-0	.000	-0		-4	-0.2
1966	KC A	0	2	.000	21	0	0	0	22	28	8	1	0	12-3	14	3.27	104	.337	.412	1-0	.000	-0		1	0.1
1967	NY N	0	0	—	11	0	0	0	16.2	14	4	0	1	8-4	9	2.16	157	.237	.333	1-0	.000	-0		2	0.1
1969	†Min A	4	1	.800	38	0	0	3-1	48.2	52	23	4	1	17-4	24	3.88	94	.281	.343	5-0	.000	0		-1	0.0
1970	Was A	3	6	.333	49	3	0	6-1	84.2	86	52	8	3	34-9	38	5.00	71	.267	.341	12-0	.000	-1	184	-14	-1.7
1971	Was A	5	2	.714	46	0	0	5-3	70.1	54	19	2	1	17-7	56	1.92	173	.217	.266	7-2	.143	-0		10	1.2
1972	StL N	1	0	1.000	30	0	0	0-0	35	46	24	1	3	17-8	15	5.66	60	.326	.410	1-0	.000	-0		-9	-0.5
Total	8	14	13	.519	219	3	0	14-5	308	323	150	20	10	120-38	173	4.00	88	.277	.346	30-2	.067	-2	184	-17	-1.3
GUANTE, CECILIO Cecilio (Magallane) B 2.1.1960 Villa Mella, D.R. BR/TR 6-3/205# d5.1																									
1982	Pit N	0	0	—	10	0	0	0-0	27	28	16	1	2	5-0	26	3.33	111	.264	.299	5-0	.000	-1		-1	-0.1
1983	Pit N	2	6	.250	49	0	0	9-0	100.1	90	45	5	2	46-6	82	3.32	112	.241	.325	22-0	.091	-1		3	0.1
1984	Pit N	2	3	.400	27	0	0	2-1	41.1	32	12	3	2	16-2	30	2.61	138	.224	.305	4-1	.000	-0		5	0.6
1985	Pit N	4	6	.400	63	0	0	5-7	109	84	34	5	5	40-9	92	2.72	132	.214	.293	17-0	.059	-1		12	1.0
1986	Pit N	5	2	.714	52	0	0	4-4	78	65	32	11	3	29-3	63	3.35	115	.225	.300	1-0	.000	-0		4	0.3
1987	NY A	3	2	.600	23	0	0	1-1	44	42	30	8	1	20-0	46	5.73	77	.247	.323	0-0	—	0		-7	-0.7
1988	NY A	5	6	.455	56	0	0	11-6	75	59	25	10	5	22-3	61	2.88	137	.213	.282	0-0	—	0		9	1.4
	Tex A	0	0	—	7	0	0	1-0	4.2	8	1	1	0	4-1	4	1.93	212	.400	.500	0-0	—	0		1	0.1
	Year	5	6	.455	63	0	0	12-6	79.2	67	33	11	5	26-4	65	2.82	140	.226	.298	0-0	—	0		11	1.5
1989	Tex A	6	6	.500	50	0	0	2-3	69	66	35	7	4	36-10	69	3.91	102	.249	.343	0-0	—	0		0	0.0

Year	Tm Lg	W	L	Pct	G	GS	CG-Sho	SV-BS	IP	H	R	HR	HB	BB-IB	SO	ERA	AERA	OAV	OOB	AB-SH	AVG	PB	Sup	APR	PW
1990	Cle A	2	3	.400	26	1	0	0-3	46.2	38	26	10	3	18-4	30	5.01	78	.220	.301	0-0	—	0	70	-5	-0.4
Total	9	29	34	.460	363	1	0	35-25	595	512	256	61	27	236-38	503	3.48	110	.232	.310	49-1	.061	-3	70	21	2.3
GUARDADO, EDDIE Edward Adrian B 10.2.1970 Stockton, CA BR/TL 6/193# d6.13																									
1993	Min A	3	8	.273	19	16	0	0-0	94.2	123	68	13	1	36-2	46	6.18	71	.319	.376	0-0	—	0	87	-17	-1.7
1994	Min A	0	2	.000	4	4	0	0-0	17	26	16	3	0	4-0	8	8.47	58	.351	.375	0-0	—	0	66	-6	-0.6
1995	Min A	4	9	.308	51	5	0	2-3	91.1	99	54	13	0	45-2	71	5.12	93	.280	.356	0-0	—	0	35	-2	-0.3
1996	Min A	6	5	.545	**83**	0	0	4-3	73.2	61	45	12	3	33-4	74	5.25	97	.228	.316	0-0	—	0		-1	-0.1
1997	Min A	0	4	.000	69	0	0	1-0	46	45	23	7	2	17-2	54	3.91	119	.251	.322	0-0	—	0		3	0.3
1998	Min A	3	1	.750	79	0	0	0-4	65.2	66	34	10	0	28-6	53	4.52	106	.265	.332	0-0	—	0		2	0.1
1999	Min A	2	5	.286	63	0	0	2-2	48	37	24	6	2	25-4	50	4.50	113	.222	.328	0-0	—	0		4	0.5
2000	Min A	7	4	.636	70	0	0	9-2	61.2	55	27	14	1	25-3	52	3.94	131	.238	.313	0-0	—	0		9	1.5
2001	Min A	7	1	.875	67	0	0	12-2	66.2	47	27	5	1	23-4	67	3.51	131	.197	.268	0-0	—	0		8	1.1
2002	†Min A★	1	3	.250	68	0	0	**45-6**	67.2	53	22	9	1	18-2	70	2.93	154	.215	.269	0-0	—	0		13	2.1
2003	†Min A★	3	5	.375	66	0	0	41-4	65.1	50	22	7	0	14-2	60	2.89	157	.207	.249	0-0	—	0		12	2.3
Total	11	36	47	.434	639	25	0	116-26	697.2	662	362	99	11	268-31	605	4.50	105	.252	.320	0-0	—	0	70	25	5.2
GUBICZA, MARK Mark Steven B 8.14.1962 Philadelphia, PA BR/TR 6-5/220# d4.6																									
1984	KC A	10	14	.417	29	29	4-2	0-0	189	172	90	13	5	75-0	111	4.05	100	.243	.317	0-0	—	0	89	1	0.2
1985	†KC A	14	10	.583	29	28	0	0-0	177.1	160	88	14	5	77-0	99	4.06	102	.238	.319	0-0	—	0	100	3	0.4
1986	KC A	12	6	.667	35	24	3-2	0-0	180.2	155	77	8	5	84-2	118	3.64	117	.233	.321	0-0	—	0	114	14	1.4
1987	KC A	13	18	.419	35	35	10-2	0-0	241.2	231	114	18	6	120-3	166	3.98	115	.259	.347	0-0	—	0	82	18	2.3
1988	KC A★	20	8	.714	35	35	8-4	0-0	269.2	237	94	11	6	83-3	183	2.70	148	.234	.294	0-0	—	0	113	37	3.9
1989	KC A★	15	11	.577	36	**36**	8-2	0-0	255	252	100	10	5	63-8	173	3.04	127	.259	.305	0-0	—	0	102	21	2.2
1990	KC A	4	7	.364	16	16	2	0-0	94	101	48	5	4	38-4	71	4.50	85	.283	.355	0-0	—	0	98	-4	-0.5
1991	KC A	9	12	.429	26	26	0	0-0	133	168	90	10	6	42-1	89	5.68	73	.308	.361	0-0	—	0	92	-21	-2.7
1992	KC A	7	6	.538	18	18	2-1	0-0	111.1	110	47	8	1	36-3	81	3.72	109	.259	.316	0-0	—	0	91	6	0.6
1993	KC A	5	8	.385	49	6	0	2-1	104.1	128	61	2	2	43-8	80	4.66	99	.307	.370	0-0	—	0	87	-2	-0.3
1994	KC A	7	9	.438	22	22	0	0-0	130	158	74	11	0	26-5	59	4.50	111	.301	.331	0-0	—	0	90	6	0.6
1995	KC A	12	14	.462	33	**33**	3-2	0-0	213.1	222	97	21	6	62-2	81	3.75	128	.272	.326	0-0	—	0	77	24	2.6
1996	KC A	4	12	.250	19	19	2-1	0-0	119.1	132	70	22	7	34-0	55	5.13	98	.284	.339	0-0	—	0	68	0	0.0
1997	Ana A	0	1	.000	2	2	0	0-0	4.2	13	13	2	0	3-0	5	25.07	18	.481	.533	0-0	—	0	110	-10	-1.3
Total	14	132	136	.493	384	329	42-16	2-1	2223.1	2239	1063	155	58	786-39	1371	3.96	109	.264	.327	0-0	—	0	93	93	9.4
GUDAT, MARV Marvin John B 8.27.1903 Goliad, TX D 3.1.1954 Los Angeles, CA BL/TL 5-11/162# d5.21 ▲																									
1929	Cin N	1	1	.500	7	2	2	0	26.2	29	12	0	0	4	0	3.38	135	.282	.308	10-0	.200	-0*	48	3	0.1
1932	†Chi N	0	0	—	1	0	0	0	1	1	0	0	0	0	2	0.00	—	.250	.250	94-1	.255	0*		0	0.0
Total	2	1	1	.500	8	2	2	0	27.2	30	12	0	0	4	2	3.25	139	.280	.306	104-1	.250	-0	48	3	0.1
GUESE, WHITEY Theodore B 1.24.1872 New Bremen, OH D 4.8.1951 Wapakoneta, OH BR/TR 6-0.5/200# d7.13																									
1901	Cin N	1	4	.200	6	5	4	0	44.1	62	48	5	3	14	11	6.09	53	.328	.383	15-0	.200	1	137	-17	-1.5
GUETTERMAN, LEE Arthur Lee B 11.22.1958 Chattanooga, TN BL/TL 6-8/227# d9.12																									
1984	Sea A	0	0	—	3	0	0	0-0	4.1	9	2	0	0	2-0	2	4.15	96	.450	.500	0-0	—	0		0	0.0
1986	Sea A	0	4	.000	41	4	1	0-3	76	108	67	7	4	30-3	38	7.34	58	.347	.406	0-0	—	0	112	-25	-1.2
1987	Sea A	11	4	.733	25	17	2-1	0-0	113.1	117	60	13	2	35-2	42	3.81	124	.267	.320	0-0	—	0	107	8	1.0
1988	NY A	1	2	.333	20	2	0	0-1	40.2	49	21	2	1	14-0	15	4.65	85	.306	.364	0-0	—	0	23	-2	-0.2
1989	NY A	5	5	.500	70	0	0	13-0	103	98	31	6	0	26-9	51	2.45	158	.258	.304	0-0	—	0		16	2.0
1990	NY A	11	7	.611	64	0	0	2-5	93	80	37	6	0	26-7	48	3.39	118	.236	.288	0-0	—	0		7	1.3
1991	NY A	3	4	.429	64	0	0	6-3	88	91	42	6	3	25-5	35	3.68	113	.268	.320	0-0	—	0		3	0.3
1992	NY A	1	1	.500	15	0	0	0-0	22.2	35	24	5	0	13-3	5	9.53	41	.354	.421	0-0	—	0		-13	-1.0
	NY N	3	4	.429	43	0	0	2-1	43.1	57	28	5	1	14-5	15	5.82	60	.324	.371	2-0	.000	-0		-10	-1.7
1993	StL N	3	3	.500	40	0	0	1-3	46	41	18	1	2	16-5	19	2.93	135	.240	.309	2-0	.500	1		5	0.6
1995	Sea A	0	0	—	23	0	0	1-1	17	21	13	1	3	11-0	11	6.88	69	.300	.417	0-0	—	0		-3	-0.1
1996	Sea A	0	2	.000	17	0	0	0-0	11	11	8	0	0	10-2	6	4.09	121	.275	.420	0-0	—	0		0	0.0
Total	11	38	36	.514	425	23	3-1	25-17	658.1	717	351	52	16	222-41	287	4.33	96	.282	.340	4-0	.250	0	112	-14	1.0
GUIDRY, RON Ronald Ames B 8.28.1950 Lafayette, LA BL/TL 5-11/162# d7.27																									
1975	NY A	0	1	.000	10	1	0	0-0	15.2	15	6	0	1	9-0	15	3.45	107	.259	.362	0-0	—	0	96	1	0.0
1976	†NY A	0	0	—	7	0	0	0-0	16	20	12	1	0	4-0	12	5.63	61	.294	.333	0-0	—	0		-4	-0.2
1977	†NY A	16	7	.696	31	25	9-5	1-0	210.2	174	72	12	0	65-2	176	2.82	140	.224	.283	0-0	—	0*	107	28	2.9
1978	†NY A★	**25**	3	**.893**	35	35	16-**9**	0-0	273.2	187	61	13	1	72-1	248	**1.74**	**208**	**.193**	**.249**	0-0	—	0*	117	**59**	**6.4**
1979	NY A★	18	8	.692	33	30	15-2	2-0	236.1	203	83	20	0	71-0	201	**2.78**	147	.236	.292	0-0	—	0*	101	34	3.6
1980	†NY A	17	10	.630	37	29	5-3	1-1	219.2	215	97	19	1	80-1	166	3.56	110	.260	.322	0-0	—	0	119	10	1.2
1981	†NY A	11	5	.688	23	21	0	0-0	127	100	41	12	1	26-0	104	2.76	129	.214	**.256**	0-0	—	0	99	13	1.7
1982	NY A☆	14	8	.636	34	33	6-1	0-0	222	216	104	22	1	69-3	162	3.81	105	.254	.309	0-0	—	0	125	5	0.3
1983	NY A✤	21	9	.700	31	31	**21**-3	0-0	250.1	232	99	26	2	60-3	156	3.42	114	.244	.288	0-0	—	0*	106	17	1.9
1984	NY A	10	11	.476	29	28	5-1	0-0	195.2	223	102	24	2	44-3	127	4.51	84	.287	.323	0-0	—	0*	110	-14	-1.3
1985	NY A	**22**	6	**.786**	34	33	11-2	0-0	259	243	104	28	0	42-3	143	3.27	123	.248	.277	0-0	—	0	127	23	2.2
1986	NY A	9	12	.429	30	30	5	0-0	192.1	202	94	28	1	38-2	140	3.98	103	.265	.300	0-0	—	0	90	3	0.3
1987	NY A	5	8	.385	22	17	2	0-0	117.2	111	50	14	1	38-3	96	3.67	120	.248	.307	0-0	—	0	87	10	1.0
1988	NY A	2	3	.400	12	10	0	0-0	56	57	28	7	2	15-3	32	4.18	94	.259	.311	0-0	—	0*	95	-1	-0.1
Total	14	170	91	.651	368	323	95-26	4-1	2392	2198	953	226	13	633-24	1778	3.29	119	.244	.292	0-0	—	0	109	184	19.9
GUINN, SKIP Drannon Eugene B 10.25.1944 St.Charles, MO BR/TL 5-10/180# d5.7																									
1968	Atl N	0	0	—	3	0	0	0	5	3	2	0	0	3-0	4	3.60	83	.167	.286	0-0	—	0*		0	0.0
1969	Hou N	1	2	.333	28	0	0	0-2	27	34	22	3	1	21-2	33	6.67	53	.304	.412	3-0	.000	-0		-9	-1.0
1971	Hou N	0	0	—	4	0	0	1-0	4.2	1	0	0	0	3-1	3	0.00	—	.067	.222	0-0	—	0		2	0.1
Total	3	1	2	.333	35	0	0	1-2	36.2	38	24	3	1	27-3	40	5.40	64	.262	.377	3-0	.000	-0		-7	-0.9
GUISE, LEFTY Witt Orison B 9.18.1909 Driggs, AR D 8.13.1968 Little Rock, AR BL/TL 6-2/172# d9.3																									
1940	Cin N	0	0	—	2	0	0	0	7.2	8	2	0	1	5	1	1.17	323	.296	.424	3-0	.333	0		2	0.1
GULLETT, DON Donald Edward B 1.6.1951 Lynn, KY BR/TL 6/190# d4.10 C11																									
1970	†Cin N	5	2	.714	44	2	0	6-0	77.2	54	23	4	0	44-6	76	2.43	166	.196	.306	19-0	.211	1	89	14	1.5
1971	Cin N	16	6	**.727**	35	31	4-3	0-3	217.2	196	73	14	2	64-6	107	2.65	127	.242	.298	75-5	.120	-2*	95	16	1.2
1972	†Cin N	9	10	.474	31	16	2	2-2	134.2	127	61	15	1	43-5	96	3.94	82	.250	.309	38-5	.211	2	129	-10	-1.2
1973	†Cin N	18	8	.692	45	30	7-4	2-0	228.1	198	95	24	3	69-8	153	3.51	97	.232	.290	64-7	.188	3*	129	-1	0.2
1974	Cin N	17	11	.607	36	35	10-3	0-1	243	201	93	22	2	88-8	183	3.04	115	.222	.291	80-10	.237	4*	131	13	1.8
1975	†Cin N	15	4	**.789**	22	22	8-3	0-0	159.2	127	49	11	2	56-4	98	2.42	149	.218	.287	62-3	.226	3	125	20	2.6
1976	†Cin N	11	3	.786	23	20	4	1-0	126	119	48	8	0	48-3	64	3.00	117	.253	.321	44-6	.182	-0*	130	6	0.7
1977	†NY A	14	4	.778	22	22	7-1	0-0	158.1	137	67	14	1	69-1	116	3.58	110	.232	.312	0-0	—	0	131	8	0.8
1978	NY A	4	2	.667	8	8	2	0-0	44.2	46	19	3	1	20-1	28	3.63	100	.269	.347	0-0	—	0	130	1	0.1
Total	9	109	50	.686	266	186	44-14	11-6	1390	1205	528	115	12	501-42	921	3.11	113	.233	.301	382-36	.194	10	123	67	7.7
GULLICKSON, BILL William Lee B 2.20.1959 Marshall, MN BR/TR 6-3/215# d9.26																									
1979	Mon N	0	0	—	1	0	0	0-0	1	2	0	0	0	0-0	0	0.00	—	.500	.500	0-0	—	0		0	0.0
1980	Mon N	10	5	.667	24	19	5-2	0-0	141	127	53	6	2	50-2	120	3.00	119	.238	.303	40-10	.175	0	113	9	1.0
1981	†Mon N	7	9	.438	22	22	3-2	0-0	157.1	142	54	3	4	34-4	115	2.80	125	.239	.283	46-4	.152	0	89	12	1.2
1982	Mon N	12	14	.462	34	34	6	0-0	236.2	231	101	25	4	61-2	155	3.57	102	.254	.302	82-9	.122	-2	109	5	0.0
1983	Mon N	17	12	.586	34	34	10-1	0-0	242.1	230	108	19	4	59-4	120	3.75	96	.251	.297	82-9	.134	1	114	-3	-0.2
1984	Mon N	12	9	.571	32	32	3	0-0	226.2	230	100	27	1	37-7	100	3.61	95	.265	.294	73-6	.110	-2	106	-4	-0.8
1985	Mon N	14	12	.538	29	29	4-1	0-0	181.1	187	78	8	1	47-9	68	3.52	96	.271	.315	64-4	.188	2	92	-2	-0.2
1986	Cin N	15	12	.556	37	37	6-2	0-0	244.2	245	103	24	2	60-10	121	3.38	115	.264	.306	79-9	.076	-4	98	13	0.8

Year	Tm Lg	W	L	Pct	G	GS	CG-Sho	SV-BS	IP	H	R	HR	HB	BB-IB	SO	ERA	AERA	OAV	OOB	AB-SH	AVG	PB	Sup	APR	PW
1987	Cin N	10	11	.476	27	27	3-1	0-0	165	172	99	33	2	39-6	89	4.85	88	.267	.308	53-4	.208	2	100	-11	-1.1
	NY A	4	2	.667	8	8	1	0-0	48	46	29	7	1	11-1	28	4.88	90	.253	.296	0-0	—	0	124	-3	-0.3
1990	Hou N	10	14	.417	32	32	2-1	0-0	193.1	221	100	21	2	61-14	73	3.82	97	.287	.338	57-7	.158	2	89	-6	-0.7
1991	Det A	**20**	9	.690	35	**35**	4	0-0	226.1	256	109	22	4	44-13	91	3.90	107	.288	.321	0-1	—	0	124	5	0.5
1992	Det A	14	13	.519	34	34	4-1	0-0	221.2	228	109	35	0	50-5	64	4.34	91	.267	.305	0-0	—	0	117	-6	-0.7
1993	Det A	13	9	.591	28	28	2	0-0	159.1	186	106	28	3	44-3	70	5.37	80	.291	.336	0-0	—	0	122	-19	-2.2
1994	Det A	4	5	.444	21	19	1	0-0	115.1	156	79	24	4	25-2	65	5.93	82	.322	.360	0-0	—	0	132	-12	-0.7
Total	14	162	136	.544	398	390	54-11	0-0	2560	2659	1228	282	34	622-82	1279	3.93	98	.268	.311	576-63	.141	-1	109	-22	-3.4
GUMBERT, AD Addison Courtney B 10.10.1868 Pittsburgh, PA D 4.23.1925 Pittsburgh, PA BR/TR 5-10/200# d9.15 b-Billy																									
1888	Chi N	3	3	.500	6	6	5	0	48.2	44	24	0	5	10	16	3.14	96	.234	.291	24	.333	2*	111	1	0.2
1889	Chi N	16	13	.552	31	28	25-2	0	246.1	258	148	16	14	76	91	3.62	115	.261	.323	153	.288	11*	112	17	2.4
1890	Bos P	23	12	.657	39	33	27-1	0	277.1	338	189	18	11	86	81	3.96	111	.288	.342	145	.241	5*	115	15	1.8
1891	Chi N	17	11	.607	32	31	24-1	0	256.1	282	149	5	10	90	73	3.58	93	.269	.332	105	.305	12*	103	-4	0.8
1892	Chi N	22	19	.537	46	45	39	0	382.2	399	220	11	14	107	118	3.41	97	.258	.312	178	.236	4*	100	0	0.4
1893	Pit N	11	7	.611	22	20	16-2	0	162.2	207	119	5	5	78	40	5.15	88	.301	.376	95	.221	1*	121	-6	-0.4
1894	Pit N	15	14	.517	38	32	26	0	271	376	245	14	6	85	67	6.04	87	.325	.374	114-1	.298	6*	103	-25	-1.4
1895	Bro N	11	16	.407	33	26	20	1	234	288	183	11	12	69	45	5.08	87	.298	.352	97-0	.361	11*	102	-23	-1.0
1896	Bro N	0	4	.000	5	4	2	0	31	34	18	2	0	11	3	3.77	109	.276	.336	11-0	.182	-0	43	1	0.2
	Phi N	5	3	.625	11	10	7-1	0	77.1	99	55	0	4	23	14	4.54	95	.308	.362	34-1	.265	1	132	-2	-0.1
	Year	5	7	.417	16	14	9-1	0	108.1	133	63	2	4	34	17	4.32	99	.300	.355	45-1	.244	1	107	-1	0.1
Total	9	123	102	.547	263	235	191-7	1	1987.1	2325	1350	82	81	635	548	4.28	96	.284	.341	956-2	.274	53	107	-26	2.9
GUMBERT, HARRY Harry Edwards "Gunboat" B 11.5.1909 Elizabeth, PA D 1.4.1995 Wimberley, TX BR/TR 6-2/185# d9.12 Mil 1945																									
1935	NY N	1	2	.333	6	3	1	0	23.2	35	27	1	0	10	11	6.08	63	.330	.388	8-0	.000	-1	73	-10	-1.1
1936	†NY N	11	3	.786	39	15	3	0	140.2	157	77	7	2	54	52	3.90	100	.281	.346	44-0	.250	2	121	-3	0.1
1937	†NY N	10	11	.476	34	24	10-1	1	200.1	194	92	11	4	62	65	3.68	106	.257	.317	72-2	.181	-1	95	6	0.8
1938	NY N	15	13	.536	38	33	14-1	0	235.2	238	114	13	7	84	84	4.01	94	.261	.328	84-3	.155	-3*	93	-3	-0.2
1939	NY N	18	11	.621	36	34	14-2	0	243.2	257	132	21	1	81	81	4.32	91	.271	.329	90-6	.200	-0*	107	-10	-0.8
1940	NY N	12	14	.462	35	30	14-2	2	237	230	110	17	3	81	77	3.76	103	.252	.316	87-2	.195	2	86	5	0.8
1941	NY N	1	1	.500	5	5	1	0	32.1	34	20	3	0	18	9	4.45	83	.266	.356	12-1	.167	-0	129	-3	-0.2
	StL N	11	5	.688	33	17	8-3	1	144.1	139	52	7	1	30	53	2.74	137	.251	.291	53-1	.321	6*	94	16	2.4
	Year	12	6	.667	38	22	9-3	1	176.2	173	56	10	1	48	62	3.06	123	.254	.304	65-2	.292	5	102	12	2.2
1942	†StL N	9	5	.643	38	19	5	5	163	156	67	3	1	59	52	3.26	105	.250	.315	54-1	.111	-2	115	4	0.4
1943	StL N	10	5	.667	21	19	7-2	0	133	115	46	4	0	32	40	2.84	118	.237	.284	45-6	.156	-2	97	9	0.9
1944	StL N	4	2	.667	10	7	3	1	61.1	60	23	1	0	19	16	2.49	141	.258	.313	21-0	.190	-0	102	6	0.6
	Cin N	10	8	.556	24	19	11-2	2	155.1	157	61	7	2	40	40	3.30	106	.262	.310	52-5	.096	-2	96	6	0.5
	Year	14	10	.583	34	26	14-2	3	216.2	217	65	8	2	59	56	3.07	114	.261	.311	73-5	.123	-2	98	13	1.1
1946	Cin N	6	8	.429	36	10	5	4	119	112	48	8	1	42	44	3.25	103	.248	.314	32-1	.250	1	67	2	0.4
1947	Cin N	10	10	.500	46	0	0	10	90.1	88	42	3	0	47	43	3.89	106	.260	.351	22-2	.273	1		3	0.7
1948	Cin N	10	8	.556	**61**	0	0	**17**	106.1	123	50	5	0	34	25	3.47	113	.291	.344	25-1	.040	-1		4	0.7
1949	Cin N	4	3	.571	29	0	0	2	40.2	58	28	5	1	8	12	5.53	76	.341	.374	2-0	.000	-0		-6	-0.9
	Pit N	1	4	.200	16	0	0	3	27.2	30	20	5	0	18	5	5.86	72	.270	.372	4-0	.250	0		-5	-0.8
	Year	5	7	.417	45	0	0	5	68.1	88	51	10	1	26	17	5.66	74	.313	.373	6-0	.167	-0		-10	-1.7
1950	Pit N	0	0	—	1	0	0	0	1.2	3	3	0	0	2	0	5.40	81	.333	.455	1-0	1.000	0		-1	0.0
Total	15	143	113	.559	508	235	96-13	48	2156	2186	1012	121	23	721	709	3.68	102	.263	.323	708-31	.184	-2	98	20	4.3
GUMBERT, BILLY William Skeen B 8.8.1865 Pittsburgh, PA D 4.13.1946 Pittsburgh, PA BR/TR 6-1.5/200# d6.19 b-Ad																									
1890	Pit N	4	6	.400	10	10	8	0	79.1	96	71	0	8	31	18	5.22	63	.290	.365	37	.243	3	134	-18	-1.4
1892	Pit N	3	2	.600	6	3	2	0	39.2	30	15	0	1	23	3	1.36	242	.201	.312	18	.111	-1*	64	7	0.7
1893	Lou N	0	0	—	1	1	0	0	0.2	2	6	0	0	5	0	27.00	16	.500	.778	1	1.000	1	175	-3	-0.1
Total	3	7	8	.467	17	14	10	0	119.2	128	92	0	9	59	21	4.06	81	.264	.355	56	.214	3	124	-14	-0.8
GUMPERT, DAVE David Lawrence B 5.5.1958 South Haven, MI BR/TR 6-1/190# d7.25																									
1982	Det A	0	0	—	5	1	0	1-1	2	7	6	1	0	2-0	0	27.00	15	.700	.750	0-0	—	0	90	-5	-0.5
1983	Det A	0	2	.000	26	0	0	2-0	44.1	43	16	1	0	7-3	14	2.64	149	.257	.281	0-0	—	0		6	0.2
1985	Chi N	1	0	1.000	9	0	0	0-0	10.1	12	7	0	0	7-1	4	3.48	115	.279	.365	1-0	.000	-0		-1	-0.1
1986	Chi N	2	0	1.000	38	0	0	2-2	59.2	60	32	4	1	28-7	45	4.37	93	.267	.349	5-0	.000	-1		-2	-0.2
1987	KC A	0	0	—	8	0	0	0-0	19.1	27	16	3	0	6-0	13	6.05	76	.333	.375	0-0	—	0		-4	-0.2
Total	5	3	2	.600	86	1	0	5-3	135.2	149	77	9	1	50-11	76	4.31	95	.283	.342	6-0	.000	-1	90	-6	-0.8
GUMPERT, RANDY Randall Pennington B 1.23.1918 Monocacy, PA BR/TR 6-3/205# d6.13 Mil 1943-45																									
1936	Phi A	1	2	.333	22	3	2	2	62.1	74	42	2	0	32	9	4.76	107	.295	.375	22-0	.273	0	46	0	0.0
1937	Phi A	0	0	—	10	1	0	0	12	16	17	1	1	15	5	12.00	39	.333	.500	3-0	.333	0	111	-9	-0.4
1938	Phi A	0	2	.000	4	2	0	0	12.1	24	18	1	0	10	1	10.95	44	.393	.479	4-0	.250	0	91	-8	-0.9
1946	NY A	11	3	.786	33	12	4	1	132.2	113	44	8	0	32	63	2.31	150	.229	.276	47-1	.128	-2	151	15	1.2
1947	NY A	4	1	.800	24	6	2	0	56.1	71	36	4	0	28	25	5.43	65	.311	.387	14-2	.071	-1*	108	-12	-1.1
1948	NY A	1	0	1.000	15	0	0	0	25	27	10	0	1	6	12	2.88	142	.267	.315	0-0	—	0		3	0.1
	Chi A	2	6	.250	16	11	6-1	0	97.1	103	43	6	2	13	31	3.79	112	.275	.303	29-3	.138	-2	50	6	0.2
	Year	3	6	.333	31	11	6-1	0	122.1	130	45	6	3	19	43	3.60	117	.273	.305	29-3	.138	-2	51	9	0.3
1949	Chi A	13	16	.448	34	32	18-3	1	234	223	111	22	1	83	78	3.81	110	.253	.318	84-6	.190	-1	92	10	1.0
1950	Chi A	5	12	.294	40	17	6-1	0	155.1	165	87	15	4	58	48	4.75	94	.275	.343	42-4	.071	-4*	73	-2	-0.6
1951	Chi A☆	9	8	.529	33	16	7-1	2	141.2	156	74	20	1	34	45	4.32	93	.272	.314	45-4	.333	3*	128	-2	-0.1
1994	Tor A	12	11	.522	25	**25**	2	0-0	147.1	165	102	20	3	76-1	124	5.68	85	.282	.364	0-0	—	0	118	-15	-1.9
1995	Tor A	4	14	.222	24	24	3	0-0	135.1	151	101	13	3	73-6	94	6.32	75	.281	.369	0-0	—	0	68	-22	-2.4
1996	Tor A	11	8	.579	27	27	4-1	0-0	187.2	158	68	20	7	53-3	165	**2.93**	**171**	**.228**	**.289**	0-0	—	0	75	43	3.8
1997	Tor A	3	6	.333	13	13	0	0-0	60	48	42	14	2	31-0	52	4.95	93	.213	.312	0-0	—	0	78	-5	-0.6
1998	Tor A	6	12	.333	22	22	2	0-0	145	133	83	19	6	65-1	113	4.41	106	.239	.324	2-0	.000	-0	82	2	0.1
	Bal A	4	4	.500	11	11	0	0-0	66	60	34	4	2	33-1	55	4.23	108	.241	.332	0-0	—	0	95	2	0.1
	Year	10	16	.385	33	33	2	0-0	211	193	39	23	8	98-2	168	4.35	107	.240	.326	2-0	.000	-0	86	4	0.2
1999	Bal A	5	9	.357	21	21	1-1	0-0	122.2	124	63	18	3	65-3	95	4.18	112	.264	.356	6-0	.167	-0	89	6	0.6
	Cin N	6	3	.667	12	12	1	0-0	77.1	70	33	10	1	21-3	60	3.03	154	.238	.290	26-3	.115	-1	125	12	1.1
2000	TB A	0	1	.000	1	1	0	0-0	1.2	7	8	2	0	2-0	3	43.20	11	.636	.692	0-0	—	0	95	-7	-0.8
Total	10	91	79	.535	240	240	17-3	0-0	1483.1	1360	750	149	35	667-22	1243	4.08	112	.243	.325	34-3	.118	-1	97	71	5.1
GUZMAN, SANTIAGO Santiago Donovan (b: Santiago Donovan (Guzman)) B 7.25.1949 San Pedro De Macoris, D.R. BR/TR 6-2/180# d9.30																									
1969	StL N	0	1	.000	1	1	0	0-0	7.1	9	4	2	0	3-1	7	4.91	73	.321	.387	3-0	.333	0	74	-1	-0.1
1970	StL N	1	1	.500	8	3	1	0-0	13.2	14	12	1	0	13-0	9	7.24	57	.275	.422	5-0	.200	-0	167	-5	-0.6
1971	StL N	0	0	—	2	1	0	0-0	10	6	1	0	0	2-0	13	0.00	—	.162	.205	1-1	.000	-0	148	3	0.2
1972	StL N	0	0	—	1	0	0	0-0	1	1	1	1	0	0-0	0	9.00	38	.250	.250	0-0	—	0		-1	0.0
Total	4	1	2	.333	12	5	1	0-0	32	30	18	4	0	18-1	29	4.50	85	.250	.348	9-1	.222	0	150	-4	-0.5
HAAS, BRUNO Bruno Philip "Boon" B 5.5.1891 Worcester, MA D 6.5.1952 Sarasota, FL BB/TL 5-10/180# d6.23																									
1915	Phi A	0	1	.000	6	2	1	0	14.1	23	27	0	0	28	7	11.93	25	.404	.600	18-0	.056	-1*	150	-15	-0.9
HAAS, MOOSE Bryan Edmund B 4.22.1956 Baltimore, MD BR/TR 6/180# d9.8																									
1976	Mil A	0	1	.000	5	2	0	0-0	16	12	8	0	0	12-0	9	3.94	89	.207	.338	0-0	—	0	75	-1	0.0
1977	Mil A	10	12	.455	32	32	6	0-0	197.2	195	104	21	2	84-8	113	4.33	94	.261	.334	0-0	—	0*	90	-5	-0.6
1978	Mil A	2	3	.400	7	6	2	1-0	30.2	33	22	6	0	8-0	32	6.16	61	.273	.315	0-0	—	0	183	-8	-1.1
1979	Mil A	11	11	.500	29	28	8-1	0-0	184.2	198	112	26	0	59-2	95	4.78	88	.275	.327	0-0	—	0	113	-13	-1.4
1980	Mil A	16	15	.516	33	33	14-3	0-0	252.1	246	96	25	1	56-6	146	3.10	125	.258	.297	0-0	—	0	82	24	2.7
1981	†Mil A	11	7	.611	24	22	5	0-1	137.1	146	69	10	1	40-4	64	4.46	77	.275	.324	0-0	—	0	120	-15	-1.8
1982	†Mil A	11	8	.579	32	27	3	1-0	193.1	232	101	15	3	39-4	104	4.47	85	.302	.334	0-0	—	0	132	-13	-1.2

Year	Tm Lg	W	L	Pct	G	GS	CG-Sho	SV-BS	IP	H	R	HR	HB	BB-IB	SO	ERA	AERA	OAV	OOB	AB-SH	AVG	PB	Sup	APR	PW
1983	Mil A	13	3	.813	25	25	7-3	0-0	179	170	66	12	1	42-5	75	3.27	115	.251	.294	0-0	—	0*	119	13	1.0
1984	Mil A	9	11	.450	31	30	4	0-0	189.1	205	91	15	0	43-3	84	3.99	97	.279	.316	0-0	—	0	88	-1	0.0
1985	Mil A	8	8	.500	27	26	6-1	0-0	161.2	165	85	21	1	25-3	78	3.84	108	.260	.287	0-0	—	0	97	3	0.2
1986	Oak A	7	2	.778	12	12	1	0-0	72.1	58	23	4	1	19-1	40	2.74	142	.218	.271	0-0	—	0	174	11	1.2
1987	Oak A	2	2	.500	9	9	0	0-0	40.2	57	29	7	0	9-0	13	5.75	72	.335	.367	0-0	—	0	135	-8	-0.7
Total	12	100	83	.546	266	252	56-8	2-1	1655	1717	806	162	10	436-36	853	4.01	97	.269	.314	0-0	—	0	109	-13	-1.7
HAAS, DAVID Robert David B 10.19.1965 Independence, MO BR/TR 6-1/200# d9.8																									
1991	Det A	1	0	1.000	11	0	0	0-1	10.2	8	8	1	1	12-3	6	6.75	62	.242	.438	0-0	—	0		-3	-0.2
1992	Det A	5	3	.625	12	11	1-1	0-0	61.2	68	30	8	1	16-1	29	3.94	100	.276	.323	0-0	—	0	111	0	0.0
1993	Det A	1	2	.333	20	0	0	0-0	28	45	20	9	0	8-5	17	6.11	70	.375	.411	0-0	—	0		-5	-0.5
Total	3	7	5	.583	43	11	1-1	0-1	100.1	121	58	18	2	36-9	52	4.84	84	.303	.361	0-0	—	0	111	-8	-0.7
HABENICHT, BOB Robert Julius "Hobby" B 2.13.1926 St.Louis, MO D 12.24.1980 Richmond, VA BR/TR 6-2/185# d4.17																									
1951	StL N	0	0	—	3	0	0	0	5	5	4	0	0	9	1	7.20	55	.278	.519	1-0	.000	0		-2	-0.1
1953	StL A	0	0	—	1	0	0	0	1.2	1	1	0	1	1	1	5.40	78	.167	.375	0-0	—	0		0	0.0
Total	2	0	0	—	4	0	0	0	6.2	6	5	0	1	10	2	6.75	60	.250	.486	1-0	.000	0		-2	-0.1
HABYAN, JOHN John Gabriel B 1.29.1964 Bay Shore, NY BR/TR 6-2/195# d9.29																									
1985	Bal A	1	0	1.000	2	0	0	0-0	2.2	3	1	0	0	0-0	2	0.00	—	.250	.250	0-0	—	0		1	0.2
1986	Bal A	1	3	.250	6	5	0	0-0	26.1	24	17	3	0	18-2	14	4.44	93	.250	.365	0-0	—	0	61	-2	-0.3
1987	Bal A	6	7	.462	27	13	0	1-0	116.1	110	67	20	2	40-1	64	4.80	92	.248	.311	0-0	—	0	83	-5	-0.4
1988	Bal A	1	0	1.000	7	0	0	0-0	14.2	22	10	2	0	4-0	4	4.30	91	.355	.382	0-0	—	0		-2	-0.1
1990	NY A	0	0	—	6	0	0	0-1	8.2	10	2	0	1	2-0	4	2.08	192	.294	.351	0-0	—	0		2	0.1
1991	NY A	4	2	.667	66	0	0	2-2	90	73	28	2	2	20-2	70	2.30	180	.225	.274	0-0	—	0		17	1.1
1992	NY A	5	6	.455	56	0	0	7-5	72.2	84	32	6	2	21-5	44	3.84	102	.295	.344	0-0	—	0		2	0.3
1993	NY A	2	1	.667	36	0	0	1-2	42.1	45	20	5	0	16-2	29	4.04	103	.276	.337	0-0	—	0		1	0.1
	KC A	0	0	—	12	0	0	0-0	14	14	7	1	0	4-2	10	4.50	102	.259	.310	0-0	—	0		0	0.0
	Year	2	1	.667	48	0	0	1-2	56.1	59	31	6	0	20-4	39	4.15	103	.272	.331	0-0	—	0		2	0.1
1994	StL N	1	0	1.000	52	0	0	1-2	47.1	50	17	2	0	20-8	46	3.23	129	.275	.347	0-0	—	0		5	0.3
1995	StL N	3	2	.600	31	0	0	0-1	40.2	32	18	0	1	15-4	35	2.88	146	.222	.298	2-0	.000	-0		5	0.5
	Cal A	1	2	.333	28	0	0	0-1	32.2	36	16	2	1	12-0	25	4.13	114	.279	.340	0-0	—	0		2	0.1
1996	Col N	1	1	.500	19	0	0	0-0	24	34	19	4	1	14-1	25	7.13	73	.347	.430	3-0	.000	-0		-3	-0.3
Total	11	26	24	.520	348	18	0	12-14	532.1	537	254	47	10	186-27	372	3.85	111	.265	.327	5-0	.000	-0	79	23	1.6
HACKER, WARREN Warren Louis B 11.21.1924 Marissa, IL D 5.22.2002 Lenzburg, IL BR/TR 6-1/185# d9.24																									
1948	Chi N	0	1	.000	3	1	0	0	3	7	7	0	0	3	0	21.00	19	.438	.526	0-0	—	0	68	-5	-0.9
1949	Chi N	5	8	.385	30	12	3	0	125.2	141	68	7	4	53	40	4.23	95	.283	.356	38-0	.184	-1*	82	-3	-0.3
1950	Chi N	0	1	.000	5	3	1	1	15.1	20	11	3	0	8	5	5.28	80	.313	.389	5-0	.000	-1	77	-2	-0.2
1951	Chi N	0	0	—	2	0	0	0	1.1	3	2	0	1	0	2	13.50	30	.500	.571	0-0	—	0		-1	-0.1
1952	Chi N	15	9	.625	33	20	12-5	1	185	144	56	17	1	31	84	2.58	149	**.212**	**.247**	58-6	.121	-2*	88	27	3.1
1953	Chi N	12	19	.387	39	32	9	2	221.2	225	123	35	3	54	106	4.38	101	.254	.299	78-5	.218	0*	92	2	0.2
1954	Chi N	6	13	.316	39	18	4-1	2	158.2	157	89	28	4	37	80	4.25	99	.257	.299	55-3	.236	1*	99	-3	-0.3
1955	Chi N	11	15	.423	35	30	13	3	213	202	112	38	2	43-7	80	4.27	96	.245	.282	72-0	.250	2	79	-4	-0.4
1956	Chi N	3	13	.188	34	24	4	0	168	190	103	28	1	44-11	65	4.66	81	.285	.327	54-1	.148	-2	97	-18	-1.8
1957	Cin N	3	2	.600	15	6	0	0	43.1	50	26	5	3	13-3	18	5.19	79	.294	.347	8-0	.125	-0	111	-4	-0.5
	Phi N	4	4	.500	20	10	1	0	74	72	40	10	1	18-2	33	4.50	85	.257	.303	23-1	.261	1	88	-5	-0.4
	Year	7	6	.538	35	16	1	0	117.1	122	44	15	4	31-5	51	4.76	82	.271	.320	31-1	.226	1	97	-9	-0.9
1958	Phi N	0	1	.000	9	1	0	0	17	24	17	2	0	8-1	4	7.41	53	.329	.395	1-0	.000	-0	45	-7	-0.4
1961	Chi A	3	3	.500	42	0	0	8	57.1	62	26	8	1	8-1	40	3.77	104	.272	.297	9-0	.111	-1		1	0.0
Total	12	62	89	.411	306	157	47-6	17	1283.1	1297	680	181	21	320-25	557	4.21	96	.259	.305	401-16	.195	-2	90	-22	-2.0
HACKETT, JIM James Joseph "Sunny Jim" B 10.1.1877 Jacksonville, IL D 3.28.1961 Douglas, MI BR/TR 6-2/185# d9.14 ▲																									
1902	StL N	0	3	.000	4	3	3	0	30.1	46	26	0	1	16	7	6.23	44	.348	.423	21-0	.286	1*	107	-10	-0.8
1903	StL N	1	3	.250	7	6	5	1	48.1	47	28	0	3	18	21	3.72	88	.249	.324	351-2	.228	1*	86	-1	0.0
Total	2	1	6	.143	11	9	8	1	78.2	93	54	0	4	34	28	4.69	65	.290	.365	372-2	.231	2	93	-11	-0.8
HACKMAN, LUTHER Luther Gean B 10.10.1974 Columbus, MS BR/TR 6-4/195# d9.1																									
1999	Col N	1	2	.333	5	3	0	0-0	16	26	19	5	0	12-0	10	10.69	54	.371	.463	5-0	.200	-0	74	-6	-0.9
2000	StL N	0	0	—	1	0	0	0-0	2.2	4	3	0	1	4-1	0	10.13	46	.400	.600	0-0	—	0		-2	-0.1
2001	StL N	1	2	.333	35	0	0	1-2	35.2	28	18	7	2	14-0	24	4.29	100	.212	.297	1-2	.000	-0		0	0.0
2002	StL N	5	4	.556	43	6	0	0-1	81	90	42	7	4	39-3	46	4.11	96	.287	.366	16-0	.063	-1	152	-2	-0.4
2003	SD N	2	2	.500	65	0	0	0-2	76.2	78	51	7	8	36-2	48	5.17	76	.261	.354	2-0	.000	-0		-13	-0.7
Total	5	9	10	.474	149	9	0	1-5	212	226	133	26	15	105-6	128	5.09	81	.274	.363	24-2	.083	-1	132	-23	-2.1
HADDIX, HARVEY Harvey "The Kitten" B 9.18.1925 Medway, OH D 1.8.1994 Springfield, OH BL/TL 5-9.5/170# d8.20 C14																									
1952	StL N	2	2	.500	7	6	3	0	42	31	18	4	2	10	31	2.79	133	.201	.259	14-0	.214	0*	148	3	0.3
1953	StL N☆	20	9	.690	36	33	19-**6**	1	253	220	97	24	4	69	163	3.06	139	.232	.287	97-3	.289	10*	122	33	4.5
1954	StL N❖	18	13	.581	43	35	13-3	4	259.2	247	114	26	3	77	184	3.57	115	.249	.303	93-0	.194	3*	120	17	2.2
1955	StL N★	12	16	.429	37	30	9-2	1	208	216	111	27	5	62-7	150	4.46	91	.268	.322	73-1	.164	0	89	-9	-0.9
1956	StL N	1	0	1.000	4	4	1-1	0	23.2	28	15	3	0	10-0	16	5.32	71	.298	.362	9-0	.222	1*	175	-4	-0.1
	Phi N	12	8	.600	31	26	11-2	2	206.2	196	98	23	6	55-9	154	3.48	107	.247	.299	93-0	.237	4*	121	3	0.7
	Year	13	8	.619	35	30	12-3	2	230.1	224	103	26	6	65-9	170	3.67	102	.253	.306	102-0	.235	5	128	-3	0.6
1957	Phi N	10	13	.435	27	25	8-1	0	170.2	176	84	18	1	39-4	136	4.06	94	.264	.303	68-2	.309	7*	80	-4	0.1
1958	Cin N	8	7	.533	29	26	8-1	0	184	191	79	28	7	43-7	110	3.52	118	.268	.314	61-6	.180	3*	102	12	1.2
1959	Pit N	12	12	.500	31	29	14-2	0	224.1	189	88	26	2	49-12	149	3.13	124	.228	**.271**	83-1	.145	-0	94	19	1.9
1960	†Pit N	11	10	.524	29	28	4	1	172.1	189	87	13	1	38-8	101	3.97	94	.277	.315	67-0	.254	4	110	-6	-0.1
1961	Pit N	10	6	.625	29	22	5-2	0	156	159	72	15	2	41-6	99	4.10	97	.266	.313	56-5	.143	0*	124	2	0.2
1962	Pit N	9	6	.600	28	20	4	0	141.1	146	74	17	2	42-6	101	4.20	94	.264	.318	52-0	.250	4	94	-3	0.1
1963	Pit N	3	4	.429	49	1	0	1	70	67	27	7	4	20-4	70	3.34	99	.256	.314	11-0	.182	1*	105	1	0.2
1964	Bal A	5	5	.500	49	0	0	10	89.2	68	26	4	2	23-8	90	2.31	155	.211	.265	19-2	.000	-2		13	1.5
1965	Bal A	3	2	.600	24	0	0	1	33.2	31	22	5	2	23-6	21	3.48	100	.248	.371	2-0	.000	-0		-3	-0.4
Total	14	136	113	.546	453	285	99-20	21	2235	2154	1012	240	43	601-77	1575	3.63	108	.252	.303	798-20	.212	35	109	74	11.4
HADDOCK, GEORGE George Silas "Gentleman George" B 12.25.1866 Portsmouth, NH D 4.18.1926 Boston, MA BR/TR 5-11/155# d9.27																									
1888	Was N	0	2	.000	2	2	2	0	16	9	8	0	1	2	3	2.25	123	.148	.188	5	.200	0	55	0	0.1
1889	Was N	11	19	.367	33	31	30	0	276.1	299	203	10	9	123	106	4.20	94	.268	.345	112	.223	7*	94	-9	0.0
1890	Buf P	9	26	.257	35	34	31	0	290.2	366	307	15	14	149	123	5.76	71	.295	.377	146	.247	7*	97	-62	-4.1
1891	Bos AA	34	11	.756	51	47	37-**5**	1	379.2	330	172	8	14	137	169	2.49	140	.226	.299	185	.243	9*	128	45	5.3
1892	Bro N	29	13	.690	46	44	39-3	1	381.1	340	190	11	14	163	153	3.14	101	.229	.311	158	.177	-1*	111	2	0.2
1893	Bro N	8	9	.471	23	20	12	0	151	193	145	10	7	89	37	5.60	79	.302	.393	85	.282	4*	102	-24	-1.7
1894	Phi N	4	3	.571	10	7	5	0	56	63	46	0	1	34	7	5.79	89	.281	.378	29-0	.172	-1	116	-3	-0.3
	Was N	0	4	.000	4	4	4	0	29	50	40	2	1	17	1	8.69	61	.373	.447	16-0	.188	-1*	87	-9	-0.8
	Year	4	7	.364	14	11	9	0	85	113	47	2	2	51	8	6.78	77	.316	.404	45-0	.178	-1	106	-13	-1.1
Total	7	95	87	.522	204	189	160-8	2	1580	1650	1111	56	61	714	599	4.07	93	.259	.340	736-0	.227	25	108	-60	-1.3
HADLEY, BUMP Irving Darius B 7.5.1904 Lynn, MA D 2.15.1963 Lynn, MA BR/TR 5-11/190# d4.20																									
1926	Was A	0	0	—	1	0	0	0	3	6	5	0	0	2	0	12.00	32	.429	.500	0-0	—	0		-3	-0.1
1927	Was A	14	6	.700	30	27	13	0	198.2	177	72	2	9	86	60	2.85	142	.244	.332	70-2	.271	2	107	28	2.7
1928	Was A	12	13	.480	33	31	16-3	0	231.2	236	105	4	8	100	80	3.54	113	.268	.348	81-3	.210	1	99	13	1.4
1929	Was A	6	16	.273	37	27	7-1	0	195.1	196	139	10	5	85	98	5.62	75	.263	.342	62-4	.097	-4	97	-28	-2.9
1930	Was A	15	11	.577	42	34	15-1	2	260.1	242	123	6	6	105	162	3.73	123	.247	.323	93-1	.226	1	99	25	2.2
1931	Was A	11	10	.524	**55**	11	2-1	8	179.2	145	81	4	1	92	124	3.06	140	**.218**	.314	54-5	.167	-1	82	21	2.3
1932	Chi A	1	1	.500	3	2	1	1	18.2	17	8	2	0	8	13	3.86	112	.262	.342	6-0	.167	-0	39	2	0.2

Year	Tm Lg	W	L	Pct	G	GS	CG-Sho	SV-BS	IP	H	R	HR	HB	BB-IB	SO	ERA	AERA	OAV	OOB	AB-SH	AVG	PB	Sup	APR	PW
	StL A	13	20	.394	40	33	12-1	1	229.2	244	160	21	8	163	132	5.53	88	.274	.391	78-6	.282	4	94	-14	-1.4
	Year	14	21	.400	43	35	13-1	2	248.1	261	165	23	8	171	145	5.40	89	.273	.388	84-6	.274	4	92	-10	-1.2
1933	StL A	15	20	.429	45	36	19-2	3	**316.2**	309	152	17	3	141	149	3.92	119	.256	.335	109-6	.156	-4	75	25	2.0
1934	StL A	10	16	.385	39	32	7-2	1	213	212	120	14	6	127	79	4.35	115	.257	.361	64-6	.203	-1	67	15	1.4
1935	Was A	10	15	.400	35	32	13	0	230.1	268	143	18	4	102	77	4.92	88	.292	.366	77-7	.195	1	110	-17	-1.3
1936	†NY A	14	4	.778	31	17	8-1	1	173.2	194	97	12	1	89	74	4.35	107	.283	.366	68-4	.235	2	129	5	0.6
1937	†NY A	11	8	.579	29	25	6	0	178.1	199	122	16	3	83	70	5.30	84	.281	.358	65-0	.169	1	127	-16	-1.4
1938	NY A	9	8	.529	29	17	8-1	1	167.1	165	79	13	3	66	61	3.60	126	.254	.325	54-3	.093	-1	113	18	1.6
1939	†NY A	12	6	.667	26	18	7-1	2	154	132	62	10	3	85	65	2.98	146	.237	.342	62-2	.177	-1	98	23	2.4
1940	NY A	3	5	.375	25	2	0	2	80	88	62	4	1	52	39	5.74	70	.276	.379	27-2	.111	-1	44	-19	-1.7
1941	NY N	1	0	1.000	3	2	0	0	13	19	10	1	0	9	4	6.23	59	.345	.438	3-1	.000	-0	161	-3	-0.3
	Phi A	4	6	.400	25	9	1	3	102.1	131	69	13	2	47	31	5.01	84	.310	.381	31-1	.129	-1	83	-11	-1.0
Total	16	161	165	.494	528	355	135-14	25	2945.2	2980	1609	167	63	1442	1318	4.24	105	.263	.350	1004-53	.189	-1	97	64	6.7
HAEFNER, MICKEY Milton Arnold B 10.9.1912 Lenzburg, IL D 1.3.1995 New Athens, IL BL/TL 5-8/160# d4.22																									
1943	Was A	11	5	.688	36	13	8-1	6	165.1	126	56	4	4	60	65	2.29	140	.208	.283	45-7	.133	0	138	15	1.6
1944	Was A	12	15	.444	31	28	18-3	1	228	221	94	7	4	71	86	3.04	107	.251	.310	70-8	.157	-1	91	6	0.7
1945	Was A	16	14	.533	37	28	19-1	3	238.1	226	103	10	7	69	83	3.47	89	.247	.305	82-6	.244	4	102	-6	-0.3
1946	Was A	14	11	.560	33	27	17-2	1	227.2	220	86	10	5	80	85	2.85	118	.251	.317	74-4	.203	4	97	14	1.9
1947	Was A	10	14	.417	31	28	14-4	1	193	195	86	8	4	85	77	3.64	102	.264	.343	59-3	.136	-1	59	3	0.1
1948	Was A	5	13	.278	28	20	4	0	147.2	151	86	7	6	61	45	4.02	108	.265	.342	43-1	.163	-1	58	0	0.0
1949	Was A	5	5	.500	19	12	4-1	0	91.2	85	51	7	2	53	23	4.42	96	.249	.353	25-3	.200	1*	86	-2	0.0
	Chi A	4	6	.400	14	12	4-1	1	80.1	84	40	9	5	41	17	4.37	95	.275	.370	23-6	.261	2	75	0	0.2
	Year	9	11	.450	33	24	8-2	1	172	169	44	16	7	94	40	4.40	96	.261	.361	48-9	.229	2	81	-2	0.2
1950	Chi A	1	6	.143	24	9	2	0	70.2	83	49	11	2	45	17	5.73	78	.299	.400	20-3	.200	0	80	-9	-0.8
	Bos N	0	2	.000	8	2	1	0	24	23	15	3	0	12	10	5.63	68	.247	.333	7-1	.286	1	92	-4	-0.2
Total	8	78	91	.462	261	179	91-13	13	1466.2	1414	666	76	39	577	508	3.50	102	.252	.326	448-42	.188	8	86	17	3.2
HAFFORD, LEO Leo Edgar B 9.17.1883 Somerville, MA D 10.2.1911 Willimantic, CT TR 6/170# d4.15																									
1906	Cin N	1	1	.500	3	1	1	0	19	13	9	0	1	11	5	0.95	291	.191	.313	9-0	.222	-0	212	2	0.1
HAFNER, FRANK Francis R. B 8.14.1867 Hannibal, MO D 3.2.1957 Hannibal, MO TR d5.5																									
1888	KC AA	0	2	.000	2	2	2	0	18	24	23	2	1	16	5	7.00	49	.308	.432	6	.000	-1	68	-6	-0.6
HAGAN, ART Arthur Charles B 3.17.1863 Providence, RI D 3.25.1936 Providence, RI TR d6.30																									
1883	Phi N	1	14	.067	17	16	15	0	137	207	151	2		33	39	5.45	57	.342	.376	59	.102	-5	75	-39	-3.5
	Buf N	0	2	.000	2	2	1	0	15	17	12	0		6	7	3.60	88	.270	.333	7	.000	-1	51	-1	-0.2
	Year	1	16	.059	19	18	16	0	152	224	15	2		39	46	5.27	59	.335	.371	66	.091	-7	72	-33	-3.7
1884	Buf N	1	2	.333	3	3	3	0	26	53	38	1		4	4	5.88	54	.384	.401	13	.308	0	135	-9	-0.7
Total	2	2	18	.100	22	21	19	0	178	277	201	3		43	50	5.36	58	.343	.376	79	.127	-6	81	-49	-4.4
HAGEMAN, CASEY Kurt Moritz B 5.12.1887 Mt.Oliver, PA D 4.1.1964 New Bedford, PA BL/TR 5-10.5/186# d9.18																									
1911	Bos A	0	2	.000	2	2	2	0	17	16	8	2	1	5	8	2.12	155	.262	.328	4-0	.000	-0	33	2	0.1
1912	Bos A	0	0	—	2	1	0	0	1.1	5	5	0	0	3	1	27.00	13	.500	.615	0-0	—	0	174	-3	-0.1
1914	StL N	2	4	.333	12	7	2	0	55.1	43	24	0	5	20	21	2.44	115	.215	.302	16-0	.125	-1	84	1	0.1
	Chi N	1	1	.500	16	1	0	1	46.2	44	26	0	3	12	17	3.47	80	.254	.314	15-0	.467	3	103	-3	0.1
	Year	3	5	.375	28	8	2	1	102	87	30	0	8	32	38	2.91	96	.233	.308	31-0	.290	2	87	-1	0.2
Total	3	3	7	.300	32	11	4	1	120.1	108	63	2	9	40	47	3.07	93	.243	.318	35-0	.257	2	86	-3	0.2
HAGEN, KEVIN Kevin Eugene B 3.8.1960 Renton, WA BR/TR 6-2/185# d6.4																									
1983	StL N	2	2	.500	9	4	0	0-0	22.1	34	15	0	0	7-0	7	4.84	75	.362	.406	5-0	.000	-1	73	-4	-0.6
1984	StL N	1	0	1.000	4	0	0	0-0	7.1	9	2	0	0	1-0	2	2.45	142	.300	.323	0-0	—	0		1	0.1
Total	2	3	2	.600	13	4	0	0-0	29.2	43	17	0	0	8-0	9	4.25	85	.347	.386	5-0	.000	-1	73	-3	-0.5
HAGERMAN, RIP Zerah Zequiel B 6.20.1888 Lyndon, KS D 1.30.1930 Albuquerque, NM BR/TR 6-2/200# d4.16																									
1909	Chi N	4	4	.500	13	7	4-1	0	79	64	29	0	2	28	32	1.82	139	.225	.298	23-0	.130	-0	79	4	0.4
1914	Cle A	9	15	.375	37	26	12-3	0	198	189	98	3	5	118	112	3.09	93	.265	.374	61-2	.016	-5	80	-5	-1.3
1915	Cle A	6	14	.300	29	22	7	0	151	156	85	4	6	77	69	3.52	87	.277	.370	38-2	.105	-2	86	-8	-1.4
1916	Cle A	0	0	—	2	0	0	0	3.2	5	6	1	2	2	1	12.27	25	.333	.474	1-0	.000	-0		-3	-0.2
Total	4	19	33	.365	81	55	23-4	0	431.2	414	218	8	15	225	214	3.09	93	.263	.360	123-4	.065	-9	83	-12	-2.5
HAHN, NOODLES Frank George B 4.29.1879 Nashville, TN D 2.6.1960 Candler, NC BL/TL 5-9/160# d4.18																									
1899	Cin N	23	8	.742	38	34	32-4	0	309	280	128	3	10	68	**145**	2.68	146	.242	.289	109-4	.147	-4	98	41	2.9
1900	Cin N	16	20	.444	39	37	29-**4**	0	311.1	306	145	4	7	89	**132**	3.27	112	.256	.312	115-3	.209	0	85	18	1.7
1901	Cin N	22	19	.537	42	42	**41**-2	0	**375.1**	370	159	12	9	69	**239**	2.71	118	.256	.294	141-4	.170	-1	95	21	2.0
1902	Cin N	23	12	.657	36	36	35-6	0	321	282	97	2	6	58	142	1.77	170	.236	.275	119-1	.185	0*	99	41	4.4
1903	Cin N	22	12	.647	34	34	34-5	0	296	297	125	3	8	47	127	2.52	141	.262	.297	112-4	.161	-2	101	32	3.1
1904	Cin N	16	18	.471	35	34	33-2	0	297.2	258	101	3	7	35	98	2.06	143	.234	.262	99-3	.172	1	70	27	3.2
1905	Cin N	5	3	.625	13	8	5-1	0	77	85	44	0	2	9	17	2.81	118	.272	.297	24-2	.167	-1	101	2	0.0
1906	NY A	3	2	.600	6	6	3-1	0	42	38	22	0	3	6	17	3.86	77	.245	.287	12-0	.333	1	113	-3	-0.3
Total	8	130	94	.580	243	231	212-25	0	2029.1	1916	821	27	52	381	917	2.55	133	.249	.289	731-21	.176	-5	92	179	17.0
HAHN, FRED Frederick Aloys B 2.16.1929 Nyack, NY D 8.16.1984 Valhalla, NY BR/TL 6-3/174# d4.19																									
1952	StL N	0	0	—	1	0	0	0	2	2	2	0	0	1	0	0.00	—	.250	.333	0-0	—	0		0	0.0
HAID, HAL Harold Augustine B 12.21.1897 Barberton, OH D 8.13.1952 Los Angeles, CA BR/TR 5-10.5/150# d9.5																									
1919	StL A	0	0	—	1	0	0	0	2	5	5	0	0	3	1	18.00	18	.556	.667	0-0	—	0		-3	-0.1
1928	StL N	2	2	.500	27	0	0	**5**	47	39	24	1	1	11	21	2.30	174	.218	.267	8-0	.375	1		5	0.6
1929	StL N	9	9	.500	38	14	8	4	154.2	171	90	8	5	66	41	4.07	115	.284	.360	49-3	.082	-4	101	6	0.2
1930	StL N	3	2	.600	20	0	0	2	33	38	17	1	3	14	13	4.09	123	.297	.379	3-0	.000	-0*		4	0.5
1931	Bos N	0	2	.000	27	0	0	1	56	59	36	3	3	16	20	4.50	84	.263	.321	8-0	.125	-1		-6	-0.3
1933	Chi A	0	0	—	6	0	0	0	14.2	18	15	2	2	13	7	7.98	53	.310	.452	4-0	.250	0		-6	-0.3
Total	6	14	15	.483	119	14	8	12	307.1	330	187	15	14	123	103	4.16	106	.275	.349	72-3	.125	-3	101	0	0.6
HAINES, JESSE Jesse Joseph "Pop" B 7.22.1893 Clayton, OH D 8.5.1978 Dayton, OH BR/TR 6/190# d7.20 C1 HF1970																									
1918	Cin N	0	0	—	1	0	0	0	5	5	1	0	0	1	2	1.80	148	.294	.333	1-0	1.000	0		1	0.1
1920	StL N	13	20	.394	**47**	37	19-4	2	301.2	303	136	9	9	80	120	2.98	100	.270	.324	108-4	.176	-1*	109	-5	-0.9
1921	StL N	18	12	.600	37	29	13-**3**	0	244.1	261	112	15	8	56	84	3.50	105	.286	.333	94-4	.181	-3*	141	7	0.5
1922	StL N	11	9	.550	29	26	11-2	0	183	207	103	10	4	45	62	3.84	101	.284	.329	72-1	.167	-2*	101	-3	-0.4
1923	StL N	20	13	.606	37	36	23-1	0	266	283	125	7	5	75	73	3.11	125	.275	.328	99-4	.202	-2	97	18	1.8
1924	StL N	8	19	.296	35	31	16-1	0	222.2	275	129	14	5	66	69	4.41	86	.309	.360	74-6	.189	-2	91	-15	-1.9
1925	StL N	13	14	.481	29	25	15	0	207	234	116	11	1	52	63	4.57	95	.290	.334	74-3	.176	-2	95	-2	-0.5
1926	†StL N	13	4	.765	33	20	14-3	1	183	186	76	10	2	48	46	3.25	120	.265	.314	61-2	.213	-1	112	14	1.0
1927	StL N	24	10	.706	38	36	**25-6**	1	300.2	273	114	11	5	77	89	2.72	145	.245	.297	114-4	.202	-1	98	39	4.1
1928	†StL N	20	8	.714	33	28	20-1	0	240.1	238	98	14	6	72	77	3.18	126	.266	.324	87-7	.184	-1	116	23	2.2
1929	StL N	13	10	.565	28	25	12	0	179.2	230	123	21	2	73	59	5.71	82	.313	.376	69-3	.159	-3	108	-18	-2.2
1930	†StL N	13	8	.619	29	24	14	1	182	215	107	15	1	54	68	4.30	117	.298	.348	65-4	.246	1	108	12	1.1
1931	StL N	12	3	.800	19	17	8-2	0	122.1	134	48	2	0	28	27	3.02	131	.278	.318	45-4	.133	-2	133	12	1.0
1932	StL N	3	5	.375	20	10	4-1	0	85.1	116	51	4	1	16	27	4.75	83	.326	.357	27-4	.185	0	83	-7	-0.6
1933	StL N	9	6	.600	32	10	5	1	115.1	113	46	3	1	37	37	2.50	139	.252	.311	30-1	.067	-2*	93	9	0.8
1934	†StL N	4	4	.500	37	6	0	1	90	86	42	6	4	19	17	3.50	121	.262	.311	19-1	.158	-1	126	**6**	0.5
1935	StL N	6	5	.545	30	11	3	2	115.1	110	49	4	1	28	24	3.59	114	.252	.299	33-2	.273	1	116	8	0.8
1936	StL N	7	5	.583	25	9	4	1	99.1	110	44	4	1	21	19	3.90	101	.284	.323	30-5	.167	-1	117	3	0.2
1937	StL N	3	3	.500	16	6	2	0	65.2	81	36	5	1	23	18	4.52	88	.303	.361	22-0	.182	-0	101	-3	-0.3
Total	19	210	158	.571	555	386	208-24	10	3208.2	3460	1556	165	57	871	981	3.64	108	.280	.330	1124-59	.186	-22	108	99	7.3

Year	Tm Lg	W	L	Pct	G	GS	CG-Sho	SV-BS	IP	H	R	HR	HB	BB-IB	SO	ERA	AERA	OAV	OOB	AB-SH	AVG	PB	Sup	APR	PW
HAISLIP, JIM James Clifton "Slim" B 8.4.1891 Farmersville, TX D 1.22.1970 Dallas, TX BR/TR 6-1/186# d8.27																									
1913	Phi N	0	0	—	1	0	0	0	3	4	4	0	0	3	0	6.00	56	.400	.538	1-0	.000	-0		-1	-0.1
HALAMA, JOHN John Thadeuz B 2.22.1972 Brooklyn, NY BL/TL 6-5/200# d4.2																									
1998	Hou N	1	1	.500	6	6	0	0-0	32.1	37	21	0	2	13-0	21	5.85	69	.296	.361	10-1	.000	-0	106	-6	-0.4
1999	Sea A	11	10	.524	38	24	1-1	0-0	179	193	88	20	7	56-3	105	4.22	112	.281	.338	5-0	.200	1	94	12	1.3
2000	†Sea A	14	9	.609	30	30	1-1	0-0	166.2	206	108	19	2	56-0	87	5.08	93	.308	.361	2-1	.500	0	117	-10	-1.1
2001	†Sea A	10	7	.588	31	17	0	0-0	110.1	132	69	18	6	26-0	50	4.73	88	.296	.340	1-1	.000	-0	143	-11	-1.3
2002	Sea A	6	5	.545	31	10	0	0-0	101	112	45	9	1	33-5	70	3.56	119	.281	.336	0-0	—	0	134	7	0.7
2003	Oak A	3	5	.375	35	13	0	0-0	108.2	117	68	18	2	36-2	51	4.22	107	.268	.325	0-0	—	0	108	-2	-0.1
Total	6	45	37	.549	171	100	2-2	0-0	698	797	399	84	20	220-10	384	4.49	100	.289	.342	18-3	.111	1	115	-10	-0.9
HALBRITER, ED Edward L. B 2.2.1860 Auburn, NY D 8.9.1936 Los Angeles, CA d5.23																									
1882	Phi AA	0	1	.000	1	1	1	0	8	17	12	1		4	4	7.88	36	.405	.457	4	.000	-1	146	-4	-0.4
HALE, DAD Ray Luther B 2.18.1880 Allegan, MI D 2.1.1946 Allegan, MI BR/TR 5-10/180# d4.21																									
1902	Bos N	1	3	.250	8	5	3	0	40	57	38	1	1	16	11	6.07	47	.333	.394	14-0	.000	-1	104	-14	-1.3
	Bal A	0	1	.000	3	2	1	0	14	21	14	0	1	6	6	4.50	84	.344	.412	6-0	.000	-1	124	-2	-0.2
Total	1	1	4	.200	11	7	4	0	54	78	52	1	2	22	17	5.67	54	.336	.398	20-0	.000	-2	110	-16	-1.5
HALICKI, ED Edward Louis B 10.4.1950 Newark, NJ BR/TR 6-7/220# d7.8																									
1974	SF N	1	8	.111	16	11	2	0-0	74.1	84	49	6	2	31-8	40	4.24	90	.275	.341	25-2	.240	1	69	-6	-0.6
1975	SF N	9	13	.409	24	23	7-2	0-0	159.2	143	76	6	3	59-7	153	3.49	109	.240	.307	53-5	.113	-2	82	3	0.2
1976	SF N	12	14	.462	32	31	8-4	0-0	186.1	171	86	10	2	61-7	130	3.62	100	.246	.308	53-7	.170	1	83	2	0.3
1977	SF N	16	12	.571	37	37	7-2	0-0	257.2	241	105	27	7	70-5	168	3.32	118	.244	.298	85-5	.176	3	98	20	2.2
1978	SF N	9	10	.474	29	28	9-4	1-0	199	166	74	11	7	45-9	105	2.85	121	.221	**.270**	66-8	.136	-2	102	12	0.8
1979	SF N	5	8	.385	33	19	3-1	0-0	125.2	134	82	12	3	47-8	81	4.58	76	.266	.330	34-2	.206	1	97	-21	-1.8
1980	SF N	0	0	—	11	2	0	0-0	25	29	15	5	0	10-1	14	5.40	66	.293	.355	6-0	.167	-0	101	-4	-0.2
	Cal A	3	1	.750	10	6	0	0-0	35.1	39	22	5	0	11-0	16	4.84	81	.279	.327	0-0	—	0	114	-4	-0.4
Total	7	55	66	.455	192	157	36-13	1-0	1063	1007	509	82	24	334-45	707	3.62	102	.247	.306	322-29	.165	3	92	2	0.5
HALL, DREW Andrew Clark B 3.27.1963 Louisville, KY BL/TL 6-4/205# d9.14																									
1986	Chi N	1	2	.333	5	4	1	1-0	23.2	24	12	3	0	10-0	21	4.56	89	.267	.340	7-0	.143	0	110	-1	-0.1
1987	Chi N	1	1	.500	21	0	0	0-1	32.2	40	31	4	0	14-0	20	6.89	62	.308	.370	4-0	.000	-0		-11	-0.6
1988	Chi N	1	1	.500	19	0	0	1-2	22.1	26	20	4	1	9-2	22	7.66	47	.295	.360	1-0	.000	0		-9	-0.8
1989	Tex A	2	1	.667	38	0	0	0-0	58.1	42	24	3	3	33-1	45	3.70	107	.207	.325	0-0	—	0		3	0.2
1990	Mon N	4	7	.364	42	0	0	3-2	58.1	52	35	6	0	29-5	40	5.09	72	.242	.327	4-1	.000	-0		-9	-1.7
Total	5	9	12	.429	125	4	1	5-5	195.1	184	122	20	4	95-8	148	5.21	75	.253	.339	16-1	.063	-1	110	-27	-3.0
HALL, CHARLEY Charles Louis "Sea Lion" (b: Carlos Clolo) B 7.27.1885 Ventura, CA D 12.6.1943 Ventura, CA BL/TR 6-1/187# d7.12																									
1906	Cin N	4	8	.333	14	9	9-1	1	95	86	56	1	8	50	49	3.32	83	.258	.368	47-1	.128	-1*	94	-8	-1.1
1907	Cin N	4	2	.667	11	8	5	0	68	51	22	0	4	43	25	2.51	103	.226	.359	26-1	.269	1*	110	2	0.3
1909	Bos A	6	4	.600	11	7	3	0	59.2	59	24	0	3	17	27	2.56	98	.271	.332	19-2	.158	-1	109	-1	-0.2
1910	Bos A	12	9	.571	35	16	13	2	188.2	142	68	6	9	73	95	1.91	134	.207	.292	82-5	.207	3*	100	10	1.6
1911	Bos A	8	7	.533	32	10	6	**4**	146.1	149	79	3	5	72	83	3.75	87	.279	.370	64-6	.141	-1*	134	-3	-0.5
1912	†Bos A	15	8	.652	34	20	9-2	2	191	178	85	3	4	70	83	3.02	113	.257	.329	75-3	.267	5	120	8	1.4
1913	Bos A	5	4	.556	35	4	2	2	105	97	67	1	5	46	48	3.43	86	.238	.322	42-1	.214	1	76	-10	-0.8
1916	StL N	0	4	.000	10	5	2	1	42.2	45	27	1	0	14	15	5.48	48	.280	.337	14-0	.143	-1	68	-11	-1.1
1918	Det A	0	1	.000	6	1	0	0	13.1	14	10	1	0	6	2	6.75	39	.269	.345	2-0	.000	-0	0	-5	-0.4
Total	9	54	47	.535	188	80	49-3	12	909.2	821	438	16	38	391	427	3.09	95	.248	.334	371-19	.197	7	107	-18	-0.8
HALL, BERT Herbert Ernest B 10.15.1888 Portland, OR D 7.18.1948 Seattle, WA BR/TR 5-10/178# d8.21																									
1911	Phi N	0	1	.000	7	1	0	0	18	19	11	0	1	13	8	4.00	86	.297	.423	3-0	.333	0	218	-1	-0.1
HALL, HERB Herbert Silas "Iron Duke" B 6.5.1893 Steeleville, IL D 7.1.1970 Fresno, CA BB/TR 6-4/220# d4.28																									
1918	Det A	0	0	—	3	0	0	0	6	12	11	0	2	7	1	15.00	18	.500	.636	1-0	.000	-0		-8	-0.4
HALL, JOHN John Sylvester B 1.9.1924 Muskogee, OK D 1.17.1995 Midwest City, OK BR/TR 6-2.5/170# d4.21																									
1948	Bro N	0	0	—	3	0	0	0	4.1	4	3	1	0	2	2	6.23	64	.267	.353	0-0	—	0		-1	0.0
HALL, JOSH Joshua Alan B 12.16.1980 Lynchburg, VA BR/TR 6-2/190# d8.2																									
2003	Cin N	0	2	.000	6	5	0	0-0	24.2	33	22	4	0	15-1	18	6.57	65	.314	.397	6-1	.167	-0	84	-7	-0.5
HALL, MARC Marcus B 8.12.1887 Joplin, MO D 2.24.1915 Joplin, MO BR/TR 6-1.5/190# d8.20																									
1910	StL A	1	7	.125	8	7	5	0	46.1	50	33	0	3	31	25	4.27	58	.289	.406	15-0	.067	-2	77	-9	-1.5
1913	Det A	10	12	.455	30	21	8-1	0	165	154	79	1	2	79	69	3.27	89	.259	.348	45-7	.089	-3	98	-5	-0.9
1914	Det A	4	6	.400	25	8	1	0	90.1	88	38	1	0	27	18	2.69	104	.267	.322	23-0	.043	-2	88	1	-0.2
Total	3	15	25	.375	63	36	14-1	0	301.2	292	150	2	5	137	112	3.25	87	.266	.350	83-7	.072	-7	92	-13	-2.6
HALL, DARREN Michael Darren B 7.14.1964 Marysville, OH BR/TR 6-3/205# d4.30																									
1994	Tor A	2	3	.400	30	0	0	17-3	31.2	26	12	3	1	14-1	28	3.41	141	.226	.315	0-0	—	0		5	1.0
1995	Tor A	0	2	.000	17	0	0	3-1	16.1	21	9	2	0	9-0	11	4.41	107	.309	.390	0-0	—	0		0	0.1
1996	LA N	0	2	.000	9	0	0	0-1	12	13	9	2	0	5-0	12	6.00	64	.271	.340	0-0	—	0		-3	-0.4
1997	LA N	3	2	.600	63	0	0	2-3	54.2	58	15	3	0	26-7	39	2.30	167	.283	.362	0-0	—	0		10	1.0
1998	LA N	0	3	.000	11	0	0	0-1	11.1	17	14	2	1	5-0	8	10.32	38	.347	.411	0-0	—	0		-8	-1.5
Total	5	5	12	.294	130	0	0	22-9	126	135	59	12	2	59-8	98	3.93	107	.278	.358	0-0	—	0		4	0.2
HALL, DICK Richard Wallace B 9.27.1930 St.Louis, MO BR/TR 6-6/200# d4.15.1952 ▲																									
1955	Pit N	6	6	.500	15	13	4	1	94.1	92	43	8	2	28-4	46	3.91	105	.253	.308	40-1	.175	1*	88	4	0.5
1956	Pit N	0	7	.000	19	9	1	1	62.1	64	36	8	0	21-3	27	4.76	79	.270	.327	29-0	.345	2*	62	-6	-0.3
1957	Pit N	0	0	—	8	0	0	0	10	17	12	4	1	5-1	7	10.80	35	.362	.434	1-0	.000	-0*		-7	-0.4
1959	Pit N	0	0	—	2	1	0	0	8.2	12	5	1	0	1-1	3	3.12	124	.333	.342	2-0	.000	-0	92	0	0.0
1960	KC A	8	13	.381	29	28	9-1	0	182.1	183	96	28	3	38-4	79	4.05	98	.261	.299	56-8	.107	-2*	97	-3	-0.6
1961	Bal A	7	5	.583	29	13	4-2	4	122.1	102	47	10	0	30-5	92	3.09	124	.227	.273	36-4	.139	-0*	103	11	1.0
1962	Bal A	6	6	.500	43	6	1	6	118.1	102	31	9	0	19-2	71	2.28	162	.230	.261	24-2	.167	1*	80	21	2.4
1963	Bal A	5	5	.500	47	3	0	12	111.2	91	39	12	4	16-6	74	2.98	116	.224	.258	28-2	.464	6*	102	7	1.5
1964	Bal A	9	1	.900	45	0	0	7	87.2	58	19	8	0	16-5	52	1.85	193	.188	.226	16-3	.125	-0		17	2.2
1965	Bal A	11	8	.579	48	0	0	12	93.2	84	34	8	0	11-7	79	3.07	113	.243	.265	15-2	.333	3*		6	1.4
1966	Bal A	6	2	.750	32	0	0	7	66	59	30	8	3	8-4	44	3.95	84	.233	.263	12-4	.167	0		-4	-0.5
1967	Phi N	10	8	.556	48	1	1	8	86	83	28	5	2	12-8	49	2.20	155	.255	.286	14-2	.071	-1	103	10	2.2
1968	Phi N	4	1	.800	32	0	0	0	46	53	26	6	1	5-3	31	4.89	61	.296	.316	3-0	.333	0		-9	-0.9
1969	†Bal A	5	2	.714	39	0	0	6-2	65.2	49	14	3	1	9-6	31	1.92	186	.213	.244	7-2	.286	1		13	1.7
1970	†Bal A	10	5	.667	32	0	0	3-4	61.1	51	25	8	0	6-2	30	3.08	118	.229	.247	12-1	.083	-1		3	0.5
1971	†Bal A	6	6	.500	27	0	0	1-3	43.1	52	27	4	1	11-9	26	4.98	67	.302	.342	5-1	.400	1		-8	-1.6
Total	16	93	75	.554	495	74	20-3	68-9	1259.2	1152	512	130	18	236-70	741	3.32	110	.244	.280	300-32	.203	10	97	55	9.1
HALL, BOB Robert Lewis B 12.22.1923 Swissvale, PA D 3.12.1983 St.Petersburg, FL BR/TR 6-2/195# d4.23																									
1949	Bos N	6	4	.600	31	6	2	0	74.1	77	40	7	1	41	43	4.36	87	.272	.366	22-0	.364	3	109	-4	-0.4
1950	Bos N	0	2	.000	21	4	0	0	50.1	58	43	8	2	33	22	6.97	55	.293	.399	12-0	.083	-1	172	-18	-0.9
1953	Pit N	3	12	.200	37	17	6-1	1	152	172	99	17	1	72	68	5.39	83	.286	.364	38-1	.158	0	74	-13	-1.1
Total	3	9	18	.333	89	27	8-1	1	276.2	307	182	32	4	146	133	5.40	77	.284	.371	72-1	.208	2	95	-35	-2.4
HALL, TOM Tom Edward B 11.23.1947 Thomasville, NC BL/TL 6/155# d6.9																									
1968	Min A	2	1	.667	8	4	0	0	29.2	27	15	1	1	12-2	18	2.43	127	.239	.317	9-1	.000	-1*	127	0	-0.1
1969	†Min A	8	7	.533	31	18	5-2	0-1	140.2	129	63	12	0	50-4	92	3.33	110	.243	.308	43-3	.186	1*	108	4	0.4
1970	†Min A	11	6	.647	52	11	1	4-0	155.1	94	46	11	2	66-4	184	2.55	146	.173	.262	44-6	.182	-0*	111	22	2.3

Year	Tm Lg	W	L	Pct	G	GS	CG-Sho	SV-BS	IP	H	R	HR	HB	BB-IB	SO	ERA	AERA	OAV	OOB	AB-SH	AVG	PB	Sup	APR	PW
1971	Min A	4	7	.364	48	11	0	9-1	129.2	104	54	13	0	58-5	137	3.33	107	.216	.297	34-1	.265	2*	96	3	0.5
1972	†Cin N	10	1	.909	47	7	1-1	8-0	124.1	77	43	13	2	56-1	134	2.61	123	.173	.268	30-3	.100	-1	126	7	0.6
1973	†Cin N	8	5	.615	54	7	0	8-6	103.2	74	43	13	0	48-10	96	3.47	98	.202	.293	22-0	.045	-2*	118	0	-0.3
1974	Cin N	3	1	.750	40	1	0	1-1	64	54	32	9	0	30-0	48	4.08	86	.232	.317	5-3	.000	-1	225	-4	-0.3
1975	Cin N	0	0	—	2	0	0	0-0	2	2	0	0	0	2-0	3	0.00	—	.250	.400	0-0	—	0		1	0.0
	NY N	4	3	.571	34	4	0	1-1	60.2	58	39	10	3	31-3	48	4.75	73	.254	.348	5-1	.400	1*	140	-10	-1.1
	Year	4	3	.571	36	4	0	1-1	62.2	60	45	10	3	33-3	51	4.60	75	.254	.350	5-1	.400	1	140	-9	-1.1
1976	NY N	1	1	.500	5	0	0	0-0	4.2	5	3	0	0	5-2	2	5.79	57	.250	.400	0-0	—	0		-1	-0.2
	†KC A	1	1	.500	31	0	0	1-0	30.1	28	19	4	0	18-1	25	4.45	79	.246	.346	0-0	—	0*		-4	-0.2
1977	KC A	0	0	—	6	0	0	0-1	7.2	4	3	2	0	6-0	10	3.52	115	.154	.313	0-0	—	0		1	0.0
Total	10	52	33	.612	358	63	7-3	32-11	852.2	656	360	88	8	382-32	797	3.27	107	.211	.297	192-18	.161	-1	114	19	1.6

HALL, BILL William Bernard "Beanie" B 2.22.1894 Charleston, WV D 8.15.1947 Newport, KY BR/TR 6-2/250# d7.4

Year	Tm Lg	W	L	Pct	G	GS	CG-Sho	SV-BS	IP	H	R	HR	HB	BB-IB	SO	ERA	AERA	OAV	OOB	AB-SH	AVG	PB	Sup	APR	PW
1913	Bro N	0	0	—	3	0	0	0	4.2	4	3	0	1	5	3	5.79	57	.267	.476	1-0	.000	-0		-1	-0.1

HALLA, JOHN John Arthur B 5.13.1884 St.Louis, MO D 9.30.1947 ElSegundo, CA BL/TL 5-11/175# d8.18

Year	Tm Lg	W	L	Pct	G	GS	CG-Sho	SV-BS	IP	H	R	HR	HB	BB-IB	SO	ERA	AERA	OAV	OOB	AB-SH	AVG	PB	Sup	APR	PW
1905	Cle A	0	0	—	3	0	0	0	12.2	12	6	0	1	0	4	2.84	92	.250	.265	5-0	.200	-0		-1	0.0

HALLADAY, ROY Harry Leroy B 5.14.1977 Denver, CO BR/TR 6-6/205# d9.20

Year	Tm Lg	W	L	Pct	G	GS	CG-Sho	SV-BS	IP	H	R	HR	HB	BB-IB	SO	ERA	AERA	OAV	OOB	AB-SH	AVG	PB	Sup	APR	PW
1998	Tor A	1	0	1.000	2	2	1	0-0	14	9	4	2	0	2-0	13	1.93	242	.176	.208	0-0	—	0	90	4	0.3
1999	Tor A	8	7	.533	36	18	1-1	1-0	149.1	156	76	19	4	79-1	82	3.92	126	.270	.359	2-1	.000	-0	83	15	1.2
2000	Tor A	4	7	.364	19	13	0	0-0	67.2	107	87	14	2	42-0	44	10.64	48	.357	.435	0-0	—	0	111	-40	-4.7
2001	Tor A	5	3	.625	17	16	1-1	0-0	105.1	97	41	3	1	25-0	96	3.16	145	.241	.287	1-1	.000	-0	82	16	1.1
2002	Tor A★	19	7	.731	34	34	2-1	0-0	**239.1**	223	93	10	7	62-6	168	2.93	157	.244	.297	6-0	.000	-1	104	39	4.0
2003	Tor A☆	**22**	7	**.759**	36	**36**	**9-2**	0-0	**266**	253	111	26	9	32-1	204	3.25	142	.247	.275	9-0	.111	-0	112	37	3.9
Total	6	59	31	.656	144	119	14-5	1-0	841.2	845	412	74	23	242-8	607	3.84	123	.258	.313	18-2	.056	-1	101	71	5.8

HALLAHAN, BILL William Anthony "Wild Bill" B 8.4.1902 Binghamton, NY D 7.8.1981 Binghamton, NY BR/TL 5-10.5/170# d4.16

Year	Tm Lg	W	L	Pct	G	GS	CG-Sho	SV-BS	IP	H	R	HR	HB	BB-IB	SO	ERA	AERA	OAV	OOB	AB-SH	AVG	PB	Sup	APR	PW
1925	StL N	1	0	1.000	6	0	0	0	15.1	14	6	0	0	11	8	3.52	123	.259	.385	3-0	.333	0		2	0.1
1926	†StL N	1	4	.200	19	3	0	0	56.2	45	27	1	1	32	28	3.65	107	.260	.379	16-0	.250	0	78	**2**	0.1
1929	StL N	4	4	.500	20	12	5	0	93.2	94	51	6	0	60	52	4.42	106	.269	.376	26-2	.154	-1	83	3	0.2
1930	†StL N	15	9	.625	35	32	13-2	2	237.1	233	135	15	0	126	**177**	4.66	108	.260	.351	81-11	.123	-6	100	13	0.5
1931	†StL N	**19**	9	.679	37	30	16-3	4	248.2	242	102	10	1	112	**159**	3.29	120	.259	.339	81-10	.099	-4	125	19	1.5
1932	StL N	12	7	.632	25	22	13-1	1	176.1	169	79	10	0	69	108	3.11	126	.253	.323	56-4	.214	2*	96	12	1.4
1933	StL N★	16	13	.552	36	32	16-2	0	244.1	245	114	6	0	98	93	3.50	99	.260	.330	80-6	.150	-0*	107	-2	-0.4
1934	†StL N	8	12	.400	32	26	10-2	0	162.2	195	93	2	0	66	70	4.26	99	.294	.358	55-4	.182	-1	109	-2	-0.4
1935	StL N	15	8	.652	40	23	8-2	1	181.1	196	91	7	1	57	73	3.42	120	.275	.329	56-4	.143	-2	123	8	0.8
1936	StL N	2	2	.500	9	6	1	0	37	58	28	4	0	17	16	6.32	62	.360	.421	9-3	.556	3	151	-9	-0.6
	Cin N	5	9	.357	23	19	5-2	0	135	150	78	3	1	57	32	4.33	88	.287	.359	47-1	.191	1	99	-9	-0.6
	Year	7	11	.389	32	25	6-2	0	172	208	82	7	1	74	48	4.76	81	.305	.373	56-4	.250	3	112	-15	-1.2
1937	Cin N	3	9	.250	21	9	2	0	63	90	52	3	2	29	18	6.14	61	.345	.414	21-1	.095	-1	90	-18	-2.9
1938	Phi N	1	8	.111	21	10	1	0	89	107	59	4	2	45	22	5.46	71	.295	.376	26-0	.192	-0	59	-14	-1.2
Total	12	102	94	.520	324	224	90-14	8	1740.1	1838	915	71	8	779	856	4.03	102	.274	.351	557-46	.162	-9	105	5	-1.5

HALLETT, JACK Jack Price B 11.13.1914 Toledo, OH D 6.11.1982 Toledo, OH BR/TR 6-4/215# d9.13 Mil 1943-45

Year	Tm Lg	W	L	Pct	G	GS	CG-Sho	SV-BS	IP	H	R	HR	HB	BB-IB	SO	ERA	AERA	OAV	OOB	AB-SH	AVG	PB	Sup	APR	PW
1940	Chi A	1	1	.500	2	2	1	0	14	15	10	1	1	6	9	6.43	69	.273	.355	5-0	.400	0	139	-2	-0.2
1941	Chi A	5	5	.500	22	6	3	0	74.2	96	57	7	3	38	25	6.03	68	.306	.386	26-1	.154	0	116	-16	-1.7
1942	Pit N	0	1	.000	3	3	2	0	22.1	23	12	0	0	8	16	4.84	70	.274	.337	8-0	.375	2	91	-3	0.0
1943	Pit N	1	2	.333	9	4	2-1	0	47.2	36	11	0	1	11	11	1.70	205	.212	.264	14-0	.286	2	98	9	0.7
1946	Pit N	5	7	.417	35	9	3-1	0	115	107	48	0	0	39	64	3.29	107	.267	.332	26-2	.231	0	40	4	0.4
1948	NY N	0	0	—	2	0	0	0	4	3	3	0	0	4	3	4.50	87	.214	.389	1-0	.000	-0		-1	0.0
Total	6	12	16	.429	73	24	11-2	0	277.2	280	141	8	5	106	128	4.05	92	.270	.340	80-3	.237	4	86	-9	-0.8

HALLSTROM, CHARLIE Charles E. "Swedish Wonder" B 1.22.1864 Jonkoping, Sweden D 5.6.1949 Chicago, IL d9.23

Year	Tm Lg	W	L	Pct	G	GS	CG-Sho	SV-BS	IP	H	R	HR	HB	BB-IB	SO	ERA	AERA	OAV	OOB	AB-SH	AVG	PB	Sup	APR	PW
1885	Pro N	0	1	.000	1	1	1	0	9	18	16	3		6	0	11.00	24	.409	.480	4	.000	-1	169	-8	-0.6

HAMANN, DOC Elmer Joseph B 12.21.1900 New Ulm, MN D 1.11.1973 Milwaukee, WI BR/TR 6-1/180# d9.21

Year	Tm Lg	W	L	Pct	G	GS	CG-Sho	SV-BS	IP	H	R	HR	HB	BB-IB	SO	ERA	AERA	OAV	OOB	AB-SH	AVG	PB	Sup	APR	PW
1922	Cle A	0	0	—	1	0	0	0	0	3	6	0	1	3	0	∞	—	1.000	1.000	0-0	—	0		-6	-0.4

HAMBRIGHT, ROGER Roger Dee B 3.26.1949 Sunnyside, WA BR/TR 5-10/180# d7.19

Year	Tm Lg	W	L	Pct	G	GS	CG-Sho	SV-BS	IP	H	R	HR	HB	BB-IB	SO	ERA	AERA	OAV	OOB	AB-SH	AVG	PB	Sup	APR	PW
1971	NY A	3	1	.750	18	0	0	2-0	26.2	22	13	5	0	10-2	14	4.39	74	.224	.294	2-0	.500	0		-3	-0.4

HAMILL, JOHN John Alexander Charles B 12.18.1860 New York, NY D 12.6.1911 Bristol, RI BR/TR 5-8/158# d5.1

Year	Tm Lg	W	L	Pct	G	GS	CG-Sho	SV-BS	IP	H	R	HR	HB	BB-IB	SO	ERA	AERA	OAV	OOB	AB-SH	AVG	PB	Sup	APR	PW
1884	Was AA	2	17	.105	19	19	18-1	0	156.2	197	158	8	5	43	50	4.48	68	.287	.333	71	.099	-3*	95	-28	-2.9

HAMILTON, DAVE David Edward B 12.13.1947 Seattle, WA BL/TL 6/190# d5.29

Year	Tm Lg	W	L	Pct	G	GS	CG-Sho	SV-BS	IP	H	R	HR	HB	BB-IB	SO	ERA	AERA	OAV	OOB	AB-SH	AVG	PB	Sup	APR	PW
1972	†Oak A	6	6	.500	25	14	1	0-0	101.1	94	34	7	1	31-2	55	2.93	97	.249	.304	26-1	.154	2	115	1	0.3
1973	Oak A	6	4	.600	16	11	1	0-0	69.2	74	37	8	1	24-0	34	4.39	81	.274	.334	0-0	—	0	101	-6	-0.8
1974	Oak A	7	4	.636	29	18	1-1	0-0	117	104	45	10	5	48-3	69	3.15	105	.241	.322	0-0	—	0	115	4	0.3
1975	Oak A	1	2	.333	11	4	0	0-0	35.2	42	19	4	0	18-1	20	4.04	90	.290	.366	0-0	—	0	61	-2	-0.2
	Chi A	6	5	.545	30	1	0	6-2	69.2	63	23	4	0	29-2	51	2.84	137	.246	.327	0-0	—	0	68	8	1.4
	Year	7	7	.500	41	5	0	6-2	105.1	105	26	8	0	47-3	71	3.25	117	.262	.338	0-0	—	0	60	7	1.2
1976	Chi A	6	6	.500	45	1	0	10-3	90.1	81	38	4	4	45-6	62	3.59	99	.243	.335	0-0	—	0	172	0	0.0
1977	Chi A	4	5	.444	55	0	0	9-6	67.1	71	33	6	0	33-4	45	3.61	114	.270	.344	0-0	—	0		3	0.4
1978	StL N	0	0	—	13	0	0	0-1	14	16	13	5	0	6-0	8	6.43	55	.296	.367	1-0	.000	-0		-5	-0.3
	Pit N	0	2	.000	16	0	0	1-1	26.1	23	16	2	0	12-2	15	3.42	108	.221	.302	6-0	.000	-1		-1	-0.2
	Year	0	2	.000	29	0	0	1-2	40.1	39	36	7	0	18-2	23	4.46	82	.247	.324	7-0	.000	-1		-7	-0.5
1979	Oak A	3	4	.429	40	7	1	5-1	82.2	80	42	5	1	43-2	52	3.70	110	.261	.349	0-0	—	0	67	2	0.2
1980	Oak A	0	3	.000	21	1	0	0-0	30	44	39	6	3	28-2	23	11.40	33	.344	.466	0-0	—	0	95	-25	-2.2
Total	9	39	41	.488	301	57	4-1	31-14	704	692	339	61	15	317-24	434	3.85	93	.259	.338	33-1	.121	1	96	-21	-1.1

HAMILTON, EARL Earl Andrew B 7.19.1891 Gibson City, IL D 11.17.1968 Anaheim, CA BL/TL 5-8/160# d4.14 Mil 1918

Year	Tm Lg	W	L	Pct	G	GS	CG-Sho	SV-BS	IP	H	R	HR	HB	BB-IB	SO	ERA	AERA	OAV	OOB	AB-SH	AVG	PB	Sup	APR	PW
1911	StL A	5	12	.294	32	17	10-1	0	177	191	103	4	4	69	55	3.97	85	.284	.354	56-1	.107	-1	99	-9	-0.8
1912	StL A	11	14	.440	41	26	17-1	2	249.2	228	117	2	9	86	139	3.24	102	.248	.319	73-6	.178	-0	56	4	0.3
1913	StL A	13	12	.520	31	24	19-3	1	217.1	197	95	3	9	83	101	2.57	114	.244	.321	74-2	.135	-2	100	5	0.3
1914	StL A	16	18	.471	44	35	20-5	2	302.1	265	111	5	10	100	111	2.50	108	.239	.307	85-7	.176	4	85	8	1.3
1915	StL A	9	17	.346	35	28	13-1	0	204	203	98	4	12	69	63	2.87	100	.274	.346	62-2	.113	-2	85	-2	-0.6
1916	StL A	0	0	—	1	0	0	0	4	4	5	0	0	4	0	9.00	31	.250	.400	0-0	—	0		-3	-0.2
	Det A	1	2	.333	5	5	3	0	37.1	34	14	0	4	22	7	2.65	108	.254	.375	13-0	.077	-1	121	1	0.0
	StL A	5	7	.417	22	12	3	0	91.1	97	44	2	2	26	25	3.05	90	.284	.339	24-0	.000	-1	90	-5	-0.8
	Year	6	9	.400	28	17	6	0	132.2	135	47	2	6	52	32	3.12	89	.275	.352	37-0	.027	-2	99	-7	-1.0
1917	StL A	0	9	.000	27	8	2	1	83	86	46	1	2	41	19	3.14	83	.274	.361	19-2	.368	3	38	-7	-0.5
1918	Pit N	6	0	1.000	6	6	6-1	0	54	47	7	0	0	13	20	0.83	344	.242	.290	21-0	.286	1	141	12	1.6
1919	Pit N	8	11	.421	28	19	9-1	1	160.1	167	73	3	5	49	39	3.31	91	.280	.340	52-1	.135	-2	83	-7	-1.0
1920	Pit N	10	13	.435	39	23	12	3	230.1	223	99	2	9	69	74	3.24	99	.258	.314	67-7	.149	-3	94	0	-0.3
1921	Pit N	13	15	.464	35	30	12-2	0	225	237	103	5	8	58	59	3.36	114	.272	.323	75-5	.160	-0	95	11	1.3
1922	Pit N	11	7	.611	33	14	9-1	2	160	183	84	6	1	40	34	3.99	102	.296	.339	58-3	.155	-2	126	2	0.0
1923	Pit N	7	9	.438	28	15	5	1	141	148	67	6	1	42	42	3.77	106	.271	.324	52-1	.173	-2	83	5	0.4
1924	Phi N	0	1	.000	3	0	0	0	6	9	9	0	1	2	2	10.50	42	.391	.462	2-0	.000	-0		-4	-0.5
Total	14	115	147	.439	410	262	140-16	13	2342.2	2319	1075	43	70	773	790	3.16	102	.265	.329	733-37	.153	-9	89	11	0.5

HAMILTON, JACK Jack Edwin B 12.25.1938 Burlington, IA BR/TR 6/200# d4.13

Year	Tm Lg	W	L	Pct	G	GS	CG-Sho	SV-BS	IP	H	R	HR	HB	BB-IB	SO	ERA	AERA	OAV	OOB	AB-SH	AVG	PB	Sup	APR	PW
1962	Phi N	9	12	.429	41	26	4-1	2	182	185	115	18	5	107-8	101	5.09	76	.268	.366	54-5	.056	-4	97	-25	-2.8
1963	Phi N	2	1	.667	19	1	0	1	30	22	19	3	0	17-2	23	5.40	60	.200	.307	3-0	.000	-0	27	-7	-0.7
1964	Det A	0	1	.000	5	1	0	0	15	24	17	2	1	8-0	5	8.40	44	.364	.434	3-0	.000	-0	49	-9	-0.5

Year	Tm Lg	W	L	Pct	G	GS	CG-Sho	SV-BS	IP	H	R	HR	HB	BB-IB	SO	ERA	AERA	OAV	OOB	AB-SH	AVG	PB	Sup	APR	PW
1965	Det A	1	1	.500	4	1	0	0	4.1	6	7	1	0	4-0	3	14.54	24	.316	.417	0-0	—	0	76	-5	-0.9
1966	NY N	6	13	.316	57	13	3-1	13	148.2	138	89	13	5	88-4	93	3.93	92	.248	.354	38-1	.132	-1	102	-11	-1.6
1967	NY N	2	0	1.000	17	1	0	1	31.1	24	15	2	1	16-5	22	3.73	91	.205	.306	5-0	.200	1	233	-1	0.0
	Cal A	9	6	.600	26	20	0	0	119.1	104	47	6	1	63-3	74	3.24	97	.239	.334	38-2	.158	-0	110	0	-0.1
1968	Cal A	3	1	.750	21	2	1	2	38	34	15	0	0	15-1	18	3.32	88	.246	.316	7-0	.143	-0	105	-1	-0.2
1969	Cle A	0	2	.000	20	0	0	1-2	30.2	37	17	2	0	23-4	13	4.40	86	.316	.426	2-0	.000	-0		-2	-0.2
	Chi A	0	3	.000	8	0	0	0-0	12.1	23	16	1	0	7-3	5	11.68	33	.411	.476	0-0	—	0		-10	-1.8
	Year	0	5	.000	28	0	0	1-2	43	60	37	3	0	30-7	18	6.49	59	.347	.441	2-0	.000	-0		-11	-2.0
Total	8	32	40	.444	218	65	8-2	20-2	611.2	597	357	48	13	348-30	357	4.53	78	.259	.356	150-8	.107	-6	102	-71	-8.8
HAMILTON, JOEY Johns Joseph B 9.9.1970 Statesboro, GA BR/TR 6-4/220# d5.24																									
1994	SD N	9	6	.600	16	16	1-1	0-0	108.2	98	40	7	6	29-3	61	2.98	138	.241	.300	40-5	.000	-4	104	14	1.4
1995	SD N	6	9	.400	31	30	2-2	0-0	204.1	189	89	17	11	56-5	123	3.08	131	.246	.305	65-5	.108	-2	99	18	1.0
1996	†SD N	15	9	.625	34	33	3-1	0-0	211.2	206	100	19	9	83-3	184	4.17	95	.256	.330	68-11	.162	1	102	-1	0.1
1997	SD N	12	7	.632	31	29	1	0-0	192.2	199	100	22	12	69-2	124	4.25	91	.271	.340	54-9	.130	1	122	-8	-0.7
1998	†SD N	13	13	.500	34	34	0	0-0	217.1	220	113	15	8	106-10	147	4.27	92	.267	.353	71-2	.141	0*	83	-10	-1.1
1999	Tor A	7	8	.467	22	18	0	0-0	98	118	73	13	3	39-0	56	6.52	76	.298	.364	2-0	.000	-0	107	-15	-1.9
2000	Tor A	2	1	.667	6	6	0	0-0	33	28	13	3	2	12-0	15	3.55	143	.233	.311	0-0	—	0	114	6	0.4
2001	Tor A	5	8	.385	22	22	0	0-0	122.1	170	88	17	3	38-1	82	5.89	78	.339	.384	3-0	.333	1	101	-18	-1.5
	Cin N	1	2	.333	4	4	0	0-0	17.1	23	12	3	1	6-0	10	6.23	73	.329	.390	5-0	.000	-1	71	-3	-0.4
2002	Cin N	4	10	.286	39	17	0	1-1	124.2	136	78	11	6	50-2	85	5.27	81	.279	.351	28-4	.250	2	96	-12	-1.1
2003	Cin N	0	0	—	3	0	0	0-0	10.2	21	15	3	0	5-0	7	12.66	34	.404	.456	3-0	.000	-0		-9	-0.5
Total	10	74	73	.503	242	209	7-4	1-1	1340.2	1408	721	130	61	493-26	894	4.44	94	.273	.341	339-36	.127	-2	101	-38	-4.3
HAMILTON, STEVE Steve Absher B 11.30.1935 Columbia, KY D 12.2.1997 Morehead, KY BL/TL 6-7/195# d4.23 C1																									
1961	Cle A	0	0	—	2	0	0	0	3	2	1	0	0	3-0	4	3.00	131	.200	.385	1-0	1.000	0		0	0.1
1962	Was A	3	8	.273	41	10	1	2	107.1	103	51	10	3	39-5	83	3.77	107	.248	.317	26-3	.077	-1*	88	2	0.2
1963	Was A	0	1	.000	3	0	0	0	2	5	3	0	0	2-0	1	13.50	27	.556	.583	0-0	—	0		-2	-0.4
	†NY A	5	1	.833	34	0	0	5	62.1	49	19	3	1	24-2	63	2.60	135	.220	.296	14-5	.286	1		7	1.0
	Year	5	2	.714	37	0	0	5	64.1	54	26	3	1	26-2	64	2.94	120	.233	.309	14-5	.286	1		5	0.6
1964	†NY A	7	2	.778	30	3	1	3	60.1	55	24	6	0	15-0	49	3.28	110	.246	.289	20-0	.200	1*	164	2	0.4
1965	NY A	3	1	.750	46	1	0	5	58.1	47	12	2	0	16-5	51	1.39	245	.214	.265	6-0	.167	0	103	12	1.0
1966	NY A	8	3	.727	44	3	1-1	3	90	69	32	8	3	22-3	57	3.00	111	.218	.273	19-2	.053	-2	62	4	0.3
1967	NY A	2	4	.333	44	0	0	4	62	57	25	7	1	23-4	55	3.48	90	.250	.320	9-1	.111	-0		-1	-0.2
1968	NY A	2	2	.500	40	0	0	11	50.2	37	13	0	1	13-4	42	2.13	136	.211	.268	3-0	.000	0		5	0.7
1969	NY A	3	4	.429	38	0	0	2-2	57	39	22	7	0	21-5	39	3.32	105	.194	.269	5-0	.000	-1		2	0.1
1970	NY A	4	3	.571	35	0	0	3-1	45.1	36	16	3	1	16-5	33	2.78	127	.222	.294	6-0	.000	-1		4	0.6
	Chi A	0	0	—	3	0	0	0-0	3	4	2	0	0	1-0	3	6.00	65	.333	.385	0-0	—	0		-1	0.0
	Year	4	3	.571	38	0	0	3-1	48.1	40	20	3	1	17-5	36	2.98	119	.230	.301	6-0	.000	-1		3	0.6
1971	†SF N	2	2	.500	39	0	0	4-3	44.2	29	15	4	1	11-6	38	3.02	113	.186	.238	2-0	.000	-0		3	0.3
1972	Chi N	1	0	1.000	22	0	0	0-0	17	24	9	1	1	8-3	13	4.76	80	.333	.398	1-0	.000	-0		-1	-0.1
Total	12	40	31	.563	421	17	3-1	42-6	663	556	244	51	12	214-42	531	3.05	114	.229	.293	112-11	.125	-2	106	36	4.0
HAMLIN, LUKE Luke Daniel "Hot Potato" B 7.3.1904 Ferris Center, MI D 2.18.1978 Clare, MI BL/TR 6-2/168# d9.18																									
1933	Det A	1	0	1.000	3	3	0	0	16.2	20	11	3	0	10	10	4.86	89	.294	.385	5-1	.400	1	118	-1	0.0
1934	Det A	2	3	.400	20	5	1	1	75.1	87	48	11	0	44	30	5.38	82	.289	.380	26-3	.231	-0	174	-7	-0.4
1937	Bro N	11	13	.458	39	25	11-1	1	185.2	183	96	4	0	48	93	3.59	113	.252	.298	59-5	.186	-1*	85	7	0.6
1938	Bro N	12	15	.444	44	30	10-3	6	237.1	243	111	14	2	65	97	3.68	106	.263	.313	78-4	.141	-3	92	7	0.3
1939	Bro N	20	13	.606	40	**36**	19-2	0	269.2	255	115	27	0	54	88	3.64	111	.248	.285	103-6	.126	-5	102	15	0.9
1940	Bro N	9	8	.529	33	25	9-2	0	182.1	183	77	17	2	34	91	3.06	131	.256	.292	58-8	.086	-4*	79	15	0.6
1941	Bro N	8	8	.500	30	20	5-1	1	136	139	75	14	2	41	58	4.24	87	.261	.316	41-3	.146	-1	130	-9	-1.1
1942	Pit N	4	4	.500	23	14	6-1	0	112	128	58	3	1	19	38	3.94	86	.281	.312	37-3	.243	1	115	-7	-0.5
1944	Phi A	6	12	.333	29	23	9-2	0	190	204	94	13	3	38	58	3.74	93	.271	.309	56-4	.232	3	88	-6	-0.5
Total	9	73	76	.490	261	181	70-12	9	1405	1442	685	106	10	353	563	3.77	103	.262	.308	463-37	.164	-8	99	14	-0.1
HAMM, PETE Peter Whitfield B 9.20.1947 Buffalo, NY BR/TR 6-5/210# d7.29																									
1970	Min A	0	2	.000	10	0	0	0-0	16.1	17	10	3	0	7-1	3	5.51	68	.262	.333	1-0	.000	-0		-3	-0.3
1971	Min A	2	4	.333	13	8	1	0-0	44	55	33	7	1	18-1	16	6.75	53	.309	.372	11-1	.273	1	126	-14	-1.6
Total	2	2	6	.250	23	8	1	0-0	60.1	72	43	10	1	25-2	19	6.41	56	.296	.362	12-1	.250	1	126	-17	-1.9
HAMMAKER, ATLEE Charlton Atlee B 1.24.1958 Carmel, CA BB/TL 6-3/200# d8.13																									
1981	KC A	1	3	.250	10	6	0	0-0	39	44	24	2	0	12-1	11	5.54	65	.286	.335	0-0	—	0	95	-7	-0.7
1982	SF N	12	8	.600	29	27	4-1	0-0	175	189	86	16	2	28-8	102	4.11	88	.278	.307	59-1	.068	-4	95	-7	-1.1
1983	SF N★	10	9	.526	23	23	8-3	0-0	172.1	147	57	9	3	32-12	127	**2.25**	**158**	.228	**.266**	59-3	.102	-1	88	22	2.4
1984	SF N	2	0	1.000	6	6	0	0-0	33	32	10	2	0	9-1	24	2.18	161	.256	.301	11-0	.182	1	113	5	0.4
1985	SF N	5	12	.294	29	29	1-1	0-0	170.2	161	81	17	0	47-5	100	3.74	92	.247	.295	47-6	.085	-3	87	-5	-0.7
1987	†SF N	10	10	.500	31	27	2	0-0	168.1	159	73	22	3	57-10	107	3.58	107	.248	.312	57-2	.123	-1	114	6	0.5
1988	SF N	9	9	.500	43	17	3-1	5-2	144.2	136	68	11	3	41-9	65	3.73	88	.248	.302	33-4	.121	-0	91	-8	-0.9
1989	†SF N	6	6	.500	28	9	0	0-1	76.2	78	34	5	1	23-2	30	3.76	90	.271	.323	19-4	.368	2	128	-2	-0.1
1990	SF N	4	5	.444	25	6	0	0-0	67.1	69	33	7	0	21-4	28	4.28	85	.273	.324	17-1	.059	-1	120	-4	-0.6
	SD N	0	4	.000	9	1	0	0-0	19.1	16	11	1	0	6-1	16	4.66	82	.213	.272	2-0	.500	0	118	-2	-0.3
	Year	4	9	.308	34	7	0	0-0	86.2	85	16	8	0	27-5	44	4.36	85	.259	.312	19-1	.105	-0	119	-5	-0.9
1991	SD N	0	1	.000	1	1	0	0-0	4.2	8	7	0	0	3-0	1	5.79	66	.364	.440	1-0	.000	-0	24	-3	-0.4
1994	Chi A	0	0	—	2	0	0	0-0	1.1	1	0	0	0	0-0	1	0.00	—	.200	.200	0-0	—	0		1	0.0
1995	Chi A	0	0	—	13	0	0	0-0	6.1	11	9	2	1	8-1	3	12.79	35	.393	.541	0-0	—	0		-6	-0.3
Total	12	59	67	.468	249	152	18-6	5-3	1078.2	1051	493	94	13	287-54	615	3.66	97	.255	.304	305-21	.118	-7	99	-10	-1.8
HAMMOND, CHRIS Christopher Andrew B 1.21.1966 Atlanta, GA BL/TL 6-1/195# d7.16 b-Steve																									
1990	Cin N	0	2	.000	3	3	0	0-0	11.1	13	9	2	0	12-1	4	6.35	62	.302	.455	3-0	.000	-0	91	-3	-0.5
1991	Cin N	7	7	.500	20	18	0	0-0	99.2	92	51	4	2	48-3	50	4.06	94	.250	.339	34-1	.353	5	77	-3	0.1
1992	Cin N	7	10	.412	28	26	0	0-0	147.1	149	75	13	3	55-6	79	4.21	86	.266	.333	44-3	.136	2*	90	-10	-0.8
1993	Fla N	11	12	.478	32	32	1	0-0	191	207	106	18	1	66-2	108	4.66	93	.277	.336	63-5	.190	4*	87	-6	-0.2
1994	Fla N	4	4	.500	13	13	1-1	0-0	73.1	79	30	5	1	23-1	40	3.07	143	.281	.336	22-3	.136	0	88	10	0.9
1995	Fla N	9	6	.600	25	24	3-2	0-0	161	157	73	17	9	47-2	126	3.80	111	.256	.315	48-5	.271	6	113	8	1.3
1996	Fla N	5	8	.385	38	9	0	0-0	81	104	65	14	4	27-3	50	6.56	62	.315	.370	15-2	.067	-1	106	-23	-3.2
1997	Bos A	3	4	.429	29	8	0	1-1	65.1	81	45	5	2	27-4	48	5.92	78	.310	.375	0-0	—	0	121	-8	-0.8
1998	Fla N	0	2	.000	3	3	0	0-0	13.2	20	11	3	1	8-0	8	6.59	62	.357	.446	5-0	.200	0	68	-4	-0.5
2002	†Atl N	7	2	.778	63	0	0	0-2	76	53	15	1	1	31-9	63	0.95	433	.195	.278	1-0	.000	0		24	2.7
2003	†NY A	3	2	.600	62	0	0	1-3	63	65	23	5	2	11-0	45	2.86	153	.270	.304	0-0	—	0		11	0.7
Total	11	56	59	.487	316	136	5-3	2-6	982.2	1020	503	87	26	355-31	621	4.16	99	.270	.335	235-19	.204	16	94	-4	-0.3
HAMNER, GRANNY Granville Wilbur B 4.26.1927 Richmond, VA D 9.12.1993 Philadelphia, PA BR/TR 5-10/163# d9.14.1944 Mil 1945 b-Garvin ▲																									
1956	Phi N	0	1	.000	3	1	0	0	8.1	10	4	0	0	2-0	4	4.32	86	.294	.333	401-3	.224	1*	71	0	0.0
1957	Phi N	0	0	—	1	0	0	0	1	1	0	0	0	0-0	1	0.00	—	.250	.250	502-7	.227	0*		0	0.0
1962	KC A	0	1	.000	3	0	0	0	4	10	6	0	0	6-1	0	9.00	47	.476	.593	0-0	—	0		-3	-0.5
Total	3	0	2	.000	7	1	0	0	13.1	21	10	0	0	8-1	5	5.40	72	.356	.433	903-10	.226	1	71	-3	-0.5
HAMNER, RALPH Ralph Conant "Bruz" B 9.12.1916 Gibsland, LA D 5.22.2001 Little Rock, AR BR/TR 6-3/165# d4.28																									
1946	Chi A	2	7	.222	25	7	1	1	71.1	80	47	2	5	39	29	4.42	77	.276	.371	18-2	.167	0	54	-10	-1.2
1947	Chi N	1	2	.333	3	3	2	0	25	24	10	0	0	16	14	2.52	157	.267	.377	8-0	.125	-0	52	3	0.3
1948	Chi N	5	9	.357	27	17	5	0	111.1	110	63	12	5	69	53	4.69	83	.259	.369	33-1	.182	1	106	-8	-0.7
1949	Chi N	0	2	.000	6	1	0	0	12.1	22	13	2	1	8	3	8.76	46	.407	.492	2-1	.000	-0	44	-6	-0.8
Total	4	8	20	.286	61	28	8	1	220	236	133	16	11	132	99	4.58	82	.275	.378	61-4	.164	0	86	-21	-2.4

Year	Tm Lg	W	L	Pct	G	GS	CG-Sho	SV-BS	IP	H	R	HR	HB	BB-IB	SO	ERA	AERA	OAV	OOB	AB-SH	AVG	PB	Sup	APR	PW
HAMPTON, MIKE Michael William B 9.9.1972 Brooksville, FL BR/TL 5-10/180# d4.17																									
1993	Sea A	1	3	.250	13	3	0	1-0	17	28	20	3	0	17-3	8	9.53	46	.368	.479	0-0	—	0	90	-10	-1.8
1994	Hou N	2	1	.667	44	0	0	0-1	41.1	46	19	4	2	16-1	24	3.70	107	.282	.354	1-0	.000	-0		1	0.1
1995	Hou N	9	8	.529	24	24	0	0-0	150.2	141	73	13	4	49-3	115	3.35	116	.247	.308	48-4	.146	1	129	5	0.6
1996	Hou N	10	10	.500	27	27	2-1	0-0	160.1	175	79	12	3	49-1	101	3.59	108	.280	.333	42-7	.238	4*	116	2	0.7
1997	†Hou N	15	10	.600	34	34	7-2	0-0	223	217	105	16	2	77-2	139	3.83	104	.257	.318	73-10	.137	1	123	5	0.8
1998	†Hou N	11	7	.611	32	32	1-1	0-0	211.2	227	92	18	5	81-1	137	3.36	121	.278	.344	61-7	.262	7	110	14	2.0
1999	†Hou N★	**22**	4	**.846**	34	34	3-2	0-0	239	206	86	12	5	101-2	177	2.90	152	.241	.322	74-5	.311	11	140	40	**5.3**
2000	†NY N	15	10	.600	33	33	3-1	0-0	217.2	194	89	10	8	99-5	151	3.14	140	.241	.328	73-4	.274	6*	114	30	3.7
2001	Col N★	14	13	.519	32	32	2-1	0-0	203	236	138	31	8	85-7	122	5.41	99	.296	.367	79-5	.291	8*	105	-4	0.5
2002	Col N	7	15	.318	30	30	0	0-0	178.2	228	135	24	7	91-4	74	6.15	78	.313	.390	64-1	.344	7*	86	-24	-1.9
2003	†Atl N	14	8	.636	31	31	1	0-0	190	186	91	14	1	78-4	110	3.84	110	.255	.326	60-9	.183	5*	115	8	1.6
Total	11	120	89	.574	334	280	19-8	1-1	1832.1	1884	927	157	45	743-33	1158	3.96	110	.269	.340	575-52	.247	48	115	67	11.6
HANCOCK, JOSH Joshua Morgan B 4.11.1978 Cleveland, MS BR/TR 6-3/217# d9.10																									
2002	Bos A	0	1	.000	3	1	0	0-0	7.1	5	3	1	0	2-0	6	3.68	122	.200	.259	0-0	—	0	41	1	0.1
2003	Phi N	0	0	—	2	0	0	0-0	3	2	1	0	0	0-0	4	3.00	133	.182	.182	0-0	—	0		0	0.0
Total	2	0	1	.000	5	1	0	0-0	10.1	7	4	1	0	2-0	10	3.48	125	.194	.237	0-0	—	0	41	1	0.1
HANCOCK, LEE Leland David B 6.27.1967 N.Hollywood, CA BL/TL 6-4/215# d9.3																									
1995	Pit N	0	0	—	11	0	0	0-0	14	10	3	0	0	2-0	6	1.93	223	.192	.222	0-0	—	0		4	0.2
1996	Pit N	0	0	—	13	0	0	0-0	18.1	21	18	5	2	10-3	13	6.38	68	.276	.375	0-0	—	0		-6	-0.2
Total	2	0	0	—	24	0	0	0-0	32.1	31	21	5	2	12-3	19	4.45	97	.242	.317	0-0	—	0		-2	0.0
HANCOCK, RYAN Ryan Lee B 11.11.1971 Santa Clara, CA BR/TR 6-2/220# d6.8																									
1996	Cal A	4	1	.800	11	4	0	0-0	27.2	34	23	2	2	17-1	19	7.48	67	.306	.408	1-0	1.000	0	116	-6	-0.9
HAND, RICH Richard Allen B 7.10.1948 Bellevue, WA BR/TR 6-1/195# d4.9																									
1970	Cle A	6	13	.316	35	25	3-1	3-0	159.2	132	71	27	4	69-3	110	3.83	103	.228	.313	41-5	.146	-1	83	3	0.2
1971	Cle A	2	6	.250	15	12	0	0-0	60.2	74	43	6	4	38-1	26	5.79	66	.311	.413	16-2	.125	-0*	117	-12	-1.6
1972	Tex A	10	14	.417	30	28	2-1	0-0	170.2	139	66	12	3	103-8	109	3.32	91	.226	.336	52-3	.154	1	96	-3	-0.2
1973	Tex A	2	3	.400	8	7	1	0-0	41.2	49	29	2	2	19-5	14	5.40	69	.290	.363	0-0	—	0	92	-8	-0.9
	Cal A	4	3	.571	16	6	0	0-0	54.2	58	29	5	1	21-0	19	3.62	98	.274	.336	0-0	—	0	92	-2	-0.2
	Year	6	6	.500	24	13	1	0-0	96.1	107	33	7	3	40-5	33	4.39	83	.281	.348	0-0	—	0	93	-11	-1.1
Total	4	24	39	.381	104	78	6-2	3-0	487.1	452	238	52	14	250-17	278	4.01	88	.249	.341	109-10	.147	-0	94	-22	-2.7
HANDIBOE, JIM James Edward "Nick" B 7.17.1866 Columbus, OH D 11.8.1942 Columbus, OH BR/TR 5-11/160# d5.28																									
1886	Pit AA	7	7	.500	14	14	12-1	0	114	82	65	1	12	33	83	3.32	102	.195	.273	44	.114	-2	94	3	0.0
HANDRAHAN, VERN James Vernon B 11.27.1938 Charlottetown, PE, CAN BL/TR 6-2/185# d4.14																									
1964	KC A	0	1	.000	18	1	0	0	35.2	33	24	9	2	25-0	18	6.06	63	.252	.377	9-0	.222	0	23	-7	-0.4
1966	KC A	0	1	.000	16	1	0	1	25.1	20	12	5	1	15-1	18	4.26	80	.227	.343	3-0	.000	-0	26	-2	-0.1
Total	2	0	2	.000	34	2	0	1	61	53	36	14	3	40-1	36	5.31	69	.242	.364	12-0	.167	-0	24	-9	-0.5
HANDS, BILL William Alfred B 5.6.1940 Hackensack, NJ BR/TR 6-2/185# d6.3																									
1965	SF N	0	2	.000	4	2	0	0	6	13	11	0	0	6-2	5	16.50	22	.433	.528	1-0	.000	-0	36	-8	-1.4
1966	Chi N	8	13	.381	41	26	0	2	159	168	91	17	5	59-6	93	4.58	80	.272	.338	49-4	.041	-3	110	-15	-2.1
1967	Chi N	7	8	.467	49	11	3-1	6	150	134	46	9	2	48-15	84	2.46	144	.239	.301	38-4	.105	-1	95	17	1.7
1968	Chi N	16	10	.615	38	34	11-4	0	258.2	221	91	26	6	36-0	148	2.89	109	.231	.262	82-7	.061	-5	109	8	0.2
1969	Chi N	20	14	.588	41	41	18-3	0-0	300	268	102	21	6	73-8	181	2.49	162	.237	.286	98-11	.092	-5	80	43	4.4
1970	Chi N	18	15	.545	39	38	12-2	1-0	265	278	121	20	4	76-8	170	3.70	122	.269	.321	75-9	.133	1	99	22	2.8
1971	Chi N	12	18	.400	36	35	14-1	0-0	242.1	248	112	27	2	50-6	128	3.42	115	.260	.297	72-9	.083	-3	89	9	0.7
1972	Chi N	11	8	.579	32	28	6-3	0-0	189	168	73	12	2	47-7	96	3.00	127	.237	.285	57-4	.018	-4	111	15	0.9
1973	Min A	7	10	.412	39	15	3-1	2-3	142	138	69	14	2	41-2	78	3.49	114	.252	.305	0-0	—	0	90	5	0.5
1974	Min A	4	5	.444	35	10	0	3-4	115.1	130	57	9	4	25-0	74	4.45	84	.284	.326	0-0	—	0	99	-6	-0.5
	Tex A	2	0	1.000	2	2	1-1	0-0	14	11	3	0	0	3-0	4	1.93	185	.208	.250	0-0	—	0	123	3	0.4
	Year	6	5	.545	37	12	1-1	3-4	129.1	141	8	9	4	28-0	78	4.18	89	.276	.319	0-0	—	0	103	-4	-0.1
1975	Tex A	6	7	.462	18	18	4-1	0-0	109.2	118	58	12	3	28-1	67	4.02	94	.271	.318	0-0	—	0	123	-4	-0.4
Total	11	111	110	.502	374	260	72-17	14-7	1951	1895	834	167	36	492-55	1128	3.35	114	.253	.301	472-48	.078	-20	99	89	7.2
HANEY, CHRIS Christopher Deane B 11.16.1968 Baltimore, MD BL/TL 6-3/195# d6.21 f-Larry																									
1991	Mon N	3	7	.300	16	16	0	0-0	84.2	94	49	6	1	43-1	51	4.04	90	.280	.362	27-2	.074	-2	79	-7	-0.9
1992	Mon N	2	3	.400	9	6	1-1	0-0	38	40	25	6	4	10-0	27	5.45	64	.270	.327	9-1	.222	0*	143	-8	-1.0
	KC A	2	3	.400	7	7	1-1	0-0	42	35	18	5	0	16-2	27	3.86	105	.226	.293	0-0	—	0	51	2	0.1
1993	KC A	9	9	.500	23	23	1-1	0-0	124	141	87	13	3	53-2	65	6.02	76	.286	.356	0-0	—	0	97	-18	-2.1
1994	KC A	2	2	.500	6	6	0	0-0	28.1	36	25	2	1	11-1	18	7.31	69	.333	.387	0-0	—	0	113	-7	-0.7
1995	KC A	3	4	.429	16	13	1	0-0	81.1	78	35	7	2	33-0	31	3.65	131	.262	.335	0-0	—	0	69	10	0.8
1996	KC A	10	14	.417	35	35	4-1	0-0	228	267	136	29	6	51-0	115	4.70	107	.291	.330	0-0	—	0	82	4	0.3
1997	KC A	1	2	.333	8	3	0	0-0	24.2	29	16	1	2	5-2	16	4.38	108	.290	.333	0-0	—	0	71	0	0.0
1998	KC A	6	6	.500	33	12	0	0-1	97.1	125	78	18	5	36-0	51	7.03	69	.316	.371	0-0	—	0	100	-21	-2.0
	Chi N	0	0	—	5	0	0	0-0	5	3	4	2	0	1-0	4	7.20	61	.167	.211	0-0	—	0		-1	-0.1
1999	Cle A	0	2	.000	13	4	0	0-0	40.1	43	22	3	3	16-0	22	4.69	108	.270	.348	0-0	—	0	83	2	0.1
2000	Cle A	0	0	—	1	0	0	0-0	1	1	1	0	0	1-0	0	9.00	55	.333	.400	0-0	—	0		0	0.0
2002	Bos A	0	0	—	24	0	0	1-0	30	32	14	2	4	10-2	15	4.20	107	.274	.343	0-0	—	0		2	0.1
Total	11	38	52	.422	196	125	8-4	1-1	824.2	924	510	94	31	286-10	442	5.07	91	.284	.344	36-3	.111	-1	87	-42	-5.4
HANKINS, DON Donald Wayne B 2.9.1902 Pendleton, IN D 5.16.1963 Winston-Salem, NC BR/TR 6-3/183# d4.23																									
1927	Det A	2	1	.667	20	1	0	2	42.2	67	39	1	0	13	10	6.33	67	.383	.426	7-0	.143	-1	119	-10	-0.8
HANKINSON, FRANK Frank Edward B 4.29.1856 New York, NY D 4.5.1911 Palisades Park, NJ BR/TR 5-11/168# d5.1 ▲																									
1878	Chi N	0	1	.000	1	1	1	0	9	11	9	0		0	4	6.00	40	.282	.282	240	.267	0*	108	-2	-0.2
1879	Chi N	15	10	.600	26	25	25-2	0	230.2	248	134	0		27	69	2.50	103	.255	.275	171	.181	-4*	92	1	-0.1
1880	Cle N	1	1	.500	4	2	2	1	25	20	10	0		3	8	1.08	217	.215	.240	263	.209	-0*	74	3	0.2
1885	NY AA	0	0	—	1	0	0	0	2	2	1	1	0	1	0	4.50	69	.250	.333	362	.224	0*		0	0.0
Total	4	16	12	.571	32	28	28-2	1	266.2	281	154	1	0	31	81	2.50	102	.252	.273	1036	.223	-4	92	2	-0.1
HANLEY, JIM James Patrick B 10.13.1885 Providence, RI D 5.1.1961 Elmhurst, NY BR/TL 5-11/165# d7.3																									
1913	NY A	0	0	—	1	0	0	0	4	5	3	0	0	4	2	6.75	44	.313	.450	1-0	.000	-0		-1	-0.1
HANNA, PRESTON Preston Lee B 9.10.1954 Pensacola, FL BR/TR 6-1/195# d9.13																									
1975	Atl N	0	0	—	4	0	0	0-0	5.2	7	1	0	2	5-0	2	1.59	238	.304	.467	0-0	—	0		1	0.1
1976	Atl N	0	0	—	5	0	0	0-0	8	11	5	0	0	4-0	3	4.50	84	.333	.405	1-0	.000	-0		-1	-0.1
1977	Atl N	2	6	.250	17	9	1	1-0	60	69	40	6	2	34-1	37	4.95	90	.285	.378	14-1	.071	-0	80	-4	-0.4
1978	Atl N	7	13	.350	29	28	0	0-0	140.1	132	89	10	3	93-5	90	5.13	79	.251	.362	49-2	.184	1	81	-14	-1.8
1979	Atl N	1	1	.500	6	4	0	0-0	24.1	27	11	1	0	15-1	15	2.96	137	.284	.382	6-0	.000	-0	60	2	0.2
1980	Atl N	2	0	1.000	32	2	0	0-0	79.1	63	28	3	3	44-4	35	3.18	118	.224	.331	14-0	.143	0	107	6	0.3
1981	Atl N	2	1	.667	20	1	0	0-0	35.1	45	27	2	0	23-2	22	6.37	56	.341	.425	4-0	.250	0	25	-10	-0.7
1982	Atl N	3	0	1.000	20	1	0	0-0	36	36	15	3	0	28-2	17	3.75	100	.277	.405	5-0	.400	1	94	1	0.1
	Oak A	0	4	.000	23	2	1	0-0	48.1	54	34	3	1	33-1	32	5.59	70	.287	.389	0-0	—	0	35	-10	-0.7
Total	8	17	25	.405	156	47	2	1-0	437.1	444	250	28	11	279-16	253	4.61	86	.269	.374	93-3	.161	1	80	-29	-3.0
HANNAHS, GERRY Gerald Ellis B 3.6.1953 Binghamton, NY BL/TL 6-3/210# d9.8																									
1976	Mon N	2	0	1.000	3	3	0	0-0	16	20	14	2	0	12-0	10	6.75	55	.323	.421	8-0	.375	1	166	-5	-0.5
1977	Mon N	1	5	.167	8	7	0	0-0	37	43	27	7	0	17-0	21	4.86	78	.291	.364	7-2	.000	-0	73	-7	-0.9
1978	LA N	0	0	—	1	0	0	0-0	2	3	2	0	0	0-0	5	9.00	39	.333	.333	0-0	—	0		-1	-0.1

Year	Tm Lg	W	L	Pct	G	GS	CG-Sho	SV-BS	IP	H	R	HR	HB	BB-IB	SO	ERA	AERA	OAV	OOB	AB-SH	AVG	PB	Sup	APR	PW
1979	LA N	0	2	.000	4	2	0	1-0	16	10	8	2	0	13-1	6	3.38	108	.175	.324	4-0	.250	0	49	0	0.0
Total	4	3	7	.300	16	12	0	1-0	71	76	51	11	0	42-1	42	5.07	74	.275	.368	19-2	.211	1	93	-13	-1.5
HANNAN, JIM James John B 1.7.1940 Jersey City, NJ BR/TR 6-3/205# d4.17																									
1962	Was A	2	4	.333	42	3	0	4	68	56	27	6	0	49-4	39	3.31	122	.230	.355	11-0	.091	-1	118	6	0.5
1963	Was A	2	2	.500	13	2	0	0	27.2	23	18	2	0	17-0	14	4.88	76	.228	.336	6-0	.000	-0	72	-4	-0.5
1964	Was A	4	7	.364	49	7	0	3	106	108	60	13	0	45-4	67	4.16	89	.266	.338	20-1	.150	-1	75	-7	-0.8
1965	Was A	1	1	.500	4	1	1-1	0	14.2	18	8	0	1	6-1	5	4.91	71	.340	.417	3-1	.000	-0	227	-2	-0.3
1966	Was A	3	9	.250	30	18	2	0	114	125	58	9	3	59-5	68	4.26	81	.288	.374	30-2	.067	-2	86	-9	-1.1
1967	Was A	1	1	.500	8	2	0	0	21.2	28	14	3	1	7-0	14	5.40	59	.315	.367	4-0	.000	-0	41	-5	-0.5
1968	Was A	10	6	.625	25	22	4-1	0	140.1	147	53	4	4	50-1	75	3.01	97	.272	.338	47-3	.064	-2	105	-1	-0.4
1969	Was A	7	6	.538	35	28	1-1	0-1	158.1	138	73	17	2	91-2	72	3.64	95	.238	.342	52-3	.115	-2	93	-3	-0.5
1970	Was A	9	11	.450	42	17	1-1	0-0	128	119	65	17	1	54-8	61	4.01	89	.250	.326	31-2	.129	-0	88	-7	-1.1
1971	Det A	1	0	1.000	7	0	0	0-0	11	7	4	1	1	7-0	6	3.27	110	.189	.333	2-0	.000	-0		1	0.1
	Mil A	1	1	.500	21	1	0	0-1	32.1	38	23	7	1	21-4	17	5.01	69	.295	.395	3-0	.000	-0	181	-7	-0.4
	Year	2	1	.667	28	1	0	0-1	43.1	45	30	8	2	28-4	23	4.57	77	.271	.381	5-0	.000	-1	179	-6	-0.3
Total	10	41	48	.461	276	101	9-4	7-2	822	807	403	79	14	406-29	438	3.88	89	.261	.348	209-12	.091	-9	92	-38	-5.0
HANNING, LOY Loy Vernon B 10.18.1917 Bunker, MO D 6.24.1986 Anaconda, MO BR/TR 6-2/175# d9.20																									
1939	StL A	0	1	.000	4	1	0	0	10	6	5	1	0	4	8	3.60	135	.158	.238	1-0	.000	-0	91	1	0.1
1942	StL A	1	1	.500	11	0	0	0	17.1	26	15	2	1	12	9	7.79	48	.356	.453	4-0	.250	0		-7	-0.7
Total	2	1	2	.333	15	1	0	0	27.1	32	20	3	1	16	17	6.26	66	.288	.383	5-0	.200	-0	91	-6	-0.6
HANSELL, GREG Gregory Michael B 3.12.1971 Bellflower, CA BR/TR 6-5/215# d4.28																									
1995	LA N	0	1	.000	20	0	0	0-1	19.1	29	17	5	2	6-1	13	7.45	51	.349	.402	0-0	—	0		-8	-0.4
1996	Min A	3	0	1.000	50	0	0	3-1	74.1	83	48	14	2	31-1	46	5.69	90	.285	.356	0-0	—	0		-4	-0.2
1997	Mil A	0	0	—	3	0	0	0-0	4.2	5	5	1	1	1-0	5	9.64	48	.263	.333	0-0	—	0		-2	-0.1
1999	Pit N	1	3	.250	33	0	0	0-3	39.1	42	20	5	3	11-3	34	3.89	118	.280	.339	2-0	.000	-0		3	0.2
Total	4	4	4	.500	106	0	0	3-5	137.2	159	90	25	8	49-5	98	5.56	85	.293	.358	2-0	.000	-0		-11	-0.5
HANSEN, ANDY Andrew Viggo "Swede" B 11.12.1924 Lake Worth, FL D 2.2.2002 Lake Worth, FL BR/TR 6-3/190# d6.30 Mil 1945-46																									
1944	NY N	3	3	.500	23	4	0	1	52.2	63	39	3	3	32	15	6.49	56	.301	.402	12-0	.167	0*	86	-14	-1.4
1945	NY N	4	3	.571	23	13	4	3	92.2	98	52	7	2	28	37	4.66	84	.273	.329	25-4	.000	-3	103	-7	-0.7
1947	NY N	1	5	.167	27	9	1	0	82.1	78	45	8	0	38	18	4.37	93	.248	.330	21-0	.190	-0	77	-3	-0.2
1948	NY N	5	3	.625	36	9	3	1	100	96	40	4	0	36	27	2.97	133	.255	.320	20-3	.050	-0	138	10	0.7
1949	NY N	2	6	.250	33	2	0	1	66.1	58	35	7	0	28	26	4.61	86	.234	.312	12-1	.000	-1	133	-2	-0.3
1950	NY N	0	1	.000	31	1	0	3	57	64	37	8	1	26	19	5.53	74	.279	.355	7-2	.000	-1	151	-8	-0.5
1951	Phi N	3	1	.750	24	0	0	0	39	34	14	4	1	7	11	2.54	152	.228	.268	3-0	.333	1		5	0.6
1952	Phi N	5	6	.455	43	0	0	4	77.1	76	36	6	3	27	18	3.26	112	.259	.328	11-2	.182	1		2	0.4
1953	Phi N	0	2	.000	30	1	0	3	51.1	60	30	6	1	24	17	4.03	104	.296	.373	7-0	.286	0	0	-1	0.0
Total	9	23	30	.434	270	39	8	16	618.2	627	328	53	11	246	188	4.22	93	.263	.335	118-12	.102	-3	105	-18	-1.4
HANSEN, SNIPE Roy Emil Frederick B 2.21.1907 Chicago, IL D 9.11.1978 Chicago, IL BB/TL 6-3/195# d7.5																									
1930	Phi N	0	7	.000	22	9	1	0	84.1	123	76	8	2	38	25	6.72	81	.364	.431	27-0	.111	-2	71	-12	-1.0
1932	Phi N	10	10	.500	39	23	5	2	191	215	103	13	6	51	56	3.72	118	.278	.328	63-4	.127	-4	104	8	0.4
1933	Phi N	6	14	.300	32	22	8	1	168.1	199	103	12	4	30	47	4.44	86	.294	.328	58-2	.155	-3*	91	-12	-1.7
1934	Phi N	6	12	.333	50	16	5-2	3	151	194	112	15	3	61	40	5.42	87	.307	.371	43-0	.233	-0	99	-13	-1.3
1935	Phi N	0	1	.000	2	1	0	0	4.1	8	7	0	0	5	0	12.46	36	.421	.542	2-0	.000	-0	94	-3	-0.6
	StL A	0	1	.000	10	0	0	0	26.2	44	28	2	1	9	8	8.78	55	.364	.412	7-0	.143	-1		-10	-0.5
Total	5	22	45	.328	155	71	19-2	6	625.2	783	429	50	16	194	176	5.01	90	.306	.358	200-6	.155	-10	93	-42	-4.7
HANSEN, ROY Roy Inglof "Ing" B 3.6.1898 Beloit, WI D 2.9.1977 Beloit, WI BR/TR 6/165# d5.28																									
1918	Was A	1	0	1.000	5	0	0	0	9	10	4	0	1	3	2	3.00	91	.278	.350	0-0	—	0		0	0.0
HANSFORD, FRANK Frank Cicero B 12.26.1874 DuQuoin, IL D 12.14.1952 Fort Scott, KS TL 6/180# d6.9																									
1898	Bro N	0	0	—	1	0	0	0	7	10	4	0	0	5	0	3.86	93	.333	.429	3-0	.000	-1		0	-0.1
HANSON, OLLIE Earl Sylvester B 1.19.1896 Holbrook, MA D 8.19.1951 Clifton, NJ BR/TR 5-11/178# d4.27																									
1921	Chi N	0	2	.000	2	2	1	0	9	9	7	0	1	6	2	7.00	55	.265	.390	3-0	.000	-0	86	-3	-0.5
HANSON, ERIK Erik Brian B 5.18.1965 Kinnelon, NJ BR/TR 6-6/210# d9.5																									
1988	Sea A	2	3	.400	6	6	0	0-0	41.2	35	17	4	1	12-1	36	3.24	129	.230	.291	0-0	—	0	66	4	0.4
1989	Sea A	9	5	.643	17	17	1	0-0	113.1	103	44	7	5	32-1	75	3.18	127	.243	.304	0-0	—	0	94	11	1.3
1990	Sea A	18	9	.667	33	33	5-1	0-0	236	205	88	15	2	68-6	211	3.24	122	.232	.287	0-0	—	0	94	23	2.4
1991	Sea A	8	8	.500	27	27	2-1	0-0	174.2	182	82	16	2	56-2	143	3.81	108	.269	.323	0-0	—	0	103	6	0.4
1992	Sea A	8	17	.320	31	30	6-1	0-0	186.2	209	110	14	7	57-1	112	4.82	83	.287	.341	0-0	—	0	83	-18	-2.1
1993	Sea A	11	12	.478	31	30	7	0-0	215	215	91	17	5	60-6	163	3.47	127	.263	.315	0-0	—	0*	86	21	2.1
1994	Cin N	5	5	.500	22	21	0	0-0	122.2	137	60	10	3	23-3	101	4.11	101	.283	.317	39-2	.154	-1	108	2	0.1
1995	†Bos A☆	15	5	.750	29	29	1-1	0-0	186.2	187	94	17	1	59-0	139	4.24	115	.258	.311	0-0	—	0	108	14	1.3
1996	Tor A	13	17	.433	35	35	4-1	0-0	214.2	243	143	26	2	102-2	156	5.41	93	.289	.365	0-0	—	0	82	-10	-1.3
1997	Tor A	0	0	—	3	2	0	0-0	15	15	13	3	0	6-0	18	7.80	59	.254	.323	0-0	—	0	120	-5	-0.2
1998	Tor A	0	3	.000	11	8	0	0-0	49	73	34	10	1	29-1	21	6.24	75	.348	.429	0-0	—	0	80	-7	-0.3
Total	11	89	84	.514	245	238	26-5	0-0	1555.1	1604	776	139	29	504-23	1175	4.15	105	.267	.325	39-2	.154	-1	93	41	4.1
HANYZEWSKI, ED Edward Michael B 9.18.1920 Union Mills, IN D 10.8.1991 Fargo, ND BR/TR 6-1/200# d5.12																									
1942	Chi N	1	1	.500	6	1	0	0	19	17	9	2	0	8	6	3.79	84	.254	.333	5-0	.200	-0	26	-1	-0.1
1943	Chi N	8	7	.533	33	16	3	0	130	120	54	2	2	45	55	2.56	130	.243	.309	41-2	.049	-4	97	7	0.4
1944	Chi N	2	5	.286	14	7	3	0	58.1	61	33	6	1	20	19	4.47	79	.261	.322	17-0	.059	-1	71	-5	-0.5
1945	Chi N	0	0	—	2	1	0	0	4.2	7	4	1	0	1	0	5.79	63	.350	.381	1-0	.000	0	116	-1	0.0
1946	Chi N	1	0	1.000	3	0	0	0	6	8	3	0	1	5	1	4.50	74	.348	.483	1-0	.000	-0		-1	-0.1
Total	5	12	13	.480	58	25	6	0	218	213	103	11	4	79	81	3.30	102	.254	.321	65-2	.062	-5	88	-1	-0.3
HARANG, AARON Aaron Michael B 5.9.1978 San Diego, CA BR/TR 6-7/240# d5.25																									
2002	Oak A	5	4	.556	16	15	0	0-0	78.1	78	44	7	3	45-2	64	4.83	91	.261	.359	3-0	.000	-0	94	-3	-0.3
2003	Oak A	1	3	.250	7	6	0	0-0	30.1	41	19	5	0	9-0	16	5.34	85	.331	.373	1-0	.000	-0	85	-2	-0.3
	Cin N	4	3	.571	9	9	0	0-0	46	48	28	6	1	10-0	26	5.28	81	.271	.314	17-0	.059	-1	107	-5	-0.8
Total	2	10	10	.500	32	30	0	0-0	154.2	167	91	18	4	64-2	106	5.06	87	.278	.349	21-0	.048	-2	96	-10	-1.4
HARDEN, RICH James Richard B C., , CAN BL/TR 6-1/180# d7.21																									
2003	†Oak A	5	4	.556	15	13	0	0-0	74.2	72	38	5	1	40-1	67	4.46	101	.259	.351	0-0	—	0	106	2	0.2
HARDER, MEL Melvin Leroy "Chief" B 10.15.1909 Beemer, NE D 10.20.2002 Chardon, OH BR/TR 6-1/195# d4.24 M2 C23																									
1928	Cle A	0	2	.000	23	1	0	1	49	64	42	4	0	32	15	6.61	63	.335	.430	8-0	.000	-1	82	-12	-0.8
1929	Cle A	1	0	1.000	11	0	0	0	17.2	24	15	2	3	5	4	5.60	79	.333	.400	1-0	.000	-0		-3	-0.2
1930	Cle A	11	10	.524	36	19	7	2	175.1	205	108	9	4	68	45	4.21	115	.295	.361	63-2	.143	-4	106	9	0.5
1931	Cle A	13	14	.481	40	24	9	1	194	229	119	8	6	72	63	4.36	106	.289	.352	75-4	.253	1	101	3	0.4
1932	Cle A	15	13	.536	39	32	17-1	0	254.2	277	125	9	3	68	90	3.75	127	.272	.319	94-2	.181	-0	103	27	2.7
1933	Cle A	15	17	.469	43	31	14-2	4	253	254	113	10	3	67	81	2.95	**151**	.259	.309	84-2	.190	-1*	57	**35**	**4.4**
1934	Cle A★	20	12	.625	44	29	17-**6**	4	255.1	246	97	6	7	81	91	2.61	**174**	.254	.316	87-9	.161	-1	92	50	**5.7**
1935	Cle A★	22	11	.667	42	35	17-4	2	287.1	313	120	6	0	53	95	3.29	137	.275	.307	102-7	.206	-1	89	39	4.1
1936	Cle A★	15	15	.500	36	30	13	1	224.2	294	155	13	6	71	84	5.17	97	.313	.365	80-6	.138	-4	88	-6	-1.0
1937	Cle A★	15	12	.556	38	30	13	2	233.2	269	127	9	4	86	95	4.28	108	.288	.350	86-7	.174	-1	105	9	0.8
1938	Cle A	17	10	.630	38	29	15-2	4	240	257	115	16	5	62	102	3.83	121	.271	.319	88-2	.114	-5*	87	23	1.8
1939	Cle A	15	9	.625	29	26	12-1	1	208	213	89	15	3	64	67	3.50	126	.269	.326	72-6	.139	-2	99	23	2.1
1940	Cle A	12	11	.522	31	25	5	0	186.1	200	96	16	5	59	76	4.06	104	.278	.337	62-5	.177	-1	98	4	0.4

Year	Tm Lg	W	L	Pct	G	GS	CG-Sho	SV-BS	IP	H	R	HR	HB	BB-IB	SO	ERA	AERA	OAV	OOB	AB-SH	AVG	PB	Sup	APR	PW
1941	Cle A	5	4	.556	15	10	1	1	68.2	76	43	8	2	37	21	5.24	75	.279	.370	25-0	.080	-2	99	-10	-1.2
1942	Cle A	13	14	.481	29	29	13-4	0	198.2	179	83	8	3	82	74	3.44	100	.240	.317	67-3	.119	-3	77	3	0.1
1943	Cle A	8	7	.533	19	18	6-1	0	135.1	126	57	7	1	61	40	3.06	102	.254	.337	47-4	.213	2	110	-1	0.1
1944	Cle A	12	10	.545	30	27	12-2	0	196.1	211	95	5	3	69	64	3.71	89	.278	.341	74-2	.216	1	120	-9	-0.9
1945	Cle A	3	7	.300	11	11	2	0	76	93	37	3	0	23	16	3.67	88	.303	.352	25-3	.080	-2	76	-4	-0.7
1946	Cle A	5	4	.556	13	12	4-1	0	92.1	85	37	4	0	31	21	3.41	97	.249	.311	35-0	.086	-2	95	0	-0.3
1947	Cle A	6	4	.600	15	15	4-1	0	80	91	41	3	1	27	17	4.50	77	.289	.347	28-5	.179	0	141	-8	-1.0
Total	20	223	186	.545	582	433	181-25	23	3426.1	3706	1714	161	59	1118	1161	3.80	113	.276	.334	1203-69	.165	-27	94	172	17.0

HARDIN, JIM James Warren B 8.6.1943 Morris Chapel, TN D 3.9.1991 Key West, FL BR/TR 6/175# d6.23

Year	Tm Lg	W	L	Pct	G	GS	CG-Sho	SV-BS	IP	H	R	HR	HB	BB-IB	SO	ERA	AERA	OAV	OOB	AB-SH	AVG	PB	Sup	APR	PW
1967	Bal A	8	3	.727	19	14	5-2	0	111	85	30	5	3	27-0	64	2.27	139	.211	.266	37-1	.135	-0	122	12	1.1
1968	Bal A	18	13	.581	35	35	16-2	0	244	188	79	20	10	70-5	160	2.51	117	.212	.277	82-11	.085	-3	97	11	1.1
1969	Bal A	6	7	.462	30	20	3-1	1-1	137.2	128	62	18	6	43-7	64	3.60	99	.248	.311	45-4	.156	2	120	-1	0.0
1970	Bal A	6	5	.545	36	19	3-2	1-1	145.1	150	60	13	1	26-3	78	3.53	103	.267	.299	45-2	.067	-1	102	4	0.0
1971	Bal A	0	0	—	6	0	0	0-0	5.2	12	5	0	0	3-1	3	4.76	70	.480	.536	0-0	—	0		-2	-0.1
	NY A	0	2	.000	12	3	0	0-0	28.1	35	19	3	1	9-3	14	5.08	64	.313	.366	4-0	.000	-0	129	-6	-0.5
	Year	0	2	.000	18	3	0	0-0	34	47	24	3	1	12-4	17	5.03	65	.343	.397	4-0	.000	-0	129	-9	-0.6
1972	Atl N	5	2	.714	26	9	1	2-1	79.2	93	47	11	2	24-4	25	4.41	86	.287	.337	21-3	.095	1	140	-6	-0.5
Total	6	43	32	.573	164	100	28-7	4-3	751.2	691	302	70	23	202-23	408	3.18	104	.244	.299	234-21	.103	-3	111	12	1.1

HARDING, CHARLIE Charles Harold "Slim" B 1.3.1891 Nashville, TN D 10.30.1971 Bold Spring, TN BR/TR 6-2.5/172# d9.18

Year	Tm Lg	W	L	Pct	G	GS	CG-Sho	SV-BS	IP	H	R	HR	HB	BB-IB	SO	ERA	AERA	OAV	OOB	AB-SH	AVG	PB	Sup	APR	PW
1913	Det A	0	0	—	1	0	0	0	2	3	1	0	0	1	0	4.50	65	.375	.444	0-0	—	0		0	0.0

HARDY, ALEX David Alexander "Dooney" B 1877 Toronto, ON, CAN D 4.22.1940 Toronto, ON, CAN BR/TL 5-10.5/175# d9.4

Year	Tm Lg	W	L	Pct	G	GS	CG-Sho	SV-BS	IP	H	R	HR	HB	BB-IB	SO	ERA	AERA	OAV	OOB	AB-SH	AVG	PB	Sup	APR	PW
1902	Chi N	2	2	.500	4	4	4-1	0	35	29	19	0	0	12	12	3.60	75	.227	.293	14-0	.214	0	151	-2	-0.2
1903	Chi N	1	1	.500	3	3	1	0	12.2	21	10	0	1	7	4	6.39	49	.375	.453	6-0	.167	0	129	-3	-0.4
Total	2	3	3	.500	7	7	5-1	0	47.2	50	29	0	1	19	16	4.34	65	.272	.343	20-0	.200	1	144	-5	-0.6

HARDY, RED Francis Joseph B 1.6.1923 Marmarth, ND D 8.15.2003 Phoenix, AZ BR/TR 5-11/175# d6.20

Year	Tm Lg	W	L	Pct	G	GS	CG-Sho	SV-BS	IP	H	R	HR	HB	BB-IB	SO	ERA	AERA	OAV	OOB	AB-SH	AVG	PB	Sup	APR	PW
1951	NY N	0	0	—	2	0	0	0	1.1	4	1	0	1	1	0	6.75	58	.571	.667	0-0	—	0		0	0.0

HARDY, HARRY Harry B 11.5.1875 Steubenville, OH D 9.4.1943 Steubenville, OH BL/TL 5-6/155# d9.26

Year	Tm Lg	W	L	Pct	G	GS	CG-Sho	SV-BS	IP	H	R	HR	HB	BB-IB	SO	ERA	AERA	OAV	OOB	AB-SH	AVG	PB	Sup	APR	PW
1905	Was A	1	1	.500	3	2	2	0	24	20	9	0	0	6	10	1.88	141	.227	.277	9-0	.111	-1	67	1	0.0
1906	Was A	0	3	.000	5	3	2	0	20	35	27	0	0	12	4	9.00	29	.385	.456	6-0	.000	-1	64	-14	-1.7
Total	2	1	4	.200	8	5	4	0	44	55	36	0	0	18	14	5.11	52	.307	.371	15-0	.067	-2	65	-13	-1.7

HARDY, LARRY Howard Lawrence B 1.10.1948 Goose Creek, TX BR/TR 5-10/180# d4.28 C7

Year	Tm Lg	W	L	Pct	G	GS	CG-Sho	SV-BS	IP	H	R	HR	HB	BB-IB	SO	ERA	AERA	OAV	OOB	AB-SH	AVG	PB	Sup	APR	PW
1974	SD N	9	4	.692	76	1	0	2-4	101.2	129	58	9	0	44-14	57	4.69	76	.317	.380	10-0	.000	-1	73	-12	-1.5
1975	SD N	0	0	—	3	0	0	0-0	2.2	8	6	3	0	2-0	3	13.50	26	.500	.556	0-0	—	0		-4	-0.2
1976	Hou N	0	0	—	15	0	0	3-0	21.2	34	19	2	0	10-2	10	7.06	45	.362	.423	2-0	.000	-0		-10	-0.5
Total	3	9	4	.692	94	1	0	5-4	126	171	83	14	0	56-16	70	5.29	66	.331	.393	12-0	.000	-1	73	-26	-2.2

HARDY, JACK John Graydon B 10.8.1959 St.Petersburg, FL BR/TR 6-2/175# d5.23

Year	Tm Lg	W	L	Pct	G	GS	CG-Sho	SV-BS	IP	H	R	HR	HB	BB-IB	SO	ERA	AERA	OAV	OOB	AB-SH	AVG	PB	Sup	APR	PW
1989	Chi A	0	0	—	5	0	0	0-0	12.1	14	9	1	1	5-0	4	6.57	58	.286	.357	0-0	—	0		-3	-0.1

HAREN, DANNY Daniel John B 9.17.1980 Monterey Park, CA BR/TR 6-5/220# d6.30

Year	Tm Lg	W	L	Pct	G	GS	CG-Sho	SV-BS	IP	H	R	HR	HB	BB-IB	SO	ERA	AERA	OAV	OOB	AB-SH	AVG	PB	Sup	APR	PW
2003	StL N	3	7	.300	14	14	0	0-0	72.2	84	44	9	5	22-0	43	5.08	80	.293	.351	25-1	.080	-0*	94	-9	-1.1

HARGAN, STEVE Steven Lowell B 9.8.1942 Ft.Wayne, IN BR/TR 6-3/180# d8.3

Year	Tm Lg	W	L	Pct	G	GS	CG-Sho	SV-BS	IP	H	R	HR	HB	BB-IB	SO	ERA	AERA	OAV	OOB	AB-SH	AVG	PB	Sup	APR	PW
1965	Cle A	4	3	.571	17	8	1	2	60.1	55	26	2	1	28-2	37	3.43	101	.246	.331	19-2	.053	-1	107	0	-0.1
1966	Cle A	13	10	.565	38	21	7-3	0	192	173	60	9	1	45-8	132	2.48	138	.241	.286	58-3	.121	-2	81	20	2.2
1967	Cle A☆	14	13	.519	30	29	15-**6**	0	223	180	79	9	3	72-7	141	2.62	125	.224	.288	67-7	.164	1	84	14	1.9
1968	Cle A	8	15	.348	32	27	4-2	0	158.1	139	81	11	5	81-8	78	4.15	71	.241	.336	51-1	.176	1	86	-19	-2.8
1969	Cle A	5	14	.263	32	23	1-1	0-0	143.2	145	95	14	3	81-9	76	5.70	66	.265	.359	44-1	.159	-1*	69	-26	-3.1
1970	Cle A	11	3	.786	23	19	8-1	0-0	142.2	101	47	14	3	53-0	72	2.90	137	.201	.279	45-8	.111	-2*	101	17	1.4
1971	Cle A	1	13	.071	37	16	1	1-1	113.1	138	83	18	6	56-5	52	6.19	62	.304	.387	32-1	.063	-3	85	-26	-3.3
1972	Cle A	0	3	.000	12	1	0	0-0	20	23	16	1	0	15-2	10	5.85	55	.291	.392	3-0	.000	-0	27	-6	-0.9
1974	Tex A	12	9	.571	37	27	8-2	0-0	186.2	202	103	15	5	48-4	98	3.95	90	.275	.320	0-0	—	0	97	-12	-1.2
1975	Tex A	9	10	.474	33	26	8-1	0-1	189.1	203	96	17	6	62-7	93	3.80	99	.275	.334	0-0	—	0	102	-2	-0.1
1976	Tex A	8	8	.500	35	8	2-1	1-2	124.1	127	63	8	3	38-3	63	3.62	99	.261	.317	0-0	—	0	70	-3	-0.4
1977	Tor A	1	3	.250	6	5	1	0-0	29.1	36	17	2	0	14-2	11	5.22	81	.308	.382	0-0	—	0	77	-2	-0.2
	Tex A	1	0	1.000	6	0	0	0-0	12.1	22	13	2	0	5-0	10	8.76	47	.393	.429	0-0	—	0		-6	-0.4
	Year	2	3	.400	12	5	1	0-0	41.2	58	34	4	0	19-2	21	6.26	67	.335	.397	0-0	—	0	78	-8	-0.6
	Atl N	0	3	.000	16	5	0	0-0	36.2	49	31	3	0	16-1	18	6.87	65	.325	.385	6-0	.000	-1	112	-8	-0.6
Total	12	87	107	.448	354	215	56-17	4-4	1632	1593	810	125	36	614-58	891	3.92	91	.257	.326	325-23	.129	-7	88	-59	-7.6

HARGESHEIMER, ALAN Alan Robert B 11.21.1954 Chicago, IL BR/TR 6-3/195# d7.14

Year	Tm Lg	W	L	Pct	G	GS	CG-Sho	SV-BS	IP	H	R	HR	HB	BB-IB	SO	ERA	AERA	OAV	OOB	AB-SH	AVG	PB	Sup	APR	PW
1980	SF N	4	6	.400	15	13	0	0-0	75	82	38	3	0	32-2	40	4.32	82	.285	.355	22-1	.182	0	89	-5	-0.6
1981	SF N	1	2	.333	6	3	0	0-0	18.2	20	9	1	1	9-2	6	4.34	79	.299	.385	5-1	.200	0	69	-1	-0.2
1983	Chi N	0	0	—	5	0	0	0-0	4	6	4	0	0	2-0	5	9.00	42	.375	.444	0-0	—	0		-2	-0.1
1986	KC A	0	1	.000	5	1	0	0-0	13	18	9	1	1	7-2	4	6.23	68	.340	.426	0-0	—	0	192	-2	-0.2
Total	4	5	9	.357	31	17	0	0-0	110.2	126	60	5	2	50-6	55	4.72	77	.297	.372	27-2	.185	1	92	-10	-1.1

HARIKKALA, TIM Timothy Allan B 7.15.1971 W.Palm Beach, FL BR/TR 6-2/185# d5.27

Year	Tm Lg	W	L	Pct	G	GS	CG-Sho	SV-BS	IP	H	R	HR	HB	BB-IB	SO	ERA	AERA	OAV	OOB	AB-SH	AVG	PB	Sup	APR	PW
1995	Sea A	0	0	—	1	0	0	0-0	3.1	7	6	1	0	1-0	1	16.20	29	.412	.444	0-0	—	0		-4	-0.2
1996	Sea A	0	1	.000	1	1	0	0-0	4.1	4	6	1	1	2-0	1	12.46	40	.250	.368	0-0	—	0	37	-3	-0.5
1999	Bos A	1	1	.500	7	0	0	0-0	13	15	9	0	1	6-1	7	6.23	80	.306	.393	0-0	—	0		-1	-0.2
Total	3	1	2	.333	9	1	0	0-0	20.2	26	21	2	2	9-1	9	9.15	54	.317	.398	0-0	—	0	37	-8	-0.9

HARKEY, MIKE Michael Anthony B 10.25.1966 San Diego, CA BR/TR 6-5/220# d9.5

Year	Tm Lg	W	L	Pct	G	GS	CG-Sho	SV-BS	IP	H	R	HR	HB	BB-IB	SO	ERA	AERA	OAV	OOB	AB-SH	AVG	PB	Sup	APR	PW
1988	Chi N	0	3	.000	5	5	0	0-0	34.2	33	14	0	2	15-3	18	2.60	139	.248	.333	11-2	.091	-1	59	2	0.1
1990	Chi N	12	6	.667	27	27	2-1	0-0	173.2	153	71	14	7	59-8	94	3.26	125	.234	.303	56-8	.250	3	98	14	1.7
1991	Chi N	0	2	.000	4	4	0	0-0	18.2	21	11	3	0	6-1	15	5.30	73	.273	.321	5-0	.400	1	121	-2	-0.1
1992	Chi N	4	0	1.000	7	7	0	0-0	38	34	13	4	1	15-0	21	1.89	190	.243	.316	15-0	.267	1*	136	5	0.6
1993	Chi N	10	10	.500	28	28	1	0-0	157.1	187	100	17	3	43-4	67	5.26	76	.305	.349	54-5	.093	-2	104	-22	-2.7
1994	Col N	1	6	.143	24	13	0	0-0	91.2	125	61	10	1	35-4	39	5.79	86	.336	.393	22-4	.182	-1	70	-6	-0.4
1995	Oak A	4	6	.400	14	12	0	0-0	66	75	46	12	3	31-0	28	6.27	71	.292	.372	0-0	—	0	82	-12	-1.4
	Cal A	4	3	.571	12	8	1	0-0	61.1	80	32	12	1	16-2	28	4.55	103	.311	.351	0-0	—	0	84	2	0.1
	Year	8	9	.471	26	20	1	0-0	127.1	155	36	24	4	47-2	56	5.44	84	.302	.362	0-0	—	0	82	-11	-1.3
1997	LA N	1	0	1.000	10	0	0	0-0	14.2	12	8	3	0	5-0	6	4.30	90	.211	.274	1-2	.000	-0		-1	-0.1
Total	8	36	36	.500	131	104	4-1	0-0	656	720	356	75	18	225-22	316	4.49	94	.281	.341	164-21	.183	1	93	-20	-2.2

HARKINS, JOHN John Joseph "Pa" B 4.12.1859 New Brunswick, NJ D 11.20.1940 New Brunswick, NJ BR/TR 6-1/205# d5.2

Year	Tm Lg	W	L	Pct	G	GS	CG-Sho	SV-BS	IP	H	R	HR	HB	BB-IB	SO	ERA	AERA	OAV	OOB	AB-SH	AVG	PB	Sup	APR	PW
1884	Cle N	12	32	.273	46	45	42-3	0	391	399	300	7		108	192	3.68	86	.249	.297	229	.205	-4*	71	-21	-2.3
1885	Bro AA	14	20	.412	34	34	33-1	0	293	303	224	7	7	56	141	3.75	88	.250	.287	159	.264	5*	101	-19	-1.1
1886	Bro AA	15	16	.484	34	33	33	0	292.1	286	203	6	5	114	118	3.30	97	.244	.313	142	.225	3*	90	-3	0.2
1887	Bro AA	10	14	.417	24	24	22	0	199	262	184	6	5	77	36	6.02	72	.309	.369	98	.235	-0*	95	-30	-2.6
1888	Bal AA	0	1	.000	1	1	1	0	8	12	12	0	0	3	2	6.75	44	.333	.385	3	.000	-0	136	-4	-0.4
Total	5	51	83	.381	139	137	131-4	0	1183.1	1262	923	26	17	358	489	4.09	85	.259	.312	631	.228	4	88	-77	-6.2

HARKNESS, SPEC Frederick Harvey B 12.13.1887 Los Angeles, CA D 5.16.1952 Compton, CA BR/TR 5-11/180# d6.13

Year	Tm Lg	W	L	Pct	G	GS	CG-Sho	SV-BS	IP	H	R	HR	HB	BB-IB	SO	ERA	AERA	OAV	OOB	AB-SH	AVG	PB	Sup	APR	PW
1910	Cle A	10	7	.588	26	16	6-1	1	136.1	132	61	2	3	55	60	3.04	85	.268	.345	50-1	.140	-1	94	-6	-0.9
1911	Cle A	2	2	.500	12	6	3	0	53.1	62	36	1	0	21	25	4.22	81	.310	.376	19-0	.316	1	162	-5	-0.3
Total	2	12	9	.571	38	22	9-1	1	189.2	194	97	3	3	76	85	3.37	84	.280	.354	69-1	.188	-0	115	-11	-1.2

Year	Tm Lg	W	L	Pct	G	GS	CG-Sho	SV-BS	IP	H	R	HR	HB	BB-IB	SO	ERA	AERA	OAV	OOB	AB-SH	AVG	PB	Sup	APR	PW
HARLEY, DICK Henry Risk B 8.18.1874 Springfield, OH D 5.16.1961 Springfield, OH BR/TR d4.15																									
1905	Bos N	2	5	.286	9	4	4-1	0	65.2	72	45	5	1	19	19	4.66	67	.286	.338	22-1	.045	-2	35	-11	-1.1
HARMAN, BILL William Bell B 1.2.1919 Bridgewater, VA BR/TR 6-4/200# d6.17 Mil 1942 ▲																									
1941	Phi N	0	0	—	5	0	0	0	13	15	8	0	0	8	3	4.85	76	.319	.418	14-0	.071	-0*		-2	-0.2
HARMON, BOB Robert Green "Hickory Bob" B 10.15.1887 Liberal, MO D 11.27.1961 Monroe, LA BB/TR 6/187# d6.23																									
1909	StL N	6	11	.353	21	17	10	0	159	155	85	6	4	65	48	3.68	69	.265	.342	51-4	.255	4	94	-19	-1.5
1910	StL N	13	15	.464	43	33	15	2	236	227	128	1	7	133	87	4.46	67	.258	.360	76-4	.184	2	129	-31	-3.1
1911	StL N	23	16	.590	51	**41**	28-2	4	348	290	155	10	7	181	144	3.13	108	.235	.336	111-9	.153	0	98	10	1.2
1912	StL N	18	18	.500	43	34	15-3	0	268	284	156	4	3	116	73	3.93	87	.281	.357	99-2	.232	1*	93	-11	-1.1
1913	StL N	8	21	.276	42	27	16-1	2	273.1	291	135	6	6	99	66	3.92	83	.286	.353	92-3	.261	5*	72	-18	-1.2
1914	Pit N	13	17	.433	37	30	19-2	3	245	226	84	4	7	55	61	2.53	105	.252	.300	86-5	.140	-1*	64	5	0.4
1915	Pit N	16	17	.485	37	32	25-5	1	269.2	242	106	6	3	62	86	2.50	109	.247	.294	95-3	.147	1*	100	4	0.7
1916	Pit N	8	11	.421	31	17	10-2	0	172.2	175	78	4	1	39	62	2.81	95	.267	.309	55-0	.109	-3*	103	-5	-0.6
1918	Pit N	2	7	.222	16	9	5	0	82.1	76	30	3	0	12	7	2.62	109	.254	.283	27-1	.148	-1*	79	3	0.2
Total	9	107	133	.446	321	240	143-15	12	2054	1966	957	44	38	762	634	3.33	90	.260	.331	692-31	.184	7	94	-62	-5.0
HARNISCH, PETE Peter Thomas B 9.23.1966 Commack, NY BB/TR 6/207# d9.13																									
1988	Bal A	0	2	.000	2	2	0	0-0	13	13	8	1	0	9-1	10	5.54	71	.260	.373	0-0	—	0	70	-2	-0.3
1989	Bal A	5	9	.357	18	17	2	0-0	103.1	97	55	10	5	64-3	70	4.62	82	.249	.358	0-0	—	0	83	-9	-1.1
1990	Bal A	11	11	.500	31	31	3	0-0	188.2	189	96	17	1	86-5	122	4.34	88	.261	.339	0-0	—	0	115	-11	-1.2
1991	Hou N★	12	9	.571	33	33	4-2	0-0	216.2	169	71	14	5	83-3	172	2.70	130	**.212**	.288	62-7	.097	-1	88	21	1.7
1992	Hou N	9	10	.474	34	34	0	0-0	206.2	182	92	18	5	64-3	164	3.70	91	.233	.294	67-5	.164	2	121	-7	-0.6
1993	Hou N	16	9	.640	33	33	5-**4**	0-0	217.2	171	84	20	6	79-5	185	2.98	130	**.214**	.289	67-10	.104	-1	108	21	1.9
1994	Hou N	8	5	.615	17	17	1	0-0	95	100	59	13	3	39-1	62	5.40	73	.269	.341	35-2	.171	1*	136	-14	-1.6
1995	NY N	2	8	.200	18	18	0	0-0	110	111	55	13	3	24-4	82	3.68	110	.261	.301	33-3	.091	-2	98	2	0.0
1996	NY N	8	12	.400	31	31	2-1	0-0	194.2	195	103	30	7	61-5	114	4.21	95	.260	.318	55-10	.091	-2*	103	-3	-0.7
1997	NY N	0	1	.000	6	5	0	0-0	25.2	35	24	5	1	11-1	12	8.06	50	.327	.388	8-1	.000	-1	123	-11	-0.6
	Mil A	1	1	.500	4	3	0	0-0	14	13	9	1	0	12-0	10	5.14	90	.245	.385	0-0	—	0	46	-1	-0.1
1998	Cin N	14	7	.667	32	32	2-1	0-0	209	176	79	24	6	64-4	157	3.14	136	.228	.291	66-9	.106	-3	115	26	2.0
1999	Cin N	16	10	.615	33	33	2-2	0-0	198.1	190	86	25	5	57-2	120	3.68	127	.252	.306	66-8	.152	1	111	23	2.5
2000	Cin N	8	6	.571	22	22	3-1	0-0	131	133	76	23	1	46-1	71	4.74	99	.261	.321	43-6	.186	1*	86	-1	0.0
2001	Cin N	1	3	.250	7	7	0	0-0	35.1	48	29	9	1	17-0	17	6.37	72	.318	.384	11-1	.273	1*	101	-7	-0.7
Total	14	111	103	.519	321	318	24-11	0-0	1959	1822	926	223	49	716-38	1368	3.89	103	.245	.313	513-62	.129	-5	106	27	1.2
HARPER, JACK Charles William B 4.2.1878 Galloway, PA D 9.30.1950 Jamestown, NY BR/TR 6/178# d9.18																									
1899	Cle N	1	4	.200	5	5	5	0	37	44	33	3	3	12	14	3.89	95	.295	.360	11-0	.182	1	101	-5	-0.4
1900	StL N	0	1	.000	1	1	0	0	3	4	7	0	0	2	0	12.00	30	.308	.400	1-0	.000	-0	114	-3	-0.5
1901	StL N	23	13	.639	39	37	28-1	0	308.2	294	158	7	16	99	128	3.62	88	.249	.316	116-3	.172	1	128	-13	-1.2
1902	StL A	15	11	.577	29	26	20-2	0	222.1	224	131	8	8	81	74	4.13	85	.262	.332	83-3	.205	-0	89	-14	-1.3
1903	Cin N	8	9	.471	17	15	13	0	135	143	87	2	10	70	45	4.33	82	.271	.367	56-0	.250	2*	97	-7	-0.5
1904	Cin N	23	9	.719	35	35	31-6	0	293.2	262	113	2	9	85	125	2.30	128	.234	.293	113-3	.159	-2	127	19	1.5
1905	Cin N	9	13	.409	26	23	15-1	1	179.1	189	116	2	8	69	70	3.86	86	.271	.344	60-4	.167	1	105	-10	-1.1
1906	Cin N	1	4	.200	5	5	3	0	36.2	38	23	1	2	20	10	4.17	66	.286	.387	11-1	.273	1	90	-5	-0.6
	Chi N	0	0	—	1	1	0	0	1	0	0	0	0	0	0	0.00	—	.000	.000	0-0	—	0	304	0	0.0
	Year	1	4	.200	6	6	3	0	37.2	38	11	1	2	20	10	4.06	68	.279	.380	11-1	.273	1	124	-5	-0.6
Total	8	80	64	.556	158	148	115-10	1	1216.2	1198	668	25	56	438	466	3.55	92	.256	.327	451-14	.186	3	111	-38	-4.1
HARPER, GEORGE George B. B 8.17.1866 Milwaukee, WI D 12.11.1931 Stockton, CA BR/TR 5-10/165# d7.11																									
1894	Phi N	6	6	.500	12	9	7	0	86.1	128	84	3	2	49	24	5.32	97	.340	.418	40-0	.150	-4	127	-7	-0.9
1896	Bro N	4	8	.333	16	11	7	0	86	106	72	4	3	39	22	5.55	74	.300	.375	37-0	.162	0	96	-13	-1.3
Total	2	10	14	.417	28	20	14	0	172.1	234	156	7	5	88	46	5.43	85	.321	.397	77-0	.156	-4	110	-20	-2.2
HARPER, HARRY Harry Clayton B 4.24.1895 Hackensack, NJ D 4.23.1963 New York, NY BL/TL 6-2/165# d6.27																									
1913	Was A	0	0	—	4	0	0	0	12.2	10	11	1	1	5	9	3.55	83	.213	.302	4-0	.250	0		-2	-0.1
1914	Was A	2	1	.667	23	3	1	2	57	45	29	1	5	35	50	3.47	81	.211	.336	12-0	.250	0	95	-4	-0.3
1915	Was A	4	4	.500	19	10	5-2	2	86.1	66	26	1	1	40	54	1.77	168	.222	.317	25-2	.000	-4	81	10	0.5
1916	Was A	14	10	.583	36	34	13-2	0	249.2	209	82	4	8	101	149	2.45	114	.235	.319	87-1	.207	1	95	11	1.0
1917	Was A	11	12	.478	31	31	10-4	0	179.1	145	85	1	5	106	99	3.01	87	.230	.345	60-2	.117	-3	117	-10	-1.8
1918	Was A	11	10	.524	35	32	14-3	1	244	182	77	1	8	104	78	2.18	125	.212	.303	82-3	.134	-4*	103	17	0.8
1919	Was A	6	21	.222	35	31	8	0	208	220	119	3	8	97	87	3.72	86	.284	.370	65-2	.169	-2	72	-14	-1.9
1920	Bos A	5	14	.263	27	22	11-1	0	162.2	163	73	9	2	66	71	3.04	120	.275	.349	50-2	.120	-3	58	8	0.4
1921	†NY A	4	3	.571	8	7	4	0	52.2	52	23	3	2	25	22	3.76	113	.263	.351	16-0	.125	-1	76	4	0.3
1923	Bro N	0	1	.000	1	1	0	0	3.2	8	6	2	0	3	4	14.73	26	.421	.500	1-0	.000	-0	127	-4	-0.6
Total	10	57	76	.429	219	171	66-12	5	1256	1100	531	26	40	582	623	2.87	105	.244	.335	402-12	.147	-16	88	16	-1.7
HARPER, JACK John Wesley B 8.5.1893 Hendricks, WV D 6.18.1927 Halstead, KS BR/TR 5-11/180# d4.17																									
1915	Phi A	0	0	—	3	0	0	0	8.2	5	4	0	0	1	3	3.12	94	.161	.188	2-0	.000	-0		0	0.0
HARPER, TRAVIS Travis Boyd B 5.21.1976 Harrisonburg, VA BR/TR 6-4/190# d8.4																									
2000	TB A	1	2	.333	6	5	1-1	0-0	32	30	17	5	1	15-0	14	4.78	103	.244	.329	0-0	—	0	99	1	0.1
2001	TB A	0	2	.000	2	2	0	0-0	7	15	11	5	0	3-0	2	7.71	58	.455	.500	0-0	—	0	21	-4	-0.7
2002	TB A	5	9	.357	37	7	0	1-1	85.2	101	54	14	9	27-3	60	5.46	82	.289	.352	0-0	—	0	71	-8	-1.3
2003	TB A	4	8	.333	61	0	0	1-5	93	86	45	9	6	31-8	64	3.77	120	.252	.323	0-0	—	0		7	0.7
Total	4	10	21	.323	106	14	1-1	2-6	217.2	232	127	33	16	76-11	140	4.71	97	.274	.342	0-0	—	0	75	-4	-1.2
HARPER, BILL William Homer "Blue Sleeve" B 6.14.1889 Bertrand, MO D 6.17.1951 Somerville, TN BB/TR 6-1/180# d6.10																									
1911	StL A	0	0	—	2	0	0	0	8	9	9	0	1	4	6	6.75	50	.300	.400	3-0	.000	-0		-3	-0.2
HARRELL, SLIM Oscar Martin B 7.31.1890 Grandview, TX D 4.30.1971 Hillsboro, TX BR/TR 6-3/180# d6.21																									
1912	Phi A	0	0	—	1	0	0	0	3	4	0	0	0	0	1	0.00	—	.364	.364	1-0	.000	-0		1	0.0
HARRELL, RAY Raymond James "Cowboy" B 2.16.1912 Petrolia, TX D 1.28.1984 Alexandria, LA BR/TR 6-1/185# d4.16																									
1935	StL N	1	1	.500	11	1	0	0	29.2	39	26	4	0	11	13	6.67	61	.320	.376	4-1	.000	-1	124	-9	-0.6
1937	StL N	3	7	.300	35	15	1-1	1	96.2	99	73	7	2	59	41	5.87	68	.263	.366	22-2	.045	-2	110	-19	-2.0
1938	StL N	2	3	.400	32	3	1	2	63	78	37	6	3	29	32	4.86	81	.308	.386	10-0	.000	-1	143	-4	-0.5
1939	Chi N	0	2	.000	4	2	0	0	17.1	29	16	2	0	6	5	8.31	47	.387	.432	5-0	.000	-1	33	-7	-0.8
	Phi N	3	7	.300	22	10	4	0	94.2	101	77	6	4	56	35	5.42	74	.270	.371	26-0	.115	-1	54	-20	-2.0
	Year	3	9	.250	26	12	4	0	112	130	80	8	4	62	40	5.87	68	.290	.381	31-0	.097	-2	51	-27	-2.8
1940	Pit N	0	0	—	3	0	0	0	3.1	5	5	0	0	2	3	8.10	47	.333	.412	0-0	—	0		-2	-0.1
1945	NY N	0	0	—	12	0	0	0	25.1	34	22	1	1	14	7	4.97	79	.343	.430	5-0	.200	1		-6	-0.2
Total	6	9	20	.310	119	31	6-1	3	330	385	256	26	10	177	136	5.70	70	.293	.381	72-3	.069	-5	91	-67	-6.2
HARRELSON, BILL William Charles B 11.17.1945 Tahlequah, OK BB/TR 6-5/215# d7.31																									
1968	Cal A	1	6	.143	10	5	1	0	33.2	28	23	4	1	26-0	22	5.08	57	.226	.359	10-0	.100	-0	60	-9	-1.8
HARRIGER, DENNY Dennis Scott B 7.21.1969 Kittanning, PA BR/TR 5-11/185# d6.16																									
1998	Det A	0	3	.000	4	2	0	0-0	12	17	12	1	0	8-2	3	6.75	70	.327	.417	0-0	—	0	98	-4	-0.6
HARRINGTON, ANDY Andrew Francis B 11.13.1888 Wakefield, MA D 11.12.1938 Malden, MA BR/TR 6/193# d9.8																									
1913	Cin N	0	0	—	1	0	0	0	4	6	5	0	0	1	1	9.00	36	.353	.389	2-0	.500	0		-2	-0.1
HARRINGTON, BILL William Womble B 10.3.1927 Sanford, NC BR/TR 5-11/160# d4.16 Mil 1953																									
1953	Phi A	0	0	—	1	0	0	0	2	5	3	0	0	0	0	13.50	32	.500	.500	0-0	—	0		-2	-0.1
1955	KC A	3	3	.500	34	1	0	2	76.2	69	41	6	2	41-4	26	4.11	102	.246	.339	17-0	.118	-1	21	0	-0.1

Year	Tm Lg	W	L	Pct	G	GS	CG-Sho	SV-BS	IP	H	R	HR	HB	BB-IB	SO	ERA	AERA	OAV	OOB	AB-SH	AVG	PB	Sup	APR	PW
1956	KC A	2	2	.500	23	1	0	1	37.2	40	27	3	0	26-1	14	6.45	67	.274	.384	7-2	.000	-1	144	-7	-0.8
Total	3	5	5	.500	58	2	0	3	116.1	114	71	9	2	67-5	40	5.03	84	.261	.357	24-2	.083	-1	84	-9	-1.0
HARRIS, BEN Ben Franklin B 12.17.1889 Donelson, TN D 4.29.1927 St.Louis, MO BR/TR 6/220# d4.19																									
1914	KC F	7	7	.500	31	14	5	1	154	179	89	7	6	41	40	4.09	68	.303	.354	45-3	.200	1	102	-22	-1.7
1915	KC F	0	0	—	1	0	0	0	2	1	0	0	0	0	0	0.00	—	.143	.143	0-0	—	0		1	0.0
Total	2	7	7	.500	32	14	5	1	156	180	89	7	6	41	40	4.04	69	.301	.352	45-3	.200	1	102	-21	-1.7
HARRIS, LUM Chalmer Luman B 1.17.1915 New Castle, AL D 11.11.1996 Pell City, AL BR/TR 6-1/180# d4.19 Mil 1945 M8 C14																									
1941	Phi A	4	4	.500	33	10	5	2	131.2	134	77	16	2	51	49	4.78	88	.260	.329	40-2	.275	2	101	-7	-0.3
1942	Phi A	11	15	.423	26	20	10-1	0	166	146	80	14	1	70	60	3.74	101	.234	.313	62-1	.161	-2	66	1	0.0
1943	Phi A	7	21	.250	32	27	15-1	1	216.1	241	122	17	3	63	55	4.20	81	.279	.330	70-4	.171	-1	71	-22	-2.7
1944	Phi A	10	9	.526	23	22	12-2	0	174.1	193	70	8	0	26	33	3.30	105	.281	.308	59-2	.169	-1	77	6	0.5
1946	Phi A	3	14	.176	34	12	4	0	125.1	153	78	11	0	48	33	5.24	68	.308	.369	36-4	.222	1	75	-20	-2.2
1947	Was A	0	0	—	3	0	0	0	6.1	7	2	0	0	7	2	2.84	131	.318	.483	1-0	.000	-0		1	0.1
Total	6	35	63	.357	151	91	46-4	3	820	874	429	66	6	265	232	4.16	88	.273	.329	268-13	.190	-0	75	-41	-4.6
HARRIS, BUBBA Charles B 2.15.1926 Sulligent, AL BR/TR 6-4/204# d4.29																									
1948	Phi A	5	2	.714	45	0	0	5	93.2	89	51	2	1	35	32	4.13	104	.249	.317	24-2	.125	-1		0	-0.1
1949	Phi A	1	1	.500	37	0	0	3	84.1	92	57	12	1	42	18	5.44	75	.286	.370	24-3	.125	-2		-12	-0.7
1951	Phi A	0	0	—	3	0	0	0	4	4	4	0	1	5	2	9.00	48	.250	.455	0-0	—	0		-2	-0.1
	Cle A	0	0	—	2	0	0	0	4	5	2	0	0	4	1	4.50	84	.333	.474	0-0	—	0		0	0.0
	Year	0	0	—	5	0	0	0	8	9	9	0	1	9	3	6.75	60	.290	.463	0-0	—	0		-2	-0.1
Total	3	6	3	.667	87	0	0	8	186	190	114	14	3	86	53	4.84	87	.267	.349	48-5	.125	-3		-14	-0.9
HARRIS, GREG Greg Allen B 11.2.1955 Lynwood, CA BB/TR 6/175# d5.20																									
1981	NY N	3	5	.375	16	14	0	1-0	68.2	65	36	8	2	28-2	54	4.46	78	.245	.321	22-0	.182	0*	109	-6	-0.6
1982	Cin N	2	6	.250	34	10	1	1-0	91.1	96	56	12	2	37-1	67	4.83	77	.274	.344	18-0	.167	-0*	83	-12	-1.0
1983	Cin N	0	0	—	1	0	0	0-0	1	2	3	0	1	3-2	1	27.00	14	.500	.750	1-0	.000	-0		-2	-0.1
1984	Mon N	0	1	.000	15	0	0	2-0	17.2	10	4	0	2	7-1	15	2.04	168	.172	.284	1-0	.000	-0		3	0.2
	†SD N	2	1	.667	19	1	0	1-0	36.2	28	14	3	2	18-0	30	2.70	132	.209	.306	8-0	.375	1	173	3	0.3
	Year	2	2	.500	34	1	0	3-0	54.1	38	21	3	4	25-1	45	2.48	142	.198	.299	9-0	.333	1	176	6	0.5
1985	Tex A	5	4	.556	58	0	0	11-4	113	74	35	7	5	43-3	111	2.47	171	.186	.273	0-0	—	0		21	2.0
1986	Tex A	10	8	.556	73	0	0	20-11	111.1	103	40	12	1	42-6	95	2.83	152	.251	.318	0-0	—	0		17	3.2
1987	Tex A	5	10	.333	42	19	0	0-4	140.2	157	92	18	4	56-3	106	4.86	92	.281	.349	0-0	—	0	125	-8	-0.7
1988	Phi N	4	6	.400	66	1	0	1-1	107	80	34	7	4	52-14	71	2.36	151	.209	.309	9-1	.333	1	100	13	1.3
1989	Phi N	2	2	.500	44	0	0	1-0	75.1	64	34	7	2	43-7	51	3.58	99	.234	.340	6-1	.167	1		0	0.1
	Bos A	2	2	.500	15	0	0	0-1	28	21	12	1	0	15-2	25	2.57	160	.208	.308	0-0	—	0		3	0.4
1990	†Bos A	13	9	.591	34	30	1	0-0	184.1	186	90	13	6	77-7	117	4.00	102	.265	.338	0-0	—	0	100	2	0.4
1991	Bos A	11	12	.478	53	21	1	2-3	173	157	79	13	5	69-5	127	3.85	112	.243	.318	0-0	—	0	80	10	1.3
1992	Bos A	4	9	.308	70	2	1	4-6	107.2	82	38	6	4	60-11	73	2.51	168	.215	.324	0-0	—	0	32	18	2.1
1993	Bos A	6	7	.462	**80**	0	0	8-10	112.1	95	55	7	10	60-14	103	3.77	123	.232	.341	0-0	—	0		9	1.1
1994	Bos A	3	4	.429	35	0	0	2-4	45.2	60	44	8	1	23-6	44	8.28	61	.321	.396	0-0	—	0		-15	-1.9
	NY A	0	1	.000	3	0	0	0-1	5	4	5	1	2	3-1	4	5.40	85	.222	.375	0-0	—	0		-1	-0.2
	Year	3	5	.375	38	0	0	2-5	50.2	64	51	9	3	26-7	48	7.99	62	.312	.394	0-0	—	0		-16	-2.1
1995	Mon N	2	3	.400	45	0	0	0-1	48.1	45	18	6	1	16-1	47	2.61	165	.245	.308	3-0	.333	1		8	0.7
Total	15	74	90	.451	703	98	4	54-46	1467	1329	689	129	54	652-86	1141	3.69	112	.243	.327	68-2	.221	3	98	63	8.6
HARRIS, GREG Gregory Wade B 12.1.1963 Greensboro, NC BR/TR 6-2/187# d9.14																									
1988	SD N	2	0	1.000	3	1	1	0-0	18	13	3	0	0	3-0	15	1.50	227	.200	.235	7-0	.000	-1	235	4	0.4
1989	SD N	8	9	.471	56	8	0	6-2	135	106	43	8	2	52-9	106	2.60	135	.215	.291	19-4	.053	-1	95	14	1.8
1990	SD N	8	8	.500	73	0	0	9-7	117.1	92	35	6	4	49-13	97	2.30	166	.220	.303	12-1	.083	-0		19	2.8
1991	SD N	9	5	.643	20	20	3-2	0-0	133	116	42	16	1	27-6	95	2.23	170	.233	.273	36-7	.083	-1	86	20	1.9
1992	SD N	4	8	.333	20	20	1	0-0	118	113	62	13	2	35-2	66	4.12	87	.252	.307	31-5	.129	1	98	-8	-0.7
1993	SD N	10	9	.526	22	22	4	0-0	152	151	65	18	3	39-6	83	3.67	113	.257	.306	53-4	.170	1	95	10	1.4
	Col N	1	8	.111	13	13	0	0-0	73.1	88	62	15	4	30-3	40	6.50	73	.299	.370	20-1	.050	-2	70	-13	-1.5
	Year	11	17	.393	35	35	4	0-0	225.1	239	66	33	7	69-9	123	4.59	95	.271	.328	73-5	.137	-0	85	-5	-0.1
1994	Col N	3	12	.200	29	19	1	1-0	130	154	99	22	5	52-4	82	6.65	75	.300	.366	40-4	.175	-0	67	-19	-1.8
1995	Min A	0	5	.000	7	6	0	0-0	32.2	50	35	5	0	16-0	21	8.82	54	.355	.415	0-0	—	0	75	-15	-1.7
Total	8	45	64	.413	243	109	10-2	16-9	909.1	883	446	103	21	303-43	605	3.98	102	.255	.317	218-26	.119	-3	87	12	2.6
HARRIS, HERB Herbert Benjamin "Hub" or "Lefty" B 4.24.1913 Chicago, IL D 1.18.1991 Crystal Lake, IL BL/TL 6-1/175# d7.21																									
1936	Phi N	0	0	—	4	0	0	0	7	14	8	0	1	5	0	10.29	44	.438	.526	1-0	.000	-0		-3	-0.2
HARRIS, PEP Hernando Petrocelli B 9.23.1972 Lancaster, SC BR/TR 6-2/185# d8.14																									
1996	Cal A	2	0	1.000	11	3	0	0-0	32.1	31	16	4	3	17-2	20	3.90	129	.254	.349	0-0	—	0	173	4	0.2
1997	Ana A	5	4	.556	61	0	0	0-3	79.2	82	33	7	2	38-6	56	3.62	127	.274	.356	0-0	—	0		9	0.9
1998	Ana A	3	1	.750	49	0	0	0-1	60	55	32	7	0	23-4	34	4.35	108	.239	.307	0-0	—	0		2	0.2
Total	3	10	5	.667	121	3	0	0-4	172	168	81	18	5	78-12	110	3.92	120	.258	.338	0-0	—	0	173	15	1.3
HARRIS, JOE Joseph White B 2.1.1882 Melrose, MA D 4.12.1966 Melrose, MA BR/TR 6-1/198# d9.22																									
1905	Bos A	1	2	.333	3	3	3	0	23	16	6	0	0	8	14	2.35	115	.198	.270	9-0	.111	-1	52	2	0.1
1906	Bos A	2	21	.087	30	24	20-1	2	235	211	130	5	7	67	99	3.52	78	.243	.303	81-1	.160	-2	44	-22	-2.0
1907	Bos A	0	7	.000	12	5	3	0	59	57	28	0	1	13	24	3.05	84	.256	.300	21-0	.190	-0	58	-3	-0.3
Total	3	3	30	.091	45	32	26-1	2	317	284	164	5	8	88	137	3.35	81	.242	.300	111-1	.162	-3	47	-23	-2.2
HARRIS, MICKEY Maurice Charles B 1.30.1917 New York, NY D 4.15.1971 Farmington, MI BL/TL 6/195# d4.23 Mil 1942-45																									
1940	Bos A	4	2	.667	13	9	3	0	68.1	83	40	8	2	26	36	5.00	90	.292	.356	22-1	.273	2	119	-3	0.0
1941	Bos A	8	14	.364	35	22	11-1	1	194	189	86	6	2	86	111	3.25	128	.250	.328	55-4	.109	2	114	18	2.0
1946	†Bos A☆	17	9	.654	34	30	15	0	222.2	236	105	18	3	76	131	3.64	101	.268	.329	78-5	.231	4	121	-1	0.2
1947	Bos A	5	4	.556	15	6	1	0	51.2	42	20	3	0	23	35	2.44	159	.225	.310	12-1	.417	3	95	6	1.4
1948	Bos A	7	10	.412	20	17	6-1	0	113.2	120	73	10	1	59	42	5.30	83	.273	.360	32-2	.063	-1	94	-11	-1.5
1949	Bos A	2	3	.400	7	6	2	0	37.2	53	26	3	1	20	14	5.02	87	.323	.400	12-2	.083	-1	113	-4	-0.5
	Was A	2	12	.143	23	19	4	0	129	151	82	8	0	55	54	5.16	82	.292	.360	39-2	.205	1	69	-12	-1.0
	Year	4	15	.211	30	25	6	0	166.2	204	85	11	1	75	68	5.13	83	.299	.369	51-4	.176	1	79	-16	-1.5
1950	Was A	5	9	.357	**53**	0	0	**15**	98	93	56	9	1	46	41	4.78	94	.247	.330	17-0	.235	1		-1	-0.2
1951	Was A	6	8	.429	41	0	0	4	87.1	87	45	6	1	43	47	3.81	107	.260	.347	16-1	.188	0		1	0.2
1952	Was A	0	0	—	1	0	0	0	1	1	1	1	0	0	0	9.00	40	.250	.250	0-0	—	0		-1	0.0
	Cle A	3	0	1.000	29	0	0	1	46.2	42	26	6	1	21	23	4.63	72	.249	.335	5-0	.200	-0		-6	-0.4
	Year	3	0	1.000	30	0	0	1	47.2	43	27	7	1	21	23	4.72	71	.249	.333	5-0	.200	-0		-7	-0.4
Total	9	59	71	.454	271	109	42-2	21	1050	1097	560	78	12	455	534	4.18	98	.267	.342	288-18	.188	11	104	-14	0.2
HARRIS, REGGIE Reginald Allen B 8.12.1968 Waynesboro, VA BR/TR 6-1/180# d7.4																									
1990	Oak A	1	0	1.000	16	1	0	0-0	41.1	25	16	5	2	21-1	31	3.48	107	.176	.287	0-0	—	0	98	2	0.1
1991	Oak A	0	0	—	2	0	0	0-0	3	5	4	0	0	3-1	2	12.00	32	.455	.533	0-0	—	0		-3	-0.1
1996	Bos A	0	0	—	4	0	0	0-1	4.1	7	6	2	1	5-0	4	12.46	41	.389	.542	0-0	—	0		-3	-0.1
1997	Phi N	1	3	.250	50	0	0	0-0	54.1	55	33	1	5	43-1	45	5.30	80	.263	.395	0-0	—	0		-5	-0.4
1998	Hou N	0	0	—	6	0	0	0-0	6	6	4	1	0	2-0	2	6.00	68	.261	.308	0-0	—	0		-1	-0.1
1999	Mil N	0	0	—	8	0	0	0-0	12	8	4	1	2	7-0	11	3.00	151	.186	.321	1-0	.000	-0		2	0.1
Total	6	2	3	.400	86	1	0	0-1	121	106	67	10	10	81-3	95	4.91	84	.238	.361	1-0	.000	-0	98	-8	-0.5
HARRIS, BOB Robert Arthur B 5.1.1917 Gillette, WY D 8.8.1989 North Platte, NE BR/TR 6/185# d9.19 Mil 1943-45																									
1938	Det A	1	0	1.000	3	1	1	0	10	14	9	0	0	4	7	7.20	69	.318	.375	3-0	.333	0	176	-2	-0.1
1939	Det A	1	1	.500	5	1	0	0	18	18	8	4	0	8	9	4.00	122	.269	.347	5-0	.400	0	90	2	0.2
	StL A	3	12	.200	28	16	6	0	126	162	88	5	0	71	48	5.71	85	.321	.405	37-2	.189	-0*	67	-10	-0.9

Year	Tm Lg	W	L	Pct	G	GS	CG-Sho	SV-BS	IP	H	R	HR	HB	BB-IB	SO	ERA	AERA	OAV	OOB	AB-SH	AVG	PB	Sup	APR	PW
	Year	4	13	.235	33	17	6	0	144	180	92	9	0	79	57	5.50	89	.315	.398	42-2	.214	-0	68	-8	-0.7
1940	StL A	11	15	.423	35	28	8-1	1	193.2	225	120	24	3	85	49	4.93	93	.290	.362	60-5	.250	3	86	-7	-0.5
1941	StL A	12	14	.462	34	29	9-2	1	186.2	237	117	18	2	85	57	5.21	83	.312	.383	61-14	.115	-3	104	-16	-2.2
1942	StL A	1	5	.167	6	6	0	0	33.2	37	24	2	0	17	9	5.61	66	.268	.348	10-2	.000	-1	69	-7	-1.1
	Phi A	1	5	.167	16	8	2-1	0	78	77	31	5	0	24	26	2.88	131	.253	.308	26-0	.269	1	79	7	0.7
	Year	2	10	.167	22	14	2-1	0	111.2	114	35	7	0	41	35	3.71	101	.258	.321	36-2	.194	0	75	0	-0.4
Total	5	30	52	.366	127	89	26-4	2	646	770	397	58	5	294	205	4.96	89	.297	.370	202-23	.193	1	87	-33	-3.9
HARRIS, GENE Tyrone Eugene B 12.5.1964 Sebring, FL BR/TR 5-11/190# d4.5																									
1989	Mon N	1	1	.500	11	0	0	0-2	20	16	11	1	0	10-0	11	4.95	71	.242	.338	1-1	.000	-0		-3	-0.2
	Sea A	1	4	.200	10	6	0	1-0	33.1	47	27	3	1	15-1	14	6.48	62	.353	.414	0-0	—	0*	97	-9	-1.2
1990	Sea A	1	2	.333	25	0	0	0-1	38	31	25	5	1	30-5	43	4.74	84	.217	.352	0-0	—	0		-4	-0.3
1991	Sea A	0	0	—	8	0	0	1-0	13.1	15	8	1	0	10-3	6	4.05	102	.273	.385	0-0	—	0		-1	0.0
1992	Sea A	0	0	—	8	0	0	0-0	9	8	7	3	0	6-0	6	7.00	57	.235	.350	0-0	—	0		-3	-0.2
	SD N	0	2	.000	14	1	0	0-0	21.1	15	8	0	1	9-0	19	2.95	121	.195	.287	3-0	.333	0*	126	1	0.1
1993	SD N	6	6	.500	59	0	0	23-8	59.1	57	27	3	1	37-8	39	3.03	136	.254	.360	1-0	.000	-0		5	1.1
1994	SD N	1	1	.500	13	0	0	0-3	12.1	21	11	2	0	8-2	9	8.03	51	.389	.468	1-0	.000	-0		-5	-0.7
	Det A	0	0	—	11	0	0	1-1	11.1	13	10	1	1	4-1	10	7.15	68	.271	.340	0-0	—	0		-3	-0.1
1995	Phi N	2	2	.500	21	0	0	0-1	19	19	9	2	0	8-0	9	4.26	99	.260	.333	0-0	—	0		0	0.1
	Bal A	0	0	—	3	0	0	0-1	4	4	2	0	0	1-0	4	4.50	106	.267	.313	0-0	—	0		0	0.0
Total	7	12	18	.400	183	7	0	26-17	241	246	145	21	5	138-20	170	4.71	86	.267	.363	6-1	.167	-0	99	-22	-1.4
HARRIS, BUDDY Walter Francis B 12.5.1948 Philadelphia, PA BR/TR 6-7/245# d9.10																									
1970	Hou N	0	0	—	2	0	0	0-0	6.1	6	4	3	0	0-0	2	5.68	68	.240	.240	1-0	.000	-0		-1	-0.1
1971	Hou N	1	1	.500	20	0	0	0-0	30.2	33	22	3	0	16-1	21	6.46	52	.275	.358	2-0	.000	-0		-10	-0.7
Total	2	1	1	.500	22	0	0	0-0	37	39	26	6	0	16-1	23	6.32	55	.269	.340	3-0	.000	-0		-11	-0.8
HARRIS, BILL William Milton B 6.23.1900 Wylie, TX D 8.21.1965 Charlotte, NC BR/TR 6-1/180# d4.22																									
1923	Cin N	3	2	.600	22	3	1	0	69.2	79	42	3	3	18	18	5.17	75	.292	.342	17-1	.353	1	71	-7	-0.3
1924	Cin N	0	0	—	3	0	0	0	7	10	7	0	0	2	5	9.00	42	.323	.364	1-0	1.000	0		-4	-0.1
1931	Pit N	2	2	.500	4	4	3-1	0	31	21	6	0	0	9	10	0.87	442	.194	.256	11-0	.091	-1	67	9	1.2
1932	Pit N	10	9	.526	37	17	4	2	168	178	84	6	6	38	63	3.64	105	.271	.317	55-0	.182	-1	88	3	0.2
1933	Pit N	4	4	.500	31	0	0	5	58.2	68	28	1	1	14	19	3.22	103	.289	.332	9-0	.000	-1		0	-0.2
1934	Pit N	0	0	—	11	1	0	0	19	28	15	2	1	7	8	6.63	62	.350	.409	2-0	.500	0	231	-5	-0.2
1938	Bos A	5	5	.500	13	11	5-1	1	80.1	83	39	5	1	21	26	4.03	122	.268	.316	28-2	.214	-0	115	9	0.9
Total	7	24	22	.522	121	36	13-2	8	433.2	467	221	17	12	109	149	3.92	101	.276	.324	123-3	.203	-1	102	5	1.5
HARRIS, BILL William Thomas B 12.3.1931 Duguayville, NB, CAN BL/TR 5-8/187# d9.27																									
1957	Bro N	0	1	.000	1	1	0	0	7	9	3	1	0	1-0	3	3.86	108	.321	.345	2-0	.500	0	42	0	0.1
1959	LA N	0	0	—	1	0	0	0	1.2	0	0	0	0	3-1	0	0.00	—	.000	.375	0-0	—	0		1	0.0
Total	2	0	1	.000	2	1	0	0	8.2	9	3	1	0	4-1	3	3.12	134	.273	.351	2-0	.500	0	42	1	0.1
HARRISON, BOB Robert Lee B 9.22.1930 St.Louis, MO BL/TR 5-11/178# d9.23																									
1955	Bal A	0	0	—	1	0	0	0	2	3	2	0	0	4-0	0	9.00	42	.500	.700	0-0	—	0		-1	-0.1
1956	Bal A	0	0	—	1	1	0	0	1.2	3	3	0	0	5-0	0	16.20	24	.375	.615	0-0	—	0	136	-2	-0.1
Total	2	0	0	—	2	1	0	0	3.2	6	5	0	0	9-0	0	12.27	31	.429	.652	0-0	—	0	136	-3	-0.2
HARRISON, RORIC Roric Edward B 9.20.1946 Los Angeles, CA BR/TR 6-3/195# d4.18																									
1972	Bal A	3	4	.429	39	2	0	4-1	94	68	24	2	4	34-9	62	2.30	134	.209	.291	17-1	.118	1	101	9	0.9
1973	Atl N	11	8	.579	38	22	3	5-2	177.1	161	90	15	3	98-6	130	4.16	95	.242	.339	54-5	.056	-2*	134	-3	-0.6
1974	Atl N	6	11	.353	20	20	3	0-0	126	148	70	12	3	49-1	46	4.71	80	.294	.358	38-6	.184	2	90	-11	-1.2
1975	Atl N	3	4	.429	15	7	2	1-0	54.2	58	33	7	0	19-1	22	4.77	79	.266	.324	15-0	.200	1	83	-5	-0.6
	Cle A	7	7	.500	19	19	4	0-0	126	137	71	9	4	46-4	52	4.79	79	.275	.338	0-0	—	0	108	-11	-1.2
1978	Min A	0	1	.000	9	0	0	0-0	12	18	10	0	0	11-0	7	7.50	51	.346	.453	0-0	—	0		-4	-0.3
Total	5	30	35	.462	140	70	12	10-3	590	590	298	45	14	257-21	319	4.24	88	.261	.338	124-12	.121	2	112	-25	-3.0
HARRISON, TOM Thomas James B 1.18.1945 Trail, BC, CAN BR/TR 6-3/200# d5.7																									
1965	KC A	0	0	—	1	0	0	0	1	2	1	0	0	1-0	0	9.00	39	.667	.750	0-0	—	0*		-1	0.0
HARRISS, SLIM William Jennings Bryan B 12.11.1896 Brownwood, TX D 9.19.1963 Temple, TX BR/TR 6-6/180# d4.19																									
1920	Phi A	9	14	.391	31	25	11-1	0	192	226	111	5	5	57	60	4.08	99	.305	.359	66-3	.106	-7	70	2	-0.3
1921	Phi A	11	16	.407	39	28	14	2	227.2	258	136	16	9	73	92	4.27	104	.290	.350	81-5	.148	-7	84	4	-0.3
1922	Phi A	9	20	.310	47	32	13	3	229.2	262	148	19	3	94	102	5.02	85	.290	.359	74-4	.176	-4	99	-17	-2.2
1923	Phi A	10	16	.385	46	28	9	6	209.1	221	114	9	2	95	89	4.00	103	.280	.359	61-5	.066	-8	85	3	-0.2
1924	Phi A	6	10	.375	36	12	4-1	2	123	138	78	5	3	62	45	4.68	92	.291	.377	42-0	.167	-3	62	-6	-0.8
1925	Phi A	19	12	.613	46	**33**	15-2	1	252.2	263	118	8	6	95	95	3.49	133	.268	.336	88-7	.205	-3	105	31	3.2
1926	Phi A	3	5	.375	12	10	2	0	57	66	34	0	0	22	13	4.11	102	.289	.352	17-1	.059	-2	81	0	-0.2
	Bos A	6	10	.375	21	18	6-1	0	113	135	66	0	2	33	34	4.46	91	.311	.362	34-1	.206	-0	84	-5	-0.6
	Year	9	15	.375	33	28	8-1	0	170	201	70	0	2	55	47	4.34	95	.304	.359	51-2	.157	-2	83	-6	-0.8
1927	Bos A	14	21	.400	44	27	11-1	1	217.2	253	127	8	9	66	77	4.18	101	.298	.355	66-6	.121	-5	75	-2	-0.7
1928	Bos A	8	11	.421	27	15	4-1	1	128.1	141	74	5	2	33	37	4.63	89	.287	.335	36-5	.139	-3	64	-6	-1.1
Total	9	95	135	.413	349	228	89-7	16	1750.1	1963	1006	75	41	630	644	4.25	100	.290	.354	565-37	.145	-40	84	4	-3.2
HARRIST, EARL Earl "Irish" B 8.20.1919 Dubach, LA D 9.1.1998 Simsboro, LA BR/TR 6/178# d8.18																									
1945	Cin N	2	4	.333	14	5	1	0	62.1	60	30	2	1	27	15	3.61	104	.249	.327	15-3	.000	-2	59	0	-0.2
1947	Chi A	3	8	.273	33	4	0	5	93.2	85	48	3	3	49	55	3.56	103	.248	.347	24-2	.208	-0	97	-1	-0.1
1948	Chi A	1	3	.250	11	1	0	0	23	23	17	4	3	13	14	5.87	73	.267	.382	4-0	.000	-1	127	-4	-0.7
	Was A	3	3	.500	23	4	0	0	60.2	70	35	1	3	37	21	4.60	94	.293	.394	18-0	.167	-1	73	-2	-0.3
	Year	4	6	.400	34	5	0	0	83.2	93	39	5	6	50	35	4.95	87	.286	.391	22-0	.136	-2	84	-6	-1.0
1952	StL A	2	8	.200	36	9	1	5	116.2	119	61	7	10	47	49	4.01	98	.269	.352	31-4	.097	-2	67	-2	-0.4
1953	Chi A	1	0	1.000	7	0	0	0	8.1	9	7	1	0	5	1	7.56	53	.290	.389	1-0	.000	-0		-3	-0.3
	Det A	0	2	.000	8	1	0	0	18.2	25	19	2	0	15	7	8.68	47	.333	.444	3-0	.000	-0	22	-9	-0.8
	Year	1	2	.333	15	1	0	0	27	34	20	3	0	20	8	8.33	49	.321	.429	4-0	.000	-0	22	-12	-1.1
Total	5	12	28	.300	132	24	2	10	383.1	391	217	20	20	193	162	4.34	90	.268	.361	96-9	.115	-7	72	-21	-2.8
HARSHMAN, JACK John Elvin B 7.12.1927 San Diego, CA BL/TL 6-2/185# d9.16.1948																									
1952	NY N	0	2	.000	2	2	0	0	6.1	12	10	2	0	6	6	14.21	26	.429	.529	2-0	.000	-0*	48	-7	-1.0
1954	Chi A	14	8	.636	35	21	9-4	1	177	157	61	7	5	96	134	2.95	127	.238	.339	56-3	.143	3*	106	17	2.4
1955	Chi A	11	7	.611	32	23	9	0	179.1	144	74	16	4	97-3	116	3.36	117	.224	.327	60-5	.183	4	122	11	1.3
1956	Chi A	15	11	.577	34	30	15-4	0	226.2	183	85	14	3	102-4	143	3.10	132	.221	.305	71-4	.169	6*	98	26	3.3
1957	Chi A	8	8	.500	30	26	6	1	151.1	142	78	16	5	82-2	83	4.10	91	.250	.344	45-2	.222	5	108	-8	-0.3
1958	Bal A	12	15	.444	34	29	17-3	4	236.1	204	89	20	3	75-1	161	2.89	124	.231	.292	82-1	.195	8*	67	17	3.3
1959	Bal A	0	6	.000	14	8	0	0	47.1	58	39	6	2	28-5	24	6.85	55	.319	.409	10-0	.200	1*	67	-16	-1.5
	Bos A	2	3	.400	8	2	0	0	24.2	29	19	2	0	10-0	14	6.57	62	.284	.348	7-1	.143	0*	54	-6	-1.1
	Cle A	5	1	.833	13	6	5-1	1	66	46	21	6	0	13-0	35	2.59	142	.179	.218	34-0	.206	2*	128	9	1.0
	Year	7	10	.412	35	16	5-1	1	138	133	26	14	2	51-5	73	4.76	79	.246	.311	51-1	.196	3	87	-14	-1.6
1960	Cle A	2	4	.333	15	8	0	0	54.1	50	32	7	0	30-2	25	3.98	94	.243	.333	17-2	.176	-0	106	-4	-0.4
Total	8	69	65	.515	217	155	61-12	7	1169.1	1025	508	96	22	539-17	741	3.50	109	.235	.320	384-18	.182	29	98	39	7.0
HARSTAD, OSCAR Oscar Theander B 5.24.1892 Parkland, WA D 11.14.1985 Corvallis, OR BR/TR 6/174# d4.23																									
1915	Cle A	3	5	.375	32	7	4	1	82	81	45	1	1	35	35	3.40	90	.270	.348	16-1	.125	-1	102	-4	-0.4
HART, BILLY Robert Lee B 5.16.1866 Palmyra, MO D 5.14.1944 Hannibal, MO 5-8/?# d7.13																									
1890	StL AA	12	8	.600	26	24	20	0	201.1	188	111	6	16	66	95	3.67	118	.240	.312	78	.192	-1*	92	17	1.1

Year	Tm Lg	W	L	Pct	G	GS	CG-Sho	SV-BS	IP	H	R	HR	HB	BB-IB	SO	ERA	AERA	OAV	OOB	AB-SH	AVG	PB	Sup	APR	PW
HART, BILL William Franklin B 7.19.1865 Louisville, KY D 9.19.1936 Cincinnati, OH TR 5-10/163# d7.26 U2																									
1886	Phi AA	9	13	.409	22	22	22-2	0	186	183	144	7	7	66	78	3.19	110	.234	.299	73	.137	-5	79	-2	-0.6
1887	Phi AA	1	2	.333	3	3	3	0	26	28	22	1	1	17	4	4.50	95	.272	.380	13	.077	-2	99	-2	-0.3
1892	Bro N	9	12	.429	28	23	16-2	1	195	188	109	3	7	96	65	3.28	97	.243	.332	125	.192	3*	97	-5	-0.1
1895	Pit N	14	17	.452	36	29	24	1	261.2	293	186	4	15	135	85	4.75	95	.279	.369	106-3	.236	-2	88	-1	0.0
1896	StL N	12	29	.293	42	41	37	0	336	411	271	11	15	141	65	5.12	85	.299	.370	161-4	.186	-5*	72	-31	-3.0
1897	StL N	9	27	.250	39	38	31	0	294.2	395	292	10	16	148	67	6.26	70	.318	.398	156-0	.250	-1*	76	-62	-5.4
1898	Pit N	5	9	.357	16	15	13-1	1	125	141	81	4	7	44	19	4.82	74	.282	.348	50-0	.240	0	64	-14	-1.3
1901	Cle A	7	11	.389	20	19	16	0	157.2	180	109	3	10	57	48	3.77	94	.283	.352	64-1	.219	-2	83	-7	-0.7
Total	8	66	120	.355	206	190	162-5	3	1582	1819	1214	43	78	704	431	4.65	86	.282	.359	748-8	.207	-14	80	-124	-11.4
HARTENSTEIN, CHUCK Charles Oscar "Twiggy" B 5.26.1942 Seguin, TX BR/TR 5-11/165# d9.11.1965 C4																									
1966	Chi N	0	0	—	5	0	0	0	9.1	8	2	0	1	3-0	4	1.93	191	.222	.300	0-0	—	0		2	0.1
1967	Chi N	9	5	.643	45	0	0	10	73	74	27	4	1	17-7	20	3.08	115	.278	.321	16-1	.063	-1		4	0.7
1968	Chi N	2	4	.333	28	0	0	1	35.2	41	19	3	1	11-2	17	4.54	70	.291	.346	2-0	.000	-0		-5	-0.9
1969	Pit N	5	4	.556	56	0	0	10-3	95.2	84	42	9	4	27-3	44	3.95	88	.241	.300	14-1	.071	-1		-3	-0.3
1970	Pit N	1	1	.500	17	0	0	1-0	23.2	25	15	3	0	8-4	14	4.56	86	.278	.333	1-0	.000	-0		-3	-0.2
	StL N	0	0	—	6	0	0	0-1	13.1	24	13	1	0	5-0	9	8.78	47	.375	.414	2-0	.000	0		-6	-0.3
	Year	1	1	.500	23	0	0	1-1	37	49	33	4	0	13-4	23	6.08	66	.318	.367	3-0	.000	-0		-9	-0.5
	Bos A	0	3	.000	17	0	0	1-2	19	21	17	6	1	12-5	12	8.05	49	.288	.395	2-0	.000	0		-7	-1.1
1977	Tor A	0	2	.000	13	0	0	0-1	27.1	40	22	8	1	6-0	15	6.59	64	.348	.385	0-0	—	0		-7	-0.4
Total	6	17	19	.472	187	0	0	23-7	297	317	157	34	9	89-21	135	4.52	80	.280	.335	37-2	.054	-2		-25	-2.4
HARTER, FRANK Franklin Pierce "Chief" B 9.19.1886 Keyesport, IL D 4.14.1959 Breese, IL BR/TR 5-11/165# d8.31																									
1912	Cin N	1	2	.333	6	3	1	0	29.1	25	16	1	0	11	12	3.07	110	.234	.305	11-0	.091	-1	44	0	-0.1
1913	Cin N	1	1	.500	17	2	0	0	46.2	47	23	3	0	19	10	3.86	84	.272	.344	14-0	.143	-1	116	-2	-0.2
1914	Ind F	1	2	.333	6	1	1	0	24.2	33	12	0	0	7	8	4.01	78	.330	.374	8-0	.000	-1	154	-1	-0.3
Total	3	3	5	.375	29	6	2	0	100.2	105	51	4	0	37	30	3.67	89	.276	.341	33-0	.091	-3	86	-3	-0.6
HARTGRAVES, DEAN Dean Charles B 8.12.1966 Bakersfield, CA BR/TL 6/185# d5.3																									
1995	Hou N	2	0	1.000	40	0	0	0-3	36.1	30	14	2	0	16-2	24	3.22	120	.227	.309	2-1	.000	-0		3	0.1
1996	Hou N	0	0	—	19	0	0	0-0	19	18	11	1	1	16-3	16	5.21	74	.257	.398	0-1	—	0		-2	-0.1
	Atl N	1	0	1.000	20	0	0	0-0	18.2	16	10	3	1	7-0	14	4.34	102	.232	.308	1-0	.000	-0		0	0.0
	Year	1	0	1.000	39	0	0	0-0	37.2	34	25	4	2	23-3	30	4.78	87	.245	.355	1-1	.000	-0		-2	-0.1
1998	SF N	0	0	—	5	0	0	0-0	5.2	10	7	1	0	4-0	4	9.53	42	.385	.438	0-0	—	0		-4	-0.2
Total	3	3	0	1.000	84	0	0	0-3	79.2	74	42	7	2	43-5	58	4.41	91	.249	.343	3-2	.000	-0		-3	-0.2
HARTLEY, MIKE Michael Edward B 8.31.1961 Hawthorne, CA BR/TR 6-1/197# d9.10																									
1989	LA N	0	1	.000	5	0	0	0-1	6	2	1	0	0	0-0	4	1.50	228	.100	.100	1-0	.000	-0		1	0.2
1990	LA N	6	3	.667	32	6	1-1	1-1	79.1	58	32	7	2	30-2	76	2.95	124	.200	.279	13-3	.077	-1	82	5	0.5
1991	LA N	2	0	1.000	40	0	0	1-0	57	53	29	7	3	37-7	44	4.42	81	.245	.362	4-0	.000	-0		-4	-0.3
	Phi N	2	1	.667	18	0	0	1-2	26.1	21	11	4	3	10-1	19	3.76	98	.219	.312	1-0	.000	-0		0	0.0
	Year	4	1	.800	58	0	0	2-2	83.1	74	43	11	6	47-8	63	4.21	86	.237	.347	5-0	.000	-1		-4	-0.3
1992	Phi N	7	6	.538	46	0	0	0-4	55	54	23	5	2	23-6	53	3.44	102	.255	.332	4-0	.000	-0*		0	0.0
1993	Min A	1	2	.333	53	0	0	1-2	81	86	38	4	7	36-3	57	4.00	109	.281	.363	0-0	—	0		4	0.1
1995	Bos A	0	0	—	5	0	0	0-0	7	8	7	1	2	2-0	2	9.00	54	.308	.375	0-0	—	0		-3	-0.1
	Bal A	1	0	1.000	3	0	0	0-0	7	5	1	0	0	1-0	4	1.29	370	.217	.250	0-0	—	0		3	0.4
	Year	1	0	1.000	8	0	0	0-0	14	13	8	1	2	3-0	6	5.14	94	.265	.321	0-0	—	0		0	0.3
Total	6	19	13	.594	202	6	1-1	4-10	318.2	287	142	28	19	139-19	259	3.70	104	.241	.328	23-3	.043	-2	82	6	0.8
HARTMAN, CHARLIE Charles Otto B 8.10.1888 Los Angeles, CA D 10.22.1960 Los Angeles, CA TL d6.24																									
1908	Bos A	0	0	—	1	0	0	0	2	1	1	0	0	2	1	4.50	55	.143	.333	0-0	—	0		0	0.0
HARTMAN, BOB Robert Louis B 8.28.1937 Kenosha, WI BR/TL 5-11/185# d4.26																									
1959	Mil N	0	0	—	3	0	0	0	1.2	6	5	0	0	2-0	1	27.00	13	.545	.615	0-0	—	0		-4	-0.2
1962	Cle A	0	1	.000	8	2	0	0	17.1	14	10	1	0	8-0	11	3.12	124	.209	.289	7-0	.000	-1	104	0	-0.1
Total	2	0	1	.000	11	2	0	0	19	20	15	1	0	10-0	12	5.21	74	.256	.337	7-0	.000	-1	104	-4	-0.3
HARTRANFT, RAY Raymond Joseph B 9.19.1890 Quakertown, PA D 2.10.1955 Spring City, PA BL/TL 6-1/195# d6.16																									
1913	Phi N	0	0	—	1	0	0	0	1	3	1	0	0	1	1	9.00	37	.500	.571	0-0	—	0		-1	0.0
HARTSOCK, JEFF Jeffrey Roger B 11.19.1966 Fairfield, OH BR/TR 6/190# d9.12																									
1992	Chi N	0	0	—	4	0	0	0-0	9.1	15	7	2	0	4-0	6	6.75	53	.375	.422	2-0	.000	-0		-3	-0.2
HARTUNG, CLINT Clinton Clarence "Floppy" or "The Hondo Hurricane" B 8.10.1922 Hondo, TX BR/TR 6-4/215# d4.15 ▲																									
1947	NY N	9	7	.563	23	20	8-1	0	138	140	76	15	2	69	54	4.57	89	.263	.350	94-0	.309	9*	107	-6	0.3
1948	NY N	8	8	.500	36	19	6-2	1	153.1	146	89	15	5	72	42	4.75	83	.258	.347	56-0	.179	2*	123	-11	-0.9
1949	NY N	9	11	.450	33	25	8	0	154.2	156	98	17	4	86	48	5.00	80	.260	.357	63-0	.190	4*	114	-16	-1.4
1950	NY N	3	3	.500	20	8	1	0	65.1	87	56	10	2	44	23	6.61	62	.326	.425	43-0	.302	4*	108	-19	-1.0
Total	4	29	29	.500	112	72	23-3	1	511.1	529	319	57	13	271	167	5.02	80	.269	.361	256-0	.250	19	114	-52	-3.0
HARTZELL, PAUL Paul Franklin B 11.2.1953 Bloomsburg, PA BR/TR 6-5/200# d4.10																									
1976	Cal A	7	4	.636	37	15	7-2	2-1	166	166	64	6	10	43-5	51	2.77	120	.266	.321	0-0	—	0	120	8	0.6
1977	Cal A	8	12	.400	41	23	6	4-0	189.1	200	92	14	4	38-6	79	3.57	110	.274	.309	0-0	—	0	98	6	0.6
1978	Cal A	6	10	.375	54	12	5	6-2	157	168	67	8	5	41-9	55	3.44	105	.278	.328	0-0	—	0	72	4	0.4
1979	Min A	6	10	.375	28	26	4	0-0	163	193	102	18	4	44-4	44	5.36	82	.301	.346	0-0	—	0	92	-15	-1.3
1980	Bal A	0	2	.000	6	0	0	0-0	17.2	22	14	3	0	9-2	5	6.62	60	.310	.387	0-0	—	0		-5	-0.5
1984	Mil A	0	1	.000	4	1	0	0-0	10.1	17	11	0	0	6-0	3	7.84	49	.370	.426	0-0	—	0	70	-5	-0.4
Total	6	27	39	.409	170	77	22-2	12-3	703.1	766	350	49	23	181-26	237	3.90	98	.282	.329	0-0	—	0	98	-7	-0.6
HARVEY, BRYAN Bryan Stanley B 6.2.1963 Soddy-Daisy, TN BR/TR 6-2/212# d5.16																									
1987	Cal A	0	0	—	3	0	0	0-0	5	6	0	0	0	2-0	3	0.00	—	.300	.364	0-0	—	0		2	0.1
1988	Cal A	7	5	.583	50	0	0	17-6	76	59	22	4	1	20-6	67	2.13	181	.214	.267	0-0	—	0		14	2.6
1989	Cal A	3	3	.500	51	0	0	25-7	55	36	21	6	0	41-1	78	3.44	111	.183	.321	0-0	—	0		3	0.6
1990	Cal A	4	4	.500	54	0	0	25-6	64.1	45	24	4	0	35-6	82	3.22	119	.201	.304	0-0	—	0		6	1.0
1991	Cal A☆	2	4	.333	67	0	0	**46-6**	78.2	51	20	6	1	17-3	101	1.60	257	.178	.225	0-0	—	0		20	3.3
1992	Cal A	0	4	.000	25	0	0	13-3	28.2	22	12	4	0	11-1	34	2.83	141	.208	.275	0-0	—	0		3	0.5
1993	Fla N★	1	5	.167	59	0	0	45-4	69	45	14	4	0	13-2	73	1.70	255	.186	.222	0-0	—	0		19	3.7
1994	Fla N	0	0	—	12	0	0	6-0	10.1	12	6	1	0	4-0	10	5.23	84	.279	.340	0-0	—	0		-1	-0.1
1995	Fla N	0	0	—	1	0	0	0-0	0	2	3	1	0	1-0	0	∞	—	1.000	1.000	0-0	—	0		-3	-0.2
Total	9	17	25	.405	322	0	0	177-32	387	278	122	30	2	144-19	448	2.49	161	.199	.271	0-0	—	0		63	11.5
HARVEY, ZAZA Ervin King B 1.5.1879 Saratoga, CA D 6.3.1954 Santa Monica, CA BL/TL 6/190# d5.3 ▲																									
1900	Chi N	0	0	—	1	0	0	0	4	3	0	0	0	1	0	0.00	—	.214	.267	3-0	.000	-1*		2	0.0
1901	Chi A	3	7	.300	16	9	5	1	92	91	59	2	5	34	27	3.62	96	.255	.328	40-2	.250	2*	108	-2	0.1
Total	2	3	7	.300	17	9	5	1	96	94	59	2	5	35	27	3.47	101	.253	.326	43-2	.233	2	108	0	0.1
HARVILLE, CHAD Chad Ashley B 9.16.1976 Selmer, TN BR/TR 5-9/180# d6.23																									
1999	Oak A	0	2	.000	15	0	0	0-0	14.1	18	11	2	0	10-1	15	6.91	67	.310	.406	0-0	—	0		-3	-0.4
2001	Oak A	0	0	—	3	0	0	0-0	3	2	0	0	0	0-0	2	0.00	—	.182	.182	0-0	—	0		1	0.1
2003	Oak A	1	0	1.000	21	0	0	1-0	21.2	25	15	3	1	17-1	18	5.82	78	.294	.413	0-0	—	0		-3	-0.2
Total	3	1	2	.333	39	0	0	1-0	39	45	26	5	1	27-2	35	5.77	79	.292	.397	0-0	—	0		-5	-0.5
HASEGAWA, SHIGETOSHI Shigetoshi B 8.1.1968 Kobe, Japan BR/TR 5-11/160# d4.5																									
1997	Ana A	3	7	.300	50	7	0	0-1	116.2	118	60	14	3	46-6	83	3.93	116	.269	.339	0-0	—	0	92	6	0.5

Year	Tm Lg	W	L	Pct	G	GS	CG-Sho	SV-BS	IP	H	R	HR	HB	BB-IB	SO	ERA	AERA	OAV	OOB	AB-SH	AVG	PB	Sup	APR	PW
1998	Ana A	8	3	.727	61	0	0	5-2	97.1	86	37	14	2	32-2	73	3.14	149	.241	.302	0-0	—	0		17	1.8
1999	Ana A	4	6	.400	64	1	0	2-3	77	80	45	14	2	34-2	44	4.91	99	.276	.352	0-0	—	0	0	0	0.0
2000	Ana A	10	5	.667	66	0	0	9-9	95.2	100	42	11	2	38-6	59	3.48	146	.270	.339	1-0	.000	-0		15	2.3
2001	Ana A	5	6	.455	46	0	0	0-6	55.2	52	28	5	2	20-5	41	4.04	113	.248	.316	0-0	—	0		3	0.5
2002	Sea A	8	3	.727	53	0	0	1-4	70.1	60	26	4	2	30-8	39	3.20	132	.238	.323	0-0	—	0		9	1.3
2003	Sea A★	2	4	.333	63	0	0	16-1	73	62	12	5	0	18-3	32	1.48	293	.235	.284	0-0	—	0		25	2.8
Total	7	40	34	.541	403	8	0	33-26	585.2	558	250	67	13	218-32	371	3.47	134	.256	.324	1-0	.000	-0	80	75	9.2
HASH, HERB Herbert Howard B 2.13.1911 Woolwine, VA BR/TR 6-1/180# d4.19																									
1940	Bos A	7	7	.500	34	12	3-1	3	120	123	68	11	5	84	36	4.95	91	.266	.385	40-3	.175	-0*	103	-4	-0.4
1941	Bos A	1	0	1.000	4	0	0	1	8.1	7	5	1	0	7	3	5.40	77	.226	.368	2-0	.000	-0		-1	-0.1
Total	2	8	7	.533	38	12	3-1	4	128.1	130	73	12	5	91	39	4.98	90	.264	.384	42-3	.167	-1	103	-5	-0.5
HASSLER, ANDY Andrew Earl B 10.18.1951 Texas City, TX BL/TL 6-5/220# d5.30																									
1971	Cal A	0	3	.000	6	4	0	0-0	18.2	25	10	0	1	15-2	13	3.86	84	.333	.446	5-1	.000	-1	48	-2	-0.3
1973	Cal A	0	4	.000	7	4	1	0-0	31.2	33	23	0	3	19-0	19	3.69	96	.262	.369	0-0	—	0	82	-4	-0.5
1974	Cal A	7	11	.389	23	22	10-2	1-0	162	132	64	10	9	79-2	76	2.61	132	.225	.325	0-0	—	0	104	12	1.3
1975	Cal A	3	12	.200	30	18	6-1	0-0	133.1	158	94	12	6	53-0	82	5.94	60	.303	.369	0-0	—	0	100	-34	-3.3
1976	Cal A	0	6	.000	14	4	0	0-0	47.1	50	31	3	0	17-2	16	5.13	65	.284	.342	0-0	—	0	73	-10	-1.2
	†KC A	5	6	.455	19	14	4-1	0-1	99.2	89	37	2	0	39-0	45	2.89	121	.242	.311	0-0	—	0	79	7	0.8
	Year	5	12	.294	33	18	4-1	0-1	147	139	40	5	0	56-2	61	3.61	95	.256	.321	0-0	—	0	78	-3	-0.4
1977	†KC A	9	6	.600	29	27	3-1	0-0	156.1	166	88	7	5	75-3	83	4.20	96	.270	.352	0-0	—	0*	125	-5	-0.4
1978	KC A	1	4	.200	11	9	1	0-0	58.1	76	36	1	2	24-0	26	4.32	89	.317	.381	0-0	—	0	109	-5	-0.4
	Bos A	2	1	.667	13	2	0	1-0	30	38	13	0	0	13-2	23	3.00	138	.302	.367	0-0	—	0	141	3	0.3
	Year	3	5	.375	24	11	1	1-0	88.1	114	20	1	2	37-2	49	3.87	102	.311	.376	0-0	—	0	114	-2	-0.1
1979	Bos A	1	2	.333	8	0	0	0-0	15.1	23	17	0	1	7-0	7	8.80	50	.365	.431	0-0	—	0		-7	-1.2
	NY N	4	5	.444	29	8	1	4-0	80.1	74	35	5	0	42-8	53	3.70	99	.252	.344	22-0	.000	-2	82	0	-0.2
1980	Pit N	0	0	—	6	0	0	0-0	11.2	9	6	2	0	4-0	4	3.86	95	.243	.310	2-0	.000	-0		0	0.0
	Cal A	5	1	.833	41	0	0	10-2	83	67	25	8	1	37-8	75	2.49	158	.214	.298	0-0	—	0		14	1.3
1981	Cal A	4	3	.571	42	0	0	5-2	75.2	72	29	8	0	33-8	44	3.21	114	.262	.339	0-0	—	0		4	0.5
1982	†Cal A	2	1	.667	54	0	0	4-2	71.1	58	24	5	4	40-5	38	2.78	146	.232	.343	0-0	—	0		10	0.6
1983	Cal A	0	5	.000	42	0	0	4-3	36.1	42	22	2	0	17-8	20	5.45	74	.302	.378	0-0	—	0		-5	-0.7
1984	StL N	1	0	1.000	3	0	0	0-0	2.1	4	3	2	0	2-1	1	11.57	30	.364	.462	0-0	—	0		-2	-0.4
1985	StL N	0	1	.000	10	0	0	0-0	10	9	5	0	0	4-0	5	1.80	197	.225	.289	0-0	—	0		1	0.1
Total	14	44	71	.383	387	112	26-5	29-10	1123.1	1125	562	67	32	520-49	630	3.83	97	.264	.346	29-1	.000	-3	101	-23	-3.7
HASTINGS, CHARLIE Charles Morton B 11.11.1870 Ironton, OH D 8.3.1934 Parkersburg, WV 5-11/179# d5.3																									
1893	Cle N	4	5	.444	15	9	6	1	92	128	81	5	5	33	14	4.70	104	.320	.379	39	.179	0*	100	0	0.0
1896	Pit N	5	10	.333	17	13	9	1	104	126	86	1	7	44	19	5.88	71	.296	.372	37-0	.216	-0	79	-18	-1.9
1897	Pit N	5	4	.556	16	10	9	0	118	138	84	3	7	47	42	4.58	91	.289	.362	43-1	.233	3	108	-6	-0.1
1898	Pit N	4	10	.286	19	13	12	0	137.1	142	76	2	10	52	40	3.41	104	.265	.341	43-1	.233	2	64	1	0.3
Total	4	18	29	.383	67	45	36	2	451.1	534	327	11	29	176	115	4.55	91	.291	.362	162-2	.216	5	87	-23	-1.7
HASTY, BOB Robert Keller B 5.3.1896 Canton, GA D 5.28.1972 Dallas, GA BR/TR 6-3/210# d9.11																									
1919	Phi A	0	2	.000	2	2	1	0	12	15	10	1	0	4	5	5.25	65	.306	.358	3-1	.333	0	46	-3	-0.4
1920	Phi A	1	3	.250	19	4	1	0	71.2	91	53	5	0	28	12	5.02	80	.323	.384	24-0	.250	0	94	-7	-0.2
1921	Phi A	5	16	.238	35	22	9	0	179.1	238	120	8	2	40	46	4.87	92	.331	.368	68-1	.294	2	63	-8	-0.5
1922	Phi A	9	14	.391	28	26	14-1	0	192.1	225	110	20	3	41	33	4.26	100	.298	.336	75-0	.200	-2	95	-1	-0.3
1923	Phi A	13	15	.464	44	36	10-1	1	243.1	274	146	11	9	72	56	4.44	93	.291	.347	88-6	.193	-3	82	-8	-1.1
1924	Phi A	1	3	.250	18	4	0	0	52.2	57	36	4	1	30	15	5.64	76	.282	.378	13-0	.077	-1	59	-7	-0.5
Total	6	29	53	.354	146	94	35-2	1	751.1	900	475	49	15	215	167	4.65	91	.305	.355	271-8	.221	-3	80	-34	-3.0
HATFIELD, GIL Gilbert "Colonel" B 1.27.1855 Hoboken, NJ D 5.26.1921 Hoboken, NJ TR 5-9.5/168# d9.24.1885 b-John ▲																									
1889	NY N	2	4	.333	6	5	5	0	52	53	43	2	1	25	28	3.98	99	.256	.339	125	.184	-0*	163	-2	-0.2
1890	NY P	1	1	.500	3	0	0	1	7.2	8	8	1	1	4	3	3.52	129	.258	.361	287	.279	0*		0	0.0
1891	Was AA	0	0	—	4	0	0	0	18	29	28	1	0	14	3	11.00	34	.349	.443	500	.256	1*		-12	-0.5
Total	3	3	5	.375	13	5	5	1	77.2	90	79	4	2	43	34	5.56	71	.280	.369	912	.253	1	163	-14	-0.7
HATHAWAY, HILLY Hillary Houston B 9.12.1969 Jacksonville, FL BL/TL 6-4/195# d9.8																									
1992	Cal A	0	0	—	2	1	0	0-0	5.2	8	5	1	0	3-0	1	7.94	50	.333	.393	0-0	—	0	92	-2	-0.1
1993	Cal A	4	3	.571	11	11	0	0-0	57.1	71	35	6	5	26-1	11	5.02	90	.326	.405	0-0	—	0	98	-3	-0.3
Tctal	2	4	3	.571	13	12	0	0-0	63	79	40	7	5	29-1	12	5.29	85	.326	.404	0-0	—	0	98	-5	-0.4
HATHAWAY, RAY Ray Wilson B 10.13.1916 Greenville, OH BR/TR 6/165# d4.20																									
1945	Bro N	0	1	.000	4	1	0	0	9	11	7	1	0	6	3	4.00	94	.297	.395	2-0	.000	-0	68	-1	-0.1
HATTEN, JOE Joseph Hilarian B 11.17.1916 Bancroft, IA D 12.16.1988 Redding, CA BR/TL 6/176# d4.21																									
1946	Bro N	14	11	.560	42	30	13-1	2	222	207	79	10	7	110	85	2.84	119	.253	.347	79-4	.076	-6	107	15	0.9
1947	†Bro N	17	8	.680	42	32	11-3	0	225.1	211	95	9	5	105	76	3.63	114	.252	.339	83-3	.205	0	104	16	1.8
1948	Bro N	13	10	.565	42	30	11-1	0	208.2	228	93	9	3	94	73	3.58	112	.283	.360	63-8	.206	1*	112	11	1.4
1949	†Bro N	12	8	.600	37	29	11-2	2	187.1	194	102	15	2	69	58	4.18	98	.271	.337	67-3	.179	-1*	122	-5	-0.6
1950	Bro N	2	2	.500	23	8	2-1	0	68.2	82	45	10	0	31	29	4.59	89	.294	.365	18-1	.111	-1*	97	-7	-0.5
1951	Bro N	1	0	1.000	11	6	0	0	49.1	55	25	3	0	21	22	4.56	86	.281	.350	15-1	.133	-1	139	-2	-0.2
	Chi N	2	6	.250	23	6	1	0	75.1	82	48	8	1	37	23	5.14	80	.281	.364	17-1	.235	0	58	-8	-0.8
	Year	3	6	.333	34	12	1	0	124.2	137	51	11	1	58	45	4.91	82	.281	.358	32-2	.188	-1	97	-9	-1.0
1952	Chi N	4	4	.500	13	8	2	0	50.1	65	35	6	1	25	15	6.08	63	.314	.391	15-1	.067	-1*	75	-10	-1.5
Total	7	65	49	.570	233	149	51-8	4	1087	1124	522	70	19	492	381	3.87	101	.271	.351	357-22	.160	-8	107	10	0.5
HATTER, CLYDE Clyde Melno B 8.7.1908 Poplar Hills, KY D 10.16.1937 Yosemite, KY BR/TL 5-11/170# d4.23																									
1935	Det A	0	0	—	8	2	0	0	33.1	44	33	2	1	30	15	7.56	55	.319	.444	10-1	.300	0	156	-14	-0.6
1937	Det A	1	0	1.000	3	0	0	0	9.1	17	12	0	1	11	4	11.57	40	.415	.547	3-0	.000	-0		-6	-0.5
Total	2	1	0	1.000	11	2	0	0	42.2	61	45	2	2	41	19	8.44	51	.341	.468	13-1	.231	0	156	-20	-1.1
HAUGHEY, CHRIS Christopher Francis "Bud" B 10.3.1925 Astoria, NY BR/TR 6-1/180# d10.3 Mil 1944-45																									
1943	Bro N	0	1	.000	1	0	0	0	7	5	6	0	0	10	0	3.86	87	.238	.484	3-0	.000	-0		-2	-0.2
HAUGHT, GARY Gary Allen B 9.29.1970 Tacoma, WA BB/TR 6-1/190# d7.16																									
1997	Oak A	0	0	—	6	0	0	0-0	11.1	12	9	3	2	6-0	11	7.15	63	.279	.385	0-0	—	0		-3	-0.1
HAUGSTAD, PHIL Philip Donald B 2.23.1924 Black River Falls, WI D 10.21.1998 Black River Falls, WI BR/TR 6-2/165# d9.1																									
1947	Bro N	1	0	1.000	6	1	0	0	12.2	14	4	1	0	4	4	2.84	145	.298	.353	2-0	.000	-0	43	2	0.1
1948	Bro N	0	0	—	1	0	0	0	1	1	0	0	0	0	0	0.00	—	.333	.333	0-0	—	0		0	0.0
1951	Bro N	0	1	.000	21	1	0	0	30.2	28	25	4	3	24	22	6.46	61	.233	.374	1-0	.000	0	270	-9	-0.4
1952	Cin N	0	0	—	9	0	0	0	12	8	9	1	1	13	2	6.75	56	.190	.393	1-0	.000	-0		-4	-0.2
Total	4	1	1	.500	37	2	0	0	56.1	51	38	6	4	41	28	5.59	70	.241	.374	4-0	.000	-0	157	-11	-0.5
HAUSMAN, TOM Thomas Matthew B 3.31.1953 Mobridge, SD BR/TR 6-5/200# d4.26																									
1975	Mil A	3	6	.333	29	9	1	0-0	112	110	57	7	6	47-7	46	4.10	94	.258	.338	0-0	—	0	76	-2	-0.2
1976	Mil A	0	0	—	3	0	0	0-0	3.1	3	2	0	0	3-1	1	5.40	65	.250	.400	0-0	—	0		-1	0.0
1978	NY N	3	3	.500	10	10	0	0-0	51.2	58	28	6	1	9-1	16	4.70	74	.287	.318	17-1	.176	1	95	-6	-0.6
1979	NY N	2	6	.250	19	10	1	2-1	78.2	65	25	6	4	19-1	33	2.75	133	.226	.282	26-1	.115	-1	70	9	0.8
1980	NY N	6	5	.545	55	4	0	1-0	122	125	63	12	3	26-8	53	3.98	89	.266	.307	16-1	.063	-1	88	-7	-0.7
1981	NY N	0	1	.000	20	0	0	0-0	33	28	8	2	0	7-1	13	2.18	160	.235	.273	2-0	.000	0		5	0.3
1982	NY N	1	2	.333	21	0	0	0-0	36.2	44	26	4	2	6-1	16	4.42	82	.295	.323	2-0	.000	-0		-5	-0.5
	Atl N	0	0	—	3	0	0	0-0	3.2	6	2	0	0	4-2	2	4.91	76	.500	.588	0-0	—	0		0	0.0

Year	Tm Lg	W	L	Pct	G	GS	CG-Sho	SV-BS	IP	H	R	HR	HB	BB-IB	SO	ERA	AERA	OAV	OOB	AB-SH	AVG	PB	Sup	APR	PW
	Year	1	2	.333	24	0	0	0-0	40.1	50	32	4	2	10-3	18	4.46	82	.311	.348	2-0	.000	-0		-6	-0.5
Total	7	15	23	.395	160	33	2	3-1	441	439	211	37	16	121-22	180	3.80	96	.262	.315	63-3	.111	-2	81	-7	-0.9
HAUSMANN, CLEM Clemens Raymond B 8.17.1919 Houston, TX D 8.29.1972 Baytown, TX BR/TR 5-9/165# d4.28																									
1944	Bos A	4	7	.364	32	12	3	2	137	139	55	6	3	69	43	3.42	99	.266	.355	38-1	.079	-3	74	2	-0.1
1945	Bos A	5	7	.417	31	13	4-2	2	125	131	77	5	2	60	30	5.04	68	.270	.352	39-0	.103	-3	65	-21	-2.1
1949	Phi A	0	0	—	1	0	0	0	1	0	1	0	0	2	0	9.00	46	.000	.500	0-0	—	0		0	0.0
Total	3	9	14	.391	64	25	7-2	4	263	270	133	11	5	131	73	4.21	81	.267	.354	77-1	.091	-5	69	-19	-2.2
HAVENS, BRAD Bradley David B 11.17.1959 Highland Park, MI BL/TL 6-1/196# d6.5																									
1981	Min A	3	6	.333	14	12	1-1	0-0	78	76	33	6	1	24-4	43	3.58	110	.257	.314	0-0	—	0	61	4	0.4
1982	Min A	10	14	.417	33	32	4-1	0-1	208.2	201	112	32	0	80-4	129	4.31	99	.250	.317	0-0	—	0	86	-3	-0.5
1983	Min A	5	8	.385	16	14	1	0-0	80.1	110	75	11	0	38-3	40	8.18	52	.333	.393	0-0	—	0	111	-31	-4.0
1985	Bal A	0	1	.000	8	1	0	0-0	14.1	20	14	4	0	10-1	19	8.79	46	.333	.429	0-0	—	0	45	-7	-0.4
1986	Bal A	3	3	.500	46	0	0	1-1	71	64	37	7	0	29-1	57	4.56	91	.248	.323	0-0	—	0		-2	-0.1
1987	LA N	0	0	—	31	1	0	1-1	35.1	30	18	2	1	23-11	23	4.33	92	.227	.346	2-0	.000	-0	91	-1	-0.1
1988	LA N	0	0	—	9	0	0	0-0	9.2	15	5	1	0	4-0	8	4.66	72	.357	.404	1-0	.000	-0		-1	0.0
	Cle A	2	3	.400	28	0	0	1-1	57.1	62	22	7	0	17-3	30	3.14	131	.273	.321	0-0	—	0		6	0.5
1989	Cle A	0	0	—	7	0	0	0-0	13.1	18	6	3	0	7-2	6	4.05	98	.353	.417	0-0	—	0		0	0.0
	Det A	1	2	.333	13	1	0	0-1	22.2	28	14	3	3	14-2	15	5.56	69	.308	.409	0-0	—	0	0	-4	-0.4
	Year	1	2	.333	20	1	0	0-1	36	46	14	6	3	21-4	21	5.00	78	.324	.412	0-0	—	0	0	-4	-0.4
Total	8	24	37	.393	205	61	6-2	3-5	590.2	624	336	76	5	246-31	370	4.81	86	.272	.341	3-0	.000	-0	86	-39	-4.6
HAWBLITZEL, RYAN Ryan Wade B 4.30.1971 West Palm Beach, FL BR/TR 6-2/170# d6.9																									
1996	Col N	0	1	.000	8	0	0	0-0	15	18	12	2	0	6-0	7	6.00	87	.290	.348	1-0	.000	-0		-1	-0.1
HAWK, ED Edward B 5.11.1890 Neosho, MO D 3.26.1936 Neosho, MO BL/TR 5-11/175# d9.7																									
1911	StL A	0	4	.000	5	4	4	0	37.2	38	18	1	4	8	14	3.35	101	.253	.309	13-0	.154	-1	16	1	0.0
HAWKE, BILL William Victor "Dick" B 4.28.1870 Elsmere, DE D 12.11.1902 Wilmington, DE BR/TR 5-8.5/169# d7.28																									
1892	StL N	5	5	.500	14	11	10-1	0	97.1	108	59	2	8	45	55	3.70	86	.270	.355	45	.089	-4*	103	-6	-0.9
1893	StL N	0	1	.000	1	1	0	0	5.1	9	9	0	0	3	1	5.06	93	.360	.429	3	.333	0	74	-2	-0.2
	Bal N	11	16	.407	29	29	22-1	0	225	248	175	8	9	108	69	4.76	100	.271	.354	93	.172	-4	90	-2	-0.5
	Year	11	17	.393	30	30	22-1	0	230.1	257	181	8	9	111	70	4.77	100	.274	.356	96	.177	-4	89	2	-0.7
1894	†Bal N	16	9	.640	32	25	17	3	206	264	174	9	12	78	68	5.81	94	.308	.374	92-5	.304	2	112	-7	-0.5
Total	3	32	31	.508	76	66	49-2	3	533.2	629	417	19	29	234	193	4.98	95	.286	.363	233-5	.210	-7	101	-17	-2.1
HAWKINS, LA TROY La Troy B 12.21.1972 Gary, IN BR/TR 6-5/195# d4.29																									
1995	Min A	2	3	.400	6	6	1	0-0	27	39	29	3	1	12-0	9	8.67	55	.339	.397	0-0	—	0	94	-12	-1.6
1996	Min A	1	1	.500	7	6	0	0-0	26.1	42	24	8	0	9-0	24	8.20	62	.372	.415	0-0	—	0	130	-8	-0.5
1997	Min A	6	12	.333	20	20	0	0-0	103.1	134	71	19	4	47-0	58	5.84	80	.317	.389	1-0	.000	-0	86	-13	-1.8
1998	Min A	7	14	.333	33	33	0	0-0	190.1	227	126	27	5	61-1	105	5.25	91	.299	.350	1-0	.000	-0	91	-13	-1.2
1999	Min A	10	14	.417	33	33	1	0-0	174.1	238	136	29	1	60-2	103	6.66	77	.323	.373	2-0	.000	-0	81	-28	-3.2
2000	Min A	2	5	.286	66	0	0	14-0	87.2	85	34	7	1	32-1	59	3.39	152	.256	.322	1-0	.000	-0		17	1.6
2001	Min A	1	5	.167	62	0	0	28-9	51.1	59	34	3	1	39-3	36	5.96	77	.291	.401	0-0	—	0		-7	-1.3
2002	†Min A	6	0	1.000	65	0	0	0-3	80.1	63	23	5	0	15-1	63	2.13	211	.217	.253	0-0	—	0		20	1.3
2003	†Min A	9	3	.750	74	0	0	2-6	77.1	69	20	4	1	15-1	75	1.86	244	.239	.278	0-1	—	0		22	3.0
Total	9	44	57	.436	366	98	2	44-18	818	956	497	105	14	290-9	532	5.05	95	.293	.350	5-1	.000	-1	90	-22	-3.7
HAWKINS, ANDY Melton Andrew B 1.21.1960 Waco, TX BR/TR 6-3/223# d7.17																									
1982	SD N	2	5	.286	15	10	1	0-0	63.2	66	33	4	2	27-3	25	4.10	84	.274	.345	15-3	.000	-2	123	-5	-0.7
1983	SD N	5	7	.417	21	19	4-1	0-0	119.2	106	50	8	5	48-4	59	2.93	119	.244	.324	31-6	.065	-1	87	5	0.4
1984	†SD N	8	9	.471	36	22	2-1	0-0	146	143	90	13	2	72-2	77	4.68	76	.254	.339	41-3	.195	1	123	-20	-2.2
1985	SD N	18	8	.692	33	33	5-2	0-0	228.2	229	88	18	4	65-8	69	3.15	113	.267	.317	77-13	.078	-4	113	11	0.8
1986	SD N	10	8	.556	37	35	3-1	0-0	209.1	218	111	24	5	75-7	117	4.30	85	.268	.332	67-6	.149	-1	113	-14	-1.3
1987	SD N	3	10	.231	24	20	0	0-0	117.2	131	71	16	2	49-2	51	5.05	78	.287	.356	32-5	.156	-0	112	-13	-1.3
1988	SD N	14	11	.560	33	33	4-2	0-0	217.2	196	88	16	6	76-4	91	3.35	102	.244	.312	62-10	.113	-2	83	2	-0.1
1989	NY A	15	15	.500	34	34	5-2	0-0	208.1	238	127	23	6	76-6	98	4.80	81	.290	.354	0-0	—	0	98	-23	-3.0
1990	NY A	5	12	.294	28	26	2-1	0-0	157.2	156	101	20	2	82-3	74	5.37	74	.260	.349	0-0	—	0	86	-23	-2.3
1991	NY A	0	2	.000	4	3	0	0-0	12.2	23	15	5	0	6-0	5	9.95	42	.383	.439	0-0	—	0	88	-8	-0.9
	Oak A	4	4	.500	15	14	1	0-0	77	68	41	5	5	36-0	40	4.79	80	.237	.329	0-0	—	0	121	-8	-0.7
	Year	4	6	.400	19	17	1	0-0	89.2	91	46	10	5	42-0	45	5.52	70	.262	.348	0-0	—	0	115	-14	-1.6
Total	10	84	91	.480	280	249	27-10	0-0	1558.1	1574	815	152	39	612-39	706	4.22	87	.265	.335	325-46	.117	-8	104	-96	-11.3
HAWKINS, WYNN Wynn Firth "Hawk" B 2.20.1936 E.Palestine, OH BR/TR 6-3/195# d4.22																									
1960	Cle A	4	4	.500	15	9	1	0	66	68	32	10	1	39-2	39	4.23	88	.269	.366	20-1	.100	-1	86	-2	-0.3
1961	Cle A	7	9	.438	30	21	3-1	1	133	139	72	16	2	59-1	51	4.06	97	.270	.344	37-3	.108	-2	95	-4	-0.6
1962	Cle A	1	0	1.000	3	0	0	0	3.2	9	5	1	0	1-0	0	7.36	53	.429	.455	0-0	—	0		-2	-0.4
Total	3	12	13	.480	48	30	4-1	1	202.2	216	109	27	3	99-3	90	4.17	93	.274	.354	57-4	.105	-2	93	-8	-1.3
HAWLEY, PINK Emerson P. B 12.5.1872 Beaver Dam, WI D 9.19.1938 Beaver Dam, WI BL/TR 5-10/185# d8.13																									
1892	StL N	6	14	.300	20	20	18	0	166.1	160	116	4	11	63	63	3.19	100	.243	.319	71	.169	-2	86	-10	-1.3
1893	StL N	5	17	.227	31	24	21	1	227	249	184	5	20	103	73	4.60	103	.270	.356	91	.286	7	80	1	0.5
1894	StL N	19	27	.413	53	41	36	0	392.2	481	306	14	21	149	120	4.90	111	.298	.365	163-5	.264	2	73	20	1.8
1895	Pit N	31	22	.585	**56**	50	44-4	1	**444.1**	449	242	7	33	122	142	3.18	142	.258	.319	185-3	.308	14*	93	66	**7.4**
1896	Pit N	22	21	.512	49	43	37-2	0	378	382	197	2	28	157	137	3.57	118	.260	.343	163-3	.239	2*	82	29	2.9
1897	Pit N	18	18	.500	40	39	33	0	311.1	362	221	7	26	94	88	4.80	87	.288	.350	130-0	.231	-2	87	-19	-1.8
1898	Cin N	27	11	.711	43	37	32-3	0	331	357	163	5	22	91	69	3.37	114	.273	.331	130-5	.185	-4	90	18	1.1
1899	Cin N	14	17	.452	34	29	25	1	250.1	289	161	7	20	65	46	4.24	92	.289	.344	101-0	.218	-1	108	-9	-1.1
1900	NY N	18	18	.500	41	38	**34**-2	0	329.1	377	204	7	20	89	80	3.53	103	.287	.341	123-4	.203	-2	104	2	0.2
1901	Mil A	7	14	.333	26	23	17	0	182.1	228	133	3	9	41	50	4.59	78	.302	.346	73-4	.260	2*	77	-18	-1.4
Total	10	167	179	.483	393	344	297-11	3	3012.2	3334	1927	61	210	974	868	3.96	107	.277	.342	1230-24	.241	15	87	80	8.3
HAWLEY, SCOTT Marvin Hiram B Painesville, OH D 4.28.1904 Alliance, OH d9.22																									
1894	Bos N	0	1	.000	1	1	1	0	7	10	6	0	2	7	1	7.71	74	.333	.487	3-0	.000	-1	50	-1	-0.1
HAYDEL, HAL John Harold B 7.9.1944 Houma, LA BR/TR 6/190# d9.7																									
1970	Min A	2	0	1.000	4	0	0	0-0	9	7	3	2	0	4-0	4	3.00	124	.226	.306	3-0	.667	2		1	0.4
1971	Min A	4	2	.667	31	0	0	1-2	40	33	19	3	2	20-1	29	4.27	83	.243	.346	3-0	.333	0		-2	-0.3
Total	2	6	2	.750	35	0	0	1-2	49	40	22	5	2	24-1	33	4.04	89	.240	.338	6-0	.500	2		-1	0.1
HAYDEN, LEFTY Eugene Franklin B 4.14.1935 San Francisco, CA BL/TL 6-2/175# d6.26																									
1958	Cin N	0	0	—	3	0	0	0	3.2	5	2	0	0	1-0	3	4.91	84	.313	.353	0-0	—	0		0	0.0
HAYES, BEN Ben Joseph B 8.4.1957 Niagara Falls, NY BR/TR 6-1/180# d6.25																									
1982	Cin N	2	0	1.000	26	0	0	2-1	45.2	37	12	3	0	22-5	38	1.97	188	.219	.307	4-2	.000	-0		8	0.3
1983	Cin N	4	6	.400	60	0	0	7-3	69.1	82	53	8	1	37-6	44	6.49	59	.301	.381	5-0	.000	-1		-19	-2.9
Total	2	6	6	.500	86	0	0	9-4	115	119	65	11	1	59-11	82	4.70	80	.270	.353	9-2	.000	-1		-11	-2.6
HAYES, JIM James Millard "Whitey" B 2.25.1912 Montevallo, AL D 11.27.1993 Decatur, GA BL/TR 6-1/168# d7.13																									
1935	Was A	2	4	.333	7	4	1	0	28	38	28	0	0	23	9	8.36	52	.322	.433	8-2	.250	-0	90	-12	-2.0
HAYNER, FRED Fred Ames B 11.3.1871 Janesville, WI D 1.14.1929 Lake Forest, IL 6/160# d8.19																									
1890	Pit N	0	0	—	1	0	0	0	4	7	9	2	0	5	1	13.50	24	.368	.500	2	.000	-0		-5	-0.2
HAYNES, HEATH Heath Burnett B 11.30.1968 Wheeling, WV BR/TR 6/175# d6.1																									
1994	Mon N	0	0	—	4	0	0	0-0	3.2	3	1	0	0	3-0	1	0.00	—	.231	.353	0-0	—	0		1	0.1

Year	Tm Lg	W	L	Pct	G	GS	CG-Sho	SV-BS	IP	H	R	HR	HB	BB-IB	SO	ERA	AERA	OAV	OOB	AB-SH	AVG	PB	Sup	APR	PW
HAYNES, JIMMY Jimmy Wayne B 9.5.1972 LaGrange, GA BR/TR 6-4/185# d9.13																									
1995	Bal A	2	1	.667	4	3	0	0-0	24	11	6	2	0	12-1	22	2.25	211	.136	.247	0-0	—	0	98	7	0.8
1996	Bal A	3	6	.333	26	11	0	1-0	89	122	84	14	2	58-1	65	8.29	59	.333	.422	0-0	—	0	118	-32	-2.6
1997	Oak A	3	6	.333	13	13	0	0-0	73.1	74	38	7	2	40-1	65	4.42	103	.262	.354	2-0	.000	-0	89	1	0.1
1998	Oak A	11	9	.550	33	33	1-1	0-0	194.1	229	124	25	5	88-4	134	5.09	90	.298	.370	3-0	.000	0	120	-11	-1.0
1999	Oak A	7	12	.368	30	25	0	0-0	142	158	112	21	2	80-3	93	6.34	73	.282	.370	4-1	.000	-0	91	-28	-3.1
2000	Mil N	12	13	.480	33	33	0	0-0	199.1	228	128	21	7	100-7	88	5.33	86	.295	.378	64-5	.125	-1	98	-17	-1.8
2001	Mil N	8	17	.320	31	29	0	0-0	172.2	182	98	20	4	78-17	112	4.85	89	.279	.356	52-5	.154	0*	87	-9	-1.1
2002	Cin N	15	10	.600	34	34	0	0-0	196.2	210	97	21	3	81-4	126	4.12	103	.278	.348	61-10	.164	-0*	87	4	0.4
2003	Cin N	2	12	.143	18	18	1	0-0	94.1	118	74	14	3	57-3	49	6.30	68	.311	.404	23-7	.261	1	92	-22	-2.6
Total	9	63	86	.423	222	199	2-1	1-0	1185.2	1332	761	145	28	594-41	754	5.32	84	.288	.370	209-28	.153	-0	97	-107	-10.9
HAYNES, JOE Joseph Walton B 9.21.1917 Lincolnton, GA D 1.6.1967 Hopkins, MN BR/TR 6-2.5/190# d4.24 C3																									
1939	Was A	8	12	.400	27	20	10-1	0	173	186	118	10	1	78	64	5.36	81	.276	.352	67-2	.209	0	90	-20	-1.9
1940	Was A	3	6	.333	22	7	1	0	63.1	85	50	4	1	34	23	6.54	64	.327	.407	19-1	.105	-2	114	-16	-2.0
1941	Chi A	0	0	—	8	0	0	0	28	30	13	0	0	11	18	3.86	106	.280	.347	11-0	.273	0		1	0.1
1942	Chi A	8	5	.615	**40**	1	1	6	103	88	37	6	3	47	35	2.62	137	.234	.324	28-1	.179	0	95	10	1.4
1943	Chi A	7	2	.778	35	2	1	3	109.1	114	51	2	2	32	37	2.96	113	.263	.316	34-0	.265	2	126	1	0.3
1944	Chi A	5	6	.455	33	12	8	2	154.1	148	55	5	0	43	44	2.57	134	.254	.306	50-1	.200	1	67	14	1.2
1945	Chi A	5	5	.500	14	13	8-1	1	104	92	44	5	1	29	34	3.55	94	.237	.291	40-0	.175	-2*	126	-1	-0.3
1946	Chi A	7	9	.438	32	23	9	2	177.1	203	80	14	4	60	60	3.76	91	.289	.349	57-3	.246	3	88	-2	0.2
1947	Chi A	14	6	.700	29	22	7-2	0	182	174	65	5	2	61	50	**2.42**	**151**	.250	.312	65-1	.262	2	86	22	2.6
1948	Chi A☆	9	10	.474	27	22	6	0	149.2	167	79	13	2	52	40	3.97	107	.284	.344	50-3	.160	-1	77	2	0.0
1949	Was A	2	9	.182	37	10	0	2	96.1	106	77	6	3	55	19	6.26	68	.283	.380	25-0	.240	1	93	-21	-2.1
1950	Was A	7	5	.583	27	10	1-1	0	101.2	124	73	14	5	46	15	5.84	77	.305	.382	35-1	.200	1	119	-14	-1.2
1951	Was A	1	4	.200	26	3	1	2	73	85	46	9	1	37	18	4.56	90	.290	.372	21-1	.333	2	130	-6	-0.2
1952	Was A	0	3	.000	22	2	0	3	66	70	35	2	1	35	18	4.50	79	.275	.364	19-0	.105	-1	86	-6	-0.4
Total	14	76	82	.481	379	147	53-5	21	1581	1672	823	95	26	620	475	4.01	96	.272	.342	521-14	.213	7	94	-36	-2.3
HAYWARD, RAY Raymond Alton B 4.27.1961 Enid, OK BL/TL 6-1/190# d9.20																									
1986	SD N	0	2	.000	3	3	0	0-0	10	16	12	1	0	4-0	6	9.00	41	.340	.392	4-0	.000	-0*	106	-6	-1.0
1987	SD N	0	0	—	4	0	0	0-0	6	12	11	3	0	3-0	2	16.50	24	.444	.500	1-0	.000	-0		-8	-0.4
1988	Tex A	4	6	.400	12	12	1-1	0-0	62.2	63	44	6	0	35-0	37	5.46	75	.276	.367	0-0	—	0	87	-10	-1.3
Total	3	4	8	.333	19	15	1-1	0-0	78.2	91	67	10	0	42-0	45	6.75	60	.301	.382	5-0	.000	-1	90	-24	-2.7
HAYWOOD, BILL William Kiernan B 4.21.1937 Colon, Panama BR/TR 6-3/205# d7.28																									
1968	Was A	0	0	—	14	0	0	0	23	27	16	1	2	12-0	10	4.70	62	.314	.406	0-0	—	0		-6	-0.3
HEAD, ED Edward Marvin B 1.25.1918 Selma, LA D 1.31.1980 Bastrop, LA BR/TR 6-1/175# d7.27 Mil 1944-45																									
1940	Bro N	1	2	.333	13	5	2	0	39.1	40	21	0	0	18	13	4.12	97	.260	.337	11-0	.182	-0*	113	-1	-0.2
1942	Bro N	10	6	.625	36	15	5-1	4	136.2	118	60	11	3	47	78	3.56	92	.231	.300	39-4	.333	4	124	-3	0.0
1943	Bro N	9	10	.474	47	18	7-3	6	169.2	166	75	8	0	66	83	3.66	92	.250	.318	46-9	.152	-2	111	-4	-0.6
1944	Bro N	4	3	.571	9	8	5-1	0	63.1	54	21	2	0	19	17	2.70	132	.232	.290	19-4	.263	1	86	7	0.8
1946	Bro N	3	2	.600	13	7	3-1	1	56	56	24	3	0	24	17	3.21	105	.267	.342	16-0	.313	2	109	1	0.2
Total	5	27	23	.540	118	53	22-6	11	465	434	201	24	3	174	208	3.48	98	.245	.314	131-17	.244	5	111	0	0.2
HEAD, RALPH Ralph B 8.30.1893 Tallapoosa, GA D 10.8.1962 Muscadine, AL BR/TR 5-10/175# d4.18																									
1923	Phi N	2	9	.182	35	13	5	0	132.1	185	111	13	1	57	24	6.66	69	.341	.404	42-0	.071	-5	91	-23	-2.1
HEALEY, TOM Thomas F. B 1853 Cranston, RI D 2.6.1891 Lewiston, ME TR d6.13																									
1878	Pro N	0	3	.000	3	3	3	0	24	27	17	1		7	2	3.00	74	.278	.327	9	.222	0	40	-2	-0.2
	Ind N	6	4	.600	11	10	9	1	89	98	50	1		13	18	2.22	91	.270	.295	45	.178	-1*	92	-3	-0.3
	Year	6	7	.462	14	13	12	**1**	113	125	54	2		20	20	2.39	87	.272	.302	54	.185	-1	79	-4	-0.5
HEALY, JOHN John J. "Egyptian" or "Long John" B 10.27.1866 Cairo, IL D 3.16.1899 St.Louis, MO BR/TR 6-2/158# d9.11																									
1885	StL N	1	7	.125	8	8	8	0	66	54	37	0		20	32	3.00	92	.210	.267	24	.042	-3	26	-2	-0.5
1886	StL N	17	23	.425	43	41	39-3	0	353.2	315	213	5		118	213	2.88	112	.230	.291	145	.097	-12	83	12	0.0
1887	Ind N	12	29	.293	41	41	40-3	0	341	415	292	24	15	108	75	5.17	80	.294	.350	138	.174	-4	74	-37	-3.6
1888	Ind N	12	24	.333	37	37	36-1	0	321.1	347	199	13	15	87	124	3.89	76	.267	.320	131	.229	4	102	-32	-2.6
1889	Was N	1	11	.083	13	12	10	0	101	139	111	2	5	38	49	6.24	63	.317	.378	45	.222	1	84	-27	-2.1
	Chi N	1	4	.200	5	5	5	0	46	48	35	4	4	18	22	4.50	92	.261	.340	20	.100	-2	77	-1	-0.3
	Year	2	15	.118	18	17	15	0	147	187	40	6	9	56	71	5.69	70	.301	.367	65	.185	-1	82	-30	-2.4
1890	Tol AA	22	21	.512	46	46	44-2	0	389	326	201	5	24	127	225	2.89	137	.221	.293	156	.218	7*	76	40	4.3
1891	Bal AA	8	10	.444	23	22	19	0	170.1	179	124	6	5	57	54	3.75	99	.261	.322	64	.141	-2	102	-1	-0.5
1892	Bal N	3	6	.333	9	8	5	0	68.1	82	51	4	2	21	24	4.74	72	.286	.339	27	.222	0	90	-7	-0.7
	Lou N	1	1	.500	2	2	2	0	18.1	15	7	0	0	5	4	1.96	156	.214	.267	7	.286	1	82	2	0.3
	Year	4	7	.364	11	10	7	0	86.2	97	11	4	2	26	28	4.15	81	.272	.325	34	.235	1	89	-5	-0.4
Total	8	78	136	.364	227	222	208-9	0	1875	1920	1270	63	70	599	822	3.84	94	.257	.318	757	.174	-9	83	-53	-5.7
HEARD, CHARLIE Charles B 1.30.1872 Philadelphia, PA D 2.20.1945 Philadelphia, PA BR/TR 6-2/190# d7.14 ▲																									
1890	Pit N	0	6	.000	6	6	5	0	44	75	65	5	2	32	13	8.39	39	.364	.454	43	.186	-1*	67	-27	-2.5
HEARD, JAY Jehosie B 1.17.1920 Athens, GA D 11.18.1999 Birmingham, AL BL/TL 5-7/155# d4.24																									
1954	Bal A	0	0	—	2	0	0	0	3.1	6	5	1	0	3	2	13.50	27	.375	.474	0-0	—	0		-4	-0.2
HEARN, BUNNY Charles Bunn B 5.21.1891 Chapel Hill, NC D 10.10.1959 Wilson, NC BL/TL 5-11/190# d9.17																									
1910	StL N	1	3	.250	5	5	4	0	39	49	22	2	1	16	14	5.08	59	.322	.391	15-0	.133	-0	130	-7	-0.6
1911	StL N	0	0	—	2	0	0	0	2.2	7	4	1	0	0	1	13.50	25	.538	.538	1-0	.000	-0		-3	-0.1
1913	NY N	1	1	.500	2	2	1	0	13	13	6	0	0	7	8	2.77	113	.277	.370	5-0	.400	1	96	0	0.1
1915	Pit F	6	11	.353	29	17	8-1	0	175.2	187	74	6	2	37	49	3.38	80	.285	.326	53-2	.189	-0	68	-10	-1.0
1918	Bos N	5	6	.455	17	12	9-1	0	126.1	119	43	2	0	29	30	2.49	108	.256	.300	45-1	.178	-1	68	4	0.3
1920	Bos N	0	3	.000	11	4	2	0	43	54	34	3	1	11	9	5.65	54	.329	.375	14-0	.143	-1	84	-13	-0.9
Total	6	13	24	.351	66	40	24-2	0	399.2	429	183	14	4	100	111	3.56	78	.287	.333	133-3	.180	-2	80	-29	-2.2
HEARN, BUNNY Elmer Lafayette B 1.13.1904 Brooklyn, NY D 3.31.1974 Venice, FL BL/TL 5-8/160# d4.13																									
1926	Bos N	4	9	.308	34	12	3	2	117.1	121	63	2	0	56	40	4.22	84	.276	.358	30-2	.100	-2	102	-9	-1.0
1927	Bos N	0	2	.000	8	0	0	0	12.2	16	9	0	0	9	5	4.26	87	.327	.431	5-0	.400	1		-2	-0.2
1928	Bos N	1	0	1.000	7	0	0	0	10	6	8	0	1	8	8	6.30	62	.167	.333	1-0	.000	-0		-3	-0.2
1929	Bos N	2	0	1.000	10	1	0	0	18.1	18	10	2	0	9	12	4.42	106	.277	.365	2-1	.000	0	112	1	0.1
Total	4	7	11	.389	59	13	3	2	158.1	161	90	4	1	82	65	4.38	85	.273	.363	38-3	.132	-2	101	-13	-1.3
HEARN, JIM James Tolbert B 4.11.1921 Atlanta, GA D 6.10.1998 Boca Grande, FL BR/TR 6-3/205# d4.17																									
1947	StL N	12	7	.632	37	21	4-1	1	162	151	67	9	1	63	57	3.22	128	.248	.319	55-2	.145	-1	111	16	1.5
1948	StL N	8	6	.571	34	13	3	1	89.2	92	44	9	2	35	27	4.22	97	.271	.342	25-1	.200	-0*	88	0	-0.2
1949	StL N	1	3	.250	17	4	0	0	42	48	27	3	2	23	18	5.14	81	.294	.388	10-0	.100	-0	79	-4	-0.4
1950	StL N	0	1	.000	6	0	0	0	9	12	11	1	0	6	4	10.00	43	.333	.429	1-0	1.000	0		-5	-0.5
	NY N	11	3	.786	16	16	11-5	0	125	72	33	8	0	38	54	1.94	211	.169	.237	44-2	.136	-0	113	29	3.2
	Year	11	4	.733	22	16	11-**5**	0	134	84	38	9	0	44	58	**2.49**	165	.182	.253	45-2	.156	0	113	23	2.7
1951	†NY N	17	9	.654	34	34	11	0	211.1	204	102	21	2	82	66	3.62	108	.251	.321	74-9	.162	-0	124	6	0.9
1952	NY N☆	14	7	.667	37	34	11-1	1	223.2	208	113	16	5	97	89	3.78	98	.245	.326	77-5	.182	4	128	-3	0.3
1953	NY N	9	12	.429	36	32	6	0	196.2	206	111	22	3	84	77	4.53	95	.266	.341	66-6	.136	0*	110	-4	-0.3
1954	NY N	8	8	.500	29	18	3-2	1	130	137	71	10	2	66	45	4.15	97	.272	.357	45-5	.111	-1	119	-3	-0.3
1955	NY N	14	16	.467	39	33	11-1	0	226.2	225	107	27	3	66-7	86	3.73	108	.260	.312	77-4	.156	1*	95	8	1.2
1956	NY N	5	11	.313	30	19	2	1	129.1	124	74	17	3	44-4	66	3.97	95	.254	.317	41-0	.098	-3*	76	-7	-1.1
1957	Phi N	5	1	.833	36	4	1	3	74	79	35	7	2	18-4	46	3.65	104	.274	.320	17-1	.000	-2	150	1	-0.1

Year	Tm Lg	W	L	Pct	G	GS	CG-Sho	SV-BS	IP	H	R	HR	HB	BB-IB	SO	ERA	AERA	OAV	OOB	AB-SH	AVG	PB	Sup	APR	PW
1958	Phi N	5	3	.625	39	1	0	0	73.1	88	45	6	0	27-6	33	4.17	95	.292	.348	14-0	.000	-1	91	-5	-0.6
1959	Phi N	0	2	.000	6	0	0	0	11	15	7	2	0	6-1	1	5.73	72	.333	.412	2-0	.000	0		-2	-0.2
Total	13	109	89	.551	396	229	63-10	8	1703.2	1661	847	158	25	655-22	669	3.81	105	.255	.325	548-35	.141	-3	110	27	3.4
HEATH, SPENCER Spencer Paul B 11.5.1894 Chicago, IL D 1.25.1930 Chicago, IL BB/TR 6/170# d5.4																									
1920	Chi A	0	0	—	4	0	0	0	7	19	12	1	0	2	0	15.43	24	.475	.500	3-0	.000	-1		-8	-0.4
HEATHCOCK, JEFF Ronald Jeffrey B 11.18.1959 Covina, CA BR/TR 6-4/205# d9.3																									
1983	Hou N	2	1	.667	6	3	0	1-0	28	19	14	1	1	4-0	12	3.21	106	.181	.216	6-3	.000	-1	121	-1	-0.1
1985	Hou N	3	1	.750	14	7	1	1-0	56.1	50	25	9	1	13-0	25	3.36	103	.239	.286	16-0	.063	0	193	0	0.1
1987	Hou N	4	2	.667	19	2	0	1-1	42.2	44	15	4	1	9-1	15	3.16	124	.277	.314	10-1	.000	-1	81	4	0.5
1988	Hou N	0	5	.000	17	1	0	0-0	31	33	25	2	1	16-6	12	5.81	57	.275	.360	3-0	.000	-0	0	-10	-1.5
Total	4	9	9	.500	56	13	1	3-1	158	146	79	16	4	42-7	64	3.76	95	.246	.297	35-4	.029	-2	143	-7	-1.0
HEATHCOTT, MIKE Michael Joseph B 5.16.1969 Chicago, IL BR/TR 6-3/180# d8.28																									
1998	Chi A	0	0	—	1	0	0	0-0	3	2	1	0	0	1-0	3	3.00	152	.182	.250	0-0	—	0		1	0.0
HEATON, NEAL Neal B 3.3.1960 South Ozone Park, NY BL/TL 6-1/205# d9.3																									
1982	Cle A	0	2	.000	8	4	0	0-0	31	32	21	1	0	16-0	14	5.23	78	.260	.340	0-0	—	0	45	-4	-0.3
1983	Cle A	11	7	.611	39	16	4-3	7-2	149.1	157	79	11	1	44-10	75	4.16	102	.269	.319	0-0	—	0	101	0	0.0
1984	Cle A	12	15	.444	38	34	4-1	0-0	198.2	231	128	21	0	75-5	75	5.21	79	.293	.350	0-0	—	0	110	-25	-3.0
1985	Cle A	9	17	.346	36	33	5-1	0-1	207.2	244	119	19	7	80-2	82	4.90	84	.298	.362	0-0	—	0	86	-15	-1.7
1986	Cle A	3	6	.333	12	12	2	0-0	74.1	73	42	8	1	34-4	24	4.24	98	.254	.335	0-0	—	0	97	-2	-0.2
	Min A	4	9	.308	21	17	3	1-0	124.1	128	60	18	1	47-4	66	3.98	108	.273	.337	0-0	—	0	66	5	0.4
	Year	7	15	.318	33	29	5	1-0	198.2	201	63	26	2	81-8	90	4.08	104	.266	.336	0-0	—	0	78	3	0.2
1987	Mon N	13	10	.565	32	32	3-1	0-0	193.1	207	103	25	3	37-3	105	4.52	93	.273	.308	67-6	.209	2	103	-3	-0.2
1988	Mon N	3	10	.231	32	11	0	2-0	97.1	98	54	14	3	43-5	43	4.99	72	.271	.351	21-4	.143	-0	101	-11	-1.5
1989	Pit N	6	7	.462	42	18	1	0-1	147.1	127	55	12	6	55-12	67	3.05	110	.233	.309	42-2	.214	1*	97	6	0.6
1990	Pit N☆	12	9	.571	30	24	0	0-1	146	143	66	17	2	38-1	68	3.45	105	.263	.311	43-3	.047	-2*	107	2	0.0
1991	Pit N	3	3	.500	42	1	0	0-1	68.2	72	37	6	4	21-2	34	4.33	83	.275	.334	14-0	.286	2*	25	-6	-0.3
1992	KC A	3	1	.750	31	0	0	0-2	41	43	21	5	1	22-2	29	4.17	97	.274	.361	0-0	—	0		-1	-0.1
	Mil A	0	0	—	1	0	0	0-0	1	0	0	0	0	1-0	2	0.00	—	.000	.250	0-0	—	0		0	0.0
	Year	3	1	.750	32	0	0	0-2	42	43	22	5	1	23-2	31	4.07	100	.269	.358	0-0	—	0		0	-0.1
1993	NY A	1	0	1.000	18	0	0	0-0	27	34	19	6	3	11-1	15	6.00	69	.301	.375	0-0	—	0		-5	-0.2
Total	12	80	96	.455	382	202	22-6	10-8	1507	1589	804	163	32	524-51	699	4.37	91	.273	.334	187-15	.171	2	96	-59	-6.5
HEAVERLO, DAVE David Wallace B 8.25.1950 Ellensburg, WA BR/TR 6-1/210# d4.14																									
1975	SF N	3	1	.750	42	0	0	1-1	64	62	18	2	1	31-4	35	2.39	159	.262	.348	4-0	.500	1		10	0.7
1976	SF N	4	4	.500	61	0	0	1-2	75	85	45	2	2	15-3	40	4.44	82	.289	.324	3-0	.333	0		-7	-0.6
1977	SF N	5	1	.833	56	0	0	1-1	98.2	92	36	10	3	21-8	58	2.55	153	.251	.294	5-2	.000	-0		13	0.8
1978	Oak A	3	6	.333	69	0	0	10-3	130	141	56	11	3	41-9	71	3.25	112	.281	.333	0-0	—	0		6	0.6
1979	Oak A	4	11	.267	62	0	0	9-8	85.2	97	42	7	4	42-18	40	4.20	97	.294	.376	1-0	.000	-0		0	0.0
1980	Sea A	6	3	.667	60	0	0	4-5	78.2	75	37	9	5	35-12	42	3.89	106	.253	.338	0-0	—	0		3	0.2
1981	Oak A	1	0	1.000	6	0	0	0-1	5.2	7	1	0	0	3-1	2	1.59	219	.292	.370	0-0	—	0		1	0.2
Total	7	26	26	.500	356	0	0	26-21	537.2	559	235	41	18	188-55	288	3.41	113	.273	.335	13-2	.231	0		26	1.9
HEBERT, WALLY Wallace Andrew "Preacher" B 8.21.1907 Lake Charles, LA D 12.8.1999 Westlake, LA BL/TL 6-1/195# d5.1																									
1931	StL A	6	7	.462	23	13	5	0	103	128	70	11	3	43	26	5.07	91	.306	.375	43-1	.209	-1	116	-5	-0.7
1932	StL A	1	12	.077	35	15	2	1	108.1	145	99	6	2	45	29	6.48	75	.322	.386	34-2	.353	2	74	-21	-1.9
1933	StL A	4	6	.400	33	10	3	0	88.1	114	58	4	1	35	19	5.30	88	.308	.369	23-4	.391	3	71	-6	-0.3
1943	Pit N	10	11	.476	34	23	12-1	0	184	197	75	3	2	45	41	2.98	117	.272	.316	59-5	.220	1*	101	10	1.4
Total	4	21	36	.368	125	61	22-1	1	483.2	584	302	24	8	168	115	4.63	91	.298	.355	159-12	.270	5	92	-22	-1.5
HEBSON, BRYAN Bryan McCall B 3.12.1976 Columbus, GA BR/TR 6-5/210# d7.6																									
2003	Mon N	0	0	—	2	0	0	0-0	2	4	3	1	1	1-0	1	13.50	35	.444	.500	0-0	—	0		-2	-0.1
HECKER, GUY Guy Jackson B 4.3.1856 Youngsville, PA D 12.3.1938 Wooster, OH BR/TR 6/190# d5.2 M1 U1 ▲																									
1882	Lou AA	6	6	.500	13	11	10	0	104	75	49	0		5	33	1.30	191	**.188**	**.199**	340	.276	4*	100	11	1.6
1883	Lou AA	28	23	.549	53	52	51-3	0	469	526	298	4		75	164	3.34	90	.266	.292	332	.271	12*	101	-24	-0.8
1884	Lou AA	**52**	20	.722	**75**	**73**	**72**-6	0	**670.2**	526	230	4	16	56	**385**	**1.80**	**172**	.204	**.226**	316	.297	28*	98	**103**	**12.9**
1885	Lou AA	30	23	.566	53	53	51-2	0	480	454	252	6	18	54	209	2.18	148	.237	.265	297	.273	9*	102	51	6.0
1886	Lou AA	26	23	.531	49	48	45-2	0	420.2	390	273	6	10	118	133	2.87	127	.231	.285	343	.341	18*	131	31	4.8
1887	Lou AA	18	12	.600	34	32	32-2	1	285.1	325	214	9	10	50	58	4.16	105	.272	.307	370	.319	11*	119	9	1.8
1888	Lou AA	8	17	.320	26	25	25	0	223.1	251	154	5	10	43	63	3.39	91	.274	.313	211	.227	2*	94	-5	-0.2
1889	Lou AA	5	13	.278	19	16	15	0	151.1	215	145	7	5	47	33	5.59	69	.324	.373	327	.284	4*	98	-26	-1.9
1890	Pit N	2	9	.182	14	12	11	0	119.2	160	111	9	3	44	32	5.11	65	.311	.368	340	.226	2*	75	-27	-1.7
Total	9	175	146	.545	336	322	312-15	1	2924	2922	1726	50	72	492	1110	2.93	113	.247	.281	2876	.282	90	106	123	22.5
HEDGPETH, HARRY Harry Malcolm B 9.4.1888 Fayetteville, NC D 7.30.1966 Richmond, VA BL/TL 6-1.5/194# d10.3																									
1913	Was A	0	0	—	1	0	0	1	1	1	0	0	0	0	0	0.00	—	.250	.250	0-0	—	0		0	0.1
HEDLUND, MIKE Michael David "Red" B 8.11.1946 Dallas, TX BR/TR 6-1/190# d5.8																									
1965	Cle A	0	0	—	6	0	0	0	5.1	6	4	0	0	5-1	4	5.06	69	.286	.407	1-0	.000	-0		-1	-0.1
1968	Cle A	0	0	—	3	0	0	0	1.2	6	2	0	1	2-0	0	10.80	27	.545	.643	0-0	—	0		-1	-0.1
1969	KC A	3	6	.333	34	16	1	2-0	125	123	53	8	1	40-2	74	3.24	114	.259	.314	33-1	.152	-1	87	5	0.4
1970	KC A	2	3	.400	9	0	0	0-0	15	18	13	6	0	7-0	5	7.20	52	.300	.373	4-1	.000	-0		-5	-1.1
1971	KC A	15	8	.652	32	30	7-1	0-0	205.2	168	68	15	1	72-1	76	2.71	127	.227	.295	68-5	.088	-4	90	17	1.6
1972	KC A	5	7	.417	29	16	1	0-0	113	119	67	10	4	41-1	52	4.78	64	.275	.341	32-3	.188	-0	127	-23	-2.3
Total	6	25	24	.510	113	62	9-1	2-0	465.2	440	207	39	7	167-5	211	3.56	96	.253	.318	138-10	.123	-5	97	-8	-1.6
HEFFNER, BOB Robert Frederic B 9.13.1938 Allentown, PA BR/TR 6-4/205# d6.19																									
1963	Bos A	4	9	.308	20	19	3-1	0	124.2	131	61	15	2	36-1	77	4.26	89	.267	.318	43-2	.116	-1*	74	-5	-0.6
1964	Bos A	7	9	.438	55	10	1-1	6	158.2	152	81	20	3	44-6	112	4.08	94	.251	.305	44-1	.159	0	113	-4	-0.4
1965	Bos A	0	2	.000	27	1	0	0	49	59	42	9	1	18-1	42	7.16	52	.304	.364	6-1	.000	-1	188	-16	-0.9
1966	Cle A	0	1	.000	5	1	0	0	13	12	6	1	0	3-0	7	3.46	99	.240	.283	1-0	.000	0	51	0	0.0
1968	Cal A	0	0	—	7	0	0	0	8	6	2	0	0	6-1	3	2.25	129	.240	.375	0-0	—	0		1	0.1
Total	5	11	21	.344	114	31	4-2	6	353.1	360	192	45	6	107-9	241	4.51	84	.264	.319	94-4	.128	-1	90	-24	-1.8
HEFLIN, BRONSON Bronson Wayne B 8.29.1971 Clarksville, TN BR/TR 6-3/195# d8.1																									
1996	Phi N	0	0	—	3	0	0	0-0	6.2	11	7	1	0	3-0	4	6.75	64	.367	.412	0-0	—	0		-2	-0.1
HEFLIN, RANDY Randolph Rutherford B 9.11.1918 Fredericksburg, VA D 8.17.1999 Fredericksburg, VA BL/TR 6/185# d6.9																									
1945	Bos A	4	10	.286	20	14	6-2	0	102	102	52	3	4	61	39	4.06	84	.272	.380	35-1	.086	-3	73	-7	-1.2
1946	Bos A	0	1	.000	5	1	0	0	14.2	16	5	0	1	12	6	2.45	149	.296	.433	3-0	.667	1	210	2	0.2
Total	2	4	11	.267	25	15	6-2	0	116.2	118	57	3	5	73	45	3.86	89	.275	.387	38-1	.132	-2	83	-5	-1.0
HEHL, JAKE Herman Jacob B 12.8.1899 Brooklyn, NY D 7.4.1961 Brooklyn, NY BR/TR 5-11/180# d6.20																									
1918	Bro N	0	0	—	1	0	0	0	1	0	0	0	1	0	0	0.00	—	.000	.250	0-0	—	0		0	0.0
HEILMAN, AARON Aaron Michael B 11.12.1978 Logansport, IN BR/TR 6-5/220# d6.26																									
2003	NY N	2	7	.222	14	13	0	0-0	65.1	79	53	13	3	41-2	51	6.75	62	.300	.397	22-0	.045	-2	80	-20	-2.3
HEIMACH, FRED Frederick Amos "Lefty" B 1.27.1901 Camden, NJ D 6.1.1973 Ft.Myers, FL BL/TL 6/175# d10.1																									
1920	Phi A	0	1	.000	1	1	0	0	5	13	9	0	0	1	0	14.40	28	.542	.560	1-0	.000	-0	59	-5	-0.6
1921	Phi A	1	0	1.000	1	1	1-1	0	9	7	0	0	0	1	1	0.00	—	.226	.250	4-0	.250	-0	75	4	0.6
1922	Phi A	7	11	.389	37	19	7	1	171.2	220	117	18	3	63	47	5.03	85	.316	.375	60-3	.250	2	86	-15	-1.1
1923	Phi A	6	12	.333	40	19	10	0	208.1	238	120	14	6	69	63	4.32	95	.292	.352	118-5	.254	2*	75	-4	0.0

Year	Tm Lg	W	L	Pct	G	GS	CG-Sho	SV-BS	IP	H	R	HR	HB	BB-IB	SO	ERA	AERA	OAV	OOB	AB-SH	AVG	PB	Sup	APR	PW
1924	Phi A	14	12	.538	40	26	10	0	198	243	122	2	4	60	60	4.73	91	.306	.357	90-3	.322	6*	101	-9	-0.3
1925	Phi A	0	1	.000	10	0	0	0	20.1	24	10	2	1	9	6	3.98	117	.312	.391	6-0	.167	-0*		2	0.1
1926	Phi A	1	0	1.000	13	1	0	0	31.2	28	14	1	0	5	8	2.84	147	.239	.270	10-0	.100	-1*	121	4	0.2
	Bos A	2	9	.182	20	13	6	0	102	119	72	5	0	42	17	5.65	72	.303	.370	44-1	.295	2*	88	-16	-1.1
	Year	3	9	.250	33	14	6	0	133.2	147	76	6	0	47	25	4.98	82	.288	.348	54-1	.259	2	90	-13	-0.9
1928	NY A	2	3	.400	13	9	5	0	68	66	30	3	1	16	25	3.31	114	.250	.295	30-1	.167	-1*	143	4	0.1
1929	NY A	11	6	.647	35	10	3-3	4	134.2	141	72	4	3	29	26	4.01	96	.272	.314	49-0	.184	1*	107	-2	-0.1
1930	Bro N	0	2	.000	9	0	0	1	7.1	14	5	0	0	3	1	4.91	100	.424	.472	4-0	.250	-0*		0	0.0
1931	Bro N	9	7	.563	31	10	7-1	1	135.1	145	66	6	1	23	43	3.46	110	.274	.306	61-0	.197	1*	81	3	0.6
1932	Bro N	9	4	.692	36	15	7	0	167.2	203	85	7	6	28	30	3.97	96	.299	.333	55-3	.164	1*	103	-3	-0.1
1933	Bro N	0	1	.000	10	3	0	0	29.2	49	33	2	2	11	7	10.01	32	.374	.431	10-0	.200	-0	138	-20	-1.0
Total	13	62	69	.473	296	127	56-5	7	1288.2	1510	755	64	27	360	334	4.46	90	.296	.346	542-16	.236	12	96	-57	-2.7

HEIMUELLER, GORMAN Gorman John B 9.24.1955 Los Angeles, CA BL/TL 6-4/195# d7.12

Year	Tm Lg	W	L	Pct	G	GS	CG-Sho	SV-BS	IP	H	R	HR	HB	BB-IB	SO	ERA	AERA	OAV	OOB	AB-SH	AVG	PB	Sup	APR	PW
1983	Oak A	3	5	.375	16	14	2-1	0-0	83.2	93	43	8	1	29-2	31	4.41	88	.286	.346	0-0	—	0	99	-4	-0.2
1984	Oak A	0	1	.000	6	0	0	0-0	14.2	21	14	2	0	7-1	3	6.14	61	.344	.400	0-0	—	0		-5	-0.3
Total	2	3	6	.333	22	14	2-1	0-0	98.1	114	57	10	1	36-3	34	4.67	83	.295	.354	0-0	—	0	99	-9	-0.5

HEINKEL, DON Donald Elliott B 10.20.1959 Racine, WI BL/TR 6/185# d4.7

Year	Tm Lg	W	L	Pct	G	GS	CG-Sho	SV-BS	IP	H	R	HR	HB	BB-IB	SO	ERA	AERA	OAV	OOB	AB-SH	AVG	PB	Sup	APR	PW
1988	Det A	0	0	—	21	0	0	1-0	36.1	30	17	4	1	12-1	30	3.96	96	.219	.285	0-0	—	0		0	0.0
1989	StL N	1	1	.500	7	5	0	0-0	26.1	40	19	2	0	7-0	16	5.81	63	.348	.379	6-2	.000	-0	102	-6	-0.4
Total	2	1	1	.500	28	5	0	1-0	62.2	70	36	6	1	19-1	46	4.74	79	.278	.327	6-2	.000	-0	102	-6	-0.4

HEINTZELMAN, KEN Kenneth Alphonse B 10.14.1915 Peruque, MO D 8.14.2000 St.Peters, MO BR/TL 5-11.5/185# d10.3 Mil 1943-45 s-Tom

Year	Tm Lg	W	L	Pct	G	GS	CG-Sho	SV-BS	IP	H	R	HR	HB	BB-IB	SO	ERA	AERA	OAV	OOB	AB-SH	AVG	PB	Sup	APR	PW
1937	Pit N	1	0	1.000	1	1	1	0	9	6	3	0	1	3	4	2.00	193	.207	.303	4-0	.000	-1	89	2	0.1
1938	Pit N	0	0	—	1	0	0	0	2	1	2	0	0	3	1	9.00	42	.167	.444	0-0	—	0		-1	0.0
1939	Pit N	1	1	.500	17	2	1-1	0	35.2	35	23	2	0	18	18	5.05	76	.250	.335	9-0	.222	0	102	-5	-0.2
1940	Pit N	8	8	.500	39	16	5-2	3	165	193	86	7	4	65	71	4.47	85	.292	.359	54-3	.167	-1*	104	-8	-0.7
1941	Pit N	11	11	.500	35	24	13-2	0	196	206	91	8	1	83	81	3.44	105	.272	.345	63-5	.127	-2	110	4	0.2
1942	Pit N	8	11	.421	27	18	5-3	0	130	143	69	9	0	63	39	4.57	74	.281	.361	35-2	.086	-2	79	-13	-2.0
1946	Pit N	8	12	.400	32	24	6-2	1	157.2	165	84	7	0	86	57	3.77	94	.271	.362	44-6	.136	-1	91	-7	-0.8
1947	Pit N	0	0	—	2	1	0	0	4	9	11	2	0	6	2	20.25	21	.409	.536	0-0	—	0	167	-7	-0.3
	Phi N	7	10	.412	24	19	8	1	136	144	72	12	2	46	55	4.04	99	.277	.338	43-6	.116	-2	92	-1	-0.5
	Year	7	10	.412	26	20	8	1	140	153	76	14	2	52	57	4.50	89	.282	.347	43-6	.116	-2	96	-9	-0.8
1948	Phi N	6	11	.353	27	16	5-2	2	130	117	66	10	1	45	57	4.29	92	.241	.307	37-6	.135	-1	77	-2	-0.4
1949	Phi N	17	10	.630	33	32	15-**5**	0	250	239	96	19	1	93	65	3.02	130	.255	.323	83-5	.157	-1	88	25	2.3
1950	†Phi N	3	9	.250	23	17	4-1	0	125.1	122	66	10	0	54	39	4.09	99	.250	.325	38-3	.053	-3	86	-1	-0.5
1951	Phi N	6	12	.333	35	12	3	2	118.1	119	61	13	4	53	55	4.18	92	.267	.350	28-3	.107	-1	67	-5	-0.8
1952	Phi N	1	3	.250	23	1	0	1	42.2	41	16	1	0	12	20	3.16	115	.266	.319	2-3	.000	-0	49	3	0.2
Total	13	77	98	.440	319	183	66-18	10	1501.2	1540	746	100	14	630	564	3.93	96	.267	.341	440-42	.127	-16	90	-16	-3.4

HEISE, CLARENCE Clarence Edward "Lefty" B 8.7.1907 Topeka, KS D 5.30.1999 Winter Park, FL BL/TL 5-10/172# d4.22

Year	Tm Lg	W	L	Pct	G	GS	CG-Sho	SV-BS	IP	H	R	HR	HB	BB-IB	SO	ERA	AERA	OAV	OOB	AB-SH	AVG	PB	Sup	APR	PW
1934	StL N	0	0	—	1	0	0	0	2	3	3	1	0	0	1	4.50	94	.300	.300	0-0	—	0		-1	0.0

HEISE, JIM James Edward B 10.2.1932 Scottdale, PA BR/TR 6-1/185# d6.29

Year	Tm Lg	W	L	Pct	G	GS	CG-Sho	SV-BS	IP	H	R	HR	HB	BB-IB	SO	ERA	AERA	OAV	OOB	AB-SH	AVG	PB	Sup	APR	PW
1957	Was A	0	3	.000	8	2	0	0	19	25	19	2	0	16-1	8	8.05	48	.329	.441	4-0	.000	-0	46	-9	-1.2

HEISER, ROY Le Roy Barton B 6.22.1942 Baltimore, MD BR/TR 6-4/190# d9.2

Year	Tm Lg	W	L	Pct	G	GS	CG-Sho	SV-BS	IP	H	R	HR	HB	BB-IB	SO	ERA	AERA	OAV	OOB	AB-SH	AVG	PB	Sup	APR	PW
1961	Was A	0	0	—	3	0	0	0	5.2	6	5	1	1	9-0	1	6.35	63	.261	.485	2-0	.000	-0		-2	-0.1

HEISERMAN, RICK Richard Michael B 2.22.1973 Atlantic, IA BR/TR 6-7/225# d5.23

Year	Tm Lg	W	L	Pct	G	GS	CG-Sho	SV-BS	IP	H	R	HR	HB	BB-IB	SO	ERA	AERA	OAV	OOB	AB-SH	AVG	PB	Sup	APR	PW
1999	StL N	0	0	—	3	0	0	0-0	4.1	8	4	2	0	4-0	4	8.31	55	.400	.500	1-0	.000	-0		-2	-0.1

HEISMANN, CRESE Christian Ernest B 4.16.1880 Cincinnati, OH D 11.19.1951 Cincinnati, OH BL/TL 6/150# d9.25

Year	Tm Lg	W	L	Pct	G	GS	CG-Sho	SV-BS	IP	H	R	HR	HB	BB-IB	SO	ERA	AERA	OAV	OOB	AB-SH	AVG	PB	Sup	APR	PW
1901	Cin N	0	1	.000	3	2	1	0	13.2	18	9	1	3	6	6	5.93	54	.316	.409	5-0	.400	1	33	-3	-0.1
1902	Cin N	2	1	.667	5	3	2	0	33	33	18	1	5	10	15	2.45	122	.260	.338	14-0	.214	0	204	1	0.1
	Bal A	0	3	.000	3	3	2	0	16	20	17	1	2	12	2	8.44	45	.308	.430	7-0	.143	-1	76	-6	-0.9
Total	2	2	5	.286	11	8	5	0	62.2	71	44	3	10	28	23	4.74	69	.285	.380	26-0	.231	1	113	-8	-0.9

HEITMANN, HARRY Henry Anton B 10.6.1896 Albany, NY D 12.15.1958 Brooklyn, NY BR/TR 6/175# d7.27 Mil 1918

Year	Tm Lg	W	L	Pct	G	GS	CG-Sho	SV-BS	IP	H	R	HR	HB	BB-IB	SO	ERA	AERA	OAV	OOB	AB-SH	AVG	PB	Sup	APR	PW
1918	Bro N	0	1	.000	1	1	0	0	0.1	4	4	0	0	0	0	108.00	3	1.000	1.000	0-0	—	0	190	-3	-0.5

HELD, MEL Melvin Nicholas "Country" B 4.12.1929 Edon, OH BR/TR 6-1/178# d4.27

Year	Tm Lg	W	L	Pct	G	GS	CG-Sho	SV-BS	IP	H	R	HR	HB	BB-IB	SO	ERA	AERA	OAV	OOB	AB-SH	AVG	PB	Sup	APR	PW
1956	Bal A	0	0	—	4	0	0	0	7	7	4	1	0	3-1	4	5.14	76	.318	.385	0-0	—	0		-1	0.0

HELLING, RICK Ricky Allen B 12.15.1970 Devils Lake, ND BR/TR 6-3/215# d4.10

Year	Tm Lg	W	L	Pct	G	GS	CG-Sho	SV-BS	IP	H	R	HR	HB	BB-IB	SO	ERA	AERA	OAV	OOB	AB-SH	AVG	PB	Sup	APR	PW
1994	Tex A	3	2	.600	9	9	1-1	0-0	52	62	34	14	0	18-0	25	5.88	82	.295	.351	0-0	—	0	108	-4	-0.4
1995	Tex A	0	2	.000	3	3	0	0-0	12.1	17	11	2	2	8-0	5	6.57	74	.340	.435	0-0	—	0	71	-3	-0.4
1996	Tex A	1	2	.333	6	2	0	0-0	20.1	23	17	7	0	9-0	16	7.52	70	.280	.348	0-0	—	0	71	-4	-0.5
	Fla N	2	1	.667	5	4	0	0-0	27.2	14	6	2	0	7-0	26	1.95	209	.143	.200	9-0	.111	-0	61	7	0.7
1997	Fla N	2	6	.250	31	8	0	0-1	76	61	38	12	4	48-2	53	4.38	92	.232	.351	11-1	.091	-1	83	-2	-0.3
	Tex A	3	3	.500	10	8	0	0-0	55	47	29	5	2	21-0	46	4.58	105	.235	.311	3-0	.000	-0	86	2	0.1
1998	†Tex A	**20**	7	.741	33	33	4-2	0-0	216.1	209	109	27	1	78-6	164	4.41	109	.253	.314	5-1	.200	0	113	13	1.2
1999	†Tex A	13	11	.542	35	**35**	3	0-0	219.1	228	127	41	6	85-5	131	4.84	105	.272	.340	2-0	.000	-0	102	5	0.3
2000	Tex A	16	13	.552	35	**35**	0	0-0	217	212	122	29	9	99-2	146	4.48	112	.252	.334	5-0	.000	-1	104	12	1.2
2001	Tex A	12	11	.522	34	34	2-1	0-0	215.2	256	134	38	4	63-2	154	5.17	90	.297	.344	4-0	.000	-0	111	-13	-1.3
2002	†Ari N	10	12	.455	30	30	0	0-0	175.2	180	94	31	6	48-6	120	4.51	99	.264	.316	46-6	.043	-2	99	-1	-0.4
2003	Bal A	7	8	.467	24	24	0	0-0	138.2	156	90	30	12	40-0	86	5.71	77	.286	.347	1-0	.000	-0	120	-19	-1.8
	†Fla N	1	0	1.000	11	0	0	0-0	16.1	11	1	1	0	5-0	12	0.55	745	.193	.258	2-0	.500	1		7	0.4
Total	10	90	78	.536	266	225	10-4	0-1	1442.1	1476	812	239	46	529-23	984	4.77	99	.266	.332	88-8	.068	-3	105	0	-1.2

HELMBOLD, HORACE Horace B Philadelphia, PA d10.11

Year	Tm Lg	W	L	Pct	G	GS	CG-Sho	SV-BS	IP	H	R	HR	HB	BB-IB	SO	ERA	AERA	OAV	OOB	AB-SH	AVG	PB	Sup	APR	PW
1890	Phi AA	0	1	.000	1	1	1	0	7	17	15	0	0	6	3	14.14	27	.447	.523	3	.000	-1	70	-8	-0.7

HEMAN, RUSS Russell Frederick B 2.10.1933 Olive, CA BR/TR 6-4/200# d4.20

Year	Tm Lg	W	L	Pct	G	GS	CG-Sho	SV-BS	IP	H	R	HR	HB	BB-IB	SO	ERA	AERA	OAV	OOB	AB-SH	AVG	PB	Sup	APR	PW
1961	Cle A	0	0	—	6	0	0	1	10	8	4	0	1	8-0	4	3.60	109	.216	.370	1-0	.000	-0		1	0.0
	LA A	0	0	—	6	0	0	0	10	4	3	1	1	2-0	2	1.80	251	.125	.189	1-0	.000	-0		2	0.1
	Year	0	0	—	12	0	0	1	20	12	11	1	2	10-0	6	2.70	156	.174	.289	2-0	.000	-0		3	0.1

HEMMING, GEORGE George Earl "Old Wax Figger" B 12.15.1868 Carrollton, OH D 6.3.1930 Springfield, MA BR/TR 5-11/170# d4.21

Year	Tm Lg	W	L	Pct	G	GS	CG-Sho	SV-BS	IP	H	R	HR	HB	BB-IB	SO	ERA	AERA	OAV	OOB	AB-SH	AVG	PB	Sup	APR	PW
1890	Cle P	0	1	.000	3	1	1	0	21	25	23	1	2	19	3	6.86	58	.284	.422	11	.182	-1	61	-5	-0.2
	Bro P	8	4	.667	19	11	11	3	123	117	86	3	3	59	32	3.80	117	.240	.325	57	.158	-4	88	9	0.4
	Year	8	5	.615	22	12	12	**3**	144	142	92	4	5	78	35	4.25	103	.247	.341	68	.162	-5	87	3	0.2
1891	Bro N	8	15	.348	27	22	19-1	1	199.2	231	173	11	11	84	83	4.96	67	.279	.353	82	.159	-1	109	-37	-3.3
1892	Cin N	0	1	.000	1	0	0	0	6	10	6	1	0	2	0	7.50	44	.357	.400	3	.333	0		-2	-0.3
	Lou N	2	2	.500	4	4	4	0	35	36	25	1	0	17	12	4.63	66	.255	.335	13	.077	-1	98	-5	-0.5
	Year	2	3	.400	5	4	4	0	41	46	30	2	0	19	12	5.05	61	.272	.346	16	.125	-1	97	-7	-0.8
1893	Lou N	18	17	.514	41	32	32-1	1	332	369	245	7	15	175	79	5.10	86	.273	.363	158	.203	-2*	96	-26	-2.0
1894	Lou N	13	19	.406	35	32	32-1	1	294.1	358	213	7	9	133	66	4.37	117	.297	.371	131-0	.252	2*	73	26	2.1
	†Bal N	4	0	1.000	6	6	4	0	45.1	48	22	0	2	26	4	3.57	153	.268	.367	21-0	.286	1	97	10	0.7
	Year	17	19	.472	41	38	36-1	1	339.2	406	30	7	11	159	70	4.27	121	.293	.370	152-0	.257	3	77	33	2.8
1895	Bal N	20	13	.606	34	31	26-1	0	262.1	288	155	10	6	96	43	4.05	118	.275	.339	117-1	.282	3*	96	22	2.2
1896	Bal N	15	6	.714	25	21	20-3	0	202	233	113	9	3	54	33	4.19	102	.287	.333	97-2	.258	4*	149	8	0.8
1897	Lou N	3	4	.429	9	8	7	0	67	80	59	5	1	25	7	5.10	84	.294	.356	28-0	.179	-1*	77	-7	-0.6
Total	8	91	82	.526	204	168	156-7	6	1587.2	1795	1120	55	52	690	362	4.53	98	.279	.353	718-3	.223	-0	97	-7	-0.7

Year	Tm Lg	W	L	Pct	G	GS	CG-Sho	SV-BS	IP	H	R	HR	HB	BB-IB	SO	ERA	AERA	OAV	OOB	AB-SH	AVG	PB	Sup	APR	PW
HENDERSON, BERNIE Bernard "Barnyard" B 4.12.1899 Douglassville, TX D 6.6.1966 Linden, TX BR/TR 5-9/175# d9.5																									
1921	Cle A	0	1	.000	2	1	0	0	3	5	5	0	0	0	1	9.00	47	.333	.333	1-0	.000	0*	78	-2	-0.4
HENDERSON, ED Edward J. (b: Eugene J. Ball) B 12.25.1884 Newark, NJ D 1.15.1964 New York, NY BL/TL 5-9/168# d5.15																									
1914	Pit F	0	1	.000	6	1	1	0	16	14	8	2	0	8	4	3.94	73	.241	.333	3-0	.000	-0	0	-2	-0.1
	Ind F	1	0	1.000	2	1	1	0	10	8	7	0	3	4	1	4.50	69	.229	.357	4-0	.000	-1	110	-2	-0.2
	Year	1	1	.500	8	2	2	0	26	22	12	2	3	12	5	4.15	71	.237	.343	7-0	.000	-1	58	-3	-0.3
HENDERSON, HARDIE James Harding B 10.31.1862 Philadelphia, PA D 2.6.1903 Philadelphia, PA BR/TR ?/200# d5.2 U2																									
1883	Phi N	0	1	.000	1	1	1	0	9	26	24	0		2	2	19.00	16	.481	.500	8	.250	0*	104	-14	-0.8
	Bal AA	10	32	.238	45	42	38	0	358.1	383	315	4		87	145	4.02	87	.256	.297	191	.162	-6*	82	-22	-2.5
1884	Bal AA	27	23	.540	52	52	50-4	0	439.1	382	235	9	16	116	346	2.62	132	.216	.271	203	.227	2*	94	37	3.9
1885	Bal AA	25	35	.417	61	61	59	0	539.1	539	311	7	19	117	263	3.19	102	.253	.298	229	.223	3	91	3	0.7
1886	Bal AA	3	15	.167	19	19	19	0	171.1	188	147	0	9	66	88	4.62	74	.252	.320	68	.235	2	102	-25	-1.7
	Bro AA	10	4	.714	14	14	14	0	124	112	82	2	0	51	49	2.90	120	.232	.306	50	.180	-1	132	5	0.3
	Year	13	19	.406	33	33	33	0	295.1	300	90	2	9	117	137	3.90	88	.244	.314	118	.212	1	115	-20	-1.4
1887	Bro AA	5	8	.385	13	12	12	0	111.2	127	85	3	5	63	28	3.95	109	.281	.375	41	.122	-3	107	2	-0.1
1888	Pit N	1	3	.250	5	5	4	0	35.1	43	31	0	2	20	9	5.35	49	.289	.380	18	.278	1	149	-11	-0.9
Total	6	81	121	.401	210	206	197-4	0	1788.1	1800	1230	25	51	522	930	3.50	98	.247	.302	808	.204	-2	96	-25	-1.1
HENDERSON, JOE Joseph Lee B 7.4.1946 Lake Cormorant, MS BL/TR 6-2/195# d6.7																									
1974	Chi A	1	0	1.000	5	3	0	0-0	15	21	15	2	0	11-0	12	8.40	44	.328	.427	1-0	.000	-0	165	-7	-0.4
1976	Cin N	2	0	1.000	4	0	0	0-0	11	9	1	0	0	8-3	7	0.00	—	.225	.354	0-0	—	0		4	0.8
1977	Cin N	0	2	.000	7	0	0	0-0	9	17	13	2	0	6-0	8	12.00	33	.386	.460	1-0	.000	-0		-8	-1.5
Total	3	3	2	.600	16	3	0	0-0	35	47	29	4	0	25-3	27	6.69	56	.318	.416	2-0	.000	-0	165	-11	-1.1
HENDERSON, ROD Rodney Wood B 3.11.1971 Greensburg, KY BR/TR 6-4/195# d4.19																									
1994	Mon N	0	1	.000	3	2	0	0-0	6.2	9	9	1	0	7-0	3	9.45	45	.333	.471	1-0	.000	-0	129	-4	-0.5
1998	Mil N	0	0	—	2	0	0	0-0	3.2	5	4	2	1	0-0	1	9.82	43	.313	.353	0-0	—	0		-2	-0.1
Total	2	0	1	.000	5	2	0	0-0	10.1	14	13	3	1	7-0	4	9.58	44	.326	.431	1-0	.000	-0	129	-6	-0.6
HENDERSON, BILL William Maxwell B 11.4.1901 Pensacola, FL D 10.6.1966 Pensacola, FL BR/TR 6/190# d6.20																									
1930	NY A	0	0	—	3	0	0	0	8	7	6	1	0	4	2	4.50	96	.250	.344	2-0	.500	0		-1	0.0
HENDLEY, BOB Charles Robert B 4.30.1939 Macon, GA BR/TL 6-2/190# d6.23																									
1961	Mil N	5	7	.417	19	13	3	0	97	96	46	8	0	39-2	44	3.90	96	.262	.332	31-2	.032	-3	100	-2	-0.4
1962	Mil N	11	13	.458	35	29	7-2	1	200	188	90	17	0	59-2	112	3.60	105	.247	.299	59-3	.119	1*	98	5	0.7
1963	Mil N	9	9	.500	41	24	7-3	3	169.1	153	80	16	1	64-4	105	3.93	82	.244	.312	47-5	.106	-1*	133	-12	-1.3
1964	SF N	10	11	.476	30	29	4-1	0	163.1	161	71	18	2	59-9	104	3.64	98	.258	.322	47-5	.106	-1	92	0	-0.2
1965	SF N	0	0	—	8	2	0	0	15	27	22	6	1	13-2	8	12.60	29	.397	.500	3-0	.000	-0	158	-14	-0.7
	Chi N	4	4	.500	18	10	2	0	62	59	39	9	1	25-0	38	4.35	85	.244	.317	14-3	.000	-1	102	-6	-0.8
	Year	4	4	.500	26	12	2	0	77	86	43	15	2	38-2	46	5.96	62	.277	.360	17-3	.000	-2	111	-21	-1.5
1966	Chi N	4	5	.444	43	6	0	7	89.2	98	46	10	0	39-6	65	3.91	94	.285	.353	18-0	.167	1	124	-3	-0.2
1967	Chi N	2	0	1.000	7	0	0	1	12.1	17	10	4	0	3-0	10	6.57	54	.315	.351	6-0	.000	-1		-4	-0.7
	NY N	3	3	.500	15	13	2	0	70.2	65	35	11	1	28-4	36	3.44	99	.241	.312	18-4	.111	-0	92	-2	-0.3
	Year	5	3	.625	22	13	2	1	83	82	39	15	1	31-4	46	3.90	87	.253	.318	24-4	.083	-1	91	-6	-1.0
Total	7	48	52	.480	216	126	25-6	12	879.1	864	439	99	6	329-29	522	3.97	90	.257	.323	243-22	.095	-6	104	-38	-3.9
HENDRICKS, ED Edward "Big Ed" B 6.20.1885 Zeeland, MI D 11.28.1930 Jackson, MI BL/TL 6-3/200# d9.15																									
1910	NY N	0	1	.000	4	1	1	1	12	12	7	0	0	4	2	3.75	79	.261	.320	4-0	.000	-1	25	-1	-0.2
HENDRICKSON, DON Donald William B 7.14.1913 Kewanna, IN D 1.19.1977 Norfolk, VA BR/TR 6-2/204# d7.4																									
1945	Bos N	4	8	.333	37	2	1	5	73.1	74	46	8	1	39	14	4.91	78	.261	.353	18-0	.167	-0	210	-8	-1.4
1946	Bos N	0	1	.000	2	0	0	0	2	4	2	0	0	2	2	4.50	76	.364	.462	1-0	.000	-0		-1	-0.1
Total	2	4	9	.308	39	2	1	5	75.1	78	48	8	1	41	16	4.90	78	.265	.357	19-0	.158	-0	210	-9	-1.5
HENDRICKSON, MARK Mark Allan B 6.23.1974 Mount Vernon, WA BL/TL 6-9/230# d8.6																									
2002	Tor A	3	0	1.000	16	4	0	0-1	36.2	25	11	1	2	12-3	21	2.45	188	.202	.279	0-0	—	0	106	8	0.6
2003	Tor A	9	9	.500	30	30	1-1	0-0	158.1	207	111	24	0	40-3	76	5.51	83	.317	.352	4-0	.250	1	133	-18	-1.6
Total	2	12	9	.571	46	34	1-1	0-1	195	232	122	25	2	52-6	97	4.94	93	.298	.340	4-0	.250	1	130	-10	-1.0
HENDRIX, CLAUDE Claude Raymond B 4.13.1889 Olathe, KS D 3.22.1944 Allentown, PA BR/TR 6/195# d6.7																									
1911	Pit N	4	6	.400	22	12	6-1	1	118.2	85	52	1	1	53	57	2.73	126	.204	.295	41-0	.098	-1	89	7	0.6
1912	Pit N	24	9	**.727**	39	32	25-4	1	288.2	256	110	6	9	105	176	2.59	126	.246	.320	121-2	.322	16*	121	21	4.0
1913	Pit N	14	15	.483	42	25	17-2	3	241	216	95	3	5	89	138	2.84	106	.248	.321	99-2	.273	10*	111	6	1.8
1914	Chi F	**29**	10	.744	**49**	37	**34**-6	5	362	262	91	6	5	77	189	1.69	157	**.203**	**.251**	130-6	.231	4*	118	**42**	**5.4**
1915	Chi F	16	15	.516	40	31	26-5	4	285	256	120	7	2	84	107	3.00	84	.241	.298	113-3	.265	11*	125	-15	-0.7
1916	Chi N	8	16	.333	36	24	15-3	2	218	193	81	4	6	67	117	2.68	108	.242	.306	80-2	.200	2*	70	6	1.1
1917	Chi N	10	12	.455	40	21	13-1	1	215	202	94	3	4	72	81	2.60	112	.257	.322	86-4	.256	3*	106	4	0.8
1918	†Chi N	20	7	**.741**	32	27	21-3	0	233	229	87	2	5	54	86	2.78	100	.259	.305	91-5	.264	8*	140	4	1.5
1919	Chi N	10	14	.417	33	25	15-2	0	206.1	208	79	3	9	42	69	2.62	110	.266	.311	78-0	.192	-0*	86	6	0.7
1920	Chi N	9	12	.429	27	23	12	0	203.2	216	101	6	3	54	72	3.58	90	.273	.322	83-1	.181	-2*	108	-8	-0.9
Total	10	144	116	.554	360	257	184-27	17	2371.1	2123	910	41	49	697	1092	2.65	110	.243	.303	922-25	.241	50	109	73	14.3
HENION, LAFAYETTE Lafayette Marion B 6.7.1899 Eureka, CA D 7.22.1955 San Luis Obispo, CA BR/TR 5-11/154# d9.10																									
1919	Bro N	0	0	—	1	0	0	0	3	2	2	0	0	2	2	6.00	50	.200	.333	1-0	.000	-0		-1	-0.1
HENKE, TOM Thomas Anthony B 12.21.1957 Kansas City, MO BR/TR 6-5/215# d9.10																									
1982	Tex A	1	0	1.000	8	0	0	0-1	15.2	14	2	0	1	8-2	9	1.15	338	.246	.348	0-0	—	0		5	0.3
1983	Tex A	1	0	1.000	8	0	0	1-0	16	16	6	1	0	4-0	17	3.38	119	.262	.308	0-0	—	0		2	0.1
1984	Tex A	1	1	.500	25	0	0	2-2	28.1	36	21	0	1	20-2	25	6.35	65	.313	.407	0-0	—	0		-6	-0.5
1985	†Tor A	3	3	.500	28	0	0	13-1	40	29	12	4	0	8-2	42	2.02	208	.206	.245	0-0	—	0		9	1.7
1986	Tor A	9	5	.643	63	0	0	27-8	91.1	63	39	6	1	32-4	118	3.35	126	.191	.261	0-0	—	0		8	1.5
1987	Tor A★	0	6	.000	72	0	0	**34-8**	94	62	27	10	0	25-3	128	2.49	181	.188	.242	0-0	—	0		**21**	2.9
1988	Tor A	4	4	.500	52	0	0	25-4	68	60	23	6	2	24-3	66	2.91	135	.237	.306	0-0	—	0		8	1.5
1989	†Tor A	8	3	.727	64	0	0	20-4	89	66	20	5	2	25-4	116	1.92	197	.205	.264	0-0	—	0		19	3.1
1990	Tor A	2	4	.333	61	0	0	32-6	74.2	58	18	8	1	19-2	75	2.17	182	.213	.266	0-0	—	0		15	2.2
1991	†Tor A	0	2	.000	49	0	0	32-3	50.1	33	13	4	0	11-2	53	2.32	181	.184	.232	0-0	—	0		11	1.5
1992	†Tor A	3	2	.600	57	0	0	34-3	55.2	40	19	5	0	22-2	46	2.26	181	.197	.272	0-0	—	0		9	1.7
1993	Tex A	5	5	.500	66	0	0	40-7	74.1	55	25	7	1	27-3	79	2.91	143	.205	.278	0-0	—	0		11	2.3
1994	Tex A	3	6	.333	37	0	0	15-6	38	33	16	6	0	12-0	39	3.79	127	.232	.290	0-0	—	0		5	1.0
1995	StL N★	1	1	.500	52	0	0	36-2	54.1	42	11	2	0	18-0	48	1.82	230	.209	.274	1-0	.000	-0		15	2.2
Total	14	41	42	.494	642	0	0	311-55	789.2	607	252	64	9	255-29	861	2.67	156	.211	.275	1-0	.000	-0		132	21.5
HENLEY, WELDON Weldon B 10.25.1880 Jasper, GA D 11.16.1960 Palatka, FL BR/TR 6/175# d4.23																									
1903	Phi A	12	10	.545	29	21	13-1	0	186.1	186	108	3	12	67	86	3.91	78	.259	.333	68-1	.132	-3*	124	-18	-2.3
1904	Phi A	15	17	.469	36	34	31-5	0	295.2	245	126	3	19	76	130	2.53	106	.226	.289	108-3	.222	2	117	2	0.6
1905	Phi A	4	11	.267	25	19	13-1	0	183.2	155	74	4	9	67	82	2.60	102	.231	.309	65-2	.169	-1	97	2	0.3
1907	Bro N	1	5	.167	7	7	5	0	56	54	31	2	1	21	11	3.05	77	.273	.345	20-2	.200	1*	83	-6	-0.5
Total	4	32	43	.427	97	81	62-7	0	721.2	640	339	12	41	231	309	2.94	93	.240	.310	261-8	.184	-2	112	-20	-1.9
HENNEMAN, MIKE Michael Alan B 12.11.1961 St.Charles, MO BR/TR 6-4/195# d5.11																									
1987	†Det A	11	3	.786	55	0	0	7-4	96.2	86	36	8	3	30-5	75	2.98	142	.238	.300	1-0	.000	-0		14	2.0
1988	Det A	9	6	.600	65	0	0	22-7	91.1	72	23	7	2	24-10	58	1.87	204	.218	.273	0-0	—	0		**20**	3.9
1989	Det A☆	11	4	.733	60	0	0	8-4	90	84	46	4	5	51-15	69	3.70	103	.251	.355	0-0	—	0		-1	-0.1

Year	Tm Lg	W	L	Pct	G	GS	CG-Sho	SV-BS	IP	H	R	HR	HB	BB-IB	SO	ERA	AERA	OAV	OOB	AB-SH	AVG	PB	Sup	APR	PW
1990	Det A	8	6	.571	69	0	0	22-6	94.1	90	36	4	3	33-12	50	3.05	130	.253	.320	0-0	—	0		9	1.6
1991	Det A	10	2	.833	60	0	0	21-3	84.1	81	29	2	0	34-8	61	2.88	144	.258	.326	0-0	—	0		12	2.1
1992	Det A	2	6	.250	60	0	0	24-4	77.1	75	36	6	0	20-10	58	3.96	100	.256	.299	0-0	—	0		0	0.1
1993	Det A	5	3	.625	63	0	0	24-5	71.2	69	28	4	2	32-8	58	2.64	163	.251	.331	0-0	—	0		11	1.7
1994	Det A	1	3	.250	30	0	0	8-5	34.2	43	27	5	2	17-7	27	5.19	93	.297	.376	0-0	—	0		-4	-0.5
1995	Det A	0	1	.000	29	0	0	18-2	29.1	24	5	0	0	9-1	24	1.53	310	.222	.282	0-0	—	0		11	1.4
	Hou N	0	1	.000	21	0	0	8-1	21	21	7	1	2	4-1	19	3.00	129	.266	.310	0-0	—	0		3	0.3
1996	†Tex A	0	7	.000	49	0	0	31-6	42	41	28	6	0	17-5	34	5.79	91	.258	.326	0-0	—	0		-2	-0.4
Total	10	57	42	.576	561	0	0	193-47	732.2	686	301	47	19	271-82	533	3.21	130	.249	.318	1-0	.000	-0		73	12.1
HENNESSEY, GEORGE George "Three Star" B 10.28.1907 Slatington, PA D 1.15.1988 Princeton, NJ BR/TR 5-10/168# d9.2																									
1937	StL A	0	1	.000	5	0	0	0	7	15	8	2	0	6	4	10.29	47	.500	.583	0-1	—	0		-4	-0.4
1942	Phi N	1	1	.500	5	1	0	0	17	11	5	1	0	10	2	2.65	125	.180	.296	5-0	.000	-1	25	2	0.1
1945	Chi N	0	0	—	2	0	0	0	3.2	7	3	0	0	1	2	7.36	50	.438	.471	0-0	—	0		-1	-0.1
Total	3	1	2	.333	12	1	0	0	27.2	33	16	3	0	17	8	5.20	72	.308	.403	5-1	.000	-1	25	-3	-0.4
HENNIGAN, PHIL Phillip Winston B 4.10.1946 Jasper, TX BR/TR 5-11.5/185# d9.2																									
1969	Cle A	2	1	.667	9	0	0	0-2	16.1	14	6	0	1	4-1	10	3.31	114	.241	.297	2-0	.000	-0		1	0.1
1970	Cle A	6	3	.667	42	1	0	3-0	71.2	69	34	7	4	44-6	43	4.02	99	.263	.376	7-2	.143	1	225	0	0.1
1971	Cle A	4	3	.571	57	0	0	14-2	82	80	45	13	3	51-4	69	4.94	78	.261	.365	6-2	.000	-0		-7	-1.0
1972	Cle A	5	3	.625	38	1	0	6-0	67.1	54	20	8	2	18-4	44	2.67	121	.226	.281	12-0	.083	-0	82	5	0.6
1973	NY N	0	4	.000	30	0	0	3-1	43.1	50	30	6	1	16-6	22	6.23	58	.289	.353	3-0	.333	0		-11	-1.1
Total	5	17	14	.548	176	2	0	26-5	280.2	267	135	34	11	133-21	188	4.26	86	.257	.344	30-4	.100	1	157	-12	-1.3
HENNING, PETE Ernest Herman B 12.28.1887 Crown Point, IN D 11.4.1939 Dyer, IN BR/TR 5-11/185# d4.17																									
1914	KC F	5	10	.333	28	14	7	2	138	153	88	5	7	58	45	4.83	58	.291	.369	44-0	.182	0	129	-29	-2.8
1915	KC F	9	15	.375	40	20	15-1	2	207	181	88	5	3	76	73	3.17	83	.235	.307	68-4	.206	-1	72	-10	-1.2
Total	2	14	25	.359	68	34	22-1	4	345	334	176	10	10	134	118	3.83	70	.258	.332	112-4	.196	-1	96	-39	-4.0
HENNINGER, RICK Richard Lee B 1.11.1948 Hastings, NE BR/TR 6-6/225# d9.3																									
1973	Tex A	1	0	1.000	6	2	0	0-0	23	23	8	1	0	11-0	6	2.74	136	.261	.333	0-0	—	0	132	3	0.1
HENNIS, RANDY Randall Philip B 12.16.1965 Clearlake, CA BR/TR 6-6/220# d9.17																									
1990	Hou N	0	0	—	3	1	0	0-0	9.2	1	0	0	1	3-0	4	0.00	—	.033	.147	2-0	.000	-0	73	4	0.2
HENRIQUEZ, OSCAR Oscar Eduardo B 1.28.1974 LaGuaira, Venezuela BR/TR 6-6/220# d9.7																									
1997	Hou N	0	1	.000	4	0	0	0-0	4	2	2	0	1	3-0	3	4.50	89	.167	.375	0-0	—	0		0	0.0
1998	Fla N	0	0	—	15	0	0	0-0	20	26	22	4	1	12-0	19	8.55	47	.306	.390	1-0	.000	-0		-11	-0.6
2002	Det A	1	1	.500	30	0	0	2-0	28	19	14	5	1	15-4	23	4.50	96	.196	.307	0-0	—	0		0	0.0
Total	3	1	2	.333	49	0	0	2-0	52	47	38	9	3	30-4	45	6.06	69	.242	.348	1-0	.000	-0		-11	-0.6
HENRY, DWAYNE Dwayne Allen B 2.16.1962 Elkton, MD BR/TR 6-3/205# d9.7																									
1984	Tex A	0	1	.000	3	0	0	0-1	4.1	5	4	0	0	7-0	2	8.31	50	.294	.500	0-0	—	0		-2	-0.3
1985	Tex A	2	2	.500	16	0	0	3-3	21	16	7	0	0	7-0	20	2.57	165	.211	.274	0-0	—	0		4	0.7
1986	Tex A	1	0	1.000	19	0	0	0-0	19.1	14	11	1	1	22-0	17	4.66	93	.209	.402	0-0	—	0		-1	0.0
1987	Tex A	0	0	—	5	0	0	0-1	10	12	10	2	0	9-0	7	9.00	50	.293	.420	0-0	—	0		-4	-0.2
1988	Tex A	0	1	.000	11	0	0	1-1	10.1	15	10	1	3	9-1	10	8.71	47	.326	.458	0-0	—	0		-5	-0.5
1989	Atl N	0	2	.000	12	0	0	1-1	12.2	12	6	2	0	5-1	16	4.26	86	.250	.321	0-0	—	0		0	-0.1
1990	Atl N	2	2	.500	34	0	0	0-1	38.1	41	26	3	0	25-0	34	5.63	72	.273	.375	0-0	—	0		-6	-0.6
1991	Hou N	3	2	.600	52	0	0	2-0	67.2	51	25	7	2	39-7	51	3.19	110	.219	.333	1-0	.000	-0		3	0.2
1992	Cin N	3	3	.500	60	0	0	0-2	83.2	59	31	4	1	44-6	72	3.33	108	.199	.301	4-0	.250	0		4	0.3
1993	Cin N	0	1	.000	3	0	0	0-0	4.2	6	8	0	0	4-1	2	3.86	105	.273	.385	1-0	.000	-0		-3	-0.5
	Sea A	2	1	.667	31	1	0	2-0	54	56	40	6	2	35-4	35	6.67	66	.273	.378	0-0	—	0	334	-12	-0.7
1995	Det A	1	0	1.000	10	0	0	5-0	8.2	11	6	0	0	10-2	9	6.23	76	.306	.457	0-0	—	0		-1	-0.2
Total	11	14	15	.483	256	1	0	14-10	334.2	298	184	26	9	216-22	275	4.65	85	.241	.354	6-0	.167	-0	334	-23	-1.9
HENRY, EARL Earl Clifford "Hook" B 6.10.1917 Roseville, OH D 12.10.2002 Zanesville, OH BL/TL 5-11/172# d9.23																									
1944	Cle A	1	1	.500	2	2	1	0	17.2	18	9	0	0	3	5	4.58	72	.269	.300	5-0	.000	-0*	101	-2	-0.2
1945	Cle A	0	3	.000	15	1	0	0	21.2	20	13	0	1	20	10	5.40	60	.253	.410	4-0	.500	1*	105	-5	-0.5
Total	2	1	4	.200	17	3	1	0	39.1	38	22	0	1	23	15	5.03	65	.260	.365	9-0	.222	0	103	-7	-0.7
HENRY, BUTCH Floyd Bluford B 10.7.1968 ElPaso, TX BL/TL 6-1/205# d4.9																									
1992	Hou N	6	9	.400	28	28	2-1	0-0	165.2	185	81	16	1	41-7	96	4.02	84	.285	.325	54-5	.148	1	89	-12	-0.9
1993	Col N	2	8	.200	20	15	1	0-0	84.2	117	66	14	1	24-2	39	6.59	72	.331	.370	22-2	.091	-1	82	-13	-1.5
	Mon N	1	1	.500	10	1	0	0-0	18.1	18	10	1	0	4-0	8	3.93	106	.250	.286	2-1	.000	-0	129	0	0.0
	Year	3	9	.250	30	16	1	0-0	103	135	16	15	1	28-2	47	6.12	76	.317	.356	24-3	.083	-2	86	-13	-1.5
1994	Mon N	8	3	.727	24	15	0	1-0	107.1	97	30	10	2	20-1	70	2.43	174	.241	.278	31-5	.290	3	104	22	2.5
1995	Mon N	7	9	.438	21	21	1-1	0-0	126.2	133	47	11	2	28-3	60	2.84	151	.275	.315	42-5	.048	-4	77	18	1.9
1997	Bos A	7	3	.700	36	5	0	6-2	84.1	89	36	6	0	19-2	51	3.52	132	.277	.315	0-1	—	0	75	10	1.3
1998	Bos A	0	0	—	2	2	0	0-0	9	8	4	2	1	3-0	6	4.00	118	.235	.316	0-0	—	0	138	1	0.1
1999	Sea A	2	0	1.000	7	4	0	0-0	25	30	15	1	2	10-0	15	5.04	94	.303	.375	0-0	—	0	211	-1	-0.1
Total	7	33	33	.500	148	91	4-2	7-2	621	677	289	61	9	149-15	345	3.83	109	.280	.322	151-19	.139	-2	93	25	3.3
HENRY, DUTCH Frank John B 5.12.1902 Cleveland, OH D 8.23.1968 Cleveland, OH BL/TL 6-1/175# d9.16																									
1921	StL A	0	0	—	1	0	0	0	2	2	1	0	0	0	1	4.50	100	.250	.250	1-0	1.000	0		0	0.0
1922	StL A	0	0	—	4	0	0	0	5	7	3	0	0	5	3	5.40	77	.280	.400	0-0	—	0		0	0.0
1923	Bro N	4	6	.400	17	9	5-2	0	94.1	105	55	9	2	28	28	3.91	99	.281	.334	35-0	.229	1	82	-1	-0.1
1924	Bro N	1	2	.333	16	4	0	0	46	69	33	0	0	15	11	5.67	66	.352	.398	20-0	.250	1	192	-9	-0.5
1927	NY N	11	6	.647	45	15	7-1	4	163.2	184	93	6	0	31	40	4.23	91	.278	.311	55-1	.236	1	137	-8	-0.7
1928	NY N	3	6	.333	17	8	4	1	64	82	36	4	1	25	23	3.80	103	.325	.388	19-0	.158	-1	100	-1	-0.2
1929	NY N	5	6	.455	27	9	4	1	101.1	129	52	10	1	31	27	3.82	120	.316	.366	28-1	.250	2	133	8	0.9
	Chi A	1	0	1.000	2	1	1	0	15	20	12	1	0	7	2	6.00	71	.308	.375	7-0	.143	0	276	-3	-0.2
1930	Chi A	2	17	.105	35	16	4	0	155	211	116	12	4	48	35	4.88	95	.331	.381	51-0	.235	1	62	-9	-0.7
Total	8	27	43	.386	164	62	25-3	6	646.1	809	401	42	8	190	170	4.39	95	.308	.356	216-2	.231	6	108	-23	-1.5
HENRY, JIM James Francis B 6.26.1910 Danville, VA D 8.15.1976 Memphis, TN BR/TR 6-2/175# d4.23																									
1936	Bos A	5	1	.833	21	8	2	0	76.1	75	43	10	2	40	36	4.60	116	.255	.348	26-0	.115	-1*	108	6	0.3
1937	Bos A	1	0	1.000	3	2	1	0	15.1	15	9	2	0	11	8	5.28	90	.263	.382	5-0	.000	-0	101	0	-0.1
1939	Phi N	0	1	.000	9	1	0	1	23	24	13	3	1	8	7	5.09	79	.276	.344	5-0	.000	-1	218	-2	-0.2
Total	3	6	2	.750	33	11	3	1	114.2	114	65	15	3	59	51	4.79	104	.260	.352	36-0	.083	-2	117	4	0.0
HENRY, JOHN John Michael B 9.2.1863 Springfield, MA D 6.11.1939 Hartford, CT TL d8.13 ▲																									
1884	Cle N	1	4	.200	5	5	5-1	0	42	46	39	2		26	23	3.64	87	.257	.351	26	.154	-1*	27	-4	-0.4
1885	Bal AA	2	7	.222	9	9	9	0	71	71	55	0	2	13	31	4.31	76	.247	.284	34	.265	1*	60	-8	-0.6
1886	Was N	1	3	.250	4	4	4	0	27.2	35	27	1		15	19	4.23	76	.285	.362	14	.357	1	99	-5	-0.5
Total	3	4	14	.222	18	18	18-1	0	140.2	152	121	3	2	54	73	4.09	79	.258	.322	74	.243	1	59	-17	-1.5
HENRY, DOUG Richard Douglas B 12.10.1963 Sacramento, CA BR/TR 6-4/205# d7.15																									
1991	Mil A	2	1	.667	32	0	0	15-1	36	16	4	1	0	14-1	28	1.00	398	.133	.221	0-0	—	0		12	1.8
1992	Mil A	1	4	.200	68	0	0	29-4	65	64	34	6	0	24-4	52	4.02	96	.256	.319	0-0	—	0		-2	-0.3
1993	Mil A	4	4	.500	54	0	0	17-7	55	67	37	7	3	25-8	38	5.56	77	.300	.373	0-0	—	0		-8	-1.4
1994	Mil A	2	3	.400	25	0	0	0-0	31.1	32	17	7	1	23-1	20	4.60	110	.271	.394	1-0	.000	-0		2	0.2
1995	NY N	3	6	.333	51	0	0	4-3	67	48	23	7	1	25-6	62	2.96	137	.198	.274	1-1	1.000	0		9	1.2
1996	NY N	2	8	.200	58	0	0	9-5	75	82	48	7	1	36-6	58	4.68	86	.273	.350	5-0	.000	-1		-7	-1.1
1997	†SF N	4	5	.444	75	0	0	3-3	70.2	70	45	5	1	41-6	69	4.71	87	.261	.358	4-0	.000	-0		-7	-0.9
1998	†Hou N	8	2	.800	59	0	0	2-3	71	55	25	9	0	35-5	59	3.04	133	.216	.307	4-1	.000	-0		9	1.1

Year	Tm Lg	W	L	Pct	G	GS	CG-Sho	SV-BS	IP	H	R	HR	HB	BB-IB	SO	ERA	AERA	OAV	OOB	AB-SH	AVG	PB	Sup	APR	PW
1999	†Hou N	2	3	.400	35	0	0	2-2	40.2	45	24	8	3	24-0	36	4.65	95	.281	.385	1-0	.000	-0		-2	-0.2
2000	Hou N	1	3	.250	45	0	0	1-1	53	39	26	10	3	28-2	46	4.42	110	.204	.314	1-0	.000	-0		4	0.2
	†SF N	3	1	.750	27	0	0	0-2	25.1	18	10	2	1	21-1	16	2.49	170	.214	.374	0-0	—	0		4	0.6
	Year	4	4	.500	72	0	0	1-3	78.1	57	39	12	4	49-3	62	3.79	123	.207	.333	1-0	.000	-0		7	0.8
2001	KC A	2	2	.500	53	0	0	0-2	75.2	75	53	14	3	45-2	57	6.07	81	.262	.365	0-0	—	0		-8	-0.4
Total	11	34	42	.447	582	0	0	82-33	665.2	611	346	83	17	341-42	541	4.19	102	.245	.337	17-2	.059	-1		6	0.8
HENRY, BILL William Francis B 2.15.1942 Long Beach, CA BL/TL 6-3/195# d9.13																									
1966	NY A	0	0	—	2	0	0	0	3	0	0	0	0	2-0	3	0.00	—	.000	.200	0-0	—	0		1	0.1
HENRY, BILL William Rodman B 10.15.1927 Alice, TX BL/TL 6-2/180# d4.17																									
1952	Bos A	5	4	.556	13	10	5	0	76.2	75	40	7	2	36	23	3.87	102	.254	.339	31-0	.258	2*	120	-1	0.1
1953	Bos A	5	5	.500	21	12	4-1	1	85.2	86	39	4	4	33	56	3.26	129	.260	.334	32-0	.188	-0	95	7	0.7
1954	Bos A	3	7	.300	24	13	3-1	0	95.2	104	56	9	1	49	38	4.52	91	.270	.351	34-0	.118	-1*	96	-4	-0.6
1955	Bos A	2	4	.333	17	7	0	0	59.2	56	28	7	0	21-2	23	3.32	129	.247	.306	19-0	.105	-1	112	5	0.3
1958	Chi N	5	4	.556	44	0	0	6	81.1	63	27	8	1	17-6	58	2.88	136	.214	.259	17-0	.235	1		11	1.4
1959	Chi N	9	8	.529	**65**	0	0	12	134.1	111	42	19	1	26-3	115	2.68	147	.227	.264	31-1	.194	0		**20**	2.7
1960	Cin N★	1	5	.167	51	0	0	17	67.2	62	25	8	4	20-5	58	3.19	120	.247	.313	8-0	.000	-1		5	0.7
1961	†Cin N	2	1	.667	47	0	0	16	53.1	50	18	8	0	15-4	53	2.19	185	.244	.294	5-0	.000	-1*		10	1.1
1962	Cin N	4	2	.667	40	0	0	11	37.1	40	21	5	1	20-5	35	4.58	88	.280	.365	3-0	.333	0		-2	-0.4
1963	Cin N	1	3	.250	47	0	0	14	52	55	30	4	1	11-2	45	4.15	81	.279	.316	6-1	.167	-0		-6	-0.8
1964	Cin N	2	2	.500	37	0	0	6	52	31	9	2	3	12-4	28	0.87	418	.170	.231	6-0	.500	1*		14	1.6
1965	Cin N	2	0	1.000	3	0	0	0	5	3	0	0	0	1-0	5	0.00	—	.176	.222	0-0	—	0		2	0.4
	SF N	2	2	.500	35	0	0	4	42	40	18	2	1	8-3	35	3.64	99	.248	.287	5-0	.200	0		0	0.0
	Year	4	2	.667	38	0	0	4	47	43	23	2	1	9-3	40	3.26	111	.242	.280	5-0	.200	0		2	0.4
1966	SF N	1	1	.500	35	0	0	1	22	15	6	3	1	10-3	15	2.45	149	.190	.286	2-0	.000	-0		3	0.3
1967	SF N	2	0	1.000	28	1	0	2	21.2	16	5	1	2	9-4	23	2.08	158	.198	.290	1-0	.000	-0	27	3	0.4
1968	SF N	0	2	.000	7	1	0	0	5	4	3	0	1	3-1	0	5.40	55	.250	.400	0-0	—	0	29	-1	-0.2
	Pit N	0	0	—	10	0	0	0	16.2	29	18	2	2	3-1	9	8.10	36	.382	.420	3-0	.000	-0		-10	-0.6
	Year	0	2	.000	17	1	0	0	21.2	33	22	2	3	6-2	9	7.48	39	.359	.416	3-0	.000	-0	30	-12	-0.8
1969	Hou N	0	0	—	3	0	0	0-0	5	2	1	0	0	2-0	2	0.00	—	.111	.200	0-0	—	0		2	0.1
Total	16	46	50	.479	527	44	12-2	90-0	913	842	386	89	25	296-43	621	3.26	119	.244	.306	203-2	.177	-0	106	58	7.2
HENSHAW, ROY Roy Knikelbine B 7.29.1911 Chicago, IL D 6.8.1993 LaGrange, IL BR/TL 5-8/155# d4.15																									
1933	Chi N	2	1	.667	21	0	0	0	38.2	32	22	0	2	20	16	4.19	78	.230	.335	10-0	.200	-0		-4	-0.4
1935	†Chi N	13	5	.722	31	18	7-3	1	142.2	135	60	6	4	68	53	3.28	120	.249	.337	51-5	.255	2	118	11	1.2
1936	Chi N	6	5	.545	39	14	6-2	1	129.1	152	67	8	5	56	69	3.97	100	.296	.370	44-2	.136	-2	102	-1	-0.5
1937	Bro N	5	12	.294	42	16	5	2	156.1	176	110	14	4	69	98	5.07	80	.278	.352	48-4	.167	-2*	77	-18	-1.9
1938	StL N	5	11	.313	27	15	4	0	130	132	63	7	1	48	34	4.02	99	.266	.332	41-1	.220	-0	84	2	0.2
1942	Det A	2	4	.333	23	2	0	1	61.2	63	32	3	1	27	24	4.09	97	.269	.347	12-0	.083	-1	32	0	-0.1
1943	Det A	0	2	.000	26	3	0	2	71.1	75	35	2	3	33	33	3.79	93	.276	.360	18-0	.111	-1	160	-2	-0.2
1944	Det A	0	0	—	7	1	0	0	12.1	17	12	0	0	6	10	8.76	41	.315	.383	5-0	.000	-1	117	-6	-0.4
Total	8	33	40	.452	216	69	22-5	7	742.1	782	401	40	20	327	337	4.16	94	.271	.349	229-12	.179	-5	98	-18	-2.1
HENSIEK, PHIL Philip Frank "Sid" B 10.13.1901 St.Louis, MO D 2.21.1972 St.Louis, MO BR/TR 6/160# d8.15																									
1935	Was A	0	3	.000	6	1	0	1	13	21	15	2	0	9	6	9.69	45	.356	.441	3-0	.667	1	80	-8	-1.2
HENSLEY, CHUCK Charles Floyd B 3.11.1959 Tulare, CA BL/TL 6-3/190# d5.10																									
1986	SF N	0	0	—	11	0	0	1-1	7.1	5	2	2	0	2-0	6	2.45	144	.179	.233	0-0	—	0		1	0.1
HENTGEN, PAT Patrick George B 11.13.1968 Detroit, MI BR/TR 6-2/200# d9.3																									
1991	Tor A	0	0	—	3	1	0	0-0	7.1	5	2	1	2	3-0	3	2.45	172	.208	.345	0-0	—	0	65	1	0.1
1992	Tor A	5	2	.714	28	2	0	0-1	50.1	49	30	7	0	32-5	39	5.36	76	.254	.357	0-0	—	0	45	-6	-0.7
1993	†Tor A☆	19	9	.679	34	32	3	0-0	216.1	215	103	27	7	74-0	122	3.87	112	.258	.322	0-0	—	0	122	11	1.1
1994	Tor A★	13	8	.619	24	24	6-3	0-0	174.2	158	74	21	3	59-1	147	3.40	142	.240	.305	0-0	—	0	90	26	2.8
1995	Tor A	10	14	.417	30	30	2	0-0	200.2	236	129	24	5	90-6	135	5.11	92	.290	.363	0-0	—	0	92	-10	-1.1
1996	Tor A	20	10	.667	35	35	**10-3**	0-0	**265.2**	238	105	20	5	94-3	177	3.22	156	.241	.308	0-0	—	0	103	**53**	**5.2**
1997	Tor A★	15	10	.600	35	**35**	**9-3**	0-0	**264**	253	116	31	7	71-2	160	3.68	125	.254	.308	7-0	.000	-1	96	28	2.3
1998	Tor A	12	11	.522	29	29	0	0-0	177.2	208	109	28	5	69-1	94	5.17	90	.293	.357	5-1	.000	-1	108	-8	-1.0
1999	Tor A	11	12	.478	34	34	1	0-0	199	225	115	32	3	65-1	118	4.79	103	.286	.338	6-0	.167	-0	97	4	0.3
2000	†StL N	15	12	.556	33	33	1-1	0-0	194.1	202	107	24	3	89-4	118	4.72	98	.276	.353	60-8	.133	-1	120	0	-0.1
2001	Bal A	2	3	.400	9	9	1	0-0	62.1	51	25	7	0	19-3	33	3.47	124	.221	.279	0-0	—	0	77	7	0.5
2002	Bal A	0	4	.000	4	4	0	0-0	22	31	20	6	0	10-0	11	7.77	55	.337	.398	0-0	—	0	49	-9	-1.2
2003	Bal A	7	8	.467	28	22	1	1-0	160.2	150	74	25	5	58-1	100	4.09	107	.247	.316	5-0	.000	-0	68	8	0.5
Total	13	129	103	.556	326	290	34-10	1-1	1995	2021	1009	253	45	733-27	1257	4.21	110	.264	.329	83-9	.108	-3	99	105	8.7
HEPLER, BILL William Lewis B 9.25.1945 Covington, VA BL/TL 6/160# d4.23																									
1966	NY N	3	3	.500	37	3	0	0	69	71	30	3	3	51-6	25	3.52	103	.274	.397	14-1	.214	0	65	1	0.1
HERBEL, RON Ronald Samuel B 1.16.1938 Denver, CO D 1.20.2000 Tacoma, WA BR/TR 6-1/195# d9.10																									
1963	SF N	0	0	—	2	0	0	0	1.1	1	1	0	0	1-0	1	6.75	47	.200	.333	0-0	—	0		0	0.0
1964	SF N	9	9	.500	40	22	7-2	1	161	162	65	7	3	61-9	98	3.07	116	.259	.327	47-5	.000	-4*	94	7	0.4
1965	SF N	12	9	.571	47	21	1	1	170.2	172	80	16	3	47-7	106	3.85	94	.261	.311	49-2	.020	-4	107	-3	-0.7
1966	SF N	4	5	.444	32	18	0	1	129.2	149	70	15	2	39-9	55	4.16	88	.291	.343	38-0	.026	-4	119	-7	-0.9
1967	SF N	4	5	.444	42	11	1-1	1	125.2	125	54	10	2	35-10	52	3.08	107	.268	.320	28-3	.107	-0	66	1	0.3
1968	SF N	0	0	—	28	2	0	0	42.2	55	26	5	1	15-8	18	3.38	87	.309	.364	3-0	.000	-0	103	-5	-0.3
1969	SF N	4	1	.800	39	4	2	1-0	87.1	92	43	7	1	23-5	34	4.02	87	.275	.320	17-1	.000	-2	221	-4	-0.4
1970	SD N	7	5	.583	64	1	0	9-6	111	114	69	14	4	39-5	53	4.95	80	.266	.330	13-0	.000	-1	23	-12	-1.5
	NY N	2	2	.500	12	0	0	1-1	13	14	3	1	0	2-1	8	1.38	291	.275	.302	0-0	—	0		4	0.7
	Year	9	7	.563	**76**	1	0	10-7	124	128	73	15	4	41-6	61	4.57	87	.267	.327	13-0	.000	-1	23	-9	-0.8
1971	Atl N	0	1	.000	25	0	0	1-0	51.2	61	31	6	4	23-1	22	5.23	71	.300	.381	11-0	.091	-1		-7	-0.4
Total	9	42	37	.532	331	79	11-3	16-7	894	945	442	81	20	285-55	447	3.83	94	.273	.330	206-11	.029	-15	105	-26	-2.8
HERBERT, ERNIE Ernie Albert "Tex" B 1.30.1887 Hale, MO D 1.13.1968 Dallas, TX BR/TR 5-10/165# d7.27																									
1913	Cin N	0	0	—	6	0	0	0	17.1	12	12	0	1	5	5	2.08	156	.179	.247	4-0	.250	0		0	0.0
1914	StL F	1	0	1.000	18	1	0	1	50.1	56	33	2	4	27	24	3.58	85	.293	.392	13-0	.538	2*	45	-6	-0.2
1915	StL F	1	0	1.000	11	1	1	0	48	48	21	1	3	18	23	3.38	85	.253	.327	18-0	.278	1*	122	-2	0.0
Total	3	2	0	1.000	35	2	1	1	115.2	116	66	3	8	50	52	3.27	92	.259	.344	35-0	.371	3	70	-8	-0.2
HERBERT, FRED Frederick (b: Herbert Frederick Kemman) B 3.4.1887 LaGrange, IL D 5.29.1963 Tice, FL BR/TR 6/185# d9.25																									
1915	NY N	1	1	.500	2	2	1	0	17	12	5	0	0	4	6	1.06	242	.197	.246	6-0	.167	-0	87	2	0.2
HERBERT, RAY Raymond Ernest B 12.15.1929 Detroit, MI BR/TR 5-11/185# d8.27 Mil 1951																									
1950	Det A	1	2	.333	8	3	1	1	22.1	20	11	1	0	12	5	3.63	129	.244	.340	7-0	.286	0	90	2	0.3
1951	Det A	4	0	1.000	5	0	0	0	12.2	8	2	0	0	9	9	1.42	294	.190	.333	4-0	.000	-0		4	0.8
1953	Det A	4	6	.400	43	3	0	6	87.2	109	58	5	0	46	37	5.24	78	.308	.387	19-0	.158	-0	102	-12	-1.2
1954	Det A	3	6	.333	42	4	0	0	84.1	114	64	6	2	50	44	5.87	63	.334	.419	17-0	.176	2	101	-21	-1.8
1955	KC A	1	8	.111	23	11	2	0	87.2	99	65	10	1	40-9	30	6.26	67	.292	.361	21-1	.190	0*	81	-18	-1.5
1958	KC A	8	8	.500	42	16	5	3	175	161	76	20	4	55-3	108	3.50	112	.248	.309	52-2	.192	1	79	7	0.9
1959	KC A	11	11	.500	37	26	10-2	1	183.2	196	108	24	1	62-4	99	4.85	83	.275	.330	57-3	.211	2	99	-14	-1.4
1960	KC A	14	15	.483	37	33	14	1	252.2	256	106	17	7	72-6	122	3.28	121	.267	.320	76-9	.171	1	78	18	2.3
1961	KC A	3	6	.333	13	12	1	0	83.2	103	56	10	2	30-1	34	5.38	78	.303	.360	28-2	.107	-1	79	-10	-1.0
	Chi A	9	6	.600	21	20	4	0	137.2	142	69	15	0	36-2	50	4.05	97	.265	.308	53-1	.226	4	98	-2	0.2
	Year	12	12	.500	34	32	5	0	221.1	245	73	25	2	66-3	84	4.55	88	.280	.328	81-3	.185	3	91	-13	-0.8

Year	Tm Lg	W	L	Pct	G	GS	CG-Sho	SV-BS	IP	H	R	HR	HB	BB-IB	SO	ERA	AERA	OAV	OOB	AB-SH	AVG	PB	Sup	APR	PW
1962	Chi A★	20	9	**.690**	35	35	12-2	0	236.2	228	90	13	1	74-4	115	3.27	119	.255	.310	82-3	.195	5	109	19	2.9
1963	Chi A	13	10	.565	33	33	14-**7**	0	224.2	230	86	12	2	35-5	105	3.24	108	.265	.295	63-10	.222	6	115	9	1.7
1964	Chi A	6	7	.462	20	19	1-1	0	111.2	117	50	14	2	17-2	40	3.47	100	.275	.303	36-2	.139	-1	93	-1	-0.2
1965	Phi N	5	8	.385	25	19	4-1	1	130.2	162	60	13	1	19-2	51	3.86	90	.309	.333	41-4	.268	3	92	-4	0.0
1966	Phi N	2	5	.286	23	2	0	2	50.1	55	26	7	1	14-2	15	4.29	84	.293	.341	13-0	.077	-1	73	-4	-0.6
Total	14	104	107	.493	407	236	68-13	15	1881.1	2000	927	167	24	571-40	864	4.01	96	.276	.328	569-37	.192	20	95	-27	1.4
HEREDIA, FELIX Felix (Perez) B 6.18.1975 Barahona, D.R. BL/TL 6/160# d8.9																									
1996	Fla N	1	1	.500	21	0	0	0-0	16.2	21	8	1	0	10-1	10	4.32	94	.313	.397	0-0	—	0		0	0.0
1997	†Fla N	5	3	.625	56	0	0	0-1	56.2	53	30	3	5	30-1	54	4.29	94	.241	.342	2-1	.500	0		-2	-0.3
1998	Fla N	0	3	.000	41	2	0	2-1	41	38	30	1	1	32-2	38	5.49	74	.241	.368	3-0	.000	-0	91	-8	-0.6
	†Chi N	3	0	1.000	30	0	0	0-2	17.2	19	9	1	0	6-1	16	4.08	108	.279	.338	0-0	—	0		0	0.0
	Year	3	3	.500	71	2	0	2-3	58.2	57	43	2	1	38-3	54	5.06	82	.252	.360	3-0	.000	-0	88	-8	-0.6
1999	Chi N	3	1	.750	69	0	0	1-6	52	56	35	7	1	25-2	50	4.85	93	.272	.347	4-0	.500	1		-4	-0.2
2000	Chi N	7	3	.700	74	0	0	2-3	58.2	46	31	6	2	33-4	52	4.76	95	.220	.329	2-0	.000	-0		0	-0.1
2001	Chi N	2	2	.500	48	0	0	0-3	35	45	27	6	2	16-1	28	6.17	67	.315	.384	1-0	.000	-0		-9	-0.9
2002	Tor A	1	2	.333	53	0	0	0-2	52.1	51	29	5	2	26-3	31	3.61	128	.256	.345	0-0	—	0		3	0.2
2003	Cin N	5	2	.714	57	0	0	1-3	72	61	27	9	2	28-5	41	3.00	142	.228	.304	3-0	.333	0		10	0.8
	†NY A	0	1	.000	12	0	0	0-1	15	13	5	1	0	5-2	4	1.20	365	.228	.290	0-0	—	0		4	0.3
Total	8	27	18	.600	461	2	0	6-22	417	403	231	40	15	211-22	324	4.27	101	.253	.342	15-1	.267	1	86	-6	-0.8
HEREDIA, GIL Gilbert B 10.26.1965 Nogales, AZ BR/TR 6-1/190# d9.1																									
1991	SF N	0	2	.000	7	4	0	0-0	33	27	14	4	0	7-2	13	3.82	94	.233	.274	7-0	.429	1	88	0	0.1
1992	SF N	2	3	.400	13	4	0	0-0	30	32	20	3	1	16-1	15	5.40	61	.278	.371	6-1	.167	0	82	-7	-1.2
	Mon N	0	0	—	7	1	0	0-0	14.2	12	3	1	0	4-0	7	1.84	189	.250	.302	3-0	.000	-0	26	3	0.1
	Year	2	3	.400	20	5	0	0-0	44.2	44	4	4	1	20-1	22	4.23	79	.270	.351	9-1	.111	-0	70	-5	-1.1
1993	Mon N	4	2	.667	20	9	1	2-1	57.1	66	28	4	2	14-2	40	3.92	106	.293	.339	13-4	.154	-0	110	2	0.3
1994	Mon N	6	3	.667	39	3	0	0-0	75.1	85	34	7	2	13-3	62	3.46	122	.281	.311	16-0	.313	1	137	5	0.7
1995	Mon N	5	6	.455	40	18	0	1-2	119	137	60	7	5	21-1	74	4.31	100	.291	.326	33-5	.182	-0	95	1	0.1
1996	Tex A	2	5	.286	44	0	0	1-3	73.1	91	50	12	1	14-2	43	5.89	89	.301	.332	0-0	—	0		-4	-0.4
1998	Oak A	3	3	.500	8	6	0	0-0	42.2	43	14	4	3	3-0	27	2.74	167	.256	.282	0-0	—	0	61	9	1.2
1999	Oak A	13	8	.619	33	33	1	0-0	200.1	228	119	22	8	34-4	117	4.81	97	.283	.318	6-1	.000	-0	115	-4	-0.3
2000	†Oak A	15	11	.577	32	32	2	0-0	198.2	214	106	24	4	66-5	101	4.12	115	.274	.332	2-1	.500	0	107	12	1.4
2001	Oak A	7	8	.467	24	18	0	0-0	109.2	144	75	27	2	29-3	48	5.58	79	.316	.357	3-0	.333	0	113	-14	-1.6
Total	10	57	51	.528	267	128	4	4-6	954	1079	523	115	28	221-23	547	4.46	101	.285	.327	89-12	.213	2	105	3	0.4
HEREDIA, UBALDO Ubaldo José (Martinez) B 5.4.1956 Ciudad Bolivar, Venezuela BR/TR 6-2/180# d5.12																									
1987	Mon N	0	1	.000	2	2	0	0-0	10	10	6	2	1	3-1	6	5.40	78	.263	.333	2-0	.000	-0	107	-1	-0.1
HEREDIA, WILSON Wilson B 3.30.1972 LaRomana, D.R. BR/TR 6/175# d4.27																									
1995	Tex A	0	1	.000	6	0	0	0-0	12	9	5	2	0	15-2	6	3.75	129	.225	.429	0-0	—	0		2	0.1
1997	Tex A	1	0	1.000	10	0	0	0-0	19.2	14	9	2	0	16-0	8	3.20	150	.197	.337	0-0	—	0		3	0.1
Total	2	1	1	.500	16	0	0	0-0	31.2	23	14	4	0	31-2	14	3.41	141	.207	.372	0-0	—	0		5	0.2
HERGES, MATT Matthew Tyler B 4.1.1970 Champaign, IL BL/TR 6/200# d8.3																									
1999	LA N	0	2	.000	17	0	0	0-2	24.1	24	13	5	1	8-0	18	4.07	105	.255	.320	1-0	.000	-0		0	0.0
2000	LA N	11	3	.786	59	4	0	1-2	110.2	100	43	7	6	40-5	75	3.17	137	.249	.323	13-1	.077	-1	58	15	1.6
2001	LA N	9	8	.529	75	0	0	1-7	99.1	97	39	8	8	46-12	76	3.44	117	.259	.350	9-1	.444	2		8	1.4
2002	Mon N	2	5	.286	62	0	0	6-8	64.2	80	33	10	2	26-8	50	4.04	111	.305	.370	1-0	.000	0		3	0.3
2003	SD N	2	2	.500	40	0	0	3-2	44	40	16	2	2	20-2	40	2.86	138	.244	.325	1-0	.000	-0		5	0.5
	†SF N	1	0	1.000	27	0	0	0-1	35	28	11	1	1	9-0	28	2.31	178	.219	.273	2-0	.500	0		7	0.4
	Year	3	2	.600	67	0	0	3-3	79	68	30	3	3	29-2	68	2.62	153	.233	.303	3-0	.333	0		12	0.9
Total	5	25	20	.556	280	4	0	11-22	378	369	155	33	20	149-27	287	3.33	126	.259	.335	27-2	.222	1	58	38	4.2
HERMAN, ART Arthur B 5.11.1871 Louisville, KY D 9.20.1955 Los Angeles, CA d6.29																									
1896	Lou N	4	6	.400	14	12	9	0	94.1	122	73	4	2	36	13	5.63	77	.310	.371	36-0	.139	-4	89	-8	-1.0
1897	Lou N	0	1	.000	3	2	1	0	18	23	14	1	0	5	4	4.00	107	.307	.350	6-0	.333	1	125	0	0.2
Total	2	4	7	.364	17	14	10	0	112.1	145	87	5	2	41	17	5.37	81	.310	.368	42-0	.167	-2	94	-8	-0.8
HERMANSON, DUSTIN Dustin Michael B 12.21.1972 Springfield, OH BR/TR 6-3/195# d5.8																									
1995	SD N	3	1	.750	26	0	0	0-0	31.2	35	26	8	1	22-1	19	6.82	59	.280	.392	0-0	—	0		-10	-1.0
1996	SD N	1	0	1.000	8	0	0	0-0	13.2	18	15	3	0	4-0	11	8.56	46	.340	.367	0-0	—	0		-8	-0.5
1997	Mon N	8	8	.500	32	28	1-1	0-0	158.1	134	68	15	1	66-2	136	3.69	114	.234	.311	48-5	.104	-0	89	11	0.9
1998	Mon N	14	11	.560	32	30	1	0-0	187	163	80	21	3	56-3	154	3.13	134	.234	.292	52-5	.115	2	91	20	2.7
1999	Mon N	9	14	.391	34	34	0	0-0	216.1	225	110	20	7	69-4	145	4.20	107	.271	.330	64-8	.047	-5	78	9	0.4
2000	Mon N	12	14	.462	38	30	2-1	4-3	198	226	128	26	4	75-5	94	4.77	101	.290	.352	55-8	.145	-1	86	-5	-0.6
2001	†StL N	14	13	.519	33	33	0	0-0	192.1	195	106	34	8	73-3	123	4.45	96	.264	.335	62-5	.081	-3*	109	-5	-1.1
2002	Bos A	1	1	.500	12	1	0	0-1	22	35	19	3	0	7-0	13	7.77	58	.354	.393	0-0	—	0	248	-7	-0.6
2003	StL N	1	2	.333	23	0	0	1-5	29.2	35	18	4	1	14-2	12	5.46	75	.315	.394	0-0	—	0		-4	-0.4
	†SF N	2	1	.667	9	6	0	0-0	39	35	14	5	2	10-2	27	3.00	137	.238	.294	11-3	.000	-1	107	5	0.2
	Year	3	3	.500	32	6	0	1-5	68.2	70	19	9	3	24-4	39	4.06	101	.271	.338	11-3	.000	-1	107	1	-0.2
Total	9	65	65	.500	247	162	4-2	5-9	1088	1101	584	139	27	396-22	734	4.28	102	.265	.331	292-34	.092	-7	92	6	-0.0
HERNAIZ, JESUS Jesus Rafael (Rodriguez) B 1.8.1945 Santurce, P.R. BR/TR 6-2/175# d6.14																									
1974	Phi N	2	3	.400	27	0	0	1-3	41.1	53	31	6	0	25-1	16	5.88	64	.323	.411	2-0	.000	-0		-10	-1.2
HERNANDEZ, ADRIAN Adrian B 3.25.1975 Havana, Cuba BR/TR 6-1/185# d4.21																									
2001	NY A	0	3	.000	6	3	0	0-0	22	15	10	7	2	10-1	10	3.68	122	.190	.297	0-0	—	0	41	2	0.2
2002	NY A	0	1	.000	2	1	0	0-0	6	10	8	2	0	6-0	9	12.00	36	.357	.471	0-0	—	0	64	-5	-0.6
Total	2	0	4	.000	8	4	0	0-0	28	25	18	9	2	16-1	19	5.46	82	.234	.344	0-0	—	0	47	-3	-0.4
HERNANDEZ, CARLOS Carlos E. B 4.22.1980 Guacara, Venezuela BL/TL 5-10/145# d8.18																									
2001	Hou N	1	0	1.000	3	3	0	0-0	17.2	11	2	1	0	7-0	17	1.02	449	.177	.261	5-1	.200	0	74	7	0.4
2002	Hou N	7	5	.583	23	21	0	0-0	111	112	56	11	3	61-5	93	4.38	98	.261	.357	35-4	.171	0*	91	0	0.1
Total	2	8	5	.615	26	24	0	0-0	128.2	123	58	12	3	68-5	110	3.92	110	.251	.345	40-5	.175	0	88	7	0.5
HERNANDEZ, LIVAN Eisler Livan B 2.20.1975 Villa Clara, Cuba BR/TR 6-2/220# d9.24 b-Orlando																									
1996	Fla N	0	0	—	1	0	0	0-0	3	3	0	0	0	2-0	2	0.00	—	.273	.385	1-0	1.000	0		1	0.1
1997	†Fla N	9	3	.750	17	17	0	0-0	96.1	81	39	5	3	38-1	72	3.18	127	.229	.304	29-3	.172	1	126	9	1.1
1998	Fla N	10	12	.455	33	33	9	0-0	234.1	265	133	37	6	104-8	162	4.72	86	.289	.363	82-1	.195	2*	103	-17	-1.2
1999	Fla N	5	9	.357	20	20	2	0-0	136	161	78	17	2	55-3	97	4.76	92	.294	.358	45-1	.289	5	97	-6	0.0
	SF N	3	3	.500	10	10	0	0-0	63.2	66	32	6	0	21-2	47	4.38	96	.267	.322	18-6	.222	1*	94	0	0.1
	Year	8	12	.400	30	30	2	0-0	199.2	227	36	23	2	76-5	144	4.64	93	.286	.347	63-7	.270	7	96	-7	0.1
2000	†SF N	17	11	.607	33	33	5-2	0-0	240	254	114	22	4	73-3	165	3.75	113	.273	.325	89-9	.236	6*	113	12	1.9
2001	SF N	13	15	.464	34	34	2	0-0	226.2	266	143	24	3	85-7	138	5.24	76	.297	.355	81-4	.296	9*	99	-34	-2.6
2002	†SF N	12	16	.429	33	33	5-3	0-0	216	233	113	19	4	71-5	134	4.38	89	.283	.340	64-10	.234	4*	103	-12	-0.7
2003	Mon N	15	10	.600	33	33	**8**	0-0	**233.1**	225	92	27	10	57-3	178	3.20	146	.253	.304	74-6	.189	-0	104	36	3.7
Total	8	84	79	.515	214	213	31-5	0-0	1449.1	1554	744	157	32	506-32	995	4.22	99	.277	.337	483-40	.234	28	105	-11	2.4
HERNANDEZ, FERNANDO Fernando B 6.16.1971 Santiago, D.R. BR/TR 6-2/185# d4.3																									
1997	Det A	0	0	—	2	0	0	0-0	1.1	5	6	0	1	3-1	2	40.50	11	.556	.692	0-0	—	0		-5	-0.2
HERNANDEZ, XAVIER Francis Xavier B 8.16.1965 Port Arthur, TX BL/TR 6-2/185# d6.4																									
1989	Tor A	1	0	1.000	7	0	0	0-0	22.2	25	15	2	1	8-0	7	4.76	79	.278	.337	0-0	—	0		-3	-0.2
1990	Hou N	2	1	.667	34	1	0	0-1	62.1	60	34	8	4	24-5	24	4.62	80	.256	.331	3-0	.333	0*	49	-5	-0.3

Year	Tm Lg	W	L	Pct	G	GS	CG-Sho	SV-BS	IP	H	R	HR	HB	BB-IB	SO	ERA	AERA	OAV	OOB	AB-SH	AVG	PB	Sup	APR	PW
1991	Hou N	2	7	.222	32	6	0	3-3	63	66	34	6	0	32-7	55	4.71	74	.263	.345	10-1	.000	-0	43	-8	-1.1
1992	Hou N	9	1	.900	77	0	0	7-3	111	81	31	5	3	42-7	96	2.11	160	.200	.279	9-0	.000	-1		15	1.3
1993	Hou N	4	5	.444	72	0	0	9-8	96.2	75	37	6	1	28-3	101	2.61	149	.212	.269	5-2	.000	-1		12	1.1
1994	NY A	4	4	.500	31	0	0	6-2	40	48	27	7	2	21-3	37	5.85	78	.300	.384	0-0	—	0		-5	-0.9
1995	†Cin N	7	2	.778	59	0	0	3-1	90	95	47	8	4	31-1	84	4.60	90	.273	.338	8-0	.000	-1		-4	-0.5
1996	Cin N	0	0	—	3	0	0	0-0	3.1	8	6	2	0	2-0	3	13.50	31	.471	.526	0-0	—	0		-4	-0.2
	Hou N	5	5	.500	58	0	0	6-4	74.2	69	39	11	2	26-5	78	4.22	92	.245	.310	2-1	.000	-0		-3	-0.4
	Year	5	5	.500	61	0	0	6-4	78	77	47	13	2	28-5	81	4.62	84	.258	.322	2-1	.000	-0		-7	-0.6
1997	Tex A	0	4	.000	44	0	0	0-1	49.1	51	27	7	2	22-4	36	4.56	105	.262	.341	0-0	—	0		1	0.1
1998	Tex A	6	6	.500	46	0	0	1-5	58	43	27	5	1	30-1	41	3.57	135	.207	.307	0-0	—	0		7	1.2
Total	10	40	35	.533	463	7	0	35-28	671	621	324	67	20	266-36	562	3.90	101	.244	.318	37-4	.027	-3	39	3	0.1

HERNANDEZ, EVELIO Gregorio Evelio (Lopez) B 12.24.1931 Guanabacoa, Cuba BR/TR 6-1/195# d9.12

Year	Tm Lg	W	L	Pct	G	GS	CG-Sho	SV-BS	IP	H	R	HR	HB	BB-IB	SO	ERA	AERA	OAV	OOB	AB-SH	AVG	PB	Sup	APR	PW
1956	Was A	1	1	.500	4	4	1	0	22.2	24	12	2	0	8-0	9	4.76	91	.276	.333	11-0	.182	-0	103	0	-0.1
1957	Was A	0	0	—	14	2	0	0	36	38	18	2	0	20-1	15	4.25	92	.268	.356	6-0	.000	-1	115	-1	-0.2
Total	2	1	1	.500	18	6	1	0	58.2	62	30	4	0	28-1	24	4.45	91	.271	.347	17-0	.118	-1	110	-1	-0.3

HERNANDEZ, WILLIE Guillermo (Villanueva) B 11.14.1954 Aguada, P.R. BL/TL 6-3/180# d4.9

Year	Tm Lg	W	L	Pct	G	GS	CG-Sho	SV-BS	IP	H	R	HR	HB	BB-IB	SO	ERA	AERA	OAV	OOB	AB-SH	AVG	PB	Sup	APR	PW
1977	Chi N	8	7	.533	67	1	0	4-7	110	94	42	11	1	28-9	78	3.03	145	.234	.284	16-3	.063	-1	20	15	2.0
1978	Chi N	8	2	.800	54	0	0	3-1	59.2	57	26	6	1	35-7	38	3.77	107	.263	.363	1-0	.000	-0*		2	0.4
1979	Chi N	4	4	.500	51	2	0	0-0	79	85	50	8	4	39-12	53	5.01	82	.281	.364	8-1	.250	0*	129	-7	-0.6
1980	Chi N	1	9	.100	53	7	0	0-2	108.1	115	58	8	2	45-4	75	4.40	89	.276	.347	19-1	.211	0	49	-4	-0.3
1981	Chi N	0	0	—	12	0	0	2-0	13.2	14	7	0	0	8-2	13	3.95	94	.280	.367	0-0	—	0*		0	0.0
1982	Chi N	4	6	.400	75	0	0	10-2	75	74	26	3	1	24-11	54	3.00	125	.268	.326	3-1	.000	-0		7	1.2
1983	Chi N	1	0	1.000	11	1	0	1-0	19.2	16	8	0	0	6-1	18	3.20	119	.222	.282	2-0	.500	0	140	1	0.1
	†Phi N	8	4	.667	63	0	0	7-3	95.2	93	39	9	1	26-7	75	3.29	109	.254	.305	13-0	.385	2		4	0.7
	Year	9	4	.692	74	1	0	8-3	115.1	109	53	9	1	32-8	93	3.28	110	.249	.301	15-0	.400	2	147	4	0.8
1984	†Det A★	9	3	.750	**80**	0	0	32-1	140.1	96	30	6	4	36-8	112	1.92	204	.194	.252	0-0	—	0		**34**	**4.2**
1985	Det A★	8	10	.444	74	0	0	31-9	106.2	82	38	13	1	14-2	76	2.70	151	.210	.236	1-0	.000	-0		16	3.1
1986	Det A☆	8	7	.533	64	0	0	24-6	88.2	87	35	13	5	21-1	77	3.55	116	.251	.301	0-0	—	0		7	1.5
1987	†Det A	3	4	.429	45	0	0	8-5	49	53	27	8	0	20-7	30	3.67	115	.276	.340	0-0	—	0		1	0.2
1988	Det A	6	5	.545	63	0	0	10-5	67.2	50	24	8	4	31-6	59	3.06	125	.208	.306	0-0	—	0		7	1.2
1989	Det A	2	2	.500	32	0	0	15-2	31.1	36	21	4	1	16-2	30	5.74	67	.293	.379	0-0	—	0		-6	-1.2
Total	13	70	63	.526	744	11	0	147-43	1044.2	952	431	97	25	349-79	788	3.38	118	.245	.308	63-6	.206	1	70	77	12.5

HERNANDEZ, JEREMY Jeremy Stuart B 7.6.1966 Burbank, CA BR/TR 6-6/195# d9.2

Year	Tm Lg	W	L	Pct	G	GS	CG-Sho	SV-BS	IP	H	R	HR	HB	BB-IB	SO	ERA	AERA	OAV	OOB	AB-SH	AVG	PB	Sup	APR	PW
1991	SD N	0	0	—	9	0	0	2-0	14.1	8	1	0	0	5-0	9	0.00	—	.157	.232	2-0	.000	-0		5	0.3
1992	SD N	1	4	.200	26	0	0	1-1	36.2	39	17	4	1	11-5	25	4.17	86	.291	.338	2-0	.000	-0		-2	-0.2
1993	SD N	0	2	.000	21	0	0	0-0	34.1	41	19	2	0	7-1	26	4.72	88	.301	.333	1-0	.000	-0		-1	-0.1
	Cle A	6	5	.545	49	0	0	8-5	77.1	75	33	12	0	27-6	44	3.14	138	.261	.320	0-0	—	0		9	1.3
1994	Fla N	3	3	.500	21	0	0	9-3	23.1	16	9	0	2	14-3	13	2.70	162	.205	.337	1-0	.000	-0		4	0.7
1995	Fla N	0	0	—	7	0	0	0-1	7	12	9	2	1	3-1	5	11.57	36	.400	.457	1-0	.000	-0		-5	-0.3
Total	5	10	14	.417	133	0	0	20-10	193	191	88	20	4	67-16	122	3.64	113	.267	.327	7-0	.000	-1		10	1.7

HERNANDEZ, MANNY Manuel Antonio (Montas) B 5.7.1961 LaRomana, D.R. BR/TR 6/150# d6.5

Year	Tm Lg	W	L	Pct	G	GS	CG-Sho	SV-BS	IP	H	R	HR	HB	BB-IB	SO	ERA	AERA	OAV	OOB	AB-SH	AVG	PB	Sup	APR	PW
1986	Hou N	2	3	.400	9	4	0	0-0	27.2	33	15	2	0	12-3	9	3.90	92	.306	.372	6-1	.000	-1	62	-2	-0.3
1987	Hou N	0	4	.000	6	3	0	0-0	21.2	25	15	1	1	5-1	12	5.40	73	.301	.341	5-0	.000	-1	85	-4	-0.7
1989	NY N	0	0	—	1	0	0	0-0	1	0	0	0	0	0-0	1	0.00	—	.000	.000	0-0	—	0		0	0.0
Total	3	2	7	.222	16	7	0	0-0	50.1	58	30	3	1	17-4	22	4.47	84	.299	.353	11-1	.000	-1	72	-6	-1.0

HERNANDEZ, ORLANDO Orlando P. "El Duque" B 10.11.1965 Villa Clara, Cuba BR/TR 6-2/210# d6.3 b-Livan

Year	Tm Lg	W	L	Pct	G	GS	CG-Sho	SV-BS	IP	H	R	HR	HB	BB-IB	SO	ERA	AERA	OAV	OOB	AB-SH	AVG	PB	Sup	APR	PW
1998	†NY A	12	4	.750	21	21	3-1	0-0	141	113	53	11	6	52-1	131	3.13	140	.222	.299	7-1	.000	-1	145	20	2.1
1999	†NY A★	17	9	.654	33	33	2-1	0-0	214.1	187	108	24	8	87-2	157	4.12	115	.233	.311	3-0	.333	0	105	15	1.6
2000	†NY A	12	13	.480	29	29	3	0-0	195.2	186	104	34	6	51-2	141	4.51	107	.247	.298	9-1	.000	-1	81	8	0.8
2001	†NY A	4	7	.364	17	16	0	0-0	94.2	90	51	19	5	42-1	77	4.85	93	.248	.333	0-0	—	0	69	-1	-0.2
2002	†NY A	8	5	.615	24	22	0	1-0	146	131	63	17	8	36-2	113	3.64	120	.236	.289	0-0	—	0	106	13	1.1
Total	5	53	38	.582	124	121	8-2	1-0	791.2	707	379	105	33	268-8	619	4.04	114	.237	.304	19-2	.053	-1	101	55	5.4

HERNANDEZ, RAMON Ramon (Gonzalez) B 8.31.1940 Carolina, P.R. BB/TL 5-9/170# d4.11

Year	Tm Lg	W	L	Pct	G	GS	CG-Sho	SV-BS	IP	H	R	HR	HB	BB-IB	SO	ERA	AERA	OAV	OOB	AB-SH	AVG	PB	Sup	APR	PW
1967	Atl N	0	2	.000	46	0	0	5	51.2	60	27	5	2	14-3	28	4.18	79	.296	.345	4-0	.000	-0		-5	-0.3
1968	Chi N	0	0	—	8	0	0	0	9	14	11	1	1	0-0	3	9.00	35	.350	.366	0-0	—	0		-6	-0.3
1971	Pit N	0	1	.000	10	0	0	4-0	12.1	5	1	0	0	2-1	7	0.73	464	.122	.163	2-0	.500	0		4	0.7
1972	†Pit N	5	0	1.000	53	0	0	14-1	70	50	14	3	3	22-2	47	1.67	199	.194	.264	12-0	.167	0		14	1.7
1973	Pit N	4	5	.444	59	0	0	11-1	89.2	71	27	5	4	25-8	64	2.41	146	.218	.282	8-0	.125	0		12	1.5
1974	†Pit N	5	2	.714	58	0	0	2-3	68.2	68	21	3	2	18-8	33	2.75	126	.258	.310	4-0	.250	1		7	0.8
1975	†Pit N	7	2	.778	46	0	0	5-3	64	62	21	0	0	28-14	43	2.95	120	.252	.325	6-2	.000	-0		6	0.9
1976	Pit N	2	2	.500	37	0	0	3-3	43	42	17	3	1	16-5	17	3.56	98	.262	.326	3-0	.000	-0		1	0.0
	Chi N	0	0	—	2	0	0	0-0	1.2	2	0	0	0	0-0	1	0.00	—	.333	.333	0-0	—	0		1	0.0
	Year	2	2	.500	39	0	0	3-3	44.2	44	22	3	1	16-5	18	3.43	102	.265	.326	3-0	.000	-0		1	0.0
1977	Chi N	0	0	—	6	0	0	1-0	7.2	11	9	1	0	3-0	4	8.22	53	.306	.359	1-0	.000	-0		-3	-0.2
	Bos A	0	1	.000	12	0	0	1-0	12.2	14	10	2	1	7-1	8	5.68	79	.280	.379	0-0	—	0		-2	-0.2
Total	9	23	15	.605	337	0	0	46-11	430.1	399	158	23	14	135-42	255	3.03	115	.245	.307	40-2	.125	1		29	4.6

HERNANDEZ, ROBERTO Roberto Manuel (Rodriguez) B 11.11.1964 Santurce, P.R. BR/TR 6-4/235# d9.2

Year	Tm Lg	W	L	Pct	G	GS	CG-Sho	SV-BS	IP	H	R	HR	HB	BB-IB	SO	ERA	AERA	OAV	OOB	AB-SH	AVG	PB	Sup	APR	PW
1991	Chi A	1	0	1.000	9	3	0	0-0	15	18	15	1	0	7-0	6	7.80	51	.290	.362	0-0	—	0	153	-7	-0.4
1992	Chi A	7	3	.700	43	0	0	12-4	71	45	15	4	4	20-1	68	1.65	235	.180	.249	0-0	—	0		18	2.9
1993	†Chi A	3	4	.429	70	0	0	38-6	78.2	66	21	6	0	20-1	71	2.29	183	.228	.276	0-0	—	0		18	2.9
1994	Chi A	4	4	.500	45	0	0	14-6	47.2	44	29	5	1	19-1	50	4.91	95	.238	.311	0-0	—	0		-1	-0.3
1995	Chi A	3	7	.300	60	0	0	32-10	59.2	63	30	9	3	28-4	84	3.92	114	.266	.351	0-0	—	0		3	0.6
1996	Chi A★	6	5	.545	72	0	0	38-8	84.2	65	21	2	0	38-5	85	1.91	248	.208	.292	0-0	—	0		27	5.1
1997	Chi A	5	1	.833	46	0	0	27-4	48	38	15	5	1	24-4	47	2.44	180	.216	.312	0-0	—	0		11	2.1
	†SF N	5	2	.714	28	0	0	4-4	32.2	29	9	2	0	14-1	35	2.48	165	.238	.316	2-0	.500	0		6	1.3
1998	TB A	2	6	.250	67	0	0	26-9	71.1	55	33	5	5	41-4	55	4.04	119	.212	.330	0-0	—	0		6	1.0
1999	TB A	2	3	.400	72	0	0	43-4	73.1	68	27	1	4	33-1	69	3.07	162	.244	.329	0-0	—	0		16	2.5
2000	TB A	4	7	.364	68	0	0	32-8	73.1	76	33	9	3	23-1	61	3.19	155	.272	.331	0-0	—	0		12	2.3
2001	KC A	5	6	.455	63	0	0	28-6	67.2	69	34	7	1	26-3	46	4.12	119	.266	.336	0-0	—	0		5	1.0
2002	KC A	1	3	.250	53	0	0	26-7	52	62	29	6	3	12-2	39	4.33	116	.300	.345	0-0	—	0		3	0.4
2003	†Atl N	5	3	.625	66	0	0	0-4	60	61	36	10	3	43-7	45	4.35	97	.263	.385	0-0	—	0		-2	-0.3
Total	13	53	54	.495	762	3	0	320-80	835	759	347	72	28	348-35	761	3.30	139	.241	.320	2-0	.500	0	153	115	21.1

HERNANDEZ, RUDY Rudolph Albert (Fuentes) B 12.10.1931 Santiago, D.R. BR/TR 6-3/185# d7.3

Year	Tm Lg	W	L	Pct	G	GS	CG-Sho	SV-BS	IP	H	R	HR	HB	BB-IB	SO	ERA	AERA	OAV	OOB	AB-SH	AVG	PB	Sup	APR	PW
1960	Was A	4	1	.800	21	0	0	0	34.2	34	24	2	1	21-3	22	4.41	88	.262	.366	6-1	.167	-0*		-4	-0.5
1961	Was A	0	1	.000	7	0	0	0	9	8	5	0	0	3-0	4	3.00	134	.250	.306	0-0	—	0		0	0.1
Total	2	4	2	.667	28	0	0	0	43.2	42	29	2	1	24-3	26	4.12	95	.259	.354	6-1	.167	-0		-4	-0.4

HERNANDEZ, RUNELVYS Runelvys Antonio B 4.27.1978 Santo Domingo, D.R. BR/TR 6-3/185# d7.15

Year	Tm Lg	W	L	Pct	G	GS	CG-Sho	SV-BS	IP	H	R	HR	HB	BB-IB	SO	ERA	AERA	OAV	OOB	AB-SH	AVG	PB	Sup	APR	PW
2002	KC A	4	4	.500	12	12	0	0-0	74.1	79	36	8	1	22-0	45	4.36	115	.273	.324	0-0	—	0	105	6	0.6
2003	KC A	7	5	.583	16	16	0	0-0	91.2	87	51	9	6	37-0	48	4.61	112	.249	.328	0-0	—	0	94	5	0.5
Total	2	11	9	.550	28	28	0	0-0	166	166	87	17	7	59-0	93	4.50	113	.260	.326	0-0	—	0	99	11	1.1

HERNDON, JUNIOR Harry Francis B 9.11.1978 Liberal, KS BR/TR 6-1/190# d8.2

Year	Tm Lg	W	L	Pct	G	GS	CG-Sho	SV-BS	IP	H	R	HR	HB	BB-IB	SO	ERA	AERA	OAV	OOB	AB-SH	AVG	PB	Sup	APR	PW
2001	SD N	2	6	.250	12	8	0	0-0	42.2	55	34	5	3	25-5	14	6.33	63	.322	.417	12-1	.000	-1	78	-12	-1.9

Year	Tm Lg	W	L	Pct	G	GS	CG-Sho	SV-BS	IP	H	R	HR	HB	BB-IB	SO	ERA	AERA	OAV	OOB	AB-SH	AVG	PB	Sup	APR	PW
HERRELL, WALT Walter William "Reds" B 2.19.1889 Rockville, MD D 1.23.1949 Front Royal, VA d6.10																									
1911	Was A	0	0	—	1	0	0	0	2	5	4	0	0	2	0	18.00	18	.556	.636	1-0	.000	-0		-3	-0.1
HERRERA, ALEX Alexander J. B 11.5.1979 Maracaibo, Venezuela BL/TL 5-11/175# d9.13																									
2002	Cle A	0	0	—	5	0	0	0-0	5.1	3	0	0	0	1-0	5	0.00	—	.158	.200	0-0	—	0		3	0.1
2003	Cle A	0	0	—	10	0	0	0-0	7	7	7	3	0	8-1	6	9.00	49	.250	.417	0-0	—	0		-3	-0.2
Total	2	0	0	—	15	0	0	0-0	12.1	10	7	3	0	9-1	11	5.11	86	.213	.339	0-0	—	0		0	-0.1
HERRERA, BOBBY Procopio Rodriguez "Tito" (b: Procopio Rodriguez (Herrera)) B 7.26.1926 Nuevo Laredo, Mexico BR/TR 6/184# d4.19																									
1951	StL A	0	0	—	3	0	0	0	2.1	6	7	2	1	4	1	27.00	16	.462	.611	0-0	—	0		-5	-0.2
HERRIAGE, TROY William Troy "Dutch" B 12.20.1930 Tipton, OK BR/TR 6-1/170# d4.25																									
1956	KC A	1	13	.071	31	16	1	0	103	135	83	16	6	64-6	59	6.64	65	.321	.414	25-2	.120	-1*	63	-24	-3.0
HERRIN, TOM Thomas Edward B 9.12.1929 Shreveport, LA D 11.29.1999 Homer, LA BR/TR 6-3/190# d4.13																									
1954	Bos A	1	2	.333	14	1	0	0	28.1	34	23	2	0	22	8	7.31	56	.315	.424	8-0	.125	-0	0	-8	-0.7
HERRING, ART Arthur L "Red" or "Sandy" B 3.10.1906 Altus, OK D 12.2.1995 Marion, IN BR/TR 5-7/168# d9.12																									
1929	Det A	2	1	.667	4	4	2	0	32	38	17	0	1	19	15	4.78	90	.302	.397	14-0	.214	1	103	0	0.1
1930	Det A	3	3	.500	23	6	1	0	77.2	97	54	2	3	36	16	5.33	90	.315	.392	23-2	.130	-2	89	-4	-0.5
1931	Det A	7	13	.350	35	16	9	1	165	186	95	8	8	67	64	4.31	106	.281	.355	55-3	.200	-1	93	4	0.5
1932	Det A	1	2	.333	12	0	0	2	22.1	25	18	2	1	15	12	5.24	90	.284	.394	4-0	.000	-0		-2	-0.3
1933	Det A	1	2	.333	24	3	1	0	61	61	34	6	1	20	20	3.84	112	.264	.325	13-0	.077	-1	171	2	0.0
1934	Bro N	2	4	.333	14	4	2	0	49.1	63	36	2	0	29	15	6.20	63	.307	.393	14-0	.143	1	111	-11	-1.1
1939	Chi A	0	0	—	7	0	0	0	14.1	13	9	2	1	5	8	5.65	84	.250	.328	4-0	.000	-0		-1	-0.1
1944	Bro N	3	4	.429	12	6	3-1	1	55.1	59	28	3	1	17	19	3.42	104	.277	.333	15-3	.200	0	122	-1	0.0
1945	Bro N	7	4	.636	22	15	7-2	2	124	103	60	11	3	43	34	3.48	108	.222	.292	42-4	.095	-2*	126	4	0.1
1946	Bro N	7	2	.778	35	2	0	5	86	91	39	2	1	29	34	3.35	101	.277	.338	22-1	.182	0	76	0	0.1
1947	Pit N	1	3	.250	11	0	0	2	10.2	18	11	3	0	4	6	8.44	50	.360	.407	2-0	.000	-0		-5	-0.9
Total	11	34	38	.472	199	56	25-3	13	697.2	754	401	41	20	284	243	4.32	96	.276	.349	208-13	.149	-4	110	-14	-2.1
HERRING, HERB Herbert Lee B 7.22.1891 Danville, AR D 4.22.1964 Tucson, AZ BR/TR 5-11/178# d9.4																									
1912	Was A	0	0	—	1	0	0	0	1	1	0	0	0	1	0	0.00	—	.250	.400	0-0	—	0		0	0.0
HERRING, BILL William Francis "Smoke" B 10.31.1893 New York, NY D 9.10.1962 Honesdale, PA BR/TR 6-3/185# d6.26																									
1915	Bro F	0	0	—	3	0	0	0	3	5	6	1	1	2	3	15.00	18	.385	.500	0-0	—	0		-4	-0.2
HERRMANN, LEROY Leroy George B 2.27.1906 Steward, IL D 7.3.1972 Livermore, CA BR/TR 5-10/185# d7.30																									
1932	Chi N	2	1	.667	7	0	0	0	12.2	18	9	0	0	9	5	6.39	59	.346	.443	2-0	.500	0		-3	-0.6
1933	Chi N	0	1	.000	9	1	0	1	21	26	19	3	4	8	4	5.57	59	.299	.384	6-0	.167	-0	102	-7	-0.4
1935	Cin N	3	5	.375	29	8	2	0	108	124	53	9	8	31	30	3.58	111	.297	.357	30-0	.267	1	117	4	0.4
Total	3	5	7	.417	45	9	2	1	141.2	168	81	12	12	48	39	4.13	93	.302	.370	38-0	.263	1	117	-6	-0.6
HERRMANN, MARTY Martin John "Lefty" B 1.10.1893 Oldenburg, IN D 9.11.1956 Cincinnati, OH BL/TL 5-10/150# d7.10 gs-Ed																									
1918	Bro N	0	0	—	1	0	0	0	1	0	0	0	0	1	0	0.00	—	.000	.250	0-0	—	0		0	0.0
HERSHEY, FRANK Frank B 12.13.1877 Gorham, NY D 12.15.1949 Canandaigua, NY TR 5-10/175# d4.20																									
1905	Bos N	0	1	.000	1	1	0	0	4	5	4	0	0	2	1	6.75	46	.313	.389	1-0	.000	-0	47	-2	-0.3
HERSHISER, OREL Orel Leonard B 9.16.1958 Buffalo, NY BR/TR 6-3/192# d9.1 C1																									
1983	LA N	0	0	—	8	0	0	1-0	8	7	6	1	0	6-0	5	3.38	107	.233	.361	0-0	—	0		-1	0.0
1984	LA N	11	8	.579	45	20	8-**4**	2-2	189.2	160	65	9	4	50-8	150	2.66	133	.225	.278	50-8	.200	2	104	19	2.1
1985	†LA N	19	3	**.864**	36	34	9-5	0-0	239.2	179	72	8	6	68-5	157	2.03	172	.206	.267	76-10	.197	3*	114	37	3.8
1986	LA N	14	14	.500	35	35	8-1	0-0	231.1	213	112	13	5	86-11	153	3.85	90	.243	.312	71-10	.239	4*	97	-12	-0.8
1987	LA N★	16	16	.500	37	35	10-1	1-0	**264.2**	247	105	17	9	74-5	190	3.06	130	.247	.304	90-10	.211	4*	92	26	**3.5**
1988	†LA N★	**23**	8	.742	35	34	**15-8**	1-0	**267**	208	73	18	4	73-10	178	2.26	148	.213	.269	85-19	.129	-0*	107	**34**	**4.5**
1989	LA N☆	15	15	.500	35	33	8-4	0-0	**256.2**	226	75	9	3	77-14	178	2.31	148	.240	.298	77-10	.182	3	85	**32**	**4.4**
1990	LA N	1	1	.500	4	4	0	0-0	25.1	26	12	1	1	4-0	16	4.26	86	.260	.295	7-1	.000	-1	92	-1	-0.2
1991	LA N	7	2	.778	21	21	0	0-0	112	112	43	3	5	32-6	73	3.46	104	.259	.316	31-4	.258	3	141	4	0.8
1992	LA N	10	15	.400	33	33	1	0-0	210.2	209	101	15	8	69-13	130	3.67	94	.257	.320	68-6	.221	4*	82	-6	0.0
1993	LA N	12	14	.462	33	33	5-1	0-0	215.2	201	106	17	7	72-13	141	3.59	106	.246	.311	73-8	.356	10*	107	3	1.5
1994	LA N	6	6	.500	21	21	1	0-0	135.1	146	67	15	2	42-6	72	3.79	104	.279	.333	44-3	.205	2*	116	0	0.3
1995	†Cle A	16	6	.727	26	26	1-1	0-0	167.1	151	76	21	5	51-1	111	3.87	121	.244	.304	0-0	—	0	109	17	2.0
1996	†Cle A	15	9	.625	33	33	1	0-0	206	238	115	21	12	58-4	125	4.24	115	.287	.341	0-0	—	0	113	11	1.3
1997	†Cle A	14	6	.700	32	32	1	0-0	195.1	199	105	26	11	69-2	107	4.47	105	.272	.340	3-1	.000	-0	109	5	0.5
1998	SF N	11	10	.524	34	34	0	0-0	202	200	105	22	13	85-7	126	4.41	90	.259	.341	66-8	.152	1	100	-10	-0.7
1999	†NY N	13	12	.520	32	32	0	0-0	179	175	92	14	11	77-2	89	4.58	96	.260	.342	62-3	.145	-1	96	-3	-0.3
2000	LA N	1	5	.167	10	6	0	0-1	24.2	42	36	5	11	14-1	13	13.14	33	.389	.493	7-0	.000	-1	88	-24	-3.8
Total	18	204	150	.576	510	466	68-25	5-3	3130.1	2939	1366	235	117	1007-108	2014	3.48	111	.248	.312	810-101	.201	33	104	131	18.9
HESKETH, JOE Joseph Thomas B 2.15.1959 Lackawanna, NY BR/TL 6-2/170# d8.7																									
1984	Mon N	2	2	.500	11	5	1-1	1-0	45	38	12	2	0	15-3	32	1.80	190	.233	.294	10-0	.100	0	98	8	0.7
1985	Mon N	10	5	.667	25	25	2-1	0-0	155.1	125	52	10	0	45-2	113	2.49	136	.222	.279	44-5	.091	-1*	96	14	1.2
1986	Mon N	6	5	.545	15	15	0	0-0	82.2	92	46	11	2	31-4	67	5.01	74	.283	.347	23-3	.000	-2	95	-10	-1.4
1987	Mon N	0	0	—	18	0	0	1-0	28.2	23	12	2	2	15-3	31	3.14	134	.211	.317	4-1	.000	-0		3	0.1
1988	Mon N	4	3	.571	60	0	0	9-2	72.2	63	30	1	0	35-9	64	2.85	126	.242	.328	2-0	.000	0		4	0.6
1989	Mon N	6	4	.600	43	0	0	3-1	48.1	54	34	5	0	26-6	44	5.77	61	.292	.376	2-0	.500	0		-12	-2.3
1990	Mon N	1	0	1.000	2	0	0	0-0	3	2	0	0	0	2-1	3	0.00	—	.200	.333	0-0	—	0		1	0.3
	Atl N	0	2	.000	31	0	0	5-4	31	30	23	5	1	12-0	21	5.81	70	.248	.319	1-0	.000	-0		-6	-0.5
	Year	1	2	.333	33	0	0	5-4	34	32	27	5	1	14-1	24	5.29	76	.244	.320	1-0	.000	-0		-5	-0.2
	Bos A	0	4	.000	12	2	0	0-0	25.2	37	12	2	0	11-1	26	3.51	117	.333	.393	0-0	—	0	11	1	0.2
1991	Bos A	12	4	.750	39	17	0	0-0	153.1	142	59	19	0	53-3	104	3.29	131	.250	.313	0-0	—	0	104	18	1.7
1992	Bos A	8	9	.471	30	25	1	1-0	148.2	162	84	15	2	58-9	104	4.36	97	.276	.339	0-0	—	0	94	-3	-0.3
1993	Bos A	3	4	.429	28	5	0	1-0	53.1	62	35	4	0	29-4	34	5.06	91	.294	.376	0-0	—	0	80	-3	-0.3
1994	Bos A	8	5	.615	25	20	0	0-0	114	117	70	9	2	46-3	83	4.26	118	.267	.334	0-0	—	0	100	5	0.4
Total	11	60	47	.561	339	114	4-2	21-7	961.2	947	469	85	9	378-48	726	3.78	107	.259	.328	86-9	.070	-2	96	20	0.4
HESS, OTTO Otto C. B 10.10.1878 Bern, Switzerland D 2.25.1926 Tucson, AZ BL/TL 6-1/170# d8.3 ▲																									
1902	Cle A	2	4	.333	7	4	4	0	43.2	67	42	0	1	23	13	5.98	58	.351	.423	14-0	.071	-1	104	-12	-1.3
1904	Cle A	8	7	.533	21	16	15-4	0	151.1	134	60	2	5	31	64	1.67	152	.238	.284	100-1	.120	-3*	102	8	0.4
1905	Cle A	10	15	.400	26	25	22-4	0	213.2	179	97	1	9	72	109	3.16	83	.229	.302	173-3	.254	5*	88	-11	-0.7
1906	Cle A	20	17	.541	43	36	33-7	**3**	333.2	274	104	4	24	85	167	1.83	143	.227	.291	154-1	.201	1*	109	28	3.3
1907	Cle A	6	6	.500	17	14	7	1	93.1	84	37	1	12	37	36	2.89	87	.243	.337	30-1	.133	0*	94	-1	-0.2
1908	Cle A	0	0	—	4	0	0	0	7	11	6	0	0	1	2	5.14	46	.407	.429	14-0	.000	-1*		-2	-0.2
1912	Bos N	12	17	.414	33	31	21	0	254	270	142	3	15	90	80	3.76	95	.283	.354	94-6	.245	3	103	-5	-0.3
1913	Bos N	7	17	.292	29	27	19-2	0	218.1	231	123	13	7	70	80	3.83	86	.279	.340	83-4	.313	8*	104	-10	-0.2
1914	Bos N	5	6	.455	14	11	7-1	1	89	89	39	2	5	33	24	3.03	91	.271	.347	47-2	.234	1*	116	-3	-0.1
1915	Bos N	0	1	.000	4	1	1	0	14	16	13	0	2	6	5	3.86	67	.286	.375	5-0	.400	1*	115	-4	-0.2
Total	10	70	90	.438	198	165	129-18	5	1418	1355	663	26	80	448	580	2.98	98	.257	.324	714-18	.216	14	103	-12	0.5
HESSELBACHER, GEORGE George Edward B 1.18.1895 Philadelphia, PA D 2.18.1980 Rydal, PA BR/TR 6-2/175# d6.29																									
1916	Phi A	0	4	.000	6	4	2	0	26	37	33	3	0	22	6	7.27	39	.349	.461	8-0	.125	-0	86	-15	-1.8
HESTERFER, LARRY Lawrence B 6.9.1878 Newark, NJ D 9.22.1943 Cedar Grove, NJ BR/TL 5-8/145# d9.5																									
1901	NY N	0	1	.000	1	1	1	0	6	15	15	0	0	3	2	7.50	44	.469	.514	2-0	.000	0	150	-6	-0.6

Year	Tm Lg	W	L	Pct	G	GS	CG-Sho	SV-BS	IP	H	R	HR	HB	BB-IB	SO	ERA	AERA	OAV	OOB	AB-SH	AVG	PB	Sup	APR	PW
HETKI, JOHNNY John Edward B 5.12.1922 Leavenworth, KS BR/TR 6-1/205# d9.14																									
1945	Cin N	1	2	.333	5	2	2	0	32.2	28	13	1	0	11	9	3.58	105	.235	.300	11-0	.091	-1	79	1	0.1
1946	Cin N	6	6	.500	32	11	4	1	126.1	121	44	3	1	31	41	2.99	112	.253	.300	33-5	.333	3	88	7	1.0
1947	Cin N	3	4	.429	37	5	2	0	96	110	72	7	1	48	33	5.81	71	.287	.368	27-0	.222	1	69	-19	-1.1
1948	Cin N	0	1	.000	3	0	0	0	6.2	8	7	0	0	3	3	9.45	41	.286	.355	1-0	.000	0		-4	-0.5
1950	Cin N	1	2	.333	22	1	0	0	53	53	33	9	3	27	21	5.09	83	.265	.361	9-2	.222	0	42	-5	-0.2
1952	StL A	0	1	.000	3	1	0	0	9.1	15	7	2	0	2	4	3.86	101	.357	.386	1-0	.000	0	67	-1	-0.1
1953	Pit N	3	6	.333	54	2	0	3	118.1	120	60	9	1	33	37	3.95	113	.266	.318	24-1	.208	1	80	6	0.6
1954	Pit N	4	4	.500	58	1	0	9	83	102	53	11	0	30	27	4.99	84	.297	.349	9-1	.222	-0	21	-7	-0.8
Total	8	18	26	.409	214	23	8	13	525.1	557	289	42	6	185	175	4.39	91	.272	.334	115-9	.235	5	72	-22	-1.0
HETZEL, ERIC Eric Paul B 9.25.1963 Crowley, LA BR/TR 6-3/175# d7.1																									
1989	Bos A	2	3	.400	12	11	0	0-0	50.1	61	39	7	2	28-1	33	6.26	66	.296	.382	0-0	—	0	132	-11	-1.0
1990	Bos A	1	4	.200	9	8	0	0-0	35	39	28	3	1	21-0	20	5.91	69	.281	.377	0-0	—	0	72	-8	-1.0
Total	2	3	7	.300	21	19	0	0-0	85.1	100	67	10	3	49-1	53	6.12	67	.290	.380	0-0	—	0	107	-19	-2.0
HEUSSER, ED Edward Burlton "The Wild Elk Of The Wasatch" B 5.7.1909 Salt Lake County, UT D 3.1.1956 Aurora, CO BB/TR 6-0.5/187# d4.25																									
1935	StL N	5	5	.500	33	11	2	2	123.1	125	50	5	2	27	39	2.92	140	.263	.305	34-1	.118	-1	90	14	0.9
1936	StL N	7	3	.700	42	3	0	3	104.1	130	73	6	4	38	26	5.43	73	.310	.373	26-0	.269	3	72	-18	-1.4
1938	Phi N	0	0	—	1	0	0	0	1	2	3	1	0	1	0	27.00	14	.400	.500	0-0	—	0		-2	-0.1
1940	Phi A	6	13	.316	41	6	2	5	110	144	84	11	2	42	39	4.99	89	.308	.368	30-1	.167	1	119	-11	-1.6
1943	Cin N	4	3	.571	26	10	2-1	0	91	97	40	4	0	23	28	3.46	96	.275	.319	27-1	.185	-1	120	-2	-0.3
1944	Cin N	13	11	.542	30	23	17-4	2	192.2	165	59	9	1	42	42	**2.38**	**146**	.231	.275	69-1	.217	1	68	25	3.1
1945	Cin N	11	16	.407	31	30	18-4	1	223	248	105	10	3	60	56	3.71	101	.280	.328	77-5	.247	4	73	1	0.6
1946	Cin N	7	14	.333	29	21	9-1	2	167.2	167	68	11	1	39	47	3.22	104	.260	.304	53-4	.208	2	83	4	0.5
1948	Phi N	3	2	.600	33	0	0	3	74	89	46	9	0	28	22	4.99	79	.299	.359	19-0	.158	-1		-8	-0.6
Total	9	56	67	.455	266	104	50-10	18	1087	1167	528	66	13	300	299	3.69	101	.274	.324	335-13	.206	8	81	3	1.1
HEVING, JOE Joseph William B 9.2.1900 Covington, KY D 4.11.1970 Covington, KY BR/TR 6-1/185# d4.29 b-Johnnie																									
1930	NY N	7	5	.583	41	2	0	6	89.2	109	57	7	1	27	37	5.22	91	.309	.360	22-2	.227	-0	120	-3	-0.3
1931	NY N	1	6	.143	22	0	0	3	42.1	48	27	4	2	11	26	4.89	76	.277	.328	8-2	.125	-0		-6	-0.9
1933	Chi A	7	5	.583	40	6	3-1	6	118	113	50	6	2	27	47	2.67	159	.249	.295	38-1	.211	0	50	17	1.8
1934	Chi A	1	7	.125	33	2	0	4	88	133	85	12	3	48	40	7.26	65	.343	.419	27-0	.185	1	92	-25	-1.9
1937	Cle A	8	4	.667	40	0	0	5	72.2	92	53	6	2	30	35	4.83	95	.311	.378	19-2	.263	0		-5	-0.7
1938	Cle A	1	1	.500	3	0	0	0	6	10	8	0	0	5	0	9.00	52	.370	.469	1-0	.000	-0		-4	-0.6
	Bos A	8	1	.889	16	11	7-1	2	82	94	35	5	1	22	34	3.73	132	.283	.330	30-3	.133	-1	135	12	1.2
	Year	9	2	.818	19	11	7-1	2	88	104	43	5	1	27	34	4.09	120	.290	.341	31-3	.129	-2	135	9	0.6
1939	Bos A	11	3	.786	46	5	1	7	107	124	65	8	2	34	43	3.70	128	.295	.350	32-3	.188	-1	116	6	0.6
1940	Bos A	12	7	.632	39	7	4	3	119	129	63	7	3	42	55	4.01	112	.272	.335	40-2	.200	0	179	4	0.6
1941	Cle A	5	2	.714	27	3	2-1	5	70.2	63	21	2	1	31	18	2.29	172	.240	.323	15-1	.000	-1	73	13	1.4
1942	Cle A	5	3	.625	27	2	0	3	46.1	52	28	4	2	25	13	4.86	71	.278	.369	7-1	.000	-1	62	-7	-1.3
1943	Cle A	1	1	.500	30	1	0	9	72	58	23	1	2	34	34	2.75	113	.230	.326	14-2	.071	-0	54	4	0.3
1944	Cle A	8	3	.727	**63**	1	0	10	119.2	106	42	2	2	41	46	1.96	169	.239	.307	22-2	.182	-1	25	14	1.4
1945	Bos N	1	0	1.000	3	0	0	0	5.1	5	2	0	1	3	1	3.38	114	.294	.429	1-1	.000	-0		0	0.1
Total	13	76	48	.613	430	40	17-3	63	1038.2	1136	559	64	24	380	429	3.90	108	.279	.344	276-22	.170	-4	120	20	1.7
HEWITT, JAKE Charles Jacob B 6.6.1870 Maidsville, WV D 5.18.1959 Morgantown, WV BL/TL 5-7/150# d8.6																									
1895	Pit N	1	0	1.000	4	2	1	2	13	13	6	0	1	2	4	4.15	108	.255	.296	6-0	.167	-1	103	2	0.1
HEYDEMAN, GREG Gregory George B 1.2.1952 Carmel, CA BR/TR 6/180# d9.2																									
1973	LA N	0	0	—	1	0	0	0-0	2	2	1	0	1	1-0	1	4.50	77	.222	.364	0-0	—	0		0	0.0
HIBBARD, GREG James Gregory B 9.13.1964 New Orleans, LA BL/TL 6/190# d5.31																									
1989	Chi A	6	7	.462	23	23	2	0-0	137.1	142	58	5	2	41-0	55	3.21	119	.268	.321	0-0	—	0	109	8	0.8
1990	Chi A	14	9	.609	33	33	3-1	0-0	211	202	80	11	6	55-2	92	3.16	121	.255	.305	0-0	—	0	85	16	1.7
1991	Chi A	11	11	.500	32	29	5	0-0	194	196	107	23	2	57-1	71	4.31	92	.266	.320	0-0	—	0	114	-10	-1.0
1992	Chi A	10	7	.588	31	28	0	1-0	176	187	92	17	7	57-2	69	4.40	88	.277	.337	0-0	—	0	103	-9	-0.7
1993	Chi N	15	11	.577	31	31	1	0-0	191	209	96	19	3	47-9	82	3.96	101	.286	.327	65-3	.092	-3*	105	-1	-0.4
1994	Sea A	1	5	.167	15	14	0	0-0	80.2	115	78	11	2	31-1	39	6.69	73	.328	.383	0-0	—	0	101	-20	-1.2
Total	6	57	50	.533	165	158	11-1	1-0	990	1051	511	86	22	288-15	408	4.05	98	.275	.327	65-3	.092	-3	103	-16	-0.8
HIBBARD, JOHN John Denison B 12.2.1864 Chicago, IL D 11.17.1937 Hollywood, CA TL d7.31																									
1884	Chi N	1	1	.500	2	2	2-1	0	17	18	10	1		9	4	2.65	118	.300	.391	7	.000	-1	102	1	0.0
HICKERSON, BRYAN Bryan David B 10.13.1963 Bemidji, MN BL/TL 6-2/203# d7.25																									
1991	SF N	2	2	.500	17	6	0	0-0	50	53	20	3	0	17-3	43	3.60	100	.275	.333	12-1	.000	-1	92	1	-0.2
1992	SF N	5	3	.625	61	1	0	0-5	87.1	74	31	7	1	21-2	68	3.09	107	.236	.282	4-0	.000	-0	191	3	0.2
1993	SF N	7	5	.583	47	15	0	0-0	120.1	137	58	14	1	39-3	69	4.26	92	.291	.344	28-4	.143	-0	120	-3	-0.4
1994	SF N	4	8	.333	28	14	0	1-0	98.1	118	60	20	1	38-6	59	5.40	74	.301	.363	27-2	.185	1	106	-14	-1.4
1995	Chi N	2	3	.400	38	0	0	1-2	31.2	36	28	3	0	15-4	28	6.82	60	.283	.359	2-0	.500	1		-10	-1.4
	Col N	1	0	1.000	18	0	0	0-1	16.2	33	24	5	1	13-1	12	11.88	45	.407	.495	1-1	1.000	1		-9	-0.4
	Year	3	3	.500	56	0	0	1-3	48.1	69	57	8	1	28-5	40	8.57	53	.332	.414	3-1	.667	1		-20	-1.8
Total	5	21	21	.500	209	36	0	2-8	404.1	451	221	52	4	143-19	279	4.72	81	.286	.345	74-8	.149	1	113	-32	-3.6
HICKEY, JIM James Robert "Sid" B 10.22.1920 N.Abington, MA D 9.20.1997 Manchester, CT BR/TR 6-1/204# d4.25 Mil 1944-45																									
1942	Bos N	0	1	.000	1	1	0	0	1.1	4	4	1	0	2	0	20.25	16	.500	.600	1-0	.000	-0	25	-3	-0.5
1944	Bos N	0	0	—	8	0	0	0	9.1	15	9	0	1	5	3	4.82	79	.366	.447	1-0	.000	-0		-2	-0.1
Total	2	0	1	.000	9	1	0	0	10.2	19	13	1	1	7	3	6.75	56	.388	.474	2-0	.000	-0	25	-5	-0.6
HICKEY, JACK John William B 11.3.1881 Minneapolis, MN D 12.28.1941 Seattle, WA BR/TL 5-10/170# d4.16																									
1904	Cle A	0	1	.000	2	2	1	0	12.1	14	13	0	0	11	5	7.30	35	.286	.417	5-0	.000	-1	141	-6	-0.5
HICKEY, KEVIN Kevin John B 2.25.1957 Chicago, IL BL/TL 6-1/200# d4.14																									
1981	Chi A	0	2	.000	41	0	0	3-0	44.1	38	22	3	1	18-5	17	3.65	98	.232	.308	0-0	—	0		-1	0.0
1982	Chi A	4	4	.500	60	0	0	6-2	78	73	32	4	2	30-6	38	3.00	135	.256	.327	0-0	—	0		8	1.0
1983	Chi A	1	2	.333	23	0	0	5-3	20.2	23	14	5	0	11-2	8	5.23	80	.264	.347	0-0	—	0		-3	-0.5
1989	Bal A	2	3	.400	51	0	0	2-0	49.1	38	16	3	1	23-4	28	2.92	130	.220	.315	0-0	—	0		5	0.5
1990	Bal A	1	3	.250	37	0	0	1-0	26.1	26	16	3	0	13-2	17	5.13	74	.265	.348	0-0	—	0		-4	-0.6
1991	Bal A	1	0	1.000	19	0	0	0-1	14	15	14	3	0	6-0	10	9.00	44	.278	.339	0-0	—	0		-8	-0.5
Total	6	9	14	.391	231	0	0	17-6	232.2	213	114	21	4	101-19	118	3.91	99	.247	.326	0-0	—	0		-3	-0.1
HICKMAN, CHARLIE Charles Taylor "Cheerful Charlie" or "Piano Legs" B 3.4.1876 Taylortown, PA D 4.19.1934 Morgantown, WV BR/TR 5-9/180# d9.8 ▲																									
1897	†Bos N	0	0	—	2	0	0	1	7.2	10	5	0	0	5	0	5.87	76	.313	.405	3-0	.667	2		-1	0.1
1898	Bos N	1	2	.333	6	3	3-1	2	33	22	8	0	0	13	9	2.18	169	.188	.269	58-1	.259	0*	83	6	0.6
1899	Bos N	6	0	1.000	11	9	5-2	1	66.1	52	38	3	8	40	14	4.48	93	.216	.346	63-1	.397	6*	167	0	0.3
1901	NY N	3	5	.375	9	9	6	0	65	76	42	1	3	26	11	4.57	72	.290	.361	406-0	.278	2*	64	-7	-0.5
1902	Cle A	0	1	.000	1	1	1	0	8	11	8	0	1	5	1	7.88	44	.324	.425	426-8	.378	1*	146	-3	-0.3
1907	Was A	0	0	—	1	0	0	0	5	4	4	0	0	5	2	3.60	67	.222	.391	198-1	.278	0*		-1	0.0
Total	6	10	8	.556	30	22	15-3	4	185	175	105	4	12	94	37	4.28	86	.249	.347	1154-11	.321	11	117	-6	0.2
HICKMAN, ERNIE Ernest P. B 1856 E.St.Louis, IL D 11.19.1891 E.St.Louis, IL d6.7																									
1884	KC U	4	13	.235	17	17	15	0	137.1	172	146	5		36	68	4.52	49	.287	.328	72	.167	-7*	67	-41	-4.1
HICKMAN, JESSE Jesse Owens B 2.18.1939 Lecompte, LA BR/TR 6-2/186# d6.5																									
1965	KC A	0	1	.000	12	0	0	0	15.1	9	10	3	0	8-0	16	5.87	59	.184	.293	0-0	—	0*		-3	-0.2
1966	KC A	0	0	—	1	0	0	0	1	0	0	0	0	1-0	0	0.00	—	.000	.333	0-0	—	0		0	0.0

Year	Tm Lg	W	L	Pct	G	GS	CG-Sho	SV-BS	IP	H	R	HR	HB	BB-IB	SO	ERA	AERA	OAV	OOB	AB-SH	AVG	PB	Sup	APR	PW
Total	2	0	1	.000	13	0	0	0	16.1	9	10	3	0	9-0	16	5.51	63	.176	.295	0-0	—	0		-3	-0.2
HIGBE, KIRBY Walter Kirby B 4.8.1915 Columbia, SC D 5.6.1985 Columbia, SC BR/TR 5-11/190# d10.3 Mil 1944-45																									
1937	Chi N	1	0	1.000	1	0	0	0	5	4	3	1	0	1	2	5.40	74	.182	.217	3-0	.000	-0		-1	-0.2
1938	Chi N	0	0	—	2	2	0	0	10	10	6	1	0	6	4	5.40	71	.263	.364	3-0	.000	-0	111	-1	-0.1
1939	Chi N	2	1	.667	9	2	0	0	22.2	12	9	0	0	22	16	3.18	124	.158	.347	7-1	.286	1	177	2	0.3
	Phi N	10	14	.417	34	26	14-1	2	187.1	208	113	10	10	101	79	4.85	83	.283	.378	66-6	.167	-2	92	-17	-2.3
	Year	12	15	.444	43	28	14-1	2	210	220	117	10	10	123	95	4.67	86	.272	.374	73-7	.178	-2	98	-14	-2.0
1940	Phi N☆	14	19	.424	41	36	20-1	1	283	242	126	12	3	121	**137**	3.72	105	.232	.313	103-3	.165	-2	77	8	0.7
1941	†Bro N	**22**	9	.710	**48**	**39**	19-2	3	298	244	123	17	6	132	121	3.14	117	.220	.306	112-6	.188	1	126	17	1.4
1942	Bro N	16	11	.593	38	32	13-2	0	221.2	180	89	17	2	106	115	3.25	100	.223	.315	77-7	.104	-4	127	2	-0.3
1943	Bro N	13	10	.565	35	27	8-1	0	185	189	81	4	5	95	108	3.70	91	.264	.354	65-4	.138	-2	95	-5	-0.8
1946	Bro N★	17	8	.680	42	29	11-3	1	210.2	178	82	6	1	107	134	3.03	111	.229	.323	77-6	.130	-4	121	9	0.7
1947	Bro N	2	0	1.000	4	3	0	0	15.2	18	9	0	1	12	10	5.17	80	.295	.419	5-0	.200	0	171	-1	-0.1
	Pit N	11	17	.393	46	30	10-1	5	225	204	108	22	3	110	99	3.72	113	.240	.329	72-6	.139	-1	90	11	1.0
	Year	13	17	.433	50	33	10-1	5	240.2	222	112	22	4	122	109	3.81	111	.243	.335	77-6	.143	-1	97	10	0.9
1948	Pit N	8	7	.533	56	8	3	10	158	140	75	11	3	83	86	3.36	121	.240	.337	48-0	.208	1	82	8	0.8
1949	Pit N	0	2	.000	7	1	0	0	15.1	25	24	2	0	12	5	13.50	31	.379	.474	3-0	.000	-0	126	-15	-1.5
	NY N	2	0	1.000	37	2	0	2	80.1	72	42	11	1	41	38	3.47	115	.242	.335	15-0	.067	-0	122	2	0.0
	Year	2	2	.500	44	3	0	2	95.2	97	48	13	1	53	43	5.08	79	.266	.361	18-0	.056	-1	124	-12	-1.5
1950	NY N	0	3	.000	18	1	0	0	34.2	37	19	2	0	30	17	4.93	83	.285	.419	4-0	.250	0	129	-2	-0.1
Total	12	118	101	.539	418	238	98-11	24	1952.1	1763	909	116	35	979	971	3.69	102	.241	.333	660-39	.153	-14	104	17	-0.5
HIGGINBOTHAM, IRV Irving Clinton B 4.26.1882 Homer, NE D 6.12.1959 Seattle, WA BR/TR 6-1/196# d8.11																									
1906	StL N	1	4	.200	7	6	4	0	47.1	50	23	1	1	11	14	3.23	81	.266	.310	18-0	.222	0	46	-3	-0.3
1908	StL N	3	8	.273	19	11	7-1	0	107	113	51	0	3	33	38	3.20	74	.270	.328	38-1	.132	-1	81	-8	-1.0
1909	StL N	1	0	1.000	3	1	1	0	11.1	5	3	0	0	2	2	1.59	159	.143	.189	3-0	.000	-0	138	1	0.0
	Chi N	5	2	.714	19	6	4	1	78	64	32	0	3	20	32	2.19	116	.213	.269	26-1	.231	1	202	1	0.1
	Year	6	2	.750	22	7	5	1	89.1	69	39	0	3	22	34	2.12	120	.205	.260	29-1	.207	0	193	2	0.1
Total	3	10	14	.417	48	24	16-1	1	243.2	232	109	1	7	66	86	2.81	88	.246	.300	85-2	.176	-1	106	-9	-1.2
HIGGINS, DENNIS Dennis Dean B 8.4.1939 Jefferson City, MO BR/TR 6-4/190# d4.12																									
1966	Chi A	1	0	1.000	42	1	0	5	93	66	27	9	5	33-4	86	2.52	126	.202	.283	17-0	.176	0	195	9	0.5
1967	Chi A	1	2	.333	9	0	0	0	12.1	13	9	0	3	10-0	8	5.84	53	.271	.426	1-0	.000	-0		-4	-0.8
1968	Was A	4	4	.500	59	0	0	13	99.2	81	40	9	3	46-9	66	3.25	90	.226	.313	15-1	.133	-0		-3	-0.5
1969	Was A	10	9	.526	55	0	0	16-10	85.1	79	42	7	3	56-7	71	3.48	100	.252	.364	11-1	.091	-1		-2	-0.5
1970	Cle A	4	6	.400	58	0	0	11-2	90.1	82	43	8	2	54-8	82	3.99	99	.248	.356	12-1	.250	1		0	0.1
1971	StL N	1	0	1.000	3	0	0	0-0	7	6	3	0	0	2-0	6	3.86	93	.240	.286	1-0	.000	-0		0	0.0
1972	StL N	1	2	.333	15	1	0	1-0	22.2	19	14	0	0	22-0	20	3.97	86	.226	.387	1-0	.000	-0	104	-3	-0.4
Total	7	22	23	.489	241	2	0	46-12	410.1	346	178	33	16	223-28	339	3.42	98	.233	.335	58-3	.155	0	144	-3	-1.6
HIGGINS, EDDIE Thomas Edward "Doc" or "Irish" B 3.18.1888 Nevada, IL D 2.14.1959 Elgin, IL BR/TR 6-0.5/174# d5.14																									
1909	StL N	3	3	.500	16	5	5	0	66	68	36	4	1	17	15	4.50	56	.273	.322	21-0	.190	-0	55	-11	-1.0
1910	StL N	0	1	.000	2	0	0	0	10.1	15	8	0	0	7	1	4.35	68	.349	.440	5-0	.400	1*		-2	-0.1
Total	2	3	4	.429	18	5	5	0	76.1	83	44	4	1	24	16	4.48	58	.284	.341	26-0	.231	1	55	-13	-1.1
HIGH, ED Edward T. "Lefty" B 12.26.1876 Baltimore, MD D 2.10.1926 Baltimore, MD TL d7.4																									
1901	Det A	1	0	1.000	4	1	1	0	18	21	9	0	1	6	4	3.50	110	.288	.350	7-0	.000	-1	88	1	0.0
HIGUERA, TEDDY Teodoro Valenzuela (Valenzuela) B 11.9.1958 Los Mochis, Mexico BB/TL 5-10/178# d4.23																									
1985	Mil A	15	8	.652	32	30	7-2	0-0	212.1	186	105	22	3	63-0	127	3.90	107	.235	.290	0-0	—	0	97	6	0.5
1986	Mil A★	20	11	.645	34	34	15-4	0-0	248.1	226	84	26	3	74-5	207	2.79	155	.241	.296	0-0	—	0	83	43	5.1
1987	Mil A	18	10	.643	35	35	14-3	0-0	261.2	236	120	24	2	87-2	240	3.85	119	.241	.301	0-0	—	0	110	22	1.9
1988	Mil A	16	9	.640	31	31	8-1	0-0	227.1	168	66	15	6	59-4	192	2.45	162	.207	**.263**	0-0	—	0	97	40	4.4
1989	Mil A	9	6	.600	22	22	2-1	0-0	135.1	125	56	9	4	48-2	91	3.46	111	.248	.316	0-0	—	0	99	7	0.6
1990	Mil A	11	10	.524	27	27	4-1	0-0	170	167	80	16	3	50-2	129	3.76	103	.256	.310	0-0	—	0	102	3	0.3
1991	Mil A	3	2	.600	7	6	0	0-0	36.1	37	18	2	1	10-0	33	4.46	89	.262	.314	0-0	—	0	138	-1	-0.1
1993	Mil A	1	3	.250	8	8	0	0-0	30	43	24	4	1	16-2	27	7.20	59	.333	.408	0-0	—	0	119	-9	-1.0
1994	Mil A	1	5	.167	17	12	0	0-0	58.2	74	55	13	2	36-0	35	7.06	71	.311	.403	0-0	—	0	90	-14	-1.2
Total	9	94	64	.595	213	205	50-12	0-0	1380	1262	608	131	25	443-17	1081	3.61	117	.243	.303	0-0	—	0	99	97	10.5
HILCHER, WHITEY Walter Frank B 2.28.1909 Chicago, IL D 11.21.1962 Minneapolis, MN BR/TR 6/174# d9.17																									
1931	Cin N	0	1	.000	2	1	0	0	12	16	5	0	1	4	5	3.00	125	.320	.382	4-0	.000	-1	69	1	0.0
1932	Cin N	0	3	.000	11	2	0	0	18.2	24	19	3	0	10	4	7.71	50	.316	.395	3-0	.333	1	76	-8	-1.0
1935	Cin N	2	0	1.000	4	2	1-1	0	19.1	19	6	0	0	5	9	2.79	142	.264	.312	6-0	.167	-0	75	3	0.3
1936	Cin N	1	2	.333	14	1	0	0	35	44	31	3	1	14	10	6.17	62	.299	.364	8-0	.000	-1	178	-11	-0.9
Total	4	3	6	.333	31	6	1-1	0	85	103	61	6	2	33	28	5.29	73	.299	.363	21-0	.095	-2	92	-15	-1.6
HILDEBRAND, ORAL Oral Clyde B 4.7.1907 Indianapolis, IN D 9.8.1977 Southport, IN BR/TR 6-3/175# d9.8																									
1931	Cle A	2	1	.667	5	2	2	0	26.2	25	16	0	3	13	6	4.39	105	.243	.345	11-0	.182	-1	64	0	0.0
1932	Cle A	8	6	.571	27	15	7	0	129.1	124	69	7	0	62	49	3.69	129	.249	.333	48-3	.146	-3	84	12	0.7
1933	Cle A☆	16	11	.593	36	31	15-**6**	0	220.1	205	110	8	1	88	90	3.76	118	.245	.318	84-0	.190	-1	93	16	1.6
1934	Cle A	11	9	.550	33	28	10-1	1	198	225	112	14	3	99	72	4.50	101	.282	.364	76-4	.171	-1	124	3	0.1
1935	Cle A	9	8	.529	34	20	8	5	171.1	171	85	12	3	63	49	3.94	114	.263	.331	55-6	.164	-2	97	11	0.8
1936	Cle A	10	11	.476	36	21	9	4	174.2	197	107	10	4	83	65	4.90	103	.283	.362	63-2	.190	0	116	4	0.4
1937	StL A	8	17	.320	30	27	12-1	1	201.1	228	127	18	3	87	75	5.14	94	.284	.356	70-9	.200	-1	90	-6	-0.7
1938	StL A	8	10	.444	23	23	10	0	163	194	104	18	3	73	66	5.69	87	.297	.370	59-4	.254	1*	82	-8	-0.7
1939	†NY A	10	4	.714	21	15	7-1	2	126.2	102	44	11	1	41	50	3.06	143	.219	.284	44-3	.182	-1	113	21	2.0
1940	NY A	1	1	.500	13	0	0	0	19.1	19	7	1	1	14	5	1.86	217	.268	.395	3-0	.000	-0		4	0.3
Total	10	83	78	.516	258	182	80-9	13	1430.2	1490	781	99	22	623	527	4.35	107	.267	.343	513-31	.187	-9	99	57	4.5
HILGENDORF, TOM Thomas Eugene B 3.10.1942 Clinton, IA BB/TL 6-1/190# d8.15																									
1969	StL N	0	0	—	6	0	0	2-1	6.1	3	1	0	0	2-0	2	1.42	252	.150	.217	1-0	1.000	1		2	0.2
1970	StL N	0	4	.000	23	0	0	3-0	20.2	22	11	0	0	13-5	13	3.92	105	.272	.368	1-0	.000	-0		0	0.0
1972	Cle A	3	1	.750	19	5	1	0-2	47	51	16	4	2	21-7	25	2.68	120	.283	.361	13-0	.077	-1	148	3	0.1
1973	Cle A	5	3	.625	48	1	1	6-2	94.2	87	38	9	3	36-6	58	3.14	125	.242	.316	0-0	—	0	46	7	0.8
1974	Cle A	4	3	.571	35	0	0	3-3	48.1	58	26	6	1	17-6	23	4.84	75	.302	.353	0-0	—	0		-5	-0.7
1975	Phi N	7	3	.700	53	0	0	0-2	96.2	81	32	6	1	38-3	52	2.14	175	.230	.303	12-2	.250	1		14	1.5
Total	6	19	14	.576	184	6	2	14-10	313.2	302	124	25	7	127-27	173	3.04	122	.255	.327	27-2	.185	1	115	21	1.9
HILJUS, ERIK Erik Kristian B 12.25.1972 Panorama City, CA BR/TR 6-5/230# d9.10																									
1999	Det A	0	0	—	6	0	0	0-0	8.2	7	5	2	0	5-0	1	5.19	95	.241	.343	0-0	—	0		0	0.0
2000	Det A	0	0	—	3	0	0	0-0	3.2	5	3	1	0	1-0	2	7.36	66	.333	.375	0-0	—	0		-1	0.0
2001	†Oak A	5	0	1.000	16	11	0	0-0	66	70	29	7	0	21-1	67	3.41	130	.263	.316	0-0	—	0	166	7	0.4
2002	Oak A	3	3	.500	9	9	0	0-0	45.2	52	36	11	0	21-1	29	6.50	68	.284	.356	0-0	—	0	96	-11	-1.2
Total	4	8	3	.727	34	20	0	0-0	124	134	73	21	0	48-2	99	4.79	93	.272	.335	0-0	—	0	133	-5	-0.8
HILL, CARMEN Carmen Proctor "Specs" or "Bunker" B 10.1.1895 Royalton, MN D 1.1.1990 Indianapolis, IN BR/TR 6-1/180# d8.24																									
1915	Pit N	2	1	.667	8	3	2-1	0	47	42	8	0	2	13	24	1.15	238	.255	.317	13-0	.154	0	91	8	0.6
1916	Pit N	0	0	—	2	0	0	0	6.1	11	10	0	1	5	5	8.53	31	.611	.708	0-0	—	0		-5	-0.2
1918	Pit N	2	3	.400	6	4	3	0	43.2	24	11	0	0	17	15	1.24	232	.160	.246	12-1	.167	0	79	6	0.9
1919	Pit N	0	0	—	4	0	0	0	5	12	6	0	0	1	1	9.00	33	.480	.500	0-0	—	0		-3	-0.2
1922	NY N	2	1	.667	8	4	0	0	28.1	33	15	0	0	5	6	4.76	84	.295	.325	11-0	.182	-0	112	-1	-0.1
1926	Pit N	3	3	.500	6	6	4-1	0	39.2	42	17	2	2	9	8	3.40	116	.288	.338	17-0	.176	-1	123	3	0.4

Year	Tm Lg	W	L	Pct	G	GS	CG-Sho	SV-BS	IP	H	R	HR	HB	BB-IB	SO	ERA	AERA	OAV	OOB	AB-SH	AVG	PB	Sup	APR	PW
1927	†Pit N	22	11	.667	43	31	22-2	3	277.2	260	125	12	4	80	95	3.24	127	.249	.305	104-3	.212	2*	107	22	2.6
1928	Pit N	16	10	.615	36	31	16-1	2	237	229	110	16	4	81	73	3.53	115	.259	.324	86-4	.233	2	107	14	1.4
1929	Pit N	2	3	.400	27	3	0	3	79	94	45	4	0	35	28	3.99	120	.297	.366	28-0	.036	-3	85	5	0.0
	StL N	0	0	—	3	1	0	0	8.2	10	10	2	1	8	1	8.31	56	.303	.452	3-0	.000	-0	262	-4	-0.2
	Year	2	3	.400	30	4	0	3	87.2	104	24	6	1	43	29	4.41	108	.297	.376	31-0	.032	-4	128	**1**	-0.2
1930	StL N	0	1	.000	4	2	0	0	14.2	12	12	2	0	13	8	7.36	68	.240	.397	3-0	.333	0	122	-3	-0.2
Total	10	49	33	.598	147	85	47-5	8	787	769	369	38	14	267	264	3.44	116	.261	.326	277-8	.191	-0	109	42	5.0
HILL, RED Clifford Joseph B 1.20.1893 Marshall, TX D 8.11.1938 ElPaso, TX BB/TL d4.21																									
1917	Phi A	0	0	—	1	0	0	0	2.2	5	4	0	0	1	0	6.75	41	.385	.429	0-0	—	0		-2	-0.1
HILL, DAVE David Burnham B 11.11.1937 New Orleans, LA BR/TL 6-2/170# d8.22																									
1957	KC A	0	0	—	2	0	0	0	2.1	6	7	3	0	3-0	1	27.00	15	.462	.563	0-0	—	0		-5	-0.3
HILL, GARRY Garry Alton B 11.3.1946 Rutherfordton, NC BR/TR 6-2/195# d6.12																									
1969	Atl N	0	1	.000	1	1	0	0-0	2.1	6	4	1	0	1-0	2	15.43	23	.462	.500	0-0	—	0	147	-3	-0.5
HILL, HERBERT Herbert Lee B 8.19.1891 Hutchins, TX D 9.2.1970 Farmers Branch, TX BR/TR 5-11.5/175# d7.17																									
1915	Cle A	0	0	—	1	0	0	0	2	1	0	0	0	2	0	0.00	—	.250	.500	0-0	—	0		1	0.0
HILL, JEREMY Jeremy Dee B 8.8.1977 Dallas, TX BR/TR 5-10/200# d9.7																									
2002	KC A	0	1	.000	10	0	0	0-0	9.1	8	4	1	0	8-1	7	3.86	130	.235	.372	0-0	—	0		1	0.1
2003	KC A	0	0	—	1	0	0	0-0	1	1	0	0	0	0-0	0	0.00	—	.250	.250	0-0	—	0		1	0.0
Total	2	0	1	.000	11	0	0	0-0	10.1	9	4	1	0	8-1	7	3.48	145	.237	.362	0-0	—	0		2	0.1
HILL, KEN Kenneth Wade B 12.14.1965 Lynn, MA BR/TR 6-2/175# d9.3																									
1988	StL N	0	1	.000	4	1	0	0-0	14	16	9	0	0	6-0	6	5.14	68	.286	.355	3-0	.000	-0	51	-3	-0.2
1989	StL N	7	15	.318	33	33	2-1	0-0	196.2	186	92	9	5	99-6	112	3.80	96	.252	.342	59-8	.153	-0	93	-3	-0.4
1990	StL N	5	6	.455	17	14	1	0-0	78.2	79	49	7	1	33-1	58	5.49	70	.264	.334	19-5	.211	1	103	-12	-1.4
1991	StL N	11	10	.524	30	30	0	0-0	181.1	147	76	15	6	67-4	121	3.57	104	.224	.299	50-7	.100	-1	93	4	0.4
1992	Mon N	16	9	.640	33	33	3-3	0-0	218	187	76	13	3	75-4	150	2.68	129	.230	.297	62-10	.177	5	100	17	2.7
1993	Mon N	9	7	.563	28	28	2	0-0	183.2	163	84	7	6	74-7	90	3.23	129	.238	.315	52-14	.115	-1*	98	16	1.4
1994	Mon N★	**16**	5	.762	23	23	2-1	0-0	154.2	145	61	12	6	44-7	85	3.32	127	.248	.304	48-16	.146	-0*	124	17	2.1
1995	StL N	6	7	.462	18	18	0	0-0	110.1	125	71	16	0	45-4	50	5.06	83	.286	.351	31-5	.194	1	101	-11	-1.0
	†Cle A	4	1	.800	12	11	1	0-0	74.2	77	36	5	1	32-0	48	3.98	118	.268	.343	0-0	—	0	137	6	0.4
1996	†Tex A	16	10	.615	35	35	7-**3**	0-0	250.2	250	110	19	6	95-3	170	3.63	145	.263	.332	0-0	—	0	103	42	3.8
1997	Tex A	5	8	.385	19	19	0	0-0	111	129	69	11	2	56-3	68	5.19	92	.298	.376	0-0	—	0	89	-4	-0.3
	Ana A	4	4	.500	12	12	1	0-0	79	65	34	8	1	39-0	38	3.65	126	.223	.315	2-1	.500	1	84	9	0.8
	Year	9	12	.429	31	31	1	0-0	190	194	38	19	3	95-3	106	4.55	103	.268	.352	2-1	.500	1	87	3	0.5
1998	Ana A	9	6	.600	19	19	0	0-0	103	123	60	6	3	47-0	57	4.98	94	.311	.384	1-0	.000	-0	99	-2	-0.2
1999	Ana A	4	11	.267	26	22	0	0-0	128.1	129	72	14	4	76-1	76	4.77	102	.270	.369	3-0	.000	-0	80	2	0.2
2000	Ana A	5	7	.417	16	16	0	0-0	78.2	102	59	16	2	53-1	50	6.52	78	.323	.415	3-1	.333	0	90	-11	-1.3
	Chi A	0	1	.000	2	1	0	0-0	3	5	8	0	0	6-0	0	24.00	21	.455	.611	0-0	—	0	94	-6	-0.9
	Year	5	8	.385	18	17	0	0-0	81.2	107	13	16	2	59-1	50	7.16	71	.327	.424	3-1	.333	0	90	-16	-2.2
2001	TB A	0	1	.000	5	0	0	0-1	7.1	10	11	4	1	5-2	2	12.27	37	.333	.444	0-0	—	0		-6	-0.7
Total	14	117	109	.518	332	315	19-8	0-1	1973	1938	977	162	47	852-43	1181	4.06	106	.260	.337	333-67	.150	4	99	55	5.4
HILL, MILT Milton Giles B 8.22.1965 Atlanta, GA BR/TR 6/180# d8.1																									
1991	Cin N	1	1	.500	22	0	0	0-1	33.1	36	14	1	0	8-2	20	3.78	101	.295	.331	1-0	.000	-0		1	0.0
1992	Cin N	0	0	—	14	0	0	1-0	20	15	9	1	1	5-2	10	3.15	114	.211	.269	0-0	—	0		0	0.0
1993	Cin N	3	0	1.000	19	0	0	0-0	28.2	34	18	5	0	9-1	23	5.65	71	.301	.344	2-0	.000	-0		-4	-0.5
1994	Atl N	0	0	—	10	0	0	0-0	11.1	18	10	3	0	6-1	10	7.94	53	.367	.436	0-0	—	0		-4	-0.2
	Sea A	1	0	1.000	13	0	0	0-0	23.2	30	19	4	0	11-3	16	6.46	76	.306	.373	0-0	—	0		-4	-0.2
Total	4	5	1	.833	78	0	0	1-1	117	133	70	14	1	39-9	79	5.08	81	.294	.345	3-0	.000	-0		-11	-0.9
HILL, BILL William Cicero "Still Bill" B 8.2.1874 Chattanooga, TN D 1.28.1938 Cincinnati, OH BL/TL 6-1/201# d4.18 b-Hugh																									
1896	Lou N	9	28	.243	43	39	32	2	319.2	353	229	14	18	155	104	4.31	101	.278	.364	116-4	.207	-5	73	2	-0.1
1897	Lou N	7	17	.292	27	26	20-1	0	199	209	127	6	17	69	55	3.62	118	.268	.341	74-2	.095	-8	81	13	0.6
1898	Cin N	13	14	.481	33	32	26-2	0	262	261	146	3	17	119	75	3.98	96	.258	.346	98-0	.133	-7	94	0	-0.6
1899	Cle N	3	6	.333	11	10	7	0	72.1	96	67	0	4	39	26	6.97	53	.318	.403	31-0	.129	-2	88	-23	-2.3
	Bal N	3	4	.429	8	7	6	0	61	64	35	1	3	18	17	3.25	122	.269	.328	24-0	.292	1	122	4	0.4
	Bro N	1	0	1.000	2	1	1	1	11	11	3	0	0	6	3	0.82	478	.262	.354	5-0	.600	2	257	3	0.5
	Year	7	10	.412	21	18	14	1	144.1	171	17	1	7	63	46	4.93	78	.294	.370	60-0	.233	0	111	-13	-1.4
Total	4	36	69	.343	124	115	92-3	3	925	994	607	24	59	406	280	4.16	99	.273	.355	348-6	.167	-20	85	-1	-1.5
HILLEBRAND, HOMER Homer Hiller Henry B 10.10.1879 Freeport, IL D 1.20.1974 Elsinore, CA BR/TL 5-8/165# d4.24 ▲																									
1905	Pit N	5	2	.714	10	6	4	1	60.2	43	20	0	2	19	37	2.82	107	.198	.269	110-4	.236	1*	124	3	0.4
1906	Pit N	3	2	.600	7	5	4-1	0	53	42	19	1	1	21	32	2.21	121	.220	.300	21-0	.238	1	125	2	0.4
1908	Pit N	0	0	—	1	0	0	0	1	1	0	0	0	0	1	0.00	—	.333	.333	0-0	—	0		0	0.0
Total	3	8	4	.667	18	11	8-1	1	114.2	86	39	1	3	40	70	2.51	113	.209	.284	131-4	.237	2	125	5	0.8
HILLEGAS, SHAWN Shawn Patrick B 8.21.1964 Dos Palos, CA BR/TR 6-2/208# d8.9																									
1987	LA N	4	3	.571	12	10	0	0-0	58	52	27	5	0	31-0	51	3.57	111	.241	.335	14-1	.000	-1	100	2	0.1
1988	LA N	3	4	.429	11	10	0	0-0	56.2	54	26	5	3	17-1	30	4.13	81	.250	.311	15-2	.133	0	85	-4	-0.5
	Chi A	3	2	.600	6	6	0	0-0	40	30	16	4	1	18-0	26	3.15	126	.207	.295	0-0	—	0	88	4	0.4
1989	Chi A	7	11	.389	50	13	0	3-0	119.2	132	67	12	3	51-4	76	4.74	80	.279	.352	0-0	—	0	102	-11	-1.6
1990	Chi A	0	0	—	7	0	0	0-0	11.1	4	1	0	0	5-1	5	0.79	483	.111	.214	0-0	—	0		4	0.2
1991	Cle A	3	4	.429	51	3	0	7-2	83	67	42	7	2	46-7	66	4.34	96	.223	.324	0-0	—	0	73	0	0.0
1992	NY A	1	8	.111	21	9	1-1	0-0	78.1	96	52	12	0	33-1	46	5.51	71	.306	.369	0-0	—	0	72	-14	-1.4
	Oak A	0	0	—	5	0	0	0-0	7.2	8	5	1	0	4-1	3	2.35	160	.276	.364	0-0	—	0		0	0.0
	Year	1	8	.111	26	9	1-1	0-0	86	104	60	13	0	37-2	49	5.23	75	.303	.368	0-0	—	0	73	-13	-1.4
1993	Oak A	3	6	.333	18	11	0	0-0	60.2	78	48	8	4	33-1	29	6.97	59	.317	.404	0-0	—	0	113	-19	-2.4
Total	7	24	38	.387	181	62	1-1	10-2	515.1	521	284	54	13	238-16	332	4.61	84	.264	.344	29-3	.069	-1	93	-38	-5.2
HILLER, FRANK Frank Walter "Dutch" B 7.13.1920 Irvington, NJ D 1.10.1987 West Chester, PA BR/TR 6/200# d5.25																									
1946	NY A	0	2	.000	3	1	0	0	11.1	13	7	2	0	6	4	4.76	72	.295	.380	4-1	.250	0	75	-2	-0.3
1948	NY A	5	2	.714	22	5	1	0	62.1	59	29	8	1	30	25	4.04	101	.244	.330	16-1	.375	2	133	1	0.3
1949	NY A	0	2	.000	4	0	0	1	7.2	9	5	0	0	7	3	5.87	69	.290	.421	2-0	.500	0		-1	-0.2
1950	Chi N	12	5	.706	38	17	9-2	1	153	153	68	16	4	32	55	3.53	119	.258	.300	44-4	.114	-3	96	12	1.0
1951	Chi N	6	12	.333	24	21	6-2	1	141.1	147	83	17	9	31	50	4.84	85	.268	.317	48-1	.125	-2	88	-10	-1.3
1952	Cin N	5	8	.385	28	15	6-1	1	124.1	129	67	7	6	37	50	4.63	81	.271	.331	30-7	.167	1*	124	-11	-1.0
1953	NY N	2	1	.667	19	1	0	0	33.2	43	29	6	4	15	10	6.15	70	.303	.385	4-0	.500	1	104	-8	-0.5
Total	7	30	32	.484	138	60	22-5	4	533.2	553	288	56	24	158	197	4.42	92	.266	.325	148-14	.176	-1	103	-19	-2.0
HILLER, JOHN John Frederick B 4.8.1943 Toronto, ON, CAN BR/TL 6/195# d9.6																									
1965	Det A	0	0	—	5	0	0	1	6	5	0	0	0	1-0	4	0.00	—	.227	.261	0-0	—	0		2	0.1
1966	Det A	0	0	—	1	0	0	0	2	2	2	0	0	2-0	1	9.00	39	.286	.400	0-0	—	0		-1	-0.1
1967	Det A	4	3	.571	23	6	2-2	3	65	57	20	4	0	9-0	49	2.63	124	.233	.259	15-1	.133	-0	80	5	0.6
1968	†Det A	9	6	.600	39	12	4-1	2	128	92	37	9	0	51-4	78	2.39	126	.200	.279	37-0	.081	-2	123	9	0.9
1969	Det A	4	4	.500	40	8	1-1	4-3	99.1	97	50	13	1	44-2	74	3.99	94	.257	.334	21-2	.286	2*	101	-3	-0.1
1970	Det A	6	6	.500	47	5	1-1	3-3	104	82	39	12	2	46-4	89	3.03	123	.219	.302	23-1	.000	-2	72	8	0.6
1972	†Det A	1	2	.333	24	3	1	3-0	44.1	39	13	4	3	13-2	26	2.03	156	.232	.299	4-0	.000	-0	94	5	0.4
1973	Det A	10	5	.667	**65**	0	0	**38-4**	125.1	89	21	7	0	39-7	124	1.44	285	.198	.260	0-0	—	0		**35**	**6.7**
1974	Det A☆	17	14	.548	59	0	0	13-9	150	127	51	10	3	62-19	134	2.64	144	.231	.309	0-0	—	0		18	3.8
1975	Det A	2	3	.400	36	0	0	14-5	70.2	52	20	6	0	36-4	87	2.17	186	.205	.300	0-0	—	0		14	1.6

Year	Tm Lg	W	L	Pct	G	GS	CG-Sho	SV-BS	IP	H	R	HR	HB	BB-IB	SO	ERA	AERA	OAV	OOB	AB-SH	AVG	PB	Sup	APR	PW
1976	Det A	12	8	.600	56	1	1-1	13-13	121	93	37	7	2	67-9	117	2.38	156	.219	.323	1-0	.000	-0	118	17	3.2
1977	Det A	8	14	.364	45	8	3	7-9	124	120	59	15	1	61-8	115	3.56	121	.258	.342	0-0	—	0	71	8	1.3
1978	Det A	9	4	.692	51	0	0	15-7	92.1	64	27	6	0	35-4	74	2.34	166	.202	.277	0-0	—	0		15	2.6
1979	Det A	4	7	.364	43	0	0	9-7	79.1	83	47	14	0	55-7	46	5.22	83	.274	.382	0-0	—	0		-6	-0.9
1980	Det A	1	0	1.000	11	0	0	0-0	30.2	38	15	3	0	14-1	18	4.40	94	.309	.374	0-0	—	0		0	0.0
Total	15	87	76	.534	545	43	13-6	125-60	1242	1040	438	110	12	535-71	1036	2.83	134	.229	.309	101-4	.109	-3	87	126	20.7
HILLMAN, DAVE Darius Dutton B 9.14.1927 Dungannon, VA BR/TR 5-11/168# d4.30																									
1955	Chi N	0	0	—	25	3	0	0	57.2	63	36	10	1	25-0	23	5.31	77	.283	.352	10-1	.100	0*	182	-7	-0.3
1956	Chi N	0	2	.000	2	2	0	0	12.1	11	7	0	0	5-0	6	2.19	172	.216	.286	4-0	.000	-1	35	1	0.1
1957	Chi N	6	11	.353	32	14	1	1	103.1	115	52	13	0	37-2	53	4.35	89	.280	.338	24-2	.000	-2*	86	-4	-0.8
1958	Chi N	4	8	.333	31	16	3	1	125.2	132	57	12	0	31-4	65	3.15	124	.265	.305	41-2	.146	-1*	85	8	0.6
1959	Chi N	8	11	.421	39	24	4-1	0	191	178	84	17	1	43-3	88	3.53	112	.248	.290	60-4	.150	1*	87	8	0.9
1960	Bos A	0	3	.000	16	3	0	0	36.2	41	27	6	0	12-1	14	5.65	72	.281	.333	6-1	.000	-0	80	-7	-0.5
1961	Bos A	3	2	.600	28	1	0	0	78	70	26	8	0	23-0	39	2.77	151	.242	.296	17-2	.000	-2	42	12	0.6
1962	Cin N	0	0	—	2	0	0	0	3.2	8	4	0	0	1-0	0	9.82	41	.421	.450	0-0	—	0		-2	-0.1
	NY N	0	0	—	13	1	0	1	15.2	21	12	5	1	8-0	8	6.32	66	.333	.405	1-0	.000	-0	42	-3	-0.2
	Year	0	0	—	15	1	0	1	19.1	29	14	5	1	9-0	8	6.98	59	.354	.415	1-0	.000	-0	42	-5	-0.3
Total	8	21	37	.362	188	64	8-1	3	624	639	305	71	3	185-10	296	3.87	103	.264	.315	163-12	.098	-5	86	6	0.3
HILLMAN, ERIC John Eric B 4.27.1966 Gary, IN BL/TL 6-10/225# d5.18																									
1992	NY N	2	2	.500	11	8	0	0-0	52.1	67	31	9	2	10-2	16	5.33	65	.318	.353	13-5	.077	-1	91	-9	-0.8
1993	NY N	2	9	.182	27	22	3-1	0-0	145	173	83	12	4	24-2	60	3.97	101	.299	.326	44-6	.159	-0	95	-3	-0.2
1994	NY N	0	3	.000	11	6	0	0-0	34.2	45	30	9	2	11-3	20	7.79	54	.321	.377	8-1	.000	-1	91	-12	-1.0
Total	3	4	14	.222	49	36	3-1	0-0	232	285	144	30	8	45-7	96	4.85	81	.306	.340	65-12	.123	-2	93	-24	-2.0
HILSEY, CHARLIE Charles T. B 3.23.1864 Philadelphia, PA D 10.31.1918 Philadelphia, PA 5-7/180# d9.27																									
1883	Phi N	0	3	.000	3	3	3	0	26	36	26	0		4	8	5.54	56	.305	.328	10	.100	-1	41	-7	-0.7
1884	Phi AA	2	1	.667	3	3	3	0	27	29	19	0	0	5	10	4.67	73	.257	.288	24	.208	0*	172	-3	-0.2
Total	2	2	4	.333	6	6	6	0	53	65	45	0	0	9	18	5.09	64	.281	.308	34	.176	-1	105	-10	-0.9
HILTON, HOWARD Howard James B 1.3.1964 Oxnard, CA BR/TR 6-3/230# d4.9																									
1990	StL N	0	0	—	2	0	0	0-0	3	2	0	0	0	3-0	2	0.00	—	.182	.357	0-0	—	0		1	0.1
HINCHLIFFE, BRETT Brett B 7.21.1974 Detroit, MI BR/TR 6-5/190# d4.5																									
1999	Sea A	0	4	.000	11	4	0	0-0	30.2	41	31	10	4	21-0	14	8.80	54	.323	.434	0-0	—	0	64	-14	-1.4
2000	Ana A	0	0	—	2	0	0	0-0	1.2	1	1	0	0	1-0	0	5.40	94	.167	.286	0-0	—	0		0	0.0
2001	NY N	0	1	.000	1	1	0	0-0	2	9	8	2	1	1-0	2	36.00	11	.643	.688	1-0	.000	-0	179	-7	-0.9
Total	3	0	5	.000	14	5	0	0-0	34.1	51	40	12	5	23-0	16	10.22	46	.347	.451	1-0	.000	-0	83	-21	-2.3
HINDS, SAM Samuel Russell B 7.11.1953 Frederick, MD BR/TR 6-6/215# d5.21																									
1977	Mil A	0	3	.000	29	1	0	2-1	72.1	72	42	5	2	40-3	46	4.73	86	.266	.355	0-0	—	0	0	-5	-0.3
HINRICHS, PAUL Paul Edwin "Herky" B 8.31.1925 Marengo, IA BR/TR 6/180# d5.16																									
1951	Bos A	0	0	—	4	0	0	0	3.1	7	8	1	0	4	1	21.60	21	.412	.524	0-0	—	0		-5	-0.3
HINRICHS, DUTCH William Louis B 4.27.1889 Orange, CA D 8.18.1972 Kingsburg, CA BR/TR 6-3/195# d6.25																									
1910	Was A	0	1	.000	3	0	0	1	7	10	7	0	0	3	5	2.57	97	.357	.419	4-0	.000	-1		-1	-0.3
HINSLEY, JERRY Jerry Dean B 4.9.1944 Hugo, OK BR/TR 5-11/165# d4.18																									
1964	NY N	0	2	.000	9	2	0	0	15.1	21	17	0	0	7-0	11	8.22	44	.313	.373	1-0	.000	-0	61	-8	-1.0
1967	NY N	0	0	—	2	0	0	0	5	6	2	0	0	4-0	3	3.60	94	.316	.435	0-0	—	0		0	0.0
Total	2	0	2	.000	11	2	0	0	20.1	27	19	0	0	11-0	14	7.08	50	.314	.388	1-0	.000	-0	61	-8	-1.0
HINTON, RICH Richard Michael B 5.22.1947 Tucson, AZ BL/TL 6-2/185# d7.17																									
1971	Chi A	3	4	.429	18	2	0	0-2	24.1	27	12	1	1	6-1	15	4.44	81	.310	.358	1-2	.000	-0	62	-1	-0.2
1972	NY A	1	0	1.000	7	3	0	0-0	16.2	20	11	2	0	8-2	13	4.86	61	.299	.364	3-0	.000	-0	160	-4	-0.3
	Tex A	0	1	.000	5	0	0	0-0	11.1	7	10	1	0	10-1	4	2.38	127	.171	.327	2-0	.500	1		-2	-0.1
	Year	1	1	.500	12	3	0	0-0	28	27	26	3	0	18-3	17	3.86	77	.250	.349	5-0	.200	1	158	-6	-0.4
1975	Chi A	1	0	1.000	15	0	0	0-1	37.1	41	22	2	0	15-1	30	4.82	81	.270	.331	0-0	—	0		-4	-0.1
1976	Cin N	1	2	.333	12	1	0	0-1	17.2	30	15	4	0	11-3	8	7.64	46	.380	.451	1-0	.000	-0	201	-7	-1.2
1978	Chi A	2	6	.250	29	4	2	1-2	80.2	78	38	5	2	28-2	48	4.02	95	.261	.326	0-0	—	0	124	-1	-0.1
1979	Chi A	1	2	.333	16	2	0	2-0	41.2	57	30	4	2	8-1	27	6.05	71	.331	.362	0-0	—	0	53	-7	-0.5
	Sea A	0	2	.000	14	1	0	0-1	20	23	14	4	2	5-1	7	5.40	81	.284	.337	0-0	—	0	41	-2	-0.2
	Year	1	4	.200	30	3	0	2-1	61.2	80	16	8	4	13-2	34	5.84	74	.316	.354	0-0	—	0	49	-10	-0.7
Total	6	9	17	.346	116	13	2	3-7	249.2	283	152	23	7	91-12	152	4.87	78	.289	.350	7-2	.143	0	103	-28	-2.7
HIPPAUF, HERB Herbert August B 5.9.1939 New York, NY D 7.17.1995 Santa Clara, CA BR/TL 6/180# d4.27																									
1966	Atl N	0	1	.000	3	0	0	0	2.2	6	5	0	0	1-0	1	13.50	27	.462	.500	0-0	—	0		-3	-0.6
HISNER, HARLEY Harley Parnell B 11.6.1926 Maples, IN BR/TR 6-1/185# d9.30																									
1951	Bos A	0	1	.000	1	1	0	0	6	7	3	0	0	4	3	4.50	99	.292	.393	2-0	.500	0	0	0	0.0
HITCHCOCK, STERLING Sterling Alex B 4.29.1971 Fayetteville, NC BL/TL 6-1/192# d9.11																									
1992	NY A	0	2	.000	3	3	0	0-0	13	23	12	2	1	6-0	6	8.31	47	.377	.441	0-0	—	0	124	-6	-0.7
1993	NY A	1	2	.333	6	6	0	0-0	31	32	18	4	1	14-1	26	4.65	90	.271	.348	0-0	—	0	118	-2	-0.2
1994	NY A	4	1	.800	23	5	1	2-0	49.1	48	24	3	0	29-1	37	4.20	109	.265	.355	0-0	—	0	100	3	0.2
1995	†NY A	11	10	.524	27	27	4-1	0-0	168.1	155	91	22	5	68-1	121	4.70	98	.245	.319	0-0	—	0	99	-1	-0.2
1996	Sea A	13	9	.591	35	35	0	0-0	196.2	245	131	27	7	73-4	132	5.35	93	.309	.368	0-0	—	0	104	-11	-1.0
1997	SD N	10	11	.476	32	28	1	0-0	161	172	102	24	4	55-2	106	5.20	75	.276	.337	50-8	.100	-1	114	-25	-2.9
1998	†SD N	9	7	.563	39	27	2-1	1-1	176.1	169	83	29	9	48-2	158	3.93	100	.251	.308	50-5	.140	-1	111	0	-0.2
1999	SD N	12	14	.462	33	33	1	0-0	205.2	202	99	29	5	76-6	194	4.11	102	.254	.320	61-7	.082	-3	96	5	0.2
2000	SD N	1	6	.143	11	11	0	0-0	65.2	69	38	12	5	26-1	61	4.93	88	.267	.345	22-1	.000	-3	91	-4	-0.6
2001	SD N	2	1	.667	3	3	0	0-0	19	22	9	1	1	3-0	15	3.32	121	.275	.310	8-0	.125	-0	192	1	0.1
	†NY A	4	4	.500	10	9	1	0-0	51.1	67	37	5	2	18-0	28	6.49	69	.315	.367	0-0	—	0	119	-10	-1.2
2002	NY A	1	2	.333	20	2	0	0-0	39.1	57	29	4	1	15-3	31	5.49	80	.326	.380	0-0	—	0	138	-6	-0.4
2003	NY A	1	3	.250	27	1	0	0-0	49.2	57	33	6	0	18-3	36	5.44	81	.285	.341	0-0	—	0	105	-6	-0.4
	StL N	5	1	.833	8	6	0	0-0	38	34	17	8	1	14-1	32	3.79	107	.238	.308	12-2	.083	-1	100	1	0.0
Total	12	74	73	.503	277	196	10-2	3-1	1264.1	1352	723	176	42	463-25	983	4.77	91	.273	.338	203-23	.094	-8	106	-61	-7.3
HITT, BRUCE Bruce Smith B 3.14.1897 Comanche, TX D 11.10.1973 Portland, OR BR/TR 6-1/190# d9.23 Mil 1918																									
1917	StL N	0	0	—	2	0	0	0	4	7	6	1	0	1	1	9.00	30	.368	.400	1-0	.000	-0		-3	-0.2
HITT, ROY Roy Wesley "Rhino" B 6.22.1884 Carleton, NE D 2.8.1956 Pomona, CA BL/TL 5-10/200# d4.27																									
1907	Cin N	6	10	.375	21	18	14-2	0	153.1	143	76	2	12	56	63	3.40	76	.258	.339	56-1	.179	-0	107	-11	-1.2
HITTLE, LLOYD Lloyd Eldon "Red" B 2.21.1924 Lodi, CA BR/TL 5-10.5/164# d6.12																									
1949	Was A	5	7	.417	36	9	3-2	0	109	123	62	2	0	57	32	4.21	101	.285	.369	28-2	.143	-2	61	-1	-0.3
1950	Was A	2	4	.333	11	4	1	0	43.1	60	27	1	0	17	9	4.98	90	.326	.383	13-1	.077	-1	55	-2	-0.3
Total	2	7	11	.389	47	13	4-2	0	152.1	183	89	3	0	74	41	4.43	98	.298	.373	41-3	.122	-3	59	-3	-0.6
HOBAUGH, ED Edward Russell B 6.27.1934 Kittanning, PA BR/TR 6/176# d4.19																									
1961	Was A	7	9	.438	26	18	3	0	126.1	142	68	12	1	64-3	67	4.42	91	.281	.362	41-5	.098	-2*	92	-4	-0.7
1962	Was A	2	1	.667	26	2	0	1	69.1	66	36	9	0	25-2	37	3.76	107	.258	.320	12-0	.167	0	88	0	0.0
1963	Was A	0	0	—	9	1	0	0	16	20	13	3	2	6-2	11	6.19	60	.308	.368	2-0	.500	2	192	-4	-0.1
Total	3	9	10	.474	61	21	3	1	211.2	228	117	24	3	95-7	115	4.34	92	.276	.350	55-5	.127	-1	96	-8	-0.8

Year	Tm Lg	W	L	Pct	G	GS	CG-Sho	SV-BS	IP	H	R	HR	HB	BB-IB	SO	ERA	AERA	OAV	OOB	AB-SH	AVG	PB	Sup	APR	PW
HOBBIE, GLEN Glen Frederick B 4.24.1936 Witt, IL BR/TR 6-2/195# d9.20																									
1957	Chi N	0	0	—	2	0	0	0	4.1	6	5	0	0	5-0	3	10.38	37	.333	.458	2-0	.000	-0		-3	-0.2
1958	Chi N	10	6	.625	55	16	2-1	2	168.1	163	80	13	7	93-8	91	3.74	105	.252	.352	48-1	.146	-2	106	3	0.3
1959	Chi N	16	13	.552	46	33	10-3	0	234	204	105	15	6	106-1	138	3.69	107	.236	.322	79-3	.114	-3	106	7	0.6
1960	Chi N	16	20	.444	46	36	16-4	1	258.2	253	130	27	9	101-7	134	3.97	95	.256	.328	86-1	.151	1	92	-5	-0.4
1961	Chi N	7	13	.350	36	29	7-2	2	198.2	207	113	26	6	54-7	103	4.26	98	.268	.319	66-3	.167	2	105	-3	0.1
1962	Chi N	5	14	.263	42	23	5	0	162	198	112	18	3	62-8	87	5.22	79	.304	.365	49-1	.122	-1	85	-20	-2.2
1963	Chi N	7	10	.412	36	24	4-1	0	165.1	172	80	17	6	49-2	94	3.92	90	.270	.327	50-3	.080	-2	94	-6	-0.9
1964	Chi N	0	3	.000	8	4	0	0	27.1	39	29	4	1	10-1	14	7.90	47	.325	.382	5-0	.000	0	65	-13	-1.2
	StL N	1	2	.333	13	5	1	1	44.1	41	23	4	1	15-1	18	4.26	89	.241	.305	13-1	.154	1	125	-1	0.0
	Year	1	5	.167	21	9	1	1	71.2	80	28	8	2	25-2	32	5.65	67	.276	.336	18-1	.111	1	98	-14	-1.2
Total 8		62	81	.434	284	170	45-11	6	1263	1283	677	124	39	495-35	682	4.20	93	.264	.335	398-13	.131	-5	98	-41	-3.9
HOBBS, JOHN John Douglas B 11.11.1956 Philadelphia, PA BR/TL 6-3/190# d8.31																									
1981	Min A	0	0	—	4	0	0	0-0	5.2	5	2	0	2	6-1	1	3.18	124	.238	.448	0-0	—	0		1	0.0
HOCH, HARRY Harry Keller B 1.9.1887 Woodside, DE D 10.26.1981 Lewes, DE BR/TR 5-10.5/165# d4.16																									
1908	Phi N	2	1	.667	3	3	2	0	26	20	10	0	2	13	4	2.77	88	.211	.318	5-3	.200	1	126	-1	0.0
1914	StL A	0	2	.000	15	2	1	0	54	55	31	1	2	27	13	3.00	90	.284	.377	18-0	.056	-2	13	-4	-0.3
1915	StL A	0	4	.000	12	3	1	0	40	52	49	2	3	26	9	7.20	40	.311	.413	10-1	.200	0	17	-21	-1.8
Total 3		2	7	.222	30	8	4	0	120	127	90	3	7	66	26	4.35	62	.279	.378	33-4	.121	-1	54	-26	-2.1
HOCKENBERY, CHUCK Charles Marion B 12.15.1950 LaCrosse, WI BB/TR 6-1/195# d7.4																									
1975	Cal A	0	5	.000	16	4	0	1-0	41	48	27	3	3	19-2	15	5.27	68	.296	.378	0-0	—	0	37	-8	-0.9
HOCKETTE, GEORGE George Edward "Lefty" B 4.7.1908 Perth, MS D 1.20.1974 Plantation, FL BL/TL 6/174# d9.17																									
1934	Bos A	2	1	.667	3	3	3-2	0	27.1	22	5	3	0	6	14	1.65	292	.218	.262	11-0	.273	0	72	9	1.0
1935	Bos A	2	3	.400	23	4	0	0	61	83	43	6	1	12	11	5.16	92	.329	.362	14-3	.143	-1	91	-3	-0.1
Total 2		4	4	.500	26	7	3-2	0	88.1	105	48	9	1	18	25	4.08	117	.297	.333	25-3	.200	-0	83	6	0.9
HODGE, SHOVEL Clarence Clemet B 7.6.1893 Mount Andrew, AL D 12.31.1967 Ft.Walton Beach, FL BL/TR 6-4/190# d9.6																									
1920	Chi A	1	1	.500	4	2	1	0	19.2	15	14	0	0	12	5	2.29	165	.224	.342	6-0	.000	-1	53	0	-0.1
1921	Chi A	6	8	.429	36	10	5	2	142.2	191	118	7	5	54	25	6.56	65	.335	.397	52-3	.327	3	116	-37	-2.6
1922	Chi A	7	6	.538	35	8	2	1	139	154	73	3	2	65	37	4.14	98	.300	.381	58-3	.207	-1	91	-2	-0.2
Total 3		14	15	.483	75	20	8	3	301.1	360	205	10	7	131	67	5.17	80	.313	.387	116-6	.250	1	100	-39	-2.9
HODGE, ED Ed Oliver B 4.19.1958 Bellflower, CA BL/TL 6-2/192# d5.1																									
1984	Min A	4	3	.571	25	15	0	0-0	100	116	59	13	1	29-1	59	4.77	88	.291	.338	0-0	—	0	107	-6	-0.5
HODGES, KEVIN Kevin Jon B 6.24.1973 Houston, TX BR/TR 6-4/200# d4.24																									
2000	Sea A	0	0	—	13	0	0	0-0	17.1	18	10	4	2	12-0	7	5.19	91	.310	.438	0-0	—	0		-1	0.0
HODGES, TREY Trey Alan B 6.29.1978 Houston, TX BR/TR 6-3/187# d9.10																									
2002	Atl N	2	0	1.000	4	0	0	0-0	11.2	16	7	2	1	2-0	6	5.40	76	.348	.373	3-0	.000	-0		-1	-0.2
2003	Atl N	3	3	.500	52	1	0	0-2	65.2	69	38	11	3	31-7	66	4.66	91	.268	.350	5-1	.000	-1	133	-3	-0.3
Total 2		5	3	.625	56	1	0	0-2	77.1	85	45	13	4	33-7	72	4.77	88	.281	.354	8-1	.000	-1	133	-4	-0.5
HODKEY, ELI Aloysius Joseph B 11.3.1917 Lorain, OH BL/TL 6-4/185# d9.12																									
1946	Phi N	0	1	.000	2	1	0	0	4.1	9	6	0	0	5	0	12.46	28	.391	.500	2-0	.000	-0	50	-4	-0.7
HODNETT, CHARLIE Charles B 1861 , IA D 4.25.1890 St.Louis, MO d5.3																									
1883	StL AA	2	2	.500	4	4	3	0	32	28	10	1		7	6	1.41	248	.220	.261	11	.182	-0	45	7	0.7
1884	StL U	12	2	.857	14	14	12-1	0	121	121	56	0		16	41	2.01	119	.243	.267	58	.207	-1*	173	5	0.1
Total 2		14	4	.778	18	18	15-1	0	153	149	66	1		23	47	1.88	139	.239	.266	69	.203	-1	143	12	0.8
HODSON, GEORGE George S. (b: George S. Hodgdon) B 6.1870 , PA D 1.9.1924 San Rafael, CA TR 5-7/150# d8.9																									
1894	Bos N	4	4	.500	12	11	8	0	74	103	66	4	5	35	12	5.84	97	.326	.402	30-0	.100	-4	101	0	-0.4
1895	Phi N	1	2	.333	4	2	1	0	17	27	23	4	0	9	6	9.53	50	.355	.424	5-0	.000	-1	52	-8	-1.0
Total 2		5	6	.455	16	13	9	0	91	130	89	8	5	44	18	6.53	84	.332	.406	35-0	.086	-5	95	-8	-1.4
HOEFT, BILLY William Frederick B 5.17.1932 Oshkosh, WI BL/TL 6-3/205# d4.18																									
1952	Det A	2	7	.222	34	10	1	4	125	123	66	14	5	63	67	4.32	88	.260	.353	40-1	.150	-1	99	-6	-0.5
1953	Det A	9	14	.391	29	27	9	2	197.2	223	113	24	4	58	90	4.83	84	.283	.335	64-3	.172	0*	97	-14	-1.5
1954	Det A	7	15	.318	34	25	10-4	1	175	180	93	22	4	59	114	4.58	81	.266	.327	52-0	.192	4*	78	-14	-1.2
1955	Det A☆	16	7	.696	32	29	17-**7**	0	220	187	75	17	6	75-1	133	2.99	129	.229	.296	82-4	.207	3*	129	25	2.7
1956	Det A	20	14	.588	38	34	18-4	0	248	276	127	22	5	104-12	172	4.06	101	.287	.356	80-5	.250	6*	108	1	0.6
1957	Det A	9	11	.450	34	28	10-1	1	207	188	85	15	5	69-2	111	3.48	111	.244	.308	67-5	.149	2*	85	10	1.0
1958	Det A	10	9	.526	36	21	6	3	143	148	70	15	1	49-3	94	4.15	97	.268	.326	44-1	.273	3*	103	0	0.2
1959	Det A	1	1	.500	2	2	0	0	9	6	5	0	1	4-0	2	5.00	81	.188	.297	3-2	.333	0*	65	-1	-0.1
	Bos A	0	3	.000	5	3	0	0	17.2	22	12	1	1	8-1	8	5.60	72	.319	.383	3-0	.000	-0*	80	-3	-0.4
	Bal A	1	1	.500	16	3	0	0	41	50	29	6	0	19-3	30	5.71	66	.307	.375	12-0	.250	1	70	-9	-0.4
	Year	2	5	.286	23	8	0	0	67.2	78	32	7	2	31-4	40	5.59	70	.295	.368	18-2	.222	0	74	-12	-0.9
1960	Bal A	2	1	.667	19	0	0	0	18.2	18	10	2	0	14-1	14	4.34	88	.240	.360	1-0	.000	-0		-1	-0.1
1961	Bal A	7	4	.636	35	12	3-1	3	138	106	37	7	1	55-3	100	2.02	190	.216	.295	39-2	.179	1	90	**28**	2.4
1962	Bal A	4	8	.333	57	4	0	7	113.2	103	62	7	1	43-5	73	4.59	81	.243	.311	19-1	.158	3	91	-10	-0.8
1963	SF N	2	0	1.000	23	0	0	4	24.1	26	12	5	0	10-2	8	4.44	72	.271	.340	1-1	1.000	1		-3	-0.2
1964	Mil N	4	0	1.000	42	0	0	4	73.1	76	35	9	1	18-6	47	3.80	93	.271	.318	9-3	.222	1		-2	0.0
1965	Chi N	2	2	.500	29	2	1	1	51.1	41	21	3	0	20-2	44	2.81	131	.215	.285	11-0	.273	1	83	4	0.3
1966	Chi N	1	2	.333	36	0	0	3	41	43	28	4	1	14-3	30	4.61	80	.264	.326	4-0	.250	0		-6	-0.4
	SF N	0	2	.000	4	0	0	0	3.2	4	3	0	0	3-1	3	7.36	50	.250	.368	0-0	—	0		-1	-0.3
	Year	1	4	.200	40	0	0	3	44.2	47	35	4	1	17-4	33	4.84	76	.263	.330	4-0	.250	0		-8	-0.7
Total 15		97	101	.490	505	200	75-17	33	1847.1	1820	883	173	36	685-45	1140	3.94	98	.259	.325	531-28	.202	24	100	-2	1.3
HOELSKOETTER, ART Arthur "Holley" or "Hoss" (a.k.a. Arthur H. Hostetter) B 9.30.1882 St.Louis, MO D 8.3.1954 St.Louis, MO BR/TR 6-2/?# d9.10 ▲																									
1905	StL N	0	1	.000	1	1	1	0	6	6	6	1	0	5	4	1.50	199	.273	.407	83-2	.241	0*	73	-1	-0.1
1906	StL N	1	4	.200	12	3	2	0	58.1	53	37	1	1	34	20	4.63	57	.240	.344	317-7	.224	1*	129	-12	-0.9
1907	StL N	0	0	—	2	0	0	0	11	9	16	0	2	10	8	5.73	44	.209	.382	397-8	.247	0*		-6	-0.3
Total 3		1	5	.167	15	4	3	0	75.1	68	59	2	3	49	32	4.54	58	.238	.355	797-17	.237	1	117	-19	-1.3
HOERNER, JOE Joseph Walter B 11.12.1936 Dubuque, IA D 10.4.1996 Hermann, MO BR/TL 6-1/200# d9.27																									
1963	Hou N	0	0	—	1	0	0	0	3	2	0	0	0	0-0	2	0.00	—	.182	.182	1-0	.000	-0		1	0.1
1964	Hou N	0	0	—	7	0	0	0	11	13	11	3	0	6-1	4	4.91	70	.310	.380	1-0	.000	-0		-4	-0.2
1966	StL N	5	1	.833	57	0	0	13	76	57	16	5	4	21-8	63	1.54	233	.212	.274	8-3	.125	1		17	2.0
1967	†StL N	4	4	.500	57	0	0	15	66	52	25	5	1	20-6	50	2.59	127	.225	.283	11-2	.182	0		4	0.6
1968	†StL N	8	2	.800	47	0	0	17	48.2	34	9	2	0	12-4	42	1.48	196	.192	.241	6-1	.000	-1		8	1.8
1969	StL N	2	3	.400	45	0	0	15-2	53.1	44	18	5	1	9-4	35	2.87	125	.230	.263	5-0	.000	-1		5	0.7
1970	Phi N☆	9	5	.643	44	0	0	9-3	57.2	53	20	5	1	20-7	39	2.65	151	.247	.307	10-0	.200	1		8	1.6
1971	Phi N	4	5	.444	49	0	0	9-5	73	57	19	6	1	21-3	57	1.97	179	.215	.272	10-0	.100	-1		12	1.7
1972	Phi N	0	2	.000	15	0	0	3-4	21.2	21	6	2	1	5-5	12	2.08	173	.259	.297	1-1	.000	-0		3	0.4
	Atl N	1	3	.250	25	0	0	2-6	23.1	34	18	4	1	8-2	19	6.56	58	.351	.394	4-0	.000	-0		-6	-1.2
	Year	1	5	.167	40	0	0	5-10	45	55	28	6	2	13-7	31	4.40	84	.309	.350	5-1	.000	-1		-3	-0.8
1973	Atl N	2	2	.500	20	0	0	2-3	12.2	17	9	1	0	4-0	10	6.39	62	.333	.382	0-0	—	0		-3	-0.6
	KC A	2	0	1.000	22	0	0	4-2	19.1	28	11	0	0	13-5	15	5.12	80	.329	.418	0-0	—	0		-1	-0.2
1974	KC A	2	3	.400	30	0	0	2-3	35.1	32	15	3	4	12-5	24	3.82	100	.244	.320	0-0	—	0		1	0.1
1975	Phi N	0	0	—	25	0	0	0-0	21	25	6	3	1	8-2	20	2.57	146	.298	.358	2-0	.000	-0		3	0.1

Year	Tm Lg	W	L	Pct	G	GS	CG-Sho	SV-BS	IP	H	R	HR	HB	BB-IB	SO	ERA	AERA	OAV	OOB	AB-SH	AVG	PB	Sup	APR	PW
1976	Tex A	0	4	.000	41	0	0	8-3	35	41	22	3	0	19-6	15	5.14	70	.315	.395	0-0	—	0		-6	-0.9
1977	Cin N	0	0	—	8	0	0	0-2	5.2	9	8	3	3	3-1	5	12.71	31	.375	.469	0-0	—	0		-5	-0.3
Total	14	39	34	.534	493	0	0	99-33	562.2	519	213	50	18	181-59	412	2.99	120	.249	.309	59-7	.102	-1		37	5.7

HOERST, LEFTY Frank Joseph B 8.11.1917 Philadelphia, PA D 2.18.2000 Maple Shade, NJ BL/TL 6-3/192# d4.26 Mil 1943-45

Year	Tm Lg	W	L	Pct	G	GS	CG-Sho	SV-BS	IP	H	R	HR	HB	BB-IB	SO	ERA	AERA	OAV	OOB	AB-SH	AVG	PB	Sup	APR	PW
1940	Phi N	1	0	1.000	6	0	0	0	12	12	7	1	0	8	3	5.25	74	.250	.357	2-0	.000	-0		-1	-0.1
1941	Phi N	3	10	.231	37	11	1	0	105.2	111	70	7	1	50	33	5.20	71	.275	.357	22-2	.182	0	58	-17	-1.8
1942	Phi N	4	16	.200	33	22	5	1	150.2	162	99	11	1	78	52	5.20	64	.271	.357	46-3	.152	-0	70	-31	-3.7
1946	Phi N	1	6	.143	18	7	2	0	68.1	77	42	4	1	36	17	4.61	74	.288	.375	17-2	.059	-1	96	-9	-1.1
1947	Phi N	1	1	.500	4	1	0	0	11.1	19	12	1	0	3	0	7.94	50	.358	.393	4-0	.500	1	66	-5	-0.7
Total	5	10	33	.233	98	41	8	1	348	381	230	24	3	175	105	5.17	68	.279	.362	91-7	.154	-1	70	-63	-7.4

HOFF, CHET Chester Cornelius "Red" B 5.8.1891 Ossining, NY D 9.17.1998 Daytona Beach, FL BL/TL 5-9/162# d9.6

Year	Tm Lg	W	L	Pct	G	GS	CG-Sho	SV-BS	IP	H	R	HR	HB	BB-IB	SO	ERA	AERA	OAV	OOB	AB-SH	AVG	PB	Sup	APR	PW
1911	NY A	0	1	.000	5	1	0	0	20.2	21	8	0	0	7	10	2.18	165	.262	.322	7-0	.286	0	80	3	0.2
1912	NY A	0	1	.000	5	1	0	0	15.2	20	14	0	0	6	14	6.89	52	.303	.361	5-0	.200	-0	82	-4	-0.3
1913	NY A	0	0	—	2	0	0	0	3	0	0	0	0	1	2	0.00	—	.000	.111	1-0	.000	-0		1	0.0
1915	StL A	2	2	.500	11	3	2	0	43.2	26	16	0	1	24	23	1.24	232	.169	.285	17-0	.176	-1	76	5	0.4
Total	4	2	4	.333	23	5	2	0	83	67	38	0	1	38	49	2.49	127	.218	.305	30-0	.200	-1	78	5	0.3

HOFFER, BILL William Leopold "Chick" or "Wizard" B 11.8.1870 Cedar Rapids, IA D 7.21.1959 Cedar Rapids, IA BR/TR 5-9/155# d4.26

Year	Tm Lg	W	L	Pct	G	GS	CG-Sho	SV-BS	IP	H	R	HR	HB	BB-IB	SO	ERA	AERA	OAV	OOB	AB-SH	AVG	PB	Sup	APR	PW
1895	†Bal N	31	6	**.838**	41	38	32-4	0	314	296	146	9	19	124	80	3.21	148	.245	.325	126-3	.214	-3	122	56	4.6
1896	†Bal N	25	7	**.781**	35	35	32-3	0	309	317	151	1	12	95	93	3.38	127	.263	.323	125-3	.304	11	128	35	3.9
1897	†Bal N	22	11	.667	38	33	29-1	0	303.1	350	188	5	17	104	62	4.30	97	.287	.351	139-2	.237	2*	110	2	0.2
1898	Bal N	0	4	.000	4	4	4	0	34.1	62	44	0	1	16	5	7.34	49	.387	.446	24-0	.208	0*	164	-16	-1.3
	Pit N	3	0	1.000	4	3	3	0	31	26	7	0	0	15	11	1,74	204	.226	.315	11-0	.091	-1	66	7	0.5
	Year	3	4	.429	8	7	7	0	65.1	88	10	0	1	31	16	4.68	76	.320	.391	35-0	.171	-0	122	-9	-0.8
1899	Pit N	8	10	.444	23	19	15-2	0	163.2	169	98	5	10	64	44	3.63	105	.266	.343	91-0	.198	-1*	112	1	0.0
1901	Cle A	3	8	.273	16	10	10	**3**	99	113	78	2	1	35	19	4.55	78	.283	.343	44-0	.136	-1*	86	-12	-1.2
Total	6	92	46	.667	161	142	125-10	3	1254.1	1333	712	22	60	453	314	3.75	112	.270	.339	560-8	.229	6	118	73	6.7

HOFFMAN, FRANK Frank J. "The Texas Wonder" B Houston, TX TR 5-9.5/163# d8.13

Year	Tm Lg	W	L	Pct	G	GS	CG-Sho	SV-BS	IP	H	R	HR	HB	BB-IB	SO	ERA	AERA	OAV	OOB	AB-SH	AVG	PB	Sup	APR	PW
1888	KC AA	3	9	.250	12	12	12	0	104	102	71	3	6	42	38	2.77	124	.248	.326	39	.154	-1	66	2	0.1

HOFFMAN, GUY Guy Alan B 7.9.1956 Ottawa, IL BL/TL 5-9/185# d7.4

Year	Tm Lg	W	L	Pct	G	GS	CG-Sho	SV-BS	IP	H	R	HR	HB	BB-IB	SO	ERA	AERA	OAV	OOB	AB-SH	AVG	PB	Sup	APR	PW
1979	Chi A	0	5	.000	24	0	0	2-1	30.1	30	18	0	1	23-5	18	5.34	80	.261	.388	0-0	—	0		-2	-0.4
1980	Chi A	1	0	1.000	23	1	0	1-0	37.2	38	12	1	0	17-2	24	2.63	154	.268	.344	0-0	—	0	89	6	0.3
1983	Chi A	1	0	1.000	11	0	0	0-0	6	14	5	1	0	2-0	2	7.50	56	.483	.500	0-0	—	0		-2	-0.3
1986	Chi N	6	2	.750	32	8	1	0-0	84	92	37	6	2	29-7	47	3.86	105	.288	.348	15-3	.067	-1*	110	2	0.1
1987	Cin N	9	10	.474	36	22	0	0-0	158.2	160	83	20	4	49-5	87	4.37	97	.265	.322	45-3	.111	-2	105	-1	-0.4
1988	Tex A	0	0	—	11	0	0	0-0	22.1	22	14	5	1	8-0	9	5.24	78	.247	.313	0-0	—	0		-2	-0.1
Total	6	17	17	.500	137	31	1	3-1	339	356	169	33	8	128-19	187	4.25	98	.274	.341	60-6	.100	-2	107	1	-0.8

HOFFMAN, TREVOR Trevor William B 10.13.1967 Bellflower, CA BR/TR 6/205# d4.6 b-Glenn

Year	Tm Lg	W	L	Pct	G	GS	CG-Sho	SV-BS	IP	H	R	HR	HB	BB-IB	SO	ERA	AERA	OAV	OOB	AB-SH	AVG	PB	Sup	APR	PW
1993	Fla N	2	2	.500	28	0	0	2-1	35.2	24	13	5	0	19-7	26	3.28	132	.185	.287	2-0	.000	-0		4	0.5
	SD N	2	4	.333	39	0	0	3-2	54.1	56	30	5	1	20-6	53	4.31	96	.264	.325	5-0	.200	0		-1	-0.1
	Year	4	6	.400	67	0	0	5-3	90	80	48	10	1	39-13	79	3.90	108	.234	.310	7-0	.143	-0		3	0.4
1994	SD N	4	4	.500	47	0	0	20-3	56	39	16	4	0	20-6	68	2.57	160	.193	.263	3-1	.000	-0		11	2.0
1995	SD N	7	4	.636	55	0	0	31-7	53.1	48	25	10	0	14-3	52	3.88	104	.235	.284	2-0	.500	1		1	0.3
1996	†SD N	9	5	.643	70	0	0	42-7	88	50	23	6	2	31-5	111	2.25	177	.161	.240	8-1	.000	-1		19	3.6
1997	SD N	6	4	.600	70	0	0	37-7	81.1	59	25	9	0	24-4	111	2.66	146	.200	.259	3-0	.333	0		13	2.5
1998	†SD N★	4	2	.667	66	0	0	**53-1**	73	41	12	2	1	21-2	86	1.48	265	.165	.232	3-0	.000	-0		22	4.4
1999	SD N★	2	3	.400	64	0	0	40-3	67.1	48	23	5	0	15-2	73	2.14	196	.197	.240	3-0	.333	1		14	2.4
2000	SD N★	4	7	.364	70	0	0	43-7	72.1	61	29	7	0	11-4	85	2.99	145	.224	.250	0-0	—	0		10	2.0
2001	SD N	3	4	.429	62	0	0	43-3	60.1	48	25	10	1	21-2	63	3.43	117	.216	.285	4-0	.000	-0		5	0.8
2002	SD N★	2	5	.286	61	0	0	38-3	59.1	52	20	2	1	18-2	69	2.73	138	.234	.292	0-0	—	0		7	1.5
2003	SD N	0	0	—	9	0	0	0-0	9	7	2	1	0	3-0	11	2.00	197	.212	.278	0-0	—	0		2	0.1
Total	11	45	44	.506	641	0	0	352-44	710	533	243	66	6	217-43	808	2.78	146	.205	.266	33-2	.121	-1		107	20.0

HOFFMAN, BILL William Joseph B 3.3.1918 Philadelphia, PA BL/TL 5-9/170# d8.13

Year	Tm Lg	W	L	Pct	G	GS	CG-Sho	SV-BS	IP	H	R	HR	HB	BB-IB	SO	ERA	AERA	OAV	OOB	AB-SH	AVG	PB	Sup	APR	PW
1939	Phi N	0	0	—	3	0	0	0	6	8	9	2	3	7	1	13.50	30	.333	.529	1-0	.000	-0		-6	-0.3

HOFFORD, JOHN John William B 5.25.1863 Philadelphia, PA D 12.16.1915 Philadelphia, PA d9.26

Year	Tm Lg	W	L	Pct	G	GS	CG-Sho	SV-BS	IP	H	R	HR	HB	BB-IB	SO	ERA	AERA	OAV	OOB	AB-SH	AVG	PB	Sup	APR	PW
1885	Pit AA	0	3	.000	3	3	3	0	25	28	16	1	0	9	21	3.60	89	.275	.333	8	.125	-1	61	-1	-0.1
1886	Pit AA	3	6	.333	9	9	9	0	81	88	66	1	2	40	25	4.33	78	.261	.343	34	.294	3	91	-9	-0.5
Total	2	3	9	.250	12	12	12	0	106	116	82	2	2	49	46	4.16	80	.264	.341	42	.262	2	84	-10	-0.6

HOGAN, GEORGE George A. B 9.25.1885 Marion, OH D 2.22.1922 Bartlesville, OK BR/TR 6/160# d4.18 b-Willie

Year	Tm Lg	W	L	Pct	G	GS	CG-Sho	SV-BS	IP	H	R	HR	HB	BB-IB	SO	ERA	AERA	OAV	OOB	AB-SH	AVG	PB	Sup	APR	PW
1914	KC F	0	1	.000	4	1	0	0	13	12	9	1	1	7	7	4.15	67	.255	.364	4-0	.000	-1	74	-2	-0.2

HOGG, BRAD Carter Bradley B 3.26.1889 Buena Vista, GA D 4.2.1935 Buena Vista, GA BR/TR 6/185# d9.1

Year	Tm Lg	W	L	Pct	G	GS	CG-Sho	SV-BS	IP	H	R	HR	HB	BB-IB	SO	ERA	AERA	OAV	OOB	AB-SH	AVG	PB	Sup	APR	PW
1911	Bos N	0	3	.000	8	3	2	1	25.2	33	20	0	1	14	8	6.66	57	.337	.425	9-1	.444	1	118	-6	-0.5
1912	Bos N	1	1	.500	10	1	0	1	31	37	32	2	2	16	12	6.97	51	.308	.399	11-0	.091	-1	164	-11	-0.8
1915	Chi N	1	0	1.000	2	2	1-1	0	13	12	3	1	1	6	0	2.08	134	.245	.339	3-1	.000	-0	120	1	0.1
1918	Phi N	13	13	.500	29	25	17-3	1	228	201	83	3	6	61	81	2.53	119	.245	.302	79-4	.228	3*	80	10	1.8
1919	Phi N	5	12	.294	22	19	13	0	150.1	163	85	7	5	55	48	4.43	73	.292	.360	60-1	.283	3*	86	-17	-1.6
Total	5	20	29	.408	71	50	33-4	3	448	446	223	13	15	152	149	3.70	85	.271	.338	162-7	.247	5	87	-23	-1.0

HOGG, BILL William Johnston "Buffalo Bill" B 9.11.1881 Port Huron, MI D 12.8.1909 New Orleans, LA BR/TR 6/200# d4.25

Year	Tm Lg	W	L	Pct	G	GS	CG-Sho	SV-BS	IP	H	R	HR	HB	BB-IB	SO	ERA	AERA	OAV	OOB	AB-SH	AVG	PB	Sup	APR	PW
1905	NY A	9	13	.409	39	22	9-3	1	205	178	104	1	13	101	125	3.20	92	.236	.336	67-1	.060	-6	79	-6	-1.5
1906	NY A	14	13	.519	28	25	15-3	0	206	171	77	5	12	72	107	2.93	101	.229	.307	72-5	.125	-5	97	4	-0.2
1907	NY A	10	8	.556	25	21	13	0	166.2	173	84	3	6	83	64	3.08	91	.270	.359	60-5	.183	-0*	101	-5	-0.6
1908	NY A	4	16	.200	24	21	6	0	152.1	155	89	4	4	63	72	3.01	82	.262	.337	43-1	.093	-3	63	-13	-2.1
Total	4	37	50	.425	116	89	43-6	1	730	677	354	13	35	319	368	3.06	92	.248	.334	242-12	.116	-14	86	-20	-4.4

HOGSETT, CHIEF Elon Chester B 11.2.1903 Brownell, KS D 7.17.2001 Hays, KS BL/TL 6/190# d9.18

Year	Tm Lg	W	L	Pct	G	GS	CG-Sho	SV-BS	IP	H	R	HR	HB	BB-IB	SO	ERA	AERA	OAV	OOB	AB-SH	AVG	PB	Sup	APR	PW
1929	Det A	1	2	.333	4	4	2-1	0	28.2	34	10	0	1	9	9	2.83	152	.312	.370	10-0	.200	-0	84	5	0.4
1930	Det A	9	8	.529	33	17	4	1	146	174	102	9	9	63	54	5.42	88	.300	.377	58-0	.293	3	83	-9	-0.6
1931	Det A	3	9	.250	22	12	5	2	112.1	150	80	8	5	33	47	5.93	77	.324	.375	47-0	.234	0	94	-13	-1.1
1932	Det A	11	9	.550	47	15	7	7	178	201	97	8	5	66	56	3.54	133	.286	.351	57-4	.246	3*	87	17	2.2
1933	Det A	6	10	.375	45	2	0	9	116	137	78	7	4	56	39	4.50	96	.296	.377	38-0	.211	-0	128	-6	-0.8
1934	†Det A	3	2	.600	26	0	0	3	50.1	61	34	4	1	19	23	4.29	102	.303	.367	13-0	.231	-0		-2	-0.2
1935	†Det A	6	6	.500	40	0	0	5	96.2	109	45	1	5	49	39	3.54	118	.288	.377	23-0	.261	2		7	1.1
1936	Det A	0	1	.000	3	0	0	0	4	8	7	1	0	1	1	9.00	55	.400	.429	0-0	—	0		-3	-0.4
	StL A	13	15	.464	39	29	10	1	215.1	278	153	15	15	90	67	5.52	97	.310	.383	70-2	.143	-2*	88	-4	-0.6
	Year	13	16	.448	42	29	10	1	219.1	286	158	16	15	91	68	5.58	96	.312	.384	70-2	.143	-2	88	-6	-1.0
1937	StL A	6	19	.240	37	26	8-1	2	177.1	245	144	19	5	75	68	6.29	77	.328	.393	62-0	.210	0*	56	-29	-3.3
1938	Was A	5	6	.455	31	9	1	3	91	107	73	12	8	36	33	6.03	75	.292	.368	23-0	.304	3*	102	-17	-1.4
1944	Det A	0	0	—	3	0	0	0	6.1	7	6	1	2	4	5	0.00	—	.250	.382	2-0	.000	-0		0	0.0
Total	11	63	87	.420	330	114	37-2	33	1222	1511	829	85	60	501	441	5.02	94	.305	.376	403-6	.226	8	84	-54	-4.7

HOGUE, CAL Calvin Grey B 10.24.1927 Dayton, OH BR/TR 6/185# d7.15

Year	Tm Lg	W	L	Pct	G	GS	CG-Sho	SV-BS	IP	H	R	HR	HB	BB-IB	SO	ERA	AERA	OAV	OOB	AB-SH	AVG	PB	Sup	APR	PW
1952	Pit N	1	8	.111	19	12	3	0	83.2	79	56	7	4	68	34	4.84	82	.258	.399	24-1	.250	1	71	-10	-0.9
1953	Pit N	1	1	.500	3	2	2	0	19	19	13	4	1	16	10	5.21	86	.250	.387	5-1	.000	-1	100	-2	-0.2
1954	Pit N	0	1	.000	3	2	0	0	11	11	6	1	0	12	7	4.91	85	.282	.442	3-1	.000	-0	75	0	-0.1
Total	3	2	10	.167	25	16	5	0	113.2	109	75	12	5	96	51	4.91	83	.259	.402	32-3	.188	0	75	-12	-1.2

Year	Tm Lg	W	L	Pct	G	GS	CG-Sho	SV-BS	IP	H	R	HR	HB	BB-IB	SO	ERA	AERA	OAV	OOB	AB-SH	AVG	PB	Sup	APR	PW
HOGUE, BOBBY Robert Clinton B 4.5.1921 Miami, FL D 12.22.1987 Miami, FL BR/TR 5-10/195# d4.24																									
1948	Bos N	8	2	.800	40	1	0	2	86.1	88	34	4	2	19	43	3.23	119	.265	.309	21-7	.095	-1	162	6	0.5
1949	Bos N	2	2	.500	33	0	0	3	72	78	30	4	2	25	23	3.13	121	.280	.343	21-3	.286	1		5	0.5
1950	Bos N	3	5	.375	36	1	0	7	62.2	69	35	8	4	31	15	5.03	77	.280	.370	13-1	.231	1	115	-6	-0.7
1951	Bos N	0	0	—	3	0	0	0	5	4	3	1	0	3	0	5.40	68	.235	.350	2-0	.500	0		-1	0.0
	StL A	1	1	.500	18	0	0	1	29.2	31	17	1	0	23	11	5.16	85	.279	.403	3-0	.667	1		-2	0.1
	†NY A	1	0	1.000	7	0	0	0	7.1	4	0	0	0	3	2	0.00	—	.174	.269	0-0	—	0		3	0.4
	Year	2	1	.667	25	0	0	1	37	35	22	1	0	26	13	4.14	104	.261	.381	3-0	.667	1		2	0.5
1952	NY A	3	5	.375	27	0	0	4	47.1	52	30	6	1	25	12	5.32	62	.294	.384	11-0	.273	0		-11	-1.8
	StL A	0	1	.000	8	1	0	0	16.1	10	5	1	0	13	2	2.76	142	.179	.333	2-0	.000	-0	22	2	0.1
	Year	3	6	.333	35	1	0	4	63.2	62	6	7	1	38	14	4.66	74	.266	.371	13-0	.231	0	25	-7	-1.7
Total	5	18	16	.529	172	3	0	17	326.2	336	154	25	9	142	108	3.97	96	.271	.350	73-11	.233	3	101	-4	-0.9
HOLBOROW, WALLY Walter Albert B 11.30.1913 New York, NY D 7.14.1986 Ft.Lauderdale, FL BR/TR 5-11/187# d9.27																									
1944	Was A	0	0	—	1	0	0	0	3	0	0	0	0	2	1	0.00	—	.000	.182	0-0	—	0		1	0.1
1945	Was A	1	1	.500	15	1	1-1	0	31.1	20	9	0	0	16	14	2.30	135	.189	.295	2-2	.000	-0	110	3	0.1
1948	Phi A	1	2	.333	5	1	1	0	17.1	32	12	1	0	7	3	5.71	75	.421	.470	4-1	.500	1	147	-3	-0.2
Total	3	2	3	.400	21	2	2-1	0	51.2	52	21	1	0	25	18	3.31	106	.272	.356	6-3	.333	1	137	1	0.0
HOLCOMBE, KEN Kenneth Edward B 8.23.1918 Burnsville, NC BR/TR 5-11.5/169# d4.27																									
1945	NY A	3	3	.500	23	2	0	0	55.1	43	19	2	0	27	20	1.79	194	.226	.323	15-0	.133	-1	74	7	0.7
1948	Cin N	0	0	—	2	0	0	0	2.1	3	2	0	0	0	2	7.71	51	.300	.300	0-0	—	0		-1	0.0
1950	Chi A	3	10	.231	24	15	5	1	96	122	68	10	0	45	37	4.59	98	.307	.378	32-2	.156	-2	87	-7	-1.0
1951	Chi A	11	12	.478	28	23	12-2	0	159.1	142	69	9	1	68	39	3.78	107	.241	.321	44-10	.250	1	77	9	1.3
1952	Chi A	0	5	.000	7	7	1	0	35	38	24	3	2	18	12	6.17	59	.286	.379	10-1	.000	-1	58	-9	-1.2
	StL A	0	2	.000	12	1	0	0	21	20	10	1	0	9	7	3.86	101	.263	.341	3-0	.333	0	0	0	0.1
	Year	0	7	.000	19	8	1	0	56	58	10	4	2	27	19	5.30	71	.278	.366	13-1	.077	-1	49	-8	-1.1
1953	Bos A	1	0	1.000	3	0	0	1	6	9	4	0	0	3	1	6.00	70	.333	.400	2-1	.000	-0		-1	-0.2
Total	6	18	32	.360	99	48	18-2	2	375	377	196	25	3	170	118	3.98	101	.265	.345	106-14	.179	-3	77	-2	-0.3
HOLDRIDGE, DAVID David Allen B 2.5.1969 Wayne, MI BR/TR 6-3/190# d8.8																									
1998	Sea A	0	0	—	7	0	0	0-0	6.2	6	3	0	0	4-0	6	4.05	115	.231	.323	0-0	—	0		1	0.0
HOLDSWORTH, FRED Fredrick William B 5.29.1952 Detroit, MI BR/TR 6-1/190# d7.27																									
1972	Det A	0	1	.000	2	2	0	0-0	7	13	10	0	0	2-0	5	12.86	25	.419	.441	3-0	.333	0	154	-7	-0.8
1973	Det A	0	1	.000	5	2	0	0-0	14.2	13	11	3	0	6-0	9	6.75	61	.236	.311	0-0	—	0	87	-4	-0.2
1974	Det A	0	3	.000	8	5	0	0-0	35.2	40	20	4	1	14-3	16	4.29	89	.286	.355	0-0	—	0	51	-2	-0.2
1976	Bal A	4	1	.800	16	0	0	2-2	39.2	24	9	0	0	13-1	24	2.04	160	.179	.250	0-0	—	0		6	0.8
1977	Bal A	0	1	.000	12	0	0	0-1	14.1	17	11	0	1	16-2	4	6.28	61	.333	.479	0-0	—	0		-4	-0.3
	Mon N	3	3	.500	14	6	0	0-0	42.1	35	17	6	0	18-0	21	3.19	120	.230	.306	10-0	.000	-1	109	3	0.3
1978	Mon N	0	0	—	6	0	0	0-0	8.2	16	10	3	0	8-3	3	7.27	49	.381	.480	0-0	—	0		-5	-0.2
1980	Mil A	0	0	—	9	0	0	0-0	19.2	24	12	2	0	9-0	12	4.58	85	.286	.355	0-0	—	0		-2	-0.1
Total	7	7	10	.412	72	15	0	2-3	182	182	100	18	2	86-9	94	4.40	84	.264	.344	13-0	.077	-1	93	-15	-0.7
HOLLAND, AL Alfred Willis B 8.16.1952 Roanoke, VA BR/TL 5-11/207# d9.5																									
1977	Pit N	0	0	—	2	0	0	0-0	2.1	4	2	0	0	0-0	1	7.71	52	.400	.400	0-0	—	0		-1	0.0
1979	SF N	0	0	—	3	0	0	0-0	7	3	0	0	0	5-0	7	0.00	—	.125	.276	0-0	—	0		3	0.1
1980	SF N	5	3	.625	54	0	0	7-4	82.1	71	21	2	1	34-8	65	1.75	203	.233	.308	5-2	.200	1		15	1.9
1981	SF N	7	5	.583	47	3	0	7-1	100.2	87	31	4	2	44-11	78	2.41	142	.233	.314	16-5	.063	-1	78	11	1.4
1982	SF N	7	3	.700	58	7	0	5-0	129.2	115	56	12	1	40-6	97	3.33	108	.231	.288	34-3	.059	-3	109	4	0.0
1983	†Phi N	8	4	.667	68	0	0	25-7	91.2	63	26	8	0	30-12	100	2.26	158	.188	.254	7-1	.000	-1		14	2.4
1984	Phi N☆	5	10	.333	68	0	0	29-7	98.1	82	38	14	1	30-6	61	3.39	107	.225	.283	5-0	.000	-1		5	0.9
1985	Phi N	0	1	.000	3	0	0	1-0	4	5	2	0	0	4-2	1	4.50	82	.333	.450	0-0	—	0		0	0.0
	Pit N	1	3	.250	38	0	0	4-4	58.2	48	22	5	0	17-6	47	3.38	106	.227	.281	5-1	.400	2		2	0.3
	Year	1	4	.200	41	0	0	5-4	62.2	53	28	5	0	21-8	48	3.45	104	.235	.295	5-1	.400	2		3	0.3
	Cal A	0	1	.000	15	0	0	0-1	24.1	17	4	4	0	10-1	14	1.48	278	.193	.276	0-0	—	0		7	0.4
1986	NY A	1	0	1.000	25	1	0	0-1	40.2	44	29	5	0	9-2	37	5.09	80	.268	.301	0-0	—	0	266	-6	-0.3
1987	NY A	0	0	—	3	0	0	0-0	6.1	9	10	1	0	9-0	5	14.21	31	.321	.486	0-0	—	0		-7	-0.3
Total	10	34	30	.531	384	11	0	78-25	646	548	241	55	5	232-54	513	2.98	122	.227	.293	72-12	.083	-2	116	47	6.8
HOLLAND, MUL Howard Arthur B 1.6.1903 Franklin, VA D 2.16.1969 Winchester, VA BR/TR 6-4/185# d5.25																									
1926	Cin N	0	0	—	3	0	0	0	6.2	3	1	0	0	5	0	1.35	273	.136	.296	2-0	.500	0		2	0.2
1927	NY N	1	0	1.000	2	0	0	0	2	0	0	0	0	3	0	0.00	—	.000	.333	0-0	—	0		1	0.2
1929	StL N	0	1	.000	8	0	0	0	14.1	13	15	3	1	7	5	9.42	50	.232	.328	4-0	.250	0		-7	-0.4
Total	3	1	1	.500	13	0	0	0	23	16	16	3	1	15	5	6.26	69	.190	.320	6-0	.333	1		-4	0.0
HOLLAND, BILL William David "Dutch" B 6.4.1915 Varina, NC D 4.5.1997 Goldsboro, NC BL/TL 6-1/190# d9.17																									
1939	Was A	0	1	.000	3	0	0	0	4	6	5	1	0	5	2	11.25	39	.400	.550	0-0	—	0		-3	-0.5
HOLLEY, ED Edward Edgar B 7.23.1899 Benton, KY D 10.26.1986 Paducah, KY BR/TR 6-1.5/195# d5.24																									
1928	Chi N	0	0	—	13	1	0	0	31	31	15	1	2	16	10	3.77	102	.265	.363	5-0	.000	-0	154	0	0.0
1932	Phi N	11	14	.440	34	30	16-2	0	228	247	114	15	6	55	87	3.95	112	.273	.319	91-2	.132	-6	85	11	0.4
1933	Phi N	13	15	.464	30	28	12-3	0	206.2	219	93	18	13	62	56	3.53	108	.273	.335	74-2	.162	-2	83	7	0.5
1934	Phi N	1	8	.111	15	13	2	0	72.2	85	62	10	4	31	14	7.18	66	.294	.370	24-0	.208	-1*	91	-15	-1.7
	Pit N	0	3	.000	5	4	0	0	9.1	20	16	1	2	6	2	15.43	27	.426	.509	2-0	1.000	2	126	-11	-1.6
	Year	1	11	.083	20	17	2	0	82	105	22	11	6	37	16	8.12	57	.313	.391	26-0	.269	1	97	-24	-3.3
Total	4	25	40	.385	97	76	30-5	0	547.2	602	300	45	27	170	169	4.40	95	.279	.339	196-4	.158	-8	89	-8	-2.4
HOLLING, CARL Carl B 7.9.1896 Dana, CA D 7.18.1962 Santa Rosa, CA BR/TR 6-1/172# d4.19																									
1921	Det A	3	7	.300	35	11	4	4	136	162	95	8	4	58	38	4.30	99	.305	.378	48-2	.271	1	98	-6	-0.2
1922	Det A	1	1	.500	5	1	0	0	9.1	21	16	1	2	5	2	15.43	25	.525	.596	2-0	.000	-0*	88	-11	-1.7
Total	2	4	8	.333	40	12	4	4	145.1	183	111	9	6	63	40	5.02	85	.320	.394	50-2	.260	1	97	-17	-1.9
HOLLINGSWORTH, AL Albert Wayne "Boots" B 2.25.1908 St.Louis, MO D 4.28.1996 Austin, TX BL/TL 6/174# d4.16 C2																									
1935	Cin N	6	13	.316	38	22	8	0	173.1	165	90	5	1	76	89	3.89	102	.243	.321	54-3	.148	-2*	76	1	-0.1
1936	Cin N	9	10	.474	29	25	9	0	184	204	97	4	5	66	76	4.16	92	.281	.345	73-1	.315	7*	108	-6	0.1
1937	Cin N	9	15	.375	43	24	11-1	5	202.1	224	108	8	2	73	74	3.91	95	.278	.339	76-0	.250	3*	110	-6	-0.3
1938	Cin N	2	2	.500	9	4	1	0	34	43	28	2	0	12	13	7.15	51	.307	.362	12-0	.250	1	139	-12	-1.1
	Phi N	5	16	.238	24	21	11-1	0	174.1	177	89	4	0	77	80	3.82	102	.264	.340	67-1	.224	-0	78	0	-0.1
	Year	7	18	.280	33	25	12-1	0	208.1	220	93	6	0	89	93	4.36	88	.272	.344	79-1	.228	1	87	-11	-1.2
1939	Phi N	1	9	.100	15	10	3	0	60	78	48	2	0	27	24	5.85	69	.317	.385	20-0	.100	-1	92	-14	-2.1
	Bro N	1	2	.333	8	5	1	0	27.1	33	17	1	1	11	11	5.27	76	.311	.381	8-1	.125	-1*	95	-3	-0.3
	Year	2	11	.154	23	15	4	0	87.1	111	21	3	1	38	35	5.67	71	.315	.384	28-1	.107	-2	93	-16	-2.4
1940	Was A	1	0	1.000	3	2	0	0	18	18	12	0	0	11	7	5.50	76	.261	.363	6-0	.167	0	158	-2	-0.1
1942	StL A	10	6	.625	33	18	7-1	4	161	173	70	4	2	52	60	2.96	125	.272	.329	56-1	.179	0*	138	10	1.0
1943	StL A	6	13	.316	35	20	9-1	3	154	169	81	7	2	51	63	4.21	79	.281	.339	50-2	.140	-1*	91	-14	-1.9
1944	†StL A	5	7	.417	26	10	3-2	1	92.2	108	51	3	1	37	22	4.47	81	.291	.357	28-0	.071	-2	65	-7	-1.1
1945	StL A	12	9	.571	26	22	15-1	1	173.1	164	60	4	0	68	64	2.70	130	.251	.322	61-3	.197	1*	88	15	2.0
1946	StL A	0	0	—	5	0	0	0	11	23	8	1	0	4	3	6.55	57	.411	.450	2-0	.000	-0		-3	-0.2
	Chi A	3	2	.600	21	2	0	1	55	63	29	2	0	22	22	4.58	74	.288	.353	12-2	.000	-1	63	-5	-0.6
	Year	3	2	.600	26	2	0	1	66	86	32	3	0	26	25	4.91	71	.313	.372	14-2	.000	-1	62	-9	-0.8
Total	11	70	104	.402	315	185	78-7	15	1520.1	1642	788	47	14	587	608	3.99	93	.275	.341	525-14	.196	3	97	-46	-4.8

Year	Tm Lg	W	L	Pct	G	GS	CG-Sho	SV-BS	IP	H	R	HR	HB	BB-IB	SO	ERA	AERA	OAV	OOB	AB-SH	AVG	PB	Sup	APR	PW
HOLLINGSWORTH, BONNIE John Burnette B 12.26.1895 Jacksboro, TN D 1.4.1990 Knoxville, TN BR/TR 5-10/170# d5.30																									
1922	Pit N	0	0	—	9	0	0	0	13.2	17	14	0	1	8	7	7.90	52	.315	.413	0-0	—	0		-6	-0.3
1923	Was A	3	7	.300	17	8	1	0	72.2	72	43	3	3	50	26	4.09	92	.272	.393	22-0	.091	-1	77	-4	-0.6
1924	Bro N	1	0	1.000	3	1	1	0	8.2	8	6	0	0	10	7	6.23	60	.267	.450	3-0	.000	-1	91	-2	-0.2
1928	Bos N	0	2	.000	7	2	0	0	22.1	30	19	2	0	13	10	5.24	75	.341	.426	6-0	.167	-0	130	-5	-0.4
Total	4	4	9	.308	36	11	2	0	117.1	127	82	5	4	81	50	4.91	78	.291	.406	31-0	.097	-2	87	-17	-1.5
HOLLINS, JESSIE Jessie Edward B 1.27.1970 Conroe, TX BR/TR 6-3/190# d9.19																									
1992	Chi N	0	0	—	4	0	0	0-0	4.2	8	7	1	0	5-0	0	13.50	27	.400	.481	0-0	—	0		-5	-0.2
HOLLISON, JOHN John Henry "Swede" B 5.3.1870 Chicago, IL D 8.19.1969 Chicago, IL BR/TL 5-8/162# d8.13																									
1892	Chi N	0	0	—	1	0	0	0	4	1	1	1	0	0	2	2.25	148	.077	.077	3	.000	-0		1	0.0
HOLLOMAN, BOBO Alva Lee B 3.7.1925 Thomaston, GA D 5.1.1987 Athens, GA BR/TR 6-2/207# d4.18																									
1953	StL A	3	7	.300	22	10	1-1	0	65.1	69	41	2	1	50	25	5.23	80	.275	.397	19-3	.105	-2	72	-6	-1.0
HOLLOWAY, JIM James Madison B 9.22.1908 Plaquemine, LA D 4.15.1997 Baton Rouge, LA BR/TR 6-1/165# d5.17																									
1929	Phi N	0	0	—	3	0	0	0	4.2	10	7	2	0	5	1	13.50	38	.455	.556	1-0	1.000	0		-4	-0.1
HOLLOWAY, KEN Kenneth Eugene (b: Kenneth Eugene Hollaway) B 8.8.1897 Barwick, GA D 9.25.1968 Thomasville, GA BR/TR 6/185# d8.27																									
1922	Det A	0	0	—	1	0	0	0	1	1	1	0	0	0	1	0.00	—	.250	.250	0-0	—	0		0	0.0
1923	Det A	11	10	.524	42	24	7-1	1	194	232	117	12	10	75	55	4.45	87	.302	.372	65-3	.123	-5	106	-14	-1.8
1924	Det A	14	6	.700	49	13	5	3	181.1	209	105	6	6	61	46	4.07	101	.299	.361	58-2	.190	-1	118	-1	-0.2
1925	Det A	13	4	.765	38	14	6	2	157.2	170	90	8	2	67	29	4.62	93	.282	.356	48-4	.229	-0	120	-4	-0.5
1926	Det A	4	6	.400	36	12	3	2	139	192	94	2	8	42	43	5.12	79	.343	.397	46-1	.239	0	126	-15	-1.0
1927	Det A	11	12	.478	36	23	11-1	6	183.1	210	103	10	4	61	36	4.07	103	.299	.359	62-6	.129	-5	94	3	-0.1
1928	Det A	4	8	.333	30	11	5	2	120.1	137	67	2	5	32	32	4.34	95	.291	.343	33-5	.121	-2	69	-2	-0.3
1929	Cle A	6	5	.545	25	11	6-2	0	119	118	52	2	2	37	32	3.03	147	.264	.323	41-0	.171	-2	74	16	1.1
1930	Cle A	1	1	.500	12	2	0	2	30	49	32	5	0	14	8	8.40	57	.374	.434	12-2	.000	-2	98	-10	-0.8
	NY A	0	0	—	16	0	0	0	34.1	52	23	3	0	8	11	5.24	82	.374	.408	13-0	.231	-0		-3	-0.2
	Year	1	1	.500	28	2	0	2	64.1	101	61	8	0	22	19	6.72	68	.374	.421	25-2	.120	-3	104	-15	-1.0
Total	9	64	52	.552	285	110	43-4	18	1160	1370	684	50	37	397	293	4.40	95	.303	.364	378-23	.167	-18	101	-30	-3.8
HOLLY, JEFF Jeffrey Owen B 3.1.1953 San Pedro, CA BL/TL 6-5/210# d5.1																									
1977	Min A	2	3	.400	18	5	0	0-0	48.1	57	37	8	1	12-0	32	6.89	58	.300	.343	0-0	—	0	131	-14	-1.3
1978	Min A	1	1	.500	15	1	0	0-0	35.1	28	15	1	0	18-3	12	3.57	108	.222	.313	0-0	—	0	70	1	0.1
1979	Min A	0	0	—	6	0	0	0-0	6.1	10	7	0	0	3-0	5	7.11	62	.385	.419	0-0	—	0		-3	-0.1
Total	3	3	4	.429	39	6	0	0-0	90	95	59	9	1	33-3	49	5.60	71	.278	.338	0-0	—	0	121	-16	-1.3
HOLMAN, BRAD Bradley Thomas B 2.9.1968 Kansas City, MO BR/TR 6-5/200# d7.4 b-Brian																									
1993	Sea A	1	3	.250	19	0	0	3-0	36.1	27	17	1	5	16-2	17	3.72	119	.208	.318	0-0	—	0		2	0.2
HOLMAN, BRIAN Brian Scott B 1.25.1965 Denver, CO BR/TR 6-4/185# d6.25 b-Brad																									
1988	Mon N	4	8	.333	18	16	1-1	0-0	100.1	101	39	3	0	34-2	58	3.23	112	.264	.323	28-4	.107	-1*	69	5	0.4
1989	Mon N	1	2	.333	10	3	0	0-0	31.2	34	18	2	1	15-0	23	4.83	73	.270	.350	8-0	.125	-0	108	-4	-0.4
	Sea A	8	10	.444	23	22	6-2	0-0	159.2	160	68	9	6	62-6	82	3.44	117	.261	.333	0-0	—	0	91	11	1.2
1990	Sea A	11	11	.500	28	28	3	0-0	189.2	188	92	17	6	66-2	121	4.03	98	.260	.324	1-0	.000	-0	87	1	0.0
1991	Sea A	13	14	.481	30	30	5-3	0-0	195.1	199	86	16	10	77-0	108	3.69	112	.268	.343	0-0	—	0	77	10	1.4
Total	4	37	45	.451	109	99	15-6	0-0	676.2	682	303	47	23	254-10	392	3.71	107	.263	.333	37-4	.108	-1	83	23	2.6
HOLMAN, SCOTT Randy Scott B 9.18.1958 Santa Paula, CA BR/TR 6-1/190# d9.20																									
1980	NY N	0	0	—	4	0	0	0-0	7	6	2	0	0	1-1	3	1.29	277	.250	.269	0-0	—	0		1	0.1
1982	NY N	2	1	.667	4	4	1	0-0	26.2	23	10	2	0	7-0	11	2.36	154	.232	.280	9-1	.222	0	79	3	0.4
1983	NY N	1	7	.125	35	10	0	0-0	101	90	48	7	1	52-8	44	3.74	97	.242	.333	23-2	.217	0	71	-1	0.1
Total	3	3	8	.273	43	14	1	0-0	134.2	119	60	9	1	60-9	58	3.34	109	.240	.320	32-3	.219	1	73	3	0.6
HOLMAN, SHAWN Shawn Leroy B 11.10.1964 Sewickley, PA BR/TR 6-2/185# d9.5																									
1989	Det A	0	0	—	5	0	0	0-0	10	8	2	0	0	11-1	9	1.80	212	.211	.380	0-0	—	0		2	0.1
HOLMES, DARREN Darren Lee B 4.25.1966 Asheville, NC BR/TR 6/199# d9.1																									
1990	LA N	0	1	.000	14	0	0	0-0	17.1	15	10	1	0	11-3	19	5.19	71	.238	.342	0-0	—	0		-2	-0.1
1991	Mil A	1	4	.200	40	0	0	3-3	76.1	90	43	6	1	27-1	59	4.72	84	.295	.351	0-0	—	0		-6	-0.4
1992	Mil A	4	4	.500	41	0	0	6-2	42.1	35	12	1	2	11-4	31	2.55	151	.224	.284	0-0	—	0		7	1.4
1993	Col N	3	3	.500	62	0	0	25-4	66.2	56	31	6	2	20-1	60	4.05	118	.222	.285	0-0	—	0		6	0.8
1994	Col N	0	3	.000	29	0	0	3-5	28.1	35	25	5	1	24-4	33	6.35	78	.313	.435	1-0	.000	-0		-5	-0.6
1995	†Col N	6	1	.857	68	0	0	14-4	66.2	59	26	3	1	28-3	61	3.24	166	.237	.313	1-3	.000	-0		13	1.7
1996	Col N	5	4	.556	62	0	0	1-7	77	78	41	8	1	28-2	73	3.97	131	.259	.323	2-0	.000	-0		7	0.7
1997	Col N	9	2	.818	42	6	0	3-1	89.1	113	58	12	0	36-3	70	5.34	97	.314	.373	19-3	.158	-0	148	-1	-0.1
1998	NY A	0	3	.000	34	0	0	2-1	51.1	53	19	4	2	14-3	31	3.33	132	.270	.321	0-0	—	0		7	0.4
1999	†Ari N	4	3	.571	44	0	0	0-2	48.2	50	21	3	1	25-8	35	3.70	124	.262	.350	2-0	.000	-0		5	0.6
2000	Ari N	0	0	—	4	0	0	1-0	2.1	5	3	0	0	1-0	2	11.57	41	.455	.462	0-0	—	0		-2	-0.1
	StL N	0	1	.000	5	0	0	0-1	8.1	12	9	2	1	3-0	5	9.72	47	.364	.410	1-0	.000	-0		-4	-0.4
	Bal A	0	0	—	5	0	0	0-0	4.2	13	13	3	0	5-0	6	25.07	19	.481	.563	0-0	—	0		-11	-0.5
	Ari N	0	0	—	4	0	0	0-0	4	7	3	1	1	0-0	3	6.75	70	.389	.421	0-0	—	0		-1	0.0
	Year	0	1	.000	13	0	0	1-1	14.2	24	15	3	2	4-0	10	9.20	50	.387	.423	1-0	.000	-0		-7	-0.5
2002	†Atl N	2	2	.500	55	0	0	1-1	54.2	41	12	3	2	12-4	47	1.81	226	.210	.262	2-0	.000	-0		14	1.0
2003	Atl N	1	2	.333	48	0	0	0-1	42	47	22	5	0	11-0	46	4.29	99	.280	.322	0-0	—	0		0	0.0
Total	13	35	33	.515	557	6	0	59-32	680	709	348	63	15	256-36	581	4.25	109	.269	.334	28-6	.107	-1	148	27	4.4
HOLMES, CHICK Elwood Marter B 3.22.1896 Beverly, NJ D 4.15.1954 Camden, NJ TR d6.27																									
1918	Phi A	0	0	—	2	0	0	0	2	4	5	0	1	1	0	13.50	22	.400	.500	0-0	—	0		-3	-0.1
HOLMES, JIM James Scott B 8.2.1882 Lawrenceburg, KY D 3.10.1960 Jacksonville, FL d9.8																									
1906	Phi A	0	1	.000	3	1	0	0	9	10	11	0	1	8	1	4.00	68	.286	.432	5-0	.600	1	106	-3	-0.2
1908	Bro N	1	4	.200	13	1	1	0	40	37	19	0	3	20	10	3.37	69	.270	.375	13-0	.077	-1	150	-4	-0.7
Total	2	1	5	.167	16	2	1	0	49	47	30	0	4	28	11	3.49	69	.273	.387	18-0	.222	0	132	-7	-0.9
HOLMES, DUCKY James William B 1.28.1869 Des Moines, IA D 8.6.1932 Truro, IA BL/TR 5-6/170# d8.8 ▲																									
1895	Lou N	1	0	1.000	2	1	1	0	14	16	11	1	1	4	0	5.79	80	.281	.339	161-3	.373	1*	138	-1	0.0
1896	Lou N	0	1	.000	2	1	0	0	12	26	23	0	0	8	3	7.50	58	.433	.500	141-4	.270	0*	213	-7	-0.4
Total	2	1	1	.500	4	2	1	0	26	42	34	1	1	12	3	6.58	68	.359	.423	302-7	.325	1	174	-8	-0.4
HOLSHOUSER, HERM Herman Alexander B 1.20.1907 Rockwell, NC D 7.26.1994 Concord, NC BR/TR 6/170# d4.15																									
1930	StL A	0	1	.000	25	1	0	1	62.1	103	63	8	3	28	37	7.80	63	.376	.439	16-0	.125	-1	211	-20	-0.9
HOLT, CHRIS Christopher Michael B 9.18.1971 Dallas, TX BR/TR 6-4/205# d9.1																									
1996	Hou N	0	1	.000	4	0	0	0-0	4.2	5	3	0	0	3-1	0	5.79	67	.263	.364	1-0	.000	-0		-1	-0.2
1997	Hou N	8	12	.400	33	32	0	0-0	209.2	211	98	17	8	61-4	95	3.52	114	.263	.320	67-9	.090	-3	94	8	0.4
1999	†Hou N	5	13	.278	32	26	0	1-1	164	193	92	12	8	57-1	115	4.66	95	.303	.363	45-7	.067	-2	89	-5	-0.7
2000	Hou N	8	16	.333	34	32	3-1	0-0	207	247	131	22	8	75-2	136	5.35	91	.303	.363	60-5	.100	-2	101	-9	-1.1
2001	Det A	7	9	.438	30	22	1	0-0	151.1	197	102	18	8	57-5	80	5.77	75	.319	.381	4-0	.250	1	107	-22	-2.0
Total	5	28	51	.354	133	112	4-1	1-1	736.2	853	426	69	32	253-13	426	4.76	92	.295	.355	177-21	.090	-7	98	-29	-3.6
HOLTGRAVE, VERN Lavern George "Woody" B 10.18.1942 Aviston, IL BR/TR 6-1/183# d9.26																									
1965	Det A	0	0	—	1	0	0	0	3	4	2	0	0	2-0	2	6.00	58	.308	.400	0-0	—	0		-1	0.0

Year	Tm Lg	W	L	Pct	G	GS	CG-Sho	SV-BS	IP	H	R	HR	HB	BB-IB	SO	ERA	AERA	OAV	OOB	AB-SH	AVG	PB	Sup	APR	PW
HOLTON, BRIAN Brian John B 11.29.1959 McKeesport, PA BR/TR 6/193# d9.9																									
1985	LA N	1	1	.500	3	0	0	0-0	4	9	7	0	0	1-0	1	9.00	39	.450	.476	0-0	—	0		-4	-0.7
1986	LA N	2	3	.400	12	3	0	0-1	24.1	28	13	1	1	6-2	24	4.44	78	.292	.337	5-0	.000	-1	52	-3	-0.5
1987	LA N	3	2	.600	53	1	0	2-1	83.1	87	39	11	0	32-11	58	3.89	102	.269	.332	5-0	.200	0	114	1	0.1
1988	†LA N	7	3	.700	45	0	0	1-0	84.2	69	19	1	1	26-7	49	1.70	196	.228	.289	10-0	.000	-1		15	1.8
1989	Bal A	5	7	.417	39	12	0	0-1	116.1	140	63	11	1	39-1	51	4.02	94	.300	.352	0-0	—	0	111	-7	-0.6
1990	Bal A	2	3	.400	33	0	0	0-1	58	68	31	7	0	21-6	27	4.50	85	.292	.348	0-0	—	0		-5	-0.3
Total	6	20	19	.513	185	16	0	3-4	370.2	401	172	31	3	125-27	210	3.62	102	.278	.334	20-0	.050	-1	102	-3	-0.2
HOLTZ, MIKE Michael James B 10.10.1972 Arlington, VA BL/TL 5-9/172# d7.11																									
1996	Cal A	3	3	.500	30	0	0	0-0	29.1	21	11	1	3	19-2	31	2.45	204	.204	.341	0-0	—	0		7	1.3
1997	Ana A	3	4	.429	66	0	0	2-6	43.1	38	21	7	2	15-4	40	3.32	138	.228	.296	1-0	.000	-0		4	0.7
1998	Ana A	2	2	.500	53	0	0	1-1	30.1	38	16	0	1	15-1	29	4.75	99	.322	.397	0-0	—	0		0	0.0
1999	Ana A	2	3	.400	28	0	0	0-0	22.1	26	20	3	2	15-1	17	8.06	60	.295	.410	0-0	—	0		-7	-1.3
2000	Ana A	3	4	.429	61	0	0	0-0	41	37	26	4	2	18-2	40	5.05	101	.248	.331	0-0	—	0		0	0.0
2001	Ana A	1	2	.333	63	0	0	0-1	37	40	24	5	2	15-4	38	4.86	94	.274	.348	0-0	—	0		-2	-0.1
2002	Oak A	0	0	—	16	0	0	0-1	14	24	11	3	1	9-0	7	6.43	68	.358	.442	0-0	—	0		-3	-0.2
	SD N	2	2	.500	33	0	0	0-3	21	18	14	2	1	21-3	19	4.71	80	.237	.396	2-0	.000	-0		-3	-0.6
Total	7	16	20	.444	350	0	0	3-12	238.1	242	143	25	14	127-17	221	4.68	100	.265	.359	3-0	.000	-0		-4	-0.2
HOLTZMAN, KEN Kenneth Dale B 11.3.1945 St.Louis, MO BR/TL 6-2/175# d9.4 Mil 1967																									
1965	Chi N	0	0	—	3	0	0	0	4	2	4	1	0	3-0	3	2.25	164	.143	.294	0-0	—	0		-1	0.0
1966	Chi N	11	16	.407	34	33	9	0	220.2	194	104	27	4	68-6	171	3.79	97	.235	.295	73-6	.123	-3	87	-1	-0.5
1967	Chi N	9	0	1.000	12	12	3	0	92.2	76	31	11	2	44-7	62	2.53	140	.222	.314	35-6	.200	1	165	9	1.0
1968	Chi N	11	14	.440	34	32	6-3	1	215	201	89	17	6	76-7	151	3.35	94	.248	.316	80-1	.125	-2*	99	-4	-0.7
1969	Chi N	17	13	.567	39	39	12-6	0-0	261.1	248	117	18	5	93-8	176	3.58	112	.247	.313	100-5	.150	-1	109	12	1.1
1970	Chi N	17	11	.607	39	38	15-1	0-0	287.2	271	125	30	3	94-6	202	3.38	133	.248	.307	105-8	.200	1*	105	31	3.0
1971	Chi N	9	15	.375	30	29	9-3	0-1	195	213	108	18	2	64-7	143	4.48	88	.276	.331	69-2	.130	-1	89	-10	-1.3
1972	†Oak A☆	19	11	.633	39	37	16-4	0-1	265.1	232	83	23	4	52-6	134	2.51	114	.236	.276	90-11	.178	2*	139	11	1.5
1973	†Oak A★	21	13	.618	40	40	16-4	0-0	297.1	275	109	22	4	66-5	157	2.97	120	.243	.286	0-0	—	0*	114	23	2.5
1974	†Oak A	19	17	.528	39	38	9-3	0-0	255.1	273	111	14	3	51-3	117	3.07	108	.272	.308	0-0	—	0	108	3	0.5
1975	†Oak A	18	14	.563	39	38	13-2	0-0	266.1	217	111	16	7	108-1	122	3.14	116	.222	.301	2-0	.000	-0	105	13	1.7
1976	Bal A	5	4	.556	13	13	6-1	0-0	97.2	100	34	4	1	35-2	25	2.86	115	.271	.333	0-0	—	0	97	5	0.5
	NY A	9	7	.563	21	21	10-2	0-0	149	165	74	14	0	35-0	41	4.17	82	.283	.322	0-0	—	0	114	-11	-1.1
	Year	14	11	.560	34	34	16-3	0-0	246.2	265	78	18	1	70-2	66	3.65	92	.278	.326	0-0	—	0	108	-6	-0.6
1977	NY A	2	3	.400	18	11	0	0-0	71.2	105	55	7	1	24-2	14	5.78	68	.362	.410	0-0	—	0	120	-17	-0.9
1978	NY A	1	0	1.000	5	3	0	0-0	17.2	21	8	2	0	9-0	3	4.08	89	.313	.395	0-0	—	0	115	0	0.0
	Chi N	0	3	.000	23	6	0	2-0	53	61	40	10	1	35-3	36	6.11	66	.286	.388	10-1	.200	0	93	-11	-0.6
1979	Chi N	6	9	.400	23	20	3-2	0-0	117.2	133	70	15	6	53-7	44	4.59	90	.287	.366	43-0	.233	2*	96	-6	-0.6
Total	15	174	150	.537	451	410	127-31	3-2	2867.1	2787	1273	249	49	910-70	1601	3.49	105	.255	.313	607-40	.163	-1	108	46	6.1
HOLZEMER, MARK Mark Harold B 8.20.1969 Littleton, CO BL/TL 6/165# d8.21																									
1993	Cal A	0	3	.000	5	4	0	0-0	23.1	34	24	2	3	13-0	10	8.87	51	.340	.431	0-0	—	0	81	-10	-1.0
1995	Cal A	0	1	.000	12	0	0	0-0	8.1	11	6	1	1	7-1	5	5.40	87	.306	.432	0-0	—	0		-1	-0.1
1996	Cal A	1	0	1.000	25	0	0	0-0	24.2	35	28	7	3	8-1	20	8.76	57	.327	.387	0-0	—	0		-11	-0.5
1997	Sea A	0	0	—	14	0	0	1-0	9	9	6	0	0	8-0	7	6.00	75	.250	.386	0-0	—	0		-1	0.0
1998	Oak A	1	0	1.000	13	0	0	0-0	9.2	13	6	1	1	3-0	3	5.59	82	.333	.386	0-0	—	0		-1	-0.1
2000	Phi N	0	1	.000	25	0	0	0-1	25.2	36	23	4	1	8-1	19	7.71	60	.336	.388	1-0	.000	-0		-8	-0.4
Total	6	2	5	.286	94	4	0	1-1	100.2	138	93	15	9	47-3	64	7.69	61	.325	.402	1-0	.000	-0	81	-32	-2.1
HONEYCUTT, RICK Frederick Wayne B 6.29.1954 Chattanooga, TN BL/TL 5-11/190# d8.24																									
1977	Sea A	0	1	.000	10	3	0	0-0	29	26	16	7	3	11-2	17	4.34	95	.239	.320	0-0	—	0	73	-1	-0.1
1978	Sea A	5	11	.313	26	24	4-1	0-0	134.1	150	81	12	3	49-5	50	4.89	78	.285	.345	0-0	—	0	96	-15	-1.6
1979	Sea A	11	12	.478	33	28	8-1	0-0	194	201	103	22	6	67-7	83	4.04	108	.268	.331	0-0	—	0	90	4	0.4
1980	Sea A☆	10	17	.370	30	30	9-1	0-0	203.1	221	99	22	3	60-7	79	3.94	105	.280	.330	0-0	—	0	70	5	0.6
1981	Tex A	11	6	.647	20	20	8-2	0-0	127.2	120	49	12	0	17-1	40	3.31	105	.246	.272	0-0	—	0	110	4	0.5
1982	Tex A	5	17	.227	30	26	4-1	0-1	164	201	103	20	3	54-4	64	5.27	74	.305	.356	0-0	—	0	80	-26	-2.9
1983	Tex A★	14	8	.636	25	25	5-2	0-0	174.2	168	59	9	6	37-2	56	**2.42**	**166**	.262	.306	0-0	—	0	101	29	3.7
	†LA N	2	3	.400	9	7	1	0-0	39	46	26	6	2	13-4	18	5.77	62	.297	.359	12-2	.083	-1	116	-8	-0.9
1984	LA N	10	9	.526	29	28	6-2	0-0	183.2	180	72	11	2	51-11	75	2.84	124	.258	.308	56-9	.143	-0	88	12	1.4
1985	†LA N	8	12	.400	31	25	1	1-0	142	141	71	9	1	49-7	67	3.42	102	.261	.321	38-8	.132	0*	94	-2	-0.1
1986	LA N	11	9	.550	32	28	0	0-0	171	164	71	9	3	45-4	100	3.32	104	.249	.300	43-6	.070	0	104	3	0.4
1987	LA N	2	12	.143	27	20	1-1	0-0	115.2	133	74	10	2	45-4	92	4.59	87	.278	.343	30-3	.233	2	59	-12	-1.1
	Oak A	1	4	.200	7	4	0	0-0	23.2	25	17	3	2	9-0	10	5.32	78	.275	.343	0-0	—	0	88	-4	-0.7
1988	†Oak A	3	2	.600	55	0	0	7-2	79.2	74	36	6	3	25-2	47	3.50	108	.253	.312	0-0	—	0		2	0.2
1989	†Oak A	2	2	.500	64	0	0	12-4	76.2	56	26	5	1	26-3	52	2.35	157	.207	.277	0-0	—	0		11	0.9
1990	†Oak A	2	2	.500	63	0	0	7-3	63.1	46	23	2	1	22-2	38	2.70	138	.204	.272	2-0	.000	-0*		7	0.5
1991	Oak A	2	4	.333	43	0	0	0-4	37.2	37	16	3	2	20-3	26	3.58	107	.261	.358	0-0	—	0		1	0.2
1992	†Oak A	1	4	.200	54	0	0	3-4	39	41	19	2	3	10-3	32	3.69	102	.272	.327	0-0	—	0		0	-0.1
1993	Oak A	1	4	.200	52	0	0	1-2	41.2	30	18	2	1	20-6	21	2.81	146	.211	.305	0-0	—	0		4	0.5
1994	Tex A	1	2	.333	42	0	0	1-1	25	37	21	4	2	9-1	18	7.20	67	.349	.410	0-0	—	0		-6	-0.6
1995	Oak A	5	1	.833	49	0	0	2-3	44.2	37	13	5	1	9-0	21	2.42	185	.231	.275	0-0	—	0		11	1.3
	NY A	0	0	—	3	0	0	0-0	1	2	3	1	0	1-0	0	27.00	17	.400	.500	0-0	—	0		-2	-0.1
	Year	5	1	.833	52	0	0	2-3	45.2	39	20	6	1	10-0	21	2.96	151	.236	.282	0-0	—	0		8	1.2
1996	†StL N	2	1	.667	61	0	0	4-3	47.1	42	15	3	0	7-3	30	2.85	147	.240	.265	1-0	.000	1		8	0.6
1997	StL N	0	0	—	2	0	0	0-0	2	5	3	0	0	1-0	2	13.50	31	.500	.545	0-0	—	0		-2	-0.1
Total	21	109	143	.433	797	268	47-11	38-27	2160	2183	1034	185	50	657-81	1038	3.72	104	.264	.320	182-28	.132	2	89	23	2.9
HOOD, DON Donald Harris B 10.16.1949 Florence, SC BL/TL 6-2/180# d7.16																									
1973	†Bal A	3	2	.600	8	4	1-1	1-0	32.1	31	17	1	1	6-0	18	3.90	96	.256	.295	0-0	—	0	72	-1	-0.2
1974	Bal A	1	1	.500	20	2	0	1-1	57.1	47	26	1	0	20-1	26	3.45	100	.223	.289	0-0	—	0*	64	0	0.0
1975	Cle A	6	10	.375	29	19	2	0-0	135.1	136	76	16	0	57-6	51	4.39	86	.268	.340	0-0	—	0*	88	-9	-1.0
1976	Cle A	3	5	.375	33	6	0	1-0	77.2	89	46	5	4	41-3	32	4.87	72	.296	.386	0-0	—	0*	71	-12	-1.1
1977	Cle A	2	1	.667	41	5	1	0-2	105	87	42	3	4	49-7	62	3.00	132	.224	.317	0-0	—	0*	73	10	0.4
1978	Cle A	5	6	.455	36	19	1	0-0	154.2	166	82	13	1	77-5	73	4.48	84	.278	.357	0-0	—	0	111	-11	-0.7
1979	Cle A	1	0	1.000	13	0	0	1-1	22	13	9	1	1	14-1	7	3.68	116	.169	.304	0-0	—	0		2	0.1
	NY A	3	1	.750	27	6	0	1-0	67.1	62	24	3	2	30-1	22	3.07	133	.252	.333	0-0	—	0	133	8	0.5
	Year	4	1	.800	40	6	0	2-1	89.1	75	30	4	3	44-2	29	3.22	128	.232	.326	0-0	—	0	132	11	0.6
1980	StL N	4	6	.400	33	8	1	0-1	82.1	90	39	2	2	34-5	35	3.39	109	.288	.359	20-2	.200	-0*	127	1	0.1
1982	KC A	4	0	1.000	30	3	0	1-1	66.2	71	31	7	2	22-1	31	3.51	117	.276	.333	0-0	—	0	111	3	0.2
1983	KC A	2	3	.400	27	0	0	0-1	47.2	48	20	5	2	14-2	17	2.27	180	.273	.328	0-0	—	0		7	0.7
Total	10	34	35	.493	297	72	6-1	6-7	848.1	840	412	57	19	364-32	374	3.79	101	.263	.339	20-2	.200	-0	99	-2	-1.0
HOOD, WALLY Wallace James Jr. B 9.24.1925 Los Angeles, CA D 6.16.2001 Glendale, CA BR/TR 6-1/190# d9.23 f-Wally																									
1949	NY A	0	0	—	2	0	0	0	2.1	0	0	0	0	1	2	0.00	—	.000	.143	0-0	—	0		1	0.1
HOOK, CHRIS Christopher Wayne B 8.4.1968 San Diego, CA BR/TR 6-5/230# d4.30																									
1995	SF N	5	1	.833	45	0	0	0-0	52.1	55	33	7	3	29-3	40	5.50	74	.274	.369	3-0	.000	-0		-7	-0.8
1996	SF N	0	1	.000	10	0	0	0-0	13.1	16	13	3	2	14-2	4	7.43	55	.308	.464	2-0	.500	0		-5	-0.3
Total	2	5	2	.714	55	0	0	0-0	65.2	71	46	10	5	43-5	44	5.89	69	.281	.390	5-0	.200	0		-12	-1.1
HOOK, JAY James Wesley B 11.18.1936 Waukegan, IL BL/TR 6-2/182# d9.3																									
1957	Cin N	0	1	.000	3	2	0	0	10	6	7	0	0	8-0	6	4.50	91	.176	.326	3-0	.000	-0	86	-1	-0.1

Year	Tm Lg	W	L	Pct	G	GS	CG-Sho	SV-BS	IP	H	R	HR	HB	BB-IB	SO	ERA	AERA	OAV	OOB	AB-SH	AVG	PB	Sup	APR	PW
1958	Cin N	0	1	.000	1	1	0	0	3	3	4	2	0	2-0	5	12.00	35	.250	.357	1-0	.000	-0	22	-2	-0.4
1959	Cin N	5	5	.500	17	15	4	0	79	79	46	10	3	39-1	37	5.13	79	.266	.356	24-2	.125	-1*	100	-7	-0.9
1960	Cin N	11	18	.379	36	33	10-2	0	222	222	119	31	5	73-7	103	4.50	85	.263	.323	72-6	.083	-3	106	-14	-2.0
1961	Cin N	1	3	.250	22	5	0	0	62.2	83	55	14	5	22-2	36	7.76	52	.322	.382	15-0	.133	-1	100	-23	-1.4
1962	NY N	8	19	.296	37	34	13	0	213.2	230	137	31	8	71-4	113	4.84	86	.273	.332	69-6	.203	2*	88	-15	-1.5
1963	NY N	4	14	.222	41	20	3	1	152.2	168	104	21	9	53-2	89	5.48	64	.281	.346	38-2	.237	2	86	-29	-3.1
1964	NY N	0	1	.000	3	2	0	0	9.2	17	10	2	0	7-0	5	9.31	38	.395	.471	3-0	.000	-0	74	-5	-0.5
Total	8	29	62	.319	160	112	30-2	1	752.2	808	482	111	30	275-16	394	5.23	75	.276	.341	225-16	.151	-2	94	-96	-9.9
HOOKER, BUCK William Edward B 8.28.1880 Richmond, VA D 7.2.1929 Richmond, VA TR 5-6/?# d9.5																									
1902	Cin N	0	1	.000	1	1	1	0	8	11	5	1	0	0	0	4.50	67	.324	.324	3-0	.000	-0	68	-1	-0.2
1903	Cin N	0	0	—	1	0	0	0	2.1	2	0	0	0	2	0	0.00	—	.250	.400	1-0	.000	-0*		1	0.0
Total	2	0	1	.000	2	1	1	0	10.1	13	5	1	0	2	0	3.48	90	.310	.341	4-0	.000	-1	68	0	-0.2
HOOPER, BOB Robert Nelson B 5.30.1922 Leamington, ON, CAN D 3.17.1980 New Brunswick, NJ BR/TR 5-11/195# d4.19																									
1950	Phi A	15	10	.600	45	20	3	5	170.1	181	108	15	1	91	58	5.02	91	.272	.361	56-4	.125	-2	132	-10	-1.3
1951	Phi A	12	10	.545	38	23	9	5	189	192	98	13	3	61	64	4.38	98	.267	.327	72-2	.208	-1	103	0	-0.1
1952	Phi A	8	15	.348	43	14	4	6	144.1	158	100	13	4	68	40	5.18	76	.279	.361	41-3	.195	1	60	-21	-2.9
1953	Cle A	5	4	.556	43	0	0	7	69.1	50	37	4	2	38	16	4.02	93	.206	.318	12-0	.083	-1		-3	-0.5
1954	Cle A	0	0	—	17	0	0	2	34.2	39	22	3	1	16	12	4.93	74	.289	.364	5-0	.000	-1		-5	-0.3
1955	Cin N	0	2	.000	8	0	0	0	13	20	12	2	0	6-0	6	7.62	56	.357	.419	1-0	.000	-0		-4	-0.6
Total	6	40	41	.494	194	57	16	25	620.2	640	377	50	11	280-0	196	4.80	87	.268	.348	187-9	.166	-4	106	-43	-5.7
HOOTEN, LEON Michael Leon B 4.4.1948 Downey, CA BR/TR 5-11/180# d4.13																									
1974	Oak A	0	0	—	6	0	0	0-0	8.1	6	3	1	1	4-0	1	3.24	103	.207	.314	0-0	—	0		0	0.0
HOOTON, BURT Burt Carlton B 2.7.1950 Greenville, TX BR/TR 6-1/210# d6.17 C4																									
1971	Chi N	2	0	1.000	3	3	2-1	0-0	21.1	8	5	2	0	10-0	22	2.11	187	.111	.220	7-0	.000	-1	98	4	0.3
1972	Chi N	11	14	.440	33	31	9-3	0-1	218.1	201	78	13	1	81-7	132	2.80	136	.246	.313	72-5	.125	-1	85	22	2.5
1973	Chi N	14	17	.452	42	34	9-2	0-1	239.2	248	107	12	4	73-7	134	3.68	107	.270	.325	70-5	.129	-0	95	8	0.9
1974	Chi N	7	11	.389	48	21	3-1	1-2	176.1	214	112	16	3	51-6	94	4.80	80	.299	.344	50-7	.060	-4	109	-19	-2.0
1975	Chi N	0	2	.000	3	3	0	0-0	11	18	12	2	0	4-0	5	8.18	47	.383	.431	3-0	.000	-0	76	-5	-0.8
	LA N	18	7	.720	31	30	12-4	0-0	223.2	172	76	16	0	64-2	148	2.82	121	.210	.265	70-13	.129	1	115	17	1.8
	Year	18	9	.667	34	33	12-4	0-0	234.2	190	80	18	0	68-2	153	3.07	112	.219	.274	73-13	.123	0	112	13	1.0
1976	LA N	11	15	.423	33	33	8-4	0-0	226.2	203	93	16	1	60-6	116	3.26	104	.241	.290	62-13	.097	-2	99	2	0.0
1977	†LA N	12	7	.632	32	31	6-2	1-0	223.1	184	74	14	3	60-5	153	2.62	146	.225	.279	67-14	.164	-0	108	30	2.4
1978	†LA N	19	10	.655	32	32	10-3	0-0	236	196	74	17	0	61-4	104	2.71	130	.226	.275	67-18	.149	1	94	25	3.1
1979	LA N	11	10	.524	29	29	12-1	0-0	212	191	85	11	2	63-4	129	2.97	123	.244	.298	75-8	.147	-1*	117	14	1.3
1980	LA N	14	8	.636	34	33	4-2	1-0	206.2	194	90	22	0	64-1	118	3.66	96	.249	.305	64-14	.063	-3	107	-2	-0.6
1981	†LA N★	11	6	.647	23	23	5-4	0-0	142.1	124	42	3	2	33-2	74	2.28	146	.237	.281	42-7	.190	2	103	16	2.1
1982	LA N	4	7	.364	21	21	2-2	0-0	120.2	130	57	5	2	33-2	51	4.03	86	.275	.325	35-6	.086	-1	98	-6	-0.6
1983	LA N	9	8	.529	33	27	2	0-0	160	156	86	21	2	59-4	87	4.22	85	.254	.319	50-4	.160	1	112	-9	-0.9
1984	LA N	3	6	.333	54	6	0	4-1	110	109	43	5	0	43-6	62	3.44	103	.263	.331	14-3	.071	-1	79	4	0.2
1985	Tex A	5	8	.385	29	20	2	0-0	124	149	78	18	0	40-2	62	5.23	81	.297	.346	0-0	—	0	86	-13	-1.2
Total	15	151	136	.526	480	377	86-29	7-5	2652	2497	1112	193	20	799-58	1491	3.38	108	.250	.304	748-117	.123	-9	101	88	8.5
HOOVER, JOHN John Nicklaus B 11.22.1962 Fresno, CA BR/TR 6-2/190# d5.23																									
1990	Tex A	0	0	—	2	0	0	0-0	4.2	8	6	0	0	3-0	0	11.57	34	.364	.440	0-0	—	0		-4	-0.2
HOOVER, DICK Richard Lloyd B 12.11.1925 Columbus, OH D 4.12.1981 Lake Placid, FL BL/TL 6/170# d4.16																									
1952	Bos N	0	0	—	2	0	0	0	4.2	8	4	1	0	3	0	7.71	47	.348	.423	0-0	—	0		-2	-0.1
HOPE, JOHN John Alan B 12.21.1970 Ft.Lauderdale, FL BR/TR 6-3/195# d8.29																									
1993	Pit N	0	2	.000	7	7	0	0-0	38	47	19	2	2	8-3	8	4.03	101	.313	.354	13-0	.077	-1	117	0	-0.1
1994	Pit N	0	0	—	9	0	0	0-0	14	18	12	1	2	4-0	6	5.79	75	.310	.375	3-0	.333	0		-3	-0.1
1995	Pit N	0	0	—	3	0	0	0-0	2.1	8	8	0	3	4-0	2	30.86	14	.615	.714	0-0	—	0		-6	-0.3
1996	Pit N	1	3	.250	5	4	0	0-0	19.1	17	18	5	2	11-1	13	6.98	63	.243	.357	5-1	.200	-0	83	-6	-1.0
Total	4	1	5	.167	24	11	0	0-0	73.2	90	57	8	9	27-4	29	5.99	70	.309	.382	21-1	.143	-1	104	-15	-1.5
HOPE, SAM Samuel B 12.4.1878 Brooklyn, NY D 6.30.1946 Greenport, NY BR/TR 5-10/?# d8.5																									
1907	Phi A	0	0	—	1	0	0	0	0.1	3	1	0	0	0	0	0.00	—	.750	.750	0-0	—	0		0	0.0
HOPKINS, PAUL Paul Henry B 9.25.1904 Chester, CT D 1.2.03 Deep River, CT BR/TR 6/175# d9.29																									
1927	Was A	1	0	1.000	2	1	0	0	9	13	6	1	0	4	5	5.00	81	.361	.425	3-0	.667	1	185	-1	0.0
1929	Was A	0	1	.000	7	0	0	0	16.1	15	5	1	0	9	5	2.20	192	.250	.348	3-0	.000	-1		4	0.1
	StL A	0	0	—	2	0	0	0	2	0	0	0	0	2	1	0.00	—	.000	.286	0-0	—	0		1	0.0
	Year	0	1	.000	9	0	0	0	18.1	15	14	1	0	11	6	1.96	217	.231	.342	3-0	.000	-1		5	0.1
Total	2	1	1	.500	11	1	0	0	27.1	28	11	2	0	15	11	2.96	142	.277	.371	6-0	.333	1	185	4	0.1
HOPPER, LEFTY Clarence F. B 5.27.1875 Jersey City, NJ D 9.27.1959 San Diego, CA TL d10.10																									
1898	Bro N	0	2	.000	2	2	2	0	11	14	11	0	0	5	5	4.91	73	.304	.373	4-0	.000	-1	59	-3	-0.4
HOPPER, JIM James McDaniel B 9.1.1919 Charlotte, NC D 1.23.1982 Charlotte, NC BR/TR 6-1/175# d4.21																									
1946	Pit N	0	1	.000	2	1	0	0	4	6	5	1	0	3	1	11.25	31	.316	.409	0-0	—	0	49	-3	-0.5
HOPPER, BILL William Booth "Bird Dog" B 10.26.1890 Jackson, TN D 1.14.1965 Allen Park, MI BR/TR 6/175# d9.11																									
1913	StL N	0	3	.000	3	3	2	0	24	20	14	2	3	8	3	3.75	86	.230	.316	8-0	.375	1	39	-2	-0.1
1914	StL N	0	0	—	3	0	0	0	5	6	3	0	0	5	1	3.60	78	.286	.423	0-0	—	0		0	0.0
1915	Was A	0	1	.000	13	0	0	1	31.1	39	23	0	1	16	8	4.60	65	.348	.434	5-0	.200	0		-6	-0.3
Total	3	0	4	.000	19	3	2	1	60.1	65	40	2	4	29	12	4.18	73	.295	.387	13-0	.308	1	39	-8	-0.4
HORAN, JOHN Patrick J. B 1863 , Ireland 5-10.5/160# d5.17																									
1884	CP U	3	6	.333	13	10	9	0	98	94	73	0		24	55	3.49	70	.236	.279	68	.088	-8*	91	-11	-1.4
HORLEN, JOE Joel Edward B 8.14.1937 San Antonio, TX BR/TR 6/175# d9.4																									
1961	Chi A	1	3	.250	5	4	0	0	17.2	25	15	2	0	13-0	11	6.62	59	.338	.437	7-1	.000	-1	107	-6	-1.1
1962	Chi A	7	6	.538	20	19	5-1	0	108.2	108	62	10	2	43-2	63	4.89	80	.262	.333	38-4	.053	-3	120	-11	-1.3
1963	Chi A	11	7	.611	33	21	3	0	124	122	50	10	2	55-8	61	3.27	107	.261	.339	40-2	.225	1	121	4	0.7
1964	Chi A	13	9	.591	32	28	9-2	0	210.2	142	54	11	4	55-4	138	1.88	184	**.190**	**.248**	69-8	.159	-1	75	37	4.0
1965	Chi A	13	13	.500	34	34	7-4	0	219	203	88	16	3	39-9	125	2.88	111	.245	.279	68-8	.132	0	95	4	0.5
1966	Chi A	10	13	.435	37	29	4-2	1	211	185	64	14	6	53-11	124	2.43	130	.233	.285	60-4	.067	-4*	83	20	2.2
1967	Chi A☆	19	7	**.731**	35	35	13-**6**	0	258	188	66	13	4	58-4	103	**2.06**	**151**	.203	**.253**	83-8	.169	1*	107	**34**	**3.8**
1968	Chi A	12	14	.462	35	35	4-1	0	223.2	197	75	16	14	70-7	102	2.37	127	.238	.307	67-5	.104	-1*	72	14	1.6
1969	Chi A	13	16	.448	36	35	7-2	0-1	235.2	237	105	20	5	77-10	121	3.78	102	.261	.321	77-7	.182	-1	80	3	0.1
1970	Chi A	6	16	.273	28	26	4	0-0	172.1	198	99	18	4	41-4	77	4.86	80	.287	.330	52-5	.115	-2	70	-15	-1.7
1971	Chi A	8	9	.471	34	18	3	2-1	137.1	150	72	12	5	30-2	82	4.26	84	.284	.325	40-2	.100	-2*	116	-8	-1.1
1972	†Oak A	3	4	.429	32	6	0	1-0	84	74	33	3	4	20-4	58	3.00	95	.236	.291	17-0	.176	-0	88	-2	-0.2
Total	12	116	117	.498	361	290	59-18	4-2	2002	1829	783	145	53	554-65	1065	3.11	110	.243	.299	618-54	.134	-12	92	74	7.5
HORNE, TRADER Berlyn Dale "Sonny" B 4.12.1899 Bachman, OH D 2.3.1983 Franklin, OH BB/TR 5-9/155# d4.24																									
1929	Chi N	1	1	.500	11	1	0	0	23	24	20	3	0	21	6	5.09	91	.273	.413	5-1	.400	0	76	-3	-0.2
HORNER, JACK William Frank B 9.21.1863 Baltimore, MD D 7.14.1910 New Orleans, LA BR d5.7																									
1894	Bal N	0	1	.000	2	1	1	1	11	15	12	0	1	7	2	9.00	61	.319	.418	6-0	.167	-0	91	-3	-0.3
HORSEY, HANSON Hanson B 11.26.1889 Galena, MD D 12.1.1949 Millington, MD BR/TR 5-11/165# d4.27																									
1912	Cin N	0	0	—	1	0	0	0	4	14	10	0	0	3	0	22.50	15	.609	.654	2-0	.000	-0		-7	-0.3

Year	Tm Lg	W	L	Pct	G	GS	CG-Sho	SV-BS	IP	H	R	HR	HB	BB-IB	SO	ERA	AERA	OAV	OOB	AB-SH	AVG	PB	Sup	APR	PW
HORSMAN, VINCE Vincent Stanley Joseph B 3.9.1967 Halifax, NS, CAN BR/TL 6-2/180# d9.5																									
1991	Tor A	0	0	—	4	0	0	0-0	4	2	0	0	0	3-1	2	0.00	—	.167	.333	0-0	—	0		2	0.1
1992	Oak A	2	1	.667	58	0	0	1-1	43.1	39	13	3	0	21-4	18	2.49	150	.252	.339	0-0	—	0		7	0.4
1993	Oak A	2	0	1.000	40	0	0	0-0	25	25	15	2	3	15-1	17	5.40	76	.255	.371	0-0	—	0		-3	-0.3
1994	Oak A	0	1	.000	33	0	0	0-0	29.1	29	17	2	1	11-2	20	4.91	90	.266	.331	0-0	—	0		-1	0.0
1995	Min A	0	0	—	6	0	0	0-0	9	12	8	2	0	4-1	4	7.00	68	.333	.390	0-0	—	0		-2	-0.1
Total	5	4	2	.667	141	0	0	1-1	110.2	107	53	9	4	54-9	61	4.07	101	.261	.349	0-0	—	0		3	0.1
HORSTMANN, OSCAR Oscar Theodore B 6.2.1891 Alma, MO D 5.11.1977 Salina, KS BR/TR 5-11/165# d4.18 Mil 1918																									
1917	StL N	9	4	.692	35	11	4-1	1	138.2	111	67	5	4	54	50	3.44	78	.225	.307	46-2	.196	1	132	-13	-1.2
1918	StL N	0	2	.000	9	2	0	0	23	29	18	0	0	14	6	5.48	49	.349	.443	4-0	.000	-0	70	-7	-0.6
1919	StL N	0	1	.000	6	2	0	0	15	14	6	0	0	12	5	3.00	93	.264	.400	2-1	.500	0	114	0	0.0
Total	3	9	7	.563	50	15	4-1	1	176.2	154	91	5	4	80	61	3.67	74	.245	.334	52-3	.192	1	121	-20	-1.8
HORTON, ELMER Elmer E. "Herky Jerky" B 9.4.1869 Hamilton, OH D 8.12.1920 Vienna, NY d9.24																									
1896	Pit N	0	2	.000	2	2	2	0	15	22	18	0	1	9	3	9.60	44	.338	.427	7-0	.000	-1	68	-8	-0.8
1898	Bro N	0	1	.000	1	1	1	0	9	16	13	0	0	6	0	10.00	36	.381	.458	4-0	.250	-0	59	-6	-0.5
Total	2	0	3	.000	3	3	3	0	24	38	31	0	1	15	3	9.75	41	.355	.439	11-0	.091	-1	66	-14	-1.3
HORTON, RICKY Ricky Neal B 7.30.1959 Poughkeepsie, NY BL/TL 6-2/195# d4.7																									
1984	StL N	9	4	.692	37	18	1-1	1-1	125.2	140	53	14	1	39-2	76	3.44	101	.285	.337	31-6	.065	-2*	126	1	0.1
1985	†StL N	3	2	.600	49	3	0	1-1	89.2	84	30	5	3	34-13	59	2.91	122	.251	.324	16-2	.063	-0	108	8	0.5
1986	StL N	4	3	.571	42	9	1	3-0	100.1	77	25	7	1	26-7	49	2.24	163	.218	.271	18-2	.056	0	68	17	1.4
1987	†StL N	8	3	.727	67	6	0	7-1	125	127	58	15	0	42-10	55	3.82	109	.263	.321	29-0	.172	0*	91	4	0.6
1988	Chi A	6	10	.375	52	9	1	2-1	109.1	120	64	6	5	36-4	28	4.86	82	.291	.349	0-0	—	0	99	-9	-1.2
	†LA N	1	1	.500	12	0	0	0-2	9	11	7	2	0	2-0	8	5.00	67	.306	.333	0-0	—	0		-2	-0.5
1989	LA N	0	0	—	23	0	0	0-1	26.2	35	15	1	1	11-2	12	5.06	68	.343	.405	1-0	.000	-0		-4	-0.2
	StL N	0	3	.000	11	8	0	0-0	45.2	50	24	2	3	10-2	14	4.73	77	.282	.328	11-2	.273	1	61	-4	-0.2
	Year	0	3	.000	34	8	0	0-1	72.1	85	27	3	4	21-4	26	4.85	73	.305	.357	12-2	.250	1	62	-8	-0.4
1990	StL N	1	1	.500	32	0	0	1-1	42	52	25	3	1	22-7	18	4.93	78	.315	.397	4-1	.000	-0		-5	-0.2
Total	7	32	27	.542	325	53	3-1	15-8	673.1	696	301	55	15	222-47	319	3.76	100	.273	.331	110-13	.109	-1	95	6	0.3
HOSKINS, DAVE David Taylor B 8.3.1925 Greenwood, MS D 4.2.1970 Flint, MI BL/TR 6-1/180# d4.18																									
1953	Cle A	9	3	.750	26	7	3	1	112.2	102	57	9	4	38	55	3.99	94	.243	.312	58-1	.259	4*	162	-4	0.1
1954	Cle A	0	1	.000	14	1	0	0	26.2	29	10	3	0	10	9	3.04	121	.284	.342	8-0	.000	-1*	312	2	0.0
Total	2	9	4	.692	40	8	3	1	139.1	131	67	12	4	48	64	3.81	98	.251	.318	66-1	.227	3	181	-2	0.1
HOST, GENE Eugene Earl "Twinkles" or "Slick" B 1.1.1933 Leeper, PA D 8.20.1998 Nashville, TN BB/TL 5-11/190# d9.16																									
1956	Det A	0	0	—	1	1	0	0	4.2	9	4	2	0	2-0	5	7.71	53	.409	.458	2-0	.000	-0	173	-2	-0.1
1957	KC A	0	2	.000	11	2	0	0	23.2	29	19	5	0	14-0	9	7.23	55	.315	.398	5-0	.000	-1	90	-7	-0.6
Total	2	0	2	.000	12	3	0	0	28.1	38	23	7	0	16-0	14	7.31	55	.333	.409	7-0	.000	-1	119	-9	-0.7
HOUCK, BYRON Byron Simon "Duke" B 8.28.1891 Prosper, MN D 6.17.1969 Santa Cruz, CA BR/TR 6/175# d5.15																									
1912	Phi A	8	8	.500	30	17	10	1	180.2	148	79	1	12	74	75	2.94	105	.234	.326	62-4	.065	-7	144	3	-0.5
1913	Phi A	14	6	.700	41	19	4-1	0	176	147	93	3	6	122	71	4.14	67	.237	.368	60-5	.083	-4	127	-26	-3.1
1914	Phi A	0	0	—	3	3	0	0	11	14	9	0	0	6	4	3.27	80	.318	.400	3-0	.333	0	195	-3	-0.1
	Bro F	2	6	.250	17	9	3	0	92	95	48	4	2	43	45	3.13	92	.272	.355	30-1	.233	2	95	-5	-0.3
1918	StL A	2	4	.333	27	2	0	2	71.2	58	24	0	0	29	29	2.39	115	.225	.303	20-0	.150	-1	96	**3**	0.2
Total	4	26	24	.520	118	50	17-1	3	531.1	462	253	8	20	274	224	3.30	87	.243	.344	175-10	.114	-9	130	-28	-3.8
HOUGH, CHARLIE Charles Oliver B 1.5.1948 Honolulu, HI BR/TR 6-2/190# d8.12 C4																									
1970	LA N	0	0	—	8	0	0	2-0	17	18	11	7	0	11-0	8	5.29	72	.265	.367	3-0	.333	0		-3	-0.1
1971	LA N	0	0	—	4	0	0	0-0	4.1	3	3	1	0	3-0	4	4.15	78	.200	.333	0-0	—	0		-1	0.0
1972	LA N	0	0	—	2	0	0	0-0	2.2	2	1	0	1	2-0	4	3.38	99	.200	.385	0-0	—	0		0	0.0
1973	LA N	4	2	.667	37	0	0	5-2	71.2	52	24	3	6	45-2	70	2.76	125	.207	.338	14-1	.214	0		6	0.6
1974	†LA N	9	4	.692	49	0	0	1-2	96	65	45	12	4	40-2	63	3.75	91	.196	.285	12-3	.000	-1		-3	-0.6
1975	LA N	3	7	.300	38	0	0	4-2	61	43	25	3	8	34-0	34	2.95	116	.195	.323	6-1	.333	1		2	0.4
1976	LA N	12	8	.600	77	0	0	18-4	142.2	102	43	6	8	77-3	81	2.21	153	.200	.314	21-0	.286	2		**17**	**3.1**
1977	†LA N	6	12	.333	70	1	0	22-5	127.1	98	53	10	7	70-6	105	3.32	115	.213	.323	22-0	.182	1	46	7	1.2
1978	†LA N	5	5	.500	55	0	0	7-4	93.1	69	38	6	5	48-4	66	3.28	107	.205	.313	12-0	.333	1		3	0.5
1979	LA N	7	5	.583	42	14	0	0-1	151.1	152	88	16	8	66-2	76	4.76	77	.264	.346	38-5	.158	-0	144	-17	-1.3
1980	LA N	1	3	.250	19	1	0	1-0	32.1	37	21	4	2	21-0	25	5.57	63	.291	.392	2-0	.500	0	102	-7	-0.8
	Tex A	2	2	.500	16	2	2-1	0-0	61.1	54	30	2	3	37-2	47	3.96	98	.240	.353	0-0	—	0	126	0	0.0
1981	Tex A	4	1	.800	21	5	2	1-1	82	61	30	4	3	31-1	69	2.96	117	.207	.289	0-0	—	0	124	5	0.2
1982	Tex A	16	13	.552	34	34	12-2	0-0	228	217	111	21	7	72-5	128	3.95	98	.251	.313	0-0	—	0	101	-3	-0.2
1983	Tex A	15	13	.536	34	33	11-3	0-0	252	219	96	22	3	95-0	152	3.18	126	.238	.309	0-0	—	0	92	26	2.9
1984	Tex A	16	14	.533	36	**36**	**17**-1	0-0	266	260	127	26	9	94-3	164	3.76	111	.255	.322	0-0	—	0	94	11	1.3
1985	Tex A	14	16	.467	34	34	14-1	0-0	250.1	198	102	23	7	83-1	141	3.31	128	.215	.283	0-0	—	0	78	25	2.8
1986	Tex A★	17	10	.630	33	33	7-2	0-0	230.1	188	115	32	9	89-2	146	3.79	114	.221	.301	0-0	—	0	105	10	1.1
1987	Tex A	18	13	.581	40	**40**	13	0-0	**285.1**	238	159	36	19	124-1	223	3.79	119	.223	.311	0-0	—	0	107	13	1.3
1988	Tex A	15	16	.484	34	34	10	0-0	252	202	111	20	12	126-1	174	3.32	123	.221	.321	0-0	—	0	81	18	2.3
1989	Tex A	10	13	.435	30	30	5-1	0-0	182	168	97	28	6	95-2	94	4.35	91	.245	.340	0-0	—	0	90	-6	-0.8
1990	Tex A	12	12	.500	32	32	5	0-0	218.2	190	108	24	11	119-2	114	4.07	96	.235	.338	0-0	—	0	102	-2	-0.2
1991	Chi A	9	10	.474	31	29	4-1	0-0	199.1	167	98	21	11	94-0	107	4.02	99	.229	.320	0-0	—	0	96	-1	-0.1
1992	Chi A	7	12	.368	27	27	4	0-0	176.1	160	88	19	7	66-2	76	3.93	98	.239	.311	0-0	—	0	87	-2	-0.3
1993	Fla N	9	16	.360	34	34	0	0-0	204.1	202	109	20	8	71-2	126	4.27	101	.259	.325	63-4	.032	-5	62	0	-0.5
1994	Fla N	5	9	.357	21	21	1-1	0-0	113.2	118	74	17	10	52-1	65	5.15	85	.274	.359	33-4	.121	-1	78	-10	-1.1
Total	25	216	216	.500	858	440	107-13	61-21	3801.1	3283	1807	383	174	1665-44	2362	3.75	106	.233	.319	226-18	.146	-2	95	88	11.7
HOUSE, CRAIG Craig Michael B 7.8.1977 Naha A.F.B., Okinawa BR/TR 6-2/210# d8.6																									
2000	Col N	1	1	.500	16	0	0	0-0	13.2	13	11	3	2	17-0	8	7.24	80	.265	.464	0-0	—	0		-1	-0.2
HOUSE, PAT Patrick Lory B 9.1.1940 Boise, ID BL/TL 6-3/185# d9.6																									
1967	Hou N	1	0	1.000	6	0	0	1	4	3	2	0	1	0-0	2	4.50	74	.214	.267	0-0	—	0		0	-0.1
1968	Hou N	1	1	.500	18	0	0	0	16.1	21	15	0	2	6-3	6	7.71	38	.323	.392	0-0	—	0		-8	-1.0
Total	2	2	1	.667	24	0	0	1	20.1	24	17	0	3	6-3	8	7.08	43	.304	.371	0-0	—	0		-8	-1.1
HOUSE, TOM Thomas Ross B 4.29.1947 Seattle, WA BL/TL 5-11/190# d6.23 C8																									
1971	Atl N	1	0	1.000	11	1	0	0-0	20.2	20	8	2	1	3-0	11	3.05	122	.263	.296	5-0	.400	1	143	1	0.1
1972	Atl N	0	0	—	8	0	0	2-0	9.1	7	3	1	1	6-0	7	2.89	131	.226	.368	1-0	.000	-0		1	0.0
1973	Atl N	4	2	.667	52	0	0	4-2	67.1	58	37	13	2	31-7	42	4.68	84	.243	.326	10-2	.200	0		-4	-0.4
1974	Atl N	6	2	.750	56	0	0	11-5	102.2	74	26	5	3	27-8	64	1.93	197	.203	.261	10-3	.400	1		20	2.2
1975	Atl N	7	7	.500	58	0	0	11-4	79.1	79	39	2	2	36-10	36	3.18	119	.262	.342	9-0	.111	-0		3	0.6
1976	Bos A	1	3	.250	36	0	0	4-2	43.2	39	22	4	2	19-4	27	4.33	90	.241	.324	0-0	—	0		-1	0.0
1977	Bos A	1	0	1.000	8	0	0	0-0	7.2	15	11	0	0	6-0	6	12.91	35	.405	.488	0-0	—	0		-6	-0.7
	Sea A	4	5	.444	26	11	1	1-0	89.1	94	42	12	4	19-2	39	3.93	105	.268	.310	0-0	—	0	63	2	0.2
	Year	5	5	.500	34	11	1	1-0	97	109	45	12	4	25-2	45	4.64	90	.281	.329	0-0	—	0	63	-4	-0.5
1978	Sea A	5	4	.556	34	9	3	0-0	116	130	70	10	5	35-2	29	4.66	82	.289	.339	0-0	—	0	128	-12	-0.8
Total	8	29	23	.558	289	21	4	33-13	536	516	258	49	20	182-33	261	3.79	103	.256	.320	35-5	.257	1	94	4	1.2
HOUSE, FRED Willard Edwin B 10.3.1890 Cabool, MO D 11.16.1923 Kansas City, MO BR/TR 6-3/190# d4.22																									
1913	Det A	1	2	.333	19	2	0	0	53.2	64	40	1	2	17	16	5.20	56	.328	.388	10-0	.000	-1	127	-12	-0.7
HOUSEMAN, FRANK Frank B , Netherlands d9.2																									
1886	Bal AA	0	1	.000	1	1	1	0	8	6	3	0	1	1	5	3.38	101	.182	.229	4	.250	-0	35	1	0.1

Year	Tm Lg	W	L	Pct	G	GS	CG-Sho	SV-BS	IP	H	R	HR	HB	BB-IB	SO	ERA	AERA	OAV	OOB	AB-SH	AVG	PB	Sup	APR	PW
HOUSER, JOE Joseph William B 7.3.1891 Steubenville, OH D 1.3.1953 Orlando, FL BL/TL 5-9.5/160# d4.24																									
1914	Buf F	0	1	.000	7	2	0	0	23	21	16	1	0	20	6	5.48	54	.250	.394	7-0	.143	-0*	127	-6	-0.3
HOUTTEMAN, ART Arthur Joseph B 8.7.1927 Detroit, MI D 5.6.2003 Rochester Hills, MI BR/TR 6-2/188# d4.29 Mil 1951																									
1945	Det A	0	2	.000	13	0	0	0	25.1	27	17	1	1	11	9	5.33	66	.270	.348	5-0	.000	-1		-4	-0.4
1946	Det A	0	1	.000	1	1	0	0	8	15	8	1	0	0	2	9.00	41	.385	.385	2-1	.500	0	164	-4	-0.4
1947	Det A	7	2	.778	23	9	7-2	0	110.2	106	51	6	1	36	58	3.42	110	.247	.306	40-0	.300	2	123	3	0.4
1948	Det A	2	16	.111	43	20	4	10	164.1	186	101	11	2	52	74	4.66	94	.287	.342	56-1	.196	-2	69	-7	-0.8
1949	Det A	15	10	.600	34	25	13-2	0	203.2	227	101	19	5	59	85	3.71	112	.282	.335	78-2	.244	1*	108	7	1.1
1950	Det A★	19	12	.613	41	34	21-**4**	4	274.2	257	112	29	8	99	88	3.54	132	.251	.322	93-11	.151	-3	100	38	3.7
1952	Det A	8	20	.286	35	28	10-2	1	221	218	116	19	5	65	109	4.36	87	.253	.309	69-6	.101	-4*	71	-11	-1.7
1953	Det A	2	6	.250	16	9	3-1	1	68.2	87	50	11	4	29	28	5.90	69	.309	.381	19-2	.158	0	80	-14	-1.4
	Cle A	7	7	.500	22	13	6-1	3	109	113	56	4	5	25	40	3.80	99	.269	.318	34-2	.147	-1*	133	-3	-0.4
	Year	9	13	.409	38	22	9-2	4	177.2	200	62	15	9	54	68	4.61	84	.285	.344	53-4	.151	-1	111	-18	-1.8
1954	†Cle A	15	7	.682	32	25	11-1	0	188	198	80	14	3	59	68	3.35	110	.273	.328	65-8	.277	5	131	7	1.3
1955	Cle A	10	6	.625	35	12	3-1	0	124.1	126	63	15	2	44-1	53	3.98	100	.265	.328	38-4	.158	-1	89	0	0.1
1956	Cle A	2	2	.500	22	4	0	1	46.2	60	39	5	4	31-2	19	6.56	64	.317	.417	12-1	.167	-1*	95	-12	-1.0
1957	Cle A	0	0	—	3	0	0	0	4	6	3	1	0	3-0	3	6.75	55	.353	.450	0-0	—	0		-1	-0.1
	Bal A	0	0	—	5	1	0	0	6.2	20	13	0	0	3-0	3	17.55	20	.513	.548	2-0	.500	0	149	-10	-0.5
	Year	0	0	—	8	1	0	0	10.2	26	19	1	0	6-0	6	13.50	27	.464	.516	2-0	.500	0	147	-12	-0.6
Total	12	87	91	.489	325	181	78-14	20	1555	1646	810	136	40	516-3	639	4.14	99	.272	.333	513-38	.193	-4	99	-11	-0.1
HOVLIK, ED Edward Charles B 8.20.1891 Cleveland, OH D 3.19.1955 Painesville, OH BR/TR 6/180# d7.14 b-Joe																									
1918	Was A	2	1	.667	8	2	1	0	28	25	10	0	0	10	10	1.29	212	.272	.343	8-0	.125	-1	207	3	0.2
1919	Was A	0	0	—	3	0	0	0	5.2	12	10	0	0	9	3	12.71	25	.480	.618	2-0	.000	-0		-6	-0.3
Total	2	2	1	.667	11	2	1	0	33.2	37	20	0	0	19	13	3.21	88	.316	.412	10-0	.100	-1	207	-3	-0.1
HOVLIK, JOE Joseph B 8.16.1884 , Czechoslovakia D 11.3.1951 Oxford Junction, IA BR/TR 5-10.5/194# d7.10 b-Ed																									
1909	Was A	0	0	—	3	0	0	0	6	13	10	0	1	3	1	4.50	54	.419	.486	2-0	.000	0		-3	-0.1
1910	Was A	0	0	—	1	0	0	0	1.2	6	5	0	1	0	0	16.20	15	.500	.538	0-0	—	0		-3	-0.1
1911	Chi A	2	0	1.000	12	3	1-1	0	47	47	21	1	0	20	24	3.06	105	.257	.330	13-0	.077	-0	104	1	0.1
Total	3	2	0	1.000	16	3	1-1	0	54.2	66	36	1	2	23	25	3.62	86	.292	.363	15-0	.067	-0	104	-5	-0.1
HOWARD, BEN Benjamin Richard B 1.15.1979 Danville, IL BR/TR 6-2/190# d4.28																									
2002	SD N	0	1	.000	3	2	0	0-0	10.2	13	11	4	0	14-1	10	9.28	41	.302	.466	4-1	.000	-0	73	-7	-0.6
2003	SD N	1	3	.250	6	6	0	0-0	34.2	31	17	10	0	15-1	24	3.63	109	.235	.313	11-0	.091	-1	87	0	0.0
Total	2	1	4	.200	9	8	0	0-0	45.1	44	28	14	0	29-2	34	4.96	79	.251	.356	15-1	.067	-1	84	-7	-0.6
HOWARD, BRUCE Bruce Ernest B 3.23.1943 Salisbury, MD BB/TR 6-2/180# d9.4 s-David																									
1963	Chi A	2	1	.667	7	0	0	1	17	12	7	0	0	14-0	9	2.65	132	.207	.361	4-0	.250	0		1	0.2
1964	Chi A	2	1	.667	3	3	1-1	0	22.1	10	2	0	1	8-1	17	0.81	429	.139	.235	8-0	.000	-1	69	7	0.9
1965	Chi A	9	8	.529	30	22	1-1	0	148	123	61	13	1	72-5	120	3.47	92	.224	.315	41-6	.146	2	106	-3	-0.2
1966	Chi A	9	5	.643	27	21	4-2	0	149	110	48	14	1	44-2	85	2.30	138	.202	.262	43-2	.070	-1	95	14	1.2
1967	Chi A	3	10	.231	30	17	1	0	112.2	102	55	9	3	52-1	76	3.43	90	.240	.325	28-3	.179	1	68	-6	-0.5
1968	Bal A	0	2	.000	10	5	0	0	31	30	16	2	2	26-2	19	3.77	78	.268	.406	7-2	.286	2	71	-3	0.0
	Was A	1	4	.200	13	7	0	0	48.2	62	30	7	0	23-2	23	5.36	54	.330	.401	16-0	.000	-2	68	-12	-1.3
	Year	1	6	.143	23	12	0	0	79.2	92	32	9	2	49-4	42	4.74	62	.307	.403	23-2	.087	0	70	-15	-1.3
Total	6	26	31	.456	120	75	7-4	1	528.2	449	219	45	8	239-13	349	3.18	99	.231	.316	147-13	.116	2	87	-2	0.3
HOWARD, CHRIS Christian B 11.18.1965 Lynn, MA BR/TL 6/185# d9.21																									
1993	Chi A	1	0	1.000	3	0	0	0-0	2.1	2	0	0	0	3-1	1	0.00	—	.286	.500	0-0	—	0		1	0.2
1994	Bos A	1	0	1.000	37	0	0	1-1	39.2	35	17	5	0	12-4	22	3.63	139	.233	.287	0-0	—	0		6	0.3
1995	Tex A	0	0	—	4	0	0	0-0	4	3	0	0	0	1-0	2	0.00	—	.231	.267	0-0	—	0		2	0.1
Total	3	2	0	1.000	44	0	0	1-1	46	40	17	5	0	16-5	25	3.13	159	.235	.296	0-0	—	0		9	0.6
HOWARD, EARL Earl Nycum B 6.25.1893 Everett, PA D 4.4.1937 Everett, PA BR/TR 6-1/160# d4.18																									
1918	StL N	0	0	—	1	0	0	0	2	0	0	0	0	2	0	0.00	—	.000	.286	0-0	—	0		1	0.1
HOWARD, FRED Fred Irving B 9.2.1956 Portland, ME BR/TR 6-3/190# d5.26																									
1979	Chi A	1	5	.167	28	6	0	0-0	68	73	34	5	1	32-2	36	3.57	119	.283	.357	0-0	—	0	92	4	0.3
HOWARD, LEE Lee Vincent B 11.11.1923 Staten Island, NY BL/TL 6-2/175# d9.22																									
1946	Pit N	0	1	.000	3	2	1	0	13.1	14	3	0	0	9	6	2.03	174	.286	.397	5-0	.000	-1	24	2	0.1
1947	Pit N	0	0	—	2	0	0	0	2.2	4	1	1	0	0	2	3.38	125	.333	.333	0-0	—	0		0	0.0
Total	2	0	1	.000	5	2	1	0	16	18	4	1	0	9	8	2.25	162	.295	.386	5-0	.000	-1	24	2	0.1
HOWE, CAL Calvin Earl B 11.27.1924 Rock Falls, IL BL/TL 6-3/230# d9.26																									
1952	Chi N	0	0	—	1	0	0	0	2	0	0	0	0	1	2	0.00	—	.000	.143	0-0	—	0		1	0.0
HOWE, LES Lester Curtis "Lucky" B 8.24.1895 Brooklyn, NY D 7.16.1976 Woodmere, NY BR/TR 5-11.5/170# d8.18																									
1923	Bos A	1	0	1.000	12	2	0	0	30	23	10	0	1	7	7	2.40	171	.211	.265	6-0	.000	-1	111	6	0.2
1924	Bos A	1	0	1.000	4	0	0	0	7.1	11	6	1	1	2	3	7.36	59	.423	.483	2-0	.500	0		-2	-0.2
Total	2	2	0	1.000	16	2	0	0	37.1	34	16	1	2	9	10	3.38	123	.252	.308	8-0	.125	-1	111	4	0.0
HOWE, STEVE Steven Roy B 3.10.1958 Pontiac, MI BL/TL 6-1/180# d4.11																									
1980	LA N	7	9	.438	59	0	0	17-9	84.2	83	33	1	2	22-10	39	2.66	132	.256	.305	11-0	.091	-1		6	1.2
1981	†LA N	5	3	.625	41	0	0	8-2	54	51	17	2	0	18-7	32	2.50	133	.254	.309	1-0	.000	0		5	0.8
1982	LA N★	7	5	.583	66	0	0	13-9	99.1	87	27	3	0	17-11	49	2.08	167	.240	.272	7-1	.000	-1		15	2.1
1983	LA N	4	7	.364	46	0	0	18-5	68.2	55	15	2	1	12-7	52	1.44	250	.217	.253	8-0	.125	0		16	3.4
1985	LA N	1	1	.500	19	0	0	3-0	22	30	17	2	1	5-2	11	4.91	71	.319	.353	0-0	—	0		-5	-0.5
	Min A	2	3	.400	13	0	0	0-3	19	28	16	1	0	7-2	10	6.16	72	.333	.372	0-0	—	0		-4	-0.8
1987	Tex A	3	3	.500	24	0	0	1-2	31.1	33	15	2	3	8-1	19	4.31	104	.280	.341	0-0	—	0		2	0.3
1991	NY A	3	1	.750	37	0	0	3-0	48.1	39	12	1	3	7-2	34	1.68	247	.222	.262	0-0	—	0		12	1.0
1992	NY A	3	0	1.000	20	0	0	6-1	22	9	7	1	0	3-1	12	2.45	160	.122	.154	0-0	—	0		3	0.6
1993	NY A	3	5	.375	51	0	0	4-3	50.2	58	31	7	3	10-4	19	4.97	84	.297	.338	0-0	—	0		-5	-0.7
1994	NY A	3	0	1.000	40	0	0	15-4	40	28	8	2	0	7-1	18	1.80	254	.194	.232	0-0	—	0		13	1.8
1995	†NY A	6	3	.667	56	0	0	2-1	49	66	29	7	4	17-3	28	4.96	93	.324	.383	0-0	—	0		-2	-0.3
1996	NY A	0	1	.000	25	0	0	1-1	17	19	12	1	1	6-3	5	6.35	78	.284	.351	0-0	—	0		-2	-0.1
Total	12	47	41	.534	497	0	0	91-40	606	586	239	32	18	139-54	328	3.03	129	.255	.300	27-1	.074	-1		54	8.8
HOWELL, HARRY Henry Harry B 11.14.1876 , NJ D 5.22.1956 Spokane, WA BR/TR 5-9/?# d10.10 U1																									
1898	Bro N	2	0	1.000	2	2	2	0	18	15	11	0	1	11	2	5.00	72	.224	.342	8-1	.250	0	188	-2	-0.1
1899	Bal N	13	8	.619	28	25	21	1	209.1	248	126	1	10	69	58	3.91	101	.294	.355	82-3	.146	-3	103	3	-0.1
1900	†Bro N	6	5	.545	21	10	7-2	1	110.1	131	69	4	3	36	26	3.75	102	.294	.351	42-0	.286	4*	88	-1	0.3
1901	Bal A	14	21	.400	37	34	32-1	0	294.2	333	188	5	7	79	93	3.67	106	.281	.330	188-4	.218	1*	94	6	0.6
1902	Bal A	9	15	.375	26	23	19-1	0	199	243	136	5	7	48	33	4.12	92	.301	.346	347-8	.268	5*	93	-8	-0.1
1903	NY A	9	6	.600	25	15	13	0	155.2	140	79	4	6	44	62	3.53	89	.240	.300	106-3	.217	2*	119	-5	-0.1
1904	StL A	13	21	.382	34	33	32-2	0	299.2	254	99	1	13	60	122	2.19	113	.230	.278	113-4	.221	5*	81	10	2.4
1905	StL A	15	22	.405	38	37	**35**-4	0	323	252	109	2	12	101	198	1.98	129	.217	.286	135-1	.193	3*	91	19	3.6
1906	StL A	15	14	.517	35	33	30-6	1	276.2	233	98	1	10	61	140	2.11	122	.231	.282	103-3	.126	-3	113	14	1.6
1907	StL A	16	15	.516	42	35	26-2	3	316.1	258	112	3	8	88	118	1.93	130	.225	.285	114-9	.237	6*	94	14	2.6
1908	StL A	18	18	.500	41	32	27-2	1	324.1	279	103	1	17	70	117	1.89	127	.240	.293	120-1	.183	1	94	16	2.2
1909	StL A	1	1	.500	10	3	0	0	37.1	42	21	0	3	8	16	3.13	77	.294	.344	34-3	.176	0*	136	-5	-0.2
1910	StL A	0	0	—	1	0	0	0	3.1	7	7	0	0	2	1	10.80	23	.467	.529	2-0	.000	-0		-3	-0.2
Total	13	131	146	.473	340	282	244-20	6	2567.2	2435	1158	27	97	677	986	2.74	108	.252	.307	1394-40	.217	21	98	58	12.5

Year	Tm Lg	W	L	Pct	G	GS	CG-Sho	SV-BS	IP	H	R	HR	HB	BB-IB	SO	ERA	AERA	OAV	OOB	AB-SH	AVG	PB	Sup	APR	PW
HOWELL, JAY Jay Canfield B 11.26.1955 Miami, FL BR/TR 6-3/205# d8.10																									
1980	Cin N	0	0	—	5	0	0	0-0	3.1	8	5	0	1	0-0	1	13.50	27	.471	.474	0-0	—	0		-4	-0.2
1981	Chi N	2	0	1.000	10	2	0	0-0	22.1	23	13	3	2	10-2	10	4.84	76	.277	.365	2-2	.000	0	168	-2	-0.1
1982	NY A	2	3	.400	6	6	0	0-0	28	42	25	1	0	13-0	21	7.71	52	.341	.399	0-0	—	0	148	-11	-1.6
1983	NY A	1	5	.167	19	12	2	0-0	82	89	53	7	3	35-0	61	5.38	73	.275	.346	0-0	—	0	99	-13	-0.8
1984	NY A	9	4	.692	61	1	0	7-2	103.2	86	33	5	0	34-3	109	2.69	141	.223	.284	0-0	—	0	190	14	1.9
1985	Oak A☆	9	8	.529	63	0	0	29-7	98	98	32	5	1	31-3	68	2.85	136	.261	.316	0-0	—	0		13	2.6
1986	Oak A	3	6	.333	38	0	0	16-4	53.1	53	23	3	1	23-4	42	3.38	115	.262	.339	0-0	—	0		3	0.5
1987	Oak A★	3	4	.429	36	0	0	16-8	44.1	48	30	6	1	21-1	35	5.89	70	.277	.355	0-0	—	0		-8	-1.5
1988	†LA N	5	3	.625	50	0	0	21-6	65	44	16	1	1	21-2	70	2.08	161	.188	.255	2-0	.000	-0		10	1.8
1989	LA N★	5	3	.625	56	0	0	28-4	79.2	60	15	3	0	22-6	55	1.58	216	.211	.266	3-0	.000	-0		17	2.8
1990	LA N	5	5	.500	45	0	0	16-8	66	59	17	5	6	20-3	59	2.18	168	.242	.315	2-0	.000	-0		12	2.2
1991	LA N	6	5	.545	44	0	0	16-2	51	39	19	3	1	11-3	40	3.18	113	.213	.259	0-0	—	0		3	0.7
1992	LA N	1	3	.250	41	0	0	4-2	46.2	41	9	2	1	18-5	36	1.54	224	.230	.303	0-0	—	0		10	1.1
1993	Atl N	3	3	.500	54	0	0	0-3	58.1	48	16	3	0	16-4	37	2.31	174	.229	.278	0-0	—	0		11	1.0
1994	Tex A	4	1	.800	40	0	0	2-3	43	44	29	10	1	16-2	22	5.44	89	.262	.324	0-0	—	0		-3	-0.3
Total	15	58	53	.523	568	21	2	155-49	844.2	782	335	57	19	291-38	666	3.34	114	.246	.310	9-2	.000	-1	127	52	10.1
HOWELL, KEN Kenneth B 11.28.1960 Detroit, MI BR/TR 6-3/228# d6.25																									
1984	LA N	5	5	.500	32	1	0	6-4	51.1	51	21	1	1	9-4	54	3.33	106	.267	.298	5-1	.000	-1	0	2	0.3
1985	†LA N	4	7	.364	56	0	0	12-3	86	66	41	8	0	35-3	85	3.77	92	.208	.287	4-0	.000	-0		-2	-0.4
1986	LA N	6	12	.333	62	0	0	12-9	97.2	86	48	7	3	63-9	104	3.87	89	.239	.354	5-0	.000	-1		-5	-1.2
1987	LA N	3	4	.429	40	2	0	1-5	55	54	32	7	0	29-2	60	4.91	81	.265	.356	4-0	.250	0	137	-5	-0.6
1988	LA N	0	1	.000	4	1	0	0-0	12.2	16	10	0	0	4-1	12	6.39	52	.320	.370	1-1	.000	-0	53	-4	-0.3
1989	Phi N	12	12	.500	33	32	1-1	0-0	204	155	84	11	2	86-6	164	3.44	103	.215	.297	65-10	.092	-2	101	4	0.2
1990	Phi N	8	7	.533	18	18	2	0-0	106.2	106	60	12	3	49-6	70	4.64	82	.260	.343	30-8	.067	-1	93	-9	-1.3
Total	7	38	48	.442	245	54	3-1	31-21	613.1	534	296	46	9	275-31	549	3.95	91	.237	.320	114-20	.079	-5	98	-19	-3.3
HOWELL, DIXIE Millard B 1.7.1920 Bowman, KY D 3.18.1960 Hollywood, FL BL/TR 6-2/210# d9.14																									
1940	Cle A	0	0	—	3	0	0	0	5	2	1	0	0	4	2	1.80	234	.143	.333	0-0	—	0		1	0.1
1949	Cin N	0	1	.000	5	1	0	0	13.1	21	12	3	0	8	7	8.10	52	.362	.439	9-0	.111	-0*	84	-5	-0.3
1955	Chi A	8	3	.727	35	0	0	9	73.2	70	27	1	0	25-5	25	2.93	135	.250	.308	21-1	.381	2		8	1.6
1956	Chi A	5	6	.455	34	1	0	4	64.1	79	39	3	2	36-10	28	4.62	89	.309	.398	17-0	.235	2	130	-5	-0.6
1957	Chi A	6	5	.545	37	0	0	6	68.1	64	25	6	0	30-4	37	3.29	113	.255	.332	27-0	.185	4*		4	1.2
1958	Chi A	0	0	—	1	0	0	0	1.2	0	0	0	0	0-0	0	0.00	—	.000	.000	0-0	—	0		1	0.0
Total	6	19	15	.559	115	2	0	19	226.1	236	104	13	2	103-19	99	3.78	104	.273	.350	74-1	.243	8	113	4	2.0
HOWELL, ROLAND Roland Boatner "Billiken" B 1.3.1892 Napoleonville, LA D 3.31.1973 Baton Rouge, LA BR/TR 6-4/210# d6.14																									
1912	StL N	0	0	—	3	0	0	0	1.2	5	5	0	0	5	0	27.00	13	.556	.714	0-0	—	0		-4	-0.2
HOWRY, BOB Bobby Dean B 8.4.1973 Phoenix, AZ BL/TR 6-5/215# d6.21																									
1998	Chi A	0	3	.000	44	0	0	9-2	54.1	37	20	7	2	19-2	51	3.15	145	.194	.270	0-0	—	0		9	0.7
1999	Chi A	5	3	.625	69	0	0	28-6	67.2	58	34	8	3	38-3	80	3.59	136	.229	.336	0-0	—	0		8	1.3
2000	†Chi A	2	4	.333	65	0	0	7-5	71	54	26	6	4	29-2	60	3.17	158	.216	.303	0-0	—	0		15	1.3
2001	Chi A	4	5	.444	69	0	0	5-6	78.2	85	41	11	4	30-9	64	4.69	98	.279	.348	0-0	—	0		1	0.1
2002	Chi A	2	2	.500	47	0	0	0-0	50.2	45	22	7	3	17-2	31	3.91	116	.245	.313	0-0	—	0		4	0.3
	Bos A	1	3	.250	20	0	0	0-1	18	22	15	2	2	4-2	14	5.00	90	.306	.350	0-0	—	0		-3	-0.5
	Year	3	5	.375	67	0	0	0-1	68.2	67	42	9	5	21-4	45	4.19	108	.262	.323	0-0	—	0		2	-0.2
2003	Bos A	0	0	—	4	0	0	0-1	4.1	11	6	1	0	3-1	4	12.46	37	.478	.519	0-0	—	0		-3	-0.2
Total	6	14	20	.412	318	0	0	49-21	344.2	312	164	42	18	140-21	304	3.92	120	.244	.323	0-0	—	0		31	3.0
HOY, PETER Peter Alexander B 6.29.1966 Brockville, ON, CAN BL/TR 6-7/220# d4.11																									
1992	Bos A	0	0	—	5	0	0	0-1	3.2	8	3	0	0	2-1	2	7.36	57	.471	.526	0-0	—	0		-1	0.0
HOYLE, TEX Roland Edison B 7.17.1921 Carbondale, PA D 7.4.1994 Carbondale, PA BR/TR 6-4/170# d4.18																									
1952	Phi A	0	0	—	3	0	0	0	2.1	9	7	2	0	1	1	27.00	15	.563	.588	0-0	—	0		-5	-0.2
HOYT, LA MARR Dewey La Marr B 1.1.1955 Columbia, SC BR/TR 6-1/222# d9.14																									
1979	Chi A	0	0	—	2	0	0	0-0	3	2	0	0	0	0-0	0	0.00	—	.200	.200	0-0	—	0		1	0.1
1980	Chi A	9	3	.750	24	13	3-1	0-0	112.1	123	66	8	2	41-3	55	4.57	88	.281	.340	0-0	—	0*	94	-7	-0.7
1981	Chi A	9	3	.750	43	1	0	10-1	90.2	80	40	10	3	28-1	60	3.57	100	.240	.303	0-0	—	0	0	1	0.1
1982	Chi A	**19**	15	.559	39	32	14-2	0-1	239.2	248	104	17	2	48-3	124	3.53	115	.266	.301	0-0	—	0	120	16	2.0
1983	†Chi A	**24**	10	.706	36	36	11-1	0-0	260.2	236	115	27	1	31-4	148	3.66	115	.238	**.260**	0-0	—	0	116	16	2.2
1984	Chi A	13	18	.419	34	34	11-1	0-0	235.2	244	127	31	5	43-3	126	4.47	93	.266	.301	0-0	—	0*	85	-7	-0.8
1985	SD N★	16	8	.667	31	31	8-3	0-0	210.1	210	85	20	2	20-2	83	3.47	102	.261	.280	64-12	.063	-4	112	5	0.1
1986	SD N	8	11	.421	35	25	1	0-1	159	170	100	27	3	68-8	85	5.15	71	.276	.350	46-3	.130	-1	105	-26	-2.9
Total	8	98	68	.590	244	172	48-8	10-3	1311.1	1313	637	140	18	279-24	681	3.99	99	.260	.300	110-15	.091	-5	106	-1	0.1
HOYT, WAITE Waite Charles "Schoolboy" B 9.9.1899 Brooklyn, NY D 8.25.1984 Cincinnati, OH BR/TR 6/180# d7.24 HF1969																									
1918	NY N	0	0	—	1	0	0	0	1	0	0	0	0	0	2	0.00	—	.000	.000	1-0	.000	-0		0	0.0
1919	Bos A	4	6	.400	13	11	6-1	0	105.1	99	42	1	0	22	28	3.25	93	.262	.303	38-2	.132	-3	83	-1	-0.3
1920	Bos A	6	6	.500	22	11	6-2	1	121.1	123	72	2	1	47	45	4.38	83	.270	.339	43-2	.116	-3	103	-11	-1.3
1921	†NY A	19	13	.594	43	32	21-1	3	282.1	301	121	3	5	81	102	3.09	137	.276	.329	99-9	.222	-2	102	35	3.3
1922	†NY A	19	12	.613	37	31	17-3	0	265	271	114	13	9	76	95	3.43	117	.269	.326	92-3	.217	1	94	19	2.0
1923	†NY A	17	9	.654	37	28	19-1	1	238.2	227	97	9	4	66	60	3.02	131	.253	.307	84-6	.190	-2	91	21	1.8
1924	NY A	18	13	.581	46	32	14-2	4	247	295	117	8	3	76	71	3.79	110	.300	.352	75-12	.133	-5	96	11	0.7
1925	NY A	11	14	.440	46	30	17-1	6	243	283	124	14	1	78	86	4.00	107	.292	.346	79-8	.304	6	95	8	1.3
1926	†NY A	16	12	.571	40	28	12-1	4	217.2	224	112	4	2	62	79	3.85	100	.264	.316	76-7	.211	-0	115	1	-0.1
1927	†NY A	**22**	7	**.759**	36	32	23-3	1	256.1	242	90	10	4	54	86	2.63	146	.251	.294	99-9	.222	0	145	38	3.8
1928	†NY A	23	7	.767	42	31	19-3	**8**	273	279	118	16	1	60	67	3.36	112	.272	.313	109-3	.257	2	146	15	1.6
1929	NY A	10	9	.526	30	25	12	1	201.2	219	115	9	3	69	57	4.24	91	.279	.339	76-8	.224	1	134	-9	-0.7
1930	NY A	2	2	.500	8	7	2	0	47.2	64	27	7	0	9	10	4.53	95	.317	.346	16-1	.063	-2	137	0	-0.2
	Det A	9	8	.529	26	20	8-1	4	135.2	176	89	7	2	47	25	4.78	100	.313	.368	46-2	.196	-2	81	-1	-0.5
	Year	11	10	.524	34	27	10-1	4	183.1	240	94	14	2	56	35	4.71	99	.314	.363	62-3	.161	-4	95	-1	-0.7
1931	Det A	3	8	.273	16	12	5	0	92	124	70	2	2	32	10	5.87	78	.319	.374	30-0	.133	-2	71	-12	-1.4
	†Phi A	10	5	.667	16	14	9-2	0	111	130	60	9	0	37	30	4.22	107	.298	.353	43-2	.302	3	109	4	0.7
	Year	13	13	.500	32	26	14-2	0	203	254	66	11	2	69	40	4.97	91	.308	.363	73-2	.233	0	91	-7	-0.7
1932	Bro N	1	3	.250	8	4	0	1	26.2	38	27	3	0	12	7	7.76	49	.342	.407	6-0	.000	-1	61	-12	-1.6
	NY N	5	7	.417	18	12	3	0	97.1	103	43	6	5	25	29	3.42	109	.275	.328	31-2	.097	-2	83	4	0.3
	Year	6	10	.375	26	16	3	1	124	141	47	9	5	37	36	4.35	86	.290	.347	37-2	.081	-3	77	-8	-1.3
1933	Pit N	5	7	.417	36	8	4-1	4	117	118	45	3	1	19	44	2.92	114	.262	.293	32-0	.156	-1	66	6	0.6
1934	Pit N	15	6	.714	48	17	8-3	5	190.2	184	75	6	2	43	105	2.93	141	.252	.296	56-2	.179	-1	95	23	2.3
1935	Pit N	7	11	.389	39	11	5	6	164	187	72	8	1	27	63	3.40	121	.285	.315	54-3	.259	2	75	15	1.7
1936	Pit N	7	5	.583	22	9	6	1	116.2	115	44	5	3	20	37	2.70	150	.255	.291	39-2	.154	-1	81	16	1.5
1937	Pit N	1	2	.333	11	0	0	2	28	31	14	3	0	6	21	4.50	86	.270	.306	12-0	.083	-1		-1	-0.2
	Bro N	7	7	.500	27	19	10-1	0	167	180	83	5	0	30	44	3.23	125	.270	.301	48-8	.083	-2	93	11	0.6
	Year	8	9	.471	38	19	10-1	2	195	211	87	8	0	36	65	3.42	117	.270	.302	60-8	.083	-3	94	9	0.4
1938	Bro N	0	3	.000	6	1	0	0	16.1	24	9	1	0	5	3	4.96	79	.333	.377	3-0	.000	-0	43	-1	-0.2
Total	21	237	182	.566	674	425	226-26	52	3762.1	4037	1780	154	49	1003	1206	3.59	112	.276	.325	1287-91	.198	-17	104	179	15.7
HRABOSKY, AL Alan Thomas B 7.21.1949 Oakland, CA BR/TL 5-11/185# d6.16 Mil 1971																									
1970	StL N	2	1	.667	16	1	0	0-1	19	22	10	2	0	7-1	12	4.74	87	.286	.345	3-0	.000	-0	65	-1	-0.2
1971	StL N	0	0	—	1	0	0	0-0	2	2	0	0	0	0-0	2	0.00	—	.250	.250	0-0	—	0		1	0.0

Year	Tm Lg	W	L	Pct	G	GS	CG-Sho	SV-BS	IP	H	R	HR	HB	BB-IB	SO	ERA	AERA	OAV	OOB	AB-SH	AVG	PB	Sup	APR	PW
1972	StL N	1	0	1.000	5	0	0	0-0	7	2	0	0	0	3-0	9	0.00	—	.087	.185	1-0	.000	-0		3	0.4
1973	StL N	2	4	.333	44	0	0	5-1	56	45	15	2	2	21-6	57	2.09	175	.220	.297	4-1	.000	-0		10	1.1
1974	StL N	8	1	.889	65	0	0	9-4	88.1	71	34	3	1	38-7	82	2.95	121	.221	.302	13-1	.308	1*		6	0.8
1975	StL N	13	3	.813	65	0	0	**22-6**	97.1	72	27	3	1	33-8	82	1.66	226	.205	.273	15-3	.200	1		**20**	4.2
1976	StL N	8	6	.571	68	0	0	13-4	95.1	89	42	5	4	39-9	73	3.30	107	.252	.328	7-3	.000	0		2	0.3
1977	StL N	6	5	.545	65	0	0	10-6	86.1	82	44	12	3	41-7	68	4.38	88	.256	.340	8-0	.000	-1		-4	-0.6
1978	†KC A	8	7	.533	58	0	0	20-3	75	52	24	6	1	35-2	60	2.88	133	.200	.290	0-0	—	0		9	2.0
1979	KC A	9	4	.692	58	0	0	11-2	65	67	31	3	1	41-10	39	3.74	114	.272	.377	0-0	—	0		4	0.7
1980	Atl N	4	2	.667	45	0	0	3-3	59.2	50	27	8	0	31-5	31	3.62	104	.223	.313	1-0	.000	-0		1	0.0
1981	Atl N	1	1	.500	24	0	0	1-0	33.2	24	5	1	0	9-1	13	1.07	335	.207	.260	1-0	.000	-0		9	0.5
1982	Atl N	2	1	.667	31	0	0	3-2	37.1	41	25	5	0	17-2	20	5.54	67	.285	.354	3-0	.333	0		-7	-0.6
Total	13	64	35	.646	545	1	0	97-32	722	619	284	50	13	315-58	548	3.10	121	.234	.314	56-8	.143	0	65	53	8.6

HUBBELL, CARL Carl Owen "King Carl" or "The Mealticket" B 6.22.1903 Carthage, MO D 11.21.1988 Scottsdale, AZ BR/TL 6/170# d7.26 HF1947

Year	Tm Lg	W	L	Pct	G	GS	CG-Sho	SV-BS	IP	H	R	HR	HB	BB-IB	SO	ERA	AERA	OAV	OOB	AB-SH	AVG	PB	Sup	APR	PW
1928	NY N	10	6	.625	20	14	8-1	1	124	117	49	7	3	21	37	2.83	138	.248	.284	47-1	.106	-3	101	13	1.4
1929	NY N	18	11	.621	39	35	19-1	1	268	273	128	17	6	67	106	3.69	124	.265	.313	93-7	.129	-6	116	28	2.2
1930	NY N	17	12	.586	37	32	17-3	2	241.2	263	120	11	11	58	117	3.87	122	.278	.327	86-10	.151	-5	104	25	1.9
1931	NY N	14	12	.538	36	30	21-4	3	248	211	88	14	4	67	155	2.65	139	**.227**	**.282**	83-6	.241	4	100	30	**3.4**
1932	NY N	18	11	.621	40	32	22	2	284	260	96	20	4	40	137	2.50	148	.238	**.268**	108-4	.241	4	107	40	**4.7**
1933	†NY N★	**23**	12	.657	45	33	22-**10**	5	**308.2**	256	69	6	3	47	156	**1.66**	**193**	.227	**.260**	109-5	.183	1	75	**55**	**7.3**
1934	NY N★	21	12	.636	49	35	**25**-5	**8**	313	286	100	17	2	37	118	**2.30**	**168**	.239	**.263**	117-3	.197	-1	103	**55**	5.9
1935	NY N☆	23	12	.657	42	35	24-1	0	302.2	314	125	27	3	49	150	3.27	118	.263	.294	109-2	.239	4	104	21	2.8
1936	†NY N★	**26**	6	**.813**	42	34	25-3	3	304	265	81	7	5	57	123	**2.31**	**169**	.236	**.276**	110-10	.227	1	92	**60**	**6.2**
1937	†NY N★	**22**	8	**.733**	39	32	18-4	4	261.2	261	108	18	3	55	**159**	3.20	122	.257	.298	97-3	.216	1	115	20	2.2
1938	NY N☆	13	10	.565	24	22	13-1	1	179	171	70	16	2	33	104	3.07	123	.249	**.285**	58-10	.155	-2	96	15	1.5
1939	NY N	11	9	.550	29	18	10	2	154	150	60	11	2	24	62	2.75	143	.249	**.280**	53-3	.151	-1	77	18	2.1
1940	NY N★	11	12	.478	31	28	11-2	0	214.1	220	102	22	2	59	86	3.65	106	.259	.309	81-2	.185	-0	111	5	0.5
1941	NY N☆	11	9	.550	26	22	11-1	1	164	169	73	10	2	53	75	3.57	104	.266	.325	57-2	.140	-2	90	3	0.0
1942	NY N☆	11	8	.579	24	20	11	0	157.1	158	75	17	1	34	61	3.95	85	.259	.299	60-3	.183	-0	124	-7	-0.9
1943	NY N	4	4	.500	12	11	3	0	66	87	36	7	0	24	31	4.91	70	.322	.378	20-4	.200	-0	116	-9	-1.0
Total	16	253	154	.622	535	433	260-36	33	3590.1	3461	1380	227	53	725	1677	2.98	130	.251	.291	1288-75	.191	-5	102	372	40.2

HUBBELL, BILL Wilbert William B 6.17.1897 San Francisco, CA D 8.3.1980 Lakewood, CO BR/TR 6-1.5/195# d9.24

Year	Tm Lg	W	L	Pct	G	GS	CG-Sho	SV-BS	IP	H	R	HR	HB	BB-IB	SO	ERA	AERA	OAV	OOB	AB-SH	AVG	PB	Sup	APR	PW
1919	NY N	1	1	.500	2	2	2	0	18.1	19	4	0	2	2	3	1.96	143	.260	.299	8-0	.125	-1	128	2	0.2
1920	NY N	0	1	.000	14	0	0	2	30	26	12	2	1	15	8	2.10	143	.239	.336	5-0	.200	-0		2	0.1
	Phi N	9	9	.500	24	18	9-1	2	150	176	77	3	4	42	26	3.84	89	.301	.352	53-2	.132	-3	83	-5	-1.0
	Year	9	10	.474	38	18	9-1	4	180	202	81	5	5	57	34	3.55	94	.291	.349	58-2	.138	-3	85	-5	-0.9
1921	Phi N	9	16	.360	36	30	15-1	2	220.1	269	146	18	3	38	43	4.33	98	.306	.337	75-1	.160	-2	83	-3	-0.4
1922	Phi N	7	15	.318	35	26	11-1	1	189	257	136	14	4	41	33	5.00	93	.317	.353	70-2	.171	-2	85	-6	-0.7
1923	Phi N	1	6	.143	22	5	1	0	55	102	70	13	2	17	8	8.35	55	.394	.435	17-2	.235	0*	79	-22	-2.3
1924	Phi N	10	9	.526	36	22	9-2	2	179	233	103	9	2	45	30	4.83	92	.324	.365	59-3	.220	-1	107	-3	-0.3
1925	Phi N	0	0	—	2	0	0	0	2.2	5	4	0	0	1	0	0.00	—	.385	.429	1-1	.000	-0		0	0.0
	Bro N	3	6	.333	33	5	3	1	86.2	120	59	8	2	24	16	5.30	79	.337	.382	20-1	.150	0	77	-10	-0.8
	Year	3	6	.333	35	5	3	1	89.1	125	63	8	2	25	16	5.14	82	.339	.384	21-2	.143	0	76	-9	-0.8
Total	7	40	63	.388	204	108	50-5	10	931	1207	611	67	20	225	167	4.68	89	.317	.359	308-12	.172	-8	90	-45	-5.2

HUCKLEBERRY, EARL Earl Eugene B 5.23.1910 Konawa, OK D 2.25.1999 Seminole, OK BR/TR 5-11/165# d9.13

Year	Tm Lg	W	L	Pct	G	GS	CG-Sho	SV-BS	IP	H	R	HR	HB	BB-IB	SO	ERA	AERA	OAV	OOB	AB-SH	AVG	PB	Sup	APR	PW
1935	Phi A	1	0	1.000	1	1	0	0	6.2	8	7	1	0	4	2	9.45	48	.296	.387	3-0	.000	-0	363	-3	-0.3

HUDEK, JOHN John Raymond B 8.8.1966 Tampa, FL BB/TR 6-1/200# d4.23

Year	Tm Lg	W	L	Pct	G	GS	CG-Sho	SV-BS	IP	H	R	HR	HB	BB-IB	SO	ERA	AERA	OAV	OOB	AB-SH	AVG	PB	Sup	APR	PW
1994	Hou N★	0	2	.000	42	0	0	16-2	39.1	24	14	5	1	18-2	39	2.97	133	.174	.270	0-0	—	0		5	0.5
1995	Hou N	2	2	.500	19	0	0	7-2	20	19	12	3	0	5-0	29	5.40	72	.247	.293	1-0	1.000	1		-3	-0.5
1996	Hou N	2	0	1.000	15	0	0	2-0	16	12	5	2	0	5-2	14	2.81	138	.207	.270	0-0	—	0		2	0.3
1997	Hou N	1	3	.250	40	0	0	4-4	40.2	38	27	8	3	33-2	36	5.98	67	.252	.396	0-0	—	0		-8	-0.8
1998	NY N	1	4	.200	28	0	0	0-0	27	23	13	2	2	19-3	28	4.00	103	.237	.367	0-0	—	0		0	0.1
	Cin N	4	2	.667	30	0	0	0-1	37	27	14	6	2	28-1	40	2.43	176	.206	.348	3-1	.000	-0		6	0.8
	Year	5	6	.455	58	0	0	0-1	64	50	46	8	4	47-4	68	3.09	136	.219	.356	3-1	.000	-0		6	0.9
1999	Cin N	0	1	.000	2	0	0	0-1	1	4	3	1	0	3-0	0	27.00	17	.667	.778	0-0	—	0		-2	-0.4
	Atl N	0	1	.000	15	0	0	0-0	16.2	21	14	1	1	11-0	18	6.48	69	.296	.393	1-0	.000	-0		-4	-0.2
	Year	0	2	.000	17	0	0	0-1	17.2	25	17	2	1	14-0	18	7.64	59	.325	.430	1-0	.000	-0		-7	-0.6
	Tor A	0	0	—	3	0	0	0-0	3.2	8	5	1	0	1-0	2	12.27	40	.471	.474	0-0	—	0		-3	-0.1
Total	6	10	15	.400	194	0	0	29-10	201.1	176	107	29	9	123-10	206	4.43	93	.236	.347	5-1	.200	0		-7	-0.3

HUDLIN, WILLIS George Willis "Ace" B 5.23.1906 Wagoner, OK D 8.5.2002 Little Rock, AR BR/TR 6/190# d8.15 Mil 1944 C3

Year	Tm Lg	W	L	Pct	G	GS	CG-Sho	SV-BS	IP	H	R	HR	HB	BB-IB	SO	ERA	AERA	OAV	OOB	AB-SH	AVG	PB	Sup	APR	PW
1926	Cle A	1	3	.250	8	2	1	0	32.1	25	13	1	2	13	6	2.78	146	.227	.320	8-1	.125	0	83	4	0.5
1927	Cle A	18	12	.600	43	30	18-1	0	264.2	291	132	3	11	83	65	4.01	105	.283	.343	96-6	.250	2	105	9	1.2
1928	Cle A	14	14	.500	42	26	10	7	220.1	231	114	7	7	90	62	4.04	103	.279	.355	72-2	.194	-0	97	5	0.7
1929	Cle A	17	15	.531	40	33	22-2	1	280.1	299	122	7	1	73	60	3.34	133	.272	.318	97-8	.196	-3	81	34	3.5
1930	Cle A	13	16	.448	37	33	13-1	1	216.2	255	133	12	1	76	60	4.57	106	.293	.351	73-3	.219	-1	101	7	0.9
1931	Cle A	15	14	.517	44	34	15-1	4	254.1	313	155	14	1	88	83	4.60	100	.301	.356	100-2	.200	1	112	1	0.3
1932	Cle A	12	8	.600	33	21	12	2	181.2	204	108	10	1	59	65	4.71	101	.278	.332	64-3	.203	1	114	3	0.4
1933	Cle A	5	13	.278	34	17	6	1	147.1	161	85	7	3	61	44	3.97	112	.275	.346	41-5	.146	-1	72	5	0.6
1934	Cle A	15	10	.600	36	26	15-1	4	195	210	109	8	5	65	58	4.75	96	.277	.338	68-5	.206	3	108	1	0.6
1935	Cle A	15	11	.577	36	29	14-3	5	231.2	252	107	8	3	61	45	3.69	122	.277	.324	86-1	.279	6*	113	22	2.8
1936	Cle A	1	5	.167	27	7	1	0	64	112	74	1	2	31	20	9.00	56	.397	.460	18-0	.111	-1	80	-28	-2.0
1937	Cle A	12	11	.522	35	23	10-2	2	175.2	213	106	8	2	43	31	4.10	112	.295	.337	59-5	.169	-1	96	4	0.5
1938	Cle A	8	8	.500	29	15	8	1	127	158	80	13	2	45	27	4.89	95	.303	.361	43-2	.116	-2	119	-4	-0.6
1939	Cle A	9	10	.474	27	20	7	3	143	175	85	6	1	42	28	4.91	90	.303	.352	48-3	.188	1	88	-7	-0.5
1940	Cle A	2	1	.667	4	4	2	0	23.2	31	13	3	0	2	8	4.94	85	.316	.330	8-0	.125	-0	115	-1	-0.1
	Was A	1	2	.333	8	6	1	0	37.1	50	33	9	2	5	9	6.51	64	.314	.343	10-2	.100	-1	133	-11	-0.8
	StL A	0	1	.000	6	1	0	0	11.1	19	16	0	0	8	4	11.12	41	.358	.443	2-0	.500	0	77	-8	-0.5
	Year	3	4	.429	18	11	3	0	72.1	100	20	12	2	15	21	6.72	63	.323	.358	20-2	.150	-1	120	-20	-1.4
	NY N	0	1	.000	1	1	0	0	5	9	6	1	0	1	1	10.80	36	.409	.435	1-0	.000	-0	22	-3	-0.5
1944	StL A	0	1	.000	1	0	0	0	2	3	2	0	0	0	1	4.50	80	.300	.300	0-0	—	0		-1	-0.1
Total	16	158	156	.503	491	328	155-11	31	2613.1	3011	1493	118	44	846	677	4.41	102	.289	.345	894-48	.201	4	101	32	6.9

HUDSON, CHARLIE Charles B 8.18.1949 Ada, OK BL/TL 6-3/185# d5.21

Year	Tm Lg	W	L	Pct	G	GS	CG-Sho	SV-BS	IP	H	R	HR	HB	BB-IB	SO	ERA	AERA	OAV	OOB	AB-SH	AVG	PB	Sup	APR	PW
1972	StL N	1	0	1.000	12	0	0	0-0	12.1	10	8	0	1	7-0	4	5.11	67	.233	.353	0-0	—	0		-2	-0.2
1973	Tex A	4	2	.667	25	4	1-1	1-1	62.1	59	35	3	0	31-2	34	4.62	81	.254	.335	0-0	—	0	90	-6	-0.5
1975	Cal A	0	1	.000	3	1	0	0-0	5.2	7	6	0	0	4-0	0	9.53	37	.304	.407	0-0	—	0	99	-4	-0.5
Total	3	5	3	.625	40	5	1-1	1-1	80.1	76	49	3	1	42-2	38	5.04	73	.255	.343	0-0	—	0	92	-12	-1.2

HUDSON, CHARLES Charles Lynn B 3.16.1959 Ennis, TX BB/TR 6-3/185# d5.31

Year	Tm Lg	W	L	Pct	G	GS	CG-Sho	SV-BS	IP	H	R	HR	HB	BB-IB	SO	ERA	AERA	OAV	OOB	AB-SH	AVG	PB	Sup	APR	PW
1983	†Phi N	8	8	.500	26	26	3	0-0	169.1	158	73	13	0	53-6	101	3.35	107	.248	.304	54-5	.093	-2*	126	5	0.2
1984	Phi N	9	11	.450	30	30	1-1	0-0	173.2	181	101	12	2	52-4	94	4.04	90	.265	.316	56-4	.089	-2	98	-12	-1.6
1985	Phi N	8	13	.381	38	26	3	0-0	193	188	92	23	1	74-7	122	3.78	98	.252	.319	57-3	.140	-1	117	-2	-0.4
1986	Phi N	7	10	.412	33	23	0	0-0	144	165	87	20	0	58-1	82	4.94	78	.291	.355	43-7	.047	-3*	91	-15	-2.0
1987	NY A	11	7	.611	35	16	6-2	0-0	154.2	137	63	19	3	57-1	100	3.61	122	.239	.308	0-0	—	0	110	16	1.5
1988	NY A	6	6	.500	28	12	1	2-0	106.1	93	53	9	4	36-4	58	4.49	88	.235	.301	0-0	—	0	117	-4	-0.5
1989	Det A	1	5	.167	18	7	0	0-0	66.2	75	49	14	2	31-3	23	6.35	60	.288	.367	0-0	—	0*	98	-17	-1.4
Total	7	50	60	.455	208	140	14-3	2-0	1007.2	997	518	110	12	361-26	580	4.14	93	.258	.321	210-19	.095	-8	108	-29	-4.2

Year	Tm Lg	W	L	Pct	G	GS	CG-Sho	SV-BS	IP	H	R	HR	HB	BB-IB	SO	ERA	AERA	OAV	OOB	AB-SH	AVG	PB	Sup	APR	PW
HUDSON, HAL Hal Campbell "Bud" or "Lefty" B 5.4.1927 Grosse Pointe, MI BL/TL 5-10/175# d4.20																									
1952	StL A	0	0	—	3	0	0	0	5.2	9	8	0	0	6	0	12.71	31	.360	.484	1-0	.000	-0		-5	-0.3
	Chi A	0	0	—	2	0	0	0	4	7	2	0	0	1	4	2.25	162	.389	.421	0-0	—	0		0	0.0
	Year	0	0	—	5	0	0	0	9.2	16	15	0	0	7	4	8.38	45	.372	.460	1-0	.000	-0		-5	-0.3
1953	Chi A	0	0	—	1	0	0	0	0.2	0	0	0	0	0	0	0.00	—	.000	.000	0-0	—	0		0	0.0
Total	2	0	0	—	6	0	0	0	10.1	16	10	0	0	7	4	7.84	49	.364	.451	1-0	.000	-0		-5	-0.3
HUDSON, JESSE Jesse James B 7.22.1948 Mansfield, LA BL/TL 6-2/165# d9.19																									
1969	NY N	0	0	—	1	0	0	0-0	2	2	1	0	0	2-0	3	4.50	81	.250	.400	0-0	—	0		0	0.0
HUDSON, JOE Joseph Paul B 9.29.1970 Philadelphia, PA BR/TR 6-1/175# d6.10																									
1995	†Bos A	0	1	.000	39	0	0	1-3	46	53	21	2	2	23-1	29	4.11	119	.301	.386	0-0	—	0		5	0.2
1996	Bos A	3	5	.375	36	0	0	1-4	45	57	35	4	0	32-4	19	5.40	94	.318	.418	0-0	—	0		-3	-0.5
1997	Bos A	3	1	.750	26	0	0	0-0	35.2	39	16	1	4	14-2	14	3.53	131	.289	.373	0-0	—	0		4	0.4
1998	Mil N	0	0	—	1	0	0	0-0	0.1	2	6	0	0	4-1	0	162.00	3	1.000	.857	0-0	—	0		-6	-0.2
Total	4	6	7	.462	102	0	0	2-7	127	151	78	7	6	73-8	62	4.82	101	.307	.400	0-0	—	0		0	-0.1
HUDSON, LUKE Luke Stephen B 5.2.1977 Fountain Valley, CA BR/TR 6-3/195# d7.1																									
2002	Cin N	0	0	—	3	0	0	0-0	6	5	5	1	0	6-0	7	4.50	94	.227	.393	0-1	—	0		-1	-0.1
HUDSON, NAT Nathaniel P. B 1.12.1859 Chicago, IL D 3.14.1928 Chicago, IL BR/TR d4.18																									
1886	†StL AA	16	10	.615	29	27	25	**1**	234.1	224	122	3	2	62	100	3.03	113	.243	.293	150	.233	1*	119	15	1.3
1887	StL AA	4	4	.500	9	9	7	0	67	91	57	2	4	20	15	4.97	91	.305	.357	48	.250	0*	89	-3	-0.3
1888	StL AA	25	10	**.714**	39	37	36-5	0	333	283	155	8	15	59	130	2.54	128	.222	.264	196	.255	5*	120	28	2.9
1889	StL AA	3	2	.600	9	5	4	0	60	71	47	2	4	15	13	4.20	101	.285	.336	52	.250	0*	82	0	0.0
Total	4	48	26	.649	86	78	72-5	1	694.1	669	381	15	25	156	258	3.08	114	.244	.291	446	.247	6	113	40	3.9
HUDSON, REX Rex Haughton B 8.11.1953 Tulsa, OK BB/TR 5-11/165# d7.27																									
1974	LA N	0	0	—	1	0	0	0-0	2	6	5	2	0	0-0	0	22.50	15	.500	.500	0-0	—	0		-4	-0.2
HUDSON, SID Sidney Charles B 1.3.1915 Coalfield, TN BR/TR 6-4/180# d4.18 Mil 1943-45 C14																									
1940	Was A	17	16	.515	38	31	19-3	1	252	272	149	20	3	81	96	4.57	91	.274	.330	93-2	.237	2	93	-11	-1.0
1941	Was A★	13	14	.481	33	33	17-3	0	249.2	242	124	12	1	97	108	3.46	117	.253	.322	86-6	.186	-0	95	12	1.3
1942	Was A☆	10	17	.370	35	31	19-1	2	239.1	266	140	9	5	70	72	4.36	84	.276	.328	89-2	.213	1*	94	-20	-1.7
1946	Was A	8	11	.421	31	15	6-1	1	142.1	160	75	9	4	37	35	3.60	93	.280	.328	43-1	.279	3	89	-7	-0.5
1947	Was A	6	9	.400	20	17	5-1	0	106	113	66	8	1	58	37	5.60	66	.272	.363	39-0	.308	2	73	-18	-2.0
1948	Was A	4	16	.200	39	29	4	1	182	217	128	11	6	107	53	5.88	74	.299	.394	59-3	.237	2	77	-28	-2.2
1949	Was A	8	17	.320	40	27	11-2	1	209	234	117	11	5	91	54	4.22	101	.283	.357	67-5	.239	2	74	-1	0.2
1950	Was A	14	14	.500	30	30	17	0	237.2	261	129	17	6	98	75	4.09	110	.284	.356	93-3	.215	-1*	92	9	0.9
1951	Was A	5	12	.294	23	19	8	0	138.2	168	90	8	4	52	43	5.13	80	.302	.365	44-1	.273	2*	71	-17	-1.5
1952	Was A	3	4	.429	7	7	6	0	62.2	59	22	4	0	29	24	2.73	130	.257	.340	24-1	.167	-0	77	6	0.7
	Bos A	7	9	.438	21	18	7	0	134.1	145	64	9	7	36	50	3.62	109	.276	.330	46-0	.174	-1	89	3	0.5
	Year	10	13	.435	28	25	13	0	197	204	68	13	7	65	74	3.34	114	.270	.333	70-1	.171	-1	86	10	1.2
1953	Bos A	6	9	.400	30	17	4	2	156	164	65	13	4	49	60	3.52	120	.269	.327	50-2	.140	-2	80	14	1.0
1954	Bos A	3	4	.429	33	5	0	5	71.1	83	43	5	2	30	27	4.42	93	.296	.363	13-0	.154	-1	77	-3	-0.4
Total	12	104	152	.406	380	279	123-11	13	2181	2384	1212	136	48	835	734	4.28	95	.278	.345	746-26	.220	9	85	-61	-4.7
HUDSON, TIM Timothy Adam B 7.14.1975 Columbus, GA BR/TR 6/160# d6.8																									
1999	Oak A	11	2	.846	21	21	1	0-0	136.1	121	56	8	4	62-2	132	3.23	144	.237	.323	4-0	.250	1*	127	22	2.0
2000	†Oak A★	**20**	6	**.769**	32	32	2-2	0-0	202.1	169	100	24	7	82-5	169	4.14	115	.227	.306	3-0	.000	-0*	120	16	1.7
2001	†Oak A	18	9	.667	35	**35**	3	0-0	235	216	100	20	6	71-5	181	3.37	131	.245	.303	8-0	.000	-1*	99	27	2.8
2002	†Oak A	15	9	.625	34	34	4-2	0-0	238.1	237	87	19	8	62-9	152	2.98	147	.263	.314	5-0	.200	1	92	38	3.6
2003	†Oak A	16	7	.696	34	34	3-**2**	0-0	240	197	84	15	10	61-9	162	2.70	167	.223	.280	3-0	.333	0	112	47	4.4
Total	5	80	33	.708	156	156	13-6	0-0	1052	940	427	86	35	338-30	796	3.26	139	.239	.304	23-0	.130	0	109	150	14.5
HUENKE, AL Albert Alfred B 6.26.1891 New Bremen, OH D 9.20.1974 St.Marys, OH BR/TR 6/175# d10.6																									
1914	NY N	0	0	—	1	0	0	0	2	2	1	0	0	0	2	4.50	59	.250	.250	1-0	.000	-0		0	0.0
HUFFMAN, PHIL Phillip Lee B 6.20.1958 Freeport, TX BR/TR 6-2/180# d4.10																									
1979	Tor A	6	18	.250	31	31	2-1	0-0	173	220	130	25	0	68-0	56	5.77	75	.304	.361	0-0	—	0	87	-28	-3.3
1985	Bal A	0	0	—	2	1	0	0-0	4.2	7	8	1	0	5-1	2	15.43	26	.350	.480	0-0	—	0	203	-6	-0.3
Total	2	6	18	.250	33	32	2-1	0-0	177.2	227	138	26	0	73-1	58	6.03	72	.305	.365	0-0	—	0	90	-34	-3.6
HUGHES, ED Edward J. B 10.5.1880 Chicago, IL D 10.14.1927 McHenry, IL BR/TR 6-1/180# d8.29.1902 b-Tom																									
1905	Bos A	3	2	.600	6	4	2	0	33.1	38	27	0	1	9	8	4.59	59	.288	.338	14-0	.214	-0	144	-9	-1.2
1906	Bos A	0	0	—	2	0	0	0	10	15	7	0	0	3	3	5.40	51	.349	.391	3-0	.000	-0		-2	-0.2
Total	2	3	2	.600	8	4	2	0	43.1	53	34	0	1	12	11	4.78	57	.303	.351	17-0	.176	-1	144	-11	-1.4
HUGHES, JAY James Jay B 1.22.1874 Sacramento, CA D 6.2.1924 Sacramento, CA BR/TR ?/185# d4.18 b-Mickey																									
1898	Bal N	23	12	.657	38	35	31-5	0	300.2	268	152	4	18	100	81	3.20	112	.237	.309	164-3	.226	4*	126	14	1.9
1899	Bro N	**28**	6	**.824**	35	35	30-3	0	291.2	250	121	6	14	119	99	2.68	146	.231	.316	107-2	.252	5	119	40	4.6
1901	Bro N	17	12	.586	31	29	24	0	250.2	265	125	3	12	102	96	3.27	103	.269	.345	91-5	.176	-1	125	4	0.3
1902	Bro N	15	10	.600	30	29	26	0	245	223	114	3	9	51	92	2.87	97	.243	.289	91-1	.209	4*	104	-5	0.0
Total	4	83	40	.675	134	128	111-8	0	1088	1006	512	16	53	372	368	3.00	114	.245	.315	453-11	.219	13	120	53	6.8
HUGHES, JIM James Michael B 7.2.1951 Los Angeles, CA BR/TR 6-3/190# d9.14																									
1974	Min A	0	2	.000	2	2	1	0-0	10.1	8	8	2	0	4-0	8	5.23	71	.216	.293	0-0	—	0	47	-2	-0.4
1975	Min A	16	14	.533	37	34	12-2	0-0	249.2	241	119	17	13	127-3	130	3.82	100	.255	.350	0-0	—	0	99	1	0.2
1976	Min A	9	14	.391	37	26	3	0-0	177	190	113	17	8	73-2	87	4.98	72	.281	.354	0-0	—	0	116	-27	-3.2
1977	Min A	0	0	—	2	0	0	0-0	4.1	4	1	0	0	1-0	1	2.08	192	.250	.278	0-0	—	0		1	0.0
Total	4	25	30	.455	78	62	16-2	0-0	441.1	443	241	36	21	205-5	226	4.30	87	.265	.350	0-0	—	0	104	-27	-3.4
HUGHES, JIM James Robert B 3.21.1923 Chicago, IL D 8.13.2001 Palos Heights, IL BR/TR 6-1/200# d9.13																									
1952	Bro N	2	1	.667	6	0	0	0	18.2	16	4	0	0	11	8	1.45	252	.235	.342	4-1	.000	-0		4	0.6
1953	†Bro N	4	3	.571	48	0	0	9	85.2	80	33	6	1	41	49	3.47	123	.245	.332	14-1	.286	1		9	0.9
1954	Bro N	8	4	.667	**60**	0	0	**24**	86.2	76	36	7	0	44	58	3.22	127	.239	.326	16-1	.188	-0		8	1.3
1955	Bro N	0	2	.000	24	0	0	6	42.2	41	22	10	0	19-1	20	4.22	96	.256	.333	10-0	.000	-2		0	-0.2
1956	Bro N	0	0	—	5	0	0	0	12	10	7	3	0	4-1	8	5.25	76	.233	.298	2-0	.000	-0		-1	-0.1
	Chi N	1	3	.250	25	1	0	0	45.1	43	35	4	4	30-5	20	5.16	73	.259	.379	7-0	.286	1	70	-9	-0.7
	Year	1	3	.250	30	1	0	0	57.1	53	38	7	4	34-6	28	5.18	74	.254	.364	9-0	.222	0	69	-11	-0.8
1957	Chi A	0	0	—	4	0	0	0	5	12	6	0	0	3-0	2	10.80	35	.462	.517	0-0	—	0		-4	-0.2
Total	6	15	13	.536	172	1	0	39	296	278	143	30	5	152-7	165	3.83	106	.251	.341	53-3	.170	-1	66	7	1.6
HUGHES, MICKEY Michael J. B 10.25.1866 New York, NY D 4.10.1931 Jersey City, NJ TR 5-6/165# d4.22 b-Jay																									
1888	Bro AA	25	13	.658	40	40	40-2	0	363	281	163	5	6	98	159	2.13	140	.206	.262	139	.137	-7	105	31	2.1
1889	†Bro AA	9	8	.529	20	17	13	0	153	172	120	6	7	86	54	4.35	86	.275	.369	68	.176	-3	135	-16	-1.6
1890	Bro N	4	4	.500	9	8	6	0	66.1	77	46	1	4	30	22	5.16	67	.281	.360	26	.038	-4	89	-8	-1.1
	Phi AA	1	3	.250	6	5	4	0	41.1	64	56	0	5	21	15	5.44	71	.344	.425	16	.125	-1	73	-14	-1.1
Total	3	39	28	.582	75	70	63-2	0	623.2	594	385	12	22	235	250	3.22	102	.243	.314	249	.137	-14	109	-7	-1.7
HUGHES, DICK Richard Henry B 2.13.1938 Stephens, AR BR/TR 6-3/195# d9.11																									
1966	StL N	2	1	.667	6	2	1-1	1	21	12	4	0	2	7-3	20	1.71	209	.162	.253	5-1	.400	1	98	5	0.8
1967	†StL N	16	6	**.727**	37	27	12-3	3	222.1	164	72	22	5	48-6	161	2.67	123	**.203**	**.251**	78-4	.128	-1*	101	17	1.4
1968	†StL N	2	2	.500	25	5	0	4	64	45	25	7	0	21-3	49	3.52	82	.202	.269	15-1	.000	-1	150	-3	-0.3
Total	3	20	9	.690	68	34	13-4	8	307.1	221	101	29	7	76-12	230	2.78	116	.200	.255	98-6	.122	-2	108	19	1.9

Year	Tm Lg	W	L	Pct	G	GS	CG-Sho	SV-BS	IP	H	R	HR	HB	BB-IB	SO	ERA	AERA	OAV	OOB	AB-SH	AVG	PB	Sup	APR	PW
HUGHES, TOM Thomas Edward B 9.13.1934 Ancon, Canal Zone BL/TR 6-2/180# d9.13																									
1959	StL N	0	2	.000	2	2	0	0	4	9	9	2	0	2-0	2	15.75	27	.409	.458	1-0	.000	-0	32	-5	-0.9
HUGHES, TOM Thomas James "Long Tom" B 11.29.1878 Chicago, IL D 2.8.1956 Chicago, IL BR/TR 6-1/175# d9.7 b-Ed																									
1900	Chi N	1	1	.500	3	3	3	0	21	31	14	0	1	7	12	5.14	70	.341	.394	6-0	.000	-0	77	-2	-0.2
1901	Chi N	10	23	.303	37	35	32-1	0	308.1	309	166	4	17	115	225	3.24	100	.259	.333	118-4	.119	-8*	89	1	-0.8
1902	Bal A	7	5	.583	13	13	12-1	0	108.1	120	57	2	2	32	45	3.90	97	.281	.334	43-4	.140	-2	119	2	0.0
	Bos A	3	3	.500	9	8	4	0	49.1	51	31	0	1	24	15	3.28	109	.267	.352	30-0	.367	2*	136	0	0.2
	Year	10	8	.556	22	21	16-1	0	157.2	171	38	2	3	56	60	3.71	100	.277	.340	73-4	.233	0	125	2	0.2
1903	†Bos A	20	7	.741	33	31	25-5	0	244.2	232	95	5	9	60	112	2.57	118	.249	.301	93-4	.280	7	132	13	1.9
1904	NY A	7	11	.389	19	18	12-1	0	136.1	141	72	3	5	48	75	3.70	73	.268	.334	54-2	.241	1*	105	-13	-1.7
	Was A	3	12	.200	16	14	14	0	124.1	133	67	4	6	34	48	3.47	77	.274	.330	57-2	.228	3*	73	-12	-1.0
	Year	10	23	.303	35	32	26-1	0	260.2	274	70	7	11	82	123	3.59	75	.271	.332	111-4	.234	4	91	-23	-2.7
1905	Was A	17	20	.459	39	35	26-6	0	291.1	239	113	3	10	79	149	2.35	113	.225	.285	104-1	.212	4	104	8	1.3
1906	Was A	7	17	.292	30	24	18-1	0	204	230	118	5	3	81	90	3.62	73	.287	.355	66-2	.212	3	84	-24	-2.6
1907	Was A	7	14	.333	34	23	18-2	**4**	211	206	104	1	12	47	102	3.11	78	.258	.309	80-3	.237	3*	94	-16	-1.2
1908	Was A	18	15	.545	43	31	24-3	4	276.1	224	91	3	6	77	165	2.21	103	.227	.287	87-8	.195	2	81	6	1.0
1909	Was A	4	7	.364	22	13	7-2	1	120.1	113	56	1	5	33	77	2.69	90	.246	.303	36-3	.083	-2	98	-6	-0.7
1911	Was A	11	17	.393	34	27	17-2	0	223	251	128	7	4	77	86	3.47	95	.288	.348	81-2	.185	-1	90	-6	-0.9
1912	Was A	13	10	.565	31	26	11-1	0	196	201	99	8	6	78	108	2.94	113	.270	.344	67-3	.194	1	102	6	0.7
1913	Was A	4	12	.250	36	12	4	6	129.2	129	81	6	15	61	59	4.30	69	.265	.365	36-1	.111	-1	84	-19	-2.4
Total	13	132	174	.431	399	313	227-25	15	2644	2610	1292	52	102	853	1368	3.09	93	.260	.324	958-39	.198	12	99	-62	-6.4
HUGHES, TOM Thomas L. "Salida Tom" B 1.28.1884 Coal Creek, CO D 11.1.1961 Los Angeles, CA BR/TR 6-2/175# d9.18																									
1906	NY A	1	0	1.000	3	1	1	0	15	11	8	2	0	1	5	4.20	71	.208	.222	5-0	.200	0	121	-1	-0.1
1907	NY A	2	0	1.000	4	3	2	0	27	16	10	0	2	11	10	2.67	105	.174	.276	7-1	.143	-0	121	1	0.0
1909	NY A	7	8	.467	24	15	9-2	2	118.2	109	42	3	4	37	69	2.65	95	.249	.313	39-1	.128	0	104	2	0.2
1910	NY A	7	9	.438	23	15	11	1	151.2	153	77	2	3	37	64	3.50	76	.271	.320	55-2	.164	-1	89	-12	-1.3
1914	Bos N	2	0	1.000	2	2	1	0	17	14	7	0	0	4	11	2.65	104	.226	.273	7-0	.000	-1	156	0	-0.1
1915	Bos N	16	14	.533	**50**	25	17-4	**9**	280.1	208	88	4	11	58	171	2.12	122	.213	.265	90-5	.100	-3	72	16	1.3
1916	Bos N	16	3	**.842**	40	13	7-1	5	161	121	46	2	8	51	97	2.35	106	.215	.290	52-2	.192	2	123	6	1.0
1917	Bos N	5	3	.625	11	8	6-2	0	74	54	21	1	3	30	40	1.95	131	.216	.307	24-1	.000	-3*	118	5	0.2
1918	Bos N	0	2	.000	3	3	1	0	18.1	17	10	1	0	6	9	3.44	78	.250	.311	6-0	.333	1	66	-2	0.0
Total	9	56	39	.589	160	85	55-9	17	863	703	309	15	31	235	476	2.56	102	.229	.291	285-12	.130	-4	97	15	1.2
HUGHES, TOMMY Thomas Owen B 10.7.1919 Wilkes-Barre, PA D 11.28.1990 Wilkes-Barre, PA BR/TR 6-1/190# d4.19 Mil 1943-45																									
1941	Phi N	9	14	.391	34	24	5-2	0	170	187	106	12	4	82	59	4.45	83	.280	.362	55-4	.200	0*	74	-18	-2.0
1942	Phi N	12	18	.400	40	31	19	1	253	224	105	8	0	99	77	3.06	108	.238	.310	80-7	.100	-5*	61	4	0.1
1946	Phi N	6	9	.400	29	13	3-2	1	111	123	64	5	1	44	34	4.38	78	.281	.349	31-2	.097	-1	58	-12	-1.7
1947	Phi N	4	11	.267	29	15	4-1	1	127	121	52	5	0	59	44	3.47	115	.265	.350	40-1	.050	-4*	57	10	0.7
1948	Cin N	0	4	.000	12	4	0	0	27	43	28	3	0	24	7	9.00	43	.364	.472	7-0	.143	-0	28	-14	-1.8
Total	5	31	56	.356	144	87	31-5	3	688	698	355	33	5	308	221	3.92	91	.266	.344	213-14	.117	-10	62	-30	-4.7
HUGHES, VERN Vernon Alexander "Lefty" B 4.15.1893 Etna, PA D 9.26.1961 Sewickley, PA BL/TL 5-10/155# d7.6																									
1914	Bal F	0	0	—	3	0	0	0	5.2	5	4	0	0	3	0	3.18	95	.250	.348	1-0	.000	-0		-1	-0.1
HUGHES, BILL William Nesbert B 11.18.1896 Philadelphia, PA D 2.25.1963 Birmingham, AL BR/TR 5-10.5/155# d9.15																									
1921	Pit N	0	0	—	1	0	0	0	2	3	1	0	1	1	2	4.50	85	.375	.500	0-0	—	0		0	0.0
HUGHES, BILL William R. B 11.25.1866 Blandinsville, IL D 8.25.1943 Santa Ana, CA BL/TL d9.28.1884 ▲																									
1885	Phi AA	0	2	.000	2	2	2	0	16.2	18	17	0	2	10	4	4.86	71	.269	.380	16	.188	0*	137	-2	-0.2
HUGHEY, JIM James Ulysses "Coldwater Jim" B 3.8.1869 Wakeshma, MI D 3.29.1945 Coldwater, MI TR 6/?# d9.29																									
1891	Mil AA	1	0	1.000	2	1	1	0	15	18	6	0	0	3	9	3.00	146	.286	.318	7	.143	-1	113	3	0.1
1893	Chi N	0	1	.000	2	2	1	0	9	14	16	0	1	3	4	11.00	42	.341	.400	2	.000	0	113	-6	-0.4
1896	Pit N	6	8	.429	25	14	11	0	155	171	108	3	7	67	48	4.99	84	.278	.355	65-0	.215	-1	121	-12	-1.0
1897	Pit N	6	10	.375	25	17	13	1	149.1	193	115	3	7	45	38	5.06	82	.310	.364	63-1	.127	-5	93	-15	-1.7
1898	StL N	7	24	.226	35	33	31	0	283.2	325	169	2	11	71	74	3.93	96	.285	.333	97-3	.113	-5	66	-3	-0.8
1899	Cle N	4	30	.118	36	34	32	0	283	403	244	9	22	88	54	5.41	68	.334	.389	111-3	.162	-5	76	-59	-6.0
1900	StL N	5	7	.417	20	12	11	0	112.2	147	90	4	6	40	23	5.19	70	.314	.375	41-0	.171	0	97	-18	-1.6
Total	7	29	80	.266	145	113	100	1	1007.2	1271	748	21	54	317	250	4.87	80	.306	.363	386-7	.153	-17	85	-110	-11.4
HUGHSON, TEX Cecil Carlton B 2.9.1916 Buda, TX D 8.6.1993 San Marcos, TX BR/TR 6-3/198# d4.16 Mil 1944-45																									
1941	Bos A	5	3	.625	12	8	4	0	61	70	30	3	1	13	22	4.13	101	.289	.328	17-3	.059	-1	86	1	0.1
1942	Bos A☆	**22**	6	.786	38	30	**22**-4	4	**281**	258	92	10	1	75	**113**	2.59	144	.245	.296	102-7	.176	1	123	**35**	3.7
1943	Bos A★	12	15	.444	35	32	**20**-4	2	266	242	87	23	2	73	114	2.64	126	.247	.300	86-10	.105	-4	85	20	1.6
1944	Bos A★	18	5	**.783**	28	23	19-2	5	203.1	172	57	4	2	41	112	2.26	151	.225	**.267**	66-10	.152	-1	140	27	3.1
1946	†Bos A	20	11	.645	39	35	21-6	3	278	252	89	15	2	51	172	2.75	133	.238	.274	91-10	.132	-2	90	30	3.0
1947	Bos A	12	11	.522	29	26	13-3	0	189.1	173	86	17	2	71	119	3.33	117	.244	.314	61-4	.033	-6	95	8	0.3
1948	Bos A	3	1	.750	15	0	0	0	19.1	21	14	0	0	7	6	5.12	86	.276	.337	2-1	.000	-0		-2	-0.5
1949	Bos A	4	2	.667	29	2	0	3	77.2	82	49	5	1	41	35	5.33	82	.268	.356	22-4	.045	-3	113	-7	-0.9
Total	8	96	54	.640	225	156	99-19	17	1375.2	1270	504	77	11	372	693	2.94	125	.245	.297	447-49	.119	-15	103	112	10.4
HUISMAN, RICK Richard Allen B 5.17.1969 Oak Park, IL BR/TR 6-3/200# d9.4																									
1995	KC A	0	0	—	7	0	0	0-0	9.2	14	8	2	0	1-0	12	7.45	64	.333	.349	0-0	—	0		-3	-0.1
1996	KC A	2	1	.667	22	0	0	1-0	29.1	25	15	4	0	18-2	23	4.60	109	.231	.336	0-0	—	0		2	0.2
Total	2	2	1	.667	29	0	0	1-0	39	39	23	6	0	19-2	35	5.31	93	.260	.339	0-0	—	0		-1	0.1
HUISMANN, MARK Mark Lawrence B 5.11.1958 Littleton, CO BR/TR 6-3/195# d8.16																									
1983	KC A	2	1	.667	13	0	0	0-1	30.2	29	20	1	0	17-3	20	5.58	73	.250	.343	0-0	—	0		-4	-0.4
1984	†KC A	3	3	.500	38	0	0	3-1	75	84	38	7	1	21-3	54	4.20	96	.286	.330	0-0	—	0		-1	-0.1
1985	KC A	1	0	1.000	9	0	0	0-0	18.2	14	4	1	0	3-0	9	1.93	216	.219	.246	0-0	—	0		5	0.2
1986	KC A	0	1	.000	10	0	0	1-2	17.1	18	8	1	0	6-0	13	4.15	103	.269	.324	0-0	—	0		1	0.1
	Sea A	3	3	.500	36	1	0	4-3	80	80	39	18	1	19-0	59	3.71	115	.256	.299	0-0	—	0	64	4	0.3
	Year	3	4	.429	46	1	0	5-5	97.1	98	42	19	1	25-0	72	3.79	112	.259	.304	0-0	—	0	64	4	0.4
1987	Sea A	0	0	—	6	0	0	0-0	14.2	10	10	1	2	4-0	15	4.91	96	.196	.276	0-0	—	0		-1	0.0
	Cle A	2	3	.400	20	0	0	2-2	35.1	38	22	6	0	8-0	23	5.09	89	.271	.307	0-0	—	0		-2	-0.2
	Year	2	3	.400	26	0	0	2-2	50	48	32	7	2	12-0	38	5.04	91	.251	.298	0-0	—	0		-3	-0.2
1988	Det A	1	0	1.000	5	0	0	0-0	5.1	6	3	0	0	2-1	6	5.06	76	.286	.348	0-0	—	0		-1	-0.1
1989	Bal A	0	0	—	8	0	0	1-1	11.1	13	8	0	0	0-0	13	6.35	60	.277	.271	0-0	—	0		-3	-0.1
1990	Pit N	1	0	1.000	2	0	0	0-0	3	6	5	2	1	1-0	2	9.00	40	.462	.533	0-0	—	0		-3	-0.5
1991	Pit N	0	0	—	5	0	0	0-0	5	7	6	0	0	2-1	5	7.20	50	.304	.360	0-0	—	0		-3	-0.1
Total	9	13	11	.542	152	1	0	11-10	296.1	305	163	37	5	83-8	219	4.40	95	.266	.314	0-0	—	0	65	-8	-0.9
HULIHAN, HARRY Harry Joseph B 4.18.1899 Rutland, VT D 9.11.1980 Rutland, VT BR/TL 5-11/170# d8.16																									
1922	Bos N	2	3	.400	7	6	2	0	40	40	23	0	4	26	16	3.15	127	.274	.398	13-1	.154	-0	115	2	0.1
HULVEY, HANK James Hensel B 7.18.1897 Mount Sidney, VA D 4.9.1982 Mount Sidney, VA BB/TR 6/180# d9.5																									
1923	Phi A	0	1	.000	1	1	0	0	7	10	6	1	0	2	2	7.71	53	.357	.400	2-0	.500	0	60	-2	-0.2
HUME, TOM Thomas Hubert B 3.29.1953 Cincinnati, OH BR/TR 6-1/185# d5.25 C8																									
1977	Cin N	3	3	.500	14	5	0	0-0	43	54	36	5	0	17-3	22	7.12	55	.305	.364	10-2	.200	1	122	-15	-1.7
1978	Cin N	8	11	.421	42	23	3	1-2	174	198	89	12	4	50-9	90	4.14	86	.289	.339	45-8	.067	-3*	108	-11	-1.4
1979	†Cin N	10	9	.526	57	12	2	17-3	163	162	54	12	0	33-9	80	2.76	**136**	.262	.295	46-1	.174	0	105	19	2.5
1980	Cin N	9	10	.474	78	0	0	25-10	137	121	44	6	3	38-14	68	2.56	140	.240	.296	16-1	.188	1		15	2.7

Year	Tm Lg	W	L	Pct	G	GS	CG-Sho	SV-BS	IP	H	R	HR	HB	BB-IB	SO	ERA	AERA	OAV	OOB	AB-SH	AVG	PB	Sup	APR	PW
1981	Cin N	9	4	.692	51	0	0	13-5	67.2	63	27	7	1	31-9	27	3.46	103	.259	.343	4-0	.000	-0		1	0.2
1982	Cin N★	2	6	.250	46	0	0	17-2	63.2	57	24	2	1	21-8	22	3.11	119	.245	.306	5-0	.000	-1		4	0.6
1983	Cin N	3	5	.375	48	0	0	9-3	66	66	40	8	3	41-11	34	4.77	80	.264	.369	5-1	.000	-1		-7	-1.0
1984	Cin N	4	13	.235	54	8	0	3-4	113.1	142	83	14	1	41-9	59	5.64	67	.309	.363	22-0	.136	-0	64	-24	-3.4
1985	Cin N	3	5	.375	56	0	0	3-2	80	65	33	7	3	35-5	50	3.26	116	.224	.313	5-0	.000	-1		4	0.4
1986	Phi N	4	1	.800	48	1	0	4-1	94.1	89	37	5	3	34-5	51	2.77	140	.252	.317	11-5	.000	-1	139	9	0.5
1987	Phi N	1	4	.200	38	6	0	0-1	70.2	75	48	10	4	41-5	29	5.60	76	.277	.377	15-0	.200	0	114	-10	-0.6
	Cin N	1	0	1.000	11	0	0	0-0	13.1	14	6	0	1	2-0	4	4.05	105	.292	.321	0-0	—	0		1	0.0
	Year	2	4	.333	49	6	0	0-1	84	89	59	10	5	43-5	33	5.36	79	.279	.369	15-0	.200	0	114	-9	-0.6
Total	11	57	71	.445	543	55	5	92-33	1086	1106	521	88	24	384-87	536	3.85	97	.268	.330	184-18	.120	-5	103	-14	-1.2
HUMPHREY, BILL Byron William B 6.17.1911 Vienna, MO D 2.13.1992 Springfield, MO BR/TR 6/180# d4.24																									
1938	Bos A	0	0	—	2	0	0	0	2	5	2	0	0	1	0	9.00	55	.500	.545	0-0	—	0		-1	0.0
HUMPHREYS, BOB Robert William B 8.18.1935 Covington, VA BR/TR 5-11/170# d9.8																									
1962	Det A	0	1	.000	4	0	0	1	5	8	4	3	0	2-0	3	7.20	57	.381	.435	0-0	—	0		-1	-0.3
1963	StL N	0	1	.000	9	0	0	0	10.2	11	8	4	1	7-1	8	5.06	70	.282	.404	0-0	—	0		-2	-0.2
1964	†StL N	2	0	1.000	28	0	0	2	42.2	32	14	3	1	15-3	36	2.53	150	.213	.287	4-2	.250	1		6	0.4
1965	Chi N	2	0	1.000	41	0	0	0	65.2	59	25	6	2	27-6	38	3.15	117	.244	.322	3-1	.000	-0		5	0.2
1966	Was A	7	3	.700	58	1	0	3	111.2	91	38	6	4	28-5	88	2.82	123	.229	.285	12-5	.167	1	229	9	0.9
1967	Was A	6	2	.750	48	2	0	4	105.2	93	54	13	2	41-3	54	4.17	76	.238	.310	15-2	.133	1	69	-11	-0.9
1968	Was A	5	7	.417	56	0	0	2	92.2	78	40	13	0	30-2	56	3.69	79	.233	.293	5-1	.400	1		-7	-0.8
1969	Was A	3	3	.500	47	0	0	5-0	79.2	69	37	3	1	38-2	43	3.05	114	.233	.320	13-0	.077	-1		1	0.0
1970	Was A	0	0	—	5	0	0	0-0	6.2	4	2	1	0	9-0	6	1.35	263	.200	.448	0-0	—	0		1	0.1
	Mil A	2	4	.333	23	1	0	3-2	45.2	37	18	3	2	22-3	32	3.15	120	.222	.314	9-1	.000	-1	71	3	0.3
	Year	2	4	.333	28	1	0	3-2	52.1	41	21	4	2	31-3	38	2.92	129	.219	.332	9-1	.000	-1	71	5	0.4
Total	9	27	21	.563	319	4	0	20-2	566	482	240	55	13	219-25	364	3.36	101	.234	.309	61-12	.131	1	110	4	-0.3
HUMPHRIES, BERT Albert B 9.26.1880 California, PA D 9.21.1945 Orlando, FL BR/TR 5-11.5/182# d4.16																									
1910	Phi N	0	0	—	5	0	0	2	9.2	13	8	0	1	3	3	4.66	67	.317	.378	2-0	.000	0		-2	-0.1
1911	Phi N	3	1	.750	11	5	2	1	41	56	25	1	6	10	13	4.17	83	.339	.398	15-0	.333	3	161	-3	-0.1
	Cin N	4	3	.571	14	7	3	0	65	62	25	3	6	18	16	2.35	141	.266	.335	16-2	.063	-1	101	6	0.6
	Year	7	4	.636	25	12	5	1	106	118	29	4	12	28	29	3.06	110	.296	.361	31-2	.194	2	127	2	0.5
1912	Cin N	9	11	.450	30	15	9-1	2	158.2	162	77	6	8	36	58	3.23	104	.270	.319	51-2	.137	-2	74	3	0.1
1913	Chi N	16	4	**.800**	28	20	13-2	1	181	169	70	10	2	24	61	2.69	118	.250	.277	62-4	.194	1	143	10	1.1
1914	Chi N	10	11	.476	34	21	8-2	0	171	162	80	5	2	37	62	2.68	104	.250	.293	55-3	.236	2*	96	1	0.4
1915	Chi N	8	13	.381	31	22	10-4	3	171.2	183	69	6	5	23	45	2.31	120	.280	.309	46-6	.174	0	72	4	0.4
Total	6	50	43	.538	153	90	45-9	9	798	807	354	31	30	151	258	2.79	110	.267	.309	247-17	.186	3	101	19	2.4
HUMPHRIES, JOHNNY John William B 6.23.1915 Clifton Forge, VA D 6.24.1965 New Orleans, LA BR/TR 6-1/185# d5.8																									
1938	Cle A	9	8	.529	**45**	6	1	6	103.1	105	69	6	1	63	56	5.23	89	.264	.367	29-2	.103	-1	76	-7	-1.2
1939	Cle A	2	4	.333	15	1	0	2	28.1	30	30	0	1	32	12	8.26	53	.294	.467	7-0	.000	-1	60	-13	-2.3
1940	Cle A	0	2	.000	19	1	1	1	33.2	35	35	5	2	29	17	8.29	51	.269	.410	6-1	.000	-1	21	-16	-0.9
1941	Chi A	4	2	.667	14	6	4-4	1	73.1	63	18	2	1	22	25	1.84	223	.230	.290	23-1	.087	-1	39	18	1.3
1942	Chi A	12	12	.500	28	28	17-2	0	228.1	227	85	9	7	59	71	2.68	134	.257	.309	80-3	.225	5	104	21	2.6
1943	Chi A	11	11	.500	28	27	8-2	0	188.1	198	86	7	6	54	51	3.30	101	.268	.322	69-0	.290	5	93	-1	0.5
1944	Chi A	8	10	.444	30	20	8	1	169	170	75	9	4	57	42	3.67	93	.267	.331	53-3	.189	0	80	-1	-0.3
1945	Chi A	6	14	.300	22	21	10-1	1	153	172	83	11	3	48	33	4.24	78	.282	.337	54-3	.148	-3	84	-16	-2.3
1946	Phi N	0	0	—	10	1	0	0	24.2	24	17	1	1	9	10	4.01	85	.258	.330	8-0	.250	0	75	-3	-0.2
Total	9	52	63	.452	211	111	49-9	12	1002	1024	498	50	26	373	317	3.78	97	.265	.334	329-13	.191	4	84	-18	-2.8
HUNT, BEN Benjamin Franklin "High Pockets" B 11.10.1888 Eufaula, OK D 9.27.1927 Greybull, WY BL/TL 6-5/190# d8.24																									
1910	Bos A	2	3	.400	7	7	3	0	46.2	45	22	4	0	20	19	4.05	63	.266	.344	18-1	.056	-2	105	-5	-0.7
1913	StL N	0	1	.000	2	1	0	0	8	6	5	0	1	9	6	3.38	96	.240	.457	2-0	.000	-0	23	-1	-0.1
Total	2	2	4	.333	9	8	3	0	54.2	51	27	4	1	29	25	3.95	67	.263	.362	20-1	.050	-2	93	-6	-0.8
HUNT, KEN Kenneth Raymond B 12.14.1938 Ogden, UT BR/TR 6-4/200# d4.16																									
1961	†Cin N	9	10	.474	29	22	4	0	136.1	130	70	13	6	66-1	75	3.96	103	.257	.348	39-3	.179	0	95	1	0.0
HUNTER, GEORGE George Henry B 7.8.1887 Buffalo, NY D 1.11.1968 Harrisburg, PA BB/TL 5-8.5/165# d5.4 twb-Bill ▲																									
1909	Bro N	4	10	.286	16	13	10	0	113.1	104	48	2	3	38	43	2.46	105	.254	.322	123-2	.228	2*	87	-1	0.2
HUNTER, CATFISH James Augustus "Jim" B 4.8.1946 Hertford, NC D 9.9.1999 Hertford, NC BR/TR 6/195# d5.13 HF1987																									
1965	KC A	8	8	.500	32	20	3-2	0	133	124	68	21	2	46-5	82	4.26	82	.246	.309	40-6	.150	-1	103	-10	-1.3
1966	KC A☆	9	11	.450	30	25	4	0	176.2	158	87	17	2	64-4	103	4.02	84	.239	.306	59-3	.153	1	95	-11	-1.3
1967	KC A★	13	17	.433	35	35	13-5	0	259.2	209	91	16	2	84-6	196	2.81	113	.219	.283	92-2	.196	4*	91	11	1.5
1968	Oak A	13	13	.500	36	34	11-2	1	234	210	99	29	4	69-10	172	3.35	84	.238	.295	82-8	.232	5*	126	-14	-1.2
1969	Oak A	12	15	.444	38	35	10-3	0-0	247	210	99	34	5	85-1	150	3.35	103	.234	.302	85-1	.224	4*	93	4	0.8
1970	Oak A★	18	14	.563	40	**40**	9-1	0-0	262.1	253	124	32	9	74-3	178	3.81	93	.250	.304	90-6	.200	4*	106	-8	-0.6
1971	†Oak A	21	11	.656	37	37	16-4	0-0	273.2	225	103	27	4	80-7	181	2.96	113	.223	.281	103-4	.350	13*	110	11	2.5
1972	†Oak A☆	21	7	**.750**	38	37	16-5	0-0	295.1	200	74	21	3	70-6	191	2.04	140	.189	.241	105-9	.219	3*	123	29	3.1
1973	†Oak A★	21	5	**.808**	36	36	11-3	0-0	256.1	222	105	39	1	69-1	124	3.34	106	.232	.282	1-0	1.000	1*	138	9	0.7
1974	†Oak A★	**25**	12	.676	41	41	23-6	0-0	318.1	268	97	25	4	46-2	143	**2.49**	134	.229	**.258**	0-0	—	0	122	35	3.8
1975	NY A★	**23**	14	.622	39	39	**30**-7	0-0	**328**	248	107	25	5	83-4	177	2.58	143	**.208**	**.261**	0-0	—	0	110	41	4.3
1976	†NY A★	17	15	.531	36	36	21-2	0-0	298.2	268	126	28	3	68-5	173	3.53	97	.241	.283	1-0	.000	-0	116	-2	-0.3
1977	†NY A	9	9	.500	22	22	8-1	0-0	143.1	137	83	29	3	47-3	52	4.71	84	.250	.310	0-0	—	0	127	-12	-1.5
1978	†NY A	12	6	.667	21	20	5-1	0-0	118	98	49	16	1	35-0	56	3.58	101	.226	.283	0-0	—	0	120	3	0.3
1979	NY A	2	9	.182	19	19	1	0-0	105	128	68	15	1	34-0	34	5.31	77	.312	.361	0-0	—	0	88	-15	-1.4
Total	15	224	166	.574	500	476	181-42	1-0	3449.1	2958	1380	374	49	954-57	2012	3.26	104	.231	.285	658-39	.226	33	112	71	9.4
HUNTER, JIM James Mac Gregor B 6.22.1964 Jersey City, NJ BR/TR 6-3/205# d5.17																									
1991	Mil A	0	5	.000	8	6	0	0-0	31	45	26	3	4	17-0	14	7.26	55	.349	.437	0-0	—	0	88	-11	-1.4
HUNTER, RICH Richard Thomas B 9.25.1974 Pasadena, CA BR/TR 6-1/185# d4.6																									
1996	Phi N	3	7	.300	14	14	0	0-0	69.1	84	54	10	5	33-2	32	6.49	67	.303	.382	18-4	.167	0*	82	-16	-1.8
HUNTER, BILL Willard Mitchell "Hawk" B 3.8.1934 Newark, NJ BR/TL 6-2/180# d4.16																									
1962	LA N	0	0	—	1	0	0	0	2	6	10	1	0	4-0	1	40.50	9	.545	.625	0-0	—	0		-9	-0.4
	NY N	1	6	.143	27	6	1	0	63	67	41	9	1	34-0	40	5.57	75	.270	.360	13-0	.231	0	66	-7	-0.7
	Year	1	6	.143	28	6	1	0	65	73	44	10	1	38-0	41	6.65	63	.282	.375	13-0	.231	0	67	-16	-1.1
1964	NY N	3	3	.500	41	0	0	5	49	54	25	4	2	9-1	22	4.41	81	.284	.322	1-2	1.000	0		-3	-0.4
Total	2	4	9	.308	69	6	1	5	114	127	76	14	3	47-1	63	5.68	69	.283	.353	14-2	.286	1	71	-19	-1.5
HUNTZINGER, WALT Walter Henry "Shakes" B 2.6.1899 Pottsville, PA D 8.11.1981 Upper Darby, PA BR/TR 6/150# d9.29																									
1923	NY N	0	1	.000	2	1	0	0	8	9	7	0	0	1	2	7.88	49	.290	.313	2-0	.000	-0	22	-3	-0.4
1924	NY N	1	1	.500	12	2	0	1	32.1	41	19	3	0	9	6	4.45	82	.318	.362	8-0	.500	1	58	-3	-0.1
1925	NY N	5	1	.833	26	1	0	0	64.1	68	30	3	0	17	19	3.50	115	.281	.328	11-0	.091	-1	230	**4**	0.2
1926	StL N	0	4	.000	9	4	2	0	34	35	19	4	0	14	9	4.24	92	.267	.338	8-0	.000	-1	75	-1	-0.2
	Chi N	1	1	.500	11	0	0	2	28.2	26	8	0	3	8	4	0.94	408	.260	.333	7-0	.143	-1		7	0.5
	Year	1	5	.167	20	4	2	2	62.2	61	31	4	3	22	13	2.73	142	.264	.336	15-0	.067	-2	75	6	0.3
Total	4	7	8	.467	60	8	2	3	167.1	179	83	10	3	49	40	3.60	108	.283	.337	36-0	.167	-1	83	4	0.0
HURD, TOM Thomas Carr "Whitey" B 5.27.1924 Danville, VA D 9.5.1982 Waterloo, IA BR/TR 5-9/155# d7.30																									
1954	Bos A	2	0	1.000	16	0	0	1	29.2	21	11	2	0	12	14	3.03	135	.198	.277	3-0	.333	0		3	0.3
1955	Bos A	8	6	.571	43	0	0	5	80.2	72	32	7	1	38-10	48	3.01	142	.242	.326	14-1	.071	-1		10	1.6

Year	Tm Lg	W	L	Pct	G	GS	CG-Sho	SV-BS	IP	H	R	HR	HB	BB-IB	SO	ERA	AERA	OAV	OOB	AB-SH	AVG	PB	Sup	APR	PW
1956	Bos A	3	4	.429	40	0	0	5	76	84	52	5	3	47-2	34	5.33	87	.289	.386	12-1	.500	2		-5	-0.4
Total 3		13	10	.565	99	0	0	11	186.1	177	95	14	4	97-12	96	3.96	111	.255	.345	29-2	.276	1		8	1.5
HURST, BRUCE Bruce Vee B 3.24.1958 St.George, UT BL/TL 6-3/215# d4.12																									
1980	Bos A	2	2	.500	12	7	0	0-0	30.2	39	33	4	2	16-0	16	9.10	46	.307	.388	0-0	—	0	145	-16	-1.7
1981	Bos A	2	0	1.000	5	5	0	0-0	23	23	11	1	1	12-2	11	4.30	90	.258	.346	0-0	—	0	116	0	-0.1
1982	Bos A	3	7	.300	28	19	0	0-0	117	161	87	16	3	40-2	53	5.77	75	.333	.383	0-0	—	0	96	-20	-1.4
1983	Bos A	12	12	.500	33	32	6-2	0-0	211.1	241	102	22	3	62-5	115	4.09	107	.290	.340	0-0	—	0	94	8	0.9
1984	Bos A	12	12	.500	33	33	9-2	0-0	218	232	106	25	6	88-3	136	3.92	106	.271	.341	0-0	—	0	105	7	0.7
1985	Bos A	11	13	.458	35	31	6-1	0-3	229.1	243	123	31	3	70-4	189	4.51	95	.273	.327	0-0	—	0	127	-4	-0.4
1986	†Bos A	13	8	.619	25	25	11-4	0-0	174.1	169	63	18	3	50-2	167	2.99	139	.256	.310	0-0	—	0	91	24	2.6
1987	Bos A☆	15	13	.536	33	33	15-3	0-0	238.2	239	124	35	1	76-5	190	4.41	103	.262	.317	0-0	—	0	96	5	0.5
1988	†Bos A	18	6	.750	33	32	7-1	0-0	216.2	222	98	21	2	65-1	166	3.66	113	.264	.316	0-0	—	0	133	10	1.1
1989	SD N	15	11	.577	33	33	**10**-2	0-0	244.2	214	84	16	0	66-7	179	2.69	130	.237	.288	70-8	.071	-2	94	22	2.2
1990	SD N	11	9	.550	33	33	9-**4**	0-0	223.2	188	85	21	1	63-5	162	3.14	122	.228	.284	67-7	.090	-2	89	18	1.3
1991	SD N	15	8	.652	31	31	4	0-0	221.2	201	89	17	3	59-3	141	3.29	116	.241	.292	67-12	.134	-0	103	13	1.2
1992	SD N	14	9	.609	32	32	6-4	0-0	217.1	223	96	22	0	51-3	131	3.85	93	.267	.308	69-9	.159	1*	110	-4	-0.2
1993	SD N	0	1	.000	2	2	0	0-0	4.1	9	7	0	0	3-0	3	12.46	33	.409	.480	0-1	—	0	120	-4	-0.7
	Col N	0	1	.000	3	3	0	0-0	8.2	6	5	1	0	3-0	6	5.19	92	.194	.265	1-0	.000	-0	107	0	0.0
	Year	0	2	.000	5	5	0	0-0	13	15	11	1	0	6-0	9	7.62	60	.283	.356	1-1	.000	-0	111	-4	-0.7
1994	Tex A	2	1	.667	8	8	0	0-0	38	53	30	8	0	16-0	24	7.11	68	.342	.394	0-0	—	0	152	-8	-0.5
Total 15		145	113	.562	379	359	83-23	0-3	2417.1	2463	1143	258	28	740-42	1689	3.92	104	.265	.319	274-37	.113	-3	107	51	5.5
HURST, JAMES James Lavon B 6.1.1967 Plantation, FL BL/TL 6/160# d4.4																									
1994	Tex A	0	0	—	8	0	0	0-0	10.2	17	12	1	0	8-1	5	10.13	48	.362	.446	0-0	—	0		-6	-0.3
HURST, JONATHAN Jonathan B 10.20.1966 New York, NY BR/TR 6-3/175# d6.9																									
1992	Mon N	1	1	.500	3	3	0	0-0	16.1	18	10	1	1	7-0	4	5.51	63	.281	.361	4-2	.000	-0	96	-3	-0.4
1994	NY N	0	1	.000	7	0	0	0-1	10	15	14	5	0	5-0	6	12.60	33	.341	.400	0-0	—	0		-9	-0.7
Total 2		1	2	.333	10	3	0	0-1	26.1	33	24	6	1	12-0	10	8.20	46	.306	.377	4-2	.000	-0	96	-12	-1.1
HURST, BILL William Hansel B 4.28.1970 Miami Beach, FL BR/TR 6-7/220# d9.18																									
1996	Fla N	0	0	—	2	0	0	0-0	2	3	0	0	0	1-0	1	0.00	—	.333	.400	0-0	—	0		1	0.0
HURTADO, EDWIN Edwin Amilgar B 2.1.1970 Barquisimeto, Venezuela BR/TR 6-3/215# d5.22																									
1995	Tor A	5	2	.714	14	10	1	0-0	77.2	81	50	11	5	40-3	33	5.45	87	.275	.367	0-0	—	0	134	-5	-0.4
1996	Sea A	2	5	.286	16	4	0	2-1	47.2	61	42	10	0	30-3	36	7.74	64	.324	.408	0-0	—	0	84	-14	-1.7
1997	Sea A	1	2	.333	13	1	0	0-0	19	25	19	5	2	15-0	10	9.00	50	.329	.447	0-0	—	0	143	-9	-1.1
Total 3		8	9	.471	43	15	1	2-1	144.1	167	111	26	7	85-6	79	6.67	71	.299	.392	0-0	—	0	121	-28	-3.2
HUSTED, BILL William J. B 10.11.1866 Gloucester, NJ D 5.17.1941 Gloucester, NJ d4.29																									
1890	Phi P	5	10	.333	18	17	12	0	129	148	105	2	5	67	33	4.88	88	.276	.361	56	.107	-6	97	-6	-1.0
HUSTING, BERT Berthold Juneau "Pete" B 3.6.1878 Fond Du Lac, WI D 9.3.1948 Milwaukee, WI BR/TR 5-10.5/185# d8.16																									
1900	Pit N	0	0	—	2	0	0	0	8	10	5	2	1	5	7	5.63	65	.303	.410	3-0	.000	-1		-1	-0.1
1901	Mil A	9	15	.375	34	26	19	1	217.1	234	151	5	13	95	67	4.27	84	.272	.353	94-4	.202	-1*	113	-15	-1.3
1902	Bos A	0	1	.000	1	1	1	0	8	15	15	0	0	8	4	9.00	40	.395	.500	4-0	.250	1	80	-6	-0.5
	Phi A	14	5	.737	32	27	17-1	0	204	240	126	7	9	91	44	3.79	97	.293	.370	82-4	.159	-3	142	-4	-0.5
	Year	14	6	.700	33	28	18-1	0	212	255	133	7	9	99	48	3.99	92	.298	.377	86-4	.163	-3	140	-9	-1.0
Total 3		23	21	.523	69	54	37-1	1	437.1	499	297	14	23	199	122	4.16	87	.285	.366	183-8	.180	-4	126	-26	-2.4
HUTCHINGS, JOHNNY John Richard Joseph B 4.14.1916 Chicago, IL D 4.27.1963 Indianapolis, IN BB/TR 6-2/250# d4.26																									
1940	†Cin N	2	1	.667	19	4	0	0	54	53	21	3	1	18	18	3.50	108	.260	.323	13-0	.154	0	75	3	0.1
1941	Cin N	0	0	—	8	0	0	0	11	12	6	0	0	4	5	4.09	88	.279	.340	0-0	—	0		-1	0.0
	Bos N	1	6	.143	36	7	1-1	2	95.2	110	59	6	4	22	36	4.14	86	.287	.333	27-1	.148	0	75	-9	-0.6
	Year	1	6	.143	44	7	1-1	2	106.2	122	62	6	4	26	41	4.13	86	.286	.333	27-1	.148	0	75	-10	-0.6
1942	Bos N	1	0	1.000	20	3	0	0	65.2	66	33	2	2	34	27	4.39	76	.260	.352	20-0	.050	-2	101	-6	-0.6
1944	Bos N	1	4	.200	14	7	1	1	56.2	55	30	3	1	26	26	3.97	96	.252	.335	15-0	.067	-1	75	-1	-0.2
1945	Bos N	7	6	.538	57	12	3-2	3	185	173	87	21	4	75	99	3.75	102	.244	.320	54-1	.241	2	138	3	0.4
1946	Bos N	0	1	.000	1	1	0	0	3	5	3	1	0	1	1	9.00	38	.357	.400	1-0	.000	-0	25	-2	-0.3
Total 6		12	18	.400	155	34	5-3	6	471	474	239	36	12	180	212	3.96	93	.260	.330	130-2	.162	-1	99	-13	-1.2
HUTCHINSON, CHAD Chad Martin B 2.21.1977 Boulder, CO BR/TR 6-5/230# d4.4																									
2001	StL N	0	0	—	3	0	0	0-0	4	9	11	3	1	6-0	2	24.75	17	.450	.593	1-0	.000	-0		-9	-0.4
HUTCHINSON, FRED Frederick Charles B 8.12.1919 Seattle, WA D 11.12.1964 Bradenton, FL BL/TR 6-2/200# d5.2 Mil 1942-45 M12																									
1939	Det A	3	6	.333	13	12	3	0	84.2	95	56	9	0	51	22	5.21	94	.287	.382	34-0	.382	3	89	-2	0.1
1940	†Det A	3	7	.300	17	10	1	0	76	85	52	6	2	26	32	5.68	84	.281	.342	30-0	.267	0	91	-6	-0.6
1946	Det A	14	11	.560	28	26	16-3	2	207	184	78	14	0	66	138	3.09	118	.236	.295	89-2	.315	8*	112	14	2.7
1947	Det A	18	10	.643	33	25	18-3	2	219.2	211	84	14	2	61	113	3.03	124	.251	.304	106-1	.302	11*	104	18	3.7
1948	Det A	13	11	.542	33	28	15	0	221	223	119	32	1	48	92	4.32	101	.258	**.297**	112-2	.205	4*	103	2	0.8
1949	Det A	15	7	.682	33	21	9-4	1	188.2	167	70	18	1	52	54	2.96	141	.237	**.290**	73-4	.247	4*	118	25	3.3
1950	Det A	17	8	.680	39	26	10-1	0	231.2	269	119	18	5	48	71	3.96	118	.290	.329	95-4	.326	10*	126	15	2.5
1951	Det A★	10	10	.500	31	20	9-2	2	188.1	204	84	12	2	27	53	3.68	113	.275	.302	85-2	.188	-2*	98	11	1.0
1952	Det A	2	1	.667	12	1	0	0	37.1	40	16	4	1	9	12	3.38	113	.276	.323	18-0	.056	-1*	69	2	0.1
1953	Det A	0	0	—	3	0	0	0	9.2	9	3	0	0	0	4	2.79	146	.243	.243	6-0	.167	0*		1	0.1
Total 10		95	71	.572	242	169	81-13	7	1464	1487	681	127	14	388	591	3.73	113	.262	.311	648-15	.264	39	108	80	13.7
HUTCHINSON, IRA Ira Kendall B 8.31.1910 Chicago, IL D 8.21.1973 Chicago, IL BR/TR 5-10.5/180# d9.24																									
1933	Chi A	0	0	—	1	1	0	0	4	7	6	1	0	3	2	13.50	31	.368	.455	2-0	.500	0	161	-4	-0.1
1937	Bos N	4	6	.400	31	8	1	0	91.2	99	44	4	1	35	29	3.73	96	.286	.353	26-1	.115	-1	78	-2	-0.3
1938	Bos N	9	8	.529	36	12	4-1	4	151	150	58	3	4	61	38	2.74	125	.258	.332	52-2	.173	-1	80	11	1.2
1939	Bro N	5	2	.714	41	1	0	1	105.2	103	54	9	1	51	46	4.34	93	.265	.352	27-1	.037	-3	217	-2	-0.4
1940	StL N	4	2	.667	20	2	1	1	63.1	68	27	3	0	19	19	3.13	128	.271	.322	18-1	.222	0	120	5	0.5
1941	StL N	1	5	.167	29	0	0	5	46.2	32	23	3	2	19	19	3.86	98	.196	.288	8-0	.250	0		0	0.0
1944	Bos N	9	7	.563	40	8	1-1	1	119.2	136	59	8	3	53	22	4.21	91	.296	.373	29-2	.138	-1	104	-2	-0.3
1945	Bos N	2	3	.400	11	0	0	1	28.2	33	18	2	1	8	4	5.02	76	.277	.328	9-1	.000	-1		-3	-0.7
Total 8		34	33	.507	209	32	7-2	13	610.2	628	289	33	12	249	179	3.76	100	.270	.344	171-8	.140	-7	94	3	-0.1
HUTCHISON, BILL William Forrest "Wild Bill" B 12.17.1859 New Haven, CT D 3.19.1926 Kansas City, MO BR/TR 5-9/175# d6.10																									
1884	KC U	1	1	.500	2	2	2	0	17	14	11	0		1	5	2.65	84	.209	.221	8	.250	-0	143	-1	-0.1
1889	Chi N	16	17	.485	37	36	33-3	0	318	306	206	11	8	117	136	3.54	118	.245	.314	133	.158	-5	90	19	1.3
1890	Chi N	**42**	25	.627	**71**	**66**	**65**-5	**2**	**603**	505	315	20	13	199	289	2.70	136	.220	.286	261	.203	-4	90	51	4.5
1891	Chi N	**44**	19	.698	**66**	**58**	**56**-4	1	**561**	508	283	26	7	178	261	2.81	119	.232	.292	243	.185	-1*	101	29	2.4
1892	Chi N	**36**	36	.500	**75**	**70**	**67**-5	1	**622**	571	316	11	13	190	**314**	2.76	120	.234	.293	263	.217	3*	79	36	4.0
1893	Chi N	16	24	.400	44	40	38-2	0	348.1	420	266	9	13	156	80	4.75	97	.289	.364	162	.253	1*	97	-4	-0.3
1894	Chi N	14	16	.467	37	34	28	0	279	374	257	9	18	140	60	6.03	93	.318	.399	136-2	.309	6*	97	-6	-0.1
1895	Chi N	13	21	.382	38	35	30-2	0	291	371	218	13	13	129	85	4.73	108	.306	.378	126-0	.198	-7	72	11	0.3
1897	StL N	1	4	.200	6	5	2	0	40	55	41	5	2	22	5	6.07	72	.324	.407	18-0	.278	1	55	-8	-0.7
Total 9		183	163	.529	376	346	321-21	4	3079.1	3124	1913	104	87	1132	1235	3.59	111	.255	.323	1350-2	.216	-6	90	127	11.3
HUTSON, HERB George Herbert B 7.17.1949 Savannah, GA BR/TR 6-2/205# d4.10																									
1974	Chi N	0	2	.000	20	2	0	0-0	28.2	24	15	3	1	15-1	22	3.45	111	.233	.325	2-0	.000	-0	11	0	0.0
HUTTON, MARK Mark Steven B 2.6.1970 South Adelaide, Australia BR/TR 6-6/240# d7.23																									
1993	NY A	1	1	.500	7	4	0	0-0	22	24	17	2	1	17-0	12	5.73	73	.293	.412	0-0	—	0	138	-5	-0.4

Year	Tm Lg	W	L	Pct	G	GS	CG-Sho	SV-BS	IP	H	R	HR	HB	BB-IB	SO	ERA	AERA	OAV	OOB	AB-SH	AVG	PB	Sup	APR	PW
1994	NY A	0	0	—	2	0	0	0-0	3.2	4	3	0	0	0-0	1	4.91	93	.250	.250	0-0	—	0		-1	0.0
1996	NY A	0	2	.000	12	2	0	0-0	30.1	32	19	3	1	18-1	25	5.04	98	.269	.364	0-0	—	0	38	-1	-0.1
	Fla N	5	1	.833	13	9	0	0-0	56.1	47	23	6	3	18-0	31	3.67	111	.222	.291	19-1	.316	2	96	4	0.5
1997	Fla N	3	1	.750	32	0	0	0-2	47.2	50	24	7	2	19-3	29	3.78	107	.286	.357	0-0	—	0		0	0.1
	Col N	0	1	.000	8	1	0	0-1	12.2	22	10	3	4	7-0	10	7.11	73	.407	.500	3-0	.000	-0	71	-2	-0.2
	Year	3	2	.600	40	1	0	0-3	60.1	72	14	10	6	26-3	39	4.48	95	.314	.392	3-0	.000	-0	86	-2	-0.1
1998	Cin N	0	1	.000	10	2	0	0-0	17	24	14	2	1	17-0	3	7.41	58	.348	.483	1-0	1.000	0	54	-5	-0.2
Total	5	9	7	.563	84	18	0	0-3	189.2	203	110	23	12	96-4	111	4.75	91	.279	.368	23-1	.304	3	91	-10	-0.3
HYDE, DICK Richard Elde B 8.3.1928 Hindsboro, IL BR/TR 5-11/170# d4.23																									
1955	Was A	0	0	—	3	0	0	0	2	2	1	0	0	1-1	1	4.50	85	.286	.375	0-0	—	0		0	0.0
1957	Was A	4	3	.571	52	2	0	1	109.1	104	54	4	7	56-7	46	4.12	95	.261	.356	18-0	.167	-0	92	-2	-0.1
1958	Was A	10	3	.769	53	0	0	18	103	82	26	1	2	35-7	49	1.75	218	.220	.288	18-3	.000	-2		**21**	3.4
1959	Was A	2	5	.286	37	0	0	4	54.1	56	34	5	2	27-3	29	4.97	79	.269	.354	6-1	.000	-1		-6	-0.8
1960	Was A	0	1	.000	9	0	0	0	8.2	11	4	2	1	5-1	4	4.15	94	.355	.459	0-0	—	0		0	0.0
1961	Bal A	1	2	.333	15	0	0	0	21	18	14	1	1	13-3	15	5.57	69	.228	.344	1-0	1.000	0		-4	-0.4
Total	6	17	14	.548	169	2	0	23	298.1	273	133	13	13	137-22	144	3.56	109	.249	.336	43-4	.093	-2	92	9	2.1
HYNDMAN, JIM James Harvey B 7.9.1866 Hamilton, ON, CAN D 1.16.1934 Alamosa, CO d7.23																									
1886	Phi AA	0	1	.000	1	1	0	0	2	5	10	1	1	5	1	27.00	13	.455	.647	4	.000	-1	288	-5	-0.6
HYNES, PAT Patrick J. B 3.12.1884 St.Louis, MO D 3.12.1907 St.Louis, MO TL d9.27 ▲																									
1903	StL N	0	1	.000	1	1	1	0	9	10	6	0	0	6	1	4.00	82	.294	.400	3-0	.000	-0	62	-1	-0.1
1904	StL A	1	0	1.000	5	2	1	0	26	35	21	1	0	7	6	6.23	40	.321	.362	254-6	.236	0*	187	-10	-0.5
Total	2	1	1	.500	6	3	2	0	35	45	27	1	0	13	7	5.66	47	.315	.372	257-6	.233	0	140	-11	-0.6
IBURG, HAM Herman Edward B 10.29.1877 San Francisco, CA D 2.11.1945 San Francisco, CA BR/TR 5-11/165# d4.17																									
1902	Phi N	11	18	.379	30	29	20-1	0	236	286	141	1	11	62	106	3.89	72	.299	.349	87-0	.138	-5*	94	-28	-3.5
IGNASIAK, GARY Gary Raymond B 9.1.1949 Anchorville, MI BR/TL 5-11/185# d9.20 b-Mike																									
1973	Det A	0	0	—	3	0	0	0-0	4.2	5	2	0	0	3-0	4	3.86	106	.278	.364	0-0	—	0		0	0.0
IGNASIAK, MIKE Michael James B 3.12.1966 Mt.Clemens, MI BB/TR 5-11/175# d8.22 b-Gary																									
1991	Mil A	2	1	.667	4	1	0	0-0	12.2	7	8	2	0	8-0	10	5.68	70	.163	.294	0-0	—	0	92	-2	-0.4
1993	Mil A	1	1	.500	27	0	0	0-2	37	32	17	2	2	21-4	28	3.65	117	.241	.350	0-0	—	0		2	0.1
1994	Mil A	3	1	.750	23	5	0	0-1	47.2	51	25	5	1	13-2	24	4.53	111	.276	.325	0-0	—	0	66	3	0.2
1995	Mil A	4	1	.800	25	0	0	0-1	39.2	51	27	5	2	23-3	26	5.90	85	.325	.411	0-0	—	0		-3	-0.4
Total	4	10	4	.714	79	6	0	0-4	137	141	77	14	5	65-9	88	4.80	98	.272	.356	0-0	—	0	72	0	-0.5
ILSLEY, BLAISE Blaise Francis B 4.9.1964 Alpena, MI BL/TL 6-1/195# d4.4																									
1994	Chi N	0	0	—	10	0	0	0-0	15	25	13	2	0	9-2	9	7.80	53	.385	.459	1-0	.000	-0		-6	-0.3
IMLAY, DOC Harry Miller B 1.12.1889 Allentown, NJ D 10.7.1948 Bordentown, NJ BR/TR 5-11/168# d7.7																									
1913	Phi N	0	0	—	9	0	0	0	13.2	19	13	1	0	7	7	7.24	46	.358	.433	3-0	.000	-0		-5	-0.3
INGERSOLL, BOB Robert Randolph B 1.8.1883 Rapid City, SD D 1.13.1927 Minneapolis, MN BR/TR 5-11.5/175# d4.23																									
1914	Cin N	0	0	—	4	0	0	0	6	5	2	0	1	5	2	3.00	98	.250	.423	1-0	1.000	0		0	0.1
INKS, BERT Albert John B 1.27.1871 Ligonier, IN D 10.3.1941 Ligonier, IN BL/TL 6-3/175# d9.2																									
1891	Bro N	3	10	.231	13	13	11-1	0	96.1	99	70	2	6	43	47	4.02	82	.256	.339	35	.286	2	74	-8	-0.7
1892	Bro N	4	2	.667	9	8	4-1	0	58	48	34	0	4	33	25	3.88	82	.216	.328	25	.400	3	155	-4	0.0
	Was N	1	2	.333	3	3	3	0	21	29	27	0	2	10	11	5.14	63	.315	.394	10	.300	1	136	-6	-0.6
	Year	5	4	.556	12	11	7-1	0	79	77	34	0	6	43	36	4.22	76	.245	.347	35	.371	4	150	-9	-0.6
1894	Bal N	9	4	.692	22	14	10	1	133	181	108	4	11	54	30	5.55	99	.321	.391	57-1	.316	2*	95	-1	0.0
	Lou N	2	6	.250	8	8	8	0	59.2	87	70	2	1	34	8	6.49	79	.336	.415	27-0	.444	3	83	-11	-0.8
	Year	11	10	.524	30	22	18	1	192.2	268	76	6	12	88	38	5.84	92	.326	.399	84-1	.357	5	91	-10	-0.8
1895	Lou N	7	20	.259	28	27	21	0	205.1	294	197	3	15	78	42	6.40	72	.331	.394	84-1	.250	-0	81	-35	-3.1
1896	Phi N	0	1	.000	3	1	0	0	10.1	21	13	1	1	5	2	7.84	55	.412	.474	5-0	.200	-0	66	-4	-0.4
	Cin N	1	1	.500	3	3	2	0	20	21	13	0	1	9	2	4.50	103	.269	.352	7-0	.000	-1	62	0	-0.1
	Year	1	2	.333	6	4	2	0	30.1	42	17	1	2	14	4	5.64	80	.326	.400	12-0	.083	-1	63	-3	-0.5
Total	5	27	46	.370	89	77	59-2	1	603.2	780	532	12	41	266	167	5.52	81	.307	.382	250-2	.300	9	89	-69	-5.7
INNIS, JEFF Jeffrey David B 7.5.1962 Decatur, IL BR/TR 6/170# d5.16																									
1987	NY N	0	1	.000	17	1	0	0-0	25.2	29	9	5	1	4-1	28	3.16	120	.279	.312	3-0	.000	-0	72	2	0.1
1988	NY N	1	1	.500	12	0	0	0-0	19	19	6	0	0	2-1	14	1.89	170	.250	.266	0-0	—	0		2	0.2
1989	NY N	0	1	.000	29	0	0	0-0	39.2	38	16	2	1	8-0	16	3.18	103	.255	.296	2-0	.000	-0		0	0.0
1990	NY N	1	3	.250	18	0	0	1-1	26.1	19	9	4	1	10-3	12	2.39	157	.209	.288	0-1	—	0		3	0.5
1991	NY N	0	2	.000	69	0	0	0-3	84.2	66	30	2	0	23-6	47	2.66	137	.219	.270	2-0	.000	-0		9	0.6
1992	NY N	6	9	.400	76	0	0	1-3	88	85	32	4	6	36-4	39	2.86	121	.266	.347	2-0	.000	-0		6	1.0
1993	NY N	2	3	.400	67	0	0	3-2	76.2	81	39	5	6	38-12	36	4.11	98	.278	.372	0-2	—	0		0	0.0
Total	7	10	20	.333	288	1	0	5-9	360	337	141	22	15	121-27	192	3.05	119	.253	.319	9-3	.000	-1	72	22	2.4
IOTT, HOOKS Clarence Eugene B 12.3.1919 Mountain Grove, MO D 8.17.1980 St.Petersburg, FL BB/TL 6-2/200# d9.6 Mil 1943-45																									
1941	StL A	0	0	—	2	0	0	0	2	2	2	0	0	1	1	9.00	48	.250	.333	0-0	—	0		-1	0.0
1947	StL A	0	1	.000	4	0	0	0	8.1	15	16	4	0	14	6	16.20	24	.375	.537	2-0	.000	-0		-10	-1.0
	NY N	3	8	.273	20	9	2-1	0	71.1	67	50	3	1	52	46	5.93	69	.251	.375	21-2	.143	1	132	-13	-1.6
Total	2	3	9	.250	26	9	2-1	0	81.2	84	68	7	1	67	53	7.05	58	.267	.397	23-2	.130	1	132	-24	-2.6
IRABU, HIDEKI Hideki B 5.5.1969 Hyogo, Japan BR/TR 6-4/240# d7.10																									
1997	NY A	5	4	.556	13	9	0	0-0	53.1	69	47	15	1	20-0	56	7.09	63	.311	.367	1-0	.000	-0	144	-16	-2.2
1998	NY A	13	9	.591	29	28	2-1	0-0	173	148	79	27	9	76-1	126	4.06	108	.233	.321	4-1	.250	0	105	9	0.9
1999	†NY A	11	7	.611	32	27	2-1	0-0	169.1	180	98	26	6	46-0	133	4.84	98	.267	.317	4-2	.000	-0	144	-1	-0.2
2000	Mon N	2	5	.286	11	11	0	0-0	54.2	77	45	9	1	14-0	42	7.24	66	.339	.377	16-2	.125	-1	106	-13	-1.4
2001	Mon N	0	2	.000	3	3	0	0-0	16.2	22	9	3	0	3-0	18	4.86	92	.314	.338	3-0	.000	-0	34	0	0.0
2002	Tex A	3	8	.273	38	2	0	16-4	47	51	30	11	1	16-2	30	5.74	82	.279	.337	0-0	—	0	69	-4	-0.8
Total	6	34	35	.493	126	80	4-2	16-4	514	547	308	91	18	175-3	405	5.15	89	.272	.333	28-5	.107	-1	119	-25	-3.7
IRVINE, DARYL Daryl Keith B 11.15.1964 Harrisonburg, VA BR/TR 6-3/195# d4.28																									
1990	Bos A	1	1	.500	11	0	0	0-0	17.1	15	10	0	0	10-3	9	4.67	87	.246	.338	0-0	—	0		-1	-0.1
1991	Bos A	0	0	—	9	0	0	0-0	18	25	13	2	2	9-1	8	6.00	72	.321	.404	0-0	—	0		-3	-0.1
1992	Bos A	3	4	.429	21	0	0	0-3	28	31	20	1	2	14-2	10	6.11	69	.287	.370	0-0	—	0		-5	-0.9
Total	3	4	5	.444	41	0	0	0-3	63.1	71	43	3	4	33-6	27	5.68	74	.287	.372	0-0	—	0		-9	-1.1
IRWIN, BILL William Franklin "Phil" B 9.16.1859 Neville, OH D 8.7.1933 Ft.Thomas, KY BR/TR 6/195# d8.30																									
1886	Cin AA	0	2	.000	2	2	2	0	17	18	19	2	0	8	6	5.82	60	.247	.321	6	.000	-0	59	-5	-0.4
ISBELL, FRANK William Frank "Bald Eagle" B 8.21.1875 Delevan, NY D 7.15.1941 Wichita, KS BL/TR 5-11/190# d5.1 ▲																									
1898	Chi N	4	7	.364	13	9	7	0	81	86	54	0	7	42	16	3.56	101	.270	.368	159-6	.233	-0*	101	-1	-0.1
1901	Chi A	0	0	—	1	0	0	0	1	2	1	0	0	0	0	9.00	39	.400	.400	556-13	.257	0*		0	0.0
1902	Chi A	0	0	—	1	1	0	0	1	3	2	0	0	1	1	9.00	38	.500	.571	515-23	.252	0*	212	-1	0.0
1906	†Chi A	0	0	—	1	0	0	0	2	1	0	0	0	0	2	0.00	—	.143	.143	549-31	.279	0*		1	0.0
1907	Chi A	0	0	—	1	0	0	1	0.1	0	0	0	0	0	0	0.00	—	.000	.000	486-24	.243	0*		0	0.0
Total	5	4	7	.364	17	10	7	1	85.1	92	57	0	7	43	19	3.59	99	.273	.367	2265-97	.257	1	112	-1	-0.1
ISHII, KAZUHISA Kazuhisa B 9.9.1973 Tokyo, Japan BL/TL 6/187# d4.6																									
2002	LA N	14	10	.583	28	28	0	0-0	154	137	82	20	4	106-3	143	4.27	90	.240	.360	50-4	.100	-2	114	-10	-1.5
2003	LA N	9	7	.563	27	27	0	0-0	147	129	72	16	6	101-4	140	3.86	104	.238	.363	34-9	.029	-3	84	1	-0.2

Year	Tm Lg	W	L	Pct	G	GS	CG-Sho	SV-BS	IP	H	R	HR	HB	BB-IB	SO	ERA	AERA	OAV	OOB	AB-SH	AVG	PB	Sup	APR	PW
Total	2	23	17	.575	55	55	0	0-0	301	266	154	36	10	207-7	283	4.07	96	.239	.362	84-13	.071	-4	99	-9	-1.7
ISRINGHAUSEN, JASON Jason Derik B 9.7.1972 Brighton, IL BR/TR 6-3/195# d7.17																									
1995	NY N	9	2	.818	14	14	1	0-0	93	88	29	6	2	31-2	55	2.81	144	.254	.317	27-4	.148	1	96	15	1.7
1996	NY N	6	14	.300	27	27	2-1	0-0	171.2	190	103	13	8	73-5	114	4.77	84	.284	.357	51-2	.255	6	90	-14	-0.8
1997	NY N	2	2	.500	6	6	0	0-0	29.2	40	27	3	1	22-0	25	7.58	53	.336	.438	7-1	.143	-0	148	-12	-1.3
1999	NY N	1	3	.250	13	5	0	1-0	39.1	43	29	7	2	22-2	31	6.41	68	.279	.374	12-1	.083	-0	134	-9	-0.9
	Oak A	0	1	.000	20	0	0	8-0	25.1	21	6	2	1	12-2	20	2.13	218	.223	.318	0-0	—	0		8	0.7
2000	†Oak A★	6	4	.600	66	0	0	33-7	69	67	34	6	3	32-5	57	3.78	126	.252	.338	0-0	—	0		7	1.3
2001	†Oak A	4	3	.571	65	0	0	34-9	71.1	54	24	5	0	23-5	74	2.65	167	.203	.266	0-0	—	0		14	2.3
2002	†StL N	3	2	.600	60	0	0	32-5	65.1	46	22	0	1	18-1	68	2.48	160	.199	.257	0-0	—	0		10	1.5
2003	StL N	0	1	.000	40	0	0	22-3	42	31	14	2	0	18-1	41	2.36	173	.200	.283	2-0	.500	1		7	0.9
Total	8	31	32	.492	311	52	3-1	130-24	606.2	580	288	44	18	251-23	485	3.83	110	.252	.328	99-8	.202	7	100	26	5.4
IZQUIERDO, HANSEL Hansel B 1.2.1977 Havana, Cuba BR/TR 6-2/205# d4.21																									
2002	Fla N	2	0	1.000	20	2	0	0-0	29.2	33	17	2	5	21-3	20	4.55	87	.289	.413	2-0	.000	-0	70	-2	-0.2
JACKSON, AL Alvin Neill B 12.26.1935 Waco, TX BL/TL 5-10/169# d6.1 C8																									
1959	Pit N	0	0	—	8	3	0	0	18	30	14	1	0	8-3	13	6.50	60	.405	.463	5-0	.200	0	239	-5	-0.3
1961	Pit N	1	0	1.000	3	2	1	0	23.2	20	10	2	0	4-1	15	3.42	117	.233	.267	8-0	.000	-1*	167	2	0.0
1962	NY N	8	20	.286	36	33	12-4	0	231.1	244	132	16	5	78-5	118	4.40	95	.273	.333	73-6	.068	-5*	83	-5	-0.7
1963	NY N	13	17	.433	37	34	11	1	227	237	128	25	12	84-2	142	3.96	88	.267	.336	79-3	.203	2*	82	-15	-1.6
1964	NY N	11	16	.407	40	31	11-3	1	213.1	229	115	18	4	60-3	112	4.26	84	.272	.323	72-2	.153	2*	72	-16	-1.6
1965	NY N	8	20	.286	37	31	7-3	1	205.1	217	111	17	8	61-4	120	4.34	81	.271	.328	60-8	.117	-1*	64	-17	-2.2
1966	StL N	13	15	.464	36	30	11-3	0	232.2	222	82	18	3	45-10	90	2.51	143	.250	.288	74-5	.176	2*	75	25	3.5
1967	StL N	9	4	.692	38	11	1-1	1	107	117	61	7	1	29-5	43	3.95	83	.279	.322	31-1	.258	2*	172	-12	-1.0
1968	NY N	3	7	.300	25	9	0	3	92.2	88	42	5	2	17-6	59	3.69	82	.249	.285	28-1	.250	1*	86	-7	-0.6
1969	NY N	0	0	—	9	0	0	0-0	11	18	13	1	1	4-0	10	10.64	34	.353	.397	1-0	.000	-0		-8	-0.4
	Cin N	1	0	1.000	33	0	0	3-0	27.1	27	17	5	3	17-3	16	5.27	71	.260	.376	4-0	.250	0		-4	-0.2
	Year	1	0	1.000	42	0	0	3-0	38.1	45	33	6	4	21-3	26	6.81	55	.290	.383	5-0	.200	0		-11	-0.6
Total	10	67	99	.404	302	184	54-14	10-0	1389.1	1449	725	115	39	407-42	738	3.98	91	.268	.322	435-26	.159	3	86	-62	-5.1
JACKSON, CHARLIE Charles Bernard B 8.4.1876 Versailles, OH D 11.23.1957 Scottsbluff, NE TR d8.11																									
1905	Det A	0	2	.000	2	2	1	0	11	14	12	1	0	7	3	5.73	48	.311	.404	4-0	.250	0	39	-4	-0.6
JACKSON, DANNY Danny Lynn B 1.5.1962 San Antonio, TX BR/TL 6/205# d9.11																									
1983	KC A	1	1	.500	4	3	0	0-0	19	26	12	1	0	6-0	9	5.21	78	.325	.372	0-0	—	0	111	-2	-0.2
1984	KC A	2	6	.250	15	11	1	0-0	76	84	41	4	5	35-0	40	4.26	95	.285	.370	0-0	—	0	81	-3	-0.3
1985	†KC A	14	12	.538	32	32	4-3	0-0	208	209	94	7	6	76-2	114	3.42	122	.261	.328	0-0	—	0	83	15	1.7
1986	KC A	11	12	.478	32	27	4-1	1-0	185.2	177	83	13	4	79-1	115	3.20	133	.256	.334	0-0	—	0	62	17	1.9
1987	KC A	9	18	.333	36	34	11-2	0-1	224	219	115	11	7	109-1	152	4.02	114	.258	.344	0-0	—	0	67	13	1.3
1988	Cin N☆	**23**	8	.742	35	35	**15**-6	0-0	260.2	206	86	13	2	71-6	161	2.73	132	.218	.273	90-8	.144	-0	114	24	3.1
1989	Cin N	6	11	.353	20	20	1	0-0	115.2	122	78	10	1	57-7	70	5.60	64	.271	.351	36-4	.222	1*	87	-23	-3.0
1990	†Cin N	6	6	.500	22	21	0	0-0	117.1	119	54	11	2	40-4	76	3.61	110	.266	.325	37-4	.054	-2*	87	3	0.0
1991	Chi N	1	5	.167	17	14	0	0-0	70.2	89	59	8	1	48-4	31	6.75	58	.309	.407	23-2	.087	-1	119	-21	-1.8
1992	Chi N	4	9	.308	19	19	0	0-0	113	117	59	5	3	48-3	51	4.22	85	.270	.343	36-4	.083	-2	79	-7	-1.1
	†Pit N	4	4	.500	15	15	0	0-0	88.1	94	40	1	1	29-3	46	3.36	103	.276	.330	24-5	.083	-1	121	-1	-0.2
	Year	8	13	.381	34	34	0	0-0	201.1	211	45	6	4	77-6	97	3.84	92	.272	.337	60-9	.083	-3	97	-9	-1.3
1993	†Phi N	12	11	.522	32	32	2-1	0-0	210.1	214	105	12	4	80-2	120	3.77	105	.263	.329	65-12	.077	-2	116	3	0.0
1994	Phi N★	14	6	.700	25	25	4-1	0-0	179.1	183	71	13	2	46-1	129	3.26	132	.266	.312	57-9	.158	1*	123	21	2.4
1995	StL N	2	12	.143	19	19	2-1	0-0	100.2	120	82	10	6	48-1	52	5.90	71	.303	.381	31-4	.161	0	85	-22	-2.5
1996	†StL N	1	1	.500	13	4	0	0-0	36.1	33	18	3	1	16-1	27	4.46	94	.243	.325	9-1	.333	1	118	0	0.2
1997	StL N	1	2	.333	4	4	0	0-0	18.2	26	17	3	2	8-1	13	7.71	54	.347	.414	7-0	.143	-0	105	-7	-0.9
	SD N	1	7	.125	13	9	0	0-0	49	72	47	8	3	20-2	19	7.53	52	.353	.413	13-1	.077	-0	92	-22	-2.9
	Year	2	9	.182	17	13	0	0-0	67.2	98	51	11	5	28-3	32	7.58	52	.351	.413	20-1	.100	-1	97	-30	-3.8
Total	15	112	131	.461	353	324	44-15	1-1	2072.2	2110	1061	133	50	816-39	1225	4.01	100	.266	.336	428-54	.126	-6	93	-12	-2.3
JACKSON, DARRELL Darrell Preston B 4.3.1956 Los Angeles, CA BB/TL 5-10/150# d6.16																									
1978	Min A	4	6	.400	19	15	1-1	0-0	92.1	89	53	9	2	48-1	54	4.48	86	.256	.347	0-0	—	0	91	-7	-0.7
1979	Min A	4	4	.500	24	8	1	0-1	69.1	89	36	5	1	26-0	43	4.28	103	.319	.377	0-0	—	0*	106	1	0.1
1980	Min A	9	9	.500	32	25	1	1-0	172	161	81	15	2	69-2	90	3.87	113	.250	.323	0-0	—	0*	81	10	1.0
1981	Min A	3	3	.500	14	5	0	0-0	32.2	35	16	1	1	19-2	26	4.41	90	.282	.382	0-0	—	0	50	-1	-0.2
1982	Min A	0	5	.000	13	7	0	0-0	44.2	51	33	6	1	24-3	16	6.25	68	.297	.384	0-0	—	0	37	-9	-0.9
Total	5	20	27	.426	102	60	3-1	1-1	411	425	219	36	7	186-8	229	4.38	96	.272	.349	0-0	—	0	79	-6	-0.7
JACKSON, EDWIN Edwin B 9.9.1983 Neu-Ulm, Germany BR/TR 6-3/190# d9.9																									
2003	LA N	2	1	.667	4	3	0	0-0	22	17	6	2	1	11-1	19	2.45	164	.221	.322	6-1	.000	-0	70	4	0.5
JACKSON, GRANT Grant Dwight "Buck" B 9.28.1942 Fostoria, OH BB/TL 6/190# d9.3 C4																									
1965	Phi N	1	1	.500	6	2	0	0	13.2	17	11	4	0	5-0	15	7.24	48	.304	.361	4-0	.000	-0	101	-5	-0.7
1966	Phi N	0	0	—	2	0	0	0	1.2	2	1	0	0	3-0	0	5.40	67	.333	.556	0-0	—	0		0	0.0
1967	Phi N	2	3	.400	43	4	0	1	84.1	86	40	3	2	43-7	83	3.84	89	.267	.352	15-0	.133	-0	103	-3	-0.3
1968	Phi N	1	6	.143	33	6	1	1	61	59	28	4	0	20-3	49	2.95	102	.248	.302	10-1	.300	1*	149	-2	-0.1
1969	Phi N☆	14	18	.438	38	35	13-4	1-0	253	237	114	16	5	92-3	180	3.34	106	.249	.316	86-6	.140	-0*	87	2	0.1
1970	Phi N	5	15	.250	32	23	1	0-0	149.2	170	94	17	1	61-3	104	5.29	76	.288	.354	44-1	.091	-2*	50	-21	-2.6
1971	†Bal A	4	3	.571	29	9	0	0-0	77.2	72	31	7	2	20-5	51	3.13	107	.249	.299	22-0	.091	0	107	2	0.2
1972	Bal A	1	1	.500	32	0	0	8-0	41	33	14	1	0	9-0	34	2.63	117	.217	.261	4-0	.000	-0		2	0.1
1973	†Bal A	8	0	1.000	45	0	0	9-2	80.1	54	18	5	0	24-4	47	1.90	196	.198	.260	0-0	—	0		17	2.1
1974	†Bal A	6	4	.600	49	0	0	12-7	66.2	48	19	7	1	22-4	56	2.57	135	.198	.265	0-0	—	0		8	1.5
1975	Bal A	4	3	.571	41	0	0	7-1	48.1	42	18	3	1	21-6	39	3.35	105	.241	.322	0-0	—	0		2	0.3
1976	Bal A	1	1	.500	13	0	0	3-0	19.1	19	11	1	2	9-2	14	5.12	64	.268	.361	0-0	—	0		-4	-0.5
	†NY A	6	0	1.000	21	2	1-1	1-0	58.2	38	11	1	1	16-0	25	1.69	203	.186	.244	0-0	—	0	206	12	1.2
	Year	7	1	.875	34	2	1-1	4-0	78	57	19	2	3	25-2	39	2.54	133	.207	.276	0-0	—	0	208	9	0.7
1977	Pit N	5	3	.625	49	2	0	4-2	91	81	44	11	1	39-8	41	3.86	103	.240	.318	18-0	.333	2	111	1	0.2
1978	Pit N	7	5	.583	60	0	0	5-3	77.1	89	32	5	1	32-9	45	3.26	114	.298	.362	12-0	.250	1		4	0.7
1979	†Pit N	8	5	.615	72	0	0	14-5	82	67	32	9	2	35-5	39	2.96	131	.230	.311	9-0	.000	-1		7	1.2
1980	Pit N	8	4	.667	61	0	0	9-3	71	71	24	4	0	20-3	31	2.92	125	.275	.322	10-0	.000	-1		6	1.1
1981	Pit N	1	2	.333	35	0	0	4-2	32.1	30	10	1	0	10-3	17	2.51	144	.248	.301	2-0	.000	-0		4	0.4
	Mon N	1	0	1.000	10	0	0	0-0	10.2	14	9	2	0	9-2	4	7.59	46	.333	.451	0-0	—	0		-4	-0.4
	Year	2	2	.500	45	0	0	4-2	43	44	24	3	0	19-5	21	3.77	95	.270	.342	2-0	.000	-0		0	0.0
1982	KC A	3	1	.750	20	0	0	0-2	38.1	42	27	7	2	21-4	15	5.17	79	.271	.363	0-0	—	0		-6	-0.5
	Pit N	0	0	—	1	0	0	0-0	0.2	1	1	1	0	0-0	0	13.50	28	.333	.333	0-0	—	0		-1	0.0
Total	18	86	75	.534	692	83	16-5	79-27	1358.2	1272	589	109	21	511-71	889	3.46	104	.251	.318	236-8	.136	-2	86	21	4.0
JACKSON, JOHN John Lewis B 7.15.1909 Philadelphia, PA D 10.22.1956 Somers Point, NJ BR/TR 6-2/180# d6.20																									
1933	Phi N	2	2	.500	10	7	1	0	54	74	42	3	5	35	11	6.00	64	.329	.430	21-0	.143	-1	112	-11	-1.0
JACKSON, LARRY Lawrence Curtis B 6.2.1931 Nampa, ID D 8.28.1990 Boise, ID BR/TR 6-2/190# d4.17																									
1955	StL N	9	14	.391	37	25	4-1	2	177.1	189	93	25	9	72-11	88	4.31	94	.277	.351	57-1	.053	-6	86	-5	-1.2
1956	StL N	2	2	.500	51	1	0	9	85.1	75	44	5	1	45-8	50	4.11	92	.240	.337	11-0	.091	-0	70	-3	-0.1
1957	StL N★	15	9	.625	41	22	6-2	1	210.1	196	84	21	4	57-8	96	3.47	114	.248	.301	72-3	.181	0	99	14	1.8
1958	StL N★	13	13	.500	49	23	11-1	8	198	211	93	21	10	51-11	124	3.68	112	.272	.324	60-2	.150	-2*	101	8	0.7
1959	StL N	14	13	.519	40	37	12-3	0	256	271	103	13	4	64-3	145	3.30	128	.270	.315	80-7	.112	-3*	88	25	2.1
1960	StL N★	18	13	.581	43	**38**	14-3	0	**282**	277	123	22	3	70-4	171	3.48	118	.257	.302	95-5	.211	2*	96	17	1.8

Year	Tm Lg	W	L	Pct	G	GS	CG-Sho	SV-BS	IP	H	R	HR	HB	BB-IB	SO	ERA	AERA	OAV	OOB	AB-SH	AVG	PB	Sup	APR	PW
1961	StL N	14	11	.560	33	28	12-3	0	211	203	99	20	4	56-5	113	3.75	117	.252	.301	74-6	.176	0*	93	16	1.8
1962	StL N	16	11	.593	36	35	11-2	0	252.1	267	121	25	6	64-6	112	3.75	114	.269	.316	89-5	.169	2	104	13	1.5
1963	Chi N★	14	18	.438	37	37	13-4	0	275	256	102	11	6	54-3	153	2.55	137	.245	.284	87-9	.195	2	79	23	3.1
1964	Chi N	**24**	11	.686	40	38	19-3	0	297.2	265	114	17	1	58-8	148	3.14	118	.235	.272	114-5	.175	1	110	18	2.5
1965	Chi N	14	21	.400	39	39	12-4	0	257.1	268	126	28	5	57-8	131	3.85	96	.267	.309	86-4	.128	1*	81	-3	-0.2
1966	Chi N	0	2	.000	3	2	0	0	8	14	13	3	0	4-0	5	13.50	27	.368	.429	3-0	.000	-0	12	-8	-1.3
	Phi N	15	13	.536	35	33	12-5	0	247	243	93	22	5	58-5	107	2.99	120	.259	.305	89-5	.146	-0*	93	16	1.8
	Year	15	15	.500	38	35	12-**5**	0	255	257	97	25	5	62-5	112	3.32	108	.264	.310	92-5	.141	-1	88	6	0.5
1967	Phi N	13	15	.464	40	37	11-4	0	261.2	242	111	17	6	54-11	139	3.10	110	.241	.283	87-4	.161	0*	89	6	0.9
1968	Phi N	13	17	.433	34	34	12-2	0	243.2	229	86	9	4	60-15	127	2.77	109	.248	.296	85-2	.141	-0*	91	6	0.8
Total	14	194	183	.515	558	429	149-37	20	3262.2	3206	1405	259	68	824-106	1709	3.40	113	.256	.304	1089-58	.156	-5	93	143	16.0
JACKSON, MIKE Michael Ray B 12.22.1964 Houston, TX BR/TR 6/200# d8.11																									
1986	Phi N	0	0	—	9	0	0	0-1	13.1	12	5	2	2	4-1	3	3.38	114	.250	.333	0-0	—	0		1	0.0
1987	Phi N	3	10	.231	55	7	0	1-1	109.1	88	55	16	3	56-6	93	4.20	101	.219	.316	17-3	.118	-0	107	1	0.1
1988	Sea A	6	5	.545	62	0	0	4-7	99.1	74	37	10	2	43-10	76	2.63	159	.209	.291	0-0	—	0		14	1.5
1989	Sea A	4	6	.400	65	0	0	7-3	99.1	81	43	8	6	54-6	94	3.17	127	.223	.332	0-0	—	0		8	0.8
1990	Sea A	5	7	.417	63	0	0	3-9	77.1	64	42	8	2	44-12	69	4.54	87	.229	.333	0-0	—	0		-4	-0.5
1991	Sea A	7	7	.500	72	0	0	14-8	88.2	64	35	5	6	34-11	74	3.25	127	.201	.290	0-0	—	0		9	1.4
1992	SF N	6	6	.500	67	0	0	2-1	82	76	35	7	4	33-10	80	3.73	89	.252	.331	2-0	.000	-0		-3	-0.5
1993	SF N	6	6	.500	**81**	0	0	1-5	77.1	58	28	7	3	24-6	70	3.03	129	.204	.272	3-0	.667	2		8	1.3
1994	SF N	3	2	.600	36	0	0	4-2	42.1	23	8	4	2	11-0	51	1.49	270	.164	.234	1-1	.000	-0		12	1.5
1995	†Cin N	6	1	.857	40	0	0	2-2	49	38	13	5	1	19-1	41	2.39	173	.213	.291	4-0	.250	0		10	1.3
1996	Sea A	1	1	.500	73	0	0	6-2	72	61	32	11	6	24-3	70	3.63	137	.225	.301	0-0	—	0		10	0.5
1997	†Cle A	2	5	.286	71	0	0	15-2	75	59	33	3	4	29-5	74	3.24	145	.215	.297	0-0	—	0		10	1.3
1998	†Cle A	1	1	.500	69	0	0	40-5	64	43	11	4	4	13-0	55	1.55	309	.195	.252	0-0	—	0		**23**	3.0
1999	†Cle A	3	4	.429	72	0	0	39-4	68.2	60	32	11	2	26-1	55	4.06	124	.232	.304	0-0	—	0		8	1.5
2001	†Hou N	5	3	.625	67	0	0	4-5	69	68	36	14	2	22-3	46	4.70	97	.260	.319	1-0	.000	-0		0	0.0
2002	†Min A	2	3	.400	58	0	0	0-2	55	59	20	5	4	13-3	29	3.27	137	.284	.333	0-0	—	0		8	0.7
Total	16	60	67	.472	960	7	0	142-59	1141.2	928	465	120	53	449-78	980	3.35	127	.223	.304	28-4	.179	1	107	115	13.9
JACKSON, MIKE Michael Warren B 3.27.1946 Paterson, NJ BL/TL 6-3/190# d5.10																									
1970	Phi N	1	1	.500	5	0	0	0-0	6.1	6	1	0	0	4-0	4	1.42	281	.286	.400	1-0	1.000	0		2	0.4
1971	StL N	0	0	—	1	0	0	0-0	0.2	1	0	0	0	1-0	0	0.00	—	.333	.500	1-0	.000	-0		0	0.0
1972	KC A	1	2	.333	7	3	0	0-0	19.2	24	14	0	0	14-1	15	6.41	47	.320	.422	5-1	.000	-1	87	-7	-1.0
1973	KC A	0	0	—	9	0	0	0-0	22.1	25	17	3	1	20-1	13	6.85	60	.301	.438	0-0	—	0		-6	-0.3
	Cle A	0	0	—	1	0	0	0-0	0.2	1	0	0	0	0-0	1	0.00	—	.333	.333	0-0	—	0		0	0.0
	Year	0	0	—	10	0	0	0-0	23	26	20	3	1	20-1	14	6.65	62	.302	.435	0-0	—	0		-5	-0.3
Total	4	2	3	.400	23	3	0	0-0	49.2	57	32	3	1	39-2	33	5.80	63	.308	.427	7-1	.143	-0	87	-11	-0.9
JACKSON, ROY LEE Roy Lee B 5.1.1954 Opelika, AL BR/TR 6-2/194# d9.13																									
1977	NY N	0	2	.000	4	4	0	0-0	24	25	16	2	3	15-1	13	6.00	62	.263	.377	6-1	.000	-1	95	-6	-0.5
1978	NY N	0	0	—	4	2	0	0-0	12.2	21	13	2	2	6-0	6	9.24	38	.429	.500	3-0	.667	1	90	-8	-0.3
1979	NY N	1	0	1.000	8	0	0	0-1	16.1	11	4	1	1	5-0	10	2.20	165	.200	.279	1-0	1.000	0		3	0.2
1980	NY N	1	7	.125	24	8	1	1-0	70.2	78	37	4	0	20-4	58	4.20	85	.287	.331	16-0	.188	1*	104	-5	-0.6
1981	Tor A	1	2	.333	39	0	0	7-1	62	65	23	5	1	25-7	27	2.61	151	.275	.346	0-0	—	0		8	0.5
1982	Tor A	8	8	.500	48	2	0	6-5	97	77	37	7	2	31-4	71	3.06	147	.218	.281	0-0	—	0	112	14	2.3
1983	Tor A	8	3	.727	49	0	0	7-5	92	92	48	6	3	41-2	48	4.50	96	.267	.344	0-0	—	0		-1	-0.1
1984	Tor A	7	8	.467	54	0	0	10-7	86	73	40	12	1	31-4	58	3.56	115	.230	.299	0-0	—	0		4	0.7
1985	SD N	2	3	.400	22	2	0	2-0	40	32	13	4	1	13-1	28	2.70	131	.224	.289	5-1	.000	-1	62	4	0.5
1986	Min A	0	1	.000	28	0	0	1-0	58.1	57	29	7	3	16-0	32	3.86	112	.256	.308	0-0	—	0		2	0.1
Total	10	28	34	.452	280	18	1	34-19	559	531	260	50	17	203-23	351	3.77	108	.254	.322	31-2	.194	1	89	15	2.8
JACOBS, TONY Anthony Robert B 8.5.1925 Dixmoor, IL D 12.21.1980 Nashville, TN BB/TR 5-9/150# d9.19																									
1948	Chi N	0	0	—	1	0	0	0	2	3	1	1	0	0	2	4.50	87	.333	.333	0-0	—	0		0	0.0
1955	StL N	0	0	—	1	0	0	0	2	6	4	1	0	1-0	1	18.00	23	.500	.538	1-0	.000	-0		-3	-0.1
Total	2	0	0	—	2	0	0	0	4	9	5	2	0	1-0	3	11.25	35	.429	.455	1-0	.000	-0		-3	-0.1
JACOBS, ART Arthur Edward B 8.28.1902 Luckey, OH D 6.8.1967 Inglewood, CA BL/TL 5-10/170# d6.18																									
1939	Cin N	0	0	—	1	0	0	1	1	2	1	0	0	1	0	9.00	43	.400	.500	0-0	—	0		-1	-0.1
JACOBS, BUCKY Newton Smith B 3.21.1913 Altavista, VA D 6.15.1990 Richmond, VA BR/TR 5-11/155# d6.27																									
1937	Was A	1	1	.500	11	1	0	0	22.1	26	12	0	0	11	8	4.84	92	.295	.374	5-0	.000	-1	39	0	-0.1
1939	Was A	0	0	—	2	0	0	0	3	1	0	0	0	0	1	0.00	—	.100	.100	0-0	—	0		2	0.1
1940	Was A	0	1	.000	9	0	0	0	15	16	11	1	2	9	6	6.00	69	.271	.386	1-1	.000	-0		-3	-0.1
Total	3	1	2	.333	22	1	0	0	40.1	43	23	1	2	20	15	4.91	88	.274	.363	6-1	.000	-1	39	-1	-0.1
JACOBS, ELMER William Elmer B 8.10.1892 Salem, MO D 2.10.1958 Salem, MO BR/TR 6/165# d4.23																									
1914	Phi N	1	3	.250	14	7	1	0	50.2	65	38	2	3	20	17	4.80	61	.342	.413	14-0	.000	-2	104	-9	-0.8
1916	Pit N	6	10	.375	34	17	8	0	153	151	70	2	4	38	46	2.94	91	.258	.308	40-1	.075	-2	95	-5	-0.8
1917	Pit N	6	19	.240	38	25	10-1	2	227.1	214	87	3	5	76	58	2.81	101	.262	.329	67-3	.179	-1	69	1	0.1
1918	Pit N	0	1	.000	8	4	0	0	23.1	31	18	0	0	14	2	5.79	50	.344	.433	7-0	.286	0	151	-7	-0.3
	Phi N	9	5	.643	18	14	12-4	1	123	91	39	3	4	42	33	2.41	124	.210	.285	38-2	.158	-1	94	8	0.8
	Year	9	6	.600	26	18	12-4	1	146.1	122	43	3	4	56	35	2.95	101	.233	.312	45-2	.178	-1	106	2	0.5
1919	Phi N	6	10	.375	17	15	13	0	128.2	150	66	5	6	44	37	3.85	84	.304	.368	45-1	.178	-1	86	-8	-1.0
	StL N	3	6	.333	17	8	4-1	1	85.1	81	30	2	5	25	31	2.53	110	.264	.329	23-1	.348	3	89	3	0.7
	Year	9	16	.360	34	23	17-1	1	214	231	33	7	11	69	68	3.32	92	.289	.353	68-2	.235	2	87	-5	-0.3
1920	StL N	4	8	.333	23	9	1	1	77.2	91	56	2	5	33	21	5.21	57	.296	.374	26-3	.192	-0	105	-20	-2.8
1924	Chi N	11	12	.478	38	22	13-1	1	190.1	181	93	9	2	72	50	3.74	104	.258	.329	54-6	.111	-4	92	4	0.1
1925	Chi N	2	3	.400	18	4	1-1	1	55.2	63	37	9	1	22	19	5.17	84	.274	.340	13-0	.231	-0	112	-5	-0.4
1927	Chi A	2	4	.333	25	8	2-1	0	74.1	105	49	3	4	37	22	4.60	88	.354	.432	20-4	.150	-1	95	-6	-0.5
Total	9	50	81	.382	250	133	65-9	7	1189.1	1223	583	40	39	423	336	3.55	91	.275	.343	347-21	.161	-8	91	-44	-4.9
JACOBSON, BEANY Albert L. (b: Albin L. Jacobson) B 6.5.1881 Port Washington, WI D 1.31.1933 Decatur, IL BL/TL 6/170# d4.30																									
1904	Was A	5	23	.179	33	30	23-1	0	253.2	276	135	6	3	57	75	3.55	75	.278	.319	88-1	.091	-6	66	-24	-3.0
1905	Was A	7	8	.467	22	17	12	0	144.1	139	83	1	5	35	50	3.30	80	.255	.305	44-0	.159	1	96	-13	-1.3
1906	StL A	9	9	.500	24	15	12	0	155	146	68	3	4	27	53	2.50	103	.252	.290	55-1	.091	-4	93	0	-0.5
1907	StL A	1	6	.143	7	7	6	0	57.1	55	28	1	0	26	16	2.98	84	.255	.335	18-1	.222	-0	54	-4	-0.5
	Bos A	0	0	—	2	1	0	0	2	2	3	0	0	3	1	9.00	29	.250	.455	0-0	—	0	52	-1	-0.1
	Year	1	6	.143	9	8	6	0	59.1	57	5	1	0	29	17	3.19	79	.254	.340	18-1	.222	-0	54	-5	-0.6
Total	4	22	46	.324	88	70	53-1	0	612.1	618	317	11	12	148	195	3.19	82	.264	.311	205-3	.117	-9	78	-42	-5.4
JACOBUS, LARRY Stuart Louis B 12.18.1893 Cincinnati, OH D 8.19.1965 N.College Hill, OH BB/TR 6-2/186# d7.15																									
1918	Cin N	0	1	.000	5	0	0	0	17.1	25	12	0	0	1	8	5.71	47	.368	.377	5-0	.000	-1		-5	-0.4
JACOME, JASON Jason James B 11.24.1970 Tulsa, OK BL/TL 6-1/155# d7.2																									
1994	NY N	4	3	.571	8	8	1-1	0-0	54	54	17	3	0	17-2	30	2.67	157	.269	.324	16-1	.063	-1	76	10	1.1
1995	NY N	0	4	.000	5	5	0	0-0	21	33	24	3	1	15-0	11	10.29	39	.359	.450	7-1	.000	-1	112	-14	-1.9
	KC A	4	6	.400	15	14	1	0-0	84	101	52	15	1	21-2	39	5.36	89	.300	.340	0-0	—	0	99	-4	-0.3
1996	KC A	0	4	.000	49	2	0	1-3	47.2	67	27	5	2	22-5	32	4.72	106	.337	.408	0-0	—	0	129	1	0.2
1997	KC A	0	0	—	7	0	0	0-0	6.2	13	7	2	1	5-1	3	9.45	50	.448	.543	0-0	—	0		-3	-0.1
	Cle A	2	0	1.000	21	4	0	0-1	42.2	45	26	8	0	15-4	24	5.27	89	.269	.328	0-0	—	0	113	-2	-0.1
	Year	2	0	1.000	28	4	0	0-1	49.1	58	32	10	1	20-5	27	5.84	80	.296	.362	0-0	—	0	112	-5	-0.2
1998	Cle A	0	1	.000	1	1	0	0-0	5	10	8	2	0	3-0	2	14.40	33	.435	.500	0-0	—	0	78	-5	-0.6

Year	Tm Lg	W	L	Pct	G	GS	CG-Sho	SV-BS	IP	H	R	HR	HB	BB-IB	SO	ERA	AERA	OAV	OOB	AB-SH	AVG	PB	Sup	APR	PW
Total	5	10	18	.357	106	34	2-1	1-4	261	323	161	38	5	98-14	141	5.34	87	.308	.368	23-2	.043	-2	97	-17	-1.7
JACQUEZ, PAT Patrick Thomas B 4.23.1947 Stockton, CA BR/TR 6/200# d4.18																									
1971	Chi A	0	0	—	2	0	0	0-0	2	4	1	0	0	2-0	1	4.50	80	.444	.500	1-0	.000	-0		0	0.0
JACQUEZ, THOMAS Thomas Patrick B 12.29.1975 Stockton, CA BL/TL 6-2/195# d9.9																									
2000	Phi N	0	0	—	9	0	0	1-0	7.1	10	9	2	0	3-1	6	11.05	42	.333	.382	0-0	—	0		-5	-0.2
JAECKEL, JAKE Paul Henry B 4.1.1942 E.Los Angeles, CA BR/TR 5-10/170# d9.19																									
1964	Chi N	1	0	1.000	4	0	0	1	8	4	0	0	0	3-0	2	0.00	—	.160	.250	1-0	.000	-0		3	0.5
JAEGER, CHARLIE Charles Thomas B 4.17.1875 Ottawa, IL D 9.27.1942 Ottawa, IL BR/TR d9.9																									
1904	Det A	3	3	.500	8	6	5	0	49	49	29	0	6	15	13	2.57	99	.261	.335	17-0	.059	-2	65	-3	-0.6
JAEGER, JOE Joseph Peter "Zip" B 3.3.1895 St.Cloud, MN D 12.13.1963 Hampton, IA BR/TR 6-1/190# d7.28																									
1920	Chi N	0	0	—	2	0	0	0	3	6	6	0	0	4	0	12.00	27	.500	.625	1-0	.000	-0		-3	-0.2
JAKUCKI, SIG Sigmund "Jack" B 8.20.1909 Camden, NJ D 5.28.1979 Galveston, TX BR/TR 6-2.5/198# d8.30																									
1936	StL A	0	3	.000	7	2	0	0	20.2	32	22	2	1	12	9	8.71	62	.348	.429	6-0	.000	-1	90	-7	-0.8
1944	†StL A	13	9	.591	35	24	12-4	3	198	211	89	17	3	54	67	3.55	101	.268	.318	73-2	.151	-2*	109	3	0.2
1945	StL A	12	10	.545	30	24	15-1	2	192.1	188	84	9	1	65	55	3.51	100	.257	.318	70-3	.186	0	105	1	0.1
Total	3	25	22	.532	72	50	27-5	5	411	431	195	28	5	131	131	3.79	96	.268	.325	149-5	.161	-2	106	-3	-0.5
JAMERSON, LEFTY Charles Dewey "Charlie" B 1.26.1900 Enfield, IL D 8.4.1980 Mocksville, NC BL/TL 6-1/195# d8.16																									
1924	Bos A	0	0	—	1	0	0	0	1	1	2	0	0	3	0	18.00	24	.250	.571	0-0	—	0		-1	-0.1
JAMES, DELVIN Delvin Dewayne B 1.3.1978 Nacogdoches, TX BR/TR 6-4/222# d4.16																									
2002	TB A	0	3	.000	8	6	0	0-0	34.1	40	25	5	1	15-1	17	6.55	68	.301	.373	0-0	—	0	59	-7	-0.5
JAMES, JEFF Jeffrey Lynn "Jesse" B 9.29.1941 Indianapolis, IN BR/TR 6-3/195# d4.13																									
1968	Phi N	4	4	.500	29	13	1-1	0	116	112	61	8	4	46-2	83	4.27	70	.256	.330	33-1	.121	-1	102	-15	-1.2
1969	Phi N	2	2	.500	6	5	1	0-0	31.2	36	20	5	0	14-1	21	5.40	66	.288	.357	11-0	.182	-0	105	-6	-0.7
Total	2	6	6	.500	35	18	2-1	0-0	147.2	148	81	13	4	60-3	104	4.51	69	.263	.336	44-1	.136	-1	104	-21	-1.9
JAMES, JOHNNY John Phillip B 7.23.1933 Bonners Ferry, ID BL/TR 5-10/160# d9.6																									
1958	NY A	0	0	—	1	0	0	0	3	2	0	0	0	4-0	1	0.00	—	.250	.500	1-0	.000	-0		1	0.1
1960	NY A	5	1	.833	28	0	0	2	43.1	38	22	3	3	26-2	29	4.36	82	.248	.362	3-0	.000	-0		-3	-0.4
1961	NY A	0	0	—	1	0	0	0	1.1	1	0	0	0	0-0	2	0.00	—	.250	.250	0-0	—	0		1	0.0
	LA A	0	2	.000	36	3	0	0	71.1	66	44	12	2	54-1	41	5.30	85	.246	.375	13-0	.000	-1*	85	-4	-0.3
	Year	0	2	.000	37	3	0	0	72.2	67	48	12	2	54-1	43	5.20	86	.246	.374	13-0	.000	-1	85	-4	-0.3
Total	3	5	3	.625	66	3	0	2	119	107	66	15	5	84-3	73	4.76	87	.247	.373	17-0	.000	-2	93	-5	-0.6
JAMES, MIKE Michael Elmo B 8.15.1967 Ft.Walton Beach, FL BR/TR 6-4/215# d4.29																									
1995	Cal A	3	0	1.000	46	0	0	1-1	55.2	49	27	6	3	26-2	36	3.88	121	.238	.332	0-0	—	0		5	0.2
1996	Cal A	5	5	.500	69	0	0	1-5	81	62	27	7	10	42-7	65	2.67	188	.214	.329	0-0	—	0		21	2.2
1997	Ana A	5	5	.500	58	0	0	7-6	62.2	69	32	3	5	28-4	57	4.31	106	.283	.367	0-0	—	0		2	0.3
1998	Ana A	0	0	—	11	0	0	0-0	14	10	3	0	0	7-0	12	1.93	243	.208	.309	0-0	—	0		4	0.2
2000	†StL N	2	2	.500	51	0	0	2-3	51.1	40	22	7	3	24-2	41	3.16	146	.219	.318	1-0	.000	-0*		7	0.5
2001	StL N	1	2	.333	40	0	0	0-0	38	43	24	5	5	17-2	26	5.21	82	.293	.382	1-0	.000	-0		-4	-0.3
2002	Col N	0	0	—	13	0	0	0-0	11.1	12	9	2	1	5-0	10	5.56	86	.267	.353	0-0	—	0		-1	-0.1
Total	7	16	14	.533	288	0	0	11-15	314	285	144	30	27	149-17	247	3.67	128	.245	.342	2-0	.000	-0		34	3.0
JAMES, RICK Richard Lee B 10.11.1947 Sheffield, AL BR/TR 6-2.5/205# d9.20																									
1967	Chi N	0	1	.000	3	1	0	0	4.2	9	8	1	0	2-0	2	13.50	26	.529	.550	1-0	.000	-0	74	-5	-0.9
JAMES, BOB Robert Harvey B 8.15.1958 Glendale, CA BR/TR 6-4/230# d9.7																									
1978	Mon N	0	1	.000	4	1	0	0-0	4	4	4	1	0	4-0	3	9.00	39	.267	.421	0-0	—	0	102	-2	-0.4
1979	Mon N	0	0	—	2	0	0	0-0	2	2	3	0	0	3-1	1	13.50	27	.250	.455	0-0	—	0		-2	-0.1
1982	Mon N	0	0	—	7	0	0	0-0	9	10	6	0	0	8-1	11	6.00	61	.294	.409	0-0	—	0		-2	-0.1
	Det A	0	2	.000	12	1	0	0-1	19.2	22	13	4	0	8-0	20	5.03	81	.278	.345	0-0	—	0	157	-2	-0.2
1983	Det A	0	0	—	4	0	0	0-0	4	5	5	2	0	3-0	4	11.25	35	.313	.421	0-0	—	0		-3	-0.2
	Mon N	1	0	1.000	27	0	0	7-0	50	37	17	3	3	23-2	56	2.88	125	.210	.312	7-0	.286	0		4	0.3
1984	Mon N	6	6	.500	62	0	0	10-9	96	92	47	6	4	45-7	91	3.66	94	.251	.333	14-0	.143	-0		-4	-0.7
1985	Chi A	8	7	.533	69	0	0	32-9	110	90	31	5	2	23-4	88	2.13	203	.226	.268	0-0	—	0		**25**	4.5
1986	Chi A	5	4	.556	49	0	0	14-8	58.1	61	36	8	4	23-3	32	5.25	82	.268	.340	0-0	—	0		-5	-1.0
1987	Chi A	4	6	.400	43	0	0	10-2	54	54	32	10	4	17-6	34	4.67	99	.256	.321	0-0	—	0		-1	-0.2
Total	8	24	26	.480	279	2	0	73-29	407	377	194	39	17	157-24	340	3.80	105	.246	.319	21-0	.190	0	124	8	1.9
JAMES, LEFTY William A. B 7.1.1889 Glen Roy, OH D 5.3.1933 Glen Roy, OH BL/TL 5-11.5/175# d4.13																									
1912	Cle A	0	1	.000	3	1	0	1	6	8	9	0	2	4	2	7.50	45	.348	.483	3-0	.000	-0	22	-3	-0.6
1913	Cle A	2	3	.400	11	4	3	0	39	42	27	0	3	9	18	3.00	101	.275	.327	13-1	.231	-0	116	-3	-0.4
1914	Cle A	0	3	.000	17	6	1	0	50.2	44	23	0	2	32	16	3.20	90	.251	.373	12-0	.000	-1	97	-1	-0.1
Total	3	2	7	.222	31	11	4	1	95.2	94	59	0	7	45	36	3.39	88	.268	.362	28-1	.107	-1	96	-7	-1.1
JAMES, BILL William Henry "Big Bill" B 1.20.1887 Detroit, MI D 5.25.1942 Venice, CA BB/TR 6-4/195# d6.12																									
1911	Cle A	2	4	.333	8	6	4	0	51.2	58	37	1	2	32	21	4.88	70	.284	.387	17-1	.059	-1	99	-8	-0.9
1912	Cle A	0	0	—	3	0	0	0	13.2	15	11	0	0	9	5	4.61	74	.288	.393	3-1	.000	-0		-2	-0.2
1914	StL A	15	14	.517	44	35	20-3	1	284	269	121	4	6	109	109	2.85	95	.257	.330	89-4	.112	-3	97	-4	-0.5
1915	StL A	6	10	.375	34	22	8	1	170.1	155	89	2	7	92	58	3.59	80	.255	.359	42-6	.190	1	86	-11	-0.8
	Det A	7	3	.700	11	9	3-1	0	67	57	26	1	0	33	24	2.42	125	.243	.336	21-1	.286	2	110	4	0.8
	Year	13	13	.500	45	31	11-1	1	237.1	212	31	3	7	125	82	3.26	89	.251	.352	63-7	.222	2	93	-10	0.0
1916	Det A	8	12	.400	30	20	8	1	151.2	141	76	1	11	79	61	3.68	78	.255	.360	44-6	.068	-3	90	-12	-2.0
1917	Det A	13	10	.565	34	23	10-2	1	198	163	71	2	12	96	62	2.09	127	.229	.330	57-2	.211	2	108	11	1.6
1918	Det A	6	11	.353	19	18	8-1	0	122	127	68	3	5	68	42	3.76	71	.279	.379	46-0	.109	-3	97	-17	-2.4
1919	Det A	1	0	1.000	2	1	0	0	9.1	12	6	0	0	7	3	5.79	55	.324	.432	4-0	.250	0	343	-2	-0.2
	Bos A	3	5	.375	13	7	4	0	72.2	74	42	2	3	39	12	4.09	74	.280	.379	21-3	.143	-1	100	-10	-1.0
	†Chi A	3	2	.600	5	5	3-2	0	39.1	39	12	0	2	14	11	2.52	126	.281	.355	14-1	.143	-1	103	4	0.3
	Year	7	7	.500	20	13	7-2	0	121.1	125	16	2	5	60	26	3.71	83	.284	.376	39-4	.154	-2	121	-8	-0.9
Total	8	64	71	.474	203	146	68-9	4	1179.2	1110	559	16	48	578	408	3.20	88	.258	.352	358-25	.142	-8	99	-47	-5.3
JAMES, BILL William Lawrence "Seattle Bill" B 3.12.1892 Iowa Hill, CA D 3.10.1971 Oroville, CA BR/TR 6-3/196# d4.17																									
1913	Bos N	6	10	.375	24	14	10-1	0	135.2	134	75	4	7	57	73	2.79	118	.264	.347	47-2	.255	1	59	2	0.4
1914	†Bos N	26	7	**.788**	46	37	30-4	3	332.1	261	91	7	13	118	156	1.90	145	.225	.304	129-5	.256	4*	118	**31**	**3.6**
1915	Bos N	5	4	.556	13	9	4	0	68.1	68	28	3	2	22	23	3.03	86	.269	.332	21-1	.048	-2*	128	-2	-0.4
1919	Bos N	0	0	—	1	0	0	0	5.1	6	2	0	0	2	1	3.38	85	.273	.333	2-0	.000	-0		0	0.0
Total	4	37	21	.638	84	60	44-5	3	541.2	469	196	14	22	199	253	2.28	126	.242	.319	199-8	.231	4	104	31	3.6
JAMIESON, CHARLIE Charles Devine "Cuckoo" B 2.7.1893 Paterson, NJ D 10.27.1969 Paterson, NJ BL/TL 5-8.5/165# d9.20.1915 ▲																									
1916	Was A	0	0	—	1	0	0	0	4	2	2	0	0	3	2	4.50	62	.143	.294	145-5	.248	0*		-1	0.0
1917	Was A	0	0	—	1	0	0	0	2.1	10	10	0	0	2	1	38.57	7	.625	.667	35-0	.171	0*		-8	-0.4
1918	Phi A	2	1	.667	5	2	1	0	23	24	17	0	2	13	2	4.30	68	.261	.364	416-1	.202	0*	103	-4	-0.5
1919	Cle A	0	0	—	4	1	0	0	13	12	9	0	0	8	0	5.54	60	.250	.357	17-0	.353	0*	141	-2	0.0
1922	Cle A	0	0	—	2	0	0	0	5.2	7	3	0	0	4	2	3.18	126	.318	.423	567-14	.323	1*		0	0.0
Total	5	2	1	.667	13	3	1	0	48	55	41	0	2	30	7	6.19	51	.286	.388	1180-20	.267	2	115	-15	-0.9
JANESKI, JERRY Gerard Joseph B 4.18.1946 Pasadena, CA BR/TR 6-4/205# d4.10																									
1970	Chi A	10	17	.370	35	35	4-1	0-0	205.2	247	125	22	5	63-10	79	4.77	82	.300	.351	66-7	.076	-4	106	-20	-2.7
1971	Was A	1	5	.167	23	10	0	1-1	61.2	72	38	5	3	34-4	19	4.96	67	.304	.395	14-2	.214	1	89	-12	-1.0

Year	Tm Lg	W	L	Pct	G	GS	CG-Sho	SV-BS	IP	H	R	HR	HB	BB-IB	SO	ERA	AERA	OAV	OOB	AB-SH	AVG	PB	Sup	APR	PW
1972	Tex A	0	1	.000	4	1	0	0-0	12.2	11	5	0	0	7-0	7	2.84	106	.229	.321	2-0	.000	-0	29	0	0.0
Total	3	11	23	.324	62	46	4-1	1-1	280	330	168	27	8	104-14	105	4.72	79	.298	.360	82-9	.098	-4	102	-32	-3.7
JANSEN, LARRY Lawrence Joseph B 7.16.1920 Verboort, OR BR/TR 6-2/190# d4.17 C14																									
1947	NY N	21	5	**.808**	42	30	20-1	1	248	241	102	23	1	57	104	3.16	129	.262	.306	86-9	.186	-0	126	24	2.2
1948	NY N	18	12	.600	42	36	15-4	2	277	283	125	25	3	54	126	3.61	109	.265	.303	95-7	.137	-2	115	12	1.1
1949	NY N	15	16	.484	37	35	17-3	0	259.2	271	130	36	2	62	113	3.85	104	.263	.306	97-6	.165	-0	114	5	0.6
1950	NY N★	19	13	.594	40	35	21-**5**	3	275	238	106	31	1	55	161	3.01	136	.232	**.271**	96-9	.167	-0	101	33	3.6
1951	†NY N☆	**23**	11	.676	39	34	18-3	0	278.2	254	102	26	3	56	145	3.04	129	.239	.279	96-12	.094	-5	101	31	3.2
1952	NY N	11	11	.500	34	27	8-1	2	167.1	183	91	16	6	47	74	4.09	91	.281	.335	45-6	.178	3	103	-8	-0.6
1953	NY N	11	16	.407	36	26	6	1	184.2	185	96	24	2	55	88	4.14	104	.256	.311	60-3	.133	-1	99	4	0.3
1954	NY N	2	2	.500	13	7	0	0	40.2	57	32	5	1	15	15	5.98	68	.337	.388	14-0	.286	1	98	-9	-0.6
1956	Cin N	2	3	.400	8	7	2	1	34.2	39	20	5	1	9-1	16	5.19	77	.281	.327	11-0	.000	-1	133	-4	-0.6
Total	9	122	89	.578	291	237	107-17	10	1765.2	1751	804	191	20	410-1	842	3.58	112	.258	.302	600-52	.150	-6	109	88	9.2
JANZEN, MARTY Martin Thomas B 5.31.1973 Homestead, FL BR/TR 6-3/197# d5.12																									
1996	Tor A	4	6	.400	15	11	0	0-0	73.2	95	65	16	2	38-3	47	7.33	68	.317	.394	0-0	—	0	99	-18	-2.0
1997	Tor A	2	1	.667	12	0	0	0-0	25	23	11	4	0	13-0	17	3.60	128	.250	.343	0-0	—	0		3	0.3
Total	2	6	7	.462	27	11	0	0-0	98.2	118	76	20	2	51-3	64	6.39	77	.301	.382	0-0	—	0	99	-15	-1.7
JARVIS, KEVIN Kevin Thomas B 8.1.1969 Lexington, KY BL/TR 6-2/200# d4.6																									
1994	Cin N	1	1	.500	6	3	0	0-0	17.2	22	14	4	0	5-0	10	7.13	58	.301	.346	4-2	.250	0	147	-5	-0.5
1995	Cin N	3	4	.429	19	11	1-1	0-0	79	91	56	13	3	32-2	33	5.70	72	.292	.358	21-1	.143	-0	116	-15	-1.1
1996	Cin N	8	9	.471	24	20	2-1	0-0	120.1	152	93	17	2	43-5	63	5.98	71	.305	.361	36-8	.167	-0	109	-25	-3.0
1997	Cin N	0	1	.000	9	0	0	1-0	13.1	21	16	4	1	7-0	12	10.13	42	.344	.420	1-0	.000	-0		-8	-0.7
	Min A	0	0	—	6	2	0	0-0	13	23	18	4	0	8-0	9	12.46	37	.371	.443	0-0	—	0	158	-10	-0.5
	Det A	0	3	.000	17	3	0	0-0	41.2	55	28	9	0	14-0	27	5.40	85	.318	.367	0-0	—	0	47	-4	-0.3
	Year	0	3	.000	23	5	0	0-0	54.2	78	30	13	0	22-0	36	7.08	65	.332	.388	0-0	—	0	92	-15	-0.8
1999	Oak A	0	1	.000	4	1	0	0-0	14	28	19	6	1	6-0	11	11.57	40	.418	.467	0-0	—	0	60	-11	-0.6
2000	Col N	3	4	.429	24	19	0	0-0	115	138	83	26	4	33-3	60	5.95	98	.300	.351	34-3	.088	-2*	119	-2	-0.3
2001	SD N	12	11	.522	32	32	1-1	0-0	193.1	189	107	37	5	49-4	133	4.79	84	.254	.303	61-5	.180	4*	117	-14	-1.0
2002	SD N	2	4	.333	7	7	0	0-0	35	36	19	5	1	10-1	24	4.37	86	.269	.322	9-1	.333	2	70	-3	-0.3
2003	SD N	4	8	.333	16	16	0	0-0	92	113	65	15	2	32-5	49	5.87	67	.304	.358	22-3	.136	1*	89	-22	-2.2
Total	9	33	46	.418	164	114	4-3	1-0	734.1	868	518	140	19	239-20	431	5.83	75	.294	.348	188-23	.160	5	109	-119	-10.5
JARVIS, RAY Raymond Arnold B 5.10.1946 Providence, RI BR/TR 6-2/198# d4.15																									
1969	Bos A	5	6	.455	29	12	2	1-0	100.1	105	59	8	3	43-1	36	4.75	80	.274	.349	29-3	.069	-2	110	-9	-1.1
1970	Bos A	0	1	.000	15	0	0	0-1	16	17	12	1	2	14-1	8	3.94	101	.274	.418	0-1	—	0		-2	-0.1
Total	2	5	7	.417	44	12	2	1-1	116.1	122	71	9	5	57-2	44	4.64	82	.274	.359	29-4	.069	-2	110	-11	-1.2
JARVIS, PAT Robert Patrick B 3.18.1941 Carlyle, IL BR/TR 5-10.5/180# d8.4																									
1966	Atl N	6	2	.750	10	9	3-1	0	62.1	46	16	1	1	12-2	41	2.31	157	.206	.250	22-1	.000	-2	150	10	1.0
1967	Atl N	15	10	.600	32	30	7-1	0	194	195	86	15	4	62-14	118	3.66	91	.260	.317	71-3	.085	-3	105	-6	-1.1
1968	Atl N	16	12	.571	34	34	14-1	0	256	202	82	15	2	50-5	157	2.60	115	.214	.252	85-10	.141	0	102	12	1.3
1969	†Atl N	13	11	.542	37	33	4-1	0-0	217.1	204	113	25	1	73-7	123	4.43	81	.246	.306	71-5	.113	-2	110	-17	-2.0
1970	Atl N	16	16	.500	36	34	11-1	0-1	254	240	110	21	0	72-5	173	3.61	119	.247	.296	82-11	.183	-0	83	20	2.4
1971	Atl N	6	14	.300	35	23	3-3	1-0	162.1	162	81	16	3	51-11	68	4.10	91	.261	.320	47-4	.106	-2	88	-5	-0.8
1972	Atl N	11	7	.611	37	6	0	2-1	98.2	94	50	7	0	44-7	56	4.10	92	.260	.337	24-3	.125	-0	132	-3	-0.5
1973	Mon N	2	1	.667	28	0	0	0-1	39.1	37	21	6	1	16-4	19	3.20	119	.250	.325	3-0	.000	-0		1	0.0
Total	8	85	73	.538	249	169	42-8	3-3	1284	1180	559	106	12	380-55	755	3.58	101	.243	.298	405-37	.121	-10	101	12	0.3
JASPER, HI Henry W. B 11.15.1880 St.Louis, MO D 5.22.1937 St.Louis, MO BR/TR 5-11/180# d4.19																									
1914	Chi A	1	0	1.000	16	0	0	0	32.1	22	22	0	1	20	19	3.34	80	.210	.341	5-0	.000	-1		-4	-0.2
1915	Chi A	0	1	.000	3	2	1	0	15.2	8	8	2	0	9	15	4.60	65	.157	.283	7-0	.286	0	98	-2	0.0
1916	StL N	5	6	.455	21	9	2	1	107	97	54	0	7	42	37	3.28	81	.254	.339	33-0	.212	1	97	-8	-0.7
1919	Cle A	4	5	.444	12	10	5	0	82.2	83	41	1	0	28	25	3.59	93	.269	.330	29-2	.103	-2	117	-1	-0.3
Total	4	10	12	.455	52	21	8	1	237.2	210	125	3	8	99	96	3.48	84	.248	.333	74-2	.162	-2	110	-15	-1.2
JASTER, LARRY Larry Edward B 1.13.1944 Midland, MI BL/TL 6-3.5/205# d9.17																									
1965	StL N	3	0	1.000	4	3	3	0	28	21	5	1	0	7-0	10	1.61	239	.206	.255	10-1	.200	0	144	7	0.8
1966	StL N	11	5	.688	26	21	6-**5**	0	151.2	124	57	17	5	45-5	92	3.26	110	.227	.290	45-2	.178	1	83	8	0.9
1967	†StL N	9	7	.563	34	23	2-1	3	152.1	141	57	12	2	44-6	87	3.01	109	.244	.297	50-1	.100	-1*	109	5	0.3
1968	†StL N	9	13	.409	31	21	3-1	0	154.1	153	63	13	6	38-5	70	3.50	83	.262	.311	43-6	.140	0	73	-8	-1.2
1969	Mon N	1	6	.143	24	11	1	0-0	77	95	60	17	2	28-6	39	5.49	67	.302	.359	19-0	.421	3	81	-18	-1.2
1970	Atl N	1	1	.500	14	0	0	0-2	22.1	33	18	5	0	8-0	9	6.85	63	.359	.402	3-0	.000	-0		-6	-0.4
1972	Atl N	1	1	.500	5	1	0	0-0	12.1	12	7	4	0	8-0	6	5.11	74	.267	.377	1-0	.000	-0	23	-1	-0.2
Total	7	35	33	.515	138	80	15-7	3-2	598	579	267	69	15	178-22	313	3.64	93	.256	.312	171-10	.170	3	89	-13	-1.0
JAVERY, AL Alva William "Beartracks" B 6.5.1918 Worcester, MA D 8.16.1977 Putnam, CT BR/TR 6-3/183# d4.23																									
1940	Bos N	2	4	.333	29	4	1	1	83.1	99	62	2	2	36	42	5.51	68	.293	.364	23-1	.087	-1	76	-19	-1.5
1941	Bos N	10	11	.476	34	23	9-1	1	160.2	181	88	5	6	65	54	4.31	83	.283	.355	58-1	.103	-4	102	-12	-1.8
1942	Bos N	12	16	.429	42	**37**	19-5	0	261	251	106	8	3	78	85	3.03	110	.251	.307	86-9	.105	-5	81	7	0.3
1943	Bos N★	17	16	.515	41	35	19-5	0	**303**	288	130	13	4	99	134	3.21	106	.248	.309	104-11	.163	-3	84	7	0.6
1944	Bos N☆	10	19	.345	40	33	11-3	3	254	248	119	12	2	118	137	3.54	108	.262	.345	79-4	.152	-3	71	7	0.4
1945	Bos N	2	7	.222	17	14	2-1	0	77.1	92	59	4	0	51	18	6.28	61	.295	.394	29-0	.207	-0	95	-19	-1.9
1946	Bos N	0	1	.000	2	1	0	0	3.1	5	5	0	0	5	0	13.50	25	.417	.588	1-0	.000	-0	125	-3	-0.6
Total	7	53	74	.417	205	147	61-15	5	1142.2	1164	569	44	17	452	470	3.80	94	.264	.335	380-26	.137	-15	84	-32	-4.5
JAY, JOEY Joseph Richard B 8.15.1935 Middletown, CT BB/TR 6-4/228# d7.21																									
1953	Mil N	1	0	1.000	3	1	1-1	0	10	6	0	0	0	5	4	0.00	—	.188	.297	3-0	.000	-0	68	5	0.4
1954	Mil N	1	0	1.000	15	1	0	0	18	21	13	2	1	16	13	6.50	57	.304	.437	0-0	—	0	96	-5	-0.3
1955	Mil N	0	0	—	12	1	0	0	19	23	11	2	0	13-2	3	4.74	79	.324	.419	3-0	.667	1	190	-2	0.0
1957	Mil N	0	0	—	1	0	0	1	0.2	0	0	0	0	0-0	0	0.00	—	.000	.000	0-0	—	0		0	0.1
1958	Mil N	7	5	.583	18	12	6-3	0	96.2	60	25	8	1	43-3	74	2.14	164	.177	.271	32-1	.094	-1	70	17	1.9
1959	Mil N	6	11	.353	34	19	4-1	0	136.1	130	71	11	5	64-6	88	4.09	87	.248	.334	35-1	.086	-1	101	-9	-1.1
1960	Mil N	9	8	.529	32	11	3	1	133.1	128	60	10	6	59-5	90	3.24	106	.254	.336	45-3	.156	0	131	0	0.0
1961	†Cin N☆	**21**	10	.677	34	34	14-**4**	0	247.1	217	102	25	5	92-1	157	3.53	115	.236	.308	89-2	.090	-5	95	18	1.4
1962	Cin N	21	14	.600	39	37	16-4	0	273	269	121	26	4	100-5	155	3.76	107	.260	.325	90-7	.167	3	97	11	1.5
1963	Cin N	7	18	.280	30	22	4-1	1	170	172	91	19	3	73-2	116	4.29	78	.266	.340	50-2	.160	0	75	-17	-2.4
1964	Cin N	11	11	.500	34	23	10	2	183	167	75	17	3	36-6	134	3.39	107	.245	.284	53-5	.057	-3	87	6	0.3
1965	Cin N	9	8	.529	37	24	4-1	1	155.2	150	83	21	4	63-0	102	4.22	89	.252	.324	49-4	.041	-3	113	-8	-1.2
1966	Cin N	6	2	.750	12	10	1-1	0	73.2	78	33	8	3	23-1	44	3.91	100	.275	.335	26-2	.115	-1	108	1	-0.1
	Atl N	0	4	.000	9	8	0	1	29.2	39	29	4	1	20-3	19	7.89	46	.315	.405	8-0	.125	-0	94	-14	-1.7
	Year	6	6	.500	21	18	1-1	1	103.1	117	33	12	4	43-4	63	5.05	76	.287	.358	34-2	.118	-1	101	-13	-1.8
Total	13	99	91	.521	310	203	63-16	7	1546.1	1460	714	153	36	607-34	999	3.77	99	.251	.323	483-27	.114	-10	97	3	-1.2
JEAN, DOMINGO Domingo (Luisa) B 1.9.1969 San Pedro De Macoris, D.R. BR/TR 6-2/175# d8.8																									
1993	NY A	1	1	.500	10	6	0	0-0	40.1	37	20	7	0	19-1	20	4.46	93	.237	.318	0-0	—	0	107	-1	0.0
JEFFCOAT, GEORGE George Edward B 12.24.1913 New Brookland, SC D 10.13.1978 Leesville, SC BR/TR 5-11.5/175# d4.20 b-Hal																									
1936	Bro N	5	6	.455	40	5	3	3	95.2	84	58	7	8	63	46	4.52	92	.239	.366	23-1	.130	-1	78	-4	-0.6
1937	Bro N	1	3	.250	21	3	1-1	0	54.1	58	33	4	1	27	29	5.13	79	.274	.358	12-0	.000	-2	85	-4	-0.5
1939	Bro N	0	0	—	1	0	0	0	2	2	0	0	0	0	1	0.00	—	.286	.286	0-0	—	0		1	0.0
1943	Bos N	1	2	.333	8	1	0	0	17.2	15	10	1	0	10	10	3.06	112	.217	.316	4-1	.500	1	124	0	0.0

Year	Tm Lg	W	L	Pct	G	GS	CG-Sho	SV-BS	IP	H	R	HR	HB	BB-IB	SO	ERA	AERA	OAV	OOB	AB-SH	AVG	PB	Sup	APR	PW
Total	4	7	11	.389	70	9	4-1	3	169.2	159	101	12	9	100	86	4.51	89	.248	.358	39-2	.128	-2	85	-7	-1.1
JEFFCOAT, HAL Harold Bentley B 9.6.1924 W.Columbia, SC BR/TR 5-10.5/185# d4.20.1948 b-George ▲																									
1954	Chi N	5	6	.455	43	3	1	7	104	110	63	12	4	58	35	5.19	81	.276	.368	31-0	.258	2*	85	-9	-0.7
1955	Chi N	8	6	.571	50	1	0	6	100.2	107	46	5	4	53-12	32	2.95	139	.276	.367	23-2	.174	1*	65	8	1.3
1956	Cin N	8	2	.800	38	16	2	2	171	189	79	12	5	55-4	55	3.84	104	.281	.337	54-3	.148	-1*	112	3	0.2
1957	Cin N	12	13	.480	37	31	10-1	0	207	236	117	29	7	46-7	63	4.52	91	.294	.335	69-8	.203	6*	111	-11	-0.6
1958	Cin N	6	8	.429	49	0	0	9	75	76	34	8	2	26-8	35	3.72	111	.268	.329	9-0	.556	2*		3	0.9
1959	Cin N	0	1	.000	17	0	0	1	21.2	21	8	3	0	10-2	12	3.32	122	.253	.333	1-0	1.000	1		2	0.2
	StL N	0	1	.000	11	0	0	0	17.2	33	18	4	0	9-2	7	9.17	46	.402	.462	3-0	.000	-0*		-8	-0.4
	Year	0	2	.000	28	0	0	1	39.1	54	31	7	0	19-4	19	5.95	70	.327	.397	4-0	.250	0		-6	-0.2
Total	6	39	37	.513	245	51	13-1	25	697	772	365	73	22	257-35	239	4.22	97	.285	.349	190-13	.211	10	109	-12	0.9
JEFFCOAT, MIKE James Michael B 8.3.1959 Pine Bluff, AR BL/TL 6-2/187# d8.21																									
1983	Cle A	1	3	.250	11	2	0	0-0	32.2	32	13	1	1	13-1	9	3.31	129	.256	.331	0-0	—	0	21	3	0.4
1984	Cle A	5	2	.714	63	1	0	1-5	75.1	82	28	7	1	24-7	41	2.99	137	.281	.330	0-0	—	0	287	9	0.8
1985	Cle A	0	0	—	9	0	0	0-0	9.2	8	5	1	0	6-1	4	2.79	148	.235	.333	0-0	—	0		1	0.1
	SF N	0	2	.000	19	1	0	0-0	22	27	13	4	2	6-3	10	5.32	65	.307	.361	1-0	.000	0	231	-4	-0.3
1987	Tex A	0	1	.000	2	2	0	0-0	7	11	10	4	0	4-0	1	12.86	35	.355	.429	0-0	—	0	91	-6	-0.6
1988	Tex A	0	2	.000	5	2	0	0-0	10	19	13	1	2	5-1	5	11.70	35	.432	.510	0-0	—	0	22	-7	-1.2
1989	Tex A	9	6	.600	22	22	2-2	0-0	130.2	139	65	7	4	33-0	64	3.58	111	.270	.317	0-0	—	0	111	3	0.4
1990	Tex A	5	6	.455	44	12	1	5-5	110.2	122	57	12	2	28-5	58	4.47	88	.283	.328	0-0	—	0	83	-4	-0.5
1991	Tex A	5	3	.625	70	0	0	1-4	79.2	104	46	8	4	25-3	43	4.63	87	.320	.372	1-0	1.000	1		-6	-0.4
1992	Tex A	0	1	.000	6	3	0	0-0	19.2	28	17	2	0	5-0	6	7.32	52	.350	.379	0-0	—	0	144	-7	-0.4
1994	Fla N	0	0	—	4	0	0	0-0	2.2	4	3	2	0	0-0	1	10.13	43	.364	.333	0-0	—	0		-1	-0.1
Total	10	25	26	.490	255	45	3-2	7-14	500	576	270	49	16	149-21	242	4.37	91	.292	.342	2-0	.500	1	103	-19	-1.8
JEFFERSON, JESSE Jesse Harrison B 3.3.1949 Midlothian, VA BR/TR 6-3/195# d6.23																									
1973	Bal A	6	5	.545	18	15	3	0-0	100.2	104	53	15	0	46-1	52	4.11	91	.267	.342	0-0	—	0	116	-5	-0.5
1974	Bal A	1	0	1.000	20	2	0	0-0	57.1	55	30	2	0	38-2	31	4.40	79	.261	.371	0-0	—	0	191	-5	-0.3
1975	Bal A	0	2	.000	4	0	0	0-0	7.2	5	3	0	0	8-2	4	2.35	150	.227	.433	0-0	—	0		1	0.2
	Chi A	5	9	.357	22	21	1	0-0	107.2	100	69	11	2	94-1	67	5.10	76	.249	.391	0-0	—	0	82	-15	-1.7
	Year	5	11	.313	26	21	1	0-0	115.1	105	73	11	2	102-3	71	4.92	79	.248	.394	0-0	—	0	83	-13	-1.5
1976	Chi A	2	5	.286	19	9	0	0-0	62.1	86	62	4	2	42-0	30	8.52	42	.339	.429	0-0	—	0	115	-33	-3.1
1977	Tor A	9	17	.346	33	33	8	0-0	217	224	123	23	1	83-4	114	4.31	98	.269	.332	0-0	—	0	78	-5	-0.5
1978	Tor A	7	16	.304	31	30	9-2	0-0	211.2	214	109	28	3	86-5	97	4.38	90	.267	.337	0-0	—	0	75	-9	-0.9
1979	Tor A	2	10	.167	34	10	2	1-2	116	150	75	19	2	45-2	43	5.51	79	.328	.387	0-0	—	0	56	-12	-1.1
1980	Tor A	4	13	.235	29	18	2-2	0-0	121.2	130	78	12	2	52-2	53	5.47	79	.281	.353	0-0	—	0	65	-13	-1.5
	Pit N	1	0	1.000	1	1	0	0-0	6.2	3	1	0	0	2-0	4	1.35	270	.143	.217	1-1	.000	-0	73	2	0.3
1981	Cal A	2	4	.333	26	5	0	0-2	77	80	39	4	2	24-4	27	3.62	101	.269	.322	0-0	—	0	39	-1	-0.2
Total	9	39	81	.325	237	144	25-4	1-4	1085.2	1151	642	118	14	520-23	522	4.81	83	.277	.356	1-1	.000	-0	81	-95	-9.3
JENKINS, FERGIE Ferguson Arthur B 12.13.1942 Chatham, ON, CAN BR/TR 6-5/210# d9.10 C2 HF1991																									
1965	Phi N	2	1	.667	7	0	0	1	12.1	7	3	2	0	2-0	10	2.19	158	.159	.196	1-0	.000	-0		2	0.4
1966	Phi N	0	0	—	1	0	0	0	2.1	3	2	0	0	1-1	2	3.86	93	.273	.333	0-0	—	0		0	0.0
	Chi N	6	8	.429	60	12	2-1	5	182	147	75	24	3	51-11	148	3.31	111	.219	.275	51-3	.137	1	100	8	0.6
	Year	6	8	.429	61	12	2-1	5	184.1	150	79	24	3	52-12	150	3.32	111	.220	.276	51-3	.137	1	100	6	0.6
1967	Chi N★	20	13	.606	38	38	**20**-3	0	289.1	230	101	30	4	83-8	236	2.80	127	.217	.276	93-8	.151	1*	101	22	2.8
1968	Chi N	20	15	.571	40	**40**	20-3	0	308	255	96	26	3	65-7	260	2.63	120	.222	.265	100-6	.160	2	92	19	2.5
1969	Chi N	21	15	.583	43	**42**	23-7	1-0	311.1	284	122	27	8	71-15	**273**	3.21	126	.242	.289	108-4	.139	-1	93	27	3.0
1970	Chi N	22	16	.579	40	39	**24**-3	0-1	313	265	128	30	7	60-6	274	3.39	133	.224	**.264**	113-10	.124	-3	98	37	3.9
1971	Chi N★	**24**	13	.649	39	**39**	**30**-3	0-0	**325**	304	114	29	5	37-6	263	2.77	142	.246	.269	115-8	.243	10	92	36	5.6
1972	Chi N☆	20	12	.625	36	36	23-5	0-0	289.1	253	111	32	7	62-7	184	3.20	119	.234	.278	109-3	.183	1	105	20	2.6
1973	Chi N	14	16	.467	38	38	7-2	0-0	271	267	133	35	4	57-10	170	3.89	102	.259	.298	84-7	.119	-1	88	1	0.2
1974	Tex A	**25**	12	.676	41	41	**29**-6	0-0	328.1	286	117	27	8	45-3	225	2.82	126	.232	.262	2-0	.500	0	103	28	3.1
1975	Tex A	17	18	.486	37	37	22-4	0-0	270	261	130	37	9	56-7	157	3.93	96	.251	.294	0-0	—	0	106	-2	-0.3
1976	Bos A	12	11	.522	30	29	12-2	0-0	209	201	85	20	5	43-6	142	3.27	120	.253	.292	0-0	—	0	97	15	1.5
1977	Bos A	10	10	.500	28	28	11-1	0-0	193	190	91	30	0	36-2	105	3.68	122	.257	.290	0-0	—	0	103	13	1.3
1978	Tex A	18	8	.692	34	30	16-4	0-0	249	228	92	21	3	41-2	157	3.04	124	.245	.278	0-0	—	0	118	22	2.3
1979	Tex A	16	14	.533	37	37	10-3	0-0	259	252	127	40	3	81-6	164	4.07	102	.256	.311	0-0	—	0	114	5	0.7
1980	Tex A	12	12	.500	29	29	12	0-0	198	190	90	22	4	52-8	129	3.77	103	.250	.299	0-0	—	0	108	6	0.6
1981	Tex A	5	8	.385	19	16	1	0-0	106	122	55	14	0	40-4	63	4.50	77	.290	.351	0-0	—	0	113	-11	-1.2
1982	Chi N	14	15	.483	34	34	4-1	0-0	217.1	221	92	19	5	68-2	134	3.15	119	.264	.319	67-12	.149	-1	105	11	1.2
1983	Chi N	6	9	.400	33	29	1-1	0-1	167.1	176	89	19	6	46-5	96	4.30	88	.275	.327	53-5	.245	3	94	-9	-0.5
Total	19	284	226	.557	664	594	267-49	7-2	4500.2	4142	1853	484	84	997-116	3192	3.34	115	.243	.287	896-66	.165	13	101	250	30.3
JENKINS, JACK Warren Washington B 12.22.1942 Covington, VA D 6.18.2002 Tampa, FL BR/TR 6-2/195# d9.13																									
1962	Was A	0	1	.000	3	1	1	0	13.1	12	6	4	0	7-0	10	4.05	100	.245	.339	4-0	.000	-0	22	0	0.0
1963	Was A	0	2	.000	4	2	0	0	12.1	16	8	2	0	12-0	5	5.84	64	.340	.475	3-0	.333	0	48	-2	-0.3
1969	LA N	0	0	—	1	0	0	0-0	1	0	0	0	0	0-0	1	0.00	—	.000	.000	0-0	—	0		0	0.0
Total	3	0	3	.000	8	3	1	0-0	26.2	28	14	6	0	19-0	16	4.73	82	.283	.398	7-0	.143	-0	38	-2	-0.3
JENNINGS, JASON Jason Ryan B 7.17.1978 Dallas, TX BR/TR 6-2/242# d8.23																									
2001	Col N	4	1	.800	7	7	1-1	0-0	39.1	42	21	2	1	19-0	26	4.58	117	.276	.358	15-1	.267	1	124	3	0.5
2002	Col N	16	8	.667	32	32	0	0-0	185.1	201	102	26	8	70-2	127	4.52	106	.280	.349	62-2	.306	4	99	4	1.0
2003	Col N	12	13	.480	32	32	1	0-0	181.1	212	115	20	5	88-7	119	5.11	96	.299	.377	54-5	.222	2*	94	-5	-0.4
Total	3	32	22	.593	71	71	2-1	0-0	406	455	238	48	14	177-9	272	4.79	102	.288	.363	131-8	.267	8	100	2	1.1
JENSEN, RYAN Larry Ryan B 9.17.1975 Salt Lake City, UT BR/TR 6/205# d5.19																									
2001	SF N	1	2	.333	10	7	0	0-0	42.1	44	21	5	4	25-0	26	4.25	94	.268	.378	12-0	.167	0	113	-1	0.0
2002	SF N	13	8	.619	32	30	1	0-0	171.2	183	93	21	5	66-4	105	4.51	86	.278	.345	56-9	.107	-2	123	-12	-1.5
2003	SF N	0	0	—	6	2	0	0-0	13.1	21	16	6	1	5-0	3	10.80	38	.404	.450	5-0	.400	1	251	-10	-0.4
Total	3	14	10	.583	48	39	1	0-0	227.1	248	130	32	10	96-4	134	4.83	81	.284	.358	73-9	.137	-1	128	-23	-1.9
JENSEN, WILLIE William Christian B 11.17.1889 Philadelphia, PA D 3.27.1917 Philadelphia, PA BL/TR 5-11.5/170# d9.10																									
1912	Det A	1	2	.333	5	4	1	0	33	43	23	1	2	18	8	4.91	66	.339	.429	11-0	.000	-2	130	-6	-0.6
1914	Phi A	0	1	.000	1	1	1	0	9	7	4	1	0	2	1	2.00	131	.226	.273	2-0	.000	0	84	0	0.0
Total	2	1	3	.250	6	5	2	0	42	50	27	2	2	20	9	4.29	73	.316	.400	13-0	.000	-2	123	-6	-0.6
JERZEMBECK, MIKE Michael Joseph B 5.18.1972 Queens, NY BR/TR 6-1/185# d8.8																									
1998	NY A	0	1	.000	3	2	0	0-0	6.1	9	9	2	0	4-0	1	12.79	34	.346	.419	0-0	—	0	127	-6	-0.7
JESTER, VIRGIL Virgil Milton B 7.23.1927 Denver, CO BR/TR 5-11/188# d6.18																									
1952	Bos N	3	5	.375	19	8	4-1	0	73	80	31	5	1	23	25	3.33	108	.283	.339	19-2	.211	1	86	2	0.2
1953	Mil N	0	0	—	2	0	0	0	2	4	5	1	0	4	0	22.50	17	.400	.571	0-0	—	0		-4	-0.2
Total	2	3	5	.375	21	8	4-1	0	75	84	36	6	1	27	25	3.84	94	.287	.349	19-2	.211	1	86	-2	0.0
JIMENEZ, GERMAN German (Camarena) B 12.5.1962 Santiago, Mexico BL/TL 5-11/200# d6.28																									
1988	Atl N	1	6	.143	15	9	0	0-0	55.2	65	39	4	1	12-0	26	5.01	73	.294	.326	17-0	.059	-1	72	-9	-1.3
JIMENEZ, JASON Jason Jon B 1.10.1976 Modesto, CA BR/TL 6-2/206# d6.3																									
2002	TB A	0	0	—	5	0	0	0-0	6.2	9	4	2	0	1-0	5	5.40	83	.333	.345	0-0	—	0		-1	0.0
	Det A	0	0	—	1	0	0	0-0	0.2	3	4	0	0	1-0	0	27.00	16	.500	.571	0-0	—	0		-3	-0.1
	Year	0	0	—	6	0	0	0-0	7.1	12	11	2	0	2-0	5	7.36	60	.364	.389	0-0	—	0		-3	-0.1

Year	Tm Lg	W	L	Pct	G	GS	CG-Sho	SV-BS	IP	H	R	HR	HB	BB-IB	SO	ERA	AERA	OAV	OOB	AB-SH	AVG	PB	Sup	APR	PW
JIMENEZ, JOSE Jose B 7.7.1973 San Pedro De Macoris, D.R. BR/TR 6-3/170# d9.9																									
1998	StL N	3	0	1.000	4	3	0	0-0	21.1	22	8	0	0	8-0	12	2.95	142	.262	.323	6-2	.000	-1	146	3	0.3
1999	StL N	5	14	.263	29	28	2-2	0-1	163	173	114	16	11	71-2	113	5.85	78	.275	.356	53-2	.094	-3*	82	-22	-2.3
2000	Col N	5	2	.714	72	0	0	24-6	70.2	63	27	4	3	28-6	44	3.18	182	.239	.316	4-1	.500	0		16	2.4
2001	Col N	6	1	.857	56	0	0	17-5	55	56	27	6	0	22-4	37	4.09	131	.264	.332	1-0	.000	-0		6	1.1
2002	Col N	2	10	.167	74	0	0	41-6	73.1	76	34	7	3	11-4	47	3.56	134	.265	.297	0-0	—	0		8	1.6
2003	Col N	2	10	.167	63	7	0	20-3	101.2	137	62	7	6	32-5	45	5.22	94	.322	.375	17-2	.176	-0	63	-2	-0.4
Total	6	23	37	.383	298	38	2-2	102-21	485	527	272	40	23	172-21	298	4.66	106	.277	.342	81-7	.123	-3	77	9	2.7
JIMENEZ, JUAN Juan Antonio (Martes) B 3.8.1949 LaTorre, D.R. BR/TR 6-1/165# d9.9																									
1974	Pit N	0	0	—	4	0	0	0-0	4	6	4	0	0	2-0	2	6.75	51	.353	.421	0-0	—	0		-2	-0.1
JIMENEZ, MIGUEL Miguel Anthony B 8.19.1969 New York, NY BR/TR 6-2/205# d9.12																									
1993	Oak A	1	0	1.000	5	4	0	0-0	27	27	12	5	1	16-0	13	4.00	102	.262	.367	0-0	—	0	130	1	0.0
1994	Oak A	1	4	.200	8	7	0	0-0	34	38	33	9	1	32-2	22	7.41	60	.275	.413	0-0	—	0	119	-13	-1.5
Total	2	2	4	.333	13	11	0	0-0	61	65	45	14	2	48-2	35	5.90	73	.270	.394	0-0	—	0	123	-12	-1.5
JODIE, BRETT Brett Paul B 3.25.1977 Columbia, SC BR/TR 6-4/208# d7.20																									
2001	NY A	0	1	.000	1	1	0	0-0	2	7	6	3	0	1-0	0	27.00	17	.583	.615	0-0	—	0	82	-5	-0.6
	SD N	0	1	.000	7	2	0	0-0	23.1	19	12	7	0	12-1	13	4.63	87	.229	.326	4-0	.000	-0	23	-1	-0.1
Total	1	0	2	.000	8	3	0	0-0	25.1	26	18	10	0	13-1	13	6.39	63	.274	.361	4-0	.000	-0	46	-6	-0.7
JOHN, TOMMY Thomas Edward B 5.22.1943 Terre Haute, IN BR/TL 6-3/185# d9.6																									
1963	Cle A	0	2	.000	6	3	0	0	20.1	23	10	1	0	6-1	9	2.21	164	.284	.330	6-0	.000	-1	74	1	0.0
1964	Cle A	2	9	.182	25	14	2-1	0	94.1	97	53	10	0	35-4	65	3.91	92	.262	.324	24-3	.208	0	101	-7	-0.7
1965	Chi A	14	7	.667	39	27	6-1	3	183.2	162	67	12	2	58-6	126	3.09	103	.237	.298	59-6	.169	2	133	4	0.9
1966	Chi A	14	11	.560	34	33	10-**5**	0	223	195	76	13	7	57-4	138	2.62	121	.235	.289	69-4	.145	2	89	15	2.0
1967	Chi A	10	13	.435	31	29	9-**6**	0	178.1	143	62	12	5	47-7	110	2.47	126	.219	.275	51-5	.157	-0	76	12	1.9
1968	Chi A★	10	5	.667	25	25	5-1	0	177.1	135	45	10	12	49-4	117	1.98	153	.212	.280	62-5	.194	2	109	21	2.5
1969	Chi A	9	11	.450	33	33	6-2	0-0	232.1	230	91	16	1	90-10	128	3.25	119	.261	.329	79-1	.114	-2	80	14	1.5
1970	Chi A	12	17	.414	37	37	10-3	0-0	269.1	253	117	19	9	101-16	138	3.27	119	.251	.323	84-9	.202	1*	85	15	2.0
1971	Chi A	13	16	.448	38	35	10-3	0-0	229.1	244	115	17	5	58-5	131	3.61	100	.274	.318	69-9	.145	-1	89	-3	-0.5
1972	LA N	11	5	.688	29	29	4-1	0-0	186.2	172	68	14	3	40-1	117	2.89	115	.244	.286	63-7	.159	-1	109	12	1.1
1973	LA N	16	7	**.696**	36	31	4-2	0-0	218	202	88	16	4	50-2	116	3.10	111	.246	.291	74-7	.203	2	119	8	1.4
1974	LA N	13	3	.813	22	22	5-3	0-0	153	133	51	4	1	42-0	78	2.59	132	.235	.287	51-9	.118	-1	129	15	1.5
1976	LA N	10	10	.500	31	31	6-2	0-0	207	207	76	7	0	61-4	91	3.09	110	.261	.312	64-10	.109	-2	91	8	0.5
1977	†LA N	20	7	.741	31	31	11-3	0-0	220.1	225	82	12	3	50-3	123	2.78	138	.267	.310	79-6	.177	1	119	23	2.9
1978	†LA N☆	17	10	.630	33	30	7	1-0	213	230	95	11	5	53-7	124	3.30	107	.271	.317	66-12	.121	-1	124	3	0.3
1979	NY A☆	21	9	.700	37	36	17-3	0-0	276.1	268	109	9	4	65-1	111	2.96	138	.260	.305	0-0	—	0	106	31	3.2
1980	†NY A★	22	9	.710	36	36	16-**6**	0-0	265.1	270	115	13	6	56-1	78	3.43	115	.268	.309	0-0	—	0	120	15	1.7
1981	†NY A	9	8	.529	20	20	7	0-0	140.1	135	50	10	3	39-2	50	2.63	136	.256	.309	0-0	—	0	93	13	1.7
1982	NY A	10	10	.500	30	26	9-2	0-0	186.2	190	84	11	3	34-1	54	3.66	109	.266	.299	0-0	—	0	103	7	0.8
	†Cal A	4	2	.667	7	7	1	0-0	35	49	18	4	0	5-0	14	3.86	105	.336	.358	0-0	—	0	103	0	0.0
	Year	14	12	.538	37	33	10-2	0-0	221.2	239	23	15	3	39-1	68	3.69	108	.278	.309	0-0	—	0	103	7	0.8
1983	Cal A	11	13	.458	34	34	9	0-0	234.2	287	126	20	2	49-5	65	4.33	93	.304	.337	0-0	—	0	95	-9	-0.7
1984	Cal A	7	13	.350	32	29	4-1	0-0	181.1	223	97	15	4	56-3	47	4.52	88	.306	.356	0-0	—	0	96	-10	-1.0
1985	Cal A	2	4	.333	12	6	0	0-0	38.1	51	22	3	1	15-1	17	4.70	88	.329	.387	0-0	—	0	77	-2	-0.3
	Oak A	2	6	.250	11	11	0	0-0	48	66	37	6	1	13-0	8	6.19	62	.332	.372	0-0	—	0	73	-14	-1.8
	Year	4	10	.286	23	17	0	0-0	86.1	117	40	9	2	28-1	25	5.53	72	.331	.379	0-0	—	0	74	-16	-2.1
1986	NY A	5	3	.625	13	10	1	0-0	70.2	73	27	8	2	15-1	28	2.93	140	.275	.316	0-0	—	0	95	9	1.0
1987	NY A	13	6	.684	33	33	3-1	0-0	187.2	212	95	12	6	47-7	63	4.03	109	.288	.335	0-0	—	0	121	6	0.5
1988	NY A	9	8	.529	35	32	0	0-0	176.1	221	96	11	6	46-4	81	4.49	88	.308	.354	0-0	—	0	112	-11	-0.8
1989	NY A	2	7	.222	10	10	0	0-0	63.2	87	45	6	3	22-2	18	5.80	67	.336	.392	0-0	—	0	72	-13	-1.5
Total	26	288	231	.555	760	700	162-46	4-0	4710.1	4783	2017	302	98	1259-102	2245	3.34	110	.265	.315	900-93	.157	1	103	163	20.1
JOHNS, AUGIE Augustus Francis "Lefty" B 9.10.1899 St.Louis, MO D 9.12.1975 San Antonio, TX BL/TL 5-8.5/170# d4.16																									
1926	Det A	6	4	.600	35	14	3-1	1	112.2	117	77	6	5	69	40	5.35	76	.271	.377	28-3	.143	-1	110	-14	-1.3
1927	Det A	0	0	—	1	0	0	0	1	1	1	0	0	1	1	9.00	47	.333	.500	0-0	—	0		0	0.0
Total	2	6	4	.600	36	14	3-1	1	113.2	118	78	6	5	70	41	5.38	75	.271	.378	28-3	.143	-1	110	-14	-1.3
JOHNS, DOUG Douglas Alan B 12.19.1967 South Bend, IN BR/TL 6-2/185# d7.8																									
1995	Oak A	5	3	.625	11	9	1-1	0-0	54.2	44	32	5	5	26-1	25	4.61	97	.226	.330	0-0	—	0	88	-2	-0.2
1996	Oak A	6	12	.333	40	23	1	1-1	158	187	112	21	6	69-5	71	5.98	82	.297	.370	0-0	—	0*	117	-19	-1.6
1998	Bal A	3	3	.500	31	10	0	1-0	86.2	108	46	9	4	32-2	34	4.57	100	.321	.381	2-0	1.000	1	114	0	0.2
1999	Bal A	6	4	.600	32	5	0	0-0	86.2	81	45	9	8	25-2	50	4.47	105	.248	.311	1-0	.000	-0	68	3	0.3
Total	4	20	22	.476	114	47	2-1	2-1	386	420	235	44	23	152-10	180	5.13	92	.282	.354	3-0	.667	1	106	-18	-1.3
JOHNS, OLLIE Oliver Tracy B 8.21.1879 Trenton, OH D 6.17.1961 Hamilton, OH BL/TL d9.24																									
1905	Cin N	1	0	1.000	4	1	1	1	18	31	22	1	0	4	8	3.50	94	.369	.398	5-1	.200	-0	175	-4	-0.3
JOHNSON, ABE Abraham B Chicago, IL d7.16																									
1893	Chi N	0	0	—	1	0	0	1	1	2	4	0	1	2	0	36.00	13	.400	.625	0	—	0		-3	-0.4
JOHNSON, ADAM Adam Bryant B 7.12.1979 San Jose, CA BR/TR 6-2/210# d7.16																									
2001	Min A	1	2	.333	7	4	0	0-0	25	32	25	6	5	13-0	17	8.28	56	.323	.424	2-0	.000	-0	70	-10	-1.0
2003	Min A	0	1	.000	2	0	0	0-0	1.1	8	8	1	0	1-0	0	47.25	10	.667	.692	0-0	—	0		-7	-1.0
Total	2	1	3	.250	9	4	0	0-0	26.1	40	33	7	5	14-0	17	10.25	45	.360	.450	2-0	.000	-0	70	-17	-2.0
JOHNSON, RANKIN Adam Rankin Jr. B 3.1.1917 Hayden, AZ BR/TR 6-3/177# d4.17 Mil 1942-45 f-Rankin																									
1941	Phi A	1	0	1.000	7	0	0	0	10	14	10	0	0	3	0	3.60	116	.326	.370	1-0	.000	-0		-2	-0.1
JOHNSON, RANKIN Adam Rankin Sr. "Tex" B 2.4.1888 Burnet, TX D 7.2.1972 Williamsport, PA BR/TR 6-1.5/185# d4.20 s-Rankin																									
1914	Bos A	3	9	.250	16	13	4-2	0	99.1	92	41	2	3	34	24	3.08	87	.265	.336	30-2	.133	-1	52	-2	-0.5
	Chi F	9	5	.643	16	14	12-2	0	120	88	29	5	4	29	60	**1.58**	169	.209	.267	37-0	.108	-3	70	15	1.3
1915	Chi F	2	4	.333	11	6	3	1	57	58	34	2	1	23	19	4.42	57	.270	.343	22-0	.045	-3	153	-12	-1.6
	Bal F	7	11	.389	23	19	12-2	1	150.2	143	68	3	1	58	62	3.35	86	.255	.326	51-3	.157	-2	94	-6	-1.1
	Year	9	15	.375	34	25	15-2	2	207.2	201	72	5	2	81	81	3.64	76	.259	.331	73-3	.123	-5	107	-17	-2.7
1918	StL N	1	1	.500	6	1	0	0	23	20	10	0	0	7	4	2.74	99	.263	.325	4-2	.250	0	28	0	0.0
Total	3	22	30	.423	72	53	31-6	2	450	401	182	12	9	151	169	2.92	93	.248	.315	144-7	.125	-9	83	-5	-1.9
JOHNSON, ART Arthur Gilbert B 2.15.1897 Warren, PA D 6.7.1982 Sarasota, FL BB/TL 6-1/167# d9.18																									
1927	NY N	0	0	—	1	0	0	0	3	1	1	0	0	1	0	0.00	—	.125	.222	0-0	—	0		1	0.0
JOHNSON, ART Arthur Henry "Lefty" B 7.16.1916 Winchester, MA BL/TL 6-2/185# d9.22 Mil 1942-45																									
1940	Bos N	0	1	.000	2	1	0	0	6	10	7	0	1	3	1	10.50	35	.345	.424	1-0	.000	-0	23	-4	-0.6
1941	Bos N	7	15	.318	43	18	6	1	183.1	189	92	7	5	71	70	3.53	101	.270	.342	55-5	.145	-2*	65	-2	-0.4
1942	Bos N	0	0	—	4	0	0	0	6.1	4	1	0	1	5	0	1.42	235	.190	.370	1-0	.000	-0		1	0.1
Total	3	7	16	.304	49	19	6	1	195.2	203	100	7	7	79	71	3.68	97	.271	.346	57-5	.140	-2	63	-5	-0.9
JOHNSON, BEN Benjamin Franklin B 5.16.1931 Greenwood, SC BR/TR 6-2/190# d9.6																									
1959	Chi N	0	0	—	4	2	0	0	16.2	17	5	1	0	4-0	6	2.16	183	.262	.304	4-1	.000	-0	113	3	0.1
1960	Chi N	2	1	.667	17	0	0	1	29.1	39	21	3	1	11-0	9	4.91	77	.355	.408	2-1	.000	-0		-5	-0.5
Total	2	2	1	.667	21	2	0	1	46	56	26	4	1	15-0	15	3.91	98	.320	.371	6-2	.000	-1	113	-2	-0.4
JOHNSON, CHET Chester Lillis "Chesty Chet" B 8.1.1917 Redmond, WA D 4.10.1983 Seattle, WA BL/TL 6/175# d9.12 b-Earl																									
1946	StL A	0	0	—	5	3	0	0	18	20	12	0	0	13	8	5.00	75	.286	.398	6-0	.000	-1	184	-3	-0.2

Year	Tm Lg	W	L	Pct	G	GS	CG-Sho	SV-BS	IP	H	R	HR	HB	BB-IB	SO	ERA	AERA	OAV	OOB	AB-SH	AVG	PB	Sup	APR	PW
JOHNSON, BART Clair Barth B 1.3.1950 Torrance, CA BR/TR 6-5/215# d9.8																									
1969	Chi A	1	3	.250	4	3	0	0-0	22.1	22	11	2	0	6-0	18	3.22	120	.259	.308	6-0	.167	0	84	0	0.1
1970	Chi A	4	7	.364	18	15	2-1	0-0	89.2	92	53	11	2	46-2	71	4.82	81	.268	.358	29-2	.276	2	98	-8	-0.7
1971	Chi A	12	10	.545	53	16	4	14-5	178	148	67	9	6	111-6	153	2.93	123	.227	.342	57-3	.193	0	123	13	1.8
1972	Chi A	0	3	.000	9	0	0	1-1	13.2	18	20	2	1	13-2	9	9.22	34	.327	.464	1-0	.000	-0		-11	-2.1
1973	Chi A	3	3	.500	22	9	0	0-0	80.2	76	39	6	2	40-0	56	4.13	96	.252	.338	0-0	—	0	103	0	0.0
1974	Chi A	10	4	.714	18	18	8-2	0-0	121.2	105	42	6	1	32-2	76	2.74	136	.229	.280	0-0	—	0	89	13	1.3
1976	Chi A	9	16	.360	32	32	8-3	0-0	211.1	231	115	19	1	62-1	91	4.73	75	.282	.329	0-0	—	0	75	-24	-2.6
1977	Chi A	4	5	.444	29	4	0	2-1	92	114	48	5	2	38-3	46	4.01	102	.302	.365	0-0	—	0	104	0	0.0
Total	8	43	51	.457	185	97	22-6	17-7	809.1	806	395	60	15	348-16	520	3.94	95	.261	.336	93-5	.215	3	93	-17	-2.2
JOHNSON, CONNIE Clifford B 12.27.1922 Stone Mountain, GA BR/TR 6-4/200# d4.17																									
1953	Chi A	4	4	.500	14	10	2-1	0	60.2	55	27	4	2	38	44	3.56	113	.238	.351	20-1	.050	-2*	102	3	0.1
1955	Chi A	7	4	.636	17	16	5-2	0	99	95	40	5	1	52-0	72	3.45	114	.251	.342	33-2	.152	-1*	110	6	0.4
1956	Chi A	0	1	.000	5	2	0	0	12.1	11	5	1	0	7-0	6	3.65	112	.234	.333	3-0	.000	-0	43	1	0.0
	Bal A	9	10	.474	26	25	9-2	0	183.2	165	79	12	1	62-3	130	3.43	114	.239	.301	58-6	.259	3	90	10	1.2
	Year	9	11	.450	31	27	9-2	0	196	176	83	13	1	69-3	136	3.44	114	.239	.303	61-6	.246	3	86	11	1.2
1957	Bal A	14	11	.560	35	30	14-3	0	242	212	93	17	3	66-1	177	3.20	112	.235	.287	89-6	.135	-4	116	11	0.5
1958	Bal A	6	9	.400	26	17	4	1	118.1	116	58	13	0	32-3	68	3.88	93	.260	.309	34-1	.206	1	82	-5	-0.5
Total	5	40	39	.506	123	100	34-8	1	716	654	302	52	7	257-7	497	3.44	109	.243	.309	237-16	.169	-3	100	26	1.7
JOHNSON, DANE Dane Edward B 2.10.1963 Coral Gables, FL BR/TR 6-5/205# d5.30																									
1994	Chi A	2	1	.667	15	0	0	0-0	12.1	16	9	2	0	11-1	7	6.57	71	.327	.443	0-0	—	0		-2	-0.4
1996	Tor A	0	0	—	10	0	0	0-0	9	5	3	0	0	5-0	7	3.00	167	.161	.278	0-0	—	0		2	0.1
1997	Oak A	4	1	.800	38	0	0	2-2	45.2	49	28	4	2	31-4	43	4.53	100	.272	.378	0-0	—	0		-2	-0.2
Total	3	6	2	.750	63	0	0	2-2	67	70	40	6	2	47-5	57	4.70	98	.269	.379	0-0	—	0		-2	-0.5
JOHNSON, DAVE David Charles B 10.4.1948 Abilene, TX BR/TR 6-1/183# d7.2																									
1974	Bal A	2	2	.500	11	0	0	2-0	15.1	17	5	1	0	5-3	6	2.93	118	.274	.328	0-0	—	0		1	0.3
1975	Bal A	0	1	.000	6	0	0	0-2	8.2	8	4	0	0	7-1	4	4.15	85	.250	.385	0-0	—	0		0	-0.1
1977	Min A	2	5	.286	30	6	0	0-1	72.2	86	42	7	5	23-1	33	4.58	87	.299	.358	0-0	—	0	109	-5	-0.5
1978	Min A	0	2	.000	6	1	0	0-0	12	15	11	1	0	9-0	7	7.50	51	.313	.421	0-0	—	0	47	-5	-0.7
Total	4	4	10	.286	53	7	0	2-3	108.2	126	62	9	5	44-5	50	4.64	83	.293	.364	0-0	—	0	103	-9	-1.0
JOHNSON, DAVE David Wayne B 10.24.1959 Baltimore, MD BR/TR 5-11/183# d5.29																									
1987	Pit N	0	0	—	5	0	0	0-0	6.1	13	7	1	0	2-0	4	9.95	41	.448	.484	0-0	—	0		-4	-0.2
1989	Bal A	4	7	.364	14	14	4	0-0	89.1	90	44	11	4	28-1	26	4.23	90	.265	.325	0-0	—	0	71	-4	-0.5
1990	Bal A	13	9	.591	30	29	3	0-0	180	196	83	30	3	43-2	68	4.10	93	.280	.321	0-0	—	0	105	-4	-0.6
1991	Bal A	4	8	.333	22	14	0	0-0	84	127	68	18	4	24-3	38	7.07	56	.349	.394	0-0	—	0	91	-29	-3.4
1993	Det A	1	1	.500	6	0	0	0-0	8.1	13	13	3	2	5-1	7	12.96	33	.342	.435	0-0	—	0		-8	-1.4
Total	5	22	25	.468	77	57	7	0-0	368	439	215	63	13	102-7	143	5.11	75	.298	.347	0-0	—	0	93	-49	-6.1
JOHNSON, DON Donald Roy B 11.12.1926 Portland, OR BR/TR 6-3/200# d4.20																									
1947	NY A	4	3	.571	15	8	2	0	54.1	57	26	2	1	23	16	3.64	97	.270	.345	13-4	.000	-2	128	-2	-0.4
1950	NY A	1	0	1.000	8	0	0	0	18	35	21	2	0	12	9	10.00	43	.398	.470	3-0	.000	-0		-12	-0.6
	StL A	5	6	.455	25	12	4-1	1	96	126	72	14	1	55	31	6.09	81	.325	.410	29-3	.069	-3	77	-10	-1.3
	Year	6	6	.500	33	12	4-1	1	114	161	76	16	1	67	40	6.71	72	.338	.421	32-3	.063	-4	79	-21	-1.9
1951	StL A	0	1	.000	6	3	0	0	15	27	26	4	1	18	8	12.60	35	.391	.523	3-1	.333	0	108	-14	-0.8
	Was A	7	11	.389	21	20	8-1	0	143.2	138	67	9	2	58	52	3.95	104	.255	.329	47-6	.085	-5	93	4	-0.1
	Year	7	12	.368	27	23	8-1	0	158.2	165	71	13	3	76	60	4.76	87	.270	.354	50-7	.100	-5	96	-10	-0.9
1952	Was A	0	5	.000	29	6	0	2	69	80	41	4	4	33	37	4.43	80	.287	.370	13-2	.077	-1	74	-8	-0.7
1954	Chi A	8	7	.533	46	16	3-3	7	144	129	53	14	0	43	68	3.13	119	.243	.298	35-7	.029	-3	96	11	0.8
1955	Bal A	2	4	.333	31	5	0	1	68	89	46	4	0	35-2	27	5.82	65	.333	.404	10-0	.000	-1	70	-14	-1.2
1958	SF N	0	1	.000	17	0	0	1	23	31	19	2	2	8-1	14	6.26	61	.323	.383	2-1	.000	-0		-7	-0.4
Total	7	27	38	.415	198	70	17-5	12	631	712	371	55	11	285-3	262	4.78	84	.288	.363	155-24	.058	-16	93	-52	-4.7
JOHNSON, EARL Earl Douglas "Lefty" B 4.2.1919 Redmond, WA D 12.3.1994 Seattle, WA BL/TL 6-3/190# d7.20 Mil 1942-45 b-Chet																									
1940	Bos A	6	2	.750	17	10	2	0	70.1	69	33	0	2	39	26	4.09	110	.260	.359	27-0	.074	-3*	107	4	0.2
1941	Bos A	4	5	.444	17	12	4	0	93.2	90	57	4	3	51	46	4.52	92	.247	.344	34-3	.294	2	125	-4	-0.1
1946	†Bos A	5	4	.556	29	5	0	3	80	78	39	5	2	39	40	3.71	99	.250	.337	22-1	.227	2	61	-1	0.1
1947	Bos A	12	11	.522	45	17	6-3	8	142.1	129	63	7	2	62	65	2.97	131	.246	.328	44-2	.273	1*	68	10	1.9
1948	Bos A	10	4	.714	35	3	1	5	91.1	98	49	7	0	42	45	4.53	97	.276	.353	31-1	.097	-3	137	-1	-0.3
1949	Bos A	3	6	.333	19	3	0	0	49.1	65	45	1	4	29	20	7.48	58	.327	.422	11-0	.000	-1	75	-16	-2.6
1950	Bos A	0	0	—	11	0	0	0	13.2	18	11	0	1	8	6	7.24	68	.333	.429	2-0	.000	-0		-3	-0.1
1951	Det A	0	0	—	6	0	0	1	5.2	9	5	0	0	2	2	6.35	66	.375	.423	0-0	—	0		-2	-0.1
Total	8	40	32	.556	179	50	13-3	17	546.1	556	302	24	14	272	250	4.30	96	.265	.353	171-7	.187	-2	95	-13	-1.0
JOHNSON, WALT Ellis Walter B 12.8.1892 Minneapolis, MN D 1.14.1965 Minneapolis, MN BR/TR 6-0.5/180# d7.6																									
1912	Chi A	0	0	—	3	0	0	0	11.2	11	6	0	1	7	7	3.86	83	.262	.380	3-0	.000	-0		-1	-0.1
1915	Chi A	0	0	—	1	0	0	0	2	3	2	0	0	0	3	9.00	33	.333	.333	0-0	—	0		-1	-0.1
1917	Phi A	0	2	.000	4	2	0	0	13.2	15	12	0	0	5	8	7.24	38	.294	.357	1-0	.000	0	78	-5	-0.7
Total	3	0	2	.000	8	2	0	0	27.1	29	20	0	1	12	18	5.93	50	.284	.365	4-0	.000	0	78	-7	-0.9
JOHNSON, ERNIE Ernest Thorwald B 6.16.1924 Brattleboro, VT BR/TR 6-4/195# d4.28																									
1950	Bos N	2	0	1.000	16	1	0	0	20.2	37	21	1	0	13	15	6.97	55	.394	.467	2-0	.500	0	344	-9	-0.6
1952	Bos N	6	3	.667	29	10	2-1	1	92	100	53	8	2	31	45	4.11	88	.270	.329	22-4	.091	-0	155	-8	-0.7
1953	Mil N	4	3	.571	36	1	0	0	81	79	34	4	3	22	36	2.67	147	.263	.320	14-1	.071	-1	23	9	0.6
1954	Mil N	5	2	.714	40	4	1	2	99.1	77	34	11	1	34	68	2.81	133	.219	.289	13-5	.231	0	138	11	0.9
1955	Mil N	5	7	.417	40	2	0	4	92	81	38	5	2	55-8	43	3.42	110	.240	.348	20-1	.100	-1	95	4	0.4
1956	Mil N	4	3	.571	36	0	0	6	51	54	21	9	1	21-2	26	3.71	93	.270	.341	4-0	.250	0		0	0.1
1957	†Mil N	7	3	.700	30	0	0	4	65	67	29	9	1	26-5	44	3.88	90	.265	.335	17-1	.353	3		-2	0.1
1958	Mil N	3	1	.750	15	0	0	1	23.1	35	21	4	1	10-3	13	8.10	43	.357	.418	2-0	.000	0		-12	-1.9
1959	Bal A	4	1	.800	31	1	0	1	50.1	57	32	6	3	19-2	29	4.11	92	.286	.353	6-0	.333	0	47	-5	-0.4
Total	9	40	23	.635	273	19	3-1	19	574.2	587	283	57	14	231-20	319	3.77	98	.266	.338	100-12	.180	2	142	-12	-1.5
JOHNSON, FRED Frederick Edward "Deacon" or "Cactus" B 3.10.1894 Tolar, TX D 6.14.1973 Kerrville, TX BR/TR 6/185# d9.27																									
1922	NY N	0	2	.000	2	2	1	0	18	20	8	3	0	1	8	4.00	100	.294	.304	4-1	.000	-1	31	1	0.0
1923	NY N	2	0	1.000	3	2	1	0	17	11	8	2	0	7	5	4.24	90	.177	.261	6-0	.000	-1	108	0	-0.1
1938	StL A	3	7	.300	17	6	3	3	69	91	50	7	1	27	24	5.61	89	.316	.377	25-1	.240	-0	112	-6	-0.8
1939	StL A	0	1	.000	5	2	1	0	14	23	12	0	0	9	2	6.43	76	.383	.464	4-1	.000	-1	100	-3	-0.2
Total	4	5	10	.333	27	12	6	3	118	145	78	12	1	44	39	5.26	88	.303	.363	39-3	.154	-2	96	-8	-1.1
JOHNSON, CHIEF George Howard "Murphy" or "Big Murph" B 3.30.1886 Winnebago, NE D 6.12.1922 Des Moines, IA BR/TR 5-11.5/190# d4.16																									
1913	Cin N	14	16	.467	44	31	13-3	0	269	251	137	8	7	86	107	3.01	108	.256	.320	88-3	.114	-3	95	1	-0.1
1914	Cin N	0	0	—	1	1	0	0	4	6	4	0	0	2	1	6.75	43	.333	.400	0-0	—	0	122	-2	-0.1
	KC F	9	10	.474	20	19	12-2	0	134	157	76	2	4	33	78	3.16	88	.298	.345	49-1	.122	-2	117	-11	-1.8
1915	KC F	17	17	.500	46	34	19-4	2	281.1	253	121	5	8	71	118	2.75	96	.242	.295	87-4	.126	-4	103	-8	-1.2
Total	3	40	43	.482	111	85	44-9	2	688.1	667	338	15	19	192	304	2.95	98	.259	.315	224-8	.121	-9	103	-20	-3.2
JOHNSON, HANK Henry Ward B 5.21.1906 Bradenton, FL D 8.20.1982 Bradenton, FL BR/TR 5-11.5/175# d4.17																									
1925	NY A	1	3	.250	24	4	2-1	0	67	88	58	3	8	37	25	6.85	62	.319	.414	17-2	.059	-1	99	-19	-1.0
1926	NY A	0	0	—	1	0	0	1	1	2	2	0	0	2	0	18.00	21	.400	.571	0-0	—	0		-1	-0.2
1928	NY A	14	9	.609	31	22	10-1	0	199	188	107	16	12	104	110	4.30	88	.250	.351	79-4	.241	2	122	-10	-0.9
1929	NY A	3	3	.500	12	8	2	0	42.2	37	28	5	0	39	24	5.06	76	.237	.390	14-2	.071	-1*	123	-6	-0.8
1930	NY A	14	11	.560	44	15	7-1	2	175.1	177	112	12	2	104	115	4.67	92	.265	.366	64-5	.266	5*	130	-9	-0.5

Year	Tm Lg	W	L	Pct	G	GS	CG-Sho	SV-BS	IP	H	R	HR	HB	BB-IB	SO	ERA	AERA	OAV	OOB	AB-SH	AVG	PB	Sup	APR	PW
1931	NY A	13	8	.619	40	23	8	4	196.1	176	114	13	1	102	106	4.72	84	.234	.326	77-1	.195	2	145	-16	-1.5
1932	NY A	2	2	.500	5	4	2	0	31.1	34	18	7	0	15	27	4.88	83	.266	.343	13-0	.231	0*	131	-2	-0.2
1933	Bos A	8	6	.571	25	21	7	1	155.1	156	84	13	3	74	65	4.06	108	.263	.348	52-2	.231	3*	93	5	0.7
1934	Bos A	6	8	.429	31	14	7-1	1	124.1	162	95	12	5	53	66	5.36	90	.316	.385	43-1	.233	1	92	-10	-0.9
1935	Bos A	2	1	.667	13	2	0	1	31	41	21	3	0	14	14	5.52	86	.331	.399	8-1	.000	-1	119	-2	-0.3
1936	Phi A	0	2	.000	3	3	0	0	11.2	16	16	4	1	10	6	7.71	66	.296	.415	4-1	.250	-0	75	-5	-0.7
1939	Cin N	0	3	.000	20	0	0	1	31.1	30	10	1	0	13	10	2.01	191	.268	.344	5-0	.400	1		6	0.5
Total	12	63	56	.529	249	116	45-4	11	1066.1	1107	665	89	32	567	568	4.75	88	.268	.361	376-19	.215	9	116	-69	-5.8
JOHNSON, JIM James Brian B 11.3.1945 Muskegon, MI D 12.6.1987 North Muskegon, MI BL/TL 5-11/175# d4.13																									
1970	SF N	1	0	1.000	3	0	0	0-0	6.2	8	6	0	0	5-1	2	8.10	49	.320	.419	2-0	.000	0		-3	-0.3
JOHNSON, JASON Jason Michael B 10.27.1973 Santa Barbara, CA BR/TR 6-6/220# d8.27																									
1997	Pit N	0	0	—	3	0	0	0-0	6	10	4	2	0	1-0	3	6.00	72	.400	.407	1-0	.000	-0		-1	-0.1
1998	TB A	2	5	.286	13	13	0	0-0	60	74	38	9	3	27-0	36	5.70	84	.306	.381	2-0	.000	-0	85	-5	-0.5
1999	Bal A	8	7	.533	22	21	0	0-0	115.1	120	74	16	3	55-0	71	5.46	86	.266	.347	2-0	.000	-0	117	-10	-1.1
2000	Bal A	1	10	.091	25	13	0	0-0	107.2	119	95	21	4	61-2	79	7.02	67	.278	.369	3-2	.000	-0	76	-31	-2.6
2001	Bal A	10	12	.455	32	32	2	0-0	196	194	109	28	13	77-3	114	4.09	105	.257	.334	3-0	.333	1	91	0	-0.1
2002	Bal A	5	14	.263	22	22	1	0-0	131.1	141	68	19	6	41-2	97	4.59	93	.276	.335	3-0	.000	-0	69	-3	-0.4
2003	Bal A	10	10	.500	32	32	0	0-0	189.2	216	100	22	10	80-8	118	4.18	105	.283	.358	5-0	.200	0	100	2	0.2
Total	7	36	58	.383	149	133	3	0-0	806	874	488	117	39	342-15	518	4.91	91	.275	.351	19-2	.105	-0	92	-48	-4.6
JOHNSON, JERRY Jerry Michael B 12.3.1943 Miami, FL BR/TR 6-3/200# d7.17																									
1968	Phi N	4	4	.500	16	11	2	0	80.2	82	33	5	2	29-2	40	3.24	93	.264	.328	25-1	.080	-0	87	-2	-0.2
1969	Phi N	6	13	.316	33	21	4-2	1-2	147.1	151	76	18	3	57-11	82	4.28	83	.268	.335	43-3	.209	2	79	-11	-1.2
1970	StL N	2	0	1.000	7	0	0	1-1	11.1	6	4	1	0	3-0	5	3.18	130	.146	.205	1-0	.000	0		1	0.3
	SF N	3	4	.429	33	1	0	3-2	65.1	67	39	5	1	38-2	44	4.27	93	.266	.364	15-0	.067	-1	90	-4	-0.6
	Year	5	4	.556	40	1	0	4-3	76.2	73	43	6	1	41-2	49	4.11	97	.249	.343	16-0	.063	-1	90	-3	-0.3
1971	†SF N	12	9	.571	67	0	0	18-5	109	93	42	9	1	48-9	85	2.97	114	.230	.310	13-1	.154	-0		6	1.2
1972	SF N	8	6	.571	48	0	0	8-6	73.1	73	40	4	0	40-10	57	4.42	79	.261	.350	9-1	.000	-1		-7	-1.6
1973	Cle A	5	6	.455	39	1	0	5-6	59.2	70	48	7	0	39-8	45	6.18	63	.299	.396	0-0	—	0	91	-16	-2.8
1974	Hou N	2	1	.667	34	0	0	0-0	45	47	26	2	0	24-7	32	4.80	72	.276	.360	1-0	.000	-0		-6	-0.4
1975	SD N	3	1	.750	21	4	0	0-0	54	60	37	3	0	31-3	18	5.17	67	.282	.368	12-0	.083	-0	120	-10	-0.8
1976	SD N	1	3	.250	24	1	0	0-0	39	39	27	0	0	26-6	27	5.31	62	.260	.367	3-0	.000	-0	27	-10	-1.0
1977	Tor A	2	4	.333	43	0	0	5-2	86	91	50	9	0	54-4	54	4.60	91	.279	.375	0-0	—	0		-4	-0.3
Total	10	48	51	.485	365	39	6-2	41-24	770.2	779	422	63	7	389-62	489	4.31	83	.265	.348	122-6	.123	-2	80	-63	-7.4
JOHNSON, JOHNNY John Clifford "Swede" B 9.29.1914 Belmore, OH D 6.26.1991 Iron Mountain, MI BL/TL 6/182# d4.19																									
1944	NY A	0	2	.000	22	1	0	3	26.2	25	14	0	1	24	11	4.05	86	.243	.391	6-0	.500	1	24	-2	-0.1
1945	Chi A	3	0	1.000	29	0	0	4	69.2	85	39	2	1	35	38	4.26	78	.306	.385	14-1	.286	2		-8	-0.2
Total	2	3	2	.600	51	1	0	7	96.1	110	53	2	2	59	49	4.20	80	.289	.387	20-1	.350	3	24	-10	-0.3
JOHNSON, YOUNGY John Godfred B 7.22.1877 San Francisco, CA D 8.28.1936 Berkeley, CA TR d4.29																									
1897	Phi N	1	2	.333	5	2	1	0	29	39	24	0	2	12	7	4.66	90	.320	.390	13-0	.077	-2	93	-3	-0.4
1899	NY N	0	0	—	1	0	0	0	2	0	0	0	0	2	1	0.00	—	.000	.250	1-0	.000	-0		1	0.0
Total	2	1	2	.333	6	2	1	0	31	39	24	0	2	14	8	4.35	96	.305	.382	14-0	.071	-2	93	-2	-0.4
JOHNSON, JOHN HENRY John Henry B 8.21.1956 Houston, TX BL/TL 6-2/190# d4.10																									
1978	Oak A	11	10	.524	33	30	7-2	0-0	186	164	81	18	0	82-6	91	3.39	108	.238	.317	0-0	—	0*	108	7	0.6
1979	Oak A	2	8	.200	14	13	1	0-0	84.2	89	45	13	1	36-0	50	4.36	93	.269	.341	0-0	—	0	65	-2	-0.3
	Tex A	2	6	.250	17	12	1	0-0	82.1	79	50	12	1	36-3	46	4.92	85	.255	.330	0-0	—	0	87	-7	-0.6
	Year	4	14	.222	31	25	2	0-0	167	168	54	25	2	72-3	96	4.63	89	.262	.335	0-0	—	0	76	-9	-0.9
1980	Tex A	2	2	.500	33	0	0	4-3	38.2	27	12	2	1	15-4	44	2.33	168	.199	.281	0-0	—	0		7	0.8
1981	Tex A	3	1	.750	24	0	0	2-1	23.2	19	7	2	1	6-1	8	2.66	130	.232	.283	0-0	—	0		3	0.5
1983	Bos A	3	2	.600	34	1	0	1-1	53.1	58	28	3	1	20-4	51	3.71	118	.283	.342	0-0	—	0	21	2	0.2
1984	Bos A	1	2	.333	30	3	0	1-0	63.2	64	26	7	0	27-1	57	3.53	118	.260	.333	0-0	—	0	65	5	0.3
1986	Mil A	2	1	.667	19	0	0	1-0	44	43	15	2	0	10-1	42	2.66	163	.251	.293	0-0	—	0		8	0.5
1987	Mil A	0	1	.000	10	2	0	0-0	26.1	42	30	1	0	18-1	18	9.57	48	.365	.451	0-0	—	0	99	-14	-0.6
Total	8	26	33	.441	214	61	9-2	9-5	602.2	585	294	60	5	250-21	407	3.90	102	.256	.328	0-0	—	0	88	9	1.4
JOHNSON, JOHN John Louis (b: John Louis Mercer) B 11.18.1869 Pekin, IL D 1.28.1941 Kansas City, MO TL 5-10/165# d9.11																									
1894	Phi N	1	1	.500	4	3	2	0	32.2	44	30	3	1	15	10	6.06	85	.319	.390	16-1	.188	-1	166	-3	-0.2
JOHNSON, JONATHAN Jonathan Kent B 7.16.1974 LaGrange, GA BR/TR 6/180# d9.27																									
1998	Tex A	0	0	—	1	1	0	0-0	4.1	5	4	0	0	5-0	3	8.31	58	.313	.455	0-0	—	0	231	-1	-0.1
1999	Tex A	0	0	—	1	0	0	0-0	3	9	5	0	1	2-0	3	15.00	34	.529	.571	0-0	—	0		-3	-0.1
2000	Tex A	1	1	.500	15	0	0	0-0	29	34	23	3	6	19-2	23	6.21	81	.291	.410	0-0	—	0		-4	-0.2
2001	Tex A	0	0	—	5	0	0	0-0	10.1	13	11	2	1	7-1	11	9.58	49	.317	.404	0-0	—	0		-5	-0.3
2002	SD N	1	2	.333	16	0	0	0-0	15.1	15	8	2	1	5-1	21	4.11	92	.250	.318	0-0	—	0		-1	-0.2
2003	Hou N	0	1	.000	4	3	0	0-0	15.1	20	11	2	0	15-3	7	5.87	76	.323	.449	4-0	.000	-0	63	-2	-0.2
Total	6	2	4	.333	42	4	0	0-0	77.1	96	62	9	9	53-7	68	6.63	69	.307	.413	4-0	.000	-0	107	-16	-1.1
JOHNSON, JOE Joseph Richard B 10.30.1961 Brookline, MA BR/TR 6-2/195# d7.25																									
1985	Atl N	4	4	.500	15	14	1	0-0	85.2	95	44	9	3	24-5	34	4.10	94	.285	.336	23-3	.043	-1	98	-2	-0.3
1986	Atl N	6	7	.462	17	15	2	0-0	87	101	58	8	2	35-4	49	4.97	80	.289	.357	26-2	.115	-1	97	-10	-1.4
	Tor A	7	2	.778	16	15	0	0-0	88	94	39	3	3	22-1	39	3.89	109	.281	.327	0-0	—	0	104	4	0.4
1987	Tor A	3	5	.375	14	14	0	0-0	66.2	77	44	10	2	18-0	27	5.13	88	.289	.338	0-0	—	0	100	-6	-0.6
Total	3	20	18	.526	62	58	3	0-0	327.1	367	185	30	10	99-10	149	4.48	92	.286	.340	49-5	.082	-2	100	-14	-1.9
JOHNSON, KEN Kenneth Travis B 6.16.1933 W.Palm Beach, FL BR/TR 6-4/210# d9.13																									
1958	KC A	0	0	—	2	0	0	0	2.1	6	7	1	0	3-0	1	27.00	14	.429	.529	0-0	—	0		-5	-0.3
1959	KC A	1	1	.500	2	2	0	0	11	11	6	2	0	5-0	8	4.09	98	.268	.340	3-0	.000	-0	132	0	-0.1
1960	KC A	5	10	.333	42	6	2	3	120.1	120	68	16	7	45-6	83	4.26	93	.263	.336	30-3	.167	-1	85	-5	-0.6
1961	KC A	0	4	.000	6	1	0	0	9.1	11	11	2	0	7-0	4	10.61	39	.297	.409	1-0	.000	-0	0	-6	-1.0
	†Cin N	6	2	.750	15	11	3-1	1	83	71	33	11	2	22-1	42	3.25	125	.229	.283	25-1	.240	1	105	8	0.8
1962	Hou N	7	16	.304	33	31	5-1	0	197	195	100	18	7	46-1	178	3.84	97	.257	.302	52-9	.077	-3	71	-3	-0.6
1963	Hou N	11	17	.393	37	32	6-1	1	224	204	86	12	8	50-4	148	2.65	119	.242	.290	74-5	.068	-4*	77	9	0.8
1964	Hou N	11	16	.407	35	35	7-1	0	218	209	100	15	7	44-6	117	3.63	94	.250	.291	76-4	.079	-2	75	-5	-0.6
1965	Hou N	3	2	.600	8	8	1	0	51.2	52	25	4	4	11-1	28	4.18	80	.267	.315	18-0	.111	-0	111	-4	-0.3
	Mil N	13	8	.619	29	26	8-1	2	179.2	165	75	15	3	37-7	123	3.21	110	.240	.280	61-3	.115	-2	108	5	0.2
	Year	16	10	.615	37	34	9-1	2	231.1	217	79	19	7	48-8	151	3.42	102	.246	.288	79-3	.114	-2	108	1	-0.1
1966	Atl N	14	8	.636	32	31	11-2	0	215.2	213	89	24	0	46-6	105	3.30	110	.262	.300	70-10	.143	0	114	8	0.8
1967	Atl N	13	9	.591	29	29	6	0	210.1	191	78	19	7	38-8	85	2.74	121	.244	.284	71-6	.127	-0	121	12	1.1
1968	Atl N	5	8	.385	31	16	1	0	135	145	58	10	9	25-10	57	3.47	86	.279	.323	40-3	.175	-0	81	-6	-0.7
1969	Atl N	0	1	.000	9	2	0	1-1	29	32	17	4	0	9-1	20	4.97	73	.283	.328	6-0	.000	-0	74	-4	-0.2
	NY A	1	2	.333	12	0	0	0-0	26	19	11	1	0	11-2	21	3.46	101	.202	.286	3-0	.000	-0		0	0.1
	Chi N	1	2	.333	9	1	0	1-1	19	17	8	2	0	13-3	18	2.84	142	.230	.345	4-1	.000	-0	44	2	0.2
1970	Mon N	0	0	—	3	0	0	0-0	6	9	6	1	2	1-0	4	7.50	55	.321	.387	0-0	—	0		-2	-0.1
Total	13	91	106	.462	334	231	50-7	9-2	1737.1	1670	778	157	56	413-56	1042	3.46	101	.253	.301	534-45	.114	-12	92	4	-0.5
JOHNSON, KEN Kenneth Wandersee "Hook" B 1.14.1923 Topeka, KS BL/TL 6-1/185# d9.18																									
1947	StL N	1	0	1.000	2	1	1	0	10	2	1	0	1	5	8	0.00	—	.063	.211	4-0	.500	1	64	4	0.5
1948	StL N	2	4	.333	13	4	0	0	45.1	43	27	1	1	30	20	4.76	86	.262	.379	20-0	.300	2*	60	-4	-0.3
1949	StL N	0	1	.000	14	2	0	0	33.2	29	28	1	3	35	18	6.42	65	.250	.435	8-0	.250	0*	106	-8	-0.3
1950	StL N	0	0	—	2	0	0	0	2	1	1	0	0	3	1	0.00	—	.167	.444	0-0	—	0		0	0.0

Year	Tm Lg	W	L	Pct	G	GS	CG-Sho	SV-BS	IP	H	R	HR	HB	BB-IB	SO	ERA	AERA	OAV	OOB	AB-SH	AVG	PB	Sup	APR	PW
	†Phi N	4	1	.800	14	8	3-1	0	60.2	61	32	3	1	43	32	4.01	101	.260	.376	19-0	.158	-0*	126	0	0.0
	Year	4	1	.800	16	8	3-1	0	62.2	62	38	3	1	46	33	3.88	105	.257	.378	19-0	.158	-0	126	0	0.0
1951	Phi N	5	8	.385	20	18	4-3	0	106.1	103	56	8	3	68	58	4.57	84	.259	.371	35-1	.143	-1*	74	-7	-0.9
1952	Det A	0	0	—	9	1	0	0	11.1	12	11	1	0	11	10	6.35	60	.273	.418	3-0	.333	0	183	-4	-0.2
Total	6	12	14	.462	74	34	8-4	0	269.1	251	156	14	9	195	147	4.58	87	.252	.379	89-1	.213	1	90	-19	-1.2

JOHNSON, LLOYD Lloyd William "Eppa" B 12.24.1910 Santa Rosa, CA D 10.8.1980 Stockton, CA BL/TL 6-4/204# d4.21

Year	Tm Lg	W	L	Pct	G	GS	CG-Sho	SV-BS	IP	H	R	HR	HB	BB-IB	SO	ERA	AERA	OAV	OOB	AB-SH	AVG	PB	Sup	APR	PW
1934	Pit N	0	0	—	1	0	0	0	1	1	0	0	0	0	0	0.00	—	.333	.333	0-0	—	0		0	0.0

JOHNSON, MARK Mark J. B 5.2.1975 Dayton, OH BR/TR 6-3/226# d4.7

Year	Tm Lg	W	L	Pct	G	GS	CG-Sho	SV-BS	IP	H	R	HR	HB	BB-IB	SO	ERA	AERA	OAV	OOB	AB-SH	AVG	PB	Sup	APR	PW
2000	Det A	0	1	.000	9	3	0	0-0	24	25	23	3	1	16-1	11	7.50	64	.266	.365	0-0	—	0	136	-8	-0.3

JOHNSON, MIKE Michael Keith B 10.3.1975 Edmonton, AL, CAN BL/TR 6-2/175# d4.6

Year	Tm Lg	W	L	Pct	G	GS	CG-Sho	SV-BS	IP	H	R	HR	HB	BB-IB	SO	ERA	AERA	OAV	OOB	AB-SH	AVG	PB	Sup	APR	PW
1997	Bal A	0	1	.000	14	5	0	2-0	39.2	52	36	12	1	16-2	29	7.94	56	.317	.377	0-0	—	0	117	-15	-0.7
	Mon N	2	5	.286	11	11	0	0-0	50	54	34	8	0	21-2	28	5.94	71	.277	.344	13-2	.077	-1	86	-8	-1.1
1998	Mon N	0	2	.000	2	2	0	0-0	7.1	16	12	4	1	2-0	4	14.73	29	.432	.475	3-0	.333	0	109	-8	-1.1
1999	Mon N	0	0	—	3	1	0	0-0	8.1	12	8	2	0	7-1	6	8.64	52	.324	.432	4-0	.250	0	287	-3	-0.1
2000	Mon N	5	6	.455	41	13	0	0-0	101.1	107	73	18	9	53-1	70	6.39	75	.269	.366	22-3	.182	0	116	-14	-1.3
2001	Mon N	0	0	—	10	0	0	0-2	11.1	13	6	3	2	4-0	10	4.76	94	.295	.380	1-0	.000	-0		0	0.0
Total	5	7	14	.333	81	32	0	2-2	218	254	169	47	13	103-6	147	6.85	66	.290	.371	43-5	.163	-1	110	-48	-4.3

JOHNSON, MIKE Michael Norton B 3.2.1951 Slayton, MN BR/TR 6-1/185# d7.25

Year	Tm Lg	W	L	Pct	G	GS	CG-Sho	SV-BS	IP	H	R	HR	HB	BB-IB	SO	ERA	AERA	OAV	OOB	AB-SH	AVG	PB	Sup	APR	PW
1974	SD N	0	2	.000	18	0	0	0-0	21.1	29	13	1	1	15-5	15	4.64	77	.326	.421	0-0	—	0		-3	-0.3

JOHNSON, RANDY Randall David "The Big Unit" B 9.10.1963 Walnut Creek, CA BR/TL 6-10/225# d9.15

Year	Tm Lg	W	L	Pct	G	GS	CG-Sho	SV-BS	IP	H	R	HR	HB	BB-IB	SO	ERA	AERA	OAV	OOB	AB-SH	AVG	PB	Sup	APR	PW
1988	Mon N	3	0	1.000	4	4	1	0-0	26	23	8	3	0	7-0	25	2.42	149	.225	.275	9-0	.111	-0	154	3	0.3
1989	Mon N	0	4	.000	7	6	0	0-0	29.2	29	25	2	0	26-1	26	6.67	53	.264	.393	7-2	.143	-0	79	-11	-1.2
	Sea A	7	9	.438	22	22	2	0-0	131	118	75	11	3	70-1	104	4.40	92	.244	.338	0-0	—	0	91	-6	-0.6
1990	Sea A☆	14	11	.560	33	33	5-2	0-0	219.2	174	103	26	5	120-2	194	3.65	109	.216	.319	0-0	—	0	95	7	0.7
1991	Sea A	13	10	.565	33	33	2-1	0-0	201.1	151	96	15	12	152-0	228	3.98	104	.213	.358	0-0	—	0	103	4	0.4
1992	Sea A	12	14	.462	31	31	6-2	0-0	210.1	154	104	13	18	144-1	**241**	3.77	106	**.206**	.344	0-0	—	0	91	2	0.1
1993	Sea A★	19	8	.704	35	34	10-3	1-0	255.1	185	97	22	16	99-1	**308**	3.24	136	**.203**	.290	0-0	—	0*	105	34	3.3
1994	Sea A★	13	6	.684	23	23	**9-4**	0-0	172	132	65	14	6	72-2	**204**	3.19	153	.216	.304	0-0	—	0	104	34	3.5
1995	†Sea A★	18	2	**.900**	30	30	6-3	0-0	214.1	159	65	12	6	65-1	**294**	**2.48**	**191**	**.201**	**.266**	0-0	—	0	109	**54**	**4.6**
1996	Sea A	5	0	1.000	14	8	0	1-1	61.1	48	27	8	2	25-0	85	3.67	135	.211	.294	0-0	—	0	122	9	0.6
1997	†Sea A★	20	4	**.833**	30	29	5-2	0-0	213	147	60	20	10	77-2	291	2.28	197	**.194**	.277	0-0	—	0	91	53	5.6
1998	Sea A	9	10	.474	23	23	6-2	0-0	160	146	90	19	11	60-0	213	4.33	107	.240	.319	7-0	.143	-0	98	3	0.3
	†Hou N	10	1	.909	11	11	4-4	0-0	84.1	57	12	4	3	26-1	116	1.28	317	.191	.261	32-3	.063	-2	99	28	3.5
1999	†Ari N★	17	9	.654	35	**35**	**12**-2	0-0	**271.2**	207	86	30	9	70-3	**364**	**2.48**	**184**	.208	.266	97-7	.124	-3	102	**61**	5.1
2000	Ari N★	19	7	**.731**	35	**35**	**8-3**	0-0	248.2	202	89	23	6	76-1	**347**	2.64	**178**	.224	.288	83-5	.157	-0	80	**51**	4.8
2001	†Ari N★	21	6	.778	35	34	3-2	0-0	249.2	181	74	19	18	71-2	**372**	**2.49**	**184**	.203	.274	80-7	.100	-3	104	**55**	**5.3**
2002	†Ari N☆	**24**	5	**.828**	35	35	**8-4**	0-0	**260**	197	78	26	13	71-1	**334**	**2.32**	**191**	**.208**	.273	89-6	.135	-2	115	**54**	**5.6**
2003	Ari N	6	8	.429	18	18	1-1	0-0	114	125	61	16	8	27-3	125	4.26	110	.280	.330	36-2	.194	1	83	4	0.5
Total	16	230	114	.669	454	444	88-35	2-1	3122.1	2435	1215	283	146	1258-223	871	3.10	143	.215	.300	440-32	.130	-11	99	439	42.4

JOHNSON, BOB Robert Dale B 4.25.1943 Aurora, IL BL/TR 6-4/220# d9.19

Year	Tm Lg	W	L	Pct	G	GS	CG-Sho	SV-BS	IP	H	R	HR	HB	BB-IB	SO	ERA	AERA	OAV	OOB	AB-SH	AVG	PB	Sup	APR	PW
1969	NY N	0	0	—	2	0	0	1-0	1.2	1	0	0	0	1-0	1	0.00	—	.167	.286	0-0	—	0		1	0.1
1970	KC A	8	13	.381	40	26	10-1	4-2	214	178	82	18	11	82-4	206	3.07	122	.228	.307	57-8	.105	-1	80	17	1.5
1971	†Pit N	9	10	.474	31	27	7-1	0-0	174.2	170	73	19	7	55-8	101	3.45	98	.259	.321	48-4	.063	-1	95	-1	-0.3
1972	†Pit N	4	4	.500	31	11	1	3-1	115.2	98	40	14	4	46-8	79	2.96	112	.231	.309	35-1	.143	-0	114	7	0.4
1973	Pit N	4	2	.667	50	2	0	4-0	92	98	41	12	5	34-7	68	3.62	97	.276	.346	14-1	.000	-1	138	0	-0.3
1974	Cle A	3	4	.429	14	10	0	0-0	72	75	42	12	3	37-5	36	4.38	83	.273	.362	0-0	—	0	127	-7	-0.6
1977	Atl N	0	1	.000	15	0	0	0-0	22.1	24	18	7	2	14-1	16	7.25	61	.270	.377	3-0	.333	0		-5	-0.3
Total	7	28	34	.452	183	76	18-2	12-3	692.1	644	296	82	32	269-33	507	3.48	102	.249	.325	157-14	.096	-4	97	12	0.5

JOHNSON, ROY Roy "Hardrock" B 10.1.1895 Madill, OK D 1.10.1986 Scottsdale, AZ BR/TR 6/185# d8.7 M1 C15

Year	Tm Lg	W	L	Pct	G	GS	CG-Sho	SV-BS	IP	H	R	HR	HB	BB-IB	SO	ERA	AERA	OAV	OOB	AB-SH	AVG	PB	Sup	APR	PW
1918	Phi A	1	5	.167	10	8	3	0	50	47	32	0	2	34	12	3.42	86	.254	.376	15-0	.067	-2	77	-5	-0.8

JOHNSON, JING Russell Conwell B 10.9.1894 Parker Ford, PA D 12.6.1950 Pottstown, PA BR/TR 5-9/172# d6.27 Mil 1918

Year	Tm Lg	W	L	Pct	G	GS	CG-Sho	SV-BS	IP	H	R	HR	HB	BB-IB	SO	ERA	AERA	OAV	OOB	AB-SH	AVG	PB	Sup	APR	PW
1916	Phi A	2	9	.182	12	12	8	0	84.1	90	46	3	0	39	25	3.74	76	.288	.368	27-1	.074	-1	88	-8	-0.9
1917	Phi A	9	12	.429	34	23	13	0	191	184	76	3	5	56	55	2.78	99	.260	.319	59-3	.203	2*	101	2	0.5
1919	Phi A	9	15	.375	34	25	12	0	202	222	106	8	3	62	67	3.61	95	.291	.346	72-4	.194	0*	82	-5	-0.3
1927	Phi A	4	2	.667	17	3	2	0	51.2	42	20	2	4	16	16	3.48	122	.235	.312	12-3	.167	-0	130	6	0.6
1928	Phi A	0	0	—	3	0	0	0	10.2	13	8	1	0	5	3	5.06	79	.310	.383	4-0	.500	1		-2	0.0
Total	5	24	38	.387	100	63	35	0	539.2	551	256	17	12	178	166	3.35	95	.275	.338	174-11	.184	2	91	-7	-0.1

JOHNSON, SI Silas Kenneth B 10.5.1906 Danway, IL D 5.12.1994 Sheridan, IL BR/TR 5-11.5/185# d5.2 Mil 1943-45

Year	Tm Lg	W	L	Pct	G	GS	CG-Sho	SV-BS	IP	H	R	HR	HB	BB-IB	SO	ERA	AERA	OAV	OOB	AB-SH	AVG	PB	Sup	APR	PW
1928	Cin N	0	0	—	3	0	0	0	10.1	9	5	0	0	5	1	4.35	91	.250	.341	4-0	.250	0		0	0.0
1929	Cin N	0	0	—	1	0	0	0	2	2	1	0	0	1	0	4.50	101	.250	.333	0-0	—	0		0	0.0
1930	Cin N	3	1	.750	35	3	0	0	78.1	86	54	5	4	31	47	4.94	98	.286	.360	17-0	.235	-0	157	-3	-0.2
1931	Cin N	11	19	.367	42	33	14	0	262.1	273	131	5	6	74	95	3.77	99	.269	.323	87-3	.149	-3	77	-2	-0.7
1932	Cin N	13	15	.464	42	27	14-2	2	245	246	109	8	2	57	94	3.27	118	.259	.302	80-2	.125	-4	77	16	1.2
1933	Cin N	7	18	.280	34	28	14-4	1	211.1	212	101	7	3	54	51	3.49	97	.263	.312	72-3	.042	-7	63	-2	-1.0
1934	Cin N	7	22	.241	46	31	9	3	215.2	264	150	15	7	84	89	5.22	78	.297	.362	72-0	.139	-3	76	-26	-3.4
1935	Cin N	5	11	.313	30	20	4-1	0	130	155	106	14	3	59	40	6.23	64	.293	.367	41-1	.024	-4	78	-32	-3.7
1936	Cin N	0	0	—	2	0	0	0	4	7	6	1	0	0	2	13.50	28	.368	.368	0-0	—	0		-4	-0.2
	StL N	5	3	.625	12	9	3-1	0	61.2	82	30	4	1	11	21	4.38	90	.314	.344	21-1	.190	-0	100	-1	-0.2
	Year	5	3	.625	14	9	3-1	0	65.2	89	35	5	1	11	23	4.93	80	.318	.346	21-1	.190	-0	101	-4	-0.4
1937	StL N	12	12	.500	38	21	12-1	1	192.1	222	92	14	1	43	64	3.32	120	.292	.330	65-3	.138	-3	109	11	0.8
1938	StL N	0	3	.000	6	3	0	0	15.2	27	17	0	0	6	4	7.47	53	.380	.429	1-1	.000	-0	43	-6	-1.0
1940	Phi N	5	14	.263	37	14	5	1	138.1	145	81	13	2	42	58	4.88	80	.268	.323	43-2	.140	-2	62	-13	-1.9
1941	Phi N	5	12	.294	39	21	6-1	2	163.1	207	91	8	1	54	80	4.52	82	.309	.362	47-2	.149	-2	71	-13	-1.5
1942	Phi N	8	19	.296	39	26	10-1	0	195.1	198	96	6	1	72	78	3.69	90	.266	.332	58-5	.103	-4	66	-10	-1.8
1943	Phi N	8	3	.727	21	14	9-1	2	113	110	48	4	0	25	46	3.27	103	.252	.292	33-3	.182	0	122	1	0.1
1946	Phi N	0	0	—	1	0	0	0	3	7	4	1	0	0	2	3.00	114	.538	.538	1-0	1.000	0		-1	0.0
	Bos N	6	5	.545	28	12	5-1	1	127	134	47	8	4	35	41	2.76	124	.272	.325	37-4	.135	-2	121	9	0.5
	Year	6	5	.545	29	12	5-1	1	130	141	52	9	4	35	43	2.77	124	.279	.330	38-4	.158	-1	121	8	0.5
1947	Bos N	6	8	.429	36	10	3	2	112.2	124	57	7	1	34	27	4.23	92	.275	.327	30-0	.033	-3	97	-3	-0.5
Total	17	101	165	.380	492	272	108-13	15	2281.1	2510	1226	120	36	687	840	4.09	92	.279	.333	709-30	.123	-37	82	-79	-13.5

JOHNSON, SYL Sylvester W (Born Sylvester Johnson) B 12.31.1900 Portland, OR D 2.20.1985 Portland, OR BR/TR 5-11/180# d4.24 C4

Year	Tm Lg	W	L	Pct	G	GS	CG-Sho	SV-BS	IP	H	R	HR	HB	BB-IB	SO	ERA	AERA	OAV	OOB	AB-SH	AVG	PB	Sup	APR	PW
1922	Det A	7	3	.700	29	8	3	1	97	99	52	7	4	30	29	3.71	105	.273	.336	36-1	.222	-0	183	0	-0.1
1923	Det A	12	7	.632	37	18	7	0	176.1	181	82	12	3	47	93	3.98	97	.274	.325	62-2	.161	-1	106	2	-0.1
1924	Det A	5	4	.556	29	9	2	3	104	117	63	8	5	42	55	4.93	83	.287	.360	34-2	.206	-0	107	-7	-0.6
1925	Det A	0	2	.000	6	0	0	0	13	11	7	1	0	10	5	3.46	124	.250	.389	3-0	.000	-1		1	0.1
1926	StL N	0	3	.000	19	6	1	1	49	54	27	3	2	15	10	4.22	92	.297	.357	12-0	.000	-2	68	-2	-0.3
1927	StL N	0	0	—	2	0	0	0	3	3	2	1	0	0	2	6.00	66	.250	.250	0-0	—	0		0	0.0
1928	†StL N	8	4	.667	34	6	2	3	120	117	53	6	4	33	66	3.90	103	.259	.315	38-0	.158	-0	92	5	0.4
1929	StL N	13	7	.650	42	19	12-3	3	182.1	186	88	11	7	56	80	3.60	129	.265	.325	60-3	.117	-2	95	20	1.4
1930	†StL N	12	10	.545	32	24	9-2	2	187.2	215	105	13	4	38	92	4.65	108	.293	.332	70-1	.214	-0	113	11	0.9
1931	†StL N	11	9	.550	32	24	12-2	2	186	186	73	9	2	29	82	3.00	131	.255	.286	60-1	.233	2	103	18	1.9
1932	StL N	5	14	.263	32	22	7	2	164.2	199	103	14	4	35	70	4.92	80	.299	.338	51-3	.196	-1	93	-17	-1.9
1933	StL N	3	3	.500	35	1	0	3	84	89	45	7	3	16	28	4.29	81	.271	.311	21-1	.238	0	144	-6	-0.6
1934	Cin N	0	0	—	2	0	0	0	6.2	9	6	2	0	0	0	2.70	151	.310	.310	2-0	.500	1		0	0.1

Year	Tm Lg	W	L	Pct	G	GS	CG-Sho	SV-BS	IP	H	R	HR	HB	BB-IB	SO	ERA	AERA	OAV	OOB	AB-SH	AVG	PB	Sup	APR	PW
	Phi N	5	9	.357	42	10	4-3	3	133.2	122	58	14	1	24	54	3.50	135	.242	.277	41-2	.195	-1	86	16	1.4
	Year	5	9	.357	44	10	4-3	3	140.1	131	63	16	1	24	54	3.46	136	.245	.279	43-2	.209	1	86	16	1.5
1935	Phi N	10	8	.556	37	18	8-1	6	174.2	182	79	15	3	31	89	3.56	128	.265	.299	58-6	.241	1	88	18	1.8
1936	Phi N	5	7	.417	39	8	1	7	111	129	60	10	3	29	48	4.30	106	.288	.335	36-0	.250	-0	105	**5**	0.4
1937	Phi N	4	10	.286	32	15	4	3	138	155	81	19	2	22	46	5.02	86	.288	.318	48-2	.146	-3	72	-7	-1.0
1938	Phi N	2	7	.222	22	6	2	0	83	87	43	4	0	11	21	4.23	92	.267	.291	29-1	.034	-3	47	-2	-0.6
1939	Phi N	8	8	.500	22	13	6	2	111	112	50	10	1	15	37	3.81	105	.264	.291	33-4	.152	-1	84	4	0.3
1940	Phi N	2	2	.500	17	2	2	2	40.2	37	22	6	0	5	13	4.20	93	.236	.259	8-1	.000	-1	123	-2	-0.3
Total	19	112	117	.489	542	209	82-11	43	2165.2	2290	1099	172	48	488	920	4.06	104	.273	.316	702-30	.181	-10	98	57	3.2
JOHNSON, TOM Thomas Raymond B 4.2.1951 St.Paul, MN BR/TR 6-1/185# d9.10																									
1974	Min A	2	0	1.000	4	0	0	1-0	7	4	1	0	0	0-0	4	0.00	—	.167	.167	0-0	—	0		2	0.5
1975	Min A	1	2	.333	18	0	0	3-2	38.2	40	23	4	2	21-4	17	4.19	92	.263	.356	0-0	—	0		-3	-0.2
1976	Min A	3	1	.750	18	1	0	0-0	48.1	44	14	2	0	8-1	37	2.61	137	.243	.275	0-0	—	0	74	6	0.5
1977	Min A	16	7	.696	71	0	0	15-7	146.2	152	57	11	5	47-8	87	3.13	128	.272	.329	0-0	—	0		14	2.4
1978	Min A	1	4	.200	18	0	0	3-1	32.2	42	22	2	2	17-4	21	5.51	70	.318	.399	0-0	—	0		-6	-0.9
Total	5	23	14	.622	129	1	0	22-10	273.1	282	117	19	9	93-17	166	3.39	114	.269	.330	0-0	—	0	74	13	2.3
JOHNSON, VIC Victor Oscar B 8.3.1920 Eau Claire, WI BR/TL 6/160# d5.3																									
1944	Bos A	0	3	.000	7	5	0	0	27.1	42	22	0	0	15	7	6.26	54	.362	.435	10-0	.000	-1	123	-9	-1.0
1945	Bos A	6	4	.600	26	9	4-1	2	85.1	90	41	4	2	46	21	4.01	85	.276	.369	30-0	.167	-1	100	-5	-0.6
1946	Cle A	0	1	.000	9	1	0	0	13.2	20	14	1	0	8	3	9.22	36	.357	.438	2-0	.000	-0	52	-9	-0.6
Total	3	6	8	.429	42	15	4-1	2	126.1	152	77	5	2	69	31	5.06	67	.305	.392	42-0	.119	-3	105	-23	-2.2
JOHNSON, WALTER Walter Perry "Barney" or "The Big Train" B 11.6.1887 Humboldt, KS D 12.10.1946 Washington, DC BR/TR 6-1/200# d8.2 M7 HF1936																									
1907	Was A	5	9	.357	14	12	11-2	0	110.1	100	35	1	2	20	71	1.88	129	.244	.282	36-0	.111	-2	58	7	0.5
1908	Was A	14	14	.500	36	30	23-6	1	256.1	194	75	0	11	53	160	1.65	139	.211	.262	79-5	.165	3	79	17	2.1
1909	Was A	13	25	.342	40	36	27-4	1	296.1	247	112	1	15	84	164	2.22	110	.221	.284	101-3	.129	-3	52	4	0.1
1910	Was A	25	17	.595	**45**	**42**	**38**-8	1	**370**	262	92	1	13	76	**313**	1.36	183	.205	.257	137-1	.175	1	104	43	5.5
1911	Was A	25	13	.658	40	37	**36-6**	1	322.1	292	119	8	8	70	207	1.90	173	.238	.283	128-6	.234	3*	106	**43**	5.4
1912	Was A	33	12	.733	50	37	34-7	2	369	259	89	2	16	76	**303**	**1.39**	**240**	**.196**	**.248**	144-6	.264	9*	102	**77**	**10.6**
1913	Was A	**36**	7	**.837**	48	36	**29-11**	2	**346**	232	56	9	9	38	**243**	**1.14**	**258**	**.190**	**.220**	134-1	.261	10*	97	**70**	**10.9**
1914	Was A	**28**	18	.609	**51**	**40**	**33-9**	1	**371.2**	287	88	3	11	74	**225**	1.72	164	.217	.265	136-5	.221	8*	89	**45**	**7.2**
1915	Was A	**27**	13	.675	47	**39**	**35-7**	4	**336.2**	258	83	1	19	56	**203**	1.55	**192**	.214	**.260**	147-5	.231	6*	94	**51**	**7.4**
1916	Was A	**25**	20	.556	48	38	**36**-3	1	**369.2**	290	105	0	9	82	**228**	1.90	147	.220	.270	142-4	.225	8*	88	35	5.2
1917	Was A	23	16	.590	47	34	30-8	3	326	248	105	3	14	68	**188**	2.21	119	.211	.263	130-2	.254	10*	102	15	3.1
1918	Was A	**23**	13	.639	39	29	29-**8**	3	326	241	71	2	8	70	**162**	**1.27**	**215**	.210	**.260**	150-4	.267	6*	92	**51**	**7.6**
1919	Was A	20	14	.588	39	29	27-**7**	2	290.1	235	73	0	7	51	**147**	**1.49**	**216**	**.219**	**.259**	125-4	.192	2*	90	**52**	**6.7**
1920	Was A	8	10	.444	21	15	12-4	3	143.2	135	68	5	5	27	78	3.13	119	.245	.286	64-2	.266	4*	67	8	1.3
1921	Was A	17	14	.548	35	32	25-1	1	264	265	122	7	2	92	**143**	3.51	117	.263	.326	111-2	.270	4*	103	19	2.3
1922	Was A	15	16	.484	41	31	23-4	4	280	283	115	8	7	99	105	2.99	129	.267	.334	108-2	.204	-1*	77	28	2.8
1923	Was A	17	12	.586	42	34	18-3	4	261	263	112	9	20	73	**130**	3.48	108	.269	.333	93-6	.194	1	94	14	1.4
1924	†Was A	**23**	7	**.767**	38	**38**	20-**6**	0	277.2	233	97	10	10	77	**158**	**2.72**	148	**.224**	**.284**	113-2	.283	7*	117	**44**	**4.9**
1925	†Was A	20	7	.741	30	29	16-3	0	229	217	95	7	7	78	108	3.07	138	**.250**	.317	97-6	.433	17*	126	30	**4.6**
1926	Was A	15	16	.484	33	33	22-2	0	260.2	259	120	13	5	73	125	3.63	107	.263	.317	103-3	.194	1*	108	8	0.7
1927	Was A	5	6	.455	18	15	7-1	0	107.2	113	70	7	7	26	48	5.10	80	.278	.332	46-1	.348	6*	96	-12	-0.4
Total	21	417	279	.599	802	666	531-110	34	5914.1	4913	1902	97	205	1363	3509	2.17	147	.227	.279	2324-70	.235	99	96	649	89.9
JOHNSON, BILL William Charles B 10.6.1960 Wilmington, DE BR/TR 6-5/205# d9.6																									
1983	Chi N	1	0	1.000	10	0	0	0-0	12.1	17	6	0	0	3-1	4	4.38	87	.347	.377	0-0	—	0		0	0.0
1984	Chi N	0	0	—	4	0	0	0-0	5.1	4	1	0	0	1-1	3	1.69	232	.235	.278	0-0	—	0		1	0.1
Total	2	1	0	1.000	14	0	0	0-0	17.2	21	7	0	0	4-2	7	3.57	108	.318	.352	0-0	—	0		1	0.1
JOHNSON, JEFF William Jeffrey B 8.4.1966 Durham, NC BR/TL 6-3/200# d6.5																									
1991	NY A	6	11	.353	23	23	0	0-0	127	156	89	15	6	33-1	62	5.95	70	.305	.351	0-0	—	0	90	-24	-2.7
1992	NY A	2	3	.400	13	8	0	0-0	52.2	71	44	4	2	23-0	14	6.66	59	.329	.395	0-0	—	0	105	-17	-1.4
1993	NY A	0	2	.000	2	2	0	0-0	2.2	12	10	1	0	2-0	0	30.38	14	.600	.636	0-0	—	0	44	-8	-1.2
Total	3	8	16	.333	38	33	0	0-0	182.1	239	143	20	8	58-1	76	6.52	63	.320	.372	0-0	—	0	91	-49	-5.3
JOHNSTON, JOEL Joel Raymond B 3.8.1967 West Chester, PA BR/TR 6-4/220# d9.5																									
1991	KC A	1	0	1.000	13	0	0	0-0	22.1	9	1	0	0	9-3	21	0.40	1024	.120	.214	0-0	—	0		9	0.5
1992	KC A	0	0	—	5	0	0	0-0	2.2	3	4	2	0	2-0	0	13.50	30	.273	.385	0-0	—	0		-3	-0.1
1993	Pit N	2	4	.333	33	0	0	2-1	53.1	38	20	7	0	19-5	31	3.38	120	.203	.277	6-1	.333	1		5	0.6
1994	Pit N	0	0	—	4	0	0	0-0	3.1	14	12	0	2	4-0	5	29.70	15	.583	.667	0-0	—	0		-9	-0.4
1995	Bos A	0	1	.000	4	0	0	0-0	4	2	5	1	1	3-0	4	11.25	43	.143	.333	0-0	—	0		-3	-0.5
Total	5	3	5	.375	59	0	0	2-1	85.2	66	42	10	3	37-8	61	4.31	96	.212	.302	6-1	.333	1		-1	0.1
JOHNSTONE, JOHN John William B 11.25.1968 Liverpool, NY BR/TR 6-3/195# d9.3																									
1993	Fla N	0	2	.000	7	0	0	0-0	10.2	16	8	1	0	7-0	5	5.91	73	.340	.426	0-0	—	0		-2	-0.3
1994	Fla N	1	2	.333	17	0	0	0-0	21.1	23	20	4	1	16-5	23	5.91	74	.264	.385	0-1	—	0		-5	-0.6
1995	Fla N	0	0	—	4	0	0	0-0	4.2	7	2	1	0	2-1	3	3.86	109	.333	.391	0-0	—	0		0	0.0
1996	Hou N	1	0	1.000	9	0	0	0-0	13	17	8	2	0	5-0	5	5.54	70	.321	.367	0-0	—	0		-2	-0.2
1997	SF N	0	0	—	10	0	0	0-0	16.2	12	4	0	4	6-0	14	2.16	189	.218	.324	2-0	.000	-0		4	0.2
	Oak A	0	0	—	5	0	0	0-0	6.1	7	2	0	0	7-0	4	2.84	159	.292	.438	0-0	—	0		1	0.1
	SF N	0	0	—	3	0	0	0-0	2	3	3	1	0	1-0	1	13.50	30	.333	.400	0-0	—	0		-2	-0.1
1998	SF N	6	5	.545	70	0	0	0-1	88	72	32	10	1	38-8	86	3.07	129	.224	.303	2-1	.000	-0		10	1.0
1999	SF N	4	6	.400	62	0	0	3-4	65.2	48	24	8	1	20-5	56	2.60	161	.203	.267	0-0	—	0		11	1.5
2000	SF N	3	4	.429	47	0	0	0-3	50	64	35	11	2	13-2	37	6.30	67	.322	.362	2-0	.000	-0		-11	-1.3
Total	8	15	19	.441	234	0	0	3-8	278.1	269	138	38	9	115-21	234	4.01	103	.255	.329	6-2	.000	-1		4	0.3
JOINER, ROY Roy Merrill "Pop" B 10.30.1906 Red Bluff, CA D 12.26.1989 Red Bluff, CA BL/TL 6/170# d4.30																									
1934	Chi N	0	1	.000	20	2	0	0	34	61	33	3	0	8	9	8.21	47	.391	.421	10-0	.200	-0	100	-16	-0.8
1935	Chi N	0	0	—	2	0	0	0	3.1	6	4	0	0	2	0	5.40	73	.429	.500	1-0	.000	-0		-1	-0.1
1940	NY N	3	2	.600	30	2	0	1	53	66	26	8	5	17	25	3.40	114	.308	.373	11-1	.273	1	67	2	0.2
Total	3	3	3	.500	52	4	0	1	90.1	133	63	11	5	27	34	5.28	74	.346	.397	22-1	.227	0	84	-15	-0.7
JOLLY, DAVE David "Gabby" B 10.14.1924 Stony Point, NC D 5.27.1963 Durham, NC BR/TR 6/165# d5.9																									
1953	Mil N	0	1	.000	24	0	0	0	38.1	34	16	4	1	27	23	3.52	111	.239	.365	2-0	.500	1		3	0.2
1954	Mil N	11	6	.647	47	1	0	10	111.1	87	36	6	2	64	62	2.43	154	.215	.321	31-2	.290	3*	24	17	3.0
1955	Mil N	2	3	.400	36	0	0	1	58.1	58	42	6	1	51-7	23	5.71	66	.258	.396	6-0	.167	0		-14	-1.0
1956	Mil N	2	3	.400	29	0	0	7	45.2	39	21	7	0	35-4	20	3.74	92	.228	.356	4-1	.000	-0		-1	-0.2
1957	Mil N	1	1	.500	23	0	0	1	37.2	37	22	4	3	21-0	27	5.02	70	.264	.367	5-0	.600	1		-6	-0.2
Total	5	16	14	.533	159	1	0	19	291.1	255	137	27	7	198-11	155	3.77	98	.236	.354	48-3	.292	5	24	-1	1.8
JONES, COWBOY Albert Edward "Bronco" B 8.23.1874 Golden, CO D 2.9.1958 Inglewood, CA BL/TL 5-11/160# d6.24																									
1898	Cle N	4	4	.500	9	9	7	0	72	76	44	0	4	29	26	3.00	121	.269	.345	28-1	.071	-3	100	2	-0.2
1899	StL N	6	5	.545	12	12	9	0	85.1	111	51	1	6	22	28	3.59	111	.314	.364	29-1	.172	0	80	3	0.5
1900	StL N	13	19	.406	39	36	29-3	0	292.2	334	185	10	19	82	68	3.54	103	.286	.343	117-3	.179	-3	106	-2	-0.3
1901	StL N	2	6	.250	10	9	7	0	76.1	97	51	4	3	22	25	4.48	71	.307	.358	27-1	.148	0	114	-12	-0.9
Total	4	25	34	.424	70	66	52-3	0	526.1	618	331	15	32	155	147	3.61	100	.292	.349	201-6	.159	-5	101	-9	-0.9
JONES, ALEX Alexander B 12.25.1869 Pittsburgh, PA D 4.4.1941 Woodville, PA BL/TL 5-6/135# d9.25																									
1889	Pit N	1	0	1.000	1	1	1	0	9	7	5	0	0	1	10	3.00	125	.206	.229	5	.200	0	143	1	0.1
1892	Lou N	5	11	.313	18	16	13-1	0	146.2	130	90	3	9	56	44	3.31	93	.228	.307	55	.145	-1	84	-5	-0.5
	Was N	0	3	.000	4	4	3	0	27	33	23	0	2	14	7	4.00	81	.289	.377	11	.273	0	44	-3	-0.3

Year	Tm Lg	W	L	Pct	G	GS	CG-Sho	SV-BS	IP	H	R	HR	HB	BB-IB	SO	ERA	AERA	OAV	OOB	AB-SH	AVG	PB	Sup	APR	PW
	Year	5	14	.263	22	20	16-1	0	173.2	163	25	3	11	70	51	3.42	91	.238	.319	66	.167	-1	76	-7	-0.8
1894	Phi N	1	0	1.000	1	1	1	0	9	10	4	0	0	0	2	2.00	257	.278	.278	4-0	.250	-0	83	3	0.2
1903	Det A	0	1	.000	2	2	0	0	8.2	19	15	0	0	6	2	12.46	23	.432	.500	4-0	.000	-1	184	-8	-0.8
Total	4	7	15	.318	26	24	18-1	0	200.1	199	137	3	11	77	65	3.73	86	.249	.324	79-0	.165	-1	86	-12	-1.3
JONES, AL Alfornia B 2.10.1959 Charleston, MS BR/TR 6-4/210# d8.6																									
1983	Chi A	0	0	—	2	0	0	0-0	2.1	3	1	0	0	2-0	2	3.86	109	.375	.500	0-0	—	0		0	0.0
1984	Chi A	1	1	.500	20	0	0	5-1	20.1	23	10	3	1	11-0	15	4.43	94	.299	.385	0-0	—	0		0	0.0
1985	Chi A	1	0	1.000	5	0	0	0-0	6	3	2	0	0	3-0	2	1.50	288	.167	.286	0-0	—	0		1	0.2
Total	3	2	1	.667	27	0	0	5-1	28.2	29	13	3	1	16-0	19	3.77	112	.282	.377	0-0	—	0		1	0.2
JONES, ART Arthur Lennox B 2.7.1906 Kershaw, SC D 11.25.1980 Columbia, SC BR/TR 6/165# d4.23																									
1932	Bro N	0	0	—	1	0	0	0	1	2	2	0	0	1	0	18.00	21	.667	.750	0-0	—	0		-1	-0.1
JONES, BARRY Barry Louis B 2.15.1963 Centerville, IN BR/TR 6-4/225# d7.18																									
1986	Pit N	3	4	.429	26	0	0	3-4	37.1	29	16	3	0	21-2	29	2.89	133	.215	.318	5-1	.200	0		3	0.5
1987	Pit N	2	4	.333	32	0	0	1-3	43.1	55	34	6	0	23-6	28	5.61	73	.314	.390	3-0	.000	-0		-9	-1.1
1988	Pit N	1	1	.500	42	0	0	2-3	56.1	57	21	3	1	21-6	31	3.04	112	.271	.335	5-0	.000	-0		2	0.1
	Chi A	2	2	.500	17	0	0	1-0	26	15	7	3	0	17-1	17	2.42	164	.170	.302	0-0	—	0		5	0.8
1989	Chi A	3	2	.600	22	0	0	1-0	30.1	22	12	2	1	8-0	17	2.37	161	.208	.265	0-0	—	0		4	0.6
1990	Chi A	11	4	.733	65	0	0	1-7	74	62	20	2	1	33-7	45	2.31	166	.235	.317	0-0	—	0		13	2.6
1991	Mon N	4	9	.308	**77**	0	0	13-8	88.2	76	35	8	1	33-8	46	3.35	108	.246	.318	1-1	.000	-0		4	0.6
1992	Phi N	5	6	.455	44	0	0	0-6	54.1	65	30	3	2	24-4	19	4.64	75	.305	.378	2-0	.000	-0		-7	-1.3
	NY N	2	0	1.000	17	0	0	1-0	15.1	20	16	0	0	11-3	11	9.39	37	.317	.413	0-0	—	0		-9	-1.3
	Year	7	6	.538	61	0	0	1-6	69.2	85	50	3	2	35-7	30	5.68	61	.308	.386	2-0	.000	-0		-16	-2.6
1993	Chi A	0	1	.000	6	0	0	0-0	7.1	14	8	2	0	3-0	7	8.59	49	.412	.459	0-0	—	0		-4	-0.4
Total	8	33	33	.500	348	0	0	23-31	433	415	199	32	6	194-37	250	3.66	102	.260	.338	16-2	.063	-1		2	1.1
JONES, CALVIN Calvin Douglas B 9.26.1963 Compton, CA BR/TR 6-3/185# d6.14																									
1991	Sea A	2	2	.500	27	0	0	2-1	46.1	33	14	0	1	29-5	42	2.53	163	.209	.335	0-0	—	0		8	0.7
1992	Sea A	3	5	.375	38	1	0	0-2	61.2	50	39	8	2	47-1	49	5.69	70	.226	.361	0-0	—	0	92	-10	-1.2
Total	2	5	7	.417	65	1	0	2-3	108	83	53	8	3	76-6	91	4.33	93	.219	.351	0-0	—	0	92	-2	-0.5
JONES, DEACON Carroll Elmer B 12.20.1892 Arcadia, KS D 12.28.1952 Pittsburg, KS BR/TR 6-1/174# d9.23																									
1916	Det A	0	0	—	1	0	0	0	7	7	3	0	0	5	2	2.57	111	.269	.387	2-0	.000	-0		0	0.0
1917	Det A	4	4	.500	24	6	2	0	77	69	34	0	6	26	28	2.92	91	.256	.334	15-2	.000	-1	131	-2	-0.2
1918	Det A	3	2	.600	21	4	1	0	67	60	35	0	1	38	15	3.09	86	.244	.347	27-0	.185	-1*	198	-6	-0.4
Total	3	7	6	.538	46	10	3	0	151	136	72	0	7	69	45	2.98	89	.251	.343	44-2	.114	-2	158	-8	-0.6
JONES, BUMPUS Charles Leander B 1.1.1870 Cedarville, OH D 6.25.1938 Xenia, OH BR/TR d10.15																									
1892	Cin N	1	0	1.000	1	1	1	0	9	0	1	0	0	4	3	0.00	—	.000	.129	2	.000	-0	19	3	0.3
1893	Cin N	1	3	.250	6	5	2	0	28.2	37	37	1	5	23	6	10.05	48	.303	.433	16	.250	1	88	-14	-1.3
	NY N	0	1	.000	1	1	0	0	4	5	5	0	1	10	1	11.25	41	.294	.571	0	—	0	30	-2	-0.3
	Year	1	4	.200	7	6	2	0	32.2	42	7	1	6	33	7	10.19	47	.302	.455	16	.250	1	78	-14	-1.6
Total	2	2	4	.333	8	7	3	0	41.2	42	43	1	6	37	10	7.99	56	.253	.407	18	.222	1	73	-13	-1.3
JONES, DALE Dale Eldon "Nubs" B 12.17.1918 Marquette, NE D 11.8.1980 Orlando, FL BR/TR 6-1/172# d9.7 Mil 1942-45																									
1941	Phi N	0	1	.000	2	1	0	0	8.1	13	11	0	0	6	2	7.56	49	.342	.432	3-0	.333	0	138	-5	-0.4
JONES, JACK Daniel Albion "Jumping Jack" B 10.23.1860 Litchfield, CT D 10.19.1936 Wallingford, CT TR d7.9																									
1883	Det N	6	5	.545	12	12	9-1	0	92.2	103	63	0		19	33	3.50	89	.259	.293	42	.190	-2	78	-3	-0.5
	Phi AA	5	2	.714	7	7	7	0	65	58	38	1		6	28	2.63	135	.223	.241	25	.240	-0	95	6	0.5
Total	1	11	7	.611	19	19	16-1	0	157.2	161	101	1		25	61	3.14	104	.245	.273	67	.209	-2	84	3	0.0
JONES, DICK Decatur Poindexter B 5.22.1902 Meadville, MS D 8.2.1994 Burlingame, CA BL/TR 6/184# d9.11																									
1926	Was A	2	1	.667	4	3	1	0	21	20	10	0	0	11	3	4.29	90	.263	.356	10-1	.200	-0*	123	0	-0.1
1927	Was A	0	0	—	2	0	0	0	3.1	8	11	0	0	5	1	21.60	19	.444	.565	0-0	—	0		-7	-0.3
Total	2	2	1	.667	6	3	1	0	24.1	28	21	0	0	16	4	6.66	58	.298	.400	10-1	.200	-0	123	-7	-0.4
JONES, DOUG Douglas Reid B 6.24.1957 Lebanon, IN BR/TR 6-2/195# d4.9																									
1982	Mil A	0	0	—	4	0	0	0-0	2.2	5	3	1	0	1-0	1	10.13	37	.385	.429	0-0	—	0		-2	-0.1
1986	Cle A	1	0	1.000	11	0	0	1-1	18	18	5	0	1	6-1	12	2.50	166	.257	.321	0-0	—	0		4	0.2
1987	Cle A	6	5	.545	49	0	0	8-4	91.1	101	45	4	6	24-5	87	3.15	144	.281	.332	0-0	—	0		10	1.3
1988	Cle A★	3	4	.429	51	0	0	37-6	83.1	69	26	1	2	16-3	72	2.27	182	.218	.260	0-0	—	0		15	2.5
1989	Cle A★	7	10	.412	59	0	0	32-9	80.2	76	25	4	1	13-4	65	2.34	169	.251	.279	0-0	—	0		14	2.9
1990	Cle A☆	5	5	.500	66	0	0	43-8	84.1	66	26	5	2	22-4	55	2.56	153	.218	.274	0-0	—	0		13	2.5
1991	Cle A	4	8	.333	36	4	0	7-5	63.1	87	42	7	0	17-5	48	5.54	75	.320	.357	0-0	—	0	99	-9	-1.6
1992	Hou N★	11	8	.579	80	0	0	36-6	111.2	96	29	5	5	17-5	93	1.85	182	.235	.274	4-0	.000	-0		18	3.8
1993	Hou N	4	10	.286	71	0	0	26-8	85.1	102	46	7	5	21-6	66	4.54	85	.298	.344	0-0	—	0		-5	-1.1
1994	Phi N★	2	4	.333	47	0	0	27-2	54	55	14	2	0	6-0	38	2.17	198	.255	.275	1-0	1.000	0		**13**	2.5
1995	Bal A	0	4	.000	52	0	0	22-3	46.2	55	30	6	2	16-2	42	5.01	95	.286	.348	0-0	—	0		-3	-0.4
1996	Chi N	2	2	.500	28	0	0	2-5	32.1	41	20	4	1	7-4	26	5.01	87	.306	.345	0-0	—	0		-2	-0.3
	Mil A	5	0	1.000	24	0	0	1-3	31.2	31	13	3	2	13-2	34	3.41	152	.254	.331	0-0	—	0		6	0.8
1997	Mil A	6	6	.500	75	0	0	36-2	80.1	62	20	4	3	9-1	82	2.02	229	.215	.242	0-0	—	0		23	4.5
1998	Mil N	3	4	.429	46	0	0	12-8	54	65	32	15	4	11-1	43	5.17	83	.298	.339	2-0	.000	-0		-5	-0.7
	†Cle A	1	2	.333	23	0	0	1-1	31.1	34	12	2	0	6-3	28	3.45	138	.279	.305	0-0	—	0		5	0.5
1999	Oak A	5	5	.500	70	0	0	10-6	104	106	43	10	3	24-3	63	3.55	131	.267	.311	0-0	—	0		15	1.4
2000	†Oak A	4	2	.667	54	0	0	2-0	73.1	86	34	6	2	18-4	54	3.93	121	.292	.334	0-0	—	0		8	0.6
Total	16	69	79	.466	846	4	0	303-77	1128.1	1155	465	86	39	247-53	909	3.30	129	.264	.307	7-0	.143	0	99	118	19.3
JONES, EARL Earl Leslie "Lefty" B 6.11.1919 Fresno, CA D 1.24.1989 Fresno, CA BL/TL 5-10.5/190# d7.6																									
1945	StL A	0	0	—	10	0	0	1	28.1	18	10	0	0	18	13	2.54	139	.184	.310	10-0	.200	1		3	0.2
JONES, ELIJAH Elijah Albert "Bumpus" B 1.27.1882 Oxford, MI D 4.29.1943 Pontiac, MI BR/TR 5-11.5/?# d4.13																									
1907	Det A	0	1	.000	4	1	1	1	16	23	15	0	1	4	9	5.06	51	.338	.384	4-0	.000	-1	104	-5	-0.4
1909	Det A	1	1	.500	2	2	0	0	10	10	3	0	0	0	2	2.70	93	.278	.278	4-0	.250	0	154	0	0.0
Total	2	1	2	.333	6	3	1	1	26	33	18	0	1	4	11	4.15	62	.317	.349	8-0	.125	-0	133	-5	-0.4
JONES, GARY Gareth Howell B 6.12.1945 Huntington Park, CA BL/TL 6/191# d9.25 b-Steve																									
1970	NY A	0	0	—	2	0	0	0-0	2	3	0	0	0	1-0	2	0.00	—	.375	.444	0-0	—	0		1	0.0
1971	NY A	0	0	—	12	0	0	0-0	14	19	14	1	0	7-1	10	9.00	36	.317	.382	1-0	.000	-0		-9	-0.5
Total	2	0	0	—	14	0	0	0-0	16	22	14	1	0	8-1	12	7.88	42	.324	.390	1-0	.000	-0		-8	-0.5
JONES, GORDON Gordon Bassett B 4.2.1930 Portland, OR D 4.25.1994 Lodi, CA BR/TR 6/190# d8.6 C2																									
1954	StL N	4	4	.500	11	10	4-2	0	81	78	25	3	1	19	48	2.00	206	.248	.292	24-4	.125	-1	74	17	1.5
1955	StL N	1	4	.200	15	9	0	0	57	66	38	10	1	28-5	46	5.84	70	.286	.363	14-3	.071	-1	88	-10	-0.9
1956	StL N	0	2	.000	5	1	0	0	11.1	14	9	2	0	5-0	6	5.56	68	.311	.380	2-0	.000	-0	116	-3	-0.4
1957	NY N	0	1	.000	10	0	0	0	11.2	16	9	1	1	3-1	5	6.17	64	.320	.364	2-0	.500	0		-3	-0.2
1958	SF N	3	1	.750	11	1	0	1	30.1	33	11	2	1	5-1	8	2.37	161	.284	.320	7-0	.000	-1	188	4	0.5
1959	SF N	3	2	.600	31	0	0	2	43.2	45	23	6	1	19-5	29	4.33	88	.280	.355	4-1	.000	-0		-2	-0.3
1960	Bal A	1	1	.500	29	0	0	2	55	59	28	9	1	13-1	30	4.42	86	.281	.324	5-0	.400	1		-3	-0.1
1961	Bal A	0	0	—	3	0	0	1	5	5	3	3	0	0-0	4	5.40	71	.250	.250	0-0	—	0		-1	0.0
1962	KC A	3	2	.600	21	0	0	6	32.2	31	23	10	0	14-1	28	6.34	67	.252	.324	5-1	.000	-1		-6	-1.2
1964	Hou N	0	1	.000	34	0	0	0	50	58	24	3	0	14-2	28	4.14	83	.290	.333	4-0	.250	0		-3	-0.2
1965	Hou N	0	0	—	1	0	0	0	1	0	0	0	0	0-0	0	0.00	—	.000	.000	0-0	—	0		0	0.0
Total	11	15	18	.455	171	21	4-2	12	378.2	405	193	49	6	120-16	232	4.16	94	.275	.330	67-9	.119	-3	90	-10	-1.3

Year	Tm Lg	W	L	Pct	G	GS	CG-Sho	SV-BS	IP	H	R	HR	HB	BB-IB	SO	ERA	AERA	OAV	OOB	AB-SH	AVG	PB	Sup	APR	PW
JONES, GREG Greg Alan B 11.15.1976 Clearwater, FL BR/TR 6-2/190# d7.30																									
2003	Ana A	0	0	—	18	0	0	0-0	27.2	29	15	3	2	14-0	28	4.88	88	.261	.354	0-0	—	0		-1	-0.1
JONES, HENRY Henry "Baldy" B Pittsburgh, PA ?/150# d4.22																									
1890	Pit N	2	1	.667	5	4	2	0	31	35	25	1	0	14	13	3.48	95	.276	.348	9	.222	-0	110	-3	-0.3
JONES, JIMMY James Condia B 4.20.1964 Dallas, TX BR/TR 6-2/190# d9.21																									
1986	SD N	2	0	1.000	3	3	1-1	0-0	18	10	6	1	0	3-0	15	2.50	147	.164	.203	6-0	.167	-0	114	2	0.2
1987	SD N	9	7	.563	30	22	2-1	0-0	145.2	154	85	14	5	54-2	51	4.14	96	.270	.336	49-8	.163	1*	114	-8	-0.6
1988	SD N	9	14	.391	29	29	3	0-0	179	192	98	14	3	44-3	82	4.12	82	.277	.319	55-9	.164	2*	95	-18	-1.9
1989	NY A	2	1	.667	11	6	0	0-0	48	56	29	7	2	16-1	25	5.25	74	.293	.352	0-0	—	0	168	-6	-0.3
1990	NY A	1	2	.333	17	7	0	0-0	50	72	42	8	1	23-0	25	6.30	63	.344	.405	0-0	—	0	105	-14	-0.8
1991	Hou N	6	8	.429	26	22	1-1	0-0	135.1	143	73	9	3	51-3	88	4.39	80	.270	.336	38-2	.184	2	92	-14	-1.1
1992	Hou N	10	6	.625	25	23	0	0-0	139.1	135	64	13	5	39-3	69	4.07	83	.258	.313	36-9	.167	2*	112	-9	-0.8
1993	Mon N	4	1	.800	12	6	0	0-0	39.2	47	34	6	0	9-0	21	6.35	66	.285	.322	9-3	.111	0	173	-10	-1.0
Total	8	43	39	.524	153	118	7-3	0-0	755	809	431	72	19	239-12	376	4.46	82	.275	.331	193-31	.166	7	111	-77	-6.3
JONES, JIM James Tilford "Sheriff" B 12.25.1876 London, KY D 5.6.1953 London, KY BR/TR 6-3/210# d7.23.2003 ▲																									
1897	Lou N	0	0	—	1	0	0	0	6.2	19	22	1	2	5	0	18.90	23	.500	.578	4-0	.250	1*		-11	-0.4
1901	NY N	0	1	.000	1	1	1	0	5	6	6	0	0	2	3	10.80	31	.300	.364	91-0	.209	0*	107	-3	-0.4
Total	2	0	1	.000	2	1	1	0	11.2	25	28	1	2	7	3	15.43	25	.431	.507	95-0	.211	1	107	-14	-0.8
JONES, JEFF Jeffrey Allen B 7.29.1956 Detroit, MI BR/TR 6-3/210# d4.10 C3																									
1980	Oak A	1	3	.250	35	0	0	5-3	44.1	32	21	2	1	26-2	34	2.84	133	.204	.316	0-0	—	0		2	0.3
1981	†Oak A	4	1	.800	33	0	0	3-1	61	51	27	7	3	40-7	43	3.39	103	.233	.355	0-0	—	0		0	-0.1
1982	Oak A	3	1	.750	18	2	0	0-1	37	44	29	6	1	26-1	18	5.11	77	.306	.415	0-0	—	0	151	-8	-0.8
1983	Oak A	1	1	.500	13	1	0	0-1	29.2	43	19	7	2	8-1	14	5.76	67	.339	.387	0-0	—	0	94	-6	-0.3
1984	Oak A	0	3	.000	13	0	0	0-0	33	31	14	4	0	12-1	19	3.55	106	.258	.323	0-0	—	0		1	0.1
Total	5	9	9	.500	112	3	0	8-6	205	201	110	26	7	112-12	128	3.95	94	.262	.358	0-0	—	0	137	-11	-0.8
JONES, BROADWAY Jesse Frank B 11.15.1898 Millsboro, DE D 9.7.1977 Lewes, DE BR/TR 5-9/154# d7.4																									
1923	Phi N	0	0	—	3	0	0	0	8	5	8	0	0	7	1	9.00	51	.185	.353	2-0	.500	0		-3	-0.1
JONES, JOHNNY John Paul "Admiral" B 8.25.1892 Arcadia, LA D 6.5.1980 Ruston, LA BR/TR 6-1/151# d4.24																									
1919	NY N	0	0	—	2	0	0	1	6.2	9	4	0	1	3	3	5.40	52	.310	.394	3-0	.000	-0		-2	-0.1
1920	Bos N	1	0	1.000	3	1	0	0	9.2	16	7	1	0	5	6	6.52	47	.372	.438	4-0	.250	1	206	-3	-0.2
Total	2	1	0	1.000	5	1	0	1	16.1	25	11	1	1	8	9	6.06	49	.347	.420	7-0	.143	0	206	-5	-0.3
JONES, STACY Joseph Stacy B 5.26.1967 Gadsden, AL BR/TR 6-6/225# d7.30																									
1991	Bal A	0	0	—	4	1	0	0-0	11	11	6	1	0	5-0	10	4.09	97	.256	.327	0-0	—	0	185	0	0.0
1996	Chi A	0	0	—	2	0	0	0-0	2	0	0	0	0	1-0	1	0.00	—	.000	.143	0-0	—	0		1	0.0
Total	2	0	0	—	6	1	0	0-0	13	11	6	1	0	6-0	11	3.46	118	.224	.304	0-0	—	0	185	1	0.0
JONES, KEN Kenneth Frederick "Broadway" B 4.13.1903 Dover, NJ D 5.15.1991 Hartford, CT BR/TR 6-3/193# d5.19																									
1924	Det A	0	0	—	1	0	0	0	2	1	0	0	0	1	0	0.00	—	.143	.250	0-0	—	0		1	0.0
1930	Bos N	0	1	.000	8	1	0	0	19.2	28	16	1	0	4	4	5.95	83	.359	.390	5-0	.200	-0	71	-3	-0.1
Total	2	0	1	.000	9	1	0	0	21.2	29	16	1	0	5	4	5.40	90	.341	.378	5-0	.200	-0	71	-2	-0.1
JONES, MARCUS Marcus Ray B 3.29.1975 Bellflower, CA BR/TR 6-5/235# d7.17																									
2000	Oak A	0	0	—	1	1	0	0-0	2.1	5	4	1	0	3-0	1	15.43	31	.417	.533	2-0	.000	-0	217	-3	-0.1
JONES, MIKE Michael B 7.6.1865 Hamilton, ON, CAN D 3.24.1894 Hamilton, ON, CAN BL/TL 5-11.5/168# d8.1																									
1890	Lou AA	2	0	1.000	3	3	2	0	22	21	12	2	0	9	6	3.27	118	.244	.316	9	.444	2	181	2	0.3
JONES, MIKE Michael Carl B 7.30.1959 Penfield, NY BL/TL 6-6/215# d9.6																									
1980	KC A	0	1	.000	3	1	0	0-0	4.2	6	7	0	0	5-1	2	11.57	35	.333	.478	0-0	—	0	0	-4	-0.7
1981	†KC A	6	3	.667	12	11	0	0-0	75.2	74	30	7	2	28-0	29	3.21	112	.256	.324	0-0	—	0	131	3	0.4
1984	†KC A	2	3	.400	23	12	0	0-0	81	86	48	10	1	36-1	43	4.89	83	.270	.343	0-0	—	0	99	-8	-0.5
1985	KC A	3	3	.500	33	1	0	0-0	64	62	40	6	0	39-4	32	4.78	87	.257	.353	0-0	—	0	66	-5	-0.4
Total	4	11	10	.524	71	25	0	0-0	225.1	228	125	23	3	108-6	106	4.43	89	.263	.343	0-0	—	0	105	-14	-1.2
JONES, ODELL Odell B 1.13.1953 Tulare, CA BR/TR 6-3/175# d9.11																									
1975	Pit N	0	0	—	2	0	0	0-0	3	1	0	0	0	0-0	2	0.00	—	.100	.100	0-0	—	0		1	0.1
1977	Pit N	3	7	.300	34	15	1	0-1	108	118	63	14	3	31-2	66	5.08	78	.278	.330	28-0	.143	-1	85	-11	-1.1
1978	Pit N	2	0	1.000	3	1	0	0-0	9	7	3	0	0	4-0	10	2.00	185	.206	.289	1-0	.000	-0	121	1	0.3
1979	Sea A	3	11	.214	25	19	3	0-0	118.2	151	90	16	3	58-8	72	6.07	72	.317	.390	0-0	—	0	93	-22	-2.3
1981	Pit N	4	5	.444	13	8	0	0-0	54.1	51	23	3	0	23-6	30	3.31	109	.250	.325	10-3	.200	-0	77	2	0.3
1983	Tex A	3	6	.333	42	0	0	10-5	67	56	28	4	2	22-1	50	3.09	130	.223	.289	0-0	—	0		6	0.9
1984	Tex A	2	4	.333	33	0	0	2-3	59.1	62	28	7	2	23-3	28	3.64	114	.281	.351	0-0	—	0		3	0.3
1986	Bal A	2	2	.500	21	0	0	0-0	49.1	58	22	4	0	23-6	32	3.83	108	.305	.373	0-0	—	0		2	0.1
1988	Mil A	5	0	1.000	28	2	0	1-0	80.2	75	47	8	1	29-6	48	4.35	92	.251	.313	0-0	—	0	126	-5	-0.3
Total	9	24	35	.407	201	45	4	13-9	549.1	579	304	56	11	213-32	338	4.42	92	.275	.341	39-3	.154	-1	90	-23	-1.7
JONES, OSCAR Oscar Lafayette "Flip Flap" B 10.22.1879 Carter Co., MO D 3.16.1953 Fort Worth, TX BR/TR 5-7/163# d4.20																									
1903	Bro N	19	14	.576	38	36	31-4	0	324.1	320	159	4	19	77	95	2.94	109	.260	.313	125-3	.256	3	105	7	0.7
1904	Bro N	17	25	.405	46	41	38	0	377	387	175	7	17	92	96	2.75	100	.270	.321	137-4	.175	-1	86	0	-0.5
1905	Bro N	8	15	.348	29	20	14	1	174	197	121	6	9	56	66	4.66	62	.285	.347	65-1	.200	-0*	85	-33	-4.0
Total	3	44	54	.449	113	97	83-4	1	875.1	904	455	17	45	225	257	3.20	92	.269	.324	327-8	.211	2	94	-26	-3.8
JONES, PERCY Percy Lee B 10.28.1899 Harwood, TX D 3.18.1979 Dallas, TX BR/TL 5-11.5/175# d8.6																									
1920	Chi N	0	0	—	4	0	0	0	7	15	10	1	1	3	0	11.57	28	.455	.514	2-0	.000	-0		-6	-0.3
1921	Chi N	3	5	.375	32	3	1	0	98.2	116	57	2	4	39	46	4.56	84	.295	.365	27-0	.222	-0	72	-8	-0.6
1922	Chi N	8	9	.471	44	24	7-2	1	162	197	104	10	5	68	45	4.78	88	.314	.385	47-4	.085	-4	94	-11	-1.3
1925	Chi N	6	6	.500	28	13	6-1	0	124	123	74	12	5	71	60	4.65	93	.263	.366	39-1	.154	-3	87	-5	-0.5
1926	Chi N	12	7	.632	30	20	10-2	2	160.1	151	64	3	5	90	80	3.09	125	.256	.359	50-4	.260	3	87	14	1.8
1927	Chi N	7	8	.467	30	11	5-1	0	112.2	123	67	3	6	72	37	4.07	95	.285	.394	40-1	.350	3	84	-6	-0.3
1928	Chi N	10	6	.625	39	19	9-1	3	154	167	80	4	7	56	41	4.03	95	.288	.358	56-2	.196	-0	130	-3	-0.3
1929	Bos N	7	15	.318	35	22	11-1	0	188.1	219	112	15	4	84	69	4.64	101	.298	.373	61-4	.148	-3*	72	0	-0.2
1930	Pit N	0	1	.000	9	2	0	0	19	26	20	3	3	11	3	6.63	75	.329	.430	2-0	.000	-0	105	-5	-0.3
Total	9	53	57	.482	251	114	49-8	6	1026	1137	588	53	40	494	381	4.34	95	.289	.374	324-16	.194	-5	92	-30	-2.0
JONES, RANDY Randall Leo B 1.12.1950 Fullerton, CA BR/TL 6/178# d6.16																									
1973	SD N	7	6	.538	20	19	6-1	0-0	139.2	129	58	13	1	37-9	77	3.16	110	.241	.289	48-4	.167	0	96	5	0.5
1974	SD N	8	22	.267	40	34	4-1	2-0	208.1	217	118	16	5	78-12	124	4.45	80	.270	.336	65-3	.154	-1*	75	-22	-2.9
1975	SD N★	20	12	.625	37	36	18-6	0-0	285	242	94	17	0	56-9	103	**2.24**	**155**	.232	.269	83-17	.133	-1*	94	37	4.5
1976	SD N★	**22**	14	.611	40	**40**	**25**-5	0-0	**315.1**	274	109	15	4	50-9	93	2.74	120	.234	**.265**	103-15	.058	-6	116	20	2.1
1977	SD N	6	12	.333	27	25	1	0-0	147.1	173	85	12	0	36-10	44	4.58	77	.291	.329	43-4	.116	-1*	73	-18	-1.9
1978	SD N	13	14	.481	37	36	7-2	0-1	253	263	104	6	0	64-20	71	2.88	116	.272	.314	82-6	.183	1*	95	8	1.1
1979	SD N	11	12	.478	39	39	6	0-0	263	257	120	17	3	64-10	112	3.63	97	.259	.304	86-7	.174	0*	93	-3	0.1
1980	SD N	5	13	.278	24	24	4-3	0-0	154.1	165	71	14	0	29-5	53	3.91	88	.276	.309	45-7	.067	-3*	78	-7	-0.9
1981	NY N	1	8	.111	13	12	0	0-0	59.1	65	48	8	1	38-1	14	4.85	72	.274	.373	17-1	.118	-1	74	-13	-1.8
1982	NY N	7	10	.412	28	20	2-1	0-0	107.2	130	68	11	4	51-3	44	4.60	79	.304	.380	27-2	.148	0	91	-13	-1.7
Total	10	100	123	.448	305	285	73-19	2-1	1933	1915	875	129	18	503-88	735	3.42	101	.260	.306	599-66	.132	-12	91	-6	-0.9
JONES, BOBBY Robert Joseph B 2.10.1970 Fresno, CA BR/TR 6-4/225# d8.14																									
1993	NY N	2	4	.333	9	9	0	0-0	61.2	61	35	6	2	22-3	35	3.65	110	.262	.327	20-2	.050	-2	95	0	-0.2

Year	Tm Lg	W	L	Pct	G	GS	CG-Sho	SV-BS	IP	H	R	HR	HB	BB-IB	SO	ERA	AERA	OAV	OOB	AB-SH	AVG	PB	Sup	APR	PW
1994	NY N	12	7	.632	24	24	1-1	0-0	160	157	75	10	4	56-9	80	3.15	133	.257	.322	46-8	.109	-2	91	13	1.3
1995	NY N	10	10	.500	30	30	3-1	0-0	195.2	209	107	20	7	53-6	127	4.19	97	.274	.325	56-18	.161	-1	112	-6	-0.6
1996	NY N	12	8	.600	31	31	3-1	0-0	195.2	219	102	26	3	46-6	116	4.42	91	.288	.329	60-9	.117	-1	114	-5	-0.5
1997	NY N★	15	9	.625	30	30	2-1	0-0	193.1	177	88	24	2	63-3	125	3.63	111	.242	.303	62-4	.129	-0	102	8	1.0
1998	NY N	9	9	.500	30	30	0	0-0	195.1	192	94	23	8	53-2	115	4.05	102	.262	.316	48-12	.188	1	98	1	0.3
1999	NY N	3	3	.500	12	9	0	0-0	59.1	69	37	3	2	11-0	31	5.61	78	.295	.328	16-1	.313	2	114	-8	-0.5
2000	†NY N	11	6	.647	27	27	1	0-0	154.2	171	90	25	5	49-3	85	5.06	87	.281	.336	44-7	.045	-3	120	-9	-1.2
2001	SD N	8	19	.296	33	33	1	0-0	195	250	137	37	4	38-6	113	5.12	78	.305	.335	57-2	.140	1	91	-32	-3.7
2002	SD N	7	8	.467	19	18	0	0-0	108	134	68	20	1	21-1	60	5.50	69	.300	.331	33-1	.152	-1	106	-20	-2.5
Total	10	89	83	.517	245	241	11-4	0-0	1518.2	1639	833	194	38	412-39	887	4.36	94	.276	.325	442-64	.133	-5	104	-58	-6.6

JONES, BOBBY Robert Mitchell B 4.11.1972 Orange, NJ BR/TL 6/185# d5.18

1997	Col N	1	1	.500	4	4	0	0-0	19.1	30	18	2	0	12-0	5	8.38	62	.380	.447	5-1	.200	0	98	-5	-0.4
1998	Col N	7	8	.467	35	20	1	0-0	141.1	153	87	12	6	66-0	109	5.22	99	.282	.362	45-5	.178	-1	95	0	-0.2
1999	Col N	6	10	.375	30	20	0	0-0	112.1	132	91	24	6	77-0	74	6.33	92	.292	.399	27-4	.148	-1	79	-7	-1.0
2000	NY N	0	1	.000	11	1	0	0-0	21.2	18	11	2	3	14-1	20	4.15	106	.222	.354	2-1	.500	1	167	1	0.1
2002	NY N	0	0	—	12	0	0	0-0	17	20	11	3	1	11-2	11	5.29	75	.299	.405	0-0	—	0*		-2	-0.1
	SD N	0	0	—	4	2	0	0-0	9.2	10	7	1	0	7-0	7	6.52	58	.270	.378	2-1	.000	-0	159	-3	-0.2
	Year	0	0	—	16	2	0	0-0	26.2	30	14	4	1	18-2	18	5.74	68	.288	.395	2-1	.000	-0	154	-6	-0.3
Total	5	14	20	.412	96	47	1	0-0	321.1	363	225	44	16	187-3	226	5.77	91	.288	.383	81-12	.173	-2	93	-16	-1.8

JONES, SAM Samuel "Toothpick Sam" B 12.14.1925 Stewartsville, OH D 11.5.1971 Morgantown, WV BR/TR 6-4/200# d9.22

1951	Cle A	0	1	.000	2	1	0	0	8.2	4	2	0	0	5	4	2.08	182	.143	.273	2-0	.000	-0	23	2	0.2
1952	Cle A	2	3	.400	14	4	0	1	36	38	30	6	4	37	28	7.25	46	.270	.434	10-0	.100	-1	98	-15	-2.0
1955	Chi N★	14	20	.412	36	34	12-4	0	241.2	175	118	22	14	185-5	**198**	4.10	100	**.206**	.355	77-5	.182	-2	76	2	0.0
1956	Chi N	9	14	.391	33	28	8-2	0	188.2	155	93	21	8	115-6	**176**	3.91	96	.221	.337	57-10	.175	0	93	-2	-0.3
1957	StL N	12	9	.571	28	27	10-2	0	182.2	164	77	17	6	71-1	154	3.60	110	.239	.315	63-4	.159	-1	103	9	0.9
1958	StL N	14	13	.519	35	35	14-2	0	250	204	95	23	6	107-5	**225**	2.88	143	.223	.307	90-2	.100	-6	85	**31**	2.5
1959	SF N★	**21**	15	.583	50	35	16-**4**	4	270.2	232	99	18	8	109-6	209	**2.83**	135	**.228**	.306	85-11	.129	-2	102	30	**3.6**
1960	SF N	18	14	.563	39	35	13-3	0	234	200	112	18	4	91-5	190	3.19	109	.230	.305	80-7	.200	1	104	2	0.3
1961	SF N	8	8	.500	37	17	2	1	128.1	134	72	12	8	57-7	105	4.49	85	.264	.347	36-5	.139	-1	107	-10	-1.3
1962	Det A	2	4	.333	30	6	1	1	81.1	77	39	13	2	35-1	73	3.65	111	.254	.330	21-0	.095	-1	66	3	0.1
1963	StL N	2	0	1.000	11	0	0	2	11	15	12	0	0	5-1	8	9.00	39	.319	.385	1-0	.000	0		-6	-1.2
1964	Bal A	0	0	—	7	0	0	0	10.1	5	3	1	0	5-0	6	2.61	137	.152	.263	0-0	—	0		1	0.1
Total	12	102	101	.502	322	222	76-17	9	1643.1	1403	752	151	60	822-37	1376	3.59	108	.230	.326	522-44	.149	-11	93	47	2.9

JONES, SAM Samuel Pond "Sad Sam" B 7.26.1892 Woodsfield, OH D 7.6.1966 Barnesville, OH BR/TR 6/170# d6.13

1914	Cle A	0	0	—	1	0	0	0	3.1	2	1	0	0	2	0	2.70	107	.200	.333	2-0	.500	0		0	0.0
1915	Cle A	4	9	.308	48	9	2	4	145.2	131	78	0	1	63	42	3.65	84	.252	.334	32-3	.156	-0	82	-8	-0.7
1916	Bos A	0	1	.000	12	0	0	1	27	25	14	0	0	10	7	3.67	76	.272	.343	6-0	.333	0*		-3	-0.1
1917	Bos A	0	1	.000	9	1	0	1	16.1	15	9	1	0	6	5	4.41	59	.259	.328	4-1	.000	-1	56	-3	-0.3
1918	†Bos A	16	5	**.762**	24	21	16-5	0	184	151	66	1	8	70	44	2.25	119	.230	.312	57-3	.175	2	114	7	1.0
1919	Bos A	12	20	.375	35	31	21-5	1	245	258	120	4	7	95	67	3.75	81	.278	.350	81-5	.136	-0	103	-19	-2.2
1920	Bos A	13	16	.448	37	33	21-3	0	274	302	143	9	4	79	86	3.94	93	.288	.340	92-5	.217	1*	88	-10	-0.9
1921	Bos A	23	16	.590	40	38	25-**5**	1	298.2	318	122	1	6	78	98	3.22	131	.279	.329	100-2	.240	5*	79	34	4.3
1922	†NY A	13	13	.500	45	28	20	**8**	260	270	132	16	3	76	81	3.67	109	.275	.329	87-4	.264	8	97	6	1.4
1923	†NY A	21	8	.724	39	27	18-3	4	243	239	114	11	6	69	68	3.63	109	.257	.312	85-3	.224	2	136	6	0.9
1924	NY A	9	6	.600	36	21	8-3	3	178.2	187	85	6	1	76	53	3.63	115	.276	.350	51-6	.176	-0	82	10	0.7
1925	NY A	15	21	.417	43	31	14-1	2	246.2	267	147	14	3	104	92	4.63	92	.281	.354	80-10	.162	-3*	84	-10	-1.5
1926	†NY A	9	8	.529	39	23	6-1	5	161	186	104	6	4	80	69	4.98	77	.298	.381	49-5	.204	1*	124	-19	-1.9
1927	StL A	8	14	.364	30	26	11	0	189.2	211	121	13	3	102	72	4.32	101	.282	.371	55-0	.109	-2*	88	-3	-0.6
1928	Was A	17	7	.708	30	27	19-4	0	224.2	209	89	5	3	78	63	2.84	141	.252	.319	79-9	.253	6*	111	27	3.3
1929	Was A	9	9	.500	24	24	8-1	0	153.2	156	80	5	3	49	36	3.92	108	.264	.324	51-3	.157	0*	99	5	0.5
1930	Was A	15	7	.682	25	25	14-1	0	183.1	195	95	4	3	61	60	4.07	113	.277	.337	61-4	.148	-1*	126	11	0.9
1931	Was A	9	10	.474	25	24	8-1	1	148	185	88	10	4	47	58	4.32	99	.304	.358	48-6	.313	4*	97	-2	0.2
1932	Chi A	10	15	.400	30	28	10	0	200.1	217	123	9	3	75	64	4.22	102	.270	.335	57-8	.193	2*	93	0	0.3
1933	Chi A	10	12	.455	27	25	11-2	0	176.2	181	80	13	4	65	60	3.36	126	.265	.333	58-1	.155	-0*	79	17	1.8
1934	Chi A	8	12	.400	27	26	11-1	0	183.1	217	120	16	2	60	60	5.11	93	.289	.343	60-4	.200	2*	100	-7	-0.5
1935	Chi A	8	7	.533	21	19	7	0	140	162	77	8	1	51	38	4.05	114	.284	.343	48-3	.167	0*	109	6	0.6
Total	22	229	217	.513	647	487	250-36	31	3883	4084	2008	152	69	1396	1223	3.84	104	.274	.339	1243-85	.197	25	100	45	7.2

JONES, SHELDON Sheldon Leslie "Available" B 2.2.1922 Tecumseh, NE D 4.18.1991 Greenville, NC BR/TR 6/180# d9.9

1946	NY N	1	2	.333	6	4	1	0	28	21	10	4	1	17	24	3.21	107	.208	.328	8-0	.250	0	44	1	0.2
1947	NY N	2	2	.500	15	6	0	0	55.2	51	27	2	3	29	24	3.88	105	.250	.352	16-1	.125	-1	116	1	-0.1
1948	NY N	16	8	.667	55	21	8-1	5	201.1	204	89	16	6	90	82	3.35	117	.263	.344	64-9	.203	1	124	13	1.6
1949	NY N	15	12	.556	42	27	11-1	0	207.1	198	93	19	10	88	79	3.34	119	.248	.331	66-6	.121	-3	99	14	1.3
1950	NY N	13	16	.448	40	28	11-2	2	199	188	114	26	7	90	97	4.61	89	.249	.335	57-10	.105	-2	93	-11	-1.7
1951	†NY N	6	11	.353	41	12	2	4	120.1	119	77	12	4	52	58	4.26	92	.260	.340	31-0	.097	-1	73	-9	-1.3
1952	Bos N	1	4	.200	39	1	0	1	70	81	45	7	1	31	40	4.76	76	.286	.359	8-1	.125	-0	74	-11	-0.8
1953	Chi N	0	2	.000	22	2	0	0	38.1	47	24	3	5	16	9	5.40	82	.299	.382	7-0	.000	-1	60	-3	-0.2
Total	8	54	57	.486	260	101	33-4	12	920	909	479	89	37	413	413	3.96	100	.258	.342	257-27	.136	-7	98	-5	-1.0

JONES, SHERMAN Sherman Jarvis "Roadblock" B 2.10.1935 Winton, NC BL/TR 6-4/205# d8.2

1960	SF N	1	1	.500	16	0	0	1	32	37	17	3	1	11-1	10	3.09	112	.291	.353	7-0	.286	0		0	0.0
1961	†Cin N	1	1	.500	24	2	0	2	55	51	32	6	2	27-6	32	4.42	92	.256	.340	11-0	.182	0	76	-3	-0.1
1962	NY N	0	4	.000	8	3	0	0	23.1	31	22	3	2	8-2	11	7.71	54	.326	.373	7-0	.429	1	70	-8	-1.0
Total	3	2	6	.250	48	5	0	3	110.1	119	71	12	5	46-9	53	4.73	83	.283	.351	25-0	.280	1	77	-11	-1.1

JONES, STEVE Steven Howell B 4.22.1941 Huntington Park, CA BL/TL 5-10/175# d8.15 b-Gary

1967	Chi A	2	2	.500	11	3	0	0	25.2	21	13	1	0	12-0	17	4.21	74	.223	.311	4-0	.250	0	84	-3	-0.4
1968	Was A	1	2	.333	7	0	0	0	10.2	8	8	3	0	7-0	11	5.91	49	.205	.326	1-0	.000	-0		-4	-0.8
1969	KC A	2	3	.400	20	4	0	0-0	44.2	45	25	3	3	24-2	31	4.23	87	.260	.358	8-0	.125	0	126	-3	-0.3
Total	3	5	7	.417	38	7	0	0-0	81	74	46	7	3	43-2	59	4.44	76	.242	.340	13-0	.154	1	111	-10	-1.5

JONES, RICK Thomas Fredrick B 4.16.1955 Jacksonville, FL BL/TL 6-5/190# d4.18

1976	Bos A	5	3	.625	24	14	1	0-0	104.1	133	48	6	1	26-1	45	3.36	116	.311	.348	0-0	—	0	112	5	0.3
1977	Sea A	1	4	.200	10	10	0	0-0	42.1	47	25	10	0	37-2	16	5.10	81	.283	.414	0-0	—	0	98	-4	-0.4
1978	Sea A	0	2	.000	3	2	0	0-0	12.1	17	8	1	0	7-0	11	5.84	65	.315	.393	0-0	—	0	47	-2	-0.3
Total	3	6	9	.400	37	26	1	0-0	159	197	81	17	1	70-3	72	4.02	99	.304	.370	0-0	—	0	102	-1	-0.4

JONES, TIM Timmothy Byron B 1.24.1954 Sacramento, CA BB/TR 6-5/220# d9.4

1977	Pit N	1	0	1.000	3	1	0	0-0	10	4	0	0	0	3-0	5	0.00	—	.118	.189	2-0	.000	-0	111	4	0.4

JONES, TODD Todd Barton Givin B 4.24.1968 Marietta, GA BL/TR 6-3/200# d7.7

1993	Hou N	1	2	.333	27	0	0	2-1	37.1	28	14	4	1	15-2	25	3.13	124	.214	.297	0-0	—	0		4	0.3
1994	Hou N	5	2	.714	48	0	0	5-4	72.2	52	23	3	1	26-4	63	2.72	145	.202	.277	5-0	.400	1		11	1.1
1995	Hou N	6	5	.545	68	0	0	15-5	99.2	89	38	8	6	52-17	96	3.07	126	.237	.336	5-0	.200	0		10	1.2
1996	Hou N	6	3	.667	51	0	0	17-6	57.1	61	30	5	5	32-6	44	4.40	88	.274	.375	1-0	.000	-0		-3	-0.6
1997	Det A	5	4	.556	68	0	0	31-5	70	60	29	3	1	35-2	70	3.09	149	.231	.320	0-0	—	0		10	1.9
1998	Det A	1	4	.200	65	0	0	28-4	63.1	58	38	7	2	36-4	57	4.97	95	.249	.347	0-0	—	0		-2	-0.2
1999	Det A	4	4	.500	65	0	0	30-5	66.1	64	30	7	1	35-1	64	3.80	130	.259	.352	0-0	—	0		8	1.4
2000	Det A★	2	4	.333	67	0	0	**42-4**	64	67	28	6	1	25-1	67	3.52	137	.276	.344	0-0	—	0		9	1.7
2001	Det A	4	5	.444	45	0	0	11-6	48.2	60	31	6	0	22-1	39	4.62	94	.303	.368	0-0	—	0		-3	-0.6
	Min A	1	0	1.000	24	0	0	2-2	19.1	27	8	3	0	7-0	15	3.26	141	.333	.386	0-0	—	0		3	0.1

Year	Tm Lg	W	L	Pct	G	GS	CG-Sho	SV-BS	IP	H	R	HR	HB	BB-IB	SO	ERA	AERA	OAV	OOB	AB-SH	AVG	PB	Sup	APR	PW
	Year	5	5	.500	69	0	0	13-8	68	87	44	9	0	29-1	54	4.24	104	.312	.373	0-0	—	0		0	-0.5
2002	Col N	1	4	.200	79	0	0	1-2	82.1	84	43	10	3	28-3	73	4.70	102	.269	.332	3-0	.000	-0		2	0.1
2003	Col N	1	4	.200	33	1	0	0-5	39.1	61	39	8	1	18-0	28	8.24	60	.361	.421	2-0	.000	-0	96	-13	-1.4
	†Bos A	2	1	.667	26	0	0	0-0	29.1	32	19	2	0	13-2	31	5.52	83	.269	.338	0-0	—	0		-3	-0.2
Total	11	39	42	.481	666	1	0	184-49	749.2	743	370	72	22	344-43	672	4.06	109	.261	.342	16-0	.188	0	96	33	4.8
JONNARD, CLAUDE Claude Alfred B 11.23.1897 Nashville, TN D 8.27.1959 Nashville, TN BR/TR 6-1/165# d10.1 twb-Bubber																									
1921	NY N	0	0	—	1	0	0	1	4	4	0	0	0	0	7	0.00	—	.267	.267	1-0	.000	-0		2	0.1
1922	NY N	6	1	.857	33	0	0	**5**	96	96	45	7	3	28	44	3.84	104	.272	.331	24-2	.042	-3		4	0.0
1923	†NY N	4	3	.571	**45**	1	1	**5**	96	105	45	6	0	35	45	3.28	116	.279	.340	26-1	.038	-3	86	4	-0.1
1924	†NY N	3	5	.375	34	3	1	5	89.2	80	33	2	2	24	40	2.41	152	.229	.282	22-1	.045	-3	123	**11**	0.7
1926	StL A	0	2	.000	12	3	0	1	36	46	29	1	0	24	13	6.00	71	.313	.409	7-1	.000	-1	79	-7	-0.4
1929	Chi N	0	1	.000	12	2	0	0	27.2	41	27	4	1	11	11	7.48	62	.320	.379	10-0	.200	1	76	-9	-0.3
Total	6	13	12	.520	137	9	2	17	349.1	372	179	20	6	122	160	3.79	104	.272	.334	90-5	.056	-9	94	5	-0.0
JORDAN, CHARLIE Charles T. "Kid" B 10.4.1871 Baltimore, MD D 6.1.1928 Hazleton, PA d7.31																									
1896	Phi N	0	0	—	2	0	0	0	4.2	9	4	0	0	2	3	7.71	56	.409	.458	2-0	.500	0		-1	0.0
JORDAN, HARRY Harry J. B 2.14.1873 Pittsburgh, PA D 3.1.1920 Pittsburgh, PA d9.25																									
1894	Pit N	1	0	1.000	1	1	1	0	9	10	7	0	1	2	1	4.00	131	.278	.333	3-0	.000	-0	135	1	0.0
1895	Pit N	0	2	.000	2	2	2	0	17	24	15	0	1	6	4	4.24	106	.329	.387	7-0	.286	-0	87	-1	-0.1
Total	2	1	2	.333	3	3	3	0	26	34	22	0	2	8	5	4.15	115	.312	.370	10-0	.200	-0	105	0	-0.1
JORDAN, MILT Milton Mignot B 5.24.1927 Mineral Springs, PA D 5.13.1993 Ithaca, NY BR/TR 6-2.5/207# d4.16																									
1953	Det A	0	1	.000	8	1	0	0	17	26	13	3	0	5	4	5.82	70	.366	.408	2-0	.500	0	153	-4	-0.1
JORDAN, NILES Niles Chapman B 12.1.1925 Lyman, WA BL/TL 5-11/180# d8.26																									
1951	Phi N	2	3	.400	5	5	2-1	0	36.2	35	15	4	0	8	11	3.19	121	.250	.291	13-0	.077	-1	55	2	0.2
1952	Cin N	0	1	.000	3	1	0	0	6.1	14	7	1	0	3	2	9.95	38	.452	.500	1-1	.000	-0	47	-4	-0.5
Total	2	2	4	.333	8	6	2-1	0	43	49	22	5	0	11	13	4.19	92	.287	.330	14-1	.071	-1	54	-2	-0.3
JORDAN, RIP Raymond Willis "Lanky" B 9.28.1889 Portland, ME D 6.5.1960 Meriden, CT BL/TR 6/172# d6.25																									
1912	Chi A	0	0	—	4	0	0	0	12.1	13	8	2	1	3	1	5.11	63	.289	.347	4-0	.000	-1		-2	-0.2
1919	Was A	0	0	—	1	1	0	0	4	6	5	1	0	2	2	11.25	29	.353	.421	1-0	.000	-0	171	-3	-0.2
Total	2	0	0	—	5	1	0	0	16.1	19	13	3	1	5	3	6.61	48	.306	.368	5-0	.000	-1	171	-5	-0.4
JORDAN, RICARDO Ricardo B 6.27.1970 Boynton Beach, FL BL/TL 5-11/165# d6.23																									
1995	Tor A	1	0	1.000	15	0	0	1-0	15	18	11	3	2	13-1	10	6.60	71	.305	.434	0-0	—	0		-3	-0.2
1996	Phi N	2	2	.500	26	0	0	0-0	25	18	6	0	0	12-0	17	1.80	240	.202	.294	1-0	.000	-0		7	0.9
1997	NY N	1	2	.333	22	0	0	0-0	27	31	17	1	2	15-2	19	5.33	76	.304	.397	1-0	.000	-0		-4	-0.4
1998	Cin N	1	0	1.000	6	0	0	0-0	3.1	4	9	2	0	7-0	1	24.30	18	.308	.524	0-0	—	0		-7	-1.2
Total	4	5	4	.556	69	0	0	1-0	70.1	71	43	6	4	47-3	47	5.25	82	.270	.381	2-0	.000	-0		-7	-0.9
JORGENS, ORVILLE Orville Edward B 6.4.1908 Rockford, IL D 1.11.1992 Colorado Springs, CO BR/TR 6-1/180# d4.19 b-Art																									
1935	Phi N	10	15	.400	**53**	24	6	2	188.1	216	129	12	8	96	57	4.83	94	.283	.370	62-3	.097	-5	105	-8	-1.3
1936	Phi N	8	8	.500	39	21	4	0	167.1	196	110	16	7	69	58	4.79	95	.290	.361	60-2	.200	-1	105	-4	-0.4
1937	Phi N	3	4	.429	52	9	1	3	140.2	159	83	12	5	68	34	4.41	98	.298	.383	35-1	.143	-1	93	-3	-0.2
Total	3	21	27	.438	144	54	11	5	496.1	571	322	40	20	233	149	4.70	95	.290	.370	157-6	.146	-7	104	-15	-1.9
JOSEPH, KEVIN Kevin John B 8.1.1976 Camp Hill, PA BR/TR 6-4/200# d8.1																									
2002	StL N	0	1	.000	11	0	0	0-0	11	16	7	1	2	6-0	2	4.91	81	.364	.462	0-0	—	0		-1	-0.1
JOSS, ADDIE Adrian B 4.12.1880 Woodland, WI D 4.14.1911 Toledo, OH BR/TR 6-3/185# d4.26 HF1978																									
1902	Cle A	17	13	.567	32	29	28-**5**	0	269.1	225	120	2	13	75	106	2.77	124	.228	.291	103-7	.117	-5*	102	23	2.0
1903	Cle A	18	13	.581	32	31	31-3	0	283.2	232	105	3	9	37	120	2.19	130	.223	**.256**	114-1	.193	0*	105	22	2.5
1904	Cle A	14	10	.583	25	24	20-5	0	192.1	160	51	0	7	30	83	**1.59**	159	.227	.266	76-3	.132	-4*	114	20	2.2
1905	Cle A	20	12	.625	33	32	31-3	0	286	246	90	4	11	46	132	2.01	131	.234	.273	97-6	.134	-0*	101	18	2.3
1906	Cle A	21	9	.700	34	31	28-9	1	282	220	81	3	3	43	106	1.72	152	.218	.252	100-10	.210	2*	110	28	3.5
1907	Cle A	**27**	11	.711	42	38	34-6	2	338.2	279	100	3	7	54	127	1.83	137	.227	.263	114-6	.114	-5	94	27	3.0
1908	Cle A	24	11	.686	42	35	29-9	2	325	232	77	2	2	30	130	**1.16**	**205**	**.197**	**.218**	97-3	.155	2	87	38	5.0
1909	Cle A	14	13	.519	33	28	24-4	0	242.2	198	71	0	4	31	67	1.71	150	.226	.255	80-2	.100	-3	76	21	2.1
1910	Cle A	5	5	.500	13	12	9-1	0	107.1	96	35	2	2	18	49	2.26	114	.245	.282	36-1	.111	-1	67	5	0.4
Total	9	160	97	.623	286	260	234-45	5	2327	1888	730	19	58	364	920	1.89	142	.223	.260	817-39	.144	-14	96	202	23.0
JOURNELL, JIMMY James Richard B 12.29.1977 Springfield, OH BR/TR ht/wt 6-4/200# d6.29																									
2003	StL N	0	0	—	7	0	0	0-0	9	10	7	0	0	11-0	8	6.00	68	.278	.438	0-0	—	0		-2	-0.1
JOYCE, MIKE Michael Lewis B 2.12.1941 Detroit, MI BR/TR 6-2/193# d7.2																									
1962	Chi A	2	1	.667	25	1	0	2	43.1	40	17	2	0	14-2	9	3.32	118	.247	.305	7-0	.429	1	137	3	0.3
1963	Chi A	0	0	—	6	0	0	0	10.2	13	10	1	0	8-2	7	8.44	42	.289	.396	0-1	—	0		-5	-0.3
Total	2	2	1	.667	31	1	0	2	54	53	27	3	0	22-4	16	4.33	88	.256	.326	7-1	.429	1	137	-2	0.0
JOYCE, DICK Richard Edward B 11.18.1943 Portland, ME BL/TL 6-5/225# d9.3																									
1965	KC A	0	1	.000	5	3	0	0	13	12	7	0	0	4-0	7	2.77	126	.240	.291	4-0	.000	-0	84	0	-0.1
JOYCE, BOB Robert Emmett B 1.14.1915 Stockton, CA D 12.10.1981 San Francisco, CA BR/TR 6-1/180# d5.4																									
1939	Phi A	3	5	.375	30	6	1	0	107.2	156	91	13	1	37	25	6.69	70	.337	.387	35-1	.086	-3	53	-22	-1.5
1946	NY N	3	4	.429	14	7	2	0	60.2	79	43	3	0	20	24	5.34	64	.315	.365	19-1	.158	0	139	-13	-1.3
Total	2	6	9	.400	44	13	3	0	168.1	235	134	16	1	57	49	6.20	69	.329	.380	54-2	.111	-3	89	-35	-2.8
JUDD, MIKE Michael Galen B 6.30.1975 San Diego, CA BR/TR 6-2/200# d9.28																									
1997	LA N	0	0	—	1	0	0	0-0	2.2	4	0	0	0	0-0	4	0.00	—	.364	.364	1-0	.000	-0		1	0.0
1998	LA N	0	0	—	7	0	0	0-0	11.1	19	19	4	1	9-1	14	15.09	26	.373	.475	1-0	.000	-0		-14	-0.6
1999	LA N	3	1	.750	7	4	0	0-0	28	30	17	4	1	12-0	22	5.46	78	.280	.358	5-3	.000	-0	113	-3	-0.4
2000	LA N	0	1	.000	1	1	0	0-0	4	4	7	2	1	3-0	5	15.75	28	.250	.400	1-1	1.000	1	127	-5	-0.7
2001	TB A	1	0	1.000	8	2	0	0-0	20	19	14	2	1	10-0	11	4.05	111	.250	.333	0-0	—	0	155	-1	-0.1
	Tex A	0	1	.000	4	1	0	0-0	9	15	10	2	0	5-0	5	8.00	58	.357	.426	1-0	.000	-0	79	-4	-0.4
	Year	1	1	.500	12	3	0	0-0	29	34	14	4	1	15-0	16	5.28	86	.288	.365	1-0	.000	-0	129	-5	-0.5
Total	5	4	3	.571	28	8	0	0-0	75	91	67	14	4	39-1	61	7.20	60	.300	.384	9-4	.111	-0	123	-26	-2.2
JUDD, RALPH Ralph Wesley B 12.7.1901 Perrysburg, OH D 5.6.1957 Lapeer, MI BL/TR 5-10/170# d10.2																									
1927	Was A	0	0	—	1	0	0	1	4	8	3	0	0	2	2	6.75	60	.400	.455	1-0	.000	-0		-1	-0.1
1929	NY N	3	0	1.000	18	0	0	0	50.2	49	19	4	0	11	21	2.66	172	.261	.302	14-0	.000	-2		10	0.3
1930	NY N	0	0	—	2	0	0	0	7.2	13	8	0	0	3	0	5.87	81	.394	.444	3-0	.000	-1		-2	-0.1
Total	3	3	0	1.000	21	0	0	1	62.1	70	30	4	0	16	23	3.32	138	.290	.335	18-0	.000	-3		7	0.1
JUDD, OSCAR Thomas William Oscar "Ossie" B 2.14.1908 London, ON, CAN D 12.27.1995 Ingersoll, ON, CAN BL/TL 6-0.5/180# d4.16																									
1941	Bos A	0	0	—	7	0	0	1	12.1	15	12	1	0	10	5	8.76	48	.300	.417	4-0	.500	2*		-5	-0.1
1942	Bos A	8	10	.444	31	19	11	2	150.1	135	72	3	2	90	70	3.89	96	.239	.346	67-3	.269	6*	133	-2	0.4
1943	Bos A☆	11	6	.647	23	20	8-1	0	155.1	131	58	2	3	69	53	2.90	114	.230	.317	54-3	.259	4*	89	6	1.1
1944	Bos A	1	1	.500	9	6	1	0	30	30	16	1	0	15	9	3.60	94	.261	.346	11-0	.182	1*	188	-2	-0.1
1945	Bos A	0	1	.000	2	1	0	0	6.1	10	8	1	0	3	5	8.53	40	.333	.394	2-0	.500	0	50	-4	-0.5
	Phi N	5	4	.556	23	9	3-1	2	82.2	80	47	3	1	40	36	3.81	101	.254	.340	30-1	.267	3*	64	-1	0.2
1946	Phi N	11	12	.478	30	24	12-1	2	173.1	169	86	6	1	90	65	3.53	97	.260	.350	79-4	.316	8*	95	-5	0.5
1947	Phi N	4	15	.211	32	19	8-1	0	146.2	155	86	6	3	69	54	4.60	87	.279	.361	64-0	.188	2*	73	-10	-0.8
1948	Phi N	0	2	.000	4	1	0	0	14.1	19	14	1	0	11	7	6.91	57	.317	.423	6-0	.167	0	90	-5	-0.6
Total	8	40	51	.440	161	99	43-4	7	771.1	744	399	24	10	397	304	3.90	93	.256	.347	317-11	.262	26	98	-28	0.1

Year	Tm Lg	W	L	Pct	G	GS	CG-Sho	SV-BS	IP	H	R	HR	HB	BB-IB	SO	ERA	AERA	OAV	OOB	AB-SH	AVG	PB	Sup	APR	PW
JUDEN, JEFF Jeffrey Daniel B 1.19.1971 Salem, MA BR/TR 6-8/265# d9.15																									
1991	Hou N	0	2	.000	4	3	0	0-0	18	19	14	3	0	7-1	11	6.00	59	.275	.329	5-0	.000	-1	60	-6	-0.6
1993	Hou N	0	1	.000	2	0	0	0-0	5	4	3	1	0	4-1	7	5.40	72	.222	.348	0-0	—	0		-1	-0.1
1994	Phi N	1	4	.200	6	5	0	0-0	27.2	29	25	4	1	12-0	22	6.18	69	.276	.350	9-2	.111	-0	72	-7	-1.1
1995	Phi N	2	4	.333	13	10	1	0-0	62.2	53	31	6	5	31-0	47	4.02	105	.235	.335	18-3	.056	-1	94	1	0.0
1996	SF N	4	0	1.000	36	0	0	0-0	41.2	39	23	7	1	20-2	35	4.10	100	.250	.335	3-0	.000	-0		-1	-0.1
	Mon N	1	0	1.000	22	0	0	0-0	32.2	22	12	1	4	14-0	26	2.20	196	.188	.294	0-1	—	0		6	0.3
	Year	5	0	1.000	58	0	0	0-0	74.1	61	39	8	5	34-2	61	3.27	128	.223	.317	3-1	.000	-0		5	0.2
1997	Mon N	11	5	.688	22	22	3	0-0	130	125	64	17	9	57-2	107	4.22	99	.255	.341	43-2	.140	0	119	1	0.1
	†Cle A	0	1	.000	8	5	0	0-0	31.1	32	21	6	1	15-0	29	5.46	86	.264	.345	0-0	—	0	94	-3	-0.1
1998	Mil N	7	11	.389	24	24	2	0-0	138.1	149	91	20	10	66-0	109	5.53	77	.277	.363	41-3	.122	-1	101	-19	-2.2
	Ana A	1	3	.250	8	6	0	0-0	40	33	32	7	2	18-0	39	6.75	70	.217	.308	0-0	—	0	92	-9	-0.7
1999	NY A	0	1	.000	2	1	0	0-0	5.2	5	9	1	1	3-0	9	1.59	298	.200	.310	0-0	—	0	39	-2	-0.2
Total	8	27	32	.458	147	76	6	0-0	533	510	325	73	34	247-6	441	4.81	89	.253	.341	119-11	.109	-3	100	-40	-4.7
JUDSON, HOWIE Howard Kolls B 2.16.1926 Hebron, IL BR/TR 6-1/195# d4.22																									
1948	Chi A	4	5	.444	40	5	1	8	107.1	102	60	7	3	56	38	4.78	89	.255	.351	29-4	.103	-2*	98	-5	-0.6
1949	Chi A	1	14	.067	26	12	3	1	108	114	65	13	1	70	36	4.58	91	.274	.380	31-3	.065	-3	61	-6	-1.0
1950	Chi A	2	3	.400	46	3	1	0	112	105	53	10	2	63	34	3.94	114	.252	.353	20-4	.100	-1	94	**8**	0.2
1951	Chi A	5	6	.455	27	14	3	1	121.2	124	67	9	2	55	43	3.77	107	.264	.343	33-5	.121	-2	108	0	-0.2
1952	Chi A	0	1	.000	21	0	0	1	34	30	17	4	0	22	15	4.24	86	.244	.359	4-0	.000	-0		-2	-0.1
1953	Cin N	0	1	.000	10	6	0	0	38.2	58	28	8	0	11	11	5.59	78	.341	.381	9-0	.111	1	137	-6	-0.2
1954	Cin N	5	7	.417	37	8	0	3	93.1	86	47	9	3	42	27	3.95	106	.251	.335	24-0	.083	-2	104	2	0.0
Total	7	17	37	.315	207	48	8	14	615	619	337	60	11	319	204	4.29	98	.265	.355	150-16	.093	-9	97	-9	-1.9
JULIO, JORGE Jorge Dandys B 3.3.1979 Caracas, Venezuela BR/TR 6-1/190# d4.26																									
2001	Bal A	1	1	.500	18	0	0	0-1	21.1	25	13	2	1	9-0	22	3.80	113	.287	.361	0-0	—	0		0	0.0
2002	Bal A	5	6	.455	67	0	0	25-6	68	55	22	5	2	27-3	55	1.99	216	.213	.292	0-0	—	0		15	3.0
2003	Bal A	0	7	.000	64	0	0	36-8	61.2	60	36	10	2	34-4	52	4.38	100	.256	.354	0-0	—	0		-2	-0.4
Total	3	6	14	.300	149	0	0	61-15	151	140	71	17	5	70-7	129	3.22	134	.242	.328	0-0	—	0		13	2.6
JUNGE, ERIC Eric Debari B 1.5.1977 Manhasset, NY BR/TR 6-5/215# d9.11																									
2002	Phi N	2	0	1.000	4	1	0	0-0	12.2	14	3	0	0	5-0	11	1.42	275	.286	.352	3-0	.000	-0	95	3	0.5
2003	Phi N	0	0	—	6	0	0	0-0	7.2	5	3	1	0	1-0	5	3.52	114	.185	.214	0-0	—	0		1	0.0
Total	2	2	0	1.000	10	1	0	0-0	20.1	19	6	1	0	6-0	16	2.21	178	.250	.305	3-0	.000	-0	95	4	0.5
JUNGELS, KEN Kenneth Peter "Curly" B 6.23.1916 Aurora, IL D 9.9.1975 West Bend, WI BR/TR 6-1/180# d9.15																									
1937	Cle A	0	0	—	2	0	0	0	3	3	1	0	0	1	0	0.00	—	.273	.333	0-0	—	0		1	0.0
1938	Cle A	1	0	1.000	9	0	0	0	15.1	21	16	1	2	18	7	8.80	53	.339	.500	5-0	.000	-1		-7	-0.4
1940	Cle A	0	0	—	2	0	0	0	3.1	3	1	0	0	1	1	2.70	156	.273	.333	1-0	.000	-0		1	0.0
1941	Cle A	0	0	—	6	0	0	0	13.2	17	12	4	1	8	6	7.24	54	.293	.388	2-0	.000	-0		-5	-0.3
1942	Pit N	0	0	—	6	0	0	0	13.2	12	11	0	0	4	7	6.59	51	.235	.291	2-0	.500	0*		-4	-0.2
Total	5	1	0	1.000	25	0	0	0	49	56	41	5	3	32	21	6.80	60	.290	.399	10-0	.100	-1		-14	-0.9
JUREWICZ, MIKE Michael Allen B 9.20.1945 Buffalo, NY BB/TL 6-3/205# d9.7																									
1965	NY A	0	0	—	2	0	0	0	2.1	5	2	0	0	1-0	2	7.71	44	.417	.462	0-0	—	0		-1	-0.1
JURISICH, AL Alvin Joseph B 8.25.1921 New Orleans, LA D 11.3.1981 New Orleans, LA BR/TR 6-2/193# d4.26																									
1944	†StL N	7	9	.438	30	14	5-2	1	130	102	53	7	5	65	53	3.39	104	.221	.323	45-1	.178	-1	78	4	0.3
1945	StL N	3	3	.500	27	6	1	0	71.2	61	45	7	1	41	42	5.15	73	.232	.338	23-0	.087	-2	143	-10	-1.0
1946	Phi N	4	3	.571	13	10	2-1	1	68.1	71	30	9	1	31	34	3.69	93	.263	.341	23-2	.130	-0	95	-1	-0.2
1947	Phi N	1	7	.125	34	12	5	3	118.1	110	69	15	1	52	48	4.94	81	.258	.340	31-4	.032	-3	81	-10	-1.0
Total	4	15	22	.405	104	42	13-3	5	388.1	344	197	38	8	189	177	4.24	87	.242	.334	122-7	.115	-6	92	-17	-1.9
JUSTIS, WALT Walter Newton "Smoke" B 8.17.1883 Moores Hill, IN D 10.4.1941 Greendale, IN BR/TR 5-11.5/195# d8.1																									
1905	Det A	0	0	—	2	0	0	0	3.1	4	3	0	1	6	0	8.10	34	.308	.550	0-0	—	0		-2	-0.1
JUUL, HEROLD Earl Herold B 5.21.1893 Chicago, IL D 1.4.1942 Chicago, IL BR/TR 5-9.5/150# d4.24																									
1914	Bro F	0	3	.000	9	3	0	0	29	26	24	0	1	31	16	6.21	46	.248	.423	9-0	.222	-0	80	-10	-0.9
JUUL, HERB Herbert Victor B 2.2.1886 Chicago, IL D 11.14.1928 Chicago, IL BL/TL 5-11/150# d7.11																									
1911	Cin N	0	0	—	1	0	0	0	4	3	2	0	0	4	2	4.50	74	.231	.412	2-0	.000	-0*		0	-0.1
KAAT, JIM James Lee B 11.7.1938 Zeeland, MI BL/TL 6-4/217# d8.2 C2																									
1959	Was A	0	2	.000	3	2	0	0	5	7	9	1	2	4-0	2	12.60	31	.350	.481	1-0	.000	-0	56	-5	-0.9
1960	Was A	1	5	.167	13	9	0	0	50	48	39	8	5	31-2	25	5.58	70	.255	.370	14-0	.143	-1	88	-10	-1.1
1961	Min A	9	17	.346	36	29	8-1	0	200.2	188	105	12	11	82-1	122	3.90	109	.248	.329	63-3	.238	3*	75	5	1.1
1962	Min A☆	18	14	.563	39	35	16-**5**	1	269	243	106	23	18	75-5	173	3.14	130	.243	.305	100-0	.180	3*	99	27	3.8
1963	Min A	10	10	.500	31	27	7-1	1	178.1	195	96	24	9	38-1	105	4.19	87	.274	.318	61-1	.131	-0*	126	-11	-1.0
1964	Min A	17	11	.607	36	34	13	1	243	231	100	23	9	60-5	171	3.22	111	.251	.301	83-3	.169	5*	117	10	1.8
1965	†Min A	18	11	.621	45	**42**	7-2	2	264.1	267	121	25	5	63-6	154	2.83	126	.258	.302	93-3	.247	6*	116	11	2.1
1966	Min A★	**25**	13	.658	41	**41**	**19**-3	0	**304.2**	271	114	29	3	55-4	205	2.75	131	.235	.270	118-1	.195	4*	103	25	3.6
1967	Min A	16	13	.552	42	38	13-2	0	263.1	269	110	21	9	42-2	211	3.04	114	.260	.294	99-1	.172	3*	96	9	1.4
1968	Min A	14	12	.538	30	29	9-2	0	208	192	78	16	3	40-0	130	2.94	105	.243	.278	77-0	.156	0*	101	4	0.6
1969	Min A	14	13	.519	40	32	10	1-1	242.1	252	114	23	9	75-15	139	3.49	105	.265	.322	87-2	.207	6*	102	2	0.7
1970	†Min A	14	10	.583	45	34	4-1	0-1	230.1	244	110	26	3	58-8	120	3.56	105	.273	.316	76-4	.197	3*	113	3	0.7
1971	Min A	13	14	.481	39	38	15-4	0-0	260.1	275	104	16	6	47-9	137	3.32	107	.268	.302	93-7	.161	-0*	107	8	0.8
1972	Min A	10	2	.833	15	15	5	0-0	113.1	94	36	6	0	20-2	64	2.06	156	.227	.260	45-1	.289	5*	114	12	2.0
1973	Min A	11	12	.478	29	28	7-2	0-0	181.2	206	101	26	4	39-1	93	4.41	90	.282	.321	0-0	—	0*	108	-9	-1.0
	Chi A	4	1	.800	7	7	3-1	0-0	42.2	44	23	4	0	4-0	16	4.22	94	.260	.277	0-0	—	0	151	-1	-0.2
	Year	15	13	.536	36	35	10-3	0-0	224.1	250	30	30	4	43-1	109	4.37	91	.278	.313	0-0	—	0	117	-11	-1.2
1974	Chi A	21	13	.618	42	39	15-3	0-0	277.1	263	106	18	6	63-3	142	2.92	128	.250	.293	1-0	.000	-0	93	22	2.6
1975	Chi A★	20	14	.588	43	41	12-1	0-0	303.2	321	121	20	9	77-0	142	3.11	125	.274	.321	0-0	—	0	99	23	2.4
1976	†Phi N	12	14	.462	38	35	7-1	0-1	227.2	241	95	21	0	32-3	83	3.48	102	.274	.298	79-1	.177	2*	106	3	0.4
1977	Phi N	6	11	.353	35	27	2	0-0	160.1	211	100	20	2	40-6	55	5.39	74	.320	.360	53-1	.189	1*	109	-21	-2.0
1978	Phi N	8	5	.615	26	24	2-1	0-0	140.1	150	67	9	5	32-6	48	4.10	87	.280	.322	48-1	.146	-1	113	-7	-0.7
1979	Phi N	1	0	1.000	3	1	0	0-0	8.1	9	4	1	0	5-2	2	4.32	89	.281	.378	1-0	.000	0	162	0	0.0
	NY A	2	3	.400	40	1	0	2-2	58.1	64	29	4	2	14-2	23	3.86	106	.287	.329	0-0	—	0	111	1	0.0
1980	NY A	0	1	.000	4	0	0	0-0	5	8	5	0	0	4-2	1	7.20	55	.381	.462	0-0	—	0		-2	-0.3
	StL N	8	7	.533	49	14	6-1	4-1	129.2	140	61	6	0	33-11	36	3.82	97	.281	.322	35-4	.143	1	121	-1	-0.1
1981	StL N	6	6	.500	41	1	0	4-5	53	60	25	2	0	17-8	8	3.40	105	.299	.345	8-0	.375	1	100	0	0.1
1982	†StL N	5	3	.625	62	2	0	2-2	75	79	40	6	2	23-9	35	4.08	89	.276	.328	12-0	.000	-1	97	-5	-0.6
1983	StL N	0	0	—	24	0	0	0-1	34.2	48	19	5	0	10-3	19	3.89	93	.327	.367	4-1	.000	-0		-2	-0.1
Total	25	283	237	.544	898	625	180-31	18-14	4530.1	4620	2038	395	122	1083-116	2461	3.45	107	.264	.309	1251-34	.185	41	105	91	16.1
KAHLER, GEORGE George Runnells "Krum" B 9.6.1889 Athens, OH D 2.7.1924 Battle Creek, MI BR/TR 6/183# d8.13																									
1910	Cle A	6	4	.600	12	12	8-2	0	95.1	80	35	0	4	46	38	1.60	161	.237	.335	35-0	.143	-2	110	6	0.4
1911	Cle A	9	8	.529	30	17	10	1	154.1	153	78	1	13	66	97	3.27	104	.270	.360	54-3	.167	-2	91	2	-0.1
1912	Cle A	12	19	.387	41	32	17-3	1	246.1	263	135	1	11	121	104	3.69	92	.291	.382	80-1	.112	-5	75	-6	-1.4
1913	Cle A	5	11	.313	24	15	5	0	117.2	118	56	1	4	32	43	3.14	97	.269	.324	33-3	.061	-3	86	-1	-0.7
1914	Cle A	0	1	.000	2	1	1	0	14	17	10	0	0	7	3	3.86	75	.309	.387	5-0	.000	-0	152	-2	-0.2
Total	5	32	43	.427	109	77	41-5	2	627.2	631	314	3	32	272	285	3.17	101	.274	.359	207-7	.121	-13	86	-1	-2.0
KAINER, DON Donald Wayne B 9.3.1955 Houston, TX BR/TR 6-3/205# d9.6																									
1980	Tex A	0	0	—	4	3	0	0-0	19.2	22	7	0	3	9-1	10	1.83	213	.289	.386	0-0	—	0	99	4	0.3

Year	Tm Lg	W	L	Pct	G	GS	CG-Sho	SV-BS	IP	H	R	HR	HB	BB-IB	SO	ERA	AERA	OAV	OOB	AB-SH	AVG	PB	Sup	APR	PW
KAISER, DON Clyde Donald "Tiger" B 2.3.1935 Byng, OK BR/TR 6-5/195# d7.20																									
1955	Chi N	0	0	—	11	0	0	0	18.1	20	11	2	1	5-0	11	5.40	76	.274	.329	2-0	.000	-0		-2	-0.2
1956	Chi N	4	9	.308	27	22	5-1	0	150.1	144	69	15	1	52-8	74	3.59	105	.247	.308	47-0	.043	-5	75	3	-0.3
1957	Chi N	2	6	.250	20	13	1	0	72	91	48	4	0	28-3	23	5.00	77	.316	.372	19-0	.105	-1	82	-10	-1.0
Total	3	6	15	.286	58	35	6-1	0	240.2	255	128	21	2	85-11	108	4.15	92	.270	.329	68-0	.059	-6	78	-9	-1.5
KAISER, JEFF Jeffrey Patrick B 7.24.1960 Wyandotte, MI BR/TL 6-3/195# d4.11																									
1985	Oak A	0	0	—	15	0	0	0-1	16.2	25	32	6	1	20-2	10	14.58	26	.342	.479	0-0	—	0		-22	-1.0
1987	Cle A	0	0	—	2	0	0	0-0	3.1	4	6	1	1	3-0	2	16.20	28	.286	.444	0-0	—	0		-4	-0.2
1988	Cle A	0	0	—	3	0	0	0-0	2.2	2	0	0	0	1-0	0	0.00	—	.286	.333	0-0	—	0		1	0.1
1989	Cle A	0	1	.000	6	0	0	0-1	3.2	5	5	1	0	5-0	4	7.36	54	.313	.455	0-0	—	0		-2	-0.4
1990	Cle A	0	0	—	5	0	0	0-0	12.2	16	5	2	0	7-1	9	3.55	111	.308	.383	0-0	—	0		1	0.0
1991	Det A	0	1	.000	10	0	0	2-0	5	6	5	1	0	5-2	4	9.00	46	.286	.423	0-0	—	0		-2	-0.5
1993	Cin N	0	0	—	3	0	0	0-0	3.1	4	1	0	0	2-1	4	2.70	149	.286	.375	0-0	—	0		1	0.0
	NY N	0	0	—	6	0	0	0-0	4.2	6	6	1	0	3-0	5	11.57	35	.353	.429	0-0	—	0		-4	-0.2
	Year	0	0	—	9	0	0	0-0	8	10	10	1	0	5-1	9	7.88	51	.323	.405	0-0	—	0		-3	-0.2
Total	7	0	2	.000	50	0	0	2-2	52	68	60	12	2	46-6	38	9.17	44	.318	.433	0-0	—	0		-31	-2.2
KAISER, BOB Robert Thomas B 4.29.1950 Cincinnati, OH BB/TL 5-10/175# d9.3																									
1971	Cle A	0	0	—	5	0	0	0-0	6	8	3	2	2	3-0	4	4.50	85	.333	.448	0-0	—	0		0	0.0
KAISERLING, GEORGE George B 5.12.1893 Steubenville, OH D 3.2.1918 Steubenville, OH BR/TR 6/175# d4.20																									
1914	Ind F	17	10	.630	37	33	20-1	0	275.1	288	119	8	17	72	75	3.11	100	.274	.330	98-3	.112	-7	121	2	-0.7
1915	New F	15	15	.500	41	29	16-5	2	261.1	246	90	1	9	73	75	2.24	114	.257	.316	79-9	.152	-3	104	10	0.7
Total	2	32	25	.561	78	62	36-6	2	536.2	534	209	9	26	145	150	2.68	106	.266	.323	177-12	.130	-10	115	12	0.0
KALFASS, BILL William Philip "Lefty" B 3.3.1916 New York, NY D 9.8.1968 Brooklyn, NY BR/TL 6-3.5/190# d9.15																									
1937	Phi A	1	0	1.000	3	1	1	0	12	10	4	0	0	10	9	3.00	157	.233	.377	4-0	.000	-1	185	3	0.1
KALLIO, RUDY Rudolph B 12.14.1892 Portland, OR D 4.6.1979 Newport, OR BR/TR 5-10/160# d4.25																									
1918	Det A	8	13	.381	30	22	10-2	0	181.1	178	91	0	1	76	70	3.62	73	.261	.336	56-4	.161	-1*	109	-20	-2.3
1919	Det A	0	0	—	12	1	0	1	22.1	28	15	0	1	8	3	5.64	57	.326	.389	4-0	.000	-1	147	-5	-0.3
1925	Bos A	1	4	.200	7	4	0	0	18.2	28	18	0	1	9	2	7.71	59	.364	.437	6-0	.333	0	97	-6	-0.9
Total	3	9	17	.346	49	27	10-2	1	222.1	234	124	0	3	93	75	4.17	69	.277	.351	66-4	.167	-1	111	-31	-3.5
KAMIENIECKI, SCOTT Scott Andrew B 4.19.1964 Mt.Clemens, MI BR/TR 6/195# d6.18																									
1991	NY A	4	4	.500	9	9	0	0-0	55.1	54	24	8	3	22-1	34	3.90	106	.256	.333	0-0	—	0	81	2	0.4
1992	NY A	6	14	.300	28	28	4	0-0	188	193	100	13	5	74-9	88	4.36	90	.269	.340	0-0	—	0	104	-9	-0.9
1993	NY A	10	7	.588	30	20	2	1-0	154.1	163	73	17	3	59-7	72	4.08	102	.277	.343	0-0	—	0	98	3	0.3
1994	NY A	8	6	.571	22	16	1	0-0	117.1	115	53	13	3	59-5	71	3.76	122	.261	.350	0-0	—	0	134	11	1.2
1995	†NY A	7	6	.538	17	16	1	0-0	89.2	83	43	8	3	49-1	43	4.01	115	.246	.346	0-0	—	0	100	6	0.7
1996	NY A	1	2	.333	7	5	0	0-1	22.2	36	30	6	2	19-1	15	11.12	44	.364	.475	0-0	—	0	135	-16	-1.5
1997	†Bal A	10	6	.625	30	30	0	0-0	179.1	179	83	20	4	67-2	109	4.01	110	.261	.328	2-0	.000	-0	99	9	0.8
1998	Bal A	2	6	.250	12	11	0	0-0	54.2	67	41	7	4	26-0	25	6.75	68	.313	.394	0-0	—	0	72	-13	-1.4
1999	Bal A	2	4	.333	43	3	0	2-0	56.1	52	32	4	4	29-2	39	4.95	95	.250	.348	0-0	—	0	86	-1	0.0
2000	Cle A	1	3	.250	26	0	0	0-0	33.1	42	22	6	1	20-5	29	5.67	88	.311	.404	0-0	—	0		-2	-0.2
	Atl N	2	1	.667	26	0	0	2-0	24.2	22	18	3	0	22-1	17	5.47	84	.239	.386	0-0	—	0		-3	-0.3
Total	10	53	59	.473	250	138	8	5-1	975.2	1006	519	105	32	446-34	542	4.52	97	.270	.351	2-0	.000	-0	102	-13	-0.9
KAMMEYER, BOB Robert Lynn B 12.2.1950 Kansas City, KS D 1.27.2003 Sacramento, CA BR/TR 6-4/210# d7.3																									
1978	NY A	0	0	—	7	0	0	0-0	21.2	24	15	1	2	6-0	11	5.82	62	.276	.327	0-0	—	0		-5	-0.2
1979	NY A	0	0	—	1	0	0	0-0	0	7	8	2	1	0-0	0	∞	—	1.000	1.000	0-0	—	0		-8	-0.6
Total	2	0	0	—	8	0	0	0-0	21.2	31	23	3	3	6-0	11	9.14	40	.330	.377	0-0	—	0		-13	-0.8
KAMP, IKE Alphonse Francis B 9.5.1900 Roxbury, MA D 2.25.1955 Boston, MA BB/TL 6/170# d9.16																									
1924	Bos N	0	1	.000	1	1	0	0	7	9	5	0	0	5	4	5.14	74	.360	.467	1-1	.000	-0	67	-1	-0.1
1925	Bos N	2	4	.333	24	4	1	0	58.1	68	38	0	0	35	20	5.09	79	.301	.395	12-1	.167	-0	116	-7	-0.6
Total	2	2	5	.286	25	5	1	0	65.1	77	43	0	0	40	24	5.10	78	.307	.402	13-2	.154	-0	106	-8	-0.7
KANE, HARRY Harry "Klondike" (b: Harry Cohen) B 7.27.1883 Hamburg, AR D 9.15.1932 Portland, OR BL/TL d8.8																									
1902	StL A	0	1	.000	4	1	1	0	23	34	21	2	0	16	7	5.48	64	.343	.435	9-0	.111	-1	82	-6	-0.4
1903	Det A	0	2	.000	3	3	2	0	18	26	22	0	1	8	10	8.50	34	.338	.407	7-0	.143	-0	106	-10	-0.9
1905	Phi N	1	1	.500	2	2	2-1	0	17	12	6	0	0	8	12	1.59	184	.203	.299	6-1	.167	-0	74	2	0.2
1906	Phi N	1	3	.250	6	3	2	0	28	28	16	0	3	18	14	3.86	68	.255	.374	8-1	.000	-1	74	-3	-0.5
Total	4	2	7	.222	15	9	7-1	0	86	100	65	2	4	50	43	4.81	62	.290	.386	30-2	.100	-2	83	-17	-1.6
KANTLEHNER, ERV Erving Leslie "Peanuts" B 7.31.1892 San Jose, CA D 2.3.1990 Santa Barbara, CA BL/TL 6/190# d4.17																									
1914	Pit N	3	2	.600	21	5	3-2	0	67	51	33	1	3	39	26	3.09	86	.218	.337	15-0	.067	-0	108	-5	-0.4
1915	Pit N	5	12	.294	29	18	10-1	3	163	135	60	1	4	58	64	2.26	121	.230	.304	52-1	.288	3	73	6	1.0
1916	Pit N	5	15	.250	34	21	7-2	2	165	151	72	1	4	57	49	3.16	85	.249	.317	46-0	.174	-0	64	-7	-0.8
	Phi N	0	0	—	3	0	0	0	4	7	4	0	0	3	2	9.00	29	.500	.588	0-0	—	0		-2	-0.1
	Year	5	15	.250	37	21	7-2	2	169	158	78	1	4	60	51	3.30	81	.254	.324	46-0	.174	-0	64	-10	-0.9
Total	3	13	29	.310	87	44	20-5	5	399	344	169	3	11	157	141	2.84	95	.239	.318	113-1	.212	2	72	-8	-0.3
KARCHNER, MATT Matthew Dean B 6.28.1967 Berwick, PA BR/TR 6-4/245# d7.18																									
1995	Chi A	4	2	.667	31	0	0	0-0	32	33	8	2	1	12-2	24	1.69	264	.275	.336	0-0	—	0		10	1.6
1996	Chi A	7	4	.636	50	0	0	1-8	59.1	61	42	10	2	41-8	46	5.76	82	.266	.377	0-0	—	0		-8	-1.2
1997	Chi A	3	1	.750	52	0	0	15-1	52.2	50	18	4	0	26-4	30	2.91	151	.258	.344	0-0	—	0		9	1.1
1998	Chi A	2	4	.333	32	0	0	11-4	36.2	33	21	2	5	19-6	30	5.15	88	.243	.348	0-0	—	0		-1	-0.3
	†Chi N	3	1	.750	29	0	0	0-3	28	30	18	6	2	14-2	22	5.14	86	.263	.354	0-0	—	0		-3	-0.3
1999	Chi N	1	0	1.000	16	0	0	0-1	18	16	5	3	2	9-0	9	2.50	181	.235	.342	0-0	—	0		4	0.2
2000	Chi N	1	1	.500	13	0	0	0-0	14.2	19	11	3	0	11-0	5	6.14	74	.311	.411	0-1	—	0		-3	-0.3
Total	6	21	13	.618	223	0	0	27-17	241.1	242	123	30	12	132-22	166	4.21	108	.262	.357	0-1	—	0		8	0.8
KARDOW, PAUL Paul Otto "Tex" B 9.19.1915 Humble, TX D 4.27.1968 San Antonio, TX BR/TR 6-6 /210# d7.1																									
1936	Cle A	0	0	—	2	0	0	0	2	1	1	0	0	2	0	4.50	112	.167	.375	0-0	—	0		0	0.0
KARGER, ED Edwin "Loose" B 5.6.1883 San Angelo, TX D 9.9.1957 Delta, CO BL/TL 5-11/185# d4.15																									
1906	Pit N	2	3	.400	6	2	0	0	28	21	11	0	2	9	8	1.93	139	.204	.281	11-0	.091	-1	95	1	0.3
	StL N	5	16	.238	25	20	17	1	191.2	193	85	0	7	43	73	2.72	97	.271	.319	73-0	.233	4	73	-5	0.0
	Year	7	19	.269	31	22	17	1	219.2	214	88	0	9	52	81	2.62	100	.263	.314	84-0	.214	3	75	-4	0.3
1907	StL N	15	19	.441	39	32	29-6	1	314	257	102	2	10	65	137	2.04	123	.223	.270	112-4	.179	1	65	17	2.4
1908	StL N	4	9	.308	22	15	9-1	0	141.1	148	77	1	2	50	34	3.06	77	.260	.322	54-0	.241	3*	70	-12	-0.8
1909	Cin N	1	3	.250	9	5	1	0	34.1	26	22	0	2	30	8	4.46	58	.217	.382	11-0	.273	2	156	-6	-0.5
	Bos A	5	2	.714	12	6	3	0	68	71	29	0	3	22	17	3.18	79	.273	.337	24-1	.125	-0	132	-3	-0.4
1910	Bos A	11	7	.611	27	25	16-1	1	183.1	162	75	5	5	53	81	3.19	80	.230	.289	68-3	.294	6	142	-6	-0.1
1911	Bos A	5	8	.385	25	18	6-1	0	131	134	70	4	4	42	57	3.37	97	.272	.334	47-2	.234	3	109	1	0.4
Total	6	48	67	.417	165	123	81-9	3	1091.2	1012	471	12	35	314	415	2.79	94	.246	.305	400-10	.220	18	99	-13	1.3
KARL, ANDY Anton Andrew B 4.8.1914 Mt.Vernon, NY D 4.8.1989 LaJolla, CA BR/TR 6-1.5/175# d4.24																									
1943	Bos A	1	1	.500	11	0	0	1	26	31	11	0	0	13	6	3.46	96	.310	.389	7-0	.286	0		0	0.1
	Phi N	1	2	.333	9	2	0	0	26.2	44	22	0	0	11	4	7.09	48	.383	.437	8-0	.250	1*	63	-10	-0.9
1944	Phi N	3	2	.600	38	0	0	2	89	76	32	1	1	21	26	2.33	155	.237	.287	15-0	.200	1*		**11**	0.7
1945	Phi N	8	8	.500	**67**	2	1	**15**	180.2	175	80	7	3	50	51	2.99	128	.253	.306	49-0	.143	-2	88	**15**	1.3
1946	Phi N	3	7	.300	39	0	0	5	65.1	84	37	6	1	22	15	4.96	69	.321	.375	10-2	.100	-0		-9	-1.5
1947	Bos N	2	3	.400	27	0	0	3	35	41	18	2	0	13	5	3.86	101	.318	.380	6-0	.167	-0		0	0.0

Year	Tm Lg	W	L	Pct	G	GS	CG-Sho	SV-BS	IP	H	R	HR	HB	BB-IB	SO	ERA	AERA	OAV	OOB	AB-SH	AVG	PB	Sup	APR	PW
Total	5	18	23	.439	191	4	1	26	422.2	451	200	16	5	130	107	3.51	104	.279	.334	95-2	.168	-0	75	7	-0.3
KARL, SCOTT Randall Scott B 8.9.1971 Fontana, CA BL/TL 6-2/195# d5.4																									
1995	Mil A	6	7	.462	25	18	1	0-0	124	141	65	10	3	50-6	59	4.14	121	.288	.356	0-0	—	0	93	10	0.9
1996	Mil A	13	9	.591	32	32	3-1	0-0	207.1	220	124	29	11	72-0	121	4.86	107	.271	.336	0-0	—	0	108	6	0.5
1997	Mil A	10	13	.435	32	32	1	0-0	193.1	212	103	23	4	67-1	119	4.47	103	.279	.339	4-0	.000	-0	79	5	0.5
1998	Mil N	10	11	.476	33	33	0	0-0	192.1	219	104	21	4	66-4	102	4.40	97	.290	.349	56-9	.071	-2*	88	-4	-0.5
1999	Mil N	11	11	.500	33	33	0	0-0	197.2	246	121	21	8	69-4	74	4.78	95	.312	.370	60-12	.183	3	90	-9	-0.4
2000	Col N	2	3	.400	17	9	0	0-0	65.2	95	56	14	3	33-3	29	7.68	76	.343	.415	14-2	.286	1	102	-10	-0.6
	Ana A	2	2	.500	6	4	0	0-0	21.2	31	21	2	0	12-0	9	6.65	76	.337	.413	0-0	—	0	83	-5	-0.8
Total	6	54	56	.491	178	161	5-1	0-0	1002	1164	594	120	33	369-18	513	4.81	99	.293	.356	134-23	.142	1	92	-7	-0.4
KARNS, BILL William Arthur B 12.28.1875 Richmond, IA D 11.15.1941 Seattle, WA BL/TL d8.14																									
1901	Bal A	1	0	1.000	3	1	1	0	17	30	18	0	0	9	5	6.35	61	.380	.443	7-1	.143	-1*	175	-4	-0.3
KARNUTH, JASON Jason Andre B 5.15.1976 LaGrange, IL BR/TR 6-2/190# d4.20																									
2001	StL N	0	0	—	4	0	0	0-0	5	6	1	1	1	4-0	1	1.80	237	.316	.458	0-0	—	0		1	0.1
KARP, RYAN Ryan Jason B 4.5.1970 Los Angeles, CA BL/TL 6-4/220# d6.23																									
1995	Phi N	0	0	—	1	0	0	0-0	2	1	1	0	0	3-0	2	4.50	94	.143	.400	0-0	—	0		0	0.0
1997	Phi N	1	1	.500	15	1	0	0-1	15	12	12	2	2	9-0	18	5.40	79	.218	.348	0-0	—	0	130	-3	-0.3
Total	2	1	1	.500	16	1	0	0-1	17	13	13	2	2	12-0	20	5.29	80	.210	.355	0-0	—	0	130	-3	-0.3
KARPEL, HERB Herbert "Lefty" B 12.27.1917 Brooklyn, NY D 1.24.1995 San Diego, CA BL/TL 5-9.5/180# d4.19																									
1946	NY A	0	0	—	2	0	0	0	1.2	4	2	0	0	0	0	10.80	32	.500	.500	0-0	—	0		-1	-0.1
KARR, BENN Benjamin Joyce "Baldy" B 11.28.1893 Mt.Pleasant, MS D 12.8.1968 Memphis, TN BL/TR 6/175# d4.20																									
1920	Bos A	3	8	.273	26	2	0	1	91.2	109	55	3	1	24	21	4.81	76	.304	.349	75-1	.280	6*	54	-11	-0.7
1921	Bos A	8	7	.533	26	7	5	0	117.2	123	53	8	1	38	37	3.67	115	.283	.342	62-4	.258	1*	96	8	1.0
1922	Bos A	5	12	.294	41	13	7	1	183.1	212	115	10	5	45	41	4.47	92	.302	.348	98-1	.214	-1*	107	-11	-1.0
1925	Cle A	11	12	.478	32	24	12-1	0	197.2	248	127	8	6	80	41	4.78	92	.317	.385	92-7	.261	4*	98	-9	-0.4
1926	Cle A	5	6	.455	30	7	4	1	113.1	137	72	9	6	41	23	5.00	81	.291	.355	45-1	.222	2*	119	-11	-0.7
1927	Cle A	3	3	.500	22	5	1	2	76.2	92	49	5	1	32	17	5.05	83	.315	.385	20-1	.200	1	87	-6	-0.3
Total	6	35	48	.422	177	58	29-1	5	780.1	921	471	43	20	260	180	4.60	90	.303	.362	392-15	.245	12	101	-40	-2.1
KARSAY, STEVE Stefan Andrew B 3.24.1972 Flushing, NY BR/TR 6-3/210# d8.17																									
1993	Oak A	3	3	.500	8	8	0	0-0	49	49	23	4	2	16-1	33	4.04	101	.258	.319	0-0	—	0	93	1	0.0
1994	Oak A	1	1	.500	4	4	1	0-0	28	26	8	1	1	8-0	15	2.57	172	.252	.310	0-0	—	0	125	7	0.4
1997	Oak A	3	12	.200	24	24	0	0-0	132.2	166	92	20	9	47-3	92	5.77	79	.304	.366	0-0	—	0*	83	-19	-1.8
1998	Cle A	0	2	.000	11	1	0	0-0	24.1	31	16	3	2	6-1	13	5.92	81	.310	.355	0-0	—	0	19	-2	-0.2
1999	†Cle A	10	2	.833	50	3	0	1-2	78.2	71	29	6	2	30-3	68	2.97	170	.247	.320	0-0	—	0	154	17	2.3
2000	Cle A	5	9	.357	72	0	0	20-9	76.2	79	33	5	3	25-4	66	3.76	132	.266	.327	1-0	.000	-0		11	2.0
2001	Cle A	0	1	.000	31	0	0	1-0	43.1	29	6	1	0	8-2	44	1.25	363	.188	.227	0-0	—	0		16	0.8
	†Atl N	3	4	.429	43	0	0	7-4	44.2	44	21	4	1	17-8	39	3.43	129	.265	.332	2-0	.000	-0		4	0.6
2002	†NY A	6	4	.600	78	0	0	12-4	88.1	87	33	7	2	30-14	65	3.26	134	.258	.320	1-0	.000	-0		12	1.6
Total	8	31	38	.449	321	40	1	41-19	565.2	582	261	51	22	187-36	435	3.88	118	.267	.328	4-0	.000	-0	91	47	5.7
KASHIWADA, TAKASHI Takashi B 5.14.1971 Tokyo, Japan BL/TL 5-11/165# d5.1																									
1997	NY N	3	1	.750	35	0	0	0-2	31.1	35	15	4	3	18-0	19	4.31	94	.289	.389	1-0	.000	-0		0	0.0
KATOLL, JACK John "Big Jack" B 6.24.1872 , Germany D 6.18.1955 Hartland, IL BR/TR 5-11/195# d9.9																									
1898	Chi N	0	1	.000	2	1	1	0	11	8	4	0	0	1	3	0.82	438	.200	.220	4-0	.000	-1	59	3	0.1
1899	Chi N	1	1	.500	2	2	2	0	18	17	15	0	1	4	1	6.00	62	.250	.301	7-0	.000	-1	125	-4	-0.4
1901	Chi A	11	10	.524	27	25	19	0	208	231	126	3	11	53	59	2.81	124	.278	.330	80-1	.125	-4	107	8	0.3
1902	Chi A	0	0	—	1	0	0	0	1	1	0	0	0	0	2	0.00	—	.250	.250	1-0	.000	-0		0	0.0
	Bal A	5	10	.333	15	13	13	0	123	175	106	5	2	32	25	4.02	94	.334	.375	57-0	.175	-0*	76	-12	-1.0
	Year	5	10	.333	16	13	13	0	124	176	110	5	2	32	27	3.99	94	.333	.374	58-0	.172	-0	76	-12	-1.0
Total	4	17	22	.436	47	41	35	0	361	432	251	8	14	90	90	3.32	109	.294	.341	149-1	.134	-6	97	-5	-1.0
KATZ, BOB Robert Clyde B 1.30.1911 Lancaster, PA D 12.14.1962 St.Joseph, MI BR/TR 5-11.5/190# d5.12																									
1944	Cin N	0	1	.000	6	2	0	0	18.1	17	9	0	0	7	4	3.93	89	.254	.324	4-0	.000	-1	60	-1	-0.1
KAUFMAN, CURT Curt Gerrard B 7.19.1957 Omaha, NE BR/TR 6-2/175# d9.10																									
1982	NY A	1	0	1.000	7	0	0	0-0	8.2	9	5	2	0	6-1	1	5.19	77	.265	.375	0-0	—	0		-1	-0.1
1983	NY A	0	0	—	4	0	0	0-0	8.2	10	3	0	0	4-0	8	3.12	125	.303	.359	0-0	—	0		1	0.0
1984	Cal A	2	3	.400	29	1	0	1-0	69	68	37	13	0	20-4	41	4.57	87	.254	.302	0-0	—	0	136	-4	-0.3
Total	3	3	3	.500	40	1	0	1-0	86.1	87	45	15	0	30-5	50	4.48	89	.260	.316	0-0	—	0	136	-4	-0.4
KAUFMANN, TONY Anthony Charles B 12.16.1900 Chicago, IL D 6.4.1982 Elgin, IL BR/TR 5-11/165# d9.23 C4 ▲																									
1921	Chi N	1	0	1.000	2	1	1	1	13	12	6	0	0	3	6	4.15	92	.240	.283	5-0	.400	1	280	0	0.1
1922	Chi N	7	13	.350	37	14	4-1	3	153	161	81	15	5	57	45	4.06	103	.273	.343	45-5	.200	1*	100	3	0.4
1923	Chi N	14	10	.583	33	24	18-2	3	206.1	209	97	14	11	67	72	3.10	129	.264	.330	74-2	.216	3	106	16	2.0
1924	Chi N	16	11	.593	34	26	16-3	0	208.1	218	104	21	4	66	79	4.02	97	.272	.330	76-0	.316	6*	95	0	0.5
1925	Chi N	13	13	.500	31	23	14-2	2	196	221	107	9	7	77	49	4.50	96	.292	.363	78-1	.192	1	97	-1	0.0
1926	Chi N	9	7	.563	26	22	14-1	2	169.2	169	71	6	6	44	52	3.02	127	.262	.316	60-2	.250	2*	103	14	1.4
1927	Chi N	3	3	.500	9	6	3	0	53.1	75	44	8	4	19	21	6.41	60	.338	.400	16-2	.313	3	125	-15	-1.1
	Phi N	0	3	.000	5	5	1	0	18.2	37	25	2	0	8	4	10.61	39	.425	.474	7-0	.143	0*	87	-13	-1.5
	StL N	0	0	—	1	0	0	0	0.1	4	3	0	0	1	0	81.00	5	1.000	1.000	0-0	—	0		-3	-0.1
	Year	3	6	.333	15	11	4	0	72.1	116	32	10	4	28	25	7.84	50	.371	.429	23-2	.261	3	108	-29	-2.7
1928	StL N	0	0	—	4	1	0	0	4.2	8	5	1	1	4	2	9.64	41	.444	.565	0-0	—	0*	85	-3	-0.1
1930	StL N	0	1	.000	2	1	0	0	10.1	15	9	2	0	4	2	7.84	64	.357	.413	3-0	.333	0	139	-3	-0.2
1931	StL N	1	1	.500	15	1	0	1	49	65	34	3	1	17	13	6.06	65	.319	.374	18-0	.111	-1*	131	-10	-0.6
1935	StL N	0	0	—	3	0	0	0	3.2	4	1	0	0	1	0	2.45	167	.286	.333	0-0	—	0*		1	0.0
Total	11	64	62	.508	202	124	71-9	12	1086.1	1198	587	81	39	368	345	4.18	97	.284	.347	382-12	.236	17	102	-14	0.8
KAYE, JUSTIN Justin Malcolm B 6.9.1976 Fort Lauderdale, FL BR/TR 6-4/195# d5.9																									
2002	Sea A	0	0	—	3	0	0	0-0	3	6	4	0	0	1-0	3	12.00	35	.429	.467	0-0	—	0		-3	-0.1
KEAGLE, GREG Gregory Charles B 6.28.1971 Corning, NY BR/TR 6-1/185# d4.1																									
1996	Det A	3	6	.333	26	6	0	0-0	87.2	104	76	13	9	68-5	70	7.39	68	.298	.418	0-0	—	0	79	-21	-1.8
1997	Det A	3	5	.375	11	10	0	0-0	45.1	58	33	9	5	18-0	33	6.55	70	.309	.382	1-0	.000	-0	90	-9	-1.3
1998	Det A	0	5	.000	9	7	0	0-0	38.2	46	26	5	4	20-0	25	5.59	85	.295	.389	0-0	—	0	84	-4	-0.4
Total	3	6	16	.273	46	23	0	0-0	171.2	208	135	27	18	106-5	128	6.76	72	.300	.402	1-0	.000	-0	84	-34	-3.5
KEALEY, STEVE Steven William B 5.13.1947 Torrance, CA BR/TR 6/185# d9.9																									
1968	Cal A	0	1	.000	6	0	0	0	10	10	3	0	0	5-2	4	2.70	108	.256	.341	0-0	—	0		0	0.0
1969	Cal A	2	0	1.000	15	3	1-1	0-0	36.2	48	18	4	1	13-1	17	3.93	89	.322	.380	9-0	.000	-1	110	-2	-0.2
1970	Cal A	1	0	1.000	17	0	0	1-0	21.2	19	11	2	0	6-2	14	4.15	87	.260	.305	4-0	.250	0		-1	-0.1
1971	Chi A	2	2	.500	54	1	0	6-0	77.1	69	40	10	0	26-6	50	3.84	94	.239	.299	10-1	.200	1	100	-2	-0.1
1972	Chi A	3	2	.600	40	0	0	4-2	57.1	50	21	4	0	12-1	37	3.30	95	.234	.273	3-0	.000	-0		0	-0.1
1973	Chi A	0	0	—	7	0	0	0-0	11.1	23	22	2	0	7-1	4	15.09	26	.418	.469	0-0	—	0		-14	-0.7
Total	6	8	5	.615	139	4	1-1	11-2	214.1	219	115	22	1	69-13	126	4.28	80	.267	.322	26-1	.115	-0	110	-19	-1.2
KEAS, ED Edward James B 2.2.1863 Dubuque, IA D 1.12.1940 Dubuque, IA d8.25																									
1888	Cle AA	3	3	.500	6	6	6	0	51	53	28	1	1	12	18	2.29	135	.259	.303	23	.087	-2	106	3	0.1

Year	Tm Lg	W	L	Pct	G	GS	CG-Sho	SV-BS	IP	H	R	HR	HB	BB-IB	SO	ERA	AERA	OAV	OOB	AB-SH	AVG	PB	Sup	APR	PW
KEATING, RAY Raymond Herbert B 7.21.1891 Bridgeport, CT D 12.28.1963 Sacramento, CA BR/TR 5-11/185# d9.12																									
1912	NY A	0	3	.000	6	5	3	0	35.2	36	27	0	1	18	21	5.80	62	.265	.355	16-0	.375	1	119	-6	-0.3
1913	NY A	6	12	.333	28	21	9-2	0	151.1	147	77	3	2	51	83	3.21	93	.256	.318	43-3	.070	-3	80	-5	-1.0
1914	NY A	8	11	.421	34	25	14	0	210	198	94	1	5	67	109	2.96	93	.253	.316	71-3	.169	-0*	102	-8	-0.5
1915	NY A	3	6	.333	11	10	8-1	0	79.1	66	41	3	3	45	37	3.63	81	.228	.337	26-0	.154	-1	109	-7	-0.7
1916	NY A	5	6	.455	14	11	6	0	91	91	42	4	2	37	35	3.07	94	.272	.349	29-1	.241	1	116	-3	-0.1
1918	NY A	2	2	.500	15	6	1	0	48.1	39	27	0	2	30	16	3.91	72	.238	.362	16-1	.188	-0	84	-6	-0.5
1919	Bos N	7	11	.389	22	14	9-1	0	136	129	61	2	2	45	48	2.98	96	.261	.325	46-3	.152	-1*	78	-4	-0.5
Total	7	31	51	.378	130	92	50-4	0	751.2	706	369	13	17	293	349	3.29	88	.254	.329	247-11	.170	-2	97	-39	-3.6
KEATING, BOB Robert M. B 9.22.1862 Springfield, MA D 1.19.1922 Springfield, MA BL/TL 6-4/190# d8.27																									
1887	Bal AA	0	1	.000	1	1	1	0	9	16	16	0	0	6	0	11.00	37	.372	.449	4	.250	-0	31	-7	-0.4
KECK, CACTUS Frank Joseph B 1.13.1899 St.Louis, MO D 2.6.1981 Kirkwood, MO BR/TR 5-11/170# d5.26																									
1922	Cin N	7	6	.538	27	15	5-1	1	131	138	71	4	5	29	27	3.37	119	.276	.322	44-3	.159	-1	105	5	0.1
1923	Cin N	3	6	.333	35	6	1	2	87	84	49	5	3	32	16	3.72	104	.254	.325	17-1	.059	-1	106	0	-0.1
Total	2	10	12	.455	62	21	6-1	3	218	222	120	9	8	61	43	3.51	112	.267	.323	61-4	.131	-2	106	5	0.0
KEEFE, DAVE David Edwin B 1.9.1897 Williston, VT D 2.4.1978 Kansas City, MO BL/TR 5-9/165# d4.21 Mil 1918 C10																									
1917	Phi A	1	0	1.000	3	0	0	0	5	5	4	0	0	4	1	1.80	153	.278	.409	1-0	.000	-0		0	-0.1
1919	Phi A	0	1	.000	1	1	1	0	9	8	4	0	0	3	5	4.00	86	.242	.306	3-0	.000	-0	46	0	-0.1
1920	Phi A	6	7	.462	31	13	7-1	0	130.1	129	60	2	6	30	41	2.97	136	.262	.313	40-1	.250	-0*	58	14	1.3
1921	Phi A	2	9	.182	44	12	4	1	173	214	126	19	5	64	68	4.68	95	.311	.374	57-0	.175	-3	94	-10	-0.9
1922	Cle A	0	0	—	18	1	0	0	36.1	47	30	2	0	12	11	6.19	65	.333	.386	6-0	.333	1	106	-9	-0.4
Total	5	9	17	.346	97	27	12-1	1	353.2	403	224	23	11	113	126	4.15	101	.294	.352	107-1	.206	-3	76	-5	-0.2
KEEFE, GEORGE George W. B 1.7.1867 Washington, DC D 8.24.1935 Washington, DC BL/TL 5-9/168# d7.30																									
1886	Was N	0	3	.000	4	4	4	0	31.1	28	22	0		15	5	5.17	62	.233	.319	14	.000	-2	109	-5	-0.6
1887	Was N	0	1	.000	1	1	1	0	8	16	20	1	2	4	0	9.00	45	.364	.440	3	.000	-1	16	-7	-0.5
1888	Was N	6	7	.462	13	13	13-1	0	114	87	55	2	4	43	52	2.84	98	.206	.286	42	.214	1	70	-1	0.2
1889	Was N	8	18	.308	30	27	24	0	230	266	182	6	4	143	90	5.13	77	.281	.378	98	.163	-2	84	-23	-2.2
1890	Buf P	6	16	.273	25	22	22	0	196	280	229	11	5	138	55	6.52	63	.321	.417	79	.203	1	87	-58	-4.2
1891	Was AA	0	3	.000	5	4	4	1	37	44	42	0	1	17	11	2.68	140	.286	.360	14	.143	-0	62	-3	-0.2
Total	6	20	48	.294	78	71	68-1	1	616.1	721	550	20	16	360	213	5.05	74	.282	.374	250	.172	-3	82	-97	-7.5
KEEFE, JOHN John Thomas B 5.5.1867 Fitchburg, MA D 8.9.1937 Fitchburg, MA TL d4.28																									
1890	Syr AA	17	24	.415	43	41	36-2	0	352.1	355	234	9	25	148	120	4.32	82	.254	.336	157	.191	-5	90	-34	-3.4
KEEFE, BOBBY Robert Francis B 6.16.1882 Folsom, CA D 12.6.1964 Sacramento, CA BR/TR 5-11/155# d4.15																									
1907	NY A	3	5	.375	19	3	0	3	57.2	60	18	1	1	20	20	2.50	112	.270	.333	19-0	.053	-2	32	3	0.4
1911	Cin N	12	13	.480	39	26	15	3	234.1	196	88	7	3	76	105	2.69	123	.229	.294	70-5	.086	-2	96	19	1.4
1912	Cin N	1	3	.250	17	6	0	2	68.2	78	52	0	4	33	29	5.24	64	.289	.375	18-2	.167	-1	65	-14	-0.8
Total	3	16	21	.432	75	35	15	8	360.2	334	158	8	8	129	154	3.14	103	.248	.317	107-7	.093	-5	86	8	1.0
KEEFE, TIM Timothy John "Smiling Tim" or "Sir Timothy" B 1.1.1857 Cambridge, MA D 4.23.1933 Cambridge, MA BR/TR 5-10.5/185# d8.6 U3 HF1964																									
1880	Tro N	6	6	.500	12	12	12	0	105	68	27	0		16	39	**0.86**	**294**	**.178**	**.212**	43	.233	-0	67	16	1.8
1881	Tro N	18	27	.400	45	45	45-4	0	403	434	241	4		83	103	3.24	91	.270	.305	152	.230	4*	87	-12	-0.7
1882	Tro N	17	26	.395	43	42	41-1	0	376	367	221	4		78	111	2.49	114	.243	.280	189	.228	5*	89	11	1.8
1883	NY AA	41	27	.603	**68**	**68**	**68**-5	0	**619**	488	244	6		108	**359**	2.41	138	**.203**	**.237**	259	.220	4*	83	61	6.0
1884	†NY AA	37	17	.685	58	58	56-4	0	483	380	196	5	15	71	334	2.25	138	**.204**	.239	210	.238	12*	112	46	5.5
1885	NY N	32	13	.711	46	46	45-7	0	400	300	154	6		102	227	**1.58**	**170**	.203	.255	166	.163	-1*	123	46	4.5
1886	NY N	**42**	20	.677	**64**	**64**	**62**-2	0	**535**	479	250	9		102	297	2.56	125	.231	.267	205	.171	1	119	39	3.8
1887	NY N	35	19	.648	56	56	54-2	0	476.2	428	260	11	11	108	189	3.12	121	**.230**	**.276**	191	.220	8	105	39	4.2
1888	†NY N	**35**	12	**.745**	51	51	48-**8**	0	434.1	317	140	5	12	90	**335**	**1.74**	**157**	**.196**	.243	181	.127	-6	108	**53**	4.7
1889	†NY N	28	13	.683	47	45	39-3	1	364	319	216	9	18	151	225	3.36	117	**.228**	.312	149	.154	-4	109	24	1.9
1890	NY P	17	11	.607	30	30	23-1	0	229	225	137	6	8	89	89	3.38	134	.246	.318	92	.109	-5	105	28	2.2
1891	NY N	2	5	.286	8	7	4	0	55	70	57	1	4	27	30	5.24	61	.299	.381	21	.095	-1	117	-13	-1.3
	Phi N	3	6	.333	11	10	9	1	78.1	82	55	2	4	30	34	3.91	87	.259	.331	29	.172	0	79	-5	-0.5
	Year	5	11	.313	19	17	13	1	133.1	152	60	3	8	57	64	4.45	75	.276	.353	50	.140	-1	94	-15	-1.8
1892	Phi N	19	16	.543	39	38	31-2	0	313.1	279	142	4	13	98	136	2.36	138	.229	.293	117	.085	-7	98	26	1.8
1893	Phi N	10	7	.588	22	22	17	0	178	202	131	3	13	80	56	4.40	104	.277	.359	79	.228	0	133	-1	-0.1
Total	14	342	225	.603	600	594	554-39	2	5049.2	4438	2471	75	98	1233	2564	2.63	125	.226	.275	2083	.187	11	104	358	35.6
KEEGAN, ED Edward Charles B 7.8.1939 Camden, NJ BR/TR 6-3/165# d8.24																									
1959	Phi N	0	3	.000	3	3	0	0	9	19	18	2	1	13-0	3	18.00	23	.432	.569	3-0	.000	-0	44	-12	-1.8
1961	KC A	0	0	—	6	0	0	1	6	6	5	0	0	5-0	3	4.50	93	.261	.393	0-0	—	0		-1	0.0
1962	Phi N	0	0	—	4	0	0	0	8	6	2	1	1	5-0	5	2.25	172	.214	.353	0-0	—	0*		2	0.1
Total	3	0	3	.000	13	3	0	1	23	31	25	3	2	23-0	11	9.00	45	.326	.467	3-0	.000	-0	44	-11	-1.7
KEEGAN, BOB Robert Charles "Smiley" B 8.4.1920 Rochester, NY D 6.20.2001 Rochester, NY BR/TR 6-2.5/207# d5.24																									
1953	Chi A	7	5	.583	22	11	4-2	1	98.2	80	34	4	2	33	32	2.74	147	.223	.293	28-2	.321	2	96	14	1.8
1954	Chi A★	16	9	.640	31	27	14-2	2	209.2	211	84	16	1	82	61	3.09	121	.266	.334	75-1	.120	-2*	114	13	1.2
1955	Chi A	2	5	.286	18	11	1	0	58.2	83	39	4	1	28-1	29	5.83	68	.336	.400	18-2	.333	2	102	-11	-1.0
1956	Chi A	5	7	.417	20	16	4	0	105.1	119	56	15	2	35-2	32	3.93	104	.286	.342	32-4	.125	-1	100	0	-0.2
1957	Chi A	10	8	.556	30	20	6-2	2	142.2	131	62	22	2	37-2	36	3.53	106	.243	.292	39-10	.103	-1	106	3	0.1
1958	Chi A	0	2	.000	14	2	0	0	29.2	44	25	9	0	18-4	8	6.07	60	.358	.437	4-1	.000	-1	124	-10	-0.6
Total	6	40	36	.526	135	87	29-6	5	644.2	668	300	70	8	233-9	198	3.66	105	.270	.332	196-20	.163	-2	106	9	1.3
KEELEY, BURT Burton Elwood "Speed" B 11.2.1879 Wilmington, IL D 5.3.1952 Ely, MN BR/TR 5-9/170# d4.18																									
1908	Was A	6	11	.353	28	15	12-1	1	169	173	87	3	4	48	68	2.98	77	.259	.313	49-6	.102	-3*	102	-15	-1.8
1909	Was A	0	0	—	2	0	0	0	7	12	13	0	1	1	0	11.57	21	.364	.400	2-0	.500	0		-7	-0.3
Total	2	6	11	.353	30	15	12-1	1	176	185	100	3	5	49	68	3.32	69	.264	.317	51-6	.118	-3	102	-22	-2.1
KEEN, VIC Howard Victor B 3.16.1899 Bel Air, MD D 12.10.1976 Salisbury, MD BR/TR 5-9/165# d8.13																									
1918	Phi A	0	1	.000	1	1	0	0	8	9	3	1	0	1	1	3.38	87	.300	.323	1-1	.000	-0	77	0	0.0
1921	Chi N	0	3	.000	5	4	1	0	25	29	17	0	1	9	9	4.68	82	.319	.386	5-1	.000	-0	59	-3	-0.4
1922	Chi N	1	2	.333	7	2	2	1	34.2	36	20	4	1	10	11	3.89	108	.275	.331	12-1	.333	1	78	0	0.1
1923	Chi N	12	8	.600	35	17	10	1	177	169	70	8	5	57	46	3.00	133	.255	.319	53-8	.151	-3	85	20	1.7
1924	Chi N	15	14	.517	40	28	15	3	234.2	242	112	17	4	80	75	3.80	103	.272	.335	77-4	.156	-4	89	5	0.0
1925	Chi N	2	6	.250	30	8	1	1	83.1	125	61	8	0	41	19	6.26	69	.359	.427	25-1	.240	0	115	-15	-1.2
1926	†StL N	10	9	.526	26	21	12-1	0	152	179	89	15	1	42	29	4.56	86	.295	.342	53-2	.057	-6	110	-10	-1.7
1927	StL N	2	1	.667	21	0	0	0	33.2	39	21	3	2	8	12	4.81	82	.293	.343	4-0	.250	0		-3	-0.2
Total	8	42	44	.488	165	81	41-1	6	748.1	828	393	56	14	248	202	4.11	97	.287	.346	230-18	.148	-12	94	-6	-1.7
KEENAN, KID Harry Leon B 1875 Louisville, KY D 6.11.1903 Covington, KY TR 5-2/?# d8.11																									
1891	Cin AA	0	1	.000	1	1	1	0	8	6	9	0	1	4	5	0.00	—	.200	.314	4	.500	0	46	1	0.2
KEENAN, JIM James William B 2.10.1858 New Haven, CT D 9.21.1926 Cincinnati, OH BR/TR 5-10/186# d5.17.1875 ▲																									
1884	Ind AA	0	0	—	1	0	0	0	3	2	1	0	0	0	0	3.00	110	.182	.182	249	.293	0*		0	0.0
1885	Cin AA	0	0	—	1	0	0	0	8	7	2	0	0	1	0	1.13	290	.233	.258	132	.265	0*		2	0.1
1886	Cin AA	0	1	.000	2	0	0	0	8	8	5	0	0	3	2	3.38	104	.258	.324	148	.270	0*		0	0.0
Total	3	0	1	.000	4	0	0	0	19	17	8	0	0	4	2	2.37	142	.236	.276	529	.280	1		2	0.1
KEENAN, JIMMIE James William "Sparkplug" B 5.25.1898 Avon, NY D 6.5.1980 Seminole, FL BL/TL 5-7/155# d9.9																									
1920	Phi N	0	0	—	1	0	0	0	3	3	1	0	0	1	2	3.00	114	.333	.400	1-0	.000	-0		0	0.0
1921	Phi N	1	2	.333	15	2	0	0	32.1	48	31	3	1	15	7	6.68	63	.364	.432	9-0	.000	-1	29	-7	-0.7

Year	Tm Lg	W	L	Pct	G	GS	CG-Sho	SV-BS	IP	H	R	HR	HB	BB-IB	SO	ERA	AERA	OAV	OOB	AB-SH	AVG	PB	Sup	APR	PW
Total	2	1	2	.333	16	2	0	0	35.1	51	32	3	1	16	9	6.37	65	.362	.430	10-0	.000	-2	29	-7	-0.7
KEENER, JEFF Jeffrey Bruce B 1.14.1959 Pana, IL BL/TR 6/170# d6.8																									
1982	StL N	1	1	.500	19	0	0	0-0	22.1	19	8	1	0	19-4	25	1.61	225	.235	.373	0-0	—	0		3	0.3
1983	StL N	0	0	—	4	0	0	0-0	4.1	6	4	0	1	1-0	4	8.31	44	.333	.381	0-0	—	0		-2	-0.1
Total	2	1	1	.500	23	0	0	0-0	26.2	25	12	1	1	20-4	29	2.70	134	.253	.374	0-0	—	0		1	0.2
KEENER, JOE Joseph Donald B 4.21.1953 San Pedro, CA BR/TR 6-4/200# d9.18																									
1976	Mon N	0	1	.000	2	2	0	0-0	4.1	7	7	0	1	8-0	1	10.38	36	.389	.593	1-1	.000	-0	95	-4	-0.6
KEENER, HARRY Joshua Harry "Beans" B 9.1869 Easton, PA D 3.5.1912 Easton, PA TR d6.27																									
1896	Phi N	3	11	.214	16	13	11	0	113.1	144	102	5	9	39	28	5.88	73	.307	.371	51-0	.314	2	94	-20	-1.6
KEETON, RICKEY Rickey B 3.18.1957 Cincinnati, OH BR/TR 6-2/190# d5.27																									
1980	Mil A	2	2	.500	5	5	0	0-0	28.1	35	15	4	0	9-0	8	4.76	81	.307	.352	0-0	—	0	97	-2	-0.2
1981	Mil A	1	0	1.000	17	0	0	0-0	35.1	47	21	4	0	11-4	9	5.09	67	.329	.374	0-0	—	0		-7	-0.3
Total	2	3	2	.600	22	5	0	0-0	63.2	82	36	8	0	20-4	17	4.95	73	.319	.364	0-0	—	0	97	-9	-0.5
KEFFER, FRANK Frank B Harrisburg, PA d4.19																									
1890	Syr AA	1	1	.500	2	1	1	0	16	15	13	0	0	9	4	5.63	63	.242	.338	7	.143	-1	76	-4	-0.4
KEHN, CHET Chester Lawrence B 10.30.1921 San Diego, CA D 4.5.1984 San Diego, CA BR/TR 5-11/168# d4.30 Mil 1943-45																									
1942	Bro N	0	0	—	3	1	0	0	7.2	8	6	2	0	4	3	7.04	46	.267	.353	2-0	1.000	1	283	-3	0.0
KEIFER, KATSY Sherman Carl B 9.3.1891 California, PA D 2.19.1927 Outwood, KY BB/TL d10.8																									
1914	Ind F	1	0	1.000	1	1	1	0	9	6	2	0	0	2	2	2.00	156	.194	.242	3-0	.333	0	88	1	0.2
KEISLER, RANDY Randy Dean B 2.24.1976 Richards, TX BL/TL 6-3/190# d9.10																									
2000	NY A	1	0	1.000	4	1	0	0-0	10.2	16	14	1	0	8-0	6	11.81	41	.364	.462	0-0	—	0	116	-8	-0.6
2001	NY A	1	2	.333	10	10	0	0-0	50.2	52	36	12	0	34-0	36	6.22	72	.259	.364	2-0	.000	-0	140	-9	-0.5
2003	SD N	0	1	.000	2	2	0	0-0	6	7	9	3	1	7-0	5	12.00	33	.292	.455	2-0	.000	-0*	119	-6	-0.7
Total	3	2	3	.400	16	13	0	0-0	67.1	75	59	16	1	49-0	47	7.62	59	.279	.389	4-0	.000	-0	133	-23	-1.8
KEKICH, MIKE Michael Dennis B 4.2.1945 San Diego, CA BR/TL 6-1/200# d6.9																									
1965	LA N	0	1	.000	5	1	0	0	10.1	10	12	2	0	13-0	9	9.58	34	.263	.451	2-1	.000	-0	80	-8	-0.7
1968	LA N	2	10	.167	25	20	1-1	0	115	116	54	9	1	46-0	84	3.91	71	.267	.336	37-2	.081	-2	78	-14	-1.6
1969	NY A	4	6	.400	28	13	1	1-0	105	91	58	11	2	49-5	66	4.54	77	.236	.323	27-3	.111	-1	72	-12	-1.2
1970	NY A	6	3	.667	26	14	1	0-0	98.2	103	59	12	1	55-3	63	4.83	73	.267	.358	32-2	.094	-1	110	-14	-1.4
1971	NY A	10	9	.526	37	24	3	0-0	170.1	167	89	13	4	82-11	93	4.07	80	.257	.341	52-8	.154	-0	118	-17	-1.7
1972	NY A	10	13	.435	29	28	2	0-0	175.1	172	77	13	4	76-5	78	3.70	80	.263	.343	59-6	.136	-1	107	-13	-1.8
1973	NY A	1	1	.500	5	4	0	0-0	14.2	20	15	1	2	14-0	4	9.20	40	.351	.486	0-0	—	0	146	-8	-0.9
	Cle A	1	4	.200	16	6	0	0-0	50	73	47	6	0	35-0	26	7.02	56	.349	.437	0-0	—	0*	83	-18	-1.7
	Year	2	5	.286	21	10	0	0-0	64.2	93	51	7	2	49-0	30	7.52	51	.350	.449	0-0	—	0	106	-27	-2.6
1975	Tex A	0	0	—	23	0	0	2-2	31.1	33	16	2	0	21-2	19	3.73	101	.282	.388	0-0	—	0		0	0.0
1977	Sea A	5	4	.556	41	2	0	3-1	90	90	58	11	3	51-3	55	5.60	74	.265	.363	0-0	—	0	22	-13	-1.2
Total	9	39	51	.433	235	112	8-1	6-3	860.2	875	485	80	17	442-29	497	4.59	73	.268	.355	209-22	.120	-5	95	-117	-12.2
KELB, GEORGE George Francis "Pugger" or "Lefty" B 7.17.1870 Toledo, OH D 10.20.1936 Toledo, OH BL/TL d4.17																									
1898	Cle N	0	1	.000	3	1	1	0	16.1	23	17	0	4	1	8	4.41	82	.329	.373	5-0	.200	-0	20	-3	-0.2
KELLEHER, HAL Harold Joseph B 6.24.1913 Philadelphia, PA D 8.27.1989 Cape May Court House, NJ BR/TR 6/165# d9.17																									
1935	Phi N	2	0	1.000	3	3	2-1	0	25	26	7	0	1	12	12	1.80	252	.260	.345	8-0	.375	1	56	6	0.6
1936	Phi N	0	5	.000	14	4	1	0	44	60	38	2	3	29	13	5.32	85	.331	.432	12-0	.167	-0	33	-5	-0.6
1937	Phi N	2	4	.333	27	2	1	0	58.1	72	51	3	7	31	20	6.63	65	.308	.404	17-0	.176	-0*	20	-15	-1.3
1938	Phi N	0	0	—	6	0	0	0	7.1	16	15	0	0	9	4	18.41	21	.432	.543	2-0	.500	0		-11	-0.5
Total	4	4	9	.308	50	9	4-1	0	134.2	174	111	5	11	81	49	5.95	74	.315	.413	39-0	.231	0	39	-25	-1.8
KELLER, KRIS Kristopher Shane B 3.1.1978 Williamsport, PA BR/TR 6-2/225# d5.24																									
2002	Det A	0	0	—	1	0	0	0-0	1	2	3	1	0	3-0	1	27.00	16	.400	.625	0-0	—	0		-2	-0.1
KELLER, RON Ronald Lee B 6.3.1943 Indianapolis, IN BR/TR 6-2/200# d7.9 Mil 1968																									
1966	Min A	0	0	—	2	0	0	0	5.1	7	4	1	0	1-0	1	5.06	71	.318	.348	1-0	.000	-0*		-1	-0.1
1968	Min A	0	1	.000	7	1	0	0	16	18	6	2	1	4-1	11	2.81	110	.305	.354	1-0	.000	-0*	28	0	0.0
Total	2	0	1	.000	9	1	0	0	21.1	25	10	3	1	5-1	12	3.38	95	.309	.352	2-0	.000	-0	28	-1	-0.1
KELLETT, AL Alfred Henry B 10.30.1901 Red Bank, NJ D 7.14.1960 New York, NY BR/TR 6-3/200# d6.29																									
1923	Phi A	0	1	.000	5	0	0	0	10	11	9	0	0	8	1	6.30	65	.282	.404	3-0	.333	0		-3	-0.2
1924	Bos A	0	0	—	1	0	0	0	0	0	2	0	0	2	0	∞	—	—	1.000	0-0	—	0		-2	-0.2
Total	2	0	1	.000	6	0	0	0	10	11	11	0	0	10	1	8.10	51	.282	.429	3-0	.333	0		-5	-0.4
KELLEY, HARRY Harry Leroy B 2.13.1906 Parkin, AR D 3.23.1958 Parkin, AR BR/TR 5-9.5/170# d4.16																									
1925	Was A	1	1	.500	6	1	0	0	16	30	23	0	0	12	7	9.00	47	.405	.488	4-0	.000	-1	40	-10	-1.0
1926	Was A	0	0	—	7	1	0	0	10	17	10	0	1	8	6	8.10	48	.405	.510	1-0	.000	-0	131	-5	-0.2
1936	Phi A	15	12	.556	35	27	20-1	3	235.1	250	112	21	2	75	82	3.86	132	.275	.332	91-7	.198	-1*	91	34	3.1
1937	Phi A	13	21	.382	41	29	14	0	205	267	154	16	3	79	68	5.36	88	.306	.365	71-1	.225	1	78	-18	-2.3
1938	Phi A	0	2	.000	4	3	0	0	8	17	16	0	0	10	3	16.88	29	.436	.551	2-0	.000	-0	67	-10	-1.5
	Was A	9	8	.529	38	14	7-2	1	148.1	162	90	12	1	46	44	4.49	100	.276	.330	48-1	.250	1	103	-1	0.0
	Year	9	10	.474	42	17	7-2	1	156.1	179	95	12	1	56	47	5.12	88	.286	.346	50-1	.240	1	97	-13	-1.5
1939	Was A	4	3	.571	15	3	2	1	53.2	69	32	2	3	14	20	4.70	93	.314	.363	15-2	.267	1	88	-2	-0.2
Total	6	42	47	.472	146	78	43-3	5	676.1	812	437	51	10	244	230	4.86	98	.296	.356	232-11	.216	0	88	-12	-2.1
KELLEY, DICK Richard Anthony B 1.8.1940 Boston, MA D 12.11.1991 Northridge, CA BR/TL 6/175# d4.15																									
1964	Mil N	0	0	—	2	0	0	0	2	2	4	0	0	3-0	2	18.00	20	.250	.455	0-0	—	0		-3	-0.2
1965	Mil N	1	1	.500	21	4	0	0	45	37	15	5	0	20-2	31	3.00	117	.226	.310	8-0	.000	-1*	81	3	0.1
1966	Atl N	7	5	.583	20	13	2-2	0	81	75	36	6	3	21-2	50	3.22	113	.247	.301	28-1	.036	-3	112	2	0.0
1967	Atl N	2	9	.182	39	9	1-1	2	98	88	48	8	1	42-7	75	3.77	88	.247	.324	16-2	.250	1	85	-5	-0.4
1968	Atl N	2	4	.333	31	11	1-1	1	98	86	36	4	1	45-2	73	2.76	109	.238	.323	23-1	.043	-1	63	2	0.1
1969	SD N	4	8	.333	27	23	1-1	0-1	136	113	60	11	5	61-8	96	3.57	99	.230	.320	47-1	.106	-2	76	0	-0.1
1971	SD N	2	3	.400	48	1	0	2-3	59.2	52	26	5	4	23-5	42	3.47	95	.232	.312	3-0	.333	0	215	-1	0.0
Total	7	18	30	.375	188	61	5-5	5-4	519.2	453	225	39	14	215-26	369	3.39	100	.237	.317	125-5	.096	-5	87	-2	-0.5
KELLEY, TOM Thomas Henry B 1.5.1944 Manchester, CT BR/TR 6/191# d5.5																									
1964	Cle A	0	0	—	6	0	0	0	9.2	9	9	1	1	9-2	7	5.59	64	.237	.396	0-0	—	0		-3	-0.2
1965	Cle A	2	1	.667	4	4	1	0	30	19	8	3	0	13-0	31	2.40	145	.186	.278	9-1	.222	0	95	4	0.5
1966	Cle A	4	8	.333	31	7	1	0	95.1	97	55	14	0	42-1	64	4.34	79	.264	.336	28-0	.143	-1	92	-11	-1.5
1967	Cle A	0	0	—	1	0	0	0	1	0	0	0	0	2-0	0	0.00	—	.000	.500	0-0	—	0		0	0.0
1971	Atl N	9	5	.643	28	20	5	0-0	143	140	56	8	1	69-6	68	2.96	126	.262	.347	43-2	.047	-4	94	10	0.5
1972	Atl N	5	7	.417	27	14	2-1	0-1	116.1	122	65	12	0	65-4	59	4.56	83	.272	.363	34-2	.088	-2	98	-9	-1.2
1973	Atl N	0	1	.000	7	0	0	0-0	12.2	13	5	0	0	7-3	5	2.84	139	.289	.370	2-0	.000	-0		1	0.0
Total	7	20	22	.476	104	45	9-1	0-1	408	400	198	38	2	207-16	234	3.75	98	.260	.347	116-5	.095	-6	96	-8	-1.9
KELLNER, ALEX Alexander Raymond B 8.26.1924 Tucson, AZ D 5.3.1996 Tucson, AZ BR/TL 6/200# d4.29 b-Walt																									
1948	Phi A	0	0	—	13	1	0	0	23	21	20	0	2	16	14	7.83	55	.239	.368	5-0	.000	-1	211	-8	-0.5
1949	Phi A☆	20	12	.625	38	27	19	1	245	243	120	18	2	129	94	3.75	110	.261	.352	92-4	.217	1	120	8	1.1
1950	Phi A	8	20	.286	36	29	15	2	225.1	253	157	28	2	112	85	5.47	83	.282	.363	80-0	.200	-1	78	-25	-2.8
1951	Phi A	11	14	.440	33	29	11-1	2	209.2	218	118	20	4	93	94	4.46	96	.272	.350	79-2	.228	-1	97	-6	-0.7
1952	Phi A	12	14	.462	34	33	14-2	0	231.1	223	124	21	4	86	105	4.36	91	.252	.321	82-4	.207	0	100	-8	-0.9
1953	Phi A	11	12	.478	25	25	14-2	0	201.2	210	98	8	4	51	81	3.93	109	.269	.317	69-5	.217	1	81	7	0.7

Year	Tm Lg	W	L	Pct	G	GS	CG-Sho	SV-BS	IP	H	R	HR	HB	BB-IB	SO	ERA	AERA	OAV	OOB	AB-SH	AVG	PB	Sup	APR	PW
1954	Phi A	6	17	.261	27	27	8-1	0	173.2	204	118	16	6	88	69	5.39	72	.301	.381	55-5	.182	-0	70	-28	-3.2
1955	KC A	11	8	.579	30	24	6-3	0	162.2	164	81	18	5	60-2	75	4.20	99	.265	.332	56-2	.214	2	87	1	0.3
1956	KC A	7	4	.636	20	17	5	0	91.2	103	49	15	2	33-3	44	4.32	100	.289	.351	30-3	.200	-0*	76	0	0.0
1957	KC A	6	5	.545	28	21	3	0	132.2	141	65	18	2	41-3	72	4.27	93	.278	.332	47-1	.234	4	98	-2	0.3
1958	KC A	0	2	.000	7	6	0	0	33.2	40	24	5	0	8-0	22	5.88	66	.315	.353	11-2	.091	-0*	84	-7	-0.4
	Cin N	7	3	.700	18	7	4	0	82	74	24	8	3	20-1	42	2.30	180	.243	.294	28-0	.357	3	93	15	2.0
1959	StL N	2	1	.667	12	4	0	0	37	31	17	9	1	10-2	19	3.16	134	.220	.275	9-0	.222	0	95	3	0.2
Total	12	101	112	.474	321	250	99-9	5	1849.1	1925	1015	184	37	747-11	816	4.41	95	.270	.342	643-28	.215	7	90	-50	-3.9
KELLNER, WALT Walter Joseph B 4.26.1929 Tucson, AZ BR/TR 6/200# d9.6 b-Alex																									
1952	Phi A	0	0	—	1	0	0	0	4	4	3	0	0	3	2	6.75	59	.250	.368	1-0	.000	-0		-1	-0.1
1953	Phi A	0	0	—	2	0	0	0	3	1	2	0	1	4	4	6.00	71	.111	.429	0-0	—	0		0	0.0
Total	2	0	0	—	3	0	0	0	7	5	5	0	1	7	6	6.43	64	.200	.394	1-0	.000	-0		-1	-0.1
KELLOGG, AL Albert C. B 9.9.1886 Providence, RI D 7.21.1953 Portland, OR TL 6-3/208# d9.25																									
1908	Phi A	0	2	.000	3	3	2	0	17	20	19	1	1	9	8	5.82	44	.294	.385	8-0	.125	-0	89	-7	-0.7
KELLUM, WIN Winford Ansley B 4.11.1876 Waterford, ON, CAN D 8.10.1951 Big Rapids, MI BB/TL 5-10/190# d4.26																									
1901	Bos A	2	3	.400	6	6	5	0	48	61	42	3	3	7	8	6.38	55	.305	.338	18-0	.167	-1	124	-13	-1.0
1904	Cin N	15	10	.600	31	24	22-1	2	224.2	206	98	1	10	46	70	2.60	113	.244	.291	82-3	.159	2*	135	7	1.0
1905	StL N	3	3	.500	11	7	5-1	0	74	70	30	1	1	10	19	2.92	102	.255	.283	25-1	.200	1	132	1	0.3
Total	3	20	16	.556	48	37	32-2	2	346.2	337	170	5	14	63	97	3.19	95	.255	.297	125-4	.168	2	133	-5	0.3
KELLY, BRYAN Bryan Keith B 2.24.1959 Silver Spring, MD BR/TR 6-2/195# d9.2																									
1986	Det A	1	2	.333	6	4	0	0-0	20	21	11	4	0	10-1	18	4.50	92	.269	.352	0-0	—	0	126	-1	-0.1
1987	Det A	0	1	.000	5	0	0	0-0	10.2	12	6	2	0	7-4	10	5.06	84	.286	.388	0-0	—	0		-1	-0.1
Total	2	1	3	.250	11	4	0	0-0	30.2	33	17	6	0	17-5	28	4.70	89	.275	.365	0-0	—	0	126	-2	-0.2
KELLY, ED Edward Leo B 12.10.1888 Pawtucket, RI D 11.4.1928 Red Lodge, MT BR/TR 5-11.5/173# d4.14																									
1914	Bos A	0	0	—	3	0	0	0	2.1	1	1	0	0	1	4	0.00	—	.100	.182	1-0	.000	-0		0	0.0
KELLY, HERB Herbert Barrett "Moke" B 6.4.1892 Mobile, AL D 5.18.1973 Torrance, CA BL/TL 5-9/160# d9.25																									
1914	Pit N	0	2	.000	5	2	2	0	25.2	24	11	0	0	7	6	2.45	108	.253	.304	9-0	.222	0	40	0	0.0
1915	Pit N	1	1	.500	5	1	0	0	11	10	9	0	1	4	6	4.09	67	.250	.333	2-0	.500	1	54	-3	-0.3
Total	2	1	3	.250	10	3	2	0	36.2	34	20	0	1	11	12	2.95	91	.252	.313	11-0	.273	1	45	-3	-0.3
KELLY, MIKE Michael J. B 11.9.1902 St.Louis, MO BR/TR 6-1/178# d9.3																									
1926	Phi N	0	0	—	4	0	0	0	6.2	9	7	0	1	4	2	9.45	44	.346	.452	3-0	.000	-0		-3	-0.2
KELLY, KING Michael Joseph B 12.31.1857 Troy, NY D 11.8.1894 Boston, MA BR/TR 5-10/170# d5.1.1878 M3 HF1945 ▲																									
1880	Chi N	0	0	—	1	0	0	0	3	3	2	0		1	1	0.00	—	.250	.308	344	.291	0*		0	0.0
1883	Chi N	0	0	—	1	0	0	0	1	1	0	0		0	0	0.00	—	.333	.333	428	.255	0*		0	0.0
1884	Chi N	0	1	.000	2	0	0	0	5.1	12	11	2		2	1	8.44	37	.400	.438	452	.354	1*		-3	-0.4
1887	Bos N	1	0	1.000	3	0	0	0	13	17	16	1	0	14	0	3.46	118	.298	.437	484	.322	1*		-2	-0.1
1890	Bos P	1	0	1.000	1	0	0	0	2	1	1	0	0	2	2	4.50	98	.143	.333	340	.326	0*		0	0.0
1891	Cin AA	0	1	.000	3	0	0	0	15.1	21	15	2	1	7	0	5.28	77	.313	.387	283	.297	1*		-1	0.0
1892	†Bos N	0	0	—	1	0	0	0	6	8	4	0	3	4	0	1.50	234	.308	.455	281	.189	0*		0	0.0
Total	7	2	2	.500	12	0	0	0	45.2	63	49	5	4	30	4	4.14	92	.312	.411	2612	.296	4		-6	-0.5
KELLY, REN Reynolds Joseph B 11.18.1899 San Francisco, CA D 8.24.1963 Millbrae, CA BR/TR 6/183# d9.18 b-George																									
1923	Phi A	0	0	—	1	0	0	0	7	7	3	0	0	4	1	2.57	160	.259	.355	3-0	.000	-0		1	0.0
KELLY, BOB Robert Edward B 10.4.1927 Cleveland, OH BR/TR 6/180# d5.4																									
1951	Chi N	7	4	.636	35	11	4	0	123.2	130	70	8	1	55	48	4.66	88	.275	.352	31-3	.161	-1	106	-7	-0.6
1952	Chi N	4	9	.308	31	15	3-2	0	125.1	114	62	7	3	46	50	3.59	107	.236	.306	37-1	.216	0	99	1	0.2
1953	Chi N	0	1	.000	14	0	0	0	17	27	19	2	1	9	6	9.53	47	.375	.451	1-0	.000	-0		-8	-0.4
	Cin N	1	2	.333	28	5	0	2	66.1	71	36	7	0	26	29	4.34	100	.276	.343	17-1	.118	-1	131	0	-0.1
	Year	1	3	.250	42	5	0	2	83.1	98	42	9	1	35	35	5.40	81	.298	.367	18-1	.111	-1	131	-9	-0.5
1958	Cin N	0	0	—	2	1	0	0	2	3	1	0	0	3-1	1	4.50	92	.500	.667	0-0	—	0	87	0	0.0
	Cle A	0	2	.000	13	3	0	0	27.2	29	18	4	1	13-0	12	5.20	70	.282	.368	4-0	.250	0	115	-5	-0.3
Total	4	12	18	.400	123	35	7-2	2	362	374	206	28	6	152-1	146	4.50	90	.268	.343	90-5	.178	-1	106	-19	-1.2
KELSO, BILL William Eugene B 2.19.1940 Kansas City, MO BR/TR 6-4/215# d7.31																									
1964	LA A	2	0	1.000	10	1	1-1	0	23.2	19	6	3	1	9-0	21	2.28	144	.218	.299	6-0	.000	-0	54	3	0.2
1966	Cal A	1	1	.500	5	0	0	0	11.1	11	3	1	1	6-1	11	2.38	141	.244	.346	1-0	.000	-0		1	0.2
1967	Cal A	5	3	.625	69	1	0	11	112	85	41	6	4	63-10	91	2.97	106	.219	.329	19-2	.105	-1	28	3	0.2
1968	Cin N	4	1	.800	35	0	0	1	54	56	26	6	3	15-5	39	4.00	79	.277	.325	8-0	.000	-1		-4	-0.6
Total	4	12	5	.706	119	2	1-1	12	201	171	76	16	9	93-16	162	3.13	102	.237	.325	34-2	.059	-2	41	3	0.0
KEMMERER, RUSS Russell Paul "Rusty" or "Dutch" B 11.1.1931 Pittsburgh, PA BR/TR 6-3/200# d6.27																									
1954	Bos A	5	3	.625	19	9	2-1	0	75.1	71	35	4	2	41	37	3.82	108	.257	.352	21-2	.143	-0	79	3	0.3
1955	Bos A	1	1	.500	7	2	0	0	17.1	18	14	3	0	15-1	13	7.27	59	.269	.402	3-0	.000	-0	145	-5	-0.5
1957	Bos A	0	0	—	1	0	0	0	4	5	2	0	0	2-1	1	4.50	89	.333	.389	1-0	.000	-0		0	0.0
	Was A	7	11	.389	39	26	6	0	172.1	214	110	20	2	71-4	81	4.96	79	.309	.373	45-7	.067	-1	122	-23	-2.3
	Year	7	11	.389	40	26	6	0	176.1	219	115	20	2	73-5	82	4.95	79	.310	.373	46-7	.065	-1	122	-23	-2.3
1958	Was A	6	15	.286	40	30	6	0	224.1	234	122	25	4	74-5	111	4.61	83	.270	.327	69-2	.159	-2	82	-19	-1.8
1959	Was A	8	17	.320	37	28	8	0	206	221	116	20	4	71-3	89	4.50	87	.276	.335	60-5	.133	-1	81	-12	-1.4
1960	Was A	0	2	.000	3	3	0	0	17.1	18	15	2	1	10-0	10	7.79	50	.269	.367	4-1	.000	0	98	-6	-0.6
	Chi A	6	3	.667	36	7	2-1	2	120.2	111	45	5	1	45-4	76	2.98	127	.248	.315	29-7	.000	-3	147	11	0.5
	Year	6	5	.545	39	10	2-1	2	138	129	51	7	2	55-4	86	3.59	106	.250	.322	33-8	.000	-3	132	4	-0.1
1961	Chi A	3	3	.500	47	2	0	2	96.2	102	53	10	0	26-1	35	4.38	89	.278	.323	15-0	.200	1	136	-5	-0.2
1962	Chi A	2	1	.667	20	0	0	0	28	30	14	3	0	11-1	17	3.86	101	.270	.336	2-1	.500	1		0	0.1
	Hou N	5	3	.625	36	2	0	3	68	72	34	10	3	15-1	23	4.10	91	.272	.318	9-0	.333	1	0	-2	-0.1
1963	Hou N	0	0	—	17	0	0	1	36.2	48	28	1	0	8-0	12	5.65	56	.320	.350	7-0	.286	0		-11	-0.5
Total	9	43	59	.422	302	109	24-2	8	1066.2	1144	588	103	17	389-21	505	4.46	86	.277	.339	265-25	.128	-5	97	-69	-6.5
KEMNER, DUTCH Herman John B 3.4.1899 Quincy, IL D 1.16.1988 Quincy, IL BR/TR 5-10.5/175# d4.19																									
1929	Cin N	0	0	—	9	0	0	1	15.1	19	13	0	0	8	10	7.63	60	.328	.409	4-0	.250	0		-5	-0.2
KENNA, ED Edward Benninghaus "The Pitching Poet" B 10.17.1877 Charleston, WV D 3.22.1912 Grant, FL TR 6/180# d5.5																									
1902	Phi A	1	1	.500	2	1	1	0	17	19	15	1	1	11	5	5.29	69	.284	.392	8-0	.125	-0	118	-3	-0.3
KENNEDY, JOE Joseph Darley B 5.24.1979 LaMesa, CA BR/TL 6-4/227# d6.6																									
2001	TB A	7	8	.467	20	20	0	0-0	117.2	122	63	16	3	34-0	78	4.44	101	.269	.321	4-0	.250	0	83	2	0.2
2002	TB A	8	11	.421	30	30	5-1	0-0	196.2	204	114	23	16	55-0	109	4.53	99	.269	.328	7-0	.429	1	97	-4	-0.4
2003	TB A	3	12	.200	32	22	1-1	1-1	133.2	167	101	19	11	47-1	77	6.13	74	.303	.364	0-0	—	0	80	-25	-2.3
Total	3	18	31	.367	82	72	6-2	1-1	448	493	278	58	30	136-1	264	4.98	90	.279	.338	11-0	.364	1	88	-27	-2.5
KENNEDY, VERN Lloyd Vernon B 3.20.1907 Kansas City, MO D 1.28.1993 Mendon, MO BL/TR 6/175# d9.18																									
1934	Chi A	0	2	.000	3	3	1	0	19.1	21	8	1	0	9	7	3.72	127	.300	.380	7-0	.286	0	25	3	0.3
1935	Chi A	11	11	.500	31	25	16-2	1	211.2	211	110	17	4	95	65	3.91	118	.262	.343	73-7	.247	1	94	14	1.4
1936	Chi A☆	21	9	.700	35	34	20-1	0	274.1	282	167	13	3	147	99	4.63	112	.268	.360	113-6	.283	5*	111	14	1.7
1937	Chi A	14	13	.519	32	30	15-1	0	221	238	150	16	3	124	114	5.09	90	.273	.366	87-3	.230	2	116	-14	-1.2
1938	Det A☆	12	9	.571	33	26	11	2	190.1	215	123	13	1	113	53	5.06	99	.287	.381	79-7	.291	3*	105	-3	0.0
1939	Det A	0	3	.000	4	4	1	0	21	25	15	4	1	9	9	6.43	76	.301	.376	7-0	.286	0	59	-2	-0.2
	StL A	9	17	.346	33	27	12-1	0	191.2	229	130	18	1	115	55	5.73	85	.297	.389	67-10	.149	-2*	94	-14	-1.8

Year	Tm Lg	W	L	Pct	G	GS	CG-Sho	SV-BS	IP	H	R	HR	HB	BB-IB	SO	ERA	AERA	OAV	OOB	AB-SH	AVG	PB	Sup	APR	PW
	Year	9	20	.310	37	31	13-1	0	212.2	254	135	22	2	124	64	5.80	84	.297	.388	74-10	.162	-2	89	-17	-2.0
1940	StL A	12	17	.414	34	32	18	0	222.1	263	149	18	3	122	70	5.59	82	.298	.385	84-3	.298	6*	105	-21	-1.5
1941	StL A	2	4	.333	6	6	2	0	45	44	27	5	0	27	6	4.40	98	.259	.360	15-1	.400	2	91	-1	0.1
	Was A	1	7	.125	17	7	2	0	66.1	77	49	5	2	39	22	5.70	71	.297	.393	21-0	.143	-1*	61	-12	-1.3
	Year	3	11	.214	23	13	4	0	111.1	121	52	10	2	66	28	5.17	80	.282	.380	36-1	.250	2	75	-13	-1.2
1942	Cle A	4	8	.333	28	12	4	1	108	99	57	1	1	50	37	4.08	84	.244	.328	30-2	.200	1*	70	-8	-0.7
1943	Cle A	10	7	.588	28	17	8-1	0	146.2	130	47	4	2	59	63	2.45	127	.242	.319	52-8	.231	1*	99	11	1.5
1944	Cle A	2	5	.286	12	10	2	0	59	66	36	0	0	37	17	5.03	66	.289	.389	23-0	.087	-2*	89	-11	-1.3
	Phi N	1	5	.167	12	7	3	0	55.1	60	31	3	0	20	23	4.23	85	.269	.329	21-2	.286	1*	113	-4	-0.3
1945	Phi N	0	3	.000	12	3	0	0	36	43	29	2	0	14	13	5.50	70	.297	.358	11-0	.182	0*	133	-7	-0.5
	Cin N	5	12	.294	24	20	11-1	1	157.2	170	74	10	3	69	38	4.00	94	.280	.356	53-1	.226	2	66	-2	0.1
	Year	5	15	.250	36	23	11-1	1	193.2	213	77	12	3	83	51	4.28	88	.283	.356	64-1	.219	2	75	-10	-0.4
Total	12	104	132	.441	344	263	126-7	5	2025.2	2173	1202	130	24	1049	691	4.67	94	.277	.363	743-50	.244	19	98	-57	-3.7
KENNEDY, MONTE Monty Calvin B 5.11.1922 Amelia, VA D 3.1.1997 Midlothian, VA BR/TL 6-2/185# d4.18																									
1946	NY N	9	10	.474	38	27	10-1	1	186.2	153	80	14	4	116	71	3.42	101	.224	.340	64-2	.234	2	100	2	0.4
1947	NY N	9	12	.429	34	24	9	0	148.1	158	90	8	4	88	60	4.85	84	.272	.372	48-1	.167	-1	116	-13	-1.6
1948	NY N	3	9	.250	25	16	7-1	0	114.1	118	64	10	3	57	63	4.01	98	.264	.351	31-2	.129	-1*	69	-3	-0.4
1949	NY N	12	14	.462	38	32	14-4	1	223.1	208	105	13	3	100	95	3.43	116	.242	.323	83-5	.145	-1*	106	12	1.1
1950	NY N	5	4	.556	36	17	5	2	114.1	120	65	14	3	53	41	4.72	87	.269	.351	36-2	.056	-3	96	-7	-0.8
1951	†NY N	1	2	.333	29	5	1	0	68	68	25	0	0	31	22	2.25	174	.270	.350	15-3	.200	0	81	11	0.5
1952	NY N	3	4	.429	31	6	2-1	0	83.1	73	37	6	2	31	48	3.02	122	.230	.303	22-1	.091	-1*	112	4	0.2
1953	NY N	0	0	—	18	0	0	0	22.2	30	18	2	1	19	11	7.15	60	.337	.459	2-0	.000	-0*		-6	-0.3
Total	8	42	55	.433	249	127	48-7	4	961	928	484	67	20	495	411	3.84	101	.253	.344	301-16	.153	-5	100	0	-0.9
KENNEDY, TED Theodore A. B 2.7.1865 Henry, IL D 10.31.1907 St.Louis, MO BL/TR 5-8/178# d6.12																									
1885	Chi N	7	2	.778	9	9	8	0	78.2	91	54	5		28	36	3.43	88	.288	.346	36	.083	-4	146	-3	-0.6
1886	Phi AA	5	15	.250	20	19	19	0	172.2	197	143	4	8	65	68	4.53	77	.272	.339	68	.044	-9	81	-17	-2.2
	Lou AA	0	4	.000	4	4	4	0	32	53	43	1	1	16	14	5.34	68	.351	.417	13	.077	-1	82	-7	-0.8
	Year	5	19	.208	24	23	23	0	204.2	250	48	5	9	81	82	4.66	76	.286	.353	81	.049	-10	81	-29	-3.0
Total	2	12	21	.364	33	32	31	0	283.1	341	240	10	9	109	118	4.32	78	.287	.351	117	.060	-14	98	-27	-3.6
KENNEDY, BILL William Aulton "Lefty" B 3.14.1921 Carnesville, GA D 4.9.1983 Seattle, WA BL/TL 6-2/195# d4.26																									
1948	Cle A	1	0	1.000	6	3	0	0	11.1	16	14	0	0	13	12	11.12	37	.333	.475	3-1	.667	1	200	-9	-0.5
	StL A	7	8	.467	26	20	3	0	132	132	82	10	5	104	77	4.70	97	.259	.389	44-3	.250	1	93	-4	-0.4
	Year	8	8	.500	32	23	3	0	143.1	148	87	10	5	117	89	5.21	87	.265	.397	47-4	.277	2	105	-12	-0.9
1949	StL A	4	11	.267	48	16	2	1	153.2	172	97	12	3	73	69	4.69	97	.285	.365	40-2	.150	-2	88	-4	-0.5
1950	StL A	0	0	—	1	0	0	0	2	1	1	0	0	2	1	0.00	—	.143	.333	0-0	—	0		1	0.0
1951	StL A	1	5	.167	19	5	1	0	56	76	37	4	1	37	29	5.79	76	.332	.427	16-0	.125	-2	85	-7	-0.7
1952	Chi A	2	2	.500	**47**	1	0	5	70.2	54	27	4	1	38	46	2.80	130	.213	.318	13-1	.231	0	24	6	0.4
1953	Bos A	0	0	—	16	0	0	2	24.1	24	13	2	1	17	14	3.70	114	.255	.375	2-1	.500	0		1	0.1
1956	Cin N	0	0	—	1	0	0	0	2	6	4	1	0	0-0	0	18.00	22	.667	.600	0-0	—	0		-3	-0.1
1957	Cin N	0	2	.000	8	0	0	3	12.2	16	9	1	1	5-1	8	6.39	64	.314	.379	2-0	.000	0		-3	-0.5
Total	8	15	28	.349	172	45	6	11	464.2	497	284	34	12	289-1	256	4.73	92	.275	.379	120-8	.208	-1	98	-22	-2.2
KENNEDY, BILL William Gorman B 12.22.1918 Alexandria, VA D 8.20.1995 Alexandria, VA BL/TL 6-1/175# d5.1 Mil 1943-45																									
1942	Was A	0	1	.000	8	2	1	2	18	21	18	1	0	10	4	8.00	46	.296	.383	4-0	.000	-1	82	-8	-0.6
1946	Was A	1	2	.333	21	2	0	3	39	40	29	1	0	29	18	6.00	56	.270	.390	8-1	.125	-0	102	-11	-1.0
1947	Was A	0	0	—	2	0	0	0	6.2	10	8	1	0	5	1	8.10	46	.370	.469	2-0	.000	-0		-4	-0.2
Total	3	1	3	.250	31	4	1	5	63.2	71	55	3	0	44	23	6.79	51	.289	.397	14-1	.071	-1	93	-23	-1.8
KENNEDY, BRICKYARD William Park B 10.7.1867 Bellaire, OH D 9.23.1915 Bellaire, OH BR/TR 5-11/160# d4.26																									
1892	Bro N	13	8	.619	26	21	18	1	191	189	115	3	4	95	108	3.86	82	.248	.334	85	.165	-1	117	-14	-1.4
1893	Bro N	25	20	.556	46	44	40-2	1	382.2	376	238	15	7	168	107	3.72	119	.249	.327	157	.248	2	90	28	2.9
1894	Bro N	24	20	.545	48	41	34	2	360.2	445	291	15	11	149	107	4.92	101	.300	.368	161-6	.304	4	105	-3	0.1
1895	Bro N	19	12	.613	40	34	27-2	1	288.2	341	199	14	7	95	41	5.05	87	.289	.346	131-1	.305	4*	112	-17	-1.0
1896	Bro N	17	20	.459	42	38	28-1	1	305.2	334	211	12	12	130	76	4.42	93	.276	.352	122-4	.189	-7	85	-10	-1.4
1897	Bro N	18	20	.474	44	40	36-2	1	343.1	370	206	6	8	149	81	3.91	105	.273	.348	147-2	.272	4*	90	7	1.0
1898	Bro N	16	22	.421	40	39	38	0	339.1	360	183	12	5	123	73	3.37	106	.270	.334	135-1	.252	3	84	6	1.1
1899	Bro N	22	9	.710	40	33	27-2	2	277.1	297	133	11	3	86	55	2.79	140	.273	.329	109-1	.248	4	101	31	3.3
1900	Bro N	20	13	.606	42	35	26-2	0	292	316	160	5	8	111	75	3.91	98	.276	.344	123-2	.301	7*	112	2	0.9
1901	Bro N	3	5	.375	14	8	6	0	85.1	80	40	1	1	24	28	3.06	110	.246	.300	36-0	.167	-1	98	3	0.1
1902	NY N	1	4	.200	6	6	4-1	0	38.2	44	25	0	0	16	9	3.96	71	.286	.353	15-0	.267	1	65	-5	-0.5
1903	†Pit N	9	6	.600	18	15	10-1	0	125.1	130	62	0	2	57	39	3.45	94	.277	.357	58-2	.362	8*	135	0	0.7
Total	12	187	159	.540	406	354	294-13	9	3030	3282	1863	94	68	1203	799	3.96	103	.273	.343	1279-19	.261	27	99	28	5.8
KENNEY, ART Arthur Joseph B 4.29.1916 Milford, MA BL/TL 6/175# d7.1																									
1938	Bos N	0	0	—	2	0	0	0	2.1	3	4	0	0	8	2	15.43	22	.300	.611	0-0	—	0		-3	-0.1
KENT, ED Edward C. B 1859 , NY BR/TR 5-6.5/152# d8.14																									
1884	Tol AA	0	1	.000	1	1	1	0	9	14	11	0	1	3	4	6.00	57	.298	.353	4	.000	-1	124	-3	-0.2
KENT, MAURY Maurice Allen B 9.17.1885 Marshalltown, IA D 4.19.1966 Iowa City, IA BR/TR 6/168# d4.15																									
1912	Bro N	5	5	.500	20	9	2-1	0	93	107	74	3	1	46	24	4.84	69	.296	.377	35-0	.229	1	122	-18	-1.5
1913	Bro N	0	0	—	3	0	0	0	7.1	5	2	0	0	3	1	2.45	134	.192	.276	3-0	.000	-0*		1	0.0
Total	2	5	5	.500	23	9	2-1	0	100.1	112	76	3	1	49	25	4.66	72	.289	.371	38-0	.211	1	122	-17	-1.5
KENT, STEVE Steven Patrick B 10.3.1978 Frankfurt, Germany BB/TL 5-11/170# d4.4																									
2002	TB A	0	2	.000	34	0	0	1-1	57.1	67	41	6	3	38-0	41	5.65	79	.294	.399	0-0	—	0		-8	-0.4
KEOUGH, MATT Matthew Lon B 7.3.1955 Pomona, CA BR/TR 6-3/190# d9.3 f-Marty																									
1977	Oak A	1	3	.250	7	6	0	0-0	42.2	39	25	4	1	22-0	23	4.85	83	.247	.341	0-0	—	0*	74	-3	-0.3
1978	Oak A★	8	15	.348	32	32	6	0-0	197.1	178	90	9	4	85-2	108	3.24	113	.241	.322	0-0	—	0*	74	7	0.9
1979	Oak A	2	17	.105	30	28	7-1	0-0	176.2	220	115	18	7	78-2	95	5.04	80	.315	.385	0-0	—	0	66	-21	-1.9
1980	Oak A	16	13	.552	34	32	20-2	0-1	250	218	94	24	5	94-3	121	2.92	130	.236	.308	0-0	—	0	95	24	2.6
1981	†Oak A	10	6	.625	19	19	10-2	0-0	140.1	125	56	11	0	45-0	60	3.40	102	.239	.298	0-0	—	0	122	3	0.2
1982	Oak A	11	18	.379	34	34	10-2	0-0	209.1	233	144	38	5	101-1	75	5.72	68	.284	.362	0-0	—	0	102	-42	-4.9
1983	Oak A	2	3	.400	14	4	0	0-0	44	50	29	7	0	31-1	28	5.52	70	.284	.388	0-0	—	0	106	-8	-0.8
	NY A	3	4	.429	12	12	0	0-0	55.2	59	42	12	2	20-0	26	5.17	75	.266	.331	0-0	—	0	126	-11	-1.2
	Year	5	7	.417	26	16	0	0-0	99.2	109	47	19	2	51-1	54	5.33	73	.274	.357	0-0	—	0	121	-19	-2.0
1985	StL N	0	1	.000	4	1	0	0-0	10	10	5	0	1	4-1	10	4.50	79	.278	.366	2-0	.000	-0	75	-1	-0.1
1986	Chi N	2	2	.500	19	2	0	0-1	29	36	17	4	1	12-2	19	4.97	82	.316	.386	5-0	.400	1	44	-3	-0.2
	Hou N	3	2	.600	10	5	0	0-0	35	22	14	5	1	18-2	25	3.09	117	.180	.289	11-0	.364	1	134	2	0.4
	Year	5	4	.556	29	7	0	0-1	64	58	19	9	2	30-4	44	3.94	97	.246	.335	16-0	.375	2	104	-1	0.2
Total	9	58	84	.408	215	175	53-7	0-2	1190	1190	631	132	27	510-14	590	4.17	91	.262	.338	18-0	.333	2	92	-53	-5.3
KEPSHIRE, KURT Kurt David B 7.3.1959 Bridgeport, CT BL/TR 6-1/180# d7.4																									
1984	StL N	6	5	.545	17	16	2-2	0-0	109	100	47	7	0	44-4	71	3.30	105	.249	.321	36-5	.056	-2	110	1	-0.2
1985	StL N	10	9	.526	32	29	0	0-0	153.1	155	89	16	0	71-3	67	4.75	75	.264	.339	51-7	.118	-1	123	-20	-2.4
1986	StL N	0	1	.000	2	1	0	0-0	8	8	4	2	0	4-0	6	4.50	81	.258	.343	1-1	.000	-0	49	-1	-0.1
Total	3	16	15	.516	51	46	2-2	0-0	270.1	263	140	25	0	119-7	144	4.16	85	.258	.332	88-13	.091	-3	117	-20	-2.7
KERFELD, CHARLIE Charles Patrick B 9.28.1963 Knob Noster, MO BR/TR 6-6/225# d7.27																									
1985	Hou N	4	2	.667	11	6	0	0-0	44.1	44	22	2	0	25-2	30	4.06	85	.268	.359	14-2	.000	-1	110	-2	-0.5
1986	†Hou N	11	2	.846	61	0	0	7-5	93.2	71	32	5	2	42-3	77	2.59	139	.213	.299	9-0	.111	-0		10	1.4

Year	Tm Lg	W	L	Pct	G	GS	CG-Sho	SV-BS	IP	H	R	HR	HB	BB-IB	SO	ERA	AERA	OAV	OOB	AB-SH	AVG	PB	Sup	APR	PW
1987	Hou N	0	2	.000	21	0	0	0-0	29.2	34	22	3	1	21-2	17	6.67	59	.309	.421	3-0	.000	-0		-8	-0.5
1990	Hou N	0	2	.000	5	0	0	0-0	3.1	9	6	0	0	6-1	4	16.20	23	.529	.652	0-0	—	0		-4	-0.8
	Atl N	3	1	.750	25	0	0	2-0	30.2	31	22	2	0	23-3	27	5.58	72	.270	.386	0-0	—	0		-5	-0.7
	Year	3	3	.500	30	0	0	2-0	34	40	32	2	0	29-4	31	6.62	61	.303	.423	0-0	—	0		-9	-1.5
Total	4	18	9	.667	123	6	0	9-5	201.2	189	104	12	3	117-11	155	4.20	88	.256	.354	26-2	.038	-2	110	-9	-1.1
KERIAZAKOS, GUS Constantine Nicholas B 7.28.1931 W.Orange, NJ D 5.4.1996 Hilton Head, SC BR/TR 6-3/187# d10.1																									
1950	Chi A	0	1	.000	1	1	0	0	2.1	7	5	0	0	5	1	19.29	23	.500	.632	1-0	1.000	0	121	-4	-0.5
1954	Was A	2	3	.400	22	3	2	0	59.2	59	29	4	0	30	33	3.77	94	.262	.346	15-2	.067	-1	99	-2	-0.2
1955	KC A	0	1	.000	5	1	0	0	11.2	15	16	4	0	7-0	8	12.34	34	.333	.415	3-0	.000	-0	149	-9	-0.7
Total	3	2	5	.286	28	5	2	0	73.2	81	50	8	0	42-0	42	5.62	65	.285	.374	19-2	.105	-1	120	-15	-1.4
KERKSIECK, BILL Wayman William B 12.6.1913 Ulm, AR D 3.11.1970 Stuttgart, AR BR/TR 6-1/183# d6.21																									
1939	Phi N	0	2	.000	23	2	1	0	62.2	81	52	13	0	32	13	7.18	56	.328	.405	12-0	.083	-0*	33	-20	-1.0
KERN, JIM James Lester B 3.15.1949 Gladwin, MI BR/TR 6-5/205# d9.6																									
1974	Cle A	0	1	.000	4	3	1	0-0	15.1	16	9	1	0	14-1	11	4.70	77	.262	.395	0-0	—	0	106	-2	-0.1
1975	Cle A	1	2	.333	13	7	0	0-0	71.2	60	31	5	5	45-3	55	3.77	101	.233	.356	0-0	—	0	100	2	0.1
1976	Cle A	10	7	.588	50	2	0	15-1	117.2	91	38	2	5	50-7	111	2.37	147	.222	.309	0-0	—	0	113	13	2.3
1977	Cle A★	8	10	.444	60	0	0	18-9	92	85	39	3	6	47-8	91	3.42	116	.260	.359	0-0	—	0		6	1.1
1978	Cle A★	10	10	.500	58	0	0	13-4	99.1	77	36	4	3	58-7	95	3.08	122	.224	.338	1-0	.000	-0		8	1.8
1979	Tex A★	13	5	.722	71	0	0	29-9	143	99	35	5	2	62-6	136	1.57	265	.199	.288	0-0	—	0		**39**	**6.3**
1980	Tex A	3	11	.214	38	1	0	2-7	63.1	65	38	4	2	45-10	40	4.83	81	.279	.392	0-0	—	0	0	-6	-1.2
1981	Tex A	1	2	.333	23	0	0	6-0	30	21	10	0	1	22-3	20	2.70	129	.204	.346	0-0	—	0		3	0.4
1982	Cin N	3	5	.375	50	0	0	2-4	76	61	27	3	2	48-14	43	2.84	130	.222	.338	7-0	.000	-0		7	0.7
	Chi A	2	1	.667	13	1	0	3-1	28	20	16	3	0	12-0	23	5.14	79	.204	.288	0-0	—	0	90	-2	-0.3
1983	Chi A	0	0	—	1	0	0	0-0	0.2	1	1	0	0	0-0	0	0.00	—	.333	.333	0-0	—	0		0	0.0
1984	Phi N	0	1	.000	8	0	0	0-0	13.1	20	16	3	0	10-1	8	10.13	36	.339	.435	1-0	.000	-0		-9	-0.6
	Mil A	1	0	1.000	6	0	0	0-0	4.2	6	0	0	0	3-0	4	0.00	—	.300	.391	0-0	—	0		2	0.4
1985	Mil A	0	1	.000	5	0	0	0-0	11	14	8	1	0	5-1	3	6.55	64	.318	.388	0-0	—	0		-2	-0.2
1986	Cle A	1	1	.500	16	0	0	0-1	27.1	34	28	1	3	23-0	11	7.90	53	.298	.429	0-0	—	0		-12	-0.7
Total	13	53	57	.482	416	14	1	88-36	793.1	670	332	35	29	444-61	651	3.32	116	.235	.341	9-0	.000	-1	93	47	10.0
KERR, DICKIE Richard Henry B 7.3.1893 St.Louis, MO D 5.4.1963 Houston, TX BL/TL 5-7/155# d4.25																									
1919	†Chi A	13	7	.650	39	17	10-1	0	212.1	208	78	2	2	64	79	2.88	110	.259	.316	68-9	.250	5	119	10	1.5
1920	Chi A	21	9	.700	45	27	19-3	**5**	253.2	266	116	7	4	72	72	3.37	112	.278	.331	90-4	.156	-4*	105	10	0.8
1921	Chi A	19	17	.528	44	37	25-3	1	308.2	357	182	12	11	96	80	4.72	90	.295	.352	105-5	.238	5*	89	-15	-1.0
1925	Chi A	0	1	.000	12	2	0	0	36.2	45	23	3	1	18	4	5.15	81	.304	.383	12-1	.333	1*	91	-4	-0.1
Total	4	53	34	.609	140	83	54-7	6	811.1	876	399	24	18	250	235	3.84	99	.281	.338	275-19	.218	7	101	1	1.2
KERRIGAN, JOE Joseph Thomas B 11.30.1954 Philadelphia, PA BR/TR 6-5/205# d7.9 M1 C15																									
1976	Mon N	2	6	.250	38	0	0	1-2	56.2	63	27	3	2	23-5	22	3.81	98	.289	.362	2-0	.000	-0		0	0.0
1977	Mon N	3	5	.375	66	0	0	11-5	89.1	80	37	4	3	33-3	43	3.22	118	.241	.310	8-2	.000	-1		5	0.5
1978	Bal A	3	1	.750	26	2	0	3-0	71.2	75	44	10	2	36-5	41	4.77	74	.273	.361	0-0	—	0	115	-12	-0.6
1980	Bal A	0	0	—	1	0	0	0-0	2.1	3	1	0	0	0-0	1	3.86	103	.273	.273	0-0	—	0		0	0.0
Total	4	8	12	.400	131	2	0	15-7	220	221	109	17	7	92-13	107	3.89	95	.264	.340	10-2	.000	-1	115	-7	-0.1
KERSHNER, JASON Jason Ashley B 12.19.1976 Scottsdale, AZ BL/TL 6-2/165# d7.25																									
2002	SD N	0	1	.000	15	0	0	0-0	18.2	15	14	2	2	10-0	11	5.79	65	.217	.333	0-1	—	0		-5	-0.3
	Tor A	0	0	—	10	0	0	1-1	5.1	5	2	1	0	4-1	7	1.69	274	.227	.346	0-0	—	0		1	0.1
2003	Tor A	3	3	.500	40	0	0	0-1	54	43	21	5	2	15-2	32	3.17	145	.217	.275	0-0	—	0		8	0.8
Total	2	3	4	.429	65	0	0	1-2	78	63	37	8	4	29-3	50	3.69	119	.218	.295	0-1	—	0		4	0.6
KESTER, RICK Richard Lee B 7.7.1946 Iola, KS BR/TR 6/190# d8.18																									
1968	Atl N	0	0	—	5	0	0	0	6.1	8	4	0	0	3-0	9	5.68	53	.308	.379	0-0	—	0		-2	-0.1
1969	Atl N	0	0	—	1	0	0	0-0	2	5	3	1	0	0-0	2	13.50	27	.455	.455	0-0	—	0		-2	-0.1
1970	Atl N	0	0	—	15	0	0	0-0	32.1	36	24	3	0	19-0	20	5.57	77	.283	.374	9-0	.000	-1		-5	-0.4
Total	3	0	0	—	21	0	0	0-0	40.2	49	31	4	0	22-0	31	5.98	68	.299	.380	9-0	.000	-1		-9	-0.6
KETCHUM, GUS Augustus Franklin B 3.21.1897 Royse City, TX D 9.6.1980 Oklahoma City, OK BR/TR 5-9.5/170# d8.7																									
1922	Phi A	0	1	.000	6	0	0	0	16	19	12	2	1	8	4	5.63	76	.302	.389	4-0	.000	-1		-2	-0.2
KEUPPER, HENRY Henry J. B 6.24.1887 Staunton, IL D 8.14.1960 Marion, IL BL/TL 6-1/185# d4.19																									
1914	StL F	8	20	.286	42	25	12-1	0	213	256	132	3	4	49	70	4.27	71	.291	.332	68-4	.250	1	86	-29	-3.1
KEY, JIMMY James Edward B 4.22.1961 Huntsville, AL BR/TL 6-1/190# d4.6																									
1984	Tor A	4	5	.444	63	0	0	10-7	62	70	37	8	1	32-8	44	4.65	88	.286	.369	0-0	—	0		-4	-0.7
1985	†Tor A★	14	6	.700	35	32	3	0-0	212.2	188	77	22	2	50-1	85	3.00	140	.237	.282	0-0	—	0*	101	29	2.7
1986	Tor A	14	11	.560	36	35	4-2	0-0	232	222	98	24	3	74-1	141	3.57	118	.256	.315	0-0	—	0	110	18	1.9
1987	Tor A	17	8	.680	36	36	8-1	0-0	261	210	93	24	2	66-6	161	**2.76**	**163**	**.221**	**.272**	0-0	—	0	93	47	4.3
1988	Tor A	12	5	.706	21	21	2-2	0-0	131.1	127	55	13	5	30-2	65	3.29	120	.250	.296	0-0	—	0	107	9	1.1
1989	†Tor A	13	14	.481	33	33	5-1	0-0	216	226	99	18	3	27-2	118	3.88	98	.270	.292	0-0	—	0	96	0	0.1
1990	Tor A	13	7	.650	27	27	0	0-0	154.2	169	79	20	1	22-2	88	4.25	93	.281	.304	0-0	—	0	114	-6	-0.6
1991	†Tor A★	16	12	.571	33	33	2-2	0-0	209.1	207	84	12	3	44-3	125	3.05	138	.254	.293	0-0	—	0	91	23	3.1
1992	†Tor A	13	13	.500	33	33	4-2	0-0	216.2	205	88	24	4	59-0	117	3.53	116	.248	.298	0-0	—	0	112	15	1.7
1993	NY A★	18	6	**.750**	34	34	4-2	0-0	236.2	219	84	26	1	43-1	173	3.00	139	.246	.279	0-0	—	0	128	33	3.1
1994	NY A★	**17**	4	.810	25	**25**	1	0-0	168	177	68	10	3	52-0	97	3.27	140	.273	.329	0-0	—	0	134	25	2.9
1995	NY A	1	2	.333	5	5	0	0-0	30.1	40	20	3	0	6-1	14	5.64	82	.323	.351	0-0	—	0	129	-3	-0.3
1996	†NY A	12	11	.522	30	30	0	0-0	169.1	171	93	21	2	58-1	116	4.68	106	.266	.326	0-0	—	0	96	5	0.7
1997	†Bal A❖	16	10	.615	34	34	1-1	0-0	212.1	210	90	24	5	82-1	141	3.43	128	.261	.331	2-1	.000	-0	98	22	2.5
1998	Bal A	6	3	.667	25	11	0	0-1	79.1	77	39	5	3	23-0	53	4.20	109	.258	.316	0-0	—	0	93	3	0.3
Total	15	186	117	.614	470	389	34-13	10-8	2591.2	2518	1104	254	38	668-29	1538	3.51	122	.255	.303	2-1	.000	-0	106	216	22.8
KEYSER, BRIAN Brian Lee B 10.31.1966 Castro Valley, CA BR/TR 6-1/180# d6.2																									
1995	Chi A	5	6	.455	23	10	0	0-1	92.1	114	53	10	2	27-1	48	4.97	90	.306	.354	0-0	—	0	84	-4	-0.4
1996	Chi A	1	2	.333	28	0	0	1-1	59.2	78	35	3	0	28-8	19	4.98	95	.328	.394	0-0	—	0		-1	0.0
Total	2	6	8	.429	51	10	0	1-2	152	192	88	13	2	55-9	67	4.97	92	.314	.370	0-0	—	0	84	-5	-0.4
KIDA, MASAO Masao B 9.12.1968 Tokyo, Japan BR/TR 6-2/209# d4.5																									
1999	Det A	1	0	1.000	49	0	0	1-0	64.2	73	48	6	4	30-3	50	6.26	79	.289	.368	0-0	—	0		-9	-0.4
2000	Det A	0	0	—	2	0	0	0-0	2.2	5	3	1	0	0-0	0	10.13	48	.385	.385	0-0	—	0		-1	-0.1
2003	LA N	0	1	.000	3	2	0	0-0	12	15	5	0	0	3-0	8	3.00	134	.300	.340	4-0	.250	0	47	1	0.1
Total	3	1	1	.500	54	2	0	1-0	79.1	93	56	7	4	33-3	58	5.90	81	.294	.364	4-0	.250	0	47	-9	-0.4
KIECKER, DANA Dana Ervin B 2.25.1961 Sleepy Eye, MN BR/TR 6-3/180# d4.12																									
1990	†Bos A	8	9	.471	32	25	0	0-0	152	145	74	7	9	54-2	93	3.97	103	.253	.325	0-0	—	0	95	2	0.3
1991	Bos A	2	3	.400	18	5	0	0-0	40.1	56	34	6	2	23-4	21	7.36	58	.344	.429	0-0	—	0	136	-12	-1.2
Total	2	10	12	.455	50	30	0	0-0	192.1	201	108	13	11	77-6	114	4.68	88	.273	.349	0-0	—	0	101	-10	-0.9
KIEFER, JOE Joseph William "Harlem Joe" or "Smoke" B 7.19.1899 W.Leyden, NY D 7.5.1975 Utica, NY BR/TR 5-11/190# d10.1																									
1920	Chi A	0	1	.000	2	1	0	0	4.2	7	8	0	1	5	1	15.43	24	.333	.481	2-0	.000	-0	148	-5	-0.8
1925	Bos A	0	2	.000	2	2	0	0	15	20	12	0	1	9	4	6.00	76	.351	.448	4-0	.000	-1	46	-2	-0.3
1926	Bos A	0	2	.000	11	1	0	0	30	29	19	2	2	16	4	4.80	85	.266	.370	7-0	.143	-0	41	-3	-0.1
Total	3	0	5	.000	15	4	0	0	49.2	56	39	2	4	30	9	6.16	68	.299	.407	13-0	.077	-1	70	-10	-1.2

Year	Tm Lg	W	L	Pct	G	GS	CG-Sho	SV-BS	IP	H	R	HR	HB	BB-IB	SO	ERA	AERA	OAV	OOB	AB-SH	AVG	PB	Sup	APR	PW
KIEFER, MARK Mark Andrew B 11.13.1968 Orange, CA BR/TR 6-4/175# d9.20 b-Steve																									
1993	Mil A	0	0	—	6	0	0	1-1	9.1	3	0	0	1	5-0	7	0.00	—	.097	.243	0-0	—	0		4	0.2
1994	Mil A	1	0	1.000	7	0	0	0-0	10.2	15	12	4	0	8-0	8	8.44	60	.357	.442	0-0	—	0		-4	-0.3
1995	Mil A	4	1	.800	24	0	0	0-0	49.2	37	20	6	0	27-2	41	3.44	145	.203	.306	0-0	—	0		8	0.7
1996	Mil A	0	0	—	7	0	0	0-0	10	15	9	1	0	5-1	5	8.10	64	.366	.426	0-0	—	0		-3	-0.1
Total	4	5	1	.833	44	0	0	1-1	79.2	70	41	11	1	45-3	61	4.29	115	.236	.336	0-0	—	0		5	0.5
KIELY, JOHN John Francis B 10.4.1964 Boston, MA BR/TR 6-3/210# d7.26																									
1991	Det A	0	1	.000	7	0	0	0-0	6.2	13	11	0	1	9-2	1	14.85	28	.448	.575	0-0	—	0		-7	-0.9
1992	Det A	4	2	.667	39	0	0	0-1	55	44	14	2	0	28-3	18	2.13	186	.224	.317	0-0	—	0		11	1.2
1993	Det A	0	2	.000	8	0	0	0-0	11.2	13	11	2	1	13-5	5	7.71	56	.295	.466	0-0	—	0		-4	-0.6
Total	3	4	5	.444	54	0	0	0-1	73.1	70	36	4	2	50-10	24	4.17	97	.260	.375	0-0	—	0		0	-0.3
KIELY, LEO Leo Patrick "Kiki" B 11.30.1929 Hoboken, NJ D 1.18.1984 Montclair, NJ BL/TL 6-2/180# d6.27 Mil 1952																									
1951	Bos A	7	7	.500	17	16	4	0	113.1	106	48	9	2	39	46	3.34	134	.251	.317	35-0	.143	-1*	75	13	1.4
1954	Bos A	5	8	.385	28	19	4-1	0	131	153	74	12	1	58	59	3.50	117	.295	.365	50-1	.180	0	91	2	0.2
1955	Bos A	3	3	.500	33	4	0	6	90	91	31	5	0	37-5	36	2.80	153	.269	.341	26-1	.192	-0	93	14	1.1
1956	Bos A	2	2	.500	23	0	0	3	31.1	47	25	1	2	14-5	9	5.17	89	.362	.429	6-0	.167	-0		-3	-0.5
1958	Bos A	5	2	.714	47	0	0	12	81	77	31	3	2	18-3	26	3.00	134	.254	.299	13-2	.000	-2		9	0.9
1959	Bos A	3	3	.500	41	0	0	7	55.2	67	26	8	1	18-3	30	4.20	97	.299	.352	8-0	.000	-1		0	0.0
1960	KC A	1	2	.333	20	0	0	1	20.2	21	4	1	1	5-0	6	1.74	229	.266	.318	1-0	.000	0		5	0.9
Total	7	26	27	.491	209	39	8-1	29	523	562	239	39	9	189-16	212	3.37	125	.279	.342	139-4	.144	-4	86	40	4.0
KIESCHNICK, BROOKS Michael Brooks B 6.6.1972 Robstown, TX BL/TR 6-4/225# d4.3.1996 ▲																									
2003	Mil N	1	1	.500	42	0	0	0-0	53	66	32	5	6	13-4	39	5.26	81	.299	.354	70-0	.300	8*		-5	0.7
KILE, DARRYL Darryl Andrew B 12.2.1968 Garden Grove, CA D 6.22.2002 Chicago, IL BR/TR 6-5/185# d4.8																									
1991	Hou N	7	11	.389	37	22	0	0-1	153.2	144	81	16	6	84-4	100	3.69	95	.246	.344	38-4	.000	-3	106	-8	-1.3
1992	Hou N	5	10	.333	22	22	2	0-0	125.1	124	61	8	4	63-4	90	3.95	85	.261	.348	32-5	.156	1	83	-9	-1.0
1993	Hou N☆	15	8	.652	32	26	4-2	0-0	171.2	152	73	12	15	69-1	141	3.51	110	.239	.324	53-8	.094	-1	121	8	0.9
1994	Hou N	9	6	.600	24	24	0	0-0	147.2	153	84	13	9	82-6	105	4.57	87	.275	.375	47-9	.149	1	123	-11	-0.9
1995	Hou N	4	12	.250	25	21	0	0-0	127	114	81	5	12	73-2	113	4.96	78	.240	.353	36-5	.111	0	104	-18	-1.8
1996	Hou N	12	11	.522	35	33	4	0-0	219	233	113	16	16	97-8	219	4.19	92	.276	.359	73-7	.137	1*	113	-8	-0.6
1997	†Hou N☆	19	7	.731	34	34	6-4	0-0	255.2	208	87	19	10	94-2	205	2.57	156	.225	.300	89-10	.124	0	110	40	4.0
1998	Col N	13	17	.433	36	**35**	4-1	0-0	230.1	257	141	28	7	96-4	158	5.20	100	.287	.358	71-9	.254	2*	87	0	0.3
1999	Col N	8	13	.381	32	32	1	0-0	190.2	225	150	33	6	109-5	116	6.61	88	.298	.387	52-8	.135	-2	88	-13	-1.4
2000	†StL N★	20	9	.690	34	34	5-1	0-0	232.1	215	109	33	13	58-1	192	3.91	118	.247	.301	73-8	.123	0	98	19	2.1
2001	†StL N	16	11	.593	34	34	2-1	0-0	227.1	228	83	22	11	65-3	179	3.09	138	.265	.322	71-5	.127	1	87	31	3.6
2002	StL N	5	4	.556	14	14	0	0-0	84.2	82	36	9	8	28-1	50	3.72	107	.257	.330	22-3	.091	-1	100	3	0.3
Total	12	133	119	.528	359	331	28-9	0-1	2165.1	2135	1099	214	117	918-41	1668	4.12	103	.260	.341	657-81	.132	-1	100	34	4.2
KILGUS, PAUL Paul Nelson B 2.2.1962 Bowling Green, KY BL/TL 6-1/185# d6.7																									
1987	Tex A	2	7	.222	25	12	0	0-0	89.1	95	45	14	2	31-2	42	4.13	109	.271	.334	0-0	—	0	86	4	0.3
1988	Tex A	12	15	.444	32	32	5-3	0-0	203.1	190	105	18	10	71-2	88	4.16	98	.243	.313	0-0	—	0	89	-1	-0.1
1989	†Chi N	6	10	.375	35	23	0	2-0	145.2	164	90	9	5	49-6	61	4.39	86	.283	.342	41-4	.073	-3	97	-14	-1.7
1990	Tor A	0	0	—	11	0	0	0-0	16.1	19	11	2	1	7-1	7	6.06	65	.306	.370	0-0	—	0		-3	-0.2
1991	Bal A	0	2	.000	38	0	0	1-0	62	60	38	8	3	24-2	32	5.08	78	.256	.328	0-0	—	0		-8	-0.3
1993	StL N	1	0	1.000	22	1	0	1-0	28.2	18	2	1	1	8-1	21	0.63	632	.180	.248	5-0	.200	0	23	11	0.6
Total	6	21	34	.382	163	68	5-3	4-0	545.1	546	291	52	22	190-14	251	4.19	97	.259	.325	46-4	.087	-2	90	-11	-1.4
KILKENNY, MIKE Michael David B 4.11.1945 Bradford, ON, CAN BR/TL 6-3.5/175# d4.11																									
1969	Det A	8	6	.571	39	15	6-4	2-0	128.1	99	54	13	4	63-1	97	3.37	111	.211	.309	37-3	.054	-2	104	5	0.3
1970	Det A	7	6	.538	36	21	3	0-1	129	141	77	10	2	70-0	105	5.16	72	.279	.368	39-4	.077	-3*	92	-18	-1.9
1971	Det A	4	5	.444	30	11	2	1-0	86.1	83	52	8	2	44-3	47	5.00	72	.247	.337	24-1	.083	-2	77	-13	-1.5
1972	Det A	0	0	—	1	0	0	0-0	1	1	1	1	0	0-0	0	9.00	35	.250	.250	0-0	—	0		-1	0.0
	Oak A	0	0	—	1	0	0	0-0	1	0	0	0	0	0-0	0	0.00	—	.000	.000	0-0	—	0		0	0.0
	SD N	0	0	—	5	0	0	0-0	4.1	7	4	1	0	3-0	5	8.31	40	.350	.435	0-0	—	0		-2	-0.1
	Cle A	4	1	.800	22	7	1	1-0	58	51	23	5	0	39-4	44	3.41	95	.237	.353	14-2	.071	-1	82	0	-0.1
	Year	4	1	.800	24	7	1	1-0	60	52	27	6	0	39-4	44	3.45	94	.234	.348	14-2	.071	-1	82	-1	-0.2
1973	Cle A	0	0	—	5	0	0	0-0	2	5	5	1	1	5-0	3	22.50	17	.455	.647	0-0	—	0		-4	-0.2
Total	5	23	18	.561	139	54	12-4	4-1	410	387	216	39	9	224-8	301	4.43	82	.248	.344	114-10	.070	-8	92	-33	-3.5
KILLEEN, EVANS Evans Henry B 2.27.1936 Brooklyn, NY BR/TR 6/190# d9.7																									
1959	KC A	0	0	—	4	0	0	0	5.2	4	3	0	0	4-0	1	4.76	84	.211	.348	0-0	—	0		0	0.0
KILLEEN, HENRY Henry F. B 5.1872 Troy, NY D 10.16.1916 Waterbury, CT 5-9/150# d9.11																									
1891	Cle N	0	1	.000	1	1	1	0	8.2	11	8	1	0	8	3	6.23	56	.297	.422	3	.000	-0	34	-2	-0.2
KILLEN, FRANK Frank Bissell "Lefty" B 11.30.1870 Pittsburgh, PA D 12.3.1939 Pittsburgh, PA BL/TL 6-1/200# d8.27																									
1891	Mil AA	7	4	.636	11	11	11-2	0	96.2	73	42	1	3	51	38	1.68	262	.202	.306	35	.229	1	126	22	2.3
1892	Was N	29	26	.527	60	52	46-2	0	459.2	448	286	15	20	182	147	3.31	98	.245	.321	186	.199	10*	90	-2	1.0
1893	Pit N	**36**	14	.720	55	48	38-2	0	415	401	235	12	15	140	99	3.64	125	.246	.312	171	.275	14	125	46	5.5
1894	Pit N	14	11	.560	28	28	20-1	0	204	261	148	3	5	86	62	4.50	117	.308	.375	80-1	.262	0	99	13	1.1
1895	Pit N	5	5	.500	13	11	6	0	95	113	77	2	1	57	25	5.49	82	.291	.383	38-0	.342	4*	83	-8	-0.2
1896	Pit N	**30**	18	.625	**52**	**50**	**44-5**	0	**432.1**	476	244	7	14	119	134	3.41	123	.277	.329	173-3	.231	9*	117	29	3.4
1897	Pit N	17	23	.425	42	41	**38**-1	0	337.1	417	246	4	8	76	99	4.46	94	.301	.341	129-0	.248	5	83	-16	-1.1
1898	Pit N	10	11	.476	23	23	17	0	177.2	201	106	3	11	41	48	3.75	95	.283	.332	65-4	.262	2*	93	-5	-0.3
	Was N	6	9	.400	17	16	15	0	128.1	149	80	4	2	29	43	3.58	102	.288	.328	55-0	.273	3*	110	-1	0.2
	Year	16	20	.444	40	39	32	0	306	350	86	7	13	70	91	3.68	98	.285	.330	120-4	.267	5	100	-5	-0.1
1899	Was N	0	2	.000	2	2	1	0	12	18	11	0	1	4	3	6.00	65	.346	.404	5-0	.200	-0	64	-3	-0.4
	Bos N	7	5	.583	12	12	11	0	99.1	108	65	3	3	26	23	4.26	98	.276	.326	41-0	.171	-2	101	-2	-0.4
	Year	7	7	.500	14	14	12	0	111.1	126	71	3	4	30	26	4.45	93	.284	.335	46-0	.174	-3	96	-2	-0.8
1900	Chi N	3	3	.500	6	6	6	0	54	65	38	1	2	11	4	4.67	77	.297	.336	20-1	.150	-1	96	-2	-0.2
Total	10	164	131	.556	321	300	253-13	0	2511.1	2730	1571	55	85	822	725	3.78	109	.272	.332	998-9	.241	44	104	71	10.9
KILLIAN, ED Edwin Henry "Twilight Ed" B 11.12.1876 Racine, WI D 7.18.1928 Detroit, MI BL/TL 5-11/170# d8.25																									
1903	Cle A	3	4	.429	9	8	7-3	0	61.2	61	24	1	4	13	18	2.48	115	.257	.307	28-0	.179	-1*	113	3	0.3
1904	Det A	15	20	.429	40	34	32-4	0	331.2	293	118	0	17	93	124	2.44	104	.238	.301	126-2	.143	-3	89	8	0.2
1905	Det A	23	14	.622	39	37	33-**8**	0	313.1	263	108	0	13	102	110	2.27	120	.230	.300	118-7	.271	6	90	17	2.6
1906	Det A	10	6	.625	21	16	14	2	149.2	165	71	0	5	54	47	3.43	81	.283	.348	53-3	.170	-1	133	-9	-1.2
1907	†Det A	25	13	.658	42	34	29-3	0	314	286	103	2	11	91	96	1.78	147	.245	.306	122-3	.320	10*	104	25	4.2
1908	†Det A	12	9	.571	27	23	15	1	180.2	170	78	3	8	53	47	2.99	81	.252	.314	73-0	.137	-3*	118	-8	-1.1
1909	Det A	11	9	.550	25	19	14-3	1	173.1	150	45	1	6	49	54	1.71	147	.236	.297	62-3	.161	-1	97	15	1.7
1910	Det A	4	3	.571	11	9	5-1	0	74	75	38	2	6	27	20	3.04	87	.268	.345	27-1	.148	-1	150	-5	-0.6
Total	8	103	78	.569	214	180	149-22	4	1598.1	1463	585	9	70	482	516	2.38	110	.246	.310	609-19	.209	6	105	46	6.1
KILLILAY, JACK John William B 5.24.1887 Leavenworth, KS D 10.21.1968 Tulsa, OK BR/TR 5-11/165# d5.13																									
1911	Bos A	4	2	.667	14	7	1	0	61	65	26	0	10	36	28	3.54	93	.302	.425	24-0	.042	-2	116	2	-0.1
KILROY, MATT Matthew Aloysius "Matches" B 6.21.1866 Philadelphia, PA D 3.2.1940 Philadelphia, PA BL/TL 5-9/175# d4.17 b-Mike																									
1886	Bal AA	29	34	.460	**68**	**68**	**66**-5	0	583	476	350	10	19	182	**513**	3.37	102	.210	.274	218	.174	-5	76	3	0.1
1887	Bal AA	**46**	19	.708	**69**	**69**	**66-6**	0	**589.1**	585	326	9	20	157	217	3.07	134	.253	.306	239	.247	9*	113	**72**	**7.2**
1888	Bal AA	17	21	.447	40	40	35-2	0	321	347	224	5	23	79	135	4.04	74	.266	.319	145	.179	-0*	100	-40	-3.8
1889	Bal AA	29	25	.537	59	56	**55**-5	0	480.2	476	283	8	27	142	217	2.85	139	.250	.312	208	.274	10*	89	49	5.7
1890	Bos P	9	15	.375	30	27	18	1	217.2	268	161	14	15	87	48	4.26	103	.290	.361	93	.215	-0*	98	4	0.3

Year	Tm Lg	W	L	Pct	G	GS	CG-Sho	SV-BS	IP	H	R	HR	HB	BB-IB	SO	ERA	AERA	OAV	OOB	AB-SH	AVG	PB	Sup	APR	PW
1891	Cin AA	1	4	.200	7	6	4	0	45.1	51	42	1	8	19	6	2.98	137	.274	.366	20	.150	-1*	73	2	0.1
1892	Was N	1	1	.500	4	3	2	0	26.1	20	11	0	2	15	1	2.39	136	.202	.319	10	.200	-0	45	3	0.3
1893	Lou N	3	2	.600	5	5	5-1	0	35	57	41	2	4	23	4	9.00	49	.354	.447	16	.438	3	105	-17	-1.3
1894	Lou N	0	5	.000	8	7	3	0	37	46	34	2	2	20	11	3.89	131	.301	.389	17-0	.118	-2	97	2	0.1
1898	Chi N	6	7	.462	13	11	10	0	100.1	119	67	2	11	30	18	4.31	83	.292	.357	96-2	.229	2*	108	-5	-0.3
Total	10	141	133	.515	303	292	264-19	1	2435.2	2445	1539	53	131	754	1170	3.47	109	.252	.314	1062-2	.222	15	95	73	8.4
KILROY, MIKE Michael Joseph B 11.4.1872 Philadelphia, PA D 10.2.1960 Philadelphia, PA BR/TR 5-11/180# d9.1 b-Matt																									
1888	Bal AA	0	1	.000	1	1	1	0	9	12	9	1	0	5	1	8.00	37	.308	.386	4	.000	-1	0	-4	-0.4
1891	Phi N	0	2	.000	3	1	0	0	10	15	14	1	2	4	3	9.90	34	.333	.412	5	.400	1	175	-6	-0.8
Total	2	0	3	.000	4	2	1	0	19	27	23	2	2	9	4	9.00	36	.321	.400	9	.222	0	92	-10	-1.2
KIM, BYUNG-HYUN Byung-Hyun B 1.19.1979 Kwangju, South Korea BR/TR 5-11/176# d5.29																									
1999	Ari N	1	2	.333	25	0	0	1-3	27.1	20	15	2	5	20-2	31	4.61	99	.211	.375	1-0	.000	-0		0	0.0
2000	Ari N	6	6	.500	61	1	0	14-6	70.2	52	39	9	9	46-5	111	4.46	106	.200	.336	3-0	.000	-0	117	1	0.2
2001	†Ari N	5	6	.455	78	0	0	19-4	98	58	32	10	8	44-3	113	2.94	156	.173	.284	6-0	.167	-0		18	2.5
2002	†Ari N★	8	3	.727	72	0	0	36-6	84	64	20	5	6	26-2	92	2.04	218	.208	.281	2-0	.500	0		21	4.2
2003	Ari N	1	5	.167	7	7	0	0-0	43	34	17	6	4	15-0	33	3.56	131	.214	.298	13-2	.154	-0	52	6	0.8
	†Bos A	8	5	.615	49	5	0	16-3	79.1	70	38	6	8	18-3	69	3.18	144	.230	.288	7-0	.286	0	185	9	1.7
Total	5	29	27	.518	292	13	0	86-22	402.1	298	161	38	40	169-15	449	3.24	141	.204	.302	32-2	.188	0	108	55	9.4
KIM, SUN-WOO Sun-Woo B 9.4.1977 Inchon, South Korea BR/TR 6-2/180# d6.15																									
2001	Bos A	0	2	.000	20	2	0	0-0	41.2	54	27	1	4	21-5	27	5.83	77	.312	.399	0-0	—	0	93	-5	-0.2
2002	Bos A	2	0	1.000	15	2	0	0-0	29	34	24	5	1	7-0	18	7.45	60	.288	.328	0-0	—	0	144	-8	-0.5
	Mon N	1	0	1.000	4	3	0	0-0	20.1	18	2	0	1	7-2	11	0.89	505	.250	.325	8-0	.250	0	131	8	0.4
2003	Mon N	0	1	.000	4	3	0	0-0	14	24	13	6	4	8-0	5	8.36	56	.407	.500	3-0	.000	-0	107	-5	-0.3
Total	3	3	3	.500	43	10	0	0-0	105	130	66	12	10	43-7	61	5.66	80	.308	.383	11-0	.182	-0	119	-10	-0.6
KIMBALL, NEWT Newell W. B 3.27.1915 Logan, UT D 3.22.2001 Las Vegas, NV BR/TR 6-2.5/190# d5.7																									
1937	Chi N	0	0	—	2	0	0	0	5	12	8	1	0	1	0	10.80	37	.444	.464	1-0	.000	-0		-4	-0.2
1938	Chi N	0	0	—	1	0	0	0	1	3	1	0	0	0	1	9.00	43	.500	.500	0-0	—	0		-1	0.0
1940	Bro N	3	1	.750	21	0	0	1	33.2	29	15	2	0	15	21	3.21	125	.238	.321	5-0	.000	-1		2	0.2
	StL N	1	0	1.000	2	1	1	0	14	11	5	1	0	6	6	2.57	155	.208	.288	6-0	.333	1	109	2	0.2
	Year	4	1	.800	23	1	1	1	47.2	40	10	3	0	21	27	3.02	132	.229	.311	11-0	.182	0	109	4	0.4
1941	Bro N	3	1	.750	15	5	1	1	52	43	22	0	0	29	17	3.63	101	.225	.327	14-0	.214	0	93	1	0.1
1942	Bro N	2	0	1.000	14	1	0	0	29.1	27	13	0	1	19	8	3.68	89	.265	.385	5-0	.200	-0	232	-1	-0.1
1943	Bro N	1	1	.500	5	0	0	1	11	9	2	0	0	5	2	1.64	205	.214	.298	3-0	.000	-0		2	0.4
	Phi N	1	6	.143	34	6	2	2	89.2	85	47	4	1	42	33	4.12	82	.253	.338	16-2	.188	1	101	-7	-0.5
	Year	2	7	.222	39	6	2	3	100.2	94	51	4	1	47	35	3.84	88	.249	.333	19-2	.158	1	101	-5	-0.1
Total	6	11	9	.550	94	13	4	5	235.2	219	113	8	2	117	88	3.78	94	.249	.339	50-2	.180	1	107	-6	0.1
KIMBER, SAM Samuel Jackson B 10.29.1852 Philadelphia, PA D 11.7.1925 Philadelphia, PA BR/TR 5-10.5/165# d5.1																									
1884	Bro AA	18	20	.474	41	41	41-4	0	361.1	364	240	6	15	72	122	3.81	87	.247	.289	142	.148	-5	94	-18	-2.0
1885	Pro N	0	1	.000	1	1	1	0	8	15	13	1		5	4	11.25	24	.405	.476	3	.000	-0	21	-6	-0.5
Total	2	18	21	.462	42	42	42-4	0	369.1	379	253	7	15	77	126	3.97	83	.251	.294	145	.145	-6	92	-24	-2.5
KIMBERLIN, HARRY Harry Lydle "Murphy" or "Mule Trader" B 3.13.1909 Sullivan, MO D 12.31.1999 Poplar Bluff, MO BR/TR 6-3/175# d7.11																									
1936	StL A	0	0	—	13	0	0	0	20	24	13	3	0	16	4	5.40	100	.296	.412	1-0	.000	-0		0	0.0
1937	StL A	0	2	.000	3	2	1	0	15.1	16	13	2	0	9	5	2.35	206	.254	.347	5-0	.200	0	63	0	0.1
1938	StL A	0	0	—	1	1	1	0	8	8	3	1	0	3	1	3.38	147	.286	.355	1-2	.000	-0	53	2	0.0
1939	StL A	1	2	.333	17	3	0	0	41	59	35	6	2	19	11	5.49	89	.326	.396	9-0	.333	0	42	-6	-0.3
Total	4	1	4	.200	34	6	2	0	84.1	107	64	12	2	47	21	4.70	106	.303	.388	16-2	.250	0	50	-4	-0.2
KIME, HAL Harold Lee "Lefty" B 3.15.1899 W.Salem, OH D 5.16.1939 Columbus, OH BL/TL 5-9/160# d6.19																									
1920	StL N	0	0	—	4	0	0	0	7	9	4	0	1	2	1	2.57	116	.333	.400	1-0	.000	-0		0	0.0
KIMSEY, CHAD Clyde Elias B 8.6.1906 Copperhill, TN D 12.3.1942 Pryor, OK BL/TR 6-2/200# d4.21																									
1929	StL A	3	6	.333	24	3	1	1	64.1	83	42	2	0	19	13	5.04	88	.340	.388	30-1	.267	3*	57	-5	-0.2
1930	StL A	6	10	.375	42	4	1	1	113.1	139	87	8	2	45	32	6.35	77	.312	.377	70-0	.343	7*	79	-16	-1.1
1931	StL A	4	6	.400	42	1	0	7	94.1	121	60	1	2	27	27	4.39	106	.312	.360	37-1	.270	5*	109	**1**	0.7
1932	StL A	4	2	.667	33	0	0	3	78.1	85	45	3	0	33	13	4.02	121	.281	.352	18-0	.333	1*		5	0.5
	Chi A	1	1	.500	7	0	0	2	11	8	4	0	1	5	6	2.45	176	.211	.318	2-0	.000	-0		2	0.5
	Year	5	3	.625	40	0	0	5	89.1	93	55	3	1	38	19	3.83	125	.274	.348	20-0	.300	1		**8**	1.0
1933	Chi A	4	1	.800	28	2	0	0	96	124	67	7	4	36	19	5.53	77	.318	.381	33-0	.152	-2	120	-12	-0.7
1936	Det A	2	3	.400	22	0	0	3	52	58	36	2	1	29	11	4.85	102	.284	.376	16-0	.313	2		-1	0.1
Total	6	24	29	.453	198	10	2	17	509.1	618	341	23	10	194	121	5.07	92	.307	.371	206-2	.282	16	83	-26	-0.2
KINDER, ELLIS Ellis Raymond "Old Folks" B 7.26.1914 Atkins, AR D 10.16.1968 Jackson, TN BR/TR 6/195# d4.30																									
1946	StL A	3	3	.500	33	7	1	1	86.2	78	35	8	0	36	59	3.32	112	.241	.318	19-2	.053	-1	95	5	0.1
1947	StL A	8	15	.348	34	26	10-2	1	194.1	201	105	11	0	82	110	4.49	86	.264	.336	62-4	.129	-4	67	-11	-1.7
1948	Bos A	10	7	.588	28	22	10-1	0	178	183	84	10	2	63	53	3.74	117	.266	.330	62-3	.097	-4	122	12	0.4
1949	Bos A	23	6	**.793**	43	30	19-**6**	4	252	251	103	21	2	99	138	3.36	130	.260	.330	92-9	.130	-4	134	27	2.2
1950	Bos A	14	12	.538	48	23	11-1	9	207	212	105	23	1	78	95	4.26	115	.263	.328	71-4	.183	-1	136	14	1.4
1951	Bos A	11	2	.846	**63**	2	1	**14**	127	108	42	8	0	46	84	2.55	175	.230	.298	34-0	.118	-3	149	**24**	2.5
1952	Bos A	5	6	.455	23	10	4	4	97.2	85	33	11	1	28	50	2.58	153	.234	.290	32-0	.000	-4	53	13	1.1
1953	Bos A	10	6	.625	**69**	0	0	**27**	107	84	30	8	2	38	39	1.85	227	.215	.288	29-1	.379	3		**25**	**5.2**
1954	Bos A	8	8	.500	48	2	0	15	107	106	47	7	0	36	67	3.62	114	.260	.318	27-5	.185	0	172	6	1.0
1955	Bos A	5	5	.500	43	0	0	18	66.2	57	22	4	1	15-4	31	2.84	151	.229	.274	12-1	.250	0		11	2.1
1956	StL N	2	0	1.000	22	0	0	6	25.2	23	11	3	0	9-3	4	3.51	108	.245	.305	2-0	.000	-0		1	0.0
	Chi A	3	1	.750	29	0	0	3	29.2	33	10	2	0	8-0	19	2.73	150	.277	.318	2-0	.000	-0		5	0.6
1957	Chi A	0	0	—	1	0	0	0	1	0	0	0	0	1-1	0	0.00	—	.000	.250	0-0	—	0		0	0.0
Total	12	102	71	.590	484	122	56-10	102	1479.2	1421	627	116	9	539-8	749	3.43	125	.252	.318	444-29	.142	-19	112	132	14.9
KING, SILVER Charles Frederick (b: Charles Frederick Koenig) B 1.11.1868 St.Louis, MO D 5.21.1938 St.Louis, MO BR/TR 6/170# d9.28																									
1886	KC N	1	3	.250	5	5	5	0	39	43	35	1		9	23	4.85	78	.243	.280	22	.045	-2*	58	-5	-0.5
1887	†StL AA	32	12	.727	46	44	43-2	1	390	401	231	4	17	109	128	3.78	120	.260	.316	222	.207	-4*	107	36	2.4
1888	†StL AA	**45**	20	.692	**66**	**64**	**64-6**	0	**584.2**	435	203	6	30	76	258	**1.63**	**200**	.200	**.237**	207	.208	9	89	**95**	**10.2**
1889	StL AA	35	16	.686	56	53	47-2	1	458	462	257	15	21	125	188	3.14	134	.254	.309	189	.228	1	117	52	4.4
1890	Chi P	30	22	.577	56	**56**	48-**4**	0	461	420	233	5	15	163	185	**2.69**	**161**	**.232**	.301	185	.168	-6*	84	**82**	**6.6**
1891	Pit N	14	29	.326	48	44	40-3	1	384.1	382	243	7	18	144	160	3.11	105	.250	.321	148	.169	-1*	71	11	0.8
1892	NY N	22	24	.478	51	47	45-1	0	410.1	392	250	15	21	171	170	3.29	98	.242	.322	163	.209	6	104	-2	0.3
1893	NY N	3	4	.429	7	7	4	0	49	69	58	4	2	26	13	8.63	54	.322	.401	17	.176	1	124	-18	-1.6
	Cin N	5	6	.455	17	15	8-1	1	105	119	69	2	7	56	30	4.89	98	.277	.369	37	.162	-0	80	2	0.1
	Year	8	10	.444	24	22	12-1	1	154	188	74	6	9	82	43	6.08	78	.292	.380	54	.167	1	94	-11	-1.5
1896	Was N	10	7	.588	22	16	12	1	145.1	179	106	3	4	43	35	4.09	108	.300	.351	58-3	.276	3	129	5	0.6
1897	Was N	6	9	.400	23	19	12	1	154	196	118	7	11	45	32	4.79	91	.307	.363	57-0	.193	0*	121	-5	-0.3
Total	10	203	152	.572	397	370	328-19	6	3180.2	3098	1803	69	146	967	1222	3.18	122	.247	.308	1305-3	.198	7	98	253	23.0
KING, CLYDE Clyde Edward B 5.23.1924 Goldsboro, NC BB/TR 6-1/175# d6.21 M5 C7																									
1944	Bro N	2	1	.667	14	3	1	0	43.2	42	18	1	1	12	14	3.09	115	.256	.311	10-1	.200	-0	79	2	0.0
1945	Bro N	5	5	.500	42	2	0	3	112.1	131	64	8	0	48	29	4.09	92	.295	.364	32-2	.125	-2*	68	-4	-0.5
1947	Bro N	6	5	.545	29	9	2	0	87.2	85	34	11	0	29	31	2.77	149	.252	.311	26-1	.115	-1	121	12	1.2
1948	Bro N	0	1	.000	9	0	0	0	12.1	14	11	3	1	6	5	8.03	50	.286	.375	2-0	.000	-0		-5	-0.4
1951	Bro N	14	7	.667	48	3	1	6	121.1	118	64	15	3	50	33	4.15	94	.263	.341	29-4	.138	0	217	-4	-0.7
1952	Bro N	2	0	1.000	23	0	0	0	42.2	56	25	5	1	12	17	5.06	72	.318	.365	5-0	.000	-1		-6	-0.3

Year	Tm Lg	W	L	Pct	G	GS	CG-Sho	SV-BS	IP	H	R	HR	HB	BB-IB	SO	ERA	AERA	OAV	OOB	AB-SH	AVG	PB	Sup	APR	PW
1953	Cin N	3	6	.333	35	4	0	2	76	78	47	15	2	32	21	5.21	84	.271	.348	10-1	.000	-1	118	-6	-0.7
Total	7	32	25	.561	200	21	4	11	496	524	263	58	8	189	150	4.14	95	.275	.343	114-9	.114	-4	126	-11	-1.4
KING, CURTIS Curtis Albert B 10.25.1970 Norristown, PA BR/TR 6-5/205# d8.1																									
1997	StL N	4	2	.667	30	0	0	0-3	29.1	38	14	0	1	11-0	13	2.76	150	.325	.379	1-0	.000	-0		3	0.5
1998	StL N	2	0	1.000	36	0	0	2-6	51	50	20	5	3	20-4	28	3.53	119	.262	.338	5-0	.000	-1		5	0.2
1999	StL N	0	0	—	2	0	0	0-0	1	3	2	0	0	0-0	1	18.00	25	.500	.500	0-0	—	0		-1	-0.1
Total	3	6	2	.750	68	0	0	2-9	81.1	91	36	5	4	31-4	42	3.43	122	.290	.356	6-0	.000	-1		7	0.6
KING, ERIC Eric Steven B 4.10.1964 Oxnard, CA BR/TR 6-2/215# d5.15																									
1986	Det A	11	4	.733	33	16	3-1	3-2	138.1	108	54	11	8	63-3	79	3.51	118	.216	.312	0-0	—	0	124	12	1.3
1987	†Det A	6	9	.400	55	4	0	9-6	116	111	67	15	4	60-10	89	4.89	87	.251	.343	0-0	—	0	59	-7	-0.8
1988	Det A	4	1	.800	23	5	0	3-0	68.2	60	28	5	5	34-2	45	3.41	112	.233	.332	0-0	—	0	143	4	0.2
1989	Chi A	9	10	.474	25	25	1-1	0-0	159.1	144	69	13	4	64-1	72	3.39	113	.244	.320	0-0	—	0	114	7	0.7
1990	Chi A	12	4	.750	25	25	2-2	0-0	151	135	59	10	6	40-0	70	3.28	117	.237	.293	0-0	—	0	110	10	0.9
1991	Cle A	6	11	.353	25	24	2-1	0-0	150.2	166	83	7	3	44-4	59	4.60	90	.279	.328	0-0	—	0	101	-6	-0.7
1992	Det A	4	6	.400	17	14	0	1-0	79.1	90	47	12	1	28-1	45	5.22	76	.285	.343	0-0	—	0	114	-10	-1.2
Total	7	52	45	.536	203	113	8-5	16-8	863.1	814	407	73	31	333-21	459	3.97	101	.249	.322	0-0	—	0	110	10	0.4
KING, KEVIN Kevin Ray B 2.11.1969 Atwater, CA BL/TL 6-4/170# d9.2																									
1993	Sea A	0	1	.000	13	0	0	0-1	11.2	9	8	3	1	4-1	8	6.17	72	.231	.304	0-0	—	0		-2	-0.2
1994	Sea A	0	2	.000	19	0	0	0-1	15.1	21	13	0	1	17-3	6	7.04	69	.333	.481	0-0	—	0		-3	-0.4
1995	Sea A	0	0	—	2	0	0	0-0	3.2	7	5	0	1	1-0	3	12.27	39	.412	.450	0-0	—	0		-3	-0.1
Total	3	0	3	.000	34	0	0	0-2	30.2	37	26	3	3	22-4	17	7.34	64	.311	.422	0-0	—	0		-8	-0.7
KING, NELLIE Nelson Joseph B 3.15.1928 Shenandoah, PA BR/TR 6-6/185# d4.15																									
1954	Pit N	0	0	—	4	0	0	0	7	10	5	0	0	1	3	5.14	81	.400	.367	0-0	—	0		-1	0.0
1955	Pit N	1	3	.250	17	4	0	0	54.1	60	24	2	2	14-3	21	2.98	138	.286	.332	12-2	.000	-2	76	5	0.2
1956	Pit N	4	1	.800	38	0	0	5	60	54	24	8	1	19-5	25	3.15	120	.241	.302	6-2	.000	-1		4	0.3
1957	Pit N	2	1	.667	36	0	0	1	52	69	27	7	2	16-6	23	4.50	84	.337	.387	5-1	.000	-1		-3	-0.2
Total	4	7	5	.583	95	4	0	6	173.1	193	80	17	5	50-14	72	3.58	109	.291	.340	23-5	.000	-3	76	5	0.3
KING, RAY Raymond Keith B 1.15.1974 Chicago, IL BL/TL 6-1/225# d5.21																									
1999	Chi N	0	0	—	10	0	0	0-0	10.2	11	8	2	1	10-0	5	5.91	76	.289	.449	1-0	.000	-0		-2	-0.1
2000	Mil N	3	2	.600	36	0	0	0-1	28.2	18	7	1	0	10-1	19	1.26	363	.180	.252	0-0	—	0		9	1.5
2001	Mil N	0	4	.000	82	0	0	1-3	55	49	22	5	1	25-7	49	3.60	119	.241	.325	2-0	.000	-0		5	0.4
2002	Mil N	3	2	.600	76	0	0	0-1	65	61	24	5	3	24-6	50	3.05	135	.255	.328	0-0	—	0		8	0.7
2003	†Atl N	3	4	.429	80	0	0	0-1	59	46	30	3	1	27-2	43	3.51	120	.213	.301	0-0	—	0		3	0.3
Total	5	9	12	.429	284	0	0	1-6	218.1	185	91	16	6	96-16	166	3.22	133	.232	.317	3-0	.000	-0		23	2.8
KINGMAN, BRIAN Brian Paul B 7.27.1954 Los Angeles, CA BR/TR 6-2/200# d6.28																									
1979	Oak A	8	7	.533	18	17	5-1	0-1	112.2	113	59	10	3	33-1	58	4.31	94	.258	.313	0-0	—	0	95	-2	-0.4
1980	Oak A	8	20	.286	32	30	10-1	0-0	211.1	209	105	21	4	82-5	116	3.83	99	.256	.325	0-0	—	0	68	-3	-0.5
1981	†Oak A	3	6	.333	18	15	3-1	0-0	100.1	112	48	10	4	32-2	52	3.95	88	.286	.345	0-0	—	0	93	-5	-0.5
1982	Oak A	4	12	.250	23	20	3	1-0	122.2	131	64	11	7	57-0	46	4.48	87	.279	.360	0-0	—	0	85	-6	-0.8
1983	SF N	0	0	—	3	0	0	0-0	4.2	10	6	0	0	1-0	1	7.71	46	.417	.440	0-0	—	0		-3	-0.2
Total	5	23	45	.338	94	82	21-3	1-1	551.2	575	282	52	18	205-8	273	4.13	92	.269	.336	0-0	—	0	82	-19	-2.4
KINNEY, DENNIS Dennis Paul B 2.26.1952 Toledo, OH BL/TL 6-1/190# d4.9																									
1978	Cle A	0	2	.000	18	0	0	5-2	38.2	37	21	3	1	14-1	19	4.42	85	.259	.325	0-0	—	0		-3	-0.2
	SD N	0	1	.000	7	0	0	0-1	7	6	5	3	0	4-0	2	6.43	52	.222	.323	1-0	.000	-0		-2	-0.3
1979	SD N	0	0	—	13	0	0	0-0	18	17	8	2	1	8-3	11	3.50	101	.250	.338	1-0	.000	-0		0	0.0
1980	SD N	4	6	.400	50	0	0	1-2	82.2	79	45	3	1	37-15	40	4.25	81	.252	.331	12-1	.083	-0		-9	-1.1
1981	Det A	0	0	—	6	0	0	0-0	3.2	5	4	0	0	4-1	3	9.82	38	.313	.450	0-0	—	0		-2	-0.1
1982	Oak A	0	0	—	3	0	0	0-0	4.1	9	4	1	0	4-0	0	8.31	47	.474	.565	0-0	—	0		-2	-0.1
Total	5	4	9	.308	97	0	0	6-5	154.1	153	87	12	3	71-20	75	4.55	78	.261	.341	14-1	.071	-1		-18	-1.8
KINNEY, MATT Matthew John B 12.16.1976 Bangor, ME BR/TR 6-5/220# d8.18																									
2000	Min A	2	2	.500	8	8	0	0-0	42.1	41	26	7	0	25-1	24	5.10	101	.261	.355	0-0	—	0	100	0	0.0
2002	Min A	2	7	.222	14	12	0	0-0	66	78	39	13	1	33-0	45	4.64	97	.295	.371	2-0	.000	-0	64	-2	-0.3
2003	Mil N	10	13	.435	33	31	1	0-0	190.2	201	121	27	6	80-4	152	5.19	82	.272	.343	55-5	.036	-4	105	-21	-2.6
Total	3	14	22	.389	55	51	1	0-0	299	320	186	47	7	138-5	221	5.06	88	.276	.351	57-5	.035	-4	95	-23	-2.9
KINNEY, WALT Walter William B 9.9.1893 Denison, TX D 7.1.1971 Escondido, CA BL/TL 6-2/186# d7.26																									
1918	Bos A	0	0	—	5	0	0	0	15	5	3	0	2	8	4	1.80	149	.106	.263	5-0	.000	-1*		2	0.0
1919	Phi A	9	15	.375	43	21	13	2	202.2	199	110	7	8	91	97	3.64	94	.262	.347	88-2	.284	5*	73	-7	0.2
1920	Phi A	2	4	.333	10	8	5-1	0	61	59	38	3	1	28	19	3.10	130	.261	.345	26-0	.346	2*	109	3	0.5
1923	Phi A	0	1	.000	5	1	0	0	12	11	13	0	0	9	9	7.50	55	.229	.351	6-0	.167	1	201	-5	-0.3
Total	4	11	20	.355	63	30	18-1	2	290.2	274	164	10	11	136	129	3.59	99	.254	.343	125-2	.280	7	90	-7	0.4
KINNUNEN, MIKE Michael John B 4.1.1958 Seattle, WA BL/TL 6-1/185# d6.12																									
1980	Min A	0	0	—	21	0	0	0-0	24.2	29	18	1	1	9-1	8	5.11	86	.290	.348	0-0	—	0		-3	-0.1
1986	Bal A	0	0	—	9	0	0	0-0	7	8	6	1	0	5-0	1	6.43	64	.308	.419	0-0	—	0		-2	-0.1
1987	Bal A	0	0	—	18	0	0	0-0	20	27	14	3	0	16-1	14	4.95	89	.338	.443	0-0	—	0		-2	-0.1
Total	3	0	0	—	48	0	0	0-0	51.2	64	38	5	1	30-2	23	5.23	84	.311	.396	0-0	—	0		-7	-0.3
KINSELLA, ED Edward William "Rube" B 1.15.1882 Lexington, IL D 1.17.1976 Bloomington, IL BR/TR 6-1.5/175# d9.16																									
1905	Pit N	0	1	.000	3	2	2	0	17	19	6	0	1	3	11	2.65	113	.292	.333	3-0	.000	-0	36	1	0.0
1910	StL A	1	3	.250	10	5	2	0	50	62	30	0	2	16	10	3.78	65	.321	.379	12-1	.250	2	114	-7	-0.3
Total	2	1	4	.200	13	7	4	0	67	81	36	0	3	19	21	3.49	75	.314	.368	15-1	.200	2	90	-6	-0.3
KINZER, MATT Matthew Roy B 6.17.1963 Indianapolis, IN BR/TR 6-2/210# d5.18																									
1989	StL N	0	2	.000	8	1	0	0-0	13.1	25	20	3	0	4-2	8	12.83	28	.403	.433	1-1	.000	-0	97	-13	-1.6
1990	Det A	0	0	—	1	0	0	0-0	1.2	3	3	0	0	3-0	1	16.20	24	.375	.545	0-0	—	0		-2	-0.1
Total	2	0	2	.000	9	1	0	0-0	15	28	23	3	0	7-2	9	13.20	28	.400	.449	1-1	.000	-0	97	-15	-1.7
KINZY, HARRY Harry Hersel "Slim" B 7.19.1910 Hallsville, TX D 6.22.2003 Ft.Worth, TX BR/TR 6-4/185# d6.8																									
1934	Chi A	0	1	.000	13	2	1	0	34.1	38	23	1	4	31	12	4.98	95	.290	.440	10-0	.300	1	83	-1	0.0
KIPP, FRED Fred Leo B 10.1.1931 Piqua, KS BL/TL 6-4/200# d9.10																									
1957	Bro N	0	0	—	1	0	0	0	4	6	4	2	0	0-0	3	9.00	46	.333	.333	1-0	.000	-0		-2	-0.1
1958	LA N	6	6	.500	40	9	0	0	102.1	107	60	16	1	45-7	58	5.01	82	.273	.349	36-0	.250	1*	80	-8	-0.7
1959	LA N	0	0	—	2	0	0	0	2.2	2	0	0	0	3-1	1	0.00	—	.222	.417	0-0	—	0		1	0.1
1960	NY A	0	1	.000	4	0	0	0	4.1	4	3	0	0	0-0	2	6.23	57	.250	.250	0-0	—	0		-1	-0.2
Total	4	6	7	.462	47	9	0	0	113.1	119	67	18	1	48-8	64	5.08	80	.274	.346	37-0	.243	1	80	-10	-0.9
KIPPER, BOB Robert Wayne B 7.8.1964 Aurora, IL BR/TL 6-2/200# d4.12 C1																									
1985	Cal A	0	1	.000	2	1	0	0-0	3.1	7	8	1	0	3-0	0	21.60	19	.467	.500	0-0	—	0	199	-6	-0.9
	Pit N	1	2	.333	5	4	0	0-0	24.2	21	16	4	0	7-0	13	5.11	70	.221	.272	8-2	.250	0	92	-4	-0.5
1986	Pit N	6	8	.429	20	19	0	0-0	114	123	60	17	2	34-3	81	4.03	95	.271	.323	33-3	.030	-3*	84	-4	-0.7
1987	Pit N	5	9	.357	24	20	1-1	0-0	110.2	117	74	25	2	52-4	83	5.94	69	.271	.350	33-3	.242	2*	98	-19	-1.9
1988	Pit N	2	6	.250	50	0	0	0-0	65	54	33	7	2	26-4	39	3.74	91	.234	.313	4-1	.000	-0		-4	-0.4
1989	Pit N	3	4	.429	52	0	0	4-4	83	55	29	5	0	33-6	58	2.93	115	.188	.267	9-1	.111	-0		5	0.4
1990	Pit N	5	2	.714	41	1	0	3-1	62.2	44	24	7	3	26-1	35	3.02	120	.195	.283	7-0	.143	-0	274	4	0.5
1991	†Pit N	2	2	.500	52	0	0	4-2	60	66	34	7	0	22-3	38	4.65	77	.276	.335	1-1	.000	-0		-7	-0.6
1992	Min A	3	3	.500	25	0	0	0-2	38.2	40	23	8	3	14-3	22	4.42	92	.268	.343	0-0	—	0		-3	-0.4

Year	Tm Lg	W	L	Pct	G	GS	CG-Sho	SV-BS	IP	H	R	HR	HB	BB-IB	SO	ERA	AERA	OAV	OOB	AB-SH	AVG	PB	Sup	APR	PW
Total	8	27	37	.422	271	45	1-1	11-9	562	527	301	81	12	217-24	369	4.34	86	.247	.317	95-11	.137	-1	103	-38	-4.5
KIPPER, THORNTON Thornton John B 9.27.1928 Bagley, WI BR/TR 6-3/190# d6.7																									
1953	Phi N	3	3	.500	20	3	0	0	45.2	59	26	8	0	12	15	4.73	89	.319	.360	11-2	.091	-1	35	-2	-0.3
1954	Phi N	0	0	—	11	0	0	1	13.2	22	13	0	1	12	5	7.90	51	.379	.493	2-0	.000	-0		-6	-0.3
1955	Phi N	0	1	.000	24	0	0	0	39.2	47	23	4	1	22-4	15	4.99	80	.301	.389	3-0	.333	0		-4	-0.2
Total	3	3	4	.429	55	3	0	1	99	128	62	12	2	46-4	35	5.27	78	.321	.393	16-2	.125	-1	35	-12	-0.8
KIRBY, CLAY Clayton Laws B 6.25.1948 Washington, DC D 10.11.1991 Arlington, VA BR/TR 6-3/185# d4.11																									
1969	SD N	7	20	.259	35	35	2	0-0	215.2	204	108	18	6	100-13	113	3.80	93	.252	.337	66-2	.061	-2	74	-9	-1.4
1970	SD N	10	16	.385	36	34	6-1	0-0	214.2	198	118	29	9	120-5	154	4.53	88	.248	.348	74-3	.149	-0	92	-12	-1.4
1971	SD N	15	13	.536	38	36	13-2	0-0	267.1	213	99	20	3	103-14	231	2.83	117	.216	.291	86-5	.093	-3*	87	15	1.2
1972	SD N	12	14	.462	34	34	9-2	0-0	238.2	197	87	21	2	116-11	175	3.13	105	.226	.317	74-6	.068	-4*	83	8	0.3
1973	SD N	8	18	.308	34	31	4-2	0-0	191.2	214	122	30	1	66-7	129	4.79	73	.282	.338	54-11	.093	-3*	101	-31	-4.0
1974	Cin N	12	9	.571	36	35	7-1	0-0	230.2	210	97	15	2	91-3	160	3.28	107	.242	.313	74-8	.095	-3	114	5	0.0
1975	Cin N	10	6	.625	26	19	1	0-0	110.2	113	63	13	5	54-3	48	4.72	76	.263	.351	32-4	.188	1	136	-14	-1.9
1976	Mon N	1	8	.111	22	15	0	0-0	78.2	81	61	10	2	63-1	51	5.72	65	.273	.399	18-6	.056	-1	101	-18	-2.0
Total	8	75	104	.419	261	239	42-8	0-0	1548	1430	755	156	30	713-57	1061	3.84	92	.246	.329	478-45	.098	-15	96	-56	-9.2
KIRBY, JOHN John F. B 1.13.1865 St.Louis, MO D 10.6.1931 St.Louis, MO TR 5-8/172# d8.1																									
1884	KC U	0	1	.000	2	2	1	0	11	13	10	0		2	1	4.09	55	.277	.306	7	.143	-1	86	-3	-0.2
1885	StL N	5	8	.385	14	14	14	0	129.1	118	66	0		44	46	3.55	77	.241	.303	50	.060	-6	82	-6	-1.1
1886	StL N	11	26	.297	41	41	38-1	0	325	329	222	9		134	129	3.30	98	.252	.322	136	.110	-9*	81	-4	-1.3
1887	Ind N	1	6	.143	8	8	5	0	62	70	64	3	2	43	7	6.10	68	.272	.381	29	.138	-2	78	-13	-1.3
	Cle AA	0	5	.000	5	5	5	0	41	62	53	1	2	28	6	9.00	48	.339	.432	18	.167	-1	38	-16	-1.3
1888	KC AA	1	4	.200	5	5	5	0	43	48	36	0	1	7	11	4.19	82	.273	.304	16	.063	-2	24	-4	-0.5
Total	5	18	50	.265	75	75	68-1	0	611.1	640	451	13	5	258	200	4.09	80	.260	.332	256	.105	-21	74	-46	-5.7
KIRBY, LA RUE La Rue B 12.30.1889 Eureka, MI D 6.10.1961 Lansing, MI BB/TR 6/185# d8.7 ▲																									
1912	NY N	1	0	1.000	3	1	1	0	11	13	7	1	1	6	2	5.73	59	.295	.392	5-0	.200	0	152	-2	-0.1
1915	StL F	0	0	—	1	0	0	0	7	7	5	1	0	2	7	5.14	56	.269	.321	178-9	.213	0*		-2	-0.1
Total	2	1	0	1.000	4	1	1	0	18	20	12	2	1	8	9	5.50	58	.286	.367	183-9	.213	0	152	-4	-0.2
KIRCHER, MIKE Michael Andrew (b: Wolfgang Andrew Kerscher) B 9.30.1897 Rochester, NY D 6.26.1972 Rochester, NY BB/TR 6/180# d8.8																									
1919	Phi A	0	0	—	2	0	0	0	8	15	8	0	0	3	2	7.88	44	.429	.474	3-0	.000	-0		-3	-0.2
1920	StL N	2	1	.667	9	3	1	0	36.2	50	23	0	2	5	5	5.40	55	.333	.363	11-0	.273	0	88	-8	-0.7
1921	StL N	0	1	.000	3	0	0	0	3.1	4	3	0	1	1	2	8.10	45	.364	.462	0-0	—	0		-1	-0.3
Total	3	2	2	.500	14	3	1	0	48	69	34	0	3	9	9	6.00	52	.352	.389	14-0	.214	-0	88	-12	-1.2
KIRK, BILL William Partlemore B 7.19.1935 Coatesville, PA BL/TL 6/165# d9.23																									
1961	KC A	0	0	—	1	1	0	0	3	6	4	2	0	1-0	3	12.00	35	.375	.412	0-0	—	0	106	-2	-0.1
KIRKWOOD, DON Donald Paul B 9.24.1949 Pontiac, MI BR/TR 6-3/188# d9.13																									
1974	Cal A	0	0	—	3	0	0	0-0	7.1	12	8	0	0	6-0	4	8.59	40	.375	.474	0-0	—	0		-4	-0.2
1975	Cal A	6	5	.545	44	2	0	7-5	84	85	38	6	0	28-2	49	3.11	115	.270	.323	0-0	—	0*	99	2	0.3
1976	Cal A	6	12	.333	28	26	4	0-0	157.2	167	91	12	1	57-9	78	4.62	72	.278	.337	0-0	—	0	94	-23	-2.4
1977	Cal A	1	0	1.000	13	0	0	1-2	17.2	20	12	3	0	9-3	10	5.09	77	.290	.372	0-0	—	0		-3	-0.1
	Chi A	1	1	.500	16	0	0	0-0	40	49	27	3	1	10-2	24	5.17	79	.310	.349	0-0	—	0		-5	-0.3
	Year	2	1	.667	29	0	0	1-2	57.2	69	43	6	1	19-5	34	5.15	79	.304	.356	0-0	—	0		-8	-0.4
1978	Tor A	4	5	.444	16	9	3	0-0	68	76	36	6	0	25-1	29	4.24	93	.289	.348	0-0	—	0*	86	-3	-0.3
Total	5	18	23	.439	120	37	7	8-7	374.2	409	212	30	2	135-17	194	4.37	82	.284	.342	0-0	—	0	90	-36	-3.0
KIRSCH, HARRY Harry Louis "Casey" B 10.17.1887 Pittsburgh, PA D 12.25.1925 Philadelphia, PA BR/TR 5-11/170# d4.16																									
1910	Cle A	0	0	—	2	0	0	0	3	5	2	0	0	1	5	6.00	43	.385	.429	0-0	—	0		-1	-0.1
KISER, GARLAND Garland Routhard B 7.8.1968 Charlotte, NC BL/TL 6-3/190# d9.9																									
1991	Cle A	0	0	—	7	0	0	0-0	4.2	7	5	0	1	4-0	3	9.64	43	.368	.500	0-0	—	0		-3	-0.1
KISINGER, RUBE Charles Samuel B 12.13.1876 Adrian, MI D 7.14.1941 Huron, OH BR/TR 6/190# d9.10																									
1902	Det A	2	3	.400	5	5	5	0	43.1	48	20	0	3	14	7	3.12	117	.281	.346	19-0	.158	-1	71	3	0.2
1903	Det A	7	9	.438	16	14	13-2	0	118.2	118	58	0	2	27	33	2.96	98	.259	.303	47-0	.128	-3	67	-1	-0.4
Total	2	9	12	.429	21	19	18-2	0	162	166	78	0	5	41	40	3.00	103	.265	.315	66-0	.136	-4	68	2	-0.2
KISON, BRUCE Bruce Eugene B 2.18.1950 Pasco, WA BR/TR 6-4/178# d7.4 C8																									
1971	†Pit N	6	5	.545	18	13	2-1	0-0	95.1	93	40	6	6	36-5	60	3.40	100	.259	.335	31-1	.065	-1	121	0	-0.1
1972	†Pit N	9	7	.563	32	18	6-1	3-2	152	123	61	11	9	69-2	102	3.26	102	.220	.316	53-2	.189	2	123	2	0.5
1973	Pit N	3	0	1.000	7	7	0	0-0	43.2	36	17	4	1	24-3	26	3.09	114	.232	.339	12-0	.083	0	129	2	0.2
1974	†Pit N	9	8	.529	40	16	1	2-2	129	123	64	8	11	57-7	71	3.49	99	.247	.335	37-2	.108	-0	126	-4	-0.4
1975	†Pit N	12	11	.522	33	29	6	0-0	192	160	89	10	4	92-9	89	3.23	110	.227	.317	59-10	.119	-2*	108	3	0.3
1976	Pit N	14	9	.609	31	29	6-1	1-0	193	180	83	10	3	52-4	98	3.08	113	.247	.297	59-8	.203	4	111	6	1.1
1977	Pit N	9	10	.474	33	32	3-1	0-0	193	209	113	25	6	55-6	122	4.90	81	.278	.328	69-3	.261	5*	115	-17	-1.1
1978	Pit N	6	6	.500	28	11	0	0-1	96	81	40	3	5	39-0	62	3.19	116	.229	.311	29-0	.138	1	88	5	0.7
1979	†Pit N	13	7	.650	33	25	3-1	0-1	172.1	157	70	13	4	45-5	105	3.19	122	.246	.298	55-7	.145	0*	102	13	1.4
1980	Cal A	3	6	.333	13	13	2-1	0-0	73.1	73	46	5	3	32-2	28	4.91	80	.264	.344	0-0	—	0	121	-9	-1.0
1981	Cal A	1	1	.500	11	4	0	0-0	44	40	18	8	0	14-1	19	3.48	105	.241	.300	0-0	—	0	80	1	0.1
1982	†Cal A	10	5	.667	33	16	3-1	1-0	142	120	54	15	5	44-3	86	3.17	128	.226	.291	0-0	—	0	130	14	1.5
1983	Cal A	11	5	.688	26	17	4-1	2-1	126.2	128	59	13	4	43-4	83	4.05	99	.264	.328	0-0	—	0	111	1	0.2
1984	Cal A	4	5	.444	20	7	0	2-1	65.1	72	42	10	6	28-3	66	5.37	74	.280	.362	0-0	—	0	110	-10	-1.3
1985	Bos A	5	3	.625	22	9	0	1-1	92	98	43	9	1	32-4	56	4.11	104	.274	.332	0-0	—	0	113	3	0.3
Total	15	115	88	.567	380	246	36-8	12-9	1809.2	1693	839	150	68	662-58	1073	3.66	102	.248	.319	404-33	.163	8	113	10	2.4
KISSINGER, BILL William Francis "Shang" B 8.15.1871 Dayton, KY D 4.20.1929 Cincinnati, OH BR/TR 5-11/185# d5.30 ▲																									
1895	Bal N	1	0	1.000	2	2	1	0	11.1	18	11	0	0	2	3	3.97	120	.353	.377	5-0	.200	-0	120	-1	-0.1
	StL N	4	12	.250	24	14	9	0	140.2	222	145	8	8	51	31	6.72	72	.352	.408	97-1	.247	-2*	64	-28	-2.4
	Year	5	12	.294	26	16	10	0	152	240	149	8	8	53	34	6.51	74	.352	.406	102-1	.245	-2	71	-27	-2.5
1896	StL N	2	9	.182	20	12	11	1	136	209	136	5	8	55	22	6.49	67	.349	.411	73-2	.301	1*	69	-32	-1.8
1897	StL N	0	4	.000	7	4	2	0	31.1	51	50	2	8	15	5	11.49	38	.362	.451	39-0	.333	2*	61	-22	-1.8
Total	3	7	25	.219	53	32	23	1	319.1	500	342	15	24	123	61	6.99	66	.352	.413	214-3	.280	1	69	-83	-6.1
KITSON, FRANK Frank R. B 9.11.1869 Hopkins, MI D 4.14.1930 Allegan, MI BL/TR 5-11/165# d5.19																									
1898	Bal N	8	5	.615	17	13	13-1	0	119.1	123	71	0	8	35	32	3.24	110	.265	.327	86-0	.314	4*	92	2	0.5
1899	Bal N	22	16	.579	40	37	34-2	0	326.2	327	144	6	12	65	75	2.78	142	.260	.303	134-1	.201	-2*	81	42	3.9
1900	†Bro N	15	13	.536	40	30	21-2	**4**	253.1	283	152	12	9	56	55	4.19	92	.282	.326	109-1	.294	5*	106	-7	-0.4
1901	Bro N	19	11	.633	38	32	26-5	2	280.2	312	135	9	10	67	127	2.98	112	.279	.326	133-1	.263	5*	104	10	1.4
1902	Bro N	19	13	.594	32	31	29-3	0	268.2	256	105	4	7	52	109	2.85	97	.251	.292	116-1	.276	8*	107	2	1.1
1903	Det A	15	16	.484	31	28	28-2	0	257.2	277	112	8	5	38	102	2.58	113	.274	.303	116-5	.181	-1*	118	8	0.7
1904	Det A	9	13	.409	26	24	19	0	199.2	211	100	7	7	38	69	3.07	83	.272	.312	72-1	.208	1*	110	-13	-1.3
1905	Det A	12	14	.462	33	27	21-3	1	225.2	230	120	3	11	57	78	3.47	79	.266	.319	87-0	.184	-1	80	-17	-2.1
1906	Was A	6	14	.300	30	21	15-1	0	197	196	97	2	6	57	59	3.65	72	.262	.320	90-0	.244	8*	101	-18	-0.8
1907	Was A	0	3	.000	5	3	2	0	32	41	20	1	2	9	11	3.94	61	.313	.366	10-0	.100	-0	84	-5	-0.6
	NY A	4	0	1.000	12	4	3	0	61	75	31	0	4	17	14	3.10	90	.305	.360	25-1	.280	1	163	-2	-0.1
	Year	4	3	.571	17	7	5	0	93	116	38	1	6	26	25	3.39	79	.308	.362	35-1	.229	0	130	-7	-0.7
Total	10	129	118	.522	304	250	211-19	7	2221.2	2331	1087	52	81	491	731	3.18	99	.270	.315	978-11	.240	27	100	2	2.3
KLAERNER, HUGO Hugo Emil "Dutch" B 10.15.1908 Fredericksburg, TX D 2.3.1982 Fredericksburg, TX BR/TR 5-11/190# d9.10																									
1934	Chi A	0	2	.000	3	3	1	0	17.1	24	21	4	0	16	9	10.90	43	.329	.449	6-0	.333	1	98	-10	-0.7

Year	Tm Lg	W	L	Pct	G	GS	CG-Sho	SV-BS	IP	H	R	HR	HB	BB-IB	SO	ERA	AERA	OAV	OOB	AB-SH	AVG	PB	Sup	APR	PW
KLAGES, FRED	Frederick Albert Anthony B 10.31.1943 Ambridge, PA BR/TR 6-2/185# d9.11																								
1966	Chi A	1	0	1.000	3	3	0	0	15.2	9	4	0	0	7-0	6	1.72	184	.167	.262	6-0	.500	1	102	3	0.3
1967	Chi A	4	4	.500	11	9	0	0	44.2	43	19	6	1	16-1	17	3.83	81	.256	.323	12-1	.000	-1*	94	-2	-0.5
Total	2	5	4	.556	14	12	0	0	60.1	52	23	6	1	23-1	23	3.28	95	.234	.308	18-1	.167	-0	96	1	-0.2
KLAWITTER, AL	Albert "Dutch" B 4.12.1888 Wilkes-Barre, PA D 5.2.1950 Milwaukee, WI BR/TR 5-11.5/187# d9.20																								
1909	NY N	1	1	.500	6	3	2	1	27	24	11	1	0	13	6	2.00	128	.247	.336	9-0	.333	1	173	1	0.3
1910	NY N	0	0	—	1	0	0	0	1	2	1	0	0	2	0	9.00	33	.400	.571	0-0	—	0		-1	0.0
1913	Det A	1	2	.333	8	3	1	0	32	39	25	0	0	15	10	5.91	49	.307	.380	11-0	.000	-2	144	-9	-0.9
Total	3	2	3	.400	15	6	3	1	60	65	37	1	0	30	16	4.20	66	.284	.367	20-0	.150	-0	157	-9	-0.6
KLAWITTER, TOM	Thomas Carl B 6.24.1958 LaCrosse, WI BR/TL 6-2/190# d4.14																								
1985	Min A	0	0	—	7	2	0	0-0	9.1	7	7	2	0	13-0	5	6.75	65	.226	.455	0-0	—	0	155	-2	-0.1
KLEINE, HAL	Harold John B 6.8.1923 St.Louis, MO D 12.10.1957 St.Louis, MO BL/TL 6-2/193# d4.26																								
1944	Cle A	1	2	.333	11	6	1	0	40.2	38	29	0	0	36	13	5.75	57	.248	.392	14-1	.143	-1*	110	-11	-0.8
1945	Cle A	0	0	—	3	0	0	0	7	8	4	0	0	7	5	3.86	84	.286	.429	3-0	.333	1		-1	0.0
Total	2	1	2	.333	14	6	1	0	47.2	46	33	0	0	43	18	5.48	60	.254	.397	17-1	.176	-0	110	-12	-0.8
KLEINHANS, TED	Theodore Otto (b: Traugott Otto Kleinhans) B 4.8.1899 Deer Park, WI D 7.24.1985 Redington Beach, FL BR/TL 6/170# d4.20																								
1934	Phi N	0	0	—	5	0	0	0	6	11	8	1	0	3	2	9.00	52	.379	.438	1-0	.000	-0		-3	-0.1
	Cin N	2	6	.250	24	9	0	0	80	107	63	2	1	38	23	5.74	71	.321	.392	23-2	.130	-1*	61	-15	-1.3
	Year	2	6	.250	29	9	0	0	86	118	66	3	1	41	25	5.97	69	.326	.396	24-2	.125	-1	60	-19	-1.4
1936	NY A	1	1	.500	19	0	0	1	29.1	36	25	0	0	23	10	5.83	80	.300	.413	6-0	.167	-0		-6	-0.4
1937	Cin N	1	2	.333	7	3	1	0	27.1	29	13	1	1	12	13	2.30	162	.271	.350	8-0	.250	0	85	2	0.2
1938	Cin N	0	0	—	1	0	0	0	1	2	1	0	0	0	0	9.00	41	.400	.400	0-0	—	0		-1	0.0
Total	4	4	9	.308	56	12	1	1	143.2	185	110	4	2	76	48	5.26	79	.311	.391	38-2	.158	-1	64	-23	-1.6
KLEINKE, NUB	Norbert George B 5.19.1911 Fond Du Lac, WI D 3.16.1950 Off Marin Coast, CA BR/TR 6-1/170# d4.25																								
1935	StL N	0	0	—	4	2	0	0	12.2	19	8	1	0	3	5	4.97	82	.358	.393	2-0	.000	-0	155	-1	-0.1
1937	StL N	1	1	.500	5	2	1	0	20.2	25	14	0	0	7	9	4.79	83	.321	.376	8-0	.000	-1	141	-2	-0.3
Total	2	1	1	.500	9	4	1	0	33.1	44	22	1	0	10	14	4.86	83	.336	.383	10-0	.000	-1	149	-3	-0.4
KLEPFER, ED	Edward Lloyd "Big Ed" B 3.17.1888 Summerville, PA D 8.9.1950 Tulsa, OK BR/TR 6/185# d7.4 Mil 1918																								
1911	NY A	0	0	—	2	0	0	0	4	5	3	0	0	2	4	6.75	53	.250	.318	1-0	.000	-0		-1	-0.1
1913	NY A	0	1	.000	8	1	0	0	24.2	38	22	2	2	12	10	7.66	39	.376	.452	6-0	.167	0	0	-10	-0.5
1915	Chi A	1	0	1.000	3	2	1	0	12.2	11	4	0	0	5	3	2.84	105	.234	.308	3-0	.000	-0	122	1	0.0
	Cle A	1	6	.143	8	7	2	0	43	47	25	0	0	11	13	2.09	146	.283	.328	12-1	.167	-0	79	1	0.1
	Year	2	6	.250	11	9	3	0	55.2	58	28	0	0	16	16	2.26	134	.272	.323	15-1	.133	-0	88	1	0.1
1916	Cle A	6	6	.500	31	13	4-1	2	143	136	52	0	4	46	62	2.52	119	.262	.327	40-2	.025	-4	79	8	0.2
1917	Cle A	14	4	.778	41	27	9	1	213	208	84	0	0	55	66	2.37	120	.264	.312	62-5	.032	-6	109	8	-0.1
1919	Cle A	0	0	—	5	0	0	0	7.1	12	14	1	0	6	7	7.36	45	.375	.474	1-0	.000	-0		-5	-0.3
Total	6	22	17	.564	98	50	16-1	3	447.2	457	204	3	6	137	165	2.81	104	.273	.330	125-8	.048	-11	95	2	-0.7
KLIEMAN, ED	Edward Frederick "Specs" or "Babe" B 3.21.1918 Norwood, OH D 11.15.1979 Homosassa, FL BR/TR 6-1/190# d9.24																								
1943	Cle A	0	1	.000	1	1	1	0	9	8	1	0	0	5	2	1.00	311	.286	.394	3-0	.000	-0	0	2	0.2
1944	Cle A	11	13	.458	47	19	5-1	5	178.1	185	73	4	7	70	44	3.38	98	.274	.348	57-2	.105	-3	125	1	-0.2
1945	Cle A	5	8	.385	38	12	4-1	4	126.1	123	60	3	4	49	33	3.85	84	.261	.336	40-2	.200	1	76	-8	-0.6
1946	Cle A	0	0	—	9	0	0	0	15	18	13	0	0	10	2	6.60	50	.290	.389	1-0	.000	-0		-6	-0.4
1947	Cle A	5	4	.556	**58**	0	0	**17**	92	78	32	5	2	39	21	3.03	115	.231	.315	19-1	.105	-1		6	0.8
1948	†Cle A	3	2	.600	44	0	0	4	79.2	62	26	3	2	46	18	2.60	156	.229	.345	14-0	.143	-0		**14**	0.9
1949	Was A	0	0	—	2	0	0	0	3	8	6	0	0	3	1	18.00	24	.500	.579	1-0	1.000	0		-4	-0.2
	Chi A	2	0	1.000	18	0	0	3	33	33	15	2	0	15	9	3.00	139	.273	.353	8-2	.250	0		3	0.3
	Year	2	0	1.000	20	0	0	3	36	41	24	2	0	18	10	4.25	98	.299	.381	9-2	.333	1		-1	0.1
1950	Phi A	0	0	—	5	0	0	0	5.2	10	6	0	2	2	0	9.53	48	.357	.438	1-0	.000	-0		-3	-0.2
Total	8	26	28	.481	222	32	10-2	33	542	525	232	17	17	239	130	3.49	100	.261	.345	144-7	.146	-3	100	5	0.6
KLIMKOWSKI, RON	Ronald Bernard B 3.1.1944 Jersey City, NJ BR/TR 6-2/190# d9.15																								
1969	NY A	0	0	—	3	1	0	0-0	14	6	1	0	0	5-1	3	0.64	542	.130	.212	3-0	.000	-0	0	5	0.2
1970	NY A	6	7	.462	45	3	1-1	1-1	98.1	80	36	7	3	33-7	40	2.65	132	.223	.293	19-4	.053	-2	135	9	1.0
1971	Oak A	2	2	.500	26	0	0	2-0	45.1	37	19	3	1	23-8	25	3.38	99	.220	.316	5-0	.400	1		0	0.1
1972	NY A	0	3	.000	16	2	0	1-0	31.1	32	15	3	1	15-7	11	4.02	74	.271	.356	6-0	.000	-1	30	-3	-0.4
Total	4	8	12	.400	90	6	1-1	4-1	189	155	71	13	5	76-23	79	2.90	116	.224	.304	33-4	.091	-2	79	11	0.9
KLINE, BOB	Robert George "Junior" B 12.9.1909 Enterprise, OH D 3.16.1987 Westerville, OH BR/TR 6-3/200# d9.17																								
1930	Bos A	0	0	—	1	0	0	0	1	1	0	0	0	0	0	0.00	—	.333	.333	0-0	—	0		1	0.0
1931	Bos A	5	5	.500	28	10	3	0	98	110	54	3	3	35	25	4.41	98	.298	.364	27-1	.333	2	102	-1	0.3
1932	Bos A	11	13	.458	47	19	4-1	2	172	203	117	10	1	76	31	5.28	85	.294	.365	54-4	.130	-3	78	-13	-1.7
1933	Bos A	7	8	.467	46	8	1	4	127	127	70	5	6	67	16	4.54	97	.265	.362	34-3	.176	-1	104	0	0.1
1934	Phi A	6	2	.750	20	0	0	1	39.2	50	34	6	0	13	14	6.35	69	.314	.366	9-1	.333	1		-10	-1.5
	Was A	1	0	1.000	6	0	0	0	4	10	8	0	1	4	1	15.75	27	.500	.600	0-0	—	0		-5	-0.9
	Year	7	2	.778	26	0	0	1	43.2	60	47	6	1	17	15	7.21	61	.335	.396	9-1	.333	1		-15	-2.4
Total	5	30	28	.517	148	37	8-1	7	441.2	501	283	24	11	195	87	5.05	87	.291	.367	124-9	.202	-1	90	-28	-3.7
KLINE, RON	Ronald Lee B 3.9.1932 Callery, PA D 6.22.2002 Callery, PA BR/TR 6-3/205# d4.21 Mil 1953																								
1952	Pit N	0	7	.000	27	11	0	0	78.2	74	55	3	6	66	27	5.49	73	.253	.401	19-0	.000	-2	67	-13	-1.3
1955	Pit N	6	13	.316	36	19	2-1	2	136.2	161	78	13	5	53-5	48	4.15	99	.298	.363	38-1	.132	-2*	60	-3	-0.5
1956	Pit N	14	18	.438	44	39	9-2	2	264	263	110	26	5	81-8	125	3.38	112	.263	.319	79-5	.127	-3	80	13	1.2
1957	Pit N	9	16	.360	40	31	11-2	0	205	214	107	27	1	61-6	88	4.04	94	.268	.319	66-3	.061	-6	79	-6	-1.3
1958	Pit N	13	16	.448	32	32	11-2	0	237.1	220	96	25	0	92-14	109	3.53	110	.252	.321	74-9	.027	-6*	74	13	0.8
1959	Pit N	11	13	.458	33	29	7	0	186	186	95	23	2	70-9	91	4.26	91	.263	.329	59-5	.136	-2*	99	-6	-0.9
1960	StL N	4	9	.308	34	17	1	1	117.2	133	86	21	0	43-5	54	6.04	68	.284	.341	35-1	.143	-2	75	-23	-2.4
1961	LA A	3	6	.333	26	12	0	1	104.2	119	62	16	1	44-5	70	4.90	92	.288	.357	31-3	.097	-2	83	-3	-0.4
	Det A	5	3	.625	10	8	3-1	0	56.1	53	25	3	0	17-1	27	2.72	151	.245	.297	18-3	.167	0	92	6	0.8
	Year	8	9	.471	36	20	3-1	1	161	172	29	19	1	61-6	97	4.14	106	.273	.336	49-6	.122	-2	86	2	0.4
1962	Det A	3	6	.333	36	4	0	2	77.1	88	40	9	2	28-2	47	4.31	94	.284	.347	16-1	.125	-1	27	-1	-0.2
1963	Was A	3	8	.273	62	1	0	17	93.2	85	36	3	3	30-7	49	2.79	133	.249	.312	11-0	.091	-0	72	8	1.2
1964	Was A	10	7	.588	61	0	0	14	81.1	81	29	4	2	21-9	40	2.32	159	.262	.310	6-2	.167	0		10	2.2
1965	Was A	7	6	.538	74	0	0	**29**	99.1	106	36	7	2	32-14	52	2.63	132	.275	.329	7-3	.000	-1		8	1.4
1966	Was A	6	4	.600	63	0	0	23	90.1	79	32	12	0	17-7	46	2.39	145	.237	.274	6-0	.167	0		8	1.3
1967	Min A	7	1	.875	54	0	0	5	71.2	71	33	10	1	15-7	36	3.77	92	.261	.302	5-1	.000	-1		-2	-0.3
1968	Pit N	12	5	.706	56	0	0	7	112.2	94	26	3	2	31-11	48	1.68	174	.234	.291	16-1	.000	-1		**15**	2.5
1969	Pit N	1	3	.250	20	0	0	3-2	31	37	23	3	1	5-2	15	5.81	60	.296	.326	5-1	.000	-1		-8	-1.2
	SF N	0	2	.000	7	0	0	0-2	11	16	6	1	0	6-3	7	4.09	86	.364	.440	0-0	—	0		-1	-0.1
	Year	1	5	.167	27	0	0	3-4	42	53	32	4	1	11-5	22	5.36	65	.314	.357	5-1	.000	-1		-9	-1.3
	Bos A	0	1	.000	16	0	0	1-1	17	24	11	4	0	17-3	7	4.76	80	.329	.451	0-0	—	0		-2	-0.1
1970	Atl N	0	0	—	5	0	0	1-0	6.1	9	5	4	0	2-0	3	7.11	60	.321	.367	0-0	—	0		-2	-0.1
Total	17	114	144	.442	736	203	44-8	108-5	2078	2113	991	217	33	731-**118**	989	3.75	101	.266	.329	491-39	.092	-28	81	11	2.6
KLINE, STEVE	Steven Jack B 10.6.1947 Wenatchee, WA BR/TR 6-3/205# d7.10																								
1970	NY A	6	6	.500	16	15	5	0-0	100.1	99	42	8	0	24-3	49	3.41	103	.254	.296	28-4	.179	2	90	2	0.4
1971	NY A	12	13	.480	31	30	15-1	0-0	222.1	206	87	21	0	37-7	81	2.96	109	.244	.275	66-5	.136	-0	97	6	0.8
1972	NY A	16	9	.640	32	32	11-4	0-0	236.1	210	79	11	10	44-6	58	2.40	123	.237	.279	76-12	.092	-3	102	12	1.1
1973	NY A	4	7	.364	14	13	2-1	0-0	74	76	39	5	1	31-3	19	4.01	91	.270	.342	0-0	—	0	86	-3	-0.5
1974	NY A	2	2	.500	4	4	0	0-0	26	26	12	3	1	5-0	6	3.46	102	.263	.305	0-0	—	0	100	0	0.0

Year	Tm Lg	W	L	Pct	G	GS	CG-Sho	SV-BS	IP	H	R	HR	HB	BB-IB	SO	ERA	AERA	OAV	OOB	AB-SH	AVG	PB	Sup	APR	PW
	Cle A	3	8	.273	16	11	1	0-0	71	70	44	9	4	31-2	17	5.07	71	.266	.350	0-0	—	0	64	-11	-1.5
	Year	5	10	.333	20	15	1	0-0	97	96	47	12	5	36-2	23	4.64	78	.265	.338	0-0	—	0	74	-12	-1.5
1977	Atl N	0	0	—	16	0	0	1-0	20.1	21	15	4	0	12-3	10	6.64	67	.259	.355	0-0	—	0		-4	-0.2
Total	6	43	45	.489	129	105	34-6	1-0	750.1	708	318	61	16	184-24	240	3.26	101	.249	.297	170-21	.124	-1	92	2	0.1
KLINE, STEVE Steven James B 8.22.1972 Sunbury, PA BB/TL 6-2/200# d4.2																									
1997	Cle A	3	1	.750	20	1	0	0-2	26.1	42	19	6	1	13-1	17	5.81	81	.365	.434	0-0	—	0	59	-3	-0.5
	Mon N	1	3	.250	26	0	0	0-1	26.1	31	18	4	1	10-3	20	6.15	68	.304	.365	1-0	.000	-0		-5	-0.6
1998	Mon N	3	6	.333	78	0	0	1-1	71.2	62	25	4	3	41-7	76	2.76	152	.228	.333	4-1	.000	-0		11	1.3
1999	Mon N	7	4	.636	**82**	0	0	0-2	69.2	56	32	8	3	33-6	69	3.75	120	.218	.313	1-1	.000	-0		6	0.9
2000	Mon N	1	5	.167	**83**	0	0	14-4	82.1	88	36	8	3	27-2	64	3.50	137	.278	.340	2-0	.000	-0		11	1.0
2001	†StL N	3	3	.500	**89**	0	0	9-1	75	53	16	3	4	29-7	54	1.80	237	.203	.288	2-0	.500	0		21	2.0
2002	†StL N	2	1	.667	66	0	0	6-2	58.1	54	23	3	1	21-2	41	3.39	117	.251	.318	1-0	.000	-0		4	0.2
2003	StL N	5	5	.500	78	0	0	3-4	63.2	56	29	5	3	30-5	31	3.82	107	.237	.328	2-1	.500	1		2	0.4
Total	7	25	28	.472	522	1	0	33-17	473.1	442	198	41	19	204-33	372	3.46	125	.249	.331	13-3	.154	0	59	47	4.7
KLING, BILL William B 1.14.1867 Kansas City, MO D 8.26.1934 Kansas City, MO BL/TR 6/190# d8.13 b-Johnny																									
1891	Phi N	4	2	.667	12	7	4	0	75	91	61	2	2	32	26	4.32	79	.289	.358	31	.194	1*	153	-10	-0.6
1892	Bal N	0	2	.000	2	2	0	0	11	17	16	1	2	7	7	11.45	30	.340	.441	4	.250	1	111	-7	-0.8
1895	Lou N	0	0	—	1	0	0	0	1	0	0	0	0	1	0	0.00	—	.000	.250	1-0	.000	-0		1	0.0
Total	3	4	4	.500	15	9	4	0	87	108	77	3	4	40	33	5.17	66	.293	.369	36-0	.194	1	143	-16	-1.4
KLINGENBECK, SCOTT Scott Edward B 2.3.1971 Cincinnati, OH BR/TR 6-2/205# d6.2																									
1994	Bal A	1	0	1.000	1	1	0	0-0	7	6	4	1	1	4-1	5	3.86	130	.240	.355	0-0	—	0	202	0	0.0
1995	Bal A	2	2	.500	6	5	0	0-0	31.1	32	17	6	0	18-0	15	4.88	97	.269	.365	0-0	—	0	98	0	0.0
	Min A	0	2	.000	18	4	0	0-0	48.1	69	48	16	4	24-0	27	8.57	56	.338	.416	0-0	—	0	93	-19	-0.9
	Year	2	4	.333	24	9	0	0-0	79.2	101	53	22	4	42-0	42	7.12	67	.313	.397	0-0	—	0	95	-20	-0.9
1996	Min A	1	1	.500	10	3	0	0-1	28.2	42	28	5	1	10-0	15	7.85	65	.339	.390	0-0	—	0	169	-9	-0.5
1998	Cin N	1	3	.250	4	4	0	0-0	22.2	26	17	6	1	7-0	13	5.96	72	.286	.340	6-0	.000	-1	75	-5	-0.7
Total	4	5	8	.385	39	17	0	0-1	138	175	114	34	7	63-1	75	6.91	69	.311	.385	6-0	.000	-1	111	-33	-2.1
KLINGER, BOB Robert Harold B 6.4.1908 Allenton, MO D 8.19.1977 Villa Ridge, MO BR/TR 6/180# d4.19 Mil 1944-45																									
1938	Pit N	12	5	.706	28	21	10-1	1	159.1	152	63	7	6	42	58	2.99	127	.253	.308	60-1	.167	-2	119	14	1.2
1939	Pit N	14	17	.452	37	33	10-2	0	225	251	120	11	3	81	64	4.36	88	.284	.346	84-1	.202	0	112	-11	-1.2
1940	Pit N	8	13	.381	39	22	3	3	142	196	102	5	5	53	48	5.39	71	.329	.388	42-1	.143	-2	85	-26	-3.6
1941	Pit N	9	4	.692	35	9	3	4	116.2	127	58	5	1	30	36	3.93	92	.276	.322	32-1	.250	2	123	-3	-0.1
1942	Pit N	8	11	.421	37	19	8-1	1	152.2	151	69	6	3	45	58	3.24	104	.252	.307	40-5	.200	1	107	0	0.3
1943	Pit N	11	8	.579	33	25	14-3	0	195	185	77	6	0	58	65	2.72	128	.252	.307	65-4	.246	3	121	15	1.7
1946	†Bos A	3	2	.600	28	1	0	**9**	57	49	16	1	1	25	16	2.37	155	.238	.323	16-3	.313	1	47	8	1.1
1947	Bos A	1	1	.500	28	0	0	5	42	42	20	5	1	24	12	3.86	101	.253	.351	9-2	.111	-1		0	-0.1
Total	8	66	61	.520	265	130	48-7	23	1089.2	1153	525	46	20	358	357	3.68	100	.271	.331	348-18	.204	3	110	-3	-0.7
KLINK, JOE Joseph Charles B 2.3.1962 Johnstown, PA BL/TL 5-11/175# d4.9																									
1987	Min A	0	1	.000	12	0	0	0-0	23	37	18	4	0	11-0	17	6.65	70	.359	.417	0-0	—	0		-5	-0.2
1990	†Oak A	0	0	—	40	0	0	1-0	39.2	34	9	1	0	18-0	19	2.04	182	.233	.317	0-0	—	0		8	0.4
1991	Oak A	10	3	.769	62	0	0	2-2	62	60	30	4	5	21-5	34	4.35	88	.259	.333	0-0	—	0		-3	-0.6
1993	Fla N	0	2	.000	59	0	0	0-0	37.2	37	22	0	0	24-4	22	5.02	86	.266	.367	2-1	.000	-0		-2	-0.2
1996	Sea A	0	0	—	3	0	0	0-0	2.1	3	1	1	0	1-0	2	3.86	128	.300	.364	0-0	—	0		0	0.0
Total	5	10	6	.625	176	0	0	3-2	164.2	171	80	10	5	75-9	94	4.26	95	.271	.352	2-1	.000	-0		-2	-0.6
KLIPPSTEIN, JOHNNY John Calvin B 10.17.1927 Washington, DC D 10.10.2003 Elgin, IL BR/TR 6-1/185# d5.3																									
1950	Chi N	2	9	.182	33	11	3	1	104.2	112	69	9	4	64	51	5.25	80	.279	.383	33-0	.333	4*	80	-11	-0.6
1951	Chi N	6	6	.500	35	11	1-1	2	123.2	125	71	10	6	53	56	4.29	95	.263	.344	37-0	.108	-2	65	-5	-0.6
1952	Chi N	9	14	.391	41	25	7-2	3	202.2	208	110	17	6	89	110	4.44	87	.265	.344	63-7	.175	1	83	-11	-1.0
1953	Chi N	10	11	.476	48	19	5	6	167.2	169	115	15	8	107	113	4.83	92	.258	.369	58-3	.155	-1	88	-11	-1.5
1954	Chi N	4	11	.267	36	21	4	1	148	155	104	13	4	96	69	5.29	79	.272	.373	45-2	.133	-2	101	-20	-2.0
1955	Cin N	9	10	.474	39	14	3-2	0	138	120	66	13	4	60-5	68	3.39	125	.233	.317	31-4	.065	-2	90	10	1.0
1956	Cin N	12	11	.522	37	29	11	1	211	219	103	26	10	82-13	86	4.09	97	.275	.346	71-8	.099	-4	110	-1	-0.5
1957	Cin N	8	11	.421	46	18	3-1	3	146	146	84	17	3	68-6	99	5.05	81	.261	.342	41-2	.073	-3	86	-12	-1.8
1958	Cin N	3	2	.600	12	4	0	1	33	37	20	5	1	14-1	22	4.91	84	.285	.356	8-1	.125	-0	76	-3	-0.5
	LA N	3	5	.375	45	0	0	9	90	81	40	12	2	44-8	73	3.80	108	.248	.338	20-1	.050	-2		4	0.2
	Year	6	7	.462	57	4	0	10	123	118	64	17	3	58-9	95	4.10	100	.259	.343	28-2	.071	-2	76	1	-0.3
1959	†LA N	4	0	1.000	28	0	0	2	45.2	48	31	8	2	33-5	30	5.91	72	.276	.392	7-0	.143	-0		-7	-0.6
1960	Cle A	5	5	.500	49	0	0	**14**	74.1	53	30	8	1	35-3	46	2.91	129	.205	.302	14-2	.143	-0		6	1.0
1961	Was A	2	2	.500	42	1	0	0	71.2	83	59	13	4	43-1	41	6.78	59	.297	.395	7-0	.143	-0	66	-21	-1.0
1962	Cin N	7	6	.538	40	7	0	4	108.2	113	66	13	4	64-5	67	4.47	90	.278	.377	24-1	.125	0	72	-8	-0.8
1963	Phi N	5	6	.455	49	1	0	8	112	80	28	3	3	46-9	86	1.93	168	.204	.291	26-2	.038	-2	53	16	1.6
1964	Phi N	2	1	.667	11	0	0	1	22.1	22	10	6	2	8-1	13	4.03	86	.250	.327	4-0	.000	-0		-1	-0.1
	Min A	0	4	.000	33	0	0	2	45.2	44	12	4	1	20-7	39	1.97	181	.260	.340	2-0	.000	0		8	0.8
1965	†Min A	9	3	.750	56	0	0	5	76.1	59	22	8	3	31-4	59	2.24	159	.217	.302	8-2	.000	-1		11	1.7
1966	Min A	1	1	.500	26	0	0	3	39.2	35	15	2	2	20-2	26	3.40	106	.238	.335	3-0	.000	-0		2	0.1
1967	Det A	0	0	—	5	0	0	0	6.2	6	4	1	0	1-0	4	5.40	60	.250	.269	0-0	—	0		-1	-0.1
Total	18	101	118	.461	711	161	37-6	66	1967.2	1915	1059	203	70	978-70	1158	4.24	94	.258	.347	502-35	.125	-14	92	-55	-4.7
KLOBEDANZ, FRED Frederick Augustus "Duke" B 6.13.1871 Waterbury, CT D 4.12.1940 Waterbury, CT BL/TL 5-11/190# d8.20																									
1896	Bos N	6	4	.600	10	9	9	0	80.2	69	41	5	7	31	26	3.01	151	.229	.316	41-0	.317	2*	115	14	1.5
1897	†Bos N	26	7	**.788**	38	37	30-2	0	309.1	344	198	13	23	125	92	4.60	97	.279	.357	148-3	.324	9*	129	2	0.8
1898	Bos N	19	10	.655	35	33	25	0	270.2	281	168	13	12	99	51	3.89	95	.266	.336	127-6	.213	0*	116	-8	-0.8
1899	Bos N	1	4	.200	5	5	4	0	33.1	39	22	2	2	9	8	4.86	86	.291	.345	11-0	.182	1	69	-2	-0.1
1902	Bos N	1	0	1.000	1	1	1	0	8	9	1	0	1	2	4	1.13	251	.281	.343	2-1	.500	1	289	2	0.3
Total	5	53	25	.679	89	85	69-2	0	702	742	430	33	45	266	181	4.12	101	.269	.343	329-10	.277	13	120	8	1.7
KLOPP, STAN Stanley Harold "Betz" B 12.22.1910 Womelsdorf, PA D 3.11.1980 Robesonia, PA BR/TR 6-1.5/180# d4.29																									
1944	Bos N	1	2	.333	24	0	0	0	46.1	47	36	1	0	33	17	4.27	89	.272	.388	7-0	.286	0		-6	-0.4
KNACKERT, BRENT Brent Bradley B 8.1.1969 Los Angeles, CA BR/TR 6-3/185# d4.10																									
1990	Sea A	1	1	.500	24	2	0	0-0	37.1	50	28	5	2	21-2	28	6.51	61	.313	.395	0-0	—	0	57	-9	-0.5
1996	Bos A	0	1	.000	8	0	0	0-0	10	16	12	1	0	7-1	5	9.00	56	.356	.434	0-0	—	0		-5	-0.3
Total	2	1	2	.333	32	2	0	0-0	47.1	66	40	6	2	28-3	33	7.04	60	.322	.403	0-0	—	0	57	-14	-0.8
KNAPP, CHRIS Robert Christian B 9.16.1953 Cherry Point, NC BR/TR 6-5/195# d9.4																									
1975	Chi A	0	0	—	2	0	0	0-0	2	2	1	0	0	4-0	3	4.50	86	.250	.500	0-0	—	0		0	0.0
1976	Chi A	3	1	.750	11	6	1	0-0	52.1	54	31	5	1	32-1	41	4.82	74	.273	.375	0-0	—	0	131	-7	-0.5
1977	Chi A	12	7	.632	27	26	4	0-0	146.1	166	90	16	7	61-1	103	4.80	85	.283	.355	0-0	—	0	116	-12	-1.4
1978	Cal A	14	8	.636	30	29	6	0-0	188.1	178	94	25	2	67-6	126	4.21	86	.250	.313	0-0	—	0	112	-10	-1.2
1979	†Cal A	5	5	.500	20	18	3	0-0	98	109	73	8	2	35-1	36	5.51	74	.275	.334	0-0	—	0	155	-19	-1.6
1980	Cal A	2	11	.154	32	20	1	1-0	117.1	133	83	18	8	51-1	46	6.14	64	.289	.365	0-0	—	0	95	-27	-2.7
Total	6	36	32	.529	122	99	15	1-0	604.1	642	372	72	20	250-10	355	4.99	78	.272	.344	0-0	—	0	119	-75	-7.4
KNAUSS, FRANK Frank H. B 1868 Cleveland, OH BL/TL 5-10/170# d6.25																									
1890	Col AA	17	12	.586	37	34	28-3	2	275.2	206	131	3	21	106	148	2.81	128	**.202**	.290	106	.226	5	111	26	2.7
1891	Cle N	0	3	.000	3	3	1	0	15	23	29	2	4	8	6	7.20	48	.338	.438	6	.167	-0	115	-8	-1.1
1892	Cin N	0	0	—	1	0	0	0	8	13	9	0	0	5	2	3.38	97	.351	.429	3	.333	0		-2	0.0
1894	Cle N	0	1	.000	2	2	1	0	11	7	9	0	3	14	2	5.73	96	.179	.429	4-1	.000	-1	129	0	0.0
1895	NY N	0	0	—	1	1	0	0	3.2	9	7	0	0	2	1	17.18	27	.450	.500	1-0	.000	-0	153	-4	-0.2

Year	Tm Lg	W	L	Pct	G	GS	CG-Sho	SV-BS	IP	H	R	HR	HB	BB-IB	SO	ERA	AERA	OAV	OOB	AB-SH	AVG	PB	Sup	APR	PW
Total	5	17	16	.515	44	40	30-3	2	313.1	258	185	5	28	135	159	3.30	111	.218	.312	120-1	.217	4	115	12	1.4
KNEISCH, RUDY Rudolph Frank B 4.10.1899 Baltimore, MD D 4.6.1965 Baltimore, MD BR/TL 5-10.5/175# d9.21																									
1926	Det A	0	1	.000	2	2	1	0	17	18	7	2	2	6	4	2.65	153	.273	.351	5-0	.000	-1	73	2	0.1
KNELL, PHIL Philip Louis B 3.12.1865 San Francisco, CA D 6.5.1944 Santa Monica, CA BR/TL 5-7.5/154# d7.6																									
1888	Pit N	1	2	.333	3	3	3	0	26.1	20	19	1	5	18	15	3.76	70	.217	.374	11	.091	-1	77	-4	-0.5
1890	Phi P	22	11	.667	35	31	30-2	0	286.2	287	199	10	28	166	99	3.83	112	.249	.358	132	.220	-1*	124	14	1.1
1891	Col AA	28	27	.509	58	52	47-**5**	0	462	363	228	4	54	226	228	2.92	118	**.209**	.319	215	.158	-9*	84	30	2.2
1892	Was N	9	13	.409	22	21	17-1	0	170	156	114	4	11	76	74	3.65	89	.234	.323	68	.118	-5	90	-6	-1.1
	Phi N	5	5	.500	11	9	7	0	80	87	47	0	11	35	43	4.05	80	.266	.357	34	.088	-3	100	-5	-0.8
	Year	14	18	.438	33	30	24-1	0	250	243	52	4	22	111	117	3.78	86	.245	.334	102	.108	-7	93	-9	-1.9
1894	Pit N	0	0	—	1	0	0	0	7	11	9	0	1	6	0	11.57	45	.355	.474	3-0	.000	-1		-4	-0.2
	Lou N	7	21	.250	32	28	25	0	247	330	237	8	14	104	67	5.32	96	.317	.387	113-1	.274	0	73	-12	-1.0
	Year	7	21	.250	33	28	25	0	254	341	242	8	15	110	67	5.49	93	.318	.389	116-1	.267	-0	73	-20	-1.2
1895	Lou N	0	6	.000	10	6	3	0	56.2	75	66	3	6	21	19	6.51	71	.314	.383	26-0	.231	0	108	-14	-1.0
	Cle N	7	5	.583	20	13	9	0	116.2	149	100	7	6	53	30	5.40	92	.306	.381	55-1	.200	-3	105	-5	-0.6
	Year	7	11	.389	30	19	12	0	173.1	224	107	10	12	74	49	5.76	85	.309	.382	81-1	.210	-3	106	-19	-1.6
Total	6	79	90	.467	192	163	141-8	0	1452.1	1478	1019	37	136	705	575	4.05	99	.256	.351	657-2	.187	-20	94	-6	-1.9
KNEPPER, CHARLIE Charles B 2.18.1871 Anderson, IN D 2.6.1946 Muncie, IN BR/TR 6-4/190# d5.26																									
1899	Cle N	4	22	.154	27	26	26	0	219.2	307	190	11	15	77	43	5.78	64	.329	.390	89-0	.135	-5	74	-51	-4.9
KNEPPER, BOB Robert Wesley B 5.25.1954 Akron, OH BL/TL 6-2/200# d9.10																									
1976	SF N	1	2	.333	4	4	0	0-0	25	26	9	0	0	7-1	11	3.24	112	.277	.327	9-0	.111	-0	79	2	0.2
1977	SF N	11	9	.550	27	27	6-2	0-0	166	151	73	14	3	72-2	100	3.36	116	.242	.321	55-5	.182	1	103	10	1.2
1978	SF N	17	11	.607	36	35	16-**6**	0-0	260	218	85	10	4	85-11	147	2.63	131	.229	.292	79-8	.063	-3	92	24	2.1
1979	SF N	9	12	.429	34	34	6-2	0-0	207.1	241	117	30	3	77-8	123	4.64	75	.289	.350	66-9	.182	3*	121	-26	-2.1
1980	SF N	9	16	.360	35	33	8-1	0-0	215.1	242	114	15	8	61-10	103	4.10	87	.281	.333	66-9	.152	-0	94	-14	-1.4
1981	†Hou N★	9	5	.643	22	22	6-5	0-0	156.2	128	41	5	4	38-1	75	2.18	151	.226	.278	47-5	.149	1	77	21	2.1
1982	Hou N	5	15	.250	33	29	4	1-0	180	193	100	14	3	60-4	108	4.45	75	.278	.335	52-6	.058	-2	85	-24	-2.6
1983	Hou N	6	13	.316	35	29	4-3	0-0	203	202	93	12	4	71-3	125	3.19	107	.261	.323	66-4	.182	3	90	1	0.5
1984	Hou N	15	10	.600	35	34	11-3	0-0	233.2	223	93	26	1	55-5	140	3.20	104	.251	.295	76-6	.171	4	127	6	1.0
1985	Hou N	15	13	.536	37	37	4	0-0	241	253	119	21	3	54-5	131	3.55	98	.271	.310	78-8	.141	0*	103	-6	-0.8
1986	†Hou N	17	12	.586	40	38	8-**5**	0-0	258	232	100	19	4	62-13	143	3.14	115	.242	.289	91-4	.099	-3*	103	14	1.3
1987	Hou N	8	17	.320	33	31	1	0-0	177.2	226	118	26	4	54-3	76	5.27	74	.313	.362	51-9	.098	-1	95	-29	-3.5
1988	Hou N★	14	5	.737	27	27	3-2	0-0	175	156	70	13	2	67-2	103	3.14	106	.243	.314	48-14	.125	-1	124	3	0.4
1989	Hou N	4	10	.286	22	20	0	0-1	113	135	78	12	2	60-4	45	5.89	58	.303	.386	31-2	.226	5	100	-30	-2.8
	SF N	3	2	.600	13	6	1-1	0-0	52	55	20	4	1	15-2	19	3.46	98	.270	.318	12-1	.083	1	105	1	0.1
	Year	7	12	.368	35	26	1-1	0-1	165	190	24	16	3	75-6	64	5.13	66	.292	.365	43-3	.186	6	101	-30	-2.7
1990	SF N	3	3	.500	12	7	0	0-0	44.1	56	28	7	1	19-4	24	5.68	64	.311	.376	13-0	.231	1	166	-9	-1.0
Total	15	146	155	.485	445	413	78-30	1-1	2708	2737	1258	228	47	857-78	1473	3.68	95	.264	.321	840-90	.137	7	103	-56	-5.3
KNERR, LOU Wallace Luther B 8.21.1921 Strasburg, PA D 3.23.1980 Denver, PA BR/TR 6-1/210# d4.17																									
1945	Phi A	5	11	.313	27	17	5	0	130	142	77	6	1	74	41	4.22	81	.283	.376	47-1	.191	-1*	72	-14	-1.8
1946	Phi A	3	16	.158	30	22	6	0	148.1	171	95	13	1	67	58	5.40	66	.288	.361	50-1	.180	0	75	-26	-3.0
1947	Was A	0	0	—	6	0	0	0	9	17	13	1	0	8	5	11.00	34	.405	.500	1-0	1.000	0		-8	-0.3
Total	3	8	27	.229	63	39	11	0	287.1	330	185	20	2	149	104	5.04	69	.290	.373	98-2	.194	-1	73	-48	-5.1
KNETZER, ELMER Elmer Ellsworth "Baron" B 7.22.1885 Carrick, PA D 10.3.1975 Pittsburgh, PA BR/TR 5-10/180# d9.11																									
1909	Bro N	1	3	.250	5	4	3	0	35.2	33	22	2	0	22	7	3.03	86	.252	.359	12-0	.000	-2	61	-4	-0.6
1910	Bro N	7	5	.583	20	15	10-3	0	132.2	122	63	1	1	60	56	3.19	95	.255	.339	38-3	.053	-3	121	-3	-0.6
1911	Bro N	11	12	.478	35	20	11-3	0	204	202	101	1	1	93	66	3.49	96	.277	.359	62-5	.097	-4	85	-4	-0.8
1912	Bro N	7	9	.438	33	16	4-1	0	140.1	135	86	6	4	70	61	4.55	74	.254	.345	37-4	.135	-1	112	-15	-1.6
1914	Pit F	20	12	.625	37	30	20-3	1	272	257	123	9	2	88	146	2.88	100	.254	.315	91-9	.099	-9	113	-5	-1.4
1915	Pit F	18	14	.563	41	33	22-3	3	279	256	105	5	1	89	120	2.58	105	.251	.311	91-8	.132	-7	106	1	-0.6
1916	Bos N	0	2	.000	2	0	0	0	5	11	9	0	0	2	2	7.20	35	.524	.565	0-0	—	0		-4	-0.7
	Cin N	5	12	.294	36	16	12	1	171.1	161	76	6	3	48	70	2.89	90	.252	.307	52-4	.154	-1*	92	-8	-0.8
	Year	5	14	.263	38	16	12	1	176.1	172	79	6	3	50	72	3.01	86	.261	.316	52-4	.154	-1	92	-12	-1.5
1917	Cin N	0	0	—	11	0	0	1	27.1	29	18	0	2	12	7	2.96	88	.282	.368	3-0	.000	-0		-3	-0.2
Total	8	69	69	.500	220	134	82-13	6	1267.1	1206	603	30	14	484	535	3.15	93	.258	.330	386-33	.109	-26	104	-45	-7.3
KNIGHT, LON Alonzo P. B 6.16.1853 Philadelphia, PA D 4.23.1932 Philadelphia, PA BR/TR 5-11.5/165# d9.4 M2 U3 ▲																									
1875	Ath NA	6	5	.545	13	13	12	0	107	114	73	0		12	15	2.27	105	.259	.278	47	.128	-3	86	-2	-0.3
1876	Phi N	10	22	.313	34	32	27	0	282	383	288	0		34	12	2.62	93	.297	.315	240	.250	-1*	128	-17	-1.5
1884	Phi AA	0	1	.000	2	1	1	0	14	24	19	0	1	4	2	9.00	38	.348	.392	484	.271	0*	125	-8	-0.4
1885	Phi AA	0	0	—	1	0	0	0	5	4	1	0	0	2	1	1.80	191	.211	.286	119	.210	-0*		1	0.1
	Pro N	0	0	—	1	0	0	0	4	4	4	1		4	1	6.75	40	.235	.381	81	.160	-0*		-1	-0.1
Total	3	10	23	.303	38	33	28	0	305	415	312	1	1	44	16	2.95	84	.297	.319	924	.248	-1	128	-25	-1.9
KNIGHT, BRANDON Brandon Michael B 10.1.1975 Oxnard, CA BL/TR 6/175# d6.5																									
2001	NY A	0	0	—	4	0	0	0-0	10.2	18	12	5	0	3-0	7	10.13	44	.367	.404	0-0	—	0		-6	-0.3
2002	NY A	0	0	—	7	0	0	0-0	8.2	11	12	2	0	5-0	7	11.42	38	.306	.390	0-0	—	0		-7	-0.3
Total	2	0	0	—	11	0	0	0-0	19.1	29	24	7	0	8-0	14	10.71	42	.341	.398	0-0	—	0		-13	-0.6
KNIGHT, JACK Elmer Russell B 1.12.1895 Pittsboro, MS D 7.30.1976 San Antonio, TX BL/TR 6/175# d9.20																									
1922	StL N	0	0	—	1	1	0	0	4	9	4	0	0	3	1	9.00	43	.474	.545	2-0	.500	0	274	-2	-0.1
1925	Phi N	7	6	.538	33	11	4	3	105.1	161	100	14	1	36	19	6.84	70	.354	.402	44-0	.205	-1*	135	-22	-2.4
1926	Phi N	3	12	.200	35	15	5	2	142.2	206	122	14	0	48	29	6.62	63	.347	.396	56-2	.214	0*	86	-35	-2.9
1927	Bos N	0	0	—	3	0	0	0	3	6	5	0	0	2	0	15.00	25	.429	.500	0-0	—	0		-4	-0.1
Total	4	10	18	.357	72	27	9	5	255	382	231	28	1	89	49	6.85	64	.353	.403	102-2	.216	0	114	-63	-5.5
KNIGHT, GEORGE George Henry B 11.24.1855 Lakeville, CT D 10.4.1912 Lakeville, CT d9.28																									
1875	NH NA	1	0	1.000	1	1	1	0	9	12	6	0		0	0	3.00	69	.293	.293	4	.000	-1	136	0	-0.1
KNIGHT, JOE Joseph William "Quiet Joe" B 9.28.1859 Port Stanley, ON, CAN D 10.16.1938 Lynhurst, ON, CAN BL/TL 5-11/185# d5.16 ▲																									
1884	Phi N	2	4	.333	6	6	6	0	51	66	53	2		21	8	5.47	55	.293	.354	24	.250	1	68	-12	-1.0
KNOLLS, HUB Oscar Edward B 12.18.1883 Valparaiso, IN D 7.1.1946 Chicago, IL TR 6-2/190# d5.1																									
1906	Bro N	0	0	—	2	0	0	0	6.2	13	5	0	0	2	3	4.05	62	.382	.417	1-1	1.000	1		-2	0.0
KNOTT, ERIC Eric James B 9.23.1974 Harvey, IL BL/TL 6/188# d9.1																									
2001	Ari N	0	1	.000	3	1	0	0-0	4.2	8	9	0	2	0-0	4	1.93	237	.348	.400	1-0	.000	-0	101	-2	-0.4
2003	Mon N	1	2	.333	13	1	0	0-0	19.1	23	12	2	0	6-0	17	5.12	92	.295	.341	5-0	.000	-1	20	-1	-0.2
Total	2	1	3	.250	16	2	0	0-0	24	31	21	2	2	6-0	21	4.50	104	.307	.355	6-0	.000	-1	60	-3	-0.6
KNOTT, JACK John Henry B 3.2.1907 Dallas, TX D 10.13.1981 Brownwood, TX BR/TR 6-2.5/200# d4.13 Mil 1942-45																									
1933	StL A	1	8	.111	20	9	0	0	82.2	88	51	11	2	33	19	5.01	93	.269	.340	23-1	.304	1	75	-3	-0.2
1934	StL A	10	3	.769	45	10	2	4	138	149	86	17	1	67	56	4.96	101	.278	.359	30-3	.133	-1	82	2	0.1
1935	StL A	11	8	.579	48	19	7-2	**7**	187.2	219	119	8	1	78	45	4.60	104	.287	.353	61-8	.115	-5	95	0	-0.4
1936	StL A	9	17	.346	47	23	9	6	192.2	272	174	15	4	93	60	7.29	74	.330	.401	57-8	.070	-5	89	-37	-4.5
1937	StL A	8	18	.308	38	22	8	2	191.1	220	117	25	5	91	74	4.89	99	.291	.370	57-4	.140	-4	76	-1	-0.6
1938	StL A	1	2	.333	7	4	0	0	30	35	19	3	0	15	8	4.80	104	.285	.362	10-1	.100	-1	84	0	-0.1
	Chi A	5	10	.333	20	18	9	0	131	135	70	8	0	54	35	4.05	121	.271	.342	40-7	.125	-2	68	12	0.9
	Year	6	12	.333	27	22	9	0	161	170	74	11	0	69	43	4.19	117	.273	.346	50-8	.120	-3	71	11	0.8
1939	Chi A	11	6	.647	25	23	8	0	149.2	157	71	13	1	41	56	4.15	114	.269	.318	53-5	.151	-3	92	12	0.8

Year	Tm Lg	W	L	Pct	G	GS	CG-Sho	SV-BS	IP	H	R	HR	HB	BB-IB	SO	ERA	AERA	OAV	OOB	AB-SH	AVG	PB	Sup	APR	PW
1940	Chi A	11	9	.550	25	23	4-2	0	158	166	88	12	2	52	44	4.56	97	.265	.324	57-4	.088	-4	98	0	-0.4
1941	Phi A	13	11	.542	27	26	11	0	194.1	212	108	20	2	81	54	4.40	95	.279	.350	65-5	.077	-3	109	-4	-0.9
1942	Phi A	2	10	.167	20	14	4	0	95.1	127	84	7	1	36	31	5.57	68	.310	.367	29-2	.138	-1	78	-24	-2.6
1946	Phi A	0	1	.000	3	1	0	0	6.1	7	4	1	1	1	2	5.68	62	.280	.333	0-1	—	0	0	-1	-0.2
Total	11	82	103	.443	325	192	62-4	19	1557	1787	991	140	20	642	484	4.97	95	.287	.355	482-49	.120	-29	87	-44	-8.1
KNOTTS, GARY Gary Everett B 2.12.1977 Decatur, AL BR/TR 6-4/235# d7.28																									
2001	Fla N	0	1	.000	2	1	0	0-0	6	7	4	1	2	1-0	9	6.00	70	.280	.357	2-0	.500	0	66	-1	-0.1
2002	Fla N	3	1	.750	28	0	0	0-1	30.2	21	15	6	1	16-0	21	4.40	90	.193	.299	1-0	.000	-0		-1	-0.2
2003	Det A	3	8	.273	20	18	0	0-0	95.1	111	70	14	4	47-0	51	6.04	71	.288	.367	1-0	.000	-0	82	-19	-1.8
Total	3	6	10	.375	50	19	0	0-1	132	139	89	21	7	64-0	81	5.66	75	.267	.352	4-0	.250	0	83	-21	-2.1
KNOUFF, ED Edward "Fred" B 6.1868 Philadelphia, PA D 9.14.1900 Philadelphia, PA BR/TR ?/210# d7.1 ▲																									
1885	Phi AA	7	6	.538	14	13	12	0	106	103	76	0	9	44	43	3.65	94	.228	.309	48	.188	-2	111	-1	-0.2
1886	Bal AA	0	1	.000	1	1	1	0	9	2	5	0	3	5	8	2.00	171	.067	.263	3	.000	-0	17	1	0.1
1887	Bal AA	2	6	.250	9	9	6	0	63	79	79	0	13	41	27	7.57	54	.295	.413	31	.290	0	123	-23	-1.9
	StL AA	4	2	.667	6	6	6-1	0	50	40	34	0	3	36	18	4.50	101	.225	.364	56	.179	-1*	103	1	0.0
	Year	6	8	.429	15	15	12-1	0	113	119	41	0	16	77	45	6.21	69	.267	.393	87	.218	-1	114	-17	-1.9
1888	StL AA	5	4	.556	9	9	9	0	81	66	45	0	8	37	25	2.67	122	.214	.314	31	.097	-2	93	4	0.1
	Cle AA	0	1	.000	2	2	1	0	9	8	2	0	1	3	2	1.00	309	.229	.308	6	.167	0	66	2	0.3
	Year	5	5	.500	11	11	10	0	90	74	6	0	9	40	27	2.50	130	.216	.314	37	.108	-2	88	7	0.4
1889	Phi AA	2	0	1.000	3	3	2	0	25	37	17	2	1	9	5	3.96	96	.333	.388	12	.250	0	131	0	0.0
Total	5	20	20	.500	44	43	37-1	0	343	335	258	2	38	175	128	4.17	89	.242	.344	187	.187	-4	106	-16	-1.6
KNOWLES, DAROLD Darold Duane B 12.9.1941 Brunswick, MO BL/TL 6/190# d4.18 Mil 1968 C3																									
1965	Bal A	0	1	.000	5	1	0	0	14.2	14	15	2	3	10-2	12	9.20	38	.250	.391	4-0	.000	-0	0	-8	-0.5
1966	Phi N	6	5	.545	69	0	0	13	100.1	98	38	4	7	46-10	88	3.05	118	.260	.347	16-0	.250	0		6	1.0
1967	Was A	6	8	.429	61	1	0	14	113.1	91	37	5	4	52-12	85	2.70	117	.228	.319	16-0	.063	-1	0	7	1.1
1968	Was A	1	1	.500	32	0	0	4	41.1	38	11	0	1	12-2	37	2.18	134	.241	.293	4-1	.250	1		4	0.4
1969	Was A★	9	2	.818	53	0	0	13-9	84.1	73	25	8	4	31-3	59	2.24	155	.236	.311	13-0	.077	0		12	1.9
1970	Was A	2	14	.125	71	0	0	27-11	119.1	100	36	4	4	58-16	71	2.04	175	.231	.325	20-2	.050	-1		18	3.1
1971	Was A	2	2	.500	12	0	0	2-2	15.1	17	6	2	0	6-1	16	3.52	94	.266	.329	2-0	.000	-0		0	0.0
	†Oak A	5	2	.714	43	0	0	7-3	52.2	40	22	3	3	16-4	40	3.59	93	.221	.289	8-1	.125	-0		-1	-0.1
	Year	7	4	.636	55	0	0	9-5	68	57	28	5	3	22-5	56	3.57	93	.233	.299	10-1	.100	-1		-1	-0.1
1972	Oak A	5	1	.833	54	0	0	11-3	65.2	49	12	1	0	37-4	36	1.37	208	.212	.319	12-1	.250	1		11	1.8
1973	†Oak A	6	8	.429	52	5	1-1	9-5	99	87	44	7	3	49-3	46	3.09	115	.246	.338	0-0	—	0*	131	3	0.6
1974	Oak A	3	3	.500	45	1	0	3-2	53.1	61	29	6	2	35-3	18	4.22	79	.296	.397	0-0	—	0	212	-6	-0.6
1975	Chi N	6	9	.400	58	0	0	15-7	88.1	107	61	3	3	36-9	63	5.81	66	.298	.364	15-2	.067	-1		-17	-3.1
1976	Chi N	5	7	.417	58	0	0	9-8	71.2	61	30	6	2	22-4	39	2.89	134	.242	.302	7-2	.143	1		5	1.2
1977	Tex A	5	2	.714	42	0	0	4-4	50.1	50	22	3	2	23-2	14	3.22	127	.272	.354	0-0	—	0		4	0.6
1978	Mon N	3	3	.500	60	0	0	6-3	72	63	20	5	0	30-3	34	2.38	149	.250	.323	6-1	.167	-0		10	1.1
1979	StL N	2	5	.286	48	0	0	6-4	48.2	54	27	5	0	17-7	22	4.07	93	.277	.333	2-0	.000	-0		-3	-0.5
1980	StL N	0	1	.000	2	0	0	0-1	1.2	3	2	1	0	0-0	1	10.80	34	.375	.375	0-0	—	0		-1	-0.2
Total	16	66	74	.471	765	8	1-1	143-62	1092	1006	437	65	38	480-85	681	3.12	112	.250	.332	125-10	.120	-2	108	44	7.8
KNOWLSON, TOM Thomas Herbert "Doc" B 4.23.1895 Pittsburgh, PA D 4.11.1943 Miami Shores, FL BB/TR 5-11/178# d7.3																									
1915	Phi A	4	6	.400	18	9	8	0	100.2	99	53	1	6	60	24	3.49	84	.273	.386	36-0	.083	-3	91	-6	-0.9
KNOWLTON, BILL William Young B 8.18.1892 Philadelphia, PA D 2.25.1944 Philadelphia, PA BR/TR d9.3																									
1920	Phi A	0	1	.000	1	1	0	0	5.2	9	9	0	3	3	5	4.76	84	.346	.469	2-0	.000	-0	99	-2	-0.3
KNUDSEN, KURT Kurt David B 2.20.1967 Arlington Heights, IL BR/TR 6-3/200# d5.16																									
1992	Det A	2	3	.400	48	1	0	5-2	70.2	70	39	9	1	41-9	51	4.58	86	.264	.362	0-0	—	0	69	-5	-0.4
1993	Det A	3	2	.600	30	0	0	2-2	37.2	41	22	9	4	16-2	29	4.78	90	.281	.361	0-0	—	0		-2	-0.2
1994	Det A	1	0	1.000	4	0	0	0-1	5.1	7	8	2	0	11-1	1	13.50	36	.304	.529	0-0	—	0		-5	-0.7
Total	3	6	5	.545	82	1	0	7-5	113.2	118	69	20	5	68-12	81	5.07	81	.272	.373	0-0	—	0	69	-12	-1.3
KNUDSON, MARK Mark Richard B 10.28.1960 Denver, CO BR/TR 6-5/215# d7.8																									
1985	Hou N	0	2	.000	2	2	0	0-0	11	21	11	0	0	3-0	4	9.00	39	.429	.462	2-0	.000	0	64	-6	-0.8
1986	Hou N	1	5	.167	9	7	0	0-0	42.2	48	23	5	1	15-5	20	4.22	85	.279	.340	10-3	.000	-1	106	-3	-0.5
	Mil A	0	1	.000	4	1	0	0-0	17.2	22	15	7	0	5-1	9	7.64	57	.286	.329	0-0	—	0	21	-5	-0.3
1987	Mil A	4	4	.500	15	8	1	0-1	62	88	46	7	0	14-1	26	5.37	85	.331	.358	0-0	—	0	104	-8	-0.9
1988	Mil A	0	0	—	5	0	0	0-0	16	17	3	1	0	2-0	7	1.13	354	.279	.302	0-0	—	0		5	0.2
1989	Mil A	8	5	.615	40	7	1	0-2	123.2	110	50	15	3	29-2	47	3.35	115	.237	.286	0-0	—	0	158	8	0.7
1990	Mil A	10	9	.526	30	27	4-2	0-0	168.1	187	84	14	3	40-1	56	4.12	94	.282	.321	0-0	—	0	96	-2	-0.3
1991	Mil A	1	3	.250	12	7	0	0-0	35	54	33	8	1	15-0	23	7.97	50	.355	.409	0-0	—	0	118	-16	-1.5
1993	Col N	0	0	—	4	0	0	0-0	5.2	16	14	4	0	5-0	3	22.24	21	.471	.538	1-0	.000	-0		-9	-0.4
Total	8	24	29	.453	121	59	6-2	0-3	482	563	279	61	8	128-10	195	4.72	84	.290	.334	13-3	.000	-1	106	-36	-3.8
KOBEL, KEVIN Kevin Richard B 10.2.1953 Buffalo, NY BR/TL 6-1/195# d9.8																									
1973	Mil A	0	1	.000	2	1	0	0-0	8.1	9	8	2	0	8-0	4	8.64	44	.273	.415	0-0	—	0	71	-4	-0.4
1974	Mil A	6	14	.300	34	24	3-2	0-1	169.1	166	84	16	2	54-1	74	3.99	91	.258	.314	0-0	—	0	80	-8	-0.8
1976	Mil A	0	1	.000	3	0	0	0-1	4	6	5	3	1	3-1	1	11.25	31	.375	.476	0-0	—	0		-3	-0.6
1978	NY N	5	6	.455	32	11	1	0-1	108.1	95	42	9	2	30-9	51	2.91	120	.239	.291	25-4	.160	0	89	6	0.6
1979	NY N	6	8	.429	30	27	1-1	0-0	161.2	169	74	14	3	46-4	67	3.51	104	.274	.325	46-9	.196	0	79	1	0.2
1980	NY N	1	4	.200	14	1	0	0-0	24.1	36	21	5	0	11-3	8	7.03	51	.353	.416	2-0	.000	-0	75	-9	-1.7
Total	6	18	34	.346	115	64	5-3	0-3	476	481	234	49	8	152-18	205	3.88	93	.266	.322	73-13	.178	0	81	-17	-2.7
KOCH, ALAN Alan Goodman B 3.25.1938 Decatur, AL BR/TR 6-4/195# d7.26																									
1963	Det A	1	1	.500	7	1	0	0	10	21	12	3	1	9-0	5	10.80	35	.467	.564	3-0	.667	1*	71	-7	-1.1
1964	Det A	0	0	—	3	0	0	0	4	6	3	1	0	3-0	1	6.75	54	.375	.474	0-0	—	0		-1	-0.1
	Was A	3	10	.231	32	14	1	0	114	110	64	18	3	43-2	67	4.89	76	.253	.320	32-3	.250	2	87	-12	-1.1
	Year	3	10	.231	35	14	1	0	118	116	68	19	3	46-2	68	4.96	75	.258	.325	32-3	.250	2	88	-13	-1.2
Total	2	4	11	.267	42	15	1	0	128	137	79	22	4	55-2	73	5.41	68	.277	.349	35-3	.286	3	86	-20	-2.3
KOCH, BILLY William Christopher B 12.14.1974 Rockville Centre, NY BR/TR 6-3/218# d5.5																									
1999	Tor A	0	5	.000	56	0	0	31-4	63.2	55	26	5	3	30-5	57	3.39	146	.235	.328	1-0	.000	-0		11	1.6
2000	Tor A	9	3	.750	68	0	0	33-5	78.2	78	28	6	2	18-4	60	2.63	193	.258	.304	1-0	.000	-0		20	3.7
2001	Tor A	2	5	.286	69	0	0	36-8	69.1	69	39	7	6	33-7	55	4.80	96	.265	.356	0-0	—	0		-1	-0.2
2002	†Oak A	11	4	.733	**84**	0	0	44-6	93.2	73	38	7	4	46-6	93	3.27	135	.214	.314	0-0	—	0		12	2.3
2003	Chi A	5	5	.500	55	0	0	11-4	53	59	36	10	1	28-1	42	5.77	79	.281	.364	0-0	—	0		-7	-1.3
Total	5	27	22	.551	332	0	0	155-27	358.1	334	167	35	16	155-23	307	3.82	123	.248	.331	2-0	.000	-0		35	6.1
KOECHER, DICK Richard Finlay "Highpockets" B 3.30.1926 Philadelphia, PA BL/TL 6-5/196# d9.29																									
1946	Phi N	0	1	.000	1	1	0	0	2.2	7	3	0	0	1	2	10.13	34	.467	.500	1-0	.000	-0	25	-2	-0.3
1947	Phi N	0	2	.000	3	2	1	0	17	20	12	1	1	10	4	4.76	84	.299	.397	4-0	.000	-1	22	-2	-0.3
1948	Phi N	0	1	.000	3	0	0	0	6	4	2	0	0	3	2	3.00	132	.235	.350	0-0	—	0		1	0.1
Total	3	0	4	.000	7	3	1	0	25.2	31	17	1	1	14	8	4.91	80	.313	.404	5-0	.000	-1	22	-3	-0.5
KOENIG, MARK Mark Anthony B 7.19.1904 San Francisco, CA D 4.22.1993 Willows, CA BB/TR 6/180# d9.8.1925 ▲																									
1930	Det A	0	1	.000	2	1	0	0	9	11	10	0	1	8	6	10.00	48	.314	.455	267-13	.240	0*	89	-4	-0.4
1931	Det A	0	0	—	3	0	0	0	7	7	5	0	0	11	3	6.43	71	.280	.500	364-2	.253	0*		-1	0.0
Total	2	0	1	.000	5	1	0	0	16	18	15	0	1	19	9	8.44	56	.300	.475	631-15	.247	0	89	-5	-0.4

Year	Tm Lg	W	L	Pct	G	GS	CG-Sho	SV-BS	IP	H	R	HR	HB	BB-IB	SO	ERA	AERA	OAV	OOB	AB-SH	AVG	PB	Sup	APR	PW
KOENIGSMARK, WILL Willis Thomas B 2.27.1896 Waterloo, IL D 7.1.1972 Waterloo, IL BR/TR 6-4/180# d9.10																									
1919	StL N	0	0	—	1	0	0	0	0	2	2	0	0	1	0	∞	—	1.000	1.000	0-0	—	0		-2	-0.2
KOESTNER, ELMER Elmer Joseph "Bob" B 11.30.1885 Piper City, IL D 10.27.1959 Fairbury, IL BR/TR 6-1.5/175# d4.23																									
1910	Cle A	5	10	.333	27	13	8-1	2	145	145	76	0	6	63	44	3.04	85	.282	.367	48-6	.313	2	106	-10	-0.8
1914	Chi N	0	0	—	4	0	0	0	6.1	6	5	0	0	4	6	2.84	98	.261	.370	1-0	.000	-0		-1	-0.1
	Cin N	0	0	—	5	1	0	0	18.1	18	15	0	0	9	6	4.42	66	.265	.351	5-0	.400	1	171	-4	-0.1
	Year	0	0	—	9	1	0	0	24.2	24	22	0	0	13	12	4.01	72	.264	.356	6-0	.333	1	173	-4	-0.2
Total	2	5	10	.333	36	14	8-1	2	169.2	169	96	0	6	76	56	3.18	83	.279	.365	54-6	.315	3	110	-15	-1.0
KOHLMAN, JOE Joseph James "Blackie" B 1.28.1913 Philadelphia, PA D 3.16.1974 Philadelphia, PA BR/TR 6/160# d9.26																									
1937	Was A	1	0	1.000	2	2	1	0	13	15	7	0	0	3	3	4.15	107	.283	.321	5-0	.200	-0	108	0	0.0
1938	Was A	0	0	—	7	0	0	0	14.1	12	10	1	0	11	5	6.28	72	.240	.377	3-0	.000	-0		-2	-0.1
Total	2	1	0	1.000	9	2	1	0	27.1	27	17	1	0	14	8	5.27	85	.262	.350	8-0	.125	-1	108	-2	-0.1
KOHLMEIER, RYAN Ryan Lyle B 6.25.1977 Salina, KS BR/TR 6-2/195# d7.29																									
2000	Bal A	0	1	.000	25	0	0	13-1	26.1	30	9	1	0	15-2	17	2.39	198	.291	.378	0-0	—	0		6	0.7
2001	Bal A	1	2	.333	34	1	0	6-4	40.2	48	33	13	2	19-2	29	7.30	59	.291	.371	0-0	—	0	0	-13	-1.1
Total	2	1	3	.250	59	1	0	19-5	67	78	42	14	2	34-4	46	5.37	83	.291	.374	0-0	—	0	0	-7	-0.4
KOLB, BRANDON Brandon Charles B 11.20.1973 Oakland, CA BR/TR 6-1/190# d5.12																									
2000	SD N	0	1	.000	11	0	0	0-1	14	16	8	0	0	11-1	12	4.50	96	.296	.409	1-0	.000	-0		0	-0.1
2001	Mil N	0	0	—	10	0	0	0-0	9.2	16	16	6	0	8-0	8	13.03	33	.372	.453	1-0	.000	-0		-10	-0.5
Total	2	0	1	.000	21	0	0	0-1	23.2	32	24	6	0	19-1	20	7.99	54	.330	.429	2-0	.000	-0		-10	-0.6
KOLB, DAN Daniel Lee B 3.29.1975 Sterling, IL BR/TR 6-4/185# d6.4																									
1999	Tex A	2	1	.667	16	0	0	0-0	31	33	18	2	1	15-0	15	4.65	109	.268	.353	0-0	—	0		1	0.1
2000	Tex A	0	0	—	1	0	0	0-0	0.2	5	5	0	0	2-0	0	67.50	7	.833	.778	0-0	—	0		-4	-0.2
2001	Tex A	0	0	—	17	0	0	0-0	15.1	15	8	2	0	10-1	15	4.70	99	.259	.362	0-0	—	0		0	0.0
2002	Tex A	3	6	.333	34	0	0	1-3	32	27	17	1	1	22-2	20	4.22	112	.227	.347	0-0	—	0		1	0.3
2003	Mil N	1	2	.333	37	0	0	21-2	41.1	34	10	2	1	19-3	39	1.96	217	.221	.310	0-0	—	0		10	1.6
Total	5	6	9	.400	105	0	0	22-5	120.1	114	58	7	3	68-6	89	3.96	117	.248	.346	0-0	—	0		8	1.8
KOLB, EDDIE Edward William B 7.20.1880 Cincinnati, OH BR/TR d10.15																									
1899	Cle N	0	1	.000	1	1	1	0	8	18	19	0	1	5	1	10.13	36	.439	.511	4-0	.250	-0	59	-8	-0.6
KOLP, RAY Raymond Carl "Jockey" B 10.1.1894 New Berlin, OH D 7.29.1967 New Orleans, LA BR/TR 5-10.5/187# d4.16																									
1921	StL A	8	7	.533	37	18	5-1	0	166.2	208	111	12	0	51	43	4.97	90	.314	.363	55-8	.127	-5*	109	-9	-1.2
1922	StL A	14	4	.778	32	18	9-1	0	169.2	199	89	10	5	36	54	3.93	106	.292	.332	57-11	.298	5	153	5	0.7
1923	StL A	5	12	.294	34	17	11-1	1	171.1	178	91	11	6	54	44	3.89	107	.273	.335	54-5	.111	-4	70	4	-0.1
1924	StL A	5	7	.417	25	12	5-1	0	96.2	131	65	4	4	25	29	5.68	79	.329	.375	30-2	.200	-0	76	-9	-1.0
1927	Cin N	3	3	.500	24	5	2-1	3	82.1	86	38	5	1	29	28	3.06	124	.278	.342	30-1	.200	-0	90	5	0.4
1928	Cin N	13	10	.565	44	23	12-1	3	209	219	87	9	4	55	61	3.19	124	.280	.330	70-4	.214	3	98	17	2.0
1929	Cin N	8	10	.444	30	16	4-1	0	145.1	151	75	8	1	39	27	4.03	113	.278	.328	49-4	.163	-2	82	8	0.8
1930	Cin N	7	12	.368	37	19	5-2	3	168.1	180	86	10	0	34	40	4.22	114	.278	.314	49-1	.245	1	58	13	1.4
1931	Cin N	4	9	.308	30	10	2	1	107	144	66	8	4	39	24	4.96	75	.332	.392	32-3	.125	-1	96	-14	-1.6
1932	Cin N	6	10	.375	32	18	7-2	1	159.2	176	80	13	3	27	42	3.89	99	.280	.313	49-2	.184	-1	84	1	-0.1
1933	Cin N	6	9	.400	30	14	4	3	150.1	168	73	7	1	23	28	3.53	96	.290	.318	45-3	.156	-1	81	-2	-0.2
1934	Cin N	0	2	.000	28	2	0	3	61.2	78	36	1	2	12	19	4.52	90	.312	.348	12-0	.083	-1	53	-2	-0.1
Total	12	79	95	.454	383	172	66-11	18	1688	1918	897	98	31	424	439	4.08	102	.292	.338	532-44	.184	-7	91	17	1.0
KOLSTAD, HAL Harold Everette B 6.1.1935 Rice Lake, WI BR/TR 5-9/190# d4.22																									
1962	Bos A	0	2	.000	27	2	0	2	61.1	65	44	11	2	35-1	36	5.43	76	.269	.363	18-2	.056	-2	97	-10	-0.6
1963	Bos A	0	2	.000	7	0	0	0	11	16	16	4	2	6-0	6	13.09	29	.340	.436	1-1	.000	-0		-10	-1.6
Total	2	0	4	.000	34	2	0	2	72.1	81	60	15	4	41-1	42	6.59	62	.280	.375	19-3	.053	-2	97	-20	-2.2
KOMIYAMA, SATORU Satoru B 9.15.1965 Chiba, Japan BR/TR 6/183# d4.4																									
2002	NY N	0	3	.000	25	0	0	0-0	43.1	53	29	7	3	12-4	33	5.61	71	.301	.351	1-1	.000	0		-8	-0.5
KONETCHY, ED Edward Joseph "Big Ed" B 9.3.1885 LaCrosse, WI D 5.27.1947 Ft.Worth, TX BR/TR 6-2.5/195# d6.29.1907 ▲																									
1910	StL N	0	0	—	1	0	0	0	4	4	2	0	0	1	0	4.50	66	.267	.313	520-11	.302	0*		0	0.0
1913	StL N	1	0	1.000	1	0	0	0	4.2	1	0	0	0	4	3	0.00	—	.071	.278	504-19	.276	0*		2	0.4
1918	Bos N	0	1	.000	1	1	1	0	8	14	8	0	0	2	3	6.75	40	.378	.410	437-16	.236	0*	0	-4	-0.4
Total	3	1	1	.500	3	1	1	0	16.2	19	10	0	0	7	6	4.32	67	.288	.356	1461-46	.273	1	0	-2	0.0
KONIECZNY, DOUG Douglas James B 9.27.1951 Detroit, MI BR/TR 6-4/220# d9.11																									
1973	Hou N	0	1	.000	2	2	0	0-0	13	12	8	0	0	4-0	6	5.54	66	.279	.333	4-0	.000	-0	85	-2	-0.2
1974	Hou N	0	3	.000	6	3	0	0-0	16	18	15	0	2	12-1	8	7.88	44	.290	.421	4-0	.000	-1	50	-8	-1.3
1975	Hou N	6	13	.316	32	29	4-1	0-0	171	184	93	15	1	87-1	89	4.47	76	.280	.361	50-5	.160	1	105	-23	-2.3
1977	Hou N	1	1	.500	4	4	0	0-0	21	26	15	1	1	8-0	7	6.00	60	.302	.361	7-1	.143	-0	100	-6	-0.5
Total	4	7	18	.280	44	38	4-1	0-0	221	240	131	16	4	111-2	110	4.93	69	.283	.364	65-6	.138	-0	99	-39	-4.3
KONIKOWSKI, ALEX Alexander James "Whitey" B 6.8.1928 Throop, PA D 9.28.1997 Seymour, CT BR/TR 6-1/187# d6.16 Mil 1952																									
1948	NY N	2	3	.400	22	1	0	1	33.1	46	34	7	0	17	9	7.56	52	.346	.420	2-1	.000	0	23	-14	-1.8
1951	†NY N	0	0	—	3	0	0	0	4	2	0	0	0	0	5	0.00	—	.154	.154	0-0	—	0		2	0.1
1954	NY N	0	0	—	10	0	0	0	12	10	10	1	0	12	6	7.50	54	.244	.415	1-0	.000	-0		-4	-0.2
Total	3	2	3	.400	35	1	0	1	49.1	58	44	8	0	29	20	6.93	57	.310	.403	3-1	.000	0	23	-16	-1.9
KONSTANTY, JIM Casimir James B 3.2.1917 Strykersville, NY D 6.11.1976 Oneonta, NY BR/TR 6-1.5/202# d6.18 Mil 1945																									
1944	Cin N	6	4	.600	20	12	5-1	0	112.2	113	46	11	1	33	19	2.80	125	.266	.320	34-3	.294	2	108	7	0.8
1946	Bos N	0	1	.000	10	1	0	0	15.1	17	9	2	0	7	9	5.28	65	.283	.358	2-0	.000	0	175	-3	-0.1
1948	Phi N	1	0	1.000	6	0	0	2	9.2	7	1	0	0	2	7	0.93	424	.233	.281	3-0	.000	-0		3	0.4
1949	Phi N	9	5	.643	53	0	0	7	97	98	38	9	1	29	43	3.25	121	.280	.337	17-1	.176	-0		**8**	1.2
1950	†Phi N★	16	7	.696	**74**	0	0	**22**	152	108	51	11	0	50	56	2.66	152	.205	.274	37-2	.108	-2		**24**	**3.8**
1951	Phi N	4	11	.267	58	1	0	9	115.2	127	58	9	0	31	27	4.05	95	.282	.328	19-3	.158	-0	46	-3	-0.4
1952	Phi N	5	3	.625	42	2	2-1	6	80	87	44	9	0	21	16	3.94	93	.274	.319	14-1	.071	-0	97	-4	-0.5
1953	Phi N	14	10	.583	48	19	7	5	170.2	198	90	18	3	42	45	4.43	95	.290	.334	50-3	.220	-0	115	-1	-0.2
1954	Phi N	2	3	.400	33	1	0	3	50.1	62	27	7	0	12	11	3.75	108	.316	.352	13-0	.000	-2	88	0	-0.2
	NY A	1	1	.500	9	0	0	2	18.1	11	2	0	0	6	3	0.98	350	.183	.254	3-0	.000	-0		6	0.7
1955	NY A	7	2	.778	45	0	0	11	73.2	68	28	5	0	24-2	19	2.32	161	.247	.305	8-3	.125	-0		10	1.4
1956	NY A	0	0	—	8	0	0	2	11	15	6	3	0	6-0	6	4.91	79	.319	.396	2-0	.000	-0		-1	-0.1
	StL N	1	1	.500	27	0	0	5	39.1	46	20	4	0	6-1	7	4.58	83	.301	.325	0-0	—	0		-2	-0.2
Total	11	66	48	.579	433	36	14-2	74	945.2	957	420	88	5	269-3	268	3.46	112	.268	.319	202-16	.163	-5	112	44	6.6
KONUSZEWSKI, DENNIS Dennis John B 2.4.1971 Bridgeport, MI BR/TR 6-3/210# d8.4																									
1995	Pit N	0	0	—	1	0	0	0-0	0.1	3	2	0	0	1-0	0	54.00	8	1.000	1.000	0-0	—	0		-2	-0.1
KOOB, ERNIE Ernest Gerald B 9.11.1892 Keeler, MI D 11.12.1941 Lemay, MO BL/TL 5-10/160# d6.23 Mil 1918																									
1915	StL A	4	5	.444	28	13	6	1	133.2	119	50	2	10	50	37	2.36	122	.254	.339	37-2	.135	-1	86	8	0.3
1916	StL A	11	8	.579	33	20	10-2	2	166.2	153	54	1	6	56	26	2.54	108	.252	.321	41-1	.000	-1	85	7	0.6
1917	StL A	6	14	.300	39	18	3-1	1	133.2	139	81	1	6	57	47	3.91	67	.280	.361	35-3	.114	-1	95	-20	-3.0
1919	StL A	2	4	.333	25	4	0	0	66	77	37	3	2	23	11	4.64	72	.296	.358	15-1	.000	-2	83	-7	-0.8
Total	4	23	31	.426	125	55	19-3	4	500	488	222	7	24	186	121	3.13	90	.266	.342	128-7	.070	-5	87	-12	-2.9
KOONCE, CAL Calvin Lee B 11.18.1940 Fayetteville, NC D 10.28.1993 Winston-Salem, NC BR/TR 6-1/185# d4.14																									
1962	Chi N	10	10	.500	35	30	3-1	0	190.2	200	93	17	7	86-3	84	3.97	105	.271	.350	64-3	.094	-4	88	5	0.1

Year	Tm Lg	W	L	Pct	G	GS	CG-Sho	SV-BS	IP	H	R	HR	HB	BB-IB	SO	ERA	AERA	OAV	OOB	AB-SH	AVG	PB	Sup	APR	PW
1963	Chi N	2	6	.250	21	13	0	0	72.2	75	43	9	2	32-2	44	4.58	77	.273	.353	19-3	.105	-0	57	-8	-0.8
1964	Chi N	3	0	1.000	6	2	0	0	31	30	8	1	0	7-1	17	2.03	183	.254	.294	10-0	.000	-1	95	5	0.5
1965	Chi N	7	9	.438	38	23	3-1	0	173	181	83	17	6	52-8	88	3.69	100	.271	.327	49-3	.102	-0	94	0	0.0
1966	Chi N	5	5	.500	45	5	0	2	108.2	113	57	13	1	35-9	65	3.81	97	.268	.321	23-3	.130	0	153	-3	-0.2
1967	Chi N	2	2	.500	34	0	0	2	51	52	27	2	1	21-6	28	4.59	77	.268	.341	7-0	.000	-1		-5	-0.5
	NY N	3	3	.500	11	6	2-1	0	45	45	16	2	0	7-1	24	2.80	121	.259	.287	13-1	.154	-0*	73	3	0.4
	Year	5	5	.500	45	6	2-1	2	96	97	19	4	1	28-7	52	3.75	93	.264	.317	20-1	.100	-1	72	-2	-0.1
1968	NY N	6	4	.600	55	2	0	11	97	80	27	4	1	32-11	50	2.41	125	.235	.301	14-0	.000	-1	115	7	0.9
1969	NY N	6	3	.667	40	0	0	7-4	83	85	53	8	3	42-8	48	4.99	73	.269	.358	17-0	.235	0		-13	-1.4
1970	NY N	0	2	.000	13	0	0	0-0	22	25	9	2	1	14-5	10	3.27	123	.301	.408	1-0	.000	-0		2	0.1
	Bos A	3	4	.429	23	8	1	2-2	76.1	64	32	7	3	29-3	37	3.54	112	.231	.309	21-1	.095	-0	107	4	0.5
1971	Bos A	0	1	.000	13	1	0	0-1	21	22	16	3	0	11-0	9	5.57	66	.278	.367	1-0	.000	0	242	-5	-0.2
Total	10	47	49	.490	334	90	9-3	24-7	971.1	972	464	85	25	368-57	504	3.78	98	.264	.333	239-14	.100	-6	95	-8	-0.6

KOOSMAN, JERRY Jerome Martin B 12.23.1942 Appleton, MN BR/TL 6-2/208# d4.14

Year	Tm Lg	W	L	Pct	G	GS	CG-Sho	SV-BS	IP	H	R	HR	HB	BB-IB	SO	ERA	AERA	OAV	OOB	AB-SH	AVG	PB	Sup	APR	PW
1967	NY N	0	2	.000	9	3	0	0	22.1	22	17	3	0	19-4	11	6.04	56	.259	.390	2-0	.000	0	52	-7	-0.5
1968	NY N★	19	12	.613	35	34	17-7	0	263.2	221	72	16	8	69-7	178	2.08	145	.228	.283	91-3	.077	-3	101	25	2.8
1969	†NY N★	17	9	.654	32	32	16-6	0-0	241	187	66	14	4	68-11	180	2.28	161	.216	.275	84-4	.048	-7	82	37	3.2
1970	NY N	12	7	.632	30	29	5-1	0-0	212	189	87	22	2	71-14	118	3.14	128	.237	.299	70-8	.086	-2	108	19	1.3
1971	NY N	6	11	.353	26	24	4	0-0	165.2	160	66	12	1	51-4	96	3.04	112	.256	.309	50-6	.160	0	88	6	0.6
1972	NY N	11	12	.478	34	24	4-1	1-0	163	155	81	14	6	52-7	147	4.14	81	.250	.310	47-9	.085	-3	85	-13	-2.0
1973	†NY N	14	15	.483	35	35	12-3	0-0	263	234	93	18	4	76-6	156	2.84	128	.242	.298	78-15	.103	-3	78	23	2.0
1974	NY N	15	11	.577	35	35	13	0-0	265	258	113	16	7	85-7	188	3.36	106	.257	.316	86-10	.186	2	96	7	0.9
1975	NY N	14	13	.519	36	34	11-4	2-0	239.2	234	106	19	4	98-6	173	3.42	101	.261	.335	78-7	.179	1	100	0	0.2
1976	NY N	21	10	.677	34	32	17-3	0-1	247.1	205	81	19	1	66-7	200	2.69	123	.226	.278	79-13	.215	3	109	19	2.8
1977	NY N	8	20	.286	32	32	6-1	0-0	226.2	195	102	17	4	81-8	192	3.49	107	.232	.301	72-5	.111	-3	77	4	0.1
1978	NY N	3	15	.167	38	32	3	2-1	235.1	221	110	17	8	84-11	160	3.75	93	.255	.323	70-5	.086	-3	84	-8	-0.8
1979	Min A	20	13	.606	37	36	10-2	0-0	263.2	268	108	19	3	83-4	157	3.38	130	.268	.325	0-0	—	0	95	28	3.4
1980	Min A	16	13	.552	38	34	8	2-0	243.1	252	119	24	5	69-5	149	4.03	108	.272	.324	0-0	—	0	87	11	1.2
1981	Min A	3	9	.250	19	13	2-1	5-0	94.1	98	49	8	0	34-7	55	4.20	94	.272	.331	0-0	—	0	61	-2	-0.3
	Chi A	1	4	.200	8	3	1	0-1	27	27	10	2	0	7-0	21	3.33	107	.260	.306	0-0	—	0	134	1	0.2
	Year	4	13	.235	27	16	3-1	5-1	121.1	125	15	10	0	41-7	76	4.01	97	.269	.325	0-0	—	0	74	-1	-0.1
1982	Chi A	11	7	.611	42	19	3-1	3-1	173.1	194	81	9	2	38-3	88	3.84	105	.287	.325	0-0	—	0	127	6	0.6
1983	†Chi A	11	7	.611	37	24	2-1	2-0	169.2	176	96	19	6	53-2	90	4.77	88	.266	.324	0-0	—	0	107	-9	-0.9
1984	Phi N	14	15	.483	36	34	3-1	0-0	224	232	95	8	3	60-5	137	3.25	112	.267	.315	74-14	.108	-3	109	10	0.8
1985	Phi N	6	4	.600	19	18	3-1	0-0	99.1	107	56	14	3	34-3	60	4.62	80	.276	.336	34-1	.088	-2	122	-9	-1.0
Total	19	222	209	.515	612	527	140-33	17-4	3839.1	3635	1608	290	71	1198-121	2556	3.36	110	.252	.310	915-100	.119	-22	95	148	14.6

KOPLITZ, HOWIE Howard Dean B 5.4.1938 Oshkosh, WI BR/TR 5-11/195# d9.8

Year	Tm Lg	W	L	Pct	G	GS	CG-Sho	SV-BS	IP	H	R	HR	HB	BB-IB	SO	ERA	AERA	OAV	OOB	AB-SH	AVG	PB	Sup	APR	PW
1961	Det A	2	0	1.000	4	1	1	0	12	16	6	0	0	8-1	9	2.25	182	.327	.414	4-0	.000	-1	129	1	0.1
1962	Det A	3	0	1.000	10	6	1	0	37.2	54	24	5	0	10-1	10	5.26	77	.342	.379	13-0	.231	1*	183	-4	-0.2
1964	Was A	0	0	—	6	1	0	0	17	20	9	3	0	13-1	9	4.76	78	.290	.402	4-0	.000	-0	144	-1	-0.1
1965	Was A	4	7	.364	33	11	0	1	106.2	97	51	11	3	48-4	59	4.05	86	.249	.333	30-1	.100	-1	108	-5	-0.6
1966	Was A	0	0	—	1	0	0	0	2	0	0	0	0	1-0	0	0.00	—	.000	.200	0-0	—	0		1	0.0
Total	5	9	7	.563	54	19	2	1	175.1	187	90	19	3	80-7	87	4.21	87	.280	.356	51-1	.118	-1	138	-8	-0.8

KOPLOVE, MIKE Michael Paul B 8.30.1976 Philadelphia, PA BR/TR 6/160# d9.6

Year	Tm Lg	W	L	Pct	G	GS	CG-Sho	SV-BS	IP	H	R	HR	HB	BB-IB	SO	ERA	AERA	OAV	OOB	AB-SH	AVG	PB	Sup	APR	PW
2001	Ari N	0	1	.000	9	0	0	0-0	10	8	7	1	2	9-1	14	3.60	127	.211	.388	1-0	.000	-0		0	0.0
2002	†Ari N	6	1	.857	55	0	0	0-0	61.2	47	24	2	0	23-4	46	3.36	132	.213	.286	1-0	.000	-0		7	0.8
2003	Ari N	3	0	1.000	31	0	0	0-1	37.2	31	11	3	5	10-1	27	2.15	217	.225	.297	0-0	—	0		9	0.7
Total	3	9	2	.818	95	0	0	0-1	109.1	86	42	6	7	42-6	87	2.96	153	.217	.301	2-0	.000	-0		16	1.5

KORINCE, GEORGE George Eugene "Moose" B 1.10.1946 Ottawa, ON, CAN BR/TR 6-3/210# d9.10

Year	Tm Lg	W	L	Pct	G	GS	CG-Sho	SV-BS	IP	H	R	HR	HB	BB-IB	SO	ERA	AERA	OAV	OOB	AB-SH	AVG	PB	Sup	APR	PW
1966	Det A	0	0	—	2	0	0	0	3	1	0	0	1	3-0	2	0.00	—	.091	.333	0-0	—	0		1	0.1
1967	Det A	1	0	1.000	9	0	0	0	14	10	8	1	0	11-1	11	5.14	63	.204	.339	1-0	.000	-0		-3	-0.2
Total	2	1	0	1.000	11	0	0	0	17	11	8	1	1	14-1	13	4.24	78	.183	.338	1-0	.000	-0		-2	-0.1

KORWAN, JIM James "Long Jim" B 3.4.1874 Brooklyn, NY D 7.24.1899 Brooklyn, NY BR/TR 6-1/181# d4.24

Year	Tm Lg	W	L	Pct	G	GS	CG-Sho	SV-BS	IP	H	R	HR	HB	BB-IB	SO	ERA	AERA	OAV	OOB	AB-SH	AVG	PB	Sup	APR	PW
1894	Bro N	0	0	—	1	0	0	0	5	9	14	1	0	5	2	14.40	34	.391	.500	2-0	.000	-0		-7	-0.2
1897	Chi N	1	2	.333	5	4	3	0	34	47	36	1	1	28	12	5.82	77	.324	.437	12-0	.000	-2	92	-6	-0.5
Total	2	1	2	.333	6	4	3	0	39	56	50	2	1	33	14	6.92	66	.333	.446	14-0	.000	-2	92	-13	-0.7

KOSKI, BILL William John "T-Bone" B 2.6.1932 Madera, CA BR/TR 6-4/185# d4.28 Mil 1952

Year	Tm Lg	W	L	Pct	G	GS	CG-Sho	SV-BS	IP	H	R	HR	HB	BB-IB	SO	ERA	AERA	OAV	OOB	AB-SH	AVG	PB	Sup	APR	PW
1951	Pit N	0	1	.000	13	1	0	0	27	26	23	2	0	28	6	6.67	63	.257	.419	4-0	.000	-1	63	-7	-0.4

KOSLO, DAVE George Bernard (b: George Bernard Koslowski) B 3.31.1920 Menasha, WI D 12.1.1975 Menasha, WI BL/TL 5-11/180# d9.12 Mil 1943-45

Year	Tm Lg	W	L	Pct	G	GS	CG-Sho	SV-BS	IP	H	R	HR	HB	BB-IB	SO	ERA	AERA	OAV	OOB	AB-SH	AVG	PB	Sup	APR	PW
1941	NY N	1	2	.333	4	3	2	0	23.2	17	6	0	0	10	12	1.90	194	.202	.287	9-0	.111	-1	46	5	0.5
1942	NY N	3	6	.333	19	11	3-1	0	78	79	49	7	1	32	42	5.08	66	.261	.333	25-0	.120	-0	89	-13	-1.5
1946	NY N	14	19	.424	40	**35**	17-3	1	265.1	251	119	15	5	101	121	3.63	95	.249	.320	88-1	.125	-3*	86	-3	-0.6
1947	NY N	15	10	.600	39	31	10-3	0	217.1	223	118	23	3	82	86	4.39	93	.259	.326	78-1	.128	-1	132	-7	-0.8
1948	NY N	8	10	.444	35	18	5-3	3	149	168	69	7	1	62	58	3.87	102	.290	.359	44-3	.114	-1	85	4	0.3
1949	NY N	11	14	.440	38	23	15	4	212	193	72	13	0	43	64	**2.50**	**159**	.239	**.278**	69-6	.145	1*	76	34	4.1
1950	NY N	13	15	.464	40	22	7-1	3	186.2	190	89	18	5	68	56	3.91	105	.268	.337	65-1	.123	-1	107	5	0.6
1951	†NY N	10	9	.526	39	16	5-2	3	149.2	153	68	18	2	45	54	3.31	118	.258	.313	50-0	.100	-1	130	9	1.0
1952	NY N	10	7	.588	41	17	8-2	5	166.1	154	66	10	2	47	67	3.19	116	.242	.296	54-3	.037	-4	117	11	0.8
1953	NY N	6	12	.333	37	12	2	2	111.2	135	70	8	1	36	36	4.76	90	.296	.349	30-3	.033	-3	87	-6	-1.2
1954	Bal A	0	1	.000	3	1	0	0	14.1	20	7	1	0	3	3	3.14	114	.333	.365	3-0	.000	-0	0	0	-0.1
	Mil N	1	1	.500	12	0	0	1	17.1	13	6	0	0	9	7	3.12	120	.228	.324	1-0	.000	-0		2	0.1
1955	Mil N	0	1	.000	1	0	0	0	0	1	1	1	0	0-0	0	∞	—	1.000	1.000	0-0	—	0		-1	-0.1
Total	12	92	107	.462	348	189	74-15	22	1591.1	1597	740	121	20	538-0	606	3.68	105	.260	.321	516-18	.109	-15	101	40	3.1

KOSTAL, JOE Joseph William "Cudgey" B 3.17.1876 Chicago, IL D 10.17.1933 Guelph, ON, CAN BR/TR 5-6/130# d7.14

Year	Tm Lg	W	L	Pct	G	GS	CG-Sho	SV-BS	IP	H	R	HR	HB	BB-IB	SO	ERA	AERA	OAV	OOB	AB-SH	AVG	PB	Sup	APR	PW
1896	Lou N	0	0	—	2	0	0	0	2	4	4	0	0	0	0	0.00	—	.400	.400	0-0	—	0		0	0.0

KOUFAX, SANDY Sanford (b: Sanford Braun) B 12.30.1935 Brooklyn, NY BR/TL 6-2/210# d6.24 HF1972

Year	Tm Lg	W	L	Pct	G	GS	CG-Sho	SV-BS	IP	H	R	HR	HB	BB-IB	SO	ERA	AERA	OAV	OOB	AB-SH	AVG	PB	Sup	APR	PW
1955	Bro N	2	2	.500	12	5	2-2	0	41.2	33	15	2	1	28-1	30	3.02	134	.216	.341	12-0	.000	-2	75	5	0.3
1956	Bro N	2	4	.333	16	10	0	0	58.2	66	37	10	0	29-0	30	4.91	81	.286	.365	17-0	.118	-0	80	-7	-0.7
1957	Bro N	5	4	.556	34	13	2	0	104.1	83	49	14	2	51-1	122	3.88	107	.216	.309	26-1	.000	-3	91	4	-0.1
1958	LA N	11	11	.500	40	26	5	1	158.2	132	89	19	1	105-6	131	4.48	91	**.220**	.335	49-5	.122	-2	96	-7	-1.1
1959	†LA N	8	6	.571	35	23	6-1	2	153.1	136	74	23	0	92-4	173	4.05	104	.235	.338	54-2	.111	-1	117	4	0.2
1960	LA N	8	13	.381	37	26	7-2	1	175	133	83	20	1	100-6	197	3.91	102	**.207**	.314	57-4	.123	-2	91	2	0.0
1961	LA N★	18	13	.581	42	35	15-2	1	255.2	212	117	27	3	96-6	**269**	3.52	123	**.222**	.295	77-8	.065	-5	100	20	1.5
1962	LA N☆	14	7	.667	28	26	11-2	1	184.1	134	61	13	2	57-4	216	**2.54**	143	**.197**	**.261**	69-2	.087	-3	119	24	2.2
1963	†LA N☆	**25**	5	.833	40	40	20-**11**	0	311	214	68	18	3	58-7	**306**	**1.88**	161	**.189**	**.230**	110-7	.064	-4	123	**47**	4.1
1964	LA N☆	19	5	**.792**	29	28	15-**7**	1	223	154	49	13	0	53-5	223	**1.74**	**187**	**.191**	**.240**	74-3	.095	-2	97	41	4.3
1965	†LA N★	**26**	8	**.765**	43	41	**27**-8	2	**335.2**	216	90	26	5	71-4	**382**	**2.04**	160	**.179**	**.227**	113-3	.177	5	108	48	5.5
1966	†LA N★	**27**	9	.750	41	**41**	**27**-5	0	**323**	241	74	19	0	77-4	**317**	**1.73**	**191**	.205	.252	118-0	.076	-5	113	**60**	**6.1**
Total	12	165	87	.655	397	314	137-40	9	2324.1	1754	806	204	18	817-48	2396	2.76	131	.205	.275	776-35	.097	-25	106	241	22.3

KOUKALIK, JOE Joseph B 3.3.1880 Chicago, IL D 12.27.1945 Chicago, IL 5-8/160# d9.1

Year	Tm Lg	W	L	Pct	G	GS	CG-Sho	SV-BS	IP	H	R	HR	HB	BB-IB	SO	ERA	AERA	OAV	OOB	AB-SH	AVG	PB	Sup	APR	PW
1904	Bro N	0	1	.000	1	1	1	0	8	10	3	0	0	4	1	1.13	244	.333	.412	3-0	.000	-0	0	1	0.0

KOUPAL, LOU Louis Laddie B 12.19.1898 Tabor, SD D 12.8.1961 San Gabriel, CA BR/TR 5-11/175# d4.17

Year	Tm Lg	W	L	Pct	G	GS	CG-Sho	SV-BS	IP	H	R	HR	HB	BB-IB	SO	ERA	AERA	OAV	OOB	AB-SH	AVG	PB	Sup	APR	PW
1925	Pit N	0	0	—	6	0	0	0	9	14	10	1	0	7	0	9.00	50	.378	.477	1-0	.000	-0*		-4	-0.2

Year	Tm Lg	W	L	Pct	G	GS	CG-Sho	SV-BS	IP	H	R	HR	HB	BB-IB	SO	ERA	AERA	OAV	OOB	AB-SH	AVG	PB	Sup	APR	PW
1926	Pit N	0	2	.000	6	2	1	0	19.2	22	9	0	1	8	7	3.20	123	.289	.365	4-0	.250	0	32	1	0.1
1928	Bro N	1	0	1.000	17	1	1	1	37.1	43	22	0	1	15	10	2.41	165	.303	.373	9-0	.111	-1	170	3	0.1
1929	Bro N	0	1	.000	18	3	0	4	40.1	49	36	3	0	25	17	5.36	86	.308	.402	14-0	.071	-2	57	-7	-0.5
	Phi N	5	5	.500	15	11	3	2	86.2	106	56	5	2	29	18	4.78	109	.305	.362	32-2	.125	-2	95	2	-0.1
	Year	5	6	.455	33	14	3	6	127	155	62	8	2	54	35	4.96	101	.306	.375	46-2	.109	-4	88	-5	-0.6
1930	Phi N	0	4	.000	13	4	1	0	36.2	52	35	4	1	17	11	8.59	64	.344	.414	12-0	.083	-1	92	-9	-0.9
1937	StL A	4	9	.308	26	13	6	0	105.2	150	87	10	0	55	24	6.56	74	.339	.412	32-2	.094	-3	90	-20	-2.2
Total	6	10	21	.323	101	34	12	7	335.1	436	255	23	5	156	87	5.58	86	.322	.394	104-4	.106	-9	90	-34	-3.7
KOWALIK, FABIAN Fabian Lorenz B 4.22.1908 Falls City, TX D 8.14.1954 Karnes City, TX BR/TR 5-11/185# d9.4																									
1932	Chi A	0	1	.000	2	1	0	0	10.1	16	11	2	1	4	2	6.97	62	.340	.404	13-0	.385	1*	98	-4	-0.2
1935	†Chi N	2	2	.500	20	2	1	1	55	60	31	2	0	19	20	4.42	89	.280	.339	15-0	.200	-0	184	-3	-0.2
1936	Chi N	0	2	.000	6	0	0	1	16	24	12	1	0	7	1	6.75	59	.358	.419	5-0	.000	-1		-4	-0.6
	Phi N	1	5	.167	22	8	2	0	77	100	57	5	2	31	19	5.38	84	.308	.372	57-1	.228	-0*	103	-6	-0.5
	Bos N	0	1	.000	1	1	1	0	9	18	8	0	0	2	0	8.00	48	.419	.444	5-0	.400	1*	133	-4	-0.3
	Year	1	8	.111	29	9	3	1	102	142	14	6	2	40	20	5.82	75	.326	.386	67-1	.224	-0	107	-13	-1.4
Total	3	3	11	.214	51	12	4	2	167.1	218	119	10	3	63	42	5.43	78	.313	.373	95-1	.242	-0	120	-21	-1.8
KOZLOWSKI, BEN Benjamin Anthony B 8.16.1980 St.Petersburg, FL BL/TL 6-6/220# d9.19																									
2002	Tex A	0	0	—	2	2	0	0-0	10	11	7	3	1	11-0	6	6.30	75	.289	.460	0-0	—	0	196	-1	-0.1
KRAEMER, JOE Joseph Wayne B 9.10.1964 Olympia, WA BL/TL 6-2/185# d8.22																									
1989	Chi N	0	1	.000	1	1	0	0-0	3.2	7	6	0	0	2-1	5	4.91	77	.368	.429	1-0	.000	-0	47	-2	-0.4
1990	Chi N	0	0	—	18	0	0	0-1	25	31	25	2	2	14-2	16	7.20	57	.310	.398	0-0	—	0		-9	-0.5
Total	2	0	1	.000	19	1	0	0-1	28.2	38	31	2	2	16-3	21	6.91	59	.319	.403	1-0	.000	-0	47	-11	-0.9
KRAKAUSKAS, JOE Joseph Victor Lawrence B 3.28.1915 Montreal, PQ, CAN D 7.8.1960 Hamilton, ON, CAN BL/TL 6-1/203# d9.9 Mil 1943-45																									
1937	Was A	4	1	.800	5	4	3	0	40	33	14	0	0	22	18	2.70	164	.226	.327	16-0	.125	-0	103	8	0.8
1938	Was A	7	5	.583	29	10	5-1	0	121.1	99	61	4	3	88	104	3.12	145	.220	.352	33-3	.182	1	100	15	1.3
1939	Was A	11	17	.393	39	29	12	1	217.1	230	125	13	1	114	110	4.60	95	.276	.364	77-3	.208	3	101	-5	-0.4
1940	Was A	1	6	.143	32	10	2	2	109	137	90	7	0	73	68	6.44	65	.309	.406	32-0	.250	1	110	-28	-1.4
1941	Cle A	1	2	.333	12	5	0	0	41.2	39	25	3	0	29	25	4.10	96	.245	.362	13-0	.077	-1	123	-3	-0.2
1942	Cle A	0	0	—	3	0	0	0	7	7	3	1	0	4	2	3.86	89	.259	.355	2-0	.000	-0		0	0.0
1946	Cle A	2	5	.286	29	5	0	1	47.1	60	31	2	0	25	20	5.51	60	.314	.394	10-0	.000	-1	83	-11	-1.7
Total	7	26	36	.419	149	63	22-1	4	583.2	605	349	30	4	355	347	4.53	93	.269	.369	183-6	.180	2	103	-24	-1.6
KRALICK, JACK John Francis B 6.1.1935 Youngstown, OH BL/TL 6-2/180# d4.15																									
1959	Was A	0	0	—	6	0	0	0	12.1	13	9	5	0	6-0	7	6.57	60	.289	.373	2-0	.000	-0		-3	-0.1
1960	Was A	8	6	.571	35	18	7-2	1	151	139	54	12	4	45-4	71	3.61	128	.245	.304	41-3	.122	-1	92	17	1.4
1961	Min A	13	11	.542	33	33	11-2	0	242	257	101	21	3	64-1	137	3.61	118	.274	.321	86-6	.151	-2	90	20	1.7
1962	Min A	12	11	.522	39	37	7-1	0	242.2	239	121	31	3	61-2	139	3.86	106	.258	.302	89-3	.202	3	96	4	0.7
1963	Min A	1	4	.200	5	5	1-1	0	25.2	28	16	2	1	8-0	13	3.86	94	.280	.339	6-1	.167	1*	39	-2	-0.3
	Cle A	13	9	.591	28	27	10-3	0	197.1	187	70	19	0	41-2	116	2.92	124	.249	.286	60-9	.183	1	106	17	1.9
	Year	14	13	.519	33	32	11-4	0	223	215	74	21	1	49-2	129	3.03	120	.253	.292	66-10	.182	2	95	15	1.6
1964	Cle A☆	12	7	.632	30	29	8-3	0	190.2	196	79	17	9	51-8	119	3.21	112	.267	.320	64-3	.156	-1	101	7	0.6
1965	Cle A	5	11	.313	30	16	1	0	86	106	58	9	2	21-3	34	4.92	71	.298	.338	21-3	.143	-1	93	-15	-2.7
1966	Cle A	3	4	.429	27	4	0	0	68.1	69	30	9	1	20-8	31	3.82	90	.268	.319	13-1	.077	-1	70	-2	-0.2
1967	Cle A	0	2	.000	2	0	0	0	2	4	3	0	0	1-0	1	9.00	36	.444	.500	0-0	—	0		-2	-0.3
Total	9	67	65	.508	235	169	45-12	1	1218	1238	541	125	23	318-28	668	3.56	108	.264	.312	382-29	.162	0	94	41	2.7
KRALY, STEVE Steve Charles "Lefty" B 4.18.1929 Whiting, IN BL/TL 5-10/152# d8.9																									
1953	NY A	0	2	.000	5	3	0	1	25	19	10	2	2	16	8	3.24	114	.209	.339	7-0	.000	-1	40	1	0.0
KRAMER, JACK John Henry B 1.5.1918 New Orleans, LA D 5.18.1995 Metairie, LA BR/TR 6-2/190# d4.25 Def 1942, Mil 1943																									
1939	StL A	9	16	.360	40	31	10-2	0	211.2	269	150	18	3	127	68	5.83	84	.318	.409	66-7	.136	-1	103	-19	-2.0
1940	StL A	3	7	.300	16	9	1	0	64.2	86	48	4	0	26	12	6.26	73	.327	.388	20-1	.050	-1	89	-10	-1.4
1941	StL A	4	3	.571	29	3	0	2	59.1	69	48	5	0	40	20	5.16	83	.289	.391	8-1	.000	1	101	-10	-0.9
1943	StL A	0	0	—	3	0	0	0	9	11	8	0	1	8	4	8.00	42	.297	.435	2-0	.500	1		-4	-0.1
1944	†StL A	17	13	.567	33	31	18-1	0	257	233	94	3	1	75	124	2.49	145	.241	.297	85-1	.165	1	90	27	3.4
1945	StL A✣	10	15	.400	29	25	15-3	2	193	190	85	13	0	73	99	3.36	105	.254	.320	61-7	.148	-0	80	2	0.3
1946	StL A★	13	11	.542	31	28	13-3	0	194.2	190	84	6	0	68	69	3.19	117	.257	.319	59-8	.136	-1	96	10	1.0
1947	StL A☆	11	16	.407	33	28	9-1	1	199.1	206	123	16	2	89	77	4.97	78	.270	.348	62-5	.113	-2	101	-22	-2.8
1948	Bos A	18	5	**.783**	29	29	14-2	0	205	233	104	12	0	64	72	4.35	101	.284	.336	73-7	.151	-1	152	3	0.1
1949	Bos A	6	8	.429	21	18	7-2	1	111.2	126	70	8	1	49	24	5.16	85	.286	.358	35-2	.257	3	117	-9	-0.8
1950	NY N	3	6	.333	35	9	1	1	86.2	91	46	6	2	39	27	3.53	116	.268	.346	20-1	.100	1	98	2	0.3
1951	NY N	0	0	—	4	1	0	0	4.2	11	8	0	0	3	2	15.43	25	.524	.583	0-0	—	0	271	-5	-0.3
	NY A	1	3	.250	19	3	0	0	40.2	46	27	1	0	21	15	4.65	82	.280	.362	10-0	.100	-0	162	-5	-0.6
Total	12	95	103	.480	322	215	88-14	7	1637.1	1761	895	92	10	682	613	4.24	96	.276	.347	501-40	.144	0	107	-40	-3.8
KRAMER, RANDY Randall John B 9.20.1960 Palo Alto, CA BR/TR 6-2/170# d9.11																									
1988	Pit N	1	2	.333	5	1	0	0-0	10	12	6	1	1	1-0	7	5.40	63	.316	.341	2-0	.000	-0	182	-2	-0.4
1989	Pit N	5	9	.357	35	15	1-1	2-4	111.1	90	53	10	7	61-4	52	3.96	85	.224	.334	33-2	.152	-0*	100	-7	-0.9
1990	Pit N	0	1	.000	12	2	0	0-0	25.2	27	15	3	2	9-4	15	4.91	74	.273	.345	5-0	.000	-1	87	-3	-0.2
	Chi N	0	2	.000	10	2	0	0-0	20.1	20	10	3	1	12-2	12	3.98	102	.253	.359	1-1	.000	-0	89	0	0.0
	Year	0	3	.000	22	4	0	0-0	46	47	14	6	3	21-6	27	4.50	85	.264	.351	6-1	.000	-1	89	-3	-0.2
1992	Sea A	0	1	.000	4	4	0	0-0	16.1	30	14	2	1	7-0	6	7.71	52	.400	.458	0-0	—	0	126	-6	-0.3
Total	4	6	15	.286	66	24	1-1	2-4	183.2	179	98	19	12	90-10	92	4.51	78	.259	.352	41-3	.122	-1	106	-18	-1.8
KRAMER, TOMMY Thomas Joseph B 1.9.1968 Cincinnati, OH BB/TR 6/185# d9.12																									
1991	Cle A	0	0	—	4	0	0	0-0	4.2	10	9	1	0	6-0	4	17.36	24	.476	.533	0-0	—	0		-6	-0.3
1993	Cle A	7	3	.700	39	16	1	0-2	121	126	60	19	2	59-7	71	4.02	108	.269	.352	0-0	—	0	122	4	0.3
Total	2	7	3	.700	43	16	1	0-2	125.2	136	69	20	2	65-7	75	4.51	96	.278	.361	0-0	—	0	122	-2	0.0
KRAPP, GENE Eugene Hamlet "Rubber Arm" B 5.12.1887 Rochester, NY D 4.13.1923 Detroit, MI BR/TR 5-5/165# d4.14																									
1911	Cle A	13	9	.591	35	26	14-1	1	222	188	115	1	13	138	132	3.41	100	.232	.353	74-3	.230	4*	109	0	0.6
1912	Cle A	2	5	.286	9	7	4	0	58.2	57	39	0	4	42	22	4.60	74	.273	.404	22-1	.318	1*	96	-7	-0.5
1914	Buf F	16	14	.533	36	29	18-1	0	252.2	198	83	4	12	115	106	2.49	119	.210	.304	77-2	.143	-2*	89	14	1.7
1915	Buf F	9	19	.321	38	30	14-1	0	231	188	106	6	4	123	93	3.51	80	.230	.333	70-2	.129	-3*	77	-15	-1.7
Total	4	40	47	.460	118	92	50-3	1	764.1	631	343	11	33	418	353	3.23	95	.227	.335	243-8	.181	-1	92	-8	0.1
KRAUS, JACK John William "Tex" or "Texas Jack" B 4.26.1918 San Antonio, TX D 1.2.1976 San Antonio, TX BR/TL 6-4/190# d4.25 Mil 1944																									
1943	Phi N	9	15	.375	34	25	10-1	2	199.2	197	83	7	0	78	48	3.16	107	.259	.328	60-9	.067	-5*	67	4	0.0
1945	Phi N	4	9	.308	19	13	0	0	81.2	96	55	3	4	40	28	5.40	71	.293	.376	25-2	.120	-1	71	-12	-1.7
1946	NY N	2	1	.667	17	1	0	0	25	25	17	4	1	15	7	6.12	56	.260	.366	3-0	.000	-0	100	-6	-0.7
Total	3	15	25	.375	70	39	10-1	2	306.1	318	155	14	5	133	83	4.00	88	.268	.345	88-11	.080	-6	70	-14	-2.4
KRAUSE, HARRY Harry William "Hal" B 7.12.1887 San Francisco, CA D 10.23.1940 San Francisco, CA BB/TL 5-10/165# d4.20																									
1908	Phi A	1	1	.500	4	2	2	0	21	20	11	0	3	4	10	2.57	100	.247	.307	7-0	.000	-1	80	-1	-0.2
1909	Phi A	18	8	.692	32	21	16-7	0	213	151	49	2	13	49	139	**1.39**	**173**	.204	.266	77-2	.156	-1	112	23	2.7
1910	Phi A	6	6	.500	16	11	9-2	0	112.1	99	46	4	8	42	60	2.88	82	.254	.339	38-4	.211	1	103	-3	-0.4
1911	Phi A	11	8	.579	27	19	12-1	2	169	155	65	2	9	47	85	3.04	104	.251	.313	59-4	.254	2	107	6	0.7
1912	Phi A	0	2	.000	4	2	0	0	5.1	10	8	0	1	2	3	13.50	23	.435	.500	4-0	.250	0	36	-6	-1.0
	Cle A	0	1	.000	2	2	0	0	4.2	11	6	0	0	2	1	11.57	29	.500	.542	0-0	—	0	98	-3	-0.6
	Year	0	3	.000	6	4	0	0	10	21	11	0	1	4	4	12.60	26	.467	.520	4-0	.250	0	69	-9	-1.6
Total	5	36	26	.581	85	57	39-10	2	525.1	446	185	8	34	146	298	2.50	107	.238	.305	185-10	.195	1	105	16	1.2

Year	Tm Lg	W	L	Pct	G	GS	CG-Sho	SV-BS	IP	H	R	HR	HB	BB-IB	SO	ERA	AERA	OAV	OOB	AB-SH	AVG	PB	Sup	APR	PW
KRAUSSE, LEW Lewis Bernard Jr. B 4.25.1943 Media, PA BR/TR 5-11/186# d6.16 f-Lew																									
1961	KC A	2	5	.286	12	8	2-1	0	55.2	49	33	3	1	46-0	32	4.85	86	.243	.382	17-1	.118	-1*	90	-3	-0.5
1964	KC A	0	2	.000	5	4	0	0	14.2	22	14	1	2	9-0	9	7.36	52	.349	.434	2-0	.000	0*	93	-6	-0.7
1965	KC A	2	4	.333	7	5	0	0	25	29	14	1	0	8-0	22	5.04	69	.284	.336	7-1	.000	-1*	55	-4	-0.8
1966	KC A	14	9	.609	36	22	4-1	3	177.2	144	69	8	6	63-8	87	2.99	114	.222	.294	52-6	.154	0*	91	7	0.9
1967	KC A	7	17	.292	48	19	0	6	160	140	85	17	4	67-6	96	4.27	75	.236	.314	41-1	.146	1*	58	-19	-2.8
1968	Oak A	10	11	.476	36	25	2	4	185	147	68	16	3	62-9	105	3.11	91	.217	.283	56-2	.161	3	92	-4	-0.2
1969	Oak A	7	7	.500	43	16	4-2	7-1	140	134	75	23	5	48-8	85	4.44	78	.256	.322	48-1	.167	4	127	-16	-1.2
1970	Mil A	13	18	.419	37	35	8-1	0-0	216	235	130	33	4	67-15	130	4.75	80	.275	.328	65-7	.138	1*	103	-24	-3.0
1971	Mil A	8	12	.400	43	22	1	0-0	180.1	164	67	23	5	62-10	92	2.94	118	.239	.306	44-5	.023	-3	76	11	0.8
1972	Bos A	1	3	.250	24	7	0	1-0	60.2	74	48	9	3	28-2	35	6.38	51	.308	.387	16-0	.125	-0	94	-20	-1.4
1973	StL N	0	0	—	1	0	0	0-0	2	2	0	0	0	1-0	1	0.00	—	.250	.333	0-0	—	0		1	0.1
1974	Atl N	4	3	.571	29	4	0	0-0	66.2	65	32	3	2	32-4	27	4.18	91	.258	.345	6-2	.333	2	81	-2	0.0
Total	12	68	91	.428	321	167	21-5	21-1	1283.2	1205	635	137	35	493-62	721	4.00	85	.248	.320	354-26	.133	6	91	-79	-8.8
KRAUSSE, LEW Lewis Bernard Sr. B 6.8.1912 Media, PA D 9.6.1988 Sarasota, FL BR/TR 6-0.5/167# d6.11 s-Lew																									
1931	Phi A	1	0	1.000	3	1	1	0	11	6	6	2	0	6	1	4.09	110	.150	.261	2-0	.000	0	132	0	0.1
1932	Phi A	4	1	.800	20	3	2-1	0	57	64	31	3	0	24	16	4.58	99	.281	.349	15-2	.133	-0	239	0	0.0
Total	2	5	1	.833	23	4	3-1	0	68	70	37	5	0	30	17	4.50	100	.261	.336	17-2	.118	0	212	0	0.1
KRAVEC, KEN Kenneth Peter B 7.29.1951 Cleveland, OH BL/TL 6-2/185# d9.4																									
1975	Chi A	0	1	.000	2	1	0	0-0	4.1	1	3	0	0	8-0	1	6.23	62	.071	.409	0-0	—	0	0	-1	-0.2
1976	Chi A	1	5	.167	9	8	1	0-0	49.2	49	28	3	1	32-0	38	4.89	73	.257	.366	0-0	—	0	74	-7	-0.7
1977	Chi A	11	8	.579	26	25	6-1	0-0	166.2	161	87	12	6	57-0	125	4.10	100	.250	.317	0-0	—	0	112	-1	0.0
1978	Chi A	11	16	.407	30	30	7-2	0-0	203	188	104	22	10	95-1	154	4.08	94	.245	.334	0-0	—	0	77	-7	-0.9
1979	Chi A	15	13	.536	36	35	10-3	1-0	250	208	115	20	14	111-3	132	3.74	114	.233	.323	0-0	—	0	94	17	1.7
1980	Chi A	3	6	.333	20	15	0	0-0	81.2	100	71	13	5	44-3	37	6.94	58	.298	.382	0-0	—	0	90	-26	-2.4
1981	Chi N	1	6	.143	24	12	0	0-0	78.1	80	48	5	4	39-6	50	5.06	73	.268	.355	15-4	.000	-1*	60	-10	-1.0
1982	Chi N	1	1	.500	13	2	0	0-0	25	27	20	3	0	18-2	20	6.12	61	.267	.375	3-0	.000	-0	130	-7	-0.5
Total	8	43	56	.434	160	128	24-6	1-0	858.2	814	476	78	40	404-15	557	4.47	90	.251	.339	18-4	.000	-1	89	-42	-4.0
KRAWCZYK, RAY Raymond Allen B 10.9.1959 Pittsburgh, PA BR/TR 6-1/186# d6.29																									
1984	Pit N	0	0	—	4	0	0	0-0	5.1	7	2	0	0	4-2	3	3.38	107	.350	.440	0-0	—	0		0	0.0
1985	Pit N	0	2	.000	8	0	0	0-2	8.1	20	13	1	1	6-3	9	14.04	26	.455	.529	0-0	—	0		-9	-1.7
1986	Pit N	0	1	.000	12	0	0	0-0	12.1	17	13	3	0	10-0	7	7.30	53	.321	.422	0-0	—	0		-5	-0.4
1988	Cal A	0	1	.000	14	1	0	1-0	24.1	29	13	2	2	8-1	17	4.81	80	.299	.361	0-0	—	0	94	-2	-0.1
1989	Mil A	0	0	—	1	0	0	0-0	2	4	3	0	0	1-0	6	13.50	28	.400	.455	0-0	—	0		-2	-0.1
Total	5	0	4	.000	39	1	0	1-2	52.1	77	44	6	3	29-6	42	7.05	54	.344	.421	0-0	—	0	94	-18	-2.3
KREEGER, FRANK Frank D 7.14.1899 Shelby Co., IL d7.28																									
1884	KC U	0	1	.000	1	1	0	0	7	9	8	0		5	3	0.00	—	.290	.389	3	.000	-1	38	0	-0.1
KREMER, RAY Remy Peter "Wiz" B 3.23.1893 Oakland, CA D 2.8.1965 Pinole, CA BR/TR 6-1/190# d4.18																									
1924	Pit N	18	10	.643	**41**	30	17-**4**	1	259.1	262	102	7	4	51	64	3.19	120	.265	.304	86-5	.151	-4*	109	21	1.6
1925	†Pit N	17	8	.680	40	27	14	2	214.2	232	106	19	9	47	62	3.69	121	.278	.323	71-5	.197	1	117	18	1.8
1926	Pit N	**20**	6	**.769**	37	26	18-3	5	231.1	221	79	9	4	51	74	**2.61**	**151**	.252	.296	83-6	.253	2	106	**34**	**3.9**
1927	†Pit N	19	8	.704	35	28	18-3	2	226	205	73	9	0	53	63	**2.47**	**166**	.244	.289	83-3	.169	-1	104	39	4.2
1928	Pit N	15	13	.536	34	31	17-1	0	219	253	124	15	4	68	61	4.64	87	.297	.352	78-3	.179	0	114	-10	-1.3
1929	Pit N	18	10	.643	34	27	14	0	221.2	226	114	21	1	60	66	4.26	112	.271	.320	86-1	.128	-2	103	16	1.3
1930	Pit N	**20**	12	.625	39	**38**	18-1	0	**276**	366	181	29	1	63	58	5.02	99	.322	.359	102-8	.157	-4	112	-2	-0.7
1931	Pit N	11	15	.423	30	30	15-1	0	230	246	110	6	5	65	58	3.33	116	.271	.323	75-3	.227	4	80	11	1.3
1932	Pit N	4	3	.571	11	10	3-1	0	56.2	61	35	5	1	16	6	4.29	89	.270	.321	19-2	.105	-1	106	-4	-0.6
1933	Pit N	1	0	1.000	7	0	0	0	20	36	26	2	0	9	4	10.35	32	.387	.441	4-0	.000	-1		-15	-0.8
Total	10	143	85	.627	308	247	134-14	10	1954.2	2108	950	122	29	483	516	3.76	113	.278	.323	687-36	.178	-7	107	108	10.7
KREMMEL, JIM James Louis B 2.28.1948 Belleville, IL BL/TL 6/175# d7.4																									
1973	Tex A	0	2	.000	4	2	0	0-0	9	15	10	1	2	6-1	6	9.00	41	.366	.460	0-0	—	0	60	-5	-0.9
1974	Chi N	0	2	.000	23	2	0	0-1	31	37	21	3	1	18-0	22	5.23	73	.303	.386	3-0	.000	-0	68	-4	-0.3
Total	2	0	4	.000	27	4	0	0-1	40	52	31	4	3	24-1	28	6.07	63	.319	.405	3-0	.000	-0	63	-9	-1.2
KRESS, RED Ralph B 1.2.1905 Columbia, CA D 11.29.1962 Los Angeles, CA BR/TR 5-11.5/165# d9.24.1927 C15 ▲																									
1935	Was A	0	0	—	3	0	0	0	5.2	8	9	0	0	5	5	12.71	34	.333	.448	252-2	.298	1*		-5	-0.2
1946	NY N	0	0	—	1	0	0	0	3.2	5	5	1	1	1	1	12.27	28	.333	.412	1-0	.000	0		-3	-0.1
Total	2	0	0	—	4	0	0	0	9.1	13	14	1	1	6	6	12.54	32	.333	.435	253-2	.296	1		-8	-0.3
KRETLOW, LOU Louis Henry "Lena" B 6.27.1921 Apache, OK BR/TR 6-2/185# d9.26																									
1946	Det A	1	0	1.000	1	1	1	0	9	7	3	2	0	2	4	3.00	122	.206	.250	4-0	.500	1	141	1	0.2
1948	Det A	2	1	.667	5	2	1	0	23.1	21	14	1	0	11	9	4.63	94	.233	.317	8-1	.500	1	41	-1	0.0
1949	Det A	3	2	.600	25	10	1	0	76	85	58	5	1	69	40	6.16	68	.290	.427	26-1	.000	-4	153	-17	-1.2
1950	StL A	0	2	.000	9	2	0	0	14.1	25	19	2	2	18	10	11.93	41	.403	.549	3-0	.000	-0*	100	-9	-1.1
	Chi A	0	0	—	11	1	0	0	21.1	17	13	1	0	27	14	3.80	118	.221	.423	4-0	.000	-1	141	0	-0.1
	Year	0	2	.000	20	3	0	0	35.2	42	20	3	2	45	24	7.07	66	.302	.478	7-0	.000	-1	116	-9	-1.2
1951	Chi A	6	9	.400	26	18	7-1	0	137	129	77	7	3	74	89	4.20	96	.250	.347	48-1	.083	-5	82	-4	-0.9
1952	Chi A	4	4	.500	19	11	4-2	1	79	52	31	5	1	56	63	2.96	123	.186	.323	20-2	.050	-1	83	5	0.4
1953	Chi A	0	0	—	9	3	0	0	20.2	12	11	2	1	30	15	3.48	116	.171	.426	4-0	.000	-0	133	0	0.0
	StL A	1	5	.167	22	11	0	0	81	93	56	5	0	52	37	5.11	82	.286	.385	25-2	.200	-1	83	-9	-0.8
	Year	1	5	.167	31	14	0	0	101.2	105	60	7	1	82	52	4.78	87	.266	.393	29-2	.172	-1	93	-10	-0.8
1954	Bal A	6	11	.353	32	20	5	0	166.2	169	83	12	1	82	82	4.37	82	.269	.349	51-4	.157	-0	81	-11	-1.0
1955	Bal A	0	4	.000	15	5	0	0	38.1	50	39	3	1	27-0	26	8.22	46	.316	.411	11-1	.091	-1	98	-19	-1.7
1956	KC A	4	9	.308	25	20	3	0	118.2	121	75	17	0	74-4	61	5.31	82	.262	.362	33-4	.061	-3	78	-11	-1.3
Total	10	27	47	.365	199	104	22-3	1	785.1	781	479	62	10	522-4	450	4.87	82	.261	.370	237-16	.114	-13	91	-75	-7.5
KREUGER, RICK Richard Allen B 11.3.1948 Grand Rapids, MI BR/TL 6-2/185# d9.6																									
1975	Bos A	0	0	—	2	0	0	0-0	4	3	2	0	0	1-0	1	4.50	91	.200	.250	0-0	—	0		0	0.0
1976	Bos A	2	1	.667	8	4	1	0-0	31	31	14	3	0	16-0	12	4.06	96	.272	.359	0-0	—	0	129	0	0.1
1977	Bos A	0	1	.000	1	0	0	0-0	0	2	2	0	0	0-0	0	∞	—	1.000	1.000	0-0	—	0		-2	-0.2
1978	Cle A	0	0	—	6	0	0	0-0	9.1	6	4	1	0	3-0	7	3.86	97	.194	.243	0-0	—	0		0	0.0
Total	4	2	2	.500	17	4	1	0-0	44.1	42	22	4	0	20-0	20	4.47	87	.259	.333	0-0	—	0	129	-2	-0.1
KREUTZER, FRANK Franklin James B 2.7.1939 Buffalo, NY BR/TL 6-1/190# d9.20																									
1962	Chi A	0	0	—	1	0	0	0	1.1	0	0	0	0	1-0	1	0.00	—	.000	.200	0-0	—	0		1	0.0
1963	Chi A	1	0	1.000	1	1	0	0	5	3	1	1	0	1-0	0	1.80	195	.188	.235	2-0	.000	-0	177	1	0.2
1964	Chi A	3	1	.750	17	2	0	1	40.1	37	15	1	0	18-3	32	3.35	103	.239	.316	8-2	.125	-0	64	1	0.2
	Was A	2	6	.250	13	9	0	0	45.1	48	26	6	1	23-0	27	4.76	78	.267	.351	11-2	.000	-1	77	-5	-0.9
	Year	5	7	.417	30	11	0	1	85.2	85	29	7	1	41-3	59	4.10	87	.254	.335	19-4	.053	-1	77	-3	-0.7
1965	Was A	2	6	.250	33	14	2-1	0	85.1	73	48	7	2	54-1	65	4.32	80	.232	.344	22-0	.045	-1	108	-8	-0.9
1966	Was A	0	5	.000	9	6	0	0	31.1	30	24	9	1	10-1	24	6.03	57	.236	.297	8-0	.250	0	64	-9	-1.2
1969	Was A	0	0	—	4	0	0	0-0	2	3	1	0	0	2-0	2	4.50	77	.333	.455	0-0	—	0		0	0.0
Total	6	8	18	.308	78	32	2-1	1-0	210.2	194	115	24	4	109-5	151	4.40	80	.241	.332	51-4	.078	-2	91	-19	-2.6
KRIEGER, KURT Kurt Ferdinand "Dutch" B 9.16.1926 Traisen, Austria D 8.16.1970 St.Louis, MO BR/TR 6-3/212# d4.21																									
1949	StL N	0	0	—	1	0	0	0	1	0	0	0	0	1	0	0.00	—	.000	.250	0-0	—	0		0	0.0
1951	StL N	0	0	—	2	0	0	0	4	6	7	1	0	5	3	15.75	25	.353	.500	0-0	—	0		-5	-0.2
Total	2	0	0	—	3	0	0	0	5	6	7	1	0	6	3	12.60	32	.300	.462	0-0	—	0		-5	-0.2

Year	Tm Lg	W	L	Pct	G	GS	CG-Sho	SV-BS	IP	H	R	HR	HB	BB-IB	SO	ERA	AERA	OAV	OOB	AB-SH	AVG	PB	Sup	APR	PW
KRIST, HOWIE Howard Wilbur "Spud" B 2.28.1916 W.Henrietta, NY D 4.23.1989 Buffalo, NY BL/TR 6-1/175# d9.12 Mil 1944-45																									
1937	StL N	3	1	.750	6	4	1	0	27.2	34	13	0	0	10	6	4.23	94	.304	.361	9-1	.000	-1	135	0	-0.1
1938	StL N	0	0	—	2	0	0	0	1.1	1	0	0	0	0	1	0.00	—	.250	.250	0-0	—	0		1	0.0
1941	StL N	10	0	1.000	37	8	2	2	114	107	57	10	1	35	36	4.03	93	.246	.304	38-2	.237	1	163	-2	-0.1
1942	StL N	13	3	.813	34	8	3	1	118.1	103	34	2	2	43	47	2.51	136	.233	.304	42-1	.143	-1*	144	14	1.6
1943	†StL N	11	5	.688	34	17	9-2	3	164.1	141	57	5	4	62	57	2.90	116	.233	.309	60-4	.167	-2	114	11	0.6
1946	StL N	0	2	.000	15	0	0	0	18.2	22	15	3	1	8	3	6.75	51	.306	.383	0-0	—	0		-6	-0.6
Total	6	37	11	.771	128	37	15-2	6	444.1	408	176	20	8	158	150	3.32	106	.244	.313	149-8	.168	-3	134	18	1.4
KRIVDA, RICK Rick Michael B 1.19.1970 McKeesport, PA BR/TL 6-1/180# d7.7																									
1995	Bal A	2	7	.222	13	13	1	0-0	75.1	76	40	9	4	25-1	53	4.54	105	.266	.329	0-0	—	0	74	2	0.1
1996	Bal A	3	5	.375	22	11	0	0-0	81.2	89	48	14	1	39-2	54	4.96	99	.283	.361	0-0	—	0	87	0	0.0
1997	Bal A	4	2	.667	10	10	0	0-0	50	67	36	7	0	18-1	29	6.30	70	.328	.379	0-0	—	0	127	-10	-1.0
1998	Cle A	2	0	1.000	11	1	0	0-0	25	24	10	2	0	16-1	10	3.24	147	.250	.357	0-0	—	0	156	4	0.3
	Cin N	0	2	.000	16	1	0	0-1	26.1	41	34	7	3	19-1	19	11.28	38	.366	.467	4-0	.000	-0	64	-20	-1.3
Total	4	11	16	.407	72	36	1	0-1	258.1	297	168	39	8	117-6	165	5.57	84	.293	.368	4-0	.000	-0	94	-24	-1.9
KROCK, GUS August H. B 5.9.1866 Milwaukee, WI D 3.22.1905 Pasadena, CA BR/TR 6/196# d4.24																									
1888	Chi N	25	14	.641	39	39	39-4	0	339.2	295	143	20	9	45	161	2.44	124	.227	.258	134	.164	-3	102	24	2.0
1889	Chi N	3	3	.500	7	7	5	0	60.2	86	43	10	2	14	16	4.90	85	.323	.362	24	.167	-1	113	-2	-0.3
	Ind N	2	2	.500	4	4	3	0	32	48	38	2	0	14	10	7.31	57	.336	.395	14	.357	1	117	-11	-0.9
	Was N	2	4	.333	6	6	6	0	48	65	50	1	1	22	17	5.25	75	.314	.383	23	.087	-2	128	-9	-1.0
	Year	7	9	.438	17	17	14	0	140.2	199	58	13	3	50	43	5.57	73	.323	.377	61	.180	-2	119	-23	-2.2
1890	Buf P	0	3	.000	4	3	3	0	25	43	37	1	0	15	5	6.12	67	.364	.436	12	.083	-1	84	-9	-0.8
Total	3	32	26	.552	60	59	56-4	0	505.1	537	311	34	12	110	209	3.49	97	.264	.306	207	.164	-7	106	-7	-1.0
KROH, RUBE Floyd Myron B 8.25.1886 Friendship, NY D 3.17.1944 New Orleans, LA BL/TL 6-2/186# d9.30																									
1906	Bos A	1	0	1.000	1	1	1-1	0	9	2	0	0	0	4	5	0.00	—	.074	.194	3-0	.000	-0	52	3	0.3
1907	Bos A	1	4	.200	7	5	1	0	34.1	33	13	0	2	8	8	2.62	98	.256	.309	11-0	.273	0	52	0	0.1
1908	Chi N	0	0	—	2	1	0	0	12	9	3	0	0	4	11	1.50	157	.200	.265	4-0	.000	-0	90	1	0.1
1909	Chi N	9	4	.692	17	13	10-2	0	120.1	97	26	2	1	30	51	1.65	154	.224	.276	40-1	.150	-0	108	14	1.6
1910	Chi N	3	1	.750	6	4	1	0	34.1	33	19	1	2	15	16	4.46	65	.254	.340	12-1	.250	0	110	-5	-0.5
1912	Bos N	0	0	—	3	1	0	0	6.1	8	4	0	0	6	1	5.68	63	.364	.500	2-0	.500	0	102	-1	0.0
Total	6	14	9	.609	36	25	13-3	0	216.1	182	65	3	5	67	92	2.29	115	.232	.296	72-2	.181	-0	94	12	1.6
KROLL, GARY Gary Melvin B 7.8.1941 Culver City, CA BR/TR 6-6/220# d7.26																									
1964	Phi N	0	0	—	2	0	0	0	3	3	1	0	0	2-0	2	3.00	116	.250	.357	0-0	—	0		0	0.0
	NY N	0	1	.000	8	2	0	0	21.2	19	11	1	1	15-0	24	4.15	86	.241	.365	3-0	.333	0	86	-1	0.0
	Year	0	1	.000	10	2	0	0	24.2	22	15	1	1	17-0	26	4.01	89	.242	.364	3-0	.333	0	86	-1	0.0
1965	NY N	6	6	.500	32	11	1	1	87	83	48	12	6	41-0	62	4.45	79	.249	.340	26-3	.115	-1	119	-8	-1.2
1966	Hou N	0	0	—	10	0	0	0	23.2	26	10	2	0	11-0	22	3.80	90	.280	.356	3-0	.000	-0		0	-0.1
1969	Cle A	0	0	—	19	0	0	0-0	24	16	14	3	0	22-0	28	4.13	91	.188	.352	0-0	—	0		-2	-0.1
Total	4	6	7	.462	71	13	1	1-0	159.1	147	84	18	7	91-0	138	4.24	84	.244	.348	32-3	.125	-1	114	-11	-1.4
KROON, MARC Marc Jason B 4.2.1973 Bronx, NY BB/TR 6-2/195# d7.7																									
1995	SD N	0	1	.000	2	0	0	0-0	1.2	1	2	0	0	2-0	2	10.80	37	.200	.429	0-0	—	0		-1	-0.2
1997	SD N	0	1	.000	12	0	0	0-0	11.1	14	9	2	1	5-0	12	6.35	61	.280	.357	0-0	—	0		-3	-0.3
1998	SD N	0	0	—	2	0	0	0-0	2.1	0	0	0	0	1-0	2	0.00	—	.000	.125	0-0	—	0		1	0.1
	Cin N	0	0	—	4	0	0	0-0	5.1	7	8	0	1	8-0	4	13.50	32	.333	.533	0-0	—	0		-5	-0.2
	Year	0	0	—	6	0	0	0-0	7.2	7	13	0	1	9-0	6	9.39	44	.250	.447	0-0	—	0		-4	-0.1
Total	3	0	2	.000	20	0	0	0-0	20.2	22	19	2	2	16-0	20	7.84	51	.265	.396	0-0	—	0		-8	-0.6
KRUEGER, BILL William Culp B 4.24.1958 Waukegan, IL BL/TL 6-5/210# d4.10																									
1983	Oak A	7	6	.538	17	16	2	0-0	109.2	104	54	7	2	53-1	58	3.61	107	.252	.336	0-0	—	0	114	1	0.0
1984	Oak A	10	10	.500	26	24	1	0-0	142	156	95	9	2	85-2	61	4.75	79	.285	.378	0-0	—	0	118	-22	-2.7
1985	Oak A	9	10	.474	32	23	2	0-0	151.1	165	95	13	2	69-1	56	4.52	85	.276	.351	0-0	—	0	130	-17	-1.9
1986	Oak A	1	2	.333	11	3	0	1-0	34.1	40	25	4	0	13-0	10	6.03	64	.301	.358	0-0	—	0	156	-9	-0.7
1987	Oak A	0	3	.000	9	0	0	0-0	5.2	9	7	0	0	8-3	2	9.53	43	.360	.515	0-0	—	0		-4	-0.7
	LA N	0	0	—	2	0	0	0-0	2.1	3	2	0	0	1-0	2	0.00	—	.250	.308	0-0	—	0		0	0.0
1988	LA N	0	0	—	1	1	0	0-0	2.1	4	3	0	1	2-1	1	11.57	29	.364	.500	0-0	—	0	133	-2	-0.1
1989	Mil A	3	2	.600	34	5	0	3-0	93.2	96	43	9	0	33-3	72	3.84	100	.264	.324	0-0	—	0	108	1	0.0
1990	Mil A	6	8	.429	30	17	0	0-0	129	137	70	10	3	54-6	64	3.98	98	.276	.345	0-0	—	0	121	-3	-0.3
1991	Sea A	11	8	.579	35	25	1	0-0	175	194	82	15	4	60-4	91	3.60	115	.289	.346	0-0	—	0	89	8	0.8
1992	Min A	10	6	.625	27	27	2-2	0-0	161.1	166	82	18	3	46-2	86	4.30	95	.263	.316	0-0	—	0	127	-3	-0.4
	Mon N	0	2	.000	9	2	0	0-0	17.1	23	13	0	1	7-0	13	6.75	51	.315	.383	3-1	.000	-0	169	-6	-0.7
1993	Det A	6	4	.600	32	7	0	0-3	82	90	43	6	4	30-5	60	3.40	126	.285	.351	0-0	—	0	159	4	0.5
1994	Det A	0	2	.000	16	2	0	0-2	19.2	26	24	3	1	17-1	17	9.61	50	.321	.431	0-0	—	0	133	-11	-0.9
	SD N	3	2	.600	8	7	1	0-0	41	42	24	5	1	7-1	30	4.83	85	.259	.292	12-2	.500	3	111	-3	-0.1
1995	SD N	0	0	—	6	0	0	0-0	7.2	13	6	1	0	4-1	6	7.04	57	.371	.436	0-0	—	0		-2	-0.1
	Sea A	2	1	.667	6	5	0	0-0	20	37	17	4	0	4-1	10	5.85	81	.407	.432	0-0	—	0	153	-4	-0.5
Total	13	68	66	.507	301	164	9-2	4-5	1194.1	1305	685	104	24	493-32	639	4.35	92	.280	.349	15-3	.400	2	121	-72	-7.8
KRUGER, ABE Abraham B 2.14.1885 Morris Run, PA D 7.4.1962 Elmira, NY BR/TR 6-2/190# d10.6																									
1908	Bro N	0	1	.000	2	1	0	0	6.1	5	5	0	3	3	2	4.26	55	.238	.407	2-0	.000	-0	60	-2	-0.2
KRUKOW, MIKE Michael Edward B 1.21.1952 Long Beach, CA BR/TR 6-5/205# d9.6																									
1976	Chi N	0	0	—	2	0	0	0-0	4.1	6	4	0	0	2-0	1	8.31	47	.333	.400	1-0	.000	-0		-2	-0.1
1977	Chi N	8	14	.364	34	33	1-1	0-0	172	195	96	16	3	61-8	106	4.40	100	.281	.340	55-7	.200	-0	85	-1	-0.1
1978	Chi N	9	3	.750	27	20	3-1	0-0	138.1	125	62	11	5	53-4	81	3.90	103	.243	.318	45-3	.244	3	99	3	0.6
1979	Chi N	9	9	.500	28	28	0	0-0	164.2	172	84	13	3	81-12	119	4.21	98	.275	.359	51-7	.314	5	84	0	0.4
1980	Chi N	10	15	.400	34	34	3	0-0	205	200	117	13	8	80-5	130	4.39	89	.258	.329	65-7	.246	2	102	-11	-1.2
1981	Chi N	9	9	.500	25	**25**	2-1	0-0	144.1	146	68	11	2	55-6	101	3.68	101	.264	.330	50-6	.180	-0	105	0	0.0
1982	Phi N	13	11	.542	33	33	7-2	0-0	208	211	87	8	3	82-10	138	3.12	118	.268	.336	72-5	.181	-0	99	10	1.1
1983	SF N	11	11	.500	31	31	2-1	0-0	184.1	189	95	17	3	76-8	136	3.95	90	.261	.332	63-4	.254	5	118	-9	-0.6
1984	SF N	11	12	.478	35	33	3-1	1-0	199.1	234	117	22	5	78-5	141	4.56	77	.290	.353	72-2	.139	-1*	130	-25	-2.8
1985	SF N	8	11	.421	28	28	6-1	0-0	194.2	176	80	19	3	49-10	150	3.38	102	.238	.287	55-8	.218	5	74	4	0.8
1986	SF N★	20	9	.690	34	34	10-2	0-0	245	204	90	24	4	55-4	178	3.05	116	.223	.269	82-12	.146	0*	129	16	1.8
1987	†SF N	5	6	.455	30	28	3	0-0	163	182	98	24	2	46-6	104	4.80	80	.288	.334	54-5	.167	1	133	-19	-1.0
1988	SF N	7	4	.636	20	20	1	0-0	124.2	111	51	13	5	31-3	75	3.54	92	.236	.289	41-4	.073	-0	109	-2	-0.2
1989	SF N	4	3	.571	8	8	0	0-0	43	37	20	5	1	18-3	18	3.98	85	.236	.316	16-0	.063	-1	108	-2	-0.5
Total	14	124	117	.515	369	355	41-10	1-0	2190.2	2188	1069	196	47	767-84	1478	3.90	96	.260	.323	722-70	.193	17	106	-38	-1.8
KRUMM, AL Albert B 1.13.1865 Pittsburgh, PA D 6.15.1937 San Diego, CA TR d5.17																									
1889	Pit N	0	1	.000	1	1	1	0	9	8	11	0	0	10	4	10.00	37	.229	.400	4	.000	-1	125	-6	-0.4
KUBENKA, JEFF Jeffrey Scot B 8.24.1974 Weimar, TX BR/TL 6-2/191# d9.6																									
1998	LA N	1	0	1.000	6	0	0	0-1	9.1	4	1	0	0	8-0	10	0.96	411	.138	.316	0-0	—	0		3	0.3
1999	LA N	0	1	.000	6	0	0	0-0	7.2	13	12	1	0	4-0	2	11.74	37	.371	.425	1-0	1.000	1		-7	-0.7
Total	2	1	1	.500	12	0	0	0-1	17	17	13	1	0	12-0	12	5.82	71	.266	.372	1-0	1.000	1		-4	-0.4
KUBINSKI, TIM Timothy Mark B 1.20.1972 Pullman, WA BL/TL 6-4/205# d7.16																									
1997	Oak A	0	0	—	11	0	0	0-0	12.2	12	9	2	1	6-1	10	5.68	80	.255	.339	0-0	—	0		-2	-0.1
1999	Oak A	0	0	—	14	0	0	0-1	12.1	14	8	3	1	5-1	7	5.84	80	.280	.351	0-0	—	0		-1	0.0
Total	2	0	0	—	25	0	0	0-1	25	26	17	5	2	11-2	17	5.76	80	.268	.345	0-0	—	0		-3	-0.1

Year	Tm Lg	W	L	Pct	G	GS	CG-Sho	SV-BS	IP	H	R	HR	HB	BB-IB	SO	ERA	AERA	OAV	OOB	AB-SH	AVG	PB	Sup	APR	PW
KUCAB, JOHNNY John Albert B 12.17.1919 Olyphant, PA D 5.26.1977 Youngstown, OH BR/TR 6-2/185# d9.14																									
1950	Phi A	1	1	.500	4	2	2	0	26	29	10	4	0	8	8	3.46	131	.282	.333	9-0	.111	-0	59	4	0.2
1951	Phi A	4	3	.571	30	1	0	4	74.2	76	37	9	1	23	23	4.22	101	.265	.322	16-0	.000	-2	21	1	-0.1
1952	Phi A	0	1	.000	25	0	0	2	51.1	64	37	5	1	20	17	5.26	75	.312	.376	10-0	.200	-0*		-8	-0.5
Total	3	5	5	.500	59	3	2	6	152	169	84	18	2	51	48	4.44	95	.284	.343	35-0	.086	-2	49	-3	-0.4
KUCEK, JACK John Andrew Charles B 6.8.1953 Warren, OH BR/TR 6-2/200# d8.8																									
1974	Chi A	1	4	.200	9	7	0	0-0	37.2	48	25	3	1	21-0	25	5.26	71	.320	.402	0-0	—	0	71	-6	-0.7
1975	Chi A	0	0	—	2	0	0	0-0	3.2	9	2	0	0	4-0	2	4.91	79	.500	.591	0-0	—	0		0	0.0
1976	Chi A	0	0	—	2	0	0	0-0	4.2	9	5	2	0	4-0	2	9.64	37	.429	.500	0-0	—	0		-3	-0.2
1977	Chi A	0	1	.000	8	3	0	0-0	34.2	35	20	4	2	10-0	25	3.63	113	.267	.324	0-0	—	0	183	0	0.0
1978	Chi A	2	3	.400	10	5	3	1-0	52	42	23	5	0	27-2	30	3.29	116	.220	.315	0-0	—	0	61	2	0.2
1979	Chi A	0	0	—	1	0	0	0-0	0.2	0	4	0	0	3-0	0	0.00	—	.000	.500	0-0	—	0		-1	-0.1
	Phi N	1	0	1.000	4	0	0	0-0	4.1	6	4	2	0	1-1	2	8.31	46	.333	.368	0-0	—	0		-2	-0.4
1980	Tor A	3	8	.273	23	12	0	1-0	68	83	56	9	1	41-1	35	6.75	64	.300	.391	0-0	—	0	83	-17	-2.4
Total	7	7	16	.304	59	27	3	2-0	205.2	232	139	25	4	111-4	121	5.12	78	.287	.373	0-0	—	0	88	-27	-3.6
KUCKS, JOHNNY John Charles B 7.27.1933 Hoboken, NJ BR/TR 6-3/184# d4.17																									
1955	†NY A	8	7	.533	29	13	3-1	0	126.2	122	54	8	2	44-6	49	3.41	110	.252	.315	40-2	.050	-4	111	6	0.2
1956	†NY A☆	18	9	.667	34	31	12-3	0	224.1	223	113	19	10	72-0	67	3.85	100	.261	.323	77-6	.143	-2	127	-2	-0.3
1957	†NY A	8	10	.444	37	23	4-1	2	179.1	169	82	13	8	59-2	78	3.56	101	.251	.316	55-11	.109	-2	123	0	0.0
1958	†NY A	8	8	.500	34	15	4-1	4	126	132	67	14	6	39-2	46	3.93	90	.269	.328	40-6	.125	-1	122	-7	-0.9
1959	NY A	0	1	.000	9	1	0	0	16.2	21	16	5	0	9-0	9	8.64	42	.323	.405	2-0	.000	-0	97	-9	-0.5
	KC A	8	11	.421	33	23	6-1	1	151.1	163	76	10	12	42-0	51	3.87	104	.278	.336	47-3	.085	-3	75	2	0.0
	Year	8	12	.400	42	24	6-1	1	168	184	79	15	12	51-0	60	4.34	91	.282	.343	49-3	.082	-3	76	-7	-0.5
1960	KC A	4	10	.286	31	17	1	0	114	140	85	22	1	43-2	38	6.00	66	.306	.361	30-3	.133	-1	79	-24	-2.7
Total	6	54	56	.491	207	123	30-7	7	938.1	970	493	91	39	308-12	338	4.10	92	.269	.330	291-31	.110	-12	107	-34	-4.2
KUCZYNSKI, BERT Bernard Carl B 1.8.1920 Philadelphia, PA D 1.19.1997 Allentown, PA BR/TR 6/195# d6.2 Mil 1943-45																									
1943	Phi A	0	1	.000	6	1	0	0	24.2	36	15	2	2	9	8	4.01	85	.336	.398	6-0	.000	-0	50	-3	-0.2
KUHAULUA, FRED Fred Mahele B 2.23.1953 Honolulu, HI BL/TL 5-11/175# d8.2																									
1977	Cal A	0	0	—	3	1	0	0-0	6.1	15	11	1	0	7-0	3	15.63	25	.455	.550	0-0	—	0	69	-8	-0.4
1981	SD N	1	0	1.000	5	4	0	0-0	29.1	28	10	1	0	9-1	16	2.45	133	.257	.314	9-1	.111	-0	89	2	0.0
Total	2	1	0	1.000	8	5	0	0-0	35.2	43	21	2	0	16-1	19	4.79	70	.303	.373	9-1	.111	-0	84	-6	-0.4
KUHN, BUB Bernard Daniel B 10.12.1899 Vicksburg, MI D 11.20.1956 Detroit, MI BL/TR 6-1.5/182# d9.1																									
1924	Cle A	0	1	.000	1	0	0	0	1	4	3	1	0	0	0	27.00	16	.667	.667	0-0	—	0		-2	-0.3
KULL, JOHN John A. (b: John A Kolonauski) B 6.24.1882 Shenandoah, PA D 3.30.1936 Schuylkill Haven, PA BL/TL 6-2/190# d10.2																									
1909	Phi A	1	0	1.000	1	0	0	0	3	3	1	0	1	5	4	3.00	80	.250	.500	1-0	1.000	0		0	0.0
KUME, MIKE John Michael B 5.19.1926 Premier, WV BR/TR 6-1/195# d8.26																									
1955	KC A	0	2	.000	6	4	0	0	23.2	35	23	1	3	15-0	7	7.99	52	.354	.445	8-0	.125	-0	64	-9	-0.7
KUNKEL, BILL William Gustave James B 7.7.1936 Hoboken, NJ D 5.4.1985 Red Bank, NJ BR/TR 6-1/187# d4.15 U17 s-Jeff																									
1961	KC A	3	4	.429	58	2	0	4	88.2	103	58	11	0	32-2	46	5.18	81	.289	.345	8-1	.125	-0	0	-9	-0.7
1962	KC A	0	0	—	9	0	0	0	7.2	8	7	3	0	4-0	6	3.52	120	.258	.333	0-0	—	0		-1	-0.1
1963	NY A	3	2	.600	22	0	0	0	46.1	42	15	3	0	13-3	31	2.72	129	.239	.289	6-0	.333	1		4	0.5
Total	3	6	6	.500	89	2	0	4	142.2	153	80	17	0	49-5	83	4.29	92	.272	.327	14-1	.214	1	0	-6	-0.3
KUNZ, EARL Earl Dewey "Pinches" B 12.25.1899 Sacramento, CA D 4.14.1963 Sacramento, CA BR/TR 5-10/170# d4.19																									
1923	Pit N	1	2	.333	21	2	1	1	45.2	48	33	2	0	24	12	5.52	73	.293	.383	12-0	.083	-1	72	-8	-0.6
KUROSAKI, RYAN Ryan Yoshitomo B 7.3.1952 Honolulu, HI BR/TR 5-10/160# d5.20																									
1975	StL N	0	0	—	7	0	0	0-0	13	15	11	3	0	7-1	6	7.62	49	.283	.361	1-0	.000	-0		-5	-0.3
KURTZ, HAL Harold James "Bud" B 8.20.1943 Washington, DC BR/TR 6-3/205# d4.18																									
1968	Cle A	1	0	1.000	28	0	0	1	38	37	24	2	5	15-6	16	5.21	57	.255	.343	4-0	.000	-0*		-9	-0.6
KUSEL, ED Edward D. B 2.15.1886 Cleveland, OH D 10.20.1948 Cleveland, OH TR 6/165# d9.18																									
1909	StL A	0	3	.000	3	3	3	0	24	43	28	1	0	1	2	7.13	34	.384	.389	10-0	.300	1	126	-14	-1.3
KUSH, EMIL Emil Benedict B 11.4.1916 Chicago, IL D 11.26.1969 River Grove, IL BR/TR 5-11/185# d9.21 Mil 1943-45																									
1941	Chi N	0	0	—	2	0	0	0	4	2	1	0	0	0	2	2.25	156	.143	.143	1-0	.000	-0		1	0.0
1942	Chi N	0	0	—	1	0	0	0	2	1	0	0	0	1	1	0.00	—	.167	.286	1-0	.000	-0		1	0.0
1946	Chi N	9	2	.818	40	6	1-1	2	129.2	120	47	4	3	43	50	3.05	109	.253	.319	38-0	.211	0	120	6	0.6
1947	Chi N	8	3	.727	47	1	1	5	91	80	38	8	3	53	44	3.36	117	.247	.358	20-0	.250	1	112	7	1.0
1948	Chi N	1	4	.200	34	1	0	3	72	70	39	5	2	37	31	4.38	89	.253	.345	13-0	.154	0	68	-3	-0.2
1949	Chi N	3	3	.500	26	0	0	2	47.2	51	21	7	2	24	22	3.78	107	.283	.374	9-0	.333	1		2	0.4
Total	6	21	12	.636	150	8	2-1	12	346.1	324	146	24	10	158	150	3.48	106	.254	.341	82-0	.220	2	106	14	1.8
KUTYNA, MARTY Marion John B 11.14.1932 Philadelphia, PA BR/TR 6/190# d9.19																									
1959	KC A	0	0	—	4	0	0	1	7.1	7	0	0	0	1-0	1	0.00	—	.250	.276	0-0	—	0		3	0.2
1960	KC A	3	2	.600	51	0	0	4	61.2	64	33	7	0	32-3	20	3.94	101	.274	.358	5-1	.200	-0		-1	-0.1
1961	Was A	6	8	.429	50	6	0	3	143	147	79	12	2	48-2	64	3.97	101	.271	.330	34-4	.206	-0	92	-2	0.0
1962	Was A	5	6	.455	54	0	0	0	78	83	42	9	0	27-2	25	4.04	100	.275	.329	8-0	.125	-0		-2	-0.2
Total	4	14	16	.467	159	6	0	8	290	301	154	28	2	108-7	110	3.88	103	.272	.335	47-5	.191	-0	92	-2	-0.1
KUTZLER, JERRY Jerry Scott B 3.25.1965 Waukegan, IL BL/TR 6-1/175# d4.28																									
1990	Chi A	2	1	.667	7	7	0	0-0	31.1	38	23	2	0	14-1	21	6.03	64	.304	.371	0-0	—	0	119	-8	-0.7
KUZAVA, BOB Robert Leroy "Sarge" B 5.28.1923 Wyandotte, MI BB/TL 6-2/204# d9.21																									
1946	Cle A	1	0	1.000	2	2	0	0	12	9	7	0	1	11	4	3.00	110	.191	.356	5-0	.200	-0	155	-1	0.0
1947	Cle A	1	1	.500	4	4	1-1	0	21.2	22	10	1	1	9	9	4.15	84	.265	.344	9-0	.111	-1	108	-1	-0.1
1949	Chi A	10	6	.625	29	18	9-1	0	156.2	139	76	6	1	91	83	4.02	104	.240	.344	56-5	.036	-6	101	4	-0.4
1950	Chi A	1	3	.250	10	7	1	0	44.1	43	28	5	0	27	21	5.68	79	.257	.361	12-2	.083	-0	112	-4	-0.4
	Was A	8	7	.533	22	22	8-1	0	155	156	80	8	1	75	84	3.95	114	.263	.346	50-3	.100	-2	86	9	0.5
	Year	9	10	.474	32	29	9-1	0	199.1	199	84	13	1	102	105	4.33	104	.261	.350	62-5	.097	-2	92	4	0.1
1951	Was A	3	3	.500	8	8	3	0	52.1	57	34	5	2	28	22	5.50	74	.284	.377	17-0	.176	-0	100	-7	-0.7
	†NY A	8	4	.667	23	8	4-1	5	82.1	76	27	5	1	27	50	2.40	159	.241	.303	22-0	.136	0*	113	13	1.9
	Year	11	7	.611	31	16	7-1	5	134.2	133	32	10	3	55	72	3.61	109	.258	.333	39-0	.154	0	107	5	1.2
1952	†NY A	8	8	.500	28	12	6-1	3	133	115	53	7	1	63	67	3.45	96	.240	.329	43-0	.093	-1	112	1	-0.1
1953	†NY A	6	5	.545	33	6	2-2	4	92.1	92	35	9	0	34	48	3.31	111	.264	.330	21-1	.048	-1	80	6	0.5
1954	NY A	1	3	.250	20	3	0	1	39.2	46	30	3	0	18	22	5.45	63	.297	.366	6-0	.000	-0	103	-11	-1.1
	Bal A	1	3	.250	4	4	0	0	23.2	30	11	0	0	11	15	4.18	86	.323	.387	7-1	.000	-1	62	-1	-0.3
	Year	2	6	.250	24	7	0	1	63.1	76	14	3	0	29	37	4.97	70	.306	.374	13-1	.000	-1	79	-12	-1.4
1955	Bal A	0	1	.000	6	1	0	0	12.1	10	7	0	0	4-1	5	3.65	105	.222	.280	1-0	.000	-0	0	0	-0.1
	Phi N	1	0	1.000	17	4	0	0	32.1	47	26	5	0	12-1	13	7.24	55	.333	.386	7-0	.143	-0	118	-10	-0.5
1957	Pit N	0	0	—	4	0	0	0	2	3	2	0	0	3-0	1	9.00	42	.333	.500	0-0	—	0		-1	-0.1
	StL N	0	0	—	3	0	0	0	2.1	4	1	0	0	2-0	2	3.86	103	.364	.462	0-0	—	0		0	0.0
	Year	0	0	—	7	0	0	0	4.1	7	8	0	0	5-0	3	6.23	62	.350	.480	0-0	—	0		-1	-0.1
Total	10	49	44	.527	213	99	34-7	13	862	849	427	54	8	415-2	446	4.05	97	.260	.344	256-12	.086	-14	100	-3	-0.9
LABINE, CLEM Clement Walter B 8.6.1926 Lincoln, RI BR/TR 6/180# d4.18																									
1950	Bro N	0	0	—	1	0	0	0	2	2	1	0	0	1	0	4.50	91	.286	.375	0-0	—	0		0	0.0
1951	Bro N	5	1	.833	14	6	5-2	0	65.1	52	17	4	0	20	39	2.20	178	.223	.285	21-0	.143	-1	146	13	1.0

Year	Tm Lg	W	L	Pct	G	GS	CG-Sho	SV-BS	IP	H	R	HR	HB	BB-IB	SO	ERA	AERA	OAV	OOB	AB-SH	AVG	PB	Sup	APR	PW
1952	Bro N	8	4	.667	25	9	0	0	77	76	44	3	1	47	43	5.14	71	.259	.364	22-3	.045	-2*	125	-11	-1.7
1953	†Bro N	11	6	.647	37	7	0	7	110.1	92	39	9	0	30	44	2.77	154	.225	.278	28-3	.071	-1	81	18	2.5
1954	Bro N	7	6	.538	47	2	0	5	108.1	101	60	7	1	56	43	4.15	98	.247	.337	30-0	.033	-2	87	-3	-0.5
1955	†Bro N	13	5	.722	**60**	8	1	11	144.1	121	61	12	0	55-4	67	3.24	125	.229	.300	31-3	.097	1	82	13	1.8
1956	†Bro N☆	10	6	.625	62	3	1	**19**	115.2	111	48	11	3	39-8	75	3.35	119	.253	.317	23-0	.087	-1	96	7	1.1
1957	Bro N★	5	7	.417	58	0	0	**17**	104.2	104	50	8	1	27-6	67	3.44	121	.259	.301	20-0	.100	-1		6	0.8
1958	LA N	6	6	.500	52	2	0	14	104	112	55	8	1	33-8	43	4.15	99	.283	.336	18-1	.056	-1	110	-1	-0.3
1959	†LA N	5	10	.333	56	0	0	9	84.2	91	39	11	1	25-10	37	3.93	108	.282	.332	16-1	.000	-2		4	0.6
1960	LA N	0	1	.000	13	0	0	1	17	26	12	1	0	8-3	15	5.82	68	.356	.420	2-0	.500	1		-3	-0.2
	Det A	0	3	.000	14	0	0	2	19.1	19	12	2	0	12-4	6	5.12	77	.257	.360	2-0	.000	-0		-2	-0.4
	†Pit N	3	0	1.000	15	0	0	3	30.1	29	5	0	1	11-3	21	1.48	253	.254	.323	4-2	.000	-0		8	0.9
1961	Pit N	4	1	.800	56	1	0	8	92.2	102	43	4	2	31-8	49	3.69	108	.284	.343	10-0	.100	-0	111	3	0.1
1962	NY N	0	0	—	3	0	0	0	4	5	6	1	0	1-0	2	11.25	37	.278	.316	0-0	—	0		-3	-0.1
Total	13	77	56	.579	513	38	7-2	96	1079.2	1043	492	81	11	396-54	551	3.63	112	.256	.322	227-13	.075	-11	103	49	5.6
LACEY, BOB Robert Joseph B 8.25.1953 Fredericksburg, VA BR/TL 6-5/210# d5.13																									
1977	Oak A	6	8	.429	64	0	0	7-3	121.2	100	46	13	0	43-11	69	3.03	133	.234	.301	0-0	—	0		14	1.9
1978	Oak A	8	9	.471	**74**	0	0	5-6	119.2	126	52	10	1	35-13	60	3.01	121	.270	.320	0-0	—	0		7	1.1
1979	Oak A	1	5	.167	42	0	0	4-5	47.2	66	34	7	1	24-8	33	5.85	69	.327	.397	0-0	—	0		-9	-1.2
1980	Oak A	3	2	.600	47	1	1-1	6-6	79.2	68	29	7	1	21-5	45	2.94	129	.234	.284	0-0	—	0	95	8	0.6
1981	Cle A	0	0	—	14	0	0	0-0	21.1	36	20	5	0	3-0	11	7.59	48	.371	.379	0-0	—	0		-10	-0.5
	Tex A	0	0	—	1	0	0	0-0	1	1	1	1	0	0-0	0	9.00	39	.250	.250	0-0	—	0		-1	0.0
	Year	0	0	—	15	0	0	0-0	22.1	37	25	6	0	3-0	11	7.66	47	.366	.374	0-0	—	0		-10	-0.5
1983	Cal A	1	2	.333	8	0	0	0-2	8.2	12	5	1	0	0-0	7	5.19	78	.343	.343	0-0	—	0		-1	-0.2
1984	SF N	1	3	.250	34	1	0	0-1	51	55	26	5	0	13-4	26	3.88	91	.276	.318	6-0	.333	1	75	-3	-0.1
Total	7	20	29	.408	284	2	1-1	22-23	450.2	464	213	49	3	139-41	251	3.67	104	.269	.322	6-0	.333	1	82	5	1.6
LACHEMANN, MARCEL Marcel Ernest B 6.13.1941 Los Angeles, CA BR/TR 6/185# d6.4 M3 C15 b-Rene																									
1969	Oak A	4	1	.800	28	0	0	2-1	43.1	43	24	1	2	19-2	16	3.95	87	.261	.340	2-1	.000	-0		-4	-0.5
1970	Oak A	3	3	.500	41	0	0	3-1	58.1	58	20	6	2	18-6	39	2.78	128	.266	.326	8-0	.000	-1		5	0.6
1971	Oak A	0	0	—	1	0	0	0-0	0.1	2	2	0	0	1-0	0	54.00	6	1.000	1.000	0-0	—	0		-2	-0.1
Total	3	7	4	.636	70	0	0	5-2	102	103	46	7	4	38-8	55	3.44	102	.268	.337	10-1	.000	-1		-1	0.0
LACHOWICZ, AL Allen Robert B 9.6.1960 Pittsburgh, PA BR/TR 6-3/198# d9.13																									
1983	Tex A	0	1	.000	2	1	0	0-0	8	9	2	0	0	2-0	8	2.25	179	.281	.324	0-0	—	0	0	2	0.2
LACKEY, JOHN John Derran B 10.23.1978 Abilene, TX BR/TR 6-6/200# d6.24																									
2002	†Ana A	9	4	.692	18	18	1	0-0	108.1	113	52	10	4	33-0	69	3.66	121	.267	.323	0-0	—	0	121	7	0.8
2003	Ana A	10	16	.385	33	33	2-**2**	0-0	204	223	117	31	10	66-4	151	4.63	93	.278	.339	3-0	.000	-0	91	-9	-1.0
Total	2	19	20	.487	51	51	3-2	0-0	312.1	336	169	41	14	99-4	220	4.29	102	.274	.333	3-0	.000	-0	102	-2	-0.2
LACKEY, BILL William D. B 12.8.1870 St.Albans, WV D 5.15.1941 Columbus, OH d10.2																									
1890	Phi AA	0	0	—	1	0	0	0	2	1	4	0	0	3	1	9.00	43	.143	.400	1	.000	-0		-2	-0.1
LaCORTE, FRANK Frank Joseph B 10.13.1951 San Jose, CA BR/TR 6-1/180# d9.8																									
1975	Atl N	0	3	.000	3	2	0	0-0	13.2	13	10	1	0	6-0	10	5.27	72	.245	.322	5-0	.000	-1	70	-2	-0.5
1976	Atl N	3	12	.200	19	17	1	0-0	105.1	97	58	6	6	53-2	79	4.70	81	.249	.344	33-3	.091	-2*	52	-8	-1.3
1977	Atl N	1	8	.111	14	7	0	0-0	37	67	51	10	2	29-1	28	11.68	38	.394	.485	10-2	.200	-0	71	-25	-4.2
1978	Atl N	0	1	.000	2	2	0	0-0	14.2	9	6	0	0	4-1	7	3.68	110	.180	.236	4-1	.000	-0	33	1	0.0
1979	Atl N	0	0	—	6	0	0	0-0	8.1	9	7	2	0	5-1	6	7.56	54	.273	.368	1-0	.000	-0		-3	-0.2
	Hou N	1	2	.333	12	3	0	0-0	27	21	16	3	0	10-1	24	5.00	70	.208	.277	3-0	.000	-0	67	-4	-0.5
	Year	1	2	.333	18	3	0	0-0	35.1	30	19	5	0	15-2	30	5.60	65	.224	.300	4-0	.000	-0	65	-7	-0.7
1980	†Hou N	8	5	.615	55	0	0	11-3	83	61	29	4	0	43-5	66	2.82	117	.210	.307	6-2	.167	0		5	0.8
1981	†Hou N	4	2	.667	37	0	0	5-3	42	41	18	1	0	21-3	40	3.64	90	.258	.339	3-0	.333	0		-1	-0.2
1982	Hou N	1	5	.167	55	0	0	7-4	76.1	71	44	5	0	46-5	51	4.48	74	.247	.344	7-1	.000	-1		-11	-1.2
1983	Hou N	4	4	.500	37	0	0	3-2	53.1	35	32	8	2	28-3	48	5.06	67	.190	.302	5-1	.200	0		-9	-1.4
1984	Cal A	1	2	.333	13	1	0	0-0	29.1	33	26	9	0	13-4	13	7.06	56	.282	.351	0-0	—	0	136	-11	-1.0
Total	10	23	44	.343	253	32	1	26-12	490	457	297	49	10	258-26	372	5.01	72	.249	.341	77-10	.104	-4	66	-68	-9.7
LaCOSS, MIKE Michael James (b: Michael James Marks) B 5.30.1956 Glendale, CA BR/TR 6-4/190# d7.18																									
1978	Cin N	4	8	.333	16	15	2-1	0-0	96	104	56	5	1	46-9	31	4.50	79	.288	.365	30-6	.067	-2*	88	-11	-1.5
1979	†Cin N★	14	8	.636	35	32	6-1	0-0	205.2	202	92	13	2	79-8	73	3.50	107	.263	.331	70-5	.129	-1	98	4	0.3
1980	Cin N	10	12	.455	34	29	4-2	0-1	169.1	207	101	9	1	68-8	59	4.62	78	.303	.366	55-6	.091	-3	102	-23	-3.0
1981	Cin N	4	7	.364	20	13	1-1	1-0	78	102	55	7	1	30-4	22	6.12	58	.325	.380	19-7	.000	-2	86	-20	-2.8
1982	Hou N	6	6	.500	41	8	0	0-2	115	107	41	3	4	54-6	51	2.90	115	.252	.342	24-3	.250	2	100	6	0.8
1983	Hou N	5	7	.417	38	17	2	1-1	138	142	81	10	2	56-11	53	4.43	77	.273	.342	35-4	.086	-2	105	-18	-1.6
1984	Hou N	7	5	.583	39	18	2-1	3-0	132	132	64	3	0	55-5	86	4.02	83	.261	.333	31-6	.129	-1	100	-9	-0.8
1985	KC A	1	1	.500	21	0	0	1-0	40.2	49	25	2	0	29-6	26	5.09	82	.304	.411	0-0	—	0		-4	-0.2
1986	SF N	10	13	.435	37	31	4-1	0-0	204.1	179	99	14	6	70-8	86	3.57	99	.240	.309	61-5	.230	6	130	-4	0.2
1987	†SF N	13	10	.565	39	26	2-1	0-2	171	184	78	16	2	63-12	79	3.68	104	.283	.346	50-4	.060	-2	102	3	0.3
1988	SF N	7	7	.500	19	19	1-1	0-0	114.1	99	55	5	1	47-3	70	3.62	90	.234	.311	33-4	.242	3	90	-6	-0.3
1989	†SF N	10	10	.500	45	18	1	6-3	150.1	143	62	3	7	65-4	78	3.17	106	.255	.336	41-3	.073	-1	132	2	0.2
1990	SF N	6	4	.600	13	12	1	0-0	77.2	75	37	5	0	39-2	39	3.94	93	.259	.342	23-8	.043	-1	136	-3	-0.5
1991	SF N	1	5	.167	18	5	0	0-1	47.1	61	39	4	2	24-0	30	7.23	50	.314	.392	9-0	.222	1	105	-19	-2.1
Total	14	98	103	.488	415	243	26-9	12-10	1739.2	1786	885	99	29	725-86	783	4.02	88	.270	.343	481-61	.125	-4	107	-102	-11.0
LACY, KERRY Kerry Ardeen B 8.7.1972 Chattanooga, TN BR/TR 6-2/195# d8.16																									
1996	Bos A	2	0	1.000	11	0	0	0-2	10.2	15	5	2	1	8-0	9	3.38	150	.333	.444	0-0	—	0		2	0.3
1997	Bos A	1	1	.500	33	0	0	3-0	45.2	60	34	7	0	22-4	18	6.11	76	.314	.381	0-0	—	0		-7	-0.4
Total	2	3	1	.750	44	0	0	3-2	56.1	75	39	9	1	30-4	27	5.59	84	.318	.394	0-0	—	0		-5	-0.1
LADD, PETE Peter Linwood B 7.17.1956 Portland, ME BR/TR 6-3/240# d8.17																									
1979	Hou N	1	1	.500	10	0	0	0-0	12.1	8	5	1	2	8-0	6	2.92	121	.178	.327	1-0	.000	-0		1	0.1
1982	†Mil A	1	3	.250	16	0	0	3-2	18	16	8	5	0	6-3	12	4.00	95	.239	.297	0-0	—	0		0	0.0
1983	Mil A	3	4	.429	44	0	0	25-6	49.1	30	17	3	1	16-2	41	2.55	147	.172	.242	0-0	—	0		6	1.2
1984	Mil A	4	9	.308	54	1	0	3-7	91	94	58	16	1	38-6	75	5.24	74	.266	.336	0-0	—	0	47	-14	-1.9
1985	Mil A	0	0	—	29	0	0	2-1	45.2	58	26	5	2	10-0	22	4.53	92	.315	.347	0-0	—	0		-2	-0.1
1986	Sea A	8	6	.571	52	0	0	6-3	70.2	69	33	10	3	18-3	53	3.82	111	.258	.306	0-0	—	0		4	0.6
Total	6	17	23	.425	205	1	0	39-19	287	275	147	40	9	96-14	209	4.14	96	.252	.313	1-0	.000	-0	47	-5	-0.1
LADE, DOYLE Doyle Marion "Porky" B 2.17.1921 Fairbury, NE D 5.18.2000 Lincoln, NE BR/TR 5-10/183# d9.18																									
1946	Chi N	0	2	.000	3	2	0	0	15.1	15	8	0	1	3	8	4.11	81	.238	.284	5-1	.200	-0	52	-1	-0.2
1947	Chi N	11	10	.524	34	25	7-1	0	187.1	202	105	15	1	79	62	3.94	100	.276	.347	60-3	.217	2*	89	-3	0.0
1948	Chi N	5	6	.455	19	12	6	0	87.1	99	44	4	1	31	29	4.02	97	.283	.343	32-0	.156	-1	110	0	-0.1
1949	Chi N	4	5	.444	36	13	5-1	1	129.2	141	73	13	2	58	43	5.00	81	.274	.350	32-4	.219	2	103	-10	-0.5
1950	Chi N	5	6	.455	34	12	2	2	117.2	126	68	14	2	50	36	4.74	89	.275	.349	35-2	.286	3	121	-5	0.1
Total	5	25	29	.463	126	64	20-2	3	537.1	583	298	46	7	221	178	4.39	91	.275	.346	164-10	.220	6	101	-19	-0.7
LAFFERTY, FLIP Frank Bernard B 5.4.1854 Scranton, PA D 2.8.1910 Wilmington, DE TR d9.15 ▲																									
1876	Phi N	0	1	.000	1	1	1	0	9	5	3	0		0	0	0.00	—	.152	.152	3	.000	-1	0	2	0.1
LAFITTE, ED Edward Francis "Doc" B 4.7.1886 New Orleans, LA D 4.12.1971 Jenkintown, PA BR/TR 6-2/188# d4.16																									
1909	Det A	0	1	.000	3	1	1	1	14	22	14	2	1	2	11	3.86	65	.344	.373	4-0	.250	0	56	-4	-0.3
1911	Det A	11	8	.579	29	20	15	1	172.1	205	113	2	5	52	63	3.92	88	.302	.356	70-2	.157	-2*	102	-13	-1.6
1912	Det A	0	0	—	1	0	0	0	1.2	2	4	0	0	2	0	16.20	20	.333	.500	0-0	—	0		-2	-0.1

Year	Tm Lg	W	L	Pct	G	GS	CG-Sho	SV-BS	IP	H	R	HR	HB	BB-IB	SO	ERA	AERA	OAV	OOB	AB-SH	AVG	PB	Sup	APR	PW
1914	Bro F	18	15	.545	42	33	23	2	290.2	260	110	7	16	127	137	2.63	109	.248	.338	101-4	.257	3	92	9	1.4
1915	Bro F	6	9	.400	17	15	7	1	117.2	126	66	6	1	57	34	3.90	70	.288	.371	53-0	.264	2	90	-15	-1.7
	Buf F	2	2	.500	14	5	1-1	1	50.1	53	25	1	2	22	17	3.40	82	.286	.368	17-0	.118	-1	110	-4	-0.4
	Year	8	11	.421	31	20	8-1	2	168	179	29	7	3	79	51	3.75	73	.287	.370	70-0	.229	1	95	-18	-2.1
Total	5	37	35	.514	106	74	47-1	6	646.2	668	332	18	25	262	262	3.33	90	.276	.353	245-6	.220	1	95	-29	-2.7
LAGGER, ED Edwin Joseph B 7.14.1912 Joliet, IL D 11.10.1981 Joliet, IL BR/TR 6-3/200# d6.15																									
1934	Phi A	0	0	—	8	0	0	0	18	27	23	1	1	14	2	11.00	40	.342	.447	6-0	.000	-1		-13	-0.6
LaGROW, LERRIN Lerrin Harris B 7.8.1948 Phoenix, AZ BR/TR 6-5/220# d7.28																									
1970	Det A	0	1	.000	10	0	0	0-1	12.1	16	11	2	0	6-0	7	7.30	51	.308	.373	1-0	.000	-0		-5	-0.4
1972	†Det A	0	1	.000	16	0	0	2-0	27.1	22	4	0	0	6-2	9	1.32	240	.222	.264	0-0	—	0		6	0.3
1973	Det A	1	5	.167	21	3	0	3-0	54	54	26	8	1	23-2	33	4.33	94	.263	.335	0-0	—	0	87	0	0.0
1974	Det A	8	19	.296	37	34	11	0-0	216.1	245	132	21	3	80-8	85	4.66	82	.287	.349	0-0	—	0	82	-21	-2.3
1975	Det A	7	14	.333	32	26	7-2	0-0	164.1	183	105	15	2	66-5	75	4.38	92	.280	.344	0-0	—	0	83	-10	-1.3
1976	StL N	0	1	.000	8	2	1	0-0	24.1	21	4	0	1	7-2	10	1.48	239	.241	.302	5-0	.000	-1	25	6	0.2
1977	Chi A	7	3	.700	66	0	0	25-3	98.2	81	32	10	1	35-3	63	2.46	166	.230	.299	0-0	—	0		17	2.6
1978	Chi A	6	5	.545	52	0	0	16-6	88	85	47	9	3	38-0	41	4.40	87	.260	.340	0-0	—	0		-5	-0.8
1979	Chi A	0	3	.000	11	2	0	1-3	17.2	27	21	2	1	16-1	9	9.17	46	.346	.463	0-0	—	0	85	-10	-1.5
	LA N	5	1	.833	31	0	0	4-3	37	38	16	2	0	18-2	22	3.41	107	.270	.350	3-0	.333	0		1	0.2
1980	Phi N	0	2	.000	25	0	0	3-1	39	42	22	5	0	17-2	21	4.15	91	.276	.343	4-0	.250	0		-2	-0.1
Total	10	34	55	.382	309	67	19-2	54-17	779	814	420	74	12	312-27	375	4.11	94	.271	.339	13-0	.154	-0	82	-23	-3.1
LAHTI, JEFF Jeffrey Allen B 10.8.1956 Oregon City, OR BR/TR 6/180# d6.27																									
1982	†StL N	5	4	.556	33	1	0	0-1	56.2	53	27	3	2	21-8	22	3.81	95	.245	.314	13-0	.077	-1	97	-1	-0.2
1983	StL N	3	3	.500	53	0	0	0-3	74	64	31	2	1	29-12	26	3.16	115	.240	.314	10-0	.000	-1		3	0.2
1984	StL N	4	2	.667	63	0	0	1-2	84.2	69	36	6	2	34-12	45	3.72	93	.225	.303	6-1	.167	-0		-1	-0.1
1985	†StL N	5	2	.714	52	0	0	19-1	68.1	63	15	3	0	26-10	41	1.84	192	.251	.321	9-0	.000	-1		13	2.0
1986	StL N	0	0	—	4	0	0	0-0	2.1	3	0	0	0	1-0	3	0.00	—	.333	.400	0-0	—	0		1	0.0
Total	5	17	11	.607	205	1	0	20-7	286	252	109	14	5	111-42	137	3.12	114	.240	.313	38-1	.053	-3	97	15	1.9
LAKE, EDDIE Edward Erving "Sparky" B 3.18.1916 Antioch, CA D 6.7.1995 Castro Valley, CA BR/TR 5-7/160# d9.26.1939 ▲																									
1944	Bos A	0	0	—	6	0	0	0	19.1	20	13	2	3	11	7	4.19	81	.278	.395	126-4	.206	1*		-3	-0.1
LAKE, JOE Joseph Henry B 1.6.1881 Brooklyn, NY D 6.30.1950 Brooklyn, NY BR/TR 6/185# d4.21																									
1908	NY A	9	22	.290	38	27	19-2	0	269.1	252	157	6	6	77	118	3.17	78	.242	.298	112-1	.188	0*	79	-25	-3.0
1909	NY A	14	11	.560	31	26	17-3	1	215.1	180	81	2	5	59	117	1.88	135	.225	.283	81-0	.173	1	107	10	1.7
1910	StL A	11	17	.393	35	29	24-1	2	261.1	243	116	2	1	77	141	2.20	112	.248	.304	91-0	.231	2*	78	2	0.6
1911	StL A	10	15	.400	30	25	14-2	0	215.1	245	115	3	4	40	69	3.30	102	.282	.316	80-1	.262	2	83	1	0.6
1912	StL A	1	7	.125	11	6	4	0	57	70	41	0	1	16	28	4.42	75	.314	.363	20-0	.150	-1	74	-8	-1.0
	Det A	9	11	.450	26	14	11	1	162.2	190	94	3	3	39	86	3.10	105	.296	.340	62-2	.145	-3	76	-3	-0.7
	Year	10	18	.357	37	20	15	1	219.2	260	97	3	4	55	114	3.44	95	.301	.346	82-2	.146	-5	76	-11	-1.7
1913	Det A	8	7	.533	28	12	6	1	137	149	67	3	0	24	35	3.28	89	.279	.310	45-1	.267	4	104	-5	0.1
Total	6	62	90	.408	199	139	95-8	5	1318	1329	671	19	20	332	594	2.85	99	.261	.309	491-5	.206	4	86	-28	-1.7
LAMABE, JACK John Alexander B 10.3.1936 Farmingdale, NY BR/TR 6-1/198# d4.17																									
1962	Pit N	3	1	.750	46	0	0	2	78	70	35	4	0	40-8	56	2.88	136	.238	.329	9-0	.000	-1		7	0.3
1963	Bos A	7	4	.636	65	2	0	6	151.1	139	63	8	4	46-11	93	3.15	120	.247	.306	32-1	.094	-1	82	8	0.6
1964	Bos A	9	13	.409	39	25	3	1	177.1	235	123	25	2	57-5	109	5.89	65	.318	.367	52-1	.115	-1	106	-35	-4.0
1965	Bos A	0	3	.000	14	0	0	0	25.1	34	24	5	3	14-2	17	8.17	46	.340	.432	4-1	.000	-0		-10	-1.2
	Hou N	0	2	.000	3	2	0	0	12.2	17	9	3	0	3-1	6	4.26	79	.315	.351	4-0	.250	0	52	-2	-0.3
1966	Chi A	7	9	.438	34	17	3-2	0	121.1	116	55	9	1	35-1	67	3.93	81	.251	.304	35-4	.057	-2	116	-8	-1.2
1967	Chi A	1	0	1.000	3	0	0	0	5	7	2	0	0	1-1	3	1.80	172	.318	.348	0-0	—	0		0	0.1
	NY N	0	3	.000	16	2	0	1	31.2	24	15	4	0	8-1	23	3.98	85	.200	.248	5-0	.000	-0	52	-2	-0.2
	†StL N	3	4	.429	23	1	1-1	4	47.2	43	16	2	0	10-3	30	2.83	116	.244	.282	10-1	.200	0	160	3	0.5
	Year	3	7	.300	39	3	1-1	5	79.1	67	22	6	0	18-4	53	3.29	101	.226	.268	15-1	.133	-0	88	1	0.3
1968	Chi N	3	2	.600	42	0	0	1	61.1	68	33	7	1	24-7	30	4.26	74	.289	.350	5-1	.200	0		-7	-0.6
Total	7	33	41	.446	285	49	7-3	15	711.2	753	375	67	11	238-40	434	4.24	85	.272	.330	156-9	.096	-6	104	-46	-6.0
LaMACCHIA, AL Alfred Anthony B 7.22.1921 St.Louis, MO BR/TR 5-10.5/190# d9.27																									
1943	StL A	0	1	.000	1	1	0	0	4	9	6	0	0	2	2	11.25	30	.450	.500	2-0	.000	-0	101	-4	-0.6
1945	StL A	2	0	1.000	5	0	0	0	9	6	2	0	0	3	2	2.00	176	.207	.281	1-0	.000	-0		2	0.3
1946	StL A	0	0	—	8	0	0	0	15	17	10	2	0	7	3	6.00	62	.279	.353	3-0	.000	-0		-3	-0.2
	Was A	0	1	.000	2	0	0	0	2.2	6	5	1	0	2	0	16.88	20	.462	.533	0-0	—	0		-4	-0.7
	Year	0	1	.000	10	0	0	0	17.2	23	19	3	0	9	3	7.64	48	.311	.386	3-0	.000	-0		-7	-0.9
Total	3	2	2	.500	16	1	0	0	30.2	38	23	3	0	14	7	6.46	55	.309	.380	6-0	.000	-1	101	-9	-1.2
LaMANNA, FRANK Frank "Hank" B 8.22.1919 Waterton, PA D 9.1.1980 Syracuse, NY BR/TR 6-2.5/195# d4.16 Mil 1943-45																									
1940	Bos N	1	0	1.000	5	1	1	0	13.1	13	8	1	0	8	3	4.73	79	.271	.375	5-0	.200	0	117	-2	-0.1
1941	Bos N	5	4	.556	35	4	0	1	72.2	77	52	5	1	56	23	5.33	67	.285	.410	32-0	.281	1*	119	-15	-1.5
1942	Bos N	0	1	.000	5	0	0	0	6.2	5	4	1	0	3	2	5.40	62	.208	.296	2-0	.000	-0*		-1	-0.2
Total	3	6	5	.545	45	5	1	1	92.2	95	64	7	1	67	28	5.24	68	.278	.398	39-0	.256	1	119	-18	-1.8
LAMANSKE, FRANK Frank James "Lefty" B 9.30.1906 Oglesby, IL D 8.4.1971 Olney, IL BL/TL 5-11/170# d4.27																									
1935	Bro N	0	0	—	2	0	0	0	3.2	5	3	0	0	1	1	7.36	54	.313	.353	1-0	.000	-0		-1	-0.1
LaMASTER, WAYNE Noble Wayne B 2.13.1907 Speed, IN D 8.4.1989 New Albany, IN BL/TL 5-8/170# d4.19																									
1937	Phi N	15	19	.441	50	30	10-1	4	220.1	255	139	24	2	82	135	5.31	82	.290	.352	79-2	.190	-2*	95	-19	-3.0
1938	Phi N	4	7	.364	18	12	1-1	0	63.2	80	58	8	3	31	35	7.77	50	.301	.380	22-3	.409	4	120	-25	-3.1
	Bro N	0	1	.000	3	0	0	0	11.1	17	6	0	0	3	3	4.76	82	.340	.377	6-0	.167	-0*		-1	-0.1
	Year	4	8	.333	21	12	1-1	0	75	97	70	8	3	34	38	7.32	53	.307	.380	28-3	.357	4	120	-24	-3.2
Total	2	19	27	.413	71	42	11-2	4	295.1	352	203	32	5	116	173	5.82	72	.295	.360	107-5	.234	1	101	-45	-6.2
LAMB, JOHN John Andrew B 7.20.1946 Sharon, CT BR/TR 6-3/180# d8.12																									
1970	Pit N	0	1	.000	23	0	0	3-2	32.1	23	10	2	2	13-1	24	2.78	140	.209	.304	3-0	.000	-0		5	0.2
1971	Pit N	0	0	—	2	0	0	0-0	4.1	3	0	0	0	1-0	1	0.00	—	.188	.235	1-0	.000	-0		2	0.1
1973	Pit N	0	1	.000	22	0	0	2-0	29.2	37	24	3	0	10-3	11	6.07	58	.308	.359	3-0	.000	-0		-9	-0.5
Total	3	0	2	.000	47	0	0	5-2	66.1	63	34	5	2	24-4	36	4.07	91	.256	.326	7-0	.000	-1		-2	-0.2
LAMB, RAY Raymond Richard B 12.28.1944 Glendale, CA BR/TR 6-1/175# d8.1																									
1969	LA N	0	1	.000	10	0	0	1-0	15	12	3	2	0	7-0	11	1.80	185	.235	.328	1-0	.000	-0		3	0.2
1970	LA N	6	1	.857	35	0	0	0-0	57	59	27	4	4	27-9	32	3.79	101	.277	.366	4-0	.000	-0		0	-0.1
1971	Cle A	6	12	.333	43	21	3-1	1-0	158.1	147	67	11	1	69-7	91	3.35	114	.247	.323	43-4	.093	-2	92	7	0.4
1972	Cle A	5	6	.455	34	9	0	0-0	107.2	101	42	5	1	29-5	64	3.09	104	.248	.299	21-1	.000	-1	88	1	0.0
1973	Cle A	3	3	.500	32	1	0	2-1	86	98	44	7	2	42-6	60	4.60	85	.291	.369	0-0	—	0	205	-4	-0.3
Total	5	20	23	.465	154	31	3-1	4-1	424	417	183	29	8	174-27	258	3.54	104	.260	.333	69-5	.058	-4	94	7	0.2
LAMBERT, CLAYTON Clayton Patrick B 3.26.1917 Summit, IL D 4.3.1981 Ogden, UT BR/TR 6-2/185# d4.22																									
1946	Cin N	2	2	.500	23	4	2	1	52.2	48	27	3	1	20	20	4.27	78	.251	.325	13-0	.154	-1	109	-4	-0.5
1947	Cin N	0	0	—	3	0	0	0	5.2	12	10	3	0	6	1	15.88	26	.444	.545	1-0	.000	-0		-7	-0.3
Total	2	2	2	.500	26	4	2	1	58.1	60	37	6	1	26	21	5.40	63	.275	.355	14-0	.143	-1	109	-11	-0.8
LAMBERT, GENE Eugene Marion B 4.26.1921 Crenshaw, MS D 2.10.2000 Germantown, TN BR/TR 5-11/175# d9.14 Mil 1943-45																									
1941	Phi N	0	1	.000	2	1	0	0	9	11	2	0	0	2	3	2.00	185	.297	.333	2-0	.000	-0	0	2	0.2
1942	Phi N	0	0	—	1	0	0	0	1	3	1	0	0	0	1	9.00	37	.500	.500	0-0	—	0		-1	0.0
Total	2	0	1	.000	3	1	0	0	10	14	3	0	0	2	4	2.70	136	.326	.356	2-0	.000	-0	0	1	0.2

Year	Tm Lg	W	L	Pct	G	GS	CG-Sho	SV-BS	IP	H	R	HR	HB	BB-IB	SO	ERA	AERA	OAV	OOB	AB-SH	AVG	PB	Sup	APR	PW
LAMBETH, OTIS Otis Samuel B 5.13.1890 Berlin, KS D 6.5.1976 Moran, KS BR/TR 6/175# d7.16 Mil 1918																									
1916	Cle A	4	4	.500	15	9	3	1	74	69	33	1	3	38	28	2.92	103	.256	.354	27-1	.111	-1*	92	0	-0.2
1917	Cle A	7	6	.538	26	10	2	2	97.1	97	48	2	11	30	27	3.14	90	.274	.349	32-3	.188	-0	112	-4	-0.6
1918	Cle A	0	0	—	2	0	0	0	7	10	5	0	0	6	3	6.43	47	.370	.485	1-0	1.000	0		-2	-0.1
Total	3	11	10	.524	43	19	5	3	178.1	176	86	3	14	74	58	3.18	92	.270	.357	60-4	.167	-1	102	-6	-0.9
LAMLEIN, FRED Frederick Arthur "Dutch" B 8.14.1887 Port Huron, MI D 9.20.1970 Port Huron, MI BR/TR 5-11/171# d9.18																									
1912	Chi A	0	0	—	1	0	0	0	2	7	7	0	0	2	1	31.50	10	.583	.643	0-0	—	0		-6	-0.2
1915	StL N	0	0	—	4	0	0	0	19	21	4	0	2	3	11	1.42	196	.300	.347	8-0	.125	-0		3	0.1
Total	2	0	0	—	5	0	0	0	21	28	11	0	2	5	12	4.29	66	.341	.393	8-0	.125	-0		-3	-0.1
LAMP, DENNIS Dennis Patrick B 9.23.1952 Los Angeles, CA BR/TR 6-3/210# d8.21																									
1977	Chi N	0	2	.000	11	3	0	0-0	30	43	21	3	2	8-4	12	6.30	70	.344	.390	8-0	.375	1	68	-5	-0.2
1978	Chi N	7	15	.318	37	36	6-3	0-0	223.2	221	96	16	4	56-8	73	3.30	122	.258	.306	73-3	.205	0	82	14	1.5
1979	Chi N	11	10	.524	38	32	6-1	0-0	200.1	223	96	14	5	46-9	86	3.50	118	.287	.329	58-7	.155	-1	95	9	1.0
1980	Chi N	10	14	.417	41	37	2-1	0-1	202.2	259	123	16	1	82-7	83	5.20	76	.317	.378	61-7	.098	-3	95	-22	-2.6
1981	Chi A	7	6	.538	27	10	3	0-0	127	103	41	4	1	43-1	71	2.41	149	.222	.289	0-0	—	0	75	16	1.7
1982	Chi A	11	8	.579	44	27	3-2	5-2	189.2	206	96	9	6	59-3	78	3.99	101	.279	.337	0-0	—	0	117	1	0.2
1983	†Chi A	7	7	.500	49	5	1	15-5	116.1	123	52	6	4	29-7	44	3.71	113	.275	.324	0-0	—	0	78	6	0.9
1984	Tor A	8	8	.500	56	4	0	9-5	85	97	53	9	1	38-7	45	4.55	90	.285	.358	0-0	—	0	154	-7	-1.2
1985	†Tor A	11	0	1.000	53	1	0	2-5	105.2	96	42	7	0	27-3	68	3.32	127	.247	.292	0-0	—	0	43	11	1.1
1986	Tor A	2	6	.250	40	2	0	2-1	73	93	50	5	0	23-6	30	5.05	84	.309	.357	0-0	—	0	86	-9	-0.9
1987	Oak A	1	3	.250	36	5	0	0-0	56.2	76	38	5	1	22-3	36	5.08	81	.326	.382	0-0	—	0	115	-7	-0.5
1988	Bos A	7	6	.538	46	0	0	0-1	82.2	92	39	3	2	19-3	49	3.48	118	.284	.326	0-0	—	0		4	0.6
1989	Bos A	4	2	.667	42	0	0	2-1	112.1	96	37	4	0	27-6	61	2.32	177	.235	.280	0-0	—	0		19	1.1
1990	†Bos A	3	5	.375	47	1	0	0-2	105.2	114	61	10	3	30-8	49	4.68	87	.279	.330	0-0	—	0	45	-7	-0.4
1991	Bos A	6	3	.667	51	0	0	0-0	92	100	54	8	3	31-7	57	4.70	92	.275	.335	0-0	—	0		-4	-0.4
1992	Pit N	1	1	.500	21	0	0	0-1	28	33	16	3	2	9-4	15	5.14	67	.292	.355	1-0	.000	-0		-5	-0.3
Total	16	96	96	.500	639	163	21-7	35-24	1830.2	1975	915	122	35	549-86	857	3.93	104	.278	.331	201-17	.164	-3	95	14	1.6
LAMPE, HENRY Henry Joseph B 9.19.1872 Boston, MA D 9.16.1936 Dorchester, MA BR/TL 5-11.5/175# d5.14																									
1894	Bos N	0	1	.000	2	1	0	0	5.1	17	19	5	0	7	1	11.81	48	.531	.615	2-0	.000	-0	337	-6	-0.7
1895	Phi N	0	2	.000	7	3	2	0	44	68	54	3	1	33	18	7.57	63	.347	.443	16-0	.125	-1	94	-15	-0.7
Total	2	0	3	.000	9	4	2	0	49.1	85	73	8	1	40	19	8.03	61	.373	.468	18-0	.111	-1	168	-21	-1.4
LANAHAN, DICK Richard Anthony B 9.27.1911 Washington, DC D 3.12.1975 Rochester, MN BL/TL 6/186# d9.15																									
1935	Was A	0	3	.000	3	3	0	0	20.2	27	13	2	2	17	10	5.66	76	.314	.438	6-1	.167	-0	40	-2	-0.3
1937	Was A	0	1	.000	6	2	0	0	11.1	16	16	2	1	13	2	12.71	35	.320	.469	1-0	.000	0	177	-10	-0.6
1940	Pit N	6	8	.429	40	8	4	2	108	121	63	8	1	42	45	4.25	90	.279	.345	34-1	.118	-2	103	-7	-1.0
1941	Pit N	0	1	.000	7	0	0	0	12	13	9	1	2	3	5	5.25	69	.283	.353	1-0	.000	-0		-2	-0.2
Total	4	6	13	.316	56	13	4	2	152	177	101	13	6	75	62	5.15	76	.288	.371	42-2	.119	-2	102	-21	-2.1
LANCASTER, LES Lester Wayne B 4.21.1962 Dallas, TX BR/TR 6-2/200# d4.7																									
1987	Chi N	8	3	.727	27	18	0	0-0	132.1	138	76	14	1	51-5	78	4.90	87	.268	.332	49-1	.082	-2	101	-7	-0.8
1988	Chi N	4	6	.400	44	3	1	5-3	85.2	89	42	4	1	34-7	36	3.78	95	.273	.337	20-3	.050	-1	147	-3	-0.5
1989	†Chi N	4	2	.667	42	0	0	8-3	72.2	60	12	2	0	15-1	56	1.36	276	.226	.263	11-0	.182	0		**18**	1.9
1990	Chi N	9	5	.643	55	6	1-1	6-4	109	121	57	11	1	40-8	65	4.62	88	.283	.342	20-1	.050	-1	85	-4	-0.5
1991	Chi N	9	7	.563	64	11	1	3-3	156	150	68	13	4	49-7	102	3.52	110	.256	.315	28-6	.179	0	114	6	0.6
1992	Det A	3	4	.429	41	1	0	0-3	86.2	101	66	11	3	51-12	35	6.33	63	.294	.386	0-0	—	0	0	-23	-1.7
1993	StL N	4	1	.800	50	0	0	0-0	61.1	56	24	5	1	21-5	36	2.93	135	.242	.307	4-0	.000	-0		6	0.4
Total	7	41	28	.594	323	39	3-1	22-16	703.2	715	345	60	11	261-45	408	4.05	98	.265	.329	132-11	.098	-4	105	-7	-0.6
LANCE, GARY Gary Dean B 9.21.1948 Greenville, SC BB/TR 6-3/195# d9.28																									
1977	KC A	0	1	.000	1	0	0	0-0	2	2	1	0	0	2-0	0	4.50	90	.286	.444	0-0	—	0		0	0.0
LANDIS, DOC Samuel H. B 8.16.1854 Philadelphia, PA BR 5-11/172# d5.2																									
1882	Phi AA	1	1	.500	2	2	2	0	17	16	12	1		1	13	3.18	88	.232	.243	12	.167	-0*	101	-1	-0.1
	Bal AA	11	28	.282	42	40	35	0	343	416	257	7		46	62	3.38	81	.281	.302	175	.166	-6*	79	-29	-3.1
	Year	12	29	.293	44	42	37	0	360	432	261	8		47	75	3.38	82	.278	.300	187	.166	-7	80	-26	-3.2
LANDIS, BILL William Henry B 10.8.1942 Hanford, CA BL/TL 6-2/178# d9.28 Mil 1968																									
1963	KC A	0	0	—	1	0	0	0	1.2	0	0	0	0	1-0	3	0.00	—	.000	.167	0-0	—	0		1	0.0
1967	Bos A	1	0	1.000	18	1	0	0	25.2	24	16	6	0	11-3	23	5.26	66	.253	.330	2-0	.000	-0*	125	-4	-0.3
1968	Bos A	3	3	.500	38	1	0	3	60	48	22	4	2	30-2	59	3.15	100	.223	.320	6-0	.000	-1	55	1	0.0
1969	Bos A	5	5	.500	45	5	0	1-1	82.1	82	53	7	3	49-3	50	5.25	73	.269	.370	11-0	.000	-0*	51	-12	-1.3
Total	4	9	8	.529	102	7	0	4-1	169.2	154	91	17	5	91-8	135	4.46	79	.248	.345	19-0	.000	-1	64	-14	-1.6
LANDRETH, LARRY Larry Robert B 3.11.1955 Stratford, ON, CAN BR/TR 6-1/175# d9.16																									
1976	Mon N	1	2	.333	3	3	0	0-0	11	13	8	1	0	10-0	7	4.09	91	.310	.434	3-0	.000	-0	71	-1	-0.3
1977	Mon N	0	2	.000	4	1	0	0-0	9.1	16	11	0	0	8-1	5	9.64	40	.381	.471	2-0	.000	-0	70	-6	-1.1
Total	2	1	4	.200	7	4	0	0-0	20.1	29	19	1	0	18-1	12	6.64	57	.345	.452	5-0	.000	-1	70	-7	-1.4
LANDRUM, JOE Joseph Butler B 12.13.1928 Columbia, SC BR/TR 5-11/180# d7.13 s-Bill																									
1950	Bro N	0	0	—	7	0	0	1	6.2	12	8	2	1	1	5	8.10	51	.414	.452	0-1	—	0		-4	-0.2
1952	Bro N	1	3	.250	9	5	2	0	38	46	24	3	1	10	17	5.21	70	.301	.348	8-3	.125	-0	113	-7	-0.7
Total	2	1	3	.250	16	5	2	1	44.2	58	32	5	2	11	22	5.64	66	.319	.364	8-4	.125	-0	113	-11	-0.9
LANDRUM, BILL Thomas William B 8.17.1957 Columbia, SC BR/TR 6-2/200# d8.31 f-Joe																									
1986	Cin N	0	0	—	10	0	0	0-0	13.1	23	11	0	0	4-0	14	6.75	57	.390	.422	2-0	.000	-0		-4	-0.2
1987	Cin N	3	2	.600	44	2	0	2-1	65	68	35	3	0	34-6	42	4.71	90	.292	.379	5-1	.200	0	128	-2	-0.1
1988	Chi N	1	0	1.000	7	0	0	0-0	12.1	19	8	1	0	3-0	6	5.84	62	.365	.400	2-0	.000	-0		-3	-0.2
1989	Pit N	2	3	.400	56	0	0	26-3	81	60	18	2	0	28-8	51	1.67	202	.205	.273	3-0	.000	-0		15	1.9
1990	†Pit N	7	3	.700	54	0	0	13-3	71.2	69	22	4	0	21-5	39	2.13	170	.262	.314	9-0	.111	0		11	1.9
1991	†Pit N	4	4	.500	61	0	0	17-5	76.1	76	32	4	0	19-5	45	3.18	112	.252	.296	4-1	.000	-0		3	0.3
1992	Mon N	1	1	.500	18	0	0	0-0	20	27	16	3	2	9-2	7	7.20	48	.325	.404	0-0	—	0		-8	-0.7
1993	Cin N	0	2	.000	18	0	0	0-0	21.2	18	9	1	0	6-1	14	3.74	108	.231	.286	0-1	—	0		1	0.1
Total	8	18	15	.545	268	2	0	58-12	361.1	360	151	18	2	124-27	218	3.39	109	.265	.325	25-3	.080	-1	128	13	3.0
LANE, JERRY Gerald Hal B 2.7.1926 Ashland, NY D 7.24.1988 Chattanooga, TN BR/TR 6-0.5/205# d7.7																									
1953	Was A	1	4	.200	20	2	0	0	56.2	64	33	3	1	16	26	4.92	79	.288	.339	9-1	.111	0	46	-6	-0.4
1954	Cin N	1	0	1.000	3	0	0	0	10.2	9	2	0	0	3	2	1.69	248	.237	.293	4-0	.000	-0		3	0.2
1955	Cin N	0	2	.000	8	0	0	1	11	11	6	2	0	6-2	5	4.91	86	.289	.386	0-0	—	0		0	-0.1
Total	3	2	6	.250	31	2	0	1	78.1	84	41	5	1	25-2	33	4.48	89	.282	.340	13-1	.077	0	46	-3	-0.3
LANFORD, SAM Lewis Grover B 1.8.1886 Woodruff, SC D 9.14.1970 Woodruff, SC BR/TR 5-7/155# d8.19																									
1907	Was A	0	1	.000	2	1	0	0	7	10	10	0	3	5	2	5.14	47	.333	.474	3-0	.333	0	56	-4	-0.4
LANFRANCONI, WALT Walter Oswald B 11.9.1916 Barre, VT D 8.18.1986 Barre, VT BR/TR 5-7.5/155# d9.12 Mil 1942-45																									
1941	Chi N	0	1	.000	2	1	0	0	6	7	3	0	0	2	1	3.00	117	.280	.333	1-0	.000	-0	0	0	0.0
1947	Bos N	4	4	.500	36	4	1	1	64	65	23	2	0	27	18	2.95	132	.272	.346	10-1	.000	-1*	57	**7**	0.8
Total	2	4	5	.444	38	5	1	1	70	72	26	2	0	29	19	2.96	131	.273	.345	11-1	.000	-1	46	7	0.8
LANG, MARTY Martin John B 9.27.1905 Hooper, NE D 1.13.1968 Lakewood, CO BR/TL 5-11/160# d7.4																									
1930	Pit N	0	0	—	2	0	0	0	1.2	9	10	2	0	3	2	54.00	9	.692	.750	0-0	—	0		-8	-0.3
LANG, CHIP Robert David B 8.21.1952 Pittsburgh, PA BR/TR 6-4/205# d9.8																									
1975	Mon N	0	0	—	1	1	0	0-0	1.2	2	2	0	0	3-0	2	10.80	36	.333	.556	0-0	—	0	138	-1	-0.1

Year	Tm Lg	W	L	Pct	G	GS	CG-Sho	SV-BS	IP	H	R	HR	HB	BB-IB	SO	ERA	AERA	OAV	OOB	AB-SH	AVG	PB	Sup	APR	PW
1976	Mon N	1	3	.250	29	2	0	0-0	62.1	56	32	3	3	34-2	30	4.19	89	.242	.346	6-2	.167	-0	35	-3	-0.2
Total	2	1	3	.250	30	3	0	0-0	64	58	34	3	3	37-2	32	4.36	86	.245	.353	6-2	.167	-0	71	-4	-0.3
LANGE, ERV Erwin Henry B 8.12.1887 Forest Park, IL D 4.24.1971 Maywood, IL BR/TR 5-10/170# d4.19																									
1914	Chi F	12	11	.522	36	22	10-2	2	190	162	69	3	3	55	87	2.23	119	.224	.282	51-1	.176	2	107	7	0.9
LANGE, FRANK Frank Herman "Seagan" B 10.28.1883 Columbus, WI D 12.26.1945 Madison, WI BR/TR 5-11/180# d5.16																									
1910	Chi A	9	4	.692	23	15	6-1	0	130.2	93	48	2	9	54	98	1.65	145	.204	.301	51-0	.255	3	121	7	1.0
1911	Chi A	8	8	.500	29	22	8-1	0	161.2	151	77	3	3	77	104	3.23	100	.251	.339	76-2	.289	8*	105	1	0.9
1912	Chi A	10	10	.500	31	20	11-2	3	165.1	165	85	4	4	68	96	3.27	98	.270	.347	65-3	.215	2*	112	-2	-0.1
1913	Chi A	1	3	.250	12	3	0	0	40.2	46	24	0	1	20	20	4.87	60	.299	.383	18-1	.167	1*	76	-6	-0.4
Total	4	28	25	.528	95	60	25-4	3	498.1	455	234	9	17	219	318	2.96	100	.250	.336	210-6	.248	14	110	0	1.4
LANGE, DICK Richard Otto B 9.1.1948 Harbor Beach, MI BR/TR 5-10/185# d9.9																									
1972	Cal A	0	0	—	2	1	0	0-0	7.2	7	4	0	0	2-0	8	4.70	62	.233	.281	3-0	.000	-0	61	-1	-0.1
1973	Cal A	2	1	.667	17	4	1	0-1	52.2	61	30	9	1	21-2	27	4.44	80	.292	.356	0-0	—	0	120	-6	-0.3
1974	Cal A	3	8	.273	21	18	1	0-0	113.2	111	63	10	4	47-0	57	3.80	91	.248	.323	0-0	—	0*	98	-8	-0.8
1975	Cal A	4	6	.400	30	8	1	1-0	102	119	70	12	1	53-3	45	5.21	68	.292	.371	0-0	—	0	87	-21	-1.9
Total	4	9	15	.375	70	31	3	1-1	276	298	167	31	6	123-5	137	4.47	78	.272	.346	3-0	.000	-0	96	-36	-3.1
LANGFORD, RICK James Rick B 3.20.1952 Farmville, VA BR/TR 6/180# d6.13 C1																									
1976	Pit N	0	1	.000	12	1	0	0-1	23	27	17	2	0	14-0	17	6.26	56	.307	.398	5-0	.200	0	76	-7	-0.3
1977	Oak A	8	19	.296	37	31	6-1	0-0	208.1	223	107	18	2	73-3	141	4.02	100	.273	.332	0-0	—	0	76	1	0.1
1978	Oak A	7	13	.350	37	24	4-2	0-1	175.2	169	77	15	3	56-8	92	3.43	106	.253	.311	0-0	—	0*	61	6	0.7
1979	Oak A	12	16	.429	34	29	14-1	0-1	218.2	233	114	22	4	57-6	101	4.28	95	.273	.319	0-0	—	0	81	-4	-0.3
1980	Oak A	19	12	.613	35	33	**28**-2	0-0	**290**	276	119	29	1	64-6	102	3.26	116	.255	.294	0-0	—	0	106	17	1.7
1981	†Oak A	12	10	.545	24	24	**18**-2	0-0	195.1	190	81	14	3	58-2	84	2.99	116	.255	.308	0-0	—	0	103	7	0.6
1982	Oak A	11	16	.407	32	31	15-2	0-0	237.1	265	121	33	2	49-1	79	4.21	93	.281	.316	1-0	.000	-0*	99	-7	-0.7
1983	Oak A	0	4	.000	7	7	0	0-0	20	43	28	4	2	10-1	2	12.15	32	.448	.495	0-0	—	0	114	-18	-2.7
1984	Oak A	0	0	—	3	2	0	0-0	8.2	15	8	2	0	2-0	2	8.31	45	.366	.395	0-0	—	0	108	-4	-0.2
1985	Oak A	3	5	.375	23	3	0	0-0	59	60	24	8	0	15-2	21	3.51	110	.261	.306	0-0	—	0	63	3	0.4
1986	Oak A	1	10	.091	16	11	0	0-0	55	69	49	13	1	18-0	30	7.36	53	.300	.351	0-0	—	0*	51	-23	-3.6
Total	11	73	106	.408	260	196	85-10	0-3	1491	1570	745	160	18	416-29	671	4.01	95	.271	.319	6-0	.167	0	87	-29	-4.3
LANGSTON, MARK Mark Edward B 8.20.1960 San Diego, CA BR/TL 6-2/190# d4.7																									
1984	Sea A	17	10	.630	35	33	5-2	0-1	225	188	99	16	8	118-5	**204**	3.40	118	.230	.330	0-0	—	0	86	13	1.5
1985	Sea A	7	14	.333	24	24	2	0-0	126.2	122	85	22	2	91-2	72	5.47	77	.255	.375	0-0	—	0	85	-18	-2.3
1986	Sea A	12	14	.462	37	36	9	0-0	239.1	234	142	30	4	123-1	**245**	4.85	88	.255	.343	0-0	—	0	89	-15	-1.4
1987	Sea A★	19	13	.594	35	35	14-3	0-0	272	242	132	30	5	114-0	**262**	3.84	123	.238	.317	0-0	—	0	88	24	2.6
1988	Sea A	15	11	.577	35	35	9-3	0-0	261.1	222	108	32	3	110-2	235	3.34	125	.233	.313	0-0	—	0	91	23	2.4
1989	Sea A	4	5	.444	10	10	2-1	0-0	73.1	60	30	3	4	19-0	60	3.56	113	.221	.279	0-0	—	0	88	5	0.6
	Mon N	12	9	.571	24	24	6-4	0-0	176.2	138	57	13	0	93-6	175	2.39	148	.218	.316	64-1	.172	0	90	20	2.4
1990	Cal A	10	17	.370	33	33	5-1	0-0	223	215	120	13	5	104-1	195	4.40	87	.259	.343	0-0	—	0	94	-12	-1.2
1991	Cal A☆	19	8	.704	34	34	7	0-0	246.1	190	89	30	2	96-3	183	3.00	137	.215	.291	0-0	—	0	96	31	3.3
1992	Cal A★	13	14	.481	32	32	9-2	0-0	229	206	103	14	6	74-2	174	3.66	109	.242	.305	2-0	.000	-0*	81	8	0.9
1993	Cal A★	16	11	.593	35	35	7	0-0	256.1	220	100	22	1	85-2	196	3.20	142	.234	.295	0-0	—	0	72	37	3.7
1994	Cal A	7	8	.467	18	18	2-1	0-0	119.1	121	67	19	0	54-1	109	4.68	105	.268	.340	0-0	—	0	81	2	0.4
1995	Cal A	15	7	.682	31	31	2-1	0-0	200.1	212	109	21	3	64-1	142	4.63	102	.272	.329	0-0	—	0	126	3	0.4
1996	Cal A	6	5	.545	18	18	2	0-0	123.1	116	68	18	2	45-0	83	4.82	104	.247	.315	0-0	—	0	97	5	0.5
1997	Ana A	2	4	.333	9	9	0	0-0	47.2	61	34	8	0	29-1	30	5.85	78	.316	.402	0-0	—	0	103	-7	-0.7
1998	†SD N	4	6	.400	22	16	0	0-1	81.1	107	55	11	1	41-1	56	5.86	67	.325	.397	24-4	.083	-0*	132	-18	-1.9
1999	Cle A	1	2	.333	25	5	0	0-1	61.2	69	40	9	0	29-6	43	5.25	96	.287	.362	2-0	.500	0	67	-2	0.0
Total	16	179	158	.531	457	428	81-18	0-3	2962.2	2723	1438	311	46	1289-34	2464	3.97	108	.246	.325	92-5	.152	-0	92	99	11.2
LANIER, MAX Hubert Max B 8.18.1915 Denton, NC BR/TL 5-10/187# d4.20 Mil 1945 s-Hal																									
1938	StL N	0	3	.000	18	3	1	0	45	57	30	1	2	28	14	4.20	94	.317	.414	10-0	.100	-0	93	-3	-0.2
1939	StL N	2	1	.667	7	6	2	0	37.2	29	11	0	1	13	14	2.39	172	.220	.295	14-1	.286	1	110	7	0.6
1940	StL N	9	6	.600	35	11	4-2	3	105	113	50	1	1	38	49	3.34	119	.276	.339	30-1	.200	-0	91	6	0.8
1941	StL N	10	8	.556	35	18	8-2	3	153	126	59	4	1	59	93	2.82	133	.225	.300	52-2	.192	-1	115	14	1.7
1942	†StL N	13	8	.619	34	20	8-2	2	161	137	55	4	2	60	93	2.96	116	.234	.308	47-4	.255	2	98	11	1.8
1943	†StL N☆	15	7	.682	32	25	14-2	3	213.1	195	62	3	2	75	123	1.90	**177**	.246	.312	73-11	.164	-2	112	31	3.1
1944	†StL N✣	17	12	.586	33	30	16-5	0	224.1	192	82	5	3	71	141	2.65	133	.234	.297	77-6	.182	-0	105	20	2.4
1945	StL N	2	2	.500	4	3	3	0	26	22	10	0	0	8	16	1.73	216	.222	.280	11-0	.182	-0	83	4	0.6
1946	StL N	6	0	1.000	6	6	6-2	0	56	45	13	1	1	19	36	1.93	179	.228	.300	25-0	.200	-0	153	10	1.1
1949	StL N	5	4	.556	15	15	4-1	0	92	92	42	5	0	35	37	3.82	109	.261	.328	27-4	.074	-2	95	5	0.2
1950	StL N	11	9	.550	27	27	10-2	0	181.1	173	70	13	1	68	89	3.13	137	.249	.317	68-4	.162	-1	99	23	2.2
1951	StL N	11	9	.550	31	23	9-2	1	160	149	60	14	1	50	59	3.26	122	.248	.306	53-3	.151	-2	66	14	1.5
1952	NY N	7	12	.368	37	16	6-1	5	137	124	64	11	3	65	47	3.94	94	.244	.333	41-5	.268	3*	71	-1	0.3
1953	NY N	0	0	—	3	0	0	0	5.1	8	4	1	0	3	2	6.75	64	.381	.458	1-0	.000	-0		-1	-0.1
	StL A	0	1	.000	10	1	0	0	22.1	28	18	2	0	19	8	7.25	58	.322	.443	6-0	.167	-0	42	-6	-0.3
Total	14	108	82	.568	327	204	91-21	17	1619.1	1490	630	65	18	611	821	3.01	125	.247	.318	535-41	.185	-3	97	134	15.7
LANKFORD, FRANK Frank Greenfield B 3.26.1971 Atlanta, GA BR/TR 6-2/190# d3.31																									
1998	LA N	0	2	.000	12	0	0	1-0	19.2	23	13	2	2	7-0	7	5.95	67	.287	.360	2-0	.000	-0		-4	-0.3
LANNING, JOHNNY John Young "Tobacco Chewin' Johnny" B 9.6.1910 Asheville, NC D 11.8.1989 Asheville, NC BR/TR 6-1/185# d4.17 Mil 1943-45 b-Tom																									
1936	Bos N	7	11	.389	28	20	3-1	0	153	154	75	9	0	55	33	3.65	105	.263	.326	52-2	.135	-2	81	2	-0.1
1937	Bos N	5	7	.417	32	11	4-1	2	116.2	107	59	10	1	40	37	3.93	91	.236	.300	33-2	.121	-1	57	-5	-0.6
1938	Bos N	8	7	.533	32	18	4-1	0	138	146	74	5	1	52	39	3.72	92	.267	.332	48-2	.188	-1	103	-8	-0.9
1939	Bos N	5	6	.455	37	6	3	4	129	120	53	6	2	53	45	3.42	108	.252	.329	42-2	.143	-1	43	6	0.4
1940	Pit N	8	4	.667	38	7	2	2	115.2	119	59	8	0	39	42	4.05	94	.268	.327	35-3	.200	1	150	-2	-0.1
1941	Pit N	11	11	.500	34	23	9	1	175.2	175	72	6	0	47	41	3.13	116	.256	.304	56-6	.107	-2	88	10	1.1
1942	Pit N	6	8	.429	34	8	2-1	1	119.1	125	52	7	1	26	31	3.32	102	.274	.314	29-2	.138	-0	59	1	0.1
1943	Pit N	4	1	.800	12	2	0	2	27	23	10	0	0	9	11	2.33	149	.223	.286	6-0	.167	-0	61	3	0.5
1945	Pit N	0	0	—	1	0	0	0	2	8	8	1	0	0	0	36.00	11	.571	.571	0-0	—	0		-6	-0.3
1946	Pit N	4	5	.444	27	9	3	1	91	97	36	3	1	31	16	3.07	115	.269	.329	21-3	.143	-0	70	5	0.4
1947	Bos N	0	0	—	3	0	0	0	3.2	4	5	0	0	6	0	9.82	40	.400	.625	0-0	—	0		-3	-0.1
Total	11	58	60	.492	278	104	30-4	13	1071	1078	503	55	6	358	295	3.58	101	.261	.321	322-22	.146	-7	83	3	0.4
LANNING, RED Lester Alfred B 5.13.1895 Harvard, IL D 6.13.1962 Bristol, CT BL/TL 5-9/165# d6.20 ▲																									
1916	Phi A	0	3	.000	6	3	1	0	24.1	38	27	1	2	17	9	8.14	35	.362	.460	33-1	.182	1*	53	-13	-1.3
LANNING, TOM Thomas Newton B 4.22.1907 Asheville, NC D 11.4.1967 Marietta, GA BL/TL 6-1/165# d9.14 b-Johnny																									
1938	Phi N	0	1	.000	3	1	0	0	7	9	7	0	0	2	2	6.43	60	.300	.344	1-0	1.000	0	22	-2	-0.3
LANSING, GENE Eugene Hewitt "Jigger" B 1.11.1898 Albany, NY D 1.18.1945 Rensselaer, NY BR/TR 6-1/185# d4.27																									
1922	Bos N	0	1	.000	15	1	0	0	40.2	46	28	1	0	22	14	5.98	67	.301	.389	11-0	.000	-1	61	-7	-0.4
LaPALME, PAUL Paul Edmore "Lefty" B 12.14.1923 Springfield, MA BL/TL 5-10/184# d5.28																									
1951	Pit N	1	5	.167	22	8	1-1	0	54.1	79	48	6	1	31	24	6.29	67	.333	.413	10-0	.100	-0	104	-13	-1.3
1952	Pit N	1	2	.333	31	2	0	0	59.2	56	33	6	1	37	25	3.92	102	.253	.363	10-1	.100	-0	123	-1	-0.1
1953	Pit N	8	16	.333	35	24	7-1	2	176.1	191	107	20	0	64	86	4.59	97	.272	.333	59-3	.085	-5	76	-5	-1.1
1954	Pit N	4	10	.286	33	15	2	0	120.2	147	79	15	0	54	57	5.52	76	.302	.368	35-3	.143	-0	97	-15	-1.5
1955	StL N	4	3	.571	56	0	0	3	91.2	76	36	10	1	34-9	39	2.75	148	.228	.297	19-0	.211	0		11	0.9

Year	Tm Lg	W	L	Pct	G	GS	CG-Sho	SV-BS	IP	H	R	HR	HB	BB-IB	SO	ERA	AERA	OAV	OOB	AB-SH	AVG	PB	Sup	APR	PW
1956	StL N	0	0	—	1	0	0	0	0.2	4	6	0	0	2-0	0	81.00	5	.667	.750	0-0	—	0		-5	-0.2
	Cin N	2	4	.333	11	2	0	0	27	26	14	7	0	4-0	4	4.67	85	.257	.283	4-2	.500	1	100	-1	-0.2
	Year	2	4	.333	12	2	0	0	27.2	30	19	7	0	6-0	4	6.51	61	.280	.316	4-2	.500	1	100	-6	-0.4
	Chi A	3	1	.750	29	0	0	2	45.2	31	14	2	0	27-2	23	2.36	173	.195	.310	6-1	.000	-1		9	0.7
1957	Chi A	1	4	.200	35	0	0	7	40.1	35	16	5	1	19-1	19	3.35	112	.235	.325	4-1	.500	1*		2	0.5
Total	7	24	45	.348	253	51	10-2	14	616.1	645	353	71	4	272-12	277	4.42	95	.269	.343	147-11	.136	-4	92	-18	-2.3

LAPIHUSKA, ANDY Andrew "Apples" B 11.1.1922 Delmont, NJ D 2.17.1996 Millville, NJ BL/TR 5-10.5/175# d9.12 Mil 1944-45

Year	Tm Lg	W	L	Pct	G	GS	CG-Sho	SV-BS	IP	H	R	HR	HB	BB-IB	SO	ERA	AERA	OAV	OOB	AB-SH	AVG	PB	Sup	APR	PW
1942	Phi N	0	2	.000	3	2	0	0	20.2	17	13	0	2	13	8	5.23	63	.221	.348	7-0	.286	0	13	-4	-0.3
1943	Phi N	0	0	—	1	0	0	0	2.1	5	6	1	0	3	0	23.14	15	.417	.533	2-0	.000	-0		-5	-0.2
Total	2	0	2	.000	4	2	0	0	23	22	19	1	2	16	8	7.04	47	.247	.374	9-0	.222	0	13	-9	-0.5

LaPOINT, DAVE David Jeffrey B 7.29.1959 Glens Falls, NY BL/TL 6-3/215# d9.10

Year	Tm Lg	W	L	Pct	G	GS	CG-Sho	SV-BS	IP	H	R	HR	HB	BB-IB	SO	ERA	AERA	OAV	OOB	AB-SH	AVG	PB	Sup	APR	PW
1980	Mil A	1	0	1.000	5	3	0	1-0	15	17	14	2	0	13-1	5	6.00	65	.293	.411	0-0	—	0	215	-5	-0.4
1981	StL N	1	0	1.000	3	2	0	0-0	10.2	12	5	1	1	2-0	4	4.22	84	.293	.341	5-0	.000	-1	175	-1	-0.1
1982	†StL N	9	3	.750	42	21	0	0-0	152.2	170	63	8	3	52-8	81	3.42	106	.290	.348	38-8	.053	-3	116	4	-0.1
1983	StL N	12	9	.571	37	29	1	0-0	191.1	191	92	12	4	84-7	113	3.95	92	.267	.342	59-5	.153	1	111	-5	-0.5
1984	StL N	12	10	.545	33	33	2-1	0-0	193	205	94	9	1	77-8	130	3.96	88	.278	.346	59-9	.068	-3	100	-10	-1.5
1985	SF N	7	17	.292	31	31	2-1	0-0	206.2	215	99	18	0	74-6	122	3.57	96	.269	.329	60-5	.167	2	79	-5	-0.4
1986	Det A	3	6	.333	16	8	0	0-1	67.2	85	49	11	0	32-3	36	5.72	72	.307	.377	0-0	—	0	102	-13	-1.4
	SD N	1	4	.200	24	4	0	0-0	61.1	67	37	8	1	24-4	41	4.26	86	.276	.342	8-4	.000	-1	91	-6	-0.6
1987	StL N	1	1	.500	6	2	0	0-0	16	26	12	4	0	5-0	8	6.75	62	.351	.392	4-0	.000	-0	131	-4	-0.5
	Chi A	6	3	.667	14	12	2-1	0-0	82.2	69	29	7	1	31-0	43	2.94	156	.224	.297	0-0	—	0	106	15	1.6
1988	Chi A	10	11	.476	25	25	1-1	0-0	161.1	151	69	10	2	47-1	79	3.40	117	.245	.299	0-0	—	0	89	11	1.2
	Pit N	4	2	.667	8	8	1	0-0	52	54	18	4	0	10-2	19	2.77	123	.271	.305	16-1	.063	-1	104	4	0.3
1989	NY A	6	9	.400	20	20	0	0-0	113.2	146	73	12	2	45-4	51	5.62	69	.310	.370	0-0	—	0	101	-19	-2.3
1990	NY A	7	10	.412	28	27	2	0-0	157.2	180	84	11	1	57-3	67	4.11	97	.292	.347	0-0	—	0	88	-4	-0.4
1991	Phi N	0	1	.000	2	2	0	0-0	5	10	10	0	1	6-0	3	16.20	23	.435	.548	2-0	.000	-0	159	-7	-1.0
Total	12	80	86	.482	294	227	11-4	1-1	1486.2	1598	748	117	17	559-47	802	4.02	93	.277	.340	251-32	.104	-6	101	-45	-6.1

LARA, YOVANNY Yovanny B. B 9.20.1975 San Cristobal, D.R. BR/TR 6-4/180# d6.28

Year	Tm Lg	W	L	Pct	G	GS	CG-Sho	SV-BS	IP	H	R	HR	HB	BB-IB	SO	ERA	AERA	OAV	OOB	AB-SH	AVG	PB	Sup	APR	PW
2000	Mon N	0	0	—	6	0	0	0-0	5.2	5	4	0	0	8-0	3	6.35	76	.250	.448	0-0	—	0		-1	0.0

LARKIN, ANDY Andrew Dane B 6.27.1974 Chelan, WA BR/TR 6-4/180# d9.29

Year	Tm Lg	W	L	Pct	G	GS	CG-Sho	SV-BS	IP	H	R	HR	HB	BB-IB	SO	ERA	AERA	OAV	OOB	AB-SH	AVG	PB	Sup	APR	PW
1996	Fla N	0	0	—	1	1	0	0-0	5	3	1	0	1	4-0	2	1.80	226	.176	.364	2-0	.000	-0	88	1	0.0
1998	Fla N	3	8	.273	17	14	0	0-0	74.2	101	87	12	4	55-3	43	9.64	42	.329	.435	29-2	.138	-1	120	-48	-5.3
2000	Cin N	0	0	—	3	0	0	0-0	6.2	6	4	1	0	5-0	7	5.40	87	.240	.367	1-0	.000	-0		0	0.0
	KC A	0	3	.000	18	0	0	1-2	19.1	29	20	5	0	11-2	17	8.84	58	.349	.421	0-0	—	0		-8	-1.0
Total	3	3	11	.214	39	15	0	1-2	105.2	139	112	18	5	75-5	69	8.86	48	.322	.425	32-2	.125	-1	112	-55	-6.3

LARKIN, TERRY Frank S. D 9.16.1894 Brooklyn, NY BR/TR d5.20 ▲

Year	Tm Lg	W	L	Pct	G	GS	CG-Sho	SV-BS	IP	H	R	HR	HB	BB-IB	SO	ERA	AERA	OAV	OOB	AB-SH	AVG	PB	Sup	APR	PW
1876	NY N	0	1	.000	1	1	1	0	9	9	7	0		0	0	3.00	71	.231	.231	4	.000	-1	72	-1	-0.1
1877	Har N	29	25	.537	56	56	55-4	0	501	510	285	2		53	96	2.14	114	**.245**	.264	228	.228	6*	111	14	1.6
1878	Chi N	29	26	.527	56	56	56-1	0	506	511	288	4		31	163	2.24	108	.246	.257	226	.288	13*	107	10	1.9
1879	Chi N	31	23	.574	58	58	57-4	0	513.1	514	277	5		30	142	2.44	105	.240	**.250**	228	.219	1*	96	8	0.5
1880	Tro N	0	5	.000	5	5	3	0	38	83	65	1		10	5	8.76	29	.421	.449	20	.150	-0*	90	-23	-2.1
Total	5	89	80	.527	176	176	172-9	0	1567.1	1627	922	12		124	406	2.43	102	.249	.263	706	.241	19	103	8	1.8

LARKIN, PAT Patrick Clibborn B 6.14.1960 Arcadia, CA BL/TL 6/180# d7.16

Year	Tm Lg	W	L	Pct	G	GS	CG-Sho	SV-BS	IP	H	R	HR	HB	BB-IB	SO	ERA	AERA	OAV	OOB	AB-SH	AVG	PB	Sup	APR	PW
1983	SF N	0	0	—	5	0	0	0-0	10.1	13	6	1	2	3-1	6	4.35	81	.317	.383	1-0	.000	-0		-1	-0.1

LARKIN, STEVE Stephen Patrick B 12.9.1910 Cincinnati, OH D 5.2.1969 Norristown, PA BR/TR 6-1/195# d5.6

Year	Tm Lg	W	L	Pct	G	GS	CG-Sho	SV-BS	IP	H	R	HR	HB	BB-IB	SO	ERA	AERA	OAV	OOB	AB-SH	AVG	PB	Sup	APR	PW
1934	Det A	0	0	—	2	1	0	0	6	8	7	0	0	5	8	1.50	293	.296	.406	3-0	.333	1	79	-1	0.1

LaROCHE, DAVE David Eugene B 5.14.1948 Colorado Springs, CO BL/TL 6-2/200# d5.11 C5

Year	Tm Lg	W	L	Pct	G	GS	CG-Sho	SV-BS	IP	H	R	HR	HB	BB-IB	SO	ERA	AERA	OAV	OOB	AB-SH	AVG	PB	Sup	APR	PW
1970	Cal A	4	1	.800	38	0	0	4-2	49.2	41	20	6	4	21-6	44	3.44	105	.224	.316	8-0	.250	1		2	0.3
1971	Cal A	5	1	.833	56	0	0	9-3	72	55	21	3	1	27-10	63	2.50	130	.212	.285	11-1	.091	-0		7	0.7
1972	Min A	5	7	.417	62	0	0	10-3	95.1	72	33	9	6	39-6	79	2.83	114	.209	.300	11-1	.091	0		5	0.8
1973	Chi N	4	1	.800	45	0	0	4-1	54.1	55	37	7	1	29-3	34	5.80	68	.274	.362	4-0	.500	1		-9	-0.8
1974	Chi N	5	6	.455	49	4	0	5-6	92	103	54	9	3	47-7	49	4.79	80	.286	.371	27-0	.333	3*	80	-8	-0.7
1975	Cle A	5	3	.625	61	0	0	17-3	82.1	61	26	5	2	57-8	94	2.19	173	.210	.344	0-0	—	0		13	1.9
1976	Cle A☆	1	4	.200	61	0	0	21-3	96.1	57	25	2	1	49-11	104	2.24	156	.175	.282	0-0	—	0		14	1.4
1977	Cle A	2	2	.500	13	0	0	4-1	18.2	15	13	3	0	7-1	18	5.30	75	.234	.301	0-0	—	0		-3	-0.6
	Cal A★	6	5	.545	46	0	0	13-2	81.1	64	31	8	2	37-8	61	3.10	127	.218	.306	0-0	—	0		8	1.3
	Year	8	7	.533	59	0	0	17-3	100	79	48	11	2	44-9	79	3.51	112	.221	.305	0-0	—	0		5	0.7
1978	Cal A	10	9	.526	59	0	0	25-6	95.2	73	35	7	2	48-11	70	2.82	128	.215	.315	0-0	—	0		8	1.7
1979	†Cal A	7	11	.389	53	1	0	10-5	85.2	107	54	13	2	32-4	59	5.57	73	.314	.372	0-0	—	0	0	-12	-2.3
1980	Cal A	3	5	.375	52	9	1	4-4	128	122	62	14	3	39-3	89	4.08	97	.256	.314	0-0	—	0*	111	-1	-0.1
1981	†NY A	4	1	.800	26	1	0	0-2	47	38	16	3	1	16-1	24	2.49	144	.229	.291	0-0	—	0	125	5	0.5
1982	NY A	4	2	.667	25	0	0	0-0	50	54	19	4	1	11-2	31	3.42	117	.273	.313	0-0	—	0		4	0.4
1983	NY A	0	0	—	1	0	0	0-0	1	2	2	1	0	0-0	0	18.00	22	.400	.400	0-0	—	0		-2	-0.1
Total	14	65	58	.528	647	15	1	126-41	1049.1	919	448	94	29	459-81	819	3.53	106	.239	.322	61-2	.246	4	101	31	4.4

LaROSE, JOHN Henry John B 10.25.1951 Pawtucket, RI BL/TL 6-1/185# d9.20

Year	Tm Lg	W	L	Pct	G	GS	CG-Sho	SV-BS	IP	H	R	HR	HB	BB-IB	SO	ERA	AERA	OAV	OOB	AB-SH	AVG	PB	Sup	APR	PW
1978	Bos A	0	0	—	1	0	0	0-0	2	3	5	1	0	3-1	0	22.50	18	.375	.545	0-0	—	0		-3	-0.2

LARSEN, DON Don James B 8.7.1929 Michigan City, IN BR/TR 6-4/227# d4.18

Year	Tm Lg	W	L	Pct	G	GS	CG-Sho	SV-BS	IP	H	R	HR	HB	BB-IB	SO	ERA	AERA	OAV	OOB	AB-SH	AVG	PB	Sup	APR	PW
1953	StL A	7	12	.368	38	22	7-2	2	192.2	201	99	11	4	64	96	4.16	101	.267	.328	81-0	.284	5*	95	2	0.9
1954	Bal A	3	21	.125	29	28	12-1	0	201.2	213	106	18	1	89	80	4.37	82	.274	.346	88-2	.250	8*	64	-16	-0.9
1955	†NY A	9	2	.818	19	13	5-1	2	97	81	38	8	2	51-3	44	3.06	122	.229	.328	41-0	.146	2*	139	8	1.0
1956	†NY A	11	5	.688	38	20	6-1	1	179.2	133	72	19	7	96-0	107	3.26	119	.204	.312	79-1	.241	6*	131	14	1.7
1957	†NY A	10	4	.714	27	20	4-1	0	139.2	113	68	12	0	87-0	81	3.74	96	.220	.332	56-0	.250	5*	133	-3	0.2
1958	†NY A	9	6	.600	19	19	5-3	0	114.1	100	43	4	4	52-3	55	3.07	115	.233	.320	49-2	.306	9*	134	7	1.8
1959	NY A	6	7	.462	25	18	3-1	0	124.2	122	65	14	2	76-2	69	4.33	84	.260	.361	47-1	.255	4*	147	-8	-0.4
1960	KC A	1	10	.091	22	15	0	0	83.2	97	55	11	0	42-1	43	5.38	74	.293	.370	29-0	.207	0*	69	-12	-1.4
1961	KC A	1	0	1.000	8	1	0	0	15	21	9	2	1	11-0	13	4.20	100	.344	.452	20-1	.300	1*	127	0	0.1
	Chi A	7	2	.778	25	3	0	2	74.1	64	36	5	1	29-2	53	4.12	95	.231	.306	25-1	.320	3	128	-1	0.2
	Year	8	2	.800	33	4	0	2	89.1	85	42	7	2	40-2	66	4.13	96	.251	.334	45-2	.311	4	128	-1	0.3
1962	†SF N	5	4	.556	49	0	0	11	86.1	83	44	9	2	47-7	58	4.38	87	.256	.352	25-1	.200	1*		-4	-0.5
1963	SF N	7	7	.500	46	0	0	3	62	46	23	8	0	30-9	44	3.05	105	.203	.296	11-1	.182	0		2	0.4
1964	SF N	0	1	.000	6	0	0	0	10.1	10	5	0	0	6-1	6	4.35	82	.256	.356	1-0	.000	-0		-1	-0.1
	Hou N	4	8	.333	30	10	2-1	1	103.1	92	36	4	1	20-4	58	2.26	151	.233	.270	31-1	.097	0*	67	11	1.3
	Year	4	9	.308	36	10	2-1	1	113.2	102	39	4	1	26-5	64	2.45	140	.235	.279	32-1	.094	0	67	10	1.2
1965	Hou N	0	0	—	1	1	0	0	5.1	8	3	0	0	3-1	1	5.06	66	.348	.423	2-0	.000	-0	104	-1	0.0
	Bal A	1	2	.333	27	1	0	1	54	53	22	4	1	20-2	40	2.67	130	.255	.322	11-0	.273	1	101	3	0.3
1967	Chi N	0	0	—	3	0	0	0	4	5	4	1	0	2-0	1	9.00	39	.333	.412	0-0	—	0		-2	-0.1
Total	14	81	91	.471	412	171	44-11	23	1548	1442	728	130	26	725-35	849	3.78	99	.247	.331	596-11	.242	46	109	-1	4.5

LARSON, DAN Daniel James B 7.4.1954 Los Angeles, CA BR/TR 6/180# d7.18

Year	Tm Lg	W	L	Pct	G	GS	CG-Sho	SV-BS	IP	H	R	HR	HB	BB-IB	SO	ERA	AERA	OAV	OOB	AB-SH	AVG	PB	Sup	APR	PW
1976	Hou N	5	8	.385	13	13	5	0-0	92.1	81	40	3	1	28-1	42	3.02	106	.236	.291	31-2	.290	4*	112	0	0.4
1977	Hou N	1	7	.125	32	10	1	1-1	97.2	108	72	13	2	45-2	44	5.81	62	.280	.355	28-0	.214	1*	112	-27	-1.9
1978	Phi N	0	0	—	1	0	0	0-0	1	1	1	1	0	1-0	2	9.00	40	.250	.400	0-0	—	0		-1	0.0
1979	Phi N	1	1	.500	3	3	0	0-0	19	17	9	1	1	9-0	9	4.26	90	.250	.342	5-1	.000	-1	115	-1	-0.1
1980	Phi N	0	5	.000	12	7	0	0-0	45.2	46	24	4	0	24-6	17	3.15	120	.271	.359	13-0	.154	-1	67	1	0.0
1981	Phi N	3	0	1.000	5	4	1	0-0	28	27	13	4	0	15-1	15	4.18	87	.260	.350	9-1	.111	0	214	-1	-0.1

Year	Tm Lg	W	L	Pct	G	GS	CG-Sho	SV-BS	IP	H	R	HR	HB	BB-IB	SO	ERA	AERA	OAV	OOB	AB-SH	AVG	PB	Sup	APR	PW
1982	Chi N	0	4	.000	12	6	0	0-0	39.2	51	30	4	2	18-0	22	5.67	66	.327	.397	11-0	.273	0	90	-9	-0.7
Total	7	10	25	.286	78	43	7	1-1	323.1	331	189	30	6	140-10	151	4.40	81	.269	.342	97-4	.216	4	111	-38	-2.4
LARY, AL Alfred Allen B 9.26.1928 Northport, AL D 7.10.2001 Northport, AL BR/TR 6-3/185# d9.6 b-Frank																									
1954	Chi N	0	0	—	1	1	0	0	6	3	2	0	0	7	4	3.00	140	.150	.370	2-0	.500	0*	85	1	0.1
1962	Chi N	0	1	.000	15	3	0	0	34	42	27	5	0	15-0	18	7.15	58	.311	.370	6-2	.167	0*	56	-9	-0.4
Total	2	0	1	.000	16	4	0	0	40	45	29	5	0	22-0	22	6.52	64	.290	.370	8-2	.250	1	63	-8	-0.3
LARY, FRANK Frank Strong "Mule" or "The Yankee Killer" B 4.10.1930 Northport, AL BR/TR 5-11/180# d9.14																									
1954	Det A	0	0	—	3	0	0	0	3.2	4	1	0	0	3	5	2.45	150	.286	.412	0-0	—	0		1	0.0
1955	Det A	14	15	.483	36	31	16-2	1	235	232	100	10	6	89-3	98	3.10	124	.262	.331	82-5	.195	1	100	16	2.0
1956	Det A	**21**	13	.618	41	**38**	20-3	1	**294**	289	116	20	12	116-4	165	3.15	131	.257	.331	103-6	.184	0	115	32	3.4
1957	Det A	11	16	.407	40	35	12-2	3	237.2	250	111	23	12	72-9	107	3.98	97	.276	.336	73-9	.123	-3	103	-1	-0.5
1958	Det A	16	15	.516	39	34	**19**-3	1	**260.1**	249	91	20	12	68-4	131	2.90	139	.251	.305	88-9	.170	-1	94	32	3.5
1959	Det A	17	10	.630	32	32	11-3	0	223	225	109	23	11	46-4	137	3.55	114	.261	.305	80-8	.125	-2	98	9	0.7
1960	Det A★	15	15	.500	38	**36**	**15**-2	1	**274.1**	262	125	25	19	62-3	149	3.51	113	.249	.301	93-8	.183	4*	104	12	1.5
1961	Det A★	23	9	.719	36	36	**22**-4	0	275.1	252	117	24	6	66-2	146	3.24	127	.243	.290	108-3	.231	4*	119	25	3.3
1962	Det A	2	6	.250	17	14	2-1	0	80	98	59	17	4	21-1	41	5.74	71	.297	.345	24-0	.167	1*	100	-15	-1.3
1963	Det A	4	9	.308	16	14	6	0	107.1	90	40	15	5	26-0	46	3.27	114	.226	.280	35-2	.229	1	107	7	1.0
1964	Det A	0	2	.000	6	4	0	0	18	24	15	3	3	10-1	6	7.00	52	.316	.416	7-0	.000	-1	103	-6	-0.7
	NY N	2	3	.400	13	8	3-1	1	57.1	62	33	7	4	14-2	27	4.55	79	.279	.332	17-1	.118	1	89	-6	-0.5
	Mil N	1	0	1.000	5	2	0	0	12.1	15	7	4	0	0-0	4	4.38	80	.306	.306	3-0	.000	-0	187	-1	-0.1
	Year	3	3	.500	18	10	3-1	1	69.2	77	15	11	4	14-2	31	4.52	79	.284	.328	20-1	.100	0	108	-7	-0.6
1965	NY N	1	3	.250	14	7	0	1	57.1	48	24	2	1	16-0	23	2.98	118	.233	.288	19-0	.211	0	85	3	0.2
	Chi A	1	0	1.000	14	1	0	2	26.2	23	12	4	2	7-2	14	4.05	79	.230	.294	2-1	.500	0	110	-2	-0.1
Total	12	128	116	.525	350	292	126-21	11	2162.1	2123	960	197	97	616-35	1099	3.49	113	.257	.314	734-52	.177	5	105	106	12.4
LASHER, FRED Frederick Walter B 8.19.1941 Poughkeepsie, NY BR/TR 6-4/210# d4.12																									
1963	Min A	0	0	—	11	0	0	0	11.1	12	10	1	0	11-1	10	4.76	76	.286	.426	1-0	.000	-0		-3	-0.1
1967	Det A	2	1	.667	17	0	0	9	30	25	14	1	1	11-1	28	3.90	84	.221	.296	9-1	.111	-0		-2	-0.4
1968	†Det A	5	1	.833	34	0	0	5	48.2	37	19	5	0	22-7	32	3.33	90	.215	.303	9-0	.111	-0		-1	-0.2
1969	Det A	2	1	.667	32	0	0	0-1	44	34	16	5	2	22-1	26	3.07	122	.224	.326	4-1	.000	-0		4	0.2
1970	Det A	1	3	.250	12	0	0	3-1	9	10	6	0	1	12-1	8	5.00	75	.278	.460	1-0	.000	-0		-1	-0.3
	Cle A	1	7	.125	43	1	0	5-4	57.2	57	34	6	3	30-1	44	4.06	98	.264	.354	8-1	.000	-1	45	-3	-0.6
	Year	2	10	.167	55	1	0	8-5	66.2	67	36	6	4	42-2	52	4.18	94	.266	.372	9-1	.000	-1	45	-3	-0.9
1971	Cal A	0	0	—	2	0	0	0-0	1.1	4	4	0	0	2-0	0	27.00	12	.667	.667	0-0	—	0		-4	-0.2
Total	6	11	13	.458	151	1	0	22-6	202	179	103	18	7	110-12	148	3.88	91	.243	.342	32-3	.063	-2	50	-10	-1.6
LASKEY, BILL William Alan B 12.20.1957 Toledo, OH BR/TR 6-5/190# d4.23																									
1982	SF N	13	12	.520	32	31	7-1	0-0	189.1	186	74	14	2	43-2	88	3.14	115	.261	.302	62-4	.129	-2	106	11	1.1
1983	SF N	13	10	.565	25	25	1	0-0	148.1	151	75	18	3	45-4	81	4.19	85	.266	.321	47-1	.106	0*	109	-9	-1.3
1984	SF N	9	14	.391	35	34	2	0-0	207.2	222	112	20	6	50-6	71	4.33	81	.273	.317	63-4	.063	-3	95	-19	-2.4
1985	SF N	5	11	.313	19	19	0	0-0	114	110	55	10	0	39-0	42	3.55	97	.255	.314	30-5	.133	1	73	-3	-0.3
	Mon N	0	5	.000	11	7	0	0-0	34.1	55	36	9	2	14-1	18	9.44	36	.362	.420	7-3	.143	-0	104	-23	-2.7
	Year	5	16	.238	30	26	0	0-0	148.1	165	40	19	2	53-1	60	4.91	70	.283	.342	37-8	.135	0	81	-25	-3.0
1986	SF N	1	1	.500	20	0	0	1-0	27.1	28	14	5	0	13-1	8	4.28	82	.275	.353	1-0	.000	-0		-2	-0.1
1988	Cle A	1	0	1.000	17	0	0	1-0	24.1	32	16	0	0	6-0	17	5.18	80	.320	.349	0-0	—	0		-3	-0.2
Total	6	42	53	.442	159	116	10-1	2-0	745.1	784	382	76	13	210-14	325	4.14	86	.272	.322	210-17	.105	-4	97	-48	-5.9
LASLEY, BILL Willard Almond B 7.13.1902 Gallipolis, OH D 8.21.1990 Seattle, WA BB/TR 6/175# d9.19																									
1924	StL A	0	0	—	2	0	0	0	4	7	3	0	0	2	0	6.75	67	.412	.474	1-0	.000	-0		-1	-0.1
LASORDA, TOM Thomas Charles B 9.22.1927 Norristown, PA BL/TL 5-10/175# d8.5 M21 C4 HF1997																									
1954	Bro N	0	0	—	4	0	0	0	9	8	5	2	0	5	5	5.00	82	.242	.333	1-0	.000	-0		-1	-0.1
1955	Bro N	0	0	—	4	1	0	0	4	5	6	1	1	6-0	4	13.50	30	.313	.500	0-0	—	0	88	-4	-0.2
1956	KC A	0	4	.000	18	5	0	1	45.1	40	38	6	3	45-3	28	6.15	70	.240	.406	13-0	.077	-1*	86	-10	-0.9
Total	3	0	4	.000	26	6	0	1	58.1	53	49	9	4	56-3	37	6.48	66	.245	.404	14-0	.071	-2	87	-15	-1.2
LATHAM, BILL William Carol B 8.29.1960 Birmingham, AL BL/TL 6-2/190# d4.15																									
1985	NY N	1	3	.250	7	3	0	0-0	22.2	21	10	1	0	7-1	10	3.97	87	.250	.304	3-1	.333	1	77	-1	0.0
1986	Min A	0	1	.000	7	2	0	0-1	16	24	14	1	1	6-0	8	7.31	59	.358	.408	0-0	—	0	95	-5	-0.3
Total	2	1	4	.200	14	5	0	0-1	38.2	45	24	2	1	13-1	18	5.35	71	.298	.351	3-1	.333	1	85	-6	-0.3
LATHROP, BILL William George B 8.12.1891 Hanover, WI D 11.20.1958 Janesville, WI BR/TR 6-2.5/184# d7.29																									
1913	Chi A	0	1	.000	6	0	0	0	17	16	11	0	1	12	9	4.24	69	.267	.397	4-0	.000	-1		-2	-0.2
1914	Chi A	1	2	.333	19	1	0	0	47.2	41	20	0	2	19	7	2.64	102	.241	.325	12-1	.000	-1	54	0	-0.1
Total	2	1	3	.250	25	1	0	0	64.2	57	31	0	3	31	16	3.06	90	.248	.345	16-1	.000	-2	54	-2	-0.3
LATMAN, BARRY Arnold Barry B 5.21.1936 Los Angeles, CA BR/TR 6-3/210# d9.10																									
1957	Chi A	1	2	.333	7	2	0	1	12.1	12	11	2	1	13-0	9	8.03	47	.267	.441	1-0	.000	-0	120	-6	-1.1
1958	Chi A	3	0	1.000	13	3	1-1	0	47.2	27	7	1	1	17-0	28	0.76	481	.162	.242	12-1	.083	-0	66	15	0.8
1959	Chi A	8	5	.615	37	21	5-2	0	156	138	71	15	4	72-3	97	3.75	100	.235	.321	47-2	.128	-1	136	1	-0.2
1960	Cle A	7	7	.500	31	20	4	0	147.1	146	78	19	6	72-2	94	4.03	93	.258	.345	41-7	.220	1	120	-6	-0.5
1961	Cle A☆	13	5	.722	45	18	4-2	5	176.2	163	84	23	5	54-3	108	4.02	98	.244	.303	55-1	.073	-3	104	1	-0.4
1962	Cle A	8	13	.381	45	21	7-1	5	179.1	179	96	23	5	72-9	117	4.17	93	.261	.334	53-3	.189	2	82	-7	-0.6
1963	Cle A	7	12	.368	38	21	4-2	2	149.1	146	90	23	6	52-3	133	4.94	73	.257	.323	44-3	.182	2	83	-21	-2.1
1964	LA A	6	10	.375	40	18	2-1	2	138	128	72	15	7	52-6	81	3.85	85	.244	.319	40-2	.125	-1	101	-11	-1.3
1965	Cal A	1	1	.500	18	0	0	0	31.2	30	12	3	0	16-3	18	2.84	120	.254	.343	2-0	.000	-0		2	0.0
1966	Hou N	2	7	.222	31	9	1-1	1	103	88	42	5	7	35-4	74	2.71	126	.233	.310	26-0	.154	0	57	6	0.5
1967	Hou N	3	6	.333	39	1	0	0	77.2	73	42	13	6	34-2	70	4.52	73	.252	.338	11-1	.091	-1	53	-9	-1.1
Total	11	59	68	.465	344	134	28-10	16	1219	1130	605	142	48	489-35	829	3.91	94	.246	.323	332-20	.145	-1	101	-35	-6.0
LATTIMORE, BILL William Hershel "Slothful Bill" B 5.25.1884 Roxton, TX D 10.30.1919 Colorado Springs, CO BL/TL 5-9/165# d4.17																									
1908	Cle A	1	2	.333	4	4	1-1	0	24	24	16	0	0	7	5	4.50	53	.247	.298	9-2	.444	1	150	-5	-0.5
LAUER, CHUCK John Charles B 4.5.1865 Pittsburgh, PA D 5.14.1915 Buffalo, NY TR d7.17 ▲																									
1884	Pit AA	0	2	.000	3	3	2	0	19	23	25	0	3	9	8	7.58	44	.277	.368	44	.114	-1*	85	-9	-0.8
LAUZERIQUE, GEORGE George Albert B 7.22.1947 Havana, Cuba BR/TR 6-1/180# d9.17																									
1967	KC A	0	2	.000	3	2	0	0	16	11	4	2	1	6-0	10	2.25	142	.193	.281	3-0	.000	-0	27	2	0.3
1968	Oak A	0	0	—	1	0	0	0	1	0	0	0	0	1-0	0	0.00	—	.000	.333	0-0	—	0		0	0.0
1969	Oak A	3	4	.429	19	8	1	0-1	61.1	58	32	14	2	27-0	39	4.70	73	.250	.331	20-0	.100	-1	100	-7	-0.8
1970	Mil A	1	2	.333	11	4	1	0-1	35	41	27	7	1	14-1	24	6.94	55	.295	.357	10-3	.200	1	176	-11	-0.7
Total	4	4	8	.333	34	14	2	0-2	113.1	110	63	23	4	48-1	73	5.00	70	.256	.333	33-3	.121	-0	114	-16	-1.2
LAVELLE, GARY Gary Robert B 1.3.1949 Scranton, PA BB/TL 6-1/200# d9.10																									
1974	SF N	0	3	.000	10	0	0	0-0	16.2	14	7	1	0	10-2	12	2.16	176	.222	.329	2-2	.000	-0		2	0.3
1975	SF N	6	3	.667	65	0	0	8-5	82.1	80	30	3	3	48-12	51	2.95	129	.260	.364	9-0	.111	-0		8	1.0
1976	SF N	10	6	.625	65	0	0	12-8	110.1	102	37	6	2	52-10	71	2.69	135	.246	.331	13-2	.077	-1		12	1.9
1977	SF N★	7	7	.500	73	0	0	20-8	118.1	106	35	4	0	37-18	93	2.05	191	.239	.295	14-0	.000	-2		23	3.2
1978	SF N	13	10	.565	67	0	0	14-10	97.2	96	41	3	2	44-11	63	3.32	104	.263	.341	15-1	.067	-1		1	0.1
1979	SF N	7	9	.438	70	0	0	20-9	96.2	86	31	5	2	42-15	80	2.51	139	.247	.327	4-2	.250	0		11	2.3
1980	SF N	6	8	.429	62	0	0	9-7	100	106	43	4	0	36-11	66	3.42	104	.275	.333	11-3	.000	-1		2	0.1
1981	SF N	2	6	.250	34	3	0	4-3	65.2	58	33	3	2	23-4	45	3.84	89	.244	.316	11-2	.273	1	95	-4	-0.3
1982	SF N	10	7	.588	68	0	0	8-5	104.2	97	35	6	1	29-12	76	2.67	135	.247	.298	13-2	.154	0		11	2.1

Year	Tm Lg	W	L	Pct	G	GS	CG-Sho	SV-BS	IP	H	R	HR	HB	BB-IB	SO	ERA	AERA	OAV	OOB	AB-SH	AVG	PB	Sup	APR	PW
1983	SF N☆	7	4	.636	56	0	0	20-9	87	73	33	4	0	19-8	68	2.59	137	.229	.270	14-0	.000	-2		8	1.2
1984	SF N	5	4	.556	77	0	0	12-7	101	92	34	5	1	42-14	71	2.76	127	.246	.321	5-0	.000	-0		9	0.9
1985	†Tor A	5	7	.417	69	0	0	8-8	72.2	54	30	5	0	36-5	50	3.10	136	.214	.310	0-0	—	0		8	1.3
1987	Tor A	2	3	.400	23	0	0	1-0	27.2	36	20	2	0	19-4	17	5.53	82	.313	.407	0-0	—	0		-4	-0.6
	Oak A	0	0	—	6	0	0	0-1	4.1	4	4	0	0	3-0	6	8.31	50	.267	.368	0-0	—	0		-2	-0.1
	Year	2	3	.400	29	0	0	1-1	32	40	28	2	0	22-4	23	5.91	75	.308	.403	0-0	—	0		-6	-0.7
Total	13	80	77	.510	745	3	0	136-80	1085	1004	413	51	13	440-126	769	2.93	125	.249	.322	111-14	.081	-6	95	85	13.4
LAVENDER, JIMMY James Sanford B 3.25.1884 Barnesville, GA D 1.12.1960 Cartersville, GA BR/TR 5-11/165# d4.23																									
1912	Chi N	16	13	.552	42	31	15-3	3	251.2	240	116	8	10	89	109	3.04	109	.257	.328	87-3	.149	-3	105	5	0.3
1913	Chi N	10	14	.417	40	20	10	2	204	206	111	6	13	98	91	3.66	87	.267	.359	68-3	.118	-4	116	-12	-1.9
1914	Chi N	11	11	.500	37	28	11-2	0	214.1	191	106	11	11	87	87	3.07	91	.247	.331	63-3	.175	2	103	-5	-0.1
1915	Chi N	10	16	.385	41	24	13-1	4	220	178	77	5	10	67	117	2.58	108	.228	.298	67-2	.134	-2	89	6	0.7
1916	Chi N	10	14	.417	36	25	9-4	2	188	163	76	3	9	62	91	2.82	103	.240	.312	53-3	.151	-2	78	2	0.0
1917	Phi N	6	8	.429	28	14	7	1	129.1	119	61	5	3	44	52	3.55	79	.250	.317	36-2	.139	-1	100	-8	-1.1
Total	6	63	76	.453	224	142	65-10	12	1207.1	1097	547	38	56	447	547	3.09	97	.249	.325	374-16	.144	-9	98	-12	-2.1
LAW, RON Ronald David B 3.14.1946 Hamilton, ON, CAN BR/TR 6-2/165# d6.29																									
1969	Cle A	3	4	.429	35	1	0	1-2	52.1	68	34	2	2	34-5	29	4.99	76	.325	.419	7-0	.143	-0	141	-7	-0.9
LAW, VERN Vernon Sanders "Deacon" B 3.12.1930 Meridian, ID BR/TR 6-2/195# d6.11 Mil 1952 C2 s-Vance																									
1950	Pit N	7	9	.438	27	17	5-1	0	128	137	83	11	4	49	57	4.92	89	.272	.341	41-0	.073	-2	104	-9	-1.2
1951	Pit N	6	9	.400	28	14	2-1	2	114	109	66	9	6	51	41	4.50	94	.253	.341	32-3	.344	5	85	-3	0.1
1954	Pit N	9	13	.409	39	18	7	3	161.2	201	109	20	3	56	57	5.51	76	.311	.362	52-6	.231	3*	70	-21	-2.1
1955	Pit N	10	10	.500	43	24	8-1	1	200.2	221	98	19	1	61-7	82	3.81	108	.280	.331	63-2	.254	3*	88	7	1.0
1956	Pit N	8	16	.333	39	32	6	2	195.2	218	110	24	6	49-10	60	4.32	87	.281	.326	57-3	.175	1	98	-13	-1.4
1957	Pit N	10	8	.556	31	25	9-3	1	172.2	172	72	18	2	32-8	55	2.87	132	.256	.290	63-4	.190	1*	110	14	1.5
1958	Pit N	14	12	.538	35	29	6-1	3	202.1	235	103	16	1	39-5	56	3.96	98	.297	.326	62-7	.194	6*	119	-4	0.1
1959	Pit N	18	9	.667	34	33	20-2	1	266	245	91	25	2	53-11	110	2.98	130	.243	.281	96-7	.167	1*	106	**31**	3.1
1960	†Pit N★	20	9	.690	35	35	**18**-3	0	271.2	266	104	25	4	40-8	120	3.08	122	.257	.286	94-7	.181	3	120	19	2.4
1961	Pit N	3	4	.429	11	10	1	0	59.1	72	33	10	1	18-3	20	4.70	85	.305	.355	19-2	.263	1	120	-4	-0.2
1962	Pit N	10	7	.588	23	20	7-2	0	139.1	156	67	21	1	27-4	78	3.94	100	.276	.310	45-7	.311	5	128	2	0.7
1963	Pit N	4	5	.444	18	12	1-1	0	76.2	91	45	11	0	13-0	31	4.93	67	.296	.321	23-1	.217	1*	118	-12	-1.2
1964	Pit N	12	13	.480	35	29	7-5	0	192	203	85	18	1	32-6	93	3.61	97	.270	.299	61-5	.311	8*	110	-1	0.7
1965	Pit N	17	9	.654	29	28	13-4	0	217.1	182	66	17	3	35-2	101	2.15	163	.229	.261	82-4	.244	4*	120	31	4.3
1966	Pit N	12	8	.600	31	28	8-4	0	177.2	203	85	19	4	24-1	88	4.05	88	.292	.318	66-4	.242	5*	136	-8	-0.2
1967	Pit N	2	6	.250	25	10	1	0	97	122	57	5	1	18-9	43	4.18	81	.308	.335	27-1	.111	-0*	107	-11	-0.9
Total	16	162	147	.524	483	364	119-28	13	2672	2833	1274	268	40	597-74	1092	3.77	101	.272	.312	883-63	.216	45	109	18	6.7
LAWRENCE, BRIAN Brian Michael B 5.14.1976 Fort Collins, CO BR/TR 6/195# d4.15																									
2001	SD N	5	5	.500	27	15	1	0-0	114.2	107	53	10	5	34-5	84	3.45	116	.244	.304	26-2	.115	-0	88	6	0.5
2002	SD N	12	12	.500	35	31	2-2	0-0	210	230	97	16	11	52-6	149	3.69	102	.281	.331	63-3	.095	-1	103	1	0.1
2003	SD N	10	15	.400	33	33	1	0-0	210.2	206	106	27	11	57-8	116	4.19	94	.258	.314	67-2	.224	5	101	-7	-0.1
Total	3	27	32	.458	95	79	4-2	0-0	535.1	543	256	53	27	143-19	349	3.83	101	.264	.318	156-7	.154	4	99	0	0.5
LAWRENCE, BROOKS Brooks Ulysses "Bull" B 1.30.1925 Springfield, OH D 4.27.2000 Springfield, OH BR/TR 6/205# d6.24																									
1954	StL N	15	6	.714	35	18	8	1	158.2	141	71	17	8	72	72	3.74	110	.243	.333	53-1	.189	0	125	8	1.0
1955	StL N	3	8	.273	46	10	2-1	1	96	102	73	11	7	58-7	52	6.56	62	.278	.384	21-2	.095	-2	99	-25	-2.7
1956	Cin N☆	19	10	.655	49	30	11-1	0	218.2	210	109	26	2	71-4	96	3.99	100	.256	.315	70-6	.157	-1	131	-1	0.0
1957	Cin N	16	13	.552	49	32	12-1	4	250.1	234	111	26	8	76-5	121	3.52	117	.247	.306	82-6	.171	-0	90	14	1.5
1958	Cin N	8	13	.381	46	23	6-2	5	181	194	89	12	4	55-7	74	4.13	100	.275	.330	53-1	.113	-2	98	1	-0.1
1959	Cin N	7	12	.368	43	14	3	10	128.1	144	74	17	4	45-9	64	4.77	85	.281	.343	40-2	.150	-1	99	-9	-1.4
1960	Cin N	1	0	1.000	7	0	0	1	7.2	9	12	1	0	8-1	2	10.57	36	.310	.447	0-0	—	0		-6	-0.9
Total	7	69	62	.527	275	127	42-5	22	1040.2	1034	539	110	33	385-33	481	4.25	96	.261	.330	319-18	.154	-5	108	-18	-2.6
LAWRENCE, BOB Robert Andrew "Larry" B 12.14.1899 Brooklyn, NY D 11.6.1983 Jamaica, NY BR/TR 5-11/180# d7.19																									
1924	Chi A	0	0	—	1	0	0	0	1	1	1	0	0	1	1	9.00	46	.250	.400	0-0	—	0		0	0.0
LAWRENCE, SEAN Sean Christopher B 9.2.1970 Oak Park, IL BL/TL 6-4/215# d8.25																									
1998	Pit N	2	1	.667	7	3	0	0-0	19.2	25	16	4	0	10-0	12	7.32	59	.313	.380	6-0	.000	-1	121	-6	-0.8
LAWSON, ROXIE Alfred Voyle B 4.13.1906 Donnellson, IA D 4.9.1977 Stockport, IA BR/TR 6/170# d8.3																									
1930	Cle A	1	2	.333	7	4	2	0	33.2	46	27	1	0	23	10	6.15	79	.324	.418	11-1	.091	-1	129	-4	-0.4
1931	Cle A	0	2	.000	17	3	0	0	55.2	72	50	5	0	36	20	7.60	61	.304	.396	14-0	.143	-0	85	-15	-0.7
1933	Det A	0	1	.000	4	2	0	0	16	17	16	2	0	17	6	7.31	59	.270	.425	5-0	.000	-1	118	-5	-0.3
1935	Det A	3	1	.750	7	4	4-2	2	40	34	11	3	0	24	16	1.57	265	.233	.341	13-1	.308	1	109	11	1.2
1936	Det A	8	6	.571	41	8	3	3	128	139	87	13	4	71	34	5.48	90	.281	.376	45-0	.222	1	140	-6	-0.5
1937	Det A	18	7	.720	37	29	15	1	217.1	236	141	17	1	115	68	5.26	89	.271	.357	81-5	.259	3	118	-13	-1.0
1938	Det A	8	9	.471	27	16	5	1	127	154	85	13	0	82	39	5.46	92	.299	.395	45-1	.044	-5	81	-6	-1.1
1939	Det A	1	1	.500	2	1	0	0	11.1	7	7	1	0	7	4	4.76	103	.167	.286	4-1	.000	-1	108	0	0.0
	StL A	3	7	.300	36	14	5	0	150.2	181	93	10	2	83	43	5.32	92	.307	.394	43-5	.186	-1*	80	-4	-0.3
	Year	4	8	.333	38	15	5	0	162	188	97	11	2	90	47	5.28	92	.297	.387	47-6	.170	-2	82	-4	-0.3
1940	StL A	5	3	.625	30	2	0	4	72	77	45	5	0	54	18	5.13	89	.278	.396	22-0	.045	-3	96	-4	-0.6
Total	9	47	39	.547	208	83	34-2	11	851.2	963	562	70	7	512	258	5.37	89	.285	.380	283-14	.173	-6	105	-46	-3.7
LAWSON, AL Alfred William B 3.24.1869 London, England D 11.29.1954 San Antonio, TX BR/TR 5-11/161# d5.13																									
1890	Bos N	0	1	.000	1	1	1	0	9	12	7	0	0	4	1	4.00	94	.308	.372	2	.000	-0	34	-1	-0.1
	Pit N	0	2	.000	2	2	1	0	10	15	20	0	0	10	2	9.00	37	.333	.455	4	.000	-1	105	-8	-1.1
	Year	0	3	.000	3	3	2	0	19	27	26	0	0	14	3	6.63	53	.321	.418	6	.000	-1	78	-9	-1.2
LAWSON, BOB Robert Baker B 8.23.1875 Lynchburg, VA D 10.28.1952 Durham, NC BR/TR 5-10/170# d5.7																									
1901	Bos N	2	2	.500	6	4	4	0	46	45	28	0	3	28	12	3.33	109	.254	.365	27-2	.148	-0*	103	0	0.0
1902	Bal A	0	2	.000	3	2	1	0	13	21	11	0	2	3	5	4.85	78	.362	.413	6-0	.167	-0	76	-2	-0.2
Total	2	2	4	.333	9	6	5	0	59	66	39	0	5	31	17	3.66	100	.281	.376	33-2	.152	-1	94	-2	-0.2
LAWSON, STEVE Steven George B 12.28.1950 Oakland, CA BR/TL 6-1/175# d8.3																									
1972	Tex A	0	0	—	13	0	0	1-1	16	13	6	1	0	10-0	13	2.81	107	.213	.324	1-0	1.000	0		0	0.1
LAXTON, BRETT Brett William B 10.5.1973 Stratford, NJ BL/TR 6-2/205# d6.21 f-Bill																									
1999	Oak A	0	1	.000	3	2	0	0-0	9.2	12	12	1	2	7-1	9	7.45	62	.316	.420	0-0	—	0	110	-5	-0.4
2000	KC A	0	1	.000	6	1	0	0-0	16.2	23	15	0	2	10-1	14	8.10	63	.348	.449	0-0	—	0	0	-5	-0.3
Total	2	0	2	.000	9	3	0	0-0	26.1	35	27	1	4	17-2	23	7.86	63	.337	.438	0-0	—	0	69	-10	-0.7
LAXTON, BILL William Harry B 1.5.1948 Camden, NJ BL/TL 6-1/190# d9.15 s-Brett																									
1970	Phi N	0	0	—	2	0	0	0-0	2	2	3	2	1	2-0	2	13.50	30	.250	.455	0-0	—	0		-2	-0.1
1971	SD N	0	2	.000	18	0	0	0-0	27.2	32	25	4	1	26-0	23	6.83	48	.305	.444	0-0	—	0		-11	-0.8
1974	SD N	0	1	.000	30	1	0	0-0	44.2	37	22	5	3	38-8	40	4.03	89	.226	.375	5-0	.200	0	49	-2	-0.1
1976	Det A	0	5	.000	26	3	0	2-1	94.2	77	49	13	6	51-1	74	4.09	91	.221	.329	0-0	—	0	24	-4	-0.3
1977	Sea A	3	2	.600	43	0	0	3-1	72.2	62	44	10	4	39-5	49	4.95	83	.233	.335	0-0	—	0		-6	-0.5
	Cle A	0	0	—	2	0	0	0-0	1.2	2	1	0	0	2-0	1	5.40	73	.286	.444	0-0	—	0		0	0.0
	Year	3	2	.600	45	0	0	3-1	74.1	64	46	10	4	41-5	50	4.96	83	.234	.339	0-0	—	0		-6	-0.5
Total	5	3	10	.231	121	4	0	5-2	243.1	212	144	34	15	158-14	189	4.73	80	.236	.356	5-0	.200	0	29	-25	-1.8
LAYANA, TIM Timothy Joseph B 3.2.1964 Inglewood, CA D 6.26.1999 Bakersfield, CA BR/TR 6-2/195# d4.9																									
1990	Cin N	5	3	.625	55	0	0	2-0	80	71	33	7	2	44-5	53	3.49	113	.244	.344	5-0	.000	-1		4	0.4
1991	Cin N	0	2	.000	22	0	0	0-1	20.2	23	18	1	0	11-0	14	6.97	55	.277	.362	1-0	.000	-0*		-7	-0.6

Year	Tm Lg	W	L	Pct	G	GS	CG-Sho	SV-BS	IP	H	R	HR	HB	BB-IB	SO	ERA	AERA	OAV	OOB	AB-SH	AVG	PB	Sup	APR	PW
1993	SF N	0	0	—	1	0	0	0-0	2	7	5	1	0	1-1	1	22.50	17	.538	.571	0-1	—	0		-4	-0.2
Total	3	5	5	.500	78	0	0	2-1	102.2	101	56	9	2	56-6	68	4.56	86	.261	.355	6-1	.000	-1		-7	-0.4
LAZAR, DANNY John Daniel B 11.14.1943 East Chicago, IN BL/TL 6-1/190# d6.21																									
1968	Chi A	0	1	.000	8	1	0	0	13.1	14	6	1	0	4-0	11	4.05	75	.269	.316	2-0	.000	0	29	-1	-0.1
1969	Chi A	0	0	—	9	3	0	0-0	20.2	21	15	5	1	11-2	9	6.53	59	.280	.371	4-1	.000	-0	107	-5	-0.3
Total	2	0	1	.000	17	4	0	0-0	34	35	21	6	1	15-2	20	5.56	63	.276	.349	6-1	.000	-0	94	-6	-0.4
LAZORKO, JACK Jack Thomas B 3.30.1956 Hoboken, NJ BR/TR 5-11/200# d6.4																									
1984	Mil A	0	1	.000	15	1	0	1-0	39.2	37	19	7	1	22-2	24	4.31	89	.245	.343	0-0	—	0	70	-1	0.0
1985	Sea A	0	0	—	15	0	0	1-0	20.1	23	10	1	3	8-1	7	3.54	119	.291	.378	0-0	—	0		1	0.1
1986	Det A	0	0	—	3	0	0	0-0	6.2	8	3	0	0	4-1	3	4.05	102	.296	.387	0-0	—	0		0	0.0
1987	Cal A	5	6	.455	26	11	2	0-0	117.2	108	68	20	2	44-5	55	4.59	94	.248	.318	0-0	—	0	100	-4	-0.2
1988	Cal A	0	1	.000	10	3	0	0-0	37.2	37	15	5	1	16-0	19	3.35	116	.255	.331	0-0	—	0	118	2	0.1
Total	5	5	8	.385	69	15	2	2-0	222	213	115	33	7	94-9	108	4.22	98	.254	.333	0-0	—	0	103	-2	0.0
LEA, CHARLIE Charles William B 12.25.1956 Orleans, France BR/TR 6-4/197# d6.12																									
1980	Mon N	7	5	.583	21	19	0	0-0	104	103	51	5	2	55-4	56	3.72	96	.262	.353	37-0	.081	-2	115	-3	-0.6
1981	Mon N	5	4	.556	16	11	2-2	0-0	64.1	63	34	4	1	26-0	31	4.62	76	.268	.341	15-4	.133	-0	95	-7	-0.9
1982	Mon N	12	10	.545	27	27	4-2	0-0	177.2	145	70	16	0	56-6	115	3.24	113	.222	.283	65-1	.123	-1	108	9	0.9
1983	Mon N	16	11	.593	33	33	8-4	0-0	222	195	87	15	1	84-4	137	3.12	115	.238	.307	70-12	.114	-2	107	11	1.0
1984	Mon N★	15	10	.600	30	30	8	0-0	224.1	198	82	19	3	68-3	123	2.89	119	.239	.296	72-12	.111	-3	100	13	1.1
1987	Mon N	0	1	.000	1	1	0	0-0	1	4	4	1	0	2-0	1	36.00	12	.571	.667	0-0	—	0	0	-3	-0.5
1988	Min A	7	7	.500	24	23	0	0-0	130	156	79	19	5	50-2	72	4.85	84	.301	.364	0-0	—	0	123	-13	-1.2
Total	7	62	48	.564	152	144	22-8	0-0	923.1	864	407	79	12	341-19	535	3.54	102	.250	.317	259-29	.112	-7	108	7	-0.2
LEACH, TERRY Terry Hester B 3.13.1954 Selma, AL BR/TR 6/215# d8.12																									
1981	NY N	1	1	.500	21	1	0	0-1	35.1	26	11	2	0	12-1	16	2.55	137	.205	.273	1-0	.000	1	76	4	0.3
1982	NY N	2	1	.667	21	1	1-1	3-1	45.1	46	22	2	0	18-5	30	4.17	87	.271	.339	8-1	.125	-0	24	-2	-0.2
1985	NY N	3	4	.429	22	4	1-1	1-0	55.2	48	19	3	1	14-3	30	2.91	119	.235	.285	12-1	.167	1	204	4	0.6
1986	NY N	0	0	—	6	0	0	0-0	6.2	6	3	0	0	3-0	4	2.70	131	.222	.300	0-0	—	0		0	0.0
1987	NY N	11	1	.917	44	12	1-1	0-2	131.1	132	54	14	1	29-5	61	3.22	117	.262	.303	33-4	.061	-2	153	8	0.6
1988	†NY N	7	2	.778	52	0	0	3-1	92	95	32	5	3	24-4	51	2.54	127	.268	.318	14-0	.143	0		6	0.8
1989	NY N	0	0	—	10	0	0	0-0	21.1	19	11	1	1	4-0	2	4.22	78	.244	.282	4-0	.000	-0		-2	-0.1
	KC A	5	6	.455	30	3	0	0-0	73.2	78	46	4	1	36-9	34	4.15	93	.278	.357	0-0	—	0	63	-6	-0.8
1990	Min A	2	5	.286	55	0	0	2-4	81.2	84	31	2	1	21-10	46	3.20	130	.268	.315	0-0	—	0		9	0.7
1991	†Min A	1	2	.333	50	0	0	0-2	67.1	82	28	3	0	14-5	32	3.61	118	.299	.332	0-0	—	0		5	0.3
1992	Chi A	6	5	.545	51	0	0	0-0	73.2	57	17	2	4	20-5	22	1.95	198	.215	.279	0-0	—	0		16	2.3
1993	Chi A	0	0	—	14	0	0	1-0	16	15	5	0	1	2-1	3	2.81	149	.250	.281	0-0	—	0		3	0.1
Total	11	38	27	.585	376	21	3-3	10-11	700	688	279	38	13	197-48	331	3.15	119	.259	.311	72-6	.097	-1	138	45	4.6
LEAL, LUIS Luis Enrique (Alvarado) B 3.21.1957 Barquisimeto, Venezuela BR/TR 6-3/205# d5.25																									
1980	Tor A	3	4	.429	13	10	1	0-0	59.2	72	35	6	1	31-2	26	4.53	95	.314	.394	0-0	—	0	114	-2	-0.2
1981	Tor A	7	13	.350	29	19	3	1-0	129.2	127	63	8	5	44-5	71	3.68	107	.254	.317	0-0	—	0	69	3	0.4
1982	Tor A	12	15	.444	38	38	10	0-0	249.2	250	113	24	3	79-3	111	3.93	114	.262	.317	0-0	—	0	86	17	1.7
1983	Tor A	13	12	.520	35	35	7-1	0-0	217.1	216	113	23	6	65-5	116	4.31	100	.257	.314	0-0	—	0	108	1	0.0
1984	Tor A	13	8	.619	35	35	6-2	0-0	222.1	221	106	27	4	77-6	134	3.89	106	.258	.320	0-0	—	0	115	5	0.4
1985	Tor A	3	6	.333	15	14	0	0-0	67.1	82	46	13	3	24-3	33	5.75	73	.303	.361	0-0	—	0	86	-11	-1.2
Total	6	51	58	.468	165	151	27-3	1-0	946	968	476	101	22	320-24	491	4.14	103	.265	.325	0-0	—	0	97	13	1.1
LEAR, KING Charles Bernard B 1.23.1891 Greencastle, PA D 10.31.1976 Waynesboro, PA BR/TR 6/175# d5.2																									
1914	Cin N	1	2	.333	17	4	3-1	1	55.2	55	23	3	2	19	20	3.07	95	.271	.339	16-0	.188	1	79	1	0.1
1915	Cin N	6	10	.375	40	15	9	0	167.2	169	73	7	6	45	46	3.01	95	.270	.324	47-7	.170	-1	92	-3	-0.6
Total	2	7	12	.368	57	19	12-1	1	223.1	224	96	10	8	64	66	3.02	95	.270	.328	63-7	.175	-0	89	-2	-0.5
LEARY, FRANK Francis Patrick B 2.26.1881 Wayland, MA D 10.4.1907 Natick, MA TR 5-10/190# d4.30																									
1907	Cin N	0	1	.000	2	1	0	0	8	7	2	0	0	6	4	1.13	231	.269	.406	2-0	.000	-0	302	1	0.1
LEARY, JACK John J. B 1858 New Haven, CT TL 5-11/186# d8.21 ▲																									
1880	Bos N	0	1	.000	1	1	0	0	3	8	5	0		0	1	15.00	15	.727	.727	3	.000	-0	43	-3	-0.5
1881	Det N	0	2	.000	2	2	1	0	13	13	6	0		2	2	4.15	70	.255	.283	11	.273	1*	9	0	0.0
1882	Pit AA	1	0	1.000	3	2	1	0	18.2	28	22	0		3	5	6.75	39	.326	.348	257	.292	1*	197	-7	-0.3
	Bal AA	2	1	.667	3	3	3	0	26	29	22	1		8	2	1.04	265	.264	.314	18	.222	0*	137	0	0.1
	Year	3	1	.750	6	5	4	0	44.2	57	29	1		11	7	3.43	79	.291	.329	275	.287	1	160	-7	-0.2
1884	Alt U	0	3	.000	3	3	2	0	24	31	30	0		2	7	5.25	51	.292	.306	33	.091	-2*	43	-7	-0.8
	CP U	0	2	.000	2	1	1	0	10	14	14	0		5	6	5.40	45	.311	.380	40	.175	-1*	52	-4	-0.6
	Year	0	5	.000	5	4	3	0	34	45	17	0		7	13	5.29	49	.298	.329	73	.137	-3	45	-11	-1.4
Total	4	3	9	.250	14	12	8	0	94.2	123	99	1		20	23	4.56	59	.301	.333	362	.254	-2	84	-21	-2.1
LEARY, TIM Timothy James B 12.23.1958 Santa Monica, CA BR/TR 6-3/205# d4.12																									
1981	NY N	0	0	—	1	1	0	0-0	2	0	0	0	0	1-0	3	0.00	—	.000	.143	1-0	.000	-0	51	1	0.0
1983	NY N	1	1	.500	2	2	1	0-0	10.2	15	10	0	0	4-0	9	3.38	108	.319	.365	3-0	.333	0	146	-2	-0.3
1984	NY N	3	3	.500	20	7	0	0-0	53.2	61	28	2	2	18-3	29	4.02	88	.285	.343	10-3	.300	2	82	-3	-0.2
1985	Mil A	1	4	.200	5	5	0	0-0	33.1	40	18	5	1	8-0	29	4.05	103	.296	.340	0-0	—	0	44	0	0.0
1986	Mil A	12	12	.500	33	30	3-2	0-0	188.1	216	97	20	7	53-4	110	4.21	103	.289	.339	0-0	—	0	93	4	0.5
1987	LA N	3	11	.214	39	12	0	1-1	107.2	121	62	15	2	36-5	61	4.76	83	.285	.343	23-3	.304	2	80	-9	-0.8
1988	†LA N	17	11	.607	35	34	9-6	0-0	228.2	201	87	13	6	56-4	180	2.91	115	.234	.284	67-13	.269	6*	93	10	1.9
1989	LA N	6	7	.462	19	17	2	0-0	117.1	107	45	9	2	37-7	59	3.38	101	.247	.306	33-6	.061	-2	75	3	0.0
	Cin N	2	7	.222	14	14	0	0-0	89.2	98	39	8	3	31-8	64	3.71	97	.278	.338	26-3	.192	2	67	0	0.2
	Year	8	14	.364	33	31	2	0-0	207	205	42	17	5	68-15	123	3.52	99	.261	.321	59-9	.119	-1	71	2	0.2
1990	NY A	9	19	.321	31	31	6-1	0-0	208	202	105	18	7	78-1	138	4.11	97	.257	.328	0-0	—	0	70	-3	-0.3
1991	NY A	4	10	.286	28	18	1	0-0	120.2	150	89	20	4	57-1	83	6.49	64	.312	.388	0-0	—	0	105	-28	-2.8
1992	NY A	5	6	.455	18	15	2	0-0	97	84	62	9	4	57-2	34	5.57	70	.245	.354	0-0	—	0	98	-16	-1.6
	Sea A	3	4	.429	8	8	1	0-0	44	47	27	3	5	30-3	12	4.91	81	.280	.394	0-0	—	0	106	-5	-0.6
	Year	8	10	.444	26	23	3	0-0	141	131	32	12	9	87-5	46	5.36	74	.256	.367	0-0	—	0	101	-19	-2.2
1993	Sea A	11	9	.550	33	27	0	0-1	169.1	202	104	21	8	58-5	68	5.05	87	.300	.362	0-0	—	0	103	-12	-1.2
1994	Tex A	1	1	.500	6	3	0	0-0	21	26	19	4	1	11-2	9	8.14	59	.306	.380	0-0	—	0	95	-7	-0.5
Total	13	78	105	.426	292	224	25-9	1-2	1491.1	1570	792	147	52	535-45	888	4.36	90	.273	.338	163-28	.221	9	89	-67	-5.7
LeCLAIR, GEORGE George Lewis "Frenchy" B 10.18.1886 Milton, VT D 10.10.1918 Farnham, PQ, CAN BR/TR 5-9/170# d6.5																									
1914	Pit F	5	2	.714	22	7	5-1	0	103.1	99	52	0	1	25	49	4.01	72	.262	.309	34-1	.147	-2	109	-10	-0.9
1915	Pit F	1	2	.333	14	3	1	1	45.2	43	20	1	0	13	10	3.35	81	.253	.306	13-0	.154	-1	232	-3	-0.3
	Buf F	0	0	—	1	0	0	0	3	4	2	0	0	1	2	6.00	47	.333	.385	0-0	—	0		-1	-0.1
	Bal F	1	8	.111	18	9	6-1	1	84	76	43	2	0	22	30	2.46	116	.246	.296	24-2	.083	-2	68	-2	-0.4
	Year	2	10	.167	33	12	7-1	2	132.2	123	46	3	0	36	42	2.85	99	.251	.302	37-2	.108	-3	108	-4	-0.8
Total	2	7	12	.368	55	19	12-2	2	236	222	117	3	1	61	91	3.36	85	.255	.305	71-3	.127	-5	108	-16	-1.7
LEDBETTER, RAZOR Ralph Overton B 12.8.1894 Rutherford College, NC D 2.1.1969 W.Palm Beach, FL BR/TR 6-3/190# d4.16																									
1915	Det A	0	0	—	1	0	0	0	1	1	0	0	0	0	0	0.00	—	.333	.333	0-0	—	0		0	0.0
LEDEZMA, WIL Wilfredo Jose B 1.21.1981 Guarico, Venezuela BL/TL 6-3/150# d4.2																									
2003	Det A	3	7	.300	34	8	0	0-1	84	99	55	12	3	35-3	49	5.79	75	.297	.365	0-0	—	0	59	-12	-1.3
LEE, CLIFF Clifton Phifer B 8.30.1978 Benton, AR BL/TL 6-3/190# d9.15																									
2002	Cle A	0	1	.000	2	2	0	0-0	10.1	6	2	0	0	8-1	6	1.74	253	.171	.326	0-0	—	0	21	3	0.3

Year	Tm Lg	W	L	Pct	G	GS	CG-Sho	SV-BS	IP	H	R	HR	HB	BB-IB	SO	ERA	AERA	OAV	OOB	AB-SH	AVG	PB	Sup	APR	PW
2003	Cle A	3	3	.500	9	9	0	0-0	52.1	41	28	7	2	20-1	44	3.61	122	.220	.301	0-0	—	0	99	3	0.3
Total	2	3	4	.429	11	11	0	0-0	62.2	47	30	7	2	28-2	50	3.30	134	.213	.306	0-0	—	0	85	6	0.6
LEE, COREY Corey Wayne B 12.26.1974 Raleigh, NC BB/TL 6-2/180# d8.24																									
1999	Tex A	0	1	.000	1	0	0	0-0	1	2	3	1	0	1-0	0	27.00	19	.400	.500	0-0	—	0		-2	-0.3
LEE, DAVID David Emmer B 3.12.1973 Pittsburgh, PA BR/TR 6-1/200# d5.22																									
1999	Col N	3	2	.600	36	0	0	0-0	49	43	21	4	4	29-1	38	3.67	158	.247	.364	5-0	.200	-0		9	0.8
2000	Col N	0	0	—	7	0	0	1-0	5.2	10	9	3	1	6-0	6	11.12	52	.357	.486	0-0	—	0		-3	-0.2
2001	SD N	1	0	1.000	41	0	0	0-0	48.2	52	20	6	6	27-1	42	3.70	108	.278	.385	1-0	.000	-0		3	0.1
2003	Cle A	1	0	1.000	8	0	0	0-0	7.2	4	4	1	0	6-1	7	4.70	94	.143	.294	0-0	—	0		0	0.0
Total	4	5	2	.714	92	0	0	1-0	111	109	54	14	11	68-3	93	4.14	119	.261	.377	6-0	.167	-0		9	0.7
LEE, DON Donald Edward B 2.26.1934 Globe, AZ BR/TR 6-4/210# d4.23 Mil 1970 f-Thornton																									
1957	Det A	1	3	.250	11	6	0	0	38.2	48	22	6	1	18-0	19	4.66	83	.308	.379	12-1	.167	-0	116	-3	-0.4
1958	Det A	0	0	—	1	0	0	0	2	1	2	1	1	1-0	0	9.00	45	.143	.333	0-0	—	0		-1	-0.1
1960	Was A	8	7	.533	44	20	1	3	165	160	72	16	3	64-3	88	3.44	113	.258	.328	43-1	.116	-0	110	9	0.8
1961	Min A	3	6	.333	37	10	4	3	115	93	49	12	4	35-1	65	3.52	120	.221	.286	30-3	.067	-3	77	10	0.6
1962	Min A	3	3	.500	9	9	1	0	52	51	27	8	7	24-0	28	4.50	91	.256	.355	19-0	.211	0	102	-1	-0.1
	LA A	8	8	.500	27	22	4-2	2	153.1	153	64	12	3	39-1	74	3.11	124	.256	.304	49-2	.184	-0	105	12	1.1
	Year	11	11	.500	36	31	5-2	2	205.1	204	69	20	10	63-1	102	3.46	113	.256	.317	68-2	.191	0	104	9	1.0
1963	LA A	8	11	.421	40	22	3-2	1	154	148	74	12	9	51-4	89	3.68	93	.251	.317	45-7	.156	-1	104	-5	-0.7
1964	LA A	5	4	.556	33	8	0	2	89.1	99	39	6	1	25-1	73	2.72	121	.279	.326	23-0	.261	2	91	3	0.5
1965	Cal A	0	1	.000	10	0	0	0	14	21	11	4	1	5-2	12	6.43	53	.350	.409	3-0	.333	1		-5	-0.3
	Hou N	0	0	—	7	0	0	0	8	8	3	0	1	3-0	3	3.38	99	.267	.353	1-0	.000	-0		0	0.0
1966	Hou N	2	0	1.000	9	0	0	0	18	17	5	1	0	4-1	9	2.50	137	.250	.292	1-0	1.000	1		2	0.3
	Chi N	2	1	.667	16	0	0	0	19	28	19	3	0	12-1	7	7.11	52	.346	.421	0-0	—	0		-8	-1.1
	Year	4	1	.800	25	0	0	0	37	45	27	4	0	16-2	16	4.86	73	.302	.365	1-0	1.000	1		-7	-0.8
Total	9	40	44	.476	244	97	13-4	11	828.1	827	387	81	31	281-14	467	3.61	104	.260	.324	226-14	.164	-1	102	13	0.6
LEE, MARK Mark Linden B 6.14.1953 Inglewood, CA BR/TR 6-4/225# d4.23																									
1978	SD N	5	1	.833	56	0	0	2-0	85	74	34	2	2	36-13	31	3.28	101	.240	.321	5-1	.000	-1		1	0.1
1979	SD N	2	4	.333	46	1	0	5-3	65	88	34	3	2	25-5	25	4.29	82	.332	.392	6-1	.333	1	175	-5	-0.4
1980	Pit N	0	1	.000	4	0	0	0-0	5.2	5	3	0	0	3-0	2	4.76	77	.227	.320	0-0	—	0		-1	0.0
1981	Pit N	0	2	.000	12	0	0	2-1	19.2	17	6	1	0	5-1	5	2.75	131	.233	.282	2-0	.500	0		2	0.4
Total	4	7	8	.467	118	1	0	9-4	175.1	184	77	6	4	69-19	63	3.64	95	.275	.345	13-2	.231	1	175	-3	0.1
LEE, MARK Mark Owen B 7.20.1964 Williston, ND BL/TL 6-3/198# d9.8																									
1988	KC A	0	0	—	4	0	0	0-0	5	6	2	0	0	1-0	0	3.60	111	.300	.333	0-0	—	0		0	0.0
1990	Mil A	1	0	1.000	11	0	0	0-0	21.1	20	5	1	0	4-0	14	2.11	184	.256	.286	0-0	—	0		5	0.2
1991	Mil A	2	5	.286	62	0	0	1-6	67.2	72	33	10	1	31-7	43	3.86	103	.283	.362	0-0	—	0		0	0.1
1995	Bal A	2	0	1.000	39	0	0	1-1	33.1	31	18	5	1	18-3	27	4.86	98	.246	.340	0-0	—	0		0	0.0
Total	4	5	5	.500	116	0	0	2-7	127.1	129	58	16	2	54-10	84	3.82	109	.270	.343	0-0	—	0		5	0.3
LEE, MIKE Michael Randall B 5.19.1941 Bell, CA BL/TL 6-5/220# d5.6																									
1960	Cle A	0	0	—	7	0	0	0	9	6	2	1	1	11-0	6	2.00	187	.207	.439	0-0	—	0		2	0.1
1963	LA A	1	1	.500	6	4	0	0	26	30	11	3	1	14-0	11	3.81	90	.300	.391	7-0	.000	-1	78	0	-0.1
Total	2	1	1	.500	13	4	0	0	35	36	13	4	2	25-0	17	3.34	105	.279	.404	7-0	.000	-1	78	2	0.0
LEE, BOB Robert Dean "Moose" or "Horse" B 11.26.1937 Ottumwa, IA BR/TR 6-3/230# d4.15																									
1964	LA A	6	5	.545	64	5	0	19	137	87	31	6	1	58-8	111	1.51	217	.182	.270	22-0	.000	-2	70	**28**	2.7
1965	Cal A☆	9	7	.563	69	0	0	23	131.1	95	35	11	1	42-8	89	1.92	177	.205	.269	21-4	.143	1		20	3.2
1966	Cal A	5	4	.556	61	0	0	16	101.2	90	39	8	1	31-2	46	2.74	122	.237	.294	11-3	.000	-0		5	0.5
1967	LA N	0	0	—	4	0	0	0	6.2	6	8	2	1	3-0	2	5.40	57	.222	.313	0-0	—	0		-4	-0.2
	Cin N	3	3	.500	27	1	0	2	50.2	51	26	0	0	25-7	33	4.44	84	.262	.338	8-0	.375	1	351	-3	-0.3
	Year	3	3	.500	31	1	0	2	57.1	57	41	2	1	28-7	35	4.55	81	.257	.335	8-0	.375	1	359	-5	-0.5
1968	Cin N	2	4	.333	44	1	0	3	65.1	73	38	4	1	37-10	34	5.10	62	.302	.387	5-0	.200	0	192	-12	-1.3
Total	5	25	23	.521	269	7	0	63	492.2	402	177	31	5	196-35	315	2.70	125	.225	.300	67-7	.104	-1	131	34	4.6
LEE, ROY Roy Edwin B 9.28.1917 Elmira, NY D 11.11.1985 St.Louis, MO BL/TL 5-11.5/175# d9.23																									
1945	NY N	0	2	.000	3	1	0	0	7	8	9	3	0	3	0	11.57	34	.267	.333	1-0	.000	-0	87	-5	-0.9
LEE, SANG-HOON Sang-Hoon B 3.11.1971 Seoul, South Korea BL/TL 6-1/190# d6.29																									
2000	Bos A	0	0	—	9	0	0	0-0	11.2	11	4	2	1	4-0	6	3.09	164	.262	.327	0-0	—	0		3	0.1
LEE, TOM Thomas Frank B 6.8.1862 Philadelphia, PA D 3.4.1886 Milwaukee, WI d6.14																									
1884	Chi N	1	4	.200	5	5	5	0	45.1	55	43	12		15	14	3.77	83	.272	.323	24	.125	-2*	95	-5	-0.5
	Bal U	5	8	.385	15	14	12	0	122	121	88	1		29	81	3.39	79	.242	.283	82	.280	-2*	89	-8	-0.8
Total	1	6	12	.333	20	19	17	0	167.1	176	131	13		44	95	3.50	80	.250	.295	106	.245	-4	90	-13	-1.3
LEE, THORNTON Thornton Starr "Lefty" B 9.13.1906 Sonoma, CA D 6.9.1997 Tucson, AZ BL/TL 6-3/205# d9.19 s-Don																									
1933	Cle A	1	1	.500	3	2	2	0	17.1	13	9	1	0	11	7	4.15	107	.203	.320	8-0	.375	1	115	1	0.2
1934	Cle A	1	1	.500	24	6	0	0	85.2	105	57	8	3	44	41	5.04	90	.308	.392	21-0	.095	-1	124	-5	-0.3
1935	Cle A	7	10	.412	32	20	8-1	1	180.2	179	90	6	4	71	81	4.04	112	.259	.331	61-3	.197	-1	85	11	0.9
1936	Cle A	3	5	.375	43	8	2	3	127	138	86	2	2	67	49	4.89	103	.271	.358	41-0	.122	-2	107	-1	-0.2
1937	Chi A	12	10	.545	30	25	13-2	0	204.2	209	91	17	1	60	80	3.52	131	.260	.312	71-5	.211	1	77	26	2.4
1938	Chi A	13	12	.520	33	30	18-1	1	245.1	252	123	12	3	94	77	3.49	140	.263	.331	97-4	.258	6*	91	33	3.4
1939	Chi A	15	11	.577	33	29	15-2	3	235	260	121	14	3	70	81	4.21	112	.285	.338	91-0	.165	-3	95	14	1.1
1940	Chi A	12	13	.480	28	27	24-1	0	228	223	100	13	2	56	87	3.47	127	.254	.300	84-5	.274	4	98	25	2.7
1941	Chi A★	22	11	.667	35	34	**30**-3	1	300.1	258	98	18	4	92	130	**2.37**	**173**	.232	**.293**	114-1	.254	5	83	**56**	**6.5**
1942	Chi A	2	6	.250	11	8	6-1	0	76	82	38	4	2	31	25	3.32	109	.278	.351	30-0	.200	0	45	0	0.0
1943	Chi A	5	9	.357	19	19	7-1	0	127	129	66	8	4	50	35	4.18	80	.266	.340	42-1	.071	-4	84	-10	-1.6
1944	Chi A	3	9	.250	15	14	6	0	113.1	105	51	3	1	25	39	3.02	114	.246	.290	42-1	.095	-3	68	3	0.0
1945	Chi A✤	15	12	.556	29	28	19-1	0	228.1	208	81	6	10	76	108	2.44	136	.245	.314	78-2	.179	-1	92	18	2.0
1946	Chi A	2	4	.333	7	7	2	0	43.1	39	24	1	1	23	23	3.53	97	.244	.342	15-0	.267	1	72	-2	-0.2
1947	Chi A	3	7	.300	21	11	2-1	1	86.2	86	50	5	2	56	57	4.47	82	.261	.372	29-0	.207	0	79	-8	-0.8
1948	NY N	1	3	.250	11	4	1	0	32.2	41	20	3	1	12	17	4.41	89	.304	.365	11-0	.091	-1	96	-2	-0.3
Total	16	117	124	.485	374	272	155-14	10	2331.1	2327	1105	121	43	838	937	3.56	119	.260	.326	835-22	.200	1	87	159	15.8
LEE, BILL William Crutcher "Big Bill" B 10.21.1909 Plaquemine, LA D 6.15.1977 Plaquemine, LA BR/TR 6-3/195# d4.29																									
1934	Chi N	13	14	.481	35	29	16-4	1	214.1	218	91	9	2	74	104	3.40	114	.263	.325	76-3	.132	-2*	97	12	1.2
1935	†Chi N	20	6	**.769**	39	32	18-3	1	252	241	106	11	5	84	100	2.96	133	.251	.314	102-3	.235	2	133	24	2.4
1936	Chi N	18	11	.621	43	33	20-**4**	1	258.2	238	106	14	3	93	102	3.31	121	.246	.314	87-9	.138	-3	94	19	1.7
1937	Chi N	14	15	.483	42	**34**	17-2	3	272.1	289	122	14	0	73	108	3.54	113	.273	.320	87-12	.172	-1	93	12	1.2
1938	†Chi N★	**22**	9	**.710**	44	**37**	19-**9**	2	291	281	95	18	2	74	121	**2.66**	**144**	.252	.299	101-7	.198	1	102	**39**	**4.1**
1939	Chi N★	19	15	.559	37	**36**	20-1	0	282.1	295	125	18	1	85	105	3.44	114	.272	.325	103-8	.126	-4	101	15	1.4
1940	Chi N	9	17	.346	37	30	9-1	0	211.1	246	129	12	2	70	70	5.03	75	.294	.350	76-2	.132	-2	107	-27	-3.2
1941	Chi N	8	14	.364	28	22	12	1	167.1	179	87	6	2	43	62	3.76	93	.270	.316	59-9	.186	1	120	-7	-0.6
1942	Chi N	13	13	.500	32	30	18-1	0	219.2	221	99	4	1	67	75	3.85	83	.258	.312	69-5	.159	1	90	-11	-1.1
1943	Chi N	3	7	.300	13	12	4	0	78.1	83	37	4	0	27	18	3.56	94	.273	.332	26-2	.269	1	76	-2	-0.2
	Phi N	1	5	.167	13	7	2	3	60.2	70	35	4	1	21	17	4.60	73	.298	.358	17-0	.059	-2	65	-8	-1.0
	Year	4	12	.250	26	19	6	3	139	153	38	8	1	48	35	4.01	84	.284	.344	43-2	.186	-0	72	-10	-1.2
1944	Phi N	10	11	.476	31	28	11-3	1	208.1	199	88	9	3	57	50	3.15	115	.248	.300	72-3	.194	-0	84	9	1.0
1945	Phi N	3	6	.333	13	13	2	0	77.1	107	52	0	0	30	13	4.66	82	.318	.374	24-3	.167	-1	100	-8	-0.8
	Bos N	6	3	.667	16	13	6-1	0	106.1	112	43	6	0	36	12	2.79	137	.279	.338	31-5	.129	-1	90	10	0.8

Year	Tm Lg	W	L	Pct	G	GS	CG-Sho	SV-BS	IP	H	R	HR	HB	BB-IB	SO	ERA	AERA	OAV	OOB	AB-SH	AVG	PB	Sup	APR	PW
	Year	9	9	.500	29	26	8-1	0	183.2	219	47	6	0	66	25	3.58	107	.297	.354	55-8	.145	-1	95	0	0.0
1946	Bos N	10	9	.526	25	21	8	0	140	148	73	7	1	45	32	4.18	82	.273	.330	47-3	.170	-1	90	-11	-1.4
1947	Chi N	0	2	.000	14	2	0	0	24	26	16	2	1	14	9	4.50	88	.268	.366	3-0	.333	0	101	-2	-0.1
Total	14	169	157	.518	462	379	182-29	13	2864	2953	1304	138	24	893	998	3.54	106	.266	.322	980-74	.168	-10	99	64	5.4
LEE, BILL William Francis "Spaceman" B 12.28.1946 Burbank, CA BL/TL 6-3/210# d6.25 Mil 1970																									
1969	Bos A	1	3	.250	20	1	0	0-1	52	56	27	9	2	28-0	45	4.50	85	.281	.372	10-0	.000	-1	46	-3	-0.3
1970	Bos A	2	2	.500	11	5	0	1-0	37	48	20	3	0	14-1	19	4.62	86	.320	.378	11-0	.000	-1	90	-2	-0.3
1971	Bos A	9	2	.818	47	3	0	2-2	102	102	35	7	1	46-7	74	2.74	135	.256	.333	23-3	.217	0	113	10	1.1
1972	Bos A	7	4	.636	47	0	0	5-2	84.1	75	31	5	1	32-8	43	3.20	101	.248	.320	16-0	.188	1		2	0.5
1973	Bos A☆	17	11	.607	38	33	18-1	1-0	284.2	275	100	20	5	76-2	120	2.75	146	.257	.307	0-0	—	0	87	37	3.6
1974	Bos A	17	15	.531	38	37	16-1	0-0	282.1	320	123	25	4	67-0	95	3.51	110	.290	.331	0-0	—	0	97	9	1.2
1975	†Bos A	17	9	.654	41	34	17-4	0-0	260	274	123	20	3	69-1	78	3.95	104	.273	.319	0-0	—	0	105	5	0.6
1976	Bos A	5	7	.417	24	14	1	3-0	96	124	68	13	3	28-1	29	5.63	70	.307	.354	0-0	—	0*	101	-16	-1.9
1977	Bos A	9	5	.643	27	16	4	1-0	128	155	67	14	0	29-1	31	4.43	102	.306	.341	0-0	—	0	101	1	0.2
1978	Bos A	10	10	.500	28	24	8-1	0-0	177	198	89	20	2	59-2	44	3.46	119	.285	.340	0-0	—	0	98	7	0.8
1979	Mon N	16	10	.615	33	33	6-3	0-0	222	230	91	20	1	46-1	59	3.04	121	.265	.302	74-7	.216	2	102	14	1.8
1980	Mon N	4	6	.400	24	18	2	0-0	118	156	71	13	3	22-1	34	4.96	72	.319	.349	41-0	.220	1*	122	-18	-1.3
1981	†Mon N	5	6	.455	31	7	0	6-0	88.2	90	33	6	2	14-2	34	2.94	119	.265	.297	22-0	.364	3	87	5	1.2
1982	Mon N	0	0	—	7	0	0	0-0	12.1	19	7	1	0	1-0	8	4.38	83	.352	.357	0-0	—	0		-1	0.0
Total	14	119	90	.569	416	225	72-10	19-5	1944.1	2122	885	176	27	531-27	713	3.62	107	.280	.327	197-10	.208	5	100	50	7.2
LEE, WATTY Wyatt Arnold B 8.12.1879 Lynch Station, VA D 3.6.1936 Washington, DC BL/TL 5-10.5/171# d4.30 ▲																									
1901	Was A	16	16	.500	36	33	25-2	0	262	328	184	14	11	45	63	4.40	83	.303	.337	129-1	.256	4*	95	-22	-1.6
1902	Was A	5	6	.455	13	10	10	0	98	118	66	5	8	20	24	5.05	73	.298	.344	391-7	.256	3*	116	-11	-0.8
1903	Was A	8	12	.400	22	20	15-2	0	166.2	169	86	5	7	40	70	3.08	102	.262	.313	231-4	.208	1*	87	-3	0.0
1904	Pit N	1	2	.333	5	3	1	0	22.2	34	25	0	3	9	5	8.74	31	.337	.407	12-0	.333	1*	92	-13	-1.3
Total	4	30	36	.455	76	66	51-4	0	549.1	649	361	24	29	114	162	4.29	81	.292	.334	763-12	.242	10	96	-49	-3.7
LEEVER, SAM Samuel "Deacon" or "The Goshen Schoolmaster" B 12.23.1871 Goshen, OH D 5.19.1953 Goshen, OH BR/TR 5-10.5/175# d5.26																									
1898	Pit N	1	0	1.000	5	3	2	0	33	26	10	0	1	5	15	2.45	145	.215	.252	12-0	.250	0	113	5	0.3
1899	Pit N	21	23	.477	**51**	39	35-4	**3**	**379**	353	191	7	11	122	121	3.18	120	.247	.311	146-6	.226	3	97	25	2.8
1900	†Pit N	15	13	.536	30	29	25-3	0	232.2	236	101	2	8	48	84	2.71	134	.263	.306	88-0	.205	0	88	25	2.5
1901	Pit N	14	5	.737	21	20	18-2	0	176	182	82	2	7	39	82	2.86	114	.265	.311	71-2	.183	-0	141	9	0.8
1902	Pit N	15	7	.682	28	26	23-4	2	222	203	73	2	8	31	86	2.39	115	.243	.277	90-0	.178	-0*	116	11	0.8
1903	†Pit N	25	7	**.781**	36	34	30-**7**	1	284.1	255	98	2	5	60	90	**2.06**	**157**	.238	.282	115-4	.165	-4	115	37	3.4
1904	Pit N	18	11	.621	34	32	26-1	0	253.1	224	85	2	5	54	63	2.17	127	.237	.282	99-2	.263	7	116	15	2.3
1905	Pit N	20	5	**.800**	33	29	20-3	1	229.2	199	94	3	12	54	81	2.70	111	.231	.286	88-2	.102	-4	143	6	0.2
1906	Pit N	22	7	.759	36	31	25-6	0	260.1	232	84	3	7	48	76	2.32	115	.243	.284	95-1	.211	2	128	14	1.4
1907	Pit N	14	9	.609	31	24	17-5	0	216.2	182	70	3	8	46	65	1.66	147	.229	.278	73-4	.151	-1	109	15	1.2
1908	Pit N	15	7	.682	38	20	14-4	2	192.2	179	60	1	6	41	28	2.10	110	.249	.295	61-2	.148	0	106	5	0.4
1909	Pit N	8	1	.889	19	4	2	2	70	74	30	0	4	14	23	2.83	96	.276	.322	24-0	.167	0	96	-1	-0.1
1910	Pit N	6	5	.545	26	8	4	2	111	104	45	2	6	25	33	2.76	112	.259	.313	31-2	.065	-3	117	4	0.1
Total	13	194	100	.660	388	299	241-39	13	2660.2	2449	1023	29	88	587	847	2.47	123	.245	.293	993-25	.184	1	114	170	16.1
LEFEBVRE, BILL Wilfred Henry "Lefty" B 11.11.1915 Natick, RI BL/TL 5-11.5/180# d6.10 Mil 1945 ▲																									
1938	Bos A	0	0	—	1	0	0	0	4	8	6	2	1	0	0	13.50	37	.400	.429	1-0	1.000	1		-3	0.0
1939	Bos A	1	1	.500	5	3	0	0	26.1	35	17	2	0	14	8	5.81	81	.333	.412	10-0	.300	1*	118	-2	-0.1
1943	Was A	2	0	1.000	6	3	1	0	32.1	33	18	3	0	16	10	4.45	72	.268	.353	14-0	.286	2*	123	-4	0.0
1944	Was A	2	4	.333	24	4	2	3	69.2	86	48	3	1	21	18	4.52	72	.305	.355	62-0	.258	3*	109	-12	-0.5
Total	4	5	5	.500	36	10	3	3	132.1	162	89	10	2	51	36	5.03	71	.306	.369	87-0	.276	7	119	-21	-0.6
LEFFERTS, CRAIG Craig Lindsay B 9.29.1957 Munich, W.Germany BL/TL 6-1/210# d4.7																									
1983	Chi N	3	4	.429	56	5	0	1-0	89	80	35	13	2	29-3	60	3.13	121	.243	.308	18-1	.111	-1	65	6	0.4
1984	†SD N	3	4	.429	62	0	0	10-2	105.2	88	29	4	1	24-1	56	2.13	168	.229	.272	17-1	.294	1		17	1.4
1985	SD N	7	6	.538	60	0	0	2-3	83.1	75	34	7	0	30-4	48	3.35	106	.244	.311	4-0	.250	0		2	0.4
1986	SD N	9	8	.529	**83**	0	0	4-3	107.2	98	41	7	1	44-11	72	3.09	118	.253	.327	8-1	.125	1*		7	1.3
1987	SD N	2	2	.500	33	0	0	2-2	51.1	56	29	9	2	15-5	39	4.38	90	.272	.327	3-0	.333	0		-3	-0.2
	†SF N	3	3	.500	44	0	0	4-5	47.1	36	18	4	0	18-6	18	3.23	119	.216	.289	4-0	.250	1		4	0.5
	Year	5	5	.500	77	0	0	6-7	98.2	92	50	13	2	33-11	57	3.83	102	.247	.310	7-0	.286	1		1	0.3
1988	SF N	3	8	.273	64	0	0	11-3	92.1	74	33	7	1	23-5	58	2.92	112	.225	.275	9-0	.000	-1		4	0.4
1989	†SF N	2	4	.333	70	0	0	20-4	107	93	38	11	1	22-5	71	2.69	126	.233	.272	7-0	.000	-1		8	0.5
1990	SD N	7	5	.583	56	0	0	23-8	78.2	68	26	10	1	22-4	60	2.52	152	.228	.283	4-2	.250	0		11	2.2
1991	SD N	1	6	.143	54	0	0	23-7	69	74	35	5	1	14-3	48	3.91	97	.285	.318	6-0	.000	-1		-1	-0.3
1992	SD N	13	9	.591	27	27	0	0-0	163.1	180	76	16	0	35-2	81	3.69	97	.285	.320	52-9	.077	-3	109	-3	-0.7
	Bal A	1	3	.250	5	5	1	0-0	33	34	19	3	0	6-0	23	4.09	99	.268	.299	0-0	—	0	54	-2	-0.2
1993	Tex A	3	9	.250	52	8	0	0-0	83.1	102	57	17	1	28-3	58	6.05	69	.304	.357	0-0	—	0	113	-16	-2.0
1994	Cal A	1	1	.500	30	0	0	1-0	34.2	50	20	7	0	12-3	27	4.67	105	.350	.392	0-0	—	0		0	0.0
Total	12	58	72	.446	696	45	1	101-37	1145.2	1108	490	120	11	322-55	719	3.43	108	.257	.308	132-14	.121	-3	98	34	3.7
LEFTWICH, PHIL Philip Dale B 5.19.1969 Lynchburg, VA BR/TR 6-5/205# d7.29																									
1993	Cal A	4	6	.400	12	12	1	0-0	80.2	81	35	5	3	27-1	31	3.79	119	.262	.326	0-0	—	0	102	7	0.8
1994	Cal A	5	10	.333	20	20	1	0-0	114	127	75	16	3	42-2	67	5.68	86	.283	.346	0-0	—	0	73	-9	-1.0
1996	Cal A	0	1	.000	2	2	0	0-0	7.1	12	9	1	0	3-0	4	7.36	68	.375	.429	0-0	—	0	93	-3	-0.3
Total	3	9	17	.346	34	34	2	0-0	202	220	119	22	6	72-3	102	4.99	95	.279	.342	0-0	—	0	84	-5	-0.5
LEHENY, REGIS Regis Francis B 1.5.1908 Pittsburgh, PA D 11.2.1976 Pittsburgh, PA BL/TL 6-0.5/180# d5.21																									
1932	Bos A	0	0	—	2	0	0	0	2.2	5	5	0	0	3	1	16.88	27	.417	.533	1-0	.000	-0		-3	-0.1
LEHEW, JIM James Anthony B 8.19.1937 Baltimore, MD BR/TR 6/185# d9.13																									
1961	Bal A	0	0	—	2	0	0	0	2	1	0	0	0	0-0	0	0.00	—	.167	.167	0-0	—	0		1	0.0
1962	Bal A	0	0	—	6	0	0	0	9.2	10	3	0	0	3-0	2	1.86	199	.303	.351	1-0	.000	-0		2	0.1
Total	2	0	0	—	8	0	0	0	11.2	11	3	0	0	3-0	2	1.54	241	.282	.326	1-0	.000	-0		3	0.1
LEHMAN, KEN Kenneth Karl B 6.10.1928 Seattle, WA BL/TL 6/186# d9.5																									
1952	†Bro N	1	2	.333	4	3	0	0	15.1	19	11	1	0	6	7	5.28	69	.297	.357	4-0	.000	0	106	-3	-0.5
1956	Bro N	2	3	.400	25	4	0	0	49.1	65	35	11	0	23-2	29	5.66	70	.325	.389	10-0	.300	1	61	-9	-0.7
1957	Bro N	0	0	—	3	0	0	0	7	7	0	0	0	1-0	3	0.00	—	.259	.286	2-0	.500	0		3	0.2
	Bal A	8	3	.727	30	3	1	6	68	57	21	1	0	22-2	32	2.78	129	.232	.294	20-0	.200	1*	50	7	1.4
1958	Bal A	2	1	.667	31	1	1	0	62	64	26	5	2	18-4	36	3.48	103	.276	.326	14-0	.071	-1	0	1	-0.1
1961	Phi N	1	1	.500	41	2	0	1	63.1	61	32	6	1	25-8	27	4.26	96	.260	.331	6-0	.000	-1*	76	-1	-0.1
Total	5	14	10	.583	134	13	2	7	265	273	125	24	3	95-16	134	3.91	97	.272	.333	56-0	.161	1	67	-2	0.2
LEHR, NORM Norman Carl Michael "King" B 5.28.1901 Rochester, NY D 7.17.1968 Livonia, NY BR/TR 6/168# d5.20																									
1926	Cle A	0	0	—	4	0	0	0	14.2	11	5	0	0	4	4	3.07	132	.216	.273	4-0	.000	-1		2	0.1
LEIBER, HANK Henry Edward B 1.17.1911 Phoenix, AZ D 11.8.1993 Tucson, AZ BR/TR 6-1.5/205# d4.16.1933 ▲																									
1942	NY N	0	1	.000	1	1	1	0	9	9	9	0	1	5	5	6.00	56	.290	.405	147-1	.218	0*	25	-3	-0.3
LEIBRANDT, CHARLIE Charles Louis B 10.4.1956 Chicago, IL BR/TL 6-3/200# d9.17																									
1979	†Cin N	0	0	—	3	0	0	0-0	4.1	2	2	0	0	2-0	1	0.00	—	.154	.250	0-0	—	0		1	0.0
1980	Cin N	10	9	.526	36	27	5-2	0-0	173.2	200	84	15	2	54-4	62	4.25	84	.292	.345	56-4	.196	1	104	-11	-0.9
1981	Cin N	1	1	.500	7	4	1-1	0-0	30	28	12	0	0	15-2	9	3.60	99	.262	.347	8-0	.000	-0	81	0	0.0
1982	Cin N	5	7	.417	36	11	0	2-0	107.2	130	68	4	2	48-9	34	5.10	73	.308	.380	25-4	.080	-1	97	-16	-1.9
1984	†KC A	11	7	.611	23	23	0	0-0	143.2	158	65	11	3	38-2	53	3.63	111	.277	.322	0-0	—	0	93	6	0.6

Year	Tm Lg	W	L	Pct	G	GS	CG-Sho	SV-BS	IP	H	R	HR	HB	BB-IB	SO	ERA	AERA	OAV	OOB	AB-SH	AVG	PB	Sup	APR	PW
1985	†KC A	17	9	.654	33	33	8-3	0-0	237.2	223	86	17	2	68-3	108	2.69	155	.248	.301	0-0	—	0	100	36	4.0
1986	KC A	14	11	.560	35	34	8-1	0-0	231.1	238	112	18	4	63-0	108	4.09	104	.268	.317	0-0	—	0	94	6	0.7
1987	KC A	16	11	.593	35	35	8-3	0-0	240.1	235	104	23	1	74-2	151	3.41	134	.253	.307	0-0	—	0	92	30	3.3
1988	KC A	13	12	.520	35	35	7-2	0-0	243	244	98	20	4	62-3	125	3.19	125	.264	.311	0-0	—	0	93	21	2.2
1989	KC A	5	11	.313	33	27	3-1	0-0	161	196	98	13	2	54-4	73	5.14	75	.304	.358	0-0	—	0	114	-21	-1.9
1990	Atl N	9	11	.450	24	24	5-2	0-0	162.1	164	72	9	4	35-3	76	3.16	128	.261	.302	50-5	.180	1	93	12	1.5
1991	†Atl N	15	13	.536	36	36	1-1	0-0	229.2	212	105	18	4	56-3	128	3.49	112	.245	.292	70-12	.043	-4	92	8	0.8
1992	†Atl N	15	7	.682	32	31	5-2	0-0	193	191	78	9	5	42-4	104	3.36	109	.258	.301	58-8	.121	-1	103	7	0.8
1993	Tex A	9	10	.474	26	26	1	0-0	150.1	169	84	15	4	45-5	89	4.55	91	.284	.336	0-0	—	0	120	-7	-0.5
Total	14	140	119	.541	394	346	52-18	2-0	2308	2390	1068	172	37	656-44	1121	3.71	108	.268	.319	267-33	.120	-5	99	72	8.7
LEIFIELD, LEFTY Albert Peter B 9.5.1883 Trenton, IL D 10.10.1970 Alexandria, VA BL/TL 6-1/165# d9.3 C9																									
1905	Pit N	5	2	.714	8	7	6-1	0	56	52	24	0	4	14	10	2.89	104	.248	.307	20-0	.350	3	106	0	0.4
1906	Pit N	18	13	.581	37	31	24-8	1	255.2	214	90	3	14	68	111	1.87	143	.231	.294	88-4	.125	-3	106	17	1.8
1907	Pit N	20	16	.556	40	33	24-6	1	286	270	107	1	12	100	112	2.33	105	.256	.328	102-2	.147	0	112	4	0.6
1908	Pit N	15	14	.517	34	26	18-5	2	218.2	168	69	1	12	86	87	2.10	110	.212	.299	75-3	.227	3	96	6	1.2
1909	†Pit N	19	8	.704	32	26	13-3	0	201.2	172	76	4	6	54	43	2.37	115	.229	.286	73-2	.192	2	131	7	0.9
1910	Pit N	15	13	.536	40	30	13-3	2	218.1	197	84	6	10	67	64	2.64	117	.253	.320	60-9	.183	0	76	11	1.6
1911	Pit N	16	16	.500	42	37	26-2	1	318	301	114	7	16	82	111	2.63	131	.260	.318	102-3	.235	6*	90	30	3.4
1912	Pit N	1	2	.333	6	1	1	0	23.2	29	15	0	2	10	8	4.18	78	.302	.380	7-0	.143	0	0	-3	-0.2
	Chi N	7	2	.778	13	9	4-1	0	70.2	68	26	0	3	21	23	2.42	137	.258	.319	26-3	.115	-1	115	7	0.7
	Year	8	4	.667	19	10	5-1	0	94.1	97	31	0	5	31	31	2.86	116	.269	.336	33-3	.121	-1	104	4	0.5
1913	Chi N	0	1	.000	6	1	0	0	21.1	28	14	0	0	5	4	5.48	58	.329	.367	7-0	.000	-1*	189	-4	-0.3
1918	StL A	2	6	.250	15	6	3-1	0	67	61	23	1	2	19	22	2.55	107	.252	.312	19-0	.053	-2	46	2	0.1
1919	StL A	6	4	.600	19	9	6-2	0	92	96	40	4	4	25	18	2.93	113	.270	.325	30-0	.100	-2	108	3	0.1
1920	StL A	0	0	—	4	0	0	0	9	17	12	0	0	3	3	7.00	56	.405	.444	2-0	.000	-0		-4	-0.2
Total	12	124	97	.561	296	216	138-32	7	1838	1673	694	27	85	554	616	2.47	116	.248	.313	611-26	.175	6	100	76	10.1
LEIPER, DAVE David Paul B 6.18.1962 Whittier, CA BL/TL 6-1/160# d9.2																									
1984	Oak A	1	0	1.000	8	0	0	0-1	7	12	7	2	0	5-0	3	9.00	42	.353	.436	0-0	—	0		-4	-0.5
1986	Oak A	2	2	.500	33	0	0	1-2	31.2	28	17	3	2	18-4	15	4.83	80	.252	.358	0-0	—	0		-3	-0.3
1987	Oak A	2	1	.667	45	0	0	1-3	52.1	49	28	6	1	18-0	33	3.78	109	.246	.306	0-0	—	0		1	0.1
	SD N	1	0	1.000	12	0	0	1-0	16	16	8	2	0	5-0	10	4.50	88	.267	.323	0-0	—	0		-1	0.0
1988	SD N	3	0	1.000	35	0	0	1-0	54	45	19	1	0	14-5	33	2.17	157	.231	.276	2-0	.500	0		5	0.4
1989	SD N	0	1	.000	22	0	0	0-0	28.2	40	19	2	2	20-4	7	5.02	70	.333	.437	1-0	.000	-0		-5	-0.3
1994	Oak A	0	0	—	26	0	0	1-0	18.2	13	4	0	1	6-1	14	1.93	230	.206	.278	0-0	—	0		6	0.3
1995	Oak A	1	1	.500	24	0	0	0-0	22.2	23	10	3	1	13-1	10	3.57	125	.258	.359	0-0	—	0		2	0.2
	Mon N	0	2	.000	26	0	0	2-1	22	16	8	2	0	6-0	12	2.86	150	.200	.256	1-0	.000	-0		3	0.3
1996	Phi N	2	0	1.000	26	0	0	0-0	21	31	16	4	0	7-2	10	6.43	67	.348	.396	0-0	—	0		-5	-0.4
	Mon N	0	1	.000	7	0	0	0-0	4	9	5	0	0	2-0	3	11.25	38	.474	.524	0-0	—	0		-3	-0.5
	Year	2	1	.667	33	0	0	0-0	25	40	25	4	0	9-2	13	7.20	60	.370	.419	0-0	—	0		-7	-0.9
Total	8	12	8	.600	264	0	0	7-7	278	282	141	25	7	114-17	150	3.98	100	.266	.338	4-0	.250	0		-4	-0.7
LEIPER, JACK John Henry Thomas B 12.23.1867 Chester, PA D 8.23.1960 West Goshen, PA BL/TL 5-11/?# d9.4																									
1891	Col AA	2	2	.500	6	5	4	0	45	41	43	3	4	39	19	5.40	64	.234	.385	21	.143	-2	101	-11	-0.9
LEISTER, JOHN John William B 1.3.1961 San Antonio, TX BR/TR 6-2/200# d5.28																									
1987	Bos A	0	2	.000	8	6	0	0-0	30.1	49	31	9	0	12-1	16	9.20	50	.368	.418	0-0	—	0	140	-14	-0.8
1990	Bos A	0	0	—	2	1	0	0-0	5.2	7	5	0	0	4-0	3	4.76	86	.304	.393	0-0	—	0	111	-1	-0.1
Total	2	0	2	.000	10	7	0	0-0	36	56	36	9	0	16-1	19	8.50	53	.359	.414	0-0	—	0	137	-15	-0.9
LEITER, AL Alois Terry B 10.23.1965 Toms River, NJ BL/TL 6-3/215# d9.15 b-Mark																									
1987	NY A	2	2	.500	4	4	0	0-0	22.2	24	16	2	0	15-0	28	6.35	69	.273	.379	0-0	—	0	73	-4	-0.6
1988	NY A	4	4	.500	14	14	0	0-0	57.1	49	27	7	5	33-0	60	3.92	101	.231	.348	0-0	—	0	102	0	0.1
1989	NY A	1	2	.333	4	4	0	0-0	26.2	23	20	1	2	21-0	22	6.08	64	.235	.377	0-0	—	0	99	-7	-0.6
	Tor A	0	0	—	1	1	0	0-0	6.2	9	3	1	0	2-0	4	4.05	93	.310	.355	0-0	—	0	96	0	0.0
	Year	1	2	.333	5	5	0	0-0	33.1	32	7	2	2	23-0	26	5.67	68	.252	.373	0-0	—	0	99	-7	-0.6
1990	Tor A	0	0	—	4	0	0	0-0	6.1	1	0	0	0	2-0	5	0.00	—	.050	.136	0-0	—	0		3	0.1
1991	Tor A	0	0	—	3	0	0	0-0	1.2	3	5	0	0	5-0	1	27.00	16	.429	.667	0-0	—	0		-4	-0.2
1992	Tor A	0	0	—	1	0	0	0-0	1	1	1	0	0	2-0	0	9.00	45	.200	.429	0-0	—	0		0	0.0
1993	†Tor A	9	6	.600	34	12	1-1	2-1	105	93	52	8	4	56-2	66	4.11	105	.240	.339	0-0	—	0	92	3	0.3
1994	Tor A	6	7	.462	20	20	1	0-0	111.2	125	68	6	2	65-3	100	5.08	95	.285	.374	0-0	—	0	84	-3	-0.3
1995	Tor A	11	11	.500	28	28	2-1	0-0	183	162	80	15	6	108-1	153	3.64	130	.238	.345	0-0	—	0	72	23	2.3
1996	Fla N★	16	12	.571	33	33	2-1	0-0	215.1	153	74	14	11	119-3	200	2.93	139	**.202**	.318	70-7	.100	-2	103	30	3.3
1997	†Fla N	11	9	.550	27	27	0	0-0	151.1	133	78	13	12	91-4	132	4.34	93	.241	.359	48-2	.104	-1	96	-5	-0.7
1998	NY N	17	6	.739	28	28	4-2	0-0	193	151	55	8	11	71-2	174	2.47	167	.216	.298	57-5	.105	0	105	37	4.2
1999	†NY N	13	12	.520	32	32	1-1	0-0	213	209	107	19	9	93-8	162	4.23	104	.262	.342	57-11	.105	-2	99	2	-0.1
2000	†NY N★	16	8	.667	31	31	2-1	0-0	208	176	84	19	11	76-1	200	3.20	138	.228	.304	58-9	.052	-4	93	28	2.6
2001	NY N	11	11	.500	29	29	0	0-0	187.1	178	81	18	4	46-3	142	3.31	125	.252	.299	62-0	.065	-3	85	15	1.2
2002	NY N	13	13	.500	33	33	2-2	0-0	204.1	194	99	23	8	69-5	172	3.48	114	.250	.317	53-3	.151	2	96	7	1.0
2003	NY N	15	9	.625	30	30	1-1	0-0	180.2	176	83	15	9	94-11	139	3.99	104	.260	.355	53-5	.019	-5	99	5	0.1
Total	17	145	112	.564	356	326	16-10	2-1	2075	1860	933	169	94	968-43	1760	3.69	115	.241	.331	458-42	.087	-14	93	130	12.7
LEITER, MARK Mark Edward B 4.13.1963 Joliet, IL BR/TR 6-3/210# d7.24 b-Al																									
1990	NY A	1	1	.500	8	3	0	0-0	26.1	33	20	5	2	9-0	21	6.84	58	.314	.376	0-0	—	0	130	-7	-0.4
1991	Det A	9	7	.563	38	15	1	1-1	134.2	125	66	16	6	50-4	103	4.21	99	.245	.316	0-0	—	0	108	0	0.0
1992	Det A	8	5	.615	35	14	1	0-0	112	116	57	9	3	43-5	75	4.18	95	.277	.342	0-0	—	0	150	-3	-0.3
1993	Det A	6	6	.500	27	13	1	0-1	106.2	111	61	17	3	44-5	70	4.73	91	.267	.338	0-0	—	0	97	-4	-0.5
1994	Cal A	4	7	.364	40	7	0	2-1	95.1	99	56	13	9	35-6	71	4.72	104	.265	.340	0-0	—	0	89	1	0.1
1995	SF N	10	12	.455	30	29	7-1	0-0	195.2	185	91	19	17	55-4	129	3.82	107	.254	.318	61-9	.098	-2	87	7	0.3
1996	SF N	4	10	.286	23	22	1	0-0	135.1	151	93	25	9	50-7	118	5.19	79	.283	.353	42-7	.143	-0	112	-19	-1.8
	Mon N	4	2	.667	12	12	1	0-0	69.2	68	35	12	7	19-1	46	4.39	98	.254	.316	25-2	.080	-1	116	1	0.0
	Year	8	12	.400	35	34	2	0-0	205	219	41	37	16	69-8	164	4.92	85	.273	.341	67-9	.119	-2	114	-19	-1.8
1997	Phi N	10	17	.370	31	31	3	0-0	182.2	216	132	25	9	64-4	148	5.67	75	.292	.352	51-10	.118	-1	104	-31	-3.9
1998	Phi N	7	5	.583	69	0	0	23-12	88.2	67	36	8	8	47-5	84	3.55	122	.216	.331	2-0	.000	-0		8	1.3
1999	Sea A	0	0	—	2	0	0	0-0	1.1	2	1	0	0	0-0	1	6.75	70	.333	.333	0-0	—	0		0	0.0
2001	Mil N	2	1	.667	20	3	0	0-0	36	32	16	6	2	8-2	26	3.75	115	.232	.284	7-0	.143	-0	143	2	0.2
Total	11	65	73	.471	335	149	15-1	26-15	1184.1	1205	664	155	75	424-43	892	4.57	92	.265	.334	188-28	.112	-6	106	-45	-5.0
LEITH, BILL William "Shady Bill" B 5.31.1873 Matteawan, NY D 7.16.1940 Beacon, NY TR 6-1/208# d9.25																									
1899	Was N	0	0	—	1	0	0	0	2	4	5	0	1	2	1	18.00	22	.400	.538	1-0	.000	-0		-3	-0.1
LEITNER, DOC George Aloysius B 9.14.1865 Piermont, NY D 5.18.1937 New York, NY BR/TR 5-11.5/185# d8.10																									
1887	Ind N	2	6	.250	8	8	8	0	65	69	66	6	0	41	27	5.68	73	.259	.358	27	.148	-3	90	-12	-1.3
LEITNER, DUMMY George Michael B 6.19.1872 Parkton, MD D 2.20.1960 Baltimore, MD BL/TR 5-7/120# d6.29																									
1901	Phi A	0	0	—	1	0	0	0	2	1	0	0	0	1	1	0.00	—	.143	.250	1-0	.000	-0		1	0.0
	NY N	0	2	.000	2	2	2	0	18	27	9	0	1	4	3	4.50	73	.342	.381	7-0	.143	-0	32	-1	-0.2
1902	Cle A	0	0	—	1	1	0	0	8	11	4	0	0	1	0	4.50	77	.324	.343	4-0	.250	0	84	0	0.0
	Chi A	0	0	—	1	0	0	0	4	9	7	0	2	2	0	13.50	25	.450	.542	3-0	.000	-0		-4	-0.2
	Year	0	0	—	2	1	0	0	12	20	15	0	2	3	0	7.50	46	.370	.424	7-0	.143	-0	84	-4	-0.2
Total	2	0	2	.000	5	3	2	0	32	48	20	0	3	8	4	5.34	63	.343	.391	15-0	.133	-1	49	-4	-0.4

Year	Tm Lg	W	L	Pct	G	GS	CG-Sho	SV-BS	IP	H	R	HR	HB	BB-IB	SO	ERA	AERA	OAV	OOB	AB-SH	AVG	PB	Sup	APR	PW
LELIVELT, BILL William John B 10.21.1884 Chicago, IL D 2.14.1968 Chicago, IL BR/TR 5-10/168# d7.19 b-Jack																									
1909	Det A	0	1	.000	4	2	1	1	20	27	12	0	0	2	4	4.50	56	.325	.341	6-0	.333	1	84	-4	-0.1
1910	Det A	0	1	.000	1	1	1	0	9	6	4	0	0	3	2	1.00	263	.207	.281	2-0	.500	1	0	1	0.1
Total	2	0	2	.000	5	3	2	1	29	33	16	0	0	5	6	3.41	75	.295	.325	8-0	.375	2	54	-3	0.0
LEMANCZYK, DAVE David Lawrence B 8.17.1950 Syracuse, NY BR/TR 6-4/235# d4.15																									
1973	Det A	0	0	—	1	0	0	0-0	2.1	4	3	0	0	0-0	0	11.57	35	.364	.364	0-0	—	0		-2	-0.1
1974	Det A	2	1	.667	22	3	0	0-0	78.2	79	43	12	2	44-6	52	4.00	95	.261	.357	0-0	—	0	85	-3	-0.1
1975	Det A	2	7	.222	26	6	4	0-1	109	120	62	8	3	46-5	67	4.46	90	.281	.352	0-0	—	0	33	-4	-0.3
1976	Det A	4	6	.400	20	10	1	0-0	81.1	86	47	7	0	34-0	51	5.09	73	.271	.341	0-0	—	0	83	-9	-1.0
1977	Tor A	13	16	.448	34	34	11	0-0	252	278	143	20	4	87-6	105	4.25	99	.282	.340	0-0	—	0	85	-5	-0.5
1978	Tor A	4	14	.222	29	20	3	0-0	136.2	170	97	16	3	65-1	62	6.26	63	.313	.388	0-0	—	0	74	-32	-3.6
1979	Tor A☆	8	10	.444	22	20	11-3	0-0	143	137	65	12	6	45-2	63	3.71	117	.258	.321	0-0	—	0	63	11	1.2
1980	Tor A	2	5	.286	10	8	0	0-0	43.1	57	29	4	0	15-0	10	5.40	80	.322	.371	0-0	—	0	65	-5	-0.7
	Cal A	2	4	.333	21	2	0	0-0	66.2	81	40	8	2	27-2	19	4.32	91	.301	.367	0-0	—	0	125	-5	-0.5
	Year	4	9	.308	31	10	0	0-0	110	138	46	12	2	42-2	29	4.75	86	.309	.368	0-0	—	0	79	-9	-1.2
Total	8	37	63	.370	185	103	30-3	0-1	913	1012	529	87	20	363-22	429	4.62	88	.284	.351	0-0	—	0	75	-54	-5.6
LEMASTER, DENNY Denver Clayton B 2.25.1939 Corona, CA BR/TL 6-1/185# d7.15																									
1962	Mil N	3	4	.429	17	12	4-1	0	86.2	75	36	11	3	32-1	69	3.01	126	.233	.308	33-2	.121	-1	116	6	0.3
1963	Mil N	11	14	.440	46	31	10-1	1	237	199	87	30	1	85-14	190	3.04	106	.227	.295	74-6	.189	3	78	6	0.9
1964	Mil N	17	11	.607	39	35	9-3	1	221	216	112	27	4	75-4	185	4.15	85	.252	.313	67-7	.134	0	115	-14	-1.6
1965	Mil N	7	13	.350	32	23	4-1	0	146.1	140	75	12	3	58-7	111	4.43	80	.251	.324	45-2	.089	-1	95	-12	-1.7
1966	Atl N	11	8	.579	27	27	10-3	0	171	170	78	25	1	41-5	139	3.74	97	.258	.301	59-4	.119	-1	124	-1	-0.3
1967	Atl N❖	9	9	.500	31	31	8-2	0	215.1	184	86	20	3	72-7	148	3.34	99	.229	.293	67-7	.104	-2	82	2	0.0
1968	Hou N	10	15	.400	33	32	7-2	0	224	231	79	11	4	72-11	146	2.81	105	.262	.319	65-9	.031	-3	86	3	-0.1
1969	Hou N	13	17	.433	38	37	11-1	1-0	244.2	232	97	20	1	72-8	173	3.16	112	.246	.298	88-6	.170	3	87	12	1.7
1970	Hou N	7	12	.368	39	21	3	3-2	162	169	88	22	2	65-9	103	4.56	85	.268	.335	45-3	.178	2	86	-11	-1.0
1971	Hou N	0	2	.000	42	0	0	2-1	60	59	23	4	1	22-6	28	3.45	98	.262	.331	6-1	.167	-0		1	0.0
1972	Mon N	2	0	1.000	13	0	0	0-0	19.2	28	17	2	1	6-1	13	7.78	46	.329	.376	3-0	.333	1		-8	-0.8
Total	11	90	105	.462	357	249	66-14	8-3	1787.2	1703	778	184	24	600-73	1305	3.58	96	.249	.310	552-47	.130	1	96	-16	-2.6
LeMAY, DICK Richard Paul B 8.28.1938 Cincinnati, OH BL/TL 6-3/190# d6.13																									
1961	SF N	3	6	.333	27	5	1	3	83.1	65	35	11	4	36-7	54	3.56	107	.217	.307	26-1	.077	-2	140	3	0.2
1962	SF N	0	1	.000	9	0	0	1	9.1	9	8	2	0	9-1	5	7.71	49	.265	.419	0-0	—	0		-4	-0.4
1963	Chi N	0	1	.000	9	1	0	0	15.1	26	9	1	0	4-2	10	5.28	66	.394	.429	2-0	.000	-0	123	-2	-0.2
Total	3	3	8	.273	45	6	1	4	108	100	52	14	4	49-10	69	4.17	91	.250	.336	28-1	.071	-1	136	-3	-0.4
LEMON, BOB Robert Granville B 9.22.1920 San Bernardino, CA D 1.11.2000 Long Beach, CA BL/TR 6/185# d9.9.1941 Mil 1943-45 M8 C6 HF1976 ▲																									
1946	Cle A	4	5	.444	32	5	1	1	94	77	40	1	0	68	39	2.49	133	.229	.359	89-3	.180	2*	83	4	0.7
1947	Cle A	11	5	.688	37	15	6-1	3	167.1	150	68	7	4	97	65	3.44	101	.242	.348	56-2	.321	9*	119	2	1.5
1948	†Cle A☆	20	14	.588	43	37	**20-10**	2	**293.2**	231	104	12	3	129	147	2.82	144	.216	.302	119-2	.286	14*	122	42	**6.6**
1949	Cle A☆	22	10	.688	37	33	22-2	1	279.2	211	101	19	6	137	138	2.99	133	.211	.309	108-5	.269	16*	115	34	**5.6**
1950	Cle A★	**23**	11	.676	44	**37**	**22**-3	3	**288**	281	144	28	2	146	**170**	3.84	113	.257	.345	136-3	.272	17*	114	15	3.4
1951	Cle A★	17	14	.548	42	**34**	17-1	2	263.1	244	119	18	2	124	132	3.52	108	.244	.328	102-1	.206	5*	92	8	1.4
1952	Cle A★	22	11	.667	42	**36**	**28**-5	4	**309.2**	236	104	15	6	105	131	2.50	134	**.208**	.279	124-6	.226	7*	134	30	4.4
1953	Cle A☆	21	15	.583	41	36	23-5	1	**286.2**	283	119	16	11	110	98	3.36	112	.262	.336	112-6	.232	8*	114	14	3.0
1954	†Cle A★	**23**	7	.767	36	33	**21**-2	0	258.1	228	95	12	4	92	110	2.72	135	.237	.303	98-8	.214	6*	134	25	3.7
1955	Cle A	**18**	10	.643	35	31	5	2	211.1	218	103	17	5	74-3	100	3.88	103	.266	.329	78-6	.244	6*	115	3	1.1
1956	Cle A	20	14	.588	39	35	**21**-2	3	255.1	230	103	23	6	89-2	94	3.03	139	.239	.305	93-7	.194	5*	95	31	4.6
1957	Cle A	6	11	.353	21	17	2	0	117.1	129	70	9	7	64-6	45	4.60	81	.287	.379	46-0	.065	-3*	98	-12	-1.7
1958	Cle A	0	1	.000	11	1	0	0	25.1	41	15	3	1	16-2	8	5.33	68	.376	.457	13-0	.231	0*	148	-4	-0.1
Total	13	207	128	.618	460	350	188-31	22	2850	2559	1185	180	57	1251-**13**	1277	3.23	119	.241	.323	1174-49	.233	90	114	192	34.2
LEMONDS, DAVE David Lee B 7.5.1948 Charlotte, NC BL/TL 6-1.5/180# d6.30																									
1969	Chi N	0	1	.000	2	1	0	0-0	4.2	5	2	0	0	5-0	0	3.86	104	.313	.476	1-0	.000	-0	44	0	0.0
1972	Chi A	4	7	.364	31	18	0	0-0	94.2	87	39	6	1	38-3	69	2.95	106	.247	.319	25-2	.120	-1*	93	0	-0.1
Total	2	4	8	.333	33	19	0	0-0	99.1	92	41	6	1	43-3	69	2.99	106	.250	.327	26-2	.115	-1	90	0	-0.1
LEMONGELLO, MARK Mark B 7.21.1955 Jersey City, NJ BR/TR 6-1/180# d9.14																									
1976	Hou N	3	1	.750	4	4	1	0-0	29	26	12	2	0	7-2	9	2.79	115	.236	.282	8-1	.000	-1	90	1	0.1
1977	Hou N	9	14	.391	34	30	5	0-0	214.2	237	88	20	3	52-4	83	3.48	103	.281	.323	69-5	.087	-4*	71	5	0.1
1978	Hou N	9	14	.391	33	30	9-1	1-0	210.1	204	100	20	9	66-5	77	3.94	84	.259	.318	64-6	.172	1	107	-16	-1.5
1979	Tor A	1	9	.100	18	10	2	0-0	83	97	64	14	3	34-8	40	6.29	69	.299	.365	0-0	—	0	75	-17	-1.7
Total	4	22	38	.367	89	74	17-1	1-0	537	564	264	56	15	159-19	209	4.06	88	.273	.326	141-12	.121	-3	86	-27	-3.0
LENNON, ED Edward Francis B 8.17.1897 Philadelphia, PA D 9.13.1947 Philadelphia, PA BR/TR 5-11/170# d6.30																									
1928	Phi N	0	0	—	5	0	0	0	12.1	19	14	0	0	10	6	8.76	49	.373	.475	4-0	.000	-1		-6	-0.4
LEON, DANNY Danilo Enrique (Lineco) B 4.3.1967 LaConcepcion, Venezuela BR/TR 6-1/170# d6.6																									
1992	Tex A	1	1	.500	15	0	0	0-0	18.1	18	14	5	3	10-0	15	5.89	65	.254	.369	0-0	—	0		-5	-0.5
LEON, IZZY Isidoro (Becerra) B 1.4.1911 Cruces, Cuba D 7.25.2002 Miami, FL BR/TR 5-10/160# d6.21																									
1945	Phi N	0	4	.000	14	4	0	0	38.2	49	25	3	0	19	11	5.35	72	.312	.386	9-0	.111	-0	44	-5	-0.5
LEON, MAX Maximino (Molino) B 2.4.1950 Pozo Hondo, Mexico BR/TR 6/170# d7.18																									
1973	Atl N	2	2	.500	12	1	1	0-2	27	30	18	6	3	9-1	18	5.33	74	.278	.344	7-1	.286	0*	157	-4	-0.5
1974	Atl N	4	7	.364	34	2	1-1	3-1	75	68	22	5	1	14-3	38	2.64	144	.242	.280	15-1	.133	-1	81	10	1.5
1975	Atl N	2	1	.667	50	1	0	6-3	85	90	52	5	7	33-8	53	4.13	92	.274	.349	9-1	.333	1	186	-5	-0.1
1976	Atl N	2	4	.333	30	0	0	3-3	36	32	15	2	2	15-3	16	2.75	138	.234	.314	2-0	.000	-0		3	0.5
1977	Atl N	4	4	.500	31	9	0	1-1	81.2	89	42	9	9	25-2	44	3.97	112	.280	.347	19-3	.316	1*	102	4	0.4
1978	Atl N	0	0	—	5	0	0	0-0	5.2	6	4	1	1	4-0	1	6.35	64	.273	.393	0-0	—	0*		-1	-0.1
Total	6	14	18	.438	162	13	2-1	13-10	310.1	315	153	28	23	100-17	170	3.71	107	.264	.330	52-6	.250	1	116	7	1.7
LEONARD, DENNIS Dennis Patrick B 5.8.1951 Brooklyn, NY BR/TR 6-1/190# d9.4																									
1974	KC A	0	4	.000	5	4	0	0-0	22	28	15	0	3	12-0	8	5.32	72	.329	.430	0-0	—	0	40	-3	-0.5
1975	KC A	15	7	.682	32	30	8	0-1	212.1	212	98	18	9	90-4	146	3.77	102	.263	.342	0-0	—	0	110	4	0.4
1976	†KC A	17	10	.630	35	34	16-2	0-0	259	247	113	16	11	70-5	150	3.51	100	.255	.309	0-0	—	0	135	2	0.0
1977	†KC A	**20**	12	.625	38	37	21-5	1-0	292.2	246	117	18	8	79-0	244	3.04	133	.227	.283	0-0	—	0*	99	31	3.0
1978	†KC A	21	17	.553	40	**40**	20-4	0-0	294.2	283	125	27	9	78-7	183	3.33	115	.254	.307	0-0	—	0	107	17	2.1
1979	KC A	14	12	.538	32	32	12-**5**	0-0	236	226	117	33	2	56-3	126	4.08	105	.253	.297	0-0	—	0	109	7	0.7
1980	†KC A	20	11	.645	38	**38**	9-3	0-0	280.1	271	127	30	1	80-5	155	3.79	107	.253	.304	0-0	—	0	117	10	1.0
1981	†KC A	13	11	.542	26	**26**	9-2	0-0	**201.2**	202	79	15	3	41-5	107	2.99	121	.258	.296	0-0	—	0	84	12	1.4
1982	KC A	10	6	.625	21	21	2	0-0	130.2	145	82	20	2	46-3	58	5.10	80	.279	.337	0-0	—	0	132	-15	-1.5
1983	KC A	6	3	.667	10	10	1	0-0	63	69	29	3	0	19-1	31	3.71	110	.277	.326	0-0	—	0	73	3	0.4
1985	KC A	0	0	—	2	0	0	0-0	2	1	0	0	0	0-0	1	0.00	—	.143	.143	0-0	—	0		1	0.0
1986	KC A	8	13	.381	33	30	5-2	0-0	192.2	207	106	22	4	51-6	114	4.44	96	.275	.321	0-0	—	0	80	-4	-0.4
Total	12	144	106	.576	312	302	103-23	1-1	2187	2137	1008	202	52	622-39	1323	3.70	107	.257	.310	0-0	—	0	106	65	6.6
LEONARD, ELMER Elmer Ellsworth "Tiny" B 11.12.1888 Napa, CA D 5.27.1981 Napa, CA BR/TR 6-3.5/210# d6.22																									
1911	Phi A	2	2	.500	5	1	1	0	19	26	11	0	2	10	10	2.84	111	.329	.418	7-1	.286	1	274	-1	-0.1
LEONARD, DUTCH Emil John B 3.25.1909 Auburn, IL D 4.17.1983 Springfield, IL BR/TR 6/175# d8.31 C3																									
1933	Bro N	2	3	.400	10	3	2	0	40	42	17	0	0	10	6	2.93	110	.261	.304	11-2	.000	-1	95	1	-0.1

Year	Tm Lg	W	L	Pct	G	GS	CG-Sho	SV-BS	IP	H	R	HR	HB	BB-IB	SO	ERA	AERA	OAV	OOB	AB-SH	AVG	PB	Sup	APR	PW
1934	Bro N	14	11	.560	44	21	11-2	5	183.2	210	90	12	4	33	58	3.28	119	.286	.320	67-5	.179	-1	128	8	1.1
1935	Bro N	2	9	.182	43	11	4	**8**	137.2	152	67	11	1	29	41	3.92	101	.280	.318	39-1	.026	-4	83	3	-0.2
1936	Bro N	0	0	—	16	0	0	1	32	34	18	2	0	5	8	3.66	113	.262	.289	5-1	.400	0		1	0.1
1938	Was A	12	15	.444	33	31	15-3	0	223.1	221	109	11	7	53	68	3.43	132	.256	**.305**	82-2	.232	3	97	24	2.8
1939	Was A	20	8	.714	34	34	21-2	0	269.1	273	124	16	5	59	88	3.54	123	.262	.305	95-13	.221	0	94	25	2.3
1940	Was A☆	14	19	.424	35	35	23-2	0	289	328	136	19	2	78	124	3.49	120	.286	.332	101-8	.158	-5	84	21	1.9
1941	Was A	18	13	.581	34	33	19-4	0	256	271	117	6	3	54	91	3.45	117	.270	.309	88-11	.102	-5	108	17	1.3
1942	Was A	2	2	.500	6	5	1-1	0	35	28	16	1	0	5	15	4.11	89	.214	.243	10-1	.100	-0	89	-1	-0.1
1943	Was A★	11	13	.458	31	30	15-2	1	219.2	218	96	9	4	46	51	3.28	98	.257	.298	67-11	.104	-4	102	-1	-0.5
1944	Was A☆	14	14	.500	32	31	17-3	0	229.1	222	97	8	3	37	62	3.06	106	.252	.284	79-5	.228	2	108	5	0.9
1945	Was A✣	17	7	.708	31	29	12-4	1	216	208	72	5	2	35	96	2.13	146	.248	.279	78-8	.231	1	125	21	2.5
1946	Was A	10	10	.500	26	23	7-2	0	161.2	182	85	9	4	36	62	3.56	94	.281	.323	53-5	.170	-1	106	-7	-0.7
1947	Phi N	17	12	.586	32	29	19-3	0	235	224	86	14	2	57	103	2.68	149	.258	.306	80-6	.175	-1	87	33	3.9
1948	Phi N	12	17	.414	34	30	16-1	0	225.2	226	85	9	4	54	92	2.51	157	.265	.312	83-2	.145	-3	80	31	3.7
1949	Chi N	7	16	.304	33	28	10-1	0	180	198	94	4	7	43	83	4.15	97	.272	.319	59-2	.203	0	73	-2	-0.1
1950	Chi N	5	1	.833	35	1	0	6	74	70	41	7	2	27	28	3.77	111	.248	.318	16-1	.063	-2	147	2	0.0
1951	Chi N☆	10	6	.625	41	1	0	3	81.2	69	30	3	2	28	30	2.64	155	.234	.305	21-1	.000	-3	129	11	2.0
1952	Chi N	2	2	.500	45	0	0	11	66.2	56	18	3	3	24	37	2.16	178	.235	.313	10-0	.200	-0		12	1.3
1953	Chi N	2	3	.400	45	0	0	8	62.2	72	34	9	1	24	27	4.60	97	.289	.354	10-0	.300	1		0	0.1
Total	20	191	181	.513	640	375	192-30	44	3218.1	3304	1432	158	56	737	1170	3.25	119	.265	.309	1054-85	.168	-21	97	204	22.2

LEONARD, DUTCH Hubert Benjamin B 4.16.1892 Birmingham, OH D 7.11.1952 Fresno, CA BL/TL 5-10.5/185# d4.12 Mil 1918

Year	Tm Lg	W	L	Pct	G	GS	CG-Sho	SV-BS	IP	H	R	HR	HB	BB-IB	SO	ERA	AERA	OAV	OOB	AB-SH	AVG	PB	Sup	APR	PW
1913	Bos A	14	17	.452	42	28	14-3	1	259.1	245	108	0	4	94	144	2.39	123	.255	.324	83-3	.181	1	120	11	1.2
1914	Bos A	19	5	.792	36	25	17-7	3	224.2	139	34	3	8	60	176	**0.96**	**280**	**.180**	**.246**	68-9	.147	-1	115	43	4.8
1915	†Bos A	15	7	.682	32	21	10-2	0	183.1	130	57	3	14	67	116	2.36	118	**.208**	.299	53-3	.264	5	105	12	1.7
1916	†Bos A	18	12	.600	48	34	17-6	6	274	244	87	6	8	66	144	2.36	117	.247	.300	85-4	.200	2	90	13	1.4
1917	Bos A	16	17	.485	37	36	26-4	1	294.1	257	88	4	5	72	144	2.17	119	.236	.286	104-2	.087	-6	83	16	0.8
1918	Bos A	8	6	.571	16	16	12-3	0	125.2	119	51	0	2	53	47	2.72	99	.254	.332	43-2	.186	0	133	-1	-0.2
1919	Det A	14	13	.519	29	28	18-4	0	217.1	212	89	7	7	65	102	2.77	115	.254	.313	71-6	.155	-3	94	8	0.4
1920	Det A	10	17	.370	28	27	10-3	0	191.1	192	107	8	8	63	76	4.33	86	.271	.338	57-3	.211	2	64	-7	-0.7
1921	Det A	11	13	.458	36	32	16-1	1	245	273	125	15	10	63	120	3.75	114	.286	.336	82-5	.171	-4	101	16	0.8
1924	Det A	3	2	.600	9	7	3	1	51.1	68	32	1	1	18	26	4.56	90	.327	.383	19-1	.211	-0	108	-3	-0.3
1925	Det A	11	4	.733	18	18	9	0	125.2	143	73	7	1	43	65	4.51	95	.289	.347	50-1	.200	-1	135	-3	-0.4
Total	11	139	113	.552	331	272	152-33	13	2192	2022	851	54	68	664	1160	2.76	115	.249	.312	715-39	.173	-5	102	105	9.5

LEONHARD, DAVE David Paul B 1.22.1941 Arlington, VA BR/TR 5-11/165# d9.21

Year	Tm Lg	W	L	Pct	G	GS	CG-Sho	SV-BS	IP	H	R	HR	HB	BB-IB	SO	ERA	AERA	OAV	OOB	AB-SH	AVG	PB	Sup	APR	PW
1967	Bal A	0	0	—	3	2	0	1	14.1	11	5	1	1	6-0	9	3.14	100	.200	.290	5-0	.000	-1	83	0	0.0
1968	Bal A	7	7	.500	28	18	5-2	1	126.1	95	46	10	2	57-3	61	3.13	93	.216	.307	31-6	.129	-1*	129	-1	-0.1
1969	†Bal A	7	4	.636	37	3	1-1	1-0	94	78	28	8	0	38-8	37	2.49	143	.228	.304	21-4	.095	-0*	83	12	1.3
1970	Bal A	0	0	—	23	0	0	1-0	28.1	32	18	5	0	18-3	14	5.08	72	.294	.385	1-0	.000	0*		-5	-0.2
1971	†Bal A	2	3	.400	12	6	1-1	1-1	54	51	18	5	1	19-0	18	2.83	118	.252	.318	18-1	.278	1*	80	4	0.5
1972	Bal A	0	0	—	14	0	0	0-0	20	20	10	3	0	12-0	7	4.50	69	.260	.356	1-0	1.000	1*		-3	0.0
Total	6	16	14	.533	117	29	7-4	5-1	337	287	125	32	4	150-14	146	3.15	103	.234	.318	77-11	.156	1	105	7	1.5

LEOPOLD, RUDY Rudolph Matas B 7.27.1905 Grand Cane, LA D 9.3.1965 Baton Rouge, LA BL/TL 6/160# d7.4

Year	Tm Lg	W	L	Pct	G	GS	CG-Sho	SV-BS	IP	H	R	HR	HB	BB-IB	SO	ERA	AERA	OAV	OOB	AB-SH	AVG	PB	Sup	APR	PW
1928	Chi A	0	0	—	2	0	0	0	2.1	3	3	0	0	0	0	3.86	105	.273	.273	1-0	.000	-0		-1	-0.1

LERCH, RANDY Randy Louis B 10.9.1954 Sacramento, CA BL/TL 6-5/190# d9.14

Year	Tm Lg	W	L	Pct	G	GS	CG-Sho	SV-BS	IP	H	R	HR	HB	BB-IB	SO	ERA	AERA	OAV	OOB	AB-SH	AVG	PB	Sup	APR	PW
1975	Phi N	0	0	—	3	0	0	0-0	7	6	5	1	0	1-0	8	6.43	58	.231	.259	0-0	—	0		-2	-0.1
1976	Phi N	0	0	—	1	0	0	1-0	3	3	1	0	0	0-0	0	3.00	118	.250	.250	1-0	1.000	1		0	0.1
1977	Phi N	10	6	.625	32	28	3	0-0	168.2	207	102	20	1	75-3	81	5.07	79	.312	.379	54-2	.167	-0*	110	-18	-1.4
1978	†Phi N	11	8	.579	33	28	5	0-0	184	183	89	15	1	70-3	96	3.96	90	.263	.329	60-2	.250	7*	135	-8	0.1
1979	Phi N	10	13	.435	37	35	6-1	0-0	214	228	98	20	3	60-4	92	3.74	102	.281	.328	72-3	.153	1*	99	1	0.3
1980	Phi N	4	14	.222	30	22	2	0-1	150	178	98	15	0	55-5	57	5.16	74	.302	.356	45-4	.267	3*	89	-22	-2.0
1981	†Mil A	7	9	.438	23	18	1	0-0	110.2	134	63	8	0	43-2	53	4.31	80	.303	.361	0-0	—	0	95	-15	-1.9
1982	Mil A	8	7	.533	21	20	1-1	0-0	108.2	123	68	12	3	51-1	33	4.97	76	.286	.361	0-0	—	0	139	-16	-2.0
	Mon N	2	0	1.000	6	4	0	0-0	23.2	26	11	0	0	8-1	4	3.42	107	.289	.343	8-0	.250	0	133	0	0.0
1983	Mon N	1	3	.250	19	5	0	0-0	38.2	45	29	6	1	18-2	24	6.75	53	.292	.368	9-1	.222	1	113	-12	-1.1
	SF N	1	0	1.000	7	0	0	0-0	10.2	9	4	1	0	8-1	6	3.38	105	.231	.354	0-0	—	0		0	0.0
	Year	2	3	.400	26	5	0	0-0	49.1	54	38	7	1	26-3	30	6.02	60	.280	.365	9-1	.222	1	113	-12	-1.1
1984	SF N	5	3	.625	37	4	0	2-1	72.1	80	36	3	1	36-3	48	4.23	83	.287	.362	15-0	.133	1	88	-5	-0.4
1986	Phi N	1	1	.500	4	0	0	0-0	8	10	8	0	0	7-1	5	7.88	49	.286	.405	3-0	.333	1		-3	-0.6
Total	11	60	64	.484	253	164	18-2	3-2	1099.1	1232	612	101	10	432-26	507	4.53	82	.289	.351	267-12	.206	15	111	-100	-9.0

LeROY, JOHN John Michael B 4.19.1975 Bellevue, WA D 6.26.2001 Sioux City, IA BR/TR 6-3/175# d9.26

Year	Tm Lg	W	L	Pct	G	GS	CG-Sho	SV-BS	IP	H	R	HR	HB	BB-IB	SO	ERA	AERA	OAV	OOB	AB-SH	AVG	PB	Sup	APR	PW
1997	Atl N	1	0	1.000	1	0	0	0-0	2	1	0	0	0	3-1	3	0.00	—	.143	.400	0-0	—	0		1	0.2

LeROY, LOUIS Louis Paul "Chief" B 2.18.1879 Omro, WI D 10.10.1944 Shawano, WI BR/TR 5-10/180# d9.22

Year	Tm Lg	W	L	Pct	G	GS	CG-Sho	SV-BS	IP	H	R	HR	HB	BB-IB	SO	ERA	AERA	OAV	OOB	AB-SH	AVG	PB	Sup	APR	PW
1905	NY A	1	1	.500	3	3	2	0	24	26	14	2	1	1	8	3.75	78	.277	.292	8-1	.125	-0	113	-2	-0.2
1906	NY A	2	0	1.000	11	2	1	1	44.2	33	19	0	2	12	28	2.22	134	.209	.273	14-1	.143	-1	170	2	0.1
1910	Bos A	0	0	—	1	0	0	0	4	7	9	1	0	2	3	11.25	23	.389	.450	1-0	.000	-0		-4	-0.2
Total	3	3	1	.750	15	5	3	1	72.2	66	42	3	3	15	39	3.22	91	.244	.292	23-2	.130	-1	136	-4	-0.3

LERSCH, BARRY Barry Lee B 9.7.1944 Denver, CO BB/TR 6/180# d4.8

Year	Tm Lg	W	L	Pct	G	GS	CG-Sho	SV-BS	IP	H	R	HR	HB	BB-IB	SO	ERA	AERA	OAV	OOB	AB-SH	AVG	PB	Sup	APR	PW
1969	Phi N	0	3	.000	10	0	0	2-1	17.2	20	14	6	1	10-2	13	7.13	50	.286	.383	3-0	.000	-0		-6	-1.1
1970	Phi N	6	3	.667	42	11	3	3-0	138	119	52	17	1	47-5	92	3.26	123	.232	.295	31-5	.065	-2	92	12	0.6
1971	Phi N	5	14	.263	38	30	3	0-0	214.1	203	97	28	3	50-2	113	3.78	93	.252	.297	59-6	.169	2*	85	-4	-0.2
1972	Phi N	4	6	.400	36	8	3-1	0-0	100.2	86	37	8	3	33-7	48	3.04	118	.231	.297	23-0	.000	-2*	77	6	0.4
1973	Phi N	3	6	.333	42	4	0	1-0	98.1	105	49	10	2	27-4	51	4.39	87	.279	.324	17-0	.176	0*	75	-4	-0.4
1974	StL N	0	0	—	1	0	0	0-0	1.1	3	6	1	0	5-0	0	40.50	9	.429	.667	0-0	—	0		-5	-0.2
Total	6	18	32	.360	169	53	9-1	6-1	570.1	536	255	70	10	172-20	317	3.82	97	.250	.306	133-11	.113	-3	84	-1	-0.9

LESHNOCK, DON Donald Lee B 11.25.1946 Youngstown, OH BR/TL 6-3/195# d6.7

Year	Tm Lg	W	L	Pct	G	GS	CG-Sho	SV-BS	IP	H	R	HR	HB	BB-IB	SO	ERA	AERA	OAV	OOB	AB-SH	AVG	PB	Sup	APR	PW
1972	Det A	0	0	—	1	0	0	0-0	1	2	0	0	0	0-0	2	0.00	—	.400	.400	0-0	—	0		0	0.0

LESKANIC, CURTIS Curtis John B 4.2.1968 Homestead, PA BR/TR 6/180# d6.27

Year	Tm Lg	W	L	Pct	G	GS	CG-Sho	SV-BS	IP	H	R	HR	HB	BB-IB	SO	ERA	AERA	OAV	OOB	AB-SH	AVG	PB	Sup	APR	PW
1993	Col N	1	5	.167	18	8	0	0-0	57	59	40	7	2	27-1	30	5.37	89	.266	.345	13-1	.154	0	71	-4	-0.4
1994	Col N	1	1	.500	8	3	0	0-0	22.1	27	14	2	0	10-0	17	5.64	88	.314	.385	6-0	.167	0	110	-1	-0.1
1995	†Col N	6	3	.667	**76**	0	0	10-6	98	83	38	7	0	33-1	107	3.40	159	.226	.288	7-2	.143	-0		18	1.8
1996	Col N	7	5	.583	70	0	0	6-4	73.2	82	51	12	2	38-1	76	6.23	84	.285	.369	3-1	.333	0		-5	-0.8
1997	Col N	4	0	1.000	55	0	0	2-2	58.1	59	36	8	0	24-0	53	5.55	93	.271	.337	1-0	.000	-0		-1	-0.1
1998	Col N	6	4	.600	66	0	0	2-3	75.2	75	37	9	1	40-2	55	4.40	118	.258	.349	2-1	.000	-0		6	0.7
1999	Col N	6	2	.750	63	0	0	0-3	85	87	54	7	5	49-4	77	5.08	114	.272	.374	4-0	.500	1		5	0.5
2000	Mil N	9	3	.750	73	0	0	12-1	77.1	58	23	7	3	51-5	75	2.56	178	.212	.337	2-0	.000	-0		18	2.9
2001	Mil N	2	6	.250	70	0	0	17-7	69.1	63	30	11	2	31-5	64	3.63	118	.241	.327	1-0	.000	-0		5	0.7
2003	Mil N	4	0	1.000	26	0	0	0-0	26.2	22	8	1	1	18-0	28	2.70	158	.227	.353	0-0	—	0		5	0.7
	KC A	1	0	1.000	27	0	0	2-1	26	16	7	1	0	11-1	22	1.73	299	.180	.267	0-0	—	0		8	0.4
Total	10	47	29	.618	552	11	0	51-27	669.1	631	338	72	16	332-20	604	4.30	118	.251	.340	39-5	.179	0	79	54	6.3

LESLEY, BRAD Bradley Jay B 9.11.1958 Turlock, CA BR/TR 6-6/230# d7.31

Year	Tm Lg	W	L	Pct	G	GS	CG-Sho	SV-BS	IP	H	R	HR	HB	BB-IB	SO	ERA	AERA	OAV	OOB	AB-SH	AVG	PB	Sup	APR	PW
1982	Cin N	0	2	.000	28	0	0	4-2	38.1	27	13	1	0	13-4	29	2.58	144	.197	.267	1-0	.000	-0		4	0.3
1983	Cin N	0	0	—	5	0	0	0-0	8.1	9	2	1	0	0-0	5	2.16	177	.290	.281	0-1	—	0		2	0.1
1984	Cin N	0	1	.000	16	0	0	2-1	19.1	17	11	3	0	14-1	7	5.12	74	.246	.369	2-0	.500	0		-2	-0.1
1985	Mil A	1	0	1.000	5	0	0	0-1	6.1	8	7	2	0	2-0	5	9.95	42	.296	.345	0-0	—	0		-4	-0.5

Year	Tm Lg	W	L	Pct	G	GS	CG-Sho	SV-BS	IP	H	R	HR	HB	BB-IB	SO	ERA	AERA	OAV	OOB	AB-SH	AVG	PB	Sup	APR	PW
Total	4	1	3	.250	54	0	0	6-4	72.1	61	33	7	0	29-5	46	3.86	98	.231	.305	3-1	.333	0		0	-0.2
LEVERENZ, WALT Walter Fred "Tiny" B 7.21.1888 Chicago, IL D 3.19.1973 Atascadero, CA BL/TL 5-10/175# d4.18																									
1913	StL A	6	17	.261	30	27	13-2	1	202.2	159	80	3	12	89	87	2.58	114	.225	.322	68-2	.176	-1*	72	8	0.7
1914	StL A	1	12	.077	27	16	5	0	111.1	107	67	5	4	63	41	3.80	71	.264	.368	33-0	.182	-0*	67	-15	-1.7
1915	StL A	1	2	.333	5	1	0	0	9	11	9	0	1	8	3	8.00	36	.333	.476	1-0	.000	-0	51	-4	-0.9
Total	3	8	31	.205	62	44	18-2	1	323	277	156	8	17	160	131	3.15	91	.242	.343	102-2	.176	-1	70	-11	-1.9
LEVERETT, DIXIE Gorham Vance B 3.29.1894 Georgetown, TX D 2.20.1957 Beaverton, OR BR/TR 5-11/190# d5.6																									
1922	Chi A	13	10	.565	33	27	16-4	2	223.2	224	95	11	3	79	60	3.34	122	.264	.329	83-1	.253	3	102	17	1.9
1923	Chi A	10	13	.435	38	24	9	3	192.2	212	108	6	6	64	64	4.06	97	.280	.341	60-6	.267	4	99	-5	-0.1
1924	Chi A	2	3	.400	21	11	4	0	99	123	72	2	3	41	29	5.82	71	.314	.383	32-2	.188	-1	110	-17	-0.9
1926	Chi A	1	1	.500	6	3	1	0	24	31	18	1	0	7	12	6.00	64	.316	.362	7-1	.143	-0	160	-6	-0.4
1929	Bos N	3	7	.300	24	12	3	1	97.2	135	81	5	5	30	28	6.36	74	.339	.393	32-0	.188	-0	93	-20	-1.6
Total	5	29	34	.460	122	77	33-4	6	637	725	374	25	17	221	193	4.51	92	.291	.353	214-10	.234	6	103	-31	-1.1
LEVERETTE, HOD Horace Wilbur "Levy" B 2.4.1889 Shreveport, LA D 4.10.1958 St.Petersburg, FL BR/TR 6/180# d4.22																									
1920	StL A	0	2	.000	3	2	0	0	10.1	9	6	1	0	12	0	5.23	75	.250	.438	3-0	.000	-1	71	-1	-0.2
LEVINE, AL Alan Brian B 5.22.1968 Park Ridge, IL BL/TR 6-3/180# d6.22																									
1996	Chi A	0	1	.000	16	0	0	0-1	18.1	22	14	1	1	7-1	12	5.40	88	.289	.353	0-0	—	0		-2	-0.1
1997	Chi A	2	2	.500	25	0	0	0-1	27.1	35	22	4	2	16-1	22	6.91	63	.313	.402	0-0	—	0		-7	-0.9
1998	Tex A	0	1	.000	30	0	0	0-0	58	68	30	6	0	16-1	19	4.50	107	.294	.336	0-0	—	0		3	0.1
1999	Ana A	1	1	.500	50	1	0	0-1	85	76	40	13	3	29-2	37	3.39	143	.247	.311	0-0	—	0	288	11	0.5
2000	Ana A	3	4	.429	51	5	0	2-0	95.1	98	44	10	2	49-5	42	3.87	131	.266	.352	0-0	—	0	151	12	0.8
2001	Ana A	8	10	.444	64	1	0	2-4	75.2	71	25	7	2	28-4	40	2.38	192	.257	.325	0-0	—	0	142	17	3.2
2002	Ana A	4	4	.500	52	0	0	5-2	63.2	61	35	8	2	34-3	40	4.24	105	.253	.342	0-0	—	0		0	0.0
2003	TB A	3	5	.375	36	0	0	0-2	49.2	45	23	7	2	18-0	25	2.90	156	.243	.317	0-0	—	0		6	0.9
	KC A	0	1	.000	18	0	0	1-1	21.1	22	6	2	1	11-1	5	2.53	204	.268	.362	0-0	—	0		6	0.3
	Year	3	6	.333	54	0	0	1-3	71	67	36	9	3	29-1	30	2.79	169	.251	.331	0-0	—	0		13	1.2
Total	8	21	29	.420	342	7	0	10-12	494.1	498	239	58	15	208-18	242	3.75	127	.265	.338	0-0	—	0	176	46	4.8
LEVRAULT, ALLEN Allen Harry B 8.15.1977 Fall River, MA BR/TR 6-3/240# d6.13																									
2000	Mil N	0	1	.000	5	1	0	0-0	12	10	7	0	0	7-0	9	4.50	101	.238	.340	3-0	.000	-0	81	0	-0.1
2001	Mil N	6	10	.375	32	20	1	0-0	130.2	146	93	27	7	59-7	80	6.06	71	.281	.359	33-6	.061	-2	88	-25	-2.8
2003	Fla N	1	0	1.000	19	0	0	0-0	28	38	12	3	1	15-2	21	3.86	106	.333	.409	2-0	.000	-0		1	0.0
Total	3	7	11	.389	56	21	1	0-0	170.2	194	112	30	8	81-9	110	5.59	77	.287	.367	38-6	.053	-3	89	-24	-2.9
LEVSEN, DUTCH Emil Henry B 4.29.1898 Wyoming, IA D 3.12.1972 St.Louis Park, MN BR/TR 6/180# d9.28																									
1923	Cle A	0	0	—	3	0	0	0	4.1	4	0	0	0	0	1	0.00	—	.267	.267	1-0	.000	-0		2	0.1
1924	Cle A	1	1	.500	4	1	1	0	16.1	22	8	0	0	4	3	4.41	97	.333	.371	5-0	.000	-1	237	1	0.0
1925	Cle A	1	2	.333	4	3	2	0	24.1	30	16	1	1	16	9	5.55	80	.313	.416	8-1	.250	0	70	-2	-0.2
1926	Cle A	16	13	.552	33	31	18-2	0	237.1	235	110	11	8	85	53	3.41	119	.261	.330	83-6	.205	-0	105	15	1.6
1927	Cle A	3	7	.300	25	13	2-1	0	80.1	96	54	1	2	37	15	5.49	77	.303	.379	25-0	.200	-1	84	-10	-1.0
1928	Cle A	0	3	.000	11	3	0	0	41.1	39	30	4	2	31	7	5.44	76	.258	.391	13-0	.000	-2	54	-6	-0.6
Total	6	21	26	.447	80	51	23-3	0	404	426	218	17	13	173	88	4.17	99	.276	.354	135-7	.178	-4	97	0	-0.1
LEWALLYN, DENNIS Dennis Dale B 8.11.1953 Pensacola, FL BR/TR 6-4/200# d9.21																									
1975	LA N	0	0	—	2	0	0	0-0	3	1	0	0	0	0-0	0	0.00	—	.100	.100	0-0	—	0		1	0.1
1976	LA N	1	1	.500	4	2	0	0-0	16.2	12	5	1	0	6-0	4	2.16	157	.207	.281	5-0	.000	-1	130	2	0.2
1977	LA N	3	1	.750	5	1	0	1-1	17	22	8	1	0	4-1	8	4.24	90	.306	.342	6-1	.000	-1	418	0	-0.2
1978	LA N	0	0	—	1	0	0	0-0	2	2	0	0	0	0-0	0	0.00	—	.250	.250	0-0	—	0		1	0.0
1979	LA N	0	1	.000	7	0	0	0-0	12.1	19	8	0	1	5-3	1	5.11	71	.358	.417	2-0	.500	0		-2	-0.1
1980	Tex A	0	0	—	4	0	0	0-1	5.2	7	5	0	0	4-1	1	7.94	49	.304	.407	0-0	—	0		-2	-0.1
1981	Cle A	0	0	—	7	0	0	0-0	13.1	16	8	1	0	2-0	11	5.40	67	.296	.316	0-0	—	0		-2	-0.1
1982	Cle A	0	1	.000	4	0	0	0-0	10.1	13	8	3	0	1-0	3	6.97	59	.310	.311	0-0	—	0		-3	-0.3
Total	8	4	4	.500	34	3	0	1-2	80.1	92	42	6	1	22-5	28	4.48	82	.287	.331	13-1	.077	-1	226	-5	-0.5
LEWANDOWSKI, DAN Daniel William B 1.6.1928 Buffalo, NY D 7.19.1996 Hamilton, ON, CAN BR/TR 6/180# d9.22																									
1951	StL N	0	1	.000	2	0	0	0	1	3	1	0	0	1	1	9.00	44	.500	.571	0-0	—	0		-1	-0.1
LEWIS B Brooklyn, NY d7.12																									
1890	Buf P	0	1	.000	1	1	0	0	3	13	20	3	0	7	1	60.00	7	.591	.690	5	.200	-0	238	-16	-1.4
LEWIS, COLBY Colby Preston B 8.2.1979 Bakersfield, CA BR/TR 6-4/215# d4.1																									
2002	Tex A	1	3	.250	15	4	0	0-2	34.1	42	26	4	2	26-2	28	6.29	75	.304	.422	0-0	—	0	83	-6	-0.5
2003	Tex A	10	9	.526	26	26	0	0-0	127	163	104	23	5	70-1	88	7.30	68	.317	.402	1-0	.000	-0	111	-27	-3.3
Total	2	11	12	.478	41	30	0	0-2	161.1	205	130	27	7	96-3	116	7.08	69	.314	.406	1-0	.000	-0	108	-33	-3.8
LEWIS, TED Edward Morgan "Parson" B 12.25.1872 Machynlleth, Wales D 5.24.1936 Durham, NH BR/TR 5-10.5/158# d7.6																									
1896	Bos N	1	4	.200	6	5	4	0	41.2	37	32	2	0	27	12	3.24	140	.236	.348	18-0	.111	-2	91	3	0.1
1897	†Bos N	21	12	.636	38	34	30-2	1	290	316	177	11	10	125	65	3.85	116	.275	.351	113-7	.248	-2	112	17	1.1
1898	Bos N	26	8	**.765**	41	33	29-1	2	313.1	267	131	9	9	109	72	2.90	127	.229	.300	131-5	.282	4*	130	30	3.2
1899	Bos N	17	11	.607	29	25	23-2	0	234.2	245	119	10	8	73	60	3.49	119	.269	.328	96-2	.260	0	93	16	1.4
1900	Bos N	13	12	.520	30	22	19-1	0	209	215	122	11	4	86	66	4.13	100	.265	.339	73-2	.137	-4	81	5	0.0
1901	Bos A	16	17	.485	39	34	31-1	1	316.1	299	172	14	8	91	103	3.53	100	.247	.304	121-1	.174	-2	105	4	0.0
Total	6	94	64	.595	183	153	136-7	4	1405	1379	753	57	39	511	378	3.53	113	.255	.324	552-17	.223	-5	106	75	5.8
LEWIS, JIM James Martin B 10.12.1955 Miami, FL BR/TR 6-3/190# d9.12																									
1979	Sea A	0	0	—	2	0	0	0-0	2.1	10	7	1	0	1-0	0	15.43	28	.625	.647	0-0	—	0		-4	-0.2
1982	NY A	0	0	—	1	0	0	0-0	0.2	3	7	0	0	3-0	0	54.00	7	.500	.667	0-0	—	0		-5	-0.2
1983	Min A	0	0	—	6	0	0	0-0	18	24	13	5	1	7-0	8	6.50	66	.324	.390	0-0	—	0		-4	-0.2
1985	Sea A	0	1	.000	2	1	0	0-0	4.2	8	4	1	2	1-0	1	7.71	55	.421	.500	0-0	—	0	65	-2	-0.3
Total	4	0	1	.000	11	1	0	0-0	25.2	45	31	7	3	12-0	9	8.77	49	.391	.462	0-0	—	0	65	-15	-0.9
LEWIS, JIM James Steven B 7.20.1964 Jackson, MI BR/TR 6-2/200# d8.9																									
1991	SD N	0	0	—	12	0	0	0-0	13	14	7	2	0	11-2	10	4.15	92	.275	.403	2-0	.000	-0		-1	0.0
LEWIS, RICHIE Richie Todd B 1.25.1966 Muncie, IN BR/TR 5-10/175# d7.31																									
1992	Bal A	1	1	.500	2	2	0	0-0	6.2	13	8	1	0	7-0	4	10.80	37	.406	.500	0-0	—	0	79	-5	-0.8
1993	Fla N	6	3	.667	57	0	0	0-2	77.1	68	37	7	1	43-6	65	3.26	133	.239	.336	2-1	.500	0		6	0.7
1994	Fla N	1	4	.200	45	0	0	0-0	54	62	44	7	1	38-9	45	5.67	77	.284	.391	5-0	.000	-0		-10	-0.8
1995	Fla N	0	1	.000	21	1	0	0-0	36	30	15	9	1	15-5	32	3.75	112	.224	.307	1-0	.000	0	64	3	0.1
1996	Det A	4	6	.400	72	0	0	2-4	90.1	78	45	9	4	65-9	78	4.18	121	.238	.361	1-0	.000	-0		9	0.8
1997	Oak A	2	0	1.000	14	0	0	0-0	18.2	24	21	7	1	15-0	12	9.64	47	.316	.430	0-0	—	0		-10	-0.9
	Cin N	0	0	—	4	0	0	0-0	5.2	4	5	3	0	3-0	4	6.35	67	.200	.304	1-0	1.000	0		-2	0.0
1998	Bal A	0	0	—	2	1	0	0-0	4.2	8	8	2	0	5-0	4	15.43	30	.421	.520	0-0	—	0	204	-6	-0.3
Total	7	14	15	.483	217	4	0	2-6	293.1	287	183	45	8	191-29	244	4.88	94	.258	.366	10-1	.200	1	100	-15	-1.2
LEWIS, SCOTT Scott Allen B 12.5.1965 Grants Pass, OR BR/TR 6-3/178# d9.25																									
1990	Cal A	1	1	.500	2	2	1	0-0	16.1	10	4	2	0	2-0	9	2.20	174	.172	.200	0-0	—	0	107	3	0.4
1991	Cal A	3	5	.375	16	11	0	0-0	60.1	81	43	9	2	21-0	37	6.27	66	.316	.373	0-0	—	0	121	-13	-1.5
1992	Cal A	4	0	1.000	21	2	0	0-0	38.1	36	18	3	2	14-1	18	3.99	100	.255	.325	0-0	—	0	137	0	0.1
1993	Cal A	1	2	.333	15	4	0	0-0	32	37	16	3	2	12-1	10	4.22	107	.311	.364	0-0	—	0	117	1	0.1
1994	Cal A	0	1	.000	20	0	0	0-0	31	46	23	5	2	10-2	10	6.10	80	.359	.414	0-0	—	0		-4	-0.2
Total	5	9	9	.500	74	19	1	0-0	178	210	104	22	8	59-4	84	5.01	85	.299	.356	0-0	—	0	118	-13	-1.1

Year	Tm Lg	W	L	Pct	G	GS	CG-Sho	SV-BS	IP	H	R	HR	HB	BB-IB	SO	ERA	AERA	OAV	OOB	AB-SH	AVG	PB	Sup	APR	PW
LEWIS, BERT William Burton B 10.3.1895 Tonawanda, NY D 3.24.1950 Tonawanda, NY BR/TR 6-2/176# d4.19																									
1924	Phi N	0	0	—	12	0	0	0	18	23	12	1	1	7	3	6.00	74	.315	.383	5-0	.000	-1		-2	-0.2
LEY, TERRY Terrence Richard B 2.21.1947 Portland, OR BL/TL 6/190# d8.20																									
1971	NY A	0	0	—	6	0	0	0-0	9	9	9	1	2	9-2	7	5.00	65	.257	.426	0-0	—	0		-3	-0.2
LIBKE, AL Albert Walter B 9.12.1918 Tacoma, WA D 3.7.2003 Wenatchee, WA BL/TR 6-4/215# d4.19 ▲																									
1945	Cin N	0	0	—	4	0	0	0	4.1	3	0	0	0	3	2	0.00	—	.200	.333	449-4	.283	1*		2	0.1
1946	Cin N	0	0	—	1	1	0	0	5	4	2	0	0	3	2	3.60	93	.235	.350	431-4	.253	0*	77	0	0.0
Total	2	0	0	—	5	1	0	0	9.1	7	2	0	0	6	4	1.93	183	.219	.342	880-8	.268	2	77	2	0.1
LIDDLE, DON Donald Eugene B 5.25.1925 Mt.Carmel, IL D 6.5.2000 Mt.Carmel, IL BL/TL 5-10/165# d4.17																									
1953	Mil N	7	6	.538	31	15	4	2	128.2	119	54	6	2	55	63	3.08	127	.248	.328	34-4	.088	-2	90	12	0.9
1954	†NY N	9	4	.692	28	19	4-3	0	126.2	100	48	5	3	55	44	3.06	132	.223	.308	37-2	.189	2*	100	15	1.5
1955	NY N	10	4	.714	33	13	4	1	106.1	97	54	18	4	61-7	56	4.23	95	.246	.351	27-2	.185	1	131	-1	0.0
1956	NY N	1	2	.333	11	5	1	1	41.1	45	22	5	1	14-3	21	3.92	97	.278	.333	12-3	.167	-0	112	-1	-0.1
	StL N	1	2	.333	14	2	0	0	24.2	36	25	8	0	18-5	14	8.39	45	.353	.446	2-0	.000	-0*	47	-12	-1.3
	Year	2	4	.333	25	7	1	1	66	81	27	13	1	32-8	35	5.59	68	.307	.379	14-3	.143	-0	93	-14	-1.4
Total	4	28	18	.609	117	54	13-3	4	427.2	397	203	42	10	203-15	198	3.75	106	.250	.337	112-11	.152	1	104	13	1.0
LIDGE, BRAD Bradley Thomas B 12.23.1976 Sacramento, CA BR/TR 6-5/200# d4.26																									
2002	Hou N	1	0	1.000	6	1	0	0-0	8.2	12	6	0	2	9-1	12	6.23	69	.333	.489	2-0	1.000	1	65	-2	0.0
2003	Hou N	6	3	.667	78	0	0	1-5	85	60	36	6	5	42-7	97	3.60	123	.202	.308	4-0	.000	-0		8	0.7
Total	2	7	3	.700	84	1	0	1-5	93.2	72	42	6	7	51-8	109	3.84	115	.216	.330	6-0	.333	1	65	6	0.7
LIDLE, CORY Cory Fulton B 3.22.1972 Hollywood, CA BR/TR 5-11/175# d5.8																									
1997	NY N	7	2	.778	54	2	0	2-1	81.2	86	38	7	3	20-4	54	3.53	114	.274	.320	5-0	.000	-0	194	4	0.3
1999	TB A	1	0	1.000	5	1	0	0-0	5	8	4	0	0	2-0	4	7.20	69	.364	.417	0-0	—	0	112	-1	-0.1
2000	TB A	4	6	.400	31	11	0	0-0	96.2	114	61	13	3	29-3	62	5.03	98	.294	.347	2-0	.000	-0	83	-2	-0.1
2001	†Oak A	13	6	.684	29	29	1	0-0	188	170	84	23	10	47-7	118	3.59	123	.242	.299	2-0	.000	-0	110	17	1.5
2002	†Oak A	8	10	.444	31	30	2-2	0-0	192	191	90	17	6	39-3	111	3.89	113	.258	.298	1-1	.000	-0	105	12	1.1
2003	Tor A	12	15	.444	31	31	2	0-0	192.2	216	133	24	5	60-3	112	5.75	80	.282	.337	6-0	.333	1	99	-23	-2.5
Total	6	45	39	.536	181	104	5-2	2-1	756	785	410	84	27	197-20	461	4.42	102	.268	.318	16-1	.125	-0	104	7	0.2
LIEBER, DUTCH Charles Edwin B 2.1.1910 Alameda, CA D 12.31.1961 Sawtelle, CA BR/TR 6-0.5/180# d4.18																									
1935	Phi A	1	1	.500	18	1	0	2	46.2	45	18	1	1	19	14	3.09	147	.263	.340	14-0	.143	-1*	134	8	0.3
1936	Phi A	0	1	.000	3	0	0	0	11.2	17	11	0	0	6	1	7.71	66	.362	.434	3-0	.000	-0		-3	-0.2
Total	2	1	2	.333	21	1	0	2	58.1	62	29	1	1	25	15	4.01	116	.284	.361	17-0	.118	-2	134	5	0.1
LIEBER, JON Jonathan Ray B 4.2.1970 Council Bluffs, IA BL/TR 6-3/220# d5.15																									
1994	Pit N	6	7	.462	17	17	1	0-0	108.2	116	62	12	1	25-3	71	3.73	116	.271	.311	39-2	.103	-2	97	2	0.0
1995	Pit N	4	7	.364	21	12	0	0-1	72.2	103	56	7	4	14-0	45	6.32	68	.346	.376	21-0	.048	-2	96	-16	-2.1
1996	Pit N	9	5	.643	51	15	0	1-3	142	156	70	19	3	28-2	94	3.99	109	.279	.315	36-3	.194	2	123	6	0.8
1997	Pit N	11	14	.440	33	32	1	0-0	188.1	193	102	23	1	51-8	160	4.49	96	.263	.309	58-2	.121	-0	97	-3	-0.4
1998	Pit N	8	14	.364	29	28	2	1-0	171	182	93	23	3	40-4	138	4.11	105	.269	.311	48-7	.167	0	84	2	0.2
1999	Chi N	10	11	.476	31	31	3-1	0-0	203.1	226	107	28	1	46-6	186	4.07	111	.279	.315	58-7	.121	-1	102	7	0.6
2000	Chi N	12	11	.522	35	**35**	6-1	0-0	**251**	248	130	36	10	54-3	192	4.41	103	.256	.301	82-10	.220	3*	97	4	0.7
2001	Chi N★	20	6	.769	34	34	5-1	0-0	232.1	226	104	25	7	41-4	148	3.80	109	.255	.290	76-9	.158	0*	121	11	1.2
2002	Chi N	6	8	.429	21	21	3	0-0	141	153	64	15	1	12-2	87	3.70	109	.277	.290	43-4	.163	-0	85	5	0.4
Total	9	86	83	.509	272	225	21-3	2-4	1510.1	1603	788	188	31	311-32	1121	4.18	103	.271	.308	461-44	.154	1	100	18	1.4
LIEBHARDT, GLENN Glenn Ignatius "Sandy" B 7.31.1910 Cleveland, OH D 3.14.1992 Winston-Salem, NC BR/TR 5-10.5/170# d4.22 f-Glenn																									
1930	Phi A	0	1	.000	5	0	0	0	9	14	12	2	0	8	2	11.00	42	.359	.468	2-0	.000	-0		-6	-0.6
1936	StL A	0	0	—	24	0	0	0	55.1	98	58	4	2	27	20	8.78	61	.375	.438	11-0	.000	-2		-18	-1.0
1938	StL A	0	0	—	2	0	0	0	3	4	2	1	0	0	1	6.00	83	.308	.308	0-0	—	0		0	0.0
Total	3	0	1	.000	31	0	0	0	67.1	116	72	7	2	35	23	8.96	59	.371	.437	13-0	.000	-2		-24	-1.6
LIEBHARDT, GLENN Glenn John B 3.10.1883 Milton, IN D 7.13.1956 Cleveland, OH BR/TR 5-10/175# d10.2 s-Glenn																									
1906	Cle A	2	0	1.000	2	2	2	0	18	13	4	0	0	1	9	1.50	175	.206	.219	8-0	.000	-1	192	2	0.2
1907	Cle A	18	14	.563	38	34	27-4	1	280.1	254	100	1	10	85	110	2.05	122	.244	.307	87-2	.161	-1	90	13	1.4
1908	Cle A	15	16	.484	38	26	19-3	0	262	222	93	2	3	81	146	2.20	109	.235	.297	80-10	.175	0	75	5	0.7
1909	Cle A	1	5	.167	12	4	1	1	52.1	54	28	0	1	16	15	2.92	87	.314	.376	15-1	.000	-2	76	-3	-0.6
Total	4	36	35	.507	90	66	49-7	2	612.2	543	225	3	14	183	280	2.17	113	.244	.306	190-13	.147	-4	86	17	1.7
LIGTENBERG, KERRY Kerry Dale B 5.11.1971 Rapid City, SD BR/TR 6-2/185# d8.12																									
1997	†Atl N	1	0	1.000	15	0	0	1-0	15	12	5	4	0	4-2	19	3.00	140	.211	.262	0-0	—	0		2	0.1
1998	†Atl N	3	2	.600	75	0	0	30-4	73	51	24	6	0	24-1	79	2.71	153	.193	.260	0-0	—	0		12	1.5
2000	†Atl N	2	3	.400	59	0	0	12-2	52.1	43	21	7	0	24-5	51	3.61	127	.226	.312	0-0	—	0		7	0.8
2001	†Atl N	3	3	.500	53	0	0	1-1	59.2	50	22	4	0	30-8	56	3.02	146	.226	.316	0-0	—	0		9	0.8
2002	†Atl N	3	4	.429	52	0	0	0-0	66.2	52	23	6	0	33-3	51	2.97	138	.213	.306	0-0	—	0		9	0.8
2003	Bal A	4	2	.667	68	0	0	1-3	59.1	60	23	9	2	14-3	47	3.34	132	.263	.310	0-0	—	0		7	0.7
Total	6	16	14	.533	322	0	0	45-10	326	268	118	36	2	129-22	303	3.09	139	.223	.298	0-0	—	0		46	4.7
LILLARD, GENE Robert Eugene B 11.12.1913 Santa Barbara, CA D 4.12.1991 Goleta, CA BR/TR 5-10.5/178# d5.8.1936 b-Bill ▲																									
1939	Chi N	3	5	.375	20	7	2	0	55	68	48	2	3	36	31	6.55	60	.309	.413	10-0	.100	1*	92	-17	-2.0
1940	StL N	0	1	.000	2	1	0	0	4.2	8	7	1	1	4	2	13.50	30	.364	.481	0-0	—	0	65	-4	-0.7
Total	2	3	6	.333	22	8	2	0	59.2	76	55	3	4	40	33	7.09	56	.314	.420	10-0	.100	1	89	-21	-2.7
LILLIE, JIM James J. "Grasshopper" (b: James J. Lilly) B 7.27.1861 New Haven, CT D 11.9.1890 Kansas City, MO d5.17 ▲																									
1883	Buf N	0	1	.000	3	0	0	0	12	16	12	0		2	4	3.00	106	.302	.327	201	.234	0*		-1	-0.1
1884	Buf N	0	1	.000	2	1	0	0	13	22	24	0		5	4	6.23	51	.324	.370	471	.223	-0*	84	-6	-0.3
1886	KC N	0	0	—	1	0	0	0	6	8	5	0		1	0	4.50	84	.348	.375	416	.175	-0*		-1	0.0
Total	3	0	2	.000	6	1	0	0	31	46	41	0		8	8	4.65	71	.319	.355	1088	.207	-0	84	-8	-0.4
LILLIQUIST, DEREK Derek Jansen B 2.20.1966 Winter Park, FL BL/TL 6/214# d4.13																									
1989	Atl N	8	10	.444	32	30	0	0-1	165.2	202	87	16	2	34-5	79	3.97	92	.301	.335	63-3	.190	0*	85	-7	-0.8
1990	Atl N	2	8	.200	12	11	0	0-0	61.2	75	45	10	1	19-4	34	6.28	64	.301	.348	23-0	.348	4*	71	-13	-1.5
	SD N	3	3	.500	16	7	1-1	0-0	60.1	61	29	6	2	23-1	29	4.33	88	.266	.337	20-2	.150	-0	101	-2	-0.2
	Year	5	11	.313	28	18	1-1	0-0	122	136	33	16	3	42-5	63	5.31	74	.285	.343	43-2	.256	4	83	-15	-1.7
1991	SD N	0	2	.000	6	2	0	0-0	14.1	25	14	3	0	4-1	7	8.79	43	.379	.414	2-0	.000	-0	106	-7	-0.8
1992	Cle A	5	3	.625	71	0	0	6-5	61.2	39	13	5	2	18-6	47	1.75	223	.186	.252	0-0	—	0		15	2.1
1993	Cle A	4	4	.500	56	2	0	10-3	64	64	20	5	1	19-5	40	2.25	193	.263	.317	0-0	—	0	127	14	1.9
1994	Cle A	1	3	.250	36	0	0	1-2	29.1	34	17	6	1	8-1	15	4.91	96	.304	.347	0-0	—	0		0	0.0
1995	Bos A	2	1	.667	28	0	0	0-3	23	27	17	7	0	9-2	9	6.26	78	.303	.356	0-0	—	0		-3	-0.4
1996	Cin N	0	0	—	5	0	0	0-1	3.2	5	3	1	0	0-0	1	7.36	58	.357	.357	0-0	—	0		-1	0.0
Total	8	25	34	.424	262	52	1-1	17-15	483.2	532	245	59	9	134-25	261	4.13	97	.283	.330	108-5	.213	4	83	-4	0.3
LILLY, TED Theodore Roosevelt B 1.4.1976 Lamita, CA BL/TL 6-1/180# d5.14																									
1999	Mon N	0	1	.000	9	3	0	0-0	23.2	30	20	7	3	9-0	28	7.61	59	.309	.382	5-1	.200	0	61	-7	-0.3
2000	NY A	0	0	—	7	0	0	0-0	8	8	6	1	0	5-0	11	5.63	86	.235	.333	0-0	—	0		-1	0.0
2001	NY A	5	6	.455	26	21	0	0-0	120.2	126	81	20	7	51-1	112	5.37	84	.267	.344	1-2	.000	-0	105	-13	-0.9
2002	NY A	3	6	.333	16	11	2-1	0-0	76.2	57	31	10	5	24-3	59	3.40	129	.202	.274	3-0	.000	-0	54	9	0.9
	†Oak A	2	1	.667	6	5	0	0-0	23.1	23	12	5	1	7-0	18	4.63	95	.253	.313	0-0	—	0	80	0	0.0
	Year	5	7	.417	22	16	2-1	0-0	100	80	16	15	6	31-3	77	3.69	119	.214	.283	3-0	.000	-0	62	9	0.9
2003	†Oak A	12	10	.545	32	31	0	0-0	178.1	179	92	24	5	58-3	147	4.34	104	.255	.314	5-0	.000	-0	88	5	0.4
Total	5	22	24	.478	96	71	2-1	0-0	430.2	423	242	67	21	154-7	375	4.68	96	.252	.320	14-3	.071	-1	86	-7	0.1

Year	Tm Lg	W	L	Pct	G	GS	CG-Sho	SV-BS	IP	H	R	HR	HB	BB-IB	SO	ERA	AERA	OAV	OOB	AB-SH	AVG	PB	Sup	APR	PW
LIMA, JOSE Jose Desiderio Rodriguez (b: Jose Desiderio Rodriguez (Lima)) B 9.30.1972 Santiago, D.R. BR/TR 6-2/170# d4.20																									
1994	Det A	0	1	.000	3	1	0	0-0	6.2	11	10	2	0	3-1	7	13.50	36	.355	.412	0-0	—	0	114	-6	-0.7
1995	Det A	3	9	.250	15	15	0	0-0	73.2	85	52	10	4	18-4	37	6.11	78	.288	.336	0-0	—	0	70	-10	-1.4
1996	Det A	5	6	.455	39	4	0	3-4	72.2	87	48	13	5	22-4	59	5.70	89	.296	.352	0-0	—	0	46	-4	-0.4
1997	†Hou N	1	6	.143	52	1	0	2-0	75	79	45	9	5	16-2	63	5.28	76	.271	.317	3-2	.000	-0	92	-9	-0.9
1998	Hou N	16	8	.667	33	33	3-1	0-0	233.1	229	100	34	7	32-1	169	3.70	109	.256	.285	79-9	.139	-1	127	11	1.0
1999	†Hou N★	21	10	.677	35	**35**	3	0-0	246.1	256	108	30	2	44-2	187	3.58	123	.265	.296	75-13	.080	-4*	102	23	2.0
2000	Hou N	7	16	.304	33	33	0	0-0	196.1	251	152	48	2	68-3	124	6.65	73	.313	.364	60-8	.167	-1	99	-34	-3.3
2001	Hou N	1	2	.333	14	9	0	0-0	53	77	48	12	5	16-1	41	7.30	63	.350	.400	16-1	.000	-2	108	-16	-0.9
	Det A	5	10	.333	18	18	2	0-0	112.2	120	66	23	4	22-2	43	4.71	92	.274	.311	1-0	.000	-0	82	-5	-0.7
2002	Det A	4	6	.400	20	12	0	0-0	68.1	86	60	12	2	21-0	33	7.77	55	.314	.360	0-0	—	0	95	-25	-2.9
2003	KC A	8	3	.727	14	14	0	0-0	73.1	80	40	7	5	26-0	32	4.91	105	.280	.347	2-1	.500	0	97	3	0.4
Total	10	71	77	.480	276	175	8-1	5-4	1211.1	1361	729	200	41	288-20	795	5.13	88	.284	.327	236-34	.119	-7	100	-72	-7.8
LINCOLN, EZRA Ezra Perry B 11.17.1868 Raynham, MA D 5.7.1951 Taunton, MA BL/TL 5-11/160# d5.2																									
1890	Cle N	3	11	.214	15	15	13	0	118	157	102	1	1	53	22	4.42	81	.310	.376	51	.157	-3	73	-15	-1.6
	Syr AA	0	3	.000	3	3	2	0	20	33	27	1	1	4	6	10.35	34	.359	.392	8	.000	-1	32	-15	-1.5
Total	1	3	14	.176	18	18	15	0	138	190	129	2	2	57	28	5.28	68	.317	.378	59	.136	-4	66	-30	-3.1
LINCOLN, MIKE Michael George B 4.10.1975 Carmichael, CA BR/TR 6-2/211# d4.7																									
1999	Min A	3	10	.231	18	15	0	0-0	76.1	102	59	11	1	26-0	27	6.84	75	.321	.368	1-0	.000	-0	83	-13	-1.8
2000	Min A	0	3	.000	8	4	0	0-0	20.2	36	25	10	2	13-0	15	10.89	47	.383	.468	0-0	—	0	109	-12	-1.3
2001	Pit N	2	1	.667	31	0	0	0-2	40.1	34	16	3	4	11-0	24	2.68	168	.225	.293	4-1	.250	0		7	0.5
2002	Pit N	2	4	.333	55	0	0	0-3	72.1	80	28	7	0	27-8	50	3.11	134	.290	.349	5-0	.000	-1		8	0.6
2003	Pit N	3	4	.429	36	0	0	5-3	36.1	38	22	5	1	13-0	28	5.20	84	.277	.342	0-0	—	0		-3	-0.6
Total	5	10	22	.313	148	19	0	5-8	246	290	150	36	8	90-8	144	5.16	90	.297	.357	10-1	.100	-1	97	-13	-2.6
LINDAMAN, VIVE Vivan Alexander B 10.28.1877 Charles City, IA D 2.13.1927 Charles City, IA BR/TR 6-1/200# d4.14																									
1906	Bos N	12	23	.343	39	36	32-2	0	307.1	303	132	4	11	90	115	2.43	111	.264	.324	106-3	.132	-2	73	3	0.1
1907	Bos N	11	15	.423	34	28	24-2	1	260	252	130	10	15	108	90	3.63	70	.265	.349	90-2	.122	-2	102	-28	-3.0
1908	Bos N	12	16	.429	43	30	21-2	1	270.2	246	112	7	10	70	68	2.36	102	.249	.306	85-4	.176	0	96	-3	-0.4
1909	Bos N	1	6	.143	15	6	6-1	0	66	75	44	1	1	28	13	4.64	61	.299	.371	22-0	.273	1	29	-11	-1.1
Total	4	36	60	.375	131	100	83-7	2	904	876	418	22	37	296	286	2.92	88	.263	.329	303-9	.152	-3	85	-39	-4.4
LINDBLAD, PAUL Paul Aaron B 8.9.1941 Chanute, KS BL/TL 6-1/195# d9.15																									
1965	KC A	0	1	.000	4	0	0	0	7.1	12	9	3	1	0-0	12	11.05	32	.353	.371	1-0	.000	-0		-6	-0.7
1966	KC A	5	10	.333	38	14	0	1	121	138	63	14	3	37-10	69	4.17	82	.292	.347	34-1	.147	0	89	-10	-1.1
1967	KC A	5	8	.385	46	10	1-1	6	115.2	106	59	15	6	35-9	83	3.58	89	.241	.304	34-1	.206	2*	118	-8	-0.8
1968	Oak A	4	3	.571	47	1	0	2	56.1	51	19	6	0	14-4	42	2.40	118	.237	.281	8-1	.375	1	0	2	0.5
1969	Oak A	9	6	.600	60	0	0	9-2	78.1	72	37	8	2	33-8	64	4.14	83	.240	.319	12-0	.333	1		-5	-0.9
1970	Oak A	8	2	.800	62	0	0	3-0	63.1	52	23	7	0	28-7	42	2.70	131	.222	.305	6-0	.000	-1		5	0.8
1971	Oak A	1	0	1.000	8	0	0	0-2	16	18	7	1	1	2-1	4	3.94	85	.295	.328	3-0	.333	0		-1	0.0
	Was A	6	4	.600	43	0	0	8-5	83.2	58	25	6	2	29-6	50	2.58	128	.196	.272	19-0	.158	0		8	1.2
	Year	7	4	.636	51	0	0	8-7	99.2	76	32	7	3	31-7	54	2.80	118	.213	.281	22-0	.182	1		7	1.2
1972	Tex A	5	8	.385	**66**	0	0	9-5	99.2	95	31	7	0	29-6	51	2.62	115	.257	.309	15-2	.200	0		6	0.9
1973	†Oak A	1	5	.167	36	3	0	2-0	78	89	38	8	3	28-2	33	3.69	96	.292	.354	0-0	—	0	25	-2	-0.2
1974	Oak A	4	4	.500	45	2	0	6-3	100.2	85	30	4	2	30-11	46	2.06	162	.231	.288	0-0	—	0	93	14	1.3
1975	†Oak A	9	1	.900	68	0	0	7-1	122.1	105	44	6	0	43-10	58	2.72	134	.237	.300	1-0	.000	-0		12	1.2
1976	Oak A	6	5	.545	65	0	0	5-5	114.2	111	50	5	3	24-5	37	3.06	110	.253	.292	0-0	—	0		1	0.2
1977	Tex A	4	5	.444	42	1	0	4-1	98.2	103	50	16	1	29-2	46	4.20	98	.270	.322	0-0	—	0	44	0	0.0
1978	Tex A	1	1	.500	18	0	0	2-2	39.2	41	16	2	2	15-7	25	3.63	104	.279	.349	0-0	—	0		2	0.1
	†NY A	0	0	—	7	1	0	0-0	18.1	21	9	4	0	8-0	9	4.42	82	.284	.354	0-0	—	0	99	-1	0.0
	Year	1	1	.500	25	1	0	2-2	58	62	13	6	2	23-7	34	3.88	96	.281	.351	0-0	—	0	97	1	0.1
Total	14	68	63	.519	655	32	1-1	64-26	1213.2	1157	510	112	26	384-88	671	3.29	104	.253	.312	133-5	.195	4	87	17	2.5
LINDE, LYMAN Lyman Gilbert B 9.30.1920 Rolling Prairie, WI D 10.24.1995 Beaver Dam, WI BR/TR 5-11/185# d9.11																									
1947	Cle A	0	0	—	1	0	0	0	0.2	3	2	0	0	1	0	27.00	13	.600	.667	0-0	—	0		-2	-0.1
1948	Cle A	0	0	—	3	0	0	0	10	9	6	1	0	4	0	5.40	75	.243	.317	2-0	.000	-0		-1	-0.1
Total	2	0	0	—	4	0	0	0	10.2	12	8	1	0	5	0	6.75	60	.286	.362	2-0	.000	-0		-3	-0.2
LINDELL, JOHNNY John Harlan B 8.30.1916 Greeley, CO D 8.27.1985 Newport Beach, CA BR/TR 6-4.5/217# d4.18.1941 Mil 1945 ▲																									
1942	NY A	2	1	.667	23	2	0	1	52.2	52	25	3	1	22	28	3.76	92	.254	.329	24-0	.250	1*	99	-2	0.0
1953	Pit N	5	16	.238	27	23	13-1	0	175.2	173	106	17	6	116	102	4.71	95	.262	.377	91-0	.286	6*	76	-6	1.0
	Phi N	1	1	.500	5	3	2	0	23.1	22	16	0	0	23	16	4.24	99	.259	.417	18-0	.389	2*	85	-2	0.1
	Year	6	17	.261	32	26	15-1	0	199	195	20	17	6	139	118	4.66	95	.261	.382	109-0	.303	8	77	-9	1.1
Total	2	8	18	.308	55	28	15-1	1	251.2	247	147	20	7	161	146	4.47	95	.260	.371	133-0	.293	9	81	-10	1.1
LINDEMANN, ERNIE Ernest B 6.10.1883 New York, NY D 12.27.1951 Brooklyn, NY BR/TR d6.28																									
1907	Bos N	0	0	—	1	1	0	0	6.1	6	5	0	0	4	3	5.68	45	.286	.400	2-1	.500	0	167	-2	-0.1
LINDQUIST, CARL Carl Emil B 5.9.1919 Morris Run, PA D 9.3.2001 Blossburg, PA BR/TR 6-2/185# d9.27																									
1943	Bos N	0	2	.000	2	2	0	0	13	17	10	3	0	4	1	6.23	55	.315	.362	4-0	.000	-1	37	-4	-0.5
1944	Bos N	0	0	—	5	0	0	0	8.2	8	5	1	0	2	4	3.12	123	.222	.263	1-0	.000	-0		0	0.0
Total	2	0	2	.000	7	2	0	0	21.2	25	15	4	0	6	5	4.98	72	.278	.323	5-0	.000	-1	37	-4	-0.5
LINDSEY, JIM James Kendrick B 1.24.1898 Greensburg, LA D 10.25.1963 Jackson, LA BR/TR 6-1/175# d5.1																									
1922	Cle A	4	5	.444	29	5	0	1	83.2	105	60	4	3	24	29	6.02	67	.324	.376	24-0	.167	-1	76	-17	-1.7
1924	Cle A	0	0	—	3	0	0	0	3	8	7	0	0	3	0	21.00	20	.500	.579	3-0	.000	-1		-5	-0.3
1929	StL N	1	1	.500	2	2	1	0	16.1	20	11	1	1	2	8	5.51	85	.290	.319	5-0	.200	-0	75	-1	-0.2
1930	†StL N	7	5	.583	39	6	3	5	105.2	131	59	6	4	46	50	4.43	113	.312	.385	28-3	.286	1	84	7	0.7
1931	†StL N	6	4	.600	35	2	1-1	7	74.2	77	32	2	0	45	32	2.77	142	.270	.370	9-4	.111	-0	76	**7**	1.0
1932	StL N	3	3	.500	33	5	0	3	89.1	96	53	6	2	38	31	4.94	80	.279	.354	21-3	.143	-1	154	-8	-0.7
1933	StL N	0	0	—	1	0	0	0	2	2	1	0	0	1	1	4.50	77	.286	.375	0-0	—	0		0	0.0
1934	Cin N	0	0	—	4	0	0	0	4	4	3	0	1	2	2	4.50	91	.286	.412	0-0	—	0		0	0.0
	StL N	0	1	.000	11	0	0	1	14	21	13	2	0	3	7	6.43	66	.328	.358	1-0	.000	-0		-4	-0.3
	Year	0	1	.000	15	0	0	1	18	25	23	2	1	5	9	6.00	70	.321	.369	1-0	.000	-0		-4	-0.3
1937	Bro N	0	1	.000	20	0	0	2	38.1	43	22	4	1	12	15	3.52	115	.295	.352	6-0	.167	-0		1	0.0
Total	9	21	20	.512	177	20	5-1	19	431	507	261	25	12	176	175	4.70	91	.300	.370	97-10	.186	-3	99	-20	-1.5
LINDSTROM, AXEL Axel Olaf B 8.26.1895 Gustavsberg, Sweden D 6.24.1940 Asheville, NC BR/TR 5-10/180# d10.3																									
1916	Phi A	0	0	—	1	0	0	1	4	2	2	0	1	0	1	4.50	63	.182	.250	2-0	.500	0		0	0.0
LINEBRINK, SCOTT Scott Cameron B 8.4.1976 Austin, TX BR/TR 6-3/185# d4.15																									
2000	SF N	0	0	—	3	0	0	0-0	2.1	7	3	1	0	2-0	0	11.57	37	.500	.563	0-0	—	0		-2	-0.1
	Hou N	0	0	—	8	0	0	0-0	9.2	11	5	3	3	6-0	6	4.66	105	.289	.426	1-0	1.000	0		0	0.0
	Year	0	0	—	11	0	0	0-0	12	18	13	4	3	8-0	6	6.00	79	.346	.460	1-0	1.000	0		-1	-0.1
2001	Hou N	0	0	—	9	0	0	0-0	10.1	6	4	0	2	6-0	9	2.61	175	.176	.326	0-0	—	0		2	0.1
2002	Hou N	0	0	—	22	0	0	0-0	24.1	31	21	2	1	13-4	24	7.03	61	.298	.375	0-0	—	0		-7	-0.4
2003	Hou N	1	1	.500	9	6	0	0-0	31.2	38	15	4	3	14-1	17	4.26	104	.317	.399	8-1	.000	-1	138	1	-0.1
	SD N	2	1	.667	43	0	0	0-0	60.2	55	22	5	3	22-3	51	2.82	140	.244	.314	4-0	.500	1		7	0.4
	Year	3	2	.600	52	6	0	0-0	92.1	93	44	9	6	36-4	68	3.31	124	.270	.344	12-1	.167	0	148	8	0.3
Total	4	3	2	.600	94	6	0	0-0	139	148	70	15	12	63-8	107	4.14	102	.277	.360	13-1	.231	1	143	1	-0.1
LINES, DICK Richard George B 8.17.1938 Montreal, PQ, CAN BR/TL 6-1/175# d4.16																									
1966	Was A	5	2	.714	53	0	0	2	83	63	23	4	1	24-7	49	2.28	152	.213	.273	10-2	.000	-1		11	1.0

Year	Tm Lg	W	L	Pct	G	GS	CG-Sho	SV-BS	IP	H	R	HR	HB	BB-IB	SO	ERA	AERA	OAV	OOB	AB-SH	AVG	PB	Sup	APR	PW
1967	Was A	2	5	.286	54	0	0	4	85.2	83	43	6	0	24-6	54	3.36	94	.245	.292	9-0	.111	1		-5	-0.3
Total	2	7	7	.500	107	0	0	6	168.2	146	66	10	1	48-13	103	2.83	117	.230	.283	19-2	.053	-1		6	0.7
LINK, FRED Edward Theodore "Laddie" B 3.11.1886 Columbus, OH D 5.22.1939 Houston, TX BL/TL 6/170# d4.15																									
1910	Cle A	5	6	.455	22	13	6-1	1	127.2	121	53	0	7	50	55	3.17	82	.259	.340	42-3	.167	-1	90	-5	-0.6
	StL A	0	1	.000	3	3	0	0	17	24	10	0	1	13	5	4.24	58	.375	.487	6-0	.167	-0	181	-3	-0.2
	Year	5	7	.417	25	16	6-1	1	144.2	145	17	0	8	63	60	3.30	78	.273	.359	48-3	.167	-1	106	-6	-0.8
LINKE, ED Edward Karl "Babe" B 11.9.1911 Chicago, IL D 6.21.1988 Chicago, IL BR/TR 5-11/180# d4.27																									
1933	Was A	1	0	1.000	3	2	0	0	16	15	10	0	0	11	6	5.06	83	.250	.366	6-1	.167	0	102	-2	-0.1
1934	Was A	2	2	.500	7	4	2	0	34.2	38	20	1	0	9	9	4.15	104	.277	.322	11-1	.182	0*	71	0	0.0
1935	Was A	11	7	.611	40	22	10-1	3	178	211	111	6	1	80	51	5.01	86	.296	.367	68-1	.294	6	131	-14	-0.7
1936	Was A	1	5	.167	13	6	1	0	52	73	46	4	0	14	11	7.10	67	.330	.370	15-0	.400	5	52	-13	-0.7
1937	Was A	6	1	.857	36	7	0	3	128.2	158	89	11	4	59	61	5.60	79	.304	.379	46-1	.217	1*	141	-15	-0.7
1938	StL A	1	7	.125	21	2	0	0	39.2	60	37	6	0	33	18	7.94	63	.357	.463	10-0	.200	0	124	-12	-1.8
Total	6	22	22	.500	120	43	13-1	6	449	555	313	28	5	206	156	5.61	79	.305	.377	156-4	.263	12	113	-56	-4.0
LINT, ROYCE Royce James B 1.1.1921 Birmingham, AL BL/TL 6-1/165# d4.13																									
1954	StL N	2	3	.400	30	4	1-1	0	70.1	75	46	9	0	30	36	4.86	85	.273	.342	10-1	.100	1*	152	-7	-0.2
LINTON, DOUG Douglas Warren B 2.9.1965 Santa Ana, CA BR/TR 6-1/190# d8.3																									
1992	Tor A	1	3	.250	8	3	0	0-0	24	31	23	5	0	17-0	16	8.63	47	.323	.417	0-0	—	0	97	-11	-1.5
1993	Tor A	0	1	.000	4	1	0	0-0	11	11	8	0	1	9-0	4	6.55	66	.256	.382	0-0	—	0	64	-2	-0.2
	Cal A	2	0	1.000	19	0	0	0-1	25.2	35	22	8	0	14-1	19	7.71	59	.324	.398	0-0	—	0		-8	-0.5
	Year	2	1	.667	23	1	0	0-1	36.2	46	33	8	1	23-1	23	7.36	61	.305	.393	0-0	—	0	62	-10	-0.7
1994	NY N	6	2	.750	32	3	0	0-0	50.1	74	27	4	0	20-3	29	4.47	94	.341	.395	7-2	.000	-1	131	-1	-0.3
1995	KC A	0	1	.000	7	2	0	0-0	22.1	22	21	4	2	10-1	13	7.25	66	.256	.347	0-0	—	0	29	-7	-0.3
1996	KC A	7	9	.438	21	18	0	0-0	104	111	65	13	8	26-1	87	5.02	100	.271	.325	0-0	—	0	90	-1	-0.2
1999	Bal A	1	4	.200	14	8	0	0-0	59	69	41	14	2	25-1	31	5.95	79	.296	.369	0-0	—	0	72	-8	-0.6
2003	Tor A	0	0	—	7	0	0	0-0	9	7	3	2	0	4-0	7	3.00	153	.226	.314	0-0	—	0		2	0.1
Total	7	17	20	.459	112	35	0	0-1	305.1	360	210	50	13	125-7	206	5.78	81	.294	.364	7-2	.000	-1	87	-36	-3.5
LINZY, FRANK Frank Alfred B 9.15.1940 Ft.Gibson, OK BR/TR 6-1/190# d8.14																									
1963	SF N	0	0	—	8	1	0	0	16.2	22	9	0	1	10-0	14	4.86	66	.324	.418	3-0	.000	-0	189	-2	-0.1
1965	SF N	9	3	.750	57	0	0	21	81.2	76	19	2	3	23-8	35	1.43	251	.250	.309	18-0	.222	1		**18**	4.1
1966	SF N	7	11	.389	51	0	0	16	100.1	107	40	4	2	34-9	57	2.96	124	.273	.333	20-3	.150	0		7	1.6
1967	SF N	7	7	.500	57	0	0	17	95.2	67	21	4	0	34-7	38	1.51	218	.203	.274	15-3	.000	-2		18	3.5
1968	SF N	9	8	.529	57	0	0	12	94.2	76	30	1	1	27-14	36	2.09	141	.218	.274	11-4	.000	-1		8	1.8
1969	SF N	14	9	.609	58	0	0	11-10	116.1	129	57	5	3	38-15	62	3.64	96	.283	.341	30-3	.267	3		-2	0.0
1970	SF N	2	1	.667	20	0	0	1-0	25.2	33	20	2	1	11-4	16	7.01	57	.327	.391	4-0	.000	-0		-8	-0.9
	StL N	3	5	.375	47	0	0	2-2	61.1	66	26	3	0	23-10	19	3.67	112	.282	.344	7-0	.000	-1		4	0.4
	Year	5	6	.455	67	0	0	3-2	87	99	53	5	1	34-14	35	4.66	88	.296	.358	11-0	.000	-1		-4	-0.5
1971	StL N	4	3	.571	50	0	0	6-2	59.1	49	18	2	0	27-11	24	2.12	170	.226	.311	4-0	.500	1		8	1.3
1972	Mil A	2	2	.500	47	0	0	12-2	77.1	70	30	4	2	27-12	24	3.03	101	.248	.313	9-1	.111	-0		0	0.0
1973	Mil A	2	6	.250	42	1	0	13-4	63	68	34	7	1	21-6	21	3.57	105	.282	.338	0-0	—	0	142	-1	-0.2
1974	Phi N	3	2	.600	22	0	0	0-1	24.2	27	11	1	0	7-1	12	3.28	115	.284	.333	0-0	—	0		1	0.2
Total	11	62	57	.521	516	2	0	111-21	816.2	790	315	35	14	282-97	358	2.85	122	.257	.321	121-14	.149	0	164	51	11.7
LiPETRI, ANGELO Michael Angelo B 7.6.1929 Brooklyn, NY BR/TR 6-1.5/180# d4.25																									
1956	Phi N	0	0	—	6	0	0	0	11	7	5	2	1	3-0	8	3.27	114	.175	.250	1-0	.000	-0		0	0.0
1958	Phi N	0	0	—	4	0	0	0	4	6	5	1	1	0-0	1	11.25	35	.353	.389	0-0	—	0		-3	-0.1
Total	2	0	0	—	10	0	0	0	15	13	10	3	2	3-0	9	5.40	70	.228	.290	1-0	.000	-0		-3	-0.1
LIPP, TOM Thomas Charles (b: Thomas Charles Lieb) B 6.4.1870 Baltimore, MD D 5.30.1932 Baltimore, MD 5-11.5/170# d9.18																									
1897	Phi N	0	1	.000	1	1	0	0	3	8	5	0	0	2	1	15.00	28	.471	.526	1-0	1.000	0	51	-3	-0.4
LIPSCOMB, NIG Gerard B 2.24.1911 Rutherfordton, NC D 2.27.1978 Huntersville, NC BR/TR 6/175# d4.23 ▲																									
1937	StL A	0	0	—	3	0	0	0	9.2	13	9	3	0	5	1	6.52	74	.333	.409	96-1	.323	1*		-2	-0.1
LIRA, FELIPE Antonio Felipe B 4.26.1972 Santa Teresa, Venezuela BR/TR 6/170# d4.27																									
1995	Det A	9	13	.409	37	22	0	1-2	146.1	151	74	17	8	56-7	89	4.31	111	.271	.341	0-0	—	0	76	8	1.0
1996	Det A	6	14	.300	32	32	3-2	0-0	194.2	204	123	30	10	66-2	113	5.22	97	.269	.331	0-0	—	0	80	-4	-0.2
1997	Det A	5	7	.417	20	15	1-1	0-0	92	101	61	15	2	45-2	64	5.77	80	.277	.358	0-0	—	0	105	-11	-1.1
	Sea A	0	4	.000	8	3	0	0-0	18.2	31	21	3	4	10-0	9	9.16	49	.365	.446	0-0	—	0	61	-10	-1.7
	Year	5	11	.313	28	18	1-1	0-0	110.2	132	24	18	6	55-2	73	6.34	72	.294	.375	0-0	—	0	98	-21	-2.8
1998	Sea A	1	0	1.000	7	0	0	0-0	15.2	22	10	5	0	5-0	16	4.60	101	.319	.360	0-0	—	0		-1	0.0
1999	Det A	0	0	—	2	0	0	0-0	3.1	7	5	2	0	2-0	3	10.80	46	.389	.450	0-0	—	0		-2	-0.1
2000	Mon N	5	8	.385	53	7	0	0-0	101.2	129	71	11	4	36-6	51	5.40	89	.310	.363	19-1	.211	2*	46	-8	-0.7
2001	Mon N	0	0	—	4	0	0	0-0	5	11	7	1	0	2-0	3	12.60	35	.440	.481	0-0	—	0		-4	-0.2
Total	7	26	46	.361	163	79	4-3	1-2	577.1	656	372	84	28	222-17	348	5.32	91	.286	.352	19-1	.211	2	80	-32	-3.0
LISENBEE, HOD Horace Milton B 9.23.1898 Clarksville, TN D 11.14.1987 Clarksville, TN BR/TR 5-11/170# d4.23																									
1927	Was A	18	9	.667	39	34	17-**4**	0	242	221	114	6	3	78	105	3.57	114	.245	.307	83-8	.133	-5	105	13	0.7
1928	Was A	2	6	.250	16	9	3	0	77	102	58	4	5	32	13	6.08	66	.326	.397	23-2	.174	-0	91	-16	-1.5
1929	Bos A	0	0	—	5	0	0	0	8.2	10	5	1	0	4	2	5.19	82	.294	.368	2-0	.000	-0		0	0.0
1930	Bos A	10	17	.370	37	31	15	0	237.1	254	130	20	5	86	47	4.40	105	.280	.346	75-8	.267	1	75	7	0.6
1931	Bos A	5	12	.294	41	17	6	0	164.2	190	108	13	3	49	42	5.19	83	.281	.332	53-0	.226	0	89	-16	-1.4
1932	Bos A	0	4	.000	19	6	3	0	73.1	87	55	9	1	25	13	5.65	80	.296	.353	21-3	.048	-2	60	-9	-0.6
1936	Phi A	1	7	.125	19	7	4	0	85.2	115	69	9	0	24	17	6.20	82	.322	.365	25-2	.120	-1	62	-11	-0.9
1945	Cin N	1	3	.250	31	3	0	1	80.1	97	56	12	2	16	14	5.49	68	.294	.330	19-0	.000	-3	158	-16	-1.1
Total	8	37	58	.389	207	107	48-4	1	969	1076	595	74	19	314	253	4.81	90	.282	.340	301-23	.169	-10	88	-48	-4.2
LISKA, AD Adolph James B 7.10.1906 Dwight, NE D 11.30.1998 Portland, OR BR/TR 5-11.5/160# d4.17																									
1929	Was A	3	9	.250	24	10	4	0	94.1	87	53	1	3	42	33	4.77	89	.249	.335	29-0	.172	-1	72	-3	-0.2
1930	Was A	9	7	.563	32	16	7-1	1	150.2	140	69	6	5	71	40	3.29	140	.250	.340	52-4	.096	-4	98	19	1.7
1931	Was A	0	1	.000	2	1	0	0	4	9	3	0	0	1	2	6.75	64	.450	.476	1-0	.000	-0	39	-1	-0.2
1932	Phi N	2	0	1.000	8	0	0	1	26.2	22	5	0	1	10	6	1.69	261	.239	.320	7-0	.000	-1		7	0.5
1933	Phi N	3	1	.750	45	1	0	1	75.2	96	46	5	0	26	23	4.52	84	.310	.363	14-0	.071	-1*	240	-6	-0.3
Total	5	17	18	.486	111	28	11-1	3	351.1	354	176	12	9	150	104	3.87	112	.266	.344	103-4	.107	-7	93	16	1.5
LITTELL, MARK Mark Alan B 1.17.1953 Cape Girardeau, MO BL/TR 6-3/210# d6.14																									
1973	KC A	1	3	.250	8	7	1	0-0	38	44	25	5	0	23-1	16	5.68	72	.288	.376	0-0	—	0	109	-5	-0.5
1975	KC A	1	2	.333	7	3	1	0-0	24.1	19	11	1	0	15-0	19	3.70	104	.229	.347	0-0	—	0	61	1	0.1
1976	†KC A	8	4	.667	60	1	0	16-5	104	68	26	1	0	60-4	92	2.08	169	.188	.301	1-0	.000	-0	201	**17**	2.6
1977	†KC A	8	4	.667	48	5	0	12-3	104.2	73	49	6	1	55-6	106	3.61	112	.198	.299	1-0	.000	-0	107	4	0.5
1978	StL N	4	8	.333	72	2	0	11-4	106.1	80	38	8	4	59-16	130	2.79	126	.213	.324	7-0	.000	-0	38	9	1.1
1979	StL N	9	4	.692	63	0	0	13-6	82.1	60	22	2	0	39-5	67	2.19	172	.203	.294	14-1	.000	-1		15	2.5
1980	StL N	0	2	.000	14	0	0	2-3	10.2	14	11	2	0	7-2	7	9.28	40	.318	.412	1-0	.000	-0		-6	-1.2
1981	StL N	1	3	.250	28	1	0	2-0	41	36	21	2	0	31-7	22	4.39	81	.237	.366	8-0	.250	0	75	-3	-0.3
1982	StL N	0	1	.000	16	0	0	0-0	20.2	22	14	1	0	15-5	7	5.23	69	.272	.385	2-0	.000	-0		-4	-0.3
Total	9	32	31	.508	316	19	2	56-21	532	416	217	28	5	304-46	466	3.32	112	.217	.324	34-1	.059	-2	102	28	4.5
LITTLE, JEFF Donald Jeffrey B 12.25.1954 Fremont, OH BR/TL 6-6/220# d9.6																									
1980	StL N	1	1	.500	7	2	0	0-0	18.2	18	9	0	0	9-0	17	3.86	96	.250	.333	6-0	.167	-0	72	0	-0.1
1982	Min A	2	0	1.000	33	0	0	0-2	36.1	33	20	6	0	27-3	26	4.21	101	.244	.368	0-0	—	0		-1	-0.1
Total	2	3	1	.750	40	2	0	0-2	55	51	29	6	0	36-3	43	4.09	99	.246	.357	6-0	.167	-0	72	-1	-0.2

Year	Tm Lg	W	L	Pct	G	GS	CG-Sho	SV-BS	IP	H	R	HR	HB	BB-IB	SO	ERA	AERA	OAV	OOB	AB-SH	AVG	PB	Sup	APR	PW
LITTLEFIELD, JOHN John Andrew B 1.5.1954 Covina, CA BR/TR 6-2/200# d6.8																									
1980	StL N	5	5	.500	52	0	0	9-5	66	71	31	2	1	20-9	22	3.14	118	.282	.330	11-1	.000	-1		2	0.2
1981	SD N	2	3	.400	42	0	0	2-3	64	53	28	5	1	28-5	21	3.66	89	.235	.322	1-1	.000	-0		-3	-0.3
Total	2	7	8	.467	94	0	0	11-8	130	124	59	7	2	48-14	43	3.39	103	.259	.326	12-2	.000	-1		-1	-0.1
LITTLEFIELD, DICK Richard Bernard B 3.18.1926 Detroit, MI D 11.20.1997 Detroit, MI BL/TL 6/180# d7.7																									
1950	Bos A	2	2	.500	15	2	0	1	23.1	27	25	7	1	24	13	9.26	53	.297	.448	4-0	.000	-1	46	-10	-1.5
1951	Chi A	1	1	.500	4	2	0	0	9.2	9	12	1	0	17	7	8.38	48	.243	.481	1-0	.000	0	88	-5	-0.8
1952	Det A	0	3	.000	28	1	0	1	47.2	46	24	4	0	25	32	4.34	88	.257	.348	7-0	.143	-0	229	-2	-0.2
	StL A	2	3	.400	7	5	3	0	46.1	35	18	4	0	17	34	2.72	144	.205	.277	16-0	.063	-2	76	5	0.3
	Year	2	6	.250	35	6	3	1	94	81	21	8	0	42	66	3.54	109	.231	.314	23-0	.087	-2	102	4	0.1
1953	StL A	7	12	.368	36	22	2	0	152.1	153	93	17	4	84	104	5.08	83	.264	.361	42-5	.190	-1*	80	-12	-1.5
1954	Bal A	0	0	—	3	0	0	0	6	8	7	0	1	6	5	10.50	34	.333	.484	1-0	.000	-0		-4	-0.2
	Pit N	10	11	.476	23	21	7-1	0	155	140	78	10	2	85	92	3.60	116	.239	.334	49-4	.163	0	77	7	0.8
1955	Pit N	5	12	.294	35	17	4-1	0	130	148	91	15	2	68-8	70	5.12	80	.290	.372	34-1	.176	0	71	-17	-2.0
1956	Pit N	0	0	—	6	2	0	0	12.2	14	8	2	0	6-0	10	4.26	88	.286	.364	2-0	.000	-0	93	-1	-0.1
	StL N	0	2	.000	3	2	0	0	9.2	9	9	2	0	4-1	5	7.45	51	.237	.310	2-0	.000	-0	58	-4	-0.7
	NY N	4	4	.500	31	7	0	2	97	78	45	16	0	39-5	65	4.08	93	.231	.306	24-1	.083	-2	70	-1	-0.3
	Year	4	6	.400	40	11	0	2	119.1	101	48	20	0	49-6	80	4.37	86	.238	.313	28-1	.071	-2	72	-7	-1.1
1957	Chi N	2	3	.400	48	2	0	4	65.2	76	46	12	1	37-4	51	5.35	72	.295	.380	11-0	.182	0	23	-12	-1.0
1958	Mil N	0	1	.000	4	0	0	1	6.1	7	5	2	1	1-0	7	4.26	83	.280	.333	0-0	—	0		-1	-0.3
Total	9	33	54	.379	243	83	16-2	9	761.2	750	461	92	12	413-18	495	4.71	86	.260	.353	193-11	.145	-5	77	-57	-7.5
LITTLEJOHN, CARLISLE Charles Carlisle B 10.6.1901 Irene, TX D 10.27.1977 Kansas City, MO BR/TR 5-10/175# d5.11																									
1927	StL N	3	1	.750	14	2	1	0	42	47	21	4	0	14	16	4.50	88	.292	.349	12-0	.417	2*	119	-1	0.1
1928	StL N	2	1	.667	12	2	1	0	32	36	16	2	0	14	6	3.66	109	.286	.357	11-0	.000	-2	116	1	-0.1
Total	2	5	2	.714	26	4	2	0	74	83	37	6	0	28	22	4.14	96	.289	.352	23-0	.217	-0	118	0	0.0
LIVELY, BUDDY Everett Adrian "Red" B 2.14.1925 Birmingham, AL BR/TR 6-0.5/200# d4.17 f-Jack																									
1947	Cin N	4	7	.364	38	17	3-1	0	123	126	75	16	0	63	52	4.68	88	.265	.351	32-3	.188	2	107	-9	-0.6
1948	Cin N	0	0	—	10	0	0	0	22.2	13	7	0	1	11	12	2.38	164	.165	.275	2-0	.000	-0		4	0.1
1949	Cin N	4	6	.400	31	10	3-1	1	103.1	91	47	11	0	53	30	3.92	107	.245	.339	26-1	.154	0	67	5	0.4
Total	3	8	13	.381	79	27	6-2	1	249	230	129	27	1	127	94	4.16	99	.248	.339	60-4	.167	1	93	0	-0.1
LIVELY, JACK Henry Everett B 5.29.1885 Joppa, AL D 12.5.1967 Arab, AL BR/TR 5-9/185# d4.16 s-Buddy																									
1911	Det A	7	5	.583	18	14	10	0	113.2	143	73	1	7	34	45	4.59	75	.313	.369	43-0	.256	3*	110	-12	-0.9
LIVENGOOD, WES Wesley Amos B 7.18.1910 Salisbury, NC D 9.2.1996 Winston-Salem, NC BR/TR 6-2/172# d5.30																									
1939	Cin N	0	0	—	5	0	0	0	5.2	9	6	3	0	3	4	9.53	40	.360	.429	0-0	—	0		-3	-0.2
LIVINGSTONE, JAKE Jacob M. B 1.1.1880 St.Petersburg, Russia D 3.22.1949 Wassaic, NY d9.6																									
1901	NY N	0	0	—	2	0	0	0	12	26	13	0	3	7	6	9.00	37	.433	.514	6-0	.167	0		-6	-0.3
LLEWELLYN, CLEM Clement Manly "Lew" B 8.1.1895 Dobson, NC D 11.26.1969 Concord, NC BL/TR 6-2/195# d6.18																									
1922	NY A	0	0	—	1	0	0	0	1	1	0	0	0	0	0	0.00	—	.250	.250	0-0	—	0		0	0.0
LLOYD, GRAEME Graeme John B 4.9.1967 Victoria, Australia BL/TL 6-7/234# d4.11																									
1993	Mil A	3	4	.429	55	0	0	0-4	63.2	64	24	5	3	13-3	31	2.83	151	.256	.299	0-0	—	0		9	0.9
1994	Mil A	2	3	.400	43	0	0	3-3	47	49	28	4	3	15-6	31	5.17	97	.269	.332	0-0	—	0		0	0.0
1995	Mil A	0	5	.000	33	0	0	4-2	32	28	16	4	0	8-2	13	4.50	111	.246	.286	0-0	—	0		2	0.4
1996	Mil A	2	4	.333	52	0	0	0-3	51	49	19	3	1	17-3	24	2.82	184	.254	.316	0-0	—	0		12	1.2
	†NY A	0	2	.000	13	0	0	0-2	5.2	12	11	1	0	5-1	6	17.47	28	.429	.486	0-0	—	0		-8	-1.3
	Year	2	6	.250	65	0	0	0-5	56.2	61	35	4	1	22-4	30	4.29	121	.276	.340	0-0	—	0		5	-0.1
1997	†NY A	1	1	.500	46	0	0	1-0	49	55	24	6	1	20-7	26	3.31	135	.293	.355	0-0	—	0		4	0.2
1998	†NY A	3	0	1.000	50	0	0	0-2	37.2	26	10	3	2	6-2	20	1.67	262	.191	.234	0-0	—	0		11	0.7
1999	Tor A	5	3	.625	74	0	0	3-6	72	68	36	11	4	23-4	47	3.63	136	.250	.317	0-0	—	0		8	0.8
2001	Mon N	9	5	.643	84	0	0	1-2	70.1	74	38	6	6	21-2	44	4.35	103	.272	.336	2-0	.000	0		0	0.1
2002	Mon N	2	3	.400	41	0	0	5-2	30.2	41	21	5	1	8-3	17	5.87	76	.325	.368	4-0	.000	-0		-4	-0.7
	Fla N	2	2	.500	25	0	0	0-1	26.1	26	13	1	1	11-1	20	4.44	89	.263	.336	0-0	—	0		-1	-0.2
	Year	4	5	.444	66	0	0	5-3	57	67	34	6	2	19-4	37	5.21	81	.298	.353	4-0	.000	-0		-5	-0.9
2003	NY N	1	2	.333	36	0	0	0-0	35.1	39	16	2	0	7-2	17	3.31	126	.281	.311	0-0	—	0		2	0.2
	KC A	0	2	.000	16	0	0	0-1	12.1	29	18	0	1	7-0	8	10.95	47	.453	.500	0-0	—	0		-8	-1.0
Total	10	30	36	.455	568	0	0	17-28	533	560	274	51	23	161-36	304	4.04	115	.271	.327	6-0	.000	-0		27	1.3
LOAIZA, ESTEBAN Esteban Antonio Veyna B 12.31.1971 Tijuana, Mexico BR/TR 6-4/190# d4.29																									
1995	Pit N	8	9	.471	32	**31**	1	0-0	172.2	205	115	21	5	55-3	85	5.16	83	.300	.352	52-7	.192	1*	102	-18	-1.5
1996	Pit N	2	3	.400	10	10	1-1	0-0	52.2	65	32	11	2	19-2	32	4.96	88	.308	.369	17-5	.118	-1*	111	-3	-0.3
1997	Pit N	11	11	.500	33	32	1	0-0	196.1	214	99	17	12	56-9	122	4.13	104	.279	.335	60-8	.167	-0	105	4	0.3
1998	Pit N	6	5	.545	21	14	0	0-1	91.2	96	50	13	3	30-1	53	4.52	95	.275	.332	29-3	.241	1	87	-1	0.1
	Tex A	3	6	.333	14	14	1	0-0	79.1	103	57	15	2	22-3	55	5.90	82	.316	.358	0-0	—	0	92	-9	-0.9
1999	†Tex A	9	5	.643	30	15	0	0-0	120.1	128	65	10	0	40-2	77	4.56	111	.275	.329	0-0	—	0	104	7	0.7
2000	Tex A	5	6	.455	20	17	0	1-0	107.1	133	67	21	3	31-1	75	5.37	93	.302	.349	3-0	.000	-0	87	-2	-0.2
	Tor A	5	7	.417	14	14	1-1	0-0	92	95	45	8	10	26-0	62	3.62	140	.270	.337	0-0	—	0	75	13	1.4
	Year	10	13	.435	34	31	1-1	1-0	199.1	228	49	29	13	57-1	137	4.56	111	.288	.344	3-0	.000	-0	82	11	1.2
2001	Tor A	11	11	.500	36	30	1-1	0-0	190	239	113	27	9	40-1	110	5.02	92	.307	.347	2-0	.000	-0	105	-8	-0.9
2002	Tor A	9	10	.474	25	25	3-1	0-0	151.1	192	102	18	4	38-3	87	5.71	81	.309	.350	6-0	.167	-0	120	-17	-1.8
2003	Chi A★	21	9	.700	34	34	1	0-0	226.1	196	75	17	10	56-2	**207**	2.90	157	.233	.286	5-1	.200	0	93	43	**5.4**
Total	9	90	82	.523	269	236	10-4	1-1	1480	1666	820	178	60	413-27	965	4.58	101	.286	.336	174-24	.178	0	99	9	2.3
LOCKE, CHUCK Charles Edward B 5.5.1932 Malden, MO BR/TR 5-11/185# d9.16																									
1955	Bal A	0	0	—	2	0	0	0	3	0	0	0	0	1-0	1	0.00	—	.000	.100	0-0	—	0		1	0.1
LOCKE, BOBBY Lawrence Donald B 3.3.1934 Rowes Run, PA BR/TR 5-11/185# d6.18																									
1959	Cle A	3	2	.600	24	7	0	2	77.2	66	33	6	3	41-2	40	3.13	118	.233	.333	24-2	.333	3	127	4	0.6
1960	Cle A	3	5	.375	32	11	2-2	2	123	121	51	10	2	37-3	53	3.37	111	.255	.311	38-3	.237	3*	109	6	0.8
1961	Cle A	4	4	.500	37	4	0	2	95.1	112	50	12	2	40-4	37	4.53	87	.300	.368	19-0	.211	0	129	-5	-0.3
1962	StL N	0	0	—	1	0	0	0	2	1	0	0	0	2-0	1	0.00	—	.143	.333	0-0	—	0		1	0.1
	Phi N	1	0	1.000	5	0	0	0	15.2	16	12	4	0	10-0	9	5.74	67	.262	.366	7-0	.286	0		-4	-0.1
	Year	1	0	1.000	6	0	0	0	17.2	17	18	4	0	12-0	10	5.09	77	.250	.363	7-0	.286	0		-3	0.0
1963	Phi N	0	0	—	9	0	0	0	10.2	10	7	0	0	5-1	7	5.91	55	.244	.326	1-0	.000	-0		-3	-0.2
1964	Phi N	0	0	—	8	0	0	0	19.1	21	6	2	0	6-3	11	2.79	124	.276	.329	2-1	.000	-0		2	0.1
1965	Cin N	0	1	.000	11	0	0	0	17.1	20	15	2	0	8-5	8	5.71	66	.299	.368	1-0	.000	0		-5	-0.2
1967	Cal A	3	0	1.000	9	1	0	2	19.1	14	6	1	1	3-0	7	2.33	135	.203	.243	3-0	.667	1	305	2	0.4
1968	Cal A	2	3	.400	29	0	0	2	36.1	51	29	3	1	13-3	21	6.44	45	.331	.385	3-0	.000	-0		-15	-2.2
Total	9	16	15	.516	165	23	2-2	10	416.2	432	209	40	9	165-21	194	4.02	91	.269	.339	98-6	.255	8	128	-17	-1.0
LOCKE, RON Ronald Thomas B 4.4.1942 Wakefield, RI BR/TL 5-11/168# d4.23																									
1964	NY N	1	2	.333	25	3	0	0	41.1	46	23	3	1	22-0	17	3.48	103	.289	.377	5-3	.000	-0	57	-2	-0.2
LOCKER, BOB Robert Awtry B 3.15.1938 George, IA BB/TR 6-3/200# d4.14																									
1965	Chi A	5	2	.714	51	0	0	2	91.1	71	36	6	2	30-10	69	3.15	101	.216	.281	14-0	.000	-2		0	0.0
1966	Chi A	9	8	.529	56	0	0	12	95	73	32	2	5	23-13	70	2.46	129	.206	.264	16-0	.250	1		7	1.8
1967	Chi A	7	5	.583	**77**	0	0	20	124.2	102	34	5	10	23-5	80	2.09	148	.222	.273	10-1	.000	-1		15	2.2
1968	Chi A	5	4	.556	70	0	0	10	90.1	78	27	4	1	27-13	62	2.29	132	.234	.290	8-0	.000	-1		7	1.0
1969	Chi A	2	3	.400	17	0	0	4-3	22	26	18	6	0	6-1	15	6.55	59	.292	.333	1-0	.000	-0		-6	-1.3

Year	Tm Lg	W	L	Pct	G	GS	CG-Sho	SV-BS	IP	H	R	HR	HB	BB-IB	SO	ERA	AERA	OAV	OOB	AB-SH	AVG	PB	Sup	APR	PW
	Sea A	3	3	.500	51	0	0	6-4	78.1	69	29	3	3	26-8	46	2.18	167	.234	.301	12-0	.083	-0		9	0.9
	Year	5	6	.455	68	0	0	10-7	100.1	95	49	9	3	32-9	61	3.14	117	.247	.308	13-0	.077	-1		3	-0.4
1970	Mil A	0	1	.000	28	0	0	3-1	31.2	37	18	1	5	10-1	19	3.41	111	.306	.380	1-0	.000	-0		-1	-0.1
	Oak A	3	3	.500	38	0	0	4-3	56.1	49	21	1	1	19-3	33	2.88	123	.232	.299	6-0	.167	-0		4	0.5
	Year	3	4	.429	66	0	0	7-4	88	86	39	2	6	29-4	52	3.07	118	.259	.329	7-0	.143	-0		4	0.4
1971	†Oak A	7	2	.778	47	0	0	6-5	72.1	68	28	2	1	19-9	46	2.86	117	.249	.298	6-0	.000	-0		3	0.5
1972	†Oak A	6	1	.857	56	0	0	10-3	78	69	25	1	2	16-5	47	2.65	108	.235	.277	6-0	.000	0		2	0.3
1973	Chi N	10	6	.625	63	0	0	18-6	106.1	96	40	6	4	42-10	76	2.54	156	.244	.321	15-1	.067	-1		13	2.3
1975	Chi N	0	1	.000	22	0	0	0-0	32.2	38	21	3	2	16-2	14	4.96	78	.306	.392	0-0	—	0		-4	-0.2
Total	10	57	39	.594	576	0	0	95-25	879	776	329	40	36	257-80	577	2.75	122	.237	.297	95-2	.074	-4		49	7.9

LOCKWOOD, SKIP Claude Edward B 8.17.1946 Boston, MA BR/TR 6/190# d4.23.1965 ▲

Year	Tm Lg	W	L	Pct	G	GS	CG-Sho	SV-BS	IP	H	R	HR	HB	BB-IB	SO	ERA	AERA	OAV	OOB	AB-SH	AVG	PB	Sup	APR	PW
1969	Sea A	0	1	.000	6	3	0	0-0	23	24	9	3	0	6-0	10	3.52	103	.279	.323	7-0	.000	-1	49	1	0.0
1970	Mil A	5	12	.294	27	26	3-1	0-0	173.2	173	91	22	6	79-2	93	4.30	88	.266	.347	53-12	.226	2	89	-9	-0.7
1971	Mil A	10	15	.400	33	32	5-1	0-0	208	191	93	13	5	91-6	115	3.33	104	.246	.326	62-10	.081	-1*	79	1	-0.2
1972	Mil A	8	15	.348	29	27	5-3	0-0	170	148	75	11	4	71-6	106	3.60	84	.232	.311	53-3	.132	-1*	79	-10	-1.6
1973	Mil A	5	12	.294	37	15	3	0-0	154.2	164	75	10	6	59-6	87	3.90	97	.280	.349	0-0	—	0	68	-2	-0.2
1974	Cal A	2	5	.286	37	2	0	1-4	81.1	81	42	8	5	32-4	39	4.32	80	.264	.339	0-0	—	0	141	-7	-0.6
1975	NY N	1	3	.250	24	0	0	2-1	48.1	28	9	3	1	25-6	61	1.49	232	.174	.287	6-1	.167	-0		11	1.0
1976	NY N	10	7	.588	56	0	0	19-5	94.1	62	31	6	2	34-8	108	2.67	124	.186	.265	18-3	.333	3		7	1.8
1977	NY N	4	8	.333	63	0	0	20-4	104	87	40	5	4	31-11	84	3.38	111	.227	.288	15-3	.200	-0		6	0.7
1978	NY N	7	13	.350	57	0	0	15-8	90.2	78	36	10	0	31-5	73	3.57	98	.236	.298	11-2	.182	1		1	0.2
1979	NY N	2	5	.286	27	0	0	9-0	42.1	33	7	3	0	14-5	42	1.49	245	.224	.292	2-1	.000	-0*		11	2.2
1980	Bos A	3	1	.750	24	1	0	2-1	45.2	61	31	4	0	17-3	11	5.32	79	.321	.371	0-0	—	0	85	-6	-0.6
Total	12	57	97	.370	420	106	16-5	68-23	1236	1130	539	98	33	490-62	829	3.55	100	.246	.320	227-35	.159	3	79	4	2.0

LOCKWOOD, MILO Milo Hathaway B 4.7.1858 Solon, OH D 10.9.1897 Economy, PA 5-10/160# d4.17 ▲

Year	Tm Lg	W	L	Pct	G	GS	CG-Sho	SV-BS	IP	H	R	HR	HB	BB-IB	SO	ERA	AERA	OAV	OOB	AB-SH	AVG	PB	Sup	APR	PW
1884	Was U	1	9	.100	11	10	6	0	67.2	99	95	4		15	48	7.32	33	.319	.351	67	.209	-2*	77	-36	-3.6

LOES, BILLY William B 12.13.1929 Long Island City, NY BR/TR 6-1/170# d5.18 Mil 1951

Year	Tm Lg	W	L	Pct	G	GS	CG-Sho	SV-BS	IP	H	R	HR	HB	BB-IB	SO	ERA	AERA	OAV	OOB	AB-SH	AVG	PB	Sup	APR	PW
1950	Bro N	0	0	—	10	0	0	0	12.2	16	11	5	0	5	2	7.82	52	.314	.375	1-0	.000	0		-5	-0.2
1952	†Bro N	13	8	.619	39	21	8-4	1	187.1	154	62	12	3	71	115	2.69	135	.224	.299	54-10	.093	-3*	133	20	1.8
1953	†Bro N	14	8	.636	32	25	9-1	0	162.2	165	92	21	3	53	75	4.54	94	.261	.322	56-2	.125	-2	132	-6	-0.8
1954	Bro N	13	5	.722	28	21	6	0	147.2	154	73	14	1	60	97	4.14	99	.269	.336	51-4	.118	-2	127	0	-0.3
1955	†Bro N	10	4	.714	22	19	6	0	128	116	59	16	2	46-1	85	3.59	113	.240	.308	44-3	.091	-3	104	7	0.3
1956	Bro N	0	1	.000	1	1	0	0	1.1	5	6	1	0	1-0	2	40.50	10	.556	.600	0-0	—	0	67	-5	-0.7
	Bal A	2	7	.222	21	6	1	3	56.2	65	33	4	2	23-1	22	4.76	82	.291	.360	17-1	.176	-1	64	-5	-0.8
1957	Bal A★	12	7	.632	31	18	8-3	4	155.1	142	59	8	4	37-4	86	3.24	111	.245	.292	50-7	.080	-3	138	7	0.6
1958	Bal A	3	9	.250	32	10	1	5	114	106	51	10	8	44-5	44	3.63	99	.252	.328	30-3	.067	-2	57	0	-0.3
1959	Bal A	4	7	.364	37	0	0	14	64.1	58	31	5	3	25-3	34	4.06	93	.239	.315	8-0	.125	-0		-1	-0.3
1960	SF N	3	2	.600	37	0	0	5	45.2	40	26	9	4	17-2	28	4.93	71	.247	.330	4-1	.250	0		-6	-0.7
1961	SF N	6	5	.545	26	18	3-1	0	114.2	114	62	13	5	39-4	55	4.24	90	.258	.324	32-4	.156	-0	103	-6	-0.6
Total	11	80	63	.559	316	139	42-9	32	1190.1	1135	565	118	35	421-20	645	3.89	99	.252	.319	347-35	.110	-17	118	0	-2.0

LOEWER, CARLTON Carlton Ernest B 9.24.1973 Lafayette, LA BR/TR 6-6/220# d6.14

Year	Tm Lg	W	L	Pct	G	GS	CG-Sho	SV-BS	IP	H	R	HR	HB	BB-IB	SO	ERA	AERA	OAV	OOB	AB-SH	AVG	PB	Sup	APR	PW
1998	Phi N	7	8	.467	21	21	1	0-0	122.2	154	86	18	3	39-1	58	6.09	71	.312	.360	35-5	.086	-1	99	-22	-2.4
1999	Phi N	2	6	.250	20	13	2-1	0-0	89.2	100	54	9	0	26-0	48	5.12	92	.287	.332	22-2	.227	1	84	-3	-0.3
2001	SD N	0	2	.000	2	2	0	0-0	4.1	13	12	2	0	3-0	1	24.92	16	.520	.571	0-0	—	0	35	-10	-1.4
2003	SD N	1	2	.333	5	5	0	0-0	21.2	35	17	3	1	8-1	11	6.65	59	.368	.419	5-1	.000	-0	91	-7	-0.8
Total	4	10	18	.357	48	41	3-1	0-0	238.1	302	169	32	4	76-2	118	6.12	73	.314	.361	62-8	.129	-1	89	-42	-4.9

LOFTUS, FRANK Francis Patrick B 3.10.1898 Scranton, PA D 10.27.1980 Belchertown, MA BR/TR 5-9/190# d9.26

Year	Tm Lg	W	L	Pct	G	GS	CG-Sho	SV-BS	IP	H	R	HR	HB	BB-IB	SO	ERA	AERA	OAV	OOB	AB-SH	AVG	PB	Sup	APR	PW
1926	Was A	0	0	—	1	0	0	0	1	3	2	0	0	2	0	9.00	43	.600	.714	0-0	—	0		-1	0.0

LOGAN, BOB Robert Dean "Lefty" B 2.10.1910 Thompson, NE D 5.20.1978 Indianapolis, IN BR/TL 5-10/170# d4.18

Year	Tm Lg	W	L	Pct	G	GS	CG-Sho	SV-BS	IP	H	R	HR	HB	BB-IB	SO	ERA	AERA	OAV	OOB	AB-SH	AVG	PB	Sup	APR	PW
1935	Bro N	0	1	.000	2	0	0	0	2.2	2	1	0	0	1	1	3.38	118	.182	.250	0-0	—	0		0	0.1
1937	Det A	0	0	—	1	0	0	0	0.2	1	0	0	0	1	1	0.00	—	.333	.500	0-0	—	0		0	0.0
	Chi N	0	0	—	4	0	0	1	6.1	6	1	0	0	4	2	1.42	280	.261	.370	1-0	.000	-0		2	0.1
1938	Chi N	0	2	.000	14	0	0	2	22.2	18	9	0	1	17	10	2.78	138	.222	.364	3-0	.000	-0		2	0.2
1941	Cin N	0	1	.000	2	0	0	0	3.1	5	5	0	0	5	0	8.10	44	.333	.500	0-0	—	0		-2	-0.4
1945	Bos N	7	11	.389	34	25	5-1	1	187	213	84	9	1	53	53	3.18	121	.283	.331	61-6	.213	1	95	10	1.1
Total	5	7	15	.318	57	25	5-1	4	222.2	245	100	9	2	81	67	3.15	122	.277	.339	65-6	.200	1	95	12	1.1

LOHRMAN, BILL William Le Roy B 5.22.1913 Brooklyn, NY D 9.13.1999 Poughkeepsie, NY BR/TR 6-1/185# d6.19

Year	Tm Lg	W	L	Pct	G	GS	CG-Sho	SV-BS	IP	H	R	HR	HB	BB-IB	SO	ERA	AERA	OAV	OOB	AB-SH	AVG	PB	Sup	APR	PW
1934	Phi N	0	1	.000	4	0	0	1	6	5	5	0	0	1	2	4.50	105	.217	.250	2-0	.500	0		0	0.0
1937	NY N	1	0	1.000	2	1	1	1	10	5	1	0	0	2	3	0.90	432	.152	.200	2-1	.000	-0	67	3	0.4
1938	NY N	9	6	.600	31	14	3	0	152	152	72	9	2	33	52	3.32	114	.253	.294	49-3	.082	-4	117	5	0.1
1939	NY N	12	13	.480	38	24	9-1	1	185.2	200	91	15	3	45	70	4.07	96	.282	.327	60-0	.233	4	100	-1	0.3
1940	NY N	10	15	.400	31	27	11-4	1	195	200	98	19	3	43	73	3.78	103	.264	.306	65-4	.123	-2	87	1	-0.1
1941	NY N	9	10	.474	33	20	6-2	3	159	184	87	7	0	40	61	4.02	92	.286	.327	48-3	.229	4	94	-8	-0.5
1942	StL N	1	1	.500	5	0	0	0	12.2	11	3	0	0	2	6	1.42	241	.244	.277	3-0	.667	1		2	0.5
	NY N	13	4	.765	26	19	12-2	0	158	143	52	11	2	33	41	2.56	131	.240	.282	58-3	.121	-3	118	14	1.2
	Year	14	5	.737	31	19	12-2	0	170.2	154	57	11	2	35	47	2.48	136	.240	.281	61-3	.148	-2	118	17	1.7
1943	NY N	5	6	.455	17	12	3	1	80.1	110	51	7	2	25	16	5.15	67	.324	.374	27-2	.037	-3*	107	-15	-2.2
	Bro N	0	2	.000	6	2	2	0	27.2	29	14	2	1	10	5	3.58	94	.274	.342	7-0	.143	0	88	-1	-0.1
	Year	5	8	.385	23	14	5	1	108	139	18	9	3	35	21	4.75	72	.312	.366	34-2	.059	-3	104	-15	-2.3
1944	Bro N	0	0	—	3	0	0	0	2.2	4	0	0	0	4	1	0.00	—	.500	.667	0-0	—	0		1	0.0
	Cin N	0	1	.000	2	1	0	0	1.2	5	5	0	0	2	0	27.00	13	.500	.583	0-0	—	0	0	-4	-0.7
	Year	0	1	.000	5	1	0	0	4.1	9	5	0	0	6	1	10.38	34	.500	.625	0-0	—	0	0	-3	-0.7
Total	9	60	59	.504	198	120	47-9	8	990.2	1048	479	70	13	240	330	3.69	101	.271	.315	321-16	.153	-3	100	-3	-1.1

LOHSE, KYLE Kyle Matthew B 10.4.1978 Chico, CA BR/TR 6-2/190# d6.22

Year	Tm Lg	W	L	Pct	G	GS	CG-Sho	SV-BS	IP	H	R	HR	HB	BB-IB	SO	ERA	AERA	OAV	OOB	AB-SH	AVG	PB	Sup	APR	PW
2001	Min A	4	7	.364	19	16	0	0-0	90.1	102	60	16	8	29-0	64	5.68	81	.284	.347	5-0	.400	1	93	-10	-0.9
2002	†Min A	13	8	.619	32	31	1-1	0-1	180.2	181	92	26	9	70-2	124	4.23	106	.259	.333	4-0	.250	0	108	5	0.5
2003	†Min A	14	11	.560	33	33	2-1	0-0	201	211	107	28	5	45-1	130	4.61	99	.268	.310	3-3	.333	0	99	0	-0.1
Total	3	31	26	.544	84	80	3-2	0-1	472	494	259	70	22	144-3	318	4.67	97	.268	.326	12-3	.333	1	101	-5	-0.5

LOISELLE, RICH Richard Frank B 1.12.1972 Neenah, WI BR/TR 6-5/225# d9.7

Year	Tm Lg	W	L	Pct	G	GS	CG-Sho	SV-BS	IP	H	R	HR	HB	BB-IB	SO	ERA	AERA	OAV	OOB	AB-SH	AVG	PB	Sup	APR	PW
1996	Pit N	1	0	1.000	5	3	0	0-0	20.2	22	8	3	0	8-1	9	3.05	143	.268	.333	8-0	.250	1	179	3	0.2
1997	Pit N	1	5	.167	72	0	0	29-5	72.2	76	29	7	1	24-3	66	3.10	139	.269	.326	1-0	.000	-0		9	1.2
1998	Pit N	2	7	.222	54	0	0	19-8	55	56	26	2	2	36-9	48	3.44	125	.262	.372	0-1	—	0		4	0.9
1999	Pit N	3	2	.600	13	0	0	0-1	15.1	16	9	2	2	9-2	14	5.28	87	.281	.397	0-1	—	0		-1	-0.1
2000	Pit N	2	3	.400	40	0	0	0-6	42.1	43	27	5	3	30-5	32	5.10	90	.262	.380	0-0	—	0		-2	-0.3
2001	Pit N	0	1	.000	18	0	0	1-0	18	28	24	3	4	17-4	9	11.50	39	.359	.495	0-0	—	0		-13	-0.7
Total	6	9	18	.333	202	3	0	49-20	224	241	123	22	12	124-24	178	4.38	100	.274	.370	9-2	.222	0	179	0	1.2

LOLICH, MICKEY Michael Stephen B 9.12.1940 Portland, OR BB/TL 6/210# d5.12

Year	Tm Lg	W	L	Pct	G	GS	CG-Sho	SV-BS	IP	H	R	HR	HB	BB-IB	SO	ERA	AERA	OAV	OOB	AB-SH	AVG	PB	Sup	APR	PW
1963	Det A	5	9	.357	33	18	4	0	144.1	145	64	13	5	56-1	103	3.55	105	.265	.336	36-2	.056	-1	92	3	0.2
1964	Det A	18	9	.667	44	33	12-6	2	232	196	88	26	5	64-0	192	3.26	112	.225	.282	64-9	.109	1	113	12	1.3
1965	Det A	15	9	.625	43	37	7-3	3	243.2	216	103	23	12	72-2	226	3.44	101	.236	.298	86-3	.058	-6	114	1	-0.6
1966	Det A	14	14	.500	40	33	5-1	3	203.2	204	119	24	6	83-8	173	4.77	73	.257	.329	64-2	.141	1	124	-28	-3.7
1967	Det A	14	13	.519	31	30	11-6	0	204	165	71	14	7	56-2	174	3.04	107	.221	.281	61-7	.197	3*	98	7	1.2
1968	†Det A	17	9	.654	39	32	8-4	1	220	178	84	23	11	65-4	197	3.19	94	.219	.285	70-4	.114	0*	110	-4	-0.6
1969	Det A☆	19	11	.633	37	36	15-1	1-0	280.2	214	111	22	14	122-10	271	3.14	119	.210	.302	91-12	.088	-3*	111	17	1.5

Year	Tm Lg	W	L	Pct	G	GS	CG-Sho	SV-BS	IP	H	R	HR	HB	BB-IB	SO	ERA	AERA	OAV	OOB	AB-SH	AVG	PB	Sup	APR	PW
1970	Det A	14	19	.424	40	39	13-3	0-0	272.2	272	125	27	5	109-3	230	3.80	98	.260	.330	82-7	.134	1*	80	-1	0.1
1971	Det A★	**25**	14	.641	45	**45**	**29**-4	0-0	**376**	336	133	36	7	92-2	**308**	2.92	123	.237	.285	115-16	.130	1	118	27	2.8
1972	†Det A★	22	14	.611	41	41	23-4	0-0	327.1	282	100	29	11	74-5	250	2.50	126	.234	.283	89-11	.067	-0	92	24	2.6
1973	Det A	16	15	.516	42	42	17-3	0-0	308.2	315	143	35	5	79-7	214	3.82	107	.266	.314	0-0	—	0	87	8	0.7
1974	Det A	16	21	.432	41	41	27-3	0-0	308	310	155	38	3	78-11	202	4.15	92	.268	.314	0-0	—	0	84	-8	-1.1
1975	Det A	12	18	.400	32	32	19-1	0-0	240.2	260	119	19	0	64-5	139	3.78	107	.279	.322	0-0	—	0	72	6	0.7
1976	NY N	8	13	.381	31	30	5-2	0-0	192.2	184	83	14	0	52-1	120	3.22	102	.252	.300	54-11	.130	0	86	0	0.0
1978	SD N	2	1	.667	20	2	0	1-0	34.2	30	6	0	1	11-3	13	1.56	214	.240	.307	3-0	.000	-0	54	8	0.7
1979	SD N	0	2	.000	27	5	0	0-0	49.1	59	33	4	0	22-3	20	4.74	75	.304	.372	6-1	.000	-0	140	-9	-0.5
Total	16	217	191	.532	586	496	195-41	11-0	3638.1	3366	1537	347	92	1099-67	2832	3.44	104	.246	.304	821-85	.110	-4	99	63	5.3
LOLLAR, TIM William Timothy B 3.17.1956 Poplar Bluff, MO BL/TL 6-3/200# d6.28																									
1980	NY A	1	0	1.000	14	1	0	2-0	32.1	33	14	3	0	20-2	13	3.34	118	.280	.379	0-0	—	0	46	2	0.1
1981	SD N	2	8	.200	24	11	0	1-0	76.2	87	56	4	3	51-8	38	6.10	53	.293	.399	18-0	.167	1	104	-25	-2.8
1982	SD N	16	9	.640	34	34	4-2	0-0	232.2	192	82	20	4	87-4	150	3.13	110	.224	.297	85-2	.247	9*	108	13	2.4
1983	SD N	7	12	.368	30	30	1	0-0	175.2	170	98	22	4	85-1	135	4.61	76	.258	.346	58-0	.241	6*	95	-22	-1.6
1984	†SD N	11	13	.458	31	31	3-2	0-0	195.2	168	89	18	1	105-2	131	3.91	91	.234	.331	68-1	.221	7	94	-5	0.1
1985	Chi A	3	5	.375	18	13	0	0-0	83	83	48	10	1	58-1	61	4.66	93	.266	.379	0-0	—	0	96	-3	-0.3
	Bos A	5	5	.500	16	10	1	1-0	67	57	37	9	1	40-0	44	4.57	94	.230	.338	1-0	.000	-0*	104	-2	-0.3
	Year	8	10	.444	34	23	1	1-0	150	140	42	19	2	98-1	105	4.62	93	.250	.361	1-0	.000	-0	99	-5	-0.6
1986	Bos A	2	0	1.000	32	1	0	0-1	43	51	35	7	3	34-3	28	6.91	60	.304	.421	1-0	1.000	0*	261	-12	-0.5
Total	7	47	52	.475	199	131	9-4	4-1	906	841	459	93	17	480-21	600	4.27	85	.249	.343	231-3	.234	23	100	-54	-2.9
LOMBARDI, VIC Victor Alvin B 9.20.1922 Reedley, CA D 12.7.1997 Fresno, CA BL/TL 5-7/158# d4.18																									
1945	Bro N	10	11	.476	38	24	9	4	203.2	195	106	11	5	86	64	3.31	113	.252	.331	71-3	.183	-1*	97	6	0.4
1946	Bro N	13	10	.565	41	25	13-2	3	193	170	76	10	2	84	60	2.89	117	.235	.316	61-10	.230	2*	111	10	1.3
1947	†Bro N	12	11	.522	33	20	7-3	3	174.2	156	73	12	2	65	72	2.99	138	.241	.312	66-1	.242	2*	78	19	2.6
1948	Pit N	10	9	.526	38	17	9	4	163	156	72	9	2	67	54	3.70	110	.255	.330	48-1	.208	1*	90	8	1.0
1949	Pit N	5	5	.500	34	12	4	1	134	149	74	12	3	68	64	4.57	92	.286	.372	49-0	.347	5*	114	-5	0.3
1950	Pit N	0	5	.000	39	2	0	1	76.1	93	61	14	2	48	26	6.60	66	.310	.409	16-1	.250	1*	91	-17	-0.9
Total	6	50	51	.495	223	100	42-5	16	944.2	919	462	68	16	418	340	3.68	106	.257	.337	311-16	.238	10	96	21	4.7
LOMBARDO, LOU Louis B 11.18.1928 Carlstadt, NJ D 6.11.2001 Rock Hill, SC BL/TL 6-2/210# d9.22																									
1948	NY N	0	0	—	2	0	0	0	5.1	5	4	1	1	5	0	6.75	58	.250	.423	2-0	.000	-0		-1	-0.1
LOMON, KEVIN Kevin Dale B 11.20.1971 Fort Smith, AR BR/TR 6-1/195# d4.27																									
1995	NY N	0	1	.000	6	0	0	0-0	9.1	17	8	0	0	5-1	6	6.75	60	.405	.468	0-1	—	0		-3	-0.3
1996	Atl N	0	0	—	6	0	0	0-0	7.1	7	4	0	1	3-0	1	4.91	90	.259	.355	0-0	—	0		0	0.0
Total	2	0	1	.000	12	0	0	0-0	16.2	24	12	0	1	8-1	7	5.94	71	.348	.423	0-1	—	0		-3	-0.3
LONBORG, JIM James Reynold B 4.16.1942 Santa Maria, CA BR/TR 6-5/210# d4.23																									
1965	Bos A	9	17	.346	32	31	7-1	0	185.1	193	112	20	3	65-3	113	4.47	83	.262	.323	59-5	.136	0	112	-16	-2.1
1966	Bos A	10	10	.500	45	23	3-1	2	181.2	173	86	18	7	55-5	131	3.86	98	.249	.308	54-6	.093	-2*	117	0	-0.2
1967	†Bos A☆	**22**	9	.710	39	**39**	15-2	0	273.1	228	102	23	19	83-5	**246**	3.16	110	.225	.294	99-6	.141	-1	110	12	1.0
1968	Bos A	6	10	.375	23	17	4-1	0	113.1	89	57	11	11	59-3	73	4.29	74	.216	.327	39-5	.282	3	104	-12	-1.4
1969	Bos A	7	11	.389	29	23	4	0-1	143.2	148	78	15	7	65-3	100	4.51	84	.270	.354	41-5	.098	-1	86	-9	-1.1
1970	Bos A	4	1	.800	9	4	0	0-0	34	33	12	3	0	9-0	21	3.18	125	.260	.304	9-0	.444	2	90	4	0.8
1971	Bos A	10	7	.588	27	26	5-1	0-0	167.2	167	86	15	14	67-6	100	4.13	90	.259	.341	53-2	.170	0	130	-9	-0.8
1972	Mil A	14	12	.538	33	30	11-2	1-0	223	197	75	17	11	76-11	143	2.83	108	.238	.309	69-9	.145	-1	109	7	0.6
1973	Phi N	13	16	.448	38	30	6	0-1	199.1	218	124	25	9	80-7	106	4.88	78	.279	.350	59-4	.136	0	99	-24	-3.2
1974	Phi N	17	13	.567	39	39	16-3	0-0	283	280	113	22	6	70-11	121	3.21	118	.261	.308	94-11	.096	-4	99	17	1.1
1975	Phi N	8	6	.571	27	26	6-2	0-0	159.1	161	84	12	5	45-7	72	4.12	91	.257	.310	44-6	.023	-3	112	-7	-0.9
1976	†Phi N	18	10	.643	33	32	8-1	1-0	222	210	85	18	5	50-4	118	3.08	115	.249	.292	67-6	.164	1	107	11	1.3
1977	†Phi N	11	4	.733	25	25	4-1	0-0	157.2	157	77	15	5	50-5	76	4.11	97	.261	.321	48-9	.104	-2	122	0	-0.4
1978	Phi N	8	10	.444	22	22	1	0-0	113.2	132	69	16	2	45-1	48	5.23	68	.293	.359	34-4	.176	1	106	-19	-2.6
1979	Phi N	0	1	.000	4	1	0	0-0	7.1	14	10	3	1	4-0	7	11.05	35	.389	.463	1-0	.000	-0	46	-6	-0.7
Total	15	157	137	.534	425	368	90-15	4-2	2464.1	2400	1170	233	105	823-71	1475	3.86	94	.255	.320	770-78	.136	-5	108	-51	-8.6
LONG, JOEY Joey J. B 7.15.1970 Sidney, OH BR/TL 6-2/220# d4.25																									
1997	SD N	0	0	—	10	0	0	0-0	11	17	11	1	1	8-1	8	8.18	47	.340	.441	0-0	—	0		-6	-0.3
LONG, LEP Lester B 7.12.1888 Summit, NJ D 10.21.1958 Birmingham, AL BR/TR 5-10/153# d6.29																									
1911	Phi A	0	0	—	4	0	0	0	8	15	6	0	0	5	4	4.50	70	.405	.476	3-0	.000	-0		-2	-0.1
LONG, RED Nelson B 9.28.1876 Burlington, ON, CAN D 8.11.1929 Hamilton, ON, CAN BR/TR 6-1/190# d9.11																									
1902	Bos N	0	0	—	1	1	1	0	8	4	2	0	1	3	5	1.13	251	.148	.258	1-0	.000	-0	48	1	0.0
LONG, BOB Robert Earl B 11.11.1954 Jasper, TN BR/TR 6-3/178# d9.2																									
1981	Pit N	1	2	.333	5	3	0	0-0	19.2	23	14	2	0	10-0	8	5.95	60	.299	.375	4-1	.000	-0	66	-5	-0.7
1985	Sea A	0	0	—	28	0	0	0-0	38.1	30	17	7	2	17-1	29	3.76	112	.210	.302	0-0	—	0		2	0.1
Total	2	1	2	.333	33	3	0	0-0	58	53	31	9	2	27-1	37	4.50	89	.241	.328	4-1	.000	-0	66	-3	-0.6
LONG, TOM Thomas Francis "Little Hawk" B 4.22.1898 Memphis, TN D 9.16.1973 Louisville, KY BL/TL 5-9/154# d4.26																									
1924	Bro N	0	0	—	1	0	0	0	2	2	2	0	0	2	0	9.00	42	.333	.500	0-0	—	0		-1	-0.1
LONG, BILL William Douglas B 2.29.1960 Cincinnati, OH BR/TR 6/185# d7.21																									
1985	Chi A	0	1	.000	4	3	0	0-0	14	25	17	4	0	5-2	13	10.29	42	.391	.429	0-0	—	0	112	-9	-0.5
1987	Chi A	8	8	.500	29	23	5-2	1-0	169	179	85	20	3	28-1	72	4.37	105	.272	.303	0-0	—	0	113	6	0.5
1988	Chi A	8	11	.421	47	18	3	2-1	174	187	89	21	4	43-4	77	4.03	99	.280	.323	0-0	—	0	80	-1	-0.1
1989	Chi A	5	5	.500	30	8	0	1-0	98.2	101	49	8	4	37-0	51	3.92	97	.265	.332	0-0	—	0	80	-2	-0.1
1990	Chi A	0	1	.000	4	0	0	0-0	5.2	6	5	2	0	2-0	2	6.35	60	.261	.320	0-0	—	0		-2	-0.3
	Chi N	6	1	.857	42	0	0	5-2	55.2	66	29	8	1	21-4	32	4.37	94	.301	.365	5-0	.000	-0		-1	-0.2
1991	Mon N	0	0	—	3	0	0	0-0	1.2	4	2	0	0	4-0	0	10.80	34	.500	.667	0-0	—	0		-1	-0.1
Total	6	27	27	.500	159	52	8-2	9-3	518.2	568	276	63	12	140-11	247	4.37	95	.281	.328	5-0	.000	-0	100	-10	-0.8
LOONEY, BRIAN Brian James B 9.26.1969 New Haven, CT BL/TL 5-10/180# d9.26																									
1993	Mon N	0	0	—	3	1	0	0-0	6	8	2	0	0	2-0	7	3.00	139	.308	.357	1-0	.000	-0	108	1	0.0
1994	Mon N	0	0	—	1	0	0	0-0	2	4	5	1	1	0-0	2	22.50	19	.400	.455	0-0	—	0		-4	-0.2
1995	Bos A	0	1	.000	3	1	0	0-0	4.2	12	9	1	0	4-1	2	17.36	28	.545	.571	0-0	—	0	57	-6	-0.9
Total	3	0	1	.000	7	2	0	0-0	12.2	24	16	2	1	6-1	11	11.37	39	.414	.463	1-0	.000	-0	82	-9	-1.1
LOOPER, AARON Aaron Joseph B 9.7.1976 Ada, OK BR/TR 6-2/180# d8.2																									
2003	Sea A	0	0	—	6	0	0	0-0	7	7	4	1	1	2-0	6	5.14	84	.269	.345	0-0	—	0		-1	0.0
LOOPER, BRADEN Braden La Vern B 10.28.1974 Weatherford, OK BR/TR 6-4/210# d3.31																									
1998	StL N	0	1	.000	4	0	0	0-2	3.1	5	4	1	0	1-0	4	5.40	78	.357	.375	0-0	—	0		-1	-0.2
1999	Fla N	3	3	.500	72	0	0	0-4	83	96	43	7	1	31-6	50	3.80	115	.293	.351	0-0	—	0		3	0.1
2000	Fla N	5	1	.833	73	0	0	2-3	67.1	71	41	3	5	36-6	29	4.41	101	.268	.364	2-0	.000	-0		-2	-0.2
2001	Fla N	3	3	.500	71	0	0	3-3	71	63	28	8	2	30-3	52	3.55	119	.242	.322	2-0	.000	-0		6	0.5
2002	Fla N	2	5	.286	78	0	0	13-3	86	73	31	8	1	28-3	55	3.14	126	.230	.295	1-0	.000	-0		9	0.9
2003	†Fla N	6	4	.600	74	0	0	28-6	80.2	82	34	4	1	29-1	56	3.68	111	.264	.326	1-1	1.000	0		5	0.8
Total	6	19	17	.528	372	0	0	46-21	391.1	390	181	31	10	155-19	246	3.70	114	.261	.332	6-1	.167	-0		20	1.9
LOOS, PETE Ivan B 3.23.1878 Philadelphia, PA D 2.23.1956 Darby, PA TR d5.2																									
1901	Phi A	0	1	.000	1	1	0	0	1	2	5	0	0	4	0	27.00	14	.400	.667	0-0	—	0	215	-3	-0.4

Year	Tm Lg	W	L	Pct	G	GS	CG-Sho	SV-BS	IP	H	R	HR	HB	BB-IB	SO	ERA	AERA	OAV	OOB	AB-SH	AVG	PB	Sup	APR	PW
LOPAT, ED Edmund Walter (b: Edmund Walter Lopatynski) B 6.21.1918 New York, NY D 6.15.1992 Darien, CT BL/TL 5-10/185# d4.30 M2 C3																									
1944	Chi A	11	10	.524	27	25	13-1	0	210	217	96	12	2	59	75	3.26	105	.265	.316	81-1	.309	6*	98	2	1.0
1945	Chi A	10	13	.435	26	24	17-1	1	199.1	226	101	8	6	56	74	4.11	81	.285	.336	82-1	.293	5*	109	-16	-1.2
1946	Chi A	13	13	.500	29	29	20-2	0	231	216	80	18	1	48	89	2.73	125	.248	.288	87-2	.253	6*	109	21	3.2
1947	Chi A	16	13	.552	31	31	22-3	0	252.2	241	88	17	2	73	109	2.81	130	.253	.307	96-4	.198	0*	91	26	2.9
1948	NY A	17	11	.607	33	31	13-3	0	226.2	246	106	16	2	66	83	3.65	112	.284	.336	81-4	.173	-1*	110	10	1.0
1949	†NY A	15	10	.600	31	30	14-4	1	215.1	222	93	19	5	69	70	3.26	124	.269	.330	76-1	.263	7	98	17	2.6
1950	†NY A	18	8	.692	35	32	15-3	1	236.1	244	110	19	4	65	72	3.47	124	.266	.317	82-5	.232	8*	124	18	2.5
1951	†NY A★	21	9	.700	31	31	20-4	0	234.2	209	86	12	3	71	93	2.91	131	.239	**.298**	84-4	.179	1	99	26	3.3
1952	†NY A	10	5	.667	20	19	10-2	0	149.1	127	47	11	4	53	56	2.53	131	.234	.307	52-2	.173	1	119	15	1.6
1953	†NY A	16	4	**.800**	25	24	9-3	0	178.1	169	58	13	4	32	50	**2.42**	**152**	.250	.288	63-5	.190	1*	126	25	2.9
1954	NY A	12	4	.750	26	23	7	0	170	189	74	14	6	33	54	3.55	97	.288	.326	57-4	.018	-5	117	-2	-0.7
1955	NY A	4	8	.333	16	12	3-1	0	86.2	101	45	12	1	16-3	24	3.74	100	.294	.327	29-0	.138	-1	83	-2	-0.4
	Bal A	3	4	.429	10	7	1	0	49	57	24	8	3	9-2	10	4.22	90	.294	.332	17-1	.176	0	73	-1	-0.1
	Year	7	12	.368	26	19	4-1	0	135.2	158	27	20	4	25-5	34	3.91	96	.294	.329	46-1	.152	-1	79	-3	-0.5
Total	12	166	112	.597	340	318	164-27	3	2439.1	2464	1008	179	43	650-5	859	3.21	116	.264	.315	887-34	.211	29	107	139	18.6
LOPATKA, ART Arthur Joseph B 5.28.1919 Chicago, IL BB/TL 5-10/170# d9.12																									
1945	StL N	1	0	1.000	4	1	1	0	11.2	7	4	0	1	3	5	1.54	243	.159	.229	4-0	.250	0	68	2	0.2
1946	Phi N	0	1	.000	4	1	0	0	5.1	13	11	1	0	4	4	16.88	20	.448	.515	0-0	—	0	150	-8	-1.2
Total	2	1	1	.500	8	2	1	0	17	20	15	1	1	7	9	6.35	57	.274	.346	4-0	.250	0	105	-6	-1.0
LOPEZ, ALBIE Albert Anthony B 8.18.1971 Mesa, AZ BR/TR 6-2/205# d7.6																									
1993	Cle A	3	1	.750	9	9	0	0-0	49.2	49	34	7	1	32-1	25	5.98	73	.262	.371	0-0	—	0	146	-8	-0.6
1994	Cle A	1	2	.333	4	4	1-1	0-0	17	20	11	3	1	6-0	18	4.24	112	.290	.355	0-0	—	0	92	0	0.0
1995	Cle A	0	0	—	6	2	0	0-0	23	17	8	4	1	7-1	22	3.13	150	.205	.272	0-0	—	0	99	4	0.2
1996	Cle A	5	4	.556	13	10	0	0-0	62	80	47	14	2	22-1	45	6.39	77	.311	.369	0-0	—	0	121	-10	-1.1
1997	Cle A	3	7	.300	37	6	0	0-1	76.2	101	61	11	4	40-9	63	6.93	68	.321	.402	1-0	.000	-0	124	-17	-1.8
1998	TB A	7	4	.636	54	0	0	1-4	79.2	73	31	7	3	32-4	62	2.60	185	.249	.326	1-0	.000	-0		16	2.0
1999	TB A	3	2	.600	51	0	0	1-2	64	66	40	8	1	24-2	37	4.64	107	.263	.325	0-0	—	0		1	0.1
2000	TB A	11	13	.458	45	24	4-1	2-2	185.1	199	95	24	1	70-3	96	4.13	120	.277	.341	6-1	.000	-1	74	16	1.6
2001	TB A	5	12	.294	20	20	1-1	0-0	124.2	152	87	16	4	51-1	67	5.34	84	.302	.368	5-0	.000	-1	69	-13	-1.5
	†Ari N	4	7	.364	13	13	2-2	0-0	81	74	36	10	0	24-2	69	4.00	115	.247	.301	24-2	.042	-1	82	6	0.6
2002	Atl N	1	4	.200	30	4	0	0-0	55.2	66	29	1	0	18-3	39	4.37	94	.300	.349	9-0	.111	-0	56	-1	-0.2
2003	KC A	4	2	.667	15	0	0	0-3	22.2	41	32	7	0	17-1	15	12.71	41	.383	.468	0-0	—	0		-16	-2.7
Total	11	47	58	.448	297	92	8-5	4-12	841.1	938	511	112	18	343-28	558	4.94	95	.284	.352	46-3	.043	-3	89	-22	-3.4
LOPEZ, AQUILINO Aquilino (Roa) B 4.21.1975 Villa Altagracia, D.R. BR/TR 6-3/160# d4.2																									
2003	Tor A	1	3	.250	72	0	0	14-2	73.2	58	31	5	5	34-5	64	3.42	134	.212	.309	0-0	—	0		9	0.7
LOPEZ, AURELIO Aurelio Alejandro (Rios) B 9.21.1948 Tecamachalco, Mexico D 9.22.1992 Matehuala, Mexico BR/TR 6/220# d9.1																									
1974	KC A	0	0	—	8	1	0	0-0	16	21	12	0	0	10-0	5	5.63	68	.344	.425	0-0	—	0	92	-3	-0.2
1978	StL N	4	2	.667	25	4	0	0-0	65	52	35	4	1	32-2	46	4.29	82	.218	.308	14-2	.214	0	159	-5	-0.5
1979	Det A	10	5	.667	61	0	0	21-5	127	95	37	12	3	51-3	106	2.41	180	.210	.292	0-0	—	0		27	3.8
1980	Det A	13	6	.684	67	1	0	21-5	124	125	56	15	3	45-5	97	3.77	109	.263	.328	0-0	—	0	87	5	0.8
1981	Det A	5	2	.714	29	3	0	3-2	81.2	70	34	8	2	31-2	53	3.64	104	.233	.306	0-0	—	0	103	2	0.1
1982	Det A	3	1	.750	19	0	0	3-0	41	41	27	8	0	19-4	26	5.27	77	.268	.345	0-0	—	0		-6	-0.6
1983	Det A☆	9	8	.529	57	0	0	18-8	115.1	87	36	12	1	49-7	90	2.81	140	.210	.292	0-0	—	0		17	2.7
1984	†Det A	10	1	.909	71	0	0	14-2	137.2	109	51	16	2	52-6	94	2.94	133	.221	.295	0-0	—	0		15	1.3
1985	Det A	3	7	.300	51	0	0	5-2	86.1	82	50	15	1	41-9	53	4.80	85	.250	.330	0-0	—	0		-6	-0.7
1986	†Hou N	3	3	.500	45	0	0	7-1	78	64	32	6	0	25-1	44	3.46	104	.221	.280	9-1	.000	-1		2	0.0
1987	Hou N	2	1	.667	26	0	0	1-1	38	39	22	6	2	12-0	21	4.50	87	.273	.333	1-1	.000	-0		-3	-0.2
Total	11	62	36	.633	459	9	0	93-26	910	785	392	102	15	367-39	635	3.56	111	.234	.309	24-4	.125	-1	117	45	6.5
LOPEZ, JAVIER Javier Alfonso B 6.11.1977 San Juan, P.R. BL/TL 6-4/200# d4.1																									
2003	Col N	4	1	.800	75	0	0	1-1	58.1	58	25	5	4	12-2	40	3.70	133	.258	.307	5-0	.200	-0		7	0.6
LOPEZ, RAMON Jose Ramon (Hevia) B 5.26.1933 Las Villas, Cuba D 9.4.1982 Miami, FL BR/TR 6/175# d8.21																									
1966	Cal A	0	1	.000	4	1	0	0	7	4	5	1	0	4-0	2	5.14	65	.154	.267	0-0	—	0*	105	-2	-0.2
LOPEZ, MARCELINO Marcelino Pons B 9.23.1943 Havana, Cuba BR/TL 6-3/210# d4.14																									
1963	Phi N	1	0	1.000	4	2	0	0	6	8	5	0	0	7-1	2	6.00	54	.333	.469	2-0	.000	-0*	147	-2	-0.3
1965	Cal A	14	13	.519	35	32	8-1	1	215.1	185	79	12	4	82-6	122	2.93	116	.230	.304	69-7	.203	3*	83	11	2.0
1966	Cal A	7	14	.333	37	32	6-2	1	199	188	95	20	9	68-2	132	3.93	85	.251	.319	58-3	.190	2*	85	-12	-0.9
1967	Cal A	0	2	.000	4	3	0	0	9	11	10	1	0	9-0	6	9.00	35	.324	.455	2-0	.500	0*	120	-6	-1.1
	Bal A	1	0	1.000	4	4	0	0	17.2	15	5	1	0	10-0	15	2.55	124	.227	.329	5-0	.000	-0*	131	1	0.0
	Year	1	2	.333	8	7	0	0	26.2	26	10	2	0	19-0	21	4.73	67	.260	.375	7-0	.143	0	126	-4	-1.1
1969	†Bal A	5	3	.625	27	4	0	0-3	69.1	65	34	3	2	34-4	57	4.41	81	.252	.340	14-2	.214	1	105	-5	-0.5
1970	†Bal A	1	1	.500	25	3	0	0-0	60.2	47	19	2	0	37-3	49	2.08	176	.217	.327	13-0	.077	0	179	9	0.4
1971	Mil A	2	7	.222	31	11	0	0-1	67.2	64	48	5	0	60-1	42	4.66	75	.251	.390	17-1	.059	-1*	84	-12	-1.6
1972	Cle A	0	0	—	4	2	0	0-0	8.1	8	5	0	0	10-0	1	5.40	60	.276	.462	1-0	.000	-0	41	-2	-0.1
Total	8	31	40	.437	171	93	14-3	2-4	653	591	300	44	15	317-17	426	3.62	94	.243	.331	181-13	.171	4	91	-18	-2.1
LOPEZ, RODRIGO Rodrigo (Munoz) B 12.14.1975 Tlalnepantla, Mexico BR/TR 6-1/180# d4.29																									
2000	SD N	0	3	.000	6	6	0	0-0	24.2	40	24	5	0	13-0	17	8.76	49	.377	.442	9-0	.111	-0	120	-12	-1.1
2002	Bal A	15	9	.625	33	28	1	0-0	196.2	172	83	23	5	62-4	136	3.57	120	.234	.296	3-0	.000	-0	104	17	1.7
2003	Bal A	7	10	.412	26	26	3-1	0-0	147	188	101	24	10	43-6	103	5.82	76	.313	.365	2-0	.000	-0	100	-24	-2.3
Total	3	22	22	.500	65	60	4-1	0-0	368.1	400	208	52	15	118-10	256	4.81	90	.277	.336	14-0	.071	-1	104	-19	-1.7
LORENZEN, LEFTY Adolph Andreas B 1.12.1893 Davenport, IA D 3.5.1963 Davenport, IA BL/TL 5-10/164# d9.12																									
1913	Det A	0	0	—	1	0	0	0	2	4	4	0	0	3	0	18.00	16	.667	.778	2-0	.500	0		-3	-0.1
LORRAINE, ANDREW Andrew Jason B 8.11.1972 Los Angeles, CA BL/TL 6-3/195# d7.17																									
1994	Cal A	0	2	.000	4	3	0	0-0	18.2	30	23	7	0	11-0	10	10.61	46	.366	.436	0-0	—	0	81	-11	-0.9
1995	Chi A	0	0	—	5	0	0	0-0	8	3	3	0	1	2-0	5	3.38	132	.111	.200	0-0	—	0		1	0.0
1997	Oak A	3	1	.750	12	6	0	0-0	29.2	45	22	2	1	15-0	18	6.37	71	.354	.418	0-0	—	0	149	-6	-0.7
1998	Sea A	0	0	—	4	0	0	0-0	3.2	3	1	0	0	4-0	0	2.45	189	.250	.438	0-0	—	0		1	0.0
1999	Chi N	2	5	.286	11	11	2-1	0-0	61.2	71	42	9	0	22-3	40	5.55	81	.293	.350	15-4	.133	0*	87	-7	-0.7
2000	Chi N	1	2	.333	8	5	0	0-1	32	36	25	5	0	18-1	25	6.47	70	.286	.370	8-2	.125	-0	121	-7	-0.6
	Cle A	0	0	—	10	0	0	0-0	9.1	8	4	1	0	5-0	5	3.86	129	.222	.317	0-0	—	0		1	0.1
2002	Mil N	0	1	.000	5	1	0	0-0	12	22	18	7	0	6-0	10	11.25	36	.379	.438	1-1	.000	-0	225	-10	-0.7
Total	7	6	11	.353	59	26	2-1	0-1	175	218	138	31	2	83-4	113	6.53	70	.307	.377	24-7	.125	-0	112	-38	-3.5
LOTZ, JOE Joseph Peter "Smokey" B 1.2.1891 Remsen, IA D 1.1.1971 Castro Valley, CA BR/TR 5-8.5/175# d7.15																									
1916	StL N	0	3	.000	12	3	1	0	40	31	20	1	1	17	18	4.27	62	.225	.314	12-0	.333	1	85	-5	-0.3
LOUDELL, ART Arthur (b: Arthur Laudel) B 4.10.1882 Latham, MO D 2.19.1961 Kansas City, MO BR/TR 5-11/173# d8.13																									
1910	Det A	1	1	.500	5	2	1	0	21.1	23	13	0	0	14	12	3.38	78	.284	.389	7-1	.143	-0	140	-2	-0.3
LOUGHLIN, LARRY Larry John B 8.16.1941 Tacoma, WA D 1.26.1999 Denver, CO BL/TL 6-1/190# d5.27																									
1967	Phi N	0	0	—	3	0	0	0	5.1	9	9	1	0	4-1	5	15.19	22	.375	.464	1-0	1.000	1		-6	-0.3
LOUN, DON Donald Nelson B 11.9.1940 Frederick, MD BR/TL 6-2/185# d9.23																									
1964	Was A	1	1	.500	2	2	1-1	0	13	13	4	0	0	3-0	3	2.08	178	.250	.291	4-0	.000	-0	12	2	0.3

Year	Tm Lg	W	L	Pct	G	GS	CG-Sho	SV-BS	IP	H	R	HR	HB	BB-IB	SO	ERA	AERA	OAV	OOB	AB-SH	AVG	PB	Sup	APR	PW
LOUX, SHANE Shane A. B 8.13.1979 Rapid City, SD BR/TR 6-2/205# d9.10																									
2002	Det A	0	3	.000	3	3	0	0-0	14	19	16	4	1	3-0	7	9.00	48	.317	.359	0-0	—	0	72	-8	-1.2
2003	Det A	1	1	.500	11	4	0	0-0	30.1	37	24	4	4	12-1	8	7.12	61	.303	.381	0-0	—	0	96	-9	-0.5
Total	2	1	4	.200	14	7	0	0-0	44.1	56	40	8	5	15-1	15	7.71	56	.308	.374	0-0	—	0	86	-17	-1.7
LOVE, SLIM Edward Haughton B 8.1.1890 Love, MS D 11.30.1942 Memphis, TN BL/TL 6-7/195# d9.8																									
1913	Was A	1	0	1.000	5	1	0	1	16.2	14	5	0	0	6	5	1.62	182	.233	.303	5-0	.200	0	50	2	0.1
1916	NY A	2	0	1.000	20	1	0	0	47.2	46	29	2	0	23	21	4.91	59	.274	.361	14-1	.000	-2	79	-9	-0.7
1917	NY A	6	5	.545	33	9	2	1	130.1	115	50	0	1	57	82	2.35	114	.251	.335	36-2	.167	-1	71	3	0.0
1918	NY A	13	12	.520	38	29	13-1	1	228.2	207	92	3	10	116	95	3.07	92	.253	.353	74-1	.230	2	91	-5	-0.5
1919	Det A	6	4	.600	22	8	4	1	89.2	92	40	3	6	40	46	3.01	106	.275	.363	27-1	.222	0	86	1	0.0
1920	Det A	0	0	—	1	0	0	0	4.1	6	4	0	0	4	2	8.31	45	.375	.500	0-0	—	0		-2	-0.1
Total	6	28	21	.571	119	48	19-1	4	517.1	480	220	8	17	246	251	3.04	94	.259	.351	156-5	.192	-0	85	-10	-1.2
LOVELACE, VANCE Vance Odell B 8.9.1963 Tampa, FL BL/TL 6-5/205# d9.10																									
1988	Cal A	0	0	—	3	0	0	0-0	1.1	2	2	1	0	3-0	0	13.50	29	.400	.625	0-0	—	0		-1	-0.1
1989	Cal A	0	0	—	1	0	0	0-0	1	0	0	0	0	1-1	1	0.00	—	.000	.250	0-0	—	0		0	0.0
1990	Sea A	0	0	—	5	0	0	0-0	2.1	3	1	0	1	6-0	1	3.86	103	.300	.588	0-0	—	0		0	0.0
Total	3	0	0	—	9	0	0	0-0	4.2	5	3	1	1	10-1	2	5.79	68	.278	.552	0-0	—	0		-1	-0.1
LOVENGUTH, LYNN Lynn Richard B 11.29.1922 Camden, NY D 9.29.2000 Beaverton, OR BL/TR 5-10.5/170# d4.18																									
1955	Phi N	0	1	.000	14	0	0	0	18	17	9	1	2	10-0	14	4.50	88	.258	.358	2-0	.000	-0		-1	-0.1
1957	StL N	0	1	.000	2	1	0	0	9	6	3	0	0	6-0	6	2.00	198	.182	.308	2-0	.000	-0*	44	2	0.1
Total	2	0	2	.000	16	1	0	0	27	23	12	1	2	16-0	20	3.67	108	.232	.342	4-0	.000	-1	44	1	0.0
LOVETT, JOHN John B 5.6.1877 Monday, OH D 12.5.1937 Murray City, OH d5.22																									
1903	StL N	0	0	—	3	1	0	0	5	6	5	0	1	5	3	5.40	60	.300	.462	3-0	.333	0	21	-1	0.0
LOVETT, LEN Leonard Walker B 7.17.1852 Lancaster Co., PA D 11.18.1922 Newark, DE BR/TR d8.4 ▲																									
1873	Res NA	0	1	.000	1	1	1	0	9	22	16	0		1	1	7.00	48	.400	.411	5	.400	0	85	-2	-0.1
LOVETT, TOM Thomas Joseph B 12.7.1863 Providence, RI D 3.19.1928 Providence, RI BR 5-8/162# d6.4																									
1885	Phi AA	7	8	.467	16	16	15-1	0	138.2	130	96	3	5	38	56	3.70	93	.236	.291	58	.224	-0	113	-1	-0.1
1889	†Bro AA	17	10	.630	29	28	23-1	0	229	234	132	3	8	65	92	4.32	86	.256	.311	100	.190	-1	125	-6	-0.7
1890	†Bro N	30	11	**.732**	44	41	39-4	0	372	327	195	14	17	141	124	2.78	124	.229	.305	164	.201	-1	130	24	2.0
1891	Bro N	23	19	.548	44	43	39-3	0	365.2	361	229	14	20	129	129	3.69	90	.248	.318	153	.163	-5	108	-13	-1.7
1893	Bro N	3	5	.375	14	8	6	1	96	134	92	2	6	35	15	6.56	67	.321	.381	50	.180	-2*	101	-21	-1.4
1894	Bos N	8	6	.571	15	13	10	0	104	155	96	12	3	36	23	5.97	95	.341	.394	49-0	.143	-5	100	-2	-0.6
Total	6	88	59	.599	162	149	132-9	1	1305.1	1341	840	48	59	444	439	3.94	94	.257	.322	574-0	.185	-13	116	-19	-2.5
LOVRICH, PETE Peter B 10.16.1942 Blue Island, IL BR/TR 6-4/200# d4.26 Mil 1964-65																									
1963	KC A	1	1	.500	20	1	0	0	20.2	25	23	5	1	10-1	16	7.84	50	.291	.367	0-1	—	0	46	-10	-0.9
LOWDERMILK, GROVER Grover Cleveland "Slim" B 1.15.1885 Sandborn, IN D 3.31.1968 Odin, IL BR/TR 6-4/190# d7.3 b-Lou																									
1909	StL N	0	2	.000	7	3	1	0	29	28	24	0	3	30	14	6.21	41	.292	.473	10-0	.100	-1	83	-11	-0.8
1911	StL N	0	1	.000	11	2	1-1	0	33.1	37	30	1	2	33	15	7.29	46	.301	.456	9-0	.111	-1	33	-13	-0.7
1912	Chi N	0	1	.000	2	1	1	0	13	17	18	1	0	14	8	9.69	34	.304	.443	4-0	.000	-1	22	-9	-0.6
1915	StL A	9	17	.346	38	29	14-1	0	222.1	183	110	1	16	133	130	3.12	92	.234	.357	72-0	.125	-3	79	-6	-1.0
	Det A	4	1	.800	7	5	0	0	28	17	16	0	1	24	18	4.18	73	.185	.359	8-1	.125	-0	120	-3	-0.5
	Year	13	18	.419	45	34	14-1	0	250.1	200	21	1	17	157	148	3.24	89	.229	.357	80-1	.125	-3	86	-13	-1.5
1916	Det A	0	0	—	1	0	0	0	0.1	0	0	0	0	3	0	0.00	—	.000	.750	0-0	—	0		0	0.0
	Cle A	1	5	.167	10	9	2	0	51.1	52	33	0	3	45	28	3.16	95	.277	.424	18-1	.167	-0	89	-4	-0.5
	Year	1	5	.167	11	9	2	0	51.2	52	37	0	3	48	28	3.14	96	.275	.429	18-1	.167	-0	89	-4	-0.5
1917	StL A	2	1	.667	3	2	2-1	0	19	16	5	0	0	4	9	1.42	183	.225	.267	7-0	.000	-1	97	2	0.2
1918	StL A	2	6	.250	13	11	4	0	80	74	44	1	3	38	25	3.15	87	.255	.347	28-0	.250	1	97	-6	-0.3
1919	StL A	0	0	—	7	0	0	0	12	6	2	0	5	4	6	0.75	442	.176	.349	1-0	.000	-0		3	0.1
	†Chi A	5	5	.500	20	11	5	0	96.2	95	44	0	4	43	43	2.79	114	.268	.353	34-0	.088	-3	128	2	-0.1
	Year	5	5	.500	27	11	5	0	108.2	101	49	0	9	47	49	2.57	125	.260	.353	35-0	.086	-4	127	5	0.0
1920	Chi A	0	0	—	3	0	0	0	5.1	9	4	0	0	5	0	6.75	56	.409	.519	0-0	—	0		-1	0.0
Total	9	23	39	.371	122	73	30-3	0	590.1	534	330	4	37	376	296	3.58	82	.253	.375	191-2	.131	-8	91	-46	-4.2
LOWDERMILK, LOU Louis Bailey B 2.23.1887 Sandborn, IN D 12.27.1975 Centralia, IL BR/TL 6-1/180# d4.20 b-Grover																									
1911	StL N	3	4	.429	16	3	3	0	65	72	39	0	5	29	20	3.46	98	.304	.391	18-0	.111	-1	44	-3	-0.5
1912	StL N	1	1	.500	4	1	1	1	15	14	8	0	0	9	2	3.00	114	.246	.348	4-1	.250	0	107	0	0.1
Total	2	4	5	.444	20	4	4	1	80	86	47	0	5	38	22	3.37	100	.293	.383	22-1	.136	-1	61	-3	-0.4
LOWE, DEREK Derek Christopher B 6.1.1973 Dearborn, MI BR/TR 6-6/170# d4.26																									
1997	Sea A	2	4	.333	12	9	0	0-0	53	59	43	11	2	20-2	39	6.96	65	.282	.349	2-0	.000	-0	116	-14	-1.3
	Bos A	0	2	.000	8	0	0	0-2	16	15	6	0	2	3-1	13	3.38	137	.268	.323	1-0	.000	-0		2	0.3
	Year	2	6	.250	20	9	0	0-2	69	74	55	11	4	23-3	52	6.13	74	.279	.344	3-0	.000	-0	115	-12	-1.0
1998	†Bos A	3	9	.250	63	10	0	4-5	123	126	65	5	4	42-5	77	4.02	117	.267	.329	4-0	.000	-0	65	7	0.7
1999	†Bos A	6	3	.667	74	0	0	15-5	109.1	84	35	7	4	25-1	80	2.63	189	.208	.260	0-0	—	0		28	2.6
2000	Bos A★	4	4	.500	74	0	0	**42-5**	91.1	90	27	6	2	22-5	79	2.56	197	.257	.304	1-0	.000	-0		**25**	3.9
2001	Bos A	5	10	.333	67	3	0	24-6	91.2	103	39	7	5	29-9	82	3.53	127	.283	.343	1-0	.000	-0	103	10	1.9
2002	Bos A★	21	8	.724	32	32	1-1	0-0	219.2	166	65	12	12	48-0	127	2.58	174	.211	.266	3-1	.333	1	123	**49**	**6.3**
2003	†Bos A	17	7	.708	33	33	1	0-0	203.1	216	113	17	11	72-4	110	4.47	102	.272	.339	4-1	.000	-0	131	2	0.3
Total	7	58	47	.552	363	87	2-1	85-23	907.1	859	393	65	42	261-27	607	3.57	130	.250	.309	16-2	.063	-0	115	109	14.7
LOWE, GEORGE George Wesley "Doc" B 4.25.1895 Ridgefield Park, NJ D 9.2.1981 Somers Point, NJ BR/TR 6-2/180# d7.28																									
1920	Cin N	0	0	—	1	0	0	0	2	1	0	0	0	1	0	0.00	—	.167	.286	0-0	—	0		1	0.0
LOWE, SEAN Jonathan Sean B 3.29.1971 Dallas, TX BR/TR 6-2/205# d8.29																									
1997	StL N	0	2	.000	6	4	0	0-0	17.1	27	21	2	1	10-0	8	9.35	44	.360	.432	3-0	.333	0	117	-10	-1.0
1998	StL N	0	3	.000	4	1	0	0-0	5.1	11	9	1	0	5-0	2	15.19	28	.440	.533	2-0	.000	-0	66	-6	-1.1
1999	Chi A	4	1	.800	64	0	0	0-3	95.2	90	39	10	4	46-1	62	3.67	133	.262	.347	0-0	—	0		15	0.7
2000	Chi A	4	1	.800	50	5	0	0-0	70.2	78	47	10	6	39-3	53	5.48	91	.284	.383	0-0	—	0	113	-3	-0.2
2001	Chi A	9	4	.692	45	11	0	3-0	127	123	55	12	7	32-2	71	3.61	128	.256	.308	3-0	.333	0	84	14	1.4
2002	Pit N	4	2	.667	43	1	0	0-2	69	85	45	8	7	34-6	57	5.35	78	.307	.393	13-2	.077	-1	110	-9	-0.7
	Col N	1	1	.500	8	0	0	0-0	10.1	16	13	1	0	7-0	7	8.71	55	.348	.434	1-0	.000	-0		-5	-0.8
	Year	5	3	.625	51	1	0	0-2	79.1	101	63	9	7	41-6	64	5.79	74	.313	.398	14-2	.071	-1	108	-14	-1.5
2003	KC A	1	1	.500	28	0	0	0-1	44.2	55	32	7	2	21-5	28	6.25	83	.301	.377	0-0	—	0		-4	-0.2
Total	7	23	15	.605	248	22	0	3-6	440	485	261	51	27	194-17	288	4.95	95	.284	.362	22-2	.136	-1	94	-8	-1.9
LOWN, TURK Omar Joseph B 5.30.1924 Brooklyn, NY BR/TR 6-1/185# d4.24																									
1951	Chi N	4	9	.308	31	18	3-1	0	127	125	80	14	1	90	39	5.46	75	.260	.378	39-2	.205	1	78	-16	-1.3
1952	Chi N	4	11	.267	33	19	5	0	156.2	154	87	13	3	93	73	4.37	88	.257	.359	50-5	.140	-0	86	-9	-0.7
1953	Chi N	8	7	.533	49	12	2	3	148.1	166	93	20	2	84	76	5.16	86	.282	.373	48-2	.125	-2	89	-9	-0.9
1954	Chi N	0	2	.000	15	0	0	0	22	23	18	1	0	15	16	6.14	68	.261	.365	0-0	—	0*		-5	-0.4
1956	Chi N	9	8	.529	61	0	0	13	110.2	95	49	10	1	78-12	74	3.58	105	.240	.363	23-1	.217	2		3	0.7
1957	Chi N	5	7	.417	**67**	0	0	12	93	74	45	10	0	51-4	51	3.77	103	.221	.321	10-0	.200	0		0	0.2
1958	Chi N	0	0	—	4	0	0	0	4	2	2	0	0	3-0	4	4.50	87	.154	.313	0-0	—	0		0	0.0
	Cin N	0	2	.000	11	0	0	0	11.2	12	8	2	0	12-2	9	5.40	77	.273	.421	1-0	.000	-0		-2	-0.3
	Year	0	2	.000	15	0	0	0	15.2	14	14	2	0	15-2	13	5.17	79	.246	.397	1-0	.000	-0		-2	-0.3
	Chi A	3	3	.500	27	0	0	8	40.2	49	22	1	0	28-4	40	3.98	91	.308	.405	9-1	.333	1		-3	-0.4
1959	†Chi A	9	2	.818	60	0	0	**15**	93.1	73	32	12	2	42-4	63	2.89	130	.215	.303	12-0	.250	1		10	1.6

Year	Tm Lg	W	L	Pct	G	GS	CG-Sho	SV-BS	IP	H	R	HR	HB	BB-IB	SO	ERA	AERA	OAV	OOB	AB-SH	AVG	PB	Sup	APR	PW
1960	Chi A	2	3	.400	45	0	0	5	67.1	60	31	6	0	34-6	39	3.88	98	.239	.326	5-2	.200	1		0	0.1
1961	Chi A	7	5	.583	59	0	0	11	101	87	37	13	0	35-3	50	2.76	142	.238	.300	14-1	.000	-2*		12	1.4
1962	Chi A	4	2	.667	42	0	0	6	56.1	58	21	3	1	25-5	40	3.04	129	.269	.346	3-0	.000	-0		5	0.7
Total	11	55	61	.474	504	49	10-1	73	1032	978	525	105	10	590-40	574	4.12	96	.252	.351	214-14	.164	1	86	-14	0.7
LOWRY, NOAH Noah Ryan B 10.10.1980 Ventura, CA BR/TL 6-2/190# d9.5																									
2003	SF N	0	0	—	4	0	0	0-0	6.1	1	0	0	1	2-0	5	0.00	—	.048	.167	2-0	.500	0		3	0.2
LOWRY, SAM Samuel Joseph B 3.25.1920 Philadelphia, PA D 12.1.1992 Philadelphia, PA BR/TR 5-11/170# d9.19 Mil 1944-46																									
1942	Phi A	0	0	—	1	0	0	0	3	3	2	0	0	1	0	6.00	63	.250	.308	1-0	.000	-0		-1	0.0
1943	Phi A	0	0	—	5	0	0	0	18	18	10	1	0	9	3	5.00	68	.269	.355	6-0	.167	-0		-3	-0.1
Total	2	0	0	—	6	0	0	0	21	21	12	1	0	10	3	5.14	67	.266	.348	7-0	.143	-0		-4	-0.1
LOYND, MIKE Michael Wallace B 3.26.1964 St.Louis, MO BR/TR 6-4/210# d7.24																									
1986	Tex A	2	2	.500	9	8	0	1-0	42	49	30	4	2	19-1	33	5.36	80	.290	.365	0-0	—	0	118	-6	-0.5
1987	Tex A	1	5	.167	26	8	0	1-0	69.1	82	53	14	1	38-0	48	6.10	74	.287	.370	0-0	—	0	94	-12	-1.0
Total	2	3	7	.300	35	16	0	2-0	111.1	131	83	18	3	57-1	81	5.82	76	.288	.368	0-0	—	0	106	-18	-1.5
LUBY, PAT John Perkins B 6.1869 Charleston, SC D 4.24.1899 Charleston, SC TR 6/185# d6.16																									
1890	Chi N	20	9	.690	34	31	26	1	267.2	226	129	6	15	95	85	3.19	115	.222	.297	116	.267	8*	104	19	2.3
1891	Chi N	8	11	.421	30	24	18	1	206	221	148	11	19	94	52	4.76	70	.264	.352	98	.245	7*	113	-26	-1.3
1892	Chi N	11	16	.407	31	27	24-1	0	252.1	248	157	10	10	103	66	3.07	108	.247	.323	163	.190	1*	73	1	0.2
1895	Lou N	1	5	.167	11	6	5	0	71.1	115	90	5	7	19	12	6.81	68	.357	.405	53-0	.283	3*	72	-21	-1.0
Total	4	40	41	.494	106	88	73-1	2	797.1	810	524	32	51	311	215	3.88	92	.254	.331	430-0	.235	18	95	-27	0.2
LUCAS, RED Charles Fred "The Nashville Narcissus" B 4.28.1902 Columbia, TN D 7.9.1986 Nashville, TN BL/TR 5-9.5/170# d4.19 ▲																									
1923	NY N	0	0	—	3	0	0	1	5.1	9	5	0	0	4	3	0.00	—	.346	.433	2-0	.000	-0		0	0.0
1924	Bos N	1	4	.200	27	4	1	0	83.2	112	60	5	6	18	30	5.16	74	.332	.377	33-0	.333	2*	67	-14	-0.5
1926	Cin N	8	5	.615	39	11	7-1	2	154	161	68	6	2	30	34	3.68	100	.277	.314	76-5	.303	6*	98	4	1.2
1927	Cin N	18	11	.621	37	23	19-4	2	239.2	231	96	6	0	39	51	3.38	112	.256	.287	150-6	.313	7*	97	17	3.1
1928	Cin N	13	9	.591	27	19	13-**4**	1	167.1	164	73	9	0	42	35	3.39	117	.258	.304	73-1	.315	6*	72	10	1.9
1929	Cin N	19	12	.613	32	32	**28**-2	0	270	267	119	14	1	58	72	3.60	127	**.257**	**.297**	140-2	.293	11*	101	31	**4.3**
1930	Cin N	14	16	.467	33	28	18-1	1	210.2	270	135	15	1	44	53	5.38	90	.315	.349	113-7	.336	15*	97	-10	0.2
1931	Cin N	14	13	.519	29	29	**24**-3	0	238	261	110	10	0	39	56	3.59	104	.280	.309	153-6	.281	11*	117	5	1.7
1932	Cin N	13	17	.433	31	31	**28**	0	269.1	261	110	10	1	35	63	2.94	131	.249	.274	150-3	.287	13*	82	26	4.4
1933	Cin N	10	16	.385	29	29	21-3	0	219.2	248	106	13	2	18	40	3.40	100	.289	.305	122-2	.287	12*	92	-1	1.3
1934	Pit N	10	9	.526	29	22	12-1	0	172.2	198	89	14	2	40	44	4.38	94	.283	.324	105-1	.219	3*	125	-2	0.0
1935	Pit N	8	6	.571	20	19	8-2	0	125.2	136	60	10	2	23	29	3.44	119	.272	.307	66-2	.318	8*	100	9	1.7
1936	Pit N	15	4	.789	27	22	12	0	175.2	178	70	7	3	26	53	3.18	128	.257	.287	108-3	.241	4*	121	19	2.2
1937	Pit N	8	10	.444	20	20	9-1	0	126.1	150	69	12	1	23	20	4.27	90	.290	.322	82-0	.268	5*	107	-5	-0.2
1938	Pit N	6	3	.667	13	13	4	0	84	90	33	5	1	16	19	3.54	107	.283	.319	46-2	.109	-2*	105	5	0.2
Total	15	157	135	.538	396	302	204-22	7	2542	2736	1203	136	22	455	602	3.72	107	.275	.308	1419-40	.283	98	101	94	21.5
LUCAS, GARY Gary Paul B 11.8.1954 Riverside, CA BL/TL 6-5/200# d4.16																									
1980	SD N	5	8	.385	46	18	0	3-1	150	138	59	8	1	43-14	85	3.24	106	.250	.302	35-7	.171	-0	87	4	0.3
1981	SD N	7	7	.500	**57**	0	0	13-4	90	78	26	1	3	36-15	53	2.00	163	.247	.325	10-2	.100	-1		11	2.1
1982	SD N	1	10	.091	65	0	0	16-9	97.1	89	42	5	1	29-7	64	3.24	106	.245	.298	14-3	.000	-1		1	0.1
1983	SD N	5	8	.385	62	0	0	17-6	91	85	38	9	0	34-11	60	2.87	122	.245	.310	12-0	.000	-1		4	0.5
1984	Mon N	0	3	.000	55	0	0	8-2	53	54	20	4	0	20-5	42	2.72	126	.267	.330	4-0	.000	-0		3	0.3
1985	Mon N	6	2	.750	49	0	0	1-3	67.2	63	29	6	0	24-8	31	3.19	106	.251	.314	5-0	.000	-1		0	0.0
1986	†Cal A	4	1	.800	27	0	0	2-2	45.2	45	19	1	0	6-0	31	3.15	131	.253	.276	0-0	—	0		4	0.5
1987	Cal A	1	5	.167	48	0	0	3-3	74.1	66	41	7	2	35-5	44	3.63	119	.241	.329	0-0	—	0		3	0.3
Total	8	29	44	.397	409	18	0	63-30	669	618	274	41	7	227-65	410	3.01	118	.249	.310	80-12	.087	-4	87	30	4.1
LUCAS, RAY Ray Wesley "Luke" B 10.2.1908 Springfield, OH D 10.9.1969 Harrison, MI BR/TR 6-2/175# d9.28																									
1929	NY N	0	0	—	3	0	0	1	8	3	0	0	0	3	1	0.00	—	.111	.200	2-0	.500	0		4	0.2
1930	NY N	0	0	—	6	0	0	0	10.1	9	8	2	1	10	1	6.97	68	.265	.444	1-0	.000	-0		-2	-0.1
1931	NY N	0	0	—	1	0	0	0	2	1	1	1	0	1	0	4.50	82	.143	.250	0-0	—	0		0	0.0
1933	Bro N	0	0	—	2	0	0	0	5	6	4	0	1	4	0	7.20	45	.316	.458	0-0	—	0		-2	-0.1
1934	Bro N	1	1	.500	10	2	0	0	30.2	39	24	2	3	14	3	6.75	58	.328	.412	6-1	.333	1	122	-9	-0.3
Total	5	1	1	.500	22	2	0	1	56	58	37	5	5	32	5	5.79	71	.282	.391	9-1	.333	1	122	-9	-0.3
LUCEY, JOE Joseph Earl "Scootch" B 3.27.1897 Holyoke, MA D 7.30.1980 Holyoke, MA BR/TR 6/168# d7.6.1920																									
1925	Bos A	0	1	.000	7	2	0	0	11	18	20	0	0	14	2	9.00	50	.360	.500	15-0	.133	-1*	102	-8	-0.6
LUCID, CON Cornelius Cecil B 2.24.1874 Dublin, Ireland D 6.25.1931 Houston, TX 5-7/170# d5.1																									
1893	Lou N	0	1	.000	2	1	0	0	6	10	14	0	1	10	0	15.00	29	.357	.538	3	.333	0	16	-8	-0.8
1894	Bro N	5	3	.625	10	9	7	0	71.1	87	68	6	9	44	15	6.56	76	.298	.406	33-0	.212	-2	114	-12	-1.1
1895	Bro N	10	7	.588	21	19	12-2	0	137	164	113	4	7	72	24	5.52	80	.292	.380	53-2	.245	2	114	-20	-1.6
	Phi N	6	3	.667	10	10	7-1	0	69.2	80	56	3	9	35	19	5.94	80	.284	.380	29-1	.345	4	128	-7	-0.4
	Year	16	10	.615	31	29	19-3	0	206.2	244	65	7	16	107	43	5.66	80	.289	.380	82-3	.280	6	119	-21	-2.0
1896	Phi N	1	4	.200	5	5	5	0	42	75	43	2	2	17	3	8.36	52	.383	.437	16-1	.125	-2	69	-15	-1.4
1897	StL N	1	5	.167	6	6	5	0	49	66	46	0	0	26	4	3.67	120	.319	.395	17-0	.176	-0	49	-3	-0.2
Total	5	23	23	.500	54	50	36-3	0	375	482	340	15	28	204	65	6.02	76	.308	.397	151-4	.238	2	103	-65	-5.5
LUCIER, LOU Louis Joseph B 3.23.1918 Northbridge, MA BR/TR 5-8/160# d4.23																									
1943	Bos A	3	4	.429	16	9	3	0	74	94	35	1	2	33	23	3.89	85	.322	.394	20-0	.200	-0	99	-5	-0.2
1944	Bos A	0	0	—	3	0	0	0	5.1	7	3	0	0	7	2	5.06	67	.292	.452	1-0	.000	-0		-1	-0.1
	Phi N	0	0	—	1	0	0	0	2	3	3	0	0	2	1	13.50	27	.333	.455	0-0	—	0		-2	-0.1
1945	Phi N	0	1	.000	13	0	0	1	20.1	14	9	1	0	5	5	2.21	173	.194	.247	4-0	.250	0		3	0.2
Total	3	3	5	.375	33	9	3	1	101.2	118	50	2	2	47	31	3.81	90	.297	.374	25-0	.200	-0	99	-5	-0.2
LUDOLPH, WILLIE William Francis "Wee Willie" B 1.21.1900 San Francisco, CA D 4.8.1952 Oakland, CA BR/TR 6-1.5/170# d5.28																									
1924	Det A	0	0	—	3	0	0	0	5.2	5	3	0	1	2	1	4.76	86	.250	.348	1-0	.000	-0		0	0.0
LUDWICK, ERIC Eric David B 12.14.1971 Whiteman Afb, MO BR/TR 6-5/210# d9.1																									
1996	StL N	0	1	.000	6	1	0	0-0	10	11	11	4	1	3-0	12	9.00	47	.275	.333	2-0	.000	-0	65	-5	-0.5
1997	StL N	0	1	.000	5	0	0	0-0	6.2	12	7	1	0	6-0	7	9.45	44	.400	.500	0-0	—	0		-4	-0.5
	Oak A	1	4	.200	6	5	0	0-0	24	32	24	7	1	16-1	14	8.25	55	.330	.430	2-0	.000	-0	73	-10	-1.6
1998	Fla N	1	4	.200	13	6	0	0-1	32.2	46	31	7	0	17-1	27	7.44	55	.333	.401	7-0	.000	-1	147	-13	-1.8
1999	Tor A	0	0	—	1	0	0	0-0	1	3	3	0	0	2-0	0	27.00	18	.500	.625	0-0	—	0		-2	-0.1
Total	4	2	10	.167	31	12	0	0-1	74.1	104	76	19	2	44-2	60	8.35	51	.334	.417	11-0	.000	-1	108	-34	-4.5
LUEBBER, STEVE Stephen Lee B 7.9.1949 Clinton, MO BR/TR 6-3/195# d6.27																									
1971	Min A	2	5	.286	18	12	0	1-0	68	73	42	7	4	37-3	35	5.03	71	.278	.373	19-2	.053	-2*	120	-11	-1.2
1972	Min A	0	0	—	2	0	0	0-0	2.1	3	0	0	0	2-1	1	0.00	—	.333	.417	0-0	—	0		1	0.1
1976	Min A	4	5	.444	38	12	2-1	2-0	119.1	109	57	9	1	62-3	45	4.00	90	.248	.341	0-0	—	0	129	-3	-0.3
1979	Tor A	0	0	—	1	0	0	0-0	0	2	1	0	0	1-0	0	∞	—	1.000	1.000	0-0	—	0		-1	-0.1
1981	Bal A	0	0	—	7	0	0	0-0	16.2	26	14	3	1	4-1	12	7.56	48	.366	.403	0-0	—	0		-7	-0.3
Total	5	6	10	.375	66	24	2-1	3-0	206.1	213	114	19	6	106-8	93	4.62	77	.271	.360	19-2	.053	-2	124	-21	-1.8
LUEBBERS, LARRY Larry Christopher B 10.11.1969 Cincinnati, OH BR/TR 6-6/190# d7.3																									
1993	Cin N	2	5	.286	14	14	0	0-0	77.1	74	49	7	1	38-3	38	4.54	89	.261	.345	24-1	.250	1	89	-7	-0.5
1999	StL N	3	3	.500	8	8	1	0-0	45.2	46	27	8	3	16-0	16	5.12	89	.261	.333	16-1	.125	-0	121	-2	-0.3
2000	Cin N	0	2	.000	14	1	0	1-0	20.1	27	15	1	0	12-2	9	6.20	76	.333	.419	0-0	—	0	20	-3	-0.3
Total	3	5	10	.333	36	23	1	1-0	143.1	147	91	16	4	66-5	63	4.96	87	.272	.352	40-2	.200	1	97	-12	-1.1

Year	Tm Lg	W	L	Pct	G	GS	CG-Sho	SV-BS	IP	H	R	HR	HB	BB-IB	SO	ERA	AERA	OAV	OOB	AB-SH	AVG	PB	Sup	APR	PW
LUEBKE, DICK Richard Raymond B 4.8.1935 Chicago, IL D 12.4.1974 San Diego, CA BR/TL 6-4/200# d8.11																									
1962	Bal A	0	1	.000	10	0	0	0	13.1	12	4	0	0	6-0	7	2.70	137	.250	.327	0-0	—	0		2	0.1
LUECKEN, RICK Richard Fred B 11.15.1960 McAllen, TX BR/TR 6-6/210# d6.6																									
1989	KC A	2	1	.667	19	0	0	1-0	23.2	23	9	3	0	13-4	16	3.42	113	.258	.353	0-0	—	0		2	0.2
1990	Atl N	1	4	.200	36	0	0	1-2	53	73	36	5	3	30-7	35	5.77	70	.336	.422	3-0	.333	1		-9	-0.7
	Tor A	0	0	—	1	0	0	0-0	1	2	1	1	0	1-0	0	9.00	44	.500	.600	0-0	—	0		-1	0.0
Total	2	3	5	.375	56	0	0	2-2	77.2	98	46	9	3	44-11	51	5.10	78	.316	.405	3-0	.333	1		-8	-0.5
LUFF, HENRY Henry T. B 9.14.1856 Philadelphia, PA D 10.11.1916 Philadelphia, PA 5-11/175# d4.21 ▲																									
1875	NH NA	1	6	.143	10	7	5	0	68.2	98	91	2		3	5	3.28	63	.295	.301	166	.271	3*	90	-12	-0.7
LUGO, URBANO Rafael Urbano (Colina) B 8.12.1962 Punto Fijo, Venezuela BR/TR 6/190# d4.28																									
1985	Cal A	3	4	.429	20	10	1	0-0	83	86	36	10	4	29-1	42	3.69	112	.274	.341	0-0	—	0	95	5	0.4
1986	Cal A	1	1	.500	6	3	0	0-0	21.1	21	9	4	0	6-0	9	3.80	108	.266	.318	0-0	—	0	110	1	0.1
1987	Cal A	0	2	.000	7	5	0	0-0	28	42	34	8	0	18-0	24	9.32	46	.339	.420	0-0	—	0	102	-17	-1.0
1988	Cal A	0	0	—	1	0	0	0-0	2	2	2	1	0	1-0	1	9.00	43	.250	.333	0-0	—	0		-1	-0.1
1989	Mon N	0	0	—	3	0	0	0-0	4	4	3	1	0	0-0	3	6.75	52	.250	.250	0-0	—	0		-1	-0.1
1990	Det A	2	0	1.000	13	1	0	0-1	24.1	30	19	9	3	13-1	12	7.03	56	.313	.411	0-0	—	0	115	-7	-0.5
Total	6	6	7	.462	50	19	1	0-1	162.2	185	103	33	7	67-2	91	5.31	77	.290	.363	0-0	—	0	101	-20	-1.2
LUHRSEN, WILD BILL William Ferdinand B 4.14.1884 Buckley, IL D 8.15.1973 Little Rock, AR BR/TR 5-9/165# d8.23																									
1913	Pit N	3	1	.750	5	3	2	0	29	25	10	3	2	16	11	2.48	122	.248	.361	10-1	.000	-1	91	2	0.2
LUKASIEWICZ, MARK Mark Francis B 3.8.1973 Jersey City, NJ BL/TL 6-5/240# d5.11																									
2001	Ana A	0	2	.000	24	0	0	0-0	22.1	21	17	6	2	9-2	25	6.04	76	.247	.330	0-0	—	0		-4	-0.3
2002	Ana A	2	0	1.000	17	0	0	0-0	14	17	6	0	0	9-0	15	3.86	115	.298	.388	0-0	—	0		1	0.1
Total	2	2	2	.500	41	0	0	0-0	36.1	38	23	6	2	18-2	40	5.20	87	.268	.354	0-0	—	0		-3	-0.2
LUKENS, AL Albert P. B 11.1868 , PA TR 5-9/168# d6.23																									
1894	Phi N	0	1	.000	3	2	1	0	15	26	22	0	3	10	0	10.20	50	.377	.476	8-0	.000	-2	117	-8	-0.5
LUMENTI, RALPH Raphael Anthony B 12.21.1936 Milford, MA BL/TL 6-3/185# d9.7																									
1957	Was A	0	1	.000	3	2	0	0	9.1	9	7	1	1	5-0	8	6.75	58	.250	.357	2-0	.000	-0	80	-3	-0.3
1958	Was A	1	2	.333	8	4	0	0	21	21	20	2	1	36-0	20	8.57	44	.266	.500	8-0	.250	0	71	-10	-1.2
1959	Was A	0	0	—	2	0	0	0	3	2	0	0	0	1-0	2	0.00	—	.200	.273	0-0	—	0		1	0.1
Total	3	1	3	.250	13	6	0	0	33.1	32	27	3	2	42-0	30	7.29	53	.256	.450	10-0	.200	-0	74	-12	-1.4
LUNA, MEMO Guillermo Romero B 6.25.1930 Tacubaya, Mexico BL/TL 6/168# d4.20																									
1954	StL N	0	1	.000	1	1	0	0	0.2	2	2	0	0	2	0	27.00	15	.667	.667	0-0	—	0	130	-2	-0.3
LUNDBOM, JACK John Frederick B 3.10.1877 Manistee, MI D 10.31.1949 Manistee, MI BR/TR 6-0.5/187# d5.9																									
1902	Cle A	1	1	.500	8	3	1	0	34	48	35	1	1	16	7	6.62	52	.333	.404	15-0	.267	1	104	-11	-0.5
LUNDGREN, CARL Carl Leonard B 2.16.1880 Marengo, IL D 8.21.1934 Marengo, IL BR/TR 5-11/175# d6.19																									
1902	Chi N	9	9	.500	18	18	17-1	0	160	158	59	2	6	45	68	1.97	137	.258	.315	66-2	.106	-4*	92	12	0.7
1903	Chi N	11	9	.550	27	20	16	**3**	193	191	103	1	6	60	67	2.94	107	.262	.323	61-3	.115	-1	97	3	0.0
1904	Chi N	17	9	.654	31	27	25-2	1	242	203	97	2	4	77	106	2.60	102	.226	.290	90-2	.222	4	99	3	0.6
1905	Chi N	13	5	.722	23	19	16-3	0	169.1	132	58	3	9	53	69	2.23	134	.220	.293	61-2	.180	1*	126	14	1.6
1906	Chi N	17	6	.739	27	24	21-5	2	207.2	160	63	3	8	89	103	2.21	119	.221	.313	67-6	.179	2*	107	13	1.7
1907	Chi N	18	7	.720	28	25	21-7	0	207	130	42	0	2	92	84	1.17	212	**.185**	.282	66-7	.106	-3	88	**29**	3.5
1908	Chi N	6	9	.400	23	15	9-1	0	138.2	149	72	5	0	56	38	4.22	56	.284	.353	47-5	.149	-1	112	-23	-2.7
1909	Chi N	0	1	.000	2	1	0	0	4.1	6	2	0	0	4	0	4.15	61	.353	.476	2-0	.500	0	83	0	-0.1
Total	8	91	55	.623	179	149	125-19	6	1322	1129	496	16	35	476	535	2.42	113	.235	.308	460-27	.157	-2	102	51	5.3
LUNDGREN, DEL Ebin Delmar B 9.21.1899 Lindsborg, KS D 10.19.1984 Lindsborg, KS BR/TR 5-8/160# d4.27																									
1924	Pit N	0	1	.000	8	1	0	0	16.2	25	13	0	1	3	4	6.48	59	.403	.439	3-0	.000	-1	44	-4	-0.3
1926	Bos A	0	2	.000	18	2	0	0	31	35	28	2	3	28	11	7.55	54	.307	.455	4-0	.000	-0	62	-11	-0.6
1927	Bos A	5	12	.294	30	17	5-2	0	136.1	160	100	7	4	87	39	6.27	67	.302	.405	44-3	.159	-2	91	-25	-2.8
Total	3	5	15	.250	56	20	5-2	0	184	220	141	9	8	118	54	6.51	64	.312	.416	51-3	.137	-3	86	-40	-3.7
LUNDQUIST, DAVID David Bruce B 6.4.1973 Beverly, MA BR/TR 6-2/200# d4.6																									
1999	Chi A	1	1	.500	17	0	0	0-0	22	28	21	3	1	12-0	18	8.59	57	.315	.394	0-0	—	0		-8	-0.6
2001	SD N	0	1	.000	17	0	0	0-1	19.2	20	13	1	1	7-1	19	5.95	67	.260	.326	0-0	—	0		-4	-0.2
2002	SD N	0	0	—	3	0	0	0-1	2.2	8	5	0	1	5-2	0	16.88	22	.615	.737	0-0	—	0		-4	-0.2
Total	3	1	2	.333	37	0	0	0-2	44.1	56	39	4	3	24-3	37	7.92	56	.313	.397	0-0	—	0		-16	-1.0
LUQUE, DOLF Adolfo Domingo De Guzman "The Pride Of Havana" B 8.4.1890 Havana, Cuba D 7.3.1957 Havana, Cuba BR/TR 5-7/160# d5.20 C9																									
1914	Bos N	0	1	.000	2	1	1	0	8.2	5	5	0	0	4	1	4.15	66	.167	.265	2-1	.000	-0	26	-1	-0.2
1915	Bos N	0	0	—	2	1	0	0	5	6	3	0	0	4	3	3.60	72	.286	.400	2-0	.000	-0*	115	-1	-0.1
1918	Cin N	6	3	.667	12	10	9-1	0	83	84	44	1	1	32	26	3.80	70	.277	.348	28-1	.321	5*	147	-10	-0.6
1919	†Cin N	10	3	.769	30	9	6-2	3	106	89	35	2	2	36	40	2.63	105	.237	.308	32-2	.125	-0*	118	3	0.5
1920	Cin N	13	9	.591	37	23	10-1	1	207.2	168	65	5	4	60	72	2.51	121	**.225**	.286	64-5	.266	4	114	16	2.1
1921	Cin N	17	19	.472	41	36	25-**3**	1	304	318	132	13	1	64	102	3.38	106	.273	.312	111-5	.270	6*	91	11	1.8
1922	Cin N	13	23	.361	39	33	18	0	261	266	123	7	1	72	79	3.31	121	.268	.318	86-3	.209	2	71	19	2.4
1923	Cin N	**27**	8	**.771**	41	37	28-**6**	2	322	279	90	2	5	88	151	**1.93**	**200**	**.235**	.291	104-10	.202	2*	95	**70**	**7.6**
1924	Cin N	10	15	.400	31	28	13-2	0	219.1	229	99	5	2	53	86	3.16	119	.271	.316	73-3	.178	-1*	88	13	1.3
1925	Cin N	16	18	.471	36	36	22-**4**	0	291	263	109	7	2	78	140	**2.63**	**156**	**.239**	**.291**	102-4	.255	5*	76	**48**	**5.9**
1926	Cin N	13	16	.448	34	31	16-1	0	233.2	231	123	7	2	77	83	3.43	108	.260	.321	78-7	.346	8	87	1	1.0
1927	Cin N	13	12	.520	29	27	17-2	0	230.2	225	103	10	0	56	76	3.20	118	.260	.305	83-7	.217	2	86	14	1.8
1928	Cin N	11	10	.524	33	29	11-1	1	234.1	254	112	12	2	84	72	3.57	111	.284	.347	67-5	.119	-1	90	8	0.4
1929	Cin N	5	16	.238	32	22	8-1	0	176	213	103	7	2	56	43	4.50	101	.310	.364	54-4	.278	4	73	0	0.3
1930	Bro N	14	8	.636	31	24	16-2	2	199	221	107	18	0	58	62	4.30	114	.287	.337	75-4	.240	1	128	17	1.7
1931	Bro N	7	6	.538	19	15	5	0	102.2	122	59	6	1	27	25	4.56	84	.297	.342	30-2	.133	0	106	-8	-0.9
1932	NY N	6	7	.462	38	5	1	5	110	128	53	4	0	32	32	4.01	93	.290	.338	25-0	.040	-2	50	-1	-0.3
1933	†NY N	8	2	.800	35	0	0	4	80.1	75	27	4	0	19	23	2.69	119	.251	.296	19-0	.263	1		6	0.8
1934	NY N	4	3	.571	26	0	0	7	42.1	54	20	3	1	17	12	3.83	101	.316	.381	7-1	.286	1		1	0.3
1935	NY N	1	0	1.000	2	0	0	0	3.2	1	0	0	0	1	2	0.00	—	.077	.143	1-1	1.000	0		2	0.4
Total	20	194	179	.520	550	367	206-26	28	3220.1	3231	1412	113	26	918	1130	3.24	117	.265	.318	1043-65	.227	37	92	208	26.2
LUSH, JOHNNY John Charles B 10.8.1885 Williamsport, PA D 11.18.1946 Beverly Hills, CA BL/TL 5-9.5/165# d4.22 ▲																									
1904	Phi N	0	6	.000	7	6	3	0	42.2	52	40	0	7	27	27	3.59	75	.301	.415	369-6	.276	2*	81	-9	-0.9
1905	Phi N	2	0	1.000	2	2	1	0	17	12	4	0	1	8	8	1.59	184	.194	.296	16-1	.313	1*	235	3	0.4
1906	Phi N	18	15	.545	37	35	24-5	0	281	254	128	2	16	119	151	2.37	110	.236	.321	212-0	.264	7*	123	0	1.0
1907	Phi N	3	5	.375	8	8	5-2	0	57.1	48	22	0	3	21	20	2.98	81	.227	.306	40-0	.200	1*	74	-2	-0.2
	StL N	7	10	.412	20	19	15-3	0	144	132	63	2	8	42	71	2.50	100	.246	.311	82-1	.280	5*	87	-1	0.7
	Year	10	15	.400	28	27	20-5	0	201.1	180	66	2	11	63	91	2.64	94	.241	.309	122-1	.254	6	83	-3	0.5
1908	StL N	11	18	.379	38	32	23-3	1	250.2	221	102	6	11	57	93	2.12	111	.231	.283	89-4	.169	1*	80	3	0.6
1909	StL N	11	18	.379	34	28	21-2	0	221.1	215	96	1	10	69	66	3.13	81	.260	.324	92-1	.239	4*	116	-11	-0.8
1910	StL N	14	13	.519	36	25	13-1	1	225.1	235	116	6	7	70	54	3.20	93	.276	.336	93-0	.226	4*	124	-11	-0.9
Total	7	66	85	.437	182	155	105-16	2	1239.1	1169	571	17	63	413	490	2.68	97	.249	.318	993-13	.254	24	106	-28	-0.1
LYLE, SPARKY Albert Walter B 7.22.1944 DuBois, PA BL/TL 6-1/192# d7.4																									
1967	Bos A	1	2	.333	27	0	0	5	43.1	33	13	3	2	14-1	42	2.28	153	.213	.283	8-0	.250	1		5	0.5
1968	Bos A	6	1	.857	49	0	0	11	65.2	67	25	6	0	14-2	52	2.74	115	.261	.298	8-1	.125	-0		2	0.2
1969	Bos A	8	3	.727	71	0	0	17-9	102.2	91	33	8	1	48-4	93	2.54	150	.240	.323	17-0	.118	-1		14	2.0

Year	Tm Lg	W	L	Pct	G	GS	CG-Sho	SV-BS	IP	H	R	HR	HB	BB-IB	SO	ERA	AERA	OAV	OOB	AB-SH	AVG	PB	Sup	APR	PW
1970	Bos A	1	7	.125	63	0	0	20-10	67.1	62	37	5	1	34-5	51	3.88	102	.244	.334	13-0	.000	-1		-1	-0.3
1971	Bos A	6	4	.600	50	0	0	16-4	52.1	41	16	5	0	23-2	37	2.75	134	.228	.311	3-1	1.000	1		6	1.4
1972	NY A	9	5	.643	59	0	0	**35-7**	107.2	84	25	3	0	29-7	75	1.92	154	.216	.268	21-2	.190	1		**13**	3.0
1973	NY A★	5	9	.357	51	0	0	27-6	82.1	66	30	4	0	18-2	63	2.51	146	.216	.258	0-0	—	0		9	2.0
1974	NY A	9	3	.750	66	0	0	15-7	114	93	30	6	1	43-7	89	1.66	213	.226	.297	1-0	.000	-0		22	2.9
1975	NY A	5	7	.417	49	0	0	6-6	89.1	94	34	1	2	36-5	65	3.12	118	.275	.345	0-0	—	0		6	0.9
1976	†NY A☆	7	8	.467	64	0	0	**23-8**	103.2	82	33	5	0	42-7	61	2.26	152	.225	.302	0-0	—	0		12	2.3
1977	†NY A★	13	5	.722	**72**	0	0	26-8	137	131	41	7	2	33-6	68	2.17	182	.257	.302	0-0	—	0		**26**	4.3
1978	†NY A	9	3	.750	59	0	0	9-2	111.2	116	46	6	4	33-8	33	3.47	105	.278	.332	0-0	—	0		3	0.4
1979	Tex A	5	8	.385	67	0	0	13-7	95	78	37	9	0	28-6	48	3.13	133	.226	.283	0-0	—	0		11	1.7
1980	Tex A	3	2	.600	49	0	0	8-4	80.2	97	47	9	0	28-6	43	4.69	83	.306	.359	0-0	—	0		-7	-0.5
	Phi N	0	0	—	10	0	0	2-1	14	11	5	0	0	6-1	6	1.93	197	.220	.293	0-0	—	0		2	0.1
1981	†Phi N	9	6	.600	48	0	0	2-2	75	85	40	4	1	33-9	29	4.44	82	.301	.372	5-1	.400	1		-6	-1.1
1982	Phi N	3	3	.500	34	0	0	2-5	36.2	50	23	3	0	12-3	12	5.15	71	.327	.373	2-0	.500	1		-6	-0.8
	Chi A	0	0	—	11	0	0	1-0	12	11	4	0	0	7-0	6	3.00	135	.262	.360	0-0	—	0		2	0.1
Total	16	99	76	.566	899	0	0	238-86	1390.1	1292	519	84	14	481-81	873	2.88	127	.251	.313	78-5	.192	2		113	19.1
LYLE, JIM James Charles B 7.24.1900 Lake, MS D 10.10.1977 Williamsport, PA BR/TR 6-1/180# d10.2																									
1925	Was A	0	0	—	1	0	0	0	3	5	2	0	0	1	3	6.00	70	.333	.375	0-0	—	0		0	0.0
LYNCH, ADRIAN Adrian Ryan B 2.9.1897 Laurens, IA D 3.16.1934 Davenport, IA BB/TR 6-1.5/185# d8.4																									
1920	StL A	2	0	1.000	5	3	1	0	22.1	23	15	1	1	17	8	5.24	75	.277	.406	9-0	.222	0	216	-3	-0.2
LYNCH, ED Edward Francis B 2.25.1956 Brooklyn, NY BR/TR 6-6/230# d8.31																									
1980	NY N	1	1	.500	5	4	0	0-0	19.1	24	12	0	1	5-0	9	5.12	69	.304	.349	6-0	.333	0	75	-3	-0.3
1981	NY N	4	5	.444	17	13	0	0-0	80.1	79	32	6	1	21-2	27	2.91	120	.254	.302	21-2	.143	1	86	5	0.6
1982	NY N	4	8	.333	43	12	0	2-1	139.1	145	57	6	1	40-4	51	3.55	102	.273	.323	33-3	.000	-3	87	4	-0.1
1983	NY N	10	10	.500	30	27	1	0-0	174.2	208	94	17	3	41-10	44	4.28	85	.302	.341	52-11	.154	-1	107	-12	-1.4
1984	NY N	9	8	.529	40	13	0	2-1	124	169	77	14	4	24-3	62	4.50	79	.324	.356	27-3	.222	1	88	-16	-2.0
1985	NY N	10	8	.556	31	29	6-1	0-0	191	188	76	19	1	27-1	65	3.44	101	.256	.281	52-9	.077	-2	104	3	-0.2
1986	NY N	0	0	—	1	0	0	0-0	1.2	2	0	0	0	0-0	1	0.00	—	.286	.286	0-0	—	0		1	0.0
	Chi N	7	5	.583	23	13	1-1	0-0	99.2	105	48	10	1	23-6	57	3.79	107	.279	.319	30-1	.033	-2	98	1	-0.1
	Year	7	5	.583	24	13	1-1	0-0	101.1	107	52	10	1	23-6	58	3.73	108	.279	.319	30-1	.033	-2	98	3	-0.1
1987	Chi N	2	9	.182	58	8	0	4-2	110.1	130	74	17	2	48-7	80	5.38	80	.295	.366	16-2	.188	-0	71	-13	-1.3
Total	8	47	54	.465	248	119	8-2	8-4	940.1	1050	470	89	14	229-33	396	4.00	92	.284	.326	237-31	.114	-6	94	-30	-4.8
LYNCH, JACK John H. B 2.5.1857 New York, NY D 4.20.1923 Bronx, NY BR/TR 5-8/185# d5.2																									
1881	Buf N	10	9	.526	20	19	17	0	165.2	203	112	2		29	32	3.59	77	.297	.325	78	.167	-3*	98	-11	-1.2
1883	NY AA	13	15	.464	29	29	29-1	0	255	263	161	6		25	119	4.09	82	.250	.267	107	.187	-3	89	-19	-1.9
1884	NY AA	37	15	.712	55	53	53-5	0	496	420	225	10	10	42	292	2.67	117	.215	.236	198	.152	-7	114	28	1.5
1885	NY AA	23	21	.523	44	43	43-1	0	379	410	243	17	3	42	177	3.61	86	.263	.283	153	.196	1	100	-22	-2.1
1886	NY AA	20	30	.400	51	50	50-1	0	432.2	485	307	10	12	116	193	3.95	83	.271	.320	169	.160	-5	94	-33	-3.4
1887	NY AA	7	14	.333	21	21	21	0	187	245	158	8	4	36	45	5.10	83	.305	.338	83	.169	-4*	75	-15	-1.4
1890	Bro AA	0	1	.000	1	1	1	0	9	22	18	1	0	5	1	12.00	32	.449	.500	4	.750	2	207	-8	-0.4
Total	7	110	105	.512	221	216	214-8	0	1924.1	2048	1224	54	29	295	859	3.69	89	.260	.289	792	.173	-18	98	-80	-8.9
LYNCH, MIKE Michael Joseph B 6.28.1880 Holyoke, MA D 4.2.1927 Garrison, NY BR/TR 6-2/170# d6.21																									
1904	Pit N	15	11	.577	27	24	24-1	0	222.2	200	90	1	15	91	95	2.71	101	.243	.330	87-1	.230	4*	114	1	0.4
1905	Pit N	17	8	.680	33	22	13	2	206.1	191	102	3	5	107	106	3.79	79	.254	.351	81-3	.136	-1	113	-14	-1.8
1906	Pit N	6	5	.545	18	12	7	0	119	101	48	2	8	31	48	2.42	110	.232	.295	39-4	.205	-0	100	2	0.1
1907	Pit N	2	2	.500	7	4	2	0	36	37	21	0	1	22	9	2.25	108	.282	.390	12-1	.250	1	139	-2	-0.1
	NY N	3	6	.333	12	10	7	1	72	68	35	3	0	30	34	3.38	73	.249	.323	27-0	.296	2	112	-7	-0.6
	Year	5	8	.385	19	14	9	1	108	105	39	3	1	52	43	3.00	82	.260	.346	39-1	.282	3	120	-7	-0.7
Total	4	43	32	.573	97	72	53-1	3	656	597	296	9	29	281	292	3.05	91	.248	.333	246-9	.203	5	112	-20	-2.0
LYNCH, TOM Thomas S. B 1863 Peru, IL D 5.13.1903 Peru, IL BL 5-11/175# d8.5																									
1884	Chi N	0	0	—	1	1	0	0	7	7	4	1		3	2	2.57	122	.241	.313	4	.000	-1	85	0	0.0
LYNN, RED Japhet Monroe B 12.27.1913 Kenney, TX D 10.27.1977 Bellville, TX BR/TR 6/162# d4.25 Mil 1945																									
1939	Det A	0	1	.000	4	0	0	0	8.1	11	8	2	1	3	3	8.64	57	.324	.395	2-0	.000	-0		-3	-0.3
	NY N	1	0	1.000	26	0	0	1	49.2	44	21	3	2	21	22	3.08	127	.240	.325	6-0	.000	-1		4	0.1
1940	NY N	4	3	.571	33	0	0	3	42.1	40	21	3	1	24	25	3.83	101	.247	.348	4-0	.000	-1		0	-0.1
1944	Chi N	5	4	.556	22	7	4-1	1	84.1	80	41	4	1	37	35	4.06	87	.251	.331	29-0	.207	0	143	-3	-0.2
Total	3	10	8	.556	85	7	4-1	5	184.2	175	91	12	5	85	85	3.95	96	.251	.336	41-0	.146	-1	143	-2	-0.5
LYON, BRANDON Brandon James B 8.10.1979 Salt Lake City, UT BR/TR 6-1/175# d8.4																									
2001	Tor A	5	4	.556	11	11	0	0-0	63	63	31	6	1	15-0	35	4.29	107	.266	.305	0-0	—	0	73	3	0.3
2002	Tor A	1	4	.200	15	10	0	0-1	62	78	47	14	2	19-2	30	6.53	71	.308	.359	0-0	—	0	88	-12	-0.8
2003	Bos A	4	6	.400	49	0	0	9-3	59	73	33	6	2	19-5	50	4.12	111	.296	.346	0-0	—	0		2	0.3
Total	3	10	14	.417	75	21	0	9-4	184	214	111	26	5	53-7	115	4.99	92	.290	.337	0-0	—	0	81	-7	-0.2
LYONS, AL Albert Harold B 7.18.1918 St.Joseph, MO D 12.20.1965 Inglewood, CA BR/TR 6-2/195# d4.19 Mil 1944-45																									
1944	NY A	0	0	—	11	0	0	0	39.2	43	22	2	2	24	14	4.54	77	.291	.397	26-0	.346	2*		-4	0.0
1946	NY A	0	1	.000	2	1	0	0	8.1	11	5	0	1	6	4	5.40	64	.314	.429	4-0	.000	-1	99	-1	-0.2
1947	NY A	1	0	1.000	6	0	0	0	11	18	11	2	0	9	7	9.00	39	.367	.466	6-0	.667	2*		-6	-0.3
	Pit N	1	2	.333	13	0	0	0	28.1	36	24	4	1	12	16	7.31	58	.300	.368	10-0	.200	1*		-8	-0.6
1948	Bos N	1	0	1.000	7	0	0	0	12.2	17	11	1	0	8	5	7.82	49	.309	.397	12-0	.167	0*		-5	-0.3
Total	4	3	3	.500	39	1	0	0	100	125	73	9	4	59	46	6.30	59	.307	.400	58-0	.293	5	99	-24	-1.4
LYONS, CURT Curt Russell B 10.17.1974 Greencastle, IN BR/TR 6-5/230# d9.19																									
1996	Cin N	2	0	1.000	3	3	0	0-0	16	17	8	1	1	7-0	14	4.50	94	.274	.357	5-1	.000	-1	114	0	-0.1
LYONS, GEORGE George Tony "Smooth" B 1.25.1891 Bible Grove, IL D 8.12.1981 Nevada, MO BR/TR 5-11/180# d9.6																									
1920	StL N	2	1	.667	7	2	1	0	23.1	21	8	2	1	9	5	3.09	97	.262	.344	7-0	.143	-0	105	1	0.1
1924	StL A	3	2	.600	26	6	2	0	77.2	97	52	2	5	45	25	5.21	87	.323	.420	20-2	.250	-0	131	-5	-0.2
Total	2	5	3	.625	33	8	3	0	101	118	60	4	6	54	30	4.72	88	.311	.405	27-2	.222	-0	126	-4	-0.1
LYONS, HERSH Herschel Englebert B 7.23.1915 Fresno, CA BR/TR 5-11/195# d4.17																									
1941	StL N	0	0	—	1	0	0	0	1.1	1	0	0	0	3	1	0.00	—	.200	.500	0-0	—	0		1	0.1
LYONS, TED Theodore Amar B 12.28.1900 Lake Charles, LA D 7.25.1986 Sulphur, LA BB/TR 5-11/200# d7.2 Mil 1943-45 M3 C6 HF1955																									
1923	Chi A	2	1	.667	9	1	0	0	22.2	30	21	2	1	15	6	6.35	62	.323	.422	5-0	.200	0	104	-7	-0.7
1924	Chi A	12	11	.522	41	22	12	3	216.1	279	143	10	2	72	52	4.87	85	.322	.375	77-4	.221	0	114	-20	-2.0
1925	Chi A	**21**	11	.656	43	32	19-**5**	3	262.2	274	111	7	2	83	45	3.26	128	.278	.335	97-9	.186	-3	104	28	2.8
1926	Chi A	18	16	.529	39	31	24-3	2	283.2	268	108	6	1	106	51	3.01	128	.252	.320	104-8	.212	-0*	86	29	3.3
1927	Chi A	**22**	14	.611	39	34	**30**-2	2	**307.2**	291	125	7	0	67	71	2.84	143	.251	.292	110-7	.255	5*	102	38	**4.7**
1928	Chi A	15	14	.517	39	27	21	6	240	276	133	11	2	68	60	3.98	102	.295	.344	91-5	.253	1*	100	-1	0.0
1929	Chi A	14	20	.412	37	31	21-1	2	259.1	276	136	11	2	76	57	4.10	105	.278	.331	91-4	.220	1*	88	7	1.1
1930	Chi A	22	15	.595	42	36	**29**-1	1	**297.2**	331	160	12	2	57	69	3.78	122	.285	.319	122-6	.311	8*	98	26	3.7
1931	Chi A	4	6	.400	22	12	7	0	101	117	50	6	0	33	16	4.01	106	.296	.350	33-3	.152	-1*	83	5	0.2
1932	Chi A	10	15	.400	33	26	19-1	2	230.2	243	104	10	3	71	58	3.28	132	.272	.327	73-6	.260	5*	74	28	3.1
1933	Chi A	10	21	.323	36	27	14-2	1	228	260	142	10	0	74	74	4.38	97	.280	.333	91-1	.286	6*	82	-7	-0.3
1934	Chi A	11	13	.458	30	24	21	1	205.1	249	138	15	2	66	53	4.87	97	.293	.345	97-4	.206	1*	95	-7	-0.4
1935	Chi A	15	8	.652	23	22	19-3	0	190.2	194	79	15	3	56	54	3.02	153	.262	.317	82-3	.220	-0*	84	30	3.2
1936	Chi A	10	13	.435	26	24	15-1	0	182	227	115	21	3	45	48	5.14	101	.305	.347	70-1	.157	-3	91	2	0.1

Year	Tm Lg	W	L	Pct	G	GS	CG-Sho	SV-BS	IP	H	R	HR	HB	BB-IB	SO	ERA	AERA	OAV	OOB	AB-SH	AVG	PB	Sup	APR	PW
1937	Chi A	12	7	.632	22	22	11	0	169.1	182	86	21	1	45	45	4.15	111	.278	.326	57-6	.211	1*	89	11	1.2
1938	Chi A	9	11	.450	23	23	17-1	0	194.2	238	93	13	0	52	54	3.70	132	.299	.342	72-3	.194	-1*	86	26	2.2
1939	Chi A☆	14	6	.700	21	21	16	0	172.2	162	71	7	1	26	65	2.76	171	.247	**.276**	61-6	.295	4	90	32	3.7
1940	Chi A	12	8	.600	22	22	17-**4**	0	186.1	188	85	17	0	37	72	3.24	137	.252	.287	75-2	.240	2	112	21	2.1
1941	Chi A	12	10	.545	22	22	19-2	0	187.1	199	87	9	4	37	63	3.70	111	.269	.308	74-2	.270	4	114	10	1.4
1942	Chi A	14	6	.700	20	20	20-1	0	180.1	167	52	11	2	26	50	**2.10**	**172**	.245	.275	67-2	.239	4	109	29	**3.8**
1946	Chi A	1	4	.200	5	5	5	0	42.2	38	17	2	0	9	10	2.32	147	.235	.275	14-1	.000	-1	55	4	0.3
Total	21	260	230	.531	594	484	356-27	23	4161	4489	2056	223	31	1121	1073	3.67	118	.276	.324	1563-83	.233	32	95	284	33.5
LYONS, TOBY Thomas A. B 3.27.1869 Cambridge, MA D 8.27.1920 Boston, MA d4.18																									
1890	Syr AA	0	2	.000	3	3	2	0	22.1	40	36	1	1	21	6	10.48	34	.377	.484	12	.333	1	254	-19	-1.1
LYSANDER, RICK Richard Eugene B 2.21.1953 Huntington Park, CA BR/TR 6-2/190# d4.12																									
1980	Oak A	0	0	—	5	0	0	0-0	13.2	24	13	3	0	4-0	5	7.90	48	.381	.418	0-0	—	0		-6	-0.3
1983	Min A	5	12	.294	61	4	1-1	3-5	125	132	63	8	2	43-12	58	3.38	126	.275	.332	0-0	—	0	80	7	0.9
1984	Min A	4	3	.571	36	0	0	5-2	56.2	62	23	2	0	27-7	22	3.49	121	.283	.357	0-0	—	0		5	0.6
1985	Min A	0	2	.000	35	1	0	3-2	61	72	43	3	0	22-2	26	6.05	73	.305	.362	0-0	—	0	41	-10	-0.5
Total	4	9	17	.346	137	5	1-1	11-9	256.1	290	142	16	2	96-21	111	4.28	99	.291	.350	0-0	—	0	72	-4	0.7
LYSTON, JOHN John Michael B 5.28.1867 Baltimore, MD D 10.29.1909 Baltimore, MD TR 5-11/185# d8.29																									
1891	Col AA	0	1	.000	1	1	1	0	6	10	8	0	1	6	1	10.50	33	.357	.486	2	.000	-0	36	-4	-0.4
1894	Cle N	0	0	—	1	1	0	0	3.2	5	6	1	0	4	0	9.82	56	.313	.450	2-0	.000	-0	103	-2	-0.1
Total	2	0	1	.000	2	2	1	0	9.2	15	14	1	1	10	1	10.24	41	.341	.473	4-0	.000	-0	79	-6	-0.5
MAAS, DUKE Duane Fredrick B 1.31.1929 Utica, MI D 12.7.1976 Mt.Clemens, MI BR/TR 5-10/170# d4.21																									
1955	Det A	5	6	.455	18	16	5-2	0	86.2	91	52	7	2	50-3	42	4.88	79	.271	.366	30-2	.167	0	117	-10	-1.1
1956	Det A	0	7	.000	26	7	0	0	63.1	81	51	9	6	32-3	34	6.54	63	.313	.398	16-0	.188	0	86	-17	-1.6
1957	Det A	10	14	.417	45	26	8-2	6	219.1	210	92	23	4	65-7	116	3.28	118	.252	.307	71-5	.085	-4	85	12	0.9
1958	KC A	4	5	.444	10	7	3-1	1	55.1	49	25	3	1	13-0	19	3.90	100	.241	.290	17-1	.176	0	62	1	0.2
	†NY A	7	3	.700	22	13	2-1	0	101.1	93	51	9	2	36-0	50	3.82	92	.242	.308	34-1	.088	-2	145	-4	-0.6
	Year	11	8	.579	32	20	5-2	1	156.2	142	57	12	3	49-0	69	3.85	95	.242	.302	51-2	.118	-1	114	-4	-0.4
1959	NY A	14	8	.636	38	21	3-1	4	138	149	82	14	2	53-1	67	4.43	82	.278	.342	40-5	.125	-1	114	-14	-2.2
1960	†NY A	5	1	.833	35	1	0	4	70.1	70	44	6	1	35-2	28	4.09	87	.265	.346	6-0	.000	-1	25	-8	-0.7
1961	NY A	0	0	—	1	0	0	0	0.1	2	2	0	0	0-0	0	54.00	7	1.000	1.000	0-0	—	0		-2	-0.1
Total	7	45	44	.506	195	91	21-7	15	734.2	745	399	71	18	284-16	356	4.19	90	.264	.333	214-14	.117	-7	103	-42	-5.2
MABE, BOB Robert Lee B 10.8.1929 Danville, VA BR/TR 5-11/165# d4.18																									
1958	StL N	3	9	.250	31	13	4	0	111.2	113	66	11	4	41-6	74	4.51	91	.260	.327	24-3	.042	-2*	69	-6	-0.8
1959	Cin N	4	2	.667	18	1	0	3	29.2	29	28	6	0	19-2	8	5.46	74	.254	.358	7-1	.000	-1	199	-8	-1.6
1960	Bal A	0	0	—	2	0	0	0	0.2	4	6	0	0	1-0	0	27.00	14	.571	.625	0-0	—	0		-3	-0.2
Total	3	7	11	.389	51	14	4	3	142	146	100	17	4	61-8	82	4.82	85	.263	.338	31-4	.032	-3	78	-17	-2.6
MacARTHUR, MAC Malcolm B 1.19.1862 Glasgow, Scotland D 10.18.1932 Detroit, MI TR 5-9.5/164# d5.2																									
1884	Ind AA	1	5	.167	6	6	6	0	52	57	49	1	2	21	19	5.02	66	.263	.333	21	.095	-2	67	-10	-1.0
MacCORMACK, FRANK Frank Louis B 9.21.1954 Jersey City, NJ BR/TR 6-4/210# d6.14																									
1976	Det A	0	5	.000	9	8	0	0-0	32.2	35	24	1	1	34-0	14	5.79	64	.294	.449	3-0	.000	-0	80	-7	-1.0
1977	Sea A	0	0	—	3	3	0	0-0	7	4	3	0	3	12-0	4	3.86	107	.174	.500	0-0	—	0	131	0	0.0
Total	2	0	5	.000	12	11	0	0-0	39.2	39	27	1	4	46-0	18	5.45	70	.275	.459	3-0	.000	-0	95	-7	-1.0
MacDONALD, ROB Robert Joseph B 4.27.1965 East Orange, NJ BL/TL 6-3/208# d8.14																									
1990	Tor A	0	0	—	4	0	0	0-0	2.1	0	0	0	0	2-0	0	0.00	—	.000	.250	0-0	—	0		1	0.0
1991	†Tor A	3	3	.500	45	0	0	0-4	53.2	51	19	5	0	25-4	24	2.85	148	.252	.332	0-0	—	0		8	0.8
1992	Tor A	1	0	1.000	27	0	0	0-0	47.1	50	24	4	1	16-3	26	4.37	94	.270	.330	0-0	—	0		-1	-0.1
1993	Det A	3	3	.500	68	0	0	3-3	65.2	67	42	8	1	33-5	39	5.35	80	.268	.349	0-0	—	0		-7	-0.6
1995	NY A	1	1	.500	33	0	0	0-1	46.1	50	25	7	1	22-0	41	4.86	95	.282	.365	0-0	—	0		-1	0.0
1996	NY N	0	2	.000	20	0	0	0-0	19	16	10	2	0	9-0	12	4.26	94	.235	.321	0-0	—	0		0	0.0
Total	6	8	9	.471	197	0	0	3-8	234.1	234	120	26	3	107-12	142	4.34	99	.264	.342	0-0	—	0		0	0.1
MACDONALD, BILL William Paul B 3.28.1929 Alameda, CA D 5.4.1991 Shasta Lake, CA BR/TR 5-10/170# d5.6 Mil 1951																									
1950	Pit N	8	10	.444	32	20	6-2	1	153	138	88	17	1	88	60	4.29	102	.243	.346	49-1	.122	-2	75	-1	-0.4
1953	Pit N	0	1	.000	4	1	0	0	7.1	12	10	0	1	8	4	12.27	36	.400	.538	0-1	—	0	20	-6	-0.6
Total	2	8	11	.421	36	21	6-2	1	160.1	150	98	17	2	96	64	4.66	94	.251	.356	49-2	.122	-2	72	-7	-1.0
MacDOUGAL, MIKE Robert Meiklejohn B 3.5.1977 Las Vegas, NV BR/TR 6-4/195# d9.22																									
2001	KC A	1	1	.500	3	3	0	0-0	15.1	18	10	2	1	4-0	7	4.70	105	.290	.343	0-0	—	0	82	0	0.0
2002	KC A	0	1	.000	6	0	0	0-0	9	5	5	0	0	7-1	10	5.00	101	.161	.316	0-0	—	0		0	0.0
2003	KC A☆	3	5	.375	68	0	0	27-8	64	64	36	4	8	32-0	57	4.08	127	.267	.369	0-0	—	0		5	0.9
Total	3	4	7	.364	77	3	0	27-8	88.1	87	51	6	9	43-1	74	4.28	119	.261	.359	0-0	—	0	82	5	0.9
MACE, JIMMY Harry L. B Washington, DC 5-11/185# d5.5																									
1891	Was AA	0	1	.000	3	1	1	0	16	18	14	0	1	8	3	7.31	51	.273	.360	6	.000	-1	67	-4	-0.3
MacFAYDEN, DANNY Daniel Knowles "Deacon Danny" B 6.10.1905 N.Truro, MA D 8.26.1972 Brunswick, ME BR/TR 5-11/170# d8.25																									
1926	Bos A	0	1	.000	3	1	1	0	13	10	7	0	0	7	1	4.85	84	.217	.321	3-0	.333	0	21	-1	0.0
1927	Bos A	5	8	.385	34	16	6-1	2	160.1	176	88	9	6	59	42	4.27	99	.294	.363	46-5	.283	4*	79	0	0.4
1928	Bos A	9	15	.375	33	28	9	0	195	215	123	12	7	78	61	4.75	87	.289	.361	63-1	.143	-1*	87	-15	-1.7
1929	Bos A	10	18	.357	32	27	14-**4**	0	221	225	108	8	5	81	61	3.62	118	.271	.340	74-4	.176	-3	74	15	1.5
1930	Bos A	11	14	.440	36	33	18-1	2	269.1	293	141	9	6	93	76	4.21	109	.281	.343	92-8	.141	-4	86	14	0.8
1931	Bos A	16	12	.571	35	32	17-2	0	230.2	263	121	4	7	79	74	4.02	107	.281	.341	81-6	.123	-5	96	6	0.3
1932	Bos A	1	10	.091	12	11	6	0	77.2	91	55	3	1	33	29	5.10	88	.289	.358	25-2	.120	-2	48	-6	-0.8
	NY A	7	5	.583	17	15	9	1	121.1	137	69	11	2	37	33	3.93	104	.281	.334	49-2	.102	-3	138	-1	-0.4
	Year	8	15	.348	29	26	15	1	199	228	76	14	3	70	62	4.39	97	.284	.344	74-4	.108	-4	98	-6	-1.2
1933	NY A	3	2	.600	25	6	2	0	90.1	120	62	8	2	37	28	5.88	66	.319	.383	34-1	.029	-4	131	-19	-1.3
1934	NY A	4	3	.571	22	11	4	0	96	110	57	5	2	31	41	4.50	90	.288	.345	39-1	.103	-2	148	-6	-0.6
1935	Cin N	1	2	.333	7	4	1	0	36	39	22	1	0	13	13	4.75	84	.281	.342	11-0	.091	-1	75	-3	-0.2
	Bos N	5	13	.278	28	20	7-1	0	151.2	200	96	8	5	34	46	5.10	74	.314	.354	51-1	.157	-1	91	-22	-2.1
	Year	6	15	.286	35	24	8-1	0	187.2	239	100	9	5	47	59	5.04	76	.308	.352	62-1	.145	-2	88	-23	-2.3
1936	Bos N	17	13	.567	37	31	21-2	0	266.2	268	97	5	5	66	86	2.87	134	.259	.307	83-8	.096	-5	75	30	2.8
1937	Bos N	14	14	.500	32	32	16-2	0	246	250	96	5	2	60	70	2.93	123	.268	.313	83-8	.157	-2	92	17	1.7
1938	Bos N	14	9	.609	29	29	19-5	0	219.2	208	82	6	5	64	58	2.95	116	.247	.304	77-2	.117	-4	83	14	0.9
1939	Bos N	8	14	.364	33	28	8	2	191.2	221	100	11	4	59	46	3.90	95	.291	.345	67-5	.179	-1	96	-6	-0.6
1940	Pit N	5	4	.556	35	8	0	2	91.1	112	47	5	4	27	24	3.55	107	.302	.356	28-1	.179	-0	108	0	0.0
1941	Was A	0	1	.000	5	0	0	0	7	12	9	1	0	5	3	10.29	39	.375	.459	0-0	—	0		-5	-0.5
1943	Bos N	2	1	.667	10	1	0	0	21.1	31	14	1	1	9	5	5.91	58	.344	.410	4-0	.250	0	75	-5	-0.6
Total	17	132	159	.454	465	333	158-18	9	2706	2981	1394	112	64	872	797	3.96	101	.281	.340	910-55	.142	-34	90	7	-0.4
MACHADO, JULIO Julio Segundo (Rondon) B 12.1.1965 Zulia, Venezuela BR/TR 5-9/165# d9.7																									
1989	NY N	0	1	.000	10	0	0	0-1	11	9	4	0	0	3-0	14	3.27	100	.214	.267	0-0	—	0		0	0.0
1990	NY N	4	1	.800	27	0	0	0-1	34.1	32	13	4	2	17-4	27	3.15	119	.248	.340	0-0	—	0		3	0.3
	Mil A	0	0	—	10	0	0	3-0	13	9	1	0	0	8-2	12	0.69	561	.191	.304	0-0	—	0		5	0.2
1991	Mil A	3	3	.500	54	0	0	3-3	88.2	65	36	12	3	55-1	98	3.45	115	.211	.334	0-0	—	0		6	0.4
Total	3	7	5	.583	101	0	0	6-5	147	115	54	16	5	83-7	151	3.12	124	.219	.328	0-0	—	0		14	0.9
MACHEMEHL, CHUCK Charles Walter B 4.20.1947 Brenham, TX BR/TR 6-4/200# d4.6																									
1971	Cle A	0	2	.000	14	0	0	3-2	18.1	16	16	2	0	15-3	9	6.38	60	.246	.373	2-0	.500	0		-5	-0.7

Year	Tm Lg	W	L	Pct	G	GS	CG-Sho	SV-BS	IP	H	R	HR	HB	BB-IB	SO	ERA	AERA	OAV	OOB	AB-SH	AVG	PB	Sup	APR	PW
MACK, DENNY Dennis Joseph (b: Dennis Joseph McGee) B 1851 Easton, PA D 4.10.1888 Wilkes-Barre, PA BR/TR 5-7/164# d5.6 M1 U2 ▲																									
1871	Rok NA	0	1	.000	3	1	1	0	13	20	30	0		3	1	3.46	118	.299	.329	122	.246	-0*	97	-2	-0.1
MACK, FRANK Frank George "Stubby" B 2.2.1900 Oklahoma City, OK D 7.2.1971 Clearwater, FL BR/TR 6-1.5/180# d8.16																									
1922	Chi A	2	2	.500	8	4	1-1	0	34.1	36	16	2	0	16	11	3.67	111	.281	.361	12-0	.250	1	73	1	0.2
1923	Chi A	0	1	.000	11	0	0	0	23.1	23	13	0	0	11	6	4.24	93	.284	.370	6-0	.000	-1		-1	-0.1
1925	Chi A	0	0	—	8	0	0	0	13.1	24	14	1	0	13	6	9.45	44	.444	.552	3-0	.333	0		-7	-0.3
Total	3	2	3	.400	27	4	1-1	0	71	83	43	3	0	40	23	4.94	82	.316	.406	21-0	.190	0	73	-7	-0.2
MACK, TONY Tony Lynn B 4.30.1961 Lexington, KY BR/TR 5-10/177# d7.27																									
1985	Cal A	0	1	.000	1	1	0	0-0	2.1	8	4	0	0	0-0	0	15.43	27	.571	.571	0-0	—	0	66	-3	-0.4
MACK, BILL William Francis B 2.12.1885 Elmira, NY D 9.30.1971 Elmira, NY BL/TL 6-1/155# d7.14																									
1908	Chi N	0	0	—	2	0	0	0	6	5	3	1	1	1	2	3.00	78	.263	.333	3-0	.667	1		-1	0.1
MacKENZIE, KEN Kenneth Purvis B 3.10.1934 Gore Bay, ON, CAN BR/TL 6/185# d5.2																									
1960	Mil N	0	1	.000	9	0	0	0	8.1	9	7	2	0	3-2	9	6.48	53	.281	.333	1-0	.000	-0		-3	-0.4
1961	Mil N	0	1	.000	5	0	0	0	7	8	5	1	1	2-0	5	5.14	73	.296	.367	2-0	.000	-0		-1	-0.2
1962	NY N	5	4	.556	42	1	0	1	80	87	47	10	3	34-3	51	4.95	84	.280	.353	12-1	.083	-1	0	-4	-0.5
1963	NY N	3	1	.750	34	0	0	3	58	63	35	11	2	12-2	41	4.97	70	.267	.307	10-0	.000	-1		-8	-0.8
	StL N	0	0	—	8	0	0	0	9	9	6	1	0	3-1	7	4.00	89	.250	.308	0-0	—	0		-1	-0.1
	Year	3	1	.750	42	0	0	3	67	72	41	12	2	15-3	48	4.84	72	.265	.307	10-0	.000	-1		-9	-0.9
1964	SF N	0	0	—	10	0	0	1	9	9	7	1	0	3-0	3	5.00	71	.265	.308	0-0	—	0		-2	-0.1
1965	Hou N	0	3	.000	21	0	0	0	37	46	22	7	0	6-0	26	3.89	86	.299	.325	11-0	.273	1		-4	-0.2
Total	6	8	10	.444	129	1	0	5	208.1	231	129	33	6	63-8	142	4.80	78	.278	.331	36-1	.111	-2	0	-23	-2.3
MACKINSON, JOHN John Joseph B 10.29.1923 Orange, NJ D 10.17.1989 Reseda, CA BR/TR 5-10.5/160# d4.16																									
1953	Phi A	0	0	—	1	0	0	0	1.1	1	0	0	0	2	0	0.00	—	.200	.429	0-0	—	0		1	0.0
1955	StL N	0	1	.000	8	1	0	0	20.2	24	18	3	1	10-2	8	7.84	52	.296	.372	4-0	.000	-0*	197	-8	-0.4
Total	2	0	1	.000	9	1	0	0	22	25	18	3	1	12-2	8	7.36	55	.291	.376	4-0	.000	-0	197	-7	-0.4
MacLEOD, BILLY William Daniel B 5.13.1942 Gloucester, MA BL/TL 6-2/190# d9.13																									
1962	Bos A	0	1	.000	2	0	0	0	1.2	4	1	0	0	1-0	2	5.40	76	.444	.500	0-0	—	0		0	0.0
MACON, MAX Max Cullen B 10.14.1915 Pensacola, FL D 8.5.1989 Jupiter, FL BL/TL 6-3/175# d4.21 Mil 1945-46 ▲																									
1938	StL N	4	11	.267	38	12	5-1	2	129.1	133	83	9	4	61	39	4.11	96	.268	.352	36-1	.306	2*	95	-6	-0.5
1940	Bro N	1	0	1.000	2	0	0	0	2	5	5	2	0	0	1	22.50	18	.455	.455	1-0	1.000	0		-4	-0.6
1942	Bro N	5	3	.625	14	8	4-1	1	84	67	22	3	2	33	27	1.93	169	.220	.300	43-3	.279	4*	100	12	1.6
1943	Bro N	7	5	.583	25	9	0	0	77	91	54	4	4	32	21	5.96	56	.291	.364	55-0	.164	-1*	185	-21	-3.0
1944	Bos N	0	0	—	1	0	0	0	3	10	7	2	0	1	1	21.00	18	.556	.579	366-2	.273	0*		-5	-0.2
1947	Bos N	0	0	—	1	0	0	0	2	1	0	0	0	1	1	0.00	—	.167	.286	1-0	.000	-0		1	0.0
Total	6	17	19	.472	81	29	9-2	3	297.1	307	171	20	10	128	90	4.24	85	.267	.345	502-6	.265	5	122	-23	-2.7
MacPHERSON, HARRY Harry William B 7.10.1926 N.Andover, MA BR/TR 5-10/150# d8.14																									
1944	Bos N	0	0	—	1	0	0	0	1	0	0	0	0	1	1	0.00	—	.000	.250	0-0	—	0		0	0.0
MacRAE, SCOTT Scott Patrick B 8.13.1974 Dearborn, MI BR/TR 6-3/205# d7.24																									
2001	Cin N	0	1	.000	24	0	0	0-0	31.1	33	15	0	2	8-0	18	4.02	113	.266	.316	3-0	.000	-0		2	0.0
MacWHORTER, KEITH Keith B 12.30.1955 Worcester, MA BR/TR 6-4/190# d5.10																									
1980	Bos A	0	3	.000	14	2	0	0-0	42.1	46	27	3	2	18-3	21	5.53	76	.280	.357	0-0	—	0	42	-5	-0.3
MADDEN, LEN Leonard Joseph "Lefty" B 7.2.1890 Toledo, OH D 9.9.1949 Toledo, OH BL/TL 6-2/165# d8.31																									
1912	Chi N	0	1	.000	6	2	0	0	12.1	16	10	1	1	9	5	2.92	114	.302	.413	4-0	.250	0	154	-1	-0.1
MADDEN, MIKE Michael Anthony B 1.13.1958 Denver, CO BL/TL 6-1/190# d4.5																									
1983	Hou N	9	5	.643	28	13	0	0-0	94.2	76	37	4	1	45-3	44	3.14	109	.231	.323	22-6	.045	-1	86	4	0.4
1984	Hou N	2	3	.400	17	7	0	0-0	40.2	46	27	1	0	35-3	29	5.53	60	.297	.422	6-0	.333	1	72	-10	-1.0
1985	Hou N	0	0	—	13	0	0	0-0	19	29	15	1	0	11-0	16	4.26	81	.363	.435	0-0	—	0		-4	-0.2
1986	Hou N	1	2	.333	13	6	0	0-0	39.2	47	20	3	0	22-3	30	4.08	88	.297	.381	9-4	.000	-1	95	-2	-0.2
Total	4	12	10	.545	71	26	0	0-0	194	198	99	9	1	113-9	119	3.94	87	.274	.370	37-10	.081	-1	84	-12	-1.0
MADDEN, KID Michael Joseph B 10.22.1866 Portland, ME D 3.16.1896 Portland, ME BL/TL 5-7.5/130# d5.6																									
1887	Bos N	21	14	.600	37	37	36-3	0	321	317	203	20	20	122	81	3.79	108	.251	.327	132	.242	3	106	8	0.9
1888	Bos N	7	11	.389	20	18	17-1	0	165	142	76	6	15	24	53	2.95	98	.228	.273	67	.164	-2	82	4	0.2
1889	Bos N	10	10	.500	22	19	18-1	1	178	194	131	7	16	71	64	4.40	95	.269	.348	86	.291	2*	105	-6	-0.4
1890	Bos P	3	2	.600	10	7	5-1	1	62	85	55	2	8	25	24	4.79	92	.313	.387	38	.184	-1*	109	-3	-0.3
1891	Bos AA	0	1	.000	1	1	1	0	8	10	12	2	3	6	6	6.75	52	.294	.442	3	.667	1	107	-4	-0.2
	Bal AA	13	12	.520	32	27	20-1	1	224	239	168	4	24	88	56	4.10	91	.264	.345	107	.271	5*	102	-7	-0.1
	Year	13	13	.500	33	28	21-1	1	232	249	174	6	27	94	62	4.19	89	.265	.349	110	.282	6	102	-11	-0.3
Total	5	54	50	.519	122	109	97-7	3	958	987	645	41	86	336	284	3.92	98	.259	.332	433	.245	9	102	-8	0.1
MADDEN, MORRIS Morris De Wayne B 8.31.1960 Laurens, SC BL/TL 6- /155# d6.11																									
1987	Det A	0	0	—	2	0	0	0-0	1.2	4	3	0	0	3-1	0	16.20	26	.444	.583	0-0	—	0		-2	-0.1
1988	Pit N	0	0	—	5	0	0	0-1	5.2	5	0	0	0	7-1	3	0.00	—	.294	.500	0-0	—	0*		2	0.1
1989	Pit N	2	2	.500	9	3	0	0-0	14	17	14	0	0	13-0	6	7.07	48	.327	.455	1-3	.000	-0*	140	-7	-1.4
Total	3	2	2	.500	16	3	0	0-1	21.1	26	17	0	0	23-2	9	5.91	58	.333	.480	1-3	.000	-0	140	-7	-1.4
MADDOX, NICK Nicholas B 11.9.1886 Govans, MD D 11.27.1954 Pittsburgh, PA BL/TR 6/175# d9.13																									
1907	Pit N	5	1	.833	6	6	6-1	0	54	32	8	0	4	13	38	0.83	292	.178	.249	20-0	.250	2	137	9	1.5
1908	Pit N	23	8	.742	36	32	22-4	1	260.2	209	89	5	11	90	70	2.28	101	.223	.298	94-4	.266	8	147	2	1.1
1909	†Pit N	13	8	.619	31	27	17-4	0	203.1	173	72	2	15	39	56	2.21	123	.232	.283	67-4	.224	4	117	10	1.4
1910	Pit N	2	3	.400	20	7	2	0	87.1	73	40	0	5	28	29	3.40	91	.246	.321	28-0	.214	1*	137	-2	0.0
Total	4	43	20	.683	93	72	47-9	1	605.1	487	209	7	35	170	193	2.29	112	.225	.292	209-8	.244	15	133	19	4.0
MADDUX, GREG Gregory Alan B 4.14.1966 San Angelo, TX BR/TR 6/170# d9.3 b-Mike																									
1986	Chi N	2	4	.333	6	5	1	0-0	31	44	20	3	1	11-2	20	5.52	73	.336	.392	12-1	.333	1	114	-4	-0.7
1987	Chi N	6	14	.300	30	27	1-1	0-0	155.2	181	111	17	4	74-13	101	5.61	76	.294	.373	42-7	.119	-2*	85	-24	-2.5
1988	Chi N☆	18	8	.692	34	34	9-3	0-0	249	230	97	13	9	81-16	140	3.18	114	.244	.309	96-1	.198	2*	103	11	1.5
1989	†Chi N	19	12	.613	35	35	7-1	0-0	238.1	222	90	13	6	82-13	135	2.95	128	.249	.315	81-8	.210	2	105	19	2.9
1990	Chi N	15	15	.500	35	**35**	8-2	0-0	237	242	116	11	4	71-10	144	3.46	118	.265	.319	83-4	.145	-2	85	9	1.3
1991	Chi N	15	11	.577	37	**37**	7-2	0-0	**263**	232	113	18	6	66-9	198	3.35	116	.237	.288	88-11	.205	3*	98	13	1.9
1992	Chi N★	**20**	11	.645	35	**35**	9-4	0-0	**268**	201	68	7	14	70-7	199	2.18	**165**	.210	.272	88-13	.170	2	95	**44**	**6.0**
1993	†Atl N	20	10	.667	36	**36**	**8-1**	0-0	**267**	228	85	14	6	52-7	197	**2.36**	**170**	.232	**.273**	91-10	.165	-1	90	**46**	**5.3**
1994	Atl N★	**16**	6	.727	25	25	**10-3**	0-0	**202**	150	44	4	6	31-3	156	**1.56**	**272**	**.207**	**.243**	63-9	.222	2	85	**57**	**6.8**
1995	†Atl N☆	**19**	2	**.905**	28	28	**10-3**	0-0	**209.2**	147	39	8	4	23-3	181	**1.63**	**262**	.197	**.224**	72-6	.153	-0	91	**61**	**6.4**
1996	†Atl N☆	15	11	.577	35	35	5-1	0-0	245	225	85	11	3	28-11	172	2.72	162	.241	.264	68-11	.147	-1	82	43	4.8
1997	†Atl N★	19	4	**.826**	33	33	5-2	0-0	232.2	200	58	9	6	20-6	177	2.20	191	.236	.256	67-6	.104	-1	102	54	5.3
1998	†Atl N★	18	9	.667	34	34	9-**5**	0-0	251	201	75	13	7	45-10	204	**2.22**	**187**	.220	**.260**	75-6	.240	4	98	**52**	**6.4**
1999	†Atl N	19	9	.679	33	33	4	0-0	219.1	258	103	16	4	37-8	136	3.57	126	.294	.323	64-13	.172	3	124	20	2.8
2000	†Atl N✤	19	9	.679	35	**35**	6-**3**	0-0	249.1	225	91	19	10	42-12	190	3.00	153	.238	.276	80-7	.188	2	88	45	**5.2**
2001	†Atl N	17	11	.607	34	34	3-**3**	0-0	233	220	86	20	7	27-10	173	3.05	145	.253	.278	64-13	.188	1*	80	36	4.4
2002	†Atl N	16	6	.727	34	34	0	0-0	199.1	194	67	14	4	45-7	118	2.62	157	.257	.301	59-9	.186	1*	93	32	3.7
2003	†Atl N	16	11	.593	36	**36**	1	0-0	218.1	225	112	24	8	33-7	124	3.96	107	.268	.299	68-8	.147	-0*	101	4	0.7
Total	18	289	163	.639	575	571	103-34	0-0	3968.2	3625	1460	234	109	838-154	2765	2.89	143	.244	.287	1261-143	.178	15	95	518	62.2

MADDUX, MIKE Michael Ausley B 8.27.1961 Dayton, OH BL/TR 6-2/190# d6.3 C1 b-Greg

Year	Tm Lg	W	L	Pct	G	GS	CG-Sho	SV-BS	IP	H	R	HR	HB	BB-IB	SO	ERA	AERA	OAV	OOB	AB-SH	AVG	PB	Sup	APR	PW
1986	Phi N	3	7	.300	16	16	0	0-0	78	88	56	6	3	34-4	44	5.42	71	.286	.359	22-4	.045	-1	97	-14	-1.8
1987	Phi N	2	0	1.000	7	2	0	0-0	17	17	5	0	0	5-0	15	2.65	160	.254	.306	3-1	.000	-0	96	3	0.3
1988	Phi N	4	3	.571	25	11	0	0-0	88.2	91	41	6	5	34-4	59	3.76	95	.275	.349	23-2	.130	-0*	109	-2	-0.1
1989	Phi N	1	3	.250	16	4	2-1	1-0	43.2	52	29	3	2	14-3	26	5.15	69	.304	.362	10-1	.000	-1	100	-8	-0.7
1990	LA N	0	1	.000	11	2	0	0-0	20.2	24	15	3	1	4-0	11	6.53	56	.293	.330	2-0	.000	-0	136	-6	-0.3
1991	SD N	7	2	.778	64	1	0	5-2	98.2	78	30	4	1	27-3	57	2.46	154	.221	.277	13-3	.077	-0	260	14	1.4
1992	SD N	2	2	.500	50	1	0	5-4	79.2	71	25	2	0	24-4	60	2.37	151	.236	.290	9-3	.111	-0	0	10	0.7
1993	NY N	3	8	.273	58	0	0	5-6	75	67	34	3	4	27-7	57	3.60	112	.243	.313	3-0	.000	-0		4	0.6
1994	NY N	2	1	.667	27	0	0	2-2	44	45	25	7	0	13-4	32	5.11	82	.263	.312	3-0	.000	-0		-3	-0.2
1995	Pit N	1	0	1.000	8	0	0	0-0	9	14	9	0	0	3-1	4	9.00	48	.359	.405	0-0	—	0		-4	-0.4
	†Bos A	4	1	.800	36	4	0	1-0	89.2	86	40	5	2	15-3	65	3.61	135	.247	.281	0-0	—	0	139	12	0.6
1996	Bos A	3	2	.600	23	7	0	0-0	64.1	76	37	12	5	27-2	32	4.48	113	.295	.370	0-0	—	0	99	4	0.3
1997	Sea A	1	0	1.000	6	0	0	0-0	10.2	20	12	1	1	8-2	7	10.13	44	.400	.492	0-0	—	0		-6	-0.5
1998	Mon N	3	4	.429	51	0	0	1-1	55.2	50	24	3	1	15-1	33	3.72	113	.243	.293	2-0	.000	-0		4	0.4
1999	Mon N	0	0	—	4	0	0	0-0	5	9	5	1	1	3-0	4	9.00	50	.409	.500	0-0	—	0		-2	-0.1
	LA N	1	1	.500	49	0	0	0-0	54.2	54	21	5	4	19-2	41	3.29	130	.261	.332	0-0	—	0		7	0.3
	Year	1	1	.500	53	0	0	0-0	59.2	63	31	6	5	22-2	45	3.77	114	.275	.349	0-0	—	0		4	0.2
2000	Hou N	2	2	.500	21	0	0	0-0	27.1	31	20	6	2	12-0	17	6.26	78	.282	.360	2-0	.000	-0		-4	-0.5
Total	15	39	37	.513	472	48	2-1	20-15	861.2	873	428	67	32	284-40	564	4.05	101	.265	.326	92-14	.065	-4	105	9	0.0

MADIGAN, TONY William J. "Tice" B 7.1868 Washington, DC D 12.4.1954 Washington, DC TR 5-5.5/126# d7.10

Year	Tm Lg	W	L	Pct	G	GS	CG-Sho	SV-BS	IP	H	R	HR	HB	BB-IB	SO	ERA	AERA	OAV	OOB	AB-SH	AVG	PB	Sup	APR	PW
1886	Was N	1	13	.071	14	13	13	0	114.2	154	110	3		44	29	4.87	66	.310	.366	48	.083	-4	50	-25	-2.6

MADISON, DAVE David Pledger B 2.1.1921 Brooksville, MS D 12.8.1985 Macon, MS BR/TR 6-3/190# d9.26 Mil 1951

Year	Tm Lg	W	L	Pct	G	GS	CG-Sho	SV-BS	IP	H	R	HR	HB	BB-IB	SO	ERA	AERA	OAV	OOB	AB-SH	AVG	PB	Sup	APR	PW
1950	NY A	0	0	—	1	0	0	0	3	3	2	1	0	1	1	6.00	72	.273	.333	0-0	—	0		-1	0.0
1952	StL A	4	2	.667	31	4	0	0	78	78	46	7	4	48	35	4.38	89	.264	.374	17-2	.118	-1	134	-5	-0.5
	Det A	1	1	.500	10	1	0	0	15	16	14	1	1	10	7	7.80	49	.291	.409	2-0	.000	0	0	-6	-0.7
	Year	5	3	.625	41	5	0	0	93	94	14	8	5	58	42	4.94	79	.268	.379	19-2	.105	-1	107	-10	-1.2
1953	Det A	3	4	.429	32	1	0	0	62	76	55	7	3	44	27	6.82	60	.303	.413	11-0	.091	-1	109	-20	-2.0
Total	3	8	7	.533	74	6	0	0	158	173	117	16	8	103	70	5.70	70	.282	.392	30-2	.100	-2	107	-32	-3.2

MADRID, ALEX Alexander B 4.18.1963 Springerville, AZ BR/TR 6-3/200# d7.20

Year	Tm Lg	W	L	Pct	G	GS	CG-Sho	SV-BS	IP	H	R	HR	HB	BB-IB	SO	ERA	AERA	OAV	OOB	AB-SH	AVG	PB	Sup	APR	PW
1987	Mil A	0	0	—	3	0	0	0-0	5.1	11	9	1	0	1-0	1	15.19	30	.440	.429	0-0	—	0		-6	-0.3
1988	Phi N	1	1	.500	5	2	1	0-0	16.1	15	5	0	0	6-2	2	2.76	129	.246	.304	3-0	.000	-0	25	2	0.2
1989	Phi N	1	2	.333	6	3	0	0-0	24.2	32	16	3	1	14-4	13	5.47	65	.314	.402	6-0	.000	-0	58	-5	-0.6
Total	3	2	3	.400	14	5	1	0-0	46.1	58	30	4	1	21-6	16	5.63	65	.309	.374	9-0	.000	-1	44	-9	-0.7

MADSON, RYAN Ryan Michael B 8.28.1980 Long Beach, CA BL/TR 6-6/180# d9.27

Year	Tm Lg	W	L	Pct	G	GS	CG-Sho	SV-BS	IP	H	R	HR	HB	BB-IB	SO	ERA	AERA	OAV	OOB	AB-SH	AVG	PB	Sup	APR	PW
2003	Phi N	0	0	—	1	0	0	0-0	2	0	0	0	0	0-0	0	0.00	—	.000	.000	0-0	—	0		1	0.0

MADURO, CALVIN Calvin Gregory B 9.5.1974 Santa Cruz, Aruba BR/TR 6/175# d9.8

Year	Tm Lg	W	L	Pct	G	GS	CG-Sho	SV-BS	IP	H	R	HR	HB	BB-IB	SO	ERA	AERA	OAV	OOB	AB-SH	AVG	PB	Sup	APR	PW
1996	Phi N	0	1	.000	4	2	0	0-0	15.1	13	6	1	2	3-0	11	3.52	123	.232	.295	4-0	.000	-0	63	2	0.0
1997	Phi N	3	7	.300	15	13	0	0-0	71	83	59	12	3	41-5	31	7.23	59	.294	.385	20-1	.050	-2*	87	-22	-2.6
2000	Bal A	0	0	—	15	2	0	0-0	23.1	29	25	8	2	16-1	18	9.64	49	.315	.420	0-0	—	0	199	-12	-0.6
2001	Bal A	5	6	.455	22	12	0	0-0	93.2	83	44	10	4	36-0	51	4.23	102	.240	.319	0-0	—	0	99	3	0.2
2002	Bal A	2	5	.286	12	10	0	0-0	56.2	64	37	12	1	22-1	29	5.56	77	.279	.344	0-0	—	0	78	-8	-0.9
Total	5	10	19	.345	68	39	0	0-0	260	272	171	43	12	118-7	140	5.78	75	.271	.352	24-1	.042	-2	93	-37	-3.9

MAESTRI, HECTOR Hector Anibal (Garcia) B 4.19.1935 Havana, Cuba BR/TR 5-10/158# d9.24

Year	Tm Lg	W	L	Pct	G	GS	CG-Sho	SV-BS	IP	H	R	HR	HB	BB-IB	SO	ERA	AERA	OAV	OOB	AB-SH	AVG	PB	Sup	APR	PW
1960	Was A	0	0	—	1	0	0	0	2	1	0	0	0	1-0	1	0.00	—	.167	.286	0-0	—	0		1	0.0
1961	Was A	0	1	.000	1	1	0	0	6	6	3	1	0	2-0	2	1.50	268	.250	.308	1-0	.000	-0	44	1	0.1
Total	2	0	1	.000	2	1	0	0	8	7	3	1	0	3-0	3	1.13	354	.233	.303	1-0	.000	-0	44	2	0.1

MAGEE, BILL William J. B 7.6.1875 , , CAN BR/TR 5-10/154# d5.18

Year	Tm Lg	W	L	Pct	G	GS	CG-Sho	SV-BS	IP	H	R	HR	HB	BB-IB	SO	ERA	AERA	OAV	OOB	AB-SH	AVG	PB	Sup	APR	PW
1897	Lou N	4	12	.250	23	17	13-1	0	156.1	187	137	6	10	101	44	5.41	79	.294	.399	62-1	.210	-2	75	-18	-1.5
1898	Lou N	16	15	.516	38	33	29-3	0	295.1	294	163	8	19	129	55	4.05	88	.258	.343	111-1	.126	-9	83	-11	-1.8
1899	Lou N	3	7	.300	12	10	6-1	0	71	91	58	1	9	28	13	5.20	74	.311	.388	27-2	.111	-2	108	-9	-1.2
	Phi N	3	5	.375	9	9	7	0	70	82	50	0	7	32	4	5.66	65	.292	.378	31-1	.161	-2	95	-11	-1.2
	Was N	1	4	.200	8	7	4	0	42	54	45	3	7	28	11	8.57	46	.312	.428	15-1	.333	1	74	-18	-1.4
	Year	7	16	.304	29	26	17-1	0	183	227	49	4	23	88	28	6.15	62	.304	.394	73-4	.178	-2	94	-37	-3.8
1901	StL N	0	0	—	1	1	0	0	8	8	4	0	0	4	3	4.50	71	.258	.343	4-0	.500	1	111	-1	0.1
	NY N	0	4	.000	6	5	4	0	42.1	56	36	4	4	11	14	5.95	56	.316	.370	14-0	.143	-1	90	-11	-0.9
	Year	0	4	.000	7	6	4	0	50.1	64	40	4	4	15	17	5.72	57	.308	.366	18-0	.222	1	94	-11	-0.8
1902	NY N	0	0	—	2	1	0	0	5	5	2	0	0	1	2	3.60	78	.263	.300	1-0	.000	-0	121	0	0.0
	Phi N	2	4	.333	8	7	6	0	53.2	61	28	1	3	18	15	3.69	76	.285	.349	19-0	.211	-0	64	-4	-0.5
	Year	2	4	.333	10	8	6	0	58.2	66	31	1	3	19	17	3.68	76	.283	.345	20-0	.200	-1	72	-5	-0.5
Total	5	29	51	.363	107	90	69-5	0	743.2	838	523	23	59	352	161	4.94	75	.283	.370	284-6	.169	-13	84	-83	-8.4

MAGLIE, SAL Salvatore Anthony "The Barber" B 4.26.1917 Niagara Falls, NY D 12.28.1992 Niagara Falls, NY BR/TR 6-2/180# d8.9 C6

Year	Tm Lg	W	L	Pct	G	GS	CG-Sho	SV-BS	IP	H	R	HR	HB	BB-IB	SO	ERA	AERA	OAV	OOB	AB-SH	AVG	PB	Sup	APR	PW
1945	NY N	5	4	.556	13	10	7-3	0	84.1	72	22	2	2	22	32	2.35	167	.231	.286	30-1	.167	-1*	84	15	1.5
1950	NY N	18	4	**.818**	47	16	12-**5**	1	206	169	71	14	10	86	96	2.71	**151**	.226	.314	66-3	.121	-1	110	32	3.1
1951	†NY N★	**23**	6	.793	42	37	22-3	4	298	254	110	27	6	86	146	2.93	**134**	**.230**	.289	112-9	.152	-3	117	**35**	3.0
1952	NY N☆	18	8	.692	35	31	12-5	1	216	199	80	16	6	75	112	2.92	127	.244	.312	69-12	.072	-3	113	20	2.0
1953	NY N	8	9	.471	27	24	9-3	0	145.1	158	79	19	1	47	80	4.15	103	.278	.334	48-6	.271	2	126	2	0.3
1954	†NY N	14	6	.700	34	32	9-1	2	218.1	222	83	21	3	70	117	3.26	124	.262	.319	63-13	.127	-2	99	23	1.7
1955	NY N	9	5	.643	23	21	6	0	129.2	142	67	18	3	48-2	71	3.75	107	.278	.340	40-6	.125	-2	106	2	-0.1
	Cle A	0	2	.000	10	2	0	2	25.2	26	14	0	1	7-0	11	3.86	103	.252	.306	5-0	.000	-0	67	0	-0.1
1956	Cle A	0	0	—	2	0	0	0	5	6	2	1	0	2-0	2	3.60	117	.300	.364	0-0	—	0		0	0.0
	†Bro N	13	5	.722	28	26	9-3	0	191	154	65	21	5	52-1	108	2.87	**138**	.222	.281	70-2	.129	-3	102	23	1.6
1957	Bro N	6	6	.500	19	17	4-1	1	101.1	94	42	12	4	26-1	50	2.93	142	.245	.298	29-4	.034	-3	82	11	0.9
	NY A	2	0	1.000	6	3	1-1	3	26	22	6	1	1	7-0	9	1.73	207	.227	.283	8-0	.250	0	100	6	0.6
1958	NY A	1	1	.500	7	3	0	0	23.1	27	12	3	0	9-2	7	4.63	76	.300	.364	7-0	.143	1	93	-2	-0.1
	StL N	2	6	.250	10	10	2	0	53	46	31	14	2	25-2	21	4.75	87	.232	.323	16-1	.125	-1	63	-3	-0.6
Total	10	119	62	.657	303	232	93-25	14	1723	1591	684	169	44	562-8	862	3.15	127	.245	.309	563-57	.135	-16	104	164	13.8

MAGNANTE, MIKE Michael Anthony B 6.17.1965 Glendale, CA BL/TL 6-1/190# d4.22

Year	Tm Lg	W	L	Pct	G	GS	CG-Sho	SV-BS	IP	H	R	HR	HB	BB-IB	SO	ERA	AERA	OAV	OOB	AB-SH	AVG	PB	Sup	APR	PW
1991	KC A	0	1	.000	38	0	0	0-0	55	55	19	3	0	23-3	42	2.45	168	.262	.333	0-0	—	0		9	0.5
1992	KC A	4	9	.308	44	12	0	0-3	89.1	115	53	5	2	35-5	31	4.94	82	.325	.382	0-0	—	0	96	-8	-1.0
1993	KC A	1	2	.333	7	6	0	0-0	35.1	37	16	3	1	11-1	16	4.08	113	.282	.340	0-0	—	0	57	2	0.2
1994	KC A	2	3	.400	36	1	0	0-0	47	55	27	5	0	16-1	21	4.60	109	.289	.340	0-0	—	0	73	2	0.2
1995	KC A	1	1	.500	28	0	0	0-1	44.2	45	23	6	2	16-1	28	4.23	113	.268	.335	0-0	—	0		3	0.2
1996	KC A	2	2	.500	38	0	0	0-1	54	58	38	5	4	24-1	32	5.67	88	.282	.361	0-0	—	0		-5	-0.2
1997	†Hou N	3	1	.750	40	0	0	1-4	47.2	39	16	2	0	11-2	43	2.27	177	.223	.266	3-0	.000	-0		8	0.6
1998	Hou N	4	7	.364	48	0	0	2-2	51.2	56	28	2	4	26-4	39	4.88	83	.276	.368	2-0	1.000	1		-4	-0.5
1999	Ana A	5	2	.714	53	0	0	0-3	69.1	68	30	2	3	29-4	44	3.38	144	.262	.334	0-0	—	0		11	1.0
2000	†Oak A	1	1	.500	55	0	0	0-3	39.2	50	22	3	2	19-7	17	4.31	110	.309	.388	1-0	.000	-0		2	0.1
2001	†Oak A	3	1	.750	65	0	0	0-1	55.1	50	23	7	1	13-3	23	2.77	160	.244	.287	0-0	—	0		8	0.5
2002	Oak A	0	2	.000	32	0	0	0-1	28.2	38	22	2	1	11-1	11	5.97	74	.317	.373	0-0	—	0		-6	-0.3
Total	12	26	32	.448	484	19	0	3-19	617.2	666	317	45	20	234-33	347	4.08	110	.279	.344	6-0	.333	1	78	22	1.3

MAGNUSON, JIM James Robert B 8.18.1946 Marinette, WI D 5.30.1991 Green Bay, WI BR/TL 6-2/190# d6.28

Year	Tm Lg	W	L	Pct	G	GS	CG-Sho	SV-BS	IP	H	R	HR	HB	BB-IB	SO	ERA	AERA	OAV	OOB	AB-SH	AVG	PB	Sup	APR	PW
1970	Chi A	1	5	.167	13	6	0	0-0	44.2	45	28	7	1	16-1	20	4.84	81	.263	.328	11-1	.000	-1	80	-5	-0.7
1971	Chi A	1	1	.500	15	4	0	0-0	30	30	18	0	2	16-0	11	4.50	80	.265	.366	4-0	.000	-0	100	-3	-0.2

Year	Tm Lg	W	L	Pct	G	GS	CG-Sho	SV-BS	IP	H	R	HR	HB	BB-IB	SO	ERA	AERA	OAV	OOB	AB-SH	AVG	PB	Sup	APR	PW
1973	NY A	0	1	.000	8	0	0	0-0	27.1	38	17	2	0	9-1	9	4.28	86	.342	.382	0-0	—	0		-3	-0.1
Total	3	2	7	.222	36	10	0	0-0	102	113	63	9	3	41-2	40	4.59	82	.286	.354	15-1	.000	-2	88	-11	-1.0

MAGRANE, JOE Joseph David B 7.2.1964 Des Moines, IA BR/TL 6-6/230# d4.25

Year	Tm Lg	W	L	Pct	G	GS	CG-Sho	SV-BS	IP	H	R	HR	HB	BB-IB	SO	ERA	AERA	OAV	OOB	AB-SH	AVG	PB	Sup	APR	PW
1987	†StL N	9	7	.563	27	26	4-2	0-0	170.1	157	75	9	10	60-6	101	3.54	117	.245	.318	52-6	.135	1*	90	10	1.0
1988	StL N	5	9	.357	24	24	4-3	0-0	165.1	133	57	6	2	51-4	100	**2.18**	**160**	.217	.278	48-8	.167	1*	70	18	1.9
1989	StL N	18	9	.667	34	33	9-3	0-0	234.2	219	81	5	6	72-7	127	2.91	125	.251	.310	80-8	.138	1*	110	20	2.3
1990	StL N	10	17	.370	31	31	3-2	0-0	203.1	204	86	10	8	59-7	100	3.59	107	.264	.320	55-9	.127	-0	74	7	1.0
1992	StL N	1	2	.333	5	5	0	0-0	31.1	34	15	2	2	15-0	20	4.02	84	.279	.364	10-1	.200	1	128	-2	-0.1
1993	StL N	8	10	.444	22	20	0	0-0	116	127	68	15	5	37-3	38	4.97	80	.286	.343	35-4	.114	-1	84	-11	-1.6
	Cal A	3	2	.600	8	8	0	0-0	48	48	27	4	0	21-0	24	3.94	115	.265	.337	0-0	—	0	102	1	0.2
1994	Cal A	2	6	.250	20	11	1	0-0	74	89	63	18	6	51-0	33	7.30	67	.300	.409	0-0	—	0	99	-19	-1.6
1996	Chi A	1	5	.167	19	8	0	0-0	53.2	70	45	10	3	25-1	21	6.88	69	.318	.390	0-0	—	0	85	-14	-1.2
Total	8	57	67	.460	190	166	21-10	0-0	1096.2	1081	517	79	42	391-28	564	3.81	103	.260	.327	280-36	.139	3	90	10	1.9

MAGRINI, PETE Peter Alexander B 6.8.1942 San Francisco, CA BR/TR 6/195# d4.13

Year	Tm Lg	W	L	Pct	G	GS	CG-Sho	SV-BS	IP	H	R	HR	HB	BB-IB	SO	ERA	AERA	OAV	OOB	AB-SH	AVG	PB	Sup	APR	PW
1966	Bos A	0	1	.000	3	1	0	0	7.1	8	9	0	1	8-0	3	9.82	39	.308	.459	3-0	.000	-0	23	-4	-0.6

MAHAFFEY, ART Arthur B 6.4.1938 Cincinnati, OH BR/TR 6-2/200# d7.30

Year	Tm Lg	W	L	Pct	G	GS	CG-Sho	SV-BS	IP	H	R	HR	HB	BB-IB	SO	ERA	AERA	OAV	OOB	AB-SH	AVG	PB	Sup	APR	PW
1960	Phi N	7	3	.700	14	12	5-1	0	93.1	78	29	9	1	34-1	56	2.31	168	.229	.298	30-5	.100	-2	81	15	1.3
1961	Phi N★	11	19	.367	36	32	12-3	0	219.1	205	110	27	7	70-6	158	4.10	99	.249	.311	63-12	.127	-2	79	0	-0.2
1962	Phi N★	19	14	.576	41	39	20-2	0	274	253	131	36	12	81-4	177	3.94	98	.246	.306	92-10	.141	1*	110	-1	-0.2
1963	Phi N	7	10	.412	26	22	6-1	0	149	143	73	18	5	48-1	97	3.99	81	.255	.314	50-3	.200	2	86	-11	-1.0
1964	Phi N	12	9	.571	34	29	2-2	0	157.1	161	84	17	6	82-5	80	4.52	77	.269	.361	50-5	.120	0	113	-15	-2.0
1965	Phi N	2	5	.286	22	9	1	0	71	82	53	11	7	32-2	52	6.21	56	.294	.373	21-1	.095	-1	118	-21	-2.0
1966	StL N	1	4	.200	12	5	0	1	35	37	27	7	1	21-4	19	6.43	56	.276	.373	7-0	.000	-1	74	-10	-1.5
Total	7	59	64	.480	185	148	46-9	1	999	959	507	125	39	368-23	639	4.17	89	.255	.324	313-36	.134	-2	97	-43	-5.6

MAHAFFEY, ROY Lee Roy "Popeye" B 2.9.1903 Belton, SC D 7.23.1969 Anderson, SC BR/TR 6/180# d8.31

Year	Tm Lg	W	L	Pct	G	GS	CG-Sho	SV-BS	IP	H	R	HR	HB	BB-IB	SO	ERA	AERA	OAV	OOB	AB-SH	AVG	PB	Sup	APR	PW
1926	Pit N	0	0	—	4	0	0	0	4.2	5	4	0	1	1	3	0.00	—	.294	.368	2-0	.000	-0		0	0.0
1927	Pit N	1	0	1.000	2	1	0	0	9.1	9	8	0	3	9	4	7.71	53	.300	.500	5-0	.400	0	207	-3	-0.2
1930	Phi A	9	5	.643	33	17	6	0	152.2	186	108	16	4	53	38	5.01	93	.298	.357	59-0	.119	-5	136	-10	-1.3
1931	†Phi A	15	4	.789	30	20	8	2	162.1	161	87	9	3	82	59	4.21	107	.258	.347	63-3	.190	1	107	6	0.6
1932	Phi A	13	13	.500	37	28	13	0	222.2	245	136	27	5	96	106	5.09	89	.274	.348	87-2	.172	-1	114	-13	-1.5
1933	Phi A	13	10	.565	33	23	9	0	179.1	198	114	5	4	74	66	5.17	83	.275	.346	65-2	.215	-0	130	-14	-1.6
1934	Phi A	6	7	.462	37	14	3	2	129	142	88	10	1	55	37	5.37	82	.276	.347	48-0	.271	2	101	-15	-1.1
1935	Phi A	8	4	.667	27	17	5	0	136	153	66	11	5	42	39	3.90	116	.283	.341	51-1	.176	-2	105	10	0.5
1936	StL A	2	6	.250	21	9	1	1	60	82	62	6	1	40	13	8.10	66	.315	.409	16-0	.063	-1	76	-17	-2.0
Total	9	67	49	.578	224	129	45	5	1056	1181	673	84	27	452	365	5.01	90	.280	.353	396-8	.184	-7	114	-56	-6.6

MAHAFFEY, LOU Louis Wood B 1.3.1874 , KY D 10.26.1949 Torrance, CA BR 5-9/170# d4.26

Year	Tm Lg	W	L	Pct	G	GS	CG-Sho	SV-BS	IP	H	R	HR	HB	BB-IB	SO	ERA	AERA	OAV	OOB	AB-SH	AVG	PB	Sup	APR	PW
1898	Lou N	0	1	.000	1	1	1	0	9	10	9	0	0	5	1	3.00	119	.278	.366	4-0	.000	-0	158	-1	-0.2

MAHAY, RON Ronald Matthew B 6.28.1971 Crestwood, IL BL/TL 6-2/185# d5.21.1995

Year	Tm Lg	W	L	Pct	G	GS	CG-Sho	SV-BS	IP	H	R	HR	HB	BB-IB	SO	ERA	AERA	OAV	OOB	AB-SH	AVG	PB	Sup	APR	PW
1997	Bos A	3	0	1.000	28	0	0	0-2	25	19	7	3	0	11-0	22	2.52	184	.204	.288	0-0	—	0		6	0.6
1998	Bos A	1	1	.500	29	0	0	1-1	26	26	16	2	2	15-1	14	3.46	136	.263	.358	0-0	—	0		1	0.1
1999	Oak A	2	0	1.000	6	1	0	1-0	19.1	8	4	2	0	3-0	15	1.86	250	.123	.162	0-0	—	0	60	6	0.6
2000	Oak A	0	1	.000	5	2	0	0-0	16	26	18	4	0	9-0	5	9.00	53	.366	.432	0-0	—	0*	99	-8	-0.4
	Fla N	1	0	1.000	18	0	0	0-0	25.1	31	17	6	0	16-1	27	6.04	73	.310	.402	4-0	.500	1		-4	-0.1
2001	Chi N	0	0	—	17	0	0	0-0	20.2	14	6	4	0	15-1	24	2.61	159	.197	.337	2-0	.000	-0		4	0.2
2002	Chi N	2	0	1.000	11	0	0	0-0	14.2	13	14	6	0	8-0	14	8.59	47	.228	.323	0-0	—	0		-7	-0.8
2003	Tex A	3	3	.500	35	0	0	0-3	45.1	33	19	3	0	20-7	38	3.18	156	.195	.280	0-0	—	0		7	0.9
Total	7	12	5	.706	149	3	0	2-6	192.1	170	101	30	2	97-10	159	4.21	110	.234	.324	6-0	.333	1	87	5	1.1

MAHLER, MICKEY Michael James B 7.30.1952 Montgomery, AL BB/TL 6-3/189# d9.13 b-Rick

Year	Tm Lg	W	L	Pct	G	GS	CG-Sho	SV-BS	IP	H	R	HR	HB	BB-IB	SO	ERA	AERA	OAV	OOB	AB-SH	AVG	PB	Sup	APR	PW
1977	Atl N	1	2	.333	5	5	0	0-0	23	31	19	4	1	9-0	14	6.26	71	.326	.380	6-1	.500	2	112	-4	-0.3
1978	Atl N	4	11	.267	34	21	1	0-1	134.2	130	82	16	7	66-6	92	4.68	87	.255	.345	41-5	.098	-2	96	-9	-1.2
1979	Atl N	5	11	.313	26	18	1	0-0	100	123	72	11	3	47-7	71	5.85	69	.304	.374	27-1	.111	-1	78	-17	-2.5
1980	Pit N	0	0	—	2	0	0	0-0	1	4	7	1	0	3-0	1	63.00	6	.571	.700	0-0	—	0		-6	-0.3
1981	Cal A	0	0	—	6	0	0	0-0	6.1	1	0	0	0	2-0	5	0.00	—	.056	.150	0-0	—	0		3	0.1
1982	Cal A	2	0	1.000	6	0	0	0-0	8	9	1	0	0	6-1	5	1.13	361	.300	.417	0-0	—	0		3	0.6
1985	Mon N	1	4	.200	9	7	1-1	1-0	48.1	40	22	3	1	24-1	32	3.54	96	.229	.323	16-1	.188	1	97	-1	-0.1
	Det A	1	2	.333	3	2	0	0-0	20.2	19	8	2	0	4-2	14	1.74	234	.241	.277	0-0	—	0	78	4	0.5
1986	Tex A	0	2	.000	29	5	0	3-0	63	71	31	3	3	29-2	28	4.14	104	.295	.372	0-0	—	0	105	2	0.1
	Tor A	0	0	—	2	0	0	0-0	1	1	0	0	1	0-0	0	0.00	—	.200	.333	0-0	—	0		0	0.0
	Year	0	2	.000	31	5	0	3-0	64	72	36	3	4	29-2	28	4.08	106	.293	.371	0-0	—	0	105	2	0.1
Total	8	14	32	.304	122	58	3-1	4-1	406	429	242	40	16	190-19	262	4.68	86	.274	.354	90-8	.144	-1	92	-25	-3.1

MAHLER, RICK Richard Keith B 8.5.1953 Austin, TX BR/TR 6-1/202# d4.20 b-Mickey

Year	Tm Lg	W	L	Pct	G	GS	CG-Sho	SV-BS	IP	H	R	HR	HB	BB-IB	SO	ERA	AERA	OAV	OOB	AB-SH	AVG	PB	Sup	APR	PW
1979	Atl N	0	0	—	15	0	0	0-0	22	28	16	4	0	11-2	12	6.14	66	.311	.386	2-0	.500	0		-4	-0.2
1980	Atl N	0	0	—	2	0	0	0-0	3.2	2	1	0	0	0-0	1	2.45	153	.154	.154	0-0	—	0		1	0.0
1981	Atl N	8	6	.571	34	14	1	2-0	112.1	109	41	5	1	43-5	54	2.80	128	.258	.326	27-2	.148	-1	57	9	1.0
1982	†Atl N	9	10	.474	39	33	5-2	0-1	205.1	213	105	18	1	62-5	105	4.21	89	.272	.324	58-11	.190	2	109	-9	-0.5
1983	Atl N	0	0	—	10	0	0	0-2	14.1	16	8	0	0	9-1	7	5.02	77	.296	.385	2-0	.000	-0		-1	-0.1
1984	Atl N	13	10	.565	38	29	9-1	0-0	222	209	86	13	3	62-7	106	3.12	124	.251	.303	71-3	.296	5	81	18	2.5
1985	Atl N	17	15	.531	39	**39**	6-1	0-0	266.2	272	116	24	2	79-8	107	3.48	111	.268	.321	90-11	.156	-1	108	11	1.2
1986	Atl N	14	18	.438	39	**39**	7-1	0-0	237.2	283	139	25	3	95-10	137	4.88	82	.301	.364	83-9	.193	2*	91	-19	-2.1
1987	Atl N	8	13	.381	39	28	3-1	0-0	197	212	118	24	2	85-8	95	4.98	87	.283	.356	65-7	.169	1*	93	-11	-0.8
1988	Atl N	9	16	.360	39	34	5	0-1	249	279	125	17	8	42-6	131	3.69	100	.282	.315	72-11	.125	-2	99	-4	-0.6
1989	Cin N	9	13	.409	40	31	5-2	0-0	220.2	242	113	15	10	51-13	102	3.83	94	.282	.328	62-3	.177	2	98	-8	-0.6
1990	†Cin N	7	6	.538	35	16	2-1	4-0	134.2	134	67	16	3	39-4	68	4.28	92	.261	.314	35-5	.114	-1	124	-4	-0.4
1991	Mon N	1	3	.250	10	6	0	0-1	37.1	37	17	2	0	15-0	17	3.62	100	.268	.338	9-3	.111	-0	70	0	0.0
	Atl N	1	1	.500	13	2	0	0-1	28.2	33	20	2	2	13-1	10	5.65	69	.282	.364	5-1	.200	0	173	-5	-0.3
	Year	2	4	.333	23	8	0	0-2	66	70	28	4	2	28-1	27	4.50	83	.275	.350	14-4	.143	-0	96	-6	-0.3
Total	13	96	111	.464	392	271	43-9	6-6	1951.1	2069	972	165	35	606-70	952	3.99	96	.275	.330	581-66	.179	7	97	-26	-0.9

MAHOMES, PAT Patrick Lavon B 8.9.1970 Bryan, TX BR/TR 6-4/210# d4.12

Year	Tm Lg	W	L	Pct	G	GS	CG-Sho	SV-BS	IP	H	R	HR	HB	BB-IB	SO	ERA	AERA	OAV	OOB	AB-SH	AVG	PB	Sup	APR	PW
1992	Min A	3	4	.429	14	13	0	0-0	69.2	73	41	5	0	37-0	44	5.04	81	.279	.364	0-0	—	0	119	-7	-0.6
1993	Min A	1	5	.167	12	5	0	0-0	37.1	47	34	8	1	16-0	23	7.71	57	.309	.372	0-0	—	0	30	-13	-1.7
1994	Min A	9	5	.643	21	21	0	0-0	120	121	68	22	1	62-1	53	4.72	103	.269	.357	0-0	—	0*	120	2	0.2
1995	Min A	4	10	.286	47	7	0	3-4	94.2	100	74	22	2	47-1	67	6.37	75	.271	.355	0-0	—	0	125	-17	-2.2
1996	Min A	1	4	.200	20	5	0	0-0	45	63	38	10	0	27-0	30	7.20	71	.330	.409	0-0	—	0	83	-10	-0.9
	Bos A	2	0	1.000	11	0	0	2-0	12.1	9	8	3	0	6-0	6	5.84	87	.209	.306	0-0	—	0		-1	-0.1
	Year	3	4	.429	31	5	0	2-0	57.1	72	51	13	0	33-0	36	6.91	74	.308	.390	0-0	—	0	83	-11	-1.0
1997	Bos A	1	0	1.000	10	0	0	0-0	10	15	10	2	2	10-1	5	8.10	57	.366	.500	0-0	—	0		-4	-0.3
1999	†NY N	8	0	1.000	39	0	0	0-1	63.2	44	26	7	2	37-5	51	3.68	119	.197	.314	16-0	.313	2*		6	0.8
2000	NY N	5	3	.625	53	5	0	0-1	94	96	63	15	2	66-4	76	5.46	81	.263	.376	17-2	.235	1	83	-12	-0.7
2001	Tex A	7	6	.538	56	4	0	0-1	107.1	115	71	17	0	55-9	61	5.70	82	.280	.359	1-0	1.000	0	84	-11	-1.1
2002	Chi N	1	1	.500	16	2	0	0-1	32.2	36	15	3	1	17-3	23	3.86	104	.286	.375	5-0	.000	-1*	80	1	0.0
2003	Pit N	0	1	.000	9	1	0	0-0	22.1	19	13	2	0	12-1	13	4.84	91	.241	.326	4-0	.250	0	86	-1	0.0
Total	11	42	39	.519	308	63	0	5-8	709	738	461	116	11	392-25	452	5.47	84	.272	.363	43-2	.256	3	104	-67	-6.6

MAHON, AL Alfred Gwinn "Lefty" B 9.23.1909 Albion, NE D 12.26.1977 New Haven, CT BL/TL 5-11/160# d4.22

Year	Tm Lg	W	L	Pct	G	GS	CG-Sho	SV-BS	IP	H	R	HR	HB	BB-IB	SO	ERA	AERA	OAV	OOB	AB-SH	AVG	PB	Sup	APR	PW
1930	Phi A	0	0	—	3	0	0	0	4.1	11	11	0	0	7	0	22.85	20	.579	.692	1-0	.000	0		-8	-0.3

Year	Tm Lg	W	L	Pct	G	GS	CG-Sho	SV-BS	IP	H	R	HR	HB	BB-IB	SO	ERA	AERA	OAV	OOB	AB-SH	AVG	PB	Sup	APR	PW
MAHONEY, CHRIS Christopher John B 6.11.1885 Milton, MA D 7.15.1954 Visalia, CA BR/TR 5-9/160# d7.12																									
1910	Bos A	0	1	.000	2	1	0	1	11	16	11	1	0	5	6	3.27	78	.327	.389	7-0	.143	-0*	131	-3	-0.3
MAHONEY, BOB Robert Paul B 6.20.1928 LeRoy, MN D 8.27.2000 Lincoln, NE BR/TR 6-1/185# d5.3																									
1951	Chi A	0	0	—	3	0	0	0	6.2	5	4	1	0	5	3	5.40	75	.208	.345	0-0	—	0		-1	0.0
	StL A	2	5	.286	30	4	0	0	81	86	47	7	0	41	30	4.44	99	.274	.358	18-1	.222	-0	71	-1	-0.1
	Year	2	5	.286	33	4	0	0	87.2	91	51	8	0	46	33	4.52	97	.269	.357	18-1	.222	-0	71	-2	-0.1
1952	StL A	0	0	—	3	0	0	0	3	8	6	0	0	4	1	18.00	22	.500	.600	0-0	—	0		-4	-0.2
Total	2	2	5	.286	36	4	0	0	90.2	99	57	8	0	50	34	4.96	88	.280	.369	18-1	.222	-0	71	-6	-0.3
MAILS, DUSTER John Walter "Walter" or "The Great" B 10.1.1894 San Quentin, CA D 7.5.1974 San Francisco, CA BL/TL 6/195# d9.28 Mil 1917-18																									
1915	Bro N	0	1	.000	2	0	0	0	5	6	5	2	0	5	3	3.60	77	.333	.478	1-0	.000	-0		-1	-0.2
1916	Bro N	0	1	.000	11	0	0	0	17.1	15	9	1	0	9	13	3.63	74	.242	.338	4-0	.250	0		-2	-0.1
1920	†Cle A	7	0	1.000	9	8	6-2	0	63.1	54	18	1	0	18	25	1.85	206	.230	.285	20-3	.200	0	115	13	1.3
1921	Cle A	14	8	.636	34	24	10-2	2	194.1	210	103	4	2	89	87	3.94	108	.283	.361	64-8	.094	-4	130	6	0.1
1922	Cle A	4	7	.364	26	13	4-1	0	104	122	69	8	4	40	54	5.28	76	.291	.359	31-1	.161	-0	99	-14	-1.3
1925	StL N	7	7	.500	21	16	9	0	131	145	78	11	7	58	49	4.60	94	.279	.360	45-2	.133	-2	101	-4	-0.6
1926	StL N	0	1	.000	1	0	0	0	1	2	1	0	0	1	1	0.00	—	.400	.500	0-0	—	0		0	0.0
Total	7	32	25	.561	104	61	29-5	2	516	554	283	27	13	220	232	4.10	100	.277	.352	165-14	.133	-7	115	-2	-0.8
MAIN, WOODY Forrest Harry B 2.12.1922 Delano, CA D 6.27.1992 Whittier, CA BR/TR 6-3.5/195# d4.21																									
1948	Pit N	1	1	.500	17	0	0	0	27	35	27	4	0	19	12	8.33	49	.324	.425	2-0	.000	-0		-12	-0.8
1950	Pit N	1	0	1.000	12	0	0	1	20.1	21	12	2	1	11	12	4.87	90	.256	.351	5-0	.400	0		-1	0.0
1952	Pit N	2	12	.143	48	11	2	2	153.1	149	78	14	0	52	79	4.46	90	.253	.314	37-3	.054	-3	59	-4	-0.9
1953	Pit N	0	0	—	2	0	0	0	4	5	5	1	0	2	4	11.25	40	.294	.368	0-0	—	0		-3	-0.1
Total	4	4	13	.235	79	11	2	3	204.2	210	122	21	1	84	107	5.14	79	.264	.335	44-3	.091	-3	59	-20	-1.8
MAIN, ALEX Miles Grant B 5.13.1884 Montrose, MI D 12.29.1965 Royal Oak, MI BL/TR 6-5/195# d4.18																									
1914	Det A	6	6	.500	32	12	5-1	3	138.1	131	51	2	3	59	55	2.67	105	.259	.340	40-0	.100	-2	93	4	0.4
1915	KC F	13	14	.481	35	28	18-2	3	230	181	88	4	5	75	91	2.54	103	.222	.291	76-3	.197	-0*	82	1	0.2
1918	Phi N	2	2	.500	8	4	1-1	0	35	30	20	1	5	16	14	4.63	65	.240	.349	11-1	.091	-1*	82	-5	-0.6
Total	3	21	22	.488	75	44	24-4	6	403.1	342	159	7	13	150	160	2.77	98	.236	.313	127-4	.157	-3	85	0	0.0
MAINS, JIM James Royal B 6.12.1922 Bridgton, ME D 3.17.1969 Bridgton, ME BR/TR 6-2/190# d8.22																									
1943	Phi A	0	1	.000	1	1	1	0	8	9	5	0	0	3	4	5.63	60	.281	.343	2-0	.000	0	50	-2	-0.2
MAINS, WILLARD Willard Eben "Grasshopper" B 7.7.1868 N.Windham, ME D 5.23.1923 Bridgton, ME TR 6-2/190# d8.3																									
1888	Chi N	1	1	.500	2	2	1	0	11	8	10	0	1	6	5	4.91	62	.211	.333	7	.143	-0	101	-2	-0.3
1891	Cin AA	12	12	.500	30	23	19	0	204	196	127	3	12	107	76	2.69	152	.244	.342	90	.244	1*	83	26	2.7
	Mil AA	0	2	.000	2	2	1	0	10	14	19	1	0	10	2	10.80	41	.318	.444	5	.600	1	64	-5	-0.7
	Year	12	14	.462	32	25	20	0	214	210	24	4	12	117	78	3.07	134	.248	.347	95	.263	2	82	16	2.0
1896	Bos N	3	2	.600	8	5	3	1	42.2	43	35	1	2	31	13	5.48	83	.261	.384	22-0	.273	-0*	119	-3	-0.3
Total	3	16	17	.485	42	32	24	1	267.2	261	191	5	15	154	96	3.53	117	.249	.353	124-0	.258	2	88	16	1.4
MAIRENA, OSWALDO Oswaldo Antonio B 7.30.1975 Chinandega, Nicaragua BL/TL 5-11/165# d9.5																									
2000	Chi N	0	0	—	2	0	0	0-0	2	7	4	1	0	2-0	0	18.00	25	.583	.643	0-0	—	0		-3	-0.1
2002	Fla N	2	3	.400	31	0	0	0-0	33.2	38	21	7	0	12-0	21	5.35	74	.288	.345	0-0	—	0		-5	-0.7
Total	2	2	3	.400	33	0	0	0-0	35.2	45	25	8	0	14-0	21	6.06	66	.313	.371	0-0	—	0		-8	-0.8
MAKOSKY, FRANK Frank B 1.20.1910 Boonton, NJ D 1.10.1987 Stroudsburg, PA BR/TR 6-1/185# d4.30																									
1937	NY A	5	2	.714	26	1	1	3	58	64	42	6	0	24	27	4.97	90	.277	.345	16-1	.313	1	59	-5	-0.4
MAKOWSKI, TOM Thomas Anthony B 12.22.1950 Buffalo, NY BR/TL 5-11/185# d5.1																									
1975	Det A	0	0	—	3	0	0	0-0	9.1	10	11	2	0	9-0	3	4.82	84	.278	.404	0-0	—	0		-3	-0.1
MALARKEY, JOHN John S. "Liz" B 5.4.1872 Springfield, OH D 10.29.1949 Cincinnati, OH TR 5-11/155# d9.21																									
1894	Was N	2	1	.667	3	3	3	0	26	42	22	1	0	5	3	4.15	127	.359	.385	14-0	.071	-2*	54	3	0.0
1895	Was N	0	8	.000	22	8	5	2	100.2	135	113	3	8	60	32	5.99	80	.316	.410	37-0	.135	-4	85	-15	-1.3
1896	Was N	0	1	.000	1	1	0	0	7	9	7	1	0	3	0	1.29	343	.310	.375	2-0	.500	1	97	1	0.1
1899	Chi N	0	1	.000	1	1	1	0	9	19	13	0	1	5	7	13.00	29	.422	.490	5-0	.200	0	38	-7	-0.5
1902	Bos N	8	10	.444	21	19	17-1	1	170.1	158	82	0	0	58	39	2.59	109	.246	.309	62-1	.210	2*	106	0	0.4
1903	Bos N	11	16	.407	32	27	25-2	0	253	266	150	5	11	96	98	3.09	104	.272	.344	87-1	.161	1	93	-3	-0.1
Total	6	21	37	.362	80	59	51-3	3	566	629	387	10	20	227	179	3.64	96	.281	.353	207-2	.169	-2	90	-21	-1.4
MALARKEY, BILL William John B 11.26.1878 Port Byron, IL D 12.12.1956 Phoenix, AZ BR/TR 5-10/185# d4.16																									
1908	NY N	0	2	.000	15	0	0	2	35	31	16	1	1	10	12	2.57	94	.242	.302	6-0	.000	-1		-2	-0.2
MALASKA, MARK Dennis Mark B 1.17.1978 Youngstown, OH BL/TL 6-3/190# d7.17																									
2003	TB A	2	1	.667	22	0	0	0-3	16	13	7	0	1	12-3	17	2.81	161	.232	.377	0-0	—	0		2	0.4
MALDONADO, CARLOS Carlos Cesar (Delgado) B 10.18.1966 Chepo, Panama BB/TR 6-2/210# d9.16																									
1990	KC A	0	0	—	4	0	0	0-0	6	9	6	0	0	4-0	9	9.00	43	.346	.419	0-0	—	0		-3	-0.2
1991	KC A	0	0	—	5	0	0	0-0	7.2	11	9	0	0	9-1	1	8.22	50	.333	.476	0-0	—	0		-4	-0.2
1993	Mil A	2	2	.500	29	0	0	1-0	37.1	40	20	2	0	17-5	18	4.58	93	.282	.350	0-0	—	0		-1	-0.1
Total	3	2	2	.500	38	0	0	1-0	51	60	35	2	0	30-6	28	5.65	74	.299	.381	0-0	—	0		-8	-0.5
MALIS, CY Cyrus Sol B 2.26.1907 Philadelphia, PA D 1.12.1971 N.Hollywood, CA BR/TR 5-11/175# d8.17																									
1934	Phi N	0	0	—	1	0	0	0	3.2	4	2	0	0	2	1	4.91	96	.267	.353	0-0	—	0		0	0.0
MALLETTE, BRIAN Brian Drew B 1.19.1975 Dublin, GA BR/TR 6/185# d4.12																									
2002	Mil N	0	0	—	5	0	0	0-0	5	7	6	3	1	3-1	5	10.80	38	.350	.458	0-0	—	0		-4	-0.2
MALLETTE, MAL Malcolm Francis B 1.30.1922 Syracuse, NY BL/TL 6-2/200# d9.25																									
1950	Bro N	0	0	—	2	0	0	0	1.1	2	0	0	0	1	2	0.00	—	.333	.429	0-0	—	0		1	0.0
MALLICOAT, ROB Robbin Dale B 11.16.1964 St.Helens, OR BL/TL 6-3/180# d9.11																									
1987	Hou N	0	0	—	4	1	0	0-0	6.2	8	5	0	0	6-0	4	6.75	58	.320	.452	0-0	—	0	161	-2	-0.1
1991	Hou N	0	2	.000	24	0	0	1-0	23.1	22	10	2	2	13-1	18	3.86	91	.259	.363	1-0	.000	-0		0	-0.1
1992	Hou N	0	0	—	23	0	0	0-0	23.2	26	19	2	5	19-2	20	7.23	47	.283	.427	1-0	.000	-0*		-10	-0.5
Total	3	0	2	.000	51	1	0	1-0	53.2	56	34	4	7	38-3	42	5.70	61	.277	.404	2-0	.000	-0	161	-12	-0.7
MALLOY, ALEX Archibald Alexander "Lick" B 10.31.1886 Laurinburg, NC D 3.1.1961 Ferris, TX BR/TR 6-2/180# d9.10																									
1910	StL A	0	6	.000	7	6	4	0	52.2	47	26	0	2	17	27	2.56	97	.261	.332	16-0	.063	-1	18	-1	-0.3
MALLOY, HERM Herman "Tug" B 6.1.1885 Massillon, OH D 5.9.1942 Louisville, OH BR/TR 6/?# d10.6																									
1907	Det A	0	1	.000	1	1	1	0	8	13	10	1	0	5	6	5.63	46	.371	.450	4-0	.250	0	78	-3	-0.3
1908	Det A	0	2	.000	3	2	2	0	17	20	11	1	2	4	8	3.71	65	.278	.333	9-0	.333	1	42	-3	-0.2
Total	2	0	3	.000	4	3	3	0	25	33	21	2	2	9	14	4.32	57	.308	.373	13-0	.308	1	55	-6	-0.5
MALLOY, BOB Robert Paul B 5.28.1918 Canonsburg, PA BR/TR 5-11/185# d5.4 Mil 1944-46																									
1943	Cin N	0	0	—	6	0	0	0	10	14	8	1	0	8	4	6.30	53	.778	.846	3-0	.667	1		-3	-0.1
1944	Cin N	1	1	.500	9	0	0	0	23.1	22	10	0	0	11	4	3.09	113	.265	.351	7-0	.000	-1		1	0.0
1946	Cin N	2	5	.286	27	3	1	2	72	71	29	2	2	26	24	2.75	122	.265	.334	18-0	.278	1	94	4	0.4
1947	Cin N	0	0	—	1	0	0	0	1	3	2	1	0	0	1	18.00	23	.600	.600	0-0	—	0		-1	-0.1
1949	StL A	1	1	.500	5	0	0	0	9.2	6	3	0	0	7	2	2.79	162	.200	.351	3-0	.000	-0		2	0.3
Total	5	4	7	.364	48	3	1	2	116	116	52	4	2	52	35	3.26	106	.287	.371	31-0	.226	1	94	3	0.5
MALLOY, BOB Robert William B 11.24.1964 Arlington, VA BR/TR 6-5/200# d5.26																									
1987	Tex A	0	0	—	2	2	0	0-0	11	13	11	6	0	3-0	8	6.55	69	.271	.314	0-0	—	0	183	-3	-0.2

Year	Tm Lg	W	L	Pct	G	GS	CG-Sho	SV-BS	IP	H	R	HR	HB	BB-IB	SO	ERA	AERA	OAV	OOB	AB-SH	AVG	PB	Sup	APR	PW
1990	Mon N	0	0	—	1	0	0	0-0	2	1	0	0	0	1-0	1	0.00	—	.143	.250	0-0	—	0		1	0.0
Total	2	0	0	—	3	2	0	0-0	13	14	11	6	0	4-0	9	5.54	79	.255	.305	0-0	—	0	183	-2	-0.2
MALONE, CHUCK Charles Ray B 7.8.1965 Harrisburg, AR BR/TR 6-7/250# d9.6																									
1990	Phi N	1	0	1.000	7	0	0	0-0	7.1	3	4	1	0	11-0	7	3.68	104	.130	.412	0-0	—	0		0	0.0
MALONE, MARTIN Martin d6.20 ▲																									
1872	Eck NA	0	2	.000	2	2	2	0	18	51	50	1		4	0	10.50	32	.443	.462	16	.375	1*	90	-14	-0.8
MALONE, PAT Perce Leigh B 9.25.1902 Altoona, PA D 5.13.1943 Altoona, PA BL/TR 6/200# d4.12																									
1928	Chi N	18	13	.581	42	25	16-2	2	250.2	218	99	15	6	99	155	2.84	136	.236	.314	95-3	.189	1	118	27	3.1
1929	†Chi N	**22**	10	.688	40	30	19-**5**	2	267	283	120	12	6	102	**166**	3.57	129	.276	.345	105-0	.210	2	111	33	3.5
1930	Chi N	**20**	9	.690	45	35	**22**-1	4	271.2	290	145	14	6	96	142	3.94	124	.271	.334	105-4	.248	5	117	26	2.6
1931	Chi N	16	9	.640	36	30	12-2	0	228.1	229	115	9	4	88	112	3.90	99	.258	.328	79-9	.215	2	132	-1	0.0
1932	†Chi N	15	17	.469	37	32	17-2	0	237	222	111	13	6	78	120	3.38	111	.244	.308	78-8	.179	0	93	8	0.8
1933	Chi N	10	14	.417	31	26	13-2	0	186.1	186	91	10	5	59	72	3.91	84	.258	.318	63-3	.159	-2	105	-11	-1.6
1934	Chi N	14	7	.667	34	21	8-1	0	191	200	85	14	3	55	111	3.53	110	.270	.322	64-8	.172	-2	100	7	0.5
1935	NY A	3	5	.375	29	2	0	3	56.1	53	45	7	1	33	25	5.43	75	.252	.357	15-1	.000	-3	193	-12	-1.7
1936	†NY A	12	4	.750	35	9	5	**9**	134.2	144	60	4	4	60	72	3.81	122	.273	.352	51-2	.196	-1	160	16	1.6
1937	NY A	4	4	.500	28	9	3	6	92	109	65	5	4	35	49	5.48	81	.291	.357	33-2	.030	-5	146	-10	-1.4
Total	10	134	92	.593	357	219	115-15	26	1915	1934	936	103	45	705	1024	3.74	111	.262	.330	688-40	.188	-2	115	83	7.4
MALONEY, CHARLIE Charles Michael B 5.22.1886 Cambridge, MA D 1.17.1967 Arlington, MA BR/TR 5-8/155# d8.10																									
1908	Bos N	0	0	—	1	0	0	0	2	3	1	0	0	1	0	4.50	54	.429	.500	0-0	—	0		0	0.0
MALONEY, JIM James William B 6.2.1940 Fresno, CA BL/TR 6-2/207# d7.27																									
1960	Cin N	2	6	.250	11	10	2-1	0	63.2	61	35	5	2	37-2	48	4.66	82	.255	.360	18-1	.111	-0	90	-5	-0.6
1961	†Cin N	6	7	.462	27	11	1	2	94.2	86	54	16	1	59-4	57	4.37	93	.242	.349	29-1	.379	4*	117	-4	-0.1
1962	Cin N	9	7	.563	22	17	3	1	115.1	90	52	11	2	66-3	105	3.51	115	.214	.320	43-0	.186	0*	96	6	0.7
1963	Cin N	23	7	.767	33	33	13-6	0	250.1	183	84	17	6	88-1	265	2.77	121	.202	.275	89-5	.169	1*	131	17	2.0
1964	Cin N	15	10	.600	31	31	11-2	0	216	175	72	16	1	83-5	214	2.71	133	.222	.296	73-1	.151	1	96	22	2.5
1965	Cin N★	20	9	.690	33	33	14-5	0	255.1	189	77	13	5	110-3	244	2.54	148	.206	.294	89-8	.225	7*	111	34	4.6
1966	Cin N	16	8	.667	32	32	10-**5**	0	224.2	174	75	18	10	90-4	216	2.80	139	.214	.299	81-3	.222	3*	92	26	3.0
1967	Cin N	15	11	.577	30	29	6-3	0	196.1	181	76	8	3	72-5	153	3.25	115	.247	.315	69-2	.159	-0*	85	11	1.5
1968	Cin N	16	10	.615	33	32	8-5	0	207	183	100	17	2	80-6	181	3.61	88	.239	.310	74-4	.243	6*	125	-12	-0.9
1969	Cin N	12	5	.706	30	27	6-3	0-0	178.2	135	64	11	1	86-4	102	2.77	136	.208	.301	55-6	.200	6	112	18	2.3
1970	Cin N	0	1	.000	7	3	0	1-0	16.2	26	22	3	2	15-0	7	11.34	36	.366	.478	3-0	.000	-0	148	-13	-0.8
1971	Cal A	0	3	.000	13	4	0	0-0	30.1	35	18	3	1	24-2	13	5.04	64	.294	.414	5-0	.200	0	62	-6	-0.6
Total	12	134	84	.615	302	262	74-30	4-0	1849	1518	729	138	36	810-39	1605	3.19	115	.224	.308	628-31	.201	26	106	94	13.6
MALONEY, SEAN Sean Patrick B 5.25.1971 South Kingstown, RI BR/TR 6-7/210# d4.28																									
1997	Mil A	0	0	—	3	0	0	0-0	7	7	4	1	2	2-0	5	5.14	90	.304	.379	0-0	—	0		0	0.0
1998	LA N	0	1	.000	11	0	0	0-0	12.2	13	7	2	2	5-0	11	4.97	80	.265	.357	1-0	.000	-0		-1	-0.1
Total	2	0	1	.000	14	0	0	0-0	19.2	20	11	3	4	7-0	16	5.03	83	.278	.365	1-0	.000	-0		-1	-0.1
MALOY, PAUL Paul Augustus "Biff" B 6.4.1892 Bascom, OH D 3.18.1976 Sandusky, OH BR/TR 5-11/185# d7.11																									
1913	Bos A	0	0	—	2	0	0	0	2	2	2	0	2	1	0	9.00	33	.286	.500	0-0	—	0		-1	-0.1
MALTZBERGER, GORDON Gordon Ralph "Maltzy" B 9.4.1912 Utopia, TX D 12.11.1974 Rialto, CA BR/TR 6/170# d4.27 Mil 1945-46 C3																									
1943	Chi A	7	4	.636	37	0	0	**14**	98.2	86	29	8	2	24	48	2.46	136	.236	.287	25-2	.120	0		11	1.6
1944	Chi A	10	5	.667	46	0	0	**12**	91.1	81	31	2	1	19	49	2.96	116	.235	.277	22-2	.136	-1		7	1.2
1946	Chi A	2	0	1.000	19	0	0	2	39.2	30	7	3	1	6	17	1.59	215	.205	.242	6-0	.000	-0		9	0.5
1947	Chi A	1	4	.200	33	0	0	5	63.2	61	26	4	1	25	22	3.39	108	.257	.331	7-1	.143	1		3	0.4
Total	4	20	13	.606	135	0	0	33	293.1	258	93	17	5	74	136	2.70	128	.236	.288	60-5	.117	0		30	3.7
MAMAUX, AL Albert Leon B 5.30.1894 Pittsburgh, PA D 12.31.1962 Santa Monica, CA BR/TR 6-0.5/168# d9.23 Mil 1918																									
1913	Pit N	0	0	—	1	0	0	0	3	2	1	0	0	2	2	3.00	101	.167	.286	1-0	.000	-0		0	0.0
1914	Pit N	5	2	.714	13	6	4-2	0	63	41	19	1	2	24	30	1.71	155	.186	.272	20-0	.250	1	117	5	0.8
1915	Pit N	21	8	.724	38	30	17-8	0	251.2	182	70	3	9	96	152	2.04	134	.208	.293	92-5	.163	-2	116	21	2.0
1916	Pit N	21	15	.583	45	37	26-1	2	310	264	123	3	9	136	163	2.53	106	.239	.327	110-2	.191	1	101	3	0.5
1917	Pit N	2	11	.154	16	13	5	0	85.2	92	59	1	3	50	22	5.25	54	.278	.378	31-1	.226	0	98	-21	-2.9
1918	Bro N	0	1	.000	2	1	0	0	8	14	6	0	0	2	2	6.75	41	.438	.471	2-0	.000	-0	54	-3	-0.3
1919	Bro N	10	12	.455	30	22	16-2	0	199.1	174	89	2	4	66	80	2.66	112	.245	.312	63-2	.175	0	88	2	0.3
1920	†Bro N	12	8	.600	41	17	9-2	4	190.2	172	70	2	4	63	101	2.69	119	.255	.322	60-2	.167	-0	98	11	1.2
1921	Bro N	3	3	.500	12	1	0	1	43	36	17	1	1	13	21	3.14	124	.240	.305	11-1	.182	-0	63	4	0.5
1922	Bro N	1	4	.200	37	7	1	3	87.2	97	46	7	2	33	35	3.70	110	.290	.358	17-2	.235	3	92	3	0.5
1923	Bro N	0	2	.000	5	1	0	0	13	20	13	0	0	6	5	8.31	47	.385	.448	2-0	.500	0	0	-6	-0.7
1924	NY A	1	1	.500	14	2	0	0	38	44	28	2	1	20	12	5.68	73	.308	.396	13-0	.077	-1	223	-7	-0.5
Total	12	76	67	.531	254	137	78-15	10	1293	1138	541	22	35	511	625	2.90	104	.245	.325	422-15	.182	2	100	12	1.4
MANDERS, HAL Harold Carl B 6.14.1917 Waukee, IA BR/TR 6/187# d8.12																									
1941	Det A	1	0	1.000	8	0	0	0	15.1	13	5	0	1	8	7	2.35	194	.236	.344	4-0	.000	-1		3	0.1
1942	Det A	2	0	1.000	18	0	0	0	33	39	19	4	1	15	14	4.09	97	.307	.385	4-0	.250	0		-1	0.0
1946	Det A	0	0	—	2	0	0	0	6	8	7	1	1	2	3	10.50	35	.364	.440	2-0	.500	0		-4	-0.2
	Chi N	0	1	.000	2	1	0	0	6	11	6	1	1	3	4	9.00	37	.423	.500	2-0	.000	-0	26	-3	-0.5
Total	3	3	1	.750	30	1	0	0	60.1	71	37	6	4	28	28	4.77	84	.309	.393	12-0	.167	-0	26	-5	-0.6
MANGUM, LEO Leo Allan "Blackie" B 5.24.1896 Durham, NC D 7.9.1974 Lima, OH BR/TR 6-1/187# d7.11																									
1924	Chi A	1	4	.200	13	7	1	0	47	69	43	3	1	25	12	7.09	58	.359	.436	14-0	.071	-1	117	-15	-1.4
1925	Chi A	1	0	1.000	7	0	0	0	15	25	15	0	0	6	6	7.80	53	.373	.425	4-0	.500	1		-6	-0.3
1928	NY N	0	0	—	1	1	0	0	3	6	5	0	0	5	1	15.00	26	.500	.647	1-0	1.000	0	260	-3	-0.1
1932	Bos N	0	0	—	7	0	0	0	10.1	17	8	1	0	0	3	5.23	72	.333	.333	2-0	.000	-0		-2	-0.1
1933	Bos N	4	3	.571	25	5	2-1	0	84	93	33	2	0	11	28	3.32	92	.280	.303	22-2	.091	-2	92	-1	-0.2
1934	Bos N	5	3	.625	29	3	1	1	94.1	127	67	9	0	23	28	5.72	67	.315	.352	32-0	.281	2	38	-20	-1.3
1935	Bos N	0	0	—	3	0	0	0	4.2	6	3	0	0	2	0	3.86	98	.300	.364	0-0	—	0		0	0.0
Total	7	11	10	.524	85	16	4-1	1	258.1	343	174	15	1	72	78	5.37	68	.318	.362	75-2	.200	0	108	-47	-3.4
MANN, JIM James Joseph B 11.17.1974 Brockton, MA BR/TR 6-3/225# d5.29																									
2000	NY N	0	0	—	2	0	0	0-0	2.2	6	3	1	0	1-0	0	10.13	44	.429	.467	0-0	—	0		-2	-0.1
2001	Hou N	0	0	—	4	0	0	0-0	5.1	3	2	0	2	4-0	5	3.38	136	.176	.391	0-0	—	0		1	0.0
2002	Hou N	0	1	.000	17	0	0	0-0	22	19	10	3	5	7-1	19	4.09	104	.235	.333	1-0	.000	-0		1	0.0
2003	Pit N	0	0	—	2	0	0	0-0	1.2	5	4	1	0	1-0	1	10.80	41	.455	.500	0-0	—	0		-2	-0.1
Total	4	0	1	.000	25	0	0	0-0	31.2	33	19	5	7	13-1	25	4.83	90	.268	.371	1-0	.000	-0		-2	-0.2
MANNING, DAVID David Anthony B 8.14.1972 Buffalo, NY BR/TR 6-3/210# d8.2																									
2003	Mil N	0	2	.000	2	2	0	0-0	6.2	11	13	1	0	8-0	2	16.20	26	.393	.514	1-0	.000	-0	22	-9	-1.3
MANNING, ERNIE Ernest Devon "Ed" B 10.9.1890 Florala, AL D 4.28.1973 Pensacola, FL BL/TR 6/175# d5.3																									
1914	StL A	0	0	—	4	0	0	0	10	11	6	0	0	3	3	3.60	75	.297	.350	4-1	.000	-0*		-1	-0.1
MANNING, JIM James Benjamin B 7.21.1943 L'Anse, MI BR/TR 6-1/185# d4.15																									
1962	Min A	0	0	—	5	1	0	0	7	14	10	0	1	1-0	3	5.14	79	.389	.410	1-0	.000	-0	153	-3	-0.2
MANNING, JACK John E. B 12.20.1853 Braintree, MA D 8.15.1929 Boston, MA BR/TR 5-8.5/158# d4.23.1873 M1 ▲																									
1874	Bal NA	4	16	.200	22	20	17	0	176.2	222	168	2		12	12	2.09	107	.266	.277	174	.351	7*	50	-1	0.5
1875	Bos NA	16	2	.889	27	18	8-1	6	144	152	86	1		14	34	2.38	90	.247	.263	348	.270	4*	173	-4	-0.3
1876	Bos N	18	5	.783	34	20	13	**5**	197.1	213	139	1		32	24	2.14	105	.252	.279	288	.264	3*	153	-1	0.0

Year	Tm Lg	W	L	Pct	G	GS	CG-Sho	SV-BS	IP	H	R	HR	HB	BB-IB	SO	ERA	AERA	OAV	OOB	AB-SH	AVG	PB	Sup	APR	PW
1877	Cin N	0	4	.000	10	4	2	1	44	83	65	1		7	6	6.95	38	.379	.398	252	.317	4*	55	-21	-1.3
1878	Bos N	1	0	1.000	3	1	1	0	11.1	24	19	1		5	2	14.29	17	.393	.439	248	.254	0*	111	-11	-0.7
Total	2 NA	20	18	.526	49	38	25-1	6	320.2	374	254	3		26	46	2.22	99	.258	.271	522	.297	11	101	-5	0.2
Total	3	19	9	.679	47	25	16	6	252.2	320	223	3		44	32	3.53	66	.284	.311	788	.278	7	137	-33	-2.0

MANNING, RUBE Walter S. B 4.29.1883 Chambersburg, PA D 4.23.1930 Williamsport, PA BR/TR 6/180# d9.25

Year	Tm Lg	W	L	Pct	G	GS	CG-Sho	SV-BS	IP	H	R	HR	HB	BB-IB	SO	ERA	AERA	OAV	OOB	AB-SH	AVG	PB	Sup	APR	PW
1907	NY A	0	1	.000	1	1	1	0	9	8	3	0	1	3	3	3.00	93	.242	.324	3-0	.000	-0	24	0	0.0
1908	NY A	13	16	.448	41	26	19-2	1	245	228	114	4	18	86	113	2.94	84	.256	.334	91-1	.187	0*	77	-11	-1.3
1909	NY A	7	11	.389	26	21	11-2	1	173	167	76	2	9	48	71	3.17	80	.265	.326	60-3	.183	-0	102	-8	-0.8
1910	NY A	2	4	.333	16	9	4	0	75	80	43	4	4	25	25	3.72	71	.283	.349	26-0	.192	0	123	-9	-0.7
Total	4	22	32	.407	84	57	35-4	2	502	483	236	10	32	162	212	3.14	81	.263	.333	180-4	.183	-0	93	-28	-2.8

MANON, JULIO Julio Alberto B 6.10.1973 Guerra, D.R. BL/TR 6/200# d6.5

Year	Tm Lg	W	L	Pct	G	GS	CG-Sho	SV-BS	IP	H	R	HR	HB	BB-IB	SO	ERA	AERA	OAV	OOB	AB-SH	AVG	PB	Sup	APR	PW
2003	Mon N	1	2	.333	23	0	0	1-0	28.1	26	13	3	1	17-1	15	4.13	114	.252	.358	1-0	.000	-0		2	0.2

MANON, RAMON Ramon (Reyes) B 1.20.1968 Santo Domingo, D.R. BR/TR 6/150# d4.19

Year	Tm Lg	W	L	Pct	G	GS	CG-Sho	SV-BS	IP	H	R	HR	HB	BB-IB	SO	ERA	AERA	OAV	OOB	AB-SH	AVG	PB	Sup	APR	PW
1990	Tex A	0	0	—	1	0	0	0-0	2	3	3	0	0	3-1	0	13.50	29	.333	.500	0-0	—	0		-2	-0.1

MANSKE, LOU Louis Hugo B 7.4.1884 Milwaukee, WI D 4.27.1963 Milwaukee, WI BL/TL 6/?# d8.31

Year	Tm Lg	W	L	Pct	G	GS	CG-Sho	SV-BS	IP	H	R	HR	HB	BB-IB	SO	ERA	AERA	OAV	OOB	AB-SH	AVG	PB	Sup	APR	PW
1906	Pit N	0	0	—	2	1	0	0	8	12	6	0	0	5	6	5.63	48	.387	.472	4-0	.000	-1	191	-2	-0.2

MANTEI, MATT Matthew Bruce B 7.7.1973 Tampa, FL BR/TR 6-1/180# d6.18

Year	Tm Lg	W	L	Pct	G	GS	CG-Sho	SV-BS	IP	H	R	HR	HB	BB-IB	SO	ERA	AERA	OAV	OOB	AB-SH	AVG	PB	Sup	APR	PW
1995	Fla N	0	1	.000	12	0	0	0-0	13.1	12	8	1	0	13-0	15	4.73	89	.245	.397	0-0	—	0		-1	0.0
1996	Fla N	1	0	1.000	14	0	0	0-1	18.1	13	13	2	1	21-1	25	6.38	64	.197	.398	1-0	.000	-0		-4	-0.2
1998	Fla N	3	4	.429	42	0	0	9-3	54.2	38	19	1	7	23-3	63	2.96	137	.203	.308	3-0	.333	0		7	1.1
1999	Fla N	1	2	.333	35	0	0	10-2	36.1	24	11	4	2	25-1	50	2.72	160	.186	.325	1-0	.000	-0		7	0.9
	†Ari N	0	1	.000	30	0	0	22-3	29	20	10	1	3	19-0	49	2.79	164	.192	.333	0-0	—	0		6	0.9
	Year	1	3	.250	65	0	0	32-5	65.1	44	28	5	5	44-1	99	2.76	162	.189	.329	1-0	.000	-0		13	1.8
2000	Ari N	1	1	.500	47	0	0	17-3	45.1	31	24	4	2	35-1	53	4.57	103	.193	.343	0-0	—	0		1	0.1
2001	Ari N	0	0	—	8	0	0	2-0	7	6	2	2	0	4-0	12	2.57	178	.222	.323	0-0	—	0		2	0.1
2002	†Ari N	2	2	.500	31	0	0	0-1	26.2	28	15	3	1	12-0	26	4.73	94	.257	.336	0-0	—	0		-1	-0.1
2003	Ari N	5	4	.556	50	0	0	29-3	55	37	17	6	2	18-1	68	2.62	178	.191	.264	0-0	—	0		12	2.3
Total	8	13	15	.464	269	0	0	89-16	285.2	209	119	24	18	170-7	361	3.56	124	.204	.325	5-0	.200	0		29	5.1

MANUEL, BARRY Barry Paul B 8.12.1965 Mamou, LA BR/TR 5-11/180# d9.6

Year	Tm Lg	W	L	Pct	G	GS	CG-Sho	SV-BS	IP	H	R	HR	HB	BB-IB	SO	ERA	AERA	OAV	OOB	AB-SH	AVG	PB	Sup	APR	PW
1991	Tex A	1	0	1.000	8	0	0	0-0	16	7	2	0	0	6-0	5	1.13	359	.143	.224	0-0	—	0		5	0.3
1992	Tex A	1	0	1.000	3	0	0	0-0	5.2	6	3	2	1	1-0	9	4.76	80	.261	.320	0-0	—	0		0	-0.1
1996	Mon N	4	1	.800	53	0	0	0-0	86	70	34	10	7	26-4	62	3.24	133	.219	.291	7-1	.000	-0		10	0.4
1997	NY N	0	1	.000	19	0	0	0-0	25.2	35	18	6	1	13-1	21	5.26	77	.324	.402	2-0	.000	-0		-4	-0.3
1998	Ari N	1	0	1.000	13	0	0	0-0	15.2	17	14	5	1	14-3	12	7.47	56	.266	.405	0-0	—	0		-6	-0.3
Total	5	7	2	.778	96	0	0	0-0	149	135	71	23	10	60-8	109	3.87	109	.240	.321	9-1	.000	-1		5	0.0

MANUEL, MOXIE Mark Garfield B 10.16.1881 Metropolis, IL D 4.26.1924 Memphis, TN BR/TR 5-11/170# d9.25

Year	Tm Lg	W	L	Pct	G	GS	CG-Sho	SV-BS	IP	H	R	HR	HB	BB-IB	SO	ERA	AERA	OAV	OOB	AB-SH	AVG	PB	Sup	APR	PW
1905	Was A	0	0	—	3	1	1	0	10	9	9	0	1	3	3	5.40	49	.243	.317	4-0	.250	0	80	-3	-0.2
1908	Chi A	3	4	.429	18	6	3	1	60.1	52	25	0	2	25	25	3.28	71	.243	.328	16-1	.063	-1	98	-5	-0.7
Total	2	3	4	.429	21	7	4	1	70.1	61	34	0	3	28	28	3.58	66	.243	.326	20-1	.100	-1	96	-8	-0.9

MANVILLE, DICK Richard Wesley B 12.25.1926 Des Moines, IA BR/TR 6-4/192# d4.30

Year	Tm Lg	W	L	Pct	G	GS	CG-Sho	SV-BS	IP	H	R	HR	HB	BB-IB	SO	ERA	AERA	OAV	OOB	AB-SH	AVG	PB	Sup	APR	PW
1950	Bos N	0	0	—	1	0	0	0	2	0	0	0	0	3	2	0.00	—	.000	.300	0-0	—	0		1	0.0
1952	Chi N	0	0	—	11	0	0	0	17	25	17	2	0	12	6	7.94	48	.362	.457	2-0	.500	0		-7	-0.3
Total	2	0	0	—	12	0	0	0	19	25	17	2	0	15	8	7.11	54	.329	.440	2-0	.500	0		-6	-0.3

MANZANILLO, JOSIAS Josias (Adams) B 10.16.1967 San Pedro De Macoris, D.R. BR/TR 6/190# d10.5 b-Ravelo

Year	Tm Lg	W	L	Pct	G	GS	CG-Sho	SV-BS	IP	H	R	HR	HB	BB-IB	SO	ERA	AERA	OAV	OOB	AB-SH	AVG	PB	Sup	APR	PW
1991	Bos A	0	0	—	1	0	0	0-0	1	2	2	0	0	3-0	1	18.00	24	.400	.625	0-0	—	0		-1	-0.1
1993	Mil A	1	1	.500	10	1	0	1-1	17	22	20	1	2	10-3	10	9.53	45	.314	.405	0-0	—	0	86	-10	-1.1
	NY N	0	0	—	6	0	0	0-0	12	8	7	1	0	9-0	11	3.00	134	.186	.321	1-0	.000	-0		0	0.0
1994	NY N	3	2	.600	37	0	0	2-3	47.1	34	15	4	3	13-2	48	2.66	157	.200	.269	4-1	.000	-0		8	0.8
1995	NY N	1	2	.333	12	0	0	0-0	16	18	15	3	0	6-2	14	7.88	51	.273	.329	0-0	—	0		-7	-1.1
	NY A	0	0	—	11	0	0	0-0	17.1	19	4	1	2	9-2	11	2.08	222	.279	.380	0-0	—	0		5	0.3
1997	Sea A	0	1	.000	16	0	0	0-1	18.1	19	13	3	0	17-1	18	5.40	83	.275	.409	1-0	.000	-0		-2	-0.1
1999	NY N	0	0	—	12	0	0	0-0	18.2	19	12	5	2	4-1	25	5.79	76	.264	.316	1-0	1.000	0*		-3	-0.1
2000	Pit N	2	2	.500	43	0	0	0-2	58.2	50	23	6	0	32-4	39	3.38	136	.240	.339	3-1	.000	-0		9	0.4
2001	Pit N	3	2	.600	71	0	0	2-5	79.2	60	32	4	5	26-3	80	3.39	133	.211	.281	1-0	.000	-0		10	0.5
2002	Pit N	0	0	—	13	0	0	0-1	13	20	11	5	1	5-0	4	7.62	55	.364	.426	0-0	—	0		-4	-0.2
2003	Cin N	0	2	.000	9	0	0	0-1	10.2	21	20	7	0	4-0	12	12.66	34	.389	.431	0-0	—	0		-12	-1.8
Total	10	10	12	.455	241	1	0	5-14	309.2	292	174	40	15	138-18	273	4.56	96	.251	.333	11-2	.091	-1	86	-7	-2.5

MANZANILLO, RAVELO Ravelo (Adams) B 10.17.1963 San Pedro De Macoris, D.R. BL/TL 6/210# d9.25 b-Josias

Year	Tm Lg	W	L	Pct	G	GS	CG-Sho	SV-BS	IP	H	R	HR	HB	BB-IB	SO	ERA	AERA	OAV	OOB	AB-SH	AVG	PB	Sup	APR	PW
1988	Chi A	0	1	.000	2	2	0	0-0	9.1	7	6	1	1	12-0	10	5.79	69	.212	.435	0-0	—	0	92	-1	-0.1
1994	Pit N	4	2	.667	46	0	0	1-2	50	45	30	4	3	42-5	39	4.14	104	.245	.385	3-0	.667	1		-1	0.0
1995	Pit N	0	0	—	5	0	0	0-0	3.2	3	3	0	1	2-0	1	4.91	88	.231	.375	1-0	.000	-0		-1	0.0
Total	3	4	3	.571	53	2	0	1-2	63	55	39	5	5	56-5	50	4.43	96	.239	.392	4-0	.500	1	92	-3	-0.1

MAPEL, ROLLA Rolla Hamilton "Lefty" B 3.9.1890 Lees Summit, MO D 4.6.1966 San Diego, CA BL/TL 5-11.5/165# d8.31

Year	Tm Lg	W	L	Pct	G	GS	CG-Sho	SV-BS	IP	H	R	HR	HB	BB-IB	SO	ERA	AERA	OAV	OOB	AB-SH	AVG	PB	Sup	APR	PW
1919	StL A	0	3	.000	4	3	2	0	20	17	12	0	3	17	2	4.50	74	.262	.435	6-0	.167	-0	8	-2	-0.3

MARAK, PAUL Paul Patrick B 8.2.1965 Lakenheath, England BR/TR 6-2/175# d9.1

Year	Tm Lg	W	L	Pct	G	GS	CG-Sho	SV-BS	IP	H	R	HR	HB	BB-IB	SO	ERA	AERA	OAV	OOB	AB-SH	AVG	PB	Sup	APR	PW
1990	Atl N	1	2	.333	7	7	1-1	0-0	39	39	16	2	3	19-3	15	3.69	109	.267	.361	11-1	.091	-0	83	2	0.2

MARANDA, GEORGES Georges Henri B 1.15.1932 Levis, PQ, CAN D 7.14.2000 Levis, PQ, CAN BR/TR 6-2/195# d4.26

Year	Tm Lg	W	L	Pct	G	GS	CG-Sho	SV-BS	IP	H	R	HR	HB	BB-IB	SO	ERA	AERA	OAV	OOB	AB-SH	AVG	PB	Sup	APR	PW
1960	SF N	1	4	.200	17	4	0	0	50.2	50	32	6	0	30-7	28	4.62	75	.254	.351	12-0	.167	-0	51	-8	-0.6
1962	Min A	1	3	.250	32	4	0	0	72.2	69	43	10	4	35-3	36	4.46	92	.252	.343	16-0	.250	1	87	-4	0.0
Total	2	2	7	.222	49	8	0	0	123.1	119	75	16	4	65-10	64	4.52	85	.253	.346	28-0	.214	1	70	-12	-0.6

MARBERRY, FIRPO Fredrick B 11.30.1898 Streetman, TX D 6.30.1976 Mexia, TX BR/TR 6-1/190# d8.11 U1

Year	Tm Lg	W	L	Pct	G	GS	CG-Sho	SV-BS	IP	H	R	HR	HB	BB-IB	SO	ERA	AERA	OAV	OOB	AB-SH	AVG	PB	Sup	APR	PW
1923	Was A	4	0	1.000	11	4	2	0	44.2	42	16	1	3	17	18	2.82	133	.258	.339	14-1	.143	-1	148	5	0.3
1924	†Was A	11	12	.478	**50**	14	6	**15**	195.1	190	88	3	9	70	68	3.09	131	.262	.335	59-8	.136	-4	97	18	1.7
1925	†Was A	9	5	.643	**55**	0	0	**15**	93.1	84	50	4	4	45	53	3.47	122	.246	.341	19-2	.263	1		**5**	1.0
1926	Was A	12	7	.632	**64**	5	3	**22**	138	120	55	4	3	66	43	3.00	129	.243	.336	34-2	.176	-1	105	13	2.0
1927	Was A	10	7	.588	56	10	2	9	155.1	177	92	4	3	68	74	4.64	88	.296	.371	41-1	.122	-3	113	-9	-1.4
1928	Was A	13	13	.500	**48**	11	7-1	3	161.1	160	79	4	3	42	76	3.85	104	.268	.319	46-3	.109	-4	90	4	0.1
1929	Was A	19	12	.613	**49**	26	16	**11**	250.1	233	100	6	6	69	121	3.06	139	.252	**.308**	81-5	.235	2	99	33	**4.0**
1930	Was A	15	5	.750	33	22	9-2	1	185	190	92	15	0	53	56	4.09	113	.270	.321	73-4	.329	5	132	12	1.5
1931	Was A	16	4	.800	45	25	11-1	7	219	211	92	13	3	63	88	3.45	124	.252	.307	82-3	.232	1	125	24	2.1
1932	Was A	8	4	.667	**54**	15	8-1	**13**	197.2	202	98	13	2	72	66	4.01	108	.268	.333	60-6	.167	-2	105	7	0.3
1933	Det A	16	11	.593	37	32	15-1	2	238.1	232	98	13	1	61	84	3.29	131	.254	**.302**	90-3	.122	-5	100	29	2.3
1934	†Det A	15	5	.750	38	19	6-1	3	155.2	174	92	12	0	48	64	4.57	96	.276	.327	55-1	.218	2	151	-4	-0.3
1935	Det A	0	1	.000	5	2	1	0	19	22	11	2	0	9	7	4.26	98	.289	.365	5-0	.200	0	62	-1	0.0
1936	NY N	0	0	—	1	0	0	0	0.1	1	1	0	0	0	0	0.00	—	.500	.500	1-0	.000	-0		0	0.0
	Was A	0	2	.000	5	1	0	0	14	11	7	2	1	3	4	3.86	124	.208	.263	2-1	.000	-0	37	2	0.1
Total	14	148	88	.627	551	186	86-7	101	2067.1	2049	971	96	38	686	822	3.63	116	.262	.325	668-34	.192	-8	114	138	13.7

MARBET, WALT Walter William B 9.13.1890 Plymouth Co., IA D 9.24.1956 Hohenwald, TN BR/TR 6-1/175# d6.17

Year	Tm Lg	W	L	Pct	G	GS	CG-Sho	SV-BS	IP	H	R	HR	HB	BB-IB	SO	ERA	AERA	OAV	OOB	AB-SH	AVG	PB	Sup	APR	PW
1913	StL N	0	1	.000	3	1	0	0	3.1	9	7	0	0	4	1	16.20	20	.500	.591	0-0	—	0	116	-5	-0.8

MARCHILDON, PHIL Philip Joseph "Babe" B 10.25.1913 Penetanguishene, ON, CAN D 1.10.1997 Toronto, ON, CAN BR/TR 5-11/175# d9.22 Mil 1943-45

Year	Tm Lg	W	L	Pct	G	GS	CG-Sho	SV-BS	IP	H	R	HR	HB	BB-IB	SO	ERA	AERA	OAV	OOB	AB-SH	AVG	PB	Sup	APR	PW
1940	Phi A	0	2	.000	2	2	1	0	10	12	9	1	0	8	4	7.20	62	.286	.400	2-1	.000	-0	30	-3	-0.4

Year	Tm Lg	W	L	Pct	G	GS	CG-Sho	SV-BS	IP	H	R	HR	HB	BB-IB	SO	ERA	AERA	OAV	OOB	AB-SH	AVG	PB	Sup	APR	PW
1941	Phi A	10	15	.400	30	27	14-1	0	204.1	188	94	15	3	118	74	3.57	117	.245	.348	66-8	.167	1	92	13	1.4
1942	Phi A	17	14	.548	38	31	18-1	1	244	215	126	14	4	140	110	4.20	90	.235	.339	84-5	.238	3	91	-8	-0.7
1945	Phi A	0	1	.000	3	2	0	0	9	5	5	0	0	11	2	4.00	86	.179	.410	2-0	.500	1	112	-1	0.0
1946	Phi A	13	16	.448	36	29	16-1	1	226.2	197	104	14	4	114	95	3.49	101	.237	.332	75-7	.067	-6	92	1	-0.6
1947	Phi A	19	9	.679	35	35	21-2	0	276.2	228	110	15	7	141	128	3.22	118	.224	.323	98-12	.153	-2	120	19	1.5
1948	Phi A	9	15	.375	33	30	12-1	0	226.1	214	133	19	4	131	66	4.53	95	.251	.353	72-3	.069	-5	92	-10	-1.5
1949	Phi A	0	3	.000	7	6	0	0	16	24	23	3	1	19	2	11.81	35	.358	.506	6-0	.167	-0	105	-14	-2.0
1950	Bos A	0	0	—	1	0	0	0	1.1	1	1	0	0	2	0	6.75	73	.200	.429	0-0	—	0		0	0.0
Total	9	68	75	.476	185	162	82-6	2	1214.1	1084	605	81	23	684	481	3.93	100	.240	.342	405-36	.143	-10	97	-3	-2.3
MARCUM, JOHNNY John Alfred "Footsie" B 9.9.1909 Campbellsburg, KY D 9.10.1984 Louisville, KY BL/TR 5-11/197# d9.7																									
1933	Phi A	3	2	.600	5	5	4-2	0	37	28	12	0	0	20	14	1.95	220	.200	.300	12-0	.167	0	115	9	1.1
1934	Phi A	14	11	.560	37	31	17-2	0	232	257	131	13	4	88	92	4.50	97	.280	.346	112-2	.268	6*	116	-3	0.2
1935	Phi A	17	12	.586	39	27	19-2	3	242.2	256	125	9	2	83	99	4.08	111	.268	.328	119-4	.311	9*	116	13	2.1
1936	Bos A	8	13	.381	31	23	9-1	1	174	194	100	14	0	52	57	4.81	110	.281	.332	88-3	.205	1*	78	12	1.2
1937	Bos A	13	11	.542	37	23	9-1	3	183.2	230	104	17	2	47	59	4.85	98	.306	.348	86-2	.267	5*	95	2	0.7
1938	Bos A	5	6	.455	15	11	7	0	92.1	113	49	11	0	25	25	4.09	120	.298	.342	37-0	.135	-1*	86	8	0.7
1939	StL A	2	5	.286	12	6	2	0	47.2	66	43	12	1	10	14	7.74	63	.332	.367	22-0	.455	3*	66	-13	-1.2
	Chi A	3	3	.500	19	6	2	0	90	125	66	15	0	19	32	6.00	79	.326	.357	57-0	.281	2*	140	-12	-0.5
	Year	5	8	.385	31	12	4	0	137.2	191	74	27	1	29	46	6.60	72	.328	.361	79-0	.329	6	103	-25	-1.7
Total	7	65	63	.508	195	132	69-8	7	1099.1	1269	630	91	9	344	392	4.66	101	.287	.340	533-11	.265	25	101	16	4.3
MARENTETTE, LEO Leo John B 2.18.1941 Detroit, MI BR/TR 6-2/200# d9.26																									
1965	Det A	0	0	—	2	0	0	0	3	1	0	0	0	1-0	3	0.00	—	.111	.200	0-0	—	0		1	0.1
1969	Mon N	0	0	—	3	0	0	0-1	5.1	9	4	1	0	1-1	4	6.75	55	.391	.400	1-0	.000	-0		-2	-0.1
Total	2	0	0	—	5	0	0	0-1	8.1	10	4	1	0	2-1	7	4.32	83	.313	.343	1-0	.000	-0		-1	0.0
MARGONERI, JOE Joseph Emanuel B 1.13.1930 Somerset, PA BL/TL 6/185# d4.25																									
1956	NY N	6	6	.500	23	13	2	0	91.2	88	45	12	0	49-3	49	3.93	96	.254	.343	29-3	.103	-1	91	-1	-0.3
1957	NY N	1	1	.500	13	2	1	0	34.1	44	23	1	1	21-2	18	5.24	75	.314	.402	8-1	.000	-1	101	-5	-0.4
Total	2	7	7	.500	36	15	3	0	126	132	68	13	1	70-5	67	4.29	89	.271	.361	37-4	.081	-2	92	-6	-0.7
MARICHAL, JUAN Juan Antonio (Sanchez) "Manito" B 10.20.1937 Laguna Verde, D.R. BR/TR 6/185# d7.19 HF1983																									
1960	SF N	6	2	.750	11	11	6-1	0	81.1	59	29	5	0	28-1	58	2.66	131	.200	.269	31-1	.129	0	131	8	0.7
1961	SF N	13	10	.565	29	27	9-3	0	185	183	88	24	2	48-5	124	3.89	98	.257	.305	59-5	.119	-2*	117	-1	-0.4
1962	†SF N★	18	11	.621	37	36	18-3	1	262.2	233	112	34	3	90-5	153	3.36	113	.234	.299	89-7	.236	4*	108	12	1.6
1963	SF N☆	**25**	8	.758	41	40	18-5	0	**321.1**	259	102	27	2	61-6	248	2.41	133	.216	.255	112-4	.179	3*	116	29	3.1
1964	SF N★	21	8	.724	33	33	**22**-4	0	269	241	89	18	1	52-8	206	2.48	144	.236	.272	97-6	.144	-1	132	30	3.1
1965	SF N★	22	13	.629	39	37	24-**10**	1	295.1	224	78	27	4	46-4	240	2.13	**169**	.205	.239	98-9	.173	1	92	**48**	**6.0**
1966	SF N★	25	6	**.806**	37	36	25-4	0	307.1	228	88	32	5	36-3	222	2.23	165	**.202**	**.230**	112-5	.250	6	111	49	5.8
1967	SF N★	14	10	.583	26	26	18-2	0	202.1	195	79	20	1	42-9	166	2.76	119	.249	.287	79-2	.177	3	138	9	1.3
1968	SF N★	**26**	9	.743	38	38	**30**-5	0	**326**	295	106	21	6	46-9	218	2.43	121	.238	.268	123-9	.163	1	144	19	2.5
1969	SF N☆	21	11	.656	37	36	27-**8**	0-0	299.2	244	90	15	6	54-7	205	**2.10**	**167**	.222	.261	109-3	.138	-1*	92	45	5.0
1970	SF N	12	10	.545	34	33	14-1	0-0	242.2	269	128	28	1	48-3	123	4.12	97	.277	.309	85-5	.059	-6	129	-5	-0.9
1971	†SF N★	18	11	.621	37	37	18-4	0-0	279	244	113	27	3	56-6	159	2.94	116	.233	.273	105-7	.133	0	132	13	1.5
1972	SF N	6	16	.273	25	24	6	0-0	165	176	82	15	3	46-7	72	3.71	94	.277	.327	51-1	.196	1	84	-6	-0.7
1973	SF N	11	15	.423	34	32	9-2	0-0	207.1	231	104	22	1	37-7	87	3.82	100	.277	.307	69-7	.188	1	100	-1	0.2
1974	Bos A	5	1	.833	11	9	0	0-0	57.1	61	32	3	2	14-1	21	4.87	79	.270	.317	0-0	—	0	137	-5	-0.5
1975	LA N	0	1	.000	2	2	0	0-0	6	11	9	2	0	5-1	1	13.50	25	.407	.500	2-0	.000	-0	155	-7	-0.8
Total	16	243	142	.631	471	457	244-52	2-0	3507.1	3153	1329	320	40	709-82	2303	2.89	122	.237	.277	1221-71	.165	10	116	237	27.5
MARION, DAN Donald G. "Rube" B 7.31.1890 Cleveland, OH D 1.18.1933 Milwaukee, WI BR/TR 6-1/187# d4.23																									
1914	Bro F	3	2	.600	17	9	4	0	89.1	97	52	1	6	38	41	3.93	73	.281	.362	36-0	.194	-2	125	-11	-0.8
1915	Bro F	12	9	.571	35	25	15-2	0	208.1	193	92	1	3	64	46	3.20	85	.248	.308	74-2	.176	-2	147	-9	-1.1
Total	2	15	11	.577	52	34	19-2	0	297.2	290	144	2	9	102	87	3.42	81	.258	.325	110-2	.182	-3	140	-20	-1.9
MARKELL, DUKE Harry Duquesne (b: Harry Duquesne Makowsky) B 8.17.1923 Paris, France D 6.14.1984 Ft.Lauderdale, FL BR/TR 6-1.5/209# d9.6																									
1951	StL A	1	1	.500	5	2	1	0	21.1	25	16	3	0	20	10	6.33	69	.298	.433	6-0	.167	-0	81	-4	-0.3
MARKLE, CLIFF Clifford Monroe B 5.3.1894 Dravosburg, PA D 5.24.1974 Temple City, CA BR/TR 5-9/163# d9.18																									
1915	NY A	2	0	1.000	3	2	2	0	23	15	3	1	0	6	12	0.39	750	.185	.241	4-1	.000	0	124	6	0.5
1916	NY A	4	3	.571	11	7	3-1	0	45.2	41	26	0	4	31	14	4.53	64	.256	.390	13-1	.000	-1	138	-7	-1.2
1921	Cin N	2	6	.250	10	6	5	0	67	75	36	0	0	20	23	3.76	95	.291	.342	24-0	.125	-2	69	-2	-0.4
1922	Cin N	4	5	.444	25	3	2-1	0	75.2	75	41	3	0	33	34	3.81	105	.268	.345	20-0	.150	-0	95	1	0.1
1924	NY A	0	3	.000	7	3	0	0	23.1	29	26	5	0	20	7	8.87	47	.333	.458	8-0	.000	-1	95	-12	-1.4
Total	5	12	17	.414	56	21	12-2	0	234.2	235	132	9	4	110	90	4.10	87	.271	.356	69-2	.087	-5	99	-14	-2.4
MARLOWE, DICK Richard Burton B 6.27.1929 Hickory, NC D 12.30.1968 Toledo, OH BR/TR 6-2/170# d9.19																									
1951	Det A	0	1	.000	2	1	0	0	1.2	5	6	0	0	2	1	32.40	13	.500	.583	0-0	—	0	21	-5	-0.8
1952	Det A	0	2	.000	4	1	0	0	11	21	10	1	0	3	3	7.36	52	.420	.453	2-0	.000	-0	23	-4	-0.7
1953	Det A	6	7	.462	42	11	2	0	119.2	152	74	13	2	42	52	5.26	77	.319	.377	32-1	.219	-0	77	-14	-1.4
1954	Det A	5	4	.556	38	2	0	2	84	76	45	11	0	40	39	4.18	88	.244	.326	18-0	.167	0	60	-5	-0.5
1955	Det A	1	0	1.000	4	1	1	1	15	12	4	1	0	4-1	9	1.80	213	.218	.271	4-0	.000	-0	231	3	0.2
1956	Det A	1	1	.500	7	1	0	0	11	12	8	1	0	9-0	4	5.73	72	.279	.404	1-0	.000	-0	43	-2	-0.3
	Chi A	0	0	—	1	0	0	0	1	2	1	1	0	1-0	0	9.00	46	.500	.600	0-0	—	0		-1	0.0
	Year	1	1	.500	8	1	0	0	12	14	11	2	0	10-0	4	6.00	69	.298	.421	1-0	.000	-0	43	-3	-0.3
Total	6	13	15	.464	98	17	3	3	243.1	280	148	28	2	101-1	108	4.99	78	.295	.362	57-1	.175	-1	77	-28	-3.5
MARONE, LOU Louis Stephen B 12.3.1945 San Diego, CA BR/TL 5-11/185# d5.30																									
1969	Pit N	1	1	.500	29	0	0	0-1	35.1	24	10	2	2	13-2	25	2.55	137	.195	.281	0-0	—	0		4	0.2
1970	Pit N	0	0	—	1	0	0	0-0	2.1	2	1	1	0	0-0	0	3.86	101	.222	.222	0-0	—	0		0	0.0
Total	2	1	1	.500	30	0	0	0-1	37.2	26	11	3	2	13-2	25	2.63	134	.197	.277	0-0	—	0		4	0.2
MAROTH, MIKE Michael Warren B 8.17.1977 Orlando, FL BL/TL 6/180# d6.8																									
2002	Det A	6	10	.375	21	21	0	0-0	128.2	136	68	7	2	36-1	58	4.48	96	.276	.326	6-0	.167	-0	71	-1	-0.1
2003	Det A	9	21	.300	33	33	1	0-0	193.1	231	131	34	8	50-2	87	5.73	75	.299	.344	2-1	.500	1	100	-30	-3.6
Total	2	15	31	.326	54	54	1	0-0	322	367	199	41	10	86-3	145	5.23	83	.290	.337	8-1	.250	1	89	-31	-3.7
MARQUARD, RUBE Richard William B 10.9.1886 Cleveland, OH D 6.1.1980 Baltimore, MD BB/TL 6-3/180# d9.25 HF1971																									
1908	NY N	0	1	.000	1	1	0	0	5	6	5	0	1	2	2	3.60	67	.316	.409	1-0	.000	-0	29	-1	-0.3
1909	NY N	5	13	.278	29	21	8	1	173	155	81	2	9	73	109	2.60	98	.248	.335	54-3	.148	-1	76	-3	-0.5
1910	NY N	4	4	.500	13	8	2	0	70.2	65	35	2	4	40	52	4.46	67	.254	.363	27-2	.111	-2	122	-7	-0.9
1911	†NY N	24	7	**.774**	45	33	22-5	3	277.2	221	98	9	4	106	**237**	2.50	135	.219	.296	104-3	.163	-1	110	28	2.7
1912	†NY N	**26**	11	.703	43	38	22-1	1	294.2	286	112	9	3	80	175	2.57	132	.255	.306	96-9	.219	2	119	30	3.5
1913	†NY N	23	10	.697	42	33	20-4	3	288	248	100	10	3	49	151	2.50	125	.237	.273	105-2	.219	2	106	23	2.4
1914	NY N	12	22	.353	39	33	15-4	2	268	261	117	9	2	47	92	3.06	87	.262	.297	84-5	.179	-1	79	-14	-1.8
1915	NY N	9	8	.529	27	21	10-2	2	169	178	85	8	1	33	79	3.73	69	.272	.308	55-2	.109	-3	130	-21	-2.4
	Bro N	2	2	.500	6	3	0	1	24.2	29	17	0	0	5	13	6.20	45	.276	.309	8-1	.125	-0	80	-7	-1.1
	Year	11	10	.524	33	24	10-2	3	193.2	207	20	8	1	38	92	4.04	64	.273	.308	63-3	.111	-3	123	-27	-3.5
1916	†Bro N	13	6	.684	36	21	15-2	5	205	169	54	2	0	38	107	1.58	170	.229	.267	63-2	.143	-1	102	23	2.1
1917	Bro N	19	12	.613	37	29	14-2	0	232.2	200	84	5	0	60	117	2.55	110	.232	.282	75-3	.200	0	83	6	0.6
1918	Bro N	9	18	.333	34	29	19-4	0	239	231	97	7	1	59	89	2.64	106	.260	.307	76-1	.171	-2	80	2	-0.1
1919	Bro N	3	3	.500	8	7	3	0	59	54	17	1	0	10	29	2.29	130	.244	.277	23-1	.261	1	88	5	0.6
1920	†Bro N	10	7	.588	28	26	10-1	0	189.2	181	83	5	1	35	89	3.23	99	.251	.287	59-3	.169	-1	110	1	-0.3

Year	Tm Lg	W	L	Pct	G	GS	CG-Sho	SV-BS	IP	H	R	HR	HB	BB-IB	SO	ERA	AERA	OAV	OOB	AB-SH	AVG	PB	Sup	APR	PW
1921	Cin N	17	14	.548	39	36	18-2	0	265.2	291	123	8	7	50	88	3.39	106	.285	.323	95-3	.200	-1	105	6	0.4
1922	Bos N	11	15	.423	39	25	7	1	198	255	131	12	0	66	57	5.09	79	.322	.374	63-3	.222	-1	71	-21	-2.3
1923	Bos N	11	14	.440	38	29	11-3	0	239	265	127	10	2	65	78	3.73	107	.288	.337	86-5	.140	-6	102	4	-0.2
1924	Bos N	1	2	.333	6	6	1	0	36	33	17	3	1	13	10	3.00	127	.254	.326	11-0	.273	0	70	2	0.2
1925	Bos N	2	8	.200	26	8	0	0	72	105	60	5	0	27	19	5.75	70	.341	.394	22-0	.136	-1	108	-17	-2.1
Total	18	201	177	.532	536	407	197-30	19	3306.2	3233	1443	107	39	858	1593	3.08	103	.260	.310	1107-48	.179	-17	99	39	0.5
MARQUEZ, ISIDRO Isidro (Espinoza) B 5.15.1965 Navojoa, Mexico BR/TR 6-3/190# d4.26																									
1995	Chi A	0	1	.000	7	0	0	0-0	6.2	9	5	3	0	2-0	8	6.75	66	.321	.367	0-0	—	0		-2	-0.2
MARQUIS, JIM James Milburn B 11.18.1900 Yoakum, TX D 8.5.1992 Jackson, CA BR/TR 5-11/174# d8.8																									
1925	NY A	0	0		2	0	0	0	7.1	12	8	1	0	6	0	9.82	43	.414	.514	2-0	.000	-0		-4	-0.2
MARQUIS, JASON Jason Scott B 8.21.1978 Manhasset, NY BL/TR 6-1/185# d6.6																									
2000	Atl N	1	0	1.000	15	0	0	0-1	23.1	23	16	4	1	12-1	17	5.01	91	.261	.353	2-0	.000	-0		-2	-0.1
2001	Atl N	5	6	.455	38	16	0	0-2	129.1	113	62	14	4	59-4	98	3.48	127	.234	.320	31-2	.032	-2*	65	10	0.6
2002	Atl N	8	9	.471	22	22	0	0-0	114.1	127	66	19	3	49-3	84	5.04	81	.283	.356	38-3	.132	-0*	100	-10	-1.3
2003	Atl N	0	0	—	21	2	0	1-0	40.2	43	27	3	2	18-2	19	5.53	76	.270	.346	2-2	.500	1	167	-6	-0.2
Total	4	14	15	.483	96	40	0	1-3	307.2	306	171	40	10	138-10	218	4.45	96	.260	.340	73-7	.096	-2	88	-8	-1.0
MARRERO, CONNIE Conrado Eugenio (Ramos) B 5.1.1911 Las Villas, Cuba BR/TR 5-5/158# d4.21																									
1950	Was A	6	10	.375	27	19	8-1	1	152	159	84	17	4	55	63	4.50	100	.269	.335	49-5	.122	-1	85	1	-0.1
1951	Was A☆	11	9	.550	25	25	16-2	0	187	198	87	8	3	71	66	3.90	105	.268	.335	61-3	.164	-2	100	6	0.3
1952	Was A	11	8	.579	22	22	16-2	0	184.1	175	68	9	4	53	77	2.88	123	.249	.305	63-5	.079	-5	85	14	0.7
1953	Was A	8	7	.533	22	20	10-2	2	145.2	130	56	14	5	48	65	3.03	129	.241	.309	48-1	.125	-2	100	14	1.1
1954	Was A	3	6	.333	22	8	1	0	66.1	74	37	12	0	22	26	4.75	75	.287	.340	15-0	.000	-1	102	-8	-1.1
Total	5	39	40	.494	118	94	51-7	3	735.1	736	332	60	16	249	297	3.67	108	.260	.323	236-14	.114	-11	94	27	0.9
MARROW, BUCK Charles Kennon B 8.29.1909 Tarboro, NC D 11.21.1982 Newport News, VA BR/TR 6-4/200# d7.3																									
1932	Det A	2	5	.286	18	7	2	1	63.2	70	40	6	6	29	31	4.81	98	.278	.366	19-1	.158	-0	67	0	0.0
1937	Bro N	1	2	.333	6	3	1	0	16.1	19	13	2	0	9	2	6.61	61	.284	.368	5-0	.000	-1	107	-4	-0.7
1938	Bro N	0	1	.000	15	0	0	0	19.2	23	10	1	3	11	6	4.58	85	.291	.398	1-0	.000	-0		-1	0.0
Total	3	3	8	.273	39	10	3	1	99.2	112	63	9	9	49	39	5.06	88	.281	.373	25-1	.120	-1	79	-5	-0.7
MARS, ED Edward M. B 12.4.1866 Chicago, IL D 12.9.1941 Chicago, IL 5-9/166# d8.12																									
1890	Syr AA	9	5	.643	16	14	14	0	121.1	132	80	2	5	49	59	4.67	76	.269	.341	51	.275	4	151	-14	-0.9
MARSHALL, CUDDLES Clarence Westly B 4.28.1925 Bellingham, WA BR/TR 6-3/200# d4.24																									
1946	NY A	3	4	.429	23	11	1	0	81	96	49	4	0	56	32	5.33	65	.308	.413	28-1	.143	-1	138	-14	-1.2
1948	NY A	0	0	—	1	0	0	0	1	0	0	0	0	3	0	0.00	—	.000	.500	0-0	—	0		0	0.0
1949	NY A	3	0	1.000	21	2	0	3	49.1	48	31	3	2	48	13	5.11	79	.259	.417	9-1	.111	-0	100	-6	-0.4
1950	StL A	1	3	.250	28	2	0	1	53.2	72	52	1	1	51	24	7.88	63	.321	.449	12-0	.333	0	118	-15	-1.0
Total	4	7	7	.500	73	15	1	4	185	216	132	8	3	158	69	5.98	67	.298	.426	49-2	.184	-1	121	-35	-2.6
MARSHALL, MIKE Michael Grant B 1.15.1943 Adrian, MI BR/TR 5-10/180# d5.31																									
1967	Det A	1	3	.250	37	0	0	10	59	51	15	6	2	20-1	41	1.98	165	.233	.303	9-2	.222	0		8	0.9
1969	Sea A	3	10	.231	20	14	3-1	0-0	87.2	99	54	8	2	35-2	47	5.13	71	.281	.347	27-1	.259	3*	87	-13	-1.3
1970	Hou N	0	1	.000	4	0	0	0-0	5.1	8	5	0	1	4-0	5	8.44	46	.400	.520	0-0	—	0		-3	-0.4
	Mon N	3	7	.300	24	5	0	3-0	64.2	56	34	4	0	29-4	38	3.48	118	.225	.305	11-2	.091	0	87	2	0.4
	Year	3	8	.273	28	5	0	3-0	70	64	38	4	1	33-4	43	3.86	106	.238	.322	11-2	.091	0	88	0	0.0
1971	Mon N	5	8	.385	66	0	0	23-7	111.1	100	56	9	4	50-13	85	4.28	82	.247	.333	16-2	.188	0		-8	-1.1
1972	Mon N	14	8	.636	**65**	0	0	18-7	116	82	26	3	2	47-7	95	1.78	199	.202	.286	22-0	.136	0		**22**	4.9
1973	Mon N	14	11	.560	**92**	0	0	**31-12**	179	163	62	10	4	75-12	124	2.66	143	.252	.331	33-4	.242	1		**22**	4.1
1974	†LA N★	15	12	.556	**106**	0	0	**21-12**	208.1	191	66	9	1	56-1	143	2.42	141	.247	.297	34-2	.235	1		**24**	3.6
1975	LA N☆	9	14	.391	57	0	0	13-8	109.1	98	46	8	4	39-4	64	3.29	104	.242	.311	15-4	.067	-1*		1	0.2
1976	LA N	4	3	.571	30	0	0	8-5	62.2	64	33	2	1	25-2	39	4.45	76	.270	.340	5-0	.000	0		-7	-0.8
	Atl N	2	1	.667	24	0	0	6-2	36.2	35	15	4	1	14-0	17	3.19	119	.259	.329	6-1	.167	0		2	0.3
	Year	6	4	.600	54	0	0	14-7	99.1	99	48	6	2	39-2	56	3.99	89	.266	.336	11-1	.091	1		-4	-0.5
1977	Atl N	1	0	1.000	4	0	0	0-0	6	12	6	1	0	2-0	6	9.00	50	.400	.438	1-0	1.000	0		-2	-0.3
	Tex A	2	2	.500	12	4	0	1-3	35.2	42	19	0	2	13-1	18	4.04	101	.304	.373	0-0	—	0	170	0	0.0
1978	Min A	10	12	.455	54	0	0	21-6	99	80	31	3	1	37-1	56	2.45	156	.225	.299	0-0	—	0		15	3.2
1979	Min A	10	15	.400	**90**	1	0	**32-10**	142.2	132	47	8	4	48-2	81	2.65	166	.254	.319	0-0	—	0	62	26	5.4
1980	Min A	1	3	.250	18	0	0	1-2	32.1	42	23	2	2	12-1	13	6.12	71	.323	.381	0-0	—	0		-5	-0.5
1981	NY N	3	2	.600	20	0	0	0-0	31	26	10	2	0	8-1	8	2.61	133	.224	.272	0-0	—	0		3	0.6
Total	14	97	112	.464	723	24	3-1	188-74	1386.2	1281	548	79	31	514-52	880	3.14	118	.249	.319	179-18	.196	6	103	87	19.2
MARSHALL, RUBE Roy De Verne "Cy" B 1.19.1890 Salineville, OH D 6.11.1980 Dover, OH BR/TR 5-11/170# d9.28																									
1912	Phi N	0	1	.000	2	1	0	0	3	12	11	0	0	1	2	21.00	17	.632	.650	0-0	—	0	40	-6	-0.9
1913	Phi N	0	1	.000	14	1	0	1	45.1	54	29	2	1	22	18	4.57	73	.297	.376	11-0	.091	-1	45	-6	-0.4
1914	Phi N	6	7	.462	27	17	7	1	134.1	144	77	2	5	50	49	3.75	78	.279	.349	43-3	.140	-2	123	-10	-1.1
1915	Buf F	2	1	.667	21	4	2	0	59.1	62	34	1	2	33	21	3.94	71	.281	.379	17-1	.294	1*	100	-8	-0.4
Total	4	8	10	.444	64	23	9	2	242	272	151	5	8	106	90	4.17	72	.290	.367	71-4	.169	-2	112	-30	-2.8
MARTE, DAMASO Damaso (Sabinon) B 2.14.1975 Santo Domingo, D.R. BL/TL 6/170# d6.30																									
1999	Sea A	0	1	.000	5	0	0	0-0	8.2	16	9	3	0	6-0	3	9.35	51	.390	.468	0-0	—	0		-4	-0.4
2001	Pit N	0	1	.000	23	0	0	0-0	36.1	34	21	5	3	12-3	39	4.71	95	.250	.320	4-0	.000	-0		-1	-0.1
2002	Chi A	1	1	.500	68	0	0	10-2	60.1	44	19	5	4	18-2	72	2.83	159	.204	.276	1-0	.000	-0		12	0.7
2003	Chi A	4	2	.667	71	0	0	11-7	79.2	50	16	3	3	34-6	87	1.58	288	.185	.280	0-0	—	0		**26**	2.4
Total	4	5	5	.500	167	0	0	21-9	185	144	65	16	10	70-11	201	2.97	153	.217	.299	5-0	.000	-1		33	2.6
MARTIN, PHONNEY Alphonse Case B 8.4.1845 New York, NY D 5.24.1933 Hollis, NY 5-7/148# d4.26 M1 ▲																									
1872	Tro NA	1	2	.333	8	3	0	0	37.1	70	59	0		2	2	4.82	75	.350	.356	119	.303	1*	95	-5	-0.2
	Eck NA	2	7	.222	10	9	9	0	85	143	106	1		9	3	3.92	87	.326	.339	78	.192	-1*	59	-7	-0.5
	Year	3	9	.250	18	12	9	0	122.1	213	111	1		11	5	4.19	83	.333	.345	197	.259	-0	68	-14	-0.7
1873	Mut NA	0	1	.000	6	1	1	0	34	50	37	0		6	1	3.44	92	.292	.316	140	.221	-0*	113	-1	-0.1
Total	2 NA	3	10	.231	24	13	10	0	156.1	263	202	1		17	6	4.03	84	.325	.339	337	.243	-1	72	-13	-0.8
MARTIN, BARNEY Barnes Robertson B 3.3.1923 Columbia, SC D 10.30.1997 Columbia, SC BR/TR 5-11/170# d4.22 s-Jerry																									
1953	Cin N	0	0	—	1	0	0	0	2	3	2	0	0	1	1	9.00	48	.333	.400	0-0	—	0		-1	0.0
MARTIN, RENIE Donald Renie B 8.30.1955 Dover, DE BR/TR 6-4/190# d5.9																									
1979	KC A	0	3	.000	25	0	0	5-2	34.2	32	20	1	1	14-3	25	5.19	82	.248	.322	0-0	—	0		-2	-0.2
1980	†KC A	10	10	.500	32	20	2	2-0	137.1	133	84	18	1	70-2	68	4.39	92	.255	.342	0-0	—	0	116	-9	-1.2
1981	†KC A	4	5	.444	29	0	0	4-1	61.2	55	25	2	0	29-7	25	2.77	130	.244	.322	0-0	—	0		4	0.7
1982	SF N	7	10	.412	29	25	1	0-0	141.1	148	91	14	0	64-9	63	4.65	77	.274	.347	49-6	.265	3*	119	-20	-1.8
1983	SF N	2	4	.333	37	6	0	1-0	94.1	95	50	11	3	51-9	43	4.20	84	.268	.363	26-1	.346	4	108	-7	0.1
1984	SF N	1	1	.500	12	0	0	0-1	23.1	29	13	2	0	16-0	8	3.86	91	.305	.405	6-0	.500	1		-2	0.0
	Phi N	0	2	.000	9	0	0	0-1	15.2	17	12	2	0	12-4	5	4.60	79	.274	.392	2-0	.000	-0		-3	-0.3
	Year	1	3	.250	21	0	0	0-2	39	46	29	4	0	28-4	13	4.15	86	.293	.400	8-0	.375	1		-5	-0.3
Total	6	24	35	.407	173	51	3	12-5	508.1	509	295	50	5	256-34	237	4.27	88	.264	.348	83-7	.301	8	117	-39	-2.7
MARTIN, SPEED Elwood Good B 9.15.1893 Wawawai, WA D 6.14.1983 Lemon Grove, CA BR/TR 6/165# d7.5																									
1917	StL A	0	2	.000	9	2	0	0	15.2	20	13	0	0	5	5	5.74	45	.339	.391	2-0	.000	-0*	125	-5	-0.6
1918	Chi N	5	2	.714	9	5	4-1	1	53.2	47	19	0	1	14	16	1.84	151	.246	.301	16-1	.188	-0	54	4	0.6
1919	Chi N	8	8	.500	35	14	7-2	2	163.2	158	58	2	4	52	54	2.47	117	.259	.321	44-5	.182	-1	95	8	0.8
1920	Chi N	4	15	.211	35	13	6	2	136	165	96	2	1	50	44	4.83	66	.305	.365	44-1	.159	-0	102	-26	-3.3

Year	Tm Lg	W	L	Pct	G	GS	CG-Sho	SV-BS	IP	H	R	HR	HB	BB-IB	SO	ERA	AERA	OAV	OOB	AB-SH	AVG	PB	Sup	APR	PW
1921	Chi N	11	15	.423	37	28	13-1	1	217.1	245	115	12	2	68	86	4.35	88	.298	.353	73-2	.233	1	91	-10	-0.8
1922	Chi N	1	0	1.000	1	1	0	0	6	10	5	0	0	2	2	7.50	56	.385	.429	1-0	.000	0	136	-2	-0.2
Total	6	29	42	.408	126	63	30-4	6	592.1	645	306	16	8	191	207	3.78	87	.287	.344	180-9	.194	-0	95	-31	-3.5
MARTIN, FRED Fred Turner B 6.27.1915 Williams, OK D 6.11.1979 Chicago, IL BR/TR 6-1/185# d4.21 C6																									
1946	StL N	2	1	.667	6	3	2	0	28.2	29	13	0	0	8	19	4.08	85	.254	.303	11-0	.273	0	149	-1	-0.1
1949	StL N	6	0	1.000	21	5	3	0	70	65	24	3	0	20	30	2.44	170	.243	.295	20-1	.300	1	144	12	1.0
1950	StL N	4	2	.667	30	2	0	0	63.1	87	43	4	1	30	19	5.12	84	.331	.401	15-1	.267	1*	31	-7	-0.4
Total	3	12	3	.800	57	10	5	0	162	181	80	7	1	58	68	3.78	108	.281	.341	46-2	.283	2	118	4	0.5
MARTIN, DOC Harold Winthrop B 9.23.1887 Roxbury, MA D 4.14.1935 Milton, MA BR/TR 5-11/165# d10.7																									
1908	Phi A	0	1	.000	1	1	0	0	2	2	4	0	1	3	2	13.50	19	.286	.545	1-0	.000	-0	27	-2	-0.4
1911	Phi A	1	1	.500	11	3	1	0	38	40	26	1	5	17	21	4.50	70	.272	.367	14-0	.214	0	145	-7	-0.3
1912	Phi A	0	0	—	2	0	0	0	4.1	5	5	0	1	5	4	10.38	30	.333	.524	3-0	.000	-1		-3	-0.2
Total	3	1	2	.333	14	4	1	0	44.1	47	35	1	7	25	27	5.48	57	.278	.393	18-0	.167	-0	115	-12	-0.9
MARTIN, JOHN John Robert B 4.11.1956 Wyandotte, MI BB/TL 6/190# d8.27																									
1980	StL N	2	3	.400	9	5	1	0-0	42	39	20	1	0	9-1	23	4.29	86	.247	.284	11-0	.273	1	77	-2	-0.1
1981	StL N	8	5	.615	17	15	4	0-0	102.2	85	43	10	2	26-0	36	3.42	104	.228	.281	33-7	.212	2*	120	1	0.4
1982	StL N	4	5	.444	24	7	0	0-1	66	56	33	6	0	30-3	21	4.23	86	.230	.314	11-2	.091	-0	104	-4	-0.6
1983	StL N	3	1	.750	26	5	0	0-0	66.1	60	31	6	2	26-4	29	3.53	103	.242	.315	18-2	.222	1	146	0	0.1
	Det A	0	0	—	15	0	0	1-0	13.1	15	11	2	0	4-1	11	7.43	53	.294	.339	0-0	—	0		-5	-0.2
Total	4	17	14	.548	91	32	5	1-1	290.1	255	138	25	4	95-9	120	3.94	92	.238	.300	73-11	.205	3	113	-10	-0.4
MARTIN, MORRIE Morris Webster "Lefty" B 9.3.1922 Dixon, MO BL/TL 6/180# d4.25																									
1949	Bro N	1	3	.250	10	4	0	0	30.2	39	25	5	2	15	15	7.04	58	.320	.403	10-0	.200	-0	43	-9	-1.0
1951	Phi A	11	4	.733	35	13	3-1	0	138	139	70	13	5	63	35	3.78	113	.259	.343	50-4	.220	-1	136	5	0.5
1952	Phi A	0	2	.000	5	5	0	0	25.1	32	19	1	2	15	13	6.39	62	.302	.398	9-0	.111	-1	97	-6	-0.5
1953	Phi A	10	12	.455	58	11	2	7	156.1	158	85	12	8	59	64	4.43	97	.262	.336	42-2	.095	-4	85	-3	-0.8
1954	Phi A	2	4	.333	13	6	2	0	52.2	57	32	9	2	19	24	5.47	71	.278	.339	17-1	.235	0	49	-7	-0.7
	Chi A	5	4	.556	35	2	1	5	70	52	18	5	1	24	31	2.06	182	.210	.281	15-2	.133	-0	106	13	1.7
	Year	7	8	.467	48	8	3	5	122.2	109	23	14	3	43	55	3.52	108	.241	.308	32-3	.188	-0	64	6	1.0
1955	Chi A	2	3	.400	37	0	0	2	52	50	27	4	2	20-2	22	3.63	109	.259	.332	10-0	.300	0		0	0.1
1956	Chi A	1	0	1.000	10	0	0	0	18.1	21	10	1	0	7-0	9	4.91	84	.292	.350	5-0	.200	0		-1	0.0
	Bal A	1	1	.500	9	0	0	0	5	10	6	1	1	2-0	3	10.80	36	.400	.464	0-0	—	0		-4	-0.7
	Year	2	1	.667	19	0	0	0	23.1	31	16	2	1	9-0	12	6.17	66	.320	.380	5-0	.200	0		-5	-0.7
1957	StL N	0	0	—	4	1	0	0	10.2	5	3	0	1	4-0	7	2.53	157	.143	.244	2-0	.000	-0	89	2	0.1
1958	StL N	3	1	.750	17	0	0	0	24.2	19	13	3	2	12-0	16	4.74	87	.211	.317	5-0	.000	-1		-1	-0.2
	Cle A	2	0	1.000	14	0	0	1	18.2	20	7	0	0	8-0	5	2.41	151	.294	.364	0-0	—	0		2	0.2
1959	Chi N	0	0	—	3	0	0	0	2.1	5	5	2	1	1-0	1	19.29	20	.455	.538	0-0	—	0		-4	-0.2
Total	10	38	34	.528	250	42	8-1	15	604.2	607	320	56	27	249-2	245	4.29	95	.262	.340	165-9	.170	-6	96	-13	-1.5
MARTIN, PAT Patrick Francis B 4.13.1892 Brooklyn, NY D 2.4.1949 Brooklyn, NY BL/TL 5-11.5/170# d9.20																									
1919	Phi A	0	2	.000	2	2	1	0	11	11	8	0	0	8	6	4.09	84	.256	.373	3-0	.000	-0	23	-1	-0.3
1920	Phi A	1	4	.200	8	5	2	0	32.1	48	36	2	4	25	14	6.12	66	.364	.478	10-2	.400	1	71	-9	-1.1
Total	2	1	6	.143	10	7	3	0	43.1	59	44	2	4	33	20	5.61	69	.337	.453	13-2	.308	1	58	-10	-1.4
MARTIN, PAUL Paul Charles B 3.10.1932 Brownstown, PA BR/TR 6-6/235# d7.2																									
1955	Pit N	0	1	.000	7	1	0	0	7	13	12	0	1	17-0	3	14.14	29	.464	.633	0-0	—	0	22	-7	-0.9
MARTIN, RAY Raymond Joseph B 3.13.1925 Norwood, MA BR/TR 6-2/177# d8.15 Mil 1943-46																									
1943	Bos N	0	0	—	2	0	0	0	3.1	3	3	0	0	1	1	8.10	42	.231	.286	1-0	.000	-0		-1	-0.1
1947	Bos N	1	0	1.000	1	1	1	0	9	7	1	0	0	4	2	1.00	389	.212	.297	3-0	.000	-0	45	3	0.4
1948	Bos N	0	0	—	2	0	0	0	2.1	0	0	0	0	1	0	0.00	—	.000	.125	0-0	—	0		1	0.0
Total	3	1	0	1.000	5	1	1	0	14.2	10	4	0	0	6	3	2.45	154	.189	.271	4-0	.000	-0	45	3	0.3
MARTIN, TOM Thomas Edgar B 5.21.1970 Charleston, SC BL/TL 6-1/185# d4.2																									
1997	†Hou N	5	3	.625	55	0	0	2-1	56	52	13	2	1	23-2	36	2.09	191	.254	.330	3-0	.000	-0		13	1.7
1998	Cle A	1	1	.500	14	0	0	0-0	14.2	29	21	3	0	12-0	9	12.89	37	.408	.488	0-0	—	0		-12	-1.3
1999	Cle A	0	1	.000	6	0	0	0-0	9.1	13	9	2	0	3-1	8	8.68	58	.325	.364	0-0	—	0		-3	-0.3
2000	Cle A	1	0	1.000	31	0	0	0-0	33.1	32	16	3	1	15-2	21	4.05	123	.254	.336	0-0	—	0		3	0.2
2001	NY N	1	0	1.000	14	0	0	0-0	17	23	22	4	1	10-2	12	10.06	41	.319	.405	3-0	.000	-0		-12	-0.7
2002	TB A	0	0	—	2	0	0	0-0	1.2	5	3	0	0	1-0	1	16.20	28	.500	.545	0-0	—	0		-2	-0.1
2003	LA N	1	2	.333	80	0	0	0-1	51	36	21	6	2	24-4	51	3.53	114	.198	.295	1-0	.000	-0		3	0.2
Total	7	9	7	.563	202	0	0	2-2	183	190	105	20	5	88-11	138	4.92	88	.269	.351	7-0	.000	-1		-10	-0.3
MARTINA, JOE Joseph John "Oyster Joe" B 7.8.1889 New Orleans, LA D 3.22.1962 New Orleans, LA BR/TR 6/183# d4.19																									
1924	†Was A	6	8	.429	24	14	8	0	125.1	129	69	7	6	56	57	4.67	86	.271	.355	43-1	.326	3*	94	-5	-0.3
MARTINEZ, ALFREDO Alfredo B 3.15.1957 Los Angeles, CA BR/TR 6-3/185# d4.20																									
1980	Cal A	7	9	.438	30	23	4-1	0-0	149.1	150	81	14	1	59-2	57	4.52	87	.259	.326	0-0	—	0	97	-9	-0.9
1981	Cal A	0	0	—	2	0	0	0-0	6	5	2	1	0	3-0	4	3.00	122	.227	.320	0-0	—	0		1	0.0
Total	2	7	9	.438	32	23	4-1	0-0	155.1	155	83	15	1	62-2	61	4.46	88	.257	.326	0-0	—	0	97	-8	-0.9
MARTINEZ, TIPPY Felix Anthony B 5.31.1950 LaJunta, CO BL/TL 5-10/180# d8.9																									
1974	NY A	0	0	—	10	0	0	0-0	12.2	14	7	0	1	9-2	10	4.26	83	.286	.400	0-0	—	0		-1	-0.1
1975	NY A	1	2	.333	23	2	0	8-0	37	27	15	2	1	32-3	20	2.68	138	.208	.364	0-0	—	0	36	3	0.4
1976	NY A	2	0	1.000	11	0	0	2-0	28	18	6	1	0	14-0	14	1.93	177	.191	.296	0-0	—	0		5	0.5
	Bal A	3	1	.750	28	0	0	8-0	41.2	32	13	0	1	28-3	31	2.59	126	.222	.349	0-0	—	0		4	0.6
	Year	5	1	.833	39	0	0	10-0	69.2	50	21	1	1	42-3	45	2.33	143	.210	.329	0-0	—	0		9	1.1
1977	Bal A	5	1	.833	41	0	0	9-2	50	47	17	2	0	27-2	29	2.70	141	.266	.359	0-0	—	0		6	1.0
1978	Bal A	3	3	.500	42	0	0	5-3	69	77	41	4	1	40-2	57	4.83	73	.281	.373	0-0	—	0*		-11	-1.0
1979	†Bal A	10	3	.769	39	0	0	3-4	78	59	29	0	1	31-4	61	2.88	139	.210	.288	0-0	—	0		10	1.6
1980	Bal A	4	4	.500	53	0	0	10-1	80.2	69	30	5	1	34-5	68	3.01	132	.240	.320	0-0	—	0*		8	1.1
1981	Bal A	3	3	.500	37	0	0	11-3	59	48	21	4	0	32-6	50	2.90	125	.231	.329	0-0	—	0		5	0.8
1982	Bal A	8	8	.500	76	0	0	16-7	95	81	39	6	1	37-5	78	3.41	119	.240	.312	0-0	—	0		6	1.2
1983	†Bal A☆	9	3	.750	65	0	0	21-6	103.1	76	30	10	0	37-3	81	2.35	169	.211	.280	0-0	—	0		19	3.0
1984	Bal A	4	9	.308	55	0	0	17-6	89.2	88	42	9	0	51-13	72	3.91	99	.260	.352	0-0	—	0		0	0.1
1985	Bal A	3	3	.500	49	0	0	4-8	70	70	48	8	0	37-8	47	5.40	75	.261	.346	0-0	—	0		-12	-1.0
1986	Bal A	0	2	.000	14	0	0	1-0	16	18	10	1	0	12-1	11	5.63	74	.295	.405	0-0	—	0		-2	-0.3
1988	Min A	0	0	—	3	0	0	0-0	4	8	9	1	1	4-0	3	18.00	23	.471	.542	0-0	—	0		-6	-0.3
Total	14	55	42	.567	546	2	0	115-40	834	732	357	53	8	425-57	632	3.45	111	.242	.333	0-0	—	0	36	34	7.6
MARTINEZ, JAVIER Javier Antonio B 2.5.1977 Bayamon, PR. BR/TR 6-2/210# d4.2																									
1998	Pit N	0	1	.000	37	0	0	0-0	41	39	32	5	4	34-1	42	4.83	89	.248	.389	1-0	.000	-0		-5	-0.3
MARTINEZ, DENNIS Jose Dennis (Emilia) "El Presidente" B 5.14.1955 Granada, Nicaragua BR/TR 6-1/185# d9.14																									
1976	Bal A	1	2	.333	4	2	1	0-0	27.2	23	8	1	0	8-0	18	2.60	126	.237	.295	0-0	—	0	40	3	0.3
1977	Bal A	14	7	.667	42	13	5	4-1	166.2	157	86	10	8	64-5	107	4.10	93	.253	.327	0-0	—	0	140	-8	-0.9
1978	Bal A	16	11	.593	40	38	15-2	0-0	276.1	257	121	20	3	93-4	142	3.52	100	.250	.312	0-0	—	0	117	0	0.1
1979	†Bal A	15	16	.484	40	**39**	**18**-3	0-0	**292.1**	279	129	28	1	78-1	132	3.66	110	.253	.300	0-0	—	0	89	14	1.5
1980	Bal A	6	4	.600	25	12	2	1-0	99.2	103	44	12	2	44-6	42	3.97	100	.272	.349	0-0	—	0*	100	2	0.1
1981	Bal A	**14**	5	.737	25	24	9-2	0-0	179	173	84	10	2	62-1	88	3.32	109	.254	.316	0-0	—	0	108	2	0.4
1982	Bal A	16	12	.571	40	39	10-2	0-0	252	262	123	30	7	87-2	111	4.21	96	.267	.329	0-0	—	0	106	-4	-0.4
1983	Bal A	7	16	.304	32	25	4	0-1	153	209	108	21	2	45-0	71	5.53	72	.330	.374	0-0	—	0	95	-29	-3.5

Year	Tm Lg	W	L	Pct	G	GS	CG-Sho	SV-BS	IP	H	R	HR	HB	BB-IB	SO	ERA	AERA	OAV	OOB	AB-SH	AVG	PB	Sup	APR	PW
1984	Bal A	6	9	.400	34	20	2	0-0	141.2	145	81	26	5	37-2	77	5.02	77	.263	.312	0-0	—	0	91	-15	-1.4
1985	Bal A	13	11	.542	33	31	3-1	0-0	180	203	110	29	9	63-3	68	5.15	78	.288	.349	0-0	—	0	139	-21	-2.4
1986	Bal A	0	0	—	4	0	0	0-0	6.2	11	5	0	0	2-0	2	6.75	61	.367	.394	0-0	—	0		-2	-0.1
	Mon N	3	6	.333	19	15	1-1	0-0	98	103	52	11	3	28-4	63	4.59	81	.274	.328	30-0	.100	-0	72	-8	-0.7
1987	Mon N	11	4	.733	22	22	2-1	0-0	144.2	133	59	9	6	40-2	84	3.30	128	.244	.301	46-4	.065	-2	113	15	1.2
1988	Mon N	15	13	.536	34	34	9-2	0-0	235.1	215	94	21	6	55-3	120	2.72	133	.239	.286	78-10	.192	2	107	17	2.3
1989	Mon N	16	7	.696	34	33	5-2	0-0	232	227	88	21	7	49-4	142	3.18	111	.257	.300	72-9	.125	-1	112	10	1.1
1990	Mon N★	10	11	.476	32	32	7-2	0-0	226	191	80	16	6	49-9	156	2.95	124	.228	.274	68-12	.103	-2	107	19	1.5
1991	Mon N★	14	11	.560	31	31	**9-5**	0-0	222	187	70	9	4	62-3	123	**2.39**	151	.226	.282	72-10	.153	1*	87	29	3.6
1992	Mon N★	16	11	.593	32	32	6	0-0	226.1	172	75	12	9	60-3	147	2.47	141	.211	.271	74-10	.189	1	101	22	2.9
1993	Mon N	15	9	.625	35	34	2	1-0	224.2	211	110	27	11	64-7	138	3.85	109	.246	.306	69-9	.159	-0*	96	10	1.1
1994	Cle A	11	6	.647	24	24	7-3	0-0	176.2	166	75	14	7	44-2	92	3.52	134	.247	.298	0-0	—	0	103	26	2.2
1995	†Cle A★	12	5	.706	28	28	3-2	0-0	187	174	71	17	12	46-2	99	3.08	153	.247	.302	0-0	—	0	105	33	2.9
1996	Cle A	9	6	.600	20	20	1-1	0-0	112	122	63	12	2	37-2	48	4.50	109	.278	.335	0-0	—	0	120	4	0.6
1997	Sea A	1	5	.167	9	9	0	0-0	49	65	46	8	7	29-1	17	7.71	58	.327	.424	0-0	—	0	120	-18	-1.7
1998	†Atl N	4	6	.400	53	5	1-1	2-2	91	109	53	8	3	19-5	62	4.45	93	.295	.332	11-1	.091	-0	128	-4	-0.4
Total	23	245	193	.559	692	562	122-30	8-4	3999.2	3897	1835	372	122	1165-71	2149	3.70	106	.256	.312	520-65	.142	-3	106	97	10.3
MARTINEZ, JOSE Jose Miguel (Martinez) B 4.1.1971 Guayubin, D.R. BR/TR 6-2/180# d5.10																									
1994	SD N	0	2	.000	4	1	0	0-0	12	18	9	2	0	5-2	7	6.75	61	.375	.434	2-0	.000	-0	0	-3	-0.5
MARTINEZ, LUIS Luis B 1.20.1980 Santo Domingo, D.R. BL/TL 6-6/200# d9.3																									
2003	Mil N	0	3	.000	4	4	0	0-0	16.1	25	18	3	0	15-2	10	9.92	43	.373	.488	4-0	.000	-0	110	-10	-1.4
MARTINEZ, PEDRO Pedro (Aquino) B 11.29.1968 Villa Mella, D.R. BL/TL 6-2/185# d6.29 b-Ramon																									
1993	SD N	3	1	.750	32	0	0	0-1	37	23	11	4	1	13-1	32	2.43	170	.172	.250	4-2	.000	-0		7	0.6
1994	SD N	3	2	.600	48	1	0	3-2	68.1	52	31	4	1	49-9	52	2.90	142	.210	.341	5-0	.000	-1	177	7	0.5
1995	Hou N	0	0	—	25	0	0	0-0	20.2	29	18	3	2	16-1	17	7.40	52	.330	.439	0-0	—	0		-8	-0.4
1996	NY N	0	0	—	5	0	0	0-0	7	8	7	1	0	7-4	6	6.43	62	.296	.429	0-0	—	0		-3	-0.1
	Cin N	0	0	—	4	0	0	0-0	3	5	2	1	0	1-0	3	6.00	71	.357	.400	0-0	—	0		0	0.0
	Year	0	0	—	9	0	0	0-0	10	13	17	2	0	8-4	9	6.30	65	.317	.420	0-0	—	0		-3	-0.1
1997	Cin N	1	1	.500	8	0	0	0-0	6.2	8	9	1	1	7-0	4	9.45	45	.286	.432	0-0	—	0		-4	-0.8
Total	5	7	4	.636	122	1	0	3-3	142.2	125	78	14	5	93-15	114	3.97	103	.232	.348	9-2	.000	-1	177	-1	-0.2
MARTINEZ, PEDRO Pedro Jaime (b: Pedro Jaime (Martinez)) B 10.25.1971 Manoguayabo, D.R. BR/TR 5-11/170# d9.24																									
1992	LA N	0	1	.000	2	1	0	0-0	8	6	2	0	0	1-0	8	2.25	153	.200	.226	2-0	.000	-0	26	1	0.1
1993	LA N	10	5	.667	65	2	0	2-1	107	76	34	5	4	57-4	119	2.61	147	.201	.309	4-2	.000	-0*	106	16	2.0
1994	Mon N	11	5	.688	24	23	1-1	1-0	144.2	115	58	11	11	45-3	142	3.42	124	.220	.294	44-5	.091	-1	99	14	1.3
1995	Mon N	14	10	.583	30	30	2-2	0-0	194.2	158	79	21	11	66-1	174	3.51	122	.227	.302	63-5	.111	-3	96	18	1.7
1996	Mon N★	13	10	.565	33	33	4-1	0-0	216.2	189	100	19	3	70-3	222	3.70	117	.232	.294	64-16	.094	-2	105	14	1.0
1997	Mon N★	17	8	.680	31	31	**13**-4	0-0	241.1	158	65	16	9	67-5	305	**1.90**	**221**	**.184**	**.249**	69-9	.116	-1	79	**58**	**5.9**
1998	†Bos A☆	19	7	.731	33	33	3-2	0-0	233.2	188	82	26	8	67-3	251	2.89	163	.217	.278	7-0	.000	-1	100	47	4.6
1999	†Bos A★	**23**	4	**.852**	31	29	5-1	0-0	213.1	160	56	9	9	37-1	**313**	**2.07**	**241**	**.205**	**.248**	2-0	.000	-0	103	**67**	**8.0**
2000	Bos A❖	18	6	.750	29	29	7-**4**	0-0	217	128	44	17	14	32-0	**284**	**1.74**	**290**	**.167**	**.213**	0-0	—	0	83	**79**	**8.4**
2001	Bos A	7	3	.700	18	18	1	0-0	116.2	84	33	5	6	25-0	163	2.39	188	.199	.253	0-0	—	0	84	28	2.1
2002	Bos A☆	20	4	**.833**	30	30	2	0-0	199.1	144	62	13	15	40-1	**239**	**2.26**	**199**	**.198**	**.254**	5-1	.000	-0	121	46	5.3
2003	†Bos A	14	4	.778	29	29	3	0-0	186.2	147	52	7	9	47-0	206	**2.22**	**206**	**.215**	**.272**	3-0	.000	-0	104	**48**	4.3
Total	12	166	67	.712	355	288	41-15	3-1	2079	1553	667	149	99	554-21	2426	2.58	174	.206	.268	263-38	.095	-8	98	436	44.7
MARTINEZ, RAMON Ramon Jaime (b: Ramon Jaime (Martinez)) B 3.22.1968 Santo Domingo, D.R. BR/TR 6-4/173# d8.13 b-Pedro																									
1988	LA N	1	3	.250	9	6	0	0-0	35.2	27	17	0	0	22-1	23	3.79	88	.216	.333	7-1	.000	-1	53	-2	-0.3
1989	LA N	6	4	.600	15	15	2-2	0-0	98.2	79	39	11	5	41-1	89	3.19	107	.219	.308	37-2	.162	0*	128	3	0.3
1990	LA N★	20	6	.769	33	33	**12**-3	0-0	234.1	191	89	22	4	67-5	223	2.92	126	.220	.278	80-9	.125	-2	122	19	1.8
1991	LA N	17	13	.567	33	33	6-4	0-0	220.1	190	89	18	7	69-4	150	3.27	110	.229	.293	77-8	.117	-1	111	9	1.0
1992	LA N	8	11	.421	25	25	1-1	0-0	150.2	141	82	11	5	69-4	101	4.00	86	.245	.331	50-5	.120	-1*	94	-11	-1.5
1993	LA N	10	12	.455	32	32	4-3	0-0	211.2	202	88	15	4	104-9	127	3.44	111	.255	.342	70-7	.129	-2	94	12	1.0
1994	LA N	12	7	.632	24	24	4-**3**	0-0	170	160	83	18	6	56-2	119	3.97	99	.249	.312	66-5	.273	5	125	-2	0.2
1995	†LA N	17	7	.708	30	30	4-2	0-0	206.1	176	95	19	5	81-5	138	3.66	104	.231	.308	64-13	.172	1	115	4	0.6
1996	†LA N	15	6	.714	28	27	2-2	0-0	168.2	153	76	12	8	86-5	133	3.42	113	.245	.341	59-8	.119	-2*	113	8	0.8
1997	LA N	10	5	.667	22	22	1	0-0	133.2	123	64	14	6	68-1	120	3.64	106	.243	.337	42-5	.190	1	125	1	0.2
1998	LA N	7	3	.700	15	15	1	0-0	101.2	76	41	8	3	41-1	91	2.83	140	.206	.288	34-5	.176	1	91	11	1.2
1999	†Bos A	2	1	.667	4	4	0	0-0	20.2	14	8	2	2	8-0	15	3.05	163	.192	.286	0-0	—	0	122	4	0.6
2000	Bos A	10	8	.556	27	27	0	0-0	127.2	143	94	16	9	67-3	89	6.13	82	.283	.372	5-0	.200	0	109	-15	-1.7
2001	Pit N	0	2	.000	4	4	0	0-0	15.2	16	15	4	2	16-0	9	8.62	52	.276	.442	5-0	.000	-1	98	-6	-0.7
Total	14	135	88	.605	301	297	37-20	0-0	1895.2	1691	880	170	66	795-41	1427	3.67	105	.239	.319	596-68	.153	-0	111	35	3.5
MARTINEZ, ROGELIO Rogelio (Ulloa) "Limonar" B 11.5.1918 Cidra, Cuba BR/TR 6/180# d7.13																									
1950	Was A	0	1	.000	2	1	0	0	1.1	4	4	0	0	2	0	27.00	17	.500	.600	0-0	—	0	161	-3	-0.5
MARTINEZ, SILVIO Silvio Ramon (Cabrera) B 8.19.1955 Santiago, D.R. BR/TR 5-10/170# d4.9																									
1977	Chi A	0	1	.000	10	0	0	1-0	21	28	14	4	0	12-2	10	5.57	74	.337	.408	0-0	—	0		-3	-0.2
1978	StL N	9	8	.529	22	22	5-2	0-0	138.1	114	65	11	2	71-7	45	3.64	97	.228	.322	47-6	.170	0	124	-2	-0.3
1979	StL N	15	8	.652	32	29	7-2	0-1	206.2	204	92	14	0	67-2	102	3.27	115	.259	.314	62-10	.129	-2*	103	8	0.5
1980	StL N	5	10	.333	25	20	2	0-0	119.2	127	75	8	2	48-3	39	4.81	77	.273	.340	35-3	.086	-2	97	-16	-2.1
1981	StL N	2	5	.286	18	16	0	0-0	97	95	48	4	1	39-3	34	3.99	89	.260	.329	35-1	.200	1	95	-5	-0.3
Total	5	31	32	.492	107	87	14-4	1-1	582.2	568	294	41	5	237-17	230	3.88	95	.258	.328	179-20	.145	-3	105	-18	-2.4
MARTINEZ, WILLIE William Jose B 1.4.1978 Barquisimeto, Venezuela BR/TR 6-2/180# d6.14																									
2000	Cle A	0	0	—	1	0	0	0-0	3	1	1	0	0	1-0	1	3.00	166	.111	.182	0-0	—	0		1	0.0
MARTINI, WEDO Guido Joe "Southern" B 7.1.1913 Birmingham, AL D 10.28.1970 Philadelphia, PA BR/TR 5-10/165# d7.28																									
1935	Phi A	0	2	.000	3	2	0	0	6.1	8	13	0	0	11	1	17.05	27	.333	.543	2-0	.000	-0	29	-8	-1.3
MARTZ, RANDY Randy Carl B 5.28.1956 Harrisburg, PA BL/TR 6-4/210# d9.6																									
1980	Chi N	1	2	.333	6	6	0	0-0	30.1	28	14	1	0	11-1	5	2.08	189	.241	.302	9-0	.111	-1	72	3	0.3
1981	Chi N	5	7	.417	33	14	1	6-1	107.2	103	49	6	1	49-1	32	3.68	101	.256	.336	28-2	.214	1*	70	1	0.2
1982	Chi N	11	10	.524	28	24	1	1-1	147.2	157	80	17	3	36-4	40	4.21	89	.272	.317	42-7	.143	1	103	-8	-1.0
1983	Chi A	0	0	—	1	1	0	0-0	5	4	2	0	0	4-0	1	3.60	117	.211	.348	0-0	—	0	86	0	0.0
Total	4	17	19	.472	68	45	2	7-2	290.2	292	145	24	4	100-6	78	3.78	99	.262	.323	79-9	.165	1	89	-4	-0.5
MASAOKA, ONAN Onan Kainoa Satoshi B 10.27.1977 Hilo, HI BR/TL 6/186# d4.5																									
1999	LA N	2	4	.333	54	0	0	1-1	66.2	55	33	8	2	47-3	61	4.32	99	.222	.348	4-1	.000	-0		1	0.0
2000	LA N	1	1	.500	29	0	0	0-0	27	23	12	2	1	15-1	27	4.00	108	.230	.336	0-0	—	0		2	0.1
Total	2	3	5	.375	83	0	0	1-1	93.2	78	45	10	3	62-4	88	4.23	102	.224	.345	4-1	.000	-0		3	0.1
MASON, DEL Adelbert William B 10.29.1883 Newfane, NY D 12.31.1962 Winter Park, FL BR/TR 6/160# d4.23																									
1904	Was A	0	3	.000	5	3	2	0	33	45	30	1	2	13	16	6.00	44	.326	.392	15-0	.000	-2	107	-12	-1.2
1906	Cin N	0	1	.000	2	1	1	0	12	10	6	1	1	6	4	4.50	61	.250	.362	5-0	.000	-1	79	-1	-0.2
1907	Cin N	5	12	.294	25	17	13-1	0	146	144	68	2	6	55	45	3.14	83	.277	.353	44-5	.182	-0	57	-7	-0.8
Total	3	5	16	.238	32	21	16-1	0	191	199	104	4	9	74	65	3.72	70	.286	.362	64-5	.125	-3	65	-20	-2.2
MASON, ERNIE Ernest B New Orleans, LA D 7.30.1904 Covington, LA 6/150# d7.17																									
1894	StL N	0	3	.000	4	2	2	0	22.2	34	29	1	0	10	3	7.15	76	.343	.404	12-0	.250	-0	59	-6	-0.5

Year	Tm Lg	W	L	Pct	G	GS	CG-Sho	SV-BS	IP	H	R	HR	HB	BB-IB	SO	ERA	AERA	OAV	OOB	AB-SH	AVG	PB	Sup	APR	PW
MASON, HANK Henry B 6.19.1931 Marshall, MO BR/TR 6/185# d9.12																									
1958	Phi N	0	0	—	1	0	0	0	5	7	7	0	1	2-0	3	10.80	37	.368	.417	2-0	.000	-0		-4	-0.2
1960	Phi N	0	0	—	3	0	0	0	5.2	9	6	1	0	5-1	3	9.53	41	.375	.467	1-0	.000	-0		-3	-0.2
Total	2	0	0	—	4	0	0	0	10.2	16	13	1	1	7-1	6	10.13	39	.372	.444	3-0	.000	-0		-7	-0.4
MASON, MIKE Michael Paul B 11.21.1958 Faribault, MN BL/TL 6-2/205# d9.13																									
1982	Tex A	1	2	.333	4	4	0	0-0	23	21	13	3	0	9-1	8	5.09	76	.244	.316	0-0	—	0	112	-3	-0.3
1983	Tex A	0	2	.000	5	0	0	0-1	10.2	10	7	0	1	6-0	9	5.91	68	.244	.354	0-0	—	0		-2	-0.3
1984	Tex A	9	13	.409	36	24	4	0-0	184.1	159	78	18	2	51-4	113	3.61	115	.233	.285	0-0	—	0	74	13	1.4
1985	Tex A	8	15	.348	38	30	1-1	0-1	179	212	113	22	3	73-4	92	4.83	88	.299	.362	0-0	—	0	87	-15	-1.7
1986	Tex A	7	3	.700	27	22	2-1	0-0	135	135	71	11	0	56-3	85	4.33	99	.257	.327	0-0	—	0	128	0	0.1
1987	Tex A	0	2	.000	8	6	0	0-0	29	37	20	6	4	22-2	21	5.59	80	.322	.444	0-0	—	0	125	-3	-0.2
	Chi N	4	1	.800	17	4	0	0-0	38	43	25	4	1	23-0	28	5.68	75	.303	.396	9-3	.222	0*	180	-5	-0.5
1988	Min A	0	1	.000	5	0	0	0-0	6.2	8	8	1	0	9-0	7	10.80	38	.286	.459	0-0	—	0		-5	-0.6
Total	7	29	39	.426	140	90	7-2	0-2	605.2	625	335	65	11	249-14	363	4.53	93	.268	.338	9-3	.222	0	102	-20	-2.1
MASON, ROGER Roger Le Roy B 9.18.1958 Bellaire, MI BR/TR 6-6/220# d9.4																									
1984	Det A	1	1	.500	5	2	0	1-0	22	23	11	1	0	10-0	15	4.50	87	.271	.340	0-0	—	0	92	-1	-0.1
1985	SF N	1	3	.250	5	5	1-1	0-0	29.2	28	13	1	0	11-1	26	2.12	162	.243	.310	11-0	.091	-0	67	2	0.3
1986	SF N	3	4	.429	11	11	1	0-0	60	56	35	5	3	30-3	43	4.80	74	.250	.342	21-1	.048	-2	99	-8	-1.1
1987	SF N	1	1	.500	5	5	0	0-0	26	30	15	4	0	10-0	18	4.50	86	.303	.367	8-0	.125	0	132	-2	-0.1
1989	Hou N	0	0	—	2	0	0	0-0	1.1	2	3	0	0	2-0	3	20.25	17	.333	.500	0-0	—	0		-2	-0.1
1991	†Pit N	3	2	.600	24	0	0	3-0	29.2	21	11	2	1	6-1	21	3.03	118	.200	.248	0-1	—	0		2	0.4
1992	†Pit N	5	7	.417	65	0	0	8-2	88	80	41	11	4	33-8	56	4.09	84	.246	.320	10-0	.000	-1		-5	-1.0
1993	SD N	0	7	.000	34	0	0	0-0	50	43	20	1	2	18-4	39	3.24	128	.242	.313	3-0	.000	-0		5	0.6
	†Phi N	5	5	.500	34	0	0	0-3	49.2	47	28	9	0	16-1	32	4.89	81	.246	.301	3-0	.333	0		-4	-0.7
	Year	5	12	.294	68	0	0	0-3	99.2	90	54	10	2	34-5	71	4.06	100	.244	.307	6-0	.167	-0		1	-0.1
1994	Phi N	1	1	.500	6	0	0	0-0	8.2	11	6	2	0	5-1	7	5.19	83	.306	.390	0-0	—	0		-1	-0.2
	NY N	2	4	.333	41	0	0	1-1	51.1	44	23	6	2	20-4	26	3.51	119	.232	.310	0-0	—	0		4	0.3
	Year	3	5	.375	47	0	0	1-1	60	55	29	8	2	25-5	33	3.75	112	.243	.323	0-0	—	0		2	0.1
Total	9	22	35	.386	232	23	2-1	13-6	416.1	385	206	42	12	161-23	286	4.02	94	.248	.320	56-2	.071	-2	96	-10	-1.7
MASTERS, WALT Walter Thomas B 3.28.1907 Pen Argyl, PA D 7.10.1992 Ottawa, ON, CAN BR/TR 5-10.5/180# d7.9																									
1931	Was A	0	0	—	3	0	0	1	9	7	2	0	0	4	1	2.00	215	.226	.314	2-0	.000	-0		2	0.1
1937	Phi N	0	0	—	1	0	0	0	1	5	4	0	0	1	0	36.00	12	.714	.750	0-0	—	0		-3	-0.1
1939	Phi A	0	0	—	4	0	0	0	11	15	9	0	0	8	2	6.55	72	.306	.404	2-0	.000	-0		-2	-0.1
Total	3	0	0	—	8	0	0	1	21	27	15	0	0	13	3	6.00	75	.310	.400	4-0	.000	-1		-3	-0.1
MASTERSON, PAUL Paul Nicholas "Lefty" (b: Paul Nicholas Nastasowski) B 10.16.1915 Chicago, IL D 11.27.1997 Chicago, IL BL/TL 5-11/165# d9.15																									
1940	Phi N	0	0	—	2	0	0	0	5	5	4	0	0	2	3	7.20	54	.263	.333	1-0	.000	-0		-2	-0.1
1941	Phi N	1	0	1.000	2	1	1	0	11.1	11	6	0	0	6	8	4.76	78	.250	.340	4-1	.000	-1	183	-1	-0.1
1942	Phi N	0	0	—	4	0	0	0	8.1	10	6	1	0	5	3	6.48	51	.303	.395	0-0	—	0		-3	-0.1
Total	3	1	0	1.000	8	1	1	0	24.2	26	16	1	0	13	14	5.84	62	.271	.358	5-1	.000	-1	183	-6	-0.3
MASTERSON, WALT Walter Edward B 6.22.1920 Philadelphia, PA BR/TR 6-2/189# d5.8 Mil 1943-45																									
1939	Was A	2	2	.500	24	5	1	0	58.1	66	44	2	2	48	12	5.55	78	.293	.422	13-0	.154	-0	122	-10	-0.6
1940	Was A	3	13	.188	31	19	3	2	130.1	128	92	6	3	88	68	4.90	85	.257	.371	38-3	.184	0	79	-15	-1.6
1941	Was A	4	3	.571	34	6	1	3	78.1	101	56	3	1	53	40	5.97	68	.321	.420	19-2	.105	-1	128	-15	-1.3
1942	Was A	5	9	.357	25	15	8-4	2	142.2	138	75	6	2	54	63	3.34	109	.251	.321	45-3	.156	-0*	105	0	-0.1
1945	Was A	1	2	.333	4	2	1-1	0	25	21	8	1	0	10	14	1.08	287	.228	.304	9-0	.111	-1	220	4	0.4
1946	Was A	5	6	.455	29	9	2	1	91.1	105	70	8	3	67	61	6.01	56	.295	.411	25-1	.080	-1	137	-26	-3.0
1947	Was A★	12	16	.429	35	31	14-4	1	253	215	98	11	2	97	135	3.13	119	.234	.309	83-3	.133	-3*	67	17	1.7
1948	Was A★	8	15	.348	33	27	9-2	2	188	171	88	12	4	122	72	3.83	113	.247	.363	57-9	.193	-0	72	12	1.2
1949	Was A	3	2	.600	10	7	3	0	53	42	22	4	3	21	17	3.23	132	.216	.303	18-1	.056	-1*	87	6	0.4
	Bos A	3	4	.429	18	5	1	4	55	58	30	2	0	35	19	4.25	102	.283	.387	17-0	.118	-0	148	0	-0.1
	Year	6	6	.500	28	12	4	4	108	100	37	6	3	56	36	3.75	115	.251	.347	35-1	.086	-2	113	6	0.3
1950	Bos A	8	6	.571	33	15	6	1	129.1	145	91	15	1	82	60	5.64	87	.287	.387	44-0	.136	-3	118	-11	-1.2
1951	Bos A	3	0	1.000	30	1	0	2	59.1	53	24	1	0	32	39	3.34	134	.228	.322	11-1	.182	-1	100	7	0.3
1952	Bos A	1	1	.500	5	1	0	0	9.1	18	12	1	0	11	3	11.57	34	.400	.518	2-0	.000	0	22	-7	-1.2
	Was A	9	8	.529	24	21	11	2	160.2	153	71	11	3	72	89	3.70	96	.253	.336	50-8	.120	-1	99	-1	-0.2
	Year	10	9	.526	29	22	11	2	170	171	75	12	3	83	92	4.13	87	.263	.350	52-8	.115	-1	95	-7	-1.4
1953	Was A	10	12	.455	29	20	10-4	0	166.1	145	79	16	3	62	95	3.63	107	.232	.304	51-3	.137	-1	78	3	0.3
1956	Det A	1	1	.500	35	0	0	0	49.2	54	28	2	1	32-1	28	4.17	99	.289	.390	4-0	.250	0		-1	-0.1
Total	14	78	100	.438	399	184	70-15	20	1649.2	1613	888	101	28	886-1	815	4.15	96	.258	.353	486-34	.140	-14	92	-37	-5.1
MATARAZZO, LEN Leonard B 9.12.1928 New Castle, PA BR/TR 6-4/195# d9.6																									
1952	Phi A	0	0	—	1	0	0	0	1	1	0	0	0	1	0	0.00	—	.250	.400	0-0	—	0		0	0.0
MATEO, JULIO Julio Cesar B 8.22.1978 Bani, D.R. BR/TR 6/180# d5.7																									
2002	Sea A	0	0	—	12	0	0	0-0	21	20	10	2	1	12-0	15	4.29	99	.247	.351	0-0	—	0		0	0.0
2003	Sea A	4	0	1.000	50	0	0	1-0	85.2	69	32	14	5	13-1	71	3.15	137	.220	.259	0-0	—	0		12	0.5
Total	2	4	0	1.000	62	0	0	1-0	106.2	89	42	16	6	25-1	86	3.38	128	.225	.279	0-0	—	0		12	0.5
MATHEWS, GREG Gregory Inman B 5.17.1962 Harbor City, CA BR/TL 6-2/180# d6.3																									
1986	StL N	11	8	.579	23	22	1	0-0	145.1	139	61	15	2	44-3	67	3.65	100	.259	.317	43-7	.047	-3	84	2	-0.1
1987	†StL N	11	11	.500	32	32	2-1	0-0	197.2	184	87	17	0	71-5	108	3.73	111	.249	.314	68-7	.191	1	89	10	1.1
1988	StL N	4	6	.400	13	13	1	0-0	68	61	34	4	2	33-5	31	4.24	82	.247	.337	23-1	.174	0	84	-5	-0.6
1990	StL N	0	5	.000	11	10	0	0-0	50.2	53	34	2	2	30-1	18	5.33	72	.277	.378	14-1	.214	1*	85	-9	-0.6
1992	Phi N	2	3	.400	14	7	0	0-0	52.1	54	31	7	1	24-2	27	5.16	68	.270	.350	14-2	.000	-1	74	-9	-0.9
Total	5	28	33	.459	93	84	4-1	0-0	514	491	247	45	7	202-16	251	4.08	94	.256	.328	162-18	.136	-1	86	-11	-1.1
MATHEWS, BOBBY Robert T. B 11.21.1851 Baltimore, MD D 4.17.1898 Baltimore, MD BR/TR 5-5.5/140# d5.4 U3 ▲																									
1871	Kek NA	6	11	.353	19	19	19-**1**	0	169	261	243	5		21	17	5.17	88	.305	.322	89	.270	-3	63	-10	-0.7
1872	Bal NA	25	18	.581	49	47	39	0	406	480	356	3		52	**57**	3.19	115	.257	.277	222	.225	-8*	96	26	1.0
1873	Mut NA	29	23	.558	52	52	47-2	0	443	489	348	5		62	**79**	2.58	123	.251	.274	223	.193	-2	90	**37**	2.5
1874	Mut NA	42	22	.656	65	65	62-**4**	0	578	652	371	3		41	**101**	1.90	118	.261	.273	298	.242	-2	100	22	1.5
1875	Mut NA	29	38	.433	70	**70**	**69**-3	0	**625.2**	711	421	4		20	75	2.49	94	.260	.265	264	.182	-10	69	-10	-2.0
1876	NY N	21	34	.382	56	56	55-2	0	516	693	395	8		24	37	2.86	75	.301	.308	218	.183	-10	83	-46	-4.5
1877	Cin N	3	12	.200	15	15	13	0	129.1	208	132	0		17	9	4.04	66	.339	.357	59	.169	-3	101	-25	-2.4
1879	Pro N	12	6	.667	27	25	15-1	**1**	189	194	85	4		26	90	2.29	103	.258	.282	173	.202	-0*	135	3	0.2
1881	Pro N	4	8	.333	14	14	10-1	0	102.1	121	81	2		21	28	3.17	84	.268	.300	57	.193	-2*	106	-7	-0.8
	Bos N	1	0	1.000	5	1	1	2	23	22	11	0		11	5	2.35	113	.239	.320	71	.169	-1*	204	1	0.0
	Year	5	8	.385	19	15	11-1	**2**	125.1	143	21	2		32	33	3.02	88	.263	.304	128	.180	-3	113	-6	-0.8
1882	Bos N	19	15	.559	34	32	31	0	285	278	151	5		22	153	2.87	100	.232	.246	169	.225	-2*	91	2	-0.1
1883	Phi AA	30	13	.698	44	44	41-1	0	381	396	224	11		31	203	2.46	144	.251	.265	167	.186	-7*	101	38	2.8
1884	Phi AA	30	18	.625	49	49	48-3	0	430.2	401	238	10	12	49	286	3.32	102	.232	.258	184	.185	-5	114	4	-0.3
1885	Phi AA	30	17	.638	48	48	46-2	0	422.1	394	229	3	20	57	286	2.43	142	.233	.267	179	.168	-7	104	42	3.3
1886	Phi AA	13	9	.591	24	24	22	0	197.2	226	148	3	13	53	93	3.96	88	.267	.320	88	.239	-0	119	-9	-0.8
1887	Phi AA	3	4	.429	7	7	7	0	58	75	64	4	3	25	9	6.67	64	.298	.368	25	.200	-0	121	-16	-1.3
Total	5 NA	131	112	.539	255	253	236-10	0	2221.2	2593	1739	20	0	196	329	2.69	108	.262	.276	1096	.216	-25	86	65	2.3
Total	10	166	136	.550	323	315	289-10	3	2734.1	3008	1758	50	48	336	1199	3.00	100	.261	.285	1390	.192	-38	104	-13	-3.9
MATHEWS, TERRY Terry Alan B 10.5.1964 Alexandria, LA BL/TR 6-2/225# d6.21																									
1991	Tex A	4	0	1.000	34	2	0	1-2	57.1	54	24	5	1	18-3	51	3.61	112	.251	.312	0-0	—	0	227	3	0.2

Year	Tm Lg	W	L	Pct	G	GS	CG-Sho	SV-BS	IP	H	R	HR	HB	BB-IB	SO	ERA	AERA	OAV	OOB	AB-SH	AVG	PB	Sup	APR	PW
1992	Tex A	2	4	.333	40	0	0	0-4	42.1	48	29	4	1	31-3	26	5.95	64	.294	.404	0-0	—	0		-9	-1.2
1994	Fla N	2	1	.667	24	2	0	0-1	43	45	16	4	1	9-1	21	3.35	131	.268	.309	6-0	.500	1	135	6	0.5
1995	Fla N	4	4	.500	57	0	0	3-4	82.2	70	32	9	1	27-4	72	3.38	125	.235	.300	13-0	.462	3		9	1.1
1996	Fla N	2	4	.333	57	0	0	4-1	55	59	33	7	1	27-5	49	4.91	83	.273	.355	4-0	.000	-0		-5	-0.6
	†Bal A	2	2	.500	14	0	0	0-1	18.2	20	7	3	0	7-0	13	3.38	146	.282	.346	0-0	—	0		4	0.6
1997	†Bal A	4	4	.500	57	0	0	1-1	63.1	63	35	8	0	36-2	39	4.41	100	.267	.359	0-0	—	0		-1	-0.1
1998	Bal A	0	1	.000	17	0	0	0-1	20.1	26	15	6	0	8-3	10	6.20	74	.342	.400	0-0	—	0		-4	-0.2
1999	KC A	2	1	.667	24	1	0	1-2	39	44	21	4	2	17-1	19	4.38	114	.289	.360	1-0	.000	-0	316	3	0.2
Total	8	22	21	.512	324	5	0	10-17	421.2	429	212	50	7	180-22	300	4.25	101	.269	.343	24-0	.375	3	213	6	0.5
MATHEWS, T. J. Timothy Jay B 1.9.1970 Belleville, IL BR/TR 6-2/200# d7.28 f-Nelson																									
1995	StL N	1	1	.500	23	0	0	2-0	29.2	21	7	1	0	11-1	28	1.52	276	.200	.276	2-0	.000	-0		8	0.6
1996	†StL N	2	6	.250	67	0	0	6-5	83.2	62	32	8	2	32-4	80	3.01	139	.203	.282	4-0	.000	-0		10	0.9
1997	StL N	4	4	.500	40	0	0	0-3	46	41	14	4	1	18-3	46	2.15	193	.238	.314	1-0	.000	-0		10	1.5
	Oak A	6	2	.750	24	0	0	3-3	28.2	34	18	5	1	12-1	24	4.40	103	.293	.362	0-0	—	0		-1	-0.2
1998	Oak A	7	4	.636	66	0	0	1-3	72.2	71	44	6	4	29-3	53	4.58	100	.258	.328	0-0	—	0		-1	-0.2
1999	Oak A	9	5	.643	50	0	0	3-2	59	46	28	9	2	20-4	42	3.81	122	.215	.287	0-0	—	0		6	1.1
2000	Oak A	2	3	.400	50	0	0	0-1	59.2	73	40	10	2	25-5	42	6.03	79	.303	.368	0-0	—	0		-7	-0.4
2001	Oak A	0	1	.000	20	0	0	1-0	23	28	14	2	0	11-3	19	5.09	87	.295	.368	0-0	—	0		-2	-0.1
	StL N	1	0	1.000	10	0	0	0-0	14.2	11	6	2	0	1-0	10	3.07	139	.204	.214	3-0	.000	-0		2	0.1
2002	Hou N	0	0	—	12	0	0	0-0	18.1	19	7	2	0	5-3	13	3.44	124	.271	.320	1-0	.000	-0		2	0.1
Total	8	32	26	.552	362	0	0	16-17	435.1	406	210	49	12	164-27	357	3.82	116	.246	.316	11-0	.000	-1		27	3.4
MATHEWSON, CHRISTY Christopher "Matty" or "Big Six" B 8.12.1880 Factoryville, PA D 10.7.1925 Saranac Lake, NY BR/TR 6-1.5/195# d7.17 M3 C2 HF1936 b-Henry																									
1900	NY N	0	3	.000	6	1	1	0	33.2	37	32	1	4	20	15	5.08	71	.278	.389	11-0	.182	0	96	-6	-0.4
1901	NY N	20	17	.541	40	38	36-5	0	336	288	131	3	13	97	221	2.41	137	.230	.292	130-4	.215	-1*	81	32	3.6
1902	NY N	14	17	.452	35	33	30-**8**	0	284.2	246	118	3	10	77	164	2.12	132	.233	.292	130-2	.200	1*	73	16	2.1
1903	NY N	30	13	.698	45	42	37-3	2	366.1	321	136	4	10	100	**267**	2.26	148	.231	.287	124-16	.226	3	105	39	**4.6**
1904	NY N	33	12	.733	48	**46**	33-4	1	367.2	306	120	7	4	78	**212**	2.03	134	.226	.270	133-9	.226	6	135	27	4.2
1905	†NY N	**31**	9	.775	43	37	32-**8**	3	338.2	252	85	4	1	64	**206**	**1.28**	**230**	.205	**.245**	127-1	.236	10*	127	**57**	**8.5**
1906	NY N	22	12	.647	38	35	22-6	1	266.2	262	100	3	3	77	128	2.97	88	.259	.313	91-3	.264	7	124	-3	0.6
1907	NY N	**24**	12	.667	41	36	31-**8**	2	315	250	88	5	2	53	**178**	2.00	124	.212	**.247**	107-3	.187	3	89	19	2.7
1908	NY N	**37**	11	.771	**56**	**44**	**34-11**	**5**	**390.2**	281	85	5	3	42	**259**	**1.43**	**169**	.197	**.222**	129-7	.155	1	107	**41**	**6.5**
1909	NY N	25	6	**.806**	37	33	26-8	2	275.1	192	57	2	0	36	149	**1.14**	**223**	.200	**.228**	95-1	.263	7	100	42	**6.6**
1910	NY N	**27**	9	.750	38	35	**27**-2	0	318.1	292	100	5	3	60	184	1.89	157	.248	.286	107-4	.234	7	125	**35**	**5.3**
1911	†NY N	26	13	.667	45	37	29-5	3	307	303	102	5	1	38	141	**1.99**	**169**	.259	.283	112-3	.196	0	112	**42**	**5.7**
1912	†NY N	23	12	.657	43	34	27	5	310	311	107	5	2	34	134	2.12	159	.260	**.281**	110-3	.264	5	117	**43**	**5.3**
1913	†NY N	25	11	.694	40	35	25-4	2	306	291	94	8	0	21	93	**2.06**	**152**	.252	**.266**	103-4	.184	-0	107	**37**	**4.6**
1914	NY N	24	13	.649	41	35	29-5	2	312	314	133	16	2	23	80	3.00	88	.263	.278	105-4	.219	6	124	-13	-0.8
1915	NY N	8	14	.364	27	24	11-1	0	186	199	97	9	1	20	57	3.58	72	.277	.298	51-3	.157	3	81	-23	-2.3
1916	NY N	3	4	.429	12	6	4-1	2	65.2	59	27	3	0	7	16	2.33	104	.243	.264	17-2	.000	-1	102	-2	-0.2
	Cin N	1	0	1.000	1	1	1	0	9	15	8	1	0	1	3	8.00	32	.366	.381	5-0	.600	1	288	-5	-0.3
	Year	4	4	.500	13	7	5-1	2	74.2	74	18	4	0	8	19	3.01	81	.261	.281	22-2	.136	1	131	-6	-0.5
Total	17	373	188	.665	636	552	435-79	30	4788.2	4219	1620	89	59	848	2507	2.13	136	.236	.273	1687-69	.215	59	108	378	56.3
MATHEWSON, HENRY Henry B 12.24.1886 Factoryville, PA D 7.1.1917 Factoryville, PA BR/TR 6-3/175# d9.28 b-Christy																									
1906	NY N	0	1	.000	2	1	1	1	10	7	7	0	1	14	2	5.40	48	.194	.431	2-1	.000	-0	28	-3	-0.3
1907	NY N	0	0	—	1	0	0	1	1	1	0	0	0	0	0	0.00	—	.250	.250	0-0	—	0		0	0.1
Total	2	0	1	.000	3	1	1	2	11	8	7	0	1	14	2	4.91	53	.200	.418	2-1	.000	-0	28	-3	-0.2
MATHIAS, CARL Carl Lynwood "Stubby" B 6.13.1936 Bechtelsville, PA BB/TL 5-11/195# d7.31																									
1960	Cle A	0	1	.000	7	0	0	0	15.1	14	7	2	0	8-0	13	3.52	106	.233	.324	1-0	.000	-0		0	0.0
1961	Was A	0	1	.000	4	3	0	0	13.2	22	19	3	1	4-0	7	11.20	36	.361	.403	5-0	.200	-0	176	-11	-0.6
Total	2	0	2	.000	11	3	0	0	29	36	26	5	1	12-0	20	7.14	54	.298	.363	6-0	.167	-0	176	-11	-0.6
MATHIS, RON Ronald Vance B 9.25.1958 Kansas City, MO BR/TR 6/175# d4.13																									
1985	Hou N	3	5	.375	23	8	0	1-0	70	83	54	7	1	27-1	34	6.04	57	.293	.352	14-2	.071	-1	115	-20	-2.2
1987	Hou N	0	1	.000	8	0	0	0-0	12	10	8	2	0	11-0	8	5.25	75	.233	.389	2-0	.000	-0		-2	-0.2
Total	2	3	6	.333	31	8	0	1-0	82	93	62	9	1	38-1	42	5.93	60	.285	.358	16-2	.063	-1	115	-22	-2.4
MATLACK, JON Jonathan Trumpbour B 1.19.1950 West Chester, PA BL/TL 6-3/205# d7.11 C1																									
1971	NY N	0	3	.000	7	6	0	0-0	37	31	18	2	0	15-0	24	4.14	83	.228	.303	11-0	.273	1	104	-3	-0.1
1972	NY N	15	10	.600	34	32	8-4	0-0	244	215	79	14	2	71-14	169	2.32	145	.234	.289	78-5	.128	1	93	25	2.7
1973	†NY N	14	16	.467	34	34	14-3	0-0	242	210	93	16	2	99-14	205	3.20	113	.236	.312	65-12	.138	2*	76	13	1.8
1974	NY N★	13	15	.464	34	34	14-**7**	0-0	265.1	221	82	8	5	76-11	195	2.41	148	.226	.283	79-11	.101	-4	78	35	3.3
1975	NY N★	16	12	.571	33	32	8-3	0-0	228.2	224	105	15	1	58-6	154	3.38	102	.254	.299	70-5	.100	0	106	-1	-0.2
1976	NY N☆	17	10	.630	35	35	16-**6**	0-0	262	236	94	18	3	57-5	153	2.95	112	.242	.284	88-7	.193	4	122	12	1.6
1977	NY N	7	15	.318	26	26	5-3	0-0	169	175	86	19	2	43-7	123	4.21	89	.273	.317	50-1	.060	-2	78	-9	-1.1
1978	Tex A	15	13	.536	35	33	18-2	1-0	270	252	93	14	4	51-4	157	2.27	166	.245	.283	0-0	—	0	72	38	4.0
1979	Tex A	5	4	.556	13	13	2	0-0	85	98	43	9	1	15-1	35	4.13	101	.293	.323	0-0	—	0	97	1	0.1
1980	Tex A	10	10	.500	35	34	8-1	1-0	234.2	265	111	17	0	48-1	142	3.68	106	.287	.321	0-0	—	0	98	6	0.3
1981	Tex A	4	7	.364	17	16	1-1	0-0	104.1	101	59	8	1	41-1	43	4.14	84	.258	.326	0-0	—	0	111	-11	-1.1
1982	Tex A	7	7	.500	33	14	1	1-1	147.2	158	64	14	2	37-4	78	3.53	110	.275	.319	0-0	—	0	81	6	0.5
1983	Tex A	2	4	.333	25	9	2	0-0	73.1	90	43	7	3	27-1	38	4.66	86	.307	.366	0-0	—	0	88	-5	-0.4
Total	13	125	126	.498	361	318	97-30	3-1	2363	2276	970	161	26	638-69	1516	3.18	114	.254	.303	441-41	.129	2	91	107	11.4
MATTERN, AL Alonzo Albert B 6.16.1883 W.Rush, NY D 11.6.1958 West Rush, NY BL/TL 5-10/165# d9.16																									
1908	Bos N	1	2	.333	5	3	1-1	0	30.1	30	10	0	0	6	8	2.08	116	.265	.303	8-2	.125	-0	68	1	0.1
1909	Bos N	15	21	.417	47	32	24-2	3	316.1	322	142	4	3	108	98	2.85	99	.268	.330	101-7	.168	-1	83	-2	-0.1
1910	Bos N	16	19	.457	**51**	37	17-**6**	1	305	288	145	5	6	121	94	2.98	112	.257	.332	98-10	.163	-4	62	10	0.6
1911	Bos N	4	15	.211	33	21	11	0	186.1	228	129	13	1	63	51	4.97	77	.320	.376	63-5	.175	-2	89	-19	-1.8
1912	Bos N	0	1	.000	2	1	0	0	6.1	10	9	0	0	1	3	7.11	50	.313	.333	2-0	.000	-0	102	-3	-0.4
Total	5	36	58	.383	138	94	53-9	4	844.1	878	435	22	10	299	254	3.37	95	.276	.340	272-24	.165	-8	77	-13	-1.6
MATTES, TROY Troy Walter B 8.26.1975 Champaign, IL BR/TR 6-8/230# d6.19																									
2001	Mon N	3	3	.500	8	8	0	0-0	45	51	33	9	4	21-2	26	6.00	74	.285	.371	15-1	.467	3	127	-8	-0.6
MATTESON, C. V. Clifford Virgil B 11.24.1861 Seville, OH D 12.18.1931 Seville, OH d6.13																									
1884	StL U	1	0	1.000	1	1	0	0	6	9	11	1		3	3	9.00	27	.321	.387	4	.000	-1	285	-4	-0.5
MATTESON, EDDIE Henry Edson "Matty" B 9.7.1884 Guys Mills, PA D 9.1.1943 Westfield, NY BR/TR 5-10.5/160# d5.30																									
1914	Phi N	3	2	.600	15	3	2	0	58	58	29	1	1	23	28	3.10	95	.278	.352	22-0	.182	-0	105	-1	-0.2
1918	Was A	5	3	.625	14	6	2	0	67.2	57	20	2	1	15	17	1.73	158	.238	.286	19-0	.105	-2	69	7	0.6
Total	2	8	5	.615	29	9	4	0	125.2	115	49	3	2	38	45	2.36	120	.257	.318	41-0	.146	-2	81	6	0.4
MATTHEWS, JOE John Joseph "Lefty" B 9.29.1898 Baltimore, MD D 2.8.1968 Hagerstown, MD BB/TL 6/170# d9.18																									
1922	Bos N	0	1	.000	3	1	0	0	10	5	6	1	1	6	0	3.60	111	.143	.286	2-0	.000	-0	0	0	0.0
MATTHEWS, MIKE Michael Scott B 10.24.1973 Fredericksburg, VA BL/TL 6-2/175# d5.31																									
2000	StL N	0	0	—	14	0	0	0-0	9.1	15	12	2	1	10-2	8	11.57	40	.349	.481	0-0	—	0		-7	-0.3
2001	†StL N	3	4	.429	51	10	0	1-2	89	74	32	11	4	33-4	72	3.24	132	.227	.305	17-1	.118	0*	89	12	0.8
2002	StL N	2	1	.667	43	0	0	0-2	41.2	40	21	5	2	22-2	32	3.89	102	.260	.352	6-0	.167	-0		0	0.0
	Mil N	0	0	—	4	0	0	0-0	4	3	2	0	0	7-1	2	4.50	91	.214	.476	0-1	—	0		0	0.0
	Year	2	1	.667	47	0	0	0-2	45.2	43	27	5	2	29-3	34	3.94	101	.256	.365	6-1	.167	-0		0	0.0
2003	SD N	6	4	.600	77	0	0	0-3	64.2	65	34	4	4	29-5	44	4.45	89	.271	.353	2-1	.000	-0		-4	-0.5

Year	Tm Lg	W	L	Pct	G	GS	CG-Sho	SV-BS	IP	H	R	HR	HB	BB-IB	SO	ERA	AERA	OAV	OOB	AB-SH	AVG	PB	Sup	APR	PW
Total 4		11	9	.550	189	10	0	1-7	208.2	197	101	22	11	101-14	158	4.14	99	.254	.344	25-3	.120	-0	89	1	0.0
MATTHEWS, WILLIAM William Calvin B 1.12.1878 Mahanoy City, PA D 1.23.1946 Mt.Carbon, PA TR d8.28																									
1909	Bos A	0	0	—	5	1	0	0	16.2	16	8	1	0	10	6	3.24	77	.271	.377	8-0	.000	-1	113	-1	-0.2
MATTHEWSON, DALE Dale Wesley B 5.15.1923 Catasauqua, PA D 2.20.1984 Blairsville, GA BR/TR 5-11.5/145# d7.3																									
1943	Phi N	0	3	.000	11	1	0	0	26	26	14	1	0	8	8	4.85	70	.271	.327	2-1	.000	-0*	0	-3	-0.4
1944	Phi N	0	0	—	17	0	0	0	32	27	14	1	0	16	8	3.94	92	.237	.331	3-0	.333	0		0	0.0
Total 2		0	3	.000	28	1	0	0	58	53	28	2	0	24	16	4.34	81	.252	.329	5-1	.200	-0	0	-3	-0.4
MATTIMORE, MIKE Michael Joseph B 1859 Renovo, PA D 4.28.1931 Butte, MT BL/TL 5-8.5/160# d5.3 ▲																									
1887	NY N	3	3	.500	7	7	6-1	0	57.1	47	39	2	4	28	12	2.35	160	.218	.319	32	.250	-0*	135	5	0.3
1888	Phi AA	15	10	.600	26	24	24-4	0	221	221	146	6	13	65	80	3.38	88	.251	.312	142	.268	7*	142	-8	-0.1
1889	Phi AA	2	1	.667	5	1	1	1	31	42	27	0	1	13	6	5.81	65	.313	.378	73	.233	1*	131	-5	-0.3
	KC AA	0	0	—	1	0	0	0	3	3	3	1	0	2	1	3.00	139	.250	.357	75	.160	-0*		0	0.0
	Year	2	1	.667	6	1	1	1	34	45	38	1	1	15	7	5.56	69	.308	.377	148	.196	1	130	-5	-0.3
1890	Bro AA	6	13	.316	19	19	19	0	178.1	201	149	3	13	76	33	4.54	86	.276	.355	129	.132	-3*	93	-15	-1.4
Total 4		26	27	.491	58	51	50-5	1	490.2	514	364	12	31	184	132	3.83	90	.261	.333	451	.204	5	121	-23	-1.5
MATTINGLY, EARL Laurence Earl B 11.4.1904 Newport, MD D 9.8.1993 Brookeville, MD BR/TR 5-10.5/164# d4.15																									
1931	Bro N	0	1	.000	8	0	0	0	14.1	15	4	0	2	10	6	2.51	152	.268	.397	3-0	.000	-0		2	0.1
MATULA, RICK Richard Carlton B 11.22.1953 Wharton, TX BR/TR 6/190# d4.8																									
1979	Atl N	8	10	.444	28	28	1	0-0	171.1	193	90	14	3	64-9	67	4.15	98	.286	.348	53-6	.094	-3	90	-1	-0.4
1980	Atl N	11	13	.458	33	30	3-1	0-0	176.2	195	100	17	0	60-9	62	4.58	82	.286	.339	57-5	.105	-3	79	-16	-2.2
1981	Atl N	0	0	—	5	0	0	0-0	7	8	5	1	0	2-0	0	6.43	56	.286	.333	1-0	.000	-0		-2	-0.1
Total 3		19	23	.452	66	58	4-1	0-0	355	396	195	32	3	126-18	129	4.41	88	.286	.343	111-11	.099	-6	85	-19	-2.7
MATUZAK, HARRY Harry George "Matty" B 1.27.1910 Omer, MI D 11.16.1978 Fairhope, AL BR/TR 5-11.5/185# d4.19																									
1934	Phi A	0	3	.000	11	0	0	0	24	28	16	2	1	10	9	4.88	90	.292	.364	6-1	.167	0		-2	-0.2
1936	Phi A	0	1	.000	6	1	0	0	15	21	14	0	0	4	8	7.20	71	.318	.357	3-1	.000	-0	207	-4	-0.2
Total 2		0	4	.000	17	1	0	0	39	49	30	2	1	14	17	5.77	81	.302	.362	9-2	.111	-0	207	-6	-0.4
MAUCK, HAL Alfred Maris B 3.6.1869 Princeton, IN D 4.27.1921 Princeton, IN BR/TR 5-11/185# d4.29																									
1893	Chi N	8	10	.444	23	18	12-1	0	143	168	112	2	9	60	23	4.41	105	.284	.359	61	.148	-5	84	0	-0.4
MAUL, AL Albert Joseph "Smiling Al" B 10.9.1865 Philadelphia, PA D 5.3.1958 Philadelphia, PA BR/TR 6/175# d6.20 ▲																									
1884	Phi U	0	1	.000	1	1	1	0	8	10	7	0		1	7	4.50	52	.286	.306	4	.000	-1	55	-2	-0.3
1887	Phi N	4	2	.667	7	5	4	0	50.1	72	50	2	2	15	18	5.54	77	.326	.374	56	.304	3*	174	-7	-0.4
1888	Pit N	0	2	.000	3	1	1	0	17	26	20	0	0	5	12	6.35	42	.342	.383	259	.208	1*	23	-8	-0.7
1889	Pit N	1	4	.200	6	4	4	0	42	64	53	3	1	28	11	9.86	38	.340	.429	257	.276	2*	148	-26	-1.9
1890	Pit P	16	12	.571	30	28	26-2	0	246.2	258	189	13	12	104	81	3.79	103	.257	.335	162	.259	7*	124	0	0.7
1891	Pit N	1	2	.333	8	3	3	1	39	44	22	0	3	16	13	2.31	142	.273	.350	149	.188	1*	97	4	0.3
1893	Was N	12	21	.364	37	33	29-1	0	297	355	254	17	18	144	72	5.30	87	.288	.370	134	.254	10*	92	-22	-0.9
1894	Was N	11	15	.423	28	26	21	0	201.2	272	200	12	10	73	34	5.98	88	.319	.379	124-1	.242	3*	99	-9	-0.5
1895	Was N	10	5	.667	16	16	14	0	135.2	136	67	5	3	37	34	**2.45**	**196**	.257	.309	72-2	.250	1*	98	33	3.0
1896	Was N	5	2	.714	8	8	7	0	62	75	50	0	4	20	18	3.63	122	.296	.357	28-0	.286	2	149	2	0.3
1897	Was N	0	1	.000	1	1	0	0	2	4	2	0	0	1	0	9.00	48	.400	.455	1-0	.000	-0	66	-1	-0.1
	Bal N	0	0	—	2	2	0	0	7.2	9	8	0	4	8	2	7.04	59	.290	.488	3-0	.333	0	162	-2	-0.1
	Year	0	1	.000	3	3	0	0	9.2	13	18	0	4	9	2	7.45	56	.317	.481	4-0	.250	-0	130	-3	-0.2
1898	Bal N	20	7	.741	28	28	26-1	0	239.2	207	74	3	4	49	31	2.10	170	.231	.274	93-1	.204	4*	127	42	4.4
1899	Bro N	2	0	1.000	4	4	2	0	26	35	19	1	2	6	2	4.50	87	.321	.368	11-0	.273	0	161	-2	-0.1
1900	Phi N	2	3	.400	5	4	3	0	38	53	31	2	2	3	6	6.16	59	.329	.349	15-0	.200	0	72	-9	-0.9
1901	NY N	0	3	.000	3	3	2	0	19	39	27	1	2	8	5	11.37	29	.419	.476	8-0	.375	1	57	-15	-1.5
Total 15		84	80	.512	187	167	143-4	1	1431.2	1659	1073	59	67	518	346	4.43	96	.284	.349	1376-4	.241	32	112	-22	1.3
MAUN, ERNIE Ernest Gerald B 2.3.1901 Clearwater, KS D 1.1.1987 Corpus Christi, TX BR/TR 6/165# d5.16																									
1924	NY N	2	1	.667	22	0	0	1	35	46	24	2	1	10	5	5.91	62	.326	.375	3-0	.667	1		-8	-0.6
1926	Phi N	1	4	.200	14	5	0	0	37.2	57	36	4	1	18	9	6.45	64	.339	.406	12-0	.250	-0	101	-10	-1.2
Total 2		3	5	.375	36	5	0	1	72.2	103	60	6	2	28	14	6.19	63	.333	.392	15-0	.333	1	101	-18	-1.8
MAUNEY, DICK Richard B 1.26.1920 Concord, NC D 2.6.1970 Albemarle, NC BR/TR 5-11.5/164# d6.13																									
1945	Phi N	6	10	.375	20	16	6-2	1	122.2	127	54	7	2	27	35	3.08	124	.268	.310	41-1	.146	-0*	79	9	1.2
1946	Phi N	6	4	.600	24	7	3-1	2	90	98	36	4	3	18	31	2.70	127	.279	.320	24-3	.167	-1*	125	5	0.6
1947	Phi N	0	0	—	9	1	0	1	16.1	15	8	1	1	7	6	3.86	104	.288	.383	2-0	.000	-0*	66	0	0.0
Total 3		12	14	.462	53	24	9-3	4	229	240	98	12	6	52	72	2.99	123	.274	.319	67-4	.149	-1	92	14	1.8
MAUPIN, HARRY Harry Carr B 7.11.1872 Wellsville, MO D 8.25.1952 Parsons, KS 5-7/150# d10.5																									
1898	StL N	0	2	.000	2	2	2	0	18	22	11	0	3	3	3	5.50	69	.297	.350	7-1	.429	1	94	-2	-0.1
1899	Cle N	0	3	.000	5	3	2	0	25	55	36	0	1	7	3	12.60	29	.437	.470	10-0	.000	-2	91	-21	-1.9
Total 2		0	5	.000	7	5	4	0	43	77	47	0	4	10	6	9.63	39	.385	.425	17-1	.176	-1	92	-23	-2.0
MAURER, DAVE David Charles B 2.23.1975 Minneapolis, MN BR/TL 6-2/205# d7.22																									
2000	SD N	1	0	1.000	14	0	0	0-1	14.2	15	8	2	2	5-1	13	3.68	117	.263	.344	0-0	—	0		0	0.0
2001	SD N	0	0	—	3	0	0	0-0	5	8	6	1	0	4-0	4	10.80	37	.348	.444	1-0	.000	-0		-4	-0.2
2002	Cle A	0	1	.000	2	0	0	0-0	1.1	3	2	1	0	0-0	0	13.50	33	.429	.429	0-0	—	0		-1	-0.2
Total 3		1	1	.500	19	0	0	0-1	21	26	16	4	2	9-1	17	6.00	71	.299	.378	1-0	.000	-0		-5	-0.4
MAURIELLO, RALPH Ralph "Tami" B 8.25.1934 Brooklyn, NY BR/TR 6-3/195# d9.13																									
1958	LA N	1	1	.500	3	2	0	0	11.2	10	6	1	0	8-0	11	4.63	89	.238	.360	4-0	.000	-1	99	0	-0.1
MAUSER, TIM Timothy Edward B 10.4.1966 Fort Worth, TX BR/TR 6/185# d7.7																									
1991	Phi N	0	0	—	3	0	0	0-0	10.2	18	10	3	0	3-0	6	7.59	48	.367	.404	3-0	.000	-0		-5	-0.3
1993	Phi N	0	0	—	8	0	0	0-0	16.1	15	9	1	1	7-0	14	4.96	80	.238	.324	4-0	.000	-0		-1	0.0
	SD N	0	1	.000	28	0	0	0-0	37.2	36	19	5	0	17-5	32	3.58	116	.248	.325	2-0	.000	-0		1	0.1
	Year	0	1	.000	36	0	0	0-0	54	51	33	6	1	24-5	46	4.00	102	.245	.325	6-0	.000	-0		0	0.1
1994	SD N	2	4	.333	35	0	0	2-0	49	50	21	3	1	19-3	32	3.49	118	.269	.335	4-1	.250	0		4	0.4
1995	SD N	0	1	.000	5	0	0	0-0	5.2	4	6	0	0	9-0	9	9.53	42	.190	.433	1-0	.000	-0		-3	-0.5
Total 4		2	6	.250	79	0	0	2-0	119.1	123	65	12	2	55-8	93	4.37	93	.265	.343	14-1	.071	-0		-4	-0.3
MAXCY, BRIAN David Brian B 5.4.1971 Amory, MS BR/TR 6-1/170# d5.27																									
1995	Det A	4	5	.444	41	0	0	0-2	52.1	61	48	6	2	31-7	20	6.88	69	.293	.385	0-0	—	0		-14	-2.0
1996	Det A	0	0	—	2	0	0	0-0	3.1	8	5	2	0	2-0	1	13.50	37	.471	.526	0-0	—	0		-3	-0.1
Total 2		4	5	.444	43	0	0	0-2	55.2	69	53	8	2	33-7	21	7.28	66	.307	.395	0-0	—	0		-17	-2.1
MAXIE, LARRY Larry Hans B 10.10.1940 Upland, CA BR/TR 6-4/220# d8.30																									
1969	Atl N	0	0	—	2	0	0	0-0	3	1	1	0	1	1-1	1	3.00	120	.111	.250	0-0	—	0		0	0.0
MAXWELL, BERT James Albert B 10.17.1886 Texarkana, AR D 12.10.1961 Brady, TX BB/TR 6/180# d9.12																									
1906	Pit N	0	1	.000	1	1	0	0	8	8	6	0	0	2	1	5.63	48	.286	.333	3-0	.000	-0	136	-2	-0.3
1908	Phi A	0	0	—	4	0	0	0	13	23	21	0	2	9	7	11.08	23	.348	.442	5-0	.000	-1		-11	-0.6
1911	NY N	1	2	.333	4	3	3	0	31	37	15	0	2	7	8	2.90	116	.311	.359	9-1	.111	-0	104	1	0.1
1914	Bro F	3	4	.429	12	8	6-1	1	71.1	76	31	0	1	24	19	3.28	88	.276	.337	23-1	.087	-2	92	-2	-0.4
Total 4		4	7	.364	21	12	9-1	1	123.1	144	73	0	5	42	35	4.16	71	.295	.357	40-2	.075	-3	99	-14	-1.2
MAY, DARRELL Darrell Kevin B 6.13.1972 San Bernardino, CA BL/TL 6-2/170# d9.10																									
1995	Atl N	0	0	—	2	0	0	0-0	4	10	5	0	0	0-0	1	11.25	38	.500	.476	0-0	—	0		-3	-0.1
1996	Pit N	0	1	.000	5	2	0	0-0	8.2	15	10	5	1	4-0	5	9.35	47	.357	.426	3-0	.333	0	83	-5	-0.4

Year	Tm Lg	W	L	Pct	G	GS	CG-Sho	SV-BS	IP	H	R	HR	HB	BB-IB	SO	ERA	AERA	OAV	OOB	AB-SH	AVG	PB	Sup	APR	PW
	Cal A	0	0	—	5	0	0	0-0	2.2	3	3	1	0	2-0	1	10.13	49	.333	.385	0-0	—	0		-1	-0.1
1997	Ana A	2	1	.667	29	2	0	0-1	51.2	56	31	6	0	25-2	42	5.23	88	.277	.351	2-0	.000	-0	171	-3	-0.2
2002	KC A	4	10	.286	30	21	2-1	0-1	131.1	144	83	28	1	50-3	95	5.35	94	.277	.339	4-0	.000	-0	80	-4	-0.4
2003	KC A	10	8	.556	35	32	2-1	0-1	210	197	98	31	2	53-1	115	3.77	137	.246	.292	4-1	.000	-0	90	27	1.9
Total	5	16	20	.444	106	57	4-2	0-3	408.1	425	230	71	4	134-6	259	4.69	107	.266	.322	13-1	.077	-1	90	11	0.7
MAY, JAKIE Frank Spruiell B 11.25.1895 Youngsville, NC D 6.3.1970 Wendell, NC BR/TL 5-8/178# d6.26 Mil 1918																									
1917	StL N	0	0	—	15	1	0	0	29.1	29	13	0	3	11	18	3.38	80	.302	.391	4-0	.000	-1	56	-2	-0.1
1918	StL N	5	6	.455	29	15	6	0	152.2	149	83	2	13	69	61	3.83	71	.264	.358	45-4	.067	-1	113	-18	-1.5
1919	StL N	3	12	.200	28	19	8-1	0	125.2	99	64	1	14	87	58	3.22	87	.230	.377	37-3	.162	-1	82	-9	-1.3
1920	StL N	1	4	.200	16	5	3	0	70.2	65	38	0	7	37	33	3.06	98	.251	.360	22-0	.227	1	74	-4	-0.2
1921	StL N	1	3	.250	5	5	1	0	21	29	14	0	0	12	5	4.71	78	.333	.414	6-0	.333	1	90	-3	-0.4
1924	Cin N	3	3	.500	38	3	2	**6**	99	104	39	2	6	29	59	3.00	126	.276	.337	27-1	.111	-2	68	9	0.4
1925	Cin N	8	9	.471	36	12	7-1	2	137.1	146	74	3	7	45	74	3.87	106	.272	.337	43-0	.186	0	104	4	0.4
1926	Cin N	13	9	.591	45	15	9-1	3	167.2	175	66	4	7	44	103	3.22	115	.276	.329	48-6	.146	-1	99	12	1.3
1927	Cin N	15	12	.556	44	28	17-2	1	235.2	242	110	4	14	70	121	3.51	108	.274	.337	76-7	.184	0	103	8	0.9
1928	Cin N	3	5	.375	21	11	1-1	1	79.1	99	44	1	1	35	39	4.42	89	.315	.386	27-3	.296	1	101	-4	-0.3
1929	Cin N	10	14	.417	41	24	10	3	199	219	111	7	5	75	92	4.61	99	.285	.352	64-3	.203	-1	76	1	0.0
1930	Cin N	3	11	.214	26	18	5-1	0	112.1	147	83	6	6	41	44	5.77	84	.320	.383	39-1	.128	-1	84	-13	-1.3
1931	Chi N	5	5	.500	31	4	1	2	79	81	35	2	3	43	38	3.87	100	.275	.372	22-1	.227	1	122	2	0.3
1932	†Chi N	2	2	.500	35	0	0	1	53.2	61	34	3	2	19	20	4.36	86	.281	.345	8-0	.125	-0		-5	-0.4
Total	14	72	95	.431	410	160	70-7	19	1562.1	1645	808	35	88	617	765	3.88	97	.278	.355	468-29	.171	-4	93	-22	-2.2
MAY, RUDY Rudolph B 7.18.1944 Coffeyville, KS BL/TL 6-3/207# d4.18																									
1965	Cal A	4	9	.308	30	19	2-1	0	124	111	59	7	4	78-1	76	3.92	87	.245	.359	30-2	.200	3	71	-7	-0.4
1969	Cal A	10	13	.435	43	25	4	2-0	180.1	142	81	20	3	66-5	133	3.44	101	.220	.295	49-1	.082	-2*	76	0	-0.2
1970	Cal A	7	13	.350	38	34	2-2	0-0	208.2	190	102	20	3	81-7	164	4.01	90	.245	.318	69-2	.087	-2	71	-9	-1.0
1971	Cal A	11	12	.478	32	31	7-2	0-1	208.1	160	74	12	2	87-6	156	3.02	107	.213	.296	68-2	.147	0	77	8	0.9
1972	Cal A	12	11	.522	35	30	10-3	1-0	205.1	162	79	15	0	82-6	169	2.94	99	.215	.292	62-2	.113	-1	82	-2	-0.4
1973	Cal A	7	17	.292	34	28	10-4	0-2	185	177	101	20	3	80-9	134	4.38	81	.254	.330	0-0	—	0	108	-18	-1.9
1974	Cal A	0	1	.000	18	3	0	2-0	27	29	24	2	1	10-0	12	7.00	49	.274	.331	0-0	—	0	137	-11	-0.5
	NY A	8	4	.667	17	15	8-2	0-0	114.1	75	36	5	4	48-0	90	2.28	155	.188	.280	0-0	—	0	130	15	1.5
	Year	8	5	.615	35	18	8-2	2-0	141.1	104	41	7	5	58-0	102	3.18	110	.206	.290	0-0	—	0	131	3	1.0
1975	NY A	14	12	.538	32	31	13-1	0-0	212	179	87	9	2	99-2	145	3.06	121	.231	.317	0-0	—	0	108	13	1.4
1976	NY A	4	3	.571	11	11	2-1	0-0	68	49	32	5	1	28-2	38	3.57	96	.206	.291	0-0	—	0	140	-2	-0.2
	Bal A	11	7	.611	24	21	5-1	0-1	152.1	156	73	11	0	42-3	71	3.78	87	.267	.314	0-0	—	0	124	-10	-1.1
	Year	15	10	.600	35	32	7-2	0-1	220.1	205	78	16	1	70-5	109	3.72	89	.249	.307	0-0	—	0	130	-11	-1.3
1977	Bal A	18	14	.563	37	37	11-4	0-0	251.2	243	114	25	5	78-2	105	3.61	105	.255	.313	0-0	—	0	105	3	0.3
1978	Mon N	8	10	.444	27	23	4-1	0-0	144	141	73	15	6	42-1	87	3.88	91	.255	.313	42-7	.143	0	126	-8	-0.9
1979	Mon N	10	3	.769	33	7	2-1	0-1	93.2	88	30	4	4	31-4	67	2.31	159	.255	.320	21-1	.143	-0	90	13	1.8
1980	†NY A	15	5	.750	41	17	3-1	3-2	175.1	144	56	14	0	39-2	133	**2.46**	**160**	.224	**.268**	0-0	—	0	95	29	3.2
1981	†NY A	6	11	.353	27	22	4	1-0	147.2	137	71	10	2	41-0	79	4.14	86	.246	.298	0-0	—	0	96	-7	-0.7
1982	NY A	6	6	.500	41	6	0	3-3	106	109	43	4	1	14-5	85	2.89	138	.267	.289	0-0	—	0	87	11	1.2
1983	NY A	1	5	.167	15	0	0	0-2	18.1	22	15	1	1	12-1	16	6.87	57	.293	.398	0-0	—	0		-6	-1.1
Total	16	152	156	.494	535	360	87-24	12-12	2622	2314	1150	199	42	958-56	1760	3.46	102	.238	.308	341-17	.123	-2	97	12	1.9
MAY, SCOTT Scott Francis B 11.11.1961 West Bend, WI BR/TR 6-1/185# d9.2																									
1988	Tex A	0	0	—	3	1	0	0-0	7.1	8	7	3	0	4-1	4	8.59	48	.296	.364	0-0	—	0	134	-3	-0.2
1991	Chi N	0	0	—	2	0	0	0-0	2	6	4	0	0	1-0	1	18.00	22	.545	.583	0-0	—	0		-3	-0.1
Total	2	0	0	—	5	1	0	0-0	9.1	14	11	3	0	5-1	5	10.61	38	.368	.422	0-0	—	0	134	-6	-0.3
MAY, BUCKSHOT William Herbert B 12.13.1899 Bakersfield, CA D 3.15.1984 Bakersfield, CA BR/TR 6-2/169# d5.9																									
1924	Pit N	0	0	—	1	0	0	0	1	2	0	0	0	0	1	0.00	—	.500	.500	0-0	—	0		0	0.0
MAYER, ED Edwin David B 11.30.1931 San Francisco, CA BL/TL 6-2/185# d9.15																									
1957	Chi N	0	0	—	3	1	0	0	7.2	8	5	2	1	2-0	3	5.87	66	.258	.324	2-0	.500	0	159	-1	0.0
1958	Chi N	2	2	.500	19	0	0	1	23.2	15	12	0	3	16-1	14	3.80	103	.190	.343	5-0	.200	-0		0	0.0
Total	2	2	2	.500	22	1	0	1	31.1	23	17	2	4	18-1	17	4.31	91	.209	.338	7-0	.286	0	159	-1	0.0
MAYER, ERSKINE Erskine John (b: James Erskine) B 1.16.1889 Atlanta, GA D 3.10.1957 Los Angeles, CA BR/TR 6/168# d9.4 b-Sam																									
1912	Phi N	0	1	.000	7	1	0	0	21.1	27	15	1	1	7	5	6.33	57	.318	.376	3-0	.000	-0	20	-4	-0.2
1913	Phi N	9	9	.500	39	19	7-2	1	170.2	172	77	6	9	46	51	3.11	107	.272	.330	50-0	.120	-2	86	3	0.1
1914	Phi N	21	19	.525	48	38	24-4	2	321	308	135	8	13	91	116	2.58	114	.256	.315	108-3	.194	2	95	12	2.0
1915	†Phi N	21	15	.583	43	33	20-2	2	274.2	240	94	9	14	59	114	2.36	116	.243	.295	88-5	.239	5	90	14	2.5
1916	Phi N	7	7	.500	28	16	7-2	0	140	148	58	7	4	33	62	3.15	84	.281	.328	38-2	.132	-1	92	-5	-0.4
1917	Phi N	11	6	.647	28	18	11-1	0	160	160	62	6	4	33	64	2.76	102	.268	.310	51-5	.196	-0	144	2	0.2
1918	Phi N	7	4	.636	13	13	7	0	104	108	46	2	4	26	16	3.12	96	.276	.328	37-3	.216	1	113	-1	-0.1
	Pit N	9	3	.750	15	14	11-1	0	123.1	122	40	1	4	27	25	2.26	127	.268	.314	42-1	.167	2	139	8	0.9
	Year	16	7	.696	28	27	18-1	0	227.1	230	45	3	8	53	41	2.65	110	.272	.320	79-4	.190	2	126	6	0.8
1919	Pit N	5	3	.625	18	10	6	1	88.1	100	50	2	2	12	20	4.48	67	.267	.294	29-1	.207	0	156	-13	-1.2
	†Chi A	1	3	.250	6	2	0	0	23.2	30	23	1	0	11	9	8.37	38	.316	.387	7-0	.000	-1	123	-12	-1.7
Total	8	91	70	.565	245	164	93-12	6	1427	1415	600	43	55	345	482	2.96	99	.264	.316	453-20	.185	5	106	4	2.1
MAYS, AL Albert C. B 5.17.1865 Canal Dover, OH D 5.7.1905 Parkersburg, WV BR d5.10																									
1885	Lou AA	6	11	.353	17	17	17	0	150	129	102	3	8	43	61	2.76	117	.219	.282	61	.213	0	78	5	0.5
1886	NY AA	11	27	.289	41	40	39-1	0	350	330	231	7	14	140	163	3.39	96	.240	.317	135	.119	-9	80	-10	-1.6
1887	NY AA	17	34	.333	52	52	50	0	441.1	551	359	11	20	136	124	4.73	90	.298	.353	221	.204	-1*	77	-22	-1.6
1888	Bro AA	9	9	.500	18	18	17-1	0	160.2	150	81	1	11	32	67	2.80	107	.238	.287	63	.079	-4	95	5	0.2
1889	Col AA	10	7	.588	21	19	13-1	0	140	167	119	4	4	56	52	4.82	75	.287	.354	54	.130	-1	103	-20	-1.8
1890	Col AA	0	1	.000	1	1	1	0	9	14	13	0	1	8	2	8.00	45	.341	.460	3	.000	-0	56	-5	-0.4
Total	6	53	89	.373	150	147	137-3	0	1251	1341	905	26	58	415	469	3.91	92	.265	.328	537	.160	-15	83	-47	-4.7
MAYS, CARL Carl William "Sub" B 11.12.1891 Liberty, KY D 4.4.1971 ElCajon, CA BL/TR 5-11.5/195# d4.15																									
1915	Bos A	6	5	.545	38	6	2	**7**	131.2	119	54	0	5	21	65	2.60	107	.244	.282	38-2	.237	2	118	2	0.4
1916	†Bos A	18	13	.581	44	24	14-2	3	245	208	79	3	9	74	76	2.39	116	.234	.299	77-3	.234	7*	97	11	2.8
1917	Bos A	22	9	.710	35	33	27-2	0	289	230	81	1	14	74	91	1.74	148	.221	.282	107-2	.252	6	108	25	4.0
1918	†Bos A	21	13	.618	35	33	**30-8**	0	293.1	230	94	2	11	81	114	2.21	121	.221	.284	104-4	.288	10*	119	16	3.7
1919	Bos A	5	11	.313	21	16	14-2	2	146	131	57	2	5	40	53	2.47	123	.247	.306	53-2	.151	-2*	78	6	0.6
	NY A	9	3	.750	13	13	12-1	0	120	96	34	3	5	37	54	1.65	193	.216	.283	45-1	.311	3	128	18	2.3
	Year	14	14	.500	34	29	26-3	2	266	227	39	5	10	77	107	2.10	148	.233	.295	98-3	.224	1	101	25	2.9
1920	NY A	26	11	.703	45	37	26-**6**	2	312	310	127	13	7	84	92	3.06	125	.263	.316	109-8	.239	2	133	28	3.5
1921	†NY A	**27**	9	**.750**	**49**	38	30-1	**7**	**336.2**	332	145	11	9	76	70	3.05	139	.257	.303	143-8	.343	12*	152	43	5.4
1922	†NY A	13	14	.481	34	29	21-1	2	240	257	111	12	7	50	41	3.60	111	.285	.327	92-3	.250	1*	110	11	1.5
1923	NY A	5	2	.714	23	7	2	0	81.1	119	59	8	4	32	16	6.20	64	.357	.420	27-1	.148	1	138	-19	-1.2
1924	Cin N	20	9	.690	37	27	15-2	0	226	238	97	3	4	36	63	3.15	120	.270	.302	83-0	.289	7*	107	15	3.0
1925	Cin N	3	5	.375	12	5	3	2	51.2	60	22	0	2	13	10	3.31	124	.294	.342	16-0	.250	1	66	5	0.9
1926	Cin N	19	12	.613	39	33	**24**-3	1	281	286	112	3	4	53	58	3.14	118	.269	.306	98-7	.224	2	114	21	2.9
1927	Cin N	3	7	.300	14	9	6	0	82	89	39	1	1	10	17	3.51	108	.276	.300	32-1	.406	5	52	2	1.0
1928	Cin N	4	1	.800	14	6	4-1	1	62.2	67	33	3	0	22	10	3.88	102	.275	.335	27-0	.296	1	119	0	0.1
1929	NY N	7	2	.778	37	8	1	4	123	140	67	8	2	31	32	4.32	106	.287	.333	34-2	.353	4	119	5	0.8
Total	15	208	126	.623	490	324	231-29	31	3021.1	2912	1211	73	89	734	862	2.92	119	.257	.307	1085-44	.268	64	117	189	31.7
MAYS, JOE Joseph Emerson B 12.10.1975 Flint, MI BB/TR 6-1/160# d4.7																									
1999	Min A	6	11	.353	49	20	2-1	0-0	171	179	92	24	2	67-2	115	4.37	117	.270	.336	3-0	.000	0	56	12	1.0

Year	Tm Lg	W	L	Pct	G	GS	CG-Sho	SV-BS	IP	H	R	HR	HB	BB-IB	SO	ERA	AERA	OAV	OOB	AB-SH	AVG	PB	Sup	APR	PW
2000	Min A	7	15	.318	31	28	2-1	0-0	160.1	193	105	20	2	67-1	102	5.56	93	.299	.364	5-1	.400	1	70	-6	-0.6
2001	Min A★	17	13	.567	34	34	4-2	0-0	233.2	205	87	25	5	64-2	123	3.16	**146**	.235	.289	1-1	.000	-0	88	**36**	**4.2**
2002	†Min A	4	8	.333	17	17	1-1	0-0	95.1	113	60	14	2	25-0	38	5.38	84	.292	.337	0-0	—	0	92	-9	-0.9
2003	Min A	8	8	.500	31	21	0	0-1	130	159	92	21	4	39-2	50	6.30	72	.302	.353	3-1	.333	1	114	-23	-2.3
Total	5	42	55	.433	162	120	9-5	0-1	790.1	849	436	104	15	262-7	428	4.69	102	.274	.331	12-3	.250	2	83	10	1.4
MAYSEY, MATT Matthew Samuel B 1.8.1967 Hamilton, ON, CAN BR/TR 6-4/225# d7.8																									
1992	Mon N	0	0	—	2	0	0	0-0	2.1	4	1	1	1	0-0	1	3.86	90	.364	.417	0-0	—	0		0	0.0
1993	Mil A	1	2	.333	23	0	0	1-1	22	28	14	4	1	13-1	10	5.73	74	.322	.408	1-0	1.000	0		-3	-0.4
Total	2	1	2	.333	25	0	0	1-1	24.1	32	15	5	2	13-1	11	5.55	75	.327	.409	1-0	1.000	0		-3	-0.4
McADAMS, JACK George D. B 12.17.1886 Benton, AR D 5.21.1937 San Francisco, CA BR/TR 6-1.5/170# d7.22																									
1911	StL N	0	0	—	6	0	0	0	9.2	7	5	0	2	5	4	3.72	91	.226	.368	1-0	.000	-0		0	0.0
McAFEE, BILL William Fort B 9.7.1907 Smithville, GA D 7.8.1958 Culpeper, VA BR/TR 6-2/186# d5.12																									
1930	Chi N	0	0	—	2	0	0	0	1	3	5	0	0	2	0	0.00	—	.375	.500	0-0	—	0		-2	-0.1
1931	Bos N	0	1	.000	18	1	0	0	29.2	39	22	2	0	10	9	6.37	59	.333	.386	3-0	.000	-0	45	-8	-0.4
1932	Was A	6	1	.857	8	5	2	0	41.1	47	22	3	0	22	10	3.92	110	.287	.371	18-2	.111	-2	130	1	0.0
1933	Was A	3	2	.600	27	1	0	5	53	64	40	3	1	21	14	6.62	63	.296	.361	15-2	.267	2	102	-13	-1.1
1934	StL A	1	0	1.000	28	0	0	0	61.2	84	48	4	3	26	11	5.84	86	.332	.401	16-0	.188	-0		-5	-0.3
Total	5	10	4	.714	83	7	2	5	186.2	237	137	12	4	81	44	5.69	78	.313	.382	52-4	.173	0	111	-27	-1.9
McALLISTER, SPORT Lewis William B 7.23.1874 Austin, MS D 7.17.1962 Wyandotte, MI BB/TR 5-11/180# d8.7 ▲																									
1896	Cle N	0	0	—	1	0	0	0	4	9	3	0	0	2	0	6.75	67	.450	.500	27-1	.222	-0*		-1	0.0
1897	Cle N	1	2	.333	4	3	3	0	28	29	20	3	0	9	10	4.50	100	.266	.322	137-4	.219	-0*	106	0	0.0
1898	Cle N	3	4	.429	9	7	6	0	65.1	73	43	2	3	23	9	4.55	80	.281	.346	57-1	.228	1*	95	-5	-0.4
1899	Cle N	0	1	.000	3	1	1	0	16	29	22	0	4	10	2	9.56	39	.387	.483	418-12	.237	0*	20	-10	-0.5
Total	4	4	7	.364	17	11	10	0	113.1	140	88	5	7	44	21	5.32	73	.302	.371	639-18	.232	1	92	-16	-0.9
McANALLY, ERNIE Ernest Lee B 8.15.1946 Pittsburg, TX BR/TR 6-1/190# d4.11																									
1971	Mon N	11	12	.478	31	25	8-2	0-0	177.2	150	85	9	8	87-2	98	3.90	91	.228	.324	60-3	.117	-2	87	-7	-1.0
1972	Mon N	6	15	.286	29	27	4-2	0-0	170	165	79	13	4	71-6	102	3.81	93	.259	.332	53-5	.113	-2	74	-5	-0.6
1973	Mon N	7	9	.438	27	24	4	0-0	147	158	84	13	3	54-6	72	4.04	95	.274	.337	49-4	.184	-1	113	-6	-0.8
1974	Mon N	6	13	.316	25	21	5-2	0-0	128.2	126	73	10	4	56-5	79	4.48	86	.256	.336	42-2	.119	-2	80	-8	-1.3
Total	4	30	49	.380	112	97	21-6	0-0	623.1	599	321	45	19	268-19	351	4.03	91	.253	.332	204-14	.132	-6	89	-26	-3.7
McANDREW, JAMIE James Brian B 9.2.1967 Williamsport, PA BR/TR 6-2/190# d7.17 f-Jim																									
1995	Mil A	2	3	.400	10	4	0	0-0	36.1	37	21	2	1	12-2	19	4.71	106	.266	.329	0-0	—	0	103	1	0.1
1997	Mil A	1	1	.500	5	4	0	0-0	19.1	24	19	1	2	23-0	8	8.38	55	.304	.471	0-0	—	0	94	-8	-0.6
Total	2	3	4	.429	15	8	0	0-0	55.2	61	40	3	3	35-2	27	5.98	81	.280	.387	0-0	—	0	98	-7	-0.5
McANDREW, JIM James Clement B 1.11.1944 Lost Nation, IA BR/TR 6-2/185# d7.21 s-Jamie																									
1968	NY N	4	7	.364	12	12	2-1	0	79	66	20	5	4	17-4	46	2.28	133	.230	.281	22-2	.045	-1	38	7	0.9
1969	NY N	6	7	.462	27	21	4-2	0-0	135	112	57	12	2	44-6	90	3.47	106	.225	.288	37-5	.135	0	95	3	0.2
1970	NY N	10	14	.417	32	27	9-3	2-0	184.1	166	77	18	2	38-6	111	3.56	113	.239	.279	54-8	.148	1	85	12	1.4
1971	NY N	2	5	.286	24	10	0	0-1	90.1	78	50	10	1	32-5	42	4.38	78	.227	.292	23-1	.043	-1	96	-10	-0.9
1972	NY N	11	8	.579	28	23	4	1-0	160.2	133	54	12	5	38-5	81	2.80	120	.225	.276	43-10	.047	-2	91	11	1.0
1973	NY N	3	8	.273	23	12	0	1-0	80.1	109	60	9	3	31-8	38	5.38	67	.330	.386	15-2	.133	2*	106	-19	-2.2
1974	SD N	1	4	.200	15	5	1	0-0	41.2	48	30	7	0	13-2	16	5.62	64	.284	.332	7-2	.143	0	103	-10	-1.1
Total	7	37	53	.411	161	110	20-6	4-1	771.1	712	348	73	17	213-36	424	3.65	98	.245	.297	201-30	.100	-3	88	-6	-0.7
McARTHUR, DIXIE Oland Alexander B 2.1.1892 Vernon, AL D 5.31.1986 West Point, MS BR/TR 6-1/185# d7.10																									
1914	Pit N	0	0	—	1	0	0	0	1	1	1	0	0	0	1	0.00	—	.250	.250	0-0	—	0		0	0.0
McAVOY, TOM Thomas John B 8.12.1936 Brooklyn, NY BL/TL 6-3/200# d9.27																									
1959	Was A	0	0	—	1	0	0	0	2.2	1	0	0	0	2-0	0	0.00	—	.125	.300	1-0	.000	-0		1	0.0
McBEAN, AL Alvin O'Neal B 5.15.1938 Charlotte Amalie, V.I. BR/TR 6/180# d7.2																									
1961	Pit N	3	2	.600	27	2	0	0	74.1	72	35	4	4	42-5	49	3.75	106	.263	.365	15-1	.267	1*	33	2	0.4
1962	Pit N	15	10	.600	33	29	6-2	0	189.2	212	93	11	7	65-2	119	3.70	106	.285	.346	67-4	.209	2*	96	4	0.6
1963	Pit N	13	3	.813	55	7	2-1	11	122.1	100	42	5	2	39-9	74	2.57	128	.222	.287	31-1	.194	2*	131	10	1.7
1964	Pit N	8	3	.727	58	0	0	22	89.2	76	23	4	4	17-8	41	1.91	184	.234	.279	12-2	.083	-1		**15**	2.9
1965	Pit N	6	6	.500	62	1	0	18	114	111	33	5	3	42-11	54	2.29	153	.260	.327	27-2	.222	1	199	16	2.4
1966	Pit N	4	3	.571	47	0	0	3	86.2	95	38	9	2	24-6	54	3.22	111	.280	.330	10-0	.100	-1*		2	0.1
1967	Pit N	7	4	.636	51	8	5	4	131	118	41	6	1	43-6	54	2.54	132	.248	.310	29-1	.207	2	98	13	1.4
1968	Pit N	9	12	.429	36	28	9-2	0	198.1	204	88	10	5	63-5	100	3.58	82	.269	.327	67-2	.194	2*	119	-13	-0.9
1969	SD N	0	1	.000	1	1	0	0-0	7	10	4	1	0	2-0	1	5.14	69	.345	.387	2-0	.500	0	25	-1	-0.1
	LA N	2	6	.250	31	0	0	4-0	48.1	46	22	6	2	21-4	26	3.91	85	.258	.340	3-0	.000	0		-3	-0.5
	Year	2	7	.222	32	1	0	4-0	55.1	56	27	7	2	23-4	27	4.07	82	.271	.346	5-0	.200	0	26	-4	-0.6
1970	LA N	0	0	—	1	0	0	0-0	1	1	0	0	0	0-0	0	0.00	—	.333	.333	0-0	—	0		0	0.0
	Pit N	0	0	—	7	0	0	1-0	10	13	11	2	0	7-0	3	8.10	48	.317	.417	1-0	.000	-0		-5	-0.3
	Year	0	0	—	8	0	0	1-0	11	14	11	2	0	7-0	3	7.36	53	.318	.412	1-0	.000	-0		-5	-0.3
Total	10	67	50	.573	409	76	22-5	63-0	1072.1	1058	430	63	30	365-56	575	3.13	111	.262	.325	264-13	.197	9	104	40	7.7
McBEE, PRYOR Pryor Edward "Lefty" B 6.20.1901 Blanco, OK D 4.19.1963 Roseville, CA BR/TL 6-1/190# d5.22																									
1926	Chi A	0	0	—	1	0	0	0	1.1	1	2	0	0	3	1	6.75	57	.250	.571	0-0	—	0		-1	0.0
McBRIDE, DICK James Dickson B 1845 Philadelphia, PA D 10.10.1916 Philadelphia, PA TR 5-9/150# d5.20 M5																									
1871	Ath NA	18	5	**.783**	25	25	25	0	222	285	223	3		40	15	4.58	88	.280	.307	132	.235	-4	137	-15	-1.2
1872	Ath NA	30	14	.682	47	47	47-1	0	419.1	508	349	3		26	44	2.85	124	.265	.275	258	.287	5	124	34	2.6
1873	Ath NA	24	19	.558	46	46	38-**3**	0	382.2	453	325	3		47	25	3.34	102	.262	.281	253	.281	3*	96	15	1.2
1874	Ath NA	33	22	.600	55	55	55	0	487	514	344	6		32	37	**1.64**	**141**	**.240**	**.251**	263	.217	-7	101	**34**	1.9
1875	Ath NA	44	14	.759	60	60	59-6	0	538	607	297	4		24	27	2.33	103	.267	.275	270	.270	3	142	5	0.3
1876	Bos N	0	4	.000	4	4	3	0	33	53	35	1		5	2	2.73	83	.353	.374	16	.188	-1	56	-4	-0.4
Total	5 NA	149	74	.668	233	233	224-10	0	2049	2367	1538	19		169	148	2.71	111	.261	.274	1176	.260	0	117	73	4.8
McBRIDE, KEN Kenneth Faye B 8.12.1935 Huntsville, AL BR/TR 6/195# d8.4 C1																									
1959	Chi A	0	1	.000	11	2	0	1	22.2	20	11	1	0	17-0	12	3.18	118	.230	.356	6-0	.167	-0	70	1	0.0
1960	Chi A	0	1	.000	5	0	0	0	4.2	6	2	0	1	3-0	4	3.86	98	.333	.435	0-0	—	0		0	0.0
1961	LA A☆	12	15	.444	38	36	11-1	1	241.2	229	114	28	7	102-4	180	3.65	124	.252	.331	83-6	.084	-5*	82	20	1.7
1962	LA A✢	11	5	.688	24	23	6-4	0	149.1	136	66	9	9	70-3	83	3.50	110	.249	.341	55-0	.164	0	110	7	1.0
1963	LA A★	13	12	.520	36	36	11-2	0	251	198	101	22	14	82-1	147	3.26	105	.218	.291	87-5	.172	2*	116	7	1.0
1964	LA A	4	13	.235	29	21	0	1	116.1	104	77	14	16	75-0	66	5.26	62	.239	.369	28-2	.214	3	101	-27	-3.1
1965	Cal A	0	3	.000	8	4	0	0	22	24	17	1	2	14-0	11	6.14	55	.270	.377	5-0	.000	-0	77	-7	-0.9
Total	7	40	50	.444	151	122	28-7	3	807.2	717	388	75	49	363-8	503	3.79	101	.240	.330	264-13	.144	-0	99	1	-0.3
McBRIDE, PETE Peter William B 7.9.1875 Adams, MA D 7.3.1944 N.Adams, MA BR/TR 5-10/170# d9.20																									
1898	Cle N	0	1	.000	1	1	1	0	7	9	6	0	1	4	6	6.43	56	.310	.412	2-0	1.000	2	98	-2	-0.1
1899	StL N	2	4	.333	11	6	4	0	64	65	46	4	4	40	26	4.08	98	.263	.375	27-0	.185	0*	93	-2	-0.1
Total	2	2	5	.286	12	7	5	0	71	74	52	4	5	44	32	4.31	92	.268	.378	29-0	.241	2	94	-4	-0.2
McCABE, RALPH Ralph Herbert "Mack" B 10.21.1918 Napanee, ON, CAN D 5.3.1974 Windsor, ON, CAN BR/TR 6-4/195# d9.18																									
1946	Cle A	0	1	.000	1	1	0	0	4	5	5	3	1	2	3	11.25	29	.313	.421	1-0	.000	-0	26	-3	-0.5
McCABE, DICK Richard James B 2.21.1896 Mamaroneck, NY D 4.11.1950 Buffalo, NY BR/TR 5-10.5/159# d5.30																									
1918	Bos A	0	1	.000	3	1	0	0	9.2	13	4	0	0	2	3	2.79	96	.351	.385	2-0	.000	-0	0	0	0.0

Year	Tm Lg	W	L	Pct	G	GS	CG-Sho	SV-BS	IP	H	R	HR	HB	BB-IB	SO	ERA	AERA	OAV	OOB	AB-SH	AVG	PB	Sup	APR	PW
1922	Chi A	1	0	1.000	3	0	0	0	3.1	4	2	0	0	0	1	5.40	75	.308	.308	0-0	—	0		0	-0.1
Total	2	1	1	.500	6	1	0	0	13	17	6	0	0	2	4	3.46	88	.340	.365	2-0	.000	-0	0	0	-0.1
McCABE, TIM Timothy J. B 10.19.1894 Ironton, MO D 4.12.1977 Ironton, MO BR/TR 6/190# d8.16																									
1915	StL A	3	1	.750	7	4	4-1	0	41.2	25	11	1	1	9	17	1.30	221	.177	.232	15-0	.067	-1	115	7	0.5
1916	StL A	2	0	1.000	13	0	0	0	25.2	29	20	0	2	7	7	3.16	87	.282	.339	4-0	.000	-0		-4	-0.3
1917	StL A	0	0	—	1	0	0	0	2.1	4	6	1	0	4	2	23.14	11	.400	.571	0-0	—	0		-5	-0.2
1918	StL A	0	0	—	1	0	0	0	1.1	2	2	0	0	1	0	13.50	20	.333	.429	0-0	—	0		-1	-0.1
Total	4	5	1	.833	22	4	4-1	0	71	60	39	2	3	21	26	2.92	96	.231	.296	19-0	.053	-1	115	-3	-0.1
McCAFFERY, HARRY Harry Charles B 11.25.1858 St.Louis, MO D 4.19.1928 St.Louis, MO BR/TR 5-10.5/185# d6.15.1882 U1 ▲																									
1885	Cin AA	1	0	1.000	1	1	1	0	9	13	9	1	2	2	2	6.00	54	.342	.405	5	.000	-1	199	-3	-0.3
McCAHAN, BILL William Glenn B 6.7.1921 Philadelphia, PA D 7.3.1986 Fort Worth, TX BR/TR 5-11/200# d9.15																									
1946	Phi A	1	1	.500	4	2	2-1	0	18	16	2	0	0	9	6	1.00	355	.246	.338	5-0	.400	1	36	5	0.7
1947	Phi A	10	5	.667	29	19	10-1	0	165.1	160	73	7	0	62	47	3.32	115	.252	.318	55-3	.164	-1	99	7	0.6
1948	Phi A	4	7	.364	17	15	5	0	86.2	98	58	8	0	65	20	5.71	75	.284	.398	31-0	.258	1	91	-13	-1.3
1949	Phi A	1	1	.500	7	4	0	0	20.2	23	9	0	0	9	3	2.61	157	.291	.364	5-0	.200	-0	93	3	0.2
Total	4	16	14	.533	57	40	17-2	0	290.2	297	142	15	0	145	76	3.84	103	.264	.348	96-3	.208	1	93	2	0.2
McCALL, WINDY John William B 7.18.1925 San Francisco, CA BL/TL 6/180# d4.25																									
1948	Bos A	0	1	.000	1	1	0	0	1.1	6	3	1	0	1	0	20.25	22	.600	.636	0-0	—	0	82	-2	-0.3
1949	Bos A	0	0	—	5	0	0	0	9.1	13	12	2	0	10	8	11.57	38	.333	.469	3-1	.667	1		-7	-0.3
1950	Pit N	0	0	—	2	0	0	0	6.2	12	7	2	0	4	5	9.45	46	.387	.457	2-0	.000	0		-3	-0.1
1954	NY N	2	5	.286	33	4	0	2	61	50	26	5	3	29	38	3.25	124	.219	.314	11-0	.000	-1	83	5	0.4
1955	NY N	6	5	.545	42	6	4	3	95	86	45	8	6	37-6	50	3.69	109	.244	.325	17-3	.118	-1	100	4	0.4
1956	NY N	3	4	.429	46	4	0	7	77.1	74	36	7	1	20-5	41	3.61	105	.252	.301	15-0	.200	-0	76	1	0.0
1957	NY N	0	0	—	5	0	0	0	3	8	5	1	1	2-0	2	15.00	26	.533	.579	0-0	—	0		-3	-0.2
Total	7	11	15	.423	134	15	4	12	253.2	249	134	26	11	103-11	144	4.22	94	.257	.334	48-4	.146	-1	88	-5	-0.1
McCALL, LARRY Larry Stephen B 9.8.1952 Asheville, NC BL/TR 6-2/195# d9.10																									
1977	NY A	0	1	.000	2	0	0	0-0	6	12	7	1	0	1-0	0	7.50	53	.375	.394	0-0	—	0*		-3	-0.4
1978	NY A	1	1	.500	5	1	0	0-0	16	20	10	2	1	6-0	7	5.63	65	.323	.391	0-0	—	0	49	-3	-0.3
1979	Tex A	1	0	1.000	2	1	0	0-0	8.1	7	2	0	0	3-0	3	2.16	193	.226	.286	0-0	—	0	87	2	0.2
Total	3	2	2	.500	9	2	0	0-0	30.1	39	19	3	1	10-0	10	5.04	76	.312	.365	0-0	—	0	70	-4	-0.5
McCALL, DUTCH Robert Leonard B 12.27.1920 Columbia, TN D 1.7.1996 Little Rock, AR BL/TL 6-1/184# d4.27																									
1948	Chi N	4	13	.235	30	20	5	0	151.1	158	93	14	1	85	89	4.82	81	.268	.361	53-2	.170	1	97	-15	-1.3
McCAMENT, RANDY Larry Randall B 7.29.1962 Albuquerque, NM BR/TR 6-3/195# d6.28																									
1989	SF N	1	1	.500	25	0	0	0-0	36.2	32	22	4	1	23-2	12	3.93	86	.241	.354	3-0	.333	0		-4	-0.2
1990	SF N	0	0	—	3	0	0	0-0	6	8	2	0	0	5-0	5	3.00	122	.333	.433	1-0	.000	-0		1	0.0
Total	2	1	1	.500	28	0	0	0-0	42.2	40	24	4	1	28-2	17	3.80	90	.255	.367	4-0	.250	0		-3	-0.2
McCANN, GENE Henry Eugene "Mike" B 6.13.1876 Baltimore, MD D 4.26.1943 New York, NY TR 5-10/185# d4.19																									
1901	Bro N	2	3	.400	6	5	3	0	34	34	25	1	4	16	9	3.44	97	.260	.358	10-1	.000	-1	127	-3	-0.4
1902	Bro N	1	2	.333	3	3	3	0	30	32	18	0	0	12	9	2.40	115	.274	.341	12-0	.083	-1	82	-1	-0.2
Total	2	3	5	.375	9	8	6	0	64	66	43	1	4	28	18	2.95	104	.266	.350	22-1	.045	-2	113	-4	-0.6
McCARTHY, ARCH Archibald Joseph B Ypsilanti, MI TR 6/160# d8.14																									
1902	Det A	2	7	.222	10	8	8	0	72	90	57	2	4	31	10	6.13	60	.306	.380	28-0	.071	-3	72	-15	-1.8
McCARTHY, GREG Gregory O'Neil B 10.30.1968 Norwalk, CT BL/TL 6-2/195# d8.28																									
1996	Sea A	0	0	—	10	0	0	0-0	9.2	8	2	0	4	4-0	7	1.86	266	.229	.364	0-0	—	0		3	0.2
1997	Sea A	1	1	.500	37	0	0	0-0	29.2	26	21	4	1	16-0	34	5.46	82	.230	.331	0-0	—	0		-4	-0.2
1998	Sea A	1	2	.333	29	0	0	0-1	23.1	18	13	6	3	17-2	25	5.01	92	.214	.365	0-0	—	0		0	0.0
Total	3	2	3	.400	76	0	0	0-1	62.2	52	36	10	8	37-2	66	4.74	98	.224	.349	0-0	—	0		-1	0.0
McCARTHY, TOMMY Thomas Francis Michael B 7.24.1863 Boston, MA D 8.5.1922 Boston, MA BR/TR 5-7/170# d7.10 M1 HF1946 ▲																									
1884	Bos U	0	7	.000	7	6	5	0	56	73	53	2		14	18	4.82	49	.296	.333	209	.215	-2*	69	-14	-1.4
1886	Phi N	0	0	—	1	0	0	0	1	0	0	0		1	1	0.00	—	.000	.250	27	.185	0*		0	0.0
1888	†StL AA	0	1	.000	2	1	0	0	5.1	5	5	1	0	2	1	5.06	64	.238	.304	511	.274	0*	53	-1	-0.1
1889	StL AA	0	0	—	1	0	0	0	5	4	4	0	0	6	1	7.20	59	.211	.400	604	.291	0*		-1	0.0
1891	StL AA	0	0	—	1	0	0	0	1	2	2	0	0	0	0	9.00	47	.400	.400	570	.309	0*		-1	0.0
1894	Bos N	0	0	—	1	0	0	0	2	1	1	0	0	3	0	4.50	126	.143	.400	539-9	.349	0*		0	0.0
Total	6	0	8	.000	13	7	5	0	70.1	85	65	3	0	26	21	4.99	54	.281	.338	2460-9	.297	-1	65	-17	-1.5
McCARTHY, TOM Thomas Michael B 6.18.1961 Lundstahl, W.Germany BR/TR 6/180# d7.5																									
1985	Bos A	0	0	—	3	0	0	0-0	5	7	6	1	0	4-0	2	10.80	40	.350	.440	0-0	—	0		-3	-0.2
1988	Chi A	2	0	1.000	6	0	0	1-0	13	9	2	0	2	2-0	5	1.38	287	.191	.255	0-0	—	0		4	0.6
1989	Chi A	1	2	.333	31	0	0	0-0	66.2	72	32	8	2	20-0	27	3.51	109	.280	.333	0-0	—	0		1	0.1
Total	3	3	2	.600	40	0	0	1-0	84.2	88	40	9	4	26-0	34	3.61	107	.272	.330	0-0	—	0		2	0.5
McCARTHY, TOM Thomas Patrick B 5.22.1884 Ft.Wayne, IN D 3.28.1933 Mishawaka, IN TR 5-7/170# d5.10																									
1908	Cin N	0	1	.000	1	1	0	0	3.2	6	5	0	0	3	3	9.82	23	.300	.391	2-0	.000	-0	214	-3	-0.5
	Pit N	0	0	—	2	1	0	0	6	3	1	0	0	6	1	0.00	—	.176	.391	4-0	.000	-0*	398	1	0.0
	Bos N	7	3	.700	14	11	7-2	0	94	77	24	0	1	28	27	1.63	148	.235	.298	35-4	.171	0	135	8	1.0
	Year	7	4	.636	17	13	7-2	0	103.2	86	29	0	1	37	31	1.82	132	.236	.308	41-4	.146	-1	160	6	0.5
1909	Bos N	0	5	.000	8	7	3	0	46.1	47	28	3	2	28	11	3.50	81	.272	.379	16-1	.125	-0*	78	-4	-0.5
Total	2	7	9	.438	25	20	10-2	0	150	133	58	3	3	65	42	2.34	108	.248	.332	57-5	.140	-1	129	2	0.0
McCARTHY, BILL William Thomas B 4.11.1882 Ashland, MA D 5.29.1939 Boston, MA BR/TR 5-11/180# d4.21																									
1906	Bos N	0	0	—	1	0	0	0	2	2	6	0	0	3	0	9.00	30	.182	.357	1-0	.000	-0		-3	-0.1
McCARTY, JOHN John A. B St.Louis, MO TR d4.18																									
1889	KC AA	8	6	.571	15	14	13	0	119.2	147	108	4	6	61	36	3.91	107	.293	.376	79	.228	-2*	122	-1	-0.2
McCASKILL, KIRK Kirk Edward B 4.9.1961 Kapuskasing, ON, CAN BR/TR 6-1/196# d5.1																									
1985	Cal A	12	12	.500	30	29	6-1	0-0	189.2	189	105	23	4	64-1	102	4.70	88	.258	.319	0-0	—	0	108	-10	-1.2
1986	†Cal A	17	10	.630	34	33	10-2	0-0	246.1	207	98	19	5	92-1	202	3.36	123	.229	.302	0-0	—	0	101	23	2.2
1987	Cal A	4	6	.400	14	13	1-1	0-0	74.2	84	52	14	2	34-0	56	5.67	76	.286	.363	0-0	—	0*	78	-11	-1.2
1988	Cal A	8	6	.571	23	23	4-2	0-0	146.1	155	78	9	1	61-3	98	4.31	90	.274	.342	0-0	—	0	130	-8	-0.7
1989	Cal A	15	10	.600	32	32	6-4	0-0	212	202	73	16	3	59-1	107	2.93	130	.254	.307	0-0	—	0	88	22	2.7
1990	Cal A	12	11	.522	29	29	2-1	0-0	174.1	161	77	9	2	72-1	78	3.25	118	.244	.320	0-0	—	0	94	9	1.2
1991	Cal A	10	19	.345	30	30	1	0-0	177.2	193	93	19	3	66-1	71	4.26	97	.283	.347	0-0	—	0	65	-3	-0.4
1992	Chi A	12	13	.480	34	34	0	0-0	209	193	116	11	6	95-5	109	4.18	93	.242	.325	0-0	—	0	105	-11	-1.1
1993	†Chi A	4	8	.333	30	14	0	2-0	113.2	144	71	12	1	36-6	65	5.23	80	.313	.362	0-0	—	0	102	-13	-1.1
1994	Chi A	1	4	.200	40	0	0	3-3	52.2	51	22	6	0	22-4	37	3.42	137	.252	.322	0-0	—	0		8	0.7
1995	Chi A	6	4	.600	55	1	0	2-3	81	97	50	10	5	33-4	50	4.89	91	.302	.373	0-0	—	0	125	-5	-0.5
1996	Chi A	5	5	.500	29	4	0	0-1	51.2	72	41	6	2	31-8	28	6.97	68	.344	.432	0-0	—	0	151	-12	-1.9
Total	12	106	108	.495	380	242	30-11	7-7	1729	1748	876	154	34	665-35	1003	4.12	99	.264	.332	0-0	—	0	97	-11	-1.3
McCATTY, STEVE Steven Earl B 3.20.1954 Detroit, MI BR/TR 6-3/205# d9.17 C1																									
1977	Oak A	0	0	—	4	2	0	0-0	14.1	16	9	1	1	7-0	9	5.02	80	.276	.364	0-0	—	0	89	-1	-0.1
1978	Oak A	0	0	—	9	0	0	0-0	20	26	14	1	0	9-1	10	4.50	81	.310	.361	0-0	—	0		-3	-0.2
1979	Oak A	11	12	.478	31	23	8	0-0	185.2	207	106	17	10	80-8	87	4.22	96	.284	.359	0-0	—	0	91	-7	-0.8
1980	Oak A	14	14	.500	33	31	11-1	0-1	221.2	202	104	27	8	99-2	114	3.86	98	.240	.323	0-0	—	0	122	-1	-0.2

Year	Tm Lg	W	L	Pct	G	GS	CG-Sho	SV-BS	IP	H	R	HR	HB	BB-IB	SO	ERA	AERA	OAV	OOB	AB-SH	AVG	PB	Sup	APR	PW
1981	†Oak A	**14**	7	.667	22	22	16-**4**	0-0	185.2	140	50	12	2	61-1	91	**2.33**	150	**.211**	.277	0-0	—	0	111	**27**	3.0
1982	Oak A	6	3	.667	21	20	2	0-0	128.2	124	62	16	4	70-0	66	3.99	98	.255	.351	0-0	—	0	131	0	-0.1
1983	Oak A	6	9	.400	38	24	3-2	5-1	167	156	79	16	1	82-4	65	3.99	97	.247	.331	0-0	—	0*	87	-1	-0.2
1984	Oak A	8	14	.364	33	30	4	0-0	179.2	206	101	24	1	71-0	63	4.76	79	.289	.353	0-0	—	0	116	-19	-2.1
1985	Oak A	4	4	.500	30	9	1	0-0	85.2	95	56	10	4	41-4	36	5.57	69	.286	.368	0-0	—	0	144	-16	-1.3
Total	9	63	63	.500	221	161	45-7	5-2	1188.1	1172	581	124	31	520-20	541	3.99	95	.258	.336	0-0	—	0	112	-21	-2.0
McCAULEY, AL Allen A. B 3.4.1863 Indianapolis, IN D 8.24.1917 Wayne Twnshp., IN BL/TL 6/180# d6.21 ▲																									
1884	Ind AA	2	7	.222	10	9	9	0	76	87	74	2	0	25	34	5.09	65	.261	.313	53	.189	2*	90	-15	-1.1
McCLAIN, JOE Joseph Fred B 5.5.1933 Johnson City, TN BR/TR 6/183# d4.14																									
1961	Was A	8	18	.308	33	29	7-2	1	212	221	105	22	4	48-7	76	3.86	104	.270	.309	68-2	.206	1	71	4	0.4
1962	Was A	0	4	.000	10	4	0	0	24	33	25	8	2	11-1	6	9.38	43	.327	.397	7-0	.143	-0	72	-13	-1.8
Total	2	8	22	.267	43	33	7-2	1	236	254	130	30	6	59-8	82	4.42	91	.276	.319	75-2	.200	1	71	-9	-1.4
McCLELLAN, PAUL Paul William B 2.3.1966 San Mateo, CA BR/TR 6-2/180# d9.2																									
1990	SF N	0	1	.000	4	1	0	0-0	7.2	14	10	3	1	6-0	2	11.74	31	.389	.488	2-0	.500	0	149	-7	-0.7
1991	SF N	3	6	.333	13	12	1	0-0	71	68	41	12	1	25-1	44	4.56	79	.252	.316	21-2	.143	-0	123	-9	-1.1
Total	2	3	7	.300	17	13	1	0-0	78.2	82	51	15	2	31-1	46	5.26	68	.268	.338	23-2	.174	0	125	-16	-1.8
McCLOSKEY, JIM James Ellwood "Irish" B 5.26.1910 Danville, PA D 8.18.1971 Jersey City, NJ BL/TL 5-9.5/180# d4.21																									
1936	Bos N	0	0	—	4	1	0	0	8	14	10	1	1	3	2	11.25	34	.378	.439	1-0	.000	-0	133	-6	-0.3
McCLOSKEY, JOHN James John B 8.20.1882 Wyoming, PA D 6.5.1919 Wilkes-Barre, PA d5.3																									
1906	Phi N	3	2	.600	9	4	3	0	41	46	21	2	1	9	6	2.85	92	.280	.322	15-0	.200	0	146	-2	-0.2
1907	Phi N	0	0	—	3	0	0	0	9	15	9	0	1	6	3	7.00	35	.417	.512	4-0	.000	-0		-4	-0.3
Total	2	3	2	.600	12	4	3	0	50	61	30	2	2	15	9	3.60	72	.305	.359	19-0	.158	-0	146	-6	-0.5
McCLUNG, SETH Michael Seth B 2.7.1981 Lewisburg, WV BR/TR 6-6/230# d3.31																									
2003	TB A	4	1	.800	12	5	0	0-0	38.2	33	23	6	3	25-1	25	5.35	85	.241	.367	0-0	—	0	93	-3	-0.3
McCLURE, BOB Robert Craig B 4.29.1952 Oakland, CA BR/TL 5-11/170# d8.13 C1																									
1975	KC A	1	0	1.000	12	0	0	1-0	15.1	4	0	0	0	14-2	15	0.00	—	.077	.273	0-0	—	0		6	0.5
1976	KC A	0	0	—	8	0	0	0-0	4	3	4	0	0	8-0	3	9.00	39	.214	.500	0-0	—	0*		-2	-0.1
1977	Mil A	2	1	.667	68	0	0	6-1	71.1	64	25	2	1	34-5	57	2.52	162	.249	.333	0-0	—	0		11	0.7
1978	Mil A	2	6	.250	44	0	0	9-4	65	53	30	8	6	30-4	47	3.74	101	.223	.322	0-0	—	0		0	0.0
1979	Mil A	5	2	.714	36	0	0	5-1	51	53	29	6	3	24-0	37	3.88	108	.269	.352	0-0	—	0		0	-0.1
1980	Mil A	5	8	.385	52	5	2-1	10-5	90.2	83	34	6	2	37-2	47	3.08	126	.241	.314	0-0	—	0	88	9	1.3
1981	†Mil A	0	0	—	4	0	0	0-0	7.2	7	3	1	0	4-1	6	3.52	97	.233	.324	0-0	—	0		0	0.0
1982	†Mil A	12	7	.632	34	26	5	0-0	172.2	160	90	21	4	74-4	99	4.22	90	.248	.327	0-0	—	0	143	-9	-0.9
1983	Mil A	9	9	.500	24	23	4	0-0	142	152	75	11	5	68-1	68	4.50	83	.277	.360	0-0	—	0	115	-12	-1.3
1984	Mil A	4	8	.333	39	18	1	1-0	139.2	154	76	9	2	52-4	68	4.38	88	.282	.342	0-0	—	0	124	-8	-0.6
1985	Mil A	4	1	.800	38	1	0	3-1	85.2	91	43	10	3	30-2	57	4.31	97	.274	.338	0-0	—	0	87	0	0.0
1986	Mil A	2	1	.667	13	0	0	0-0	16.1	18	7	2	0	10-1	11	3.86	112	.286	.378	0-0	—	0		1	0.2
	Mon N	2	5	.286	52	0	0	6-2	62.2	53	22	2	1	23-2	42	3.02	123	.232	.303	4-0	.250	0		5	0.7
1987	Mon N	6	1	.857	52	0	0	5-1	52.1	47	30	8	0	20-3	33	3.44	122	.241	.309	2-0	.000	-0		1	0.2
1988	Mon N	1	3	.250	19	0	0	2-0	19	23	13	3	1	6-0	12	6.16	58	.307	.357	2-0	.000	-0		-4	-0.9
	NY N	1	0	1.000	14	0	0	1-0	11	12	5	1	1	2-0	7	4.09	79	.279	.326	0-0	—	-0		-1	-0.1
	Year	2	3	.400	33	0	0	3-0	30	35	22	4	2	8-0	19	5.40	64	.297	.346	2-0	.000	-0		-5	-1.0
1989	Cal A	6	1	.857	48	0	0	3-0	52.1	39	14	2	1	15-1	36	1.55	247	.212	.270	0-0	—	0		12	1.5
1990	Cal A	2	0	1.000	11	0	0	0-1	7	7	6	0	0	3-0	6	6.43	60	.269	.345	0-0	—	0		-2	-0.4
1991	Cal A	0	0	—	13	0	0	0-0	9.2	13	11	3	1	5-0	5	9.31	44	.317	.396	0-0	—	0		-6	-0.3
	StL N	1	1	.500	32	0	0	0-4	23	24	8	1	1	8-2	15	3.13	119	.282	.340	1-0	1.000	0		2	0.2
1992	StL N	2	2	.500	71	0	0	0-0	54	52	21	6	2	25-5	24	3.17	107	.261	.345	0-0	—	0		1	0.1
1993	Fla N	1	1	.500	14	0	0	0-2	6.1	13	5	2	0	5-0	6	7.11	61	.419	.500	0-0	—	0		-2	-0.3
Total	19	68	57	.544	698	73	12-1	52-22	1158.2	1125	551	104	34	497-39	701	3.81	101	.257	.334	9-0	.222	0	122	2	0.4
McCLUSKEY, HARRY Harry Robert B 3.29.1892 Clay Center, OH D 6.7.1962 Toledo, OH BL/TL 5-11.5/173# d7.29																									
1915	Cin N	0	0	—	3	0	0	0	5	4	3	0	0	0	2	5.40	53	.182	.182	2-0	.000	-0		-1	-0.1
McCOLL, ALEX Alexander Boyd "Red" B 3.29.1894 Eagleville, OH D 2.6.1991 Kingsville, OH BB/TR 6-1/178# d8.27																									
1933	†Was A	1	0	1.000	4	1	1	0	17	13	5	0	0	7	5	2.65	158	.210	.290	6-0	.333	1	61	3	0.2
1934	Was A	3	4	.429	42	2	1	1	112	129	56	6	1	36	29	3.86	112	.291	.345	31-0	.097	-2	40	5	0.2
Total	2	4	4	.500	46	3	2	1	129	142	61	6	1	43	34	3.70	116	.281	.338	37-0	.135	-1	47	8	0.4
McCONNAUGHEY, RALPH Ralph James B 8.5.1889 Vandergrift, PA D 6.4.1966 Detroit, MI BR/TR 5-8.5/166# d7.8																									
1914	Ind F	0	2	.000	7	2	1	0	26	23	15	3	1	16	7	4.85	64	.245	.360	8-0	.125	-0	55	-3	-0.3
McCONNELL, GEORGE George Neely "Slats" B 9.16.1877 Shelbyville, TN D 5.10.1964 Chattanooga, TN BR/TR 6-3/190# d4.13 ▲																									
1909	NY A	0	1	.000	2	1	0	0	4	3	2	0	0	3	4	2.25	112	.231	.375	43-1	.209	0*	28	0	0.0
1912	NY A	8	12	.400	23	20	19	0	176.2	172	96	3	4	52	91	2.75	131	.269	.328	91-1	.297	3*	65	8	1.6
1913	NY A	4	15	.211	35	20	8	3	180	162	90	2	7	60	72	3.20	94	.247	.317	67-3	.179	-1*	83	-5	-0.4
1914	Chi N	0	1	.000	1	1	0	0	7	3	1	0	0	3	3	1.29	216	.125	.222	2-0	.000	-0	0	1	0.2
1915	Chi F	**25**	10	**.714**	44	35	23-4	1	303	262	103	8	8	89	151	2.20	114	.232	.292	125-3	.248	4*	124	9	1.7
1916	Chi N	4	12	.250	28	21	8-1	0	171.1	137	66	8	5	35	82	2.57	113	.223	.271	57-2	.158	-2	65	5	0.4
Total	6	41	51	.446	133	98	58-5	4	842	739	358	21	24	242	403	2.60	112	.240	.301	385-10	.229	4	86	18	3.5
McCOOL, BILLY William John B 7.14.1944 Batesville, IN BR/TL 6-2/203# d4.24																									
1964	Cin N	6	5	.545	40	3	0	7	89.1	66	27	3	1	29-5	87	2.42	150	.206	.272	17-1	.000	-2	49	12	1.4
1965	Cin N	9	10	.474	62	2	0	21	105.1	93	53	9	4	47-7	120	4.27	88	.237	.324	27-0	.037	-2	70	-5	-1.2
1966	Cin N☆	8	8	.500	57	0	0	18	105.1	76	32	5	3	41-7	104	2.48	157	.205	.288	18-0	.167	-0		15	3.0
1967	Cin N	3	7	.300	31	11	0	2	97.1	92	45	8	5	56-7	83	3.42	110	.246	.351	26-1	.077	-1	83	2	0.1
1968	Cin N	3	4	.429	30	4	0	2	50.2	59	35	4	0	41-4	30	4.97	64	.294	.408	8-1	.125	-0	130	-11	-1.7
1969	SD N	3	5	.375	54	0	0	7-2	58.2	59	32	2	6	42-8	35	4.30	82	.266	.393	1-0	.000	-0		-5	-0.9
1970	StL N	0	3	.000	18	0	0	1-1	21.2	20	15	0	0	16-0	12	6.23	66	.250	.367	4-1	.000	-0		-4	-0.6
Total	7	32	42	.432	292	20	0	58-3	528.1	465	239	31	19	272-38	471	3.59	103	.237	.334	101-4	.069	-6	83	4	0.1
McCORMICK, JIM James B 11.3.1856 Glasgow, Scotland D 3.10.1918 Paterson, NJ BR/TR 5-10.5/215# d5.20 M3																									
1878	Ind N	5	8	.385	14	14	12-1	0	117	128	47	0		15	36	1.69	120	.269	.292	56	.143	-3*	106	5	0.4
1879	Cle N	20	40	.333	62	60	59-3	0	546.1	582	308	3		74	197	2.42	103	.259	.282	282	.220	-1*	68	6	0.6
1880	Cle N	**45**	28	.616	**74**	**74**	**72**-7	0	**657.2**	585	274	2		75	260	1.85	127	.226	.247	289	.246	1*	101	**39**	**4.2**
1881	Cle N	26	30	.464	59	58	**57**-2	0	526	484	267	4		84	178	2.45	107	.235	.265	309	.256	6*	104	9	1.2
1882	Cle N	**36**	30	.545	**68**	**67**	**65**-4	0	**595.2**	550	274	14		103	200	2.37	118	.238	.271	262	.218	-4*	92	30	2.3
1883	Cle N	28	12	**.700**	43	41	36-1	1	342	316	151	1		65	145	**1.84**	**171**	.233	.268	157	.236	-1	102	47	4.8
1884	Cle N	19	22	.463	42	41	39-3	0	359	357	206	16		75	182	2.86	110	.247	.285	190	.263	2*	76	13	1.4
	Cin U	21	3	**.875**	24	24	24-**7**	0	210	151	57	3		14	161	**1.54**	**166**	**.188**	**.202**	110	.245	-6*	114	**26**	1.9
1885	Pro N	1	3	.250	4	4	4	0	37	34	26	1		20	8	2.43	110	.234	.327	14	.214	0	68	-1	0.1
	†Chi N	20	4	.833	24	24	24-3	0	215	187	103	8		40	88	2.43	124	.224	.260	103	.223	0*	158	14	1.4
	Year	21	7	.750	28	28	28-3	0	252	221	111	9		60	96	2.43	122	.226	.271	117	.222	1	146	10	1.5
1886	†Chi N	31	11	.738	42	42	38-2	0	347.2	341	165	18		100	172	2.82	128	.253	.304	174	.236	2	134	35	3.8
1887	Pit N	13	23	.361	36	36	36	0	322.1	377	217	12	12	84	77	4.30	89	.285	.334	136	.243	-0	75	-15	-1.0
Total	10	265	214	.553	492	485	466-33	1	4275.2	4092	2095	82	12	749	1704	2.43	117	.242	.274	2082	.236	-3	98	208	21.1
McCORMICK, MIKE Michael Francis B 9.29.1938 Pasadena, CA BL/TL 6-2/195# d9.3																									
1956	NY N	0	1	.000	3	2	0	0	6.2	7	7	1	0	10-0	4	9.45	40	.269	.472	1-0	.000	-0	105	-4	-0.5
1957	NY N	3	1	.750	24	5	1	0	74.2	79	37	7	3	32-2	50	4.10	96	.280	.357	22-1	.273	1	99	-1	0.0

Year	Tm Lg	W	L	Pct	G	GS	CG-Sho	SV-BS	IP	H	R	HR	HB	BB-IB	SO	ERA	AERA	OAV	OOB	AB-SH	AVG	PB	Sup	APR	PW
1958	SF N	11	8	.579	42	28	8-2	1	178.1	192	103	20	3	60-6	82	4.59	83	.276	.332	54-3	.222	1	98	-16	-1.3
1959	SF N	12	16	.429	47	31	7-3	4	225.2	213	117	24	1	86-13	151	3.99	96	.248	.314	66-11	.106	-2	104	-5	-0.7
1960	SF N★	15	12	.556	40	34	15-4	3	253	228	87	15	1	65-12	154	**2.70**	129	.241	.290	88-5	.182	1	111	25	3.0
1961	SF N★	13	16	.448	40	35	13-3	0	250	235	99	33	2	75-3	163	3.20	119	.249	.305	80-5	.188	1	108	18	2.0
1962	SF N	5	5	.500	28	15	1	0	98.2	112	64	18	1	45-2	42	5.38	71	.286	.356	28-0	.107	0*	122	-17	-1.5
1963	Bal A	6	8	.429	25	21	2	0	136	132	70	18	0	66-4	75	4.30	81	.256	.340	46-3	.174	1	106	-12	-1.1
1964	Bal A	0	2	.000	4	2	0	0	17.1	21	10	1	0	8-0	13	5.19	69	.288	.358	6-0	.167	-0	112	-3	-0.3
1965	Was A	8	8	.500	44	21	3-1	1	158	158	64	17	0	36-4	88	3.36	103	.260	.300	41-4	.073	-1*	91	4	0.2
1966	Was A	11	14	.440	41	32	8-3	0	216	193	98	23	2	51-8	101	3.46	100	.236	.281	66-5	.212	3	87	-2	0.1
1967	SF N	**22**	10	.688	40	35	14-5	0	262.1	220	88	25	5	81-18	150	2.85	115	.226	.289	84-6	.119	0*	115	17	1.9
1968	SF N	12	14	.462	38	28	9-2	1	198.1	196	92	17	2	49-13	121	3.58	82	.254	.298	58-5	.103	1	102	-13	-1.7
1969	SF N	11	9	.550	32	28	9	0-1	196.2	175	81	20	1	77-8	76	3.34	105	.237	.308	66-5	.136	1	110	6	0.6
1970	SF N	3	4	.429	23	11	1	2-1	78.1	80	58	15	3	36-7	37	6.20	64	.262	.343	25-2	.160	0	152	-18	-1.5
	NY A	2	0	1.000	9	4	0	0-0	20.2	26	15	2	0	13-1	12	6.10	58	.295	.386	5-0	.200	0	127	-6	-0.5
1971	KC A	0	0	—	4	1	0	0-0	9.2	14	10	0	0	5-0	2	9.31	37	.350	.422	2-0	.000	-0	261	-6	-0.3
Total	16	134	128	.511	484	333	91-23	12-2	2380.1	2281	1100	256	24	795-101	1321	3.73	95	.251	.312	738-55	.156	9	107	-33	-1.6
McCORMICK, HARRY Patrick Henry B 10.25.1855 Syracuse, NY D 8.8.1889 Syracuse, NY BR/TR 5-9/155# d5.1																									
1879	Syr N	18	33	.353	54	54	49-5	0	457.1	517	291	3		31	96	2.99	79	.266	.277	230	.222	-0*	79	-30	-2.8
1881	Wor N	1	8	.111	9	9	9-1	0	78.1	89	50	1		15	7	3.56	85	.275	.307	45	.133	-2*	62	-4	-0.6
1882	Cin AA	14	11	.560	25	25	24-3	0	219.2	177	87	4		42	33	1.52	174	.206	.243	93	.129	-5*	88	25	1.8
1883	Cin AA	8	6	.571	15	15	14-1	0	128.2	139	70	1		27	21	2.87	113	.258	.294	55	.309	4	121	7	1.0
Total	4	41	58	.414	103	103	96-10	0	884	922	498	9		115	157	2.66	98	.252	.274	423	.203	-4	86	-2	-0.6
McCORRY, BILL William Charles B 7.9.1887 Saranac Lake, NY D 3.22.1973 Augusta, GA BL/TR 5-9/157# d9.17																									
1909	StL A	0	2	.000	2	2	2	0	15	29	21	1	0	6	10	9.00	27	.397	.443	5-0	.000	-0	15	-12	-1.2
McCRABB, LES Lester William "Buster" B 11.4.1914 Wakefield, PA BR/TR 5-11/175# d9.7 C5																									
1939	Phi A	1	2	.333	5	4	2	0	35.2	42	20	4	1	10	11	4.04	117	.290	.340	13-2	.000	-2	103	2	0.0
1940	Phi A	0	0	—	4	0	0	0	11.2	19	13	2	1	2	4	6.94	64	.365	.400	4-0	.250	0		-4	-0.2
1941	Phi A	9	13	.409	26	23	11-1	2	157.1	188	105	16	3	49	40	5.49	76	.293	.346	56-1	.143	-2	77	-20	-2.7
1942	Phi A	0	0	—	1	0	0	0	4	14	14	2	1	2	0	31.50	12	.560	.607	1-0	.000	-0		-11	-0.4
1950	Phi A	0	0	—	2	0	0	0	1.1	7	4	0	0	0	2	27.00	17	.636	.636	0-0	—	0		-3	-0.1
Total	5	10	15	.400	38	27	13-1	2	210	270	156	24	6	63	57	5.96	72	.309	.359	74-3	.122	-4	81	-36	-3.4
McCREERY, ED Esley Porterfield "Big Ed" B 12.24.1889 Cripple Creek, CO D 10.19.1960 Sacramento, CA BR/TR 6/190# d8.16																									
1914	Det A	1	0	1.000	3	1	0	0	4	6	5	0	0	3	4	11.25	25	.316	.409	1-0	.000	-0	337	-3	-0.6
McCREERY, TOM Thomas Livingston B 10.19.1874 Beaver, PA D 7.3.1941 Beaver, PA BB/TR 5-11/180# d6.8 ▲																									
1895	Lou N	3	1	.750	8	4	3-1	1	48.2	51	40	0	5	38	14	5.36	86	.266	.400	108-2	.324	1*	108	-3	0.0
1896	Lou N	0	1	.000	1	1	0	0	1	4	10	1	0	5	0	36.00	12	.571	.750	441-9	.351	0*	49	-5	-0.6
1900	Pit N	0	0	—	1	0	0	0	3	3	4	2	0	1	0	12.00	30	.250	.308	132-6	.220	0*		-2	-0.1
Total	3	3	2	.600	10	5	3-1	1	52.2	58	54	3	5	44	14	6.32	72	.275	.412	681-17	.322	2	97	-10	-0.7
McCULLERS, LANCE Lance Graye B 3.8.1964 Tampa, FL BB/TR 6-1/218# d8.12																									
1985	SD N	0	2	.000	21	0	0	5-2	35	23	15	3	1	16-3	27	2.31	153	.195	.296	4-2	.000	-0		3	0.2
1986	SD N	10	10	.500	70	7	0	5-5	136	103	46	12	4	58-9	92	2.78	132	.216	.304	22-3	.091	0*	73	14	2.1
1987	SD N	8	10	.444	78	0	0	16-11	123.1	115	60	11	2	59-11	126	3.72	106	.244	.330	14-1	.071	-1		2	0.3
1988	SD N	3	6	.333	60	0	0	10-5	97.2	70	29	8	0	55-12	81	2.49	137	.205	.313	8-0	.250	1		10	1.2
1989	NY A	4	3	.571	52	1	0	3-3	84.2	83	46	9	3	37-4	82	4.57	85	.255	.332	0-0	—	0	47	-6	-0.5
1990	NY A	1	0	1.000	11	0	0	0-1	15	14	8	2	0	6-2	11	3.60	111	.241	.308	0-0	—	0		0	0.0
	Det A	1	0	1.000	9	1	0	0-0	29.2	18	11	2	0	13-1	20	2.73	145	.170	.256	0-0	—	0	230	3	0.1
	Year	2	0	1.000	20	1	0	0-1	44.2	32	21	4	0	19-3	31	3.02	131	.195	.274	0-0	—	0	229	4	0.1
1992	Tex A	1	0	1.000	5	0	0	0-0	5	1	4	0	0	8-0	3	5.40	70	.067	.391	0-0	—	0		-1	-0.2
Total	7	28	31	.475	306	9	0	39-27	526.1	427	219	47	10	252-42	442	3.25	115	.223	.315	48-6	.104	0	88	25	3.2
McCULLOUGH, CHARLIE Charles F. B 1867 Dublin, Ireland TR 6-1/185# d4.23																									
1890	Bro AA	4	21	.160	26	25	24	0	215.2	247	174	5	16	102	61	4.59	85	.279	.364	86	.023	-12	62	-16	-2.6
	Syr AA	1	2	.333	3	3	3	0	26	29	25	1	0	14	8	7.27	49	.274	.358	9	.111	0	108	-10	-0.8
	Year	5	23	.179	29	28	27	0	241.2	276	31	6	16	116	69	4.88	79	.278	.363	95	.032	-12	66	-34	-3.4
McCULLOUGH, PAUL Paul Willard B 7.28.1898 New Castle, PA D 11.7.1970 New Castle, PA BR/TR 5-9.5/190# d7.2																									
1929	Was A	0	0	—	3	0	0	0	7.1	7	7	1	0	2	3	8.59	49	.250	.300	1-0	.000	-0		-3	-0.2
McCULLOUGH, PHIL Pinson Lamar B 7.22.1917 Stockbridge, GA D 1.16.2003 Decatur, GA BR/TR 6-4/204# d4.22 Mil 1943-45																									
1942	Was A	0	0	—	1	0	0	0	3	5	4	0	0	2	2	6.00	61	.333	.412	1-0	.000	-0		-1	-0.1
McCURRY, JEFF Jeffrey Dee B 1.21.1970 Tokyo, Japan BR/TR 6-7/210# d5.6																									
1995	Pit N	1	4	.200	55	0	0	1-1	61	82	38	9	5	30-4	27	5.02	86	.337	.421	3-0	.000	-0		-5	-0.4
1996	Det A	0	0	—	2	0	0	0-0	3.1	9	9	3	0	2-0	0	24.30	21	.474	.524	0-0	—	0		-7	-0.3
1997	Col N	1	4	.200	33	0	0	0-2	40.2	43	22	7	0	20-0	19	4.43	117	.277	.358	1-0	.000	-0		3	0.3
1998	Pit N	1	3	.250	16	0	0	0-0	19.1	24	14	4	1	9-0	11	6.52	66	.324	.400	0-0	—	0		-4	-0.7
1999	Hou N	0	1	.000	5	0	0	0-0	4	11	8	1	0	2-0	3	15.75	28	.478	.520	0-0	—	0		-5	-0.9
Total	5	3	12	.200	111	0	0	1-3	128.1	169	91	24	6	63-4	60	5.89	78	.329	.407	4-0	.000	-0		-18	-2.0
McDANIEL, LINDY Lyndall Dale B 12.13.1935 Hollis, OK BR/TR 6-3/195# d9.2 b-Von																									
1955	StL N	0	0	—	4	2	0	0	19	22	10	4	0	7-1	7	4.74	86	.293	.349	5-0	.200	-0	110	-1	-0.1
1956	StL N	7	6	.538	39	7	1	0	116.1	121	60	7	0	42-7	59	3.40	111	.273	.333	32-0	.219	2	123	1	0.3
1957	StL N	15	9	.625	30	26	10-1	0	191	196	87	13	3	53-4	75	3.49	114	.266	.316	74-3	.257	4*	109	8	1.4
1958	StL N	5	7	.417	26	17	2-1	0	108.2	139	76	17	2	31-2	47	5.80	71	.305	.351	30-2	.067	-3	118	-18	-2.0
1959	StL N	14	12	.538	62	7	1	**15**	132	144	61	11	1	41-8	86	3.82	111	.283	.335	29-3	.034	-2	66	6	1.1
1960	StL N★	12	4	.750	65	2	1	**26**	116.1	85	28	8	1	24-3	105	2.09	196	.207	.249	26-0	.231	1	86	**25**	**4.7**
1961	StL N	10	6	.625	55	0	0	9	94.1	117	57	11	2	31-11	65	4.87	90	.305	.359	17-3	.235	-0		-3	-0.5
1962	StL N	3	10	.231	55	2	0	14	107	96	53	12	1	29-8	79	4.12	104	.239	.288	21-1	.095	-1	164	3	0.4
1963	Chi N	13	7	.650	57	0	0	**22**	88	82	32	9	0	27-5	75	2.86	123	.251	.304	22-1	.091	-0		6	1.3
1964	Chi N	1	7	.125	63	0	0	15	95	104	43	4	1	23-4	71	3.88	96	.276	.318	16-1	.125	-1		-1	-0.1
1965	Chi N	5	6	.455	71	0	0	2	128.2	115	45	12	0	47-20	92	2.59	142	.241	.307	8-0	.000	-1		14	1.3
1966	SF N	10	5	.667	64	0	0	6	121.2	103	48	5	0	35-9	93	2.66	138	.228	.282	22-4	.091	-1		11	1.3
1967	SF N	2	6	.250	41	3	0	3	72.2	69	34	5	2	24-10	48	3.72	88	.248	.310	11-0	.091	-1	53	-3	-0.4
1968	SF N	0	0	—	12	0	0	0	19.1	30	16	2	0	5-0	9	7.45	40	.357	.393	2-0	.000	-0		-8	-0.5
	NY A	4	1	.800	24	0	0	10	51.1	30	10	5	1	12-3	43	1.75	165	.166	.221	13-2	.000	-1		7	1.1
1969	NY A	5	6	.455	51	0	0	5-4	83.2	84	37	4	0	23-6	60	3.55	98	.261	.305	8-2	.000	-1		0	0.0
1970	NY A	9	5	.643	62	0	0	29-6	111.2	88	29	7	0	23-5	81	2.01	175	.217	.258	24-1	.167	0		20	**3.4**
1971	NY A	5	10	.333	44	0	0	4-7	69.2	82	41	12	0	24-6	39	5.04	64	.296	.350	9-1	.111	-0		-13	-2.7
1972	NY A	3	1	.750	37	0	0	0-0	68	54	23	4	0	25-5	47	2.25	131	.217	.287	7-1	.286	1		4	0.4
1973	NY A	12	6	.667	47	3	1	10-4	160.1	148	54	11	1	49-9	93	2.86	128	.250	.304	2-0	.000	-0	49	17	2.2
1974	KC A	1	4	.200	38	5	2	1-2	106.2	109	50	6	0	24-5	47	3.46	111	.265	.303	0-0	—	0	65	3	0.2
1975	KC A	5	1	.833	40	0	0	1-2	78	81	40	3	0	24-5	40	4.15	93	.273	.323	0-0	—	0		-2	-0.2
Total	21	141	119	.542	987	74	18-2	172-25	2139.1	2099	934	172	15	623-136	1361	3.45	109	.258	.309	378-25	.148	-4	107	76	12.6
McDANIEL, VON Max Von B 4.18.1939 Hollis, OK D 8.20.1995 Lawton, OK BR/TR 6-2.5/180# d6.13 b-Lindy																									
1957	StL N	7	5	.583	17	13	4-2	0	86.2	71	37	7	1	31-3	45	3.22	123	.225	.293	26-1	.000	-3	68	6	0.4
1958	StL N	0	0	—	2	1	0	0	2	5	3	0	0	5-0	0	13.50	31	.500	.667	0-1	—	0	174	-2	-0.1
Total	2	7	5	.583	19	14	4-2	0	88.2	76	40	7	1	36-3	45	3.45	115	.233	.309	26-2	.000	-3	76	4	0.3

Year	Tm Lg	W	L	Pct	G	GS	CG-Sho	SV-BS	IP	H	R	HR	HB	BB-IB	SO	ERA	AERA	OAV	OOB	AB-SH	AVG	PB	Sup	APR	PW
McDERMOTT, JOE Joseph d5.4.1871																									
1872	Eck NA	0	7	.000	7	7	7	0	63	143	144	3		14	1	8.14	42	.376	.398	32	.281	2	66	-35	-2.0
McDERMOTT, MICKEY Maurice Joseph "Maury" B 8.29.1929 Poughkeepsie, NY D 8.7.2003 Phoenix, AZ BL/TL 6-2/170# d4.24 C1 ▲																									
1948	Bos A	0	0	—	7	0	0	0	23.1	16	18	2	1	35	17	6.17	71	.208	.460	8-0	.375	1		-5	-0.1
1949	Bos A	5	4	.556	12	12	6-2	0	80	63	37	5	3	52	50	4.05	108	.220	.345	33-0	.212	1	120	4	0.5
1950	Bos A	7	3	.700	38	15	4	5	130	119	80	8	2	124	96	5.19	94	.249	.406	44-0	.364	6*	135	-3	0.4
1951	Bos A	8	8	.500	34	19	9-1	3	172	141	72	9	5	92	127	3.35	133	.226	.330	66-1	.273	2*	95	20	2.0
1952	Bos A	10	9	.526	30	21	7-2	0	162	139	70	14	3	92	117	3.72	106	.234	.340	62-3	.226	3*	95	6	0.9
1953	Bos A	18	10	.643	32	30	8-4	0	206.1	169	82	9	2	109	92	3.01	140	.224	.323	93-0	.301	7*	92	25	4.1
1954	Was A	7	15	.318	30	26	11-1	1	196.1	172	95	8	3	110	95	3.44	103	.239	.339	95-2	.200	3*	93	-1	0.2
1955	Was A	10	10	.500	31	20	8-1	1	156	140	75	9	9	100-2	78	3.75	102	.243	.361	95-1	.263	7*	96	1	1.0
1956	†NY A	2	6	.250	23	9	1	0	87	85	46	10	0	47-2	38	4.24	91	.261	.350	52-1	.212	3*	92	-4	-0.1
1957	KC A	1	4	.200	29	4	0	0	69	68	47	9	0	50-2	29	5.48	72	.266	.382	49-0	.245	3*	141	-11	0.0
1958	Det A	0	0	—	2	0	0	0	2	6	4	0	0	2-0	0	9.00	45	.500	.571	3-0	.333	0*		-2	-0.1
1961	StL N	1	0	1.000	19	0	0	4	27	29	17	3	0	15-2	15	3.67	120	.271	.358	14-0	.071	-1*		0	-0.1
	KC A	0	0	—	4	0	0	0	5.2	14	12	0	0	10-0	3	14.29	29	.452	.585	5-0	.200	1*		-7	-0.3
Total	12	69	69	.500	291	156	54-11	14	1316.2	1161	655	86	28	838-8	757	3.91	105	.240	.354	619-8	.252	36	102	23	8.4
McDERMOTT, MIKE Michael H. B 5.6.1864 Fall River, MA D 5.7.1947 Fall River, MA 5-10/152# d9.2																									
1889	Lou AA	1	8	.111	9	9	9	0	84.1	108	65	4	2	34	22	4.16	92	.302	.365	33	.182	-1	68	-3	-0.3
McDERMOTT, MIKE Michael Joseph B 9.7.1862 St.Louis, MO D 6.30.1943 St.Louis, MO TR 5-8/145# d4.20																									
1895	Lou N	4	19	.174	33	26	18	0	207.1	258	203	8	11	103	42	5.99	77	.300	.382	82-0	.159	-2	106	-32	-2.6
1896	Lou N	2	7	.222	12	10	4-1	0	65	87	77	4	6	44	12	7.34	59	.318	.423	27-1	.296	1	82	-21	-1.9
1897	Cle N	4	5	.444	9	7	4	0	62	75	44	2	3	25	12	4.50	100	.296	.367	25-0	.320	1	68	0	0.0
	StL N	1	2	.333	4	4	1	0	21.1	23	23	2	0	19	3	9.28	47	.274	.408	9-0	.222	-0	73	-9	-0.8
	Year	5	7	.417	13	11	5	0	83.1	98	28	4	3	44	15	5.72	78	.291	.378	34-0	.294	1	70	-9	-0.8
Total	3	11	33	.250	58	47	27-1	0	355.2	443	347	16	20	191	69	6.17	74	.301	.389	143-1	.217	0	92	-62	-5.3
McDEVITT, DANNY Daniel Eugene B 11.18.1932 New York, NY BL/TL 5-10/175# d6.17																									
1957	Bro N	7	4	.636	22	17	5-2	0	119	105	55	5	6	72-1	90	3.25	128	.238	.351	39-4	.154	-0	97	9	0.8
1958	LA N	2	6	.250	13	10	2	0	48.1	71	43	6	0	31-1	26	7.45	55	.355	.438	15-0	.133	-0	118	-17	-2.3
1959	LA N	10	8	.556	39	22	6-2	4	145	149	83	16	14	51-5	106	3.97	106	.263	.335	46-2	.109	-2	92	-1	-0.3
1960	LA N	0	4	.000	24	7	0	0	53	51	26	7	6	42-3	30	4.25	93	.260	.406	10-2	.200	0	89	-1	0.0
1961	NY A	1	2	.333	8	2	0	1	13	18	11	2	1	8-0	8	7.62	49	.353	.443	1-0	.000	0	83	-6	-1.0
	Min A	1	0	1.000	16	1	0	0	26.2	20	11	1	4	19-0	15	2.36	179	.213	.368	3-0	.000	-0	125	4	0.2
	Year	2	2	.500	24	3	0	1	39.2	38	17	3	5	27-0	23	4.08	100	.262	.393	4-0	.000	-0	94	-1	-0.8
1962	KC A	0	3	.000	33	1	0	2	51	47	37	5	1	41-2	28	5.82	73	.250	.385	9-0	.222	0	63	-9	-0.5
Total	6	21	27	.438	155	60	13-4	7	456	461	266	42	32	264-12	303	4.40	94	.265	.370	123-8	.138	-3	97	-21	-3.1
McDILL, ALLEN Allen Gabriel B 8.23.1971 Greenville, MS BL/TL 6/155# d5.15																									
1997	KC A	0	0	—	3	0	0	0-0	4	3	6	1	1	8-0	2	13.50	35	.214	.522	0-0	—	0		-4	-0.2
1998	KC A	0	0	—	7	0	0	0-0	6	9	7	3	0	2-0	3	10.50	46	.333	.379	0-0	—	0		-3	-0.2
2000	Det A	0	0	—	13	0	0	0-0	10	13	9	2	1	1-0	7	7.20	67	.317	.349	0-0	—	0		-3	-0.1
2001	Bos A	0	0	—	15	0	0	0-1	14.2	13	9	2	1	7-1	16	5.52	81	.236	.328	0-0	—	0		-1	-0.1
Total	4	0	0	—	38	0	0	0-1	34.2	38	31	8	3	18-1	28	7.79	60	.277	.371	0-0	—	0		-11	-0.6
McDONALD, HANK Henry Monroe B 1.16.1911 Santa Monica, CA D 10.17.1982 Hemet, CA BR/TR 6-3/200# d4.16																									
1931	Phi A	2	4	.333	19	10	1-1	0	70.1	62	43	3	1	41	23	3.71	121	.239	.346	21-0	.095	-1	111	2	0.0
1933	Phi A	1	1	.500	4	1	0	0	12.1	14	12	0	0	4	1	5.11	84	.264	.316	4-0	.000	-0	60	-3	-0.4
	StL A	0	4	.000	25	5	0	0	58.1	83	59	6	3	34	22	8.64	54	.332	.418	14-0	.143	-1	66	-22	-1.4
	Year	1	5	.167	29	6	0	0	70.2	97	63	6	3	38	23	8.02	57	.320	.401	18-0	.111	-1	65	-24	-1.8
Total	2	3	9	.250	48	16	1-1	0	141	159	114	9	4	79	46	5.87	77	.283	.375	39-0	.103	-2	93	-23	-1.8
McDONALD, JIM Jimmie Le Roy "Hot Rod" B 5.17.1927 Grants Pass, OR BR/TR 5-10.5/185# d7.27																									
1950	Bos A	1	0	1.000	9	0	0	0	19	23	9	1	1	10	5	3.79	129	.329	.420	3-0	.333	1		2	0.2
1951	StL A	4	7	.364	16	11	5	1	84	84	48	5	2	46	28	4.07	108	.260	.356	29-1	.207	-0*	81	1	0.1
1952	NY A	3	4	.429	26	5	1	0	69.1	71	31	1	2	40	20	3.50	95	.268	.368	19-0	.316	3	131	-1	0.4
1953	†NY A	9	7	.563	27	18	6-2	0	129.2	128	64	4	1	39	43	3.82	97	.260	.316	41-3	.098	-3*	122	-3	-0.5
1954	NY A	4	1	.800	16	10	3-1	0	71	54	28	3	1	45	20	3.17	108	.213	.332	19-2	.211	2	159	2	0.4
1955	Bal A	3	5	.375	21	8	0	0	51.2	76	48	5	0	30-1	20	7.14	53	.345	.421	11-1	.182	1	84	-20	-2.5
1956	Chi A	0	2	.000	8	3	0	0	18.2	29	18	2	1	7-0	10	8.68	47	.377	.425	5-0	.000	-0	36	-9	-0.8
1957	Chi A	0	1	.000	10	0	0	0	22.1	18	8	2	0	10-1	12	2.01	185	.234	.315	1-0	.000	0		3	0.2
1958	Chi A	0	0	—	3	0	0	0	2.1	6	8	1	0	4-0	0	19.29	19	.429	.556	0-0	—	0		-5	-0.3
Total	9	24	27	.471	136	55	15-3	1	468	489	262	24	8	231-2	158	4.27	89	.273	.357	128-7	.180	4	109	-30	-2.8
McDONALD, JOHN John Joseph (b: John Joseph McDonnell) B 1.27.1883 Throop, PA D 4.9.1950 Roselle, NJ BR/TR 6-1/170# d9.3																									
1907	Was A	0	0	—	1	0	0	0	6	12	11	0	0	2	3	9.00	27	.414	.452	3-0	.333	1		-5	-0.2
McDONALD, BEN Larry Benard B 11.24.1967 Baton Rouge, LA BR/TR 6-7/213# d9.6																									
1989	Bal A	1	0	1.000	6	0	0	0-0	7.1	8	7	2	0	4-0	3	8.59	44	.286	.364	0-0	—	0		-4	-0.4
1990	Bal A	8	5	.615	21	15	3-2	0-0	118.2	88	36	9	0	35-0	65	2.43	157	.205	.262	0-0	—	0	77	18	1.9
1991	Bal A	6	8	.429	21	21	1	0-0	126.1	126	71	16	1	43-2	85	4.84	82	.261	.321	0-0	—	0	108	-12	-1.2
1992	Bal A	13	13	.500	35	35	4-2	0-0	227	213	113	32	9	74-5	158	4.24	95	.247	.311	0-0	—	0	115	-5	-0.4
1993	Bal A	13	14	.481	34	34	7-1	0-0	220.1	185	92	17	5	86-4	171	3.39	132	.228	.304	0-0	—	0	85	25	2.9
1994	Bal A	14	7	.667	24	24	5-1	0-0	157.1	151	75	14	2	54-2	94	4.06	123	.255	.319	0-0	—	0	98	15	1.8
1995	Bal A	3	6	.333	14	13	1	0-0	80	67	40	10	3	38-3	62	4.16	114	.224	.316	0-0	—	0	80	5	0.5
1996	Mil A	12	10	.545	35	35	2	0-0	221.1	228	104	25	6	67-0	146	3.90	133	.264	.319	0-0	—	0	97	31	2.6
1997	Mil A	8	7	.533	21	21	1	0-0	133	120	68	13	5	36-2	110	4.06	114	.237	.294	1-0	.000	-0	84	7	0.7
Total	9	78	70	.527	211	198	24-6	0-0	1291.1	1186	606	138	31	437-18	894	3.91	115	.243	.308	1-0	.000	-0	95	80	8.4
McDOOLAN d4.14																									
1873	Mar NA	0	1	.000	1	1	1	0	9	18	24	0		0	0	3.00	108	.305	.305	4	.000	-1	33	-2	-0.2
McDOUGAL, DEWEY James H. B 9.19.1871 Aledo, IL D 4.28.1935 Galesburg, IL TR 5-10/188# d4.24																									
1895	StL N	3	10	.231	18	14	10	0	114.2	187	146	11	10	46	23	8.32	58	.360	.423	41-0	.146	-2	90	-43	-3.5
1896	StL N	0	1	.000	3	1	0	0	10	13	11	2	1	4	0	8.10	54	.310	.383	3-0	.000	-1	65	-4	-0.3
Total	2	3	11	.214	21	15	10	0	124.2	200	157	13	11	50	23	8.30	58	.357	.420	44-0	.136	-3	89	-47	-3.8
McDOUGAL, SANDY John Auchanbolt B 5.21.1874 Buffalo, NY D 10.2.1910 Buffalo, NY BR/TR 5-10/155# d6.12																									
1895	Bro N	0	0	—	1	0	0	1	3	3	4	0	0	5	2	12.00	37	.250	.471	1-0	.000	-0		-2	-0.1
1905	StL N	1	4	.200	5	5	5	0	44.2	50	24	0	0	12	10	3.43	87	.301	.348	15-1	.133	-1	58	-3	-0.2
Total	2	1	4	.200	6	5	5	1	47.2	53	28	0	0	17	12	3.97	78	.298	.359	16-1	.125	-1	58	-5	-0.3
McDOWELL, JACK Jack Burns B 1.16.1966 Van Nuys, CA BR/TR 6-5/180# d9.15																									
1987	Chi A	3	0	1.000	4	4	0	0-0	28	16	6	1	2	6-0	15	1.93	238	.168	.233	0-0	—	0	94	8	0.9
1988	Chi A	5	10	.333	26	26	1	0-0	158.2	147	85	12	7	68-5	84	3.97	100	.245	.326	0-0	—	0	82	-2	-0.2
1990	Chi A	14	9	.609	33	33	4	0-0	205	189	93	20	7	77-0	165	3.82	100	.244	.316	0-0	—	0	104	1	0.1
1991	Chi A★	17	10	.630	35	**35**	**15**-3	0-0	253.2	212	97	19	4	82-2	191	3.41	117	.228	.292	0-0	—	0	117	20	2.0
1992	Chi A★	20	10	.667	34	34	**13**-1	0-0	260.2	247	95	21	7	75-9	178	3.18	122	.251	.307	0-0	—	0	115	24	2.5
1993	†Chi A★	**22**	10	.688	34	34	10-**4**	0-0	256.2	261	104	20	3	69-6	158	3.37	125	.266	.314	0-0	—	0	107	25	3.0
1994	Chi A	10	9	.526	25	**25**	6-2	0-0	181	186	82	12	5	42-2	127	3.73	125	.266	.310	0-0	—	0	90	20	1.8
1995	†NY A	15	10	.600	30	30	**8-2**	0-0	217.2	211	106	25	5	78-1	157	3.93	118	.254	.320	0-0	—	0	99	14	1.4
1996	†Cle A	13	9	.591	30	30	5-1	0-0	192	214	119	22	4	67-2	141	5.11	96	.282	.341	0-0	—	0	102	-4	-0.4

Year	Tm Lg	W	L	Pct	G	GS	CG-Sho	SV-BS	IP	H	R	HR	HB	BB-IB	SO	ERA	AERA	OAV	OOB	AB-SH	AVG	PB	Sup	APR	PW
1997	Cle A	3	3	.500	8	6	0	0-0	40.2	44	25	6	1	18-1	38	5.09	92	.282	.356	0-0	—	0	101	-2	-0.2
1998	Ana A	5	3	.625	14	14	0	0-0	76	96	45	11	1	19-1	45	5.09	92	.311	.350	0-0	—	0	93	-3	-0.2
1999	Ana A	0	4	.000	4	4	0	0-0	19	31	17	4	2	5-0	12	8.05	60	.369	.413	0-0	—	0	38	-6	-0.9
Total	12	127	87	.593	277	275	62-13	0-0	1889	1854	874	173	48	606-29	1311	3.85	111	.257	.317	0-0	—	0	101	95	9.8
McDOWELL, ROGER Roger Alan B 12.21.1960 Cincinnati, OH BR/TR 6-1/182# d4.11																									
1985	NY N	6	5	.545	62	2	0	17-6	127.1	108	43	9	1	37-8	70	2.83	122	.230	.286	19-2	.158	0	89	10	1.2
1986	†NY N	14	9	.609	75	0	0	22-6	128	107	48	4	3	42-5	65	3.02	117	.228	.294	18-1	.278	1		8	1.9
1987	NY N	7	5	.583	56	0	0	25-7	88.2	95	41	7	2	28-4	32	4.16	91	.276	.330	13-0	.231	1		-2	-0.1
1988	†NY N	5	5	.500	62	0	0	16-4	89	80	31	1	3	31-7	46	2.63	123	.238	.304	9-0	.333	2*		6	1.1
1989	NY N	1	5	.167	25	0	0	4-1	35.1	34	21	1	2	16-3	15	3.31	99	.254	.340	2-0	.500	0		-3	-0.4
	Phi N	3	3	.500	44	0	0	19-4	56.2	45	15	2	1	22-5	32	1.11	319	.220	.298	1-0	.000	-0		12	2.1
	Year	4	8	.333	69	0	0	23-5	92	79	40	3	3	38-8	47	1.96	176	.233	.315	3-0	.333	0		9	1.7
1990	Phi N	6	8	.429	72	0	0	22-6	86.1	92	41	2	2	35-9	39	3.86	99	.286	.355	2-1	.000	-0		0	0.0
1991	Phi N	3	6	.333	38	0	0	3-3	59	61	28	1	2	32-12	28	3.20	115	.266	.360	2-0	.000	-0		1	0.1
	LA N	6	3	.667	33	0	0	7-2	42.1	39	12	3	0	16-8	22	2.55	141	.257	.324	0-0	—	0*		6	1.3
	Year	9	9	.500	71	0	0	10-5	101.1	100	40	4	2	48-20	50	2.93	124	.262	.346	2-0	.000	-0		6	1.4
1992	LA N	6	10	.375	65	0	0	14-8	83.2	103	46	3	1	42-13	50	4.09	84	.306	.381	3-1	.000	1		-7	-1.3
1993	LA N	5	3	.625	54	0	0	2-1	68	76	32	2	2	30-10	27	2.25	170	.288	.364	2-0	.500	0		7	1.0
1994	LA N	0	3	.000	32	0	0	0-1	41.1	50	25	3	1	22-6	29	5.23	75	.303	.388	1-0	.000	-0		-6	-0.4
1995	Tex A	7	4	.636	64	0	0	4-4	85	86	39	5	6	34-7	49	4.02	120	.277	.354	0-0	—	0		8	1.1
1996	Bal A	1	1	.500	41	0	0	4-2	59.1	69	32	7	2	23-1	20	4.25	116	.296	.363	0-0	—	0		4	0.2
Total	12	70	70	.500	723	2	0	159-55	1050	1045	454	50	28	410-98	524	3.30	114	.263	.334	72-5	.222	6	89	44	7.8
McDOWELL, SAM Samuel Edward Thomas "Sudden Sam" B 9.21.1942 Pittsburgh, PA BL/TL 6-5/218# d9.15																									
1961	Cle A	0	0	—	1	1	0	0	6.1	3	0	0	0	5-0	5	0.00	—	.136	.296	2-0	.000	-0	45	3	0.1
1962	Cle A	3	7	.300	25	13	0	1	87.2	81	64	9	4	70-1	70	6.06	64	.243	.379	26-1	.154	-1	99	-21	-2.2
1963	Cle A	3	5	.375	14	12	3-1	0	65	63	37	6	0	44-0	63	4.85	75	.256	.368	19-4	.211	0*	100	-8	-0.8
1964	Cle A	11	6	.647	31	24	6-2	1	173.1	148	60	8	3	100-6	177	2.70	133	.229	.334	56-3	.143	0	97	17	1.6
1965	Cle A★	17	11	.607	42	35	14-3	4	273	178	80	9	6	132-7	**325**	**2.18**	**160**	**.185**	.286	95-5	.126	-3*	88	**37**	3.8
1966	Cle A✧	9	8	.529	35	28	8-**5**	3	194.1	130	66	12	6	102-3	**225**	2.87	120	**.188**	.297	60-3	.200	1*	93	14	1.4
1967	Cle A	13	15	.464	37	37	10-1	0	236.1	201	112	21	7	123-3	236	3.85	85	.233	.331	82-4	.183	1	98	-13	-1.4
1968	Cle A★	15	14	.517	38	37	11-3	0	269	181	78	13	10	110-9	**283**	1.81	164	.189	.278	85-6	.153	0	84	28	3.3
1969	Cle A★	18	14	.563	39	38	18-4	1-0	285	222	111	13	7	102-9	**279**	2.94	128	.213	.286	92-11	.174	-1	84	23	2.5
1970	Cle A★	20	12	.625	39	39	19-1	0-0	**305**	236	108	25	7	131-10	**304**	2.92	136	.213	.299	105-8	.124	-3*	92	32	2.8
1971	Cle A✧	13	17	.433	35	31	8-2	1-1	214.2	160	89	22	3	153-13	192	3.40	113	.207	.338	73-6	.178	-1	71	9	1.1
1972	SF N	10	8	.556	28	25	4	0-1	164.1	155	86	12	6	86-6	122	4.33	81	.253	.348	59-4	.119	-1	128	-13	-1.5
1973	SF N	1	2	.333	18	3	0	3-0	40	45	23	4	0	29-0	35	4.50	85	.285	.392	12-1	.167	-0	85	-3	-0.3
	NY A	5	8	.385	16	15	2-1	0-0	95.2	73	47	4	0	64-2	75	3.95	93	.212	.332	0-0	—	0	83	-3	-0.3
1974	NY A	1	6	.143	13	7	0	0-0	48	42	27	6	0	41-2	33	4.69	75	.236	.379	0-0	—	0	64	-5	-0.8
1975	Pit N	2	1	.667	14	1	0	0-0	34.2	30	11	0	0	20-3	29	2.86	124	.242	.345	8-0	.000	-1	223	4	0.2
Total	15	141	134	.513	425	346	103-23	14-2	2492.1	1948	999	164	59	1312-74	2453	3.17	112	.215	.317	774-56	.154	-8	91	101	9.5
McELROY, CHUCK Charles Dwayne B 10.1.1967 Port Arthur, TX BL/TL 6/195# d9.4																									
1989	Phi N	0	0	—	11	0	0	0-0	10.1	12	2	1	0	4-1	8	1.74	204	.286	.348	0-0	—	0		2	0.1
1990	Phi N	0	1	.000	16	0	0	0-0	14	24	13	0	0	10-2	16	7.71	50	.369	.447	0-0	—	0		-6	-0.4
1991	Chi N	6	2	.750	71	0	0	3-3	101.1	73	33	7	0	57-7	92	1.95	199	.210	.317	10-0	.300	1		**17**	1.5
1992	Chi N	4	7	.364	72	0	0	6-5	83.2	73	40	5	0	51-10	83	3.55	102	.237	.341	6-0	.667	3		-1	0.2
1993	Chi N	2	2	.500	49	0	0	0-0	47.1	51	30	4	1	25-5	31	4.56	88	.280	.368	6-0	.000	-1		-5	-0.4
1994	Cin N	1	2	.333	52	0	0	5-6	57.2	52	15	3	0	15-2	38	2.34	177	.244	.294	6-0	.167	-0		13	0.7
1995	Cin N	3	4	.429	44	0	0	0-3	40.1	46	29	5	1	15-3	27	6.02	68	.291	.350	3-0	.000	-0		-9	-1.3
1996	Cin N	2	0	1.000	12	0	0	0-0	12.1	13	10	2	0	10-1	13	6.57	65	.265	.390	2-0	.000	-0		-3	-0.5
	Cal A	5	1	.833	40	0	0	0-2	36.2	32	12	2	2	13-2	32	2.95	170	.239	.313	0-0	—	0		9	1.3
1997	Ana A	0	0	—	13	0	0	0-2	15.2	17	7	2	0	3-0	18	3.45	133	.270	.303	0-0	—	0		2	0.1
	Chi A	1	3	.250	48	0	0	1-3	59.1	56	29	3	2	19-1	44	3.94	111	.247	.307	0-0	—	0*		3	0.2
	Year	1	3	.250	61	0	0	1-5	75	73	40	5	2	22-1	62	3.84	115	.252	.306	0-0	—	0		4	0.3
1998	Col N	6	4	.600	78	0	0	2-4	68.1	68	23	3	0	24-0	61	2.90	179	.268	.327	5-1	.200	-0		14	1.9
1999	Col N	3	1	.750	41	0	0	0-3	40.2	48	29	9	0	28-3	37	6.20	94	.296	.396	1-1	.000	-0		-1	-0.1
	NY N	0	0	—	15	0	0	0-0	13.1	12	5	0	1	8-1	7	3.38	130	.250	.362	0-0	—	0		2	0.1
	Year	3	1	.750	56	0	0	0-3	54	60	34	9	1	36-4	44	5.50	99	.286	.388	1-1	.000	-0		1	0.0
2000	Bal A	3	0	1.000	43	2	0	0-1	63.1	60	36	6	2	34-2	50	4.69	101	.247	.340	0-0	—	0	149	0	0.0
2001	Bal A	1	2	.333	18	5	0	0-0	45.1	49	29	8	2	28-2	22	5.36	80	.269	.371	0-0	—	0	104	-5	-0.2
	SD N	1	1	.500	31	0	0	0-3	29.2	38	24	6	0	18-4	25	5.16	78	.306	.392	3-0	.000	-0		-7	-0.4
Total	13	38	30	.559	654	7	0	17-35	739.1	724	366	66	11	362-46	604	3.90	112	.258	.342	42-2	.214	2	117	25	2.8
McELROY, JIM James D. B 11.5.1862 Napa Co., CA D 7.24.1889 Needles, CA 5-10/170# d5.26																									
1884	Phi N	1	12	.077	13	13	13	0	111	115	112	1		54	45	4.86	61	.254	.333	48	.146	-3*	49	-22	-2.2
	Wil U	0	1	.000	1	1	0	0	5	10	6	0		0	3	10.80	25	.385	.385	2	.000	-0	16	-3	-0.3
Total	1	1	13	.071	14	14	13	0	116	125	118	1		54	48	5.12	58	.261	.336	50	.140	-4	47	-25	-2.5
McENANEY, WILL William Henry B 2.14.1952 Springfield, OH BL/TL 6/180# d7.3																									
1974	Cin N	2	1	.667	24	0	0	2-1	27	24	16	4	0	9-1	13	4.33	81	.250	.311	0-0	—	0		-3	-0.4
1975	†Cin N	5	2	.714	70	0	0	15-4	91	92	29	6	2	23-7	48	2.47	146	.264	.310	14-0	.000	-2		11	1.0
1976	†Cin N	2	6	.250	55	0	0	7-2	72.1	97	44	3	1	23-8	28	4.85	72	.323	.370	6-1	.167	1		-11	-1.4
1977	Mon N	3	5	.375	69	0	0	3-5	86.2	92	39	6	2	22-4	38	3.95	97	.271	.314	8-0	.000	-1		0	-0.1
1978	Pit N	0	0	—	6	0	0	0-0	8.2	15	11	3	1	2-0	6	10.38	36	.395	.429	0-0	—	0		-6	-0.3
1979	StL N	0	3	.000	45	0	0	2-2	64	60	26	3	2	16-8	15	2.95	128	.251	.299	3-0	.000	-0		5	0.3
Total	6	12	17	.414	269	0	0	29-14	349.2	380	165	25	8	95-28	148	3.76	97	.279	.326	31-1	.032	-2		-4	-0.9
McEVOY, LOU Louis Anthony B 5.30.1902 Williamsburg, KS D 12.17.1953 Webster Groves, MO BR/TR 6-2.5/203# d4.28																									
1930	NY A	1	3	.250	28	1	0	3	52.1	64	51	4	2	29	14	6.71	64	.288	.375	16-0	.125	-1	20	-17	-1.4
1931	NY A	0	0	—	6	0	0	1	12.1	19	17	1	1	12	3	12.41	32	.358	.485	4-0	.000	-1		-12	-0.6
Total	2	1	3	.250	34	1	0	4	64.2	83	68	5	3	41	17	7.79	54	.302	.398	20-0	.100	-2	20	-29	-2.0
McFADDEN, BARNEY Bernard Joseph B 3.20.1877 Eckley, PA D 4.28.1924 Mauch Chunk, PA BR/TR 6-1/195# d4.24																									
1901	Cin N	3	4	.429	8	5	4	0	46	54	39	2	6	40	11	6.07	53	.290	.431	20-0	.150	-1	111	-14	-1.7
1902	Phi N	0	1	.000	1	1	1	0	9	14	13	0	0	7	3	8.00	35	.350	.447	3-0	.000	-0	72	-6	-0.5
Total	2	3	5	.375	9	6	5	0	55	68	52	2	6	47	14	6.38	49	.301	.434	23-0	.130	-2	105	-20	-2.2
McFARLAN, DAN Anderson Daniel B 11.1.1873 Gainesville, TX D 9.23.1924 Louisville, KY ?/178# d9.2 b-Alex																									
1895	Lou N	0	7	.000	7	7	6	0	46	80	56	4	5	15	10	6.65	70	.376	.429	21-0	.238	-1	77	-13	-1.3
1899	Bro N	0	0	—	1	0	0	0	6	6	1	0	0	1	0	1.50	261	.261	.346	2-0	.000	-0		2	0.1
	Was N	8	18	.308	32	28	22-1	0	211.2	268	166	5	11	64	41	4.76	82	.308	.363	86-1	.186	-0	72	-24	-2.4
	Year	8	18	.308	33	28	22-1	0	217.2	274	170	6	11	67	41	4.67	84	.307	.363	88-1	.182	-1	72	-17	-2.3
Total	2	8	25	.242	40	35	28-1	0	263.2	354	223	10	16	82	51	5.02	81	.320	.375	109-1	.193	-1	74	-35	-3.6
McFARLAND, CHAPPIE Charles A. B 3.13.1875 White Hall, IL D 12.14.1924 Houston, TX TR 6-1/?# d9.15 b-Monte																									
1902	StL N	0	1	.000	2	1	1	0	11	11	7	1	0	3	3	5.73	48	.262	.311	4-0	.000	-1	99	-3	-0.2
1903	StL N	9	19	.321	28	26	25-1	0	229	253	133	2	6	48	76	3.07	106	.284	.325	74-3	.108	-4	73	2	0.0
1904	StL N	14	18	.438	32	31	28-1	0	269.1	266	149	7	4	56	111	3.21	84	.248	.288	99-2	.131	-2	123	-18	-1.9
1905	StL N	8	18	.308	31	28	22-3	1	250.1	281	145	3	6	65	85	3.81	78	.284	.332	85-1	.165	1	88	-24	-2.1
1906	StL N	2	1	.667	6	4	2	1	37.1	33	18	1	0	8	16	1.93	136	.219	.258	15-0	.133	-1	104	0	0.0
	Pit N	1	3	.250	6	5	2-1	0	35.1	39	14	0	2	7	11	2.55	105	.298	.343	13-0	.385	1	109	0	0.2

Year	Tm Lg	W	L	Pct	G	GS	CG-Sho	SV-BS	IP	H	R	HR	HB	BB-IB	SO	ERA	AERA	OAV	OOB	AB-SH	AVG	PB	Sup	APR	PW
	Bro N	0	1	.000	1	1	1	0	9	10	8	1	0	5	5	8.00	32	.286	.375	3-0	.000	-0	29	-5	-0.4
	Year	3	5	.375	13	10	5-1	1	81.2	82	9	2	2	20	32	2.87	92	.259	.307	31-0	.226	0	100	-4	-0.2
Total	5	34	61	.358	106	96	81-6	2	841.1	893	474	15	18	192	307	3.35	87	.270	.313	293-6	.143	-6	95	-48	-4.4
McFARLAND, MONTE Lamont Amos B 11.7.1872 White Hall, IL D 11.15.1913 Peoria, IL 5-10/175# d9.14 b-Chappie																									
1895	Chi N	2	0	1.000	2	2	2	0	14	21	11	0	0	5	5	5.14	99	.339	.388	7-1	.143	-1	182	0	-0.1
1896	Chi N	0	4	.000	4	3	2	0	25	32	25	0	2	21	3	7.20	63	.308	.433	12-1	.000	-2	37	-6	-0.8
Total	2	2	4	.333	6	5	4	0	39	53	36	0	2	26	8	6.46	73	.319	.418	19-2	.053	-3	99	-6	-0.9
McFETRIDGE, JACK John Reed B 8.25.1869 Philadelphia, PA D 1.10.1917 Philadelphia, PA 6/175# d6.7																									
1890	Phi N	1	0	1.000	1	1	1	0	9	5	1	0	0	2	4	1.00	366	.156	.206	4	.750	1	69	3	0.4
1903	Phi N	1	11	.083	14	13	11	0	103	120	71	2	3	49	31	4.89	67	.299	.379	34-3	.176	0	92	-16	-1.5
Total	2	2	11	.154	15	14	12	0	112	125	72	2	3	51	35	4.58	72	.288	.367	38-3	.237	2	90	-13	-1.1
McGAFFIGAN, ANDY Andrew Joseph B 10.25.1956 W.Palm Beach, FL BR/TR 6-3/195# d9.22																									
1981	NY A	0	0	—	2	0	0	0-0	7	5	3	1	0	3-0	2	2.57	139	.200	.267	0-0	—	0		0	0.0
1982	SF N	1	0	1.000	4	0	0	0-0	8	5	1	0	1	1-0	4	0.00	—	.179	.233	1-0	.000	-0		3	0.3
1983	SF N	3	9	.250	43	16	0	2-0	134.1	131	67	17	1	39-5	93	4.29	83	.255	.308	30-2	.067	-1	75	-8	-1.0
1984	Mon N	3	4	.429	21	3	0	1-1	46	37	14	2	0	15-2	39	2.54	135	.220	.283	8-1	.000	-1	138	5	0.6
	Cin N	0	2	.000	9	3	0	0-1	23	23	14	2	0	8-0	18	5.48	69	.261	.323	2-2	.000	-0	86	-3	-0.3
	Year	3	6	.333	30	6	0	1-2	69	60	18	4	0	23-2	57	3.52	101	.234	.296	10-3	.000	-1	112	1	0.3
1985	Cin N	3	3	.500	15	15	2	0-0	94.1	88	40	4	2	30-4	83	3.72	102	.247	.309	29-1	.034	-2	87	2	-0.1
1986	Mon N	10	5	.667	48	14	1-1	2-1	142.2	114	49	9	2	55-8	104	2.65	140	.223	.298	33-4	.061	-2*	121	16	1.3
1987	Mon N	5	2	.714	69	0	0	12-1	120.1	105	38	5	3	42-7	100	2.39	176	.235	.303	17-2	.000	-1		23	1.5
1988	Mon N	6	0	1.000	63	0	0	4-5	91.1	81	31	4	2	37-7	71	2.76	131	.233	.309	5-0	.000	-0		9	0.6
1989	Mon N	3	5	.375	57	0	0	2-3	75	85	40	3	3	30-4	40	4.68	76	.293	.361	1-0	1.000	0		-8	-0.9
1990	SF N	0	0	—	4	0	0	0-0	4.2	10	9	2	0	4-0	4	17.36	21	.455	.538	0-0	—	0		-7	-0.4
	KC A	4	3	.571	24	11	0	1-0	78.2	75	40	6	2	28-1	49	3.09	124	.248	.313	0-0	—	0	116	3	0.2
1991	KC A	0	0	—	4	0	0	0-0	8	14	5	0	0	2-0	3	4.50	92	.389	.410	0-0	—	0		-1	0.0
Total	11	38	33	.535	363	62	3-1	24-12	833.1	773	351	55	16	294-38	610	3.38	111	.247	.312	126-12	.048	-7	98	34	1.8
McGEACHY, JACK John Charles B 5.23.1864 Clinton, MA D 4.5.1930 Cambridge, MA BR/TR 5-8/165# d6.17.1886 ▲																									
1887	Ind N	0	1	.000	1	0	0	0	6.1	13	17	2	0	4	3	11.37	37	.351	.415	405	.269	0*		-7	-0.6
1888	Ind N	0	0	—	1	0	0	0	5	5	5	1	0	3	0	7.20	41	.238	.333	452	.219	0*		-2	-0.1
1889	Ind N	0	0	—	3	0	0	0	4.2	7	9	2	0	6	3	11.57	36	.333	.481	532	.267	0*		-4	-0.2
Total	3	0	1	.000	5	0	0	0	16	25	31	5	0	13	6	10.13	37	.316	.413	1389	.252	0		-13	-0.9
McGEE, BILL William Henry "Fiddler Bill" B 11.16.1909 Batchtown, IL D 2.11.1987 St.Louis, MO BR/TR 6-1/215# d9.29																									
1935	StL N	1	0	1.000	1	1	1	0	9	3	1	0	0	1	2	1.00	410	.103	.133	3-0	.333	0	41	3	0.4
1936	StL N	1	1	.500	7	2	0	0	16	23	14	3	0	4	8	7.88	50	.359	.397	4-0	.250	0	118	-6	-0.6
1937	StL N	1	0	1.000	4	1	1	0	14	13	4	1	1	4	9	2.57	155	.255	.321	5-0	.200	-0	325	2	0.2
1938	StL N	7	12	.368	47	25	10-1	5	216	216	101	4	1	78	104	3.21	123	.257	.321	67-4	.209	1	83	14	1.3
1939	StL N	12	5	.706	43	17	5-4	0	156	155	68	14	0	59	56	3.81	108	.261	.328	55-2	.145	-2	109	8	0.6
1940	StL N	16	10	.615	38	31	11-3	0	218	222	108	13	2	96	78	3.80	105	.263	.340	73-10	.178	-1	108	5	0.3
1941	StL N	0	1	.000	4	3	0	0	14	17	9	1	1	13	2	5.14	73	.298	.437	4-1	.000	-1	105	-2	-0.2
	NY N	2	9	.182	22	14	1	0	106	117	68	9	0	54	41	4.92	75	.285	.368	31-1	.161	-1	98	-15	-1.6
	Year	2	10	.167	26	17	1	0	120	134	72	10	1	67	43	4.95	75	.286	.377	35-2	.143	-2	100	-17	-1.8
1942	NY N	6	3	.667	31	8	2-1	1	104	95	50	8	1	46	40	2.94	114	.244	.326	29-2	.103	-2	100	1	-0.2
Total	8	46	41	.529	197	102	31-9	6	853	861	423	53	6	355	340	3.74	104	.263	.336	271-20	.170	-6	102	10	0.2
McGEEHAN, CONNY Cornelius Bernard B 8.25.1882 Drifton, PA D 7.4.1907 Hazleton, PA TR d7.15 b-Dan																									
1903	Phi A	1	0	1.000	3	0	0	0	10	9	5	0	1	1	4	4.50	68	.237	.275	6-0	.000	-1*		-1	-0.1
McGEHEE, KEVIN George Kevin B 1.18.1969 Alexandria, LA BR/TR 6/190# d8.23																									
1993	Bal A	0	0	—	5	0	0	0-0	16.2	18	11	5	2	7-2	7	5.94	76	.281	.365	0-0	—	0		-2	-0.1
McGEHEE, PAT Patrick Henry B 7.2.1888 Meadville, MS D 12.30.1946 Paducah, KY BL/TR 6-2.5/180# d8.23																									
1912	Det A	0	0	—	1	1	0	0	0	1	0	0	0	1	0	—	—	1.000	1.000	0-0	—	0	91	0	0.0
McGILBERRY, RANDY Randall Kent B 10.29.1953 Mobile, AL BB/TR 6-1/195# d9.6																									
1977	KC A	0	1	.000	3	0	0	0-0	7	7	4	1	0	1-0	1	5.14	79	.280	.308	0-0	—	0		-1	-0.1
1978	KC A	0	1	.000	18	0	0	0-1	25.2	27	16	2	0	18-1	12	4.21	91	.276	.388	0-0	—	0		-2	-0.1
Total	2	0	2	.000	21	0	0	0-1	32.2	34	20	3	0	19-1	13	4.41	88	.276	.373	0-0	—	0		-3	-0.2
McGILL, BILL William John "Parson" B 6.29.1880 Galva, KS D 8.7.1959 Alva, OK BR/TR 6-2/185# d9.16																									
1907	StL A	1	0	1.000	2	2	1	0	18.1	22	8	0	0	2	8	3.44	73	.301	.320	9-0	.000	-1	121	-1	-0.2
McGILL, WILLIE William Vaness "Kid" B 11.10.1873 Atlanta, GA D 8.29.1944 Indianapolis, IN TL 5-6.5/170# d5.8																									
1890	Cle P	11	9	.550	24	20	19	0	183.2	222	146	5	12	96	82	4.12	97	.286	.373	68	.147	2	114	1	0.4
1891	Cin AA	2	5	.286	8	8	6	0	65	69	56	1	3	37	19	4.98	82	.263	.361	20	.100	0	72	-3	-0.3
	StL AA	18	9	.667	33	29	20-1	1	233	207	140	10	12	126	146	2.70	155	.230	.332	83	.157	-0	109	29	2.5
	Year	20	14	.588	41	37	26-1	1	298	276	147	11	15	163	165	3.20	130	.238	.339	103	.146	-0	101	24	2.2
1892	Cin N	1	1	.500	3	3	1	0	17	18	14	0	0	5	7	5.29	62	.261	.311	7	.286	0	129	-3	-0.3
1893	Chi N	17	18	.486	39	34	26-1	0	302.2	311	206	6	14	181	91	4.61	101	.258	.361	124	.234	2*	103	8	0.7
1894	Chi N	7	19	.269	27	23	22	0	208	272	195	2	10	117	58	5.84	97	.312	.400	82-1	.244	0	81	-4	-0.4
1895	Phi N	10	8	.556	20	20	13	0	146	177	122	2	4	81	70	5.55	86	.295	.382	63-1	.222	-0	104	-12	-1.1
1896	Phi N	5	4	.556	12	11	7	0	79.2	87	62	0	4	53	29	5.31	81	.275	.386	29-2	.207	-0	141	-8	-0.7
Total	7	71	73	.493	166	148	114-2	1	1235	1363	941	26	59	696	502	4.57	100	.273	.368	476-4	.202	4	102	8	0.8
McGILLEN, JOHN John Joseph B 8.6.1917 Eddystone, PA D 8.11.1987 Upland, PA BL/TL 6-1/175# d4.20																									
1944	Phi A	0	0	—	2	0	0	0	1	1	2	0	0	2	0	18.00	19	.333	.600	0-0	—	0		-1	-0.1
McGINLEY, JIM James William B 10.2.1878 Groveland, MA D 9.20.1961 Haverhill, MA BR/TR 5-9.5/165# d9.22																									
1904	StL N	2	1	.667	3	3	3	0	27	28	8	0	3	6	6	2.00	135	.267	.325	11-0	.091	-1	94	2	0.1
1905	StL N	0	1	.000	1	1	0	0	3	5	6	1	0	2	0	15.00	20	.333	.412	1-0	1.000	0	145	-4	-0.5
Total	2	2	2	.500	4	4	3	0	30	33	14	1	3	8	6	3.30	83	.275	.336	12-0	.167	-0	108	-2	-0.4
McGINN, DAN Daniel Michael B 11.29.1943 Omaha, NE BL/TL 6/190# d9.3																									
1968	Cin N	0	1	.000	14	0	0	0	12	13	7	1	1	11-2	16	5.25	60	.271	.417	2-0	.000	-0		-2	-0.2
1969	Mon N	7	10	.412	74	1	0	6-3	132.1	123	67	8	5	65-8	112	3.94	93	.245	.337	29-0	.172	1	48	-4	-0.4
1970	Mon N	7	10	.412	52	19	3-2	0-0	130.2	154	88	13	7	78-4	83	5.44	76	.296	.394	35-3	.114	-2	83	-19	-2.2
1971	Mon N	1	4	.200	28	6	1	0-0	71	74	51	7	1	42-4	40	5.96	59	.274	.374	17-0	.235	0	92	-18	-1.1
1972	Chi N	0	5	.000	42	2	0	4-2	62.2	78	46	5	4	29-6	42	5.89	65	.301	.379	8-0	.250	1*	12	-13	-1.1
Total	5	15	30	.333	210	28	4-2	10-5	408.2	442	259	34	18	225-24	293	5.11	74	.276	.371	91-3	.165	-0	81	-56	-5.0
McGINNIS, JUMBO George Washington B 2.22.1864 Alton, MO D 5.18.1934 St.Louis, MO 5-10/197# d5.2																									
1882	StL AA	25	18	.581	45	45	43-3	0	388.1	391	241	2		53	134	2.60	108	.245	.269	203	.217	1*	112	10	0.8
1883	StL AA	28	16	.636	45	45	41-**6**	0	382.2	325	174	3		69	128	2.33	150	.215	.249	180	.200	-6	89	49	4.2
1884	StL AA	24	16	.600	40	40	39-5	0	354.1	331	196	4	12	35	141	2.84	115	.233	.258	146	.233	3	108	19	1.9
1885	StL AA	6	6	.500	13	13	12-3	0	112	98	65	1	6	19	41	3.38	97	.225	.267	50	.220	0	99	0	0.0
1886	StL AA	5	5	.500	10	10	10-1	0	87.2	107	75	2	7	27	30	3.80	91	.288	.347	37	.189	-1	133	-7	-0.6
	Bal AA	11	13	.458	26	25	24	0	209.1	235	141	6	14	48	70	3.48	98	.280	.329	85	.188	-1	70	-5	-0.5
	Year	16	18	.471	36	35	34-1	0	297	342	145	8	21	75	100	3.58	96	.282	.335	122	.189	-2	88	-11	-1.1
1887	Cin AA	3	5	.375	8	8	8	0	69.1	85	66	3	8	43	18	5.45	80	.296	.402	31	.194	-0	126	-8	-0.7
Total	6	102	79	.564	187	186	177-18	0	1603.2	1572	958	21	47	294	562	2.95	112	.243	.281	732	.210	-5	101	58	5.1

Year	Tm Lg	W	L	Pct	G	GS	CG-Sho	SV-BS	IP	H	R	HR	HB	BB-IB	SO	ERA	AERA	OAV	OOB	AB-SH	AVG	PB	Sup	APR	PW
McGINNIS, GUS Gus B 8.1870 Barnesville, OH D 4.20.1904 Barnesville, OH TL 5-11/168# d4.27																									
1893	Chi N	2	5	.286	13	5	3	0	67.1	85	67	2	3	31	13	5.35	87	.299	.374	25	.240	2	106	-8	-0.5
	Phi N	1	3	.250	5	4	4-1	0	37.1	39	20	0	2	17	12	4.34	106	.262	.345	15	.200	-1	72	3	0.2
	Year	3	8	.273	18	9	7-1	0	104.2	124	25	2	5	48	25	4.99	93	.286	.364	40	.225	1	91	-3	-0.3
McGINNITY, JOE Joseph Jerome "Iron Man" (b: Joseph Jerome McGinty) B 3.19.1871 Rock Island, IL D 11.14.1929 Brooklyn, NY BR/TR 5-11/206# d4.18 C1 HF1946																									
1899	Bal N	**28**	16	.636	48	41	38-4	2	366.1	358	164	3	26	93	74	2.68	148	.256	.314	145-5	.193	-5*	102	48	4.5
1900	†Bro N	**28**	8	**.778**	44	37	32-1	0	**343**	350	179	5	40	113	93	2.94	131	.264	.340	145-5	.193	-5*	105	23	1.4
1901	Bal A	26	20	.565	**48**	**43**	**39**-1	1	**382**	412	219	7	21	96	75	3.56	109	.272	.324	148-8	.209	-4	91	17	1.3
1902	Bal A	13	10	.565	25	23	19	0	198.2	219	100	3	8	46	39	3.44	110	.280	.327	87-4	.287	4*	104	10	1.4
	NY N	8	8	.500	19	16	16-1	0	153	122	52	1	9	32	67	2.06	136	.219	.273	66-8	.121	-4*	92	13	0.9
1903	NY N	**31**	20	.608	**55**	**48**	**44**-3	2	**434**	391	162	4	19	109	171	2.43	138	.236	.291	165-13	.206	-2	96	**42**	4.0
1904	NY N	**35**	8	**.814**	**51**	44	38-**9**	**5**	**408**	307	103	8	13	86	144	**1.61**	**169**	.206	.256	142-12	.176	-1	113	**50**	**5.4**
1905	†NY N	21	15	.583	**46**	38	26-2	3	320.1	289	131	6	14	71	125	2.87	102	.240	.290	120-1	.233	6	115	6	1.3
1906	NY N	**27**	12	.692	**45**	37	32-3	2	339.2	316	127	1	7	71	105	2.25	116	.246	.289	115-12	.130	-3	114	10	0.7
1907	NY N	18	18	.500	**47**	34	23-3	**4**	310.1	320	126	6	15	58	120	3.16	78	.266	.308	103-8	.175	0	121	-15	-1.8
1908	NY N	11	7	.611	37	20	7-5	**5**	186	192	73	8	7	37	55	2.27	106	.267	.310	61-5	.180	-0	120	-1	-0.2
Total	10	246	142	.634	465	381	314-32	24	3441.1	3276	1436	52	179	812	1068	2.66	120	.249	.302	1297-81	.194	-14	105	203	18.9
McGLINCHY, KEVIN Kevin Michael B 6.28.1977 Malden, MA BR/TR 6-5/220# d4.5																									
1999	†Atl N	7	3	.700	64	0	0	0-2	70.1	66	25	6	1	30-7	67	2.82	160	.255	.330	2-0	.000	-0		13	1.5
2000	Atl N	0	0	—	10	0	0	0-0	8.1	11	4	1	0	6-1	9	2.16	212	.314	.415	0-0	—	0		1	0.1
Total	2	7	3	.700	74	0	0	0-2	78.2	77	29	7	1	36-8	76	2.75	164	.262	.340	2-0	.000	-0		14	1.6
McGLOTHEN, LYNN Lynn Everatt B 3.27.1950 Monroe, LA D 8.14.1984 Dubach, LA BL/TR 6-2/195# d6.25																									
1972	Bos A	8	7	.533	22	22	4-1	0-0	145	135	66	9	7	59-1	112	3.41	94	.247	.326	53-3	.189	1	106	-4	-0.1
1973	Bos A	1	2	.333	6	3	0	0-1	23	39	23	6	1	8-0	16	8.22	49	.386	.429	0-0	—	0	133	-10	-1.1
1974	StL N★	16	12	.571	31	31	8-3	0-0	237.1	212	80	12	2	89-14	142	2.69	133	.241	.312	83-3	.181	-1	93	24	2.7
1975	StL N	15	13	.536	35	34	9-2	0-0	239	231	110	21	4	97-11	146	3.92	96	.254	.326	80-10	.087	-5	97	2	-0.5
1976	StL N	13	15	.464	33	32	10-4	0-0	205	209	96	10	4	68-6	106	3.91	91	.268	.328	71-7	.211	2	93	-5	-0.6
1977	SF N	2	9	.182	21	15	2	0-0	80	94	62	9	1	52-4	42	5.62	70	.299	.397	19-1	.105	-1	83	-17	-2.1
1978	SF N	0	0	—	5	1	0	0-0	12.2	15	9	0	0	4-0	9	4.97	69	.313	.358	3-0	.000	-0	182	-3	-0.2
	Chi N	5	3	.625	49	1	0	0-5	80	77	33	7	0	39-5	60	3.04	133	.257	.341	13-0	.231	1	67	7	0.6
	Year	5	3	.625	54	2	0	0-5	92.2	92	36	7	0	43-5	69	3.30	120	.264	.344	16-0	.188	0	114	4	0.4
1979	Chi N	13	14	.481	42	29	6-1	2-0	212	236	103	27	3	55-8	147	4.12	100	.283	.327	71-4	.225	1	93	3	0.4
1980	Chi N	12	14	.462	39	27	2-2	0-0	182.1	211	105	24	1	64-7	119	4.79	82	.293	.348	51-8	.196	2*	91	-14	-1.8
1981	Chi N	1	4	.200	20	6	0	0-0	54.2	71	32	1	1	28-4	26	4.77	77	.317	.394	12-0	.083	-1	72	-6	-0.5
	Chi A	0	0	—	11	0	0	0-0	21.2	14	10	0	1	7-3	12	4.15	86	.189	.268	0-0	—	0		-1	-0.1
1982	NY A	0	0	—	4	0	0	0-0	5	9	6	1	0	2-0	2	10.80	37	.375	.423	0-0	—	0		-4	-0.2
Total	11	86	93	.480	318	201	41-13	2-6	1497.2	1553	735	127	25	572-63	939	3.98	94	.270	.336	456-36	.173	-1	94	-28	-3.5
McGLOTHIN, PAT Ezra Mac B 10.20.1920 Coalfield, TN BL/TR 6-3.5/180# d4.25																									
1949	Bro N	1	1	.500	7	0	0	0	15.2	13	8	2	0	5	11	4.60	89	.224	.286	3-0	.000	-0		-1	-0.1
1950	Bro N	0	0	—	1	0	0	0	2	5	3	0	0	1	2	13.50	30	.455	.500	0-0	—	0		-2	-0.1
Total	2	1	1	.500	8	0	0	0	17.2	18	11	2	0	6	13	5.60	73	.261	.320	3-0	.000	-0		-3	-0.2
McGLOTHLIN, JIM James Milton "Red" B 10.6.1943 Los Angeles, CA D 12.23.1975 Union, KY BR/TR 6-1/185# d9.20																									
1965	Cal A	0	3	.000	3	3	1	0	18	18	9	1	0	7-1	9	3.50	97	.261	.329	6-0	.000	-1	34	-1	-0.2
1966	Cal A	3	1	.750	19	11	0	0	67.2	79	37	9	1	19-0	41	4.52	74	.292	.338	17-1	.059	-0	134	-9	-0.5
1967	Cal A★	12	8	.600	32	29	9-**6**	0	197.1	163	74	13	4	56-2	137	2.96	106	.226	.284	57-7	.140	-0	105	5	0.5
1968	Cal A	10	15	.400	40	32	8	3	208.1	187	87	19	8	60-5	135	3.54	82	.244	.304	63-6	.111	-1	99	-13	-1.6
1969	Cal A	8	16	.333	37	35	4-1	0-0	201	188	86	19	5	58-1	96	3.18	110	.249	.306	58-5	.121	-1	72	5	0.6
1970	†Cin N	14	10	.583	35	34	5-3	0-0	210.2	192	91	19	3	86-8	97	3.59	113	.245	.319	66-4	.121	1	95	13	1.7
1971	Cin N	8	12	.400	30	26	6	0-0	170.2	151	65	15	4	47-4	93	3.22	104	.243	.300	51-3	.137	1	87	3	0.5
1972	†Cin N	9	8	.529	31	21	3-1	0-1	145	165	71	15	0	49-6	69	3.91	82	.287	.341	46-1	.174	3	143	-13	-1.1
1973	Cin N	3	3	.500	24	9	0	0-0	63.1	91	52	13	0	23-3	18	6.68	51	.340	.390	16-1	.125	0	144	-25	-2.0
	Chi A	0	1	.000	5	1	0	0-0	18.1	13	8	2	0	13-0	14	3.93	101	.203	.333	0-0	—	0	23	1	0.0
Total	9	67	77	.465	256	201	36-11	3-1	1300.1	1247	580	125	25	418-30	709	3.61	94	.255	.315	380-28	.126	2	100	-34	-2.1
McGLYNN, STONEY Ulysses Simpson Grant B 5.26.1872 Lancaster, PA D 8.26.1941 Manitowoc, WI BR/TR 5-11/185# d9.20																									
1906	StL N	2	2	.500	6	6	6	0	48	43	16	0	1	15	25	2.44	108	.249	.312	17-0	.059	-1	97	1	0.1
1907	StL N	14	25	.359	45	**39**	**33**-3	1	**352.1**	329	159	6	4	112	109	2.91	86	.251	.312	125-6	.200	3*	85	-12	-1.1
1908	StL N	1	6	.143	16	6	4	1	75.2	76	40	0	2	17	23	3.45	68	.256	.301	26-1	.077	-1	75	-8	-0.8
Total	3	17	33	.340	67	51	43-3	2	476	448	215	6	7	144	157	2.95	85	.252	.310	168-7	.167	0	86	-19	-1.8
McGOWAN, MICKEY Tullis Earl B 11.26.1921 Dothan, AL D 3.8.2003 Georgia BL/TL 6-2/200# d4.22																									
1948	NY N	0	0	—	3	0	0	0	3.2	3	3	1	0	4	2	7.36	53	.231	.412	1-0	.000	-0		-1	-0.1
McGRANER, HOWARD Howard "Muck" B 9.11.1889 Hamley Run, OH D 10.22.1952 Zaleski, OH BL/TL 5-7/155# d9.12																									
1912	Cin N	1	0	1.000	4	0	0	0	19	22	17	2	1	7	5	7.11	47	.293	.361	8-0	.250	1		-7	-0.2
McGRAW, TUG Frank Edwin B 8.30.1944 Martinez, CA D 1.05.2004 Brentwood, TN BR/TL 6/185# d4.18																									
1965	NY N	2	7	.222	37	9	2	1	97.2	88	47	8	3	48-2	57	3.32	106	.249	.341	23-0	.130	-1*	66	0	-0.1
1966	NY N	2	9	.182	15	12	1	0	62.1	72	38	11	0	25-2	34	5.34	68	.294	.355	17-2	.235	1	75	-10	-1.5
1967	NY N	0	3	.000	4	4	0	0	17.1	13	16	3	0	13-2	18	7.79	44	.206	.338	4-1	.250	0	84	-8	-1.1
1969	†NY N	9	3	.750	42	4	1	12-0	100.1	89	31	6	0	47-7	92	2.24	163	.243	.329	24-0	.167	0*	164	**14**	2.1
1970	NY N	4	6	.400	57	0	0	10-2	90.2	77	40	6	1	49-17	81	3.28	123	.231	.328	13-0	.308	1		6	1.0
1971	NY N	11	4	.733	51	1	0	8-2	111	73	22	4	3	41-11	109	1.70	200	.189	.271	18-2	.222	2	52	**22**	3.6
1972	NY N★	8	6	.571	54	0	0	27-5	106	71	26	3	3	40-11	92	1.70	198	.197	.279	20-2	.100	-0		19	3.6
1973	†NY N	5	6	.455	60	2	0	25-7	118.2	106	53	11	3	55-9	81	3.87	94	.243	.329	24-3	.167	1	122	-2	-0.1
1974	NY N	6	11	.353	41	4	1-1	3-6	88.2	96	43	12	0	32-6	54	4.16	86	.279	.338	14-1	.071	-0	85	-4	-0.8
1975	Phi N☆	9	6	.600	56	0	0	14-3	102.2	84	38	6	3	36-6	55	2.98	126	.226	.299	13-1	.154	-0		9	1.4
1976	†Phi N	7	6	.538	58	0	0	11-6	97.1	81	34	4	0	42-10	76	2.50	142	.226	.304	7-0	.143	0		9	1.5
1977	†Phi N	7	3	.700	45	0	0	9-3	79	62	25	6	1	24-5	58	2.62	153	.221	.282	10-0	.400	2		12	1.9
1978	†Phi N	8	7	.533	55	1	0	9-2	89.2	82	39	6	0	23-7	63	3.21	111	.245	.292	4-2	.000	-0	0	2	0.3
1979	Phi N	4	3	.571	65	1	0	16-2	83.2	83	56	9	2	29-7	57	5.16	74	.259	.321	6-1	.167	-0	139	-14	-1.7
1980	†Phi N	5	4	.556	57	0	0	20-5	92.1	62	16	3	2	23-9	75	1.46	260	.194	.250	8-3	.250	0		**23**	3.3
1981	†Phi N	2	4	.333	34	0	0	10-1	44	35	13	2	0	14-3	26	2.66	136	.219	.278	1-1	.000	0		5	0.9
1982	Phi N	3	3	.500	34	0	0	5-6	39.2	50	19	3	1	12-6	25	4.31	85	.305	.356	2-0	.000	-0		-2	-0.3
1983	Phi N	2	1	.667	34	1	0	0-0	55.2	58	24	4	0	19-4	30	3.56	100	.271	.326	3-2	.333	0	124	1	0.1
1984	Phi N	2	0	1.000	25	0	0	0-0	38	36	17	1	0	10-4	26	3.79	96	.245	.289	3-0	.333	0		0	0.0
Total	19	96	92	.511	824	39	5-1	180-50	1514.2	1318	597	108	22	582-128	1109	3.14	116	.237	.309	214-21	.182	5	86	82	14.1
McGRAW, JOHN John (b: Roy Elmer Hoar) B 12.8.1890 Intercourse, PA D 4.27.1967 Torrance, CA BR/TR 5-9/160# d7.29																									
1914	Bro F	0	0	—	1	0	0	0	2	0	0	0	1	0	2	0.00	—	.000	.143	0-0	—	0		1	0.0
McGRAW, BOB Robert Emmett B 4.10.1895 LaVeta, CO D 6.2.1978 Boise, ID BR/TR 6-2/160# d9.25 Mil 1918-19																									
1917	NY A	0	1	.000	2	2	1	0	11	9	5	0	0	3	3	0.82	328	.257	.316	3-0	.000	-0	67	1	0.0
1918	NY A	0	1	.000	1	1	0	0	0	0	4	0	0	4	0	∞	—	—	1.000	0-0	—	0	107	-4	-0.3
1919	NY A	1	0	1.000	6	0	0	0	16.1	11	6	1	1	10	3	3.31	97	.216	.355	3-0	.000	-0		0	0.0
	Bos A	0	2	.000	10	1	0	0	26.2	33	23	0	3	17	6	6.75	45	.347	.461	10-1	.100	-1	182	-11	-0.9
	Year	1	2	.333	16	1	0	0	43	44	30	1	4	27	9	5.44	57	.301	.424	13-1	.077	-1	178	-10	-0.9
1920	NY A	0	0	—	15	0	0	0	27	24	18	1	1	20	11	4.67	82	.240	.372	7-0	.000	-1		-3	-0.3
1925	Bro N	0	2	.000	2	2	2	0	19.2	14	9	0	0	13	3	3.20	130	.222	.355	6-1	.167	-0	61	2	0.1

Year	Tm Lg	W	L	Pct	G	GS	CG-Sho	SV-BS	IP	H	R	HR	HB	BB-IB	SO	ERA	AERA	OAV	OOB	AB-SH	AVG	PB	Sup	APR	PW
1926	Bro N	9	13	.409	33	21	10	1	174.1	197	104	12	2	67	49	4.59	83	.292	.358	55-6	.145	-2	95	-13	-1.7
1927	Bro N	0	1	.000	1	1	0	0	4	5	5	1	0	2	2	9.00	44	.313	.389	1-0	.000	-0	64	-2	-0.4
	StL N	4	5	.444	18	12	4-1	0	94	121	65	3	0	30	37	5.07	78	.323	.373	33-4	.182	1	120	-12	-0.9
	Year	4	6	.400	19	13	4-1	0	98	126	71	4	0	32	39	5.23	75	.322	.374	34-4	.176	1	116	-14	-1.3
1928	Phi N	7	8	.467	39	3	0	1	120	148	86	7	2	56	28	5.18	83	.317	.392	36-3	.111	-2	106	-14	-1.8
1929	Phi N	5	5	.500	41	4	0	4	86.1	113	68	6	2	43	22	5.73	91	.324	.401	20-1	.200	0	126	-7	-0.7
Total	9	26	38	.406	168	47	17-1	6	579.1	675	393	31	11	265	164	5.00	81	.303	.380	174-16	.138	-6	101	-63	-6.9
McGRAW, TOM Thomas Virgil B 12.8.1967 Portland, OR BL/TL 6-2/195# d5.7																									
1997	StL N	0	0	—	2	0	0	0-0	1.2	2	0	0	0	1-0	0	0.00	—	.333	.375	0-0	—	0		1	0.0
McGREGOR, SCOTT Scott Houston B 1.18.1954 Inglewood, CA BB/TL 6-1/190# d9.19																									
1976	Bal A	0	1	.000	3	2	0	0-0	14.2	17	7	0	0	5-0	6	3.68	89	.293	.349	0-0	—	0	67	-1	0.0
1977	Bal A	3	5	.375	29	5	1	4-0	114	119	57	8	7	30-2	55	4.42	86	.275	.328	0-0	—	0	104	-7	-0.5
1978	Bal A	15	13	.536	35	32	13-4	1-1	233	217	98	19	1	47-3	94	3.32	106	.248	.286	0-0	—	0	92	4	0.5
1979	†Bal A	13	6	.684	27	23	7-2	0-0	174.2	165	70	19	2	23-0	81	3.35	120	.248	**.273**	0-0	—	0	110	15	1.4
1980	Bal A	20	8	.714	36	36	12-4	0-0	252	254	101	16	2	58-3	119	3.32	119	.265	.306	0-0	—	0*	122	18	1.7
1981	Bal A☆	13	5	.722	24	22	8-3	0-0	160	167	63	13	0	40-5	82	3.26	111	.273	.315	0-0	—	0	109	8	0.9
1982	Bal A	14	12	.538	37	37	7-1	0-0	226.1	238	126	31	1	52-6	84	4.61	88	.267	.306	0-0	—	0	107	-16	-1.6
1983	†Bal A	18	7	.720	36	36	12-2	0-0	260	271	101	24	1	45-2	86	3.18	125	.269	.298	0-0	—	0	124	24	2.1
1984	Bal A	15	12	.556	30	30	10-3	0-0	196.1	216	93	18	5	54-2	67	3.94	98	.280	.329	0-0	—	0	99	0	0.1
1985	Bal A	14	14	.500	35	34	8-1	0-0	204	226	118	34	1	65-2	86	4.81	84	.283	.334	0-0	—	0	111	-17	-2.0
1986	Bal A	11	15	.423	34	33	4-2	0-0	203	216	110	35	3	57-0	95	4.52	92	.270	.319	0-0	—	0	103	-7	-0.8
1987	Bal A	2	7	.222	26	15	1-1	0-0	85.1	112	69	15	3	35-1	39	6.64	66	.326	.388	0-0	—	0	91	-21	-1.7
1988	Bal A	0	3	.000	4	4	0	0-0	17.1	27	18	3	0	7-0	10	8.83	44	.370	.415	0-0	—	0	70	-9	-1.2
Total	13	138	108	.561	356	309	83-23	5-1	2140.2	2245	1031	235	26	518-26	904	3.99	98	.271	.313	0-0	—	0	108	-9	-1.1
McGREW, SLIM Walter Howard B 8.5.1899 Yoakum, TX D 8.21.1967 Houston, TX BR/TR 6-7.5/235# d4.18																									
1922	Was A	0	0	—	1	0	0	0	1.2	4	6	0	0	2	1	10.80	36	.500	.600	1-0	.000	-0		-3	-0.1
1923	Was A	0	0	—	3	0	0	0	5	11	9	0	0	3	1	12.60	30	.440	.500	1-0	.000	-0		-5	-0.3
1924	Was A	0	1	.000	6	2	0	0	23.1	25	15	1	0	12	8	5.01	80	.281	.366	8-0	.000	-1	84	-2	-0.3
Total	3	0	1	.000	10	2	0	0	30	40	30	1	0	17	10	6.60	60	.328	.410	10-0	.000	-2	84	-10	-0.7
McGUIRE d6.16																									
1894	Cin N	0	0	—	1	0	0	0	6	15	9	0	0	5	1	10.50	53	.469	.541	4-0	.250	-0		-3	-0.1
McGUIRE, TOM Thomas Patrick "Elmer" B 2.1.1892 Chicago, IL D 12.7.1959 Phoenix, AZ BR/TR 6/175# d4.18 Mil 1918																									
1914	Chi F	5	6	.455	24	12	7	0	131.1	143	76	7	4	57	37	3.70	72	.288	.366	70-0	.271	4*	131	-18	-0.8
1919	Chi A	0	0	—	1	0	0	0	3	5	4	0	0	3	0	9.00	35	.500	.615	1-0	.000	-0		-2	-0.1
Total	2	5	6	.455	25	12	7	0	134.1	148	80	7	4	60	37	3.82	70	.292	.371	71-0	.268	3	131	-20	-0.9
McGUNNIGLE, BILL William Henry "Gunner" B 1.1.1855 Boston, MA D 3.9.1899 Brockton, MA BR/TR 5-9/155# d5.2 M5 ▲																									
1879	Buf N	9	5	.643	14	13	13-2	0	120	113	66	0		16	62	2.63	99	**.235**	.260	171	.175	-2*	99	1	-0.1
1880	Buf N	2	3	.400	5	5	4-1	0	37	43	19	0		8	3	3.41	72	.279	.315	22	.182	-1*	48	-2	-0.3
Total	2	11	8	.579	19	18	17-3	0	157	156	85	0		24	65	2.81	92	.246	.274	193	.176	-3	86	-1	-0.4
McHALE, MARTY Martin Joseph B 10.30.1888 Stoneham, MA D 5.7.1979 Hempstead, NY BR/TR 5-11.5/174# d9.28																									
1910	Bos A	0	2	.000	2	2	1	0	13.2	15	8	0	1	6	14	4.61	55	.259	.338	6-0	.000	-1	105	-2	-0.4
1911	Bos A	0	0	—	4	1	0	0	9.1	19	12	1	1	3	3	9.64	34	.475	.523	3-0	.000	-0	198	-6	-0.3
1913	NY A	2	4	.333	7	6	4-1	0	48.2	49	21	1	1	10	11	2.96	101	.268	.309	15-0	.000	-1	54	0	-0.1
1914	NY A	6	16	.273	31	23	12	1	191	195	82	3	4	33	75	2.97	93	.268	.303	60-2	.200	2*	73	-6	-0.6
1915	NY A	3	7	.300	13	11	6	0	78.1	86	45	1	0	19	25	4.25	69	.277	.318	21-2	.143	1	102	-11	-1.2
1916	Bos A	0	1	.000	2	1	0	0	6	7	7	0	1	4	1	3.00	92	.280	.400	0-0	—	0	0	-2	-0.3
	Cle A	0	0	—	5	0	0	0	11.1	10	7	1	0	6	2	5.56	54	.270	.372	2-0	.000	-0		-2	-0.2
	Year	0	1	.000	7	1	0	0	17.1	17	14	1	1	10	3	4.67	63	.274	.384	2-0	.000	0	0	-4	-0.5
Total	6	11	30	.268	64	44	23-1	1	358.1	381	182	7	8	81	131	3.57	80	.276	.320	107-4	.140	-0	81	-29	-3.1
McILREE, VANCE Vance Elmer B 10.14.1897 Riverside, IA D 5.6.1959 Kansas City, MO BR/TR 6/160# d9.13																									
1921	Was A	0	0	—	1	0	0	0	1	1	1	0	0	0	0	9.00	46	.200	.200	0-0	—	0		0	0.0
McILWAIN, STOVER Stover William "Smokey" (b: William Stover McIlwain) B 9.22.1939 Savannah, GA D 1.15.1966 Buffalo, NY BR/TR 6-4/195# d9.25																									
1957	Chi A	0	0	—	1	0	0	0	1	2	0	0	0	1-0	0	0.00	—	.500	.600	0-0	—	0		0	0.0
1958	Chi A	0	0	—	1	1	0	0	4	4	1	1	0	0-0	4	2.25	162	.250	.250	1-0	.000	-0	272	1	0.0
Total	2	0	0	—	2	1	0	0	5	6	1	1	0	1-0	4	1.80	203	.300	.333	1-0	.000	-0	272	1	0.0
McINTIRE, HARRY John Reid B 1.11.1879 Dayton, OH D 1.9.1949 Daytona Beach, FL BR/TR 5-11/180# d4.14																									
1905	Bro N	8	25	.242	40	35	29-1	1	308.2	340	188	6	20	101	135	3.70	78	.285	.351	138-3	.246	7*	69	-31	-2.4
1906	Bro N	13	21	.382	39	31	25-4	3	276	254	123	2	14	89	121	2.97	85	.247	.316	103-1	.175	1*	74	-15	-1.8
1907	Bro N	7	15	.318	28	22	19-3	0	199.2	178	82	6	7	79	49	2.39	98	.248	.329	69-2	.217	5*	58	-3	0.2
1908	Bro N	11	20	.355	40	35	26-4	2	288	259	106	5	20	90	108	2.69	87	.252	.324	100-1	.200	2	89	-7	-0.7
1909	Bro N	7	17	.292	32	26	20-2	1	228	200	114	5	21	91	84	3.63	71	.246	.337	76-3	.171	1	84	-24	-2.3
1910	†Chi N	13	9	.591	28	19	10-2	0	176	152	70	5	10	50	65	3.07	94	.240	.305	66-3	.258	3*	106	-1	0.3
1911	Chi N	11	7	.611	25	17	9-1	0	149	147	81	5	4	33	56	4.11	81	.257	.302	53-3	.264	4*	128	-10	-0.6
1912	Chi N	1	2	.333	4	3	2	0	23.2	22	11	0	0	6	8	3.80	87	.256	.304	10-1	.300	1*	51	-1	0.1
1913	Cin N	0	1	.000	1	0	0	0	1	3	3	0	0	0	0	27.00	12	.600	.600	0-0	—	0		-2	-0.4
Total	9	71	117	.378	237	188	140-17	7	1650	1555	778	34	96	539	626	3.22	83	.256	.326	615-17	.218	24	84	-94	-7.6
McINTOSH, JOE Joseph Anthony B 8.4.1951 Billings, MT BB/TR 6-2/185# d4.5																									
1974	SD N	0	4	.000	10	5	0	0-0	37.1	36	19	3	1	17-2	22	3.62	99	.250	.329	10-1	.000	-1	49	-1	-0.3
1975	SD N	8	15	.348	37	28	4-1	0-1	183	195	88	14	2	60-9	71	3.69	94	.273	.330	48-5	.188	2*	87	-4	-0.2
Total	2	8	19	.296	47	33	4-1	0-1	220.1	231	107	17	3	77-11	93	3.68	95	.270	.330	58-6	.155	1	81	-5	-0.5
McINTYRE, FRANK Frank W. B 7.12.1859 Walled Lake, MI D 7.8.1887 Detroit, MI d5.16																									
1883	Det N	1	0	1.000	1	1	1	0	11	11	10	0		1	0	0.82	379	.234	.250	4	.000	-0	190	1	0.0
	Col AA	1	1	.500	2	2	2	0	19	20	19	0		7	6	5.21	59	.253	.314	7	.000	-0	178	-5	-0.4
Total	1	2	1	.667	3	3	3	0	30	31	29	0		8	6	3.60	86	.246	.291	11	.000	-1	181	-4	-0.4
McJAMES, DOC James McCutchen (b: James Mc Cutchen James) B 8.27.1873 Williamsburg, SC D 9.23.1901 Charleston, SC TR d9.24																									
1895	Was N	1	1	.500	2	2	2	0	17	17	11	0	0	16	9	1.59	302	.258	.402	7-0	.143	-1	96	4	0.3
1896	Was N	12	20	.375	37	33	29	1	280.1	310	208	2	6	135	103	4.27	103	.278	.359	111-3	.162	-9	93	5	-0.3
1897	Was N	15	23	.395	44	39	33-**3**	2	323.2	361	212	7	21	137	**156**	3.61	120	.280	.358	124-0	.169	-7	72	22	1.4
1898	Bal N	27	15	.643	45	42	40-2	0	374	327	148	5	12	113	178	2.36	152	.234	.296	149-1	.181	-4	114	49	4.3
1899	Bro N	18	15	.545	37	34	27-1	1	275.1	295	166	4	10	122	105	3.50	112	.274	.353	112-0	.170	-5	96	8	0.4
1901	Bro N	5	6	.455	13	12	6	0	91	104	71	1	7	40	42	4.75	71	.285	.367	34-0	.029	-4	125	-15	-1.9
Total	6	78	80	.494	178	162	137-6	4	1361.1	1414	816	19	56	563	593	3.43	116	.266	.343	537-4	.162	-30	95	73	4.2
McKAIN, ARCHIE Archie Richard "Happy" B 5.12.1911 Delphos, KS D 5.21.1985 Salina, KS BB/TL 5-10/175# d4.25																									
1937	Bos A	8	8	.500	36	18	3	2	137	152	84	7	0	64	66	4.66	102	.273	.348	49-1	.265	3*	97	0	0.2
1938	Bos A	5	4	.556	37	5	1	6	99.2	119	60	6	2	44	27	4.52	109	.297	.369	31-2	.065	-2	96	3	0.2
1939	Det A	5	6	.455	32	11	4-1	4	129.2	120	66	6	0	54	49	3.68	133	.247	.322	41-0	.220	4	90	15	1.5
1940	†Det A	5	0	1.000	27	0	0	3	51	48	18	2	0	25	24	2.82	168	.247	.333	7-1	.143	0		10	1.1
1941	Det A	2	1	.667	15	0	0	0	43	58	24	3	0	11	14	5.02	90	.330	.369	11-0	.000	-1		-1	0.0
	StL A	0	1	.000	8	0	0	1	10	16	9	2	1	4	2	8.10	53	.364	.429	2-0	.000	-0		-4	-0.4
	Year	2	2	.500	23	0	0	1	53	74	38	5	1	15	16	5.60	80	.336	.381	13-0	.000	-1		-4	-0.4
1943	StL A	1	1	.500	10	0	0	0	16	16	9	0	0	6	6	3.94	84	.242	.306	1-0	.000	-0		-1	-0.2
Total	6	26	21	.553	165	34	8-1	16	486.1	529	270	26	3	208	188	4.26	112	.275	.347	142-4	.176	3	96	22	2.4

Year	Tm Lg	W	L	Pct	G	GS	CG-Sho	SV-BS	IP	H	R	HR	HB	BB-IB	SO	ERA	AERA	OAV	OOB	AB-SH	AVG	PB	Sup	APR	PW
McKAIN, HAL Harold Le Roy B 7.10.1906 Logan, IA D 1.24.1970 Sacramento, CA BL/TR 5-11/185# d9.22																									
1927	Cle A	0	1	.000	2	1	0	0	11	18	6	0	0	4	5	4.09	103	.391	.440	4-0	.000	-1	40	0	0.0
1929	Chi A	6	9	.400	34	10	4-1	1	158	158	84	10	10	85	33	3.65	117	.275	.378	44-1	.227	2	71	8	1.1
1930	Chi A	6	4	.600	32	5	0	5	89	108	67	0	3	42	52	5.56	83	.299	.377	31-2	.419	7*	138	-9	-0.2
1931	Chi A	6	9	.400	27	8	3	0	112	134	82	10	3	57	39	5.71	75	.295	.377	42-1	.119	-1*	74	-17	-1.8
1932	Chi A	0	0	—	8	0	0	0	11.1	17	15	1	0	5	7	11.12	39	.340	.400	1-0	.000	-0		-8	-0.4
Total	5	18	23	.439	103	24	7-1	6	381.1	435	254	21	16	193	136	4.93	88	.293	.380	122-4	.230	8	85	-26	-1.3
McKAY, REEVE Reeve Stewart "Rip" B 11.16.1881 Morgan, TX D 1.18.1946 Dallas, TX TR 6-1.5/168# d10.2																									
1915	StL A	0	0	—	1	0	0	0	1	1	1	0	0	0	0	9.00	32	.500	.500	0-0	—	0		-1	0.0
McKEE, JIM James Marion B 2.1.1947 Columbus, OH D 9.14.2002 Pickaway County, OH BR/TR 6-7/215# d9.15																									
1972	Pit N	1	0	1.000	2	0	0	0-0	5	2	0	0	0	1-0	4	0.00	—	.125	.176	0-0	—	0		2	0.4
1973	Pit N	0	1	.000	15	1	0	0-0	27	31	21	2	1	17-0	13	5.67	62	.287	.389	4-0	.000	-0	325	-7	-0.4
Total	2	1	1	.500	17	1	0	0-0	32	33	21	2	1	18-0	17	4.78	73	.266	.364	4-0	.000	-0	325	-5	0.0
McKEE, ROGERS Rogers Hornsby B 9.16.1926 Shelby, NC BL/TL 6-1/160# d8.18 Mil 1945-46																									
1943	Phi N	1	0	1.000	4	1	1	0	13.1	12	9	0	0	5	1	6.08	56	.226	.293	5-0	.200	0	277	-3	-0.2
1944	Phi N	0	0	—	1	0	0	0	2	2	1	1	0	1	0	4.50	80	.250	.333	0-0	—	0		0	0.0
Total	2	1	0	1.000	5	1	1	0	15.1	14	10	1	0	6	1	5.87	58	.230	.299	5-0	.200	0	277	-3	-0.2
McKEITHAN, TIM Emmett James B 11.2.1906 Lawndale, NC D 8.20.1969 Forest City, NC BR/TR 6-2/182# d7.21																									
1932	Phi A	0	1	.000	4	2	0	0	12.2	18	11	0	0	5	0	7.11	64	.340	.397	3-0	.000	0	85	-4	-0.2
1933	Phi A	1	0	1.000	3	1	0	0	9	10	4	0	0	4	3	4.00	107	.278	.350	3-0	.333	0	218	1	0.1
1934	Phi A	0	0	—	3	0	0	0	4	7	7	2	0	5	0	15.75	28	.389	.522	1-0	.000	-0		-5	-0.2
Total	3	1	1	.500	10	3	0	0	25.2	35	22	2	0	14	3	7.36	60	.327	.405	7-0	.143	0	129	-8	-0.3
McKELVY, RUSS Russell Errett B 9.8.1854 Swissvale, PA D 10.19.1915 Omaha, NE BR/TR d5.1 ▲																									
1878	Ind N	0	2	.000	4	1	1	0	25	38	23	1		3	3	2.16	94	.322	.339	253	.225	0*	107	-3	-0.1
McKENNA, KIT James William B 2.10.1873 Lynchburg, VA D 3.31.1941 Lynchburg, VA TR 5-9/180# d7.7																									
1898	Bro N	2	6	.250	14	9	7	0	100.2	118	75	4	17	57	27	5.63	64	.290	.399	40-1	.225	0	66	-18	-1.1
1899	Bal N	2	3	.400	8	4	4	1	45	66	38	1	3	19	7	4.60	86	.340	.407	17-0	.059	-1*	118	-5	-0.5
Total	2	4	9	.308	22	13	11	1	145.2	184	113	5	20	76	34	5.31	70	.306	.402	57-1	.175	-0	83	-23	-1.6
McKENRY, LIMB Frank Gordon "Big Pete" B 8.13.1888 Piney Flats, TN D 11.1.1956 Fresno, CA BR/TR 6-4/205# d8.27																									
1915	Cin N	5	5	.500	21	11	5	0	110.1	94	43	2	3	39	37	2.94	97	.238	.311	33-3	.152	0	83	0	0.1
1916	Cin N	1	1	.500	6	1	0	0	14.2	14	8	0	2	8	2	4.30	60	.259	.375	5-0	.400	2	115	-2	-0.2
Total	2	6	6	.500	27	12	5	0	125	108	51	2	5	47	39	3.10	91	.241	.319	38-3	.184	2	85	-2	-0.1
McKEON, JOEL Joel Jacob B 2.25.1963 Covington, KY BL/TL 6/185# d5.6																									
1986	Chi A	3	1	.750	30	0	0	1-2	33	18	10	2	0	17-2	18	2.45	176	.165	.273	0-0	—	0		7	0.7
1987	Chi A	1	2	.333	13	0	0	0-0	21	27	22	8	0	15-0	14	9.43	49	.318	.416	0-0	—	0		-10	-1.2
Total	2	4	3	.571	43	0	0	1-2	54	45	32	10	0	32-2	32	5.17	86	.232	.336	0-0	—	0		-3	-0.5
McKEON, LARRY Lawrence G. B 3.25.1866 , NY D 7.18.1915 Indianapolis, IN 5-10/168# d5.1																									
1884	Ind AA	18	41	.305	61	60	59-2	0	512	488	350	20	18	94	308	3.50	94	.235	.275	250	.212	-3*	74	-14	-1.2
1885	Cin AA	20	13	.606	33	33	32-2	0	290	273	143	5	13	50	117	2.86	114	.241	.281	121	.165	-5	94	14	0.8
1886	Cin AA	8	8	.500	19	19	16	0	156	174	118	6	3	54	46	5.08	69	.276	.336	75	.253	1	132	-22	-1.6
	KC N	0	2	.000	3	3	3	0	21	44	32	0		8	3	10.71	35	.411	.452	9	.000	-1	54	-13	-0.9
Total	3	46	64	.418	116	115	110-4	0	979	979	643	31	34	206	474	3.71	90	.248	.291	455	.202	-9	90	-35	-2.9
McKNIGHT, TONY Tony Mark B 6.29.1977 Texarkana, AR BL/TR 6-5/205# d8.10																									
2000	Hou N	4	1	.800	6	6	1	0-0	35	35	19	4	2	9-0	23	3.86	126	.245	.297	13-1	.000	-2	164	3	0.2
2001	Hou N	1	0	1.000	3	3	0	0-0	18	21	8	4	2	3-0	10	4.00	114	.288	.329	7-0	.000	-1	141	1	0.0
	Pit N	2	6	.250	12	12	0	0-0	69.1	88	44	15	3	21-4	36	5.19	87	.307	.358	17-4	.000	-1	81	-6	-0.7
	Year	3	6	.333	15	15	0	0-0	87.1	109	48	19	5	24-4	46	4.95	91	.303	.352	24-4	.000	-2	93	-4	-0.7
Total	2	7	7	.500	21	21	1	0-0	122.1	144	71	23	7	33-4	69	4.63	99	.286	.336	37-5	.000	-4	114	-2	-0.5
McLAIN, DENNY Dennis Dale B 3.29.1944 Chicago, IL BR/TR 6-1/185# d9.21																									
1963	Det A	2	1	.667	3	3	2	0	21	20	12	2	0	16-0	22	4.29	87	.253	.375	5-1	.200	1	103	-2	-0.1
1964	Det A	4	5	.444	19	16	3	0	100	84	48	16	1	37-0	70	4.05	90	.225	.296	37-4	.135	-1*	126	-4	-0.6
1965	Det A	16	6	.727	33	29	13-4	1	220.1	174	73	25	2	62-1	192	2.61	133	.216	.273	74-4	.054	-4	117	20	1.6
1966	Det A★	20	14	.588	38	38	14-4	0	264.1	205	120	42	3	104-3	192	3.92	89	.214	.292	93-5	.183	2	110	-9	-1.0
1967	Det A	17	16	.515	37	37	10-3	0	235	209	110	35	3	73-3	161	3.79	86	.237	.295	85-5	.118	-3*	96	-14	-2.3
1968	†Det A★	**31**	6	**.838**	41	**41**	**28**-6	0	**336**	241	86	31	6	63-2	280	1.96	154	.200	.243	111-16	.162	0*	146	36	4.4
1969	Det A★	**24**	9	.727	42	**41**	23-**9**	0-0	**325**	288	105	25	4	67-7	181	2.80	134	.237	.278	106-13	.160	-1	100	**36**	3.2
1970	Det A	3	5	.375	14	14	1	0-0	91.1	100	51	19	3	28-0	52	4.63	80	.273	.327	31-3	.065	-2	113	-9	-0.9
1971	Was A	10	22	.313	33	32	9-3	0-0	216.2	233	115	31	3	72-8	103	4.28	77	.281	.337	58-9	.103	-1	74	-24	-3.3
1972	Oak A	1	2	.333	5	5	0	0-0	22.1	32	17	4	0	8-0	8	6.04	47	.323	.374	4-2	.000	-0	118	-9	-1.1
	Atl N	3	5	.375	15	8	2	1-0	54	60	41	12	1	18-0	21	6.50	58	.279	.335	12-2	.167	0	99	-14	-1.9
Total	10	131	91	.590	280	264	105-29	2-0	1886	1646	778	242	26	548-24	1282	3.39	101	.234	.290	616-64	.133	-9	109	7	-2.0
McLAUGHLIN, BARNEY Bernard B 1857 , Ireland D 2.13.1921 Lowell, MA BR/TR d8.2 b-Frank ▲																									
1884	KC U	1	3	.250	7	4	4	0	48.2	62	44	2		15	14	5.36	42	.291	.338	162	.228	-1*	43	-15	-0.9
McLAUGHLIN, BYRON Byron Scott B 9.29.1955 Van Nuys, CA BR/TR 6-1/185# d9.18																									
1977	Sea A	0	0	—	1	0	0	0-0	1.1	5	4	1	0	0-0	1	27.00	15	.625	.625	0-0	—	0		-3	-0.1
1978	Sea A	4	8	.333	20	17	4	0-0	107	97	58	15	6	39-0	87	4.37	87	.238	.312	0-0	—	0	79	-6	-0.7
1979	Sea A	7	7	.500	47	7	1	14-3	123.2	114	58	13	2	60-8	74	4.22	104	.251	.337	0-0	—	0	145	5	0.5
1980	Sea A	3	6	.333	45	4	0	2-3	90.2	124	74	15	2	50-14	41	6.85	60	.331	.410	0-0	—	0	38	-25	-2.4
1983	Cal A	2	4	.333	16	7	0	0-2	55.2	63	32	3	2	22-3	45	5.17	78	.286	.351	0-0	—	0	119	-6	-0.6
Total	5	16	25	.390	129	35	5	16-8	378.1	403	226	47	12	171-25	248	5.11	80	.275	.353	0-0	—	0	94	-35	-3.3
McLAUGHLIN, FRANK Francis Edward B 6.19.1856 Lowell, MA D 4.5.1917 Lowell, MA BR/TR 5-9/160# d8.9.1882 b-Barney ▲																									
1883	Pit AA	0	0	—	2	0	0	0	9	14	21	0		3	1	13.00	25	.333	.378	114	.219	0*		-10	-0.4
1884	KC U	0	0	—	2	1	0	0	10	15	12	0		2	3	5.40	41	.326	.354	123	.228	-0*	229	-4	-0.2
Total	2	0	0	—	4	1	0	0	19	29	33	0		5	4	9.00	30	.330	.366	237	.224	-0	229	-14	-0.6
McLAUGHLIN, JOEY Joey Richard B 7.11.1956 Tulsa, OK BR/TR 6-2/205# d6.11																									
1977	Atl N	0	0	—	3	2	0	0-0	6	10	10	3	0	3-0	0	15.00	30	.385	.448	1-0	.000	-0	150	-6	-0.3
1979	Atl N	5	3	.625	37	0	0	5-0	69	54	23	3	1	34-4	40	2.48	164	.224	.319	11-0	.182	0		11	1.4
1980	Tor A	6	9	.400	55	10	0	4-3	135.2	159	79	16	4	53-11	70	4.51	96	.302	.366	0-0	—	0	91	-4	-0.5
1981	Tor A	1	5	.167	40	0	0	10-1	60	55	24	2	0	21-2	38	2.85	138	.249	.313	0-0	—	0		6	0.8
1982	Tor A	8	6	.571	44	0	0	8-6	70	54	27	7	1	30-3	49	3.21	140	.212	.296	0-0	—	0		9	1.9
1983	Tor A	7	4	.636	50	0	0	9-11	64.2	63	33	11	0	37-7	47	4.45	97	.259	.353	0-0	—	0		0	0.0
1984	Tor A	0	0	—	6	0	0	0-0	10.2	12	6	0	0	7-1	3	2.53	162	.286	.380	0-0	—	0		1	0.1
	Tex A	2	1	.667	15	0	0	0-2	32.2	33	17	4	0	13-1	21	4.41	94	.260	.326	0-0	—	0		0	-0.1
	Year	2	1	.667	21	0	0	0-2	43.1	45	27	4	0	20-2	24	3.95	105	.266	.340	0-0	—	0		0	0.0
Total	7	29	28	.509	250	12	0	36-23	448.2	440	219	46	6	198-29	268	3.85	110	.262	.339	12-0	.167	-0	104	17	3.3
McLAUGHLIN, JUD Justin Theodore B 3.24.1912 Brighton, MA D 9.27.1964 Cambridge, MA BL/TL 5-11/155# d6.23																									
1931	Bos A	0	0	—	9	0	0	0	12	23	16	1	0	8	3	12.00	36	.397	.470	0-0	—	0		-9	-0.4
1932	Bos A	0	0	—	1	0	0	0	3	5	5	0	0	4	0	15.00	30	.385	.529	1-0	.000	-0		-3	-0.1
1933	Bos A	0	0	—	6	0	0	0	8.2	14	7	1	0	5	1	6.23	70	.359	.432	0-0	—	0		-2	-0.1
Total	3	0	0	—	16	0	0	0	23.2	42	28	2	0	17	4	10.27	42	.382	.465	1-0	.000	-0		-14	-0.6

Year	Tm Lg	W	L	Pct	G	GS	CG-Sho	SV-BS	IP	H	R	HR	HB	BB-IB	SO	ERA	AERA	OAV	OOB	AB-SH	AVG	PB	Sup	APR	PW
McLAUGHLIN, BO Michael Duane B 10.23.1953 Oakland, CA BR/TR 6-5/210# d7.20																									
1976	Hou N	4	5	.444	17	11	4-2	1-0	79	71	31	6	2	17-1	32	2.85	112	.244	.288	19-2	.000	-1	68	2	0.1
1977	Hou N	4	7	.364	46	6	0	5-2	84.2	81	44	6	6	34-6	59	4.25	84	.260	.341	9-2	.000	-1	83	-7	-0.9
1978	Hou N	0	1	.000	12	1	0	2-0	23.1	30	17	2	2	16-2	10	5.01	66	.313	.417	3-0	.000	-0	108	-6	-0.4
1979	Hou N	1	2	.333	12	0	0	0-1	16.1	22	15	2	0	4-0	12	5.51	64	.314	.347	1-0	.000	-0		-6	-0.9
	Atl N	1	1	.500	37	1	0	0-0	49.2	63	33	2	2	16-6	45	4.89	83	.303	.357	5-1	.000	-1	44	-5	-0.4
	Year	2	3	.400	49	1	0	0-1	66	85	35	4	2	20-6	57	5.05	78	.306	.354	6-1	.000	-1	45	-11	-1.3
1981	Oak A	0	0	—	11	0	0	1-0	11.2	17	15	1	1	9-0	3	11.57	30	.333	.443	0-0	—	0		-10	-0.5
1982	Oak A	0	4	.000	21	2	1	0-0	48.1	51	31	3	1	27-1	27	4.84	81	.267	.359	0-0	—	0	70	-6	-0.4
Total	6	10	20	.333	156	21	5-2	9-3	313	335	186	22	14	123-16	188	4.49	80	.275	.346	37-5	.000	-3	70	-38	-3.4
McLAUGHLIN, PAT Patrick Elmer B 8.17.1910 Taylor, TX D 11.1.1999 Houston, TX BR/TR 6-2/175# d4.25																									
1937	Det A	0	2	.000	10	3	0	0	32.2	39	23	3	0	16	8	6.34	74	.291	.367	10-0	.100	-1*	124	-5	-0.3
1940	Phi A	0	0	—	1	0	0	0	1.2	4	3	1	0	1	0	16.20	27	.444	.500	0-0	—	0		-2	-0.1
1945	Det A	0	0	—	1	0	0	0	1	2	2	0	0	0	0	9.00	39	.400	.400	0-0	—	0		-1	-0.1
Total	3	0	2	.000	12	3	0	0	35.1	45	28	4	0	17	8	6.88	67	.304	.376	10-0	.100	-1	124	-8	-0.5
McLAUGHLIN, WARREN Warren A. B 1.22.1876 N.Plainfield, NJ D 10.22.1923 Plainfield, NJ TL d7.7																									
1900	Phi N	0	0	—	1	0	0	0	6	4	4	0	0	6	1	4.50	80	.190	.370	2-0	.500	1		-1	0.0
1902	Pit N	3	0	1.000	3	3	3	0	26	27	13	0	1	9	13	2.77	99	.267	.333	11-0	.364	1	199	-1	0.0
1903	Phi N	0	3	.000	3	2	2	0	23	38	24	0	1	11	3	7.04	46	.376	.442	10-0	.200	0	41	-9	-0.9
Total	3	3	3	.500	7	5	5	0	55	69	41	0	2	26	17	4.75	64	.309	.386	23-0	.304	2	124	-11	-0.9
McLAUGHLIN, BILL William B 11.18.1860 Cleveland, OH D 11.16.1895 Cleveland, OH BL/TL ?/157# d5.30																									
1884	Bal AA	1	2	.333	3	2	2	0	22	27	22	2	0	11	8	3.68	94	.300	.376	22	.227	0*	104	-2	-0.2
McLEAN, AL Albert Eldon "Elrod" B 9.20.1912 Chicago, IL D 9.29.1990 Asheboro, NC BR/TR 6/175# d7.16																									
1935	Was A	0	0	—	4	0	0	0	8.2	12	8	0	0	5	3	7.27	59	.324	.405	2-0	.000	-0		-3	-0.2
McLELAND, WAYNE Wayne Gaffney "Nubbin" B 8.29.1924 Milton, IA BR/TR 6/180# d4.20																									
1951	Det A	0	1	.000	6	1	0	0	11	20	10	1	1	4	0	8.18	51	.400	.455	1-1	.000	-0	64	-4	-0.3
1952	Det A	0	0	—	4	0	0	0	2.2	4	3	0	0	6	0	10.13	38	.444	.667	0-0	—	0		-2	-0.1
Total	2	0	1	.000	10	1	0	0	13.2	24	13	1	1	10	0	8.56	48	.407	.500	1-1	.000	-0	64	-6	-0.4
McLISH, CAL Calvin Coolidge Julius Caesar Tuskahoma "Buster" B 12.1.1925 Anadarko, OK BB/TR 6-1/200# d5.13 Mil 1945-46 C16																									
1944	Bro N	3	10	.231	23	13	3	0	84	110	81	10	1	48	24	7.82	45	.321	.406	32-1	.219	0*	118	-39	-4.9
1946	Bro N	0	0	—	1	0	0	0	0	1	2	0	0	0	0	∞	—	1.000	1.000	0-0	—	0		-2	-0.2
1947	Pit N	0	0	—	1	0	0	0	1	2	2	0	1	0	0	18.00	23	.400	.500	0-0	—	0		-1	-0.1
1948	Pit N	0	0	—	2	1	0	0	5	8	5	0	0	2	1	9.00	45	.400	.455	1-0	.000	-0*	174	-2	-0.1
1949	Chi N	1	1	.500	8	2	0	0	23	31	21	6	0	12	6	5.87	69	.341	.417	9-0	.333	2*	153	-6	-0.3
1951	Chi N	4	10	.286	30	17	5-1	0	145.2	159	76	16	3	52	46	4.45	92	.283	.347	42-0	.119	-1*	72	-3	-0.4
1956	Cle A	2	4	.333	37	2	0	1	61.2	67	36	5	0	32-5	27	4.96	85	.282	.364	9-0	.111	1*	64	-4	-0.2
1957	Cle A	9	7	.563	42	7	2	1	144.1	118	55	11	2	67-10	88	2.74	135	.220	.308	43-4	.186	3*	130	14	1.9
1958	Cle A	16	8	.667	39	30	13	1	225.2	214	92	25	1	70-4	97	2.99	122	.251	.307	64-4	.094	-1	137	13	1.3
1959	Cle A★	19	8	.704	35	32	13	1	235.1	253	110	26	5	72-6	113	3.63	101	.270	.325	74-9	.189	1	118	0	0.3
1960	Cin N	4	14	.222	37	21	2-1	0	151.1	170	85	16	7	48-8	56	4.16	92	.287	.345	41-1	.049	-3	78	-9	-1.2
1961	Chi A	10	13	.435	31	27	4	1	162.1	178	87	21	1	47-1	80	4.38	89	.280	.328	54-3	.167	-1	86	-8	-1.0
1962	Phi N	11	5	.688	32	24	5-1	1	154.2	184	84	15	2	45-6	71	4.25	91	.293	.341	51-1	.078	-2	107	-8	-0.9
1963	Phi N	13	11	.542	32	32	10-2	0	209.2	184	85	14	4	56-3	98	3.26	99	.239	.292	69-4	.203	4*	110	1	0.6
1964	Phi N	0	1	.000	2	1	0	0	5.1	6	3	0	0	1-1	6	3.38	103	.261	.292	1-0	.000	-0	76	0	0.0
Total	15	92	92	.500	352	209	57-5	6	1609	1685	824	165	27	552-44	713	4.01	93	.270	.331	490-27	.149	4	106	-54	-5.2
McMACKIN, SAM Samuel B 1872 Cleveland, OH D 2.11.1903 Columbus, OH BR/TL d9.4																									
1902	Chi A	0	0	—	1	0	0	0	3	1	1	0	0	0	2	0.00	—	.100	.100	1-0	.000	-0		1	0.0
	Det A	0	1	.000	1	1	1	0	8.1	9	5	0	1	4	2	3.24	113	.273	.368	4-0	.500	1	79	0	0.1
	Year	0	1	.000	2	1	1	0	11.1	10	9	0	1	4	4	2.38	150	.233	.313	5-0	.400	0	80	1	0.1
McMAHAN, JACK Jack Wally B 7.22.1932 Hot Springs, AR BR/TL 6/175# d4.18																									
1956	Pit N	0	0	—	11	0	0	0	13.1	18	9	1	0	9-0	9	6.08	62	.340	.435	1-0	.000	-0		-3	-0.1
	KC A	0	5	.000	23	9	0	0	61.2	69	40	7	2	31-0	13	4.82	90	.290	.374	14-0	.000	-2	69	-4	-0.5
Total	1	0	5	.000	34	9	0	0	75	87	49	8	2	40-0	22	5.04	84	.299	.385	15-0	.000	-2	69	-7	-0.6
McMAHON, DON Donald John B 1.4.1930 Brooklyn, NY D 7.22.1987 Los Angeles, CA BR/TR 6-2/222# d6.30 C11																									
1957	†Mil N	2	3	.400	32	0	0	9	46.2	33	13	0	0	29-4	46	1.54	227	.196	.312	8-0	.250	1		9	1.5
1958	†Mil N☆	7	2	.778	38	0	0	8	58.2	50	25	4	2	29-5	37	3.68	96	.235	.328	9-1	.111	0		0	-0.1
1959	Mil N	5	3	.625	60	0	0	**15**	80.2	81	26	5	1	37-5	55	2.57	138	.259	.335	9-0	.222	1		10	1.3
1960	Mil N	3	6	.333	48	0	0	10	63.2	66	48	9	2	32-4	50	5.94	58	.263	.350	11-0	.000	-1		-20	-3.3
1961	Mil N	6	4	.600	53	0	0	8	92	84	35	4	2	51-6	55	2.84	132	.249	.349	16-1	.188	0		8	1.0
1962	Mil N	0	1	.000	2	0	0	0	3	3	2	1	0	0-0	3	6.00	63	.250	.250	0-0	—	0		-1	-0.1
	Hou N	5	5	.500	51	0	0	8	76.2	53	14	4	1	33-1	69	1.53	245	.201	.288	12-0	.083	-1		20	2.9
	Year	5	6	.455	53	0	0	8	79.2	56	19	5	1	33-1	72	1.69	221	.203	.287	12-0	.083	-1		19	2.8
1963	Hou N	1	5	.167	49	2	0	5	80	83	38	10	0	26-2	51	4.05	78	.270	.323	12-0	.083	0	68	-7	-0.5
1964	Cle A	6	4	.600	70	0	0	16	101	67	31	7	2	52-5	92	2.41	150	.189	.293	14-0	.143	-0		13	1.6
1965	Cle A	3	3	.500	58	0	0	11	85	79	36	8	1	37-7	60	3.28	106	.248	.328	9-1	.222	0		2	0.2
1966	Cle A	1	1	.500	12	0	0	1	12.1	8	4	1	0	6-0	5	2.92	118	.190	.286	2-0	.000	-0		1	0.1
	Bos A	8	7	.533	49	0	0	9	78	65	29	7	3	38-8	57	2.65	143	.232	.326	11-0	.091	-0		8	1.7
	Year	9	8	.529	61	0	0	10	90.1	73	36	8	3	44-8	62	2.69	140	.227	.321	13-0	.077	-0		9	1.8
1967	Bos A	1	2	.333	11	0	0	2	17.2	14	8	3	0	13-0	10	3.57	98	.215	.346	2-0	.000	-0		0	-0.1
	Chi A	5	0	1.000	52	0	0	3	91.2	54	21	5	6	27-4	74	1.67	186	.173	.251	11-0	.182	0		15	0.9
	Year	6	2	.750	63	0	0	5	109.1	68	29	8	6	40-4	84	1.98	160	.180	.269	13-0	.154	-0		14	0.8
1968	Chi A	2	1	.667	25	0	0	0	46	31	10	2	3	20-6	32	1.96	155	.190	.287	3-0	.333	0		6	0.4
	†Det A	3	1	.750	20	0	0	1	35.2	22	8	2	0	10-1	33	2.02	149	.180	.241	4-0	.000	-0		4	0.5
	Year	5	2	.714	45	0	0	1	81.2	53	18	4	3	30-7	65	1.98	152	.186	.268	7-0	.143	-0		11	0.9
1969	Det A	3	5	.375	34	0	0	11-2	37	25	17	2	1	18-1	38	3.89	96	.192	.293	6-0	.000	-1		0	-0.1
	SF N	3	1	.750	13	0	0	2-3	23.2	13	9	1	0	9-0	21	3.04	115	.157	.239	3-1	.333	0		1	0.3
1970	SF N	9	5	.643	61	0	0	19-5	94.1	70	32	9	2	45-13	74	2.96	135	.202	.297	14-1	.143	0		12	2.2
1971	†SF N	10	6	.625	61	0	0	4-5	82	73	40	9	7	37-6	71	4.06	84	.242	.335	7-1	.000	-1		-4	-0.9
1972	SF N	3	3	.500	44	0	0	5-2	63	46	26	8	1	21-3	45	3.71	94	.206	.274	4-1	.250	0		0	0.0
1973	SF N	4	0	1.000	22	0	0	6-0	30.1	21	5	1	0	7-3	20	1.48	258	.189	.237	1-0	1.000	0		8	1.4
1974	SF N	0	0	—	9	0	0	0-0	11.2	13	5	2	0	2-0	5	3.09	124	.283	.306	0-0	—	0		1	0.0
Total	18	90	68	.570	874	2	0	153-17	1310.2	1054	482	104	34	579-84	1003	2.96	119	.221	.308	168-7	.137	-1	68	86	10.9
McMAHON, DOC Henry John B 12.19.1886 Woburn, MA D 12.11.1929 Woburn, MA TR d10.6																									
1908	Bos A	1	0	1.000	1	1	1	0	9	14	3	0	0	0	3	3.00	82	.350	.350	5-0	.400	1	306	0	0.0
McMAHON, SADIE John Joseph B 9.19.1867 Wilmington, DE D 2.20.1954 Wilmington, DE BR/TR 5-9.5/165# d7.5																									
1889	Phi AA	14	12	.538	28	27	27-2	0	242	230	160	5	14	102	117	3.53	107	.243	.325	104	.154	-6*	109	6	0.1
1890	Phi AA	29	18	.617	48	46	44	1	410	414	238	5	20	133	225	3.34	116	.254	.318	175	.229	3*	109	18	2.3
	Bal AA	7	3	.700	12	11	11-1	0	99	84	49	1	6	33	66	3.00	135	.223	.296	39	.103	-4	86	10	0.5
	Year	**36**	21	.632	**60**	**57**	**55**-1	1	**509**	498	54	6	26	166	**291**	3.27	120	.248	.314	214	.206	-1	104	24	2.8
1891	Bal AA	**35**	24	.593	61	**58**	**53-5**	1	**503**	493	259	13	17	149	219	2.81	133	.248	.306	210	.205	-3	92	54	4.9
1892	Bal N	19	25	.432	48	46	44-2	1	397	430	260	9	9	145	118	3.24	106	.265	.329	177	.141	-9*	109	1	-0.8
1893	Bal N	23	18	.561	43	40	35	1	346.1	378	232	6	9	156	79	4.37	109	.269	.346	148	.243	-3	101	17	1.3
1894	Bal N	25	8	.758	35	33	26	0	275.2	317	175	7	9	111	60	4.21	130	.285	.355	126-8	.286	0	135	36	3.1

Year	Tm Lg	W	L	Pct	G	GS	CG-Sho	SV-BS	IP	H	R	HR	HB	BB-IB	SO	ERA	AERA	OAV	OOB	AB-SH	AVG	PB	Sup	APR	PW
1895	†Bal N	10	4	.714	15	15	15-**4**	0	122.1	110	54	1	4	32	37	2.94	162	.237	.291	51-1	.314	1	97	25	2.3
1896	Bal N	11	9	.550	22	22	19	0	175.2	195	109	4	3	55	33	3.48	123	.279	.334	73-0	.123	-7	118	10	0.3
1897	Bro N	0	6	.000	9	7	5	0	63	75	56	1	3	29	13	5.86	70	.293	.372	25-0	.200	-1	77	-13	-1.0
Total	9	173	127	.577	321	305	279-14	4	2634	2726	1592	52	94	945	967	3.51	118	.260	.326	1128-9	.204	-29	107	164	13.0
McMAKIN, JOHN John Weaver "Spartanburg John" B 3.6.1878 Spartanburg, SC D 9.25.1956 Lyman, SC BR/TL 5-11/165# d4.19																									
1902	Bro N	2	2	.500	4	4	4	0	32	34	18	0	2	11	6	3.09	89	.272	.341	11-0	.182	1	129	-2	-0.2
McMANUS, JOE Joab Logan B 9.7.1887 Palmyra, IL D 12.23.1955 Beckley, WV BR/TR 5-11/180# d4.12																									
1913	Cin N	0	0	—	1	0	0	0	2	3	4	0	0	4	1	18.00	18	.375	.583	0-0	—	0		-3	-0.1
McMANUS, PAT Patrick B 1858 , Ireland d5.22																									
1879	Tro N	0	2	.000	2	2	2	0	21	24	21	1		1	6	3.00	83	.258	.266	8	.125	-1	102	-2	-0.2
McMICHAEL, GREG Gregory Winston B 12.1.1966 Knoxville, TN BR/TR 6-3/215# d4.12																									
1993	†Atl N	2	3	.400	74	0	0	19-2	91.2	68	22	3	0	29-4	89	2.06	195	.206	.269	4-0	.000	-0		21	1.8
1994	Atl N	4	6	.400	51	0	0	21-10	58.2	66	29	1	0	19-6	47	3.84	111	.280	.332	1-0	.000	-0		2	0.3
1995	†Atl N	7	2	.778	67	0	0	2-2	80.2	64	27	8	0	32-9	74	2.79	153	.213	.289	6-0	.000	-0		13	1.3
1996	†Atl N	5	3	.625	73	0	0	2-6	86.2	84	37	4	1	27-7	78	3.22	137	.253	.309	0-0	—	0		10	0.9
1997	NY N	7	10	.412	73	0	0	7-11	87.2	73	34	8	2	27-6	81	2.98	136	.233	.295	3-0	.667	1		10	2.0
1998	NY N	1	2	.333	22	0	0	0-0	22.2	23	12	1	1	14-2	22	3.97	104	.271	.380	0-0	—	0		0	0.0
	LA N	0	1	.000	12	0	0	1-2	14.1	17	8	1	1	6-3	11	4.40	90	.309	.381	0-0	—	0		-1	0.0
	NY N	4	1	.800	30	0	0	1-3	31	41	19	7	2	15-5	22	4.06	102	.318	.392	1-0	.000	-0		-2	-0.3
	Year	5	4	.556	64	0	0	2-5	68	81	45	9	4	35-10	55	4.10	100	.301	.386	1-0	.000	-0		-3	-0.3
1999	NY N	1	1	.500	19	0	0	0-1	18.2	20	10	3	0	8-3	18	4.82	91	.270	.337	0-0	—	0		-1	-0.1
	Oak A	0	0	—	17	0	0	0-0	15	15	9	3	2	12-2	3	5.40	86	.283	.426	0-0	—	0		-1	-0.1
2000	Atl N	0	0	—	15	0	0	0-0	16.1	12	8	3	0	4-1	14	4.41	104	.214	.262	0-0	—	0		1	0.0
Total	8	31	29	.517	453	0	0	53-37	523.1	483	215	42	9	193-48	459	3.25	130	.246	.314	15-0	.133	-0		52	5.8
McMULLEN, GEORGE George B , CA d7.2																									
1887	NY AA	2	1	.667	3	3	2	0	21	25	25	2	0	19	2	7.71	55	.269	.393	12	.083	-2	130	-7	-0.7
McMULLIN, JOHN John F. "Lefty" B 1848 Philadelphia, PA D 4.11.1881 Philadelphia, PA BR/TL 5-9/160# d5.9 ▲																									
1871	Tro NA	12	15	.444	29	29	28	0	249	430	362	4		75	12	5.53	76	.342	.379	136	.279	1	114	-37	-2.1
1872	Mut NA	1	0	1.000	3	1	1	1	15	18	15	0		2	1	3.60	94	.247	.267	236	.254	0*	125	-1	0.0
1873	Ath NA	1	0	1.000	1	1	1	0	8	10	5	0		1	2	2.25	152	.303	.324	227	.273	0*	178	1	0.1
1875	Phi NA	0	0	—	4	0	0	0	11.1	32	23	0		1	0	7.94	29	.464	.471	222	.257	1*		-7	-0.3
Total	4 NA	14	15	.483	37	31	30	1	283.1	490	405	4		79	15	5.43	75	.342	.376	821	.264	2	118	-44	-2.3
McMURTRY, CRAIG Joe Craig B 11.5.1959 Troy, TX BR/TR 6-5/195# d4.10																									
1983	Atl N	15	9	.625	36	35	6-3	0-0	224.2	204	86	13	1	88-1	105	3.08	126	.243	.314	70-12	.086	-4	109	18	1.6
1984	Atl N	9	17	.346	37	30	0	0-0	183.1	184	100	16	1	102-4	99	4.32	89	.268	.359	52-8	.115	-1*	72	-9	-1.1
1985	Atl N	0	3	.000	17	6	0	1-0	45	56	36	6	1	27-1	28	6.60	58	.306	.394	14-1	.071	-1	61	-12	-0.9
1986	Atl N	1	6	.143	37	5	0	0-1	79.2	82	46	7	2	43-5	50	4.74	84	.265	.357	16-1	.125	-0*	90	-6	-0.5
1988	Tex A	3	3	.500	32	0	0	3-4	60	37	16	5	1	24-4	35	2.25	182	.180	.266	0-0	—	0		12	1.3
1989	Tex A	0	0	—	19	0	0	0-1	23	29	21	3	2	13-1	14	7.43	53	.312	.400	0-0	—	0		-8	-0.4
1990	Tex A	0	3	.000	23	3	0	0-0	41.2	43	25	4	1	30-0	14	4.32	91	.281	.398	0-0	—	0	54	-3	-0.2
1995	Hou N	0	1	.000	11	0	0	0-1	10.1	15	11	0	1	9-1	4	7.84	49	.357	.463	1-0	.000	-0		-5	-0.4
Total	8	28	42	.400	212	79	6-3	4-7	667.2	650	341	54	10	336-17	349	4.08	96	.259	.345	153-22	.098	-6	88	-13	-0.6
McNABB, EDGAR Edgar J. "Texas" B 10.24.1865 Coshocton, OH D 2.28.1894 Pittsburgh, PA BR/TR 5-11.5/170# d5.12																									
1893	Bal N	8	7	.533	21	14	12	0	142	167	109	5	8	53	18	4.12	115	.284	.352	67	.194	-2	100	4	0.2
McNALLY, DAVE David Arthur B 10.31.1942 Billings, MT D 12.1.2002 Billings, MT BR/TL 5-11/190# d9.26																									
1962	Bal A	1	0	1.000	1	1	1-1	0	9	2	0	0	0	3-0	4	0.00	—	.071	.161	3-0	.000	-0	72	4	0.5
1963	Bal A	7	8	.467	29	20	2	1	125.2	133	67	9	5	55-4	78	4.58	76	.276	.352	38-3	.053	-2	104	-14	-1.8
1964	Bal A	9	11	.450	30	23	5-3	0	159.1	157	72	15	9	51-1	88	3.67	97	.260	.325	51-2	.137	0	84	-2	-0.2
1965	Bal A	11	6	.647	35	29	6-2	0	198.2	163	69	15	6	73-6	116	2.85	122	.222	.297	65-3	.092	-3	100	16	1.0
1966	†Bal A	13	6	.684	34	33	5-1	0	213	212	91	22	4	64-1	158	3.17	105	.256	.311	77-4	.195	3	136	0	0.4
1967	Bal A	7	7	.500	24	22	3-1	0	119	134	65	13	2	39-1	70	4.54	69	.295	.353	38-7	.158	0	122	-18	-2.1
1968	Bal A	22	10	.688	35	35	18-5	0	273	175	67	24	10	55-1	202	1.95	150	.182	**.232**	86-8	.128	4	110	31	4.3
1969	†Bal A★	20	7	.741	41	40	11-4	0-0	268.2	232	103	21	5	84-6	166	3.22	111	.234	.296	94-8	.085	-2	127	13	0.8
1970	†Bal A☆	**24**	9	.727	40	**40**	16-1	0-0	296	277	114	29	7	78-3	185	3.22	113	.250	.301	105-6	.133	4*	125	16	2.1
1971	†Bal A	21	5	**.808**	30	30	11-1	0-0	224.1	188	75	24	5	58-2	91	2.89	116	.229	.282	74-14	.162	3	153	15	2.0
1972	Bal A★	13	17	.433	36	36	12-6	0-0	241	220	85	15	2	68-15	120	2.95	105	.247	.301	79-2	.152	2	83	5	0.8
1973	†Bal A	17	17	.500	38	38	17-4	0-0	266	247	100	16	5	81-6	87	3.21	116	.251	.310	0-0	—	0	91	19	2.4
1974	†Bal A	16	10	.615	39	37	13-4	1-0	259	260	112	19	8	81-6	111	3.58	97	.270	.330	0-0	—	0	110	-1	0.0
1975	Mon N	3	6	.333	12	12	0	0-0	77.1	88	50	8	4	36-4	36	5.24	73	.280	.362	21-1	.190	2	90	-11	-1.0
Total	14	184	119	.607	424	396	120-33	2-0	2730	2488	1070	230	72	826-56	1512	3.24	106	.245	.305	731-58	.133	10	112	73	9.2
McNAMARA, TIM Timothy Augustine B 11.20.1898 Millville, MA D 11.5.1994 N.Smithfield, RI BR/TR 5-11/170# d4.27																									
1922	Bos N	3	4	.429	24	5	4-2	0	70.2	55	26	2	1	26	16	2.42	165	.225	.303	17-1	.118	-1	110	**12**	0.9
1923	Bos N	3	13	.188	32	16	3	0	139.1	185	95	8	5	29	32	4.91	81	.320	.357	39-0	.179	1	101	-15	-1.5
1924	Bos N	8	12	.400	35	21	6-2	0	179	242	119	9	3	31	35	5.18	74	.334	.364	43-6	.140	-1	82	-27	-2.6
1925	Bos N	0	0	—	1	0	0	0	0.2	6	6	0	0	2	1	81.00	5	.857	.889	0-0	—	0		-6	-0.2
1926	NY N	0	0	—	6	0	0	0	6	7	6	0	0	4	4	9.00	42	.304	.407	0-0	—	0		-3	-0.1
Total	5	14	29	.326	98	42	13-4	0	395.2	495	252	19	9	92	88	4.78	82	.314	.355	99-7	.152	-1	93	-39	-3.5
McNAUGHTON, GORDON Gordon Joseph B 7.31.1910 Chicago, IL D 8.6.1942 Chicago, IL BR/TR 6-1/190# d8.13																									
1932	Bos A	0	1	.000	6	2	0	0	21	21	15	1	3	22	6	6.43	70	.259	.434	8-0	.250	0	133	-3	-0.1
McNEAL, HARRY John Harley B 8.13.1878 Iberia, OH D 1.11.1945 Cleveland, OH BL/TR 6-2/175# d8.5																									
1901	Cle A	5	5	.500	12	10	9	0	85.1	120	68	4	8	30	15	4.43	80	.328	.391	37-1	.162	-2	108	-10	-1.1
McNICHOL, BRIAN Brian David B 5.20.1974 Fairfax, VA BL/TL 6-5/225# d9.7																									
1999	Chi N	0	2	.000	4	2	0	0-0	10.2	15	8	4	1	7-0	12	6.75	67	.333	.426	2-1	.000	-0	41	-2	-0.4
McNICHOL, ED Edwin Briggs B 1.10.1879 Martins Ferry, OH D 11.1.1952 Salineville, OH BR/TR 5-5/170# d7.9																									
1904	Bos N	2	12	.143	17	15	12-1	0	122	120	70	3	5	74	39	4.28	64	.262	.371	43-0	.093	-4	65	-16	-2.0
McPARTLIN, FRANK Frank B 2.16.1872 Hoosick Falls, NY D 11.13.1943 New York, NY TR 6/180# d8.22																									
1899	NY N	0	0	—	1	0	0	0	4	4	4	0	2	3	2	4.50	83	.267	.450	1-0	.000	-0		-1	0.0
McPHERSON, JOHN John Jacob B 3.9.1869 Easton, PA D 9.30.1941 Easton, PA TR d7.12																									
1901	Phi A	0	1	.000	1	1	0	0	4	7	5	0	1	4	0	11.25	34	.368	.500	1-0	.000	-0	54	-3	-0.4
1904	Phi N	1	12	.077	15	12	11-1	0	128	130	82	1	6	46	32	3.66	73	.264	.334	47-1	.064	-4	49	-15	-1.7
Total	2	1	13	.071	16	13	11-1	0	132	137	87	1	7	50	32	3.89	70	.268	.341	48-1	.063	-4	51	-18	-2.1
McQUAID, HERB Herbert George B 3.29.1899 San Francisco, CA D 4.4.1966 Richmond, CA BR/TR 6-2/185# d6.22																									
1923	Cin N	1	0	1.000	12	1	0	0	34.1	31	11	0	3	10	9	2.36	164	.238	.308	7-0	.000	-1	106	6	0.2
1926	NY A	1	0	1.000	17	1	0	0	38.1	48	34	5	2	13	6	6.10	63	.329	.391	7-1	.000	-1	87	-11	-0.6
Total	2	2	0	1.000	29	2	0	0	72.2	79	45	5	5	23	15	4.33	89	.286	.352	14-1	.000	-2	97	-5	-0.4
McQUEEN, MIKE Michael Robert B 8.30.1950 Oklahoma City, OK BL/TL 5-11/190# d10.2																									
1969	Atl N	0	0	—	1	1	0	0-0	3	2	1	0	0	3-0	3	3.00	120	.182	.357	0-0	—	0	74	0	0.0
1970	Atl N	1	5	.167	22	8	1	1-0	66	67	48	10	1	31-2	54	5.59	77	.266	.345	20-0	.300	2	68	-10	-0.7
1971	Atl N	4	1	.800	17	3	0	1-0	56	47	24	7	2	23-4	38	3.54	105	.228	.309	19-2	.211	0	183	1	0.1

Year	Tm Lg	W	L	Pct	G	GS	CG-Sho	SV-BS	IP	H	R	HR	HB	BB-IB	SO	ERA	AERA	OAV	OOB	AB-SH	AVG	PB	Sup	APR	PW
1972	Atl N	0	5	.000	23	7	1	1-0	78.1	79	45	11	1	44-3	40	4.60	83	.260	.352	23-0	.087	-2	57	-6	-0.6
1974	Cin N	0	0	—	10	0	0	0-0	15	17	10	4	0	11-0	5	5.40	65	.288	.394	1-0	1.000	0		-3	-0.1
Total	5	5	11	.313	73	19	2	3-0	218.1	212	128	32	4	112-9	140	4.66	84	.255	.343	63-2	.206	1	83	-18	-1.3
McQUILLAN, GEORGE George Watt B 5.1.1885 Brooklyn, NY D 3.30.1940 Columbus, OH BR/TR 5-11.5/175# d5.8																									
1907	Phi N	4	0	1.000	6	5	5-3	0	41	21	3	0	1	11	28	0.66	368	.158	.228	11-1	.364	3	82	9	1.3
1908	Phi N	23	17	.575	48	42	32-7	2	359.2	263	88	1	6	91	114	1.53	159	.207	.263	119-6	.151	-1	99	33	3.8
1909	Phi N	13	16	.448	41	28	16-4	2	247.2	202	87	5	1	54	96	2.14	121	.226	.271	76-7	.118	-3	103	10	0.7
1910	Phi N	9	6	.600	24	17	13-3	1	152.1	109	42	2	3	50	71	**1.60**	196	.204	.276	47-5	.149	-1	113	23	2.2
1911	Cin N	2	6	.250	19	5	2	0	77	92	60	2	4	31	28	4.68	71	.308	.380	22-1	.091	-1	77	-14	-1.4
1913	Pit N	8	6	.571	25	16	7	1	141.2	144	60	1	1	35	59	3.43	88	.273	.319	39-3	.103	-1	108	-3	-0.4
1914	Pit N	13	17	.433	45	28	15	4	259.1	248	100	8	8	60	96	2.98	89	.261	.310	73-8	.068	-4	87	-6	-1.1
1915	Pit N	8	10	.444	30	20	9	1	149	160	64	1	2	39	56	2.84	96	.284	.332	44-3	.091	-3	79	-3	-0.6
	Phi N	4	3	.571	9	8	5	0	63.2	60	31	1	1	11	13	2.12	129	.247	.282	23-1	.043	-2	149	1	-0.2
	Year	12	13	.480	39	28	14	1	212.2	220	37	2	3	50	69	2.62	104	.273	.317	67-4	.075	-5	99	-1	-0.8
1916	Phi N	1	7	.125	21	3	1	2	62	58	33	2	3	15	22	2.76	96	.251	.305	11-4	.091	-1	19	-3	-0.6
1918	Cle A	0	1	.000	5	1	0	1	23	25	10	0	0	4	7	2.35	128	.284	.315	4-0	.000	-0	0	1	0.0
Total	10	85	89	.489	273	173	105-17	14	1576.1	1382	578	23	30	401	590	2.38	114	.241	.294	469-39	.117	-14	96	48	3.7
McQUILLAN, HUGH Hugh A. "Handsome Hugh" B 9.15.1897 New York, NY D 8.26.1947 New York, NY BR/TR 6/170# d7.26																									
1918	Bos N	1	0	1.000	1	1	1	0	9	7	3	0	0	5	1	3.00	90	.219	.324	4-0	.250	0	338	0	0.0
1919	Bos N	2	3	.400	16	7	2	1	60	66	34	3	1	14	13	3.45	83	.288	.332	18-1	.222	0*	155	-6	-0.5
1920	Bos N	11	15	.423	38	26	17-1	5	225.2	230	110	3	2	70	53	3.55	86	.273	.330	74-6	.257	6	96	-13	-0.8
1921	Bos N	13	17	.433	45	31	13-2	5	250	284	137	9	2	90	94	4.00	91	.291	.352	88-5	.205	1	113	-14	-1.3
1922	Bos N	5	10	.333	28	17	7	0	136	154	70	3	1	56	33	4.24	94	.299	.369	42-5	.167	-1*	77	1	0.0
	†NY N	6	5	.545	15	13	5	1	94.1	111	48	7	0	34	24	3.82	105	.301	.360	37-0	.189	-1	95	2	0.1
	Year	11	15	.423	43	30	12	1	230.1	265	53	10	1	90	57	4.06	98	.300	.365	79-5	.177	-2	85	1	0.1
1923	†NY N	15	14	.517	38	32	15-5	0	229.2	224	96	12	5	66	75	3.41	112	.259	.315	82-3	.171	-2*	85	12	1.1
1924	†NY N	14	8	.636	27	23	14-1	3	184	179	68	8	2	43	49	2.69	136	.259	.304	67-4	.209	-1*	124	19	2.0
1925	NY N	2	3	.400	14	11	2	1	70	95	49	9	1	23	23	6.04	67	.343	.395	21-1	.143	-1*	99	-14	-0.9
1926	NY N	11	10	.524	33	22	12-1	0	167	171	72	7	1	42	47	3.72	101	.271	.318	53-1	.132	-3*	95	5	0.4
1927	NY N	5	4	.556	11	9	5	0	58	73	32	4	1	22	17	4.50	86	.309	.371	19-0	.211	1	147	-3	-0.4
	Bos N	3	5	.375	13	12	2	0	78	109	65	2	2	24	17	5.54	67	.332	.381	22-5	.227	0	113	-20	-1.7
	Year	8	9	.471	24	21	7	0	136	182	70	6	3	46	34	5.10	74	.323	.377	41-5	.220	1	128	-22	-2.1
Total	10	88	94	.484	279	204	95-10	16	1561.2	1703	784	67	18	489	446	3.83	95	.284	.340	527-31	.195	0	104	-31	-2.0
McRAE, NORM Norman B 9.26.1947 Elizabeth, NJ D 7.25.2003 Garland, TX BR/TR 6-1/195# d9.13																									
1969	Det A	0	0	—	3	0	0	0-0	3	2	2	0	0	1-0	3	6.00	62	.200	.250	0-0	—	0		-1	0.0
1970	Det A	0	0	—	19	0	0	0-0	31.1	26	13	1	1	25-0	16	2.87	130	.226	.366	1-1	.000	-0		2	0.1
Total	2	0	0	—	22	0	0	0-0	34.1	28	15	1	1	26-0	19	3.15	119	.224	.357	1-1	.000	-0		1	0.1
McTIGUE, BILL William Patrick "Rebel" B 1.3.1891 Nashville, TN D 5.8.1920 Nashville, TN BL/TL 6-1.5/175# d5.2																									
1911	Bos N	0	5	.000	14	8	0	0	37	37	32	3	2	49	23	7.05	54	.280	.481	12-0	.083	-1	74	-10	-1.2
1912	Bos N	2	0	1.000	10	1	1	0	34.2	39	26	0	0	18	17	5.45	66	.289	.373	13-0	.077	-1	225	-6	-0.4
1916	Det A	0	0	—	3	0	0	0	5.1	5	6	0	0	5	1	5.06	57	.278	.435	1-0	.000	-0		-2	-0.1
Total	3	2	5	.286	27	9	1	0	77	81	64	3	2	72	41	6.19	59	.284	.432	26-0	.077	-2	93	-18	-1.7
McVEY, CAL Calvin Alexander B 8.30.1850 Montrose, IA D 8.20.1926 San Francisco, CA BR/TR 5-9/170# d5.5.1871 M3 ▲																									
1875	Bos NA	1	0	1.000	3	2	0	1	11	15	9	0		1	1	4.91	44	.294	.308	389	.355	2*	148	-2	-0.2
1876	Chi N	5	2	.714	11	6	5	2	59.1	57	22	0		2	9	1.52	161	.235	.241	308	.347	3*	119	6	0.7
1877	Chi N	4	8	.333	17	10	6	**2**	92	129	87	2		11	20	4.50	66	.301	.319	266	.368	6*	93	-15	-1.3
1879	Cin N	0	2	.000	3	1	1	0	14	34	23	1		2	7	8.36	28	.453	.468	354	.297	1*	119	-8	-0.8
Total	3	9	12	.429	31	17	12	4	165.1	220	132	3		15	36	3.76	73	.295	.309	928	.334	10	104	-17	-1.4
McWEENY, DOUG Douglas Lawrence "Buzz" B 8.17.1896 Chicago, IL D 1.1.1953 Melrose Park, IL BR/TR 6-2/190# d4.24																									
1921	Chi A	3	6	.333	27	8	3	2	97.2	127	76	7	0	45	46	6.08	70	.325	.394	31-1	.032	-4	86	-20	-2.0
1922	Chi A	0	1	.000	4	1	0	0	10.2	13	8	0	0	7	5	5.91	69	.325	.426	1-0	.000	0	0	-2	-0.2
1924	Chi A	1	3	.250	13	5	2	0	43.1	47	25	2	2	17	18	4.57	90	.294	.369	9-1	.000	-0	78	-2	0.0
1926	Bro N	11	13	.458	42	24	10-1	1	216.1	213	97	6	8	84	96	3.04	126	.258	.333	64-4	.109	-4	77	16	1.1
1927	Bro N	4	8	.333	34	22	6	1	164.1	167	80	13	8	70	73	3.56	111	.266	.347	47-6	.043	-4	88	7	0.1
1928	Bro N	14	14	.500	42	32	12-**4**	1	244	218	108	11	5	114	79	3.17	125	.235	.322	81-3	.173	-1	85	22	2.4
1929	Bro N	4	10	.286	36	22	4	1	146	167	119	17	3	93	59	6.10	76	.288	.390	48-3	.104	-2	127	-25	-2.2
1930	Cin N	0	2	.000	8	2	0	0	25.2	28	23	0	0	20	10	7.36	66	.283	.403	7-0	.143	-0	72	-7	-0.4
Total	8	37	57	.394	206	116	37-5	6	948	980	536	56	26	450	386	4.17	98	.269	.353	288-18	.104	-16	92	-11	-1.2
McWILLIAMS, LARRY Larry Dean B 2.10.1954 Wichita, KS BL/TL 6-5/180# d7.17																									
1978	Atl N	9	3	.750	15	15	3-1	0-0	99.1	84	38	11	2	35-4	42	2.81	144	.224	.294	32-4	.063	-2	120	11	1.2
1979	Atl N	3	2	.600	13	13	1	0-0	66.1	69	41	4	4	22-2	32	5.56	73	.272	.338	24-2	.208	1	117	-8	-0.3
1980	Atl N	9	14	.391	30	30	4-1	0-0	163.2	188	97	27	7	39-2	77	4.95	76	.285	.331	51-4	.157	-0	91	-20	-2.5
1981	Atl N	2	1	.667	6	5	2-1	0-0	37.2	31	13	2	0	8-0	23	3.11	115	.230	.269	10-1	.100	-0	109	3	0.2
1982	Atl N	2	3	.400	27	2	0	0-1	37.2	52	30	3	2	20-5	24	6.21	60	.327	.407	6-1	.167	0	94	-10	-1.1
	Pit N	6	5	.545	19	18	2-2	1-0	121.2	106	49	9	4	24-1	94	3.11	120	.232	.275	32-9	.188	-0*	90	7	0.7
	Year	8	8	.500	46	20	2-2	1-1	159.1	158	53	12	6	44-6	118	3.84	97	.256	.311	38-10	.184	-0	90	-3	-0.4
1983	Pit N	15	8	.652	35	35	8-4	0-0	238	205	99	19	3	87-7	199	3.25	114	.230	.298	79-10	.114	-3	100	11	0.8
1984	Pit N	12	11	.522	34	32	7-2	1-1	227.1	226	86	18	2	78-7	149	2.93	123	.263	.324	74-12	.122	-3*	108	15	1.2
1985	Pit N	7	9	.438	30	19	2	0-0	126.1	139	70	9	7	62-11	52	4.70	76	.283	.369	40-4	.125	-1*	113	-14	-1.7
1986	Pit N	3	11	.214	49	15	0	0-1	122.1	129	75	16	7	49-5	80	5.15	75	.268	.345	29-3	.138	0*	108	-16	-1.7
1987	Atl N	0	1	.000	9	2	0	0-0	20.1	25	15	2	2	7-1	13	5.75	76	.301	.366	5-0	.200	0	94	-3	-0.1
1988	StL N	6	9	.400	42	17	2-1	1-1	136	130	64	10	4	45-7	70	3.90	89	.253	.317	37-1	.162	1*	93	-6	-0.5
1989	Phi N	2	11	.154	40	16	2-1	0-1	120.2	123	67	3	4	49-4	54	4.10	87	.265	.337	27-3	.111	-1*	95	-9	-1.0
	KC A	2	2	.500	8	5	1	0-0	32.2	31	15	2	3	8-1	24	4.13	93	.254	.313	0-0	—	0	61	0	0.0
1990	KC A	0	0	—	13	0	0	0-0	8.1	10	9	2	1	9-1	7	9.72	40	.313	.476	0-0	—	0		-5	-0.2
Total	13	78	90	.464	370	224	34-13	3-5	1558.1	1548	768	137	52	542-58	940	3.99	93	.259	.324	446-54	.135	-8	102	-44	-5.0
MEACHAM, RUSTY Russell Loren B 1.27.1968 Stuart, FL BR/TR 6-2/175# d6.29																									
1991	Det A	2	1	.667	10	4	0	0-0	27.2	35	17	4	0	11-0	14	5.20	80	.315	.368	0-0	—	0	148	-3	-0.3
1992	KC A	10	4	.714	64	0	0	2-4	101.2	88	39	5	1	21-5	64	2.74	148	.233	.269	0-0	—	0		12	1.7
1993	KC A	2	2	.500	15	0	0	0-0	21	31	15	2	3	5-1	13	5.57	82	.326	.375	0-0	—	0		-3	-0.4
1994	KC A	3	3	.500	36	0	0	4-1	50.2	51	23	7	2	12-1	36	3.73	134	.263	.307	0-0	—	0		7	0.8
1995	KC A	4	3	.571	49	0	0	2-1	59.2	72	36	6	1	19-5	30	4.98	96	.304	.352	0-0	—	0		-1	-0.1
1996	Sea A	1	1	.500	15	5	0	1-0	42.1	57	28	9	4	13-1	25	5.74	86	.328	.385	0-0	—	0	135	-3	-0.2
2000	Hou N	0	0	—	5	0	0	0-0	4.2	8	6	3	0	2-0	3	11.57	42	.381	.435	0-0	—	0		-3	-0.1
2001	TB A	1	3	.250	24	0	0	0-0	35.1	39	24	3	2	10-0	13	5.60	80	.277	.325	0-0	—	0		-4	-0.4
Total	8	23	17	.575	218	9	0	9-6	343	381	188	39	13	93-13	198	4.43	102	.282	.328	0-0	—	0	142	2	1.0
MEADOR, JOHNNY John Davis B 12.4.1892 Madison, NC D 4.11.1970 Winston-Salem, NC BR/TR 5-10.5/165# d4.24																									
1920	Pit N	0	2	.000	12	2	0	0	36.1	48	18	1	0	7	5	4.21	76	.340	.372	6-0	.167	-0	61	-3	-0.1
MEADOWS, LEE Henry Lee "Specs" B 7.12.1894 Oxford, NC D 1.29.1963 Daytona Beach, FL BL/TR 6/190# d4.19																									
1915	StL N	13	11	.542	39	26	14-1	0	244	232	112	5	5	88	104	2.99	93	.259	.329	83-1	.096	-4	104	-7	-1.2
1916	StL N	12	23	.343	**51**	36	11-1	2	289	261	117	3	14	119	120	2.58	102	.247	.332	95-3	.158	-1	84	-1	-0.2
1917	StL N	15	9	.625	43	37	18-4	2	265.2	253	99	5	4	90	100	3.08	87	.262	.328	89-7	.101	-6	109	-7	-1.5
1918	StL N	8	14	.364	30	23	12	1	165.1	176	91	1	10	56	49	3.59	75	.280	.348	55-2	.127	-2*	95	-17	-2.5
1919	StL N	4	10	.286	22	12	3-1	0	92	100	44	3	2	30	28	3.03	92	.292	.352	29-1	.103	-2	81	-5	-0.7

Year	Tm Lg	W	L	Pct	G	GS	CG-Sho	SV-BS	IP	H	R	HR	HB	BB-IB	SO	ERA	AERA	OAV	OOB	AB-SH	AVG	PB	Sup	APR	PW
	Phi N	8	10	.444	18	17	15-3	0	158.1	128	55	3	7	49	88	2.33	138	.229	.300	51-4	.118	-3*	65	12	1.0
	Year	12	20	.375	40	29	18-4	0	250.1	228	58	6	9	79	116	2.59	118	.253	.320	80-5	.112	-5	71	10	0.3
1920	Phi N	16	14	.533	35	33	19-3	0	247	249	104	5	8	90	95	2.84	120	.270	.341	82-2	.171	-3*	89	13	1.3
1921	Phi N	11	16	.407	28	27	15-2	0	194.1	226	118	10	4	62	52	4.31	98	.288	.343	62-4	.210	2	81	1	0.6
1922	Phi N	12	18	.400	33	33	19-2	0	237	264	127	8	11	71	62	4.03	116	.288	.346	86-5	.314	3	77	18	2.6
1923	Phi N	1	3	.250	8	5	0	1	19.2	40	32	0	0	15	10	13.27	35	.430	.509	10-0	.400	2	129	-15	-2.3
	Pit N	16	10	.615	31	25	17-1	0	227	250	97	3	1	44	66	3.01	133	.284	.319	88-3	.250	3	112	22	2.6
	Year	17	13	.567	39	30	17-1	1	246.2	290	102	3	1	59	76	3.83	106	.298	.339	98-3	.265	5	117	2	0.3
1924	Pit N	13	12	.520	36	30	15-3	0	229.1	240	99	7	4	51	61	3.26	118	.278	.322	82-2	.195	-1	88	14	1.1
1925	†Pit N	19	10	.655	35	31	20-1	1	255.1	272	128	11	8	67	87	3.67	122	.273	.323	97-5	.175	-1	124	21	2.0
1926	Pit N	**20**	9	.690	36	31	15-1	0	226.2	254	125	10	4	52	54	3.97	99	.287	.329	88-1	.227	-1	130	-2	-0.2
1927	†Pit N	19	10	.655	40	**38**	**25**-2	0	299.1	315	131	11	8	66	84	3.40	121	.273	.317	115-3	.157	-5	118	23	1.4
1928	Pit N	1	1	.500	4	2	1	0	10	18	11	0	0	5	3	8.10	50	.383	.442	4-0	.500	1	156	-5	-0.7
1929	Pit N	0	0	—	1	0	0	0	0.2	2	1	0	0	1	0	13.50	35	.500	.600	1-0	.000	-0		-1	0.0
Total	15	188	180	.511	490	406	219-25	7	3160.2	3280	1491	85	90	956	1063	3.37	106	.274	.332	1117-43	.180	-19	101	64	3.3

MEADOWS, BRIAN Matthew Brian B 11.21.1975 Montgomery, AL BR/TR 6-4/210# d4.4

1998	Fla N	11	13	.458	31	31	1	0-0	174.1	222	106	20	3	46-3	88	5.21	78	.315	.358	54-2	.130	-1	77	-21	-2.5
1999	Fla N	11	15	.423	31	31	0	0-0	178.1	214	117	31	5	57-5	72	5.60	78	.302	.354	50-7	.140	0	87	-24	-2.8
2000	SD N	7	8	.467	22	22	0	0-0	124.2	150	80	24	8	50-6	53	5.34	81	.301	.373	40-4	.150	-1	120	-14	-1.5
	KC A	6	2	.750	11	10	2	0-0	71.2	84	39	8	0	14-0	26	4.77	107	.293	.322	0-0	—	0	104	3	0.3
2001	KC A	1	6	.143	10	10	0	0-0	50.1	73	41	12	1	12-2	21	6.97	70	.351	.386	0-0	—	0	87	-10	-1.1
2002	Pit N	1	6	.143	11	11	0	0-0	62.2	62	29	7	1	14-8	31	3.88	108	.256	.300	18-3	.000	-2	54	2	0.0
2003	Pit N	2	1	.667	34	7	0	1-0	76.1	91	45	8	1	11-2	38	4.72	93	.290	.315	14-3	.071	-1	122	-4	-0.3
Total	6	39	51	.433	150	122	3	1-0	738.1	896	457	110	19	204-26	329	5.24	84	.302	.349	176-19	.119	-4	91	-68	-7.9

MEADOWS, RUFUS Rufus Rivers B 8.25.1907 Chase City, VA D 5.10.1970 Wichita, KS BL/TL 5-11/175# d4.23

1926	Cin N	0	0	—	1	0	0	0	0.1	0	0	0	0	0	0	0.00	—	.000	.000	1-0	.000	-0		0	0.0

MEADS, DAVE David Donald B 1.7.1964 Montclair, NJ BL/TL 6- /175# d4.13

1987	Hou N	5	3	.625	45	0	0	0-1	48.2	60	31	8	1	16-2	32	5.55	71	.321	.372	3-0	.333	1		-8	-1.2
1988	Hou N	3	1	.750	22	2	0	0-0	39.2	37	20	4	0	14-0	27	3.18	105	.240	.302	4-0	.250	1	27	-1	0.0
Total	2	8	4	.667	67	2	0	0-1	88.1	97	51	12	1	30-2	59	4.48	82	.284	.340	7-0	.286	1	27	-9	-1.2

MEAKIM, GEORGE George Clinton B 7.11.1865 Brooklyn, NY D 2.17.1923 Queens, NY BR/TR 5-7.5/154# d5.2

1890	†Lou AA	12	7	.632	28	21	16-3	1	192	173	100	4	5	63	123	2.91	133	.233	.298	72	.153	-2*	73	22	1.6
1891	Phi AA	1	4	.200	6	6	4	0	35	51	45	1	1	22	13	6.94	55	.329	.416	15	.200	0	109	-14	-1.3
1892	Chi N	0	1	.000	1	1	1	0	9	18	14	0	0	2	0	11.00	30	.400	.426	5	.400	0	190	-6	-0.5
	Cin N	1	1	.500	3	3	1	0	13.2	19	18	1	2	9	4	8.56	38	.317	.423	5	.000	-1	142	-8	-0.9
	Year	1	2	.333	4	4	2	0	22.2	37	25	1	2	11	4	9.53	35	.352	.424	10	.200	-0	154	-13	-1.4
1895	Lou N	1	0	1.000	1	1	1	0	7	7	2	0	0	4	2	2.57	180	.259	.355	3-0	.333	0	77	2	0.2
Total	4	15	13	.536	39	32	23-3	1	256.2	268	179	6	8	100	142	4.03	95	.260	.331	100-0	.170	-2	90	-4	-0.9

MEARS, CHRIS Christopher Peter B 1.20.1978 Ottawa, ON, CAN BR/TR 6-4/190# d6.29

2003	Det A	1	3	.250	29	3	0	5-0	41.1	50	28	5	3	11-0	21	5.44	79	.307	.360	0-0	—	0	28	-6	-0.6

MECHE, GIL Gilbert Allen B 9.8.1978 Lafayette, LA BR/TR 6-3/180# d7.6

1999	Sea A	8	4	.667	16	15	0	0-0	85.2	73	48	9	2	57-1	47	4.73	100	.237	.357	0-0	—	0	79	0	0.0
2000	Sea A	4	4	.500	15	15	1-1	0-0	85.2	75	37	7	1	40-0	60	3.78	125	.240	.324	0-0	—	0	89	10	0.8
2003	Sea A	15	13	.536	32	32	1	0-0	186.1	187	97	30	3	63-2	130	4.59	94	.263	.324	5-0	.200	0	101	-4	-0.5
Total	3	27	21	.563	63	62	2-1	0-0	357.2	335	182	46	6	160-3	237	4.43	102	.252	.332	5-0	.200	0	92	6	0.3

MECIR, JIM James Jason B 5.16.1970 Bayside, NY BB/TR 6-1/195# d9.4

1995	Sea A	0	0	—	2	0	0	0-0	4.2	5	1	0	0	2-0	3	0.00	—	.263	.333	0-0	—	0		2	0.1
1996	NY A	1	1	.500	26	0	0	0-0	40.1	42	24	6	0	23-4	38	5.13	96	.275	.361	0-0	—	0		-1	0.0
1997	NY A	0	4	.000	25	0	0	0-1	33.2	36	23	5	2	10-1	25	5.88	76	.279	.338	0-0	—	0		-5	-0.5
1998	TB A	7	2	.778	68	0	0	0-3	84	68	30	6	3	33-5	77	3.11	154	.225	.306	1-0	.000	-0		16	1.5
1999	TB A	0	1	.000	17	0	0	0-2	20.2	15	7	0	1	14-0	15	2.61	191	.203	.330	0-0	—	0		5	0.3
2000	TB A	7	2	.778	38	0	0	1-3	49.2	35	17	2	1	22-0	33	3.08	161	.201	.293	0-0	—	0		11	1.7
	†Oak A	3	1	.750	25	0	0	4-5	35.1	35	14	2	1	14-2	37	2.80	170	.255	.327	0-0	—	0		7	0.8
	Year	10	3	.769	63	0	0	5-8	85	70	36	4	2	36-2	70	2.96	164	.225	.308	0-0	—	0		18	2.5
2001	†Oak A	2	8	.200	54	0	0	3-5	63	54	25	4	1	26-7	61	3.43	129	.231	.310	0-0	—	0		8	1.2
2002	†Oak A	6	4	.600	61	0	0	1-5	67.2	68	36	5	4	29-4	53	4.26	103	.259	.337	0-0	—	0		1	0.2
2003	†Oak A	2	3	.400	41	0	0	1-1	37	40	25	4	1	16-1	25	5.59	81	.280	.352	0-0	—	0		-4	-0.5
Total	9	28	26	.519	357	0	0	10-25	436	398	202	34	14	189-24	367	3.86	121	.244	.325	1-0	.000	-0		40	4.8

MEDICH, DOC George Francis B 12.9.1948 Aliquippa, PA BR/TR 6-5/227# d9.5

1972	NY A	0	0	—	1	1	0	0-0	0	2	2	0	0	2-0	0	∞	—	1.000	1.000	0-0	—	0	210	-2	-0.2
1973	NY A	14	9	.609	34	32	11-3	0-0	235	217	84	20	3	74-6	145	2.95	124	.241	.299	0-0	—	0	106	22	1.9
1974	NY A	19	15	.559	38	38	17-4	0-0	279.2	275	122	24	8	91-8	154	3.60	98	.259	.321	0-0	—	0*	108	1	0.1
1975	NY A	16	16	.500	38	37	15-2	0-0	272.1	271	115	25	1	72-5	132	3.50	105	.264	.309	0-0	—	0	105	8	0.7
1976	Pit N	8	11	.421	29	26	3	0-0	179	193	80	10	2	48-9	86	3.52	99	.281	.326	52-8	.096	-2	83	0	-0.2
1977	Oak A	10	6	.625	26	25	1	0-0	147.2	155	89	19	3	49-3	74	4.69	86	.265	.322	0-0	—	0	118	-11	-1.1
	Sea A	2	0	1.000	3	3	1	0-0	22.1	26	9	1	2	4-0	3	3.63	114	.286	.327	0-0	—	0	145	2	0.1
	Year	12	6	.667	29	28	2	0-0	170	181	16	20	5	53-3	77	4.55	89	.268	.323	0-0	—	0	121	-10	-1.0
	NY N	0	1	.000	1	1	0	0-0	7	6	3	0	0	1-0	3	3.86	97	.261	.280	2-0	.000	-0	48	0	0.0
1978	Tex A	9	8	.529	28	22	6-2	2-0	171	166	78	10	3	52-2	71	3.74	101	.255	.311	0-0	—	0	102	2	0.2
1979	Tex A	10	7	.588	29	19	4-1	0-1	149	156	78	9	4	49-3	58	4.17	100	.269	.328	0-0	—	0	111	0	0.1
1980	Tex A	14	11	.560	34	32	6	0-0	204.1	230	104	13	3	56-1	91	3.92	100	.285	.333	0-0	—	0*	120	-1	-0.2
1981	Tex A	10	6	.625	20	20	4-**4**	0-0	143.1	136	51	8	2	33-5	65	3.08	113	.252	.296	0-0	—	0	119	8	0.9
1982	Tex A	7	11	.389	21	21	2	0-0	122.2	146	73	8	3	61-5	37	5.06	77	.307	.383	0-0	—	0	83	-16	-2.0
	†Mil A	5	4	.556	10	10	1	0-0	63	57	37	4	1	32-1	36	5.00	76	.242	.332	0-0	—	0	108	-8	-1.0
	Year	12	15	.444	31	31	3	0-0	185.2	203	42	12	4	93-6	73	5.04	76	.286	.366	0-0	—	0	91	-23	-3.0
Total	11	124	105	.541	312	287	71-16	2-1	1996.1	2036	925	151	35	624-48	955	3.78	99	.266	.321	54-8	.093	-2	107	5	-0.7

MEDINA, RAFAEL Rafael Eduardo B 2.15.1975 Panama City, Panama BR/TR 6-3/194# d4.2

1998	Fla N	2	6	.250	12	12	0	0-0	67.1	76	50	8	3	52-3	49	6.01	67	.289	.407	19-6	.053	-2	91	-15	-1.7
1999	Fla N	1	1	.500	20	0	0	0-0	23.1	20	15	3	1	20-2	16	5.79	75	.227	.376	0-0	—	0		-3	-0.3
Total	2	3	7	.300	32	12	0	0-0	90.2	96	65	11	4	72-5	65	5.96	69	.274	.399	19-6	.053	-2	91	-18	-2.0

MEDLINGER, IRV Irving John B 6.18.1927 Chicago, IL D 9.3.1975 Wheeling, IL BL/TL 5-11/185# d4.20

1949	StL A	0	0	—	3	0	0	0	4	11	13	1	0	3	4	27.00	17	.478	.538	0-0	—	0		-9	-0.4
1951	StL A	0	0	—	6	0	0	0	9.2	10	10	1	0	12	5	8.38	52	.270	.449	0-0	—	0		-4	-0.2
Total	2	0	0	—	9	0	0	0	13.2	21	23	2	0	15	9	13.83	32	.350	.480	0-0	—	0		-13	-0.6

MEDVIN, SCOTT Scott Howard B 9.16.1961 North Olmsted, OH BR/TR 6-1/195# d5.11

1988	Pit N	3	0	1.000	17	0	0	0-0	27.2	23	16	1	1	9-2	16	4.88	70	.230	.297	3-1	.000	-0		-4	-0.5
1989	Pit N	0	1	.000	6	0	0	0-0	6.1	6	5	0	0	5-2	4	5.68	59	.240	.367	0-0	—	0		-2	-0.3
1990	Sea A	0	1	.000	5	0	0	0-1	4.1	7	4	0	1	2-0	1	6.23	64	.368	.455	0-0	—	0		-1	-0.3
Total	3	3	2	.600	28	0	0	0-1	38.1	36	25	1	2	16-4	21	5.17	67	.250	.331	3-1	.000	-0		-7	-1.1

MEEGAN, PETE Peter James "Steady Pete" B 11.13.1863 San Francisco, CA D 3.15.1905 San Francisco, CA d8.12

1884	Ric AA	7	12	.368	22	22	22-1	0	179	177	130	7	14	29	106	4.32	77	.246	.288	75	.160	-2*	77	-18	-1.6
1885	Pit AA	7	8	.467	18	16	14-1	0	146	146	90	1	10	38	58	3.39	95	.247	.303	67	.194	-1*	95	-3	-0.4
Total	2	14	20	.412	40	38	36-2	0	325	323	220	8	24	67	164	3.90	84	.246	.295	142	.176	-3	85	-21	-2.0

Year	Tm Lg	W	L	Pct	G	GS	CG-Sho	SV-BS	IP	H	R	HR	HB	BB-IB	SO	ERA	AERA	OAV	OOB	AB-SH	AVG	PB	Sup	APR	PW
MEEHAN, BILL William Thomas B 9.4.1889 Osceola Mills, PA D 10.8.1982 Douglas, WY BR/TR 5-9/155# d9.17																									
1915	Phi A	0	1	.000	1	1	0	0	4	7	5	0	0	3	4	11.25	26	.389	.476	1-0	1.000	0	150	-3	-0.4
MEEKER, ROY Charles Roy B 9.15.1900 Lead Mine, MO D 3.25.1929 Orlando, FL BL/TL 5-9/175# d9.22																									
1923	Phi A	3	0	1.000	5	2	2	0	25	24	10	0	0	13	12	3.60	114	.253	.343	9-0	.111	-1	171	2	0.2
1924	Phi A	5	12	.294	30	14	5-1	0	146	166	86	7	5	81	37	4.68	91	.288	.381	48-5	.229	-0	76	-5	-0.5
1926	Cin N	0	2	.000	7	1	1	0	21	24	18	1	0	9	5	6.43	57	.324	.398	6-0	.000	-1	23	-7	-0.6
Total	3	8	14	.364	42	17	8-1	0	192	214	114	8	5	103	54	4.73	89	.287	.377	63-5	.190	-2	85	-10	-0.9
MEEKIN, JOUETT George Jouett B 2.21.1867 New Albany, IN D 12.14.1944 New Albany, IN BR/TR 6-1/180# d6.13																									
1891	Lou AA	9	16	.360	28	25	24-2	0	221	223	154	2	6	106	141	4.28	85	.253	.338	94	.223	4*	88	-13	-0.9
1892	Lou N	7	10	.412	19	18	17	0	156.1	168	108	3	6	78	67	4.03	76	.264	.350	64	.078	-5*	101	-16	-1.8
	Was N	3	10	.231	14	14	13-1	0	112	112	91	2	4	48	58	3.46	94	.250	.328	45	.133	-1	97	-8	-0.8
	Year	10	20	.333	33	32	30-1	0	268.1	280	96	5	10	126	125	3.79	83	.258	.341	109	.101	-5	99	-22	-2.6
1893	Was N	10	15	.400	31	28	24-1	0	245	289	201	6	7	140	91	4.96	93	.285	.376	113	.257	3*	85	-10	-0.5
1894	†NY N	33	9	**.786**	53	49	41-1	2	418	414	240	13	11	176	137	3.70	142	.256	.333	174-1	.276	6	90	81	6.2
1895	NY N	16	11	.593	29	29	24-1	0	225.2	296	170	10	9	73	76	5.30	88	.312	.366	96-0	.292	4*	99	-9	-0.5
1896	NY N	26	14	.650	42	41	34	0	334.1	378	205	8	15	127	110	3.82	110	.283	.351	144-0	.299	12*	119	14	2.2
1897	NY N	20	11	.645	37	34	30-2	0	303.2	328	176	9	8	99	83	3.76	110	.273	.333	137-0	.299	6*	105	19	1.9
1898	NY N	16	18	.471	38	37	34-1	0	320	329	185	9	12	108	82	3.77	92	.264	.328	129-0	.209	1	102	-3	-0.5
1899	NY N	5	11	.313	18	18	16	0	148.1	169	103	4	8	70	30	4.37	86	.286	.369	58-0	.207	1	92	-11	-1.0
	Bos N	7	6	.538	13	13	12	0	108	111	52	0	2	23	23	2.83	147	.266	.307	41-0	.171	-1	66	12	1.0
	Year	12	17	.414	31	31	28	0	256.1	280	56	4	10	93	53	3.72	105	.278	.344	99-0	.192	-1	80	7	0.0
1900	Pit N	0	2	.000	2	2	1	0	13	20	21	1	1	8	3	6.92	53	.351	.439	4-0	.000	-1	38	-7	-0.8
Total	10	152	133	.533	324	308	270-9	2	2605.1	2837	1706	67	89	1056	901	4.07	103	.273	.345	1099-1	.243	29	97	49	4.5
MEELER, PHIL Charles Phillip B 7.3.1948 South Boston, VA BR/TR 6-5/215# d5.10																									
1972	Det A	0	1	.000	7	0	0	0-0	8.1	10	6	0	0	7-1	5	4.32	73	.303	.405	2-0	.000	-0		-2	-0.2
MEERS, RUSS Russell Harlan "Babe" B 11.28.1918 Tilton, IL D 11.16.1994 Lancaster, PA BL/TL 5-10/170# d9.28 Mil 1942-45																									
1941	Chi N	0	1	.000	1	1	0	0	8	5	2	0	1	0	5	1.13	312	.172	.200	2-0	.000	-0	24	2	0.2
1946	Chi N	1	2	.333	7	2	0	0	11.1	10	6	0	0	10	2	3.18	104	.238	.385	1-1	1.000	0	155	0	0.0
1947	Chi N	2	0	1.000	35	1	0	0	64.1	61	34	5	2	38	28	4.48	88	.263	.371	14-0	.143	-1	179	-2	-0.2
Total	3	3	3	.500	43	4	0	0	83.2	76	42	5	3	48	35	3.98	96	.251	.359	17-1	.176	-0	120	0	0.0
MEINE, HEINIE Henry William "The Count Of Luxemburg" B 5.1.1896 St.Louis, MO D 3.18.1968 St.Louis, MO BR/TR 5-11/180# d8.16																									
1922	StL A	0	0	—	1	0	0	0	4	5	3	1	0	2	0	4.50	92	.313	.389	1-0	.000	-0		0	0.0
1929	Pit N	7	6	.538	22	13	7-1	1	108	120	62	4	7	34	19	4.50	106	.291	.355	39-3	.103	-2	107	4	0.1
1930	Pit N	6	8	.429	20	16	4	1	117.1	168	89	6	5	44	18	6.14	81	.346	.406	41-2	.122	-3	84	-13	-1.3
1931	Pit N	**19**	13	.594	36	**35**	22-3	0	**284**	278	121	8	7	87	58	2.98	129	.254	.313	96-7	.146	-2	90	25	2.4
1932	Pit N	12	9	.571	28	25	13-1	1	172.1	193	92	6	3	45	32	3.86	99	.278	.324	61-5	.164	-2	110	-1	-0.4
1933	Pit N	15	8	.652	32	29	12-2	0	207.1	227	99	10	2	50	50	3.65	91	.278	.321	75-6	.173	-1	117	-6	-0.9
1934	Pit N	7	6	.538	26	14	2	0	106.1	134	60	12	1	25	22	4.32	95	.306	.345	28-2	.107	-1	79	-3	-0.5
Total	7	66	50	.569	165	132	60-7	3	999.1	1125	526	47	25	287	199	3.95	101	.284	.337	341-25	.144	-12	98	6	-0.6
MEINKE, FRANK Frank Louis B 10.18.1863 Chicago, IL D 11.8.1931 Chicago, IL BR 5-10.5/172# d5.1 s-Bob ▲																									
1884	Det N	8	23	.258	35	31	31-1	0	289	341	217	10		63	124	3.18	91	.275	.310	341	.164	-3*	72	-13	-1.4
1885	Det N	0	1	.000	1	1	0	0	5	13	12	0		4	0	3.60	79	.433	.500	3	.000	-0	20	-3	-0.4
Total	2	8	24	.250	36	32	31-1	0	294	354	229	10		67	124	3.18	91	.279	.315	344	.163	-3	70	-16	-1.8
MELENDEZ, JOSE Jose Luis (Garcia) B 9.2.1965 Naguabo, P.R. BR/TR 6-2/175# d9.11																									
1990	Sea A	0	0	—	3	0	0	0-0	5.1	8	8	2	1	3-0	7	11.81	34	.333	.429	0-0	—	0		-5	-0.2
1991	SD N	8	5	.615	31	9	0	3-1	93.2	77	35	11	1	24-3	60	3.27	116	.221	.269	20-0	.100	-0	84	7	0.8
1992	SD N	6	7	.462	56	3	0	0-2	89.1	82	32	9	3	20-7	82	2.92	123	.249	.295	5-1	.000	-0	59	6	0.8
1993	Bos A	2	1	.667	9	0	0	0-1	16	10	4	2	0	5-3	14	2.25	206	.179	.238	0-0	—	0		4	0.7
1994	Bos A	0	1	.000	10	0	0	0-0	16.1	20	11	3	2	8-2	9	6.06	83	.323	.417	0-0	—	0		-1	-0.1
Total	5	16	14	.533	109	12	0	3-4	220.2	197	90	27	7	60-15	172	3.47	111	.241	.294	25-1	.080	-1	76	11	2.0
MELTER, STEVE Stephen Blazius B 1.2.1886 Cherokee, IA D 1.28.1962 Mishawaka, IN BR/TR 6-2/180# d6.27																									
1909	StL N	0	1	.000	23	1	0	3	64.1	79	49	1	2	20	24	3.50	72	.322	.378	15-0	.133	-0	166	-12	-0.6
MELTON, CLIFF Clifford George "Mickey Mouse" or "Mountain Music" B 1.3.1912 Brevard, NC D 7.28.1986 Baltimore, MD BL/TL 6-5.5/203# d4.25																									
1937	†NY N	20	9	.690	46	27	14-2	**7**	248	216	90	9	6	55	142	2.61	149	.233	.280	82-10	.122	-5	105	33	3.4
1938	NY N	14	14	.500	36	31	10-1	0	243	266	126	19	1	61	101	3.89	97	.276	.319	80-13	.175	-1	110	-5	-0.5
1939	NY N	12	15	.444	41	23	9-2	5	207.1	214	94	7	4	65	95	3.56	110	.269	.327	66-8	.182	-1	101	8	1.0
1940	NY N	10	11	.476	37	21	4-1	2	166.2	185	103	9	3	68	91	4.91	79	.285	.355	54-6	.222	2	113	-18	-1.8
1941	NY N	8	11	.421	42	22	9-3	1	194.1	181	83	14	2	61	100	3.01	123	.246	.305	61-8	.115	-3	95	11	0.9
1942	NY N✣	11	5	.688	23	17	12-2	1	143.2	122	51	9	2	33	61	2.63	128	.229	.276	47-2	.234	2	112	11	1.6
1943	NY N	9	13	.409	34	28	6-2	0	186.1	184	85	7	3	69	55	3.19	108	.257	.325	54-3	.148	0	97	1	0.3
1944	NY N	2	2	.500	13	10	1	0	64.1	78	40	5	1	19	15	4.06	90	.294	.344	25-1	.120	-2	133	-5	-0.4
Total	8	86	80	.518	272	179	65-13	16	1453.2	1446	672	79	22	431	660	3.42	109	.259	.314	469-51	.164	-9	106	36	4.5
MELTON, RUBE Reuben Franklin B 2.27.1917 Cramerton, NC D 9.11.1971 Greer, SC BR/TR 6-5/205# d4.17 Mil 1945-46																									
1941	Phi N	1	5	.167	25	5	2	0	83.2	81	48	7	0	47	57	4.73	78	.258	.355	19-2	.105	-1	55	-8	-0.7
1942	Phi N	9	20	.310	42	29	10-1	4	209.1	180	95	7	3	114	107	3.70	89	.234	.335	65-0	.123	-1	61	-7	-1.2
1943	Bro N	5	8	.385	30	17	4-2	0	119.1	106	62	3	5	79	63	3.92	86	.243	.365	38-5	.105	-2	126	-9	-1.2
1944	Bro N	9	13	.409	37	23	6-1	0	187.1	178	92	1	2	96	91	3.46	103	.254	.345	57-9	.123	-3	83	-1	-0.4
1946	Bro N	6	3	.667	24	12	3-2	1	99.2	72	27	3	3	52	44	1.99	170	.206	.314	28-3	.107	-2	101	15	1.2
1947	Bro N	0	1	.000	4	1	0	0	4.2	7	7	1	0	7	1	13.50	31	.350	.519	1-0	1.000	0	0	-4	-0.7
Total	6	30	50	.375	162	87	25-6	5	704	624	331	22	13	395	363	3.62	95	.241	.344	208-19	.120	-9	83	-14	-3.0
MENDOZA, MIKE Michael Joseph B 11.26.1955 Inglewood, CA BR/TR 6-5/215# d9.7																									
1979	Hou N	0	0	—	1	0	0	0-0	1	0	0	0	0	0-0	0	0.00	—	.000	.000	0-0	—	0*		0	0.0
MENDOZA, RAMIRO Ramiro B 6.15.1972 Los Santos, Panama BR/TR 6-2/154# d5.25																									
1996	NY A	4	5	.444	12	11	0	0-0	53	80	43	5	4	10-1	34	6.79	73	.343	.379	0-0	—	0	75	-11	-1.5
1997	†NY A	8	6	.571	39	15	0	2-2	133.2	157	67	15	5	28-2	82	4.24	105	.292	.330	0-0	—	0	128	4	0.5
1998	†NY A	10	2	.833	41	14	1-1	1-3	130.1	131	50	9	9	30-6	56	3.25	135	.264	.314	0-1	—	0	141	17	1.5
1999	†NY A	9	9	.500	53	6	0	3-3	123.2	141	68	13	3	27-3	80	4.29	110	.284	.323	0-0	—	0	82	5	0.7
2000	NY A	7	4	.636	14	9	1-1	0-1	65.2	66	32	9	4	20-1	30	4.25	114	.260	.321	0-0	—	0	138	5	0.7
2001	†NY A	8	4	.667	56	2	0	6-2	100.2	89	44	9	2	23-3	70	3.75	120	.241	.287	2-0	.000	-0	134	9	1.0
2002	†NY A	8	4	.667	62	0	0	4-4	91.2	102	43	8	2	16-2	61	3.44	127	.275	.305	1-0	.000	-0		8	1.1
2003	Bos A	3	5	.375	37	5	0	0-1	66.2	98	51	10	5	20-4	36	6.75	68	.349	.397	0-0	—	0	133	-14	-1.4
Total	8	57	39	.594	314	62	2-2	16-16	765.1	864	398	78	34	174-22	449	4.32	106	.284	.327	3-1	.000	-0	120	23	2.6
MENEFEE, JOCK John B 1.15.1868 Rowlesburg, WV D 3.11.1953 Belle Vernon, PA BR/TR 6/165# d8.17 ▲																									
1892	Pit N	0	0	—	1	0	0	0	4	10	6	0	0	2	0	11.25	29	.455	.500	3	.000	-0*		-3	-0.1
1893	Lou N	8	7	.533	15	15	14-1	0	129.1	150	95	3	3	40	30	4.24	103	.281	.335	73	.274	4*	102	-3	0.1
1894	Lou N	8	17	.320	28	24	20-1	0	211.2	258	153	4	9	50	43	4.29	119	.297	.342	79-8	.165	-6*	77	19	1.3
	Pit N	5	8	.385	13	13	13	0	111.2	159	95	3	2	39	33	5.40	97	.331	.383	47-2	.255	0	92	-4	-0.2
	Year	13	25	.342	41	37	33-1	0	323.1	417	102	7	11	89	76	4.68	110	.309	.357	126-10	.198	-5	83	15	1.1
1895	Pit N	0	1	.000	2	1	0	0	1.2	2	8	0	1	7	0	16.20	28	.286	.667	0-0	—	0	0	-4	-0.5
1898	NY N	0	1	.000	1	1	1	0	9.1	11	8	0	2	2	3	4.82	72	.289	.357	5-0	.000	-1	163	-2	-0.2
1900	Chi N	9	4	.692	16	13	11	0	117	140	74	1	10	35	30	3.85	94	.296	.357	46-2	.109	-3*	109	-1	-0.4
1901	Chi N	8	12	.400	21	20	19	0	182.1	201	102	4	6	34	55	3.80	85	.278	.315	152-7	.257	4*	92	-7	-0.2

Year	Tm Lg	W	L	Pct	G	GS	CG-Sho	SV-BS	IP	H	R	HR	HB	BB-IB	SO	ERA	AERA	OAV	OOB	AB-SH	AVG	PB	Sup	APR	PW
1902	Chi N	12	10	.545	22	21	20-3	0	197.1	201	81	1	6	26	60	2.42	112	.264	.293	216-14	.231	3*	122	8	1.1
1903	Chi N	8	10	.444	20	17	13-1	0	147	157	85	3	6	38	39	3.00	105	.275	.327	64-2	.203	1*	99	-1	0.1
Total	9	58	70	.453	139	125	111-6	0	1111.1	1289	707	19	45	273	293	3.81	101	.288	.335	685-35	.222	2	96	2	1.0
MENENDEZ, TONY Antonio Gustavo (Remon) B 2.20.1965 Havana, Cuba BR/TR 6-2/190# d6.22																									
1992	Cin N	1	0	1.000	3	0	0	0-0	4.2	1	1	1	0	0-0	5	1.93	187	.067	.067	0-0	—	0		1	0.2
1993	Pit N	2	0	1.000	14	0	0	0-0	21	20	8	4	1	4-0	13	3.00	135	.256	.298	1-0	.000	-0		2	0.2
1994	SF N	0	1	.000	6	0	0	0-1	3.1	8	8	2	0	2-0	2	21.60	19	.471	.526	0-0	—	0		-6	-1.2
Total	3	3	1	.750	23	0	0	0-1	29	29	17	7	1	6-0	20	4.97	80	.264	.305	1-0	.000	-0		-3	-0.8
MENHART, PAUL Paul Gerard B 3.25.1969 St.Louis, MO BR/TR 6-2/190# d4.27																									
1995	Tor A	1	4	.200	21	9	1	0-0	78.2	72	49	9	6	47-4	50	4.92	96	.248	.360	0-0	—	0	86	-2	-0.1
1996	Sea A	2	2	.500	11	6	0	0-0	42	55	36	9	2	25-0	18	7.29	68	.327	.421	0-0	—	0	122	-11	-0.8
1997	SD N	2	3	.400	9	8	0	0-0	44	42	23	6	0	13-0	22	4.70	83	.256	.309	12-2	.000	-1	139	-3	-0.4
Total	3	5	9	.357	41	23	1	0-0	164.2	169	108	24	8	85-4	90	5.47	83	.272	.364	12-2	.000	-1	111	-16	-1.3
MEOLA, MIKE Emile Michael B 10.19.1905 New York, NY D 9.1.1976 Fair Lawn, NJ BR/TR 5-11/175# d4.24																									
1933	Bos A	0	0	—	3	0	0	0	2.1	5	6	0	0	2	1	23.14	19	.417	.500	0-0	—	0		-4	-0.2
1936	StL A	0	1	.000	9	0	0	0	19.1	29	20	0	1	13	6	9.31	58	.358	.453	2-0	.500	1		-7	-0.2
	Bos A	0	2	.000	6	3	1	1	21.1	29	17	0	1	10	8	5.48	97	.326	.400	7-0	.143	-0	50	-1	-0.1
	Year	0	3	.000	15	3	1	1	40.2	58	20	0	2	23	14	7.30	73	.341	.426	9-0	.222	0	49	-8	-0.3
Total	2	0	3	.000	18	3	1	1	43	63	43	0	2	25	15	8.16	65	.346	.431	9-0	.222	0	50	-12	-0.5
MERCADO, HECTOR Hector Luis B 4.29.1974 Catano, P.R. BL/TL 6-3/205# d4.4																									
2000	Cin N	0	0	—	12	0	0	0-0	14	12	7	2	0	8-0	13	4.50	105	.240	.339	1-0	.000	-0		1	0.0
2001	Cin N	3	2	.600	56	0	0	0-2	53	55	27	6	0	30-1	59	4.08	112	.266	.356	2-0	.000	-0		3	0.2
2002	Phi N	2	2	.500	31	3	0	0-0	39	32	21	2	3	25-2	40	4.62	85	.224	.349	4-0	.250	0	95	-3	-0.3
2003	Phi N	0	0	—	13	0	0	1-1	18.2	18	12	5	1	12-0	15	5.79	69	.254	.360	2-0	.000	-0		-4	-0.2
Total	4	5	4	.556	112	3	0	1-3	124.2	117	67	15	4	75-3	127	4.55	94	.248	.353	9-0	.111	-0	95	-3	-0.3
MERCEDES, JOSE Jose Miguel (Santana) B 3.5.1971 ElSeibo, D.R. BR/TR 6-1/180# d5.31																									
1994	Mil A	2	0	1.000	19	0	0	0-1	31	22	9	4	2	16-1	11	2.32	217	.216	.333	0-0	—	0		9	0.5
1995	Mil A	0	1	.000	5	0	0	0-2	7.1	12	9	1	0	8-0	6	9.82	51	.375	.476	0-0	—	0		-4	-0.4
1996	Mil A	0	2	.000	11	0	0	0-1	16.2	20	18	6	0	5-0	6	9.18	57	.294	.338	0-0	—	0		-7	-0.7
1997	Mil A	7	10	.412	29	23	2-1	0-0	159	146	76	24	5	53-2	80	3.79	122	.248	.314	2-0	.000	-0	79	14	1.2
1998	Mil N	2	2	.500	7	5	0	0-0	32	42	25	5	1	9-1	11	6.75	63	.316	.359	11-0	.091	-0	95	-8	-0.9
2000	Bal A	14	7	.667	36	20	1	0-0	145.2	150	71	15	3	64-1	70	4.02	118	.270	.345	1-0	.000	-0	108	11	1.3
2001	Bal A	8	17	.320	33	31	2	0-0	184	219	125	20	10	63-3	123	5.82	74	.294	.354	5-0	.000	-0	90	-29	-3.4
2003	Mon N	0	0	—	5	0	0	0-0	7.1	6	3	0	0	5-0	3	0.00	—	.231	.355	0-0	—	0		2	0.1
Total	8	33	39	.458	145	79	5-1	0-4	583	617	336	75	21	223-8	310	4.75	96	.274	.342	19-0	.053	-1	90	-12	-2.3
MERCER, WIN George Barclay B 6.20.1874 Chester, WV D 1.12.1903 San Francisco, CA BR/TR 5-7/140# d4.21 ▲																									
1894	Was N	17	23	.425	50	39	30	3	339.1	445	285	9	14	126	72	3.85	137	.313	.375	165-1	.291	3*	95	41	3.8
1895	Was N	13	23	.361	44	38	32	2	313.1	432	281	17	18	96	85	4.42	109	.322	.376	201-5	.254	-0*	90	3	0.3
1896	Was N	25	18	.581	46	45	38-2	0	366.1	456	266	10	20	117	94	4.13	107	.302	.360	156-2	.244	0*	100	11	1.1
1897	Was N	21	20	.512	**47**	**43**	35-**3**	**3**	342	403	219	5	28	104	91	3.18	136	.291	.353	139-4	.317	8*	89	33	3.9
1898	Was N	12	18	.400	33	30	24	0	233.2	309	181	3	18	71	52	4.81	76	.316	.373	249-9	.321	8*	90	-30	-2.5
1899	Was N	7	14	.333	23	21	21	0	186	234	128	2	6	53	28	4.60	85	.307	.356	375-6	.299	5*	98	-13	-0.5
1900	NY N	13	17	.433	33	29	26-1	0	242.2	303	138	5	20	58	39	3.86	94	.305	.355	248-3	.294	7*	89	1	0.8
1901	Was A	9	13	.409	24	22	19-1	1	179.2	217	126	8	10	50	31	4.56	80	.295	.348	140-3	.300	6*	86	-16	-0.9
1902	Det A	15	18	.455	35	33	28-4	1	281.2	282	129	5	10	80	40	3.04	120	.261	.318	100-3	.180	-2	65	20	2.0
Total	9	132	164	.446	335	300	253-11	10	2484.2	3081	1753	64	144	755	532	3.98	107	.302	.358	1773-36	.285	35	90	50	8.0
MERCER, JACK Harry Vernon B 3.10.1889 Zanesville, OH D 6.25.1945 Dayton, OH d8.2																									
1910	Pit N	0	0	—	1	0	0	0	1	0	0	0	0	2	1	0.00	—	.000	.500	0-0	—	0		0	0.0
MERCER, MARK Mark Kenneth B 5.22.1954 Fort Bragg, NC BL/TL 6-5/220# d9.1																									
1981	Tex A	0	1	.000	7	0	0	2-1	7.2	7	4	1	0	7-0	8	4.70	74	.241	.389	0-0	—	0		-1	-0.2
MERCKER, KENT Kent Franklin B 2.1.1968 Indianapolis, IN BL/TL 6-2/195# d9.22																									
1989	Atl N	0	0	—	2	1	0	0-0	4.1	8	6	0	0	6-0	4	12.46	29	.400	.538	1-0	.000	-0	121	-4	-0.2
1990	Atl N	4	7	.364	36	0	0	7-3	48.1	43	22	6	2	24-3	39	3.17	128	.236	.329	3-0	.000	-0		3	0.6
1991	†Atl N	5	3	.625	50	4	0	6-2	73.1	56	23	5	1	35-3	62	2.58	151	.211	.303	10-0	.100	-0	87	11	1.2
1992	†Atl N	3	2	.600	53	0	0	6-3	68.1	51	27	4	3	35-1	49	3.42	107	.207	.312	5-0	.000	-0		3	0.1
1993	†Atl N	3	1	.750	43	6	0	0-3	66	52	24	2	2	36-3	59	2.86	140	.212	.318	13-0	.000	-1	75	8	0.2
1994	Atl N	9	4	.692	20	17	2-1	0-0	112.1	90	46	16	0	45-3	111	3.45	123	.220	.295	37-3	.054	-2	97	11	0.9
1995	†Atl N	7	8	.467	29	26	0	0-0	143	140	73	16	3	61-2	102	4.15	103	.258	.332	48-6	.104	-2	111	1	0.0
1996	Bal A	3	6	.333	14	12	0	0-0	58	73	56	12	3	35-1	22	7.76	64	.307	.396	0-0	—	0	99	-20	-2.3
	Cle A	1	0	1.000	10	0	0	0-0	11.2	10	4	1	0	3-1	7	3.09	159	.244	.283	0-0	—	0		3	0.2
	Year	4	6	.400	24	12	0	0-0	69.2	83	65	13	3	38-2	29	6.98	71	.297	.380	0-0	—	0	99	-17	-2.1
1997	Cin N	8	11	.421	28	25	0	0-0	144.2	135	65	16	2	62-6	75	3.92	109	.250	.327	45-4	.156	1*	67	7	0.9
1998	StL N	11	11	.500	30	29	0	0-0	161.2	199	99	11	3	53-4	72	5.07	83	.310	.361	54-5	.148	1*	121	-15	-1.7
1999	StL N	6	5	.545	25	18	0	0-0	103.2	125	73	16	2	51-3	64	5.12	89	.303	.380	28-4	.179	1*	118	-10	-0.8
	†Bos A	2	0	1.000	5	5	0	0-0	25.2	23	12	0	1	13-0	17	3.51	142	.235	.327	0-0	—	0	82	4	0.3
2000	Ana A	1	3	.250	21	7	0	0-0	48.1	57	35	12	2	29-3	30	6.52	78	.300	.396	0-0	—	0	106	-6	-0.4
2002	Col N	3	1	.750	58	0	0	0-3	44	55	33	12	2	22-2	37	6.14	78	.299	.380	1-0	.000	-0		-6	-0.5
2003	Cin N	0	2	.000	49	0	0	0-3	38.1	31	13	5	0	25-2	41	2.35	182	.225	.344	0-0	—	0		7	0.4
	†Atl N	0	0	—	18	0	0	1-1	17	15	3	1	0	7-2	7	1.06	399	.231	.301	1-0	.000	-0		6	0.2
	Year	0	2	.000	67	0	0	1-4	55.1	46	22	6	0	32-4	48	1.95	218	.227	.331	1-0	.000	-0		13	0.6
Total	14	66	64	.508	491	150	2-1	20-18	1168.2	1163	614	135	26	542-39	798	4.27	101	.261	.342	246-22	.114	-4	102	3	-0.9
MERENA, SPIKE John Joseph B 11.18.1909 Paterson, NJ D 3.9.1977 Bridgeport, CT BL/TL 6/185# d9.16																									
1934	Bos A	1	2	.333	4	3	2-1	0	24.2	20	8	2	1	16	7	2.92	165	.222	.346	7-2	.143	-0	60	5	0.5
MERIDITH, RON Ronald Knox B 11.26.1956 San Pedro, CA BL/TL 6/175# d9.16																									
1984	Chi N	0	0	—	3	0	0	0-0	5.1	6	5	1	0	2-1	4	3.38	116	.273	.320	0-0	—	0		-1	0.0
1985	Chi N	3	2	.600	32	0	0	1-3	46.1	53	24	3	1	24-6	23	4.47	90	.301	.382	4-0	.250	0		-2	-0.1
1986	Tex A	1	0	1.000	5	0	0	0-0	3	2	1	0	0	1-1	2	3.00	144	.286	.333	0-0	—	0		0	0.1
1987	Tex A	1	0	1.000	11	0	0	0-1	20.2	25	18	7	0	12-2	17	6.10	74	.298	.385	0-0	—	0		-5	-0.2
Total	4	5	2	.714	51	0	0	1-4	75.1	86	48	11	1	39-10	46	4.78	87	.298	.377	4-0	.250	0		-8	-0.2
MERRIMAN, BRETT Brett Alan B 7.15.1966 Jacksonville, IL BR/TR 6-2/180# d4.8																									
1993	Min A	1	1	.500	19	0	0	0-0	27	36	29	3	3	23-2	14	9.67	45	.343	.466	0-0	—	0		-15	-0.9
1994	Min A	0	1	.000	15	0	0	0-1	17	18	13	0	4	14-0	10	6.35	77	.269	.414	0-0	—	0		-3	-0.2
Total	2	1	2	.333	34	0	0	0-1	44	54	42	3	7	37-2	24	8.39	54	.314	.445	0-0	—	0		-18	-1.1
MERRITT, GEORGE George Washington B 4.14.1880 Paterson, NJ D 2.21.1938 Memphis, TN TR 6/160# d9.6 ▲																									
1901	Pit N	3	0	1.000	3	3	3	0	24	28	18	0	2	5	5	4.88	67	.289	.337	11-0	.273	1*	260	-4	-0.3
1903	Pit N	0	0	—	1	0	0	0	4	4	3	0	0	1	2	2.25	144	.267	.313	27-1	.148	0*		0	0.0
Total	2	3	0	1.000	4	3	3	0	28	32	21	0	2	6	7	4.50	73	.286	.333	38-1	.184	1	260	-4	-0.3
MERRITT, JIM James Joseph B 12.9.1943 Altadena, CA BL/TL 6-2/180# d8.2																									
1965	†Min A	5	4	.556	16	9	1	2	76.2	68	29	11	0	20-1	61	3.17	112	.239	.287	22-1	.136	0	121	4	0.6
1966	Min A	7	14	.333	31	18	5-1	3	144	112	57	17	0	33-3	124	3.38	107	.212	.257	39-2	.103	-1	64	6	0.8
1967	Min A	13	7	.650	37	28	11-4	0	227.2	196	72	21	7	30-6	161	2.53	137	.230	.260	74-3	.135	0	100	23	2.0
1968	Min A	12	16	.429	38	34	11-1	1	238.1	207	102	21	7	52-1	181	3.25	95	.232	.277	71-4	.141	0	99	-4	-0.4

Year	Tm Lg	W	L	Pct	G	GS	CG-Sho	SV-BS	IP	H	R	HR	HB	BB-IB	SO	ERA	AERA	OAV	OOB	AB-SH	AVG	PB	Sup	APR	PW
1969	Cin N	17	9	.654	42	36	8-1	0-0	251	269	127	33	5	61-8	144	4.37	86	.273	.316	77-15	.143	0	116	-11	-1.2
1970	†Cin N★	20	12	.625	35	35	12-1	0-0	234	248	114	21	1	53-12	136	4.08	99	.270	.310	83-6	.169	3	109	2	0.4
1971	Cin N	1	11	.083	28	11	0	0-0	107	115	55	14	3	31-8	38	4.37	77	.279	.332	29-2	.138	0*	62	-12	-1.3
1972	Cin N	1	0	1.000	4	1	0	0-0	8	13	4	1	0	2-1	4	4.50	71	.361	.395	2-0	.000	-0	55	-1	-0.1
1973	Tex A	5	13	.278	35	19	8-1	1-0	160	191	79	18	1	34-3	65	4.05	92	.296	.327	0-0	—	0	92	-4	-0.5
1974	Tex A	0	0	—	26	1	0	0-0	32.2	46	17	3	0	6-2	18	4.13	86	.329	.349	0-0	—	0	74	-2	-0.1
1975	Tex A	0	0	—	5	0	0	0-0	3.2	3	1	0	1	0-0	0	0.00	—	.214	.267	0-0	—	0		1	0.0
Total	11	81	86	.485	297	192	56-9	7-0	1483	1468	657	160	25	322-45	932	3.65	98	.257	.297	397-33	.141	3	99	2	0.2
MERRITT, LLOYD Lloyd Wesley B 4.8.1933 St.Louis, MO BR/TR 6/189# d4.22																									
1957	StL N	1	2	.333	44	0	0	7	65.1	60	29	7	4	28-5	35	3.31	120	.251	.337	7-0	.000	-0		4	0.2
MERTZ, JIM James Verlin B 8.10.1916 Lima, OH D 2.4.2003 Waycross, GA BR/TR 5-10.5/170# d5.1 Mil 1944-46																									
1943	Was A	5	7	.417	33	10	2	3	116.2	109	65	7	0	58	53	4.63	69	.251	.339	38-3	.184	0	166	-16	-1.6
MESA, JOSE Jose Ramon Nova (b: Jose Ramon Nova (Mesa)) B 5.22.1966 Pueblo Viejo, D.R. BR/TR 6-3/225# d9.10																									
1987	Bal A	1	3	.250	6	5	0	0-0	31.1	38	23	7	0	15-0	17	6.03	73	.297	.371	0-0	—	0	74	-6	-0.6
1990	Bal A	3	2	.600	7	7	0	0-0	46.2	37	20	2	1	27-2	24	3.86	99	.218	.325	0-0	—	0	106	0	0.0
1991	Bal A	6	11	.353	23	23	2-1	0-0	123.2	151	86	11	3	62-2	64	5.97	66	.307	.385	0-0	—	0*	113	-28	-3.2
1992	Bal A	3	8	.273	13	12	0	0-0	67.2	77	41	9	2	27-1	22	5.19	78	.287	.353	0-0	—	0	83	-8	-1.2
	Cle A	4	4	.500	15	15	1-1	0-0	93	92	45	5	2	43-0	40	4.16	94	.262	.344	0-0	—	0	118	-1	-0.1
	Year	7	12	.368	28	27	1-1	0-0	160.2	169	50	14	4	70-1	62	4.59	86	.273	.348	0-0	—	0	102	-8	-1.3
1993	Cle A	10	12	.455	34	33	3	0-0	208.2	232	122	21	7	62-2	118	4.92	88	.286	.339	0-0	—	0	103	-12	-1.1
1994	Cle A	7	5	.583	51	0	0	2-4	73	71	33	3	3	26-7	63	3.82	124	.254	.321	0-0	—	0		8	1.2
1995	†Cle A★	3	0	1.000	62	0	0	**46-2**	64	49	9	3	0	17-2	58	1.13	418	.216	.268	0-0	—	0		**25**	4.3
1996	†Cle A☆	2	7	.222	69	0	0	39-5	72.1	69	32	6	3	28-4	64	3.73	131	.257	.331	0-0	—	0		10	1.8
1997	†Cle A	4	4	.500	66	0	0	16-5	82.1	83	28	7	3	28-3	69	2.40	195	.259	.322	0-0	—	0		19	2.2
1998	Cle A	3	4	.429	44	0	0	1-2	54	61	36	7	4	20-3	35	5.17	92	.282	.351	0-0	—	0		-3	-0.4
	SF N	5	3	.625	32	0	0	0-1	30.2	30	14	1	0	18-2	28	3.52	113	.256	.356	0-0	—	0		1	0.2
1999	Sea A	3	6	.333	68	0	0	33-5	68.2	84	42	11	4	40-4	42	4.98	95	.305	.396	0-0	—	0		-2	-0.4
2000	†Sea A	4	6	.400	66	0	0	1-2	80.2	89	48	11	5	41-0	84	5.36	88	.280	.365	0-0	—	0		-4	-0.4
2001	Phi N	3	3	.500	71	0	0	42-4	69.1	65	26	4	2	20-2	59	2.34	182	.246	.301	0-0	—	0		12	2.3
2002	Phi N	4	6	.400	74	0	0	45-9	75.2	65	26	5	4	39-7	64	2.97	131	.231	.332	0-0	—	0		9	1.8
2003	Phi N	5	7	.417	61	0	0	24-4	58	71	44	7	1	31-2	45	6.52	61	.296	.379	0-0	—	0		-17	-3.3
Total	15	70	91	.435	762	95	6-2	249-43	1299.2	1364	675	120	44	544-43	896	4.32	100	.271	.345	0-0	—	0	99	3	3.1
MESSENGER, BUD Andrew Warren B 2.1.1898 Grand Blanc, MI D 11.4.1971 Lansing, MI BR/TR 6/175# d7.31																									
1924	Cle A	2	0	1.000	5	2	1	0	25	28	13	4	0	14	4	4.32	99	.283	.372	8-2	.125	-0	237	1	0.0
MESSERSMITH, ANDY John Alexander B 8.6.1945 Toms River, NJ BR/TR 6-1/200# d7.4																									
1968	Cal A	4	2	.667	28	5	2-1	4	81.1	44	21	3	1	35-4	74	2.21	132	.157	.252	20-4	.100	-1*	78	7	0.6
1969	Cal A	16	11	.593	40	33	10-2	2-0	250	169	81	17	5	100-7	211	2.52	138	**.190**	.274	77-6	.156	2*	101	28	3.2
1970	Cal A	11	10	.524	37	26	6-1	5-0	194.2	144	75	21	6	78-6	162	3.01	120	**.205**	.289	70-5	.157	0*	91	12	1.4
1971	Cal A☆	20	13	.606	38	38	14-4	0-0	276.2	224	112	16	7	121-6	179	2.99	108	.218	.303	93-6	.172	4*	103	4	1.0
1972	Cal A	8	11	.421	25	21	10-3	2-0	169.2	125	56	5	2	68-8	142	2.81	104	.207	.288	53-2	.189	2*	75	4	0.8
1973	LA N	14	10	.583	33	33	10-3	0-0	249.2	196	90	24	6	77-3	177	2.70	127	.214	.278	89-5	.169	2*	117	20	2.0
1974	†LA N★	**20**	6	**.769**	39	39	13-3	0-0	292.1	227	93	24	3	94-0	221	2.59	132	.212	**.277**	96-4	.240	9	119	30	3.8
1975	LA N☆	19	14	.576	42	**40**	**19-7**	1-0	**321.2**	244	92	22	5	96-2	213	2.29	149	**.213**	.275	108-5	.157	2*	93	**42**	4.5
1976	Atl N❖	11	11	.500	29	28	12-3	1-0	207.1	166	83	14	2	74-1	135	3.04	125	.219	.287	67-6	.179	0	85	15	1.6
1977	Atl N	5	4	.556	16	16	1	0-0	102.1	101	54	12	2	39-5	69	4.40	101	.256	.323	34-2	.118	-0	96	2	0.2
1978	NY A	0	3	.000	6	5	0	0-0	22.1	24	21	7	1	15-0	16	5.64	64	.267	.377	0-0	—	0	94	-8	-0.9
1979	LA N	2	4	.333	11	11	1	0-0	62.1	55	34	9	0	34-2	26	4.91	74	.244	.342	22-1	.091	-1	124	-7	-0.7
Total	12	130	99	.568	344	295	98-27	15-0	2230.1	1719	812	174	40	831-44	1625	2.86	121	.212	.287	729-46	.170	20	101	149	17.5
METCALF, TOM Thomas John B 7.16.1940 Amherst, WI BR/TR 6-2.5/174# d8.4																									
1963	NY A	1	0	1.000	8	0	0	0	13	12	4	1	0	3-1	3	2.77	127	.250	.294	0-0	—	0		1	0.1
METIVIER, DEWEY George Dewey B 5.6.1898 Cambridge, MA D 3.2.1947 Cambridge, MA BL/TR 5-11/175# d9.15																									
1922	Cle A	2	0	1.000	2	2	2	0	18	18	9	1	1	3	1	4.50	89	.265	.306	6-0	.167	-0	138	0	0.0
1923	Cle A	4	2	.667	26	5	1	1	73.1	111	66	1	6	38	9	6.50	61	.368	.448	20-0	.150	-0	159	-21	-1.5
1924	Cle A	1	5	.167	26	6	1	3	76.1	110	50	3	0	34	14	5.31	81	.358	.422	24-0	.125	-2	89	-6	-0.7
Total	3	7	7	.500	54	13	4	4	167.2	239	125	5	7	75	24	5.74	72	.353	.423	50-0	.140	-2	122	-27	-2.2
METZGER, BUTCH Clarence Edward B 5.23.1952 Lafayette, IN BR/TR 6-1/185# d9.8																									
1974	SF N	1	0	1.000	10	0	0	0-0	12.2	11	5	0	0	12-7	5	3.55	107	.239	.397	0-0	—	0		1	0.0
1975	SD N	1	0	1.000	4	0	0	0-0	4.2	6	4	1	0	4-1	6	7.71	45	.316	.417	0-0	—	0		-2	-0.4
1976	SD N	11	4	.733	77	0	0	16-8	123.1	119	44	5	3	52-14	89	2.92	112	.258	.335	8-2	.000	-0		6	0.8
1977	SD N	0	0	—	17	1	0	0-1	22.2	27	16	5	1	12-4	6	5.56	64	.307	.388	3-0	.000	-0	276	-6	-0.3
	StL N	4	2	.667	58	0	0	7-3	92.2	78	36	8	1	38-2	48	3.11	124	.228	.305	4-2	.000	-0		8	0.5
	Year	4	2	.667	75	1	0	7-4	115.1	105	63	13	2	50-6	54	3.59	106	.244	.323	7-2	.000	-1	258	2	0.2
1978	NY N	1	3	.250	25	0	0	0-0	37.1	48	28	4	1	22-7	21	6.51	54	.324	.406	0-0	—	0		-12	-1.2
Total	5	18	9	.667	191	1	0	23-12	293.1	289	133	23	6	140-35	175	3.74	94	.262	.344	15-4	.000	-1	276	-5	-0.6
MEYER, BRIAN Brian Scott B 1.29.1963 Camden, NJ BR/TR 6/190# d9.3																									
1988	Hou N	0	0	—	8	0	0	0-0	12.1	9	2	2	0	4-0	10	1.46	228	.225	.295	0-0	—	0		3	0.2
1989	Hou N	0	1	.000	12	0	0	1-0	18	16	13	0	1	13-3	13	4.50	75	.239	.366	0-1	—	0		-4	-0.2
1990	Hou N	0	4	.000	14	0	0	1-0	20.1	16	7	3	0	6-0	6	2.21	168	.211	.268	1-0	.000	-0		3	0.6
Total	3	0	5	.000	34	0	0	2-0	50.2	41	22	5	1	23-3	29	2.84	123	.224	.313	1-1	.000	-0		2	0.6
MEYER, JACK John Robert B 3.23.1932 Philadelphia, PA D 3.9.1967 Philadelphia, PA BR/TR 6-1/175# d4.16																									
1955	Phi N	6	11	.353	50	5	0	**16**	110.1	75	50	14	3	66-6	97	3.43	116	.190	.310	20-1	.100	0	67	6	0.9
1956	Phi N	7	11	.389	41	7	2	2	96	86	49	8	4	51-11	66	4.41	84	.242	.343	20-2	.200	1	51	-5	-0.8
1957	Phi N	0	2	.000	19	2	0	0	37.2	44	30	6	1	28-2	34	5.73	66	.297	.408	6-1	.167	0	139	-10	-0.4
1958	Phi N	3	6	.333	37	5	1	2	90.1	77	38	8	1	33-3	87	3.59	110	.232	.301	18-1	.278	1	136	5	0.5
1959	Phi N	5	3	.625	47	1	1	1	93.2	76	43	9	1	53-2	71	3.36	122	.222	.326	14-0	.071	-1	0	6	0.4
1960	Phi N	3	1	.750	7	4	0	0	25	25	13	2	0	11-0	18	4.32	90	.272	.336	8-1	.125	-0	97	-1	-0.1
1961	Phi N	0	0	—	1	0	0	0	2	2	2	1	0	2-0	2	9.00	45	.286	.444	0-0	—	0		-1	-0.1
Total	7	24	34	.414	202	24	4	21	455	385	225	48	10	244-24	375	3.92	100	.230	.330	86-6	.163	1	84	0	0.4
MEYER, BOB Robert Bernard B 8.4.1939 Toledo, OH BR/TL 6-2/185# d4.20																									
1964	NY A	0	3	.000	7	1	0	0	18.1	16	12	1	0	12-0	12	4.91	74	.235	.350	4-0	.000	-0	0	-3	-0.5
	LA A	1	1	.500	6	5	0	0	18	25	10	2	1	13-0	13	5.00	66	.333	.438	5-2	.000	-1	162	-3	-0.4
	KC A	1	4	.200	9	7	2	0	42	37	23	2	0	33-0	30	3.86	99	.248	.378	12-1	.000	-1*	77	-2	-0.3
	Year	2	8	.200	22	13	2	0	78.1	78	26	5	1	58-0	55	4.37	84	.267	.387	21-3	.000	-2	99	-7	-1.2
1969	Sea A	0	3	.000	6	5	1	0-0	32.2	30	14	4	2	10-0	17	3.31	110	.252	.316	11-0	.091	-1	73	1	0.0
1970	Mil A	0	1	.000	10	0	0	0-0	18.1	24	13	2	0	12-0	20	6.38	59	.329	.424	3-2	.333	0		-5	-0.2
Total	3	2	12	.143	38	18	3	0-0	129.1	132	72	11	3	80-0	92	4.38	84	.273	.376	35-5	.057	-3	92	-12	-1.4
MEYER, RUSS Russell Charles "Rowdy" or "The Mad Monk" B 10.25.1923 Peru, IL D 11.16.1998 Oglesby, IL BB/TR 6-1/185# d9.13 C1																									
1946	Chi N	0	0	—	4	1	0	1	17	21	7	2	0	10	10	3.18	104	.309	.397	5-0	.200	0	129	0	0.0
1947	Chi N	3	2	.600	23	2	1	0	45	43	17	4	1	14	22	3.40	116	.257	.319	12-0	.250	0	67	4	0.4
1948	Chi N	10	10	.500	29	26	8-3	0	164.2	157	75	8	1	77	89	3.66	107	.254	.338	56-7	.107	-3	107	6	0.3
1949	Phi N	17	8	.680	37	28	14-2	1	213	199	84	14	1	70	78	3.08	128	.250	.311	70-6	.143	-1	93	19	1.9
1950	†Phi N	9	11	.450	32	25	3	1	159.2	193	108	21	2	67	74	5.30	76	.304	.373	50-7	.140	-1	99	-23	-2.5
1951	Phi N	8	9	.471	28	24	7-2	0	168	172	69	13	2	55	65	3.48	111	.263	.322	48-13	.104	-2	112	8	0.4

Year	Tm Lg	W	L	Pct	G	GS	CG-Sho	SV-BS	IP	H	R	HR	HB	BB-IB	SO	ERA	AERA	OAV	OOB	AB-SH	AVG	PB	Sup	APR	PW
1952	Phi N	13	14	.481	37	32	14-1	1	232.1	235	99	10	2	65	92	3.14	116	.260	.311	79-5	.089	-2	110	12	0.9
1953	†Bro N	15	5	.750	34	32	10-2	0	191.1	201	109	25	1	63	106	4.56	93	.269	.327	75-6	.147	-2	143	-8	-1.0
1954	Bro N	11	6	.647	36	28	6-2	0	180.1	193	89	17	2	49	70	3.99	102	.275	.322	47-14	.043	-3	122	2	-0.3
1955	†Bro N	6	2	.750	18	11	2-1	0	73	86	46	8	0	31-6	26	5.42	75	.300	.364	27-2	.037	-3	171	-9	-1.1
1956	Chi N	1	6	.143	20	9	0	0	57	71	41	11	2	26-4	28	6.32	60	.313	.384	12-2	.083	-1	96	-14	-1.5
	Cin N	0	0	—	1	0	0	0	1	1	0	0	0	0-0	1	0.00	—	.250	.250	0-0	—	0		0	0.0
	Year	1	6	.143	21	9	0	0	58	72	45	11	2	26-4	29	6.21	61	.312	.382	12-2	.083	-1	96	-14	-1.5
1957	Bos A	0	0	—	2	1	0	0	5	10	5	0	0	3-0	1	5.40	74	.417	.464	1-0	1.000	0	90	-1	0.0
1959	KC A	1	0	1.000	18	0	0	1	24	24	12	3	1	11-0	10	4.50	89	.261	.340	2-0	.000	-0		0	-0.1
Total	13	94	73	.563	319	219	65-13	5	1531.1	1606	761	136	15	541-10	672	3.99	99	.271	.333	484-62	.114	-18	116	-4	-2.6
MEYERLE, LEVI Levi Samuel "Long Levi" B 7.1845 Philadelphia, PA D 11.4.1921 Philadelphia, PA BR/TR 6-1/177# d5.20 ▲																									
1871	Ath NA	0	0	—	1	0	0	0	1	1	1	0		2	0	9.00	45	.250	.500	130	.492	1*		0	0.0
1876	Phi N	0	2	.000	2	2	2	0	18	28	23	0		1	0	5.00	48	.337	.345	256	.340	1*	64	-4	-0.3
MIADICH, BART John Barton B 2.3.1976 Torrance, CA BR/TR 6-4/205# d9.2																									
2001	Ana A	0	0	—	11	0	0	0-0	10	6	5	2	0	8-0	11	4.50	101	.182	.341	0-0	—	0		0	0.0
2003	Ana A	0	0	—	1	0	0	0-0	2	5	4	0	1	1-0	3	18.00	24	.500	.583	0-0	—	0		-3	-0.1
Total	2	0	0	—	12	0	0	0-0	12	11	9	2	1	9-0	14	6.75	67	.256	.396	0-0	—	0		-3	-0.1
MICELI, DAN Daniel B 9.9.1970 Newark, NJ BR/TR 6/207# d9.9																									
1993	Pit N	0	0	—	9	0	0	0-0	5.1	6	3	0	0	3-0	4	5.06	80	.273	.360	0-0	—	0		-1	0.0
1994	Pit N	2	1	.667	28	0	0	2-1	27.1	28	19	5	2	11-2	27	5.93	73	.267	.342	3-0	.000	-0		-4	-0.5
1995	Pit N	4	4	.500	58	0	0	21-6	58	61	30	7	4	28-5	56	4.66	93	.270	.355	1-0	.000	-0		-1	-0.2
1996	Pit N	2	10	.167	44	9	0	1-0	85.2	99	65	15	3	45-5	66	5.78	76	.291	.372	13-0	.000	-1	87	-15	-2.0
1997	Det A	3	2	.600	71	0	0	3-5	82.2	77	49	13	1	38-4	79	5.01	92	.248	.330	0-0	—	0		-4	-0.2
1998	†SD N	10	5	.667	67	0	0	2-6	72.2	64	28	6	1	27-4	70	3.22	122	.238	.308	1-0	1.000	1		6	1.2
1999	SD N	4	5	.444	66	0	0	2-2	68.2	67	39	7	2	36-5	59	4.46	94	.266	.360	1-0	.000	-0		-3	-0.4
2000	Fla N	6	4	.600	45	0	0	0-3	48.2	45	23	4	1	18-2	40	4.25	104	.242	.311	0-0	—	0		2	0.3
2001	Fla N	0	5	.000	29	0	0	0-3	24.2	29	21	5	0	11-2	31	6.93	61	.287	.354	0-0	—	0		-8	-1.4
	Col N	2	0	1.000	22	0	0	1-0	20.1	18	8	2	0	5-0	17	2.21	241	.231	.274	0-0	—	0		5	0.4
	Year	2	5	.286	51	0	0	1-3	45	47	33	7	0	16-2	48	4.80	98	.263	.320	0-0	—	0		-2	-1.0
2002	Tex A	0	2	.000	9	0	0	0-1	8.1	13	8	1	0	3-0	5	8.64	55	.333	.381	0-0	—	0		-3	-0.6
2003	Col N	0	2	.000	14	0	0	0-0	20.2	24	13	7	1	9-1	18	5.66	87	.286	.362	0-0	—	0		-1	-0.1
	Cle A	1	1	.500	13	0	0	0-1	15	9	4	1	0	6-1	19	1.20	368	.164	.246	0-0	—	0		5	0.6
	NY A	0	0	—	7	0	0	1-0	4.2	4	3	2	0	3-0	1	5.79	76	.211	.318	0-0	—	0		-1	0.0
	Year	1	1	.500	20	0	0	1-1	19.2	13	7	3	0	9-1	20	2.29	193	.176	.265	0-0	—	0		4	0.6
	Hou N	1	1	.500	23	0	0	0-0	30	22	7	3	1	7-1	20	2.10	211	.208	.263	1-0	.000	-0		8	0.4
Total	11	35	42	.455	505	9	0	33-28	572.2	566	320	78	16	250-32	512	4.59	95	.258	.335	20-0	.050	-2	87	-15	-2.5
MICHAELS, JOHN John Joseph B 7.10.1907 Bridgeport, CT D 11.18.1996 Sebring, FL BL/TL 5-10.5/154# d4.16																									
1932	Bos A	1	6	.143	28	8	2	0	80.2	101	59	4	3	27	16	5.13	88	.304	.362	21-0	.143	-1*	71	-7	-0.6
MICHAELSON, JOHN John August "Mike" B 8.12.1893 Tivalkoski, Finland D 4.16.1968 Woodruff, WI BR/TR 5-9/165# d8.28																									
1921	Chi A	0	0	—	2	0	0	0	2.2	4	3	0	0	1	1	10.13	42	.400	.455	0-0	—	0		-2	-0.1
MICHALAK, CHRIS Christian Matthew B 1.4.1971 Joliet, IL BL/TL 6-2/195# d8.22																									
1998	Ari N	0	0	—	5	0	0	0-0	5.1	9	7	1	0	4-0	5	11.81	36	.375	.448	0-0	—	0		-4	-0.2
2001	Tor A	6	7	.462	24	18	0	0-0	115	133	66	14	12	49-5	57	4.62	100	.296	.377	3-2	.333	1	84	-1	0.1
	Tex A	2	2	.500	11	0	0	1-1	21.2	24	8	5	1	6-0	10	3.32	141	.279	.333	0-0	—	0		3	0.6
	Year	8	9	.471	35	18	0	1-1	136.2	157	78	19	13	55-5	67	4.41	104	.293	.371	3-2	.333	1	84	3	0.7
2002	Tex A	0	2	.000	13	0	0	0-0	14.1	20	7	1	1	10-2	5	4.40	108	.339	.437	0-0	—	0		1	0.1
Total	3	8	11	.421	53	18	0	1-1	156.1	186	88	21	14	69-7	77	4.66	99	.301	.380	3-2	.333	1	84	-1	0.6
MICKENS, GLENN Glenn Roger B 7.26.1930 Wilmar, CA BR/TR 6/175# d7.19																									
1953	Bro N	0	1	.000	4	2	0	0	6.1	11	9	2	0	4	5	11.37	37	.393	.469	2-0	.000	-0	178	-5	-0.7
MIDDLEBROOK, JASON Jason Douglas B 6.26.1975 Jackson, MI BR/TR 6-3/215# d9.17																									
2001	SD N	2	1	.667	4	3	0	0-0	19.1	18	11	6	1	10-1	10	5.12	78	.247	.345	7-0	.143	-0	131	-2	-0.3
2002	SD N	1	3	.250	12	2	0	0-0	35.1	31	20	1	1	15-2	28	5.09	74	.244	.322	6-1	.333	1	86	-5	-0.4
	NY N	1	0	1.000	3	3	0	0-0	16	13	7	1	0	7-0	14	3.94	101	.220	.303	5-0	.000	-0	109	0	0.0
	Year	2	3	.400	15	5	0	0-0	51.1	44	12	2	1	22-2	42	4.73	81	.237	.316	11-1	.182	0	101	-4	-0.4
2003	NY N	0	0	—	5	0	0	0-0	7	13	8	0	0	4-0	3	10.29	40	.433	.486	0-0	—	0		-5	-0.2
Total	3	4	4	.500	24	8	0	0-0	77.2	75	46	8	2	36-3	55	5.33	73	.260	.341	18-1	.167	0	113	-12	-0.9
MIDDLETON, JIM James Blaine "Rifle Jim" B 5.28.1889 Argos, IN D 1.12.1974 Argos, IN BR/TR 5-11.5/165# d4.18																									
1917	NY N	1	1	.500	13	0	0	1	36	35	18	1	1	8	9	2.75	93	.255	.301	8-0	.000	-1		-3	-0.3
1921	Det A	6	11	.353	38	10	2	**7**	121.2	149	83	5	2	44	31	5.03	85	.302	.361	34-4	.147	-2	117	-9	-1.3
Total	2	7	12	.368	51	10	2	8	157.2	184	101	6	3	52	40	4.51	86	.292	.348	42-4	.119	-3	117	-12	-1.6
MIDDLETON, JOHN John Wayne "Lefty" B 4.11.1900 Mt.Calm, TX D 11.3.1986 Amarillo, TX BL/TL 6-1/185# d9.6																									
1922	Cle A	0	1	.000	2	1	0	0	7.1	8	7	1	0	6	2	7.36	54	.286	.412	3-0	.333	0	106	-3	-0.3
MIDKIFF, DICK Richard B 9.28.1914 Gonzales, TX D 10.30.1956 Temple, TX BR/TR 6-2/185# d4.24																									
1938	Bos A	1	1	.500	13	2	0	0	35.1	43	30	5	0	21	10	5.09	97	.305	.395	10-0	.200	0	107	-4	-0.2
MIELKE, GARY Gary Roger B 1.28.1963 St.James, MN BR/TR 6-3/185# d8.19																									
1987	Tex A	0	0	—	3	0	0	0-0	3	3	2	2	0	1-0	3	6.00	75	.250	.308	0-0	—	0		0	0.0
1989	Tex A	1	0	1.000	43	0	0	1-1	49.2	52	18	4	2	25-3	26	3.26	122	.280	.369	0-0	—	0		5	0.2
1990	Tex A	0	3	.000	33	0	0	0-1	41	42	17	4	2	15-5	13	3.73	105	.271	.343	0-0	—	0		2	0.1
Total	3	1	3	.250	79	0	0	1-2	93.2	97	37	10	4	41-8	42	3.56	112	.275	.356	0-0	—	0		7	0.3
MIKKELSEN, PETE Peter James B 10.25.1939 Staten Island, NY BR/TR 6-2/220# d4.17																									
1964	†NY A	7	4	.636	50	0	0	12	86	79	35	3	4	41-5	63	3.56	102	.247	.338	16-4	.063	-1		2	0.2
1965	NY A	4	9	.308	41	3	0	1	82.1	78	40	10	3	36-9	69	3.28	104	.249	.332	10-1	.100	-0	9	-2	-0.2
1966	Pit N	9	8	.529	71	0	0	14	126	106	45	8	5	51-9	76	3.07	116	.234	.318	20-2	.150	-0		8	1.3
1967	Pit N	1	2	.333	32	0	0	2	56.1	50	29	7	3	19-5	30	4.31	78	.237	.308	4-2	.000	-0		-5	-0.4
	Chi N	0	0	—	7	0	0	0	7	9	6	1	1	5-0	0	6.43	55	.333	.455	0-0	—	0		-2	-0.1
	Year	1	2	.333	39	0	0	2	63.1	59	35	8	4	24-5	30	4.55	74	.248	.326	4-2	.000	-0		-7	-0.5
1968	Chi N	0	0	—	3	0	0	0	4.2	7	4	3	0	1-0	5	7.71	41	.350	.381	1-0	1.000	0		-2	-0.1
	StL N	0	0	—	5	0	0	0	16	10	5	0	0	7-3	8	1.13	257	.179	.270	3-0	.000	-0		2	0.1
	Year	0	0	—	8	0	0	0	20.2	17	9	3	0	8-3	13	2.61	113	.224	.298	4-0	.250	0		0	0.0
1969	LA N	7	5	.583	48	0	0	4-0	81.1	57	34	9	4	30-8	51	2.77	120	.193	.277	6-1	.167	-0		3	0.4
1970	LA N	4	2	.667	33	0	0	6-3	62	48	20	5	4	20-4	47	2.76	139	.211	.286	6-1	.333	1		8	1.0
1971	LA N	8	5	.615	41	0	0	5-6	74	67	38	10	1	17-5	46	3.65	89	.242	.286	10-0	.200	0		-6	-1.0
1972	LA N	5	5	.500	33	0	0	5-1	57.2	65	32	3	5	23-4	41	4.06	82	.283	.360	7-0	.000	-0		-5	-1.0
Total	9	45	40	.529	364	3	0	49-10	653.1	576	288	59	30	250-52	436	3.38	102	.237	.315	83-11	.133	-2	9	1	0.2
MIKLOS, HANK John Joseph B 11.27.1910 Chicago, IL D 3.29.2000 Adrian, MI BL/TL 5-11/175# d4.23																									
1944	Chi N	0	0	—	2	0	0	0	7	9	6	1	0	3	0	7.71	46	.333	.400	2-0	.000	-0		-3	-0.1
MILACKI, BOB Robert B 7.28.1964 Trenton, NJ BR/TR 6-4/234# d9.18																									
1988	Bal A	2	0	1.000	3	3	1-1	0-0	25	9	2	1	0	9-0	18	0.72	543	.110	.198	0-0	—	0	70	9	0.8
1989	Bal A	14	12	.538	37	**36**	3-2	0-0	243	233	105	21	2	88-4	113	3.74	102	.254	.318	0-0	—	0	94	3	0.3
1990	Bal A	5	8	.385	27	24	1-1	0-0	135.1	143	73	18	0	61-2	60	4.46	85	.273	.346	0-0	—	0	93	-11	-0.9
1991	Bal A	10	9	.526	31	26	3-1	0-0	184	175	86	17	1	53-3	108	4.01	99	.253	.305	0-0	—	0	93	0	0.0

Year	Tm Lg	W	L	Pct	G	GS	CG-Sho	SV-BS	IP	H	R	HR	HB	BB-IB	SO	ERA	AERA	OAV	OOB	AB-SH	AVG	PB	Sup	APR	PW
1992	Bal A	6	8	.429	23	20	0	1-0	115.2	140	78	16	2	44-2	51	5.84	69	.296	.356	0-0	—	0	102	-22	-2.4
1993	Cle A	1	1	.500	5	2	0	0-0	16	19	8	3	0	11-0	7	3.38	129	.302	.405	0-0	—	0	42	1	0.1
1994	KC A	0	5	.000	10	10	0	0-0	55.2	68	43	6	1	20-3	17	6.14	82	.298	.352	0-0	—	0	90	-7	-0.5
1996	Sea A	1	4	.200	7	4	0	0-0	21	30	20	3	0	15-3	13	6.86	72	.330	.425	0-0	—	0	112	-6	-1.0
Total	8	39	47	.453	143	125	8-5	1-0	795.2	817	415	85	6	301-17	387	4.38	91	.266	.330	0-0	—	0	94	-33	-3.6
MILCHIN, MIKE Michael Wayne B 2.28.1968 Knoxville, TN BL/TL 6-3/190# d5.14																									
1996	Min A	2	1	.667	26	0	0	0-1	21.2	31	21	6	0	12-1	19	8.31	62	.341	.417	0-0	—	0		-7	-0.8
	Bal A	1	0	1.000	13	0	0	0-0	11	13	7	0	0	5-1	10	5.73	86	.325	.375	0-0	—	0		-1	0.0
	Year	3	1	.750	39	0	0	0-1	32.2	44	32	6	0	17-2	29	7.44	68	.336	.404	0-0	—	0		-8	-0.8
MILES, CARL Carl Thomas B 3.22.1918 Trenton, MO BB/TL 5-11/178# d6.8																									
1940	Phi A	0	0	—	2	0	0	0	8	9	12	2	0	8	6	13.50	33	.281	.425	4-0	.750	2		-7	-0.2
MILES, JIM James Charlie B 8.8.1943 Grenada, MS BR/TR 6-2/210# d9.7																									
1968	Was A	0	0	—	3	0	0	0	4.1	8	6	0	0	2-0	5	12.46	23	.421	.455	0-0	—	0		-4	-0.2
1969	Was A	0	1	.000	10	1	0	0-0	20.1	19	15	2	4	15-1	15	6.20	56	.257	.400	3-0	.333	0*	76	-6	-0.2
Total	2	0	1	.000	13	1	0	0-0	24.2	27	21	2	4	17-1	20	7.30	46	.290	.410	3-0	.333	0	76	-10	-0.4
MILITELLO, SAM Sam Salvatore B 11.26.1969 Tampa, FL BR/TR 6-3/200# d8.9																									
1992	NY A	3	3	.500	9	9	0	0-0	60	43	24	6	2	32-1	42	3.45	114	.195	.302	0-0	—	0	101	4	0.3
1993	NY A	1	1	.500	3	2	0	0-0	9.1	10	8	1	2	7-1	5	6.75	62	.270	.413	0-0	—	0	111	-3	-0.5
Total	2	4	4	.500	12	11	0	0-0	69.1	53	32	7	4	39-2	47	3.89	102	.205	.319	0-0	—	0	103	1	-0.2
MILJUS, JOHNNY John Kenneth "Jovo" or "Big Serb" B 6.30.1895 Pittsburgh, PA D 2.11.1976 Fort Harrison, MT BR/TR 6-1/178# d10.2 Mil 1918																									
1915	Pit F	0	0	—	1	0	0	0	1	1	0	0	0	0	0	0.00	—	.250	.250	0-0	—	0		0	0.0
1917	Bro N	0	1	.000	4	1	1	0	15	14	3	0	3	8	9	0.60	466	.250	.373	5-0	.000	-1	27	3	0.1
1920	Bro N	1	0	1.000	9	0	0	0	23.1	24	10	2	0	4	9	3.09	104	.267	.298	6-0	.333	1*		0	0.2
1921	Bro N	6	3	.667	28	9	3	1	93.2	115	49	1	2	27	37	4.23	92	.312	.362	30-0	.167	-2	106	-2	-0.3
1927	†Pit N	8	3	.727	19	6	3-2	0	75.2	62	21	0	0	17	24	1.90	216	.228	.273	28-1	.179	-1	79	17	2.3
1928	Pit N	5	7	.417	21	10	3	1	69.2	90	48	2	3	33	26	5.30	77	.313	.389	26-0	.308	1	94	-9	-1.3
	Cle A	1	4	.200	11	4	1	1	50.2	46	25	1	0	20	19	2.66	156	.243	.316	15-0	.200	-0	51	5	0.5
1929	Cle A	8	8	.500	34	15	4	2	128.1	174	93	10	3	64	42	5.19	86	.331	.406	43-2	.256	1	96	-12	-1.1
Total	7	29	26	.527	127	45	15-2	5	457.1	526	249	16	11	173	166	3.92	104	.293	.359	153-3	.222	0	92	2	0.4
MILLER, DYAR Dyar K B 5.29.1946 Batesville, IN BR/TR 6-1/195# d6.9 C2																									
1975	Bal A	6	3	.667	30	0	0	8-4	46.1	32	14	3	0	16-4	33	2.72	129	.199	.267	0-0	—	0		5	1.0
1976	Bal A	2	4	.333	49	0	0	7-3	88.2	79	31	5	1	36-5	37	2.94	111	.246	.321	0-0	—	0		4	0.3
1977	Bal A	2	2	.500	12	0	0	1-1	22.1	25	14	6	0	10-1	9	5.64	67	.278	.350	0-0	—	0		-4	-0.7
	Cal A	4	4	.500	41	0	0	4-3	92.1	81	35	10	0	30-7	49	3.02	130	.242	.300	0-0	—	0		10	0.8
	Year	6	6	.500	53	0	0	5-4	114.2	106	53	16	0	40-8	58	3.53	111	.249	.311	0-0	—	0		6	0.1
1978	Cal A	6	2	.750	41	0	0	1-0	84.2	85	29	3	5	41-3	34	2.66	136	.264	.352	0-0	—	0		9	0.7
1979	Cal A	1	0	1.000	14	1	0	0-0	35.1	44	14	2	2	13-0	16	3.31	123	.319	.376	0-0	—	0	111	3	0.1
	Tor A	0	0	—	10	0	0	0-0	15.1	27	18	3	0	5-0	7	10.57	41	.391	.427	0-0	—	0		-9	-0.4
	Year	1	0	1.000	24	1	0	0-0	50.2	71	37	5	2	18-0	23	5.51	76	.343	.392	0-0	—	0	109	-6	-0.3
1980	NY N	1	2	.333	31	0	0	1-1	42	37	9	1	0	11-3	28	1.93	185	.242	.289	1-1	.000	-0		8	0.5
1981	NY N	1	0	1.000	23	0	0	0-1	38.1	49	20	2	1	15-2	22	3.29	106	.327	.387	3-0	.333	0		-1	0.0
Total	7	23	17	.575	251	1	0	22-13	465.1	459	184	35	9	177-25	235	3.23	113	.264	.331	4-1	.250	0	122	25	2.3
MILLER, ELMER Elmer Joseph "Lefty" B 4.17.1903 Detroit, MI D 1.8.1987 Corona, CA BL/TL 5-11/189# d6.21 ▲																									
1929	Phi N	0	1	.000	8	2	0	0	11.1	12	18	1	3	21	5	11.12	47	.279	.537	38-0	.237	0*	118	-8	-0.5
MILLER, FRANK Frank Lee "Bullet" B 5.13.1886 Allegan, MI D 2.19.1974 Allegan, MI BR/TR 6/188# d7.12																									
1913	Chi A	0	1	.000	1	1	0	0	1.2	4	5	0	0	3	2	27.00	11	.571	.700	0-0	—	0	0	-4	-0.6
1916	Pit N	7	10	.412	30	20	10-2	1	173	135	55	4	7	49	88	2.29	117	.226	.292	51-7	.137	-1	97	9	0.8
1917	Pit N	10	19	.345	38	28	14-5	1	224	216	98	1	5	60	92	3.13	91	.251	.304	76-5	.118	-4*	76	-7	-1.4
1918	Pit N	11	8	.579	23	23	14-2	0	170.1	152	60	1	7	37	47	2.38	121	.250	.301	57-7	.105	-3	109	9	0.6
1919	Pit N	13	12	.520	32	26	16-3	0	201.2	170	79	6	5	34	59	3.03	99	.234	.272	66-6	.106	-5	106	0	-0.5
1922	Bos N	11	13	.458	31	23	14-2	1	200	213	100	7	2	60	65	3.51	114	.279	.333	68-5	.118	-5	85	10	0.6
1923	Bos N	0	3	.000	8	6	0	1	39.1	54	26	2	3	11	6	4.58	87	.335	.389	7-1	.143	-0	93	-3	-0.3
Total	7	52	66	.441	163	127	68-14	4	1010	944	423	21	29	254	359	3.01	104	.253	.306	325-31	.117	-18	92	14	-0.8
MILLER, FRED Frederick Holman "Speedy" B 6.28.1886 Fairfield, IN D 5.2.1953 Brookville, IN BL/TL 6-2/190# d7.8																									
1910	Bro N	1	1	.500	6	2	0	0	21	25	19	1	3	13	2	4.71	64	.309	.423	8-0	.250	0	86	-6	-0.4
MILLER, BERT Herbert A. B 10.26.1875 Riley, MI D 6.14.1937 Flint, MI d7.15																									
1897	Lou N	0	1	.000	4	1	1	0	17	32	23	0	0	3	3	7.94	54	.395	.417	6-0	.167	-1	0	-7	-0.3
MILLER, OX John Anthony B 5.4.1915 Gause, TX BR/TR 6-1/190# d8.7																									
1943	Was A	0	0	—	3	0	0	0	6	10	7	1	0	5	1	10.50	31	.370	.469	1-0	.000	-0		-4	-0.2
	StL A	0	0	—	2	0	0	0	6	7	8	2	2	3	3	12.00	28	.304	.429	1-0	.000	-0		-5	-0.2
	Year	0	0	—	5	0	0	0	12	17	15	3	2	8	4	11.25	29	.340	.450	2-0	.000	-0		-10	-0.4
1945	StL A	2	1	.667	4	3	3	0	28.1	23	5	2	0	5	4	1.59	222	.219	.255	11-1	.182	-0*	65	6	0.6
1946	StL A	1	3	.250	11	3	0	1	35.1	52	28	5	0	15	12	6.88	54	.338	.396	7-1	.286	1	100	-10	-1.0
1947	Chi N	1	2	.333	4	4	1	0	16	31	18	2	0	5	7	10.13	39	.397	.434	7-0	.429	2	101	-10	-1.2
Total	4	4	6	.400	24	10	4	1	91.2	123	66	12	2	33	27	6.38	57	.318	.374	27-2	.259	2	92	-23	-2.0
MILLER, JOHN John Ernest B 5.30.1941 Baltimore, MD BR/TR 6-2/210# d9.22																									
1962	Bal A	1	1	.500	2	1	0	0	10	2	1	0	0	5-0	4	0.90	411	.065	.194	3-0	.000	-0	0	3	0.7
1963	Bal A	1	1	.500	3	2	0	0	17	12	6	0	0	14-0	16	3.18	109	.194	.342	6-0	.000	-1	90	1	0.0
1965	Bal A	6	4	.600	16	16	1	0	93.1	75	38	4	1	58-0	71	3.18	109	.223	.336	30-1	.100	-1	120	3	0.3
1966	Bal A	4	8	.333	23	16	0	0	100.2	92	59	15	0	58-3	81	4.74	70	.241	.340	34-4	.118	-1	104	-16	-1.9
1967	Bal A	0	0	—	2	0	0	0	6	7	5	1	2	3-0	6	7.50	42	.304	.429	0-0	—	0		-3	-0.1
Total	5	12	14	.462	46	35	1	0	227	188	109	20	3	138-3	178	3.89	88	.225	.336	73-5	.096	-3	108	-12	-1.0
MILLER, CYCLONE Joseph H. B 9.24.1859 Springfield, MA D 10.13.1916 New London, CT TL 5-9.5/165# d7.11																									
1884	CP U	1	0	1.000	1	1	1	0	9	4	2	0		0	13	1.00	244	.125	.125	4	.250	-0	175	1	0.1
	Pro N	3	2	.600	6	5	2	0	34.2	36	24	0		11	12	2.08	137	.259	.313	23	.043	-3	149	1	-0.1
	Phi N	0	1	.000	1	1	1	0	9	17	19	5		6	1	10.00	30	.386	.460	4	.000	-1	124	-7	-0.5
	Year	3	3	.500	7	6	3	0	43.2	53	26	5		17	13	3.71	78	.290	.350	27	.037	-4	144	-6	-0.6
1886	Phi AA	10	8	.556	19	19	19-1	0	169.2	158	109	6	4	59	99	2.97	118	.239	.305	66	.136	-1*	84	7	0.6
Total	2	14	11	.560	27	26	23-1	0	222.1	215	154	11	4	76	125	3.04	110	.245	.308	97	.113	-5	100	2	0.1
MILLER, JUSTIN Justin Mark B 8.27.1977 Torrance, CA BR/TR 6-2/209# d4.12																									
2002	Tor A	9	5	.643	25	18	0	0-0	102.1	103	70	12	11	66-2	68	5.54	83	.268	.385	2-0	.000	-0	95	-11	-1.3
MILLER, WHITEY Kenneth Albert B 5.2.1915 St.Louis, MO D 4.3.1991 St.Louis, MO BR/TR 6-1/195# d9.15																									
1944	NY N	0	1	.000	4	0	0	0	5	1	2	0	0	4	2	0.00	—	.059	.238	1-0	.000	-0*		1	0.2
MILLER, KURT Kurt Everett B 8.24.1972 Tucson, AZ BR/TR 6-5/205# d6.11																									
1994	Fla N	1	3	.250	4	4	0	0-0	20	26	18	3	2	7-0	11	8.10	54	.317	.380	6-1	.167	-0	57	-7	-1.1
1996	Fla N	1	3	.250	26	5	0	0-2	46.1	57	41	5	2	33-8	30	6.80	60	.313	.422	8-1	.375	1	173	-16	-1.1
1997	Fla N	0	1	.000	7	0	0	0-0	7.1	12	8	2	1	7-0	7	9.82	41	.364	.488	0-0	—	0		-5	-0.5
1998	Chi N	0	0	—	3	0	0	0-0	4	3	0	0	0	0-0	6	0.00	—	.200	.200	0-0	—	0		2	0.1
1999	Chi N	0	0	—	4	0	0	0-0	3	6	6	1	0	3-0	1	18.00	25	.462	.563	0-0	—	0		-4	-0.2
Total	5	2	7	.222	44	9	0	0-2	80.2	104	73	11	5	50-8	55	7.48	56	.320	.416	14-2	.286	1	121	-30	-2.8

Year	Tm Lg	W	L	Pct	G	GS	CG-Sho	SV-BS	IP	H	R	HR	HB	BB-IB	SO	ERA	AERA	OAV	OOB	AB-SH	AVG	PB	Sup	APR	PW
MILLER, LARRY Larry Don B 6.19.1937 Topeka, KS BL/TL 6/195# d6.21																									
1964	LA N	4	8	.333	16	14	1	0	79.2	87	44	1	2	28-4	50	4.18	78	.275	.334	26-2	.269	2	107	-9	-1.1
1965	NY N	1	4	.200	28	5	0	0	57.1	66	32	6	1	25-0	36	5.02	70	.289	.357	11-0	.182	0	40	-8	-0.6
1966	NY N	0	2	.000	4	1	0	0	8.1	9	7	3	0	4-0	7	7.56	48	.273	.351	2-0	.500	0	0	-3	-0.6
Total	3	5	14	.263	48	20	1	0	145.1	162	83	10	3	57-4	93	4.71	72	.281	.344	39-2	.256	2	82	-20	-2.3
MILLER, RED Leo Alphonso B 2.11.1897 Philadelphia, PA D 10.20.1973 Orlando, FL BR/TR 5-11/195# d7.13																									
1923	Phi N	0	0	—	1	0	0	0	1.2	6	6	0	0	1	0	32.40	14	.545	.583	1-0	.000	-0		-4	-0.2
MILLER, MATT Matt Jacob B 11.23.1971 Greenwood, MS BR/TR 6-3/210# d6.27																									
2003	Col N	0	0	—	4	0	0	0-0	4.1	5	1	0	0	2-0	5	2.08	237	.313	.389	0-0	—	0		1	0.1
MILLER, MATT Matthew Lincoln B 8.2.1974 Lubbock, TX BL/TL 6-3/175# d5.8																									
2001	Det A	0	0	—	13	0	0	0-0	9.2	16	8	0	1	4-0	6	7.45	58	.372	.438	0-0	—	0		-3	-0.1
2002	Det A	0	0	—	2	0	0	0-1	0.2	4	2	1	0	1-0	1	13.50	32	.571	.625	0-0	—	0		-1	-0.1
Total	2	0	0	—	15	0	0	0-1	10.1	20	10	1	1	5-0	7	7.84	55	.400	.464	0-0	—	0		-4	-0.2
MILLER, PAUL Paul Robert B 4.27.1965 Burlington, WI BR/TR 6-5/215# d7.30																									
1991	Pit N	0	0	—	1	1	0	0-0	5	4	3	0	0	3-0	2	5.40	66	.222	.333	3-0	.000	-0	75	-1	-0.1
1992	Pit N	1	0	1.000	6	0	0	0-0	11.1	11	3	0	0	1-0	5	2.38	145	.256	.267	3-0	.000	-0		1	0.1
1993	Pit N	0	0	—	3	2	0	0-0	10	15	6	2	0	2-0	2	5.40	75	.349	.378	2-0	.000	-0	100	-1	-0.1
Total	3	1	0	1.000	10	3	0	0-0	26.1	30	12	2	0	6-0	9	4.10	90	.288	.324	8-0	.000	-1	98	-1	-0.1
MILLER, RALPH Ralph Darwin B 3.15.1873 Cincinnati, OH D 5.8.1973 Cincinnati, OH BR/TR 5-11/170# d5.4 b-Bing																									
1898	Bro N	4	14	.222	23	21	16	0	151.2	161	119	4	13	86	43	5.34	67	.270	.374	62-1	.194	-1*	85	-27	-2.6
1899	Bal N	1	3	.250	6	4	3	1	37	44	28	0	4	14	3	4.38	91	.295	.371	11-0	.182	1	86	-2	-0.1
Total	2	5	17	.227	29	25	19	1	188.2	205	147	4	17	100	46	5.15	71	.275	.374	73-1	.192	1	85	-29	-2.7
MILLER, RALPH Ralph Henry "Moose" or "Lefty" B 1.14.1899 Vinton, IA D 2.18.1967 White Bear Lake, MN BR/TL 6-1.5/190# d9.16																									
1921	Was A	0	0	—	1	0	0	0	1	0	0	0	0	0	0	0.00	—	.000	.000	0-0	—	0		0	0.0
MILLER, RANDY Randall Scott B 3.18.1953 Oxnard, CA BR/TR 6-1/180# d9.7																									
1977	Bal A	0	0	—	1	0	0	0-0	0.2	4	3	0	0	0-0	0	40.50	9	.800	.667	0-0	—	0		-3	-0.1
1978	Mon N	0	1	.000	5	0	0	0-0	7	11	9	1	0	3-1	6	10.29	34	.393	.424	1-0	.000	-0		-5	-0.7
Total	2	0	1	.000	6	0	0	0-0	7.2	15	12	1	0	3-1	6	12.91	28	.455	.462	1-0	.000	-0		-8	-0.8
MILLER, BOB Robert Gerald B 7.15.1935 Berwyn, IL BR/TL 6-1/185# d6.25																									
1953	Det A	1	2	.333	13	1	0	0	36.1	43	25	2	1	21	9	5.94	68	.289	.380	8-0	.125	-1	66	-7	-0.5
1954	Det A	1	1	.500	32	1	0	1	69.2	62	25	1	0	26	27	2.45	150	.244	.312	15-0	.133	-0*	72	8	0.3
1955	Det A	2	1	.667	7	3	1	0	25.1	26	12	4	0	12-1	11	2.49	154	.263	.339	9-0	.222	0*	123	2	0.2
1956	Det A	0	2	.000	11	3	0	0	31.2	37	23	5	0	22-2	16	5.68	72	.308	.413	7-0	.143	0	108	-6	-0.3
1962	Cin N	0	0	—	6	0	0	0	5.1	14	13	1	2	3-0	4	21.94	18	.538	.576	1-0	.000	-0		-10	-0.5
	NY N	2	2	.500	17	0	0	1	20.1	24	16	2	1	8-0	8	7.08	59	.312	.379	1-0	.000	-0		-5	-0.9
	Year	2	2	.500	23	0	0	1	25.2	38	34	3	3	11-0	12	10.17	41	.369	.433	2-0	.000	-0		-15	-1.4
Total	5	6	8	.429	86	8	1	2	188.2	206	114	15	4	92-3	75	4.72	83	.284	.365	41-0	.146	-1	104	-18	-1.7
MILLER, BOB Robert John B 6.16.1926 Detroit, MI BR/TR 6-3/190# d9.16																									
1949	Phi N	0	0	—	3	0	0	0	2.2	2	0	0	0	2	0	0.00	—	.200	.333	0-0	—	0		1	0.1
1950	†Phi N	11	6	.647	35	22	7-2	1	174	190	78	9	5	57	44	3.57	113	.277	.337	61-2	.180	-1	98	10	0.9
1951	Phi N	2	1	.667	17	3	0	0	34.1	47	33	2	1	18	10	6.82	56	.331	.410	7-0	.429	1	168	-14	-1.0
1952	Phi N	0	1	.000	3	1	0	0	9	13	6	2	0	1	2	6.00	61	.351	.368	1-0	.000	-0	0	-2	-0.2
1953	Phi N	8	9	.471	35	20	8-3	2	157.1	169	76	14	2	42	63	4.00	105	.271	.319	55-1	.182	-1	89	6	0.4
1954	Phi N	7	9	.438	30	16	5	0	150	176	84	14	3	39	42	4.56	89	.300	.340	50-3	.160	0	116	-8	-0.7
1955	Phi N	8	4	.667	40	0	0	1	89.2	80	26	6	1	28-6	28	2.41	165	.242	.300	18-1	.278	1		16	2.1
1956	Phi N	3	6	.333	49	6	3-1	5	122.1	115	55	14	3	34-11	53	3.24	115	.248	.301	22-2	.091	-1	79	5	0.2
1957	Phi N	2	5	.286	32	1	0	6	60.1	61	18	4	1	17-5	12	2.69	142	.265	.315	8-0	.250	2	116	9	1.3
1958	Phi N	1	1	.500	17	0	0	0	22.1	36	30	7	0	9-2	9	11.69	34	.360	.402	1-1	.000	-0		-18	-1.4
Total	10	42	42	.500	261	69	23-6	15	822	889	406	72	16	247-24	263	3.96	101	.277	.329	223-10	.184	1	101	5	1.7
MILLER, BOB Robert Lane (b: Robert Lane Gemeinweiser) B 2.18.1939 St.Louis, MO D 8.6.1993 Rancho Bernardo, CA BR/TR 6-1/182# d6.26 C4																									
1957	StL N	0	0	—	5	0	0	0	9	13	9	2	0	5-0	7	7.00	57	.325	.391	0-0	—	0*		-3	-0.2
1959	StL N	4	3	.571	11	10	3	0	70.2	66	31	2	1	21-2	43	3.31	128	.248	.303	24-1	.208	0	91	6	0.6
1960	StL N	4	3	.571	15	7	0	0	52.2	53	21	2	1	17-2	33	3.42	120	.262	.320	14-1	.143	-1*	102	4	0.5
1961	StL N	1	3	.250	34	5	0	3	74.1	82	41	6	0	46-7	39	4.24	104	.290	.388	14-2	.357	2*	52	1	0.3
1962	NY N	1	12	.077	33	21	1	0	143.2	146	98	20	6	62-2	91	4.89	86	.259	.335	41-2	.122	-1*	57	-13	-1.0
1963	LA N	10	8	.556	42	23	2	1	187	171	71	7	3	65-9	125	2.89	105	.244	.310	57-5	.070	-3	119	3	0.3
1964	LA N	7	7	.500	**74**	2	0	9	137.2	115	49	1	2	63-16	94	2.62	124	.226	.312	19-2	.158	1	122	9	1.3
1965	†LA N	6	7	.462	61	1	0	9	103	82	37	9	3	26-3	77	2.97	110	.225	.277	16-1	.000	-1	54	4	0.6
1966	†LA N	4	2	.667	46	0	0	5	84.1	70	31	5	1	29-7	58	2.77	119	.230	.297	13-2	.077	-1		5	0.2
1967	LA N	2	9	.182	52	4	0	0	85.2	88	46	9	3	27-9	32	4.31	72	.273	.332	8-1	.125	-0	21	-12	-1.5
1968	Min A	0	3	.000	45	0	0	2	72.1	65	26	1	5	24-7	41	2.74	113	.239	.311	7-0	.143	-0		3	0.2
1969	†Min A	5	5	.500	48	11	1	3-3	119.1	118	42	9	0	32-7	57	3.02	121	.264	.311	31-2	.000	-3	130	10	0.6
1970	Cle A	2	2	.500	15	2	0	1-0	28	35	14	1	0	15-2	15	4.18	95	.310	.388	5-0	.200	0	135	-1	-0.1
	Chi A	4	6	.400	15	12	0	0-0	70	88	42	11	4	33-3	36	5.01	78	.315	.391	23-2	.174	0*	90	-7	-0.8
	Year	6	8	.429	30	14	0	1-0	98	123	46	12	4	48-5	51	4.78	82	.314	.390	28-2	.179	1	96	-7	-0.9
	Chi N	0	0	—	7	1	0	2-0	9	6	5	3	0	6-1	4	5.00	90	.194	.316	0-0	—	0	100	0	0.0
1971	Chi N	0	0	—	2	0	0	0-0	7	10	4	0	0	1-0	2	5.14	77	.357	.367	1-0	.000	-0		-1	0.0
	SD N	7	3	.700	38	0	0	7-2	63.2	53	12	0	1	26-7	36	1.41	234	.227	.308	10-2	.000	-1		14	2.5
	†Pit N	1	2	.333	16	0	0	3-4	28	20	8	1	0	13-4	13	1.29	263	.200	.292	1-0	.000	0		5	0.7
	Year	8	5	.615	56	0	0	10-6	98.2	83	29	1	1	40-11	51	1.64	205	.230	.308	12-2	.000	-1		18	3.2
1972	†Pit N	5	2	.714	36	0	0	3-1	54.1	54	19	3	1	24-7	18	2.65	125	.263	.343	4-1	.000	-0		4	0.5
1973	SD N	0	0	—	18	0	0	0-0	30.2	29	18	4	0	12-1	15	4.11	85	.244	.311	2-0	.000	-0		-3	-0.2
	NY N	0	0	—	1	0	0	0-0	1	0	0	0	0	0-0	1	0.00	—	.000	.000	0-0	—	0		0	0.0
	Year	0	0	—	19	0	0	0-0	31.2	29	18	4	0	12-1	16	3.98	88	.238	.304	2-0	.000	-0		-3	-0.2
	Det A	4	2	.667	22	0	0	1-1	42	34	16	3	0	22-2	23	3.43	119	.230	.324	0-0	—	0		3	0.5
1974	NY N	2	2	.500	58	0	0	2-2	78	89	39	2	1	39-13	35	3.58	100	.296	.375	9-0	.111	-0		-1	-0.1
Total	17	69	81	.460	694	99	7	51-13	1551.1	1487	679	101	32	608-111	895	3.37	105	.255	.326	299-24	.110	-8	95	30	4.9
MILLER, BOB Robert W. B 1862 D 5.23.1931 Newark, NJ d8.30																									
1890	Roc AA	3	7	.300	13	12	11	1	92.1	89	58	2	3	26	20	4.29	83	.246	.302	40	.150	-1*	54	-5	-0.5
1891	Was AA	2	5	.286	7	7	3	0	42	53	51	3	6	24	13	4.29	87	.298	.399	18	.111	-2	69	-8	-1.1
Total	2	5	12	.294	20	19	14	1	134.1	142	109	5	9	50	33	4.29	84	.263	.336	58	.138	-3	60	-13	-1.6
MILLER, ROGER Roger Wesley B 8.1.1954 Connellsville, PA D 4.26.1993 Mill Run, PA BR/TR 6-3/200# d9.8																									
1974	Mil A	0	0	—	2	0	0	0-0	2.1	3	3	1	1	0-0	2	11.57	31	.300	.364	0-0	—	0		-2	-0.1
MILLER, RONNIE Roland Arthur B 8.28.1918 Mason City, IA D 1.6.1998 Ferguson, MO BB/TR 5-11/167# d9.10 Mil 1942-45																									
1941	Was A	0	0	—	1	0	0	0	2	2	1	0	0	1	0	4.50	90	.333	.429	0-0	—	0		0	0.0
MILLER, ROSCOE Roscoe Clyde "Roxy" or "Rubberlegs" B 12.2.1876 Greenville, IN D 4.18.1913 Corydon, IN BR/TR 6-2/190# d4.25																									
1901	Det A	23	13	.639	38	36	35-3	1	332	339	168	1	13	98	79	2.95	130	.261	.320	130-2	.208	0	106	33	3.3
1902	Det A	6	12	.333	20	18	15-1	1	148.2	158	85	3	9	57	39	3.69	99	.273	.347	60-0	.183	-2	65	-1	-0.2
	NY N	1	8	.111	10	9	7	0	72.2	77	40	1	5	11	15	4.58	61	.271	.310	21-2	.048	-2	51	-9	-1.3
1903	NY N	2	5	.286	15	8	6	**3**	85	101	53	1	1	24	30	4.13	81	.302	.351	31-0	.161	-1	70	-7	-0.7
1904	Pit N	7	7	.500	19	17	11-2	0	134.1	133	67	4	4	39	35	3.35	82	.256	.313	46-0	.043	-4	103	-9	-1.3
Total	4	39	45	.464	102	88	74-6	5	772.2	808	413	10	32	229	198	3.45	100	.268	.326	288-4	.160	-8	89	7	-0.2

Year	Tm Lg	W	L	Pct	G	GS	CG-Sho	SV-BS	IP	H	R	HR	HB	BB-IB	SO	ERA	AERA	OAV	OOB	AB-SH	AVG	PB	Sup	APR	PW
MILLER, RUSS Russell Lewis B 3.25.1900 Etna, OH D 4.30.1962 Bucyrus, OH BR/TR 5-11/165# d9.24 b-Jake																									
1927	Phi N	1	1	.500	2	2	1	0	15.1	21	9	2	1	3	4	5.28	78	.339	.379	3-3	.333	0	93	-1	-0.1
1928	Phi N	0	12	.000	33	12	1	1	108	137	79	14	0	34	19	5.42	79	.315	.365	27-1	.148	-1*	89	-15	-1.6
Total	2	1	13	.071	35	14	2	1	123.1	158	88	16	1	37	23	5.40	79	.318	.366	30-4	.167	-1	90	-16	-1.7
MILLER, STU Stuart Leonard B 12.26.1927 Northampton, MA BR/TR 5-11.5/165# d8.12																									
1952	StL N	6	3	.667	12	11	6-2	0	88	63	25	3	2	26	64	2.05	182	.197	.262	25-6	.120	-1	74	15	1.6
1953	StL N	7	8	.467	40	18	8-2	4	137.2	161	86	19	2	47	79	5.56	77	.293	.351	43-4	.186	1*	99	-17	-1.4
1954	StL N	2	3	.400	19	4	0	2	46.2	55	36	5	3	29	22	5.79	71	.307	.405	13-0	.308	1*	157	-9	-0.8
1956	StL N	0	1	.000	3	0	0	1	7.1	12	6	3	0	5-0	5	4.91	77	.387	.459	1-0	.000	-0*		-2	-0.2
	Phi N	5	8	.385	24	15	2	0	106.2	109	65	16	4	51-12	55	4.47	83	.263	.347	25-1	.160	2*	87	-11	-1.0
	Year	5	9	.357	27	15	2	1	114	121	69	19	4	56-12	60	4.50	83	.271	.356	26-1	.154	2	87	-14	-1.2
1957	NY N	7	9	.438	38	13	0	1	124	110	53	15	3	45-6	60	3.63	108	.242	.313	35-1	.057	-3	91	6	0.4
1958	SF N	6	9	.400	41	20	4-1	0	182	160	60	16	2	49-3	119	**2.47**	**154**	.233	**.286**	50-5	.120	-0*	105	27	2.1
1959	SF N	8	7	.533	59	9	2	8	167.2	164	66	15	5	57-13	95	2.84	134	.260	.322	45-4	.044	-3	117	17	1.4
1960	SF N	7	6	.538	47	3	2	2	101.2	100	49	9	3	31-5	65	3.90	89	.256	.312	25-3	.200	1	93	-4	-0.3
1961	SF N★	14	5	.737	63	0	0	**17**	122	95	41	4	1	37-11	89	2.66	143	.215	.277	20-1	.200	2*		**16**	3.1
1962	†SF N	5	8	.385	59	0	0	19	107	107	55	8	2	42-7	78	4.12	92	.268	.337	16-1	.125	-0*		-4	-0.6
1963	Bal A	5	8	.385	**71**	0	0	**27**	112.1	93	36	5	3	53-13	114	2.24	155	.232	.323	16-2	.313	2		14	2.6
1964	Bal A	7	7	.500	66	0	0	23	97	77	37	7	3	34-14	87	3.06	117	.222	.295	9-2	.111	-0		5	1.0
1965	Bal A	14	7	.667	67	0	0	24	119.1	87	26	5	1	32-10	104	1.89	184	.207	.265	16-4	.063	-1		22	**4.9**
1966	Bal A	9	4	.692	51	0	0	18	92	65	24	5	4	22-6	67	2.25	148	.201	.259	19-2	.105	-1		12	2.1
1967	Bal A	3	10	.231	42	0	0	8	81.1	63	28	5	1	36-12	60	2.55	124	.220	.307	11-0	.000	-1		4	0.6
1968	Atl N	0	0	—	2	0	0	0	1.1	1	4	0	0	4-2	1	27.00	11	.500	.833	0-0	—	0		-3	-0.2
Total	16	105	103	.505	704	93	24-5	154	1694	1522	697	140	39	600-**114**	1164	3.24	115	.242	.311	369-36	.133	-2	103	88	15.3
MILLER, TRAVIS Travis Eugene B 11.2.1972 Dayton, OH BR/TL 6-3/205# d8.25																									
1996	Min A	1	2	.333	7	7	0	0-0	26.1	45	29	7	0	9-0	15	9.23	55	.388	.432	0-0	—	0	103	-12	-1.0
1997	Min A	1	5	.167	13	7	0	0-0	48.1	64	49	8	1	23-2	26	7.63	61	.320	.389	0-0	—	0	93	-18	-1.8
1998	Min A	0	2	.000	14	0	0	0-0	23.1	25	10	0	0	11-1	23	3.86	124	.272	.346	0-0	—	0		3	0.2
1999	Min A	2	2	.500	52	0	0	0-2	49.2	55	19	3	0	16-3	40	2.72	187	.284	.335	0-0	—	0		11	0.8
2000	Min A	2	3	.400	67	0	0	1-3	67	83	35	4	1	32-2	62	3.90	133	.297	.368	0-0	—	0		7	0.5
2001	Min A	1	4	.200	45	0	0	0-0	48.2	54	30	5	1	20-1	30	4.81	96	.283	.347	0-0	—	0		-2	-0.3
2002	Min A	0	0	—	5	0	0	0-0	4	5	2	0	0	2-2	3	4.50	100	.294	.368	0-0	—	0		0	0.0
Total	7	7	18	.280	203	14	0	1-5	267.1	331	174	27	3	113-11	199	5.05	97	.304	.367	0-0	—	0	99	-11	-1.6
MILLER, TREVER Trever Douglas B 5.29.1973 Louisville, KY BR/TL 6-3/175# d9.4																									
1996	Det A	0	4	.000	5	4	0	0-0	16.2	28	17	3	2	9-0	8	9.18	55	.384	.453	0-0	—	0	46	-7	-1.1
1998	†Hou N	2	0	1.000	37	1	0	1-1	53.1	57	21	4	1	20-1	30	3.04	133	.266	.332	3-0	.333	1	91	6	0.3
1999	†Hou N	3	2	.600	47	0	0	1-0	49.2	58	29	6	5	29-1	37	5.07	87	.299	.400	3-2	.000	-0		-3	-0.3
2000	Phi N	0	0	—	14	0	0	0-0	14	19	16	3	1	9-1	10	8.36	56	.317	.408	0-0	—	0		-7	-0.3
	LA N	0	0	—	2	0	0	0-0	2.1	8	6	0	1	3-0	1	23.14	19	.571	.667	0-0	—	0		-5	-0.2
	Year	0	0	—	16	0	0	0-0	16.1	27	26	3	2	12-1	11	10.47	44	.365	.461	0-0	—	0		-11	-0.5
2003	Tor A	2	2	.500	**79**	0	0	4-1	52.2	46	30	7	5	28-3	44	4.61	100	.231	.341	0-0	—	0		0	0.0
Total	5	7	8	.467	184	5	0	6-2	188.2	216	119	23	15	98-6	130	5.20	85	.286	.377	6-2	.167	0	58	-16	-1.6
MILLER, WADE Wade T. B 9.13.1976 Reading, PA BR/TR 6-2/185# d7.7																									
1999	Hou N	0	1	.000	5	1	0	0-0	10.1	17	11	4	0	5-0	8	9.58	46	.362	.423	1-0	.000	-0	146	-6	-0.5
2000	Hou N	6	6	.500	16	16	2	0-0	105	104	66	14	3	42-1	89	5.14	95	.257	.331	40-1	.100	-2	111	-3	-0.5
2001	†Hou N	16	8	.667	32	32	1	0-0	212	183	91	31	4	76-3	183	3.40	135	.234	.304	66-10	.167	0	96	25	2.7
2002	Hou N	15	4	.789	26	26	1-1	0-0	164.2	151	63	14	6	62-9	144	3.28	130	.249	.322	62-6	.177	0	118	18	2.0
2003	Hou N	14	13	.519	33	33	1	0-0	187.1	168	96	17	10	77-1	161	4.13	107	.242	.323	63-5	.159	0*	102	5	0.6
Total	5	51	32	.614	112	108	5-1	0-0	679.1	623	327	80	23	262-14	585	3.93	115	.246	.320	232-22	.155	-2	106	39	4.3
MILLER, JAKE Walter B 2.28.1898 Wagram, OH D 8.20.1975 Venice, FL BL/TL 6-2/170# d9.11 b-Russ																									
1924	Cle A	0	1	.000	2	2	1	0	12	13	6	0	0	5	4	3.00	142	.265	.333	5-0	.000	-1	99	1	0.0
1925	Cle A	10	13	.435	32	22	13	2	190.1	207	85	4	7	62	51	3.31	133	.279	.340	71-3	.183	-3	80	23	2.1
1926	Cle A	7	4	.636	18	11	5-3	1	82.2	99	34	1	2	18	24	3.27	124	.307	.348	24-0	.083	-2	70	8	0.7
1927	Cle A	10	8	.556	34	23	11	0	185.1	189	80	4	6	48	53	3.21	131	.271	.324	58-3	.138	-4	86	20	1.3
1928	Cle A	8	9	.471	25	24	8	0	158	203	89	6	5	43	37	4.44	93	.332	.381	52-6	.135	-4	75	-3	-0.7
1929	Cle A	14	12	.538	29	29	14-2	0	206	227	98	7	7	60	58	3.58	124	.279	.334	75-7	.200	-3	81	19	1.9
1930	Cle A	4	4	.500	24	9	1	0	88.1	147	89	6	4	38	31	7.13	68	.373	.433	33-5	.303	1	105	-23	-1.5
1931	Cle A	2	1	.667	10	5	1-1	0	41.1	45	26	2	0	19	17	4.35	106	.273	.348	13-0	.077	-1	143	0	-0.1
1933	Chi A	5	6	.455	26	14	4-2	0	105.2	130	75	3	6	47	30	5.62	75	.297	.373	37-3	.189	-1*	102	-15	-1.3
Total	9	60	58	.508	200	139	58-8	3	1069.2	1260	582	33	37	340	305	4.09	106	.298	.355	368-27	.171	-19	86	30	2.4
MILLER, WALT Walter W. B 10.19.1884 Spiceland, IN D 3.1.1956 Marion, IN BR/TR 5-11.5/180# d9.20																									
1911	Bro N	0	1	.000	3	2	0	0	11	16	14	0	1	6	0	6.55	51	.356	.442	4-0	.000	-1	56	-6	-0.5
MILLER, BILL William Francis "Wild Bill" B 4.12.1910 Hannibal, MO D 2.26.1982 Hannibal, MO BR/TR 6/180# d10.2																									
1937	StL A	0	1	.000	1	1	0	0	4	7	6	1	1	4	1	13.50	36	.389	.522	1-0	.000	-0	36	-3	-0.5
MILLER, BILL William Paul "Lefty" or "Hooks" B 7.26.1927 Minersville, PA D 7.1.2003 Lititz, PA BL/TL 6/175# d4.20																									
1952	NY A	4	6	.400	21	13	5-2	0	88	78	43	5	2	49	45	3.48	96	.241	.345	28-2	.214	1	125	-3	-0.3
1953	NY A	2	1	.667	13	3	0	1	34	46	19	3	1	19	17	4.76	77	.324	.407	10-1	.200	0	112	-4	-0.3
1954	NY A	0	1	.000	2	1	0	0	5.2	9	4	0	0	1	6	6.35	54	.375	.385	1-0	.000	-0	51	-2	-0.3
1955	Bal A	0	1	.000	5	1	0	0	4	3	6	0	0	10-1	4	13.50	28	.200	.520	1-0	1.000	0	163	-4	-0.7
Total	4	6	9	.400	41	18	5-2	1	131.2	136	72	8	3	79-1	72	4.24	81	.270	.371	40-3	.225	1	121	-13	-1.6
MILLIGAN, JOHN John Alexander B 1.22.1904 Schuylerville, NY D 5.15.1972 Fort Pierce, FL BR/TL 5-10/172# d8.11																									
1928	Phi N	2	5	.286	13	7	3	0	68	69	39	2	1	32	22	4.37	98	.274	.358	20-4	.050	-2	96	-1	-0.3
1929	Phi N	0	1	.000	8	3	0	0	9.2	29	19	0	2	10	2	16.76	31	.527	.612	3-0	.333	0	140	-11	-0.8
1930	Phi N	1	2	.333	9	2	1	0	28.1	26	16	0	2	21	7	3.18	172	.255	.392	9-0	.111	-1	88	5	0.4
1931	Phi N	0	0	—	3	0	0	0	8	11	5	0	1	4	6	3.38	126	.324	.410	2-0	.000	-0		0	0.0
1934	Was A	0	0	—	2	0	0	0	2.2	6	3	0	0	0	1	10.13	43	.500	.500	0-0	—	0		-2	-0.1
Total	5	3	8	.273	35	12	4	0	116.2	141	82	2	6	67	38	5.17	90	.310	.405	34-4	.088	-3	108	-9	-0.8
MILLIGAN, BILLY William Joseph B 8.19.1878 Buffalo, NY D 10.14.1928 Buffalo, NY BR/TL 5-7/?# d4.30																									
1901	Phi A	0	3	.000	6	3	2	0	33	43	24	1	2	14	5	4.36	86	.312	.383	15-1	.333	2*	137	-3	0.0
1904	NY N	0	1	.000	5	1	1	2	25	36	22	2	1	4	6	5.40	51	.310	.339	9-0	.111	0	0	-8	-0.4
Total	2	0	4	.000	11	4	3	2	58	79	46	3	3	18	11	4.81	69	.311	.364	24-1	.250	2	118	-11	-0.4
MILLIKEN, BOB Robert Fogle "Bobo" B 8.25.1926 Majorsville, WV BR/TR 6/195# d4.22 C7																									
1953	†Bro N	8	4	.667	37	10	3	2	117.2	94	52	13	0	42	65	3.37	127	.214	.283	34-2	.118	-1	107	10	0.7
1954	Bro N	5	2	.714	24	3	0	2	62.2	58	31	12	2	18	25	4.02	102	.246	.304	17-0	.176	-0	80	0	-0.1
Total	2	13	6	.684	61	13	3	4	180.1	152	83	25	2	60	90	3.59	117	.225	.290	51-2	.137	-2	101	10	0.6
MILLS, ALAN Alan Bernard B 10.18.1966 Lakeland, FL BR/TR 6-1/192# d4.14																									
1990	NY A	1	5	.167	36	0	0	0-2	41.2	48	21	4	1	33-6	24	4.10	97	.298	.418	0-0	—	0		-1	0.0
1991	NY A	1	1	.500	6	2	0	0-0	16.1	16	9	1	0	8-0	11	4.41	94	.254	.333	0-0	—	0	44	-1	0.0
1992	Bal A	10	4	.714	35	3	0	2-1	103.1	78	33	5	1	54-10	60	2.61	154	.215	.315	0-0	—	0	106	15	2.1
1993	Bal A	5	4	.556	45	0	0	4-3	100.1	80	39	14	4	51-5	68	3.23	139	.225	.324	0-0	—	0		13	1.1
1994	Bal A	3	3	.500	47	0	0	2-2	45.1	43	26	7	2	24-2	44	5.16	97	.251	.348	0-0	—	0		0	-0.1
1995	Bal A	3	0	1.000	21	0	0	0-1	23	30	20	4	2	18-4	16	7.43	64	.309	.424	0-0	—	0		-7	-0.8
1996	†Bal A	3	2	.600	49	0	0	3-5	54.2	40	26	10	1	35-2	50	4.28	115	.208	.330	0-0	—	0		5	0.4

Year	Tm Lg	W	L	Pct	G	GS	CG-Sho	SV-BS	IP	H	R	HR	HB	BB-IB	SO	ERA	AERA	OAV	OOB	AB-SH	AVG	PB	Sup	APR	PW
1997	†Bal A	2	3	.400	39	0	0	0-0	38.2	41	23	5	1	33-1	32	4.89	90	.268	.399	0-0	—	0		-2	-0.3
1998	Bal A	3	4	.429	72	0	0	2-3	77	55	32	8	1	50-8	57	3.74	122	.203	.326	0-0	—	0		8	0.6
1999	LA N	3	4	.429	68	0	0	0-5	72.1	70	33	10	4	43-4	49	3.73	115	.261	.367	2-0	.000	-0		5	0.3
2000	LA N	2	1	.667	18	0	0	1-0	25.2	31	12	3	1	16-0	18	4.21	103	.304	.403	3-0	.000	-0		1	0.1
	Bal A	2	0	1.000	23	0	0	1-0	23.2	25	17	6	1	19-1	18	6.46	73	.263	.391	0-0	—	0		-4	-0.3
2001	Bal A	1	1	.500	15	0	0	0-0	14	20	15	6	2	11-3	9	9.64	45	.333	.452	0-0	—	0		-8	-1.0
Total	12	39	32	.549	474	5	0	15-22	636	577	306	83	21	395-46	456	4.12	108	.245	.356	5-0	.000	-0	75	24	2.1
MILLS, ART Arthur Grant B 3.2.1903 Utica, NY D 7.23.1975 Utica, NY BR/TR 5-10/155# d4.16 C5 f-Willie																									
1927	Bos N	0	1	.000	15	1	0	0	37.2	41	19	1	3	18	7	3.82	97	.287	.378	7-0	.000	-1	229	-1	-0.1
1928	Bos N	0	0	—	4	0	0	0	7.2	17	11	3	2	8	0	12.91	30	.472	.587	1-0	.000	-0		-7	-0.3
Total	2	0	1	.000	19	1	0	0	45.1	58	30	4	5	26	7	5.36	70	.324	.424	8-0	.000	-1	229	-8	-0.4
MILLS, LEFTY Howard Robinson B 5.12.1910 Dedham, MA D 9.23.1982 Riverside, CA BL/TL 6-1/187# d6.10																									
1934	StL A	0	0	—	4	0	0	0	8.2	10	4	0	0	11	2	4.15	120	.303	.477	3-0	.333	0		1	0.0
1937	StL A	1	1	.500	2	2	1	0	12.2	16	13	1	0	10	10	6.39	75	.286	.394	5-0	.000	-1	81	-3	-0.5
1938	StL A	10	12	.455	30	27	15-1	0	210.1	216	139	16	8	116	134	5.31	94	.262	.358	66-5	.091	-3	90	-8	-1.0
1939	StL A	4	11	.267	34	14	4	2	144.1	147	114	16	8	113	103	6.55	74	.264	.395	47-2	.234	1	69	-24	-2.0
1940	StL A	0	6	.000	26	5	1	0	59	64	55	7	3	52	18	7.78	59	.275	.413	13-0	.154	-0	31	-19	-1.6
Total	5	15	30	.333	96	48	21-1	2	435	453	325	40	19	302	267	6.06	81	.266	.382	134-7	.149	-3	78	-53	-5.1
MILLS, DICK Richard Alan B 1.29.1945 Boston, MA BR/TR 6-3/195# d9.7																									
1970	Bos A	0	0	—	2	0	0	0-0	3.2	6	4	0	1	3-0	3	2.45	161	.353	.476	0-0	—	0		-1	0.0
MILLS, WILLIE William Grant "Wee Willie" B 8.15.1877 Schenevus, NY D 7.5.1914 Norwood, NY BR/TR 5-7/150# d7.13 s-Art																									
1901	NY N	0	2	.000	2	2	2	0	16	21	15	2	1	4	3	8.44	39	.313	.361	6-0	.167	0	64	-7	-0.7
MILLWOOD, KEVIN Kevin Austin B 12.24.1974 Gastonia, NC BR/TR 6-4/205# d7.14																									
1997	Atl N	5	3	.625	12	8	0	0-0	51.1	55	26	1	2	21-1	42	4.03	104	.281	.348	12-1	.000	-1	131	1	0.0
1998	Atl N	17	8	.680	31	29	3-1	0-0	174.1	175	86	18	3	56-3	163	4.08	102	.258	.316	50-6	.080	-1	112	3	0.2
1999	†Atl N★	18	7	.720	33	33	2	0-0	228	168	80	24	4	59-2	205	2.68	168	**.202**	**.258**	78-6	.154	0	99	45	4.4
2000	†Atl N	10	13	.435	36	**35**	0	0-0	212.2	213	115	26	3	62-2	168	4.66	99	.258	.311	59-14	.119	-1	96	1	-0.2
2001	Atl N	7	7	.500	21	21	0	0-0	121	121	66	20	1	40-6	84	4.31	102	.260	.319	43-1	.093	-2	119	1	-0.2
2002	†Atl N	18	8	.692	35	34	1-1	0-0	217	186	83	16	8	65-7	178	3.24	127	.230	.292	70-11	.200	3	101	22	2.7
2003	Phi N	14	12	.538	35	35	5-**3**	0-0	222	210	103	19	4	68-6	169	4.01	100	.250	.307	68-6	.059	-3	101	1	-0.2
Total	7	89	58	.605	203	195	11-5	0-0	1226.1	1128	559	124	25	371-27	1009	3.78	113	.243	.301	380-45	.118	-5	104	74	6.7
MILNAR, AL Albert Joseph "Happy" (b: Albert Joseph Mlinar) B 12.26.1913 Cleveland, OH BL/TL 6-2/195# d4.30 Mil 1944-45																									
1936	Cle A	1	2	.333	4	3	1	0	22	26	20	0	0	18	9	7.36	68	.286	.404	10-0	.300	0	70	-5	-0.5
1938	Cle A	3	1	.750	23	5	2	1	68.1	90	48	5	0	26	29	5.00	93	.320	.378	26-0	.154	-0*	121	-5	-0.3
1939	Cle A	14	12	.538	37	26	12-2	3	209	212	96	11	0	99	76	3.79	116	.264	.345	79-0	.253	4*	109	17	2.2
1940	Cle A☆	18	10	.643	37	33	15-**4**	3	242.1	242	120	14	1	99	99	3.27	129	.257	.328	94-3	.181	-1	112	18	1.5
1941	Cle A	12	19	.387	35	30	9-1	0	229.1	236	128	9	1	116	82	4.36	90	.266	.352	82-1	.171	2	89	-13	-1.4
1942	Cle A	6	8	.429	28	19	8-2	0	157	146	82	3	4	85	35	4.13	84	.251	.350	70-1	.171	2*	120	-11	-0.7
1943	Cle A	1	3	.250	16	6	0	0	39	51	38	0	1	35	12	8.08	38	.329	.455	19-0	.211	0*	99	-21	-2.0
	StL A	1	2	.333	3	2	1	0	14.2	23	11	0	0	9	7	5.52	60	.354	.432	6-1	.333	1	190	-4	-0.6
	Year	2	5	.286	19	8	1	0	53.2	74	19	0	1	44	19	7.38	43	.336	.449	25-1	.240	1	123	-25	-2.6
1946	StL A	1	1	.500	4	2	1-1	0	14.2	15	4	1	0	6	1	2.45	152	.278	.350	4-0	.750	1	57	2	0.4
	Phi N	0	0	—	1	1	0	0	0	2	4	0	0	2	0	∞	—	1.000	1.000	0-0	—	0	225	-4	-0.3
Total	8	57	58	.496	188	127	49-10	7	996.1	1043	551	43	7	495	350	4.22	96	.270	.354	390-6	.203	9	106	-26	-1.7
MILSTEAD, GEORGE George Earl "Cowboy" B 6.26.1903 Cleburne, TX D 8.9.1977 Cleburne, TX BL/TL 5-10/144# d6.27																									
1924	Chi N	1	1	.500	13	2	1	0	29.2	41	25	3	1	13	6	6.07	64	.328	.396	6-0	.167	0	76	-8	-0.4
1925	Chi N	1	1	.500	5	3	1	0	21	26	12	0	0	8	7	3.00	144	.310	.370	7-0	.000	-1	98	1	0.0
1926	Chi N	1	5	.167	18	4	0	2	55.1	63	30	0	1	24	14	3.58	107	.309	.384	19-0	.053	-2	65	0	-0.1
Total	3	3	7	.300	36	9	2	2	106	130	67	3	2	45	27	4.16	95	.315	.385	32-0	.063	-3	80	-7	-0.5
MILTON, ERIC Eric Robert B 8.4.1975 State College, PA BL/TL 6-3/200# d4.5																									
1998	Min A	8	14	.364	32	32	1	0-0	172.1	195	113	25	2	70-0	107	5.64	85	.282	.347	9-0	.444	1	90	-15	-1.5
1999	Min A	7	11	.389	34	34	5-2	0-0	206.1	190	111	28	3	63-2	163	4.49	113	.243	.299	2-0	.000	0	88	13	0.8
2000	Min A	13	10	.565	33	33	0	0-0	200	205	123	35	7	44-0	160	4.86	106	.260	.303	2-0	.000	-0	94	3	0.2
2001	Min A☆	15	7	.682	35	34	2-1	0-0	220.2	222	109	35	5	61-0	157	4.32	106	.257	.308	2-0	.000	-0	104	8	0.5
2002	†Min A	13	9	.591	29	29	2-1	0-0	171	173	96	24	3	30-0	121	4.84	93	.258	.291	5-0	.400	1*	85	-5	-0.6
2003	†Min A	1	0	1.000	3	3	0	0-0	17	15	5	2	0	1-0	7	2.65	172	.234	.242	0-0	—	0	108	4	0.2
Total	6	57	51	.528	166	165	10-4	0-0	987.1	1000	557	149	20	269-2	715	4.76	101	.259	.308	20-0	.300	2	92	8	-0.4
MILTON, LARRY Samuel Lawrence "Tug" B 5.4.1879 Owensboro, KY D 5.16.1942 Hannibal, MO TR d5.7																									
1903	StL N	0	0	—	1	0	0	0	4	3	1	0	0	1	0	2.25	145	.200	.250	2-0	.500	0		1	0.1
MIMBS, MIKE Michael Randall B 2.13.1969 Macon, GA BL/TL 6-2/180# d5.6																									
1995	Phi N	9	7	.563	35	19	2-1	1-0	136.2	127	70	10	6	75-2	93	4.15	102	.250	.348	35-8	.143	-1	85	1	0.0
1996	Phi N	3	9	.250	21	17	0	0-0	99.1	116	66	13	2	41-1	56	5.53	78	.294	.361	33-2	.121	-1	79	-12	-1.4
1997	Phi N	0	3	.000	17	1	0	0-0	28.2	31	27	6	3	27-1	29	7.53	56	.272	.424	2-0	.000	-0	22	-11	-1.0
Total	3	12	19	.387	73	37	2-1	1-0	264.2	274	163	29	11	143-4	178	5.03	85	.270	.362	70-10	.129	-2	81	-22	-2.4
MINAHAN, COTTON Edmund Joseph B 12.10.1882 Springfield, OH D 5.20.1958 E.Orange, NJ BR/TR 6/190# d4.21																									
1907	Cin N	0	2	.000	2	2	1	0	14	12	8	0	1	13	4	1.29	202	.261	.433	5-0	.000	-1	82	0	-0.1
MINARCIN, RUDY Rudolph Anthony "Buster" B 3.25.1930 N.Vandergrift, PA BR/TR 6/195# d4.11																									
1955	Cin N	5	9	.357	41	12	3-1	1	115.2	116	73	17	3	51-7	45	4.90	86	.261	.339	28-0	.179	-1	100	-9	-0.9
1956	Bos A	1	0	1.000	3	1	0	0	9.2	9	4	2	1	8-0	5	2.79	165	.250	.400	2-0	.500	1	96	2	0.2
1957	Bos A	0	0	—	26	0	0	2	44.2	44	30	5	1	30-4	20	4.43	90	.267	.375	2-0	.000	0		-4	-0.2
Total	3	6	9	.400	70	13	3-1	3	170	169	107	24	5	89-11	70	4.66	90	.262	.352	32-0	.188	0	101	-11	-0.9
MINCHEY, NATE Nathan Derek B 8.31.1969 Austin, TX BR/TR 6-8/225# d9.12																									
1993	Bos A	1	2	.333	5	5	1	0-0	33	35	16	5	0	8-2	18	3.55	131	.265	.307	0-0	—	0	103	3	0.2
1994	Bos A	2	3	.400	6	5	0	0-0	23	44	26	1	0	14-2	15	8.61	59	.427	.483	0-0	—	0	58	-10	-1.5
1996	Bos A	0	2	.000	2	2	0	0-0	6	16	11	1	0	5-0	4	15.00	34	.533	.583	0-0	—	0	91	-6	-0.9
1997	Col N	0	0	—	2	0	0	0-0	2	5	3	0	0	1-0	1	13.50	38	.556	.600	0-0	—	0		-1	-0.1
Total	4	3	7	.300	15	12	1	0-0	64	100	56	7	0	28-4	38	6.75	72	.365	.418	0-0	—	0	82	-14	-2.3
MINER, RAY Raymond Theadore "Lefty" B 4.4.1897 Glens Falls, NY D 9.15.1963 Glenridge, NY BR/TL 5-11/160# d9.15																									
1921	Phi A	0	0	—	1	0	0	0	1	2	4	0	0	3	0	36.00	12	.400	.625	0-0	—	0		-3	-0.1
MINETTO, CRAIG Craig Stephen B 4.25.1954 Stockton, CA BL/TL 6/185# d7.4																									
1978	Oak A	0	0	—	4	1	0	0-0	12	13	10	1	2	7-0	3	3.75	97	.283	.393	0-0	—	0	221	-2	-0.1
1979	Oak A	1	5	.167	36	13	0	0-1	118.1	131	85	16	3	58-3	64	5.55	73	.282	.360	0-0	—	0	91	-22	-1.1
1980	Oak A	0	2	.000	7	1	0	1-0	8	11	7	2	0	3-1	5	7.88	48	.324	.368	0-0	—	0	47	-3	-0.7
1981	Oak A	0	0	—	8	0	0	0-0	6.2	7	2	0	1	4-0	4	2.70	129	.280	.387	0-0	—	0		1	0.0
Total	4	1	7	.125	55	15	0	1-1	145	162	104	19	6	72-4	76	5.40	74	.284	.364	0-0	—	0	97	-26	-1.9
MINGORI, STEVE Stephen Bernard B 2.29.1944 Kansas City, MO BL/TL 5-10/170# d8.5																									
1970	Cle A	1	0	1.000	21	0	0	1-0	20.1	17	8	2	1	12-5	16	2.66	149	.227	.341	1-0	.000	-0		2	0.1
1971	Cle A	1	2	.333	54	0	0	4-2	56.2	31	10	2	1	24-6	45	1.43	268	.166	.259	2-0	.500	0		14	1.0
1972	Cle A	0	6	.000	41	0	0	10-3	57	67	28	4	2	36-8	47	3.95	82	.293	.392	8-0	.125	-0*		-4	-0.7
1973	Cle A	0	0	—	5	0	0	0-1	11.2	10	8	3	0	10-1	4	6.17	64	.233	.377	0-0	—	0		-2	-0.1

Year	Tm Lg	W	L	Pct	G	GS	CG-Sho	SV-BS	IP	H	R	HR	HB	BB-IB	SO	ERA	AERA	OAV	OOB	AB-SH	AVG	PB	Sup	APR	PW
	KC A	3	3	.500	19	1	0	1-0	56.1	59	21	6	3	23-6	46	3.04	136	.267	.344	0-0	—	0	0	6	0.6
	Year	3	3	.500	24	1	0	1-1	68	69	21	9	3	33-7	50	3.57	114	.261	.350	0-0	—	0	0	4	0.5
1974	KC A	2	3	.400	36	0	0	2-4	67.1	53	31	4	2	23-5	43	2.81	136	.212	.282	0-0	—	0		4	0.4
1975	KC A	0	3	.000	36	0	0	2-2	50.1	42	21	2	1	20-4	25	2.50	154	.226	.300	1-0	.000	-0		5	0.4
1976	†KC A	5	5	.500	55	0	0	10-2	85.1	73	23	3	3	25-8	38	2.32	151	.238	.301	0-0	—	0		12	1.9
1977	†KC A	2	4	.333	43	0	0	4-2	64	59	26	4	1	19-4	19	3.09	131	.254	.307	0-0	—	0		6	0.7
1978	†KC A	1	4	.200	45	0	0	7-1	69	64	25	5	3	16-4	28	2.74	140	.242	.290	0-0	—	0		8	0.7
1979	KC A	3	3	.500	30	1	0	1-0	46.2	69	36	10	1	17-2	18	5.79	74	.348	.401	0-0	—	0	85	-9	-1.0
Total	10	18	33	.353	385	2	0	42-17	584.2	544	237	45	18	225-53	329	3.03	126	.248	.321	12-0	.167	-0	47	42	4.0
MINNER, PAUL Paul Edison "Lefty" B 7.30.1923 New Wilmington, PA BL/TL 6-5/210# d9.12																									
1946	Bro N	0	1	.000	3	0	0	0	4	6	4	1	0	3	3	6.75	50	.333	.429	0-0	—	0		-2	-0.3
1948	Bro N	4	3	.571	28	2	0	1	62.2	61	23	5	0	26	23	2.44	164	.257	.331	21-0	.190	1*	155	9	1.1
1949	†Bro N	3	1	.750	27	1	0	2	47.1	49	22	7	1	18	17	3.80	108	.272	.342	14-0	.214	-0	172	1	0.1
1950	Chi N	8	13	.381	39	24	9-1	4	190.1	217	105	18	1	72	99	4.11	102	.287	.350	65-1	.215	2*	89	1	0.5
1951	Chi N	6	17	.261	33	28	14-3	1	201.2	219	97	20	0	64	68	3.79	108	.277	.331	71-2	.254	5*	85	6	1.4
1952	Chi N	14	9	.609	28	27	12-2	0	180.2	180	84	13	1	54	61	3.74	103	.258	.312	64-3	.234	6*	117	3	1.1
1953	Chi N	12	15	.444	31	27	9-2	1	201	227	109	15	3	40	64	4.21	106	.283	.320	68-3	.221	2	71	5	1.0
1954	Chi N	11	11	.500	32	29	12	1	218	236	107	19	1	50	79	3.96	106	.280	.317	76-1	.171	3*	109	6	0.9
1955	Chi N	9	9	.500	22	22	7-1	0	157.2	173	67	15	1	47-10	53	3.48	117	.283	.333	56-1	.232	2	102	11	1.5
1956	Chi N	2	5	.286	10	9	1	0	47	60	38	9	2	19-2	14	6.89	55	.324	.389	12-0	.250	2	101	-15	-1.7
Total	10	69	84	.451	253	169	64-9	10	1310.1	1428	656	122	10	393-12	481	3.94	105	.279	.331	447-11	.219	22	96	25	5.6
MINNICK, DON Donald Athey B 4.14.1931 Lynchburg, VA BR/TR 6-3/195# d9.23																									
1957	Was A	0	1	.000	2	1	0	0	9.1	14	8	1	0	2-0	7	4.82	81	.341	.372	2-0	.000	-0	23	-2	-0.2
MINOR, BLAS Blas B 3.20.1966 Merced, CA BR/TR 6-3/203# d7.28																									
1992	Pit N	0	0	—	1	0	0	0-0	2	3	2	0	0	0-0	0	4.50	77	.333	.333	0-0	—	0		-1	0.0
1993	Pit N	8	6	.571	65	0	0	2-1	94.1	94	43	8	4	26-3	84	4.10	99	.263	.316	10-0	.200	1		1	0.2
1994	Pit N	0	1	.000	17	0	0	1-0	19	27	17	4	1	9-2	17	8.05	54	.351	.420	0-1	—	0		-7	-0.4
1995	NY N	4	2	.667	35	0	0	1-0	46.2	44	21	6	1	13-1	43	3.66	111	.253	.309	2-0	.000	-0		2	0.2
1996	NY N	0	0	—	17	0	0	0-1	25.2	23	11	4	0	6-2	20	3.51	115	.237	.279	1-0	.000	-0		2	0.1
	Sea A	0	1	.000	11	0	0	0-0	25.1	27	14	6	0	11-0	14	4.97	100	.276	.349	0-0	—	0		0	0.0
1997	Hou N	1	0	1.000	11	0	0	1-2	12	13	7	1	1	5-0	6	4.50	89	.277	.352	0-0	—	0		-1	-0.1
Total	6	13	10	.565	157	0	0	5-4	225	231	115	29	7	70-8	184	4.40	95	.269	.326	13-1	.154	0		-4	0.0
MINSHALL, JIM James Edward B 7.4.1947 Covington, KY BR/TR 6-6/215# d9.14																									
1974	Pit N	0	1	.000	5	0	0	0-1	4.1	1	1	0	0	2-1	3	0.00	—	.083	.200	0-0	—	0		1	0.3
1975	Pit N	0	0	—	1	0	0	0-0	1	0	0	0	0	2-0	2	0.00	—	.000	.400	0-0	—	0		0	0.0
Total	2	0	1	.000	6	0	0	0-1	5.1	1	1	0	0	4-1	5	0.00	—	.067	.250	0-0	—	0		1	0.3
MINTON, GREG Gregory Brian B 7.29.1951 Lubbock, TX BB/TR 6-2/190# d9.7																									
1975	SF N	1	1	.500	4	2	0	0-0	17	19	14	1	1	11-3	6	6.88	55	.288	.397	6-1	.000	-1	92	-5	-0.6
1976	SF N	0	3	.000	10	2	0	0-0	25.2	32	18	0	1	12-1	7	4.91	74	.317	.388	5-0	.200	-0*	109	-4	-0.4
1977	SF N	1	1	.500	2	2	0	0-0	14	14	8	0	0	4-0	5	4.50	87	.264	.316	3-1	.333	1*	91	-1	0.0
1978	SF N	0	1	.000	11	0	0	0-1	15.2	22	14	3	1	8-1	6	8.04	43	.338	.413	1-0	.000	-0		-8	-0.5
1979	SF N	4	3	.571	46	0	0	4-3	79.2	59	25	0	2	27-7	33	1.81	194	.215	.289	4-1	.000	-0		13	1.3
1980	SF N	4	6	.400	68	0	0	19-6	91.1	81	28	0	0	34-6	42	2.46	144	.243	.312	8-2	.125	-0		11	1.8
1981	SF N	4	5	.444	55	0	0	21-4	84.1	84	28	0	0	36-8	29	2.88	119	.267	.340	12-1	.000	-1		6	1.0
1982	SF N★	10	4	.714	78	0	0	30-7	123	108	29	5	2	42-17	58	1.83	197	.244	.310	17-1	.176	0		**24**	**3.9**
1983	SF N	7	11	.389	73	0	0	22-6	106.2	117	51	6	0	47-13	38	3.54	100	.283	.352	11-0	.545	4		-1	0.3
1984	SF N	4	9	.308	74	1	0	19-5	124.1	130	60	6	0	57-20	48	3.76	93	.267	.341	21-1	.048	-1	50	-4	-0.6
1985	SF N	5	4	.556	68	0	0	4-3	96.2	98	42	6	0	54-18	37	3.54	97	.272	.364	8-0	.000	-1		0	0.0
1986	SF N	4	4	.500	48	0	0	5-4	68.2	63	35	4	1	34-15	34	3.93	90	.251	.339	5-0	.400	2		-4	-0.2
1987	SF N	1	0	1.000	15	0	0	1-0	23.1	30	9	2	1	10-3	9	3.47	111	.323	.394	2-1	.000	-0		2	0.1
	Cal A	5	4	.556	41	0	0	10-2	76	71	28	4	1	29-4	35	3.08	140	.257	.328	0-0	—	0		11	1.6
1988	Cal A	4	5	.444	44	0	0	7-10	79	67	37	1	3	34-10	46	2.85	136	.233	.317	0-0	—	0		5	0.7
1989	Cal A	4	3	.571	62	0	0	8-3	90	76	22	4	2	37-4	42	2.20	174	.230	.310	0-0	—	0		17	1.6
1990	Cal A	1	1	.500	11	0	0	0-0	15.1	11	4	1	1	7-1	4	2.35	163	.212	.317	0-0	—	0		3	0.3
Total	16	59	65	.476	710	7	0	150-54	1130.2	1082	452	43	16	483-131	479	3.10	118	.257	.334	103-9	.146	2	94	65	10.3
MINTZ, STEVE Stephen Wayne B 11.24.1968 Wilmington, NC BL/TR 5-11/190# d5.18																									
1995	SF N	1	2	.333	14	0	0	0-1	19.1	26	16	4	2	12-3	7	7.45	55	.329	.426	3-0	.000	-0		-7	-0.9
1999	Ana A	0	0	—	3	0	0	0-0	5	8	2	1	0	2-0	2	3.60	135	.381	.435	0-0	—	0		1	0.0
Total	2	1	2	.333	17	0	0	0-1	24.1	34	18	5	2	14-3	9	6.66	64	.340	.427	3-0	.000	-0		-6	-0.9
MINUTELLI, GINO Gino Michael B 5.23.1964 Wilmington, DE BL/TL 6/180# d9.18																									
1990	Cin N	0	0	—	2	0	0	0-0	1	0	1	0	1	2-0	0	9.00	44	.000	.500	0-0	—	0		-1	0.0
1991	Cin N	0	2	.000	16	3	0	0-0	25.1	30	17	5	0	18-1	21	6.04	63	.288	.387	3-0	.000	-0	95	-5	-0.4
1993	SF N	0	1	.000	9	0	0	0-1	14.1	7	9	2	0	15-0	10	3.77	104	.152	.349	4-0	.000	-0		-1	-0.1
Total	3	0	3	.000	27	3	0	0-1	40.2	37	27	7	1	35-1	31	5.31	73	.242	.378	7-0	.000	-1	95	-7	-0.5
MIRABELLA, PAUL Paul Thomas B 3.20.1954 Belleville, NJ BL/TL 6-2/196# d7.28																									
1978	Tex A	3	2	.600	10	4	0	1-0	28	30	18	2	0	17-0	23	5.79	65	.286	.379	0-0	—	0	155	-5	-0.9
1979	NY A	0	4	.000	10	1	0	0-0	14.1	16	15	3	1	10-1	4	8.79	46	.276	.391	0-0	—	0	67	-8	-1.4
1980	Tor A	5	12	.294	33	22	3-1	0-1	130.2	151	73	11	3	66-3	53	4.34	99	.294	.375	0-0	—	0	81	-2	-0.2
1981	Tor A	0	0	—	8	1	0	0-0	14.2	20	16	2	1	7-0	9	7.36	54	.313	.384	0-0	—	0	137	-6	-0.3
1982	Tex A	1	1	.500	40	0	0	3-3	50.2	46	28	4	2	22-5	29	4.80	81	.241	.324	0-0	—	0		-5	-0.2
1983	Bal A	0	0	—	3	2	0	0-0	9.2	9	6	1	0	7-0	4	5.59	71	.243	.364	0-0	—	0	137	-1	-0.1
1984	Sea A	2	5	.286	52	1	0	3-3	68	74	39	6	1	32-6	41	4.37	91	.282	.359	0-0	—	0	23	-4	-0.4
1985	Sea A	0	0	—	10	0	0	0-0	13.2	9	4	0	2	4-1	8	1.32	320	.188	.268	0-0	—	0		4	0.2
1986	Sea A	0	0	—	8	0	0	0-0	6.1	13	7	1	0	3-0	6	8.53	50	.419	.471	0-0	—	0		-3	-0.1
1987	Mil A	2	1	.667	29	0	0	2-2	29.1	30	20	0	0	16-3	14	4.91	93	.268	.351	0-0	—	0		-2	-0.2
1988	Mil A	2	2	.500	38	0	0	4-0	60	44	12	3	0	21-5	33	1.65	242	.204	.272	0-0	—	0		16	1.2
1989	Mil A	0	0	—	13	0	0	0-0	15.1	18	14	1	1	7-3	6	7.63	50	.290	.356	0-0	—	0		-6	-0.3
1990	Mil A	4	2	.667	44	2	0	0-1	59	66	32	9	2	27-2	28	3.97	98	.281	.357	0-0	—	0	82	-1	-0.1
Total	13	19	29	.396	298	33	3-1	13-10	499.2	526	284	43	13	239-29	258	4.45	92	.272	.352	0-0	—	0	95	-23	-2.8
MIRANDA, ANGEL Angel Luis (Andujar) B 11.9.1969 Arecibo, P.R. BL/TL 6-1/195# d6.5																									
1993	Mil A	4	5	.444	22	17	2	0-0	120	100	53	12	2	52-4	88	3.30	129	.226	.309	0-0	—	0	94	11	0.7
1994	Mil A	2	5	.286	8	8	1	0-0	46	39	28	8	0	27-0	24	5.28	95	.234	.338	0-0	—	0	82	0	-0.1
1995	Mil A	4	5	.444	30	10	0	1-2	74	83	47	8	0	49-2	45	5.23	95	.291	.391	0-0	—	0	88	-2	-0.2
1996	Mil A	7	6	.538	46	12	0	1-1	109.1	116	68	12	2	69-4	78	4.94	105	.277	.376	0-0	—	0	97	2	0.1
1997	Mil A	0	0	—	10	0	0	0-0	14	17	6	1	3	9-2	8	3.86	120	.309	.433	0-0	—	0		1	0.1
Total	5	17	21	.447	116	47	3	2-3	363.1	355	202	41	7	206-12	243	4.46	108	.260	.356	0-0	—	0	91	12	0.6
MISURACA, MIKE Michael William B 8.21.1968 Long Beach, CA BR/TR 6/190# d7.27																									
1997	Mil A	0	0	—	5	0	0	0-0	10.1	15	13	5	0	7-1	10	11.32	41	.333	.423	0-0	—	0		-7	-0.3
MITCHELL, ROY Albert Roy B 4.19.1885 Belton, TX D 9.8.1959 Temple, TX BR/TR 5-9.5/170# d9.10																									
1910	StL A	4	2	.667	6	6	6	0	52	43	24	0	2	12	23	2.60	95	.244	.300	19-0	.211	0	113	-1	-0.1
1911	StL A	4	8	.333	28	12	8-1	0	133.1	134	79	4	6	45	40	3.85	88	.273	.341	49-1	.224	1*	82	-6	-0.3
1912	StL A	3	4	.429	13	7	5	0	62	81	36	2	4	17	22	4.65	71	.323	.375	19-0	.316	3	95	-6	-0.3
1913	StL A	13	16	.448	33	27	21-4	1	245.1	265	111	6	5	47	59	3.01	97	.282	.320	88-2	.148	-1*	99	-2	-0.4
1914	StL A	4	5	.444	28	9	4	**4**	103.1	134	77	1	6	38	38	4.35	62	.320	.384	34-0	.206	1	84	-22	-1.9

Year	Tm Lg	W	L	Pct	G	GS	CG-Sho	SV-BS	IP	H	R	HR	HB	BB-IB	SO	ERA	AERA	OAV	OOB	AB-SH	AVG	PB	Sup	APR	PW
1918	Chi A	0	1	.000	2	2	0	0	12	18	14	1	0	4	3	7.50	36	.346	.393	2-1	.000	-0	124	-7	-0.5
	Cin N	4	0	1.000	5	3	3-2	0	36.1	27	3	0	0	5	9	0.74	359	.208	.237	14-0	.214	0	189	8	1.1
1919	Cin N	0	1	.000	7	1	0	0	31	32	16	0	0	9	10	2.32	119	.276	.328	10-0	.000	-2	0	-1	-0.2
Total	7	32	37	.464	122	67	47-7	5	675.1	734	360	14	23	177	204	3.42	86	.285	.337	235-4	.187	3	98	-37	-2.6

MITCHELL, CHARLIE Charles Ross B 6.24.1962 Dickson, TN BR/TR 6-3/170# d8.9 b-John

Year	Tm Lg	W	L	Pct	G	GS	CG-Sho	SV-BS	IP	H	R	HR	HB	BB-IB	SO	ERA	AERA	OAV	OOB	AB-SH	AVG	PB	Sup	APR	PW
1984	Bos A	0	0	—	10	0	0	0-0	16.1	14	7	1	2	6-3	7	2.76	151	.226	.314	0-0	—	0		2	0.1
1985	Bos A	0	0	—	2	0	0	0-1	1.2	5	3	1	0	0-0	2	16.20	26	.500	.500	0-0	—	0		-2	-0.1
Total	2	0	0	—	12	0	0	0-1	18	19	10	2	2	6-3	9	4.00	105	.264	.338	0-0	—	0		0	0.0

MITCHELL, CLARENCE Clarence Elmer B 2.22.1891 Franklin, NE D 11.6.1963 Grand Island, NE BL/TL 5-11.5/190# d6.2 Mil 1918 C2 ▲

Year	Tm Lg	W	L	Pct	G	GS	CG-Sho	SV-BS	IP	H	R	HR	HB	BB-IB	SO	ERA	AERA	OAV	OOB	AB-SH	AVG	PB	Sup	APR	PW
1911	Det A	1	0	1.000	5	1	0	0	14.1	20	13	1	0	7	4	8.16	42	.351	.422	4-0	.500	1	125	-6	-0.3
1916	Cin N	11	10	.524	29	24	17-1	0	194.2	211	87	4	10	45	52	3.14	83	.285	.334	117-1	.239	2*	132	-12	-0.9
1917	Cin N	9	15	.375	32	20	10-2	1	159.1	166	73	4	2	34	37	3.22	81	.268	.308	90-2	.278	4*	91	-8	-0.7
1918	Bro N	0	1	.000	1	1	0	0	0.1	4	4	0	0	0	0	108.00	3	1.000	1.000	24-1	.250	0*	136	-3	-0.5
1919	Bro N	7	5	.583	23	11	9	0	108.2	123	49	0	0	23	43	3.06	97	.297	.334	49-0	.367	6*	129	-1	0.6
1920	†Bro N	5	2	.714	19	7	3-1	1	78.2	85	35	1	0	23	18	3.09	104	.288	.340	107-1	.234	1*	102	1	0.2
1921	Bro N	11	9	.550	37	18	13-**3**	2	190	206	91	7	5	46	39	2.89	135	.280	.327	91-0	.264	3*	102	14	1.9
1922	Bro N	0	3	.000	5	3	0	0	12.2	28	24	0	1	7	1	14.21	29	.467	.529	155-3	.290	2*	153	-14	-2.1
1923	Phi N	9	10	.474	29	19	8-1	0	139.1	170	93	8	4	46	41	4.72	98	.299	.355	78-0	.269	3*	93	-3	-0.1
1924	Phi N	6	13	.316	30	26	9-1	1	165	223	113	10	6	58	36	5.62	79	.321	.379	102-2	.255	-1*	84	-16	-1.5
1925	Phi N	10	17	.370	32	26	12-1	1	199.1	245	130	23	5	51	46	5.28	90	.302	.347	92-4	.196	-2*	85	-5	-0.5
1926	Phi N	9	14	.391	28	25	12	1	178.2	232	111	7	4	55	52	4.58	90	.318	.369	78-1	.244	1*	94	-9	-0.6
1927	Phi N	6	3	.667	13	12	8-1	0	94.2	99	44	7	2	28	17	4.09	101	.271	.327	42-2	.238	2*	115	2	0.4
1928	Phi N	0	0	—	3	0	0	0	5.2	13	6	0	0	2	0	9.53	45	.542	.577	4-0	.250	0*		-3	-0.1
	†StL N	8	9	.471	19	18	9-1	0	150	149	59	8	3	38	31	3.30	121	.265	.315	56-5	.125	-3	81	15	1.3
	Year	8	9	.471	22	18	9-1	0	155.2	162	63	8	3	40	31	3.53	114	.276	.326	60-5	.133	-3	81	10	1.2
1929	StL N	8	11	.421	25	22	16	0	173	221	89	13	5	60	39	4.27	109	.320	.379	66-6	.273	4*	99	10	1.2
1930	StL N	1	0	1.000	1	1	0	0	3	5	2	0	0	2	1	6.00	84	.357	.438	2-0	.500	0	139	0	0.0
	NY N	10	3	.769	24	16	5	0	129	151	68	10	1	36	40	3.98	119	.298	.346	47-2	.255	0	138	11	1.0
	Year	11	3	.786	25	17	5	0	132	156	76	10	1	38	41	4.02	118	.300	.349	49-2	.265	1	139	9	1.0
1931	NY N	13	11	.542	27	25	13	0	190.1	221	103	12	3	52	39	4.07	91	.285	.332	73-0	.219	2	128	-8	-0.8
1932	NY N	1	3	.250	8	3	1	2	30.1	41	21	1	1	11	7	4.15	89	.325	.384	10-0	.200	0	174	-3	-0.4
Total	18	125	139	.473	390	278	145-12	9	2217	2613	1215	116	52	624	543	4.12	95	.297	.347	1287-30	.252	26	105	-38	-1.9

MITCHELL, CRAIG Craig Seton B 4.14.1954 Santa Rosa, CA BR/TR 6-3/180# d9.25

Year	Tm Lg	W	L	Pct	G	GS	CG-Sho	SV-BS	IP	H	R	HR	HB	BB-IB	SO	ERA	AERA	OAV	OOB	AB-SH	AVG	PB	Sup	APR	PW
1975	Oak A	0	1	.000	1	1	0	0-0	3.2	6	5	0	0	2-0	2	12.27	30	.375	.444	0-0	—	0	48	-3	-0.5
1976	Oak A	0	0	—	1	0	0	0-0	3.1	3	1	0	0	0-0	0	2.70	124	.231	.231	0-0	—	0		0	0.0
1977	Oak A	0	1	.000	3	1	0	0-0	5.2	9	6	1	0	2-0	1	7.94	51	.346	.393	0-0	—	0	22	-3	-0.4
Total	3	0	2	.000	5	2	0	0-0	12.2	18	12	1	0	4-0	3	7.82	48	.327	.373	0-0	—	0	36	-6	-0.9

MITCHELL, FRED Frederick Francis (b: Frederick Francis Yapp) B 6.5.1878 Cambridge, MA D 10.13.1970 Newton, MA BR/TR 5-9.5/185# d4.27 M7 C3 ▲

Year	Tm Lg	W	L	Pct	G	GS	CG-Sho	SV-BS	IP	H	R	HR	HB	BB-IB	SO	ERA	AERA	OAV	OOB	AB-SH	AVG	PB	Sup	APR	PW
1901	Bos A	6	6	.500	17	13	10	0	108.2	115	67	2	11	51	34	3.81	93	.268	.360	44-0	.159	-1*	96	-3	-0.4
1902	Bos A	0	1	.000	1	0	0	0	4	8	5	1	0	5	2	11.25	32	.421	.542	1-0	.000	-0		-3	-0.4
	Phi A	5	8	.385	18	14	9	1	107.2	120	71	4	8	59	22	3.59	102	.282	.380	48-3	.188	-1*	98	-2	-0.2
	Year	5	9	.357	19	14	9	1	111.2	128	76	5	8	64	24	3.87	95	.288	.388	49-3	.184	-1	98	-5	-0.6
1903	Phi N	11	16	.407	28	28	24-1	0	227	250	155	4	19	102	69	4.48	73	.284	.370	95-2	.200	-1*	111	-30	-3.1
1904	Phi N	4	7	.364	13	13	11	0	108.2	133	62	3	7	25	29	3.40	79	.306	.353	82-3	.207	1*	117	-8	-0.5
	Bro N	2	5	.286	8	8	8-1	0	66	73	37	0	3	23	16	3.82	72	.291	.357	24-1	.292	2	91	-6	-0.3
	Year	6	12	.333	21	21	19-1	0	174.2	206	41	3	10	48	45	3.56	76	.300	.355	106-4	.226	4	107	-16	-0.8
1905	Bro N	3	7	.300	12	10	9	0	96.1	107	73	2	5	38	44	4.76	61	.285	.358	79-1	.190	0*	90	-21	-1.8
Total	5	31	50	.383	97	86	71-2	1	718.1	806	470	16	53	303	216	4.10	78	.286	.366	373-10	.198	1	103	-73	-6.7

MITCHELL, JOHN John Kyle B 8.11.1965 Dickson, TN BR/TR 6-2/195# d9.8 b-Charlie

Year	Tm Lg	W	L	Pct	G	GS	CG-Sho	SV-BS	IP	H	R	HR	HB	BB-IB	SO	ERA	AERA	OAV	OOB	AB-SH	AVG	PB	Sup	APR	PW
1986	NY N	0	1	.000	4	1	0	0-0	10	10	4	1	0	4-0	2	3.60	98	.278	.350	2-0	.000	-0	25	0	0.0
1987	NY N	3	6	.333	20	19	1	0-0	111.2	124	64	6	2	36-3	57	4.11	92	.279	.333	35-5	.114	-1	115	-8	-0.6
1988	NY N	0	0	—	1	0	0	0-0	1	2	0	0	0	1-0	1	0.00	—	.500	.600	1-0	.000	-0		0	0.0
1989	NY N	0	1	.000	2	0	0	0-0	3	3	7	0	0	4-1	4	6.00	54	.231	.412	0-0	—	0		-3	-0.6
1990	Bal A	6	6	.500	24	17	0	0-0	114.1	133	63	7	3	48-3	43	4.64	82	.300	.366	0-0	—	0	111	-11	-1.0
Total	5	9	14	.391	51	37	1	0-0	240	272	138	14	5	93-7	107	4.35	87	.289	.352	38-5	.105	-1	111	-22	-2.2

MITCHELL, LARRY Larry Paul B 10.16.1971 Flint, MI BR/TR 6-1/200# d8.11

Year	Tm Lg	W	L	Pct	G	GS	CG-Sho	SV-BS	IP	H	R	HR	HB	BB-IB	SO	ERA	AERA	OAV	OOB	AB-SH	AVG	PB	Sup	APR	PW
1996	Phi N	0	0	—	7	0	0	0-0	12	14	6	1	0	5-1	7	4.50	96	.311	.373	2-0	.000	-0		0	0.0

MITCHELL, MONROE Monroe Barr B 9.11.1901 Starkville, MS D 9.4.1976 Valdosta, GA BR/TL 6-1.5/170# d7.11

Year	Tm Lg	W	L	Pct	G	GS	CG-Sho	SV-BS	IP	H	R	HR	HB	BB-IB	SO	ERA	AERA	OAV	OOB	AB-SH	AVG	PB	Sup	APR	PW
1923	Was A	2	4	.333	10	6	3-1	2	41.2	57	35	0	1	22	8	6.48	58	.350	.430	12-0	.250	1	84	-13	-1.5

MITCHELL, PAUL Paul Michael B 8.19.1949 Worcester, MA BR/TR 6-1/195# d7.1

Year	Tm Lg	W	L	Pct	G	GS	CG-Sho	SV-BS	IP	H	R	HR	HB	BB-IB	SO	ERA	AERA	OAV	OOB	AB-SH	AVG	PB	Sup	APR	PW
1975	Bal A	3	0	1.000	11	4	1	0-1	57	41	23	8	0	19-4	31	3.63	97	.204	.271	0-0	—	0	225	0	0.0
1976	Oak A	9	7	.563	26	26	4-1	0-0	142	169	74	15	1	30-0	67	4.25	79	.294	.328	0-0	—	0	124	-14	-1.5
1977	Oak A	0	3	.000	5	3	0	0-0	13.2	21	16	3	0	7-0	5	10.54	38	.339	.406	0-0	—	0	45	-9	-1.5
	Sea A	3	3	.500	9	9	0	0-0	39.2	50	26	7	1	16-1	20	4.99	83	.311	.370	0-0	—	0	80	-4	-0.6
	Year	3	6	.333	14	12	0	0-0	53.1	71	30	10	1	23-1	25	6.41	64	.318	.380	0-0	—	0	71	-13	-2.1
1978	Sea A	8	14	.364	29	29	4-2	0-0	168	173	86	21	2	79-1	75	4.18	91	.270	.350	0-0	—	0	80	-6	-0.8
1979	Sea A	1	4	.200	10	6	1	0-0	36.2	46	26	4	0	15-0	18	4.42	99	.309	.370	0-0	—	0	69	-3	-0.3
	Mil A	3	3	.500	18	8	0	0-0	75	81	50	11	3	10-0	32	5.76	73	.276	.301	0-0	—	0	122	-12	-0.8
	Year	4	7	.364	28	14	1	0-0	111.2	127	56	15	3	25-0	50	5.32	80	.287	.325	0-0	—	0	99	-14	-1.1
1980	Mil A	5	5	.500	17	11	1-1	1-0	89.1	92	40	7	1	15-3	29	3.53	110	.267	.298	0-0	—	0	97	4	0.4
Total	6	32	39	.451	125	96	11-4	1-1	621.1	673	341	76	8	191-9	277	4.45	85	.278	.330	0-0	—	0	100	-44	-5.1

MITCHELL, BOBBY Robert McKasha B 2.6.1856 Cincinnati, OH D 5.1.1933 Springfield, OH BL/TL 5-5/135# d9.6

Year	Tm Lg	W	L	Pct	G	GS	CG-Sho	SV-BS	IP	H	R	HR	HB	BB-IB	SO	ERA	AERA	OAV	OOB	AB-SH	AVG	PB	Sup	APR	PW
1877	Cin N	6	5	.545	12	12	11-1	0	100	123	69	0		11	41	3.51	75	.281	.299	49	.204	-0*	86	-8	-0.6
1878	Cin N	7	2	.778	9	9	9-1	0	80	69	32	1		18	51	2.14	100	**.223**	.265	49	.245	1*	116	3	0.4
1879	Cle N	7	15	.318	23	22	20	0	194.2	236	153	1		42	90	3.28	76	.283	.317	109	.147	-4*	84	-17	-2.1
1882	StL AA	0	1	.000	1	1	0	0	7	12	13	0		2	2	7.71	36	.353	.389	4	.000	-1	110	-4	-0.4
Total	4	20	23	.465	45	44	40-2	0	381.2	440	267	2		73	184	3.18	77	.272	.304	211	.180	-5	91	-26	-2.7

MITCHELL, WILLIE William B 12.1.1889 Pleasant Grove, MS D 11.23.1973 Sardis, MS BR/TL 6/176# d9.22 Mil 1918

Year	Tm Lg	W	L	Pct	G	GS	CG-Sho	SV-BS	IP	H	R	HR	HB	BB-IB	SO	ERA	AERA	OAV	OOB	AB-SH	AVG	PB	Sup	APR	PW
1909	Cle A	1	2	.333	3	3	3	0	23	18	6	0	4	10	8	1.57	163	.225	.340	7-0	.286	1	46	2	0.4
1910	Cle A	12	8	.600	35	18	11-1	0	183.2	155	77	2	15	55	102	2.60	100	.236	.310	63-3	.159	-3	120	-1	-0.6
1911	Cle A	7	14	.333	30	22	9	0	177.1	190	102	1	13	60	78	3.76	91	.284	.354	64-2	.109	-5*	84	-7	-1.3
1912	Cle A	5	8	.385	29	15	8	1	163.2	149	88	0	7	56	94	2.80	121	.240	.309	53-1	.113	-4	105	5	-0.2
1913	Cle A	14	8	.636	35	22	14-4	0	217	153	62	1	8	88	141	1.91	159	.202	.292	70-6	.143	-2	108	27	2.3
1914	Cle A	11	17	.393	39	32	16-3	0	257	228	127	3	7	124	179	3.19	91	.238	.330	81-8	.086	-3	103	-7	-1.4
1915	Cle A	11	14	.440	36	30	12-1	0	236	210	103	1	2	84	149	2.82	108	.241	.309	79-6	.127	-5	96	6	-0.1
1916	Cle A	2	5	.286	12	6	1	1	43.2	55	35	1	0	19	24	5.15	58	.309	.376	11-1	.000	-1	101	-11	-1.7
	Det A	7	5	.583	23	17	7-2	0	127.2	119	53	1	5	48	60	3.31	86	.253	.329	36-1	.250	2	121	-4	-0.3
	Year	9	10	.474	35	23	8-2	1	171.1	174	58	2	5	67	84	3.78	77	.269	.342	47-2	.191	1	116	-15	-2.0
1917	Det A	12	8	.600	30	22	12-5	0	185.1	172	66	2	13	46	80	2.19	121	.250	.309	59-4	.119	-3*	106	9	0.5
1918	Det A	0	1	.000	1	1	0	0	4	3	4	0	0	5	2	9.00	30	.200	.400	2-0	.000	-0	85	-3	-0.4
1919	Det A	1	2	.333	3	2	0	0	13.2	12	8	2	1	10	4	5.27	61	.255	.397	5-0	.200	0	110	-2	-0.4
Total	11	83	92	.474	276	190	93-16	4	1632	1464	731	14	75	605	921	2.88	103	.244	.320	530-32	.130	-24	102	14	-3.2

MITRE, SERGIO Sergio Armando B 2.16.1981 Los Angeles, CA BR/TR 6-4/210# d7.22

Year	Tm Lg	W	L	Pct	G	GS	CG-Sho	SV-BS	IP	H	R	HR	HB	BB-IB	SO	ERA	AERA	OAV	OOB	AB-SH	AVG	PB	Sup	APR	PW
2003	Chi N	0	1	.000	3	2	0	0-0	8.2	15	8	1	0	4-1	3	8.31	51	.395	.442	2-0	.500	0	67	-4	-0.3

Year	Tm Lg	W	L	Pct	G	GS	CG-Sho	SV-BS	IP	H	R	HR	HB	BB-IB	SO	ERA	AERA	OAV	OOB	AB-SH	AVG	PB	Sup	APR	PW
MIZELL, VINEGAR BEND Wilmer David B 8.13.1930 Leakesville, MS D 2.21.1999 Kerrville, TX BR/TL 6-3.5/205# d4.22 Mil 1954																									
1952	StL N	10	8	.556	30	30	7-2	0	190	171	89	12	1	103	146	3.65	102	.237	.333	68-4	.044	-5	103	1	-0.6
1953	StL N	13	11	.542	33	33	10-1	0	224.1	193	93	12	4	114	173	3.49	122	.227	.321	83-3	.084	-4	89	20	1.5
1956	StL N	14	14	.500	33	33	11-3	0	208.2	172	93	20	7	92-5	153	3.62	104	.222	.310	75-5	.107	-3	94	5	0.4
1957	StL N	8	10	.444	33	21	7-2	0	149.1	136	69	18	1	51-4	87	3.74	106	.241	.303	45-1	.089	-2	89	4	0.3
1958	StL N	10	14	.417	30	29	8-2	0	189.2	178	81	17	2	91-9	80	3.42	121	.252	.335	61-5	.115	-3	59	14	1.3
1959	StL N✣	13	10	.565	31	30	8-1	0	201.1	196	104	21	8	89-7	108	4.20	101	.252	.333	75-5	.187	1	109	1	0.0
1960	StL N	1	3	.250	9	9	0	0	55.1	64	31	7	0	28-4	42	4.55	90	.291	.369	18-1	.111	-1	84	-3	-0.2
	†Pit N	13	5	.722	23	23	8-3	0	155.2	141	59	7	3	46-6	71	3.12	120	.247	.305	51-4	.137	-1	107	11	1.0
	Year	14	8	.636	32	32	8-3	0	211	205	64	14	3	74-10	113	3.50	110	.259	.323	69-5	.130	-1	101	10	0.8
1961	Pit N	7	10	.412	25	17	2-1	0	100	120	61	16	0	31-8	37	5.04	79	.299	.348	23-5	.130	-1	75	-11	-1.7
1962	Pit N	1	1	.500	4	3	0	0	16.1	15	10	3	1	10-0	6	4.96	79	.254	.366	6-0	.000	-0	82	-2	-0.2
	NY N	0	2	.000	17	2	0	0	38	48	35	10	1	25-0	15	7.34	57	.324	.416	8-0	.250	0	105	-12	-0.6
	Year	1	3	.250	21	5	0	0	54.1	63	40	13	2	35-0	21	6.63	62	.304	.402	14-0	.143	-0	90	-15	-0.8
Total	9	90	88	.506	268	230	61-15	0	1528.2	1434	725	143	28	680-43	918	3.85	104	.247	.328	513-33	.111	-19	91	28	1.2
MLICKI, DAVE David John B 6.8.1968 Cleveland, OH BR/TR 6-4/190# d9.12																									
1992	Cle A	0	2	.000	4	4	0	0-0	21.2	23	14	3	1	16-0	16	4.98	78	.280	.404	0-0	—	0	111	-3	-0.2
1993	Cle A	0	0	—	3	3	0	0-0	13.1	11	6	2	2	6-0	7	3.38	129	.220	.328	0-0	—	0	99	1	0.1
1995	NY N	9	7	.563	29	25	0	0-0	160.2	160	82	23	4	54-2	123	4.26	95	.256	.317	39-12	.051	-1	111	-3	-0.4
1996	NY N	6	7	.462	51	2	0	1-2	90	95	46	9	6	33-8	83	3.30	122	.277	.348	10-0	.100	-0	90	4	0.4
1997	NY N	8	12	.400	32	32	1-1	0-0	193.2	194	89	21	5	76-7	157	4.00	101	.259	.329	48-3	.188	2*	104	4	0.5
1998	NY N	1	4	.200	10	10	1	0-0	57	68	38	8	5	25-4	39	5.68	73	.297	.374	16-3	.188	1	120	-10	-0.7
	LA N	7	3	.700	20	20	2-1	0-0	124.1	120	64	15	2	38-1	78	4.05	98	.253	.308	34-7	.059	-2	114	-2	-0.3
	Year	8	7	.533	30	30	3-1	0-0	181.1	188	69	23	7	63-5	117	4.57	88	.267	.330	50-10	.100	-1	116	-13	-1.0
1999	LA N	0	1	.000	2	0	0	0-0	7.1	10	4	1	0	2-0	1	4.91	87	.323	.364	1-2	1.000	1		0	0.0
	Det A	14	12	.538	31	31	2	0-0	191.2	209	108	24	12	70-1	119	4.60	108	.276	.344	4-0	.000	0	82	6	0.6
2000	Det A	6	11	.353	24	21	0	0-0	119.1	143	79	17	3	44-1	57	5.58	87	.291	.349	2-0	.000	-0	82	-9	-1.1
2001	Det A	4	8	.333	15	15	0	0-0	81	118	69	19	6	41-2	48	7.33	59	.348	.424	1-0	.000	-0	85	-26	-3.0
	†Hou N	7	3	.700	19	14	0	0-0	86.2	85	53	18	9	33-1	49	5.09	90	.260	.339	26-4	.115	-1	114	-5	-0.6
2002	Hou N	4	10	.286	22	16	0	0-0	86	101	57	11	3	34-5	57	5.34	80	.290	.356	27-0	.185	0	72	-11	-1.6
Total	10	66	80	.452	262	193	6-2	1-2	1232.2	1337	709	171	58	472-32	834	4.72	92	.276	.344	208-31	.125	-0	97	-54	-6.3
MMAHAT, KEVIN Kevin Paul B 11.9.1964 Memphis, TN BL/TL 6-5/220# d9.9																									
1989	NY A	0	2	.000	4	2	0	0-0	7.2	13	12	2	1	8-0	3	12.91	30	.406	.500	0-0	—	0	82	-8	-1.3
MODAK, MIKE Michael B 5.18.1922 Campbell, OH D 12.12.1995 Lakeland, FL BR/TR 5-10.5/195# d7.4 Mil 1946																									
1945	Cin N	1	2	.333	20	3	1-1	1	42.1	52	27	0	0	23	7	5.74	65	.308	.391	10-0	.100	-1	68	-8	-0.7
MOEHLER, BRIAN Brian Merritt B 12.31.1971 Rockingham, NC BR/TR 6-3/195# d9.22																									
1996	Det A	0	1	.000	2	2	0	0-0	10.1	11	10	1	0	8-1	2	4.35	116	.262	.380	0-0	—	0	82	-1	-0.1
1997	Det A	11	12	.478	31	31	2-1	0-0	175.1	198	97	22	5	61-1	97	4.67	98	.285	.343	3-0	.000	-0	107	-1	-0.1
1998	Det A	14	13	.519	33	33	4-3	0-0	221.1	220	103	30	2	56-1	123	3.90	121	.259	.306	4-0	.000	-0	85	20	2.2
1999	Det A	10	16	.385	32	32	2-2	0-0	196.1	229	116	22	7	59-5	106	5.04	98	.294	.347	1-0	.000	0	86	-1	0.0
2000	Det A	12	9	.571	29	29	2	0-0	178	222	99	20	2	40-0	103	4.50	107	.305	.342	4-0	.000	-0	111	6	0.6
2001	Det A	0	0	—	1	1	0	0-0	8	6	3	0	0	1-0	2	3.38	129	.207	.233	0-0	—	0	107	1	0.1
2002	Det A	1	1	.500	3	3	0	0-0	19.2	17	5	3	0	2-0	13	2.29	188	.233	.250	0-0	—	0	79	5	0.4
	Cin N	2	4	.333	10	9	0	0-0	43.1	61	34	8	1	11-0	18	6.02	71	.330	.369	14-1	.000	-1	121	-9	-1.1
2003	Hou N	0	0	—	3	3	0	0-0	13.2	22	12	4	0	6-0	5	7.90	56	.379	.431	4-0	.000	-0	120	-5	-0.2
Total	8	50	56	.472	144	143	10-6	0-0	866	986	479	110	17	244-8	469	4.57	104	.287	.335	30-1	.000	-3	98	15	1.8
MOELLER, DENNIS Dennis Michael B 9.15.1967 Tarzana, CA BR/TL 6-2/195# d7.28																									
1992	KC A	0	3	.000	5	4	0	0-0	18	24	17	5	0	11-2	6	7.00	58	.333	.407	0-0	—	0	96	-6	-0.9
1993	Pit N	1	0	1.000	10	0	0	0-0	16.1	26	20	2	1	7-1	13	9.92	41	.356	.420	0-0	—	0		-11	-0.6
Total	2	1	3	.250	15	4	0	0-0	34.1	50	37	7	1	18-3	19	8.39	48	.345	.413	0-0	—	0	96	-17	-1.5
MOELLER, JOE Joseph Douglas B 2.15.1943 Blue Island, IL BR/TR 6-5/208# d4.12 Mil 1962																									
1962	LA N	6	5	.545	19	15	1	1	85.2	87	55	10	0	58-1	46	5.25	69	.266	.375	33-1	.212	1	145	-15	-1.6
1964	LA N	7	13	.350	27	24	1	0	145.1	153	89	14	4	31-4	97	4.21	77	.265	.305	45-4	.067	-2	78	-21	-2.9
1966	†LA N	2	4	.333	29	8	0	0	78.2	73	31	4	3	14-8	31	2.52	131	.244	.283	12-3	.167	1	83	5	0.5
1967	LA N	0	0	—	6	0	0	0	5	9	5	1	0	3-1	2	9.00	34	.409	.462	0-0	—	0		-3	-0.2
1968	LA N	1	1	.500	3	3	0	0	16	17	10	1	1	2-0	11	5.06	55	.270	.299	7-0	.000	-1	94	-4	-0.6
1969	LA N	1	0	1.000	23	4	0	1-0	51.1	54	23	4	0	13-0	25	3.33	100	.278	.322	10-0	.200	0	146	-1	0.0
1970	LA N	7	9	.438	31	19	2-1	4-0	135.1	131	63	16	1	43-3	63	3.92	98	.248	.305	39-3	.154	0	78	0	-0.1
1971	LA N	2	4	.333	28	1	0	1-1	66.1	72	32	5	0	12-2	32	3.80	85	.279	.307	9-0	.000	-0	55	-5	-0.4
Total	8	26	36	.419	166	74	4-1	7-1	583.2	596	308	55	9	176-19	307	4.01	86	.263	.316	155-11	.129	-2	97	-44	-5.3
MOELLER, RON Ronald Ralph "The Kid" B 10.13.1938 Cincinnati, OH BL/TL 6/180# d9.8 Mil 1962																									
1956	Bal A	0	1	.000	4	1	0	0	8.2	10	5	0	0	3-0	2	4.15	94	.286	.333	1-0	.000	-0	23	-1	-0.1
1958	Bal A	0	0	—	4	0	0	0	4.1	6	2	0	0	3-0	3	4.15	87	.333	.429	0-0	—	0		0	0.0
1961	LA A	4	8	.333	33	18	1-1	0	112.2	122	80	15	2	83-0	87	5.83	77	.275	.391	29-1	.207	2*	103	-14	-1.0
1963	LA A	0	0	—	3	0	0	0	2.2	5	2	1	0	1-0	2	6.75	51	.385	.429	0-0	—	0		-1	0.0
	Was A	2	0	1.000	8	3	0	0	24.1	31	17	4	1	10-0	10	6.29	59	.316	.385	9-0	.222	0	128	-6	-0.5
	Year	2	0	1.000	11	3	0	0	27	36	22	5	1	11-0	12	6.33	58	.324	.390	9-0	.222	0	129	-7	-0.5
Total	4	6	9	.400	52	22	1-1	0	152.2	174	106	20	3	100-0	104	5.78	74	.287	.389	39-1	.205	2	105	-22	-1.6
MOFFETT, SAM Samuel R. B 3.14.1857 Wheeling, WV D 5.5.1907 Butte, MT BR/TR 6/175# d5.15 b-Joe ▲																									
1884	Cle N	3	19	.136	24	22	21	0	197.2	236	165	9		58	84	3.87	81	.284	.330	256	.184	-3*	60	-16	-1.5
1887	Ind N	1	5	.167	6	6	6	0	50	47	45	1	4	23	3	3.78	110	.242	.335	41	.122	-2*	65	-2	-0.4
1888	Ind N	2	5	.286	7	7	6-1	0	56	62	40	3	2	17	7	4.66	64	.278	.335	35	.114	-1*	151	-10	-1.1
Total	3	6	29	.171	37	35	33-1	0	303.2	345	250	13	6	98	94	4.00	82	.276	.332	332	.169	-6	76	-28	-3.0
MOFFITT, RANDY Randall James B 10.13.1948 Long Beach, CA BR/TR 6-3/190# d6.11																									
1972	SF N	1	5	.167	40	0	0	4-2	70.2	72	31	5	2	30-6	37	3.69	94	.266	.341	8-2	.000	-1		-1	-0.2
1973	SF N	4	4	.500	60	0	0	14-4	100.1	86	30	9	1	31-4	65	2.42	158	.225	.284	17-1	.059	-1		15	1.4
1974	SF N	5	7	.417	61	1	0	15-4	102	99	52	9	2	29-4	49	4.50	85	.256	.308	16-2	.313	2	69	-4	-0.4
1975	SF N	4	5	.444	55	0	0	11-6	74	73	35	6	3	32-6	39	3.89	98	.257	.336	14-0	.214	1		0	0.0
1976	SF N	6	6	.500	58	0	0	14-2	103	92	36	6	1	35-9	50	2.27	160	.238	.300	14-0	.143	-0		13	1.8
1977	SF N	4	9	.308	64	0	0	11-7	87.2	91	41	4	3	39-13	68	3.59	109	.273	.348	3-1	.000	-0		3	0.5
1978	SF N	8	4	.667	70	0	0	12-9	81.2	79	35	5	3	33-13	52	3.31	104	.258	.331	7-1	.143	0		1	0.0
1979	SF N	2	5	.286	28	0	0	2-1	35	53	33	5	2	14-6	16	7.71	45	.356	.416	4-0	.000	-0*		-17	-3.2
1980	SF N	1	1	.500	13	0	0	0-1	16.2	18	10	2	1	4-2	10	4.86	73	.281	.333	1-0	.000	-0		-2	-0.3
1981	SF N	0	0	—	10	0	0	0-0	11.1	15	10	2	0	2-1	11	7.94	43	.313	.333	0-0	—	0		-5	-0.3
1982	Hou N	2	4	.333	30	0	0	3-3	41.2	36	15	3	5	13-3	20	3.02	110	.228	.305	2-1	.000	-0		2	0.2
1983	Tor A	6	2	.750	45	0	0	10-3	57.1	52	27	5	1	24-6	38	3.77	115	.243	.318	0-0	—	0		3	0.5
Total	12	43	52	.453	534	1	0	96-42	781.1	766	355	61	24	286-73	455	3.65	102	.257	.324	86-8	.140	-1	69	8	-0.0
MOFORD, HERB Herbert B 8.6.1928 Brooksville, KY BR/TR 6-1/175# d4.12																									
1955	StL N	1	1	.500	14	1	0	2	24	29	23	5	1	15-3	8	7.88	52	.299	.395	2-0	.000	-0	66	-10	-0.9
1958	Det A	4	9	.308	25	11	6	1	109.2	83	45	10	9	42-6	58	3.61	112	.214	.304	37-3	.027	-4	73	7	0.4
1959	Bos A	0	2	.000	4	2	0	0	8.2	10	11	3	0	6-0	7	11.42	36	.286	.390	1-0	.000	-0	98	-6	-1.1
1962	NY N	0	1	.000	7	0	0	0	15	21	15	3	0	1-0	5	7.20	58	.318	.324	4-0	.250	0		-5	-0.3
Total	4	5	13	.278	50	14	6	3	157.1	143	94	21	10	64-9	78	5.03	81	.244	.327	44-3	.045	-4	76	-14	-1.9

Year	Tm Lg	W	L	Pct	G	GS	CG-Sho	SV-BS	IP	H	R	HR	HB	BB-IB	SO	ERA	AERA	OAV	OOB	AB-SH	AVG	PB	Sup	APR	PW
MOGRIDGE, GEORGE George Anthony B 2.18.1889 Rochester, NY D 3.4.1962 Rochester, NY BL/TL 6-2/165# d8.17																									
1911	Chi A	0	2	.000	4	1	0	0	12.2	12	10	1	0	1	5	4.97	65	.255	.271	5-0	.400	0	179	-3	-0.3
1912	Chi A	3	4	.429	17	8	2	3	64.2	69	32	2	1	15	31	4.04	79	.264	.307	16-0	.125	-0	78	-3	-0.4
1915	NY A	2	3	.400	6	5	3-1	0	41	33	11	0	3	11	11	1.76	167	.219	.285	12-0	.083	-1	89	5	0.5
1916	NY A	6	12	.333	30	21	10-2	0	194.2	174	71	3	7	45	66	2.31	125	.252	.305	66-2	.212	1	72	9	1.0
1917	NY A	9	11	.450	29	25	15-1	0	196.1	185	82	5	9	39	46	2.98	90	.255	.301	69-4	.159	-1	94	-5	-0.6
1918	NY A	16	13	.552	**45**	19	13-1	**7**	239.1	232	78	6	8	43	62	2.18	130	.263	.304	79-6	.190	-0*	125	14	2.0
1919	NY A	10	9	.526	35	18	13-3	0	169	159	68	6	7	46	58	2.77	115	.250	.307	48-2	.125	-1	100	7	0.7
1920	NY A	5	9	.357	26	15	7	1	125.1	146	83	4	3	36	35	4.31	89	.287	.338	42-1	.167	-1	103	-10	-1.0
1921	Was A	18	14	.563	38	36	21-4	0	288	301	119	12	7	66	101	3.00	137	.269	.313	98-3	.153	-5	75	36	3.0
1922	Was A	18	13	.581	34	32	18-3	0	251.2	300	120	12	11	72	61	3.58	108	.304	.358	86-9	.244	4	97	9	1.4
1923	Was A	13	13	.500	33	30	17-3	1	211	228	90	10	3	56	62	3.11	121	.285	.334	75-6	.227	1	105	16	2.0
1924	†Was A	16	11	.593	30	30	13-2	0	213	217	97	2	7	61	48	3.76	107	.270	.327	74-4	.176	-2	86	11	1.0
1925	Was A	3	4	.429	10	8	3	0	53	58	27	2	4	18	12	4.08	104	.291	.362	19-1	.105	-2	97	2	0.0
	StL A	1	1	.500	2	2	1	0	15.1	17	10	2	1	5	8	5.87	80	.279	.343	4-0	.000	-0	99	-1	-0.1
	Year	4	5	.444	12	10	4	0	68.1	75	16	4	5	23	20	4.48	97	.288	.358	23-1	.087	-2	97	1	-0.1
1926	Bos N	6	10	.375	39	10	2	3	142	173	82	6	3	36	46	4.50	79	.311	.356	46-5	.174	-1*	120	-15	-1.6
1927	Bos N	6	4	.600	20	1	0	5	48.2	48	23	4	2	15	26	3.70	100	.257	.319	15-0	.200	-0	23	0	0.1
Total	15	132	133	.498	398	261	138-20	20	2265.2	2352	1003	77	76	565	678	3.23	109	.273	.323	754-43	.182	-8	95	72	7.7
MOHART, GEORGE George Benjamin B 3.6.1892 Buffalo, NY D 10.2.1970 Silver Creek, NY BR/TR 5-9/165# d4.15																									
1920	Bro N	0	1	.000	13	1	0	0	35.2	33	17	0	3	7	13	1.77	181	.250	.303	8-0	.125	-0	123	2	0.2
1921	Bro N	0	0	—	2	0	0	0	7	8	5	0	1	1	1	3.86	101	.296	.345	2-0	.500	0		-1	0.0
Total	2	0	1	.000	15	1	0	0	42.2	41	22	0	4	8	14	2.11	157	.258	.310	10-0	.200	0	123	1	0.2
MOHLER, MIKE Michael Ross B 7.26.1968 Dayton, OH BR/TL 6-2/195# d4.7																									
1993	Oak A	1	6	.143	42	9	0	0-1	64.1	57	45	10	2	44-4	42	5.60	73	.241	.361	0-0	—	0	80	-13	-1.2
1994	Oak A	0	1	.000	1	1	0	0-0	2.1	2	3	1	0	2-0	4	7.71	57	.167	.286	0-0	—	0	83	-1	-0.2
1995	Oak A	1	1	.500	28	0	0	1-1	23.2	16	8	0	0	18-1	15	3.04	147	.198	.343	0-0	—	0		4	0.3
1996	Oak A	6	3	.667	72	0	0	7-6	81	79	36	9	1	41-6	64	3.67	134	.263	.350	0-0	—	0		11	1.3
1997	Oak A	1	10	.091	62	10	0	1-3	101.2	116	65	11	7	54-8	66	5.13	88	.301	.391	0-0	—	0*	73	-8	-0.7
1998	Oak A	3	3	.500	57	0	0	0-1	61	70	38	6	4	26-3	42	5.16	89	.289	.365	0-0	—	0		-3	-0.3
1999	StL N	1	1	.500	48	0	0	1-1	49.1	47	26	3	1	23-2	31	4.38	104	.254	.338	3-0	.000	-0		1	0.0
2000	StL N	1	1	.500	22	0	0	0-2	19	26	20	1	2	15-1	8	9.00	51	.321	.439	1-0	1.000	0		-9	-0.8
	Cle A	0	1	.000	2	0	0	0-1	1	1	1	1	0	0-0	2	9.00	55	.250	.250	0-0	—	0		0	-0.1
2001	Ari N	0	0	—	13	0	0	0-2	13.2	14	11	3	0	9-0	7	7.24	63	.286	.390	0-0	—	0		-3	-0.2
Total	9	14	27	.341	347	20	0	10-18	417	428	253	45	17	232-25	281	4.99	91	.272	.368	4-0	.250	0	73	-21	-1.9
MOHORCIC, DALE Dale Robert B 1.25.1956 Cleveland, OH BR/TR 6-3/220# d5.31																									
1986	Tex A	2	4	.333	58	0	0	7-5	79	86	25	5	1	15-6	29	2.51	172	.279	.315	0-0	—	0		15	1.3
1987	Tex A	7	6	.538	74	0	0	16-7	99.1	88	34	11	2	19-6	48	2.99	150	.244	.285	0-0	—	0		18	2.8
1988	Tex A	2	6	.250	43	0	0	5-3	52	62	35	6	5	20-5	25	4.85	84	.295	.363	0-0	—	0		-6	-0.9
	NY A	2	2	.500	13	0	0	1-2	22.2	21	7	1	3	9-2	19	2.78	142	.239	.327	0-0	—	0		3	0.5
	Year	4	8	.333	56	0	0	6-5	74.2	83	46	7	8	29-7	44	4.22	96	.279	.352	0-0	—	0		-3	-0.4
1989	NY A	2	1	.667	32	0	0	2-3	57.2	65	41	8	6	18-3	24	4.99	78	.286	.352	0-0	—	0		-10	-0.5
1990	Mon N	1	2	.333	34	0	0	2-2	53	56	21	6	4	18-3	29	3.23	113	.286	.350	8-1	.125	-0		2	0.1
Total	5	16	21	.432	254	0	0	33-22	363.2	378	163	37	21	99-25	174	3.49	119	.272	.327	8-1	.125	-0		22	3.3
MOISAN, BILL William Joseph B 7.30.1925 Bradford, MA BL/TR 6-1/170# d9.17																									
1953	Chi N	0	0	—	3	0	0	0	5	5	3	0	1	2	1	5.40	82	.278	.381	0-0	—	0		0	0.0
MOLESWORTH, CARLTON Carlton B 2.15.1876 Frederick, MD D 7.25.1961 Frederick, MD BL/TL 5-7.5/162# d9.14																									
1895	Was N	0	2	.000	4	3	1	0	16	33	34	1	4	15	7	14.63	33	.418	.531	7-0	.143	-1	124	-15	-1.3
MOLINA, GABE Cruz Gabriel B 5.3.1975 Denver, CO BR/TR 5-11/190# d5.1																									
1999	Bal A	1	2	.333	20	0	0	0-1	23	22	19	4	0	16-1	14	6.65	71	.256	.373	0-0	—	0		-6	-0.6
2000	Bal A	0	0	—	9	0	0	0-0	13	25	14	2	0	9-0	8	9.00	53	.397	.459	0-0	—	0		-6	-0.3
	Atl N	0	0	—	2	0	0	0-0	2	3	4	1	1	1-0	1	9.00	51	.375	.455	0-0	—	0		-2	-0.1
2002	StL N	1	0	1.000	12	0	0	0-0	11.1	6	2	1	0	6-0	4	1.59	250	.162	.279	0-0	—	0		3	0.3
2003	StL N	0	0	—	3	0	0	0-0	2.2	5	4	1	0	1-0	1	13.50	30	.385	.429	0-0	—	0		-3	-0.1
Total	4	2	2	.500	46	0	0	0-1	52	61	43	9	1	33-1	28	6.58	69	.295	.389	0-0	—	0		-14	-0.8
MOLONEY, RICHIE Richard Henry B 6.7.1950 Brookline, MA BR/TR 6-3/185# d9.20																									
1970	Chi A	0	0	—	1	0	0	0-0	1	2	0	0	0	0-0	1	0.00	—	.400	.400	0-0	—	0		0	0.0
MOLYNEAUX, VINCE Vincent Leo B 8.17.1888 Lewiston, NY D 5.4.1950 Stamford, CT BR/TR 6/180# d7.5																									
1917	StL A	0	0	—	7	0	0	0	22	18	15	0	0	20	4	4.91	53	.237	.396	4-0	.000	-1		-5	-0.3
1918	Bos A	1	0	1.000	6	0	0	0	10.2	3	4	0	0	8	1	3.38	80	.086	.256	2-0	.000	-0		0	-0.1
Total	2	1	0	1.000	13	0	0	0	32.2	21	19	0	0	28	5	4.41	60	.189	.353	6-0	.000	-1		-5	-0.4
MONAHAN, RINTY Edward Francis B 4.28.1928 Brooklyn, NY BR/TR 6-1.5/195# d8.9																									
1953	Phi A	0	0	—	4	0	0	0	10.2	11	5	0	0	7	2	4.22	102	.275	.383	2-0	.000	-0		0	0.0
MONBOUQUETTE, BILL William Charles B 8.11.1936 Medford, MA BR/TR 5-11/195# d7.18 C3																									
1958	Bos A	3	3	.429	10	8	3	0	54.1	52	25	4	0	20-4	30	3.31	121	.251	.313	17-2	.176	-1	98	3	0.3
1959	Bos A	7	7	.500	34	17	4	0	151.2	165	86	15	3	33-1	87	4.15	98	.285	.323	46-3	.065	-4*	96	-5	-0.9
1960	Bos A★	14	11	.560	35	30	12-3	0	215	217	91	18	2	68-9	134	3.64	111	.263	.319	65-8	.092	-3*	91	12	0.9
1961	Bos A	14	14	.500	32	32	12-1	0	236.1	233	106	24	0	100-1	161	3.39	123	.254	.326	69-14	.130	-1*	88	18	1.9
1962	Bos A☆	15	13	.536	35	35	11-4	0	235.1	227	100	22	3	65-1	153	3.33	124	.251	.302	73-8	.096	-3	91	19	1.6
1963	Bos A☆	20	10	.667	37	36	13-1	0	266.2	258	119	31	0	42-6	174	3.81	99	.250	.279	88-10	.114	-3	119	2	-0.2
1964	Bos A	13	14	.481	36	35	7-5	0	234	258	114	34	1	40-4	120	4.04	95	.277	.306	72-5	.083	-2*	95	-3	-0.6
1965	Bos A	10	18	.357	35	35	10-2	0	228.2	239	114	32	1	40-5	110	3.70	101	.269	.299	68-10	.059	-3*	92	-1	-0.4
1966	Det A	7	8	.467	30	14	2-1	0	102.2	120	60	14	3	22-4	61	4.73	74	.293	.330	26-4	.154	-0	107	-14	-1.9
1967	Det A	0	0	—	2	0	0	0	2	1	0	0	0	0-0	2	0.00	—	.143	.143	0-0	—	0		1	0.0
	NY A	6	5	.545	33	10	2-1	1	133.1	122	39	6	4	17-7	53	2.36	132	.246	.274	32-3	.156	-0	86	12	1.0
	Year	6	5	.545	35	10	2-1	1	135.1	123	42	6	4	17-7	55	2.33	134	.245	.273	32-3	.156	-0	86	13	1.0
1968	NY A	5	7	.417	17	11	2	0	89.1	92	47	7	3	13-2	32	4.43	65	.264	.293	26-2	.115	0	98	-14	-1.7
	SF N	0	1	.000	7	0	0	1	12.1	11	9	4	0	2-0	5	3.65	81	.239	.265	0-0	—	0		-2	-0.2
Total	11	114	112	.504	343	263	78-18	3	1961.2	1995	910	211	20	462-44	1122	3.68	104	.263	.305	582-69	.103	-20	97	28	-0.2
MONGE, SID Isidro Pedroza B 4.11.1951 Agua Prieta, Mexico BB/TL 6-2/195# d9.12																									
1975	Cal A	0	2	.000	4	2	2	0-0	23.2	22	12	3	1	10-0	17	4.18	85	.242	.324	0-0	—	0	62	-1	-0.1
1976	Cal A	6	7	.462	32	13	2	0-0	117.2	108	50	10	1	49-0	53	3.37	99	.248	.324	0-0	—	0	89	0	-0.1
1977	Cal A	0	1	.000	4	0	0	1-0	12.1	14	6	2	0	6-0	4	2.92	135	.304	.377	0-0	—	0		1	0.1
	Cle A	1	2	.333	33	0	0	3-1	39	47	31	6	0	27-4	25	6.23	63	.309	.407	0-0	—	0		-11	-0.9
	Year	1	3	.250	37	0	0	4-1	51.1	61	40	8	0	33-4	29	5.44	73	.308	.400	0-0	—	0		-10	-0.8
1978	Cle A	4	3	.571	48	2	0	6-4	84.2	71	36	4	0	51-6	54	2.76	136	.225	.330	0-0	—	0	108	6	0.6
1979	Cle A☆	12	10	.545	76	0	0	19-7	131	96	37	9	1	64-8	108	2.40	177	.209	.300	0-0	—	0		28	5.1
1980	Cle A	3	5	.375	67	0	0	14-7	94.1	80	39	12	3	40-6	61	3.53	116	.227	.310	0-0	—	0		6	0.6
1981	Cle A	3	5	.375	31	0	0	4-2	58	58	31	9	0	21-2	41	4.34	84	.266	.326	0-0	—	0		-5	-0.7
1982	Phi N	7	1	.875	47	0	0	2-3	72	70	35	8	2	22-3	43	3.75	98	.256	.312	9-2	.111	-0		-1	-0.1
1983	Phi N	3	0	1.000	14	0	0	0-0	11.2	20	10	4	0	6-1	7	6.94	51	.377	.433	1-0	.000	-0		-4	-0.9
	SD N	7	3	.700	47	0	0	7-1	68.2	65	24	4	1	31-6	32	3.15	111	.257	.338	10-1	.100	-0		4	0.6
	Year	10	3	.769	61	0	0	7-1	80.1	85	39	8	1	37-7	39	3.70	95	.278	.354	11-1	.091	-1		-1	-0.3

Year	Tm Lg	W	L	Pct	G	GS	CG-Sho	SV-BS	IP	H	R	HR	HB	BB-IB	SO	ERA	AERA	OAV	OOB	AB-SH	AVG	PB	Sup	APR	PW
1984	SD N	2	1	.667	13	0	0	0-1	15	17	10	3	0	17-3	7	4.80	74	.293	.447	1-0	.000	-0		-3	-0.5
	Det A	1	0	1.000	19	0	0	0-0	36	40	21	5	2	12-0	19	4.25	92	.282	.340	0-0	—	0		-2	-0.1
Total	10	49	40	.551	435	17	4	56-26	764	708	342	79	11	356-39	471	3.53	107	.248	.331	21-3	.095	-1	81	18	3.6
MONROE, ED Edward Oliver "Peck" B 2.22.1895 Louisville, KY D 4.29.1969 Louisville, KY BR/TR 6-5/187# d5.29 Mil 1918																									
1917	NY A	1	0	1.000	9	1	1	1	28.2	35	15	1	2	6	12	3.45	78	.310	.355	12-0	.167	-0	134	-3	-0.2
1918	NY A	0	0	—	1	0	0	0	2	1	2	0	0	2	1	4.50	63	.143	.333	0-0	—	0		-1	0.0
Total	2	1	0	1.000	10	1	1	1	30.2	36	17	1	2	8	13	3.52	77	.300	.354	12-0	.167	-0	134	-4	-0.2
MONROE, LARRY Lawrence James B 6.20.1956 Detroit, MI BR/TR 6-4/200# d8.23																									
1976	Chi A	0	1	.000	8	2	0	0-0	21.2	23	11	0	0	13-0	9	4.15	86	.284	.379	0-0	—	0	49	-1	-0.1
MONROE, ZACH Zachary Charles B 7.8.1931 Peoria, IL BR/TR 6/198# d6.27																									
1958	†NY A	4	2	.667	21	6	1	1	58	57	29	8	0	27-1	18	3.26	108	.263	.344	17-0	.118	-1	199	0	-0.1
1959	NY A	0	0	—	3	0	0	0	3.1	3	2	2	0	2-0	1	5.40	67	.231	.333	0-0	—	0		-1	0.0
Total	2	4	2	.667	24	6	1	1	61.1	60	31	10	0	29-1	19	3.38	105	.261	.344	17-0	.118	-1	199	-1	-0.1
MONTAGUE, JOHN John Evans B 9.12.1947 Newport News, VA BR/TR 6-2/213# d9.9																									
1973	Mon N	0	0	—	4	0	0	0-0	7.2	8	3	0	1	2-2	7	3.52	109	.286	.344	1-0	.000	-0		0	0.0
1974	Mon N	3	4	.429	46	1	0	3-2	82.2	73	37	5	4	38-5	43	3.16	122	.241	.329	10-0	.100	-0	23	5	0.3
1975	Mon N	0	1	.000	12	0	0	2-0	17.2	23	11	4	2	6-1	9	5.60	68	.324	.383	1-0	.000	-0*		-3	-0.2
	Phi N	0	0	—	3	0	0	0-0	5	8	5	1	0	4-1	1	9.00	42	.400	.500	0-0	—	0		-3	-0.1
	Year	0	1	.000	15	0	0	2-0	22.2	31	17	5	2	10-2	10	6.35	60	.341	.410	1-0	.000	-0		-5	-0.3
1977	Sea A	8	12	.400	47	15	2	4-1	182.1	193	95	20	4	75-5	98	4.29	96	.272	.343	0-0	—	0	80	-3	-0.2
1978	Sea A	1	3	.250	19	0	0	2-1	43.2	52	31	2	0	24-4	14	6.18	62	.308	.386	0-0	—	0		-10	-1.0
1979	Sea A	6	4	.600	41	1	0	1-3	116.1	125	73	14	2	47-13	60	5.57	79	.284	.349	0-0	—	0	21	-12	-0.9
	†Cal A	2	0	1.000	14	0	0	6-2	17.2	16	12	3	0	9-0	6	5.09	80	.242	.333	0-0	—	0		-2	-0.5
	Year	8	4	.667	55	1	0	7-5	134	141	86	17	2	56-13	66	5.51	79	.279	.347	0-0	—	0	21	-14	-1.4
1980	Cal A	4	2	.667	37	0	0	3-1	73.2	97	47	8	1	21-1	22	5.13	77	.324	.365	0-0	—	0		-10	-0.8
Total	7	24	26	.480	223	17	2	21-10	546.2	595	314	57	14	226-32	260	4.76	86	.283	.351	12-0	.083	-0	74	-38	-3.4
MONTALVO, RAFAEL Rafael Edgardo (Torres) B 3.31.1964 Rio Piedras, P.R. BR/TR 6/185# d4.13																									
1986	Hou N	0	0	—	1	0	0	0-0	1	1	1	0	0	2-0	0	9.00	40	.250	.500	0-0	—	0		-1	0.0
MONTEAGUDO, AURELIO Aurelio Faustino (Cintra) B 11.19.1943 Caibarien, Cuba D 11.10.1990 Saltillo, Mexico BR/TR 5-11/185# d9.1 f-Rene																									
1963	KC A	0	0	—	4	0	0	0	7	4	2	0	0	3-0	3	2.57	152	.182	.269	0-0	—	0		1	0.1
1964	KC A	0	4	.000	11	6	0	0	31.1	40	32	11	1	10-0	14	8.90	43	.317	.370	7-0	.286	1	70	-16	-1.7
1965	KC A	0	0	—	4	0	0	0	7	5	4	1	0	4-1	5	3.86	90	.185	.290	0-0	—	0*		-1	0.0
1966	KC A	0	0	—	6	0	0	0	12.2	12	4	0	0	7-0	3	2.84	120	.261	.352	0-0	—	0		1	0.1
	Hou N	0	0	—	10	0	0	1	15.1	14	8	1	0	11-1	7	4.70	73	.241	.362	1-0	.000	-0		-2	-0.1
1967	Chi A	0	1	.000	1	1	0	0	1.1	4	3	1	0	2-0	0	20.25	15	.500	.600	0-0	—	0	0	-2	-0.4
1970	KC A	1	1	.500	21	0	0	0-0	27.1	20	11	2	1	9-0	18	2.96	126	.200	.273	2-0	.000	-0		2	0.1
1973	Cal A	2	1	.667	15	0	0	3-2	30	23	18	2	4	16-3	8	4.20	85	.215	.336	0-0	—	0		-3	-0.4
Total	7	3	7	.300	72	7	0	4-2	132	122	82	18	6	62-5	58	5.05	72	.247	.336	10-0	.200	1	63	-20	-2.3
MONTEAGUDO, RENE Rene (Miranda) B 3.12.1916 Havana, Cuba D 9.14.1973 Hialeah, FL BL/TL 5-7/165# d9.6 s-Aurelio ▲																									
1938	Was A	1	1	.500	5	3	2	0	22	26	15	3	0	15	13	5.73	79	.286	.387	6-1	.500	1	143	-3	-0.1
1940	Was A	2	6	.250	27	8	3	2	100.2	128	70	7	3	52	64	6.08	69	.316	.398	33-0	.182	0	97	-18	-1.3
1945	Phi N	0	0	—	14	0	0	0	45.2	67	42	1	2	28	16	7.49	51	.347	.435	193-4	.301	2*		-16	-0.6
Total	3	3	7	.300	46	11	5	2	168.1	221	127	11	5	95	93	6.42	64	.321	.407	232-5	.289	4	113	-37	-2.0
MONTEFUSCO, JOHN John Joseph "Count" B 5.25.1950 Long Branch, NJ BR/TR 6-1/180# d9.3																									
1974	SF N	3	2	.600	7	5	1-1	0-1	39.1	41	22	3	0	19-0	34	4.81	79	.256	.335	14-0	.286	3	101	-3	-0.1
1975	SF N	15	9	.625	35	34	10-4	0-0	243.2	210	85	11	8	86-12	215	2.88	132	.233	.303	80-9	.087	-2	93	25	2.1
1976	SF N★	16	14	.533	37	36	11-**6**	0-0	253.1	224	90	11	4	74-8	172	2.84	128	.238	.294	78-6	.103	-2*	81	24	2.3
1977	SF N	7	12	.368	26	25	4	0-0	157.1	170	82	10	3	46-6	110	3.49	112	.273	.321	49-4	.122	-1	82	3	0.1
1978	SF N	11	9	.550	36	36	3	0-0	238.2	233	110	25	4	68-6	177	3.81	91	.255	.308	70-9	.057	-3*	108	-9	-1.1
1979	SF N	3	8	.273	22	22	0	0-0	137	145	64	15	2	51-7	76	3.94	89	.279	.343	42-2	.167	2*	83	-5	-0.2
1980	SF N	4	8	.333	22	17	1	0-0	113.1	120	61	15	2	39-6	85	4.37	81	.265	.325	30-3	.033	-2	93	-10	-1.3
1981	Atl N	2	3	.400	26	9	0	1-0	77.1	75	32	9	0	27-2	34	3.49	103	.260	.321	15-0	.067	-1	107	1	0.0
1982	SD N	10	11	.476	32	32	1	0-0	184.1	177	93	17	3	41-2	83	4.00	86	.251	.290	58-6	.086	-2	101	-12	-1.5
1983	SD N	9	4	.692	31	10	1	4-1	95.1	94	38	6	1	32-6	52	3.30	106	.265	.326	19-4	.053	-1	114	2	0.2
	NY A	5	0	1.000	6	6	0	0-0	38	39	14	3	1	10-0	15	3.32	118	.271	.318	0-0	—	0	109	3	0.4
1984	NY A	5	3	.625	11	11	0	0-0	55.1	55	26	5	1	13-2	23	3.58	106	.253	.295	0-0	—	0	104	1	0.0
1985	NY A	0	0	—	3	1	0	0-0	7	12	8	3	0	2-0	2	10.29	39	.387	.412	0-0	—	0	227	-5	-0.2
1986	NY A	0	0	—	4	0	0	0-1	12.1	9	3	2	0	5-0	3	2.19	187	.200	.280	0-0	—	0		3	0.2
Total	13	90	83	.520	298	244	32-11	5-3	1652.1	1604	728	135	29	513-57	1081	3.54	103	.255	.311	455-43	.097	-10	95	18	0.9
MONTEJO, MANNY Manuel (Bofill) B 10.16.1935 Caibarien, Cuba BR/TR 5-11/150# d7.25																									
1961	Det A	0	0	—	12	0	0	0	16.1	13	7	2	2	6-1	15	3.86	106	.217	.309	0-0	—	0		1	0.0
MONTELEONE, RICH Richard B 3.22.1963 Tampa, FL BR/TR 6-2/234# d4.15 C2																									
1987	Sea A	0	0	—	3	0	0	0-0	7	10	5	2	1	4-0	2	6.43	74	.345	.441	0-0	—	0		-1	0.0
1988	Cal A	0	0	—	3	0	0	0-0	4.1	4	0	0	1	1-1	3	0.00	—	.222	.300	0-0	—	0		2	0.1
1989	Cal A	2	2	.500	24	0	0	0-2	39.2	39	15	3	1	13-1	27	3.18	120	.255	.314	0-0	—	0		3	0.3
1990	NY A	0	1	.000	5	0	0	0-0	7.1	8	5	0	0	2-0	8	6.14	65	.276	.323	0-0	—	0		-1	-0.2
1991	NY A	3	1	.750	26	0	0	0-0	47	42	27	5	0	19-3	34	3.64	114	.236	.307	0-0	—	0		0	0.0
1992	NY A	7	3	.700	47	0	0	0-2	92.2	82	35	7	0	27-3	62	3.30	119	.235	.289	0-0	—	0		7	0.7
1993	NY A	7	4	.636	42	0	0	0-1	85.2	85	52	14	0	35-10	50	4.94	84	.262	.329	0-0	—	0		-8	-0.9
1994	SF N	4	3	.571	39	0	0	0-1	45.1	43	18	6	0	13-2	16	3.18	126	.253	.299	3-0	.000	-0		4	0.5
1995	Cal A	1	0	1.000	9	0	0	0-1	9	8	2	1	0	3-0	5	2.00	235	.267	.314	0-0	—	0		3	0.3
1996	Cal A	0	3	.000	12	0	0	0-0	15.1	23	11	5	1	2-0	5	5.87	85	.348	.377	0-0	—	0		-1	-0.2
Total	10	24	17	.585	210	0	0	0-7	353.1	344	170	43	4	119-20	212	3.87	106	.255	.314	3-0	.000	-0		8	0.6
MONTGOMERY, JEFF Jeffrey Thomas B 1.7.1962 Wellston, OH BR/TR 5-11/180# d8.1																									
1987	Cin N	2	2	.500	14	1	0	0-0	19.1	25	15	2	0	9-1	13	6.52	65	.313	.382	2-0	.000	-0	43	-5	-0.8
1988	KC A	7	2	.778	45	0	0	1-2	62.2	54	25	6	2	30-1	47	3.45	116	.231	.321	0-0	—	0		5	0.6
1989	KC A	7	3	.700	63	0	0	18-6	92	66	16	3	2	25-4	94	1.37	282	.198	.257	0-0	—	0		**25**	3.5
1990	KC A	6	5	.545	73	0	0	24-10	94.1	81	36	6	5	34-8	94	2.39	161	.227	.302	0-0	—	0		12	1.9
1991	KC A	4	4	.500	67	0	0	33-6	90	83	32	6	2	28-2	77	2.90	142	.246	.305	0-0	—	0		13	1.8
1992	KC A★	1	6	.143	65	0	0	39-7	82.2	61	23	5	3	27-2	69	2.18	187	.205	.277	0-0	—	0		16	2.7
1993	KC A★	7	5	.583	69	0	0	**45-6**	87.1	65	22	3	2	23-4	66	2.27	203	.206	.263	0-0	—	0		**22**	4.5
1994	KC A	2	3	.400	42	0	0	27-5	44.2	48	21	5	1	15-1	50	4.03	124	.276	.335	0-0	—	0		5	0.9
1995	KC A	2	3	.400	54	0	0	31-7	65.2	60	27	7	2	25-4	49	3.43	140	.252	.322	0-0	—	0		10	1.4
1996	KC A☆	4	6	.400	48	0	0	24-10	63.1	59	31	14	3	19-3	45	4.26	118	.251	.314	0-0	—	0		6	1.1
1997	KC A	1	4	.200	55	0	0	14-3	59.1	53	24	9	0	18-5	48	3.49	135	.240	.295	0-0	—	0		8	0.9
1998	KC A	2	5	.286	56	0	0	36-5	56	58	35	8	2	22-2	54	4.98	97	.264	.335	0-0	—	0		-1	-0.3
1999	KC A	1	4	.200	49	0	0	12-7	51.1	72	40	7	2	21-3	27	6.84	73	.343	.404	0-0	—	0		-9	-1.0
Total	13	46	52	.469	700	1	0	304-74	868.2	785	347	81	26	296-40	733	3.27	134	.241	.308	2-0	.000	-0	43	107	17.2
MONTGOMERY, MONTY Monty Bryson B 9.1.1946 Albemarle, NC BR/TR 6-3/200# d9.14																									
1971	KC A	3	0	1.000	3	2	0	0-0	21.1	16	5	0	0	3-0	12	2.11	163	.205	.235	7-1	.000	-0	130	3	0.5
1972	KC A	3	3	.500	9	8	1-1	0-0	56.1	55	21	2	0	17-2	24	3.04	100	.263	.316	17-3	.176	1	106	0	0.0
Total	2	6	3	.667	12	10	1-1	0-0	77.2	71	26	2	0	20-2	36	2.78	113	.247	.294	24-4	.125	0	110	3	0.5

Year	Tm Lg	W	L	Pct	G	GS	CG-Sho	SV-BS	IP	H	R	HR	HB	BB-IB	SO	ERA	AERA	OAV	OOB	AB-SH	AVG	PB	Sup	APR	PW
MONTGOMERY, STEVE Steven Lewis B 12.25.1970 Westminster, CA BR/TR 6-4/210# d4.3																									
1996	Oak A	1	0	1.000	8	0	0	0-0	13.2	18	14	5	0	13-2	8	9.22	53	.310	.437	0-0	—	0		-6	-0.4
1997	Oak A	0	1	.000	4	0	0	0-0	6.1	10	7	2	0	8-2	1	9.95	46	.385	.514	0-0	—	0		-4	-0.5
1999	Phi N	1	5	.167	53	0	0	3-0	64.2	54	25	10	0	31-3	55	3.34	141	.229	.318	1-0	1.000	0		10	0.9
2000	SD N	0	2	.000	7	0	0	0-0	5.2	6	6	3	0	4-0	3	7.94	54	.273	.385	0-0	—	0		-3	-0.5
Total	4	2	8	.200	72	0	0	3-0	90.1	88	52	20	0	56-7	67	4.98	95	.257	.361	1-0	1.000	0		-3	-0.5
MONZANT, RAMON Ramon Segundo (Espina) B 1.4.1933 Maracaibo, Venezuela BR/TR 6/165# d7.2																									
1954	NY N	0	0	—	6	1	0	0	7.2	8	5	0	0	11	5	4.70	86	.276	.463	2-0	.000	-0	199	-1	-0.1
1955	NY N	4	8	.333	28	12	3	0	94.2	98	47	11	3	43-5	54	3.99	101	.278	.357	24-2	.125	-1*	76	1	0.0
1956	NY N	1	0	1.000	4	1	1	0	13	8	7	4	0	7-0	11	4.15	91	.170	.278	4-0	.000	-1*	186	-1	-0.1
1957	NY N	3	2	.600	24	2	0	0	49.2	55	27	6	2	16-1	37	3.99	99	.286	.340	10-0	.300	1	11	-1	-0.1
1958	SF N	8	11	.421	43	16	4-1	1	150.2	160	89	20	6	57-5	93	4.72	81	.273	.339	49-1	.163	-1*	119	-15	-1.8
1960	SF N	0	0	—	1	0	0	0	1	1	1	1	0	0-0	1	9.00	39	.250	.250	0-0	—	0		-1	0.0
Total	6	16	21	.432	106	32	8-1	1	316.2	330	176	42	11	134-11	201	4.38	89	.273	.346	89-3	.157	-2	100	-18	-2.1
MOODY, ERIC Eric Lane B 1.6.1971 Greenville, SC BR/TR 6-6/185# d8.3																									
1997	Tex A	0	1	.000	10	1	0	0-1	19	26	10	4	0	2-0	12	4.26	112	.329	.341	0-0	—	0	38	1	0.0
MOON, LEO Leo "Lefty" B 6.22.1899 Bellemont, NC D 8.25.1970 New Orleans, LA BR/TL 5-11/165# d7.9																									
1932	Cle A	0	0	—	1	0	0	0	5.2	11	8	0	0	7	1	11.12	43	.379	.500	2-0	.500	0		-4	-0.1
MOONEY, JIM Jim Irving B 9.4.1906 Mooresburg, TN D 4.27.1979 Johnson City, TN BR/TL 5-11/168# d8.14																									
1931	NY N	7	1	.875	10	8	6-2	0	71.2	71	19	1	1	16	38	2.01	184	.262	.306	25-1	.160	-1	119	14	1.4
1932	NY N	6	10	.375	29	18	4-1	0	124.2	154	79	18	0	42	37	5.05	73	.299	.352	41-0	.122	-2	103	-17	-2.1
1933	StL N	2	5	.286	21	8	2	1	77.1	87	36	1	0	26	14	3.72	93	.296	.353	20-2	.050	-2	87	-1	-0.3
1934	†StL N	2	4	.333	32	7	1	1	82.1	114	59	3	4	49	27	5.47	77	.326	.414	19-1	.053	-2	99	-11	-1.0
Total	4	17	20	.459	92	41	13-3	2	356	426	193	23	5	133	116	4.25	89	.298	.360	105-4	.105	-7	102	-15	-2.0
MOONEYHAM, BILL William Craig B 8.16.1960 Livermore, CA BR/TR 6/175# d4.19																									
1986	Oak A	4	5	.444	45	6	0	2-3	99.2	103	53	4	3	67-4	75	4.52	86	.270	.382	0-0	—	0	125	-7	-0.5
MOORE, BALOR Balor Lilbon B 1.25.1951 Smithville, TX BL/TL 6-2/184# d5.21																									
1970	Mon N	0	2	.000	6	2	0	0-0	9.2	14	9	0	0	8-0	6	7.45	55	.368	.458	3-0	.333	0	44	-4	-0.6
1972	Mon N	9	9	.500	22	22	6-3	0-0	147.2	122	61	15	5	59-5	161	3.47	102	.226	.305	55-1	.145	-0	112	2	0.2
1973	Mon N	7	16	.304	35	32	3-1	0-0	176.1	151	98	18	3	109-2	151	4.49	85	.233	.343	53-2	.057	-3	79	-11	-1.6
1974	Mon N	0	2	.000	8	2	0	0-0	13.2	13	8	1	0	15-0	16	3.95	97	.245	.412	2-0	.000	-0	45	-1	-0.1
1977	Cal A	0	2	.000	7	3	0	0-0	22.2	28	19	7	3	10-1	14	3.97	99	.298	.376	0-0	—	0	137	-3	-0.3
1978	Tor A	6	9	.400	37	18	2	0-3	144.1	165	85	16	7	54-1	75	4.93	80	.294	.360	0-0	—	0	84	-15	-1.4
1979	Tor A	5	7	.417	34	16	5	0-1	139.1	135	85	17	8	79-4	51	4.84	90	.262	.366	0-0	—	0	98	-7	-0.6
1980	Tor A	1	1	.500	31	3	0	1-0	64.2	76	43	6	4	31-3	22	5.29	82	.309	.391	0-0	—	0	104	-7	-0.4
Total	8	28	48	.368	180	98	16-4	1-4	718.1	704	408	80	30	365-16	496	4.52	87	.261	.352	113-3	.106	-3	90	-46	-4.8
MOORE, BRAD Bradley Alan B 6.21.1964 Loveland, CO BR/TR 6-1/185# d6.14																									
1988	Phi N	0	0	—	5	0	0	0-0	5.2	4	0	0	0	4-1	2	0.00	—	.267	.421	0-0	—	0		2	0.1
1990	Phi N	0	0	—	3	0	0	0-0	2.2	4	1	0	0	2-1	1	3.38	113	.400	.462	0-0	—	0		0	0.0
Total	2	0	0	—	8	0	0	0-0	8.1	8	1	0	0	6-2	3	1.08	338	.320	.438	0-0	—	0		2	0.1
MOORE, CARLOS Carlos Whitman B 8.13.1906 Clinton, TN D 7.2.1958 New Orleans, LA BR/TR 6-1.5/180# d5.4																									
1930	Was A	0	0	—	4	0	0	0	11.2	9	3	0	0	4	2	2.31	199	.225	.295	4-0	.000	-1		3	0.1
MOORE, DONNIE Donnie Ray B 2.13.1954 Lubbock, TX D 7.18.1989 Anaheim, CA BL/TR 6/185# d9.14																									
1975	Chi N	0	0	—	4	1	0	0-0	8.2	12	4	1	0	4-0	8	4.15	93	.316	.381	3-0	.000	-0	114	0	0.0
1977	Chi N	4	2	.667	27	1	0	0-1	48.2	51	27	1	0	18-7	34	4.07	108	.285	.345	10-0	.300	1	182	1	0.2
1978	Chi N	9	7	.563	71	1	0	4-5	102.2	117	55	7	2	31-11	50	4.12	98	.287	.337	15-1	.267	1	178	-2	-0.2
1979	Chi N	1	4	.200	39	1	0	1-0	73	95	46	8	2	25-7	43	5.18	80	.321	.375	13-0	.154	0	64	-7	-0.4
1980	StL N	1	1	.500	11	0	0	0-0	21.2	25	15	1	1	5-1	10	6.23	59	.298	.341	4-2	.750	2		-5	-0.3
1981	Mil A	0	0	—	3	0	0	0-0	4	4	3	0	0	4-0	2	6.75	51	.286	.421	0-0	—	0		-1	-0.1
1982	†Atl N	3	1	.750	16	0	0	1-2	27.2	32	13	1	2	7-3	17	4.23	88	.294	.345	1-0	.000	-0		-1	-0.1
1983	Atl N	2	3	.400	43	0	0	6-1	68.2	72	30	6	0	10-3	41	3.67	106	.279	.300	8-1	.500	1		2	0.2
1984	Atl N	4	5	.444	47	0	0	16-3	64.1	63	27	3	1	18-6	47	2.94	131	.258	.309	3-0	.000	-0		5	0.9
1985	Cal A★	8	8	.500	65	0	0	31-8	103	91	28	9	0	21-3	72	1.92	214	.237	.275	0-0	—	0		24	**4.8**
1986	†Cal A	4	5	.444	49	0	0	21-8	72.2	60	28	10	0	22-4	53	2.97	139	.228	.285	0-0	—	0		9	1.4
1987	Cal A	2	2	.500	14	0	0	5-2	26.2	28	12	2	0	13-2	17	2.70	160	.259	.339	0-0	—	0		4	0.6
1988	Cal A	5	2	.714	27	0	0	4-3	33	48	20	4	0	8-2	22	4.91	79	.343	.373	0-0	—	0		-4	-0.8
Total	13	43	40	.518	416	4	0	89-33	654.2	698	308	53	8	186-49	416	3.67	110	.276	.325	57-4	.281	5	139	25	6.2
MOORE, EARL Earl Alonzo "Big Ebbie" or "Crossfire" B 7.29.1879 Pickerington, OH D 11.28.1961 Columbus, OH BR/TR 6/195# d4.25																									
1901	Cle A	16	14	.533	31	30	28-4	0	251.1	234	129	4	8	107	99	2.90	122	.244	.325	99-3	.162	-5	109	17	1.0
1902	Cle A	17	18	.486	36	34	29-4	1	293	304	158	8	7	101	84	2.95	117	.268	.331	113-3	.212	-0	93	12	1.2
1903	Cle A	20	8	.714	29	27	27-3	0	247.2	196	88	0	5	62	148	**1.74**	**164**	**.217**	.271	87-5	.092	-5	127	27	2.2
1904	Cle A	12	11	.522	26	24	22-1	0	227.2	186	83	2	10	61	139	2.25	113	.224	.285	86-2	.140	-2	130	7	0.1
1905	Cle A	15	15	.500	31	30	28-3	0	269	232	111	6	18	92	131	2.64	99	.234	.311	96-1	.104	-4	118	-2	-0.8
1906	Cle A	1	1	.500	5	4	2	0	29.2	27	15	1	2	18	8	3.94	66	.245	.362	10-0	.000	-1	117	-3	-0.4
1907	Cle A	1	1	.500	3	2	1	0	19.1	18	14	0	1	8	7	4.66	54	.250	.333	7-0	.000	-1	108	-4	-0.5
	NY A	2	6	.250	12	9	3	1	64	72	49	1	4	30	28	3.94	71	.286	.371	22-0	.273	1	97	-10	-1.1
	Year	3	7	.300	15	11	4	1	83.1	90	53	1	5	38	35	4.10	66	.278	.362	29-0	.207	0	99	-14	-1.6
1908	Phi N	2	1	.667	3	3	3-1	0	26	20	4	0	2	8	16	0.00	—	.217	.294	9-1	.222	0	97	5	0.8
1909	Phi N	18	12	.600	38	34	24-4	0	299.2	238	93	7	9	108	173	2.10	124	.210	.283	96-5	.094	-4	82	17	1.0
1910	Phi N	22	15	.595	46	35	18-**6**	0	283	228	98	5	10	121	**185**	2.58	121	.228	.318	87-8	.230	2	103	20	2.6
1911	Phi N	15	19	.441	42	36	21-5	1	308.1	265	123	11	12	164	174	2.63	131	.240	.345	101-3	.109	-6	84	26	1.9
1912	Phi N	9	14	.391	31	24	10-1	1	182.1	186	101	3	7	77	79	3.31	110	.275	.355	56-3	.107	-4	70	4	-0.1
1913	Phi N	1	3	.250	12	5	0	1	52	50	37	3	1	40	24	5.02	66	.254	.382	16-1	.000	-2	113	-10	-0.9
	Chi N	1	1	.500	7	2	0	0	28.1	34	19	3	0	12	12	4.45	71	.321	.390	8-0	.125	-0	71	-4	-0.3
	Year	2	4	.333	19	7	0	1	80.1	84	22	6	1	52	36	4.82	68	.277	.385	24-1	.042	-2	102	-12	-1.2
1914	Buf F	11	15	.423	36	27	14-2	2	194.2	184	109	3	10	99	96	4.30	69	.263	.362	56-3	.161	-2	91	-26	-3.5
Total	14	163	154	.514	388	326	230-34	6	2776	2474	1231	57	106	1108	1403	2.78	110	.241	.321	949-38	.141	-34	100	76	3.2
MOORE, EUEL Euel Walton "Chief" B 5.27.1908 Reagan, OK D 2.12.1989 Tishomingo, OK BR/TR 6-2/185# d7.8																									
1934	Phi N	5	7	.417	20	16	3	1	122.1	145	60	9	0	41	38	4.05	117	.288	.342	46-0	.109	-4	63	9	0.4
1935	Phi N	1	6	.143	15	8	1	1	40.1	63	40	5	2	20	15	7.81	58	.354	.425	15-1	.400	1	89	-12	-1.7
	NY N	1	0	1.000	6	0	0	0	8	9	5	0	0	4	3	5.63	69	.281	.361	2-0	.000	-0		-1	-0.2
	Year	2	6	.250	21	8	1	1	48.1	72	50	5	2	24	18	7.45	59	.343	.415	17-1	.353	1	91	-14	-1.9
1936	Phi N	2	3	.400	20	5	1	1	54.1	76	50	4	1	12	19	6.96	65	.311	.346	18-0	.222	-0	101	-12	-1.1
Total	3	9	16	.360	61	29	5	3	225	293	155	18	3	77	75	5.48	84	.306	.360	81-1	.185	-3	77	-16	-2.6
MOORE, GENE Eugene Sr. "Blue Goose" B 11.9.1885 Lancaster, TX D 8.31.1938 Dallas, TX BL/TL 6-2/185# d9.28 s-Gene																									
1909	Pit N	0	0	—	1	0	0	0	2	4	4	0	0	3	2	18.00	15	.364	.500	1-0	.000	-0		-3	-0.2
1910	Pit N	2	1	.667	4	1	0	0	17.1	19	7	1	0	7	9	3.12	99	.268	.333	6-0	.000	-1	72	0	0.0
1912	Cin N	0	1	.000	5	2	0	1	14.2	17	11	0	2	11	6	4.91	68	.304	.435	4-0	.000	-1	44	-3	-0.3
Total	3	2	2	.500	10	3	0	1	34	40	22	1	2	21	17	4.76	67	.290	.391	11-0	.000	-2	54	-6	-0.5
MOORE, FRANK Frank J. B 9.12.1877 Dover, OH D 5.20.1964 Portsmouth, OH BR/TR 6-4/200# d6.14																									
1905	Pit N	0	0	—	1	0	0	0	3	2	0	0	0	0	1	0.00	—	.200	.200	1-0	.000	-0		1	0.0

Year	Tm Lg	W	L	Pct	G	GS	CG-Sho	SV-BS	IP	H	R	HR	HB	BB-IB	SO	ERA	AERA	OAV	OOB	AB-SH	AVG	PB	Sup	APR	PW
MOORE, JIM James Stanford B 12.14.1903 Prescott, AR D 5.19.1973 Seattle, WA BR/TR 6/165# d9.21																									
1928	Cle A	0	1	.000	1	1	1	0	9	5	2	0	0	5	1	2.00	207	.161	.278	3-0	.000	-0	20	2	0.2
1929	Cle A	0	0	—	2	0	0	0	5.2	6	6	1	0	4	0	9.53	47	.273	.385	2-0	.000	-0		-3	-0.1
1930	Chi A	2	1	.667	9	5	2	1	40	42	18	0	0	12	11	3.60	128	.268	.320	13-2	.231	-0	104	5	0.3
1931	Chi A	0	2	.000	33	4	0	0	83.2	93	52	3	1	27	15	4.95	86	.282	.338	16-0	.063	-1	65	-5	-0.3
1932	Chi A	0	0	—	1	0	0	0	1	1	0	0	0	1	2	0.00	—	.250	.400	1-0	.000	-0		0	0.0
Total	5	2	4	.333	46	10	3	1	139.1	147	78	4	1	49	29	4.52	97	.270	.332	35-2	.114	-2	82	-1	0.1
MOORE, WHITEY Lloyd Albert B 6.10.1912 Tuscarawas, OH D 12.10.1987 Uhrichsville, OH BR/TR 6-1/195# d9.27 Mil 1943-45																									
1936	Cin N	1	0	1.000	1	0	0	0	5	3	3	0	0	3	4	5.40	71	.167	.286	2-1	.000	-0		-1	-0.1
1937	Cin N	0	3	.000	13	6	0	0	38.2	32	22	1	4	39	27	4.89	76	.239	.424	8-0	.000	-1	58	-4	-0.4
1938	Cin N	6	4	.600	19	11	3-1	0	90.1	66	41	4	3	42	38	3.49	105	.205	.302	26-1	.077	-2	91	1	-0.1
1939	†Cin N	13	12	.520	42	24	9-2	3	187.2	177	88	10	6	95	81	3.45	111	.254	.348	61-7	.098	-4	100	6	0.3
1940	†Cin N	8	8	.500	25	15	5-1	1	116.2	100	48	8	7	56	60	3.63	104	.231	.329	39-4	.128	-1	104	4	0.2
1941	Cin N	2	1	.667	23	4	1	0	61.2	62	35	2	3	45	17	4.38	82	.256	.379	18-0	.167	-1	165	-6	-0.4
1942	Cin N	0	0	—	1	0	0	0	1	0	0	0	0	1	0	0.00	—	.000	.250	0-0	—	0		0	0.0
	StL N	0	1	.000	9	0	0	0	12.1	10	6	0	1	11	1	4.38	78	.217	.379	2-0	.000	-0		-1	-0.1
	Year	0	1	.000	10	0	0	0	13.1	10	13	0	1	12	1	4.05	84	.204	.371	2-0	.000	-0		0	-0.1
Total	7	30	29	.508	133	60	18-4	4	513.1	450	243	25	24	292	228	3.75	100	.237	.346	156-13	.103	-10	100	-1	-0.6
MOORE, MARCUS Marcus Braymont B 11.2.1970 Oakland, CA BB/TR 6-5/195# d7.8																									
1993	Col N	3	1	.750	27	0	0	0-2	26.1	30	25	4	1	20-0	13	6.84	70	.291	.398	1-0	.000	-0		-6	-0.9
1994	Col N	1	1	.500	29	0	0	0-0	33.2	33	26	4	5	21-2	33	6.15	81	.252	.376	1-0	.000	-0		-4	-0.2
1996	Cin N	3	3	.500	23	0	0	2-0	26.1	26	21	3	2	22-1	27	5.81	73	.263	.397	3-0	.333	1		-6	-1.0
Total	3	7	5	.583	79	0	0	2-2	86.1	89	72	11	8	63-3	73	6.25	75	.267	.389	5-0	.200	0		-16	-2.1
MOORE, MIKE Michael Wayne B 11.26.1959 Eakly, OK BR/TR 6-4/205# d4.11																									
1982	Sea A	7	14	.333	28	27	1-1	0-0	144.1	159	91	21	2	79-0	73	5.36	79	.285	.373	0-0	—	0	75	-15	-1.9
1983	Sea A	6	8	.429	22	21	3-2	0-0	128	130	75	10	3	60-4	108	4.71	91	.267	.348	0-0	—	0	83	-6	-0.5
1984	Sea A	7	17	.292	34	33	6	0-0	212	236	127	16	5	85-10	158	4.97	80	.282	.350	0-0	—	0	87	-21	-2.0
1985	Sea A	17	10	.630	35	34	14-2	0-0	247	230	100	18	4	70-2	155	3.46	122	.247	.300	0-0	—	0	95	22	2.4
1986	Sea A	11	13	.458	38	**37**	11-1	1-0	266	279	141	28	12	94-6	146	4.30	99	.273	.339	0-0	—	0	103	-1	-0.1
1987	Sea A	9	19	.321	33	33	12	0-0	231	268	145	29	0	84-3	115	4.71	100	.292	.348	1-0	.000	-0	78	-4	-0.4
1988	Sea A	9	15	.375	37	32	9-3	1-1	228.2	196	104	24	3	63-6	182	3.78	110	.232	.286	0-0	—	0	81	11	1.1
1989	†Oak A★	19	11	.633	35	35	6-3	0-0	241.2	193	82	14	2	83-1	172	2.61	141	.219	.286	0-0	—	0	98	30	3.7
1990	†Oak A	13	15	.464	33	33	3	0-0	199.1	204	113	14	3	84-2	73	4.65	80	.267	.339	0-0	—	0	93	-21	-2.5
1991	Oak A	17	8	.680	33	33	3-1	0-0	210	176	75	11	5	105-1	153	2.96	130	.229	.324	0-0	—	0	95	21	2.5
1992	†Oak A	17	12	.586	36	**36**	2	0-0	223	229	113	20	8	103-5	117	4.12	91	.268	.349	0-0	—	0*	120	-9	-1.1
1993	Det A	13	9	.591	36	**36**	4-3	0-0	213.2	227	135	35	3	89-10	89	5.22	82	.271	.340	0-0	—	0	129	-21	-1.7
1994	Det A	11	10	.524	25	**25**	4	0-0	154.1	152	97	27	3	89-8	62	5.42	89	.263	.361	0-0	—	0	98	-7	-0.7
1995	Det A	5	15	.250	25	25	1	0-0	132.2	179	118	24	2	68-3	64	7.53	63	.323	.396	0-0	—	0	94	-39	-4.5
Total	14	161	176	.478	450	440	79-16	2-1	2831.2	2858	1516	291	55	1156-61	1667	4.39	95	.264	.335	1-0	.000	-0	96	-60	-5.7
MOORE, RAY Raymond Leroy "Farmer" B 6.1.1926 Meadows, MD D 3.2.1995 Clinton, MD BR/TR 6-1/205# d8.1																									
1952	Bro N	1	2	.333	14	2	0	0	28.1	29	17	3	2	26	11	4.76	76	.274	.425	3-0	.000	-0	49	-4	-0.4
1953	Bro N	0	1	.000	1	1	1	0	8	6	3	1	0	4	4	3.38	126	.214	.313	3-0	.000	-0	21	1	0.0
1955	Bal A	10	10	.500	46	14	3-1	6	151.2	128	75	14	4	80-1	80	3.92	97	.229	.327	44-2	.136	-2	100	-1	-0.4
1956	Bal A	12	7	.632	32	27	9-1	0	185	161	90	12	1	99-1	105	4.18	94	.238	.332	70-4	.271	6	89	-3	0.2
1957	Bal A	11	13	.458	34	32	7-1	0	227.1	196	99	17	2	112-5	117	3.72	97	.236	.326	84-3	.214	4	86	-2	0.1
1958	Chi A	9	7	.563	32	20	4-2	2	136.2	107	63	10	0	70-2	73	3.82	95	.220	.315	44-5	.205	2	99	-2	-0.1
1959	†Chi A	3	6	.333	29	8	0	0	89.2	86	46	10	1	46-3	49	4.12	91	.261	.348	23-1	.087	-1	59	-4	-0.5
1960	Chi A	1	1	.500	14	0	0	0	20.2	19	13	5	0	11-0	3	5.66	67	.253	.345	2-0	.000	-0		-4	-0.4
	Was A	3	2	.600	37	0	0	13	65.2	49	24	5	1	27-3	29	2.88	135	.213	.296	14-0	.071	-1		8	0.7
	Year	4	3	.571	51	0	0	13	86.1	68	40	10	1	38-3	32	3.54	109	.223	.308	16-0	.063	-1		4	0.3
1961	Min A	4	4	.500	46	0	0	14	56.1	49	23	8	1	38-3	45	3.67	115	.233	.351	4-1	.000	0		5	0.9
1962	Min A	8	3	.727	49	0	0	9	64.2	55	35	8	2	30-4	58	4.73	86	.231	.319	5-1	.000	-1		-3	-0.7
1963	Min A	1	3	.250	31	1	0	2	38.2	50	34	8	1	17-2	38	6.98	52	.309	.378	3-0	.333	0	73	-14	-1.5
Total	11	63	59	.516	365	105	24-5	46	1072.2	935	522	101	15	560-24	612	4.06	93	.238	.332	299-17	.187	6	86	-23	-2.1
MOORE, BARRY Robert Barry B 4.3.1943 Statesville, NC BL/TL 6-1/190# d5.29																									
1965	Was A	0	0	—	1	0	0	0	1	1	1	0	0	1-0	0	0.00	—	.333	.500	0-0	—	0		0	0.0
1966	Was A	3	3	.500	12	11	1	0	62.1	55	26	3	1	39-2	28	3.75	92	.240	.352	19-1	.105	-1	93	-1	-0.1
1967	Was A	7	11	.389	27	26	3-1	0	143.2	127	67	15	3	71-6	74	3.76	84	.240	.332	46-4	.130	-0	86	-9	-1.0
1968	Was A	4	6	.400	32	18	0	3	117.2	116	55	8	2	42-2	56	3.37	87	.261	.326	31-3	.097	-1*	108	-8	-0.8
1969	Was A	9	8	.529	31	25	4	0-0	134	123	70	12	2	67-1	51	4.30	81	.246	.334	43-2	.209	2*	113	-11	-1.3
1970	Cle A	3	5	.375	13	12	0	0-0	70.1	70	34	8	1	46-3	35	4.22	94	.262	.370	21-1	.095	-1	88	-1	-0.2
	Chi A	0	4	.000	24	7	0	0-0	70.2	85	56	12	8	34-0	34	6.37	61	.302	.386	19-1	.263	1	95	-18	-0.8
	Year	3	9	.250	37	19	0	0-0	141	155	60	20	9	80-3	69	5.30	74	.283	.378	40-2	.175	-0	91	-18	-1.0
Total	6	26	37	.413	140	99	8-1	3-0	599.2	577	309	58	17	300-14	278	4.16	82	.256	.345	179-12	.151	-1	98	-48	-4.2
MOORE, BOBBY Robert Devell B 11.8.1958 Jena, LA BR/TR 6-4/200# d9.11																									
1985	SF N	0	0	—	11	0	0	0-0	16.2	18	6	1	0	10-2	10	3.24	106	.269	.364	2-0	.000	-0		1	0.0
MOORE, ROY Roy Daniel B 10.26.1898 Austin, TX D 4.5.1951 Seattle, WA BB/TL 6/185# d4.15																									
1920	Phi A	1	13	.071	24	14	5	0	132.2	161	89	6	3	64	45	4.68	86	.314	.393	50-1	.200	-1*	52	-7	-0.7
1921	Phi A	10	10	.500	29	26	12	0	191.2	206	110	4	4	122	64	4.51	99	.280	.385	74-0	.257	3*	82	3	0.7
1922	Phi A	0	3	.000	15	6	0	0	50.2	65	43	1	3	32	29	7.64	56	.319	.418	19-1	.263	1	116	-15	-0.6
	Det A	0	0	—	9	0	0	2	19.2	29	14	0	5	10	9	5.95	65	.367	.468	7-0	.429	1		-4	-0.1
	Year	0	3	.000	24	6	0	2	70.1	94	63	1	8	42	38	7.17	58	.332	.432	26-1	.308	2	119	-18	-0.7
1923	Det A	0	0	—	3	0	0	1	12	15	4	0	0	11	7	3.00	129	.288	.413	5-0	.000	-0*		2	0.1
Total	4	11	26	.297	80	46	17	3	406.2	476	260	11	15	239	154	4.98	85	.300	.397	155-2	.239	4	78	-21	-0.6
MOORE, TOMMY Tommy Joe B 7.7.1948 Lynwood, CA BR/TR 5-11/175# d9.15																									
1972	NY N	0	0	—	3	1	0	0-0	12.1	12	4	1	0	1-0	5	2.92	115	.273	.283	3-0	.333	0	53	1	0.1
1973	NY N	0	1	.000	3	1	0	0-0	3.1	6	5	1	0	3-0	1	10.80	34	.400	.500	0-0	—	0*	122	-3	-0.6
1975	StL N	0	0	—	10	0	0	0-0	18.2	15	10	2	0	12-1	6	3.86	98	.203	.314	2-0	.500	0		0	0.0
	Tex A	0	2	.000	12	0	0	0-1	21	31	21	1	1	12-4	15	8.14	46	.352	.436	0-0	—	0*		-10	-0.8
1977	Sea A	2	1	.667	14	1	0	0-1	33	36	22	1	3	21-2	13	4.91	84	.281	.390	0-0	—	0	65	-4	-0.3
Total	4	2	4	.333	42	3	0	0-2	88.1	100	62	6	4	49-7	40	5.40	71	.287	.378	5-0	.400	1	77	-16	-1.6
MOORE, TREY Warren Neal B 10.2.1972 Houston, TX BL/TL 6-1/200# d4.5																									
1998	Mon N	2	5	.286	13	11	0	0-0	61	78	37	5	1	17-3	35	5.02	84	.306	.348	17-1	.235	1*	68	-5	-0.4
2000	Mon N	1	5	.167	8	8	0	0-0	35.1	55	31	7	4	21-1	24	6.62	72	.364	.455	8-2	.125	-0	77	-8	-1.1
2001	Atl N	0	0	—	2	0	0	0-0	4	7	5	0	0	2-0	1	11.25	39	.368	.429	1-0	1.000	1		-3	-0.1
Total	3	3	10	.231	23	19	0	0-0	100.1	140	73	12	5	40-4	60	5.83	76	.329	.391	26-3	.231	2	72	-16	-1.6
MOORE, CY William Austin B 2.7.1905 Elberton, GA D 3.28.1972 Augusta, GA BR/TR 6-1/178# d6.7																									
1929	Bro N	3	3	.500	32	3	0	2	68	87	45	3	0	31	17	5.56	83	.320	.389	16-1	.188	-0	63	-5	-0.5
1930	Bro N	0	0	—	1	0	0	0	0	2	1	0	0	0	0	—	—	1.000	1.000	0-0	—	0		0	0.0
1931	Bro N	1	2	.333	23	1	1	0	61.2	62	31	5	4	13	35	3.79	100	.262	.311	13-1	.154	-1	22	0	-0.1
1932	Bro N	0	3	.000	20	2	0	0	48.2	56	32	3	1	17	21	4.81	79	.293	.354	14-0	.214	0*	99	-6	-0.3
1933	Phi N	8	9	.471	36	18	9-3	1	161.1	177	74	7	3	42	53	3.74	102	.279	.326	48-1	.063	-4	81	3	-0.1
1934	Phi N	4	9	.308	35	15	3	0	126.2	163	98	11	2	65	55	6.47	73	.309	.387	42-1	.143	-3	91	-18	-1.9
Total	6	16	26	.381	147	39	13-3	3	466.1	547	281	29	10	168	181	4.86	86	.293	.355	133-4	.128	-8	84	-26	-2.9

Year	Tm Lg	W	L	Pct	G	GS	CG-Sho	SV-BS	IP	H	R	HR	HB	BB-IB	SO	ERA	AERA	OAV	OOB	AB-SH	AVG	PB	Sup	APR	PW
MOORE, BILL William Christopher B 9.3.1902 Corning, NY D 1.24.1984 Corning, NY BR/TR 6-3/195# d4.15																									
1925	Det A	0	0	—	1	0	0	0	0	0	2	0	0	3	0	∞	—	—	1.000	0-0	—	0		-2	-0.2
MOORE, WILCY William Wilcy "Cy" B 5.20.1897 Bonita, TX D 3.29.1963 Hollis, OK BR/TR 6/195# d4.14																									
1927	†NY A	19	7	.731	50	12	6-1	**13**	213	185	68	3	1	59	75	**2.28**	**169**	**.234**	**.289**	75-7	.080	-7	119	39	4.5
1928	NY A	4	4	.500	35	2	0	2	60.1	71	44	4	0	31	18	4.18	90	.286	.366	14-2	.143	-1	203	-8	-0.9
1929	NY A	6	4	.600	41	0	0	8	61	64	36	4	0	19	21	4.13	93	.268	.322	15-1	.067	-2		-3	-0.6
1931	Bos A	11	13	.458	53	15	8-1	**10**	185.1	195	88	7	1	55	37	3.88	111	.269	.322	56-2	.161	-3	64	10	1.3
1932	Bos A	4	10	.286	37	2	0	4	84.1	98	59	5	1	42	28	5.23	86	.284	.363	22-0	.045	-2	28	-7	-1.1
	†NY A	2	0	1.000	10	1	0	4	25	27	8	1	0	6	8	2.52	162	.273	.314	8-0	.000	-1	84	5	0.4
	Year	6	10	.375	47	3	0	8	109.1	125	12	6	1	48	36	4.61	95	.282	.353	30-0	.033	-4	45	-2	-0.7
1933	NY A	5	6	.455	35	0	0	8	62	92	53	1	0	20	17	5.52	70	.333	.378	15-2	.133	-1		-16	-2.9
Total	6	51	44	.537	261	32	14-2	49	691	732	356	25	3	232	204	3.70	110	.269	.327	205-14	.102	-17	91	20	0.7
MOORHEAD, BOB Charles Robert B 1.23.1938 Chambersburg, PA D 12.3.1986 Lemoyne, PA BR/TR 6-1/208# d4.11																									
1962	NY N	0	2	.000	38	7	0	0	105.1	118	69	13	4	42-4	63	4.53	92	.289	.358	22-1	.045	-1	126	-6	-0.3
1965	NY N	0	1	.000	9	0	0	0	14.1	16	7	0	0	5-0	5	4.40	80	.271	.328	0-0	—	0		-1	0.0
Total	2	0	3	.000	47	7	0	0	119.2	134	76	13	4	47-4	68	4.51	91	.287	.354	22-1	.045	-1	126	-7	-0.3
MOOSE, BOB Robert Ralph B 10.9.1947 Export, PA D 10.9.1976 Martins Ferry, OH BR/TR 6/200# d9.19																									
1967	Pit N	1	0	1.000	2	2	1	0	14.2	14	6	1	1	4-0	7	3.68	91	.259	.322	6-0	.333	1	196	0	0.1
1968	Pit N	8	12	.400	38	22	3-3	3	171.1	136	61	5	3	41-7	126	2.73	107	.218	.268	54-2	.093	-2	78	4	0.3
1969	Pit N	14	3	.824	44	19	6-1	4-1	170	149	64	9	5	62-3	165	2.91	120	.231	.302	53-4	.075	-1	166	10	0.9
1970	†Pit N	11	10	.524	28	27	9-2	0-0	189.2	186	88	14	3	64-5	119	3.99	98	.262	.325	66-4	.182	3*	93	1	0.3
1971	†Pit N	11	7	.611	30	18	3-1	1-0	140	169	73	12	2	35-11	68	4.11	82	.301	.340	39-5	.103	-1	138	-12	-1.6
1972	†Pit N	13	10	.565	31	30	6-3	1-0	226	213	84	11	4	47-9	144	2.91	114	.248	.288	71-6	.169	3*	121	11	1.5
1973	Pit N	12	13	.480	33	29	6-3	0-0	201.1	219	86	11	4	70-11	111	3.53	100	.280	.340	67-4	.134	-0*	98	2	0.3
1974	Pit N	1	5	.167	7	6	0	0-0	35.2	59	30	4	2	7-3	15	7.57	46	.386	.410	11-0	.182	0	84	-15	-1.9
1975	Pit N	2	2	.500	23	5	1	0-0	67.2	63	30	4	2	25-3	34	3.72	95	.246	.318	18-2	.167	0	104	0	0.1
1976	Pit N	3	9	.250	53	2	0	10-3	88	100	44	4	4	32-7	38	3.68	95	.294	.356	12-0	.250	2	25	-3	-0.3
Total	10	76	71	.517	289	160	35-13	19-4	1304.1	1308	566	75	30	387-59	827	3.50	98	.262	.317	397-27	.141	4	111	-2	-0.3
MOOTY, JAKE Jake T. B 4.13.1912 Millsap, TX D 4.20.1970 Fort Worth, TX BR/TR 5-10.5/170# d9.9																									
1936	Cin N	0	0	—	8	0	0	1	13.2	10	6	0	0	4	11	3.95	97	.204	.264	1-0	.000	-0		0	0.0
1937	Cin N	0	3	.000	14	2	0	1	39	54	39	2	0	22	11	8.31	45	.327	.406	8-1	.000	-1*	46	-19	-1.5
1940	Chi N	6	6	.500	20	12	6	1	114	101	45	11	1	49	42	2.92	128	.243	.325	38-3	.263	2*	77	10	1.1
1941	Chi N	8	9	.471	33	14	7-1	4	153.1	143	69	9	2	56	45	3.35	105	.251	.320	50-3	.200	1	85	2	0.4
1942	Chi N	2	5	.286	19	10	1	1	84.1	89	48	11	0	44	28	4.70	68	.265	.350	28-1	.214	0	137	-13	-1.0
1943	Chi N	0	0	—	2	0	0	0	1	2	0	0	0	1	1	0.00	—	.400	.500	0-0	—	0		0	0.0
1944	Det A	0	0	—	15	0	0	0	28.1	35	20	0	1	18	7	4.45	80	.310	.409	7-0	.143	-0		-4	-0.3
Total	7	16	23	.410	111	38	14-1	8	433.2	434	227	33	4	194	145	4.03	88	.263	.341	132-8	.205	1	92	-24	-1.3
MORAGA, DAVID David Michael B 7.8.1975 Torrance, CA BL/TL 6/184# d6.11																									
2000	Mon N	0	0	—	3	0	0	0-0	1.2	6	7	0	0	2-0	2	37.80	13	.600	.615	0-0	—	0		-6	-0.3
	Col N	0	0	—	1	0	0	0-0	1	4	5	1	1	0-0	0	45.00	13	.667	.625	0-0	—	0		-3	-0.1
	Year	0	0	—	4	0	0	0-0	2.2	10	16	1	1	2-0	2	40.50	13	.625	.619	0-0	—	0		-9	-0.4
MORAN, HIKER Albert Thomas B 1.1.1912 Rochester, NY D 1.7.1998 Saratoga Springs, NY BR/TR 6-4.5/185# d9.29																									
1938	Bos N	0	0	—	1	0	0	0	3	1	0	0	0	1	0	0.00	—	.111	.200	1-0	.000	-0		1	0.0
1939	Bos N	1	1	.500	6	2	1	0	20	21	10	3	0	11	4	4.50	82	.276	.368	5-1	.200	1	142	-1	-0.1
Total	2	1	1	.500	7	2	1	0	23	22	10	3	0	12	4	3.91	94	.259	.351	6-1	.167	0	142	0	-0.1
MORAN, BILL Carl William "Bugs" B 9.26.1950 Portsmouth, VA BR/TR 6-4/210# d4.12																									
1974	Chi A	1	3	.250	15	5	0	0-0	46.1	57	27	5	6	23-2	17	4.66	80	.302	.393	0-0	—	0	113	-5	-0.4
MORAN, CHARLIE Charles Barthell "Uncle Charlie" B 2.22.1878 Nashville, TN D 6.14.1949 Horse Cave, KY BR/TR 5-8/180# d9.9 U22 ▲																									
1903	StL N	0	1	.000	3	2	2	0	24	30	29	0	1	19	7	5.25	62	.297	.413	14-0	.429	1*	124	-7	-0.2
MORAN, HARRY Harry Edwin B 4.2.1889 Slater, WV D 11.28.1962 Beckley, WV BL/TL 6-1/165# d6.23																									
1912	Det A	0	1	.000	5	2	1	0	14.2	19	14	1	2	12	3	4.91	66	.339	.471	5-0	.200	-0	125	-4	-0.3
1914	Buf F	10	7	.588	34	16	7-2	2	154	159	87	7	11	53	73	4.27	69	.276	.348	51-3	.196	-0	114	-21	-2.2
1915	New F	13	9	.591	34	23	13-2	0	205.2	193	80	2	18	66	87	2.54	101	.262	.337	61-9	.180	-1*	96	1	0.1
Total	3	23	17	.575	73	41	21-4	2	374.1	371	181	10	31	131	163	3.34	82	.271	.348	117-12	.188	-1	105	-24	-2.4
MORAN, SAM Samuel B 9.16.1870 Rochester, NY D 8.27.1897 Rochester, NY TL ?/160# d8.28																									
1895	Pit N	2	4	.333	10	6	6	0	62.2	78	63	2	3	51	19	7.47	60	.300	.420	26-0	.154	-1*	103	-17	-1.2
MORE, FORREST Forrest B 9.30.1883 Hayden, IN D 8.17.1968 Columbus, IN BR/TR 6/180# d4.15																									
1909	StL N	1	5	.167	15	2	1	0	50	48	33	0	3	20	17	5.04	50	.258	.340	13-1	.154	1	111	-12	-1.3
	Bos N	1	5	.167	10	4	3	0	48.2	47	47	0	4	20	10	4.44	64	.270	.359	15-0	.067	-1	50	-12	-1.5
	Year	2	10	.167	25	6	4	0	98.2	95	49	0	7	40	27	4.74	56	.264	.349	28-1	.107	-1	70	-24	-2.8
MOREHEAD, DAVE David Michael "Moe" B 9.5.1942 San Diego, CA BR/TR 6-1/185# d4.13																									
1963	Bos A	10	13	.435	29	29	6-1	0	174.2	137	82	20	0	99-2	136	3.81	99	.211	.316	57-3	.105	-3	89	-1	-0.4
1964	Bos A	8	15	.348	32	30	3-1	0	166.2	156	101	14	4	112-2	139	4.97	78	.248	.358	54-2	.093	-2	86	-19	-2.6
1965	Bos A	10	18	.357	34	33	5-2	0	192.2	157	103	18	3	113-1	163	4.06	92	.217	.325	61-4	.131	0	80	-7	-1.1
1966	Bos A	1	2	.333	12	5	0	0	28	31	17	7	0	7-0	20	5.46	70	.274	.317	6-0	.500	1	120	-4	-0.3
1967	†Bos A	5	4	.556	10	9	1-1	0	47.2	48	24	0	2	22-0	40	4.34	80	.264	.348	12-3	.083	-0	111	-3	-0.7
1968	Bos A	1	4	.200	11	9	3-1	0	55	52	17	3	2	20-0	28	2.45	129	.249	.320	16-1	.125	-0	98	4	0.3
1969	KC A	2	3	.400	21	2	0	0-0	33	28	22	7	0	28-1	32	5.73	64	.239	.384	2-0	.000	0	24	-7	-0.9
1970	KC A	3	5	.375	28	17	1	1-0	121.2	121	64	9	1	62-3	69	3.62	103	.261	.347	36-3	.167	-0	100	-2	-0.2
Total	8	40	64	.385	177	134	19-6	1-0	819.1	730	430	78	12	463-9	627	4.15	90	.237	.336	244-16	.127	-5	90	-39	-5.9
MOREHEAD, SETH Seth Marvin "Moe" B 8.15.1934 Houston, TX BL/TL 6-0.5/195# d4.27																									
1957	Phi N	1	1	.500	34	1	1	1	58.2	57	27	1	2	20-4	36	3.68	103	.254	.315	6-0	.000	-1	46	1	-0.1
1958	Phi N	1	6	.143	27	11	0	0	92.1	121	67	8	1	26-3	54	5.85	68	.319	.359	22-3	.182	0	87	-19	-1.3
1959	Phi N	0	2	.000	3	3	0	0	10	15	11	3	1	3-0	8	9.90	41	.333	.388	3-0	.000	-0	138	-6	-0.9
	Chi N	0	1	.000	11	2	0	0	18.2	25	13	1	0	8-2	9	4.82	82	.313	.375	2-0	.500	1	136	-3	-0.1
	Year	0	3	.000	14	5	0	0	28.2	40	19	4	1	11-2	17	6.59	61	.320	.380	5-0	.200	0	138	-8	-1.0
1960	Chi N	2	9	.182	45	7	2	4	123.1	123	61	17	2	46-6	64	3.94	96	.258	.324	29-1	.138	-1	80	-2	-0.2
1961	Mil N	1	0	1.000	12	0	0	0	15.1	16	11	4	1	7-0	13	6.46	58	.271	.358	0-0	—	0		-4	-0.3
Total	5	5	19	.208	132	24	3	5	318.1	357	190	34	7	110-15	184	4.81	80	.282	.340	62-4	.145	-1	95	-33	-2.9
MOREL, RAMON Ramon Rafael B 8.15.1974 Villa Gonzalez, D.R. BR/TR 6-2/175# d7.6																									
1995	Pit N	0	1	.000	5	0	0	0-1	6.1	6	2	0	0	2-1	3	2.84	152	.300	.364	0-0	—	0		1	0.2
1996	Pit N	2	1	.667	29	0	0	0-0	42	57	27	4	1	19-5	22	5.36	82	.324	.391	4-1	.000	-0		-4	-0.3
1997	Pit N	0	0	—	5	0	0	0-0	7.2	11	4	2	0	4-1	4	4.70	91	.344	.417	0-0	—	0		0	0.0
	Chi N	0	0	—	3	0	0	0-0	3.2	3	2	1	0	3-0	3	4.91	88	.214	.353	0-0	—	0		0	0.0
	Year	0	0	—	8	0	0	0-0	11.1	14	10	3	0	7-1	7	4.76	90	.304	.396	0-0	—	0		0	0.0
Total	3	2	2	.500	42	0	0	0-1	59.2	77	35	7	1	28-7	32	4.98	87	.318	.390	4-1	.000	-0		-3	-0.1
MOREN, LEW Lewis Howard "Hicks" B 8.4.1883 Pittsburgh, PA D 11.2.1966 Pittsburgh, PA BR/TR 5-11/150# d9.21																									
1903	Pit N	0	1	.000	1	1	1	0	6	9	7	0	1	2	2	9.00	36	.346	.414	2-0	.000	-0	62	-3	-0.4
1904	Pit N	0	0	—	1	0	0	0	4	7	6	1	1	4	0	9.00	30	.412	.545	2-0	.000	-0		-3	-0.2
1907	Phi N	11	18	.379	37	31	21-3	1	255	202	106	3	9	101	98	2.54	95	.226	.311	74-3	.081	-2	89	-7	-1.1
1908	Phi N	8	9	.471	28	16	9-4	0	154	146	68	1	2	49	72	2.92	83	.258	.320	49-2	.245	2	67	-8	-0.8

Year	Tm Lg	W	L	Pct	G	GS	CG-Sho	SV-BS	IP	H	R	HR	HB	BB-IB	SO	ERA	AERA	OAV	OOB	AB-SH	AVG	PB	Sup	APR	PW
1909	Phi N	16	15	.516	40	31	19-2	1	257.2	226	103	6	4	93	110	2.65	98	.239	.309	90-2	.111	-3	109	-1	-0.7
1910	Phi N	13	14	.481	34	26	12-1	1	205.1	207	104	6	9	82	74	3.55	88	.269	.347	74-0	.149	-1	103	-8	-1.2
Total	6	48	57	.457	141	105	62-10	3	882	797	394	17	26	331	356	2.95	90	.248	.323	291-7	.134	-5	96	-30	-4.4
MORENO, ANGEL Angel (Veneroso) B 6.6.1955 LaMendosa Soledad, Mexico BL/TL 5-9/165# d8.15																									
1981	Cal A	1	3	.250	8	4	1	0-0	31.1	27	10	2	0	14-0	12	2.87	127	.233	.313	0-0	—	0	37	3	0.4
1982	Cal A	3	7	.300	13	8	2	1-1	49.1	55	31	7	1	23-0	22	4.74	86	.288	.364	0-0	—	0	67	-5	-0.9
Total	2	4	10	.286	21	12	3	1-1	80.2	82	41	9	1	37-0	34	4.02	97	.267	.345	0-0	—	0	58	-2	-0.5
MORENO, JUAN Juan Carlos (Vegas) B 2.28.1975 Maiquetia, Venezuela BL/TL 6-1/205# d5.17																									
2001	Tex A	3	3	.500	45	0	0	0-2	41.1	22	21	6	0	28-2	36	3.92	119	.153	.291	0-0	—	0		2	0.3
2002	SD N	0	0	—	4	0	0	0-0	6	6	6	1	0	10-1	3	7.50	50	.261	.471	0-0	—	0		-3	-0.2
Total	2	3	3	.500	49	0	0	0-2	47.1	28	27	7	0	38-3	39	4.37	104	.168	.320	0-0	—	0		-1	0.1
MORENO, JULIO Julio (Gonzalez) B 1.28.1922 Guines, Cuba D 1.2.1987 Miami, FL BR/TR 5-8/165# d9.8																									
1950	Was A	1	1	.500	4	3	1	0	21.1	22	13	1	1	12	7	4.64	97	.268	.368	8-1	.125	-1	114	-1	-0.1
1951	Was A	5	11	.313	31	18	5	2	132.2	132	82	18	1	80	37	4.88	84	.256	.357	40-3	.175	-1	95	-12	-1.4
1952	Was A	9	9	.500	26	22	7	0	147.1	154	75	10	5	52	62	3.97	90	.270	.337	49-1	.122	-2	96	-8	-1.1
1953	Was A	3	1	.750	12	2	1	0	35.1	41	11	2	0	13	13	2.80	139	.291	.351	9-0	.000	-1	125	5	0.4
Total	4	18	22	.450	73	45	14	2	336.2	349	181	31	7	157	119	4.25	91	.267	.349	106-5	.132	-5	98	-16	-2.2
MORENO, ORBER Orber (Aquiles) B 4.27.1977 Caracas, Venezuela BR/TR 6-2/190# d5.25																									
1999	KC A	0	0	—	7	0	0	0-1	8	4	5	1	0	6-0	7	5.63	89	.143	.294	0-0	—	0		0	0.0
2003	NY N	0	0	—	7	0	0	0-0	8	10	7	1	0	3-0	5	7.88	53	.313	.371	1-0	.000	-0		-3	-0.2
Total	2	0	0	—	14	0	0	0-1	16	14	12	2	0	9-0	12	6.75	68	.233	.333	1-0	.000	-0		-3	-0.2
MORET, ROGER Rogelio (Torres) B 9.16.1949 Guayama, P.R. BB/TL 6-4/175# d9.13																									
1970	Bos A	1	0	1.000	3	1	0	0-0	8.1	7	3	0	0	4-0	2	3.24	122	.226	.314	3-0	.000	-0	90	1	0.0
1971	Bos A	4	3	.571	13	7	4-1	0-0	71	50	24	5	2	40-4	47	2.92	127	.205	.321	23-0	.087	-1	104	6	0.5
1972	Bos A	0	0	—	3	0	0	0-0	5	5	3	0	0	6-0	4	3.60	90	.263	.440	1-0	.000	-0		0	0.0
1973	Bos A	13	2	.867	30	15	5-2	3-1	156.1	138	60	19	3	67-2	90	3.17	127	.238	.318	0-0	—	0	120	15	1.4
1974	Bos A	9	10	.474	31	21	10-1	2-0	173.1	158	79	15	2	79-4	111	3.74	103	.243	.323	0-0	—	0	87	2	0.1
1975	†Bos A	14	3	.824	36	16	4-1	1-0	145	132	60	8	2	76-6	80	3.60	113	.248	.341	0-0	—	0*	128	9	1.0
1976	Atl N	3	5	.375	27	12	1	1-2	77.1	84	44	7	1	27-2	30	5.00	76	.280	.339	23-2	.130	-1	118	-8	-0.9
1977	Tex A	3	3	.500	18	8	0	4-0	72.1	59	41	6	0	38-2	39	3.73	110	.220	.313	0-0	—	0	99	0	-0.1
1978	Tex A	0	1	.000	7	2	0	1-0	14.2	23	8	1	1	2-0	5	4.91	77	.390	.413	0-0	—	0	36	-1	-0.1
Total	9	47	27	.635	168	82	24-5	12-3	723.1	656	322	61	11	339-20	408	3.66	108	.245	.329	50-2	.100	-2	107	24	1.9
MOREY, DAVE David Beale B 2.25.1889 Malden, MA D 1.4.1986 Oak Bluffs, MA BL/TR 6/185# d7.4																									
1913	Phi A	0	0	—	2	0	0	0	4	2	2	0	1	2	1	4.50	61	.222	.417	1-0	.000	-0		-1	0.0
MORGAN, CY Cyril Arlon B 11.11.1895 Lakeville, MA D 9.11.1946 Lakeville, MA BR/TR 6/170# d6.8																									
1921	Bos N	1	1	.500	17	0	0	1	30.1	37	24	0	1	17	8	6.53	56	.314	.404	5-0	.000	-1		-9	-0.6
1922	Bos N	0	0	—	2	0	0	0	1.1	8	8	0	0	2	0	27.00	15	.667	.714	0-0	—	0		-5	-0.2
Total	2	1	1	.500	19	0	0	1	31.2	45	32	0	1	19	8	7.39	50	.346	.433	5-0	.000	-1		-14	-0.8
MORGAN, DAN Daniel B 5.1853 , MO D 1.30.1910 St.Louis, MO d5.4 ▲																									
1875	RS NA	1	3	.250	7	4	4-1	0	42	40	40	0		1	7	1.29	170	.212	.216	69	.261	1*	64	1	0.2
MORGAN, CY Harry Richard B 11.10.1878 Pomeroy, OH D 6.28.1962 Wheeling, WV BR/TR 6/175# d9.18																									
1903	StL A	0	2	.000	2	1	1	0	13	12	12	0	2	6	6	4.15	70	.245	.351	4-0	.250	0	49	-3	-0.4
1904	StL A	0	2	.000	8	3	2	0	51	51	23	3	2	10	24	3.71	67	.262	.304	18-0	.056	-2	57	-5	-0.4
1905	StL A	2	5	.286	13	8	5-1	0	77.1	82	59	1	9	37	44	3.61	71	.273	.370	31-0	.258	-2	153	-15	-1.0
1907	StL A	2	5	.286	10	6	4	0	55	77	43	3	2	17	14	6.05	42	.333	.384	20-0	.100	-1	103	-19	-2.2
	Bos A	6	6	.500	16	13	9-2	0	114.1	77	35	1	3	34	50	1.97	131	.193	.262	35-1	.057	-4	61	8	0.4
	Year	8	11	.421	26	19	13-2	0	169.1	154	37	4	5	51	64	3.30	78	.245	.307	55-1	.073	-5	74	-10	-1.8
1908	Bos A	14	13	.519	30	26	17-2	1	205	166	78	7	10	90	99	2.46	100	.226	.319	63-5	.127	-3	94	1	-0.1
1909	Bos A	2	6	.250	12	10	5	1	64.2	52	19	0	6	31	30	2.37	106	.240	.350	20-1	.050	-2	68	3	0.3
	Phi A	16	11	.593	28	26	21-5	0	228.2	152	56	3	16	71	81	1.65	146	.191	.271	74-8	.108	-3	103	20	2.1
	Year	18	17	.514	40	36	26-5	1	293.1	204	60	3	22	102	111	1.81	134	**.202**	.289	94-9	.096	-4	93	24	2.4
1910	Phi A	18	12	.600	36	34	23-3	0	290.2	214	92	0	18	117	134	1.55	153	.216	.310	99-12	.141	-4	125	24	2.1
1911	Phi A	15	7	.682	38	30	15-2	1	249.2	217	109	0	21	113	136	2.70	117	.243	.341	94-2	.160	-5	130	9	0.3
1912	Phi A	3	8	.273	16	14	5	0	93.2	75	56	0	5	51	47	3.75	82	.226	.338	30-2	.033	-3	84	-9	-1.1
1913	Cin N	0	1	.000	1	1	0	0	2.1	5	4	0	1	1	2	15.43	21	.500	.583	1-0	.000	-0	23	-3	-0.4
Total	10	78	78	.500	210	172	107-15	3	1445.1	1180	586	18	95	578	667	2.51	105	.229	.318	489-31	.125	-25	105	11	-0.4
MORGAN, MIKE Michael Thomas B 10.8.1959 Tulare, CA BR/TR 6-2/215# d6.11																									
1978	Oak A	0	3	.000	3	3	1	0-0	12.1	19	12	1	0	8-0	0	7.30	50	.373	.458	0-0	—	0	49	-5	-0.9
1979	Oak A	2	10	.167	13	13	2	0-0	77.1	102	57	7	3	50-0	17	5.94	68	.332	.426	0-0	—	0	60	-16	-2.0
1982	NY A	7	11	.389	30	23	2	0-0	150.1	167	77	15	2	67-5	71	4.37	91	.285	.358	0-0	—	0	90	-5	-0.5
1983	Tor A	0	3	.000	16	4	0	0-0	45.1	48	26	6	0	21-0	22	5.16	84	.273	.348	0-0	—	0	74	-3	-0.1
1985	Sea A	1	1	.500	2	2	0	0-0	6	11	8	2	0	5-0	2	12.00	35	.393	.485	0-0	—	0	227	-5	-0.8
1986	Sea A	11	17	.393	37	33	9-1	1-0	216.1	243	122	24	4	86-3	116	4.53	94	.286	.353	0-0	—	0	102	-7	-0.8
1987	Sea A	12	17	.414	34	31	8-2	0-0	207	245	117	25	5	53-3	85	4.65	102	.296	.340	0-0	—	0	92	3	0.4
1988	Bal A	1	6	.143	22	10	2	1-0	71.1	70	45	6	1	23-1	29	5.43	72	.255	.315	0-0	—	0	79	-11	-1.0
1989	LA N	8	11	.421	40	19	0	0-1	152.2	130	51	6	2	33-8	72	2.53	135	.234	.277	36-3	.083	-2	65	14	1.8
1990	LA N	11	15	.423	33	33	6-**4**	0-0	211	216	100	19	5	60-5	106	3.75	98	.266	.319	71-5	.113	-2	97	-2	-0.3
1991	LA N★	14	10	.583	34	33	5-1	1-0	236.1	197	85	12	3	61-10	140	2.78	129	.226	.278	76-8	.092	-3	90	21	1.8
1992	Chi N	16	8	.667	34	34	6-1	0-0	240	203	80	14	3	79-10	123	2.55	142	.234	.298	74-11	.108	-2	102	26	2.4
1993	Chi N	10	15	.400	32	32	1-1	0-0	207.2	206	100	15	7	74-8	111	4.03	99	.262	.329	66-5	.061	-4	75	0	-0.3
1994	Chi N	2	10	.167	15	15	1	0-0	80.2	111	65	12	4	35-2	57	6.69	62	.338	.402	24-1	.125	-1	102	-23	-2.9
1995	Chi N	2	1	.667	4	4	0	0-0	24.2	19	8	2	1	9-1	15	2.19	188	.216	.296	7-1	.143	-0	77	5	0.6
	StL N	5	6	.455	17	17	1	0-0	106.2	114	48	10	5	25-1	46	3.88	108	.283	.329	31-3	.032	-2	90	6	0.4
	Year	7	7	.500	21	21	1	0-0	131.1	133	52	12	6	34-2	61	3.56	117	.271	.323	38-4	.053	-2	88	10	1.0
1996	StL N	4	8	.333	18	18	0	0-0	103	118	63	14	0	40-0	55	5.24	80	.294	.353	33-9	.061	-3	96	-11	-1.4
	Cin N	2	3	.400	5	5	0	0-0	27.1	28	9	2	1	7-0	19	2.30	184	.267	.316	7-2	.000	-1	102	5	0.8
	Year	6	11	.353	23	23	0	0-0	130.1	146	14	16	1	47-0	74	4.63	91	.289	.346	40-11	.050	-3	97	-5	-0.6
1997	Cin N	9	12	.429	31	30	1	0-0	162	165	91	13	8	49-6	103	4.78	89	.266	.327	44-9	.091	-2	82	-8	-1.1
1998	Min A	4	2	.667	18	17	0	0-0	98	108	41	13	7	24-1	50	3.49	137	.286	.337	2-0	.500	0	102	13	0.8
	†Chi N	0	1	.000	5	5	0	0-0	22.2	30	21	8	1	15-1	10	7.15	62	.323	.422	6-1	.667	2	159	-7	-0.1
1999	Tex A	13	10	.565	34	25	1	0-1	140	184	108	25	7	48-2	61	6.24	82	.323	.380	4-0	.250	0	109	-19	-2.5
2000	Ari N	5	5	.500	60	4	0	5-1	101.2	123	55	10	1	40-5	56	4.87	97	.311	.372	16-1	.438	2	63	0	0.2
2001	†Ari N	1	0	1.000	31	1	0	0-1	38	45	20	2	0	17-4	24	4.26	107	.306	.373	0-0	—	0	161	1	0.0
2002	Ari N	1	1	.500	29	0	0	0-1	34	41	22	7	3	9-1	13	5.29	84	.289	.344	0-0	—	0		-3	-0.2
Total	22	141	186	.431	597	411	46-10	8-5	2772.1	2943	1431	270	73	938-77	1403	4.23	97	.276	.337	497-59	.109	-16	92	-31	-5.7
MORGAN, TOM Tom Stephen "Plowboy" B 5.20.1930 ElMonte, CA D 1.13.1987 Anaheim, CA BR/TR 6-2/195# d4.20 Mil 1952 C8																									
1951	†NY A	9	3	.750	27	16	4-2	2	124.2	119	56	11	3	36	57	3.68	104	.253	.310	44-1	.273	2	101	3	0.6
1952	NY A	5	4	.556	16	12	2-1	2	93.2	86	34	8	4	33	35	3.07	108	.252	.325	33-0	.182	1	155	4	0.6
1954	NY A	11	5	.688	32	17	7-4	1	143	149	58	8	5	40	34	3.34	103	.274	.327	49-1	.143	0	133	3	0.4
1955	†NY A	7	3	.700	40	1	0	10	72	72	29	3	5	24-4	17	3.25	115	.267	.337	18-1	.222	0	119	5	0.9
1956	†NY A	6	7	.462	41	0	0	11	71.1	74	41	2	3	27-4	20	4.16	93	.284	.347	13-3	.154	-0		-4	-0.8
1957	KC A	9	7	.563	46	13	5	7	143.2	160	76	19	3	61-9	32	4.64	85	.299	.370	33-4	.091	-2	90	-8	-0.9
1958	Det A	2	5	.286	39	1	0	1	62.2	70	28	7	1	4-0	32	3.16	128	.286	.299	10-1	.200	-0	111	4	0.4
1959	Det A	1	4	.200	46	1	0	9	92.2	94	48	11	6	18-3	39	3.98	102	.265	.308	23-0	.391	4	87	0	0.4

Year	Tm Lg	W	L	Pct	G	GS	CG-Sho	SV-BS	IP	H	R	HR	HB	BB-IB	SO	ERA	AERA	OAV	OOB	AB-SH	AVG	PB	Sup	APR	PW
1960	Det A	3	2	.600	22	0	0	1	29	33	17	6	0	10-1	12	4.66	85	.295	.347	0-1	—	0		-2	-0.3
	Was A	1	3	.250	14	0	0	0	24	36	15	6	1	5-3	11	3.75	104	.343	.375	5-0	.000	-1		-1	-0.2
	Year	4	5	.444	36	0	0	1	53	69	36	12	1	15-4	23	4.25	92	.318	.360	5-1	.000	-1		-3	-0.5
1961	LA A	8	2	.800	59	0	0	10	91.2	74	31	7	5	17-3	39	2.36	191	.224	.269	12-0	.083	-1		18	2.2
1962	LA A	5	2	.714	48	0	0	9	58.2	53	23	6	1	19-6	29	2.91	132	.247	.304	6-2	.000	-1		6	0.7
1963	LA A	0	0	—	13	0	0	1	16.1	20	11	1	3	6-1	7	5.51	62	.313	.392	1-0	.000	-0		-4	-0.2
Total	12	67	47	.588	443	61	18-7	64	1023.1	1040	467	95	40	300-34	364	3.61	106	.270	.326	247-14	.186	3	112	24	3.8
MORIARITY, GENE Eugene John B 1.5.1865 Holyoke, MA BL/TL 5-8/130# d6.18 ▲																									
1884	Ind AA	0	2	.000	2	2	2	0	13.2	16	13	0	1	7	4	5.27	62	.267	.353	37	.216	0*	46	-3	-0.3
1885	Det N	0	0	—	1	0	0	0	2	3	3	0		1	1	9.00	32	.300	.364	39	.026	-0*		-1	-0.1
Total	2	0	2	.000	3	2	2	0	15.2	19	16	0	1	8	5	5.74	56	.271	.354	76	.118	-0	46	-4	-0.4
MORLAN, JOHN John Glen B 11.22.1947 Columbus, OH BR/TR 6/178# d7.20																									
1973	Pit N	2	2	.500	10	7	1	0-0	41	42	18	4	0	23-3	23	3.95	89	.276	.369	11-0	.182	1	107	-1	0.0
1974	Pit N	0	3	.000	39	0	0	0-0	65	54	37	2	3	48-5	38	4.29	81	.227	.357	7-0	.000	-1		-7	-0.5
Total	2	2	5	.286	49	7	1	0-0	106	96	55	6	3	71-8	61	4.16	84	.246	.362	18-0	.111	0	107	-8	-0.5
MORMAN, ALVIN Alvin B 1.6.1969 Rockingham, NC BL/TL 6-3/210# d4.2																									
1996	Hou N	4	1	.800	53	0	0	0-2	42	43	24	8	0	24-6	31	4.93	79	.261	.353	0-0	—	0		-4	-0.4
1997	†Cle A	0	0	—	34	0	0	2-0	18.1	19	13	2	1	14-3	13	5.89	80	.268	.395	1-0	.000	-0		-2	-0.1
1998	Cle A	0	1	.000	31	0	0	0-1	22	25	13	1	0	11-1	16	5.32	90	.298	.375	0-0	—	0		-1	0.0
	SF N	0	1	.000	9	0	0	0-1	7	8	4	4	0	3-0	7	5.14	77	.276	.344	0-0	—	0		-1	-0.1
1999	KC A	2	4	.333	49	0	0	1-2	53.1	66	27	6	4	23-0	31	4.05	124	.307	.378	0-0	—	0		5	0.5
Total	4	6	7	.462	176	0	0	3-6	142.2	161	81	21	5	75-10	98	4.79	95	.285	.371	1-0	.000	-0		-3	-0.1
MOROGIELLO, DAN Daniel Joseph B 3.26.1955 Brooklyn, NY BL/TL 6-1/200# d5.20																									
1983	Bal A	0	1	.000	22	0	0	1-0	37.2	39	10	1	1	10-3	15	2.39	166	.265	.314	0-0	—	0		7	0.3
MORONEY, JIM James Francis B 12.4.1883 Boston, MA D 2.26.1929 Philadelphia, PA BL/TL 6-1/175# d4.24																									
1906	Bos N	0	3	.000	3	3	3	0	27	28	20	1	6	12	11	5.33	50	.259	.365	10-0	.100	-1	72	-7	-0.7
1910	Phi N	1	2	.333	12	2	1	1	42	43	20	1	4	11	13	2.14	146	.295	.360	10-0	.000	-1	48	2	0.0
1912	Chi N	1	1	.500	10	3	1	1	23.2	25	13	0	4	17	5	4.56	73	.316	.460	6-0	.500	1	95	-2	-0.1
Total	3	2	6	.250	25	8	5	2	92.2	96	53	2	14	40	29	3.69	83	.288	.388	26-0	.154	-1	75	-7	-0.8
MORRELL, BILL Willard Blackmer B 4.9.1893 Hyde Park, MA D 8.5.1975 Birmingham, AL BR/TR 6/172# d4.20																									
1926	Was A	3	3	.500	26	2	1	1	69.2	83	48	5	2	29	16	5.30	73	.311	.383	17-0	.235	1	109	-12	-0.9
1930	NY N	0	0	—	2	0	0	0	8	6	1	0	0	1	3	1.13	421	.214	.241	2-0	.000	-0		3	0.1
1931	NY N	5	3	.625	20	7	2	1	66	83	34	4	0	27	16	4.36	85	.306	.369	18-2	.111	-0	116	-3	-0.4
Total	3	8	6	.571	48	9	3	2	143.2	172	83	9	2	57	35	4.64	83	.304	.370	37-2	.162	-0	111	-12	-1.2
MORRILL, JOHN John Francis "Honest John" B 2.19.1855 Boston, MA D 4.2.1932 Brookline, MA BR/TR 5-10.5/155# d4.24.1876 M8 ▲																									
1880	Bos N	0	0	—	3	0	0	0	10.2	9	3	0		1	0	0.84	269	.273	.294	342	.237	0*		1	0.1
1881	†Bos N	0	1	.000	3	0	0	1	5.2	9	8	0		1	0	6.35	42	.333	.357	311	.289	1*		-3	-0.4
1882	Bos N	0	0	—	1	0	0	0	2	3	0	0		0	2	0.00	—	.375	.375	349	.289	0*		1	0.0
1883	Bos N	1	0	1.000	2	1	1	0	13	15	11	0		4	5	2.77	112	.268	.317	404	.319	1*	86	0	0.0
1884	Bos N	0	1	.000	7	1	1	**2**	23	34	23	0		6	13	7.43	39	.315	.351	438	.260	1*	37	-9	-0.4
1886	Bos N	0	0	—	1	0	0	0	4	5	1	0		0	2	0.00	—	.313	.313	430	.247	0*		1	0.1
1889	Was N	0	0	—	1	0	0	0	0.1	0	0	0	0	0	0	0.00	—	.000	.000	146	.185	0*		0	0.0
Total	7	1	2	.333	18	2	2	3	58.2	75	46	0	0	12	22	4.30	66	.301	.333	2420	.268	4	66	-9	-0.6
MORRIS, DANNY Danny Walker B 6.11.1946 Greenville, KY BR/TR 6-1/200# d9.10																									
1968	Min A	0	1	.000	3	2	0	0	10.2	11	5	0	0	4-0	6	1.69	183	.262	.326	3-0	.000	-0	113	1	0.0
1969	Min A	0	1	.000	3	1	0	0-0	5.1	5	4	1	0	4-1	1	5.06	72	.238	.360	0-0	—	0	24	-1	-0.2
Total	2	0	2	.000	6	3	0	0-0	16	16	9	1	0	8-1	7	2.81	117	.254	.338	3-0	.000	-0	80	0	-0.2
MORRIS, ED Edward "Cannonball" B 9.29.1862 Brooklyn, NY D 4.12.1937 Pittsburgh, PA BB/TL 5-7/165# d5.1																									
1884	Col AA	34	13	**.723**	52	52	47-3	0	429.2	335	159	3	13	51	302	2.18	139	.204	.234	199	.186	2*	105	46	4.5
1885	Pit AA	39	24	.619	**63**	**63**	**63-7**	0	**581**	459	245	5	14	101	**298**	2.35	137	**.208**	**.247**	237	.186	-5*	88	58	4.7
1886	Pit AA	**41**	20	.672	64	63	63-**12**	**1**	555.1	455	244	5	7	118	326	2.45	138	.214	**.258**	227	.167	-7	95	62	4.8
1887	Pit N	14	22	.389	38	38	37-1	0	317.2	375	225	13	8	71	91	4.31	89	.286	.326	126	.198	-4	78	-19	-2.0
1888	Pit N	29	23	.558	**55**	**55**	**54**-5	0	480	470	216	7	8	74	135	2.31	115	.245	.276	189	.101	-11	85	13	0.1
1889	Pit N	6	13	.316	21	21	18	0	170	196	107	4	6	48	40	4.13	91	.280	.332	72	.097	-5	78	-6	-1.1
1890	Pit P	8	7	.533	18	15	15-1	0	144.1	178	116	5	3	35	25	4.86	80	.290	.332	63	.143	-4	93	-11	-1.2
Total	7	171	122	.584	311	307	297-29	1	2678	2468	1312	42	59	498	1217	2.82	116	.235	.273	1113	.161	-34	90	143	9.8
MORRIS, JIM James Samuel B 1.19.1964 Brownwood, TX BL/TL 6-3/215# d9.18																									
1999	TB A	0	0	—	5	0	0	0-0	4.2	3	3	1	1	2-0	3	5.79	86	.167	.286	0-0	—	0		0	0.0
2000	TB A	0	0	—	16	0	0	0-0	10.1	10	9	1	0	7-1	10	4.35	114	.250	.362	0-0	—	0		-1	-0.1
Total	2	0	0	—	21	0	0	0-0	15	13	12	2	1	9-1	13	4.80	103	.224	.338	0-0	—	0		-1	-0.1
MORRIS, JACK John Scott B 5.16.1955 St.Paul, MN BR/TR 6-3/200# d7.26																									
1977	Det A	1	1	.500	7	6	1	0-0	45.2	38	20	4	0	23-0	28	3.74	115	.235	.328	0-0	—	0	73	3	0.2
1978	Det A	3	5	.375	28	7	0	0-0	106	107	57	8	3	49-5	48	4.33	90	.268	.345	0-0	—	0	116	-6	-0.4
1979	Det A	17	7	.708	27	27	9-1	0-0	197.2	179	76	19	4	59-4	113	3.28	132	.244	.301	0-0	—	0*	107	24	2.6
1980	Det A	16	15	.516	36	36	11-2	0-0	250	252	125	20	4	87-5	112	4.18	99	.262	.322	0-0	—	0*	97	-1	0.0
1981	Det A★	**14**	7	.667	25	25	15-1	0-0	198	153	69	14	2	78-11	97	3.05	124	.218	.295	0-0	—	0	126	17	1.7
1982	Det A	17	16	.515	37	37	17-3	0-0	266.1	247	131	37	0	96-7	135	4.06	100	.247	.311	0-0	—	0	91	2	0.2
1983	Det A	20	13	.606	37	37	20-1	0-0	**293.2**	257	117	30	3	83-5	**232**	3.34	117	.233	.287	0-0	—	0*	108	21	2.2
1984	†Det A★	19	11	.633	35	35	9-1	0-0	240.1	221	108	20	2	87-7	148	3.60	109	.241	.307	0-0	—	0	115	9	1.1
1985	Det A★	16	11	.593	35	35	13-4	0-0	257	212	102	21	5	110-7	191	3.33	122	.225	.307	0-0	—	0*	103	24	2.2
1986	Det A	21	8	.724	35	35	15-**6**	0-0	267	229	105	40	0	82-7	223	3.27	126	.229	.287	0-0	—	0	119	27	2.7
1987	†Det A★	18	11	.621	34	34	13	0-0	266	227	111	39	1	93-7	208	3.38	125	.228	.293	1-0	.000	-0*	112	27	2.6
1988	Det A	15	13	.536	34	34	10-2	0-0	235	225	115	20	4	83-7	168	3.94	97	.251	.317	0-0	—	0	104	-4	-0.4
1989	Det A	6	14	.300	24	24	10	0-0	170.1	189	102	23	2	59-3	115	4.86	79	.283	.339	0-0	—	0	83	-19	-1.9
1990	Det A	15	18	.455	36	**36**	**11**-3	0-0	249.2	231	144	26	6	97-13	162	4.51	88	.242	.313	0-0	—	0	110	-19	-2.3
1991	†Min A★	18	12	.600	35	**35**	10-2	0-0	246.2	226	107	18	5	92-5	163	3.43	125	.245	.315	0-0	—	0	103	20	2.3
1992	†Tor A	**21**	6	.778	34	34	6-1	0-0	240.2	222	114	18	10	80-2	132	4.04	101	.246	.312	0-0	—	0	122	3	0.3
1993	Tor A	7	12	.368	27	27	4-1	0-0	152.2	189	116	18	3	65-2	103	6.19	70	.302	.368	0-0	—	0	90	-32	-3.3
1994	Cle A	10	6	.625	23	23	1	0-0	141.1	163	96	14	4	67-2	100	5.60	84	.292	.369	0-0	—	0	127	-12	-1.1
Total	18	254	186	.577	549	527	175-28	0-0	3824	3567	1815	389	58	1390-99	2478	3.90	105	.247	.313	1-0	.000	-0	107	84	8.7
MORRIS, JOHN John Wallace B 8.23.1941 Lewes, DE BR/TL 6-1/198# d7.19																									
1966	Phi N	1	1	.500	13	0	0	0	13.2	15	8	2	1	3-1	8	5.27	68	.278	.328	0-0	—	0		-2	-0.3
1968	Bal A	2	0	1.000	19	0	0	0	31.2	19	11	4	4	17-2	22	2.56	114	.173	.303	6-0	.000	-1		1	0.0
1969	Sea A	0	0	—	6	0	0	0-0	12.2	16	10	2	0	8-1	8	6.39	57	.308	.400	1-0	1.000	1		-4	-0.1
1970	Mil A	4	3	.571	20	9	2	0-0	73.1	70	33	4	2	22-3	40	3.93	97	.253	.312	17-1	.176	0	89	0	0.1
1971	Mil A	2	2	.500	43	1	0	1-0	67.2	69	34	4	1	27-9	42	3.72	93	.270	.334	5-1	.200	0	129	-3	-0.1
1972	SF N	0	0	—	7	0	0	0-0	6.1	9	6	2	0	2-0	5	4.26	82	.310	.355	0-0	—	0		-2	-0.1
1973	SF N	1	0	1.000	7	0	0	0-1	6.1	12	8	0	0	3-0	3	8.53	45	.429	.469	1-0	.000	-0		-4	-0.5
1974	SF N	1	1	.500	17	0	0	1-0	20.2	17	7	1	0	4-1	9	3.05	125	.215	.253	1-0	1.000	0		2	0.2
Total	8	11	7	.611	132	10	2	2-1	232.1	227	117	19	8	86-17	137	3.95	90	.256	.325	31-2	.194	1	97	-12	-0.8
MORRIS, BUGS Joseph Harley (a.k.a. Joseph Harley Bennett In 1918) B 4.19.1892 Weir City, KS D 11.21.1957 Noel, MO BR/TR 5-9.5/163# d7.20																									
1918	StL A	0	2	.000	4	2	0	0	10.1	12	7	1	0	7	0	3.48	79	.308	.413	4-0	.250	0	96	-2	-0.3

Year	Tm Lg	W	L	Pct	G	GS	CG-Sho	SV-BS	IP	H	R	HR	HB	BB-IB	SO	ERA	AERA	OAV	OOB	AB-SH	AVG	PB	Sup	APR	PW
1921	Chi A	0	3	.000	3	2	1	0	17.2	19	14	1	0	16	2	6.11	69	.297	.438	6-0	.333	0	10	-4	-0.5
	StL A	0	0	—	3	1	0	0	5.2	11	10	1	2	6	3	14.29	31	.407	.543	1-0	1.000	0	93	-6	-0.2
	Year	0	3	.000	6	3	1	0	23.1	30	15	2	2	22	5	8.10	53	.330	.470	7-0	.429	1	39	-9	-0.7
Total	2	0	5	.000	10	5	1	0	33.2	42	31	3	2	29	5	6.68	57	.323	.453	11-0	.364	1	56	-12	-1.0
MORRIS, MATT Matthew Christian B 8.9.1974 Middletown, NY BR/TR 6-5/210# d4.4																									
1997	StL N	12	9	.571	33	33	3	0-0	217	208	88	12	7	69-2	149	3.19	130	.258	.319	73-2	.205	3*	96	23	2.2
1998	StL N	7	5	.583	17	17	2-1	0-0	113.2	101	37	8	3	42-6	79	2.53	166	.243	.316	29-7	.069	-0	103	21	2.0
2000	†StL N	3	3	.500	31	0	0	4-3	53	53	22	3	2	17-1	34	3.57	129	.261	.323	3-3	.333	0*		7	0.7
2001	†StL N★	**22**	8	.733	34	34	2-1	0-0	216.1	218	86	13	13	54-3	185	3.16	135	.265	.318	72-11	.139	-1	123	26	3.2
2002	†StL N☆	17	9	.654	32	32	1-1	0-0	210.1	210	86	16	6	64-3	171	3.42	116	.261	.317	71-5	.169	1	114	14	1.6
2003	StL N	11	8	.579	27	27	5-**3**	0-0	172.1	164	76	20	4	39-1	120	3.76	108	.252	.297	52-12	.192	3	127	6	0.8
Total	6	72	42	.632	174	143	13-6	4-3	982.2	954	395	72	35	285-16	738	3.28	127	.257	.315	300-40	.167	6	113	97	10.5
MORRIS, ED Walter Edward "Big Ed" B 12.7.1899 Foshee, AL D 3.3.1932 Century, FL BR/TR 6-2/185# d8.5																									
1922	Chi N	0	0	—	5	0	0	0	12	22	17	1	0	6	5	8.25	51	.386	.444	4-0	.250	-0		-7	-0.3
1928	Bos A	19	15	.559	47	29	20	5	257.2	255	118	7	5	80	104	3.53	117	.264	.323	91-2	.154	-4	95	16	1.5
1929	Bos A	14	14	.500	33	26	17-2	1	208.1	227	118	7	2	95	73	4.45	96	.282	.360	69-7	.232	2	81	-2	-0.1
1930	Bos A	4	9	.308	18	9	3	0	65.1	67	42	1	0	38	28	4.13	112	.260	.355	19-1	.316	2	35	0	0.2
1931	Bos A	5	7	.417	37	14	3	0	130.2	131	80	4	5	74	46	4.75	91	.260	.361	38-2	.158	-2	83	-7	-0.7
Total	5	42	45	.483	140	78	43-2	6	674	702	375	20	12	293	256	4.19	101	.271	.348	221-12	.195	-1	81	0	0.6
MORRISETTE, BILL William Lee B 1.17.1893 Baltimore, MD D 3.25.1966 Virginia Beach, VA BR/TR 6/176# d9.19																									
1915	Phi A	2	0	1.000	4	1	1	0	20	15	6	0	0	5	11	1.35	217	.195	.244	7-0	.286	0	174	3	0.3
1916	Phi A	0	0	—	1	0	0	0	4	6	3	0	0	5	2	6.75	42	.429	.579	1-0	.000	0		-1	0.0
1920	Det A	1	1	.500	8	3	1	0	27	25	21	0	3	19	15	4.33	86	.245	.379	8-0	.000	-1	92	-3	-0.4
Total	3	3	1	.750	13	4	2	0	51	46	30	0	3	29	28	3.35	100	.238	.347	16-0	.125	-1	115	-1	-0.1
MORRISON, JOHNNY John Dewey "Jughandle Johnny" B 10.22.1895 Pellville, KY D 3.20.1966 Louisville, KY BR/TR 5-11/188# d9.28 b-Phil																									
1920	Pit N	1	0	1.000	2	1	1-1	0	7	4	0	0	0	1	3	0.00	—	.167	.200	3-0	.000	-0	147	2	0.3
1921	Pit N	9	7	.563	21	17	11-**3**	0	144	131	49	3	1	33	52	2.88	133	.258	.305	42-4	.119	-1	76	18	1.7
1922	Pit N	17	11	.607	45	33	20-**5**	1	286.1	315	130	10	6	87	104	3.43	119	.286	.341	101-10	.198	-2	113	21	1.5
1923	Pit N	25	13	.658	42	37	27-2	2	301.2	287	136	6	5	110	114	3.49	115	.253	.321	115-6	.183	-3	103	18	1.6
1924	Pit N	11	16	.407	**41**	25	10	2	237.2	213	114	7	4	73	85	3.75	102	.245	.307	77-11	.169	-2	80	3	0.0
1925	†Pit N	17	14	.548	**44**	26	10	**4**	211	245	113	12	7	60	60	3.88	115	.291	.343	73-6	.178	-2	104	12	1.2
1926	Pit N	6	8	.429	26	13	6-2	2	122.1	119	52	2	2	44	39	3.38	116	.267	.335	39-0	.077	-4	67	9	0.5
1927	Pit N	3	2	.600	21	2	1	3	53.2	63	27	2	0	21	21	4.19	98	.304	.368	13-1	.154	-0	166	0	-0.1
1929	Bro N	13	7	.650	39	10	4	**8**	136.2	150	87	11	3	61	57	4.48	103	.279	.355	43-1	.163	-2	104	0	-0.4
1930	Bro N	1	2	.333	16	0	0	1	34.2	47	29	4	0	16	11	5.45	90	.346	.414	5-0	.000	-1		-4	-0.3
Total	10	103	80	.563	297	164	90-13	23	1535	1574	737	57	28	506	546	3.65	113	.271	.332	511-39	.164	-18	97	79	6.0
MORRISON, MIKE Michael B 2.6.1867 Erie, PA D 6.16.1955 Erie, PA BR/TR 5-8.5/156# d4.19																									
1887	Cle AA	12	25	.324	40	40	35	0	316.2	385	341	13	22	205	158	4.92	88	.294	.398	141	.191	-4*	93	-30	-2.4
1888	Cle AA	1	3	.250	4	4	4	0	35	40	35	3	1	19	14	5.40	57	.278	.366	17	.235	-0	89	-8	-0.8
1890	Syr AA	6	9	.400	17	14	13-1	0	127	131	112	4	13	81	69	5.88	60	.258	.374	120	.242	3*	97	-35	-2.7
	Bal AA	1	2	.333	4	4	3	0	26	15	20	0	2	20	13	3.81	107	.163	.325	9	.111	-1	104	-1	-0.1
	Year	7	11	.389	21	18	16-1	0	153	146	26	4	15	101	82	5.53	66	.244	.366	129	.233	3	99	-36	-2.8
Total	3	20	39	.339	65	62	55-1	0	504.2	571	508	20	38	325	254	5.14	78	.278	.387	287	.213	-2	95	-74	-6.0
MORRISON, PHIL Philip Melvin B 10.18.1894 Rockport, IN D 1.18.1955 Lexington, KY BB/TR 6-2/190# d9.30 b-Johnny																									
1921	Pit N	0	0	—	1	0	0	0	0.2	1	0	0	0	0	1	0.00	—	.333	.333	0-0	—	0		0	0.0
MORRISON, HANK Stephen Henry B 5.22.1866 Olneyville, RI D 9.30.1927 Attleboro, MA BR/TR 5-10/180# d5.28																									
1887	Ind N	3	4	.429	7	7	5	0	57	79	73	2	1	27	13	7.58	55	.307	.375	26	.115	-2	96	-21	-2.0
MORRISON, GUY Walter Guy B 8.29.1895 Hinton, WV D 8.14.1934 Grand Rapids, MI BR/TR 5-11/185# d8.31																									
1927	Bos N	1	2	.333	11	3	1	0	34.1	40	22	1	0	15	6	4.46	83	.296	.367	8-0	.125	1	138	-4	-0.2
1928	Bos N	0	0	—	1	0	0	0	3	4	4	1	0	3	0	12.00	33	.308	.438	0-0	—	0		-2	-0.1
Total	2	1	2	.333	12	3	1	0	37.1	44	26	2	0	18	6	5.06	74	.297	.373	8-0	.125	1	138	-6	-0.3
MORRISSEY, FRANK Michael Joseph "Deacon" B 5.5.1876 Baltimore, MD D 2.22.1939 Baltimore, MD TR 5-4/140# d7.13																									
1901	Bos A	0	0	—	1	0	0	0	4.1	5	1	0	2	2	1	2.08	170	.278	.409	3-0	.000	-1		1	0.0
1902	Chi N	1	3	.250	5	5	5	0	40	40	16	0	2	8	13	2.25	120	.260	.305	22-0	.091	-1*	65	2	0.1
Total	2	1	3	.250	6	5	5	0	44.1	45	17	0	4	10	14	2.23	125	.262	.317	25-0	.080	-1	65	3	0.1
MORTON, CARL Carl Wendle B 1.18.1944 Kansas City, MO D 4.12.1983 Tulsa, OK BR/TR 6/200# d4.11																									
1969	Mon N	0	3	.000	8	5	0	0-0	29.1	29	15	2	2	18-3	16	4.60	80	.264	.368	7-0	.000	-0	48	-2	-0.2
1970	Mon N	18	11	.621	43	37	10-4	0-1	284.2	281	123	27	4	125-17	154	3.60	114	.262	.339	93-11	.161	2	101	18	2.0
1971	Mon N	10	18	.357	36	35	9	1-0	213.2	252	129	22	4	83-13	84	4.80	74	.295	.358	77-2	.182	2	95	-31	-3.4
1972	Mon N	7	13	.350	27	27	3-1	0-0	172	170	84	16	3	53-6	51	3.92	91	.258	.314	52-4	.135	1*	66	-8	-0.7
1973	Atl N	15	10	.600	38	37	10-4	0-0	256.1	254	114	18	4	70-7	112	3.41	116	.259	.309	94-2	.181	4*	118	12	1.5
1974	Atl N	16	12	.571	38	38	7-1	0-0	274.2	293	110	10	2	89-12	113	3.15	120	.277	.331	89-12	.112	-4	99	18	1.3
1975	Atl N	17	16	.515	39	39	11-2	0-0	277.2	302	122	19	3	82-3	78	3.50	108	.278	.328	94-5	.160	-1	81	11	1.2
1976	Atl N	4	9	.308	26	24	1-1	0-0	140.1	172	79	6	5	45-4	42	4.17	91	.306	.359	45-5	.178	-0*	93	-8	-0.6
Total	8	87	92	.486	255	242	51-13	1-1	1648.2	1753	776	120	27	565-65	650	3.73	102	.275	.334	551-41	.156	3	94	10	1.1
MORTON, CHARLIE Charles Hazen B 10.12.1854 Kingsville, OH D 12.9.1921 Massillon, OH BR/TR ?/150# d5.2.1882 M3 U1 ▲																									
1884	Tol AA	0	1	.000	3	1	1	0	23.1	18	14	0	1	5	7	3.09	111	.209	.261	111	.162	-0*	35	1	0.0
MORTON, GUY Guy Sr. "The Alabama Blossom" B 6.1.1893 Vernon, AL D 10.18.1934 Sheffield, AL BR/TR 6-1/175# d6.20 Mil 1918 s-Guy																									
1914	Cle A	1	13	.071	25	13	5	1	128	116	62	1	3	55	80	3.02	95	.257	.341	35-2	.029	-4	56	-2	-0.7
1915	Cle A	16	15	.516	34	27	15-6	1	240	189	75	5	2	60	134	2.14	143	.216	.268	82-3	.146	-4	74	25	2.7
1916	Cle A	12	6	.667	27	18	9	0	149.2	139	63	1	3	42	88	2.89	104	.246	.302	57-2	.211	-1	116	2	0.1
1917	Cle A	10	10	.500	35	18	6-1	2	161	158	74	3	2	59	62	2.74	103	.266	.335	47-3	.085	-4	86	-1	-0.7
1918	Cle A	14	8	.636	30	28	13-1	0	214.2	189	87	1	3	77	123	2.64	114	.240	.310	77-0	.156	-1	101	6	0.5
1919	Cle A	9	9	.500	26	20	9-3	0	147.1	128	65	3	0	47	64	2.81	119	.233	.293	56-1	.161	-2	98	7	0.5
1920	Cle A	8	6	.571	29	17	6-1	1	137	140	80	2	1	57	72	4.47	85	.270	.344	46-1	.217	-1	93	-9	-1.0
1921	Cle A	8	3	.727	30	7	3-2	0	107.2	98	45	1	2	32	45	2.76	155	.244	.303	35-3	.171	-2	53	16	1.1
1922	Cle A	14	9	.609	38	23	13-3	0	202.2	218	117	7	4	85	102	4.00	100	.277	.351	68-6	.191	-2	112	-6	-0.6
1923	Cle A	6	6	.500	33	14	3-2	1	129.1	133	67	3	2	56	54	4.24	93	.276	.354	44-1	.159	-2	115	0	-0.3
1924	Cle A	0	1	.000	10	0	0	0	12.1	12	12	0	0	13	6	6.57	65	.250	.410	1-0	.000	-0		-3	-0.3
Total	11	98	86	.533	317	185	82-19	6	1629.2	1520	747	27	22	583	830	3.13	108	.251	.319	548-22	.157	-24	93	35	1.3
MORTON, KEVIN Kevin Joseph B 8.3.1968 Norwalk, CT BR/TL 6-2/185# d7.5																									
1991	Bos A	6	5	.545	16	15	1	0-0	86.1	93	49	9	1	40-2	45	4.59	94	.284	.356	0-0	—	0	127	-3	-0.3
MORTON, SPARROW William P. TL d7.15																									
1884	Phi N	0	2	.000	2	2	2	0	17	16	20	0		11	5	5.29	56	.222	.325	8	.375	1	53	-5	-0.3
MOSELEY, EARL Earl Victor "Vic" B 9.7.1884 Middleburg, OH D 7.1.1963 Alliance, OH BR/TR 5-9.5/168# d6.17																									
1913	Bos A	8	5	.615	24	15	7-3	0	120.2	105	56	1	0	49	62	3.13	94	.248	.326	37-1	.081	-2	89	-2	-0.4
1914	Ind F	19	18	.514	43	38	29-4	1	316.2	303	149	5	4	123	205	3.47	90	.258	.330	109-7	.110	-8	98	-8	-1.7
1915	New F	15	15	.500	38	32	22-5	1	268	222	87	2	2	99	142	**1.91**	134	.229	.302	88-7	.148	-4*	94	17	1.3
1916	Cin N	7	10	.412	31	15	7	1	150.1	145	75	5	0	69	60	3.89	67	.257	.338	46-2	.087	-2	123	-19	-2.5
Total	4	49	48	.505	136	100	65-12	3	855.2	775	367	13	6	340	469	3.01	94	.247	.322	280-17	.114	-17	99	-12	-3.3

Year	Tm Lg	W	L	Pct	G	GS	CG-Sho	SV-BS	IP	H	R	HR	HB	BB-IB	SO	ERA	AERA	OAV	OOB	AB-SH	AVG	PB	Sup	APR	PW
MOSER, WALTER Walter Fredrick B 2.27.1881 Concord, NC D 12.10.1946 Philadelphia, PA BR/TR 5-9/170# d9.3																									
1906	Phi N	0	4	.000	6	4	4	0	42.2	49	35	0	1	15	17	3.59	73	.295	.357	14-0	.000	-2	14	-8	-0.9
1911	Bos A	0	1	.000	6	3	1	0	24.2	37	28	0	1	11	11	4.01	82	.366	.434	7-0	.000	-1	132	-6	-0.4
	StL A	0	2	.000	2	2	0	0	3.1	11	12	0	0	4	2	21.60	16	.478	.556	1-0	1.000	0	53	-7	-1.0
	Year	0	3	.000	8	5	1	0	28	48	15	0	1	15	13	6.11	54	.387	.457	8-0	.125	-1	101	-14	-1.4
Total	2	0	7	.000	14	9	5	0	70.2	97	75	0	2	30	30	4.58	63	.334	.401	22-0	.045	-2	70	-21	-2.3
MOSKAU, PAUL Paul Richard B 12.20.1953 St.Joseph, MO BR/TR 6-2/210# d6.21																									
1977	Cin N	6	6	.500	20	19	2-2	0-0	108	116	51	10	1	40-3	71	4.00	98	.278	.338	38-1	.184	2*	106	0	0.1
1978	Cin N	6	4	.600	26	25	2-1	1-0	145	139	65	17	3	57-4	88	3.97	89	.255	.327	49-2	.204	4*	138	-4	0.0
1979	Cin N	5	4	.556	21	15	1	0-0	106.1	107	53	9	0	51-3	58	3.89	96	.263	.341	37-6	.081	-2	103	-3	-0.4
1980	Cin N	9	7	.563	33	19	2-1	2-1	152.2	147	69	13	1	41-2	94	4.01	89	.257	.305	44-8	.159	-0	108	-5	-0.6
1981	Cin N	2	1	.667	27	1	0	2-1	54.2	54	31	4	1	32-5	32	4.94	72	.258	.355	6-2	.000	-0	150	-7	-0.4
1982	Pit N	1	3	.250	13	5	0	0-1	35	43	21	7	0	8-0	15	4.37	85	.303	.338	11-1	.091	-1	119	-3	-0.4
1983	Chi N	3	2	.600	8	8	0	0-0	32	44	25	7	0	14-1	16	6.75	56	.331	.395	11-2	.182	0	116	-9	-1.2
Total	7	32	27	.542	148	92	7-4	5-3	633.2	650	315	67	6	243-18	374	4.22	87	.268	.333	196-22	.153	2	117	-31	-2.9
MOSS, MAL Charles Malcolm B 4.18.1905 Sullivan, IN D 2.5.1983 Savannah, GA BR/TL 6/175# d4.29																									
1930	Chi N	0	0	—	12	1	0	1	18.2	18	13	0	0	14	4	6.27	78	.254	.376	11-0	.273	0	214	-2	-0.1
MOSS, DAMIAN Damian Joseph B 11.24.1976 Darlinghurst, Australia BR/TL 6/187# d4.26																									
2001	Atl N	0	0	—	5	1	0	0-0	9	3	3	1	0	9-0	8	3.00	147	.097	.300	1-0	.000	0	42	2	0.1
2002	†Atl N	12	6	.667	33	29	0	0-0	179	140	80	20	6	89-5	111	3.42	120	.221	.321	50-6	.100	-1	112	11	1.0
2003	SF N	9	7	.563	21	20	0	0-0	115	121	62	12	5	63-3	57	4.70	88	.273	.367	29-7	.241	1	97	-7	-0.7
	Bal A	1	5	.167	10	9	0	0-0	50.2	63	40	12	6	29-2	22	6.22	71	.307	.405	0-0	—	0	79	-12	-1.1
Total	3	22	18	.550	69	59	0	0-0	353.2	327	185	45	17	190-10	198	4.22	98	.249	.349	80-13	.150	0	100	-6	-0.7
MOSS, RAY Raymond Earl B 12.5.1901 Chattanooga, TN D 8.9.1998 Chattanooga, TN BR/TR 6-1/185# d4.17																									
1926	Bro N	0	0	—	1	0	0	0	1	3	1	0	0	0	0	9.00	42	.600	.600	1-0	.000	-0		0	0.0
1927	Bro N	1	0	1.000	1	1	0	0	8.1	11	3	0	0	1	1	3.24	122	.333	.353	3-1	.333	1	86	1	0.2
1928	Bro N	0	3	.000	22	5	1-1	1	60.1	62	43	5	0	35	5	4.92	81	.279	.377	25-0	.320	2*	98	-7	-0.1
1929	Bro N	11	6	.647	39	20	7-2	0	182	214	115	9	7	81	59	5.04	92	.296	.373	66-2	.076	-5*	96	-6	-1.0
1930	Bro N	9	6	.600	36	11	5	1	118.1	127	78	13	4	55	30	5.10	96	.270	.352	39-2	.154	-2	100	-1	-0.4
1931	Bro N	0	0	—	1	0	0	0	1	1	0	0	0	1	0	0.00	—	.333	.500	0-0	—	0		0	0.0
	Bos N	1	3	.250	12	5	0	0	45	56	32	2	0	16	14	4.60	82	.306	.362	15-0	.133	-1	63	-7	-0.6
	Year	1	3	.250	13	5	0	0	46	57	35	2	0	17	14	4.50	84	.306	.365	15-0	.133	-1	63	-6	-0.6
Total	6	22	18	.550	112	42	13-3	2	416	474	272	29	11	189	109	4.95	91	.289	.367	149-5	.148	-5	94	-20	-1.9
MOSSI, DON Donald Louis "The Sphinx" B 1.11.1929 St.Helena, CA BL/TL 6-1/195# d4.17																									
1954	†Cle A	6	1	.857	40	5	2	7	93	56	22	5	1	39	55	1.94	190	.176	.267	19-1	.158	0	67	**19**	1.7
1955	Cle A	4	3	.571	57	1	0	9	81.2	81	28	4	1	18-2	69	2.42	164	.253	.292	9-0	.111	0	156	13	1.4
1956	Cle A	6	5	.545	48	3	0	11	87.2	79	38	6	1	33-5	59	3.59	117	.240	.311	20-0	.150	0	85	7	1.0
1957	Cle A★	11	10	.524	36	22	6-1	2	159	165	82	16	2	57-5	97	4.13	90	.265	.327	55-0	.218	2	107	-6	-0.7
1958	Cle A	7	8	.467	43	5	0	3	101.2	106	49	6	4	30-6	55	3.90	94	.269	.324	26-0	.115	-2	64	-3	-0.6
1959	Det A	17	9	.654	34	30	15-3	0	228	210	92	20	3	49-0	125	3.36	121	.243	.284	77-5	.169	0*	94	19	2.1
1960	Det A	9	8	.529	23	22	9-2	0	158.1	158	68	17	1	32-4	69	3.47	114	.258	.293	43-3	.116	-0	86	9	0.9
1961	Det A	15	7	.682	35	34	12-1	1	240.1	237	97	29	0	47-3	137	2.96	139	.258	.292	79-6	.165	1	121	28	2.5
1962	Det A	11	13	.458	35	27	8-1	1	180.1	195	92	24	1	36-1	121	4.19	97	.270	.303	55-1	.164	1*	103	-1	-0.1
1963	Det A	7	7	.500	24	16	3	2	122.2	110	58	20	4	17-0	68	3.74	100	.236	.268	39-2	.205	2	108	-1	0.2
1964	Chi A	3	1	.750	34	0	0	7	40	37	16	9	1	7-2	36	2.93	118	.240	.278	6-0	.167	-0		2	0.2
1965	KC A	5	8	.385	51	0	0	7	55.1	59	30	0	0	20-6	41	3.74	93	.278	.333	8-0	.000	-1		-3	-0.8
Total	12	101	80	.558	460	165	55-8	50	1548	1493	672	156	19	385-34	932	3.43	114	.252	.297	436-18	.163	4	103	83	7.8
MOSSOR, EARL Earl Dalton B 7.21.1925 Forbus, TN D 12.29.1988 Batavia, OH BL/TR 6-1/175# d4.30																									
1951	Bro N	0	0	—	3	0	0	0	1.2	2	6	1	0	7	1	32.40	12	.333	.692	1-0	1.000	0		-5	-0.2
MOTA, DANNY Daniel (Avila) B 10.9.1975 Seybol, D.R. BR/TR 6/180# d9.15																									
2000	Min A	0	0	—	4	0	0	0-0	5.1	10	5	1	0	1-0	3	8.44	61	.370	.393	0-0	—	0		-2	-0.1
MOTA, GUILLERMO Guillermo B 7.25.1973 San Pedro De Macoris, D.R. BR/TR 6-6/200# d5.2																									
1999	Mon N	2	4	.333	51	0	0	0-1	55.1	54	24	5	2	25-3	27	2.93	153	.257	.338	1-0	1.000	1		8	0.9
2000	Mon N	1	1	.500	29	0	0	0-0	30	27	21	3	2	12-0	24	6.00	80	.245	.328	1-0	.000	-0		-3	-0.2
2001	Mon N	1	3	.250	53	0	0	0-3	49.2	51	30	9	1	18-1	31	5.26	85	.271	.335	3-0	.333	0		-4	-0.2
2002	LA N	1	3	.250	43	0	0	0-1	60.2	45	30	4	2	27-6	49	4.15	92	.202	.292	4-0	.250	0		-2	-0.1
2003	LA N	6	3	.667	76	0	0	1-2	105	78	23	7	1	26-4	99	1.97	204	.206	.258	9-0	.222	1		26	2.2
Total	5	11	14	.440	252	0	0	1-7	300.2	255	128	28	8	108-14	230	3.53	119	.230	.301	18-0	.278	3		25	2.6
MOULDER, GLEN Glen Hubert B 9.28.1917 Cleveland, OK D 11.27.1994 Decatur, GA BR/TR 6/180# d4.28																									
1946	Bro N	0	0	—	1	0	0	0	2	2	1	1	0	1	1	4.50	75	.286	.375	0-0	—	0		0	0.0
1947	StL A	4	2	.667	32	2	0	2	73	78	37	4	0	43	23	3.82	101	.283	.379	17-1	.235	-0	114	0	0.0
1948	Chi A	3	6	.333	33	9	0	2	85.2	108	67	8	1	54	26	6.41	66	.316	.411	20-4	.300	2	78	-20	-1.8
Total	3	7	8	.467	66	11	0	4	160.2	188	105	13	1	98	50	5.21	78	.301	.396	37-5	.270	1	86	-20	-1.8
MOUNCE, TONY Anthony David B 2.8.1975 Sacramento, CA BL/TL 6-2/170# d6.13																									
2003	Tex A	1	5	.167	11	11	0	0-0	50.2	65	42	9	5	25-0	30	7.11	70	.317	.403	2-0	.000	-0	62	-11	-1.0
MOUNTAIN, FRANK Frank Henry B 5.17.1860 Ft.Edward, NY D 11.19.1939 Schenectady, NY BR/TR 5-11/185# d7.19 ▲																									
1880	Tro N	1	1	.500	2	2	2	0	17	23	17	0		6	2	5.29	48	.307	.358	9	.222	-0	157	-4	-0.4
1881	Det N	3	4	.429	7	7	7	0	60	80	63	2		18	13	5.25	56	.292	.336	25	.160	-0	114	-13	-1.3
1882	Wor N	0	5	.000	5	5	5	0	42	47	30	0		11	5	3.00	104	.255	.297	16	.063	-2	27	0	-0.2
	Phi AA	2	6	.250	8	8	8	0	69	72	49	1		11	15	3.91	72	.251	.279	36	.333	3*	89	-7	-0.3
	Wor N	2	11	.154	13	13	11	0	102	138	93	4		24	24	3.97	78	.299	.334	70	.271	2*	45	-9	-0.7
1883	Col AA	26	33	.441	59	59	57-4	0	503	546	345	8		123	159	3.60	86	.259	.300	276	.217	7*	88	-27	-1.8
1884	Col AA	23	17	.575	42	41	40-5	1	360.2	289	163	7	11	78	156	2.45	124	.209	.257	210	.238	9*	94	23	3.3
1885	Pit AA	1	4	.200	5	5	5	0	46	56	31	1	2	24	7	4.30	75	.320	.408	20	.100	-1	88	-4	-0.4
1886	Pit AA	0	2	.000	2	2	2	0	16	22	21	0	5	14	2	7.88	43	.319	.466	55	.145	0*	105	-7	-0.6
Total	7	58	83	.411	143	142	137-9	1	1215.2	1273	812	23	18	309	383	3.47	88	.254	.299	717	.220	17	86	-48	-2.4
MOUNTJOY, BILL William Henry "Medicine Bill" B 12.11.1858 London, ON, CAN D 5.19.1894 London, ON, CAN BL/TR 5-6/150# d9.29																									
1883	Cin AA	0	1	.000	1	1	1	0	8	9	4	0		2	3	2.25	144	.265	.306	3	.000	-1	18	1	0.0
1884	Cin AA	19	12	.613	33	33	32-3	0	289	274	148	5	16	43	96	2.93	114	.238	.275	119	.151	-3*	118	7	0.3
1885	Cin AA	10	7	.588	17	17	17-1	0	153.2	149	89	5	7	52	50	3.16	103	.247	.314	60	.167	0	123	1	0.0
	Bal AA	2	4	.333	6	6	6-1	0	53	72	47	1	4	13	15	5.43	60	.316	.363	18	.056	-0*	85	-11	-0.9
	Year	12	11	.522	23	23	23-2	0	206.2	221	52	6	11	65	65	3.75	87	.266	.327	78	.141	0	113	-10	-0.9
Total	3	31	24	.564	57	57	56-5	0	503.2	504	288	11	27	110	164	3.25	102	.250	.297	200	.145	-4	114	-2	-0.6
MOYER, ED Charles Edward B 8.15.1885 Andover, OH D 11.18.1962 Jacksonville, FL d7.20																									
1910	Was A	0	3	.000	6	3	2	0	25	22	15	1	3	13	3	3.24	77	.253	.369	8-0	.125	-1	90	-3	-0.3
MOYER, JAMIE Jamie B 11.18.1962 Sellersville, PA BL/TL 6/170# d6.16																									
1986	Chi N	7	4	.636	16	16	1-1	0-0	87.1	107	52	10	3	42-1	45	5.05	80	.311	.388	22-4	.091	-0	106	-9	-0.9
1987	Chi N	12	15	.444	35	33	1	0-0	201	210	127	28	5	97-9	147	5.10	84	.271	.353	61-7	.230	3*	80	-18	-1.7
1988	Chi N	9	15	.375	34	30	3-1	0-2	202	212	84	20	4	55-7	121	3.48	104	.272	.322	60-8	.083	-2	80	4	0.4
1989	Tex A	4	9	.308	15	15	1	0-0	76	84	51	10	2	33-0	44	4.86	82	.283	.354	0-0	—	0	81	-9	-1.3
1990	Tex A	2	6	.250	33	10	1	0-0	102.1	115	59	6	4	39-4	58	4.66	84	.290	.354	0-0	—	0	95	-8	-0.5
1991	StL N	0	5	.000	8	7	0	0-0	31.1	38	21	5	1	16-0	20	5.74	65	.319	.399	8-0	.000	-1	62	-7	-1.0

Year	Tm Lg	W	L	Pct	G	GS	CG-Sho	SV-BS	IP	H	R	HR	HB	BB-IB	SO	ERA	AERA	OAV	OOB	AB-SH	AVG	PB	Sup	APR	PW
1993	Bal A	12	9	.571	25	25	3-1	0-0	152	154	63	11	6	38-2	90	3.43	131	.265	.316	0-0	—	0	107	17	2.2
1994	Bal A	5	7	.417	23	23	0	0-0	149	158	81	23	2	38-3	87	4.77	105	.271	.316	0-0	—	0	85	4	0.3
1995	Bal A	8	6	.571	27	18	0	0-0	115.2	117	70	18	3	30-0	65	5.21	91	.265	.314	0-0	—	0	103	-6	-0.5
1996	Bos A	7	1	.875	23	10	0	0-0	90	111	50	14	1	27-2	50	4.50	113	.300	.347	0-0	—	0	130	6	0.5
	Sea A	6	2	.750	11	11	0	0-0	70.2	66	36	9	1	19-3	29	3.31	150	.243	.292	0-0	—	0	122	9	0.9
	Year	13	3	.813	34	21	0	0-0	160.2	177	43	23	2	46-5	79	3.98	126	.276	.323	0-0	—	0	126	14	1.4
1997	†Sea A	17	5	.773	30	30	2	0-0	188.2	187	82	21	7	43-2	113	3.86	117	.256	.303	3-0	.333	0	150	16	1.8
1998	Sea A	15	9	.625	34	34	4-3	0-0	234.1	234	99	23	10	42-2	158	3.53	131	.256	.295	2-0	.000	-0	96	29	2.7
1999	Sea A	14	8	.636	32	32	4	0-0	228	235	108	23	9	48-1	137	3.87	123	.267	.311	2-1	.500	1	89	22	2.1
2000	Sea A	13	10	.565	26	26	0	0-0	154	173	103	22	3	53-2	98	5.49	86	.281	.339	2-0	.000	-0	113	-15	-1.7
2001	†Sea A	20	6	.769	33	33	1	0-0	209.2	187	84	24	10	44-4	119	3.43	121	.239	.285	1-1	.000	-0	121	20	2.2
2002	Sea A	13	8	.619	34	34	4-2	0-0	230.2	198	89	28	9	50-4	147	3.32	128	.230	.278	5-0	.200	0	110	26	2.2
2003	Sea A★	21	7	.750	33	33	1	0-0	215	199	83	19	8	66-3	129	3.27	133	.246	.307	5-1	.400	1	116	26	3.3
Total	17	185	132	.584	472	420	26-8	0-2	2737.2	2785	1342	314	88	780-49	1657	4.07	109	.264	.318	171-22	.152	2	104	107	11.0

MROZINSKI, RON Ronald Frank B 9.16.1930 White Haven, PA BR/TL 5-11/160# d6.20

Year	Tm Lg	W	L	Pct	G	GS	CG-Sho	SV-BS	IP	H	R	HR	HB	BB-IB	SO	ERA	AERA	OAV	OOB	AB-SH	AVG	PB	Sup	APR	PW
1954	Phi N	1	1	.500	15	4	1	0	48	49	26	10	0	25	26	4.50	90	.261	.347	12-2	.083	-1	83	-2	-0.2
1955	Phi N	0	2	.000	22	1	0	1	34.1	38	26	2	4	19-2	18	6.55	61	.299	.396	4-0	.000	-1	67	-9	-0.6
Total	2	1	3	.250	37	5	1	1	82.1	87	52	12	4	44-2	44	5.36	75	.276	.368	16-2	.063	-2	80	-11	-0.8

MUDROCK, PHIL Philip Ray B 6.12.1937 Louisville, CO BR/TR 6-1/190# d4.19

Year	Tm Lg	W	L	Pct	G	GS	CG-Sho	SV-BS	IP	H	R	HR	HB	BB-IB	SO	ERA	AERA	OAV	OOB	AB-SH	AVG	PB	Sup	APR	PW
1963	Chi N	0	0	—	1	0	0	0	1	2	1	0	0	0-0	0	9.00	39	.400	.400	0-0	—	0		-1	0.0

MUELLER, GORDIE Joseph Gordon B 12.10.1922 Baltimore, MD BR/TR 6-4/200# d4.19

Year	Tm Lg	W	L	Pct	G	GS	CG-Sho	SV-BS	IP	H	R	HR	HB	BB-IB	SO	ERA	AERA	OAV	OOB	AB-SH	AVG	PB	Sup	APR	PW
1950	Bos A	0	0	—	8	0	0	0	7	11	8	1	0	13	1	10.29	48	.344	.533	1-0	.000	-0		-4	-0.2

MUELLER, LES Leslie Clyde B 3.4.1919 Belleville, IL BR/TR 6-3/190# d8.15 Mil 1942-44

Year	Tm Lg	W	L	Pct	G	GS	CG-Sho	SV-BS	IP	H	R	HR	HB	BB-IB	SO	ERA	AERA	OAV	OOB	AB-SH	AVG	PB	Sup	APR	PW
1941	Det A	0	0	—	4	0	0	0	13	9	9	1	0	10	8	4.85	94	.205	.352	3-0	.000	-0		-1	-0.1
1945	†Det A	6	8	.429	26	18	6-2	1	134.2	117	63	8	2	58	42	3.68	96	.234	.316	44-1	.182	0	79	-1	-0.1
Total	2	6	8	.429	30	18	6-2	1	147.2	126	72	9	2	68	50	3.78	95	.231	.319	47-1	.170	0	79	-2	-0.2

MUELLER, WILLIE Willard Lawrence B 8.30.1956 West Bend, WI BR/TR 6-4/220# d8.12

Year	Tm Lg	W	L	Pct	G	GS	CG-Sho	SV-BS	IP	H	R	HR	HB	BB-IB	SO	ERA	AERA	OAV	OOB	AB-SH	AVG	PB	Sup	APR	PW
1978	Mil A	1	0	1.000	5	0	0	0-0	12.2	16	11	1	0	6-0	6	6.39	59	.291	.361	0-0	—	0		-4	-0.3
1981	Mil A	0	0	—	1	0	0	0-0	2	4	1	0	0	0-0	1	4.50	76	.400	.400	0-0	—	0		0	0.0
Total	2	1	0	1.000	6	0	0	0-0	14.2	20	12	1	0	6-0	7	6.14	61	.308	.366	0-0	—	0		-4	-0.3

MUFFETT, BILLY Billy Arnold "Muff" B 9.21.1930 Hammond, IN BR/TR 6-1/198# d8.3 C18

Year	Tm Lg	W	L	Pct	G	GS	CG-Sho	SV-BS	IP	H	R	HR	HB	BB-IB	SO	ERA	AERA	OAV	OOB	AB-SH	AVG	PB	Sup	APR	PW
1957	StL N	3	2	.600	23	0	0	8	44	35	11	1	0	13-4	21	2.25	176	.222	.279	7-1	.000	-1		9	1.2
1958	StL N	4	6	.400	35	6	1	5	84	107	52	11	5	42-9	41	4.93	84	.316	.397	20-1	.200	0	91	-7	-0.9
1959	SF N	0	0	—	5	0	0	0	6.2	11	6	2	0	3-1	3	5.40	71	.407	.467	0-0	—	0		-2	-0.1
1960	Bos A	6	4	.600	23	14	4-1	0	125	116	53	6	5	36-2	75	3.24	125	.242	.299	41-1	.268	2	67	9	0.9
1961	Bos A	3	11	.214	38	11	2	2	112.2	130	87	18	2	36-2	47	5.67	73	.291	.344	23-1	.217	2	62	-20	-2.1
1962	Bos A	0	0	—	1	1	0	0	4	8	4	0	0	2-0	1	9.00	46	.471	.500	1-0	.000	-0	130	-2	-0.1
Total	6	16	23	.410	125	32	7-1	15	376.1	407	213	38	12	132-18	188	4.33	94	.277	.339	92-4	.217	3	72	-13	-1.1

MUICH, JOE Ignatius Andrew B 11.23.1903 St.Louis, MO D 7.2.1993 St.Louis, MO BR/TR 6-2/175# d9.4

Year	Tm Lg	W	L	Pct	G	GS	CG-Sho	SV-BS	IP	H	R	HR	HB	BB-IB	SO	ERA	AERA	OAV	OOB	AB-SH	AVG	PB	Sup	APR	PW
1924	Bos N	0	0	—	3	0	0	0	9	19	12	1	0	5	1	11.00	35	.432	.490	3-0	.000	-1		-7	-0.4

MUIR, JOE Joseph Allen B 11.26.1922 Oriole, MD D 6.25.1980 Baltimore, MD BL/TL 6-1/172# d4.21

Year	Tm Lg	W	L	Pct	G	GS	CG-Sho	SV-BS	IP	H	R	HR	HB	BB-IB	SO	ERA	AERA	OAV	OOB	AB-SH	AVG	PB	Sup	APR	PW
1951	Pit N	0	2	.000	9	1	0	0	16.1	11	6	2	0	7	5	2.76	153	.180	.265	1-0	.000	-0	21	2	0.3
1952	Pit N	2	3	.400	12	5	1	0	35.2	42	28	3	0	18	17	6.31	63	.288	.366	9-0	.111	-0	94	-9	-1.1
Total	2	2	5	.286	21	6	1	0	52	53	34	5	0	25	22	5.19	78	.256	.336	10-0	.100	-0	80	-7	-0.8

MULCAHY, HUGH Hugh Noyes "Losing Pitcher" B 9.9.1913 Brighton, MA D 10.19.2001 Aliquippa, PA BR/TR 6-2/190# d7.24 Mil 1941-45 C1

Year	Tm Lg	W	L	Pct	G	GS	CG-Sho	SV-BS	IP	H	R	HR	HB	BB-IB	SO	ERA	AERA	OAV	OOB	AB-SH	AVG	PB	Sup	APR	PW
1935	Phi N	1	5	.167	18	5	0	1	52.2	62	35	2	5	25	11	4.78	95	.295	.383	17-0	.000	-2*	45	-2	-0.4
1936	Phi N	1	1	.500	3	2	2	0	22.2	20	8	0	2	12	2	3.18	143	.238	.347	8-1	.250	0	84	4	0.3
1937	Phi N	8	18	.308	**56**	26	9-1	3	215.2	256	147	17	7	97	54	5.13	84	.296	.372	73-3	.151	-3	107	-21	-2.3
1938	Phi N	10	20	.333	46	34	15	1	267.1	294	162	14	6	120	90	4.61	84	.278	.354	94-7	.170	-2*	80	-23	-2.4
1939	Phi N	9	16	.360	38	32	14-1	4	225.2	246	144	19	11	93	59	4.99	80	.282	.359	76-5	.158	-3	82	-26	-2.8
1940	Phi N☆	13	22	.371	36	36	21-3	0	280	283	141	12	3	91	82	3.60	108	.261	.320	94-6	.202	1*	78	3	0.6
1945	Phi N	1	3	.250	5	4	1	0	28.1	33	17	1	0	9	2	3.81	101	.295	.347	7-1	.000	-1	55	-1	-0.1
1946	Phi N	2	4	.333	16	5	1	0	62.2	69	34	3	5	33	12	4.45	77	.295	.393	16-1	.188	1	80	-6	-0.4
1947	Pit N	0	0	—	2	1	0	0	6.2	8	7	1	0	7	2	4.05	104	.333	.484	3-0	.333	0	230	-1	0.0
Total	9	45	89	.336	220	145	63-5	9	1161.2	1271	695	69	39	487	314	4.49	89	.280	.355	388-24	.165	-9	84	-73	-7.5

MULDER, MARK Mark Alan B 8.5.1977 South Holland, IL BL/TL 6-6/200# d4.18

Year	Tm Lg	W	L	Pct	G	GS	CG-Sho	SV-BS	IP	H	R	HR	HB	BB-IB	SO	ERA	AERA	OAV	OOB	AB-SH	AVG	PB	Sup	APR	PW
2000	Oak A	9	10	.474	27	27	0	0-0	154	191	106	22	4	69-3	88	5.44	87	.308	.376	4-0	.000	-0	102	-13	-1.3
2001	†Oak A	**21**	8	.724	34	34	6-**4**	0-0	229.1	214	92	16	5	51-4	153	3.45	128	.249	.294	5-0	.200	0	110	27	3.3
2002	†Oak A	19	7	.731	30	30	2-1	0-0	207.1	182	88	21	11	55-3	159	3.47	127	.232	.290	5-0	.000	-0	103	22	2.5
2003	Oak A★	15	9	.625	26	26	**9-2**	0-0	186.2	180	66	15	2	40-2	128	3.13	144	.259	.300	4-1	.000	-0	95	31	3.8
Total	4	64	34	.653	117	117	17-7	0-0	777.1	767	352	74	22	215-12	528	3.77	119	.259	.312	18-1	.056	-1	103	67	8.3

MULHOLLAND, TERRY Terence John B 3.9.1963 Uniontown, PA BR/TL 6-3/206# d6.8

Year	Tm Lg	W	L	Pct	G	GS	CG-Sho	SV-BS	IP	H	R	HR	HB	BB-IB	SO	ERA	AERA	OAV	OOB	AB-SH	AVG	PB	Sup	APR	PW
1986	SF N	1	7	.125	15	10	0	0-0	54.2	51	33	3	1	35-2	27	4.94	71	.251	.363	19-1	.053	-1	63	-9	-1.3
1988	SF N	2	1	.667	9	6	2-1	0-0	46	50	20	3	1	7-0	18	3.72	88	.281	.312	14-0	.000	-1	118	-2	-0.2
1989	SF N	0	0	—	5	1	0	0-0	11	15	5	0	0	4-0	6	4.09	83	.319	.373	2-1	.000	-0	79	-1	0.0
	Phi N	4	7	.364	20	17	2-1	0-0	104.1	122	61	8	4	32-3	60	5.00	71	.292	.347	34-2	.059	-2	82	-15	-1.6
	Year	4	7	.364	25	18	2-1	0-0	115.1	137	64	8	4	36-3	66	4.92	72	.295	.350	36-3	.056	-2	82	-16	-1.6
1990	Phi N	9	10	.474	33	26	6-1	0-1	180.2	172	78	15	2	42-7	75	3.34	115	.252	.292	62-4	.097	-2	86	8	0.4
1991	Phi N	16	13	.552	34	34	8-3	0-0	232	231	100	15	3	49-2	142	3.61	102	.260	.299	80-5	.087	-4*	92	2	-0.2
1992	Phi N	13	11	.542	32	32	**12**-2	0-0	229	227	101	14	3	46-3	125	3.81	92	.261	.298	83-6	.096	-2	120	-6	-0.8
1993	†Phi N★	12	9	.571	29	28	7-2	0-0	191	177	80	20	3	40-2	116	3.25	122	.241	.282	62-8	.065	-4	113	15	1.0
1994	NY A	6	7	.462	24	19	2	0-0	120.2	150	94	24	3	37-1	72	6.49	71	.303	.353	0-0	—	0	135	-27	-2.3
1995	SF N	5	13	.278	29	24	2	0-0	149	190	112	25	4	38-1	65	5.80	71	.313	.354	49-3	.102	-0*	108	-31	-3.2
1996	Phi N	8	7	.533	21	21	3	0-0	133.1	157	74	17	3	21-1	52	4.66	93	.293	.320	45-4	.178	1	91	-4	-0.4
	Sea A	5	4	.556	12	12	0	0-0	69.1	75	38	5	2	28-3	34	4.67	106	.286	.356	0-0	—	0	114	3	0.3
1997	Chi N	6	12	.333	25	25	1	0-0	157	162	79	20	9	45-2	74	4.07	106	.271	.330	49-3	.163	-0	63	3	0.4
	SF N	0	1	.000	15	2	0	0-0	29.2	28	21	4	2	6-1	25	5.16	79	.248	.295	6-1	.167	0	101	-5	-0.2
	Year	6	13	.316	40	27	1	0-0	186.2	190	26	24	11	51-3	99	4.24	101	.267	.324	55-4	.164	0	66	-1	0.2
1998	†Chi N	6	5	.545	70	6	0	3-2	112	100	49	7	4	39-7	72	2.89	152	.235	.304	17-1	.294	2	94	13	1.4
1999	Chi N	6	6	.500	26	16	0	0-0	110	137	71	16	1	32-4	44	5.15	88	.309	.355	32-3	.094	-2	84	-9	-1.0
	†Atl N	4	2	.667	16	8	0	1-0	60.1	64	24	5	0	13-2	39	2.98	151	.274	.310	16-2	.125	-0	97	9	0.9
	Year	10	8	.556	42	24	0	1-0	170.1	201	29	21	1	45-6	83	4.39	103	.297	.340	48-5	.104	-2	88	0	-0.1
2000	†Atl N	9	9	.500	54	20	1	1-2	156.2	198	96	24	4	41-7	78	5.11	90	.308	.351	36-9	.250	2	102	-8	-0.7
2001	Pit N	0	0	—	22	1	0	0-0	36.1	38	15	5	1	10-1	17	3.72	121	.277	.329	3-0	.000	-0	123	4	0.2
	LA N	1	1	.500	19	3	0	0-0	29.1	40	20	7	1	7-0	25	5.83	69	.315	.356	6-0	.000	-1	69	-6	-0.4
	Year	1	1	.500	41	4	0	0-0	65.2	78	23	12	2	17-1	42	4.66	92	.295	.342	9-0	.000	-1	81	-2	-0.2
2002	LA N	0	0	—	21	0	0	0-0	32	45	29	10	2	7-0	17	7.31	52	.331	.367	1-0	.000	-0		-14	-0.7
	Cle A	3	2	.600	16	3	0	0-0	47	56	27	5	4	14-3	21	4.60	96	.301	.356	0-0	—	0	127	-2	-0.1
2003	Cle A	3	4	.429	45	3	0	0-2	99	117	60	17	6	37-6	42	4.91	90	.295	.360	1-0	.000	-0	180	-5	-0.3
Total	17	119	131	.476	592	317	46-10	5-7	2390.1	2602	1287	269	63	630-58	1246	4.37	94	.278	.325	617-53	.112	-16	99	-87	-8.8

MULLANE, TONY Anthony John "Count" or "The Apollo Of The Box" B 1.20.1859 Cork, Ireland D 4.25.1944 Chicago, IL BB/TR 5-10.5/165# d8.27 ▲

Year	Tm Lg	W	L	Pct	G	GS	CG-Sho	SV-BS	IP	H	R	HR	HB	BB-IB	SO	ERA	AERA	OAV	OOB	AB-SH	AVG	PB	Sup	APR	PW
1881	Det N	1	4	.200	5	5	5	0	44	55	42	2		17	7	4.91	59	.302	.362	19	.263	-0	100	-8	-0.7
1882	Lou AA	30	24	.556	**55**	**55**	51-5	0	460.1	418	212	3		78	**170**	1.88	132	.226	.257	303	.257	11*	107	34	5.0

Year	Tm Lg	W	L	Pct	G	GS	CG-Sho	SV-BS	IP	H	R	HR	HB	BB-IB	SO	ERA	AERA	OAV	OOB	AB-SH	AVG	PB	Sup	APR	PW
1883	StL AA	35	15	**.700**	53	49	49-3	**1**	460.2	372	222	3		74	191	2.19	**159**	.207	.238	307	.225	1*	83	60	5.5
1884	Tol AA	36	26	.581	67	65	64-**7**	0	567	481	276	5	32	89	325	2.52	135	.214	.255	352	.276	15*	77	55	7.1
1886	Cin AA	33	27	.550	63	56	55-1	0	529.2	501	315	11	18	166	250	3.70	95	.242	.303	324	.225	2*	103	-8	-0.4
1887	Cin AA	31	17	.646	48	48	47-**6**	0	416.1	414	234	11	32	121	97	3.24	134	.257	.322	199	.221	2*	100	51	4.6
1888	Cin AA	26	16	.619	44	42	41-4	**1**	380.1	341	194	9	29	75	186	2.84	112	.231	.282	175	.251	5*	110	15	1.9
1889	Cin AA	11	9	.550	33	24	17	**5**	220	218	133	4	13	89	112	2.99	131	.251	.329	196	.296	9*	87	17	1.9
1890	Cin N	12	10	.545	25	21	21	1	209	175	101	7	8	96	91	2.24	159	.220	.310	286	.276	7*	94	27	3.0
1891	Cin N	23	26	.469	51	47	42-1	0	426.1	390	250	15	18	187	124	3.23	104	.234	.318	209	.148	-5*	83	7	0.2
1892	Cin N	21	13	.618	37	34	30-3	1	295	222	131	12	12	127	109	2.59	126	**.201**	.290	118	.169	-1*	93	21	2.3
1893	Cin N	6	6	.500	15	13	11	1	122.1	130	84	4	9	65	24	4.41	108	.264	.360	52	.288	3*	81	4	0.5
	Bal N	12	16	.429	34	26	23	1	244.2	277	177	4	7	124	71	4.45	107	.277	.360	114	.228	-3*	93	7	0.4
	Year	18	22	.450	49	39	34	**2**	367	407	183	8	16	189	95	4.44	107	.273	.360	166	.247	-0	89	20	0.9
1894	Bal N	6	9	.400	21	15	9	4	122.2	155	117	4	7	90	43	6.31	87	.305	.417	53-0	.396	5	111	-13	-0.7
	Cle N	1	2	.333	4	4	3	0	33	46	35	3	0	10	3	7.64	72	.326	.371	13-1	.077	-1	120	-6	-0.4
	Year	7	11	.389	25	19	12	**4**	155.2	201	44	7	7	100	46	6.59	83	.310	.407	66-1	.333	4	113	-15	-1.1
Total	13	284	220	.563	555	504	468-30	15	4531.1	4195	2523	97	185	1408	1803	3.05	118	.235	.298	2720-1	.243	50	94	263	30.2
MULLEN, SCOTT Kenneth Scott B 1.17.1975 San Benito, TX BR/TL 6-2/190# d8.31																									
2000	KC A	0	0	—	11	0	0	0-0	10.1	10	5	2	0	3-0	7	4.35	118	.244	.295	0-0	—	0		1	0.0
2001	KC A	0	0	—	17	0	0	0-0	10	13	6	0	0	9-0	3	4.50	109	.310	.423	0-0	—	0		0	0.0
2002	KC A	4	5	.444	44	0	0	0-2	40	40	16	5	2	13-2	21	3.15	160	.267	.329	0-0	—	0		7	1.3
2003	KC A	0	0	—	2	0	0	0-0	4.1	11	8	2	0	5-0	3	16.62	31	.458	.552	0-0	—	0		-5	-0.2
	LA N	0	0	—	1	1	0	0-0	3	2	3	0	1	5-0	1	9.00	45	.200	.471	1-0	.000	-0	187	-2	-0.1
Total	4	4	5	.444	75	1	0	0-2	67.2	76	38	9	3	35-2	35	4.66	107	.285	.369	1-0	.000	-0	187	1	1.0
MULLIGAN, JOE Joseph Ignatius "Big Joe" B 7.31.1913 Weymouth, MA D 6.5.1986 W.Roxbury, MA BR/TR 6-4/210# d6.28																									
1934	Bos A	1	0	1.000	14	2	1	0	44.2	46	21	1	2	27	13	3.63	132	.279	.387	12-1	.000	-1	190	6	0.1
MULLIGAN, DICK Richard Charles B 3.18.1918 Swoyersville, PA D 12.15.1992 Victoria, TX BL/TL 6/167# d9.24 Mil 1942-45																									
1941	Was A	0	1	.000	1	1	1	0	9	11	5	0	0	2	2	5.00	81	.306	.342	3-0	.000	-0	86	-1	-0.1
1946	Phi N	2	2	.500	19	5	1	1	54.2	61	32	0	4	27	16	4.77	72	.289	.380	11-1	.000	-1	90	-7	-0.6
	Bos N	1	0	1.000	4	0	0	0	15.1	6	4	1	0	9	4	2.35	146	.122	.259	4-0	.000	0		2	0.1
	Year	3	2	.600	23	5	1	1	70	67	40	1	4	36	20	4.24	81	.258	.357	15-1	.000	-1	90	-5	-0.5
1947	Bos N	0	0	—	1	0	0	0	2	4	2	0	0	1	1	9.00	43	.400	.455	0-0	—	0		-1	-0.1
Total	3	3	3	.500	25	6	2	1	81	82	43	1	4	39	23	4.44	79	.268	.358	18-1	.000	-1	90	-7	-0.7
MULLIN, GEORGE George Joseph "Wabash George" B 7.4.1880 Toledo, OH D 1.7.1944 Wabash, IN BR/TR 5-11/188# d5.4																									
1902	Det A	13	16	.448	35	30	25	0	260	282	155	4	7	95	78	3.67	99	.277	.343	120-1	.325	9*	106	-3	0.7
1903	Det A	19	15	.559	41	36	31-6	**2**	320.2	284	128	4	8	106	170	2.25	130	.237	.303	126-4	.278	8*	110	21	3.5
1904	Det A	17	23	.425	45	44	42-7	0	382.1	345	154	1	10	131	161	2.40	106	.242	.310	155-3	.290	11*	74	3	2.4
1905	Det A	21	21	.500	44	**41**	**35**-1	0	**347.2**	303	149	4	8	138	168	2.51	109	.236	.314	135-3	.259	6*	79	4	1.7
1906	Det A	21	18	.538	40	40	35-2	0	330	315	139	3	15	108	123	2.78	99	.254	.322	142-1	.225	3*	88	-2	0.3
1907	†Det A	20	20	.500	46	42	35-5	3	357.1	346	153	1	15	106	146	2.59	100	.256	.318	157-0	.217	3*	120	1	0.8
1908	†Det A	17	13	.567	39	30	26-1	0	290.2	301	142	1	7	71	121	3.10	78	.271	.319	125-3	.256	8*	139	-20	-1.1
1909	†Det A	**29**	8	**.784**	40	35	29-3	1	303.2	258	96	1	8	78	124	2.22	113	.234	.289	126-2	.214	5*	129	12	2.3
1910	Det A	21	12	.636	38	32	27-5	0	289	260	125	7	14	102	98	2.87	92	.254	.330	129-0	.256	6*	126	-8	-0.1
1911	Det A	18	10	.643	30	29	25-2	0	234.1	245	99	7	12	61	87	3.07	113	.276	.331	98-1	.286	8*	100	13	2.1
1912	Det A	12	17	.414	30	29	22-2	0	226	214	112	3	9	92	88	3.54	92	.255	.335	90-2	.278	9*	97	-4	0.6
1913	Det A	1	6	.143	7	7	4	0	52.1	53	28	1	2	18	16	2.75	106	.270	.338	20-0	.350	3*	40	-1	0.2
	Was A	3	5	.375	11	9	3	0	57.1	69	34	1	5	25	14	5.02	59	.294	.374	21-0	.190	0*	103	-10	-1.2
	Year	4	11	.267	18	16	7	0	109.2	122	38	2	7	43	30	3.94	75	.283	.358	41-0	.268	3	76	-11	-1.0
1914	Ind F	14	10	.583	36	20	11-1	2	203	202	100	4	10	91	74	2.70	115	.261	.346	77-4	.312	8*	90	2	0.8
1915	New F	2	2	.500	5	4	3	0	32.1	41	22	0	0	16	14	5.85	44	.318	.393	10-1	.100	-0*	96	-10	-1.1
Total	14	228	196	.538	487	428	353-35	8	3686.2	3518	1636	42	130	1238	1482	2.82	101	.255	.322	1531-25	.262	87	103	-2	11.9
MULLINS, GREG Gregory Eugene B 12.13.1971 Palatka, FL BL/TL 5-10/160# d9.18																									
1998	Mil N	0	0	—	2	0	0	0-0	1	1	0	0	1	0-0	1	0.00	—	.250	.400	0-0	—	0		0	0.0
MULRENAN, DOMINIC Dominic Joseph B 12.18.1893 Woburn, MA D 7.27.1964 Melrose, MA BR/TR 5-11/170# d4.24																									
1921	Chi A	2	8	.200	12	10	3	0	56	84	52	2	2	36	10	7.23	59	.359	.449	20-1	.150	-1	77	-19	-2.7
MULRONEY, FRANK Francis Joseph B 4.8.1903 Mallard, IA D 11.11.1985 Aberdeen, WA BR/TR 6/170# d4.15																									
1930	Bos A	0	1	.000	2	0	0	0	3	3	2	0	0	0	2	3.00	154	.273	.273	0-0	—	0		0	0.0
MUNCRIEF, BOB Robert Cleveland B 1.28.1916 Madill, OK D 2.6.1996 Duncanville, TX BR/TR 6-2/190# d9.30																									
1937	StL A	0	0	—	1	1	0	0	2	3	2	1	0	2	0	4.50	107	.300	.417	0-0	—	0	180	0	0.0
1939	StL A	0	0	—	2	0	0	0	3	7	5	1	0	3	1	15.00	32	.500	.588	0-0	—	0		-3	-0.1
1941	StL A	13	9	.591	36	24	12-2	1	214.1	221	95	18	5	53	67	3.65	118	.266	.314	76-5	.237	2	102	16	1.6
1942	StL A	6	8	.429	24	18	7-1	0	134.1	149	61	11	0	31	39	3.89	95	.280	.319	45-1	.111	-1	91	0	-0.1
1943	StL A	13	12	.520	35	27	12-3	1	205	211	80	13	2	48	80	2.81	118	.264	.307	66-8	.152	-2	100	9	0.7
1944	†StL A★	13	8	.619	33	27	12-3	1	219.1	216	83	11	3	50	88	3.08	117	.258	.302	78-5	.231	1	108	15	1.5
1945	StL A	13	4	.765	27	15	10	1	145.2	132	51	8	2	44	54	2.72	130	.239	.297	45-8	.067	-4*	132	12	0.9
1946	StL A	3	12	.200	29	14	4-1	0	115.1	149	75	6	0	31	49	4.99	75	.314	.356	32-2	.031	-3	79	-15	-2.2
1947	StL A	8	14	.364	31	23	7	0	176.1	210	108	14	2	51	74	4.90	79	.299	.348	57-4	.105	-3	83	-19	-2.4
1948	†Cle A	5	4	.556	21	9	1-1	0	72.1	76	37	8	0	31	24	3.98	102	.279	.353	18-2	.111	-1	89	0	-0.1
1949	Pit N	1	5	.167	13	4	1	3	35.2	44	27	8	0	13	11	6.31	67	.310	.368	7-3	.143	-0	73	-8	-1.2
	Chi N	5	6	.455	34	3	1	2	75	80	42	7	1	31	36	4.56	88	.276	.348	14-1	.286	1	102	-4	-0.4
	Year	6	11	.353	47	7	2	5	110.2	124	47	15	1	44	47	5.12	80	.287	.354	21-4	.238	1	86	-10	-1.6
1951	NY A	0	0	—	2	0	0	0	3	5	3	0	0	4	2	9.00	43	.417	.563	0-0	—	0		-2	-0.1
Total	12	80	82	.494	288	165	67-11	9	1401.1	1503	669	106	15	392	525	3.80	100	.275	.325	438-39	.155	-10	98	1	-1.9
MUNGER, RED George David B 10.4.1918 Houston, TX D 7.23.1996 Houston, TX BR/TR 6-2/200# d5.1 Mil 1944-46																									
1943	StL N	9	5	.643	32	9	5	2	93.1	101	47	2	0	42	45	3.95	85	.281	.357	28-0	.214	1	146	-6	-0.7
1944	StL N❖	11	3	.786	21	12	7-2	2	121	92	23	2	2	41	55	1.34	263	.212	.284	44-0	.114	-3	65	29	3.4
1946	†StL N	2	2	.500	10	7	2	1	48.2	47	19	0	0	12	28	3.33	104	.255	.301	16-0	.250	1	117	2	0.3
1947	StL N☆	16	5	.762	40	31	13-6	3	224.1	218	94	12	2	76	123	3.37	123	.255	.318	81-3	.185	1	120	20	1.9
1948	StL N	10	11	.476	39	25	7-2	0	166	179	91	13	1	74	72	4.50	91	.272	.347	50-2	.160	0	101	-8	-0.8
1949	StL N★	15	8	.652	35	28	12-2	2	188.1	179	86	13	2	87	82	3.87	108	.255	.339	66-5	.258	4	122	9	1.4
1950	StL N	7	8	.467	32	20	5-1	0	154.2	158	73	15	3	70	61	3.90	110	.262	.342	51-3	.137	-2	93	7	0.5
1951	StL N	4	6	.400	23	11	3	0	94.2	106	58	13	0	46	44	5.32	74	.286	.365	29-1	.172	-0	81	-13	-1.1
1952	StL N	0	1	.000	1	1	0	0	4.1	7	6	2	1	1	1	12.46	30	.389	.450	2-0	.000	-0	24	-4	-0.6
	Pit N	0	3	.000	5	4	0	0	26.1	30	21	5	0	10	8	7.18	56	.283	.345	7-1	.000	-1	50	-8	-0.8
	Year	0	4	.000	6	5	0	0	30.2	37	23	7	1	11	9	7.92	50	.298	.360	9-1	.000	-1	45	-11	-1.4
1956	Pit N	3	4	.429	35	13	0	2	107	126	56	8	0	41-6	45	4.04	93	.299	.359	28-2	.107	-0	86	-4	-0.3
Total	10	77	56	.579	273	161	54-13	12	1228.2	1243	574	85	11	500-6	564	3.83	103	.264	.336	402-17	.174	0	104	24	3.2
MUNGO, VAN Van Lingle B 6.8.1911 Pageland, SC D 2.12.1985 Pageland, SC BR/TR 6-2/185# d9.7 C1																									
1931	Bro N	3	1	.750	5	4	2-1	0	31	27	9	0	1	13	12	2.32	164	.241	.325	12-0	.250	1	67	5	0.7
1932	Bro N	13	11	.542	39	33	11-1	2	223.1	224	120	9	6	115	107	4.43	86	.260	.351	79-4	.203	0	103	-13	-1.2
1933	Bro N	16	15	.516	41	28	18-3	0	248	223	89	7	0	84	110	2.72	118	.236	.298	84-4	.179	-0	91	15	1.8
1934	Bro N★	18	16	.529	45	**38**	22-3	3	**315.1**	300	137	15	3	104	184	3.37	116	.249	.310	121-1	.248	4*	100	20	2.6
1935	Bro N	16	10	.615	37	26	18-**4**	2	214.1	205	100	13	2	90	143	3.65	109	.252	.328	90-1	.289	5*	106	10	1.6
1936	Bro N☆	18	19	.486	45	**37**	22-2	3	311.2	275	137	8	3	118	**238**	3.35	123	**.234**	.305	123-4	.179	-4*	92	28	2.7
1937	Bro N★	9	11	.450	25	21	14	3	161	136	65	3	3	56	122	2.91	139	**.229**	.298	64-0	.250	2*	87	19	2.8

Year	Tm Lg	W	L	Pct	G	GS	CG-Sho	SV-BS	IP	H	R	HR	HB	BB-IB	SO	ERA	AERA	OAV	OOB	AB-SH	AVG	PB	Sup	APR	PW
1938	Bro N	4	11	.267	24	18	6-2	0	133.1	133	78	11	2	72	72	3.92	100	.259	.353	47-4	.191	1*	94	-4	-0.2
1939	Bro N	4	5	.444	14	10	1	0	77.1	70	36	7	3	33	34	3.26	124	.239	.322	29-1	.345	2*	95	5	0.8
1940	Bro N	1	0	1.000	7	0	0	1	22	24	6	1	0	10	9	2.45	163	.282	.358	7-0	.000	-1*		4	0.1
1941	Bro N	0	0	—	2	0	0	0	2	1	1	0	0	2	0	4.50	81	.143	.333	0-0	—	0		0	0.0
1942	NY N	1	2	.333	9	5	0	0	36.1	38	32	4	0	21	27	5.94	57	.273	.369	14-0	.214	-0	115	-12	-0.9
1943	NY N	3	7	.300	45	13	2-2	2	154.1	140	68	7	6	79	83	3.91	88	.243	.341	44-2	.159	-1*	100	-4	-0.4
1945	NY N✧	14	7	.667	26	26	7-2	0	183	161	77	4	4	71	101	3.20	122	.238	.314	73-0	.233	4*	106	13	1.7
Total	14	120	115	.511	364	259	123-20	16	2113	1957	955	89	33	868	1242	3.47	110	.245	.321	787-21	.221	13	98	86	12.1
MUNIZ, MANNY Manuel (Rodriguez) B 12.31.1947 Caguas, P.R. BR/TR 5-11/190# d9.3																									
1971	Phi N	0	1	.000	5	0	0	0-0	10.1	9	8	2	0	8-1	6	6.97	51	.225	.354	1-0	.000	-0		-3	-0.3
MUNNINGHOFF, SCOTT Scott Andrew B 12.5.1958 Cincinnati, OH BR/TR 6/175# d4.13																									
1980	Phi N	0	0	—	4	0	0	0-0	6	8	3	0	0	5-0	2	4.50	84	.320	.419	1-0	1.000	1		0	0.1
MUNNS, LES Leslie Ernest "Big Ed" or "Nemo" B 12.1.1908 Fort Bragg, CA D 2.28.1997 Cedar Rapids, IA BR/TR 6-5/212# d4.22																									
1934	Bro N	3	7	.300	33	9	4	0	99.1	106	67	7	0	60	41	4.71	83	.280	.378	29-0	.241	2*	76	-12	-0.8
1935	Bro N	1	3	.250	21	5	0	1	58.1	74	47	5	4	33	13	5.55	72	.319	.413	16-0	.188	-0*	115	-12	-0.9
1936	StL N	0	3	.000	7	1	0	1	24	23	18	2	0	12	4	3.00	131	.240	.324	9-0	.111	-1*	129	-1	-0.2
Total	3	4	13	.235	61	15	4	2	181.2	203	132	14	4	105	58	4.76	83	.287	.382	54-0	.204	1	93	-25	-1.9
MUNOZ, OSCAR Juan Oscar B 9.25.1969 Hialeah, FL BR/TR 6-3/222# d8.6																									
1995	Min A	2	1	.667	10	3	0	0-0	35.1	40	28	6	1	17-0	25	5.60	85	.276	.354	0-0	—	0	124	-5	-0.4
MUNOZ, MIKE Michael Anthony B 7.12.1965 Baldwin Park, CA BL/TL 6-2/200# d9.6																									
1989	LA N	0	0	—	3	0	0	0-0	2.2	5	5	1	0	2-0	3	16.88	20	.417	.500	0-0	—	0		-4	-0.2
1990	LA N	0	1	.000	8	0	0	0-1	5.2	6	2	0	0	3-0	2	3.18	115	.300	.391	1-0	.000	-0		0	0.1
1991	Det A	0	0	—	6	0	0	0-0	9.1	14	10	0	0	5-0	3	9.64	43	.350	.413	0-0	—	0		-5	-0.2
1992	Det A	1	2	.333	65	0	0	2-1	48	44	16	3	0	25-6	23	3.00	132	.246	.335	0-0	—	0		6	0.5
1993	Det A	0	1	.000	8	0	0	0-0	3	4	2	1	0	6-1	1	6.00	72	.308	.526	0-0	—	0		0	-0.1
	Col N	2	1	.667	21	0	0	0-2	18	21	12	1	0	9-3	16	4.50	106	.309	.380	0-0	—	0		0	0.0
1994	Col N	4	2	.667	57	0	0	1-1	45.2	37	22	3	0	31-5	32	3.74	133	.223	.343	0-0	—	0		5	0.6
1995	†Col N	2	4	.333	64	0	0	2-2	43.2	54	38	9	1	27-0	37	7.42	73	.307	.398	2-0	.500	1		-7	-0.8
1996	Col N	2	2	.500	54	0	0	0-3	44.2	55	33	4	1	16-2	45	6.65	79	.302	.360	1-0	.000	-0		-5	-0.3
1997	Col N	3	3	.500	64	0	0	2-0	45.2	52	25	4	0	13-0	26	4.53	114	.294	.339	1-0	.000	0		3	0.3
1998	Col N	2	2	.500	40	0	0	3-1	41.1	53	32	2	1	16-2	24	5.66	91	.312	.372	2-1	.000	-0		-3	-0.3
1999	Tex A	2	1	.667	56	0	0	1-2	52.2	52	24	5	1	18-2	27	3.93	129	.263	.323	0-0	—	0		7	0.4
2000	Tex A	0	1	.000	7	0	0	0-1	4	11	6	1	0	3-1	1	13.50	37	.524	.583	0-0	—	0		-3	-0.6
Total	12	18	20	.474	453	0	0	11-14	364.1	408	227	34	4	174-22	240	5.19	95	.287	.363	7-1	.143	1		-6	-0.6
MUNOZ, BOBBY Roberto (Sbert) B 3.3.1968 Rio Piedras, P.R. BR/TR 6-7/252# d5.29																									
1993	NY A	3	3	.500	38	0	0	0-2	45.2	48	27	1	0	26-5	33	5.32	78	.270	.357	0-0	—	0		-5	-0.6
1994	Phi N	7	5	.583	21	14	1	1-1	104.1	101	40	8	1	35-0	59	2.67	161	.252	.310	34-2	.206	1	89	16	1.9
1995	Phi N	0	2	.000	3	3	0	0-0	15.2	15	13	2	3	9-0	6	5.74	74	.268	.386	5-0	.000	-1	57	-4	-0.4
1996	Phi N	0	3	.000	6	6	0	0-0	25.1	42	28	5	1	7-1	8	7.82	55	.375	.413	7-1	.143	0	70	-11	-1.1
1997	Phi N	1	5	.167	8	7	0	0-0	33.1	47	35	4	2	15-1	20	8.91	48	.338	.403	10-1	.300	1	74	-17	-2.2
1998	Bal A	0	0	—	9	1	0	0-0	12	18	13	4	1	6-0	6	9.75	47	.383	.439	0-0	—	0	163	-7	-0.3
2001	Mon N	0	4	.000	15	7	0	0-0	42	53	25	6	2	21-1	21	5.14	87	.321	.404	11-0	.000	-1	44	-3	-0.3
Total	7	11	22	.333	100	38	1	1-3	278.1	324	181	30	10	119-8	153	5.17	83	.295	.364	67-4	.164	1	75	-31	-3.0
MUNRO, PETER Peter Daniel B 6.14.1975 Flushing, NY BR/TR 6-2/200# d4.6																									
1999	Tor A	0	2	.000	31	2	0	0-1	55.1	70	38	6	2	23-0	38	6.02	82	.318	.382	0-0	—	0	113	-5	-0.2
2000	Tor A	1	1	.500	9	3	0	0-0	25.2	38	22	1	3	16-0	16	5.96	85	.355	.452	1-0	.000	-0	105	-4	-0.2
2002	Hou N	5	5	.500	19	14	0	0-0	80.2	89	37	5	3	23-3	45	3.57	120	.283	.338	22-1	.136	-1	91	5	0.6
2003	Hou N	3	4	.429	40	2	0	0-1	54	63	30	7	5	26-2	27	4.67	95	.294	.382	1-2	.000	0	95	-1	-0.1
Total	4	9	12	.429	99	21	0	0-2	215.2	260	127	19	13	88-5	126	4.76	96	.304	.376	24-3	.125	-0	94	-5	0.1
MURA, STEVE Stephen Andrew B 2.12.1955 New Orleans, LA BR/TR 6-2/190# d9.5																									
1978	SD N	0	2	.000	5	2	0	0-0	7.2	15	10	1	0	5-0	5	11.74	28	.441	.500	1-0	.000	-0	54	-7	-1.3
1979	SD N	4	4	.500	38	5	0	2-3	73	57	30	6	1	37-2	59	3.08	115	.217	.314	10-3	.000	-1	80	3	0.2
1980	SD N	8	7	.533	37	23	3-1	2-1	168.2	149	74	9	3	86-4	109	3.68	93	.246	.338	51-0	.137	-0*	105	-4	-0.3
1981	SD N	5	14	.263	23	22	2	0-0	138.2	156	72	10	0	50-2	70	4.28	76	.285	.344	44-2	.136	-0*	87	-17	-2.1
1982	StL N	12	11	.522	35	30	7-1	0-0	184.1	196	89	16	0	80-4	84	4.05	90	.278	.348	53-10	.057	-4	118	-7	-1.3
1983	Chi A	0	0	—	6	0	0	0-0	12.1	13	11	1	0	6-0	4	4.38	96	.260	.333	0-0	—	0		-2	-0.1
1985	Oak A	1	1	.500	23	1	0	1-0	48	41	25	3	0	25-4	29	4.13	94	.225	.317	0-0	—	0	71	-2	-0.1
Total	7	30	39	.435	167	83	12-2	5-4	632.2	627	311	46	4	289-16	360	4.00	88	.263	.340	159-15	.101	-5	101	-36	-5.0
MURAKAMI, MASANORI Masanori B 5.6.1944 Otsuki, Japan BL/TL 6/180# d9.1																									
1964	SF N	1	0	1.000	9	0	0	1	15	8	3	1	0	1-0	15	1.80	198	.163	.176	3-0	.000	-0		3	0.2
1965	SF N	4	1	.800	45	1	0	8	74.1	57	31	9	3	22-5	85	3.75	96	.205	.271	13-0	.154	-0	364	1	0.0
Total	2	5	1	.833	54	1	0	9	89.1	65	34	10	3	23-5	100	3.43	105	.199	.257	16-0	.125	-1	364	4	0.2
MURCHISON, TIM Thomas Malcolm B 10.8.1896 Liberty, NC D 10.20.1962 Liberty, NC BR/TL 6/185# d6.21																									
1917	StL N	0	0	—	1	0	0	0	1	0	0	0	0	2	2	0.00	—	.000	.400	0-0	—	0		0	0.0
1920	Cle A	0	0	—	2	0	0	0	5	3	1	0	0	4	0	0.00	—	.200	.368	1-0	.000	-0		2	0.1
Total	2	0	0	—	3	0	0	0	6	3	1	0	0	6	2	0.00	—	.167	.375	1-0	.000	-0		2	0.1
MURFF, RED John Robert B 4.1.1921 Burlington, TX BR/TR 6-3/195# d4.21																									
1956	Mil N	0	0	—	14	1	0	1	24.1	25	14	3	0	7-0	18	4.44	78	.272	.320	5-0	.200	0	127	-3	-0.1
1957	Mil N	2	2	.500	12	1	0	2	26	31	14	3	0	11-1	13	4.85	72	.301	.368	6-1	.000	-1	252	-3	-0.6
Total	2	2	2	.500	26	2	0	3	50.1	56	28	6	0	18-1	31	4.65	75	.287	.346	11-1	.091	-1	190	-6	-0.7
MURPHY, CON Cornelius B. "Monk" or "Razzle Dazzle" B 10.15.1863 Worcester, MA D 8.1.1914 Worcester, MA TR 5-9/130# d9.11																									
1884	Phi N	0	3	.000	3	3	3	0	26	37	34	1		6	10	6.58	45	.319	.352	10	.000	-1	36	-10	-0.9
1890	Bro P	4	10	.286	20	14	11	2	139	168	134	2	6	82	29	4.79	93	.286	.379	69	.217	-1*	85	-7	-0.6
Total	2	4	13	.235	23	17	14	2	165	205	168	3	6	88	39	5.07	83	.292	.375	79	.190	-3	78	-17	-1.5
MURPHY, DANNY Daniel Francis B 8.23.1942 Beverly, MA BL/TR 5-11/185# d6.18.1960 ▲																									
1969	Chi A	2	1	.667	17	0	0	4-1	31.1	28	8	2	2	10-0	16	2.01	192	.252	.323	1-0	.000	0		6	0.8
1970	Chi A	2	3	.400	51	0	0	5-3	80.2	82	55	11	4	49-8	42	5.69	69	.273	.378	6-0	.333	2		-14	-0.8
Total	2	4	4	.500	68	0	0	9-4	112	110	63	13	6	59-8	58	4.66	83	.268	.364	7-0	.286	2		-8	0.0
MURPHY, DAN Daniel Lee B 9.18.1964 Artesia, CA BR/TR 6-2/195# d8.10																									
1989	SD N	0	0	—	7	0	0	0-0	6.1	6	6	1	0	4-1	1	5.68	62	.231	.333	0-0	—	0		-2	-0.1
MURPHY, ED Edward J. B 1.22.1877 Auburn, NY D 1.29.1935 Weedsport, NY TR 6-1/186# d4.23																									
1898	Phi N	1	2	.333	7	3	2	0	30	41	23	3	1	10	8	5.10	67	.323	.377	14-1	.357	1	96	-5	-0.3
1901	StL N	10	9	.526	23	21	16	0	165	201	105	5	1	32	42	4.20	76	.298	.331	64-1	.250	3	141	-21	-1.6
1902	StL N	10	6	.625	23	17	12-1	1	164	187	86	7	2	31	37	3.02	91	.286	.321	61-0	.262	1	123	-7	-0.4
1903	StL N	4	8	.333	15	12	9	0	106	108	62	2	6	38	16	3.31	99	.262	.333	64-2	.203	-1*	69	0	-0.1
Total	4	25	25	.500	68	53	39-1	1	465	537	276	17	10	111	103	3.64	84	.288	.331	203-4	.246	5	115	-33	-2.4
MURPHY, JOHN John Henry 5-11/165# d4.17																									
1884	Alt U	5	6	.455	14	10	10	0	111.2	141	90	3		9	46	3.87	69	.289	.302	94	.149	-7*	59	-14	-1.5
	Wil U	0	6	.000	7	6	5	0	48	52	36	3		2	27	3.00	89	.259	.266	31	.065	-4*	32	-1	-0.4
	Year	5	12	.294	21	16	15	0	159.2	193	38	6		11	73	3.61	74	.280	.291	125	.128	-11	49	-17	-1.9

MURPHY, JOHNNY John Joseph "Grandma" "Fireman" Or "Fordham Johnny" B 7.14.1908 New York, NY D 1.14.1970 New York, NY BR/TR 6-2/190# d5.19 Def 1944-45

Year	Tm Lg	W	L	Pct	G	GS	CG-Sho	SV-BS	IP	H	R	HR	HB	BB-IB	SO	ERA	AERA	OAV	OOB	AB-SH	AVG	PB	Sup	APR	PW
1932	NY A	0	0	—	2	0	0	0	3.1	7	6	0	0	3	2	16.20	25	.438	.526	1-0	1.000	1		-4	-0.2
1934	NY A	14	10	.583	40	20	10	4	207.2	193	79	11	0	76	70	3.12	130	.250	.317	71-5	.099	-3	94	26	2.5
1935	NY A	10	5	.667	40	8	4	5	117	110	67	7	0	55	28	4.08	99	.243	.325	32-2	.156	2	123	-2	-0.1
1936	†NY A	9	3	.750	27	5	2	5	88	90	38	5	1	36	34	3.38	138	.262	.334	36-0	.361	4	189	13	2.0
1937	†NY A☆	13	4	.765	39	4	0	10	110	121	59	7	1	50	36	4.17	107	.277	.352	35-3	.229	2	157	4	0.9
1938	†NY A☆	8	2	.800	32	2	1	**11**	91.1	90	47	5	1	41	43	4.24	107	.256	.336	32-2	.063	-3	87	**5**	0.4
1939	†NY A☆	3	6	.333	38	0	0	**19**	61.1	57	33	2	0	28	30	4.40	99	.252	.335	11-1	.182	1		0	0.1
1940	NY A	8	4	.667	35	1	0	9	63.1	58	27	5	0	15	23	3.69	109	.247	.292	13-2	.077	0	109	4	0.7
1941	†NY A	8	3	.727	35	0	0	**15**	77.1	68	20	1	0	40	29	1.98	199	.237	.330	18-3	.056	-1		**18**	2.9
1942	NY A	4	10	.286	31	0	0	**11**	58	66	27	2	2	23	24	3.41	101	.293	.364	13-2	.154	0		-1	-0.1
1943	†NY A	12	4	.750	37	0	0	8	68	44	22	2	0	30	31	2.51	128	.183	.273	19-1	.053	-2		6	1.0
1946	NY A	4	2	.667	27	0	0	7	45	40	22	4	0	19	19	3.40	102	.240	.317	6-1	.000	-0		-1	-0.1
1947	Bos A	0	0	—	32	0	0	3	54.2	41	17	1	0	28	9	2.80	139	.206	.304	11-0	.273	1		7	0.5
Total	13	93	53	.637	415	40	17	107	1045	985	464	52	5	444	378	3.50	117	.249	.326	298-22	.154	-0	123	75	10.5

MURPHY, JOE Joseph Akin B 9.7.1866 St.Louis, MO D 3.28.1951 Coral Gables, FL 5-11/160# d4.28

Year	Tm Lg	W	L	Pct	G	GS	CG-Sho	SV-BS	IP	H	R	HR	HB	BB-IB	SO	ERA	AERA	OAV	OOB	AB-SH	AVG	PB	Sup	APR	PW
1886	Cin AA	2	3	.400	5	5	5	0	46	50	34	0	1	21	11	4.89	72	.256	.332	18	.000	-3	54	-6	-0.8
	StL N	0	4	.000	4	4	3	0	33	45	41	3		16	11	8.18	39	.319	.389	14	.214	0	62	-15	-1.3
	StL AA	1	0	1.000	1	1	1	0	7	5	4	0	0	3	3	3.86	89	.179	.258	3	.000	-1	155	0	-0.1
1887	StL AA	1	0	1.000	1	1	1	0	9	13	8	0	0	4	5	5.00	91	.317	.378	6	.167	-1	309	-1	-0.1
Total	2	4	7	.364	11	11	10	0	95	113	87	3	1	44	30	5.97	59	.279	.351	41	.098	-4	94	-22	-2.3

MURPHY, ROB Robert Albert B 5.26.1960 Miami, FL BL/TL 6-2/215# d9.13

Year	Tm Lg	W	L	Pct	G	GS	CG-Sho	SV-BS	IP	H	R	HR	HB	BB-IB	SO	ERA	AERA	OAV	OOB	AB-SH	AVG	PB	Sup	APR	PW
1985	Cin N	0	0	—	2	0	0	0-0	3	2	2	1	0	2-0	1	6.00	63	.200	.333	0-0	—	0		-1	0.0
1986	Cin N	6	0	1.000	34	0	0	1-2	50.1	26	4	0	0	21-2	36	0.72	542	.155	.245	3-0	.000	-0		17	2.0
1987	Cin N	8	5	.615	87	0	0	3-4	100.2	91	37	7	0	32-5	99	3.04	140	.239	.297	5-1	.200	0		13	1.6
1988	Cin N	0	6	.000	**76**	0	0	3-3	84.2	69	31	3	1	38-6	74	3.08	116	.229	.317	0-0	—	0		5	0.4
1989	Bos A	5	7	.417	74	0	0	9-7	105	97	38	7	1	41-8	107	2.74	150	.251	.323	0-0	—	0		14	1.8
1990	†Bos A	0	6	.000	68	0	0	7-3	57	85	46	10	1	32-3	54	6.32	65	.348	.420	0-0	—	0		-14	-1.6
1991	Sea A	0	1	.000	57	0	0	4-0	48	47	17	4	1	19-4	34	3.00	138	.250	.322	0-0	—	0		6	0.3
1992	Hou N	3	1	.750	59	0	0	0-2	55.2	56	28	2	0	21-4	42	4.04	83	.260	.322	1-1	.000	-0		-5	-0.3
1993	StL N	5	7	.417	73	0	0	1-3	64.2	73	37	8	1	20-6	41	4.87	82	.290	.342	2-1	.500	0		-6	-0.9
1994	StL N	4	3	.571	50	0	0	2-1	40.1	35	18	7	0	13-2	25	3.79	110	.230	.291	0-0	—	0		2	0.3
	NY A	0	0	—	3	0	0	0-0	1.2	3	3	2	0	0-0	0	16.20	28	.375	.375	0-0	—	0		-2	-0.1
1995	LA N	0	1	.000	6	0	0	0-0	5	6	7	2	0	3-0	2	12.60	30	.300	.391	1-0	1.000	1		-5	-0.8
	Fla N	1	1	.500	8	0	0	0-0	7.1	8	9	1	0	5-1	5	9.82	43	.286	.394	0-0	—	0		-5	-0.8
	Year	1	2	.333	14	0	0	0-0	12.1	14	21	3	0	8-1	7	10.95	37	.292	.393	1-0	1.000	1		-10	-1.6
Total	11	32	38	.457	597	0	0	30-25	623.1	598	277	54	5	247-41	520	3.64	109	.254	.324	12-3	.250	1		19	1.9

MURPHY, BOB Robert J. B 12.26.1866 Dutchess Co., NY 6/173# d5.27

Year	Tm Lg	W	L	Pct	G	GS	CG-Sho	SV-BS	IP	H	R	HR	HB	BB-IB	SO	ERA	AERA	OAV	OOB	AB-SH	AVG	PB	Sup	APR	PW
1890	NY N	1	0	1.000	3	2	1	0	18	23	17	0	0	10	8	5.50	64	.303	.384	9	.111	-1	90	-3	-0.2
	Bro AA	3	9	.250	12	12	10	0	96	121	95	6	5	46	26	5.72	68	.299	.377	50	.180	0*	81	-19	-1.6
Total	1	4	9	.308	15	14	11	0	114	144	112	6	5	56	34	5.68	67	.299	.378	59	.169	-1	82	-22	-1.8

MURPHY, TOM Thomas Andrew B 12.30.1945 Cleveland, OH BR/TR 6-3/185# d6.13

Year	Tm Lg	W	L	Pct	G	GS	CG-Sho	SV-BS	IP	H	R	HR	HB	BB-IB	SO	ERA	AERA	OAV	OOB	AB-SH	AVG	PB	Sup	APR	PW
1968	Cal A	5	6	.455	15	15	3	0	99.1	67	30	5	5	28-0	56	2.17	134	.191	.258	28-5	.000	-3	100	7	0.4
1969	Cal A	10	16	.385	36	35	4	0-0	215.2	213	110	12	21	69-3	100	4.21	83	.260	.332	71-5	.141	-0	81	-15	-1.7
1970	Cal A	16	13	.552	39	38	5-2	0-0	227	223	114	32	7	81-10	99	4.24	85	.261	.329	76-8	.184	3	101	-14	-1.4
1971	Cal A	6	17	.261	37	36	7	0-0	243.1	228	108	24	9	82-9	89	3.77	86	.256	.323	75-6	.173	1	86	-12	-0.9
1972	Cal A	0	0	—	6	0	0	0-0	10	13	6	0	0	8-1	2	5.40	54	.342	.447	1-0	.000	-0		-3	-0.1
	KC A	4	4	.500	18	9	1-1	1-0	70.1	77	26	3	6	16-0	34	3.07	99	.287	.341	13-5	.000	-1*	142	0	-0.1
	Year	4	4	.500	24	9	1-1	1-0	80.1	90	31	3	6	24-1	36	3.36	90	.294	.356	14-5	.000	-1	143	-2	-0.2
1973	StL N	3	7	.300	19	13	2	0-0	88.2	89	38	5	3	22-0	42	3.76	97	.269	.317	23-3	.174	0	80	1	0.2
1974	Mil A	10	10	.500	70	0	0	20-7	123	97	27	6	2	51-18	47	1.90	190	.224	.306	2-0	.500	0		**24**	**4.9**
1975	Mil A	1	9	.100	52	0	0	20-9	72.1	85	43	5	5	27-5	32	4.60	83	.295	.362	0-0	—	0*		-6	-1.2
1976	Mil A	0	1	.000	15	0	0	1-2	18.1	25	18	2	2	9-3	7	7.36	47	.313	.396	0-0	—	0		-8	-0.5
	Bos A	4	5	.444	37	0	0	8-5	81	91	43	5	2	25-11	32	3.44	114	.290	.343	0-0	—	0		1	0.1
	Year	4	6	.400	52	0	0	9-7	99.1	116	64	7	4	34-14	39	4.17	92	.294	.354	0-0	—	0		-7	-0.4
1977	Bos A	0	1	.000	16	0	0	0-0	30.2	44	25	6	0	12-0	13	6.75	67	.338	.392	0-0	—	0		-7	-0.3
	Tor A	2	1	.667	19	1	0	2-0	52	63	22	6	1	18-3	26	3.63	116	.304	.358	0-0	—	0	128	4	0.2
	Year	2	2	.500	35	1	0	2-0	82.2	107	28	12	1	30-3	39	4.79	90	.318	.371	0-0	—	0	125	-3	-0.1
1978	Tor A	6	9	.400	50	0	0	7-4	94	87	43	11	0	37-10	36	3.93	100	.256	.322	0-0	—	0		1	0.2
1979	Tor A	1	2	.333	10	0	0	0-2	18.1	23	11	1	0	8-0	6	5.40	81	.311	.378	0-0	—	0		-1	-0.2
Total	12	68	101	.402	439	147	22-3	59-29	1444	1425	664	123	63	493-73	621	3.78	94	.263	.329	289-32	.145	0	89	-28	-0.4

MURPHY, WALTER Walter Joseph B 9.27.1907 New York, NY D 3.23.1976 Houston, TX BR/TR 6-1.5/180# d4.19

Year	Tm Lg	W	L	Pct	G	GS	CG-Sho	SV-BS	IP	H	R	HR	HB	BB-IB	SO	ERA	AERA	OAV	OOB	AB-SH	AVG	PB	Sup	APR	PW
1931	Bos A	0	0	—	2	0	0	0	2	4	2	0	0	1	0	9.00	48	.444	.500	0-0	—	0		-1	0.0

MURRAY, AMBY Ambrose Joseph B 6.4.1913 Fall River, MA D 2.6.1997 Port Salerno, FL BL/TL 5-7/150# d7.5

Year	Tm Lg	W	L	Pct	G	GS	CG-Sho	SV-BS	IP	H	R	HR	HB	BB-IB	SO	ERA	AERA	OAV	OOB	AB-SH	AVG	PB	Sup	APR	PW
1936	Bos N	0	0	—	4	1	0	0	11	15	5	1	0	3	2	4.09	94	.319	.360	4-0	.250	0	199	0	0.0

MURRAY, DALE Dale Albert B 2.2.1950 Cuero, TX BR/TR 6-4/205# d7.7

Year	Tm Lg	W	L	Pct	G	GS	CG-Sho	SV-BS	IP	H	R	HR	HB	BB-IB	SO	ERA	AERA	OAV	OOB	AB-SH	AVG	PB	Sup	APR	PW
1974	Mon N	1	1	.500	32	0	0	10-0	69.2	46	12	1	0	23-2	31	1.03	373	.187	.256	10-0	.000	-1		19	1.1
1975	Mon N	15	8	.652	63	0	0	9-10	111.1	134	59	0	3	39-10	43	3.96	97	.305	.361	14-0	.214	1		-3	-0.5
1976	Mon N	4	9	.308	**81**	0	0	13-8	113.1	117	47	1	0	37-12	35	3.26	114	.277	.331	8-3	.000	-1		6	0.9
1977	Cin N	7	2	.778	61	1	0	4-4	102	125	60	13	2	46-6	42	4.94	80	.314	.382	12-2	.167	-0	339	-11	-1.0
1978	Cin N	1	1	.500	15	0	0	2-0	32.2	34	20	1	1	17-4	25	4.13	86	.272	.356	3-2	.000	-0		-4	-0.3
	NY N	8	5	.615	53	0	0	5-2	86.1	85	39	4	2	36-19	37	3.65	96	.266	.340	7-0	.000	-0		-2	-0.2
	Year	9	6	.600	68	0	0	7-2	119	119	74	5	3	53-23	62	3.78	93	.268	.344	10-2	.000	-1		-6	-0.5
1979	NY N	4	8	.333	58	0	0	4-7	97	105	58	6	0	52-14	37	4.82	76	.287	.373	6-2	.000	-0		-13	-1.6
	Mon N	1	2	.333	9	0	0	1-1	13.1	14	4	1	0	3-2	4	2.70	136	.292	.327	2-0	.000	-0		2	0.3
	Year	5	10	.333	67	0	0	5-8	110.1	119	62	7	0	55-16	41	4.57	80	.287	.368	8-2	.000	-1		-11	-1.3
1980	Mon N	0	1	.000	16	0	0	0-0	29.1	39	23	3	0	12-2	16	6.14	58	.315	.372	3-0	.000	-0		-9	-0.5
1981	Tor A	1	0	1.000	11	0	0	0-0	15.1	12	2	0	0	5-0	12	1.17	336	.211	.274	0-0	—	0		5	0.3
1982	Tor A	8	7	.533	56	0	0	11-7	111	115	48	3	3	32-5	60	3.16	142	.268	.323	0-0	—	0		13	2.0
1983	NY A	2	4	.333	40	0	0	1-2	94.1	113	56	5	1	22-4	45	4.48	87	.297	.333	0-0	—	0		-8	-0.5
1984	NY A	1	2	.333	19	0	0	0-1	23.2	30	15	2	2	5-0	13	4.94	77	.306	.352	0-0	—	0		-4	-0.4
1985	NY A	0	0	—	3	0	0	0-0	2	4	3	0	0	0-0	0	13.50	30	.400	.400	0-0	—	0		-2	-0.1
	Tex A	0	0	—	1	0	0	0-0	1	3	2	0	0	0-0	0	18.00	24	.750	.750	0-0	—	0		-1	-0.1
	Year	0	0	—	4	0	0	0-0	3	7	5	0	0	0-0	0	15.00	27	.500	.500	0-0	—	0		-3	-0.2
Total	12	53	50	.515	518	1	0	60-42	902.1	976	448	40	14	329-80	400	3.85	100	.282	.343	65-9	.077	-3	339	-12	-0.6

MURRAY, DAN Daniel Saffle B 11.21.1973 Los Alamitos, CA BR/TR 6-1/193# d8.9

Year	Tm Lg	W	L	Pct	G	GS	CG-Sho	SV-BS	IP	H	R	HR	HB	BB-IB	SO	ERA	AERA	OAV	OOB	AB-SH	AVG	PB	Sup	APR	PW
1999	NY N	0	0	—	1	0	0	0-0	2	4	3	0	0	2-0	1	13.50	32	.444	.500	0-0	—	0		-2	-0.1
	KC A	0	0	—	4	0	0	0-0	8.1	9	8	4	1	4-0	8	6.48	77	.265	.359	0-0	—	0		-2	-0.1
2000	KC A	0	0	—	10	0	0	0-0	19.1	20	10	7	1	10-0	16	4.66	110	.278	.369	0-0	—	0		1	0.1
Total	2	0	0	—	15	0	0	0-0	29.2	33	21	11	2	16-0	25	5.76	88	.287	.378	0-0	—	0		-3	-0.1

MURRAY, GEORGE George King "Smiler" B 9.23.1898 Charlotte, NC D 10.18.1955 Memphis, TN BR/TR 6-2/200# d5.8

Year	Tm Lg	W	L	Pct	G	GS	CG-Sho	SV-BS	IP	H	R	HR	HB	BB-IB	SO	ERA	AERA	OAV	OOB	AB-SH	AVG	PB	Sup	APR	PW
1922	NY A	3	2	.600	22	2	0	0	56.2	53	27	0	1	26	14	3.97	101	.255	.340	18-0	.278	2	85	**1**	0.2
1923	Bos A	7	11	.389	39	18	5	0	177.2	190	111	9	7	87	40	4.91	84	.291	.380	55-6	.164	-3	69	-11	-1.3
1924	Bos A	2	9	.182	28	7	0	0	80.1	97	68	6	7	32	27	6.72	65	.307	.383	22-1	.182	-1	55	-19	-2.2

Year	Tm Lg	W	L	Pct	G	GS	CG-Sho	SV-BS	IP	H	R	HR	HB	BB-IB	SO	ERA	AERA	OAV	OOB	AB-SH	AVG	PB	Sup	APR	PW
1926	Was A	6	3	.667	12	12	5	0	81.1	89	56	1	6	37	28	5.64	69	.287	.374	36-3	.139	-2	140	-15	-1.6
1927	Was A	1	1	.500	7	3	0	0	18	18	18	1	2	15	5	7.00	58	.265	.412	6-1	.167	-0	130	-7	-0.6
1933	Chi A	0	0	—	2	0	0	0	2.1	3	2	0	0	2	0	7.71	55	.375	.500	0-0	—	0		-1	0.0
Total	6	19	26	.422	110	42	10	0	416.1	450	282	17	23	199	114	5.38	76	.288	.376	137-11	.175	-4	90	-52	-5.5
MURRAY, HEATH Heath Robertson B 4.19.1973 Troy, OH BL/TL 6-4/205# d5.24																									
1997	SD N	1	2	.333	17	3	0	0-0	33.1	50	25	3	4	21-3	16	6.75	58	.376	.472	6-0	.000	-1	111	-10	-0.9
1999	SD N	0	4	.000	22	8	0	0-0	50	60	33	7	1	26-4	25	5.76	73	.297	.377	13-1	.154	0	109	-8	-0.5
2001	Det A	1	7	.125	40	4	0	0-2	63.1	82	48	11	3	40-5	42	6.54	67	.322	.418	0-0	—	0	64	-15	-1.5
2002	Cle A	0	2	.000	9	0	0	0-0	12	12	10	3	2	7-0	11	7.50	59	.267	.389	0-0	—	0		-4	-0.5
Total	4	2	15	.118	88	15	0	0-2	158.2	204	116	24	10	94-12	94	6.41	66	.321	.415	19-1	.105	-1	97	-37	-3.4
MURRAY, JIM James Francis "Big Jim" B 12.31.1900 Scranton, PA D 7.15.1973 Queens, NY BB/TL 6-2/210# d7.3																									
1922	Bro N	0	0	—	4	0	0	1	6	8	3	0	0	3	3	4.50	90	.320	.393	2-0	.500	0		0	0.0
MURRAY, JOE Joseph Ambrose B 11.11.1920 Wilkes-Barre, PA D 10.19.2001 San Clemente, CA BL/TL 6/165# d8.17																									
1950	Phi A	0	3	.000	8	2	0	0	30	34	20	1	0	21	8	5.70	80	.283	.390	11-0	.000	-2	99	-3	-0.4
MURRAY, MATT Matthew Michael B 9.26.1970 Boston, MA BL/TR 6-6/240# d8.12																									
1995	Atl N	0	2	.000	4	1	0	0-0	10.2	10	8	3	1	5-0	3	6.75	63	.256	.356	2-0	.500	0	85	-3	-0.4
	Bos A	0	1	.000	2	1	0	0-0	3.1	11	10	1	0	3-0	1	18.90	26	.524	.583	0-0	—	0	76	-6	-0.9
Total	1	0	3	.000	6	2	0	0-0	14	21	18	4	1	8-0	4	9.64	46	.350	.435	2-0	.500	0	83	-9	-1.3
MURRAY, PAT Patrick Joseph B 7.18.1897 Scottsville, NY D 11.5.1983 Rochester, NY BR/TL 6/175# d7.1																									
1919	Phi N	0	2	.000	8	2	1	0	34.1	50	28	0	4	12	11	6.29	51	.347	.412	12-0	.000	-1	37	-10	-0.7
MUSGRAVES, DENNIS Dennis Eugene B 12.25.1943 Indianapolis, IN BR/TR 6-4/188# d7.9																									
1965	NY N	0	0	—	5	1	0	0	16	11	2	0	2	7-0	11	0.56	627	.200	.313	2-0	.000	-0	25	5	0.2
MUSSELMAN, JEFF Jeffrey Joseph B 6.21.1963 Doylestown, PA BL/TL 6/180# d9.2																									
1986	Tor A	0	0	—	6	0	0	0-0	5.1	8	7	1	0	5-1	4	10.13	42	.333	.448	0-0	—	0		-4	-0.2
1987	Tor A	12	5	.706	68	1	0	3-5	89	75	43	7	3	54-12	54	4.15	109	.237	.353	0-0	—	0	101	4	0.8
1988	Tor A	8	5	.615	15	15	0	0-0	85	80	34	4	3	30-2	39	3.18	124	.252	.320	0-0	—	0	127	7	1.0
1989	Tor A	0	1	.000	5	3	0	0-0	11	19	15	2	0	9-0	3	10.64	36	.404	.491	0-0	—	0	104	-9	-0.7
	NY N	3	2	.600	20	0	0	0-0	26.1	27	11	1	0	14-3	11	3.08	106	.267	.357	0-0	—	0		0	0.2
1990	NY N	0	2	.000	28	0	0	0-1	32	40	22	3	1	11-1	14	5.63	67	.310	.364	1-0	.000	-0		-7	-0.4
Total	5	23	15	.605	142	19	0	3-6	248.2	249	132	18	7	123-19	125	4.31	94	.266	.354	1-0	.000	0	118	-9	0.7
MUSSELMAN, RON Ralph Ronald B 11.11.1954 Wilmington, NC BR/TR 6-2/185# d8.18																									
1982	Sea A	1	0	1.000	12	0	0	0-0	15.2	18	7	2	1	6-1	9	3.45	123	.300	.362	0-0	—	0		1	0.1
1984	Tor A	0	2	.000	11	0	0	1-0	21.1	18	7	2	0	10-2	9	2.11	195	.225	.304	0-0	—	0		4	0.4
1985	Tor A	3	0	1.000	25	4	0	0-0	52.1	59	28	2	0	24-2	29	4.47	94	.284	.352	0-0	—	0	124	-1	-0.1
Total	3	4	2	.667	48	4	0	1-0	89.1	95	42	6	1	40-5	47	3.73	112	.273	.343	0-0	—	0	124	4	0.4
MUSSER, PAUL Paul B 6.24.1889 Millheim, PA D 7.7.1973 State College, PA BR/TR 6/175# d6.6 Mil 1918-19																									
1912	Was A	0	0	—	7	2	0	2	20.2	16	7	0	2	16	10	2.61	128	.225	.382	7-0	.000	-1	144	2	0.0
1919	Bos A	0	2	.000	5	4	1	0	19.2	26	16	0	0	8	14	4.12	73	.342	.405	8-0	.000	-1	123	-5	-0.6
Total	2	0	2	.000	12	6	1	2	40.1	42	23	0	2	24	24	3.35	95	.286	.393	15-0	.000	-2	127	-3	-0.6
MUSSILL, BARNEY Bernard James B 10.1.1919 Bower Hill, PA BR/TL 6-1/200# d4.20																									
1944	Phi N	0	1	.000	16	0	0	0	19.1	20	16	1	0	13	5	6.05	60	.267	.375	1-0	.000	-0		-6	-0.3
MUSSINA, MIKE Michael Cole B 12.8.1968 Williamsport, PA BR/TR 6-2/185# d8.4																									
1991	Bal A	4	5	.444	12	12	2	0-0	87.2	77	31	7	1	21-0	52	2.87	138	.239	.286	0-0	—	0	96	10	1.0
1992	Bal A★	18	5	**.783**	32	32	8-4	0-0	241	212	70	16	2	48-2	130	2.54	159	.239	**.278**	0-0	—	0	101	40	3.7
1993	Bal A☆	14	6	.700	25	25	3-2	0-0	167.2	163	84	20	3	44-2	117	4.46	101	.256	.306	0-0	—	0	120	3	0.3
1994	Bal A★	16	5	.762	24	24	3	0-0	176.1	163	63	19	1	42-1	99	3.06	164	.248	.291	0-0	—	0	96	36	4.0
1995	Bal A	**19**	9	.679	32	32	7-**4**	0-0	221.2	187	86	24	1	50-4	158	3.29	145	.226	.270	0-0	—	0	91	36	4.0
1996	†Bal A	19	11	.633	36	**36**	4-1	0-0	243.1	264	137	31	3	69-0	204	4.81	102	.275	.325	0-0	—	0	125	5	0.5
1997	†Bal A☆	15	8	.652	33	33	4-1	0-0	224.2	197	87	27	3	54-3	218	3.20	138	.234	.282	4-0	.250	0	109	31	2.8
1998	Bal A	13	10	.565	29	29	4-2	0-0	206.1	189	85	22	4	41-3	175	3.49	131	.242	.282	2-0	.000	-0	101	24	2.5
1999	Bal A★	18	7	.720	31	31	4	0-0	203.1	207	88	16	1	52-0	172	3.50	134	.268	.312	11-0	.273	1	129	26	3.2
2000	Bal A	11	15	.423	34	34	6-1	0-0	**237.2**	236	105	28	3	46-0	210	3.79	125	.255	.291	6-0	.000	-1	66	27	2.5
2001	†NY A	17	11	.607	34	34	4-3	0-0	228.2	202	87	20	4	42-2	214	3.15	143	.237	**.274**	7-0	.143	-0	85	34	3.9
2002	†NY A	18	10	.643	33	33	2-2	0-0	215.2	208	103	27	5	48-1	182	4.05	108	.253	.296	5-1	.600	1	124	10	1.4
2003	†NY A	17	8	.680	31	31	2-1	0-0	214.2	192	86	21	3	40-4	195	3.40	129	.238	.275	2-0	.000	-0	93	26	2.8
Total	13	199	110	.644	386	386	53-21	0-0	2668.2	2497	1112	278	34	597-222	126	3.53	129	.247	.290	37-1	.216	1	103	308	32.6
MUSTAIKIS, ALEX Alexander Dominick B 3.26.1909 Chelsea, MA D 1.17.1970 Scranton, PA BR/TR 6-3/180# d7.7																									
1940	Bos A	0	1	.000	6	1	0	0	15	15	18	1	0	15	6	9.00	50	.254	.405	6-0	.333	1	78	-8	-0.3
MUTIS, JEFF Jeffrey Thomas B 12.20.1966 Allentown, PA BL/TL 6-2/185# d6.15																									
1991	Cle A	0	3	.000	3	3	0	0-0	12.1	23	16	1	0	7-1	6	11.68	36	.397	.455	0-0	—	0	66	-9	-1.4
1992	Cle A	0	2	.000	3	2	0	0-0	11.1	24	14	4	0	6-0	8	9.53	41	.429	.469	0-0	—	0	58	-7	-1.0
1993	Cle A	3	6	.333	17	13	1-1	0-0	81	93	56	14	7	33-2	29	5.78	75	.289	.365	0-0	—	0	87	-12	-1.1
1994	Fla N	1	0	1.000	35	0	0	0-0	38.1	51	25	6	1	15-3	30	5.40	81	.331	.390	3-0	.000	-0		-4	-0.2
Total	4	4	11	.267	58	18	1-1	0-0	143	191	111	25	8	61-6	73	6.48	66	.324	.390	3-0	.000	-0	79	-32	-3.7
MYERS, BRETT Brett Allen B 8.17.1980 Jacksonville, FL BR/TR 6-4/215# d7.24																									
2002	Phi N	4	5	.444	12	12	1	0-0	72	73	38	11	6	29-1	34	4.25	92	.277	.359	23-3	.130	-0	104	-4	-0.4
2003	Phi N	14	9	.609	32	32	1-1	0-0	193	205	99	20	9	76-8	143	4.43	90	.272	.344	62-5	.145	-0*	128	-9	-0.9
Total	2	18	14	.563	44	44	2-1	0-0	265	278	137	31	15	105-9	177	4.38	91	.273	.348	85-8	.141	-1	121	-13	-1.3
MYERS, ELMER Elmer Glenn B 3.2.1894 York Springs, PA D 7.29.1976 Collingswood, NJ BR/TR 6-2/185# d10.6 Mil 1918																									
1915	Phi A	1	0	1.000	1	1	1-1	0	9	2	0	0	0	5	12	0.00	—	.074	.219	3-1	.000	-0	100	3	0.2
1916	Phi A	14	23	.378	44	35	31-2	1	315	280	169	7	14	168	182	3.66	78	.248	.353	126-4	.214	2*	85	-28	-2.5
1917	Phi A	9	16	.360	38	23	13-2	3	201.2	221	122	2	5	79	88	4.42	62	.283	.353	73-2	.247	2	97	-31	-3.4
1918	Phi A	4	8	.333	18	15	5-1	1	95.1	101	66	4	4	42	17	4.63	63	.283	.365	35-0	.143	-2	89	-18	-2.3
1919	Cle A	8	7	.533	23	15	6-1	1	134.2	134	68	3	10	43	38	3.74	89	.264	.334	46-1	.239	2	87	-4	-0.1
1920	Cle A	2	4	.333	16	7	2	1	71.2	93	52	1	4	23	16	4.77	80	.316	.374	25-2	.240	0	96	-10	-0.7
	Bos A	9	1	.900	12	10	9-1	0	97	90	30	1	2	24	34	2.13	171	.249	.299	38-0	.316	3	142	16	1.8
	Year	11	5	.688	28	17	11-1	1	168.2	183	37	2	6	47	50	3.25	114	.279	.333	63-2	.286	3	122	7	1.1
1921	Bos A	8	12	.400	30	20	11	0	172	217	107	11	10	53	40	4.87	87	.315	.373	65-1	.215	-2	94	-12	-1.4
1922	Bos A	0	1	.000	3	1	0	0	5.2	10	11	1	2	3	1	17.47	24	.370	.469	1-0	.000	-0	41	-7	-1.0
Total	8	55	72	.433	185	127	78-8	7	1102	1148	625	30	51	440	428	4.06	80	.275	.352	412-11	.226	4	94	-91	-9.4
MYERS, HENRY Henry C. B 5.1858 Philadelphia, PA D 4.18.1895 Philadelphia, PA BR/TR 5-9/159# d8.20.1881 M1 ▲																									
1882	Bal AA	0	2	.000	6	2	1	0	26	30	28	2		4	7	6.58	42	.270	.296	294	.180	-1*	84	-9	-0.6
MYERS, JIMMY James Xavier B 4.28.1969 Oklahoma City, OK BR/TR 6-1/190# d4.6																									
1996	Bal A	0	0	—	11	0	0	0-0	14	18	13	4	0	3-1	6	7.07	70	.305	.328	0-0	—	0		-4	-0.2
MYERS, JOSEPH Joseph William B 3.18.1882 Wilmington, DE D 2.11.1956 Delaware City, DE BR/TR 5-10.5/205# d10.7																									
1905	Phi A	0	0	—	1	1	1	0	5	3	3	0	1	3	5	3.60	74	.176	.333	2-0	.000	-0	80	-1	-0.1
MYERS, MIKE Michael Stanley B 6.26.1969 Cook County, IL BL/TL 6-3/200# d4.25																									
1995	Fla N	0	0	—	2	0	0	0-0	2	1	0	0	0	3-0	0	0.00	—	.167	.444	0-0	—	0		1	0.0
	Det A	1	0	1.000	11	0	0	0-1	6.1	10	7	1	2	4-0	4	9.95	48	.385	.485	0-0	—	0		-3	-0.4

Year	Tm Lg	W	L	Pct	G	GS	CG-Sho	SV-BS	IP	H	R	HR	HB	BB-IB	SO	ERA	AERA	OAV	OOB	AB-SH	AVG	PB	Sup	APR	PW
1996	Det A	1	5	.167	**83**	0	0	6-2	64.2	70	41	6	4	34-8	69	5.01	101	.272	.365	0-0	—	0		-1	0.0
1997	Det A	0	4	.000	**88**	0	0	2-3	53.2	58	36	12	2	25-2	50	5.70	81	.274	.351	0-0	—	0		-6	-0.4
1998	Mil N	2	2	.500	70	0	0	1-2	50	44	19	5	6	22-1	40	2.70	158	.249	.348	0-0	—	0		7	0.6
1999	Mil N	2	1	.667	71	0	0	0-3	41.1	46	24	7	3	13-1	35	5.23	87	.291	.356	1-0	.000	-0		-2	-0.1
2000	Col N	0	1	.000	78	0	0	1-1	45.1	24	10	2	2	24-3	41	1.99	292	.160	.284	0-0	—	0		16	0.8
2001	Col N	2	3	.400	73	0	0	0-2	40	32	17	2	1	24-7	36	3.60	148	.225	.339	0-0	—	0		6	0.8
2002	†Ari N	4	3	.571	69	0	0	4-5	37	39	18	2	8	17-0	31	4.38	101	.275	.381	0-0	—	0		1	0.2
2003	Ari N	0	1	.000	64	0	0	0-3	36.1	38	23	4	5	21-1	21	5.70	82	.262	.374	0-0	—	0		-3	-0.1
Total	9	12	20	.375	609	0	0	14-22	376.2	362	195	41	33	187-23	327	4.37	111	.256	.354	1-0	.000	-0		16	1.4
MYERS, RANDY Randall Kirk B 9.19.1962 Vancouver, WA BL/TL 6-1/215# d10.6																									
1985	NY N	0	0	—	1	0	0	0-0	2	0	0	0	0	1-0	2	0.00	—	.000	.143	0-0	—	0		1	0.1
1986	NY N	0	0	—	10	0	0	0-0	10.2	11	5	1	1	9-1	13	4.22	84	.256	.396	0-0	—	0		-1	0.0
1987	NY N	3	6	.333	54	0	0	6-3	75	61	36	6	0	30-5	92	3.96	96	.225	.296	7-0	.286	1		-1	-0.1
1988	†NY N	7	3	.700	55	0	0	26-3	68	45	15	5	2	17-2	69	1.72	187	.190	.248	4-0	.250	1		12	2.7
1989	NY N	7	4	.636	65	0	0	24-5	84.1	62	23	4	0	40-4	88	2.35	139	.206	.297	5-0	.000	-1		10	1.8
1990	†Cin N★	4	6	.400	66	0	0	31-6	86.2	59	24	6	3	38-8	98	2.08	190	.193	.287	4-0	.250	0		16	3.0
1991	Cin N	6	13	.316	58	12	1	6-4	132	116	61	8	1	80-5	108	3.55	107	.242	.347	29-3	.172	0	79	3	0.4
1992	SD N	3	6	.333	66	0	0	38-8	79.2	84	38	7	1	34-3	66	4.29	83	.279	.349	7-1	.143	-0		-5	-0.9
1993	Chi N	2	4	.333	73	0	0	**53-6**	75.1	65	26	7	1	26-2	86	3.11	129	.230	.295	2-1	.500	1*		9	1.8
1994	Chi N★	1	5	.167	38	0	0	21-5	40.1	40	18	3	0	16-1	32	3.79	110	.260	.327	1-0	.000	-0		2	0.3
1995	Chi N★	1	2	.333	57	0	0	**38-6**	55.2	49	25	7	0	28-1	59	3.88	106	.237	.324	0-0	—	0		2	0.4
1996	†Bal A	4	4	.500	62	0	0	31-7	58.2	60	24	7	1	29-4	74	3.53	140	.265	.347	0-0	—	0		10	1.8
1997	†Bal A★	2	3	.400	61	0	0	**45-1**	59.2	47	12	2	0	22-2	56	1.51	292	.217	.289	0-0	—	0		19	3.7
1998	Tor A	3	4	.429	41	0	0	28-5	42.1	44	21	4	2	19-4	32	4.46	105	.265	.346	1-0	.000	-0		2	0.3
	†SD N	1	3	.250	21	0	0	0-1	14.1	15	10	2	0	7-1	9	6.28	62	.273	.355	0-0	—	0		-4	-0.7
Total	14	44	63	.411	728	12	1	347-60	884.2	758	338	69	12	396-43	884	3.19	122	.233	.316	60-5	.183	2	79	75	14.6
MYERS, RODNEY Rodney Luther B 6.26.1969 Rockford, IL BR/TR 6-1/200# d4.3																									
1996	Chi N	2	1	.667	45	0	0	0-0	67.1	61	38	6	3	38-3	50	4.68	93	.243	.343	5-0	.000	-1		-2	-0.2
1997	Chi N	0	0	—	5	1	0	0-0	9	12	6	1	1	7-1	6	6.00	72	.333	.455	0-0	—	0	86	-1	-0.1
1998	Chi N	0	0	—	12	0	0	0-1	18	26	14	3	0	6-0	15	7.00	63	.342	.390	1-0	.000	-0		-5	-0.2
1999	Chi N	3	1	.750	46	0	0	0-1	63.2	71	34	10	1	25-2	41	4.38	103	.289	.354	7-0	.429	1		1	0.1
2000	SD N	0	0	—	3	0	0	0-0	2	2	1	0	0	0-0	3	4.50	96	.250	.250	0-0	—	0		0	0.0
2001	SD N	1	2	.333	37	0	0	1-1	47.1	53	31	6	4	20-0	29	5.32	75	.291	.367	2-0	.000	-0		-7	-0.5
2002	SD N	1	1	.500	14	0	0	0-0	21.1	29	20	1	3	10-0	11	5.91	64	.333	.420	1-0	.000	-0		-8	-0.7
2003	LA N	0	0	—	4	0	0	0-0	9	10	7	1	1	4-0	5	6.00	67	.270	.357	2-0	.000	-0		-2	-0.1
Total	8	7	5	.583	166	1	0	1-3	237.2	264	151	28	13	110-6	160	5.11	83	.286	.366	18-0	.167	0	86	-24	-1.7
MYETTE, AARON Aaron Kenneth B 9.26.1977 New Westminster, BC, CAN BR/TR 6-4/195# d9.7																									
1999	Chi A	0	2	.000	4	3	0	0-0	15.2	17	11	2	2	14-1	11	6.32	77	.266	.412	0-0	—	0	38	-2	-0.2
2000	Chi A	0	0	—	2	0	0	0-0	2.2	0	0	0	0	4-0	1	0.00	—	.000	.333	0-0	—	0		1	0.1
2001	Tex A	4	5	.444	19	15	0	0-0	80.2	94	65	12	11	37-0	67	7.14	65	.293	.381	0-0	—	0	111	-20	-1.9
2002	Tex A	2	5	.286	15	12	0	0-0	48.1	64	57	11	6	41-0	48	10.06	47	.325	.448	0-0	—	0	116	-27	-3.0
2003	Cle A	0	0	—	2	0	0	0-0	2.2	7	7	1	1	2-0	1	23.63	19	.467	.556	0-0	—	0		-5	-0.2
Total	5	6	12	.333	42	30	0	0-0	150	182	140	26	20	98-1	128	8.16	58	.301	.410	0-0	—	0	106	-53	-5.2
MYRICK, BOB Robert Howard B 10.1.1952 Hattiesburg, MS BR/TL 6-1/195# d5.28																									
1976	NY N	1	1	.500	21	1	0	0-0	27.2	34	13	2	0	13-1	11	3.25	101	.306	.376	3-0	.000	-0	53	-1	-0.1
1977	NY N	2	2	.500	44	4	0	2-0	87.1	86	39	5	1	33-5	49	3.61	104	.265	.331	11-0	.182	-0	83	1	0.1
1978	NY N	0	3	.000	17	0	0	0-2	24.2	18	10	3	0	13-2	13	3.28	106	.207	.310	2-0	.000	-0		1	0.1
Total	3	3	6	.333	82	5	0	2-2	139.2	138	62	10	1	59-8	73	3.48	104	.264	.337	16-0	.125	-1	79	1	0.1
NABHOLZ, CHRIS Christopher William B 1.5.1967 Harrisburg, PA BL/TL 6-5/212# d6.11																									
1990	Mon N	6	2	.750	11	11	1-1	0-0	70	43	23	6	2	32-1	53	2.83	129	.176	.274	21-2	.000	-2	88	7	0.6
1991	Mon N	8	7	.533	24	24	1	0-0	153.2	134	66	5	2	57-4	99	3.63	100	.237	.307	52-3	.115	-1	103	1	0.1
1992	Mon N	11	12	.478	32	32	1-1	0-0	195	176	80	11	5	74-2	130	3.32	104	.244	.317	65-7	.123	-1	108	3	0.4
1993	Mon N	9	8	.529	26	21	1	0-0	116.2	100	57	9	8	63-4	74	4.09	102	.236	.343	39-3	.128	-1	104	4	0.3
1994	Cle A	0	1	.000	6	4	0	0-0	11	23	16	1	1	9-0	5	11.45	41	.418	.500	0-0	—	0	127	-8	-0.6
	Bos A	3	4	.429	8	8	0	0-0	42	44	32	5	2	29-1	23	6.64	76	.282	.399	0-0	—	0	71	-6	-0.8
	Year	3	5	.375	14	12	0	0-0	53	67	36	6	3	38-1	28	7.64	65	.318	.425	0-0	—	0	88	-14	-1.4
1995	Chi N	0	1	.000	34	0	0	0-0	23.1	22	15	4	0	14-3	21	5.40	76	.253	.350	1-0	.000	-0		-3	-0.1
Total	6	37	35	.514	141	100	4-2	0-0	611.2	542	289	41	20	278-15	405	3.94	97	.240	.327	178-15	.107	-5	102	-2	-0.1
NABORS, JACK Herman John B 11.19.1887 Montevallo, AL D 11.20.1923 Wilton, AL BR/TR 6-3/185# d8.9																									
1915	Phi A	0	5	.000	10	7	2	0	54	58	46	1	5	35	18	5.50	53	.304	.424	16-1	.125	-1	93	-16	-1.4
1916	Phi A	1	20	.048	40	30	11	1	212.2	206	110	2	3	95	74	3.47	82	.266	.349	69-0	.101	-4	68	-15	-2.0
1917	Phi A	0	0	—	2	0	0	0	3	2	1	0	0	1	2	3.00	92	.200	.273	0-0	—	0		0	0.0
Total	3	1	25	.038	52	37	13	1	269.2	266	157	3	8	131	94	3.87	74	.273	.364	85-1	.106	-6	73	-31	-3.4
NAGLE, JUDGE Walter Harold "Lucky" B 3.10.1880 Santa Rosa, CA D 5.26.1971 Santa Rosa, CA BR/TR 6/176# d4.26																									
1911	Pit N	4	2	.667	8	3	1	1	27.1	33	16	3	1	6	11	3.62	95	.324	.367	7-0	.143	-0	73	-1	-0.3
	Bos A	1	1	.500	5	1	0	0	27	27	12	2	0	6	12	3.33	98	.262	.303	10-1	.100	-1	110	1	-0.1
Total	1	5	3	.625	13	4	1	1	54.1	60	28	5	1	12	23	3.48	97	.293	.335	17-1	.118	-1	82	0	-0.4
NAGY, CHARLES Charles Harrison B 5.5.1967 Bridgeport, CT BL/TR 6-3/200# d6.29																									
1990	Cle A	2	4	.333	9	8	0	0-0	45.2	58	31	7	1	21-1	26	5.91	66	.315	.386	0-0	—	0	87	-9	-1.0
1991	Cle A	10	15	.400	33	33	6-1	0-0	211.1	228	103	15	6	66-7	109	4.13	101	.275	.330	0-0	—	0	71	3	0.2
1992	Cle A★	17	10	.630	33	33	10-3	0-0	252	245	91	11	2	57-1	169	2.96	132	.260	.300	0-0	—	0	96	27	3.0
1993	Cle A	2	6	.250	9	9	1	0-0	48.2	66	38	6	2	13-1	30	6.29	69	.322	.367	0-0	—	0	113	-11	-1.3
1994	Cle A	10	8	.556	23	23	3	0-0	169.1	175	76	15	5	48-1	108	3.45	137	.265	.319	0-0	—	0	118	23	2.2
1995	†Cle A	16	6	.727	29	29	2-1	0-0	178	194	95	20	6	61-0	139	4.55	103	.278	.339	0-0	—	0	135	5	0.6
1996	†Cle A★	17	5	**.773**	32	32	5	0-0	222	217	89	21	3	61-2	167	3.41	144	.255	.306	0-0	—	0	105	39	3.5
1997	†Cle A	15	11	.577	34	34	1-1	0-0	227	253	115	27	7	77-4	149	4.28	110	.282	.342	5-0	.200	0	106	11	1.3
1998	†Cle A	15	10	.600	33	33	2	0-0	210.1	250	139	34	9	66-12	120	5.22	91	.297	.352	5-0	.000	-1	109	-14	-1.2
1999	†Cle A☆	17	11	.607	33	32	1	0-0	202	238	120	26	6	59-4	126	4.95	102	.293	.344	6-0	.000	-1*	115	2	0.3
2000	Cle A	2	7	.222	11	11	0	0-0	57	71	53	15	2	21-2	41	8.21	61	.300	.359	0-0	—	0	96	-19	-2.2
2001	Cle A	5	6	.455	15	13	0	0-0	70.1	102	53	10	0	20-1	29	6.40	71	.342	.379	1-1	1.000	0	127	-14	-1.7
2002	Cle A	1	4	.200	19	7	0	0-0	48.2	76	51	10	2	13-1	22	8.88	50	.360	.399	0-0	—	0*	75	-24	-2.1
2003	SD N	0	2	.000	5	0	0	0-0	12.1	15	7	0	0	3-0	7	4.38	90	.313	.353	2-0	.000	-0		-1	-0.2
Total	14	129	105	.551	318	297	31-6	0-0	1954.2	2188	1061	217	51	586-37	1242	4.51	101	.284	.336	19-1	.105	-1	107	18	1.4
NAGY, MIKE Michael Timothy B 3.25.1948 Bronx, NY BR/TR 6-3/200# d4.21																									
1969	Bos A	12	2	.857	33	28	7-1	0-0	196.2	183	84	10	11	106-3	84	3.11	122	.245	.347	65-4	.077	-2*	129	12	0.6
1970	Bos A	6	5	.545	23	20	4	0-0	128.2	138	71	16	2	64-2	56	4.48	89	.275	.358	44-2	.250	2	115	-6	-0.3
1971	Bos A	1	3	.250	12	7	0	0-1	38	46	29	4	0	20-1	9	6.63	56	.315	.395	12-0	.083	-1	90	-11	-1.1
1972	Bos A	0	0	—	1	0	0	0-0	2	3	2	0	1	0-0	2	9.00	36	.375	.400	0-0	—	0		-1	-0.1
1973	StL N	0	2	.000	9	7	0	0-0	40.2	44	21	4	1	15-2	14	4.20	87	.282	.345	11-0	.091	-1	86	-2	-0.2
1974	Hou N	1	1	.500	9	0	0	0-0	12.2	17	13	3	1	5-0	5	8.53	41	.309	.371	1-0	.000	-0		-7	-1.0
Total	6	20	13	.606	87	62	11-1	0-1	418.2	431	220	37	16	210-8	170	4.15	92	.267	.356	133-6	.135	-2	115	-15	-2.1
NAGY, STEVE Stephen B 5.28.1919 Franklin, NJ BL/TL 5-10/170# d4.20																									
1947	Pit N	1	3	.250	6	1	0	0	14	18	10	1	0	9	4	5.79	73	.310	.403	4-0	.250	0	21	-2	-0.4
1950	Was A	2	5	.286	9	9	2	0	53.1	69	50	5	0	29	17	6.58	68	.307	.386	22-1	.227	2*	85	-15	-1.3

Year	Tm Lg	W	L	Pct	G	GS	CG-Sho	SV-BS	IP	H	R	HR	HB	BB-IB	SO	ERA	AERA	OAV	OOB	AB-SH	AVG	PB	Sup	APR	PW
Total	2	3	8	.273	15	10	2	0	67.1	87	60	6	0	38	21	6.42	69	.307	.389	26-1	.231	2	79	-17	-1.7
NAHEM, SAM Samuel Ralph "Subway Sam" B 10.19.1915 New York, NY BR/TR 6-1.5/190# d10.2 Mil 1943-45																									
1938	Bro N	1	0	1.000	1	1	1	0	9	6	3	0	0	4	2	3.00	130	.194	.286	5-0	.400	0	152	1	0.2
1941	StL N	5	2	.714	26	8	2	1	81.2	76	35	2	2	38	31	2.98	126	.243	.329	23-6	.174	-1	135	6	0.4
1942	Phi N	1	3	.250	35	2	0	0	74.2	72	48	2	2	40	38	4.94	67	.254	.350	20-0	.100	-1	102	-14	-0.8
1948	Phi N	3	3	.500	28	1	0	0	59	68	52	4	3	45	30	7.02	56	.288	.408	13-0	.154	-0	90	-19	-1.8
Total	4	10	8	.556	90	12	3	1	224.1	222	138	8	7	127	101	4.69	78	.257	.357	61-6	.164	-2	130	-26	-2.0
NAKAMURA, MICHEAL Micheal Yoshihide B 9.6.1976 Nara, Japan BR/TR 5-10/170# d6.7																									
2003	Min A	0	0	—	12	0	0	1-0	12.2	20	11	4	1	2-0	14	7.82	58	.339	.371	0-0	—	0		-4	-0.2
NAKTENIS, PETE Peter Ernest B 6.12.1914 Aberdeen, WA BL/TL 6-1/185# d6.13																									
1936	Phi A	0	1	.000	7	1	0	0	18.2	24	26	2	2	27	18	12.54	41	.324	.515	5-0	.200	-0	34	-14	-0.6
1939	Cin N	0	0	—	3	0	0	0	4	2	1	0	2	0	1	2.25	170	.154	.267	0-0	—	0		1	0.1
Total	2	0	1	.000	10	1	0	0	22.2	26	27	2	4	27	19	10.72	45	.299	.483	5-0	.200	-0	34	-13	-0.5
NANCE, SHANE Joseph Shane B 9.7.1977 Houston, TX BL/TL 5-8/180# d8.24																									
2002	Mil N	0	0	—	4	0	0	0-0	6.1	4	3	1	0	4-0	5	4.26	96	.174	.296	3-0	.333	0		0	0.0
2003	Mil N	0	2	.000	26	0	0	0-1	24.1	34	16	5	1	10-1	25	4.81	88	.327	.385	0-0	—	0		-2	-0.2
Total	2	0	2	.000	30	0	0	0-1	30.2	38	19	6	1	14-1	30	4.70	90	.299	.368	3-0	.333	0		-2	-0.2
NAPIER, BUDDY Skelton Le Roy B 12.18.1889 Byromville, GA D 3.29.1968 Hutchins, TX BR/TR 5-11/165# d8.14																									
1912	StL A	1	2	.333	7	2	0	0	25.1	33	21	0	3	5	10	4.97	67	.317	.366	7-0	.000	-1	22	-5	-0.7
1918	Chi N	0	0	—	1	0	0	0	6.2	10	4	0	0	4	2	5.40	52	.357	.438	3-0	.333	0		-1	-0.1
1920	Cin N	4	2	.667	9	5	5-1	0	49	47	12	0	1	7	17	1.29	236	.254	.285	14-0	.214	1	119	9	1.2
1921	Cin N	0	2	.000	22	6	1	1	56.2	72	38	2	0	13	14	5.56	64	.329	.366	14-0	.143	1	100	-11	-0.4
Total	4	5	6	.455	39	13	6-1	1	137.2	162	75	2	4	29	43	3.92	84	.302	.343	38-0	.158	1	94	-8	0.0
NARANJO, CHOLLY Lazaro Ramon Gonzalo "Gonzalo" B 11.25.1934 Havana, Cuba BL/TR 5-11.5/165# d7.8																									
1956	Pit N	1	2	.333	17	3	0	0	34.1	37	22	7	1	17-1	26	4.46	85	.282	.364	7-0	.143	0	62	-4	-0.2
NARLESKI, RAY Raymond Edmond B 11.25.1928 Camden, NJ BR/TR 6-1/175# d4.17 f-Bill																									
1954	†Cle A	3	3	.500	42	2	1	13	89	59	25	8	2	44	52	2.22	165	.189	.293	16-2	.000	-2	60	15	1.2
1955	Cle A	9	1	.900	**60**	1	1	**19**	111.2	91	47	11	0	52-3	94	3.71	108	.220	.306	24-3	.292	1	67	6	0.7
1956	Cle A❖	3	2	.600	32	0	0	4	59.1	36	11	5	1	19-0	42	1.52	277	.170	.240	8-0	.250	0		**18**	1.6
1957	Cle A	11	5	.688	46	15	7-1	16	154.1	136	65	15	4	70-6	93	3.09	120	.235	.320	43-4	.093	-2	112	9	0.7
1958	Cle A★	13	10	.565	44	24	7	1	183.1	179	87	21	3	91-10	102	4.07	90	.255	.341	54-4	.204	1	126	-6	-0.8
1959	Det A	4	12	.250	42	10	1	5	104.1	105	83	21	1	59-3	71	5.78	70	.254	.343	21-4	.095	-1	100	-21	-3.3
Total	6	43	33	.566	266	52	17-1	58	702	606	318	81	11	335-22	454	3.60	106	.230	.318	166-17	.157	-2	110	21	0.1
NARUM, BUSTER Leslie Ferdinand B 11.16.1940 Philadelphia, PA BR/TR 6-1/200# d4.14																									
1963	Bal A	0	0	—	7	0	0	0	9	8	3	0	0	5-2	5	3.00	116	.242	.342	1-0	1.000	1		1	0.2
1964	Was A	9	15	.375	38	32	7-2	0	199	195	104	31	5	73-4	121	4.30	86	.259	.325	66-5	.061	-5	89	-10	-1.8
1965	Was A	4	12	.250	46	24	2	0	173.2	176	98	16	7	91-11	86	4.46	78	.267	.360	46-6	.043	-2	93	-18	-1.7
1966	Was A	0	0	—	3	0	0	0	3.1	11	9	2	0	4-0	0	21.60	16	.579	.652	0-0	—	0		-7	-0.3
1967	Was A	1	0	1.000	2	2	0	0	11.2	8	4	1	0	4-0	8	3.09	103	.195	.267	5-0	.000	-1	96	0	0.0
Total	5	14	27	.341	96	58	9-2	0	396.2	398	218	50	12	177-17	220	4.45	80	.264	.344	118-11	.059	-6	91	-34	-3.6
NASH, JIM James Edwin B 2.9.1945 Hawthorne, NV BR/TR 6-5/230# d7.3																									
1966	KC A	12	1	.923	18	17	5	1	127	95	32	6	0	47-3	98	2.06	165	.204	.276	49-3	.102	-2	140	20	1.8
1967	KC A	12	17	.414	37	34	8-2	0	222.1	200	103	21	4	87-5	186	3.76	85	.242	.314	70-3	.100	-2	93	-14	-2.0
1968	Oak A	13	13	.500	34	33	12-6	0	228.2	185	63	18	3	55-12	169	2.28	123	.219	.269	74-6	.068	-2	100	16	1.5
1969	Oak A	8	8	.500	26	19	3-1	0-0	115.1	112	53	17	2	30-3	75	3.67	94	.247	.296	36-3	.111	-1	122	-4	-0.6
1970	Atl N	13	9	.591	34	33	6-2	0-0	212.1	211	105	22	5	90-7	153	4.07	106	.257	.332	80-3	.087	-3	107	6	0.3
1971	Atl N	9	7	.563	32	19	2	2-0	133	166	81	17	0	50-3	65	4.94	75	.314	.370	47-0	.149	-1*	121	-16	-2.1
1972	Atl N	1	1	.500	11	4	0	1-0	31.1	35	20	2	0	25-1	10	5.46	70	.307	.420	9-0	.222	0	99	-5	-0.3
	Phi N	0	8	.000	9	8	0	0-0	37.1	46	33	5	3	17-2	15	6.27	57	.311	.384	10-0	.100	-0	61	-12	-2.2
	Year	1	9	.100	20	12	0	1-0	68.2	81	36	7	3	42-3	25	5.90	62	.309	.400	19-0	.158	-0	74	-16	-2.5
Total	7	68	64	.515	201	167	36-11	4-0	1107.1	1050	490	108	17	401-36	771	3.58	96	.250	.316	375-18	.101	-11	108	-9	-3.6
NASTU, PHILIP Philip B 3.8.1955 Bridgeport, CT BL/TL 6-2/180# d9.15																									
1978	SF N	0	1	.000	3	1	0	0-0	8	8	5	1	0	2-0	5	5.63	61	.258	.303	1-0	.000	-0	0	-2	-0.2
1979	SF N	3	4	.429	25	14	1	0-0	100	105	51	14	2	41-5	47	4.32	81	.272	.344	24-4	.042	-1	110	-8	-0.6
1980	SF N	0	0	—	6	0	0	0-0	6	10	9	1	0	5-1	1	6.00	59	.357	.455	0-0	—	0		-4	-0.2
Total	3	3	5	.375	34	15	1	0-0	114	123	65	16	2	48-6	53	4.50	78	.276	.349	25-4	.040	-1	103	-14	-1.0
NATHAN, JOE Joseph Michael B 11.22.1974 Houston, TX BR/TR 6-4/195# d4.21																									
1999	SF N	7	4	.636	19	14	0	1-0	90.1	84	45	17	1	46-0	54	4.18	100	.243	.333	28-5	.179	1	114	1	0.1
2000	SF N	5	2	.714	20	15	0	0-1	93.1	89	63	12	4	63-4	61	5.21	81	.255	.371	32-4	.156	3	143	-13	-0.6
2002	SF N	0	0	—	4	0	0	0-0	3.2	1	0	0	0	0-0	2	0.00	—	.083	.083	0-0	—	0		2	0.1
2003	†SF N	12	4	.750	78	0	0	0-3	79	51	26	7	3	33-3	83	2.96	139	.186	.277	1-1	.000	-0		11	2.0
Total	4	24	10	.706	121	29	0	1-4	266.1	225	134	36	8	142-7	200	4.12	102	.229	.329	61-10	.164	3	131	1	1.6
NATION, JOEY Joseph Paul B 9.28.1978 Oklahoma City, OK BL/TL 6-2/175# d9.23																									
2000	Chi N	0	2	.000	2	2	0	0-0	11.2	12	9	2	2	8-0	8	6.94	65	.279	.407	4-0	.500	1	71	-3	-0.3
NAULTY, DAN Daniel Donovan B 1.6.1970 Los Angeles, CA BR/TR 6-6/210# d4.2																									
1996	Min A	3	2	.600	49	0	0	4-5	57	43	26	5	0	35-3	56	3.79	135	.207	.321	0-0	—	0		8	0.7
1997	Min A	1	1	.500	29	0	0	1-2	30.2	29	20	8	0	10-0	23	5.87	79	.254	.305	0-0	—	0		-3	-0.2
1998	Min A	0	2	.000	19	0	0	0-1	23.2	25	16	3	0	10-1	15	4.94	97	.269	.337	0-0	—	0		-1	-0.1
1999	NY A	1	0	1.000	33	0	0	0-0	49.1	40	24	8	4	22-0	25	4.38	108	.225	.322	0-0	—	0		3	0.2
Total	4	5	5	.500	130	0	0	5-8	160.2	137	86	24	4	77-4	119	4.54	107	.231	.321	0-0	—	0		7	0.6
NAVARRO, JAIME Jaime (Cintron) B 3.27.1967 Bayamon, PR. BR/TR 6-4/210# d6.20 f-Julio																									
1989	Mil A	7	8	.467	19	17	1	0-0	109.2	119	47	6	1	32-3	56	3.12	123	.277	.327	0-0	—	0	78	7	0.9
1990	Mil A	8	7	.533	32	22	3	1-1	149.1	176	83	11	4	41-3	75	4.46	87	.293	.340	0-0	—	0	124	-9	-0.8
1991	Mil A	15	12	.556	34	34	10-2	0-0	234	237	117	18	6	73-3	114	3.92	101	.261	.318	0-0	—	0	105	-1	-0.2
1992	Mil A	17	11	.607	34	34	5-3	0-0	246	224	98	14	6	64-4	100	3.33	116	.246	.295	0-0	—	0	107	15	1.4
1993	Mil A	11	12	.478	35	34	5-1	0-0	214.1	254	135	21	11	73-4	114	5.33	80	.300	.356	0-0	—	0	102	-24	-2.2
1994	Mil A	4	9	.308	29	10	0	0-0	89.2	115	71	10	4	35-4	65	6.62	76	.314	.377	0-0	—	0	79	-14	-1.7
1995	Chi N	14	6	.700	29	29	1-1	0-0	200.1	194	79	19	3	56-7	128	3.28	125	.251	.303	65-8	.185	2	110	20	1.9
1996	Chi N	15	12	.556	35	35	4-1	0-0	236.2	244	116	25	10	72-5	158	3.92	111	.269	.327	77-8	.130	-2	99	9	0.5
1997	Chi A	9	14	.391	33	33	2	0-0	209.2	267	155	22	3	73-6	142	5.79	76	.309	.359	1-1	.000	-0	109	-36	-3.4
1998	Chi A	8	16	.333	37	27	1	1-0	172.2	223	135	30	7	77-1	71	6.36	72	.315	.384	1-0	.000	-0	103	-35	-4.0
1999	Chi A	8	13	.381	32	27	0	0-0	159.2	206	126	29	11	71-1	74	6.09	80	.313	.387	3-1	.000	-0	95	-24	-2.7
2000	Mil N	0	5	.000	5	5	0	0-0	18.2	34	31	6	0	18-3	7	12.54	36	.410	.505	5-0	.000	-1	64	-18	-2.7
	Cle A	0	1	.000	7	2	0	0-0	14.2	20	13	3	1	5-0	9	7.98	62	.328	.377	0-0	—	0	141	-5	-0.3
Total	12	116	126	.479	361	309	32-8	2-1	2055.1	2313	1206	214	67	690-44	1113	4.72	90	.285	.342	152-18	.145	-2	103	-115	-13.3
NAVARRO, JULIO Julio (Ventura) "Whiplash" B 1.9.1936 Vieques, PR. BR/TR 5-11/190# d9.3 s-Jaime																									
1962	LA A	1	1	.500	9	0	0	0	15.1	20	9	2	0	4-2	11	4.70	82	.317	.353	2-0	.500	0		-1	-0.1
1963	LA A	4	5	.444	57	0	0	12	90.1	75	36	7	2	32-6	53	2.89	119	.228	.296	15-1	.200	1		5	0.7
1964	LA A	0	0	—	5	0	0	1	9.1	5	2	0	2	5-0	8	1.93	170	.167	.324	2-0	.000	-0		2	0.1
	Det A	2	1	.667	26	0	0	2	41	40	19	9	2	16-1	36	3.95	93	.250	.324	5-0	.000	-1		-1	-0.2
	Year	2	1	.667	31	0	0	3	50.1	45	26	9	4	21-1	44	3.58	100	.237	.324	7-0	.000	-1		1	-0.1

Year	Tm Lg	W	L	Pct	G	GS	CG-Sho	SV-BS	IP	H	R	HR	HB	BB-IB	SO	ERA	AERA	OAV	OOB	AB-SH	AVG	PB	Sup	APR	PW
1965	Det A	0	2	.000	15	1	0	1	30	25	16	5	0	12-1	22	4.20	83	.238	.308	4-1	.000	-0	126	-3	-0.2
1966	Det A	0	0	—	1	0	0	0	0	2	3	2	1	0-0	0	∞	—	1.000	1.000	0-0	—	0		-3	-0.3
1970	Atl N	0	0	—	17	0	0	1-1	26.1	24	12	7	1	1-0	21	4.10	105	.233	.248	6-0	.167	-0		1	0.0
Total	6	7	9	.438	130	1	0	17-1	212.1	191	97	32	8	70-10	151	3.65	99	.241	.306	34-2	.147	-0	126	0	0.0
NAYLOR, EARL Earl Eugene B 5.19.1919 Kansas City, MO D 1.16.1990 Winter Haven, FL BR/TR 6/190# d4.15 Mil 1944-45 ▲																									
1942	Phi N	0	5	.000	20	4	1	0	60.1	68	43	5	0	29	19	6.12	54	.286	.363	168-3	.196	1*	38	-17	-1.2
NAYLOR, ROLLIE Roleine Cecil B 2.4.1892 Krum, TX D 6.18.1966 Fort Worth, TX BR/TR 6-1.5/180# d9.14 Mil 1918																									
1917	Phi A	2	2	.500	5	5	3	0	33	30	10	1	1	11	11	1.64	168	.265	.336	11-0	.091	-1	94	3	0.4
1919	Phi A	5	18	.217	31	23	17	0	204.2	210	109	2	4	64	68	3.34	103	.280	.339	71-4	.169	-2	51	-3	-0.6
1920	Phi A	10	23	.303	42	36	20	0	251.1	306	147	7	6	86	90	3.47	116	.312	.371	86-2	.163	-6	69	10	0.7
1921	Phi A	3	13	.188	32	19	6	0	169.1	214	106	10	3	55	39	4.84	92	.315	.369	52-1	.115	-4*	93	-4	-0.7
1922	Phi A	10	15	.400	35	26	11	0	171.1	212	115	7	3	51	37	4.73	90	.309	.359	55-2	.200	1*	98	-12	-1.3
1923	Phi A	12	7	.632	26	20	9-2	0	143	149	68	5	0	59	27	3.46	119	.273	.344	45-0	.244	1	104	10	1.2
1924	Phi A	0	5	.000	10	7	1	0	38.1	53	29	2	0	20	10	6.34	68	.333	.408	8-0	.375	1	43	-7	-0.7
Total	7	42	83	.336	181	136	67-2	0	1011	1174	584	34	17	346	282	3.93	102	.300	.359	328-9	.177	-11	80	-3	-1.0
NAYMICK, MIKE Michael John B 9.6.1917 Berlin, PA BR/TR 6-8/225# d9.24																									
1939	Cle A	0	1	.000	2	1	1	0	4.2	3	1	0	0	5	3	1.93	228	.188	.381	3-0	.000	-0	0	1	0.2
1940	Cle A	1	2	.333	13	4	0	0	30	36	17	1	3	17	15	5.10	83	.290	.389	6-0	.167	0	78	-2	-0.1
1943	Cle A	4	4	.500	29	4	0	2	62.2	32	23	3	3	47	41	2.30	135	.160	.328	16-2	.188	-0	61	4	0.5
1944	Cle A	0	0	—	7	0	0	0	13	16	15	1	0	10	4	9.69	34	.314	.426	1-0	.000	-0		-9	-0.5
	StL N	0	0	—	1	0	0	0	2	2	1	0	0	1	1	4.50	78	.333	.429	0-0	—	0		0	0.0
Total	4	5	7	.417	52	9	1	2	112.1	89	57	5	6	80	64	3.93	89	.224	.362	26-2	.154	-1	65	-6	0.1
NEAGLE, DENNY Dennis Edward B 9.13.1968 Gambrills, MD BL/TL 6-2/217# d7.27																									
1991	Min A	0	1	.000	7	3	0	0-0	20	28	9	3	0	7-2	14	4.05	106	.329	.380	0-0	—	0	100	1	0.0
1992	†Pit N	4	6	.400	55	6	0	2-2	86.1	81	46	9	2	43-8	77	4.48	77	.247	.335	11-2	.000	-1*	101	-10	-1.3
1993	Pit N	3	5	.375	50	7	0	1-0	81.1	82	49	10	3	37-3	73	5.31	76	.258	.340	14-2	.000	-2	89	-11	-1.2
1994	Pit N	9	10	.474	24	24	2	0-0	137	135	80	18	3	49-3	122	5.12	84	.259	.322	42-5	.190	1	83	-9	-1.0
1995	Pit N★	13	8	.619	31	**31**	5-1	0-0	**209.2**	221	91	20	3	45-3	150	3.43	125	.273	.312	74-5	.122	-0*	104	19	1.7
1996	Pit N	14	6	.700	27	27	1	0-0	182.2	186	67	21	3	34-2	131	3.05	143	.267	.303	55-16	.182	0*	93	27	2.7
	†Atl N	2	3	.400	6	6	1	0-0	38.2	40	26	5	0	14-0	18	5.59	79	.268	.329	14-0	.143	-0	82	-4	-0.5
	Year	16	9	.640	33	33	2	0-0	221.1	226	30	26	3	48-2	149	3.50	125	.267	.308	69-16	.174	-0	91	22	2.2
1997	†Atl N☆	**20**	5	.800	34	34	4-4	0-0	233.1	204	87	18	6	49-5	172	2.97	142	.233	.277	72-9	.153	1	113	32	3.3
1998	†Atl N	16	11	.593	32	31	5-2	0-0	210.1	196	91	25	6	60-3	165	3.55	117	.250	.307	63-9	.175	1	113	15	1.8
1999	Cin N	9	5	.643	20	19	0	0-0	111.2	95	54	23	4	40-3	76	4.27	109	.229	.300	37-5	.162	-0	120	7	0.6
2000	Cin N	8	2	.800	18	18	0	0-0	117.2	111	48	15	3	50-3	88	3.52	134	.247	.325	37-7	.189	1*	117	16	1.3
	†NY A	7	7	.500	16	15	1	0-0	91.1	99	61	16	2	31-1	58	5.81	83	.278	.335	0-0	—	0	112	-9	-1.1
2001	Col N	9	8	.529	30	30	0	0-0	170.2	192	107	29	7	60-3	139	5.38	99	.284	.344	56-8	.196	2	104	0	0.2
2002	Col N	8	11	.421	35	28	1	0-0	164.1	170	101	26	10	63-5	111	5.26	91	.266	.338	45-5	.267	2	83	-6	-0.4
2003	Col N	2	4	.333	7	7	0	0-0	35.1	47	31	12	1	12-0	21	7.90	62	.320	.375	11-2	.000	-1	74	-9	-1.4
Total	13	124	92	.574	392	286	20-7	3-2	1890.1	1887	948	250	53	594-44	1415	4.24	105	.260	.319	531-75	.164	3	103	59	4.7
NEAGLE, JACK John Henry B 1.2.1858 Syracuse, NY D 9.20.1904 Syracuse, NY BR/TR 5-6/155# d7.8 ▲																									
1879	Cin N	0	1	.000	2	2	1	0	13	13	12	0		5	4	3.46	67	.241	.305	12	.167	-0*	99	-2	-0.2
1883	Phi N	1	7	.125	8	7	6	0	61.1	88	77	1		21	13	6.90	45	.315	.363	73	.164	-2*	74	-25	-2.4
	Bal AA	1	4	.200	6	5	4	0	46	48	48	1		20	9	4.89	71	.251	.322	35	.286	1*	76	-7	-0.4
	Pit AA	3	12	.200	16	16	12	0	114	156	123	9		25	41	5.84	56	.306	.338	101	.188	-1*	73	-34	-3.3
	Year	4	16	.200	22	21	16	0	160	204	127	10		45	50	5.57	60	.291	.334	136	.213	-0	73	-42	-3.7
1884	Pit AA	11	26	.297	38	38	37-2	0	326	354	219	6	18	70	85	3.73	89	.255	.300	148	.149	-5*	61	-17	-2.1
Total	3	16	50	.242	70	68	60-2	0	560.1	659	479	17	18	141	152	4.59	71	.272	.317	369	.176	-8	67	-85	-8.4
NEAL, BLAINE Blaine B 4.6.1978 Marlton, NJ BL/TR 6-5/205# d9.3																									
2001	Fla N	0	0	—	4	0	0	0-0	5.1	7	4	0	0	5-0	3	6.75	62	.304	.429	0-0	—	0		-1	-0.1
2002	Fla N	3	0	1.000	32	0	0	0-0	33	32	12	1	0	14-2	33	2.73	145	.248	.322	0-0	—	0		4	0.3
2003	Fla N	0	0	—	18	0	0	0-0	21	38	20	2	1	9-1	10	8.14	50	.413	.449	0-0	—	0		-10	-0.5
Total	3	3	0	1.000	54	0	0	0-0	59.1	77	36	3	1	28-3	46	5.01	80	.316	.381	0-0	—	0		-7	-0.3
NEALE, JOE Joseph Hunt B 5.7.1866 Wadsworth, OH D 12.30.1913 Akron, OH BR/TR 5-8/153# d6.21																									
1886	Lou AA	0	1	.000	1	1	0	0	7	11	12	0	1	7	0	7.71	47	.393	.528	5	.000	-0*	82	-3	-0.3
1887	Lou AA	1	4	.200	5	4	4	0	41.1	60	50	4	2	15	11	6.97	63	.326	.383	19	.053	-2	80	-11	-1.0
1890	StL AA	5	3	.625	10	9	8	0	69	53	37	4	4	15	23	3.39	127	.206	.261	30	.067	-3*	104	7	0.3
1891	StL AA	6	4	.600	15	11	9-1	**3**	110.1	109	73	4	7	36	24	4.24	99	.249	.317	51	.118	-3	114	3	0.0
Total	4	12	12	.500	31	25	21-1	3	227.2	233	172	12	14	73	58	4.59	93	.257	.322	105	.086	-9	103	-4	-1.0
NECCIAI, RON Ronald Andrew B 6.18.1932 Gallatin, PA BR/TR 6-5/185# d8.10 Mil 1953																									
1952	Pit N	1	6	.143	12	9	0	0	54.2	63	45	5	1	32	31	7.08	56	.296	.390	17-0	.059	-1	62	-16	-1.9
NEGRAY, RON Ronald Alvin B 2.26.1930 Akron, OH BR/TR 6-1/185# d9.14																									
1952	Bro N	0	0	—	4	1	0	0	13	15	5	0	0	5	5	3.46	105	.294	.357	2-0	.000	-0	122	0	0.0
1955	Phi N	4	3	.571	19	10	2	0	71.2	71	31	13	0	21-2	30	3.52	113	.257	.308	24-2	.000	-3	92	4	0.0
1956	Phi N	2	3	.400	39	4	0	3	66.2	72	36	6	1	24-9	44	4.18	89	.280	.340	7-1	.429	1	89	-4	-0.2
1958	LA N	0	0	—	4	0	0	0	11.1	12	9	4	0	7-0	2	7.15	57	.279	.373	2-0	.000	-0		-3	-0.2
Total	4	6	6	.500	66	15	2	3	162.2	170	81	23	1	57-11	81	4.04	95	.271	.330	35-3	.086	-3	94	-3	-0.4
NEHER, JIM James Gilmore B 2.5.1889 Rochester, NY D 11.11.1951 Buffalo, NY BR/TR 5-11/185# d9.10																									
1912	Cle A	0	0	—	1	0	0	0	1	0	0	0	0	0	0	0.00	—	.000	.000	0-0	—	0		0	0.0
NEHF, ART Arthur Neukom B 7.31.1892 Terre Haute, IN D 12.18.1960 Phoenix, AZ BL/TL 5-9.5/176# d8.13																									
1915	Bos N	5	4	.556	12	10	6-4	0	78.1	60	29	0	3	21	39	2.53	103	.214	.276	28-1	.143	-1	98	1	0.0
1916	Bos N	7	5	.583	22	13	6-1	0	121	110	40	1	3	20	36	2.01	124	.244	.281	40-0	.125	-0*	113	5	0.4
1917	Bos N	17	8	.680	38	23	16-4	0	233.1	197	78	4	4	39	101	2.16	118	.231	.268	70-3	.171	5	109	7	1.4
1918	Bos N	15	15	.500	32	31	**28**-2	0	284.1	274	107	2	6	76	96	2.69	100	.259	.312	95-6	.168	1*	104	1	0.6
1919	Bos N	8	9	.471	22	19	13-1	0	168.2	151	66	6	6	40	53	3.09	92	.242	.294	63-1	.206	2*	97	-2	0.1
	NY N	9	2	.818	13	12	9-2	0	102	70	23	2	2	19	24	1.50	187	.196	.240	35-1	.229	3	130	15	2.1
	Year	17	11	.607	35	31	22-3	0	270.2	221	28	8	8	59	77	2.49	114	.225	.275	98-2	.214	5	109	13	2.2
1920	NY N	21	12	.636	40	33	22-4	0	280.2	273	113	8	1	45	79	3.08	97	.260	.291	97-4	.268	5	139	0	0.6
1921	†NY N	20	10	.667	41	34	18-2	1	260.2	266	116	18	2	55	67	3.63	101	.271	.311	89-8	.202	0*	121	4	0.6
1922	†NY N	19	13	.594	37	35	20-2	1	268.1	286	122	15	4	64	60	3.29	122	.276	.321	98-4	.255	4	107	21	2.5
1923	†NY N	13	10	.565	34	27	7-1	2	196	219	112	14	2	49	50	4.50	85	.281	.326	63-1	.190	1	141	-16	-1.5
1924	†NY N	14	4	.778	30	20	11	2	171.2	167	75	14	2	42	72	3.62	101	.254	.301	57-4	.228	6*	157	3	1.0
1925	NY N	11	9	.550	29	20	8-1	1	155	193	86	7	1	50	63	3.77	107	.308	.360	51-1	.216	1*	102	1	0.3
1926	NY N	0	0	—	2	0	0	0	1.2	2	2	0	0	1	0	10.80	35	.286	.375	1-0	.000	-0		-1	-0.1
	Cin N	0	1	.000	7	1	0	0	17	25	10	0	1	5	4	3.71	100	.379	.431	5-0	.200	-0	68	-1	0.0
	Year	0	1	.000	9	1	0	0	18.2	27	13	0	1	6	4	4.34	85	.370	.425	6-0	.167	-0	68	-2	-0.1
1927	Cin N	3	5	.375	21	5	1	4	45.1	59	33	2	0	14	21	5.56	68	.319	.367	13-1	.077	-1	90	-9	-1.5
	Chi N	1	1	.500	8	2	2-1	1	26.1	25	5	0	0	9	12	1.37	283	.260	.324	7-0	.429	1	66	7	0.7
	Year	4	6	.400	29	7	3-1	5	71.2	84	8	2	0	23	33	4.02	95	.299	.352	20-1	.200	0	83	-1	-0.8
1928	Chi N	13	7	.650	31	21	10-2	0	176.2	190	62	3	1	52	40	2.65	145	.281	.334	58-5	.190	2	102	24	2.8
1929	†Chi N	8	5	.615	32	14	4	1	120.2	148	85	11	2	39	27	5.59	83	.310	.365	45-1	.289	4	130	-12	-0.7
Total	15	184	120	.605	451	320	181-27	13	2707.2	2715	1164	107	40	640	844	3.20	105	.265	.310	915-41	.210	34	119	48	9.3

Year	Tm Lg	W	L	Pct	G	GS	CG-Sho	SV-BS	IP	H	R	HR	HB	BB-IB	SO	ERA	AERA	OAV	OOB	AB-SH	AVG	PB	Sup	APR	PW
NEIBAUER, GARY Gary Wayne B 10.29.1944 Billings, MT BR/TR 6-3/200# d4.12																									
1969	†Atl N	1	2	.333	29	0	0	0-0	57.2	42	28	9	1	31-2	42	3.90	92	.204	.310	10-0	.000	-1		-2	-0.2
1970	Atl N	0	3	.000	7	0	0	0-0	12.2	11	7	0	0	8-1	9	4.97	86	.239	.352	2-0	.000	-0		-1	-0.1
1971	Atl N	1	0	1.000	6	1	0	1-0	21	14	5	3	1	9-1	6	2.14	173	.187	.282	5-1	.000	-1	24	4	0.2
1972	Atl N	0	0	—	8	0	0	0-0	17.1	27	15	6	1	6-0	8	7.27	52	.360	.410	4-1	.000	-0		-6	-0.4
	Phi N	0	2	.000	9	2	0	0-1	18.2	17	12	1	1	14-0	7	5.30	68	.239	.372	4-0	.250	0	61	-3	-0.3
	Year	0	2	.000	17	2	0	0-1	36	44	15	7	2	20-0	15	6.25	59	.301	.391	8-1	.125	-0	60	-9	-0.7
1973	Atl N	2	1	.667	16	1	0	0-2	21.1	24	19	3	2	19-1	9	7.17	55	.282	.421	4-1	.250	1	67	-7	-0.8
Total	5	4	8	.333	75	4	0	1-3	148.2	135	86	22	6	87-5	81	4.78	78	.242	.349	29-3	.069	-1	53	-15	-1.6
NEIDLINGER, JIM James Llewellyn B 9.24.1964 Vallejo, CA BB/TR 6-4/180# d8.1																									
1990	LA N	5	3	.625	12	12	0	0-0	74	67	30	4	1	15-1	46	3.28	112	.241	.279	25-0	.120	-0	121	4	0.3
NEIGER, AL Alvin Edward B 3.26.1939 Wilmington, DE BL/TL 6/195# d7.30																									
1960	Phi N	0	0	—	6	0	0	0	12.2	16	8	2	2	4-1	3	5.68	68	.340	.393	2-0	.500	0		-2	-0.1
NEKOLA, BOTS Francis Joseph B 12.10.1906 New York, NY D 3.11.1987 Rockville, MD BL/TL 5-11.5/175# d7.19																									
1929	NY A	0	0	—	9	1	0	0	18.2	21	10	0	0	15	2	4.34	89	.296	.419	4-1	.500	1	241	-1	0.1
1933	Det A	0	0	—	2	0	0	0	1.1	4	4	1	0	1	0	27.00	16	.500	.556	0-0	—	0		-3	-0.1
Total	2	0	0	—	11	1	0	0	20	25	14	1	0	16	2	5.85	66	.316	.432	4-1	.500	1	241	-4	0.0
NELSON, RED Albert Francis (b: Albert W. Horazdovsky) B 5.19.1886 Cleveland, OH D 10.26.1956 St.Petersburg, FL BR/TR 5-11/190# d9.9																									
1910	StL A	5	1	.833	7	6	6-1	0	60	57	26	0	4	14	30	2.55	97	.261	.318	23-0	.261	2	117	0	0.4
1911	StL A	3	9	.250	16	13	6	0	81	103	68	1	7	44	24	5.22	65	.324	.417	27-1	.111	-2	85	-17	-2.3
1912	StL A	0	2	.000	8	3	0	1	18	21	14	0	0	13	9	7.00	47	.318	.430	3-0	.333	1	82	-5	-0.5
	Phi N	2	0	1.000	4	2	1	0	19.1	25	10	2	2	6	2	3.72	97	.305	.367	10-0	.100	-1	202	0	-0.1
1913	Phi N	0	0	—	2	0	0	0	8.1	9	2	0	0	4	3	2.16	154	.290	.371	3-0	.333	0		1	0.1
	Cin N	0	0	—	2	0	0	0	1.2	6	7	1	1	4	0	37.80	9	.667	.786	0-0	—	0		-5	-0.3
	Year	0	0	—	4	0	0	0	10	15	19	1	1	8	3	8.10	41	.375	.490	3-0	.333	0		-4	-0.2
Total	4	10	12	.455	39	24	13-1	1	188.1	221	127	4	14	85	68	4.54	68	.305	.389	66-1	.182	0	104	-26	-2.7
NELSON, ANDY Andrew A. "Peaches" B 11.30.1884 St.Paul, MN TL d5.26																									
1908	Chi A	0	0	—	2	1	0	0	9	11	4	0	1	4	1	2.00	116	.282	.364	2-0	.000	0	148	0	0.0
NELSON, EMMETT George Emmett "Ramrod" B 2.26.1905 Viborg, SD D 8.25.1967 Sioux Falls, SD BR/TR 6-3/180# d6.24																									
1935	Cin N	4	4	.500	19	7	3-1	1	60.1	70	31	2	2	23	14	4.33	92	.295	.363	15-1	.133	-1	79	-1	-0.2
1936	Cin N	1	0	1.000	6	1	0	0	17	24	8	1	1	4	3	3.18	120	.333	.377	6-0	.167	-0	133	1	0.0
Total	2	5	4	.556	25	8	3-1	1	77.1	94	39	3	3	27	17	4.07	97	.304	.366	21-1	.143	-1	86	0	-0.2
NELSON, JIM James Lorin B 7.4.1947 Birmingham, AL BR/TR 6/180# d5.30																									
1970	Pit N	4	2	.667	15	10	1-1	0-0	68.1	64	32	5	3	38-5	42	3.42	114	.255	.355	20-1	.200	0	117	2	0.2
1971	Pit N	2	2	.500	17	2	0	0-0	34.2	27	9	0	5	26-4	11	2.34	145	.225	.382	6-0	.500	2	26	5	0.7
Total	2	6	4	.600	32	12	1-1	0-0	103	91	41	5	8	64-9	53	3.06	122	.245	.364	26-1	.269	2	106	7	0.9
NELSON, JEFF Jeffrey Allan B 11.17.1966 Baltimore, MD BR/TR 6-8/235# d4.16																									
1992	Sea A	1	7	.125	66	0	0	6-8	81	71	34	7	6	44-12	46	3.44	116	.245	.353	0-0	—	0		5	0.5
1993	Sea A	5	3	.625	71	0	0	1-10	60	57	30	5	8	34-10	61	4.35	102	.258	.371	0-0	—	0		1	0.2
1994	Sea A	0	0	—	28	0	0	0-0	42.1	35	18	3	8	20-4	44	2.76	177	.226	.342	0-0	—	0		8	0.4
1995	†Sea A	7	3	.700	62	0	0	2-2	78.2	58	21	4	6	27-5	96	2.17	218	.209	.291	0-0	—	0		22	2.5
1996	†NY A	4	4	.500	73	0	0	2-2	74.1	75	38	6	2	36-1	91	4.36	113	.262	.348	0-0	—	0		5	0.5
1997	†NY A	3	7	.300	77	0	0	2-6	78.2	53	32	7	4	37-12	81	2.86	156	.191	.294	0-0	—	0		12	1.5
1998	†NY A	5	3	.625	45	0	0	3-3	40.1	44	18	1	8	22-4	35	3.79	116	.278	.387	1-1	.000	-0		3	0.5
1999	†NY A	2	1	.667	39	0	0	1-1	30.1	27	14	2	3	22-2	35	4.15	114	.245	.380	0-0	—	0		3	0.3
2000	†NY A	8	4	.667	73	0	0	0-4	69.2	44	24	2	2	45-1	71	2.45	197	.183	.314	1-0	.000	-0		17	2.5
2001	†Sea A★	4	3	.571	69	0	0	4-1	65.1	30	21	3	6	44-1	88	2.76	151	.136	.295	0-0	—	0		11	1.2
2002	Sea A	3	2	.600	41	0	0	2-2	45.2	36	20	4	3	27-3	55	3.94	107	.221	.335	0-0	—	0		2	0.2
2003	Sea A	3	2	.600	46	0	0	7-4	37.2	34	16	3	2	14-1	47	3.35	129	.248	.323	0-0	—	0		4	0.5
	†NY A	1	0	1.000	24	0	0	1-2	17.2	17	9	1	2	10-2	21	4.58	96	.246	.358	0-0	—	0		0	0.0
	Year	4	2	.667	70	0	0	8-6	55.1	51	29	4	4	24-3	68	3.74	116	.248	.335	0-0	—	0		4	0.5
Total	12	46	39	.541	714	0	0	31-45	721.2	581	295	48	60	382-58	771	3.32	136	.223	.333	2-1	.000	-0		93	10.8
NELSON, JOE Joseph George B 10.25.1974 Alameda, CA BR/TR 6-2/185# d6.13																									
2001	Atl N	0	0	—	2	0	0	0-0	2	7	9	1	1	2-0	0	36.00	12	.583	.625	0-0	—	0		-7	-0.3
NELSON, LUKE Luther Martin B 12.4.1893 Cable, IL D 11.14.1985 Moline, IL BR/TR 6/180# d5.25																									
1919	NY A	3	0	1.000	9	1	0	0	24.1	22	9	1	1	11	11	2.96	108	.244	.333	7-0	.143	-0	246	1	0.1
NELSON, LYNN Lynn Bernard "Line Drive" B 2.24.1905 Sheldon, ND D 2.15.1955 Kansas City, MO BL/TR 5-10.5/170# d4.18																									
1930	Chi N	3	2	.600	37	3	0	0	81.1	97	52	10	6	28	29	5.09	96	.300	.367	18-0	.222	0	149	-1	0.0
1933	Chi N	5	5	.500	24	3	3	1	75.2	65	34	2	0	30	20	3.21	102	.232	.306	21-2	.238	2*	85	0	0.2
1934	Chi N	0	1	.000	2	1	0	0	1	4	4	1	0	1	0	36.00	11	.667	.714	0-0	—	0	134	-4	-0.6
1937	Phi A	4	9	.308	30	4	1	2	116	140	78	12	2	51	49	5.90	80	.300	.371	113-1	.354	6*	111	-10	0.0
1938	Phi A	10	11	.476	32	23	13	2	191	215	142	29	5	79	75	5.65	85	.277	.347	112-0	.277	4*	108	-17	-1.1
1939	Phi A	10	13	.435	35	24	12-2	1	197.2	233	117	27	3	64	75	4.78	98	.292	.347	80-0	.188	-2*	74	1	-0.1
1940	Det A	1	1	.500	6	2	0	0	14	23	19	5	0	9	7	10.93	44	.371	.451	23-0	.348	2*	83	-9	-0.8
Total	7	33	42	.440	166	60	29-2	6	676.2	777	446	86	16	262	255	5.25	88	.287	.353	367-3	.281	13	97	-40	-2.4
NELSON, MEL Melvin Frederick B 5.30.1936 San Diego, CA BR/TL 6/185# d9.27																									
1960	StL N	0	1	.000	2	1	0	0	8	7	3	1	0	2-1	7	3.38	121	.226	.273	2-0	.500	0	43	1	0.1
1963	LA A	2	3	.400	36	3	0	1	52.2	55	34	7	2	32-5	41	5.30	65	.263	.365	11-0	.091	-1*	43	-11	-1.0
1965	Min A	0	4	.000	28	3	0	3	54.2	57	29	7	2	23-3	31	4.12	86	.261	.337	9-1	.111	-0	107	-3	-0.3
1967	Min A	0	0	—	1	0	0	0	0.1	3	2	1	0	0-0	0	54.00	6	.750	.750	0-0	—	0		-2	-0.1
1968	†StL N	2	1	.667	18	4	1	1	52.2	49	20	3	0	9-3	16	2.91	100	.254	.284	12-0	.167	0	120	0	0.0
1969	StL N	0	1	.000	8	0	0	0-0	5.1	13	7	0	0	3-0	3	11.81	30	.520	.533	0-0	—	0		-4	-0.8
Total	6	4	10	.286	93	11	1	5-0	173.2	184	95	19	4	69-12	98	4.40	76	.271	.339	34-1	.147	-1	86	-19	-2.1
NELSON, ROGER Roger Eugene "Spider" B 6.7.1944 Altadena, CA BR/TR 6-3/205# d9.9																									
1967	Chi A	0	1	.000	5	0	0	0	7	4	1	1	2	0-0	4	1.29	241	.182	.250	0-0	—	0		2	0.2
1968	Bal A	4	3	.571	19	6	0	1	71	49	21	3	1	26-3	70	2.41	121	.192	.270	16-4	.063	-0	74	5	0.4
1969	KC A	7	13	.350	29	29	8-1	0-0	193.1	170	78	12	6	65-4	82	3.31	112	.243	.309	58-5	.138	-1	82	9	0.8
1970	KC A	0	2	.000	4	2	0	0-0	9	18	10	3	1	0-0	3	10.00	37	.419	.422	0-0	—	0	119	-6	-1.0
1971	KC A	0	1	.000	13	1	0	0-0	34	35	20	1	0	5-0	29	5.29	65	.269	.294	6-0	.333	1	183	-6	-0.2
1972	KC A	11	6	.647	34	19	10-6	2-0	173.1	120	41	13	1	31-1	120	2.08	146	.196	**.234**	54-4	.093	-2	89	20	2.0
1973	†Cin N	3	2	.600	14	8	1	0-0	54.2	49	25	4	3	24-1	17	3.46	99	.246	.333	18-1	.111	-1	133	-1	-0.2
1974	Cin N	4	4	.500	14	12	1	1-0	85.1	67	36	7	1	35-1	42	3.38	104	.213	.293	28-2	.179	0	77	1	0.1
1976	KC A	0	0	—	3	0	0	0-0	8.2	4	2	0	2	4-1	4	2.08	169	.138	.278	0-0	—	0		2	0.1
Total	9	29	32	.475	135	77	20-7	4-0	636.1	516	234	44	17	190-11	371	3.06	110	.224	.286	180-16	.128	-3	91	26	2.2
NELSON, GENE Wayland Eugene B 12.3.1960 Tampa, FL BR/TR 6/174# d5.4																									
1981	NY A	3	1	.750	8	7	0	0-0	39.1	40	24	5	1	23-1	16	4.81	74	.261	.358	0-0	—	0	140	-6	-0.5
1982	Sea A	6	9	.400	22	19	2-1	0-0	122.2	133	70	16	2	60-1	71	4.62	92	.279	.360	0-0	—	0	85	-5	-0.5
1983	Sea A	0	3	.000	10	5	1	0-0	32	38	29	6	1	21-2	11	7.88	54	.295	.397	0-0	—	0	102	-11	-0.9
1984	Chi A	3	5	.375	20	9	2	1-0	74.2	72	38	9	1	17-0	36	4.46	93	.254	.297	0-0	—	0	67	-1	-0.1
1985	Chi A	10	10	.500	46	18	1	2-2	145.2	144	74	23	7	67-4	101	4.26	101	.258	.344	1-0	.000	-0*	95	2	0.2
1986	Chi A	6	6	.500	54	1	0	6-5	114.2	118	52	7	3	41-5	70	3.85	112	.271	.337	0-0	—	0	21	7	0.7
1987	Oak A	6	5	.545	54	6	0	3-3	123.2	120	58	12	5	35-0	94	3.93	105	.249	.304	0-0	—	0*	70	4	0.3

Year	Tm Lg	W	L	Pct	G	GS	CG-Sho	SV-BS	IP	H	R	HR	HB	BB-IB	SO	ERA	AERA	OAV	OOB	AB-SH	AVG	PB	Sup	APR	PW
1988	†Oak A	9	6	.600	54	1	0	3-3	111.2	93	42	9	3	38-4	67	3.06	124	.228	.296	0-0	—	0*	96	9	1.1
1989	†Oak A	3	5	.375	50	0	0	3-1	80	60	33	5	2	30-3	70	3.26	113	.203	.277	0-0	—	0*		4	0.3
1990	†Oak A	3	3	.500	51	0	0	5-3	74.2	55	14	5	3	17-1	38	1.57	238	.208	.259	0-0	—	0		19	1.6
1991	Oak A	1	5	.167	44	0	0	0-5	48.2	60	38	12	3	23-1	23	6.84	56	.306	.381	0-0	—	0		-17	-1.8
1992	Oak A	3	1	.750	28	2	0	0-1	51.2	68	37	5	0	22-5	23	6.45	58	.335	.391	0-0	—	0*	110	-14	-1.0
1993	Cal A	0	5	.000	46	0	0	4-2	52.2	50	25	3	2	23-4	31	3.08	147	.251	.329	0-0	—	0		6	0.6
	Tex A	0	0	—	6	0	0	1-1	8	10	3	0	0	1-1	4	3.38	123	.303	.324	0-0	—	0		1	0.0
	Year	0	5	.000	52	0	0	5-3	60.2	60	33	3	2	24-5	35	3.12	144	.259	.328	0-0	—	0		7	0.6
Total	13	53	64	.453	493	68	6-1	28-26	1080	1061	537	117	33	418-32	655	4.13	98	.258	.328	1-0	.000	-0	92	-2	0.0
NELSON, BILL William F. B 9.28.1863 Terre Haute, IN D 6.23.1941 Terre Haute, IN TR d9.3																									
1884	Pit AA	1	2	.333	3	3	3	0	26	26	21	1	4	8	6	4.50	73	.252	.330	12	.167	-1	97	-4	-0.4
NEN, ROBB Robert Allen B 11.28.1969 San Pedro, CA BR/TR 6-4/200# d4.10 f-Dick																									
1993	Tex A	1	1	.500	9	3	0	0-0	22.2	28	17	1	0	26-0	12	6.35	66	.326	.478	0-0	—	0	184	-5	-0.4
	Fla N	1	0	1.000	15	1	0	0-0	33.1	35	28	5	0	20-0	27	7.02	62	.255	.348	4-0	.000	-0	146	-9	-0.5
1994	Fla N	5	5	.500	44	0	0	15-0	58	46	20	6	0	17-2	60	2.95	148	.222	.280	3-0	.000	-0		10	1.9
1995	Fla N	0	7	.000	62	0	0	23-6	65.2	62	26	6	1	23-3	68	3.29	128	.244	.308	0-0	—	0		7	1.1
1996	Fla N	5	1	.833	75	0	0	35-7	83	67	21	2	1	21-6	92	1.95	209	.225	.277	2-0	.000	-0		**20**	2.7
1997	†Fla N	9	3	.750	73	0	0	35-7	74	72	35	7	0	40-7	81	3.89	104	.250	.338	0-0	—	0		1	0.2
1998	SF N★	7	7	.500	78	0	0	40-5	88.2	59	21	4	1	25-5	110	1.52	261	.180	.239	3-0	.000	-0		**23**	4.7
1999	SF N✧	3	8	.273	72	0	0	37-9	72.1	79	36	8	0	27-3	77	3.98	106	.275	.337	0-0	—	0		1	0.3
2000	†SF N	4	3	.571	68	0	0	41-5	66	37	15	4	2	19-1	92	1.50	282	.162	.230	0-0	—	0		21	4.0
2001	SF N	4	5	.444	79	0	0	**45-7**	77.2	58	28	6	1	22-6	93	3.01	132	.203	.260	1-0	.000	-0		9	1.8
2002	†SF N★	6	2	.750	68	0	0	43-8	73.2	64	19	2	1	20-8	81	2.20	177	.232	.286	2-0	.500	0		15	3.1
Total	10	45	42	.517	643	4	0	314-54	715	607	266	51	7	260-41	793	2.98	138	.227	.295	15-0	.067	-1	178	93	18.9
NEU, MIKE Michael David B 3.9.1978 Napa, CA BB/TR 5-10/190# d4.9																									
2003	Oak A	0	0	—	32	0	0	1-0	42	43	18	2	2	26-2	20	3.64	124	.261	.368	0-0	—	0		4	0.3
NEUBAUER, HAL Harold Charles B 5.13.1902 Hoboken, NJ D 9.9.1949 Providence, RI BR/TR 6-0.5/185# d6.12																									
1925	Bos A	1	0	1.000	7	0	0	0	10.1	17	18	2	0	11	4	12.19	37	.378	.500	0-0	—	0		-9	-0.7
NEUER, TEX John S. B 6.8.1877 Fremont, OH D 1.14.1966 Northumberland, PA TL d8.28																									
1907	NY A	4	2	.667	7	6	6-3	0	54	40	21	1	0	19	22	2.17	129	.208	.280	21-0	.095	-2	133	3	0.1
NEUGEBAUER, NICK Nickolas Donald B 7.15.1980 Riverside, CA BR/TR 6-3/235# d8.19																									
2001	Mil N	1	1	.500	2	2	0	0-0	6	6	5	1	0	6-0	11	7.50	57	.250	.400	3-0	.000	-0	129	-2	-0.4
2002	Mil N	1	7	.125	12	12	0	0-0	55.1	56	33	10	0	44-3	47	4.72	87	.264	.389	19-1	.105	-1	71	-5	-0.7
Total	2	2	8	.200	14	14	0	0-0	61.1	62	38	11	0	50-3	58	4.99	83	.263	.390	22-1	.091	-1	80	-7	-1.1
NEUMEIER, DAN Daniel George B 3.9.1948 Shawano, WI BR/TR 6-5/205# d9.8																									
1972	Chi A	0	0	—	3	0	0	0-0	3	2	3	0	0	3-0	0	9.00	35	.200	.385	1-0	.000	-0		-2	-0.1
NEVEL, ERNIE Ernie Wyre B 8.17.1918 Charleston, MO D 7.10.1988 Springfield, MO BR/TR 6-1/200# d9.26																									
1950	NY A	0	1	.000	3	1	0	0	6.1	10	7	0	0	6	3	9.95	43	.345	.457	1-1	.000	-0	63	-4	-0.5
1951	NY A	0	0	—	1	0	0	1	4	1	0	0	0	1	1	0.00	—	.083	.154	1-0	.000	-0		2	0.1
1953	Cin N	0	0	—	10	0	0	0	10.1	16	7	0	0	1	5	6.10	71	.390	.405	0-0	—	0		-2	-0.1
Total	3	0	1	.000	14	1	0	1	20.2	27	14	0	0	8	9	6.10	69	.329	.389	2-1	.000	-0	63	-4	-0.5
NEVERS, ERNIE Ernest Alonzo B 6.11.1902 Willow River, MN D 5.3.1976 San Rafael, CA BR/TR 6/205# d4.26																									
1926	StL A	2	4	.333	11	7	4	0	74.2	82	41	4	1	24	16	4.46	96	.290	.347	27-0	.185	-1*	67	0	0.0
1927	StL A	3	8	.273	27	5	2	2	94.2	105	61	8	2	35	22	4.94	88	.311	.379	32-1	.219	-1	65	-5	-0.5
1928	StL A	1	0	1.000	6	0	0	0	9	9	4	1	0	2	1	3.00	140	.281	.324	1-0	.000	-0		1	0.1
Total	3	6	12	.333	44	12	6	2	178.1	196	106	13	3	61	39	4.64	93	.300	.363	60-1	.200	-2	66	-4	-0.4
NEWCOMBE, DON Donald "Newk" B 6.14.1926 Madison, NJ BL/TR 6-4/225# d5.20 Mil 1952																									
1949	†Bro N★	17	8	.680	38	31	19-**5**	1	244.1	223	89	17	3	73	149	3.17	129	.243	.301	96-1	.229	3*	119	27	2.9
1950	Bro N★	19	11	.633	40	35	20-4	3	267.1	258	120	22	2	75	130	3.70	111	.254	.306	97-3	.247	7	116	12	1.9
1951	Bro N★	20	9	.690	40	36	18-3	0	272	235	115	19	6	91	**164**	3.28	120	.230	.297	103-2	.223	5	138	17	2.2
1954	Bro N	9	8	.529	29	25	6	0	144.1	158	81	24	5	49	82	4.55	90	.274	.335	47-3	.319	4*	116	-7	-0.4
1955	†Bro N★	20	5	**.800**	34	31	17-1	0	233.2	222	103	35	1	38-1	143	3.20	127	.249	**.279**	117-1	.359	20*	156	19	**4.0**
1956	†Bro N	**27**	7	**.794**	38	36	18-5	0	268	219	101	33	3	46-8	139	3.06	130	**.221**	**.257**	111-3	.234	8*	129	26	**4.1**
1957	Bro N	11	12	.478	28	28	12-4	0	198.2	199	86	28	1	33-4	90	3.49	119	.258	.288	74-1	.230	5*	106	14	2.1
1958	LA N	0	6	.000	11	8	1	0	34.1	53	37	11	0	8-1	16	7.86	52	.346	.377	12-0	.417	2	88	-15	-2.0
	Cin N	7	7	.500	20	18	7	1	133.1	159	61	20	1	28-4	53	3.85	108	.298	.333	60-0	.350	8*	107	4	1.2
	Year	7	13	.350	31	26	8	1	167.2	212	66	31	1	36-5	69	4.67	89	.309	.343	72-0	.361	10	101	-10	-0.8
1959	Cin N	13	8	.619	30	29	17-2	1	222	216	87	25	5	27-3	100	3.16	128	.253	.279	105-1	.305	15*	131	22	3.6
1960	Cin N	4	6	.400	16	15	1	0	82.2	99	48	12	3	14-0	36	4.57	84	.304	.333	36-2	.139	-0*	86	-7	-0.9
	Cle A	2	3	.400	20	2	0	1	54	61	28	6	0	8-0	27	4.33	86	.289	.315	20-0	.300	2*	83	-3	-0.1
Total	10	149	90	.623	344	294	136-24	7	2154.2	2102	956	252	30	490-21	1129	3.56	114	.254	.298	878-17	.271	79	122	109	18.6
NEWELL, TOM Thomas Dean B 5.17.1963 Monrovia, CA BR/TR 6-1/185# d9.9																									
1987	Phi N	0	0	—	2	0	0	0-0	1	4	4	1	0	3-1	1	36.00	12	.571	.700	0-0	—	0		-3	-0.2
NEWHAUSER, DON Donald Louis B 11.7.1947 Miami, FL BR/TR 6-4/200# d6.15																									
1972	Bos A	4	2	.667	31	0	0	4-1	37	30	11	2	2	25-5	27	2.43	133	.226	.354	2-0	.000	-0		3	0.6
1973	Bos A	0	0	—	9	0	0	1-0	12	9	2	0	1	13-2	8	0.00	—	.205	.390	0-0	—	0		4	0.2
1974	Bos A	0	1	.000	2	0	0	0-0	3.2	5	4	0	0	4-1	2	9.82	39	.357	.474	0-0	—	0		-2	-0.4
Total	3	4	3	.571	42	0	0	5-1	52.2	44	17	2	3	42-8	37	2.39	144	.230	.372	2-0	.000	-0		5	0.4
NEWHOUSER, HAL Harold "Prince Hal" B 5.20.1921 Detroit, MI D 11.10.1998 Detroit, MI BL/TL 6-2/192# d9.29 HF1992																									
1939	Det A	0	1	.000	1	1	1	0	5	3	3	0	0	4	4	5.40	91	.188	.350	1-0	.000	-0	0	0	0.0
1940	Det A	9	9	.500	28	20	7	0	133.1	149	81	12	2	76	89	4.86	98	.282	.374	40-4	.200	-1	88	0	0.0
1941	Det A	9	11	.450	33	27	5-1	0	173	166	109	6	1	137	106	4.79	95	.249	.378	60-5	.150	-2	108	-5	-0.6
1942	Det A☆	8	14	.364	38	23	11-1	5	183.2	137	73	4	2	114	103	2.45	161	**.207**	.325	52-3	.154	-1*	64	23	2.9
1943	Det A★	8	17	.320	37	25	10-1	1	195.2	163	88	3	0	111	144	3.04	116	.224	.327	65-4	.185	-1	79	6	0.9
1944	Det A★	**29**	9	.763	47	34	25-6	2	312.1	264	94	6	1	102	**187**	2.22	161	.230	.293	120-6	.242	3	117	45	6.1
1945	†Det A✧	**25**	9	**.735**	40	**36**	**29-8**	2	**313.1**	239	73	5	0	110	**212**	**1.81**	**194**	**.211**	.281	109-8	.257	4	106	**58**	**7.6**
1946	Det A★	**26**	9	.743	37	34	29-6	1	292.2	215	77	10	1	98	275	**1.94**	**189**	**.201**	**.269**	103-8	.126	-1	104	**51**	**6.4**
1947	Det A★	17	17	.500	40	36	**24**-3	2	285	268	105	9	2	110	176	2.87	131	.249	.320	96-3	.198	2	86	28	**3.7**
1948	Det A★	**21**	12	.636	39	35	19-2	1	272.1	249	109	10	1	99	143	3.01	145	.242	.309	92-6	.207	1	86	38	4.5
1949	Det A	18	11	.621	38	35	22-3	1	292	277	118	19	0	111	144	3.36	124	.251	.319	91-14	.198	2	106	28	2.9
1950	Det A	15	13	.536	35	30	15-1	3	213.2	232	110	23	4	81	87	4.34	108	.279	.346	74-5	.176	-2	85	10	0.9
1951	Det A	6	6	.500	15	14	7-1	0	96.1	98	47	9	3	19	37	3.92	106	.268	.310	29-4	.310	2*	102	3	0.6
1952	Det A	9	9	.500	25	19	8	0	154	148	72	13	0	47	57	3.74	102	.254	.310	46-1	.217	3*	99	1	0.5
1953	Det A	0	1	.000	7	4	0	1	21.2	31	22	4	2	8	6	7.06	58	.348	.414	8-0	.500	2	131	-8	-0.3
1954	†Cle A	7	2	.778	26	1	0	7	46.2	34	16	3	0	18	25	2.51	147	.209	.286	13-1	.154	-0	72	6	1.1
1955	Cle A	0	0	—	2	0	0	0	2.1	1	0	0	0	4-1	1	0.00	—	.125	.417	0-0	—	0		1	0.0
Total	17	207	150	.580	488	374	212-33	26	2993	2674	1197	136	19	1249-**1**	1796	3.06	130	.239	.316	999-72	.201	12	96	285	37.2
NEWKIRK, FLOYD Floyd Elmo "Three-Finger" B 7.16.1908 Norris City, IL D 4.15.1976 Clayton, MO BR/TR 5-11/178# d8.21 b-Joel																									
1934	NY A	0	0	—	1	0	0	0	1	1	0	0	0	1	0	0.00	—	.333	.500	0-0	—	0		0	0.0

Year	Tm Lg	W	L	Pct	G	GS	CG-Sho	SV-BS	IP	H	R	HR	HB	BB-IB	SO	ERA	AERA	OAV	OOB	AB-SH	AVG	PB	Sup	APR	PW
NEWKIRK, JOEL Joel Inez "Sailor" B 5.1.1896 Kyana, IN D 1.22.1966 Eldorado, IL BR/TR 6/180# d8.20 b-Floyd																									
1919	Chi N	0	0	—	1	0	0	0	2	2	3	0	1	3	1	13.50	21	.286	.545	1-0	.000	-0		-2	-0.1
1920	Chi N	0	1	.000	2	1	0	0	6.2	8	6	1	0	6	2	5.40	59	.333	.467	3-0	.000	-0	74	-2	-0.3
Total	2	0	1	.000	3	1	0	0	8.2	10	9	1	1	9	3	7.27	43	.323	.488	4-0	.000	-1	74	-4	-0.4
NEWLIN, MAURY Maurice Milton B 6.22.1914 Bloomingdale, IN D 8.14.1978 Houston, TX BR/TR 6/176# d9.20 Mil 1942-45																									
1940	StL A	1	0	1.000	1	1	0	0	6	4	4	1	0	2	3	6.00	76	.190	.261	2-0	.500	0	134	-1	-0.1
1941	StL A	0	2	.000	14	0	0	1	27.2	43	24	4	0	12	10	6.51	66	.361	.420	6-0	.000	-1		-7	-0.5
Total	2	1	2	.333	15	1	0	1	33.2	47	28	5	0	14	13	6.42	68	.336	.396	8-0	.125	-1	134	-8	-0.6
NEWMAN, AL Alan Spencer B 10.2.1969 LaHabra, CA BL/TL 6-6/240# d5.14																									
1999	TB A	2	2	.500	18	0	0	0-1	15.2	22	12	2	1	9-0	20	6.89	72	.333	.421	0-0	—	0		-3	-0.5
2000	Cle A	0	0	—	1	0	0	0-0	1.1	6	3	1	0	1-0	0	20.25	25	.667	.700	0-0	—	0		-2	-0.1
Total	2	2	2	.500	19	0	0	0-1	17	28	15	3	1	10-0	20	7.94	63	.373	.453	0-0	—	0		-5	-0.6
NEWMAN, FRED Frederick William B 2.21.1942 Boston, MA D 6.24.1987 Framingham, MA BR/TR 6-3/190# d9.16																									
1962	LA A	0	1	.000	4	1	0	0	6.1	11	7	0	0	3-1	4	9.95	39	.393	.452	1-0	.000	-0	69	-4	-0.5
1963	LA A	1	5	.167	12	8	0	0	44	56	27	6	2	15-2	16	5.32	64	.316	.374	16-0	.250	1	101	-8	-1.0
1964	LA A	13	10	.565	32	28	7-2	0	190	177	68	9	7	39-8	83	2.75	120	.246	.291	61-5	.180	2*	83	13	2.0
1965	Cal A	14	16	.467	36	36	10-2	0	260.2	225	94	15	1	64-10	109	2.93	116	.234	.282	74-7	.095	-0	82	14	2.0
1966	Cal A	4	7	.364	21	19	1	0	102.2	112	54	7	6	31-2	42	4.73	71	.289	.349	30-3	.200	1	101	-13	-1.2
1967	Cal A	1	0	1.000	3	1	0	0	6.1	8	5	1	1	2-0	0	1.42	221	.320	.393	1-0	.000	-0	55	0	-0.1
Total	6	33	39	.458	108	93	18-4	0	610	589	255	38	17	154-23	254	3.41	99	.256	.307	183-15	.153	3	87	2	1.2
NEWMAN, RAY Raymond Francis B 6.20.1945 Evansville, IN BL/TL 6-5/205# d5.16																									
1971	Chi N	1	2	.333	30	0	0	2-0	38.1	30	15	4	0	17-0	35	3.52	112	.219	.305	6-0	.000	-1		2	0.1
1972	Mil A	0	0	—	4	0	0	1-0	7	4	0	0	0	2-0	1	0.00	—	.182	.250	1-0	1.000	0		2	0.2
1973	Mil A	2	1	.667	11	0	0	1-2	18.1	19	6	2	0	5-1	10	2.95	128	.260	.304	0-0	—	0		2	0.4
Total	3	3	3	.500	45	0	0	4-2	63.2	53	21	6	0	24-1	46	2.97	128	.228	.300	7-0	.143	-0		6	0.7
NEWSOM, BOBO Louis Norman "Buck" B 8.11.1907 Hartsville, SC D 12.7.1962 Orlando, FL BR/TR 6-2/220# d9.11																									
1929	Bro N	0	3	.000	3	2	0	0	9.1	15	12	0	0	5	6	10.61	44	.375	.444	2-0	.000	-0	57	-6	-0.9
1930	Bro N	0	0	—	2	0	0	0	3	2	2	0	0	2	1	0.00	—	.167	.286	0-0	—	0		1	0.0
1932	Chi N	0	0	—	1	0	0	0	1	1	0	0	0	0	0	0.00	—	.333	.333	0-0	—	0		0	0.0
1934	StL A	16	20	.444	47	32	15-2	5	262.1	259	138	15	1	149	135	4.01	124	.261	.358	93-3	.183	-3*	67	26	2.9
1935	StL A	0	6	.000	7	6	1	1	42.2	54	29	2	0	13	22	4.85	99	.303	.351	11-2	.091	-1	39	-1	-0.3
	Was A	11	12	.478	28	23	17-2	2	198.1	222	108	9	4	84	65	4.45	97	.288	.361	73-4	.301	4	94	-2	0.1
	Year	11	18	.379	35	29	18-2	3	241	276	113	11	4	97	87	4.52	97	.291	.359	84-6	.274	3	82	-3	-0.2
1936	Was A	17	15	.531	43	**38**	24-4	2	285.2	294	160	13	3	146	156	4.32	111	.268	.355	108-4	.213	0*	102	15	1.4
1937	Was A	3	4	.429	11	10	3	0	67.2	76	49	4	3	48	39	5.85	76	.287	.402	25-0	.120	-1*	110	-10	-0.9
	Bos A	13	10	.565	30	27	14-1	0	207.2	193	114	14	3	119	127	4.46	106	.243	.344	75-4	.253	2*	82	8	0.8
	Year	16	14	.533	41	**37**	17-1	0	275.1	269	118	18	6	167	166	4.81	97	.254	.359	100-4	.220	1	89	1	-0.1
1938	StL A☆	20	16	.556	44	**40**	**31**	1	**329.2**	334	205	30	5	192	226	5.08	98	.265	.364	124-14	.250	1*	96	-3	-0.2
1939	StL A	3	1	.750	6	6	3	0	45.2	50	26	5	1	22	28	4.73	103	.266	.346	18-0	.222	-0	112	1	0.1
	Det A☆	17	10	.630	35	31	21-3	2	246	222	100	14	2	104	164	3.37	145	.238	.316	97-4	.186	-4	91	42	3.7
	Year	20	11	.645	41	**37**	**24**-3	2	291.2	272	105	19	3	126	192	3.58	136	.243	.321	115-4	.191	-4	95	42	3.8
1940	†Det A★	21	5	.808	36	34	20-3	0	264	235	110	19	3	100	164	2.83	**168**	.238	.310	107-4	.215	-1	109	47	3.9
1941	Det A	12	20	.375	43	36	12-2	2	250.1	265	140	15	3	118	175	4.60	99	.264	.343	88-5	.102	-6	70	2	-0.5
1942	Was A	11	17	.393	30	29	15-2	0	213.2	236	135	5	3	92	**113**	4.93	74	.280	.353	75-4	.160	-2	81	-28	-3.5
	Bro N	2	2	.500	6	5	2-1	0	32	28	13	1	1	14	21	3.38	97	.235	.321	11-1	.000	-1	103	0	-0.2
1943	Bro N	9	4	.692	22	12	6-1	1	125	113	51	4	2	57	75	3.02	111	.244	.329	44-3	.250	1	124	3	0.4
	StL A	1	6	.143	10	9	0	0	52.1	69	45	7	1	35	37	7.39	45	.318	.415	15-1	.333	1	87	-22	-2.4
	Was A	3	3	.500	6	6	2	0	40	38	22	1	2	21	11	3.82	84	.247	.345	15-0	.133	-1	127	-3	-0.6
	Year	4	9	.308	16	15	2	0	92.1	107	27	8	3	56	48	5.85	56	.288	.386	30-1	.233	0	103	-25	-3.0
1944	Phi A★	13	15	.464	37	33	18-2	1	265	243	100	11	4	82	142	2.82	123	.244	.304	88-9	.114	-6	68	18	1.2
1945	Phi A	8	20	.286	36	34	16-3	0	257.1	255	111	12	3	103	127	3.29	104	.260	.332	86-7	.163	-4	76	3	-0.4
1946	Phi A	3	5	.375	10	9	3-1	0	58.2	61	27	2	5	30	32	3.38	105	.266	.364	19-4	.105	-1	86	1	-0.1
	Was A	11	8	.579	24	22	14-2	1	178	163	63	5	2	60	82	2.78	120	.242	.306	62-7	.161	-2	101	13	1.0
	Year	14	13	.519	34	31	17-3	1	236.2	224	67	7	7	90	114	2.93	116	.248	.321	81-11	.148	-3	97	11	0.9
1947	Was A	4	6	.400	14	13	1	0	83.2	99	44	2	1	37	40	4.09	91	.296	.368	29-2	.241	1	88	-4	-0.4
	†NY A	7	5	.583	17	15	6-2	0	115.2	109	38	8	2	30	42	2.80	126	.250	.301	42-1	.095	-3	127	11	0.6
	Year	11	11	.500	31	28	7-2	0	199.1	208	43	10	3	67	82	3.34	108	.270	.331	71-3	.155	-3	108	7	0.2
1948	NY N	0	4	.000	11	4	0	0	25.2	35	16	1	0	13	9	4.21	94	.330	.403	7-1	.429	1	79	-2	-0.2
1952	Was A	1	1	.500	10	0	0	2	12.2	16	7	2	0	9	5	4.97	72	.302	.403	2-0	.000	-0		-2	-0.3
	Phi A	3	3	.500	14	5	1	1	47.2	38	19	2	2	23	22	3.59	110	.220	.318	15-1	.133	-1	93	3	0.3
	Year	4	4	.500	24	5	1	3	60.1	54	23	4	2	32	27	3.88	100	.239	.338	17-1	.118	-1	95	2	0.0
1953	Phi A	2	1	.667	17	2	1	0	38.2	44	24	3	5	24	16	4.89	88	.282	.395	6-1	.167	-0	124	-3	-0.2
Total	20	211	222	.487	600	483	246-31	21	3759.1	3769	1908	206	61	1732	2082	3.98	107	.261	.342	1337-86	.189	-26	89	108	5.3
NEWSOME, DICK Heber Hampton B 12.13.1909 Ahoskie, NC D 12.15.1965 Ahoskie, NC BR/TR 6/185# d4.25																									
1941	Bos A	19	10	.655	36	29	17-2	0	213.2	235	115	13	7	79	58	4.13	101	.277	.344	78-6	.244	3	112	1	0.5
1942	Bos A	8	10	.444	24	23	11	0	158	174	98	11	0	67	40	5.01	74	.278	.348	55-6	.236	2	105	-21	-1.9
1943	Bos A	8	13	.381	25	22	8-2	0	154.1	166	83	8	5	68	40	4.49	74	.274	.352	48-2	.146	-1*	90	-19	-2.5
Total	3	35	33	.515	85	74	36-4	0	526	575	296	32	12	214	138	4.50	84	.276	.347	181-14	.215	3	104	-39	-3.9
NEWTON, DOC Eustace James B 10.26.1877 Indianapolis, IN D 5.14.1931 Memphis, TN BL/TL 6/185# d4.27																									
1900	Cin N	9	15	.375	35	27	22-1	0	234.2	255	146	4	12	100	88	4.14	89	.276	.355	86-4	.198	-1	74	-12	-1.2
1901	Cin N	4	13	.235	20	18	17	0	168.1	190	117	6	14	59	65	4.12	78	.282	.353	69-1	.130	-4	90	-21	-2.2
	Bro N	6	5	.545	13	12	9	0	105	110	42	1	7	30	45	2.83	119	.268	.328	41-0	.220	1	107	8	0.8
	Year	10	18	.357	33	30	26	0	273.1	300	47	7	21	89	110	3.62	90	.277	.343	110-1	.164	-4	97	-9	-1.4
1902	Bro N	15	14	.517	31	28	26-4	2	264.1	208	95	2	11	87	107	2.42	114	**.217**	.289	109-2	.174	-1*	97	11	1.0
1905	NY A	2	2	.500	11	7	2	0	59.2	61	23	1	2	24	15	2.11	139	.266	.341	22-0	.136	-1	107	4	0.1
1906	NY A	7	5	.583	21	15	6-2	0	125	118	53	3	7	33	52	3.17	94	.252	.311	41-1	.220	-0	94	-1	-0.1
1907	NY A	7	10	.412	19	15	10	0	133	132	66	0	7	31	70	3.18	88	.261	.313	37-5	.108	-1	95	-4	-0.6
1908	NY A	4	5	.444	23	13	6-1	1	88.1	78	52	0	7	41	49	2.95	84	.242	.341	25-1	.160	-0	134	-7	-0.8
1909	NY A	0	3	.000	4	4	1	0	22.1	27	17	0	3	11	11	2.82	90	.300	.394	6-0	.167	0	63	-3	-0.3
Total	8	54	72	.429	177	139	99-8	3	1200.2	1179	611	17	70	416	502	3.22	95	.257	.329	436-14	.172	-9	93	-25	-3.3
NICHOLS, KID Charles Augustus B 9.14.1869 Madison, WI D 4.11.1953 Kansas City, MO BB/TR 5-10.5/175# d4.23 M2 HF1949																									
1890	Bos N	27	19	.587	48	47	47-**7**	0	424	374	175	8	11	112	222	2.23	169	.229	.283	174	.247	1*	75	63	5.9
1891	Bos N	30	17	.638	52	48	45-5	**3**	425.1	413	219	15	17	103	240	2.39	**153**	.245	.295	183	.197	-3	96	**48**	**4.5**
1892	†Bos N	35	16	.686	53	51	49-5	0	453	404	211	15	10	121	192	2.84	124	.229	.283	197	.203	1*	85	34	3.3
1893	Bos N	34	14	.708	52	44	43-1	1	425	426	222	15	15	118	94	3.52	140	.253	.308	177	.220	-2*	93	66	5.5
1894	Bos N	32	13	.711	50	46	40-**3**	0	407	488	308	23	9	121	113	4.75	119	.294	.345	170-2	.294	3*	104	39	3.3
1895	Bos N	26	16	.619	48	43	43-1	**3**	390.2	434	222	15	5	90	148	3.41	149	.277	.318	161-1	.230	-5*	95	67	5.2
1896	Bos N	**30**	14	.682	49	43	37-3	1	372.1	387	211	14	7	101	102	2.83	161	.266	.316	147-9	.190	-3*	103	**59**	5.4
1897	†Bos N	**31**	11	.738	46	40	37-2	**3**	**368**	362	152	9	3	68	127	2.64	**169**	.255	**.291**	147-2	.265	4	106	**70**	**6.9**
1898	Bos N	**31**	12	.721	**50**	42	40-5	**4**	388	316	136	7	14	85	138	2.13	173	**.221**	**.272**	158-3	.241	3*	95	62	**6.4**
1899	Bos N	21	19	.525	42	37	37-4	1	343.1	326	155	11	6	82	108	2.99	139	.250	.298	136-2	.191	-5	86	40	3.4
1900	Bos N	13	16	.448	29	27	25-**4**	0	231.1	215	116	11	11	72	53	3.07	134	.246	.311	90-2	.200	-2	105	23	2.3
1901	Bos N	19	16	.543	38	34	33-4	0	321	306	146	8	10	90	143	3.22	112	.250	.306	163-4	.282	9*	81	16	2.6
1904	StL N	21	13	.618	36	35	35-3	1	317	268	97	3	5	50	134	2.02	134	.222	.256	109-0	.156	-1	78	27	2.8
1905	StL N	1	5	.167	7	7	5	0	51.2	64	47	1	0	18	16	5.40	55	.296	.350	22-0	.227	0*	83	-16	-1.6

Year	Tm Lg	W	L	Pct	G	GS	CG-Sho	SV-BS	IP	H	R	HR	HB	BB-IB	SO	ERA	AERA	OAV	OOB	AB-SH	AVG	PB	Sup	APR	PW
	Phi N	10	6	.625	17	16	15-1	0	138.2	129	47	1	4	28	50	2.27	129	.250	.294	53-0	.189	0	88	11	1.0
	Year	11	11	.500	24	23	20-1	0	190.1	193	51	2	4	46	66	3.12	94	.264	.311	75-0	.200	0	87	-6	-0.6
1906	Phi N	0	1	.000	4	2	1	0	11	17	16	0	2	13	1	9.82	27	.386	.542	3-0	.000	-0	279	-8	-0.7
Total	15	361	208	.634	621	562	532-48	17	5067.1	4929	2480	156	129	1272	1881	2.96	139	.250	.300	2090-25	.226	-0	94	601	56.2

NICHOLS, CHET Chester Raymond Jr. B 2.22.1931 Pawtucket, RI D 3.27.1995 Lincoln, RI BB/TL 6-1.5/195# d4.19 Mil 1952 f-Chet

Year	Tm Lg	W	L	Pct	G	GS	CG-Sho	SV-BS	IP	H	R	HR	HB	BB-IB	SO	ERA	AERA	OAV	OOB	AB-SH	AVG	PB	Sup	APR	PW
1951	Bos N	11	8	.579	33	19	12-3	2	156	142	61	4	1	69	71	**2.88**	127	.246	.327	51-4	.137	-2	92	13	1.4
1954	Mil N	9	11	.450	35	20	5-1	1	122.1	132	68	5	4	65	55	4.41	84	.286	.376	35-4	.086	-3	109	-10	-1.7
1955	Mil N	9	8	.529	34	21	6	1	144	139	79	20	1	67-6	44	4.00	94	.253	.334	52-1	.154	-2	123	-7	-0.9
1956	Mil N	0	1	.000	2	0	0	0	4	9	3	1	0	3-1	2	6.75	51	.563	.632	1-0	.000	-0		-1	-0.3
1960	Bos A	0	2	.000	6	1	0	0	12.2	12	6	0	0	4-0	11	4.26	95	.240	.296	3-0	.000	-0	22	0	0.0
1961	Bos A	3	2	.600	26	2	0	3	51.2	40	12	3	0	26-1	20	2.09	199	.221	.317	9-0	.111	-0	42	12	1.4
1962	Bos A	1	1	.500	29	1	0	3	57	61	25	3	0	22-1	33	3.00	138	.276	.339	9-2	.000	-1	195	5	0.3
1963	Bos A	1	3	.250	21	7	0	0	52.2	61	30	8	0	24-0	27	4.78	79	.298	.365	13-1	.231	0	101	-5	-0.4
1964	Cin N	0	0	—	3	0	0	0	3	4	2	1	0	0-0	3	6.00	60	.308	.308	0-0	—	0		-1	0.0
Total	9	34	36	.486	189	71	23-4	10	603.1	600	286	45	6	280-9	266	3.64	105	.264	.344	173-12	.127	-8	104	6	-0.2

NICHOLS, CHET Chester Raymond Sr. "Nick" B 7.3.1897 Woonsocket, RI D 7.11.1982 Pawtucket, RI BR/TR 5-11/160# d7.30 s-Chet

Year	Tm Lg	W	L	Pct	G	GS	CG-Sho	SV-BS	IP	H	R	HR	HB	BB-IB	SO	ERA	AERA	OAV	OOB	AB-SH	AVG	PB	Sup	APR	PW
1926	Pit N	0	0	—	3	0	0	0	7.2	13	11	0	0	5	2	8.22	48	.342	.419	3-0	.333	0		-5	-0.2
1927	Pit N	0	3	.000	8	0	0	0	27.2	34	19	1	1	17	9	5.86	70	.309	.406	9-0	.111	-0		-4	-0.4
1928	NY N	0	0	—	3	0	0	0	2.2	11	13	0	1	3	1	23.63	17	.611	.682	0-0	—	0		-8	-0.4
1930	Phi N	1	2	.333	16	5	1	0	59.2	76	51	8	2	16	15	6.79	80	.306	.353	20-0	.300	0*	93	-7	-0.3
1931	Phi N	0	1	.000	3	0	0	0	5.2	10	6	0	0	1	1	9.53	45	.435	.458	2-0	.000	-0		-3	-0.4
1932	Phi N	0	2	.000	11	0	0	1	19.1	23	16	2	0	14	5	6.98	63	.299	.407	4-0	.000	-1		-4	-0.5
Total	6	1	8	.111	44	5	1	1	122.2	167	116	11	4	56	33	7.19	67	.325	.395	38-0	.211	-1	93	-31	-2.2

NICHOLS, DOLAN Dolan Levon "Nick" B 2.28.1930 Tishomingo, MS D 11.20.1989 Tupelo, MS BR/TR 6/195# d4.15

Year	Tm Lg	W	L	Pct	G	GS	CG-Sho	SV-BS	IP	H	R	HR	HB	BB-IB	SO	ERA	AERA	OAV	OOB	AB-SH	AVG	PB	Sup	APR	PW
1958	Chi N	0	4	.000	24	0	0	1	41.1	46	27	1	1	16-2	9	5.01	78	.295	.362	5-0	.000	-1		-5	-0.5

NICHOLS, TRICKY Frederick C. B 7.26.1850 Bridgeport, CT D 8.22.1897 Bridgeport, CT BR/TR 5-7.5/150# d4.21

Year	Tm Lg	W	L	Pct	G	GS	CG-Sho	SV-BS	IP	H	R	HR	HB	BB-IB	SO	ERA	AERA	OAV	OOB	AB-SH	AVG	PB	Sup	APR	PW
1875	NH NA	4	29	.121	34	33	30	0	288	321	245	2		9	48	2.38	87	.242	.248	119	.193	-2	56	-11	-0.7
1876	Bos N	1	0	1.000	1	1	1	0	9	7	5	0		0	0	1.00	226	.200	.200	4	.000	-1	103	1	0.0
1877	StL N	18	23	.439	42	39	35-1	0	350	376	195	2		53	80	2.60	100	.263	.289	186	.167	-6*	80	2	-0.4
1878	Pro N	4	7	.364	11	10	10	0	98	157	98	0		8	21	4.22	52	.344	.356	49	.184	-0	138	-21	-1.8
1880	Wor N	0	2	.000	2	2	2	0	17.2	29	16	0		4	4	4.08	64	.358	.388	7	.000	-1	57	-3	-0.4
1882	Bal AA	1	12	.077	16	13	12	0	118.1	155	113	2		17	21	5.02	55	.296	.319	95	.158	-2*	78	-27	-2.4
Total	5	24	44	.353	72	65	60-1	0	593	724	427	4		82	126	3.37	76	.287	.309	341	.161	-10	88	-48	-5.0

NICHOLS, ROD Rodney Lea B 12.29.1964 Burlington, IA BR/TR 6-2/200# d7.30

Year	Tm Lg	W	L	Pct	G	GS	CG-Sho	SV-BS	IP	H	R	HR	HB	BB-IB	SO	ERA	AERA	OAV	OOB	AB-SH	AVG	PB	Sup	APR	PW
1988	Cle A	1	7	.125	11	10	3	0-0	69.1	73	41	5	2	23-1	31	5.06	81	.272	.332	0-0	—	0	64	-6	-0.6
1989	Cle A	4	6	.400	15	11	0	0-0	71.2	81	42	9	2	24-0	42	4.40	90	.285	.343	0-0	—	0	83	-5	-0.6
1990	Cle A	0	3	.000	4	2	0	0-0	16	24	14	5	2	6-0	3	7.88	50	.343	.410	0-0	—	0	58	-6	-1.0
1991	Cle A	2	11	.154	31	16	3-1	1-1	137.1	145	63	6	6	30-3	76	3.54	118	.273	.316	0-0	—	0	49	8	0.7
1992	Cle A	4	3	.571	30	9	0	0-0	105.1	114	58	13	2	31-1	56	4.53	86	.273	.323	0-0	—	0	114	-7	-0.4
1993	LA N	0	1	.000	4	0	0	0-1	6.1	9	5	1	0	2-2	3	5.68	67	.360	.407	0-0	—	0		-2	-0.2
1995	Atl N	0	0	—	5	0	0	0-0	6.2	14	11	3	0	5-1	3	5.40	79	.424	.500	0-0	—	0		-4	-0.2
Total	7	11	31	.262	100	48	6-1	1-2	412.2	460	234	42	14	121-8	214	4.43	91	.282	.335	0-0	—	0	72	-22	-2.3

NICHOLSON, FRANK Frank Collins B 8.29.1889 Berlin, PA D 11.10.1972 Jersey Shore, PA BR/TR 6-2/175# d9.6

Year	Tm Lg	W	L	Pct	G	GS	CG-Sho	SV-BS	IP	H	R	HR	HB	BB-IB	SO	ERA	AERA	OAV	OOB	AB-SH	AVG	PB	Sup	APR	PW
1912	Phi N	0	0	—	2	0	0	0	4	8	3	1	0	2	1	6.75	54	.471	.526	0-0	—	0		-1	0.0

NICHTING, CHRIS Christopher Thomas B 5.13.1966 Cincinnati, OH BR/TR 6-1/205# d5.15

Year	Tm Lg	W	L	Pct	G	GS	CG-Sho	SV-BS	IP	H	R	HR	HB	BB-IB	SO	ERA	AERA	OAV	OOB	AB-SH	AVG	PB	Sup	APR	PW
1995	Tex A	0	0	—	13	0	0	0-0	24.1	36	19	1	1	13-1	6	7.03	69	.343	.413	0-0	—	0		-5	-0.2
2000	Cle A	0	0	—	7	0	0	0-1	9	13	7	0	2	5-1	7	7.00	71	.342	.435	0-0	—	0		-2	-0.1
2001	Cin N	0	3	.000	36	0	0	1-2	36.1	46	24	6	0	8-1	33	4.46	102	.307	.338	1-0	.000	-0		-1	-0.1
	Col N	0	0	—	7	0	0	0-0	6	9	3	2	0	0-0	7	4.50	119	.346	.346	0-1	—	0		1	0.1
	Year	0	3	.000	43	0	0	1-2	42.1	55	30	8	0	8-1	40	4.46	105	.313	.339	1-1	.000	-0		-1	0.0
2002	Col N	1	1	.500	29	0	0	0-0	36.1	40	18	7	1	5-0	25	4.46	107	.280	.307	3-0	.333	0		2	0.1
Total	4	1	4	.200	92	0	0	1-3	112	144	71	16	4	31-3	78	5.22	92	.312	.356	4-1	.250	0		-5	-0.2

NICKLE, DOUG Douglas Alan B 10.2.1974 Sonoma, CA BR/TR 6-4/210# d9.18

Year	Tm Lg	W	L	Pct	G	GS	CG-Sho	SV-BS	IP	H	R	HR	HB	BB-IB	SO	ERA	AERA	OAV	OOB	AB-SH	AVG	PB	Sup	APR	PW
2000	Phi N	0	0	—	4	0	0	0-0	2.2	5	4	0	1	2-0	0	13.50	35	.417	.533	0-0	—	0		-2	-0.1
2001	Phi N	0	0	—	2	0	0	0-0	2	1	0	0	0	0-0	1	0.00	—	.143	.143	0-0	—	0		1	0.0
2002	Phi N	0	0	—	4	0	0	0-0	4.1	6	3	2	0	4-0	2	6.23	63	.316	.435	1-0	.000	-0		-1	-0.1
	SD N	1	0	1.000	10	0	0	0-0	11.2	20	13	1	1	9-0	7	8.49	44	.357	.448	0-0	—	0		-7	-0.5
	Year	1	0	1.000	14	0	0	0-0	16	26	16	3	1	13-0	9	7.88	48	.347	.444	1-0	.000	-0		-8	-0.6
Total	3	1	0	1.000	20	0	0	0-0	20.2	32	20	3	2	15-0	10	7.84	50	.340	.438	1-0	.000	-0		-9	-0.7

NICOL, GEORGE George Edward B 10.17.1870 Barry, IL D 8.4.1924 Milwaukee, WI TL 5-7/155# d9.23 ▲

Year	Tm Lg	W	L	Pct	G	GS	CG-Sho	SV-BS	IP	H	R	HR	HB	BB-IB	SO	ERA	AERA	OAV	OOB	AB-SH	AVG	PB	Sup	APR	PW
1890	StL AA	2	1	.667	3	3	2	0	17	11	13	1	2	19	16	4.76	91	.180	.390	7	.286	1	161	-1	0.0
1891	Chi N	0	1	.000	3	2	0	0	11	14	20	0	1	10	12	4.91	68	.298	.431	6	.333	1	233	-5	-0.3
1894	Pit N	3	4	.429	9	5	3	0	46.1	58	38	2	5	39	13	6.22	84	.304	.434	22-2	.409	2	62	-3	-0.3
	Lou N	0	1	.000	2	2	2	0	17	35	35	4	1	16	4	13.76	37	.417	.515	112-1	.339	1*	76	-16	-0.5
	Year	3	5	.375	11	7	5	0	63.1	93	41	6	6	55	17	8.24	63	.338	.458	134-3	.351	2	66	-18	-0.8
Total	3	5	7	.417	17	12	7	0	91.1	118	106	7	9	84	45	7.19	67	.308	.443	147-3	.347	4	108	-25	-1.1

NIED, DAVID David Glen B 12.22.1968 Dallas, TX BR/TR 6-2/188# d9.1

Year	Tm Lg	W	L	Pct	G	GS	CG-Sho	SV-BS	IP	H	R	HR	HB	BB-IB	SO	ERA	AERA	OAV	OOB	AB-SH	AVG	PB	Sup	APR	PW
1992	Atl N	3	0	1.000	6	2	0	0-0	23	10	3	0	0	5-0	19	1.17	312	.130	.183	7-0	.286	0	74	6	0.9
1993	Col N	5	9	.357	16	16	1	0-0	87	99	53	8	1	42-4	46	5.17	92	.296	.369	23-3	.174	0	88	-2	-0.3
1994	Col N	9	7	.563	22	22	2-1	0-0	122	137	70	15	4	47-5	74	4.80	104	.287	.354	40-3	.100	-2	92	2	-0.1
1995	Col N	0	0	—	2	0	0	0-0	4.1	11	10	2	0	3-0	3	20.77	26	.458	.519	0-0	—	0		-5	-0.3
1996	Col N	0	2	.000	6	1	0	0-0	5.1	5	8	1	0	8-0	4	13.50	39	.250	.448	1-0	.000	-0	52	-4	-0.7
Total	5	17	18	.486	52	41	3-1	0-0	241.2	262	144	26	5	105-9	146	5.06	94	.281	.353	71-6	.141	-2	90	-3	-0.5

NIEDENFUER, TOM Thomas Edward B 8.13.1959 St.Louis Park, MN BR/TR 6-5/225# d8.15

Year	Tm Lg	W	L	Pct	G	GS	CG-Sho	SV-BS	IP	H	R	HR	HB	BB-IB	SO	ERA	AERA	OAV	OOB	AB-SH	AVG	PB	Sup	APR	PW
1981	†LA N	3	1	.750	17	0	0	2-1	26	25	11	1	1	6-2	12	3.81	87	.258	.305	0-0	—	0		-1	-0.2
1982	LA N	3	4	.429	55	0	0	9-5	69.2	71	22	3	2	25-8	60	2.71	128	.269	.333	3-0	.000	-0		7	0.8
1983	†LA N	8	3	.727	66	0	0	11-4	94.2	55	22	6	1	29-11	66	1.90	189	.170	.237	4-0	.000	-0		19	2.4
1984	LA N	2	5	.286	33	0	0	11-3	47.1	39	14	3	2	23-7	45	2.47	143	.227	.325	3-1	.000	-0		6	1.1
1985	†LA N	7	9	.438	64	0	0	19-6	106.1	86	32	6	1	24-5	102	2.71	129	.223	.268	9-1	.111	-0		12	2.1
1986	LA N	6	6	.500	60	0	0	11-6	80	86	35	11	1	29-15	55	3.71	93	.280	.341	4-1	.500	1		-2	-0.2
1987	LA N	1	0	1.000	15	0	0	1-1	16.1	13	5	1	1	9-1	10	2.76	144	.220	.329	0-0	—	0		3	0.2
	Bal A	3	5	.375	45	0	0	13-3	52.1	55	32	11	1	22-3	37	4.99	89	.266	.335	0-0	—	0		-3	-0.7
1988	Bal A	3	4	.429	52	0	0	18-5	59	59	23	8	2	19-3	40	3.51	111	.259	.320	0-0	—	0		4	0.6
1989	Sea A	0	3	.000	25	0	0	0-3	36.1	46	29	7	1	15-5	15	6.69	60	.309	.371	0-0	—	0		-10	-0.7
1990	StL N	0	6	.000	52	0	0	2-1	65	66	26	3	0	25-7	32	3.46	110	.269	.331	3-0	.000	-0		3	0.2
Total	10	36	46	.439	484	0	0	97-38	653	601	251	60	13	226-67	474	3.29	112	.247	.311	26-3	.115	-1		38	5.6

NIEHAUS, DICK Richard J. B 10.24.1892 Covington, KY D 3.12.1957 Atlanta, GA BL/TL 5-11/165# d9.9

Year	Tm Lg	W	L	Pct	G	GS	CG-Sho	SV-BS	IP	H	R	HR	HB	BB-IB	SO	ERA	AERA	OAV	OOB	AB-SH	AVG	PB	Sup	APR	PW
1913	StL N	0	2	.000	3	3	2	0	24	20	17	1	0	13	4	4.13	78	.241	.344	7-0	.286	1	62	-4	-0.2
1914	StL N	1	0	1.000	8	1	1	0	17.1	18	11	1	0	8	6	3.12	90	.269	.347	4-0	.250	1	102	-1	0.0
1915	StL N	2	1	.667	15	2	0	0	45.1	48	35	2	1	22	21	3.97	70	.281	.366	14-0	.071	-1	147	-9	-0.6
1920	Cle A	1	2	.333	19	3	0	2	40	42	21	0	1	16	12	3.60	106	.269	.341	9-0	.444	2	70	0	0.1
Total	4	4	5	.444	45	9	3	2	126.2	128	84	4	2	59	43	3.77	85	.268	.351	34-0	.235	2	87	-14	-0.7

Year	Tm Lg	W	L	Pct	G	GS	CG-Sho	SV-BS	IP	H	R	HR	HB	BB-IB	SO	ERA	AERA	OAV	OOB	AB-SH	AVG	PB	Sup	APR	PW
NIEKRO, JOE Joseph Franklin B 11.7.1944 Martins Ferry, OH BR/TR 6-1/190# d4.16 b-Phil s-Lance																									
1967	Chi N	10	7	.588	36	22	7-2	0	169.2	171	68	15	2	32-7	77	3.34	106	.257	.291	46-9	.196	1	114	4	0.5
1968	Chi N	14	10	.583	34	29	2-1	2	177	204	93	18	3	59-8	65	4.32	73	.294	.349	60-9	.100	-2	128	-21	-3.0
1969	Chi N	0	1	.000	4	3	0	0-0	19.1	24	9	3	0	6-0	7	3.72	108	.304	.349	5-1	.200	0	73	1	0.1
	SD N	8	17	.320	37	31	8-3	0-0	202	213	91	15	0	45-9	55	3.70	96	.273	.311	51-5	.118	0*	77	-3	-0.4
	Year	8	18	.308	41	34	8-3	0-0	221.1	237	94	18	0	51-9	62	3.70	97	.276	.314	56-6	.125	0	76	-2	-0.3
1970	Det A	12	13	.480	38	34	6-2	0-0	213	221	107	28	3	72-4	101	4.06	92	.266	.325	66-15	.197	4*	110	-8	-0.4
1971	Det A	6	7	.462	31	15	0	1-0	122.1	136	62	13	2	49-3	43	4.49	80	.283	.350	30-6	.133	-0*	111	-10	-1.0
1972	†Det A	3	2	.600	18	7	1	1-0	47	62	20	3	1	8-1	24	3.83	82	.330	.360	12-1	.250	1	108	-2	-0.2
1973	Atl N	2	4	.333	20	0	0	3-4	24	23	11	2	0	11-1	12	4.13	96	.277	.351	3-0	.333	0		0	0.1
1974	Atl N	3	2	.600	27	2	0	0-3	43	36	19	5	2	18-2	31	3.56	107	.237	.322	5-1	.000	-1	115	1	0.1
1975	Hou N	6	4	.600	40	4	1-1	4-0	88	79	32	3	2	39-4	54	3.07	110	.240	.320	14-2	.214	1	117	4	0.5
1976	Hou N	4	8	.333	36	13	0	0-1	118	107	60	8	1	56-1	77	3.36	95	.238	.322	27-4	.185	2	121	-7	-0.4
1977	Hou N	13	8	.619	44	14	9-2	5-3	180.2	155	66	14	1	64-3	101	3.04	117	.237	.304	50-3	.140	-1	112	13	1.4
1978	Hou N	14	14	.500	35	29	10-1	0-0	202.2	190	97	13	9	73-1	97	3.86	86	.248	.318	65-9	.138	-1*	100	-14	-2.0
1979	Hou N☆	**21**	11	.656	38	38	11-**5**	0-0	263.2	221	102	17	7	107-1	119	3.00	117	.228	.308	83-13	.120	-2	97	15	1.5
1980	†Hou N	20	12	.625	37	36	11-2	0-0	256	268	119	12	4	79-3	127	3.55	93	.270	.323	80-18	.275	8	131	-9	-0.3
1981	†Hou N	9	9	.500	24	24	5-2	0-0	166	150	60	8	0	47-4	77	2.82	117	.243	.294	51-11	.176	1	104	9	1.0
1982	Hou N	17	12	.586	35	35	16-5	0-0	270	224	79	12	5	64-1	130	2.47	135	.229	.278	89-7	.090	-4	90	30	2.8
1983	Hou N	15	14	.517	38	**38**	9-1	0-0	263.2	238	115	15	3	101-5	152	3.48	98	.241	.311	85-12	.094	-3	106	-1	-0.6
1984	Hou N	16	12	.571	38	**38**	6-1	0-0	248.1	223	104	16	4	89-4	127	3.04	109	.241	.308	83-11	.133	-2	127	6	0.5
1985	Hou N	9	12	.429	32	32	4-1	0-0	213	197	100	21	5	99-6	117	3.72	93	.247	.329	68-10	.250	4	100	-5	-0.1
	NY A	2	1	.667	3	3	0	0-0	12.1	14	8	3	0	8-0	4	5.84	69	.280	.379	0-0	—	0	144	-2	-0.4
1986	NY A	9	10	.474	25	25	0	0-0	125.2	139	84	15	1	63-3	59	4.87	84	.275	.356	0-0	—	0	110	-15	-1.9
1987	NY A	3	4	.429	8	8	1	0-0	50.2	40	25	4	4	19-0	30	3.55	124	.215	.300	0-0	—	0	70	3	0.4
	†Min A	4	9	.308	19	18	0	0-0	96.1	115	76	11	6	45-0	54	6.26	74	.296	.375	0-0	—	0	81	-18	-2.0
	Year	7	13	.350	27	26	1	0-0	147	155	80	15	10	64-0	84	5.33	85	.270	.351	0-0	—	0	78	-16	-1.6
1988	Min A	1	1	.500	5	2	0	0-0	11.2	16	13	2	0	9-0	7	10.03	41	.320	.424	0-0	—	0	123	-7	-1.0
Total	22	221	204	.520	702	500	107-29	16-11	3584	3466	1620	276	65	1262-71	1747	3.59	97	.255	.319	973-147	.156	6	106	-36	-4.8
NIEKRO, PHIL Philip Henry B 4.1.1939 Blaine, OH BR/TR 6-1/180# d4.15 HF1997 b-Joe																									
1964	Mil N	0	0	—	10	0	0	0	15	15	10	1	1	7-0	8	4.80	73	.273	.365	0-0	—	0		-3	-0.1
1965	Mil N	2	3	.400	41	1	0	6	74.2	73	32	5	3	26-3	49	2.89	122	.258	.323	10-0	.100	-0*	223	3	0.2
1966	Atl N	4	3	.571	28	0	0	2	50.1	48	32	4	2	23-5	17	4.11	88	.249	.335	8-3	.000	-1		-5	-0.7
1967	Atl N	11	9	.550	46	20	10-1	9	207	164	64	9	7	55-3	129	**1.87**	**178**	.218	.275	57-6	.123	-0	87	27	3.0
1968	Atl N	14	12	.538	37	34	15-5	2	257	228	83	16	5	45-3	140	2.59	116	.239	.276	77-18	.104	-1	89	12	1.4
1969	†Atl N★	23	13	.639	40	35	21-4	1-1	284.1	235	93	21	5	57-7	193	2.56	141	.221	.264	95-9	.211	3	102	32	4.5
1970	Atl N	12	18	.400	34	32	10-3	0-1	229.2	222	124	40	6	68-2	168	4.27	101	.248	.304	79-6	.152	-1	86	0	-0.1
1971	Atl N	15	14	.517	42	36	18-4	2-0	268.2	248	112	27	3	70-6	173	2.98	125	.245	.294	92-7	.152	-2	94	16	1.5
1972	Atl N	16	12	.571	38	36	17-1	0-1	282.1	254	112	22	5	53-3	164	3.06	124	.236	.274	93-11	.194	1	96	19	2.1
1973	Atl N	13	10	.565	42	30	9-1	4-1	245	214	103	21	5	89-4	131	3.31	119	.234	.305	82-7	.122	-1	110	15	1.4
1974	Atl N	**20**	13	.606	41	39	**18**-6	1-0	**302.1**	249	91	19	6	88-3	195	2.38	159	.225	.284	104-9	.192	-0	102	**45**	**5.0**
1975	Atl N☆	15	15	.500	39	37	13-1	0-1	275.2	285	115	29	11	72-3	144	3.20	118	.269	.321	99-4	.172	-0	80	18	1.8
1976	Atl N	17	11	.607	38	37	10-2	0-0	270.2	249	116	18	8	101-7	173	3.29	115	.242	.313	94-9	.191	1	103	12	1.4
1977	Atl N	16	20	.444	44	**43**	**20**-2	0-0	**330.1**	315	166	26	8	164-12	**262**	4.03	110	.255	.344	109-12	.174	-3	81	15	1.3
1978	Atl N★	19	18	.514	44	**42**	**22**-4	1-0	**334.1**	295	129	16	13	102-5	248	2.88	141	.235	.298	120-4	.225	2*	80	**36**	**4.6**
1979	Atl N	**21**	20	.512	44	**44**	**23**-1	0-0	**342**	311	160	41	11	113-8	208	3.39	120	.241	.306	123-7	.195	1	99	19	2.6
1980	Atl N	15	18	.455	40	**38**	11-3	1-0	275	256	119	30	3	85-3	176	3.63	103	.249	.306	90-5	.133	-2	82	5	0.4
1981	Atl N	7	7	.500	22	22	3-3	0-0	139.1	120	56	6	1	56-2	62	3.10	116	.233	.309	52-3	.077	-4	98	6	0.2
1982	†Atl N☆	17	4	**.810**	35	35	4-2	0-0	234.1	225	106	23	3	73-1	144	3.61	104	.255	.313	87-3	.195	2	128	3	0.5
1983	Atl N	11	10	.524	34	33	2	0-0	201.2	212	94	18	2	105-3	128	3.97	98	.276	.362	65-6	.185	0	100	-1	0.0
1984	NY A☆	16	8	.667	32	31	5-1	0-0	215.2	219	85	15	3	76-0	136	3.09	123	.267	.327	0-0	—	0	125	16	1.8
1985	NY A	16	12	.571	33	33	7-1	0-0	220	203	110	29	2	120-1	149	4.09	98	.245	.341	0-0	—	0	107	-1	-0.2
1986	Cle A	11	11	.500	34	32	5	0-0	210.1	241	126	24	6	95-1	81	4.32	96	.287	.362	0-0	—	0	109	-9	-0.9
1987	Tor A	0	2	.000	3	3	0	0-0	12	15	11	4	0	7-0	7	8.25	55	.306	.393	0-0	—	0	61	-5	-0.6
	Cle A	7	11	.389	22	22	2	0-0	123.2	142	83	18	4	53-1	57	5.89	77	.286	.356	0-0	—	0	85	-14	-1.7
	Year	7	13	.350	25	25	2	0-0	135.2	157	87	22	4	60-1	64	6.10	74	.288	.359	0-0	—	0	82	-21	-2.3
	Atl N	0	0	—	1	1	0	0-0	3	6	5	0	0	6-0	0	15.00	29	.429	.600	1-0	.000	-0	125	-3	-0.2
Total	24	318	274	.537	864	716	245-45	29-5	5404.1	5044	2337	482	123	1809-86	3342	3.35	115	.247	.311	1537-129	.169	-6	97	258	29.2
NIELSEN, JERRY Gerald Arthur B 8.5.1966 Sacramento, CA BL/TL 6-3/185# d7.12																									
1992	NY A	1	0	1.000	20	0	0	0-0	19.2	17	10	1	0	18-2	12	4.58	86	.243	.393	0-0	—	0		-1	0.0
1993	Cal A	0	0	—	10	0	0	0-0	12.1	18	13	1	1	4-0	8	8.03	56	.340	.377	0-0	—	0		-5	-0.2
Total	2	1	0	1.000	30	0	0	0-0	32	35	23	2	1	22-2	20	5.91	70	.285	.387	0-0	—	0		-6	-0.2
NIELSEN, SCOTT Jeffrey Scott B 12.18.1958 Salt Lake City, UT BR/TR 6-1/190# d7.7																									
1986	NY A	4	4	.500	10	9	2-2	0-0	56	66	29	12	2	12-0	20	4.02	102	.299	.340	0-0	—	0	130	0	0.0
1987	Chi A	3	5	.375	19	7	1-1	2-0	66.1	83	48	9	1	25-1	23	6.24	74	.307	.366	0-0	—	0	128	-11	-1.2
1988	NY A	1	2	.333	7	2	0	0-0	19.2	27	16	5	0	13-2	4	6.86	58	.333	.426	0-0	—	0	127	-6	-0.8
1989	NY A	1	0	1.000	2	0	0	0-0	0.2	2	1	0	0	1-0	0	13.50	29	.500	.600	0-0	—	0		-1	-0.1
Total	4	9	11	.450	38	18	3-3	2-0	142.2	178	94	26	3	51-3	47	5.49	78	.309	.367	0-0	—	0	128	-18	-2.1
NIEMANN, RANDY Randal Harold B 11.15.1955 Scotia, CA BL/TL 6-4/200# d5.20 C5																									
1979	Hou N	3	2	.600	26	7	3-2	1-0	67	68	32	1	1	22-3	24	3.76	94	.272	.326	15-1	.133	-0	108	-2	-0.2
1980	Hou N	0	1	.000	22	1	0	1-0	33	40	21	2	0	12-1	18	5.45	60	.299	.354	6-0	.333	1	108	-8	-0.3
1982	Pit N	1	1	.500	20	0	0	1-0	35.1	34	22	1	2	17-4	26	5.09	73	.254	.344	2-0	1.000	1		-5	-0.2
1983	Pit N	0	1	.000	8	1	0	0-0	13.2	20	14	2	1	7-1	8	9.22	40	.357	.431	1-0	.000	-0	95	-7	-0.5
1984	Chi A	0	0	—	5	0	0	0-0	5.1	5	1	0	0	5-1	5	1.69	247	.263	.417	0-0	—	0		1	0.1
1985	NY N	0	0	—	4	0	0	0-0	4.2	5	0	0	0	0-0	2	0.00	—	.278	.278	0-0	—	0		2	0.1
1986	NY N	2	3	.400	31	1	0	0-0	35.2	44	17	2	0	12-2	18	3.79	94	.308	.359	6-0	.333	1	227	-1	0.0
1987	Min A	1	0	1.000	6	0	0	0-0	5.1	3	5	0	2	7-0	1	8.44	55	.158	.429	0-0	—	0		-2	-0.3
Total	8	7	8	.467	122	10	3-2	3-0	200	219	112	8	6	82-12	102	4.64	77	.283	.352	30-1	.267	2	117	-22	-1.3
NIEMES, JACK Jacob Leland B 10.19.1919 Cincinnati, OH D 3.4.1966 Hamilton, OH BR/TL 6-1/180# d5.30 Mil 1944-46																									
1943	Cin N	0	0	—	3	0	0	0	3	5	3	0	0	2	1	6.00	55	.385	.467	0-0	—	0		-1	-0.1
NIESON, CHUCK Charles Bassett B 9.24.1942 Hanford, CA BR/TR 6-2/185# d9.18																									
1964	Min A	0	0	—	2	0	0	0	2	1	1	1	0	1-0	5	4.50	79	.143	.250	0-0	—	0		0	0.0
NIEVES, JUAN Juan Manuel (Cruz) B 1.5.1965 Las Lomas, P.R. BL/TL 6-3/175# d4.10																									
1986	Mil A	11	12	.478	35	33	4-3	0-0	184.2	224	124	17	1	77-0	116	4.92	88	.299	.363	0-0	—	0	102	-15	-1.7
1987	Mil A	14	8	.636	34	33	3-1	0-0	195.2	199	112	24	2	100-5	163	4.88	94	.264	.348	0-0	—	0	115	-5	-0.5
1988	Mil A	7	5	.583	25	15	1-1	1-0	110.1	84	53	13	1	50-4	73	4.08	98	.208	.295	0-0	—	0	113	0	0.0
Total	3	32	25	.561	94	81	8-5	1-0	490.2	507	289	54	4	227-9	352	4.71	92	.266	.343	0-0	—	0	110	-20	-2.2
NIGGELING, JOHNNY John Arnold B 7.10.1903 Remsen, IA D 9.16.1963 LeMars, IA BR/TR 6/170# d4.30																									
1938	Bos N	1	0	1.000	2	0	0	0	2	4	2	0	0	1	1	9.00	38	.400	.455	0-0	—	0		-1	-0.2
1939	Cin N	2	1	.667	10	5	2-1	0	40.1	51	28	2	2	13	20	5.80	66	.309	.367	13-2	.154	-0	132	-8	-0.6
1940	StL A	7	11	.389	28	20	10	0	153.2	148	88	9	5	69	82	4.45	103	.250	.333	51-1	.176	-1	81	1	0.0
1941	StL A	7	9	.438	24	20	13-1	0	168.1	168	83	17	1	63	68	3.80	113	.255	.320	60-4	.167	-1	83	8	0.5
1942	StL A	15	11	.577	28	27	16-3	0	206.1	173	76	10	11	93	107	2.66	139	.226	.319	72-5	.139	-2	86	22	2.3
1943	StL A	6	8	.429	20	20	7	0	150.1	122	61	7	6	57	73	3.17	105	.220	.299	49-5	.061	-4	92	3	-0.3
	Was A	4	2	.667	6	6	5-3	0	51	27	6	0	0	17	24	0.88	363	.153	.227	18-0	.278	1	79	14	2.1

Year	Tm Lg	W	L	Pct	G	GS	CG-Sho	SV-BS	IP	H	R	HR	HB	BB-IB	SO	ERA	AERA	OAV	OOB	AB-SH	AVG	PB	Sup	APR	PW
	Year	10	10	.500	26	26	12-3	0	201.1	149	9	7	6	74	97	2.59	127	.204	.282	67-5	.119	-3	90	16	1.8
1944	Was A	10	8	.556	24	24	14-2	0	206	164	65	5	4	88	121	2.32	141	.221	.307	69-4	.130	-2	92	23	1.7
1945	Was A	7	12	.368	26	25	8-2	0	176.2	161	80	7	3	73	90	3.16	98	.240	.318	59-0	.119	-4	96	-3	-0.8
1946	Was A	3	2	.600	8	6	3	0	38	39	22	1	1	21	10	4.03	83	.265	.361	11-2	.182	0	128	-4	-0.4
	Bos N	2	5	.286	8	8	3	0	58	54	23	2	1	21	24	3.26	105	.243	.311	18-2	.111	-1	59	2	0.1
Total	9	64	69	.481	184	161	81-12	0	1250.2	1111	534	60	34	516	620	3.22	113	.236	.316	420-25	.140	-14	89	57	4.4

NIPPER, AL Albert Samuel B 4.2.1959 San Diego, CA BR/TR 6/194# d9.6 C3

Year	Tm Lg	W	L	Pct	G	GS	CG-Sho	SV-BS	IP	H	R	HR	HB	BB-IB	SO	ERA	AERA	OAV	OOB	AB-SH	AVG	PB	Sup	APR	PW
1983	Bos A	1	1	.500	3	2	1	0-0	16	17	4	0	1	7-0	5	2.25	194	.293	.373	0-0	—	0	42	4	0.4
1984	Bos A	11	6	.647	29	24	6	0-0	182.2	183	86	18	7	52-1	84	3.89	107	.257	.313	0-0	—	0	113	7	0.7
1985	Bos A	9	12	.429	25	25	5	0-0	162	157	83	14	9	82-3	85	4.06	106	.256	.350	0-0	—	0	87	3	0.4
1986	†Bos A	10	12	.455	26	26	3	0-0	159	186	108	24	4	47-2	79	5.38	78	.290	.340	0-0	—	0	105	-22	-2.5
1987	Bos A	11	12	.478	30	30	6	0-0	174	196	115	30	7	62-1	89	5.43	84	.284	.345	0-0	—	0	111	-17	-1.9
1988	Chi N	2	4	.333	22	12	0	1-0	80	72	37	9	3	34-2	27	3.04	119	.238	.321	23-2	.087	-1	102	2	-0.1
1990	Cle A	2	3	.400	9	5	0	0-0	24	35	19	2	2	19-0	12	6.75	58	.354	.448	0-0	—	0	93	-7	-1.3
Total	7	46	50	.479	144	124	21	1-0	797.2	846	452	97	33	303-9	381	4.52	93	.271	.339	23-2	.087	-1	103	-30	-4.3

NIPPERT, MERLIN Merlin Lee B 9.1.1938 Mangum, OK BR/TR 6-1/175# d9.12

Year	Tm Lg	W	L	Pct	G	GS	CG-Sho	SV-BS	IP	H	R	HR	HB	BB-IB	SO	ERA	AERA	OAV	OOB	AB-SH	AVG	PB	Sup	APR	PW
1962	Bos A	0	0	—	4	0	0	0	6	4	3	1	0	4-1	3	4.50	92	.200	.320	0-0	—	0		0	0.0

NISCHWITZ, RON Ronald Lee B 7.1.1937 Dayton, OH BB/TL 6-3/205# d9.4

Year	Tm Lg	W	L	Pct	G	GS	CG-Sho	SV-BS	IP	H	R	HR	HB	BB-IB	SO	ERA	AERA	OAV	OOB	AB-SH	AVG	PB	Sup	APR	PW
1961	Det A	0	1	.000	6	1	0	0	11.1	13	12	2	0	8-1	8	5.56	74	.295	.382	2-0	.000	-0	108	-3	-0.3
1962	Det A	4	5	.444	48	0	0	4	64.2	73	30	5	1	26-1	28	3.90	104	.285	.351	12-0	.417	2		2	0.5
1963	Cle A	0	2	.000	14	0	0	1	16.2	17	13	3	0	8-2	10	6.48	56	.262	.342	1-0	.000	-0		-5	-0.6
1965	Det A	1	0	1.000	20	0	0	1	22.2	21	10	2	0	6-1	12	2.78	125	.259	.307	3-0	.000	-0		1	0.0
Total	4	5	8	.385	88	1	0	6	115.1	124	65	12	1	48-5	58	4.21	92	.278	.345	18-0	.278	1	108	-5	-0.4

NITCHOLAS, OTHO Otho James B 9.13.1908 McKinney, TX D 9.11.1986 McKinney, TX BR/TR 6/190# d4.18

Year	Tm Lg	W	L	Pct	G	GS	CG-Sho	SV-BS	IP	H	R	HR	HB	BB-IB	SO	ERA	AERA	OAV	OOB	AB-SH	AVG	PB	Sup	APR	PW
1945	Bro N	1	0	1.000	7	0	0	0	18.2	19	14	4	0	1	4	5.30	71	.257	.267	4-0	.250	0		-3	-0.2

NITKOWSKI, C. J. Christopher John B 3.9.1973 Suffern, NY BL/TL 6-2/185# d6.3

Year	Tm Lg	W	L	Pct	G	GS	CG-Sho	SV-BS	IP	H	R	HR	HB	BB-IB	SO	ERA	AERA	OAV	OOB	AB-SH	AVG	PB	Sup	APR	PW
1995	Cin N	1	3	.250	9	7	0	0-1	32.1	41	25	4	2	15-1	18	6.12	67	.306	.382	10-0	.200	0	72	-8	-0.8
	Det A	1	4	.200	11	11	0	0-0	39.1	53	32	7	3	20-2	13	7.09	67	.335	.413	0-0	—	0	71	-9	-1.0
1996	Det A	2	3	.400	11	8	0	0-0	45.2	62	44	7	7	38-1	36	8.08	63	.332	.457	0-0	—	0	142	-15	-1.3
1998	Hou N	3	3	.500	43	0	0	3-2	59.2	49	27	4	6	23-2	44	3.77	108	.228	.317	4-1	.000	-0		2	0.2
1999	Det A	4	5	.444	68	7	0	0-0	81.2	63	44	11	3	45-3	66	4.30	115	.213	.319	1-0	.000	-0*	105	5	0.5
2000	Det A	4	9	.308	67	11	0	0-2	109.2	124	79	13	4	49-3	81	5.25	92	.286	.358	0-0	—	0	97	-10	-0.8
2001	Det A	0	3	.000	56	0	0	0-6	45.1	51	30	7	5	31-7	38	5.56	78	.283	.401	0-0	—	0		-6	-0.3
	NY N	1	0	1.000	5	0	0	0-0	5.2	3	0	0	0	3-1	4	0.00	—	.167	.286	0-0	—	0		3	0.4
2002	Tex A	0	1	.000	12	0	0	0-0	13.2	11	4	0	0	13-0	14	2.63	180	.224	.387	0-0	—	0		3	0.2
2003	Tex A	0	0	—	6	0	0	0-0	9.2	17	8	0	0	8-1	5	7.45	67	.415	.490	0-0	—	0		-2	-0.1
Total	8	16	31	.340	288	44	0	3-11	442.2	474	293	53	30	245-21	319	5.33	87	.277	.373	15-1	.133	-1	99	-37	-3.0

NIXON, WILLARD Willard Lee B 6.17.1928 Taylorsville, GA D 12.10.2000 Rome, GA BL/TR 6-2/195# d7.7

Year	Tm Lg	W	L	Pct	G	GS	CG-Sho	SV-BS	IP	H	R	HR	HB	BB-IB	SO	ERA	AERA	OAV	OOB	AB-SH	AVG	PB	Sup	APR	PW
1950	Bos A	8	6	.571	22	15	2	2	101.1	126	75	7	2	58	57	6.04	81	.310	.398	36-3	.139	-1	103	-12	-1.6
1951	Bos A	7	4	.636	33	14	2-1	1	125	136	79	12	7	56	70	4.90	91	.285	.368	45-1	.289	3*	129	-7	-0.3
1952	Bos A	5	4	.556	23	13	5	0	103.2	115	64	12	4	61	50	4.86	81	.290	.390	53-0	.208	1*	128	-10	-0.7
1953	Bos A	4	8	.333	23	15	5-1	0	116.2	114	57	6	1	59	57	3.93	107	.254	.343	42-1	.190	0	99	4	0.4
1954	Bos A	11	12	.478	31	30	8-2	0	199.2	182	102	16	9	87	102	4.06	101	.248	.333	68-2	.265	5	88	2	0.8
1955	Bos A	12	10	.545	31	31	7-3	0	208	207	102	10	3	85-2	95	4.07	105	.259	.330	69-4	.261	5	84	7	1.3
1956	Bos A	9	8	.529	23	22	9-1	0	145.1	142	79	9	8	57-2	74	4.21	110	.255	.331	54-2	.204	-1	106	6	0.6
1957	Bos A	12	13	.480	29	29	11-1	0	191	207	86	10	7	56-3	96	3.68	108	.280	.335	75-0	.293	5*	114	7	1.3
1958	Bos A	1	7	.125	10	8	2	0	43.1	48	30	7	0	11-0	15	6.02	67	.281	.324	17-0	.294	1	73	-8	-1.2
Total	9	69	72	.489	225	177	51-9	3	1234	1277	674	89	41	530-7	616	4.39	97	.270	.348	459-13	.242	17	101	-11	0.6

NOLAN, THE ONLY Edward Sylvester B 11.7.1857 Paterson, NJ D 5.18.1913 Paterson, NJ BL/TR 5-8/171# d5.1

Year	Tm Lg	W	L	Pct	G	GS	CG-Sho	SV-BS	IP	H	R	HR	HB	BB-IB	SO	ERA	AERA	OAV	OOB	AB-SH	AVG	PB	Sup	APR	PW
1878	Ind N	13	22	.371	38	38	37-1	0	347	357	208	1		56	125	2.57	79	.253	.281	152	.243	6	99	-21	-1.0
1881	Cle N	8	14	.364	22	21	20	0	180	183	111	3		38	54	3.05	86	.251	.288	168	.244	1*	79	-9	-0.9
1883	Pit AA	0	7	.000	7	7	6	0	55	81	44	0		10	23	4.25	76	.321	.347	26	.308	1	73	-7	-0.5
1884	Wil U	1	4	.200	5	5	5	0	40	44	28	1		7	52	2.93	91	.262	.291	33	.273	-0*	32	-1	0.0
1885	Phi N	1	5	.167	7	7	6	0	54	55	43	1		24	20	4.17	67	.256	.331	26	.077	-2	49	-7	-0.7
Total	5	23	52	.307	79	78	74-1	0	676	720	434	6		135	274	2.98	80	.259	.294	405	.240	6	82	-45	-3.1

NOLAN, GARY Gary Lynn B 5.27.1948 Herlong, CA BR/TR 6-2.5/197# d4.15

Year	Tm Lg	W	L	Pct	G	GS	CG-Sho	SV-BS	IP	H	R	HR	HB	BB-IB	SO	ERA	AERA	OAV	OOB	AB-SH	AVG	PB	Sup	APR	PW
1967	Cin N	14	8	.636	33	32	8-5	0	226.2	193	73	18	5	62-7	206	2.58	145	.228	.282	67-8	.104	-1	69	27	2.4
1968	Cin N	9	4	.692	23	22	4-2	0	150	105	48	10	3	49-1	111	2.40	132	.196	.266	46-7	.130	2	122	11	1.1
1969	Cin N	8	8	.500	16	15	2-1	0-0	108.2	102	45	11	0	40-3	83	3.56	106	.247	.312	35-8	.229	3*	107	4	0.9
1970	†Cin N	18	7	.720	37	37	4-2	0-0	250.2	226	102	25	1	96-9	181	3.27	124	.240	.309	82-9	.159	1	100	23	2.0
1971	Cin N	12	15	.444	35	35	9	0-0	244.2	208	91	12	2	59-11	146	3.16	106	.227	.275	75-6	.147	-1	92	6	0.6
1972	†Cin N✣	15	5	**.750**	25	25	6-2	0-0	176	147	48	13	1	30-5	90	1.99	161	.227	.259	60-4	.117	-1	131	23	2.6
1973	Cin N	0	1	.000	2	2	0	0-0	10.1	6	4	1	0	7-1	3	3.48	98	.167	.295	2-0	.000	0	13	0	0.0
1975	†Cin N	15	9	.625	32	32	5-1	0-0	210.2	202	75	18	1	29-5	74	3.16	114	.251	.275	68-6	.176	2	123	13	1.5
1976	†Cin N	15	9	.625	34	34	7-1	0-0	239.1	232	96	28	1	27-3	113	3.46	101	.254	.275	79-6	.101	-3	119	4	-0.2
1977	Cin N	4	1	.800	8	8	0	0-0	39.1	53	22	5	0	12-1	28	4.81	82	.321	.367	15-2	.067	-1	141	-4	-0.5
	Cal A	0	3	.000	5	5	0	0-0	18.1	31	19	5	0	2-0	4	8.84	44	.365	.371	0-0	—	0*	87	-10	-1.2
Total	10	110	70	.611	250	247	45-14	0-0	1674.2	1505	623	146	14	413-46	1039	3.08	116	.239	.285	529-56	.138	0	106	97	9.2

NOLD, DICK Richard Louis B 5.4.1943 San Francisco, CA BR/TR 6-2/190# d8.19

Year	Tm Lg	W	L	Pct	G	GS	CG-Sho	SV-BS	IP	H	R	HR	HB	BB-IB	SO	ERA	AERA	OAV	OOB	AB-SH	AVG	PB	Sup	APR	PW
1967	Was A	0	2	.000	7	3	0	0	20.1	19	13	1	0	13-0	10	4.87	65	.241	.348	3-0	.000	-0	92	-4	-0.4

NOLES, DICKIE Dickie Ray B 11.19.1956 Charlotte, NC BR/TR 6-2/190# d7.5

Year	Tm Lg	W	L	Pct	G	GS	CG-Sho	SV-BS	IP	H	R	HR	HB	BB-IB	SO	ERA	AERA	OAV	OOB	AB-SH	AVG	PB	Sup	APR	PW
1979	Phi N	3	4	.429	14	14	0	0-0	90	80	40	6	2	38-2	42	3.80	101	.246	.325	30-1	.100	-1	87	1	0.0
1980	†Phi N	1	4	.200	48	3	0	6-1	81	80	42	5	1	42-11	57	3.89	98	.254	.342	13-2	.308	1	149	-2	-0.1
1981	†Phi N	2	2	.500	13	8	0	0-0	58.1	57	30	2	3	23-2	34	4.17	87	.260	.336	19-2	.105	-1	113	-4	-0.4
1982	Chi N	10	13	.435	31	30	2-2	0-0	171	180	99	11	5	61-2	85	4.42	85	.274	.336	56-4	.107	-2	97	-14	-2.0
1983	Chi N	5	10	.333	24	18	1-1	0-0	116.1	133	69	9	1	37-3	59	4.72	81	.287	.339	38-3	.237	1	89	-12	-1.3
1984	Chi N	2	2	.500	21	1	0	0-3	50.2	60	29	4	1	16-1	14	5.15	76	.305	.356	10-0	.000	-1	0	-5	-0.5
	Tex A	2	3	.400	18	6	0	0-0	57.2	60	38	6	5	30-0	39	5.15	81	.262	.360	0-0	—	0	131	-6	-0.6
1985	Tex A	4	8	.333	28	13	0	1-0	110.1	129	67	11	6	33-1	59	5.06	84	.289	.346	0-0	—	0	83	-9	-0.9
1986	Cle A	3	2	.600	32	0	0	0-0	54.2	56	33	9	5	30-4	32	5.10	81	.269	.367	0-0	—	0		-5	-0.4
1987	Chi N	4	2	.667	41	1	0	2-2	64.1	59	31	1	5	27-1	33	3.50	122	.239	.325	11-0	.000	-1	0	4	0.3
	Det A	0	0	—	4	0	0	2-1	2	2	1	0	0	1-0	0	4.50	94	.250	.333	0-0	—	0		0	0.0
1988	Bal A	0	2	.000	2	2	0	0-0	3.1	11	10	2	1	0-0	1	24.30	16	.500	.522	0-0	—	0	117	-8	-1.1
1990	Phi N	0	1	.000	1	0	0	0-0	0.1	2	1	0	0	0-0	0	27.00	14	.667	.667	0-0	—	0		-1	-0.2
Total	11	36	53	.404	277	96	3-3	11-7	860	909	490	66	35	338-27	455	4.56	86	.272	.343	177-12	.136	-3	94	-61	-7.2

NOLTE, ERIC Eric Carl B 4.28.1964 Canoga Park, CA BL/TL 6-3/205# d8.1

Year	Tm Lg	W	L	Pct	G	GS	CG-Sho	SV-BS	IP	H	R	HR	HB	BB-IB	SO	ERA	AERA	OAV	OOB	AB-SH	AVG	PB	Sup	APR	PW
1987	SD N	2	6	.250	12	12	1	0-0	67.1	57	28	6	2	36-2	44	3.21	123	.226	.326	21-3	.095	-1	78	5	0.5
1988	SD N	0	0	—	2	0	0	0-0	3	3	2	1	0	2-0	1	6.00	57	.273	.385	0-0	—	0		-1	0.0
1989	SD N	0	0	—	3	1	0	0-0	9	15	12	1	0	7-1	8	11.00	32	.375	.458	2-0	.000	-0	278	-7	-0.4
1991	SD N	3	2	.600	6	6	0	0-0	22	37	27	6	0	10-0	15	11.05	34	.378	.423	9-2	.111	-0	126	-16	-2.6
	Tex A	0	0	—	3	0	0	0-0	2.2	3	1	0	0	3-0	1	3.38	120	.273	.429	0-0	—	0		0	0.0
Total	4	5	8	.385	26	19	1	0-0	104	115	70	14	2	58-3	69	5.63	69	.279	.367	32-5	.094	-1	103	-19	-2.5

Year	Tm Lg	W	L	Pct	G	GS	CG-Sho	SV-BS	IP	H	R	HR	HB	BB-IB	SO	ERA	AERA	OAV	OOB	AB-SH	AVG	PB	Sup	APR	PW
NOMO, HIDEO Hideo B 8.31.1968 Osaka, Japan BR/TR 6-2/210# d5.2																									
1995	†LA N★	13	6	.684	28	28	4-**3**	0-0	191.1	124	63	14	5	78-2	**236**	2.54	149	**.182**	.269	66-5	.091	-4	106	29	2.1
1996	†LA N	16	11	.593	33	33	3-2	0-0	228.1	180	93	23	2	85-6	234	3.19	121	.218	.290	75-10	.133	-0	98	19	1.9
1997	LA N	14	12	.538	33	33	1	0-0	207.1	193	104	23	9	92-2	233	4.25	91	.243	.328	69-5	.159	2	121	-8	-0.9
1998	LA N	2	7	.222	12	12	2	0-0	67.2	57	39	8	3	38-0	73	5.05	78	.228	.334	20-2	.050	-1	52	-7	-0.9
	NY N	4	5	.444	17	16	1	0-0	89.2	73	49	11	1	56-2	94	4.82	86	.224	.337	30-2	.267	2	110	-6	-0.4
	Year	6	12	.333	29	28	3	0-0	157.1	130	54	19	4	94-2	167	4.92	83	.226	.336	50-4	.180	1	86	-14	-1.3
1999	Mil N	12	8	.600	28	28	0	0-0	176.1	173	96	27	3	78-2	161	4.54	100	.256	.333	56-7	.214	2*	111	0	0.2
2000	Det A	8	12	.400	32	31	1	0-0	190	191	102	31	3	89-1	181	4.74	102	.263	.344	6-0	.000	-1	90	5	0.4
2001	Bos A	13	10	.565	33	33	2-2	0-0	198	171	105	26	3	96-2	**220**	4.50	100	.231	.320	5-0	.200	0	107	2	0.2
2002	LA N	16	6	.727	34	34	0	0-0	220.1	189	92	26	2	101-5	193	3.39	113	.236	.321	63-6	.063	-1	117	10	0.7
2003	LA N	16	13	.552	33	33	2-2	0-0	218.1	175	82	24	1	98-6	177	3.09	130	.223	.309	65-6	.138	1	77	24	3.0
Total	9	114	90	.559	283	281	16-9	0-0	1787.1	1526	825	213	32	811-28	1802	3.85	107	.231	.316	455-43	.136	-0	102	68	6.3
NOMURA, TAKAHITO Takahito B 1.10.1969 Kouchi Prefecture, Japan BL/TL 5-7/175# d4.3																									
2002	Mil N	0	0	—	21	0	0	0-1	13.2	11	14	2	2	18-4	9	8.56	48	.224	.437	0-0	—	0		-7	-0.3
NOPS, JERRY Jeremiah H. B 6.23.1875 Toledo, OH D 3.26.1937 Camden, NJ BL/TL 5-8.5/168# d9.7																									
1896	Phi N	1	0	1.000	1	1	1	0	7	11	5	0	0	1	1	5.14	84	.355	.375	4-0	.000	-1	165	0	-0.1
	Bal N	2	1	.667	3	3	3	0	22	29	15	0	0	2	8	6.14	70	.315	.330	9-0	.111	-1	105	-2	-0.3
	Year	3	1	.750	4	4	4	0	29	40	21	0	0	3	9	5.90	73	.325	.341	13-0	.077	-2	120	-3	-0.4
1897	†Bal N	20	6	.769	30	25	23-1	0	220.2	235	107	5	9	52	69	2.81	148	.270	.318	92-2	.196	-3	97	31	2.5
1898	Bal N	16	9	.640	33	29	23-2	0	235	241	130	5	16	78	91	3.56	100	.263	.332	91-1	.220	2	99	2	0.1
1899	Bal N	17	11	.607	33	33	26-2	0	259	296	156	1	11	71	60	4.03	98	.287	.339	105-0	.276	1*	93	2	0.1
1900	Bro N	4	4	.500	9	8	6-1	0	68	79	45	1	2	18	22	3.84	100	.289	.338	25-0	.160	-1	104	-2	-0.3
1901	Bal A	12	10	.545	27	23	17-1	1	176.2	192	123	5	13	59	43	4.08	95	.274	.341	59-4	.220	-0	96	-3	-0.6
Total	6	72	41	.637	136	122	99-7	1	988.1	1083	581	17	51	281	294	3.70	106	.277	.333	385-7	.221	-2	97	28	1.4
NORIEGA, JOHN John Alan B 12.20.1943 Ogden, UT BR/TR 6-4/185# d5.1																									
1969	Cin N	0	0	—	5	0	0	0-0	7.2	12	6	1	0	3-0	4	5.87	64	.400	.429	0-0	—	0		-2	-0.1
1970	Cin N	0	0	—	8	0	0	0-0	18	25	17	0	2	10-1	6	8.00	51	.333	.420	4-0	.250	0		-7	-0.3
Total	2	0	0	—	13	0	0	0-0	25.2	37	23	1	2	13-1	10	7.36	54	.352	.423	4-0	.250	0		-9	-0.4
NORMAN, FRED Fredie Hubert B 8.20.1942 San Antonio, TX BB/TL 5-8/160# d9.21																									
1962	KC A	0	0	—	2	0	0	0	4	4	1	0	0	1-0	2	2.25	188	.250	.294	0-0	—	0		1	0.0
1963	KC A	0	1	.000	2	2	0	0	6.1	9	9	1	0	7-0	6	11.37	34	.346	.471	1-0	.000	-0	80	-5	-0.6
1964	Chi N	0	4	.000	8	5	0	0	31.2	34	25	9	1	21-5	20	6.54	57	.279	.389	11-0	.091	-1	62	-9	-1.1
1966	Chi N	0	0	—	2	0	0	0	4	5	2	0	0	2-1	6	4.50	82	.313	.389	0-0	—	0		0	0.0
1967	Chi N	0	0	—	1	0	0	0	1	0	0	0	0	0-0	3	0.00	—	.000	.000	0-0	—	0		0	0.0
1970	LA N	2	0	1.000	30	0	0	1-1	62	65	40	8	2	33-1	47	5.23	73	.273	.364	7-2	.143	0		-10	-0.5
	StL N	0	0	—	1	0	0	0-0	1	1	0	0	0	0-0	0	0.00	—	.333	.250	0-0	—	0		0	0.0
	Year	2	0	1.000	31	0	0	1-1	63	66	43	8	2	33-1	47	5.14	75	.274	.362	7-2	.143	0		-9	-0.5
1971	StL N	0	0	—	4	0	0	0-0	3.2	7	5	1	0	7-0	4	12.27	29	.438	.583	0-0	—	0		-3	-0.2
	SD N	3	12	.200	20	18	5	0-1	127.1	114	48	7	2	56-7	77	3.32	99	.240	.321	38-3	.237	2*	51	3	0.6
	Year	3	12	.200	24	18	5	0-1	131	121	50	8	2	63-7	81	3.57	93	.246	.332	38-3	.237	2	51	-2	0.4
1972	SD N	9	11	.450	42	28	10-6	2-0	211.2	195	88	18	2	88-12	167	3.44	96	.244	.318	64-5	.125	1*	104	-2	-0.1
1973	SD N	1	7	.125	12	11	1	0-0	74	72	35	9	1	29-2	49	4.26	82	.262	.332	22-1	.136	-0	58	-4	-0.4
	†Cin N	12	6	.667	24	24	7-3	0-0	166.1	136	67	18	1	72-9	112	3.30	103	.224	.304	58-6	.052	-4	134	2	-0.2
	Year	13	13	.500	36	35	8-3	0-0	240.1	208	72	27	2	101-11	161	3.60	95	.236	.313	80-7	.075	-4	109	-1	-0.6
1974	Cin N	13	12	.520	35	26	8-2	0-1	186.1	170	69	15	2	68-9	141	3.14	111	.241	.307	61-7	.131	-2	124	10	0.9
1975	†Cin N	12	4	.750	34	26	2	0-0	188	163	85	23	0	84-5	119	3.73	97	.235	.316	60-9	.117	-2	130	-3	-0.5
1976	†Cin N	12	7	.632	33	24	8-3	0-0	180.1	153	71	10	3	70-5	126	3.09	113	.231	.305	50-7	.140	-1	118	7	0.4
1977	Cin N	14	13	.519	35	34	8-1	0-1	221.1	200	97	28	3	98-9	160	3.38	117	.241	.322	73-6	.110	-2	100	10	0.9
1978	Cin N	11	9	.550	36	31	0	1-0	177.1	173	86	19	3	82-6	111	3.70	96	.255	.336	50-8	.140	-1	102	-5	-0.6
1979	†Cin N	11	13	.458	34	31	5	0-0	195.1	193	86	14	0	57-4	95	3.64	103	.258	.309	59-6	.153	0	105	3	0.3
1980	Mon N	4	4	.500	48	8	2	4-0	98	96	50	8	3	40-4	58	4.13	86	.259	.333	20-2	.050	-2	91	-6	-0.8
Total	16	104	103	.502	403	268	56-15	8-4	1939.2	1790	864	188	23	815-79	1303	3.64	98	.246	.321	574-62	.125	-11	105	-11	-1.9
NORRIS, MIKE Michael Kelvin B 3.19.1955 San Francisco, CA BR/TR 6-2/175# d4.10																									
1975	Oak A	1	0	1.000	4	3	1-1	0-0	16.2	6	2	0	0	8-0	5	0.00	—	.107	.215	0-0	—	0	137	6	0.4
1976	Oak A	4	5	.444	24	19	1-1	0-0	96	91	53	10	2	56-2	44	4.78	70	.250	.350	0-0	—	0	117	-14	-1.0
1977	Oak A	2	7	.222	16	12	1-1	0-0	77.1	77	45	14	4	31-1	35	4.77	85	.260	.336	1-0	.000	-0*	78	-5	-0.5
1978	Oak A	0	5	.000	14	5	1	0-0	49	46	35	2	3	35-1	36	5.51	66	.249	.373	0-0	—	0*	64	-10	-0.9
1979	Oak A	5	8	.385	29	18	3	0-0	146.1	146	87	11	9	94-9	96	4.80	85	.265	.376	0-0	—	0	83	-12	-1.0
1980	Oak A	22	9	.710	33	33	24-1	0-0	284.1	215	88	18	6	83-2	180	2.53	149	**.209**	.270	0-0	—	0	111	**43**	4.7
1981	†Oak A★	12	9	.571	23	23	12-2	0-0	172.2	145	77	17	10	63-0	78	3.75	93	.228	.305	0-0	—	0	106	-4	-0.5
1982	Oak A	7	11	.389	28	28	7-1	0-0	166.1	154	103	25	6	84-1	83	4.76	82	.242	.335	0-0	—	0*	92	-19	-1.7
1983	Oak A	4	5	.444	16	16	2	0-0	88.2	68	42	11	3	36-0	63	3.76	103	.213	.297	0-0	—	0	98	1	0.0
1990	Oak A	1	0	1.000	14	0	0	0-0	27	24	10	0	2	9-0	16	3.00	124	.242	.315	0-0	—	0		2	0.1
Total	10	58	59	.496	201	157	52-7	0-0	1124.1	972	542	108	45	499-16	636	3.89	97	.233	.319	1-0	.000	-0	99	-12	-0.4
NORTH, LOU Louis Alexander B 6.15.1891 Elgin, IL D 5.15.1974 Shelton, CT BR/TR 5-11/175# d8.22 Mil 1918																									
1913	Det A	0	1	.000	1	1	0	0	6	10	11	1	0	9	3	15.00	19	.370	.528	2-0	.000	-0	178	-7	-0.8
1917	StL N	0	0	—	5	0	0	0	11.1	14	5	1	0	4	4	3.97	68	.350	.409	3-0	.000	-0		-1	-0.1
1920	StL N	3	2	.600	24	6	3	1	88	90	42	3	2	32	37	3.27	91	.278	.346	31-1	.226	0*	145	-4	-0.3
1921	StL N	4	4	.500	40	0	0	**7**	86.1	81	39	5	1	32	28	3.54	103	.256	.327	19-0	.158	-1		**2**	0.1
1922	StL N	10	3	.769	**53**	10	4	4	149.2	164	90	4	6	64	84	4.45	87	.283	.361	47-2	.234	2	131	-10	-0.5
1923	StL N	3	4	.429	34	3	0	1	71.2	90	50	8	3	31	24	5.15	76	.308	.380	22-0	.182	-1	211	-10	-0.9
1924	StL N	0	0	—	6	1	0	0	14.2	15	12	1	0	9	8	6.75	56	.273	.375	4-0	.250	-0	135	-4	-0.2
	Bos N	1	2	.333	9	4	1	0	35.1	45	25	1	0	19	11	5.35	71	.321	.403	9-0	.111	-1	89	-6	-0.6
	Year	1	2	.333	15	5	1	0	50	60	29	2	0	28	19	5.76	66	.308	.395	13-0	.154	-1	98	-11	-0.8
Total	7	21	16	.568	172	25	8	13	463	509	274	24	12	200	199	4.43	82	.287	.363	137-3	.197	-1	139	-40	-3.3
NORTHROP, JAKE George Howard "Jerky" B 3.5.1888 Monroeton, PA D 11.16.1945 Monroeton, PA BL/TR 5-11/170# d7.29																									
1918	Bos N	5	1	.833	7	4	4-1	0	40	26	9	0	0	3	4	1.35	199	.183	.200	13-2	.154	-1	106	6	0.8
1919	Bos N	1	5	.167	11	3	2	0	37.1	43	22	2	1	10	9	4.58	62	.301	.351	8-1	.500	3	74	-7	-0.6
Total	2	6	6	.500	18	7	6-1	0	77.1	69	31	2	1	13	13	2.91	95	.242	.278	21-3	.286	2	92	-1	0.2
NORTON, EFFIE Elisha Strong "Leiter" B 8.17.1873 Conneaut, OH D 3.5.1950 Aspinwall, PA BR/TR 5-10.5/170# d8.8																									
1896	Was N	3	1	.750	8	5	2	0	44	49	25	2	6	14	13	3.07	144	.280	.354	19-0	.211	-0	87	6	0.4
1897	Was N	2	1	.667	4	2	1	0	17	31	18	0	0	11	3	6.88	63	.387	.462	18-0	.278	1*	90	-4	-0.5
Total	2	5	2	.714	12	7	3	0	61	80	43	2	6	25	16	4.13	106	.314	.388	37-0	.243	0	88	2	-0.1
NORTON, PHIL Phillip Douglas B 2.1.1976 Texarkana, TX BR/TL 6-1/190# d8.3																									
2000	Chi N	0	1	.000	2	2	0	0-0	8.2	14	10	5	0	7-0	6	9.35	49	.350	.447	3-1	.667	1	101	-5	-0.4
2003	Chi N	0	0	—	4	0	0	0-0	3.1	2	2	0	0	3-0	0	5.40	78	.182	.357	0-0	—	0		0	0.0
	Cin N	0	0	—	17	0	0	0-0	14.2	7	4	0	0	6-0	7	2.45	174	.149	.245	1-0	.000	-0		3	0.1
	Year	0	0	—	21	0	0	0-0	18	9	11	0	0	9-0	7	3.00	142	.155	.269	1-0	.000	-0		3	0.1
Total	2	0	1	.000	23	2	0	0-0	26.2	23	16	5	0	16-0	13	5.06	86	.235	.342	4-1	.500	1	101	-2	-0.3
NORTON, TOM Thomas John B 4.26.1950 Elyria, OH BR/TR 6-1/200# d4.18																									
1972	Min A	0	1	.000	21	0	0	0-0	32.1	31	14	1	1	14-0	22	2.78	116	.252	.333	0-0	—	0		1	0.1

Year	Tm Lg	W	L	Pct	G	GS	CG-Sho	SV-BS	IP	H	R	HR	HB	BB-IB	SO	ERA	AERA	OAV	OOB	AB-SH	AVG	PB	Sup	APR	PW
NOSEK, RANDY Randall William B 1.8.1967 Omaha, NE BR/TR 6-4/215# d5.27																									
1989	Det A	0	2	.000	2	2	0	0-0	5.1	7	8	2	0	10-0	4	13.50	28	.333	.548	0-0	—	0	47	-5	-0.9
1990	Det A	1	1	.500	3	2	0	0-0	7	7	7	1	0	9-1	3	7.71	51	.280	.457	0-0	—	0	103	-3	-0.6
Total	2	1	3	.250	5	4	0	0-0	12.1	14	15	3	0	19-1	7	10.22	38	.304	.500	0-0	—	0	76	-8	-1.5
NOTTEBART, DON Donald Edward B 1.23.1936 West Newton, MA BR/TR 6-1/190# d7.1																									
1960	Mil N	1	0	1.000	5	1	0	1	15.1	14	10	0	0	15-2	8	4.11	83	.233	.387	5-0	.000	-1	180	-2	-0.2
1961	Mil N	6	7	.462	38	11	2	3	126.1	117	61	11	2	48-2	66	4.06	92	.251	.321	38-1	.184	0	103	-4	-0.3
1962	Mil N	2	2	.500	39	0	0	2	64	64	30	4	4	20-3	36	3.23	117	.258	.321	6-0	.333	1		2	0.3
1963	Hou N	11	8	.579	31	27	9-2	0	193	170	80	10	1	39-1	118	3.17	99	.234	.272	66-3	.167	0	101	-1	-0.1
1964	Hou N	6	11	.353	28	24	2	0	157	165	76	12	1	37-1	90	3.90	88	.275	.314	47-5	.064	-2	89	-7	-0.8
1965	Hou N	4	15	.211	29	25	3	0	158	166	99	14	5	55-11	77	4.67	72	.273	.337	48-4	.104	-1	104	-27	-2.9
1966	Cin N	5	4	.556	59	1	0	11	111.1	97	45	11	2	43-5	69	3.07	127	.235	.309	24-1	.167	-0	45	8	0.8
1967	Cin N	0	3	.000	47	0	0	4	79.1	75	25	4	2	19-4	48	1.93	194	.253	.299	3-2	.000	-0		12	0.7
1969	NY A	0	0	—	4	0	0	0-0	6	6	3	1	1	0-0	5	4.50	77	.261	.292	0-0	—	0		-1	0.0
	Chi N	1	1	.500	16	0	0	0-0	18	28	14	2	0	7-0	8	7.00	58	.350	.398	1-0	.000	0		-5	-0.5
Total	9	36	51	.414	296	89	16-2	21-0	928.1	902	443	69	18	283-29	525	3.65	96	.256	.312	238-16	.134	-3	95	-25	-3.0
NOURSE, CHET Chester Linwood B 8.7.1887 Ipswich, MA D 4.20.1958 Clearwater, FL BR/TR 6-3/185# d7.27																									
1909	Bos A	0	0	—	3	0	0	0	5	5	5	0	0	5	3	7.20	35	.263	.417	2-0	.000	-0		-2	-0.2
NOVOA, RAFAEL Rafael Angel B 10.26.1967 New York, NY BL/TL 6/180# d7.31																									
1990	SF N	0	1	.000	7	2	0	1-0	18.2	21	14	3	0	13-1	14	6.75	54	.284	.386	5-0	.200	0	111	-6	-0.3
1993	Mil A	0	3	.000	15	7	2	0-0	56	58	32	7	4	22-2	17	4.50	95	.267	.343	0-0	—	0	68	-2	-0.1
Total	2	0	4	.000	22	9	2	1-0	74.2	79	46	10	4	35-3	31	5.06	81	.271	.354	5-0	.200	0	77	-8	-0.4
NOYES, WIN Winfield Charles B 6.16.1889 Pleasanton, NE D 4.8.1969 Cashmere, WA BR/TR 6/180# d5.19 Mil 1918																									
1913	Bos N	0	0	—	11	0	0	0	20.2	22	18	1	4	6	5	4.79	69	.289	.372	4-0	.250	0		-4	-0.2
1917	Phi A	10	10	.500	27	22	11-1	1	171	156	74	5	4	77	64	2.95	93	.258	.345	52-2	.115	-2	95	-2	-0.5
1919	Phi A	1	5	.167	10	6	3	0	49	66	34	1	1	15	20	5.69	60	.332	.381	16-0	.125	-1	88	-10	-1.1
	Chi A	0	0	—	1	1	0	0	6	10	5	0	0	0	4	7.50	42	.385	.385	2-0	.500	0	123	-2	-0.1
	Year	1	5	.167	11	7	3	0	55	76	10	1	1	15	24	5.89	58	.338	.382	18-0	.167	-1	92	-12	-1.2
Total	3	11	15	.423	49	29	14-1	1	246.2	254	131	7	9	98	93	3.76	78	.280	.356	74-2	.135	-3	93	-18	-1.9
NUNEZ, EDWIN Edwin (Martinez) B 5.27.1963 Humacao, P.R. BR/TR 6-5/237# d4.7																									
1982	Sea A	1	2	.333	8	5	0	0-0	35.1	36	18	7	0	16-0	27	4.58	93	.269	.347	0-0	—	0	107	0	0.0
1983	Sea A	0	4	.000	14	5	0	0-0	37	40	21	3	3	22-1	35	4.38	98	.278	.385	0-0	—	0	51	-1	-0.1
1984	Sea A	2	2	.500	37	0	0	7-2	67.2	55	26	8	3	21-2	57	3.19	125	.218	.283	0-0	—	0		6	0.4
1985	Sea A	7	3	.700	70	0	0	16-5	90.1	79	36	13	0	34-5	58	3.09	136	.234	.302	0-0	—	0		10	1.4
1986	Sea A	1	2	.333	14	1	0	0-2	21.2	25	15	5	0	5-1	17	5.82	73	.284	.323	0-0	—	0	64	-3	-0.4
1987	Sea A	3	4	.429	48	0	0	12-5	47.1	45	20	7	1	18-3	34	3.80	125	.262	.328	0-0	—	0		6	1.0
1988	Sea A	1	4	.200	14	3	0	0-0	29.1	45	33	4	2	14-3	19	7.98	52	.366	.427	0-0	—	0	66	-13	-1.9
	NY N	1	0	1.000	10	0	0	0-0	14	21	7	1	0	3-0	8	4.50	72	.339	.369	0-0	—	0		-2	-0.1
1989	Det A	3	4	.429	27	0	0	1-2	54	49	33	6	0	36-13	41	4.17	92	.254	.366	0-0	—	0		-4	-0.5
1990	Det A	3	1	.750	42	0	0	6-1	80.1	65	26	4	2	37-6	66	2.24	177	.218	.308	0-0	—	0		13	0.7
1991	Mil A	2	1	.667	23	0	0	8-1	25.1	28	20	6	0	13-2	24	6.04	66	.277	.353	0-0	—	0		-7	-1.0
1992	Mil A	1	1	.500	10	0	0	0-0	13.2	12	5	1	0	6-0	10	2.63	146	.231	.310	0-0	—	0		2	0.2
	Tex A	0	2	.000	39	0	0	3-1	45.2	51	29	5	2	16-0	39	5.52	69	.279	.337	0-0	—	0		-8	-0.4
	Year	1	3	.250	49	0	0	3-1	59.1	63	37	6	2	22-0	49	4.85	79	.268	.331	0-0	—	0		-6	-0.2
1993	Oak A	3	6	.333	56	0	0	1-3	75.2	89	36	2	6	29-2	58	3.81	107	.298	.369	0-0	—	0		2	0.2
1994	Oak A	0	0	—	15	0	0	0-0	15	26	20	2	0	10-0	15	12.00	37	.382	.456	0-0	—	0		-13	-0.6
Total	13	28	36	.438	427	14	0	54-22	652.1	666	345	74	19	280-38	508	4.19	98	.266	.341	0-0	—	0	78	-12	-1.1
NUNEZ, JOSE Jose (Jimenez) B 1.13.1964 Jarabacoa, D.R. BR/TR 6-3/175# d4.9																									
1987	Tor A	5	2	.714	37	9	0	0-0	97	91	57	12	0	58-8	99	5.01	90	.256	.356	0-0	—	0*	131	-5	-0.3
1988	Tor A	0	1	.000	13	2	0	0-1	29.1	28	11	3	1	17-3	18	3.07	128	.259	.365	0-0	—	0	81	3	0.1
1989	Tor A	0	0	—	6	1	0	0-0	10.2	8	3	0	0	2-0	14	2.53	149	.200	.238	0-0	—	0	120	2	0.1
1990	Chi N	4	7	.364	21	10	0	0-0	60.2	61	47	5	0	34-4	40	6.53	63	.270	.361	11-3	.000	-1	113	-14	-2.4
Total	4	9	10	.474	77	22	0	0-1	197.2	188	118	20	1	111-15	171	5.05	84	.258	.353	11-3	.000	-1	117	-14	-2.5
NUNEZ, JOSE Jose Antonio B 3.14.1979 Monte Cristi, D.R. BL/TL 6-2/173# d4.3																									
2001	LA N	0	1	.000	6	0	0	0-1	7.1	14	15	4	0	5-0	11	13.50	30	.389	.463	0-0	—	0		-10	-1.1
	SD N	4	1	.800	56	0	0	0-1	51.2	48	20	3	4	20-3	49	3.31	121	.245	.324	3-0	.000	-0		5	0.4
	Year	4	2	.667	62	0	0	0-2	59	62	41	7	4	25-3	60	4.58	88	.267	.346	3-0	.000	-0		-5	-0.7
2002	SD N	0	0	—	1	0	0	0-0	1	0	0	0	0	1-0	0	0.00	—	.000	.250	0-0	—	0		0	0.0
Total	2	4	2	.667	63	0	0	0-2	60	62	35	7	4	26-3	60	4.50	89	.264	.345	3-0	.000	-0		-5	-0.7
NUNEZ, VLADIMIR Vladimir (Zarabaza) B 3.15.1975 Havana, Cuba BR/TR 6-4/235# d9.11																									
1998	Ari N	0	0	—	4	0	0	0-0	5.1	7	6	0	0	2-0	2	10.13	42	.318	.360	0-0	—	0		-3	-0.2
1999	Ari N	3	2	.600	27	0	0	1-1	34	29	15	2	1	20-5	28	2.91	157	.242	.347	3-0	.000	-0		5	0.6
	Fla N	4	8	.333	17	12	0	0-1	74.2	66	48	9	3	34-1	58	4.58	95	.243	.330	25-2	.160	-0	81	-5	-0.7
	Year	7	10	.412	44	12	0	1-2	108.2	95	52	11	4	54-6	86	4.06	109	.242	.336	28-2	.143	-1	80	0	-0.1
2000	Fla N	0	6	.000	17	12	0	0-0	68.1	88	63	12	2	34-2	45	7.90	56	.319	.391	17-4	.118	0	88	-26	-1.8
2001	Fla N	4	5	.444	52	3	0	0-1	92	79	33	9	5	30-5	64	2.74	154	.234	.302	9-2	.111	-0	80	14	1.2
2002	Fla N	6	5	.545	77	0	0	20-8	97.2	80	38	8	0	37-1	73	3.41	116	.224	.294	5-0	.200	0		7	1.0
2003	Fla N	0	3	.000	14	0	0	0-3	10.2	21	21	7	0	7-0	10	16.03	26	.396	.452	0-0	—	0		-15	-2.7
Total	6	17	29	.370	208	27	0	21-14	382.2	370	224	47	11	164-14	280	4.68	91	.257	.333	59-8	.136	-1	87	-23	-2.6
NUNN, HOWIE Howard Ralph B 10.18.1935 Westfield, NC BR/TR 6/173# d4.11																									
1959	StL N	2	2	.500	16	0	0	0	21.1	23	18	3	0	15-5	20	7.59	56	.291	.404	1-1	.000	-0		-7	-1.1
1961	Cin N	2	1	.667	24	0	0	0	37.2	35	17	0	1	24-4	26	3.58	113	.252	.357	8-0	.250	0		2	0.1
1962	Cin N	0	0	—	6	0	0	0	9.2	15	6	0	0	3-1	4	5.59	72	.375	.400	1-0	.000	-0		-1	-0.1
Total	3	4	3	.571	46	0	0	0	68.2	73	41	3	1	42-10	50	5.11	80	.283	.378	10-1	.200	-0		-6	-1.1
NUXHALL, JOE Joseph Henry B 7.30.1928 Hamilton, OH BL/TL 6-3/219# d6.10																									
1944	Cin N	0	0	—	1	0	0	0	0.2	2	5	0	0	5	0	67.50	5	.500	.778	0-0	—	0		-5	-0.2
1952	Cin N	1	4	.200	37	5	2	1	92.1	83	33	4	3	42	52	3.22	117	.246	.334	23-0	.087	-1	71	7	0.3
1953	Cin N	9	11	.450	30	17	5-1	2	141.2	136	77	13	8	69	52	4.32	101	.252	.345	49-2	.327	7	83	0	0.7
1954	Cin N	12	5	.706	35	14	5-1	0	166.2	188	77	11	6	59	85	3.89	108	.292	.353	52-4	.173	4*	125	7	1.0
1955	Cin N★	17	12	.586	50	33	14-**5**	3	257	240	108	25	5	78-6	98	3.47	122	.249	.307	86-4	.198	4*	116	23	2.8
1956	Cin N☆	13	11	.542	44	32	10-2	3	200.2	196	96	18	6	87-6	120	3.72	107	.257	.336	59-4	.186	3	92	4	0.7
1957	Cin N	10	10	.500	39	28	6-2	1	174.1	192	104	24	7	53-3	99	4.75	87	.275	.331	59-5	.237	3*	111	-13	-1.2
1958	Cin N	12	11	.522	36	26	5	0	175.2	169	78	15	1	63-5	111	3.79	109	.257	.322	62-2	.210	0	95	7	0.9
1959	Cin N	9	9	.500	28	21	6-1	1	131.2	155	76	10	1	35-1	75	4.24	96	.292	.335	44-2	.250	3	119	-5	-0.4
1960	Cin N	1	8	.111	38	6	0	0	112	130	58	8	4	27-6	72	4.42	86	.297	.340	26-0	.077	-1*	50	-6	-0.5
1961	KC A	5	8	.385	37	13	1	1	128	135	81	12	3	65-2	81	5.34	78	.268	.352	65-5	.292	7*	85	-13	-0.5
1962	LA A	0	0	—	5	0	0	0	5.1	7	6	0	1	5-0	2	10.13	38	.304	.448	0-0	—	0		-3	-0.2
	Cin N	5	0	1.000	12	9	1	1	66	59	20	4	1	25-1	57	2.45	164	.240	.311	26-3	.269	3	160	11	1.1
1963	Cin N	15	8	.652	35	29	14-2	2	217.1	194	73	14	6	39-2	169	2.61	128	.237	.275	76-4	.158	0	110	17	1.7
1964	Cin N	9	8	.529	32	22	7-4	2	154.2	146	73	19	6	51-3	111	4.07	89	.250	.316	54-1	.130	-1*	99	-5	-0.7
1965	Cin N	11	4	.733	32	16	5-1	2	148.2	142	57	18	3	31-2	117	3.45	109	.252	.294	45-6	.178	1	112	8	0.7
1966	Cin N	6	8	.429	35	16	2-1	0	130	136	71	14	9	42-7	71	4.50	87	.270	.336	40-1	.100	-2	96	-8	-1.1
Total	16	135	117	.536	526	287	83-20	19	2302.2	2310	1093	209	70	776-44	1372	3.90	102	.262	.325	766-43	.198	28	104	26	5.1

Year	Tm Lg	W	L	Pct	G	GS	CG-Sho	SV-BS	IP	H	R	HR	HB	BB-IB	SO	ERA	AERA	OAV	OOB	AB-SH	AVG	PB	Sup	APR	PW
NYE, RICH Richard Raymond B 8.4.1944 Oakland, CA BL/TL 6-4/185# d9.16																									
1966	Chi N	0	2	.000	3	2	0	0	17	16	4	1	0	7-2	9	2.12	174	.254	.329	4-0	.250	0	0	3	0.4
1967	Chi N	13	10	.565	35	30	7	0	205	179	82	15	2	52-4	119	3.20	111	.234	.282	75-3	.213	3	92	7	1.1
1968	Chi N	7	12	.368	27	20	6-1	1	132.2	145	65	16	1	34-4	74	3.80	83	.276	.319	44-1	.182	-0	85	-10	-1.5
1969	Chi N	3	5	.375	34	5	1	3-1	68.2	72	43	13	1	21-4	39	5.11	79	.271	.324	16-0	.063	-1*	75	-7	-1.0
1970	StL N	0	0	—	6	0	0	0-0	8	13	5	2	0	6-1	5	4.50	92	.371	.452	2-0	.500	1		-1	0.0
	Mon N	3	2	.600	8	6	2	0-0	46.1	47	23	3	0	20-3	21	4.08	101	.260	.330	17-1	.176	0*	113	0	0.0
	Year	3	2	.600	14	6	2	0-0	54.1	60	28	5	0	26-4	26	4.14	99	.278	.351	19-1	.211	1	113	0	0.0
Total	5	26	31	.456	113	63	16-1	4-1	477.2	472	222	50	4	140-18	267	3.71	96	.257	.309	158-5	.190	2	86	-8	-1.0
NYE, RYAN Ryan Craig B 6.24.1973 Biloxi, MS BR/TR 6-2/195# d6.7																									
1997	Phi N	0	2	.000	4	2	0	0-0	12	20	11	2	2	9-0	7	8.25	51	.392	.484	2-1	.000	-0	43	-5	-0.7
1998	Phi N	0	0	—	1	0	0	0-0	1	3	3	1	0	0-0	3	27.00	16	.500	.500	0-0	—	0		-2	-0.1
Total	2	0	2	.000	5	2	0	0-0	13	23	14	3	2	9-0	10	9.69	44	.404	.486	2-1	.000	-0	43	-7	-0.8
NYMAN, JERRY Gerald Smith B 11.23.1942 Logan, UT BL/TL 5-10/165# d8.24																									
1968	Chi A	2	1	.667	8	7	1-1	0	40.1	38	13	1	0	16-1	27	2.01	151	.247	.314	13-1	.154	-0	74	3	0.2
1969	Chi A	4	4	.500	20	10	2-1	0-0	64.2	58	40	7	0	39-1	40	5.29	73	.244	.346	20-1	.050	-1*	110	-9	-1.2
1970	SD N	0	2	.000	2	2	0	0-0	5.1	8	9	1	0	2-0	2	15.19	26	.364	.400	0-0	—	0*	101	-6	-0.9
Total	3	6	7	.462	30	19	3-2	0-0	110.1	104	62	9	0	57-2	69	4.57	78	.251	.338	33-2	.091	-1	98	-12	-1.9
OANA, PRINCE Henry Kawaihoa B 1.22.1908 Waipahu, HI D 6.19.1976 Austin, TX BR/TR 6-2/193# d4.22.1934 ▲																									
1943	Det A	3	2	.600	10	0	0	0	34	34	21	4	2	19	15	4.50	78	.262	.364	26-0	.385	4*		-4	-0.1
1945	Det A	0	0	—	3	1	0	1	11.1	3	2	0	0	7	3	1.59	221	.086	.238	5-0	.200	-0*	48	2	0.1
Total	2	3	2	.600	13	1	0	1	45.1	37	23	4	2	26	18	3.77	93	.224	.337	31-0	.355	4	48	-2	0.0
OBERBECK, HENRY Henry A. B 5.17.1858 , MO D 8.26.1921 St.Louis, MO d5.7.1883 ▲																									
1884	Bal U	0	0	—	2	1	0	0	6	9	3	0		2	1	3.00	89	.321	.367	125	.184	-1*	80	0	0.0
	KC U	0	5	.000	6	4	3	0	29.2	47	35	0		3	6	5.76	39	.338	.352	90	.189	-1*	19	-12	-1.5
	Year	0	5	.000	8	5	3	0	35.2	56	36	0		5	7	5.30	44	.335	.355	215	.186	-2	33	-12	-1.5
OBERLANDER, DOC Hartman Louis B 5.12.1864 Waukegan, IL D 11.14.1922 Pryor, MT TL 5-10.5/165# d5.16																									
1888	Cle AA	1	2	.333	3	3	3	0	25.2	27	33	2	1	18	23	5.26	59	.260	.374	14	.214	0	200	-8	-0.7
OBERLIN, FRANK Frank Rufus "Flossie" B 3.29.1876 Elsie, MI D 1.6.1952 Ashley, IN BR/TR 6-1/165# d9.20																									
1906	Bos A	1	3	.250	4	4	4	0	34	38	20	0	2	13	13	3.18	87	.286	.358	13-0	.154	-0	79	-3	-0.3
1907	Bos A	1	5	.167	12	4	2	0	46	48	31	2	2	24	18	4.30	60	.271	.365	13-0	.154	-0	20	-8	-1.1
	Was A	2	6	.250	11	8	3	0	48.2	57	38	0	2	12	18	4.62	52	.294	.341	18-0	.056	-2*	87	-13	-2.1
	Year	3	11	.214	23	12	5	0	94.2	105	41	2	4	36	36	4.47	56	.283	.353	31-0	.097	-2	63	-22	-3.2
1909	Was A	1	4	.200	9	4	1	0	41	41	22	1	6	16	13	3.73	65	.266	.358	14-0	.143	-1*	65	-5	-0.7
1910	Was A	0	6	.000	8	6	6	0	57.1	52	32	0	2	23	18	2.98	84	.259	.341	19-0	.053	-2	45	-5	-0.7
Total	4	5	24	.172	44	26	16	0	227	236	143	3	14	88	80	3.77	67	.275	.352	77-0	.104	-4	62	-34	-4.9
OBERMUELLER, WES Wesley Mitchell B 12.22.1976 Cedar Rapids, IA BR/TR 6-2/195# d9.20																									
2002	KC A	0	2	.000	2	2	0	0-0	7.2	14	10	3	0	2-0	5	11.74	43	.378	.410	0-0	—	0	46	-5	-0.8
2003	Mil N	2	5	.286	12	11	0	0-0	65.2	81	40	10	6	25-2	34	5.07	84	.301	.371	23-2	.130	-1	82	-6	-0.6
Total	2	2	7	.222	14	13	0	0-0	73.1	95	50	13	6	27-2	39	5.77	75	.310	.375	23-2	.130	-1	77	-11	-1.4
O'BRIEN, DAN Daniel Jogues B 4.22.1954 St.Petersburg, FL BR/TR 6-4/215# d9.4																									
1978	StL N	0	2	.000	7	2	0	0-0	18	22	12	1	2	8-2	12	4.50	78	.301	.381	3-1	.000	-0	89	-3	-0.3
1979	StL N	1	1	.500	6	0	0	0-0	11	21	10	0	0	3-0	5	8.18	46	.420	.436	2-0	.000	-0		-5	-0.8
Total	2	1	3	.250	13	2	0	0-0	29	43	22	1	2	11-2	17	5.90	61	.350	.403	5-1	.000	-1	89	-8	-1.1
O'BRIEN, EDDIE Edward Joseph B 12.11.1930 S.Amboy, NJ BR/TR 5-9/165# d4.25.1953 Mil 1954 C1 twb-Johnny ▲																									
1956	Pit N	0	0	—	1	0	0	0	2	1	0	0	1	0-0	0	0.00	—	.167	.286	53-3	.264	0*		1	0.0
1957	Pit N	1	0	1.000	3	1	1	0	12.1	11	3	2	0	3-0	10	2.19	173	.229	.275	4-0	.000	-1	70	2	0.1
1958	Pit N	0	0	—	1	0	0	0	2	4	3	1	0	1-0	1	13.50	29	.444	.500	0-0	—	0		-2	-0.1
Total	3	1	0	1.000	5	1	1	0	16.1	16	6	3	1	4-0	11	3.31	115	.254	.309	57-3	.246	-0	70	1	0.0
O'BRIEN, DARBY John F. B 4.15.1867 Troy, NY D 3.11.1892 W.Troy, NY BR/TR 5-10/165# d6.23																									
1888	Cle AA	11	19	.367	30	30	30-1	0	259	245	162	5	12	99	135	3.30	94	.241	.315	109	.183	-3*	88	-5	-0.7
1889	Cle N	22	17	.564	41	41	39-1	0	346.2	345	216	9	24	167	122	4.15	97	.251	.343	140	.250	4	95	3	0.7
1890	Cle P	8	16	.333	25	25	22	0	206.1	229	171	9	19	93	54	3.40	117	.269	.354	96	.156	-6*	91	8	0.1
1891	Bos AA	18	13	.581	40	30	22	2	268.2	300	197	13	20	127	87	3.65	95	.273	.359	128	.234	1*	153	-11	-1.2
Total	4	59	65	.476	136	126	113-2	2	1080.2	1119	746	36	75	486	398	3.68	100	.258	.343	473	.211	-4	106	-5	-1.1
O'BRIEN, JOHNNY John Thomas B 12.11.1930 S.Amboy, NJ BR/TR 5-9/170# d4.19.1953 Mil 1951 twb-Eddie ▲																									
1956	Pit N	1	0	1.000	8	0	0	0	19	8	6	2	2	9-0	9	2.84	133	.133	.260	104-4	.173	-0*		2	0.1
1957	Pit N	0	3	.000	16	1	0	0	40	46	32	7	1	24-2	19	6.07	62	.293	.384	35-1	.314	2*	70	-11	-0.5
1958	StL N	0	0	—	1	0	0	0	2	7	5	0	0	2-0	2	22.50	18	.538	.600	2-0	.000	0*		-4	-0.2
Total	3	1	3	.250	25	1	0	0	61	61	43	9	3	35-2	30	5.61	68	.265	.363	141-5	.206	2	70	-13	-0.6
O'BRIEN, BOB Robert Allen B 4.23.1949 Pittsburgh, PA BL/TL 5-10/170# d4.11																									
1971	LA N	2	2	.500	14	4	1-1	0-0	42	42	18	4	1	13-1	15	3.00	108	.262	.320	9-2	.111	-0	75	0	-0.1
O'BRIEN, BUCK Thomas Joseph B 5.9.1882 Brockton, MA D 7.25.1959 Boston, MA BR/TR 5-10/188# d9.9																									
1911	Bos A	5	1	.833	6	5	5-2	0	47.2	30	9	0	1	21	31	0.38	868	.180	.275	16-0	.125	-1	66	14	1.7
1912	†Bos A	20	13	.606	37	34	25-2	0	275.2	237	107	3	10	90	115	2.58	132	.237	.306	94-4	.138	-5	91	24	2.1
1913	Bos A	4	9	.308	15	12	6	0	90.1	103	42	0	0	35	54	3.69	80	.307	.373	30-1	.167	0	99	-4	-0.5
	Chi A	0	2	.000	6	3	0	0	18.1	21	14	0	0	13	4	3.93	74	.323	.436	3-0	.000	-0	76	-3	-0.4
	Year	4	11	.267	21	15	6	0	108.2	124	17	0	0	48	58	3.73	79	.310	.384	33-1	.152	-0	94	-8	-0.9
Total	3	29	25	.537	64	54	36-4	0	432	391	172	3	11	159	204	2.63	125	.250	.323	143-5	.140	-6	89	31	2.9
O'BRIEN, BILLY William Smith B 3.14.1860 Albany, NY D 5.26.1911 Kansas City, MO BR/TR 6/185# d9.27 ▲																									
1884	StP U	1	0	1.000	2	0	0	0	10	8	5	0		3	7	1.80	73	.205	.262	30	.233	-0*		-1	-0.1
OCKEY, WALTER Walter Andrew "Footie" (b: Walter Andrew Okpych) B 1.4.1920 New York, NY D 12.4.1971 Staten Island, NY BR/TR 6/175# d5.3																									
1944	NY N	0	0	—	2	0	0	0	2.2	2	1	1	0	2	1	3.38	109	.200	.333	0-0	—	0		0	0.0
O'CONNOR, ANDY Andrew James B 9.14.1884 Roxbury, MA D 9.26.1980 Norwood, MA BR/TR 6/160# d10.6																									
1908	NY A	0	1	.000	1	1	1	0	8	15	11	0	3	7	5	10.13	24	.429	.556	3-0	.000	-0	83	-6	-0.6
O'CONNOR, BRIAN Brian Michael B 1.4.1977 Cincinnati, OH BL/TL 6-2/190# d5.13																									
2000	Pit N	0	0	—	6	1	0	0-0	12.1	12	11	2	1	11-0	7	5.11	90	.250	.393	2-0	.500	0	220	-2	-0.1
O'CONNOR, FRANK Frank Henry B 9.15.1870 Keeseville, NY D 12.26.1913 Brattleboro, VT BL/TL 6/185# d8.3																									
1893	Phi N	0	0	—	3	1	0	1	4	2	5	0	0	9	0	11.25	41	.143	.478	2	1.000	2	335	-2	0.0
O'CONNOR, JACK Jack William B 6.2.1958 Twentynine Palms, CA BL/TL 6-3/215# d4.9																									
1981	Min A	3	2	.600	28	0	0	0-3	35.1	46	27	3	2	30-6	16	5.86	67	.336	.462	0-0	—	0		-7	-0.9
1982	Min A	8	9	.471	23	19	6-1	0-0	126	122	63	13	2	57-4	56	4.29	99	.255	.336	0-0	—	0	89	0	-0.1
1983	Min A	2	3	.400	27	8	0	0-0	83	107	59	13	0	36-1	56	5.86	73	.315	.376	0-0	—	0	115	-14	-0.8
1984	Min A	0	0	—	2	0	0	0-0	4.2	1	1	1	0	4-0	0	1.93	218	.067	.263	0-0	—	0		1	0.0
1985	Mon N	0	2	.000	20	1	0	0-1	23.2	21	14	1	0	13-7	16	4.94	69	.239	.330	0-0	—	0	52	-4	-0.4
1987	Bal A	1	1	.500	29	0	0	2-1	46	46	23	5	0	23-4	33	4.30	103	.263	.343	0-0	—	0		1	0.0
Total	6	14	17	.452	129	28	6-1	2-5	318.2	343	187	36	4	163-22	177	4.89	86	.278	.361	0-0	—	0	96	-23	-2.2

Year	Tm Lg	W	L	Pct	G	GS	CG-Sho	SV-BS	IP	H	R	HR	HB	BB-IB	SO	ERA	AERA	OAV	OOB	AB-SH	AVG	PB	Sup	APR	PW
O'DAY, HANK Henry Francis B 7.8.1862 Chicago, IL D 7.2.1935 Chicago, IL TR 6/180# d5.2 M2 U30																									
1884	Tol AA	9	28	.243	41	40	35-2	**1**	326.2	335	241	6	18	66	163	3.75	91	.252	.297	242	.211	-1*	73	-12	-1.0
1885	Pit AA	5	7	.417	12	12	10	0	103	110	77	4	7	16	36	3.67	88	.258	.296	49	.245	1*	115	-8	-0.6
1886	Was N	2	2	.500	6	6	6	0	49	41	17	1		17	47	1.65	195	.219	.284	19	.053	-2	44	8	0.4
1887	Was N	8	20	.286	30	30	29	0	254.2	255	197	15	9	109	86	4.17	96	.254	.332	116	.198	-3*	87	-7	-0.7
1888	Was N	16	29	.356	46	46	46-2	0	403	359	208	19	16	117	186	3.10	89	.232	.293	166	.139	-6*	66	-12	-1.9
1889	Was N	2	10	.167	13	13	11	0	108	117	88	7	6	57	23	4.33	91	.268	.360	44	.182	-1	51	-7	-0.6
	†NY N	9	1	.900	10	10	8	0	78	83	51	2	7	35	28	4.27	92	.264	.351	31	.097	-1	135	0	-0.2
	Year	11	11	.500	23	23	19	0	186	200	59	9	13	92	51	4.31	92	.266	.356	75	.147	-2	87	-10	-0.8
1890	NY P	22	13	.629	43	35	32-1	**3**	329	355	249	11	18	161	94	4.21	108	.264	.350	150	.227	-3	110	11	0.4
Total	7	73	110	.399	201	192	177-5	4	1651.1	1655	1128	65	81	578	663	3.74	96	.251	.319	817	.190	-16	86	-27	-4.2
O'DELL, BILLY William Oliver B 2.10.1932 Whitmire, SC BB/TL 5-11/170# d6.20 Mil 1955																									
1954	Bal A	1	1	.500	7	2	1	0	16.1	15	7	0	0	5	6	2.76	130	.242	.299	3-0	.000	-0	25	1	0.1
1956	Bal A	0	0	—	4	1	0	0	8	6	1	0	0	6-1	6	1.13	349	.222	.353	1-0	.000	-0	91	3	0.1
1957	Bal A	4	10	.286	35	15	2-1	4	140.1	107	48	12	5	39-2	97	2.69	133	.212	.275	34-5	.147	-1*	58	14	1.2
1958	Bal A★	14	11	.560	41	25	12-3	8	221.1	201	83	13	4	51-6	137	2.97	121	.241	.284	72-4	.111	-1*	108	15	1.7
1959	Bal A★	10	12	.455	38	24	6-2	1	199.1	163	74	18	1	67-7	88	2.93	129	.220	.284	60-2	.083	-3*	77	19	1.7
1960	SF N	8	13	.381	43	24	6-1	2	202.2	198	80	16	2	72-8	145	3.20	109	.252	.314	56-3	.107	1*	99	9	0.9
1961	SF N	7	5	.583	46	14	4-1	2	130.1	132	63	10	1	33-6	110	3.59	106	.260	.305	39-4	.103	-2*	126	1	-0.2
1962	†SF N	19	14	.576	43	39	20-2	0	280.2	282	126	18	7	66-1	195	3.53	108	.258	.303	90-10	.133	-1*	116	7	0.6
1963	SF N	14	10	.583	36	33	10-3	1	222.1	218	90	14	7	70-12	116	3.16	101	.253	.313	78-5	.205	4*	131	2	0.3
1964	SF N	8	7	.533	36	8	1	2	85	82	55	10	4	35-6	54	5.40	66	.252	.329	22-0	.000	-2*	74	-16	-2.9
1965	Mil N	10	6	.625	62	1	0	18	111.1	87	35	10	2	30-8	78	2.18	161	.215	.269	23-2	.174	1	50	14	2.6
1966	Atl N	2	3	.400	24	0	0	6	41.1	44	14	3	2	18-1	20	2.40	152	.272	.352	8-0	.250	0*		5	0.8
	Pit N	3	2	.600	37	2	0	4	71.1	74	24	3	4	23-1	47	2.78	129	.275	.339	16-0	.063	-1	86	7	0.4
	Year	5	5	.500	61	2	0	10	112.2	118	28	6	6	41-2	67	2.64	136	.274	.344	24-0	.125	-1	86	11	1.2
1967	Pit N	5	6	.455	27	11	1	0	86.2	88	58	10	3	41-7	34	5.82	58	.265	.347	26-1	.115	-0*	138	-21	-2.5
Total	13	105	100	.512	479	199	63-13	48	1817	1697	758	137	42	556-66	1133	3.29	109	.246	.304	528-36	.125	-7	104	60	4.8
ODENWALD, TED Theodore Joseph "Lefty" B 1.4.1902 Hudson, WI D 10.23.1965 Shakopee, MN BR/TL 5-10/147# d4.13																									
1921	Cle A	1	0	1.000	10	0	0	0	17.1	16	5	0	1	6	4	1.56	274	.262	.338	3-0	.000	-1		5	0.2
1922	Cle A	0	0	—	1	0	0	0	1.1	6	6	0	0	2	2	40.50	10	.600	.667	0-0	—	0		-5	-0.2
Total	2	1	0	1.000	11	0	0	0	18.2	22	11	0	1	8	6	4.34	98	.310	.387	3-0	.000	-1		0	0.0
ODOM, DAVE David Everett "Blimp" or "Porky" B 6.5.1918 Dinuba, CA D 11.19.1987 Myrtle Beach, SC BR/TR 6-1/220# d5.31																									
1943	Bos N	0	3	.000	22	3	1	2	54.2	54	32	3	4	30	17	5.27	65	.269	.374	12-0	.000	-2	58	-8	-0.8
ODOM, BLUE MOON Johnny Lee B 5.29.1945 Macon, GA BR/TR 6/185# d9.5																									
1964	KC A	1	2	.333	5	5	1-1	0	17	29	21	5	0	11-0	10	10.06	38	.363	.440	5-0	.000	-0	135	-11	-1.6
1965	KC A	0	0	—	1	0	0	0	1	2	1	0	0	2-0	0	9.00	39	.400	.571	0-0	—	0		-1	0.0
1966	KC A	5	5	.500	14	14	4-2	0	90.1	70	31	1	2	53-2	47	2.49	136	.215	.326	31-1	.097	-1*	87	8	0.9
1967	KC A	3	8	.273	29	17	0	0	103.2	94	67	9	3	68-7	67	5.04	63	.243	.359	28-0	.286	2*	109	-22	-2.0
1968	Oak A★	16	10	.615	32	31	9-4	0	231.1	179	74	9	7	98-9	143	2.45	115	.216	.302	78-4	.218	6*	121	9	1.9
1969	Oak A★	15	6	.714	32	32	10-3	0-0	231.1	179	87	15	6	112-5	150	2.92	118	.215	.310	79-8	.266	11*	133	12	2.3
1970	Oak A	9	8	.529	29	29	4-1	0-0	156.1	128	77	14	8	100-1	88	3.80	93	.227	.348	54-1	.241	6*	97	-6	0.2
1971	Oak A	10	12	.455	25	25	3-1	0-0	140.2	147	78	13	0	71-7	69	4.29	78	.271	.352	50-1	.160	1*	92	-16	-2.3
1972	†Oak A	15	6	.714	31	30	4-2	0-0	194.1	164	62	10	3	87-2	86	2.50	114	.234	.319	66-5	.121	0*	125	8	0.9
1973	†Oak A	5	12	.294	30	24	3	0-0	150.1	153	86	14	2	67-3	83	4.49	79	.263	.339	1-0	.000	-0*	102	-17	-1.8
1974	†Oak A	1	5	.167	34	5	1	1-2	87.1	85	39	4	3	52-3	52	3.81	87	.267	.373	0-0	—	0*	48	-3	-0.2
1975	Oak A	0	2	.000	7	2	0	0-0	11	19	15	1	1	11-1	4	12.27	30	.422	.534	0-0	—	0*	145	-10	-1.5
	Cle A	1	0	1.000	3	1	1-1	0-1	10.1	4	3	1	0	8-0	10	2.61	145	.118	.286	0-0	—	0	93	2	0.1
	Year	1	2	.333	10	3	1-1	0-1	21.1	23	7	2	1	19-1	14	7.59	49	.291	.430	0-0	—	0	127	-8	-1.4
	Atl N	1	7	.125	15	10	0	0-0	56	78	46	5	0	28-0	30	7.07	54	.342	.411	13-1	.077	-1	81	-17	-2.2
1976	Chi A	2	2	.500	8	4	0	0-0	28	31	21	2	1	20-0	18	5.79	62	.282	.394	0-0	—	0	129	-7	-1.0
Total	13	84	85	.497	295	229	40-15	1-3	1509	1362	708	103	36	788-40	857	3.70	89	.244	.339	405-21	.195	26	109	-71	-6.3
O'DONNELL, GEORGE George Dana B 5.27.1929 Winchester, IL BR/TR 6-3/175# d4.18																									
1954	Pit N	3	9	.250	21	10	3	1	87.1	105	50	4	2	21	8	4.53	92	.315	.348	23-0	.087	-1	45	-3	-0.4
O'DONOGHUE, JOHN John Eugene B 10.7.1939 Kansas City, MO BR/TL 6-3/210# d9.29 s-John																									
1963	KC A	0	1	.000	1	1	0	0	6	6	2	0	0	2-0	1	1.50	260	.286	.348	2-0	.000	-0	23	1	0.1
1964	KC A	10	14	.417	39	32	2-1	0	173.2	202	104	24	3	65-4	79	4.92	78	.286	.347	55-7	.236	2*	90	-20	-2.4
1965	KC A☆	9	18	.333	34	30	4-1	0	177.2	183	92	15	1	66-8	82	3.95	88	.267	.331	55-6	.218	3*	76	-11	-1.3
1966	Cle A	6	8	.429	32	13	2	0	108	109	50	13	2	23-2	49	3.83	90	.264	.303	33-0	.152	-0	108	-4	-0.5
1967	Cle A	8	9	.471	33	17	5-2	2	130.2	120	52	10	2	33-3	81	3.24	101	.247	.296	40-1	.100	-0	89	1	0.4
1968	Bal A	0	0	—	16	0	0	2	22	34	15	2	0	7-3	11	6.14	48	.374	.414	2-0	.000	-0		-7	-0.4
1969	Sea A	2	2	.500	55	0	0	6-2	70	58	28	5	3	37-4	48	2.96	123	.230	.331	13-3	.077	-1		4	0.3
1970	Mil A	2	0	1.000	25	0	0	0-3	23.1	29	15	4	0	9-1	13	5.01	76	.299	.358	2-0	.000	-0		-3	-0.2
	Mon N	2	3	.400	9	3	0	0-1	22.1	20	14	2	2	11-1	6	5.24	79	.263	.359	4-0	.000	-0	87	-2	-0.5
1971	Mon N	0	0	—	13	0	0	0-0	17.1	19	10	3	0	7-1	7	4.67	76	.271	.333	0-0	—	0		-2	-0.1
Total	9	39	55	.415	257	96	13-4	10-6	751	780	382	78	13	260-27	377	4.07	87	.269	.330	206-17	.170	2	88	-43	-4.6
O'DONOGHUE, JOHN John Preston B 5.26.1969 Wilmington, DE BL/TL 6-6/198# d6.27 f-John																									
1993	Bal A	0	1	.000	11	1	0	0-0	19.2	22	12	4	1	10-1	16	4.58	98	.278	.367	0-0	—	0	103	-1	-0.1
O'DOUL, LEFTY Francis Joseph B 3.4.1897 San Francisco, CA D 12.7.1969 San Francisco, CA BL/TL 6/180# d4.29 ▲																									
1919	NY A	0	0	—	3	0	0	0	5	7	6	0	0	4	2	3.60	89	.304	.407	16-0	.250	0*		-2	-0.1
1920	NY A	0	0	—	2	0	0	0	3.2	4	2	0	1	2	2	4.91	78	.286	.412	12-0	.167	-0*		0	0.0
1922	NY A	0	0	—	6	0	0	0	16	24	13	0	0	12	5	3.38	119	.353	.450	9-0	.333	1*		-1	0.0
1923	Bos A	1	1	.500	23	1	0	0	53	69	50	2	4	31	10	5.43	76	.337	.433	35-2	.143	-1*	121	-11	-0.7
Total	4	1	1	.500	34	1	0	0	77.2	104	71	2	5	49	19	4.87	83	.335	.434	72-2	.194	-1	121	-14	-0.8
OELKERS, BRYAN Bryan Alois B 3.11.1961 Zaragoza, Spain BL/TL 6-3/192# d4.9																									
1983	Min A	0	5	.000	10	8	0	0-0	34.1	56	34	7	0	17-0	13	8.65	49	.376	.437	0-0	—	0	88	-15	-1.8
1986	Cle A	3	3	.500	35	4	0	1-1	69	70	38	13	6	40-2	33	4.70	88	.262	.368	0-0	—	0	104	-3	-0.3
Total	2	3	8	.273	45	12	0	1-1	103.1	126	72	20	6	57-2	46	6.01	70	.303	.392	0-0	—	0	94	-18	-2.1
OESCHGER, JOE Joseph Carl B 5.24.1892 Chicago, IL D 7.28.1986 Rohnert Park, CA BR/TR 6- /190# d4.21																									
1914	Phi N	4	8	.333	32	12	5	1	124	129	74	5	10	54	47	3.77	78	.279	.366	40-1	.075	-4	102	-10	-1.4
1915	Phi N	1	0	1.000	6	1	1	0	23.2	21	13	1	0	9	8	3.42	80	.247	.319	7-0	.000	-1	81	-2	-0.2
1916	Phi N	1	0	1.000	14	0	0	0	30.1	18	8	2	1	14	17	2.37	112	.184	.292	5-1	.000	-1		2	0.1
1917	Phi N	15	14	.517	42	30	18-5	1	262	241	108	7	6	72	123	2.75	102	.249	.305	88-2	.114	-4*	95	1	-0.6
1918	Phi N	6	18	.250	30	23	13-2	**3**	184	159	87	3	7	83	60	3.03	99	.238	.328	60-1	.083	-4	78	-4	-1.0
1919	Phi N	0	1	.000	5	4	2	0	38	52	29	1	2	16	5	5.92	54	.340	.409	15-0	.000	-2	179	-10	-0.7
	NY N	0	1	.000	5	1	0	0	8	12	4	0	0	2	3	4.50	62	.400	.438	1-0	.000	-0	57	-1	-0.2
	Bos N	4	2	.667	7	7	4-1	0	56.2	63	19	0	1	21	16	2.54	112	.300	.366	22-0	.091	-1	88	2	0.0
	Year	4	4	.500	17	12	6-1	0	102.2	127	22	1	3	39	24	3.94	76	.323	.389	38-0	.053	-4	118	-9	-0.9
1920	Bos N	15	13	.536	38	30	20-5	0	299	294	124	10	8	99	80	3.46	88	.265	.329	101-5	.178	-3	86	-7	-1.0
1921	Bos N	20	14	.588	46	36	19-**3**	0	299	303	128	11	15	97	68	3.52	104	.274	.341	110-2	.255	2	93	8	1.1
1922	Bos N	6	21	.222	46	23	10-1	1	195.2	234	137	8	8	81	51	5.06	79	.303	.375	63-1	.190	-0	73	-23	-2.6
1923	Bos N	5	15	.250	44	19	6-1	2	166.1	227	117	4	5	54	33	5.68	70	.330	.383	52-2	.231	-0	78	-27	-2.8
1924	NY N	2	0	1.000	10	2	0	0	29	35	17	1	0	14	10	3.10	118	.287	.360	7-0	.429	1	208	-1	0.0
	Phi N	2	7	.222	19	8	0	0	65.1	88	44	6	3	16	8	4.41	101	.333	.378	20-0	.250	-1	62	-2	-0.3

Year	Tm Lg	W	L	Pct	G	GS	CG-Sho	SV-BS	IP	H	R	HR	HB	BB-IB	SO	ERA	AERA	OAV	OOB	AB-SH	AVG	PB	Sup	APR	PW
	Year	4	7	.364	29	10	0	0	94.1	123	47	7	3	30	18	4.01	105	.319	.372	27-0	.296	0	89	-3	-0.3
1925	Bro N	1	2	.333	21	3	1	0	37	60	38	2	1	19	6	6.08	69	.382	.452	8-1	.125	-0	101	-11	-0.8
Total	12	82	116	.414	365	199	99-18	8	1818	1936	947	61	67	651	535	3.81	88	.281	.349	599-16	.165	-18	88	-85	-10.4
OGDEN, JACK John Mahlon B 11.5.1897 Ogden, PA D 11.9.1977 Philadelphia, PA BR/TR 6/190# d6.22 b-Curly																									
1918	NY N	0	0	—	5	0	0	0	8.2	8	4	0	2	3	1	3.12	84	.296	.406	1-0	.000	-0		-1	-0.1
1928	StL A	15	16	.484	38	31	18-1	2	242.2	257	121	23	1	80	67	4.15	101	.274	.331	85-2	.200	-1	93	5	0.3
1929	StL A	4	8	.333	34	14	7	0	131.1	154	83	8	0	44	32	4.93	90	.301	.357	45-2	.244	0	95	-7	-0.5
1931	Cin N	4	8	.333	22	9	3-1	1	89	79	42	3	0	32	24	2.93	127	.242	.310	27-1	.148	-1*	61	5	0.4
1932	Cin N	2	2	.500	24	3	1	0	57	72	40	5	0	22	20	5.21	74	.310	.370	12-0	.167	0*	58	-9	-0.5
Total	5	25	34	.424	123	57	29-2	3	528.2	570	290	39	3	181	144	4.24	97	.280	.340	170-5	.200	-1	88	-7	-0.4
OGDEN, CURLY Warren Harvey B 1.24.1901 Ogden, PA D 8.6.1964 Upland, PA BR/TR 6-1.5/180# d7.18 b-Jack																									
1922	Phi A	1	4	.200	15	6	4	0	72.1	59	29	4	5	33	20	3.11	137	.237	.338	29-0	.241	-0*	50	9	0.5
1923	Phi A	1	2	.333	18	2	0	0	46.1	63	39	2	3	32	14	5.63	73	.330	.434	17-0	.294	1*	50	-9	-0.4
1924	Phi A	0	3	.000	5	1	0	0	12.2	14	9	1	1	7	4	4.97	86	.275	.373	3-0	.000	-1	118	-1	-0.3
	†Was A	9	5	.643	16	16	9-3	0	108	83	36	3	2	51	23	2.58	156	.221	.317	47-1	.277	2*	114	19	2.4
	Year	9	8	.529	21	17	9-3	0	120.2	97	41	4	3	58	27	2.83	143	.227	.324	50-1	.260	1	114	17	2.1
1925	Was A	3	1	.750	17	4	2-1	0	42	45	24	1	2	18	6	4.50	94	.288	.369	12-0	.250	-0	124	-1	-0.1
1926	Was A	4	4	.500	22	9	4	0	96.1	114	55	2	5	45	21	4.30	90	.305	.387	27-1	.185	-1	123	-5	-0.5
Total	5	18	19	.486	93	38	19-4	0	377.2	378	192	13	18	186	88	3.79	108	.271	.364	135-2	.244	1	103	12	1.6
OGEA, CHAD Chad Wayne B 11.9.1970 Lake Charles, LA BR/TR 6-2/200# d5.3																									
1994	Cle A	0	1	.000	4	1	0	0-0	16.1	21	11	2	1	10-2	11	6.06	78	.304	.400	0-0	—	0	19	-2	-0.1
1995	†Cle A	8	3	.727	20	14	1	0-0	106.1	95	38	11	1	29-0	57	3.05	154	.233	.283	0-0	—	0	115	20	1.8
1996	†Cle A	10	6	.625	29	21	1-1	0-0	146.2	151	82	22	5	42-3	101	4.79	102	.266	.321	0-0	—	0	106	3	0.2
1997	†Cle A	8	9	.471	21	21	1	0-0	126.1	139	79	13	5	47-4	80	4.99	94	.283	.348	2-2	.000	-0	106	-5	-0.6
1998	†Cle A	5	4	.556	19	9	0	0-1	69	74	44	9	7	25-1	43	5.61	85	.273	.346	0-0	—	0	104	-5	-0.6
1999	Phi N	6	12	.333	36	28	0	0-0	168	192	110	36	4	61-1	77	5.63	84	.288	.349	44-7	.091	-2	92	-15	-1.6
Total	6	37	35	.514	129	94	3-1	0-1	632.2	672	364	93	23	214-11	369	4.88	98	.272	.333	46-9	.087	-2	102	-4	-0.9
OGRODOWSKI, JOE Joseph Anthony B 11.20.1906 Hoytville, PA D 6.24.1959 Elmira, NY BR/TR 5-11/165# d4.27																									
1925	Bos N	0	0	—	1	0	0	0	1	6	8	0	0	3	0	54.00	7	.600	.692	0-0	—	0		-6	-0.3
OHKA, TOMO Tomokazu B 3.18.1976 Kyoto, Japan BR/TR 6-1/180# d7.19																									
1999	Bos A	1	2	.333	8	2	0	0-0	13	21	12	2	0	6-0	8	6.23	80	.362	.415	0-0	—	0	112	-3	-0.5
2000	Bos A	3	6	.333	13	12	0	0-0	69.1	70	25	7	2	26-0	40	3.12	162	.263	.331	0-0	—	0	50	15	1.7
2001	Bos A	2	5	.286	12	11	0	0-0	52.1	69	40	7	2	19-0	37	6.19	73	.317	.375	3-0	.000	-0	92	-10	-1.1
	Mon N	1	4	.200	10	10	0	0-0	54.2	65	30	8	1	10-0	31	4.77	94	.302	.335	15-3	.200	0	81	-1	-0.1
2002	Mon N	13	8	.619	32	31	2	0-0	192.2	194	83	19	7	45-7	118	3.18	141	.264	.310	55-8	.127	-1	95	23	2.3
2003	Mon N	10	12	.455	34	34	2	0-0	199	233	106	24	9	45-11	118	4.16	113	.292	.335	55-8	.182	-0*	90	9	0.9
Total	5	30	37	.448	109	100	4	0-0	581	652	296	67	21	151-18	352	4.00	116	.285	.333	128-19	.156	-2	86	33	3.2
OHL, JOE Joseph Earl (b: Joseph Earl Von Ohl) B 1.10.1888 Jobstown, NJ D 12.18.1951 Camden, NJ BL/TL 6-1/175# d7.29																									
1909	Was A	0	0	—	4	0	0	0	8.2	7	4	0	1	1	2	2.08	117	.194	.237	2-0	.000	-0		0	0.0
OHMAN, WILL William McDaniel B 8.13.1977 Frankfurt, West Germany BL/TL 6-2/195# d9.19																									
2000	Chi N	1	0	1.000	6	0	0	0-0	3.1	4	3	0	0	4-1	2	8.10	56	.308	.471	0-0	—	0		-1	-0.2
2001	Chi N	0	1	.000	11	0	0	0-0	11.2	14	10	2	0	6-0	12	7.71	54	.292	.370	2-0	.000	-0		-4	-0.4
Total	2	1	1	.500	17	0	0	0-0	15	18	13	2	0	10-1	14	7.80	54	.295	.394	2-0	.000	-0		-5	-0.6
OHME, KEVIN Kevin Arthur B 4.13.1971 Palm Beach, FL BL/TL 6-1/180# d4.14																									
2003	StL N	0	0	—	2	0	0	0-0	4.1	3	0	0	0	1-1	2	0.00	—	.200	.235	1-0	1.000	1		2	0.2
OJALA, KIRT Kirt Stanley B 12.24.1968 Kalamazoo, MI BL/TL 6-2/200# d8.18																									
1997	Fla N	1	2	.333	7	5	0	0-0	28.2	28	10	4	0	18-0	19	3.14	128	.252	.354	7-1	.000	-1	101	3	0.3
1998	Fla N	2	7	.222	41	13	1	0-0	125	128	71	14	4	59-4	75	4.25	96	.267	.351	26-2	.154	1	77	-6	-0.2
1999	Fla N	0	1	.000	8	1	0	0-0	10.2	21	17	1	0	6-0	5	14.34	30	.438	.482	0-0	—	0	42	-12	-0.9
Total	3	3	10	.231	56	19	1	0-0	164.1	177	98	19	4	83-4	99	4.71	86	.277	.362	33-3	.121	0	81	-15	-0.8
OJEDA, BOB Robert Michael B 12.17.1957 Los Angeles, CA BL/TL 6-1/190# d7.13																									
1980	Bos A	1	1	.500	7	7	0	0-0	26	39	20	2	0	14-1	12	6.92	61	.361	.434	0-0	—	0	106	-7	-0.5
1981	Bos A	6	2	.750	10	10	2	0-0	66.1	50	25	6	2	25-2	28	3.12	124	.212	.292	0-0	—	0	120	6	0.7
1982	Bos A	4	6	.400	22	14	0	0-0	78.1	95	53	13	1	29-0	52	5.63	77	.296	.355	0-0	—	0	98	-11	-1.2
1983	Bos A	12	7	.632	29	28	5	0-0	173.2	173	85	15	3	73-2	94	4.04	108	.265	.336	0-0	—	0	105	6	0.7
1984	Bos A	12	12	.500	33	32	8-**5**	0-0	216.2	211	106	17	2	96-2	137	3.99	105	.259	.336	0-0	—	0	101	6	0.6
1985	Bos A	9	11	.450	39	22	5	1-0	157.2	166	74	11	2	48-9	102	4.00	107	.273	.327	0-0	—	0	81	6	0.7
1986	†NY N	18	5	**.783**	32	30	7-2	0-0	217.1	185	72	15	2	52-3	148	2.57	138	.230	.278	71-8	.113	-2	122	24	2.2
1987	NY N	3	5	.375	10	7	0	0-0	46.1	45	23	5	0	10-1	21	3.88	97	.253	.291	14-0	.071	-0	120	-1	-0.1
1988	NY N	10	13	.435	29	29	5-5	0-0	190.1	158	74	6	4	33-2	133	2.88	112	.225	.261	61-4	.164	1*	82	6	0.9
1989	NY N	13	11	.542	31	31	5-2	0-0	192	179	83	16	2	78-5	95	3.47	94	.245	.317	66-6	.106	-2*	113	-5	-0.6
1990	NY N	7	6	.538	38	12	0	0-2	118	123	53	10	2	40-4	62	3.66	102	.272	.332	30-1	.133	-0	108	1	0.3
1991	LA N	12	9	.571	31	31	2-1	0-0	189.1	181	78	15	3	70-9	120	3.18	113	.257	.323	56-6	.161	1	95	8	1.1
1992	LA N	6	9	.400	29	29	2-1	0-0	166.1	169	80	8	1	81-8	94	3.63	95	.268	.349	49-5	.102	-1	98	-4	-0.4
1993	Cle A	2	1	.667	9	7	0	0-0	43	48	22	5	0	21-0	27	4.40	99	.289	.363	0-0	—	0	106	0	0.1
1994	NY A	0	0	—	2	2	0	0-0	3	11	8	1	0	6-0	3	24.00	19	.611	.680	0-0	—	0	120	-6	-0.3
Total	15	115	98	.540	351	291	41-16	1-2	1884.1	1833	856	145	24	676-48	1128	3.65	103	.257	.321	347-30	.127	-4	102	29	4.2
OKRIE, FRANK Frank Anthony "Lefty" B 10.28.1896 Detroit, MI D 10.16.1959 Detroit, MI BL/TL 5-11/175# d4.20 s-Len																									
1920	Det A	1	2	.333	21	1	1	0	41	44	29	2	5	18	9	5.27	71	.295	.390	5-1	.200	-0	107	-6	-0.1
OLDHAM, RED John Cyrus B 7.15.1893 Zion, MD D 1.28.1961 Costa Mesa, CA BB/TL 6- /176# d8.19																									
1914	Det A	2	4	.333	9	7	3	0	45.1	42	22	1	3	8	23	3.38	83	.243	.288	15-1	.267	1	78	-2	-0.2
1915	Det A	3	0	1.000	17	2	1	4	57.2	52	22	1	4	17	17	2.81	108	.243	.311	14-0	.143	-0	84	2	0.1
1920	Det A	8	13	.381	39	22	10-1	1	215.1	248	132	5	6	91	62	3.85	97	.302	.376	69-4	.174	-1	93	-6	-0.5
1921	Det A	11	14	.440	40	28	12-1	1	229.1	258	129	11	6	81	67	4.24	101	.288	.351	85-2	.224	2*	117	3	0.6
1922	Det A	10	13	.435	43	28	9	3	212	256	130	14	11	59	72	4.67	83	.305	.358	73-1	.260	4	123	-19	-1.3
1925	†Pit N	3	2	.600	11	4	3	1	53	66	27	2	2	18	10	3.91	114	.313	.372	18-0	.333	2	80	4	0.5
1926	Pit N	2	2	.500	17	2	0	2	41.2	56	27	1	1	18	16	5.62	70	.359	.429	9-1	.222	0	85	-6	-0.5
Total	7	39	48	.448	176	93	38-2	12	854.1	978	489	35	33	292	267	4.15	93	.295	.358	283-9	.226	9	108	-24	-1.3
OLIN, STEVE Steven Robert B 10.4.1965 Portland, OR D 3.22.1993 Little Lake Nellie, FL BR/TR 6-3/185# d7.29																									
1989	Cle A	1	4	.200	25	0	0	1-0	36	35	16	1	0	14-2	24	3.75	106	.255	.325	0-0	—	0		1	0.1
1990	Cle A	4	4	.500	50	1	0	1-2	92.1	96	41	3	6	26-2	64	3.41	115	.270	.329	0-0	—	0	93	4	0.4
1991	Cle A	3	6	.333	48	0	0	17-5	56.1	61	26	2	1	23-7	38	3.36	124	.274	.344	0-0	—	0		4	0.8
1992	Cle A	8	5	.615	72	0	0	29-7	88.1	80	25	8	4	27-6	47	2.34	167	.248	.313	0-0	—	0		16	3.1
Total	4	16	19	.457	195	1	0	48-14	273	272	108	14	11	90-17	173	3.10	128	.262	.327	0-0	—	0	93	25	4.4
OLIVARES, OMAR Omar (Palqu) B 7.6.1967 Mayaguez, P.R. BR/TR 6-1/193# d8.18 f-Ed																									
1990	StL N	1	1	.500	9	6	0	0-0	49.1	45	17	2	2	17-0	20	2.92	131	.249	.320	17-0	.176	1	83	5	0.4
1991	StL N	11	7	.611	28	24	0	1-0	167.1	148	72	13	5	61-1	91	3.71	100	.243	.316	53-4	.226	3	102	2	0.6

Year	Tm Lg	W	L	Pct	G	GS	CG-Sho	SV-BS	IP	H	R	HR	HB	BB-IB	SO	ERA	AERA	OAV	OOB	AB-SH	AVG	PB	Sup	APR	PW
1992	StL N	9	9	.500	32	30	1	0-0	197	189	84	20	4	63-5	124	3.84	88	.257	.316	68-3	.235	4*	102	-7	0.0
1993	StL N	5	3	.625	58	9	0	1-4	118.2	134	60	10	9	54-7	63	4.17	95	.288	.370	26-3	.269	2*	113	-2	0.2
1994	StL N	3	4	.429	14	12	1	1-0	73.2	84	53	10	4	37-0	26	5.74	72	.294	.379	28-2	.214	2*	122	-15	-1.0
1995	Col N	1	3	.250	11	6	0	0-0	31.2	44	28	4	2	21-0	15	7.39	73	.349	.447	7-1	.143	0*	78	-5	-0.5
	Phi N	0	1	.000	5	0	0	0-0	10	11	6	1	1	2-0	7	5.40	78	.282	.326	2-0	.500	1		-1	0.0
	Year	1	4	.200	16	6	0	0-0	41.2	55	39	5	3	23-0	22	6.91	74	.333	.420	9-1	.222	1	82	-6	-0.5
1996	Det A	7	11	.389	25	25	4	0-0	160	169	90	16	9	75-4	81	4.89	103	.275	.359	0-0	—	0	89	5	0.5
1997	Det A	5	6	.455	19	19	3-2	0-0	115	110	68	8	9	53-1	74	4.70	98	.253	.344	3-0	.667	1*	107	-3	-0.1
	Sea A	1	4	.200	13	12	0	0-0	62.1	81	41	10	4	28-3	29	5.49	82	.315	.387	2-0	.500	0	100	-7	-0.5
	Year	6	10	.375	32	31	3-2	0-0	177.1	191	46	18	13	81-4	103	4.97	92	.276	.360	5-0	.600	2	105	-10	-0.6
1998	Ana A	9	9	.500	37	26	1	0-0	183	189	92	19	5	91-1	112	4.03	116	.270	.357	2-0	.000	0*	92	12	1.2
1999	Ana A	8	9	.471	20	20	3	0-0	131	135	62	11	6	49-0	49	4.05	120	.273	.342	6-1	.333	1	74	13	1.6
	Oak A	7	2	.778	12	12	1	0-0	74.2	82	43	8	3	32-0	36	4.34	107	.283	.358	0-0	—	0	125	1	0.2
	Year	15	11	.577	32	32	4	0-0	205.2	217	49	19	9	81-0	85	4.16	115	.276	.348	6-1	.333	1	93	14	1.8
2000	Oak A	4	8	.333	21	16	1	0-0	108	134	86	10	7	60-0	57	6.75	70	.309	.396	1-0	1.000	0	101	-23	-1.9
2001	Pit N	6	9	.400	45	12	1	1-1	110	123	87	17	10	42-8	69	6.55	69	.283	.356	27-0	.222	2*	108	-25	-2.7
Total	12	77	86	.472	349	229	16-2	4-5	1591.2	1678	889	159	80	685-30	853	4.67	93	.275	.353	242-14	.240	18	99	-50	-2.0
OLIVER, DARREN Darren Christopher B 10.6.1970 Rio Linda, CA BR/TL 6-2/200# d9.1 f-Bob																									
1993	Tex A	0	0	—	2	0	0	0-0	3.1	2	1	1	0	1-1	4	2.70	154	.154	.214	0-0	—	0		1	0.0
1994	Tex A	4	0	1.000	43	0	0	2-1	50	40	24	4	6	35-4	50	3.42	141	.223	.368	0-0	—	0		7	0.6
1995	Tex A	4	2	.667	17	7	0	0-0	49	47	25	3	1	32-1	39	4.22	114	.257	.369	0-0	—	0	88	3	0.4
1996	†Tex A	14	6	.700	30	30	1-1	0-0	173.2	190	97	20	10	76-3	112	4.66	112	.279	.356	0-0	—	0	104	10	1.0
1997	Tex A	13	12	.520	32	32	3-1	0-0	201.1	213	111	29	11	82-3	104	4.20	114	.271	.346	2-0	.500	1	106	9	1.0
1998	Tex A	6	7	.462	19	19	2	0-0	103.1	140	84	11	10	43-1	58	6.53	74	.325	.394	6-0	.167	0	118	-20	-2.0
	StL N	4	4	.500	10	10	0	0-0	57	64	31	7	0	23-1	29	4.26	98	.283	.347	23-0	.087	-1*	90	-1	-0.2
1999	StL N	9	9	.500	30	30	2-1	0-0	196.1	197	96	16	11	74-4	119	4.26	107	.265	.339	73-8	.274	5*	97	10	1.3
2000	Tex A	2	9	.182	21	21	0	0-0	108	151	95	16	4	42-3	49	7.42	68	.339	.397	2-0	.000	0	112	-27	-2.1
2001	Tex A	11	11	.500	28	28	1	0-0	154	189	109	23	6	65-0	104	6.02	78	.305	.374	6-2	.333	1	118	-22	-2.5
2002	Bos A	4	5	.444	14	9	1-1	0-0	58	70	30	7	6	27-0	32	4.66	97	.317	.401	1-0	.000	-0	85	0	0.0
2003	Col N	13	11	.542	33	32	1	0-0	180.1	201	108	21	8	61-3	88	5.04	98	.284	.345	67-2	.254	4*	108	-2	0.2
Total	11	84	76	.525	279	218	11-4	2-1	1334.1	1504	811	158	73	561-24	788	5.02	96	.287	.362	180-12	.239	10	106	-32	-2.3
OLIVERAS, FRANCISCO Francisco Javier (Noa) B 1.31.1963 Santurce, P.R. BR/TR 5-10/170# d5.3																									
1989	Min A	3	4	.429	12	8	1	0-0	55.2	64	28	8	1	15-0	24	4.53	92	.288	.335	0-0	—	0	115	-1	-0.2
1990	SF N	2	2	.500	33	2	0	2-0	55.1	47	22	5	2	21-6	41	2.77	132	.230	.304	5-0	.000	-1	111	4	0.2
1991	SF N	6	6	.500	55	1	0	3-1	79.1	69	36	12	1	22-4	48	3.86	93	.242	.296	10-0	.200	0	75	-2	-0.3
1992	SF N	0	3	.000	16	7	0	0-0	44.2	41	19	11	1	10-2	17	3.63	91	.250	.294	7-0	.143	0	59	-1	-0.1
Total	4	11	15	.423	116	18	1	5-1	235	221	105	36	5	68-12	130	3.71	99	.253	.307	22-0	.136	-0	94	0	-0.4
OLIVO, DIOMEDES Diomedes Antonio (Maldonado) B 1.22.1919 Guayubin, D.R. D 2.15.1977 Santo Domingo, D.R. BL/TL 6-1/195# d9.5 b-Chi-Chi s-Gilberto																									
1960	Pit N	0	0	—	4	0	0	0	9.2	8	3	1	0	5-1	10	2.79	134	.216	.310	1-0	.000	-0		1	0.0
1962	Pit N	5	1	.833	62	1	0	7	84.1	88	30	5	0	25-7	66	2.77	142	.277	.325	16-2	.188	1	89	11	1.0
1963	StL N	0	5	.000	19	0	0	0	13.1	16	9	1	1	9-1	9	5.40	66	.296	.400	0-0	—	0		-2	-0.5
Total	3	5	6	.455	85	1	0	7	107.1	112	42	7	1	39-9	85	3.10	125	.274	.334	17-2	.176	0	89	10	0.5
OLIVO, CHI-CHI Federico Emilio (Maldonado) B 3.18.1928 Guayubin, D.R. D 2.3.1977 Guayubin, D.R. BR/TR 6-2/215# d6.5 b-Diomedes																									
1961	Mil N	0	0	—	3	0	0	0	2	3	4	1	0	5-1	1	18.00	21	.500	.727	0-0	—	0		-3	-0.2
1964	Mil N	2	1	.667	38	0	0	5	60	55	25	7	0	21-5	45	3.75	94	.247	.309	4-0	.250	0		0	0.0
1965	Mil N	0	1	.000	8	0	0	0	13	12	2	1	0	5-2	11	1.38	254	.267	.327	0-0	—	0		3	0.2
1966	Atl N	5	4	.556	47	0	0	7	66	59	34	4	1	19-5	41	4.23	86	.240	.293	9-0	.111	-0		-4	-0.7
Total	4	7	6	.538	96	0	0	12	141	129	65	13	1	50-13	98	3.96	90	.248	.311	13-0	.154	-0		-4	-0.7
OLLOM, JIM James Donald B 7.8.1945 Snohomish, WA BR/TL 6-4/210# d9.3																									
1966	Min A	0	0	—	3	1	0	0	10	6	4	1	1	1-0	11	3.60	100	.167	.211	2-0	.000	-0	123	0	0.0
1967	Min A	0	1	.000	21	2	0	0	35	33	24	4	4	11-1	17	5.40	64	.258	.331	5-0	.200	0	76	-7	-0.4
Total	2	0	1	.000	24	3	0	0	45	39	28	5	5	12-1	28	5.00	70	.238	.306	7-0	.143	-0	92	-7	-0.4
OLMSTEAD, FRED Frederic William B 7.3.1881 Grand Rapids, MI D 10.22.1936 Muskogee, OK BR/TR 5-11/170# d7.2																									
1908	Chi A	0	0	—	1	0	0	0	2	6	3	0	0	1	1	13.50	17	.600	.636	1-0	.000	1		-2	-0.1
1909	Chi A	3	2	.600	8	6	5	0	54.2	52	17	1	1	12	21	1.81	129	.277	.323	21-0	.095	-1	105	3	0.1
1910	Chi A	10	12	.455	32	20	14-4	0	184.1	174	64	1	4	50	68	1.95	123	.260	.316	65-2	.154	-2	64	8	0.8
1911	Chi A	6	6	.500	25	11	7-1	2	117.2	146	78	3	6	30	45	4.21	77	.309	.358	37-1	.189	-0	124	-15	-1.4
Total	4	19	20	.487	66	37	26-5	2	358.2	378	162	5	11	93	135	2.74	97	.283	.334	124-3	.153	-3	90	-6	-0.6
OLMSTED, AL Alan Ray B 3.18.1957 St.Louis, MO BR/TL 6-2/195# d9.12																									
1980	StL N	1	1	.500	5	5	0	0-0	34.2	32	13	2	1	14-1	14	2.86	130	.244	.322	11-2	.182	-0	101	3	0.2
OLMSTED, HANK Henry Theodore B 1.12.1879 Sac Bay, MI D 1.6.1969 Bradenton, FL BR/TR 5-8.5/147# d7.15																									
1905	Bos A	1	2	.333	3	3	3	0	25	18	10	0	0	12	6	3.24	83	.205	.300	8-0	.125	-0	26	-1	-0.1
OLSEN, OLE Arthur Ole B 9.12.1894 S.Norwalk, CT D 9.12.1980 Norwalk, CT BR/TR 5-10/163# d4.12																									
1922	Det A	7	6	.538	37	15	5	3	137	147	84	8	14	40	52	4.53	86	.281	.348	39-3	.179	-1*	112	-11	-1.0
1923	Det A	1	1	.500	17	2	1	0	41.1	42	30	1	5	17	12	6.31	61	.290	.383	8-1	.125	-1	193	-10	-0.6
Total	2	8	7	.533	54	17	6	3	178.1	189	114	9	19	57	64	4.95	78	.283	.356	47-4	.170	-2	122	-21	-1.6
OLSEN, KEVIN Kevin Gary B 7.26.1976 Covina, CA BR/TR 6-2/200# d9.7																									
2001	Fla N	0	0	—	4	2	0	0-0	15	11	2	0	0	2-1	13	1.20	352	.204	.232	3-1	.000	-0	22	5	0.2
2002	Fla N	0	5	.000	17	8	0	0-0	55.2	57	31	5	1	31-1	38	4.53	87	.270	.363	12-0	.083	-1	97	-4	-0.4
2003	Fla N	0	0	—	7	0	0	0-0	12	25	18	2	0	4-1	12	12.75	32	.431	.468	0-0	—	0		-12	-0.6
Total	3	0	5	.000	28	10	0	0-0	82.2	93	51	7	1	37-3	63	5.12	79	.288	.361	15-1	.067	-1	81	-11	-0.8
OLSEN, VERN Vern Jarl B 3.16.1918 Hillsboro, OR D 7.13.1989 Maywood, IL BR/TL 6-0.5/175# d9.8 Mil 1943-45																									
1939	Chi N	1	0	1.000	4	0	0	0	7.2	2	0	0	0	7	3	0.00	—	.087	.300	1-0	.000	0		3	0.5
1940	Chi N	13	9	.591	34	20	9-4	0	172.2	172	64	5	2	62	71	2.97	126	.260	.325	57-3	.263	3*	95	16	2.5
1941	Chi N	10	8	.556	37	23	10-2	1	185.2	202	84	7	1	59	73	3.15	111	.276	.331	63-2	.238	3	108	5	0.9
1942	Chi N	6	9	.400	32	17	4-1	1	140.1	161	75	6	1	55	46	4.49	71	.283	.347	48-1	.188	1	103	-17	-1.5
1946	Chi N	0	0	—	5	0	0	0	9.2	10	3	0	0	9	8	2.79	119	.294	.442	0-0	—	0		1	0.0
Total	5	30	26	.536	112	60	23-7	2	516	547	226	18	4	192	201	3.40	103	.271	.335	169-6	.231	8	102	8	2.4
OLSON, GREGG Greggory William B 10.11.1966 Scribner, NE BR/TR 6-4/206# d9.2																									
1988	Bal A	1	1	.500	10	0	0	0-1	11	10	4	1	0	10-1	9	3.27	120	.244	.392	0-0	—	0		1	0.2
1989	Bal A	5	2	.714	64	0	0	27-6	85	57	17	1	1	46-10	90	1.69	224	.188	.295	0-0	—	0		20	2.8
1990	Bal A☆	6	5	.545	64	0	0	37-5	74.1	57	20	3	3	31-3	74	2.42	157	.213	.299	0-0	—	0		12	2.6
1991	Bal A	4	6	.400	72	0	0	31-8	73.2	74	28	1	1	29-5	72	3.18	125	.261	.331	0-0	—	0		7	1.3
1992	Bal A	1	5	.167	60	0	0	36-8	61.1	46	14	3	0	24-0	58	2.05	196	.211	.287	0-0	—	0		14	2.7
1993	Bal A	0	2	.000	50	0	0	29-6	45	37	9	1	0	18-3	44	1.60	280	.223	.296	1-0	.000	-0		14	2.1
1994	Atl N	0	2	.000	16	0	0	1-0	14.2	19	15	1	1	13-3	10	9.20	46	.317	.440	1-0	.000	-0		-7	-1.0
1995	Cle A	0	0	—	3	0	0	0-0	2.2	5	4	1	0	2-0	0	13.50	35	.417	.500	0-0	—	0		-2	-0.1
	KC A	3	3	.500	20	0	0	3-2	30.1	23	11	3	0	17-2	21	3.26	147	.215	.317	0-0	—	0		5	1.0
	Year	3	3	.500	23	0	0	3-2	33	28	19	4	0	19-2	21	4.09	117	.235	.336	0-0	—	0		3	0.9
1996	Det A	3	0	1.000	43	0	0	8-2	43	43	25	6	1	28-4	29	5.02	101	.259	.369	0-0	—	0		1	0.0
	Hou N	1	0	1.000	9	0	0	0-0	9.1	12	5	1	0	7-2	8	4.82	80	.308	.404	0-0	—	0		-1	-0.1
1997	Min A	0	0	—	11	0	0	0-0	8.1	19	17	0	0	11-1	6	18.36	25	.432	.545	0-0	—	0		-12	-0.5
	KC A	4	3	.571	34	0	0	1-3	41.2	39	18	3	1	17-3	28	3.02	156	.260	.337	0-0	—	0		6	0.9

Year	Tm Lg	W	L	Pct	G	GS	CG-Sho	SV-BS	IP	H	R	HR	HB	BB-IB	SO	ERA	AERA	OAV	OOB	AB-SH	AVG	PB	Sup	APR	PW
	Year	4	3	.571	45	0	0	1-3	50	58	35	3	1	28-4	34	5.58	84	.299	.388	0-0	—	0		-5	0.4
1998	Ari N	3	4	.429	64	0	0	30-4	68.2	56	25	4	1	25-1	55	3.01	140	.223	.295	2-0	.500	1		9	1.7
1999	†Ari N	9	4	.692	61	0	0	14-9	60.2	54	28	9	2	25-2	45	3.71	123	.238	.316	0-0	—	0		6	1.1
2000	LA N	0	1	.000	13	0	0	0-1	17.2	21	11	4	1	7-0	15	5.09	85	.296	.363	0-0	—	0		-2	-0.1
2001	LA N	0	1	.000	28	0	0	0-1	24.2	26	24	4	0	20-1	24	8.03	50	.268	.383	0-0	—	0		-12	-0.6
Total	14	40	39	.506	622	0	0	217-56	672	598	275	46	12	330-41	588	3.46	122	.239	.328	4-0	.250	1		59	14.0
OLSON, TED Theodore Otto B 8.27.1912 Quincy, MA D 12.9.1980 Weymouth, MA BR/TR 6-2.5/185# d6.21																									
1936	Bos A	1	1	.500	5	3	1	0	18.1	24	16	3	0	8	5	7.36	72	.324	.390	7-0	.143	-0	66	-3	-0.3
1937	Bos A	0	0	—	11	0	0	0	32.1	42	28	4	0	15	11	7.24	66	.318	.388	10-0	.300	1		-8	-0.3
1938	Bos A	0	0	—	2	0	0	0	7	9	5	0	0	2	2	6.43	77	.310	.355	1-0	.000	-0		-1	-0.1
Total	3	1	1	.500	18	3	1	0	57.2	75	49	7	0	25	18	7.18	69	.319	.385	18-0	.222	1	66	-12	-0.7
OLWINE, ED Edward R. B 5.28.1958 Greenville, OH BL/TL 6-2/165# d6.2																									
1986	Atl N	0	0	—	37	0	0	1-0	47.2	35	20	5	1	17-7	37	3.40	117	.207	.282	3-0	.333	1		3	0.2
1987	Atl N	0	1	.000	27	0	0	1-1	23.1	25	16	4	1	8-1	12	5.01	87	.269	.330	0-1	—	0		-2	-0.1
1988	Atl N	0	0	—	16	0	0	1-0	18.2	22	15	4	1	4-1	5	6.75	55	.286	.329	0-0	—	0		-6	-0.3
Total	3	0	1	.000	80	0	0	3-1	89.2	82	51	13	3	29-9	54	4.52	89	.242	.306	3-1	.333	1		-5	-0.2
O'NEAL, SKINNY Oran Herbert B 5.2.1899 Gatewood, MO D 6.2.1981 Springfield, MO BR/TR 5-11/160# d4.18																									
1925	Phi N	0	0	—	11	1	0	0	20.1	35	23	2	0	12	6	9.30	51	.407	.480	6-0	.167	-0	106	-8	-0.4
1927	Phi N	0	0	—	2	0	0	0	5	9	5	0	0	2	2	9.00	46	.409	.458	1-0	.000	-0		-2	-0.1
Total	2	0	0	—	13	1	0	0	25.1	44	28	2	0	14	8	9.24	50	.407	.475	7-0	.143	-0	106	-10	-0.5
O'NEAL, RANDY Randall Jeffrey B 8.30.1960 Ashland, KY BR/TR 6-2/195# d9.12																									
1984	Det A	2	1	.667	4	3	0	0-0	18.2	16	7	0	0	6-0	12	3.38	116	.222	.282	0-0	—	0	107	2	0.2
1985	Det A	5	5	.500	28	12	1	1-0	94.1	82	42	8	2	36-3	52	3.24	126	.240	.310	0-0	—	0	93	7	0.7
1986	Det A	3	7	.300	37	11	1	2-1	122.2	121	69	13	3	44-9	68	4.33	95	.260	.324	0-0	—	0	104	-4	-0.3
1987	Atl N	4	2	.667	16	10	0	0-0	61	79	41	12	2	24-3	33	5.61	78	.316	.378	19-1	.105	-1*	125	-7	-0.6
	StL N	0	0	—	1	1	0	0-0	5	2	1	0	0	2-0	4	1.80	231	.111	.200	1-0	1.000	0	22	1	0.1
	Year	4	2	.667	17	11	0	0-0	66	81	2	12	2	26-3	37	5.32	82	.302	.366	20-1	.150	-0	116	-6	-0.5
1988	StL N	2	3	.400	10	8	0	0-0	53	57	29	7	2	10-1	20	4.58	76	.274	.314	19-1	.000	-2	121	-6	-0.7
1989	Phi N	0	1	.000	20	1	0	0-1	39	46	28	5	0	9-2	29	6.23	57	.301	.333	5-0	.000	-1	399	-10	-0.6
1990	SF N	1	0	1.000	26	0	0	0-0	47	58	23	3	0	18-4	30	3.83	95	.314	.371	6-1	.167	-0		-2	-0.1
Total	7	17	19	.472	142	46	2	3-2	440.2	461	240	48	9	149-22	248	4.35	91	.272	.331	50-3	.080	-3	115	-19	-1.3
O'NEIL, ED Edward J. B 3.11.1859 Fall River, MA D 9.30.1892 Fall River, MA TR 5-11/180# d6.20																									
1890	Tol AA	0	2	.000	2	2	2	0	16	27	18	0	0	13	2	7.88	50	.365	.460	9	.000	-2	145	-6	-0.6
	Phi AA	0	6	.000	6	6	6	0	52	84	77	0	7	32	17	9.69	40	.353	.444	31	.161	-1*	58	-32	-2.5
	Year	0	8	.000	8	8	8	0	68	111	80	0	7	45	19	9.26	42	.356	.448	40	.125	-2	80	-40	-3.1
O'NEILL, J. J. B Brooklyn, NY d8.20																									
1875	Atl NA	0	4	.000	5	4	3	0	34	59	45	3		0	0	5.03	41	.343	.343	26	.077	-2*	68	-9	-0.9
O'NEILL, TIP James Edward B 5.25.1858 Woodstock, ON, CAN D 12.31.1915 Montreal, PQ, CAN BR/TR 6-1.5/167# d5.5 ▲																									
1883	NY N	5	12	.294	19	19	15	0	148	182	129	5		64	55	4.07	76	.289	.354	76	.197	-1*	83	-14	-1.4
1884	StL AA	11	4	.733	17	14	14	0	141	125	95	3	4	51	36	2.68	122	.219	.288	297	.276	5*	112	4	0.7
Total	2	16	16	.500	36	33	29	0	289	307	224	8	4	115	91	3.39	94	.256	.323	373	.260	3	95	-10	-0.7
O'NEILL, HARRY Joseph Henry B 11.20.1892 Lindsay, ON, CAN D 9.5.1969 Ridgetown, ON, CAN BR/TR 6/180# d9.15																									
1922	Phi A	0	0	—	1	0	0	0	3	2	1	0	1	1	0	3.00	142	.200	.333	1-0	.000	-0		0	0.0
1923	Phi A	0	0	—	3	0	0	0	2	1	0	0	0	3	2	0.00	—	.167	.444	0-0	—	0		1	0.0
Total	2	0	0	—	4	0	0	0	5	3	1	0	1	4	2	1.80	233	.188	.381	1-0	.000	-0		1	0.0
O'NEILL, MIKE Michael Joyce (a.k.a. Michael Joyce In 1901) B 9.7.1877 Maam, Ireland D 8.12.1959 Scranton, PA BL/TL 5-11/185# d9.20 b-Jim b-Jack b-Steve																									
1901	StL N	2	2	.500	5	4	4-1	0	41	29	12	2	5	10	16	1.32	242	.197	.272	15-0	.400	3*	139	7	1.0
1902	StL N	16	15	.516	36	32	29-2	2	288.1	297	136	3	12	66	105	2.90	94	.266	.314	135-1	.319	9*	92	-5	0.8
1903	StL N	4	13	.235	19	17	12	0	145	184	124	2	6	43	39	3.79	86	.304	.356	110-0	.227	2*	66	-17	-1.4
1904	StL N	10	14	.417	25	24	23-1	0	220	229	86	1	3	50	68	2.09	129	.262	.304	91-5	.231	5*	94	11	2.0
Total	4	32	44	.421	85	77	68-4	2	694.1	739	358	8	26	169	228	2.73	105	.269	.318	351-6	.271	19	89	-4	2.4
O'NEILL, EMMETT Robert Emmett "Pinky" B 1.13.1918 San Mateo, CA D 10.11.1993 Sparks, NV BR/TR 6-2.5/180# d8.3																									
1943	Bos A	1	4	.200	11	5	1	0	57.2	56	31	3	1	46	20	4.53	73	.256	.387	16-0	.188	1	51	-7	-0.5
1944	Bos A	6	11	.353	28	22	8-1	0	151.2	154	88	6	2	89	68	4.63	73	.265	.365	55-0	.182	-0	109	-20	-2.2
1945	Bos A	8	11	.421	24	22	10-1	0	141.2	134	87	5	5	117	55	5.15	66	.258	.399	50-1	.180	2	107	-24	-2.7
1946	Chi N	0	0	—	1	0	0	0	1	0	0	0	0	3	1	0.00	—	.000	.500	0-0	—	0		0	0.0
	Chi A	0	0	—	2	0	0	0	3.2	4	2	0	0	5	0	0.00	—	.333	.529	1-0	.000	-0		1	0.0
Total	4	15	26	.366	66	49	19-2	0	355.2	348	208	14	8	260	144	4.76	71	.261	.385	122-1	.180	2	103	-50	-5.4
ONTIVEROS, STEVE Steven B 3.5.1961 Tularosa, NM BR/TR 6/190# d6.14																									
1985	Oak A	1	3	.250	39	0	0	8-1	74.2	45	17	4	2	19-2	36	1.93	200	.174	.234	0-0	—	0		18	1.3
1986	Oak A	2	2	.500	46	0	0	10-3	72.2	72	40	10	1	25-3	54	4.71	82	.265	.322	0-0	—	0*		-6	-0.5
1987	Oak A	10	8	.556	35	22	2-1	1-3	150.2	141	78	19	4	50-3	97	4.00	103	.242	.305	0-0	—	0	119	1	0.2
1988	Oak A	3	4	.429	10	10	0	0-0	54.2	57	32	4	0	21-1	30	4.61	82	.265	.331	0-0	—	0*	161	-6	-0.6
1989	Phi N	2	1	.667	6	5	0	0-0	30.2	34	15	2	0	15-1	12	3.82	93	.288	.368	12-0	.083	-0	115	-1	0.0
1990	Phi N	0	0	—	5	0	0	0-0	10	9	3	1	0	3-0	6	2.70	142	.225	.279	0-0	—	0		1	0.1
1993	Sea A	0	2	.000	14	0	0	0-0	18	18	3	0	0	6-2	13	1.00	442	.277	.338	0-0	—	0		6	0.6
1994	Oak A	6	4	.600	27	13	2	0-0	115.1	93	39	7	6	26-1	56	**2.65**	167	.217	**.271**	0-0	—	0	86	24	1.9
1995	Oak A★	9	6	.600	22	22	2-1	0-0	129.2	144	75	12	4	38-0	77	4.37	102	.283	.335	0-0	—	0	104	-2	0.0
2000	Bos A	1	1	.500	3	1	0	0-0	5.1	9	6	1	0	4-0	1	10.13	50	.375	.464	0-0	—	0	37	-3	-0.5
Total	10	34	31	.523	207	73	6-2	19-7	661.2	622	308	60	17	207-13	382	3.67	113	.248	.307	12-0	.083	-0	113	32	2.5
OQUIST, MIKE Michael Lee B 5.30.1968 LaJunta, CO BR/TR 6-2/170# d8.14																									
1993	Bal A	0	0	—	5	0	0	0-0	11.2	12	5	0	0	4-1	8	3.86	116	.261	.320	0-0	—	0		1	0.0
1994	Bal A	3	3	.500	15	9	0	0-0	58.1	75	41	7	6	30-4	39	6.17	81	.319	.404	0-0	—	0	92	-7	-0.6
1995	Bal A	2	1	.667	27	0	0	0-1	54	51	27	6	2	41-3	27	4.17	114	.246	.370	0-0	—	0		3	0.1
1996	SD N	0	0	—	8	0	0	0-0	7.2	6	2	0	0	4-2	4	2.35	169	.231	.333	0-0	—	0		2	0.1
1997	Oak A	4	6	.400	19	17	1	0-0	107.2	111	62	15	6	43-3	72	5.02	90	.266	.340	4-1	.250	0*	107	-5	-0.4
1998	Oak A	7	11	.389	31	29	0	0-0	175	210	125	27	5	57-1	112	6.22	73	.298	.352	1-1	.000	-0	102	-27	-2.4
1999	Oak A	9	10	.474	28	24	0	0-0	140.2	158	86	18	2	64-5	89	5.37	87	.283	.358	2-0	.000	-0	104	-8	-1.0
Total	7	25	31	.446	133	79	1	0-1	555	623	348	73	21	243-19	351	5.46	85	.284	.358	7-2	.143	-0	102	-41	-4.2
O'RILEY, DON Donald Lee B 3.12.1945 Topeka, KS D 5.2.1997 Kansas City, MO BR/TR 6-3/205# d6.20																									
1969	KC A	1	1	.500	18	0	0	1-0	23.1	32	23	0	0	15-2	10	6.94	53	.311	.395	3-0	.000	-0*		-9	-0.9
1970	KC A	0	0	—	9	2	0	0-0	23.1	26	15	5	1	9-0	13	5.40	69	.277	.343	3-2	.000	-0	155	-4	-0.3
Total	2	1	1	.500	27	2	0	1-0	46.2	58	38	5	1	24-2	23	6.17	60	.294	.371	6-2	.000	-1	155	-13	-1.2
OROPESA, EDDIE Edilberto B 11.23.1971 Colon, Cuba BL/TL 6-3/215# d4.3																									
2001	Phi N	1	0	1.000	30	0	0	0-1	19	16	10	1	0	17-6	15	4.74	90	.232	.384	0-0	—	0		-1	0.0
2002	Ari N	2	0	1.000	32	0	0	0-1	25.1	39	30	6	2	15-0	18	10.30	43	.348	.431	0-0	—	0		-15	-1.0
2003	Ari N	3	3	.500	47	0	0	0-0	38.2	38	27	3	2	27-2	39	5.82	80	.257	.379	0-0	—	0		-4	-0.5
Total	3	6	3	.667	109	0	0	0-2	83	93	67	10	4	59-8	72	6.94	65	.283	.397	0-0	—	0		-20	-1.5
OROSCO, JESSE Jesse Russell B 4.21.1957 Santa Barbara, CA BR/TL 6-2/185# d4.5																									
1979	NY N	1	2	.333	18	2	0	0-0	35	33	20	4	2	22-0	22	4.89	75	.260	.377	6-1	.000	-1	97	-4	-0.4
1981	NY N	0	1	.000	8	0	0	1-0	17.1	13	4	2	0	6-2	18	1.56	224	.213	.284	2-0	.000	-0		4	0.2

Year	Tm Lg	W	L	Pct	G	GS	CG-Sho	SV-BS	IP	H	R	HR	HB	BB-IB	SO	ERA	AERA	OAV	OOB	AB-SH	AVG	PB	Sup	APR	PW
1982	NY N	4	10	.286	54	2	0	4-1	109.1	92	37	7	2	40-2	89	2.72	134	.230	.300	14-0	.143	-0	109	12	1.5
1983	NY N★	13	7	.650	62	0	0	17-5	110	76	27	3	1	38-7	84	1.47	247	.197	.269	12-2	.333	1		**24**	**5.2**
1984	NY N☆	10	6	.625	60	0	0	31-8	87	58	29	7	2	34-6	85	2.59	137	.185	.267	4-1	.250	1		9	2.1
1985	NY N	8	6	.571	54	0	0	17-8	79	66	26	6	0	34-7	68	2.73	127	.224	.303	7-2	.429	1		7	1.6
1986	†NY N	8	6	.571	58	0	0	21-8	81	64	23	6	3	35-3	62	2.33	152	.217	.304	3-0	.000	0		12	2.5
1987	NY N	3	9	.250	58	0	0	16-6	77	78	41	5	2	31-9	78	4.44	85	.266	.336	8-1	.000	-1		-5	-1.0
1988	†LA N	3	2	.600	55	0	0	9-6	53	41	18	4	2	30-3	43	2.72	123	.215	.323	2-0	.000	-0		4	0.5
1989	Cle A	3	4	.429	69	0	0	3-4	78	54	20	7	2	26-4	79	2.08	191	.198	.270	0-0	—	0		16	1.5
1990	Cle A	5	4	.556	55	0	0	2-1	64.2	58	35	9	0	38-7	55	3.90	101	.239	.338	0-0	—	0		-2	-0.2
1991	Cle A	2	0	1.000	47	0	0	0-0	45.2	52	20	4	1	15-8	36	3.74	111	.286	.338	0-0	—	0		3	0.1
1992	Mil A	3	1	.750	59	0	0	1-1	39	33	15	5	1	13-1	40	3.23	119	.232	.297	0-0	—	0		3	0.3
1993	Mil A	3	5	.375	57	0	0	8-5	56.2	47	25	2	3	17-3	67	3.18	134	.224	.289	1-0	.000	-0		6	0.9
1994	Mil A	3	1	.750	40	0	0	0-4	39	32	26	4	2	26-2	36	5.08	99	.222	.345	0-0	—	0		-1	-0.1
1995	Bal A	2	4	.333	**65**	0	0	3-3	49.2	28	19	4	1	27-7	58	3.26	146	.169	.283	0-0	—	0		8	1.0
1996	†Bal A	3	1	.750	66	0	0	0-3	55.2	42	22	5	2	28-4	52	3.40	145	.207	.308	0-0	—	0		10	0.6
1997	†Bal A	6	3	.667	71	0	0	0-4	50.1	29	13	6	0	30-0	46	2.32	190	.169	.289	0-0	—	0		13	2.0
1998	Bal A	4	1	.800	69	0	0	7-2	56.2	46	20	6	1	28-1	50	3.18	143	.221	.314	0-0	—	0		9	0.9
1999	Bal A	0	2	.000	65	0	0	1-3	32	28	21	5	2	20-3	35	5.34	88	.239	.352	0-0	—	0		-3	-0.1
2000	StL N	0	0	—	6	0	0	0-0	2.1	3	3	1	2	3-2	4	3.86	120	.273	.500	0-0	—	0		-1	0.0
2001	LA N	0	1	.000	35	0	0	0-2	16	17	7	3	0	7-1	21	3.94	102	.279	.348	0-0	—	0		0	0.0
2002	LA N	1	2	.333	56	0	0	1-0	27	24	10	4	0	12-1	22	3.00	127	.229	.305	0-0	—	0		2	0.3
2003	SD N	1	1	.500	42	0	0	2-1	25	33	22	4	2	10-0	22	7.56	52	.317	.381	0-0	—	0		-11	-0.9
	NY A	0	0	—	15	0	0	0-1	4.1	4	6	0	0	6-3	4	10.38	42	.250	.435	0-0	—	0		-3	-0.1
	Min A	1	1	.500	8	0	0	0-0	4.2	4	3	0	1	5-0	3	5.79	79	.235	.417	0-0	—	0		-1	-0.1
	Year	1	1	.500	23	0	0	0-1	9	8	14	0	1	11-3	7	8.00	56	.242	.426	0-0	—	0		-4	-0.2
Total	24	87	80	.521	1252	4	0	144-76	1295.1	1055	512	113	34	581-86	1179	3.16	125	.223	.309	59-7	.169	2	97	111	18.3

O'ROURKE d7.9

Year	Tm Lg	W	L	Pct	G	GS	CG-Sho	SV-BS	IP	H	R	HR	HB	BB-IB	SO	ERA	AERA	OAV	OOB	AB-SH	AVG	PB	Sup	APR	PW
1872	Eck NA	0	1	.000	1	1	1	0	9	16	15	0		2	0	8.00	42	.327	.353	4	.000	-1	34	-4	-0.3

O'ROURKE, JIM James Henry "Orator Jim" B 9.1.1850 Bridgeport, CT D 1.8.1919 Bridgeport, CT BR/TR 5-8/185# d4.26.1872 M5 U1 HF1945 b-John s-Queenie ▲

Year	Tm Lg	W	L	Pct	G	GS	CG-Sho	SV-BS	IP	H	R	HR	HB	BB-IB	SO	ERA	AERA	OAV	OOB	AB-SH	AVG	PB	Sup	APR	PW
1883	Buf N	0	0	—	2	0	0	1	7	10	9	0		1	1	6.43	49	.357	.379	436	.328	1*		-2	-0.1
1884	Buf N	0	1	.000	4	0	0	1	12.2	7	5	0		1	3	2.84	111	.175	.195	467	.347	2*		1	0.1
Total	2	0	1	.000	6	0	0	2	19.2	17	14	0		2	4	4.12	77	.250	.271	903	.338	2		-1	0.0

O'ROURKE, MIKE Michael J. d9.1

Year	Tm Lg	W	L	Pct	G	GS	CG-Sho	SV-BS	IP	H	R	HR	HB	BB-IB	SO	ERA	AERA	OAV	OOB	AB-SH	AVG	PB	Sup	APR	PW
1890	Bal AA	1	2	.333	5	5	5	0	41	45	19	0	3	10	8	3.95	103	.271	.324	26	.115	-1*	60	2	0.1

ORR, DAVE David L. B 9.29.1859 New York, NY D 6.2.1915 Richmond Hill, NY BR/TR 5-11/250# d5.17.1883 M1 ▲

Year	Tm Lg	W	L	Pct	G	GS	CG-Sho	SV-BS	IP	H	R	HR	HB	BB-IB	SO	ERA	AERA	OAV	OOB	AB-SH	AVG	PB	Sup	APR	PW
1885	NY AA	0	0	—	3	0	0	0	10	11	13	2	0	5	1	7.20	43	.250	.327	444	.342	2*		-5	-0.2

ORRELL, JOE Forrest Gordon B 3.6.1917 National City, CA D 1.12.1993 Chula Vista, CA BR/TR 6-4/210# d8.12

Year	Tm Lg	W	L	Pct	G	GS	CG-Sho	SV-BS	IP	H	R	HR	HB	BB-IB	SO	ERA	AERA	OAV	OOB	AB-SH	AVG	PB	Sup	APR	PW
1943	Det A	0	0	—	10	0	0	1	19.1	18	9	0	2	11	2	3.72	95	.257	.373	4-0	.250	0		0	0.0
1944	Det A	2	1	.667	10	2	0	0	22.1	26	13	0	1	11	10	2.42	147	.286	.369	4-0	.250	0	105	0	0.1
1945	Det A	2	3	.400	12	5	1	0	48	46	18	1	2	24	14	3.00	117	.260	.355	15-0	.133	-1	53	3	0.2
Total	3	4	4	.500	32	7	1	1	89.2	90	40	1	5	46	26	3.01	117	.266	.362	23-0	.174	-1	68	3	0.3

ORTEGA, PHIL Filomeno Coronado "Kemo" B 10.7.1939 Gilbert, AZ BR/TR 6-2/175# d9.10

Year	Tm Lg	W	L	Pct	G	GS	CG-Sho	SV-BS	IP	H	R	HR	HB	BB-IB	SO	ERA	AERA	OAV	OOB	AB-SH	AVG	PB	Sup	APR	PW
1960	LA N	0	0	—	3	1	0	0	6.1	12	12	1	0	5-0	4	17.05	23	.400	.486	1-0	.000	-0	178	-8	-0.4
1961	LA N	0	2	.000	4	2	1	0	13	10	9	6	0	2-0	15	5.54	78	.208	.240	4-0	.250	0	41	-2	-0.2
1962	LA N	0	2	.000	24	3	0	1	53.2	60	43	8	3	39-2	30	6.88	53	.276	.392	7-0	.000	-1	40	-19	-1.0
1963	LA N	0	0	—	1	0	0	0	1	2	2	1	0	0-0	1	18.00	17	.400	.400	0-0	—	0		-2	-0.1
1964	LA N	7	9	.438	34	25	4-3	1	157.1	149	74	22	6	56-2	107	4.00	81	.249	.317	44-7	.136	-0*	104	-11	-1.2
1965	Was A	12	15	.444	35	29	4-2	0	179.2	176	107	33	5	97-7	88	5.11	68	.262	.356	53-3	.208	4	97	-28	-3.4
1966	Was A	12	12	.500	33	31	5-1	0	197.1	158	91	29	5	53-5	121	3.92	88	.218	.274	54-8	.056	-2	96	-7	-1.2
1967	Was A	10	10	.500	34	34	5-2	0	219.2	189	77	16	6	57-3	122	3.03	104	.231	.286	66-7	.061	-3	97	7	0.3
1968	Was A	5	12	.294	31	16	1-1	0	115.2	115	70	12	5	62-8	57	4.98	59	.263	.356	24-5	.167	1	105	-26	-3.5
1969	Cal A	0	0	—	5	0	0	0-0	8	13	13	3	0	7-1	4	10.13	34	.333	.435	0-0	—	0		-7	-0.4
Total	10	46	62	.426	204	141	20-9	2-0	951.2	884	498	131	30	378-28	549	4.43	75	.246	.321	253-30	.115	-1	97	-103	-11.1

ORTH, AL Albert Lewis "Smiling Al" or "The Curveless Wonder" B 9.5.1872 Tipton, IN D 10.8.1948 Lynchburg, VA BL/TR 6/200# d8.15 U6 ▲

Year	Tm Lg	W	L	Pct	G	GS	CG-Sho	SV-BS	IP	H	R	HR	HB	BB-IB	SO	ERA	AERA	OAV	OOB	AB-SH	AVG	PB	Sup	APR	PW
1895	Phi N	8	1	.889	11	10	9	1	88	103	50	0	2	22	25	3.89	123	.288	.332	45-2	.356	4	159	9	1.0
1896	Phi N	15	10	.600	25	23	19	0	196	244	128	10	3	46	23	4.41	98	.302	.342	82-0	.256	3	103	-1	0.2
1897	Phi N	14	19	.424	36	34	29-2	0	282.1	349	194	12	6	82	64	4.62	91	.301	.350	152-2	.329	7*	104	-14	-0.4
1898	Phi N	15	13	.536	32	28	25-1	0	250	290	131	2	8	53	52	3.02	114	.288	.329	123-7	.293	8*	122	9	1.7
1899	Phi N	14	3	.824	21	15	13-3	1	144.2	149	67	0	3	19	35	**2.49**	148	.266	.294	62-1	.210	1*	105	17	1.6
1900	Phi N	14	14	.500	33	30	24-2	1	262	302	145	4	13	60	68	3.78	96	.288	.335	129-0	.310	7*	105	-2	0.5
1901	Phi N	20	12	.625	35	33	30-**6**	1	281.2	250	101	3	8	32	92	2.27	150	.237	**.264**	128-0	.281	5*	95	33	**4.4**
1902	Was A	19	18	.514	38	37	36-1	0	324	367	181	18	9	40	76	3.97	93	.286	.312	175-3	.217	1*	101	-5	-0.3
1903	Was A	10	22	.313	36	32	30-2	**2**	279.2	326	174	8	7	62	88	4.34	72	.290	.331	162-1	.302	9*	75	-34	-2.4
1904	Was A	3	4	.429	10	7	7	0	73.2	88	49	2	3	15	23	4.76	56	.297	.338	102-0	.216	0*	134	-15	-1.3
	NY A	11	6	.647	20	18	11-2	0	137.2	122	47	0	3	19	47	2.68	101	.238	.270	64-1	.297	3*	98	3	0.8
	Year	14	10	.583	30	25	18-2	0	211.1	210	51	2	6	34	70	3.41	79	.260	.295	166-1	.247	3	108	-10	-0.5
1905	NY A	18	16	.529	40	37	26-6	0	305.1	273	122	8	7	61	121	2.86	103	.241	.284	131-3	.183	-1*	99	7	0.6
1906	NY A	**27**	17	.614	45	39	**36**-3	0	**338.2**	317	115	2	1	66	133	2.34	127	.251	.289	135-3	.274	6*	90	21	3.4
1907	NY A	14	21	.400	36	33	21-2	0	248.2	244	134	2	6	53	78	2.61	107	.259	.303	105-2	.324	7*	98	-4	0.5
1908	NY A	2	13	.133	21	17	8-1	0	139.1	134	62	4	4	30	22	3.42	72	.255	.300	69-2	.290	5*	93	-9	-0.5
1909	NY A	0	0	—	1	1	0	0	3	6	4	0	0	1	1	12.00	21	.429	.467	34-1	.265	0*	251	-2	-0.1
Total	15	204	189	.519	440	394	324-31	6	3354.2	3564	1704	75	83	661	948	3.37	101	.272	.311	1698-28	.273	63	101	13	9.7

ORTIZ, RAMON Diogenes Ramon (Ortiz) B 3.23.1973 Cotui, D.R. BR/TR 6/165# d8.19

Year	Tm Lg	W	L	Pct	G	GS	CG-Sho	SV-BS	IP	H	R	HR	HB	BB-IB	SO	ERA	AERA	OAV	OOB	AB-SH	AVG	PB	Sup	APR	PW
1999	Ana A	2	3	.400	9	9	0	0-0	48.1	50	35	7	2	25-0	44	6.52	75	.265	.353	0-0	—	0	81	-8	-0.6
2000	Ana A	8	6	.571	18	18	2	0-0	111.1	96	69	18	2	55-0	73	5.09	100	.236	.327	0-0	—	0	104	-1	-0.1
2001	Ana A	13	11	.542	32	32	2	0-0	208.2	223	114	25	12	76-6	135	4.36	105	.274	.343	7-0	.000	-1	93	3	0.1
2002	†Ana A	15	9	.625	32	32	4-1	0-0	217.1	188	97	40	5	68-0	162	3.77	118	.230	.292	7-0	.000	-1	128	17	1.5
2003	Ana A	16	13	.552	32	32	1	0-0	180	209	121	28	12	63-0	94	5.20	83	.287	.350	5-1	.000	-0	114	-22	-3.0
Total	5	54	42	.563	123	123	9-1	0-0	765.2	766	436	118	33	287-6	508	4.63	99	.259	.329	19-1	.000	-2	108	-11	-2.1

ORTIZ, BABY Oliverio (Nunez) B 12.5.1919 Camaguey, Cuba D 3.27.1984 Central Senado, Cuba BR/TR 6/190# d9.23 b-Roberto

Year	Tm Lg	W	L	Pct	G	GS	CG-Sho	SV-BS	IP	H	R	HR	HB	BB-IB	SO	ERA	AERA	OAV	OOB	AB-SH	AVG	PB	Sup	APR	PW
1944	Was A	0	2	.000	2	2	1	0	13	13	11	0	0	6	4	6.23	52	.255	.333	6-0	.167	-0	103	-4	-0.6

ORTIZ, RUSS Russell Reid B 6.5.1974 Van Nuys, CA BR/TR 6-1/200# d4.2

Year	Tm Lg	W	L	Pct	G	GS	CG-Sho	SV-BS	IP	H	R	HR	HB	BB-IB	SO	ERA	AERA	OAV	OOB	AB-SH	AVG	PB	Sup	APR	PW
1998	SF N	4	4	.500	22	13	0	0-0	88.1	90	51	11	4	46-1	75	4.99	80	.269	.360	25-5	.280	3	146	-10	-0.4
1999	SF N	18	9	.667	33	33	3	0-0	207.2	189	109	24	6	125-5	164	3.81	110	.244	.351	71-7	.197	3	117	3	0.8
2000	†SF N	14	12	.538	33	32	0	0-0	195.2	192	117	28	7	112-1	167	5.01	84	.261	.361	61-6	.197	4	119	-17	-1.4
2001	SF N	17	9	.654	33	33	1-1	0-0	218.2	187	90	13	0	91-3	169	3.29	121	.232	.309	67-8	.194	5	128	17	2.4
2002	†SF N	14	10	.583	33	33	2	0-0	214.1	191	89	15	4	94-5	137	3.61	108	.241	.323	69-7	.246	8	123	9	2.0
2003	†Atl N★	**21**	7	.750	34	34	1-1	0-0	212.1	177	101	17	4	102-7	149	3.81	111	.223	.312	70-6	.257	8*	126	10	1.9
Total	6	88	51	.633	188	178	7-2	0-0	1137	1026	557	108	25	570-22	861	3.97	103	.242	.333	363-39	.223	31	124	12	5.3

ORWOLL, OSSIE Oswald Christian B 11.17.1900 Portland, OR D 5.8.1967 Decorah, IA BL/TL 6/174# d4.13 ▲

Year	Tm Lg	W	L	Pct	G	GS	CG-Sho	SV-BS	IP	H	R	HR	HB	BB-IB	SO	ERA	AERA	OAV	OOB	AB-SH	AVG	PB	Sup	APR	PW
1928	Phi A	6	5	.545	27	8	3	2	106	110	59	7	2	50	53	4.58	87	.274	.358	170-5	.306	7*	84	-4	0.0
1929	Phi A	0	2	.000	12	0	0	1	30	32	23	6	0	6	12	4.80	88	.278	.314	51-0	.255	1*		-4	-0.2
Total	2	6	7	.462	39	8	3	3	136	142	82	13	2	56	65	4.63	88	.275	.348	221-5	.294	7	84	-8	-0.2

Year	Tm Lg	W	L	Pct	G	GS	CG-Sho	SV-BS	IP	H	R	HR	HB	BB-IB	SO	ERA	AERA	OAV	OOB	AB-SH	AVG	PB	Sup	APR	PW
OSBORN, OZZIE Danny Leon B 6.19.1946 Springfield, MO BR/TR 6-2/195# d4.26																									
1975	Chi A	3	0	1.000	24	0	0	0-0	58	57	29	2	2	37-1	38	4.50	86	.265	.375	0-0	—	0		-2	-0.2
OSBORN, BOB John Bode B 4.17.1903 San Diego, TX D 4.19.1960 Paris, AR BR/TR 6-1/175# d9.16																									
1925	Chi N	0	0	—	1	0	0	0	2	6	2	0	0	0	0	0.00	—	.600	.600	0-0	—	0		0	0.0
1926	Chi N	6	5	.545	31	15	6	1	136.1	157	64	3	0	58	43	3.63	106	.301	.371	41-4	.146	-3	91	4	0.1
1927	Chi N	5	5	.500	24	12	2	0	107.2	125	54	2	1	48	45	4.18	92	.294	.367	39-1	.205	-0	112	-2	-0.2
1929	Chi N	0	0	—	3	1	0	0	9	8	3	0	0	2	1	3.00	154	.242	.286	4-0	.250	0	113	2	0.1
1930	Chi N	10	6	.625	35	13	3	1	126.2	147	74	9	1	53	42	4.97	98	.300	.369	42-3	.095	-5	136	2	-0.1
1931	Pit N	6	1	.857	27	2	0	0	64.2	85	43	3	1	20	9	5.01	77	.316	.366	18-0	.167	-0	189	-8	-0.8
Total	6	27	17	.614	121	43	11	2	446.1	528	240	17	3	181	140	4.32	97	.302	.368	144-8	.153	-8	117	-2	-0.9
OSBORNE, DONOVAN Donovan Alan B 6.21.1969 Roseville, CA BB/TL 6-2/195# d4.9																									
1992	StL N	11	9	.550	34	29	0	0-0	179	193	91	14	2	38-2	104	3.77	90	.275	.312	58-2	.121	-1	94	-12	-1.5
1993	StL N	10	7	.588	26	26	1	0-0	155.2	153	73	18	7	47-4	83	3.76	106	.257	.318	49-7	.204	2*	104	4	0.6
1995	StL N	4	6	.400	19	19	0	0-0	113.1	112	58	17	2	34-2	82	3.81	110	.260	.316	31-3	.161	2	67	3	0.4
1996	†StL N	13	9	.591	30	30	2-1	0-0	198.2	191	87	22	1	57-5	134	3.53	119	.254	.306	59-10	.220	4	86	14	1.7
1997	StL N	3	7	.300	14	14	0	0-0	80.1	84	46	10	1	23-2	51	4.93	84	.274	.323	24-1	.208	1	82	-5	-0.5
1998	StL N	5	4	.556	14	14	1-1	0-0	83.2	84	42	11	1	22-2	60	4.09	103	.256	.301	25-4	.040	-1	116	1	-0.1
1999	StL N	1	3	.250	6	6	0	0-0	29.1	34	18	4	2	10-0	21	5.52	83	.298	.362	10-1	.100	-0	114	-2	-0.3
2002	Chi N	0	1	.000	11	0	0	0-0	16	19	11	1	0	10-2	13	6.19	65	.297	.387	3-0	.000	-0		-3	-0.2
Total	8	47	46	.505	154	138	4-2	0-0	856	870	426	97	16	241-19	548	3.96	101	.264	.315	259-28	.162	5	92	0	0.1
OSBORNE, TINY Earnest Preston B 4.9.1893 Porterdale, GA D 1.5.1969 Atlanta, GA BL/TR 6-4.5/215# d4.15 s-Bobo																									
1922	Chi N	9	5	.643	41	14	7-1	3	184	183	113	7	12	95	81	4.50	93	.271	.370	67-2	.134	-4	112	-7	-1.0
1923	Chi N	8	15	.348	37	25	8-1	1	179.2	174	117	14	2	89	69	4.56	88	.255	.342	60-0	.200	-1	85	-14	-1.7
1924	Chi N	0	0	—	2	0	0	1	3	3	1	0	0	2	2	3.00	130	.300	.417	0-0	—	0		0	0.0
	Bro N	6	5	.545	21	13	6	0	104.1	123	67	1	4	54	52	5.09	74	.298	.384	36-1	.250	1	104	-14	-1.2
	Year	6	5	.545	23	13	6	1	107.1	126	72	1	4	56	54	5.03	75	.298	.385	36-1	.250	1	104	-15	-1.2
1925	Bro N	8	15	.348	41	22	10	1	175	210	111	9	4	75	59	4.94	85	.304	.375	57-1	.246	1	91	-13	-1.4
Total	4	31	40	.437	142	74	31-2	6	646	693	409	31	22	315	263	4.72	86	.280	.367	220-4	.200	-3	95	-48	-5.3
OSBORNE, FRED Frederick W. B Hampton, IA TL d7.14 ▲																									
1890	Pit N	0	5	.000	8	5	5	0	58	82	87	6	7	45	14	8.38	39	.323	.438	168	.238	1*	100	-36	-2.1
OSBORNE, WAYNE Wayne Harold "Ossie" or "Fish Hook" B 10.11.1912 Watsonville, CA D 3.13.1987 Vancouver, WA BL/TR 6-2.5/172# d4.18																									
1935	Pit N	0	0	—	2	0	0	0	1.1	1	1	0	0	0	1	6.75	61	.250	.250	0-0	—	0*		0	0.0
1936	Bos N	1	1	.500	5	3	0	0	20	31	13	1	0	9	8	5.85	66	.352	.412	8-0	.250	0	133	-4	-0.3
Total	2	1	1	.500	7	3	0	0	21.1	32	14	1	0	9	9	5.91	65	.348	.406	8-0	.250	0	133	-4	-0.3
OSBURN, PAT Larry Patrick B 5.4.1949 Murray, KY BL/TL 6-4/195# d4.13																									
1974	Cin N	0	0	—	6	0	0	0-0	9	11	9	2	0	4-0	4	8.00	44	.297	.357	2-0	.000	-0		-5	-0.2
1975	Mil A	0	1	.000	6	1	0	0-0	11.2	19	9	2	2	9-0	1	5.40	71	.404	.492	0-0	—	0	46	-2	-0.2
Total	2	0	1	.000	12	1	0	0-0	20.2	30	18	4	2	13-0	5	6.53	57	.357	.437	2-0	.000	-0	46	-7	-0.4
OSGOOD, CHARLIE Charles Benjamin B 11.23.1926 Somerville, MA BR/TR 5-10/180# d6.18																									
1944	Bro N	0	0	—	1	0	0	0	3	2	1	0	1	3	0	3.00	118	.222	.462	0-0	—	0		0	0.0
OSINSKI, DAN Daniel B 11.17.1933 Chicago, IL BR/TR 6-2/195# d4.11																									
1962	KC A	0	0	—	4	0	0	0	4.2	8	9	1	0	8-0	4	17.36	24	.381	.533	0-0	—	0		-6	-0.3
	LA A	6	4	.600	33	0	0	4	54.1	45	22	3	0	30-3	44	2.82	137	.223	.323	11-1	.000	-1		6	1.0
	Year	6	4	.600	37	0	0	4	59	53	33	4	0	38-3	48	3.97	98	.238	.347	11-1	.000	-1		-2	0.7
1963	LA A	8	8	.500	47	16	4-1	0	159.1	145	66	15	2	80-6	100	3.28	105	.242	.331	45-2	.111	-2	102	3	0.0
1964	LA A	3	3	.500	47	4	1-1	2	93	87	47	8	2	39-7	88	3.48	94	.244	.321	18-2	.056	-1	108	-4	-0.3
1965	Mil N	0	3	.000	61	0	0	6	83	81	28	4	1	40-9	54	2.82	125	.261	.347	6-0	.167	-0		7	0.3
1966	Bos A	4	3	.571	44	1	0	2	67.1	68	33	8	1	28-6	44	3.61	105	.274	.349	6-0	.333	0	46	1	0.1
1967	†Bos A	3	1	.750	34	0	0	2	63.2	61	19	5	0	14-2	38	2.54	137	.243	.283	9-0	.333	1		7	0.6
1969	Chi A	5	5	.500	51	0	0	2-2	60.2	56	28	3	0	23-5	27	3.56	108	.251	.320	3-0	.000	-0		1	0.2
1970	Hou N	0	1	.000	3	0	0	0-1	3.2	5	4	0	0	2-1	1	9.82	40	.357	.412	0-0	—	0		-2	-0.4
Total	8	29	28	.509	324	21	5-2	18-3	589.2	556	256	47	6	264-39	400	3.34	107	.250	.330	98-5	.122	-3	96	13	1.2
OSTEEN, CLAUDE Claude Wilson B 8.9.1939 Caney Spring, TN BL/TL 5-11/173# d7.6 Mil 1970 C15																									
1957	Cin N	0	0	—	3	0	0	0	4	4	1	0	0	3-0	3	2.25	183	.250	.368	1-0	.000	-0		1	0.0
1959	Cin N	0	0	—	2	0	0	0	7.2	11	10	2	0	9-1	3	7.04	58	.333	.465	2-0	.000	-0		-4	-0.2
1960	Cin N	0	1	.000	20	3	0	0	48.1	53	29	4	1	30-4	15	5.03	76	.293	.393	12-0	.083	-1*	108	-6	-0.4
1961	Cin N	0	0	—	1	0	0	0	0.1	0	0	0	0	0-0	0	0.00	—	.000	.000	0-0	—	0*		0	0.0
	Was A	1	1	.500	3	3	0	0	18.1	14	11	3	1	9-0	14	4.91	82	.219	.320	7-1	.143	-0	103	-2	-0.2
1962	Was A	8	13	.381	28	22	7-2	1	150.1	140	62	12	4	47-6	59	3.65	111	.246	.308	48-1	.208	1*	69	9	1.3
1963	Was A	9	14	.391	40	29	8-2	0	212.1	222	101	23	1	60-4	109	3.35	111	.270	.318	70-5	.171	1*	78	4	0.4
1964	Was A	15	13	.536	37	36	13	0	257	256	107	20	3	64-8	133	3.33	111	.259	.304	90-7	.156	1*	99	12	1.5
1965	†LA N	15	15	.500	40	40	9-1	0	287	253	95	19	3	78-10	162	2.79	117	.236	.290	99-6	.121	-1*	92	19	2.2
1966	†LA N	17	14	.548	39	38	8-3	0	240.1	238	92	6	2	65-13	137	2.85	116	.261	.309	76-2	.211	6	96	11	2.1
1967	LA N☆	17	17	.500	39	39	14-5	0	288.1	298	116	19	2	52-10	152	3.22	96	.270	.301	101-5	.178	6*	105	-4	0.2
1968	LA N	12	18	.400	39	36	5-3	0	253.2	267	109	14	5	54-10	119	3.09	90	.275	.314	84-9	.179	2*	85	-13	-1.2
1969	LA N	20	15	.571	41	41	16-7	0-0	321	293	103	17	6	74-8	183	2.66	125	.245	.291	111-8	.216	6*	106	27	3.8
1970	LA N★	16	14	.533	37	37	11-4	0-0	258.2	280	121	24	4	52-3	114	3.83	100	.276	.312	93-1	.204	5*	120	1	0.5
1971	LA N	14	11	.560	38	38	11-4	0-0	259	262	108	25	3	63-2	109	3.51	92	.266	.311	86-8	.186	2*	132	-6	0.1
1972	LA N	20	11	.645	33	33	14-4	0-0	252	232	82	16	4	69-4	100	2.64	126	.245	.299	88-6	.273	10*	96	23	4.2
1973	LA N★	16	11	.593	33	33	12-3	0-0	236.2	227	97	20	2	61-2	86	3.31	104	.258	.306	78-8	.154	-1	103	5	0.6
1974	Hou N	9	9	.500	23	21	7-2	0-0	138.1	158	67	8	2	47-1	45	3.71	94	.292	.348	46-2	.283	3	104	-5	-0.2
	StL N	0	2	.000	8	2	0	0-0	22.2	26	14	1	0	11-5	6	4.37	82	.286	.363	7-0	.000	-1	122	-3	-0.3
	Year	9	11	.450	31	23	7-2	0-0	161	184	19	9	2	58-6	51	3.80	92	.291	.350	53-2	.245	3	106	-7	-0.5
1975	Chi A	7	16	.304	37	37	5	0-0	204.1	237	110	16	2	92-2	63	4.36	89	.294	.365	0-0	—	0	81	-11	-1.0
Total	18	196	195	.501	541	488	140-40	1-0	3460.1	3471	1435	249	45	940-93	1612	3.30	104	.263	.313	1099-69	.188	38	99	58	13.4
OSTEEN, DARRELL Milton Darrell B 2.14.1943 Oklahoma City, OK BR/TR 6-1/170# d9.2 Mil 1970																									
1965	Cin N	0	0	—	3	0	0	0	3	2	0	0	0	4-0	1	0.00	—	.200	.429	0-0	—	0		1	0.1
1966	Cin N	0	2	.000	13	0	0	1	15	26	21	3	0	9-2	17	12.00	33	.371	.443	2-0	.500	0*		-12	-1.6
1967	Cin N	0	2	.000	10	0	0	2	14.1	10	10	1	3	13-1	13	6.28	60	.196	.388	1-1	.000	-0*		-3	-0.5
1970	Oak A	1	0	1.000	3	1	0	0-0	5.2	9	4	0	0	3-0	3	6.35	56	.346	.414	2-0	.000	-0	126	-2	-0.3
Total	4	1	4	.200	29	1	0	3-0	38	47	35	4	3	29-3	34	8.05	47	.299	.418	5-1	.200	-0	126	-16	-2.3
OSTENDORF, FRED Frederick K. B 8.5.1890 Baltimore, MD D 3.2.1965 Kecoughtan, VA BL/TL 6-0.5/169# d7.16																									
1914	Ind F	0	0	—	1	0	0	0	2	5	5	0	1	2	0	22.50	14	.500	.615	1-0	.000	-0		-3	-0.2
OSTER, BILL William Charles B 1.2.1933 New York, NY BL/TL 6-3/198# d8.23																									
1954	Phi A	0	1	.000	8	1	0	0	15.2	19	15	2	0	12	5	6.32	62	.311	.425	3-0	.333	0	45	-5	-0.3
OSTERMUELLER, FRITZ Frederick Raymond B 9.15.1907 Quincy, IL D 12.17.1957 Quincy, IL BL/TL 5-11/175# d4.21 Mil 1945																									
1934	Bos A	10	13	.435	33	23	10	3	198.2	200	93	7	1	99	75	3.49	138	.262	.348	78-0	.167	-2	72	27	2.7
1935	Bos A	7	8	.467	22	19	10	1	137.2	135	67	0	3	78	41	3.92	121	.257	.356	49-2	.286	1	80	13	1.4
1936	Bos A	10	16	.385	43	23	7-1	2	180.2	210	115	8	3	84	90	4.88	109	.288	.364	64-4	.234	0	91	7	0.9
1937	Bos A	3	7	.300	25	7	2	1	86.2	101	64	2	1	44	29	4.98	95	.286	.367	33-3	.333	3	108	-6	-0.3
1938	Bos A	13	5	.722	31	18	10-1	2	176.2	199	98	15	3	58	46	4.58	108	.275	.331	74-3	.216	2*	127	9	0.9
1939	Bos A	11	7	.611	34	20	8	4	159.1	173	86	6	2	58	61	4.24	112	.277	.341	56-5	.161	-2	122	9	0.7

Year	Tm Lg	W	L	Pct	G	GS	CG-Sho	SV-BS	IP	H	R	HR	HB	BB-IB	SO	ERA	AERA	OAV	OOB	AB-SH	AVG	PB	Sup	APR	PW
1940	Bos A	5	9	.357	31	16	5	0	143.2	166	86	7	0	70	80	4.95	91	.284	.361	54-0	.315	4*	100	-7	-0.2
1941	StL A	0	3	.000	15	2	0	0	46	45	26	3	0	23	20	4.50	96	.257	.343	14-2	.214	0*	121	-1	0.0
1942	StL A	3	1	.750	10	4	2	0	43.2	46	22	4	0	17	21	3.71	100	.266	.332	16-0	.188	-0	144	0	-0.1
1943	StL A	0	2	.000	11	3	0	0	28.2	36	16	1	0	13	4	5.02	66	.321	.392	7-0	.286	0	59	-4	-0.3
	Bro N	1	1	.500	7	1	0	0	27.1	21	11	0	0	12	15	3.29	102	.212	.297	11-1	.000	-1*	51	0	-0.1
1944	Bro N	2	1	.667	10	4	3	1	41.2	46	17	3	0	12	17	3.24	110	.267	.315	13-1	.154	-0*	94	2	0.1
	Pit N	11	7	.611	28	24	14-1	1	204.2	201	79	7	1	65	80	2.73	136	.260	.318	80-1	.250	2*	102	21	1.9
	Year	13	8	.619	38	28	17-1	2	246.1	247	84	10	1	77	97	2.81	131	.261	.317	93-2	.237	2	101	23	2.0
1945	Pit N	5	4	.556	14	11	4-1	0	80.2	74	45	6	2	37	29	4.57	86	.236	.321	28-1	.321	2	111	-4	-0.2
1946	Pit N	13	10	.565	27	25	16-2	0	193.1	193	70	5	3	56	57	2.84	124	.263	.318	64-5	.328	6*	94	15	2.5
1947	Pit N	12	10	.545	26	24	12-3	0	183	181	94	18	1	68	66	3.84	110	.254	.320	64-6	.188	0	124	6	0.5
1948	Pit N	8	11	.421	23	22	10-2	0	134.1	143	73	13	1	41	43	4.42	92	.262	.315	44-3	.182	-0	80	-5	-0.7
Total	15	114	115	.498	390	246	113-11	15	2066.2	2170	1062	105	21	835	774	3.99	109	.268	.337	749-37	.234	16	100	82	9.7

OSTING, JIMMY James Michael B 4.7.1977 Louisville, KY BR/TL 6-5/190# d5.2

Year	Tm Lg	W	L	Pct	G	GS	CG-Sho	SV-BS	IP	H	R	HR	HB	BB-IB	SO	ERA	AERA	OAV	OOB	AB-SH	AVG	PB	Sup	APR	PW
2001	SD N	0	0	—	3	0	0	0-0	2	1	0	0	0	2-1	3	0.00	—	.143	.333	0-0	—	0		1	0.0
2002	Mil N	0	2	.000	3	3	0	0-0	12	18	11	3	0	10-0	7	7.50	55	.340	.444	3-1	.000	-0	15	-5	-0.6
Total	2	0	2	.000	6	3	0	0-0	14	19	11	3	0	12-1	10	6.43	64	.317	.431	3-1	.000	-0	15	-4	-0.6

OSTROWSKI, JOE Joseph Paul "Professor" or "Specs" B 11.15.1916 W.Wyoming, PA D 1.3.2003 Wilkes-Barre, PA BL/TL 6/180# d7.18

Year	Tm Lg	W	L	Pct	G	GS	CG-Sho	SV-BS	IP	H	R	HR	HB	BB-IB	SO	ERA	AERA	OAV	OOB	AB-SH	AVG	PB	Sup	APR	PW
1948	StL A	4	6	.400	26	9	3	3	78.1	108	54	6	0	17	20	5.97	76	.333	.367	18-3	.222	1	70	-10	-1.0
1949	StL A	8	8	.500	40	13	4	2	141	185	94	16	0	27	34	4.79	95	.307	.337	37-0	.189	2	103	-6	-0.4
1950	StL A	2	4	.333	9	7	2	0	57.1	57	22	2	0	7	15	2.51	197	.251	.274	18-0	.222	1	68	13	1.4
	NY A	1	1	.500	21	4	1	3	43.2	50	26	11	0	15	15	5.15	83	.294	.351	9-1	.111	-0	147	-4	-0.2
	Year	3	5	.375	30	11	3	3	101	107	33	13	0	22	30	3.65	128	.270	.308	27-1	.185	1	95	11	1.2
1951	†NY A	6	4	.600	34	3	2	5	95.1	103	44	4	1	18	30	3.49	110	.279	.314	28-0	.107	-2	209	3	0.1
1952	NY A	2	2	.500	20	1	0	2	40	56	31	5	1	14	17	5.62	59	.327	.382	8-2	.000	-1	105	-12	-1.4
Total	5	23	25	.479	150	37	12	15	455.2	559	271	44	2	98	131	4.54	95	.300	.336	118-6	.161	1	104	-16	-1.5

OSUNA, AL Alfonso B 8.10.1965 Inglewood, CA BR/TL 6-3/200# d9.2

Year	Tm Lg	W	L	Pct	G	GS	CG-Sho	SV-BS	IP	H	R	HR	HB	BB-IB	SO	ERA	AERA	OAV	OOB	AB-SH	AVG	PB	Sup	APR	PW
1990	Hou N	2	0	1.000	12	0	0	0-1	11.1	10	6	1	3	6-1	6	4.76	78	.270	.396	0-0	—	0		-1	-0.2
1991	Hou N	7	6	.538	71	0	0	12-9	81.2	59	39	5	3	46-5	68	3.42	103	.201	.311	2-1	.000	-0		-1	-0.2
1992	Hou N	6	3	.667	66	0	0	0-2	61.2	52	29	8	1	38-5	37	4.23	80	.236	.343	0-0	—	0		-5	-0.7
1993	Hou N	1	1	.500	44	0	0	2-0	25.1	17	10	3	1	13-2	21	3.20	121	.200	.301	0-0	—	0		2	0.2
1994	LA N	2	0	1.000	15	0	0	0-1	8.2	13	6	0	0	4-0	7	6.23	63	.333	.395	0-0	—	0		-2	-0.4
1996	SD N	0	0	—	10	0	0	0-1	4	5	1	0	1	2-1	4	2.25	177	.313	.400	1-0	.000	-0		1	0.0
Total	6	18	10	.643	218	0	0	14-14	192.2	156	91	17	9	109-14	143	3.83	93	.226	.332	3-1	.000	-0		-6	-1.3

OSUNA, ANTONIO Antonio Pedro B 4.12.1973 Sinaloa, Mexico BR/TR 5-11/160# d4.25

Year	Tm Lg	W	L	Pct	G	GS	CG-Sho	SV-BS	IP	H	R	HR	HB	BB-IB	SO	ERA	AERA	OAV	OOB	AB-SH	AVG	PB	Sup	APR	PW
1995	†LA N	2	4	.333	39	0	0	0-2	44.2	39	22	5	1	20-2	46	4.43	86	.241	.326	2-0	.000	-0		-2	-0.2
1996	†LA N	9	6	.600	73	0	0	4-5	84	65	33	6	2	32-12	85	3.00	129	.220	.296	1-0	.000	0		8	1.4
1997	LA N	3	4	.429	48	0	0	0-0	61.2	46	15	6	1	19-2	68	2.19	176	.209	.274	2-0	.500	0		13	1.4
1998	LA N	7	1	.875	54	0	0	6-5	64.2	50	26	8	2	32-0	72	3.06	129	.214	.311	2-0	.000	-0		6	0.8
1999	LA N	0	0	—	5	0	0	0-0	4.2	4	5	0	1	3-0	5	7.71	56	.222	.364	0-0	—	0		-2	-0.1
2000	LA N	3	6	.333	46	0	0	0-3	67.1	57	30	7	2	35-2	70	3.74	116	.229	.325	2-0	.000	-0		5	0.6
2001	Chi A	0	0	—	4	0	0	0-1	4.1	8	10	3	1	2-1	6	20.77	22	.421	.478	0-0	—	0		-7	-0.3
2002	Chi A	8	2	.800	59	0	0	11-3	67.2	64	32	1	4	28-4	66	3.86	117	.250	.330	0-0	—	0		5	0.8
2003	NY A	2	5	.286	48	0	0	0-1	50.2	58	22	3	2	20-3	47	3.73	118	.282	.348	0-0	—	0		4	0.5
Total	9	34	28	.548	376	0	0	21-20	449.2	391	195	39	16	191-26	465	3.58	115	.236	.317	9-0	.111	-0		30	4.9

OSWALT, ROY Roy Edward B 8.29.1977 Kosciusko, MS BR/TR 6/170# d5.6

Year	Tm Lg	W	L	Pct	G	GS	CG-Sho	SV-BS	IP	H	R	HR	HB	BB-IB	SO	ERA	AERA	OAV	OOB	AB-SH	AVG	PB	Sup	APR	PW
2001	Hou N	14	3	.824	28	20	3-1	0-0	141.2	126	48	13	6	24-2	144	2.73	168	.235	.273	47-3	.191	0	126	27	3.1
2002	Hou N	19	9	.679	35	34	0	0-0	233	215	86	17	5	62-4	208	3.01	142	.247	.299	77-7	.130	-1	103	31	3.5
2003	Hou N	10	5	.667	21	21	0	0-0	127.1	116	48	15	5	29-0	108	2.97	150	.246	.296	39-7	.179	0	107	19	2.1
Total	3	43	17	.717	84	75	3-1	0-0	502	457	182	45	16	115-6	460	2.92	151	.243	.291	163-17	.160	-0	110	77	8.7

OTEY, BILL William Tilford "Steamboat Bill" B 12.16.1886 Dayton, OH D 4.23.1931 Dayton, OH BL/TL 6-2/181# d9.27

Year	Tm Lg	W	L	Pct	G	GS	CG-Sho	SV-BS	IP	H	R	HR	HB	BB-IB	SO	ERA	AERA	OAV	OOB	AB-SH	AVG	PB	Sup	APR	PW
1907	Pit N	0	1	.000	3	2	1	0	16.1	23	11	1	1	4	5	4.41	55	.319	.364	4-0	.250	0	88	-3	-0.2
1910	Was A	0	1	.000	9	1	1	0	34.2	40	17	1	1	6	12	3.38	74	.301	.336	13-0	.385	2	27	-3	0.0
1911	Was A	1	3	.250	12	2	0	0	49.2	68	44	2	3	15	16	6.34	52	.333	.387	17-1	.059	-2	66	-15	-1.1
Total	3	1	5	.167	24	5	2	0	100.2	131	72	4	5	25	33	5.01	57	.320	.367	34-1	.206	0	64	-21	-1.3

OTIS, HARRY Harry George "Cannonball" B 10.5.1886 W.New York, NJ D 1.29.1976 Teaneck, NJ BR/TL 6- /180# d9.5

Year	Tm Lg	W	L	Pct	G	GS	CG-Sho	SV-BS	IP	H	R	HR	HB	BB-IB	SO	ERA	AERA	OAV	OOB	AB-SH	AVG	PB	Sup	APR	PW
1909	Cle A	2	2	.500	5	3	0	0	26.1	26	11	0	3	18	6	1.37	187	.283	.416	9-1	.111	-0	83	2	0.2

O'TOOLE, DENNIS Dennis Joseph B 3.13.1949 Chicago, IL BR/TR 6-3/195# d9.8 b-Jim

Year	Tm Lg	W	L	Pct	G	GS	CG-Sho	SV-BS	IP	H	R	HR	HB	BB-IB	SO	ERA	AERA	OAV	OOB	AB-SH	AVG	PB	Sup	APR	PW
1969	Chi A	0	0	—	2	0	0	0-0	4	5	3	0	0	2-0	4	6.75	57	.333	.389	0-0	—	0		-1	-0.1
1970	Chi A	0	0	—	3	0	0	0-0	3.1	5	1	0	0	2-0	3	2.70	144	.357	.412	0-0	—	0		0	0.0
1971	Chi A	0	0	—	1	0	0	0-0	2	0	0	0	0	1-0	2	0.00	—	.000	.143	0-0	—	0		1	0.0
1972	Chi A	0	0	—	3	0	0	0-0	5	10	3	0	0	2-0	5	5.40	58	.417	.462	0-0	—	0		-1	-0.1
1973	Chi A	0	0	—	6	0	0	0-0	16	23	11	3	0	3-0	8	5.63	70	.329	.356	0-0	—	0		-3	-0.1
Total	5	0	0	—	15	0	0	0-0	30.1	43	18	3	0	10-0	22	5.04	75	.333	.376	0-0	—	0		-4	-0.3

O'TOOLE, JIM James Jerome B 1.10.1937 Chicago, IL BB/TL 6/198# d9.26 b-Dennis

Year	Tm Lg	W	L	Pct	G	GS	CG-Sho	SV-BS	IP	H	R	HR	HB	BB-IB	SO	ERA	AERA	OAV	OOB	AB-SH	AVG	PB	Sup	APR	PW
1958	Cin N	0	1	.000	1	1	0	0	7	4	2	0	0	5-0	4	1.29	322	.154	.290	2-0	.000	-0	22	2	0.2
1959	Cin N	5	8	.385	28	19	3-1	0	129.1	144	78	14	4	73-2	68	5.15	79	.287	.380	37-3	.135	-0*	127	-13	-1.1
1960	Cin N	12	12	.500	34	31	7-2	1	196.1	198	94	14	4	66-4	124	3.80	100	.263	.323	66-7	.106	-3	86	0	-0.5
1961	†Cin N	19	9	.679	39	35	11-3	2	252.2	229	101	16	3	93-7	178	3.10	131	.240	.309	93-4	.172	-1	109	**26**	2.6
1962	Cin N	16	13	.552	36	34	11-3	0	251.2	222	115	20	5	87-4	170	3.50	115	.238	.305	91-3	.110	-5	116	12	0.7
1963	Cin N★	17	14	.548	33	32	12-5	0	234.1	208	85	13	3	57-4	146	2.88	116	.239	.285	74-6	.149	-1	104	12	1.3
1964	Cin N	17	7	.708	30	30	9-3	0	220	194	71	8	0	51-7	145	2.66	136	.235	.277	70-7	.100	-1	91	24	2.4
1965	Cin N	3	10	.231	29	22	2	1	127.2	154	98	14	3	47-4	71	5.92	63	.294	.352	45-3	.089	-2	126	-31	-3.1
1966	Cin N	5	7	.417	25	24	2	0	142	139	65	16	3	49-6	96	3.55	110	.254	.317	47-1	.128	-2	98	3	0.0
1967	Chi A	4	3	.571	15	10	1-1	0	54.1	53	21	4	1	18-2	37	2.82	110	.251	.313	13-1	.077	-1	70	2	0.1
Total	10	98	84	.538	270	238	58-18	4	1615.1	1545	730	119	26	546-40	1039	3.57	106	.251	.313	538-35	.125	-15	104	37	2.6

O'TOOLE, MARTY Martin James B 11.27.1888 Wm.Penn, PA D 2.18.1949 Aberdeen, WA BR/TR 5-11/175# d9.21

Year	Tm Lg	W	L	Pct	G	GS	CG-Sho	SV-BS	IP	H	R	HR	HB	BB-IB	SO	ERA	AERA	OAV	OOB	AB-SH	AVG	PB	Sup	APR	PW
1908	Cin N	1	0	1.000	3	2	1	0	15	15	8	0	0	7	5	2.40	96	.273	.355	5-0	.200	-0	214	-1	-0.1
1911	Pit N	3	2	.600	5	5	3	0	38	28	17	1	0	20	34	2.37	145	.215	.320	14-0	.357	2	105	3	0.5
1912	Pit N	15	17	.469	37	36	17-**6**	0	275.1	237	110	4	2	159	150	2.71	120	.241	.348	99-2	.222	2	96	16	1.9
1913	Pit N	6	8	.429	26	16	7	1	144.2	148	69	3	3	55	58	3.30	92	.271	.341	53-1	.132	-2	136	-5	-0.7
1914	Pit N	1	8	.111	19	9	1	1	92.1	92	56	2	0	47	36	4.68	57	.270	.358	30-0	.167	0	60	-20	-1.8
	NY N	1	1	.500	10	5	2	0	34	34	17	0	0	12	13	4.24	63	.262	.324	10-1	.300	1	92	-5	-0.2
	Year	2	9	.182	29	14	3	1	126.1	126	20	2	0	59	49	4.56	58	.268	.349	40-1	.200	1	71	-20	-2.0
Total	5	27	36	.429	100	73	31-6	2	599.1	554	277	10	5	300	296	3.21	95	.254	.345	211-4	.204	2	104	-12	-0.4

OTTEN, JIM James Edward B 7.1.1951 Lewistown, MT BR/TR 6-2/195# d7.31

Year	Tm Lg	W	L	Pct	G	GS	CG-Sho	SV-BS	IP	H	R	HR	HB	BB-IB	SO	ERA	AERA	OAV	OOB	AB-SH	AVG	PB	Sup	APR	PW
1974	Chi A	0	1	.000	5	1	0	0-0	16.1	22	11	0	1	12-2	11	5.51	68	.324	.432	0-0	—	0	47	-3	-0.2
1975	Chi A	0	0	—	2	0	0	0-0	5.1	4	5	1	0	7-0	3	6.75	58	.235	.440	0-0	—	0		-2	-0.1
1976	Chi A	0	0	—	2	0	0	0-0	6	9	6	0	0	2-0	3	4.50	79	.333	.379	0-0	—	0		-2	-0.1
1980	StL N	0	5	.000	31	4	0	0-0	55.1	71	38	3	2	26-7	38	5.53	67	.323	.393	5-0	.200	-0	66	-11	-0.9
1981	StL N	1	0	1.000	24	0	0	0-0	35.2	44	23	3	0	20-5	20	5.30	67	.321	.405	2-1	.000	-0		-7	-0.4
Total	5	1	6	.143	64	5	0	0-0	118.2	150	83	7	3	67-14	75	5.46	67	.320	.404	7-1	.143	-0	63	-25	-1.7

Year	Tm Lg	W	L	Pct	G	GS	CG-Sho	SV-BS	IP	H	R	HR	HB	BB-IB	SO	ERA	AERA	OAV	OOB	AB-SH	AVG	PB	Sup	APR	PW
OTTO, DAVE David Alan B 11.12.1964 Chicago, IL BL/TL 6-7/210# d9.8																									
1987	Oak A	0	0	—	3	0	0	0-0	6	7	6	1	0	1-0	3	9.00	46	.304	.333	0-0	—	0		-3	-0.2
1988	Oak A	0	0	—	3	2	0	0-0	10	9	2	0	0	6-0	7	1.80	210	.243	.349	0-0	—	0	108	2	0.1
1989	Oak A	0	0	—	1	1	0	0-0	6.2	6	2	0	0	2-0	4	2.70	137	.261	.320	0-0	—	0	98	1	0.0
1990	Oak A	0	0	—	2	0	0	0-0	2.1	3	3	0	0	3-0	2	7.71	48	.300	.462	0-0	—	0		-1	-0.1
1991	Cle A	2	8	.200	18	14	1	0-0	100	108	52	7	4	27-6	47	4.23	98	.283	.333	0-0	—	0	77	-1	-0.1
1992	Cle A	5	9	.357	18	16	0	0-0	80.1	110	64	12	1	33-0	32	7.06	55	.333	.395	0-0	—	0	72	-26	-3.6
1993	Pit N	3	4	.429	28	8	0	0-0	68	85	40	9	3	28-1	30	5.03	81	.317	.387	18-1	.222	1	92	-7	-0.5
1994	Chi N	0	1	.000	36	0	0	0-1	45	49	20	4	1	22-4	19	3.80	109	.283	.367	2-0	.000	-0		2	0.1
Total	8	10	22	.313	109	41	1	0-1	318.1	377	189	33	9	122-11	144	5.06	80	.303	.367	20-1	.200	1	79	-33	-4.3
OVERALL, ORVAL Orval B 2.2.1881 Farmersville, CA D 7.14.1947 Fresno, CA BB/TR 6-2/214# d4.16																									
1905	Cin N	18	23	.439	42	39	32-2	0	318	290	146	4	14	147	173	2.86	116	.252	.343	117-5	.145	-2	85	16	1.7
1906	Cin N	4	5	.444	13	10	6	0	82.1	77	52	1	4	46	33	4.26	65	.253	.359	31-0	.194	0	130	-12	-1.3
	†Chi N	12	3	.800	18	14	13-2	1	144	116	43	1	4	51	94	1.88	141	.217	.290	53-3	.170	-1	118	12	1.2
	Year	16	8	.667	31	24	19-2	1	226.1	193	47	2	8	97	127	2.74	98	.230	.316	84-3	.179	-1	123	-3	-0.1
1907	†Chi N	23	7	.767	36	30	26-**8**	3	268.1	201	62	3	11	69	141	1.68	149	.208	.268	94-8	.213	3	112	28	**3.9**
1908	†Chi N	15	11	.577	37	27	16-4	4	225	165	74	3	2	78	167	1.92	123	.208	.280	70-8	.129	-0*	101	7	0.8
1909	Chi N	20	11	.645	38	32	23-**9**	3	285	204	66	1	8	80	**205**	1.42	179	**.198**	.262	96-4	.229	8	100	35	5.2
1910	†Chi N	12	6	.667	23	21	11-4	1	144.2	106	44	2	1	54	92	2.68	108	.212	.291	41-6	.122	-1*	103	8	1.0
1913	Chi N	4	5	.444	11	9	6-1	0	68	73	33	1	1	26	30	3.31	96	.284	.352	24-1	.250	2	83	-1	0.1
Total	7	108	71	.603	218	182	133-30	12	1535.1	1232	520	16	45	551	935	2.23	123	.223	.298	526-35	.179	9	101	93	12.6
OVERMIRE, STUBBY Frank W. B 5.16.1919 Moline, MI D 3.3.1977 Lakeland, FL BR/TL 5-7/170# d4.25 C4																									
1943	Det A	7	6	.538	29	18	8-3	1	147	135	56	5	1	38	48	3.18	111	.243	.293	42-5	.167	0	89	7	0.6
1944	Det A	11	11	.500	32	28	11-3	1	199.2	214	84	2	2	41	57	3.07	116	.271	.309	63-5	.175	1	101	10	1.3
1945	†Det A	9	9	.500	31	22	9	4	162.1	189	81	6	3	42	36	3.88	91	.294	.341	53-6	.189	0	102	-5	-0.5
1946	Det A	5	7	.417	24	13	3	1	97.1	106	54	6	0	29	34	4.62	79	.274	.325	33-4	.152	-1	128	-9	-1.1
1947	Det A	11	5	.688	28	17	7-3	0	140.2	142	62	9	1	44	33	3.77	100	.259	.315	47-2	.149	-1	108	3	0.2
1948	Det A	3	4	.429	37	4	0	3	66.1	89	48	5	0	31	14	5.97	73	.326	.395	14-0	.071	-1	150	-11	-1.1
1949	Det A	1	3	.250	14	1	0	0	17.1	29	21	2	1	9	3	9.87	42	.377	.448	3-0	.333	0	22	-11	-1.9
1950	StL A	9	12	.429	31	19	8-2	0	161	200	89	11	1	45	39	4.19	118	.298	.343	48-2	.167	1	69	12	1.3
1951	StL A	1	6	.143	8	7	3	0	53.1	61	26	5	0	21	13	3.54	124	.281	.345	14-3	.071	-1	40	4	0.3
	NY A	1	1	.500	15	4	1	0	44.2	50	27	2	2	18	14	4.63	83	.287	.361	7-0	.143	0	133	-5	-0.2
	Year	2	7	.222	23	11	4	0	98	111	33	7	2	39	27	4.04	102	.284	.352	21-3	.095	-0	72	0	0.1
1952	StL A	0	3	.000	17	4	0	0	41	44	21	3	0	7	10	3.73	105	.270	.300	11-0	.182	-0	50	0	0.0
Total	10	58	67	.464	266	137	50-11	10	1130.2	1259	569	56	11	325	301	3.96	98	.280	.330	335-27	.161	-1	94	-5	-1.1
OVERY, MIKE Harry Michael B 1.27.1951 Clinton, IL BR/TR 6-2/190# d8.14																									
1976	Cal A	0	2	.000	5	0	0	0-2	7.1	6	5	1	1	3-1	8	6.14	54	.214	.313	0-0	—	0		-2	-0.4
OVITZ, ERNIE Ernest Gayhart B 10.7.1885 Mineral Point, WI D 9.11.1980 Green Bay, WI BR/TR 5-8.5/156# d6.22																									
1911	Chi N	0	0	—	1	0	0	0	2	3	2	0	0	3	0	4.50	74	.375	.545	0-0	—	0		-1	0.0
OWCHINKO, BOB Robert Dennis B 1.1.1955 Detroit, MI BL/TL 6-2/195# d9.25																									
1976	SD N	0	2	.000	2	2	0	0-0	4.1	11	8	0	0	3-1	4	16.62	20	.478	.538	1-1	.000	-0	121	-6	-1.0
1977	SD N	9	12	.429	30	28	3-2	0-0	170	191	93	20	0	67-5	101	4.45	80	.287	.351	49-11	.082	-2	114	-17	-2.1
1978	SD N	10	13	.435	36	33	4-1	0-1	202.1	198	87	14	1	78-12	94	3.56	94	.263	.330	63-6	.175	1	79	-3	-0.3
1979	SD N	6	12	.333	42	20	2	0-1	149.1	144	73	16	2	55-6	66	3.74	95	.259	.327	33-7	.121	-0	90	-5	-0.5
1980	Cle A	2	9	.182	29	14	1-1	0-0	114.1	138	71	13	2	47-2	66	5.27	77	.301	.365	0-0	—	0	64	-14	-1.2
1981	†Oak A	4	3	.571	29	0	0	2-4	39.1	34	15	2	1	19-2	26	3.20	109	.245	.335	0-0	—	0		2	0.3
1982	Oak A	2	4	.333	54	0	0	3-3	102	111	60	11	0	52-5	67	5.21	75	.275	.356	0-0	—	0		-13	-0.8
1983	Pit N	0	0	—	1	0	0	0-1	0	2	1	1	0	0-0	0	o	—	1.000	1.000	0-0	—	0		-1	-0.1
1984	Cin N	3	5	.375	49	4	0	2-1	94	91	47	10	0	39-2	60	4.12	92	.253	.325	12-1	.167	1	99	-3	-0.2
1986	Mon N	1	0	1.000	3	3	0	0-0	15	17	6	1	0	3-0	6	3.60	103	.288	.323	5-0	.200	0	121	0	0.1
Total	10	37	60	.381	275	104	10-4	7-11	890.2	937	461	88	6	363-35	490	4.28	85	.274	.343	163-26	.135	-0	90	-60	-5.8
OWEN, FRANK Frank Malcolm "Yip" B 12.23.1879 Ypsilanti, MI D 11.24.1942 Dearborn, MI BB/TR 5-11/160# d4.26																									
1901	Det A	1	3	.250	8	5	3	0	56	70	43	1	4	30	17	4.34	89	.302	.391	20-2	.050	-2*	74	-3	-0.3
1903	Chi A	8	12	.400	26	20	15-1	1	167.1	167	85	1	7	44	66	3.50	80	.259	.314	57-2	.123	-1	94	-9	-1.0
1904	Chi A	21	15	.583	37	36	34-4	1	315	243	95	2	11	61	103	1.94	126	.214	.261	107-3	.215	5	114	18	3.2
1905	Chi A	21	13	.618	42	38	32-3	0	334	276	110	6	9	56	125	2.10	117	.227	.266	124-8	.145	-4	109	15	1.3
1906	†Chi A	22	13	.629	42	36	27-7	0	293	289	114	4	4	54	66	2.33	109	.261	.298	103-5	.136	-2	116	5	0.6
1907	Chi A	2	3	.400	11	4	2	0	47	43	22	1	0	13	15	2.49	96	.246	.298	16-0	.250	0	92	-2	-0.2
1908	Chi A	6	7	.462	25	14	5-1	0	140	142	79	2	3	37	48	3.41	68	.260	.310	50-1	.180	1	93	-21	-1.7
1909	Chi A	1	1	.500	3	2	1	0	16	19	8	0	1	3	3	4.50	52	.279	.319	6-0	.167	-0	120	-3	-0.4
Total	8	82	67	.550	194	155	119-16	2	1368.1	1249	556	17	39	298	443	2.55	100	.244	.290	483-21	.159	-3	106	0	1.5
OWENS, JIM James Philip "Bear" B 1.16.1934 Gifford, PA BR/TR 5-11/190# d4.19 Mil 1957-58 C6																									
1955	Phi N	0	2	.000	3	2	0	0	8.2	13	8	2	0	7-0	6	8.31	48	.382	.488	1-1	.000	-0	79	-4	-0.7
1956	Phi N	0	4	.000	10	5	0	0	29.2	35	26	3	2	22-1	22	7.28	51	.313	.431	6-1	.167	0	90	-11	-1.3
1958	Phi N	1	0	1.000	1	1	0	0	7	4	4	1	0	5-0	3	2.57	154	.154	.290	2-0	.000	0	136	0	0.0
1959	Phi N	12	12	.500	31	30	11-1	1	221.1	203	97	14	4	73-11	135	3.21	128	.244	.306	75-3	.120	-1	73	18	1.7
1960	Phi N	4	14	.222	31	22	6	0	150	182	95	21	1	64-7	83	5.04	77	.299	.365	44-3	.068	-3	78	-19	-2.4
1961	Phi N	5	10	.333	20	17	3	0	106.2	119	62	8	0	32-2	38	4.47	91	.287	.335	27-5	.074	-1*	65	-6	-0.9
1962	Phi N	2	4	.333	23	12	1	0	69.2	90	53	12	0	33-1	21	6.33	61	.318	.388	14-3	.143	0	113	-19	-1.4
1963	Cin N	0	2	.000	19	3	0	4	42.1	42	28	6	0	24-2	29	5.31	63	.259	.353	8-0	.125	0	137	-9	-0.6
1964	Hou N	8	7	.533	48	11	0	6	118	115	48	7	0	32-6	88	3.28	104	.262	.309	29-1	.103	-1	89	3	0.2
1965	Hou N	6	5	.545	50	0	0	8	71.1	64	28	4	0	29-8	53	3.28	102	.238	.310	8-1	.125	-0		1	0.2
1966	Hou N	4	7	.364	40	0	0	2	50	53	29	5	1	17-7	32	4.68	73	.273	.332	4-0	.000	-0		-7	-1.4
1967	Hou N	0	1	.000	10	0	0	0	10.2	12	5	1	0	2-1	6	4.22	78	.308	.341	0-0	—	0		-1	-0.1
Total	12	42	68	.382	286	103	21-1	21	885.1	932	483	84	8	340-46	516	4.31	88	.273	.338	218-18	.101	-7	84	-54	-6.7
OWNBEY, RICK Richard Wayne B 10.20.1957 Corona, CA BR/TR 6-3/185# d8.17																									
1982	NY N	1	2	.333	8	8	2	0-0	50.1	44	23	3	0	43-1	28	3.75	97	.242	.382	15-1	.200	1*	109	0	0.0
1983	NY N	1	3	.250	10	4	0	0-0	34.2	31	19	4	1	21-0	19	4.67	78	.240	.351	9-1	.111	-0*	67	-3	-0.4
1984	StL N	0	3	.000	4	4	0	0-0	19	23	13	1	0	8-0	11	4.74	73	.303	.360	4-2	.000	-0*	51	-4	-0.6
1986	StL N	1	3	.250	17	3	0	0-0	42.2	47	20	4	2	19-0	25	3.80	96	.294	.372	7-3	.000	-1	73	-1	-0.2
Total	4	3	11	.214	39	19	2	0-0	146.2	145	75	12	3	91-1	83	4.11	88	.265	.369	35-7	.114	-1	82	-8	-1.2
OZMER, DOC Horace Robert B 5.25.1901 Atlanta, GA D 12.28.1970 Atlanta, GA BR/TR 5-10.5/185# d5.11																									
1923	Phi A	0	0	—	1	0	0	0	2	1	1	0	0	1	1	4.50	91	.167	.286	0-0	—	0		0	0.0
PABOR, CHARLIE Charles Henry B 9.24.1846 New York, NY D 4.23.1913 New Haven, CT BL/TL 5-8/155# d5.4 M2 ▲																									
1871	Cle NA	0	2	.000	7	1	1	0	29.1	50	53	4		6	0	6.75	61	.325	.350	142	.296	0*	77	-7	-0.2
1872	Cle NA	1	1	.500	2	2	2	0	18	20	15	0		3	0	4.00	89	.247	.274	92	.207	-0*	145	-1	-0.1
1875	Atl NA	0	1	.000	1	1	0	0	4	11	12	0		1	0	9.00	23	.407	.429	153	.235	0*	102	-3	-0.4
Total	3 NA	1	4	.200	10	4	3	0	51.1	81	80	4		10	0	5.96	63	.309	.335	387	.251	-0	106	-11	-0.7
PACELLA, JOHN John Lewis B 9.15.1956 Brooklyn, NY BR/TR 6-3/195# d9.15																									
1977	NY N	0	0	—	3	0	0	0-0	4	2	2	0	0	2-0	1	0.00	—	.133	.235	0-0	—	0		1	0.0
1979	NY N	0	2	.000	4	3	0	0-0	16.1	16	8	0	0	4-0	12	4.41	83	.246	.290	4-0	.000	-0	57	-1	-0.2
1980	NY N	3	4	.429	32	15	0	0-0	84	89	51	5	2	59-2	68	5.14	69	.280	.396	20-2	.100	-1	121	-14	-1.2
1982	NY A	0	1	.000	3	1	0	0-0	10	13	8	0	1	9-1	2	7.20	55	.342	.451	0-0	—	0	23	-3	-0.3
	Min A	1	2	.333	21	1	0	2-1	51.2	61	48	14	0	37-0	20	7.32	58	.299	.402	0-0	—	0	43	-18	-1.1

Year	Tm Lg	W	L	Pct	G	GS	CG-Sho	SV-BS	IP	H	R	HR	HB	BB-IB	SO	ERA	AERA	OAV	OOB	AB-SH	AVG	PB	Sup	APR	PW
	Year	1	3	.250	24	2	0	2-1	61.2	74	50	14	1	46-1	22	7.30	58	.306	.410	0-0	—	0	32	-21	-1.4
1984	Bal A	0	1	.000	6	1	0	0-0	14.2	15	13	2	0	9-1	8	6.75	57	.268	.369	0-0	—	0	116	-5	-0.3
1986	Det A	0	0	—	5	0	0	1-0	11	10	5	0	0	13-1	5	4.09	101	.294	.469	0-0	—	0		0	0.0
Total	6	4	10	.286	74	21	0	3-1	191.2	206	135	21	3	133-5	116	5.73	67	.282	.391	24-2	.083	-1	97	-40	-3.1
PACHECO, ALEX Alexander Melchor (Lara) B 7.19.1973 Caracas, Venezuela BR/TR 6-3/200# d4.17																									
1996	Mon N	0	0	—	5	0	0	0-0	5.2	8	7	2	0	1-0	7	11.12	39	.320	.346	0-0	—	0		-4	-0.2
PACILLO, PAT Patrick Michael B 7.23.1963 Jersey City, NJ BR/TR 6-2/205# d5.23																									
1987	Cin N	3	3	.500	12	7	0	0-0	39.2	41	30	7	1	19-0	23	6.13	69	.270	.351	11-1	.091	-0*	110	-8	-1.1
1988	Cin N	1	0	1.000	6	0	0	0-0	10.2	14	7	2	0	4-0	11	5.06	71	.318	.375	1-0	.000	-0		-2	-0.2
Total	2	4	3	.571	18	7	0	0-0	50.1	55	37	9	1	23-0	34	5.90	70	.281	.356	12-1	.083	-0	110	-10	-1.3
PACKARD, GENE Eugene Milo B 7.13.1887 Colorado Springs, CO D 5.18.1959 Riverside, CA BL/TL 5-10/155# d9.27																									
1912	Cin N	1	0	1.000	1	1	1	0	9	7	3	0	0	4	2	3.00	112	.206	.289	4-0	.250	1	218	1	0.1
1913	Cin N	7	11	.389	39	21	9-2	0	190.2	208	97	2	8	64	73	2.97	109	.286	.350	61-4	.180	-0*	114	1	0.1
1914	KC F	20	14	.588	42	34	24-4	5	302	282	127	5	3	88	154	2.89	96	.246	.301	116-5	.241	2*	122	-3	0.3
1915	KC F	20	12	.625	42	31	21-5	2	281.2	250	111	3	9	74	108	2.68	98	.242	.298	95-8	.232	2*	99	-3	0.2
1916	Chi N	10	6	.625	37	16	5-2	5	155.1	154	60	4	3	38	36	2.78	105	.256	.304	54-2	.130	-1*	108	3	0.5
1917	Chi N	0	0	—	2	0	0	0	1.2	3	2	1	0	0	1	10.80	27	.375	.375	0-0	—	0		-1	-0.1
	StL N	9	6	.600	34	11	6	2	153.1	138	48	4	3	25	44	2.47	109	.246	.281	52-0	.288	3*	89	5	0.9
	Year	9	6	.600	36	11	6	2	155	141	51	5	3	25	45	2.55	105	.247	.283	52-0	.288	3	89	5	0.8
1918	StL N	12	12	.500	30	23	10-1	2	182.1	184	84	6	5	33	46	3.50	77	.266	.304	69-4	.174	-1*	119	-12	-1.7
1919	Phi N	6	8	.429	21	16	10-1	1	134.1	167	70	3	4	30	24	4.15	78	.321	.363	51-0	.137	-2*	123	-11	-1.3
Total	8	85	69	.552	248	153	86-15	17	1410.1	1393	602	28	35	356	488	3.01	95	.262	.312	502-23	.205	4	113	-20	-1.0
PACTWA, JOE Joseph Martin B 6.2.1948 Hammond, IN BL/TL 5-11/185# d9.15																									
1975	Cal A	1	0	1.000	4	3	0	0-0	16.1	23	7	0	0	10-0	3	3.86	92	.343	.423	0-0	—	0	91	0	0.0
PADILLA, VICENTE Vicente De La Cruz B 9.27.1977 Chinandega, Nicaragua BR/TR 6-2/200# d6.29																									
1999	Ari N	0	1	.000	5	0	0	0-1	2.2	7	5	1	0	3-0	0	16.88	27	.467	.556	0-0	—	0		-3	-0.6
2000	Ari N	2	1	.667	27	0	0	0-1	35	32	10	0	0	10-2	30	2.31	203	.242	.294	1-0	1.000	0		9	0.7
	Phi N	2	6	.250	28	0	0	2-4	30.1	40	23	3	1	18-5	21	5.34	87	.328	.413	0-0	—	0		-4	-0.7
	Year	4	7	.364	55	0	0	2-5	65.1	72	37	3	1	28-7	51	3.72	126	.283	.353	1-0	1.000	0		5	0.0
2001	Phi N	3	1	.750	23	0	0	0-3	34	36	18	1	0	12-0	29	4.24	100	.273	.333	3-1	.333	1		0	0.1
2002	Phi N★	14	11	.560	32	32	1-1	0-0	206	198	83	16	15	53-5	128	3.28	119	.254	.312	58-7	.052	-4	110	14	1.1
2003	Phi N	14	12	.538	32	32	1-1	0-0	208.2	196	94	22	16	62-4	133	3.62	110	.251	.317	67-3	.060	-3	117	7	0.6
Total	5	35	32	.522	147	64	2-2	2-9	516.2	509	233	43	32	158-16	341	3.61	113	.259	.323	129-11	.070	-5	110	23	1.2
PAGAN, DAVE David Percy B 9.15.1949 Nipawin, SK, CAN BR/TR 6-2/175# d7.1																									
1973	NY A	0	0	—	4	1	0	0-0	12.2	16	4	1	0	1-0	9	2.84	129	.320	.333	0-0	—	0	268	1	0.1
1974	NY A	1	3	.250	16	6	1	0-0	49.1	49	29	1	0	28-0	39	5.11	69	.265	.362	0-0	—	0	112	-7	-0.6
1975	NY A	0	0	—	13	0	0	1-0	31	30	16	2	2	13-5	18	4.06	91	.256	.336	0-0	—	0		-1	-0.1
1976	NY A	1	1	.500	7	2	1	0-0	23.2	18	7	0	0	4-0	13	2.28	150	.222	.253	0-0	—	0	77	3	0.2
	Bal A	1	4	.200	20	5	0	1-1	46.2	54	33	2	1	23-1	34	5.98	55	.298	.370	0-0	—	0	107	-14	-1.5
	Year	2	5	.286	27	7	1	1-1	70.1	72	37	2	1	27-1	47	4.73	70	.275	.336	0-0	—	0	98	-11	-1.3
1977	Sea A	1	1	.500	24	4	1-1	2-1	66	86	52	3	2	26-2	30	6.14	67	.323	.383	0-0	—	0	109	-15	-0.8
	Pit N	0	0	—	1	0	0	0-0	3	1	0	0	0	0-0	4	0.00	—	.100	.100	0-0	—	0		1	0.1
Total	5	4	9	.308	85	18	3-1	4-2	232.1	254	141	9	5	95-8	147	4.96	74	.285	.353	0-0	—	0	113	-32	-2.6
PAGE, JOE Joseph Francis "Fireman" B 10.28.1917 Cherry Valley, PA D 4.21.1980 Latrobe, PA BL/TL 6-2/205# d4.19																									
1944	NY A☆	5	7	.417	19	16	4	0	102.2	100	65	3	3	52	63	4.56	76	.258	.351	32-2	.156	-0	97	-14	-1.5
1945	NY A	6	3	.667	20	9	4	0	102	95	43	1	0	46	50	2.82	123	.246	.326	36-0	.250	1	139	5	0.4
1946	NY A	9	8	.529	31	17	6-1	3	136	126	66	7	4	72	77	3.57	97	.252	.351	43-6	.163	-0*	142	-4	-0.5
1947	†NY A★	14	8	.636	56	2	0	**17**	141.1	105	41	5	1	72	116	2.48	142	.208	.308	46-2	.217	1	163	**18**	3.3
1948	NY A☆	7	8	.467	**55**	1	0	16	107.2	116	59	6	1	66	77	4.26	96	.275	.374	24-1	.292	3	243	-3	-0.2
1949	†NY A	13	8	.619	**60**	0	0	**27**	135.1	103	44	8	5	75	99	2.59	156	.215	.328	40-0	.175	-1		**23**	4.0
1950	NY A	3	7	.300	37	0	0	13	55.1	66	34	8	0	31	33	5.04	85	.295	.380	8-0	.250	1		-5	-0.9
1954	Pit N	0	0	—	7	0	0	0	9.2	16	17	4	1	7	4	11.17	37	.364	.462	0-0	—	0		-9	-0.4
Total	8	57	49	.538	285	45	14-1	76	790	727	369	42	15	421	519	3.53	106	.247	.344	229-11	.205	5	124	11	4.2
PAGE, PHIL Philippe Rausac B 8.23.1905 Springfield, MA D 7.27.1958 Springfield, MA BR/TL 6-2/175# d9.18 C6																									
1928	Det A	2	0	1.000	3	2	2	0	22	21	9	1	0	10	3	2.45	167	.256	.337	9-0	.222	-0	124	3	0.3
1929	Det A	0	2	.000	10	4	1	0	25.1	29	24	1	1	19	6	8.17	53	.296	.415	8-0	.125	-1	147	-9	-0.7
1930	Det A	0	1	.000	12	0	0	0	12	23	16	1	0	9	2	9.75	49	.434	.516	0-0	—	0		-7	-0.4
1934	Bro N	1	0	1.000	6	0	0	0	10	13	7	1	0	6	4	5.40	72	.342	.432	1-0	.000	-0		-2	-0.1
Total	4	3	3	.500	31	6	3	0	69.1	86	56	4	1	44	15	6.23	68	.317	.415	18-0	.167	-1	140	-15	-0.9
PAGE, SAM Samuel Walter B 2.11.1916 Woodruff, SC D 5.29.2002 Greenville, SC BL/TR 6/172# d9.11																									
1939	Phi A	0	3	.000	4	3	1	0	22	34	27	1	0	15	11	6.95	68	.343	.430	7-1	.429	1	106	-8	-0.7
PAGE, VANCE Vance Linwood B 9.15.1905 Elm City, NC D 7.14.1951 Wilson, NC BR/TR 6/180# d8.6																									
1938	†Chi N	5	4	.556	13	9	3	1	68	90	33	4	0	13	18	3.84	100	.323	.353	26-1	.154	-1	93	0	0.0
1939	Chi N	7	7	.500	27	17	8-1	1	139.1	169	77	8	1	37	43	3.88	102	.298	.342	47-2	.255	3	102	-2	0.1
1940	Chi N	1	3	.250	30	1	0	2	59	65	38	1	0	26	22	4.42	85	.271	.342	13-0	.308	2*	278	-6	-0.2
1941	Chi N	2	2	.500	25	3	1	1	48.1	48	24	2	2	30	17	4.28	82	.254	.362	7-1	.286	1	64	-3	-0.1
Total	4	15	16	.484	95	30	12-1	5	314.2	372	172	15	3	106	100	4.03	95	.292	.348	93-4	.237	4	103	-11	-0.2
PAIGE, PAT George Lynn "Piggy" B 5.5.1882 Paw Paw, MI D 6.8.1939 Berlin, WI BL/TR 5-10/175# d5.20																									
1911	Cle A	1	0	1.000	2	1	1	0	16	21	12	0	0	7	6	4.50	76	.339	.406	7-0	.143	-0	169	-2	-0.1
PAIGE, SATCHEL Leroy Robert B 7.7.1906 Mobile, AL D 6.8.1982 Kansas City, MO BR/TR 6-3.5/180# d7.9 C2 HF1971																									
1948	†Cle A	6	1	.857	21	7	3-2	1	72.2	61	21	2	1	22	43	2.48	164	.228	.290	23-2	.087	-2	121	14	1.0
1949	Cle A	4	7	.364	31	5	1	5	83	70	29	4	1	33	54	3.04	131	.230	.308	16-0	.063	-1	63	10	1.2
1951	StL A	3	4	.429	23	3	0	5	62	67	39	6	1	29	48	4.79	92	.276	.355	16-1	.125	-2	61	-3	-0.6
1952	StL A☆	12	10	.545	46	6	3-2	10	138	116	51	5	3	57	91	3.07	128	.226	.307	39-4	.128	-2	56	13	2.1
1953	StL A★	3	9	.250	57	4	0	11	117.1	114	51	12	1	39	51	3.53	119	.257	.319	29-1	.069	-3	95	9	0.6
1965	KC A	0	0	—	1	1	0	0	3	1	0	0	0	0-0	1	0.00	—	.100	.100	1-0	.000	-0	50	1	0.0
Total	6	28	31	.475	179	26	7-4	32	476	429	191	29	7	180-0	288	3.29	124	.241	.313	124-8	.097	-10	80	44	4.3
PAINE, PHIL Phillips Steere "Flip" B 6.8.1930 Chepachet, RI D 2.19.1978 Lebanon, PA BR/TR 6-2/181# d7.14 Mil 1952																									
1951	Bos N	2	0	1.000	21	0	0	0	35.1	36	15	2	4	20	17	3.06	120	.271	.382	4-0	.000	-1		2	0.0
1954	Mil N	1	0	1.000	11	0	0	0	14	14	9	1	1	12	11	3.86	97	.292	.443	0-0	—	0		-1	-0.1
1955	Mil N	2	0	1.000	15	0	0	0	25.1	20	8	2	0	14-3	26	2.49	151	.225	.324	3-0	.333	0		4	0.3
1956	Mil N	0	0	—	1	0	0	0	0	3	2	0	0	0-0	0	o	—	1.000	1.000	0-0	—	0		-2	-0.2
1957	Mil N	0	0	—	1	0	0	0	2	1	0	0	0	3-0	2	0.00	—	.143	.400	0-0	—	0		1	0.1
1958	StL N	5	1	.833	46	0	0	1	73.1	70	33	7	5	31-4	45	3.56	116	.256	.342	7-1	.286	0		4	0.4
Total	6	10	1	.909	95	0	0	1	150	144	67	12	10	80-7	101	3.36	116	.260	.362	14-1	.214	-0		8	0.5
PAINTER, LANCE Lance Telford B 7.21.1967 Bedford, England BL/TL 6-1/195# d5.19																									
1993	Col N	2	2	.500	10	6	1	0-0	39	52	26	5	0	9-0	16	6.00	80	.333	.370	10-3	.300	1	116	-3	-0.2
1994	Col N	4	6	.400	15	14	0	0-0	73.2	91	51	9	1	26-2	41	6.11	81	.302	.354	21-3	.143	-1	114	-7	-0.8
1995	†Col N	3	0	1.000	33	1	0	1-0	45.1	55	23	9	2	10-0	36	4.37	124	.296	.338	9-1	.111	-0	201	4	0.3
1996	Col N	4	2	.667	34	1	0	0-1	50.2	56	37	12	3	25-3	48	5.86	89	.280	.364	15-0	.133	-1*	17	-3	-0.4
1997	StL N	1	1	.500	14	0	0	0-0	17	13	9	1	0	8-2	11	4.76	87	.213	.304	1-0	.000	-0		-1	-0.1

Year	Tm Lg	W	L	Pct	G	GS	CG-Sho	SV-BS	IP	H	R	HR	HB	BB-IB	SO	ERA	AERA	OAV	OOB	AB-SH	AVG	PB	Sup	APR	PW
1998	StL N	4	0	1.000	65	0	0	1-1	47.1	42	24	5	4	28-3	39	3.99	105	.249	.365	1-1	1.000	0		1	0.2
1999	StL N	4	5	.444	56	4	0	1-2	63.1	63	37	6	2	25-1	56	4.83	95	.265	.336	7-0	.000	-1	65	-2	-0.2
2000	Tor A	2	0	1.000	42	2	0	0-1	66.2	69	37	9	2	22-1	53	4.72	108	.271	.332	0-0	—	0	129	3	0.2
2001	Tor A	0	1	.000	10	0	0	0-0	18.1	27	17	4	1	11-0	14	7.85	59	.342	.429	0-0	—	0		-6	-0.3
	Mil N	1	0	1.000	13	0	0	0-0	10.2	11	5	3	0	7-2	6	4.22	102	.268	.375	0-0	—	0		0	0.0
2003	StL N	0	1	.000	22	0	0	0-1	18	17	12	3	0	7-1	11	5.50	74	.246	.316	1-0	.000	-0		-3	-0.1
Total	10	25	18	.581	314	28	1	3-6	450	496	278	66	15	178-15	331	5.24	92	.283	.351	65-8	.154	-1	111	-17	-1.4

PALACIOS, VICENTE Vicente (Diaz) B 7.19.1963 Veracruz, Mexico BR/TR 6-3/195# d9.4

Year	Tm Lg	W	L	Pct	G	GS	CG-Sho	SV-BS	IP	H	R	HR	HB	BB-IB	SO	ERA	AERA	OAV	OOB	AB-SH	AVG	PB	Sup	APR	PW
1987	Pit N	2	1	.667	6	4	0	0-0	29.1	27	14	1	1	9-1	13	4.30	96	.250	.314	9-0	.111	-0	121	0	-0.1
1988	Pit N	1	2	.333	7	3	0	0-0	24.1	28	18	3	0	15-1	15	6.66	51	.295	.387	8-0	.000	-0	200	-8	-0.9
1990	Pit N	0	0	—	7	0	0	3-0	15	4	0	0	0	2-0	8	0.00	—	.083	.120	4-0	.000	-0		6	0.3
1991	Pit N	6	3	.667	36	7	1-1	3-2	81.2	69	34	12	1	38-2	64	3.75	95	.228	.315	14-5	.071	-1	115	0	-0.1
1992	Pit N	3	2	.600	20	8	0	0-0	53	56	25	1	0	27-1	33	4.25	81	.280	.364	14-2	.071	-1	112	-4	-0.4
1994	StL N	3	8	.273	31	17	1-1	1-0	117.2	104	60	16	3	43-2	95	4.44	94	.245	.314	33-3	.000	-4	68	-3	-0.6
1995	StL N	2	3	.400	20	5	0	0-0	40.1	48	29	7	2	19-1	34	5.80	72	.300	.379	6-1	.167	-0	95	-7	-0.8
2000	SD N	0	1	.000	7	0	0	0-0	10.2	12	10	4	0	5-1	8	6.75	64	.308	.378	0-0	—	0		-4	-0.3
Total	8	17	20	.459	134	44	2-2	7-2	372	348	190	44	7	158-9	270	4.43	87	.253	.330	88-11	.045	-6	99	-20	-2.9

PALAGYI, MIKE Michael Raymond B 7.4.1917 Conneaut, OH BR/TR 6-2/185# d8.18

Year	Tm Lg	W	L	Pct	G	GS	CG-Sho	SV-BS	IP	H	R	HR	HB	BB-IB	SO	ERA	AERA	OAV	OOB	AB-SH	AVG	PB	Sup	APR	PW
1939	Was A	0	0	—	1	0	0	0	0	0	3	0	1	3	0	o	—	—	1.000	0-0	—	0		-3	-0.2

PALICA, ERV Ervin Martin (b: Ervin Martin Pavliecivich) B 2.9.1928 Lomita, CA D 5.29.1982 Huntington Beach, CA BR/TR 6-1.5/180# d4.21.1945 Mil 1952

Year	Tm Lg	W	L	Pct	G	GS	CG-Sho	SV-BS	IP	H	R	HR	HB	BB-IB	SO	ERA	AERA	OAV	OOB	AB-SH	AVG	PB	Sup	APR	PW
1947	Bro N	0	1	.000	3	0	0	0	3	2	1	0	1	2	1	3.00	138	.182	.357	0-0	—	0		0	0.1
1948	Bro N	6	6	.500	41	10	3	3	125.1	111	63	13	3	58	74	4.45	90	.239	.327	39-1	.128	0*	109	-3	-0.3
1949	†Bro N	8	9	.471	49	1	0	6	97	93	43	6	1	49	44	3.62	113	.261	.352	19-4	.158	0	86	5	0.9
1950	Bro N	13	8	.619	43	19	10-2	1	201.1	176	89	13	2	98	131	3.58	115	.237	.327	68-3	.221	2*	117	11	1.1
1951	Bro N	2	6	.250	19	8	0	0	53	55	28	10	0	20	15	4.75	83	.259	.323	13-1	.154	0*	98	-4	-0.5
1953	Bro N	0	0	—	4	0	0	0	6	10	8	1	0	8	3	12.00	36	.370	.514	1-0	1.000	0		-5	-0.2
1954	Bro N	3	3	.500	25	3	0	0	67.2	77	45	9	1	31	25	5.32	77	.285	.357	16-0	.250	1*	102	-10	-0.7
1955	Bal A	5	11	.313	33	25	5-1	2	169.2	165	91	10	2	83-4	68	4.14	92	.260	.342	55-2	.236	2	86	-7	-0.3
1956	Bal A	4	11	.267	29	14	2	0	116.1	117	64	10	1	50-3	62	4.49	87	.264	.336	32-0	.156	-2*	66	-8	-1.0
Total	9	41	55	.427	246	80	20-3	12	839.1	806	432	72	11	399-7	423	4.22	94	.255	.338	243-11	.198	5	94	-21	-0.9

PALL, DONN Donn Steven B 1.11.1962 Chicago, IL BR/TR 6-1/183# d8.1

Year	Tm Lg	W	L	Pct	G	GS	CG-Sho	SV-BS	IP	H	R	HR	HB	BB-IB	SO	ERA	AERA	OAV	OOB	AB-SH	AVG	PB	Sup	APR	PW
1988	Chi A	0	2	.000	17	0	0	0-0	28.2	39	11	1	0	8-1	16	3.45	115	.328	.367	0-0	—	0		2	0.2
1989	Chi A	4	5	.444	53	0	0	6-4	87	90	35	9	8	19-3	58	3.31	115	.270	.323	0-0	—	0		5	0.5
1990	Chi A	3	5	.375	56	0	0	2-1	76	63	33	7	4	24-8	39	3.32	116	.232	.301	0-0	—	0		3	0.3
1991	Chi A	7	2	.778	51	0	0	0-1	71	59	22	7	3	20-3	40	2.41	165	.231	.295	0-0	—	0		12	1.4
1992	Chi A	5	2	.714	39	0	0	1-1	73	79	43	9	2	27-8	27	4.93	78	.272	.335	0-0	—	0		-8	-0.8
1993	Chi A	2	3	.400	39	0	0	1-1	58.2	62	25	5	2	11-3	29	3.22	130	.268	.306	0-0	—	0		6	0.5
	Phi N	1	0	1.000	8	0	0	0-0	17.2	15	7	1	0	3-0	11	2.55	156	.231	.265	0-0	—	0		2	0.1
1994	NY A	1	2	.333	26	0	0	0-0	35	43	18	3	1	9-0	21	3.60	127	.295	.338	0-0	—	0		3	0.2
	Chi N	0	0	—	2	0	0	0-0	4	8	2	1	0	1-0	2	4.50	92	.444	.474	0-0	—	0		0	0.0
1996	Fla N	1	1	.500	12	0	0	0-0	18.2	16	15	3	0	9-1	9	5.79	70	.232	.316	2-0	.000	0		-4	-0.4
1997	Fla N	0	0	—	2	0	0	0-1	2.1	3	1	1	0	1-0	0	3.86	105	.300	.364	1-0	.000	-0		0	0.0
1998	Fla N	0	1	.000	23	0	0	0-0	33.1	42	19	5	1	7-2	26	5.13	79	.326	.362	2-0	.000	-0		-3	-0.2
Total	10	24	23	.511	328	0	0	10-9	505.1	519	231	52	21	139-29	278	3.63	110	.268	.322	5-0	.000	-0		18	1.8

PALM, MIKE Richard Paul B 2.13.1925 Boston, MA BR/TR 6-3.5/190# d7.11

Year	Tm Lg	W	L	Pct	G	GS	CG-Sho	SV-BS	IP	H	R	HR	HB	BB-IB	SO	ERA	AERA	OAV	OOB	AB-SH	AVG	PB	Sup	APR	PW
1948	Bos A	0	0	—	3	0	0	0	3	6	2	0	0	5	1	6.00	73	.400	.550	3-0	.000	-0		0	-0.1

PALMER, BILLY Billy B St.Louis, MO d5.28

Year	Tm Lg	W	L	Pct	G	GS	CG-Sho	SV-BS	IP	H	R	HR	HB	BB-IB	SO	ERA	AERA	OAV	OOB	AB-SH	AVG	PB	Sup	APR	PW
1885	StL N	0	4	.000	4	4	4	0	34	46	33	2		20	9	3.44	80	.311	.393	11	.091	-0	67	-6	-0.6

PALMER, DAVID David William B 10.19.1957 Glens Falls, NY BR/TR 6-1/205# d9.9

Year	Tm Lg	W	L	Pct	G	GS	CG-Sho	SV-BS	IP	H	R	HR	HB	BB-IB	SO	ERA	AERA	OAV	OOB	AB-SH	AVG	PB	Sup	APR	PW
1978	Mon N	0	1	.000	5	1	0	0-0	9.2	9	4	1	0	2-0	7	2.79	126	.243	.282	1-0	.000	-0	76	0	0.1
1979	Mon N	10	2	.833	36	11	2-1	2-1	122.2	110	41	10	2	30-7	72	2.64	139	.237	.285	31-4	.032	-3	125	15	1.1
1980	Mon N	8	6	.571	24	19	3-1	0-0	129.2	124	53	11	2	30-1	73	2.98	120	.255	.299	45-2	.200	1*	111	6	0.9
1982	Mon N	6	4	.600	13	13	1	0-0	73.2	60	34	3	2	36-2	46	3.18	115	.224	.315	24-3	.042	-2	114	2	0.0
1984	Mon N	7	3	.700	20	19	1-1	0-0	105.1	101	45	5	0	44-4	66	3.84	89	.256	.330	33-6	.152	1	99	-3	-0.1
1985	Mon N	7	10	.412	24	23	0	0-0	135.2	128	60	5	3	67-5	106	3.71	91	.250	.340	36-5	.111	-1	87	-4	-0.5
1986	Atl N	11	10	.524	35	35	2	0-0	209.2	181	98	17	5	102-8	170	3.65	109	.234	.325	66-10	.182	1	83	7	0.9
1987	Atl N	8	11	.421	28	28	0	0-0	152.1	169	94	17	7	64-4	111	4.90	89	.281	.354	48-8	.125	-0	103	-9	-1.0
1988	Phi N	7	9	.438	22	22	1-1	0-0	129	129	67	8	0	48-5	85	4.47	80	.261	.324	39-9	.256	5	85	-11	-0.8
1989	Det A	0	3	.000	5	5	0	0-0	17.1	25	19	1	0	11-0	12	7.79	49	.342	.424	0-0	—	0	137	-9	-1.2
Total	10	64	59	.520	212	176	10-4	2-1	1085	1036	515	78	21	434-36	748	3.78	99	.252	.325	323-47	.149	2	98	-6	-0.6

PALMER, JIM James Alvin B 10.15.1945 New York, NY BR/TR 6-3/196# d4.17 HF1990

Year	Tm Lg	W	L	Pct	G	GS	CG-Sho	SV-BS	IP	H	R	HR	HB	BB-IB	SO	ERA	AERA	OAV	OOB	AB-SH	AVG	PB	Sup	APR	PW
1965	Bal A	5	4	.556	27	6	0	1	92	75	49	6	2	56-1	75	3.72	93	.229	.342	26-0	.192	1*	72	-4	-0.3
1966	†Bal A	15	10	.600	30	30	6	0	208.1	176	83	21	0	91-1	147	3.46	96	.231	.311	73-2	.096	-2*	132	0	-0.3
1967	Bal A	3	1	.750	9	9	2-1	0	49	34	18	6	0	20-0	23	2.94	107	.199	.281	13-3	.077	0	154	1	0.1
1969	†Bal A	16	4	**.800**	26	23	11-6	0-0	181	131	48	11	1	64-1	123	2.34	153	.200	.272	64-2	.203	2*	135	27	3.1
1970	†Bal A★	20	10	.667	39	39	17-**5**	0-0	**305**	263	98	21	1	100-4	199	2.71	134	.231	.293	113-7	.150	-1*	109	**34**	3.1
1971	†Bal A★	20	9	.690	37	37	20-3	0-0	282	231	94	19	4	106-6	184	2.68	125	.221	.294	102-11	.196	2*	123	22	2.5
1972	Bal A★	21	10	.677	36	36	18-3	0-0	274.1	219	73	21	1	70-1	184	2.07	149	.217	.268	98-6	.224	4	118	30	4.1
1973	†Bal A	22	9	.710	38	37	19-6	1-0	296.1	225	86	16	3	113-5	158	**2.40**	156	.211	.288	0-0	—	0	112	46	4.7
1974	†Bal A	7	12	.368	26	26	5-2	0-0	178.2	176	78	12	3	69-4	84	3.27	106	.257	.326	0-0	—	0	86	2	0.3
1975	Bal A☆	**23**	11	.676	39	38	25-**10**	1-0	323	253	87	20	2	80-4	193	**2.09**	**168**	.216	.266	0-0	—	0	102	**52**	**5.6**
1976	Bal A	**22**	13	.629	40	**40**	23-6	0-0	**315**	255	101	20	8	84-5	159	2.51	130	.224	.278	0-0	—	0	91	27	3.0
1977	Bal A★	**20**	11	.645	39	**39**	**22**-3	0-0	**319**	263	106	24	3	99-1	193	2.91	131	.229	.290	0-0	—	0	99	37	3.3
1978	Bal A★	21	12	.636	38	38	19-6	0-0	**296**	246	94	19	1	97-1	138	2.46	142	.227	.290	0-0	—	0	94	35	3.9
1979	†Bal A	10	6	.625	23	22	7	0-0	155.2	144	66	12	0	43-0	67	3.30	122	.246	.295	0-0	—	0	127	12	1.1
1980	Bal A	16	10	.615	34	33	4	0-0	224	238	108	26	3	74-0	109	3.98	100	.275	.332	0-0	—	0*	114	-1	0.0
1981	Bal A	7	8	.467	22	22	5	0-0	127.1	117	60	14	2	46-1	35	3.75	97	.247	.313	0-0	—	0	102	-2	-0.1
1982	Bal A	15	5	**.750**	36	32	8-2	1-0	227	195	85	22	4	63-1	103	3.13	129	.231	**.286**	0-0	—	0	106	23	1.9
1983	†Bal A	5	4	.556	14	11	0	0-0	76.2	86	42	11	0	19-0	34	4.23	94	.281	.320	0-0	—	0	102	-3	-0.4
1984	Bal A	0	3	.000	5	3	0	0-0	17.2	22	19	2	0	17-1	4	9.17	42	.319	.443	0-0	—	0	78	-10	-1.3
Total	19	268	152	.638	558	521	211-53	4-0	3948	3349	1395	303	38	1311-37	2212	2.86	125	.230	.294	489-31	.174	7	109	328	34.3

PALMER, LOWELL Lowell Raymond B 8.18.1947 Sacramento, CA BR/TR 6-1/190# d6.21

Year	Tm Lg	W	L	Pct	G	GS	CG-Sho	SV-BS	IP	H	R	HR	HB	BB-IB	SO	ERA	AERA	OAV	OOB	AB-SH	AVG	PB	Sup	APR	PW
1969	Phi N	2	8	.200	26	9	1-1	0-0	90	91	54	12	6	47-7	68	5.20	68	.264	.356	22-2	.136	1	86	-15	-1.4
1970	Phi N	1	2	.333	38	5	0	0-0	102	98	66	15	5	55-4	85	5.47	73	.255	.353	27-1	.148	1	126	-17	-0.7
1971	Phi N	0	0	—	3	1	0	0-0	15	13	11	3	4	13-0	6	6.00	59	.236	.411	5-0	.200	-0	126	-4	-0.2
1972	StL N	0	3	.000	16	2	0	0-0	34.2	30	16	2	1	26-1	25	3.89	87	.244	.375	5-0	.000	-1*	26	-2	-0.2
	Cle A	0	0	—	1	0	0	0-0	2	2	1	0	0	2-0	3	4.50	72	.222	.364	0-0	—	0		0	0.0
1974	SD N	2	5	.286	22	8	1	0-0	73	68	48	9	7	59-6	52	5.67	63	.256	.398	23-0	.087	-1*	98	-16	-1.5
Total	5	5	18	.217	106	25	2-1	0-0	316.2	302	196	41	23	202-18	239	5.29	70	.255	.370	82-3	.122	-0	95	-54	-4.0

PALMERO, EMILIO Emilio Antonio "Pal" B 6.13.1895 Guanabacoa, Cuba D 7.15.1970 Toledo, OH BL/TL 5-11/157# d9.21

Year	Tm Lg	W	L	Pct	G	GS	CG-Sho	SV-BS	IP	H	R	HR	HB	BB-IB	SO	ERA	AERA	OAV	OOB	AB-SH	AVG	PB	Sup	APR	PW
1915	NY N	0	2	.000	3	2	1	0	11.2	10	4	0	3	9	8	3.09	83	.233	.400	4-0	.250	0	44	0	0.0
1916	NY N	0	3	.000	4	2	0	0	15.2	17	14	2	1	8	8	8.04	30	.288	.382	3-0	.000	-0*	107	-9	-1.4
1921	StL A	4	7	.364	24	9	4	0	90	109	63	1	6	49	26	5.00	90	.319	.413	37-0	.216	1*	85	-6	-0.5
1926	Was A	2	2	.500	7	3	0	0	17	22	15	1	1	15	6	4.76	81	.344	.475	3-0	.333	0	58	-4	-0.7

Year	Tm Lg	W	L	Pct	G	GS	CG-Sho	SV-BS	IP	H	R	HR	HB	BB-IB	SO	ERA	AERA	OAV	OOB	AB-SH	AVG	PB	Sup	APR	PW
1928	Bos N	0	1	.000	3	1	0	0	6.2	14	8	0	0	2	0	5.40	72	.452	.485	1-1	.000	-0	65	-2	-0.3
Total	5	6	15	.286	41	17	5	0	141	172	104	4	11	83	48	5.17	77	.319	.420	48-1	.208	1	76	-21	-2.9
PALMQUIST, ED Edwin Lee B 6.10.1933 Los Angeles, CA BR/TR 6-3/195# d6.10																									
1960	LA N	0	1	.000	22	0	0	0	39	34	16	6	1	16-5	23	2.54	156	.243	.317	7-0	.000	-1		4	0.1
1961	LA N	0	1	.000	5	0	0	1	8.2	10	8	0	2	7-0	5	6.23	70	.333	.463	0-0	—	0		-2	-0.3
	Min A	1	1	.500	9	2	0	0	21	33	23	7	3	13-3	13	9.43	45	.359	.450	3-2	.000	-0	94	-11	-0.9
Total	2	1	3	.250	36	2	0	1	68.2	77	47	13	6	36-8	41	5.11	80	.294	.383	10-2	.000	-1	94	-9	-1.1
PANIAGUA, JOSE Jose Luis (Sanchez) B 8.20.1973 San Jose De Ocoa, D.R. BR/TR 6-2/185# d4.4																									
1996	Mon N	2	4	.333	13	11	0	0-0	51	55	24	7	3	23-0	27	3.53	123	.282	.365	11-1	.000	-1	82	4	0.3
1997	Mon N	1	2	.333	9	3	0	0-0	18	29	24	2	4	16-1	8	12.00	35	.372	.495	5-0	.000	-1	146	-14	-1.9
1998	Sea A	2	0	1.000	18	0	0	1-1	22	15	5	3	3	5-0	16	2.05	227	.200	.277	0-0	—	0		7	0.6
1999	Sea A	6	11	.353	59	0	0	3-9	77.2	75	37	5	7	52-4	74	4.06	117	.264	.387	0-0	—	0		6	1.2
2000	†Sea A	3	0	1.000	69	0	0	5-3	80.1	68	31	6	7	38-3	71	3.47	136	.234	.331	1-0	.000	-0		13	0.6
2001	†Sea A	4	3	.571	60	0	0	3-1	66	59	35	7	4	38-2	46	4.36	95	.233	.341	1-0	.000	-0		-2	-0.2
2002	Det A	0	1	.000	41	0	0	1-1	41.2	50	30	10	3	15-1	34	5.83	74	.294	.356	0-0	—	0		-7	-0.4
2003	Chi A	0	0	—	1	0	0	0-0	0.1	3	4	0	0	1-0	0	108.00	4	.750	.800	0-0	—	0		-4	-0.2
Total	8	18	21	.462	270	14	0	13-15	357	354	190	40	31	188-11	276	4.49	100	.262	.362	18-1	.000	-1	93	3	0.0
PANTHER, JIM James Edward B 3.1.1945 Burlington, IA BR/TR 6-1/190# d4.5																									
1971	Oak A	0	1	.000	4	0	0	0-0	5.2	10	9	1	0	5-2	4	11.12	30	.385	.484	1-0	.000	-0		-6	-0.8
1972	Tex A	5	9	.357	58	4	0	0-1	93.2	101	55	8	5	46-8	44	4.13	73	.277	.365	8-3	.125	0	37	-14	-2.1
1973	Atl N	2	3	.400	23	0	0	0-2	30.2	45	26	3	0	9-1	8	7.63	52	.363	.391	0-0	—	0		-10	-1.6
Total	3	7	13	.350	85	4	0	0-3	130	156	90	12	5	60-11	56	5.26	62	.303	.377	9-3	.111	-0	37	-30	-4.5
PAPA, JOHN John Paul B 12.5.1940 Bridgeport, CT BR/TR 5-11/190# d4.11																									
1961	Bal A	0	0	—	2	0	0	0	1	2	2	1	0	3-0	3	18.00	21	.400	.625	0-0	—	0		-2	-0.1
1962	Bal A	0	0	—	1	0	0	0	1	3	3	0	0	1-0	0	27.00	14	.600	.571	0-0	—	0		-3	-0.1
Total	2	0	0	—	3	0	0	0	2	5	5	1	0	4-0	3	22.50	17	.500	.600	0-0	—	0		-5	-0.2
PAPAI, AL Alfred Thomas B 5.7.1917 Divernon, IL D 9.7.1995 Springfield, IL BR/TR 6-3/185# d4.24																									
1948	StL N	0	1	.000	10	0	0	0	16	14	10	3	0	7	8	5.06	81	.241	.323	2-0	.000	-0*		-2	-0.1
1949	StL A	4	11	.267	42	15	6	2	142.1	175	103	8	1	81	31	5.06	90	.298	.384	38-1	.079	-2	84	-11	-1.1
1950	Bos A	4	2	.667	16	3	2	2	50.2	61	41	5	0	28	19	6.75	73	.293	.377	17-1	.176	-0	68	-10	-1.0
	StL N	1	0	1.000	13	0	0	0	19	21	12	0	0	14	7	5.21	82	.300	.417	3-0	.000	-0		-2	-0.1
1955	Chi A	0	0	—	7	0	0	0	11.2	10	5	1	0	8-2	5	3.86	102	.244	.360	2-0	.000	-0		0	0.0
Total	4	9	14	.391	88	18	8	4	239.2	281	171	17	1	138-2	70	5.37	84	.291	.380	62-2	.097	-3	82	-25	-2.3
PAPE, LARRY Laurence Albert B 7.21.1883 Norwood, OH D 7.21.1918 Swissvale, PA BR/TR 5-11/175# d7.6																									
1909	Bos A	2	0	1.000	11	3	2-1	2	57.1	46	17	0	5	12	18	2.04	123	.221	.280	21-0	.143	-1	103	3	0.0
1911	Bos A	10	8	.556	27	19	10-1	0	176.1	167	68	3	4	63	49	2.45	134	.264	.335	64-3	.203	-1	74	19	1.8
1912	Bos A	1	1	.500	13	2	1	1	48.2	74	36	0	2	16	17	4.99	68	.366	.418	17-0	.235	1	98	-9	-0.3
Total	3	13	9	.591	51	24	13-2	3	282.1	287	121	3	11	91	84	2.81	112	.275	.340	102-3	.196	-1	80	13	1.5
PAPISH, FRANK Frank Richard "Pap" B 10.21.1917 Pueblo, CO D 8.30.1965 Pueblo, CO BR/TL 6-2/192# d5.8																									
1945	Chi A	4	4	.500	19	5	3	1	84.1	75	36	3	0	40	45	3.74	89	.241	.328	26-3	.231	1	123	-2	0.0
1946	Chi A	7	5	.583	31	15	6-2	0	138	122	52	7	1	63	66	2.74	125	.243	.328	43-3	.186	-0	107	11	0.9
1947	Chi A	12	12	.500	38	26	6-1	3	199	185	82	6	2	98	79	3.26	112	.245	.333	58-6	.086	-5	78	10	0.6
1948	Chi A	2	8	.200	32	14	2	4	95.1	97	65	7	3	75	41	5.00	85	.265	.394	27-1	.185	-1	109	-11	-1.1
1949	Cle A	1	0	1.000	25	3	1	1	62	54	24	2	0	39	23	3.19	125	.240	.352	8-3	.125	0	120	6	0.3
1950	Pit N	0	0	—	4	1	0	0	2.1	8	7	1	0	4	1	27.00	16	.533	.632	0-0	—	0	121	-5	-0.2
Total	6	26	29	.473	149	64	18-3	9	581	541	266	26	6	319	255	3.58	103	.249	.346	162-16	.154	-5	99	9	0.5
PAPPALAU, JOHN John Joseph B 4.3.1875 Albany, NY D 5.12.1944 Albany, NY BR/TR 6/175# d6.9																									
1897	Cle N	0	1	.000	2	1	1	0	12	22	16	0	2	6	3	10.50	43	.393	.469	5-0	.000	-0	95	-7	-0.4
PAPPAS, MILT Milton Stephen "Gimpy" (b: Miltiades Stergios Papastegios) B 5.11.1939 Detroit, MI BR/TR 6-3/190# d8.10																									
1957	Bal A	0	0	—	4	0	0	0	9	6	1	0	0	3-0	3	1.00	359	.200	.273	1-0	.000	-0		3	0.1
1958	Bal A	10	10	.500	31	21	3	0	135.1	135	67	8	2	48-1	72	4.06	89	.262	.326	42-3	.143	-0*	90	-7	-0.9
1959	Bal A	15	9	.625	33	27	15-4	3	209.1	175	82	8	4	75-2	120	3.27	116	.226	.297	79-1	.139	-3	98	14	1.1
1960	Bal A	15	11	.577	30	27	11-3	0	205.2	184	81	15	6	83-4	126	3.37	113	.243	.320	70-5	.043	-5	92	13	1.0
1961	Bal A	13	9	.591	26	23	11-4	1	177.2	134	67	16	7	78-5	89	3.04	127	.208	.300	66-3	.136	1	92	17	2.1
1962	Bal A★	12	10	.545	35	32	9-1	0	205.1	200	105	31	2	75-3	130	4.03	92	.257	.322	69-3	.087	-0	97	-8	-0.7
1963	Bal A	16	9	.640	34	32	11-4	0	216.2	186	80	21	5	69-6	120	3.03	115	.233	.296	71-7	.127	-0*	111	12	1.4
1964	Bal A	16	7	.696	37	36	13-7	0	251.2	225	89	21	7	48-10	157	2.97	120	.239	.280	93-2	.129	-2	120	18	1.4
1965	Bal A★	13	9	.591	34	34	9-3	0	221.1	192	81	22	3	52-3	127	2.60	133	.233	.279	70-7	.071	-3	89	19	1.3
1966	Cin N	12	11	.522	33	32	6-2	0	209.2	224	106	23	3	39-4	133	4.29	91	.275	.308	75-3	.107	-2*	101	-8	-1.0
1967	Cin N	16	13	.552	34	32	5-3	0	217.2	218	88	19	5	38-5	129	3.35	112	.259	.293	72-2	.097	-2	95	10	1.1
1968	Cin N	2	5	.286	15	11	0	0	62.2	70	41	9	2	10-3	43	5.60	56	.275	.306	16-4	.063	-1*	105	-15	-1.7
	Atl N	10	8	.556	22	19	3-1	0	121.1	111	36	8	3	22-6	75	2.37	126	.246	.283	37-2	.162	2	76	9	1.6
	Year	12	13	.480	37	30	3-1	0	184	181	39	17	5	32-9	118	3.47	88	.256	.291	53-6	.132	1	87	-7	-0.1
1969	†Atl N	6	10	.375	26	24	1	0-0	144	149	66	14	4	44-9	72	3.63	100	.267	.323	45-1	.156	3	89	-1	0.2
1970	Atl N	2	2	.500	11	3	1	0-0	35.2	44	25	6	2	7-1	25	6.06	71	.293	.331	10-0	.000	-1	84	-6	-0.7
	Chi N	10	8	.556	21	20	6-2	0-0	144.2	135	53	14	0	36-9	80	2.68	168	.248	.292	50-1	.240	4	94	25	3.4
	Year	12	10	.545	32	23	7-2	0-0	180.1	179	58	20	2	43-10	105	3.34	134	.258	.300	60-1	.200	3	93	19	2.7
1971	Chi N	17	14	.548	35	35	14-**5**	0-0	261.1	279	109	25	5	62-6	99	3.51	112	.274	.317	91-2	.154	-1	91	13	1.3
1972	Chi N	17	7	.708	29	28	10-3	0-0	195	187	72	18	8	29-3	80	2.77	138	.251	.286	68-4	.191	1	112	19	2.6
1973	Chi N	7	12	.368	30	29	1-1	0-0	162	192	82	20	4	40-9	48	4.28	92	.299	.342	48-2	.063	-3	79	-4	-0.7
Total	17	209	164	.560	520	465	129-43	4-0	3186	3046	1331	298	72	858-89	1728	3.40	110	.252	.304	1073-52	.123	-14	96	123	12.9
PARK, CHAN HO Chan Ho B 6.30.1973 Kongju, South Korea BR/TR 6-2/185# d4.8																									
1994	LA N	0	0	—	2	0	0	0-0	4	5	5	1	1	5-0	6	11.25	35	.294	.478	0-0	—	0		-3	-0.2
1995	LA N	0	0	—	2	1	0	0-0	4	2	2	1	0	2-0	7	4.50	84	.143	.250	1-0	.000	-0	95	0	0.0
1996	LA N	5	5	.500	48	10	0	0-0	108.2	82	48	7	4	71-3	119	3.64	106	.209	.335	19-3	.053	-1	91	4	0.3
1997	LA N	14	8	.636	32	29	2	0-0	192	149	80	24	8	70-1	166	3.38	114	.213	.290	51-11	.176	3	113	11	1.4
1998	LA N	15	9	.625	34	34	2	0-0	220.2	199	101	16	11	97-1	191	3.71	107	.244	.328	72-6	.194	3	117	7	0.9
1999	LA N	13	11	.542	33	33	0	0-0	194.1	208	120	31	14	100-4	174	5.23	82	.276	.369	59-6	.153	0	114	-20	-1.9
2000	LA N	18	10	.643	34	34	3-1	0-0	226	173	92	21	12	124-4	217	3.27	133	.214	.325	70-6	.214	5	100	28	3.8
2001	LA N★	15	11	.577	36	**35**	2-1	0-0	234	183	98	23	20	91-1	218	3.50	115	.216	.305	69-7	.145	2	99	15	1.8
2002	Tex A	9	8	.529	25	25	0	0-0	145.2	154	95	20	17	78-2	121	5.75	82	.273	.376	4-0	.000	-0	126	-14	-1.4
2003	Tex A	1	3	.250	7	7	0	0-0	29.2	34	26	5	6	25-0	16	7.58	66	.306	.448	0-0	—	0	85	-8	-0.8
Total	10	90	65	.581	253	208	9-2	0-0	1359	1189	667	149	93	663-16	1235	4.09	102	.237	.334	345-39	.168	11	109	20	3.9
PARK, JIM James B 11.10.1892 Richmond, KY D 12.17.1970 Lexington, KY BR/TR 6-2/175# d9.7																									
1915	StL A	2	0	1.000	3	3	1	0	22.2	18	8	1	0	9	5	1.19	240	.214	.290	10-0	.400	1	204	3	0.4
1916	StL A	1	4	.200	26	6	1	0	79	69	28	2	1	25	26	2.62	105	.244	.307	20-0	.100	-2	55	2	-0.1
1917	StL A	1	1	.500	13	0	0	0	20.1	27	20	1	0	12	9	6.64	39	.333	.419	2-0	.000	-0		-9	-0.9
Total	3	4	5	.444	42	9	2	0	122	114	56	4	1	46	40	3.02	91	.254	.325	32-0	.188	-0	109	-4	-0.6
PARKER, CHRISTIAN Christian Michael B 7.3.1975 Albuquerque, NM BR/TR 6-1/200# d4.6																									
2001	NY A	0	1	.000	1	1	0	0-0	3	8	7	2	0	1-0	1	21.00	21	.471	.500	0-0	—	0	82	-5	-0.7
PARKER, DOC Harley Park B 6.14.1872 Theresa, NY D 3.3.1941 Chicago, IL BR/TR 6-2/200# d7.11 b-Jay																									
1893	Chi N	0	0	—	1	0	0	1	2	5	3	0	0	1	0	13.50	34	.455	.500	1	.000	-0		-2	-0.1

Year	Tm Lg	W	L	Pct	G	GS	CG-Sho	SV-BS	IP	H	R	HR	HB	BB-IB	SO	ERA	AERA	OAV	OOB	AB-SH	AVG	PB	Sup	APR	PW
1895	Chi N	4	2	.667	7	6	5-1	0	51.1	65	30	1	3	9	9	3.68	138	.304	.341	22-0	.318	1	98	8	0.7
1896	Chi N	1	5	.167	9	7	7	0	73	100	71	3	3	27	15	6.16	74	.323	.382	36-0	.278	0*	74	-13	-0.8
1901	Cin N	0	1	.000	1	1	1	0	8	26	21	1	0	2	0	15.75	20	.531	.549	3-0	.000	-0	66	-12	-0.9
Total	4	5	8	.385	18	14	13-1	1	134.1	196	125	5	6	39	24	5.90	79	.336	.383	62-0	.274	0	85	-19	-1.1
PARKER, HARRY Harry William B 9.14.1947 Highland, IL BR/TR 6-3/190# d8.8																									
1970	StL N	1	1	.500	7	4	0	0-0	22.1	24	13	0	0	15-0	9	3.22	128	.276	.382	8-0	.250	0	98	0	0.1
1971	StL N	0	0	—	4	0	0	0-0	5	6	4	2	0	2-0	2	7.20	50	.286	.348	0-0	—	0		-2	-0.1
1973	†NY N	8	4	.667	38	9	0	5-1	96.2	79	40	7	3	36-3	63	3.35	108	.217	.291	23-5	.174	-0	106	3	0.3
1974	NY N	4	12	.250	40	16	1	4-3	131	145	64	10	3	46-5	58	3.92	91	.281	.342	36-3	.000	-4	56	-4	-1.0
1975	NY N	2	3	.400	18	1	0	2-0	34.2	37	17	2	0	19-5	22	4.41	78	.272	.361	2-1	.000	1	102	-3	-0.3
	StL N	0	1	.000	14	0	0	1-0	18.2	21	13	3	0	10-2	13	6.27	60	.288	.365	1-1	.000	0		-4	-0.2
	Year	2	4	.333	32	1	0	3-0	53.1	58	34	5	0	29-7	35	5.06	70	.278	.363	3-2	.000	1	99	-7	-0.5
1976	Cle A	0	0	—	3	0	0	0-0	7	3	0	0	0	0-0	5	0.00	—	.136	.136	0-0	—	0		3	0.2
Total	6	15	21	.417	124	30	1	12-4	315.1	315	151	24	6	128-15	172	3.85	94	.258	.330	70-10	.086	-3	79	-7	-1.0
PARKER, CLAY James Clayton B 12.19.1962 Columbia, LA BR/TR 6-1/185# d9.14																									
1987	Sea A	0	0	—	3	1	0	0-0	7.2	15	10	2	1	4-0	8	10.57	45	.405	.465	0-0	—	0	96	-5	-0.2
1989	NY A	4	5	.444	22	17	2	0-0	120	123	53	12	2	31-3	53	3.68	105	.264	.311	0-0	—	0	94	3	0.2
1990	NY A	1	1	.500	5	2	0	0-0	22	19	11	5	0	7-1	20	4.50	88	.229	.286	0-0	—	0	126	-1	-0.1
	Det A	2	2	.500	24	1	0	0-0	51	45	18	6	1	25-5	20	3.18	125	.242	.332	0-0	—	0	69	5	0.4
	Year	3	3	.500	29	3	0	0-0	73	64	21	11	1	32-6	40	3.58	111	.238	.318	0-0	—	0	107	5	0.3
1992	Sea A	0	2	.000	8	6	0	0-0	33.1	47	28	6	2	11-0	20	7.56	53	.338	.390	0-0	—	0	119	-12	-0.6
Total	4	7	10	.412	62	27	2	0-0	234	249	120	31	6	78-9	121	4.42	89	.273	.332	0-0	—	0	101	-10	-0.3
PARKER, JAY Jay B 7.8.1874 Theresa, NY D 6.8.1935 Hartford, MI BR/TR 5-11/185# d9.27 b-Harley																									
1899	Pit N	0	0	—	1	1	0	0	0	0	2	0	1	2	0	o	—	—	1.000	0-0	—	0	132	-2	-0.1
PARKER, ROY Roy William B 2.29.1896 Union, MO D 5.17.1954 Tulsa, OK BR/TR 6-3/200# d9.10																									
1919	StL N	0	0	—	2	0	0	0	2	6	7	0	1	1	0	31.50	9	.333	.400	0-0	—	0		-6	-0.3
PARKS, SLICKER Vernon Henry B 11.10.1895 Dallas, MI D 2.21.1978 Royal Oak, MI BR/TR 5-10/158# d7.11																									
1921	Det A	3	2	.600	10	1	0	0	25.1	33	17	2	1	16	10	5.68	75	.306	.400	9-1	.111	-1	98	-3	-0.5
PARKS, BILL William Robert B 6.4.1849 Easton, PA D 10.10.1911 Easton, PA BR/TR 5-8/150# d4.26 M1 ▲																									
1875	Was NA	4	8	.333	14	11	9	0	106.2	144	120	3		5	3	3.29	72	.280	.287	111	.180	-3*	66	-9	-1.0
	Phi NA	0	0	—	2	0	0	0	5.1	13	11	0		1	0	8.44	27	.419	.438	6	.167	-0		-3	-0.2
	Year	4	8	.333	16	11	9	0	112	157	135	3		6	3	3.54	67	.288	.295	117	.179	-3	66	-17	-1.2
PARMELEE, ROY Le Roy Earl "Tarzan" B 4.25.1907 Lambertville, MI D 8.31.1981 Monroe, MI BR/TR 6-1/190# d9.28																									
1929	NY N	1	0	1.000	2	1	0	0	7	13	7	1	1	3	1	9.00	51	.481	.548	2-0	.500	0	171	-3	-0.3
1930	NY N	0	1	.000	11	1	0	0	21	18	26	3	0	26	19	9.43	50	.228	.419	4-0	.250	1	147	-12	-0.5
1931	NY N	2	2	.500	13	5	4	0	58.2	47	25	1	3	33	30	3.68	100	.223	.336	20-1	.200	-0	74	2	0.1
1932	NY N	0	3	.000	8	3	0	0	25.1	25	18	0	2	14	23	3.91	95	.250	.353	5-0	.400	1	60	-3	-0.2
1933	NY N	13	8	.619	32	32	14-3	0	218.1	191	94	9	14	77	132	3.17	101	.232	.309	81-1	.235	4*	122	1	0.5
1934	NY N	10	6	.625	22	21	7-2	0	152.2	134	59	6	6	60	83	3.42	113	**.238**	.318	55-2	.200	2	96	13	1.4
1935	NY N	14	10	.583	34	31	13	0	226	214	117	20	9	97	79	4.22	91	.249	.332	86-0	.209	3	115	-8	-0.4
1936	StL N	11	11	.500	37	28	9	2	221	226	125	13	10	107	79	4.56	86	.270	.360	76-2	.197	-0	101	-14	-1.3
1937	Chi N	7	8	.467	33	18	8	0	145.2	165	93	13	7	79	55	5.13	78	.286	.379	52-1	.173	0*	153	-18	-1.6
1939	Phi A	1	6	.143	14	5	0	1	44.2	42	41	2	3	35	13	6.45	73	.235	.369	15-0	.133	-1*	82	-10	-1.3
Total	10	59	55	.518	206	145	55-5	3	1120.1	1075	605	68	55	531	514	4.27	89	.253	.343	396-7	.207	9	112	-52	-3.6
PARNELL, MEL Melvin Lloyd "Dusty" B 6.13.1922 New Orleans, LA BL/TL 6/180# d4.20																									
1947	Bos A	2	3	.400	15	5	1	0	50.2	60	41	1	1	27	23	6.39	61	.296	.381	18-0	.056	-2	105	-14	-1.4
1948	Bos A	15	8	.652	35	27	16-1	0	212	205	87	7	4	90	77	3.14	140	.252	.330	80-2	.162	-4	106	26	2.2
1949	Bos A★	**25**	7	.781	39	33	**27**-4	2	**295.1**	258	102	8	5	134	122	2.77	157	.237	.324	114-10	.254	2	123	**49**	5.2
1950	Bos A	18	10	.643	40	31	21-2	3	249	244	116	17	7	106	93	3.61	136	.259	.338	98-3	.194	-1	119	30	3.1
1951	Bos A★	18	11	.621	36	29	11-3	2	221	229	99	11	0	77	77	3.26	137	.272	.333	81-4	.309	4*	99	24	**3.3**
1952	Bos A	12	12	.500	33	29	15-3	2	214	207	94	13	5	89	107	3.62	109	.255	.332	84-0	.095	-3*	95	9	0.6
1953	Bos A	21	8	.724	38	34	12-5	0	241	217	98	15	4	116	136	3.06	137	.239	.328	94-6	.223	1	93	28	3.2
1954	Bos A	3	7	.300	19	15	4-1	0	92.1	104	45	7	1	35	38	3.70	111	.287	.349	34-1	.088	-2	93	3	0.2
1955	Bos A	2	3	.400	13	9	0	1	46	62	44	12	1	25-1	18	7.83	55	.318	.395	19-0	.316	1*	140	-16	-1.4
1956	Bos A	7	6	.538	21	20	6-1	0	131.1	129	71	13	0	59-2	41	3.77	123	.256	.333	46-4	.152	-2	95	8	0.5
Total	10	123	75	.621	289	232	113-20	10	1752.2	1715	797	104	28	758-3	732	3.50	125	.257	.335	668-30	.198	-7	106	147	15.5
PARNHAM, RUBE James Arthur B 2.1.1894 Heidelberg, PA D 11.25.1963 McKeesport, PA BR/TR 6-3/185# d9.20																									
1916	Phi A	2	1	.667	4	3	2	0	24.2	27	14	0	0	13	8	4.01	71	.300	.388	11-0	.273	1	150	-3	-0.2
1917	Phi A	0	1	.000	2	2	0	0	11	12	6	1	0	9	4	4.09	67	.316	.447	3-0	.000	-0	105	-1	-0.2
Total	2	2	2	.500	6	5	2	0	35.2	39	20	1	0	22	12	4.04	70	.305	.407	14-0	.214	0	132	-4	-0.4
PARONTO, CHAD Chad Michael B 7.28.1975 Woodsville, NH BR/TR 6-5/255# d4.18																									
2001	Bal A	1	3	.250	24	0	0	0-1	27	33	24	5	1	11-0	16	5.00	86	.289	.354	0-0	—	0		-6	-0.7
2002	Cle A	0	2	.000	29	0	0	0-0	35.2	34	19	3	2	11-1	23	4.04	109	.248	.305	0-0	—	0		1	0.0
2003	Cle A	0	2	.000	6	0	0	0-0	6.2	7	8	1	0	3-0	6	9.45	47	.292	.357	0-0	—	0		-4	-0.7
Total	3	1	7	.125	59	0	0	0-1	69.1	74	51	9	3	25-1	45	4.93	88	.269	.330	0-0	—	0		-9	-1.4
PARQUE, JIM Jim Vo B 2.8.1975 Norwalk, CA BL/TL 5-11/165# d5.26																									
1998	Chi A	7	5	.583	21	21	0	0-0	113	135	72	14	6	49-0	77	5.10	89	.299	.375	1-2	.000	-0	108	-7	-0.6
1999	Chi A	9	15	.375	31	30	1	0-0	173.2	210	111	23	10	79-2	111	5.13	95	.299	.374	5-1	.400	1	90	-5	-0.6
2000	†Chi A	13	6	.684	33	32	0	0-0	187	208	105	21	11	71-1	111	4.28	117	.283	.352	4-0	.000	-0	128	12	1.0
2001	Chi A	0	3	.000	5	5	1	0-0	28	36	26	7	2	10-1	15	8.04	57	.308	.369	0-0	—	0	108	-10	-0.8
2002	Chi A	1	4	.200	8	4	0	0-0	25.1	34	29	11	1	16-0	13	9.95	45	.318	.405	0-0	—	0	67	-14	-2.1
2003	TB A	1	1	.500	5	5	0	0-0	17.1	27	23	2	1	16-0	8	11.94	38	.351	.468	0-0	—	0	126	-13	-1.2
Total	6	31	34	.477	103	97	2	0-0	544.1	650	366	78	31	241-4	335	5.42	89	.297	.372	10-3	.200	0	108	-37	-4.3
PARRA, JOSE Jose Miguel B 11.28.1972 Jacagua, D.R. BR/TR 5-11/160# d5.7																									
1995	LA N	0	0	—	8	0	0	0-0	10.1	10	8	2	1	6-1	7	4.35	87	.256	.362	0-2	—	0		-2	-0.1
	Min A	1	5	.167	12	12	0	0-0	61.2	83	59	11	2	22-0	29	7.59	63	.313	.366	0-0	—	0	88	-20	-1.6
1996	Min A	5	5	.500	27	5	0	0-1	70	88	48	15	3	27-0	50	6.04	85	.308	.370	0-0	—	0	80	-6	-0.7
2000	Pit N	0	1	.000	6	2	0	0-0	11.2	17	9	3	1	7-0	9	6.94	66	.354	.446	0-0	—	1	60	-3	-0.1
2002	Ari N	0	1	.000	16	0	0	0-0	14	13	5	0	1	11-2	8	3.21	138	.255	.397	0-0	—	0		2	0.1
Total	4	6	12	.333	69	19	0	0-1	167.2	211	129	31	8	73-3	103	6.33	76	.306	.376	0-2	—	1	83	-29	-2.4
PARRETT, JEFF Jeffrey Dale B 8.26.1961 Indianapolis, IN BR/TR 6-3/193# d4.11																									
1986	Mon N	0	1	.000	12	0	0	0-0	20.1	19	11	3	0	13-0	21	4.87	76	.247	.352	2-0	.500	0		-2	-0.1
1987	Mon N	7	6	.538	45	0	0	6-5	62	53	33	8	0	30-4	56	4.21	100	.229	.317	5-0	.000	-1		0	-0.1
1988	Mon N	12	4	.750	61	0	0	6-4	91.2	66	29	8	1	45-9	62	2.65	136	.214	.311	0-0	—	0		10	1.9
1989	Phi N	12	6	.667	72	0	0	6-6	105.2	90	43	6	0	44-13	98	2.98	119	.232	.307	5-0	.000	-1		5	0.8
1990	Phi N	4	9	.308	47	5	0	1-3	81.2	92	51	10	1	36-8	69	5.18	74	.293	.366	10-2	.000	-1	94	-12	-1.8
	Atl N	1	1	.500	20	0	0	1-3	27	27	11	1	1	19-2	17	3.00	135	.281	.392	1-0	1.000	0		3	0.3
	Year	5	10	.333	67	5	0	2-6	108.2	119	66	11	2	55-10	86	4.64	84	.290	.373	11-2	.091	-1	93	-9	-1.5
1991	Atl N	1	2	.333	18	0	0	1-0	21.1	31	18	2	0	12-2	14	6.33	61	.326	.402	0-0	—	0		-6	-0.7
1992	†Oak A	9	1	.900	66	0	0	0-1	98.1	81	35	7	2	42-3	78	3.02	124	.226	.308	0-0	—	0		9	0.8
1993	Col N	3	3	.500	40	6	0	1-3	73.2	78	47	6	2	45-9	66	5.38	89	.274	.371	11-0	.091	-1	119	-3	-0.3
1995	StL N	4	7	.364	59	0	0	0-2	76.2	71	33	8	1	28-5	71	3.64	115	.243	.310	2-0	.500	0		6	0.7

Year	Tm Lg	W	L	Pct	G	GS	CG-Sho	SV-BS	IP	H	R	HR	HB	BB-IB	SO	ERA	AERA	OAV	OOB	AB-SH	AVG	PB	Sup	APR	PW
1996	StL N	2	2	.500	33	0	0	0-2	42.1	40	20	2	1	20-2	42	4.25	99	.245	.330	2-0	.000	0		1	0.1
	Phi N	1	1	.500	18	0	0	0-0	24	24	5	0	0	11-2	22	1.88	230	.270	.347	0-0	—	0		7	0.5
	Year	3	3	.500	51	0	0	0-2	66.1	64	31	2	1	31-4	64	3.39	125	.254	.336	2-0	.000	0		7	0.6
Total	10	56	43	.566	491	11	0	22-29	724.2	672	336	61	9	345-59	616	3.80	104	.249	.333	38-2	.105	-1	120	18	2.1
PARRIS, STEVE Steven Michael B 12.17.1967 Joliet, IL BR/TR 6/190# d6.21																									
1995	Pit N	6	6	.500	15	15	1-1	0-0	82	89	49	12	7	33-1	61	5.38	80	.283	.361	28-1	.250	1	85	-7	-0.8
1996	Pit N	0	3	.000	8	4	0	0-0	26.1	35	22	4	1	11-0	27	7.18	61	.321	.385	6-2	.167	0	103	-7	-0.7
1998	Cin N	6	5	.545	18	16	1-1	0-0	99	89	44	9	4	32-3	77	3.73	115	.236	.302	29-3	.138	-1	99	6	0.6
1999	Cin N	11	4	.733	22	21	2-1	0-0	128.2	124	59	16	6	52-4	86	3.50	133	.260	.338	38-5	.158	-1	92	14	1.4
2000	Cin N	12	17	.414	33	33	0	0-0	192.2	227	109	30	4	71-5	117	4.81	98	.294	.355	55-4	.127	-1*	84	-1	-0.2
2001	Tor A	4	6	.400	19	19	1	0-0	105.2	126	60	18	2	41-4	49	4.60	100	.299	.362	1-1	.000	-0	89	-1	-0.1
2002	Tor A	5	5	.500	14	14	0	0-0	75.1	96	50	13	3	35-5	48	5.97	77	.314	.387	4-0	.000	-0	108	-9	-1.1
2003	TB A	0	3	.000	10	7	0	0-0	43.2	60	32	12	0	13-0	14	6.18	73	.328	.369	1-0	.000	-0	78	-8	-0.5
Total	8	44	49	.473	139	129	5-3	0-0	753.1	846	425	114	27	288-22	479	4.75	96	.286	.353	162-16	.154	-2	91	-13	-1.4
PARRISH, JOHN John Henry B 11.26.1977 Lancaster, PA BL/TL 5-11/180# d7.24																									
2000	Bal A	2	4	.333	8	8	0	0-0	36.1	40	32	6	1	35-0	28	7.18	66	.288	.425	0-0	—	0	102	-11	-1.4
2001	Bal A	1	2	.333	16	1	0	0-0	22	22	17	5	3	17-1	20	6.14	70	.256	.396	0-0	—	0	108	-5	-0.6
2003	Bal A	0	1	.000	14	0	0	0-2	23.2	17	7	2	1	8-2	15	1.90	231	.205	.280	0-0	—	0		6	0.3
Total	3	3	7	.300	38	9	0	0-2	82	79	56	13	5	60-3	63	5.38	84	.256	.381	0-0	—	0	105	-10	-1.7
PARROTT, MIKE Michael Everett Arch B 12.6.1954 Oxnard, CA BR/TR 6-4/210# d9.5																									
1977	Bal A	0	0	—	3	0	0	0-0	4.1	4	1	0	0	2-0	2	2.08	183	.250	.333	0-0	—	0		1	0.0
1978	Sea A	1	5	.167	27	10	0	1-1	82.1	108	59	8	3	32-5	41	5.14	74	.316	.373	0-0	—	0	110	-15	-1.0
1979	Sea A	14	12	.538	38	30	13-2	0-0	229.1	231	104	17	6	86-16	127	3.77	116	.267	.336	0-0	—	0	100	16	1.8
1980	Sea A	1	16	.059	27	16	1	3-1	94	136	83	16	1	42-9	53	7.28	57	.348	.411	0-0	—	0	65	-31	-4.7
1981	Sea A	3	6	.333	24	12	0	1-0	85	102	51	3	1	28-1	43	5.08	76	.299	.350	0-0	—	0	99	-10	-1.0
Total	5	19	39	.328	119	68	14-2	5-2	495	581	298	44	11	190-31	266	4.87	85	.297	.360	0-0	—	0	93	-39	-4.9
PARROTT, TOM Thomas William "Tacky Tom" B 4.10.1868 Portland, OR D 1.1.1932 Dundee, OR BR/TR 5-10.5/170# d6.18 b-Jiggs ▲																									
1893	Chi N	0	3	.000	4	3	2	0	27	35	30	1	0	17	7	6.67	69	.304	.394	27	.259	-0*	141	-6	-0.5
	Cin N	10	7	.588	22	17	11-1	0	154	174	95	1	9	70	33	4.09	117	.276	.357	68	.191	-3*	85	12	0.8
	Year	10	10	.500	26	20	13-1	0	181	209	101	2	9	87	40	4.48	106	.281	.363	95	.211	-3	93	11	0.3
1894	Cin N	17	19	.472	41	36	31-1	1	308.2	402	268	19	11	126	61	5.60	99	.311	.377	229-1	.323	8*	83	0	0.7
1895	Cin N	11	18	.379	41	31	23	**3**	263.1	382	228	8	5	76	57	5.47	91	.334	.378	201-6	.343	10*	90	-16	-0.5
1896	StL N	1	1	.500	7	2	2	0	42	62	39	4	3	18	8	6.21	70	.339	.407	474-14	.291	1*	82	-8	-0.3
Total	4	39	48	.448	115	89	69-2	4	795	1055	660	33	28	307	166	5.33	96	.314	.376	999-21	.301	17	88	-18	0.2
PARSON, JIGGS William Edwin B 12.28.1885 Parker, SD D 5.19.1967 Los Angeles, CA BR/TR 6-2/180# d5.16																									
1910	Bos N	0	2	.000	10	4	0	0	35.1	35	23	2	2	26	7	3.82	87	.278	.409	12-0	.083	-1	162	-2	-0.3
1911	Bos N	0	1	.000	7	0	0	0	25	36	30	2	4	15	7	6.48	59	.375	.478	10-0	.200	-0		-9	-0.5
Total	2	0	3	.000	17	4	0	0	60.1	71	53	4	6	41	14	4.92	72	.320	.439	22-0	.136	-2	162	-11	-0.8
PARSONS, CHARLIE Charles James B 7.18.1863 Cherry Flats, PA D 3.24.1936 Mansfield, PA BL/TL 5-10/160# d5.29																									
1886	Bos N	0	2	.000	2	2	2	0	16	20	13	0		4	5	3.94	82	.308	.348	8	.375	1	48	-1	-0.1
1887	NY AA	1	1	.500	4	4	4	0	34	51	36	0	1	6	5	4.50	94	.319	.347	15	.200	-1	116	-4	-0.2
1890	Cle N	0	1	.000	2	1	0	0	9	12	11	0	4	6	2	6.00	60	.308	.449	4	.750	1	194	-3	-0.2
Total	3	1	4	.200	8	7	6	0	59	83	60	0	5	16	12	4.58	84	.314	.365	27	.333	2	109	-8	-0.5
PARSONS, TOM Thomas Anthony B 9.13.1939 Lakeville, CT BR/TR 6-7/210# d9.5																									
1963	Pit N	0	1	.000	1	1	0	0	4.1	7	6	1	0	2-0	2	8.31	40	.368	.429	2-0	.000	-0	0	-3	-0.5
1964	NY N	1	2	.333	4	2	1	0	19.1	20	9	1	0	6-0	10	4.19	85	.274	.321	7-0	.000	-1	74	-1	-0.2
1965	NY N	1	10	.091	35	11	1-1	1	90.2	108	53	17	0	17-2	58	4.67	76	.290	.321	18-1	.056	-1	61	-11	-1.3
Total	3	2	13	.133	40	14	2-1	1	114.1	135	68	19	0	25-2	70	4.72	75	.291	.325	27-1	.037	-2	58	-15	-2.0
PARSONS, BILL William Raymond B 8.17.1948 Riverside, CA BR/TR 6-6/195# d4.13																									
1971	Mil A	13	17	.433	36	35	12-4	0-0	244.2	219	95	19	4	93-10	139	3.20	109	.241	.312	72-8	.167	3	86	9	1.5
1972	Mil A	13	13	.500	33	30	10-2	0-0	214	194	102	27	3	68-8	111	3.91	78	.240	.299	67-6	.164	0	100	-20	-2.5
1973	Mil A	3	6	.333	20	17	0	0-0	59.2	59	50	6	0	67-1	30	6.79	55	.257	.423	0-0	—	0	96	-20	-2.6
1974	Oak A	0	0	—	4	0	0	0-0	2	1	0	0	0	3-0	2	0.00	—	.143	.400	0-0	—	0		1	0.0
Total	4	29	36	.446	93	82	22-6	0-0	520.1	473	247	52	7	231-19	282	3.89	86	.242	.322	139-14	.165	3	94	-30	-3.6
PARTENHEIMER, STAN Stanwood Wendell "Party" B 10.21.1922 Chicopee Falls, MA D 1.28.1989 Wilson, NC BR/TL 5-11/175# d5.27 f-Steve																									
1944	Bos A	0	0	—	1	1	0	0	1	3	2	0	0	2	0	18.00	19	.500	.625	1-0	.000	-0	49	-2	-0.1
1945	StL N	0	0	—	8	2	0	0	13.1	12	9	2	0	16	6	6.08	62	.250	.438	3-0	.000	-0	170	-3	-0.2
Total	2	0	0	—	9	3	0	0	14.1	15	11	2	0	18	6	6.91	54	.278	.458	4-0	.000	-1	129	-5	-0.3
PASCHALL, BILL William Herbert B 4.22.1954 Norfolk, VA BR/TR 6/175# d9.20																									
1978	KC A	0	1	.000	2	0	0	1-0	8	6	3	0	1	0-0	5	3.38	114	.207	.226	0-0	—	0		1	0.1
1979	KC A	0	1	.000	7	0	0	0-1	13.2	18	11	2	2	5-3	3	6.59	65	.300	.368	0-0	—	0		-3	-0.2
1981	KC A	0	0	—	2	0	0	0-0	2	2	1	0	0	0-0	1	4.50	80	.286	.286	0-0	—	0		0	0.0
Total	3	0	2	.000	11	0	0	1-1	23.2	26	15	2	3	5-3	9	5.32	76	.271	.321	0-0	—	0		-2	-0.1
PASCUAL, CAMILO Camilo Alberto (Lus) B 1.20.1934 Havana, Cuba BR/TR 5-11/185# d4.15 C3 b-Carlos																									
1954	Was A	4	7	.364	48	4	1	3	119.1	126	65	7	6	61	60	4.22	84	.276	.368	30-1	.133	-0	81	-9	-0.8
1955	Was A	2	12	.143	43	16	1	3	129	158	94	5	6	70-6	82	6.14	62	.311	.395	32-2	.219	0	93	-32	-3.0
1956	Was A	6	18	.250	39	27	6	2	188.2	194	131	33	6	89-4	162	5.87	74	.261	.342	58-6	.138	-2*	81	-27	-3.1
1957	Was A	8	17	.320	29	26	8-2	0	175.2	168	85	11	3	76-5	113	4.10	95	.258	.333	50-5	.140	-2*	80	-3	-0.5
1958	Was A	8	12	.400	31	27	6-2	0	177.1	166	66	14	3	60-2	146	3.15	121	.248	.311	57-4	.158	-1	75	13	1.4
1959	Was A❖	17	10	.630	32	30	**17-6**	0	238.2	202	80	10	3	69-7	185	2.64	148	.226	.282	86-5	.302	6	105	34	**4.7**
1960	Was A❖	12	8	.600	26	22	8-3	2	151.2	139	65	11	2	53-2	143	3.03	128	.240	.305	51-4	.176	3*	120	12	1.9
1961	Min A★	15	16	.484	35	33	15-**8**	0	252.1	205	114	26	3	100-1	**221**	3.46	123	.217	.293	85-5	.165	-0	102	19	2.2
1962	Min A★	20	11	.645	34	33	**18-5**	0	257.2	236	100	25	2	59-5	**206**	3.32	123	.241	.285	97-0	.268	8	107	24	3.7
1963	Min A	21	9	.700	31	31	**18**-3	0	248.1	205	76	21	3	81-4	**202**	2.46	148	.224	.288	92-5	.250	6*	129	33	4.7
1964	Min A★	15	12	.556	36	36	14-1	0	267.1	245	121	30	3	98-6	213	3.30	108	.241	.308	94-4	.181	4	112	5	0.9
1965	†Min A	9	3	.750	27	27	5-1	0	156	126	67	12	5	63-0	96	3.35	106	.217	.298	60-2	.200	3	122	4	0.7
1966	Min A	8	6	.571	21	19	2	0	103	113	63	9	2	30-0	56	4.89	73	.278	.328	37-1	.216	1	103	-13	-1.5
1967	Was A	12	10	.545	28	27	5-1	0	164.2	147	73	15	3	43-3	106	3.28	96	.237	.288	51-6	.176	1	108	-4	-0.4
1968	Was A	13	12	.520	31	31	8-4	0	201	181	72	11	4	59-4	111	2.69	109	.239	.297	65-4	.185	1	98	4	0.6
1969	Was A	2	5	.286	14	13	0	0-0	55.1	49	42	12	5	38-1	34	6.83	51	.239	.371	17-0	.235	0*	118	-19	-2.0
	Cin N	0	0	—	5	1	0	0-0	7.1	14	7	2	0	4-0	3	8.59	44	.424	.486	0-0	—	0	447	-3	-0.2
1970	LA N	0	0	—	10	0	0	0-0	14	12	4	2	1	5-1	8	2.57	149	.231	.310	0-0	—	0		2	0.1
1971	Cle A	2	2	.500	9	1	0	0-0	23.1	17	9	0	1	11-0	20	3.09	124	.205	.302	5-1	.600	1	23	2	0.5
Total	18	174	170	.506	529	404	132-36	10-0	2930.2	2703	1334	256	61	1069-**51**	2167	3.63	103	.244	.312	967-55	.205	29	103	42	9.9
PASCUAL, CARLOS Carlos Alberto (Lus) "Little Potato" B 3.13.1931 Havana, Cuba BR/TR 5-6/165# d9.24 b-Camilo																									
1950	Was A	1	1	.500	2	2	2	0	17	12	5	0	1	8	3	2.12	212	.194	.296	4-1	.250	0	60	4	0.5
PASHNICK, LARRY Larry John B 4.25.1956 Lincoln Park, MI BR/TR 6-3/205# d4.10																									
1982	Det A	4	4	.500	28	13	1	0-0	94.1	110	46	17	1	25-2	19	4.01	102	.297	.342	0-0	—	0	91	1	0.0
1983	Det A	1	3	.250	12	6	0	0-1	37.2	48	27	5	3	18-1	17	5.26	75	.308	.383	0-0	—	0	81	-7	-0.6
1984	Min A	2	1	.667	13	1	0	0-0	38.1	38	19	3	2	11-1	10	3.52	120	.260	.321	0-0	—	0	64	2	0.1
Total	3	7	8	.467	53	20	1	0-1	170.1	196	92	25	6	54-4	46	4.17	98	.292	.347	0-0	—	0	86	-4	-0.5

Year	Tm Lg	W	L	Pct	G	GS	CG-Sho	SV-BS	IP	H	R	HR	HB	BB-IB	SO	ERA	AERA	OAV	OOB	AB-SH	AVG	PB	Sup	APR	PW
PASSEAU, CLAUDE Claude William B 4.9.1909 Waynesboro, MS D 8.30.2003 Lucedale, MS BR/TR 6-3/198# d9.29																									
1935	Pit N	0	1	.000	1	1	0	0	3	7	4	0	0	2	1	12.00	34	.500	.563	1-0	.000	-0	124	-2	-0.3
1936	Phi N	11	15	.423	49	21	8-2	3	217.1	247	118	7	4	55	85	3.48	130	.280	.325	78-2	.282	3*	93	18	2.4
1937	Phi N	14	18	.438	50	**34**	18-1	2	**292.1**	348	158	16	5	79	135	4.34	100	.296	.343	107-1	.196	-0	93	0	0.0
1938	Phi N	11	18	.379	44	33	15	1	239	281	147	8	8	93	100	4.52	86	.287	.354	80-4	.162	-2*	85	-20	-2.2
1939	Phi N	2	4	.333	8	8	4-1	0	53.1	54	26	1	1	25	29	4.22	95	.263	.346	20-0	.200	-0	95	0	-0.1
	Chi N	13	9	.591	34	27	13-1	3	221	215	86	8	4	48	108	3.05	129	.254	.297	77-2	.156	-1*	109	22	2.0
	Year	15	13	.536	42	35	17-2	3	274.1	269	91	9	5	73	**137**	3.28	120	.256	.307	97-2	.165	-2	106	22	1.9
1940	Chi N	20	13	.606	46	31	20-4	5	280.2	259	97	8	4	59	124	2.50	150	.237	.278	98-3	.204	6	116	37	**5.1**
1941	Chi N★	14	14	.500	34	30	20-3	0	231	262	99	10	1	52	80	3.35	105	.281	.320	86-4	.221	5	115	6	1.1
1942	Chi N★	19	14	.576	35	34	24-3	0	278.1	284	116	13	3	74	89	2.68	119	.260	.309	105-5	.181	1	110	9	1.1
1943	Chi N☆	15	12	.556	35	31	18-1	1	257	245	96	10	4	66	93	2.91	115	.249	.299	96-6	.198	1	110	13	1.5
1944	Chi N	15	9	.625	34	27	18-2	3	227	234	80	8	1	50	89	2.89	122	.266	.306	80-7	.162	-1	85	20	2.0
1945	†Chi N❖	17	9	.654	34	27	19-**5**	1	227	205	70	4	2	59	98	2.46	149	.238	.289	91-3	.187	2	119	**33**	**3.9**
1946	Chi N★	9	8	.529	21	21	10-2	0	129.1	118	53	5	1	42	47	3.13	106	.237	.298	49-3	.204	3	108	2	0.6
1947	Chi N	2	6	.250	19	6	1-1	2	63.1	97	54	7	1	24	26	6.25	63	.353	.407	14-1	.000	-2	52	-18	-2.2
Total	13	162	150	.519	444	331	188-26	21	2719.2	2856	1204	105	39	728	1104	3.32	113	.267	.316	982-41	.192	13	102	120	14.9
PASTORE, FRANK Frank Enrico B 8.21.1957 Alhambra, CA BR/TR 6-3/205# d4.4																									
1979	†Cin N	6	7	.462	30	9	2-1	4-2	95.1	102	47	8	1	23-5	63	4.25	88	.271	.313	25-2	.160	-0	105	-4	-0.6
1980	Cin N	13	7	.650	27	27	9-2	0-0	184.2	161	72	13	0	42-3	110	3.27	110	.233	.275	64-6	.156	-1	110	7	0.5
1981	Cin N	4	9	.308	22	22	2-1	0-0	132	125	73	11	3	35-1	81	4.02	88	.247	.297	44-6	.114	-2	104	-10	-1.2
1982	Cin N	8	13	.381	31	29	3-2	0-0	188.1	210	86	13	4	57-8	94	3.97	93	.286	.338	58-5	.172	1	94	-3	-0.3
1983	Cin N	9	12	.429	36	29	4-1	0-0	184.1	207	104	20	1	64-3	93	4.88	78	.290	.346	59-3	.186	2	103	-18	-1.8
1984	Cin N	3	8	.273	24	16	1	0-0	98.1	110	74	10	3	40-3	53	6.50	58	.285	.353	28-2	.071	-2	98	-26	-2.8
1985	Cin N	2	1	.667	17	6	1	0-0	54	60	23	1	1	16-1	29	3.83	99	.287	.336	14-2	.143	-0	97	1	0.0
1986	Min A	3	1	.750	33	1	0	2-3	49.1	54	28	4	0	24-6	18	4.01	108	.283	.356	0-0	—	0	105	0	0.0
Total	8	48	58	.453	220	139	22-7	6-5	986.1	1029	507	80	13	301-30	541	4.29	87	.270	.323	292-26	.151	-2	101	-53	-6.2
PASTORIUS, JIM James W. "Sunny Jim" B 7.12.1881 Pittsburgh, PA D 5.10.1941 Pittsburgh, PA BL/TL 5-9/165# d4.15																									
1906	Bro N	10	14	.417	29	24	16-3	0	211.2	225	111	4	3	69	58	3.61	70	.274	.333	71-5	.141	-0	103	-26	-2.9
1907	Bro N	16	12	.571	28	26	20-4	0	222	218	74	2	6	77	70	2.35	100	.264	.331	73-4	.205	3*	92	3	0.8
1908	Bro N	4	20	.167	28	25	16-2	0	213.2	171	88	5	7	74	54	2.44	96	.216	.288	62-3	.129	-0	58	-6	-0.7
1909	Bro N	1	9	.100	12	9	5-1	0	79.2	91	65	4	1	58	23	5.76	45	.313	.429	25-0	.080	-1	57	-27	-3.0
Total	4	31	55	.360	97	84	57-10	0	727	705	338	15	17	278	205	3.12	78	.258	.330	231-12	.152	1	81	-56	-5.8
PATE, JOE Joseph William B 6.6.1892 Alice, TX D 12.26.1948 Fort Worth, TX BL/TL 5-10/184# d4.15																									
1926	Phi A	9	0	1.000	47	2	0	6	113	109	38	3	2	51	24	2.71	154	.262	.345	27-2	.148	-0	81	**20**	1.8
1927	Phi A	0	3	.000	32	0	0	6	53.2	67	36	3	1	21	14	5.20	82	.318	.382	10-0	.300	1		-5	-0.3
Total	2	9	3	.750	79	2	0	12	166.2	176	74	6	3	72	38	3.51	120	.281	.358	37-2	.189	1	81	15	1.5
PATRICK, BRONSWELL Bronswell Dante B 9.16.1970 Greenville, NC BR/TR 6-1/220# d5.18																									
1998	Mil N	4	1	.800	32	3	0	0-0	78.2	83	43	9	0	29-1	49	4.69	91	.279	.339	15-1	.200	2	93	-3	-0.1
1999	SF N	1	0	1.000	6	0	0	1-0	5.1	9	7	1	0	3-0	6	10.13	42	.375	.429	1-0	.000	-0		-4	-0.7
Total	2	5	1	.833	38	3	0	1-0	84	92	50	10	0	32-1	55	5.04	85	.286	.346	16-1	.188	1	93	-7	-0.8
PATTEN, CASE Case Lyman "Casey" B 5.7.1876 Westport, NY D 5.31.1935 Rochester, NY BB/TL 6/175# d5.4																									
1901	Was A	18	10	.643	32	30	26-4	0	254.1	285	163	8	17	74	109	3.93	93	.280	.339	96-6	.135	-5	115	-9	-1.2
1902	Was A	18	17	.514	36	34	33-1	0	299.2	331	186	11	11	89	92	4.05	91	.281	.337	125-3	.096	-10*	94	-13	-2.2
1903	Was A	11	22	.333	36	34	32	1	300	313	163	11	4	80	133	3.60	87	.268	.317	106-5	.132	-6	68	-16	-2.2
1904	Was A	14	23	.378	45	39	37-2	**3**	357.2	367	162	2	20	79	150	3.07	87	.266	.315	126-4	.127	-5	77	-15	-2.1
1905	Was A	14	21	.400	42	36	29-2	0	309.2	300	145	3	10	86	113	3.14	84	.256	.312	103-4	.155	-2	94	-14	-1.8
1906	Was A	19	16	.543	38	32	28-7	0	282.2	253	106	2	6	79	96	2.17	122	.242	.299	94-1	.117	-4	72	11	0.8
1907	Was A	12	16	.429	36	29	20-1	0	237.1	272	135	3	6	63	58	3.56	68	.290	.339	87-3	.126	-3	96	-30	-3.9
1908	Was A	0	2	.000	4	3	1	0	18	25	14	0	0	6	6	3.50	65	.333	.383	5-0	.200	-0	179	-4	-0.4
	Bos A	0	1	.000	1	1	0	0	3	8	5	0	0	1	0	15.00	16	.533	.563	1-0	.000	-0	139	-3	-0.5
	Year	0	3	.000	5	4	1	0	21	33	10	0	0	7	6	5.14	45	.367	.412	6-0	.167	-0	170	-7	-0.9
Total	8	106	128	.453	270	238	206-17	4	2062.1	2154	1079	40	74	557	757	3.36	88	.270	.323	743-26	.127	-35	90	-93	-13.5
PATTERSON, DANNY Danny Shane B 2.17.1971 San Gabriel, CA BR/TR 6/170# d7.26																									
1996	†Tex A	0	0	—	7	0	0	0-0	8.2	10	4	0	0	3-1	5	0.00	—	.286	.342	0-0	—	0		3	0.1
1997	Tex A	10	6	.625	54	0	0	1-7	71	70	29	3	0	23-4	69	3.42	140	.263	.318	0-0	—	0		11	2.1
1998	Tex A	2	5	.286	56	0	0	2-0	60.2	64	31	11	2	19-2	33	4.45	108	.274	.332	0-0	—	0		3	0.3
1999	†Tex A	2	0	1.000	53	0	0	0-1	60.1	77	38	5	1	19-3	43	5.67	90	.304	.353	1-0	.000	-0		-3	-0.1
2000	Det A	5	1	.833	58	0	0	0-2	56.2	69	26	4	2	14-2	29	3.97	122	.309	.353	0-0	—	0		6	0.5
2001	Det A	5	4	.556	60	0	0	1-4	64.2	64	24	4	4	12-5	27	3.06	142	.274	.316	0-0	—	0		10	1.2
2002	Det A	0	2	.000	6	0	0	0-1	3	5	5	0	1	2-0	1	15.00	29	.357	.471	0-0	—	0		-3	-0.6
2003	Det A	0	0	—	19	0	0	3-0	17.2	15	8	1	1	4-0	19	4.08	106	.227	.282	0-0	—	0		1	0.1
Total	8	24	18	.571	313	0	0	7-15	342.2	374	165	28	11	96-17	226	4.07	117	.282	.333	1-0	.000	-0		28	3.6
PATTERSON, DARYL Daryl Alan B 11.21.1943 Coalinga, CA BL/TR 6-4/195# d4.10 Mil 1969																									
1968	†Det A	2	3	.400	38	1	0	7	68	53	19	3	4	27-1	49	2.12	142	.213	.299	13-0	.000	-1	116	6	0.5
1969	Det A	0	2	.000	18	0	0	0-2	22.1	15	8	2	0	19-3	12	2.82	132	.205	.358	1-0	.000	-0		2	0.1
1970	Det A	7	1	.875	43	0	0	2-2	78	81	47	9	5	39-1	55	4.85	77	.269	.361	11-0	.000	-1		-10	-1.1
1971	Det A	0	1	.000	12	0	0	0-0	9.1	14	7	1	1	6-1	5	4.82	75	.359	.457	0-0	—	0		-2	-0.2
	Oak A	0	0	—	4	0	0	0-0	5.2	5	5	3	1	4-0	2	7.94	42	.238	.385	1-0	.000	-0		-3	-0.2
	Year	0	1	.000	16	0	0	0-0	15	19	16	4	2	10-1	7	6.00	58	.317	.431	1-0	.000	-0		-5	-0.4
	StL N	0	1	.000	13	2	0	1-0	26.2	20	14	3	0	15-1	11	4.39	82	.211	.313	5-0	.000	-0	98	-2	-0.2
1974	Pit N	2	1	.667	14	0	0	1-1	21	35	19	3	0	9-1	8	7.29	47	.376	.427	4-0	.000	-1		-9	-1.3
Total	5	11	9	.550	142	3	0	11-5	231	223	119	24	11	119-8	142	4.09	85	.256	.350	35-0	.000	-3	102	-18	-2.4
PATTERSON, DAVE David Glenn B 7.25.1956 Springfield, MO BR/TR 6/170# d6.9																									
1979	LA N	4	1	.800	36	0	0	6-1	53	62	35	5	0	22-6	34	5.26	69	.292	.356	7-2	.143	-0*		-9	-1.1
PATTERSON, GIL Gilbert Thomas B 9.5.1955 Philadelphia, PA BR/TR 6-1/185# d4.19 C3																									
1977	NY A	1	2	.333	10	6	0	1-0	33.1	38	20	3	3	20-1	29	5.40	73	.290	.396	0-0	—	0	110	-4	-0.4
PATTERSON, JEFF Jeffrey Simmons B 10.1.1968 Anaheim, CA BR/TR 6-2/200# d4.30																									
1995	NY A	0	0	—	3	0	0	0-0	3.1	3	1	1	0	3-0	3	2.70	171	.231	.375	0-0	—	0		1	0.0
PATTERSON, JOHN John Hollis B 1.30.1978 Orange, TX BR/TR 6-6/200# d7.20																									
2002	Ari N	2	0	1.000	7	5	0	0-0	30.2	27	11	7	1	7-0	31	3.23	138	.235	.285	10-1	.100	-0	175	4	0.2
2003	Ari N	1	4	.200	16	8	0	1-0	55	61	39	7	2	30-5	43	6.05	77	.281	.371	13-0	.077	-1	96	-7	-0.7
Total	2	3	4	.429	23	13	0	1-0	85.2	88	50	14	3	37-5	74	5.04	91	.265	.342	23-1	.087	-1	125	-3	-0.5
PATTERSON, KEN Kenneth Brian B 7.8.1964 Costa Mesa, CA BL/TL 6-4/210# d7.9																									
1988	Chi A	0	2	.000	9	2	0	1-0	20.2	25	11	2	0	7-0	8	4.79	83	.294	.348	0-0	—	0	92	-1	-0.1
1989	Chi A	6	1	.857	50	1	0	0-1	65.2	64	37	11	2	28-3	43	4.52	84	.257	.332	0-0	—	0	166	-5	-0.6
1990	Chi A	2	1	.667	43	0	0	2-0	66.1	58	27	6	2	34-1	40	3.39	113	.242	.335	0-0	—	0		3	0.2
1991	Chi A	3	0	1.000	43	0	0	1-1	63.2	48	22	5	1	35-1	32	2.83	141	.214	.321	0-0	—	0		8	0.4
1992	Chi N	2	3	.400	32	1	0	0-2	41.2	41	25	7	1	27-6	23	3.89	93	.268	.373	1-1	.000	-0	251	-3	-0.4
1993	Cal A	1	1	.500	46	0	0	1-1	59	54	30	7	0	35-5	36	4.58	99	.249	.352	0-0	—	0		1	0.0
1994	Cal A	0	0	—	1	0	0	0-0	0.2	0	0	0	0	0-0	1	0.00	—	.000	.000	0-0	—	0		0	0.0
Total	7	14	8	.636	224	4	0	5-5	317.2	290	152	38	6	166-16	183	3.88	102	.248	.340	1-1	.000	-0	144	3	-0.5

Year	Tm Lg	W	L	Pct	G	GS	CG-Sho	SV-BS	IP	H	R	HR	HB	BB-IB	SO	ERA	AERA	OAV	OOB	AB-SH	AVG	PB	Sup	APR	PW
PATTERSON, REGGIE Reginald Allen B 11.7.1958 Birmingham, AL BR/TR 6-4/180# d8.13																									
1981	Chi A	0	1	.000	6	1	0	0-0	7.1	14	11	1	0	6-0	2	13.50	27	.412	.500	0-0	—	0	150	-8	-0.9
1983	Chi N	1	2	.333	5	2	0	0-0	18.2	17	12	3	2	6-0	10	4.82	79	.246	.321	6-2	.000	-1	151	-2	-0.4
1984	Chi N	0	1	.000	3	1	0	0-0	6	10	7	1	0	2-0	5	10.50	37	.357	.400	2-0	.000	-0	23	-4	-0.5
1985	Chi N	3	0	1.000	8	5	1	0-0	39	36	13	2	0	10-1	17	3.00	133	.250	.297	10-2	.100	-0	111	4	0.3
Total	4	4	4	.500	22	9	1	0-0	71	77	43	7	2	24-1	34	5.20	75	.280	.340	18-4	.056	-1	114	-10	-1.5
PATTERSON, BOB Robert Chandler B 5.16.1959 Jacksonville, FL BR/TL 6-2/192# d9.2																									
1985	SD N	0	0	—	3	0	0	0-0	4	13	11	2	0	3-0	1	24.75	14	.565	.615	0-0	—	0		-9	-0.4
1986	Pit N	2	3	.400	11	5	0	0-0	36.1	49	20	0	0	5-2	20	4.95	78	.322	.342	8-2	.125	-0	79	-3	-0.4
1987	Pit N	1	4	.200	15	7	0	0-0	43	49	34	5	1	22-4	27	6.70	61	.290	.369	12-1	.083	-1	91	-12	-1.2
1989	Pit N	4	3	.571	12	3	0	1-0	26.2	23	13	3	0	8-2	20	4.05	83	.232	.287	3-2	.000	0	105	-2	-0.4
1990	†Pit N	8	5	.615	55	5	0	5-3	94.2	88	33	9	3	21-7	70	2.95	123	.249	.294	19-1	.053	-1	105	8	1.0
1991	†Pit N	4	3	.571	54	1	0	2-1	65.2	67	32	7	0	15-1	57	4.11	87	.267	.306	4-0	.250	0	101	-3	-0.3
1992	†Pit N	6	3	.667	60	0	0	9-4	64.2	59	22	7	0	23-6	43	2.92	118	.246	.309	6-0	.333	1		4	0.8
1993	Tex A	2	4	.333	52	0	0	1-1	52.2	59	28	8	1	11-0	46	4.78	87	.282	.318	0-0	—	0		-2	-0.2
1994	Cal A	2	3	.400	47	0	0	1-0	42	35	21	6	2	15-2	30	4.07	120	.229	.306	0-0	—	0		3	0.3
1995	Cal A	5	2	.714	62	0	0	0-1	53.1	48	18	6	1	13-3	41	3.04	155	.246	.295	0-0	—	0		11	1.1
1996	Chi N	3	3	.500	79	0	0	8-2	54.2	46	19	6	1	22-7	53	3.13	139	.229	.303	3-0	.333	0		8	1.0
1997	Chi N	1	6	.143	76	0	0	0-3	59.1	47	23	9	0	10-1	58	3.34	129	.222	.252	1-0	.000	-0		7	0.7
1998	Chi N	1	1	.500	33	0	0	1-1	20.1	36	20	2	0	12-3	17	7.52	59	.391	.453	0-1	—	0		-8	-0.7
Total	13	39	40	.494	559	21	0	28-16	617.1	619	294	70	9	180-38	483	4.08	98	.263	.315	56-7	.125	-1	90	2	1.3
PATTERSON, ROY Roy Lewis "Boy Wonder" B 12.17.1876 Stoddard, WI D 4.14.1953 St.Croix Falls, WI BR/TR 6/185# d4.24																									
1901	Chi A	20	15	.571	41	35	30-4	0	312.1	345	164	11	11	62	127	3.37	103	.277	.317	117-6	.222	1	109	10	1.0
1902	Chi A	19	14	.576	34	30	26-2	0	268	262	111	5	3	67	61	3.06	111	.256	.304	105-5	.190	-2	99	13	1.2
1903	Chi A	15	15	.500	34	30	26-2	1	293	275	119	5	11	69	89	2.70	104	.248	.298	105-3	.105	-6	96	8	0.2
1904	Chi A	9	9	.500	22	17	14-4	0	165	148	52	1	7	24	64	2.29	107	.241	.277	58-3	.103	-4	96	5	0.1
1905	Chi A	4	6	.400	13	9	7	0	88.2	73	34	0	0	16	29	1.83	135	.226	.263	30-1	.267	2	83	4	0.7
1906	Chi A	10	7	.588	21	18	12-3	1	142	119	46	1	4	17	45	2.09	121	.231	.261	49-4	.061	-5	88	8	0.5
1907	Chi A	4	6	.400	19	13	4-1	0	96	105	42	0	2	18	27	2.63	91	.280	.316	31-0	.097	-3	121	-4	-0.7
Total	7	81	72	.529	184	152	119-16	2	1365	1327	568	23	38	273	442	2.75	107	.255	.297	495-22	.156	-16	101	44	3.0
PATTIN, MARTY Martin William B 4.6.1943 Charleston, IL BR/TR 5-11/180# d5.14 C1																									
1968	Cal A	4	4	.500	52	4	0	3	84	67	27	7	2	37-4	66	2.79	104	.221	.307	12-1	.083	-1	127	2	0.1
1969	Sea A	7	12	.368	34	27	2-1	0-0	158.2	166	104	29	2	71-5	126	5.62	65	.268	.345	58-2	.155	-1*	110	-31	-3.5
1970	Mil A	14	12	.538	37	29	11	0-0	233.1	204	91	20	6	71-9	161	3.39	112	.235	.296	70-7	.129	-2*	83	13	1.2
1971	Mil A☆	14	14	.500	36	36	9-5	0-0	264.2	225	100	29	4	73-11	169	3.13	111	.235	.289	83-11	.084	-3	85	12	1.0
1972	Bos A	17	13	.567	38	35	13-4	0-1	253	232	102	19	9	65-3	168	3.24	100	.243	.295	86-7	.140	0	107	1	0.1
1973	Bos A	15	15	.500	34	30	11-2	1-0	219.1	238	112	31	8	69-7	119	4.31	93	.277	.335	0-0	—	0	124	-5	-0.6
1974	KC A	3	7	.300	25	11	2	0-1	117.1	121	55	10	2	28-3	50	3.99	96	.264	.306	0-0	—	0	84	0	-0.1
1975	KC A	10	10	.500	44	15	5-1	5-1	177	173	77	13	3	45-6	89	3.25	119	.253	.300	0-0	—	0*	117	10	1.1
1976	†KC A	8	14	.364	44	15	4-1	5-3	141	114	51	9	3	38-9	65	2.49	141	.216	.271	0-0	—	0	105	14	2.2
1977	†KC A	10	3	.769	31	10	4	0-0	128.1	115	56	16	2	37-2	55	3.58	113	.242	.297	0-0	—	0	100	8	0.7
1978	†KC A	3	3	.500	32	5	2	4-1	78.2	72	41	8	2	25-7	30	3.32	116	.248	.307	0-0	—	0	61	1	0.0
1979	KC A	5	2	.714	31	7	1	3-0	94.1	109	50	11	1	21-2	41	4.58	93	.293	.329	0-0	—	0	103	-1	-0.1
1980	†KC A	4	0	1.000	37	0	0	4-0	89	97	39	7	1	23-7	40	3.64	112	.277	.321	0-0	—	0		5	0.2
Total	13	114	109	.511	475	224	64-14	25-7	2038.2	1933	905	209	45	603-75	1179	3.62	102	.250	.306	309-28	.123	-7	101	29	2.3
PATTISON, JIMMY James Wells B 12.18.1908 Bronx, NY D 2.22.1991 Melbourne, FL BL/TL 6/185# d4.18																									
1929	Bro N	0	1	.000	6	0	0	0	11.2	9	6	1	0	4	5	4.63	100	.231	.302	2-0	.500	0		0	0.1
PATTON, HARRY Harry Claude B 6.29.1884 Gillespie, IL D 6.9.1930 St.Louis, MO d8.22																									
1910	StL N	0	0	—	1	0	0	0	4	4	2	0	0	2	2	2.25	132	.267	.353	0-0	—	0		0	0.0
PAUL, MIKE Michael George B 4.18.1945 Detroit, MI BL/TL 6/183# d5.27 C6																									
1968	Cle A	5	8	.385	36	7	0	3	91.2	72	42	11	5	35-5	87	3.93	75	.213	.295	24-1	.167	0	118	-8	-1.2
1969	Cle A	5	10	.333	47	12	0	2-0	117.1	104	48	12	2	54-11	98	3.61	105	.241	.325	27-1	.000	-3	45	4	0.2
1970	Cle A	2	8	.200	30	15	1	0-2	88	91	51	13	0	45-0	70	4.81	82	.271	.351	26-1	.154	-1	67	-8	-1.0
1971	Cle A	2	7	.222	17	12	1	0-0	62	78	42	8	5	14-3	33	5.95	64	.318	.365	19-1	.053	-1	64	-12	-1.7
1972	Tex A	8	9	.471	49	20	2-1	1-2	161.2	149	50	4	2	52-12	108	2.17	139	.246	.306	48-3	.167	1	73	13	1.6
1973	Tex A	5	4	.556	36	10	1	2-2	87.1	104	55	9	5	36-2	49	4.95	75	.295	.364	0-0	—	0*	84	-12	-1.1
	Chi N	0	1	.000	11	1	0	0-0	18.1	17	7	2	0	9-2	6	3.44	115	.258	.342	4-0	.000	-0	45	1	0.0
1974	Chi N	0	1	.000	2	0	0	0-0	1.1	4	4	1	0	1-1	1	27.00	14	.500	.556	0-0	—	0		-3	-0.5
Total	7	27	48	.360	228	77	5-1	8-6	627.2	619	299	60	19	246-36	452	3.91	89	.260	.331	148-7	.115	-4	71	-25	-3.7
PAULSEN, GIL Guilford Paul Hans B 11.14.1902 Graettinger, IA D 4.2.1994 Harlan, IA BR/TR 6-2.5/190# d10.3																									
1925	StL N	0	0	—	1	0	0	0	2	1	0	0	0	0	1	0.00	—	.125	.125	0-0	—	0		1	0.1
PAVANO, CARL Carl Anthony B 1.8.1976 New Britain, CT BR/TR 6-5/228# d5.23																									
1998	Mon N	6	9	.400	24	23	0	0-0	134.2	130	70	18	8	43-1	83	4.21	100	.251	.315	38-6	.158	-0	82	0	-0.1
1999	Mon N	6	8	.429	19	18	1-1	0-0	104	117	66	8	4	35-1	70	5.63	80	.285	.345	33-5	.061	-2	82	-10	-1.2
2000	Mon N	8	4	.667	15	15	0	0-0	97	89	40	8	8	34-1	64	3.06	157	.248	.324	35-3	.143	-1	100	17	1.8
2001	Mon N	1	6	.143	8	8	0	0-0	42.2	59	33	7	2	16-1	36	6.33	71	.331	.391	13-1	.077	-1	34	-9	-1.3
2002	Mon N	3	8	.273	15	14	0	0-0	74.1	98	55	14	7	31-5	51	6.30	71	.318	.391	24-3	.208	0	92	-13	-1.6
	Fla N	3	2	.600	22	8	0	0-0	61.2	76	33	5	3	14-3	41	3.79	104	.306	.348	16-2	.188	1	149	-1	-0.1
	Year	6	10	.375	37	22	0	0-0	136	174	39	19	10	45-8	92	5.16	82	.313	.372	40-5	.200	1	112	-15	-1.7
2003	†Fla N	12	13	.480	33	32	2	0-0	201	204	99	19	7	49-10	133	4.30	95	.265	.311	61-5	.098	-1	92	-3	-0.5
Total	6	39	50	.438	136	118	3-1	0-0	715.1	773	396	79	39	222-22	478	4.59	94	.277	.336	220-25	.127	-5	89	-19	-3.0
PAVLAS, DAVE David Lee B 8.12.1962 Frankfurt, W.Germany BR/TR 6-7/180# d8.21																									
1990	Chi N	2	0	1.000	13	0	0	0-0	21.1	23	7	2	0	6-2	12	2.11	194	.271	.312	1-0	.000	0		4	0.3
1991	Chi N	0	0	—	1	0	0	0-0	1	3	2	1	0	0-0	0	18.00	22	.750	.750	0-0	—	0		-1	-0.1
1995	NY A	0	0	—	4	0	0	0-0	5.2	8	2	0	0	0-0	3	3.18	145	.333	.333	0-0	—	0		1	0.0
1996	NY A	0	0	—	16	0	0	1-0	23	23	7	0	1	7-2	18	2.35	211	.264	.326	0-0	—	0		6	0.3
Total	4	2	0	1.000	34	0	0	1-0	51	57	18	3	1	13-4	33	2.65	172	.285	.329	1-0	.000	0		10	0.5
PAVLIK, ROGER Roger Allen B 10.4.1967 Houston, TX BB/TR 6-2/220# d5.2																									
1992	Tex A	4	4	.500	13	12	1	0-0	62	66	32	3	3	34-0	45	4.21	90	.280	.375	0-0	—	0	112	-3	-0.3
1993	Tex A	12	6	.667	26	26	2	0-0	166.1	151	67	18	5	80-3	131	3.41	122	.245	.334	0-0	—	0	113	16	1.6
1994	Tex A	2	5	.286	11	11	0	0-0	50.1	61	45	8	4	30-1	31	7.69	63	.300	.394	0-0	—	0	85	-14	-1.5
1995	Tex A	10	10	.500	31	31	2-1	0-0	191.2	174	96	19	4	90-5	149	4.37	111	.243	.329	0-0	—	0	84	12	1.2
1996	†Tex A★	15	8	.652	34	34	7	0-0	201	216	120	28	5	81-5	127	5.19	101	.276	.346	0-0	—	0	109	3	0.1
1997	Tex A	3	5	.375	11	11	0	0-0	57.2	59	29	7	1	31-1	35	4.37	110	.267	.358	0-0	—	0	75	3	0.4
1998	Tex A	1	1	.500	5	0	0	1-0	14	16	8	2	1	5-1	8	3.86	125	.286	.349	0-0	—	0		1	0.1
Total	7	47	39	.547	131	125	12-1	1-0	743	743	397	85	23	351-16	526	4.58	103	.262	.346	0-0	—	0	99	18	1.6
PAWLOWSKI, JOHN John B 9.6.1963 Johnson City, NY BR/TR 6-2/175# d9.19																									
1987	Chi A	0	0	—	2	0	0	0-0	3.2	7	2	0	0	3-0	2	4.91	94	.438	.500	0-0	—	0		0	0.0
1988	Chi A	1	0	1.000	6	0	0	0-0	14	20	14	2	0	3-0	10	8.36	48	.328	.354	0-0	—	0		-6	-0.4
Total	2	1	0	1.000	8	0	0	0-0	17.2	27	16	2	0	6-0	12	7.64	54	.351	.388	0-0	—	0		-6	-0.4
PAXTON, MIKE Michael De Wayne B 9.3.1953 Memphis, TN BR/TR 5-11/190# d5.25																									
1977	Bos A	10	5	.667	29	12	2-1	0-1	108	134	53	7	3	25-2	58	3.83	118	.311	.350	0-0	—	0	126	6	0.7
1978	Cle A	12	11	.522	33	27	5-2	1-2	191	179	89	13	8	63-5	96	3.86	97	.247	.313	0-0	—	0	106	-1	-0.2

Year	Tm Lg	W	L	Pct	G	GS	CG-Sho	SV-BS	IP	H	R	HR	HB	BB-IB	SO	ERA	AERA	OAV	OOB	AB-SH	AVG	PB	Sup	APR	PW
1979	Cle A	8	8	.500	33	24	3	0-0	159.2	210	118	14	2	52-1	70	5.92	72	.315	.363	0-0	—	0	123	-30	-2.5
1980	Cle A	0	0	—	4	0	0	0-1	7.2	13	11	4	0	6-1	6	12.91	32	.394	.475	0-0	—	0		-7	-0.3
Total	4	30	24	.556	99	63	10-3	1-4	466.1	536	271	38	13	146-9	230	4.71	87	.289	.342	0-0	—	0	117	-32	-2.3
PAYNE, GEORGE George Washington B 5.23.1890 Mt.Vernon, KY D 1.24.1959 Bellflower, CA BR/TR 5-11/172# d5.8																									
1920	Chi A	1	1	.500	12	0	0	0	29.2	39	24	2	0	9	7	5.46	69	.312	.358	8-0	.125	-0		-7	-0.5
PAYNE, HARLEY Harley Fenwick "Lady" B 1.9.1868 Windsor, OH D 12.29.1935 Orwell, OH BB/TL 6/160# d4.18																									
1896	Bro N	14	16	.467	34	28	24-2	0	241.2	284	129	4	8	58	52	3.39	122	.290	.335	98-4	.214	0*	72	21	2.2
1897	Bro N	14	17	.452	40	38	30-1	0	280	350	215	8	17	71	86	4.63	88	.303	.353	110-3	.236	-0*	90	-24	-2.0
1898	Bro N	1	0	1.000	1	1	1	0	9	11	8	0	0	3	2	4.00	90	.297	.350	4-0	.750	1	178	-1	0.0
1899	Pit N	1	3	.250	5	5	2	0	26.1	33	19	2	2	4	8	3.76	101	.306	.342	10-0	.100	-1	79	-1	-0.1
Total	4	30	36	.455	80	72	57-3	0	557	678	371	14	27	136	148	4.04	101	.298	.345	222-7	.230	0	83	-5	0.1
PAYNE, MIKE Michael Earl B 11.15.1961 Woonsocket, RI D 8.4.2002 Dunnellon, FL BR/TR 5-11/165# d8.22																									
1984	Atl N	0	1	.000	3	1	0	0-0	5.2	7	4	0	0	3-0	3	6.35	61	.333	.417	1-0	.000	-0	46	-1	-0.2
PAZIK, MIKE Michael Joseph B 1.26.1950 Lynn, MA BL/TL 6-2/195# d5.11 C4																									
1975	Min A	0	4	.000	5	3	0	0-0	19.2	28	20	5	0	10-0	8	8.24	47	.329	.400	0-0	—	0	54	-9	-1.5
1976	Min A	0	0	—	5	0	0	0-0	9	13	9	0	1	4-0	6	7.00	51	.342	.419	0-0	—	0		-4	-0.2
1977	Min A	1	0	1.000	3	3	0	0-0	18	18	5	1	0	6-0	6	2.50	160	.265	.320	0-0	—	0	128	3	0.2
Total	3	1	4	.200	13	6	0	0-0	46.2	59	34	6	1	20-0	20	5.79	67	.309	.376	0-0	—	0	92	-10	-1.5
PEARCE, FRANK Franklin Johnson B 3.30.1860 Jefferson County, KY D 11.13.1926 Louisville, KY d10.4																									
1876	Lou N	0	0	—	1	0	0	0	4	5	4	0		1	1	4.50	60	.263	.300	2	.000	-0		0	-0.1
PEARCE, FRANK Franklin Thomas B 8.31.1905 Middletown, KY D 9.3.1950 Van Buren, NY BR/TR 6/170# d4.20																									
1933	Phi N	5	4	.556	20	7	3-1	0	82	78	41	5	0	29	18	3.62	105	.251	.315	26-4	.192	-1	106	1	0.0
1934	Phi N	0	2	.000	7	1	0	0	20	25	16	4	0	5	4	7.20	66	.301	.341	3-0	.667	1	73	-4	-0.3
1935	Phi N	0	0	—	5	0	0	0	13	22	15	0	0	6	7	8.31	55	.361	.418	4-0	.500	1		-5	-0.2
Total	3	5	6	.455	32	8	3-1	0	115	125	72	9	0	40	29	4.77	85	.275	.333	33-4	.273	1	98	-8	-0.5
PEARCE, JIM James Madison B 6.9.1925 Zebulon, NC BR/TR 6-6/180# d9.8																									
1949	Was A	0	1	.000	2	1	0	0	5.1	9	10	1	0	5	1	8.44	50	.375	.483	2-0	.000	-0	21	-4	-0.6
1950	Was A	2	1	.667	20	3	1	0	56.2	58	40	2	1	37	18	6.04	74	.270	.379	13-0	.154	-1	141	-8	-0.5
1953	Was A	0	1	.000	4	1	0	0	9.1	15	10	3	0	6	0	7.71	51	.405	.488	1-0	.000	-0	91	-5	-0.4
1954	Cin N	1	0	1.000	2	1	1	0	11	7	1	0	1	5	3	0.00	—	.194	.310	3-1	.000	-0	64	5	0.4
1955	Cin N	0	1	.000	2	1	0	0	3.1	8	5	0	0	0-0	0	10.80	39	.471	.444	0-0	—	0	105	-2	-0.4
Total	5	3	4	.429	30	7	2	0	85.2	97	66	6	2	53-0	22	5.78	76	.295	.395	19-1	.105	-2	100	-14	-1.5
PEARCE, JOSH Joshua Ray B 8.20.1977 Yakima, WA BR/TR 6-3/215# d4.20																									
2002	StL N	0	0	—	3	3	0	0-0	13	20	13	1	1	8-0	1	7.62	52	.377	.460	4-2	.250	0	117	-6	-0.3
2003	StL N	0	0	—	7	0	0	0-0	9	11	3	0	1	2-0	4	3.00	136	.306	.359	0-0	—	0		1	0.1
Total	2	0	0	—	10	3	0	0-0	22	31	16	1	2	10-0	5	5.73	70	.348	.422	4-2	.250	0	117	-5	-0.2
PEARS, FRANK Frank H. B 8.30.1866 Louisville, KY D 11.29.1923 St.Louis, MO TR 5-9/145# d10.6 U2																									
1889	KC AA	0	2	.000	3	2	2	0	22	21	16	2	1	9	5	4.91	85	.244	.323	11	.091	-1	52	0	-0.1
1893	StL N	0	0	—	1	0	0	0	4	9	7	0	1	2	0	13.50	35	.429	.500	2	.000	-0		-3	-0.2
Total	2	0	2	.000	4	2	2	0	26	30	23	2	2	11	5	6.23	69	.280	.358	13	.077	-2	52	-3	-0.3
PEARSON, ALEX Alexander Franklin B 3.9.1877 Greensboro, PA D 10.30.1966 Rochester, PA BR/TR 5-10.5/160# d8.1																									
1902	StL N	2	6	.250	11	10	8	0	82	90	47	0	3	22	24	3.95	69	.279	.330	34-0	.265	0	79	-9	-0.8
1903	Cle A	1	2	.333	4	3	2	0	30.1	34	15	1	1	3	12	3.56	80	.281	.304	12-0	.083	-1	109	-1	-0.2
Total	2	3	8	.273	15	13	10	0	112.1	124	62	1	4	25	36	3.85	72	.279	.323	46-0	.217	-0	86	-10	-1.0
PEARSON, IKE Issac Overton B 3.1.1917 Grenada, MS D 3.17.1985 Sarasota, FL BR/TR 6-1/180# d6.6 Mil 1943-45																									
1939	Phi N	2	13	.133	26	13	4	0	125	144	84	15	5	56	29	5.76	70	.296	.374	37-4	.054	-3*	55	-21	-2.5
1940	Phi N	3	14	.176	29	20	5-1	1	145.1	160	91	13	3	57	43	5.45	72	.275	.343	44-4	.205	1	75	-21	-2.0
1941	Phi N	4	14	.222	46	10	0	6	136	139	75	8	8	70	38	3.57	104	.266	.361	40-0	.125	-2	41	-3	-0.7
1942	Phi N	1	6	.143	35	7	0	0	85.1	87	48	4	4	50	21	4.54	73	.271	.376	23-0	.043	-2	65	-11	-1.1
1946	Phi N	1	0	1.000	5	2	1-1	0	14.1	16	8	1	1	8	6	3.77	91	.271	.368	5-0	.200	1	237	-1	0.0
1948	Chi A	2	3	.400	23	2	0	1	53	62	32	8	2	27	12	4.92	87	.292	.378	10-2	.200	-0	106	-4	-0.3
Total	6	13	50	.206	164	54	10-2	8	559	608	338	49	23	268	149	4.83	79	.279	.363	159-10	.126	-6	69	-61	-6.6
PEARSON, JASON Jason John B 12.29.1975 Freeport, IL BL/TL 6/195# d6.4																									
2002	SD N	0	0	—	2	0	0	0-0	1.2	1	0	0	0	0-0	3	0.00	—	.167	.167	0-0	—	0		1	0.0
2003	StL N	0	0	—	2	0	0	0-0	1	4	7	1	0	3-0	1	63.00	6	.571	.700	0-0	—	0		-7	-0.3
Total	2	0	0	—	4	0	0	0-0	2.2	5	7	1	0	3-0	4	23.63	16	.385	.500	0-0	—	0		-6	-0.3
PEARSON, MONTE Montgomery Marcellus "Hoot" B 9.2.1909 Oakland, CA D 1.27.1978 Fresno, CA BR/TR 6/175# d4.22																									
1932	Cle A	0	0	—	8	0	0	0	8	10	9	1	0	11	5	10.13	47	.323	.500	0-0	—	0		-4	-0.1
1933	Cle A	10	5	.667	19	16	10	0	135.1	111	45	5	0	55	54	**2.33**	191	.221	.297	50-2	.260	1	98	30	3.1
1934	Cle A	18	13	.581	39	33	19	2	254.2	257	144	16	1	130	140	4.52	101	.260	.346	92-6	.272	6	106	3	0.9
1935	Cle A	8	13	.381	30	24	10-1	0	181.2	199	117	9	0	103	90	4.90	92	.279	.371	62-1	.177	-0	91	-9	-0.8
1936	†NY A☆	19	7	**.731**	33	31	15-1	1	223	191	99	13	3	135	118	3.71	125	**.233**	.343	91-6	.253	6	152	27	3.3
1937	†NY A	9	3	.750	22	20	7-1	1	144.2	145	60	6	1	64	71	3.17	140	.261	.339	51-4	.216	1	121	21	1.6
1938	†NY A	16	7	.696	28	27	17-1	0	202	198	107	12	0	113	98	3.97	114	.258	.354	76-3	.171	1	133	13	1.3
1939	†NY A	12	5	.706	22	20	8	0	146.1	151	77	9	1	70	76	4.49	97	.272	.354	53-5	.321	6	158	0	0.6
1940	NY A☆	7	5	.583	16	16	7-1	0	109.2	108	48	8	0	44	43	3.69	109	.262	.333	33-7	.121	-1	108	6	0.6
1941	Cin N	1	3	.250	7	4	1	0	24.1	22	15	3	0	15	8	5.18	69	.242	.349	5-1	.000	-1*	71	-4	-0.6
Total	10	100	61	.621	224	191	94-5	4	1429.2	1392	721	82	6	740	703	4.00	112	.256	.346	513-35	.228	19	121	83	9.9
PEARSON, TERRY Terry Bobby Gene B 11.10.1971 Tuscaloosa, AL BR/TR 6/200# d4.4																									
2002	Det A	0	0	—	4	0	0	0-0	6	8	7	2	0	2-1	4	10.50	41	.320	.370	0-0	—	0		-4	-0.2
PEASLEY, MARV Marvin Warren B 7.16.1888 Jonesport, ME D 12.27.1948 San Francisco, CA BL/TL 6-1/175# d9.27																									
1910	Det A	0	1	.000	2	1	0	0	10	13	14	0	1	11	4	8.10	32	.295	.446	3-0	.000	0	127	-6	-0.5
PEAVY, JAKE Jacob Edward B 5.3.1981 Mobile, AL BR/TR 6-1/180# d6.22																									
2002	SD N	6	7	.462	17	17	0	0-0	97.2	106	54	11	3	33-4	90	4.52	84	.274	.334	33-2	.212	2	105	-9	-0.8
2003	SD N	12	11	.522	32	32	0	0-0	194.2	173	94	33	6	82-3	156	4.11	96	.238	.318	55-8	.073	-2	98	-3	-0.6
Total	2	18	18	.500	49	49	0	0-0	292.1	279	148	44	9	115-7	246	4.25	91	.250	.324	88-10	.125	-0	100	-12	-1.4
PECHINEY, GEORGE George Adolphe "Pisch" B 9.20.1861 Cincinnati, OH D 7.14.1943 Cincinnati, OH BR/TR 5-9/184# d8.4																									
1885	Cin AA	7	4	.636	11	11	11-1	0	98	95	45	1	6	30	49	2.02	161	.247	.311	40	.150	-2	91	10	0.8
1886	Cin AA	15	21	.417	40	40	35-2	0	330.1	355	230	4	14	133	110	4.14	85	.266	.339	144	.208	-1*	104	-24	-2.3
1887	Cle AA	1	9	.100	10	10	10	0	86	118	124	8	3	44	24	7.12	61	.303	.378	36	.250	-0	88	-27	-2.1
Total	3	23	34	.404	61	61	56-3	0	514.1	568	399	13	23	207	183	4.23	85	.269	.341	220	.205	-3	99	-41	-3.6
PEEK, STEVE Stephen George B 7.30.1914 Springfield, MA D 9.20.1991 Syracuse, NY BB/TR 6-2/195# d4.16 Mil 1942-45																									
1941	NY A	4	2	.667	17	8	2	0	80	85	48	6	0	39	18	5.06	78	.276	.357	28-1	.036	-3	121	-9	-0.8
PEERY, RED George Allan B 8.15.1906 Payson, UT D 5.6.1985 Salt Lake City, UT BL/TL 5-11/160# d9.22																									
1927	Pit N	0	0	—	1	0	0	0	1	0	1	0	0	1	0	0.00	—	.000	.333	0-0	—	0		0	0.0
1929	Bos N	0	1	.000	9	1	0	0	44	53	28	1	0	9	3	5.11	91	.305	.339	14-0	.214	1*	56	-2	0.0
Total	2	0	1	.000	10	1	0	0	45	53	29	1	0	10	3	5.00	93	.301	.339	14-0	.214	1	56	-2	0.0

Year	Tm Lg	W	L	Pct	G	GS	CG-Sho	SV-BS	IP	H	R	HR	HB	BB-IB	SO	ERA	AERA	OAV	OOB	AB-SH	AVG	PB	Sup	APR	PW
PEITZ, HEINIE Henry Clement B 11.28.1870 St.Louis, MO D 10.23.1943 Cincinnati, OH BR/TR 5-11/165# d10.15.1892 C1 b-Joe ▲																									
1894	StL N	0	0	—	1	0	0	0	3	7	7	0	1	2	0	9.00	60	.438	.526	338-7	.263	0*		-2	-0.1
1897	Cin N	0	1	.000	2	1	1	0	8	9	8	0	2	4	0	7.88	58	.281	.395	266-7	.293	0*	125	-2	-0.2
1899	Cin N	0	0	—	1	0	0	0	5	6	3	0	0	1	3	5.40	73	.300	.333	293-10	.270	0*		0	0.0
Total	3	0	1	.000	4	1	1	0	16	22	18	0	3	7	3	7.31	62	.324	.410	897-24	.274	1	125	-4	-0.3
PELTY, BARNEY Barney B 9.10.1880 Farmington, MO D 5.24.1939 Farmington, MO BR/TR 5-9/175# d8.20																									
1903	StL A	3	3	.500	7	6	5	1	48.2	49	25	1	2	15	20	2.40	121	.261	.322	20-0	.150	-0	90	0	0.0
1904	StL A	15	18	.455	39	35	31-2	0	301	270	121	7	20	77	126	2.84	87	.241	.301	118-2	.127	-6*	89	-9	-1.8
1905	StL A	14	14	.500	31	28	27-1	0	258.2	222	106	3	12	68	114	2.75	93	.233	.293	98-4	.153	-3	119	-3	-0.6
1906	StL A	16	11	.593	34	30	25-4	2	260.2	189	77	1	18	59	92	1.59	163	**.206**	.267	91-3	.165	-3	110	27	2.9
1907	StL A	12	21	.364	36	31	29-5	1	273	234	101	1	18	64	85	2.57	98	.234	.292	95-3	.168	-2	79	1	0.0
1908	StL A	7	4	.636	20	13	7-1	0	122	104	44	0	10	32	36	1.99	120	.241	.309	42-4	.119	-3*	138	4	0.1
1909	StL A	11	11	.500	27	23	17-5	0	199.1	158	63	2	5	53	88	2.30	105	.222	.281	91-4	.165	0*	100	4	0.8
1910	StL A	5	11	.313	27	19	13-3	0	165.1	157	81	3	8	70	48	3.48	71	.263	.348	56-4	.089	-4*	67	-13	-1.4
1911	StL A	7	15	.318	28	22	18-1	0	197	197	87	4	4	69	59	2.97	114	.265	.331	65-2	.138	-3*	55	11	0.8
1912	StL A	1	5	.167	6	6	2	0	38.2	43	27	0	3	15	10	5.59	59	.297	.374	12-0	.000	-2	70	-8	-1.1
	Was A	1	4	.200	11	4	1	0	43.2	40	18	0	4	10	15	3.30	101	.250	.310	9-0	.222	0	55	2	0.2
	Year	2	9	.182	17	10	3	0	82.1	83	21	0	7	25	25	4.37	76	.272	.341	21-0	.095	-2	64	-6	-0.9
Total	10	92	117	.440	266	217	175-22	4	1908	1663	750	22	104	532	693	2.63	100	.239	.302	697-26	.143	-25	90	16	-0.1
PEMBER, DAVE David Joseph B 5.24.1978 Cincinnati, OH BR/TR 6-5/225# d9.3																									
2002	Mil N	0	1	.000	4	1	0	0-0	8.2	7	6	1	0	6-0	5	5.19	79	.219	.333	1-0	.000	-0	23	-1	-0.2
PENA, ALEJANDRO Alejandro (Vasquez) B 6.25.1959 Cambiaso, D.R. BR/TR 6-1/205# d9.14																									
1981	†LA N	1	1	.500	14	0	0	2-2	25.1	18	8	2	0	11-1	14	2.84	117	.194	.279	6-0	.000	-1		2	0.1
1982	LA N	0	2	.000	29	0	0	0-0	35.2	37	24	2	1	21-7	20	4.79	72	.272	.373	0-0	—	0		-7	-0.3
1983	†LA N	12	9	.571	34	26	4-3	1-1	177	152	67	7	1	51-7	120	2.75	131	.229	.283	60-1	.100	-2	90	16	1.7
1984	LA N	12	6	.667	28	28	8-**4**	0-0	199.1	186	67	7	3	46-7	135	**2.48**	**142**	.246	.291	66-4	.121	-1	95	22	1.8
1985	LA N	0	1	.000	2	1	0	0-0	4.1	7	5	1	0	3-1	2	8.31	42	.350	.435	1-0	.000	-0	127	-3	-0.5
1986	LA N	1	2	.333	24	10	0	1-0	70	74	40	6	1	30-5	46	4.89	71	.270	.343	17-3	.176	0	124	-11	-0.6
1987	LA N	2	7	.222	37	7	0	11-0	87.1	82	41	9	2	37-5	76	3.50	113	.251	.325	13-1	.077	-1	59	3	0.2
1988	†LA N	6	7	.462	60	0	0	12-2	94.1	75	29	4	1	27-6	83	1.91	175	.218	.275	6-0	.000	-1		13	1.9
1989	LA N	4	3	.571	53	0	0	5-4	76	62	20	6	2	18-4	75	2.13	160	.220	.271	1-0	1.000	0		11	1.1
1990	NY N	3	3	.500	52	0	0	5-0	76	71	31	4	1	22-5	76	3.20	117	.245	.295	6-0	.167	-0		4	0.3
1991	NY N	6	1	.857	44	0	0	4-5	63	63	20	5	0	19-4	49	2.71	134	.267	.317	0-0	—	0		7	0.8
	†Atl N	2	0	1.000	15	0	0	11-0	19.1	11	3	1	0	3-0	13	1.40	279	.167	.203	1-0	.000	-0		5	1.1
	Year	8	1	.889	59	0	0	15-5	82.1	74	26	6	0	22-4	62	2.40	154	.245	.293	1-0	.000	-0		12	1.9
1992	Atl N	1	6	.143	41	0	0	15-3	42	40	19	7	0	13-5	34	4.07	90	.255	.310	2-0	.000	-0		-1	-0.3
1994	Pit N	3	2	.600	22	0	0	7-1	28.2	22	16	4	1	10-2	27	5.02	86	.206	.280	1-0	.000	-0		-1	-0.3
1995	Bos A	1	1	.500	17	0	0	0-0	24.1	33	23	5	0	12-2	25	7.40	66	.314	.385	0-0	—	0		-7	-0.5
	Fla N	2	0	1.000	13	0	0	0-1	18	11	3	2	0	3-1	21	1.50	281	.169	.206	1-0	.000	-0		6	0.5
	†Atl N	0	0	—	14	0	0	0-0	13	11	6	1	0	4-0	18	4.15	103	.224	.283	0-0	—	0		0	0.0
	Year	2	0	1.000	27	0	0	0-1	31	22	9	3	0	7-1	39	2.61	162	.193	.240	1-0	.000	-0		6	0.5
1996	Fla N	0	1	.000	4	0	0	0-0	4	4	5	2	0	1-0	5	4.50	91	.235	.278	0-0	—	0		-1	-0.3
Total	15	56	52	.519	503	72	12-7	74-19	1057.2	959	427	75	13	331-62	839	3.11	118	.240	.299	181-9	.110	-5	92	58	6.7
PENA, HIPOLITO Hipolito (Concepcion) B 1.30.1964 Fantino, D.R. BL/TL 6-3/165# d9.1																									
1986	Pit N	0	3	.000	10	1	0	1-0	8.1	7	10	3	1	3-1	6	8.64	44	.206	.289	0-0	—	0	0	-5	-0.9
1987	Pit N	0	3	.000	16	1	0	1-0	25.2	16	14	2	0	26-3	16	4.56	90	.184	.372	6-0	.167	-0	22	-1	-0.1
1988	NY A	1	1	.500	16	0	0	0-0	14.1	10	8	1	0	9-1	10	3.14	126	.192	.306	0-0	—	0		0	0.0
Total	3	1	7	.125	42	2	0	2-0	48.1	33	32	6	1	38-5	32	4.84	83	.191	.338	6-0	.167	-0	11	-6	-1.0
PENA, JIM James Patrick B 9.17.1964 Los Angeles, CA BL/TL 6/175# d7.7																									
1992	SF N	1	1	.500	25	2	0	0-0	44	49	19	4	1	20-5	32	3.48	95	.282	.357	5-3	.200	0	205	-1	0.0
PENA, JESUS Jesus B 3.8.1975 Santo Domingo, D.R. BL/TL 6/170# d8.7																									
1999	Chi A	0	0	—	26	0	0	0-1	20.1	21	15	3	1	23-5	20	5.31	92	.259	.429	0-0	—	0		-2	-0.1
2000	Chi A	2	1	.667	20	0	0	1-0	23.1	25	18	6	1	16-0	19	5.40	93	.278	.385	0-0	—	0		-2	-0.2
	Bos A	0	0	—	2	0	0	0-0	3	3	1	1	0	3-0	1	3.00	168	.273	.429	0-0	—	0		1	0.0
	Year	2	1	.667	22	0	0	1-0	26.1	28	27	7	1	19-0	20	5.13	98	.277	.390	0-0	—	0		-1	-0.2
Total	2	2	1	.667	48	0	0	1-1	46.2	49	34	10	2	42-5	40	5.21	95	.269	.408	0-0	—	0		-3	-0.3
PENA, JOSE Jose (Gutierrez) B 12.3.1942 Ciudad Juarez, Mexico BR/TR 6-2/190# d6.1																									
1969	Cin N	1	1	.500	6	0	0	0-0	5	10	10	0	0	5-1	3	18.00	21	.400	.500	0-0	—	0		-7	-1.3
1970	LA N	4	3	.571	29	0	0	4-2	57	51	32	8	3	29-5	31	4.42	87	.241	.336	8-0	.125	0		-4	-0.5
1971	LA N	2	0	1.000	21	0	0	1-0	43	32	18	7	1	18-1	44	3.56	91	.211	.295	3-0	.667	1		-1	0.0
1972	LA N	0	0	—	5	0	0	0-0	7.1	13	8	1	0	6-1	4	8.59	39	.371	.452	0-0	—	0		-4	-0.2
Total	4	7	4	.636	61	0	0	5-2	112.1	106	68	16	4	58-8	82	4.97	72	.250	.341	11-0	.273	1		-16	-2.0
PENA, JUAN Juan Francisco B 6.27.1977 Santo Domingo, D.R. BR/TR 6-5/210# d5.8																									
1999	Bos A	2	0	1.000	2	2	0	0-0	13	9	1	0	0	3-0	15	0.69	719	.196	.245	0-0	—	0	103	6	1.0
PENA, ORLANDO Orlando Gregorio (Quevara) B 11.17.1933 Victoria De Las Tunas, Cuba BR/TR 5-11/154# d8.24																									
1958	Cin N	1	0	1.000	9	0	0	3	15	10	1	0	0	4-1	11	0.60	691	.185	.241	0-0	—	0		6	0.6
1959	Cin N	5	9	.357	46	8	1	5	136	150	80	26	0	39-5	76	4.76	85	.280	.325	34-5	.088	-0	85	-10	-1.1
1960	Cin N	0	1	.000	4	0	0	0	9.1	8	3	0	0	3-2	9	2.89	132	.222	.282	1-0	.000	-0		1	0.1
1962	KC A	6	4	.600	13	12	6-1	0	89.2	71	31	9	1	27-2	56	3.01	140	.213	.272	31-0	.161	-0	109	12	1.2
1963	KC A	12	20	.375	35	33	9-3	0	217	218	93	24	5	53-2	128	3.69	106	.260	.306	62-10	.145	0	70	7	0.9
1964	KC A	12	14	.462	40	32	5	0	219.1	231	126	40	8	73-2	184	4.43	86	.268	.329	75-3	.160	0*	90	-17	-2.0
1965	KC A	0	6	.000	12	5	0	0	35.1	42	30	4	2	13-0	24	6.88	51	.302	.368	9-0	.111	-0	65	-13	-2.0
	Det A	4	6	.400	30	0	0	4	57.1	54	18	5	1	20-5	55	2.51	138	.252	.318	8-1	.250	1		6	1.1
	Year	4	12	.250	42	5	0	4	92.2	96	51	9	3	33-5	79	4.18	83	.272	.338	17-1	.176	1	66	-6	-0.9
1966	Det A	4	2	.667	54	0	0	7	108	105	47	16	5	35-6	79	3.08	113	.252	.315	18-2	.111	-1		2	0.2
1967	Det A	0	1	.000	2	0	0	0	2	5	3	0	1	0-0	2	13.50	24	.500	.500	0-0	—	0		-2	-0.4
	Cle A	0	3	.000	48	1	0	8	88.1	67	34	8	1	22-5	72	3.36	97	.208	.259	8-1	.000	-1	27	1	-0.1
	Year	0	4	.000	50	1	0	8	90.1	72	35	8	2	22-5	74	3.59	91	.217	.267	8-1	.000	-1	27	-1	-0.5
1970	Pit N	2	1	.667	23	0	0	2-1	37.2	38	21	6	1	7-2	25	4.78	82	.268	.305	6-1	.000	-1		-3	-0.3
1971	Bal A	0	1	.000	5	0	0	0-0	14.2	16	7	0	0	5-1	4	3.07	109	.281	.339	3-0	.000	-0		0	-0.1
1973	Bal A	1	1	.500	11	2	0	1-1	44.2	36	20	10	2	8-1	23	4.03	93	.218	.260	0-0	—	0	60	0	0.0
	StL N	4	4	.500	42	0	0	6-1	62	60	17	3	0	14-4	38	2.18	168	.251	.290	7-1	.143	-0		10	1.5
1974	StL N	5	2	.714	42	0	0	1-2	45	45	15	0	1	20-3	23	2.60	138	.269	.342	2-0	.500	0		5	0.8
	Cal A	0	0	—	4	0	0	3-0	8	6	0	0	0	1-0	5	0.00	—	.214	.241	0-0	—	0		3	0.3
1975	Cal A	0	2	.000	7	0	0	0-0	12.2	13	3	0	0	8-1	4	2.13	167	.283	.382	0-0	—	0		2	0.3
Total	14	56	77	.421	427	93	21-4	40-5	1202	1175	549	151	28	352-42	818	3.71	102	.255	.309	264-24	.136	-3	86	10	1.0
PENA, RAMON Ramon Arturo (Padilla) B 5.5.1962 Santiago, D.R. BR/TR 5-10/155# d4.27 b-Tony																									
1989	Det A	0	0	—	8	0	0	0-0	18	26	13	0	2	8-3	12	6.00	64	.338	.409	0-0	—	0		-4	-0.2
PENCE, RUSTY Russell William B 3.11.1900 Marine, IL D 8.11.1971 Hot Springs, AR BR/TR 6/185# d5.13																									
1921	Chi A	0	0	—	4	0	0	0	5.1	6	5	0	1	7	2	8.44	50	.286	.483	1-0	.000	-0		-2	-0.1
PENNER, KEN Kenneth William B 4.24.1896 Boonville, IN D 5.28.1959 Sacramento, CA BL/TR 5-11.5/170# d9.11																									
1916	Cle A	1	1	.500	4	2	0	0	12.2	14	6	0	0	4	5	4.26	71	.304	.360	2-0	.000	-0	88	-1	-0.1
1929	Chi N	0	1	.000	5	0	0	0	12.2	14	11	1	0	6	3	2.84	162	.280	.357	4-0	.250	0		0	0.0

Year	Tm Lg	W	L	Pct	G	GS	CG-Sho	SV-BS	IP	H	R	HR	HB	BB-IB	SO	ERA	AERA	OAV	OOB	AB-SH	AVG	PB	Sup	APR	PW
Total	2	1	2	.333	9	2	0	0	25.1	28	17	1	0	10	8	3.55	108	.292	.358	6-0	.167	-0	88	-1	-0.1
PENNINGTON, BRAD Brad Lee B 4.14.1969 Salem, IN BL/TL 6-5/205# d4.17																									
1993	Bal A	3	2	.600	34	0	0	4-3	33	34	25	7	2	25-0	39	6.55	69	.266	.391	0-0	—	0		-7	-1.1
1994	Bal A	0	1	.000	8	0	0	0-1	6	9	8	2	0	8-0	7	12.00	42	.346	.500	0-0	—	0		-4	-0.6
1995	Bal A	0	1	.000	8	0	0	0-1	6.2	3	7	1	0	11-1	10	8.10	59	.136	.424	0-0	—	0		-3	-0.3
	Cin N	0	0	—	6	0	0	0-0	9.2	9	8	0	1	11-0	7	5.59	74	.273	.447	2-0	.000	-0		-2	-0.2
1996	Bos A	0	2	.000	14	0	0	0-0	13	6	5	1	0	15-1	13	2.77	183	.140	.356	0-0	—	0		3	0.4
	Cal A	0	0	—	8	0	0	0-0	7.1	5	10	1	0	16-0	7	12.27	41	.185	.488	0-0	—	0		-5	-0.3
	Year	0	2	.000	22	0	0	0-0	20.1	11	19	2	0	31-1	20	6.20	82	.157	.412	0-0	—	0		-3	0.1
1998	TB A	0	0	—	1	0	0	0-0	0	1	1	0	0	3-0	0	o	—	1.000	1.000	0-0	—	0		-1	-0.1
Total	5	3	6	.333	79	0	0	4-5	75.2	67	64	12	3	89-2	83	7.02	66	.239	.423	2-0	.000	-0		-19	-2.2
PENNINGTON, KEWPIE George Louis B 9.24.1896 New York, NY D 5.3.1953 Newark, NJ BR/TR 5-8.5/168# d4.14																									
1917	StL A	0	0	—	1	0	0	0	1	1	0	0	0	0	0	0.00	—	.250	.250	0-0	—	0		0	0.0
PENNOCK, HERB Herbert Jefferis "The Knight Of Kennett Square" B 2.10.1894 Kennett Square, PA D 1.30.1948 New York, NY BB/TL 6/160# d5.14 Mil 1918 C4 HF1948																									
1912	Phi A	1	2	.333	17	2	1	2	50	48	31	1	3	30	38	4.50	68	.262	.375	15-1	.133	-1	120	-8	-0.5
1913	Phi A	2	1	.667	14	3	1	0	33.1	30	24	4	0	22	17	5.13	54	.242	.356	9-0	.111	-0	223	-10	-0.8
1914	†Phi A	11	4	.733	28	14	8-3	3	151.2	136	56	1	2	65	90	2.79	94	.248	.330	56-1	.214	2	140	-3	-0.1
1915	Phi A	3	6	.333	11	8	3-1	1	44	46	34	2	2	29	24	5.32	55	.266	.377	18-0	.278	1	81	-11	-1.9
	Bos A	0	0	—	5	1	0	0	14	23	16	0	0	10	7	9.64	29	.390	.478	6-0	.167	0	262	-10	-0.5
	Year	3	6	.333	16	9	3-1	1	58	69	26	2	2	39	31	6.36	45	.297	.403	24-0	.250	1	101	-21	-2.4
1916	Bos A	0	2	.000	9	2	0	1	26.2	23	11	0	1	8	12	3.04	91	.245	.311	8-0	.125	-0*	27	-1	-0.1
1917	Bos A	5	5	.500	24	5	4-1	1	100.2	90	49	2	3	23	35	3.31	78	.243	.292	24-1	.167	2	117	-9	-0.7
1919	Bos A	16	8	.667	32	26	16-5	0	219	223	78	2	3	48	70	2.71	111	.274	.316	75-6	.173	1	120	9	1.0
1920	Bos A	16	13	.552	37	31	19-4	2	242.1	244	108	9	4	61	68	3.68	99	.264	.312	77-7	.260	4*	97	3	0.6
1921	Bos A	13	14	.481	32	31	15-1	0	222.2	268	121	7	2	59	91	4.04	105	.307	.352	85-4	.212	2	79	2	0.5
1922	Bos A	10	17	.370	32	26	15-1	1	202	230	108	7	1	74	59	4.32	95	.297	.359	65-2	.138	-3	72	-3	-0.5
1923	†NY A	19	6	**.760**	35	27	21-1	3	238.1	235	86	11	2	68	93	3.13	126	.261	.314	83-8	.193	0	121	25	2.4
1924	NY A	21	9	.700	40	34	25-4	3	286.1	302	104	13	1	64	101	2.83	147	.273	.314	101-10	.158	-2	107	43	3.8
1925	NY A	16	17	.485	47	31	21-2	2	**277**	267	117	11	2	71	88	2.96	144	.254	**.303**	99-9	.202	-3	84	36	3.3
1926	†NY A	23	11	.676	40	33	19-1	2	266.1	294	133	11	4	43	78	3.62	107	.282	**.313**	85-16	.212	3	119	6	1.0
1927	†NY A	19	8	.704	34	26	18-1	2	209.2	225	89	5	2	48	51	3.00	128	.283	.325	69-13	.217	-0	134	19	2.1
1928	NY A	17	6	.739	28	24	18-**5**	3	211	215	71	2	0	40	53	2.56	147	.267	.302	74-7	.203	-1	114	31	3.1
1929	NY A	9	11	.450	27	23	8-1	2	157.1	205	101	11	3	28	49	4.92	78	.318	.349	51-6	.176	-1	108	-19	-2.1
1930	NY A	11	7	.611	25	19	11-1	0	156.1	194	95	8	0	20	46	4.32	100	.301	.322	60-1	.183	-2	137	-2	-0.5
1931	NY A	11	6	.647	25	25	12-1	0	189.1	247	96	7	1	30	65	4.28	93	.315	.342	66-7	.152	1	147	-3	-0.2
1932	†NY A	9	5	.643	22	21	9-1	0	146.2	191	94	8	0	38	54	4.60	89	.310	.350	53-5	.151	0	143	-13	-1.0
1933	NY A	7	4	.636	23	5	2-1	4	65	96	46	4	0	21	22	5.54	70	.342	.387	21-6	.238	0	180	-13	-1.9
1934	Bos A	2	0	1.000	30	2	1	1	62	68	31	2	0	16	16	3.05	158	.276	.321	14-1	.214	-0	163	**9**	0.3
Total	22	241	162	.598	617	419	247-35	33	3571.2	3900	1699	128	36	916	1227	3.60	106	.282	.328	1214-111	.191	3	113	78	7.3
PENNY, BRAD Bradley Wayne B 5.24.1978 Broken Arrow, OK BR/TR 6-4/200# d4.7																									
2000	Fla N	8	7	.533	23	22	0	0-0	119.2	120	70	13	5	60-4	80	4.81	92	.263	.354	45-1	.111	-2*	115	-5	-0.7
2001	Fla N	10	10	.500	31	31	1-1	0-0	205	183	92	15	7	54-3	154	3.69	114	.240	.296	62-3	.161	1	85	12	1.0
2002	Fla N	8	7	.533	24	24	1-1	0-0	129.1	148	76	18	1	50-7	93	4.66	85	.288	.350	48-1	.167	0	108	-12	-1.3
2003	†Fla N	14	10	.583	32	32	0	0-0	196.1	195	96	21	3	56-6	138	4.13	99	.264	.316	68-5	.132	1*	116	-1	-0.1
Total	4	40	34	.541	110	109	2-2	0-0	650.1	646	334	67	16	220-20	465	4.22	99	.261	.324	223-10	.143	-1	105	-6	-1.1
PENSON, PAUL Paul Eugene B 7.12.1931 Kansas City, KS BR/TR 6-1/185# d4.21																									
1954	Phi N	1	1	.500	5	3	0	0	16	14	11	1	0	14	3	4.50	90	.237	.368	7-0	.000	-1	132	-2	-0.3
PENTZ, GENE Eugene David B 6.21.1953 Johnstown, PA BR/TR 6-1/200# d7.29																									
1975	Det A	0	4	.000	13	0	0	0-1	25.1	27	14	0	0	20-4	21	3.20	126	.293	.412	0-0	—	0		1	0.1
1976	Hou N	3	3	.500	40	0	0	5-2	63.2	62	26	5	1	31-2	36	2.97	108	.259	.343	5-0	.200	0		1	0.2
1977	Hou N	5	2	.714	41	4	0	2-2	87	76	41	8	1	44-5	51	3.83	93	.236	.324	13-0	.000	-2	118	-2	-0.4
1978	Hou N	0	0	—	10	0	0	0-0	15	12	13	1	1	13-3	8	6.00	55	.214	.366	1-0	.000	-0		-6	-0.3
Total	4	8	9	.471	104	4	0	7-5	191	177	94	14	3	108-14	116	3.63	96	.250	.346	19-0	.053	-1	118	-6	-0.4
PEOPLES, JIMMY James Elsworth B 10.8.1863 Big Beaver, MI D 8.29.1920 Detroit, MI TR 5-8/200# d5.29.1884 U1 ▲																									
1885	Cin AA	0	2	.000	2	2	1	0	15	30	28	0	3	2	4	12.00	27	.390	.427	22	.182	-0*	118	-13	-1.1
PEPPER, LAURIN Hugh McLaurin B 1.18.1931 Vaughan, MS BR/TR 5-11/190# d7.4																									
1954	Pit N	1	5	.167	14	8	0	0	50.2	63	53	4	0	43	17	7.99	52	.315	.429	17-0	.235	0	75	-21	-2.0
1955	Pit N	0	1	.000	14	1	0	0	20	30	24	5	2	25-0	7	10.35	40	.370	.523	2-0	.000	-0	43	-13	-0.6
1956	Pit N	1	1	.500	11	7	0	0	30	30	17	1	0	25-1	12	3.00	126	.256	.385	6-0	.000	-0	67	0	-0.1
1957	Pit N	0	1	.000	5	1	0	0	9	11	8	1	0	5-2	4	8.00	47	.297	.381	0-0	—	0*	70	-4	-0.4
Total	4	2	8	.200	44	17	0	0	109.2	134	102	11	2	98-3	40	7.06	57	.308	.433	25-0	.160	-0	69	-38	-3.1
PEPPER, BOB Robert Ernest B 5.3.1895 Rosston, PA D 4.8.1968 Ford Cliff, PA BR/TR 6-2/178# d7.23																									
1915	Phi A	0	0	—	1	0	0	0	5	6	5	0	1	4	0	1.80	163	.333	.478	2-0	.000	-0		-1	-0.1
PEPPERS, HARRISON William Harrison (b: William Harrison Pepper) B 9.1866 , KY D 11.5.1903 Webb City, MO BL d6.30																									
1894	Lou N	0	1	.000	2	1	0	0	8	10	7	0	0	4	0	6.75	76	.303	.378	4-0	.000	-1	83	-1	-0.1
PERAZA, LUIS Luis (Rios) B 6.17.1942 Rio Piedras, P.R. BR/TR 5-11/185# d4.9																									
1969	Phi N	0	0	—	8	0	0	0-0	9	12	6	1	0	2-0	7	6.00	59	.364	.378	1-0	.000	-0		-2	-0.1
PERAZA, OSWALDO Oswald Jose B 10.19.1962 Puerto Cabello, Venezuela BR/TR 6-4/172# d4.4																									
1988	Bal A	5	7	.417	19	15	1	0-0	86	98	62	10	2	37-2	61	5.55	71	.282	.352	0-0	—	0	96	-18	-2.1
PERCIVAL, TROY Troy Eugene B 8.9.1969 Fontana, CA BR/TR 6-3/200# d4.26																									
1995	Cal A	3	2	.600	62	0	0	3-3	74	37	19	6	1	26-2	94	1.95	242	.147	.229	0-0	—	0		22	1.4
1996	Cal A★	0	2	.000	62	0	0	36-3	74	38	20	8	2	31-4	100	2.31	217	.149	.246	1-0	.000	-0		23	2.4
1997	Ana A	5	5	.500	55	0	0	27-4	52	40	20	6	4	22-2	72	3.46	132	.205	.296	0-0	—	0		7	1.4
1998	Ana A★	2	7	.222	67	0	0	42-6	66.2	45	31	5	3	37-4	87	3.65	129	.186	.299	0-0	—	0		7	1.3
1999	Ana A☆	4	6	.400	60	0	0	31-8	57	38	24	9	3	22-0	58	3.79	128	.186	.274	0-0	—	0		8	1.4
2000	Ana A	5	5	.500	54	0	0	32-10	50	42	27	7	2	30-4	49	4.50	113	.228	.339	0-0	—	0		3	0.5
2001	Ana A★	4	2	.667	57	0	0	39-3	57.2	39	19	3	2	18-1	71	2.65	172	.187	.258	0-0	—	0		12	2.3
2002	†Ana A	4	1	.800	58	0	0	40-4	56.1	38	12	5	0	25-1	68	1.92	231	.188	.276	0-0	—	0		16	3.2
2003	Ana A	0	5	.000	52	0	0	33-4	49.1	33	22	7	3	23-1	48	3.47	125	.184	.286	0-0	—	0		4	0.8
Total	9	27	35	.435	527	0	0	283-45	537	350	194	56	20	234-19	647	3.00	157	.182	.276	1-0	.000	-0		102	14.7
PERDUE, HUB Herbert Rodney "The Gallatin Squash" B 6.7.1882 Bethpage, TN D 10.31.1968 Gallatin, TX BR/TR 5-10.5/192# d4.19																									
1911	Bos N	6	10	.375	24	19	9	1	137.1	180	100	10	4	41	40	4.98	77	.321	.372	48-4	.208	-1	117	-16	-1.7
1912	Bos N	13	16	.448	37	30	20-1	3	249	295	135	11	2	54	101	3.80	94	.303	.341	87-6	.138	-5	83	-4	-1.1
1913	Bos N	16	13	.552	38	32	16-3	1	212.1	201	107	7	4	39	91	3.26	101	.249	.287	67-4	.104	-5	95	1	-0.7
1914	Bos N	2	5	.286	9	9	2	0	51	60	35	5	3	11	13	5.82	47	.311	.357	14-1	.071	-0	92	-15	-1.8
	StL N	8	8	.500	22	19	12	1	153.1	160	60	3	5	35	43	2.82	99	.290	.338	48-5	.167	-1	92	3	-0.1
	Year	10	13	.435	31	28	14	1	204.1	220	64	8	8	46	56	3.57	78	.296	.343	62-6	.145	-1	92	-9	-1.9
1915	StL N	6	12	.333	31	13	5-1	1	115.1	141	66	7	2	19	29	4.21	66	.311	.341	36-1	.111	-1	96	-16	-2.5
Total	5	51	64	.443	161	122	64-5	7	918.1	1037	503	43	20	199	317	3.85	85	.293	.334	300-21	.140	-13	95	-47	-7.9
PEREZ, CARLOS Carlos Gross (b: Carlos Gross (Perez)) B 4.14.1971 Nigua, D.R. BL/TL 6-3/195# d4.27 b-Pascual b-Melido																									
1995	Mon N★	10	8	.556	28	23	2-1	0-0	141.1	142	61	18	5	28-2	106	3.69	116	.257	.299	45-4	.133	1	90	10	1.3

Year	Tm Lg	W	L	Pct	G	GS	CG-Sho	SV-BS	IP	H	R	HR	HB	BB-IB	SO	ERA	AERA	OAV	OOB	AB-SH	AVG	PB	Sup	APR	PW
1997	Mon N	12	13	.480	33	32	8-**5**	0-0	206.2	206	109	21	4	48-1	110	3.88	108	.260	.303	64-5	.172	2	98	3	0.6
1998	Mon N	7	10	.412	23	23	3	0-0	163.1	177	79	12	3	33-3	82	3.75	112	.277	.314	47-11	.191	2	70	7	0.9
	LA N	4	4	.500	11	11	4-2	0-0	77.2	67	30	9	0	30-1	46	3.24	122	.234	.307	24-3	.083	-0	76	7	0.7
	Year	11	14	.440	34	34	7-2	0-0	241	244	33	21	3	63-4	128	3.59	115	.263	.312	71-14	.155	1	72	12	1.6
1999	LA N	2	10	.167	17	16	0	0-0	89.2	116	77	23	6	39-1	40	7.43	58	.317	.389	27-3	.296	4	83	-31	-2.9
2000	LA N	5	8	.385	30	22	0	0-1	144	192	95	25	8	33-1	64	5.56	78	.324	.367	43-7	.047	-3*	102	-19	-1.7
Total	5	40	53	.430	142	127	17-8	0-1	822.2	900	451	108	26	211-9	448	4.44	95	.279	.327	250-33	.152	6	89	-23	-1.1
PEREZ, GEORGE George Thomas B 12.29.1937 San Fernando, CA BR/TR 6-2.5/200# d4.17																									
1958	Pit N	0	1	.000	4	0	0	1	8.1	9	5	1	0	4-0	2	5.40	72	.300	.371	2-0	.000	-0		-1	-0.2
PEREZ, MELIDO Melido Turpen Gross (b: Melido Turpen Gross (Perez)) B 2.15.1966 San Cristobal, D.R. BR/TR 6-4/180# d9.4 b-Pascual b-Carlos																									
1987	KC A	1	1	.500	3	3	0	0-0	10.1	18	12	2	0	5-0	5	7.84	58	.375	.434	0-0	—	0	126	-4	-0.7
1988	Chi A	12	10	.545	32	32	3-1	0-0	197	186	105	26	2	72-0	138	3.79	105	.248	.313	0-0	—	0	100	0	-0.1
1989	Chi A	11	14	.440	31	31	2	0-0	183.1	187	106	23	3	90-3	141	5.01	76	.264	.348	0-0	—	0	97	-21	-2.6
1990	Chi A	13	14	.481	35	35	3-3	0-0	197	177	111	14	2	86-1	161	4.61	83	.241	.320	0-0	—	0	103	-18	-2.3
1991	Chi A	8	7	.533	49	8	0	1-4	135.2	111	49	15	1	52-0	128	3.12	128	.224	.299	0-0	—	0	86	14	1.5
1992	NY A	13	16	.448	33	33	10-1	0-0	247.2	212	94	16	5	93-5	218	2.87	137	.235	.308	0-0	—	0	90	26	2.9
1993	NY A	6	14	.300	25	25	0	0-0	163	173	103	22	1	64-5	148	5.19	80	.267	.333	0-0	—	0	74	-20	-2.1
1994	NY A	9	4	.692	22	22	1	0-0	151.1	134	74	16	3	58-5	109	4.10	112	.238	.311	0-0	—	0	100	9	0.6
1995	NY A	5	5	.500	13	12	1	0-0	69.1	70	46	10	1	31-2	44	5.58	83	.261	.337	0-0	—	0	129	-8	-1.0
Total	9	78	85	.479	243	201	20-5	1-4	1354.2	1268	700	144	18	551-21	1092	4.17	97	.248	.321	0-0	—	0	97	-22	-3.8
PEREZ, MIKE Michael Irvin (Ortega) B 10.19.1964 Yauco, P.R. BR/TR 6/187# d9.5																									
1990	StL N	1	0	1.000	13	0	0	1-1	13.2	12	6	0	0	3-0	5	3.95	97	.240	.273	1-0	.000	-0		0	0.0
1991	StL N	0	2	.000	14	0	0	0-0	17	19	11	1	1	7-2	7	5.82	64	.288	.365	0-0	—	0		-3	-0.4
1992	StL N	9	3	.750	77	0	0	0-3	93	70	23	4	1	32-9	46	1.84	185	.210	.278	4-2	.000	-0		15	1.9
1993	StL N	7	2	.778	65	0	0	7-3	72.2	65	24	4	1	20-1	58	2.48	160	.243	.294	1-0	.000	0		12	1.5
1994	StL N	2	3	.400	36	0	0	12-2	31	52	32	5	3	10-1	20	8.71	48	.391	.430	0-0	—	0		-16	-3.0
1995	Chi N	2	6	.250	68	0	0	2-1	71.1	72	30	8	4	27-8	49	3.66	112	.268	.340	4-1	.000	0		5	0.5
1996	Chi N	1	0	1.000	24	0	0	0-0	27	29	14	2	3	13-1	22	4.67	93	.264	.357	1-0	.000	-0		0	0.0
1997	KC A	2	0	1.000	16	0	0	0-0	20.1	15	8	2	1	8-0	17	3.54	133	.214	.304	0-0	—	0		3	0.3
Total	8	24	16	.600	313	0	0	22-10	346	334	148	26	14	120-22	224	3.56	110	.257	.323	11-3	.000	-0		16	0.8
PEREZ, ODALIS Odalis Amadol B 6.11.1978 Las Matas De Farfan, D.R. BL/TL 6/175# d9.1																									
1998	†Atl N	0	1	.000	10	0	0	0-1	10.2	10	5	1	0	4-0	5	4.22	99	.244	.311	0-0	—	0		0	0.0
1999	Atl N	4	6	.400	18	17	0	0-0	93	100	65	12	1	53-2	82	6.00	75	.275	.366	30-4	.133	-1	109	-14	-1.3
2001	Atl N	7	8	.467	24	16	0	0-0	95.1	108	55	7	1	39-0	71	4.91	90	.290	.357	26-2	.192	1	92	-4	-0.5
2002	LA N★	15	10	.600	32	32	4-2	0-0	222.1	182	76	21	4	38-5	155	3.00	128	.226	.262	64-10	.156	2	110	24	3.1
2003	LA N	12	12	.500	30	30	0	0-0	185.1	191	98	28	3	46-4	141	4.52	89	.267	.313	52-10	.096	-2	93	-9	-1.1
Total	5	38	37	.507	114	95	4-2	0-1	606.2	591	299	69	9	180-11	454	4.24	96	.257	.312	172-26	.140	-1	102	-3	0.2
PEREZ, OLIVER Oliver (Martinez) B 8.15.1981 Culiacan, Mexico BL/TL 6-3/160# d6.16																									
2002	SD N	4	5	.444	16	15	0	0-0	90	71	37	13	5	48-1	94	3.50	108	.218	.325	30-3	.133	-1	91	4	0.2
2003	SD N	4	7	.364	19	19	0	0-0	103.2	103	65	20	3	65-2	117	5.38	73	.258	.365	33-3	.212	1	94	-17	-1.5
	Pit N	0	3	.000	5	5	0	0-0	23	26	15	2	1	12-1	24	5.87	75	.283	.371	6-0	.000	-1	69	-3	-0.4
	Year	4	10	.286	24	24	0	0-0	126.2	129	18	22	4	77-3	141	5.47	74	.263	.366	39-3	.179	0	89	-20	-1.9
Total	2	8	15	.348	40	39	0	0-0	216.2	200	117	35	9	125-4	235	4.65	84	.245	.349	69-6	.159	-0	90	-16	-1.7
PEREZ, PASCUAL Pascual Gross (b: Pascual Gross (Perez)) B 5.17.1957 San Cristobal, D.R. BR/TR 6-2/163# d5.7 b-Melido b-Carlos																									
1980	Pit N	0	1	.000	2	2	0	0-0	12	15	6	0	2	2-0	7	3.75	97	.341	.380	4-0	.250	0	86	0	0.0
1981	Pit N	2	7	.222	17	13	2	0-0	86.1	92	50	5	3	34-9	46	3.96	91	.273	.345	22-2	.136	-0*	84	-6	-0.7
1982	†Atl N	4	4	.500	16	11	0	0-0	79.1	85	35	4	0	17-3	29	3.06	122	.276	.311	18-5	.167	1	94	4	0.5
1983	Atl N★	15	8	.652	33	33	7-1	0-0	215.1	213	88	20	4	51-5	144	3.43	113	.260	.306	75-7	.160	-1	103	11	1.1
1984	Atl N	14	8	.636	30	30	4-1	0-0	211.2	208	96	26	3	51-5	145	3.74	103	.260	.305	66-6	.076	-2*	99	4	0.4
1985	Atl N	1	13	.071	22	22	0	0-0	95.1	115	72	10	1	57-10	57	6.14	63	.297	.386	25-4	.120	-0	88	-22	-2.9
1987	Mon N	7	0	1.000	10	10	2	0-0	70.1	52	21	5	1	16-1	58	2.30	183	.206	.256	24-1	.042	-2*	120	14	1.2
1988	Mon N	12	8	.600	27	27	4-2	0-0	188	133	59	15	7	44-6	131	2.44	148	.196	**.252**	54-6	.037	-3*	89	23	2.3
1989	Mon N	9	13	.409	33	28	2	0-1	198.1	178	85	15	4	45-13	152	3.31	107	.237	.282	54-9	.204	2*	94	3	0.6
1990	NY A	1	2	.333	3	3	0	0-0	14	8	3	0	0	3-0	12	1.29	310	.163	.212	0-0	—	0	38	4	0.8
1991	NY A	2	4	.333	14	14	0	0-0	73.2	68	26	7	0	24-1	41	3.18	131	.250	.311	0-0	—	0	83	9	0.6
Total	11	67	68	.496	207	193	21-4	0-1	1244.1	1167	541	107	25	344-53	822	3.44	110	.249	.302	342-40	.120	-5	94	44	3.9
PEREZ, YORKIS Yorkis Miguel Vargas (b: Yorkis Miguel Vargas (Perez)) B 9.30.1967 Bajos De Haina, D.R. BL/TL 6/180# d9.30																									
1991	Chi N	1	0	1.000	3	0	0	0-1	4.1	2	1	0	0	2-0	3	2.08	187	.167	.250	0-0	—	0		1	0.2
1994	Fla N	3	0	1.000	44	0	0	0-2	40.2	33	18	4	1	14-3	41	3.54	124	.220	.291	2-0	.000	-0		4	0.2
1995	Fla N	2	6	.250	69	0	0	1-3	46.2	35	29	6	2	28-4	47	5.21	81	.203	.320	2-0	.000	-0		-5	-0.8
1996	Fla N	3	4	.429	64	0	0	0-2	47.2	51	28	2	1	31-4	47	5.29	77	.274	.377	1-0	.000	-0		-5	-0.7
1997	NY N	0	1	.000	9	0	0	0-1	8.2	15	8	2	0	4-0	7	8.31	49	.375	.422	1-0	.000	-0		-4	-0.4
1998	Phi N	0	2	.000	57	0	0	0-0	52	40	23	3	0	25-0	42	3.81	114	.209	.297	2-0	.000	-0		3	0.1
1999	Phi N	3	1	.750	35	0	0	0-1	32	29	15	4	0	15-1	26	3.94	120	.244	.326	2-0	.000	-0		3	0.2
2000	Hou N	2	1	.667	33	0	0	0-2	22.2	25	18	4	0	14-2	21	5.16	94	.266	.355	1-0	.000	-0		-2	-0.3
2002	Bal A	0	0	—	23	0	0	1-0	27.1	21	12	4	0	14-1	25	3.29	130	.198	.292	0-0	—	0		3	0.1
Total	9	14	15	.483	337	0	0	2-12	282	251	152	29	4	147-15	259	4.44	98	.235	.326	11-0	.000	-1		-2	-1.4
PERISHO, MATT Matthew Alan B 6.8.1975 Burlington, IA BL/TL 6/175# d5.27																									
1997	Ana A	0	2	.000	11	8	0	0-0	45	59	34	6	3	28-0	35	6.00	76	.324	.419	1-0	.000	-0	95	-8	-0.4
1998	Tex A	0	2	.000	2	2	0	0-0	5	15	17	2	2	8-0	2	27.00	18	.500	.625	0-0	—	0	135	-12	-1.5
1999	Tex A	0	0	—	4	1	0	0-0	10.1	8	3	0	0	2-1	17	2.61	195	.211	.250	0-0	—	0	0	3	0.1
2000	Tex A	2	7	.222	34	13	0	0-1	105	136	99	20	6	67-3	74	7.37	68	.316	.411	4-0	.000	-0	85	-29	-2.0
2001	Det A	2	3	.400	30	4	0	0-2	39.1	54	29	5	4	14-1	19	5.72	76	.327	.391	0-0	—	0	75	-7	-0.8
2002	Det A	0	0	—	5	0	0	0-0	10.1	16	11	2	0	6-0	3	8.71	49	.372	.440	0-0	—	0		-5	-0.2
Total	6	4	14	.222	86	28	0	0-3	215	288	193	35	15	125-5	150	7.07	67	.324	.412	5-0	.000	-1	87	-58	-4.8
PERKINS, CECIL Cecil Boyce B 12.1.1940 Baltimore, MD BR/TR 6/175# d7.5																									
1967	NY A	0	1	.000	2	1	0	0	5	6	5	1	0	2-0	1	9.00	35	.316	.381	1-0	.000	-0	111	-3	-0.5
PERKINS, CHARLIE Charles Sullivan "Lefty" B 9.9.1905 Ensley, AL D 5.25.1988 Salem, OR BR/TL 6-1/175# d5.1																									
1930	Phi A	0	0	—	8	1	0	0	23.2	25	20	0	0	15	15	6.46	72	.313	.421	8-0	.125	-1	129	-5	-0.3
1934	Bro N	0	3	.000	11	2	0	0	24.1	37	25	3	2	14	5	8.51	46	.336	.421	7-0	.286	0	88	-12	-1.2
Total	2	0	3	.000	19	3	0	0	48	62	45	3	2	29	20	7.50	57	.326	.421	15-0	.200	-1	101	-17	-1.5
PERKINS, DAN Daniel Lee B 3.15.1975 Miami, FL BR/TR 6-2/193# d4.7																									
1999	Min A	1	7	.125	29	12	0	0-0	86.2	117	69	14	5	43-0	44	6.54	78	.326	.401	2-0	.500	0	76	-14	-1.1
PERKOVICH, JOHN John Joseph "Perky" B 3.10.1924 Chicago, IL D 9.16.2000 Little Rock, AR BR/TR 5-11/170# d5.6																									
1950	Chi A	0	0	—	1	0	0	0	5	7	4	3	0	1	3	7.20	62	.318	.348	1-0	.000	-0		-1	-0.1
PERKOWSKI, HARRY Harry Walter B 9.6.1922 Dante, VA BL/TL 6-2.5/196# d9.13																									
1947	Cin N	0	0	—	3	1	0	0	7.1	12	3	1	0	3	2	3.68	111	.375	.429	1-0	.000	0	150	1	0.0
1949	Cin N	1	1	.500	5	3	2	0	23.2	21	14	2	0	14	3	4.56	92	.236	.340	9-0	.333	1	91	-1	-0.1
1950	Cin N	0	0	—	22	0	0	0	34.1	36	21	6	1	23	19	5.24	81	.286	.400	22-0	.318	2*		-3	0.1
1951	Cin N	3	6	.333	35	7	1	1	102	96	42	2	1	46	56	2.82	144	.251	.333	25-3	.040	-3*	53	12	0.7
1952	Cin N	12	10	.545	33	24	11-1	0	194	197	91	9	3	89	86	3.80	99	.265	.347	75-1	.160	-0	119	-2	-0.1
1953	Cin N	12	11	.522	33	25	7-2	2	193	204	107	26	1	62	70	4.52	96	.271	.327	69-0	.203	1	94	-3	-0.1

Year	Tm Lg	W	L	Pct	G	GS	CG-Sho	SV-BS	IP	H	R	HR	HB	BB-IB	SO	ERA	AERA	OAV	OOB	AB-SH	AVG	PB	Sup	APR	PW
1954	Cin N	2	8	.200	28	12	3-1	0	95.2	100	71	16	1	62	32	6.11	69	.276	.379	25-2	.160	0	83	-19	-1.7
1955	Chi N	3	4	.429	25	4	0	2	47.2	53	32	3	0	25-4	28	5.29	77	.283	.366	13-0	.154	-0*	71	-7	-0.9
Total	8	33	40	.452	184	76	24-4	5	697.2	719	381	65	7	324-4	296	4.37	94	.269	.349	239-6	.180	1	95	-22	-2.1
PERLMAN, JON Jonathan Samuel B 12.13.1956 Dallas, TX BL/TR 6-3/185# d9.6																									
1985	Chi N	1	0	1.000	6	0	0	0-0	8.2	10	11	3	0	8-2	4	11.42	35	.313	.439	1-0	.000	-0		-6	-0.6
1987	SF N	0	0	—	10	0	0	0-0	11.1	11	7	1	1	4-0	3	3.97	97	.256	.320	0-0	—	0		-1	-0.1
1988	Cle A	0	2	.000	10	0	0	0-1	19.2	25	12	0	0	11-3	10	5.49	75	.309	.391	0-0	—	0		-2	-0.2
Total	3	1	2	.333	26	0	0	0-1	39.2	46	30	4	1	23-5	17	6.35	63	.295	.383	1-0	.000	-0		-9	-0.9
PERME, LEN Leonard John B 11.25.1917 Cleveland, OH BL/TL 6/170# d9.8 Mil 1943-45																									
1942	Chi A	0	1	.000	4	1	1	0	13	5	2	0	1	4	4	1.38	260	.119	.213	3-0	.333	0	0	3	0.3
1946	Chi A	0	0	—	4	0	0	0	4.1	6	4	0	0	7	2	8.31	41	.316	.500	0-0	—	0		-2	-0.1
Total	2	0	1	.000	8	1	1	0	17.1	11	6	0	1	11	6	3.12	114	.180	.315	3-0	.333	0	0	1	0.2
PERNOLL, HUB Henry Hubbard B 3.14.1888 Grants Pass, OR D 2.18.1944 Grants Pass, OR BR/TL 5-8/175# d4.25																									
1910	Det A	4	3	.571	11	5	4	0	54.2	54	20	1	5	14	25	2.96	89	.270	.333	16-1	.063	-2	122	0	-0.1
1912	Det A	0	0	—	3	0	0	0	9	9	6	0	0	4	3	6.00	54	.265	.342	3-0	.000	-0		-2	-0.1
Total	2	4	3	.571	14	5	4	0	63.2	63	26	1	5	18	28	3.39	80	.269	.335	19-1	.053	-2	122	-2	-0.2
PERRANOSKI, RON Ronald Peter (b: Ronald Peter Perzanowski) B 4.1.1936 Paterson, NJ BL/TL 6/192# d4.14 C17																									
1961	LA N	7	5	.583	53	1	0	6	91.2	82	31	5	4	41-7	56	2.65	164	.244	.330	12-0	.083	-0	245	16	2.1
1962	LA N	6	6	.500	**70**	0	0	20	107.1	103	40	1	0	36-9	68	2.85	127	.255	.314	14-1	.071	-1		10	1.3
1963	†LA N	16	3	**.842**	**69**	0	0	21	129	112	30	7	4	43-14	75	1.67	180	.231	.298	24-2	.125	0		**20**	3.9
1964	LA N	5	7	.417	72	0	0	14	125.1	128	62	5	1	46-19	79	3.09	105	.263	.325	19-3	.105	-0		-3	-0.3
1965	†LA N	6	6	.500	59	0	0	17	104.2	85	28	2	3	40-7	53	2.24	146	.226	.303	19-0	.158	1		14	2.1
1966	†LA N	6	7	.462	55	0	0	7	82	82	32	4	1	31-11	50	3.18	104	.269	.337	8-1	.250	1		2	0.6
1967	LA N	6	7	.462	**70**	0	0	16	110	97	36	4	3	45-13	75	2.45	126	.240	.318	10-0	.100	-0		8	1.2
1968	Min A	8	7	.533	66	0	0	6	87	86	36	5	0	38-12	65	3.10	100	.252	.325	7-0	.000	-1		0	-0.1
1969	†Min A	9	10	.474	75	0	0	**31-11**	119.2	85	32	4	1	52-16	62	2.11	174	.205	.292	24-4	.083	-1		20	**4.4**
1970	†Min A	7	8	.467	67	0	0	**34-11**	111	108	38	7	1	42-7	55	2.43	153	.259	.325	24-1	.042	-2		15	2.5
1971	Min A	1	4	.200	36	0	0	5-6	42.2	60	39	2	3	28-4	21	6.75	53	.337	.431	3-1	.000	-0		-16	-2.3
	Det A	0	1	.000	11	0	0	2-1	18	16	9	2	1	3-1	8	2.50	144	.254	.290	2-0	.000	-0		1	0.0
	Year	1	5	.167	47	0	0	7-7	60.2	76	60	4	4	31-5	29	5.49	65	.315	.396	5-1	.000	-1		-16	-2.3
1972	Det A	0	1	.000	17	0	0	0-0	18.2	23	16	2	1	8-1	10	7.71	41	.307	.381	1-0	.000	-1		-8	-0.5
	LA N	2	0	1.000	9	0	0	0-0	16.2	19	8	0	0	8-0	5	2.70	124	.292	.365	0-0	—	0		0	0.0
1973	Cal A	0	2	.000	8	0	0	0-0	11	11	5	0	1	7-0	5	4.09	87	.282	.404	0-0	—	0		0	0.0
Total	13	79	74	.516	737	1	0	179-29	1174.2	1097	442	50	24	468-121	687	2.79	123	.250	.323	167-13	.096	-4	245	79	14.9
PERRIN, BILL William Joseph "Lefty" B 6.23.1910 New Orleans, LA D 6.30.1974 New Orleans, LA BR/TL 5-11/172# d9.30																									
1934	Cle A	0	1	.000	1	1	0	0	5	13	9	0	1	2	3	14.40	32	.520	.571	2-0	.000	-0	96	-5	-0.6
PERRITT, POL William Dayton B 8.30.1892 Arcadia, LA D 10.15.1947 Shreveport, LA BR/TR 6-2/168# d9.7																									
1912	StL N	1	1	.500	6	3	1	0	31	25	16	0	0	10	13	3.19	107	.243	.310	9-0	.222	-0	71	1	0.0
1913	StL N	6	14	.300	36	21	8	0	175	205	123	9	8	64	64	5.25	62	.300	.367	59-1	.203	-1	82	-40	-4.0
1914	StL N	16	13	.552	41	32	18-3	2	286	248	106	7	15	93	115	2.36	118	.245	.318	92-7	.141	-2	100	14	1.0
1915	NY N	12	18	.400	35	29	16-4	0	220	226	95	6	12	59	91	2.66	96	.266	.323	68-2	.162	-1	86	-7	-1.3
1916	NY N	18	11	.621	40	29	17-5	2	251	243	82	11	7	56	115	2.62	93	.257	.304	83-5	.084	-4	133	-2	-0.8
1917	†NY N	17	7	.708	35	26	14-5	1	215	186	61	3	7	45	72	1.88	135	.237	.284	70-2	.157	-2	131	15	1.5
1918	NY N	18	13	.581	35	31	19-6	0	233	212	82	5	1	38	60	2.74	96	.246	.278	80-5	.175	-1*	92	0	-0.3
1919	NY N	1	1	.500	11	3	0	1	19	27	18	0	2	12	2	7.11	39	.386	.488	4-0	.000	-1	113	-9	-1.1
1920	NY N	0	0	—	8	0	0	2	15	9	3	0	0	4	3	1.80	167	.167	.224	4-0	.000	-1		2	0.1
1921	NY N	2	0	1.000	5	1	0	0	11.2	17	9	0	0	2	5	3.86	95	.321	.345	3-0	.000	-0	112	-2	-0.3
	Det A	1	0	1.000	4	2	0	0	13	18	9	0	1	7	3	4.85	88	.383	.473	5-0	.400	0	137	-1	0.0
Total	10	92	78	.541	256	177	93-23	8	1469.2	1416	604	41	53	390	543	2.89	94	.259	.315	477-22	.151	-13	103	-29	-5.2
PERRY, GAYLORD Gaylord Jackson B 9.15.1938 Williamston, NC BR/TR 6-4/215# d4.14 HF1991 b-Jim																									
1962	SF N	3	1	.750	13	7	1	0	43	54	29	3	0	14-2	20	5.23	73	.310	.354	13-2	.231	0	158	-8	-0.6
1963	SF N	1	6	.143	31	4	0	2	76	84	41	10	2	29-7	52	4.03	79	.279	.345	18-0	.222	1*	121	-8	-0.7
1964	SF N	12	11	.522	44	19	5-2	5	206.1	179	65	16	5	43-6	155	2.75	130	.232	.275	56-7	.054	-3*	82	21	2.0
1965	SF N	8	12	.400	47	26	6	1	195.2	194	105	21	6	70-16	170	4.19	86	.256	.322	64-5	.156	-0*	96	-13	-1.1
1966	SF N★	21	8	.724	36	35	13-3	0	255.2	242	92	15	5	40-3	201	2.99	123	.247	.279	86-6	.186	-0	105	22	2.5
1967	SF N	15	17	.469	39	37	18-3	1	293	231	98	20	4	84-17	230	2.61	126	.214	.273	91-15	.143	-1*	90	23	2.6
1968	SF N	16	15	.516	39	38	19-3	1	291	240	93	10	4	59-12	173	2.44	120	.222	.264	97-8	.113	-3	92	17	1.8
1969	SF N	19	14	.576	40	39	26-3	0-1	**325.1**	290	115	23	11	91-14	233	2.49	141	.237	.295	117-7	.120	-2	102	34	3.4
1970	SF N★	**23**	13	.639	41	**41**	23-**5**	0-0	**328.2**	292	138	27	8	84-8	214	3.20	124	.237	.289	120-10	.117	-4	111	26	2.6
1971	†SF N	16	12	.571	37	37	14-2	0-0	280	255	116	20	5	67-4	158	2.76	123	.242	.287	98-10	.102	-3*	111	15	1.1
1972	Cle A★	**24**	16	.600	41	40	**29**-5	1-0	342.2	253	79	17	12	82-16	234	1.92	168	.205	.261	110-14	.155	0	80	**49**	**6.7**
1973	Cle A	19	19	.500	41	41	**29**-7	0-0	344	315	143	34	5	115-9	238	3.38	116	.246	.310	0-0	—	0	91	20	2.2
1974	Cle A★	21	13	.618	37	37	28-4	0-0	322.1	230	98	25	6	99-7	216	2.51	**144**	.204	.270	0-0	—	0	102	**41**	4.5
1975	Cle A	6	9	.400	15	15	10-1	0-0	121.2	120	57	16	1	34-5	85	3.55	107	.256	.308	0-0	—	0	68	2	0.3
	Tex A	12	8	.600	22	22	15-4	0-0	184	157	70	12	3	36-1	148	3.03	124	.227	.267	0-0	—	0	107	16	1.6
	Year	18	17	.514	37	37	25-5	0-0	305.2	277	75	28	4	70-6	233	3.24	117	.239	.284	0-0	—	0	91	18	1.9
1976	Tex A	15	14	.517	32	32	21-2	0-0	250.1	232	93	14	0	52-3	143	3.24	111	.247	.285	0-0	—	0	94	14	1.4
1977	Tex A	15	12	.556	34	34	13-4	0-0	238	239	108	21	5	56-4	177	3.37	122	.262	.307	0-0	—	0	86	16	1.6
1978	SD N	**21**	6	**.778**	37	37	5-2	0-0	260.2	241	96	9	2	66-8	154	2.73	122	.248	.295	87-13	.092	-3	120	16	1.3
1979	SD N★	12	11	.522	32	32	10	0-0	232.2	225	90	12	4	67-10	140	3.06	116	.257	.312	71-11	.085	-2	81	13	1.1
1980	Tex A	6	9	.400	24	24	6-2	0-0	155	159	74	12	7	46-3	107	3.43	114	.268	.327	0-0	—	0	99	6	0.6
	NY A	4	4	.500	10	8	0	0-0	50.2	65	33	2	1	18-0	28	4.44	89	.320	.372	0-0	—	0	91	-5	-0.7
	Year	10	13	.435	34	32	6-2	0-0	205.2	224	37	14	8	64-3	135	3.68	106	.281	.338	0-0	—	0	97	1	-0.1
1981	Atl N	8	9	.471	23	23	3	0-0	150.2	182	70	9	4	24-1	60	3.94	91	.304	.332	48-5	.250	3*	107	-4	-0.2
1982	Sea A	10	12	.455	32	32	6	0-0	216.2	245	117	27	4	54-4	116	4.40	97	.287	.331	0-0	—	0	86	-3	-0.3
1983	Sea A	3	10	.231	16	16	2	0-0	102	116	60	18	3	23-3	42	4.94	86	.286	.327	0-0	—	0	60	-6	-0.7
	KC A	4	4	.500	14	14	1-1	0-0	84.1	98	48	6	1	26-1	40	4.27	96	.292	.342	0-0	—	0	81	-3	-0.2
	Year	7	14	.333	30	30	3-1	0-0	186.1	214	52	24	4	49-4	82	4.64	90	.289	.334	0-0	—	0	69	-9	-0.9
Total	22	314	265	.542	777	690	303-53	11-1	5350.1	4938	2128	399	108	1379-164	3534	3.11	117	.245	.296	1076-113	.131	-16	96	301	32.8
PERRY, SCOTT Herbert Scott B 4.17.1891 Denison, TX D 10.27.1959 Kansas City, MO BR/TR 6/175# d5.13																									
1915	StL A	0	0	—	1	1	0	0	2	5	3	0	1	1	0	13.50	21	.455	.538	0-0	—	0	153	-2	-0.1
1916	Chi N	2	1	.667	4	3	2-1	0	28.1	30	9	0	0	3	10	2.54	115	.291	.311	11-0	.273	1	68	2	0.3
1917	Cin N	0	0	—	4	1	0	0	13.1	17	15	0	1	8	4	6.75	39	.321	.419	5-0	.000	-1	288	-7	-0.4
1918	Phi A	20	19	.513	44	**36**	**30**-3	2	**332.1**	295	97	1	2	111	81	1.98	148	.247	.312	112-6	.134	-6	73	32	3.5
1919	Phi A	4	17	.190	25	21	12	1	183.2	193	92	4	2	72	38	3.58	96	.282	.352	59-5	.136	-3	78	-3	-0.2
1920	Phi A	11	25	.306	42	34	20-1	1	263.2	310	151	14	7	65	79	3.62	111	.300	.345	83-5	.157	-4	67	10	0.8
1921	Phi A	3	6	.333	12	8	5	1	70	77	36	4	1	24	19	4.11	108	.288	.349	26-0	.038	-4	75	4	0.1
Total	7	40	68	.370	132	104	69-5	5	893.1	927	403	23	14	284	231	3.07	113	.277	.336	296-16	.135	-17	75	36	4.0
PERRY, JIM James Evan B 10.30.1935 Williamston, NC BB/TR 6-4/200# d4.23 b-Gaylord																									
1959	Cle A	12	10	.545	44	13	8-2	4	153	122	54	10	2	55-7	79	2.65	139	.225	.295	50-1	.300	3	109	17	2.7
1960	Cle A	**18**	10	**.643**	41	**36**	10-**4**	1	261.1	257	118	35	4	91-3	120	3.62	103	.260	.321	91-5	.242	3*	97	4	0.7
1961	Cle A☆	10	17	.370	35	35	6-1	0	223.2	238	132	28	6	87-5	90	4.71	84	.273	.341	73-5	.164	-1	87	-19	-2.1
1962	Cle A	12	12	.500	35	27	7-3	0	193.2	213	94	21	2	59-1	74	4.14	94	.285	.337	60-7	.183	0	100	-3	-0.3
1963	Cle A	0	0	—	5	0	0	0	10.1	12	6	0	0	2-0	7	5.23	69	.293	.326	2-0	.000	-0		-1	-0.1

Year	Tm Lg	W	L	Pct	G	GS	CG-Sho	SV-BS	IP	H	R	HR	HB	BB-IB	SO	ERA	AERA	OAV	OOB	AB-SH	AVG	PB	Sup	APR	PW
	Min A	9	9	.500	35	25	5-1	1	168.1	167	77	17	2	57-4	65	3.74	97	.256	.315	51-1	.216	3	101	-1	0.2
	Year	9	9	.500	40	25	5-1	1	178.2	179	81	17	2	59-4	72	3.83	95	.258	.316	53-1	.208	3	101	-2	0.1
1964	Min A	6	3	.667	42	1	0	2	65.1	61	26	7	1	23-4	55	3.44	104	.245	.309	13-0	.154	-0	174	2	0.3
1965	†Min A	12	7	.632	36	19	4-2	0	167.2	142	57	18	3	47-2	88	2.63	135	.232	.286	53-4	.170	1	96	17	1.9
1966	Min A	11	7	.611	33	25	8-1	0	184.1	149	61	17	5	53-4	122	2.54	142	.222	.281	59-2	.220	4	106	20	2.4
1967	Min A	8	7	.533	37	11	3-2	0	130.2	123	51	8	3	50-5	94	3.03	114	.255	.325	42-0	.190	1*	98	6	0.7
1968	Min A	8	6	.571	32	18	3-2	1	139	113	37	8	5	26-2	69	2.27	136	.219	.262	42-4	.143	2	96	14	1.8
1969	†Min A	20	6	.769	46	36	12-3	0-0	261.2	244	87	18	9	66-10	153	2.82	130	.247	.298	93-3	.172	1*	127	27	2.6
1970	†Min A★	**24**	12	.667	40	**40**	13-4	0-0	278.2	258	112	20	9	57-10	168	3.04	123	.243	.286	97-10	.247	5*	106	20	3.1
1971	Min A☆	17	17	.500	40	39	8	1-0	270	263	135	39	5	102-10	126	4.23	84	.259	.326	92-4	.185	1	109	-17	-1.9
1972	Min A	13	16	.448	35	35	5-2	0-0	217.2	191	93	14	8	60-5	85	3.35	96	.236	.292	71-5	.155	-1	88	-1	-0.3
1973	Det A	14	13	.519	35	34	7-1	0-0	203	225	96	22	4	55-5	66	4.03	101	.282	.329	0-0	—	0	88	2	0.2
1974	Cle A	17	12	.586	36	36	8-3	0-0	252	242	94	11	5	64-10	71	2.96	122	.254	.303	0-0	—	0	96	18	2.0
1975	Cle A	1	6	.143	8	6	0	0-0	37.2	46	34	8	0	18-5	11	6.69	57	.309	.383	0-0	—	0	70	-13	-1.9
	Oak A	3	4	.429	15	11	2-1	0-1	67.2	61	43	7	7	26-1	33	4.66	78	.237	.319	0-0	—	0	90	-9	-0.9
	Year	4	10	.286	23	17	2-1	0-1	105.1	107	47	15	7	44-6	44	5.38	69	.264	.342	0-0	—	0	83	-22	-2.8
Total	17	215	174	.553	630	447	109-32	10-1	3285.2	3127	1407	308	80	998-93	1576	3.45	106	.252	.309	889-51	.199	23	100	83	11.1
PERRY, PAT William Patrick B 2.4.1959 Taylorville, IL BL/TL 6-1/170# d9.12																									
1985	StL N	1	0	1.000	6	0	0	0-0	12.1	3	0	0	0	3-1	6	0.00	—	.077	.143	2-0	.500	0		5	0.4
1986	StL N	2	3	.400	46	0	0	2-0	68.2	59	31	5	0	34-9	29	3.80	96	.239	.323	8-0	.000	-1		-1	-0.1
1987	StL N	4	2	.667	45	0	0	1-1	65.2	54	34	7	2	21-3	33	4.39	95	.222	.288	7-0	.143	-0		-1	-0.1
	Cin N	1	0	1.000	12	0	0	1-1	15.1	6	0	0	1	4-1	6	0.00	—	.122	.204	0-0	—	0		7	0.5
	Year	5	2	.714	57	0	0	2-2	81	60	38	7	3	25-4	39	3.56	117	.205	.274	7-0	.143	-0		6	0.4
1988	Cin N	2	2	.500	12	0	0	0-0	20.2	21	17	4	0	9-4	11	5.66	63	.262	.326	2-0	.000	-0		-6	-1.1
	Chi N	2	2	.500	35	0	0	1-3	38	40	15	5	1	7-0	24	3.32	109	.270	.304	1-0	1.000	1		1	0.3
	Year	4	4	.500	47	0	0	1-3	58.2	61	32	9	1	16-4	35	4.14	87	.268	.312	3-0	.333	1		-4	-0.8
1989	Chi N	0	1	.000	19	0	0	1-0	35.2	23	8	2	0	16-3	20	1.77	213	.187	.279	6-0	.167	-0		7	0.4
1990	LA N	0	0	—	7	0	0	0-0	6.2	9	7	0	1	5-1	2	8.10	45	.310	.417	1-0	.000	-0		-3	-0.2
Total	6	12	10	.545	182	0	0	6-5	263	215	112	23	5	99-22	131	3.46	110	.224	.296	27-0	.148	0		9	0.1
PERRYMAN, PARSON Emmett Key B 10.24.1888 Everett Springs, GA D 9.12.1966 Starke, FL BR/TR 6-4.5/193# d4.14																									
1915	StL A	2	4	.333	24	3	0	0	50.1	52	27	2	1	16	19	3.93	73	.281	.342	6-0	.000	-1	102	-5	-0.6
PERSON, ROBERT Robert Alan B 10.6.1969 Lowell, MA BR/TR 5-11/180# d9.18																									
1995	NY N	1	0	1.000	3	1	0	0-0	12	5	1	1	0	2-0	10	0.75	540	.119	.159	3-0	.667	1	112	5	0.4
1996	NY N	4	5	.444	27	13	0	0-0	89.2	86	50	16	2	35-3	76	4.52	89	.247	.316	21-5	.143	-0*	102	-4	-0.5
1997	Tor A	5	10	.333	23	22	0	0-0	128.1	125	86	19	5	60-2	99	5.61	82	.255	.338	4-0	.000	-0	72	-13	-1.4
1998	Tor A	3	1	.750	27	0	0	6-2	38.1	45	31	9	2	22-1	31	7.04	66	.294	.379	0-0	—	0		-9	-1.1
1999	Tor A	0	2	.000	11	0	0	2-0	11	9	12	1	4	15-1	12	9.82	50	.231	.467	0-0	—	0		-5	-0.9
	Phi N	10	5	.667	31	22	0	0-0	137	130	72	23	2	70-1	127	4.27	111	.252	.341	41-4	.073	-2	118	6	0.3
2000	Phi N	9	7	.563	28	28	1-1	0-0	173.1	144	73	13	6	95-1	164	3.63	128	.229	.332	53-8	.132	-0	89	21	1.6
2001	Phi N	15	7	.682	33	33	3-1	0-0	208.1	179	103	34	8	80-3	183	4.19	101	.234	.311	67-5	.119	1	99	2	0.2
2002	Phi N	4	5	.444	16	16	0	0-0	87.2	79	58	13	5	51-0	61	5.44	72	.241	.350	24-3	.083	1*	121	-16	-1.4
2003	Bos A	0	0	—	7	0	0	1-0	11.2	11	10	0	1	8-0	10	7.71	59	.250	.364	1-0	.000	-0		-4	-0.2
Total	9	51	42	.548	206	135	4-2	9-2	897.1	813	496	129	35	438-12	773	4.64	95	.242	.332	214-25	.117	-0	98	-17	-3.0
PERTICA, BILL William Andrew B 8.17.1898 Santa Barbara, CA D 12.28.1967 Los Angeles, CA BR/TR 5-9/165# d8.7																									
1918	Bos A	0	0	—	1	0	0	0	3	3	1	0	0	0	1	3.00	89	.273	.273	1-0	.000	-0		0	0.0
1921	StL N	14	10	.583	38	31	15-2	2	208.1	212	104	9	10	70	67	3.37	109	.267	.334	70-5	.143	-3	110	4	-0.1
1922	StL N	8	8	.500	34	15	2	0	117.1	153	94	5	3	65	30	5.91	65	.333	.419	33-0	.182	-0*	121	-28	-3.1
1923	StL N	0	0	—	1	1	0	0	2.1	2	2	0	1	3	0	3.86	101	.250	.500	1-0	.000	-0	42	0	0.0
Total	4	22	18	.550	74	47	17-2	2	331	370	201	14	14	138	98	4.27	87	.291	.367	105-5	.152	-4	112	-24	-3.2
PERZANOWSKI, STAN Stanley B 8.25.1950 East Chicago, IN BB/TR 6-2/170# d6.20																									
1971	Chi A	0	1	.000	5	0	0	1-0	6	14	10	1	0	3-0	5	12.00	30	.412	.447	2-0	.000	-0		-6	-1.0
1974	Chi A	0	0	—	2	1	0	0-0	2.1	8	7	1	0	2-0	2	19.29	19	.533	.588	0-0	—	0	94	-5	-0.2
1975	Tex A	3	3	.500	12	8	1	0-0	66	59	25	1	5	25-2	26	3.00	126	.246	.327	0-0	—	0	70	6	0.6
1976	Tex A	0	0	—	5	0	0	0-0	11.2	20	15	3	2	4-0	6	10.03	36	.385	.448	0-0	—	0		-8	-0.4
1978	Min A	2	7	.222	13	7	1	1-0	56.2	59	37	1	4	26-0	31	5.24	73	.276	.362	0-0	—	0	114	-9	-1.2
Total	5	5	11	.313	37	16	2	2-0	142.2	160	94	7	11	60-2	70	5.11	74	.288	.366	2-0	.000	-0	91	-22	-2.2
PETEREK, JEFF Jeffrey Allen B 9.22.1963 Michigan City, IN BR/TR 6-2/195# d8.14																									
1989	Mil A	0	2	.000	7	4	0	0-0	31.1	31	14	3	0	14-1	16	4.02	96	.252	.328	0-0	—	0	59	0	0.0
PETERS, CHRIS Christopher Michael B 1.28.1972 Fort Thomas, KY BL/TL 6-1/170# d7.19																									
1996	Pit N	2	4	.333	16	10	0	0-0	64	72	43	9	1	25-0	28	5.63	78	.287	.350	19-1	.211	0	70	-8	-0.6
1997	Pit N	2	2	.500	31	1	0	0-1	37.1	38	23	6	3	21-4	17	4.58	94	.277	.383	4-0	.250	0	86	-2	-0.2
1998	Pit N	8	10	.444	39	21	1	1-0	148	142	63	13	3	55-4	103	3.47	124	.252	.319	39-4	.231	1	105	14	1.7
1999	Pit N	5	4	.556	19	11	0	0-0	71	98	59	17	4	27-0	46	6.59	69	.322	.381	22-1	.273	2	117	-16	-1.4
2000	Pit N	0	1	.000	18	0	0	1-0	28.1	23	9	2	1	14-2	16	2.86	161	.221	.319	6-0	.167	-0		6	0.3
2001	Mon N	2	4	.333	13	6	0	0-1	31	47	26	7	2	15-1	14	7.55	59	.367	.435	11-0	.091	-1	90	-9	-1.5
Total	6	19	25	.432	136	49	1	2-2	379.2	420	223	54	14	157-11	224	4.81	91	.282	.353	101-6	.218	2	98	-15	-1.7
PETERS, GARY Gary Charles B 4.21.1937 Grove City, PA BL/TL 6-2/200# d9.10																									
1959	Chi A	0	0	—	2	0	0	0	1	2	0	0	0	2-0	1	0.00	—	.400	.571	0-0	—	0		0	0.0
1960	Chi A	0	0	—	2	0	0	0	3.1	4	1	0	0	1-0	4	2.70	140	.286	.333	0-0	—	0		0	0.0
1961	Chi A	0	0	—	3	0	0	1	10.1	10	2	0	0	2-0	6	1.74	225	.270	.308	3-0	.333	0		3	0.2
1962	Chi A	0	1	.000	5	0	0	0	6.1	8	5	0	1	1-0	4	5.68	69	.308	.345	0-0	—	0		-2	-0.2
1963	Chi A	19	8	.704	41	30	13-4	1	243	192	69	9	8	68-2	189	**2.33**	**150**	.216	.277	81-2	.259	9*	96	**34**	4.8
1964	Chi A☆	**20**	8	.714	37	36	11-3	0	273.2	217	89	20	7	104-9	205	2.50	138	.219	.296	120-3	.208	8*	109	29	3.9
1965	Chi A	10	12	.455	33	30	1	0	176.1	181	76	19	4	63-8	95	3.62	88	.265	.329	72-0	.181	2*	98	-7	-0.6
1966	Chi A	12	10	.545	30	27	11-4	0	204.2	156	54	11	3	45-6	129	**1.98**	**160**	.212	**.260**	81-3	.235	6*	102	**29**	**4.0**
1967	Chi A★	16	11	.593	38	36	11-3	0	260	187	81	15	11	91-8	215	2.28	136	**.199**	.276	99-4	.212	7*	109	24	3.6
1968	Chi A	4	13	.235	31	25	6-1	1	162.2	146	79	7	7	60-6	110	3.76	80	.242	.315	72-0	.208	7*	93	-13	-0.6
1969	Chi A	10	15	.400	36	32	7-3	0-0	218.2	238	118	21	5	78-1	140	4.53	85	.283	.344	71-6	.169	2*	105	-15	-1.4
1970	Bos A	16	11	.593	34	34	10-4	0-0	221.2	221	114	20	7	83-2	155	4.06	98	.257	.325	82-2	.244	6*	123	-2	0.4
1971	Bos A	14	11	.560	34	32	9-1	1-0	214	241	111	25	6	70-3	100	4.37	85	.288	.346	96-5	.271	8*	113	-14	-0.8
1972	Bos A	3	3	.500	33	4	0	1-1	85.1	91	48	10	3	38-8	67	4.32	75	.279	.356	30-0	.200	1	130	-10	-0.7
Total	14	124	103	.546	359	286	79-23	5-1	2081	1894	847	157	62	706-53	1420	3.25	106	.243	.309	807-25	.222	57	107	56	12.6
PETERS, RUBE Oscar Casper B 3.15.1885 Grantfork, IL D 2.7.1965 Pequannock, NJ BR/TR 6-1/195# d4.13																									
1912	Chi A	5	6	.455	28	11	4	0	108.2	134	73	2	6	33	39	4.14	77	.309	.366	31-2	.194	-1	86	-14	-1.1
1914	Bro F	2	2	.500	11	3	1	0	37.2	52	27	1	0	16	13	3.82	75	.335	.398	11-1	.091	-1	151	-6	-0.7
Total	2	7	8	.467	39	14	5	0	146.1	186	100	3	6	49	52	4.06	77	.316	.374	42-3	.167	-1	100	-20	-1.8
PETERS, RAY Raymond James B 8.27.1946 Buffalo, NY BR/TR 6-5.5/210# d6.4																									
1970	Mil A	0	2	.000	2	2	0	0-0	2	7	7	0	0	5-0	1	31.50	12	.583	.667	0-0	—	0	82	-6	-0.9
PETERS, STEVE Steven Bradley B 11.14.1962 Oklahoma City, OK BL/TL 5-10/170# d8.11																									
1987	StL N	0	0	—	12	0	0	1-0	15	17	3	1	0	6-1	11	1.80	231	.298	.365	2-0	.000	-0		4	0.2
1988	StL N	3	3	.500	44	0	0	0-1	45	57	34	8	0	22-7	30	6.40	54	.313	.382	3-0	.000	0		-14	-1.8
Total	2	3	3	.500	56	0	0	1-1	60	74	37	9	0	28-8	41	5.25	70	.310	.378	5-0	.000	-1		-10	-1.6

Year	Tm Lg	W	L	Pct	G	GS	CG-Sho	SV-BS	IP	H	R	HR	HB	BB-IB	SO	ERA	AERA	OAV	OOB	AB-SH	AVG	PB	Sup	APR	PW
PETERSON, ADAM Adam Charles B 12.11.1965 Long Beach, CA BR/TR 6-3/190# d9.19																									
1987	Chi A	0	0	—	1	1	0	0-0	4	8	6	1	0	3-0	1	13.50	34	.444	.500	0-0	—	0	199	-4	-0.2
1988	Chi A	0	1	.000	2	2	0	0-0	6	6	9	0	0	6-1	5	13.50	29	.240	.387	0-0	—	0	92	-6	-0.7
1989	Chi A	0	1	.000	3	2	0	0-0	5.1	13	9	1	0	2-0	3	15.19	25	.464	.500	0-0	—	0	166	-6	-0.9
1990	Chi A	2	5	.286	20	11	2	0-0	85	90	46	12	2	26-0	29	4.55	84	.278	.332	0-0	—	0	108	-7	-0.6
1991	SD N	3	4	.429	13	11	0	0-0	54.2	50	33	10	0	28-2	37	4.45	86	.242	.329	13-1	.000	-1	90	-5	-0.7
Total	5	5	11	.313	39	27	2	0-0	155	167	103	24	2	65-3	75	5.46	71	.277	.347	13-1	.000	-1	108	-28	-3.1
PETERSON, FRITZ Fritz Fred (b: Fred Ingels Peterson) B 2.8.1942 Chicago, IL BB/TL 6/200# d4.15																									
1966	NY A	12	11	.522	34	32	11-2	0	215	196	89	15	3	40-6	96	3.31	101	.241	.277	67-8	.224	4	110	1	0.6
1967	NY A	8	14	.364	36	30	6-1	0	181.1	179	88	11	3	43-9	102	3.47	90	.256	.301	48-3	.146	1	78	-10	-1.0
1968	NY A	12	11	.522	36	27	6-2	0	212.1	187	72	13	4	29-9	115	2.63	110	.241	.270	63-5	.079	-2	100	7	0.8
1969	NY A	17	16	.515	37	37	16-4	0-0	272	228	95	15	3	43-11	150	2.55	137	.229	.261	80-7	.112	-0	75	26	3.3
1970	NY A★	20	11	.645	39	37	8-2	0-0	260.1	247	102	24	3	40-6	127	2.90	121	.248	**.279**	90-7	.222	5	112	16	2.6
1971	NY A	15	13	.536	37	35	16-4	1-0	274	269	106	25	4	42-7	139	3.05	106	.258	.287	85-14	.082	-3	103	6	0.4
1972	NY A	17	15	.531	35	35	12-3	0-0	250.1	270	98	17	5	44-5	100	3.24	91	.276	.309	82-15	.232	4	122	-6	-0.3
1973	NY A	8	15	.348	31	31	6	0-0	184.1	207	93	18	7	49-10	59	3.95	93	.286	.336	0-0	—	0	74	-6	-0.7
1974	NY A	0	0	—	3	1	0	0-0	7.2	13	4	1	0	2-1	5	4.70	75	.361	.395	0-0	—	0	150	-1	0.0
	Cle A	9	14	.391	29	29	3	0-0	152.2	187	89	16	4	37-7	52	4.36	83	.305	.346	0-0	—	0	97	-15	-2.0
	Year	9	14	.391	32	30	3	0-0	160.1	200	93	17	4	39-8	57	4.38	83	.308	.349	0-0	—	0	99	-18	-2.0
1975	Cle A	14	8	.636	25	25	6-2	0-0	146.1	154	73	15	6	40-4	47	3.94	96	.275	.330	0-0	—	0	124	-2	-0.3
1976	Cle A	0	3	.000	9	9	0	0-0	47	59	31	3	0	10-0	19	5.55	63	.309	.342	0-0	—	0	129	-10	-0.6
	Tex A	1	0	1.000	4	2	0	0-1	15	21	7	0	0	7-0	4	3.60	100	.344	.412	0-0	—	0	122	0	0.0
	Year	1	3	.250	13	11	0	0-1	62	80	12	3	0	17-0	23	5.08	69	.317	.359	0-0	—	0	127	-10	-0.6
Total	11	133	131	.504	355	330	90-20	1-1	2218.1	2217	947	173	42	426-75	1015	3.30	101	.261	.298	515-59	.159	8	101	6	2.8
PETERSON, JIM James Niels B 8.18.1908 Philadelphia, PA D 4.8.1975 Palm Beach, FL BR/TR 6-0.5/200# d7.9																									
1931	Phi A	0	1	.000	6	1	1	0	13	18	10	0	0	4	7	6.23	72	.321	.367	2-0	.500	1	94	-2	-0.1
1933	Phi A	2	5	.286	32	5	0	0	90.2	114	64	6	0	36	18	4.96	86	.305	.366	27-0	.148	-1	115	-9	-0.5
1937	Bro N	0	0	—	3	0	0	0	5.2	8	5	3	0	2	4	7.94	51	.333	.385	0-0	—	0		-2	-0.1
Total	3	2	6	.250	41	6	1	0	109.1	140	79	9	0	42	29	5.27	82	.308	.367	29-0	.172	0	112	-13	-0.7
PETERSON, KENT Kent Franklin "Pete" B 12.21.1925 Goshen, UT D 4.27.1995 Highland, UT BR/TL 5-10/175# d7.15 Mil 1945-46																									
1944	Cin N	0	0	—	1	0	0	0	1	0	0	0	0	0	0	0.00	—	.000	.000	0-0	—	0		0	0.0
1947	Cin N	6	13	.316	37	17	3-1	2	152.1	156	74	8	3	62	78	4.25	96	.265	.338	44-4	.068	-3	62	1	-0.4
1948	Cin N	2	15	.118	43	17	2	1	137	146	82	10	6	59	64	4.60	85	.271	.350	36-2	.139	-2	67	-12	-1.5
1949	Cin N	4	5	.444	30	7	2	0	66.1	66	54	8	4	46	28	6.24	67	.261	.383	18-2	.056	-2	78	-15	-2.0
1950	Cin N	0	3	.000	9	2	0	0	20	25	20	4	0	17	6	7.20	59	.305	.424	3-1	.333	0	42	-7	-0.9
1951	Cin N	1	1	.500	9	0	0	0	9.2	13	8	0	1	8	5	6.52	63	.317	.440	1-0	.000	-0		-2	-0.5
1952	Phi N	0	0	—	3	0	0	2	7	2	0	0	0	2	7	0.00	—	.091	.167	1-0	.000	-0		3	0.2
1953	Phi N	0	1	.000	15	0	0	0	27	26	20	3	1	21	20	6.67	63	.252	.384	7-0	.000	-1		-6	-0.4
Total	8	13	38	.255	147	43	7-1	5	420.1	434	258	33	15	215	208	4.95	82	.266	.357	110-9	.091	-8	65	-38	-5.5
PETERSON, KYLE Kyle Johnathan B 4.9.1976 Elkhorn, NE BL/TR 6-3/215# d7.19																									
1999	Mil N	4	7	.364	17	12	0	0-1	77	87	46	3	4	25-2	34	4.56	100	.285	.344	22-2	.136	-0	91	-2	-0.3
2001	Mil N	1	2	.333	3	2	0	0-0	14.2	19	10	3	0	4-2	12	5.52	78	.302	.343	5-0	.200	0	86	-2	-0.3
Total	2	5	9	.357	20	14	0	0-1	91.2	106	56	6	4	29-4	46	4.71	95	.288	.344	27-2	.148	-0	91	-4	-0.6
PETERSON, SID Sidney Herbert B 1.31.1918 Havelock, ND D 8.29.2001 Wichita Falls, TX BR/TR 6-3/220# d5.4																									
1943	StL A	2	0	1.000	3	0	0	0	10	15	3	0	1	3	0	2.70	123	.341	.396	2-0	.000	-0		1	0.1
PETKOVSEK, MARK Mark Joseph B 11.18.1965 Beaumont, TX BR/TR 6/185# d6.8																									
1991	Tex A	0	1	.000	4	1	0	0-0	9.1	21	16	4	0	4-0	6	14.46	28	.438	.472	0-0	—	0	159	-11	-0.9
1993	Pit N	3	0	1.000	26	0	0	0-0	32.1	43	25	7	0	9-2	14	6.96	58	.328	.369	0-0	—	0		-10	-0.8
1995	StL N	6	6	.500	26	21	1-1	0-0	137.1	136	71	11	6	35-3	71	4.00	105	.262	.313	37-3	.081	-1	90	2	0.1
1996	†StL N	11	2	.846	48	6	0	0-3	88.2	83	37	9	5	35-2	45	3.55	118	.251	.331	16-0	.188	0	75	7	0.9
1997	StL N	4	7	.364	55	2	0	2-0	96	109	61	14	6	31-4	51	5.06	82	.292	.354	11-1	.091	-0	100	-10	-1.0
1998	StL N	7	4	.636	48	10	0	0-5	105.2	131	63	9	8	36-3	55	4.77	88	.312	.375	22-2	.318	2	110	-7	-0.5
1999	Ana A	10	4	.714	64	0	0	1-3	83	85	37	6	2	21-2	43	3.47	140	.269	.314	0-0	—	0		12	1.7
2000	Ana A	4	2	.667	64	1	0	2-2	81	86	40	8	3	23-6	31	4.33	117	.277	.332	0-0	—	0	37	7	0.5
2001	Tex A	1	2	.333	55	0	0	0-4	76.2	103	61	14	5	28-4	42	6.69	70	.323	.379	1-0	.000	-0		-17	-0.8
Total	9	46	28	.622	390	41	1-1	5-17	710	797	411	82	35	222-26	358	4.74	93	.288	.346	87-6	.161	1	90	-27	-0.8
PETRY, DAN Daniel Joseph B 11.13.1958 Palo Alto, CA BR/TR 6-4/200# d7.8																									
1979	Det A	6	5	.545	15	15	2	0-0	98	90	46	11	4	33-5	43	3.95	110	.254	.321	0-0	—	0	86	5	0.4
1980	Det A	10	9	.526	27	25	4-3	0-0	164.2	156	82	9	1	83-14	88	3.94	105	.253	.340	0-0	—	0	105	2	0.3
1981	Det A	10	9	.526	23	22	7-2	0-0	141	115	53	10	1	57-4	79	3.00	126	.224	.301	0-0	—	0	78	10	1.5
1982	Det A	15	9	.625	35	35	8-1	0-0	246	220	98	15	4	100-5	132	3.22	126	.241	.317	0-0	—	0	113	23	2.3
1983	Det A	19	11	.633	38	**38**	9-2	0-0	266.1	256	126	37	6	99-7	122	3.92	100	.256	.325	0-0	—	0	122	1	0.2
1984	†Det A	18	8	.692	35	35	7-2	0-0	233.1	231	94	21	3	66-4	144	3.24	121	.259	.312	0-0	—	0	121	19	2.1
1985	Det A★	15	13	.536	34	34	8	0-0	238.2	190	98	24	3	81-9	109	3.36	121	.217	.285	0-0	—	0	89	20	2.2
1986	Det A	5	10	.333	20	20	2	0-0	116	122	78	15	5	53-3	56	4.66	89	.268	.348	0-0	—	0	91	-12	-1.3
1987	†Det A	9	7	.563	30	21	0	0-0	134.2	148	101	22	10	76-5	93	5.61	75	.279	.375	0-0	—	0	150	-25	-2.4
1988	Cal A	3	9	.250	22	22	4-1	0-0	139.2	139	70	18	6	59-5	64	4.38	88	.263	.341	0-0	—	0	94	-6	-0.3
1989	Cal A	3	2	.600	19	4	0	0-0	51	53	32	8	1	23-0	21	5.47	70	.275	.347	0-0	—	0	89	-9	-0.8
1990	Det A	10	9	.526	32	23	1	0-0	149.2	148	78	14	1	77-7	73	4.45	89	.263	.349	0-0	—	0	96	-7	-0.7
1991	Det A	2	3	.400	17	6	0	0-0	54.2	66	35	9	0	19-3	18	4.94	84	.300	.356	0-0	—	0	110	-6	-0.4
	Atl N	0	0	—	10	0	0	0-0	24.1	29	17	2	1	14-1	9	5.55	70	.296	.389	5-0	.200	0		-4	-0.2
	Bos A	0	0	—	13	0	0	1-0	22.1	21	17	3	1	12-2	12	4.43	97	.250	.347	0-0	—	0		-2	-0.1
Total	13	125	104	.546	370	300	52-11	1-0	2080.1	1984	1025	218	47	852-74	1063	3.95	102	.253	.328	5-0	.200	0	106	9	2.8
PETTIBONE, JAY Harry Jonathan B 6.21.1957 Mt.Clemens, MI BR/TR 6-4/182# d9.11																									
1983	Min A	0	4	.000	4	4	1	0-0	27	28	16	8	2	8-0	10	5.33	80	.280	.345	0-0	—	0	48	-2	-0.3
PETTIT, PAUL George William Paul "Lefty" B 11.29.1931 Los Angeles, CA BL/TL 6-2/195# d5.4																									
1951	Pit N	0	0	—	2	0	0	0	2.2	2	1	1	0	1	0	3.38	125	.200	.273	1-0	.000	-0		0	0.0
1953	Pit N	1	2	.333	10	5	0	0	28	33	27	1	0	20	14	7.71	58	.297	.405	8-1	.250	1*	112	-10	-0.8
Total	2	1	2	.333	12	5	0	0	30.2	35	28	2	0	21	14	7.34	61	.289	.394	9-1	.222	1	112	-10	-0.8
PETTIT, LEON Leon Arthur "Lefty" B 6.23.1902 Waynesburg, PA D 11.21.1974 Columbia, TN BL/TL 5-10.5/165# d4.18																									
1935	Was A	8	5	.615	41	7	1	3	109	129	65	6	4	58	45	4.95	87	.301	.390	25-1	.080	0	126	-7	-0.7
1937	Phi N	0	1	.000	3	1	0	0	4	6	5	1	0	4	0	11.25	39	.353	.476	0-0	—	0	80	-3	-0.5
Total	2	8	6	.571	44	8	1	3	113	135	70	7	4	62	45	5.18	84	.303	.393	25-1	.080	0	120	-10	-1.2
PETTITTE, ANDY Andrew Eugene B 6.15.1972 Baton Rouge, LA BL/TL 6-5/235# d4.29																									
1995	†NY A	12	9	.571	31	26	3	0-0	175	183	86	15	1	63-3	114	4.17	111	.272	.333	0-0	—	0	91	9	0.9
1996	†NY A☆	**21**	8	.724	35	34	2	0-0	221	229	105	23	3	72-2	162	3.87	128	.271	.330	0-0	—	0	103	25	2.8
1997	†NY A	18	7	.720	35	**35**	4-1	0-0	240.1	233	86	7	3	65-0	166	2.88	154	.256	.307	0-0	—	0	128	42	4.1
1998	†NY A	16	11	.593	33	32	5	0-0	216.1	226	110	20	6	87-1	146	4.24	103	.274	.344	4-2	.000	-0	102	3	0.3
1999	†NY A	14	11	.560	31	31	0	0-0	191.2	216	105	20	3	89-3	121	4.70	101	.289	.364	5-0	.200	0	109	3	0.5
2000	†NY A	19	9	.679	32	32	3-1	0-0	204.2	219	111	17	4	80-4	125	4.35	111	.271	.338	5-0	.000	-0	128	9	1.1
2001	†NY A★	15	10	.600	31	31	2	0-0	200.2	224	103	14	6	41-3	164	3.99	113	.281	.319	4-1	.000	-0	108	9	1.1
2002	†NY A	13	5	.722	22	22	3-1	0-0	134.2	144	58	6	4	32-2	97	3.27	134	.272	.317	3-0	.333	1	116	15	2.0
2003	†NY A	21	8	.724	33	33	1	0-0	208.1	227	109	21	1	50-3	180	4.02	109	.272	.312	7-0	.143	-0	139	5	0.6

Year	Tm Lg	W	L	Pct	G	GS	CG-Sho	SV-BS	IP	H	R	HR	HB	BB-IB	SO	ERA	AERA	OAV	OOB	AB-SH	AVG	PB	Sup	APR	PW
Total	9	149	78	.656	283	276	23-3	0-0	1792.2	1901	873	143	31	579-21	1275	3.94	116	.273	.330	28-3	.107	-0	114	120	13.4
PETTY, CHARLIE Charles E. B 6.28.1866 Nashville, TN TR ?/175# d7.30																									
1889	Cin AA	2	3	.400	5	5	5	0	44	44	29	3	6	20	10	5.52	71	.253	.350	20	.300	1	98	-3	-0.2
1893	NY N	5	2	.714	9	6	4	0	54	66	36	0	1	28	12	3.33	140	.292	.373	22	.318	3	168	6	0.8
1894	Was N	3	8	.273	16	12	8	0	103	156	114	4	9	32	14	5.59	95	.344	.399	41-5	.195	-2	85	-6	-0.6
	Cle N	0	2	.000	4	3	2	0	27	42	37	4	3	14	4	8.67	63	.350	.431	12-0	.083	-2	103	-9	-0.6
	Year	3	10	.231	20	15	10	0	130	198	45	8	12	46	18	6.23	85	.346	.406	53-5	.170	-4	89	-21	-1.2
Total	3	10	15	.400	34	26	19	0	228	308	216	11	19	94	40	5.41	91	.317	.388	95-5	.232	-0	107	-12	-0.6
PETTY, JESSE Jesse Lee "The Silver Fox" B 11.23.1894 Orr, OK D 10.23.1971 St.Paul, MN BR/TL 6/195# d4.14																									
1921	Cle A	0	0	—	4	0	0	0	9	10	2	0	0	0	0	2.00	213	.345	.345	2-0	.000	-0		2	0.1
1925	Bro N	9	9	.500	28	21	7	0	153	188	97	15	2	47	39	4.88	86	.304	.355	50-3	.140	-3	95	-11	-1.4
1926	Bro N	17	17	.500	38	33	23-1	1	275.2	246	118	9	3	79	101	2.84	135	**.240**	.296	97-3	.175	-3	71	25	2.4
1927	Bro N	13	18	.419	42	33	19-2	1	271.2	263	108	13	4	53	101	2.98	133	.254	.293	91-1	.099	-7	53	29	2.2
1928	Bro N	15	15	.500	40	31	15-2	1	234	264	119	18	5	56	74	4.04	98	.289	.334	81-4	.111	-5	93	4	-0.3
1929	Pit N	11	10	.524	36	25	12-1	0	184.1	197	100	12	0	42	58	3.71	129	.277	.317	67-1	.104	-5	95	17	1.0
1930	Pit N	1	6	.143	10	7	0	1	41.1	67	43	8	2	13	16	8.27	60	.362	.410	12-1	.083	-1	88	-14	-2.0
	Chi N	1	3	.250	9	3	0	0	39.1	51	18	2	0	6	18	2.97	164	.317	.341	13-1	.231	0	30	7	0.6
	Year	2	9	.182	19	10	0	1	80.2	118	20	10	2	19	34	5.69	87	.341	.379	25-2	.160	-1	71	-8	-1.4
Total	7	67	78	.462	207	153	76-6	4	1208.1	1286	605	77	16	296	407	3.68	113	.275	.320	413-14	.128	-25	80	59	2.6
PETTYJOHN, ADAM Adam Christopher B 6.11.1977 Phoenix, AZ BR/TL 6-3/190# d7.16																									
2001	Det A	1	6	.143	16	9	0	0-0	65	81	48	10	4	21-2	40	5.82	75	.309	.366	2-0	.000	-0	69	-12	-1.1
PEZZULLO, PRETZEL John B 12.10.1910 Bridgeport, CT D 5.16.1990 Dallas, TX BL/TL 5-11.5/180# d4.18																									
1935	Phi N	3	5	.375	41	7	2	1	84.1	115	74	5	7	45	24	6.40	71	.321	.407	24-0	.250	0	78	-16	-1.4
1936	Phi N	0	0	—	1	0	0	0	2	1	1	0	0	6	0	4.50	101	.167	.583	0-0	—	0		0	0.0
Total	2	3	5	.375	42	7	2	1	86.1	116	75	5	7	51	24	6.36	71	.319	.412	24-0	.250	0	78	-16	-1.4
PFANN, BILL William F. B 6.1863 Hamilton, ON, CAN D 6.3.1904 Hamilton, ON, CAN 6/205# d6.16																									
1894	Cin N	0	1	.000	1	1	0	0	3	10	10	1	0	4	0	27.00	21	.526	.609	1-0	.000	-0	115	-6	-0.7
PFEFFER, JEFF Edward Joseph B 3.4.1888 Seymour, IL D 8.15.1972 Chicago, IL BR/TR 6-3/210# d4.16 Mil 1918 b-Big Jeff																									
1911	StL A	0	0	—	2	0	0	0	10	11	11	0	0	4	4	7.20	47	.297	.366	4-0	.000	-1		-4	-0.3
1913	Bro N	0	1	.000	5	2	1	0	24.1	28	16	0	4	13	13	3.33	99	.311	.421	7-1	.000	-1	103	-2	-0.2
1914	Bro N	23	12	.657	43	34	27-3	4	315	264	99	9	7	91	135	1.97	145	.232	.293	116-1	.198	-1*	104	30	3.2
1915	Bro N	19	14	.576	40	34	26-6	3	291.2	243	93	8	17	76	84	2.10	132	.231	.293	106-1	.255	5	114	22	2.9
1916	†Bro N	25	11	.694	41	36	30-6	1	328.2	274	91	5	17	63	128	1.92	140	.230	.278	122-3	.279	7*	110	30	4.1
1917	Bro N	11	15	.423	30	30	24-3	0	266	225	84	4	16	66	115	2.23	125	.234	.294	100-5	.130	-4*	92	16	1.0
1918	Bro N	1	0	1.000	1	1	1-1	0	9	2	0	0	0	3	1	0.00	—	.071	.161	4-0	.250	0	54	3	0.4
1919	Bro N	17	13	.567	30	30	26-4	0	267	270	95	7	12	49	92	2.66	112	.267	.308	97-3	.206	1	101	12	1.5
1920	†Bro N	16	9	.640	30	28	20-2	0	215	225	81	5	5	45	80	3.01	106	.273	.314	74-6	.243	1	110	8	0.8
1921	Bro N	1	5	.167	6	5	2	0	31.2	36	19	0	1	9	8	4.55	86	.310	.365	11-0	.000	-2	51	-2	-0.5
	StL N	9	3	.750	18	13	7-1	0	98.2	115	51	3	5	28	22	4.29	86	.305	.361	29-4	.138	-1	128	-4	-0.6
	Year	10	8	.556	24	18	9-1	0	130.1	151	57	3	6	37	30	4.35	86	.306	.362	40-4	.100	-2	106	-7	-1.1
1922	StL N	19	12	.613	44	32	19-1	2	261.1	286	126	12	11	58	83	3.58	108	.279	.324	98-2	.245	4*	111	9	1.4
1923	StL N	8	9	.471	26	18	7-1	0	152.1	171	80	8	9	40	32	4.02	97	.287	.341	55-1	.127	-4	98	-1	-0.5
1924	StL N	4	5	.444	16	12	3	0	78	102	52	3	1	30	20	5.31	71	.318	.378	26-1	.115	-2	82	-12	-1.5
	Pit N	5	3	.625	15	4	1	0	58.2	68	23	3	0	17	19	3.07	125	.293	.341	25-1	.240	-0	116	5	0.5
	Year	9	8	.529	31	16	4	0	136.2	170	28	6	1	47	39	4.35	88	.307	.363	51-2	.176	-3	90	-8	-1.0
Total	13	158	112	.585	347	279	194-28	10	2407.1	2320	921	67	105	592	836	2.77	114	.258	.311	874-29	.206	2	104	110	12.2
PFEFFER, BIG JEFF Francis Xavier B 3.31.1882 Champaign, IL D 12.19.1954 Kankakee, IL BR/TR 6-1/185# d4.15 b-Jeff																									
1905	Chi N	4	4	.500	15	11	9	0	101	84	36	2	4	36	56	2.50	120	.240	.318	40-1	.200	1	77	6	0.5
1906	Bos N	13	22	.371	36	36	33-4	0	302.1	270	138	4	16	114	158	2.95	91	.246	.325	158-2	.196	3*	78	-9	-0.4
1907	Bos N	6	8	.429	19	16	12-1	0	144	129	62	3	7	61	65	3.00	85	.253	.341	60-1	.250	3*	99	-7	-0.3
1908	Bos N	0	0	—	4	0	0	0	10	18	16	1	0	8	3	12.60	19	.383	.473	2-0	.000	-0		-10	-0.6
1910	Chi N	1	0	1.000	13	1	1	0	41.1	43	31	1	1	16	11	3.27	88	.281	.353	17-1	.176	1*	77	-7	-0.3
1911	Bos N	7	5	.583	26	6	4-1	2	97	116	74	3	0	57	24	4.73	81	.301	.391	46-0	.196	1*	95	-11	-1.1
Total	6	31	39	.443	113	70	59-6	2	695.2	660	357	14	28	292	317	3.30	87	.260	.342	323-5	.204	8	83	-38	-2.2
PFEFFER, FRED Nathaniel Frederick "Fritz" or "Dandelion" B 3.17.1860 Louisville, KY D 4.10.1932 Chicago, IL BR/TR 5-10.5/184# d5.1.1882 M1 ▲																									
1884	Chi N	0	0	—	1	0	0	0	1	3	2	0		1	0	9.00	35	.333	.400	467	.289	0*		-1	0.0
1885	†Chi N	2	1	.667	5	2	2	**2**	31.2	26	15	1		8	13	2.56	118	.222	.272	469	.241	1*	94	2	0.2
1892	Lou N	0	0	—	1	0	0	0	5	4	3	0	0	5	0	1.80	170	.211	.375	470	.257	0*		0	0.0
1894	Lou N	0	0	—	1	0	0	0	7	8	6	0	1	6	0	2.57	198	.286	.429	414-15	.309	0*		1	0.0
Total	4	2	1	.667	8	2	2	2	44.2	41	26	1	1	20	13	2.62	129	.237	.320	1820-15	.273	1	94	2	0.2
PFIESTER, JACK John Albert "Jack The Giant Killer" (b: John Albert Hagenbush) B 5.24.1878 Cincinnati, OH D 9.3.1953 Loveland, OH BR/TL 5-11/180# d9.8																									
1903	Pit N	0	3	.000	3	3	2	0	19	26	21	0	2	10	15	6.16	53	.321	.409	6-0	.000	-1	69	-7	-0.9
1904	Pit N	1	1	.500	3	2	1	0	20	28	18	0	0	9	6	7.20	38	.318	.381	7-0	.286	1	125	-8	-0.6
1906	†Chi N	20	8	.714	31	29	20-4	0	250.2	173	63	3	13	63	153	1.51	175	.194	.258	84-2	.048	-7	129	30	2.6
1907	†Chi N	14	9	.609	30	22	13-3	0	195	143	61	1	5	48	90	**1.15**	**216**	.207	.263	64-8	.094	-3	126	21	2.1
1908	†Chi N	12	10	.545	33	29	18-3	0	252	204	82	1	11	70	117	2.00	118	.223	.287	79-4	.101	-4	113	7	0.1
1909	Chi N	17	6	.739	29	25	13-5	0	196.2	179	67	1	5	49	73	2.43	105	.240	.291	65-3	.169	0	131	6	0.8
1910	†Chi N	6	3	.667	14	13	5-2	0	100.1	82	28	0	1	26	34	1.79	161	.225	.279	33-1	.091	-2	83	12	0.7
1911	Chi N	1	4	.200	6	5	3	0	33.2	34	25	0	2	18	15	4.01	83	.262	.360	11-1	.182	0	77	-5	-0.6
Total	8	71	44	.617	149	128	75-17	0	1067.1	869	365	6	39	293	503	2.02	128	.223	.284	349-19	.103	-15	117	56	4.2
PFISTER, DAN Daniel Albin B 12.20.1936 Plainfield, NJ BR/TR 6/187# d9.9																									
1961	KC A	0	0	—	2	0	0	0	2.1	5	4	2	0	4-0	3	15.43	27	.417	.563	0-0	—	0		-3	-0.1
1962	KC A	4	14	.222	41	25	2	1	196.1	175	112	27	9	106-2	123	4.54	93	.238	.340	65-2	.185	-1*	85	-8	-0.8
1963	KC A	1	0	1.000	3	1	0	0	9.1	8	2	1	1	3-0	9	1.93	202	.229	.308	3-0	.000	-0*	159	2	0.2
1964	KC A	1	5	.167	19	3	0	0	41.1	50	32	10	6	29-4	21	6.53	58	.311	.431	6-0	.000	-0*	93	-11	-1.6
Total	4	6	19	.240	65	29	2	1	249.1	238	150	40	16	142-6	156	4.87	85	.252	.358	74-2	.162	-2	89	-20	-2.3
PFUND, LEE Le Roy Herbert B 10.10.1918 Oak Park, IL BR/TR 6-1/185# d4.21																									
1945	Bro N	3	2	.600	15	10	2	0	62.1	69	51	4	5	35	27	5.20	72	.274	.373	22-1	.182	0	203	-12	-0.8
PHEBUS, BILL Raymond William B 8.2.1909 Cherryvale, KS D 10.11.1989 Bartow, FL BR/TR 5-9/170# d9.6																									
1936	Was A	0	0	—	2	1	0	0	7.1	4	6	1	1	4	4	2.45	195	.114	.225	1-0	.000	0	129	0	0.0
1937	Was A	3	2	.600	6	5	4-1	1	40.2	33	13	2	2	24	12	2.21	200	.232	.351	8-1	.000	1	67	10	1.2
1938	Was A	0	0	—	5	0	0	1	6.1	9	9	1	0	7	2	11.37	40	.346	.485	1-0	.000	-0		-5	-0.2
Total	3	3	2	.600	13	6	4-1	2	54.1	46	28	4	3	35	18	3.31	135	.227	.349	10-1	.000	1	78	5	1.0
PHELPS, RAY Raymond Clifford B 12.11.1903 Dunlap, TN D 7.7.1971 Fort Pierce, FL BR/TR 6-2/200# d4.23																									
1930	Bro N	14	7	.667	36	24	11-2	0	179.2	198	98	21	3	52	64	4.11	120	.280	.332	68-1	.147	-2	113	16	1.4
1931	Bro N	7	9	.438	28	26	3-1	0	149.1	184	88	3	4	44	50	5.00	76	.306	.357	51-0	.157	-1	108	-16	-1.6
1932	Bro N	4	5	.444	20	9	4-1	0	79.1	101	58	5	3	27	21	5.90	65	.323	.382	23-2	.087	-1	122	-18	-1.8
1935	Chi A	4	8	.333	27	17	4	1	125	126	77	10	3	55	38	4.82	96	.262	.341	41-1	.122	-4	90	-3	-0.5
1936	Chi A	4	6	.400	15	4	2	0	68.2	91	54	9	2	42	17	6.03	86	.331	.423	26-0	.231	1	68	-7	-0.7
Total	5	33	35	.485	126	80	24-4	1	602	700	375	48	15	220	190	4.93	90	.294	.358	209-4	.148	-8	103	-28	-3.2
PHELPS, TOMMY Thomas Allen B 3.4.1974 Seoul, South Korea BL/TL 6-3/190# d3.31																									
2003	Fla N	3	2	.600	27	7	0	0-0	63	70	32	3	2	23-1	43	4.00	103	.282	.345	11-1	.091	0	121	0	0.0

Year	Tm Lg	W	L	Pct	G	GS	CG-Sho	SV-BS	IP	H	R	HR	HB	BB-IB	SO	ERA	AERA	OAV	OOB	AB-SH	AVG	PB	Sup	APR	PW
PHELPS, TRAVIS Travis Howard B 7.25.1977 Neosho, MO BR/TR 6-2/165# d4.19																									
2001	TB A	2	2	.500	49	0	0	5-1	62	53	30	6	3	24-1	54	3.48	129	.226	.301	0-0	—	0		6	0.4
2002	TB A	1	2	.333	26	0	0	0-0	37.2	30	20	7	5	27-0	36	4.78	93	.222	.367	0-0	—	0		-1	0.0
Total	2	3	4	.429	75	0	0	5-1	99.2	83	50	13	8	51-1	90	3.97	113	.224	.326	0-0	—	0		5	0.4
PHILLIPPE, DEACON Charles Louis B 5.23.1872 Rural Retreat, VA D 3.30.1952 Avalon, PA BR/TR 6-0.5/180# d4.21																									
1899	Lou N	21	17	.553	42	38	33-2	1	321	331	178	10	7	64	68	3.17	122	.266	.306	128-5	.203	-1*	97	22	2.0
1900	†Pit N	20	13	.606	38	33	29-1	0	279	274	127	7	7	42	75	2.84	128	.257	**.289**	105-4	.181	-2	83	26	2.2
1901	Pit N	22	12	.647	37	32	30-1	2	296	274	115	7	10	38	103	2.22	147	.244	.275	113-2	.230	5*	120	33	4.1
1902	Pit N	20	9	.690	31	30	29-5	0	272	265	90	1	4	26	122	2.05	134	.255	.276	113-3	.221	3*	135	19	2.1
1903	†Pit N	25	9	.735	36	33	31-4	2	289.1	269	116	4	4	29	123	2.43	133	.241	**.263**	124-0	.210	2*	125	27	2.9
1904	Pit N	10	10	.500	21	19	17-3	1	166.2	183	82	1	3	26	82	3.24	85	.272	.302	65-1	.123	-4	77	-9	-1.4
1905	Pit N	20	13	.606	38	33	25-5	0	279	235	95	0	10	48	133	2.19	137	.233	.274	97-2	.093	-4	93	22	2.0
1906	Pit N	15	10	.600	33	24	19-3	0	218.2	216	78	3	2	26	90	2.47	108	.252	.276	82-0	.244	3	89	7	1.1
1907	Pit N	14	11	.560	35	26	17-1	2	214	214	83	2	5	36	61	2.61	93	.264	.300	65-5	.185	1	124	-2	-0.2
1908	Pit N	0	0	—	5	0	0	0	12	20	15	0	0	3	1	11.25	20	.357	.390	4-0	.250	0		-10	-0.5
1909	†Pit N	8	3	.727	22	13	7-1	0	131.2	121	41	2	4	14	38	2.32	117	.253	.280	42-1	.071	-3	101	8	0.2
1910	Pit N	14	2	.875	31	8	5-1	4	121.2	111	46	4	3	9	30	2.29	135	.239	.258	41-1	.220	1	153	9	1.1
1911	Pit N	0	0	—	3	0	0	0	6	5	5	0	0	2	3	7.50	46	.238	.304	1-0	1.000	1		-2	0.0
Total	13	189	109	.634	372	289	242-27	12	2607	2518	1071	41	59	363	929	2.59	120	.253	.283	980-24	.189	2	107	150	15.6
PHILLIPS, BUZ Albert Abernathy B 5.25.1904 Newton, NC D 11.6.1964 Baltimore, MD BR/TR 5-11.5/185# d8.5																									
1930	Phi N	0	0	—	14	1	0	0	43.2	68	44	6	1	18	9	8.04	68	.354	.412	13-0	.462	2	80	-11	-0.3
PHILLIPS, RED Clarence Lemuel B 11.3.1908 Pauls Valley, OK D 2.1.1988 Wichita, KS BR/TR 6-3.5/195# d7.24																									
1934	Det A	2	0	1.000	7	1	1	1	23.1	31	17	1	0	16	3	6.17	71	.316	.412	12-0	.250	1	317	-4	-0.3
1936	Det A	2	4	.333	22	6	3	0	87.1	124	67	12	0	22	15	6.49	76	.332	.370	33-0	.303	2	86	-13	-0.5
Total	2	4	4	.500	29	7	4	1	110.2	155	84	13	0	38	18	6.42	75	.329	.379	45-0	.289	3	117	-17	-0.8
PHILLIPS, JASON Jason Charles B 3.22.1974 Williamsport, PA BR/TR 6-6/225# d4.5																									
1999	Pit N	0	0	—	6	0	0	0-0	7	11	9	2	0	6-1	7	11.57	39	.393	.486	0-0	—	0		-5	-0.2
2002	Cle A	1	3	.250	8	6	0	0-0	41.2	41	24	7	4	20-0	23	4.97	89	.259	.353	0-0	—	0	113	-2	-0.2
2003	Cle A	0	1	.000	3	0	0	0-0	5	9	5	1	0	2-0	2	9.00	49	.409	.440	0-0	—	0		-2	-0.4
Total	3	1	4	.200	17	6	0	0-0	53.2	61	38	10	4	28-1	32	6.20	71	.293	.381	0-0	—	0	113	-9	-0.8
PHILLIPS, JACK John Stephen B 5.24.1919 St.Louis, MO D 6.16.1958 St.Louis, MO BR/TR 6-1/185# d7.13																									
1945	NY N	0	0	—	1	0	0	0	4.1	5	5	1	1	4	0	10.38	38	.294	.455	2-0	.500	0*		-3	-0.1
PHILLIPS, ED Norman Edwin B 9.20.1944 Ardmore, OK BR/TR 6-1/190# d4.9																									
1970	Bos A	0	2	.000	18	0	0	0-0	23.2	29	14	4	2	10-1	23	5.32	74	.312	.387	3-0	.000	-0		-2	-0.3
PHILLIPS, TOM Thomas Gerald B 4.5.1889 Philipsburg, PA D 4.12.1929 Philipsburg, PA BR/TR 6-2/190# d9.13																									
1915	StL A	1	3	.250	5	4	1	0	27.1	28	13	0	2	12	5	2.96	97	.283	.372	9-1	.111	-1	57	0	-0.2
1919	Cle A	3	2	.600	22	3	1	0	55	55	27	2	3	34	18	2.95	114	.272	.385	11-0	.364	1	86	**1**	0.1
1921	Was A	1	0	1.000	1	1	1	0	9	9	2	0	0	3	2	2.00	206	.290	.353	3-0	.000	-1	61	2	0.2
1922	Was A	3	7	.300	17	7	2-1	0	70	72	43	2	4	22	19	4.89	79	.273	.338	20-1	.150	-1	78	-7	-0.9
Total	4	8	12	.400	45	15	5-1	0	161.1	164	85	4	9	71	44	3.74	95	.275	.361	43-2	.186	-1	73	-4	-0.8
PHILLIPS, BILL William Corcoran "Whoa Bill" or "Silver Bill" B 11.9.1868 Allenport, PA D 10.25.1941 Charleroi, PA BR/TR 5-11/180# d8.11 M2																									
1890	Pit N	1	9	.100	10	10	9	0	82	123	97	8	1	29	25	7.57	44	.336	.386	46	.239	1*	69	-38	-3.1
1895	Cin N	6	7	.462	18	9	6	2	109	126	90	6	7	44	15	6.03	82	.285	.359	48-0	.313	2*	120	-9	-0.6
1899	Cin N	17	9	.654	33	27	18-1	1	227.2	234	121	3	14	71	43	3.32	118	.265	.330	92-4	.130	-5*	99	13	0.7
1900	Cin N	9	11	.450	29	24	17-3	0	208.1	229	140	5	13	67	51	4.28	86	.279	.343	79-1	.165	-4	115	-16	-1.3
1901	Cin N	14	18	.438	37	36	29-1	0	281.1	364	196	7	12	67	109	4.64	69	.311	.354	109-1	.202	2*	93	-45	-3.8
1902	Cin N	16	16	.500	33	33	30	0	269	267	121	3	9	55	85	2.51	119	.259	.302	114-2	.342	10*	116	12	2.6
1903	Cin N	7	6	.538	16	13	11-1	0	118.1	134	74	0	7	30	46	3.35	106	.279	.330	57-0	.175	-1*	118	1	0.0
Total	7	70	76	.479	176	152	120-6	3	1295.2	1477	839	32	63	363	374	4.09	87	.284	.338	545-8	.224	4	103	-82	-5.5
PHILLIPS, TAYLOR William Taylor "Tay" B 6.18.1933 Atlanta, GA BL/TL 5-11/185# d6.8																									
1956	Mil N	5	3	.625	23	6	3	2	87.2	69	25	6	7	33-8	36	2.26	153	.223	.310	21-1	.000	-2	81	13	1.1
1957	Mil N	3	2	.600	27	6	0	2	73	82	46	3	1	40-3	36	5.55	63	.300	.388	20-0	.100	-1	130	-16	-1.2
1958	Chi N	7	10	.412	39	27	5-1	1	170.1	178	102	22	6	79-5	102	4.76	82	.266	.348	54-5	.056	-4	106	-16	-1.8
1959	Chi N	0	2	.000	7	2	0	0	16.2	22	14	3	2	11-2	5	7.56	52	.319	.422	4-0	.000	-0	57	-6	-0.7
	Phi N	1	4	.200	32	3	1	1	63	72	35	4	4	31-1	35	5.00	82	.303	.389	11-0	.091	-1	80	-4	-0.4
	Year	1	6	.143	39	5	1	1	79.2	94	39	7	6	42-3	40	5.54	74	.306	.397	15-0	.067	-1	70	-10	-1.1
1960	Phi N	0	1	.000	10	1	0	0	14	21	13	2	1	4-0	6	8.36	46	.356	.388	1-0	.000	-0	182	-6	-0.4
1963	Chi A	0	0	—	9	0	0	0	14	16	16	2	1	13-5	13	10.29	34	.302	.441	2-0	.000	-0		-10	-0.5
Total	6	16	22	.421	147	45	9-1	6	438.2	460	251	42	22	211-24	233	4.82	78	.275	.362	113-6	.053	-9	104	-45	-3.9
PHOEBUS, TOM Thomas Harold B 4.7.1942 Baltimore, MD BR/TR 5-8/185# d9.15																									
1966	Bal A	2	1	.667	3	3	2-2	0	22	16	3	0	0	6-0	17	1.23	271	.213	.272	6-1	.167	0	62	5	0.9
1967	Bal A	14	9	.609	33	33	7-4	0	208	177	84	16	0	114-1	179	3.33	95	.227	.325	76-3	.145	1	142	-4	-0.5
1968	Bal A	15	15	.500	36	36	9-3	0	240.2	186	81	10	4	105-5	193	2.62	112	.212	.299	82-7	.183	3	98	8	1.4
1969	Bal A	14	7	.667	35	33	6-2	0-0	202	180	89	23	4	87-5	117	3.52	101	.241	.321	75-5	.200	2	119	1	0.2
1970	†Bal A	5	5	.500	27	21	3	0-1	135	106	58	11	6	62-2	72	3.07	119	.219	.312	43-3	.163	-0	120	6	0.3
1971	SD N	3	11	.214	29	21	2	0-0	133.1	144	67	14	3	64-6	80	4.45	74	.280	.361	36-2	.167	1	90	-13	-1.2
1972	SD N	0	1	.000	1	1	0	0-0	5.2	3	5	2	0	6-0	8	7.94	41	.150	.346	2-0	.000	-0	27	-3	-0.4
	Chi N	3	3	.500	37	1	0	6-3	83.1	76	40	9	2	45-4	59	3.78	101	.247	.343	15-1	.133	-1*	46	0	0.0
	Year	3	4	.429	38	2	0	6-3	89	79	42	11	2	51-4	67	4.04	93	.241	.343	17-1	.118	-1	35	-2	-0.4
Total	7	56	52	.519	201	149	29-11	6-4	1030	888	427	85	19	489-23	725	3.33	100	.233	.322	335-22	.170	6	112	0	0.7
PHOENIX, STEVE Steven Robert B 1.31.1968 Phoenix, AZ BR/TR 6-2/175# d7.30																									
1994	Oak A	0	0	—	2	0	0	0-0	4.1	4	3	0	0	2-0	3	6.23	71	.235	.316	0-0	—	0		-1	0.0
1995	Oak A	0	0	—	1	0	0	0-0	1.2	3	6	1	0	3-0	3	32.40	14	.429	.600	0-0	—	0		-5	-0.2
Total	2	0	0	—	3	0	0	0-0	6	7	9	1	0	5-0	6	13.50	33	.292	.414	0-0	—	0		-6	-0.2
PHYLE, BILL William Joseph B 6.25.1875 Duluth, MN D 8.6.1953 Los Angeles, CA TR d9.17 ▲																									
1898	Chi N	2	1	.667	3	3	3-2	0	23	24	15	0	2	6	4	0.78	458	.267	.327	9-0	.111	-0*	119	4	0.4
1899	Chi N	1	8	.111	10	9	9	1	83.2	92	58	2	4	29	10	4.20	89	.279	.344	34-0	.176	-2	77	-4	-0.5
1901	NY N	7	10	.412	24	19	16	1	168.2	208	121	2	6	54	62	4.27	77	.301	.356	66-0	.182	-1*	126	-21	-1.8
Total	3	10	19	.345	37	31	28-2	2	275.1	324	194	4	12	89	76	3.96	88	.291	.350	109-0	.174	-4	110	-21	-1.9
PIATT, DOUG Douglas William B 9.26.1965 Beaver, PA BL/TR 6-1/185# d6.11																									
1991	Mon N	0	0	—	21	0	0	0-0	34.2	29	11	3	0	17-0	29	2.60	139	.230	.322	1-0	.000	-0		4	0.2
PIATT, WILEY Wiley Harold "Iron Man" B 7.13.1874 Blue Creek, OH D 9.20.1946 Cincinnati, OH BL/TL 5-10/175# d4.22																									
1898	Phi N	24	14	.632	39	37	33-**6**	0	306	285	156	2	19	97	121	3.18	108	.245	.314	122-1	.262	4*	100	10	1.3
1899	Phi N	23	15	.605	39	38	31-2	0	305	323	173	6	23	86	89	3.45	107	.271	.332	122-3	.270	4*	115	7	0.8
1900	Phi N	9	10	.474	22	20	16-1	0	160.2	194	120	5	16	71	47	4.65	78	.298	.380	68-1	.250	2	111	-21	-2.0
1901	Phi A	5	12	.294	18	16	15	1	140	176	112	3	3	60	45	4.63	82	.303	.372	58-1	.224	0	115	-16	-1.7
	Chi A	4	2	.667	7	6	4-1	0	51.2	42	29	2	4	14	19	2.79	125	.220	.287	17-0	.118	-1	110	3	0.1
	Year	9	14	.391	25	22	19-1	1	191.2	218	35	5	7	74	64	4.13	89	.283	.351	75-1	.200	-1	114	-13	-1.6
1902	Chi A	12	12	.500	32	30	22-2	0	246	263	129	3	9	66	96	3.51	96	.274	.327	85-4	.200	2	115	-5	-0.4
1903	Bos N	9	14	.391	25	23	18	0	181	198	107	5	4	61	100	3.18	101	.280	.340	71-2	.225	2*	107	-3	-0.2
Total	6	86	79	.521	182	170	139-12	1	1390.1	1481	826	26	78	455	517	3.60	98	.272	.337	543-12	.239	13	110	-25	-2.1

Year	Tm Lg	W	L	Pct	G	GS	CG-Sho	SV-BS	IP	H	R	HR	HB	BB-IB	SO	ERA	AERA	OAV	OOB	AB-SH	AVG	PB	Sup	APR	PW
PICHARDO, HIPOLITO Hipolito Antonio (Balbina) B 8.22.1969 Jicome Esperanza, D.R. BR/TR 6-1/185# d4.21																									
1992	KC A	9	6	.600	31	24	1-1	0-0	143.2	148	71	9	3	49-1	59	3.95	103	.267	.327	0-0	—	0	117	1	0.1
1993	KC A	7	8	.467	30	25	2	0-0	165	183	85	10	6	53-2	70	4.04	114	.282	.338	0-0	—	0	86	7	0.6
1994	KC A	5	3	.625	45	0	0	3-2	67.2	82	42	4	7	24-5	36	4.92	102	.308	.378	0-0	—	0		0	0.0
1995	KC A	8	4	.667	44	0	0	1-1	64	66	34	4	4	30-7	43	4.36	110	.265	.352	2-0	.000	-0		3	0.4
1996	KC A	3	5	.375	57	0	0	3-2	68	74	41	5	2	26-5	43	5.43	92	.284	.351	0-0	—	0		-2	-0.1
1997	KC A	3	5	.375	47	0	0	11-2	49	51	24	7	1	24-8	34	4.22	112	.271	.357	0-0	—	0		3	0.6
1998	KC A	7	8	.467	27	18	0	1-0	112.1	126	73	11	4	43-2	55	5.13	94	.280	.346	2-0	.000	-0	92	-5	-0.5
2000	Bos A	6	3	.667	38	1	0	1-1	65	63	29	1	3	26-2	37	3.46	146	.260	.337	1-0	.000	-0	74	10	1.3
2001	Bos A	2	1	.667	30	0	0	0-3	34.2	42	23	3	5	10-3	17	4.93	91	.300	.363	0-0	—	0		-3	-0.1
2002	Hou N	0	1	.000	1	0	0	0-0	0.1	3	3	0	0	2-1	0	81.00	5	.750	.833	0-0	—	0		-3	-0.4
Total	10	50	44	.532	350	68	3-1	20-11	769.2	838	425	54	35	287-36	394	4.44	105	.279	.346	5-0	.000	-1	94	11	1.9
PICHE, RON Ronald Jacques B 5.22.1935 Verdun, PQ, CAN BR/TR 5-11/165# d5.30 C1																									
1960	Mil N	3	5	.375	37	0	0	9	48	48	26	3	3	23-4	38	3.56	96	.258	.346	7-0	.000	-0		-3	-0.6
1961	Mil N	2	2	.500	12	1	1	1	23.1	20	12	1	0	16-2	16	3.47	108	.238	.353	5-1	.000	-1	71	0	-0.1
1962	Mil N	3	2	.600	14	8	2	0	52	54	32	6	3	29-3	28	4.85	78	.273	.369	18-0	.056	-1*	118	-6	-0.6
1963	Mil N	1	1	.500	37	1	0	0	53	53	32	4	0	25-6	40	3.40	95	.256	.333	7-0	.000	-1	80	-5	-0.3
1965	Cal A	0	3	.000	14	1	0	0	19.2	20	15	5	0	12-2	14	6.86	50	.267	.364	1-0	.000	-0	77	-7	-1.0
1966	StL N	1	3	.250	20	0	0	2	25.1	21	13	4	1	18-4	21	4.26	84	.214	.339	4-1	.000	-0		-2	-0.3
Total	6	10	16	.385	134	11	3	12	221.1	216	130	23	7	123-21	157	4.19	84	.255	.350	42-2	.024	-3	113	-23	-2.9
PICKETT, RICKY Cecil Lee B 1.19.1970 Fort Worth, TX BL/TL 6-1/220# d4.28																									
1998	Ari N	0	0	—	2	0	0	0-0	0.2	3	6	0	0	4-0	2	81.00	5	.600	.778	0-0	—	0		-5	-0.3
PICKETT, CHARLIE Charles Albert B 3.1.1883 Delaware, OH D 5.20.1969 Springfield, OH BR/TR 6-1/175# d6.21																									
1910	StL N	0	0	—	2	0	0	0	6	7	2	0	0	2	2	1.50	199	.280	.333	0-0	—	0		1	0.1
PICKFORD, KEVIN Kevin Patrick B 3.12.1975 Fresno, CA BL/TL 6-4/200# d5.16																									
2002	SD N	0	2	.000	16	4	0	0-0	30	37	23	3	3	20-1	18	6.00	63	.314	.423	5-0	.000	-1	92	-9	-0.6
PICKREL, CLARENCE Clarence Douglas B 3.28.1911 Gretna, VA D 11.4.1983 Rocky Mount, VA BR/TR 6-1/180# d4.22																									
1933	Phi N	1	0	1.000	9	0	0	0	13.2	20	7	0	1	3	6	3.95	97	.357	.400	1-0	.000	-0		0	-0.1
1934	Bos N	0	0	—	10	1	0	0	16	24	9	0	0	7	9	5.06	76	.333	.392	2-0	.000	-0	203	-2	-0.1
Total	2	1	0	1.000	19	1	0	0	29.2	44	16	0	1	10	15	4.55	85	.344	.396	3-0	.000	-0	203	-2	-0.2
PICO, JEFF Jeffrey Mark B 2.12.1966 Antioch, CA BR/TR 6-1/190# d5.31																									
1988	Chi N	6	7	.462	29	13	3-2	1-1	112.2	108	57	6	0	37-6	57	4.15	87	.252	.309	34-2	.147	-0	104	-6	-0.8
1989	Chi N	3	1	.750	53	5	0	2-1	90.2	99	43	8	0	31-10	38	3.77	100	.278	.334	10-3	.100	-1	118	0	0.0
1990	Chi N	4	4	.500	31	8	0	2-1	92	120	53	7	1	37-10	37	4.79	85	.321	.382	22-1	.273	2	144	-6	-0.2
Total	3	13	12	.520	113	26	3-2	5-3	295.1	327	153	21	1	105-26	132	4.24	90	.282	.340	66-6	.182	1	119	-12	-1.0
PICONE, MARIO Mario Peter "Babe" B 7.5.1926 Brooklyn, NY BR/TR 5-11/180# d9.27																									
1947	NY N	0	0	—	2	1	0	0	7	10	6	1	0	2	1	7.71	53	.345	.387	2-0	.500	1	152	-2	0.0
1952	NY N	0	1	.000	2	1	0	0	9	11	8	2	0	5	3	7.00	53	.306	.390	2-1	.000	-0	72	-3	-0.3
1954	NY N	0	0	—	5	0	0	0	13.2	13	8	1	0	11	6	5.27	77	.283	.421	1-0	.000	0		-1	-0.1
	Cin N	0	1	.000	4	1	0	0	10.1	9	7	3	0	7	1	6.10	69	.243	.364	1-0	.000	0	43	-2	-0.1
	Year	0	1	.000	9	1	0	0	24	22	9	4	0	18	7	5.63	73	.265	.396	2-0	.000	0	43	-3	-0.2
Total	3	0	2	.000	13	3	0	0	40	43	29	7	0	25	11	6.30	64	.291	.393	6-1	.167	1	89	-8	-0.5
PIECHOTA, AL Aloysius Edward "Pie" B 1.19.1914 Chicago, IL D 6.13.1996 Chicago, IL BR/TR 6/195# d5.7																									
1940	Bos N	2	5	.286	21	8	2	0	61	68	45	6	0	41	18	5.75	65	.278	.381	20-1	.200	1	93	-15	-1.4
1941	Bos N	0	0	—	1	0	0	0	1	0	0	0	0	1	0	0.00	—	.000	.250	0-0	—	0		0	0.0
Total	2	2	5	.286	22	8	2	0	62	68	45	6	0	42	18	5.66	66	.274	.379	20-1	.200	1	93	-15	-1.4
PIEH, CY Edwin John B 9.29.1886 Waunakee, WI D 9.12.1945 Jacksonville, FL BR/TR 6-2/190# d9.6																									
1913	NY A	1	0	1.000	4	0	0	0	10.1	10	8	0	0	7	6	4.35	69	.256	.370	4-0	.250	0		-2	-0.1
1914	NY A	3	4	.429	18	4	1	0	62.1	68	41	6	0	29	24	5.05	55	.289	.367	17-1	.118	-0*	86	-15	-1.6
1915	NY A	4	5	.444	21	8	3-2	0	94	78	40	2	5	39	46	2.87	102	.234	.324	30-0	.067	-3	75	0	-0.4
Total	3	8	9	.471	43	12	4-2	0	166.2	156	89	8	5	75	76	3.78	76	.257	.344	51-1	.098	-3	78	-17	-2.1
PIERCE, ED Edward John B 10.6.1968 Arcadia, CA BL/TL 6-1/185# d9.6																									
1992	KC A	0	0	—	2	1	0	0-0	5.1	9	2	1	0	4-0	3	3.38	120	.429	.500	0-0	—	0	67	0	0.0
PIERCE, GEORGE George Thomas "Filbert" B 1.10.1888 Aurora, IL D 10.11.1935 Joliet, IL BL/TL 5-10.5/175# d4.16																									
1912	Chi N	0	0	—	3	2	0	0	14.2	15	13	0	0	12	9	5.52	60	.185	.290	6-0	.167	0	77	-4	-0.2
1913	Chi N	13	5	.722	25	21	14-3	0	164	137	60	4	3	59	73	2.30	138	.234	.308	55-3	.073	-3	129	14	1.1
1914	Chi N	9	12	.429	30	17	4	1	141	122	82	3	2	65	78	3.51	79	.239	.327	45-2	.089	-3	109	-11	-1.8
1915	Chi N	13	9	.591	36	20	8-2	0	176	158	83	1	4	77	96	3.32	84	.244	.328	56-3	.196	1	92	-11	-1.2
1916	Chi N	0	0	—	4	1	0	0	4.1	6	5	0	0	1	0	2.08	140	.300	.333	0-0	—	0	103	-1	-0.1
1917	StL N	1	1	.500	5	0	0	0	10.1	7	7	0	1	3	4	3.48	77	.184	.262	4-0	.000	-1		-2	-0.4
Total	6	36	27	.571	103	61	26-5	1	510.1	445	250	8	10	217	260	3.10	94	.236	.318	166-8	.120	-6	110	-15	-2.6
PIERCE, JEFF Jeffrey Charles B 6.7.1969 Poughkeepsie, NY BR/TR 6-1/190# d4.26																									
1995	Bos A	0	3	.000	12	0	0	0-1	15	16	12	0	0	14-4	12	6.60	74	.286	.423	0-0	—	0		-3	-0.5
PIERCE, RAY Raymond Lester "Lefty" B 6.6.1897 Emporia, KS D 5.4.1963 Denver, CO BL/TL 5-7/156# d5.12																									
1924	Chi N	0	0	—	6	0	0	0	7.1	7	6	2	0	4	2	7.36	53	.269	.367	0-0	—	0		-2	-0.1
1925	Phi N	5	4	.556	23	8	4	0	90	134	67	7	1	24	18	5.50	87	.356	.397	28-4	.179	-0	115	-6	-0.5
1926	Phi N	2	7	.222	37	7	1	0	84.2	128	71	3	1	35	18	5.63	74	.348	.406	24-2	.125	-2*	80	-16	-1.7
Total	3	7	11	.389	66	15	5	0	182	269	144	12	2	63	38	5.64	79	.349	.400	52-6	.154	-2	101	-24	-2.3
PIERCE, TONY Tony Michael B 1.29.1946 Brunswick, GA BR/TL 6-1/190# d4.14																									
1967	KC A	3	4	.429	49	6	0	7	97.2	79	42	6	5	30-6	61	3.04	105	.221	.290	20-1	.000	-2	77	-1	-0.3
1968	Oak A	1	2	.333	17	3	0	1	32.2	39	16	3	1	10-2	16	3.86	73	.295	.347	6-1	.000	-1	113	-4	-0.4
Total	2	4	6	.400	66	9	0	8	130.1	118	58	9	6	40-8	77	3.25	95	.241	.305	26-2	.000	-3	88	-5	-0.7
PIERCE, BILLY Walter William B 4.2.1927 Detroit, MI BL/TL 5-10/160# d6.1																									
1945	Det A	0	0	—	5	0	0	0	10	6	2	1	1	10	10	1.80	195	.182	.386	2-0	.000	-0		2	0.1
1948	Det A	3	0	1.000	22	5	0	0	55.1	47	40	5	1	51	36	6.34	69	.234	.391	17-0	.294	2	145	-10	-0.3
1949	Chi A	7	15	.318	32	26	8	0	171.2	145	89	11	0	112	95	3.88	108	.228	.344	51-6	.176	-1*	88	3	0.4
1950	Chi A	12	16	.429	33	29	15-1	1	219.1	189	112	11	2	137	118	3.98	113	.228	.339	77-4	.260	4*	82	11	1.5
1951	Chi A	15	14	.517	37	28	18-1	2	240.1	237	93	14	1	73	113	3.03	133	.258	.313	79-5	.203	-0*	94	28	3.1
1952	Chi A	15	12	.556	33	32	14-4	1	255.1	214	76	12	3	79	144	2.57	142	.227	.289	91-5	.187	0*	102	33	3.5
1953	Chi A★	18	12	.600	40	33	19-7	3	271.1	216	94	20	3	102	**186**	2.72	148	**.218**	.292	87-10	.126	-4*	82	**38**	3.5
1954	Chi A	9	10	.474	36	26	12-4	3	188.2	179	86	15	3	86	148	3.48	107	.249	.330	57-6	.193	0*	96	3	0.2
1955	Chi A★	15	10	.600	33	26	16-6	1	205.2	162	50	16	3	64-5	157	**1.97**	**200**	.213	**.277**	70-8	.171	-1*	81	**45**	**5.3**
1956	Chi A★	20	9	.690	35	33	**21**-1	1	276.1	261	108	24	3	100-7	192	3.32	123	.249	.316	102-7	.157	-4*	124	26	1.9
1957	Chi A★	**20**	12	.625	37	34	**16**-4	2	257	228	98	18	1	71-9	171	3.26	115	.234	.287	99-3	.172	-2*	96	15	1.6
1958	Chi A☆	17	11	.607	35	32	**19**-3	2	245	204	83	33	1	66-2	144	2.68	136	.227	.279	83-6	.205	2	95	26	3.0
1959	†Chi A☆	14	15	.483	34	33	12-2	0	224	217	98	26	3	62-4	114	3.62	104	.253	.305	68-6	.191	3	79	5	0.9
1960	Chi A	14	7	.667	32	30	8-1	0	196.1	201	81	24	0	46-1	108	3.62	104	.266	.307	67-3	.179	1	115	7	0.7
1961	Chi A☆	10	9	.526	39	28	5-1	3	180	190	85	17	1	54-3	106	3.80	103	.275	.326	56-6	.143	-2	104	2	0.0
1962	†SF N	16	6	.727	30	23	7-2	1	162.1	147	67	19	3	35-2	76	3.49	109	.239	.283	56-7	.214	2	131	7	1.0
1963	SF N	3	11	.214	38	13	3-1	8	99	106	49	12	1	20-1	52	4.27	75	.272	.308	31-1	.129	-0	116	-9	-1.4
1964	SF N	3	0	1.000	34	1	0	4	49	40	14	6	0	10-1	29	2.20	162	.222	.260	9-0	.333	1	123	7	0.6

Year	Tm Lg	W	L	Pct	G	GS	CG-Sho	SV-BS	IP	H	R	HR	HB	BB-IB	SO	ERA	AERA	OAV	OOB	AB-SH	AVG	PB	Sup	APR	PW
Total	18	211	169	.555	585	432	193-38	32	3306.2	2989	1325	284	30	1178-**35**	1999	3.27	119	.240	.307	1102-83	.184	0	98	239	25.6
PIERCY, BILL William Benton "Wild Bill" B 5.2.1896 ElMonte, CA D 8.28.1951 Long Beach, CA BR/TR 6-1/185# d10.3																									
1917	NY A	0	1	.000	1	1	1	0	9	9	3	0	0	2	4	3.00	90	.257	.297	2-0	.000	0	27	0	0.0
1921	†NY A	5	4	.556	14	10	5-1	0	81.2	82	40	4	7	28	35	2.98	142	.263	.337	28-0	.214	0	97	9	0.9
1922	Bos A	3	9	.250	29	12	7-1	0	121.1	140	77	2	6	62	24	4.67	88	.304	.394	34-4	.147	-1	59	-9	-0.8
1923	Bos A	8	17	.320	30	24	11	0	187.1	193	105	5	14	73	51	3.41	121	.277	.357	53-8	.132	-3	74	8	0.8
1924	Bos A	5	7	.417	23	18	3	0	121	156	87	4	10	66	20	5.95	73	.335	.429	39-5	.154	-2	108	-17	-1.5
1926	Chi N	6	5	.545	19	5	1	0	90.1	96	52	1	6	37	31	4.48	86	.280	.360	35-0	.257	1	126	-5	-0.5
Total	6	27	43	.386	116	70	28-2	0	610.2	676	364	16	43	268	165	4.26	97	.292	.376	191-17	.173	-5	88	-14	-1.1
PIERETTI, MARINO Marino Paul "Chick" B 9.23.1920 Lucca, Italy D 1.30.1981 San Francisco, CA BR/TR 5-7/158# d4.19																									
1945	Was A	14	13	.519	44	27	14-3	2	233.1	235	114	3	1	91	66	3.32	94	.257	.325	81-4	.222	2	102	-10	-0.9
1946	Was A	2	2	.500	30	2	1	0	62	70	48	9	2	40	20	5.95	56	.292	.397	14-1	.214	0	102	-18	-1.0
1947	Was A	2	4	.333	23	10	2-1	0	83.1	97	50	3	2	47	32	4.21	88	.287	.377	26-2	.231	-0	126	-7	-0.5
1948	Was A	0	2	.000	8	1	0	0	11.2	18	14	1	0	7	6	10.80	40	.375	.455	2-0	.000	-0*	83	-7	-1.1
	Chi A	8	10	.444	21	18	4	1	120	117	70	6	0	52	28	4.95	86	.262	.339	39-1	.179	-1*	80	-8	-1.0
	Year	8	12	.400	29	19	4	1	131.2	135	74	7	0	59	34	5.47	78	.273	.351	41-1	.171	-1	80	-15	-2.1
1949	Chi A	4	6	.400	39	9	0	4	116	131	77	10	0	54	25	5.51	76	.289	.364	38-1	.237	1*	93	-16	-1.2
1950	Cle A	0	1	.000	29	1	0	1	47.1	45	24	2	0	30	11	4.18	104	.253	.361	7-0	.286	0*	146	1	0.1
Total	6	30	38	.441	194	68	21-4	8	673.2	713	397	34	5	321	188	4.53	81	.272	.353	207-9	.217	2	98	-65	-5.6
PIEROTTI, AL Albert Felix B 10.24.1895 Boston, MA D 2.12.1964 Everett, MA BR/TR 5-10.5/195# d8.9																									
1920	Bos N	1	1	.500	6	2	2	0	25	23	9	2	0	9	12	2.88	106	.250	.317	8-1	.250	0	90	1	0.1
1921	Bos N	0	1	.000	2	0	0	0	1.2	3	4	0	0	3	1	21.60	17	.375	.545	1-0	.000	-0		-3	-0.6
Total	2	1	2	.333	8	2	2	0	26.2	26	13	2	0	12	13	4.05	76	.260	.339	9-1	.222	-0	90	-2	-0.5
PIERRO, BILL William Leonard "Wild Bill" B 4.15.1926 Brooklyn, NY BR/TR 6-1/155# d7.17																									
1950	Pit N	0	2	.000	12	3	0	0	29	33	34	2	2	28	13	10.55	42	.289	.438	9-0	.222	-0*	74	-17	-1.0
PIERSOLL, CHRIS Christopher Earl B 9.25.1977 Van Nuys, CA BR/TR 6-4/195# d8.31																									
2001	Cin N	0	0	—	11	0	0	0-0	11.1	12	4	0	1	6-0	7	2.38	191	.267	.365	0-0	—	0		2	0.1
PIERSON, WILLIAM William Morris B 6.14.1899 Atlantic City, NJ D 2.20.1959 Atlantic City, NJ BL/TL 6-2/180# d7.4																									
1918	Phi A	0	1	.000	8	1	0	0	21.2	20	10	0	2	20	6	3.32	88	.286	.457	4-0	.250	-0	26	-1	-0.1
1919	Phi A	0	0	—	2	1	0	0	7.2	9	3	0	0	8	4	3.52	97	.333	.486	3-0	.333	0	160	0	0.0
1924	Phi A	0	0	—	1	0	0	0	2.2	3	1	0	0	3	0	3.38	127	.300	.462	0-0	—	0		0	0.0
Total	3	0	1	.000	11	2	0	0	32	32	14	0	2	31	10	3.38	94	.299	.464	7-0	.286	0	97	-1	-0.1
PIKTUZIS, GEORGE George Richard B 1.3.1932 Chicago, IL D 11.28.1993 Long Beach, CA BR/TL 6-2/200# d4.25																									
1956	Chi N	0	0	—	2	0	0	0	5	6	4	1	0	2-0	3	7.20	52	.333	.400	0-0	—	0		-2	-0.1
PILLETTE, DUANE Duane Xavier "Dee" B 7.24.1922 Detroit, MI BR/TR 6-3/205# d7.19 f-Herman																									
1949	NY A	2	4	.333	12	3	2	0	37.1	43	20	6	0	19	9	4.34	93	.299	.380	11-2	.000	-1	89	-1	-0.2
1950	NY A	0	0	—	4	0	0	0	7	9	3	0	0	3	4	1.29	334	.321	.387	0-0	—	0		2	0.1
	StL A	3	5	.375	24	7	1	2	73.2	104	62	6	2	44	18	7.09	70	.337	.423	22-1	.136	-1*	81	-14	-1.4
	Year	3	5	.375	28	7	1	2	80.2	113	66	6	2	47	22	6.58	74	.335	.420	22-1	.136	-1	82	-13	-1.3
1951	StL A	6	14	.300	35	24	6-1	0	191	205	113	14	5	115	65	4.99	88	.276	.376	59-6	.136	-3*	60	-10	-1.3
1952	StL A	10	13	.435	30	30	9-1	0	205.1	222	94	14	7	55	62	3.59	109	.274	.325	66-6	.182	0*	99	7	0.6
1953	StL A	7	13	.350	31	25	5-1	0	166.2	181	90	16	2	62	58	4.48	94	.277	.341	53-2	.132	-1	73	-3	-0.5
1954	Bal A	10	14	.417	25	25	11-1	0	179	158	79	9	1	67	66	3.12	115	.234	.303	53-6	.132	-1	81	5	0.8
1955	Bal A	0	3	.000	7	5	0	0	20.2	31	16	0	0	14-1	13	6.53	58	.344	.433	6-0	.167	0	65	-6	-0.7
1956	Phi N	0	0	—	20	0	0	0	23.1	32	21	2	0	12-4	10	6.56	57	.330	.396	1-0	.000	-0		-8	-0.4
Total	8	38	66	.365	188	119	34-4	2	904	985	498	67	17	391-5	305	4.40	93	.277	.351	271-23	.140	-7	78	-28	-3.0
PILLETTE, HERMAN Herman Polycarp "Old Folks" B 12.26.1895 St.Paul, OR D 4.30.1960 Sacramento, CA BR/TR 6-2/190# d7.30 s-Duane																									
1917	Cin N	0	0	—	1	0	0	0	1	4	2	0	0	0	0	18.00	15	.571	.571	0-0	—	0		-1	-0.1
1922	Det A	19	12	.613	40	37	18-4	1	274.2	270	110	6	15	95	71	2.85	136	.258	.328	99-3	.172	-3	120	30	2.9
1923	Det A	14	19	.424	47	36	14	1	250.1	280	138	7	6	83	64	3.85	100	.288	.347	85-2	.247	4	106	-4	0.0
1924	Det A	1	1	.500	19	3	1	1	37.2	46	30	1	3	14	13	4.78	86	.297	.366	11-0	.364	1	150	-5	-0.2
Total	4	34	32	.515	107	76	33-4	3	563.2	600	280	14	24	192	148	3.45	113	.275	.340	195-5	.215	2	115	20	2.6
PILLION, SQUIZ Cecil Randolph B 4.13.1894 Hartford, CT D 9.30.1962 Pittsburgh, PA BL/TL 6/178# d8.20																									
1915	Phi A	0	0	—	2	0	0	0	5.1	10	5	0	1	2	0	6.75	43	.400	.464	1-0	.000	-0		-2	-0.1
PINA, HORACIO Horacio (Garcia) B 3.12.1945 Coahuila, Mexico BR/TR 6-2/177# d8.14																									
1968	Cle A	1	1	.500	12	3	0	2	31.1	24	7	0	1	15-1	24	1.72	172	.218	.315	6-2	.000	-1	108	4	0.3
1969	Cle A	4	2	.667	31	4	0	1-2	46.2	44	29	6	5	27-2	32	5.21	72	.256	.371	6-0	.500	1	100	-6	-0.7
1970	Was A	5	3	.625	61	0	0	6-4	71	66	25	4	3	35-9	41	2.79	128	.250	.341	3-0	.000	-0		6	0.8
1971	Was A	1	1	.500	56	0	0	2-2	57.2	47	26	2	4	31-7	38	3.59	92	.227	.335	1-0	.000	-0		-2	-0.1
1972	Tex A	2	7	.222	60	0	0	15-3	76	61	33	3	8	43-7	60	3.20	94	.228	.351	5-2	.200	0		-2	-0.2
1973	†Oak A	6	3	.667	47	0	0	8-2	88	58	31	8	8	34-5	41	2.76	129	.193	.290	0-0	—	0		8	1.1
1974	Chi N	3	4	.429	34	0	0	4-3	47.1	49	22	4	2	28-4	32	3.99	96	.268	.367	5-0	.200	-0		0	0.1
	Cal A	1	2	.333	11	0	0	0-1	11.2	9	3	1	0	3-2	6	2.31	149	.209	.261	0-0	—	0		2	0.4
1978	Phi N	0	0	—	2	0	0	0-0	2.1	0	0	0	0	0-0	4	0.00	—	.000	.000	1-0	.000	-0		1	0.0
Total	8	23	23	.500	314	7	0	38-17	432	358	176	28	31	216-37	278	3.25	106	.231	.334	27-4	.185	0	103	11	1.7
PINEDA, LUIS Luis A. B 10.17.1974 San Cristobal, D.R. BR/TR 6-1/160# d8.4																									
2001	Det A	0	1	.000	16	0	0	0-0	18.1	16	10	2	0	14-2	13	4.91	89	.239	.366	0-0	—	0		-1	0.0
2002	Cin N	1	3	.250	26	2	0	0-0	32.1	25	16	4	2	24-1	31	4.18	102	.221	.362	3-0	.000	-0	185	1	0.0
Total	2	1	4	.200	42	2	0	0-0	50.2	41	26	6	2	38-3	44	4.44	97	.228	.363	3-0	.000	-0	185	0	0.0
PINEIRO, JOEL Joel Alberto B 9.25.1978 Rio Piedras, P.R. BR/TR 6-1/180# d8.8																									
2000	Sea A	1	0	1.000	8	1	0	0-0	19.1	25	13	3	0	13-0	10	5.59	84	.316	.404	0-0	—	0	239	-2	-0.1
2001	Sea A	6	2	.750	17	11	0	0-0	75.1	50	24	2	3	21-0	56	2.03	205	.191	.257	0-0	—	0	81	16	1.5
2002	Sea A	14	7	.667	37	28	2-1	0-0	194.1	189	75	24	7	54-1	136	3.24	130	.256	.310	7-0	.143	-0	114	22	2.3
2003	Sea A	16	11	.593	32	32	3-**2**	0-0	211.2	192	94	19	6	76-3	151	3.78	114	.241	.309	4-1	.000	-0	113	14	1.5
Total	4	37	20	.649	94	72	5-3	0-0	500.2	456	206	48	16	164-4	353	3.38	127	.243	.306	11-1	.091	-0	110	50	5.2
PINKHAM, ED Edward B 1849 Brooklyn, NY BL/TL 5-7/142# d5.8 ▲																									
1871	Chi NA	1	0	1.000	3	0	0	1	10.1	10	8	0		3	0	3.48	132	.208	.255	95	.263	1*		**2**	0.1
PINNANCE, ED Elijah Edward "Peanuts" B 10.22.1879 Walpole Island, ON, CAN D 12.12.1944 Walpole Island, ON, CAN BL/TR 6-1/180# d9.14																									
1903	Phi A	0	0	—	2	1	0	1	7	5	2	0	0	2	2	2.57	119	.200	.259	3-0	.000	-0	117	1	0.0
PINTO, LERTON William Lerton B 4.8.1899 Chillicothe, OH D 5.13.1983 Oxnard, CA BL/TL 6/190# d5.23																									
1922	Phi N	0	1	.000	9	0	0	0	24.2	31	20	1	0	14	4	5.11	91	.320	.405	9-0	.111	-1		-2	-0.2
1924	Phi N	0	0	—	3	0	0	0	4	7	4	1	0	0	1	9.00	50	.467	.467	1-0	.000	-0		-2	-0.1
Total	2	0	1	.000	12	0	0	0	28.2	38	24	2	0	14	5	5.65	82	.339	.413	10-0	.100	-1		-4	-0.3
PIPGRAS, ED Edward John B 6.15.1904 Schleswig, IA D 4.13.1964 Currie, MN BR/TR 6-2.5/175# d8.25 b-George																									
1932	Bro N	0	1	.000	5	1	0	0	10	16	11	2	0	6	5	5.40	71	.348	.423	2-0	.000	-0	154	-4	-0.3
PIPGRAS, GEORGE George William B 12.20.1899 Ida Grove, IA D 10.19.1986 Gainesville, FL BR/TR 6-1.5/185# d6.9 U9 b-Ed																									
1923	NY A	1	3	.250	8	2	2	0	33.1	34	22	2	1	25	12	5.94	66	.276	.403	9-0	.000	-1	84	-6	-0.7
1924	NY A	0	1	.000	9	1	0	1	15.1	20	18	0	4	18	4	9.98	42	.351	.532	3-0	.333	0	101	-9	-0.6
1927	†NY A	10	3	.769	29	21	9-1	0	166.1	148	81	2	1	77	81	4.11	94	.247	.334	67-2	.239	2	156	0	0.1
1928	†NY A	**24**	13	.649	46	**38**	22-4	3	**300.2**	314	132	4	3	103	139	3.38	111	.272	.333	115-6	.157	-4	127	15	1.1

Year	Tm Lg	W	L	Pct	G	GS	CG-Sho	SV-BS	IP	H	R	HR	HB	BB-IB	SO	ERA	AERA	OAV	OOB	AB-SH	AVG	PB	Sup	APR	PW
1929	NY A	18	12	.600	39	33	13-3	0	225.1	229	132	16	5	95	125	4.23	91	.264	.340	84-4	.143	-4	129	-12	-1.8
1930	NY A	15	15	.500	44	30	15-**3**	4	221	230	133	9	8	70	111	4.11	105	.263	.324	80-6	.150	-2	143	0	-0.3
1931	NY A	7	6	.538	36	14	6-1	3	137.2	134	73	8	2	58	59	3.79	105	.251	.327	41-1	.024	-6	99	0	-0.6
1932	†NY A	16	9	.640	32	27	14-2	0	219	235	120	15	6	87	111	4.19	97	.269	.340	82-5	.220	1	130	-4	-0.4
1933	NY A	2	2	.500	4	4	3	0	33	32	13	1	0	12	14	3.27	119	.252	.317	11-0	.091	-1	99	3	0.3
	Bos A	9	8	.529	22	17	9-2	1	128.1	140	65	5	2	45	56	4.07	108	.276	.337	46-2	.196	-1	102	6	0.5
	Year	11	10	.524	26	21	12-2	1	161.1	172	70	6	2	57	70	3.90	110	.271	.333	57-2	.175	-1	101	9	0.8
1934	Bos A	0	0	—	2	1	0	0	3.1	4	3	1	0	3	0	8.10	59	.308	.438	1-0	.000	-0	109	-1	0.0
1935	Bos A	0	1	.000	5	1	0	0	5	9	9	3	1	5	2	14.40	33	.391	.517	0-1	—	0	37	-5	-0.8
Total	11	102	73	.583	276	189	93-16	12	1488.1	1529	801	66	33	598	714	4.09	98	.266	.339	539-27	.163	-15	127	-13	-3.2
PIPPEN, COTTON Henry Harold B 4.2.1911 Cisco, TX D 2.15.1981 Williams, CA BR/TR 6-2/180# d8.28																									
1936	StL N	0	2	.000	6	3	0	0	21	37	18	5	2	8	8	7.71	51	.402	.461	6-0	.167	0	72	-8	-0.6
1939	Phi A	4	11	.267	25	17	5	1	118.2	169	97	13	1	40	33	5.99	79	.329	.378	35-3	.086	-2	77	-18	-2.0
	Det A	0	1	.000	3	2	0	0	14	18	13	1	0	6	5	7.07	69	.310	.375	5-0	.400	0	108	-3	-0.2
	Year	4	12	.250	28	19	5	1	132.2	187	19	14	1	46	38	6.11	77	.327	.378	40-3	.125	-2	80	-23	-2.2
1940	Det A	1	2	.333	4	3	0	0	21.1	29	16	3	1	10	9	6.75	70	.326	.400	8-0	.000	-1	49	-3	-0.5
Total	3	5	16	.238	38	25	5	1	175	253	144	22	4	64	55	6.38	73	.336	.391	54-3	.111	-3	76	-32	-3.3
PIRTLE, GERRY Gerald Eugene B 12.3.1947 Tulsa, OK BR/TR 6-1/185# d7.2																									
1978	Mon N	0	2	.000	19	0	0	0-1	25.2	33	24	5	2	23-6	14	5.96	59	.314	.446	0-0	—	0		-9	-0.7
PISCIOTTA, MARC Marc George B 8.7.1970 Edison, NJ BR/TR 6-5/240# d6.30																									
1997	Chi N	3	1	.750	24	0	0	0-1	28.1	20	10	1	1	16-0	21	3.18	136	.200	.314	1-0	.000	-0		4	0.5
1998	Chi N	1	2	.333	43	0	0	0-0	44	44	21	4	2	32-3	31	4.09	108	.259	.380	3-0	.333	0		2	0.1
1999	KC A	0	2	.000	8	0	0	0-0	8.1	9	8	1	0	10-0	3	8.64	58	.281	.452	0-0	—	0		-3	-0.5
Total	3	4	5	.444	75	0	0	0-1	80.2	73	39	6	3	58-3	55	4.24	105	.242	.367	4-0	.250	0		3	0.1
PITLOCK, SKIP Lee Patrick Thomas B 11.6.1947 Hillside, IL BL/TL 6-2/180# d6.12																									
1970	SF N	5	5	.500	18	15	1	0-0	87	92	48	13	4	48-2	56	4.66	85	.274	.369	25-3	.080	-0	105	-5	-0.5
1974	Chi A	3	3	.500	40	5	0	1-1	105.2	103	58	7	7	55-4	68	4.43	84	.257	.353	0-0	—	0	113	-8	-0.5
1975	Chi A	0	0	—	1	0	0	0-0	0	1	0	0	0	0-0	0	—	—	1.000	1.000	0-0	—	0		0	0.0
Total	3	8	8	.500	59	20	1	1-1	192.2	196	106	20	11	103-6	124	4.53	85	.266	.361	25-3	.080	-0	109	-13	-1.0
PITTINGER, TOGIE Charles Reno B 1.12.1872 Greencastle, PA D 1.14.1909 Greencastle, PA BL/TR 6-2/175# d4.26																									
1900	Bos N	2	9	.182	18	13	8	0	114	135	97	7	8	54	27	5.13	80	.293	.377	46-0	.130	-4	88	-12	-1.4
1901	Bos N	13	16	.448	34	33	27-1	0	281.1	288	135	7	8	76	129	3.01	120	.263	.316	100-2	.110	-8	65	15	0.7
1902	Bos N	27	16	.628	46	40	36-7	0	389.1	360	139	4	16	128	174	2.52	112	.245	.313	147-4	.136	-8	100	18	0.9
1903	Bos N	18	22	.450	44	39	35-3	1	351.2	396	205	12	17	143	140	3.48	92	.294	.369	128-3	.109	-9	76	-10	-1.9
1904	Bos N	15	21	.417	38	37	35-5	0	335.1	298	149	1	14	144	146	2.66	104	.242	.329	121-3	.107	-9	74	2	-0.5
1905	Phi N	23	14	.622	**46**	37	29-4	2	337.1	311	155	3	16	104	136	3.09	94	.247	.313	122-12	.156	-3	126	-5	-1.0
1906	Phi N	8	10	.444	20	16	9-2	0	129.2	128	62	2	12	50	43	3.40	77	.252	.334	44-1	.091	-1	92	-8	-1.3
1907	Phi N	9	5	.643	16	12	8-1	0	102	101	43	3	5	35	37	3.00	81	.261	.330	36-0	.139	-1	105	-6	-0.9
Total	8	115	113	.504	262	227	187-23	3	2040.2	2017	985	39	96	734	832	3.10	98	.260	.332	744-25	.124	-43	89	-6	-5.4
PITTSLEY, JIM James Michael B 4.3.1974 DuBois, PA BR/TR 6-7/215# d5.23																									
1995	KC A	0	0	—	1	1	0	0-0	3.1	7	5	3	0	1-0	0	13.50	35	.438	.471	0-0	—	0	117	-3	-0.1
1997	KC A	5	8	.385	21	21	0	0-0	112	120	72	15	6	54-1	52	5.46	86	.277	.361	2-0	.500	1	93	-8	-0.8
1998	KC A	1	1	.500	39	2	0	0-0	68.1	88	56	13	2	37-1	44	6.59	73	.322	.401	2-1	.000	-0	39	-14	-0.6
1999	KC A	1	2	.333	5	5	0	0-0	23.1	33	22	2	1	15-0	7	6.94	72	.337	.426	0-0	—	0	97	-6	-0.6
	Mil N	0	1	.000	15	0	0	0-1	18.2	20	12	3	1	10-0	13	4.82	94	.274	.365	1-0	.000	0		-1	0.0
Total	4	7	12	.368	81	29	0	0-1	225.2	268	167	36	10	117-2	116	6.02	79	.300	.382	5-1	.200	1	91	-32	-2.1
PITULA, STAN Stanley B 3.23.1931 Hackensack, NJ D 8.15.1965 Hackensack, NJ BR/TR 5-10/170# d4.24																									
1957	Cle A	2	2	.500	23	5	1	0	59.2	67	37	8	2	32-4	17	4.98	75	.296	.384	15-0	.200	0*	130	-8	-0.5
PIZARRO, JUAN Juan Ramon (Cordova) B 2.7.1937 Santurce, P.R. BL/TL 5-11/190# d5.4																									
1957	†Mil N	5	6	.455	24	10	3	0	99.1	99	58	16	1	51-2	68	4.62	76	.261	.348	36-0	.250	3*	101	-14	-1.1
1958	†Mil N	6	4	.600	16	10	7-1	1	96.2	75	36	12	4	47-0	84	2.70	130	.212	.311	32-0	.250	3	107	8	1.1
1959	Mil N	6	2	.750	29	14	6-2	0	133.2	117	61	13	8	70-3	126	3.77	94	.237	.340	41-2	.122	-0	133	-2	-0.1
1960	Mil N	6	7	.462	21	17	3	0	114.2	105	63	13	4	72-1	88	4.55	75	.244	.354	40-1	.275	3*	123	-14	-1.2
1961	Chi A	14	7	.667	39	25	12-1	2	194.2	164	73	17	4	89-1	188	3.05	128	.226	.312	69-1	.246	5*	110	19	2.5
1962	Chi A	12	14	.462	36	32	9-1	1	203.1	182	97	16	1	97-3	173	3.81	103	.236	.320	69-3	.159	-0*	94	1	0.0
1963	Chi A★	16	8	.667	32	28	10-3	1	214.2	177	69	14	3	63-1	163	2.39	147	.224	.282	73-3	.178	3	110	25	3.0
1964	Chi A☆	19	9	.679	33	33	11-4	0	239	193	78	23	3	55-5	162	2.56	135	.219	.267	90-2	.211	5	105	24	3.3
1965	Chi A	6	3	.667	18	18	2-1	0	97	96	42	9	1	37-3	65	3.43	93	.254	.321	34-1	.235	3*	119	-3	0.1
1966	Chi A	8	6	.571	34	9	1	3	88.2	91	49	9	1	39-7	42	3.76	84	.269	.346	26-3	.154	0	120	-9	-1.3
1967	Pit N	8	10	.444	50	9	1-1	9	107	99	55	10	2	52-15	96	3.95	85	.245	.332	27-0	.259	2	67	-8	-1.2
1968	Pit N	1	1	.500	12	0	0	0	11	14	7	2	1	10-2	6	3.27	89	.311	.439	2-0	.000	-0*		-1	-0.3
	Bos A	6	8	.429	19	12	6	2	107.2	97	46	15	0	44-4	84	3.59	88	.242	.315	31-4	.161	1*	97	-4	-0.3
1969	Bos A	0	1	.000	6	0	0	2-0	9	14	7	2	0	6-0	4	6.00	63	.359	.444	3-0	.333	0		-2	-0.3
	Cle A	3	3	.500	48	4	1	4-3	82.2	67	34	6	2	49-7	44	3.16	119	.229	.335	15-1	.200	0	123	5	0.4
	Oak A	1	1	.500	3	0	0	1-0	7.2	3	2	1	0	3-0	4	2.35	147	.125	.214	2-0	.500	0		1	0.3
	Year	4	5	.444	57	4	1	7-3	99.1	84	41	9	2	58-7	52	3.35	112	.236	.339	20-1	.250	1	124	4	0.4
1970	Chi N	0	0	—	12	0	0	1-0	15.2	16	9	2	1	9-0	14	4.60	98	.262	.366	3-0	.000	-0		0	0.0
1971	Chi N	7	6	.538	16	14	6-3	0-0	101.1	78	43	10	2	40-3	67	3.46	114	.209	.288	34-2	.176	1	80	5	0.7
1972	Chi N	4	5	.444	16	7	1	1-0	59.1	66	28	7	1	32-5	24	3.94	97	.293	.384	21-0	.143	-0	63	0	0.0
1973	Chi N	0	1	.000	2	0	0	0-1	4	6	5	1	1	1-0	3	11.25	35	.353	.400	1-0	.000	-0		-3	-0.5
	Hou N	2	2	.500	15	1	0	0-0	23.1	28	17	1	1	11-3	10	6.56	56	.301	.381	3-1	.000	-0	73	-7	-1.0
	Year	2	3	.400	17	1	0	0-1	27.1	34	20	2	2	12-3	13	7.24	51	.309	.384	4-1	.000	-0	72	-9	-1.5
1974	†Pit N	1	1	.500	7	2	0	0-0	24	20	11	2	0	11-2	7	1.88	184	.220	.298	6-0	.333	0	164	2	0.2
Total	18	131	105	.555	488	245	79-17	28-4	2034.1	1807	890	201	41	888-67	1522	3.43	104	.237	.319	658-24	.202	29	105	23	4.3
PLADSON, GORDIE Gordon Cecil B 7.31.1956 New Westminster, BC, CAN BR/TR 6-4/210# d9.7																									
1979	Hou N	0	0	—	4	0	0	0-0	4	9	2	1	0	2-0	2	4.50	78	.450	.500	0-0	—	0		0	0.0
1980	Hou N	0	4	.000	12	6	0	0-0	41.1	38	23	3	0	16-0	13	4.35	76	.244	.312	10-0	.000	-1	86	-5	-0.6
1981	Hou N	0	0	—	2	0	0	0-0	4	9	4	0	0	3-0	3	9.00	37	.429	.500	0-0	—	0		-2	-0.1
1982	Hou N	0	0	—	2	0	0	0-0	1.1	10	8	0	0	2-0	0	54.00	6	.769	.750	0-0	—	0		-8	-0.4
Total	4	0	4	.000	20	6	0	0-0	50.2	66	37	4	0	23-0	18	6.04	55	.314	.379	10-0	.000	-1	86	-15	-1.1
PLANETA, EMIL Emil Joseph B 1.31.1909 Higganum, CT D 2.2.1963 Rocky Hill, CT BR/TR 6/190# d9.20																									
1931	NY N	0	0	—	2	0	0	0	5.1	7	7	0	0	4	0	10.13	36	.292	.393	1-0	.000	-0		-4	-0.2
PLANK, ED Edward Arthur B 4.9.1952 Chicago, IL BR/TR 6-1/205# d9.6																									
1978	SF N	0	0	—	5	0	0	0-0	6.2	6	3	1	0	2-1	1	4.05	85	.273	.320	0-0	—	0		0	0.0
1979	SF N	0	0	—	4	0	0	0-0	3.2	9	5	0	0	2-1	1	7.36	48	.450	.500	0-0	—	0		-2	-0.1
Total	2	0	0	—	9	0	0	0-0	10.1	15	8	1	0	4-2	2	5.23	66	.357	.404	0-0	—	0		-2	-0.1
PLANK, EDDIE Edward Stewart "Gettysburg Eddie" B 8.31.1875 Gettysburg, PA D 2.24.1926 Gettysburg, PA BL/TL 5-11.5/175# d5.13 HF1946																									
1901	Phi A	17	13	.567	33	32	28-1	0	260.2	254	133	3	7	68	90	3.31	114	.252	.304	99-2	.182	-3	96	14	0.9
1902	Phi A	20	15	.571	36	32	31-1	0	300	319	140	5	18	61	107	3.30	111	.273	.319	120-4	.292	6	107	18	2.3
1903	Phi A	23	16	.590	**43**	**40**	33-3	0	336	317	128	5	23	65	176	2.38	128	.249	.297	134-2	.187	-1*	100	20	2.0
1904	Phi A	26	17	.605	44	43	37-7	0	357.1	311	111	2	19	86	201	2.17	124	.235	.292	129-6	.240	3*	93	23	3.2
1905	†Phi A	24	12	.667	41	**41**	**35**-4	0	346.2	287	113	3	24	75	210	2.26	118	.227	.283	126-2	.230	3	108	20	2.2
1906	Phi A	19	6	**.760**	26	25	21-5	0	211.2	173	70	1	15	51	108	2.25	121	.226	.288	73-5	.233	2	126	13	1.6

Year	Tm Lg	W	L	Pct	G	GS	CG-Sho	SV-BS	IP	H	R	HR	HB	BB-IB	SO	ERA	AERA	OAV	OOB	AB-SH	AVG	PB	Sup	APR	PW
1907	Phi A	24	16	.600	43	40	33-**8**	0	343.2	282	115	5	17	85	183	2.20	118	.226	.285	123-8	.211	2	84	17	2.2
1908	Phi A	14	16	.467	34	28	21-4	1	244.2	202	71	1	9	46	135	2.17	118	.224	.269	89-1	.180	-1*	80	14	1.4
1909	Phi A	19	10	.655	34	33	24-3	0	265.1	215	74	1	8	62	132	1.76	136	.224	.277	96-2	.219	4*	111	19	2.6
1910	Phi A	16	10	.615	38	32	22-1	2	250.1	218	89	3	8	55	123	2.01	118	.237	.286	86-2	.128	-3	138	10	0.6
1911	†Phi A	23	8	.742	40	30	24-**6**	**4**	256.2	237	85	2	14	77	149	2.10	150	.255	.322	94-6	.191	-1	121	29	3.2
1912	Phi A	26	6	.813	37	30	23-5	2	259.2	234	90	1	6	83	110	2.22	139	.245	.309	90-11	.267	4	132	25	3.2
1913	†Phi A	18	10	.643	41	30	18-7	4	242.2	211	87	3	5	57	151	2.60	106	.243	.293	76-6	.105	-0	145	4	0.4
1914	†Phi A	15	7	.682	34	22	12-4	3	185.1	178	68	2	6	42	110	2.87	91	.266	.315	60-7	.150	0	142	-4	-0.6
1915	StL F	21	11	.656	42	31	23-6	3	268.1	212	75	1	3	54	147	2.08	**138**	.218	**.262**	93-4	.258	3	101	23	**3.0**
1916	StL A	16	15	.516	37	26	17-3	3	235.2	203	78	2	6	67	88	2.33	118	.237	.297	81-4	.185	-0	121	12	1.4
1917	StL A	5	6	.455	20	14	8-1	1	131	105	39	2	2	38	26	1.79	145	.225	.287	38-4	.105	-1	83	11	0.7
Total	17	326	194	.627	623	529	410-69	23	4495.2	3958	1566	42	190	1072	2246	2.35	122	.239	.293	1607-76	.206	17	109	268	30.3

PLANTENBERG, ERIK Erik John B 10.30.1968 Renton, WA BB/TL 6-1/180# d7.31

Year	Tm Lg	W	L	Pct	G	GS	CG-Sho	SV-BS	IP	H	R	HR	HB	BB-IB	SO	ERA	AERA	OAV	OOB	AB-SH	AVG	PB	Sup	APR	PW
1993	Sea A	0	0	—	20	0	0	1-0	9.2	11	7	0	1	12-1	3	6.52	68	.282	.462	0-0	—	0		-2	-0.1
1994	Sea A	0	0	—	6	0	0	0-0	7	4	0	0	1	7-0	1	0.00	—	.174	.387	0-0	—	0		4	0.2
1997	Phi N	0	0	—	35	0	0	0-0	25.2	25	14	1	1	12-0	12	4.91	87	.255	.339	0-0	—	0		-1	-0.1
Total	3	0	0	—	61	0	0	1-0	42.1	40	21	1	3	31-1	16	4.46	98	.250	.379	0-0	—	0		1	0.0

PLEIS, BILL William B 8.5.1937 St.Louis, MO BL/TL 5-10/175# d4.16

Year	Tm Lg	W	L	Pct	G	GS	CG-Sho	SV-BS	IP	H	R	HR	HB	BB-IB	SO	ERA	AERA	OAV	OOB	AB-SH	AVG	PB	Sup	APR	PW
1961	Min A	4	2	.667	37	0	0	2	56.1	59	35	4	4	34-5	32	4.95	86	.266	.370	9-0	.111	-1		-4	-0.5
1962	Min A	2	5	.286	21	4	0	3	45	46	27	7	1	14-2	31	4.40	93	.264	.319	14-0	.286	1	66	-2	-0.3
1963	Min A	6	2	.750	36	4	1	0	68	67	37	10	0	16-2	37	4.37	83	.258	.297	16-1	.125	0	165	-5	-0.6
1964	Min A	4	1	.800	47	0	0	4	50.2	43	23	6	1	31-3	42	3.91	92	.232	.342	4-1	.250	0		-1	0.0
1965	†Min A	4	4	.500	41	2	0	4	51.1	49	20	3	0	27-5	33	2.98	119	.250	.336	7-1	.000	-1	25	3	0.4
1966	Min A	1	2	.333	8	0	0	0	9.1	5	6	1	0	4-0	9	1.93	186	.152	.243	0-0	—	0		0	0.0
Total	6	21	16	.568	190	10	1	13	280.2	269	148	31	6	126-17	184	4.07	93	.251	.330	50-3	.160	0	96	-9	-1.0

PLESAC, DAN Daniel Thomas B 2.4.1962 Gary, IN BL/TL 6-5/215# d4.11

Year	Tm Lg	W	L	Pct	G	GS	CG-Sho	SV-BS	IP	H	R	HR	HB	BB-IB	SO	ERA	AERA	OAV	OOB	AB-SH	AVG	PB	Sup	APR	PW
1986	Mil A	10	7	.588	51	0	0	14-4	91	81	34	5	0	29-1	75	2.97	146	.240	.296	0-0	—	0		13	2.7
1987	Mil A★	5	6	.455	57	0	0	23-13	79.1	63	30	8	3	23-1	89	2.61	176	.213	.275	0-0	—	0		15	2.7
1988	Mil A★	1	2	.333	50	0	0	30-5	52.1	46	14	2	0	12-2	52	2.41	166	.234	.278	0-0	—	0		10	1.6
1989	Mil A★	3	4	.429	52	0	0	33-7	61.1	47	16	6	0	17-1	52	2.35	164	.213	.264	0-0	—	0		11	2.3
1990	Mil A	3	7	.300	66	0	0	24-10	69	67	36	5	3	31-6	65	4.43	88	.257	.340	0-0	—	0		-3	-0.6
1991	Mil A	2	7	.222	45	10	0	8-4	92.1	92	49	12	3	39-1	61	4.29	93	.263	.336	0-0	—	0	122	-4	-0.5
1992	Mil A	5	4	.556	44	4	0	1-2	79	64	28	5	3	35-5	54	2.96	130	.229	.317	0-0	—	0	125	8	0.8
1993	Chi N	2	1	.667	57	0	0	0-2	62.2	74	37	10	0	21-6	47	4.74	84	.298	.349	1-0	.000	-0		-6	-0.3
1994	Chi N	2	3	.400	54	0	0	1-2	54.2	61	30	9	1	13-0	53	4.61	90	.279	.321	4-0	.000	-0		-3	-0.3
1995	Pit N	4	4	.500	58	0	0	3-2	60.1	53	26	3	1	27-7	57	3.58	120	.237	.318	4-0	.250	0		5	0.6
1996	Pit N	6	5	.545	73	0	0	11-6	70.1	67	35	4	0	24-6	76	4.09	107	.247	.305	5-0	.000	-1		2	0.2
1997	Tor A	2	4	.333	73	0	0	1-4	50.1	47	22	8	0	19-4	61	3.58	128	.244	.310	0-0	—	0		6	0.6
1998	Tor A	4	3	.571	78	0	0	4-1	50	41	23	4	1	16-1	55	3.78	124	.224	.286	0-0	—	0		5	0.6
1999	Tor A	0	3	.000	30	0	0	0-2	22.2	28	21	4	0	9-1	26	8.34	59	.308	.366	0-0	—	0		-8	-0.8
	†Ari N	2	1	.667	34	0	0	1-0	21.2	22	9	3	0	8-1	27	3.32	138	.259	.323	1-0	.000	-0		3	0.4
2000	Ari N	5	1	.833	62	0	0	0-4	40	34	21	4	0	26-2	45	3.15	149	.228	.341	0-0	—	0		4	0.5
2001	Tor A	4	5	.444	62	0	0	1-1	45.1	34	18	4	1	24-5	68	3.57	129	.207	.311	0-0	—	0		6	1.0
2002	Tor A	1	2	.333	19	0	0	0-1	13.1	11	5	1	0	6-0	14	3.38	137	.216	.293	0-0	—	0		2	0.4
	Phi N	2	1	.667	41	0	0	1-2	23	16	12	5	0	12-3	27	4.70	83	.190	.292	0-0	—	0		-2	-0.2
2003	Phi N	2	1	.667	58	0	0	2-2	33.1	29	12	3	1	11-1	37	2.70	148	.228	.295	0-0	—	0		5	0.4
Total	18	65	71	.478	1064	14	0	158-74	1072	977	478	105	17	402-54	1041	3.64	117	.242	.311	15-0	.067	-1	114	69	12.1

PLITT, NORMAN Norman William B 2.21.1893 York, PA D 2.1.1954 New York, NY BR/TR 5-11/180# d4.26

Year	Tm Lg	W	L	Pct	G	GS	CG-Sho	SV-BS	IP	H	R	HR	HB	BB-IB	SO	ERA	AERA	OAV	OOB	AB-SH	AVG	PB	Sup	APR	PW
1918	Bro N	0	0	—	1	0	0	0	2	3	1	0	0	1	0	4.50	62	.429	.500	1-0	1.000	0		0	0.0
1927	Bro N	2	6	.250	19	8	1	0	62.1	73	40	3	1	36	9	4.91	81	.303	.396	18-2	.222	-0	75	-6	-0.7
	NY N	1	0	1.000	3	0	0	0	7.1	9	3	0	1	1	0	3.68	105	.310	.355	1-0	.000	-0		0	0.1
	Year	3	6	.333	22	8	1	0	69.2	82	47	3	2	37	9	4.78	83	.304	.392	19-2	.211	-0	75	-6	-0.6
Total	2	3	6	.333	23	8	1	0	71.2	85	44	3	2	38	9	4.77	82	.307	.394	20-2	.250	0	76	-6	-0.6

PLODINEC, TIM Timothy Alfred B 1.27.1947 Aliquippa, PA BR/TR 6-4/190# d6.2

Year	Tm Lg	W	L	Pct	G	GS	CG-Sho	SV-BS	IP	H	R	HR	HB	BB-IB	SO	ERA	AERA	OAV	OOB	AB-SH	AVG	PB	Sup	APR	PW
1972	StL N	0	0	—	1	0	0	0-0	0.1	3	1	0	0	0-0	0	27.00	13	.750	.750	0-0	—	0		-1	0.0

PLUNK, ERIC Eric Vaughn B 9.3.1963 Wilmington, CA BR/TR 6-5/217# d5.12

Year	Tm Lg	W	L	Pct	G	GS	CG-Sho	SV-BS	IP	H	R	HR	HB	BB-IB	SO	ERA	AERA	OAV	OOB	AB-SH	AVG	PB	Sup	APR	PW
1986	Oak A	4	7	.364	26	15	0	0-0	120.1	91	75	14	5	102-2	98	5.31	73	.214	.370	0-0	—	0	95	-19	-1.6
1987	Oak A	4	6	.400	32	11	0	2-3	95	91	53	8	2	62-3	90	4.74	87	.253	.361	0-0	—	0	94	-5	-0.6
1988	†Oak A	7	2	.778	49	0	0	5-4	78	62	27	6	1	39-4	79	3.00	126	.217	.311	0-0	—	0		8	0.9
1989	Oak A	1	1	.500	23	0	0	1-2	28.2	17	7	1	1	12-0	24	2.20	168	.172	.268	0-0	—	0		5	0.4
	NY A	7	5	.583	27	7	0	0-0	75.2	65	36	9	0	52-2	61	3.69	105	.237	.355	0-0	—	0	117	1	0.0
	Year	8	6	.571	50	7	0	1-2	104.1	82	41	10	1	64-2	85	3.28	117	.220	.333	0-0	—	0	118	6	0.4
1990	NY A	6	3	.667	47	0	0	0-1	72.2	58	27	6	2	43-4	67	2.72	146	.225	.340	0-0	—	0		9	1.1
1991	NY A	2	5	.286	43	8	0	0-0	111.2	128	69	18	1	62-1	103	4.76	87	.286	.371	0-0	—	0	69	-10	-0.6
1992	Cle A	9	6	.600	58	0	0	4-4	71.2	61	31	5	0	38-2	50	3.64	107	.229	.324	0-0	—	0		3	0.5
1993	Cle A	4	5	.444	70	0	0	15-3	71	61	29	5	0	30-4	77	2.79	156	.226	.301	0-0	—	0		10	1.4
1994	Cle A	7	2	.778	41	0	0	3-4	71	61	25	3	2	37-5	73	2.54	186	.231	.329	0-0	—	0		17	1.9
1995	†Cle A	6	2	.750	56	0	0	2-3	64	48	19	5	4	27-2	71	2.67	176	.211	.303	0-0	—	0		15	1.7
1996	†Cle A	3	2	.600	56	0	0	2-1	77.2	56	21	6	3	34-2	85	2.43	201	.203	.293	0-0	—	0		23	1.3
1997	†Cle A	4	5	.444	55	0	0	0-2	65.2	62	37	12	1	36-7	66	4.66	101	.245	.339	1-0	.000	-0*		0	0.0
1998	Cle A	3	1	.750	37	0	0	0-3	41	44	23	6	2	15-1	38	4.83	99	.282	.349	0-0	—	0		0	0.0
	Mil N	1	2	.333	26	0	0	1-2	31.2	33	14	3	3	15-1	36	3.69	115	.270	.359	1-0	.000	0		2	0.2
1999	Mil N	4	4	.500	68	0	0	0-3	75.1	71	44	15	5	43-5	63	5.02	90	.251	.357	0-0	—	0		-3	-0.4
Total	14	72	58	.554	714	41	0	35-35	1151	1009	537	122	32	647-45	1081	3.82	111	.236	.339	2-0	.000	0	88	56	6.2

PLYMPTON, JEFF Jeffrey Hunter B 11.24.1965 Framingham, MA BR/TR 6-2/205# d6.15

Year	Tm Lg	W	L	Pct	G	GS	CG-Sho	SV-BS	IP	H	R	HR	HB	BB-IB	SO	ERA	AERA	OAV	OOB	AB-SH	AVG	PB	Sup	APR	PW
1991	Bos A	0	0	—	4	0	0	0-0	5.1	5	0	0	0	4-0	2	0.00	—	.263	.375	0-0	—	0		2	0.1

POAT, RAY Raymond Willis B 12.19.1917 Chicago, IL D 4.29.1990 Oak Lawn, IL BR/TR 6-2/200# d4.15 Def 1945

Year	Tm Lg	W	L	Pct	G	GS	CG-Sho	SV-BS	IP	H	R	HR	HB	BB-IB	SO	ERA	AERA	OAV	OOB	AB-SH	AVG	PB	Sup	APR	PW
1942	Cle A	1	3	.250	4	4	1-1	0	18.1	24	11	1	1	9	8	5.40	64	.296	.374	5-0	.000	-0	93	-3	-0.6
1943	Cle A	2	5	.286	17	4	1	0	45	44	22	3	0	20	31	4.40	71	.259	.337	13-0	.154	-1	108	-5	-0.8
1944	Cle A	4	8	.333	36	6	1	1	80.2	82	50	9	0	37	40	5.13	64	.265	.343	17-2	.000	-2	105	-15	-2.3
1947	NY N	4	3	.571	7	7	5	0	60	53	18	8	0	13	25	2.55	160	.238	.280	21-1	.190	2	99	11	1.4
1948	NY N	11	10	.524	39	24	7-3	0	157.2	162	95	21	3	67	57	4.34	91	.262	.337	56-1	.125	-1	146	-10	-1.3
1949	NY N	0	0	—	2	0	0	0	2.1	8	6	0	0	1	0	19.29	21	.615	.643	0-0	—	0		-4	-0.2
	Pit N	0	1	.000	11	2	0	0	36	52	29	6	0	15	17	6.25	67	.335	.394	10-0	.100	-1	52	-8	-0.5
	Year	0	1	.000	13	2	0	0	38.1	60	32	6	0	16	17	7.04	59	.357	.413	10-0	.100	-1	53	-11	-0.7
Total	6	22	30	.423	116	47	15-4	1	400	425	231	48	4	162	178	4.55	82	.271	.340	122-4	.115	-3	124	-34	-4.3

PODBIELAN, BUD Clarence Anthony B 3.6.1924 Curlew, WA D 10.26.1982 Syracuse, NY BR/TR 6-1.5/170# d4.25

Year	Tm Lg	W	L	Pct	G	GS	CG-Sho	SV-BS	IP	H	R	HR	HB	BB-IB	SO	ERA	AERA	OAV	OOB	AB-SH	AVG	PB	Sup	APR	PW
1949	Bro N	0	1	.000	7	1	0	0	12.1	9	9	1	1	9	5	3.65	112	.205	.352	3-0	.000	-0	107	-1	-0.1
1950	Bro N	5	4	.556	20	10	2	1	72.2	93	47	10	2	29	28	5.33	77	.307	.371	28-2	.107	-1	131	-10	-1.2
1951	Bro N	2	2	.500	27	5	1	0	79.2	67	32	9	2	36	26	3.50	112	.233	.322	23-0	.304	1	103	5	0.4
1952	Bro N	0	0	—	3	0	0	0	2	4	5	1	0	3	1	18.00	20	.444	.583	0-0	—	0*		-4	-0.2
	Cin N	4	5	.444	24	7	4-1	1	86.2	78	30	8	1	26	22	2.80	135	.245	.304	25-0	.160	0	64	9	0.9
	Year	4	5	.444	27	7	4-1	1	88.2	82	33	9	1	29	23	3.15	120	.251	.314	25-0	.160	0	64	7	0.7
1953	Cin N	6	16	.273	36	24	8-1	1	186.1	214	112	21	8	67	74	4.73	92	.290	.356	56-3	.125	-3	85	-9	-1.2
1954	Cin N	7	10	.412	27	24	4	0	131	157	92	20	2	58	42	5.36	78	.300	.370	42-3	.143	-1	105	-19	-2.2

Year	Tm Lg	W	L	Pct	G	GS	CG-Sho	SV-BS	IP	H	R	HR	HB	BB-IB	SO	ERA	AERA	OAV	OOB	AB-SH	AVG	PB	Sup	APR	PW
1955	Cin N	1	2	.333	17	2	0	0	42	36	16	4	1	11-0	26	3.21	132	.234	.284	5-1	.400	1	42	5	0.4
1957	Cin N	0	1	.000	5	3	1	0	16	18	11	4	0	4-0	13	6.19	66	.290	.333	5-0	.000	-1	114	-3	-0.3
1959	Cle A	0	1	.000	6	0	0	0	12.1	17	8	1	0	2-0	5	5.84	63	.354	.380	1-0	.000	-0		-3	-0.2
Total	9	25	42	.373	172	76	20-2	3	641	693	362	79	17	245-0	242	4.49	92	.279	.347	188-9	.154	-4	98	-30	-3.7

PODGAJNY, JOHNNY John Sigmund "Specs" B 6.10.1920 Chester, PA D 3.2.1971 Chester, PA BR/TR 6-2/173# d9.15

Year	Tm Lg	W	L	Pct	G	GS	CG-Sho	SV-BS	IP	H	R	HR	HB	BB-IB	SO	ERA	AERA	OAV	OOB	AB-SH	AVG	PB	Sup	APR	PW
1940	Phi N	1	3	.250	4	4	3	0	35	33	14	0	1	1	12	2.83	138	.250	.261	12-0	.167	-0	45	3	0.4
1941	Phi N	9	12	.429	34	24	8	0	181.1	191	96	8	4	70	53	4.62	80	.270	.339	62-3	.129	-3*	88	-13	-1.6
1942	Phi N	6	14	.300	43	23	6	0	186.2	191	95	9	11	63	40	3.91	85	.268	.337	60-2	.183	-0*	84	-13	-1.4
1943	Phi N	4	4	.500	13	5	3	0	64	77	32	4	0	16	13	4.22	80	.310	.352	20-1	.250	1	116	-5	-0.4
	Pit N	0	4	.000	15	5	0	0	34.1	37	28	1	0	13	7	4.72	74	.266	.329	7-0	.143	-0*	73	-7	-0.7
	Year	4	8	.333	28	10	3	0	98.1	114	31	5	0	29	20	4.39	78	.295	.344	27-1	.222	0	95	-12	-1.1
1946	Cle A	0	0	—	6	0	0	0	9	13	8	0	0	2	4	5.00	66	.302	.333	0-0	—	0		-3	-0.1
Total	5	20	37	.351	115	61	20	0	510.1	542	273	22	16	165	129	4.20	84	.273	.334	161-6	.168	-3	85	-38	-3.8

PODRES, JOHNNY John Joseph B 9.30.1932 Witherbee, NY BL/TL 5-11/192# d4.17 Mil 1956 C13

Year	Tm Lg	W	L	Pct	G	GS	CG-Sho	SV-BS	IP	H	R	HR	HB	BB-IB	SO	ERA	AERA	OAV	OOB	AB-SH	AVG	PB	Sup	APR	PW
1953	†Bro N	9	4	.692	33	18	3-1	0	115	126	62	12	1	64	82	4.23	101	.282	.373	36-1	.306	2*	120	-1	0.1
1954	Bro N	11	7	.611	29	21	6-2	0	151.2	147	77	13	1	53	79	4.27	96	.255	.317	60-3	.283	5*	116	-2	0.2
1955	†Bro N	9	10	.474	27	24	5-2	0	159.1	160	80	15	4	57-2	114	3.95	103	.259	.325	60-4	.183	-0*	126	2	0.1
1957	Bro N	12	9	.571	31	27	10-**6**	3	196	168	64	15	1	44-1	109	**2.66**	**156**	.230	**.273**	72-3	.208	1*	95	31	3.4
1958	LA N☆	13	15	.464	39	31	10-2	1	210.1	208	96	27	2	78-8	143	3.72	110	.261	.326	71-4	.127	-3*	95	9	0.7
1959	†LA N	14	9	.609	34	29	6-2	0	195	192	93	23	3	74-7	145	4.11	103	.261	.330	65-3	.246	3	98	5	1.0
1960	LA N★	14	12	.538	34	33	8-1	0	227.2	217	88	25	1	71-9	159	3.08	129	.250	.307	66-10	.136	-1	85	21	2.1
1961	LA N	18	5	**.783**	32	29	6-1	0	182.2	192	81	27	4	51-2	124	3.74	116	.271	.322	69-4	.232	1	111	13	1.5
1962	LA N★	15	13	.536	40	40	8	0	255	270	121	20	3	71-14	178	3.81	95	.272	.321	88-5	.159	1	110	-3	-0.4
1963	†LA N	14	12	.538	37	34	10-5	1	198.1	196	91	16	3	64-13	134	3.54	85	.257	.315	64-3	.141	1	115	-12	-1.4
1964	LA N	0	2	.000	2	2	0	0	2.2	5	5	1	0	3-1	0	16.88	19	.417	.533	0-0	—	0	54	-4	-0.7
1965	LA N	7	6	.538	27	22	2-1	1	134	126	57	17	2	39-4	63	3.43	95	.247	.301	45-1	.178	1	83	-2	-0.3
1966	LA N	0	0	—	1	0	0	0	1.2	2	0	0	0	1-1	1	0.00	—	.400	.429	0-0	—	0		1	0.0
	Det A	4	5	.444	36	13	2-1	4	107.2	106	48	12	1	34-3	53	3.43	102	.259	.313	30-0	.233	2	94	0	0.2
1967	Det A	3	1	.750	21	8	0	1	63.1	58	29	12	1	11-2	34	3.84	85	.244	.280	20-0	.100	-1	117	-4	-0.4
1969	SD N	5	6	.455	17	9	1	0-1	64.2	66	34	7	1	28-3	17	4.31	82	.264	.337	16-2	.063	-1	89	-5	-1.0
Total	15	148	116	.561	440	340	77-24	11-1	2265	2239	1026	242	28	743-70	1435	3.68	105	.259	.318	762-43	.190	12	103	49	5.1

POETZ, JOE Joseph Frank "Bull Montana" B 6.22.1900 St.Louis, MO D 2.7.1942 St.Louis, MO BR/TR 5-10.5/175# d9.14

Year	Tm Lg	W	L	Pct	G	GS	CG-Sho	SV-BS	IP	H	R	HR	HB	BB-IB	SO	ERA	AERA	OAV	OOB	AB-SH	AVG	PB	Sup	APR	PW
1926	NY N	0	1	.000	2	1	0	0	8	5	3	2	1	8	0	3.38	111	.192	.400	1-0	.000	0	44	1	0.1

POFFENBERGER, BOOTS Cletus Elwood B 7.1.1915 Williamsport, MD D 9.1.1999 Williamsport, MD BR/TR 5-10/178# d6.11

Year	Tm Lg	W	L	Pct	G	GS	CG-Sho	SV-BS	IP	H	R	HR	HB	BB-IB	SO	ERA	AERA	OAV	OOB	AB-SH	AVG	PB	Sup	APR	PW
1937	Det A	10	5	.667	29	16	5	3	137.1	147	83	8	4	79	35	4.65	100	.277	.375	51-2	.216	-0	144	-1	-0.1
1938	Det A	6	7	.462	25	15	8-1	1	125	147	74	8	2	66	28	4.82	104	.297	.382	44-1	.182	-1	80	2	0.0
1939	Bro N	0	0	—	3	1	0	0	5	7	3	1	0	4	2	5.40	75	.318	.423	1-0	.000	-0	130	-1	0.0
Total	3	16	12	.571	57	32	13-1	4	267.1	301	160	17	6	149	65	4.75	101	.287	.379	96-3	.198	-2	113	0	-0.1

POHOLSKY, TOM Thomas George B 8.26.1929 Detroit, MI D 1.6.2001 Kirkwood, MO BR/TR 6-3/205# d4.20 Mil 1952

Year	Tm Lg	W	L	Pct	G	GS	CG-Sho	SV-BS	IP	H	R	HR	HB	BB-IB	SO	ERA	AERA	OAV	OOB	AB-SH	AVG	PB	Sup	APR	PW
1950	StL N	0	0	—	5	1	0	0	14.2	16	6	2	0	3	2	3.68	117	.281	.317	2-0	.000	-0	41	1	0.0
1951	StL N	7	13	.350	38	26	10-1	1	195	204	106	15	0	68	70	4.43	89	.271	.331	67-6	.209	0	125	-10	-0.8
1954	StL N	5	7	.417	25	13	4	0	106	101	43	11	4	20	55	3.06	135	.254	.293	27-6	.148	-1	120	11	1.1
1955	StL N	9	11	.450	30	24	8-2	0	151	143	71	26	2	35-4	66	3.81	106	.244	.289	44-5	.182	-0	91	3	0.3
1956	StL N	9	14	.391	33	29	7-2	0	203	210	100	27	5	44-7	95	3.59	105	.268	.309	69-3	.159	-1	88	1	0.0
1957	Chi N	1	7	.125	28	11	1	0	84	117	55	9	2	22-4	28	4.93	79	.330	.366	19-1	.105	-1	103	-11	-1.0
Total	6	31	52	.373	159	104	30-5	1	753.2	791	381	90	13	192-15	316	3.93	101	.270	.316	228-21	.171	-3	103	-5	-0.4

POINDEXTER, JENNINGS Chester Jennings "Jinx" B 9.30.1910 Pauls Valley, OK D 3.3.1983 Norman, OK BL/TL 5-10/165# d9.15

Year	Tm Lg	W	L	Pct	G	GS	CG-Sho	SV-BS	IP	H	R	HR	HB	BB-IB	SO	ERA	AERA	OAV	OOB	AB-SH	AVG	PB	Sup	APR	PW
1936	Bos A	0	2	.000	3	3	0	0	10.2	13	11	0	0	16	2	6.75	79	.302	.492	4-0	.000	-1	44	-2	-0.4
1939	Phi N	0	0	—	11	1	0	0	30.1	29	19	0	0	15	12	4.15	96	.250	.336	10-0	.200	-0	153	-2	-0.1
Total	2	0	2	.000	14	4	0	0	41	42	30	0	0	31	14	4.83	90	.264	.384	14-0	.143	-1	76	-4	-0.5

POLCHOW, LOU Louis William B 3.14.1881 Mankato, MN D 8.15.1912 Good Thunder, MN 5-9/?# d9.14

Year	Tm Lg	W	L	Pct	G	GS	CG-Sho	SV-BS	IP	H	R	HR	HB	BB-IB	SO	ERA	AERA	OAV	OOB	AB-SH	AVG	PB	Sup	APR	PW
1902	Cle A	0	1	.000	1	1	1	0	8	9	5	0	0	4	2	5.63	61	.281	.361	4-0	.000	-1	63	-1	-0.2

POLE, DICK Richard Henry B 10.13.1950 Trout Creek, MI BR/TR 6-3/210# d8.3 C15

Year	Tm Lg	W	L	Pct	G	GS	CG-Sho	SV-BS	IP	H	R	HR	HB	BB-IB	SO	ERA	AERA	OAV	OOB	AB-SH	AVG	PB	Sup	APR	PW
1973	Bos A	3	2	.600	12	7	0	0-0	54.2	70	35	4	0	18-0	24	5.60	72	.318	.370	0-0	—	0	155	-8	-0.7
1974	Bos A	1	1	.500	15	2	0	1-0	45	55	28	6	1	13-0	32	4.20	92	.304	.352	0-0	—	0	160	-4	-0.2
1975	†Bos A	4	6	.400	18	11	2-1	0-0	89.2	102	46	11	2	32-4	42	4.42	92	.290	.349	0-0	—	0	78	-2	-0.2
1976	Bos A	6	5	.545	31	15	1	0-0	120.2	131	62	8	2	48-3	49	4.33	90	.279	.346	1-0	.000	-0	82	-3	-0.3
1977	Sea A	7	12	.368	25	24	3	0-0	122.1	127	76	16	6	57-2	51	5.15	80	.270	.353	0-0	—	0	80	-13	-1.9
1978	Sea A	4	11	.267	21	18	2	0-1	98.2	122	82	16	3	41-3	41	6.48	59	.306	.371	0-0	—	0	103	-30	-3.8
Total	6	25	37	.403	122	77	8-1	1-1	531	607	329	61	14	209-12	239	5.05	79	.290	.356	1-0	.000	-0	94	-60	-7.1

POLITTE, CLIFF Clifford Anthony B 2.27.1974 Kirkwood, MO BR/TR 5-11/185# d4.2

Year	Tm Lg	W	L	Pct	G	GS	CG-Sho	SV-BS	IP	H	R	HR	HB	BB-IB	SO	ERA	AERA	OAV	OOB	AB-SH	AVG	PB	Sup	APR	PW
1998	StL N	2	3	.400	8	8	0	0-0	37	45	32	6	1	18-0	22	6.32	66	.302	.379	14-1	.071	-1	118	-10	-1.2
1999	Phi N	1	0	1.000	13	0	0	0-0	17.2	19	14	2	0	15-0	15	7.13	66	.275	.405	0-0	—	0		-4	-0.2
2000	Phi N	4	3	.571	12	8	0	0-0	59	55	24	8	0	27-1	50	3.66	127	.248	.328	15-2	.133	0	81	7	0.8
2001	Phi N	2	3	.400	23	0	0	0-0	26	24	8	2	1	8-3	23	2.42	176	.250	.306	2-0	.000	0		5	0.9
2002	Phi N	2	0	1.000	13	0	0	0-1	16.1	19	10	0	1	9-1	15	3.86	101	.288	.382	1-0	.000	-0		-1	-0.2
	Tor A	1	3	.250	55	0	0	1-2	57.1	38	23	5	1	19-1	57	3.61	128	.186	.258	0-0	—	0		7	0.4
2003	Tor A	1	5	.167	54	0	0	12-6	49.1	52	32	11	1	17-4	40	5.66	81	.268	.326	0-0	—	0		-5	-0.7
Total	6	13	17	.433	178	16	0	13-9	262.2	252	143	34	5	113-10	222	4.52	99	.252	.328	32-3	.094	-1	98	-1	-0.2

POLIVKA, KEN Kenneth Lyle "Soup" B 1.21.1921 Chicago, IL D 7.23.1988 Aurora, IL BL/TL 5-10.5/175# d4.18

Year	Tm Lg	W	L	Pct	G	GS	CG-Sho	SV-BS	IP	H	R	HR	HB	BB-IB	SO	ERA	AERA	OAV	OOB	AB-SH	AVG	PB	Sup	APR	PW
1947	Cin N	0	0	—	2	0	0	0	3	3	1	0	0	3	1	3.00	137	.250	.400	0-0	—	0		0	0.0

POLLET, HOWIE Howard Joseph B 6.26.1921 New Orleans, LA D 8.8.1974 Houston, TX BL/TL 6-1.5/175# d8.20 Mil 1944-45 C7

Year	Tm Lg	W	L	Pct	G	GS	CG-Sho	SV-BS	IP	H	R	HR	HB	BB-IB	SO	ERA	AERA	OAV	OOB	AB-SH	AVG	PB	Sup	APR	PW
1941	StL N	5	2	.714	9	8	6-2	0	70	55	18	1	1	27	37	1.93	195	.212	.289	28-1	.179	-0	107	14	1.4
1942	†StL N	7	5	.583	27	13	5-2	0	109.1	102	43	7	2	39	42	2.88	119	.242	.309	31-2	.226	3	123	6	0.9
1943	StL N❖	8	4	.667	16	14	12-5	0	118.1	83	26	2	2	32	61	**1.75**	192	.200	.261	43-1	.163	-1	83	22	2.1
1946	†StL N☆	**21**	10	.677	40	32	22-4	5	**266**	228	84	12	5	86	107	**2.10**	**165**	.234	.300	87-7	.161	-0	99	**35**	4.3
1947	StL N	9	11	.450	37	24	9	2	176.1	195	96	11	3	87	73	4.34	95	.286	.369	65-0	.231	2	103	-3	-0.1
1948	StL N	13	8	.619	36	26	11	0	186.1	216	102	10	2	67	80	4.54	90	.289	.349	68-5	.118	-3*	123	-9	-1.1
1949	StL N★	20	9	.690	39	28	17-**5**	1	230.2	228	80	9	2	59	108	2.77	150	.256	.304	82-3	.195	1	100	**35**	**4.2**
1950	StL N	14	13	.519	37	30	14-2	2	232.1	228	103	19	1	68	117	3.29	130	.256	.310	84-2	.143	-2*	96	22	2.1
1951	StL N	0	3	.000	6	2	0	1	12.1	10	10	1	0	8	10	4.38	91	.208	.321	1-0	.000	1	111	-2	-0.3
	Pit N	6	10	.375	21	21	4-1	0	128.2	149	81	24	1	51	47	5.04	84	.294	.360	36-4	.139	-0	86	-10	-1.1
	Year	6	13	.316	27	23	4-1	1	141	159	85	25	1	59	57	4.98	84	.287	.357	37-4	.135	0	88	-11	-1.4
1952	Pit N	7	16	.304	31	30	9-1	0	214	217	111	22	3	71	90	4.12	97	.266	.327	68-2	.191	2	70	-3	0.0
1953	Pit N	1	1	.500	5	2	0	0	12.2	27	15	2	0	6	8	10.66	42	.482	.532	3-1	.333	0	200	-8	-0.9
	Chi N	5	6	.455	25	17	2	1	111.1	120	62	6	1	44	45	4.12	108	.271	.338	31-3	.129	-1	78	3	0.1
	Year	6	7	.462	30	19	2	1	124	147	66	8	1	50	53	4.79	93	.295	.360	34-4	.147	-1	91	-7	-0.8
1954	Chi N	8	10	.444	20	20	4-2	0	128.1	131	60	4	0	54	58	3.58	117	.263	.332	47-3	.277	2	94	7	1.2
1955	Chi N	4	3	.571	24	7	1-1	5	61	62	41	11	0	27-3	27	5.61	73	.265	.337	15-1	.400	3	112	-10	-0.8
1956	Chi A	3	1	.750	11	4	0	0	26.1	27	15	2	0	11-0	14	4.10	100	.252	.322	8-1	.375	1*	174	-1	0.0
	Pit N	0	4	.000	19	0	0	3	23.1	18	10	3	0	8-1	10	3.09	122	.212	.277	1-1	.000	0		1	0.3
Total	14	131	116	.530	403	278	116-25	20	2107.1	2096	957	146	23	745-4	934	3.51	113	.260	.324	698-37	.185	7	99	99	12.3

Year	Tm Lg	W	L	Pct	G	GS	CG-Sho	SV-BS	IP	H	R	HR	HB	BB-IB	SO	ERA	AERA	OAV	OOB	AB-SH	AVG	PB	Sup	APR	PW
POLLEY, DALE Ezra Dale B 8.9.1965 Georgetown, KY BR/TL 6/165# d6.23																									
1996	NY A	1	3	.250	32	0	0	0-0	21.2	23	20	5	3	11-1	14	7.89	63	.264	.363	0-0	—	0		-7	-1.1
POLLI, LOU Louis Americo "Crip" B 7.9.1901 Baveno, Italy D 12.19.2000 Berlin, VT BR/TR 5-10.5/165# d4.18																									
1932	StL A	0	0	—	5	0	0	0	6.2	13	8	0	0	3	5	5.40	90	.406	.457	2-0	.500	0		-2	-0.1
1944	NY N	0	2	.000	19	0	0	3	35.2	42	25	3	0	20	6	4.54	81	.294	.380	6-0	.000	-1		-5	-0.4
Total	2	0	2	.000	24	0	0	3	42.1	55	33	3	0	23	11	4.68	82	.314	.394	8-0	.125	-1		-7	-0.5
POLONI, JOHN John Paul B 2.28.1954 Dearborn, MI BL/TL 6-5/210# d9.16																									
1977	Tex A	1	0	1.000	2	1	0	0-0	7	8	5	1	0	1-0	5	6.43	64	.286	.310	0-0	—	0	176	-2	-0.2
POMORSKI, JOHN John Leon B 12.30.1905 Brooklyn, NY D 12.6.1977 Brampton, ON, CAN BR/TR 6/178# d4.17																									
1934	Chi A	0	0	—	3	0	0	0	1.2	1	2	0	0	2	0	5.40	88	.143	.333	0-0	—	0		0	0.0
POND, ARLIE Erasmus Arlington B 1.19.1872 Saugus, MA D 9.19.1930 Cebu, Philippines BR/TR 5-10/160# d7.4 Mil 1898																									
1895	Bal N	0	1	.000	6	1	1	2	13.2	10	13	0	1	12	13	5.93	80	.200	.365	6-0	.333	1*	45	-2	-0.1
1896	Bal N	16	8	.667	28	26	21-2	0	214.1	232	133	4	6	57	80	3.49	123	.274	.324	81-5	.235	0	112	13	1.0
1897	Bal N	18	9	.667	32	28	23	0	248	267	131	4	15	72	59	3.52	118	.273	.332	90-3	.244	2*	122	21	1.9
1898	Bal N	1	1	.500	3	2	1-1	0	20	8	4	0	2	9	4	0.45	795	.123	.250	7-0	.286	1	178	6	0.6
Total	4	35	19	.648	69	57	46-3	2	496	517	281	8	24	150	156	3.45	122	.266	.327	184-8	.245	3	117	38	3.4
PONDER, ELMER Charles Elmer B 6.26.1893 Reed, OK D 4.20.1974 Albuquerque, NM BR/TR 6/178# d9.18 Mil 1918-19																									
1917	Pit N	1	1	.500	3	2	1-1	0	21.1	12	5	0	1	6	11	1.69	168	.167	.241	7-0	.000	-1	13	3	0.1
1919	Pit N	0	5	.000	9	5	0	0	47.1	55	26	0	3	6	6	3.99	76	.297	.330	15-0	.133	-1	37	-6	-0.7
1920	Pit N	11	15	.423	33	23	13-2	0	196	182	76	3	2	40	62	2.62	123	.246	.286	59-3	.119	-4	71	10	0.9
1921	Pit N	2	0	1.000	8	1	1	0	24.2	29	8	1	0	3	3	2.19	175	.305	.327	10-0	.000	-2	150	4	0.1
	Chi N	3	6	.333	16	11	5	0	89.1	117	58	7	3	17	31	4.74	81	.321	.356	33-2	.121	-2	92	-10	-1.1
	Year	5	6	.455	24	12	6	0	114	146	62	8	3	20	34	4.18	91	.317	.350	43-2	.093	-4	97	-6	-1.0
Total	4	17	27	.386	69	42	20-3	0	378.2	395	173	11	9	72	113	3.21	105	.271	.309	124-5	.105	-10	73	1	-0.7
PONSON, SIDNEY Sidney Alton B 11.2.1976 Noord, Aruba BR/TR 6-1/220# d4.19																									
1998	Bal A	8	9	.471	31	20	0	1-1	135	157	82	19	3	42-2	85	5.27	87	.293	.345	4-0	.500	1	100	-11	-1.2
1999	Bal A	12	12	.500	32	32	6	0-0	210	227	118	35	1	80-2	112	4.71	100	.282	.345	3-1	.000	-0	104	-1	-0.1
2000	Bal A	9	13	.409	32	32	6-1	0-0	222	223	125	30	1	83-0	152	4.82	98	.258	.323	1-2	.000	-0	97	-2	-0.2
2001	Bal A	5	10	.333	23	23	3-1	0-0	138.1	161	83	21	6	37-0	84	4.94	87	.289	.339	3-0	.000	-0	90	-10	-0.9
2002	Bal A	7	9	.438	28	28	3	0-0	176	172	84	26	2	63-1	120	4.09	105	.258	.323	3-0	.333	1	108	5	0.5
2003	Bal A	14	6	.700	21	21	4	0-0	148	147	65	10	4	43-2	100	3.77	117	.258	.313	5-0	.000	-0	121	11	1.3
	†SF N	3	6	.333	10	10	0	0-0	68	64	29	6	1	18-3	34	3.71	111	.255	.305	22-3	.091	-1	78	4	0.4
Total	6	58	65	.472	177	166	22-2	1-1	1097.1	1151	586	147	18	366-10	687	4.54	99	.271	.330	41-6	.122	-1	101	-4	-0.2
POOLE, ED Edward I. B 9.7.1874 Canton, OH D 3.11.1919 Malvern, OH BR/TR 5-10/175# d10.6																									
1900	Pit N	1	0	1.000	1	0	0	0	7	4	1	0	0	0	3	1.29	283	.167	.167	4-0	.500	1*		2	0.4
1901	Pit N	5	4	.556	12	10	8-1	0	80	78	45	3	6	30	26	3.60	91	.254	.332	78-0	.205	1*	126	-2	-0.1
1902	Pit N	0	0	—	1	0	0	0	8	7	4	0	0	3	2	1.13	244	.233	.303	4-0	.250	0		0	0.0
	Cin N	12	4	.750	16	16	16-2	0	138	129	47	2	8	54	55	2.15	139	.248	.328	61-0	.115	-4*	108	13	1.0
	Year	12	4	.750	17	16	16-2	0	146	136	52	2	8	57	57	2.10	142	.247	.326	65-0	.123	-4	108	12	1.0
1903	Cin N	7	13	.350	25	21	18-1	0	184	188	105	4	12	77	73	3.28	109	.270	.352	70-3	.243	0	104	5	0.6
1904	Bro N	8	14	.364	25	23	19-1	1	178	178	86	4	8	74	67	3.39	81	.268	.349	62-3	.129	-3	87	-7	-1.1
Total	5	33	35	.485	80	70	61-5	1	595	584	288	13	34	238	226	3.04	103	.260	.340	279-6	.183	-6	103	11	0.8
POOLE, JIM James Richard B 4.28.1966 Rochester, NY BL/TL 6-2/203# d6.15																									
1990	LA N	0	0	—	16	0	0	0-0	10.2	7	5	1	0	8-4	6	4.22	87	.184	.326	0-0	—	0		0	0.0
1991	Tex A	0	0	—	5	0	0	1-0	6	10	4	0	0	3-0	4	4.50	90	.370	.419	0-0	—	0		-1	0.0
	Bal A	3	2	.600	24	0	0	0-0	36	19	10	3	0	9-2	34	2.00	198	.157	.212	0-0	—	0		7	1.0
	Year	3	2	.600	29	0	0	1-0	42	29	19	3	0	12-2	38	2.36	168	.196	.252	0-0	—	0		7	1.0
1992	Bal A	0	0	—	6	0	0	0-1	3.1	3	3	0	0	1-0	3	0.00	—	.231	.286	0-0	—	0		0	0.0
1993	Bal A	2	1	.667	55	0	0	2-1	50.1	30	18	2	0	21-5	29	2.15	209	.175	.263	0-0	—	0		10	0.6
1994	Bal A	1	0	1.000	38	0	0	0-2	20.1	32	15	4	0	11-2	18	6.64	75	.372	.430	0-0	—	0		-3	-0.1
1995	†Cle A	3	3	.500	42	0	0	0-0	50.1	40	22	7	2	17-0	41	3.75	125	.217	.288	0-0	—	0		6	0.6
1996	Cle A	4	0	1.000	32	0	0	0-1	26.2	29	15	3	0	14-4	19	3.04	161	.274	.355	0-0	—	0		3	0.4
	SF N	2	1	.667	35	0	0	0-3	23.2	15	7	2	1	13-3	19	2.66	154	.188	.309	2-0	.000	-0		4	0.5
1997	SF N	3	1	.750	63	0	0	0-0	49.1	73	44	6	4	25-4	26	7.11	57	.353	.429	0-1	—	0		-17	-1.3
1998	SF N	1	3	.250	26	0	0	0-2	32.1	38	20	5	0	9-5	16	5.29	75	.302	.346	4-2	.250	1		-5	-0.5
	†Cle A	0	0	—	12	0	0	0-1	7	9	4	0	1	3-1	11	5.14	93	.300	.382	0-0	—	0		0	0.0
1999	Phi N	1	1	.500	51	0	0	1-1	35.1	48	20	3	3	15-1	22	4.33	109	.327	.400	2-0	.000	-0		1	0.0
	Cle A	1	0	1.000	3	0	0	0-0	1	2	2	0	0	3-1	0	18.00	28	.667	.714	0-0	—	0		-1	-0.2
2000	Det A	1	0	1.000	18	0	0	0-1	8.2	13	8	4	1	1-0	5	7.27	66	.361	.375	0-0	—	0		-3	-0.2
	Mon N	0	0	—	5	0	0	0-0	2	8	6	1	0	3-1	3	27.00	18	.571	.647	0-0	—	0		-4	-0.2
Total	11	22	12	.647	431	0	0	4-13	363	376	203	41	12	156-33	256	4.31	102	.271	.346	8-3	.125	0		-3	0.6
POORMAN, TOM Thomas Iverson B 10.14.1857 Lock Haven, PA D 2.18.1905 Lock Haven, PA BL/TR 5-7/135# d5.5 ▲																									
1880	Buf N	1	8	.111	11	9	9	1	85	117	90	3		19	13	4.13	59	.307	.340	70	.157	-3*	51	-18	-1.8
	Chi N	2	0	1.000	2	1	0	0	15	12	5	0		8	0	2.40	101	.203	.299	25	.200	0*	102	1	0.1
	Year	3	8	.273	13	10	9	1	100	129	10	3		27	13	3.87	63	.293	.334	95	.168	-3	56	-17	-1.7
1884	Tol AA	0	1	.000	1	1	1	0	9	13	11	1	0	2	0	3.00	114	.310	.341	382	.233	0*	18	-1	-0.1
1887	Phi AA	0	0	—	1	0	0	0	0.2	5	4	1	0	1	1	40.50	11	.714	.750	585	.265	0*		-3	-0.1
Total	3	3	9	.250	15	11	10	1	109.2	147	110	5	0	30	14	4.02	63	.301	.341	1062	.245	-2	52	-21	-1.9
POPP, BILL William Peter B 6.7.1877 St.Louis, MO D 9.5.1909 St.Louis, MO TR 5-10.5/170# d4.19																									
1902	StL N	2	6	.250	9	7	5	0	60.1	87	60	2	5	26	20	4.92	56	.337	.408	21-2	.048	-3	120	-19	-2.3
PORRAY, ED Edmund Joseph B 12.5.1888 , At Sea On Atlantic Ocean D 7.13.1954 Lackawaxen, PA BR/TR 5-11/170# d4.17																									
1914	Buf F	0	1	.000	3	3	0	0	10.1	18	9	2	0	7	0	4.35	68	.391	.472	4-0	.000	-1	147	-3	-0.3
PORTER, CHUCK Charles William B 1.12.1956 Baltimore, MD BR/TR 6-3/188# d9.14																									
1981	Mil A	0	0	—	3	0	0	0-0	4.1	6	2	0	0	1-0	1	4.15	83	.316	.350	0-0	—	0		0	0.0
1982	Mil A	0	0	—	3	0	0	0-0	3.2	3	2	0	0	1-0	3	4.91	77	.250	.308	0-0	—	0		0	0.0
1983	Mil A	7	9	.438	25	21	6-1	0-0	134	162	72	9	2	38-2	76	4.50	83	.298	.342	0-0	—	0	119	-12	-1.2
1984	Mil A	6	4	.600	17	12	1	0-0	81.1	92	37	8	0	12-2	48	3.87	100	.284	.309	0-0	—	0	111	1	0.1
1985	Mil A	0	0	—	6	1	0	0-0	13.2	15	8	1	0	2-0	8	1.98	211	.273	.298	0-0	—	0	197	1	0.0
Total	5	13	13	.500	54	34	7-1	0-0	237	278	121	18	2	54-4	136	4.14	92	.291	.328	0-0	—	0	118	-10	-1.1
PORTER, HENRY Henry B 6.1858 Vergennes, VT D 12.30.1906 Brockton, MA BR/TR ?/142# d9.27																									
1884	Mil U	3	3	.500	6	6	6-1	0	51	32	25	1		9	71	3.00	44	.168	.205	40	.275	1*	145	-20	-1.4
1885	Bro AA	33	21	.611	54	54	53-2	0	481.2	427	261	11	16	107	197	2.78	118	.223	.270	195	.205	-2	102	25	2.2
1886	Bro AA	27	19	.587	48	48	48-1	0	424	439	277	8	5	120	163	3.42	102	.252	.303	184	.179	-9	113	5	-0.5
1887	Bro AA	15	24	.385	40	40	38-1	0	339.2	416	264	7	7	96	74	4.21	102	.297	.345	146	.199	-3	92	-2	-0.5
1888	KC AA	18	37	.327	55	54	53-4	0	474	527	336	16	23	120	145	4.16	83	.272	.321	195	.144	-13	65	-29	-3.6
1889	KC AA	0	3	.000	4	4	3	0	23	52	46	0	1	14	9	12.52	33	.433	.496	10	.100	-1	85	-17	-1.5
Total	6	96	107	.473	207	206	201-9	0	1793.1	1893	1209	43	52	466	659	3.70	95	.259	.308	770	.184	-27	93	-38	-5.3
PORTER, NED Ned Swindell B 5.6.1905 Apalachicola, FL D 6.30.1968 Gainesville, FL BR/TR 6/173# d8.7																									
1926	NY N	0	0	—	2	0	0	0	2	2	1	1	0	0	1	4.50	83	.250	.250	0-0	—	0		0	0.0
1927	NY N	0	0	—	1	0	0	0	2	3	1	0	0	1	0	0.00	—	.333	.400	0-0	—	0		0	0.0
Total	2	0	0	—	3	0	0	0	4	5	2	1	0	1	1	2.25	169	.294	.333	0-0	—	0		0	0.0

Year	Tm Lg	W	L	Pct	G	GS	CG-Sho	SV-BS	IP	H	R	HR	HB	BB-IB	SO	ERA	AERA	OAV	OOB	AB-SH	AVG	PB	Sup	APR	PW
PORTER, ODIE Odie Oscar B 5.24.1877 Borden, IN D 5.2.1903 Borden, IN TL d6.16																									
1902	Phi A	0	1	.000	1	1	1	0	8	12	10	0	0	5	2	3.38	109	.343	.425	3-0	.000	-0	98	-2	-0.2
PORTERFIELD, BOB Erwin Coolidge B 8.10.1923 Newport, VA D 4.28.1980 Sealy, TX BR/TR 6/190# d8.8																									
1948	NY A	5	3	.625	16	12	2-1	0	78	85	42	5	0	34	30	4.50	91	.273	.345	24-7	.250	0	138	-3	-0.3
1949	NY A	2	5	.286	12	8	3	0	57.2	53	26	3	1	29	25	4.06	100	.251	.344	19-0	.053	-2	97	1	0.0
1950	NY A	1	1	.500	10	2	0	1	19.2	28	19	2	0	8	9	8.69	49	.341	.400	3-0	.333	1*	84	-9	-0.8
1951	NY A	0	0	—	2	0	0	0	3	5	6	0	0	3	2	15.00	26	.385	.500	0-0	—	0		-4	-0.2
	Was A	9	8	.529	19	19	10-3	0	133.1	109	51	8	0	54	53	3.24	126	.224	.302	46-0	.130	-3	78	14	1.3
	Year	9	8	.529	21	19	10-3	0	136.1	114	55	8	0	57	55	3.50	117	.228	.308	46-0	.130	-3	78	10	1.1
1952	Was A	13	14	.481	31	29	15-3	0	231.1	222	80	7	4	85	80	2.72	131	.254	.323	79-3	.190	0	68	22	2.4
1953	Was A	**22**	10	.688	34	32	**24-9**	0	255	243	99	19	1	73	77	3.35	116	.257	.310	98-4	.255	8*	119	19	3.3
1954	Was A★	13	15	.464	32	31	**21**-2	0	244	249	104	14	3	77	82	3.32	107	.266	.322	88-5	.102	-3	98	7	0.5
1955	Was A	10	17	.370	30	27	8-2	0	178	197	103	14	2	54-5	74	4.45	86	.282	.333	63-5	.190	1	100	-14	-1.8
1956	Bos A	3	12	.200	25	18	4-1	0	126	127	82	21	1	64-4	53	5.14	90	.260	.347	43-1	.326	3	83	-6	-0.4
1957	Bos A	4	4	.500	28	9	3-1	1	102.1	107	54	8	1	30-2	28	4.05	99	.272	.324	29-0	.172	-0	92	-2	-0.1
1958	Bos A	0	0	—	2	0	0	0	4	3	2	1	0	0-0	1	4.50	89	.214	.214	0-0	—	0		0	0.0
	Pit N	4	6	.400	37	6	2-1	5	87.2	78	33	7	1	19-3	39	3.29	118	.241	.281	20-0	.050	-1	93	7	0.8
1959	Pit N	0	0	—	6	0	0	0	5.1	6	2	1	0	2-1	1	1.69	229	.286	.348	0-0	—	0		1	0.0
	Chi N	0	0	—	4	0	0	0	6.1	14	9	1	0	3-0	0	11.37	35	.424	.472	1-0	.000	-0		-5	-0.3
	Pit N	1	2	.333	30	0	0	1	36	45	20	2	0	17-5	18	4.75	81	.321	.395	3-0	.000	-0		-3	-0.2
	Year	1	2	.333	40	0	0	1	47.2	65	35	4	0	22-6	19	5.29	73	.335	.403	4-0	.000	-0		-7	-0.5
Total	12	87	97	.473	318	193	92-23	8	1567.2	1571	732	113	14	552-20	572	3.79	102	.263	.326	516-25	.184	4	96	25	4.2
PORTO, AL Alfred "Lefty" B 6.27.1926 Heilwood, PA BL/TL 5-11/176# d4.22																									
1948	Phi N	0	0	—	3	0	0	0	4	2	0	0	0	1	1	0.00	—	.143	.200	0-0	—	0		2	0.1
PORTOCARRERO, ARNIE Arnold Mario B 7.5.1931 New York, NY D 6.21.1986 Kansas City, KS BR/TR 6-3/196# d4.18																									
1954	Phi A	9	18	.333	34	33	16-1	0	248	233	124	25	5	114	132	4.06	96	.249	.329	75-7	.107	-2	73	-4	-0.8
1955	KC A	5	9	.357	24	20	4-1	0	111.1	109	66	12	4	67-4	34	4.77	88	.259	.364	37-2	.108	-1	95	-7	-1.0
1956	KC A	0	1	.000	3	1	0	0	8	9	9	2	0	7-0	2	10.13	43	.300	.432	1-0	.000	-0	82	-4	-0.5
1957	KC A	4	9	.308	33	17	1	0	114.2	103	55	10	3	34-2	42	3.92	101	.240	.298	28-3	.107	-1	78	1	-0.1
1958	Bal A	15	11	.577	32	27	10-3	2	204.2	173	81	17	3	57-3	90	3.25	110	.229	.284	67-3	.164	0	93	9	0.9
1959	Bal A	2	7	.222	27	14	1	0	90	107	73	10	2	32-0	23	6.80	56	.294	.352	21-3	.000	-3	82	-29	-2.7
1960	Bal A	3	2	.600	13	5	1	0	40.2	44	23	6	0	9-0	15	4.43	86	.275	.312	11-0	.000	-1	116	-3	-0.5
Total	7	38	57	.400	166	117	33-5	2	817.1	778	431	82	17	320-9	338	4.32	89	.252	.322	240-18	.108	-9	85	-37	-4.7
PORTUGAL, MARK Mark Steven B 10.30.1962 Los Angeles, CA BR/TR 6/190# d8.14																									
1985	Min A	1	3	.250	6	4	0	0-0	24.1	24	16	3	0	14-0	12	5.55	79	.270	.362	0-0	—	0	103	-3	-0.3
1986	Min A	6	10	.375	27	15	3	1-1	112.2	112	56	10	1	50-1	67	4.31	100	.265	.342	0-0	—	0	111	2	0.2
1987	Min A	1	3	.250	13	7	0	0-1	44	58	40	13	1	24-1	28	7.77	60	.326	.407	0-0	—	0	90	-14	-1.1
1988	Min A	3	3	.500	26	0	0	3-1	57.2	60	30	11	1	17-1	31	4.53	90	.274	.325	0-0	—	0		-2	-0.3
1989	Hou N	7	1	.875	20	15	2-1	0-0	108	91	34	7	2	37-0	86	2.75	123	.232	.301	34-3	.206	3	111	9	1.0
1990	Hou N	11	10	.524	32	32	1	0-0	196.2	187	90	21	4	67-4	136	3.62	103	.250	.313	66-5	.136	-1	84	2	0.0
1991	Hou N	10	12	.455	32	27	1	1-1	168.1	163	91	19	2	59-5	120	4.49	78	.256	.318	46-6	.196	3*	120	-18	-1.9
1992	Hou N	6	3	.667	18	16	1-1	0-0	101.1	76	32	7	1	41-3	62	2.66	126	.213	.295	28-6	.107	-1	89	9	0.7
1993	Hou N	18	4	**.818**	33	33	1-1	0-0	208	194	75	10	4	77-3	131	2.77	140	.248	.318	65-10	.231	4	115	25	2.9
1994	SF N	10	8	.556	21	21	1	0-0	137.1	135	68	17	6	45-2	87	3.93	102	.260	.324	48-4	.354	8	111	0	0.7
1995	SF N	5	5	.500	17	17	1	0-0	104	106	56	10	2	34-2	63	4.15	98	.262	.323	29-7	.103	-0	113	-2	-0.2
	†Cin N	6	5	.545	14	14	0	0-0	77.2	79	35	7	2	22-0	33	3.82	108	.262	.316	29-1	.172	2	136	3	0.5
	Year	11	10	.524	31	**31**	1	0-0	181.2	185	41	17	4	56-2	96	4.01	102	.262	.320	58-8	.138	1	124	1	0.3
1996	Cin N	8	9	.471	27	26	1-1	0-0	156	146	77	20	2	42-2	93	3.98	106	.248	.297	48-7	.167	-0*	94	4	0.3
1997	Phi N	0	2	.000	3	3	0	0-0	13.2	17	8	0	0	5-0	2	4.61	92	.321	.373	4-0	.000	-0	51	-1	-0.1
1998	Phi N	10	5	.667	26	26	3	0-0	166.1	186	88	26	4	32-2	104	4.44	98	.283	.319	50-4	.260	4	105	-2	0.3
1999	Bos A	7	12	.368	31	27	1	0-0	150.1	179	100	28	4	41-1	79	5.51	90	.292	.337	3-1	.000	-0	92	-7	-0.8
Total	15	109	95	.534	346	283	16-4	5-4	1826.1	1813	896	209	36	607-27	1134	4.03	100	.261	.321	450-54	.198	20	104	5	1.9
PORZIO, MIKE Lawrence Michael B 8.20.1972 Waterbury, CT BL/TL 6-3/190# d7.9																									
1999	Col N	0	0	—	16	0	0	0-0	14.2	21	14	5	0	10-0	10	8.59	68	.328	.419	0-0	—	0		-3	-0.1
2002	Chi A	2	2	.500	32	0	0	0-0	43	40	25	10	3	23-2	33	4.81	94	.248	.347	0-0	—	0		-1	-0.1
2003	Chi A	1	1	.500	3	3	0	0-0	14	18	10	2	2	1-0	9	6.43	71	.321	.350	0-0	—	0	81	-3	-0.3
Total	3	3	3	.500	51	3	0	0-0	71.2	79	49	17	5	34-2	52	5.90	81	.281	.364	0-0	—	0	81	-7	-0.5
POSEDEL, BILL William John "Sailor Bill" or "Barnacle Bill" B 8.2.1906 San Francisco, CA D 11.28.1989 Livermore, CA BR/TR 5-11/175# d4.23 Mil 1942-45 C18																									
1938	Bro N	8	9	.471	33	17	6-1	1	140	178	96	14	2	46	49	5.66	69	.311	.365	44-4	.227	1	121	-23	-2.5
1939	Bos N	15	13	.536	33	29	18-5	1	220.2	221	103	8	0	78	73	3.92	94	.268	.331	73-5	.110	-4	94	-1	-0.6
1940	Bos N	12	17	.414	35	32	18	1	233	263	118	16	1	81	86	4.13	90	.288	.346	82-2	.171	1	89	-10	-1.0
1941	Bos N	4	4	.500	18	9	3	0	57.1	61	36	6	1	30	10	4.87	73	.279	.368	25-1	.320	2	116	-8	-0.8
1946	Bos N	2	0	1.000	19	0	0	4	28.1	34	24	4	0	13	9	6.99	49	.304	.376	3-0	.000	-0		-10	-1.1
Total	5	41	43	.488	138	87	45-6	6	679.1	757	377	48	4	248	227	4.56	82	.286	.349	227-12	.176	0	100	-52	-6.0
POSER, BOB John Falk B 3.16.1910 Columbus, WI D 5.21.2002 Columbus, WI BL/TR 6/173# d4.17																									
1932	Chi A	0	0	—	1	0	0	0	0.2	3	2	0	0	2	1	27.00	16	.600	.714	3-0	.000	-0*		-2	-0.1
1935	StL A	1	1	.500	4	1	0	0	13.2	26	15	0	0	4	1	9.22	52	.400	.435	4-1	.250	0	54	-6	-0.7
Total	2	1	1	.500	5	1	0	0	14.1	29	17	0	0	6	2	10.05	47	.414	.461	7-1	.143	0	54	-8	-0.8
POSSEHL, LOU Louis Thomas B 4.12.1926 Chicago, IL D 10.7.1997 Sarasota, FL BR/TR 6-2/180# d8.25 gf-George																									
1946	Phi N	1	2	.333	4	4	0	0	13.2	19	9	0	1	10	4	5.93	58	.339	.448	3-1	.000	-0	62	-3	-0.6
1947	Phi N	0	0	—	2	0	0	0	4.1	5	2	0	1	0	1	4.15	96	.385	.429	0-0	—	0		0	0.1
1948	Phi N	1	1	.500	3	2	1	0	14.2	17	8	3	0	4	7	4.91	80	.304	.350	4-0	.250	0*	135	-1	-0.1
1951	Phi N	0	1	.000	2	1	0	0	6	9	5	0	0	3	6	6.00	64	.333	.400	1-0	.000	-0	92	-2	-0.3
1952	Phi N	0	1	.000	4	1	0	0	12.2	12	9	3	0	7	4	4.97	73	.235	.328	2-0	.000	-0	73	-2	-0.2
Total	5	2	5	.286	15	8	1	0	51.1	62	33	6	2	24	22	5.26	71	.305	.384	10-1	.100	-0	85	-8	-1.1
POTE, LOU Louis William B 8.21.1971 Evergreen Park, IL BR/TR 6-3/190# d8.11																									
1999	Ana A	1	1	.500	20	0	0	3-0	29.1	23	9	1	0	12-1	20	2.15	226	.219	.299	0-0	—	0		8	0.6
2000	Ana A	1	1	.500	32	1	0	1-0	50.1	52	23	4	0	17-1	44	3.40	150	.267	.324	0-0	—	0	37	8	0.4
2001	Ana A	2	0	1.000	44	1	0	2-1	86.2	88	41	11	3	32-5	66	4.15	110	.258	.325	0-0	—	0	61	5	0.3
2002	Ana A	0	2	.000	31	0	0	0-1	50.1	33	20	7	3	26-2	32	3.22	138	.194	.304	0-0	—	0		7	0.4
Total	4	4	4	.500	127	2	0	6-2	216.2	196	93	23	6	87-9	162	3.49	135	.242	.317	0-0	—	0	50	28	1.7
POTT, NELLIE Nelson Adolph "Lefty" B 7.16.1899 Cincinnati, OH D 12.3.1963 Cincinnati, OH BL/TL 6/185# d4.19																									
1922	Cle A	0	0	—	2	0	0	0	2	7	7	1	0	2	0	31.50	13	.583	.643	0-0	—	0		-6	-0.3
POTTER, DYKES Maryland Dykes B 11.18.1910 Ashland, KY D 2.27.2002 Greenup, KY BR/TR 6/185# d4.26 b-Squire																									
1938	Bro N	0	0	—	2	0	0	0	2	4	1	1	0	0	1	4.50	87	.400	.400	0-0	—	0		0	0.0
POTTER, NELS Nelson Thomas "Nellie" B 8.23.1911 Mt.Morris, IL D 9.30.1990 Mt.Morris, IL BL/TR 5-11/180# d4.25																									
1936	StL N	0	0	—	1	0	0	0	1	0	0	0	0	0	0	0.00	—	.000	.000	0-0	—	0		0	0.0
1938	Phi A	2	12	.143	35	9	4	5	111.1	139	95	15	2	49	43	6.47	75	.306	.376	39-1	.256	1*	75	-20	-2.1
1939	Phi A	8	12	.400	41	25	9	2	196.1	258	163	26	5	88	60	6.60	71	.321	.391	67-4	.179	-1	106	-37	-3.2
1940	Phi A	9	14	.391	31	25	13	0	200.2	213	115	18	1	71	73	4.44	100	.269	.330	71-6	.254	2	82	1	0.3
1941	Phi A	1	1	.500	10	3	1	2	23.1	35	26	3	0	16	7	9.26	45	.337	.425	6-1	.167	0	152	-12	-1.1
	Bos A	2	0	1.000	10	0	0	0	20	21	10	0	0	16	6	4.50	93	.284	.411	3-0	.000	-0		0	0.0
	Year	3	1	.750	20	3	1	2	43.1	56	43	3	0	32	13	7.06	59	.315	.419	9-1	.111	0	152	-12	-1.1

Year	Tm Lg	W	L	Pct	G	GS	CG-Sho	SV-BS	IP	H	R	HR	HB	BB-IB	SO	ERA	AERA	OAV	OOB	AB-SH	AVG	PB	Sup	APR	PW
1943	StL A	10	5	.667	33	13	8	1	168.1	146	56	11	3	54	80	2.78	120	.235	.299	55-4	.145	-1	88	12	1.0
1944	†StL A	19	7	.731	32	29	16-3	0	232	211	79	6	1	70	91	2.83	127	.244	.301	82-5	.159	-2	137	22	2.3
1945	StL A	15	11	.577	32	32	21-3	0	255.1	212	75	10	1	68	129	2.47	143	.226	.279	92-5	.304	4	88	30	3.6
1946	StL A	8	9	.471	23	19	10	0	145	152	72	9	3	59	72	3.72	100	.268	.340	52-0	.231	2	80	-1	0.1
1947	StL A	4	10	.286	32	10	3	2	122.2	130	61	13	2	44	65	4.04	96	.277	.342	35-0	.257	3	73	-1	0.2
1948	StL A	1	1	.500	2	2	0	0	10.1	11	7	1	2	4	4	5.23	87	.262	.354	4-0	.500	1	79	-1	-0.1
	Phi A	2	2	.500	8	0	0	1	18	17	8	1	0	5	13	4.00	107	.250	.301	4-0	.250	0		1	0.2
	Year	3	3	.500	10	2	0	1	28.1	28	19	2	2	9	17	4.45	99	.255	.322	8-0	.375	1	82	0	0.1
	†Bos N	5	2	.714	18	7	3	2	85	77	27	4	0	8	47	2.33	165	.245	.264	29-2	.379	3	145	14	1.5
1949	Bos N	6	11	.353	41	3	1	7	96.2	99	49	6	1	30	57	4.19	90	.265	.321	23-0	.130	-0	93	-3	-0.5
Total	12	92	97	.487	349	177	89-6	22	1686	1721	843	123	21	582	747	3.99	99	.265	.328	562-28	.228	11	99	5	2.2
POTTER, SQUIRE Robert B 3.18.1902 Flatwoods, KY D 1.27.1983 Ashland, KY BR/TR 6-1/185# d8.7 b-Dykes																									
1923	Was A	0	0	—	1	0	0	0	3	11	9	0	0	4	1	21.00	18	.688	.750	0-0	—	0		-6	-0.3
POTTS, MIKE Michael Larry B 9.5.1970 Langdale, AL BL/TL 5-9/179# d4.6																									
1996	Mil A	1	2	.333	24	0	0	1-0	45.1	58	39	7	0	30-2	21	7.15	73	.319	.407	0-0	—	0		-9	-0.6
POUNDS, BILL Jeared Wells B 3.11.1878 Paterson, NJ D 7.7.1936 Paterson, NJ BR/TR 5-10.5/178# d5.2																									
1903	Cle A	0	0	—	1	0	0	0	5	8	7	0	0	0	2	10.80	26	.364	.364	2-0	.500	1		-4	-0.1
	Bro N	0	0	—	1	0	0	0	6	8	5	1	0	2	2	6.00	53	.348	.400	3-0	.667	1		-2	0.0
Total	1	0	0	—	2	0	0	0	11	16	12	1	0	2	4	8.18	37	.356	.383	5-0	.600	1		-6	-0.1
POWELL, ABNER Charles Abner "Ab" B 12.15.1860 Shenandoah, PA D 8.7.1953 New Orleans, LA BL/TR 5-7/160# d8.4 ▲																									
1884	Was U	6	12	.333	18	17	14-1	0	134	135	107	3		19	78	3.43	70	.245	.270	191	.283	0*	64	-19	-1.8
1886	Bal AA	2	5	.286	7	7	7	0	60	66	51	2	1	26	15	5.10	67	.264	.336	39	.179	-1*	77	-10	-0.9
	Cin AA	0	1	.000	4	1	1	0	15.1	16	13	0	0	9	4	4.70	75	.271	.368	74	.230	-0*	67	-2	-0.1
	Year	2	6	.250	11	8	8	0	75.1	82	17	2	1	35	19	5.02	69	.265	.342	113	.212	-1	75	-12	-1.0
Total	2	8	18	.308	29	25	22-1	0	209.1	217	171	5	1	54	97	4.00	69	.252	.297	304	.257	-1	68	-31	-2.8
POWELL, DENNIS Dennis Clay B 8.13.1963 Moultrie, GA BR/TL 6-3/200# d7.7																									
1985	LA N	1	1	.500	16	2	0	1-0	29.1	30	19	7	1	13-3	19	5.22	67	.263	.341	3-2	.000	-0	89	-5	-0.4
1986	LA N	2	7	.222	27	6	0	0-0	65.1	65	32	5	1	25-7	31	4.27	81	.272	.341	14-0	.214	1	64	-5	-0.5
1987	Sea A	1	3	.250	16	3	0	0-1	34.1	32	13	3	0	15-0	17	3.15	151	.250	.324	0-0	—	0	116	6	0.6
1988	Sea A	1	3	.250	12	2	0	0-0	18.2	29	20	2	2	11-2	15	8.68	48	.363	.442	0-0	—	0	153	-9	-1.6
1989	Sea A	2	2	.500	43	1	0	2-0	45	49	25	6	2	21-0	27	5.00	81	.285	.364	0-0	—	0	67	-3	-0.2
1990	Sea A	0	0	—	2	0	0	0-0	3	5	3	0	1	2-0	0	9.00	44	.357	.471	0-0	—	0		-1	-0.1
	Mil A	0	4	.000	9	7	0	0-0	39.1	59	37	0	1	19-0	23	6.86	57	.341	.405	0-0	—	0	90	-14	-1.2
	Year	0	4	.000	11	7	0	0-0	42.1	64	41	0	2	21-0	23	7.02	55	.342	.410	0-0	—	0	90	-16	-1.3
1992	Sea A	4	2	.667	49	0	0	0-0	57	49	30	5	3	29-2	35	4.58	87	.238	.340	0-0	—	0		-3	-0.3
1993	Sea A	0	0	—	33	2	0	0-0	47.2	42	22	7	1	24-2	32	4.15	106	.255	.349	0-0	—	0	63	2	0.1
Total	8	11	22	.333	207	23	0	3-1	339.2	360	201	35	12	159-16	199	4.95	80	.279	.360	17-2	.176	1	89	-32	-3.6
POWELL, GROVER Grover David B 10.10.1940 Sayre, PA D 5.21.1985 Raleigh, NC BL/TL 5-10/175# d7.13																									
1963	NY N	1	1	.500	20	4	1-1	0	49.2	37	23	2	1	32-0	39	2.72	128	.202	.323	10-0	.200	1	68	2	0.2
POWELL, JAY James Willard B 1.9.1972 Meridian, MS BR/TR 6-4/220# d9.10																									
1995	Fla N	0	0	—	9	0	0	0-0	8.1	7	2	0	2	6-1	4	1.08	391	.241	.405	0-0	—	0		2	0.1
1996	Fla N	4	3	.571	67	0	0	2-3	71.1	71	41	5	4	36-1	52	4.54	90	.255	.348	5-1	.000	-1		-4	-0.5
1997	†Fla N	7	2	.778	74	0	0	2-2	79.2	71	35	3	4	30-3	65	3.28	123	.242	.317	4-0	.500	1		5	0.7
1998	Fla N	4	4	.500	33	0	0	3-3	36.1	36	19	5	2	22-6	24	4.21	96	.263	.370	0-0	—	0		-1	-0.1
	†Hou N	3	3	.500	29	0	0	4-1	34	22	9	1	1	15-3	38	2.38	170	.182	.277	1-0	.000	-0		7	1.2
	Year	7	7	.500	62	0	0	7-4	70.1	58	31	6	3	37-9	62	3.33	122	.225	.328	1-0	.000	-0		6	1.1
1999	†Hou N	5	4	.556	67	0	0	4-3	75	82	38	3	3	40-4	77	4.32	102	.282	.372	0-0	—	0		1	0.1
2000	Hou N	1	1	.500	29	0	0	0-0	27	29	18	1	0	19-1	16	5.67	86	.271	.381	1-0	.000	-0*		-2	-0.1
2001	Hou N	2	2	.500	35	0	0	0-5	36.1	41	18	4	0	19-0	28	3.72	123	.275	.355	1-0	.000	-0		3	0.2
	Col N	3	1	.750	39	0	0	7-1	38.2	34	18	5	2	12-3	26	2.79	191	.245	.314	0-0	—	0		7	0.9
	Year	5	3	.625	74	0	0	7-6	75	75	36	9	2	31-3	54	3.24	153	.260	.335	1-0	.000	-0		10	1.1
2002	Tex A	3	2	.600	51	0	0	0-4	49.2	50	28	5	1	24-4	35	3.44	137	.253	.336	0-0	—	0		3	0.3
2003	Tex A	3	0	1.000	51	0	0	0-0	58.2	75	58	7	2	34-3	40	7.82	64	.318	.399	0-0	—	0		-18	-0.9
Total	9	35	22	.614	484	0	0	22-22	515	518	284	39	21	257-29	405	4.23	105	.262	.351	12-1	.167	-0		3	1.9
POWELL, JEREMY Jeremy Robert B 6.18.1976 Bellflower, CA BR/TR 6-5/230# d7.23																									
1998	Mon N	1	5	.167	7	6	0	0-0	25	27	25	5	4	11-0	14	7.92	53	.290	.382	6-0	.000	-1	95	-10	-1.9
1999	Mon N	4	8	.333	17	17	0	0-0	97	113	60	14	8	44-2	44	4.73	95	.302	.385	30-1	.133	0	86	-3	-0.3
2000	Mon N	0	3	.000	11	4	0	0-0	26	35	27	6	0	9-0	19	7.96	60	.321	.370	5-0	.600	1	96	-9	-0.8
Total	3	5	16	.238	35	27	0	0-0	148	175	112	25	12	64-2	77	5.84	77	.304	.381	41-1	.171	1	89	-22	-3.0
POWELL, JACK John Joseph "Red" B 7.9.1874 Bloomington, IL D 10.17.1944 Chicago, IL BR/TR 5-11/195# d6.23																									
1897	Cle N	15	10	.600	27	26	24-2	0	225	245	117	2	9	62	61	3.16	142	.275	.328	97-4	.206	-4*	111	29	2.2
1898	Cle N	23	15	.605	42	41	36-**6**	0	342	328	154	8	16	112	93	3.00	121	.251	.317	136-2	.132	-7	100	27	1.8
1899	StL N	23	19	.548	48	**43**	**40**-2	0	373	433	197	15	15	85	87	3.52	113	.290	.334	134-4	.201	-1*	87	24	2.0
1900	StL N	17	16	.515	38	37	28-3	0	287.2	325	194	9	3	77	77	4.44	82	.284	.331	109-4	.284	10	107	-21	-1.1
1901	StL N	19	19	.500	**45**	37	33-2	**3**	338.1	351	168	14	12	50	133	3.54	90	.266	.299	119-9	.176	1	108	-11	-1.2
1902	StL A	22	17	.564	42	39	36-3	**2**	328.1	320	144	12	9	93	137	3.21	110	.256	.312	127-3	.205	4*	99	16	1.7
1903	StL A	15	19	.441	38	34	33-4	**2**	306.1	294	131	11	5	58	169	2.91	100	.252	.290	120-3	.208	2*	84	3	0.5
1904	NY A	23	19	.548	47	45	38-3	0	390.1	340	154	15	10	92	202	2.44	111	.235	.286	146-4	.178	-3	90	7	0.1
1905	NY A	8	13	.381	37	23	13-1	1	203	214	107	4	6	57	84	3.50	84	.272	.326	65-0	.185	-0	95	-10	-1.4
	StL A	2	1	.667	3	3	3	0	28	22	6	0	1	5	12	1.61	158	.218	.262	10-0	.100	-0	83	3	0.3
	Year	10	14	.417	40	26	16-1	1	231	236	9	4	7	62	96	3.27	88	.266	.319	75-0	.173	-1	94	-10	-1.1
1906	StL A	13	14	.481	28	26	25-3	1	244	196	77	2	8	55	132	1.77	146	.223	.275	91-2	.231	3	74	21	2.6
1907	StL A	13	16	.448	32	31	27-4	1	255.2	229	104	4	5	62	96	2.68	94	.242	.292	91-1	.132	-3	92	-4	-1.0
1908	StL A	16	13	.552	33	32	23-5	1	256	208	73	1	6	47	85	2.11	113	.231	.274	89-4	.236	3	92	13	1.4
1909	StL A	12	16	.429	34	27	18-4	3	239	221	83	1	4	42	82	2.11	115	.250	.287	78-4	.179	0	77	5	0.4
1910	StL A	7	11	.389	21	18	8-3	0	129.1	121	45	0	1	28	52	2.30	108	.250	.292	43-1	.163	-1	63	5	0.3
1911	StL A	8	19	.296	31	27	18-1	1	207.2	224	120	7	7	44	52	3.29	102	.262	.304	73-4	.164	-3*	94	-2	-0.8
1912	StL A	9	17	.346	32	27	19	0	235.1	248	117	5	3	52	67	3.10	107	.276	.318	82-1	.183	0	83	4	0.2
Total	16	245	254	.491	578	516	422-46	15	4389	4319	1991	110	120	1021	1621	2.97	106	.258	.305	1610-50	.192	-1	94	109	8.0
POWELL, JACK Reginald Bertrand B 8.17.1891 Holcomb, MO D 3.12.1930 Memphis, TN TR 6-2/?# d6.14																									
1913	StL A	0	0	—	2	0	0	0	2	1	3	0	0	2	0	0.00	—	.143	.333	0-0	—	0		0	0.0
POWELL, ROSS Ross John B 1.24.1968 Grand Rapids, MI BL/TL 6/180# d9.5																									
1993	Cin N	0	3	.000	9	1	0	0-0	16.1	13	8	1	0	6-0	17	4.41	91	.224	.297	1-0	.000	-0	45	0	-0.1
1994	Hou N	0	0	—	12	0	0	0-0	7.1	6	1	0	1	5-0	5	1.23	322	.240	.387	0-0	—	0		2	0.1
1995	Hou N	0	0	—	15	0	0	0-0	9	16	12	1	0	11-4	8	11.00	35	.381	.500	0-0	—	0		-7	-0.4
	Pit N	0	2	.000	12	3	0	0-0	20.2	20	14	5	2	10-0	12	5.23	82	.253	.352	3-1	.000	-0	133	-2	-0.2
	Year	0	2	.000	27	3	0	0-0	29.2	36	20	6	2	21-4	20	6.98	60	.298	.407	3-1	.000	-0	137	-10	-0.6
Total	3	0	5	.000	48	4	0	0-0	53.1	55	35	7	3	32-4	42	5.40	76	.270	.375	4-1	.000	-0	116	-7	-0.6
POWELL, BRIAN William Brian B 10.10.1973 Bainbridge, GA BR/TR 6-2/205# d6.27																									
1998	Det A	3	8	.273	18	16	0	0-0	83.2	101	67	17	2	36-2	46	6.35	74	.294	.364	1-0	.000	-0	80	-16	-1.8
2000	Hou N	2	1	.667	9	5	0	0-0	31.1	34	21	8	1	13-0	14	5.74	85	.279	.348	9-0	.222	1	143	-3	-0.2
2001	Hou N	0	1	.000	1	1	0	0-0	3	5	6	1	0	3-0	3	18.00	25	.357	.471	1-0	.000	-0	101	-4	-0.6
2002	Det A	1	5	.167	13	9	0	0-0	57.2	64	34	11	1	21-0	30	4.84	89	.278	.339	0-0	—	0	65	-3	-0.3

Year	Tm Lg	W	L	Pct	G	GS	CG-Sho	SV-BS	IP	H	R	HR	HB	BB-IB	SO	ERA	AERA	OAV	OOB	AB-SH	AVG	PB	Sup	APR	PW
2003	SF N	0	1	.000	1	1	0	0-0	4.2	8	7	3	0	1-0	3	13.50	30	.381	.409	2-0	.000	-0	69	-5	-0.6
Total	5	6	16	.273	42	32	0	0-0	180.1	212	135	40	4	74-2	96	6.14	75	.290	.357	13-0	.154	0	87	-31	-3.5
POWELL, BILL William Burris "Big Bill" B 5.8.1885 Taylor County, WV D 9.28.1967 E.Liverpool, OH BR/TR 6-2.5/182# d4.16																									
1909	Pit N	0	1	.000	3	1	0	0	7.1	7	6	0	1	6	2	3.68	74	.292	.452	3-0	.333	0	77	-1	-0.2
1910	Pit N	4	6	.400	12	9	4-2	0	75	65	32	0	5	34	23	2.40	129	.242	.338	23-1	.261	1	61	4	0.6
1912	Chi N	0	0	—	1	0	0	0	2	2	2	0	0	1	0	9.00	37	.250	.333	0-0	—	0		-1	0.0
1913	Cin N	0	1	.000	1	1	0	0	0.1	2	2	0	0	2	0	54.00	6	1.000	1.000	0-0	—	0	116	-2	-0.3
Total	4	4	8	.333	17	11	4-2	0	84.2	76	42	0	6	43	25	2.87	107	.251	.355	26-1	.269	1	68	0	0.1
POWER, TED Ted Henry B 1.31.1955 Guthrie, OK BR/TR 6-4/225# d9.9																									
1981	LA N	1	3	.250	5	2	0	0-0	14.1	16	6	0	1	7-2	7	3.14	106	.286	.364	3-0	.000	-0	13	0	-0.1
1982	LA N	1	1	.500	12	4	0	0-0	33.2	38	27	4	0	23-1	15	6.68	52	.288	.391	6-1	.000	-1	127	-12	-0.7
1983	Cin N	5	6	.455	49	6	1	2-0	111	120	62	10	1	49-3	57	4.54	84	.286	.357	16-3	.000	-1	77	-9	-1.1
1984	Cin N	9	7	.563	**78**	0	0	11-4	108.2	93	37	4	0	46-8	81	2.82	134	.237	.311	5-1	.000	-0		11	1.8
1985	Cin N	8	6	.571	64	0	0	27-9	80	65	27	2	1	45-8	42	2.70	141	.227	.330	0-0	—	0		9	1.9
1986	Cin N	10	6	.625	56	10	0	1-1	129	115	59	13	1	52-10	95	3.70	105	.245	.318	24-3	.125	0	136	3	0.3
1987	Cin N	10	13	.435	34	34	2-1	0-0	204	213	115	28	3	71-7	133	4.50	94	.267	.327	59-9	.119	0*	96	-7	-0.8
1988	KC A	5	6	.455	22	12	2-2	0-0	80.1	98	54	7	3	30-3	44	5.94	67	.305	.366	0-0	—	0	122	-15	-1.8
	Det A	1	1	.500	4	2	0	0-0	18.2	23	13	1	0	8-4	13	5.79	66	.307	.373	0-0	—	0	60	-4	-0.4
	Year	6	7	.462	26	14	2-2	0-0	99	121	16	8	3	38-7	57	5.91	67	.306	.367	0-0	—	0	113	-20	-2.2
1989	StL N	7	7	.500	23	15	0	0-0	97	96	47	7	1	21-3	43	3.71	98	.255	.294	33-3	.091	-2	101	-2	-0.5
1990	†Pit N	1	3	.250	40	0	0	7-0	51.2	50	23	5	0	17-6	42	3.66	99	.255	.312	8-0	.125	0		0	0.0
1991	Cin N	5	3	.625	68	0	0	3-1	87	87	37	6	2	31-5	51	3.62	105	.265	.329	3-0	.000	-0		3	0.2
1992	Cle A	3	3	.500	64	0	0	6-5	99.1	88	33	7	4	35-9	51	2.54	154	.248	.316	0-0	—	0		14	1.0
1993	Cle A	0	2	.000	20	0	0	0-1	20	30	17	2	0	8-3	11	7.20	60	.333	.384	0-0	—	0		-6	-0.5
	Sea A	2	2	.500	25	0	0	13-2	25.1	27	11	1	0	9-1	16	3.91	113	.287	.346	0-0	—	0		2	0.3
	Year	2	4	.333	45	0	0	13-3	45.1	57	32	3	0	17-4	27	5.36	82	.310	.365	0-0	—	0		-4	-0.2
Total	13	68	69	.496	564	85	5-3	70-23	1160	1159	568	97	17	452-73	701	4.00	98	.264	.331	157-20	.089	-4	104	-13	-0.4
POWERS, JIM James T. B 1868 New York, NY 5-10/150# d4.18																									
1890	Bro AA	1	2	.333	4	2	2	0	30	38	29	1	1	16	3	5.70	68	.299	.382	13	.154	-0	43	-6	-0.5
POWERS, IKE John Lloyd B 3.13.1906 Hancock, MD D 12.22.1968 Hancock, MD BR/TR 6-0.5/188# d7.26																									
1927	Phi A	1	1	.500	11	1	0	0	26	26	16	1	0	7	3	4.50	95	.271	.320	5-0	.400	1	98	-1	0.0
1928	Phi A	1	0	1.000	9	0	0	2	12	8	6	1	1	10	4	4.50	89	.222	.404	0-0	—	0		0	0.0
Total	2	2	1	.667	20	1	0	2	38	34	22	2	1	17	7	4.50	93	.258	.347	5-0	.400	1	98	-1	0.0
PRALL, WILLIE Wilfred Anthony B 4.20.1950 Hackensack, NJ BL/TL 6-3/200# d9.3																									
1975	Chi N	0	2	.000	3	3	0	0-0	14.2	21	15	1	0	8-0	7	8.59	45	.339	.408	4-2	.000	-0	99	-7	-0.8
PRATT, AL Albert George "Uncle Al" B 11.19.1848 Allegheny, PA D 11.21.1937 Pittsburgh, PA TR 5-7/140# d5.4 M2 U2																									
1871	Cle NA	10	17	.370	28	28	22	0	224.2	296	288	9		47	**34**	3.77	110	.277	.307	130	.262	2*	83	7	0.8
1872	Cle NA	2	9	.182	15	12	8	0	105.2	150	133	3		14	7	5.79	61	.286	.305	65	.277	0*	72	-26	-1.6
Total	2 NA	12	26	.316	43	40	30	0	330.1	446	421	12		61	41	4.41	89	.280	.306	195	.267	3	80	-19	-0.8
PRATT, ANDY Andrew Elias B 8.27.1979 Mesa, AZ BL/TL 5-11/160# d9.28																									
2002	Atl N	0	0	—	1	0	0	0-0	1.1	1	1	0	0	4-0	1	6.75	61	.200	.556	0-0	—	0		0	0.0
PREGENZER, JOHN John Arthur B 8.2.1935 Burlington, WI BR/TR 6-5/220# d4.20																									
1963	SF N	0	0	—	6	0	0	1	9.1	8	5	0	1	8-2	5	4.82	66	.242	.405	0-0	—	0		-1	-0.1
1964	SF N	2	0	1.000	13	0	0	0	18.1	21	15	1	1	11-3	8	4.91	73	.296	.398	0-0	—	0		-4	-0.5
Total	2	2	0	1.000	19	0	0	1	27.2	29	20	1	2	19-5	13	4.88	70	.279	.400	0-0	—	0		-5	-0.6
PRENDERGAST, JIM James Bartholomew B 8.23.1917 Brooklyn, NY D 8.23.1994 Amherst, NY BL/TL 6-1/208# d4.25																									
1948	Bos N	1	1	.500	10	2	0	1	16.2	30	20	1	0	5	3	10.26	37	.380	.417	5-0	.000	-1	116	-12	-1.4
PRENDERGAST, MIKE Michael Thomas B 12.15.1888 Arlington, IL D 11.18.1967 Omaha, NE BR/TR 5-9.5/165# d4.26																									
1914	Chi F	5	9	.357	30	19	7-1	0	136	131	53	5	3	40	71	2.38	111	.255	.313	37-4	.108	-3	73	3	-0.1
1915	Chi F	14	12	.538	42	30	16-3	0	253.2	220	93	6	4	67	95	2.48	101	.240	.295	80-4	.075	-9	88	0	-1.0
1916	Chi N	6	11	.353	35	10	4-2	2	152	127	53	5	1	23	56	2.31	126	.228	.260	46-1	.152	-2	62	8	0.7
1917	Chi N	3	6	.333	35	8	1	1	99.1	112	42	6	0	21	43	3.35	86	.302	.339	28-0	.250	1	114	-2	0.0
1918	Phi N	13	14	.481	33	30	20	1	252.1	257	102	6	1	46	41	2.89	104	.273	.308	85-2	.082	-8	80	3	-0.6
1919	Phi N	0	1	.000	5	1	0	0	15	20	15	0	1	10	5	8.40	38	.351	.456	3-0	.333	0	25	-7	-0.4
Total	6	41	53	.436	180	98	48-6	4	908.1	867	358	28	10	207	311	2.74	102	.258	.304	279-11	.115	-19	81	5	-1.4
PRENTISS, GEORGE George Pepper (a.k.a. George Pepper Wilson In 1901) B 6.10.1876 Wilmington, DE D 9.8.1902 Wilmington, DE BB/TR 5-11/175# d9.23																									
1901	Bos A	1	0	1.000	2	1	1	0	10	7	4	0	0	6	0	1.80	196	.194	.310	3-0	.333	1	134	2	0.2
1902	Bos A	2	2	.500	7	4	3	0	41	55	31	0	0	10	9	5.27	68	.322	.359	16-0	.313	1	136	-6	-0.5
	Bal A	0	1	.000	2	2	0	0	6.2	14	10	1	0	5	1	10.80	35	.424	.500	4-0	.000	-1	124	-4	-0.6
	Year	2	3	.400	9	6	3	0	47.2	69	17	1	0	15	10	6.04	60	.338	.384	20-0	.250	-0	133	-11	-1.1
Total	2	3	3	.500	11	7	4	0	57.2	76	45	1	0	21	10	5.31	68	.317	.372	23-0	.261	1	133	-8	-0.9
PRESKO, JOE Joseph Edward "Baby Joe" B 10.7.1928 Kansas City, MO BR/TR 6/170# d5.3																									
1951	StL N	7	4	.636	15	12	5	2	88.2	86	36	9	2	20	38	3.45	115	.251	.296	37-0	.162	-1	113	6	0.5
1952	StL N	7	10	.412	28	18	5-1	0	146.2	140	74	16	1	57	63	4.05	92	.247	.317	43-3	.093	-2	99	-5	-0.8
1953	StL N	6	13	.316	34	25	4	1	161.2	165	95	19	5	65	56	5.01	85	.261	.335	59-4	.220	1*	106	-12	-1.1
1954	StL N	4	9	.308	37	6	1-1	0	71.2	97	56	14	5	41	36	6.91	60	.327	.416	16-0	.250	0*	101	-19	-3.0
1957	Det A	1	1	.500	7	0	0	0	11	10	3	0	1	4-1	3	1.64	236	.278	.357	1-0	.000	-0		2	0.4
1958	Det A	0	0	—	7	0	0	2	10.2	13	4	0	0	1-0	6	3.38	120	.317	.326	0-0	—	0		1	0.1
Total	6	25	37	.403	128	61	15-2	5	490.1	511	268	58	14	188-1	202	4.61	87	.267	.336	156-7	.173	-1	105	-27	-3.9
PRESSNELL, TOT Forest Charles B 8.8.1906 Findlay, OH D 1.6.2001 Findlay, OH BR/TR 5-10/175# d4.21																									
1938	Bro N	11	14	.440	43	19	6-1	3	192	209	86	11	8	56	57	3.56	110	.276	.332	63-1	.143	-1	91	8	0.9
1939	Bro N	9	7	.563	31	18	10-2	2	156.2	171	76	8	1	33	43	4.02	100	.273	.311	51-3	.196	-1	111	1	0.0
1940	Bro N	6	5	.545	24	4	1-1	2	68.1	58	31	4	2	17	21	3.69	108	.221	.274	17-4	.000	-2	71	2	0.1
1941	Chi N	5	3	.625	29	1	0	1	70	69	26	2	4	23	27	3.09	114	.253	.320	15-1	.200	0	73	**5**	0.5
1942	Chi N	1	1	.500	27	0	0	4	39.1	40	28	5	5	5	9	5.49	58	.260	.305	3-0	.667	1		-10	-0.6
Total	5	32	30	.516	154	42	17-4	12	526.1	547	247	30	20	134	157	3.80	101	.264	.315	149-9	.161	-3	100	6	0.9
PRICE, JOE Joseph Walter B 11.29.1956 Inglewood, CA BR/TL 6-4/220# d6.14																									
1980	Cin N	7	3	.700	24	13	2	0-0	111.1	95	45	10	1	37-0	44	3.56	101	.236	.302	39-3	.128	-2	105	1	-0.1
1981	Cin N	6	1	.857	41	0	0	4-2	53.2	42	19	3	0	18-2	41	2.52	141	.222	.286	3-0	.000	-0		5	0.7
1982	Cin N	3	4	.429	59	1	0	3-5	72.2	73	26	7	4	32-8	71	2.85	130	.263	.346	3-2	.333	0	95	7	0.6
1983	Cin N	10	6	.625	21	21	5	0-0	144	118	46	12	0	46-2	83	2.88	133	.225	.285	41-3	.098	-1	66	16	1.6
1984	Cin N	7	13	.350	30	30	3-1	0-0	171.2	176	91	19	2	61-5	129	4.19	90	.261	.322	48-9	.146	-1	92	-9	-1.1
1985	Cin N	2	2	.500	26	8	0	1-0	64.2	59	35	10	0	23-7	52	3.90	97	.242	.301	14-1	.000	-1	105	-2	-0.3
1986	Cin N	1	2	.333	25	2	0	0-1	41.2	49	30	5	0	22-2	30	5.40	72	.293	.366	7-0	.143	0	126	-8	-0.5
1987	†SF N	2	2	.500	20	0	0	1-0	35	19	10	5	1	13-2	42	2.57	150	.154	.241	6-0	.167	-0		6	0.6
1988	SF N	1	6	.143	38	3	0	4-1	61.2	59	33	5	1	27-6	49	3.94	83	.249	.328	8-2	.000	-0	127	-6	-0.8
1989	SF N	1	1	.500	7	1	0	0-1	14	16	9	3	0	4-2	10	5.79	58	.314	.357	2-0	.000	0	157	-3	-0.4
	Bos A	2	5	.286	31	5	0	0-1	70.1	71	35	8	0	30-3	52	4.35	94	.262	.332	0-0	—	0	79	0	-0.1
1990	Bal A	3	4	.429	50	0	0	0-2	65.1	62	29	8	0	24-2	54	3.58	106	.253	.319	0-0	—	0		1	0.1
Total	11	45	49	.479	372	84	10-1	13-13	906	839	408	95	9	337-41	657	3.65	103	.246	.313	171-20	.111	-5	91	8	0.3

Year	Tm Lg	W	L	Pct	G	GS	CG-Sho	SV-BS	IP	H	R	HR	HB	BB-IB	SO	ERA	AERA	OAV	OOB	AB-SH	AVG	PB	Sup	APR	PW
PRICE, BILL William B Philadelphia, PA d4.27																									
1890	Phi AA	1	0	1.000	1	1	1	0	9	6	3	0	1	7	1	2.00	194	.182	.341	4	.250	-0	87	2	0.2
PRIDDY, BOB Robert Simpson B 12.10.1939 Pittsburgh, PA BR/TR 6-1/200# d9.20																									
1962	Pit N	1	0	1.000	2	0	0	0	3	4	1	0	0	1-0	1	3.00	131	.308	.357	0-0	—	0		0	0.1
1964	Pit N	1	2	.333	19	0	0	1	34.1	35	16	2	1	15-1	23	3.93	89	.282	.354	3-0	.000	0		-1	-0.2
1965	SF N	1	0	1.000	8	0	0	0	10.1	6	2	1	0	2-0	7	1.74	207	.176	.216	1-0	.000	-0*		2	0.2
1966	SF N	6	3	.667	38	3	0	1	91	88	45	8	3	28-3	51	3.96	93	.259	.317	17-0	.176	0*	40	-2	-0.3
1967	Was A	3	7	.300	46	8	1	4	110	98	48	12	0	33-5	57	3.44	92	.240	.295	22-2	.182	1*	62	-3	-0.1
1968	Chi A	3	11	.214	35	18	2	0	114	106	50	14	4	41-1	66	3.63	83	.244	.314	24-3	.042	-1*	96	-6	-0.9
1969	Chi A	0	0	—	4	0	0	0-0	8	10	5	2	0	2-0	5	4.50	86	.303	.343	0-0	—	0		-1	0.0
	Cal A	0	1	.000	15	0	0	0-0	26.1	24	14	4	0	7-1	15	4.78	73	.242	.292	2-1	.000	0		-3	-0.1
	Year	0	1	.000	19	0	0	0-0	34.1	34	22	6	0	9-1	20	4.72	76	.258	.305	2-1	.000	0		-4	-0.1
	Atl N	0	0	—	1	0	0	0-0	2	1	0	0	0	1-0	1	0.00	—	.143	.250	0-0	—	0		1	0.0
1970	Atl N	5	5	.500	41	0	0	8-2	73	75	46	9	3	24-2	32	5.42	79	.269	.331	15-2	.200	0		-7	-1.0
1971	Atl N	4	9	.308	40	0	0	4-3	64	71	36	8	1	44-5	36	4.22	88	.289	.396	11-0	.182	0		-4	-0.8
Total	9	24	38	.387	249	29	3	18-5	536	518	263	60	12	198-18	294	4.00	88	.257	.324	95-8	.137	1	72	-24	-3.1
PRIEST, EDDIE Eddie Lee B 4.8.1974 Boaz, AL BR/TL 6-1/200# d5.27																									
1998	Cin N	0	1	.000	2	2	0	0-0	6	12	8	2	0	1-0	1	10.50	41	.444	.448	2-0	.000	-0	107	-4	-0.6
PRIETO, ARIEL Ariel B 10.22.1969 Havana, Cuba BR/TR 6-3/225# d7.2																									
1995	Oak A	2	6	.250	14	9	1	0-0	58	57	35	4	5	32-1	37	4.97	90	.264	.369	0-0	—	0	79	-4	-0.4
1996	Oak A	6	7	.462	21	21	2	0-0	125.2	130	66	9	7	54-2	75	4.15	119	.273	.352	0-0	—	0	90	9	0.8
1997	Oak A	6	8	.429	22	22	0	0-0	125	155	84	16	5	70-3	90	5.04	90	.306	.393	0-0	—	0	102	-11	-1.0
1998	Oak A	0	1	.000	2	2	0	0-0	8.1	17	11	2	1	5-1	8	11.88	38	.415	.489	0-0	—	0	92	-6	-0.6
2000	Oak A	1	2	.333	8	6	0	0-0	31.2	42	21	3	1	13-0	19	5.12	93	.321	.384	2-0	.000	-0	125	-2	-0.1
2001	TB A	0	0	—	3	0	0	0-0	3.2	6	1	0	1	2-0	2	2.45	183	.375	.474	0-0	—	0		1	0.0
Total	6	15	24	.385	70	60	3	0-0	352.1	407	218	34	20	176-7	231	4.85	97	.294	.378	2-0	.000	-0	96	-13	-1.3
PRIM, RAY Raymond Lee "Pop" B 12.30.1906 Salitpa, AL D 4.29.1995 Monte Rio, CA BR/TL 6/178# d9.24																									
1933	Was A	0	1	.000	2	1	0	0	14.1	13	6	0	0	2	6	3.14	133	.232	.259	5-1	.000	-1*	0	2	0.1
1934	Was A	0	2	.000	8	1	0	0	14.2	19	11	1	0	8	3	6.75	64	.339	.422	3-0	.000	-0	60	-4	-0.4
1935	Phi N	3	4	.429	29	6	1	0	73.1	110	54	4	0	15	27	5.77	79	.340	.369	24-0	.083	-2	69	-8	-0.9
1943	Chi N	4	3	.571	29	5	0	1	60	67	24	2	0	14	27	2.55	131	.282	.321	12-2	.167	-0	122	4	0.5
1945	†Chi N	13	8	.619	34	19	9-2	2	165.1	142	58	9	1	23	88	2.40	**153**	**.228**	**.256**	51-5	.255	3	99	21	2.9
1946	Chi N	2	3	.400	14	2	0	1	23.1	28	17	5	0	10	10	5.79	57	.289	.355	5-0	.200	0	90	-6	-1.2
Total	6	22	21	.512	116	34	10-2	4	351	379	170	21	1	72	161	3.56	107	.272	.308	100-8	.180	-0	90	9	1.0
PRINCE, DON Donald Mark B 4.5.1938 Clarkton, NC BR/TR 6-4/200# d9.21																									
1962	Chi N	0	0	—	1	0	0	0	1	0	0	0	1	1-0	0	0.00	—	.000	.500	0-0	—	0		0	0.0
PRINZ, BRET Bret Randolph B 6.15.1977 Chicago Heights, IL BR/TR 6-3/185# d4.22																									
2001	Ari N	4	1	.800	46	0	0	9-3	41	33	13	4	1	19-1	27	2.63	174	.220	.310	0-0	—	0		8	1.3
2002	Ari N	0	2	.000	20	0	0	0-2	13.1	23	14	1	1	10-1	10	9.45	47	.404	.493	0-0	—	0		-6	-0.9
2003	Ari N	0	0	—	1	0	0	0-0	1	1	0	0	0	1-1	1	0.00	—	.250	.400	0-0	—	0		0	0.0
	NY A	0	0	—	2	0	0	0-0	2	6	4	1	0	3-1	2	18.00	24	.500	.600	0-0	—	0		-3	-0.1
Total	3	4	3	.571	69	0	0	9-5	57.1	63	31	6	2	33-4	40	4.71	97	.283	.377	0-0	—	0		-1	0.3
PRIOR, MARK Mark William B 9.7.1980 San Diego, CA BR/TR 6-5/225# d5.22																									
2002	Chi N	6	6	.500	19	19	1	0-0	116.2	98	45	14	7	38-0	147	3.32	121	.226	.296	35-2	.171	2	99	10	1.1
2003	†Chi N☆	18	6	.750	30	30	3-1	0-0	211.1	183	67	15	9	50-4	245	2.43	174	.231	.283	72-7	.250	5*	104	41	**4.9**
Total	2	24	12	.667	49	49	4-1	0-0	328	281	112	29	16	88-4	392	2.74	151	.229	.288	107-9	.224	7	102	51	6.0
PROCTOR, JIM James Arthur B 9.9.1935 Brandywine, MD BR/TR 6/165# d9.14																									
1959	Det A	0	1	.000	2	1	0	0	2.2	8	5	0	0	3-0	0	16.88	24	.533	.611	0-0	—	0	109	-3	-0.6
PROCTOR, RED Noah Richard B 10.27.1900 Williamsburg, VA D 12.17.1954 Richmond, VA BR/TR 6-1/165# d8.6																									
1923	Chi A	0	0	—	2	0	0	0	4	11	8	0	0	2	0	13.50	29	.550	.591	0-0	—	0		-5	-0.2
PROESER, GEORGE George "Yatz" B 5.30.1864 Cincinnati, OH D 10.13.1941 New Burlington, OH BL/TL 5-10/190# d9.15 ▲																									
1888	Cle AA	3	4	.429	7	7	7-1	0	59	53	39	4	7	30	20	3.81	81	.231	.338	23	.304	2	83	-3	-0.2
PROKOPEC, LUKE Kenneth Luke B 2.23.1978 Blackwood, Australia BL/TR 5-11/166# d9.4																									
2000	LA N	1	1	.500	5	3	0	0-0	21	19	10	2	2	9-0	12	3.00	145	.253	.345	5-1	.000	-1*	113	2	0.1
2001	LA N	8	7	.533	29	22	0	0-0	138.1	146	80	27	4	40-1	91	4.88	82	.268	.321	36-7	.194	1*	127	-14	-1.2
2002	Tor A	2	9	.182	22	12	0	0-0	71.2	90	57	19	7	25-2	41	6.78	68	.302	.364	0-0	—	0	65	-16	-2.1
Total	3	11	17	.393	56	37	0	0-0	231	255	147	48	13	74-3	144	5.30	80	.278	.337	41-8	.171	0	104	-28	-3.2
PROLY, MIKE Michael James B 12.15.1950 Jamaica, NY BR/TR 6/185# d4.10																									
1976	StL N	1	0	1.000	14	0	0	0-1	17	21	9	0	0	6-1	4	3.71	96	.328	.370	0-1	—	0		-1	0.0
1978	Chi A	5	2	.714	14	6	2	1-0	65.2	63	24	4	0	12-0	19	2.74	139	.250	.282	0-0	—	0	122	7	0.7
1979	Chi A	3	8	.273	38	6	0	9-2	88.1	89	43	6	1	40-7	32	3.87	110	.260	.337	0-0	—	0	89	4	0.6
1980	Chi A	5	10	.333	62	3	0	8-6	146.2	136	67	7	3	58-9	56	3.07	132	.253	.323	0-0	—	0	89	12	1.3
1981	Phi N	2	1	.667	35	2	0	2-0	63	66	29	6	1	19-5	19	3.86	94	.282	.335	7-0	.000	-1	86	-1	-0.1
1982	Chi N	5	3	.625	44	1	0	1-5	82	77	22	5	2	22-5	24	2.30	162	.257	.310	14-5	.286	1	94	13	1.4
1983	Chi N	1	5	.167	60	0	0	1-2	83	79	35	5	1	38-13	31	3.58	106	.259	.339	11-2	.091	-0		3	0.2
Total	7	22	29	.431	267	18	2	22-16	545.2	531	229	33	8	195-40	185	3.23	121	.261	.324	32-8	.156	-0	100	37	4.1
PROUGH, BILL Herschel Clinton "Clint" B 11.28.1887 Markle, IN D 12.29.1936 Richmond, IN BR/TR 6-3/185# d4.27																									
1912	Cin N	0	0	—	1	0	0	0	3	7	5	0	0	1	1	6.00	56	.538	.571	1-0	.000	-0		-2	-0.1
PRUDHOMME, AUGIE John Olgus B 11.20.1902 Frierson, LA D 10.4.1992 Shreveport, LA BR/TR 6-2/186# d4.19																									
1929	Det A	1	6	.143	34	6	2	1	94	119	78	7	2	53	26	6.22	69	.322	.410	21-0	.238	1	157	-20	-1.1
PRUETT, HUB Hubert Shelby "Shucks" B 9.1.1900 Malden, MO D 1.28.1982 Ladue, MO BL/TL 5-10.5/165# d4.26																									
1922	StL A	7	7	.500	39	8	4	7	119.2	99	48	2	5	59	70	2.33	178	.235	.336	34-3	.147	-1	82	19	2.3
1923	StL A	4	7	.364	32	8	3	2	104.1	109	57	3	3	64	59	4.31	97	.279	.385	23-4	.130	-1	79	0	0.0
1924	StL A	3	4	.429	33	1	0	0	65	64	42	1	4	42	27	4.57	99	.270	.389	15-1	.200	-1	37	-2	-0.2
1927	Phi N	7	17	.292	31	28	12-1	1	186	238	147	6	12	89	90	6.05	68	.314	.395	60-5	.217	1	86	-41	-4.1
1928	Phi N	2	4	.333	13	9	4	0	71.1	78	49	2	3	49	35	4.54	94	.291	.406	24-2	.208	-0	86	-5	-0.4
1930	NY N	5	4	.556	45	8	1	3	135.2	152	83	11	4	63	49	4.78	99	.287	.367	37-2	.135	-1	94	0	-0.1
1932	Bos N	1	5	.167	18	7	4	0	63	76	42	3	6	30	27	5.14	73	.308	.396	19-0	.105	-1	48	-10	-0.8
Total	7	29	48	.377	211	69	28-1	13	745	816	468	28	37	396	357	4.63	92	.286	.380	212-17	.170	-3	80	-39	-3.3
PRUIETT, TEX Charles Le Roy B 4.10.1883 Osgood, IN D 3.6.1953 Ventura, CA BL/TR d4.26																									
1907	Bos A	3	11	.214	35	17	6-2	3	173.2	166	77	1	8	59	54	3.11	83	.254	.323	51-1	.157	-1	59	-7	-0.6
1908	Bos A	1	7	.125	13	6	1-1	2	58.2	55	26	1	2	21	28	1.99	123	.275	.350	16-0	.063	-2	32	1	-0.1
Total	2	4	18	.182	48	23	7-3	5	232.1	221	103	2	10	80	82	2.83	90	.259	.329	67-1	.134	-2	52	-6	-0.7
PUCKETT, TROY Troy Levi B 12.10.1889 Winchester, IN D 4.13.1971 Winchester, IN BL/TR 6-2/186# d10.4																									
1911	Phi N	0	0	—	1	0	0	0	2	4	3	0	1	2	1	13.50	26	.444	.583	0-0	—	0		-2	-0.1
PUENTE, MIGUEL Miguel Antonio (Aguilar) B 5.8.1948 San Luis Potosi, Mexico BR/TR 6/160# d5.3																									
1970	SF N	1	3	.250	6	4	1	0-0	18.2	25	18	5	0	11-1	14	8.20	49	.325	.409	7-1	.000	-1	130	-8	-1.5
PUFFER, BRANDON Brandon Duane B 10.5.1975 Downey, CA BR/TR 6-3/190# d4.17																									
2002	Hou N	3	3	.500	55	0	0	0-0	69	67	37	3	5	38-8	48	4.43	96	.258	.361	6-1	.000	-0		-1	-0.1

Year	Tm Lg	W	L	Pct	G	GS	CG-Sho	SV-BS	IP	H	R	HR	HB	BB-IB	SO	ERA	AERA	OAV	OOB	AB-SH	AVG	PB	Sup	APR	PW
2003	Hou N	0	0	—	13	0	0	0-1	21	24	13	2	1	16-3	10	5.14	86	.300	.423	3-0	.000	-0		-2	-0.1
Total	2	3	3	.500	68	0	0	0-1	90	91	50	5	6	54-11	58	4.60	94	.268	.376	9-1	.000	-1		-3	-0.2
PUGH, TIM Timothy Dean B 1.26.1967 S.Lake Tahoe, CA BR/TR 6-6/230# d9.1																									
1992	Cin N	4	2	.667	7	7	0	0-0	45.1	47	15	2	1	13-3	18	2.58	140	.276	.330	13-1	.077	-0	75	5	0.5
1993	Cin N	10	15	.400	31	27	3-1	0-0	164.1	200	102	19	7	59-1	94	5.26	77	.303	.363	54-7	.222	2	99	-21	-2.6
1994	Cin N	3	3	.500	10	9	1	0-0	47.2	60	37	5	3	26-0	24	6.04	68	.314	.396	14-1	.357	2	113	-11	-0.9
1995	Cin N	6	5	.545	28	12	0	0-0	98.1	100	46	13	1	32-2	38	3.84	107	.266	.324	28-4	.143	0*	117	3	0.2
1996	Cin N	1	0	1.000	9	0	0	0-0	15.1	20	18	3	1	11-2	9	10.57	40	.317	.421	0-1	—	0		-10	-0.5
	KC A	0	1	.000	19	1	0	0-0	36.1	42	24	9	2	12-1	27	5.45	92	.282	.341	0-0	—	0	111	-2	-0.1
	Cin N	0	1	.000	1	0	0	0-0	0.1	4	2	0	0	0-0	0	54.00	8	.800	.800	0-0	—	0		-2	-0.3
1997	Det A	1	1	.500	2	2	0	0-0	9	6	5	0	0	5-0	4	5.00	92	.188	.297	0-0	—	0	130	0	0.0
Total	6	25	28	.472	107	58	4-1	0-0	416.2	479	249	51	15	158-9	214	4.97	83	.291	.355	109-14	.202	4	102	-38	-3.7
PULEO, CHARLIE Charles Michael B 2.7.1955 Glen Ridge, NJ BR/TR 6-3/200# d9.16																									
1981	NY N	0	0	—	4	1	0	0-0	13.1	8	1	0	0	8-2	8	0.00	—	.182	.308	2-0	.000	-0	51	5	0.2
1982	NY N	9	9	.500	36	24	1-1	1-0	171	179	99	13	2	90-7	98	4.47	81	.275	.362	48-6	.125	-1	102	-16	-1.6
1983	Cin N	6	12	.333	27	24	0	0-0	143.2	145	86	18	5	91-9	71	4.89	78	.269	.375	50-2	.100	-2	91	-16	-2.1
1984	Cin N	1	2	.333	5	4	0	0-0	22	27	15	2	0	15-2	6	5.73	66	.297	.393	5-2	.200	0	93	-4	-0.5
1986	Atl N	1	2	.333	5	3	1	0-0	24.1	13	10	4	1	12-1	18	2.96	135	.160	.274	6-1	.333	0	90	2	0.3
1987	Atl N	6	8	.429	35	16	1	0-0	123.1	122	63	11	3	40-0	99	4.23	103	.262	.319	28-6	.179	1*	78	3	0.3
1988	Atl N	5	5	.500	53	3	0	1-1	106.1	101	46	9	3	47-7	70	3.47	106	.251	.330	13-4	.231	0	72	2	0.2
1989	Atl N	1	1	.500	15	1	0	0-0	29	26	15	2	0	16-1	17	4.66	79	.245	.333	1-1	.000	-0	24	-2	-0.2
Total	8	29	39	.426	180	76	3-1	2-1	633	621	335	59	14	319-29	387	4.25	90	.261	.348	153-22	.144	-1	90	-26	-3.4
PULIDO, ALFONSO Alfonso (Manzo) B 1.23.1957 Veracruz, Mexico BL/TL 5-11/170# d9.5																									
1983	Pit N	0	0	—	1	1	0	0-0	2	4	3	2	0	1-0	1	9.00	41	.400	.455	0-1	—	0	143	-1	-0.1
1984	Pit N	0	0	—	1	0	0	0-0	2	3	2	0	0	1-0	2	9.00	40	.333	.400	0-0	—	0		-1	-0.1
1986	NY A	1	1	.500	10	3	0	1-0	30.2	38	17	8	0	9-0	13	4.70	87	.306	.351	0-0	—	0	126	-2	-0.1
Total	3	1	1	.500	12	4	0	1-0	34.2	45	22	10	0	11-0	16	5.19	78	.315	.361	0-1	—	0	129	-4	-0.3
PULIDO, CARLOS Juan Carlos (Valera) B 8.5.1971 Caracas, Venezuela BL/TL 6/195# d4.9																									
1994	Min A	3	7	.300	19	14	0	0-0	84.1	87	57	17	1	40-1	32	5.98	82	.273	.352	0-0	—	0	96	-9	-0.8
2003	Min A	0	1	.000	7	1	0	0-0	15.2	15	9	0	0	3-0	6	4.02	113	.254	.281	0-0	—	0	121	0	0.0
Total	2	3	8	.273	26	15	0	0-0	100	102	66	17	1	43-1	38	5.67	85	.270	.341	0-0	—	0	98	-9	-0.8
PULSIPHER, BILL William Thomas B 10.9.1973 Fort Benning, GA BL/TL 6-3/210# d6.17																									
1995	NY N	5	7	.417	17	17	2	0-0	126.2	122	58	11	4	45-0	81	3.98	102	.255	.324	38-4	.105	0	88	3	0.3
1998	NY N	0	0	—	15	1	0	0-1	14.1	23	11	2	0	5-1	13	6.91	60	.371	.418	1-0	.000	-0*	156	-4	-0.2
	Mil N	3	4	.429	11	10	0	0-0	58	63	30	6	1	26-3	38	4.66	92	.289	.361	19-1	.158	-0	86	-1	-0.2
	Year	3	4	.429	26	11	0	0-1	72.1	86	34	8	1	31-4	51	5.10	83	.307	.373	20-1	.150	-1	93	-6	-0.4
1999	Mil N	5	6	.455	19	16	0	0-0	87.1	100	65	19	2	36-2	42	5.98	76	.286	.352	21-8	.143	-1	111	-15	-1.5
2000	NY N	0	2	.000	2	2	0	0-0	6.2	12	9	1	1	6-0	7	12.15	36	.387	.500	2-0	.000	-0	42	-6	-0.8
2001	Bos A	0	0	—	23	0	0	0-0	22	25	15	3	2	14-0	16	5.32	84	.294	.402	0-0	—	0		-2	-0.1
	Chi A	0	0	—	14	0	0	0-0	8	11	8	2	1	7-0	4	7.88	59	.314	.432	0-0	—	0		-3	-0.1
	Year	0	0	—	37	0	0	0-0	30	36	25	5	3	21-0	20	6.00	75	.300	.411	0-0	—	0		-5	-0.2
Total	5	13	19	.406	101	46	2	0-1	323	356	196	44	11	139-6	201	5.13	83	.283	.356	81-13	.123	-1	96	-28	-2.6
PUMPELLY, SPENCER Spencer Armstrong B 4.11.1893 Owego, NY D 12.5.1973 Sayre, PA TR 5-11/175# d7.11																									
1925	Was A	0	0	—	1	0	0	0	1	1	1	1	0	1	0	9.00	47	.333	.500	0-0	—	0		0	0.0
PURCELL, BLONDIE William Aloysius B Paterson, NJ BR/TR 5-9.5/159# d5.1 M1 ▲																									
1879	Syr N	4	15	.211	22	17	15	0	179.2	245	165	1		19	28	3.76	63	.303	.319	277	.260	3*	64	-33	-2.5
	Cin N	0	2	.000	2	2	2	0	18	27	15	0		2	3	4.00	58	.355	.372	50	.220	-0*	69	-2	-0.2
	Year	4	17	.190	24	19	17	0	197.2	272	19	1		21	31	3.78	63	.308	.324	327	.254	3	65	-39	-2.7
1880	Cin N	3	17	.150	25	21	21	0	196	235	149	1		32	47	3.21	77	.271	.297	325	.292	4*	56	-11	-0.5
1881	Buf N	4	1	.800	9	5	5	0	61.2	62	37	2		9	15	2.77	100	.248	.274	113	.292	2*	117	0	0.2
1882	Buf N	2	1	.667	6	3	2	0	31	44	30	1		4	9	4.94	59	.338	.358	380	.276	1*	138	-7	-0.5
1883	Phi N	2	6	.250	11	9	7	0	80	110	71	0		12	30	4.39	70	.306	.329	425	.268	2*	75	-13	-0.8
1884	Phi N	0	0	—	1	0	0	0	4	3	1	0		0	1	2.25	133	.188	.188	428	.252	0*		1	0.0
1885	Phi AA	0	1	.000	1	0	0	0	6	11	9	0	0	2	3	6.00	57	.423	.464	304	.296	0*		-2	-0.2
1886	Bal AA	0	0	—	1	0	0	0	1	1	1	0	0	0	0	9.00	38	.200	.200	85	.224	0*		0	0.0
1887	Bal AA	0	0	—	1	0	0	0	4	8	8	0	1	4	2	15.75	26	.381	.500	567	.250	0*		-4	-0.2
Total	9	15	43	.259	79	57	52	0	581.1	746	486	5	1	84	138	3.73	70	.292	.314	2954	.267	12	72	-71	-4.7
PURDIN, JOHN John Nolan B 7.16.1942 Lynx, OH BR/TR 6-2/185# d9.16																									
1964	LA N	2	0	1.000	3	2	1-1	0	16	6	1	1	0	6-0	8	0.56	576	.115	.207	5-0	.200	0	176	5	0.7
1965	LA N	2	1	.667	11	2	0	0	22.2	26	19	8	0	13-3	16	6.75	48	.283	.368	3-0	.000	-0	120	-9	-1.2
1968	LA N	2	3	.400	35	1	0	2	55.2	42	22	2	0	21-7	38	3.07	90	.206	.276	6-0	.500	1*	251	-2	-0.1
1969	LA N	0	0	—	9	0	0	0-0	16.1	19	11	7	0	12-1	6	6.06	55	.292	.403	2-0	.000	-0		-5	-0.3
Total	4	6	4	.600	58	5	1-1	2-0	110.2	93	53	18	0	52-11	68	3.90	77	.225	.309	16-0	.250	1	174	-11	-0.9
PURKEY, BOB Robert Thomas B 7.14.1929 Pittsburgh, PA BR/TR 6-2/195# d4.14																									
1954	Pit N	3	8	.273	36	11	0	0	131.1	145	78	3	7	62	38	5.07	83	.293	.375	26-3	.077	-1	75	-10	-0.5
1955	Pit N	2	7	.222	14	10	2	1	67.2	77	47	5	2	25-1	24	5.32	77	.287	.353	19-3	.316	2	58	-9	-0.9
1956	Pit N	0	0	—	2	0	0	0	4	2	1	1	0	0-0	1	2.25	168	.143	.143	0-0	—	0		1	0.0
1957	Pit N	11	14	.440	48	21	6-1	2	179.2	194	84	10	7	38-9	51	3.86	98	.278	.317	45-2	.111	-0	69	1	0.1
1958	Cin N☆	17	11	.607	37	34	17-3	0	250	259	106	25	4	49-3	70	3.60	115	.268	.304	81-6	.111	-2	87	15	1.5
1959	Cin N	13	18	.419	38	33	9-1	1	218	241	118	25	6	43-2	78	4.25	95	.279	.316	66-4	.167	3	90	-5	-0.4
1960	Cin N	17	11	.607	41	33	11-1	0	252.2	259	114	23	9	59-5	97	3.60	106	.265	.311	83-6	.133	-2	113	6	0.5
1961	†Cin N★	16	12	.571	36	34	13-1	1	246.1	245	118	27	6	51-4	116	3.73	109	.255	.296	80-7	.100	-3	96	8	0.8
1962	Cin N★	23	5	**.821**	37	37	18-2	0	288.1	260	109	28	14	64-3	141	2.81	143	.240	.289	107-7	.103	-2	114	**35**	3.0
1963	Cin N	6	10	.375	21	21	4-1	0	137	143	60	12	2	33-6	55	3.55	94	.272	.317	41-3	.098	-1	87	-3	-0.3
1964	Cin N	11	9	.550	34	25	9-2	1	195.2	181	77	16	7	49-4	78	3.04	119	.246	.298	58-8	.052	-4	116	11	0.8
1965	StL N	10	9	.526	32	17	3-1	2	124.1	148	83	20	7	33-4	39	5.79	66	.294	.344	35-7	.029	-3	123	-23	-3.4
1966	Pit N	0	1	.000	10	0	0	1	19.2	16	3	0	0	4-0	5	1.37	260	.235	.278	4-0	.000	-0*		5	0.3
Total	13	129	115	.529	386	276	92-13	9	2114.2	2170	998	195	71	510-41	793	3.79	103	.266	.313	645-56	.110	-13	97	32	1.5
PURNER, OSCAR Oscar E. B 12.9.1873 Washington, DC d9.2																									
1895	Was N	0	0	—	1	0	0	0	2	4	2	1	0	3	0	9.00	53	.400	.538	1-0	.000	-0		-1	0.0
PUTTMANN, AMBROSE Ambrose Nicholas "Putty" or "Brose" B 9.9.1880 Cincinnati, OH D 6.21.1936 Jamaica, NY TL 6-4/185# d9.4																									
1903	NY A	2	0	1.000	3	2	1	0	19	16	9	0	1	4	8	0.95	330	.229	.280	7-0	.143	-0	206	2	0.3
1904	NY A	2	0	1.000	9	3	2-1	0	49.1	40	21	0	0	17	26	2.74	99	.222	.289	18-0	.278	2	105	0	0.2
1905	NY A	2	7	.222	17	9	5-1	1	86.1	79	50	2	5	37	39	4.27	69	.245	.332	32-0	.313	3*	96	-9	-0.7
1906	StL N	2	2	.500	4	4	0	0	18.2	23	13	2	2	9	12	5.30	50	.303	.391	6-0	.333	0	139	-5	-0.9
Total	4	8	9	.471	33	18	8-2	1	173.1	158	93	4	8	67	85	3.58	80	.244	.322	63-0	.286	4	119	-12	-1.1
PUTZ, J.J. Joseph Jason B 2.2.1977 Trenton, MI BR/TR 6-5/220# d8.11																									
2003	Sea A	0	0	—	3	0	0	0-0	3.2	4	2	0	0	3-0	3	4.91	88	.267	.389	0-0	—	0		0	0.0
PYECHA, JOHN John Nicholas B 11.25.1931 Aliquippa, PA BR/TR 6-5/200# d4.24																									
1954	Chi N	0	1	.000	1	0	0	0	2.2	4	3	1	0	2	2	10.13	41	.333	.429	1-0	.000	-0		-2	-0.3
PYLE, EWALD Ewald "Lefty" B 8.27.1910 St.Louis, MO BL/TL 6-0.5/175# d4.23																									
1939	StL A	0	2	.000	6	1	0	0	8.1	17	15	3	0	11	5	12.96	38	.405	.528	2-0	.000	-0	145	-8	-1.3

Year	Tm Lg	W	L	Pct	G	GS	CG-Sho	SV-BS	IP	H	R	HR	HB	BB-IB	SO	ERA	AERA	OAV	OOB	AB-SH	AVG	PB	Sup	APR	PW
1942	StL A	0	0	—	2	0	0	0	5.1	6	4	0	0	4	1	6.75	55	.286	.400	3-0	.000	-0		-1	-0.1
1943	Was A	4	8	.333	18	11	2-1	1	72.2	70	38	0	1	45	25	4.09	78	.254	.360	20-1	.100	-1	60	-6	-1.2
1944	NY N	7	10	.412	31	21	3	0	164	152	89	12	6	68	79	4.34	85	.241	.321	51-1	.157	-0	95	-10	-1.0
1945	NY N	0	0	—	6	1	0	0	6.1	16	12	0	0	4	2	17.05	23	.457	.513	2-0	.000	-0	108	-8	-0.4
	Bos N	0	1	.000	4	2	0	0	13.2	16	15	1	0	18	10	7.24	53	.302	.479	6-0	.333	1	155	-6	-0.3
	Year	0	1	.000	10	3	0	0	20	32	22	1	0	22	12	10.35	37	.364	.491	8-0	.250	0	139	-15	-0.7
Total	5	11	21	.344	67	36	5-1	1	270.1	277	173	16	7	150	122	5.03	71	.262	.357	84-2	.143	-2	91	-39	-4.3
PYLE, HARLAN Harlan Albert "Firpo" B 11.29.1905 Burchard, NE D 1.13.1993 Beatrice, NE BR/TR 6-2/180# d9.21																									
1928	Cin N	0	0	—	2	1	0	0	1.1	1	3	0	0	4	1	20.25	20	.143	.455	1-0	.000	-0	128	-2	-0.1
PYLE, SHADOW Harry Thomas B 11.29.1861 Reading, PA D 12.26.1908 Reading, PA TL 5-8/136# d10.15																									
1884	Phi N	0	1	.000	1	1	1	0	9	9	8	0		6	4	4.00	75	.257	.366	4	.000	-1	0	-1	-0.2
1887	Chi N	1	3	.250	4	4	3	0	26.2	32	27	1	2	21	5	4.73	95	.291	.414	16	.188	-0	90	-2	-0.2
Total	2	1	4	.200	5	5	4	0	35.2	41	35	1	2	27	9	4.54	90	.283	.402	20	.150	-1	76	-3	-0.4
QUALTERS, TOM Thomas Francis "Money Bags" B 4.1.1935 McKeesport, PA BR/TR 6-0.5/190# d9.13																									
1953	Phi N	0	0	—	1	0	0	0	0.1	4	6	1	1	1	0	162.00	3	.800	.857	0-0	—	0		-6	-0.2
1957	Phi N	0	0	—	6	0	0	0	7.1	12	6	0	0	4-1	6	7.36	52	.400	.471	0-0	—	0		-3	-0.1
1958	Phi N	0	0	—	1	0	0	0	2	2	1	0	0	1-0	0	4.50	88	.222	.300	0-0	—	0		0	0.0
	Chi A	0	0	—	26	0	0	0	43	45	22	1	0	20-4	14	4.19	87	.281	.359	2-0	.000	0		-3	-0.1
Total	3	0	0	—	34	0	0	0	52.2	63	35	2	1	26-5	20	5.64	65	.309	.388	2-0	.000	0		-12	-0.4
QUANTRILL, PAUL Paul John B 11.3.1968 London, ON, CAN BL/TR 6-1/185# d7.20																									
1992	Bos A	2	3	.400	27	0	0	1-4	49.1	55	18	1	1	15-5	24	2.19	193	.288	.340	0-0	—	0		9	0.8
1993	Bos A	6	12	.333	49	14	1-1	1-1	138	151	73	13	2	44-14	66	3.91	118	.279	.334	0-0	—	0	68	8	0.9
1994	Bos A	1	1	.500	17	0	0	0-2	23	25	10	4	2	5-1	15	3.52	143	.278	.323	0-0	—	0		4	0.3
	Phi N	2	2	.500	18	1	0	1-1	30	39	21	3	3	10-3	13	6.00	72	.331	.394	3-0	.000	-0	64	-5	-0.6
1995	Phi N	11	12	.478	33	29	0	0-0	179.1	212	102	20	6	44-3	103	4.67	91	.295	.338	57-7	.105	-2	89	-9	-1.2
1996	Tor A	5	14	.263	38	20	0	0-2	134.1	172	90	27	2	51-3	86	5.43	92	.316	.373	0-0	—	0	82	-7	-0.7
1997	Tor A	6	7	.462	77	0	0	5-5	88	103	25	5	1	17-3	56	1.94	236	.297	.329	1-0	.000	-0		**24**	3.4
1998	Tor A	3	4	.429	82	0	0	7-7	80	88	26	5	3	22-6	59	2.59	180	.285	.334	0-0	—	0		18	1.7
1999	Tor A	3	2	.600	41	0	0	0-4	48.2	53	19	5	4	17-1	28	3.33	148	.282	.351	0-0	—	0		9	0.8
2000	Tor A	2	5	.286	68	0	0	1-2	83.2	100	45	7	2	25-1	47	4.52	113	.298	.347	0-0	—	0		6	0.4
2001	Tor A★	11	2	.846	**80**	0	0	2-7	83	86	29	6	6	12-7	58	3.04	151	.274	.311	0-0	—	0		15	2.0
2002	LA N	5	4	.556	**86**	0	0	1-2	76.2	80	27	1	3	25-7	53	2.70	142	.267	.328	3-0	.333	0		9	1.0
2003	LA N	2	5	.286	**89**	0	0	1-4	77.1	61	18	2	3	15-2	44	1.75	230	.227	.275	1-0	.000	-0		20	1.7
Total	12	59	73	.447	705	64	1-1	20-41	1091.1	1225	503	99	38	302-56	652	3.65	124	.287	.337	65-7	.108	-2	83	101	10.5
QUARLES, BILL William H. B 1869 Petersburg, VA D 3.25.1897 Petersburg, VA 6-3/?# d5.21																									
1891	Was AA	1	1	.500	3	2	2	0	22	32	27	1	2	12	10	8.18	46	.330	.414	11	.000	-2	100	-9	-0.7
1893	Bos N	2	1	.667	3	3	3	0	27	31	20	2	2	5	6	4.67	106	.279	.322	9	.222	0	127	1	0.0
Total	2	3	2	.600	6	5	5	0	49	63	47	3	4	17	16	6.24	70	.303	.367	20	.100	-2	119	-8	-0.7
QUEEN, MEL Melvin Douglas B 3.26.1942 Johnson City, NY BL/TR 6-1/197# d4.13.1964 M1 C5 s-Mel ▲																									
1966	Cin N	0	0	—	7	0	0	1	7	11	5	0	0	6-0	9	6.43	61	.367	.459	55-1	.127	0*		-2	-0.1
1967	Cin N	14	8	.636	31	24	6-2	0	195.2	155	69	17	6	52-5	154	2.76	136	.215	.271	81-3	.210	3*	80	19	2.4
1968	Cin N	0	1	.000	5	4	0	0	18.1	25	15	7	0	6-4	20	5.89	54	.333	.383	8-0	.125	0*	158	-6	-0.3
1969	Cin N	1	0	1.000	2	2	0	0-0	12	7	3	2	1	3-0	7	2.25	167	.163	.234	6-0	.167	-0	212	2	0.1
1970	Cal A	3	6	.333	34	3	0	9-3	60	58	28	5	5	28-6	44	4.20	86	.261	.354	16-0	.250	1*	49	-3	-0.4
1971	Cal A	2	2	.500	44	0	0	4-3	65.2	49	17	3	8	29-6	53	1.78	182	.212	.319	8-1	.000	-1*		10	0.7
1972	Cal A	0	0	—	17	0	0	0-0	31	31	17	2	3	19-1	19	4.35	67	.265	.376	2-0	.000	0		-5	-0.3
Total	7	20	17	.541	140	33	6-2	14-6	389.2	336	154	36	23	143-22	306	3.14	113	.233	.310	176-5	.170	3	97	15	2.1
QUEEN, MEL Melvin Joseph B 3.4.1918 Maxwell, PA D 4.4.1982 Fort Smith, AR BR/TR 6-0.5/204# d4.18 Mil 1945 f-Mel																									
1942	NY A	1	0	1.000	4	0	0	0	5.2	6	0	0	2	3	0	0.00	—	.300	.440	0-0	—	0		2	0.4
1944	NY A	6	3	.667	10	10	4-1	0	81.2	68	32	7	1	34	30	3.31	105	.227	.308	31-3	.194	0	125	3	0.2
1946	NY A	1	1	.500	14	3	1	0	30.1	40	28	2	0	21	26	6.53	53	.315	.412	7-0	.143	-0	116	-12	-0.8
1947	NY A	0	0	—	5	0	0	0	6.2	9	7	2	1	4	2	9.45	37	.321	.424	1-0	.000	-0		-4	-0.2
	Pit N	3	7	.300	14	12	2	0	74	70	39	8	1	51	34	4.01	105	.244	.360	26-1	.077	-2	106	1	-0.1
1948	Pit N	4	4	.500	25	8	0	1	66.1	82	51	8	3	40	34	6.65	61	.308	.405	17-2	.059	-2	76	-17	-2.0
1950	Pit N	5	14	.263	33	21	4-1	0	120.1	135	95	18	2	73	76	5.98	73	.284	.381	35-2	.057	-3	90	-22	-3.2
1951	Pit N	7	9	.438	39	21	4-1	0	168.1	149	90	21	1	99	123	4.44	95	.233	.337	47-6	.106	-3	100	-2	-0.6
1952	Pit N	0	2	.000	2	2	0	0	3.1	8	12	2	0	4	3	29.70	13	.381	.480	0-0	—	0	89	-9	-1.3
Total	8	27	40	.403	146	77	15-3	1	556.2	567	354	68	11	329	328	5.09	80	.262	.362	164-14	.104	-10	100	-60	-7.6
QUEVEDO, RUBEN Ruben Eduardo B 1.5.1979 Valencia, Venezuela BR/TR 6-1/190# d4.14																									
2000	Chi N	3	10	.231	21	15	1	0-0	88	96	81	21	3	54-4	65	7.47	61	.271	.370	30-1	.133	-1	78	-31	-3.7
2001	Mil N	4	5	.444	10	10	0	0-0	56.2	56	30	9	0	30-4	60	4.61	93	.257	.344	16-4	.250	1	84	-1	-0.1
2002	Mil N	6	11	.353	26	25	1-1	0-0	139	159	100	28	4	68-3	93	5.76	71	.288	.368	42-3	.095	-2	106	-27	-3.1
2003	Mil N	1	4	.200	9	8	0	0-0	42.2	53	32	12	0	23-1	19	6.75	63	.314	.390	10-1	.300	1	86	-11	-1.0
Total	4	14	30	.318	66	58	2-1	0-0	326.1	364	243	70	7	175-12	237	6.15	69	.281	.367	98-9	.153	-2	92	-70	-7.9
QUICK, EDDIE Edward B 12.1881 Baltimore, MD D 6.19.1913 Rocky Ford, CO TR 5-11/?# d9.28																									
1903	NY A	0	0	—	1	1	0	0	2	5	5	0	0	1	0	9.00	35	.455	.500	1-0	.000	-0	160	-2	-0.1
QUINN, TAD Clarence Carr B 9.21.1882 Torrington, CT D 8.6.1946 Waterbury, CT TR 6-1/210# d9.27																									
1902	Phi A	0	1	.000	1	1	1	0	8	12	9	1	0	1	3	4.50	82	.343	.361	3-0	.000	-0	78	-2	-0.2
1903	Phi A	0	0	—	2	0	0	0	9	11	6	0	1	5	1	5.00	61	.297	.395	3-0	.667	1		-2	0.1
Total	2	0	1	.000	3	1	1	0	17	23	15	1	1	6	4	4.76	70	.319	.380	6-0	.333	1	78	-4	-0.1
QUINN, FRANK Frank William B 11.27.1927 Springfield, MA D 1.11.1993 Boynton Beach, FL BR/TR 6-2/180# d5.29																									
1949	Bos A	0	0	—	8	0	0	0	22	18	7	2	1	9	4	2.86	152	.222	.308	6-0	.167	-0		4	0.1
1950	Bos A	0	0	—	1	0	0	0	2	2	2	0	0	1	0	9.00	54	.250	.333	0-0	—	0		-1	0.0
Total	2	0	0	—	9	0	0	0	24	20	9	2	1	10	4	3.38	131	.225	.310	6-0	.167	-0		3	0.1
QUINN, JACK John Picus (b: John Quinn Picus) B 7.5.1883 Janesville, PA D 4.17.1946 Pottsville, PA BR/TR 6- /196# d4.15																									
1909	NY A	9	5	.643	23	11	8	1	118.2	110	45	1	4	24	36	1.97	128	.252	.297	45-1	.156	0	119	5	0.8
1910	NY A	18	12	.600	35	31	20	0	235.2	214	88	2	6	58	82	2.37	112	.247	.299	82-4	.232	4	102	6	1.6
1911	NY A	8	10	.444	40	16	7	2	174.2	203	111	2	4	41	71	3.76	96	.297	.341	61-2	.164	-1	74	-7	-0.6
1912	NY A	5	7	.417	18	11	7	0	102.2	139	89	4	4	23	47	5.79	62	.325	.365	39-1	.205	-1	84	-22	-2.1
1913	Bos N	4	3	.571	8	7	6-1	0	56.1	55	22	1	1	7	33	2.40	137	.261	.288	20-0	.200	1*	72	5	0.9
1914	Bal F	26	14	.650	46	42	27-4	1	342.2	335	129	3	8	65	164	2.60	117	.266	.307	121-8	.273	6*	89	15	2.5
1915	Bal F	9	22	.290	44	31	21	1	273.2	289	137	9	8	63	118	3.45	83	.278	.325	110-3	.264	3*	83	-18	-1.4
1918	Chi A	5	1	.833	6	5	5	0	51	38	13	0	0	7	22	2.29	119	.216	.246	18-0	.222	1	143	4	0.7
1919	NY A	15	14	.517	38	31	18-4	0	266	242	96	8	6	65	97	2.61	123	.244	.295	91-4	.209	1	99	18	2.0
1920	NY A	18	10	.643	41	32	17-2	3	253.1	271	110	8	2	48	101	3.20	119	.273	.308	88-3	.091	-5	105	18	1.4
1921	†NY A	8	7	.533	33	13	6	0	119	158	61	2	5	32	44	3.78	112	.327	.375	41-2	.220	1	97	6	0.8
1922	Bos A	13	16	.448	40	32	16-4	0	256	263	119	9	3	59	67	3.48	118	.267	.311	91-3	.099	-5	99	16	1.4
1923	Bos A	13	17	.433	42	28	16-1	7	243	302	125	6	6	53	71	3.89	106	.316	.356	80-6	.225	0	75	9	1.0
1924	Bos A	12	13	.480	44	25	13-2	7	228.2	241	109	10	12	52	64	3.27	134	.273	.322	78-4	.179	-4	82	23	2.2
1925	Bos A	7	8	.467	19	15	8	0	105	140	68	3	3	26	24	4.37	104	.315	.357	32-2	.094	-2	89	1	0.0
	Phi A	6	3	.667	18	13	4	0	99.2	119	56	3	3	16	19	3.88	120	.296	.328	31-1	.097	-3	90	6	0.3
	Year	13	11	.542	37	28	12	0	204.2	259	61	6	6	42	43	4.13	111	.306	.343	63-3	.095	-5	89	8	0.3
1926	Phi A	10	11	.476	31	21	8-3	1	163.2	191	74	4	1	36	58	3.41	122	.296	.334	46-6	.174	-0	98	15	1.8

Year	Tm Lg	W	L	Pct	G	GS	CG-Sho	SV-BS	IP	H	R	HR	HB	BB-IB	SO	ERA	AERA	OAV	OOB	AB-SH	AVG	PB	Sup	APR	PW
1927	Phi A	15	10	.600	34	26	11-3	1	201.1	211	82	8	4	37	43	3.26	131	.278	.315	66-7	.091	-7	82	24	1.9
1928	Phi A	18	7	.720	31	28	18-4	1	211.1	239	92	3	7	34	43	2.90	139	.286	.320	79-6	.165	-3	142	22	2.1
1929	†Phi A	11	9	.550	35	18	7	2	161	182	87	8	1	39	41	3.97	107	.290	.332	60-4	.133	-4	104	3	-0.1
1930	†Phi A	9	7	.563	35	6	0	6	89.2	109	51	6	1	22	28	4.42	106	.302	.344	34-0	.265	1	61	**2**	0.5
1931	Bro N	5	4	.556	39	1	0	**15**	64.1	65	28	1	1	24	25	2.66	143	.266	.335	15-1	.200	0	90	6	1.1
1932	Bro N	3	7	.300	42	0	0	**8**	87.1	102	36	1	1	24	28	3.30	116	.296	.343	20-3	.200	0		**5**	0.7
1933	Cin N	0	1	.000	14	0	0	1	15.2	20	9	0	0	5	3	4.02	84	.323	.373	1-0	.000	-0		-1	-0.1
Total	23	247	218	.531	756	443	243-28	57	3920.1	4238	1837	102	91	860	1329	3.29	113	.280	.323	1349-71	.184	-16	95	161	19.4
QUINN, WIMPY Wellington Hunt B 5.14.1918 Birmingham, AL D 9.1.1954 Santa Monica, CA BR/TR 6-2/187# d6.8																									
1941	Chi N	0	0	—	3	0	0	0	5	3	4	0	0	3	2	7.20	49	.158	.273	2-0	.500	0		-2	-0.1
QUINTANA, LUIS Luis Joaquin (Santos) B 12.25.1951 Vega Baja, P.R. BL/TL 6-2/175# d7.9																									
1974	Cal A	2	1	.667	18	0	0	0-2	12.2	17	6	0	0	14-1	11	4.26	81	.327	.463	0-0	—	0		-1	-0.2
1975	Cal A	0	2	.000	4	0	0	0-0	7	13	6	2	0	6-1	5	6.43	55	.394	.487	0-0	—	0		-2	-0.5
Total	2	2	3	.400	22	0	0	0-2	19.2	30	12	2	0	20-2	16	5.03	69	.353	.472	0-0	—	0		-3	-0.7
QUIRICO, RAFAEL Rafael Octavio (Dottin) B 9.7.1969 Santo Domingo, D.R. BL/TL 6-3/170# d6.25																									
1996	Phi N	0	1	.000	1	1	0	0-0	1.2	4	7	1	0	5-0	1	37.80	11	.444	.643	0-0	—	0	21	-6	-0.8
QUIRK, ART Arthur Lincoln B 4.11.1938 Providence, RI BR/TL 5-11/170# d4.17																									
1962	Bal A	2	2	.500	7	5	0	0	27.1	36	20	3	0	18-0	18	5.93	62	.308	.400	7-1	.143	0	92	-7	-0.8
1963	Was A	1	0	1.000	7	3	0	0	21	23	13	3	0	8-1	12	4.29	87	.280	.341	4-0	.250	0	152	-2	-0.1
Total	2	3	2	.600	14	8	0	0	48.1	59	33	6	0	26-1	30	5.21	71	.296	.376	11-1	.182	0	114	-9	-0.9
QUISENBERRY, DAN Daniel Raymond B 2.7.1953 Santa Monica, CA D 9.30.1998 Leawood, KS BR/TR 6-2/180# d7.8																									
1979	KC A	3	2	.600	32	0	0	5-5	40	42	16	5	0	7-5	13	3.15	136	.278	.306	0-0	—	0		5	0.7
1980	†KC A	12	7	.632	**75**	0	0	**33-3**	128.1	129	47	5	1	27-15	37	3.09	132	.265	.302	0-0	—	0		15	3.0
1981	†KC A	1	4	.200	40	0	0	18-4	62.1	59	16	1	1	15-8	20	1.73	208	.258	.301	0-0	—	0		12	1.9
1982	KC A★	9	7	.563	72	0	0	**35-9**	136.2	126	43	12	0	12-2	46	2.57	159	.252	.266	0-0	—	0		**23**	4.2
1983	KC A★	5	3	.625	**69**	0	0	**45-8**	139	118	35	6	0	11-2	48	1.94	211	.229	.243	0-0	—	0		**33**	**4.0**
1984	†KC A☆	6	3	.667	72	0	0	**44-9**	129.1	121	39	10	0	12-4	41	2.64	153	.247	.264	0-0	—	0		21	2.9
1985	†KC A	8	9	.471	**84**	0	0	**37-12**	129	142	41	8	1	16-5	54	2.37	175	.280	.301	0-0	—	0		24	4.4
1986	KC A	3	7	.300	62	0	0	12-4	81.1	92	30	2	3	24-12	36	2.77	154	.291	.342	0-0	—	0		12	1.8
1987	KC A	4	1	.800	47	0	0	8-3	49	58	15	3	1	10-3	17	2.76	166	.287	.322	0-0	—	0		11	1.4
1988	KC A	0	1	.000	20	0	0	1-0	25.1	32	11	0	0	5-2	9	3.55	112	.305	.336	0-0	—	0		1	0.1
	StL N	2	0	1.000	33	0	0	0-1	38	54	26	4	0	6-1	19	6.16	57	.344	.364	1-0	.000	0		-10	-0.5
1989	StL N	3	1	.750	63	0	0	6-1	78.1	78	25	2	0	14-9	37	2.64	138	.261	.293	4-0	.250	0		9	0.7
1990	SF N	0	1	.000	5	0	0	0-1	6.2	13	12	1	0	3-2	2	13.50	27	.419	.432	1-0	.000	-0		-8	-1.0
Total	12	56	46	.549	674	0	0	244-60	1043.1	1064	356	59	7	162-70	379	2.76	146	.267	.294	6-0	.167	0		148	23.6
RABE, CHARLIE Charles Henry B 5.6.1932 Boyce, TX BL/TL 6-1/180# d9.21																									
1957	Cin N	0	1	.000	2	1	0	0	8.1	5	2	2	0	0-0	6	2.16	190	.167	.167	2-0	.000	-0	21	2	0.2
1958	Cin N	0	3	.000	9	1	0	0	18.2	25	10	3	0	9-0	10	4.34	96	.321	.391	4-0	.000	-1	43	0	-0.1
Total	2	0	4	.000	11	2	0	0	27	30	12	5	0	9-0	16	3.67	113	.278	.333	6-0	.000	-1	32	2	0.1
RACHUNOK, STEVE Stephen Stepanovich "The Mad Russian" B 12.5.1916 Rittman, OH D 5.11.2002 Corona, CA BR/TR 6-4.5/205# d9.17																									
1940	Bro N	0	1	.000	2	1	1	0	10	9	5	0	0	5	10	4.50	89	.243	.333	2-0	.000	0	87	0	0.0
RACZKA, MIKE Michael B 11.16.1962 New Britain, CT BL/TL 6/200# d8.15																									
1992	Oak A	0	0	—	8	0	0	0-0	6.1	8	7	0	0	5-0	2	8.53	44	.308	.394	0-0	—	0		-4	-0.2
RADATZ, DICK Richard Raymond "The Monster" B 4.2.1937 Detroit, MI BR/TR 6-5/235# d4.10																									
1962	Bos A	9	6	.600	**62**	0	0	**24**	124.2	95	32	9	4	40-2	144	2.24	184	.211	.278	31-2	.097	-2		**26**	**3.9**
1963	Bos A★	15	6	.714	66	0	0	25	132.1	94	31	9	5	51-13	162	1.97	192	.201	.285	29-2	.069	-2		**26**	**5.0**
1964	Bos A★	16	9	.640	79	0	0	**29**	157	103	44	13	7	58-9	181	2.29	168	.186	.269	37-2	.162	-0		26	4.9
1965	Bos A	9	11	.450	63	0	0	22	124.1	104	57	11	5	53-11	121	3.91	95	.227	.312	27-2	.185	1		0	0.1
1966	Bos A	0	2	.000	16	0	0	4	19	24	10	3	0	11-2	19	4.74	80	.304	.389	2-0	.000	-0		-1	-0.2
	Cle A	0	3	.000	39	0	0	10	56.2	49	33	6	3	34-6	49	4.61	75	.233	.344	9-0	.111	-0		-8	-0.8
	Year	0	5	.000	55	0	0	14	75.2	73	47	9	3	45-8	68	4.64	76	.253	.356	11-0	.091	-1		-8	-1.0
1967	Cle A	0	0	—	3	0	0	0	3	5	2	1	0	2-0	1	6.00	54	.357	.438	0-0	—	0		-1	0.0
	Chi N	1	0	1.000	20	0	0	5	23.1	12	21	4	5	24-2	18	6.56	54	.154	.380	4-0	.250	0		-8	-0.8
1969	Det A	2	2	.500	11	0	0	0-1	18.2	14	8	3	0	5-0	18	3.38	111	.212	.268	2-0	.000	-0		1	0.1
	Mon N	0	4	.000	22	0	0	3-1	34.2	32	22	6	1	18-1	32	5.71	64	.244	.340	4-0	.250	0		-6	-0.8
Total	7	52	43	.547	381	0	0	122-2	693.2	532	260	65	30	296-46	745	3.13	122	.212	.300	145-8	.131	-3		55	11.4
RADBOURN, CHARLEY Charles Gardner "Old Hoss" B 12.11.1854 Rochester, NY D 2.5.1897 Bloomington, IL BR/TR 5-9/168# d5.5.1880 HF1939																									
1881	Pro N	25	11	**.694**	41	36	34-3	0	325.1	309	162	1		64	117	2.43	109	**.235**	.270	270	.219	-1*	122	14	1.4
1882	Pro N	33	19	.635	54	51	50-**6**	0	466	422	213	6		51	**201**	2.11	134	.226	.247	326	.239	-1*	109	**35**	**3.2**
1883	Pro N	**48**	25	.658	**76**	68	66-4	1	632.1	563	275	7		56	315	2.05	150	.227	**.244**	381	.283	14*	118	**74**	**8.3**
1884	†Pro N	**59**	12	**.831**	**75**	**73**	**73**-11	1	**678.2**	528	216	18		98	**441**	**1.38**	**206**	.205	.234	361	.230	5*	112	**116**	**10.7**
1885	Pro N	28	21	.571	49	49	49-2	0	445.2	423	209	4		83	154	2.20	122	.241	.275	249	.233	11*	97	22	3.4
1886	Bos N	27	31	.466	58	58	57-3	0	509.1	521	300	18		111	218	3.00	107	.254	.292	253	.237	7*	101	12	2.0
1887	Bos N	24	23	.511	50	50	48-1	0	425	505	305	20	14	133	87	4.55	90	.286	.340	175	.229	2*	103	-19	-1.6
1888	Bos N	7	16	.304	24	24	24-1	0	207	187	110	8	8	45	64	2.87	100	.234	.282	79	.215	1	74	1	0.1
1889	Bos N	20	11	.645	33	31	28-1	0	277	282	151	14	8	72	99	3.67	113	.256	.306	122	.189	-1*	114	19	1.6
1890	Bos P	27	12	.692	41	38	36-1	0	343	352	183	8	11	100	80	3.31	133	.254	.309	154	.253	0*	99	46	3.9
1891	Cin N	11	13	.458	26	24	23-2	0	218	236	149	13	13	62	54	4.25	79	.266	.323	96	.177	-1*	84	-15	-1.5
Total	11	309	194	.614	527	502	488-35	2	4527.1	4328	2273	117	54	875	1830	2.68	120	.241	.278	2466	.236	38	106	305	31.5
RADBOURN, GEORGE George B. "Dordy" B 4.8.1856 Bloomington, IL D 1.1.1904 Bloomington, IL ?/160# d5.30																									
1883	Det N	1	2	.333	3	3	2	0	22	38	28	1		7	2	6.55	47	.345	.385	12	.167	-1	92	-8	-0.8
RADEBAUGH, ROY Roy B 2.22.1884 Champaign, IL D 1.17.1945 Cedar Rapids, IA BR/TR 5-7/160# d9.22																									
1911	StL N	0	0	—	2	1	0	0	10	6	3	0	0	4	1	2.70	125	.176	.263	3-0	.000	-0	67	1	0.0
RADER, DREW Drew Leon "Lefty" B 5.14.1901 Elmira, NY D 6.5.1975 Catskill, NY BR/TL 6-2/187# d7.18																									
1921	Pit N	0	0	—	1	0	0	0	2	2	0	0	0	0	0	0.00	—	.286	.286	1-0	.000	-0		1	0.0
RADFORD, PAUL Paul Revere "Shorty" B 10.14.1861 Roxbury, MA D 2.21.1945 Boston, MA BR/TR 5-6/148# d5.1.1883 ▲																									
1884	†Pro N	0	2	.000	2	2	1	0	13	27	19	0		3	2	7.62	37	.403	.429	355	.197	0*	74	-6	-0.7
1885	Pro N	0	2	.000	3	2	2	0	18.1	34	27	1		8	3	7.85	34	.378	.429	371	.243	1*	74	-10	-0.8
1887	NY AA	0	0	—	2	0	0	0	5	15	16	1	0	3	4	18.00	24	.789	.818	466	.265	1*		-8	-0.3
1890	Cle P	0	0	—	1	0	0	0	5	7	5	1	0	3	3	3.60	110	.318	.348	466	.292	0*		0	0.0
1891	Bos AA	0	0	—	1	0	0	0	1	0	0	0	0	0	0	0.00	—	.000	.000	456	.259	0*		0	0.0
1893	Was N	0	0	—	1	0	0	0	1	2	2	2	0	2	1	18.00	26	.400	.571	464	.228	0*		-1	0.0
Total	6	0	4	.000	10	4	3	0	43.1	85	69	5	0	17	13	8.52	37	.413	.457	2598	.250	2	69	-25	-1.8
RADINSKY, SCOTT Scott David B 3.3.1968 Glendale, CA BL/TL 6-3/204# d4.9																									
1990	Chi A	6	1	.857	62	0	0	4-1	52.1	47	29	1	2	36-1	46	4.82	80	.241	.362	0-0	—	0		-5	-0.7
1991	Chi A	5	5	.500	67	0	0	8-7	71.1	53	18	4	1	23-2	49	2.02	197	.206	.270	0-0	—	0		16	2.4
1992	Chi A	3	7	.300	68	0	0	15-8	59.1	54	21	3	2	34-5	48	2.73	142	.243	.347	0-0	—	0		7	1.5
1993	†Chi A	8	2	.800	73	0	0	4-1	54.2	61	33	3	1	19-3	44	4.28	98	.268	.327	0-0	—	0		-3	-0.4
1995	Chi A	2	1	.667	46	0	0	1-2	38	46	23	7	0	17-4	14	5.45	82	.309	.371	0-0	—	0		-3	-0.2
1996	†LA N	5	1	.833	58	0	0	1-3	52.1	52	19	2	0	17-5	48	2.41	161	.264	.318	1-0	.000	-0		8	0.8
1997	LA N	5	1	.833	75	0	0	3-2	62.1	54	22	4	1	21-5	44	2.89	134	.236	.298	4-0	.000	-0		7	0.6

Year	Tm Lg	W	L	Pct	G	GS	CG-Sho	SV-BS	IP	H	R	HR	HB	BB-IB	SO	ERA	AERA	OAV	OOB	AB-SH	AVG	PB	Sup	APR	PW
1998	LA N	6	6	.500	62	0	0	13-11	61.2	63	21	5	4	20-1	45	2.63	151	.272	.337	0-0	—	0		9	1.9
1999	StL N	2	1	.667	43	0	0	3-0	27.2	27	16	2	1	18-3	17	4.88	94	.270	.371	0-0	—	0		-1	-0.1
2000	StL N	0	0	—	1	0	0	0-0	0	0	0	0	0	1-0	0	—	—	—	1.000	0-0	—	0		0	0.0
2001	Cle A	0	0	—	2	0	0	0-0	2	4	6	2	0	3-0	3	27.00	17	.400	.538	0-0	—	0		-5	-0.2
Total	11	42	25	.627	557	0	0	52-35	481.2	461	208	33	12	209-29	358	3.44	117	.253	.330	5-0	.000	-1		30	5.6
RADKE, BRAD Brad William B 10.27.1972 Eau Claire, WI BR/TR 6-2/180# d4.29																									
1995	Min A	11	14	.440	29	28	2-1	0-0	181	195	112	32	4	47-0	75	5.32	90	.275	.319	0-0	—	0	93	-9	-1.0
1996	Min A	11	16	.407	35	35	3	0-0	232	231	125	40	4	57-2	148	4.46	115	.256	.302	0-0	—	0	88	15	1.3
1997	Min A	20	10	.667	35	**35**	4-1	0-0	239.2	238	114	28	3	48-1	174	3.87	120	.257	.293	3-1	.000	-0	109	19	2.1
1998	Min A★	12	14	.462	32	32	5-1	0-0	213.2	238	109	23	9	43-1	146	4.30	111	.283	.324	2-0	.000	-0	86	11	1.2
1999	Min A	12	14	.462	33	33	4	0-0	218.2	239	97	28	1	44-0	121	3.75	136	.280	.314	5-0	.000	-1	71	31	3.3
2000	Min A	12	16	.429	34	34	4-1	0-0	226.2	261	119	27	5	51-1	141	4.45	116	.286	.326	2-0	.000	-0	68	18	1.9
2001	Min A	15	11	.577	33	33	6-2	0-0	226	235	105	24	10	26-0	137	3.94	117	.271	.298	4-0	.500	1	103	16	1.8
2002	†Min A	9	5	.643	21	21	2-1	0-0	118.1	124	64	12	7	20-0	62	4.72	95	.272	.309	0-0	—	0	106	-2	-0.2
2003	†Min A	14	10	.583	33	33	3-1	0-0	212.1	242	111	32	5	28-2	120	4.49	101	.288	.314	5-0	.200	0	102	2	0.2
Total	9	116	110	.513	285	284	33-8	0-0	1868.1	2003	956	246	48	364-7	1124	4.32	112	.274	.311	21-1	.143	-0	91	101	10.6
RADLOSKY, ROB Robert Vincent B 1.7.1974 W.Palm Beach, FL BR/TR 6-2/192# d5.25																									
1999	Min A	0	1	.000	7	0	0	0-1	8.2	15	12	7	1	4-0	3	12.46	41	.375	.444	0-0	—	0		-6	-0.6
RAETHER, HAL Harold Herman "Bud" B 10.10.1932 Lake Mills, WI BR/TR 6-1/185# d7.4																									
1954	Phi A	0	0	—	1	0	0	0	2	1	1	0	0	4	0	4.50	87	.200	.556	0-0	—	0		0	0.0
1957	KC A	0	0	—	1	0	0	0	2	2	2	1	0	0-0	0	9.00	44	.250	.250	0-0	—	0		-1	-0.1
Total	2	0	0	—	2	0	0	0	4	3	3	1	0	4-0	0	6.75	58	.231	.412	0-0	—	0		-1	-0.1
RAFFENSBERGER, KEN Kenneth David B 8.8.1917 York, PA D 11.10.2002 York, PA BR/TL 6-2/185# d4.25 Mil 1945																									
1939	StL N	0	0	—	1	0	0	0	1	2	0	0	0	0	1	0.00	—	.400	.400	0-0	—	0		0	0.0
1940	Chi N	7	9	.438	43	10	3	3	114.2	120	54	10	2	29	55	3.38	111	.271	.319	30-2	.167	-1	70	3	0.3
1941	Chi N	0	1	.000	10	1	0	0	18	17	9	0	0	7	5	4.50	78	.262	.333	5-1	.000	-1	145	-1	-0.1
1943	Phi N	0	1	.000	1	1	1	0	8	7	3	0	0	2	3	1.13	300	.241	.290	3-0	.000	-0	0	1	0.1
1944	Phi N★	13	20	.394	37	31	18-3	0	258.2	257	101	9	2	45	136	3.06	118	.252	.285	80-13	.138	-3*	72	17	1.5
1945	Phi N	0	3	.000	5	4	1	0	24.1	28	19	3	0	14	6	4.44	86	.283	.372	8-0	.000	-1	88	-3	-0.4
1946	Phi N	8	15	.348	39	23	14-2	**6**	196	203	89	10	1	39	73	3.63	95	.265	.302	60-9	.167	-1	72	-3	-0.5
1947	Phi N	2	6	.250	10	7	3-1	0	41	50	30	4	1	8	16	5.49	73	.307	.343	15-0	.267	0	72	-7	-1.1
	Cin N	6	5	.545	19	15	7	1	106.2	132	54	11	0	29	38	4.13	99	.305	.348	37-2	.162	-1	86	0	-0.1
	Year	8	11	.421	29	22	10-1	1	147.2	182	58	15	1	37	54	4.51	90	.305	.347	52-2	.192	-0	82	-7	-1.2
1948	Cin N	11	12	.478	40	24	7-4	0	180.1	187	88	15	1	37	57	3.84	102	.259	.296	62-3	.113	-3	75	1	-0.3
1949	Cin N	18	17	.514	41	**38**	20-**5**	0	284	289	129	23	2	80	103	3.39	123	.264	.315	90-12	.178	0	90	21	2.3
1950	Cin N	14	19	.424	38	35	18-4	0	239	271	127	34	2	40	87	4.26	100	.279	.308	82-3	.134	-2	95	0	-0.3
1951	Cin N	16	17	.485	42	33	14-5	5	248.2	232	108	29	6	38	81	3.44	119	.246	.279	82-6	.122	-3	89	18	1.8
1952	Cin N	17	13	.567	38	33	18-**6**	1	247	247	85	18	2	45	93	2.81	134	.261	.295	75-11	.107	-2	85	26	2.7
1953	Cin N	7	14	.333	26	26	9-1	0	174	200	87	23	0	33	47	3.93	111	.289	.322	57-8	.140	-1	84	7	0.7
1954	Cin N	0	2	.000	6	1	0	0	10.1	15	10	2	0	3	5	7.84	53	.333	.367	2-0	.500	0	276	-4	-0.6
Total	15	119	154	.436	396	282	133-31	16	2151.2	2257	993	191	19	449	806	3.60	110	.267	.306	688-70	.141	-17	84	76	6.0
RAFFO, AL Albert Martin B 11.27.1941 San Francisco, CA BR/TR 6-5/210# d4.29																									
1969	Phi N	1	3	.250	45	0	0	1-0	72.1	81	35	6	4	25-3	38	4.11	86	.286	.349	6-2	.167	0		-4	-0.1
RAGAN, PAT Don Carlos Patrick B 11.15.1888 Blanchard, IA D 9.4.1956 Los Angeles, CA BR/TR 5-10.5/185# d4.21 C1																									
1909	Cin N	0	1	.000	2	0	0	0	8	7	4	0	0	4	2	3.38	77	.259	.355	2-0	.500	0		-1	0.0
	Chi N	0	0	—	2	0	0	0	3.2	4	2	0	0	1	2	2.45	104	.286	.333	2-0	.000	-0		0	0.0
	Year	0	1	.000	4	0	0	0	11.2	11	10	0	0	5	4	3.09	84	.268	.348	4-0	.250	0		-1	0.0
1911	Bro N	4	3	.571	22	7	5-1	1	93.2	81	32	0	2	31	39	2.11	158	.252	.321	29-0	.138	-1	74	11	0.6
1912	Bro N	7	18	.280	36	26	12-1	1	208	211	101	7	4	65	101	3.63	92	.270	.329	67-4	.060	-7	87	-2	-1.0
1913	Bro N	15	18	.455	44	32	14	0	264.2	284	145	10	4	64	109	3.77	87	.281	.327	91-3	.165	-2	119	-15	-1.8
1914	Bro N	10	15	.400	38	25	14-1	3	208.1	214	104	5	3	85	106	2.98	96	.270	.343	75-1	.133	-3	103	-4	-0.8
1915	Bro N	1	0	1.000	5	0	0	0	19.2	11	6	0	0	8	7	0.92	304	.164	.253	6-0	.167	-0		3	0.1
	Bos N	16	12	.571	33	26	13-3	0	227	208	71	2	7	59	81	2.46	105	.255	.311	80-1	.150	-0	105	9	0.8
	Year	17	12	.586	38	26	13-3	0	246.2	219	75	2	7	67	88	2.34	112	.248	.306	86-1	.151	-1	104	12	0.9
1916	Bos N	9	9	.500	28	23	14-3	0	182	143	53	3	0	47	94	2.08	120	.218	.270	60-2	.217	3*	93	9	1.4
1917	Bos N	6	9	.400	30	13	5-1	1	147.2	138	59	6	1	35	61	2.93	87	.250	.295	48-3	.125	-1	100	-6	-0.7
1918	Bos N	8	17	.320	30	25	15-2	0	206.1	212	95	4	4	54	68	3.23	83	.270	.320	71-4	.183	-2	121	-12	-1.6
1919	Bos N	0	2	.000	4	3	0	0	12.2	16	13	0	0	3	3	7.11	40	.281	.317	4-0	.250	0	56	-6	-0.9
	NY N	1	0	1.000	7	1	1	0	22.2	19	7	0	0	14	7	1.59	177	.247	.363	7-0	.429	1	199	2	0.3
	Year	1	2	.333	11	4	1	0	35.1	35	14	0	0	17	10	3.57	79	.261	.344	11-0	.364	1	92	-4	-0.6
	Chi A	0	0	—	1	0	0	0	1	1	0	0	0	0	0	0.00	—	.250	.250	0-0	—	0		0	0.0
1923	Phi N	0	0	—	1	0	0	0	3	6	2	1	0	0	0	6.00	77	.400	.400	2-0	.500	0		0	0.0
Total	11	77	104	.425	283	181	93-12	6	1608.1	1555	694	38	25	470	680	2.99	97	.260	.317	544-18	.154	-13	103	-12	-3.6
RAGGIO, BRADY Brady John B 9.17.1972 Los Angeles, CA BR/TR 6-4/210# d4.15																									
1997	StL N	1	2	.333	15	4	0	0-0	31.1	44	24	1	1	16-0	21	6.89	60	.336	.407	3-1	.000	-0	172	-8	-0.7
1998	StL N	1	1	.500	4	1	0	0-0	7	22	12	1	1	3-0	3	15.43	27	.579	.605	1-0	.000	-0	153	-8	-1.4
2003	Ari N	0	0	—	10	0	0	1-0	8.1	9	6	1	0	6-1	8	6.48	72	.290	.405	0-0	—	0		-1	-0.1
Total	3	2	3	.400	29	5	0	1-0	46.2	75	42	3	2	25-1	32	8.10	52	.375	.443	4-1	.000	-0	165	-17	-2.2
RAGLAND, FRANK Frank Roland B 5.26.1904 Water Valley, MS D 7.28.1959 Paris, MS BR/TR 6-1/186# d4.17																									
1932	Was A	1	0	1.000	12	1	0	0	37.2	54	33	5	3	21	11	7.41	58	.346	.433	11-0	.273	1	99	-13	-0.5
1933	Phi N	0	4	.000	11	5	0	0	38.1	51	32	1	1	10	4	6.81	56	.317	.360	10-0	.200	-0	57	-10	-0.9
Total	2	1	4	.200	23	6	0	0	76	105	65	6	4	31	15	7.11	58	.331	.398	21-0	.238	1	62	-23	-1.4
RAICH, ERIC Eric James B 11.1.1951 Detroit, MI BR/TR 6-4/225# d5.24																									
1975	Cle A	7	8	.467	18	17	2	0-0	92.2	118	61	12	1	31-6	34	5.54	69	.320	.368	0-0	—	0	94	-16	-2.3
1976	Cle A	0	0	—	1	0	0	0-0	2.2	7	5	1	0	0-0	1	16.88	21	.467	.467	0-0	—	0		-4	-0.2
Total	2	7	8	.467	19	17	2	0-0	95.1	125	66	13	1	31-6	35	5.85	65	.326	.371	0-0	—	0	94	-20	-2.5
RAIN, STEVE Steven Nicholas B 6.2.1975 Los Angeles, CA BR/TR 6-6/250# d7.17																									
1999	Chi N	0	1	.000	16	0	0	0-0	14.2	28	17	1	1	7-0	12	9.20	49	.418	.474	0-0	—	0		-8	-0.4
2000	Chi N	3	4	.429	37	0	0	0-3	49.2	46	25	10	1	27-0	54	4.35	104	.250	.347	2-0	.000	0		1	0.1
Total	2	3	5	.375	53	0	0	0-3	64.1	74	42	11	2	34-0	66	5.46	83	.295	.381	2-0	.000	0		-7	-0.3
RAINEY, CHUCK Charles David B 7.14.1954 San Diego, CA BR/TR 5-11/190# d4.8																									
1979	Bos A	8	5	.615	20	16	4-1	1-0	103.2	97	47	7	3	41-1	41	3.82	116	.250	.325	0-0	—	0	97	7	0.9
1980	Bos A	8	3	.727	16	13	2-1	0-0	87	92	49	7	2	41-3	43	4.86	87	.273	.353	0-0	—	0	114	-5	-0.6
1981	Bos A	0	1	.000	11	2	0	0-0	40	39	21	2	0	13-1	20	2.70	144	.252	.306	0-0	—	0	104	2	0.1
1982	Bos A	7	5	.583	27	25	3-3	0-0	129	146	75	14	2	63-2	57	5.02	86	.294	.373	0-0	—	0	104	-8	-0.6
1983	Chi N	14	13	.519	34	34	1-1	0-0	191	219	109	17	3	74-3	84	4.48	85	.295	.358	56-10	.161	1	105	-15	-1.8
1984	Chi N	5	7	.417	17	16	0	0-0	88.1	102	55	4	2	38-1	45	4.28	91	.290	.361	31-1	.097	-1	104	-7	-1.0
	Oak A	1	1	.500	16	0	0	1-1	30.2	43	27	2	0	17-4	10	6.75	56	.333	.403	0-0	—	0		-12	-0.8
Total	6	43	35	.551	141	106	10-6	2-1	669.2	738	383	53	12	287-15	300	4.50	90	.284	.355	87-11	.138	-1	105	-38	-3.8
RAJSICH, DAVE David Christopher B 9.28.1951 Youngstown, OH BL/TL 6-5/175# d7.2 b-Gary																									
1978	NY A	0	0	—	4	2	0	0-0	13.1	16	6	0	0	6-0	9	4.05	90	.320	.379	0-0	—	0	124	0	0.0
1979	Tex A	1	3	.250	27	3	0	0-0	53.2	56	25	7	0	18-0	32	3.52	118	.267	.325	0-0	—	0	65	3	0.3
1980	Tex A	2	1	.667	24	1	0	2-0	48.1	56	34	7	3	22-0	35	5.96	65	.295	.370	0-0	—	0	23	-10	-0.6

Year	Tm Lg	W	L	Pct	G	GS	CG-Sho	SV-BS	IP	H	R	HR	HB	BB-IB	SO	ERA	AERA	OAV	OOB	AB-SH	AVG	PB	Sup	APR	PW
Total	3	3	4	.429	55	6	0	2-0	115.1	128	65	14	3	46-0	76	4.60	87	.284	.350	0-0	—	0	75	-7	-0.3
RAKERS, JASON Jason Paul B 6.29.1973 Pittsburgh, PA BR/TR 6-2/197# d5.6																									
1998	Cle A	0	0	—	1	0	0	0-0	1	0	1	0	0	3-0	0	9.00	53	.000	.500	0-0	—	0		0	0.0
1999	Cle A	0	0	—	1	0	0	0-0	2	2	1	1	0	1-0	0	4.50	112	.250	.333	0-0	—	0		0	0.0
2000	KC A	2	0	1.000	11	0	0	0-0	21.2	33	22	5	0	7-0	16	9.14	56	.351	.392	0-0	—	0		-9	-0.7
Total	3	2	0	1.000	13	0	0	0-0	24.2	35	24	6	0	11-0	16	8.76	58	.337	.393	0-0	—	0		-9	-0.7
RAKOW, ED Edward Charles "Rock" B 5.30.1935 Pittsburgh, PA D 8.26.2000 West Palm Beach, FL BB/TR 5-11/178# d4.22																									
1960	LA N	0	1	.000	9	2	0	0	22	30	19	5	0	11-3	9	7.36	54	.323	.390	6-0	.333	0	67	-7	-0.3
1961	KC A	2	8	.200	45	11	1	1	124.2	131	80	14	8	49-1	81	4.76	88	.269	.341	29-3	.103	-2	98	-9	-0.8
1962	KC A	14	17	.452	42	35	11-2	1	235.1	232	126	31	4	98-5	159	4.25	99	.260	.334	82-5	.098	-5	92	-2	-0.7
1963	KC A	9	10	.474	34	26	7-1	0	174.1	173	85	18	5	61-4	104	3.92	99	.261	.326	57-2	.105	-2	91	-1	-0.2
1964	Det A	8	9	.471	42	13	1	3	152.1	155	70	14	6	59-1	96	3.72	98	.266	.337	39-4	.000	-4	95	-2	-0.5
1965	Det A	0	0	—	6	0	0	0	13.1	14	11	2	0	11-0	10	6.08	57	.280	.403	3-0	.000	-0		-4	-0.3
1967	Atl N	3	2	.600	17	3	0	0	39.1	36	23	4	1	15-3	25	5.26	63	.240	.311	10-0	.000	-1	132	-7	-1.0
Total	7	36	47	.434	195	90	20-3	5	761.1	771	414	88	24	304-17	484	4.33	92	.264	.336	226-14	.084	-13	94	-32	-3.8
RALEIGH, JOHN John Austin B 4.21.1890 Elkhorn, WI D 8.24.1955 Escondido, CA BR/TL d8.4																									
1909	StL N	1	10	.091	15	10	3	0	80.2	85	42	0	3	21	26	3.79	67	.285	.339	23-1	.087	-2	39	-10	-1.4
1910	StL N	0	0	—	3	1	0	0	5	8	5	0	0	0	2	9.00	33	.364	.364	1-0	.000	-0	125	-3	-0.2
Total	2	1	10	.091	18	11	3	0	85.2	93	47	0	3	21	28	4.10	62	.291	.340	24-1	.083	-2	47	-13	-1.6
RAMBERT, PEP Elmer Donald B 8.1.1916 Cleveland, OH D 11.16.1974 W.Palm Beach, FL BR/TR 6/175# d9.23																									
1939	Pit N	0	0	—	2	0	0	0	3.2	7	4	0	0	1	4	9.82	39	.389	.421	0-0	—	0		-2	-0.1
1940	Pit N	0	1	.000	3	1	0	0	8.1	12	8	0	3	4	0	7.56	50	.333	.442	2-0	.000	0	68	-3	-0.3
Total	2	0	1	.000	5	1	0	0	12	19	12	0	3	5	4	8.25	46	.352	.435	2-0	.000	0	68	-5	-0.4
RAMBO, PETE Warren Dawson B 11.1.1906 Thorofare, NJ D 6.19.1991 Camden, NJ BR/TR 5-9/150# d9.16																									
1926	Phi N	0	0	—	1	0	0	0	3.2	6	8	0	0	4	4	14.73	28	.353	.476	1-0	1.000	0		-4	-0.2
RAMIREZ, ALLAN Daniel Allan B 5.1.1957 Victoria, TX BR/TR 5-10/180# d6.8																									
1983	Bal A	4	4	.500	11	10	1	0-0	57	46	22	6	0	30-1	20	3.47	114	.229	.328	0-0	—	0	115	4	0.6
RAMIREZ, ERASMO Erasmo B 4.29.1976 Santa Ana, CA BL/TL 6/180# d4.30																									
2003	Tex A	3	1	.750	34	0	0	0-1	49	46	21	4	4	9-0	28	3.86	129	.251	.298	0-0	—	0		6	0.4
RAMIREZ, HECTOR Hector Bienvenido B 12.15.1971 ElSeibo, D.R. BR/TR 6-3/218# d8.28																									
1999	Mil N	1	2	.333	15	0	0	0-3	21	19	8	1	0	11-2	9	3.43	132	.247	.341	3-0	.000	-0		3	0.3
2000	Mil N	0	1	.000	6	0	0	0-0	9	11	10	1	0	5-0	4	10.00	46	.289	.372	1-0	1.000	0		-5	-0.4
Total	2	1	3	.250	21	0	0	0-3	30	30	18	2	0	16-2	13	5.40	84	.261	.351	4-0	.250	0		-2	-0.1
RAMIREZ, HORACIO Horacio B 11.24.1979 Carson, CA BL/TL 6-1/170# d4.2																									
2003	Atl N	12	4	.750	29	29	1	0-0	182.1	181	91	21	6	72-10	100	4.00	106	.263	.337	61-6	.098	-3	141	4	0.1
RAMIREZ, ROBERTO Roberto Sanchez B 8.17.1972 Veracruz, Mexico BL/TL 6/171# d6.12																									
1998	SD N	1	0	1.000	21	0	0	0-0	14.2	12	13	4	0	12-1	17	6.14	64	.211	.348	0-0	—	0		-5	-0.3
1999	Col N	1	5	.167	32	4	0	1-0	40.1	68	42	8	0	22-2	32	8.26	70	.368	.435	7-1	.143	-0	115	-9	-1.2
Total	2	2	5	.286	53	4	0	1-0	55	80	55	12	0	34-3	49	7.69	69	.331	.413	7-1	.143	-0	115	-14	-1.5
RAMOS, EDGAR Edgar Jose (Malave) B 3.6.1975 Cumana, Venezuela BR/TR 6-4/190# d5.21																									
1997	Phi N	0	2	.000	4	2	0	0-0	14	15	9	3	1	6-0	4	5.14	83	.288	.373	3-1	.000	-0	33	-1	-0.2
RAMOS, MARIO Mario Martin B 10.19.1977 Aurora, IL BL/TL 6-1/180# d6.19																									
2003	Tex A	1	1	.500	3	3	0	0-0	13	11	9	3	2	13-0	8	6.23	80	.224	.406	1-0	.000	-0	105	-1	-0.2
RAMOS, PEDRO Pedro (Guerra) "Pete" B 4.28.1935 Pinar Del Rio, Cuba BB/TR 6/185# d4.11																									
1955	Was A	5	11	.313	45	9	3-1	5	130	121	62	13	11	39-3	34	3.88	99	.253	.319	38-0	.079	-3*	90	0	-0.3
1956	Was A	12	10	.545	37	18	4	0	152	178	95	23	3	76-0	54	5.27	82	.299	.377	44-4	.205	0*	106	-13	-1.6
1957	Was A	12	16	.429	43	30	7-1	0	231	251	131	43	7	69-4	91	4.79	81	.271	.325	76-3	.171	-1*	93	-21	-2.4
1958	Was A	14	18	.438	43	**37**	10-4	3	259.1	277	133	38	5	77-9	132	4.23	90	.273	.325	88-7	.239	1*	98	-13	-1.4
1959	Was A☆	13	19	.406	37	35	11	0	233.2	233	127	30	9	52-4	95	4.16	94	.257	.301	75-6	.147	-0*	90	-7	-0.9
1960	Was A	11	18	.379	43	**36**	14-1	2	274	254	126	24	7	99-8	160	3.45	113	.245	.313	86-7	.116	-2*	94	12	1.1
1961	Min A	11	20	.355	42	34	9-3	2	264.1	265	134	39	4	79-6	174	3.95	107	.258	.312	93-2	.172	1*	90	8	0.8
1962	Cle A	10	12	.455	37	27	7-2	1	201.1	189	104	28	5	85-5	96	3.71	104	.246	.323	68-2	.147	2*	86	-1	0.1
1963	Cle A	9	8	.529	36	22	5	0	184.2	156	74	29	4	41-6	169	3.12	116	.226	.272	55-4	.109	1*	107	10	0.8
1964	Cle A	7	10	.412	36	19	3-1	0	133	144	84	18	4	26-6	98	5.14	70	.273	.310	39-1	.179	2*	105	-23	-2.5
	NY A	1	0	1.000	13	0	0	8	21.2	13	3	1	0	0-0	21	1.25	291	.183	.176	5-1	.000	-1		6	0.6
	Year	8	10	.444	49	19	3-1	8	154.2	157	91	19	4	26-6	119	4.60	78	.263	.294	44-2	.159	1	105	-15	-1.9
1965	NY A	5	5	.500	65	0	0	19	92.1	80	34	7	1	27-9	68	2.92	116	.237	.294	12-2	.083	-1		5	0.6
1966	NY A	3	9	.250	52	1	0	13	89.2	98	43	10	1	18-4	58	3.61	92	.283	.317	13-0	.154	-0	53	-4	-0.7
1967	Phi N	0	0	—	6	0	0	0	8	14	8	1	2	8-1	1	9.00	38	.412	.545	1-0	.000	-0		-4	-0.2
1969	Pit N	0	1	.000	5	0	0	0-0	6	8	4	2	0	0-0	4	6.00	58	.320	.320	1-0	.000	-0		-1	-0.2
	Cin N	4	3	.571	38	0	0	2-2	66.1	73	41	8	5	24-11	40	5.16	73	.284	.357	8-2	.000	-1		-9	-1.0
	Year	4	4	.500	43	0	0	2-2	72.1	81	47	10	5	24-11	44	5.23	72	.287	.354	9-2	.000	-1		-10	-1.2
1970	Was A	0	0	—	4	0	0	0-0	8.1	10	7	2	0	4-0	10	7.56	47	.294	.368	1-0	.000	0*		-3	-0.2
Total	15	117	160	.422	582	268	73-13	55-2	2355.2	2364	1210	316	68	724-76	1305	4.08	95	.261	.318	703-41	.155	-0	96	-58	-7.4
RAMSAY, ROBERT Robert Arthur B 12.3.1973 Vancouver, WA BL/TL 6-5/230# d8.27																									
1999	Sea A	0	2	.000	6	3	0	0-0	18.1	23	13	3	0	9-1	11	6.38	74	.324	.395	0-0	—	0	85	-3	-0.3
2000	†Sea A	1	1	.500	37	1	0	0-0	50.1	43	22	3	1	40-3	32	3.40	139	.234	.368	0-0	—	0	60	7	0.3
Total	2	1	3	.250	43	4	0	0-0	68.2	66	35	6	1	49-4	43	4.19	113	.259	.375	0-0	—	0	79	4	0.0
RAMSDELL, WILLIE James Willard "The Knuck" B 4.4.1916 Williamsburg, KS D 10.8.1969 Wichita, KS BR/TR 5-10/180# d9.24																									
1947	Bro N	1	1	.500	2	0	0	0	2.2	4	6	0	1	3	3	6.75	61	.333	.500	1-0	1.000	0		-2	-0.4
1948	Bro N	4	4	.500	27	1	0	4	50.1	48	35	6	3	41	34	5.19	77	.251	.391	11-0	.091	-1	22	-7	-1.2
1950	Bro N	1	2	.333	5	0	0	1	6.1	7	3	0	1	2	2	2.84	144	.292	.370	3-0	.000	-0		1	0.1
	Cin N	7	12	.368	27	22	8-1	0	157.1	151	77	17	2	75	83	3.72	114	.255	.341	50-6	.200	1	90	7	0.8
	Year	8	14	.364	32	22	8-1	1	163.2	158	81	17	3	77	85	3.68	115	.257	.342	53-6	.189	0	90	8	0.9
1951	Cin N	9	17	.346	31	31	10-1	0	196	204	103	18	8	70	88	4.04	101	.266	.333	58-5	.155	-1	73	1	-0.1
1952	Chi N	2	3	.400	19	4	0	0	67	41	22	5	5	24	30	2.42	159	.173	.263	18-0	.056	-1	69	10	0.6
Total	5	24	39	.381	111	58	18-2	5	479.2	455	246	46	20	215	240	3.83	107	.250	.335	141-11	.156	-2	79	10	-0.2
RAMSEY, TOAD Thomas A. B 8.8.1864 Indianapolis, IN D 3.27.1906 Indianapolis, IN BR/TL d9.5																									
1885	Lou AA	3	6	.333	9	9	9	0	79	44	38	1	1	28	83	1.94	167	.150	.227	31	.129	-2	87	10	0.8
1886	Lou AA	38	27	.585	67	67	**66**-3	0	**588.2**	447	297	3	12	207	499	2.45	149	**.198**	.269	241	.241	-3	87	**77**	6.7
1887	Lou AA	37	27	.578	65	64	61	0	561	544	358	9	16	167	**355**	3.43	128	.242	.299	225	.191	-10	96	58	3.7
1888	Lou AA	8	30	.211	40	40	37-1	0	342.1	362	278	10	11	86	228	3.42	90	.262	.310	142	.120	-7*	74	-19	-2.5
1889	Lou AA	1	16	.059	18	18	15	0	140	175	152	7	2	71	60	5.59	69	.297	.374	57	.263	0	62	-29	-2.6
	StL AA	3	1	.750	5	3	3	0	41	44	29	0	1	10	33	3.95	107	.265	.311	17	.294	0	108	1	0.1
	Year	4	17	.190	23	21	18	0	181	219	36	7	3	81	93	5.22	75	.290	.361	74	.270	1	68	-27	-2.5
1890	StL AA	24	17	.585	44	40	34-1	0	348.2	325	221	10	8	102	257	3.69	117	.239	.296	145	.228	-1	94	20	1.4
Total	6	114	124	.479	248	241	225-5	0	2100.2	1941	1373	40	51	671	1515	3.29	117	.234	.295	858	.204	-22	87	118	7.6
RANDALL, SCOTT Scott Philip B 10.29.1975 Fullerton, CA BR/TR 6-3/200# d8.26																									
2003	Cin N	2	5	.286	15	2	0	0-1	27.2	34	20	1	2	11-3	25	6.51	66	.304	.376	4-0	.250	0	11	-6	-1.1

RANDOLPH, STEPHEN Stephen Lecharles B 5.1.1974 Okinawa, Japan BL/TL 6-3/180# d3.31

Year	Tm Lg	W	L	Pct	G	GS	CG-Sho	SV-BS	IP	H	R	HR	HB	BB-IB	SO	ERA	AERA	OAV	OOB	AB-SH	AVG	PB	Sup	APR	PW
2003	Ari N	8	1	.889	50	0	0	0-0	60	50	28	7	2	43-3	50	4.05	115	.226	.357	3-1	.000	-0		5	0.6

RANEY, RIBS Frank Robert Donald (b: Frank Robert Donald Raniszewski) B 2.16.1923 Detroit, MI D 7.7.2003 Warren, MI BR/TR 6-4/190# d9.18

Year	Tm Lg	W	L	Pct	G	GS	CG-Sho	SV-BS	IP	H	R	HR	HB	BB-IB	SO	ERA	AERA	OAV	OOB	AB-SH	AVG	PB	Sup	APR	PW
1949	StL A	1	2	.333	3	3	1	0	16.1	23	15	2	0	12	5	7.71	59	.333	.432	6-0	.000	-1	92	-5	-0.8
1950	StL A	0	1	.000	1	0	0	0	2	2	2	0	0	2	2	4.50	110	.250	.400	1-0	.000	-0		0	-0.1
Total	2	1	3	.250	4	3	1	0	18.1	25	17	2	0	14	7	7.36	62	.325	.429	7-0	.000	-1	92	-5	-0.9

RAPP, PAT Patrick Leland B 7.13.1967 Jennings, LA BR/TR 6-3/215# d7.10

Year	Tm Lg	W	L	Pct	G	GS	CG-Sho	SV-BS	IP	H	R	HR	HB	BB-IB	SO	ERA	AERA	OAV	OOB	AB-SH	AVG	PB	Sup	APR	PW
1992	SF N	0	2	.000	3	2	0	0-0	10	8	8	0	1	6-1	3	7.20	46	.235	.366	2-1	.000	-0	41	-4	-0.7
1993	Fla N	4	6	.400	16	16	1	0-0	94	101	49	7	2	39-1	57	4.02	108	.281	.351	31-2	.194	0	81	2	0.2
1994	Fla N	7	8	.467	24	23	2-1	0-0	133.1	132	67	13	7	69-3	75	3.85	114	.266	.361	41-4	.122	-2*	90	7	0.5
1995	Fla N	14	7	.667	28	28	3-2	0-0	167.1	158	72	10	7	76-2	102	3.44	123	.253	.340	56-9	.107	-3	111	14	1.2
1996	Fla N	8	16	.333	30	29	0	0-0	162.1	184	95	12	3	91-6	86	5.10	80	.301	.390	58-0	.121	-2	103	-16	-2.2
1997	Fla N	4	6	.400	19	19	1-1	0-0	108.2	121	59	11	3	51-3	64	4.47	90	.286	.365	35-4	.143	0	112	-6	-0.4
	SF N	1	2	.333	8	6	0	0-0	33	37	24	5	2	21-1	28	6.00	68	.294	.395	12-0	.000	-1	113	-7	-0.7
	Year	5	8	.385	27	25	1-1	0-0	141.2	158	29	16	5	72-4	92	4.83	84	.288	.372	47-4	.106	-1	112	-13	-1.1
1998	KC A	12	13	.480	32	32	1-1	0-0	188.1	208	117	24	10	107-7	132	5.30	91	.285	.381	2-1	.000	-0	86	-8	-0.9
1999	†Bos A	6	7	.462	37	26	0	0-0	146.1	147	78	13	7	69-1	90	4.12	121	.263	.351	2-0	.000	-0	105	13	0.9
2000	Bal A	9	12	.429	31	30	0	0-0	174	203	125	18	5	83-5	106	5.90	80	.289	.365	3-0	.000	-0	124	-25	-2.4
2001	Ana A	5	12	.294	31	28	1	0-0	170	169	96	20	2	71-2	82	4.76	96	.261	.332	5-0	.000	-1	88	-3	-0.2
Total	10	70	91	.435	259	239	9-5	0-0	1387.1	1468	790	133	49	683-32	825	4.68	96	.276	.361	247-21	.117	-8	100	-33	-4.7

RASCHI, VIC Victor John Angelo B 3.28.1919 W.Springfield, MA D 10.14.1988 Groveland, NY BR/TR 6-1/205# d9.23

Year	Tm Lg	W	L	Pct	G	GS	CG-Sho	SV-BS	IP	H	R	HR	HB	BB-IB	SO	ERA	AERA	OAV	OOB	AB-SH	AVG	PB	Sup	APR	PW
1946	NY A	2	0	1.000	2	2	2	0	16	14	7	0	0	5	11	3.94	88	.230	.288	4-3	.250	0	137	0	0.0
1947	†NY A	7	2	.778	15	14	6-1	0	104.2	89	47	11	1	38	51	3.87	91	.226	.296	40-1	.250	2	139	-3	-0.1
1948	NY A★	19	8	.704	36	31	18-6	1	222.2	208	103	15	3	74	124	3.84	106	.247	.310	81-4	.235	2	134	8	1.0
1949	†NY A★	21	10	.677	38	**37**	21-3	0	274.2	247	120	16	6	138	124	3.34	121	.241	.334	83-11	.157	1	123	20	2.1
1950	†NY A★	21	8	**.724**	33	32	17-2	1	256.2	232	120	19	3	116	155	4.00	107	.243	.327	86-10	.198	1	116	11	1.1
1951	†NY A	21	10	.677	35	**34**	15-4	0	258.1	233	110	20	5	103	**164**	3.27	117	.242	.319	85-13	.176	-2	123	16	1.4
1952	†NY A★	16	6	.727	31	31	13-4	0	223	174	78	12	6	91	127	2.78	119	.216	.300	69-10	.188	3	113	16	1.6
1953	†NY A	13	6	.684	28	26	7-4	1	181	150	74	11	1	55	76	3.33	111	.224	**.283**	63-5	.143	-2	135	9	0.5
1954	StL N	8	9	.471	30	29	6-2	0	179	182	99	24	0	71	73	4.73	87	.268	.335	64-3	.141	-2	105	-9	-0.9
1955	StL N	0	1	.000	1	1	0	0	1.2	5	4	0	0	1-1	1	21.60	19	.556	.545	0-0	—	0	88	-3	-0.5
	KC A	4	6	.400	20	18	1	0	101.1	132	66	10	1	35-4	38	5.42	77	.312	.364	33-3	.182	-0	80	-13	-1.1
Total	10	132	66	.667	269	255	106-26	3	1819	1666	828	138	26	727-5	944	3.72	105	.244	.319	608-63	.184	3	119	52	5.1

RASMUSSEN, DENNIS Dennis Lee B 4.18.1959 Los Angeles, CA BL/TL 6-7/230# d9.16 gf-Bill Brubaker

Year	Tm Lg	W	L	Pct	G	GS	CG-Sho	SV-BS	IP	H	R	HR	HB	BB-IB	SO	ERA	AERA	OAV	OOB	AB-SH	AVG	PB	Sup	APR	PW
1983	SD N	0	0	—	4	1	0	0-0	13.2	10	5	1	0	8-0	13	1.98	177	.200	.310	3-0	.000	-0	101	2	0.1
1984	NY A	9	6	.600	24	24	1	0-0	147.2	127	79	16	4	60-0	110	4.57	83	.234	.312	0-0	—	0	130	-12	-1.1
1985	NY A	3	5	.375	22	16	2	0-0	101.2	97	56	10	1	42-1	63	3.98	101	.255	.327	0-0	—	0	105	-2	-0.2
1986	NY A	18	6	.750	31	31	3-1	0-0	202	160	91	28	2	74-0	131	3.88	106	.217	.289	0-0	—	0	129	8	0.8
1987	NY A	9	7	.563	26	25	2	0-0	146	145	78	31	4	55-1	89	4.75	93	.260	.328	0-0	—	0	121	-3	-0.3
	Cin N	4	1	.800	7	7	0	0-0	45.1	39	22	5	1	12-0	39	3.97	107	.229	.283	15-0	.067	-1	119	1	0.1
1988	Cin N	2	6	.250	11	11	1-1	0-0	56.1	68	36	8	2	22-4	27	5.75	62	.300	.364	22-0	.227	1	90	-11	-1.4
	SD N	14	4	.778	20	20	6	0-0	148.1	131	48	9	2	36-0	85	2.55	133	.238	.286	48-6	.188	2	129	14	2.1
	Year	16	10	.615	31	31	7-1	0-0	204.2	199	53	17	4	58-4	112	3.43	101	.256	.309	70-6	.200	3	115	3	0.7
1989	SD N	10	10	.500	33	33	1	0-0	183.2	190	100	18	3	72-6	87	4.26	82	.270	.335	65-3	.169	1	99	-16	-1.5
1990	SD N	11	15	.423	32	32	3-1	0-0	187.2	217	110	28	3	62-4	86	4.51	85	.292	.348	62-6	.290	5*	110	-16	-1.5
1991	SD N	6	13	.316	24	24	1-1	0-0	146.2	155	74	12	2	49-3	75	3.74	102	.271	.328	44-3	.136	1*	83	-2	0.0
1992	Chi N	0	0	—	3	1	0	0-0	5	7	6	2	1	2-1	0	10.80	33	.350	.417	0-1	—	0	100	-4	-0.2
	KC A	4	1	.800	5	5	1-1	0-0	37.2	25	7	0	0	6-0	12	1.43	283	.197	.233	0-0	—	0	63	10	1.6
1993	KC A	1	2	.333	9	4	0	0-0	29	40	25	4	1	14-1	12	7.45	62	.328	.399	0-0	—	0	125	-8	-0.7
1995	KC A	0	1	.000	5	1	0	0-0	10	13	10	3	0	8-2	6	9.00	53	.302	.412	0-0	—	0	97	-4	-0.4
Total	12	91	77	.542	256	235	21-5	0-0	1460.2	1424	747	175	26	522-23	835	4.15	93	.257	.321	259-19	.193	8	111	-43	-2.6

RASMUSSEN, ERIC Eric Ralph (Born Harold Ralph Rasmussen) B 3.22.1952 Racine, WI BR/TR 6-3/205# d7.21

Year	Tm Lg	W	L	Pct	G	GS	CG-Sho	SV-BS	IP	H	R	HR	HB	BB-IB	SO	ERA	AERA	OAV	OOB	AB-SH	AVG	PB	Sup	APR	PW
1975	StL N	5	5	.500	14	13	2-1	0-0	81	86	44	8	0	20-2	59	3.78	100	.264	.306	26-1	.154	-0	90	-1	-0.2
1976	StL N	6	12	.333	43	17	2-1	0-2	150.1	139	67	10	2	54-6	76	3.53	100	.247	.313	38-4	.105	-1	92	1	0.1
1977	StL N	11	17	.393	34	34	11-3	0-0	233	223	103	24	5	63-7	120	3.48	111	.254	.305	72-6	.139	0	84	9	1.0
1978	StL N	2	5	.286	10	10	2-1	0-0	60.1	61	32	4	0	20-2	32	4.18	84	.270	.324	18-2	.111	-1	59	-4	-0.6
	SD N	12	10	.545	27	24	3-2	0-0	146.1	154	72	16	1	43-6	59	4.06	82	.277	.327	46-8	.152	-1	102	-11	-1.6
	Year	14	15	.483	37	34	5-3	0-0	206.2	215	76	20	1	63-8	91	4.09	83	.275	.326	64-10	.141	-2	89	-18	-2.2
1979	SD N	6	9	.400	45	20	5-3	3-2	156.2	142	59	9	0	42-6	54	3.27	108	.244	.292	36-6	.056	-2*	93	8	0.5
1980	SD N	4	11	.267	40	14	0	1-3	111.1	130	60	9	3	33-6	50	4.37	79	.295	.347	21-6	.095	-1	78	-12	-1.6
1982	StL N	1	2	.333	8	3	0	0-0	18.1	21	13	2	0	8-4	15	4.42	82	.288	.354	3-1	.000	-0	49	-3	-0.4
1983	StL N	0	0	—	6	0	0	1-0	7.2	16	11	1	0	4-2	6	11.74	31	.444	.500	0-0	—	0		-7	-0.3
	KC A	3	6	.333	11	9	2-1	0-0	52.2	61	28	4	0	22-0	18	4.78	85	.289	.355	0-0	—	0	77	-2	-0.4
Total	8	50	77	.394	238	144	27-12	5-7	1017.2	1033	489	87	11	309-41	489	3.85	94	.266	.319	260-34	.119	-5	86	-22	-3.5

RASMUSSEN, HANS Henry Florian B 4.18.1895 Chicago, IL D 1.1.1949 Chicago, IL BR/TR 6-6/220# d8.11

Year	Tm Lg	W	L	Pct	G	GS	CG-Sho	SV-BS	IP	H	R	HR	HB	BB-IB	SO	ERA	AERA	OAV	OOB	AB-SH	AVG	PB	Sup	APR	PW
1915	Chi F	0	0	—	2	0	0	0	2	3	3	0	0	2	2	13.50	19	.600	.714	1-0	.000	-0		-2	-0.1

RATH, GARY Alfred Gary B 1.10.1973 Gulfport, MS BL/TL 6-2/185# d6.2

Year	Tm Lg	W	L	Pct	G	GS	CG-Sho	SV-BS	IP	H	R	HR	HB	BB-IB	SO	ERA	AERA	OAV	OOB	AB-SH	AVG	PB	Sup	APR	PW
1998	LA N	0	0	—	3	0	0	0-0	3.1	3	4	1	0	2-0	4	10.80	37	.250	.357	0-0	—	0		-2	-0.1
1999	Min A	0	1	.000	5	1	0	0-0	4.2	6	6	1	0	5-0	1	11.57	44	.300	.440	0-0	—	0	91	-3	-0.5
Total	2	0	1	.000	8	1	0	0-0	8	9	10	2	0	7-0	5	11.25	41	.281	.410	0-0	—	0	91	-5	-0.6

RATH, FRED Frederick Helsher Jr. B 1.5.1973 Dallas, TX BR/TR 6-3/220# d7.29 f-Fred

Year	Tm Lg	W	L	Pct	G	GS	CG-Sho	SV-BS	IP	H	R	HR	HB	BB-IB	SO	ERA	AERA	OAV	OOB	AB-SH	AVG	PB	Sup	APR	PW
1998	Col N	0	0	—	2	0	0	0-0	5.1	6	1	0	0	2-0	2	1.69	306	.300	.348	2-0	.000	-0		2	0.1

RATH, FRED Frederick Helsher Sr. B 9.1.1943 Little Rock, AR BR/TR 6-3/200# d9.10 s-Fred

Year	Tm Lg	W	L	Pct	G	GS	CG-Sho	SV-BS	IP	H	R	HR	HB	BB-IB	SO	ERA	AERA	OAV	OOB	AB-SH	AVG	PB	Sup	APR	PW
1968	Chi A	0	0	—	5	0	0	0	11.1	8	5	0	1	3-1	3	1.59	191	.182	.250	0-0	—	0		1	0.0
1969	Chi A	0	2	.000	3	2	0	0-0	11.2	11	10	4	0	8-1	4	7.71	50	.256	.373	3-0	.000	-0	34	-4	-0.6
Total	2	0	2	.000	8	2	0	0-0	23	19	15	4	1	11-2	7	4.70	73	.218	.313	3-0	.000	-0	34	-3	-0.6

RATLIFF, JON Jon Charles B 12.22.1971 Syracuse, NY BR/TR 6-4/195# d9.15

Year	Tm Lg	W	L	Pct	G	GS	CG-Sho	SV-BS	IP	H	R	HR	HB	BB-IB	SO	ERA	AERA	OAV	OOB	AB-SH	AVG	PB	Sup	APR	PW
2000	Oak A	0	0	—	1	0	0	0-0	1	0	0	0	0	0-0	0	0.00	—	.000	.000	0-0	—	0		1	0.0

RATZER, STEVE Steven Wayne B 9.9.1953 Paterson, NJ BR/TR 6-1/192# d10.5

Year	Tm Lg	W	L	Pct	G	GS	CG-Sho	SV-BS	IP	H	R	HR	HB	BB-IB	SO	ERA	AERA	OAV	OOB	AB-SH	AVG	PB	Sup	APR	PW
1980	Mon N	0	0	—	1	1	0	0-0	4	9	5	0	0	2-0	0	11.25	32	.450	.500	1-0	.000	-0	200	-3	-0.2
1981	Mon N	1	1	.500	12	0	0	0-0	17.1	23	14	2	0	7-1	4	6.23	56	.311	.370	2-0	.000	-0		-6	-0.6
Total	2	1	1	.500	13	1	0	0-0	21.1	32	19	2	0	9-1	4	7.17	49	.340	.398	3-0	.000	-0	200	-9	-0.8

RAU, DOUG Douglas James B 12.15.1948 Columbus, TX BL/TL 6-2/175# d9.2

Year	Tm Lg	W	L	Pct	G	GS	CG-Sho	SV-BS	IP	H	R	HR	HB	BB-IB	SO	ERA	AERA	OAV	OOB	AB-SH	AVG	PB	Sup	APR	PW
1972	LA N	2	2	.500	7	3	2	0-0	32.2	18	11	1	1	11-2	19	2.20	151	.159	.236	7-1	.143	1	62	4	0.6
1973	LA N	4	2	.667	31	3	0	3-1	63.2	64	28	5	1	28-2	51	3.96	87	.259	.336	11-2	.091	-1	34	-2	-0.3
1974	†LA N	13	11	.542	36	35	3-1	0-0	198.1	191	90	20	4	70-1	126	3.72	92	.251	.316	64-8	.141	-1	124	-5	-0.6
1975	LA N	15	9	.625	38	38	8-2	0-0	257.2	227	96	18	3	61-1	151	3.11	110	.236	.282	87-10	.195	2	116	11	1.2
1976	LA N	16	12	.571	34	32	8-3	0-0	231	221	71	18	7	69-1	98	2.57	132	.258	.317	60-8	.150	1	85	22	2.8
1977	†LA N	14	8	.636	32	32	4-2	0-0	212.1	232	87	15	6	49-2	126	3.43	112	.282	.325	71-3	.141	-0	99	11	0.9
1978	†LA N	15	9	.625	30	30	7-2	0-0	199	219	82	17	2	68-5	95	3.26	108	.284	.342	63-13	.143	-1	122	6	0.5
1979	LA N	1	5	.167	11	11	1-1	0-0	56	73	37	3	4	22-0	28	5.30	69	.320	.384	14-1	.143	1	88	-10	-0.9
1981	Cal A	1	2	.333	3	3	0	0-0	10.1	14	10	2	0	4-0	3	8.71	42	.341	.400	0-0	—	0	90	-5	-0.9
Total	9	81	60	.574	222	187	33-11	3-1	1261	1259	512	99	28	382-14	697	3.35	105	.262	.318	377-46	.154	2	106	32	3.3

Year	Tm Lg	W	L	Pct	G	GS	CG-Sho	SV-BS	IP	H	R	HR	HB	BB-IB	SO	ERA	AERA	OAV	OOB	AB-SH	AVG	PB	Sup	APR	PW
RAUCH, JON Jon Erich B 9.27.1978 Louisville, KY BR/TR 6-10/230# d4.2																									
2002	Chi A	2	1	.667	8	6	0	0-0	28.2	28	26	7	2	14-2	19	6.59	68	.248	.338	0-0	—	0	151	-8	-0.7
RAUCH, BOB Robert John B 6.16.1949 Brookings, SD BR/TR 6-4/200# d6.29																									
1972	NY N	0	1	.000	19	0	0	1-0	27	27	16	3	0	21-2	23	5.00	67	.273	.393	3-0	.000	-0		-5	-0.3
RAUTZHAN, LANCE Clarence George B 8.20.1952 Pottsville, PA BR/TL 6-1/195# d7.23																									
1977	†LA N	4	1	.800	25	0	0	2-4	20.2	25	10	0	0	7-1	13	4.35	88	.313	.364	1-0	.000	-0		-1	-0.2
1978	†LA N	2	1	.667	43	0	0	4-2	61.1	61	22	1	1	19-3	25	2.93	120	.263	.318	4-2	.000	-0		4	0.3
1979	LA N	0	2	.000	12	0	0	1-2	9.2	9	9	0	1	11-2	5	7.45	49	.273	.447	0-0	—	0		-4	-0.8
	Mil A	0	0	—	3	0	0	0-0	3	3	3	0	0	10-0	2	9.00	46	.300	.650	0-0	—	0		-1	-0.1
Total	3	6	4	.600	83	0	0	7-8	94.2	98	44	1	2	47-6	45	3.90	93	.276	.359	5-2	.000	-1		-2	-0.8
RAWLEY, SHANE Shane William B 7.27.1955 Racine, WI BR/TL 6/180# d4.6																									
1978	Sea A	4	9	.308	52	2	0	4-1	111.1	114	57	7	5	51-3	66	4.12	93	.275	.356	0-0	—	0*	71	-4	-0.4
1979	Sea A	5	9	.357	48	3	0	11-5	84.1	88	40	2	1	40-5	48	3.84	114	.278	.357	0-0	—	0*	124	5	0.9
1980	Sea A	7	7	.500	59	0	0	13-9	113.2	103	44	3	3	63-16	68	3.33	125	.257	.360	0-0	—	0		11	1.7
1981	Sea A	4	6	.400	46	0	0	8-7	68.1	64	31	1	1	38-6	35	3.95	98	.257	.354	0-0	—	0		0	0.1
1982	NY A	11	10	.524	47	17	3	3-1	164	165	79	10	2	54-5	111	4.06	98	.267	.324	0-0	—	0	98	0	0.1
1983	NY A	14	14	.500	34	33	13-2	1-0	238.1	246	111	19	3	79-1	124	3.78	103	.269	.327	0-0	—	0	97	4	0.4
1984	NY A	2	3	.400	11	10	0	0-0	42	46	33	0	0	27-0	24	6.21	61	.272	.372	0-0	—	0	79	-12	-1.3
	Phi N	10	6	.625	18	18	3	0-0	120.1	117	55	13	1	27-2	58	3.81	95	.257	.298	43-0	.116	-2*	103	0	-0.2
1985	Phi N	13	8	.619	36	31	6-2	0-0	198.2	188	82	16	2	81-6	106	3.31	112	.249	.321	58-7	.138	0	110	9	1.0
1986	Phi N☆	11	7	.611	23	23	7-1	0-0	157.2	166	67	13	1	50-4	73	3.54	109	.270	.325	52-10	.173	0	131	7	0.8
1987	Phi N	17	11	.607	36	**36**	4-1	0-0	229.2	250	118	23	5	86-8	123	4.39	97	.279	.343	79-12	.152	-0*	105	-1	-0.1
1988	Phi N	8	16	.333	32	32	4-1	0-0	198	220	111	27	4	78-7	87	4.18	85	.286	.351	57-11	.105	-1	96	-17	-2.1
1989	Min A	5	12	.294	27	25	1	0-0	145	167	89	19	0	60-1	68	5.21	80	.293	.359	0-0	—	0	85	-15	-1.6
Total	12	111	118	.485	469	230	41-7	40-23	1871.1	1934	917	153	28	734-64	991	4.02	98	.271	.338	289-40	.138	-3	101	-13	-0.7
RAY, CARL Carl Grady B 1.31.1889 Danbury, NC D 4.2.1970 Lexington, NC BL/TL 5-11/170# d9.25																									
1915	Phi A	0	1	.000	2	1	0	0	7.1	11	7	0	4	6	6	4.91	60	.333	.488	2-0	.000	0	25	-2	-0.3
1916	Phi A	0	1	.000	3	1	0	0	9.1	9	8	0	1	14	5	4.82	59	.257	.480	3-0	.000	-0	53	-3	-0.3
Total	2	0	2	.000	5	2	0	0	16.2	20	15	0	5	20	11	4.86	59	.294	.484	5-0	.000	-0	39	-5	-0.6
RAY, JIM James Francis "Sting" B 12.1.1944 Rock Hill, SC BR/TR 6-1/195# d9.16																									
1965	Hou N	0	2	.000	3	2	0	0	7.2	11	9	1	0	6-0	7	10.57	32	.355	.447	2-0	.000	-0	117	-6	-1.0
1966	Hou N	0	0	—	1	0	0	0	0	0	1	0	0	1-0	0	o	—	—	1.000	0-0	—	0		-1	-0.1
1968	Hou N	2	3	.400	41	2	1	1	80.2	65	26	5	1	25-8	71	2.68	110	.220	.278	15-1	.067	-1*	103	3	0.0
1969	Hou N	8	2	.800	40	13	0	0-0	115	105	55	11	2	48-4	115	3.91	91	.245	.322	26-3	.115	-1	92	-3	-0.4
1970	Hou N	6	3	.667	52	2	0	5-1	105	97	39	13	0	49-2	67	3.26	119	.251	.333	27-0	.185	-0	69	9	0.8
1971	Hou N	10	4	.714	47	1	0	3-1	97.2	72	27	3	2	31-5	46	2.12	159	.211	.277	18-0	.167	0	79	13	1.9
1972	Hou N	10	9	.526	54	0	0	8-9	90.1	77	50	10	3	44-6	50	4.28	79	.227	.319	16-1	.063	-1		-11	-2.5
1973	Hou N	6	4	.600	42	0	0	6-3	69	65	37	5	3	38-8	25	4.43	82	.253	.355	13-2	.231	0		-6	-0.9
1974	Det A	1	3	.250	28	0	0	2-1	52.1	49	27	4	1	29-4	26	4.47	85	.254	.350	0-0	—	0		-3	-0.2
Total	9	43	30	.589	308	20	1	25-15	617.2	541	271	52	12	271-37	407	3.61	97	.238	.320	117-7	.137	-3	92	-5	-2.4
RAY, KEN Kenneth Alan B 11.27.1974 Atlanta, GA BR/TR 6-2/200# d7.10																									
1999	KC A	1	0	1.000	13	0	0	0-0	11.1	23	12	2	1	6-0	0	8.74	57	.460	.526	0-0	—	0		-5	-0.3
RAY, FARMER Robert Henry B 9.17.1886 Ft.Lyon, CO D 3.11.1963 Electra, TX BL/TR 5-11/160# d6.13																									
1910	StL A	4	10	.286	21	16	11	0	140.2	146	77	3	7	49	35	3.58	69	.285	.356	40-3	.175	0	73	-14	-1.5
RAYDON, CURT Curtis Lowell B 11.18.1933 Bloomington, IL BR/TR 6-4/190# d4.15																									
1958	Pit N	8	4	.667	31	20	2-1	1	134.1	118	64	18	5	61-4	85	3.62	107	.236	.323	38-4	.026	-2	120	2	-0.2
RAYMOND, BUGS Arthur Lawrence B 2.24.1882 Chicago, IL D 9.7.1912 Chicago, IL BR/TR 5-10/180# d9.23																									
1904	Det A	0	1	.000	5	2	1	0	14.2	14	9	0	2	6	7	3.07	83	.250	.344	5-0	.000	-1	14	-2	-0.1
1907	StL N	2	4	.333	8	6	6-1	0	64.2	56	34	3	1	21	34	1.67	150	.230	.294	22-0	.091	-0	81	1	0.0
1908	StL N	15	25	.375	48	37	23-5	2	324.1	236	116	2	14	95	145	2.03	116	.207	.277	90-3	.189	1	61	11	1.8
1909	NY N	18	12	.600	39	30	18-2	0	270	239	98	7	6	87	121	2.47	104	.245	.311	89-5	.146	0	90	7	0.9
1910	NY N	4	11	.267	19	11	6	0	99.1	106	63	2	8	40	55	3.81	78	.280	.362	32-1	.156	-1	78	-12	-1.5
1911	NY N	6	4	.600	17	9	4-1	0	81.2	73	40	1	2	33	39	3.31	102	.248	.328	25-3	.200	-0	104	0	0.0
Total	6	45	57	.441	136	95	58-9	2	854.2	724	360	15	33	282	401	2.49	105	.235	.306	263-12	.160	-0	78	5	1.1
RAYMOND, HARRY Harry H. "Jack" B 2.20.1862 Utica, NY D 3.21.1925 San Diego, CA 5-9/179# d9.9.1888 ▲																									
1889	Lou AA	1	0	1.000	1	1	1	0	9	8	2	0	0	11	1	1.00	385	.229	.413	515	.239	0*	97	3	0.2
RAYMOND, CLAUDE Joseph Claude Marc "Frenchy" B 5.7.1937 St.Jean, PQ, CAN BR/TR 5-10/175# d4.15 C1																									
1959	Chi A	0	0	—	3	0	0	0	4	5	4	2	0	2-0	1	9.00	42	.333	.389	0-0	—	0		-2	-0.1
1961	Mil N	1	0	1.000	13	0	0	2	20.1	22	9	2	1	9-1	13	3.98	94	.275	.356	3-0	.000	-0		0	0.0
1962	Mil N	5	5	.500	26	0	0	10	42.2	37	15	5	2	15-2	40	2.74	138	.236	.309	8-1	.000	-1		5	0.9
1963	Mil N	4	6	.400	45	0	0	5	53.1	57	36	12	4	27-4	44	5.40	60	.268	.361	4-0	.500	2		-13	-2.3
1964	Hou N	5	5	.500	38	0	0	0	79.2	64	28	3	3	22-1	56	2.82	121	.229	.289	14-2	.071	-0*		6	0.7
1965	Hou N	7	4	.636	33	7	2	5	96.1	87	35	6	5	16-2	79	2.90	116	.244	.285	26-0	.115	-1*	97	5	0.6
1966	Hou N☆	7	5	.583	62	0	0	16	92	85	39	10	4	25-6	73	3.13	109	.242	.298	9-1	.111	-0		2	0.2
1967	Hou N	0	4	.000	21	0	0	5	31	31	12	5	2	7-4	17	3.19	104	.256	.305	5-0	.200	0		1	0.1
	Atl N	4	1	.800	28	0	0	5	34.1	33	11	2	0	11-5	14	2.62	127	.260	.314	2-0	.000	-0		3	0.5
	Year	4	5	.444	49	0	0	10	65.1	64	27	7	2	18-9	31	2.89	115	.258	.310	7-0	.143	0		4	0.6
1968	Atl N	3	5	.375	36	0	0	10	60.1	56	21	4	1	18-9	37	2.83	106	.256	.313	7-0	.143	-0		1	0.3
1969	Atl N	2	2	.500	33	0	0	1-1	48	56	34	4	2	13-2	15	5.25	69	.298	.346	7-1	.286	0		-10	-0.8
	Mon N	1	2	.333	15	0	0	1-1	22	21	12	2	2	8-3	11	4.09	90	.256	.333	4-0	.000	-0		-1	-0.2
	Year	3	4	.429	48	0	0	2-2	70	77	46	6	4	21-5	26	4.89	74	.285	.342	11-1	.182	-0		-11	-1.0
1970	Mon N	6	7	.462	59	0	0	23-6	83.1	76	48	13	2	27-7	68	4.43	93	.240	.300	11-2	.000	-1		-4	-0.9
1971	Mon N	1	7	.125	37	0	0	0-1	53.2	81	34	5	0	25-8	29	4.70	75	.373	.433	1-1	.000	-0		-8	-1.1
Total	12	46	53	.465	449	7	2	83-9	721	711	338	75	28	225-54	497	3.66	96	.261	.321	101-8	.109	-2	97	-15	-2.1
RAZIANO, BARRY Barry John B 2.5.1947 New Orleans, LA BB/TR 5-10/175# d8.18																									
1973	KC A	0	0	—	2	0	0	0-0	5	6	3	1	1	1-1	0	5.40	76	.316	.381	0-0	—	0		-1	0.0
1974	Cal A	1	2	.333	13	0	0	1-2	16.2	15	14	1	0	8-1	9	6.48	53	.246	.333	0-0	—	0		-6	-1.1
Total	2	1	2	.333	15	0	0	1-2	21.2	21	17	2	1	9-2	9	6.23	58	.262	.344	0-0	—	0		-7	-1.1
REAGAN, RIP Arthur (b: Arthur Edgar Ragan) B 6.5.1878 Lincoln, IL D 6.8.1953 Kansas City, MO BR/TR 5-11/170# d9.19																									
1903	Cin N	0	2	.000	3	2	2	0	18	40	30	0	1	7	7	6.00	59	.455	.500	8-0	.250	0	161	-8	-0.7
REAMES, BRITT William Britt B 8.19.1973 Seneca, SC BR/TR 5-11/175# d8.20																									
2000	†StL N	2	1	.667	8	7	0	0-0	40.2	30	17	4	1	23-1	31	2.88	160	.207	.318	12-1	.167	-0*	77	7	0.4
2001	Mon N	4	8	.333	41	13	0	0-1	95	101	68	16	5	48-3	86	5.59	80	.273	.362	17-3	.118	1	72	-13	-1.2
2002	Mon N	1	4	.200	42	6	0	0-1	68	70	42	8	3	38-6	76	5.03	89	.266	.364	9-2	.111	-0	76	-4	-0.3
2003	Mon N	0	0	—	2	0	0	0-0	1.1	4	4	0	0	2-0	1	27.00	17	.500	.600	1-0	.000	-0		-3	-0.1
Total	4	7	13	.350	93	26	0	0-2	205	205	131	28	9	111-10	194	5.00	90	.261	.357	39-6	.128	1	74	-13	-1.2
REARDON, JEFF Jeffrey James B 10.1.1955 Dalton, MA BR/TR 6-1/195# d8.25																									
1979	NY N	1	2	.333	18	0	0	2-0	20.2	12	7	2	0	9-3	10	1.74	209	.174	.266	0-0	—	0		3	0.5
1980	NY N	8	7	.533	61	0	0	6-4	110.1	96	36	10	0	47-15	101	2.61	136	.231	.306	8-0	.000	-1		12	1.5
1981	NY N	1	0	1.000	18	0	0	2-0	28.2	27	11	2	1	12-4	28	3.45	101	.245	.323	1-0	.000	-0		1	0.0
	†Mon N	2	0	1.000	25	0	0	6-1	41.2	21	6	3	1	9-0	21	1.30	270	.148	.204	4-2	.000	-0		10	0.7

Year	Tm Lg	W	L	Pct	G	GS	CG-Sho	SV-BS	IP	H	R	HR	HB	BB-IB	SO	ERA	AERA	OAV	OOB	AB-SH	AVG	PB	Sup	APR	PW
	Year	3	0	1.000	43	0	0	8-1	70.1	48	21	5	2	21-4	49	2.18	160	.190	.257	5-2	.000	-1		12	0.7
1982	Mon N	7	4	.636	75	0	0	26-8	109	87	28	6	2	36-4	86	2.06	177	.221	.287	10-1	.100	-0		19	2.7
1983	Mon N	7	9	.438	66	0	0	21-8	92	87	34	7	1	44-9	78	3.03	119	.250	.334	8-0	.125	-0		6	1.1
1984	Mon N	7	7	.500	68	0	0	23-3	87	70	31	5	3	37-7	79	2.90	118	.220	.306	9-0	.000	-1		5	0.9
1985	Mon N★	2	8	.200	63	0	0	**41-9**	87.2	68	31	7	1	26-4	67	3.18	107	.209	.269	7-2	.286	0		4	0.8
1986	Mon N☆	7	9	.438	62	0	0	35-13	89	83	42	12	1	26-2	67	3.94	94	.251	.306	8-1	.125	-0		-2	-0.4
1987	†Min A	8	8	.500	63	0	0	31-10	80.1	70	41	14	3	28-4	83	4.48	103	.232	.301	0-0	—	0		2	0.4
1988	Min A☆	2	4	.333	63	0	0	42-8	73	68	21	6	2	15-2	56	2.47	165	.245	.288	0-0	—	0		13	2.3
1989	Min A	5	4	.556	65	0	0	31-11	73	68	33	8	3	12-3	46	4.07	102	.246	.280	0-0	—	0		2	0.2
1990	†Bos A	5	3	.625	47	0	0	21-7	51.1	39	19	5	1	19-4	33	3.16	129	.206	.282	0-0	—	0		6	1.1
1991	Bos A★	1	4	.200	57	0	0	40-9	59.1	54	21	9	1	16-3	44	3.03	142	.236	.286	0-0	—	0		8	1.5
1992	Bos A	2	2	.500	46	0	0	27-8	42.1	53	20	6	1	7-0	32	4.25	99	.308	.335	0-0	—	0		1	0.2
	†Atl N	3	0	1.000	14	0	0	3-2	15.2	14	2	0	1	2-1	7	1.15	319	.241	.279	0-0	—	0		4	0.9
1993	Cin N	4	6	.400	58	0	0	8-4	61.2	66	34	4	5	10-0	35	4.09	99	.270	.308	2-1	.000	-0		-2	-0.4
1994	NY A	1	0	1.000	11	0	0	2-1	9.2	17	9	3	0	3-0	4	8.38	55	.386	.426	0-0	—	0		-4	-0.5
Total	16	73	77	.487	880	0	0	367-106	1132.1	1000	426	109	27	358-65	877	3.16	121	.236	.297	57-7	.088	-3		88	13.5

REARDON, JEREMIAH Jeremiah J. B 9.1868 D 4.22.1907 St.Louis, MO d7.17

Year	Tm Lg	W	L	Pct	G	GS	CG-Sho	SV-BS	IP	H	R	HR	HB	BB-IB	SO	ERA	AERA	OAV	OOB	AB-SH	AVG	PB	Sup	APR	PW
1886	StL N	0	1	.000	1	1	1	0	8	10	8	1		5	0	6.75	48	.323	.417	4	.250	0	57	-2	-0.2
	Cin AA	0	1	.000	1	1	0	0	2	5	4	0	0	4	0	18.00	20	.500	.643	3	.000	-1	67	-3	-0.4
Total	1	0	2	.000	2	2	1	0	10	15	12	1	0	9	0	9.00	36	.366	.480	7	.143	-1	65	-5	-0.6

REBERGER, FRANK Frank Beall "Crane" B 6.7.1944 Caldwell, ID BL/TR 6-5/200# d6.6 C3

Year	Tm Lg	W	L	Pct	G	GS	CG-Sho	SV-BS	IP	H	R	HR	HB	BB-IB	SO	ERA	AERA	OAV	OOB	AB-SH	AVG	PB	Sup	APR	PW
1968	Chi N	0	1	.000	3	1	0	0	6	9	4	1	0	2-0	3	4.50	70	.346	.393	0-0	—	0	219	-1	-0.1
1969	SD N	1	2	.333	67	0	0	6-2	87.2	83	38	6	2	41-8	65	3.59	99	.258	.342	5-0	.200	0		0	0.1
1970	SF N	7	8	.467	45	18	3	2-1	152	178	108	13	7	98-6	117	5.57	72	.293	.395	47-3	.234	1*	129	-28	-2.4
1971	SF N	3	0	1.000	13	7	0	0-0	43.2	37	20	5	2	19-0	21	3.92	87	.228	.315	13-0	.231	0*	153	-1	0.0
1972	SF N	3	4	.429	20	11	2	0-0	99.1	97	49	10	5	37-2	52	3.99	87	.257	.329	35-0	.229	2*	118	-5	-0.1
Total	5	14	15	.483	148	37	5	8-3	388.2	404	219	35	16	197-16	258	4.52	81	.270	.359	100-3	.230	4	133	-35	-2.5

RECCIUS, JOHN John B 10.29.1859 Louisville, KY D 9.1.1930 Louisville, KY 5-6.5/?# d5.2 b-Phil ▲

Year	Tm Lg	W	L	Pct	G	GS	CG-Sho	SV-BS	IP	H	R	HR	HB	BB-IB	SO	ERA	AERA	OAV	OOB	AB-SH	AVG	PB	Sup	APR	PW
1882	Lou AA	4	6	.400	13	10	9-1	0	95	106	70	3		22	31	3.03	82	.264	.303	266	.237	3*	133	-6	-0.3
1883	Lou AA	0	0	—	1	0	0	0	4	10	3	0		0	0	2.25	133	.455	.455	63	.143	-0*		0	0.0
Total	2	4	6	.400	14	10	9-1	0	99	116	73	3		22	31	3.00	83	.274	.310	329	.219	3	133	-6	-0.3

RECCIUS, PHIL Phillip B 6.7.1862 Louisville, KY D 2.15.1903 Louisville, KY 5-9/163# d9.25.1882 b-John ▲

Year	Tm Lg	W	L	Pct	G	GS	CG-Sho	SV-BS	IP	H	R	HR	HB	BB-IB	SO	ERA	AERA	OAV	OOB	AB-SH	AVG	PB	Sup	APR	PW
1884	Lou AA	6	7	.462	18	11	11	0	129.1	118	80	2	4	19	46	2.71	114	.228	.261	263	.240	2*	64	2	0.4
1885	Lou AA	0	4	.000	7	5	4	1	40	46	35	0	1	11	10	3.82	84	.253	.299	402	.241	1*	88	-3	-0.2
1886	Lou AA	0	1	.000	1	1	0	0	3	7	6	0	0	3	0	9.00	40	.467	.556	13	.308	0*	82	-2	-0.3
1887	Cle AA	0	0	—	1	0	0	0	7	8	7	0	0	5	0	7.71	56	.320	.433	229	.205	-0*		-2	-0.1
Total	4	6	12	.333	27	17	15	1	179.1	179	128	2	5	38	56	3.26	97	.242	.284	907	.233	4	73	-5	-0.2

REDDING, PHIL Philip Hayden B 1.28.1889 Crystal Springs, MS D 3.31.1928 Greenwood, MS BL/TR 5-11.5/190# d9.14

Year	Tm Lg	W	L	Pct	G	GS	CG-Sho	SV-BS	IP	H	R	HR	HB	BB-IB	SO	ERA	AERA	OAV	OOB	AB-SH	AVG	PB	Sup	APR	PW
1912	StL N	2	1	.667	3	3	2	0	25.1	31	17	2	0	11	9	4.97	69	.313	.382	8-1	.000	-1	100	-3	-0.4
1913	StL N	0	0	—	1	0	0	0	2.2	2	2	0	0	1	1	6.75	48	.286	.375	1-0	.000	-0		-1	-0.1
Total	2	2	1	.667	4	3	2	0	28	33	19	2	0	12	10	5.14	66	.311	.381	9-1	.000	-1	100	-4	-0.5

REDDING, TIM Timothy J. B 2.12.1978 Rochester, NY BR/TR 6/180# d6.24

Year	Tm Lg	W	L	Pct	G	GS	CG-Sho	SV-BS	IP	H	R	HR	HB	BB-IB	SO	ERA	AERA	OAV	OOB	AB-SH	AVG	PB	Sup	APR	PW
2001	Hou N	3	1	.750	13	9	0	0-0	55.2	62	38	11	3	24-0	55	5.50	83	.286	.360	14-2	.214	0	117	-6	-0.4
2002	Hou N	3	6	.333	18	14	0	0-0	73.1	78	49	10	0	35-3	63	5.40	79	.276	.352	20-1	.100	-1	113	-9	-1.1
2003	Hou N	10	14	.417	33	32	0	0-0	176	179	85	16	7	65-4	116	3.68	121	.261	.329	50-8	.200	2	79	11	1.6
Total	3	16	21	.432	64	55	0	0-0	305	319	172	37	10	124-7	234	4.43	100	.269	.341	84-11	.179	0	94	-4	0.1

REDFERN, PETE Peter Irvine B 8.25.1954 Glendale, CA BR/TR 6-2/195# d5.15

Year	Tm Lg	W	L	Pct	G	GS	CG-Sho	SV-BS	IP	H	R	HR	HB	BB-IB	SO	ERA	AERA	OAV	OOB	AB-SH	AVG	PB	Sup	APR	PW
1976	Min A	8	8	.500	23	23	1-1	0-0	118	105	61	6	3	63-1	74	3.51	102	.241	.339	0-0	—	0	141	-2	-0.3
1977	Min A	6	9	.400	30	28	1	0-0	137.1	164	89	13	4	66-2	73	5.18	77	.304	.382	0-0	—	0	122	-19	-1.8
1978	Min A	0	2	.000	3	2	0	0-0	9.2	10	12	2	0	6-0	4	6.52	59	.294	.381	0-0	—	0	94	-5	-0.8
1979	Min A	7	3	.700	40	6	0	1-2	108.1	106	45	8	1	35-0	85	3.49	126	.258	.315	0-0	—	0*	141	11	0.9
1980	Min A	7	7	.500	23	16	2	2-1	104.2	117	58	11	0	33-3	73	4.56	96	.283	.333	0-0	—	0	82	-1	-0.2
1981	Min A	9	8	.529	24	23	3	0-1	141.2	140	70	12	2	52-1	77	4.07	97	.261	.326	0-0	—	0	86	-1	-0.2
1982	Min A	5	11	.313	27	13	2	0-1	94.1	122	74	16	1	51-3	40	6.58	65	.322	.401	0-0	—	0	81	-23	-3.3
Total	7	42	48	.467	170	111	9-1	3-5	714	764	409	68	11	306-10	426	4.54	90	.278	.350	0-0	—	0	106	-40	-5.7

REDMAN, MARK Mark Allen B 1.5.1974 San Diego, CA BL/TL 6-5/220# d7.24

Year	Tm Lg	W	L	Pct	G	GS	CG-Sho	SV-BS	IP	H	R	HR	HB	BB-IB	SO	ERA	AERA	OAV	OOB	AB-SH	AVG	PB	Sup	APR	PW
1999	Min A	1	0	1.000	5	1	0	0-0	12.2	17	13	3	1	7-0	11	8.53	60	.298	.385	0-0	—	0	183	-5	-0.3
2000	Min A	12	9	.571	32	24	0	0-0	151.1	168	81	22	3	45-0	117	4.76	109	.281	.333	4-1	.000	-0	86	9	0.9
2001	Min A	2	4	.333	9	9	0	0-0	49	57	26	6	0	19-0	29	4.22	109	.286	.349	0-0	—	0	80	1	0.2
	Det A	0	2	.000	2	2	0	0-0	9	11	6	1	1	4-0	4	6.00	72	.306	.390	0-0	—	0	43	-1	-0.3
	Year	2	6	.250	11	11	0	0-0	58	68	8	7	1	23-0	33	4.50	101	.289	.355	0-0	—	0	74	0	-0.1
2002	Det A	8	15	.348	30	30	3	0-0	203	211	107	15	6	51-2	109	4.21	102	.268	.314	5-0	.200	0	68	2	0.1
2003	†Fla N	14	9	.609	29	29	3	0-0	190.2	172	82	16	5	61-3	151	3.59	114	.239	.301	61-4	.016	-6	112	11	0.5
Total	5	37	39	.487	107	95	6	0-0	615.2	636	315	63	16	187-5	421	4.27	105	.265	.321	70-5	.029	-6	88	17	1.1

REED, HOWIE Howard Dean "Diz" B 12.21.1936 Dallas, TX D 12.7.1984 Corpus Christi, TX BR/TR 6-1/210# d9.13

Year	Tm Lg	W	L	Pct	G	GS	CG-Sho	SV-BS	IP	H	R	HR	HB	BB-IB	SO	ERA	AERA	OAV	OOB	AB-SH	AVG	PB	Sup	APR	PW
1958	KC A	1	0	1.000	3	1	1	0	10.1	5	1	0	0	4-0	5	0.87	449	.132	.214	2-1	.000	0	46	3	0.3
1959	KC A	0	3	.000	6	3	0	0	20.2	26	19	3	0	10-0	11	7.40	54	.313	.379	3-0	.000	-0	66	-7	-0.9
1960	KC A	0	0	—	1	0	0	0	1.2	2	1	1	0	0-0	1	0.00	—	.286	.286	0-0	—	0		0	0.0
1964	LA N	3	4	.429	26	7	0	1	90	79	34	4	0	36-9	52	3.20	101	.236	.309	20-0	.100	-0	81	2	0.2
1965	†LA N	7	5	.583	38	5	0	1	78	73	31	6	3	27-6	47	3.12	105	.243	.311	12-0	.000	0	86	1	0.2
1966	LA N	0	0	—	1	0	0	0	1.2	1	0	0	0	0-0	0	0.00	—	.167	.167	1-0	.000	-0		1	0.0
	Cal A	0	1	.000	19	1	0	1	43	39	14	5	0	15-2	17	2.93	115	.247	.307	6-0	.000	-1	26	3	0.1
1967	Hou N	1	1	.500	4	2	0	0	18.1	19	8	0	0	2-0	9	3.44	96	.268	.288	4-0	.000	-0	80	0	-0.1
1969	Mon N	6	7	.462	31	15	2-1	1-0	106	119	59	7	2	50-7	59	4.84	76	.290	.365	32-3	.125	1	93	-10	-1.0
1970	Mon N	6	5	.545	57	1	0	5-1	89	81	34	7	2	40-5	42	3.13	131	.252	.336	10-1	.000	-0	153	10	1.2
1971	Mon N	2	3	.400	43	0	0	0-0	56.2	66	28	8	0	24-7	25	4.29	82	.296	.360	1-0	.000	-0		-4	-0.3
Total	10	26	29	.473	229	35	3-1	9-1	515.1	510	229	41	7	208-36	268	3.72	96	.261	.332	91-5	.066	-1	85	-1	-0.3

REED, JERRY Jerry Maxwell B 10.8.1955 Bryson City, NC BR/TR 6-1/190# d9.11

Year	Tm Lg	W	L	Pct	G	GS	CG-Sho	SV-BS	IP	H	R	HR	HB	BB-IB	SO	ERA	AERA	OAV	OOB	AB-SH	AVG	PB	Sup	APR	PW
1981	Phi N	0	1	.000	4	0	0	0-0	4.2	7	4	0	0	6-0	5	7.71	47	.333	.481	0-0	—	0		-2	-0.4
1982	Phi N	1	0	1.000	7	0	0	0-0	8.2	11	6	0	1	3-0	1	5.19	71	.324	.395	0-0	—	0		-2	-0.2
	Cle A	1	1	.500	6	1	0	0-0	15.2	15	6	1	0	3-0	10	3.45	119	.250	.286	0-0	—	0	22	1	0.2
1983	Cle A	0	0	—	7	0	0	0-0	21.1	26	19	4	0	9-1	11	7.17	59	.310	.372	0-0	—	0		-7	-0.3
1985	Cle A	3	5	.375	33	5	0	8-2	72.1	67	41	12	3	19-2	37	4.11	101	.245	.298	0-0	—	0	79	-2	-0.2
1986	Sea A	4	0	1.000	11	4	0	0-2	34.2	38	13	3	0	13-0	16	3.12	136	.273	.336	0-0	—	0	187	4	0.5
1987	Sea A	1	2	.333	39	1	0	7-1	81.2	79	32	7	3	24-3	51	3.42	139	.255	.314	0-0	—	0	58	12	0.6
1988	Sea A	1	1	.500	46	0	0	1-2	86.1	82	42	8	2	33-7	48	3.96	105	.256	.325	0-0	—	0*		2	0.1
1989	Sea A	7	7	.500	52	1	0	0-4	101.2	89	44	10	1	43-10	50	3.19	127	.235	.313	0-0	—	0	0	8	1.0
1990	Sea A	0	1	.000	4	0	0	0-0	7.1	8	4	1	0	3-0	2	4.91	81	.286	.355	0-0	—	0		-1	-0.1
	Bos A	2	1	.667	29	0	0	2-1	45	55	27	1	0	16-2	17	4.80	85	.302	.353	0-0	—	0		-4	-0.2
	Year	2	2	.500	33	0	0	2-1	52.1	63	31	2	0	19-2	19	4.82	85	.300	.353	0-0	—	0		-4	-0.3
Total	9	20	19	.513	238	12	0	18-10	479.1	477	238	47	10	172-25	248	3.94	107	.261	.325	0-0	—	0	103	9	1.0

REED, RICK Richard Allen B 8.16.1964 Huntington, WV BR/TR 6/205# d8.8

Year	Tm Lg	W	L	Pct	G	GS	CG-Sho	SV-BS	IP	H	R	HR	HB	BB-IB	SO	ERA	AERA	OAV	OOB	AB-SH	AVG	PB	Sup	APR	PW
1988	Pit N	1	0	1.000	2	2	0	0-0	12	10	4	1	0	2-0	6	3.00	114	.233	.267	4-0	.000	-0	143	1	0.0

Year	Tm Lg	W	L	Pct	G	GS	CG-Sho	SV-BS	IP	H	R	HR	HB	BB-IB	SO	ERA	AERA	OAV	OOB	AB-SH	AVG	PB	Sup	APR	PW
1989	Pit N	1	4	.200	15	7	0	0-0	54.2	62	35	5	2	11-3	34	5.60	60	.290	.326	13-0	.077	-0	64	-13	-1.1
1990	Pit N	2	3	.400	13	8	1-1	1-0	53.2	62	32	6	1	12-6	27	4.36	83	.279	.318	16-0	.250	1	115	-6	-0.4
1991	Pit N	0	0	—	1	1	0	0-0	4.1	8	6	1	0	1-0	2	10.38	34	.400	.429	2-0	.500	1	151	-4	-0.1
1992	KC A	3	7	.300	19	18	1-1	0-0	100.1	105	47	10	5	20-3	49	3.68	110	.271	.312	0-0	—	0	81	3	0.3
1993	KC A	0	0	—	1	0	0	0-0	3.2	6	4	0	1	1-0	3	9.82	47	.375	.444	0-0	—	0		-2	-0.1
	Tex A	1	0	1.000	2	0	0	0-0	4	6	1	1	1	1-0	2	2.25	185	.375	.444	0-0	—	0		1	0.2
	Year	1	0	1.000	3	0	0	0-0	7.2	12	9	1	2	2-0	5	5.87	74	.375	.444	0-0	—	0		-1	0.1
1994	Tex A	1	1	.500	4	3	0	0-0	16.2	17	13	3	1	7-0	12	5.94	81	.254	.333	0-0	—	0	140	-2	-0.2
1995	Cin N	0	0	—	4	3	0	0-0	17	18	12	5	0	3-0	10	5.82	71	.273	.304	3-2	.000	-0	161	-3	-0.2
1997	NY N	13	9	.591	33	31	2	0-0	208.1	186	76	19	5	31-4	113	2.89	140	.239	.272	57-6	.175	4	99	27	3.0
1998	NY N☆	16	11	.593	31	31	2-1	0-0	212.1	208	84	30	6	29-2	153	3.48	119	.261	.290	64-12	.125	-1	91	17	2.0
1999	†NY N	11	5	.688	26	26	1-1	0-0	149.1	163	77	23	1	47-2	104	4.58	96	.281	.334	45-8	.244	2*	122	-3	0.1
2000	†NY N	11	5	.688	30	30	0	0-0	184	192	90	28	5	34-3	121	4.11	107	.266	.302	49-14	.204	1	119	8	0.6
2001	NY N❖	8	6	.571	20	20	3-1	0-0	134.2	119	53	16	1	17-3	99	3.48	119	.236	.262	40-4	.125	-1	92	12	1.2
	Min A	4	6	.400	12	12	0	0-0	67.2	92	45	12	4	14-0	43	5.19	89	.325	.363	0-0	—	0	84	-6	-0.7
2002	†Min A	15	7	.682	33	32	2-1	0-0	188	192	89	32	6	26-0	121	3.78	119	.259	.288	4-1	.250	0	111	13	1.3
2003	†Min A	6	12	.333	27	21	2-1	0-1	135	155	80	21	5	29-2	71	5.07	90	.285	.325	0-0	—	0	69	-8	-1.0
Total	15	93	76	.550	273	245	14-7	1-1	1545.2	1601	748	213	44	285-28	970	4.03	105	.267	.303	297-47	.172	7	101	35	4.9

REED, BOB Robert Edward B 1.12.1945 Boston, MA BR/TR 5-10/175# d9.5

1969	Det A	0	0	—	8	1	0	0-0	14.2	9	3	0	0	8-0	9	1.84	203	.184	.298	2-0	.500	0	71	3	0.2
1970	Det A	2	4	.333	16	4	0	2-0	46.1	54	25	5	0	14-0	26	4.86	77	.292	.342	12-0	.083	-0*	78	-5	-0.7
Total	2	2	4	.333	24	5	0	2-0	61	63	28	5	0	22-0	35	4.13	90	.269	.332	14-0	.143	-0	76	-2	-0.5

REED, RON Ronald Lee B 11.2.1942 LaPorte, IN BR/TR 6-6/215# d9.26

1966	Atl N	1	1	.500	2	2	0	0	8.1	7	2	1	0	4-0	6	2.16	168	.226	.314	2-0	.000	-0	73	1	0.3
1967	Atl N	1	1	.500	3	3	0	0	21.1	21	8	1	2	3-0	11	2.95	112	.262	.299	8-0	.000	-1	88	1	0.0
1968	Atl N★	11	10	.524	35	28	6-1	0	201.2	189	87	10	6	49-11	111	3.35	89	.246	.294	62-9	.161	1	87	-8	-0.8
1969	†Atl N	18	10	.643	36	33	7-1	0-0	241.1	227	103	24	6	56-5	160	3.47	104	.246	.292	80-13	.125	-2*	114	4	0.2
1970	Atl N	7	10	.412	21	18	6	0-0	134.2	140	69	16	2	39-5	68	4.41	97	.266	.319	44-5	.091	-2*	91	0	-0.2
1971	Atl N	13	14	.481	32	32	8-1	0-0	222.1	221	105	26	2	54-10	129	3.72	100	.261	.304	74-6	.149	-3	78	0	-0.4
1972	Atl N	11	15	.423	31	30	11-1	0-0	213	222	109	18	6	60-7	111	3.93	97	.270	.321	73-5	.178	-1	89	-5	-0.6
1973	Atl N	4	11	.267	20	19	2	1-0	116.1	133	71	7	3	31-6	64	4.41	89	.287	.334	45-1	.200	-0*	90	-9	-1.0
1974	Atl N	10	11	.476	28	28	6-2	0-0	186	171	76	16	2	41-6	78	3.39	112	.243	.285	57-7	.105	-3	75	9	0.5
1975	Atl N	4	5	.444	10	10	1	0-0	74.2	93	39	1	0	16-2	40	4.22	90	.304	.335	26-0	.231	1	93	-2	-0.1
	StL N	9	8	.529	24	24	7-2	0-0	175.2	181	79	4	4	37-5	99	3.23	117	.263	.304	56-5	.161	-0	98	9	0.7
	Year	13	13	.500	34	34	8-2	0-0	250.1	274	83	5	4	53-7	139	3.52	107	.276	.313	82-5	.183	1	97	5	0.6
1976	†Phi N	8	7	.533	59	4	1	14-9	128	88	39	8	2	32-7	96	2.46	144	.193	.247	24-2	.167	-0	118	15	2.1
1977	†Phi N	7	5	.583	60	3	0	15-3	124.1	101	41	9	1	37-7	84	2.75	146	.223	.283	18-1	.111	-0	126	17	1.9
1978	†Phi N	3	4	.429	66	0	0	17-2	108.2	87	32	6	5	23-5	85	2.24	160	.223	.273	6-0	.000	-0		15	1.4
1979	Phi N	13	8	.619	61	0	0	5-5	102	110	52	9	2	32-9	58	4.15	92	.278	.332	10-2	.300	1		-4	-0.7
1980	†Phi N	7	5	.583	55	0	0	9-4	91.1	88	45	4	1	30-10	54	4.04	94	.253	.311	10-0	.300	1		-2	-0.1
1981	†Phi N	5	3	.625	39	0	0	8-2	61.1	54	26	6	1	17-8	40	3.08	118	.237	.290	6-0	.500	1		2	0.5
1982	Phi N	5	5	.500	57	2	0	14-2	98	85	30	4	3	24-5	57	2.66	138	.235	.286	12-1	.333	2	144	12	1.8
1983	†Phi N	9	1	.900	61	0	0	8-4	95.2	89	42	5	1	34-14	73	3.48	103	.248	.312	6-1	.167	-0		2	0.1
1984	Chi A	0	6	.000	51	0	0	12-5	73	67	29	7	1	14-2	57	3.08	135	.248	.286	1-0	.000	-0		8	0.8
Total	19	146	140	.510	751	236	55-8	103-36	2477.2	2374	1084	182	50	633-124	1481	3.46	107	.252	.301	620-58	.158	-6	92	65	6.4

REED, STEVE Steven Vincent B 3.11.1966 Los Angeles, CA BR/TR 6-2/202# d8.30

1992	SF N	1	0	1.000	18	0	0	0-0	15.2	13	5	2	1	3-0	11	2.30	144	.220	.270	0-0	—	0		2	0.1
1993	Col N	9	5	.643	64	0	0	3-3	84.1	80	47	13	3	30-5	51	4.48	107	.259	.328	9-2	.000	-1		2	0.3
1994	Col N	3	2	.600	**61**	0	0	3-7	64	79	33	9	6	26-3	51	3.94	126	.306	.374	2-0	.000	-0		5	0.3
1995	†Col N	5	2	.714	71	0	0	3-3	84	61	24	8	1	21-3	79	2.14	252	.203	.256	3-0	.333	0		**23**	1.9
1996	Col N	4	3	.571	70	0	0	0-6	75	66	38	11	6	19-0	51	3.96	132	.239	.298	3-0	.333	0		8	0.6
1997	Col N	4	6	.400	63	0	0	6-7	62.1	49	28	10	5	27-1	43	4.04	128	.219	.315	1-0	.000	-0		7	1.2
1998	SF N	2	1	.667	50	0	0	1-4	54.2	30	10	4	4	19-5	50	1.48	268	.160	.251	3-0	.333	0		16	0.8
	†Cle A	2	2	.500	20	0	0	0-1	25.2	26	19	4	1	8-0	23	6.66	72	.260	.321	0-0	—	0		-5	-0.6
1999	†Cle A	3	2	.600	63	0	0	0-3	61.2	69	33	10	3	20-5	44	4.23	119	.285	.341	0-0	—	0		5	0.3
2000	Cle A	2	0	1.000	57	0	0	0-1	56	58	30	7	1	21-4	39	4.34	115	.269	.335	0-0	—	0		3	0.2
2001	Cle A	1	1	.500	31	0	0	0-1	27.1	22	11	3	2	10-2	21	3.62	125	.212	.293	0-0	—	0*		3	0.2
	†Atl N	2	2	.500	39	0	0	1-0	31	30	14	3	1	13-3	25	3.48	127	.259	.336	0-0	—	0		3	0.4
2002	SD N	2	4	.333	40	0	0	1-2	41	33	9	2	6	10-2	36	1.98	191	.228	.304	1-0	.000	-0*		9	1.3
	NY N	0	1	.000	24	0	0	0-1	26	23	6	0	2	4-1	14	2.08	191	.240	.284	1-0	.000	-0		6	0.3
	Year	2	5	.286	64	0	0	1-3	67	56	19	2	8	14-3	50	2.01	191	.232	.297	2-0	.000	-0		15	1.6
2003	Col N	5	3	.625	67	0	0	0-2	63.1	59	24	9	8	26-3	39	3.27	150	.254	.348	0-0	—	0		10	1.2
Total	12	45	34	.570	738	0	0	18-41	772	698	331	95	50	257-37	577	3.50	137	.244	.314	23-2	.130	-1		97	8.5

REEDER, BILL William Edgar B 2.20.1922 Dike, TX D 3.12.2001 Sulphur Springs, TX BR/TR 6-5/205# d4.23

1949	StL N	1	1	.500	21	1	0	0	33.2	33	22	2	1	30	21	5.08	82	.270	.418	3-0	.000	-0	85	-3	-0.2

REES, STAN Stanley Milton "Nellie" B 2.25.1899 Cynthiana, KY D 8.30.1937 Lexington, KY BL/TL 6-3/190# d6.12

1918	Was A	1	0	1.000	2	0	0	0	2	3	0	0	0	4	1	0.00	—	.500	.700	0-0	—	0		1	0.1

REGAN, MIKE Michael John B 11.19.1888 Phoenix, NY D 5.22.1961 Albany, NY BR/TR 5-10/160# d5.13

1917	Cin N	11	10	.524	32	26	16-1	0	216	228	106	4	4	41	50	2.71	97	.273	.310	75-0	.200	1*	107	-6	-0.3
1918	Cin N	5	5	.500	22	6	4-3	2	80	77	38	0	0	29	15	3.26	82	.262	.328	27-0	.296	2*	104	-6	-0.5
1919	Cin N	0	0	—	1	0	0	0	2.1	1	1	0	0	0	1	0.00	—	.143	.143	1-0	.000	-0		0	0.0
Total	3	16	15	.516	55	32	20-4	2	298.1	306	145	4	4	70	66	2.84	93	.269	.314	103-0	.223	3	107	-12	-0.8

REGAN, PHIL Philip Raymond "The Vulture" B 4.6.1937 Otsego, MI BR/TR 6-3/200# d7.19 M1 C7

1960	Det A	0	4	.000	17	7	0	1	68	70	39	11	2	25-1	38	4.50	88	.267	.333	17-1	.059	-1	89	-4	-0.4
1961	Det A	10	7	.588	32	16	6	2	120	134	70	19	1	41-1	46	5.25	78	.281	.337	40-3	.075	-2*	101	-10	-1.6
1962	Det A	11	9	.550	35	23	6	0	171.1	169	89	23	1	64-0	87	4.04	101	.254	.318	63-4	.206	1	115	0	0.0
1963	Det A	15	9	.625	38	27	5-1	1	189	179	95	33	7	59-5	115	3.86	97	.245	.305	63-3	.143	-1	123	-4	-0.7
1964	Det A	5	10	.333	32	21	2	1	146.2	162	87	21	5	49-4	91	5.03	73	.282	.341	41-4	.317	5*	117	-21	-1.5
1965	Det A	1	5	.167	16	7	1	0	51.2	57	31	6	0	20-1	37	5.05	69	.282	.341	12-2	.083	-0	87	-8	-1.0
1966	†LA N☆	14	1	.933	65	0	0	**21**	116.2	85	24	6	0	24-9	88	1.62	203	.207	.248	21-2	.143	0		**24**	4.1
1967	LA N	6	9	.400	55	3	0	6	96.1	108	38	2	2	32-17	53	2.99	104	.284	.339	10-0	.100	-0	28	0	0.1
1968	LA N	2	0	1.000	5	0	0	0	7.2	10	3	1	0	1-0	7	3.52	78	.313	.333	1-0	.000	-0		0	-0.1
	Chi N	10	5	.667	68	0	0	25	127	109	36	9	2	24-6	60	2.20	144	.232	.271	20-3	.150	0		12	2.2
	Year	12	5	.706	73	0	0	**25**	134.2	119	40	10	2	25-6	67	2.27	138	.237	.274	21-3	.143	0		12	2.1
1969	Chi N	12	6	.667	71	0	0	17-3	112	120	49	6	2	35-13	56	3.70	109	.282	.335	15-0	.067	-0		5	0.9
1970	Chi N	5	9	.357	54	0	0	12-9	75.2	81	43	8	1	32-7	31	4.76	95	.287	.356	9-0	.000	-1		-1	-0.2
1971	Chi N	5	5	.500	48	1	0	6-4	73.1	84	37	4	2	33-13	28	3.93	100	.301	.374	8-3	.000	-1	68	0	-0.1
1972	Chi N	0	1	.000	5	0	0	0-0	4	6	1	0	0	2-0	2	2.25	169	.400	.471	0-0	—	0		1	0.1
	Chi A	0	1	.000	10	0	0	0-1	13.1	18	7	1	1	6-2	4	4.05	77	.346	.417	1-0	1.000	0		-1	0.0
Total	13	96	81	.542	551	105	20-1	92-17	1372.2	1392	649	150	26	447-79	743	3.84	97	.265	.322	321-25	.153	1	112	-7	1.8

REICHERT, DAN Daniel Robert B 7.12.1976 Monterey, CA BR/TR 6-3/175# d7.16

1999	KC A	2	2	.500	8	8	0	0-0	36.2	48	38	2	2	32-1	20	9.08	55	.327	.451	3-1	.333	0	146	-15	-1.3
2000	KC A	8	10	.444	44	18	1-1	2-4	153.1	157	92	15	7	91-1	94	4.70	109	.271	.372	1-0	.000	-0	92	4	0.4
2001	KC A	8	8	.500	27	19	0	0-0	123	131	83	14	8	67-2	77	5.63	87	.278	.374	5-0	.000	-1	95	-8	-0.9
2002	KC A	3	5	.375	30	6	0	0-0	66	77	48	10	4	25-2	36	5.32	94	.306	.373	0-0	—	0	68	-5	-0.4

Year	Tm Lg	W	L	Pct	G	GS	CG-Sho	SV-BS	IP	H	R	HR	HB	BB-IB	SO	ERA	AERA	OAV	OOB	AB-SH	AVG	PB	Sup	APR	PW
2003	Tor A	0	0	—	15	0	0	0-1	16.1	28	12	2	2	8-3	13	6.06	76	.389	.463	0-0	—	0		-3	-0.1
Total	5	21	25	.457	124	51	1-1	2-5	395.1	441	273	43	23	223-9	240	5.55	90	.290	.385	9-1	.111	-0	99	-27	-2.3

REID, EARL Earl Percy B 6.8.1913 Bangor, AL D 5.11.1984 Cullman, AL BL/TR 6-3/190# d5.8

Year	Tm Lg	W	L	Pct	G	GS	CG-Sho	SV-BS	IP	H	R	HR	HB	BB-IB	SO	ERA	AERA	OAV	OOB	AB-SH	AVG	PB	Sup	APR	PW
1946	Bos N	1	0	1.000	2	0	0	0	3	4	3	0	0	3	2	3.00	114	.308	.438	0-0	—	0		-1	-0.1

REIDY, BILL William Joseph B 10.9.1873 Cleveland, OH D 10.14.1915 Cleveland, OH BR/TR 5-10/175# d7.21

Year	Tm Lg	W	L	Pct	G	GS	CG-Sho	SV-BS	IP	H	R	HR	HB	BB-IB	SO	ERA	AERA	OAV	OOB	AB-SH	AVG	PB	Sup	APR	PW
1896	NY N	0	1	.000	2	1	1	0	13	24	11	0	3	2	1	7.62	55	.393	.439	5-0	.000	-1	34	-3	-0.3
1899	Bro N	1	0	1.000	2	1	1	1	7	9	2	0	0	2	2	2.57	152	.310	.355	3-0	.000	-1	129	1	0.2
1901	Mil A	16	20	.444	37	33	28-2	0	301.1	364	183	14	9	62	50	4.21	85	.295	.333	112-7	.143	-6	94	-11	-1.8
1902	StL A	3	5	.375	12	9	7	0	95	111	52	0	7	13	16	4.45	79	.292	.327	41-0	.195	-0*	82	-6	-0.4
1903	StL A	1	4	.200	5	5	5-1	0	43	53	31	1	3	7	8	3.98	73	.301	.339	15-0	.067	-2	59	-7	-0.9
	Bro N	6	7	.462	15	13	11	0	104	130	54	0	6	14	21	3.46	92	.315	.346	37-1	.243	1	107	-2	-0.2
1904	Bro N	0	4	.000	6	4	2	1	38.1	49	33	0	2	6	11	4.46	62	.293	.326	32-0	.156	-0*	63	-9	-0.9
Total	6	27	41	.397	79	66	55-3	2	601.2	740	366	15	30	106	109	4.17	82	.301	.337	245-8	.159	-9	90	-37	-4.3

REINHART, ART Arthur Conrad B 5.29.1899 Ackley, IA D 11.11.1946 Houston, TX BL/TL 6-1/170# d4.26

Year	Tm Lg	W	L	Pct	G	GS	CG-Sho	SV-BS	IP	H	R	HR	HB	BB-IB	SO	ERA	AERA	OAV	OOB	AB-SH	AVG	PB	Sup	APR	PW
1919	StL N	0	0	—	1	0	0	0	0	0	0	0	1	0	0	—	—	—	1.000	0-0	—	0		0	0.0
1925	StL N	11	5	.688	20	16	15-1	0	144.2	149	61	7	4	47	26	3.05	142	.278	.341	67-2	.328	5*	115	19	2.3
1926	†StL N	10	5	.667	27	11	9	0	143	159	75	5	3	47	26	4.22	93	.295	.355	63-3	.317	4*	151	-3	0.2
1927	StL N	5	2	.714	21	9	4-2	1	81.2	82	47	5	0	36	15	4.19	94	.267	.344	32-1	.313	2*	108	-2	0.0
1928	StL N	4	6	.400	23	9	3-1	2	75.1	80	39	3	0	27	12	2.87	140	.272	.333	24-0	.167	-0*	73	5	0.6
Total	5	30	18	.625	92	45	31-4	3	444.2	470	222	20	8	157	79	3.60	113	.280	.345	186-6	.301	10	114	19	3.1

REIS, JACK Harrie Crane B 6.14.1890 Cincinnati, OH D 7.20.1939 Cincinnati, OH BR/TR 5-10.5/160# d9.9

Year	Tm Lg	W	L	Pct	G	GS	CG-Sho	SV-BS	IP	H	R	HR	HB	BB-IB	SO	ERA	AERA	OAV	OOB	AB-SH	AVG	PB	Sup	APR	PW
1911	StL N	0	0	—	3	0	0	0	9.1	5	3	0	0	8	4	0.96	350	.156	.325	2-0	.000	-0		2	0.1

REIS, LAURIE Lawrence P. B 11.20.1858 , IL D 1.24.1921 Chicago, IL BR/TR ?/160# d10.1

Year	Tm Lg	W	L	Pct	G	GS	CG-Sho	SV-BS	IP	H	R	HR	HB	BB-IB	SO	ERA	AERA	OAV	OOB	AB-SH	AVG	PB	Sup	APR	PW
1877	Chi N	3	1	.750	4	4	4-1	0	36	29	8	1		6	11	0.75	396	.213	.246	16	.125	-2	111	8	0.6
1878	Chi N	1	3	.250	4	4	4	0	36	55	34	0		4	8	3.25	75	.335	.351	20	.150	-1*	148	-4	-0.5
Total	2	4	4	.500	8	8	8-1	0	72	84	42	1		10	19	2.00	135	.280	.303	36	.139	-2	129	4	0.1

REIS, BOBBY Robert Joseph Thomas B 1.2.1909 Woodside, NY D 5.1.1973 St.Paul, MN BR/TR 6-1/175# d9.19.1931 ▲

Year	Tm Lg	W	L	Pct	G	GS	CG-Sho	SV-BS	IP	H	R	HR	HB	BB-IB	SO	ERA	AERA	OAV	OOB	AB-SH	AVG	PB	Sup	APR	PW
1935	Bro N	3	2	.600	14	2	1	2	41.1	46	26	0	1	24	7	2.83	140	.277	.372	85-0	.247	1*	128	1	0.3
1936	Bos N	6	5	.545	35	5	3	0	138.2	152	77	7	5	74	25	4.48	86	.283	.375	60-0	.217	1*	75	-9	-0.4
1937	Bos N	0	0	—	4	0	0	0	5	3	1	0	0	5	0	1.80	199	.158	.333	86-0	.244	1*		1	0.1
1938	Bos N	1	6	.143	16	2	1	0	57.2	61	35	5	6	41	20	4.99	69	.271	.397	49-2	.184	-0*	62	-10	-1.0
Total	4	10	13	.435	69	9	5	2	242.2	262	139	12	12	144	52	4.27	88	.277	.379	280-2	.229	3	85	-17	-1.0

REIS, TOMMY Thomas Edward B 8.6.1914 Newport, KY BR/TR 6-2/180# d4.27

Year	Tm Lg	W	L	Pct	G	GS	CG-Sho	SV-BS	IP	H	R	HR	HB	BB-IB	SO	ERA	AERA	OAV	OOB	AB-SH	AVG	PB	Sup	APR	PW
1938	Phi N	0	1	.000	4	0	0	0	4.2	8	11	0	0	8	2	19.29	20	.364	.533	2-0	.000	-0		-8	-1.3
	Bos N	0	0	—	4	0	0	0	6.1	8	5	1	0	1	4	7.11	48	.296	.321	0-0	—	0		-2	-0.1
	Year	0	1	.000	8	0	0	0	11	16	20	1	0	9	6	12.27	30	.327	.431	2-0	.000	-0		-10	-1.4

REISIGL, BUGS Jacob B 12.12.1887 Brooklyn, NY D 2.24.1957 Amsterdam, NY BR/TR 5-10.5/175# d9.20

Year	Tm Lg	W	L	Pct	G	GS	CG-Sho	SV-BS	IP	H	R	HR	HB	BB-IB	SO	ERA	AERA	OAV	OOB	AB-SH	AVG	PB	Sup	APR	PW
1911	Cle A	0	1	.000	2	1	1	0	13	13	9	1	0	3	6	6.23	55	.271	.314	5-0	.000	-1	85	-3	-0.3

REISLING, DOC Frank Carl B 7.25.1874 Martins Ferry, OH D 3.4.1955 Tulsa, OK BR/TR 5-10/180# d9.10

Year	Tm Lg	W	L	Pct	G	GS	CG-Sho	SV-BS	IP	H	R	HR	HB	BB-IB	SO	ERA	AERA	OAV	OOB	AB-SH	AVG	PB	Sup	APR	PW
1904	Bro N	3	4	.429	7	7	6-1	0	51	45	16	0	9	10	19	2.12	130	.238	.308	13-0	.154	0	43	4	0.6
1905	Bro N	0	1	.000	2	0	0	0	3	3	1	0	0	4	2	3.00	96	.273	.467	1-0	.000	0		0	0.1
1909	Was A	2	4	.333	10	6	6-1	0	66.2	70	29	0	0	17	22	2.43	100	.270	.315	24-2	.167	0*	145	-1	-0.1
1910	Was A	10	10	.500	30	20	13-2	1	191	185	77	3	5	44	57	2.54	98	.264	.312	60-5	.200	2*	96	0	0.2
Total	4	15	19	.441	49	33	25-4	1	311.2	303	123	3	14	75	100	2.45	103	.261	.314	98-7	.184	2	92	3	0.8

REITH, BRIAN Brian Eric B 2.28.1978 Fort Wayne, IN BR/TR 6-5/220# d5.16

Year	Tm Lg	W	L	Pct	G	GS	CG-Sho	SV-BS	IP	H	R	HR	HB	BB-IB	SO	ERA	AERA	OAV	OOB	AB-SH	AVG	PB	Sup	APR	PW
2001	Cin N	0	7	.000	9	8	0	0-0	40.1	56	37	13	2	16-0	22	7.81	58	.333	.394	12-0	.250	0	51	-13	-1.8
2003	Cin N	2	3	.400	42	1	0	1-0	61.1	61	32	8	1	36-6	39	4.11	104	.263	.358	7-0	.000	-1	88	0	-0.1
Total	2	2	10	.167	51	9	0	1-0	101.2	117	69	21	3	52-6	61	5.58	79	.292	.372	19-0	.158	-0	57	-13	-1.9

REITSMA, CHRIS Christopher Michael B 12.31.1977 Minneapolis, MN BR/TR 6-5/214# d4.4

Year	Tm Lg	W	L	Pct	G	GS	CG-Sho	SV-BS	IP	H	R	HR	HB	BB-IB	SO	ERA	AERA	OAV	OOB	AB-SH	AVG	PB	Sup	APR	PW
2001	Cin N	7	15	.318	36	29	0	0-0	182	209	121	23	5	49-6	96	5.29	86	.288	.334	48-7	.104	-1*	95	-15	-1.6
2002	Cin N	6	12	.333	32	21	1-1	0-0	138.1	144	73	17	5	45-5	84	3.64	117	.267	.327	30-7	.100	-1	80	4	0.4
2003	Cin N	9	5	.643	57	3	0	12-6	84	92	41	14	0	19-6	53	4.29	100	.281	.320	8-0	.125	-0	110	1	0.1
Total	3	22	32	.407	125	53	1-1	12-6	404.1	445	235	54	10	113-17	233	4.52	97	.280	.329	86-14	.105	-3	91	-10	-1.1

REKAR, BRYAN Bryan Robert B 6.3.1972 Oak Lawn, IL BR/TR 6-3/205# d7.19

Year	Tm Lg	W	L	Pct	G	GS	CG-Sho	SV-BS	IP	H	R	HR	HB	BB-IB	SO	ERA	AERA	OAV	OOB	AB-SH	AVG	PB	Sup	APR	PW
1995	Col N	4	6	.400	15	14	1	0-0	85	95	51	11	3	24-2	60	4.98	108	.282	.332	26-4	.038	-2	74	3	0.2
1996	Col N	2	4	.333	14	11	0	0-1	58.1	87	61	11	5	26-1	25	8.95	58	.345	.413	15-1	.267	1	111	-19	-1.5
1997	Col N	1	0	1.000	2	2	0	0-0	9.1	11	7	3	0	6-0	4	5.79	89	.282	.378	4-0	.250	0	142	-1	-0.1
1998	TB A	2	8	.200	16	15	1	0-0	86.2	95	56	16	2	21-0	55	4.98	96	.282	.321	0-0	—	0	83	-4	-0.4
1999	TB A	6	6	.500	27	12	0	0-0	94.2	121	68	14	5	41-2	55	5.80	86	.313	.385	5-0	.200	0	126	-8	-0.8
2000	TB A	7	10	.412	30	27	2	0-0	173.1	200	92	22	4	39-0	95	4.41	112	.291	.328	3-0	.333	1	86	10	0.9
2001	TB A	3	13	.188	25	25	0	0-0	140.2	167	104	21	6	45-2	87	5.89	76	.294	.348	2-0	.000	-0	74	-22	-2.0
2002	KC A	0	2	.000	2	2	0	0-0	7	12	12	1	0	6-0	2	15.43	33	.387	.474	0-0	—	0	65	-7	-1.0
Total	8	25	49	.338	131	108	4	0-1	655	788	451	99	25	208-7	383	5.62	88	.299	.351	55-5	.145	-1	89	-48	-4.7

REMLINGER, MIKE Michael John B 3.23.1966 Middletown, NY BL/TL 6/195# d6.15

Year	Tm Lg	W	L	Pct	G	GS	CG-Sho	SV-BS	IP	H	R	HR	HB	BB-IB	SO	ERA	AERA	OAV	OOB	AB-SH	AVG	PB	Sup	APR	PW
1991	SF N	2	1	.667	8	6	1-1	0-0	35	36	17	5	0	20-1	19	4.37	82	.271	.364	7-4	.000	-0	184	-3	-0.2
1994	NY N	1	5	.167	10	9	0	0-0	54.2	55	30	9	1	35-4	33	4.61	91	.261	.364	16-3	.000	-1	70	-2	-0.4
1995	NY N	0	1	.000	5	0	0	0-1	5.2	7	5	1	0	2-0	6	6.35	64	.292	.346	1-0	.000	-0		-2	-0.3
	Cin N	0	0	—	2	0	0	0-0	1	2	1	0	0	3-0	1	9.00	46	.500	.714	0-0	—	0		-1	0.0
	Year	0	1	.000	7	0	0	0-1	6.2	9	9	1	0	5-0	7	6.75	60	.321	.424	1-0	.000	-0		-2	-0.3
1996	Cin N	0	1	.000	19	4	0	0-0	27.1	24	17	4	3	19-2	19	5.60	76	.242	.377	7-0	.143	0	112	-3	-0.1
1997	Cin N	8	8	.500	69	12	2	2-0	124	100	61	11	7	60-6	145	4.14	103	.223	.322	21-3	.095	0*	106	2	0.3
1998	Cin N	8	15	.348	35	28	1-1	0-0	164.1	164	96	23	5	87-1	144	4.82	89	.266	.358	47-7	.106	-2	88	-11	-1.5
1999	†Atl N	10	1	.909	73	0	0	1-2	83.2	66	24	9	1	35-5	81	2.37	190	.215	.297	2-2	.000	-0		20	2.3
2000	†Atl N	5	3	.625	71	0	0	12-4	72.2	55	29	6	3	37-1	72	3.47	132	.207	.308	3-0	.000	-0		10	1.2
2001	†Atl N	3	3	.500	74	0	0	1-4	75	67	25	9	2	23-4	93	2.76	160	.234	.296	2-0	.000	-0*		14	1.0
2002	†Atl N★	7	3	.700	73	0	0	0-5	68	48	17	3	1	28-3	69	1.99	206	.198	.284	2-0	.000	-0		16	2.1
2003	†Chi N	6	5	.545	73	0	0	0-1	69	54	30	11	2	39-4	83	3.65	115	.211	.318	1-0	.000	-0		5	0.6
Total	11	50	46	.521	512	59	4-2	16-17	780.1	678	352	91	25	388-31	765	3.78	113	.234	.328	109-19	.073	-4	98	45	5.0

REMMERSWAAL, WIN Wilhelmus Abraham B 3.8.1954 The Hague, Netherlands BR/TR 6-2/160# d8.3

Year	Tm Lg	W	L	Pct	G	GS	CG-Sho	SV-BS	IP	H	R	HR	HB	BB-IB	SO	ERA	AERA	OAV	OOB	AB-SH	AVG	PB	Sup	APR	PW
1979	Bos A	1	0	1.000	8	0	0	0-0	20.1	26	16	1	1	12-1	16	7.08	63	.317	.402	0-0	—	0		-5	-0.3
1980	Bos A	2	1	.667	14	0	0	0-0	35.1	39	18	4	0	9-1	20	4.58	92	.295	.338	0-0	—	0		-1	-0.1
Total	2	3	1	.750	22	0	0	0-0	55.2	65	34	5	1	21-2	36	5.50	78	.304	.364	0-0	—	0		-6	-0.4

REMNEAS, ALEX Alexander Norman B 2.21.1886 Minneapolis, MN D 8.27.1975 Phoenix, AZ BR/TR 6-1/180# d4.15

Year	Tm Lg	W	L	Pct	G	GS	CG-Sho	SV-BS	IP	H	R	HR	HB	BB-IB	SO	ERA	AERA	OAV	OOB	AB-SH	AVG	PB	Sup	APR	PW
1912	Det A	0	0	—	1	0	0	0	1.2	5	5	0	0	0	0	27.00	12	.455	.455	0-0	—	0		-4	-0.1
1915	StL A	0	0	—	2	0	0	0	6	3	4	0	1	3	5	1.50	191	.136	.269	1-0	.000	-0		0	0.0
Total	2	0	0	—	3	0	0	0	7.2	8	9	0	1	3	5	7.04	42	.242	.324	1-0	.000	0		-4	-0.1

RENFER, ERWIN Erwin Arthur B 12.11.1891 Elgin, IL D 10.26.1957 Sycamore, IL BR/TR 6/180# d9.18

Year	Tm Lg	W	L	Pct	G	GS	CG-Sho	SV-BS	IP	H	R	HR	HB	BB-IB	SO	ERA	AERA	OAV	OOB	AB-SH	AVG	PB	Sup	APR	PW
1913	Det A	0	1	.000	1	1	0	0	6	5	5	0	1	3	1	6.00	49	.227	.346	2-0	.000	-0	25	-2	-0.3

RENFROE, LADDIE Cohen Williams B 5.9.1962 Natchez, MS BB/TR 5-11/200# d7.3

Year	Tm Lg	W	L	Pct	G	GS	CG-Sho	SV-BS	IP	H	R	HR	HB	BB-IB	SO	ERA	AERA	OAV	OOB	AB-SH	AVG	PB	Sup	APR	PW
1991	Chi N	0	1	.000	4	0	0	0-1	4.2	11	7	1	0	2-1	4	13.50	29	.440	.481	1-0	.000	-0		-4	-0.8

Year	Tm Lg	W	L	Pct	G	GS	CG-Sho	SV-BS	IP	H	R	HR	HB	BB-IB	SO	ERA	AERA	OAV	OOB	AB-SH	AVG	PB	Sup	APR	PW
RENFROE, MARSHALL Marshall Daniel B 5.25.1936 Century, FL D 12.10.1970 Pensacola, FL BL/TL 6/180# d9.27																									
1959	SF N	0	0	—	1	1	0	0	2	3	6	1	0	3-0	3	27.00	14	.333	.500	1-0	.000	-0	188	-5	-0.2
RENIFF, HAL Harold Eugene "Porky" B 7.2.1938 Warren, OH BR/TR 6/215# d6.8																									
1961	NY A	2	0	1.000	25	0	0	2	45.1	31	14	1	0	31-3	21	2.58	144	.197	.330	5-0	.000	-1		6	0.2
1962	NY A	0	0	—	2	0	0	0	3.2	6	3	0	1	5-1	1	7.36	51	.400	.545	0-0	—	0		-1	-0.1
1963	†NY A	4	3	.571	48	0	0	18	89.1	63	31	3	2	42-5	56	2.62	134	.202	.300	15-1	.000	-1		8	1.0
1964	†NY A	6	4	.600	41	0	0	9	69.1	47	26	3	0	30-4	38	3.12	116	.199	.287	10-0	.100	-1*		4	0.6
1965	NY A	3	4	.429	51	0	0	3	85.1	74	40	4	5	48-7	74	3.80	90	.232	.340	2-1	.000	-0		-3	-0.3
1966	NY A	3	7	.300	56	0	0	9	95.1	80	37	2	5	49-8	79	3.21	104	.229	.330	14-2	.286	1		2	0.3
1967	NY A	0	2	.000	24	0	0	0	40	40	22	0	3	14-2	24	4.27	73	.256	.328	2-1	.000	-0		-5	-0.3
	NY N	3	3	.500	29	0	0	4	43	42	20	1	1	23-4	21	3.35	101	.266	.361	4-0	.000	-0		-1	-0.2
Total	7	21	23	.477	276	0	0	45	471.1	383	193	14	17	242-34	314	3.27	106	.225	.326	52-5	.096	-2		10	1.2
RENINGER, JIM James David B 3.7.1915 Aurora, IL D 8.23.1993 N.Fort Myers, FL BR/TR 6-3/210# d9.17																									
1938	Phi A	0	2	.000	4	4	1	0	22.2	28	18	3	0	14	9	7.15	68	.295	.385	7-0	.000	-0	73	-4	-0.3
1939	Phi A	0	2	.000	4	2	0	0	16.1	24	15	3	0	12	3	7.71	61	.369	.468	6-0	.167	-0	28	-5	-0.5
Total	2	0	4	.000	8	6	1	0	39	52	33	6	0	26	12	7.38	65	.325	.419	13-0	.077	-1	58	-9	-0.8
RENKO, STEVE Steven B 12.10.1944 Kansas City, KS BR/TR 6-5/230# d6.27																									
1969	Mon N	6	7	.462	18	15	4	0-0	103.1	94	54	14	2	50-6	68	4.01	92	.243	.330	36-2	.167	1	117	-4	-0.4
1970	Mon N	13	11	.542	41	33	7-1	1-0	222.2	203	121	27	6	104-7	142	4.32	95	.241	.327	80-3	.200	2	116	-6	-0.3
1971	Mon N	15	14	.517	40	37	9-3	0-1	275.2	256	128	24	3	135-11	129	3.75	94	.247	.333	100-4	.210	4*	96	-7	-0.3
1972	Mon N	1	10	.091	30	12	0	0-0	97	96	60	11	0	67-10	66	5.20	68	.262	.375	24-0	.292	1*	64	-17	-1.6
1973	Mon N	15	11	.577	36	34	9	1-0	249.2	201	94	26	1	108-12	164	2.81	136	.218	.299	88-4	.273	7*	94	26	3.5
1974	Mon N	12	16	.429	37	35	8-1	0-0	227.2	222	115	17	0	81-8	138	4.03	96	.257	.318	81-2	.210	3	92	-3	0.1
1975	Mon N	6	12	.333	31	25	3-1	1-0	170.1	175	89	20	1	76-7	99	4.07	94	.265	.340	54-5	.278	5*	95	-5	0.0
1976	Mon N	0	1	.000	5	1	0	0-1	13	15	8	2	0	3-0	4	5.54	67	.288	.327	3-0	.333	0	0	-2	-0.1
	Chi N	8	11	.421	28	27	4-1	0-0	163.1	164	79	12	0	43-8	112	3.86	100	.258	.304	53-4	.094	-3*	73	0	-0.4
	Year	8	12	.400	33	28	4-1	0-1	176.1	179	82	14	0	46-8	116	3.98	97	.260	.306	56-4	.107	-3	71	-1	-0.5
1977	Chi N	2	2	.500	13	8	0	1-0	51.1	51	32	10	1	21-6	34	4.56	96	.258	.330	12-0	.167	0	91	-2	-0.2
	Chi A	5	0	1.000	8	8	0	0-0	53.1	55	23	3	1	17-0	36	3.54	116	.274	.330	0-0	—	0	107	4	0.3
1978	Oak A	6	12	.333	27	25	3-1	0-0	151	152	77	10	2	67-4	89	4.29	85	.265	.342	0-0	—	0	72	-7	-0.8
1979	Bos A	11	9	.550	27	27	4-1	0-0	171	174	86	22	2	53-1	99	4.11	108	.260	.315	0-0	—	0	110	6	0.6
1980	Bos A	9	9	.500	32	23	1	0-0	165.1	180	86	17	1	56-4	90	4.19	101	.281	.337	0-0	—	0	93	0	-0.1
1981	Cal A	8	4	.667	22	15	0	1-0	102	93	40	7	1	42-1	50	3.44	106	.250	.323	0-0	—	0	108	4	0.4
1982	Cal A	11	6	.647	31	23	4	0-1	156	163	78	17	1	51-0	81	4.44	91	.269	.325	0-0	—	0	108	-4	-0.5
1983	KC A	6	11	.353	25	17	1	1-0	121.1	144	63	9	0	36-1	54	4.30	95	.293	.338	0-0	—	0	107	-2	-0.3
Total	15	134	146	.479	451	365	57-9	6-3	2494	2438	1233	248	22	1010-86	1455	3.99	98	.256	.327	531-24	.215	21	97	-19	-0.1
REPLOGLE, ANDY Andrew David B 10.7.1953 South Bend, IN BR/TR 6-5/205# d4.11																									
1978	Mil A	9	5	.643	32	18	3-2	0-1	149.1	177	75	14	1	47-3	41	3.92	96	.301	.350	0-0	—	0	114	-4	-0.4
1979	Mil A	0	0	—	3	0	0	0-0	8	13	5	0	0	2-0	2	5.63	74	.382	.417	0-0	—	0		-1	0.0
Total	2	9	5	.643	35	18	3-2	0-1	157.1	190	80	14	1	49-3	43	4.00	95	.305	.353	0-0	—	0	114	-5	-0.4
RESCIGNO, XAVIER Xavier Frederick "Mr. X" B 10.13.1913 New York, NY BR/TR 5-10.5/175# d4.22																									
1943	Pit N	6	9	.400	37	14	5-1	2	132.2	125	52	6	2	45	41	2.98	117	.252	.317	35-0	.143	0	94	8	0.8
1944	Pit N	10	8	.556	48	6	2	5	124	146	69	9	1	34	45	4.35	85	.291	.337	22-1	.091	-1	90	-7	-1.0
1945	Pit N	3	5	.375	44	1	0	9	78.2	95	57	6	1	34	29	5.72	69	.303	.372	15-1	.133	-0	0	-14	-1.6
Total	3	19	22	.463	129	21	7-1	16	335.1	366	178	21	4	113	115	4.13	89	.279	.338	72-2	.125	-1	85	-13	-1.8
RETTGER, GEORGE George Edward B 7.29.1868 Cleveland, OH D 6.5.1921 Lakewood, OH BR/TR 5-11/175# d8.13																									
1891	StL AA	7	3	.700	14	12	10-1	1	92.2	85	63	4	8	51	49	3.40	123	.235	.343	42	.071	-3*	104	6	0.3
1892	Cle N	1	3	.250	6	5	3	0	38	32	27	2	1	31	12	4.26	80	.219	.360	15	.133	-0	93	-3	-0.3
	Cin N	1	0	1.000	1	1	1	0	9	8	5	0	1	10	1	4.00	82	.229	.413	8	.125	-0*	310	0	0.0
	Year	2	3	.400	7	6	4	0	47	40	21	2	2	41	13	4.21	80	.221	.371	23	.130	-0	128	-3	-0.3
Total	2	9	6	.600	21	18	14-1	1	139.2	125	95	6	10	92	62	3.67	106	.231	.352	65	.092	-3	111	3	0.0
RETTIG, OTTO Adolph John B 1.29.1894 New York, NY D 6.16.1977 Stuart, FL BR/TR 5-11/165# d7.19																									
1922	Phi A	1	2	.333	4	4	1	0	18.1	18	11	0	1	12	3	4.91	87	.265	.383	6-0	.000	-1	40	-1	-0.2
REULBACH, ED Edward Marvin "Big Ed" B 12.1.1882 Detroit, MI D 7.17.1961 Glens Falls, NY BR/TR 6-1/190# d5.16																									
1905	Chi N	18	14	.563	34	29	28-5	1	291.2	208	71	1	18	73	152	1.42	210	**.201**	.266	110-2	.127	-6*	81	48	4.6
1906	†Chi N	19	4	**.826**	33	24	20-6	3	218	129	51	2	13	92	94	1.65	160	**.175**	.278	83-6	.157	-2*	123	26	2.8
1907	†Chi N	17	4	**.810**	27	22	16-4	0	192	147	48	1	9	64	96	1.69	148	.217	.294	63-4	.175	0	99	19	2.2
1908	†Chi N	24	7	**.774**	46	35	25-7	1	297.2	227	81	4	12	106	133	2.03	116	.214	.292	99-9	.232	7	143	14	2.2
1909	Chi N	19	10	.655	35	32	23-6	0	262.2	194	69	1	11	82	105	1.78	143	.212	.285	86-7	.140	-1	90	24	2.9
1910	†Chi N	12	8	.600	24	23	14-1	0	173.1	161	76	1	9	49	55	3.12	92	.250	.312	56-6	.107	-3	126	-4	-0.8
1911	Chi N	16	9	.640	33	29	15-2	0	221.2	191	97	3	4	103	79	2.96	112	.236	.325	67-7	.090	-1	106	9	1.0
1912	Chi N	10	6	.625	39	19	8	4	169	161	86	7	8	60	75	3.78	88	.259	.332	55-1	.109	-3	131	-7	-0.7
1913	Chi N	1	3	.250	10	3	1	0	38.2	41	27	1	1	21	10	4.42	72	.281	.375	12-0	.250	0	126	-6	-0.6
	Bro N	7	6	.538	15	12	8-2	0	110	77	34	3	4	34	46	2.05	161	.202	.274	29-3	.103	0	65	14	1.6
	Year	8	9	.471	25	15	9-2	0	148.2	118	37	4	5	55	56	2.66	123	.223	.303	41-3	.146	0	77	10	1.0
1914	Bro N	11	18	.379	44	29	14-3	3	256	228	108	5	10	83	119	2.64	108	.242	.310	74-3	.122	-0	89	6	0.7
1915	New F	21	10	.677	33	30	23-4	1	270	233	88	3	3	69	117	2.23	115	.236	.287	92-8	.196	-2	117	12	1.2
1916	Bos N	7	6	.538	21	11	6	0	109.1	99	38	1	4	41	47	2.47	101	.251	.328	33-2	.091	-1	101	1	0.2
1917	Bos N	0	1	.000	5	2	0	0	22.1	21	13	0	1	15	9	2.82	90	.256	.378	3-0	.000	1	89	-2	0.0
Total	13	182	106	.632	399	300	201-40	13	2632.1	2117	887	33	107	892	1137	2.28	122	.224	.299	862-58	.147	-11	107	154	17.3
REUSCHEL, PAUL Paul Richard B 1.12.1947 Quincy, IL BR/TR 6-4/225# d7.25 b-Rick																									
1975	Chi N	1	3	.250	28	0	0	5-2	36	44	15	1	1	13-2	12	3.50	110	.312	.372	4-0	.000	-0		2	0.2
1976	Chi N	4	2	.667	50	2	0	3-0	87	94	46	12	1	33-4	55	4.55	85	.278	.341	13-0	.154	-0	114	-5	-0.3
1977	Chi N	5	6	.455	69	0	0	4-5	107	105	58	9	0	40-8	62	4.37	100	.262	.326	11-1	.000	-1		0	0.0
1978	Chi N	2	0	1.000	16	0	0	0-0	28	29	16	4	1	13-3	13	5.14	78	.269	.352	4-0	.000	-0		-2	-0.2
	Cle A	2	4	.333	18	6	1	0-0	89.2	95	33	5	2	22-1	24	3.11	121	.271	.316	0-0	—	0	52	7	0.5
1979	Cle A	2	1	.667	17	1	0	1-0	45.1	73	43	7	0	11-0	22	7.94	54	.365	.398	0-0	—	0	149	-18	-1.1
Total	5	16	16	.500	198	9	1	13-7	393	440	211	38	5	132-18	188	4.51	90	.286	.342	32-1	.063	-2	73	-16	-0.9
REUSCHEL, RICK Rickey Eugene B 5.16.1949 Quincy, IL BR/TR 6-3/235# d6.19 b-Paul																									
1972	Chi N	10	8	.556	21	18	5-4	0-0	129	127	46	3	2	29-6	87	2.93	130	.259	.302	44-6	.136	-1	107	12	1.6
1973	Chi N	14	15	.483	36	36	7-3	0-0	237	244	95	15	5	62-6	168	3.00	132	.263	.312	73-9	.123	-3	73	21	2.3
1974	Chi N	13	12	.520	41	38	8-2	0-0	240.2	262	130	18	6	83-12	160	4.30	89	.276	.335	86-9	.221	2	102	-10	-0.5
1975	Chi N	11	17	.393	38	37	6	1-0	234	244	116	17	7	67-8	155	3.73	103	.268	.322	77-6	.208	2	88	0	0.4
1976	Chi N	14	12	.538	38	37	9-2	1-0	260	260	117	17	8	64-5	146	3.46	112	.265	.311	83-7	.229	4	96	9	1.5
1977	Chi N★	20	10	.667	39	37	8-4	1-0	252	233	84	13	5	74-11	166	2.79	158	.247	.304	87-6	.207	1*	72	42	5.3
1978	Chi N	14	15	.483	35	35	9-1	0-0	242.2	235	98	16	5	54-8	115	3.41	118	.254	.297	73-10	.137	-1	83	16	1.9
1979	Chi N	18	12	.600	36	36	5-1	0-0	239	251	104	16	10	75-8	125	3.62	114	.274	.333	79-5	.165	1*	106	14	2.0
1980	Chi N	11	13	.458	38	**38**	6	0-0	257	281	111	13	4	76-10	140	3.40	115	.286	.336	82-10	.159	-1*	83	14	1.4
1981	Chi N	4	7	.364	13	13	1	0-0	85.2	87	40	4	4	23-4	53	3.47	107	.267	.323	25-4	.080	-1*	79	1	0.0
	†NY A	4	4	.500	12	11	3	0-0	70.2	75	24	4	1	10-0	22	2.67	134	.280	.306	0-0	—	0	105	7	0.8
1983	Chi N	1	1	.500	4	4	0	0-0	20.2	18	9	1	0	10-2	9	3.92	97	.234	.318	7-0	.143	-0	76	0	0.0
1984	Chi N	5	5	.500	19	14	1	0-0	92.1	123	57	7	3	23-0	43	5.17	76	.339	.374	29-4	.241	2*	108	-11	-0.9
1985	Pit N	14	8	.636	31	26	9-1	1-0	194	153	58	7	3	52-10	138	2.27	158	.215	.271	59-6	.169	2	91	27	3.6
1986	Pit N	9	16	.360	35	34	4-2	0-0	215.2	232	106	20	8	57-2	125	3.96	97	.274	.322	70-8	.157	0*	97	-3	-0.2

Year	Tm Lg	W	L	Pct	G	GS	CG-Sho	SV-BS	IP	H	R	HR	HB	BB-IB	SO	ERA	AERA	OAV	OOB	AB-SH	AVG	PB	Sup	APR	PW
1987	Pit N★	8	6	.571	25	25	9-3	0-0	177	163	63	12	6	35-1	80	2.75	150	.246	.287	60-6	.150	2	98	25	2.1
	†SF N	5	3	.625	9	8	3-1	0-0	50	44	28	1	2	7-2	27	4.32	89	.230	.264	19-1	.105	-0	138	-3	-0.5
	Year	13	9	.591	34	33	**12-4**	0-0	227	207	34	13	8	42-3	107	3.09	131	.242	.282	79-7	.139	2	107	23	1.6
1988	SF N	19	11	.633	36	**36**	7-2	0-0	245	242	88	11	6	42-8	92	3.12	105	.260	.293	73-19	.110	-1	121	8	0.6
1989	†SF N★	17	8	.680	32	32	2	0-0	208.1	195	75	18	2	54-4	111	2.94	115	.247	.294	61-16	.164	1	110	11	1.4
1990	SF N	3	6	.333	15	13	0	1-0	87	102	40	8	1	31-9	49	3.93	93	.297	.353	26-3	.154	0	103	-2	-0.2
1991	SF N	0	2	.000	4	1	0	0-1	10.2	17	5	0	0	7-1	4	4.22	85	.370	.453	2-0	.000	-0	50	-1	-0.1
Total	19	214	191	.528	557	529	102-26	5-1	3548.1	3588	1494	221	88	935-117	2015	3.37	114	.264	.313	1115-135	.168	8	94	177	22.5
REUSS, JERRY Jerry B 6.19.1949 St.Louis, MO BL/TL 6-5/217# d9.27																									
1969	StL N	1	0	1.000	1	1	0	0-0	7	2	0	0	2	3-0	3	0.00	—	.091	.259	3-0	.333	0	50	3	0.6
1970	StL N	7	8	.467	20	20	5-2	0-0	127.1	132	62	9	1	49-2	74	4.10	101	.271	.337	40-5	.050	-3	83	2	-0.1
1971	StL N	14	14	.500	36	35	7-2	0-0	211	228	125	15	7	109-11	131	4.78	75	.279	.366	65-11	.123	0	120	-27	-3.3
1972	Hou N	9	13	.409	33	30	4-1	1-0	192	177	101	14	10	83-3	174	4.17	81	.246	.329	66-1	.106	-1	122	-19	-2.2
1973	Hou N	16	13	.552	41	**40**	12-3	0-0	279.1	271	123	17	3	117-6	177	3.74	97	.256	.330	95-9	.137	-1*	106	-1	-0.3
1974	†Pit N	16	11	.593	35	35	14-1	0-0	260	259	115	20	1	101-16	105	3.50	99	.261	.327	86-4	.151	0	108	-1	-0.2
1975	†Pit N★	18	11	.621	32	32	15-6	0-0	237.1	224	73	10	0	78-8	131	2.54	140	.253	.313	71-10	.197	2	93	30	4.1
1976	Pit N	14	9	.609	31	29	11-3	2-0	209.1	209	98	16	2	51-10	108	3.53	99	.256	.301	66-3	.242	6	118	-3	0.2
1977	Pit N	10	13	.435	33	33	8-2	0-0	208	225	109	11	4	71-2	116	4.11	97	.280	.339	70-4	.171	1*	102	-4	-0.2
1978	Pit N	3	2	.600	23	12	3-1	0-0	82.2	97	48	5	3	23-1	42	4.90	76	.297	.346	27-0	.185	0	127	-9	-0.5
1979	LA N	7	14	.333	39	21	4-1	3-3	160	178	88	4	3	60-7	83	3.54	103	.282	.347	42-3	.167	1	83	-5	-0.4
1980	LA N★	18	6	.750	37	29	10-**6**	3-2	229.1	193	74	12	0	40-9	111	2.51	140	.227	.260	68-4	.088	-1	111	25	2.6
1981	†LA N	10	4	.714	22	22	8-2	0-0	152.2	138	44	6	4	27-3	51	2.30	144	.243	.282	51-7	.196	0	126	17	1.8
1982	LA N	18	11	.621	39	37	8-4	0-0	254.2	232	98	11	2	50-10	138	3.11	112	.240	.277	77-16	.221	3	113	11	1.7
1983	†LA N	12	11	.522	32	31	7	0-0	223.1	233	94	12	2	50-5	143	2.94	122	.271	.311	71-10	.282	5	93	14	2.2
1984	LA N	5	7	.417	30	15	2	1-1	99	102	51	4	0	31-7	44	3.82	93	.266	.319	24-2	.167	1	93	-4	-0.4
1985	†LA N	14	10	.583	34	33	5-3	0-0	212.2	210	78	13	3	58-7	84	2.92	119	.260	.310	74-6	.135	-1	102	15	1.4
1986	LA N	2	6	.250	19	13	0	1-0	74	96	57	13	2	17-4	29	5.84	59	.313	.353	20-0	.250	2	113	-23	-2.0
1987	LA N	0	0	—	1	0	0	0-0	2	2	1	0	0	0-0	2	4.50	88	.333	.286	0-0	—	0		0	0.0
	Cin N	0	5	.000	7	7	0	0-0	34.2	52	31	2	1	12-2	10	7.79	55	.351	.404	8-2	.125	0	67	-12	-1.4
	Year	0	5	.000	8	7	0	0-0	36.2	54	34	2	1	12-2	12	7.61	56	.351	.399	8-2	.125	0	67	-12	-1.4
	Cal A	4	5	.444	17	16	1-1	0-0	82.1	112	60	16	2	17-1	37	5.25	82	.327	.361	0-0	—	0	115	-11	-1.0
1988	Chi A	13	9	.591	32	29	2	0-0	183	183	79	15	3	43-1	73	3.44	116	.263	.307	0-0	—	0	103	11	1.3
1989	Chi A	8	5	.615	23	19	1-1	0-1	106.2	135	65	12	3	21-1	27	5.06	75	.308	.340	0-0	—	0	115	-14	-1.6
	Mil A	1	4	.200	7	7	0	0-0	33.2	36	23	7	1	13-1	13	5.35	72	.273	.342	0-0	—	0	77	-6	-0.8
	Year	9	9	.500	30	26	1-1	0-1	140.1	171	26	19	4	34-2	40	5.13	74	.300	.340	0-0	—	0	105	-20	-2.4
1990	Pit N	0	0	—	4	1	0	0-0	7.2	8	3	1	0	3-1	1	3.52	103	.267	.333	0-2	—	0	75	0	0.0
Total	22	220	191	.535	628	547	127-39	11-7	3669.2	3734	1700	245	59	1127-118	1907	3.64	100	.265	.320	1024-99	.167	15	106	-11	1.5
REVENIG, TODD Todd Michael B 6.28.1969 Brainerd, MN BR/TR 6-1/185# d8.24																									
1992	Oak A	0	0	—	2	0	0	0-0	2	2	0	0	0	0-0	1	0.00	—	.286	.286	0-0	—	0		1	0.0
REYES, CARLOS Carlos Alberto B 4.4.1969 Miami, FL BB/TR 6-1/190# d4.7																									
1994	Oak A	0	3	.000	27	9	0	1-0	78	71	38	10	2	44-1	57	4.15	107	.242	.342	0-0	—	0	76	3	0.1
1995	Oak A	4	6	.400	40	1	0	0-1	69	71	43	10	5	28-4	48	5.09	88	.264	.344	0-0	—	0	83	-5	-0.6
1996	Oak A	7	10	.412	46	10	0	0-0	122.1	134	71	19	2	61-8	78	4.78	103	.281	.359	0-0	—	0	62	1	0.1
1997	Oak A	3	4	.429	37	6	0	0-1	77.1	101	52	13	2	25-2	43	5.82	78	.316	.367	0-0	—	0	68	-10	-0.8
1998	SD N	2	2	.500	22	0	0	1-1	27.2	23	11	4	2	6-0	24	3.58	109	.235	.290	0-1	—	0		2	0.2
	Bos A	1	1	.500	24	0	0	0-0	38.1	35	15	2	1	14-2	23	3.52	134	.246	.316	0-0	—	0		6	0.3
1999	SD N	2	4	.333	65	0	0	1-1	77.1	76	38	11	0	24-4	57	3.72	113	.254	.307	1-0	.000	-0		3	0.3
2000	Phi N	0	2	.000	10	0	0	0-0	10.1	10	6	2	0	5-0	4	5.23	89	.270	.357	0-0	—	0		0	-0.1
	SD N	1	1	.500	12	0	0	1-2	18	15	12	5	1	8-0	13	6.00	72	.221	.312	1-0	.000	-0		-3	-0.3
	Year	1	3	.250	22	0	0	1-2	28.1	25	21	7	1	13-0	17	5.72	78	.238	.328	1-0	.000	-0		-4	-0.4
2003	TB A	0	3	.000	10	3	0	0-0	39.2	40	23	10	2	5-0	13	5.22	87	.265	.294	1-0	.000	0	61	-2	-0.1
Total	8	20	36	.357	293	29	0	4-6	558	576	309	86	17	220-21	360	4.66	97	.267	.337	3-1	.000	-0	70	-5	-0.9
REYES, DENNYS Dennys (Valarde) B 4.19.1977 Higuera De Zaragoza, Mexico BL/TL 6-3/246# d7.13																									
1997	LA N	2	3	.400	14	5	0	0-0	47	51	21	4	1	18-3	36	3.83	101	.280	.347	9-1	.000	-1	119	1	0.1
1998	LA N	0	4	.000	11	3	0	0-0	28.2	27	17	1	0	20-4	33	4.71	84	.255	.370	5-1	.000	-1	116	-3	-0.4
	Cin N	3	1	.750	8	7	0	0-0	38.2	35	19	2	1	27-1	44	4.42	97	.255	.380	12-0	.083	-0	126	0	0.0
	Year	3	5	.375	19	10	0	0-0	67.1	62	25	3	1	47-5	77	4.54	91	.255	.375	17-1	.059	-1	124	-3	-0.4
1999	Cin N	2	2	.500	65	1	0	2-1	61.2	53	30	5	3	39-1	72	3.79	123	.232	.348	4-0	.000	-0	20	5	0.2
2000	Cin N	2	1	.667	62	0	0	0-1	43.2	43	31	5	1	29-0	36	4.53	104	.262	.371	2-0	.000	0		-2	-0.1
2001	Cin N	2	6	.250	35	6	0	0-0	53	51	35	5	1	35-1	52	4.92	93	.248	.357	11-0	.182	-0*	54	-3	-0.5
2002	Col N	0	1	.000	43	0	0	0-0	40.1	43	19	1	0	24-3	30	4.24	113	.279	.372	0-0	—	0		3	0.1
	Tex A	4	3	.571	15	5	0	0-0	42.1	55	33	9	0	21-1	29	6.38	74	.316	.390	0-0	—	0	118	-8	-1.1
2003	Pit N	0	0	—	12	0	0	0-0	10.1	10	13	1	0	9-1	11	10.45	42	.263	.388	0-0	—	0		-7	-0.3
	Ari N	0	0	—	3	0	0	0-0	2.1	5	3	1	0	1-0	5	11.57	40	.417	.462	0-0	—	0		-2	-0.1
	Year	0	0	—	15	0	0	0-0	12.2	15	22	2	0	10-1	16	10.66	42	.300	.403	0-0	—	0		-8	-0.4
Total	7	15	21	.417	268	27	0	2-2	368	373	221	34	7	223-15	348	4.77	94	.266	.366	43-2	.070	-2	98	-16	-2.1
REYES, AL Rafael Alberto B 4.10.1971 San Cristobal, D.R. BR/TR 6-1/195# d4.27																									
1995	Mil A	1	1	.500	27	0	0	1-0	33.1	19	9	3	3	18-2	29	2.43	205	.167	.292	0-0	—	0		9	0.5
1996	Mil A	1	0	1.000	5	0	0	0-0	5.2	8	5	1	0	2-0	2	7.94	65	.320	.370	0-0	—	0		-1	-0.2
1997	Mil A	1	2	.333	19	0	0	1-0	29.2	32	19	4	3	9-0	28	5.46	85	.274	.341	0-0	—	0		-2	-0.2
1998	Mil N	5	1	.833	50	0	0	0-1	57	55	26	9	2	31-1	58	3.95	108	.253	.351	5-0	.200	0		3	0.2
1999	Mil N	2	0	1.000	26	0	0	0-1	36	27	17	5	3	25-1	39	4.25	107	.206	.344	2-0	.000	-0		2	0.1
	Bal A	2	3	.400	27	0	0	0-3	29.2	23	16	4	3	16-2	28	4.85	97	.225	.341	0-0	—	0		0	0.0
2000	Bal A	1	0	1.000	13	0	0	0-1	13	13	10	2	0	11-1	10	6.92	68	.271	.393	0-0	—	0		-3	-0.2
	LA N	0	0	—	6	0	0	0-0	6.2	2	0	0	0	1-0	8	0.00	—	.087	.125	0-0	—	0		3	0.2
2001	LA N	2	1	.667	19	0	0	1-1	25.2	28	13	3	1	13-1	23	3.86	104	.269	.350	3-1	.333	0		0	0.0
2002	Pit N	0	0	—	15	0	0	0-1	17	9	5	1	2	7-0	21	2.65	158	.161	.273	0-0	—	0		3	0.2
2003	NY A	0	0	—	13	0	0	0-1	17	13	7	1	0	9-1	9	3.18	138	.203	.301	0-0	—	0		2	0.1
Total	9	15	8	.652	220	0	0	3-9	270.2	229	127	33	17	142-9	255	4.06	111	.229	.331	10-1	.200	0		16	0.7
REYNOLDS, ALLIE Allie Pierce "Superchief" B 2.10.1917 Bethany, OK D 12.26.1994 Oklahoma City, OK BR/TR 6/195# d9.17																									
1942	Cle A	0	0	—	2	0	0	0	5	5	1	0	0	4	2	0.00	—	.250	.375	2-0	.000	-0		2	0.0
1943	Cle A	11	12	.478	34	21	11-3	3	198.2	140	72	3	7	109	**151**	2.99	104	**.202**	.316	67-5	.149	-1*	112	5	0.5
1944	Cle A	11	8	.579	28	21	5-1	1	158	141	63	2	4	91	84	3.30	100	.240	.346	57-3	.123	-3*	102	2	-0.1
1945	Cle A✣	18	12	.600	44	30	16-2	4	247.1	227	102	7	5	130	112	3.20	101	.247	.343	85-7	.094	-7	108	1	-0.7
1946	Cle A	11	15	.423	31	28	9-3	0	183.1	180	93	10	1	108	107	3.88	85	.259	.359	63-6	.222	1*	96	-14	-1.7
1947	†NY A	19	8	**.704**	34	30	17-4	2	241.2	207	94	23	4	123	129	3.20	110	.227	.322	89-7	.146	-2*	153	9	0.7
1948	NY A	16	7	.696	39	31	11-1	3	236.1	240	108	17	4	111	101	3.77	108	.268	.351	83-5	.193	0*	129	10	0.7
1949	†NY A☆	17	6	.739	35	31	4-2	1	213.2	200	102	15	4	123	105	4.00	101	.250	.353	78-2	.218	6*	126	4	0.8
1950	†NY A★	16	12	.571	35	29	14-2	2	240.2	215	108	12	8	138	160	3.74	115	.242	.349	81-9	.185	1*	122	16	1.7
1951	†NY A	17	8	.680	40	26	16-**7**	7	221	171	84	12	5	100	126	3.05	125	**.213**	.304	76-5	.184	0*	140	21	2.2
1952	†NY A☆	20	8	.714	35	29	24-**6**	6	244.1	194	70	10	7	97	**160**	**2.06**	**161**	.218	.300	85-4	.153	-1*	118	35	4.1
1953	†NY A★	13	7	.650	41	15	5-1	13	145	140	64	9	5	61	86	3.41	108	.253	.333	41-0	.122	1*	106	4	0.5
1954	NY A✣	13	4	.765	36	18	5-4	7	157.1	133	65	13	3	66	100	3.32	104	.233	.314	50-5	.160	-0	185	2	0.2
Total	13	182	107	.630	434	309	137-36	49	2492.1	2193	1026	133	57	1261	1423	3.30	110	.238	.333	857-58	.163	-5	125	97	8.9

Year	Tm Lg	W	L	Pct	G	GS	CG-Sho	SV-BS	IP	H	R	HR	HB	BB-IB	SO	ERA	AERA	OAV	OOB	AB-SH	AVG	PB	Sup	APR	PW
REYNOLDS, ARCHIE Archie Edward B 1.3.1946 Glendale, CA BR/TR 6-2/205# d8.15																									
1968	Chi N	0	1	.000	7	1	0	0	13.1	14	10	1	1	7-0	6	6.75	47	.259	.355	2-0	.500	1	110	-5	-0.3
1969	Chi N	0	1	.000	2	2	0	0-0	7.1	11	5	1	0	7-1	4	2.45	164	.379	.500	1-0	.000	0	99	0	0.1
1970	Chi N	0	2	.000	7	1	0	0-0	15	17	11	2	1	9-0	9	6.60	68	.298	.403	2-0	.000	0	20	-3	-0.3
1971	Cal A	0	3	.000	15	1	0	0-0	27.1	32	15	2	0	18-5	15	4.61	70	.305	.407	2-0	.000	-0	0	-4	-0.4
1972	Mil A	0	1	.000	5	2	0	0-0	18.2	26	18	2	0	8-1	13	7.23	42	.338	.391	4-0	.500	1	102	-9	-0.5
Total	5	0	8	.000	36	7	0	0-0	81.2	100	59	8	2	49-7	47	5.73	61	.311	.403	11-0	.273	2	77	-21	-1.4
REYNOLDS, CHARLIE Charles E. B 7.31.1857 Allegany, NY D 5.1.1913 Buffalo, NY d5.18																									
1882	Phi AA	1	1	.500	2	2	1	0	12	18	11	0		3	4	5.25	53	.327	.362	8	.125	-1	110	-3	-0.4
REYNOLDS, KEN Kenneth Lee B 1.4.1947 Trevose, PA BL/TL 6/180# d9.5																									
1970	Phi N	0	0	—	4	0	0	0-0	2.1	3	0	0	0	4-0	1	0.00	—	.333	.538	0-0	—	0		1	0.1
1971	Phi N	5	9	.357	35	25	2-1	0-0	162.1	163	89	11	6	82-1	81	4.49	79	.269	.358	50-1	.200	2*	97	-16	-1.1
1972	Phi N	2	15	.118	33	23	2	0-0	154.1	149	76	17	1	60-6	87	4.26	84	.258	.327	40-1	.200	1*	75	-9	-0.8
1973	Mil A	0	1	.000	2	1	0	0-0	7.1	5	7	1	1	10-0	3	7.36	51	.200	.444	0-0	—	0	24	-3	-0.3
1975	StL N	0	1	.000	10	0	0	0-0	17	12	4	0	0	11-2	7	1.59	237	.214	.343	2-0	.000	-0		4	0.2
1976	SD N	0	3	.000	19	2	0	1-0	32.1	38	27	0	0	29-4	18	6.40	51	.309	.435	5-0	.000	-1	134	-12	-1.2
Total	6	7	29	.194	103	51	4-1	1-0	375.2	370	203	29	8	196-13	197	4.46	80	.265	.356	97-2	.186	2	87	-35	-3.1
REYNOLDS, SHANE Richard Shane B 3.26.1968 Bastrop, LA BR/TR 6-3/210# d7.20																									
1992	Hou N	1	3	.250	8	5	0	0-0	25.1	42	22	2	0	6-1	10	7.11	47	.385	.414	4-2	.500	1	134	-11	-1.4
1993	Hou N	0	0	—	5	1	0	0-0	11	11	4	0	0	6-1	10	0.82	474	.256	.347	2-0	.500	0	93	3	0.2
1994	Hou N	8	5	.615	33	14	1-1	0-0	124	128	46	10	6	21-3	110	3.05	130	.263	.302	33-7	.091	-2	107	14	1.1
1995	Hou N	10	11	.476	30	30	3-2	0-0	189.1	196	87	15	2	37-6	175	3.47	112	.263	.300	63-10	.127	-2*	117	7	0.7
1996	Hou N	16	10	.615	35	35	4-1	0-0	239	227	103	20	8	44-3	204	3.65	106	.249	.288	76-14	.184	4	98	9	1.3
1997	†Hou N	9	10	.474	30	30	2	0-0	181	189	92	19	3	47-5	152	4.23	95	.267	.313	53-7	.113	-0	112	-4	-0.3
1998	†Hou N	19	8	.704	35	**35**	3-1	0-0	233.1	257	99	25	2	53-2	209	3.51	115	.280	.318	82-7	.159	1	135	15	1.8
1999	†Hou N	16	14	.533	35	**35**	4-2	0-0	231.2	250	108	23	1	37-0	197	3.85	115	.275	.303	66-17	.167	1	94	15	2.0
2000	Hou N☆	7	8	.467	22	22	0	0-0	131	150	86	20	6	45-2	93	5.22	93	.287	.345	40-4	.225	2	102	-6	-0.4
2001	†Hou N	14	11	.560	28	28	3	0-0	182.2	208	95	24	4	36-2	102	4.34	106	.290	.327	52-10	.077	-2	98	5	0.4
2002	Hou N	3	6	.333	13	13	0	0-0	74	80	43	13	1	26-2	47	4.86	88	.274	.334	21-9	.048	-2	83	-5	-0.6
2003	Atl N	11	9	.550	30	29	0	0-0	167.1	191	104	20	8	59-6	94	5.43	78	.293	.358	54-10	.093	-3	142	-19	-2.2
Total	12	114	95	.545	304	277	20-7	0-0	1789.2	1929	889	191	41	417-33	1403	4.09	102	.275	.318	546-97	.141	-0	111	23	2.6
REYNOLDS, BOB Robert Allen B 1.21.1947 Seattle, WA BR/TR 6/205# d9.19																									
1969	Mon N	0	0	—	1	1	0	0-0	1.1	3	6	0	0	3-0	2	20.25	18	.429	.545	0-0	—	0	241	-3	-0.2
1971	StL N	0	0	—	4	0	0	0-0	7	15	8	2	1	6-1	4	10.29	35	.441	.537	1-0	.000	-0		-5	-0.3
	Mil A	0	1	.000	3	0	0	0-0	6	4	2	0	0	3-0	4	3.00	116	.222	.318	1-0	.000	-0		0	0.1
1972	Bal A	0	0	—	3	0	0	0-0	9.2	8	2	0	0	7-2	5	1.86	166	.258	.395	2-0	.000	-0		1	0.0
1973	†Bal A	7	5	.583	42	1	0	9-3	111	88	27	3	0	31-6	77	1.95	192	.219	.272	0-0	—	0	143	23	2.6
1974	†Bal A	7	5	.583	54	0	0	7-3	69.1	75	23	4	1	14-3	43	2.73	127	.278	.314	0-0	—	0		6	1.2
1975	Bal A	0	1	.000	7	0	0	0-2	6	11	6	1	0	1-0	1	9.00	39	.423	.429	0-0	—	0		-4	-0.6
	Det A	0	2	.000	21	0	0	3-1	34.2	40	20	8	1	14-1	26	4.67	86	.288	.355	0-0	—	0		-2	-0.1
	Cle A	0	2	.000	5	0	0	2-0	9.2	11	7	0	0	3-1	5	4.66	81	.289	.341	0-0	—	0		-1	-0.3
	Year	0	5	.000	33	0	0	5-3	50.1	62	39	9	1	18-2	32	5.19	76	.305	.362	0-0	—	0		-7	-1.0
Total	6	14	16	.467	140	2	0	21-9	254.2	255	101	18	3	82-14	167	3.15	116	.264	.320	4-0	.000	-0	194	15	2.4
REYNOLDS, ROSS Ross Ernest "Doc" B 8.20.1887 Barksdale, TX D 6.23.1970 Ada, OK BR/TR 6-2/185# d5.2																									
1914	Det A	5	3	.625	26	7	3-1	0	78	62	26	0	6	39	31	2.08	135	.230	.340	21-1	.048	-2	67	6	0.3
1915	Det A	0	1	.000	4	2	0	0	11.1	17	9	0	1	5	2	6.35	48	.378	.451	3-0	.000	-0	60	-3	-0.3
Total	2	5	4	.556	30	9	3-1	0	89.1	79	35	0	7	44	33	2.62	108	.251	.355	24-1	.042	-2	66	3	0.0
REYNOSO, ARMANDO Armando Martin (Gutierrez) B 5.1.1966 San Luis Potosi, Mexico BR/TR 6/196# d8.11																									
1991	Atl N	2	1	.667	6	5	0	0-0	23.1	26	18	4	3	10-1	10	6.17	63	.299	.390	7-0	.000	-0	139	-5	-0.6
1992	Atl N	1	0	1.000	3	1	0	1-0	7.2	11	4	2	1	2-1	2	4.70	78	.393	.452	2-1	.000	-0	198	-1	-0.1
1993	Col N	12	11	.522	30	30	4	0-0	189	206	101	22	9	63-7	117	4.00	119	.277	.337	63-6	.127	-1*	92	11	1.2
1994	Col N	3	4	.429	9	9	1	0-0	52.1	54	30	5	6	22-1	25	4.82	103	.278	.366	17-3	.176	-0	116	1	0.2
1995	†Col N	7	7	.500	20	18	0	0-0	93	116	61	12	5	36-3	40	5.32	101	.316	.383	30-2	.133	-2	82	0	0.0
1996	Col N	8	9	.471	30	30	0	0-0	168.2	195	97	27	9	49-0	88	4.96	105	.291	.347	52-7	.173	-1	95	6	0.6
1997	NY N	6	3	.667	16	16	1-1	0-0	91.1	95	47	7	6	29-4	47	4.53	89	.275	.338	29-0	.241	3	128	-3	0.0
1998	NY N	7	3	.700	11	11	0	0-0	68.1	64	31	4	5	32-3	40	3.82	108	.256	.351	30-1	.167	0	95	2	0.5
1999	Ari N	10	6	.625	31	27	0	0-0	167	178	90	20	6	67-7	79	4.37	105	.276	.347	49-8	.163	-0	121	3	0.3
2000	Ari N	11	12	.478	31	30	2	0-0	170.2	179	102	22	6	52-5	89	5.27	89	.273	.330	48-7	.104	-2	94	-8	-1.0
2001	Ari N	1	6	.143	9	9	0	0-0	46.2	58	32	13	4	13-2	15	5.98	77	.312	.366	10-3	.100	-0	90	-6	-0.8
2002	Ari N	0	0	—	2	0	0	0-0	1.2	3	2	0	0	1-0	2	10.80	41	.375	.444	0-0	—	0		-1	-0.1
Total	12	68	62	.523	198	186	8-1	1-0	1079.2	1185	615	138	60	376-34	554	4.74	100	.283	.349	337-38	.148	-4	101	-1	0.2
RHEM, FLINT Charles Flint "Shad" B 1.24.1901 Rhems, SC D 7.30.1969 Columbia, SC BR/TR 6-2/180# d9.6																									
1924	StL N	2	2	.500	6	3	3	1	32.1	31	18	1	0	17	20	4.45	85	.254	.345	12-0	.167	-0	135	-2	-0.3
1925	StL N	8	13	.381	30	24	8-1	1	170	204	114	16	4	58	66	4.92	88	.299	.357	59-5	.237	1	109	-13	-1.2
1926	†StL N	**20**	7	.741	34	34	20-1	0	258	241	121	12	1	75	72	3.21	122	.250	.305	96-5	.188	-2	143	15	1.2
1927	StL N	10	12	.455	27	26	9-2	0	169.1	189	102	6	4	54	51	4.41	90	.285	.342	59-3	.068	-5	97	-9	-1.6
1928	†StL N	11	8	.579	28	22	9	3	169.2	199	91	13	3	71	47	4.14	97	.296	.365	67-1	.164	-1	124	-2	-0.2
1930	†StL N	12	8	.600	26	19	9	0	139.2	173	90	11	3	37	47	4.45	113	.306	.352	52-4	.231	-1	144	5	0.3
1931	†StL N	11	10	.524	33	26	10-2	1	207.1	214	100	17	3	60	72	3.56	111	.268	.321	69-5	.130	-4	116	6	0.1
1932	StL N	4	2	.667	6	6	5-1	0	50	48	19	3	0	10	18	3.06	129	.257	.294	16-3	.188	0	128	5	0.6
	Phi N	11	7	.611	26	20	10	1	168.2	177	79	13	0	49	35	3.74	118	.269	.319	62-4	.113	-5	117	12	0.7
	Year	15	9	.625	32	26	15-1	1	218.2	225	85	16	0	59	53	3.58	120	.266	.314	78-7	.128	-5	120	18	1.3
1933	Phi N	5	14	.263	28	19	3	2	125	182	109	10	2	33	27	6.62	58	.340	.381	46-1	.087	-4	100	-34	-5.0
1934	StL N	1	0	1.000	5	1	0	1	15.2	26	12	0	0	7	6	4.60	92	.394	.452	2-0	.000	-0	163	-2	-0.2
	Bos N	8	8	.500	25	20	5-1	0	152.2	164	71	5	0	38	56	3.60	106	.273	.317	52-1	.058	-5	78	4	-0.1
	Year	9	8	.529	30	21	5-1	1	168.1	190	74	5	0	45	62	3.69	105	.285	.331	54-1	.056	-5	82	3	-0.3
1935	Bos N	0	5	.000	10	6	0	0	40.1	61	37	4	0	11	10	5.36	71	.341	.379	10-1	.000	-1	67	-12	-1.3
1936	StL N	2	1	.667	10	4	0	0	26.2	49	26	2	0	9	7	6.75	58	.405	.446	8-0	.125	-0	172	-10	-1.0
Total	12	105	97	.520	294	230	91-8	10	1725.1	1958	989	113	20	529	534	4.20	98	.287	.340	610-33	.144	-28	117	-37	-8.0
RHINES, BILLY William Pearl "Bunker" B 3.14.1869 Ridgway, PA D 1.30.1922 Ridgway, PA BR/TR 5-11/168# d4.22																									
1890	Cin N	28	17	.622	46	45	45-6	0	401.1	337	163	6	15	113	182	**1.95**	**183**	.221	**.281**	154	.188	-5	71	**68**	**6.0**
1891	Cin N	17	24	.415	48	43	40-1	1	372.2	364	224	4	22	124	138	2.87	117	.246	.314	148	.122	-9	84	12	0.4
1892	Cin N	3	7	.300	11	9	6	0	74.2	102	71	0	4	36	10	5.42	60	.313	.388	27	.185	1*	84	-19	-1.9
1893	Lou N	1	4	.200	5	5	3	0	31	49	37	3	3	19	0	8.71	50	.348	.436	11	.091	-2	86	-15	-1.6
1895	Cin N	19	10	.655	38	33	25	0	267.2	322	195	4	21	76	72	4.81	103	.293	.351	113-2	.221	-3	116	6	0.1
1896	Cin N	8	6	.571	19	17	11-3	0	143	128	52	1	9	48	32	**2.45**	**188**	**.238**	**.311**	52-1	.192	-3	71	33	2.4
1897	Cin N	21	15	.583	41	32	26-1	0	288.2	311	175	4	17	86	65	4.08	111	.273	.333	107-2	.159	-6	71	14	0.7
1898	Pit N	12	16	.429	31	29	27-2	0	258	289	143	0	13	61	48	3.52	101	.281	.329	100-1	.150	-4	80	0	-0.2
1899	Pit N	4	4	.500	9	9	4	0	54	59	42	3	4	13	6	6.00	64	.277	.330	23-1	.435	4*	113	-10	-0.9
Total	9	113	103	.523	248	222	187-13	1	1891	1961	1102	25	108	576	553	3.48	114	.262	.324	735-7	.177	-27	85	89	5.0
RHOADS, BOB Robert Barton "Dusty" (b: Barton Emory Rhoads) B 10.4.1879 Wooster, OH D 2.12.1967 San Bernardino, CA BR/TR 6-1/215# d4.19																									
1902	Chi N	4	8	.333	16	12	12-1	1	118	131	66	1	6	42	43	3.20	84	.281	.348	45-0	.222	0	61	-6	-0.6
1903	StL N	5	8	.385	17	13	12-1	0	129	154	88	3	3	47	52	4.60	71	.303	.366	50-2	.140	-2*	87	-14	-1.4
	Cle A	2	3	.400	5	5	5	0	41	55	34	2	2	3	21	5.27	54	.320	.339	17-0	.118	-1	90	-10	-1.2
1904	Cle A	10	9	.526	22	19	18	0	175.1	175	72	1	5	48	72	2.87	88	.261	.315	92-0	.196	0*	104	-4	-0.5

Year	Tm Lg	W	L	Pct	G	GS	CG-Sho	SV-BS	IP	H	R	HR	HB	BB-IB	SO	ERA	AERA	OAV	OOB	AB-SH	AVG	PB	Sup	APR	PW
1905	Cle A	16	9	.640	28	26	24-4	0	235	219	96	4	10	55	61	2.83	93	.249	.300	95-3	.221	4*	111	-4	0.1
1906	Cle A	22	10	.688	38	34	31-7	0	315	259	95	5	5	92	89	1.80	145	.227	.288	118-6	.161	-3	114	**28**	2.5
1907	Cle A	15	14	.517	35	31	23-5	1	275	258	105	0	14	84	76	2.29	109	.250	.316	92-6	.185	-1	90	7	0.5
1908	Cle A	18	12	.600	37	30	20-1	0	270	229	82	2	7	73	62	1.77	135	.239	.298	90-5	.222	4	104	16	2.5
1909	Cle A	5	9	.357	20	15	9-2	0	133.1	124	63	1	6	50	46	2.90	88	.281	.361	43-4	.163	-0	118	-5	-0.6
Total	8	97	82	.542	218	185	154-21	2	1691.2	1604	701	19	58	494	522	2.61	100	.256	.316	642-26	.188	-0	100	8	1.3
RHODEN, RICK Richard Alan B 5.16.1953 Boynton Beach, FL BR/TR 6-3/195# d7.5																									
1974	LA N	1	0	1.000	4	0	0	0-0	9	5	2	1	0	4-1	7	2.00	171	.161	.257	2-0	.500	0		2	0.2
1975	LA N	3	3	.500	26	11	1	0-1	99.1	94	40	8	1	32-1	40	3.08	111	.253	.310	28-1	.071	-2	101	3	0.0
1976	LA N★	12	3	.800	27	26	10-3	0-0	181	165	66	17	1	53-2	77	2.98	114	.242	.296	65-7	.308	7	121	8	1.3
1977	†LA N	16	10	.615	31	31	4-1	0-0	216.1	223	98	20	2	63-1	122	3.74	102	.270	.321	78-6	.231	5*	106	3	0.7
1978	†LA N	10	8	.556	30	23	6-3	0-0	164.2	160	77	13	3	51-0	79	3.66	96	.255	.311	52-6	.135	-0	128	-3	-0.4
1979	Pit N	0	1	.000	1	1	0	0-0	5	5	4	0	0	2-0	2	7.20	54	.263	.333	1-0	1.000	0	23	-2	-0.2
1980	Pit N	7	5	.583	20	19	2	0-0	126.2	133	58	9	3	40-4	70	3.84	95	.273	.330	40-4	.375	6	103	-2	0.5
1981	Pit N	9	4	.692	21	21	4-2	0-0	136.1	147	66	6	2	53-2	76	3.89	92	.283	.348	48-3	.188	1	108	-4	-0.2
1982	Pit N	11	14	.440	35	35	6-1	0-0	230.1	239	115	14	2	70-8	128	4.14	90	.267	.320	83-2	.265	8*	100	-9	0.1
1983	Pit N	13	13	.500	36	35	7-2	1-0	244.1	256	95	13	2	68-15	153	3.09	120	.276	.325	86-2	.151	-2	92	16	1.5
1984	Pit N	14	9	.609	33	33	6-3	0-0	238.1	216	81	13	1	62-0	136	2.72	133	.243	.292	84-5	.333	10*	91	23	3.4
1985	Pit N	10	15	.400	35	35	2	0-0	213.1	254	119	18	6	69-3	128	4.47	80	.296	.352	74-2	.189	2*	89	-22	-2.2
1986	Pit N☆	15	12	.556	34	34	12-1	0-0	253.2	211	82	17	2	76-8	159	2.84	135	.228	.286	90-7	.278	9*	103	30	4.3
1987	NY A	16	10	.615	30	29	4	0-0	181.2	184	84	22	3	61-5	107	3.86	114	.268	.327	0-0	—	0	84	11	1.4
1988	NY A	12	12	.500	30	30	5-1	0-0	197	206	107	20	8	56-4	94	4.29	92	.269	.322	1-0	.000	-0*	100	-10	-1.1
1989	Hou N	2	6	.250	20	17	0	0-0	96.2	108	49	7	3	41-8	41	4.28	79	.289	.361	29-2	.207	1	86	-9	-0.6
Total	16	151	125	.547	413	380	69-17	1-1	2593.2	2606	1143	198	39	801-62	1419	3.59	103	.264	.319	761-47	.238	45	100	35	8.7
RHODES, ARTHUR Arthur Lee B 10.24.1969 Waco, TX BL/TL 6-2/206# d8.21																									
1991	Bal A	0	3	.000	8	8	0	0-0	36	47	35	4	0	23-0	23	8.00	49	.320	.405	0-0	—	0	90	-17	-1.2
1992	Bal A	7	5	.583	15	15	2-1	0-0	94.1	87	39	6	1	38-2	77	3.63	111	.249	.324	0-0	—	0	103	5	0.6
1993	Bal A	5	6	.455	17	17	0	0-0	85.2	91	62	16	1	49-1	49	6.51	69	.274	.366	0-0	—	0	94	-17	-1.8
1994	Bal A	3	5	.375	10	10	3-2	0-0	52.2	51	34	8	2	30-1	47	5.81	86	.254	.352	0-0	—	0	103	-4	-0.5
1995	Bal A	2	5	.286	19	9	0	0-1	75.1	68	53	13	0	48-1	77	6.21	77	.239	.349	0-0	—	0	104	-11	-0.9
1996	†Bal A	9	1	.900	28	2	0	1-0	53	48	28	6	0	23-3	62	4.08	121	.241	.318	0-0	—	0	122	4	0.6
1997	†Bal A	10	3	.769	53	0	0	1-1	95.1	75	32	9	4	26-5	102	3.02	146	.218	.278	1-0	.000	-0*		16	2.0
1998	Bal A	4	4	.500	45	0	0	4-4	77	65	30	8	1	34-2	83	3.51	130	.233	.313	2-0	.500	0		10	0.9
1999	Bal A	3	4	.429	43	0	0	3-2	53	43	37	9	0	45-6	59	5.43	86	.221	.364	0-0	—	0		-6	-0.7
2000	†Sea A	5	8	.385	72	0	0	0-7	69.1	51	34	6	0	29-3	77	4.28	110	.205	.286	0-0	—	0		4	0.7
2001	†Sea A	8	0	1.000	71	0	0	3-4	68	46	14	5	1	12-0	83	1.72	241	.189	.230	1-0	.000	-0*		20	2.2
2002	Sea A	10	4	.714	66	0	0	2-5	69.2	45	18	4	0	13-1	81	2.33	182	.187	.227	0-0	—	0		16	3.0
2003	Sea A	3	3	.500	67	0	0	3-3	54	53	25	4	1	18-2	48	4.17	104	.256	.319	0-0	—	0		2	0.2
Total	13	69	51	.575	514	61	5-3	17-27	883.1	770	441	98	11	388-27	868	4.33	103	.235	.316	4-0	.250	0	100	22	5.1
RHODES, CHARLIE Charles Anderson "Dusty" B 4.7.1885 Caney, KS D 10.26.1918 Caney, KS BR/TR 5-7/180# d7.26																									
1906	StL N	3	4	.429	9	6	3	0	45	37	21	0	6	20	32	3.40	77	.223	.328	16-0	.188	-0	97	-3	-0.5
1908	Cin N	0	0	—	1	0	0	0	4	1	2	0	1	2	4	0.00	—	.077	.250	1-0	.000	-0		0	0.0
	StL N	1	2	.333	4	4	3	0	33	23	14	2	1	12	15	3.00	79	.200	.281	12-0	.250	1	104	-1	0.0
	Year	1	2	.333	5	4	3	0	37	24	18	2	2	14	19	2.68	88	.188	.278	13-0	.231	1	105	-2	0.0
1909	StL N	3	5	.375	12	10	4	0	61	55	36	0	2	33	25	3.98	63	.256	.360	19-0	.211	1	113	-10	-0.9
Total	3	7	11	.389	26	20	10	0	143	116	73	2	10	67	76	3.46	73	.228	.329	48-0	.208	2	107	-14	-1.4
RHODES, GORDON John Gordon "Dusty" B 8.11.1907 Winnemucca, NV D 3.22.1960 Long Beach, CA BR/TR 6/187# d4.29																									
1929	NY A	0	4	.000	10	4	0	0	42.2	57	32	3	2	16	13	4.85	80	.333	.397	10-3	.300	1	82	-7	-0.5
1930	NY A	0	0	—	3	0	0	0	2	3	3	0	0	4	1	9.00	48	.500	.700	0-0	—	0		-1	-0.1
1931	NY A	6	3	.667	18	11	4	0	87	82	49	3	0	52	36	3.41	116	.235	.334	28-4	.214	1	147	1	0.1
1932	NY A	1	2	.333	10	2	1	0	24	25	22	0	0	21	15	7.88	52	.275	.411	7-0	.286	0	230	-10	-0.9
	Bos A	1	8	.111	12	11	4	0	79.1	79	46	5	0	31	22	5.11	88	.261	.329	27-0	.074	-2	45	-2	-0.4
	Year	2	10	.167	22	13	5	0	103.1	104	48	5	0	52	37	5.75	76	.264	.350	34-0	.118	-2	72	-11	-1.3
1933	Bos A	12	15	.444	34	29	14	0	232	242	126	13	1	93	85	4.03	109	.265	.334	86-4	.267	4*	114	7	1.2
1934	Bos A	12	12	.500	44	31	10	2	219	247	133	10	4	98	79	4.56	105	.285	.360	75-1	.133	-3	103	5	0.2
1935	Bos A	2	10	.167	34	19	1	2	146.1	195	103	14	1	60	44	5.41	88	.324	.387	48-1	.146	-4*	83	-10	-1.1
1936	Phi A	9	20	.310	35	28	13-1	1	216.1	266	162	26	2	102	61	5.74	89	.304	.378	75-2	.213	-2	68	-17	-2.0
Total	8	43	74	.368	200	135	47-1	5	1048.2	1196	676	74	10	477	356	4.85	95	.286	.361	356-15	.194	-5	95	-34	-3.5
RHODES, BILL William Clarence B Pottstown, PA d6.14																									
1893	Lou N	5	12	.294	20	19	17	0	151.2	244	173	10	10	66	22	7.60	58	.352	.416	70	.129	-4	127	-59	-4.7
RIBANT, DENNIS Dennis Joseph B 9.20.1941 Detroit, MI BR/TR 5-11/175# d8.9																									
1964	NY N	1	5	.167	14	7	1-1	1	57.2	65	35	8	0	9-1	35	5.15	69	.281	.308	20-0	.100	-0*	105	-9	-0.9
1965	NY N	1	3	.250	19	1	0	3	35.1	29	16	5	0	6-0	13	3.82	92	.228	.261	6-0	.000	-1	25	-1	-0.2
1966	NY N	11	9	.550	39	26	10-1	3	188.1	184	78	20	1	40-5	84	3.20	114	.254	.291	61-4	.197	0*	99	9	1.0
1967	Pit N	9	8	.529	38	22	2	0	172	186	78	16	3	40-5	75	4.08	82	.280	.323	60-2	.267	5*	108	-9	-0.2
1968	Det A	2	2	.500	14	0	0	1	24.1	20	7	1	1	10-2	7	2.22	136	.217	.301	5-0	.200	0*		2	0.4
	Chi A	0	2	.000	17	0	0	1	31.1	42	24	3	2	17-4	20	6.03	50	.318	.399	7-0	.000	-1		-10	-0.8
	Year	2	4	.333	31	0	0	2	55.2	62	35	4	3	27-6	27	4.37	69	.277	.359	12-0	.083	-0		-8	-0.4
1969	StL N	0	0	—	1	0	0	0-0	1.1	4	2	1	0	1-0	0	13.50	26	.571	.556	0-0	—	0*		-1	-0.1
	Cin N	0	0	—	7	0	0	0-1	8.1	6	5	1	0	3-0	7	1.08	349	.188	.257	0-0	—	0		1	0.0
	Year	0	0	—	8	0	0	0-1	9.2	10	7	2	0	4-0	7	2.79	134	.256	.318	0-0	—	0		-1	-0.1
Total	6	24	29	.453	149	56	13-2	9-1	518.2	536	245	55	7	126-17	241	3.87	90	.267	.310	159-6	.195	4	103	-18	-0.8
RICCELLI, FRANK Frank Joseph B 2.24.1953 Syracuse, NY BL/TL 6-3/205# d9.11																									
1976	SF N	1	1	.500	4	3	0	0-0	16	16	10	1	0	5-0	11	5.63	65	.258	.309	6-0	.167	-0	97	-3	-0.3
1978	Hou N	0	0	—	2	0	0	0-0	3	1	0	0	0	0-0	1	0.00	—	.100	.100	0-0	—	0		1	0.1
1979	Hou N	2	2	.500	11	2	0	0-0	22	22	11	0	0	18-0	20	4.09	86	.262	.392	6-0	.333	1	138	-1	-0.1
Total	3	3	3	.500	17	5	0	0-0	41	39	21	1	0	23-0	32	4.39	81	.250	.344	12-0	.250	1	115	-3	-0.3
RICCI, CHUCK Charles Mark B 11.20.1968 Abington, PA BR/TR 6-2/180# d9.8																									
1995	Phi N	1	0	1.000	7	0	0	0-0	10	9	2	0	1	3-0	9	1.80	235	.273	.333	0-0	—	0		3	0.2
RICE, SAM Edgar Charles B 2.20.1890 Morocco, IN D 10.13.1974 Rossmoor, MD BL/TR 5-9/150# d8.7 Mil 1918 HF1963 ▲																									
1915	Was A	1	0	1.000	4	2	1	0	18	13	8	0	0	9	9	2.00	148	.213	.314	8-0	.375	1	147	1	0.1
1916	Was A	0	1	.000	5	1	0	0	21.1	18	10	0	0	10	3	2.95	95	.237	.326	197-1	.299	2*	54	-1	0.1
Total	2	1	1	.500	9	3	1	0	39.1	31	18	0	0	19	12	2.52	114	.226	.321	205-1	.302	2	121	0	0.2
RICE, PAT Patrick Edward B 11.2.1963 Rapid City, SD BR/TR 6-2/200# d5.18																									
1991	Sea A	1	1	.500	7	2	0	0-0	21	18	10	3	1	10-1	12	3.00	138	.234	.319	0-0	—	0	78	2	0.1
RICH, WOODY Woodrow Earl B 3.9.1916 Morganton, NC D 4.18.1983 Morganton, NC BL/TR 6-2/185# d4.22 Mil 1945																									
1939	Bos A	4	3	.571	21	12	3	1	77	78	46	2	5	35	24	4.91	96	.264	.352	27-1	.259	0	138	0	0.1
1940	Bos A	1	0	1.000	3	1	1	0	11.2	9	3	2	0	1	8	0.77	583	.214	.233	4-0	.000	-1	78	4	0.2
1941	Bos A	0	0	—	2	1	0	0	3.2	8	7	1	0	2	4	17.18	24	.421	.476	0-0	—	0	166	-5	-0.2
1944	Bos N	1	1	.500	7	2	1	0	25	32	17	3	3	12	6	5.76	66	.327	.416	8-1	.125	-1	110	-4	-0.4
Total	4	6	4	.600	33	16	5	1	117.1	127	73	8	8	50	42	5.06	89	.280	.361	39-2	.205	-1	135	-5	-0.3
RICHARD, J.R. James Rodney B 3.7.1950 Vienna, LA BR/TR 6-8/222# d9.5																									
1971	Hou N	2	1	.667	4	4	1	0-0	21	17	9	1	0	16-0	29	3.43	98	.215	.344	7-2	.000	-1	92	0	-0.1

Year	Tm Lg	W	L	Pct	G	GS	CG-Sho	SV-BS	IP	H	R	HR	HB	BB-IB	SO	ERA	AERA	OAV	OOB	AB-SH	AVG	PB	Sup	APR	PW
1972	Hou N	1	0	1.000	4	1	0	0-0	6	10	9	0	2	8-0	8	13.50	25	.385	.556	0-0	—	0	184	-7	-0.9
1973	Hou N	6	2	.750	16	10	2-1	0-0	72	54	37	2	1	38-0	75	4.00	91	.210	.313	28-1	.179	-0	153	-4	-0.5
1974	Hou N	2	3	.400	15	9	0	0-0	64.2	58	31	3	1	36-0	42	4.18	83	.243	.343	21-1	.143	0	109	-4	-0.3
1975	Hou N	12	10	.545	33	31	7-1	0-0	203	178	107	8	4	138-0	176	4.39	77	.238	.358	74-5	.203	4	142	-24	-2.0
1976	Hou N	20	15	.571	39	39	14-3	0-0	291	221	105	14	4	151-4	214	2.75	116	**.212**	.312	100-1	.140	0	105	15	1.7
1977	Hou N	18	12	.600	36	36	13-3	0-0	267	212	94	18	0	104-1	214	2.97	120	.218	.292	87-11	.230	6	107	22	3.2
1978	Hou N	18	11	.621	36	36	16-3	0-0	275.1	192	104	12	2	141-4	**303**	3.11	107	**.196**	.298	101-5	.178	1*	125	7	0.9
1979	Hou N	18	13	.581	38	38	19-4	0-0	292.1	220	98	13	3	98-5	**313**	**2.71**	130	**.209**	.276	95-11	.126	-0	85	**29**	2.9
1980	Hou N★	10	4	.714	17	17	4-4	0-0	113.2	65	31	2	0	40-1	119	1.90	173	.166	.242	39-4	.154	1	93	18	2.3
Total	10	107	71	.601	238	221	76-19	0-0	1606	1227	625	73	17	770-15	1493	3.15	108	.212	.305	552-41	.168	12	112	52	7.2

RICHARDS, DUANE Duane Lee B 12.16.1936 Spartanburg, IN BR/TR 6-3/200# d9.25

Year	Tm Lg	W	L	Pct	G	GS	CG-Sho	SV-BS	IP	H	R	HR	HB	BB-IB	SO	ERA	AERA	OAV	OOB	AB-SH	AVG	PB	Sup	APR	PW
1960	Cin N	0	0	—	2	0	0	0	3	5	4	0	0	2-0	2	9.00	42	.385	.438	0-0	—	0		-2	-0.1

RICHARDS, RUSTY Russell Earl B 1.27.1965 Houston, TX BL/TR 6-4/200# d9.20

Year	Tm Lg	W	L	Pct	G	GS	CG-Sho	SV-BS	IP	H	R	HR	HB	BB-IB	SO	ERA	AERA	OAV	OOB	AB-SH	AVG	PB	Sup	APR	PW
1989	Atl N	0	0	—	2	2	0	0-0	9.1	10	5	2	1	6-0	4	4.82	76	.278	.395	3-1	.000	-0	133	-1	-0.1
1990	Atl N	0	0	—	1	0	0	0-0	1	2	3	1	0	1-0	0	27.00	15	.400	.500	0-0	—	0		-2	-0.1
Total	2	0	0	—	3	2	0	0-0	10.1	12	8	3	1	7-0	4	6.97	53	.293	.408	3-1	.000	-0	133	-3	-0.2

RICHARDSON, HARDY Abram Harding "Old True Blue" B 4.21.1855 Clarksboro, NJ D 1.14.1931 Utica, NY BR/TR 5-9.5/170# d5.1.1879 ▲

Year	Tm Lg	W	L	Pct	G	GS	CG-Sho	SV-BS	IP	H	R	HR	HB	BB-IB	SO	ERA	AERA	OAV	OOB	AB-SH	AVG	PB	Sup	APR	PW
1885	Buf N	0	0	—	1	0	0	0	4	5	2	0		3	1	2.25	133	.294	.400	426	.319	0*		0	0.0
1886	Det N	3	0	1.000	4	0	0	0	12	11	8	1		10	5	4.50	74	.208	.333	538	.351	2*		-1	-0.1
Total	2	3	0	1.000	5	0	0	0	16	16	10	1		13	6	3.94	82	.229	.349	964	.337	3		-1	-0.1

RICHARDSON, DANNY Daniel B 1.25.1863 Elmira, NY D 9.12.1926 New York, NY BR/TR 5-8/165# d5.22.1884 M1 ▲

Year	Tm Lg	W	L	Pct	G	GS	CG-Sho	SV-BS	IP	H	R	HR	HB	BB-IB	SO	ERA	AERA	OAV	OOB	AB-SH	AVG	PB	Sup	APR	PW
1885	NY N	7	1	.875	9	8	7-1	0	75	58	30	0		18	21	2.40	111	.205	.252	198	.263	2*	175	5	0.5
1886	NY N	0	2	.000	5	1	1	0	25	33	24	1		11	17	5.76	56	.320	.386	237	.232	1*	19	-7	-0.3
1887	NY N	0	0	—	1	0	0	0	0	0	0	0	0	1	0	—	—	—	1.000	450	.278	0*		0	0.0
Total	3	7	3	.700	15	9	8-1	0	100	91	54	1	0	30	38	3.24	86	.236	.291	885	.262	3	154	-2	0.2

RICHARDSON, GORDIE Gordon Clark B 7.19.1938 Colquitt, GA BR/TL 6/185# d7.26

Year	Tm Lg	W	L	Pct	G	GS	CG-Sho	SV-BS	IP	H	R	HR	HB	BB-IB	SO	ERA	AERA	OAV	OOB	AB-SH	AVG	PB	Sup	APR	PW
1964	†StL N	4	2	.667	19	6	1	1	47	40	18	2	1	15-0	28	2.30	166	.231	.296	13-0	.077	-0	104	6	0.7
1965	NY N	2	2	.500	35	0	0	2	52.1	41	27	5	2	16-2	43	3.78	93	.224	.289	7-1	.000	-1		-2	-0.3
1966	NY N	0	2	.000	15	1	0	1	18.2	24	19	7	0	6-1	15	9.16	40	.312	.353	1-0	.000	-0	48	-10	-1.1
Total	3	6	6	.500	69	7	1	4	118	105	64	14	3	37-3	86	4.04	90	.242	.303	21-1	.048	-1	99	-6	-0.7

RICHARDSON, JEFF Jeffrey Scott B 8.29.1963 Wichita, KS BR/TR 6-3/185# d9.19

Year	Tm Lg	W	L	Pct	G	GS	CG-Sho	SV-BS	IP	H	R	HR	HB	BB-IB	SO	ERA	AERA	OAV	OOB	AB-SH	AVG	PB	Sup	APR	PW
1990	Cal A	0	0	—	1	0	0	0-0	0.1	1	0	0	0	0-0	0	0.00	—	.500	.500	0-0	—	0		0	0.0

RICHARDSON, JACK John William B 10.3.1891 Central City, IL D 1.18.1970 Marion, IL BB/TR 6-3/197# d9.17

Year	Tm Lg	W	L	Pct	G	GS	CG-Sho	SV-BS	IP	H	R	HR	HB	BB-IB	SO	ERA	AERA	OAV	OOB	AB-SH	AVG	PB	Sup	APR	PW
1915	Phi A	0	1	.000	3	3	2	0	24	21	13	0	1	14	11	2.63	111	.253	.367	8-0	.000	-1	116	0	-0.2
1916	Phi A	0	0	—	1	0	0	0	0.2	2	3	0	0	1	1	40.50	7	.667	.750	0-0	—	0		-2	-0.1
Total	2	0	1	.000	4	3	2	0	24.2	23	16	0	1	15	12	3.65	80	.267	.382	8-0	.000	-1	116	-2	-0.3

RICHERT, PETE Peter Gerard B 10.29.1939 Floral Park, NY BL/TL 6/184# d4.12 Mil 1968

Year	Tm Lg	W	L	Pct	G	GS	CG-Sho	SV-BS	IP	H	R	HR	HB	BB-IB	SO	ERA	AERA	OAV	OOB	AB-SH	AVG	PB	Sup	APR	PW
1962	LA N	5	4	.556	19	12	1	0	81.1	77	35	6	1	45-1	75	3.87	94	.249	.346	25-1	.080	-1	137	0	-0.1
1963	LA N	5	3	.625	20	12	1	0	78	80	40	7	1	28-3	54	4.50	67	.262	.326	22-2	.182	1	138	-11	-1.0
1964	LA N	2	3	.400	8	6	1-1	0	34.2	38	17	2	2	18-2	25	4.15	78	.271	.360	11-0	.091	-0	113	-3	-0.4
1965	Was A★	15	12	.556	34	29	6	0	194	146	64	18	2	84-7	161	2.60	134	.210	.296	64-3	.156	-0*	78	19	2.6
1966	Was A★	14	14	.500	36	34	7	0	245.2	196	106	36	1	69-6	195	3.37	103	.215	.270	86-5	.163	2*	94	1	0.3
1967	Was A	2	6	.250	11	10	1-1	0	54.1	49	29	5	1	15-0	41	4.64	68	.237	.288	17-1	.059	-1*	44	-8	-1.2
	Bal A	7	10	.412	26	19	5-1	2	132.1	107	53	11	1	41-1	90	2.99	105	.220	.279	37-5	.108	-1*	71	0	0.0
	Year	9	16	.360	37	29	6-2	2	186.2	156	56	16	2	56-1	131	3.47	91	.225	.282	54-6	.093	-2	62	-6	-1.2
1968	Bal A	6	3	.667	36	0	0	6	62.1	51	25	7	3	12-1	47	3.47	84	.225	.273	10-1	.200	0		-3	-0.3
1969	†Bal A	7	4	.636	44	0	0	12-3	57.1	42	17	7	0	14-2	54	2.20	162	.202	.249	8-2	.125	-0		8	1.7
1970	†Bal A	7	2	.778	50	0	0	13-4	54.2	36	14	5	1	24-3	66	1.98	185	.194	.284	4-0	.000	-0		10	2.1
1971	†Bal A	3	5	.375	35	0	0	4-1	36.1	26	15	3	1	22-6	35	3.47	97	.205	.325	2-1	.000	-0		0	0.0
1972	LA N	2	3	.400	37	0	0	6-3	52	42	17	3	1	18-5	38	2.25	148	.219	.286	6-1	.500	1		6	0.8
1973	LA N	3	3	.500	39	0	0	7-6	51	44	18	5	1	19-5	31	3.18	108	.234	.306	5-1	.200	0		3	0.4
1974	StL N	0	0	—	13	0	0	1-0	11.1	10	7	1	0	11-1	4	2.38	151	.244	.389	0-0	—	0		0	0.0
	Phi N	2	1	.667	21	0	0	0-0	20.1	15	6	0	0	4-3	9	2.21	171	.205	.244	0-0	—	0		3	0.4
	Year	2	1	.667	34	0	0	1-0	31.2	25	13	1	0	15-4	13	2.27	163	.219	.303	0-0	—	0		3	0.4
Total	13	80	73	.523	429	122	22-3	51-17	1165.2	959	463	116	16	424-46	925	3.19	106	.223	.294	297-23	.145	-1	92	25	5.3

RICHIE, LEW Lewis A. B 8.23.1883 Ambler, PA D 8.15.1936 South Mountain, PA BR/TR 5-8/165# d5.8

Year	Tm Lg	W	L	Pct	G	GS	CG-Sho	SV-BS	IP	H	R	HR	HB	BB-IB	SO	ERA	AERA	OAV	OOB	AB-SH	AVG	PB	Sup	APR	PW
1906	Phi N	9	11	.450	33	22	14-3	0	205.2	170	86	3	6	79	65	2.41	109	.230	.309	60-1	.050	-3	82	2	-0.3
1907	Phi N	6	6	.500	25	12	9-2	0	117	88	37	0	5	38	40	1.77	137	.215	.290	43-2	.163	0	64	6	0.6
1908	Phi N	7	10	.412	25	15	13-2	1	157.2	125	50	1	6	49	58	1.83	133	.233	.304	52-0	.212	2	62	8	1.0
1909	Phi N	1	1	.500	11	1	0	1	45	40	14	0	2	18	11	2.00	130	.263	.349	16-0	.250	1	188	3	0.2
	Bos N	7	7	.500	22	13	9-2	2	131.2	118	58	2	1	44	42	2.32	121	.247	.312	44-1	.114	-2	82	3	-0.1
	Year	8	8	.500	33	14	9-2	3	176.2	158	61	2	3	62	53	2.24	123	.251	.321	60-1	.150	-1	90	7	0.1
1910	Bos N	0	3	.000	4	2	0	0	16.1	20	11	0	0	9	7	2.76	121	.317	.403	4-0	.000	-1	34	0	-0.1
	†Chi N	11	4	.733	30	11	8-3	4	130	117	45	1	3	51	53	2.70	107	.257	.336	40-2	.225	3	131	5	0.9
	Year	11	7	.611	34	13	8-3	4	146.1	137	50	1	3	60	60	2.71	108	.264	.344	44-2	.205	2	115	4	0.8
1911	Chi N	15	11	.577	36	29	18-4	1	253	213	88	6	2	103	78	2.31	143	.235	.315	91-2	.154	-3	100	28	2.4
1912	Chi N	16	8	.667	39	27	15-4	0	238	222	102	5	6	74	69	2.95	113	.261	.324	76-6	.132	-3	100	9	0.4
1913	Chi N	2	4	.333	16	5	1	0	65	77	53	3	1	30	15	5.82	55	.304	.380	17-1	.118	-0	109	-18	-1.6
Total	8	74	65	.532	241	137	87-20	9	1359.1	1190	544	21	32	495	438	2.54	115	.246	.320	443-15	.147	-7	92	46	3.4

RICHMOND, BERYL Beryl Justice B 8.24.1907 Glen Easton, WV D 4.24.1980 Cameron, WV BB/TL 6-1/185# d4.21

Year	Tm Lg	W	L	Pct	G	GS	CG-Sho	SV-BS	IP	H	R	HR	HB	BB-IB	SO	ERA	AERA	OAV	OOB	AB-SH	AVG	PB	Sup	APR	PW
1933	Chi N	0	0	—	4	0	0	0	4.2	10	1	0	0	2	2	1.93	170	.455	.500	1-0	.000	-0*		1	0.0
1934	Cin N	1	2	.333	6	2	1	0	19.1	23	11	0	0	10	9	3.72	110	.303	.384	5-0	.000	-1	85	0	0.0
Total	2	1	2	.333	10	2	1	0	24	33	12	0	0	12	11	3.38	116	.337	.409	6-0	.000	-1	85	1	0.0

RICHMOND, LEE J Lee B 5.5.1857 Sheffield, OH D 10.1.1929 Toledo, OH TL 5-10/155# d9.27 ▲

Year	Tm Lg	W	L	Pct	G	GS	CG-Sho	SV-BS	IP	H	R	HR	HB	BB-IB	SO	ERA	AERA	OAV	OOB	AB-SH	AVG	PB	Sup	APR	PW
1879	Bos N	1	0	1.000	1	1	1	0	9	4	6	0		1	11	2.00	124	.114	.139	6	.333	0	224	0	0.0
1880	Wor N	32	32	.500	**74**	66	57-5	**3**	590.2	541	278	7		74	243	2.15	121	.232	.255	309	.227	-4*	97	25	1.8
1881	Wor N	25	26	.490	53	52	50-3	0	462.1	547	302	7		68	156	3.39	89	.284	.309	252	.250	-1*	98	-19	-1.7
1882	Wor N	14	33	.298	48	46	44	0	411	525	343	11		88	123	3.74	83	.294	.327	228	.281	7*	90	-23	-1.3
1883	Pro N	3	7	.300	12	12	8	0	92	122	67	2		27	13	3.33	93	.314	.358	194	.284	3*	88	-3	0.0
1886	Cin AA	0	2	.000	3	2	1	0	18	24	22	0	2	11	6	8.00	44	.308	.407	29	.276	0*	126	-8	-0.6
Total	6	75	100	.429	191	179	161-8	3	1583	1763	1018	27	2	269	552	3.06	95	.269	.298	1018	.257	7	96	-28	-1.8

RICHMOND, RAY Raymond Sinclair B 6.15.1896 Fillmore, IL D 10.21.1969 DeSoto, MO BR/TR 6/175# d9.25

Year	Tm Lg	W	L	Pct	G	GS	CG-Sho	SV-BS	IP	H	R	HR	HB	BB-IB	SO	ERA	AERA	OAV	OOB	AB-SH	AVG	PB	Sup	APR	PW
1920	StL A	2	0	1.000	2	2	1	0	17	18	12	0	0	9	4	6.35	62	.273	.360	6-1	.167	-0	233	-3	-0.3
1921	StL A	0	1	.000	6	2	0	0	14.1	21	19	1	3	13	6	11.30	40	.362	.500	4-0	.000	-1	93	-9	-0.6
Total	2	2	1	.667	8	4	1	0	31.1	39	31	1	3	22	10	8.62	48	.315	.430	10-1	.100	-1	161	-12	-0.9

RICHTER, REGGIE Emil Henry B 9.14.1888 Dusseldorf, Germany D 8.2.1934 Winfield, IL BR/TR 6-2/180# d5.30

Year	Tm Lg	W	L	Pct	G	GS	CG-Sho	SV-BS	IP	H	R	HR	HB	BB-IB	SO	ERA	AERA	OAV	OOB	AB-SH	AVG	PB	Sup	APR	PW
1911	Chi N	1	3	.250	22	5	0	2	54.2	62	30	1	3	20	34	3.13	106	.307	.378	10-0	.100	-1	118	-1	-0.2

RICKETTS, DICK Richard James B 12.4.1933 Pottstown, PA D 3.6.1988 Rochester, NY BL/TR 6-7/215# d6.14 b-Dave

Year	Tm Lg	W	L	Pct	G	GS	CG-Sho	SV-BS	IP	H	R	HR	HB	BB-IB	SO	ERA	AERA	OAV	OOB	AB-SH	AVG	PB	Sup	APR	PW
1959	StL N	1	6	.143	12	9	0	0	55.2	68	42	7	0	30-4	25	5.82	73	.301	.381	18-2	.056	-2	70	-10	-1.3

RIDDLE, ELMER Elmer Ray B 7.31.1914 Columbus, GA D 5.14.1984 Columbus, GA BR/TR 5-11.5/170# d10.1 b-Johnny

Year	Tm Lg	W	L	Pct	G	GS	CG-Sho	SV-BS	IP	H	R	HR	HB	BB-IB	SO	ERA	AERA	OAV	OOB	AB-SH	AVG	PB	Sup	APR	PW
1939	Cin N	0	0	—	1	0	0	0	2	1	0	0	0	0	0	0.00	—	.143	.143	0-0	—	0		1	0.0

Year	Tm Lg	W	L	Pct	G	GS	CG-Sho	SV-BS	IP	H	R	HR	HB	BB-IB	SO	ERA	AERA	OAV	OOB	AB-SH	AVG	PB	Sup	APR	PW
1940	†Cin N	1	2	.333	15	1	1	2	33.2	30	12	0	0	17	9	1.87	202	.250	.343	7-0	.143	0	23	5	0.5
1941	Cin N	19	4	**.826**	33	22	15-4	1	216.2	180	68	8	5	59	80	**2.24**	**160**	.224	.282	71-9	.225	3	115	30	3.5
1942	Cin N	7	11	.389	29	19	7-1	0	158.1	157	74	7	4	79	78	3.69	89	.260	.349	58-0	.259	3	89	-5	-0.3
1943	Cin N	**21**	11	.656	36	33	19-5	3	260.1	235	87	6	2	107	69	2.63	126	.245	.322	93-6	.194	1	112	19	2.4
1944	Cin N	2	2	.500	4	4	2	0	26.2	25	12	0	0	12	6	4.05	86	.250	.330	8-1	.125	-0	84	-1	-0.1
1945	Cin N	1	4	.200	12	3	0	0	29.2	39	27	4	0	27	5	8.19	46	.333	.458	11-0	.273	1	90	-13	-1.8
1947	Cin N	1	0	1.000	16	3	0	0	30.1	42	30	5	1	31	8	8.31	49	.333	.468	5-1	.000	-0	143	-13	-0.7
1948	Pit N☆	12	10	.545	28	27	12-3	1	191	184	83	20	3	81	63	3.49	117	.250	.327	64-6	.188	1*	86	12	1.4
1949	Pit N	1	8	.111	16	12	1	1	74.1	81	45	9	4	45	24	5.33	79	.281	.386	22-1	.136	-1	82	-7	-1.0
Total	10	65	52	.556	190	124	57-13	8	1023	974	438	59	19	458	342	3.40	107	.252	.335	339-24	.204	7	99	28	3.9
RIDDLEBERGER, DENNY Dennis Michael B 11.22.1945 Clifton Forge, VA BR/TL 6-3/195# d9.15																									
1970	Was A	0	0	—	8	0	0	0-0	9.1	7	2	1	0	2-0	5	0.96	369	.219	.257	0-0	—	0		2	0.1
1971	Was A	3	1	.750	57	0	0	1-0	69.2	67	27	9	1	32-7	56	3.23	103	.260	.341	4-0	.000	0		1	0.1
1972	Cle A	1	3	.250	38	0	0	0-1	54	45	23	5	2	22-3	34	2.50	129	.237	.319	4-0	.000	-0		1	0.1
Total	3	4	4	.500	103	0	0	1-1	133	119	52	15	3	56-10	95	2.77	119	.248	.327	8-0	.000	-0		4	0.3
RIDDLEMOSER, DORSEY Dorsey Lee B 3.25.1875 Frederick, MD D 5.11.1954 Frederick, MD BR/TR d8.22																									
1899	Was N	0	0	—	1	0	0	0	2	7	4	0	0	2	0	18.00	22	.538	.600	1-0	.000	-0		-3	-0.1
RIDGWAY, JACK Jacob A. B 7.23.1889 Philadelphia, PA D 2.23.1928 Philadelphia, PA BL/TR 5-11/174# d5.20																									
1914	Bal F	0	1	.000	4	1	0	0	9	20	11	1	1	3	2	11.00	28	.444	.490	1-0	.000	-0	136	-6	-0.6
RIDZIK, STEVE Stephen George B 4.29.1929 Yonkers, NY BR/TR 5-11/170# d9.4																									
1950	Phi N	0	0	—	1	0	0	0	3	3	2	1	0	1	2	6.00	67	.300	.364	0-0	—	0		-1	0.0
1952	Phi N	4	2	.667	24	9	2	0	92.2	74	37	11	1	37	43	3.01	121	.218	.297	22-2	.136	0	100	6	0.3
1953	Phi N	9	6	.600	42	12	1	0	124	119	61	15	5	48	53	3.77	112	.256	.332	36-2	.194	2	74	6	0.8
1954	Phi N	4	5	.444	35	6	0	0	80.2	72	42	7	0	44	45	4.13	98	.233	.326	22-1	.227	1	63	-1	0.0
1955	Phi N	0	1	.000	3	1	0	0	11	7	9	1	3	8-0	6	2.45	162	.179	.360	4-0	.000	-1	45	-1	-0.1
	Cin N	0	3	.000	13	2	0	0	30	35	16	4	1	14-1	6	4.50	94	.299	.376	6-0	.167	-0	53	0	-0.1
	Year	0	4	.000	16	3	0	0	41	42	19	5	4	22-1	12	3.95	105	.269	.372	10-0	.100	-1	50	-1	-0.2
1956	NY N	6	2	.750	41	5	1-1	0	92.1	80	42	7	5	65-5	53	3.80	99	.240	.369	28-0	.250	1*	98	1	0.1
1957	NY N	0	2	.000	15	0	0	0	26.2	19	14	3	2	19-1	13	4.73	83	.213	.360	5-0	.200	-0*		-2	-0.1
1958	Cle A	0	2	.000	6	0	0	0	8.2	9	7	1	0	5-2	6	2.08	176	.257	.341	1-0	.000	-0		-1	-0.1
1963	Was A	5	6	.455	20	10	0	1	89.2	82	53	16	5	35-0	47	4.82	77	.240	.316	29-0	.172	0	93	-10	-1.1
1964	Was A	5	5	.500	49	3	0	2	112	96	46	10	7	31-6	60	2.89	128	.236	.298	27-2	.222	1	64	8	0.8
1965	Was A	6	4	.600	63	0	0	8	109.2	108	61	18	7	43-4	72	4.02	86	.257	.333	18-2	.167	0		-9	-0.8
1966	Phi N	0	0	—	2	0	0	0	2.1	5	2	0	0	1-0	0	7.71	47	.455	.462	0-0	—	0		-1	-0.1
Total	12	39	38	.506	314	48	4-1	11	782.2	709	392	94	36	351-19	406	3.79	101	.243	.330	198-9	.192	4	83	-5	-0.4
RIEDLING, JOHN John Richard B 8.29.1975 Ft.Lauderdale, FL BR/TR 5-11/190# d8.30																									
2000	Cin N	3	1	.750	13	0	0	1-1	15.1	11	7	1	1	8-0	18	2.35	201	.208	.323	2-0	.000	-0		3	0.5
2001	Cin N	1	1	.500	29	0	0	1-2	33.2	22	9	1	2	14-0	23	2.41	189	.186	.284	1-0	.000	-0		8	0.5
2002	Cin N	2	4	.333	33	0	0	0-0	46.2	39	16	2	3	26-6	30	2.70	157	.234	.345	1-0	.000	-0		8	0.9
2003	Cin N	2	3	.400	55	8	0	1-3	101	107	61	7	3	47-0	65	4.90	87	.270	.347	18-1	.222	0	124	-8	-0.4
Total	4	8	9	.471	130	8	0	3-6	196.2	179	93	11	9	95-6	136	3.75	116	.244	.335	22-1	.182	-0	124	11	1.5
RIEGER, ELMER Elmer Jay B 2.25.1889 Perris, CA D 10.21.1959 Los Angeles, CA BB/TR 6/175# d4.20																									
1910	StL N	0	2	.000	13	1	0	0	21.1	26	16	1	1	7	9	5.48	54	.325	.386	3-0	.000	0	125	-6	-0.5
RIGBY, BRAD Bradley Kenneth B 5.14.1973 Milwaukee, WI BR/TR 6-6/203# d6.28																									
1997	Oak A	1	7	.125	14	14	0	0-0	77.2	92	44	14	2	22-2	34	4.87	93	.302	.344	3-0	.000	-0	83	-2	-0.2
1999	Oak A	3	4	.429	29	0	0	0-1	62.1	69	31	5	5	26-7	26	4.33	107	.284	.361	0-0	—	0		3	0.3
	KC A	1	2	.333	20	0	0	0-1	21.1	33	20	6	2	5-0	10	7.17	70	.351	.388	0-0	—	0		-6	-0.7
	Year	4	6	.400	49	0	0	0-2	83.2	102	55	11	7	31-7	36	5.06	94	.303	.368	0-0	—	0		-3	-0.4
2000	KC A	0	0	—	4	0	0	1-0	8.1	19	16	6	1	5-0	3	16.20	32	.422	.490	0-0	—	0		-10	-0.4
	Mon N	0	0	—	6	0	0	1-0	5.1	8	5	0	1	3-0	2	5.06	95	.348	.444	1-0	.000	-0		-1	-0.1
Total	3	5	13	.278	73	14	0	2-2	175	221	116	31	11	61-9	75	5.50	85	.311	.369	4-0	.000	-0	83	-16	-1.1
RIGDON, PAUL Paul David B 11.2.1975 Jacksonville, FL BR/TR 6-5/210# d5.21																									
2000	Cle A	1	1	.500	5	4	0	0-0	17.2	21	15	4	0	9-1	15	7.64	65	.300	.380	0-0	—	0	141	-5	-0.4
	Mil N	4	4	.500	12	12	0	0-0	69.2	68	37	14	1	26-4	48	4.52	101	.255	.318	16-7	.188	2	107	1	0.2
2001	Mil N	3	5	.375	15	15	0	0-0	79.1	86	52	13	3	46-6	49	5.79	74	.287	.385	20-5	.200	0	96	-12	-1.0
Total	2	8	10	.444	32	31	0	0-0	166.2	175	104	31	4	81-11	112	5.45	82	.275	.357	36-12	.194	2	107	-16	-1.2
RIGGAN, JERROD Jerrod Ashley B 5.16.1974 Brewster, WA BR/TR 6-3/200# d8.29																									
2000	NY N	0	0	—	1	0	0	0-0	2	3	2	0	0	0-0	1	0.00	—	.300	.300	0-0	—	0		0	0.0
2001	NY N	3	3	.500	35	0	0	0-1	47.2	42	19	5	0	24-7	41	3.40	122	.243	.330	2-0	.000	-0		4	0.5
2002	Cle A	2	1	.667	29	0	0	0-0	33	53	28	3	0	18-4	22	7.64	58	.373	.433	0-0	—	0		-11	-0.9
2003	Cle A	0	0	—	2	0	0	0-0	4	7	4	0	0	1-0	2	9.00	49	.412	.421	0-0	—	0		-2	-0.1
Total	4	5	4	.556	67	0	0	0-1	86.2	105	53	8	0	43-11	66	5.19	82	.307	.377	2-0	.000	-0		-9	-0.5
RIGHETTI, DAVE David Allan B 11.28.1958 San Jose, CA BL/TL 6-3/198# d9.16 C4																									
1979	NY A	0	1	.000	3	3	0	0-0	17.1	10	7	2	0	10-0	13	3.63	112	.182	.303	0-0	—	0	74	1	0.1
1981	†NY A	8	4	.667	15	15	2	0-0	105.1	75	25	1	0	38-0	89	2.05	175	.196	.268	0-0	—	0	97	19	2.2
1982	NY A	11	10	.524	33	27	4	1-0	183	155	88	11	6	108-4	163	3.79	105	.229	.338	0-0	—	0	95	3	0.2
1983	NY A	14	8	.636	31	31	7-2	0-0	217	194	96	12	2	67-2	169	3.44	113	.237	.296	0-0	—	0	120	10	0.9
1984	NY A	5	6	.455	64	0	0	31-9	96.1	79	29	5	0	37-7	90	2.34	163	.223	.293	0-0	—	0		16	2.7
1985	NY A	12	7	.632	74	0	0	29-10	107	96	36	5	0	45-3	92	2.78	144	.241	.316	0-0	—	0		16	3.1
1986	NY A★	8	8	.500	74	0	0	**46-10**	106.2	88	31	4	2	35-7	83	2.45	167	.226	.291	0-0	—	0		21	4.1
1987	NY A★	8	6	.571	60	0	0	31-13	95	95	45	9	2	44-4	77	3.51	126	.262	.341	0-0	—	0		7	1.4
1988	NY A	5	4	.556	60	0	0	25-9	87	86	35	5	1	37-2	70	3.52	112	.257	.332	0-0	—	0		5	0.7
1989	NY A	2	6	.250	55	0	0	25-9	69	73	32	3	1	26-6	51	3.00	129	.277	.341	0-0	—	0		4	0.6
1990	NY A	1	1	.500	53	0	0	36-3	53	48	24	8	2	26-2	43	3.57	112	.234	.325	0-0	—	0		2	0.2
1991	SF N	2	7	.222	61	0	0	24-5	71.2	64	29	4	3	28-6	51	3.39	106	.240	.317	3-1	.000	-0		2	0.3
1992	SF N	2	7	.222	54	4	0	3-2	78.1	79	47	4	0	36-5	47	5.06	65	.269	.344	7-4	.143	-0	75	-15	-1.9
1993	SF N	1	1	.500	51	0	0	1-2	47.1	58	31	11	1	17-0	31	5.70	69	.305	.365	1-0	1.000	0		-9	-0.4
1994	Oak A	0	0	—	7	0	0	0-1	7	13	13	3	1	9-0	4	16.71	27	.419	.548	0-0	—	0		-10	-0.4
	Tor A	0	1	.000	13	0	0	0-1	13.1	9	10	2	0	10-0	10	6.75	71	.188	.322	0-0	—	0		-2	-0.2
	Year	0	1	.000	20	0	0	0-2	20.1	22	26	5	1	19-0	14	10.18	46	.278	.416	0-0	—	0		-11	-0.6
1995	Chi A	3	2	.600	10	9	0	0-0	49.1	65	24	6	0	18-0	29	4.20	106	.325	.377	0-0	—	0	114	2	0.2
Total	16	82	79	.509	718	89	13-2	252-74	1403.2	1287	602	95	21	591-48	1112	3.46	113	.244	.321	11-5	.182	0	104	72	13.8
RIGHTNOWAR, RON Ronald Gene B 9.5.1964 Toledo, OH BR/TR 6-3/190# d5.20																									
1995	Mil A	2	1	.667	34	0	0	1-3	36.2	35	23	3	5	18-3	22	5.40	92	.271	.374	0-0	—	0		-1	-0.1
RIGNEY, JOHNNY John Dungan B 10.28.1914 Oak Park, IL D 10.21.1984 Lombard, IL BR/TR 6-2/190# d4.21 Mil 1942-45																									
1937	Chi A	2	5	.286	22	4	0	1	90.2	107	65	10	3	46	38	4.96	93	.290	.373	30-2	.167	-0	80	-7	-0.5
1938	Chi A	9	9	.500	38	12	7-1	1	167	164	74	16	2	72	84	3.56	138	.256	.333	55-3	.145	-3	66	26	2.1
1939	Chi A	15	8	.652	35	29	11-2	0	218.2	208	103	10	2	84	119	3.70	128	.247	.316	80-5	.200	-1	98	23	1.9
1940	Chi A	14	18	.438	39	33	19-2	3	280.2	240	117	22	2	90	141	3.11	142	.230	.292	93-12	.215	1*	82	39	4.1
1941	Chi A	13	13	.500	30	29	18-3	0	237	224	116	21	2	92	119	3.84	107	.249	.320	84-2	.202	2	92	8	0.9
1942	Chi A	3	3	.500	7	7	6	0	59	40	23	2	1	16	34	3.20	112	.185	.245	19-2	.053	-1	92	3	0.2
1946	Chi A	5	5	.500	15	11	3-2	0	82.2	76	37	6	2	35	51	4.03	85	.240	.319	26-4	.154	-1	78	-2	-0.3
1947	Chi A	2	3	.400	11	7	2	0	50.2	42	15	3	0	15	19	1.95	187	.228	.286	14-1	.000	-2	62	9	0.7

Year	Tm Lg	W	L	Pct	G	GS	CG-Sho	SV-BS	IP	H	R	HR	HB	BB-IB	SO	ERA	AERA	OAV	OOB	AB-SH	AVG	PB	Sup	APR	PW
Total	8	63	64	.496	197	132	66-10	5	1186.1	1101	550	90	14	450	605	3.59	121	.244	.314	401-31	.177	-6	85	99	9.1
RIJO, JOSE Jose Antonio (Abreu) B 5.13.1965 San Cristobal, D.R. BR/TR 6-2/200# d4.5																									
1984	NY A	2	8	.200	24	5	0	2-1	62.1	74	40	5	1	33-1	47	4.76	80	.298	.382	0-0	—	0	62	-9	-1.3
1985	Oak A	6	4	.600	12	9	0	0-1	63.2	57	26	6	1	28-2	65	3.53	109	.239	.322	0-0	—	0	86	3	0.4
1986	Oak A	9	11	.450	39	26	4	1-2	193.2	172	116	24	4	108-7	176	4.65	83	.237	.336	0-0	—	0	112	-21	-1.9
1987	Oak A	2	7	.222	21	14	1	0-0	82.1	106	67	10	2	41-1	67	5.90	70	.305	.378	0-0	—	0	87	-21	-1.8
1988	Cin N	13	8	.619	49	19	0	0-2	162	120	47	7	3	63-7	160	2.39	150	.209	.288	37-4	.054	-2	94	21	2.5
1989	Cin N	7	6	.538	19	19	1-1	0-0	111	101	39	6	2	48-3	86	2.84	127	.249	.328	38-1	.211	1	87	10	1.2
1990	†Cin N	14	8	.636	29	29	7-1	0-0	197	151	65	10	2	78-1	152	2.70	147	.212	.291	62-11	.161	-0	100	26	2.9
1991	Cin N	15	6	**.714**	30	30	3-1	0-0	204.1	165	69	8	3	55-4	172	2.51	152	.219	**.272**	67-9	.209	1*	121	26	2.8
1992	Cin N	15	10	.600	33	33	2	0-0	211	185	67	15	3	44-1	171	2.56	141	.238	.281	72-6	.194	1	100	23	3.0
1993	Cin N	14	9	.609	36	**36**	2-1	0-0	257.1	218	76	19	2	62-2	**227**	2.48	162	.230	.278	82-12	.268	7	88	45	4.8
1994	Cin N❖	9	6	.600	26	**26**	2	0-0	172.1	177	73	16	4	52-1	171	3.08	134	.265	.321	49-10	.204	2	104	18	1.7
1995	Cin N	5	4	.556	14	14	0	0-0	69	76	33	6	0	22-1	62	4.17	99	.285	.336	22-2	.136	-0	106	0	0.0
2001	Cin N	0	0	—	13	0	0	0-0	17	19	6	2	0	9-2	12	2.12	215	.271	.354	0-0	—	0		4	0.2
2002	Cin N	5	4	.556	31	9	0	0-0	77	89	48	13	1	20-1	38	5.14	83	.283	.327	16-3	.125	-1	116	-7	-0.8
Total	14	116	91	.560	376	269	22-4	3-6	1880	1710	772	147	28	663-34	1606	3.24	120	.243	.308	445-58	.191	9	100	118	13.7
RILEY, GEORGE George Michael B 10.6.1956 Philadelphia, PA BL/TL 6-2/210# d9.15																									
1979	Chi N	0	1	.000	4	1	0	0-0	13	16	9	1	2	6-1	5	5.54	75	.320	.414	2-1	.000	-0	21	-2	-0.1
1980	Chi N	0	4	.000	22	0	0	0-0	36	41	29	2	2	20-5	18	5.75	68	.293	.389	1-1	.000	-0		-8	-0.8
1984	SF N	1	0	1.000	5	4	0	0-0	29.1	39	14	1	2	7-0	12	3.99	88	.315	.358	10-1	.100	-0	94	-1	-0.1
1986	Mon N	0	0	—	10	0	0	0-0	8.2	7	4	0	1	8-3	5	4.15	89	.212	.372	0-0	—	0		0	0.0
Total	4	1	5	.167	41	5	0	0-0	87	103	56	4	7	41-9	40	4.97	76	.297	.380	13-3	.077	-1	75	-11	-1.0
RILEY, MATT Matthew Paul B 8.2.1979 Antioch, CA BL/TL 6-1/205# d9.9																									
1999	Bal A	0	0	—	3	3	0	0-0	11	17	9	4	0	13-0	6	7.36	64	.378	.508	0-0	—	0	152	-3	-0.1
2003	Bal A	1	0	1.000	2	2	0	0-0	10	7	2	1	0	5-0	8	1.80	244	.194	.293	0-0	—	0	73	3	0.3
Total	2	1	0	1.000	5	5	0	0-0	21	24	11	5	0	18-0	14	4.71	97	.296	.420	0-0	—	0	122	0	0.2
RINCON, ANDY Andrew John B 3.5.1959 Monterey Park, CA BR/TR 6-3/195# d9.15																									
1980	StL N	3	1	.750	4	4	1	0-0	31	23	9	1	0	7-1	22	2.61	142	.215	.263	12-1	.250	0	85	4	0.6
1981	StL N	3	1	.750	5	5	1-1	0-0	35.2	27	8	0	2	5-1	13	1.77	201	.214	.256	13-2	.231	1	165	7	0.9
1982	StL N	2	3	.400	11	6	1	0-0	40	35	22	1	0	25-0	11	4.72	77	.241	.351	10-1	.100	-0	93	-4	-0.5
Total	3	8	5	.615	20	15	3-1	0-0	106.2	85	39	2	2	37-2	46	3.12	116	.225	.297	35-4	.200	1	114	7	1.0
RINCON, JUAN Juan Manuel B 1.23.1979 Maracaibo, Venezuela BR/TR 5-11/190# d6.7																									
2001	Min A	0	0	—	4	0	0	0-0	5.2	7	5	1	0	5-0	4	6.35	72	.318	.444	1-0	1.000	0		-1	0.0
2002	Min A	0	2	.000	10	3	0	0-1	28.2	44	23	5	0	9-0	21	6.28	72	.352	.393	0-0	—	0	69	-6	-0.4
2003	†Min A	5	6	.455	58	0	0	0-1	85.2	74	38	5	4	38-7	63	3.68	124	.231	.315	0-0	—	0		8	0.9
Total	3	5	8	.385	72	3	0	0-2	120	125	66	11	4	52-7	88	4.43	103	.267	.342	1-0	1.000	0	69	1	0.5
RINCON, RICARDO Ricardo (Espinoza) B 4.13.1970 Veracruz, Mexico BL/TL 6/190# d4.3																									
1997	Pit N	4	8	.333	62	0	0	4-2	60	51	26	5	2	24-6	71	3.45	124	.230	.309	1-1	.000	-0		5	1.0
1998	Pit N	0	2	.000	60	0	0	14-3	65	50	31	6	0	29-2	64	2.91	148	.208	.292	2-0	.000	-0		7	0.4
1999	†Cle A	2	3	.400	59	0	0	0-2	44.2	41	22	6	1	24-5	30	4.43	114	.248	.346	0-0	—	0		4	0.4
2000	Cle A	2	0	1.000	35	0	0	0-0	20	17	7	1	1	13-1	20	2.70	184	.224	.344	0-0	—	0		5	0.4
2001	†Cle A	2	1	.667	67	0	0	2-2	54	44	18	3	0	21-5	50	2.83	160	.223	.294	0-0	—	0		10	0.6
2002	Cle A	1	4	.200	46	0	0	0-3	35.2	36	21	3	1	8-1	30	4.79	92	.263	.304	1-0	.000	-0		-2	-0.2
	†Oak A	0	0	—	25	0	0	1-1	20.1	11	7	1	0	3-0	19	3.10	142	.164	.194	0-0	—	0		3	0.2
	Year	1	4	.200	71	0	0	1-4	56	47	31	4	1	11-1	49	4.18	105	.230	.268	1-0	.000	-0		2	0.0
2003	†Oak A	8	4	.667	64	0	0	0-3	55.1	45	21	4	3	32-4	40	3.25	139	.230	.343	0-0	—	0		8	1.6
Total	7	19	22	.463	418	0	0	21-16	355	295	153	29	8	154-24	324	3.42	132	.227	.310	4-1	.000	-0		40	4.4
RINEER, JEFF Jeffrey Alan B 7.3.1955 Lancaster, PA BL/TL 6-4/205# d9.30																									
1979	Bal A	0	0	—	1	0	0	0-0	1	0	0	0	0	0-0	0	0.00	—	.000	.000	0-0	—	0		0	0.0
RING, JIMMY James Joseph B 2.15.1895 Brooklyn, NY D 7.6.1965 Queens, NY BR/TR 6-1/170# d4.13																									
1917	Cin N	3	7	.300	24	7	3	2	88	90	47	2	1	35	33	4.40	60	.272	.343	26-0	.077	-2	173	-13	-1.6
1918	Cin N	9	5	.643	21	18	13-4	0	142.1	130	57	5	3	48	26	2.85	94	.247	.314	50-4	.120	-3	161	-2	-0.7
1919	†Cin N	10	9	.526	32	18	12-2	3	183	150	53	2	3	51	61	2.26	123	.232	.291	62-2	.097	-5	86	13	1.0
1920	Cin N	17	16	.515	42	33	18-1	1	266.2	268	134	4	5	92	73	3.54	86	.264	.329	96-2	.198	-0	113	-16	-1.9
1921	Phi N	10	19	.345	34	30	21	1	246	258	161	8	5	88	88	4.24	100	.274	.340	83-5	.145	-4	86	-1	-0.4
1922	Phi N	12	18	.400	40	33	17	1	249.1	292	160	19	3	103	116	4.58	102	.297	.365	88-4	.148	-5	90	4	0.2
1923	Phi N	18	16	.529	39	36	23	0	304.1	336	151	13	1	115	112	3.87	119	.283	.347	113-9	.106	-9*	86	25	1.8
1924	Phi N	10	12	.455	32	31	16-1	0	215.1	236	123	9	4	108	72	3.97	112	.286	.371	74-5	.230	-1	95	5	0.6
1925	Phi N	14	16	.467	38	37	21-1	0	270	325	166	14	1	119	93	4.37	109	.297	.367	101-5	.109	-7	86	9	0.3
1926	NY N	11	10	.524	39	23	5	2	183.1	207	114	12	1	74	76	4.57	82	.290	.357	56-3	.143	-3	105	-18	-2.2
1927	StL N	0	4	.000	13	3	1	0	33	39	28	3	1	17	13	6.55	60	.300	.385	8-0	.375	1	93	-9	-0.8
1928	Phi N	4	17	.190	35	25	4	1	176	220	135	14	2	103	70	6.44	66	.320	.410	60-1	.183	-2	79	-36	-3.7
Total	12	118	149	.442	389	294	154-9	11	2357.1	2551	1329	105	30	953	833	4.13	95	.281	.351	817-40	.147	-40	97	-39	-7.4
RIOS, DANNY Daniel B 11.11.1972 Madrid, Spain BR/TR 6-2/190# d5.30																									
1997	NY A	0	0	—	2	0	0	0-0	2.1	9	5	3	1	2-0	1	19.29	23	.563	.632	0-0	—	0		-4	-0.2
1998	KC A	0	1	.000	5	0	0	0-0	7.1	9	9	1	1	6-0	6	6.14	79	.300	.421	0-0	—	0		-3	-0.3
Total	2	0	1	.000	7	0	0	0-0	9.2	18	14	4	2	8-0	7	9.31	51	.391	.491	0-0	—	0		-7	-0.5
RIPLEY, ALLEN Allen Stevens B 10.18.1952 Norwood, MA BR/TR 6-3/190# d4.10 f-Walt																									
1978	Bos A	2	5	.286	15	11	1	0-0	73	92	49	10	3	22-2	26	5.55	74	.311	.362	0-0	—	0	83	-10	-0.9
1979	Bos A	3	1	.750	16	3	0	1-1	64.2	77	42	9	3	25-5	34	5.15	86	.295	.362	0-0	—	0	109	-5	-0.4
1980	SF N	9	10	.474	23	20	2	0-1	112.2	119	59	10	4	36-6	65	4.15	85	.274	.331	40-3	.150	-0	93	-8	-1.2
1981	SF N	4	4	.500	19	14	1	0-0	90.2	103	45	5	3	27-2	47	4.07	84	.289	.342	30-2	.133	-1	107	-6	-0.6
1982	Chi N	5	7	.417	28	19	0	0-0	122.2	130	61	12	2	38-6	57	4.26	88	.285	.338	38-2	.132	-1	78	-5	-0.6
Total	5	23	27	.460	101	67	4	1-2	463.2	521	256	46	15	148-21	229	4.52	84	.289	.345	108-7	.139	-3	89	-34	-3.7
RIPLEY, WALT Walter Franklin B 11.26.1916 Worcester, MA D 10.7.1990 Attleboro, MA BR/TR 6/168# d8.17 s-Allen																									
1935	Bos A	0	0	—	2	0	0	0	4	7	4	0	0	3	0	9.00	53	.412	.500	0-0	—	0		-1	-0.1
RIPPELMEYER, RAY Raymond Roy B 7.9.1933 Valmeyer, IL BR/TR 6-3/200# d4.14 C9																									
1962	Was A	1	2	.333	18	1	0	0	39.1	47	24	7	0	17-2	17	5.49	74	.294	.358	6-0	.500	2	0	-5	0.0
RIPPLE, CHARLIE Charles Dawson B 12.1.1921 Bolton, NC D 5.6.1979 Wilmington, NC BL/TL 6-2/210# d9.25																									
1944	Phi N	0	0	—	1	1	0	0	2.1	6	4	0	0	4	2	15.43	23	.500	.625	1-0	1.000	0	139	-3	-0.1
1945	Phi N	0	1	.000	4	0	0	0	7.2	7	6	0	0	10	5	7.04	54	.241	.436	1-0	.000	-0		-2	-0.3
1946	Phi N	1	0	1.000	6	0	0	0	3.1	5	4	0	0	6	3	10.80	32	.385	.579	0-0	—	0		-2	-0.5
Total	3	1	1	.500	11	1	0	0	13.1	18	14	0	0	20	10	9.45	39	.333	.514	2-0	.500	0	139	-7	-0.9
RISKE, DAVID David Richard B 10.23.1976 Renton, WA BR/TR 6-2/175# d8.14																									
1999	Cle A	1	1	.500	12	0	0	0-1	14	20	15	2	0	6-0	16	8.36	60	.333	.388	0-0	—	0		-5	-0.6
2001	†Cle A	2	0	1.000	26	0	0	1-0	27.1	20	7	3	2	18-3	29	1.98	229	.206	.339	0-0	—	0		7	0.5
2002	Cle A	2	2	.500	51	0	0	1-0	51.1	49	32	8	4	35-4	65	5.26	84	.257	.378	0-0	—	0		-5	-0.3
2003	Cle A	2	2	.500	68	0	0	8-5	74.2	52	21	9	3	20-3	82	2.29	193	.196	.260	0-0	—	0		18	1.2
Total	4	7	5	.583	157	0	0	10-6	167.1	141	75	22	9	79-10	192	3.66	123	.230	.324	0-0	—	0		15	0.8

Year	Tm Lg	W	L	Pct	G	GS	CG-Sho	SV-BS	IP	H	R	HR	HB	BB-IB	SO	ERA	AERA	OAV	OOB	AB-SH	AVG	PB	Sup	APR	PW
RISLEY, BILL William Charles B 5.29.1967 Chicago, IL BR/TR 6-2/215# d7.8																									
1992	Mon N	1	0	1.000	1	1	0	0-0	5	4	1	0	0	1-0	2	1.80	193	.235	.278	2-0	.000	-0	104	1	0.2
1993	Mon N	0	0	—	2	0	0	0-0	3	2	3	1	1	2-0	2	6.00	70	.200	.385	0-0	—	0		-1	0.0
1994	Sea A	9	6	.600	37	0	0	0-2	52.1	31	20	7	0	19-4	61	3.44	142	.170	.246	0-0	—	0		9	1.8
1995	†Sea A	2	1	.667	45	0	0	1-6	60.1	55	21	7	1	18-1	65	3.13	151	.244	.300	0-0	—	0		12	0.5
1996	Tor A	0	1	.000	25	0	0	0-2	41.2	33	20	7	0	25-0	29	3.89	129	.221	.330	0-0	—	0		5	0.2
1997	Tor A	0	1	.000	3	0	0	0-1	4.1	3	4	2	0	2-0	2	8.31	55	.188	.278	0-0	—	0		-2	-0.3
1998	Tor A	3	4	.429	44	0	0	0-0	54.2	52	37	7	4	34-4	42	5.27	89	.259	.372	0-0	—	0		-4	-0.5
Total	7	15	13	.536	157	1	0	1-11	221.1	180	106	31	6	101-9	203	3.98	120	.225	.313	2-0	.000	-0	104	20	1.9
RITCHIE, JAY Jay Seay B 11.20.1936 Salisbury, NC BR/TR 6-4/190# d8.4																									
1964	Bos A	1	1	.500	21	0	0	0	46	43	21	4	0	14-2	35	2.74	141	.249	.303	9-0	.111	-1		3	0.1
1965	Bos A	1	2	.333	44	0	0	2	71	83	30	3	1	26-5	55	3.17	118	.302	.361	5-0	.200	0		4	0.2
1966	Atl N	0	1	.000	22	0	0	4	35.1	32	17	3	0	12-4	33	4.08	89	.241	.303	4-1	.500	1		-1	0.0
1967	Atl N	4	6	.400	52	0	0	2	82.1	75	32	6	4	29-11	57	3.17	105	.245	.317	10-0	.300	1		2	0.4
1968	Cin N	2	3	.400	28	2	0	0	56.2	68	32	7	1	13-2	32	4.61	69	.293	.332	7-0	.000	-1	55	-8	-0.9
Total	5	8	13	.381	167	2	0	8	291.1	301	132	23	6	94-24	212	3.49	101	.269	.327	35-1	.200	1	55	0	-0.2
RITCHIE, TODD Todd Everett B 11.7.1971 Portsmouth, VA BR/TR 6-3/205# d4.3																									
1997	Min A	2	3	.400	42	0	0	0-2	74.2	87	41	11	2	28-0	44	4.58	102	.290	.353	2-0	.000	-0		1	0.0
1998	Min A	0	0	—	15	0	0	0-0	24	30	17	1	0	9-0	21	5.63	85	.288	.345	0-0	—	0		-3	-0.2
1999	Pit N	15	9	.625	28	26	2	0-0	172.2	169	79	17	4	54-3	107	3.49	131	.259	.318	53-8	.151	-1*	114	19	2.3
2000	Pit N	9	8	.529	31	31	1-1	0-0	187	208	111	26	3	51-1	124	4.81	96	.282	.329	60-2	.217	2	104	-4	-0.1
2001	Pit N	11	15	.423	33	33	4-2	0-0	207.1	211	118	23	7	52-7	124	4.47	100	.259	.308	59-8	.153	0*	65	-3	-0.3
2002	Chi A	5	15	.250	26	23	0	0-0	133.2	176	104	18	5	52-2	77	6.06	75	.318	.378	4-0	.250	0*	95	-25	-3.0
2003	Mil N	1	2	.333	5	5	0	0-0	28.1	36	17	4	4	10-0	15	5.08	84	.319	.388	9-2	.222	0	80	-3	-0.2
Total	7	43	52	.453	180	118	7-3	0-2	827.2	917	487	100	25	256-13	512	4.66	98	.280	.335	187-20	.176	2	92	-18	-1.5
RITCHIE, WALLY Wallace Reid B 7.12.1965 Glendale, CA BL/TL 6-2/180# d5.1																									
1987	Phi N	3	2	.600	49	0	0	3-0	62.1	60	27	8	1	29-11	45	3.75	113	.254	.336	4-0	.250	0		4	0.3
1988	Phi N	0	0	—	19	0	0	0-0	26	19	14	1	1	17-2	8	3.12	114	.207	.327	0-0	—	0		0	0.0
1991	Phi N	1	2	.333	39	0	0	0-3	50.1	44	17	4	2	17-5	26	2.50	147	.234	.299	3-0	.000	-0		6	0.3
1992	Phi N	2	1	.667	40	0	0	1-1	39	44	17	3	0	17-3	19	3.00	117	.288	.359	1-0	.000	0		1	0.1
Total	4	6	5	.545	147	0	0	4-4	177.2	167	75	16	4	80-21	98	3.14	121	.250	.329	8-0	.125	0		11	0.7
RITTER, REGGIE Reggie Blake B 1.23.1960 Malvern, AR BL/TR 6-2/195# d5.17																									
1986	Cle A	0	0	—	5	0	0	0-0	10	14	10	1	1	4-0	6	6.30	66	.341	.396	0-0	—	0		-3	-0.1
1987	Cle A	1	1	.500	14	0	0	0-1	26.2	33	21	5	0	16-1	11	6.08	75	.300	.386	0-0	—	0		-5	-0.3
Total	2	1	1	.500	19	0	0	0-1	36.2	47	31	6	1	20-1	17	6.14	72	.311	.389	0-0	—	0		-8	-0.4
RITTER, HANK William Herbert B 10.12.1893 McCoysville, PA D 9.3.1964 Akron, OH BR/TR 6/180# d8.3																									
1912	Phi N	0	0	—	3	0	0	0	6	5	5	0	0	5	1	4.50	81	.192	.323	1-0	.000	-0		-1	-0.1
1914	NY N	1	0	1.000	1	0	0	0	8	4	1	0	0	4	4	1.13	236	.160	.276	3-0	.000	-0		2	0.1
1915	NY N	2	1	.667	22	1	0	2	58.1	66	38	4	5	15	35	4.63	55	.291	.348	16-0	.125	-1*	87	-14	-0.9
1916	NY N	1	0	1.000	3	0	0	0	5	3	0	0	1	0	3	0.00	—	.200	.250	0-0	—	0*		1	0.3
Total	4	4	1	.800	29	1	0	2	77.1	78	44	4	6	24	43	3.96	67	.266	.334	20-0	.100	-1	87	-12	-0.6
RITTWAGE, JIM James Michael B 10.23.1944 Cleveland, OH BR/TR 6-3/190# d9.7																									
1970	Cle A	1	1	.500	8	3	1	0-0	26	18	12	0	0	21-0	16	4.15	95	.194	.342	8-0	.375	1	105	0	0.1
RITZ, KEVIN Kevin D B 6.8.1965 Eatontown, NJ BR/TR 6-4/220# d7.15																									
1989	Det A	4	6	.400	12	12	1	0-0	74	75	41	2	1	44-5	56	4.38	87	.265	.360	0-0	—	0	91	-5	-0.6
1990	Det A	0	4	.000	4	4	0	0-0	7.1	14	12	0	0	14-2	3	11.05	36	.400	.571	0-0	—	0	69	-7	-1.1
1991	Det A	0	3	.000	11	5	0	0-1	15.1	17	22	1	2	22-1	9	11.74	35	.288	.482	0-0	—	0	119	-13	-2.0
1992	Det A	2	5	.286	23	11	0	0-0	80.1	88	52	4	3	44-4	57	5.60	71	.278	.368	0-0	—	0	103	-14	-1.1
1994	Col N	5	6	.455	15	15	0	0-0	73.2	88	49	5	4	35-4	53	5.62	89	.303	.384	20-5	.000	-2	87	-4	-0.7
1995	†Col N	11	11	.500	31	28	0	2-0	173.1	171	91	16	6	65-3	120	4.21	128	.259	.329	48-11	.188	-1	77	17	2.1
1996	Col N	17	11	.607	35	35	2	0-0	213	236	135	24	12	105-3	105	5.28	99	.282	.368	65-11	.231	2	109	-1	0.4
1997	Col N	6	8	.429	18	18	1	0-0	107.1	142	72	16	1	46-3	56	5.87	88	.330	.392	35-2	.057	-2	98	-5	-0.7
1998	Col N	0	2	.000	2	2	0	0-0	9	17	11	1	1	2-0	3	11.00	47	.395	.435	3-0	.333	0	62	-4	-0.7
Total	9	45	56	.446	151	130	4	2-1	753.1	848	485	69	30	377-25	462	5.35	92	.287	.371	171-29	.158	-3	94	-36	-4.4
RIVERA, BEN Bienvenido Santana B 1.11.1968 San Pedro De Macoris, D.R. BR/TR 6-6/210# d4.9																									
1992	Atl N	0	1	.000	8	0	0	0-0	15.1	21	8	1	2	13-2	11	4.70	78	.339	.462	1-0	.000	-0		-1	-0.1
	Phi N	7	3	.700	20	14	4-1	0-0	102	78	32	8	2	32-2	66	2.82	124	.211	.277	32-2	.094	-1	152	9	0.8
	Year	7	4	.636	28	14	4-1	0-0	117.1	99	38	9	4	45-4	77	3.07	115	.230	.307	33-2	.091	-1	151	7	0.7
1993	†Phi N	13	9	.591	30	28	1-1	0-0	163	175	99	16	6	85-4	123	5.02	79	.273	.361	51-13	.098	-2	146	-17	-2.3
1994	Phi N	3	4	.429	9	7	0	0-0	38	40	29	7	1	22-0	19	6.87	63	.274	.371	9-3	.000	-1	91	-9	-1.4
Total	3	23	17	.575	67	49	5-2	0-0	318.1	314	168	32	11	152-8	219	4.52	85	.258	.343	93-18	.086	-3	140	-18	-3.0
RIVERA, LUIS Luis (Gutierrez) B 6.21.1978 Chihuahua, Mexico BR/TR 6-3/163# d4.4																									
2000	Atl N	1	0	1.000	5	0	0	0-0	6.2	4	1	0	0	5-1	5	1.35	340	.190	.346	0-0	—	0		2	0.3
	Bal A	0	0	—	1	0	0	0-0	0.2	1	0	0	0	1-0	0	0.00	—	.333	.500	0-0	—	0		0	0.0
Total	1	1	0	1.000	6	0	0	0-0	7.1	5	1	0	0	6-1	5	1.23	375	.208	.367	0-0	—	0		2	0.3
RIVERA, MARIANO Mariano B 11.29.1969 Panama City, Panama BR/TR 6-4/170# d5.23																									
1995	†NY A	5	3	.625	19	10	0	0-1	67	71	43	11	2	30-0	51	5.51	84	.266	.342	0-0	—	0	105	-7	-0.6
1996	†NY A	8	3	.727	61	0	0	5-3	107.2	73	25	1	2	34-3	130	2.09	237	.189	.258	0-0	—	0		**35**	3.3
1997	†NY A★	6	4	.600	66	0	0	43-9	71.2	65	17	5	0	20-6	68	1.88	236	.237	.285	0-0	—	0		21	4.1
1998	†NY A	3	0	1.000	54	0	0	36-5	61.1	48	13	3	1	17-1	36	1.91	230	.215	.270	0-0	—	0		18	2.6
1999	†NY A✤	4	3	.571	66	0	0	**45-4**	69	43	15	2	3	18-3	52	1.83	260	.176	.239	0-0	—	0		23	4.5
2000	†NY A★	7	4	.636	66	0	0	36-5	75.2	58	26	4	0	25-3	58	2.85	170	.208	.271	0-0	—	0		17	3.3
2001	†NY A✤	4	6	.400	71	0	0	**50-7**	80.2	61	24	5	1	12-2	83	2.34	192	.209	.242	0-0	—	0		19	3.8
2002	†NY A★	1	4	.200	45	0	0	28-4	46	35	16	3	2	11-2	41	2.74	160	.203	.259	0-0	—	0		8	1.6
2003	†NY A	5	2	.714	64	0	0	40-6	70.2	61	15	3	4	10-1	63	1.66	265	.235	.272	0-0	—	0		22	4.3
Total	9	43	29	.597	512	10	0	283-44	649.2	515	194	37	15	177-21	582	2.49	185	.215	.271	0-0	—	0	105	156	26.9
RIVERA, ROBERTO Roberto (Diaz) B 1.1.1969 Bayamon, P.R. BL/TL 6/175# d9.3																									
1995	Chi N	0	0	—	7	0	0	0-0	5	8	3	1	0	2-0	2	5.40	76	.381	.435	0-0	—	0		-1	0.0
1999	SD N	1	2	.333	12	0	0	0-0	7	6	4	1	0	3-0	3	3.86	109	.240	.310	0-0	—	0		0	0.0
Total	2	1	2	.333	19	0	0	0-0	12	14	7	2	0	5-0	5	4.50	93	.304	.365	0-0	—	0		-1	0.0
RIVIERE, TINK Arthur Bernard B 8.2.1899 Liberty, TX D 9.27.1965 Liberty, TX BR/TR 5-10/167# d4.15																									
1921	StL N	1	0	1.000	18	2	0	0	38.1	45	30	2	2	20	15	6.10	60	.280	.366	8-0	.375	2	79	-10	-0.4
1925	Chi A	0	0	—	3	0	0	0	4.2	6	7	0	1	7	1	13.50	31	.429	.636	1-0	.000	-0		-5	-0.2
Total	2	1	0	1.000	21	2	0	0	43	51	37	2	3	27	16	6.91	54	.291	.395	9-0	.333	2	79	-15	-0.6
RIXEY, EPPA Eppa "Jeptha" B 5.3.1891 Culpeper, VA D 2.28.1963 Cincinnati, OH BR/TL 6-5/210# d6.21 Mil 1918-19 HF1963																									
1912	Phi N	10	10	.500	23	20	10-3	0	162	147	57	2	2	54	59	2.50	145	.256	.322	53-2	.170	-2	64	21	2.2
1913	Phi N	9	5	.643	35	19	9-1	2	155.2	148	67	4	6	56	75	3.12	107	.258	.331	47-3	.191	-0	106	4	0.3
1914	Phi N	2	11	.154	24	15	2	0	103	124	73	0	3	45	41	4.37	67	.313	.387	26-0	.038	-1	105	-15	-1.9
1915	†Phi N	11	12	.478	29	22	10-2	1	176.2	163	67	2	2	64	88	2.39	115	.250	.319	55-5	.164	-0	95	6	0.8
1916	Phi N	22	10	.688	38	33	20-3	0	287	239	91	2	7	74	134	1.85	143	.229	.284	97-4	.155	-2	124	21	2.5
1917	Phi N	16	21	.432	39	36	23-4	1	281.1	249	102	1	5	67	121	2.27	124	.241	.290	94-6	.191	-1	75	13	1.8
1919	Phi N	6	12	.333	23	18	11-1	0	154	160	88	4	3	50	63	3.97	81	.278	.339	47-3	.149	-2	84	-14	-1.6

Year	Tm Lg	W	L	Pct	G	GS	CG-Sho	SV-BS	IP	H	R	HR	HB	BB-IB	SO	ERA	AERA	OAV	OOB	AB-SH	AVG	PB	Sup	APR	PW
1920	Phi N	11	22	.333	41	34	25	2	284.1	288	137	5	4	69	109	3.48	98	.274	.321	101-3	.248	1*	68	0	0.3
1921	Cin N	19	18	.514	40	37	21-2	1	301	324	128	1	5	66	76	2.78	129	.282	.324	101-9	.129	-5	91	23	2.2
1922	Cin N	**25**	13	.658	40	**38**	26-2	0	**313.1**	337	146	13	4	45	80	3.53	113	.275	.303	109-11	.193	-1	102	19	1.9
1923	Cin N	20	15	.571	42	37	23-3	1	309	334	124	3	4	65	97	2.80	138	.280	.320	107-9	.159	-5	97	37	3.3
1924	Cin N	15	14	.517	35	29	15-**4**	1	238.1	219	86	3	2	47	57	2.76	137	.246	.285	84-6	.214	1	97	29	3.4
1925	Cin N	21	11	.656	39	36	22-2	1	287.1	302	109	8	7	47	69	2.88	143	.273	.307	103-5	.214	-1	102	43	4.1
1926	Cin N	14	8	.636	37	29	14-3	0	233	231	104	12	2	58	61	3.40	109	.265	.313	84-6	.226	0	128	9	0.7
1927	Cin N	12	10	.545	34	29	11-1	1	219.2	240	106	3	3	43	42	3.48	109	.287	.325	81-3	.247	4	115	6	0.9
1928	Cin N	19	18	.514	43	**37**	17-3	2	291.1	317	127	4	3	67	58	3.43	115	.288	.330	104-3	.173	-1	82	17	1.8
1929	Cin N	10	13	.435	35	24	11	1	201	235	102	6	3	60	37	4.16	110	.296	.348	65-5	.231	0	76	11	1.0
1930	Cin N	9	13	.409	32	21	5	0	164	207	103	11	7	47	37	5.10	95	.317	.370	55-3	.200	-1	88	-4	-0.5
1931	Cin N	4	7	.364	22	17	4	0	126.2	143	71	4	0	30	22	3.91	96	.291	.332	40-1	.150	-1	90	-5	-0.3
1932	Cin N	5	5	.500	25	11	6-2	0	111.2	108	50	3	4	16	14	2.66	145	.254	.288	34-0	.265	1	71	11	1.1
1933	Cin N	6	3	.667	16	12	5-1	0	94.1	118	48	1	0	12	10	3.15	108	.298	.319	35-0	.257	2	116	0	0.2
Total	21	266	251	.515	692	554	290-37	14	4494.2	4633	1986	92	76	1082	1350	3.15	116	.272	.318	1522-87	.191	-15	94	232	24.2
RIZZO, TODD Todd Michael B 5.24.1971 Media, PA BR/TL 6-3/220# d4.2																									
1998	Chi A	0	0	—	9	0	0	0-0	6.2	12	12	0	0	6-0	3	13.50	34	.387	.474	0-0	—	0		-7	-0.3
1999	Chi A	0	2	.000	3	0	0	0-0	1.1	4	2	0	0	3-1	2	6.75	72	.500	.636	0-0	—	0		-1	-0.1
Total	2	0	2	.000	12	0	0	0-0	8	16	14	0	0	9-1	5	12.38	37	.410	.510	0-0	—	0		-8	-0.4
ROA, JOE Joseph Rodger B 10.11.1971 Southfield, MI BR/TR 6-1/194# d9.20																									
1995	Cle A	0	1	.000	1	1	0	0-0	6	9	4	1	0	2-0	0	6.00	78	.360	.407	0-0	—	0	59	-1	-0.1
1996	Cle A	0	0	—	1	0	0	0-0	1.2	4	2	0	0	3-0	0	10.80	45	.500	.636	0-0	—	0		-1	0.0
1997	SF N	2	5	.286	28	3	0	0-0	65.2	86	40	8	2	20-5	34	5.21	78	.333	.380	15-0	.133	-0	128	-7	-0.6
2002	Phi N	4	4	.500	14	11	0	0-0	71.1	78	33	11	1	13-2	35	4.04	97	.279	.310	25-3	.240	2	105	0	0.0
2003	Phi N	0	2	.000	6	3	0	0-0	19.1	28	13	3	1	4-0	16	6.05	66	.341	.379	4-0	.250	0	55	-4	-0.3
	Col N	0	0	—	4	0	0	0-0	6.2	7	3	2	0	0-0	4	4.05	121	.269	.269	0-0	—	0		1	0.0
	SD N	1	1	.500	18	1	0	0-0	25.1	34	20	5	1	6-0	18	6.75	58	.315	.353	3-0	.333	0	95	-8	-0.5
	Year	1	3	.250	28	4	0	0-0	51.1	69	24	10	2	10-0	38	6.14	67	.319	.354	7-0	.286	0	63	-11	-0.8
Total	5	7	13	.350	72	19	0	0-0	196	246	115	30	5	48-7	107	5.10	79	.313	.353	47-3	.213	2	97	-20	-1.5
ROACH, JASON Jason Glenn B 4.20.1976 Kinston, NC BR/TR 6-4/190# d6.14																									
2003	NY N	0	2	.000	2	2	0	0-0	9	14	12	3	1	4-0	2	12.00	35	.350	.422	2-0	1.000	1	68	-8	-1.1
ROACH, JOHN John F. B 11.19.1867 Renovo, PA D 4.2.1934 Peoria, IL BR/TR 5-9/175# d5.14 b-Mike																									
1887	NY N	0	1	.000	1	1	1	0	8	18	17	0	1	4	3	11.25	33	.419	.479	4	.250	-0	34	-7	-0.6
ROACH, SKEL Rudolph Charles (b: Rudolph Charles Weichbrodt) B 10.20.1871 Danzig, Germany D 3.9.1958 Oak Park, IL BR/TR 6-2/?# d8.9																									
1899	Chi N	1	0	1.000	1	1	1	0	9	13	3	0	0	1	0	3.00	125	.333	.350	4-0	.000	-1	115	1	0.0
ROBBINS, BRUCE Bruce Duane B 9.10.1959 Portland, IN BL/TL 6-1/190# d7.28																									
1979	Det A	3	3	.500	10	8	0	0-0	46	45	21	3	0	21-0	22	3.91	111	.265	.342	0-0	—	0	120	2	0.3
1980	Det A	4	2	.667	15	6	0	0-0	51.2	60	40	12	0	28-0	23	6.62	62	.287	.368	0-0	—	0	130	-13	-1.3
Total	2	7	5	.583	25	14	0	0-0	97.2	105	61	15	0	49-0	45	5.34	79	.277	.356	0-0	—	0	125	-11	-1.0
ROBERGE, BERT Bertrand Roland B 10.3.1954 Lewiston, ME BR/TR 6-4/190# d5.28																									
1979	Hou N	3	0	1.000	26	0	0	4-1	32	20	6	0	0	17-0	13	1.69	209	.196	.308	2-0	.000	-0		7	0.8
1980	Hou N	2	0	1.000	14	0	0	0-0	24.1	24	16	2	2	10-1	9	5.92	56	.261	.343	3-1	.000	-0		-7	-0.5
1982	Hou N	1	2	.333	22	0	0	3-2	25.2	29	12	0	0	6-3	18	4.21	79	.284	.324	1-0	.000	-0		-2	-0.3
1984	Chi A	3	3	.500	21	0	0	0-2	40.2	36	18	2	3	15-1	25	3.76	111	.240	.320	0-0	—	0		2	0.3
1985	Mon N	3	3	.500	42	0	0	2-5	68	58	28	5	2	22-5	34	3.44	99	.232	.299	1-0	.000	-0		0	0.0
1986	Mon N	0	4	.000	21	0	0	1-0	28.2	33	20	2	1	10-3	20	6.28	59	.295	.352	2-0	.000	-0		-7	-1.0
Total	6	12	12	.500	146	0	0	10-10	219.1	200	100	11	8	80-13	119	3.98	90	.248	.320	9-1	.000	-1		-7	-0.7
ROBERSON, SID Sidney Dean B 9.7.1971 Jacksonville, FL BL/TL 5-9/170# d5.20																									
1995	Mil A	6	4	.600	26	13	0	0-0	84.1	102	55	16	8	37-3	40	5.76	87	.307	.388	0-0	—	0	99	-5	-0.6
ROBERTS, DALE Dale "Mountain Man" B 4.12.1942 Owenton, KY BR/TL 6-4/180# d9.9																									
1967	NY A	0	0	—	2	0	0	0	2	3	2	0	2	2-1	0	9.00	35	.429	.636	0-0	—	0		-1	-0.1
ROBERTS, DAVE David Arthur B 9.11.1944 Gallipolis, OH BL/TL 6-2/197# d7.6																									
1969	SD N	0	3	.000	22	5	0	1-0	48.2	65	30	5	3	19-0	19	4.81	74	.322	.387	15-0	.267	1*	70	-7	-0.4
1970	SD N	8	14	.364	43	21	3-2	1-2	181.2	182	80	16	1	43-11	102	3.81	104	.261	.304	59-4	.153	1	74	6	0.8
1971	SD N	14	17	.452	37	34	14-2	0-0	269.2	238	79	9	5	61-9	135	2.10	157	.240	.285	86-8	.221	2*	62	36	4.6
1972	Hou N	12	7	.632	35	28	7-3	2-0	192	227	100	18	2	57-3	111	4.50	75	.296	.345	67-6	.239	6	143	-22	-1.6
1973	Hou N	17	11	.607	39	36	12-6	0-1	249.1	264	92	15	2	62-8	119	2.85	128	.271	.314	85-12	.129	-3*	102	19	1.8
1974	Hou N	10	12	.455	34	30	8-2	1-0	204	216	83	6	3	65-2	72	3.40	102	.276	.332	73-2	.219	5*	101	4	1.0
1975	Hou N	8	14	.364	32	27	7	1-1	198.1	182	98	16	2	73-4	101	4.27	79	.244	.310	63-10	.143	-0	91	-19	-1.9
1976	Det A	16	17	.485	36	36	18-4	0-0	252	254	122	16	4	63-4	79	4.00	93	.264	.309	0-0	—	0	82	-5	-0.5
1977	Det A	4	10	.286	22	22	5	0-0	129.1	143	88	20	2	41-2	46	5.15	84	.274	.328	0-0	—	0	91	-14	-1.3
	Chi N	1	1	.500	17	6	1	1-0	53	55	22	1	1	12-8	23	3.23	136	.275	.315	17-0	.059	-2	74	6	0.2
1978	Chi N	6	8	.429	35	20	2-1	1-0	142.1	159	87	17	3	56-15	54	5.25	77	.288	.353	52-3	.327	6*	109	-15	-0.7
1979	SF N	0	2	.000	26	1	0	3-5	42	42	15	3	1	18-3	23	2.57	136	.262	.339	5-0	.000	-1	177	4	0.2
	†Pit N	5	2	.714	21	3	0	1-0	38.2	47	18	1	1	12-4	15	3.26	119	.318	.366	5-0	.000	-1	137	2	0.3
	Year	5	4	.556	47	4	0	4-5	80.2	89	24	4	2	30-7	38	2.90	127	.289	.352	10-0	.000	-1	150	5	0.5
1980	Pit N	0	1	.000	2	0	0	0-0	2.1	2	1	0	0	1-0	1	3.86	95	.250	.333	0-0	—	0		0	0.0
	Sea A	2	3	.400	37	4	0	3-1	80.1	86	46	7	1	27-7	47	4.37	95	.270	.324	0-0	—	0	70	-3	-0.3
1981	NY N	0	3	.000	7	4	0	0-0	15.1	26	18	5	0	5-0	10	9.39	37	.366	.408	4-0	.250	0	51	-10	-1.6
Total	13	103	125	.452	445	277	77-20	15-10	2099	2188	979	155	31	615-80	957	3.78	97	.270	.321	531-45	.194	15	93	-18	0.6
ROBERTS, GRANT Grant William B 9.13.1977 ElCajon, CA BR/TR 6-3/205# d7.27																									
2000	NY N	0	0	—	4	1	0	0-0	7	11	10	0	0	4-1	6	11.57	38	.344	.395	0-1	—	0	187	-6	-0.3
2001	NY N	1	0	1.000	16	0	0	0-1	26	24	11	2	0	8-1	29	3.81	109	.240	.294	3-0	.000	-0		1	0.0
2002	NY N	3	1	.750	34	0	0	0-0	45	43	12	3	1	16-7	31	2.20	180	.253	.317	1-0	1.000	0		9	0.8
2003	NY N	0	3	.000	18	0	0	1-0	19	19	9	0	1	3-1	10	3.79	110	.257	.295	0-0	—	0		1	0.1
Total	4	4	4	.500	72	1	0	1-1	97	97	42	5	2	31-10	76	3.62	113	.258	.314	4-1	.250	0	187	5	0.6
ROBERTS, JIM James Newson "Big Jim" B 10.13.1895 Artesia, MS D 6.24.1984 Columbus, MS BR/TR 6-3/205# d7.27																									
1924	Bro N	0	3	.000	11	5	0	0	25.1	41	28	1	2	8	10	7.46	50	.360	.411	7-0	.143	-0	72	-12	-1.2
1925	Bro N	0	0	—	1	0	0	0	1	1	1	0	0	0	0	0.00	—	.500	.500	0-0	—	0		0	0.0
Total	2	0	3	.000	12	5	0	0	26.1	42	29	1	2	8	10	7.18	52	.362	.413	7-0	.143	-0	72	-12	-1.2
ROBERTS, RAY Raymond B 8.25.1895 Cruger, MS D 1.30.1962 Cruger, MS BL/TR 5-11/180# d9.12																									
1919	Phi A	0	2	.000	3	2	0	0	14	21	14	0	0	3	2	7.71	44	.368	.400	4-0	.250	-0	114	-6	-0.7
ROBERTS, ROBIN Robin Evan B 9.30.1926 Springfield, IL BB/TR 6/190# d6.18 HF1976																									
1948	Phi N	7	9	.438	20	20	9	0	146.2	148	63	10	4	61	84	3.19	124	.278	.356	44-3	.250	4*	70	12	1.6
1949	Phi N	15	15	.500	43	31	11-3	4	226.2	229	101	15	5	75	95	3.69	107	.273	.337	67-5	.075	-3	99	7	0.4
1950	†Phi N★	20	11	.645	40	**39**	21-**5**	1	304.1	282	112	29	2	77	146	3.02	134	.248	.297	102-7	.118	-4	99	**38**	3.2
1951	Phi N★	21	15	.583	44	**39**	22-6	2	**315**	284	115	20	3	64	127	3.03	127	.237	**.278**	87-14	.172	5	99	30	**3.8**
1952	Phi N☆	**28**	7	.800	39	**37**	**30**-3	2	**330**	292	104	22	5	45	148	2.59	141	.234	.263	112-13	.125	2	122	**43**	**4.6**
1953	Phi N★	**23**	16	.590	44	**41**	**33**-5	2	**346.2**	324	119	30	2	61	**198**	2.75	153	.242	.276	123-9	.179	2	96	**59**	6.4
1954	Phi N★	**23**	15	.605	45	**38**	**29**-4	4	**336.2**	289	116	35	5	56	**185**	2.97	136	.231	**.266**	122-4	.123	-3	107	44	4.3
1955	Phi N★	**23**	14	.622	41	**38**	**26**-1	3	**305**	292	137	41	2	53-3	160	3.28	121	.246	.279	107-5	.252	14*	104	18	3.4

Year	Tm Lg	W	L	Pct	G	GS	CG-Sho	SV-BS	IP	H	R	HR	HB	BB-IB	SO	ERA	AERA	OAV	OOB	AB-SH	AVG	PB	Sup	APR	PW
1956	Phi N☆	19	18	.514	43	37	**22**-1	3	297.1	328	155	46	2	40-3	157	4.45	84	.282	.305	100-3	.200	4	103	-18	-1.7
1957	Phi N	10	22	.313	39	32	14-2	2	249.2	246	122	40	1	43-16	128	4.07	93	.252	.283	80-4	.162	0	79	-6	-0.6
1958	Phi N	17	14	.548	35	34	21-1	0	269.2	270	112	30	2	51-5	130	3.24	122	.259	.292	99-3	.202	4*	95	21	2.6
1959	Phi N	15	17	.469	35	35	19-2	0	257.1	267	137	34	5	35-4	137	4.27	96	.263	.290	89-2	.191	3	77	-4	-0.1
1960	Phi N	12	16	.429	35	33	13-2	1	237.1	256	113	31	2	34-7	122	4.02	97	.275	.300	79-4	.152	-1	81	-1	-0.3
1961	Phi N	1	10	.091	26	18	2	0	117	154	85	19	2	23-6	54	5.85	70	.326	.354	33-1	.091	-2	89	-23	-2.1
1962	Bal A	10	9	.526	27	25	6	0	191.1	176	63	17	4	41-7	102	2.78	133	.244	.288	52-7	.192	2	84	23	2.4
1963	Bal A	14	13	.519	35	35	9-2	0	251.1	230	100	35	3	40-8	124	3.33	104	.240	.272	79-8	.203	2	104	6	0.8
1964	Bal A	13	7	.650	31	31	8-4	0	204	203	69	18	3	52-6	109	2.91	123	.261	.308	68-4	.132	-1	97	17	1.4
1965	Bal A	5	7	.417	20	15	5-1	0	114.2	110	51	17	1	20-3	63	3.38	103	.252	.282	35-3	.171	1	94	1	0.2
	Hou N	5	2	.714	10	10	3-2	0	76	61	22	1	0	10-1	34	1.89	177	.216	.243	21-3	.238	3	104	11	1.4
1966	Hou N	3	5	.375	13	12	1-1	1	63.2	79	31	7	1	10-0	26	3.82	90	.307	.331	16-3	.063	-1	88	-3	-0.4
	Chi N	2	3	.400	11	9	1	0	48.1	62	35	8	0	11-0	28	6.14	60	.313	.349	10-3	.200	1	88	-12	-1.0
	Year	5	8	.385	24	21	2-1	1	112	141	39	15	1	21-0	54	4.82	73	.310	.339	26-6	.115	-0	88	-17	-1.4
Total	19	286	245	.539	676	609	305-45	25	4688.2	4582	1962	505	54	902-69	2357	3.41	113	.255	.292	1525-108	.167	34	95	263	30.3
ROBERTS, WILLIS Willis Augusto (De Leon) B 6.19.1975 San Cristobal, D.R. BR/TR 6-3/175# d7.2																									
1999	Det A	0	0	—	1	0	0	0-0	1.1	3	4	0	1	0-0	0	13.50	37	.500	.500	0-0	—	0		-2	-0.1
2001	Bal A	9	10	.474	46	18	1	6-4	132	142	75	15	11	55-1	95	4.91	87	.274	.354	4-1	.250	0	97	-7	-0.9
2002	Bal A	5	4	.556	66	0	0	1-2	75	79	34	5	4	32-3	51	3.36	127	.270	.345	0-0	—	0		6	0.6
2003	Bal A	3	1	.750	26	0	0	0-0	39.1	41	26	7	7	16-2	26	5.72	77	.273	.370	0-0	—	0		-6	-0.5
Total	4	17	15	.531	139	18	1	7-6	247.2	265	139	27	23	103-6	172	4.62	93	.274	.355	4-1	.250	0	97	-9	-0.9
ROBERTSON, CHARLIE Charles Culbertson B 1.31.1896 Dexter, TX D 8.23.1984 Fort Worth, TX BL/TR 6/175# d5.13																									
1919	Chi A	0	1	.000	1	1	0	0	2	5	2	0	0	0	1	9.00	35	.556	.556	0-0	—	0	25	-1	-0.2
1922	Chi A	14	15	.483	37	34	21-3	0	272	294	124	9	4	89	83	3.64	112	.286	.345	87-8	.184	-2	95	13	0.8
1923	Chi A	13	18	.419	38	34	18-1	0	255	262	126	8	5	104	91	3.81	104	.272	.346	85-8	.247	0	88	5	0.4
1924	Chi A	4	10	.286	17	14	5	0	97.1	108	65	2	0	54	29	4.99	83	.293	.383	33-3	.182	-1	70	-10	-1.4
1925	Chi A	8	12	.400	24	23	6-2	0	137	181	96	8	2	47	27	5.26	79	.327	.381	45-2	.222	0	91	-19	-2.3
1926	StL A	1	2	.333	8	7	1	0	28	38	27	4	2	21	13	8.36	51	.333	.445	10-0	.300	1	109	-10	-0.8
1927	Bos N	7	17	.292	28	21	6	0	154.1	188	90	2	4	46	49	4.72	79	.308	.360	50-3	.240	1	70	-16	-2.1
1928	Bos N	2	5	.286	13	7	3	1	59.1	73	40	5	0	16	17	5.31	74	.308	.352	17-2	.000	-1	114	-9	-1.0
Total	8	49	80	.380	166	141	60-6	1	1005	1149	570	38	17	377	310	4.44	90	.296	.361	327-26	.208	-2	88	-47	-6.6
ROBERTSON, JERIOME Jeriome Paul B 3.30.1977 San Jose, CA BL/TL 6-1/190# d9.2																									
2002	Hou N	0	2	.000	11	1	0	0-0	9.2	13	8	4	0	5-3	6	6.52	66	.394	.439	0-0	—	0	43	-3	-0.4
2003	Hou N	15	9	.625	32	31	0	0-0	160.2	180	98	23	6	64-8	99	5.10	87	.287	.356	52-5	.154	-0*	115	-11	-1.4
Total	2	15	11	.577	43	32	0	0-0	170.1	193	106	27	6	69-11	105	5.18	86	.292	.360	52-5	.154	-0	113	-14	-1.8
ROBERTSON, JERRY Jerry Lee B 10.13.1943 Winchester, KS D 3.24.1996 Burlington, KS BB/TR 6-2/205# d4.8																									
1969	Mon N	5	16	.238	38	27	3	1-0	179.2	186	87	17	4	81-11	133	3.96	93	.272	.348	56-2	.089	-3	67	-4	-0.8
1970	Det A	0	0	—	11	0	0	0-0	14.2	19	8	1	0	5-1	11	3.68	101	.306	.353	0-0	—	0		-1	0.0
Total	2	5	16	.238	49	27	3	1-0	194.1	205	95	18	4	86-12	144	3.94	94	.274	.348	56-2	.089	-3	67	-5	-0.8
ROBERTSON, NATE Nathan Daniel B 9.3.1977 Wichita, KS BR/TL 6-2/215# d9.7																									
2002	Fla N	0	1	.000	6	1	0	0-0	8.1	15	11	3	2	4-1	3	11.88	33	.375	.457	2-0	.000	-0	23	-7	-0.8
2003	Det A	1	2	.333	8	8	0	0-0	44.2	55	27	6	0	23-2	33	5.44	79	.306	.384	0-0	—	0	96	-5	-0.3
Total	2	1	3	.250	14	9	0	0-0	53	70	38	9	2	27-3	36	6.45	66	.318	.398	2-0	.000	-0	89	-12	-1.1
ROBERTSON, DICK Preston B 1891 Washington, DC D 10.2.1944 New Orleans, LA BR/TR 5-9/160# d9.16																									
1913	Cin N	0	1	.000	2	1	1	0	10	13	9	0	0	9	1	7.20	45	.342	.468	3-0	.000	-0	0	-4	-0.4
1918	Bro N	3	6	.333	13	9	7-1	0	87	87	34	0	0	28	18	2.59	108	.272	.330	30-0	.300	2*	60	1	0.3
1919	Was A	0	1	.000	7	4	0	0	27.2	25	11	1	0	9	7	2.28	141	.253	.315	7-0	.000	-1	61	2	0.0
Total	3	3	8	.273	22	14	8-1	0	124.2	125	54	1	0	46	26	2.89	101	.274	.340	40-0	.225	0	56	-1	-0.1
ROBERTSON, RICH Richard Paul B 10.14.1944 Albany, CA BR/TR 6-2/210# d9.10																									
1966	SF N	0	0	—	1	0	0	0	2.1	3	3	0	0	2-0	2	7.71	48	.300	.417	0-0	—	0		-1	-0.1
1967	SF N	0	0	—	1	0	0	0	2	3	1	0	0	0-0	1	4.50	73	.333	.333	0-0	—	0		0	0.0
1968	SF N	2	0	1.000	3	1	0	0	9	9	6	0	0	3-0	8	6.00	49	.265	.324	2-1	.500	0	324	-3	-0.5
1969	SF N	1	3	.250	17	7	1-1	0-0	44.1	53	32	4	1	21-1	20	5.48	64	.298	.368	10-1	.000	-1	130	-10	-0.9
1970	SF N	8	9	.471	41	26	6	1-1	183.2	199	113	22	1	96-3	121	4.85	82	.277	.359	59-7	.102	-1	108	-18	-1.6
1971	SF N	2	2	.500	23	6	1	1-0	61	66	40	5	2	31-3	32	4.57	74	.267	.351	15-0	.067	-1	113	-9	-0.8
Total	6	13	14	.481	86	40	8-1	2-1	302.1	333	195	31	4	153-7	184	4.94	76	.278	.358	86-9	.093	-2	118	-41	-3.9
ROBERTSON, RICH Richard Wayne B 9.15.1968 Nacogdoches, TX BL/TL 6-4/175# d4.30																									
1993	Pit N	0	1	.000	9	0	0	0-1	9	15	6	0	0	4-0	5	6.00	68	.385	.442	0-0	—	0		-2	-0.2
1994	Pit N	0	0	—	8	0	0	0-0	15.2	20	12	2	0	10-4	8	6.89	63	.313	.400	4-0	.250	0		-4	-0.2
1995	Min A	2	0	1.000	25	4	1	0-0	51.2	48	28	4	0	31-4	38	3.83	125	.253	.354	0-0	—	0	98	4	0.1
1996	Min A	7	17	.292	36	31	5-**3**	0-1	186.1	197	113	22	9	116-2	114	5.12	100	.273	.378	0-0	—	0	79	0	0.1
1997	Min A	8	12	.400	31	26	0	0-0	147	169	105	19	6	70-3	69	5.69	82	.292	.370	5-0	.200	0	79	-19	-2.2
1998	Ana A	0	0	—	5	0	0	0-0	5.2	11	11	3	0	2-0	3	15.88	30	.393	.419	0-0	—	0		-7	-0.3
Total	6	17	30	.362	114	61	6-3	0-2	415.1	460	275	50	15	233-13	237	5.40	90	.284	.375	9-0	.222	0	81	-28	-2.7
ROBINSON, DEWEY Dewey Everett B 4.28.1955 Evanston, IL BR/TR 6/180# d4.6 C2																									
1979	Chi A	0	1	.000	11	0	0	0-0	14.1	11	12	1	0	9-2	5	6.28	68	.212	.328	0-0	—	0		-3	-0.2
1980	Chi A	1	1	.500	15	0	0	0-1	35	26	13	2	0	16-0	28	3.09	131	.215	.302	0-0	—	0		4	0.2
1981	Chi A	1	0	1.000	4	0	0	0-0	4	5	2	1	0	3-1	2	4.50	80	.357	.471	0-0	—	0		0	-0.1
Total	3	2	2	.500	30	0	0	0-1	53.1	42	27	4	0	28-3	35	4.05	100	.225	.323	0-0	—	0		1	-0.1
ROBINSON, DON Don Allen B 6.8.1957 Ashland, KY BR/TR 6-4/231# d4.10																									
1978	Pit N	14	6	.700	35	32	9-1	1-0	228.1	203	98	20	3	57-4	135	3.47	107	.236	.283	85-4	.235	2	111	8	0.8
1979	†Pit N	8	8	.500	29	25	4	0-0	160.2	171	74	12	4	52-5	96	3.87	101	.277	.335	49-4	.204	1	115	2	0.1
1980	Pit N	7	10	.412	29	24	3-2	1-0	160.1	157	74	14	5	45-5	103	3.99	92	.257	.312	57-0	.333	6*	91	-4	0.3
1981	Pit N	0	3	.000	16	2	0	2-1	38.1	47	27	4	0	23-4	17	5.87	61	.313	.400	12-0	.250	1*	123	-9	-0.6
1982	Pit N	15	13	.536	38	30	6	0-0	227	213	123	26	3	103-11	165	4.28	87	.250	.331	85-2	.282	8*	115	-15	-0.9
1983	Pit N	2	2	.500	9	6	0	0-1	36.1	43	21	5	0	21-3	28	4.46	83	.297	.386	13-0	.154	1*	111	-3	-0.3
1984	Pit N	5	6	.455	51	1	0	10-4	122	99	45	6	0	49-4	110	3.02	119	.226	.298	31-0	.290	4*	49	8	1.3
1985	Pit N	5	11	.313	44	6	0	3-5	95.1	95	49	6	2	42-11	65	3.87	93	.255	.334	21-0	.238	3	74	-5	-0.5
1986	Pit N	3	4	.429	50	0	0	14-1	69.1	61	27	5	2	27-3	53	3.38	114	.237	.310	6-0	.667	2		4	0.8
1987	Pit N	6	6	.500	42	0	0	12-7	65.1	66	29	6	0	22-3	53	3.86	107	.267	.326	7-0	.143	0*		3	0.6
	†SF N	5	1	.833	25	0	0	7-0	42.2	39	13	1	0	18-3	26	2.74	140	.239	.311	11-0	.273	2		6	1.2
	Year	11	7	.611	67	0	0	19-7	108	105	45	7	0	40-6	79	3.42	117	.256	.320	18-0	.222	2		9	1.8
1988	SF N	10	5	.667	51	19	3-2	6-3	176.2	152	63	11	3	49-12	122	2.45	134	.231	.284	52-2	.173	3*	103	13	1.4
1989	†SF N	12	11	.522	34	32	5-1	0-0	197	184	80	22	2	37-6	96	3.43	99	.248	.283	81-0	.185	4*	113	1	0.2
1990	SF N	10	7	.588	26	25	4	0-0	157.2	173	84	18	1	41-8	78	4.57	80	.280	.324	63-3	.143	1*	103	-15	-1.5
1991	SF N	5	9	.357	34	16	0	1-0	121.1	123	64	12	1	50-7	78	4.38	82	.265	.334	40-0	.150	0*	99	-11	-1.2
1992	Cal A	1	0	1.000	3	3	0	0-0	16.1	19	4	1	0	3-0	9	2.20	181	.292	.324	0-0	—	0	76	3	0.2
	Phi N	1	4	.200	8	8	0	0-0	43.2	49	32	6	1	4-0	17	6.18	57	.290	.300	18-0	.389	3*	117	-13	-1.0
Total	15	109	106	.507	524	229	34-6	57-22	1958.1	1894	907	175	27	643-89	1251	3.79	96	.255	.314	631-15	.231	41	106	-27	0.9
ROBINSON, HUMBERTO Humberto Valentino B 6.25.1930 Colon, Panama BR/TR 6-1/155# d4.20																									
1955	Mil N	3	1	.750	13	2	1	2	38	31	13	1	4	25-2	19	3.08	122	.235	.368	13-0	.077	-1	119	4	0.3
1956	Mil N	0	0	—	1	0	0	0	2	1	0	0	0	2-0	0	0.00	—	.167	.375	0-0	—	0		1	0.1
1958	Mil N	2	4	.333	19	0	0	1	41.2	30	15	4	2	13-2	26	3.02	116	.203	.276	6-0	.167	1		3	0.5
1959	Cle A	1	0	1.000	5	0	0	0	8.2	9	4	0	0	4-1	6	4.15	89	.281	.361	0-0	—	0		0	0.0

Year	Tm Lg	W	L	Pct	G	GS	CG-Sho	SV-BS	IP	H	R	HR	HB	BB-IB	SO	ERA	AERA	OAV	OOB	AB-SH	AVG	PB	Sup	APR	PW
	Phi N	2	4	.333	31	4	1	1	73	70	36	6	0	24-6	32	3.33	123	.251	.308	13-1	.231	1	60	4	0.4
1960	Phi N	0	4	.000	33	1	0	0	49.2	48	24	6	0	22-5	31	3.44	113	.255	.333	6-0	.167	-0	23	1	0.1
Total	5	8	13	.381	102	7	2	4	213	189	92	17	6	90-16	114	3.25	119	.241	.322	38-1	.158	0	73	13	1.4
ROBINSON, JEFF Jeffrey Daniel B 12.13.1960 Santa Ana, CA BR/TR 6-4/200# d4.7																									
1984	SF N	7	15	.318	34	33	1-1	0-0	171.2	195	99	12	7	52-4	102	4.56	77	.288	.341	61-1	.115	-2	88	-21	-2.6
1985	SF N	0	0	—	8	0	0	0-0	12.1	16	11	2	0	10-1	8	5.11	67	.333	.441	0-0	—	0		-4	-0.2
1986	SF N	6	3	.667	64	1	0	8-1	104.1	92	46	8	1	32-7	90	3.36	105	.234	.291	15-1	.067	-1*	177	1	0.0
1987	SF N	6	8	.429	63	0	0	10-6	96.2	69	34	10	1	48-10	82	2.79	138	.207	.306	18-0	.111	-1		12	1.7
	Pit N	2	1	.667	18	0	0	4-1	26.2	20	9	1	0	6-1	19	3.04	135	.215	.263	4-1	.250	1		4	0.6
	Year	8	9	.471	81	0	0	14-7	123.1	89	50	11	1	54-11	101	2.85	137	.209	.297	22-1	.136	0		16	2.3
1988	Pit N	11	5	.688	75	0	0	9-4	124.2	113	44	6	3	39-5	87	3.03	112	.244	.303	16-5	.188	0		6	1.0
1989	Pit N	7	13	.350	50	19	0	4-4	141.1	161	92	14	1	59-11	95	4.58	73	.283	.347	35-5	.229	2	121	-25	-3.1
1990	NY A	3	6	.333	54	4	1	0-2	88.2	82	35	8	1	34-3	43	3.45	115	.248	.319	0-0	—	0	74	6	0.7
1991	Cal A	0	3	.000	39	0	0	3-2	57	56	34	9	2	29-4	57	5.37	77	.259	.349	0-0	—	0		-6	-0.4
1992	Chi N	4	3	.571	49	5	0	1-3	78	76	29	5	2	40-7	46	3.00	120	.263	.354	12-2	.000	-1	70	5	0.4
Total	9	46	57	.447	454	62	2-1	39-23	901.1	880	433	75	18	349-53	629	3.79	95	.258	.327	161-15	.137	-1	94	-22	-1.9
ROBINSON, JEFF Jeffrey Mark B 12.14.1961 Ventura, CA BR/TR 6-6/240# d4.12																									
1987	†Det A	9	6	.600	29	21	2-1	0-0	127.1	132	86	16	7	54-3	98	5.37	79	.262	.340	0-0	—	0	123	-17	-1.7
1988	Det A	13	6	.684	24	23	6-2	0-0	172	121	61	19	3	72-5	114	2.98	128	**.197**	.282	0-0	—	0	106	18	1.8
1989	Det A	4	5	.444	16	16	1-1	0-0	78	76	47	10	1	46-1	40	4.73	81	.259	.358	0-0	—	0	139	-8	-0.9
1990	Det A	10	9	.526	27	27	1-1	0-0	145	141	101	23	6	88-9	76	5.96	67	.255	.361	0-0	—	0	123	-30	-3.4
1991	Bal A	4	9	.308	21	19	0	0-0	104.1	119	62	12	6	51-2	65	5.18	76	.289	.375	0-0	—	0	83	-14	-1.5
1992	Tex A	4	4	.500	16	4	0	0-2	45.2	50	30	6	0	21-1	18	5.72	67	.281	.351	0-0	—	0	120	-9	-1.4
	Pit N	3	1	.750	8	7	0	0-0	36.1	33	18	2	1	15-0	14	4.46	77	.244	.322	11-2	.091	-1	165	-3	-0.4
Total	6	47	40	.540	141	117	10-5	0-2	708.2	672	405	88	24	347-21	425	4.79	82	.250	.339	11-2	.091	-1	118	-63	-7.5
ROBINSON, JACK John Edward B 2.20.1921 Orange, NJ D 3.2.2000 Ormond Beach, FL BR/TR 6/175# d5.4																									
1949	Bos A	0	0	—	3	0	0	0	4	4	1	0	1	1	1	2.25	194	.267	.353	0-0	—	0		1	0.1
ROBINSON, HANK John Henry "Rube" (b: John Henry Roberson) B 8.16.1889 Floyd, AR D 7.3.1965 N.Little Rock, AR BR/TL 5-11.5/160# d9.2																									
1911	Pit N	0	1	.000	5	0	0	0	13	13	7	0	1	5	8	2.77	124	.283	.365	3-0	.000	-0		0	0.0
1912	Pit N	12	7	.632	33	16	11	2	175	146	54	3	10	30	79	2.26	144	.237	.284	59-0	.254	3	91	21	2.4
1913	Pit N	14	9	.609	43	22	8-1	0	196.1	184	72	1	7	41	50	2.38	127	.255	.301	61-3	.180	-1	96	13	1.2
1914	StL N	7	8	.467	26	16	6-1	0	126	128	61	1	4	32	30	3.00	93	.274	.325	35-3	.171	-0	98	-3	-0.3
1915	StL N	7	8	.467	32	15	6-1	0	143	128	54	1	7	35	57	2.45	114	.245	.301	47-0	.106	-2	123	4	0.3
1918	NY A	2	4	.333	11	3	1	0	48	47	21	0	3	16	14	3.00	94	.269	.340	13-0	.000	-2	71	-1	-0.4
Total	6	42	37	.532	150	72	32-3	2	701.1	646	269	6	32	159	238	2.53	118	.253	.305	218-6	.170	-3	99	34	3.2
ROBINSON, KEN Kenneth Neal B 11.3.1969 Barberton, OH D 2.28.1999 Tucson, AZ BR/TR 5-7/175# d7.20																									
1995	Tor A	1	2	.333	21	0	0	0-0	39	25	21	7	2	22-1	31	3.69	128	.179	.295	0-0	—	0		3	0.2
1996	KC A	1	0	1.000	5	0	0	0-0	6	9	4	0	0	3-1	5	6.00	84	.346	.400	0-0	—	0		-1	-0.1
1997	Tor A	0	0	—	3	0	0	0-1	3.1	1	1	1	0	1-0	4	2.70	170	.100	.182	0-0	—	0		1	0.1
Total	3	2	2	.500	29	0	0	0-1	48.1	35	26	8	2	26-2	40	3.91	121	.199	.304	0-0	—	0		3	0.2
ROBINSON, RON Ronald Dean B 3.24.1962 Exeter, CA BR/TR 6-4/235# d8.14																									
1984	Cin N	1	2	.333	12	5	1	0-0	39.2	35	18	3	0	13-3	24	2.72	139	.232	.291	8-1	.000	-1	107	2	0.1
1985	Cin N	7	7	.500	33	12	0	1-0	108.1	107	53	11	1	32-3	76	3.99	95	.259	.311	22-5	.091	-1	74	-2	-0.4
1986	Cin N	10	3	.769	70	0	0	14-6	116.2	110	44	10	2	43-8	117	3.24	120	.253	.321	14-0	.071	-1		9	1.1
1987	Cin N	7	5	.583	48	18	0	4-2	154	148	71	14	1	43-8	99	3.68	115	.256	.305	36-5	.194	0	130	9	0.5
1988	Cin N	3	7	.300	17	16	0	0-0	78.2	88	47	5	2	26-4	38	4.12	87	.285	.339	25-1	.200	1	80	-8	-0.9
1989	Cin N	5	3	.625	15	15	0	0-0	83.1	80	36	8	2	28-2	36	3.35	108	.252	.316	28-2	.214	1	126	2	0.3
1990	Cin N	2	2	.500	6	5	0	0-0	31.1	36	18	2	0	14-0	14	4.88	81	.295	.368	11-1	.091	-1	137	-3	-0.4
	Mil A	12	5	.706	22	22	7-2	0-0	148.1	158	60	5	6	37-1	57	2.91	133	.275	.322	0-0	—	0	131	14	1.5
1991	Mil A	0	1	.000	1	1	0	0-0	4.1	6	3	0	1	3-1	0	6.23	64	.353	.476	0-0	—	0	69	-1	-0.2
1992	Mil A	1	4	.200	8	8	0	0-0	35.1	51	26	3	2	14-0	12	5.86	66	.331	.392	0-0	—	0	98	-9	-1.1
Total	9	48	39	.552	232	102	8-2	19-8	800	819	376	61	17	253-30	473	3.63	107	.267	.323	144-15	.153	-2	111	13	0.5
ROBINSON, BILL William (b: William Anderson) B Taylorsville, KY d8.12																									
1889	Lou AA	0	1	.000	1	1	1	0	8	10	10	2	0	6	2	10.13	38	.294	.400	3	.333	0	80	-4	-0.3
ROBINSON, YANK William H. B 9.19.1859 Philadelphia, PA D 8.25.1894 St.Louis, MO BR/TR 5-6.5/170# d8.24 ▲																									
1882	Det N	0	0	—	1	0	0	0	2	0	0	0		1	0	0.00	—	.000	.125	39	.179	-0*		1	0.0
1884	Bal U	3	3	.500	11	3	3	0	75	96	61	1		18	61	3.48	77	.292	.329	415	.267	-0*	101	-7	-0.6
1886	†StL AA	0	1	.000	1	1	1	0	9	10	11	0	0	7	1	3.00	115	.286	.405	481	.274	0*	121	-1	-0.1
1887	†StL AA	0	0	—	1	0	0	1	3	3	2	0	1	3	0	3.00	151	.333	.538	430	.305	0*		0	0.0
Total	4	3	4	.429	14	4	4	1	89	109	74	1	1	29	62	3.34	85	.287	.339	1365	.279	0	104	-7	-0.7
ROBITAILLE, CHICK Joseph Anthony B 3.2.1879 Whitehall, NY D 7.30.1947 Waterford, NY BR/TR 5-8/150# d9.2																									
1904	Pit N	4	3	.571	9	8	8	0	66	52	22	1	1	13	34	1.91	144	.208	.250	21-0	.095	-2	47	5	0.2
1905	Pit N	8	5	.615	17	12	10	0	120.1	126	54	1	3	28	32	2.92	103	.276	.322	45-1	.133	-2	80	0	-0.3
Total	2	12	8	.600	26	20	18	0	186.1	178	76	2	4	41	66	2.56	114	.252	.297	66-1	.121	-4	67	5	-0.1
ROCHE, ARMANDO Armando (Baez) B 12.7.1926 Havana, Cuba D 6.26.1997 Chicago, IL BR/TR 6/190# d5.10																									
1945	Was A	0	0	—	2	0	0	0	6	10	4	0	0	2	0	6.00	52	.400	.444	1-0	.000	-0		-2	-0.1
ROCHFORD, MIKE Michael Joseph B 3.14.1963 Methuen, MA BL/TL 6-4/205# d9.3																									
1988	Bos A	0	0	—	2	0	0	0-0	2.1	4	0	0	0	1-0	1	0.00	—	.364	.417	0-0	—	0		1	0.1
1989	Bos A	0	0	—	4	0	0	0-0	4	4	7	1	0	4-1	1	6.75	61	.267	.400	0-0	—	0		-3	-0.1
1990	Bos A	0	1	.000	2	1	0	0-0	4	10	10	1	0	4-0	0	18.00	23	.526	.583	0-0	—	0	156	-6	-1.0
Total	3	0	1	.000	8	1	0	0-0	10.1	18	17	2	0	9-1	2	9.58	43	.400	.482	0-0	—	0	156	-8	-1.0
ROCKER, JOHN John Loy B 10.17.1974 Statesboro, GA BR/TL 6-4/210# d5.5																									
1998	†Atl N	1	3	.250	47	0	0	2-2	38	22	10	4	3	22-4	42	2.13	195	.172	.307	0-0	—	0		9	0.9
1999	†Atl N	4	5	.444	74	0	0	38-7	72.1	47	24	5	1	37-4	104	2.49	181	.180	.284	0-0	—	0		16	3.0
2000	†Atl N	1	2	.333	59	0	0	24-3	53	42	25	5	2	48-4	77	2.89	159	.210	.368	0-0	—	0		7	0.9
2001	Atl N	2	2	.500	30	0	0	19-4	32	25	13	2	2	16-1	36	3.09	143	.216	.319	0-0	—	0		4	0.8
	†Cle A	3	7	.300	38	0	0	4-3	34.2	33	23	2	3	25-3	43	5.45	83	.250	.379	0-0	—	0		-3	-0.7
2002	Tex A	2	3	.400	30	0	0	1-3	24.1	29	19	5	0	13-1	30	6.66	71	.299	.372	0-0	—	0		-5	-0.9
2003	TB A	0	0	—	2	0	0	0-0	1	2	1	0	1	3-0	0	9.00	50	.500	.750	0-0	—	0		0	0.0
Total	6	13	22	.371	280	0	0	88-22	255.1	200	115	23	12	164-17	332	3.42	131	.213	.336	0-0	—	0		28	4.0
RODAS, RICH Richard Martin B 11.7.1959 Roseville, CA BL/TL 6-1/180# d9.6																									
1983	LA N	0	0	—	7	0	0	0-0	4.2	4	1	0	0	3-1	5	1.93	187	.222	.333	0-0	—	0		1	0.0
1984	LA N	0	0	—	3	0	0	0-0	5	5	3	2	0	1-0	1	5.40	65	.250	.286	1-0	.000	-0		-1	0.0
Total	2	0	0	—	10	0	0	0-0	9.2	9	4	2	0	4-1	6	3.72	96	.237	.310	1-0	.000	-0		0	0.0
RODNEY, FERNANDO Fernando B 3.17.1979 Samana, D.R. BR/TR 5-11/170# d5.4																									
2002	Det A	1	3	.250	20	0	0	0-4	18	25	15	2	0	10-2	10	6.00	72	.329	.402	0-0	—	0		-4	-0.8
2003	Det A	1	3	.250	27	0	0	3-3	29.2	35	20	2	1	17-1	33	6.07	71	.294	.379	0-0	—	0		-5	-0.7
Total	2	2	6	.250	47	0	0	3-7	47.2	60	35	4	1	27-3	43	6.04	71	.308	.388	0-0	—	0		-9	-1.5
RODRIGUEZ, EDUARDO Eduardo (Reyes) B 3.6.1952 Barceloneta, P.R. BR/TR 6/185# d6.20																									
1973	Mil A	9	7	.563	30	6	2	5-5	76.1	71	33	6	2	47-7	49	3.30	114	.247	.354	1-0	1.000	1	158	3	0.8
1974	Mil A	7	4	.636	43	6	0	4-4	111.2	97	49	7	5	51-5	58	3.63	100	.241	.330	0-0	—	0	73	0	0.0

Year	Tm Lg	W	L	Pct	G	GS	CG-Sho	SV-BS	IP	H	R	HR	HB	BB-IB	SO	ERA	AERA	OAV	OOB	AB-SH	AVG	PB	Sup	APR	PW
1975	Mil A	7	0	1.000	43	1	0	7-0	87.2	77	37	9	5	44-9	65	3.49	110	.235	.332	0-0	—	0	161	4	0.3
1976	Mil A	5	13	.278	45	12	3	8-3	136	124	68	10	3	65-6	77	3.64	96	.249	.334	0-0	—	0	67	-5	-0.7
1977	Mil A	5	6	.455	42	5	1-1	4-2	142.2	126	70	15	3	56-6	104	4.35	94	.236	.310	0-0	—	0	79	-1	-0.1
1978	Mil A	5	5	.500	32	8	0	2-2	105.1	107	49	9	2	26-3	51	3.93	96	.262	.306	0-0	—	0	122	-1	-0.1
1979	KC A	4	1	.800	29	1	1	2-0	74.1	79	42	9	3	34-4	26	4.84	88	.276	.355	0-0	—	0	297	-3	-0.3
Total	7	42	36	.538	264	39	7-1	32-16	734	681	348	65	23	323-40	430	3.89	98	.248	.329	1-0	1.000	1	102	-3	-0.1
RODRIGUEZ, FELIX Felix Antonio B 12.5.1972 Monte Cristi, D.R. BR/TR 6-1/170# d5.13																									
1995	LA N	1	1	.500	11	0	0	0-1	10.2	11	3	2	0	5-0	5	2.53	150	.275	.356	0-0	—	0		2	0.3
1997	Cin N	0	0	—	26	1	0	0-0	46	48	23	2	6	28-2	34	4.30	99	.271	.387	3-1	.000	-0	151	0	-0.1
1998	Ari N	0	2	.000	43	0	0	5-3	44	44	31	5	1	29-1	36	6.14	69	.259	.365	0-0	—	0		-9	-0.5
1999	SF N	2	3	.400	47	0	0	0-1	66.1	67	32	6	2	29-2	55	3.80	111	.262	.338	6-1	.333	2		3	0.4
2000	†SF N	4	2	.667	76	0	0	3-5	81.2	65	29	5	3	42-2	95	2.64	160	.220	.320	4-0	.000	-0		15	0.9
2001	SF N	9	1	.900	80	0	0	0-3	80.1	53	16	5	1	27-2	91	1.68	237	.188	.259	0-0	—	0		**23**	2.4
2002	†SF N	8	6	.571	71	0	0	0-6	69	53	33	5	4	29-1	58	4.17	93	.212	.301	1-0	1.000	1		-1	-0.3
2003	†SF N	8	2	.800	68	0	0	2-1	61	59	21	5	4	29-2	46	3.10	133	.259	.351	1-0	1.000	0		8	1.2
Total	8	32	17	.653	422	1	0	10-20	459	400	188	35	21	218-12	420	3.43	120	.235	.327	15-2	.267	2	151	41	4.3
RODRIGUEZ, FREDDY Fernando Pedro (Borrego) B 4.29.1924 Havana, Cuba BR/TR 6/180# d4.18																									
1958	Chi N	0	0	—	7	0	0	2	7.1	8	6	2	1	5-0	5	7.36	53	.267	.389	1-0	.000	-0		-2	-0.2
1959	Phi N	0	0	—	1	0	0	0	2	4	3	1	1	0-0	1	13.50	30	.400	.455	0-0	—	0		-2	-0.1
Total	2	0	0	—	8	0	0	2	9.1	12	9	3	2	5-0	6	8.68	46	.300	.404	1-0	.000	-0		-4	-0.3
RODRIGUEZ, FRANK Francisco B 12.11.1972 Brooklyn, NY BR/TR 6/190# d4.26																									
1995	Bos A	0	2	.000	9	2	0	0-0	15.1	21	19	3	0	10-1	14	10.57	46	.323	.413	0-0	—	0	201	-9	-0.9
	Min A	5	6	.455	16	16	0	0-0	90.1	93	64	8	5	47-0	45	5.38	89	.269	.361	0-0	—	0	99	-8	-0.7
	Year	5	8	.385	25	18	0	0-0	105.2	114	69	11	5	57-1	59	6.13	78	.277	.369	0-0	—	0	110	-19	-1.6
1996	Min A	13	14	.481	38	33	3	2-0	206.2	218	129	27	5	78-1	110	5.05	101	.272	.337	0-0	—	0	98	-1	-0.1
1997	Min A	3	6	.333	43	15	0	0-2	142.1	147	82	12	4	60-9	65	4.62	101	.271	.346	1-0	.000	-0	104	-1	0.0
1998	Min A	4	6	.400	20	11	0	0-0	70	88	58	6	3	30-0	62	6.56	73	.303	.369	0-0	—	0	94	-15	-1.7
1999	Sea A	2	4	.333	28	5	0	3-1	73.1	94	47	11	4	30-2	47	5.65	84	.314	.383	3-0	.333	0*	94	-6	-0.4
2000	Sea A	2	1	.667	23	0	0	0-0	47.1	60	33	8	0	22-2	19	6.27	75	.317	.383	1-0	.000	-0		-7	-0.4
2001	Cin N	0	0	—	7	0	0	0-0	8.2	16	12	1	0	5-2	9	11.42	40	.400	.457	1-0	.000	-0		-6	-0.3
Total	7	29	39	.426	184	82	3	5-3	654	737	444	76	21	282-17	371	5.53	88	.286	.358	6-0	.167	-0	102	-53	-4.5
RODRIGUEZ, FRANCISCO Francisco Jose B 1.7.1982 Caracas, Venezuela BR/TR 6/165# d9.18																									
2002	†Ana A	0	0	—	5	0	0	0-0	5.2	3	0	0	1	2-1	13	0.00	—	.167	.286	0-0	—	0		3	0.1
2003	Ana A	8	3	.727	59	0	0	2-4	86	50	30	12	2	35-5	95	3.03	142	.172	.262	0-0	—	0		14	1.6
Total	2	8	3	.727	64	0	0	2-4	91.2	53	30	12	3	37-6	108	2.85	152	.172	.263	0-0	—	0		17	1.7
RODRIGUEZ, JOSE Jose Illich (Jose) B 12.18.1974 Cayey, P.R. BL/TL 6-1/205# d5.18																									
2000	StL N	0	0	—	6	0	0	0-0	4	2	2	0	1	3-0	2	0.00	—	.143	.316	1-0	.000	-0		1	0.0
2002	StL N	0	0	—	2	0	0	0-0	0.1	4	2	0	0	2-0	0	54.00	7	.800	.857	0-0	—	0		-2	-0.1
	Min A	0	1	.000	4	0	0	0-0	3.2	8	6	0	0	4-1	1	14.73	31	.421	.522	0-0	—	0		-4	-0.7
Total	2	0	1	.000	12	0	0	0-0	8	14	10	0	1	9-1	3	9.00	50	.368	.490	1-0	.000	-0		-5	-0.8
RODRIGUEZ, NERIO Nerio B 3.4.1971 San Pedro De Macoris, D.R. BR/TR 6-1/195# d8.16																									
1996	Bal A	0	1	.000	8	1	0	0-0	16.2	18	11	2	1	7-0	12	4.32	114	.265	.338	0-0	—	0	19	0	0.0
1997	Bal A	2	1	.667	6	2	0	0-1	22	21	15	2	1	8-0	11	4.91	90	.250	.309	0-0	—	0	52	-2	-0.3
1998	Bal A	1	3	.250	6	4	0	0-0	19	25	17	0	0	9-0	8	8.05	57	.321	.382	0-0	—	0	87	-7	-1.2
	Tor A	1	0	1.000	7	0	0	0-0	8.1	10	9	1	1	8-0	3	9.72	48	.286	.432	0-0	—	0		-4	-0.4
	Year	2	3	.400	13	4	0	0-0	27.1	35	30	1	1	17-0	11	8.56	54	.310	.398	0-0	—	0	86	-11	-1.6
1999	Tor A	0	1	.000	2	0	0	0-0	2	2	3	2	0	2-0	2	13.50	37	.250	.400	0-0	—	0		-2	-0.3
2002	Cle A	0	0	—	1	0	0	0-0	0.1	0	0	0	0	0-0	0	0.00	—	.000	.000	0-0	—	0		0	0.0
	StL N	0	0	—	2	0	0	0-0	4.1	4	3	1	0	1-0	2	4.15	95	.222	.263	1-0	.000	-0		0	0.0
Total	5	4	6	.400	32	7	0	0-1	72.2	80	58	8	3	35-0	38	6.32	73	.274	.350	1-0	.000	-0	66	-15	-2.2
RODRIGUEZ, RICK Ricardo B 9.21.1960 Oakland, CA BR/TR 6-3/190# d9.17																									
1986	Oak A	1	2	.333	3	3	0	0-0	16.1	17	12	4	0	7-0	2	6.61	59	.262	.333	0-0	—	0	70	-5	-0.7
1987	Oak A	1	0	1.000	15	0	0	0-0	24.1	32	8	1	1	15-1	9	2.96	140	.337	.432	0-0	—	0		4	0.2
1988	Cle A	1	2	.333	10	5	0	0-0	33	43	28	4	1	17-1	9	7.09	58	.323	.401	0-0	—	0	97	-10	-0.8
1990	SF N	0	0	—	3	0	0	0-0	3.1	5	3	0	0	2-0	2	8.10	45	.357	.438	0-0	—	0		-2	-0.1
Total	4	3	4	.429	31	8	0	0-0	77	97	51	9	2	41-2	22	5.73	71	.316	.399	0-0	—	0	87	-13	-1.4
RODRIGUEZ, RICARDO Ricardo Antonio B 3.21.1979 Guayubin, D.R. BR/TR 6-3/195# d8.21																									
2002	Cle A	2	2	.500	7	7	0	0-0	41.1	40	27	5	8	18-3	24	5.66	78	.255	.361	0-0	—	0	106	-5	-0.5
2003	Cle A	3	9	.250	15	15	0	0-0	81.2	89	57	16	3	28-1	41	5.73	77	.275	.336	3-0	.000	-0	72	-11	-1.3
Total	2	5	11	.313	22	22	0	0-0	123	129	84	21	11	46-4	65	5.71	77	.268	.344	3-0	.000	-0	83	-16	-1.8
RODRIGUEZ, RICH Richard Anthony B 3.1.1963 Downey, CA BL/TL 6/200# d6.30																									
1990	SD N	1	1	.500	32	0	0	1-0	47.2	52	17	2	1	16-4	22	2.83	135	.287	.347	3-0	.000	-0		5	0.3
1991	SD N	3	1	.750	64	1	0	0-2	80	66	31	8	0	44-8	40	3.26	117	.234	.335	5-0	.000	-1*	24	5	0.2
1992	SD N	6	3	.667	61	1	0	0-1	91	77	28	4	0	29-4	64	2.37	151	.229	.289	6-2	.000	-0	0	11	1.1
1993	SD N	2	3	.400	34	0	0	2-3	30	34	15	2	1	9-3	22	3.30	125	.281	.336	0-0	—	0		2	0.3
	Fla N	0	1	.000	36	0	0	1-1	46	39	23	8	1	24-5	21	4.11	105	.229	.328	2-0	.000	-0		1	0.1
	Year	2	4	.333	70	0	0	3-4	76	73	38	10	2	33-8	43	3.79	112	.251	.331	2-0	.000	-0		3	0.4
1994	StL N	3	5	.375	56	0	0	0-3	60.1	62	30	6	1	26-4	43	4.03	103	.270	.345	1-0	.000	-0		0	0.0
1995	StL N	0	0	—	1	0	0	0-0	1.2	0	0	0	0	0-0	0	0.00	—	.000	.000	0-0	—	0		1	0.0
1997	†SF N	4	3	.571	71	0	0	1-4	65.1	65	24	7	1	21-4	32	3.17	129	.264	.325	3-0	.333	1		8	0.9
1998	SF N	4	0	1.000	68	0	0	2-4	65.2	69	28	7	0	20-5	44	3.70	107	.272	.322	6-1	.167	-0		3	0.2
1999	SF N	3	0	1.000	62	0	0	0-2	56.2	60	33	8	1	28-5	44	5.24	80	.274	.356	1-1	1.000	1		-6	-0.2
2000	NY N	0	1	.000	32	0	0	0-0	37	59	40	7	3	15-0	18	7.78	57	.364	.416	1-0	.000	-0		-17	-0.8
2001	Cle A	2	2	.500	53	0	0	0-2	39	41	24	2	2	17-3	31	4.15	109	.270	.349	0-0	—	0		0	0.0
2002	Tex A	3	2	.600	36	0	0	1-2	16.2	14	10	1	1	11-1	12	5.40	88	.237	.366	0-0	—	0		-1	-0.2
2003	Ana A	0	0	—	3	0	0	0-0	3.2	4	1	0	0	1-0	3	2.45	176	.308	.333	0-0	—	0		1	0.0
Total	13	31	22	.585	609	2	0	8-24	640.2	642	304	62	12	261-46	396	3.81	107	.264	.337	28-4	.107	-0	11	13	1.9
RODRIGUEZ, ROSARIO Rosario Isabel (Echavarria) B 7.8.1969 Los Mochis, Mexico BR/TL 6/185# d9.1																									
1989	Cin N	1	1	.500	7	0	0	0-1	4.1	3	2	0	0	3-1	0	4.15	87	.188	.316	0-0	—	0		0	0.0
1990	Cin N	0	0	—	9	0	0	0-0	10.1	15	7	3	1	2-0	8	6.10	65	.357	.391	0-0	—	0		-2	-0.1
1991	†Pit N	1	1	.500	18	0	0	6-0	15.1	14	7	1	1	8-0	10	4.11	87	.246	.348	1-0	.000	-0		-1	-0.1
Total	3	2	2	.500	34	0	0	6-1	30	32	16	4	2	13-1	18	4.80	77	.278	.359	1-0	.000	-0		-3	-0.2
RODRIGUEZ, WILFREDO Wilfredo Jose B 3.20.1979 Ciudad Bolivar, Venezuela BL/TL 6-3/180# d9.21																									
2001	Hou N	0	0	—	2	0	0	0-0	3	6	5	2	0	1-0	3	15.00	31	.429	.438	0-0	—	0		-3	-0.2
RODRIQUEZ, ROBERTO Roberto (Munoz) B 11.29.1941 Caracas, Venezuela BR/TR 6-3/185# d5.13																									
1967	KC A	1	1	.500	15	5	0	2	40.1	42	17	4	1	14-1	29	3.57	89	.268	.331	9-0	.000	-1	93	-1	-0.2
1970	Oak A	0	0	—	6	0	0	0-0	12.1	10	5	2	0	3-0	8	2.92	121	.227	.271	1-0	.000	-0		1	0.0
	SD N	0	0	—	10	0	0	3-1	16.1	26	16	1	0	5-0	8	6.61	60	.366	.408	3-0	.000	-0		-6	-0.3
	Chi N	3	2	.600	26	0	0	2-1	43.1	50	33	6	0	15-2	46	5.82	78	.289	.340	8-0	.125	1		-6	-0.6
	Year	3	2	.600	36	0	0	5-2	59.2	76	52	7	0	20-2	54	6.03	72	.311	.360	11-0	.091	0		-12	-0.9
Total	2	4	3	.571	57	5	0	7-2	112.1	128	71	13	1	37-3	91	4.81	80	.288	.341	21-0	.048	-1	93	-12	-1.1
ROE, PREACHER Elwin Charles B 2.26.1915 Ash Flat, AR BR/TL 6-2/170# d8.22																									
1938	StL N	0	0	—	1	0	0	0	2.2	6	4	0	0	2	1	13.50	29	.429	.500	1-0	.000	-0		-2	-0.1

Year	Tm Lg	W	L	Pct	G	GS	CG-Sho	SV-BS	IP	H	R	HR	HB	BB-IB	SO	ERA	AERA	OAV	OOB	AB-SH	AVG	PB	Sup	APR	PW
1944	Pit N	13	11	.542	39	25	7-1	1	185.1	182	82	7	2	59	88	3.11	120	.253	.311	53-6	.132	-2	92	11	1.0
1945	Pit N❖	14	13	.519	33	31	15-3	1	235	228	77	11	1	46	**148**	2.87	137	.259	.296	75-8	.107	-3	87	32	3.2
1946	Pit N	3	8	.273	21	10	1	2	70	83	50	5	2	25	28	5.14	69	.294	.356	15-0	.067	-1	83	-13	-2.0
1947	Pit N	4	15	.211	38	22	4-1	2	144	156	93	19	0	63	59	5.25	80	.276	.348	40-4	.125	-2	66	-15	-1.9
1948	Bro N	12	8	.600	34	22	8-2	2	177.2	156	60	14	2	33	86	2.63	152	.233	.271	51-9	.098	-2	104	27	2.6
1949	†Bro N★	15	6	**.714**	30	27	13-3	1	212.2	201	69	25	2	44	109	2.79	147	.252	.293	70-7	.114	-2	105	32	2.6
1950	Bro N☆	19	11	.633	36	32	16-2	1	250.2	245	96	34	4	66	125	3.30	124	.257	.308	91-8	.154	-3	102	25	2.3
1951	Bro N☆	22	3	**.880**	34	33	19-2	0	257.2	247	91	30	0	64	113	3.04	129	.258	.304	89-9	.112	-5	112	28	1.9
1952	†Bro N❖	11	2	.846	27	25	8-2	0	158.2	163	59	16	3	39	83	3.12	117	.270	.317	57-5	.070	-3	131	10	0.4
1953	†Bro N	11	3	.786	25	24	9-1	0	157	171	78	27	1	40	85	4.36	98	.278	.323	57-5	.053	-4	134	1	-0.3
1954	Bro N	3	4	.429	15	10	1	0	63	69	40	11	0	23	31	5.00	82	.279	.339	21-2	.143	-0	103	-7	-0.7
Total	12	127	84	.602	333	261	101-17	10	1914.1	1907	799	199	17	504	956	3.43	116	.261	.310	620-63	.110	-27	103	129	9.0
ROE, CLAY James Clay "Shad" B 1.7.1904 Greenbriar, TN D 4.4.1956 Cleveland, MS BL/TL 6-1/180# d10.3																									
1923	Was A	0	1	.000	1	1	0	0	1.2	0	4	0	0	6	2	0.00	—	.000	.500	0-0	—	0	176	-1	-0.2
ROEBUCK, ED Edward Jack B 7.3.1931 East Millsboro, PA BR/TR 6-2/185# d4.18																									
1955	†Bro N	5	6	.455	47	0	0	12	84	96	51	14	3	24-5	33	4.71	86	.288	.341	18-0	.111	-1		-6	-1.0
1956	†Bro N	5	4	.556	43	0	0	1	89.1	83	49	15	2	29-2	60	3.93	101	.251	.314	18-1	.333	2		-2	0.0
1957	Bro N	8	2	.800	44	1	0	8	96.1	70	37	9	2	46-6	73	2.71	154	.205	.303	21-0	.238	2	0	**13**	1.9
1958	LA N	0	1	.000	32	0	0	5	44	45	22	9	2	15-3	26	3.48	118	.271	.335	4-0	.500	1		2	0.2
1960	LA N	8	3	.727	58	0	0	8	116.2	109	42	13	0	38-11	77	2.78	143	.256	.315	24-4	.167	-0		14	1.6
1961	LA N	2	0	1.000	5	0	0	0	9	12	5	1	0	2-0	9	5.00	87	.324	.359	2-0	.000	-0		0	-0.1
1962	LA N	10	2	.833	64	0	0	9	119.1	102	60	11	6	54-6	72	3.09	117	.232	.321	28-0	.214	1		2	0.3
1963	LA N	2	4	.333	29	0	0	0	40.1	54	25	4	2	21-5	26	4.24	71	.321	.399	4-0	.250	0		-7	-1.0
	Was A	2	1	.667	26	0	0	4	57.1	63	27	5	2	29-2	25	3.30	113	.284	.369	11-1	.182	0		1	0.1
1964	Was A	0	0	—	2	0	0	0	1	0	1	0	0	2-0	0	9.00	41	.000	.333	0-0	—	0		-1	0.0
	Phi N	5	3	.625	60	0	0	12	77.1	55	21	7	4	25-6	42	2.21	157	.196	.270	6-1	.000	-1		11	1.5
1965	Phi N	5	3	.625	44	0	0	3	50.1	55	27	2	5	15-5	29	3.40	102	.288	.349	1-1	.000	-0		-2	-0.4
1966	Phi N	0	2	.000	6	0	0	0	6	9	7	0	0	2-0	5	6.00	60	.333	.367	0-0	—	0		-3	-0.6
Total	11	52	31	.627	460	1	0	62	791	753	374	90	28	302-51	477	3.35	114	.254	.326	137-8	.204	3	0	22	2.5
ROESLER, MIKE Michael Joseph B 9.12.1963 Fort Wayne, IN BR/TR 6-5/195# d8.9																									
1989	Cin N	0	1	.000	17	0	0	0-0	25	22	11	4	0	9-1	14	3.96	91	.239	.307	0-0	—	0		0	-0.1
1990	Pit N	1	0	1.000	5	0	0	0-0	6	5	2	1	0	2-0	4	3.00	121	.217	.280	1-0	.000	-0		1	0.1
Total	2	1	1	.500	22	0	0	0-0	31	27	13	5	0	11-1	18	3.77	96	.235	.302	1-0	.000	-0		1	0.0
ROETTGER, OSCAR Oscar Frederick Louis "Okkie" B 2.19.1900 St.Louis, MO D 7.4.1986 St.Louis, MO BR/TR 6/170# d7.7 b-Wally ▲																									
1923	NY A	0	0	—	5	0	0	1	11.2	16	15	3	1	12	7	8.49	46	.340	.483	2-0	.000	-0		-7	-0.4
1924	NY A	0	0	—	1	0	0	0	0	1	0	0	0	2	0		—	1.000	1.000	0-0	—	0		0	0.0
Total	2	0	0	—	6	0	0	1	11.2	17	15	3	1	14	7	8.49	46	.354	.508	2-0	.000	-0		-7	-0.4
ROGALSKI, JOE Joseph Anthony B 7.16.1915 Ashland, WI D 11.20.1951 Ashland, WI BR/TR 6-2/187# d9.14																									
1938	Det A	0	0	—	2	0	0	0	7	12	4	0	0	0	2	2.57	194	.400	.400	2-0	.000	-0		1	0.0
ROGERS, KEVIN Charles Kevin B 8.20.1968 Cleveland, MS BB/TL 6-2/190# d9.4																									
1992	SF N	0	2	.000	6	6	0	0-0	34	37	17	4	1	13-1	26	4.24	78	.280	.349	9-3	.222	0	87	-3	-0.2
1993	SF N	2	2	.500	64	0	0	0-2	80.2	71	28	3	4	28-5	62	2.68	146	.236	.308	3-0	.000	-0		10	0.4
1994	SF N	0	0	—	9	0	0	0-1	10.1	10	4	1	0	6-0	7	3.48	115	.250	.348	0-0	—	0		1	0.0
Total	3	2	4	.333	79	6	0	0-3	125	118	49	8	5	47-6	95	3.17	119	.249	.323	12-3	.167	-0	87	8	0.2
ROGERS, JIMMY James Randall B 1.3.1967 Tulsa, OK BR/TR 6-2/190# d7.30																									
1995	Tor A	2	4	.333	19	0	0	0-0	23.2	21	15	4	0	18-4	13	5.70	83	.239	.364	0-0	—	0		-2	-0.4
ROGERS, KENNY Kenneth Scott B 11.10.1964 Savannah, GA BL/TL 6-1/205# d4.6																									
1989	Tex A	3	4	.429	73	0	0	2-3	73.2	60	28	2	4	42-9	63	2.93	135	.232	.344	0-0	—	0		8	0.9
1990	Tex A	10	6	.625	69	3	0	15-8	97.2	93	40	6	1	42-5	74	3.13	125	.249	.323	0-0	—	0	62	8	1.5
1991	Tex A	10	10	.500	63	9	0	5-1	109.2	121	80	14	6	61-7	73	5.42	75	.281	.375	0-0	—	0	121	-20	-3.4
1992	Tex A	3	6	.333	**81**	0	0	6-4	78.2	80	32	7	0	26-8	70	3.09	123	.261	.318	0-0	—	0		6	0.8
1993	Tex A	16	10	.615	35	33	5	0-0	208.1	210	108	18	4	71-2	140	4.10	101	.263	.325	0-0	—	0	125	0	0.2
1994	Tex A	11	8	.579	24	24	6-2	0-0	167.1	169	93	24	3	52-1	120	4.46	108	.260	.315	0-0	—	0	107	7	0.8
1995	Tex A★	17	7	.708	31	31	3-1	0-0	208	192	87	26	2	76-1	140	3.38	143	.243	.309	0-0	—	0	99	32	3.3
1996	†NY A	12	8	.600	30	30	2-1	0-0	179	179	97	16	8	83-2	92	4.68	106	.261	.346	0-0	—	0	106	6	0.7
1997	NY A	6	7	.462	31	22	1	0-0	145	161	100	18	7	62-1	78	5.65	79	.280	.354	3-0	.000	-0	130	-20	-1.3
1998	Oak A	16	8	.667	34	34	7-1	0-0	238.2	215	96	19	7	67-0	138	3.17	144	.242	.299	4-0	.000	-0	99	37	3.7
1999	Oak A	5	3	.625	19	19	3	0-0	119.1	135	66	8	9	41-0	68	4.30	108	.288	.353	3-0	.000	-0	114	4	0.4
	†NY N	5	1	.833	12	12	2-1	0-0	76	71	35	8	4	28-1	58	4.03	109	.253	.328	25-3	.120	-0	128	3	0.3
2000	Tex A	13	13	.500	34	34	2	0-0	227.1	257	126	20	11	78-2	127	4.55	110	.285	.348	4-1	.500	1	91	12	1.5
2001	Tex A	5	7	.417	20	20	0	0-0	120.2	150	88	18	8	49-2	74	6.19	75	.307	.376	2-0	.000	-0	108	-20	-1.5
2002	Tex A	13	8	.619	33	33	2-1	0-0	210.2	212	101	21	6	70-1	107	3.84	123	.261	.324	3-0	.667	1*	88	17	1.9
2003	†Min A	13	8	.619	33	31	0	0-0	195	227	108	22	11	50-5	116	4.57	100	.292	.342	4-0	.000	-0	106	-2	0.0
Total	15	158	114	.581	622	335	33-7	28-16	2455	2532	1285	247	91	898-47	1538	4.23	108	.267	.334	48-4	.146	0	108	78	9.8
ROGERS, LEE Lee Otis "Buck" B 10.8.1913 Tuscaloosa, AL D 11.23.1995 Little Rock, AR BR/TL 5-11/170# d4.27																									
1938	Bos A	1	1	.500	14	2	0	0	27.2	32	24	4	0	18	7	6.51	76	.302	.403	6-0	.000	-0	80	-5	-0.3
	Bro N	0	2	.000	12	2	0	0	23.2	23	16	0	1	10	11	5.70	68	.256	.337	1-0	.000	0*	54	-4	-0.2
Total	1	1	3	.250	26	4	0	0	51.1	55	40	4	1	28	18	6.14	73	.281	.373	7-0	.000	0	68	-9	-0.5
ROGERS, BUCK Orlin Woodrow "Lefty" B 11.5.1912 Spring Garden, VA D 2.20.1999 Winston-Salem, NC BR/TL 5-8.5/164# d9.15																									
1935	Was A	0	1	.000	2	1	0	0	10	16	15	0	0	6	7	7.20	60	.340	.415	3-0	.000	-1	80	-6	-0.5
ROGERS, STEVE Stephen Douglas B 10.26.1949 Jefferson City, MO BR/TR 6-1/182# d7.18																									
1973	Mon N	10	5	.667	17	17	7-3	0-0	134	93	28	5	1	49-3	64	1.54	247	.199	.274	41-5	.098	-1	68	32	3.8
1974	Mon N☆	15	22	.405	38	38	11-1	0-0	253.2	255	139	19	5	80-7	154	4.47	86	.265	.322	79-7	.139	-1	75	-14	-1.9
1975	Mon N	11	12	.478	35	35	12-3	0-0	251.2	248	104	13	4	88-8	137	3.29	117	.260	.324	77-6	.169	1	88	14	1.4
1976	Mon N	7	17	.292	33	32	8-4	1-0	230	212	93	10	4	69-7	150	3.21	116	.250	.307	74-6	.149	-2*	68	13	1.4
1977	Mon N	17	16	.515	40	40	17-4	0-0	301.2	272	122	16	5	81-3	206	3.10	123	.242	.294	96-12	.104	-5	91	22	1.9
1978	Mon N★	13	10	.565	30	29	11-1	1-0	219	186	64	12	2	64-2	126	2.47	143	.235	.293	71-8	.113	-2	78	27	2.7
1979	Mon N★	13	12	.520	37	37	13-**5**	0-0	248.2	232	97	14	4	78-9	143	3.00	122	.251	.311	77-2	.156	1*	100	18	1.9
1980	Mon N	16	11	.593	37	37	**14**-4	0-0	281	247	101	16	3	85-7	147	2.98	120	.238	.296	81-15	.160	1*	107	20	2.0
1981	†Mon N	12	8	.600	22	22	7-3	0-0	160.2	149	64	7	2	41-4	87	3.42	102	.248	.296	55-4	.145	-1*	102	3	0.2
1982	Mon N★	19	8	.704	35	35	14-4	0-0	277	245	84	12	6	65-7	179	**2.40**	**152**	.237	.285	85-12	.129	0	103	**38**	3.7
1983	Mon N☆	17	12	.586	36	36	13-**5**	0-0	273	258	108	14	5	78-12	146	3.23	111	.252	.306	82-20	.146	-1	96	11	0.9
1984	Mon N	6	15	.286	31	28	1	0-0	169.1	171	93	12	2	78-5	64	4.31	80	.267	.346	49-4	.143	1	81	-19	-2.0
1985	Mon N	2	4	.333	8	7	1	0-0	38	51	25	1	0	20-1	18	5.68	60	.329	.401	14-0	.143	0	89	-9	-1.2
Total	13	158	152	.510	399	393	129-37	2-0	2837.2	2619	1122	151	43	876-75	1621	3.17	116	.248	.306	881-101	.138	-8	89	156	14.8
ROGERS, TOM Thomas Andrew "Shotgun" B 2.12.1892 Sparta, TN D 3.7.1936 Nashville, TN BR/TR 6-0.5/180# d4.14																									
1917	StL A	3	6	.333	24	8	3	0	108.2	112	58	2	3	44	27	3.89	67	.277	.352	29-2	.172	-1	76	-13	-1.2
1918	StL A	8	10	.444	29	16	11	2	154	148	66	3	3	49	29	3.27	84	.267	.330	53-3	.245	2	95	-6	-0.5
1919	StL A	0	1	.000	2	0	0	0	1	7	6	0	0	0	1	27.00	12	.700	.700	0-0	—	0		-3	-0.6
	Phi A	4	12	.250	23	18	7-1	0	140	152	82	9	3	60	37	4.31	80	.292	.369	49-1	.224	-0	83	-12	-1.0
	Year	4	13	.235	25	18	7-1	0	141	159	86	9	3	60	38	4.47	77	.300	.374	49-1	.224	-0	83	-15	-1.6
1921	†NY A	0	1	.000	5	0	0	1	11	12	9	1	1	9	0	7.36	58	.300	.440	3-0	.333	0*		-3	-0.2

Year	Tm Lg	W	L	Pct	G	GS	CG-Sho	SV-BS	IP	H	R	HR	HB	BB-IB	SO	ERA	AERA	OAV	OOB	AB-SH	AVG	PB	Sup	APR	PW
Total	4	15	30	.333	83	42	21-1	3	414.2	431	221	15	10	162	94	3.95	75	.282	.354	134-6	.224	1	86	-37	-3.5
ROGGE, CLINT Francis Clinton B 7.19.1889 Memphis, MI D 1.6.1969 Mt.Clemens, MI BL/TR 5-10/185# d4.11																									
1915	Pit F	17	11	.607	37	31	17-5	0	254.1	240	96	6	9	93	93	2.55	106	.257	.330	81-8	.173	-1	94	1	0.1
1921	Cin N	1	2	.333	6	2	0	0	35.1	43	19	2	0	9	12	4.08	88	.307	.349	10-0	.100	0	103	-2	-0.1
Total	2	18	13	.581	43	33	17-5	0	289.2	283	115	8	9	102	105	2.73	103	.264	.332	91-8	.165	-1	94	-1	0.0
ROGGENBURK, GARRY Garry Earl B 4.16.1940 Cleveland, OH BR/TL 6-6/195# d4.20																									
1963	Min A	2	4	.333	36	2	0	4	50	47	26	3	5	22-3	24	2.16	169	.253	.344	7-0	.143	0	98	3	0.4
1965	Min A	1	0	1.000	12	0	0	2	21	21	10	1	0	12-2	6	3.43	104	.266	.359	3-2	.000	-0		0	0.0
1966	Min A	1	2	.333	12	0	0	1	12.1	14	8	4	0	10-0	3	5.84	62	.292	.414	0-0	—	0		-2	-0.5
	Bos A	0	0	—	1	0	0	0	0.1	1	0	0	0	1-0	0	0.00	—	.500	.667	0-0	—	0		0	0.0
	Year	1	2	.333	13	0	0	1	12.2	15	12	4	0	11-0	3	5.68	63	.300	.426	0-0	—	0		-2	-0.5
1968	Bos A	0	0	—	4	0	0	0	8.1	9	2	0	0	3-0	4	2.16	146	.257	.316	0-0	—	0		1	0.0
1969	Bos A	0	1	.000	7	0	0	0-0	9.2	13	9	1	1	5-0	8	8.38	45	.342	.432	2-0	.000	-0		-4	-0.4
	Sea A	2	2	.500	7	4	1	0-1	24.1	27	12	6	1	11-0	11	4.44	82	.276	.351	8-1	.125	-0	85	-1	-0.3
	Year	2	3	.400	14	4	1	0-1	34	40	16	7	2	16-0	19	5.56	66	.294	.374	10-1	.100	-1	84	-6	-0.7
Total	5	6	9	.400	79	6	1	7-1	126	132	67	15	7	64-5	56	3.64	99	.272	.362	20-3	.100	-1	90	-3	-0.8
ROGOVIN, SAUL Saul Walter B 10.10.1923 Brooklyn, NY D 1.23.1995 New York, NY BR/TR 6-2/205# d4.28																									
1949	Det A	0	1	.000	5	0	0	0	5.2	13	9	1	0	7	2	14.29	29	.464	.571	0-0	—	0		-6	-0.8
1950	Det A	2	1	.667	11	5	1	0	40	39	21	5	2	26	11	4.50	104	.258	.374	16-0	.188	0	119	1	0.1
1951	Det A	1	1	.500	5	4	0	0	24	23	15	4	0	7	5	5.25	80	.247	.300	7-0	.286	1	144	-3	-0.1
	Chi A	11	7	.611	22	22	17-3	0	192.2	166	64	11	1	67	77	2.48	163	.234	.301	74-0	.203	-0*	90	33	2.9
	Year	12	8	.600	27	26	17-3	0	216.2	189	68	15	1	74	82	**2.78**	**146**	.235	.301	81-0	.210	1	99	**30**	2.8
1952	Chi A	14	9	.609	33	30	12-3	1	231.2	224	104	14	3	79	121	3.85	95	.255	.318	84-4	.202	3	106	-2	0.0
1953	Chi A	7	12	.368	22	19	4-1	1	131	151	82	17	2	48	62	5.22	77	.289	.351	37-2	.135	-0	94	-16	-2.1
1955	Bal A	1	8	.111	14	12	1	0	71	79	42	5	2	27-1	35	4.56	84	.288	.355	22-0	.091	-1*	52	-6	-0.9
	Phi N	5	3	.625	12	11	5-2	0	73	60	25	3	0	17-2	27	3.08	129	.230	.274	24-2	.250	2*	94	9	1.1
1956	Phi N	7	6	.538	22	18	3	0	106.2	122	65	22	0	27-3	48	4.98	75	.282	.324	36-3	.111	-2	128	-14	-1.8
1957	Phi N	0	0	—	4	0	0	0	8	11	8	1	0	3-1	0	9.00	42	.333	.378	0-0	—	0		-4	-0.2
Total	8	48	48	.500	150	121	43-9	2	883.2	888	435	83	10	308-7	388	4.06	96	.262	.325	300-11	.180	2	100	-8	-1.8
ROHR, LES Leslie Norvin B 3.5.1946 Lowestoft, England BL/TL 6-5/205# d9.19																									
1967	NY N	2	1	.667	3	3	0	0	17	13	7	1	0	9-0	15	2.12	160	.224	.319	6-0	.000	-1	112	1	0.1
1968	NY N	0	2	.000	2	1	0	0	6	9	4	0	0	7-3	5	4.50	67	.333	.471	0-0	—	0	57	-1	-0.2
1969	NY N	0	0	—	1	0	0	0-0	1.1	5	4	0	0	1-0	0	20.25	18	.625	.667	0-0	—	0		-3	-0.1
Total	3	2	3	.400	6	4	0	0-0	24.1	27	15	1	0	17-3	20	3.70	90	.290	.393	6-0	.000	-0	99	-3	-0.2
ROHR, BILLY William Joseph B 7.1.1945 San Diego, CA BL/TL 6-3/170# d4.14																									
1967	Bos A	2	3	.400	10	8	2-1	0	42.1	43	27	4	2	22-2	16	5.10	68	.256	.349	10-3	.000	-1	103	-7	-0.9
1968	Cle A	1	0	1.000	17	0	0	1	18.1	18	16	5	0	10-2	5	6.87	43	.265	.354	1-0	.000	-0		-8	-0.6
Total	2	3	3	.500	27	8	2-1	1	60.2	61	43	9	2	32-4	21	5.64	59	.258	.351	11-3	.000	-1	103	-15	-1.5
ROJAS, MEL Melquiades (Medrano) B 12.10.1966 Haina, D.R. BR/TR 5-11/185# d8.1																									
1990	Mon N	3	1	.750	23	0	0	1-1	40	34	17	5	2	24-4	26	3.60	101	.234	.351	3-3	.000	-0		0	0.0
1991	Mon N	3	3	.500	37	0	0	6-3	48	42	21	4	1	13-1	37	3.75	97	.228	.280	4-1	.000	-0		0	-0.1
1992	Mon N	7	1	.875	68	0	0	10-1	100.2	71	17	2	2	34-8	70	1.43	243	.199	.271	15-0	.067	-1		**23**	2.2
1993	Mon N	5	8	.385	66	0	0	10-9	88.1	80	39	6	4	30-3	48	2.95	141	.242	.308	12-0	.083	-1		10	1.4
1994	Mon N	3	2	.600	58	0	0	16-2	84	71	35	11	4	21-0	84	3.32	127	.227	.283	10-0	.200	0		8	0.7
1995	Mon N	1	4	.200	59	0	0	30-9	67.2	69	32	2	7	29-4	61	4.12	104	.262	.350	6-2	.000	-1		2	0.2
1996	Mon N	7	4	.636	74	0	0	36-4	81	56	30	5	2	28-3	92	3.22	134	.193	.265	8-0	.375	1		11	2.2
1997	Chi N	0	4	.000	54	0	0	13-6	59	54	30	11	5	30-1	61	4.42	97	.244	.346	1-0	.000	-0		0	-0.1
	NY N	0	2	.000	23	0	0	2-1	26.1	24	17	4	2	6-1	32	5.13	79	.235	.288	0-0	—	0		-4	-0.3
	Year	0	6	.000	77	0	0	15-7	85.1	78	51	15	7	36-2	93	4.64	91	.241	.329	1-0	.000	-0		-3	-0.4
1998	NY N	5	2	.714	50	0	0	2-4	58	68	39	9	3	30-5	41	6.05	68	.305	.391	0-0	—	0		-12	-1.3
1999	LA N	0	0	—	5	0	0	0-0	5	5	7	3	0	3-1	3	12.60	34	.250	.348	0-0	—	0		-5	-0.2
	Det A	0	0	—	5	0	0	0-0	6.1	12	16	3	3	4-0	6	22.74	22	.387	.487	0-0	—	0		-12	-0.5
	Mon N	0	0	—	3	0	0	0-0	2.2	5	5	0	2	2-0	1	16.88	27	.417	.529	0-0	—	0		-3	-0.2
Total	10	34	31	.523	525	0	0	126-40	667	591	305	65	37	254-31	562	3.82	106	.237	.315	59-6	.119	-2		18	4.0
ROJAS, MINNIE Minervino Alejandro (Landin) B 11.26.1933 Remidios, Cuba D 3.24.2002 Los Angeles, CA BR/TR 6-1/170# d5.30																									
1966	Cal A	7	4	.636	47	2	0	10	84.1	83	28	9	1	15-2	37	2.88	117	.262	.296	14-1	.071	-0	92	6	0.8
1967	Cal A	12	9	.571	72	0	0	**27**	121.2	106	45	7	3	38-17	83	2.52	125	.232	.292	17-3	.059	-1		6	1.2
1968	Cal A	4	3	.571	38	0	0	6	55	55	29	11	0	15-4	33	4.25	68	.252	.299	10-0	.100	-0		-8	-1.4
Total	3	23	16	.590	157	2	0	43	261	244	102	27	4	68-23	153	3.00	105	.246	.295	41-4	.073	-2	92	4	0.6
ROLAND, JIM James Ivan B 12.14.1942 Franklin, NC BR/TL 6-3/190# d9.20																									
1962	Min A	0	0	—	1	0	0	0	2	1	0	0	0	0-0	1	0.00	—	.143	.143	0-0	—	0		1	0.0
1963	Min A	4	1	.800	10	7	2-1	0	49	32	17	4	0	27-1	34	2.57	142	.185	.292	15-3	.000	-2	129	5	0.4
1964	Min A	2	6	.250	30	13	1	3	94.1	76	48	12	4	55-2	63	4.10	87	.218	.329	27-0	.148	-1	88	-5	-0.6
1966	Min A	0	0	—	1	0	0	0	2	0	0	0	0	0-0	1	0.00	—	.000	.000	0-0	—	0		1	0.0
1967	Min A	0	1	.000	25	0	0	2	35.2	33	12	3	0	17-5	16	3.03	114	.244	.325	3-0	.000	-0		2	0.1
1968	Min A	4	1	.800	28	4	1	0	61.2	55	33	3	2	24-2	36	3.50	88	.238	.314	8-2	.000	-1*	113	-5	-0.4
1969	Oak A	5	1	.833	39	3	2	1-0	86.1	59	24	2	6	46-6	48	2.19	157	.197	.314	21-0	.095	-1	154	12	0.8
1970	Oak A	3	3	.500	28	2	0	2-0	43.1	28	14	2	0	23-1	26	2.70	131	.181	.285	6-0	.000	-0	113	5	0.6
1971	Oak A	1	3	.250	31	0	0	1-0	45.1	34	18	4	5	19-3	30	3.18	105	.214	.310	3-1	.000	-0		1	0.0
1972	Oak A	0	0	—	2	0	0	0-0	2.1	5	2	0	0	0-0	0	3.86	74	.455	.455	0-0	—	0		-1	0.0
	NY A	0	1	.000	16	0	0	0-0	25	27	14	3	1	16-1	13	5.04	59	.287	.396	1-0	.000	-0		-5	-0.3
	Tex A	0	0	—	5	0	0	0-0	3.1	7	3	1	1	2-1	4	8.10	37	.412	.500	0-0	—	0		-2	-0.1
	Year	0	1	.000	23	0	0	0-0	30.2	39	24	4	2	18-2	17	5.28	56	.320	.415	1-0	.000	-0		-8	-0.4
Total	10	19	17	.528	216	29	6-1	9-0	450.1	357	185	34	19	229-22	272	3.22	106	.218	.319	84-6	.071	-5	112	9	0.5
ROMAN, JOSE Jose Rafael (Sarita) B 5.21.1963 Santo Domingo, D.R. BR/TR 6/175# d9.5																									
1984	Cle A	0	2	.000	3	2	0	0-0	6	9	12	1	0	11-0	3	18.00	23	.391	.541	0-0	—	0	77	-9	-1.3
1985	Cle A	0	4	.000	5	3	0	0-0	16.1	13	17	3	0	14-0	12	6.61	63	.200	.342	0-0	—	0	29	-6	-1.1
1986	Cle A	1	2	.333	6	5	0	0-0	22	23	20	3	1	17-0	9	6.55	63	.280	.394	0-0	—	0	92	-7	-0.8
Total	3	1	8	.111	14	10	0	0-0	44.1	45	49	7	1	42-0	24	8.12	51	.265	.400	0-0	—	0	70	-22	-3.2
ROMANICK, RON Ronald James B 11.6.1960 Burley, ID BR/TR 6-4/195# d4.5																									
1984	Cal A	12	12	.500	33	33	8-2	0-0	229.2	240	107	23	4	61-3	87	3.76	106	.270	.316	0-0	—	0	91	4	0.3
1985	Cal A	14	9	.609	31	31	6-1	0-0	195	210	101	29	4	62-1	64	4.11	100	.280	.334	0-0	—	0	106	-1	-0.2
1986	Cal A	5	8	.385	18	18	1-1	0-0	106.1	124	68	13	0	44-0	38	5.50	75	.297	.360	0-0	—	0	107	-15	-1.6
Total	3	31	29	.517	82	82	15-4	0-0	531	574	276	65	8	167-4	189	4.24	96	.279	.332	0-0	—	0	100	-12	-1.5
ROMANO, JIM James King B 4.6.1927 Brooklyn, NY D 9.12.1990 New York, NY BR/TR 6-4/190# d9.21																									
1950	Bro N	0	0	—	3	1	0	0	6.1	8	6	0	0	2	8	5.68	72	.296	.345	1-0	.000	-0	216	-2	-0.1
ROMANO, MIKE Michael Desport B 3.3.1972 New Orleans, LA BR/TR 6-2/195# d9.5																									
1999	Tor A	0	0	—	3	0	0	0-0	5.1	8	8	1	0	5-0	3	11.81	42	.364	.464	0-0	—	0		-4	-0.2
ROMBERGER, DUTCH Allen Isaiah B 5.26.1927 Klingerstown, PA D 5.26.1983 Weikert, PA BR/TR 6/185# d5.31																									
1954	Phi A	1	1	.500	10	0	0	0	15.2	28	20	3	0	12	6	11.49	34	.406	.488	2-0	.000	0		-12	-1.3
ROMERO, J.C. Juan Carlos B 6.4.1976 Rio Piedras, P.R. BB/TL 5-11/193# d9.15																									
1999	Min A	0	0	—	5	0	0	0-0	9.2	13	4	0	0	0-0	4	3.72	137	.333	.333	0-0	—	0		2	0.1

Year	Tm Lg	W	L	Pct	G	GS	CG-Sho	SV-BS	IP	H	R	HR	HB	BB-IB	SO	ERA	AERA	OAV	OOB	AB-SH	AVG	PB	Sup	APR	PW
2000	Min A	2	7	.222	12	11	0	0-0	57.2	72	51	8	1	30-0	50	7.02	74	.312	.390	0-0	—	0	86	-13	-1.5
2001	Min A	1	4	.200	14	11	0	0-0	65	71	48	10	1	24-1	39	6.23	74	.277	.339	2-0	.500	1	99	-12	-0.6
2002	†Min A	9	2	.818	81	0	0	1-4	81	62	17	3	4	36-4	76	1.89	238	.213	.308	0-0	—	0		**24**	2.9
2003	†Min A	2	0	1.000	73	0	0	0-4	63	66	37	7	6	42-7	50	5.00	91	.272	.392	1-0	.000	-0		-3	-0.1
Total	5	14	13	.519	185	22	0	1-8	276.1	284	157	28	12	132-12	219	4.76	99	.268	.354	3-0	.333	1	95	-2	0.8

ROMERO, RAMON Ramon (De Los Santos) B 1.8.1959 San Pedro De Macoris, D.R. BL/TL 6-4/170# d9.18

Year	Tm Lg	W	L	Pct	G	GS	CG-Sho	SV-BS	IP	H	R	HR	HB	BB-IB	SO	ERA	AERA	OAV	OOB	AB-SH	AVG	PB	Sup	APR	PW
1984	Cle A	0	0	—	1	0	0	0-0	3	0	0	0	1	0-0	3	0.00	—	.000	.111	0-0	—	0		1	0.1
1985	Cle A	2	3	.400	19	10	0	0-0	64.1	69	48	13	5	38-0	38	6.58	63	.276	.381	0-0	—	0	86	-16	-1.1
Total	2	2	3	.400	20	10	0	0-0	67.1	69	48	13	6	38-0	41	6.28	66	.267	.373	0-0	—	0	86	-15	-1.0

ROMMEL, EDDIE Edwin Americus B 9.13.1897 Baltimore, MD D 8.26.1970 Baltimore, MD BR/TR 6-2/197# d4.19 C2 U22

Year	Tm Lg	W	L	Pct	G	GS	CG-Sho	SV-BS	IP	H	R	HR	HB	BB-IB	SO	ERA	AERA	OAV	OOB	AB-SH	AVG	PB	Sup	APR	PW
1920	Phi A	7	7	.500	33	12	8-2	1	173.2	165	68	5	4	43	43	2.85	141	.259	.309	51-8	.216	-0*	74	24	2.0
1921	Phi A	16	23	.410	46	32	20	3	285.1	312	155	21	1	87	71	3.94	113	.284	.337	94-10	.191	-2	77	16	1.8
1922	Phi A	**27**	13	.675	**51**	33	22-3	2	294	294	128	21	5	63	54	3.28	130	.267	.309	94-6	.181	-3	91	30	3.6
1923	Phi A	18	19	.486	**56**	31	19-3	5	297.2	306	141	14	3	108	76	3.27	126	.271	.336	101-4	.238	1	75	24	3.2
1924	Phi A	18	15	.545	43	34	21-3	1	278	302	139	8	3	94	72	3.95	108	.284	.344	95-6	.158	-6*	95	13	1.0
1925	Phi A	**21**	10	.677	52	28	14-1	3	261	285	127	10	7	95	67	3.69	126	.281	.346	81-11	.185	-1	99	27	2.9
1926	Phi A	11	11	.500	37	26	12-3	0	219	225	91	10	2	54	52	3.08	135	.268	.314	61-10	.098	-4	82	27	2.2
1927	Phi A	11	3	.786	30	17	8-2	1	146.2	166	83	6	3	48	33	4.36	98	.286	.343	51-4	.157	-2	125	-1	-0.2
1928	Phi A	13	5	.722	43	11	6	4	173.2	177	70	11	2	26	37	3.06	131	.266	.295	47-4	.255	3	100	19	2.2
1929	†Phi A	12	2	.857	32	6	4	4	113.2	135	52	10	1	34	25	2.85	148	.294	.344	39-4	.205	-0	156	14	1.5
1930	Phi A	9	4	.692	35	9	5	3	130.1	142	66	11	1	27	35	4.28	109	.277	.315	38-3	.263	3	102	8	1.0
1931	†Phi A	7	5	.583	25	10	8-1	0	118	136	50	5	1	27	18	2.97	151	.291	.331	54-0	.259	2*	113	18	1.8
1932	Phi A	1	2	.333	17	0	0	2	65.1	84	43	6	0	18	16	5.51	82	.315	.358	20-0	.300	2		-7	0.0
Total	13	171	119	.590	500	249	147-18	29	2556.1	2729	1213	138	33	724	599	3.54	122	.277	.329	826-70	.199	-7	92	212	23.0

ROMO, ENRIQUE Enrique (Navarro) B 7.15.1947 Santa Rosalia, Mexico BR/TR 5-11/185# d4.7 b-Vicente

Year	Tm Lg	W	L	Pct	G	GS	CG-Sho	SV-BS	IP	H	R	HR	HB	BB-IB	SO	ERA	AERA	OAV	OOB	AB-SH	AVG	PB	Sup	APR	PW
1977	Sea A	8	10	.444	58	3	0	16-7	114.1	93	40	8	5	39-7	105	2.83	146	.227	.300	0-0	—	0	94	16	2.9
1978	Sea A	11	7	.611	56	0	0	10-12	107.1	88	46	12	5	39-6	62	3.69	104	.227	.302	0-0	—	0		3	0.5
1979	†Pit N	10	5	.667	84	0	0	5-8	129.1	122	50	11	3	43-9	106	2.99	130	.253	.317	12-4	.167	-0		12	1.5
1980	Pit N	5	5	.500	74	0	0	11-7	123.2	117	53	10	1	28-4	82	3.27	111	.252	.293	11-2	.455	3*		4	0.7
1981	Pit N	1	3	.250	33	0	0	9-1	41.2	47	27	5	0	18-7	23	4.54	79	.288	.353	4-2	.000	-0		-6	-0.8
1982	Pit N	9	3	.750	45	0	0	1-0	86.2	81	43	11	1	36-6	58	4.36	85	.245	.321	10-1	.300	1*		-4	-0.5
Total	6	44	33	.571	350	3	0	52-35	603	548	259	57	15	203-39	436	3.45	111	.245	.310	37-9	.270	4	94	25	4.3

ROMO, VICENTE Vicente (Navarro) "Huevo" B 4.12.1943 Santa Rosalia, Mexico BR/TR 6-1/195# d4.11 b-Enrique

Year	Tm Lg	W	L	Pct	G	GS	CG-Sho	SV-BS	IP	H	R	HR	HB	BB-IB	SO	ERA	AERA	OAV	OOB	AB-SH	AVG	PB	Sup	APR	PW
1968	LA N	0	0	—	1	0	0	0	1	1	1	0	0	0-0	0	0.00	—	.250	.200	0-0	—	0		0	0.0
	Cle A	5	3	.625	40	1	0	12	83.1	43	15	5	2	32-6	54	1.62	183	.154	.241	14-4	.143	-0	88	14	1.9
1969	Cle A	1	1	.500	3	0	0	0-0	8	7	3	0	0	3-1	7	2.25	168	.233	.294	2-0	.500	0		1	0.2
	Bos A	7	9	.438	52	11	4-1	11-2	127.1	116	51	14	1	50-6	89	3.18	120	.247	.319	31-3	.129	-1	91	9	1.2
	Year	8	10	.444	55	11	4-1	11-2	135.1	123	55	14	1	53-7	96	3.13	122	.246	.318	33-3	.152	-0	91	10	1.4
1970	Bos A	7	3	.700	48	10	0	6-1	108	115	51	14	0	43-6	71	4.08	97	.273	.338	27-2	.148	0	121	1	0.1
1971	Chi A	1	7	.125	45	2	0	5-0	72	52	27	5	0	37-6	48	3.38	107	.202	.300	11-1	.364	1	62	4	0.7
1972	Chi A	3	0	1.000	28	0	0	1-3	51.2	47	19	5	1	18-2	46	3.31	95	.246	.311	9-0	.000	-1		0	-0.1
1973	SD N	2	3	.400	49	1	0	7-3	87.2	85	43	11	0	46-8	51	3.70	94	.260	.347	16-2	.125	-0	51	-3	-0.2
1974	SD N	5	5	.500	54	1	0	9-5	71	78	47	6	2	37-13	26	4.56	78	.290	.374	6-1	.000	-1	49	-11	-1.8
1982	LA N	1	2	.333	15	6	0	1-0	35.2	25	12	1	2	14-0	24	3.03	115	.195	.285	5-4	.200	0	102	3	0.2
Total	8	32	33	.492	335	32	4-1	52-14	645.2	569	269	61	8	280-48	416	3.36	106	.239	.318	121-17	.149	-1	103	18	2.2

ROMONOSKY, JOHN John B 7.7.1929 Harrisburg, IL BR/TR 6-2/195# d9.6

Year	Tm Lg	W	L	Pct	G	GS	CG-Sho	SV-BS	IP	H	R	HR	HB	BB-IB	SO	ERA	AERA	OAV	OOB	AB-SH	AVG	PB	Sup	APR	PW
1953	StL N	0	0	—	2	2	0	0	7.2	9	6	1	1	4	3	4.70	91	.281	.378	2-0	.000	-0	105	-1	-0.1
1958	Was A	2	4	.333	18	5	1	0	55.1	52	42	6	0	28-4	38	6.51	59	.243	.328	13-1	.308	2*	90	-16	-1.3
1959	Was A	1	0	1.000	12	2	0	0	38.1	36	15	4	3	19-0	22	3.29	119	.254	.352	11-0	.182	0*	158	3	0.2
Total	3	3	4	.429	32	9	1	0	101.1	97	63	11	4	51-4	63	5.15	75	.250	.341	26-1	.231	2	110	-14	-1.2

RONDON, GILBERTO Gilberto B 11.18.1953 Bronx, NY BR/TR 6-2/200# d4.10 f-Diomedes

Year	Tm Lg	W	L	Pct	G	GS	CG-Sho	SV-BS	IP	H	R	HR	HB	BB-IB	SO	ERA	AERA	OAV	OOB	AB-SH	AVG	PB	Sup	APR	PW
1976	Hou N	2	2	.500	19	7	0	0-0	53.2	70	37	6	0	39-0	21	5.70	56	.315	.416	14-2	.286	1	161	-15	-1.0
1979	Chi A	0	0	—	4	0	0	0-0	9.2	11	5	2	0	6-0	3	3.72	114	.282	.370	0-0	—	0		0	0.0
Total	2	2	2	.500	23	7	0	0-0	63.1	81	42	8	0	45-0	24	5.40	62	.310	.409	14-2	.286	1	161	-15	-1.0

RONEY, MATT Matthew Stephen B 1.10.1980 Tulsa, OK BR/TR 6-3/230# d4.2

Year	Tm Lg	W	L	Pct	G	GS	CG-Sho	SV-BS	IP	H	R	HR	HB	BB-IB	SO	ERA	AERA	OAV	OOB	AB-SH	AVG	PB	Sup	APR	PW
2003	Det A	1	9	.100	45	11	0	0-2	100.2	102	67	17	4	48-4	47	5.45	79	.262	.346	2-0	.500	0	77	-14	-1.1

ROOKER, JIM James Phillip B 9.23.1942 Lakeview, OR BR/TL 6/201# d6.30

Year	Tm Lg	W	L	Pct	G	GS	CG-Sho	SV-BS	IP	H	R	HR	HB	BB-IB	SO	ERA	AERA	OAV	OOB	AB-SH	AVG	PB	Sup	APR	PW
1968	Det A	0	0	—	2	0	0	0	4.2	4	2	0	0	1-0	4	3.86	78	.235	.278	2-0	.000	-0		0	0.0
1969	KC A	4	16	.200	28	22	8-1	0-0	158.1	136	80	13	1	73-3	108	3.75	98	.229	.312	57-0	.281	8*	86	-3	0.5
1970	KC A	10	15	.400	38	29	6-3	1-0	203.2	190	99	11	1	102-4	117	3.54	106	.252	.339	70-2	.200	3*	85	1	0.5
1971	KC A	2	7	.222	20	7	1-1	0-1	54	59	35	2	1	24-1	31	5.33	64	.284	.354	10-1	.000	-1*	60	-11	-1.8
1972	KC A	5	6	.455	18	10	4-2	0-0	72	78	37	3	1	24-0	44	4.38	70	.280	.337	20-0	.100	-1	93	-10	-1.6
1973	Pit N	10	6	.625	41	18	6-3	5-0	170.1	143	59	12	2	52-10	122	2.85	124	.229	.288	49-5	.245	3*	129	15	1.7
1974	†Pit N	15	11	.577	33	33	15-1	0-0	262.2	228	93	11	4	83-6	139	2.78	125	.238	.299	95-5	.305	11	105	21	3.3
1975	†Pit N	13	11	.542	28	28	7-1	0-0	196.2	177	80	16	3	76-13	102	2.97	119	.238	.309	63-9	.095	-3	107	11	1.0
1976	Pit N	15	8	.652	30	29	10-1	1-0	198.2	201	83	12	2	72-5	92	3.35	104	.263	.325	74-5	.216	3*	130	4	0.8
1977	Pit N	14	9	.609	30	30	7-2	0-0	204.1	196	87	24	0	64-4	89	3.08	129	.253	.308	70-1	.186	0	108	16	1.7
1978	Pit N	9	11	.450	28	28	1	0-0	163.1	160	94	13	3	81-4	76	4.24	87	.259	.346	56-1	.161	0*	103	-11	-1.2
1979	†Pit N	4	7	.364	19	17	1	0-0	103.2	106	58	11	0	39-5	44	4.60	84	.266	.329	33-2	.121	-1	94	-7	-0.8
1980	Pit N	2	2	.500	4	4	0	0-0	18	16	7	0	0	12-0	8	3.50	104	.262	.378	7-1	.143	1	80	1	0.2
Total	13	103	109	.486	319	255	66-15	7-1	1810.1	1694	814	128	18	703-55	976	3.46	105	.249	.319	606-32	.201	23	103	27	4.3

ROOT, CHARLIE Charles Henry "Chinski" B 3.17.1899 Middletown, OH D 11.5.1970 Hollister, CA BR/TR 5-10.5/190# d4.18 C6

Year	Tm Lg	W	L	Pct	G	GS	CG-Sho	SV-BS	IP	H	R	HR	HB	BB-IB	SO	ERA	AERA	OAV	OOB	AB-SH	AVG	PB	Sup	APR	PW
1923	StL A	0	4	.000	27	2	0	0	60	68	45	4	6	18	27	5.70	73	.302	.369	13-0	.077	-1	50	-9	-0.7
1926	Chi N	18	17	.514	42	32	21-2	2	271.1	267	104	10	6	62	127	2.82	136	.264	.310	91-4	.143	-4	93	30	3.1
1927	Chi N	**26**	15	.634	**48**	36	21-4	2	**309**	296	148	16	9	117	145	3.76	103	.254	.326	122-5	.221	3	127	5	0.7
1928	Chi N	14	18	.438	40	30	13-1	2	237	214	109	15	7	73	122	3.57	108	.242	.305	73-8	.178	-0	67	8	0.9
1929	†Chi N	19	6	**.760**	43	31	19-4	5	272	286	120	12	3	83	124	3.47	133	.275	.330	96-5	.156	0	118	**37**	2.7
1930	Chi N	16	14	.533	37	30	15-**4**	3	220.1	247	122	17	7	63	124	4.33	113	.281	.334	80-2	.262	5	102	14	1.9
1931	Chi N	17	14	.548	39	31	19-3	2	251	240	109	7	7	71	131	3.48	111	.252	.309	90-1	.222	3	101	12	1.6
1932	†Chi N	15	10	.600	39	24	11	3	216.1	211	99	10	5	55	96	3.58	105	.253	.303	76-2	.171	-1	103	6	0.3
1933	Chi N	15	10	.600	35	30	20-2	0	242.1	232	85	14	10	61	86	2.60	126	.252	.306	85-4	.094	-4	102	18	1.2
1934	Chi N	4	7	.364	34	9	2	0	117.2	141	62	8	5	53	46	4.28	90	.298	.375	40-1	.175	2	94	-5	-0.3
1935	†Chi N	15	8	.652	38	18	11-1	2	201.1	193	85	15	3	47	94	3.08	127	.252	.298	69-12	.203	2	131	18	1.9
1936	Chi N	3	6	.333	33	4	0	1	73.2	81	34	3	2	20	32	4.15	96	.280	.331	15-0	.333	1	149	0	0.1
1937	Chi N	13	5	.722	43	15	5	5	178.2	173	71	18	4	32	74	3.38	118	.253	.290	67-2	.179	0	133	13	1.3
1938	†Chi N	8	7	.533	44	11	5	8	160.2	163	62	10	2	30	70	2.86	134	.258	.294	48-1	.167	-0	72	15	1.4
1939	Chi N	8	8	.500	35	16	8	4	167.1	189	83	11	2	34	65	4.03	98	.286	.323	57-3	.175	2	98	0	0.0
1940	Chi N	2	4	.333	36	8	1	1	112	118	61	9	1	33	50	3.86	97	.265	.317	31-0	.129	-1	125	-4	-0.3
1941	Chi N	8	7	.533	19	15	6	0	106.2	133	68	8	0	37	46	5.40	65	.306	.360	33-4	.152	2	113	-20	-2.3
Total	17	201	160	.557	632	342	177-21	40	3197.1	3252	1467	187	79	889	1459	3.59	110	.264	.318	1086-54	.180	8	105	138	13.5

ROPER, JOHN John Christopher B 11.21.1971 Southern Pines, NC BR/TR 6/175# d5.16

Year	Tm Lg	W	L	Pct	G	GS	CG-Sho	SV-BS	IP	H	R	HR	HB	BB-IB	SO	ERA	AERA	OAV	OOB	AB-SH	AVG	PB	Sup	APR	PW
1993	Cin N	2	5	.286	16	15	0	0-0	80	92	51	10	4	36-3	54	5.62	72	.295	.372	28-1	.179	-0	121	-13	-1.0
1994	Cin N	6	2	.750	16	15	0	0-0	92	90	49	16	4	30-0	51	4.50	92	.255	.318	33-2	.182	0	142	-3	-0.2
1995	Cin N	0	0	—	2	2	0	0-0	7	13	9	3	0	4-0	6	10.29	40	.406	.472	1-1	.000	-0	164	-5	-0.2

Year	Tm Lg	W	L	Pct	G	GS	CG-Sho	SV-BS	IP	H	R	HR	HB	BB-IB	SO	ERA	AERA	OAV	OOB	AB-SH	AVG	PB	Sup	APR	PW
	SF N	0	0	—	1	0	0	0-0	1	2	3	0	0	2-0	0	27.00	15	.500	.571	0-0	—	0		-2	-0.1
	Year	0	0	—	3	2	0	0-0	8	15	20	3	0	6-0	6	12.38	33	.417	.488	1-1	.000	-0	165	-7	-0.3
Total	3	8	7	.533	35	32	0	0-0	180	197	112	29	8	72-3	111	5.35	76	.281	.352	62-4	.177	0	134	-23	-1.5
ROQUE, RAFAEL Rafael Antonio B 1.1.1972 Cotui, D.R. BL/TL 6-4/186# d8.1																									
1998	Mil N	4	2	.667	9	9	0	0-0	48	42	28	9	1	24-0	34	4.88	88	.237	.332	13-4	.077	-1	125	-3	-0.4
1999	Mil N	1	6	.143	43	9	0	1-1	84.1	96	52	16	4	42-1	66	5.34	85	.286	.369	17-1	.059	-1	83	-6	-0.5
2000	Mil N	0	0	—	4	0	0	0-0	5.1	7	6	1	0	7-1	4	10.13	45	.333	.483	0-0	—	0		-3	-0.2
Total	3	5	8	.385	56	18	0	1-1	137.2	145	86	26	5	73-2	104	5.36	83	.272	.362	30-5	.067	-2	102	-12	-1.1
ROSADO, JOSE Jose Antonio B 11.9.1974 Newark, NJ BL/TL 6/175# d6.12																									
1996	KC A	8	6	.571	16	16	2-1	0-0	106.2	101	39	7	4	26-1	64	3.21	156	.249	.298	0-0	—	0	82	22	2.6
1997	KC A★	9	12	.429	33	33	2	0-0	203.1	208	117	26	4	73-3	129	4.69	101	.264	.326	2-0	.000	-0*	81	0	-0.1
1998	KC A	8	11	.421	38	25	2-1	1-0	174.2	180	106	25	5	57-2	135	4.69	103	.260	.320	2-0	.500	0	89	0	0.0
1999	KC A★	10	14	.417	33	33	5	0-0	208	197	103	24	5	72-1	141	3.85	130	.248	.314	5-0	.000	-1	91	24	2.3
2000	KC A	2	2	.500	5	5	0	0-0	27.2	29	18	4	4	9-0	15	5.86	88	.271	.347	0-0	—	0	88	-2	-0.2
Total	5	37	45	.451	125	112	11-2	1-0	720.1	715	383	86	22	237-7	484	4.27	114	.257	.318	9-0	.111	-0	86	44	4.6
ROSARIO, RODRIGO Rodrigo B 12.14.1977 LaRomana, D.R. BR/TR 6-2/160# d6.21																									
2003	Hou N	1	0	1.000	2	2	0	0-0	8	5	2	0	1	3-1	6	1.13	395	.172	.273	0-0	—	0	169	2	0.3
ROSE, BRIAN Brian Leonard B 2.13.1976 New Bedford, MA BR/TR 6-3/215# d7.25																									
1997	Bos A	0	0	—	1	1	0	0-0	3	5	4	0	0	2-0	3	12.00	39	.357	.438	0-0	—	0	99	-2	-0.1
1998	Bos A	1	4	.200	8	8	0	0-0	37.2	43	32	9	2	14-0	18	6.93	68	.285	.351	0-0	—	0	118	-9	-1.0
1999	Bos A	7	6	.538	22	18	0	0-0	98	112	59	19	2	29-2	51	4.87	102	.280	.332	2-1	.000	-0	83	1	0.2
2000	Bos A	3	5	.375	15	12	0	0-0	53	58	37	11	3	21-3	24	6.11	83	.274	.345	3-0	.000	-0	87	-5	-0.7
	Col N	4	5	.444	12	12	0	0-0	63.2	72	41	10	3	30-6	40	5.51	105	.281	.361	21-3	.048	-2	79	2	0.0
2001	NY N	0	1	.000	3	0	0	0-0	8.2	10	4	3	0	2-1	4	4.15	100	.286	.324	1-0	.000	-0		0	0.0
	TB A	0	2	.000	7	3	0	0-0	20.1	31	20	4	0	12-0	11	8.85	51	.356	.426	0-0	—	0	82	-9	-0.7
Total	5	15	23	.395	68	54	0	0-0	284.1	331	197	56	10	110-12	151	5.86	87	.287	.352	27-4	.037	-2	88	-22	-2.3
ROSE, CHUCK Charles Alfred B 9.1.1885 Macon, MO D 8.4.1961 Salina, KS BL/TL 5-8.5/158# d9.13																									
1909	StL A	1	2	.333	3	3	3	0	25	32	17	1	3	7	6	5.40	45	.330	.393	7-1	.000	-1	68	-7	-0.9
ROSE, DON Donald Gary B 3.19.1947 Covina, CA BR/TR 6-3/195# d9.15																									
1971	NY N	0	0	—	1	0	0	0-0	2	2	0	0	0	0-0	1	0.00	—	.286	.286	0-0	—	0		1	0.0
1972	Cal A	1	4	.200	16	4	0	0-0	42.2	49	25	9	0	19-5	39	4.22	69	.283	.352	10-1	.200	1	152	-8	-0.7
1974	SF N	0	0	—	2	0	0	0-1	1	4	1	0	0	1-0	0	9.00	42	.667	.714	0-0	—	0		0	0.0
Total	3	1	4	.200	19	4	0	0-1	45.2	55	26	9	0	20-5	40	4.14	72	.296	.362	10-1	.200	1	152	-7	-0.7
ROSEBRAUGH, ZEKE Eli Ethelbert B 9.8.1870 Charleston, IL D 7.16.1930 Fresno, CA TL d9.21																									
1898	Pit N	0	2	.000	4	2	2	0	21.2	23	14	0	3	9	6	3.32	107	.271	.361	8-0	.375	1	50	-1	0.0
1899	Pit N	0	1	.000	2	2	0	0	6	14	8	0	1	3	2	9.00	42	.452	.514	2-0	.000	-0	47	-3	-0.4
Total	2	0	3	.000	6	4	2	0	27.2	37	22	0	4	12	8	4.55	79	.319	.402	10-0	.300	1	49	-4	-0.4
ROSEMAN, CHIEF James John B 1856 New York, NY D 7.4.1938 Brooklyn, NY BR/TR 5-7/167# d5.1.1882 M1 ▲																									
1885	NY AA	0	1	.000	1	1	0	0	1	3	5	0	0	2	0	27.00	12	.333	.455	410	.278	0*	246	-3	-0.4
1886	NY AA	0	0	—	1	0	0	0	7	6	6	0	0	0	0	5.14	63	.240	.240	559	.227	0*		-1	0.0
1887	NY AA	0	0	—	2	0	0	0	8	11	14	0	2	5	1	7.88	54	.407	.529	241	.228	-0*		-4	-0.2
Total	3	0	1	.000	4	1	0	0	16	20	25	0	2	7	1	7.88	47	.328	.414	1210	.245	0	246	-8	-0.6
ROSENBERG, STEVE Steven Allen B 10.31.1964 Brooklyn, NY BL/TL 6/186# d6.4																									
1988	Chi A	0	1	.000	33	0	0	1-0	46	53	22	5	0	19-0	28	4.30	92	.298	.360	0-0	—	0		0	0.0
1989	Chi A	4	13	.235	38	21	2	0-0	142	148	92	14	1	58-1	77	4.94	77	.273	.339	0-0	—	0	80	-20	-2.2
1990	Chi A	1	0	1.000	6	0	0	0-0	10	10	6	2	0	5-0	4	5.40	71	.256	.341	0-0	—	0		-2	-0.1
1991	SD N	1	1	.500	10	0	0	0-1	11.2	11	9	3	0	5-1	6	6.94	55	.250	.327	1-0	.000	-0		-3	-0.6
Total	4	6	15	.286	87	21	2	1-1	209.2	222	129	24	1	87-2	115	4.94	78	.276	.343	1-0	.000	-0	80	-25	-2.9
ROSENTHAL, WAYNE Wayne Scott B 2.19.1965 Brooklyn, NY BR/TR 6-5/220# d6.26 C1																									
1991	Tex A	1	4	.200	36	0	0	1-1	70.1	72	43	9	1	36-1	61	5.25	77	.257	.341	0-0	—	0		-9	-0.6
1992	Tex A	0	0	—	6	0	0	0-0	4.2	7	4	1	0	2-0	1	7.71	49	.333	.391	0-0	—	0		-2	-0.1
Total	2	1	4	.200	42	0	0	1-1	75	79	47	10	1	38-1	62	5.40	74	.262	.344	0-0	—	0		-11	-0.7
ROSER, STEVE Emerson Corey B 1.25.1918 Rome, NY D 2.8.2002 Utica, NY BR/TR 6-4/220# d5.5																									
1944	NY A	4	3	.571	16	6	1	1	84	80	39	3	0	34	34	3.86	90	.256	.329	30-2	.100	-2	96	-2	-0.4
1945	NY A	0	0	—	11	0	0	0	27	27	15	1	0	8	11	3.67	94	.262	.315	8-0	.125	-0		-2	-0.1
1946	NY A	1	1	.500	4	1	0	0	3.1	7	6	0	0	4	1	16.20	21	.438	.550	0-0	—	0	124	-4	-0.8
	Bos N	1	1	.500	14	1	0	1	35	33	15	1	0	18	18	3.60	95	.250	.340	5-0	.000	-1	75	0	-0.1
Total	3	6	5	.545	45	8	1	2	149.1	147	75	5	0	64	64	4.04	86	.261	.336	43-2	.093	-3	97	-8	-1.4
ROSS, BUSTER Chester Franklin B 3.11.1903 Kuttawa, KY D 4.24.1982 Mayfield, KY BL/TL 6-1/195# d6.15																									
1924	Bos A	4	3	.571	30	2	1-1	1	93.1	109	49	3	0	30	16	3.47	126	.307	.361	25-0	.200	-0	145	7	0.4
1925	Bos A	3	8	.273	33	8	0	0	94.1	119	86	9	5	40	15	6.20	73	.313	.386	24-2	.125	-1	90	-18	-1.9
1926	Bos A	0	1	.000	1	0	0	0	2.2	5	7	0	0	4	0	16.88	24	.385	.529	1-0	.000	-0		-4	-0.6
Total	3	7	12	.368	64	10	1-1	1	190.1	233	142	12	5	74	31	5.01	89	.311	.377	50-2	.160	-2	102	-15	-2.1
ROSS, CLIFF Clifford Davis B 8.3.1928 Philadelphia, PA D 4.13.1999 Philadelphia, PA BL/TL 6-4/195# d9.11																									
1954	Cin N	0	0	—	4	0	0	1	2.2	0	0	0	0	0	1	0.00	—	.000	.000	0-0	—	0		1	0.1
ROSS, ERNIE Ernest Bertram "Curly" B 3.31.1880 Toronto, ON, CAN D 3.28.1950 Toronto, ON, CAN BL/TL 5-8/150# d9.17																									
1902	Bal A	1	1	.500	2	2	2	0	17	20	18	0	1	12	2	7.41	51	.294	.407	8-0	.000	-1	76	-6	-0.6
ROSS, BOB Floyd Robert B 11.2.1928 Fullerton, CA BR/TL 6/165# d6.16 Mil 1952																									
1950	Was A	0	1	.000	6	2	0	0	12.2	15	12	1	0	15	2	8.53	53	.300	.462	3-0	.000	-0	70	-5	-0.4
1951	Was A	0	1	.000	11	1	0	0	31.2	36	25	3	0	21	23	6.54	63	.295	.399	9-0	.111	-0	43	-8	-0.5
1956	Phi N	0	0	—	3	0	0	0	3.1	4	3	1	0	2-0	4	8.10	46	.333	.400	0-0	—	0		-1	-0.1
Total	3	0	2	.000	20	3	0	0	47.2	55	40	5	0	38-0	29	7.17	58	.299	.417	12-0	.083	-1	64	-14	-1.0
ROSS, GARY Gary Douglas B 9.16.1947 McKeesport, PA BR/TR 6-1/190# d6.28																									
1968	Chi N	1	1	.500	13	5	1	0	41	44	22	1	0	25-3	31	4.17	76	.288	.383	11-0	.091	-1	82	-5	-0.3
1969	Chi N	0	0	—	2	1	0	0-0	2	1	3	0	0	2-0	2	13.50	30	.143	.333	0-0	—	0	110	-2	-0.1
	SD N	3	12	.200	46	7	0	3-4	109.2	104	58	5	5	56-8	58	4.19	85	.252	.345	23-5	.000	-2	39	-9	-1.3
	Year	3	12	.200	48	8	0	3-4	111.2	105	60	5	5	58-8	60	4.35	82	.250	.345	23-5	.000	-2	50	-10	-1.4
1970	SD N	2	3	.400	33	2	0	1-1	62.1	72	37	8	3	36-10	39	5.20	77	.305	.402	8-2	.500	2	203	-7	-0.3
1971	SD N	1	3	.250	13	0	0	0-0	24.1	27	10	0	1	11-2	13	2.96	112	.300	.375	1-1	.000	-0		1	0.1
1972	SD N	4	3	.571	60	0	0	3-3	91.2	87	35	2	4	49-12	46	2.45	134	.261	.359	13-1	.154	-0		6	0.5
1973	SD N	4	4	.500	58	0	0	0-1	76.1	93	51	8	4	33-8	44	5.42	64	.304	.376	4-1	.000	-0		-16	-1.6
1974	SD N	0	0	—	9	0	0	0-0	18	23	10	1	0	6-4	11	4.50	79	.315	.363	1-0	.000	-0		-2	-0.1
1975	Cal A	0	1	.000	1	1	0	0-0	5	6	3	1	0	1-0	4	5.40	66	.273	.304	0-0	—	0	0	-1	-0.2
1976	Cal A	8	16	.333	34	31	7-2	0-0	225	224	89	12	5	58-5	100	3.00	111	.258	.306	0-0	—	0	83	7	1.0
1977	Cal A	2	4	.333	14	12	0	0-0	58.1	83	41	10	2	11-1	30	5.55	71	.337	.369	0-0	—	0	86	-11	-0.9
Total	10	25	47	.347	283	59	8-2	7-9	713.2	764	359	48	24	288-53	378	3.92	89	.278	.349	61-10	.115	-2	83	-39	-3.2
ROSS, GEORGE George Sidney B 6.27.1892 San Rafael, CA D 4.22.1935 Amityville, NY BL/TL 5-10.5/175# d6.27																									
1918	NY N	0	0	—	1	0	0	1	2.1	2	0	0	0	3	2	0.00	—	.222	.417	1-0	.000	-0		1	0.1

Year	Tm Lg	W	L	Pct	G	GS	CG-Sho	SV-BS	IP	H	R	HR	HB	BB-IB	SO	ERA	AERA	OAV	OOB	AB-SH	AVG	PB	Sup	APR	PW
ROSS, BUCK Lee Ravon B 2.2.1915 Norwood, NC D 11.23.1978 Charlotte, NC BR/TR 6-2/170# d5.7																									
1936	Phi A	9	14	.391	30	27	12-1	0	200.2	253	146	17	0	83	47	5.83	88	.304	.367	71-4	.169	-1	91	-15	-1.5
1937	Phi A	5	10	.333	28	22	7-1	0	147.1	183	102	12	2	63	37	4.89	96	.306	.373	49-0	.102	-3	92	-6	-0.8
1938	Phi A	9	16	.360	29	28	10	0	184.1	218	132	23	0	80	54	5.32	91	.289	.357	63-5	.190	-0	79	-11	-1.2
1939	Phi A	6	14	.300	29	28	6-1	0	174	216	143	17	0	95	43	6.00	78	.302	.384	58-7	.207	-1	91	-27	-2.6
1940	Phi A	5	10	.333	24	19	10	1	156.1	160	91	15	0	60	43	4.38	102	.256	.322	53-2	.132	-2	89	1	-0.2
1941	Phi A	0	1	.000	1	1	0	0	4	10	9	2	0	2	0	18.00	23	.435	.480	1-0	.000	-0	83	-6	-0.8
	Chi A	3	8	.273	20	11	7	0	108.1	99	51	6	1	43	30	3.16	130	.239	.312	32-4	.219	1	67	9	0.8
	Year	3	9	.250	21	12	7	0	112.1	109	54	8	1	45	30	3.69	111	.249	.321	33-4	.212	1	69	3	0.0
1942	Chi A	5	7	.417	22	14	4-2	1	113.1	118	63	6	0	39	37	5.00	72	.264	.323	38-2	.158	0	95	-13	-1.4
1943	Chi A	11	7	.611	21	21	7-1	0	149.1	140	61	6	2	56	41	3.19	105	.253	.324	46-4	.087	-1	101	3	0.2
1944	Chi A	2	7	.222	20	9	2	0	90.1	97	56	7	2	35	20	5.18	66	.280	.350	26-2	.077	-2	106	-15	-1.7
1945	Chi A	1	1	.500	13	2	0	0	37.1	51	28	3	0	17	8	5.79	57	.327	.393	11-0	.182	-0	51	-10	-0.6
Total	10	56	95	.371	237	182	65-6	2	1365.1	1545	882	114	7	573	360	4.94	88	.283	.351	448-30	.154	-11	90	-90	-9.8
ROSS, MARK Mark Joseph B 8.8.1957 Galveston, TX BR/TR 6/195# d9.12																									
1982	Hou N	0	0	—	4	0	0	0-0	6	3	1	0	0	0-0	4	1.50	222	.143	.143	0-0	—	0		1	0.1
1984	Hou N	1	0	1.000	2	0	0	0-0	2.1	1	0	0	0	0-0	1	0.00	—	.125	.125	0-0	—	0		1	0.2
1985	Hou N	0	2	.000	8	0	0	1-1	13	12	7	2	0	2-0	3	4.85	72	.240	.269	1-0	.000	-0		-2	-0.3
1987	Pit N	0	0	—	1	0	0	0-0	1	1	1	1	0	0-0	0	9.00	46	.250	.250	0-0	—	0		0	0.0
1988	Tor A	0	0	—	3	0	0	0-0	7.1	5	6	0	0	4-1	4	4.91	80	.185	.281	0-0	—	0		-2	-0.1
1990	Pit N	1	0	1.000	9	0	0	0-0	12.2	11	5	2	0	4-2	5	3.55	102	.244	.306	1-0	.000	-0		0	0.0
Total	6	2	2	.500	27	0	0	1-1	42.1	33	20	5	0	10-3	17	3.83	94	.213	.259	2-0	.000	-0		-2	-0.1
ROSSELLI, JOEY Joseph Donald B 5.28.1972 Burbank, CA BR/TL 6-1/170# d4.30																									
1995	SF N	2	1	.667	9	5	0	0-0	30	39	29	5	0	20-2	7	8.70	47	.342	.428	10-1	.200	0	137	-14	-1.2
ROSSO, FRANK Francis James B 3.1.1921 Agawam, MA D 1.26.1980 Springfield, MA BR/TR 5-11/180# d9.15																									
1944	NY N	0	0	—	2	0	0	0	4	11	5	0	0	3	1	9.00	41	.550	.609	0-0	—	0*		-2	-0.1
ROTBLATT, MARV Marvin "Rotty" B 10.18.1927 Chicago, IL BB/TL 5-7/160# d7.4																									
1948	Chi A	0	1	.000	7	2	0	0	18.1	19	16	0	1	23	4	7.85	54	.271	.457	4-0	.000	-0	74	-7	-0.4
1950	Chi A	0	0	—	2	0	0	0	8.2	11	7	2	0	5	6	6.23	72	.344	.432	2-0	.000	-0		-2	-0.1
1951	Chi A	4	2	.667	26	2	0	2	47.2	44	21	4	1	23	20	3.40	119	.244	.333	9-2	.000	-2	242	3	0.3
Total	3	4	3	.571	35	4	0	2	74.2	74	44	6	2	51	30	4.82	86	.262	.379	15-2	.000	-2	156	-6	-0.2
ROTHSCHILD, LARRY Lawrence Lee B 3.12.1954 Chicago, IL BL/TR 6-2/180# d9.11 M4 C9																									
1981	Det A	0	0	—	5	0	0	1-0	5.2	4	1	0	0	6-1	1	1.59	238	.200	.370	0-0	—	0		1	0.1
1982	Det A	0	0	—	2	0	0	0-0	2.2	4	4	1	0	2-0	0	13.50	30	.333	.429	0-0	—	0		-3	-0.1
Total	2	0	0	—	7	0	0	1-0	8.1	8	5	1	0	8-1	1	5.40	72	.250	.390	0-0	—	0		-2	0.0
ROUNSAVILLE, GENE Virle Gene B 9.27.1944 Konawa, OK BR/TR 6-3/205# d4.7																									
1970	Chi A	0	1	.000	8	0	0	0-0	6.1	10	8	1	0	2-0	3	9.95	39	.357	.400	0-0	—	0		-4	-0.6
ROWAN, JACK John Albert B 6.16.1887 New Castle, PA D 9.29.1966 Dayton, OH BR/TR 6-1/210# d9.6																									
1906	Det A	0	1	.000	1	1	1	0	9	15	13	0	0	6	0	11.00	25	.375	.457	4-0	.250	0	130	-7	-0.6
1908	Cin N	3	3	.500	8	7	4-1	0	49.1	46	17	0	0	16	24	1.82	126	.253	.313	14-0	.071	-0	105	2	0.2
1909	Cin N	11	12	.478	38	23	14	0	225.2	185	86	0	3	104	81	2.79	93	.233	.324	65-2	.092	-1	106	2	-0.2
1910	Cin N	14	13	.519	42	30	18-4	1	261	242	122	4	9	105	108	2.93	99	.254	.334	83-3	.229	3	100	-1	0.1
1911	Phi N	2	4	.333	12	6	2	0	45.2	59	35	3	1	20	17	4.73	73	.316	.385	13-1	.077	-1	80	-8	-0.9
	Chi N	0	0	—	1	0	0	0	2	1	4	0	1	2	0	4.50	74	.143	.400	1-0	.000	-0		-1	-0.1
	Year	2	4	.333	13	6	2	0	47.2	60	43	3	2	22	17	4.72	73	.309	.385	14-1	.071	-1	80	-9	-1.0
1913	Cin N	0	4	.000	5	5	5	0	39	37	14	0	1	9	21	3.00	108	.264	.313	11-0	.182	1	32	2	0.3
1914	Cin N	1	3	.250	12	2	0	2	39	38	22	1	0	10	16	3.46	85	.262	.310	8-0	.000	-1	73	-2	-0.4
Total	7	31	40	.437	119	74	44-5	3	670.2	623	313	8	15	272	267	3.07	92	.255	.333	199-6	.151	1	95	-13	-1.6
ROWE, DAVE David Elwood B 10.9.1854 Harrisburg, PA D 12.9.1930 Glendale, CA BR/TR 5-9/180# d5.30 M2 b-Jack ▲																									
1877	Chi N	0	1	.000	1	1	0	0	1	3	2	0		2	0	18.00	17	.600	.714	7	.286	0*	16	-1	-0.2
1882	Cle N	0	1	.000	1	1	1	0	9	29	35	3		7	0	12.00	23	.492	.545	97	.258	0*	76	-13	-0.8
1883	Bal AA	0	0	—	1	0	0	0	4	12	11	1		2	1	20.25	17	.500	.538	256	.313	0*		-5	-0.2
1884	StL U	1	0	1.000	1	1	1	0	9	10	3	0		0	2	2.00	120	.263	.263	485	.293	0*	107	1	0.1
Total	4	1	2	.333	4	3	2	0	23	54	51	4		11	3	9.78	28	.429	.474	845	.295	0	66	-18	-1.1
ROWE, DON Donald Howard B 4.3.1936 Brawley, CA BL/TL 6/180# d4.9 C8																									
1963	NY N	0	0	—	26	1	0	0	54.2	59	27	6	1	21-0	27	4.28	81	.280	.346	13-0	.231	0	148	-3	-0.2
ROWE, KEN Kenneth Darrell B 12.31.1933 Ferndale, MI BR/TR 6-2/185# d4.14 C2																									
1963	LA N	1	1	.500	14	0	0	1	27.2	28	16	2	1	11-3	12	2.93	103	.264	.336	5-0	.000	-1		-2	-0.2
1964	Bal A	1	0	1.000	6	0	0	0	4.1	10	10	1	0	1-0	4	8.31	43	.455	.478	0-0	—	0		-5	-0.9
1965	Bal A	0	0	—	6	0	0	0	13.1	17	5	0	0	2-1	3	3.38	103	.321	.333	1-0	1.000	0		1	0.0
Total	3	2	1	.667	26	0	0	1	45.1	55	31	3	1	14-4	19	3.57	90	.304	.352	6-0	.167	-0		-6	-1.1
ROWE, SCHOOLBOY Lynwood Thomas B 1.11.1910 Waco, TX D 1.8.1961 ElDorado, AR BR/TR 6-4.5/210# d4.15 Mil 1944-45 C2																									
1933	Det A	7	4	.636	19	15	8-1	0	123.1	129	60	7	1	31	75	3.58	121	.269	.315	50-2	.220	-0*	100	9	0.8
1934	†Det A	24	8	.750	45	30	20-3	1	266	259	110	12	1	81	149	3.45	127	.256	.312	109-4	.303	12*	115	31	4.5
1935	†Det A☆	19	13	.594	42	34	21-**6**	3	275.2	272	121	11	2	68	140	3.69	113	.255	**.301**	109-3	.312	14*	141	20	3.2
1936	Det A★	19	10	.655	41	35	19-4	3	245.1	266	134	15	2	64	115	4.51	110	.275	.321	90-2	.256	7*	95	16	2,3
1937	Det A	1	4	.200	10	2	1	0	31.1	49	32	7	1	9	6	8.62	54	.350	.393	10-1	.200	-0	84	-13	-1.5
1938	Det A	0	2	.000	4	3	0	0	21	20	11	1	0	11	4	3.00	167	.256	.348	6-1	.167	-0	53	3	0.3
1939	Det A	10	12	.455	28	24	8-1	0	164	192	113	17	2	61	51	4.99	98	.291	.353	61-3	.246	2*	110	-5	-0.3
1940	†Det A	16	3	**.842**	27	23	11-1	0	169	170	68	15	1	43	61	3.46	137	.259	.305	67-1	.269	5	137	26	3.1
1941	Det A	8	6	.571	27	14	4	1	139	155	70	6	0	33	54	4.14	110	.278	.318	55-1	.273	5*	95	7	1.2
1942	Det A	1	0	1.000	2	1	0	0	10.1	9	2	0	0	2	7	0.00	—	.220	.256	4-1	.000	-1	87	3	0.3
	Bro N	1	0	1.000	9	2	0	0	30.1	36	19	2	1	12	6	5.34	61	.288	.355	19-0	.211	0*	180	-6	-0.3
1943	Phi N	14	8	.636	27	25	11-3	1	199	196	73	7	3	29	52	2.94	115	.249	.279	120-1	.300	16*	112	10	3.3
1946	Phi N	11	4	.733	17	16	9-2	0	136	112	39	3	6	21	51	2.12	162	.224	.263	61-1	.180	2*	80	19	2.3
1947	Phi N★	14	10	.583	31	28	15-1	1	195.2	232	106	22	3	45	74	4.32	93	.292	.333	79-2	.278	10*	105	-6	0.3
1948	Phi N	10	10	.500	30	20	8	2	148	167	74	5	2	31	46	4.07	97	.281	.319	52-2	.192	2*	93	0	0.2
1949	Phi N	3	7	.300	23	6	2	0	65.1	68	43	2	2	17	22	4.82	82	.300	.354	17-0	.235	2	67	-8	-0.9
Total	15	158	101	.610	382	278	137-22	12	2219.1	2332	1075	132	27	558	913	3.87	110	.269	.315	909-25	.263	76	109	106	18.8
ROWLAND, MIKE Michael Evan B 1.31.1953 Chicago, IL BR/TR 6-3/205# d7.25																									
1980	SF N	1	1	.500	19	0	0	0-0	27	20	8	2	1	8-2	8	2.33	152	.206	.271	0-0	—	0		4	0.3
1981	SF N	0	1	.000	9	1	0	0-0	15.2	13	7	1	1	6-2	8	3.45	100	.232	.313	1-0	1.000	0	310	0	0.0
Total	2	1	2	.333	28	1	0	0-0	42.2	33	15	3	2	14-4	16	2.74	128	.216	.287	1-0	1.000	0	310	4	0.3
ROY, CHARLIE Charles Robert B 6.22.1884 Beaulieu, MN D 2.10.1950 Blackfoot, ID BR/TR 5-10/190# d6.27 b-Luther																									
1906	Phi N	0	1	.000	7	1	0	0	18.1	24	12	0	1	5	6	4.91	53	.316	.366	7-1	.000	-1*	84	-4	-0.3
ROY, EMIL Emil Arthur B 5.26.1907 Brighton, MA D 1.5.1997 Crystal River, FL BR/TR 5-11/180# d9.30																									
1933	Phi A	0	1	.000	1	1	0	0	2.1	4	7	0	0	4	3	27.00	16	.364	.533	0-0	—	0	20	-5	-0.7
ROY, JEAN-PIERRE Jean-Pierre B 6.26.1920 Montreal, PQ, CAN BB/TR 5-10/160# d5.5																									
1946	Bro N	0	0	—	3	1	0	0	6.1	5	7	2	0	5	6	9.95	34	.200	.333	2-0	.000	-0	177	-4	-0.2

Year	Tm Lg	W	L	Pct	G	GS	CG-Sho	SV-BS	IP	H	R	HR	HB	BB-IB	SO	ERA	AERA	OAV	OOB	AB-SH	AVG	PB	Sup	APR	PW
ROY, LUTHER Luther Franklin B 7.29.1902 Ooltewah, TN D 7.24.1963 Grand Rapids, MI BR/TR 5-10.5/161# d6.12 b-Charlie																									
1924	Cle A	0	5	.000	16	5	2	0	48.2	62	48	3	0	31	14	7.77	55	.318	.412	15-1	.267	-0	63	-17	-1.4
1925	Cle A	0	0	—	6	1	0	0	10	14	7	1	0	11	1	3.60	123	.368	.510	2-0	.000	-0	76	0	-0.1
1927	Chi N	3	1	.750	11	0	0	0	19.2	14	9	0	1	11	5	2.29	169	.209	.329	3-0	.333	0		2	0.4
1929	Phi N	3	6	.333	21	11	1	0	88.2	137	91	11	3	37	16	8.42	62	.350	.411	32-0	.281	2	108	-28	-2.0
	Bro N	0	0	—	2	0	0	0	3.2	4	2	0	0	2	0	4.91	94	.286	.375	1-0	.000	-0		0	0.0
	Year	3	6	.333	23	11	1	0	92.1	141	99	11	3	39	16	8.29	62	.348	.409	33-0	.273	2	109	-28	-2.0
Total	4	6	12	.333	56	17	3	0	170.2	231	157	15	4	92	36	7.17	66	.328	.408	53-1	.264	2	98	-43	-3.1
ROY, NORMIE Norman Brooks "Jumbo" B 11.15.1928 Newton, MA BR/TR 6/200# d4.23																									
1950	Bos N	4	3	.571	19	6	2	1	59.2	72	38	6	2	39	25	5.13	75	.305	.408	18-1	.167	0	126	-9	-0.9
ROZEK, DICK Richard Louis B 3.27.1927 Cedar Rapids, IA D 9.27.2001 LaQuinta, CA BL/TL 6-0.5/190# d4.29																									
1950	Cle A	0	0	—	12	2	0	0	25.1	28	15	3	0	19	14	4.97	87	.283	.398	5-1	.000	-1	177	-1	-0.2
1951	Cle A	0	0	—	7	1	0	0	15.1	18	12	1	1	11	5	2.93	129	.286	.400	3-0	.333	0	164	-1	-0.1
1952	Cle A	1	0	1.000	10	1	0	0	12.2	11	8	0	0	13	5	4.97	67	.224	.387	2-0	.000	-0	209	-2	-0.2
1953	Phi A	0	0	—	2	0	0	0	10.2	8	6	3	0	9	2	5.06	85	.222	.378	2-0	.000	-0		-1	0.0
1954	Phi A	0	0	—	2	0	0	0	1.1	0	1	0	1	3	0	6.75	58	.000	.500	0-0	—	0		0	0.0
Total	5	1	0	1.000	33	4	0	0	65.1	65	42	7	2	55	26	4.55	88	.260	.396	12-1	.083	-1	178	-5	-0.5
ROZEMA, DAVE David Scott B 8.5.1956 Grand Rapids, MI BR/TR 6-4/200# d4.11																									
1977	Det A	15	7	.682	28	28	16-1	0-0	218.1	222	87	25	7	34-4	92	3.09	139	.265	.298	0-0	—	0	110	27	2.5
1978	Det A	9	12	.429	28	28	11-2	0-0	209.1	205	83	17	2	41-1	57	3.14	124	.260	.297	0-0	—	0	87	16	1.4
1979	Det A	4	4	.500	16	16	4-1	0-0	97.1	101	52	12	6	30-2	33	3.51	124	.270	.329	0-0	—	0	108	4	0.3
1980	Det A	6	9	.400	42	13	2-1	4-1	144.2	152	68	11	5	49-14	49	3.92	105	.277	.339	0-0	—	0	117	3	0.4
1981	Det A	5	5	.500	28	9	2-2	3-2	104	99	42	12	3	25-8	46	3.63	104	.256	.305	0-0	—	0	58	3	0.2
1982	Det A	3	0	1.000	8	2	0	1-0	27.2	17	5	2	1	7-1	15	1.63	250	.179	.243	0-0	—	0	67	8	0.9
1983	Det A	8	3	.727	29	16	1	2-0	105	100	50	10	1	29-6	63	3.43	114	.248	.297	0-0	—	0	140	3	0.4
1984	Det A	7	6	.538	29	16	0	0-0	101	110	49	13	2	18-3	48	3.74	105	.274	.307	0-0	—	0	96	1	0.2
1985	Tex A	3	7	.300	34	4	0	7-4	88	100	45	10	2	22-3	42	4.19	101	.287	.332	0-0	—	0	64	0	0.1
1986	Tex A	0	0	—	6	0	0	0-0	10.2	19	9	1	0	3-0	3	5.91	73	.404	.423	0-0	—	0		-2	-0.1
Total	10	60	53	.531	248	132	36-7	17-7	1106	1125	490	113	29	258-42	448	3.47	117	.266	.310	0-0	—	0	102	63	6.3
RUBIO, JORGE Jorge Jesus (Chavez) B 4.23.1945 Mexicali, Mexico BR/TR 6-3/200# d4.21																									
1966	Cal A	2	1	.667	7	4	1-1	0	27.1	22	10	2	1	16-1	27	2.96	113	.220	.333	8-1	.000	-1	52	1	0.0
1967	Cal A	0	2	.000	3	3	0	0	15	18	7	2	4	9-0	4	3.60	87	.316	.443	3-0	.333	1	18	-1	0.0
Total	2	2	3	.400	10	7	1-1	0	42.1	40	17	4	5	25-1	31	3.19	103	.255	.374	11-1	.091	-0	38	0	0.0
RUCKER, DAVE David Michael B 9.1.1957 San Bernardino, CA BL/TL 6-1/190# d4.12																									
1981	Det A	0	0	—	2	0	0	0-0	4	3	4	0	1	1-0	2	6.75	56	.188	.278	0-0	—	0		-2	-0.1
1982	Det A	5	6	.455	27	4	1	0-2	64	62	26	4	2	23-3	31	3.38	121	.251	.320	0-0	—	0	78	5	0.8
1983	Det A	1	2	.333	4	3	0	0-0	9	18	17	2	1	8-0	6	17.00	23	.419	.519	0-0	—	0	147	-13	-1.9
	StL N	5	3	.625	34	0	0	0-0	37	36	14	1	1	18-0	22	2.43	149	.263	.353	4-0	.000	-0		4	0.7
1984	StL N	2	3	.400	50	0	0	0-1	73	62	23	0	1	34-2	38	2.10	166	.237	.324	7-0	.143	-0		10	0.6
1985	Phi N	3	2	.600	39	3	0	1-1	79.1	83	42	6	2	40-6	41	4.31	86	.279	.361	12-1	.333	2*	120	-5	-0.1
1986	Phi N	0	2	.000	19	0	0	0-0	25	34	19	4	0	14-3	14	5.76	67	.340	.410	1-0	.000	-0		-5	-0.4
1988	Pit N	0	2	.000	31	0	0	0-0	28.1	39	19	2	0	9-1	16	4.76	72	.328	.369	2-0	.000	-0		-5	-0.4
Total	7	16	20	.444	206	10	1	1-4	319.2	337	164	19	8	147-15	170	3.94	94	.276	.354	26-1	.192	1	115	-11	-0.8
RUCKER, NAP George B 9.30.1884 Crabapple, GA D 12.19.1970 Alpharetta, GA BR/TL 5-11/190# d4.15																									
1907	Bro N	15	13	.536	37	30	26-4	0	275.1	242	94	3	8	80	131	2.06	114	.242	.303	97-3	.155	-1	104	8	0.7
1908	Bro N	17	19	.472	42	37	30-6	1	333.1	265	107	1	19	125	199	2.08	113	.231	.317	117-1	.179	-1	75	9	1.2
1909	Bro N	13	19	.406	38	33	28-6	1	309.1	245	95	6	14	101	201	2.24	116	.228	.303	101-7	.119	-5	70	14	0.8
1910	Bro N	17	18	.486	41	**39**	**27-6**	0	**320.1**	293	112	5	9	84	147	2.58	117	.251	.306	110-4	.209	-1	77	18	1.7
1911	Bro N	22	18	.550	48	33	23-5	4	315.2	255	102	12	8	110	190	2.71	123	.226	.300	104-7	.202	2	61	30	3.9
1912	Bro N	18	21	.462	45	34	23-**6**	4	297.2	272	101	6	3	72	151	2.21	152	.250	.298	102-4	.245	2	91	37	5.1
1913	Bro N	14	15	.483	41	33	16-4	3	260	236	99	3	7	67	111	2.87	115	.249	.304	87-2	.241	2	72	14	1.6
1914	Bro N	7	6	.538	16	16	5	0	103.2	113	57	2	2	27	35	3.39	84	.275	.323	34-3	.265	2	102	-6	-0.5
1915	Bro N	9	4	.692	19	15	7-1	1	122.2	134	42	3	2	28	38	2.42	115	.279	.322	42-0	.214	1	95	6	0.9
1916	†Bro N	2	1	.667	9	4	1	0	37.1	34	14	0	1	7	14	1.69	159	.241	.282	11-0	.091	-1	118	3	0.1
Total	10	134	134	.500	336	274	186-38	14	2375.1	2089	823	41	73	701	1217	2.42	119	.243	.306	805-31	.195	1	81	133	15.5
RUDOLPH, ERNIE Ernest William B 2.13.1909 Black River Falls, WI D 1.13.2003 Black River Falls, WI BL/TR 5-8/165# d6.16																									
1945	Bro N	1	0	1.000	7	0	0	0	8.2	12	10	1	0	7	3	5.19	72	.333	.442	0-0	—	1		-3	-0.2
RUDOLPH, DON Frederick Donald B 8.16.1931 Baltimore, MD D 9.12.1968 Granada Hills, CA BL/TL 5-11/195# d9.21																									
1957	Chi A	1	0	1.000	5	0	0	0	12	6	3	2	0	2-0	2	2.25	166	.146	.186	2-0	.500	1		2	0.2
1958	Chi A	1	0	1.000	7	0	0	1	7	4	2	0	0	5-1	2	2.57	141	.190	.346	0-0	—	0		1	0.2
1959	Chi A	0	0	—	4	0	0	1	3	4	0	0	0	2-1	0	0.00	—	.333	.429	0-0	—	0		1	0.1
	Cin N	0	0	—	5	0	0	0	7.1	13	4	1	0	3-1	8	4.91	83	.394	.444	1-0	.000	-0		0	0.0
1962	Cle A	0	0	—	1	0	0	0	0.1	1	0	0	0	0-0	0	0.00	—	1.000	1.000	0-0	—	0		0	0.0
	Was A	8	10	.444	37	23	6-2	0	176.1	187	84	13	3	42-2	68	3.62	111	.274	.316	57-1	.175	1	92	5	0.6
	Year	8	10	.444	38	23	6-2	0	176.2	188	88	13	3	42-2	68	3.62	112	.275	.317	57-1	.175	1	92	6	0.6
1963	Was A	7	19	.269	37	26	4	1	174	189	98	28	6	36-3	70	4.55	82	.275	.314	45-5	.178	2	77	-15	-1.9
1964	Was A	1	3	.250	28	8	0	0	70.1	81	36	10	0	12-5	32	4.09	90	.290	.317	15-0	.067	-1	54	-3	-0.2
Total	6	18	32	.360	124	57	10-2	3	450.1	485	227	54	9	102-13	182	4.00	96	.276	.317	120-6	.167	3	81	-9	-1.0
RUDOLPH, DICK Richard "Baldy" B 8.25.1887 New York, NY D 10.20.1949 Bronx, NY BR/TR 5-9.5/160# d9.30 M1 C7																									
1910	NY N	0	1	.000	3	1	1	2	12	21	11	0	0	2	9	7.50	40	.350	.371	4-0	.250	0	50	-5	-0.6
1911	NY N	0	0	—	1	0	0	0	2	2	2	0	0	0	0	9.00	37	.250	.250	1-0	1.000	0		-1	0.0
1913	Bos N	14	13	.519	33	22	17-2	0	249.1	258	101	4	2	59	109	2.92	112	.276	.320	88-4	.239	4*	92	14	2.2
1914	†Bos N	26	10	.722	42	36	31-6	0	336.1	288	105	9	4	61	138	2.35	117	.238	.276	120-5	.125	-1*	112	18	1.9
1915	Bos N	22	19	.537	44	**43**	30-3	1	341.1	304	125	4	6	64	147	2.37	109	.242	.282	116-4	.198	6*	109	7	1.6
1916	Bos N	19	12	.613	41	38	27-5	3	312	266	93	7	3	38	133	2.16	115	.235	**.261**	101-4	.158	1	93	14	1.9
1917	Bos N	13	14	.481	31	30	22-5	0	242.2	252	104	1	4	54	96	3.41	75	.272	.314	87-7	.230	3*	123	-20	-1.8
1918	Bos N	9	10	.474	21	20	15-3	0	154	144	63	2	0	30	48	2.57	104	.255	.292	54-3	.185	-1	66	0	-0.1
1919	Bos N	13	18	.419	37	32	24-2	2	273.2	282	95	2	3	54	76	2.17	132	.276	.314	88-1	.193	3	80	16	2.3
1920	Bos N	4	8	.333	18	11	3	0	89	104	57	4	4	24	24	4.04	75	.294	.346	27-2	.185	-0	96	-13	-1.7
1922	Bos N	0	2	.000	3	3	1	0	16	22	10	2	0	5	3	5.06	79	.328	.375	5-0	.400	1	88	-1	-0.1
1923	Bos N	1	2	.333	4	4	1-1	0	19.1	27	12	0	1	10	3	3.72	107	.333	.413	7-0	.000	-1	88	0	-0.1
1927	Bos N	0	0	—	1	0	0	0	1.1	1	0	0	0	1	0	0.00	—	.200	.333	0-0	—	0		1	0.0
Total	13	121	109	.526	279	240	172-27	8	2049	1971	778	35	27	402	786	2.66	104	.258	.298	698-30	.188	14	97	30	5.5
RUEBEL, MATT Matthew Alexander B 10.16.1969 Cincinnati, OH BL/TL 6-2/180# d5.21																									
1996	Pit N	1	1	.500	26	7	0	1-0	58.2	64	38	7	6	25-0	22	4.60	95	.277	.358	13-2	.231	1	121	-4	-0.1
1997	Pit N	3	2	.600	44	0	0	0-1	62.2	77	50	8	5	27-3	50	6.32	68	.301	.372	7-1	.000	-1		-14	-1.1
1998	TB A	0	2	.000	7	1	0	0-0	8.2	11	7	3	0	4-0	6	6.23	77	.314	.385	0-0	—	0	39	-2	-0.3
Total	3	4	5	.444	77	8	0	1-1	130	152	95	18	11	56-3	78	5.54	79	.291	.367	20-3	.150	-0	113	-20	-1.5
RUETER, KIRK Kirk Wesley B 12.1.1970 Hoyleton, IL BL/TL 6-3/195# d7.7																									
1993	Mon N	8	0	1.000	14	14	1	0-0	85.2	85	33	5	0	18-1	31	2.73	153	.264	.303	26-8	.077	-1	111	12	1.1
1994	Mon N	7	3	.700	20	20	0	0-0	92.1	106	60	11	2	23-1	50	5.17	82	.294	.335	34-2	.118	-1	134	-10	-1.0
1995	Mon N	5	3	.625	9	9	1-1	0-0	47.1	38	17	3	1	9-0	28	3.23	133	.224	.267	16-2	.000	-2	96	6	0.8
1996	Mon N	5	6	.455	16	16	0	0-0	78.2	91	44	12	2	22-0	30	4.58	95	.294	.344	25-2	.120	-1	130	-2	-0.2
	SF N	1	2	.333	4	3	0	0-0	23.1	18	6	0	0	5-0	16	1.93	212	.207	.250	7-0	.143	0	51	6	0.7

Year	Tm Lg	W	L	Pct	G	GS	CG-Sho	SV-BS	IP	H	R	HR	HB	BB-IB	SO	ERA	AERA	OAV	OOB	AB-SH	AVG	PB	Sup	APR	PW
	Year	6	8	.429	20	19	0	0-0	102	109	8	12	2	27-0	46	3.97	108	.275	.324	32-2	.125	-1	119	3	0.5
1997	†SF N	13	6	.684	32	32	0	0-0	190.2	194	83	17	1	51-8	115	3.45	119	.264	.311	65-7	.138	-1	118	13	1.4
1998	SF N	16	9	.640	33	33	1	0-0	187.2	193	100	27	7	57-3	102	4.36	91	.265	.321	67-9	.209	1*	141	-10	-0.9
1999	SF N	15	10	.600	33	33	1	0-0	184.2	219	118	28	2	55-2	94	5.41	78	.297	.346	58-8	.155	1	125	-25	-2.6
2000	†SF N	11	9	.550	32	31	0	0-0	184	205	92	23	2	62-5	71	3.96	107	.290	.345	60-10	.200	2*	119	5	0.8
2001	SF N	14	12	.538	34	34	0	0-0	195.1	213	105	25	4	66-4	83	4.42	90	.283	.341	58-10	.172	2*	120	-10	-0.8
2002	†SF N	14	8	.636	33	33	0	0-0	203.2	204	83	22	1	54-7	76	3.23	120	.262	.308	62-13	.177	0*	118	14	1.5
2003	†SF N	10	5	.667	27	27	0	0-0	147	170	77	14	1	47-2	41	4.53	91	.297	.350	53-6	.132	-1	128	-6	-0.5
Total	11	119	73	.620	287	285	4-1	0-0	1620.1	1736	818	187	23	469-33	737	4.11	100	.277	.328	531-77	.154	1	123	-7	0.3
RUETHER, DUTCH Walter Henry B 9.13.1893 Alameda, CA D 5.16.1970 Phoenix, AZ BL/TL 6-1.5/180# d4.13 Mil 1918 ▲																									
1917	Chi N	2	0	1.000	10	4	1	0	36.1	37	12	0	3	12	23	2.48	117	.285	.359	44-1	.273	2*	162	2	0.4
	Cin N	1	2	.333	7	4	1-1	0	35.2	43	17	0	2	14	12	3.53	74	.323	.396	24-0	.208	1*	101	-3	-0.1
	Year	3	2	.600	17	8	2-1	0	72	80	21	0	5	26	35	3.00	92	.304	.378	68-1	.250	3	133	-1	0.3
1918	Cin N	0	1	.000	2	2	1	0	10	10	9	0	1	3	10	2.70	99	.244	.311	3-0	.000	-0	28	-2	-0.2
1919	†Cin N	19	6	**.760**	33	29	20-3	0	242.2	195	69	1	7	83	78	1.82	153	.223	.295	92-3	.261	6*	117	24	3.1
1920	Cin N	16	12	.571	37	33	23-5	3	265.2	235	87	2	9	96	99	2.47	123	.247	.321	104-2	.192	-1*	93	19	2.0
1921	Bro N	10	13	.435	36	27	12-1	2	211.1	247	116	7	7	67	78	4.26	91	.299	.356	97-2	.351	11*	89	-6	0.5
1922	Bro N	21	12	.636	35	35	26-2	0	267.1	290	123	11	6	92	89	3.53	115	.282	.345	125-5	.208	6*	96	18	2.5
1923	Bro N	15	14	.517	34	34	20	0	275	308	157	11	6	86	87	4.22	92	.287	.343	117-2	.274	4*	116	-8	-0.2
1924	Bro N	8	13	.381	30	21	13-2	3	168	190	92	4	5	45	63	3.91	96	.282	.332	62-1	.242	2*	86	-4	-0.2
1925	†Was A	18	7	.720	30	29	16-1	0	223.1	241	105	5	8	105	68	3.87	109	.281	.365	108-3	.333	6*	120	14	2.2
1926	Was A	12	6	.667	23	23	9	0	169.1	214	100	5	4	66	48	4.84	80	.311	.375	92-3	.250	4*	134	-16	-1.1
	†NY A	2	3	.400	5	5	1	0	36	32	14	0	1	18	8	3.50	110	.248	.345	21-0	.095	-2*	79	3	0.1
	Year	14	9	.609	28	28	10	0	205.1	246	18	5	5	84	56	4.60	84	.301	.370	113-3	.221	3	125	-14	-1.0
1927	NY A	13	6	.684	27	26	12-3	0	184	202	88	8	7	52	45	3.38	114	.287	.343	80-0	.262	5*	132	9	1.2
Total	11	137	95	.591	309	272	155-18	8	2124.2	2244	989	54	66	739	708	3.50	104	.277	.342	969-22	.258	45	109	50	10.2
RUFFCORN, SCOTT Scott Patrick B 12.29.1969 Austin, TX BR/TR 6-4/210# d6.19																									
1993	Chi A	0	2	.000	3	2	0	0-0	10	9	11	2	0	10-0	2	8.10	52	.265	.422	0-0	—	0	66	-5	-0.8
1994	Chi A	0	2	.000	2	2	0	0-0	6.1	15	11	1	0	5-0	3	12.79	37	.455	.513	0-0	—	0	49	-6	-0.9
1995	Chi A	0	0	—	4	0	0	0-0	8	10	7	0	2	13-0	5	7.88	57	.333	.556	0-0	—	0		-3	-0.1
1996	Chi A	0	1	.000	3	1	0	0-0	6.1	10	8	1	0	6-0	3	11.37	42	.370	.485	0-0	—	0	39	-5	-0.5
1997	Phi N	0	3	.000	18	4	0	0-0	39.2	42	40	4	7	36-1	33	7.71	55	.275	.423	6-1	.000	-0	81	-16	-1.1
Total	5	0	8	.000	30	9	0	0-0	70.1	86	77	8	9	70-1	46	8.57	51	.310	.455	6-1	.000	-0	66	-35	-3.4
RUFFIN, BRUCE Bruce Wayne B 10.4.1963 Lubbock, TX BB/TL 6-2/209# d6.28																									
1986	Phi N	9	4	.692	21	21	6	0-0	146.1	138	53	6	1	44-6	70	2.46	157	.251	.306	55-1	.073	-3	111	19	1.2
1987	Phi N	11	14	.440	35	35	3-1	0-0	204.2	236	118	17	2	73-4	93	4.35	98	.298	.355	73-6	.055	-5	83	-6	-1.1
1988	Phi N	6	10	.375	55	15	3	3-2	144.1	151	86	7	3	80-6	82	4.43	81	.275	.368	33-0	.121	-0	73	-17	-1.8
1989	Phi N	6	10	.375	24	23	1	0-0	125.2	152	69	10	0	62-6	70	4.44	80	.301	.377	34-1	.176	2	104	-12	-1.0
1990	Phi N	6	13	.316	32	25	2-1	0-0	149	178	99	14	1	62-7	79	5.38	71	.297	.361	44-6	.068	-2	100	-26	-3.0
1991	Phi N	4	7	.364	31	15	1-1	0-0	119	125	52	6	1	38-3	85	3.78	97	.272	.327	24-6	.000	-1	83	-1	-0.2
1992	Mil A	1	6	.143	25	6	1	0-2	58	66	43	7	0	41-3	45	6.67	58	.293	.398	0-0	—	0	67	-17	-1.8
1993	Col N	6	5	.545	59	12	0	2-1	139.2	145	71	10	1	69-9	126	3.87	124	.269	.350	25-3	.080	-1	110	10	0.7
1994	Col N	4	5	.444	56	0	0	16-5	55.2	55	28	6	1	30-2	65	4.04	123	.253	.343	4-0	.250	0		4	0.9
1995	†Col N	0	1	.000	37	0	0	11-1	34	26	8	1	0	19-1	23	2.12	255	.222	.331	2-0	.000	-0		10	0.8
1996	Col N	7	5	.583	71	0	0	24-5	69.2	55	35	5	0	29-3	74	4.00	130	.212	.288	1-0	.000	0		7	1.4
1997	Col N	0	2	.000	23	0	0	7-2	22	18	15	3	0	18-0	31	5.32	97	.220	.360	0-0	—	0		-1	-0.1
Total	12	60	82	.423	469	152	17-3	63-18	1268	1345	677	92	10	565-50	843	4.19	98	.275	.348	295-23	.081	-10	89	-30	-4.0
RUFFIN, JOHNNY Johnny Renando B 7.29.1971 Butler, AL BR/TR 6-3/172# d8.8																									
1993	Cin N	2	1	.667	21	0	0	2-1	37.2	36	16	4	1	11-1	30	3.58	112	.247	.304	3-0	.333	0		2	0.2
1994	Cin N	7	2	.778	51	0	0	1-2	70	57	26	7	0	27-3	44	3.09	134	.223	.295	8-0	.000	-1		9	0.9
1995	Cin N	0	0	—	10	0	0	0-0	13.1	4	3	0	0	11-0	11	1.35	305	.093	.278	2-0	.000	-0		4	0.2
1996	Cin N	1	3	.250	49	0	0	0-1	62.1	71	42	10	2	37-5	69	5.49	77	.292	.386	4-0	.500	1		-9	-0.4
2000	Ari N	0	0	—	5	0	0	0-0	9	14	9	4	0	3-1	5	9.00	52	.350	.395	0-0	—	0		-4	-0.2
2001	Fla N	0	0	—	3	0	0	0-0	3.2	5	4	0	1	4-1	4	4.91	86	.313	.476	0-0	—	0		-1	-0.1
Total	6	10	6	.625	139	0	0	3-4	196	187	100	25	4	93-11	163	4.13	101	.251	.336	17-0	.176	-0		1	0.6
RUFFING, RED Charles Herbert B 5.3.1904 Granville, IL D 2.17.1986 Mayfield Hts., OH BR/TR 6-1.5/205# d5.31 Mil 1943-44 C1 HF1967 ▲																									
1924	Bos A	0	0	—	8	2	0	0	23	29	17	0	3	9	10	6.65	66	.333	.414	7-0	.143	-0	135	-4	-0.2
1925	Bos A	9	18	.333	37	27	13-3	1	217.1	253	135	10	2	75	64	5.01	91	.299	.357	79-2	.215	-0	88	-4	-0.5
1926	Bos A	6	15	.286	37	22	6	2	166	169	96	4	5	68	58	4.39	93	.274	.351	51-2	.196	0	69	-6	-0.8
1927	Bos A	5	13	.278	26	18	10	2	158.1	160	94	7	4	87	77	4.66	91	.277	.375	55-6	.255	1*	72	-6	-0.4
1928	Bos A	10	25	.286	42	34	**25**-1	2	289.1	303	147	8	10	96	118	3.89	106	.275	.339	121-7	.314	11*	71	6	1.8
1929	Bos A	9	22	.290	35	32	18-1	1	244.1	280	162	17	2	118	109	4.86	88	.297	.376	114-3	.307	5*	76	-18	-1.1
1930	Bos A	0	3	.000	4	3	1	0	24	32	19	1	1	6	14	6.38	72	.323	.368	11-0	.273	1*	56	-5	-0.4
	NY A	15	5	.750	34	25	12-2	1	197.2	200	106	10	2	62	117	4.14	104	.260	.317	99-0	.374	17*	130	6	1.9
	Year	15	8	.652	38	28	13-2	1	221.2	232	113	11	3	68	131	4.38	99	.268	.323	110-0	.364	18	122	1	1.5
1931	NY A	16	14	.533	37	30	19-1	2	237	240	130	11	6	87	132	4.41	90	.256	.323	109-6	.330	11*	143	-11	-0.1
1932	†NY A	18	7	.720	35	29	22-3	2	259	219	102	16	3	115	**190**	3.09	132	**.226**	.311	124-2	.306	14*	129	32	4.0
1933	NY A	9	14	.391	35	28	18	3	235	230	118	7	4	93	122	3.91	99	.258	.330	115-2	.252	8*	111	0	0.7
1934	NY A★	19	11	.633	36	31	19-5	0	256.1	232	134	18	1	104	149	3.93	103	.236	.310	113-0	.248	7*	122	2	0.7
1935	NY A	16	11	.593	30	29	19-2	0	222	201	88	17	1	76	81	3.12	130	.239	.303	109-1	.339	14*	103	27	4.2
1936	†NY A	20	12	.625	33	33	25-3	0	271	274	133	22	3	90	102	3.85	121	.263	.323	127-2	.291	16*	119	25	3.9
1937	†NY A	20	7	.741	31	31	22-4	0	256.1	242	101	17	1	68	131	2.98	149	.247	.296	129-2	.202	3*	137	43	4.0
1938	†NY A☆	**21**	7	**.750**	31	31	22-3	0	247.1	246	104	16	0	82	127	3.31	137	.258	.317	107-1	.224	10*	127	**37**	**4.5**
1939	†NY A★	21	7	.750	28	28	22-**5**	0	233.1	211	88	15	2	75	95	2.93	149	.240	.301	114-3	.307	9*	152	38	4.8
1940	NY A★	15	12	.556	30	30	20-3	0	226	218	98	24	3	76	97	3.38	119	.252	.314	89-1	.124	-3*	99	17	1.3
1941	†NY A☆	15	6	.714	23	23	13-2	0	185.2	177	87	13	1	54	60	3.54	111	.252	.306	89-1	.303	12*	136	7	1.7
1942	†NY A☆	14	7	.667	24	24	16-4	0	193.2	183	72	10	3	41	80	3.21	107	.250	.292	80-2	.250	7*	142	9	1.5
1945	NY A	7	3	.700	11	11	8-1	0	87.1	85	32	2	1	20	24	2.89	120	.251	.294	46-0	.217	1*	132	6	0.6
1946	NY A	5	1	.833	8	8	4-2	0	61	37	13	2	0	23	19	1.77	195	.171	.251	25-0	.120	-1	102	12	1.0
1947	Chi A	3	5	.375	9	9	1	0	53	63	39	7	0	16	11	6.11	60	.290	.339	24-0	.208	-0*	118	-13	-1.7
Total	22	273	225	.548	624	538	335-45	16	4344	4284	2115	254	58	1541	1987	3.80	109	.258	.323	1937-43	.269	143	112	200	31.4
RUHLE, VERN Vernon Gerald B 1.25.1951 Coleman, MI BR/TR 6-1/187# d9.9 C6																									
1974	Det A	2	0	1.000	5	3	1	0-0	33	35	13	1	1	6-0	10	2.73	140	.273	.307	0-0	—	0	108	3	0.1
1975	Det A	11	12	.478	32	31	8-3	0-0	190	199	104	17	7	65-6	67	4.03	100	.266	.328	0-0	—	0	90	-1	-0.3
1976	Det A	9	12	.429	32	32	5-1	0-0	199.2	227	99	19	4	59-4	88	3.92	95	.288	.339	0-0	—	0	99	-4	-0.4
1977	Det A	3	5	.375	14	10	0	0-0	66.1	83	44	9	3	15-0	27	5.70	75	.305	.346	0-0	—	0	65	-8	-0.9
1978	Hou N	3	3	.500	13	10	2-2	0-0	68	57	17	0	1	20-1	27	2.12	156	.224	.282	18-1	.056	-1	95	10	0.7
1979	Hou N	2	6	.250	13	10	2-2	0-1	66.1	64	33	9	2	8-0	33	4.07	86	.249	.277	19-2	.053	-1	86	-4	-0.6
1980	†Hou N	12	4	.750	28	22	6-2	0-0	159.1	148	51	7	3	29-1	55	2.37	139	.251	.287	49-4	.245	4	97	17	2.1
1981	†Hou N	4	6	.400	20	15	1	1-1	102	97	36	6	1	20-1	39	2.91	113	.250	.288	24-4	.250	3	97	5	0.8
1982	Hou N	9	13	.409	31	21	3-2	1-1	149	169	81	12	4	24-4	56	3.93	85	.289	.319	41-5	.098	-0	80	-14	-2.1
1983	Hou N	8	5	.615	41	9	0	3-0	114.2	107	49	13	3	36-7	43	3.69	92	.249	.308	19-4	.105	0	107	-1	-0.1
1984	Hou N	1	9	.100	40	6	0	2-0	90.1	112	58	5	3	29-7	60	4.58	73	.309	.363	12-0	.083	0	106	-15	-1.6
1985	Cle A	2	10	.167	42	16	1	3-1	125	139	65	16	2	30-6	54	4.32	96	.283	.324	0-0	—	0	71	-2	-0.2
1986	†Cal A	1	3	.250	16	3	0	1-0	47.2	46	25	5	1	7-0	23	4.15	99	.247	.276	0-0	—	0	81	-1	0.0
Total	13	67	88	.432	327	188	29-12	11-4	1411.1	1483	675	119	35	348-37	582	3.73	97	.270	.316	182-20	.148	6	90	-15	-2.5

Year	Tm Lg	W	L	Pct	G	GS	CG-Sho	SV-BS	IP	H	R	HR	HB	BB-IB	SO	ERA	AERA	OAV	OOB	AB-SH	AVG	PB	Sup	APR	PW
RUNYAN, SEAN Sean David B 6.21.1974 Fort Smith, AR BL/TL 6-3/200# d3.31																									
1998	Det A	1	4	.200	**88**	0	0	1-2	50.1	47	23	7	2	28-3	39	3.58	132	.255	.348	0-0	—	0		6	0.5
1999	Det A	0	1	.000	12	0	0	0-0	10.2	9	4	2	1	3-1	6	3.38	147	.237	.295	0-0	—	0		2	0.2
2000	Det A	0	0	—	3	0	0	0-0	3	2	2	0	0	2-0	1	6.00	80	.222	.333	0-0	—	0		0	0.0
Total	3	1	5	.167	103	0	0	1-2	64	58	29	9	3	33-4	46	3.66	130	.251	.339	0-0	—	0		8	0.7
RUPE, RYAN Ryan Kittman B 3.31.1975 Houston, TX BR/TR 6-6/240# d5.5																									
1999	TB A	8	9	.471	24	24	0	0-0	142.1	136	81	17	12	57-2	97	4.55	109	.253	.334	4-0	.000	-0	85	7	0.6
2000	TB A	5	6	.455	18	18	0	0-0	91	121	75	19	9	31-3	61	6.92	71	.321	.381	1-0	.000	-0	100	-19	-1.9
2001	TB A	5	12	.294	28	26	0	0-1	143.1	161	111	30	11	48-0	123	6.59	68	.283	.348	3-0	.333	1	89	-30	-2.9
2002	TB A	5	10	.333	15	15	2	0-0	90	83	60	11	10	25-0	67	5.60	80	.243	.311	1-0	.000	-0	76	-11	-1.6
2003	Bos A	1	1	.500	4	1	0	0-1	10	13	9	4	0	1-0	7	6.30	72	.302	.318	0-0	—	0	81	-2	-0.4
Total	5	24	38	.387	89	84	2	0-2	476.2	514	336	81	42	162-5	355	5.85	81	.275	.343	9-0	.111	-0	88	-55	-6.2
RUSCH, GLENDON Glendon James B 11.7.1974 Seattle, WA BL/TL 6-2/170# d4.6																									
1997	KC A	6	9	.400	30	27	1	0-0	170.1	206	111	28	7	52-0	116	5.50	86	.301	.353	3-0	.000	-0	90	-13	-1.1
1998	KC A	6	15	.286	29	24	1-1	1-0	154.2	191	104	22	4	50-0	94	5.88	82	.304	.358	3-0	.000	-0	75	-15	-1.7
1999	KC A	0	1	.000	3	0	0	0-0	4	7	7	1	1	3-0	4	15.75	32	.368	.478	0-0	—	0		-4	-0.7
	NY N	0	0	—	1	0	0	0-0	1	1	0	0	0	0-0	0	0.00	—	.333	.333	0-0	—	0		1	0.0
2000	†NY N	11	11	.500	31	30	2	0-0	190.2	196	91	18	6	44-2	157	4.01	110	.267	.311	50-4	.060	-3	79	10	0.7
2001	NY N	8	12	.400	33	33	1	0-0	179	216	101	23	7	43-2	156	4.63	89	.300	.344	54-6	.056	-4	71	-11	-1.5
2002	Mil N	10	16	.385	34	34	4-1	0-0	210.2	227	118	30	5	76-1	140	4.70	87	.279	.343	66-14	.288	5*	95	-14	-1.0
2003	Mil N	1	12	.077	32	19	1	1-0	123.1	171	93	11	4	45-3	93	6.42	66	.331	.387	34-4	.206	1*	69	-29	-2.5
Total	7	42	76	.356	193	167	10-2	2-0	1033.2	1215	625	133	34	313-8	760	5.11	86	.295	.348	210-28	.152	-1	81	-75	-7.8
RUSH, ANDY Jesse Howard B 12.26.1889 Longton, KS D 3.16.1969 Fresno, CA BR/TR 6-3/180# d4.16																									
1925	Bro N	0	1	.000	4	2	0	0	9.2	16	14	3	0	5	4	9.31	45	.364	.429	3-0	.000	-0	91	-6	-0.6
RUSH, BOB Robert Ransom B 12.21.1925 Battle Creek, MI BR/TR 6-4/205# d4.22																									
1948	Chi N	5	11	.313	36	16	4	0	133.1	153	70	8	1	37	72	3.92	100	.287	.335	39-2	.128	-2*	54	-1	-0.2
1949	Chi N	10	18	.357	35	27	9-1	4	201	197	104	9	0	79	80	4.07	99	.255	.324	63-5	.032	-7	66	-1	-0.8
1950	Chi N☆	13	20	.394	39	34	19-1	1	254.2	261	124	11	6	93	93	3.71	113	.265	.332	90-1	.167	-1*	66	14	1.7
1951	Chi N	11	12	.478	37	29	12-2	2	211.1	212	108	16	3	68	129	3.83	107	.254	.312	68-4	.191	-0	100	3	0.3
1952	Chi N★	17	13	.567	34	32	17-4	0	250.1	205	99	14	6	81	157	2.70	143	.216	.282	96-2	.292	7	102	26	4.0
1953	Chi N	9	14	.391	29	28	8-1	0	166.2	177	97	17	5	66	84	4.54	98	.270	.341	54-3	.111	-2	71	-2	-0.4
1954	Chi N	13	15	.464	33	32	11	0	236.1	213	102	12	5	103	124	3.77	111	.243	.323	83-1	.277	7	84	15	2.5
1955	Chi N	13	11	.542	33	33	14-3	0	234	204	95	19	2	73-4	130	3.50	117	.234	.293	82-3	.110	-3	95	18	1.4
1956	Chi N	13	10	.565	32	32	13-1	0	239.2	210	101	30	2	59-8	104	3.19	118	.233	.280	82-4	.098	-3	93	14	0.9
1957	Chi N	6	16	.273	31	29	5	0	205.1	211	111	16	2	66-6	103	4.38	88	.265	.318	69-3	.203	2	93	-11	-1.0
1958	†Mil N	10	6	.625	28	20	5-2	0	147.1	142	59	13	1	31-7	84	3.42	103	.253	.291	45-3	.200	2	122	3	0.4
1959	Mil N	5	6	.455	31	9	1-1	0	101.1	102	39	5	1	23-2	64	2.40	148	.257	.298	32-1	.188	0	95	10	1.0
1960	Mil N	2	0	1.000	10	0	0	1	15	24	9	2	0	5-2	8	4.20	82	.369	.403	3-0	.333	1		-2	-0.2
	Chi A	0	0	—	9	0	0	0	14.1	16	10	4	0	5-2	12	5.65	67	.302	.362	1-0	1.000	0		-3	-0.1
Total	13	127	152	.455	417	321	118-16	8	2410.2	2327	1128	176	34	789-31	1244	3.65	109	.251	.311	807-32	.173	0	87	83	9.5
RUSIE, AMOS Amos Wilson "The Hoosier Thunderbolt" B 5.30.1871 Mooresville, IN D 12.6.1942 Seattle, WA BR/TR 6-1/200# d5.9 HF1977																									
1889	Ind N	12	10	.545	33	22	19-1	0	225	246	181	12	9	116	109	5.32	78	.270	.358	103	.175	-3	110	-25	-2.2
1890	NY N	29	34	.460	67	62	56-4	1	548.2	436	300	3	26	289	**341**	2.56	137	**.211**	.316	284	.278	10*	79	50	5.9
1891	NY N	33	20	.623	61	57	52-**6**	1	500.1	391	244	6	18	262	**337**	2.55	125	**.207**	.310	220	.245	4*	110	40	3.9
1892	NY N	32	31	.508	65	62	59-2	0	541	410	290	7	12	270	304	2.84	113	.202	.299	256	.215	0*	99	23	2.5
1893	NY N	33	21	.611	**56**	**52**	**50-4**	1	**482**	451	260	15	16	218	**208**	3.23	144	**.240**	.324	212	.269	3	103	**74**	**6.8**
1894	†NY N	**36**	13	.735	54	**50**	45-**3**	1	444	426	228	10	5	200	**195**	**2.78**	**189**	**.250**	**.330**	186-2	.280	2*	86	**118**	**10.2**
1895	NY N	23	23	.500	49	47	42-**4**	0	393.1	384	248	9	7	159	**201**	3.73	125	.252	.325	179-0	.246	-5*	100	37	2.8
1897	NY N	28	10	.737	38	37	35-2	0	322.1	314	143	6	10	87	135	**2.54**	163	.253	.308	144-0	.278	3*	126	58	5.9
1898	NY N	20	11	.645	37	36	33-4	1	300	288	149	6	9	103	114	3.03	115	.251	.317	138-0	.210	-1*	101	18	1.4
1901	Cin N	0	1	.000	3	2	2	0	22	43	25	1	0	3	6	8.59	37	.406	.422	8-0	.125	-0	44	-12	-0.5
Total	10	246	174	.586	463	427	393-30	5	3778.2	3389	2068	75	112	1707	1950	3.07	130	.234	.319	1730-2	.248	13	99	381	36.7
RUSKIN, SCOTT Scott Drew B 6.8.1963 Jacksonville, FL BR/TL 6-2/185# d4.9																									
1990	Pit N	2	2	.500	44	0	0	2-3	47.2	50	21	2	2	28-3	34	3.02	120	.269	.367	6-0	.333	2		2	0.3
	Mon N	1	0	1.000	23	0	0	0-3	27.2	25	7	2	0	10-3	23	2.28	160	.243	.310	2-0	.000	-0		5	0.2
	Year	3	2	.600	67	0	0	2-6	75.1	75	34	4	2	38-6	57	2.75	132	.260	.347	8-0	.250	1		7	0.5
1991	Mon N	4	4	.500	64	0	0	6-5	63.2	57	31	4	3	30-2	46	4.24	85	.241	.333	2-0	.000	0		-3	-0.4
1992	Cin N	4	3	.571	57	0	0	0-3	53.2	56	31	6	1	20-4	43	5.03	72	.275	.339	3-2	.000	-0		-8	-0.9
1993	Cin N	0	0	—	4	0	0	0-0	1	3	2	1	0	2-0	0	18.00	22	.500	.625	0-0	—	0		-1	-0.1
Total	4	11	9	.550	192	0	0	8-14	193.2	191	92	15	6	90-12	146	3.95	92	.260	.343	13-2	.154	1		-5	-0.9
RUSSELL, ALLAN Allan E. "Rubberarm" B 7.31.1893 Baltimore, MD D 10.20.1972 Baltimore, MD BB/TR 5-11/165# d9.13 b-Lefty																									
1915	NY A	1	2	.333	5	3	1	0	27	21	10	1	1	21	21	2.67	110	.228	.377	8-1	.250	0	50	1	0.1
1916	NY A	6	10	.375	34	19	8-1	6	171.1	138	83	8	7	75	104	3.20	90	.232	.324	45-6	.044	-3*	84	-8	-1.1
1917	NY A	7	8	.467	25	10	6	2	104.1	89	42	2	7	39	55	2.24	120	.236	.319	31-1	.323	3*	72	2	0.7
1918	NY A	7	11	.389	27	18	7-2	4	141	139	68	6	5	73	54	3.26	87	.267	.363	42-4	.167	-1*	90	-9	-1.3
1919	NY A	5	5	.500	23	9	4-1	1	90.2	89	48	5	2	32	50	3.47	92	.251	.317	30-1	.233	0	85	-5	-0.4
	Bos A	10	4	.714	21	11	9-1	4	121.1	105	38	1	1	39	63	2.52	120	.246	.310	41-2	.122	-1	132	9	0.8
	Year	15	9	.625	44	20	13-2	**5**	212	194	43	6	3	71	113	2.93	106	.248	.313	71-3	.169	-1	110	4	0.4
1920	Bos A	5	6	.455	16	10	7	1	107.2	100	44	3	3	38	53	3.01	121	.251	.321	41-2	.122	-2*	98	7	0.5
1921	Bos A	6	11	.353	39	14	7	3	173	204	92	10	9	77	60	4.11	103	.303	.382	57-0	.123	-5*	75	2	-0.3
1922	Bos A	6	7	.462	34	11	1	2	125.2	152	81	6	5	57	34	5.01	82	.314	.392	38-0	.079	-3	51	-12	-1.3
1923	Was A	10	7	.588	52	5	4	**9**	181.1	177	81	9	2	77	67	3.03	124	.270	.348	50-7	.200	2*	83	13	1.2
1924	†Was A	5	1	.833	37	0	0	8	82.1	83	49	1	1	45	17	4.37	92	.282	.379	18-1	.278	2		-4	-0.2
1925	Was A	2	4	.333	32	2	0	2	68.2	85	57	6	1	37	25	5.77	73	.315	.399	14-1	.143	-1	50	-14	-1.1
Total	11	70	76	.479	345	112	54-5	42	1394.1	1382	693	58	44	610	603	3.52	99	.269	.351	415-26	.157	-10	80	-18	-2.4
RUSSELL, LEFTY Clarence Dickson B 7.8.1890 Baltimore, MD D 1.22.1962 Baltimore, MD BL/TL 6-1/165# d10.1 b-Allan																									
1910	Phi A	1	0	1.000	1	1	1-1	0	9	8	0	0	0	2	5	0.00	—	.258	.303	3-0	.000	-0	85	3	0.3
1911	Phi A	0	3	.000	7	2	0	0	31.2	45	32	1	5	18	7	7.67	41	.357	.456	13-0	.385	1	126	-16	-1.1
1912	Phi A	0	2	.000	5	2	1	0	17.1	18	18	1	3	14	9	7.27	42	.265	.412	4-0	.000	-0	72	-8	-0.8
Total	3	1	5	.167	13	5	2-1	0	58	71	50	2	8	34	21	6.36	47	.316	.423	20-0	.250	0	96	-21	-1.6
RUSSELL, REB Ewell Albert B 4.12.1889 Jackson, MS D 9.30.1973 Indianapolis, IN BL/TL 5-11/185# d4.18 ▲																									
1913	Chi A	22	16	.579	**52**	36	26-8	4	316.2	250	89	2	7	79	122	1.90	154	.220	.275	106-4	.189	3*	69	38	4.7
1914	Chi A	7	12	.368	38	23	8-1	1	167.1	168	80	3	3	33	79	2.90	92	.268	.308	64-0	.266	4*	91	-5	-0.2
1915	Chi A	11	10	.524	41	25	10-3	2	229.1	215	90	0	6	47	90	2.59	115	.249	.292	86-2	.244	4*	101	9	1.1
1916	Chi A	18	11	.621	56	25	16-5	3	264.1	207	88	1	1	42	112	2.42	114	.220	**.254**	91-2	.143	-4	103	13	1.0
1917	†Chi A	15	5	**.750**	35	24	11-5	3	189.1	170	61	1	1	32	54	1.95	136	.245	.279	68-4	.279	5*	121	13	2.0
1918	Chi A	7	5	.583	19	15	10-2	0	124.2	117	45	0	0	33	38	2.60	105	.252	.302	50-4	.140	-1*	105	3	0.0
1919	Chi A	0	0	—	1	0	0	0	0	1	0	0	0	1	0	—	—	1.000	1.000	0-0	—	0		0	0.0
Total	7	80	59	.576	242	148	81-24	13	1291.2	1128	453	7	18	267	495	2.33	120	.239	.282	465-16	.209	10	95	71	8.6
RUSSELL, JACK Jack Erwin B 10.24.1905 Paris, TX D 11.3.1990 Clearwater, FL BR/TR 6-1.5/178# d5.5																									
1926	Bos A	0	5	.000	36	5	1	0	98	94	40	2	1	24	17	3.58	114	.268	.316	21-1	.190	-0	87	8	0.6
1927	Bos A	4	9	.308	34	15	4-1	0	147	172	80	5	5	40	25	4.10	103	.298	.348	48-1	.125	-3*	94	2	-0.1
1928	Bos A	11	14	.440	32	26	10-2	0	201.1	233	102	6	4	41	27	3.84	107	.294	.332	62-7	.210	-0*	78	5	0.6
1929	Bos A	6	18	.250	35	32	13	0	227.1	263	132	12	3	40	37	3.92	109	.290	.322	70-5	.129	-4*	76	3	0.1

Year	Tm Lg	W	L	Pct	G	GS	CG-Sho	SV-BS	IP	H	R	HR	HB	BB-IB	SO	ERA	AERA	OAV	OOB	AB-SH	AVG	PB	Sup	APR	PW
1930	Bos A	9	20	.310	35	30	15	0	229.2	302	162	11	3	53	35	5.45	85	.321	.359	79-2	.177	-3*	72	-23	-2.4
1931	Bos A	10	18	.357	36	31	13	0	232	298	145	7	2	65	45	5.16	83	.310	.355	82-4	.195	-0*	78	-19	-1.7
1932	Bos A	1	7	.125	11	6	1	0	39.2	61	35	2	0	15	7	6.81	66	.343	.394	11-1	.091	-1*	57	-10	-1.6
	Cle A	5	7	.417	18	11	6	1	113	146	67	5	1	27	27	4.70	101	.310	.349	40-1	.300	2	87	2	0.4
	Year	6	14	.300	29	17	7	1	152.2	207	72	7	1	42	34	5.25	89	.319	.361	51-2	.255	1	76	-7	-1.2
1933	†Was A	12	6	.667	50	3	2	**13**	124	119	45	3	1	32	28	2.69	156	.255	.305	34-2	.147	-1	122	**20**	3.1
1934	Was A☆	5	10	.333	**54**	9	3	**7**	157.2	179	86	6	2	56	38	4.17	104	.287	.348	44-2	.159	3	99	1	0.5
1935	Was A	4	9	.308	43	7	2	3	126	170	88	10	2	37	30	5.71	76	.324	.371	35-0	.200	1	121	-19	-1.6
1936	Was A	3	2	.600	18	5	1	3	49.2	66	46	3	0	25	6	6.34	75	.317	.391	15-1	.000	-2	181	-11	-1.2
	Bos A	0	3	.000	23	2	0	0	40	57	27	2	0	16	9	5.62	94	.345	.403	7-0	.286	0	8	-1	0.1
	Year	3	5	.375	41	7	1	3	89.2	123	28	5	0	41	15	6.02	83	.330	.396	22-1	.091	-2	125	-12	-1.1
1937	Det A	2	5	.286	25	0	0	4	40.1	63	35	4	1	20	10	7.59	62	.362	.431	7-1	.000	-0		-11	-1.8
1938	†Chi N	6	1	.857	42	0	0	3	102.1	100	43	1	1	30	29	3.34	115	.258	.313	32-1	.219	1		6	0.7
1939	Chi N	4	3	.571	39	0	0	3	68.2	78	32	3	0	24	32	3.67	107	.282	.339	17-0	.000	-2*		2	0.1
1940	StL N	3	4	.429	26	0	0	1	54	53	22	1	0	26	16	2.50	160	.252	.335	13-0	.000	-2		7	0.7
Total	15	85	141	.376	557	182	71-3	38	2050.2	2454	1187	83	26	571	418	4.46	97	.299	.346	617-29	.167	-11	85	-38	-3.5
RUSSELL, JEFF Jeffrey Lee B 9.2.1961 Cincinnati, OH BR/TR 6-3/210# d8.13																									
1983	Cin N	4	5	.444	10	10	2	0-0	68.1	58	30	7	0	22-3	40	3.03	126	.233	.290	21-2	.143	1	86	4	0.6
1984	Cin N	6	18	.250	33	30	4-2	0-0	181.2	186	97	15	4	65-8	101	4.26	89	.263	.327	57-5	.140	-0*	72	-10	-1.2
1985	Tex A	3	6	.333	13	13	0	0-0	62	85	55	10	2	27-1	44	7.55	56	.324	.388	0-0	—	0	96	-21	-2.5
1986	Tex A	5	2	.714	37	0	0	2-0	82	74	40	11	1	31-2	54	3.40	127	.244	.315	0-0	—	0		6	0.5
1987	Tex A	5	4	.556	52	2	0	3-1	97.1	109	56	9	2	52-5	56	4.44	101	.285	.369	0-0	—	0	61	0	0.1
1988	Tex A★	10	9	.526	34	24	5	0-0	188.2	183	86	15	7	66-3	88	3.82	107	.257	.324	1-0	.000	-0*	96	7	0.8
1989	Tex A★	6	4	.600	71	0	0	**38-6**	72.2	45	21	4	3	24-5	77	1.98	200	.182	.260	0-0	—	0		15	3.1
1990	Tex A	1	5	.167	27	0	0	10-2	25.1	23	15	1	0	16-5	16	4.26	92	.253	.361	0-0	—	0		-2	-0.3
1991	Tex A	6	4	.600	68	0	0	30-10	79.1	71	36	11	1	26-1	52	3.29	123	.235	.294	0-0	—	0		5	0.9
1992	Tex A	2	3	.400	51	0	0	28-9	56.2	51	14	3	2	22-3	43	1.91	199	.238	.313	0-0	—	0		12	2.1
	†Oak A	2	0	1.000	8	0	0	2-0	9.2	4	0	0	0	3-0	5	0.00	—	.125	.200	0-0	—	0		4	0.9
	Year	4	3	.571	59	0	0	30-9	66.1	55	18	3	2	25-3	48	1.63	233	.224	.298	0-0	—	0		16	3.0
1993	Bos A	1	4	.200	51	0	0	33-4	46.2	39	16	1	1	14-1	45	2.70	171	.231	.287	0-0	—	0		9	1.9
1994	Bos A	0	5	.000	29	0	0	12-3	28	30	17	3	1	13-2	18	5.14	98	.270	.346	0-0	—	0		0	0.0
	Cle A	1	1	.500	13	0	0	5-3	12.2	13	8	2	0	3-0	10	4.97	95	.265	.308	0-0	—	0		0	-0.1
	Year	1	6	.143	42	0	0	17-6	40.2	43	25	5	1	16-2	28	5.09	97	.269	.335	0-0	—	0		0	-0.1
1995	Tex A	1	0	1.000	37	0	0	20-4	32.2	36	12	3	0	9-1	21	3.03	159	.277	.324	0-0	—	0		6	0.8
1996	†Tex A	3	3	.500	55	0	0	3-3	56	58	22	5	4	22-3	23	3.38	155	.269	.341	0-0	—	0		11	1.1
Total	14	56	73	.434	589	79	11-2	186-45	1099.2	1065	525	100	28	415-43	693	3.75	112	.255	.323	79-7	.139	1	81	46	8.7
RUSSELL, JOHN John Albert B 10.20.1894 San Mateo, CA D 11.19.1930 Ely, NV BL/TL 6-2/195# d7.4 Mil 1918																									
1917	Bro N	0	1	.000	5	1	1	0	16	12	8	1	0	6	1	4.50	62	.222	.300	4-0	.250	0	27	-2	-0.1
1918	Bro N	0	0	—	1	0	0	0	1	2	2	0	0	1	0	18.00	15	.500	.600	0-0	—	0		-1	-0.1
1921	Chi A	2	5	.286	11	9	4	0	66.1	82	42	3	1	35	15	5.29	80	.314	.397	25-1	.400	3	112	-7	-0.3
1922	Chi A	0	1	.000	4	1	0	1	6.2	7	5	0	0	4	3	6.75	60	.280	.379	1-0	.000	-0	125	-2	-0.3
Total	4	2	7	.222	21	11	5	1	90	103	57	4	1	46	19	5.40	73	.299	.384	30-1	.367	3	110	-12	-0.8
RUSSO, MARIUS Marius Ugo "Lefty" B 7.19.1914 Brooklyn, NY BR/TL 6-1/190# d6.6 Mil 1944-45																									
1939	NY A	8	3	.727	21	11	9-2	2	116	86	37	6	1	41	55	2.41	181	.210	.283	41-2	.244	1	131	26	2.4
1940	NY A	14	8	.636	30	24	15	1	189.1	181	79	17	1	55	87	3.28	123	.249	.303	64-6	.188	2	133	17	2.1
1941	†NY A☆	14	10	.583	28	27	17-3	1	209.2	195	85	8	1	87	105	3.09	127	.247	.322	78-5	.231	3	108	20	2.4
1942	NY A	4	1	.800	9	5	2	0	45.1	41	15	2	1	14	15	2.78	124	.244	.306	17-1	.235	1	154	4	0.5
1943	†NY A	5	10	.333	24	14	5-1	1	101.2	89	53	7	2	45	42	3.72	87	.235	.319	31-2	.194	1	92	-7	-0.9
1946	NY A	0	2	.000	8	3	0	0	18.2	26	9	1	0	11	7	4.34	80	.333	.416	4-0	.000	-1*	41	-1	-0.2
Total	6	45	34	.570	120	84	48-6	5	680.2	618	278	41	6	253	311	3.13	124	.242	.312	235-16	.213	8	116	59	6.3
RUSTECK, RICH Richard Frank B 7.12.1941 Chicago, IL BR/TL 6-1/175# d6.10																									
1966	NY N	1	2	.333	8	3	1-1	0	24	24	10	1	0	8-0	9	3.00	121	.276	.337	5-0	.000	-1	113	1	0.1
RUTH, BABE George Herman "The Bambino" or "The Sultan Of Swat" B 2.6.1895 Baltimore, MD D 8.16.1948 New York, NY BL/TL 6-2/215# d7.11 C1 HF1936 ▲																									
1914	Bos A	2	1	.667	4	3	1	0	23	21	12	1	0	7	3	3.91	69	.236	.292	10-0	.200	0*	153	-3	-0.3
1915	†Bos A	18	8	.692	32	28	16-1	0	217.2	166	80	3	6	85	112	2.44	114	.212	.294	92-2	.315	16*	137	8	2.8
1916	†Bos A	23	12	.657	44	**41**	23-**9**	1	323.2	230	83	0	8	118	170	**1.75**	**158**	**.201**	.280	136-4	.272	14*	108	**35**	**5.7**
1917	Bos A	24	13	.649	41	38	**35**-6	2	326.1	244	93	2	11	108	128	2.01	128	.211	.284	123-7	.325	17*	103	22	4.9
1918	†Bos A	13	7	.650	20	19	18-1	0	166.1	125	51	1	2	49	40	2.22	121	.214	.277	317-3	.300	12*	112	10	2.9
1919	Bos A	9	5	.643	17	15	12	1	133.1	148	59	2	2	58	30	2.97	102	.290	.365	432-3	.322	14*	99	-1	1.4
1920	NY A	1	0	1.000	1	1	0	0	4	3	4	0	0	2	0	4.50	85	.200	.294	458-5	.376	1*	291	-1	-0.1
1921	†NY A	2	0	1.000	2	1	0	0	9	14	10	1	0	9	2	9.00	47	.350	.469	540-4	.378	2*	256	-4	-0.6
1930	NY A	1	0	1.000	1	1	1	0	9	11	3	0	0	2	3	3.00	143	.306	.342	518-21	.359	1*	180	2	0.3
1933	NY A★	1	0	1.000	1	1	1	0	9	12	5	0	0	3	0	5.00	78	.308	.357	459-0	.301	1*	131	-1	0.0
Total	10	94	46	.671	163	148	107-17	4	1221.1	974	400	10	29	441	488	2.28	122	.221	.297	3085-49	.338	78	117	67	17.0
RUTHERFORD, JOHNNY John William "Doc" B 5.5.1925 Belleville, ON, CAN BL/TR 5-10.5/170# d4.30																									
1952	†Bro N	7	7	.500	22	11	4	2	97.1	97	51	9	2	29	29	4.25	86	.262	.319	31-1	.290	2	98	-7	-0.7
RUTHVEN, DICK Richard David B 3.27.1951 Sacramento, CA BR/TR 6-3/190# d4.17																									
1973	Phi N	6	9	.400	25	23	3-1	1-0	128.1	125	69	10	3	75-9	98	4.21	90	.257	.358	38-6	.132	-1*	88	-6	-0.8
1974	Phi N	9	13	.409	35	35	6	0-0	212.2	182	106	11	3	116-7	153	4.02	94	.231	.329	68-5	.191	-1	84	-5	-0.7
1975	Phi N	2	2	.500	11	7	0	0-0	40.2	37	22	2	1	22-0	26	4.20	89	.243	.341	13-2	.154	-0*	101	-2	-0.3
1976	Atl N☆	14	17	.452	36	36	8-4	0-0	240.1	255	112	14	8	90-8	142	4.19	90	.275	.343	76-9	.171	-0*	84	-4	-0.4
1977	Atl N	7	13	.350	25	23	6-2	0-0	151	158	86	14	1	62-6	84	4.23	105	.267	.336	45-5	.267	3	76	1	0.4
1978	Atl N	2	6	.250	13	13	2-1	0-0	81	78	43	8	0	28-2	45	4.11	99	.257	.317	24-3	.083	-2	70	-1	-0.3
	†Phi N	13	5	.722	20	20	9-2	0-0	150.2	136	52	13	1	28-1	75	2.99	120	.248	.283	53-3	.283	4*	104	11	1.8
	Year	15	11	.577	33	33	11-3	0-0	231.2	214	56	21	1	56-3	120	3.38	111	.251	.295	77-6	.221	3	90	9	1.5
1979	Phi N	7	5	.583	20	20	3-2	0-0	122.1	121	59	10	2	37-6	58	4.27	90	.256	.311	41-2	.146	-0*	118	-4	-0.5
1980	†Phi N	17	10	.630	33	33	6-1	0-0	223.1	241	99	9	3	74-9	86	3.55	107	.283	.340	68-12	.235	4	110	6	1.0
1981	†Phi N★	12	7	.632	23	22	5	0-0	146.2	162	94	10	3	54-4	80	5.15	70	.281	.342	50-5	.140	-0	121	-25	-2.9
1982	Phi N	11	11	.500	33	31	8-2	0-0	204.1	189	99	18	6	59-10	115	3.79	97	.246	.301	64-12	.109	-2	95	-4	-0.8
1983	Phi N	1	3	.250	7	7	0	0-0	33.2	46	23	5	0	10-0	26	5.61	64	.333	.368	9-3	.111	-0	117	-7	-0.8
	Chi N	12	9	.571	25	25	5-2	0-0	149.1	156	78	17	3	28-3	73	4.10	93	.269	.304	53-4	.226	2	117	-6	-0.5
	Year	13	12	.520	32	32	5-2	0-0	183	202	83	22	3	38-3	99	4.38	86	.281	.317	62-7	.210	2	117	-14	-1.3
1984	Chi N	6	10	.375	23	22	0	0-0	126.2	154	75	14	4	41-4	55	5.04	78	.302	.357	44-5	.159	0*	88	-13	-1.5
1985	Chi N	4	7	.364	20	15	0	0-0	87.1	103	49	6	0	37-3	26	4.53	88	.299	.362	24-6	.208	0	75	-5	-0.7
1986	Chi N	0	0	—	6	0	0	0-0	10.2	12	9	4	0	6-0	3	5.06	80	.293	.383	1-0	.000	-0		-2	-0.1
Total	14	123	127	.492	355	332	61-17	1-0	2109	2155	1075	165	38	767-72	1145	4.14	92	.267	.331	671-82	.183	6	95	-66	-7.1
RYAN, JACK Jack "Gulfport" B 9.19.1884 Lawrenceville, IL D 10.16.1949 Handsboro, MS BR/TR 5-10/165# d7.2																									
1908	Cle A	1	1	.500	8	1	1	1	35.2	27	12	3	1	2	7	2.27	105	.220	.238	11-0	.091	0	143	1	0.1
1909	Bos A	3	3	.500	13	8	2	0	59.1	64	34	0	4	20	24	3.34	75	.288	.358	19-2	.211	0*	92	-7	-0.7
1911	Bro N	0	1	.000	3	1	0	0	6	9	7	1	1	4	1	3.00	111	.375	.483	1-0	.000	-0	68	-2	-0.2
Total	3	4	5	.444	24	10	3	1	101	100	53	4	6	26	32	2.94	85	.271	.329	31-2	.161	1	95	-8	-0.8
RYAN, JIMMY James Edward "Pony" B 2.11.1863 Clinton, MA D 10.26.1923 Chicago, IL BR/TL 5-9/162# d10.8.1885 ▲																									
1886	†Chi N	0	0	—	5	0	0	1	23.1	19	13	3		13	15	4.63	78	.257	.368	327	.306	1*		0	0.1
1887	Chi N	2	1	.667	8	3	2	0	45	53	36	3	6	17	14	4.20	107	.305	.386	508	.285	2*	115	1	0.2

Year	Tm Lg	W	L	Pct	G	GS	CG-Sho	SV-BS	IP	H	R	HR	HB	BB-IB	SO	ERA	AERA	OAV	OOB	AB-SH	AVG	PB	Sup	APR	PW
1888	Chi N	4	0	1.000	8	2	1	0	38.1	47	29	2	0	12	11	3.05	99	.297	.347	549	.332	4*	101	-2	0.0
1891	Chi N	0	0	—	2	0	0	1	5.2	11	7	0	0	2	2	1.59	210	.393	.433	505	.277	1*		-1	0.0
1893	Chi N	0	0	—	1	0	0	0	4.2	3	0	0	0	0	1	0.00	—	.176	.176	341	.299	0*		2	0.1
Total	5	6	1	.857	24	5	3	2	117	133	85	8	6	44	43	3.62	105	.295	.365	2230	.300	9	114	0	0.4
RYAN, JASON Jason Paul B 1.21.1976 Long Branch, NJ BB/TR 6-3/185# d8.24																									
1999	Min A	1	4	.200	8	8	1	0-0	40.2	46	23	9	3	17-0	15	4.87	105	.286	.363	0-0	—	0	59	1	0.1
2000	Min A	0	1	.000	16	1	0	0-0	26	37	24	8	1	10-0	19	7.62	68	.330	.384	0-0	—	0	55	-7	-0.3
Total	2	1	5	.167	24	9	1	0-0	66.2	83	47	17	4	27-0	34	5.94	86	.304	.371	0-0	—	0	59	-6	-0.2
RYAN, JOHN John A. B Birmingham, MI BL/TR d4.19																									
1884	Bal U	3	2	.600	6	6	5	0	51	61	42	1		16	33	3.35	80	.277	.326	25	.080	-3*	130	-5	-0.7
RYAN, JOHNNY John Joseph B 10.1853 Philadelphia, PA D 3.22.1902 Philadelphia, PA 5-7.5/150# d8.19.1873 ▲																									
1874	Bal NA	0	0	—	1	0	0	0	3.1	13	8	0		0	0	16.20	14	.565	.565	181	.193	-0*		-3	-0.1
1875	NH NA	1	5	.167	10	6	4	0	59.1	70	55	1		9	1	3.19	65	.255	.279	146	.158	-1*	45	-6	-0.5
1876	Lou N	0	0	—	1	0	0	0	8	22	20	0		0	1	5.63	48	.449	.449	241	.253	-0*		-3	-0.1
Total	2 NA	1	5	.167	11	6	4	0	62.2	83	63	1		9	1	3.88	54	.279	.301	327	.177	-1	45	-9	-0.6
RYAN, KEN Kenneth Frederick B 10.24.1968 Pawtucket, RI BR/TR 6-3/230# d8.31																									
1992	Bos A	0	0	—	7	0	0	1-0	7	4	5	2	0	5-0	5	6.43	66	.174	.310	0-0	—	0		-1	-0.1
1993	Bos A	7	2	.778	47	0	0	1-3	50	43	23	2	3	29-5	49	3.60	129	.235	.342	0-0	—	0		5	0.9
1994	Bos A	2	3	.400	42	0	0	13-3	48	46	14	1	1	17-3	32	2.44	207	.256	.323	0-0	—	0		13	1.8
1995	Bos A	0	4	.000	28	0	0	7-3	32.2	34	20	4	1	24-6	34	4.96	98	.268	.388	0-0	—	0		0	-0.1
1996	Phi N	3	5	.375	62	0	0	8-5	89	71	32	4	1	45-8	70	2.43	178	.223	.321	7-1	.143	-0		16	1.5
1997	Phi N	1	0	1.000	22	0	0	0-0	20.2	31	23	5	2	13-1	10	9.58	44	.344	.430	0-0	—	0		-12	-0.6
1998	Phi N	0	0	—	17	1	0	0-0	22.2	21	12	1	1	20-1	16	4.37	99	.253	.396	1-0	.000	-0	191	0	0.0
1999	Phi N	1	2	.333	15	0	0	0-0	15.2	16	11	2	0	11-2	9	6.32	75	.267	.380	0-0	—	0		-2	-0.4
Total	8	14	16	.467	240	1	0	30-14	285.2	266	140	21	9	164-26	225	3.91	117	.250	.352	8-1	.125	-0	191	19	3.0
RYAN, NOLAN Lynn Nolan B 1.31.1947 Refugio, TX BR/TR 6-2/195# d9.11 HF1999																									
1966	NY N	0	1	.000	2	1	0	0	3	5	5	1	0	3-1	6	15.00	24	.357	.471	0-0	—	0	48	-3	-0.6
1968	NY N	6	9	.400	21	18	3	0	134	93	50	12	4	75-4	133	3.09	98	.200	.314	44-1	.114	-1	80	-1	-0.3
1969	†NY N	6	3	.667	25	10	2	1-0	89.1	60	38	3	1	53-3	92	3.53	104	.189	.306	29-3	.103	-1	111	2	-0.1
1970	NY N	7	11	.389	27	19	5-2	1-1	131.2	86	59	10	4	97-2	125	3.42	118	.188	.333	45-2	.178	-1	79	8	0.9
1971	NY N	10	14	.417	30	26	3	0-0	152	125	78	8	15	116-4	137	3.97	86	.219	.365	47-3	.128	-0	87	-11	-1.7
1972	Cal A☆	19	16	.543	39	39	20-**9**	0-0	284	166	80	14	10	157-4	**329**	2.28	128	**.171**	.291	96-1	.135	0	85	22	2.9
1973	Cal A★	21	16	.568	41	39	26-4	1-0	326	238	113	18	7	162-2	**383**	2.87	124	.203	.302	0-0	—	0	89	29	3.1
1974	Cal A	22	16	.579	42	41	26-3	0-1	**332.2**	221	127	18	9	202-3	**367**	2.89	119	**.190**	.313	0-0	—	0	105	20	2.3
1975	Cal A☆	14	12	.538	28	28	10-5	0-0	198	152	90	13	7	132-0	186	3.45	103	.213	.339	0-0	—	0	94	1	0.1
1976	Cal A	17	18	.486	39	39	21-**7**	0-0	284.1	193	117	13	5	183-2	**327**	3.36	99	**.195**	.322	0-0	—	0	72	1	0.1
1977	Cal A❖	19	16	.543	37	37	**22**-4	0-0	299	198	110	12	9	204-7	**341**	2.77	142	**.193**	.329	0-0	—	0	91	38	4.3
1978	Cal A	10	13	.435	31	31	14-3	0-0	234.2	183	106	12	3	148-7	**260**	3.72	97	.220	.335	0-0	—	0	100	-1	-0.1
1979	†Cal A★	16	14	.533	34	34	17-**5**	0-0	222.2	169	104	15	6	114-3	**223**	3.60	114	**.212**	.311	0-0	—	0	109	10	1.2
1980	†Hou N	11	10	.524	35	35	4-2	0-0	233.2	205	100	10	3	98-1	200	3.35	98	.236	.314	70-5	.086	-1	108	-2	-0.4
1981	†Hou N★	11	5	.688	21	21	5-3	0-0	149	99	34	2	1	68-1	140	**1.69**	**195**	**.188**	.280	51-4	.216	3	96	**27**	**3.4**
1982	Hou N	16	12	.571	35	35	10-3	0-0	250.1	196	100	20	8	109-3	245	3.16	105	**.213**	.301	83-6	.120	-1	102	5	0.3
1983	Hou N	14	9	.609	29	29	5-2	0-0	196.1	134	74	9	4	101-3	183	2.98	114	**.195**	.300	69-4	.072	-4	97	10	0.7
1984	Hou N	12	11	.522	30	30	5-2	0-0	183.2	143	78	12	4	69-2	197	3.04	109	.211	.286	61-5	.098	-2	106	4	0.2
1985	Hou N★	10	12	.455	35	35	4	0-0	232	205	108	12	9	95-8	209	3.80	91	.239	.318	63-14	.111	-1	98	-6	-0.8
1986	†Hou N	12	8	.600	30	30	1	0-0	178	119	72	14	4	82-5	194	3.34	108	.188	.283	59-3	.102	-2	93	6	0.3
1987	Hou N	8	16	.333	34	34	0	0-0	211.2	154	75	14	4	87-2	**270**	**2.76**	**142**	**.199**	.284	65-7	.062	-3	77	**27**	2.4
1988	Hou N	12	11	.522	33	33	4-1	0-0	220	186	98	18	7	87-6	**228**	3.52	95	.227	.304	70-7	.057	-3	104	-5	-1.0
1989	Tex A★	16	10	.615	32	32	6-2	0-0	239.1	162	96	17	9	98-3	**301**	3.20	124	**.187**	.275	0-0	—	0	99	21	2.1
1990	Tex A	13	9	.591	30	30	5-2	0-0	204	137	86	18	7	74-2	**232**	3.44	114	**.188**	**.267**	0-0	—	0	99	12	1.1
1991	Tex A	12	6	.667	27	27	2-2	0-0	173	102	58	12	5	72-0	203	2.91	139	**.172**	**.263**	0-0	—	0	107	24	2.3
1992	Tex A	5	9	.357	27	27	2	0-0	157.1	138	75	9	12	69-0	157	3.72	102	.238	.327	0-0	—	0	92	1	0.0
1993	Tex A	5	5	.500	13	13	0	0-0	66.1	54	47	5	1	40-0	46	4.88	85	.220	.329	0-0	—	0	89	-9	-1.2
Total	27	324	292	.526	807	773	222-61	3-2	5386	3923	2178	321	158	2795-785	5714	3.19	112	.204	.307	852-65	.110	-17	95	230	21.5
RYAN, B.J. Robert Victor B 12.28.1975 Bossier City, LA BR/TR 6-6/230# d7.28																									
1999	Cin N	0	0	—	1	0	0	0-0	2	4	1	0	0	1-0	1	4.50	104	.500	.556	0-0	—	0		0	0.0
	Bal A	1	0	1.000	13	0	0	0-0	18.1	9	6	0	0	12-1	28	2.95	159	.150	.288	0-0	—	0		4	0.2
2000	Bal A	2	3	.400	42	0	0	0-3	42.2	36	29	7	0	31-1	41	5.91	80	.225	.349	0-0	—	0		-5	-0.5
2001	Bal A	2	4	.333	61	0	0	2-2	53	47	31	6	2	30-4	54	4.25	101	.233	.335	1-0	.000	-0		-1	-0.2
2002	Bal A	2	1	.667	67	0	0	1-1	57.2	51	31	7	4	33-4	56	4.68	91	.241	.353	1-0	.000	-0		-2	-0.1
2003	Bal A	4	1	.800	76	0	0	0-2	50.1	42	19	1	3	27-0	63	3.40	129	.227	.330	0-0	—	0		6	0.6
Total	5	11	9	.550	260	0	0	3-8	224	189	117	21	9	134-10	243	4.38	101	.229	.340	2-0	.000	-0		2	0.0
RYAN, ROSY Wilfred Patrick Dolan B 3.15.1898 Worcester, MA D 12.10.1980 Scottsdale, AZ BL/TR 6/185# d9.7																									
1919	NY N	1	2	.333	4	3	1	0	20.1	20	9	0	1	9	7	3.10	91	.260	.345	6-0	.000	-1	66	-1	-0.2
1920	NY N	0	1	.000	3	1	1	0	15.1	14	6	1	0	4	5	1.76	170	.259	.310	5-0	.000	-1	52	1	0.0
1921	NY N	7	10	.412	36	16	5	3	147.1	140	72	6	1	32	58	3.73	98	.255	.297	45-3	.200	1	112	-1	-0.1
1922	†NY N	17	12	.586	46	22	12-1	3	191.2	194	87	5	2	74	75	3.01	133	.269	.338	62-3	.194	1	94	18	2.5
1923	†NY N	16	5	.762	**45**	15	7	4	172.2	169	77	8	2	46	58	3.49	109	.257	.308	53-7	.208	0	176	6	0.7
1924	†NY N	8	6	.571	37	9	2	5	124.2	137	64	1	2	37	36	4.26	86	.285	.339	36-1	.139	-1	111	-7	-1.0
1925	Bos N	2	8	.200	37	7	1	2	122.2	152	103	7	0	52	48	6.31	64	.303	.368	39-0	.282	3*	150	-33	-2.1
1926	Bos N	0	2	.000	7	2	0	0	19	29	19	1	0	7	1	7.58	47	.392	.444	5-0	.200	-0	47	-9	-0.8
1928	NY A	0	0	—	3	0	0	0	6	17	11	1	0	1	5	16.50	23	.486	.500	4-0	.000	-1		-8	-0.4
1933	Bro N	1	1	.500	30	0	0	2	61.1	69	38	3	3	16	22	4.55	71	.276	.327	13-0	.154	0		-10	-0.5
Total	10	52	47	.525	248	75	29-1	19	881	941	486	33	11	278	315	4.14	91	.277	.333	268-14	.190	1	121	-44	-1.9
RYBA, MIKE Dominic Joseph B 6.9.1903 DeLancey, PA D 12.13.1971 Brookline Station, MO BR/TR 5-11.5/195# d9.22 C4																									
1935	StL N	1	1	.500	2	1	1	0	16	15	6	0	0	1	6	3.38	121	.242	.254	5-1	.400	1	62	2	0.3
1936	StL N	5	1	.833	14	0	0	0	45	55	33	3	2	16	25	5.40	73	.294	.356	18-1	.167	-0*		-8	-1.0
1937	StL N	9	6	.600	38	8	5	0	135	152	76	8	2	40	57	4.13	96	.284	.336	48-1	.313	4*	119	-3	0.1
1938	StL N	1	1	.500	3	0	0	0	5	8	3	0	0	1	0	5.40	73	.348	.375	0-0	—	0		-1	-0.1
1941	Bos A	7	3	.700	40	3	0	6	121	143	72	14	0	42	54	4.46	93	.297	.353	37-4	.216	1	166	-5	-0.2
1942	Bos A	3	3	.500	18	0	0	3	44.1	49	25	5	1	13	16	3.86	97	.278	.332	17-0	.294	1*		-2	-0.2
1943	Bos A	7	5	.583	40	8	4-1	2	143.2	142	57	4	0	57	50	3.26	102	.262	.333	43-4	.186	0	130	1	0.1
1944	Bos A	12	7	.632	42	7	2	2	138	119	57	7	0	39	50	3.33	102	.233	.287	41-5	.146	-0	116	2	0.3
1945	Bos A	7	6	.538	34	9	4-1	2	123	122	45	5	2	33	44	2.49	137	.259	.310	36-4	.250	2	106	10	1.2
1946	†Bos A	0	1	.000	9	0	0	1	12.2	12	7	1	0	5	5	3.55	103	.261	.333	2-0	1.000	1		0	0.0
Total	10	52	34	.605	240	36	16-2	16	783.2	817	381	47	7	247	307	3.66	100	.269	.326	247-20	.235	9	118	-4	0.5
RYERSON, GARY Gary Lawrence B 6.17.1948 Los Angeles, CA BR/TL 6-1/175# d6.28																									
1972	Mil A	3	8	.273	20	14	4-1	0-0	102	119	48	9	0	21-5	45	3.62	84	.290	.323	24-2	.042	-1	69	-8	-1.0
1973	Mil A	0	1	.000	9	4	0	0-0	23	32	23	0	0	7-1	10	7.83	48	.327	.364	0-0	—	0	107	-11	-0.5
Total	2	3	9	.250	29	18	4-1	0-0	125	151	71	9	0	28-6	55	4.39	72	.297	.331	24-2	.042	-1	79	-19	-1.5
SAARLOOS, KIRK Kirk Craig B 5.23.1979 Long Beach, CA BR/TR 6/185# d6.18																									
2002	Hou N	6	7	.462	17	17	1-1	0-0	85.1	100	59	12	6	27-5	54	6.01	71	.301	.362	30-5	.067	-2	112	-15	-2.0
2003	Hou N	2	1	.667	36	4	0	0-0	49.1	55	31	4	3	17-3	43	4.93	90	.281	.346	5-3	.000	-0	164	-3	-0.2
Total	2	8	8	.500	53	21	1-1	0-0	134.2	155	90	16	9	44-8	97	5.61	77	.294	.356	35-8	.057	-2	122	-18	-2.2

Year	Tm Lg	W	L	Pct	G	GS	CG-Sho	SV-BS	IP	H	R	HR	HB	BB-IB	SO	ERA	AERA	OAV	OOB	AB-SH	AVG	PB	Sup	APR	PW
SABATHIA, C.C. Carsten Charles B 7.21.1980 Vallejo, CA BL/TL 6-7/260# d4.8																									
2001	†Cle A	17	5	.773	33	33	0	0-0	180.1	149	93	19	7	95-1	171	4.39	103	.228	.330	4-1	.000	-0	109	4	0.4
2002	Cle A	13	11	.542	33	33	2	0-0	210	198	109	17	1	88-2	149	4.37	101	.252	.324	5-0	.200	0	101	1	0.1
2003	Cle A☆	13	9	.591	30	30	2-1	0-0	197.2	190	85	19	6	66-3	141	3.60	123	.255	.319	6-0	.500	1*	80	21	2.1
Total	3	43	25	.632	96	96	4-1	0-0	588	537	287	55	14	249-6	461	4.12	108	.246	.324	15-1	.267	1	97	26	2.6
SABEL, ERIK Erik Douglas B 10.14.1974 Lafayette, IN BR/TR 6-3/193# d7.9																									
1999	Ari N	0	0	—	7	0	0	0-0	9.2	12	7	1	2	6-2	6	6.52	70	.300	.417	2-0	.000	-0		-2	-0.1
2001	Ari N	3	2	.600	42	0	0	0-0	51.1	57	26	8	3	12-3	25	4.38	104	.282	.332	0-0	—	0		1	0.1
2002	Det A	0	0	—	1	0	0	0-0	0	2	2	1	0	0-0	0	o	—	1.000	1.000	0-0	—	0		-2	-0.2
Total	3	3	2	.600	50	0	0	0-0	61	71	35	10	5	18-5	31	5.02	91	.291	.352	2-0	.000	-0		-3	-0.2
SABERHAGEN, BRET Bret William B 4.11.1964 Chicago Heights, IL BR/TR 6-1/195# d4.4																									
1984	†KC A	10	11	.476	38	18	2-1	1-0	157.2	138	71	13	2	36-4	73	3.48	116	.237	.281	0-0	—	0*	77	8	0.9
1985	†KC A	20	6	.769	32	32	10-1	0-0	235.1	211	79	19	1	38-1	158	2.87	145	.241	**.271**	0-0	—	0	98	36	3.9
1986	KC A	7	12	.368	30	25	4-2	0-0	156	165	77	15	2	29-1	112	4.15	103	.268	.302	0-0	—	0	71	3	0.4
1987	KC A★	18	10	.643	33	33	15-4	0-0	257	246	99	27	6	53-2	163	3.36	136	.252	.293	0-0	—	0	105	38	3.8
1988	KC A	14	16	.467	35	35	9	0-0	260.2	271	122	18	4	59-5	171	3.80	105	.269	.309	0-0	—	0	87	6	0.6
1989	KC A	**23**	6	**.793**	36	35	**12**-4	0-0	**262.1**	209	74	13	2	43-6	193	**2.16**	**178**	.217	**.251**	0-0	—	0*	107	**48**	**5.3**
1990	KC A★	5	9	.357	20	20	5	0-0	135	146	52	9	1	28-1	87	3.27	118	.279	.314	0-0	—	0	109	11	1.2
1991	KC A	13	8	.619	28	28	7-2	0-0	196.1	165	76	12	9	45-5	136	3.07	134	.228	.280	0-0	—	0	102	23	2.4
1992	NY N	3	5	.375	17	15	1-1	0-1	97.2	84	39	6	4	27-1	81	3.50	99	.233	.292	28-3	.107	-1	82	1	0.2
1993	NY N	7	7	.500	19	19	4-1	0-0	139.1	131	55	11	3	17-4	93	3.29	122	.250	.275	45-8	.111	-0	99	13	1.3
1994	NY N☆	14	4	**.778**	24	24	4	0-0	177.1	169	58	13	4	13-0	143	2.74	153	.254	.271	58-8	.172	1	112	30	3.1
1995	NY N	5	5	.500	16	16	3	0-0	110	105	45	13	5	20-2	71	3.35	121	.251	.291	35-5	.114	-1	109	9	0.8
	†Col N	2	1	.667	9	9	0	0-0	43	60	33	8	5	13-1	29	6.28	86	.323	.382	14-0	.071	-1	104	-3	-0.3
	Year	7	6	.538	25	25	3	0-0	153	165	39	21	10	33-3	100	4.18	106	.273	.320	49-5	.102	-2	109	4	0.5
1997	Bos A	0	1	.000	6	6	0	0-0	26	30	20	5	2	10-0	14	6.58	71	.288	.353	1-0	.000	-0	116	-5	-0.3
1998	†Bos A	15	8	.652	31	31	0	0-0	175	181	82	22	6	29-1	100	3.96	119	.264	.299	5-0	.000	-1	100	15	1.7
1999	†Bos A	10	6	.625	22	22	0	0-0	119	122	43	11	2	11-0	81	2.95	169	.265	.284	4-0	.000	-0	99	27	3.2
2001	Bos A	1	2	.333	3	3	0	0-0	15	19	11	3	1	0-0	10	6.00	75	.302	.313	0-0	—	0	103	-2	-0.4
Total	16	167	117	.588	399	371	76-16	1-1	2562.2	2452	1036	218	59	471-34	1715	3.34	126	.252	.289	190-24	.121	-2	99	258	27.8
SACKINSKY, BRIAN Brian Walter B 6.22.1971 Pittsburgh, PA BR/TR 6-4/220# d4.20																									
1996	Bal A	0	0	—	3	0	0	0-0	4.2	6	2	1	0	3-0	2	3.86	128	.316	.409	0-0	—	0		1	0.0
SADECKI, RAY Raymond Michael B 12.26.1940 Kansas City, KS BL/TL 5-11/180# d5.19																									
1960	StL N	9	9	.500	26	26	7-1	0	157.1	148	76	15	1	86-1	95	3.78	109	.249	.342	57-2	.211	-0*	94	4	0.3
1961	StL N	14	10	.583	31	31	13	0	222.2	196	100	28	3	102-2	114	3.72	118	.238	.321	87-2	.253	2*	95	19	1.8
1962	StL N	6	8	.429	22	17	4-1	1	102.1	121	74	13	3	43-3	50	5.54	77	.296	.362	37-2	.081	-2*	100	-14	-1.9
1963	StL N	10	10	.500	36	28	4-1	1	193.1	198	100	25	4	78-3	136	4.10	87	.266	.338	64-7	.141	-1*	121	-10	-1.3
1964	†StL N	20	11	.645	37	32	9-2	1	220	232	104	16	1	60-4	119	3.68	103	.273	.319	75-9	.160	2*	105	4	0.6
1965	StL N	6	15	.286	36	28	4	1	172.2	192	107	26	0	64-4	122	5.21	74	.284	.344	55-3	.200	2	87	-23	-2.5
1966	StL N	2	1	.667	5	3	1	0	24.1	16	9	2	0	9-0	21	2.22	162	.188	.266	7-1	.429	2*	82	3	0.6
	SF N	3	7	.300	26	19	3-1	0	105	125	82	20	4	39-2	62	5.40	68	.293	.354	34-2	.324	5	110	-23	-1.5
	Year	5	8	.385	31	22	4-1	0	129.1	141	87	22	4	48-2	83	4.80	76	.276	.339	41-3	.341	7	106	-24	-0.9
1967	SF N	12	6	.667	35	24	10-2	0	188	165	65	8	4	58-4	145	2.78	118	.238	.298	73-1	.247	4*	100	12	1.6
1968	SF N	12	18	.400	38	36	13-6	0	254	225	94	14	3	70-17	206	2.91	101	.237	.290	85-4	.094	-1*	92	3	0.1
1969	SF N	5	8	.385	29	17	4-3	0-0	138.1	137	73	18	2	53-4	104	4.23	83	.259	.325	40-4	.125	2*	116	-10	-0.6
1970	NY N	8	4	.667	28	19	4	0-1	138.2	134	67	18	0	52-9	89	3.89	103	.255	.320	39-8	.205	1	118	2	0.1
1971	NY N	7	7	.500	34	20	5-2	0-0	163.1	139	56	10	4	44-5	120	2.92	117	.229	.283	50-5	.200	1	84	11	0.9
1972	NY N	2	1	.667	34	2	0	0-1	75.2	73	33	3	2	31-6	38	3.09	109	.257	.331	13-1	.154	-0	92	1	-0.1
1973	†NY N	5	4	.556	31	11	1	1-0	116.2	109	47	11	1	41-3	87	3.39	107	.248	.312	31-2	.226	1	104	4	0.3
1974	NY N	8	8	.500	34	10	3-1	0-1	103	107	49	7	2	35-6	46	3.41	105	.274	.332	27-0	.259	1	68	0	0.1
1975	StL N	1	0	1.000	8	0	0	0-0	11	13	7	0	0	7-2	8	3.27	115	.289	.370	0-0	—	0		0	0.0
	Atl N	2	3	.400	25	5	0	1-1	66.1	73	39	3	4	21-5	24	4.21	90	.286	.341	15-1	.200	0	93	-4	-0.3
	Year	3	3	.500	33	5	0	1-1	77.1	86	43	3	4	28-7	32	4.07	93	.287	.346	15-1	.200	0	93	-4	-0.3
	KC A	1	0	1.000	5	0	0	0-2	3	5	2	0	0	3-0	0	3.00	129	.333	.444	0-0	—	0		0	0.0
1976	KC A	0	0	—	3	0	0	0-1	4.2	7	0	0	0	3-0	1	0.00	—	.368	.455	0-0	—	0		2	0.1
	Mil A	2	0	1.000	36	0	0	1-0	37.1	38	20	2	3	20-2	27	4.34	81	.262	.363	0-0	—	0		-3	-0.2
	Year	2	0	1.000	39	0	0	1-1	42	45	20	2	3	23-2	28	3.86	91	.274	.374	0-0	—	0		-2	-0.1
1977	NY N	0	1	.000	4	0	0	0-1	3	3	2	1	0	3-0	0	6.00	62	.300	.462	0-0	—	0		-1	-0.1
Total	18	135	131	.508	563	328	85-20	7-8	2500.2	2456	1206	240	41	922-82	1614	3.78	97	.258	.324	789-54	.191	19	101	-23	-2.0
SADLER, CARL William Carl B 10.11.1976 Gainesville, FL BL/TL 6-2/180# d7.31																									
2002	Cle A	1	2	.333	24	0	0	0-1	20.1	15	10	2	0	11-0	23	4.43	99	.211	.317	0-0	—	0		0	0.0
2003	Cle A	0	0	—	18	0	0	0-0	9.2	11	2	0	2	5-0	10	1.86	237	.306	.409	0-0	—	0		3	0.1
Total	2	1	2	.333	42	0	0	0-1	30	26	12	2	2	16-0	33	3.60	122	.243	.349	0-0	—	0		3	0.1
SADOWSKI, JIM James Michael B 8.7.1951 Pittsburgh, PA BR/TR 6-3/195# d4.27																									
1974	Pit N	0	1	.000	4	0	0	0-0	9	7	6	1	0	9-0	1	6.00	58	.233	.400	1-0	.000	0		-2	-0.2
SADOWSKI, BOB Robert B 2.19.1938 Pittsburgh, PA BR/TR 6-2/195# d6.19 b-Ed b-Ted																									
1963	Mil N	5	7	.417	19	18	5-1	0	116.2	99	36	8	5	30-6	72	2.62	123	.231	.288	35-3	.057	-2	95	9	0.7
1964	Mil N	9	10	.474	51	18	5	5	166.2	159	85	18	7	56-5	96	4.10	86	.251	.317	52-6	.154	0	143	-10	-1.1
1965	Mil N	5	9	.357	34	13	3	3	123	117	62	11	3	35-5	78	4.32	82	.250	.305	35-2	.086	-2	78	-9	-1.2
1966	Bos A	1	1	.500	11	5	0	0	33.1	41	26	4	1	9-1	11	5.40	70	.311	.354	7-1	.000	-1	102	-7	-0.5
Total	4	20	27	.426	115	54	13-1	8	439.2	416	209	41	16	130-17	257	3.87	90	.250	.309	129-12	.101	-4	107	-17	-2.1
SADOWSKI, TED Theodore B 4.1.1936 Pittsburgh, PA D 7.18.1993 Shaler Twsp., PA BR/TR 6-1.5/190# d9.2 b-Ed b-Bob																									
1960	Was A	1	0	1.000	9	1	0	1	17.1	17	10	4	1	9-1	12	5.19	75	.258	.351	3-0	.000	-0	91	-2	-0.1
1961	Min A	0	2	.000	15	1	0	0	33	49	29	6	1	11-2	12	6.82	62	.348	.396	6-0	.000	-1	42	-9	-0.5
1962	Min A	1	1	.500	19	0	0	0	34	37	19	6	1	11-0	15	5.03	81	.301	.363	4-0	.500	1		-2	-0.1
Total	3	2	3	.400	43	2	0	1	84.1	103	58	16	3	31-3	39	5.76	71	.312	.374	13-0	.154	-0	65	-13	-0.7
SAGER, A. J. Anthony Joseph B 3.3.1965 Columbus, OH BR/TR 6-4/220# d4.4																									
1994	SD N	1	4	.200	22	3	0	0-0	46.2	62	34	4	2	16-5	26	5.98	69	.325	.379	10-1	.100	0	59	-10	-0.8
1995	Col N	0	0	—	10	0	0	0-1	14.2	19	16	1	0	7-1	10	7.36	73	.311	.382	3-0	.000	-0		-3	-0.2
1996	Det A	4	5	.444	22	9	0	0-0	79	91	46	10	2	29-2	52	5.01	101	.294	.355	0-0	—	0	98	1	0.1
1997	Det A	3	4	.429	38	1	0	3-1	84	81	43	10	1	24-6	53	4.18	110	.258	.307	0-0	—	0	0	3	0.3
1998	Det A	4	2	.667	31	3	0	2-1	59.1	79	47	7	1	23-4	23	6.52	72	.325	.383	1-0	.000	-0	125	-12	-1.0
Total	5	12	15	.444	123	16	0	5-3	283.2	332	186	32	6	99-18	164	5.36	88	.297	.353	14-1	.071	-0	92	-21	-1.6
SAIN, JOHNNY John Franklin B 9.25.1917 Havana, AR BR/TR 6-2/200# d4.24 Mil 1943-45 C17																									
1942	Bos N	4	7	.364	40	3	0	6	97	79	54	8	5	63	68	3.90	86	.228	.354	27-2	.074	-2	50	-8	-1.2
1946	Bos N	20	14	.588	37	34	**24**-3	2	265	225	80	8	2	87	129	2.21	155	.230	.294	94-10	.298	5*	98	34	**5.4**
1947	Bos N★	21	12	.636	38	35	22-3	1	266	265	117	19	4	79	132	3.52	111	.255	.310	107-8	.346	12*	126	12	2.7
1948	†Bos N★	**24**	15	.615	42	**39**	**28**-4	1	**314.2**	297	105	19	5	83	137	2.60	147	.245	.296	115-16	.217	3*	110	43	**5.3**
1949	Bos N	10	17	.370	37	36	16-1	0	243	285	150	15	4	75	73	4.81	78	.291	.344	97-3	.206	1*	99	-30	-2.8
1950	Bos N	20	13	.606	37	37	25-3	0	278.1	294	139	34	2	70	96	3.94	98	.269	.314	102-7	.206	4	112	-2	0.0
1951	Bos N	5	13	.278	26	22	6-1	1	160.1	195	88	16	3	45	63	4.21	87	.299	.347	52-4	.212	3	82	-11	-0.9
	†NY A	2	1	.667	7	4	1	1	37	41	17	5	0	8	21	4.14	93	.281	.318	14-0	.286	1	110	0	0.1
1952	†NY A	11	6	.647	35	16	8	7	148.1	149	70	15	2	38	57	3.46	96	.261	.310	71-1	.268	7*	144	-4	0.1

Year	Tm Lg	W	L	Pct	G	GS	CG-Sho	SV-BS	IP	H	R	HR	HB	BB-IB	SO	ERA	AERA	OAV	OOB	AB-SH	AVG	PB	Sup	APR	PW
1953	†NY A☆	14	7	.667	40	19	10-1	9	189	189	68	16	3	45	84	3.00	123	.262	.308	68-4	.250	5*	136	17	2.4
1954	NY A	6	6	.500	45	0	0	**22**	77	66	27	11	0	15	33	3.16	109	.229	.266	17-1	.353	3		4	1.1
1955	NY A	0	0	—	3	0	0	0	5.1	6	4	4	0	1-0	5	6.75	55	.300	.333	2-0	.000	-0		-2	-0.1
	KC A	2	5	.286	25	0	0	1	44.2	54	28	10	0	10-4	12	5.44	77	.297	.332	8-0	.000	-1		-5	-0.9
	Year	2	5	.286	28	0	0	1	50	60	38	14	0	11-4	17	5.58	74	.297	.332	10-0	.000	-1		-6	-1.0
Total	11	139	116	.545	412	245	140-16	51	2125.2	2145	947	180	30	619-4	910	3.49	106	.261	.315	774-56	.245	40	111	48	11.2
ST.CLAIRE, RANDY Randy Anthony B 8.23.1960 Glens Falls, NY BR/TR 6-2/190# d9.11 C1 f-Ebba																									
1984	Mon N	0	0	—	4	0	0	0-0	8	11	4	0	1	2-1	4	4.50	76	.344	.378	0-0	—	0		-1	0.0
1985	Mon N	5	3	.625	42	0	0	0-1	68.2	69	32	3	1	26-7	25	3.93	86	.265	.333	5-1	.200	1		-4	-0.3
1986	Mon N	2	0	1.000	11	0	0	1-0	19	13	5	2	0	6-1	21	2.37	156	.186	.250	1-1	.000	-0		3	0.4
1987	Mon N	3	3	.500	44	0	0	7-2	67	64	31	9	1	20-4	43	4.03	104	.249	.302	6-2	.333	0		3	0.3
1988	Mon N	0	0	—	6	0	0	0-0	7.1	11	5	2	0	5-1	6	6.14	59	.344	.421	0-0	—	0		-2	-0.1
	Cin N	1	0	1.000	10	0	0	0-0	13.2	13	8	3	0	5-2	8	2.63	136	.241	.300	1-0	.000	-0		0	0.0
	Year	1	0	1.000	16	0	0	0-0	21	24	18	5	0	10-3	14	3.86	93	.279	.347	1-0	.000	-0		-2	-0.1
1989	Min A	1	0	1.000	14	0	0	1-0	22.1	19	13	4	2	10-2	14	5.24	79	.226	.320	0-0	—	0		-2	-0.1
1991	†Atl N	0	0	—	19	0	0	0-0	28.2	31	17	4	0	9-3	30	4.08	95	.282	.333	2-0	.500	0		-1	0.0
1992	Atl N	0	0	—	10	0	0	0-0	15.1	17	11	1	0	8-3	7	5.87	62	.283	.368	0-0	—	0		-4	-0.2
1994	Tor A	0	0	—	2	0	0	0-0	2	4	4	0	0	2-1	2	9.00	54	.444	.545	0-0	—	0		-2	-0.1
Total	9	12	6	.667	162	0	0	9-3	252	252	130	28	5	93-25	160	4.14	92	.260	.325	15-4	.267	1		-10	-0.1
ST.VRAIN, JIM James Marcellin B 6.6.1883 Ralls County, MO D 6.12.1937 Butte, MT BR/TL 5-9/175# d4.20																									
1902	Chi N	4	6	.400	12	11	10-1	0	95	88	36	0	5	25	51	2.08	130	.246	.304	31-0	.097	-2	82	6	0.5
SAIPE, MIKE Michael Eric B 9.10.1973 San Diego, CA BR/TR 6-1/190# d6.25																									
1998	Col N	0	1	.000	2	2	0	0-0	10	22	12	5	2	0-0	2	10.80	48	.431	.453	1-0	.000	0	98	-5	-0.4
SALE, FREDDY Frederick Link B 5.2.1902 Chester, SC D 5.27.1956 Hermosa Beach, CA BR/TR 5-9/160# d6.30																									
1924	Pit N	0	0	—	1	0	0	0	1	2	0	0	0	0	0	0.00	—	.500	.500	0-0	—	0		0	0.0
SALISBURY, HARRY Henry H. B 5.15.1855 Providence, RI D 3.29.1933 Chicago, IL BL 5-8.5/162# d8.28																									
1879	Tro N	4	6	.400	10	10	9	0	89	103	72	0		11	31	2.22	112	.265	.285	36	.056	-4	76	-1	-0.3
1882	Pit AA	20	18	.526	38	38	38-1	0	335	315	188	1		37	135	2.63	99	.232	.253	145	.152	-6*	107	-1	-0.7
Total	2	24	24	.500	48	48	47-1	0	424	418	260	1		48	166	2.55	102	.239	.260	181	.133	-10	100	-2	-1.0
SALISBURY, BILL William Ansel "Solly" B 11.12.1876 Algona, IA D 1.17.1952 Rowena, OR BR/TR 6/180# d4.19																									
1902	Phi N	0	0	—	2	1	0	0	6	15	10	1	1	2	0	13.50	21	.469	.514	1-0	.000	-0	145	-6	-0.3
SALKELD, ROGER Roger William B 3.6.1971 Burbank, CA BR/TR 6-5/215# d9.8 gf-Bill																									
1993	Sea A	0	0	—	3	2	0	0-0	14.1	13	4	0	1	4-0	13	2.51	176	.232	.295	0-0	—	0	52	3	0.2
1994	Sea A	2	5	.286	13	13	0	0-0	59	76	47	7	1	45-1	46	7.17	68	.314	.419	0-0	—	0	107	-12	-1.2
1996	Cin N	8	5	.615	29	19	1-1	0-0	116	114	69	18	6	54-2	82	5.20	82	.261	.349	32-4	.031	-3	119	-10	-1.2
Total	3	10	10	.500	45	34	1-1	0-0	189.1	203	120	25	8	103-3	141	5.61	79	.277	.369	32-4	.031	-3	111	-19	-2.2
SALLEE, SLIM Harry Franklin "Scatter" B 2.3.1885 Higginsport, OH D 3.23.1950 Higginsport, OH BL/TL 6-3/180# d4.16																									
1908	StL N	3	8	.273	25	12	7-1	0	128.2	144	65	1	3	36	39	3.15	75	.274	.324	41-1	.049	-3	55	-10	-1.1
1909	StL N	10	11	.476	32	27	12-1	0	219	223	107	3	5	59	55	2.42	104	.264	.315	71-6	.113	-2	129	-7	-0.8
1910	StL N	7	8	.467	18	13	9-1	2	115	112	44	4	1	24	46	2.97	100	.251	.290	37-2	.108	-2	90	2	0.0
1911	StL N	15	9	.625	36	30	18-1	3	245	234	102	6	5	64	74	2.76	123	.257	.309	89-4	.169	-2	96	15	1.0
1912	StL N	16	17	.485	48	32	20-3	**6**	294	289	122	6	6	72	108	2.60	132	.266	.315	103-2	.136	-4	84	26	2.3
1913	StL N	19	15	.559	50	29	18-3	5	276	257	98	11	5	60	106	2.71	119	.255	.301	95-6	.211	2	86	16	2.2
1914	StL N	18	17	.514	46	29	18-3	**6**	282.1	252	92	5	9	72	105	2.10	133	.246	.302	91-6	.231	2	87	22	3.1
1915	StL N	13	17	.433	46	33	17-2	3	275.1	245	121	6	3	57	91	2.84	98	.238	.280	92-4	.120	-3	86	-3	-0.8
1916	StL N	5	5	.500	16	7	4-2	1	70	75	28	2	2	23	28	3.47	76	.290	.352	18-2	.167	-0	56	-3	-0.6
	NY N	9	4	.692	15	11	7-2	0	111.2	96	24	2	0	10	35	1.37	178	.234	.252	35-1	.257	2	117	13	1.8
	Year	14	9	.609	31	18	11-4	1	181.2	171	28	4	2	33	63	2.18	115	.256	.293	53-3	.226	2	92	9	1.2
1917	†NY N	18	7	.720	34	24	18-1	**4**	215.2	199	70	4	1	34	54	2.17	118	.249	.280	77-6	.221	1	149	8	0.9
1918	NY N	8	8	.500	18	16	12-1	2	132	122	44	3	0	12	33	2.25	117	.241	**.259**	41-4	.122	-2	92	5	0.3
1919	†Cin N	21	7	.750	29	28	22-4	0	227.2	221	63	4	1	20	24	2.06	135	.258	.276	74-8	.189	2	116	20	2.5
1920	Cin N	5	6	.455	21	12	6	2	116	129	57	4	2	16	13	3.34	91	.293	.320	35-1	.171	-1	121	-5	-0.7
	NY N	1	0	1.000	5	2	1	0	17	16	7	0	0	0	2	1.59	189	.239	.239	3-1	.333	1	171	1	0.1
	Year	6	6	.500	26	14	7	2	133	145	14	4	2	16	15	3.11	97	.285	.310	38-2	.184	-0	128	-5	-0.6
1921	NY N	6	4	.600	37	0	0	2	96.1	115	48	7	0	14	23	3.64	101	.307	.332	22-4	.364	2		-1	0.0
Total	14	174	143	.549	476	305	189-25	36	2821.2	2729	1092	68	43	573	836	2.56	114	.258	.299	924-58	.171	-8	99	99	10.2
SALMON, ROGER Roger Elliott B 5.11.1891 Newark, NJ D 6.17.1974 Belfast, ME BL/TL 6-2/170# d5.3																									
1912	Phi A	1	0	1.000	2	1	0	0	5	7	7	0	0	4	5	9.00	34	.318	.423	1-1	.000	-0	96	-4	-0.6
SALVE, GUS Augustus William B 12.29.1885 Boston, MA D 3.29.1971 Providence, RI BL/TL 6/190# d9.14																									
1908	Phi A	0	1	.000	2	1	1	0	15.1	17	7	1	1	9	6	4.11	62	.266	.365	5-0	.000	-1	27	-2	-0.2
SALVESON, JACK John Theodore B 1.5.1914 Fullerton, CA D 12.28.1974 Norwalk, CA BR/TR 6-0.5/180# d6.3																									
1933	NY N	0	2	.000	8	2	2	0	30.2	30	17	4	0	14	8	3.82	84	.252	.331	9-0	.111	-1	26	-3	-0.2
1934	NY N	3	1	.750	12	4	0	0	38.1	43	16	2	0	13	18	3.52	110	.281	.337	10-0	.300	0*	134	2	0.3
1935	Pit N	0	1	.000	5	0	0	0	7	11	12	1	1	5	2	9.00	46	.306	.405	2-0	.000	-0		-5	-0.6
	Chi A	1	2	.333	20	2	2	1	66.2	79	39	6	0	23	22	4.86	95	.298	.354	20-0	.300	2	150	-1	0.1
1943	Cle A	5	3	.625	23	11	4-3	3	86	87	36	5	1	26	24	3.35	93	.266	.322	26-2	.231	2	94	-2	0.0
1945	Cle A	0	0	—	19	0	0	0	44	52	23	3	1	6	11	3.68	88	.294	.321	10-0	.400	3		-3	0.2
Total	5	9	9	.500	87	19	8-3	4	272.2	302	143	21	3	87	85	3.99	91	.280	.336	77-2	.260	7	99	-12	-0.2
SALVO, MANNY Manuel "Gyp" B 6.30.1912 Sacramento, CA D 2.7.1997 Vallejo, CA BR/TR 6-4/210# d4.22																									
1939	NY N	4	10	.286	32	18	4	1	136	150	84	11	5	75	69	4.63	85	.285	.380	41-0	.098	-2	101	-12	-1.3
1940	Bos N	10	9	.526	21	20	14-**5**	0	160.2	151	63	9	2	43	60	3.08	121	.248	.300	58-0	.103	-3	95	11	0.9
1941	Bos N	7	16	.304	35	27	11-2	0	195	192	103	9	4	93	67	4.06	88	.255	.340	62-0	.113	-0	89	-10	-1.2
1942	Bos N	7	8	.467	25	14	6-1	0	130.2	129	52	7	4	41	25	3.03	110	.260	.322	41-2	.122	-1	70	4	0.3
1943	Bos N	0	1	.000	1	1	0	0	5	5	4	0	0	6	1	7.20	47	.250	.423	2-0	1.000	2	75	-2	-0.2
	Phi N	0	0	—	1	0	0	0	0.1	2	1	0	0	1	0	27.00	12	.667	.750	0-0	—	0		-1	0.0
	Bos N	5	6	.455	20	13	5-1	0	93.2	94	45	6	1	25	25	3.27	105	.261	.311	28-2	.214	0	69	0	0.0
	Year	5	7	.417	22	14	5-1	0	99	101	48	6	1	32	26	3.55	96	.264	.322	30-2	.267	2	69	-3	-0.2
Total	5	33	50	.398	135	93	40-9	1	721.1	723	352	42	16	284	247	3.69	98	.261	.334	232-4	.129	-4	87	-10	-1.5
SAMBITO, JOE Joseph Charles B 6.28.1952 Brooklyn, NY BL/TL 6-1/190# d7.20																									
1976	Hou N	3	2	.600	20	4	1-1	1	53.1	45	21	4	0	14-1	26	3.54	90	.237	.286	9-0	.222	1	110	-1	0.1
1977	Hou N	5	5	.500	54	1	0	7-4	89	77	34	6	0	24-2	67	2.33	154	.235	.286	13-0	.154	-0	0	10	1.2
1978	Hou N	4	9	.308	62	0	0	11-4	88	85	32	5	0	32-7	96	3.07	108	.260	.322	6-1	.167	0		3	0.6
1979	Hou N★	8	7	.533	63	0	0	22-6	91.1	80	20	8	4	23-4	83	1.77	198	.235	.290	7-0	.286	2		19	**4.4**
1980	†Hou N	8	4	.667	64	0	0	17-5	90.1	65	26	3	2	22-3	75	2.19	150	.200	.254	9-0	.000	-1		12	1.9
1981	†Hou N	5	5	.500	49	0	0	10-3	63.2	43	17	4	2	22-5	41	1.84	179	.192	.269	5-0	.000	-1		10	1.8
1982	Hou N	0	0	—	9	0	0	4-1	12.2	7	2	0	0	2-2	7	0.71	468	.159	.196	1-0	.000	-0*		4	0.2
1984	Hou N	0	0	—	32	0	0	0-0	47.2	39	16	5	0	16-2	26	3.02	110	.228	.289	2-0	.000	-0		3	0.1
1985	NY N	0	0	—	8	0	0	0-0	10.2	21	18	1	0	8-0	3	12.66	27	.420	.492	0-0	—	0		-12	-0.6
1986	†Bos A	2	0	1.000	53	0	0	12-0	44.2	54	26	4	2	16-3	30	4.84	86	.298	.362	0-0	—	0		-3	-0.2
1987	Bos A	2	6	.250	47	0	0	0-4	37.2	46	29	8	0	16-3	35	6.93	66	.301	.367	0-0	—	0		-9	-1.6
Total	11	37	38	.493	461	5	1-1	84-27	629	562	241	48	10	195-32	489	3.03	115	.241	.300	52-1	.135	2	82	36	7.9

Year	Tm Lg	W	L	Pct	G	GS	CG-Sho	SV-BS	IP	H	R	HR	HB	BB-IB	SO	ERA	AERA	OAV	OOB	AB-SH	AVG	PB	Sup	APR	PW
SAMPEN, BILL William Albert B 1.18.1963 Lincoln, IL BR/TR 6-2/195# d4.10																									
1990	Mon N	12	7	.632	59	4	0	2-1	90.1	94	34	7	2	33-6	69	2.99	122	.268	.332	8-2	.000	-1	235	6	1.1
1991	Mon N	9	5	.643	43	8	0	0-0	92.1	96	49	13	3	46-7	52	4.00	91	.273	.358	13-2	.231	0	99	-5	-0.8
1992	Mon N	1	4	.200	44	1	0	0-1	63.1	62	22	4	1	29-6	23	3.13	111	.268	.351	6-1	.000	-1	0	3	0.2
	KC A	0	2	.000	8	1	0	0-0	19.2	21	10	0	3	3-1	14	3.66	111	.292	.338	0-0	—	0	45	0	0.0
1993	KC A	2	2	.500	18	0	0	0-4	18.1	25	12	1	4	9-0	9	5.89	78	.338	.437	0-0	—	0		-2	-0.4
1994	Cal A	1	1	.500	10	0	0	0-0	15.1	14	11	1	3	13-0	9	6.46	76	.241	.405	0-0	—	0		-2	-0.2
Total	5	25	21	.543	182	14	0	2-6	299.1	312	138	26	16	133-20	176	3.73	101	.274	.355	27-5	.111	-1	124	0	-0.1
SAMPSON, BENJ Benjamin Damon B 4.27.1975 Des Moines, IA BR/TL 6-2/210# d9.9																									
1998	Min A	1	0	1.000	5	2	0	0-0	17.1	10	3	0	1	6-0	16	1.56	306	.172	.254	0-0	—	0	78	6	0.3
1999	Min A	3	2	.600	30	4	0	0-0	71	107	65	17	0	34-3	56	8.11	63	.351	.410	3-0	.000	-0	128	-21	-1.3
Total	2	4	2	.667	35	6	0	0-0	88.1	117	68	17	1	40-3	72	6.83	74	.322	.384	3-0	.000	-0	111	-15	-1.0
SAMUELS, JOE Joseph Jonas "Skabotch" B 3.21.1905 Scranton, PA D 10.28.1996 Bath, NY BR/TR 6-1.5/196# d4.23																									
1930	Det A	0	0	—	2	0	0	0	6	10	11	1	0	6	1	16.50	29	.417	.533	1-0	.000	-0		-7	-0.3
SAMUELS, ROGER Roger Howard B 1.5.1961 San Jose, CA BL/TL 6-5/210# d7.20																									
1988	SF N	1	2	.333	15	0	0	0-0	23.1	17	10	4	1	7-0	22	3.47	94	.202	.272	3-0	.000	-0		0	-0.1
1989	Pit N	0	0	—	5	0	0	0-0	3.2	9	4	1	0	4-0	2	9.82	34	.474	.565	0-0	—	0		-3	-0.1
Total	2	1	2	.333	20	0	0	0-0	27	26	14	5	1	11-0	24	4.33	76	.252	.330	3-0	.000	-0		-3	-0.2
SANCHEZ, ALEX Alex Anthony B 4.8.1966 Concord, CA BR/TR 6-2/185# d5.23																									
1989	Tor A	0	1	.000	4	3	0	0-0	11.2	16	13	1	0	14-0	4	10.03	38	.356	.492	0-0	—	0	136	-8	-0.5
SANCHEZ, DUANER Duaner B 10.14.1979 Cotui, D.R. BR/TR 6/160# d6.14																									
2002	Ari N	0	0	—	6	0	0	0-1	3.2	3	2	1	0	5-0	4	4.91	90	.214	.421	0-0	—	0		0	0.0
	Pit N	0	0	—	3	0	0	0-0	2.1	3	4	1	0	2-0	2	15.43	27	.300	.417	0-0	—	0		-3	-0.1
	Year	0	0	—	9	0	0	0-1	6	6	12	2	0	7-0	6	9.00	48	.250	.419	0-0	—	0		-3	-0.1
2003	Pit N	1	0	1.000	6	0	0	0-0	6	15	11	2	2	1-0	3	16.50	27	.500	.529	0-0	—	0		-8	-1.0
Total	2	1	0	1.000	15	0	0	0-1	12	21	17	4	2	8-0	9	12.75	34	.389	.477	0-0	—	0		-11	-1.1
SANCHEZ, FELIX Felix Antonio B 8.3.1981 Puerto Plata, D.R. BR/TL 6-3/180# d9.3																									
2003	Chi N	0	0	—	3	0	0	0-0	1.2	2	2	1	0	3-0	2	10.80	39	.333	.556	0-0	—	0		-1	-0.1
SANCHEZ, ISRAEL Israel (Matos) B 8.20.1963 Falcon Lasvias, Cuba BL/TL 5-9/170# d7.7																									
1988	KC A	3	2	.600	19	1	0	1-0	35.2	36	20	0	0	18-2	14	4.54	88	.265	.348	0-0	—	0	183	-2	-0.3
1990	KC A	0	0	—	11	0	0	0-0	9.2	16	9	1	1	3-0	5	8.38	46	.381	.426	0-0	—	0		-4	-0.2
Total	2	3	2	.600	30	1	0	1-0	45.1	52	29	1	1	21-2	19	5.36	74	.292	.366	0-0	—	0	183	-6	-0.5
SANCHEZ, JESUS Jesus Paulino B 10.11.1974 Nizao Bani, D.R. BL/TL 5-10/153# d3.31																									
1998	Fla N	7	9	.438	35	29	0	0-1	173	178	98	18	4	91-2	137	4.47	91	.272	.363	52-4	.135	-1*	105	-10	-0.8
1999	Fla N	5	7	.417	59	10	0	0-2	76.1	84	53	16	4	60-11	62	6.01	73	.291	.411	12-2	.083	-0*	103	-13	-1.8
2000	Fla N	9	12	.429	32	32	2-2	0-0	182	197	118	32	4	76-4	123	5.34	83	.280	.348	56-3	.232	2*	105	-19	-1.6
2001	Fla N	2	4	.333	16	9	0	0-0	62.2	61	33	7	2	31-2	46	4.74	89	.256	.346	17-2	.235	1*	107	-3	-0.2
2002	Chi N	0	0	—	8	0	0	0-0	8.1	15	12	4	1	10-1	6	12.96	31	.395	.510	1-0	.000	-0		-8	-0.4
2003	Col N	0	0	—	9	0	0	0-0	8	11	8	1	0	4-2	2	9.00	55	.324	.395	0-0	—	0		-3	-0.1
Total	6	23	32	.418	159	80	2-2	0-3	510.1	546	322	78	15	272-22	376	5.26	81	.279	.367	138-11	.181	1	105	-56	-4.9
SANCHEZ, LUIS Luis Mercedes (b: Luis Mercedes Escoba (Sanchez)) B 8.24.1953 Cariaco, Venezuela BR/TR 6-2/210# d4.10																									
1981	Cal A	0	2	.000	17	0	0	2-2	33.2	39	16	4	1	11-0	13	2.94	124	.287	.342	0-0	—	0		1	0.1
1982	†Cal A	7	4	.636	46	0	0	5-3	92.2	89	36	3	7	34-4	58	3.21	127	.259	.337	0-0	—	0		9	1.1
1983	Cal A	10	8	.556	56	1	0	7-9	98.1	92	42	6	3	40-14	49	3.66	110	.254	.332	0-0	—	0	68	5	1.0
1984	Cal A	9	7	.563	49	0	0	11-10	83.2	84	34	10	3	33-9	62	3.33	119	.268	.340	0-0	—	0		6	1.2
1985	Cal A	2	0	1.000	26	0	0	2-0	61.1	67	41	9	1	27-3	34	5.72	72	.283	.354	0-0	—	0		-10	-0.5
Total	5	28	21	.571	194	1	0	27-24	369.2	371	169	32	15	145-30	216	3.75	107	.267	.340	0-0	—	0	68	11	2.9
SANCHEZ, RAUL Raul Guadalupe (Rodriguez) B 12.12.1930 Marianao, Cuba BR/TR 6/150# d4.17																									
1952	Was A	1	1	.500	3	2	1-1	0	12.2	13	5	0	0	7	6	3.55	100	.260	.351	5-0	.000	-1	61	0	0.0
1957	Cin N	3	2	.600	38	0	0	5	62.1	61	37	7	4	25-3	37	4.76	86	.262	.341	7-1	.286	1		-5	-0.3
1960	Cin N	1	0	1.000	8	0	0	0	14.2	12	9	1	3	11-1	5	4.91	78	.226	.388	2-0	.500	0		-2	-0.1
Total	3	5	3	.625	49	2	1-1	5	89.2	86	51	8	7	43-4	48	4.62	86	.256	.351	14-1	.214	0	61	-7	-0.4
SANDERS, BEN Alexander Bennett B 2.16.1865 Catharpin, VA D 8.29.1930 Memphis, TN BR/TR 6/210# d6.6 ▲																									
1888	Phi N	19	10	.655	31	29	28-**8**	0	275.1	240	100	3	3	33	121	1.90	157	.228	.253	236	.246	5*	94	30	3.7
1889	Phi N	19	18	.514	44	39	34-1	1	349.2	406	217	9	4	96	123	3.55	122	.282	.328	169	.278	6	83	24	2.4
1890	Phi P	19	18	.514	43	40	37-2	1	346.2	412	237	13	10	69	107	3.76	114	.283	.320	189	.312	9*	92	20	2.3
1891	Phi AA	11	5	.688	19	18	15	0	145	157	85	3	8	37	40	3.79	100	.267	.319	156	.250	2*	123	1	0.3
1892	Lou N	12	19	.387	31	31	30-3	0	268.1	281	150	6	2	62	77	3.22	95	.259	.300	198	.273	10*	84	-3	0.7
Total	5	80	70	.533	168	157	144-14	2	1385	1496	789	34	27	297	468	3.24	116	.266	.306	948	.271	33	93	72	9.4
SANDERS, DAVE David Andrew B 8.29.1979 Oklahoma City, OK BL/TL 6/200# d4.23																									
2003	Chi A	0	0	—	20	0	0	0-0	22	25	16	5	1	11-0	14	6.14	74	.281	.363	0-0	—	0		-4	-0.2
SANDERS, DEE Dee Wilman B 4.8.1921 Quitman, TX BR/TR 6-3/195# d8.12																									
1945	StL A	0	0	—	2	0	0	0	1.1	7	7	0	0	1	1	40.50	9	.700	.727	0-0	—	0		-5	-0.3
SANDERS, KEN Kenneth George "Daffy" B 7.8.1941 St.Louis, MO BR/TR 5-11/185# d8.6																									
1964	KC A	0	2	.000	21	0	0	1	27	23	12	2	1	17-4	18	3.67	104	.232	.345	0-0	—	0		0	0.1
1966	Bos A	3	6	.333	24	0	0	2	47.1	36	22	2	2	28-9	33	3.80	100	.214	.332	6-3	.000	-0		0	0.1
	KC A	3	4	.429	38	1	0	1	65.1	59	28	8	1	48-7	41	3.72	91	.250	.374	8-1	.250	0	130	-1	-0.1
	Year	6	10	.375	62	1	0	3	112.2	95	33	10	3	76-16	74	3.75	95	.235	.357	14-4	.143	0	123	0	0.0
1968	Oak A	0	1	.000	7	0	0	0	10.2	8	5	1	0	8-2	6	3.38	84	.229	.372	0-0	—	0		-1	-0.1
1970	Mil A	5	2	.714	50	0	0	13-6	92.1	64	19	1	4	25-6	64	1.75	216	.201	.266	13-2	.231	1		21	2.3
1971	Mil A	7	12	.368	**83**	0	0	**31-4**	136.1	111	35	9	4	34-10	80	1.91	182	.227	.282	14-1	.000	-1		**23**	4.4
1972	Mil A	2	9	.182	62	0	0	17-4	92.1	88	38	10	2	31-13	51	3.12	98	.245	.308	7-1	.143	0		-2	-0.3
1973	Min A	2	4	.333	27	0	0	8-3	44.1	53	31	4	2	21-1	19	6.09	65	.299	.374	0-0	—	0		-9	-1.4
	Cle A	5	1	.833	15	0	0	5-1	27.1	18	6	2	0	9-2	14	1.65	238	.188	.257	0-0	—	0		7	1.4
	Year	7	5	.583	42	0	0	13-4	71.2	71	37	6	2	30-3	33	4.40	90	.260	.334	0-0	—	0		-3	0.0
1974	Cle A	0	1	.000	9	0	0	1-0	11	21	12	5	0	5-2	4	9.82	37	.404	.456	0-0	—	0		-7	-0.7
	Cal A	0	0	—	9	0	0	1-1	9.2	10	5	0	0	3-0	4	2.79	123	.278	.317	0-0	—	0		0	0.0
	Year	0	1	.000	18	0	0	2-1	20.2	31	17	5	0	8-2	8	6.53	54	.352	.398	0-0	—	0		-7	-0.7
1975	NY N	1	1	.500	29	0	0	5-1	43	31	11	2	0	14-7	8	2.30	150	.205	.271	2-0	.000	-0*		6	0.4
1976	NY N	1	2	.333	31	0	0	1-0	47	39	16	4	1	12-4	16	2.87	115	.231	.281	2-0	.000	-0		3	0.2
	KC A	0	0	—	3	0	0	0-0	3	3	0	0	0	3-0	2	0.00	—	.273	.429	0-0	—	0		1	0.1
Total	10	29	45	.392	408	1	0	86-20	656.2	564	240	50	17	258-67	360	2.97	118	.235	.312	52-8	.115	-0	126	41	6.4
SANDERS, ROY Roy Garvin "Butch" or "Pepe" B 8.1.1892 Stafford, KS D 1.17.1950 Kansas City, MO BR/TR 6-0.5/195# d4.16																									
1917	Cin N	0	1	.000	2	2	1	0	14	12	7	0	1	16	3	4.50	58	.273	.475	6-0	.000	-1*	101	-2	-0.2
1918	Pit N	7	9	.438	28	14	6-1	1	156	135	59	1	2	52	55	2.60	111	.239	.305	53-2	.151	-1	81	5	0.5
Total	2	7	10	.412	30	16	7-1	1	170	147	66	1	3	68	58	2.75	104	.241	.321	59-2	.136	-2	83	3	0.3
SANDERS, ROY Roy Lee "Simon" B 6.10.1894 , MO D 7.8.1963 Louisville, KY BR/TR 6/185# d8.6																									
1918	NY A	0	2	.000	6	2	0	0	25.2	28	15	0	2	16	8	4.21	67	.301	.414	7-0	.000	-1	27	-4	-0.5
1920	StL A	1	1	.500	8	1	0	0	17.1	20	10	1	1	17	2	5.19	75	.313	.463	4-0	.000	-1	243	-1	-0.2
Total	2	1	3	.250	14	3	0	0	43	48	25	1	3	33	10	4.60	71	.306	.435	11-0	.000	-2	110	-5	-0.7

Year	Tm Lg	W	L	Pct	G	GS	CG-Sho	SV-BS	IP	H	R	HR	HB	BB-IB	SO	ERA	AERA	OAV	OOB	AB-SH	AVG	PB	Sup	APR	PW
SANDERS, SCOTT Scott Gerald B 3.25.1969 Hannibal, MO BR/TR 6-4/220# d8.6																									
1993	SD N	3	3	.500	9	9	0	0-0	52.1	54	32	4	1	23-1	37	4.13	100	.265	.339	16-4	.063	-1	77	-2	-0.4
1994	SD N	4	8	.333	23	20	0	1-0	111	103	63	10	5	48-4	109	4.78	86	.245	.326	32-6	.125	-0	102	-7	-0.7
1995	SD N	5	5	.500	17	15	1	0-0	90	79	46	14	2	31-4	88	4.30	94	.228	.294	27-3	.296	2	109	-1	0.0
1996	†SD N	9	5	.643	46	16	0	0-0	144	117	58	10	2	48-5	157	3.38	118	.221	.284	36-4	.194	2	128	11	1.1
1997	Sea A	3	6	.333	33	6	0	2-2	65.1	73	48	16	3	38-5	62	6.47	70	.280	.371	0-0	—	0	85	-13	-1.7
	Det A	3	8	.273	14	14	1-1	0-0	74.1	79	44	14	1	24-1	58	5.33	86	.276	.329	0-0	—	0	67	-4	-0.6
	Year	6	14	.300	47	20	1-1	2-2	139.2	152	47	30	4	62-6	120	5.86	78	.278	.350	0-0	—	0	73	-18	-2.3
1998	Det A	0	2	.000	3	2	0	0-0	9.2	24	19	1	0	6-2	6	17.69	27	.471	.526	0-0	—	0	39	-13	-1.7
	SD N	3	1	.750	23	0	0	0-0	30.2	33	20	5	0	5-1	26	4.11	95	.270	.299	0-1	—	0		-3	-0.4
1999	Chi N	4	7	.364	67	6	0	2-3	104.1	112	69	19	0	53-8	89	5.52	82	.277	.358	18-2	.278	2	71	-11	-0.9
Total	7	34	45	.430	235	88	2-1	5-5	681.2	674	399	93	14	276-31	632	4.86	87	.257	.327	129-20	.194	4	94	-43	-5.3
SANDERS, WAR Warren Williams B 8.2.1877 Maynardville, TN D 8.3.1962 Chattanooga, TN BR/TL 5-10/160# d4.18																									
1903	StL N	1	6	.143	8	6	3	0	40	48	37	0	2	21	9	6.07	54	.286	.372	15-0	.067	-2	69	-11	-1.6
1904	StL N	1	2	.333	4	3	1	0	19	25	15	1	1	1	11	4.74	57	.298	.314	6-0	.000	-1	60	-4	-0.7
Total	2	2	8	.200	12	9	4	0	59	73	52	1	3	22	20	5.64	55	.290	.354	21-0	.048	-2	66	-15	-2.3
SANDERSON, SCOTT Scott Douglas B 7.22.1956 Dearborn, MI BR/TR 6-5/200# d8.6																									
1978	Mon N	4	2	.667	10	9	1-1	0-0	61	52	20	3	1	21-0	50	2.51	141	.232	.298	19-2	.105	-1	88	7	0.5
1979	Mon N	9	8	.529	34	24	5-3	1-0	168	148	69	16	3	54-4	138	3.43	107	.236	.297	50-7	.160	-0	96	7	0.5
1980	Mon N	16	11	.593	33	33	7-3	0-0	211.1	206	76	18	3	56-3	125	3.11	115	.257	.307	64-8	.078	-3	95	14	1.2
1981	†Mon N	9	7	.563	22	22	4-1	0-0	137.1	122	50	10	1	31-2	77	2.95	119	.236	.278	35-5	.114	2	124	8	1.1
1982	Mon N	12	12	.500	32	32	7	0-0	224	212	98	24	3	58-5	158	3.46	106	.251	.299	57-16	.140	1	107	5	0.4
1983	Mon N	6	7	.462	18	16	0	1-0	81.1	98	50	12	0	20-0	55	4.65	77	.303	.343	28-1	.143	-0	94	-11	-1.7
1984	†Chi N	8	5	.615	24	24	3	0-0	140.2	140	54	5	2	24-3	76	3.14	125	.264	.294	42-4	.119	-1	104	11	0.9
1985	Chi N	5	6	.455	19	19	2	0-0	121	100	49	13	0	27-4	80	3.12	128	.228	.268	31-6	.065	-2	97	9	0.7
1986	Chi N	9	11	.450	37	28	1-1	1-0	169.2	165	85	21	2	37-2	124	4.19	97	.255	.295	51-6	.059	-3*	84	-2	-0.7
1987	Chi N	8	9	.471	32	22	0	2-2	144.2	156	72	23	3	50-5	106	4.29	100	.274	.333	40-4	.075	-1	90	2	0.0
1988	Chi N	1	2	.333	11	0	0	0-2	15.1	13	9	1	0	3-1	6	5.28	68	.232	.258	0-0	—	0		-2	-0.5
1989	†Chi N	11	9	.550	37	23	2	0-0	146.1	155	69	16	2	31-6	86	3.94	96	.273	.312	43-6	.047	-2	95	-1	-0.5
1990	†Oak A	17	11	.607	34	34	2-1	0-0	206.1	205	99	27	4	66-2	128	3.88	96	.255	.312	0-0	—	0	108	-4	-0.6
1991	NY A☆	16	10	.615	34	34	2-2	0-0	208	200	95	22	3	29-0	130	3.81	109	.252	.279	0-0	—	0	101	8	0.8
1992	NY A	12	11	.522	33	33	2-1	0-0	193.1	220	116	28	4	64-5	104	4.93	80	.286	.340	0-0	—	0	119	-22	-2.4
1993	Cal A	7	11	.389	21	21	4-1	0-0	135.1	153	77	15	5	27-5	66	4.46	101	.289	.325	0-0	—	0	86	0	-0.1
	SF N	4	2	.667	11	8	0	0-0	48.2	48	20	12	1	7-2	36	3.51	111	.255	.283	14-1	.000	-1	112	3	0.2
1994	Chi A	8	4	.667	18	14	1	0-0	92	110	57	20	2	12-1	36	5.09	92	.296	.321	0-0	—	0	136	-4	-0.4
1995	Cal A	1	3	.250	7	7	0	0-0	39.1	48	23	6	2	4-1	23	4.12	114	.298	.320	0-0	—	0	102	1	0.1
1996	Cal A	0	2	.000	5	4	0	0-0	18	39	21	5	2	4-0	7	7.50	67	.433	.464	0-0	—	0	106	-7	-0.6
Total	19	163	143	.533	472	407	43-14	5-4	2561.2	2590	1209	297	43	625-51	1611	3.84	102	.263	.307	474-66	.097	-12	102	22	-1.1
SANFORD, FRED John Frederick B 8.9.1919 Garfield, UT BB/TR 6-1/200# d5.5 Mil 1944-45																									
1943	StL A	0	0	—	3	0	0	0	9.1	7	2	0	0	4	2	1.93	172	.219	.306	0-1	—	0		2	0.1
1946	StL A	2	1	.667	3	3	2-2	0	22	19	7	0	0	9	8	2.05	182	.235	.311	7-0	.286	1	46	3	0.6
1947	StL A	7	16	.304	34	23	9	4	186.2	186	89	17	0	76	62	3.71	104	.261	.332	54-7	.204	-0	66	3	0.2
1948	StL A	12	21	.364	42	33	9-1	2	227	250	123	19	2	91	79	4.64	98	.279	.347	73-2	.151	-2*	73	1	0.0
1949	NY A	7	3	.700	29	11	3	0	95.1	100	53	9	0	57	51	3.87	105	.270	.367	34-2	.118	-2	115	-1	-0.4
1950	NY A	5	4	.556	26	12	2	0	112.2	103	60	9	1	79	54	4.55	94	.252	.374	35-1	.229	1	103	-2	0.0
1951	NY A	0	3	.000	11	2	0	0	26.2	15	11	2	0	25	10	3.71	103	.169	.351	5-0	.000	-1	58	1	0.1
	Was A	2	3	.400	7	7	0	0	37	51	27	5	0	27	12	6.57	62	.329	.429	14-1	.071	-1	115	-9	-1.1
	StL A	2	4	.333	9	7	1	0	27.1	37	33	6	0	23	7	10.21	43	.308	.420	7-0	.286	1	136	-16	-2.6
	Year	4	10	.286	27	16	1	0	91	103	40	13	0	75	29	6.82	60	.283	.405	26-1	.115	-1	120	-24	-3.6
Total	7	37	55	.402	164	98	26-3	6	744	768	405	67	3	391	285	4.45	94	.268	.357	229-14	.170	-4	87	-18	-3.1
SANFORD, JACK John Stanley B 5.18.1929 Wellesley Hills, MA D 3.7.2000 Beckley, WV BR/TR 6/190# d9.16 C2																									
1956	Phi N	1	0	1.000	3	1	0	0	13	7	2	0	1	13-0	6	1.38	269	.184	.404	3-0	.333	0	95	4	0.3
1957	Phi N★	19	8	.704	33	33	15-3	0	236.2	194	94	22	3	94-2	**188**	3.08	124	**.221**	.297	89-4	.169	-1	112	18	1.8
1958	Phi N	10	13	.435	38	27	7-2	0	186.1	197	103	15	3	81-6	106	4.44	89	.274	.347	59-3	.169	1	94	-9	-1.0
1959	SF N	15	12	.556	36	31	10	1	222.1	198	90	22	7	70-4	132	3.16	121	.235	.298	72-5	.111	-1	111	17	1.8
1960	SF N	12	14	.462	37	34	11-**6**	0	219	199	111	11	2	99-6	125	3.82	91	.243	.325	74-5	.176	1	126	-9	-1.0
1961	SF N	13	9	.591	38	33	6	0	217.1	203	114	22	5	87-7	112	4.22	90	.249	.322	74-5	.216	6*	112	-10	-0.4
1962	†SF N	24	7	.774	39	38	13-2	0	265.1	233	110	23	3	92-4	147	3.43	111	.234	.300	98-4	.153	0	130	13	1.4
1963	SF N	16	13	.552	42	**42**	11	0	284.1	273	123	21	5	76-8	158	3.51	91	.251	.303	94-7	.138	3*	128	-7	-0.3
1964	SF N	5	7	.417	18	17	3-1	1	106.1	91	44	7	4	37-3	64	3.30	108	.228	.298	30-3	.133	1*	88	3	0.4
1965	SF N	4	5	.444	23	16	0	2	91	92	50	11	7	30-7	43	3.96	91	.256	.324	25-1	.120	-0	100	-5	-0.6
	Cal A	1	2	.333	9	5	0	1	29.1	35	16	2	0	10-1	13	4.60	74	.324	.381	7-1	.143	-0	114	-4	-0.4
1966	Cal A	13	7	.650	50	6	0	5	108	108	51	11	4	27-6	54	3.83	88	.271	.316	22-1	.136	1	96	-6	-0.9
1967	Cal A	3	2	.600	12	9	0	1	48.1	53	26	6	0	7-1	21	4.47	70	.288	.311	15-2	.200	1	142	-7	-0.5
	KC A	1	2	.333	10	1	0	0	22	24	18	1	2	14-4	13	6.55	49	.296	.408	3-0	.000	-0	82	-8	-1.0
	Year	4	4	.500	22	10	0	1	70.1	77	21	7	2	21-5	34	5.12	62	.291	.344	18-2	.167	1	135	-15	-1.5
Total	12	137	101	.576	388	293	76-14	11	2049.1	1907	952	174	46	737-59	1182	3.69	98	.247	.314	665-41	.158	12	115	-10	-0.4
SANFORD, MO Meredith Leroy B 12.24.1966 Americus, GA BR/TR 6-6/220# d8.9																									
1991	Cin N	1	2	.333	5	5	0	0-0	28	19	14	3	1	15-1	31	3.86	99	.186	.297	8-2	.000	-1	90	0	-0.1
1993	Col N	1	2	.333	11	6	0	0-0	35.2	37	25	4	0	27-0	36	5.30	90	.278	.395	8-1	.000	-1	82	-2	-0.3
1995	Min A	0	0	—	11	0	0	0-0	18.2	16	11	7	2	16-0	17	5.30	90	.225	.382	0-0	—	0		-1	-0.1
Total	3	2	4	.333	27	11	0	0-0	82.1	72	50	14	3	58-1	84	4.81	93	.235	.360	16-3	.000	-2	83	-3	-0.5
SANTANA, JOHAN Johan Alexander B 3.13.1979 Tovar, Venezuela BL/TL 6/195# d4.3																									
2000	Min A	2	3	.400	30	5	0	0-0	86	102	64	11	2	54-0	64	6.49	80	.302	.398	1-0	.000	-0	80	-11	-0.5
2001	Min A	1	0	1.000	15	4	0	0-0	43.2	50	25	6	3	16-0	28	4.74	97	.292	.358	0-0	—	0	151	-1	-0.1
2002	†Min A	8	6	.571	27	14	0	1-0	108.1	84	41	7	1	49-0	137	2.99	150	.212	.298	4-0	.250	0	105	17	2.0
2003	†Min A	12	3	.800	45	18	0	0-0	158.1	127	56	17	3	47-1	169	3.07	148	.216	.276	3-0	.333	0	103	26	2.2
Total	4	23	12	.657	117	41	0	1-0	396.1	363	186	41	9	166-1	398	3.97	118	.243	.320	8-0	.250	0	104	31	3.6
SANTANA, JULIO Julio Franklin B 1.20.1973 San Pedro De Macoris, D.R. BR/TR 6/175# d4.6																									
1997	Tex A	4	6	.400	30	14	0	0-1	104	141	86	16	4	49-2	64	6.75	71	.323	.392	2-0	.500	0	103	-22	-1.7
1998	Tex A	0	0	—	3	0	0	0-0	5.1	7	5	0	0	4-1	1	8.44	57	.304	.407	0-0	—	0		-2	-0.1
	TB A	5	6	.455	32	19	1	0-0	140.1	144	72	18	5	58-2	60	4.23	113	.270	.344	4-0	.000	-0	92	8	0.4
	Year	5	6	.455	35	19	1	0-0	145.2	151	77	18	5	62-3	61	4.39	109	.272	.347	4-0	.000	-0	92	7	0.3
1999	TB A	1	4	.200	22	5	0	0-0	55.1	66	49	10	7	32-0	34	7.32	68	.300	.404	1-0	1.000	0	56	-13	-1.0
2000	Mon N	1	5	.167	36	4	0	0-2	66.2	69	45	11	2	33-2	58	5.67	85	.271	.356	7-0	.000	-1	96	-6	-0.5
2002	Det A	3	5	.375	38	0	0	0-1	57	49	19	8	2	28-2	38	2.84	152	.238	.335	0-0	—	0		10	1.2
Total	5	14	26	.350	161	42	1	0-4	428.2	476	276	63	20	204-9	255	5.33	89	.284	.366	14-0	.143	-0	93	-25	-1.7
SANTANA, MARINO Marino (Castro) B 5.10.1972 San Jose De Los Llanos, D.R. BR/TR 6-1/175# d9.4																									
1998	Det A	0	0	—	7	0	0	0-0	7.1	9	3	1	1	8-2	10	3.68	128	.310	.474	0-0	—	0		1	0.0
1999	Bos A	0	0	—	3	0	0	0-0	4	8	7	3	0	3-0	4	15.75	32	.444	.500	0-0	—	0		-4	-0.2
Total	2	0	0	—	10	0	0	0-0	11.1	17	10	4	1	11-2	14	7.94	61	.362	.483	0-0	—	0		-3	-0.2
SANTIAGO, JOSE Jose Guillermo (Guzman) "Pants" B 9.4.1928 Coamo, P.R. BR/TR 5-10/175# d4.17																									
1954	Cle A	0	0	—	1	0	0	0	1.2	0	1	0	0	2	1	0.00	—	.000	.286	0-0	—	0		0	0.0
1955	Cle A	2	0	1.000	17	0	0	0	32.2	31	11	1	5	14-1	19	2.48	161	.256	.350	4-2	.500	1		5	0.4
1956	KC A	1	2	.333	9	5	0	0	21.2	36	26	8	5	17-0	9	8.31	52	.387	.500	5-1	.400	0	169	-11	-1.2

Year	Tm Lg	W	L	Pct	G	GS	CG-Sho	SV-BS	IP	H	R	HR	HB	BB-IB	SO	ERA	AERA	OAV	OOB	AB-SH	AVG	PB	Sup	APR	PW
Total	3	3	2	.600	27	5	0	0	56	67	38	9	10	33-1	29	4.66	88	.306	.414	9-3	.444	2	169	-6	-0.8
SANTIAGO, JOSE Jose Rafael (Alfonso) B 8.15.1940 Juana Diaz, P.R. BR/TR 6-2/185# d9.9																									
1963	KC A	1	0	1.000	4	0	0	0	7	8	7	4	0	2-0	6	9.00	43	.276	.323	0-0	—	0		-3	-0.4
1964	KC A	0	6	.000	34	8	0	0	83.2	84	53	9	4	35-1	64	4.73	81	.258	.336	18-2	.000	-2	102	-10	-0.9
1965	KC A	0	0	—	4	0	0	0	5	8	5	1	0	4-2	8	9.00	39	.364	.462	0-0	—	0		-3	-0.1
1966	Bos A	12	13	.480	35	28	7-1	2	172	155	87	17	2	58-0	119	3.66	104	.238	.300	56-4	.196	0*	94	0	0.0
1967	†Bos A	12	4	.750	50	11	2	5	145.1	138	61	15	2	47-3	109	3.59	97	.251	.312	42-1	.190	2	157	0	0.3
1968	Bos A✧	9	4	.692	18	18	7-2	0	124	96	34	9	3	42-0	86	2.25	140	.215	.286	43-3	.163	1*	100	12	1.5
1969	Bos A	0	0	—	10	0	0	0-0	7.2	11	5	2	0	4-0	4	3.52	108	.324	.395	0-0	—	0		0	0.0
1970	Bos A	0	2	.000	8	0	0	1-0	11.1	18	13	0	0	8-1	8	10.32	38	.353	.441	3-0	.667	1*		-7	-1.1
Total	8	34	29	.540	163	65	16-3	8-0	556	518	265	57	11	200-7	404	3.74	96	.246	.313	162-10	.173	2	107	-11	-0.7
SANTIAGO, JOSE Jose Rafael (Fuentes) B 11.5.1974 Fajardo, P.R. BR/TR 6-3/200# d6.7																									
1997	KC A	0	0	—	4	0	0	0-0	4.2	7	2	0	1	2-1	1	1.93	245	.333	.417	0-0	—	0		1	0.0
1998	KC A	0	0	—	2	0	0	0-0	2	4	2	0	0	0-0	2	9.00	54	.444	.444	0-0	—	0		-1	0.0
1999	KC A	3	4	.429	34	0	0	2-1	47.1	46	23	7	2	14-2	15	3.42	147	.251	.307	0-0	—	0		7	0.8
2000	KC A	8	6	.571	45	0	0	2-6	69	70	33	7	3	26-3	44	3.91	131	.260	.329	0-0	—	0		8	1.5
2001	KC A	2	2	.500	20	0	0	0-1	29.1	40	22	2	1	9-1	15	6.75	73	.333	.376	0-0	—	0		-5	-0.5
	Phi N	2	4	.333	53	0	0	0-1	62.1	66	25	3	2	13-1	28	3.61	118	.272	.312	3-0	.000	-0		5	0.4
2002	Phi N	1	3	.250	42	0	0	0-1	47	56	35	7	3	15-1	30	6.70	58	.290	.347	2-0	.000	0		-14	-1.1
2003	Cle A	1	3	.250	25	0	0	0-2	31.2	37	11	2	0	14-3	15	2.84	156	.298	.370	0-0	—	0		6	0.6
Total	7	17	22	.436	225	0	0	4-12	293.1	326	153	28	12	93-12	150	4.39	105	.281	.337	5-0	.000	0		7	1.7
SANTORINI, AL Alan Joel B 5.19.1948 Irvington, NJ BR/TR 6/190# d9.10																									
1968	Atl N	0	1	.000	1	1	0	0	3	4	4	1	0	0-0	0	0.00	—	.286	.286	0-0	—	0	58	-1	-0.2
1969	SD N	8	14	.364	32	30	2-1	0-0	184.2	194	95	11	7	73-10	111	3.95	90	.270	.341	63-3	.111	-1	72	-11	-1.3
1970	SD N	1	8	.111	21	12	0	1-0	75.2	91	56	11	3	43-6	41	6.07	66	.294	.382	18-0	.000	-2	79	-17	-2.0
1971	SD N	0	2	.000	18	3	0	0-1	38.1	43	19	4	0	11-1	21	3.76	88	.285	.329	5-0	.400	1	63	-2	-0.1
	StL N	0	2	.000	19	5	0	2-0	49.2	51	21	2	1	19-2	21	3.81	95	.270	.340	10-0	.300	1	98	0	0.0
	Year	0	4	.000	37	8	0	2-1	88	94	25	6	1	30-3	42	3.78	92	.276	.335	15-0	.333	1	86	-2	-0.1
1972	StL N	8	11	.421	30	19	3-3	0-1	133.2	136	63	6	1	46-7	72	4.11	83	.263	.323	40-3	.075	-2	93	-8	-1.3
1973	StL N	0	0	—	6	0	0	0-0	8.1	14	5	1	1	2-0	2	5.40	68	.400	.436	1-0	.000	-0		-1	-0.1
Total	6	17	38	.309	127	70	5-4	3-2	493.1	533	263	36	13	194-26	268	4.29	83	.276	.344	137-6	.109	-4	80	-40	-5.0
SANTOS, VICTOR Victor Irving B 10.2.1976 San Pedro De Macoris, D.R. BR/TR 6-3/175# d4.9																									
2001	Det A	2	2	.500	33	7	0	0-0	76.1	62	33	9	3	49-4	52	3.30	132	.222	.341	0-0	—	0	146	8	0.4
2002	Col N	0	4	.000	24	2	0	0-0	26	41	30	3	0	22-3	25	10.38	46	.360	.460	2-0	.500	0	135	-13	-1.7
2003	Tex A	0	2	.000	8	4	0	0-0	25.2	29	21	5	1	16-1	15	7.01	71	.296	.397	2-1	.000	-0	74	-5	-0.4
Total	3	2	8	.200	65	13	0	0-0	128	132	84	17	4	87-8	92	5.48	83	.269	.380	4-1	.250	0	121	-10	-1.7
SARMIENTO, MANNY Manuel Eduardo (Aponte) B 2.2.1956 Cagua, Venezuela BR/TR 6/170# d7.30																									
1976	†Cin N	5	1	.833	22	0	0	0-0	43.2	36	14	1	1	12-3	20	2.06	170	.222	.278	7-0	.000	-1		6	0.6
1977	Cin N	0	0	—	24	0	0	1-0	40.1	28	13	6	0	11-2	23	2.45	160	.196	.247	1-1	.000	-0		6	0.2
1978	Cin N	9	7	.563	63	4	0	5-3	127.1	109	65	16	1	54-10	72	4.38	81	.234	.310	16-1	.000	-1*	70	-10	-1.4
1979	Cin N	0	4	.000	23	1	0	0-2	38.2	47	21	2	1	7-2	23	4.66	80	.311	.337	6-1	.000	-1	213	-3	-0.4
1980	Sea A	0	1	.000	9	0	0	1-1	14.2	14	7	2	0	6-1	15	3.68	112	.255	.317	0-0	—	0		1	0.0
1982	Pit N	9	4	.692	35	17	4	1-0	164.2	153	69	7	0	46-4	81	3.39	110	.246	.295	47-7	.191	1	134	6	0.4
1983	Pit N	3	5	.375	52	0	0	4-1	84.1	74	35	8	0	36-8	49	2.99	124	.243	.318	10-2	.000	-1		5	0.4
Total	7	26	22	.542	228	22	4	12-7	513.2	461	224	42	3	172-30	283	3.49	106	.242	.301	87-12	.103	-3	127	11	-0.2
SASAKI, KAZUHIRO Kazuhiro B 2.22.1968 Tokyo, Japan BR/TR 6-4/209# d4.5																									
2000	†Sea A	2	5	.286	63	0	0	37-3	62.2	42	25	10	2	31-5	78	3.16	149	.184	.285	0-0	—	0		11	1.9
2001	†Sea A★	0	4	.000	69	0	0	45-7	66.2	48	24	6	4	11-2	62	3.24	128	.195	.241	0-0	—	0		8	1.3
2002	Sea A★	4	5	.444	61	0	0	37-8	60.2	44	24	6	2	20-4	73	2.52	168	.201	.268	0-0	—	0		9	1.9
2003	Sea A	1	2	.333	35	0	0	10-4	33.1	31	17	2	1	15-2	29	4.05	107	.238	.318	0-0	—	0		1	0.0
Total	4	7	16	.304	228	0	0	129-22	223.1	165	90	24	9	77-13	242	3.14	139	.200	.273	0-0	—	0		29	5.1
SAUCIER, KEVIN Kevin Andrew B 8.9.1956 Pensacola, FL BR/TL 6-1/196# d10.1																									
1978	Phi N	0	1	.000	1	0	0	0-0	2	4	4	0	1	1-0	2	18.00	20	.400	.500	0-0	—	0		-3	-0.5
1979	Phi N	1	4	.200	29	2	0	1-1	62.1	68	31	4	3	33-3	21	4.19	92	.291	.381	10-0	.100	-1	35	-2	-0.2
1980	†Phi N	7	3	.700	40	0	0	0-2	50	50	21	2	4	20-8	25	3.42	111	.281	.359	8-0	.000	-1		2	0.3
1981	Det A	4	2	.667	38	0	0	13-2	49	26	11	1	5	21-3	23	1.65	228	.160	.277	0-0	—	0		11	1.9
1982	Det A	3	1	.750	31	1	0	5-2	40.1	35	15	0	2	29-4	23	3.12	130	.254	.391	0-0	—	0	112	5	0.5
Total	5	15	11	.577	139	3	0	19-7	203.2	183	82	7	15	104-18	94	3.31	116	.253	.356	18-0	.056	-2	62	13	2.0
SAUERBECK, SCOTT Scott William B 11.9.1971 Cincinnati, OH BR/TL 6-3/190# d4.5																									
1999	Pit N	4	1	.800	65	0	0	2-3	67.2	53	19	6	4	38-5	55	2.00	229	.220	.336	1-1	.000	-0		18	1.3
2000	Pit N	5	4	.556	75	0	0	1-3	75.2	76	36	4	1	61-8	83	4.04	114	.270	.399	1-0	.000	-0		6	0.6
2001	Pit N	2	2	.500	70	0	0	2-2	62.2	61	41	4	2	40-6	79	5.60	80	.257	.369	2-0	.000	-0		-7	-0.5
2002	Pit N	5	4	.556	78	0	0	0-0	62.2	50	18	4	1	27-4	70	2.30	182	.220	.306	2-0	.000	-0*		13	1.7
2003	Pit N	3	4	.429	53	0	0	0-4	40	30	20	5	1	25-2	32	4.05	108	.207	.327	1-0	.000	-0		1	0.2
	†Bos A	0	1	.000	26	0	0	0-1	16.2	17	14	1	4	18-3	18	6.48	70	.266	.448	0-0	—	0		-4	-0.2
Total	5	19	16	.543	367	0	0	5-13	325.1	287	148	24	13	209-28	337	3.71	121	.240	.358	7-1	.000	-1		27	3.1
SAUNDERS, TONY Anthony Scott B 4.29.1974 Baltimore, MD BL/TL 6-2/205# d4.5																									
1997	†Fla N	4	6	.400	22	21	0	0-0	111.1	99	62	12	2	64-1	102	4.61	88	.244	.347	37-1	.081	-1	116	-7	-0.7
1998	TB A	6	15	.286	31	31	2	0-0	192.1	191	95	15	7	111-1	172	4.12	116	.265	.364	2-0	1.000	1	65	14	1.4
1999	TB A	3	3	.500	9	9	0	0-0	42	53	39	6	4	29-0	30	6.43	77	.315	.424	0-0	—	0	102	-9	-1.0
Total	3	13	24	.351	62	61	2	0-0	345.2	343	196	33	13	204-2	304	4.56	100	.265	.367	39-1	.128	0	87	-2	-0.3
SAUNDERS, DENNIS Dennis James B 1.4.1949 Alhambra, CA BB/TR 6-3/195# d5.21																									
1970	Det A	1	1	.500	8	0	0	1-2	14	16	5	1	1	5-1	8	3.21	116	.286	.355	5-0	.000	-1		1	0.1
SAUVEUR, RICH Richard Daniel B 11.23.1963 Arlington, VA BL/TL 6-4/170# d7.1																									
1986	Pit N	0	0	—	3	3	0	0-0	12	17	8	3	2	6-0	6	6.00	64	.354	.446	3-1	.333	0	116	-2	-0.1
1988	Mon N	0	0	—	4	0	0	0-0	3	3	2	1	0	2-0	3	6.00	60	.250	.357	0-0	—	0		-1	0.0
1991	NY N	0	0	—	6	0	0	0-2	3.1	7	4	1	0	2-0	4	10.80	34	.467	.529	0-0	—	0		-2	-0.1
1992	KC A	0	1	.000	8	0	0	0-0	14.1	15	7	1	2	8-1	7	4.40	92	.273	.385	0-0	—	0		0	0.0
1996	Chi A	0	0	—	3	0	0	0-0	3	3	5	1	1	5-0	1	15.00	32	.333	.600	0-0	—	0		-3	-0.1
2000	Oak A	0	0	—	10	0	0	0-0	10.1	13	5	3	0	1-0	7	4.35	109	.310	.326	0-0	—	0		1	0.0
Total	6	0	1	.000	34	3	0	0-2	46	58	31	10	5	24-1	28	6.07	69	.320	.414	3-1	.333	0	116	-7	-0.3
SAVAGE, JACK John Joseph B 4.22.1964 Louisville, KY BR/TR 6-3/190# d9.14																									
1987	LA N	0	0	—	3	0	0	0-0	3.1	4	1	0	0	0-0	0	2.70	147	.286	.286	0-0	—	0		1	0.0
1990	Min A	0	2	.000	17	0	0	1-2	26	37	26	3	0	11-1	12	8.31	50	.339	.397	0-0	—	0		-11	-0.8
Total	2	0	2	.000	20	0	0	1-2	29.1	41	27	3	0	11-1	12	7.67	54	.333	.385	0-0	—	0		-10	-0.8
SAVAGE, BOB John Robert B 12.1.1921 Manchester, NH BR/TR 6-2/180# d6.24 Mil 1943-45																									
1942	Phi A	0	1	.000	8	3	0	0	30.2	24	16	0	0	31	10	3.23	117	.220	.393	9-0	.111	0	113	1	0.0
1946	Phi A	3	15	.167	40	19	7-1	2	164	164	80	5	2	93	78	4.06	87	.259	.355	41-1	.122	1	78	-7	-0.7
1947	Phi A	8	10	.444	44	8	2-1	2	146	135	71	8	0	55	56	3.76	101	.245	.314	40-2	.050	-4	90	0	-0.5
1948	Phi A	5	1	.833	33	1	1	5	75.1	98	55	9	0	33	26	6.21	69	.318	.384	13-2	.077	-1	21	-15	-1.3
1949	StL A	0	0	—	4	0	0	0	7	12	5	1	0	3	1	6.43	70	.400	.455	1-0	.000	-0		-1	-0.1
Total	5	16	27	.372	129	31	10-2	9	423	433	227	23	2	215	171	4.32	88	.265	.352	104-5	.087	-3	80	-22	-2.6

Year	Tm Lg	W	L	Pct	G	GS	CG-Sho	SV-BS	IP	H	R	HR	HB	BB-IB	SO	ERA	AERA	OAV	OOB	AB-SH	AVG	PB	Sup	APR	PW
SAVIDGE, DON Donald Snyder B 8.28.1908 Berwick, PA D 3.22.1983 Santa Barbara, CA BR/TR 6-1/180# d8.6 f-Ralph																									
1929	Was A	0	0	—	3	0	0	0	6	12	7	1	0	2	2	9.00	47	.414	.452	0-0	—	0		-3	-0.1
SAVIDGE, RALPH Ralph Austin "The Human Whipcord" B 2.3.1879 Jerseytown, PA D 7.22.1959 Berwick, PA BR/TR 6-2/210# d9.22 s-Don																									
1908	Cin N	0	1	.000	4	1	1	0	21	18	9	0	0	8	7	2.57	90	.247	.321	7-0	.000	-1	0	-1	-0.2
1909	Cin N	0	0	—	1	0	0	0	4	10	12	1	1	3	2	22.50	12	.588	.667	1-0	.000	-0		-8	-0.4
Total	2	0	1	.000	5	1	1	0	25	28	21	1	1	11	9	5.76	41	.311	.392	8-0	.000	-1	0	-9	-0.6
SAVRANSKY, MOE Morris B 1.13.1929 Cleveland, OH BL/TL 5-11/175# d4.23																									
1954	Cin N	0	2	.000	16	0	0	0	24	23	13	6	2	8	7	4.88	86	.247	.320	2-0	.500	1		-1	0.0
SAWYER, RICK Richard Clyde B 4.7.1948 Bakersfield, CA BR/TR 6-2/205# d4.28																									
1974	NY A	0	0	—	1	0	0	0-0	1.2	2	3	0	0	1-0	1	16.20	22	.500	.600	0-0	—	0		-2	-0.1
1975	NY A	0	0	—	4	0	0	0-0	6	7	4	0	0	2-0	3	3.00	123	.304	.360	0-0	—	0		0	0.0
1976	SD N	5	3	.625	13	11	4-2	0-0	81.2	84	24	2	1	38-8	33	2.53	129	.272	.351	24-5	.208	1	110	8	0.9
1977	SD N	7	6	.538	56	9	0	0-0	111	136	77	15	7	55-11	45	5.84	61	.316	.399	20-2	.150	1	139	-28	-2.8
Total	4	12	9	.571	74	20	4-2	0-0	200.1	229	108	17	8	96-19	82	4.49	77	.299	.380	44-7	.182	2	122	-22	-2.0
SAWYER, WILL Willard Newton B 7.29.1864 Brimfield, OH D 1.5.1936 Kent, OH BL/TL d7.21																									
1883	Cle N	4	10	.286	17	15	15	0	141	119	79	1		47	76	2.36	133	**.217**	.279	47	.021	-7	52	11	0.2
SAYLES, BILL William Nisbeth B 7.27.1917 Portland, OR D 11.20.1996 Lincoln City, OR BR/TR 6-2/175# d7.17 Mil 1944-45																									
1939	Bos A	0	0	—	5	0	0	0	14	14	13	1	0	13	9	7.07	67	.264	.409	7-0	.143	-0		-4	-0.2
1943	NY N	1	3	.250	18	3	1	0	53	60	29	1	0	23	38	4.75	72	.284	.355	13-0	.308	1*	82	-6	-0.4
	Bro N	0	0	—	5	0	0	0	11.2	13	14	0	0	10	5	7.71	44	.271	.397	2-0	.500	0*		-7	-0.3
	Year	1	3	.250	23	3	1	0	64.2	73	46	1	0	33	43	5.29	65	.282	.363	15-0	.333	1	82	-13	-0.7
Total	2	1	3	.250	28	3	1	0	78.2	87	56	2	0	46	52	5.61	65	.279	.372	22-0	.273	1	78	-17	-0.9
SAYLOR, PHIL Philip Andrew "Lefty" B 1.2.1871 Van Wert Co., OH D 7.23.1937 W.Alexandria, OH TL d7.11																									
1891	Phi N	0	0	—	1	0	0	0	3	2	2	1	0	0	0	6.00	57	.182	.182	1	.000	-0		-1	0.0
SCANLAN, FRANK Frank Aloysius B 4.28.1890 Syracuse, NY D 4.9.1969 Brooklyn, NY BL/TL 6-1.5/175# d8.6 b-Doc																									
1909	Phi N	0	0	—	6	0	0	1	11	8	3	0	0	5	5	1.64	159	.211	.302	4-0	.000	-1		1	0.0
SCANLAN, BOB Robert Guy B 8.9.1966 Los Angeles, CA BR/TR 6-8/210# d5.7																									
1991	Chi N	7	8	.467	40	13	0	1-1	111	114	60	5	3	40-3	44	3.89	100	.268	.331	24-2	.042	-2	82	-3	-0.6
1992	Chi N	3	6	.333	69	0	0	14-4	87.1	76	32	4	1	30-6	42	2.89	125	.235	.301	4-0	.000	-0		7	0.9
1993	Chi N	4	5	.444	70	0	0	0-3	75.1	79	41	6	3	28-7	44	4.54	88	.278	.343	2-1	.500	0		-4	-0.5
1994	Mil A	2	6	.250	30	12	0	2-1	103	117	53	11	4	28-2	65	4.11	123	.288	.339	0-0	—	0	64	10	0.6
1995	Mil A	4	7	.364	17	14	0	0-0	83.1	101	66	9	7	44-3	29	6.59	76	.304	.391	0-0	—	0	103	-14	-1.5
1996	Det A	0	0	—	8	0	0	0-0	11	16	15	1	1	9-1	3	10.64	48	.348	.464	0-0	—	0		-7	-0.3
	KC A	0	1	.000	9	0	0	0-1	11.1	13	4	1	1	3-1	3	3.18	158	.295	.354	0-0	—	0		2	0.2
	Year	0	1	.000	17	0	0	0-1	22.1	29	25	2	2	12-2	6	6.85	73	.322	.413	0-0	—	0		-5	-0.1
1998	Hou N	0	1	.000	27	0	0	0-0	26.1	24	12	4	1	13-0	9	3.08	132	.245	.330	0-0	—	0		2	0.1
2000	Mil N	0	0	—	2	0	0	0-0	1.2	6	6	0	1	0-0	1	27.00	17	.600	.583	0-0	—	0		-4	-0.2
2001	Mon N	0	0	—	18	0	0	0-0	26.1	37	23	0	1	14-0	5	7.86	57	.339	.419	0-0	—	0		-9	-0.4
Total	9	20	34	.370	290	39	0	17-10	536.2	583	312	41	23	209-23	245	4.63	94	.281	.349	30-3	.067	-2	89	-20	-1.7
SCANLAN, DOC William Dennis B 3.7.1881 Syracuse, NY D 5.29.1949 Brooklyn, NY BL/TR 5-8/165# d9.24 b-Frank																									
1903	Pit N	0	1	.000	1	1	1	0	9	5	7	0	0	6	0	4.00	81	.167	.306	2-0	.000	0	42	-1	-0.1
1904	Pit N	1	3	.250	4	3	1	0	22	21	18	0	2	20	10	4.91	56	.236	.387	6-0	.000	-1	109	-6	-1.0
	Bro N	6	6	.500	13	12	11-3	0	104	94	39	0	2	40	40	2.16	127	.242	.316	35-5	.143	-2	88	6	0.4
	Year	7	9	.438	17	15	12-3	0	126	115	43	0	4	60	50	2.64	104	.241	.331	41-5	.122	-2	92	1	-0.6
1905	Bro N	14	12	.538	33	28	22-2	0	249.2	220	119	4	8	104	135	2.92	99	.237	.319	96-3	.167	-2	103	-2	-0.5
1906	Bro N	18	13	.581	38	33	28-6	2	288	230	128	5	6	127	120	3.19	79	.214	.301	97-3	.186	3	109	-19	-2.1
1907	Bro N	6	8	.429	17	15	10-2	0	107	90	50	1	3	61	59	3.20	73	.239	.349	34-0	.265	5	93	-9	-0.7
1909	Bro N	8	7	.533	19	17	12-2	0	141.1	125	53	2	4	65	72	2.93	88	.252	.343	44-1	.273	5	87	-3	0.3
1910	Bro N	9	11	.450	34	25	14	2	217.1	175	76	1	5	116	103	2.61	116	.234	.341	69-2	.203	1	72	12	1.1
1911	Bro N	3	10	.231	22	15	3	1	113.2	101	67	2	6	69	45	3.64	92	.256	.374	33-2	.121	-2	66	-7	-1.0
Total	8	65	71	.478	181	149	102-15	5	1252	1061	557	15	36	608	584	3.00	93	.234	.330	416-16	.188	8	90	-29	-3.6
SCANTLEBURY, PAT Patricio Athelstan B 11.11.1917 Gatun, Canal Zone D 5.24.1991 Glen Ridge, NJ BL/TL 6-1/180# d4.19																									
1956	Cin N	0	1	.000	6	2	0	0	19	24	14	5	0	5-0	10	6.63	60	.293	.333	3-1	.000	-0*	144	-5	-0.3
SCARBERY, RANDY Randy James B 6.22.1952 Fresno, CA BB/TR 6-1/185# d4.16																									
1979	Chi A	2	8	.200	45	5	0	4-0	101.1	102	56	9	3	34-3	45	4.62	92	.262	.323	0-0	—	0	43	-2	-0.2
1980	Chi A	1	2	.333	15	0	0	2-0	28.2	24	14	1	2	7-0	18	4.08	99	.238	.297	0-0	—	0		0	0.0
Total	2	3	10	.231	60	5	0	6-0	130	126	70	10	5	41-3	63	4.50	94	.257	.318	0-0	—	0	43	-2	-0.2
SCARBOROUGH, RAY Ray Wilson (b: Rae Wilson Scarborough) B 7.23.1917 Mt.Gilead, NC D 7.1.1982 Mount Olive, NC BR/TR 6/185# d6.26 Mil 1943-45 C1																									
1942	Was A	2	1	.667	17	5	1-1	0	63.1	68	32	2	0	32	16	4.12	89	.272	.355	21-1	.190	0	197	-2	-0.1
1943	Was A	4	4	.500	24	6	2	3	86	93	42	2	0	46	43	2.83	113	.273	.359	24-2	.333	2	171	0	0.2
1946	Was A	7	11	.389	32	20	6-1	1	155.2	176	85	8	1	74	46	4.05	83	.286	.364	50-4	.140	-2	83	-13	-1.4
1947	Was A	6	13	.316	33	18	8-2	0	161	165	74	5	1	67	63	3.41	109	.267	.339	50-3	.120	-3	58	3	0.0
1948	Was A	15	8	.652	31	26	9	1	185.1	166	71	10	3	72	76	2.82	154	.233	.307	64-6	.219	-0	98	29	3.4
1949	Was A	13	11	.542	34	27	11-1	0	199.2	204	115	10	7	88	81	4.60	93	.265	.346	67-7	.194	-0	94	-7	-0.7
1950	Was A	3	5	.375	8	8	4-2	0	58.1	62	30	2	2	22	24	4.01	112	.276	.345	20-0	.100	-1	63	3	0.3
	Chi A☆	10	13	.435	27	23	8-1	1	149.1	160	95	10	4	62	70	5.30	85	.274	.347	46-4	.174	-1	73	-12	-1.7
	Year	13	18	.419	35	31	12-3	1	207.2	222	99	12	6	84	94	4.94	91	.274	.347	66-4	.152	-3	71	-9	-1.4
1951	Bos A	12	9	.571	37	22	8	0	184	201	106	21	14	61	71	5.09	88	.275	.342	68-3	.191	-2	120	-7	-1.0
1952	Bos A	1	5	.167	28	8	1-1	4	76.2	79	47	8	4	35	29	4.81	82	.266	.351	18-0	.222	0	66	-7	-0.6
	†NY A	5	1	.833	9	4	1	0	34	27	11	4	1	15	13	2.91	114	.223	.314	14-0	.357	2	164	3	0.6
	Year	6	6	.500	37	12	2-1	4	110.2	106	17	12	5	50	42	4.23	89	.254	.340	32-0	.281	2	95	-5	0.0
1953	NY A	2	2	.500	25	1	0	2	54.2	52	23	4	4	26	20	3.29	112	.250	.345	12-1	.083	-0	144	2	0.2
	Det A	0	2	.000	13	0	0	2	20.2	34	24	3	3	11	12	8.27	49	.354	.436	2-0	.000	-0		-11	-1.2
	Year	2	4	.333	38	1	0	4	75.1	86	53	7	7	37	32	4.66	81	.283	.374	14-1	.071	-0	141	-10	-1.0
Total	10	80	85	.485	318	168	59-9	14	1428.2	1487	755	89	44	611	564	4.13	97	.267	.344	456-31	.186	-6	96	-19	-2.0
SCARCE, MAC Guerrant McCurdy B 4.8.1949 Danville, VA BL/TL 6-3/200# d7.10																									
1972	Phi N	1	2	.333	31	0	0	4-0	36.2	30	14	6	2	20-2	40	3.44	105	.222	.331	6-0	.000	-1		1	0.1
1973	Phi N	1	8	.111	52	0	0	12-2	70.2	54	23	3	1	47-14	57	2.42	157	.220	.347	5-1	.000	-1		10	1.4
1974	Phi N	3	8	.273	58	0	0	5-1	70.1	72	40	6	2	35-7	50	4.99	76	.275	.359	6-0	.000	-1		-8	-1.4
1975	NY N	0	0	—	1	0	0	0-0	0	1	0	0	0	0-0	0	—	—	1.000	1.000	0-0	—	0		0	0.0
1978	Min A	1	1	.500	17	0	0	0-1	32	35	19	5	3	15-0	17	3.94	97	.292	.381	0-0	—	0		-2	-0.1
Total	5	6	19	.240	159	0	0	21-4	209.2	192	96	20	8	117-23	164	3.69	102	.251	.354	17-1	.000	-2		1	0.0
SCHACHT, AL Alexander B 11.11.1892 New York, NY D 7.14.1984 Waterbury, CT BR/TR 5-11/142# d9.18 C12																									
1919	Was A	2	0	1.000	2	2	1	0	15	14	5	0	0	4	4	2.40	134	.233	.281	3-2	.000	0	244	1	0.2
1920	Was A	6	4	.600	22	11	5-1	1	99.1	130	60	2	1	30	19	4.44	84	.319	.367	26-1	.192	1	165	-7	-0.4
1921	Was A	6	6	.500	29	5	2	1	82.2	110	59	2	2	27	15	4.90	84	.332	.386	22-1	.227	1	138	-9	-1.2
Total	3	14	10	.583	53	18	8-1	2	197	254	124	4	3	61	38	4.48	86	.318	.368	51-4	.196	2	163	-15	-1.4
SCHACHT, SID Sidney B 2.3.1918 Bogota, NJ D 3.30.1991 Ft.Lauderdale, FL BR/TR 5-11/170# d4.23																									
1950	StL A	0	0	—	8	1	0	0	10.2	24	22	5	0	14	7	16.03	31	.429	.543	2-0	.000	-0*	146	-12	-0.6
1951	StL A	0	0	—	6	0	0	1	6	14	15	1	0	5	4	21.00	21	.452	.528	0-0	—	0		-10	-0.5
	Bos N	0	2	.000	5	0	0	0	4.2	6	4	0	0	2	1	1.93	191	.300	.364	0-0	—	0		0	-0.1

Year	Tm Lg	W	L	Pct	G	GS	CG-Sho	SV-BS	IP	H	R	HR	HB	BB-IB	SO	ERA	AERA	OAV	OOB	AB-SH	AVG	PB	Sup	APR	PW
Total	2	0	2	.000	19	1	0	1	21.1	44	41	6	0	21	12	14.34	31	.411	.508	2-0	.000	-0	146	-22	-1.2
SCHACKER, HAL Harold B 4.6.1925 Brooklyn, NY BR/TR 6/190# d5.9																									
1945	Bos N	0	1	.000	6	0	0	0	15.1	14	12	2	0	9	6	5.28	73	.241	.343	2-0	.000	0		-3	-0.2
SCHAEFFER, HARRY Harry Edward "Lefty" B 6.23.1924 Reading, PA BL/TL 6-2.5/175# d7.28																									
1952	NY A	0	1	.000	5	2	0	0	17	18	14	2	0	18	15	5.29	63	.265	.419	3-0	.000	-0	79	-5	-0.3
SCHAEFFER, MARK Mark Philip B 6.5.1948 Santa Monica, CA BL/TL 6-5/215# d4.18																									
1972	SD N	2	0	1.000	41	0	0	1-0	41	52	21	3	2	28-2	25	4.61	71	.319	.418	3-0	.000	-0		-5	-0.3
SCHAFFERNOTH, JOE Joseph Arthur B 8.6.1937 Trenton, NJ BR/TR 6-4.5/195# d4.15																									
1959	Chi N	1	0	1.000	5	1	0	0	7.2	11	7	1	0	4-0	3	8.22	48	.355	.429	3-0	.000	-0	158	-3	-0.4
1960	Chi N	2	3	.400	33	0	0	3	55	46	21	2	1	17-2	33	2.78	136	.235	.295	7-1	.286	0		5	0.6
1961	Chi N	0	4	.000	21	0	0	0	38.1	43	29	7	1	18-2	23	6.34	66	.293	.373	5-0	.000	-1		-8	-0.8
	Cle A	0	1	.000	15	0	0	0	17	16	11	2	1	14-1	9	4.76	83	.242	.383	1-0	.000	-0		-2	-0.1
Total	3	3	8	.273	74	1	0	3	118	116	68	12	3	53-5	68	4.58	86	.264	.345	16-1	.125	-1	158	-8	-0.7
SCHALLOCK, ART Arthur Lawrence B 4.25.1924 Mill Valley, CA BL/TL 5-9/160# d7.16																									
1951	NY A	3	1	.750	11	6	1	0	46.1	50	20	3	1	20	19	3.88	99	.272	.346	17-1	.294	1	143	1	0.2
1952	NY A	0	0	—	2	0	0	0	2	3	2	0	0	2	1	9.00	37	.375	.500	0-0	—	0		-1	-0.1
1953	†NY A	0	0	—	7	1	0	1	21.1	30	12	2	1	15	13	2.95	125	.345	.447	6-0	.333	0	144	0	0.0
1954	NY A	0	1	.000	6	1	1	0	17.1	20	10	3	1	11	9	4.15	83	.282	.386	3-0	.000	-0	26	-2	-0.2
1955	NY A	0	0	—	2	0	0	0	3	4	2	1	0	1-0	2	6.00	62	.333	.385	0-0	—	0		-1	0.0
	Bal A	3	5	.375	30	6	1	0	80.1	92	52	2	2	42-3	33	4.15	92	.294	.378	19-3	.105	-1	58	-7	-0.7
	Year	3	5	.375	32	6	1	0	83.1	96	55	3	2	43-3	35	4.21	90	.295	.378	19-3	.105	-1	58	-8	-0.7
Total	5	6	7	.462	58	14	3	1	170.1	199	98	11	5	91-3	77	4.02	94	.295	.381	45-4	.200	1	100	-10	-0.8
SCHANZ, CHARLEY Charles Murrell B 6.8.1919 Anacortes, WA D 5.28.1992 Sacramento, CA BR/TR 6-3.5/215# d4.20																									
1944	Phi N	13	16	.448	40	30	13-1	3	241.1	231	108	6	6	103	84	3.32	109	.254	.334	81-3	.148	-1	76	6	0.6
1945	Phi N	4	15	.211	35	21	5-1	5	144.2	165	99	5	9	87	56	4.35	88	.285	.387	39-5	.154	-0	66	-13	-1.6
1946	Phi N	6	6	.500	32	15	4	4	116.1	130	82	8	5	71	47	5.80	59	.286	.389	36-4	.083	-2	123	-28	-3.1
1947	Phi N	2	4	.333	34	6	1	2	101.2	107	59	7	3	47	42	4.16	96	.295	.380	27-1	.148	-1	84	-4	-0.3
1950	Bos A	3	2	.600	14	0	0	0	22.2	25	21	3	1	24	14	8.34	59	.281	.439	11-0	.091	-1		-7	-1.4
Total	5	28	43	.394	155	72	23-2	14	626.2	658	369	29	24	332	243	4.34	86	.275	.369	194-13	.134	-5	82	-46	-5.8
SCHAPPERT, JOHN John B Brooklyn, NY D 7.29.1916 Rockaway Beach, NY BR/TR 5-10/170# d5.3																									
1882	StL AA	8	7	.533	15	14	13	0	128	131	99	2		32	38	3.52	80	.248	.291	50	.180	0	135	-7	-0.8
SCHARDT, BILL Wilburt "Big Bill" B 1.20.1886 Cleveland, OH D 7.20.1964 Vermilion, OH BR/TR 6-4/210# d4.14																									
1911	Bro N	5	15	.250	39	22	10-1	4	195.1	190	102	4	8	91	77	3.59	93	.266	.355	59-3	.169	0	79	-7	-0.7
1912	Bro N	0	1	.000	7	0	0	1	20.2	25	13	1	2	6	7	4.35	77	.321	.384	6-0	.000	-1		-2	-0.1
Total	2	5	16	.238	46	22	10-1	5	216	215	115	5	10	97	84	3.67	91	.271	.358	65-3	.154	-1	79	-9	-0.8
SCHATTINGER, JEFF Jeffrey Charles B 10.25.1955 Fresno, CA BL/TR 6-5/200# d9.21																									
1981	KC A	0	0	—	1	0	0	0-0	3	2	0	0	2	1-0	1	0.00	—	.182	.357	0-0	—	0		1	0.1
SCHATZEDER, DAN Daniel Ernest B 12.1.1954 Elmhurst, IL BL/TL 6/195# d9.4																									
1977	Mon N	2	1	.667	6	3	1-1	0-0	21.2	16	6	0	0	13-0	14	2.49	153	.203	.312	6-0	.333	0	78	4	0.5
1978	Mon N	7	7	.500	29	18	2	0-0	143.2	108	54	10	2	68-5	69	3.07	115	.213	.306	45-2	.222	3*	93	8	1.0
1979	Mon N	10	5	.667	32	21	3	1-0	162	136	57	17	1	59-2	106	2.83	130	.225	.294	51-1	.216	4	115	16	1.7
1980	Det A	11	13	.458	32	26	9-2	0-0	192.2	178	88	23	3	58-9	94	4.02	103	.246	.303	0-0	—	0	91	5	0.5
1981	Det A	6	8	.429	17	14	1	0-0	71.1	74	49	13	2	29-1	20	6.06	62	.265	.334	0-0	—	0	98	-17	-2.8
1982	SF N	1	4	.200	13	3	0	0-1	33.1	47	30	3	0	12-4	18	7.29	49	.333	.383	8-0	.125	-0	65	-13	-1.8
	Mon N	0	2	.000	26	1	0	0-0	36	37	16	1	2	12-5	15	3.50	104	.276	.340	5-0	.400	1	48	1	0.1
	Year	1	6	.143	39	4	0	0-1	69.1	84	18	4	2	24-9	33	5.32	68	.305	.362	13-0	.231	1	61	-13	-1.7
1983	Mon N	5	2	.714	58	2	0	2-2	87	88	34	3	5	25-6	48	3.21	112	.265	.324	10-1	.200	0	61	4	0.3
1984	Mon N	7	7	.500	36	14	1-1	1-0	136	112	44	13	2	36-1	89	2.71	126	.224	.276	35-5	.314	5*	79	12	1.6
1985	Mon N	3	5	.375	24	15	1	0-0	104.1	101	52	13	0	31-0	64	3.80	90	.259	.311	31-1	.194	3	97	-6	-0.1
1986	Mon N	3	2	.600	30	1	0	1-0	59	53	29	6	0	19-2	33	3.20	116	.240	.298	21-0	.429	6*	169	1	0.7
	Phi N	3	3	.500	25	0	0	1-0	29.1	28	14	3	0	16-7	14	3.38	114	.252	.344	5-0	.200	0		1	0.2
	Year	6	5	.545	55	1	0	2-0	88.1	81	50	9	0	35-9	47	3.26	115	.244	.314	26-0	.385	7	166	2	0.9
1987	Phi N	3	1	.750	26	0	0	0-0	37.2	40	21	4	0	14-7	28	4.06	105	.278	.333	12-0	.167	0		0	0.0
	†Min A	3	1	.750	30	1	0	0-0	43.2	64	37	8	1	18-3	30	6.39	73	.342	.399	0-0	—	0	99	-10	-0.8
1988	Cle A	0	2	.000	15	0	0	3-1	16	26	19	6	1	2-0	10	9.56	43	.351	.377	0-0	—	0		-9	-1.4
	Min A	0	1	.000	10	0	0	0-0	10.1	8	2	1	1	5-1	7	1.74	234	.216	.326	0-0	—	0		3	0.2
	Year	0	3	.000	25	0	0	3-1	26.1	34	26	7	2	7-1	17	6.49	63	.306	.358	0-0	—	0		-7	-1.2
1989	Hou N	4	1	.800	36	0	0	1-1	56.2	64	33	2	3	28-6	46	4.45	76	.287	.374	9-0	.000	-1		-8	-0.8
1990	Hou N	1	3	.250	45	2	0	0-0	64	61	23	2	0	23-4	37	2.39	156	.261	.321	4-0	.250	0	73	8	0.5
	NY N	0	0	—	6	0	0	0-0	5.2	5	0	0	0	0-0	2	0.00	—	.263	.263	0-0	—	0		2	0.1
	Year	1	3	.250	51	2	0	0-0	69.2	66	26	2	0	23-4	39	2.20	169	.261	.317	4-0	.250	0	73	10	0.6
1991	KC A	0	0	—	8	0	0	0-0	6.2	11	9	0	0	7-1	4	9.45	44	.367	.486	0-0	—	0		-4	-0.2
Total	15	69	68	.504	504	121	18-4	10-5	1317	1257	617	128	23	475-64	748	3.74	100	.253	.319	242-10	.240	22	94	-2	-0.5
SCHAUER, RUBE Alexander John (b: Dimitri Ivanovich Dimitrihoff) B 3.19.1891 Odessa, Russia D 4.15.1957 Minneapolis, MN BR/TR 6-2/192# d8.27																									
1913	NY N	0	1	.000	3	1	1	0	12	14	11	0	0	9	7	7.50	42	.292	.404	3-0	.000	-0	24	-5	-0.4
1914	NY N	0	0	—	6	0	0	0	22.1	16	10	2	0	8	6	3.22	82	.205	.279	7-0	.143	-0		-1	-0.1
1915	NY N	2	8	.200	32	7	4	0	105.1	101	56	4	2	35	65	3.50	73	.258	.322	26-0	.077	-2	58	-13	-1.4
1916	NY N	1	4	.200	19	3	1	0	45.2	44	22	0	2	16	24	2.96	82	.257	.328	9-0	.222	0	61	-4	-0.4
1917	Phi A	7	16	.304	33	21	10	1	215	209	116	6	3	69	62	3.14	88	.263	.324	76-6	.145	-2	97	-13	-1.6
Total	5	10	29	.256	93	32	16	1	400.1	384	215	12	7	137	164	3.35	80	.259	.324	121-6	.132	-4	85	-36	-3.9
SCHEETZ, OWEN Owen Franklin B 12.24.1913 New Bedford, OH D 9.28.1994 Kirkersville, OH BR/TR 6-1/200# d4.22																									
1943	Was A	0	0	—	6	0	0	1	9	16	7	0	0	4	5	7.00	46	.381	.435	2-0	.000	-0		-3	-0.2
SCHEFFER, AARON Aaron Alvin Marcus B 10.15.1975 Ypsilanti, MI BL/TR 6-2/165# d6.13																									
1999	Sea A	0	0	—	4	0	0	0-0	4.2	6	5	0	1	3-0	4	1.93	246	.353	.417	0-0	—	0		0	0.0
SCHEGG, LEFTY Gilbert Eugene (b: Gilbert Eugene Price) B 8.28.1889 Leesville, OH D 2.27.1963 Niles, OH BL/TL 5-11/180# d8.20																									
1912	Was A	0	0	—	2	1	0	0	5.1	7	5	0	0	4	3	3.38	99	.333	.440	2-0	.000	-0	89	-1	-0.1
SCHEIB, CARL Carl Alvin B 1.1.1927 Gratz, PA BR/TR 6-1/192# d9.6 Mil 1945-46																									
1943	Phi A	0	1	.000	6	0	0	0	18.2	24	14	4	1	3	3	4.34	78	.308	.341	5-0	.000	-1		-3	-0.3
1944	Phi A	0	0	—	15	0	0	0	36.1	36	18	1	4	11	13	4.21	83	.257	.329	10-0	.300	1		-2	0.1
1945	Phi A	0	0	—	4	0	0	0	8.2	6	3	0	0	4	2	3.12	110	.207	.303	2-0	.000	-0		0	0.0
1947	Phi A	4	6	.400	21	12	6-2	0	116	121	68	11	2	55	26	5.04	76	.274	.357	45-0	.133	-2*	81	-13	-1.4
1948	Phi A	14	8	.636	32	24	15-1	0	198.2	219	90	14	1	76	44	3.94	109	.286	.351	104-0	.298	7*	105	10	2.1
1949	Phi A	9	12	.429	38	23	11-2	0	182.2	191	117	16	2	118	43	5.12	80	.275	.382	72-2	.236	3*	103	-21	-1.9
1950	Phi A	3	10	.231	43	8	1	3	106	138	96	13	0	70	37	7.22	63	.317	.411	52-0	.250	2*	92	-32	-3.3
1951	Phi A	1	12	.077	46	11	3	10	143	132	78	7	8	71	49	4.47	96	.250	.347	53-0	.396	8*	74	-3	0.8
1952	Phi A	11	7	.611	30	19	8-1	2	158	153	82	21	4	50	42	4.39	90	.253	.314	82-1	.220	-1*	131	-5	-0.6
1953	Phi A	3	7	.300	28	8	3	2	96	99	57	9	7	29	25	4.88	88	.261	.325	41-0	.195	-1*	80	-6	-0.7
1954	Phi A	0	1	.000	1	1	0	0	2	5	5	0	1	1	1	22.50	17	.500	.583	0-0	—	0	68	-4	-0.6
	StL N	0	1	.000	3	1	0	0	4.2	6	6	3	0	5	5	11.57	36	.300	.440	2-0	.000	-0	87	-3	-0.6
Total	11	45	65	.409	267	107	47-6	17	1070.2	1130	634	99	30	493	290	4.88	85	.274	.355	468-3	.250	16	100	-82	-6.4

Year	Tm Lg	W	L	Pct	G	GS	CG-Sho	SV-BS	IP	H	R	HR	HB	BB-IB	SO	ERA	AERA	OAV	OOB	AB-SH	AVG	PB	Sup	APR	PW
SCHEIBECK, FRANK Frank S. B 6.28.1865 Detroit, MI D 10.22.1956 Detroit, MI BR/TR 5-7/145# d5.9 ▲																									
1887	Cle AA	0	1	.000	1	1	1	0	9	17	18	1	1	4	3	12.00	36	.362	.423	9	.222	0*	29	-7	-0.5
SCHEIBLE, JACK John G. B 2.16.1866 Youngstown, OH D 8.9.1897 Youngstown, OH TL d9.8																									
1893	Cle N	1	1	.500	2	2	2-1	0	18	15	9	0	0	11	1	2.00	244	.221	.329	7	.143	-0	64	5	0.4
1894	Phi N	0	1	.000	1	1	0	0	0.1	6	10	0	1	2	0	189.00	3	.857	.900	0-0	—	0	55	-7	-0.8
Total	2	1	2	.333	3	3	2-1	0	18.1	21	19	0	1	13	1	5.40	91	.280	.393	7-0	.143	-0	62	-2	-0.4
SCHEID, RICH Richard Paul B 2.3.1965 Staten Island, NY BL/TL 6-3/185# d9.11																									
1992	Hou N	0	1	.000	7	1	0	0-0	12	14	8	2	0	6-1	8	6.00	56	.280	.357	1-0	.000	-0	81	-3	-0.3
1994	Fla N	1	3	.250	8	5	0	0-0	32.1	35	18	6	2	8-0	17	3.34	131	.269	.321	7-1	.000	-1	46	2	0.1
1995	Fla N	0	0	—	6	0	0	0-0	10.1	14	7	1	0	7-0	10	6.10	69	.341	.429	1-0	.000	-0		-2	-0.1
Total	3	1	4	.200	21	6	0	0-0	54.2	63	33	9	2	21-1	35	4.45	93	.285	.351	9-1	.000	-1	52	-3	-0.3
SCHELLE, JIM Gerard Anthony B 4.13.1917 Baltimore, MD D 5.4.1990 Weymouth, MA BR/TR 6-3/204# d7.23																									
1939	Phi A	0	0	—	1	0	0	0	0	1	3	0	1	3	0	o	—	1.000	1.000	0-0	—	0		-3	-0.2
SCHEMANSKE, FRED Frederick George "Buck" B 4.28.1903 Detroit, MI D 2.18.1960 Detroit, MI BR/TR 6-2/190# d9.15																									
1923	Was A	0	0	—	1	0	0	0	1	3	3	0	0	0	0	27.00	14	.600	.600	2-0	1.000	1*		-2	0.0
SCHENCK, BILL William G. B 7.1854 Brooklyn, NY D 1.29.1934 Brooklyn, NY 5-7/171# d5.29 ▲																									
1882	Lou AA	1	0	1.000	2	1	1	0	10	6	2	0		1	4	0.90	275	.162	.184	231	.260	0*	104	2	0.2
SCHENEBERG, JOHN John Bluford B 11.20.1887 Guyandotte, WV D 9.26.1950 Huntington, WV BB/TR 6-1/180# d9.23																									
1913	Pit N	0	1	.000	1	1	0	0	6	10	5	0	0	2	1	6.00	50	.400	.444	2-0	.500	0	25	-2	-0.2
1920	StL A	0	0	—	1	0	0	0	2	7	7	0	0	1	0	27.00	15	.583	.615	0-0	—	0		-5	-0.2
Total	2	0	1	.000	2	1	0	0	8	17	12	0	0	3	1	11.25	29	.459	.500	2-0	.500	0	25	-7	-0.4
SCHERMAN, FRED Frederick John B 7.25.1944 Dayton, OH BL/TL 6-1/195# d4.26																									
1969	Det A	1	0	1.000	4	0	0	0-0	4	6	3	2	0	0-0	3	6.75	55	.333	.333	0-0	—	0		-1	-0.2
1970	Det A	4	4	.500	48	0	0	1-2	69.2	61	28	5	1	28-3	58	3.23	115	.237	.314	12-0	.167	-0		4	0.4
1971	Det A	11	6	.647	69	1	1	20-7	113	91	38	11	5	49-7	46	2.71	133	.226	.317	24-2	.208	1	125	10	2.2
1972	†Det A	7	3	.700	57	3	0	12-6	94	91	43	5	5	53-9	53	3.64	87	.269	.371	22-1	.091	-1	56	-5	-0.8
1973	Det A	2	2	.500	34	0	0	1-1	61.2	59	30	6	3	30-4	28	4.23	97	.258	.350	0-0	—	0*		0	-0.1
1974	Hou N	2	5	.286	53	0	0	4-2	61.1	67	33	5	7	26-6	35	4.11	85	.284	.370	3-0	.000	-0		-5	-0.7
1975	Hou N	0	1	.000	16	0	0	0-1	16.1	21	11	4	1	4-1	13	4.96	68	.318	.361	1-0	.000	-0		-4	-0.2
	Mon N	4	3	.571	34	7	0	0-1	76.1	84	37	3	5	41-7	43	3.54	108	.283	.374	16-0	.063	-1	72	1	0.1
	Year	4	4	.500	50	7	0	0-2	92.2	105	40	7	6	45-8	56	3.79	99	.289	.371	17-0	.059	-1	74	-1	-0.1
1976	Mon N	2	2	.500	31	0	0	1-1	40	42	25	5	3	14-3	18	4.95	75	.261	.330	4-1	.250	0		-5	-0.5
Total	8	33	26	.559	346	11	1	39-21	536.1	522	248	46	30	245-40	297	3.66	99	.260	.347	82-4	.134	-1	74	-5	0.2
SCHERRER, BILL William Joseph B 1.20.1958 Tonawanda, NY BL/TL 6-4/180# d9.7																									
1982	Cin N	0	1	.000	5	2	0	0-0	17.1	17	7	0	0	0-0	7	2.60	143	.250	.250	2-1	.500	1*	83	1	0.1
1983	Cin N	2	3	.400	73	0	0	10-6	92	73	31	6	0	33-4	57	2.74	139	.225	.291	11-1	.091	-0		10	0.8
1984	Cin N	1	1	.500	36	0	0	1-1	52.1	64	31	6	0	15-3	35	4.99	76	.300	.342	3-1	.000	-0		-6	-0.3
	†Det A	1	0	1.000	18	0	0	0-0	19	14	4	1	0	8-1	16	1.89	207	.206	.289	0-0	—	0		5	0.2
1985	Det A	3	2	.600	48	0	0	0-2	66	62	35	10	1	41-13	46	4.36	93	.248	.354	0-0	—	0		-2	-0.1
1986	Det A	0	1	.000	13	0	0	0-0	21	19	19	3	1	22-4	16	7.29	57	.244	.416	0-0	—	0		-8	-0.4
1987	Cin N	1	1	.500	23	0	0	0-0	33	43	17	3	0	16-4	24	4.36	97	.328	.393	1-0	.000	-0		0	0.0
1988	Bal A	0	1	.000	4	0	0	0-0	4	8	6	2	0	3-0	3	13.50	29	.400	.478	0-0	—	0		-4	-0.7
	Phi N	0	0	—	8	0	0	0-0	6.2	7	4	0	0	2-0	3	5.40	66	.269	.321	0-0	—	0		-1	-0.1
Total	7	8	10	.444	228	2	0	11-9	311.1	307	154	31	2	140-29	207	4.08	97	.260	.336	17-3	.118	-0	83	-5	-0.5
SCHESLER, DUTCH Charles B 6.1.1900 Frankfurt, Germany D 11.19.1953 Harrisburg, PA BR/TR 6-2/185# d4.16																									
1931	Phi N	0	0	—	17	0	0	0	38.1	65	39	4	4	18	14	7.28	58	.385	.455	9-0	.111	-0		-13	-0.6
SCHETTLER, LOU Louis Martin B 6.12.1886 Pittsburgh, PA D 5.1.1960 Youngstown, OH BR/TR 5-11/160# d4.25																									
1910	Phi N	2	6	.250	27	7	3	1	107	96	53	2	2	51	62	3.20	98	.247	.337	41-1	.171	-1	92	-2	-0.3
SCHILLING, CURT Curtis Montague B 11.14.1966 Anchorage, AK BR/TR 6-4/215# d9.7																									
1988	Bal A	0	3	.000	4	4	0	0-0	14.2	22	19	3	1	10-1	4	9.82	40	.355	.434	0-0	—	0	52	-10	-1.6
1989	Bal A	0	1	.000	5	1	0	0-0	8.2	10	6	2	0	3-0	6	6.23	61	.286	.342	0-0	—	0	0	-2	-0.2
1990	Bal A	1	2	.333	35	0	0	3-6	46	38	13	1	0	19-0	32	2.54	150	.229	.302	0-0	—	0		7	0.5
1991	Hou N	3	5	.375	56	0	0	8-3	75.2	79	35	2	0	39-7	71	3.81	92	.271	.356	3-0	.333	0		-2	-0.3
1992	Phi N	14	11	.560	42	26	10-4	2-1	226.1	165	67	11	1	59-4	147	2.35	149	**.201**	**.253**	64-8	.156	-0	90	28	3.0
1993	†Phi N	16	7	.696	34	34	7-2	0-0	235.1	234	114	23	4	57-6	186	4.02	99	.259	.303	75-13	.147	-1	109	1	0.0
1994	Phi N	2	8	.200	13	13	1	0-0	82.1	87	42	10	3	28-3	58	4.48	96	.270	.333	28-1	.107	-1	85	0	-0.1
1995	Phi N	7	5	.583	17	17	1	0-0	116	96	52	12	3	26-2	114	3.57	119	.220	.267	40-5	.175	0	90	8	0.6
1996	Phi N	9	10	.474	26	26	**8-2**	0-0	183.1	149	69	16	3	50-5	182	3.19	135	.223	.278	63-7	.175	-0*	80	24	2.1
1997	Phi N★	17	11	.607	35	**35**	7-2	0-0	254.1	208	96	25	5	58-3	**319**	2.97	143	.224	.271	81-12	.173	-0	87	34	3.6
1998	Phi N☆	15	14	.517	35	**35**	**15**-2	0-0	**268.2**	236	101	23	6	61-3	**300**	3.25	133	.236	.282	76-12	.132	-1	76	33	3.2
1999	Phi N★	15	6	.714	24	24	8-1	0-0	180.1	159	74	25	5	44-0	152	3.54	133	.237	.287	50-9	.100	0	110	24	2.5
2000	Phi N	6	6	.500	16	16	4-1	0-0	112.2	110	49	17	1	32-4	96	3.91	119	.253	.305	30-2	.167	0	100	11	1.0
	Ari N	5	6	.455	13	13	4-1	0-0	97.2	94	41	10	0	13-0	72	3.69	128	.257	.280	31-7	.258	2	84	12	1.3
	Year	11	12	.478	29	29	**8-2**	0-0	210.1	204	45	27	1	45-4	168	3.81	123	.255	.294	61-9	.213	2	93	22	2.3
2001	†Ari N☆	**22**	6	**.786**	35	**35**	**6-1**	0-0	**256.2**	237	86	37	1	39-0	293	2.98	154	.245	**.273**	83-14	.133	-2	97	46	4.3
2002	†Ari N★	23	7	.767	36	35	5-1	0-0	259.1	218	95	29	3	33-1	316	3.23	138	.224	**.251**	86-8	.174	-1	113	34	3.5
2003	Ari N	8	9	.471	24	24	3-2	0-0	168	144	58	17	3	32-2	194	2.95	159	.230	.270	52-4	.058	-3	70	31	2.4
Total	16	163	117	.582	450	338	79-19	13-10	2586	2286	1017	263	39	603-41	2542	3.33	129	.236	.282	762-102	.150	-8	93	279	25.8
SCHILLINGS, RED Elbert Isaiah B 3.29.1900 Deport, TX D 1.7.1954 Oklahoma City, OK BR/TR 5-10/180# d9.11																									
1922	Phi A	0	0	—	4	0	0	0	8	10	6	1	0	11	4	6.75	63	.313	.488	2-0	.000	-0		-2	-0.1
SCHIRALDI, CALVIN Calvin Drew B 6.16.1962 Houston, TX BR/TR 6-4/200# d9.1																									
1984	NY N	0	2	.000	5	3	0	0-0	17.1	20	13	3	0	10-0	16	5.71	62	.286	.375	3-0	.000	-0	83	-4	-0.5
1985	NY N	2	1	.667	10	4	0	0-2	26.1	43	27	4	3	11-0	21	8.89	39	.368	.435	8-0	.125	-0	121	-16	-1.6
1986	†Bos A	4	2	.667	25	0	0	9-3	51	36	8	5	1	15-2	55	1.41	296	.201	.265	0-0	—	0		16	2.3
1987	Bos A	8	5	.615	62	1	0	6-4	83.2	75	45	15	1	40-5	93	4.41	103	.240	.326	0-0	—	0	20	1	0.1
1988	Chi N	9	13	.409	29	27	2-1	1-0	166.1	166	87	13	2	63-7	140	4.38	82	.257	.323	60-4	.100	-2	106	-13	-1.9
1989	Chi N	3	6	.333	54	0	0	4-4	78.2	60	34	7	1	50-2	54	3.78	100	.209	.326	9-1	.000	-1		1	0.0
	SD N	3	1	.750	5	4	0	0-0	21.1	12	6	1	0	13-0	17	2.53	138	.162	.287	7-1	.143	1	126	3	0.6
	Year	6	7	.462	59	4	0	4-4	100	72	11	8	1	63-2	71	3.51	106	.199	.319	16-2	.063	0	119	4	0.6
1990	SD N	3	8	.273	42	8	0	1-1	104	105	59	11	1	60-6	74	4.41	87	.264	.360	21-1	.190	2	86	-7	-0.6
1991	Tex A	0	1	.000	3	0	0	0-0	4.2	5	6	3	0	5-0	1	11.57	35	.263	.417	0-0	—	0		-4	-0.6
Total	8	32	39	.451	235	47	2-1	21-14	553.1	522	285	62	9	267-22	471	4.28	90	.248	.334	108-7	.111	-1	96	-23	-2.2
SCHLITZER, BIFF Victor Joseph B 12.4.1884 Rochester, NY D 1.4.1948 Wellesley Hills, MA BR/TR 5-11/175# d4.17																									
1908	Phi A	6	8	.429	24	18	11-2	0	131	110	56	1	2	45	57	3.16	81	.234	.303	46-1	.196	-1	80	-5	-0.8
1909	Phi A	0	3	.000	4	3	0	0	13.1	13	9	0	3	7	6	5.40	45	.245	.365	4-0	.250	0	88	-4	-0.7
	Bos A	4	4	.500	13	8	5	1	69.2	68	34	0	1	17	23	3.49	72	.234	.279	27-2	.185	0	109	-6	-0.7
	Year	4	7	.364	17	11	5	1	83	81	38	0	4	24	29	3.80	65	.236	.294	31-2	.194	1	103	-9	-1.4
1914	Buf F	0	0	—	3	0	0	0	3.1	7	8	3	0	2	1	16.20	18	.438	.500	1-0	1.000	0		-5	-0.2
Total	3	10	15	.400	44	29	16-2	1	217.1	198	107	4	6	71	87	3.60	71	.239	.303	78-3	.205	0	88	-20	-2.4
SCHMACK, BRIAN Brian Robert B 12.7.1973 Chicago, IL BR/TR 6-2/190# d8.24																									
2003	Det A	1	0	1.000	11	0	0	0-0	13	14	6	1	1	4-0	4	3.46	125	.292	.345	0-0	—	0		1	0.1

Year	Tm Lg	W	L	Pct	G	GS	CG-Sho	SV-BS	IP	H	R	HR	HB	BB-IB	SO	ERA	AERA	OAV	OOB	AB-SH	AVG	PB	Sup	APR	PW
SCHMELZ, AL Alan George B 11.12.1943 Whittier, CA BR/TR 6-4/210# d9.7																									
1967	NY N	0	0	—	2	0	0	0	3	4	1	1	0	1-0	2	3.00	113	.364	.417	0-0	—	0		0	0.0
SCHMIDT, CURT Curtis Allen B 3.16.1970 Miles City, MT BR/TR 6-6/200# d4.28																									
1995	Mon N	0	0	—	11	0	0	0-0	10.1	15	8	1	2	9-0	7	6.97	62	.357	.491	0-0	—	0		-3	-0.1
SCHMIDT, DAVE David Joseph B 4.22.1957 Niles, MI BR/TR 6-1/185# d5.1																									
1981	Tex A	0	1	.000	14	1	0	1-0	31.2	31	11	1	1	11-3	13	3.13	111	.258	.326	0-0	—	0	52	2	0.1
1982	Tex A	4	6	.400	33	8	0	6-2	109.2	118	45	5	5	25-5	69	3.20	121	.279	.325	0-0	—	0	79	8	0.7
1983	Tex A	3	3	.500	31	0	0	2-5	46.1	42	20	3	1	14-1	29	3.88	103	.241	.300	0-0	—	0		2	0.2
1984	Tex A	6	6	.500	43	0	0	12-4	70.1	69	30	3	0	20-9	46	2.56	162	.262	.311	0-0	—	0		9	1.8
1985	Tex A	7	6	.538	51	4	1-1	5-1	85.2	81	36	6	0	22-8	46	3.15	134	.246	.292	0-0	—	0	113	9	1.3
1986	Chi A	3	6	.333	49	1	0	8-3	92.1	94	37	10	5	27-7	67	3.31	130	.264	.322	0-0	—	0	42	10	1.0
1987	Bal A	10	5	.667	35	14	2-2	1-1	124	128	57	13	1	26-2	70	3.77	117	.263	.301	0-0	—	0	100	9	0.9
1988	Bal A	8	5	.615	41	9	0	2-1	129.2	129	58	14	3	38-5	67	3.40	115	.262	.317	0-0	—	0	106	6	0.6
1989	Bal A	10	13	.435	38	26	2	0-0	156.2	196	102	24	2	36-2	46	5.69	67	.310	.346	0-0	—	0	103	-32	-4.0
1990	Mon N	3	3	.500	34	0	0	13-4	48	58	26	3	0	13-5	22	4.31	85	.297	.340	3-0	.000	-0		-4	-0.7
1991	Mon N	0	1	.000	4	0	0	0-0	4.1	9	5	2	0	2-0	3	10.38	35	.429	.478	0-0	—	0		-3	-0.6
1992	Sea A	0	0	—	3	0	0	0-0	3.1	7	7	1	0	3-0	1	18.90	21	.438	.526	0-0	—	0		-5	-0.3
Total	12	54	55	.495	376	63	5-3	50-21	902	962	434	85	18	237-47	479	3.88	104	.274	.321	3-0	.000	-0	98	11	1.0
SCHMIDT, FREDDY Frederick Albert B 2.9.1916 Hartford, CT BR/TR 6-1/185# d4.25 Mil 1945																									
1944	†StL N	7	3	.700	37	9	3-2	5	114.1	94	48	5	1	58	58	3.15	112	.222	.317	34-1	.206	-0	119	4	0.3
1946	StL N	1	0	1.000	16	0	0	0	27.1	27	11	0	3	15	14	3.29	105	.276	.388	1-0	.000	-0		1	0.0
1947	StL N	0	0	—	2	0	0	0	4	5	2	1	0	1	2	2.25	184	.333	.375	0-0	—	0		0	0.0
	Phi N	5	8	.385	29	5	0	0	76.2	76	44	4	4	43	24	4.70	85	.285	.392	20-0	.050	-2	66	-5	-1.0
	Chi N	0	0	—	1	1	0	0	3	4	3	0	0	5	0	9.00	44	.333	.529	2-0	.000	-0	112	-1	-0.1
	Year	5	8	.385	32	6	0	0	83.2	85	8	5	4	49	26	4.73	85	.289	.398	22-0	.045	-2	73	-6	-1.1
Total	3	13	11	.542	85	15	3-2	5	225.1	206	108	10	8	122	98	3.75	98	.252	.355	57-1	.140	-2	101	-1	-0.8
SCHMIDT, BILL Frederick William B 4.1861 New Orleans, LA D 5.28.1928 New Orleans, LA TR 5-8/152# d7.6																									
1886	Det N	5	4	.556	9	9	9	0	77	81	47	0		30	36	4.09	81	.259	.324	38	.184	-1*	147	-4	-0.5
SCHMIDT, PETE Friedrich Christoph Herman B 7.23.1890 Lowden, IA D 3.11.1973 Pembroke, ON, CAN BR/TR 5-11/175# d7.14																									
1913	StL A	0	0	—	1	0	0	1	2	3	1	0	0	2	0	4.50	65	.333	.455	0-0	—	0		0	0.0
SCHMIDT, HENRY Henry Martin B 6.26.1873 Brownsville, TX D 4.23.1926 Nashville, TN BR/TR 5-11/170# d4.17																									
1903	Bro N	22	13	.629	40	36	29-5	2	301	321	167	5	21	120	96	3.83	83	.280	.359	107-5	.196	3*	109	-15	-0.9
SCHMIDT, JASON Jason David B 1.29.1973 Lewiston, ID BR/TR 6-5/185# d4.28																									
1995	Atl N	2	2	.500	9	2	0	0-1	25	27	17	2	1	18-3	19	5.76	74	.287	.393	5-1	.200	0	53	-4	-0.5
1996	Atl N	3	4	.429	13	11	0	0-0	58.2	69	48	8	0	32-0	48	6.75	65	.296	.373	19-1	.000	-2	113	-14	-1.6
	Pit N	2	2	.500	6	6	1	0-0	37.2	39	19	2	2	21-0	26	4.06	108	.271	.365	12-1	.083	-1	131	1	0.0
	Year	5	6	.455	19	17	1	0-0	96.1	108	25	10	2	53-0	74	5.70	77	.286	.370	31-2	.032	-2	120	-13	-1.6
1997	Pit N	10	9	.526	32	32	2	0-0	187.2	193	106	16	9	76-2	136	4.60	93	.265	.341	56-9	.107	-1	93	-6	-0.7
1998	Pit N	11	14	.440	33	33	0	0-0	214.1	228	106	24	4	71-3	158	4.07	106	.275	.334	62-12	.097	-2	69	7	0.4
1999	Pit N	13	11	.542	33	33	2	0-0	212.2	219	110	24	3	85-4	148	4.19	109	.262	.330	60-12	.083	-2	88	10	0.6
2000	Pit N	2	5	.286	11	11	0	0-0	63.1	71	43	6	1	41-2	51	5.40	85	.284	.384	19-2	.000	-2	100	-6	-0.7
2001	Pit N	6	6	.500	14	14	1	0-0	84	81	46	11	7	28-2	77	4.61	98	.256	.328	23-5	.174	1	91	-1	-0.1
	SF N	7	1	.875	11	11	0	0-0	66.1	57	29	2	0	33-1	65	3.39	118	.230	.319	26-1	.154	1	162	4	0.5
	Year	13	7	.650	25	25	1	0-0	150.1	138	36	13	7	61-3	142	4.07	105	.244	.324	49-6	.163	2	120	3	0.4
2002	†SF N	13	8	.619	29	29	2-2	0-0	185.1	148	78	15	2	73-1	196	3.45	113	.218	.294	56-4	.125	-1	112	9	0.8
2003	†SF N★	17	5	**.773**	29	29	5-**3**	0-0	207.2	152	56	14	5	46-1	208	**2.34**	**176**	**.200**	**.250**	61-15	.066	-4	110	**44**	3.9
Total	9	86	67	.562	220	211	13-5	0-1	1342.2	1284	658	124	34	524-19	1132	4.02	106	.251	.323	399-63	.095	-13	99	44	2.6
SCHMIDT, JEFF Jeffrey Thomas B 2.21.1971 Northfield, MN BR/TR 6-5/205# d5.17																									
1996	Cal A	2	0	1.000	9	0	0	0-0	8	13	9	2	0	8-0	2	7.88	64	.394	.500	0-0	—	0		-3	-0.6
SCHMIDT, WILLARD Willard Raymond B 5.29.1928 Hays, KS BR/TR 6-1/187# d4.19																									
1952	StL N	2	3	.400	18	3	0	1	34.2	36	20	6	2	18	30	5.19	72	.267	.361	8-0	.125	-0	64	-5	-0.6
1953	StL N	0	2	.000	6	2	0	0	17.2	21	20	1	1	13	11	9.17	46	.288	.402	4-0	.000	-1	52	-10	-0.9
1955	StL N	7	6	.538	20	15	8-1	0	129.2	89	40	7	3	57-7	86	2.78	146	.197	.289	42-2	.119	-3	88	20	1.6
1956	StL N	6	8	.429	33	21	2	1	147.2	131	69	18	1	78-7	52	3.84	99	.246	.341	43-3	.233	1	104	0	0.3
1957	StL N	10	3	.769	40	8	1	0	116.2	146	67	13	2	49-6	63	4.78	83	.312	.377	33-4	.212	0	158	-9	-0.9
1958	Cin N	3	5	.375	41	2	0	0	69.1	60	29	8	1	33-7	41	2.86	145	.235	.320	11-1	.091	-1	152	7	0.8
1959	Cin N	3	2	.600	36	4	0	0	70.2	80	36	4	1	30-4	40	3.95	103	.296	.366	12-1	.083	0	116	0	0.1
Total	7	31	29	.517	194	55	11-1	2	586.1	563	281	57	11	278-31	323	3.93	101	.258	.342	153-11	.163	-2	105	3	0.4
SCHMIT, CRAZY Frederick M. "Germany" B 2.13.1866 Chicago, IL D 10.5.1940 Chicago, IL BL/TL 5-10.5/165# d4.21																									
1890	Pit N	1	9	.100	11	10	9-1	0	83.1	108	98	3	8	42	35	5.83	57	.304	.390	33	.061	-3	69	-30	-2.7
1892	Bal N	1	4	.200	6	6	6	0	47.1	37	26	0	0	26	17	3.23	106	.207	.307	19	.105	-1*	55	2	0.1
1893	Bal N	3	2	.600	9	6	4	0	49	67	51	1	2	22	10	6.61	72	.316	.386	21	.238	-0	145	-10	-0.7
	NY N	0	2	.000	4	4	1	0	20.2	30	25	0	2	17	5	7.40	63	.330	.445	9	.444	1	146	-6	-0.3
	Year	3	4	.429	13	10	5	0	69.2	97	35	1	4	39	15	6.85	69	.320	.405	30	.300	1	145	-14	-1.0
1899	Cle N	2	17	.105	20	19	16	0	138.1	197	138	3	14	62	24	5.86	63	.334	.410	70-1	.157	-2*	61	-39	-4.1
1901	Bal A	0	2	.000	4	3	1	0	22.2	25	20	0	0	16	2	1.99	195	.278	.387	9-0	.222	0	116	1	0.1
Total	5	7	36	.163	54	48	37-1	0	361.1	464	358	7	26	185	93	5.45	69	.306	.391	161-1	.161	-4	87	-82	-7.6
SCHMITZ, JOHNNY John Albert "Bear Tracks" B 11.27.1920 Wausau, WI BR/TL 6/170# d9.6 Mil 1943-45																									
1941	Chi N	2	0	1.000	5	3	1	0	20.2	12	5	0	1	9	11	1.31	269	.182	.289	7-1	.571	2*	137	5	0.7
1942	Chi N	3	7	.300	23	10	1	2	86.2	70	41	3	3	45	51	3.43	93	.230	.335	26-2	.154	-1	113	-3	-0.2
1946	Chi N☆	11	11	.500	41	31	14-2	2	224.1	184	77	6	2	94	**135**	2.61	127	**.221**	.302	70-6	.129	-2*	92	17	1.6
1947	Chi N	13	18	.419	38	28	10-3	4	207	209	91	8	2	80	97	3.22	123	.262	.330	68-6	.132	-2	76	16	2.1
1948	Chi N★	18	13	.581	34	30	18-2	1	242	186	92	11	2	97	100	2.64	148	**.215**	.295	84-7	.131	-2	73	31	3.8
1949	Chi N	11	13	.458	36	31	9-3	3	207	227	117	11	2	92	75	4.35	93	.287	.363	70-3	.143	-1	85	-9	-0.7
1950	Chi N	10	16	.385	39	27	8-3	0	193	217	122	23	4	91	75	4.99	84	.284	.363	67-2	.119	-3	97	-15	-1.7
1951	Chi N	1	2	.333	8	3	0	0	18	22	16	1	0	15	6	8.00	51	.301	.420	6-0	.167	-0	43	-7	-0.9
	Bro N	1	4	.200	16	7	0	0	55.2	55	37	4	2	28	20	5.34	74	.259	.351	18-0	.222	2	125	-9	-0.5
	Year	2	6	.250	24	10	0	0	73.2	77	43	5	2	43	26	5.99	66	.270	.370	24-0	.208	1	100	-15	-1.4
1952	Bro N	1	1	.500	10	3	1	0	33.1	29	16	3	1	18	11	4.32	84	.238	.340	8-2	.125	-0	220	-2	-0.1
	NY A	1	1	.500	5	2	1	1	15	15	7	0	1	9	3	3.60	92	.263	.373	5-0	.600	2	105	-1	0.1
	Cin N	1	0	1.000	3	0	0	0	5	3	0	0	0	3	3	0.00	—	.188	.316	0-0	—	0		2	0.4
1953	NY A	0	0	—	3	0	0	0	4.1	2	1	1	0	3	0	2.08	178	.143	.294	0-1	—	0		1	0.1
	Was A	2	7	.222	24	13	5	4	107.2	118	52	9	4	37	39	3.68	106	.286	.351	34-3	.059	-4	86	1	-0.2
	Year	2	7	.222	27	13	5	4	112	120	56	10	4	40	39	3.62	108	.282	.349	34-4	.059	-4	86	2	-0.1
1954	Was A	11	8	.579	29	23	12-2	1	185.1	176	66	6	3	64	56	2.91	122	.255	.318	60-6	.117	-3	99	15	1.3
1955	Was A	7	10	.412	32	21	6-1	1	165	187	76	8	7	54-4	49	3.71	103	.291	.349	54-3	.185	0	96	3	0.4
1956	Bos A	0	0	—	2	0	0	0	4.1	5	2	0	0	4-0	0	0.00	—	.278	.409	1-0	.000	-0		1	0.1
	Bal A	0	3	.000	18	3	0	0	38.1	49	23	3	1	14-1	15	3.99	98	.318	.379	9-1	.000	-1	53	-2	-0.3
	Year	0	3	.000	20	3	0	0	42.2	54	25	3	1	18-1	15	3.59	111	.314	.382	10-1	.000	-2	52	-1	-0.2
Total	13	93	114	.449	366	235	86-16	19	1812.2	1766	841	97	35	757-5	746	3.55	107	.258	.335	587-43	.141	-14	91	44	6.0
SCHMUTZ, CHARLIE Charles Otto "King" B 1.1.1890 San Diego, CA D 6.27.1962 Seattle, WA BR/TR 6-1.5/195# d5.13																									
1914	Bro N	1	3	.250	18	5	1	0	57.1	57	29	1	1	13	21	3.30	87	.265	.310	16-0	.188	1	65	-2	-0.1
1915	Bro N	0	0	—	1	0	0	0	4	7	5	0	0	1	1	6.75	41	.438	.471	1-0	.000	-0		-2	-0.1

Year	Tm Lg	W	L	Pct	G	GS	CG-Sho	SV-BS	IP	H	R	HR	HB	BB-IB	SO	ERA	AERA	OAV	OOB	AB-SH	AVG	PB	Sup	APR	PW
Total	2	1	3	.250	19	5	1	0	61.1	64	34	1	1	14	22	3.52	81	.277	.321	17-0	.176	0	65	-4	-0.2
SCHNEIBERG, FRANK Frank Frederick B 3.12.1882 Milwaukee, WI D 5.18.1948 Milwaukee, WI TR d6.8																									
1910	Bro N	0	0	—	1	0	0	0	1	5	8	0	0	4	0	63.00	5	.625	.750	0-0	—	0		-6	-0.3
SCHNEIDER, DAN Daniel Louis B 8.29.1942 Evansville, IN BL/TL 6-3/170# d5.12																									
1963	Mil N	1	0	1.000	30	3	0	0	43.2	36	20	2	0	20-5	19	3.09	104	.225	.309	7-0	.000	-1	116	-1	-0.2
1964	Mil N	1	2	.333	13	5	0	0	36.1	38	25	6	0	13-2	14	5.45	65	.270	.329	8-1	.000	-1*	165	-8	-0.6
1966	Atl N	0	0	—	14	0	0	0	26.1	35	13	1	1	5-0	11	3.42	106	.324	.360	8-0	.500	1		0	0.1
1967	Hou N	0	2	.000	54	0	0	2	52.2	60	33	5	2	27-8	39	4.96	67	.296	.377	5-0	.200	0*		-10	-0.4
1969	Hou N	0	1	.000	6	0	0	0-0	7.1	16	12	2	0	5-2	3	13.50	26	.485	.553	1-0	.000	-0		-8	-0.9
Total	5	2	5	.286	117	8	0	2-0	166.1	185	103	16	3	70-17	86	4.71	72	.287	.356	29-1	.172	-0	148	-27	-2.0
SCHNEIDER, JEFF Jeffrey Theodore B 12.6.1952 Bremerton, WA BB/TL 6-3/195# d8.12																									
1981	Bal A	0	0	—	11	0	0	1-0	24	27	15	4	1	12-1	17	4.88	74	.290	.377	0-0	—	0		-3	-0.2
SCHNEIDER, PETE Peter Joseph B 8.20.1895 Los Angeles, CA D 6.1.1957 Los Angeles, CA BR/TR 6-1/194# d6.20																									
1914	Cin N	5	13	.278	29	15	11-1	1	144.1	143	71	1	7	56	62	2.81	104	.269	.347	45-1	.178	1*	54	0	0.0
1915	Cin N	14	19	.424	48	35	16-5	2	275.2	254	110	4	7	104	108	2.48	115	.251	.325	94-6	.245	5	74	7	1.4
1916	Cin N	10	19	.345	44	31	16-2	1	274.1	259	112	4	13	82	117	2.69	96	.255	.319	89-4	.236	2*	88	-6	-0.5
1917	Cin N	20	19	.513	46	42	24	0	333.2	311	128	4	11	117	138	2.10	124	.255	.326	114-2	.167	0*	97	14	1.5
1918	Cin N	10	15	.400	33	30	17-2	0	217	213	106	2	11	117	51	3.53	76	.272	.374	83-3	.289	6*	115	-20	-1.7
1919	NY A	0	1	.000	7	4	0	0	29	19	14	1	3	22	11	3.41	94	.192	.355	9-0	.111	-1	92	-1	-0.2
Total	6	59	86	.407	207	157	84-10	4	1274	1199	541	16	52	498	487	2.66	102	.257	.336	434-16	.221	14	89	-6	0.5
SCHNELL, KARL Karl Otto B 9.20.1899 Los Angeles, CA D 5.31.1992 Palo Alto, CA BR/TR 6-1/176# d4.24																									
1922	Cin N	0	0	—	10	0	0	0	20	21	10	0	0	18	5	2.70	148	.300	.443	4-0	.250	0		2	0.1
1923	Cin N	0	0	—	1	0	0	0	1	2	4	0	0	2	0	36.00	11	.667	.800	0-0	—	0		-3	-0.1
Total	2	0	0	—	11	0	0	0	21	23	14	0	0	20	5	4.29	93	.315	.462	4-0	.250	0		-1	0.0
SCHOEN, GERRY Gerald Thomas B 1.15.1947 New Orleans, LA BR/TR 6-3/215# d9.14																									
1968	Was A	0	1	.000	1	1	0	0	3.2	6	3	1	0	1-0	1	7.36	40	.400	.438	1-0	.000	-0	30	-2	-0.3
SCHOENEWEIS, SCOTT Scott David B 10.2.1973 Long Branch, NJ BL/TL 6/186# d4.7																									
1999	Ana A	1	1	.500	31	0	0	0-0	39.1	47	27	4	0	14-1	22	5.49	88	.294	.349	0-0	—	0		-3	-0.1
2000	Ana A	7	10	.412	27	27	1-1	0-0	170	183	112	21	6	67-2	78	5.45	93	.276	.346	3-0	.333	0	94	-7	-0.6
2001	Ana A	10	11	.476	32	32	1	0-0	205.1	227	122	21	14	77-2	104	5.08	90	.281	.351	0-0	—	1	91	-10	-0.7
2002	†Ana A	9	8	.529	54	15	0	1-3	118	119	68	17	5	49-4	65	4.88	91	.264	.340	2-0	.000	-0	119	-5	-0.7
2003	Ana A	1	1	.500	39	0	0	0-1	38.2	37	19	2	3	10-3	29	3.96	109	.250	.309	0-0	—	0		1	0.1
	Chi A	2	1	.667	20	0	0	0-1	26	26	16	1	1	9-2	27	4.50	101	.255	.321	0-0	—	0		-1	-0.1
	Year	3	2	.600	59	0	0	0-2	64.2	63	41	3	4	19-5	56	4.18	106	.252	.314	0-0	—	0		1	0.0
Total	5	30	32	.484	203	74	2-1	1-5	597.1	639	364	66	29	226-14	325	5.08	92	.274	.343	5-0	.200	1	98	-25	-2.1
SCHOOLER, MIKE Michael Ralph B 8.10.1962 Anaheim, CA BR/TR 6-3/220# d6.10																									
1988	Sea A	5	8	.385	40	0	0	15-6	48.1	45	21	4	1	24-4	54	3.54	118	.245	.330	0-0	—	0		3	0.7
1989	Sea A	1	7	.125	67	0	0	33-7	77	81	27	2	2	19-3	69	2.81	144	.266	.313	0-0	—	0		10	1.8
1990	Sea A	1	4	.200	49	0	0	30-4	56	47	18	5	1	16-5	45	2.25	176	.227	.283	1-0	.000	-0		10	1.7
1991	Sea A	3	3	.500	34	0	0	7-3	34.1	25	14	2	0	10-0	31	3.67	112	.198	.255	0-0	—	0		2	0.4
1992	Sea A	2	7	.222	53	0	0	13-5	51.2	55	29	7	1	24-6	33	4.70	85	.275	.351	0-0	—	0		-4	-0.7
1993	Tex A	3	0	1.000	17	0	0	0-0	24.1	30	17	3	0	10-1	16	5.55	75	.303	.367	0-0	—	0		-4	-0.4
Total	6	15	29	.341	260	0	0	98-25	291.2	283	126	23	5	103-19	248	3.49	116	.253	.316	1-0	.000	-0		17	3.5
SCHORR, ED Edward Walter B 2.14.1891 Bremen, OH D 9.12.1969 Atlantic City, NJ BR/TR 6-2.5/180# d4.26																									
1915	Chi N	0	0	—	2	0	0	0	6	9	5	0	0	5	3	7.50	37	.409	.519	2-0	.500	0		-3	-0.1
SCHOTT, GENE Arthur Eugene B 7.14.1913 Batavia, OH D 11.16.1992 Sun City Center, FL BR/TR 6-2/185# d4.16																									
1935	Cin N	8	11	.421	33	19	9-1	0	159	153	84	5	1	64	49	3.91	102	.253	.326	60-0	.200	1*	92	1	0.3
1936	Cin N	11	11	.500	31	22	8	1	180	184	93	7	4	73	65	3.80	101	.262	.335	60-1	.300	7*	90	-1	0.7
1937	Cin N	4	13	.235	37	16	7-2	1	154.1	150	69	2	1	48	56	2.97	125	.253	.310	49-2	.143	-1*	58	10	0.9
1938	Cin N	5	5	.500	31	4	0	2	83	89	47	8	1	32	21	4.45	82	.279	.347	24-0	.125	-1	116	-7	-0.9
1939	Phi N	0	1	.000	4	0	0	0	11	14	7	0	2	5	1	4.91	82	.326	.420	6-0	.333	1*		-1	0.0
Total	5	28	41	.406	136	61	24-3	4	587.1	590	300	22	9	222	192	3.72	103	.261	.329	199-3	.211	6	85	2	1.0
SCHOUREK, PETE Peter Alan B 5.10.1969 Austin, TX BL/TL 6-5/205# d4.9																									
1991	NY N	5	4	.556	35	8	1-1	2-1	86.1	82	49	7	2	43-4	67	4.27	85	.248	.334	22-0	.136	0	130	-7	-0.6
1992	NY N	6	8	.429	22	21	0	0-0	136	137	60	9	2	44-6	60	3.64	96	.261	.319	42-2	.048	-3*	83	-2	-0.6
1993	NY N	5	12	.294	41	18	0	0-1	128.1	168	90	13	3	45-7	72	5.96	67	.319	.370	32-3	.219	2	102	-25	-2.7
1994	Cin N	7	2	.778	22	10	0	0-0	81.1	90	39	11	3	29-4	69	4.09	101	.287	.351	23-1	.174	1	97	2	0.3
1995	†Cin N	18	7	.720	29	29	2	0-0	190.1	158	72	17	8	45-3	160	3.22	128	.228	.281	59-12	.220	2	111	20	2.6
1996	Cin N	4	5	.444	12	12	0	0-0	67.1	79	48	7	3	24-1	54	6.01	70	.293	.352	19-5	.263	1*	110	-12	-1.3
1997	Cin N	5	8	.385	18	17	0	0-0	84.2	78	59	18	4	38-0	59	5.42	79	.241	.327	24-6	.167	1*	88	-13	-1.6
1998	Hou N	7	6	.538	15	15	0	0-0	80	82	43	10	4	36-0	59	4.50	90	.269	.350	19-5	.211	1	107	-4	-0.5
	†Bos A	1	3	.250	10	8	0	0-0	44	45	21	7	1	14-1	36	4.30	110	.273	.328	0-0	—	0	91	3	0.2
1999	Pit N	4	7	.364	30	17	0	0-0	113	128	75	20	5	49-5	94	5.34	86	.287	.358	25-3	.000	-2	65	-9	-0.9
2000	Bos A	3	10	.231	21	21	0	0-0	107.1	116	67	17	3	38-2	63	5.11	99	.278	.341	4-0	.500	1*	80	-1	0.0
2001	Bos A	1	5	.167	33	0	0	0-1	30.1	35	19	4	1	15-3	20	4.45	101	.292	.375	0-0	—	0		-1	-0.1
Total	11	66	77	.462	288	176	3-1	2-3	1149	1198	642	140	39	420-36	813	4.59	91	.270	.335	269-37	.164	3	95	-49	-5.2
SCHREIBER, BARNEY David Henry B 5.8.1882 Waverly, OH D 10.6.1964 Chillicothe, OH BL/TL 6/185# d5.15																									
1911	Cin N	0	0	—	3	0	0	1	10	19	11	2	0	2	5	5.40	61	.413	.438	3-0	.000	-0		-3	-0.2
SCHREIBER, PAUL Paul Frederick "Von" B 10.8.1902 Jacksonville, FL D 1.28.1982 Sarasota, FL BR/TR 6-2/180# d9.2 C13																									
1922	Bro N	0	0	—	1	0	0	0	1	2	0	0	0	0	0	0.00	—	.500	.500	0-0	—	0		0	0.0
1923	Bro N	0	0	—	9	0	0	1	15	16	9	1	2	8	4	4.20	92	.276	.382	2-0	.000	-0		-1	-0.1
1945	NY A	0	0	—	2	0	0	0	4.1	4	2	0	0	2	1	4.15	83	.267	.353	1-0	.000	-0		0	0.0
Total	3	0	0	—	12	0	0	1	20.1	22	11	1	2	10	5	3.98	96	.286	.382	3-0	.000	-0		-1	-0.1
SCHRENK, STEVE Steven Wayne B 11.20.1968 Chicago, IL BR/TR 6-3/185# d7.3																									
1999	Phi N	1	3	.250	32	2	0	1-0	50.1	41	24	6	7	14-4	36	4.29	110	.223	.301	3-1	.000	-0	146	3	0.2
2000	Phi N	2	3	.400	20	0	0	0-0	23.1	25	20	3	1	13-0	19	7.33	64	.269	.361	0-0	—	0		-7	-1.2
Total	2	3	6	.333	52	2	0	1-0	73.2	66	44	9	8	27-4	55	5.25	90	.238	.322	3-1	.000	-0	146	-4	-1.0
SCHROLL, AL Albert Bringhurst "Bull" B 3.22.1932 New Orleans, LA D 11.30.1999 Alexandria, LA BR/TR 6-2/210# d4.20																									
1958	Bos A	0	0	—	5	0	0	0	10	6	5	1	0	4-0	7	4.50	89	.176	.263	1-0	1.000	0		0	0.0
1959	Phi N	1	1	.500	3	0	0	0	9.1	12	9	1	0	6-0	4	8.68	47	.353	.439	4-0	.250	0		-4	-0.7
	Bos A	1	4	.200	14	5	1	0	46	47	29	3	1	22-1	26	4.70	86	.269	.350	9-2	.111	0	70	-4	-0.4
1960	Chi N	0	0	—	2	0	0	0	2.2	3	3	1	0	5-0	2	10.13	37	.273	.500	1-0	1.000	0		-2	0.0
1961	Min A	4	4	.500	11	8	2	0	50	53	36	5	2	27-1	24	5.22	81	.266	.360	18-0	.278	2	104	-6	-0.7
Total	4	6	9	.400	35	13	3	0	118	121	82	11	3	64-2	63	5.34	77	.267	.359	33-2	.273	4	92	-16	-1.8
SCHROM, KEN Kenneth Marvin B 11.23.1954 Grangeville, ID BR/TR 6-2/195# d8.8																									
1980	Tor A	1	0	1.000	17	0	0	1-0	31	32	18	2	0	19-3	13	5.23	82	.274	.372	0-0	—	0*		-2	-0.1
1982	Tor A	1	0	1.000	6	0	0	0-0	15.1	13	11	3	0	15-3	8	5.87	76	.232	.394	0-0	—	0		-2	-0.1
1983	Min A	15	8	.652	33	28	6-1	0-0	196.1	196	92	14	9	80-3	80	3.71	115	.266	.341	0-0	—	0*	93	10	0.9
1984	Min A	5	11	.313	25	21	3	0-0	137	156	75	15	1	41-2	49	4.47	94	.285	.333	0-0	—	0	83	-4	-0.5
1985	Min A	9	12	.429	29	26	6	0-0	160.2	164	95	28	0	59-2	74	4.99	88	.272	.333	0-0	—	0	83	-8	-0.9
1986	Cle A☆	14	7	.667	34	33	3-1	0-0	206	217	118	34	12	49-3	87	4.54	91	.271	.318	0-0	—	0	114	-9	-1.0

Year	Tm Lg	W	L	Pct	G	GS	CG-Sho	SV-BS	IP	H	R	HR	HB	BB-IB	SO	ERA	AERA	OAV	OOB	AB-SH	AVG	PB	Sup	APR	PW
1987	Cle A	6	13	.316	32	29	4-1	0-0	153.2	185	126	29	3	57-1	61	6.50	70	.298	.357	0-0	—	0	92	-32	-3.4
Total	7	51	51	.500	176	137	22-3	1-0	900	963	535	125	25	320-17	372	4.81	90	.276	.338	0-0	—	0	94	-47	-5.1
SCHUELER, RON Ronald Richard B 4.18.1948 Catharine, KS BR/TR 6-4/205# d4.16 C7																									
1972	Atl N	5	8	.385	37	18	3	2-1	144.2	122	68	16	2	60-3	96	3.67	103	.227	.304	42-2	.190	0	71	1	0.0
1973	Atl N	8	7	.533	39	20	4-2	2-2	186	179	91	24	0	66-11	124	3.87	102	.255	.317	62-7	.177	-1	111	1	-0.1
1974	Phi N	11	16	.407	44	27	5	1-0	203.1	202	91	17	4	98-18	109	3.72	102	.264	.350	51-7	.118	-2	77	3	-0.1
1975	Phi N	4	4	.500	46	6	1	0-0	92.2	88	55	6	1	40-4	69	5.24	71	.258	.336	13-1	.154	-0	118	-13	-1.0
1976	Phi N	1	0	1.000	35	0	0	3-0	49.2	44	18	4	2	16-2	43	2.90	123	.243	.307	2-1	.000	-0		3	0.1
1977	Min A	8	7	.533	52	7	0	3-1	134.2	131	74	16	6	61-5	77	4.41	91	.260	.343	0-0	—	0	167	-7	-0.6
1978	Chi A	3	5	.375	30	7	0	0-2	81.2	76	50	10	7	39-2	39	4.30	89	.251	.341	0-0	—	0*	94	-7	-0.7
1979	Chi A	0	1	.000	8	1	0	0-0	19.2	19	16	3	2	13-1	6	7.32	58	.264	.382	0-0	—	0	64	-6	-0.3
Total	8	40	48	.455	291	86	13-2	11-6	912.1	861	463	96	24	393-46	563	4.08	94	.253	.331	170-18	.159	-3	95	-25	-2.7
SCHULER, DAVE David Paul B 10.4.1953 Framingham, MA BR/TL 6-4/210# d9.17																									
1979	Cal A	0	0	—	1	0	0	0-0	1.2	2	2	1	0	0-0	0	10.80	38	.333	.286	0-0	—	0		-1	-0.1
1980	Cal A	0	1	.000	8	0	0	0-0	12.2	13	5	3	0	2-1	7	3.55	111	.271	.288	0-0	—	0		1	0.0
1985	Atl N	0	0	—	9	0	0	0-0	10.2	19	8	4	0	3-0	10	6.75	57	.404	.440	0-0	—	0		-3	-0.2
Total	3	0	1	.000	18	0	0	0-0	25	34	15	8	0	5-1	17	5.40	73	.337	.358	0-0	—	0		-3	-0.3
SCHULLSTROM, ERIK Erik Paul B 3.25.1969 San Diego, CA BR/TR 6-5/220# d7.18																									
1994	Min A	0	0	—	9	0	0	1-1	13	13	7	0	1	5-0	13	2.77	176	.260	.339	0-0	—	0		2	0.1
1995	Min A	0	0	—	37	0	0	0-1	47	66	36	8	1	22-1	21	6.89	69	.332	.399	0-0	—	0		-9	-0.5
Total	2	0	0	—	46	0	0	1-2	60	79	43	8	2	27-1	34	6.00	80	.317	.387	0-0	—	0		-7	-0.4
SCHULTZ, BUDDY Charles Budd B 9.19.1950 Cleveland, OH BR/TL 6/175# d9.3																									
1975	Chi N	2	0	1.000	6	0	0	0-0	5.2	11	6	0	0	5-1	4	6.35	61	.367	.457	0-1	—	0		-2	-0.4
1976	Chi N	1	1	.500	29	0	0	2-4	23.2	37	19	3	0	9-1	15	6.08	64	.356	.400	4-0	.000	-0		-6	-0.6
1977	StL N	6	1	.857	40	3	0	1-1	85.1	76	26	5	0	24-0	66	2.32	166	.245	.298	12-2	.167	0*	139	14	1.1
1978	StL N	2	4	.333	62	0	0	6-2	83	68	36	6	0	36-6	70	3.80	93	.226	.305	5-2	.200	1		-1	0.0
1979	StL N	4	3	.571	31	0	0	3-1	42.1	40	21	7	0	14-5	38	4.46	84	.256	.312	4-0	.000	-0		-2	-0.4
Total	5	15	9	.625	168	3	0	12-8	240	232	108	21	0	88-13	193	3.68	101	.257	.320	25-5	.120	0	139	3	-0.3
SCHULTZ, BARNEY George Warren B 8.15.1926 Beverly, NJ BR/TR 6-2/200# d4.12 C6																									
1955	StL N	1	2	.333	19	0	0	4	29.2	28	27	5	4	15-3	19	7.89	52	.259	.370	4-0	.000	-1		-12	-1.4
1959	Det A	1	2	.333	13	0	0	0	18.1	17	12	1	1	14-1	17	4.42	92	.254	.390	2-0	1.000	1		-1	-0.1
1961	Chi N	7	6	.538	41	0	0	7	66.2	57	32	6	4	25-4	59	2.70	155	.228	.307	10-2	.100	-1		7	1.3
1962	Chi N	5	5	.500	51	0	0	5	77.2	66	36	8	4	23-6	58	3.82	108	.231	.296	5-2	.000	-0		3	0.4
1963	Chi N	1	0	1.000	15	0	0	2	27.1	25	11	5	0	9-2	18	3.62	97	.263	.327	4-0	.000	-0		0	0.0
	StL N	2	0	1.000	24	0	0	1	35.1	36	15	5	2	8-2	26	3.57	99	.263	.311	0-1	—	0		0	0.0
	Year	3	0	1.000	39	0	0	3	62.2	61	32	10	2	17-4	44	3.59	98	.263	.317	4-1	.000	-0		1	0.0
1964	†StL N	1	3	.250	30	0	0	14	49.1	35	14	1	0	11-3	29	1.64	232	.201	.246	6-1	.167	-0		10	1.4
1965	StL N	2	2	.500	34	0	0	2	42.1	39	22	8	0	11-3	38	3.83	100	.242	.289	2-0	.000	-0		-1	-0.1
Total	7	20	20	.500	227	0	0	35	346.2	303	169	39	15	116-24	264	3.63	109	.237	.307	33-6	.121	-1		6	1.5
SCHULTZ, BOB Robert Duffy B 11.27.1923 Louisville, KY D 3.31.1979 Nashville, TN BR/TL 6-3/200# d4.20																									
1951	Chi N	3	6	.333	17	10	2	0	77.1	75	51	9	2	51	27	5.24	78	.251	.364	29-1	.138	-1	101	-10	-1.2
1952	Chi N	6	3	.667	29	5	1	0	74	63	34	3	2	51	31	4.01	96	.232	.357	18-0	.222	0	51	0	0.0
1953	Chi N	0	2	.000	7	2	0	0	11.2	13	10	2	1	11	4	5.40	82	.289	.439	3-0	.000	-0	100	-2	-0.4
	Pit N	0	2	.000	11	2	0	0	18.2	26	19	3	2	10	5	8.20	55	.321	.409	2-1	.000	0	30	-7	-0.7
	Year	0	4	.000	18	4	0	0	30.1	39	21	5	3	21	9	7.12	63	.310	.420	5-1	.000	-0	65	-10	-1.1
1955	Det A	0	0	—	1	0	0	0	1.1	2	3	0	0	2-0	0	20.25	19	.333	.500	0-0	—	0		-2	-0.1
Total	4	9	13	.409	65	19	3	0	183	179	117	17	7	125-0	67	5.16	79	.255	.372	52-2	.154	-1	82	-21	-2.4
SCHULTZ, WEBB Wilbert Carl B 1.31.1898 Wautoma, WI D 7.26.1986 Delavan, WI BR/TR 5-11/172# d8.3																									
1924	Chi A	0	0	—	1	0	0	0	1	1	1	0	0	0	0	9.00	46	.250	.250	0-0	—	0		0	0.0
SCHULTZ, MIKE William Michael B 12.17.1920 Syracuse, NY BL/TL 6-1/175# d4.20																									
1947	Cin N	0	0	—	1	0	0	0	2	4	2	0	0	2	0	4.50	91	.444	.545	0-0	—	0		0	0.0
SCHULTZE, JOHN John F. B Burlington, NJ 6-0.5/165# d5.6																									
1891	Phi N	0	1	.000	6	1	0	0	15	18	15	1	0	11	4	6.60	52	.286	.392	6	.167	-0	18	-5	-0.3
SCHULZ, AL Albert Christopher B 5.12.1889 Toledo, OH D 12.13.1931 Gallipolis, OH BR/TL 6/182# d9.25																									
1912	NY A	1	1	.500	3	1	1	0	16.1	11	8	0	0	11	8	2.20	163	.183	.310	5-0	.000	-0	0	2	0.2
1913	NY A	7	14	.333	38	22	9	0	193	197	110	4	5	69	77	3.73	80	.269	.336	63-2	.175	0	92	-16	-1.7
1914	NY A	1	3	.250	6	4	1	0	28.1	27	17	0	2	10	18	4.76	58	.237	.310	7-0	.000	-0	79	-6	-0.7
	Buf F	9	12	.429	27	23	10	2	171	160	80	3	2	77	87	3.37	88	.259	.343	56-2	.179	-1	92	-8	-1.0
1915	Buf F	21	14	.600	42	38	25-5	0	309.2	264	125	8	6	149	160	3.08	91	.238	.332	109-3	.165	-4	106	-7	-1.1
1916	Cin N	8	19	.296	44	22	10	2	215	208	100	4	5	93	95	3.14	83	.268	.350	64-1	.125	-3	65	-15	-2.3
Total	5	47	63	.427	160	110	56-5	4	933.1	867	440	19	20	409	445	3.32	85	.254	.338	304-8	.155	-9	91	-50	-6.6
SCHULZ, WALT Walter Frederick B 4.16.1900 St.Louis, MO D 2.27.1928 Prescott, AR BR/TR 6/170# d7.8																									
1920	StL N	0	0	—	2	0	0	0	6	10	5	0	0	2	0	6.00	50	.370	.414	2-0	.000	-0		-2	-0.1
SCHULZE, DON Donald Arthur B 9.27.1962 Roselle, IL BR/TR 6-3/225# d9.13																									
1983	Chi N	0	1	.000	4	3	0	0-0	14	19	11	1	1	7-0	8	7.07	54	.322	.403	1-1	.000	0	116	-4	-0.3
1984	Chi N	0	0	—	1	1	0	0-0	3	8	4	0	0	1-0	2	12.00	33	.571	.563	0-0	—	0	136	-2	-0.1
	Cle A	3	6	.333	19	14	2	0-0	85.2	105	53	9	0	27-0	39	4.83	85	.302	.349	0-0	—	0	121	-8	-0.8
1985	Cle A	4	10	.286	19	18	1	0-0	94.1	128	75	10	4	19-2	37	6.01	69	.322	.357	0-0	—	0	98	-22	-2.7
1986	Cle A	4	4	.500	19	13	1	0-0	84.2	88	48	9	5	34-0	33	5.00	83	.266	.342	0-0	—	0	103	-6	-0.5
1987	NY N	1	2	.333	5	4	0	0-0	21.2	24	15	4	1	6-0	5	6.23	61	.296	.344	2-1	.000	0	120	-5	-0.6
1989	NY A	1	1	.500	2	2	0	0-0	11	12	5	1	1	5-0	5	4.09	95	.300	.375	0-0	—	0	70	0	0.0
	SD N	2	1	.667	7	4	0	0-0	24.1	38	20	6	0	6-0	15	5.55	63	.352	.379	4-1	.000	-0	196	-7	-0.8
Total	6	15	25	.375	76	59	4	0-0	338.2	422	231	40	12	105-2	144	5.47	74	.306	.357	7-3	.000	0	112	-54	-5.8
SCHUMACHER, HAL Harold Henry "Prince Hal" B 11.23.1910 Hinckley, NY D 4.21.1993 Cooperstown, NY BR/TR 6/190# d4.15 Mil 1943-45																									
1931	NY N	1	1	.500	8	2	1	1	18.1	31	23	3	0	14	11	10.80	34	.387	.479	7-0	.143	-0	255	-14	-1.4
1932	NY N	5	6	.455	27	13	2-1	0	101.1	119	60	3	2	39	38	3.55	104	.288	.352	31-1	.226	1*	110	-3	-0.2
1933	†NY N☆	19	12	.613	35	33	21-7	1	258.2	199	71	9	1	84	96	2.16	149	**.214**	.280	98-2	.214	1*	115	33	4.4
1934	NY N	23	10	.697	41	36	18-2	0	297	299	131	16	2	89	112	3.18	122	.259	.313	117-2	.239	10*	125	22	3.3
1935	NY N★	19	9	.679	33	33	19-3	0	261.2	235	100	11	5	70	79	2.89	133	.238	.292	107-3	.196	2*	125	27	3.2
1936	†NY N	11	13	.458	35	30	9-2	1	215.1	234	103	15	1	69	75	3.47	112	.280	.336	74-0	.216	2*	102	8	1.1
1937	†NY N	13	12	.520	38	29	10-1	1	217.2	222	100	12	0	89	100	3.60	108	.264	.335	81-1	.222	3*	98	7	1.1
1938	NY N	13	8	.619	28	28	12-3	0	185	178	81	12	2	50	54	3.50	108	.248	.299	67-1	.239	4*	100	7	1.3
1939	NY N	13	10	.565	29	27	8	0	181.2	199	106	14	3	89	58	4.81	82	.276	.358	69-4	.203	1*	127	-15	-1.6
1940	NY N	13	13	.500	34	30	12-1	1	227	218	93	14	0	96	123	3.25	119	.251	.325	78-3	.192	2*	92	16	2.2
1941	NY N	12	10	.545	30	26	12-3	1	206	187	81	11	5	79	63	3.36	110	.243	.317	66-4	.152	-1*	90	11	1.0
1942	NY N	12	13	.480	29	29	12-3	0	216	208	81	12	3	82	49	3.04	111	.251	.321	75-5	.173	1*	112	10	1.4
1946	NY N	4	4	.500	24	13	2	1	96.2	95	50	8	0	52	48	3.91	88	.255	.347	26-2	.038	-2	111	-5	-0.6
Total	13	158	121	.566	391	329	138-26	7	2482.1	2424	1080	140	24	902	906	3.36	111	.255	.321	896-28	.202	24	110	104	15.2
SCHUMANN, HACK Carl J. B 8.13.1884 Buffalo, NY D 3.25.1946 Mill Grove, NY TR 6-2/230# d9.19																									
1906	Phi A	0	2	.000	4	2	1	0	18	21	13	0	2	8	9	4.00	68	.296	.383	6-0	.000	-1	66	-3	-0.4

Year	Tm Lg	W	L	Pct	G	GS	CG-Sho	SV-BS	IP	H	R	HR	HB	BB-IB	SO	ERA	AERA	OAV	OOB	AB-SH	AVG	PB	Sup	APR	PW
SCHUPP, FERDIE Ferdinand Maurice B 1.16.1891 Louisville, KY D 12.16.1971 Los Angeles, CA BR/TR 5-10/150# d4.19																									
1913	NY N	0	0	—	5	1	0	0	12	10	3	0	0	3	2	0.75	416	.244	.295	3-0	.333	1	96	3	0.2
1914	NY N	0	0	—	8	0	0	1	17	19	11	0	2	9	9	5.82	46	.306	.411	2-0	.000	-0		-5	-0.3
1915	NY N	1	0	1.000	23	1	0	0	54.2	57	37	1	3	29	28	5.10	50	.281	.379	10-0	.200	0	203	-15	-0.8
1916	NY N	9	3	.750	30	11	8-4	1	140.1	79	22	1	5	37	86	0.90	271	.167	.235	41-0	.098	-2	87	24	1.7
1917	†NY N	21	7	**.750**	36	32	25-6	0	272	202	69	7	4	70	147	1.95	131	**.209**	.265	93-1	.161	1	142	21	2.2
1918	NY N	0	1	.000	10	2	1	0	33.1	42	34	1	3	27	22	7.56	35	.328	.456	9-0	.111	-0	173	-19	-1.0
1919	NY N	1	3	.250	9	4	0	1	32	32	24	2	0	18	17	5.63	50	.269	.365	6-2	.333	0	113	-10	-1.2
	StL N	4	4	.500	10	10	6	0	69.2	55	31	2	1	30	37	3.75	75	.221	.307	20-1	.050	-0	88	-5	-0.7
	Year	5	7	.417	19	14	6	1	101.2	87	34	4	1	48	54	4.34	64	.236	.326	26-3	.115	-0	95	-15	-1.9
1920	StL N	16	13	.552	38	37	17	0	250.2	246	118	5	9	127	119	3.52	85	.265	.358	86-4	.256	6*	139	-14	-1.0
1921	StL N	2	0	1.000	9	4	1	1	37.1	42	26	5	2	21	22	4.10	89	.276	.371	14-1	.286	0	185	-4	-0.2
	Bro N	3	4	.429	20	7	1	2	61	75	34	2	2	27	26	4.57	85	.310	.384	12-1	.083	-1	76	-3	-0.4
	Year	5	4	.556	29	11	2	3	98.1	117	38	7	4	48	48	4.39	87	.297	.379	26-2	.192	-0	114	-8	-0.6
1922	Chi A	4	4	.500	18	12	3-1	0	74	79	61	4	2	66	38	6.08	67	.284	.425	23-0	.217	1	120	-19	-1.7
Total	10	61	39	.610	216	121	62-11	6	1054	938	470	30	33	464	553	3.32	87	.244	.331	319-10	.182	5	129	-46	-3.2
SCHURR, WAYNE Wayne Allen B 8.6.1937 Garrett, IN BR/TR 6-4/185# d4.15																									
1964	Chi N	0	0	—	26	0	0	0	48.1	57	22	3	0	11-1	29	3.72	100	.298	.333	5-0	.000	-0		0	0.0
SCHUTZ, CARL Carl James B 8.22.1971 Hammond, LA BL/TL 5-11/208# d9.3																									
1996	Atl N	0	0	—	3	0	0	0-0	3.1	3	1	0	0	2-1	5	2.70	163	.273	.385	0-0	—	0		1	0.0
SCHWABE, MIKE Michael Scott B 7.12.1964 Ft.Dodge, IA BR/TR 6-4/200# d5.27																									
1989	Det A	2	4	.333	13	4	0	0-0	44.2	58	33	6	1	16-5	13	6.04	63	.307	.359	0-0	—	0	71	-11	-1.2
1990	Det A	0	0	—	1	0	0	0-0	3.2	5	1	0	0	0-0	1	2.45	162	.357	.357	0-0	—	0		1	0.1
Total	2	2	4	.333	14	4	0	0-0	48.1	63	34	6	1	16-5	14	5.77	66	.310	.359	0-0	—	0	71	-10	-1.1
SCHWALL, DON Donald Bernard B 3.2.1936 Wilkes-Barre, PA BR/TR 6-6/200# d5.21																									
1961	Bos A★	15	7	.682	25	25	10-2	0	178.2	167	76	8	6	110-1	91	3.22	129	.255	.366	61-11	.180	-0*	121	17	1.9
1962	Bos A	9	15	.375	33	32	5-1	0	182.1	180	118	18	10	121-1	89	4.94	84	.260	.377	66-5	.136	-2*	105	-18	-2.3
1963	Pit N	6	12	.333	33	24	3-2	0	167.2	158	72	13	6	74-13	86	3.33	99	.255	.338	50-0	.160	-0	87	0	0.1
1964	Pit N	4	3	.571	15	9	0	0	49.2	53	28	1	0	15-1	36	4.35	81	.269	.321	19-0	.263	2*	136	-5	-0.5
1965	Pit N	9	6	.600	43	1	0	4	77	77	37	5	2	30-4	55	2.92	120	.269	.341	15-0	.000	-2	75	2	0.3
1966	Pit N	3	2	.600	11	4	0	0	41.2	31	13	3	1	21-2	24	2.16	165	.209	.312	10-1	.100	-0	86	6	0.7
	Atl N	3	3	.500	11	8	0	0	45.1	44	23	2	2	19-2	27	4.37	83	.256	.333	13-0	.000	-2	106	-3	-0.5
	Year	6	5	.545	22	12	0	0	87	75	27	5	3	40-4	51	3.31	109	.234	.323	23-1	.043	-2	100	2	0.2
1967	Atl N	0	0	—	1	0	0	0	0.2	0	0	0	0	1-1	0	0.00	—	.000	.500	0-0	—	0		0	0.0
Total	7	49	48	.505	172	103	18-5	4	743	710	367	50	27	391-25	408	3.72	102	.257	.352	234-17	.145	-5	108	-1	-0.3
SCHWAMB, BLACKIE Ralph Richard B 8.6.1926 Lancaster, CA D 12.21.1989 Los Angeles, CA BR/TR 6-5.5/198# d7.25																									
1948	StL A	1	1	.500	12	5	0	0	31.2	44	34	3	0	21	7	8.53	53	.331	.422	10-0	.300	1	131	-13	-0.6
SCHWARZ, JEFF Jeffrey William B 5.20.1964 Fort Pierce, FL BR/TR 6-5/190# d4.24																									
1993	Chi A	2	2	.500	41	0	0	0-0	51	35	21	1	3	38-2	41	3.71	113	.201	.349	0-0	—	0		4	0.2
1994	Chi A	0	0	—	9	0	0	0-0	11.1	9	10	0	0	16-0	14	6.35	74	.205	.417	0-0	—	0		-3	-0.1
	Cal A	0	0	—	4	0	0	0-0	6.2	5	3	0	0	6-0	4	4.05	121	.250	.407	0-0	—	0		1	0.0
	Year	0	0	—	13	0	0	0-0	18	14	20	0	0	22-0	18	5.50	86	.219	.414	0-0	—	0		-2	-0.1
Total	2	2	2	.500	54	0	0	0-0	69	49	34	1	3	60-2	59	4.17	104	.206	.367	0-0	—	0		2	0.1
SCHWENCK, RUDY Rudolph Christian B 4.6.1884 Louisville, KY D 11.27.1941 Anchorage, KY BL/TL 6/174# d9.23																									
1909	Chi N	1	1	.500	3	2	0	0	4	16	7	0	1	3	3	13.50	19	.308	.357	4-0	.250	0	83	-4	-0.8
SCHWENK, HAL Harold Edward B 8.23.1890 Schuylkill Haven, PA D 9.3.1955 Kansas City, MO BL/TL 6/185# d9.4																									
1913	StL A	1	0	1.000	1	1	1	0	11	12	4	0	0	4	3	3.27	90	.333	.400	3-0	.333	1	126	0	0.1
SCOGGINS, JIM Lynn J. "Lefty" B 7.19.1891 Killeen, TX D 8.16.1923 Columbia, SC BL/TL 5-11/165# d8.26																									
1913	Chi A	0	1	.000	1	1	0	0	0	0	1	0	0	1	0	—	—	.000	.500	0-0	—	0	76	0	0.0
SCORE, HERB Herbert Jude B 6.7.1933 Rosedale, NY BL/TL 6-2/185# d4.15																									
1955	Cle A☆	16	10	.615	33	32	11-2	0	227.1	158	85	18	1	154-1	**245**	2.85	140	.194	.322	84-8	.119	-4	106	28	2.3
1956	Cle A★	20	9	.690	35	33	16-**5**	0	249.1	162	82	18	2	129-2	**263**	2.53	**166**	**.186**	.290	87-4	.184	1	98	45	4.9
1957	Cle A	2	1	.667	5	5	3-1	0	36	18	9	0	1	26-2	39	2.00	186	.149	.304	11-0	.091	-0	86	7	0.6
1958	Cle A	2	3	.400	12	5	2-1	3	41	29	19	1	0	34-1	48	3.95	92	.197	.346	11-0	.091	-0	74	-1	-0.2
1959	Cle A	9	11	.450	30	25	9-1	0	160.2	123	93	28	1	115-0	147	4.71	78	**.210**	.339	52-0	.096	-3	119	-19	-2.5
1960	Chi A	5	10	.333	23	22	5-1	0	113.2	91	54	10	2	87-0	78	3.72	102	.226	.363	30-2	.100	-0	84	0	-0.1
1961	Chi A	1	2	.333	8	5	1	0	24.1	22	19	3	0	24-1	14	6.66	59	.259	.411	6-1	.000	-1	77	-7	-0.8
1962	Chi A	0	0	—	4	0	0	0	6	6	3	1	0	4-0	3	4.50	87	.261	.370	0-0	—	0		0	0.0
Total	8	55	46	.545	150	127	47-11	3	858.1	609	364	79	7	573-7	837	3.36	117	.200	.326	281-15	.128	-8	99	53	4.2
SCOTT, DICK Amos Richard B 2.5.1883 Bethel, OH D 1.18.1911 Chicago, IL BR/TR 6/180# d6.26																									
1901	Cin N	0	2	.000	3	2	2	0	21	26	15	2	3	9	7	5.14	62	.302	.388	9-0	.000	-1	55	-4	-0.5
SCOTT, DARRYL Darryl Nelson B 8.6.1968 Fresno, CA BR/TR 6-1/185# d5.31																									
1993	Cal A	1	2	.333	16	0	0	0-0	20	19	13	1	1	11-1	13	5.85	77	.250	.344	0-0	—	0		-2	-0.3
SCOTT, ED Edward B 8.12.1870 Walbridge, OH D 11.1.1933 Toledo, OH BR/TR 6-3/?# d4.19																									
1900	Cin N	17	20	.459	42	35	31	1	315	370	192	10	14	65	87	3.86	95	.292	.334	123-2	.154	-5	88	-9	-0.9
1901	Cle A	6	6	.500	17	16	11	1	124.2	149	82	2	7	38	23	4.40	81	.293	.350	48-2	.208	1	96	-8	-0.5
Total	2	23	26	.469	59	51	42	2	439.2	519	274	12	21	103	110	4.01	91	.292	.338	171-4	.170	-4	90	-17	-1.4
SCOTT, GEORGE George William B 11.17.1896 Trenton, MO D 12.3.1962 Philomath, OR BR/TR 6-1/175# d8.17																									
1920	StL N	0	0	—	2	0	0	0	6	4	3	0	0	3	1	4.50	66	.200	.304	1-0	.000	-0		-1	-0.1
SCOTT, JIM James "Death Valley Jim" B 4.23.1888 Deadwood, SD D 4.7.1957 Jacumba, CA BR/TR 6-1/235# d4.25 Mil 1917-18 U2																									
1909	Chi A	12	12	.500	36	29	20-4	0	250.1	194	86	0	16	93	135	2.30	102	.223	.310	85-2	.106	-1	104	3	0.0
1910	Chi A	8	18	.308	41	23	14-2	1	229.2	182	99	5	4	86	135	2.43	99	.226	.303	74-2	.203	2	77	-3	0.0
1911	Chi A	14	11	.560	39	26	13-3	0	222	195	82	3	4	81	128	2.39	135	.240	.311	71-5	.155	-2	89	21	1.7
1912	Chi A	2	2	.500	6	4	2-1	0	37.2	36	16	0	1	15	23	2.15	149	.265	.342	12-0	.000	-2	52	3	0.1
1913	Chi A	20	21	.488	48	**38**	25-4	1	312.1	252	96	2	9	86	158	1.90	154	.223	.283	97-8	.072	-7	72	35	3.8
1914	Chi A	14	18	.438	43	33	12-2	1	253.1	228	109	5	5	75	138	2.84	94	.246	.306	86-2	.163	-0	89	-2	-0.2
1915	Chi A	24	11	.686	48	35	23-**7**	2	296.1	256	98	3	5	78	120	2.03	146	.238	.292	95-6	.126	-5	97	28	2.9
1916	Chi A	7	14	.333	32	21	8-1	3	165.1	155	63	3	3	53	71	2.72	101	.258	.321	52-4	.115	-3	85	2	-0.1
1917	Chi A	6	7	.462	24	17	6-2	1	125	126	37	0	6	42	37	1.87	142	.272	.341	42-0	.119	-2	91	10	0.9
Total	9	107	114	.484	317	226	123-26	9	1892	1624	686	21	53	609	945	2.30	120	.238	.305	614-29	.129	-21	87	97	9.1
SCOTT, JACK John William B 4.18.1892 Ridgeway, NC D 11.30.1959 Durham, NC BL/TR 6-2.5/199# d9.6																									
1916	Pit N	0	0	—	1	0	0	0	5	5	6	1	0	3	4	10.80	25	.278	.381	2-0	.000	0*		-4	-0.2
1917	Bos N	1	2	.333	7	3	3	0	39.2	36	12	0	3	5	21	1.82	141	.255	.295	16-0	.125	-1	39	3	0.1
1919	Bos N	6	6	.500	19	12	7	1	103.2	109	47	3	1	39	44	3.13	91	.275	.341	40-2	.175	-1*	116	-4	-0.7
1920	Bos N	10	21	.323	44	33	22-3	1	291	308	148	6	13	85	94	3.53	87	.277	.336	99-3	.212	0	95	-19	-2.1
1921	Bos N	15	13	.536	**47**	28	16-2	3	233.2	258	108	9	7	57	83	3.70	99	.283	.330	88-1	.341	10*	121	0	1.0
1922	Cin N	0	0	—	1	0	0	0	1	2	1	0	0	1	0	9.00	44	.500	.600	1-0	.000	-0		0	0.0
	†NY N	8	2	.800	17	10	5	2	79.2	83	42	7	2	23	37	4.41	91	.265	.320	30-1	.267	1	130	-1	-0.1
	Year	8	2	.800	18	10	5	2	80.2	85	48	7	2	24	37	4.46	90	.268	.324	31-1	.258	1	130	-2	-0.1
1923	†NY N	16	7	.696	40	25	9-3	1	220	223	104	15	4	65	79	3.89	98	.267	.323	79-2	.316	7	134	0	0.6

Year	Tm Lg	W	L	Pct	G	GS	CG-Sho	SV-BS	IP	H	R	HR	HB	BB-IB	SO	ERA	AERA	OAV	OOB	AB-SH	AVG	PB	Sup	APR	PW
1925	NY N	14	15	.483	36	28	18-2	3	239.2	251	98	10	4	55	87	3.15	128	.269	.313	87-0	.241	6*	88	25	3.5
1926	NY N	13	15	.464	**50**	22	13	5	226	242	118	13	3	53	82	4.34	86	.276	.319	83-0	.337	9*	99	-10	-0.3
1927	Phi N	9	21	.300	**48**	25	17-1	1	233.1	304	154	15	4	69	69	5.09	81	.330	.379	114-3	.289	8*	71	-26	-2.1
1928	NY N	4	1	.800	16	3	3	1	50.1	59	22	3	2	11	17	3.58	109	.295	.338	15-0	.267	1	144	2	0.3
1929	NY N	7	6	.538	30	6	2	1	91.2	89	44	12	0	27	40	3.53	130	.260	.314	26-0	.308	3	105	10	1.6
Total	12	103	109	.486	356	195	115-11	19	1814.2	1969	904	94	43	493	657	3.85	96	.281	.332	680-12	.275	44	103	-24	1.6
SCOTT, LEFTY Marshall B 7.15.1915 Roswell, NM D 3.3.1964 Houston, TX BR/TL 6-0.5/165# d6.15																									
1945	Phi N	0	2	.000	8	2	0	0	22.1	29	13	1	0	12	5	4.43	86	.312	.390	3-1	.000	-0	11	-1	-0.2
SCOTT, MIKE Michael Warren B 4.26.1955 Santa Monica, CA BR/TR 6-3/215# d4.18																									
1979	NY N	1	3	.250	18	9	0	0-0	52.1	59	35	4	0	20-3	21	5.33	68	.289	.351	12-1	.000	-1	121	-10	-0.8
1980	NY N	1	1	.500	6	6	1-1	0-0	29.1	40	14	1	0	8-1	13	4.30	83	.331	.369	9-0	.111	0	121	-2	-0.1
1981	NY N	5	10	.333	23	23	1	0-0	136	130	65	11	1	34-1	54	3.90	89	.261	.306	41-1	.073	-2	73	-4	-0.5
1982	NY N	7	13	.350	37	22	1	3-2	147	185	100	13	2	60-3	63	5.14	71	.321	.381	48-0	.146	0	98	-26	-3.0
1983	Hou N	10	6	.625	24	24	2-2	0-0	145	143	67	8	5	46-0	73	3.72	92	.258	.318	48-8	.167	1	124	-4	-0.4
1984	Hou N	5	11	.313	31	29	0	0-0	154	179	96	7	3	43-4	83	4.68	71	.293	.337	47-6	.128	-0	108	-26	-2.4
1985	Hou N	18	8	.692	36	35	4-2	0-0	221.2	194	91	20	3	80-4	137	3.29	106	.235	.302	72-3	.153	2	128	6	0.8
1986	†Hou N★	18	10	.643	37	37	7-**5**	0-0	**275.1**	182	73	17	2	72-6	**306**	**2.22**	**162**	**.186**	**.242**	95-10	.126	-2*	97	**45**	**4.5**
1987	Hou N★	16	13	.552	36	**36**	8-3	0-0	247.2	199	94	21	4	79-6	233	3.23	121	.217	**.281**	80-8	.125	-1	85	22	2.2
1988	Hou N	14	8	.636	32	32	8-5	0-0	218.2	162	74	19	8	53-6	190	2.92	114	.204	.260	71-7	.085	-3	113	13	1.0
1989	Hou N✤	**20**	10	.667	33	33	9-2	0-0	229	180	87	23	3	62-12	172	3.10	109	.212	.267	75-9	.133	-0	122	8	0.8
1990	Hou N	9	13	.409	32	32	4-2	0-0	205.2	194	102	27	1	66-6	121	3.81	98	.246	.302	54-6	.130	-0	76	-4	-0.5
1991	Hou N	0	2	.000	2	2	0	0-0	7	11	10	2	1	4-1	3	12.86	27	.367	.457	1-0	.000	-0	51	-7	-1.1
Total	13	124	108	.534	347	319	45-22	3-2	2068.2	1858	908	173	33	627-53	1469	3.54	100	.240	.297	653-59	.124	-6	103	11	0.5
SCOTT, MICKEY Ralph Robert B 7.25.1947 Weimar, Germany BL/TL 6-1/165# d5.6																									
1972	Bal A	0	1	.000	15	0	0	0-1	23	23	7	2	1	5-0	11	2.74	113	.277	.319	1-0	.000	1		1	0.1
1973	Bal A	0	0	—	1	0	0	0-0	1.2	2	1	1	0	2-0	2	5.40	69	.286	.444	0-0	—	0		0	0.0
	Mon N	1	2	.333	22	0	0	0-1	24	27	14	3	2	9-0	11	5.25	73	.287	.362	3-0	.000	-0		-3	-0.3
1975	Cal A	4	2	.667	50	0	0	1-4	68.1	59	34	8	1	18-5	31	3.29	108	.233	.282	0-0	—	0		0	0.0
1976	Cal A	3	0	1.000	33	0	0	3-1	39	47	17	3	0	12-4	10	3.23	103	.307	.355	0-0	—	0*		0	0.0
1977	Cal A	0	2	.000	12	0	0	0-0	16	19	16	1	0	4-2	5	5.63	70	.302	.343	0-0	—	0		-5	-0.5
Total	5	8	7	.533	133	0	0	4-7	172	177	89	18	4	50-11	70	3.72	95	.271	.323	4-0	.000	0		-7	-0.7
SCOTT, DICK Richard Lewis B 3.15.1933 Portsmouth, NH BR/TL 6-2/185# d5.8																									
1963	LA N	0	0	—	9	0	0	2	12	17	10	6	0	3-0	6	6.75	45	.340	.370	0-0	—	0		-5	-0.3
1964	Chi N	0	0	—	3	0	0	0	4.1	10	6	2	0	1-0	1	12.46	30	.417	.440	0-0	—	0		-4	-0.2
Total	2	0	0	—	12	0	0	2	16.1	27	16	8	0	4-0	7	8.27	39	.365	.392	0-0	—	0		-9	-0.5
SCOTT, TIM Timothy Dale B 11.16.1966 Hanford, CA BR/TR 6-2/205# d6.25																									
1991	SD N	0	0	—	2	0	0	0-0	1	2	2	0	0	0-0	1	9.00	42	.400	.400	0-0	—	0		-1	-0.1
1992	SD N	4	1	.800	34	0	0	0-1	37.2	39	24	4	1	21-6	30	5.26	68	.267	.361	0-0	—	0		-7	-0.9
1993	SD N	2	0	1.000	24	0	0	0-2	37.2	38	13	1	4	15-0	30	2.39	173	.260	.341	2-1	.000	-0		6	0.3
	Mon N	5	2	.714	32	0	0	1-1	34	31	15	3	0	19-2	35	3.71	113	.242	.340	2-0	.000	-0		2	0.4
	Year	7	2	.778	56	0	0	1-3	71.2	69	32	4	4	34-2	65	3.01	138	.252	.341	4-1	.000	-0		8	0.7
1994	Mon N	5	2	.714	40	0	0	1-0	53.1	51	17	0	2	18-3	37	2.70	157	.251	.318	2-0	.000	-0		9	1.0
1995	Mon N	2	0	1.000	62	0	0	2-3	63.1	52	30	6	6	23-2	57	3.98	108	.222	.307	4-0	.250	0		2	0.1
1996	Mon N	3	5	.375	45	0	0	1-2	46.1	41	18	3	2	21-2	37	3.11	139	.238	.325	4-0	.000	-0		6	0.8
	SF N	2	2	.500	20	0	0	0-2	19.2	24	18	5	1	9-0	10	8.24	50	.316	.391	1-0	.000	-0		-8	-1.4
	Year	5	7	.417	65	0	0	1-4	66	65	36	8	3	30-2	47	4.64	92	.262	.345	5-0	.000	-1		-2	-0.6
1997	SD N	1	1	.500	14	0	0	0-1	18.1	25	17	2	3	5-0	14	7.85	49	.321	.379	0-0	—	0		-8	-0.8
	Col N	0	0	—	3	0	0	0-0	2.2	5	3	0	0	2-0	2	10.13	51	.455	.538	0-0	—	0		-1	0.0
	Year	1	1	.500	17	0	0	0-1	21	30	20	2	3	7-0	16	8.14	50	.337	.400	0-0	—	0		-9	-0.8
Total	7	24	13	.649	276	0	0	5-12	314	308	157	24	19	133-15	253	4.13	100	.257	.338	15-1	.067	-1		0	-0.6
SCUDDER, SCOTT William Scott B 2.14.1968 Paris, TX BR/TR 6-2/185# d6.6																									
1989	Cin N	4	9	.308	23	17	0	0-0	100.1	91	54	14	1	61-11	66	4.49	80	.239	.345	24-4	.167	1	91	-8	-1.0
1990	†Cin N	5	5	.500	21	10	0	0-0	71.2	74	41	12	3	30-4	42	4.90	81	.265	.342	18-1	.056	-1	105	-7	-1.0
1991	Cin N	6	9	.400	27	14	0	1-0	101.1	91	52	6	6	56-4	51	4.35	87	.246	.352	29-2	.103	-0	101	-5	-0.7
1992	Cle A	6	10	.375	23	22	0	0-0	109	134	80	10	2	55-0	66	5.28	74	.303	.380	0-0	—	0	90	-21	-2.6
1993	Cle A	0	1	.000	2	1	0	0-0	4	5	4	0	1	4-0	1	9.00	48	.333	.500	0-0	—	0	64	-2	-0.3
Total	5	21	34	.382	96	64	0	1-0	386.1	395	231	42	13	206-19	226	4.80	80	.266	.358	71-7	.113	-0	95	-43	-5.6
SCURRY, ROD Rodney Grant B 3.17.1956 Sacramento, CA D 11.5.1992 Reno, NV BL/TL 6-2/180# d4.17																									
1980	Pit N	0	2	.000	20	0	0	0-0	37.2	23	12	2	2	17-3	28	2.15	170	.176	.280	4-0	.250	0		5	0.3
1981	Pit N	4	5	.444	27	7	0	7-2	74	74	33	6	3	40-2	65	3.77	95	.261	.357	19-0	.158	0	46	0	-0.1
1982	Pit N	4	5	.444	76	0	0	14-6	103.2	79	26	3	4	64-7	94	1.74	214	.212	.331	21-1	.238	1		21	2.4
1983	Pit N	4	9	.308	61	0	0	7-8	68	63	45	6	4	53-7	67	5.56	67	.249	.382	5-0	.000	-1		-13	-2.5
1984	Pit N	5	6	.455	43	0	0	4-1	46.1	28	14	1	0	22-3	48	2.53	143	.175	.275	2-0	.000	-0		6	1.2
1985	Pit N	0	1	.000	30	0	0	2-1	47.2	42	22	4	0	28-1	43	3.21	112	.236	.337	4-0	.000	-0		1	0.0
	NY A	1	0	1.000	5	0	0	1-0	12.2	5	4	2	0	10-1	17	2.84	141	.125	.300	0-0	—	0		2	0.2
1986	NY A	1	2	.333	31	0	0	2-1	39.1	38	18	1	2	22-1	36	3.66	112	.252	.354	0-0	—	0		2	0.2
1988	Sea A	0	2	.000	39	0	0	2-0	31.1	32	16	6	4	18-4	33	4.02	104	.258	.365	0-0	—	0		0	0.0
Total	8	19	32	.373	332	7	0	39-19	460.2	384	190	31	19	274-29	431	3.24	115	.227	.339	55-1	.164	0	46	24	1.7
SEALE, JOHNNIE Johnny Ray "Durango Kid" B 11.14.1938 Edgewater, CO BL/TL 5-10/155# d9.20																									
1964	Det A	1	0	1.000	4	0	0	0	10	6	4	1	0	4-0	5	3.60	102	.171	.256	1-0	.000	-0		0	0.0
1965	Det A	0	0	—	4	0	0	0	3	7	4	1	0	2-0	3	12.00	29	.500	.500	0-0	—	0		-3	-0.1
Total	2	1	0	1.000	8	0	0	0	13	13	8	2	0	6-0	8	5.54	65	.265	.333	1-0	.000	-0		-3	-0.1
SEAMAN, KIM Kim Michael B 5.6.1957 Pascagoula, MS BL/TL 6-4/205# d9.28																									
1979	StL N	0	0	—	1	0	0	0-0	2	0	0	0	0	2-0	3	0.00	—	.000	.250	0-0	—	0		1	0.0
1980	StL N	3	2	.600	26	0	0	4-1	23.2	16	9	2	0	13-1	10	3.42	108	.188	.296	1-0	.000	-0		1	0.2
Total	2	3	2	.600	27	0	0	4-1	25.2	16	9	2	0	15-1	13	3.16	117	.176	.292	1-0	.000	-0		2	0.2
SEANEZ, RUDY Rudy Caballero B 10.20.1968 Brawley, CA BR/TR 5-10/185# d9.7																									
1989	Cle A	0	0	—	5	0	0	0-0	5	1	2	0	0	4-1	7	3.60	110	.071	.250	0-0	—	0		0	0.0
1990	Cle A	2	1	.667	24	0	0	0-0	27.1	22	17	2	1	25-1	24	5.60	70	.220	.378	0-0	—	0		-4	-0.5
1991	Cle A	0	0	—	5	0	0	0-1	5	10	12	2	0	7-0	7	16.20	26	.385	.515	0-0	—	0		-7	-0.4
1993	SD N	0	0	—	3	0	0	0-0	3.1	8	6	1	0	2-0	1	13.50	31	.471	.526	0-0	—	0		-4	-0.2
1994	LA N	1	1	.500	17	0	0	0-1	23.2	24	7	2	1	9-1	18	2.66	148	.273	.340	1-0	.000	-0		4	0.3
1995	LA N	1	3	.250	37	0	0	3-1	34.2	39	27	5	1	18-3	29	6.75	56	.285	.372	1-0	.000	-0		-11	-1.3
1998	†Atl N	4	1	.800	34	0	0	2-2	36	25	13	2	1	16-0	50	2.75	151	.195	.286	1-0	.000	-0		5	0.7
1999	Atl N	6	1	.857	56	0	0	3-5	53.2	47	21	3	1	21-1	41	3.35	134	.234	.307	1-0	.000	0		7	0.9
2000	Atl N	2	4	.333	23	0	0	2-1	21	15	11	3	1	9-1	20	4.29	107	.192	.284	0-0	—	0		1	0.1
2001	SD N	0	2	.000	26	0	0	1-2	24	15	8	3	1	15-0	24	2.63	153	.176	.304	0-0	—	0		4	0.3
	†Atl N	0	0	—	12	0	0	0-0	12	8	4	1	0	4-0	17	3.00	147	.182	.250	0-0	—	0		2	0.1
	Year	0	2	.000	38	0	0	1-2	36	23	14	4	1	19-0	41	2.75	151	.178	.287	0-0	—	0		6	0.4
2002	Tex A	1	3	.250	33	0	0	0-4	33	28	25	5	0	24-1	40	5.73	83	.230	.354	0-0	—	0		-5	-0.5
2003	Bos A	0	1	.000	9	0	0	0-1	8.2	11	7	2	0	6-1	9	6.23	73	.297	.386	0-0	—	0		-2	-0.2
Total	12	17	17	.500	284	0	0	11-18	287.1	253	160	31	7	160-10	287	4.54	93	.235	.334	4-0	.000	-0		-10	-0.7

Year	Tm Lg	W	L	Pct	G	GS	CG-Sho	SV-BS	IP	H	R	HR	HB	BB-IB	SO	ERA	AERA	OAV	OOB	AB-SH	AVG	PB	Sup	APR	PW
SEARAGE, RAY Raymond Mark B 5.1.1955 Freeport, NY BL/TL 6-1/180# d6.11																									
1981	NY N	1	0	1.000	26	0	0	1-0	36.2	34	16	2	0	17-3	16	3.68	95	.252	.331	1-0	1.000	0		0	0.0
1984	Mil A	2	1	.667	21	0	0	6-1	38.1	20	3	0	1	16-3	29	0.70	547	.155	.253	0-0	—	0		14	1.5
1985	Mil A	1	4	.200	33	0	0	1-2	38	54	27	2	0	24-4	36	5.92	70	.338	.422	0-0	—	0		-7	-0.8
1986	Mil A	0	1	.000	17	0	0	1-1	22	29	17	6	1	9-1	10	6.95	62	.315	.382	0-0	—	0		-5	-0.2
	Chi A	1	0	1.000	29	0	0	0-0	29	15	3	1	0	19-3	26	0.62	696	.156	.291	0-0	—	0		11	0.6
	Year	1	1	.500	46	0	0	1-1	51	44	20	7	1	28-4	36	3.35	129	.234	.333	0-0	—	0		6	0.4
1987	Chi A	2	3	.400	58	0	0	2-3	55.2	56	28	9	1	24-3	33	4.20	109	.264	.339	0-0	—	0		2	0.2
1989	LA N	3	4	.429	41	0	0	0-1	35.2	29	15	1	0	18-6	24	3.53	97	.225	.313	0-0	—	0		0	0.0
1990	LA N	1	0	1.000	29	0	0	0-0	32.1	30	11	1	0	10-0	19	2.78	132	.250	.299	2-0	.000	-0		3	0.2
Total	7	11	13	.458	254	0	0	11-8	287.2	267	120	22	3	137-23	193	3.50	114	.249	.332	3-0	.333	0		18	1.5
SEARCY, STEVE William Steven B 6.4.1964 Knoxville, TN BL/TL 6-1/185# d8.29																									
1988	Det A	0	2	.000	2	2	0	0-0	8	8	6	3	0	4-0	5	5.63	68	.242	.324	0-0	—	0	60	-2	-0.3
1989	Det A	1	1	.500	8	2	0	0-1	22.1	27	16	3	0	12-1	11	6.04	63	.307	.390	0-0	—	0	189	-5	-0.4
1990	Det A	2	7	.222	16	12	1	0-0	75.1	76	44	9	0	51-3	66	4.66	85	.270	.375	0-0	—	0	55	-7	-0.7
1991	Det A	1	2	.333	16	5	0	0-0	40.2	52	40	8	0	30-0	32	8.41	49	.313	.412	0-0	—	0	101	-18	-1.2
	Phi N	2	1	.667	18	0	0	0-0	30.1	29	16	2	0	14-1	21	4.15	88	.252	.328	4-0	.000	-0		-2	-0.2
1992	Phi N	0	0	—	10	0	0	0-0	10.1	13	9	0	0	8-0	5	6.10	57	.325	.429	0-0	—	0		-4	-0.2
Total	5	6	13	.316	70	21	1	0-1	187	205	131	25	0	119-5	140	5.68	69	.283	.379	4-0	.000	-0	81	-38	-3.0
SEATON, TOM Thomas Gordon B 8.30.1887 Blair, NE D 4.10.1940 ElPaso, TX BB/TR 6/175# d4.13																									
1912	Phi N	16	12	.571	44	27	16-2	2	255	246	126	8	9	106	118	3.28	111	.261	.342	83-4	.217	-0	95	11	0.9
1913	Phi N	**27**	12	.692	52	35	21-5	1	**322.1**	262	117	6	10	136	**168**	2.60	128	.226	.313	110-3	.109	-5	114	25	2.3
1914	Bro F	25	14	.641	44	38	26-7	2	302.2	299	130	6	13	102	172	3.03	95	.259	.326	107-1	.206	2	100	-4	-0.2
1915	Bro F	11	11	.500	32	24	13	3	189.1	199	123	6	3	99	86	4.42	62	.273	.362	66-8	.242	3*	145	-36	-3.5
	New F	2	6	.250	12	10	7	1	75	61	26	1	2	21	28	2.28	112	.224	.285	26-0	.154	-0	98	3	0.3
	Year	13	17	.433	44	34	20	4	264.1	260	30	7	5	120	114	3.81	70	.260	.342	92-8	.217	3	132	-35	-3.2
1916	Chi N	6	6	.500	31	12	4	1	121	108	54	3	4	43	45	3.27	89	.246	.319	38-1	.184	0	122	-3	-0.3
1917	Chi N	5	4	.556	16	9	3-1	1	74.2	60	30	0	1	23	27	2.53	115	.227	.292	21-1	.238	1	92	3	0.5
Total	6	92	65	.586	231	155	90-15	11	1340	1235	606	30	42	530	644	3.12	99	.249	.327	451-18	.186	0	109	-1	-0.0
SEATS, TOM Thomas Edward B 9.24.1910 Farmington, NC D 5.10.1992 San Ramon, CA BR/TL 5-11/190# d5.4																									
1940	Det A	2	2	.500	26	2	0	1	55.2	67	43	4	0	21	25	4.69	101	.290	.349	12-0	.083	-1	129	-3	-0.3
1945	Bro N	10	7	.588	31	18	6-2	0	121.2	127	71	8	5	37	44	4.36	86	.261	.320	43-4	.209	0	135	-7	-0.8
Total	2	12	9	.571	57	20	6-2	1	177.1	194	114	12	5	58	69	4.47	91	.271	.329	55-4	.182	-1	129	-10	-1.1
SEAVER, TOM George Thomas "Tom Terrific" B 11.17.1944 Fresno, CA BR/TR 6-1/206# d4.13 HF1992																									
1967	NY N★	16	13	.552	35	34	18-2	0	251	224	85	19	5	78-6	170	2.76	123	.241	.301	77-6	.143	2*	94	18	2.4
1968	NY N★	16	12	.571	36	35	14-5	1	277.2	224	73	15	8	48-5	205	2.20	137	.222	.261	95-3	.158	0*	76	26	3.0
1969	†NY N☆	**25**	7	**.781**	36	35	18-5	0-0	273.1	202	75	24	7	82-9	208	2.21	166	**.207**	.272	91-4	.121	-0*	102	43	5.3
1970	NY N★	18	12	.600	37	36	19-2	0-0	290.2	230	103	21	4	83-8	**283**	**2.82**	**143**	.214	.272	95-7	.179	4*	88	**39**	4.4
1971	NY N☆	20	10	.667	36	35	21-4	0-1	286.1	210	61	18	4	61-2	**289**	**1.76**	**194**	.206	**.252**	92-11	.196	4*	104	**54**	**6.7**
1972	NY N☆	21	12	.636	35	35	13-3	0-0	262	215	92	23	5	77-2	249	2.92	115	.224	.284	89-6	.146	4*	80	15	2.4
1973	†NY N★	19	10	.655	36	36	**18**-3	0-0	290	219	74	23	4	64-5	**251**	**2.08**	**174**	**.206**	**.252**	93-9	.161	3*	96	**50**	**5.5**
1974	NY N	11	11	.500	32	32	12-5	0-0	236	199	89	19	3	75-10	201	3.20	112	.230	.293	71-7	.099	-2	92	14	1.1
1975	NY N★	**22**	9	.710	36	36	15-5	0-0	280.1	217	81	11	4	88-6	**243**	2.38	146	.214	.279	95-7	.179	3*	105	37	**4.5**
1976	NY N★	14	11	.560	35	34	13-5	0-0	271	211	83	14	4	77-9	**235**	2.59	127	.213	.272	82-9	.085	-2	93	**25**	2.2
1977	NY N	7	3	.700	13	13	5-3	0-0	96	79	33	7	0	28-3	72	3.00	125	.221	.275	31-2	.161	-0	97	9	1.0
	Cin N★	14	3	.824	20	20	14-4	0-0	165.1	120	45	12	0	38-3	124	2.34	168	.201	.248	55-11	.218	4	113	30	3.4
	Year	21	6	.778	33	33	19-**7**	0-0	261.1	199	50	19	0	66-6	196	2.58	150	**.209**	**.258**	86-13	.198	4	107	40	4.4
1978	Cin N☆	16	14	.533	36	36	8-1	0-0	259.2	218	97	26	0	89-11	226	2.88	124	.227	.289	74-13	.122	-0	100	18	1.9
1979	†Cin N	16	6	**.727**	32	32	9-**5**	0-0	215	187	85	16	0	61-6	131	3.14	119	.236	.289	76-4	.158	2*	115	14	1.5
1980	Cin N	10	8	.556	26	26	5-1	0-0	168	140	74	24	1	59-3	101	3.64	98	.225	.290	46-7	.130	1	111	-2	0.0
1981	Cin N★	**14**	2	**.875**	23	23	6-1	0-0	166.1	120	51	10	3	66-8	87	2.54	140	.205	.285	55-4	.200	4	125	19	2.2
1982	Cin N	5	13	.278	21	21	0	0-0	111.1	136	75	14	3	44-4	62	5.50	67	.302	.367	34-5	.176	1*	78	-21	-3.0
1983	NY N	9	14	.391	34	34	5-2	0-0	231	201	104	18	4	86-5	135	3.55	103	.235	.305	64-6	.156	2	88	3	0.4
1984	Chi A	15	11	.577	34	33	10-4	0-0	236.2	216	108	27	2	61-3	131	3.95	105	.240	.288	0-0	—	0	100	8	0.9
1985	Chi A	16	11	.593	35	33	6-1	0-0	238.2	223	103	22	8	69-6	134	3.17	136	.248	.304	0-0	—	0	86	25	2.7
1986	Chi A	2	6	.250	12	12	1	0-0	72	66	37	9	5	27-1	31	4.38	99	.242	.319	0-0	—	0	65	0	0.0
	Bos A	5	7	.417	16	16	1	0-0	104.1	114	46	8	2	29-1	72	3.80	110	.278	.326	0-0	—	0	88	6	0.6
	Year	7	13	.350	28	28	2	0-0	176.1	180	50	17	7	56-2	103	4.03	105	.264	.323	0-0	—	0	78	6	0.6
Total	20	311	205	.603	656	647	231-61	1-1	4782.2	3971	1674	380	76	1390-116	3640	2.86	127	.226	.283	1315-121	.154	28	96	430	49.1
SEAY, BOBBY Robert Michael B 6.20.1978 Sarasota, FL BL/TL 6-2/221# d8.14																									
2001	TB A	1	1	.500	12	0	0	0-0	13	13	11	3	1	5-1	12	6.23	72	.260	.339	0-0	—	0		-3	-0.4
2003	TB A	0	0	—	12	0	0	0-1	9	7	3	0	0	6-0	5	3.00	151	.226	.333	0-0	—	0		2	0.1
Total	2	1	1	.500	24	0	0	0-1	22	20	14	3	1	11-1	17	4.91	92	.247	.337	0-0	—	0		-1	-0.3
SEBRA, BOB Robert Bush B 12.11.1961 Ridgewood, NJ BR/TR 6-2/200# d6.26																									
1985	Tex A	0	2	.000	7	4	0	0-0	20.1	26	17	4	1	14-2	13	7.52	56	.306	.402	0-0	—	0	48	-7	-0.6
1986	Mon N	5	5	.500	17	13	3-1	0-0	91.1	82	39	9	3	25-2	66	3.55	104	.239	.294	29-0	.207	1*	85	2	0.3
1987	Mon N	6	15	.286	36	27	4-1	0-0	177.1	184	99	15	3	67-0	156	4.42	95	.272	.337	51-4	.157	0	72	-4	-0.5
1988	Phi N	1	2	.333	3	3	0	0-0	11.1	15	11	0	0	10-0	7	7.94	45	.333	.417	5-0	.000	-0	116	-5	-1.0
1989	Phi N	2	3	.400	6	5	0	0-0	34.1	41	20	6	4	10-2	21	4.46	80	.295	.357	10-1	.000	-0	80	-4	-0.5
	Cin N	0	0	—	15	0	0	1-0	21	24	16	2	3	18-1	14	6.43	56	.296	.433	1-0	.000	-0		-6	-0.3
	Year	2	3	.400	21	5	0	1-0	55.1	65	39	8	7	28-3	35	5.20	69	.295	.388	11-1	.000	-1	79	-10	-0.8
1990	Mil A	1	2	.333	10	0	0	0-0	11	20	10	1	1	5-1	4	8.18	47	.408	.456	0-0	—	0		-5	-0.9
Total	6	15	29	.341	94	52	7-2	1-0	366.2	392	212	37	15	149-8	281	4.71	84	.276	.347	96-5	.146	-0	76	-29	-3.5
SECHRIST, DOC Theodore O'Hara B 2.10.1876 Williamstown, KY D 4.2.1950 Louisville, KY BR/TR 5-9/160# d4.28																									
1899	NY N	0	0	—	1	0	0	0	0	0	0	0	0	2	0	—	—	—	1.000	0-0	—	0		0	0.0
SECRIST, DON Donald Laverne B 2.26.1944 Seattle, WA BL/TL 6-2/195# d4.11																									
1969	Chi A	0	1	.000	19	0	0	0-0	40	35	28	7	1	14-2	23	6.07	64	.227	.296	7-0	.143	0		-9	-0.4
1970	Chi A	0	0	—	9	0	0	0-0	14.2	19	9	2	0	12-0	9	5.52	71	.333	.437	0-0	—	0		-2	-0.1
Total	2	0	1	.000	28	0	0	0-0	54.2	54	37	9	1	26-2	32	5.93	65	.256	.338	7-0	.143	0		-11	-0.5
SEDGWICK, DUKE Henry Kenneth B 6.1.1898 Martins Ferry, OH D 12.4.1982 Clearwater, FL BR/TR 6/175# d7.12																									
1921	Phi N	1	3	.250	16	5	1	0	71.1	81	48	3	4	32	21	4.92	86	.283	.363	24-0	.208	-1	82	-3	-0.3
1923	Was A	0	1	.000	5	2	1	0	16	27	17	1	0	6	4	7.88	48	.415	.465	5-0	.000	-1	99	-8	-0.4
Total	2	1	4	.200	21	7	2	0	87.1	108	65	4	4	38	25	5.46	76	.308	.382	29-0	.172	-2	85	-11	-0.7
SEDLACEK, SHAWN Shawn Patrick B 6.29.1977 Cedar Rapids, IA BR/TR 6-4/200# d6.18																									
2002	KC A	3	5	.375	16	14	0	0-0	84.1	99	64	16	6	36-2	52	6.72	75	.303	.375	6-0	.000	-1	90	-13	-1.1
SEELBACH, CHUCK Charles Frederick B 3.20.1948 Lakewood, OH BR/TR 6/180# d6.29																									
1971	Det A	0	0	—	5	0	0	0-0	4	6	6	2	1	7-0	1	13.50	27	.375	.583	0-0	—	0		-4	-0.2
1972	†Det A	9	8	.529	61	3	0	14-3	112	96	39	6	3	39-4	76	2.89	109	.238	.308	21-1	.143	1	75	4	0.8
1973	Det A	1	0	1.000	5	0	0	0-0	7	7	3	1	0	2-1	2	3.86	106	.250	.300	0-0	—	0		0	0.1
1974	Det A	0	0	—	4	0	0	0-0	7.2	9	4	2	1	3-0	0	4.70	81	.300	.382	0-0	—	0		0	0.0
Total	4	10	8	.556	75	3	0	14-3	130.2	118	52	11	5	51-5	79	3.38	97	.247	.325	21-1	.143	1	75	0	0.7

Year	Tm Lg	W	L	Pct	G	GS	CG-Sho	SV-BS	IP	H	R	HR	HB	BB-IB	SO	ERA	AERA	OAV	OOB	AB-SH	AVG	PB	Sup	APR	PW
SEELBACH, CHRIS Christopher Don B 12.18.1972 Lufkin, TX BR/TR 6-4/180# d9.9																									
2000	Atl N	0	1	.000	2	0	0	0-0	1.2	3	2	0	0	0-0	1	10.80	42	.500	.429	0-0	—	0		-1	-0.2
2001	Atl N	0	0	—	5	0	0	0-0	8	9	7	3	0	5-1	8	7.88	56	.273	.368	0-0	—	0		-3	-0.1
Total	2	0	1	.000	7	0	0	0-0	9.2	12	9	3	0	5-1	9	8.38	53	.308	.378	0-0	—	0		-4	-0.3
SEGELKE, HERMAN Herman Neils B 4.24.1958 San Mateo, CA BR/TR 6-4/200# d4.7																									
1982	Chi N	0	0	—	3	0	0	0-0	4.1	6	4	1	0	6-0	4	8.31	45	.316	.480	0-0	—	0		-2	-0.1
SEGUI, DIEGO Diego Pablo (Gonzalez) B 8.17.1937 Holguin, Cuba BR/TR 6/190# d4.12 s-David																									
1962	KC A	8	5	.615	37	13	2	6	116.2	89	53	16	1	46-2	71	3.86	109	.211	.288	34-1	.235	2	106	5	0.8
1963	KC A	9	6	.600	38	23	4-1	0	167	173	84	17	2	73-7	116	3.77	103	.267	.341	55-4	.218	1	95	0	0.1
1964	KC A	8	17	.320	40	35	5-2	0	217	219	118	30	1	94-3	155	4.56	84	.260	.333	71-3	.155	0	89	-16	-1.6
1965	KC A	5	15	.250	40	25	5-1	0	163	166	102	18	2	67-3	119	4.64	75	.261	.331	47-4	.191	2*	94	-24	-2.5
1966	Was A	3	7	.300	21	13	1-1	0	72	82	42	8	0	24-1	54	5.00	69	.291	.345	18-0	.111	-1	61	-11	-1.5
1967	KC A	3	4	.429	36	3	0	1	70	62	30	4	2	31-5	52	3.09	103	.238	.323	9-0	.000	-1	27	-1	-0.2
1968	Oak A	6	5	.545	52	0	0	6	83	51	25	7	0	32-8	72	2.39	118	.173	.254	9-0	.111	0		4	0.6
1969	Sea A	12	6	.667	66	8	2	12-3	142.1	127	62	14	2	61-9	113	3.35	109	.238	.317	27-3	.148	-0	106	4	0.5
1970	Oak A	10	10	.500	47	19	3-2	2-0	162	130	54	9	2	68-4	95	**2.56**	**139**	.222	.303	43-6	.116	-2	99	18	1.8
1971	†Oak A	10	8	.556	26	21	5	0-0	146.1	122	59	13	4	63-4	81	3.14	106	.229	.315	47-1	.085	-1	106	3	0.1
1972	Oak A	0	1	.000	7	3	0	0-0	22.2	25	10	2	0	7-1	11	3.57	80	.287	.340	7-0	.143	-0	155	-2	-0.1
	StL N	3	1	.750	33	0	0	9-2	55.2	47	23	2	0	32-10	54	3.07	111	.229	.332	7-0	.143	0		1	0.2
1973	StL N	7	6	.538	65	0	0	17-6	100.1	78	35	6	0	53-12	93	2.78	131	.211	.310	10-0	.000	-1		10	1.4
1974	Bos A	6	8	.429	58	0	0	10-6	108	106	54	9	1	49-10	76	4.00	96	.257	.334	0-0	—	0		-2	-0.3
1975	†Bos A	2	5	.286	33	1	1	6-1	71	71	41	10	0	43-3	45	4.82	85	.270	.373	0-0	—	0	0	-5	-0.6
1977	Sea A	0	7	.000	40	7	0	2-0	110.2	108	75	20	1	43-4	91	5.69	72	.251	.319	0-0	—	0	56	-18	-1.1
Total	15	92	111	.453	639	171	28-7	71-18	1807.2	1656	867	185	18	786-86	1298	3.81	96	.243	.322	384-22	.151	-1	92	-34	-2.4
SEGURA, JOSE Jose Altagracia (Mota) B 1.26.1963 Fundacion, D.R. BR/TR 5-11/180# d4.10																									
1988	Chi A	0	0	—	4	0	0	0-0	8.2	19	17	1	0	8-0	2	13.50	29	.432	.519	0-0	—	0		-10	-0.5
1989	Chi A	0	1	.000	7	0	0	0-1	6	13	11	2	0	3-1	4	15.00	25	.464	.500	0-0	—	0		-8	-1.0
1991	SF N	0	1	.000	11	0	0	0-1	16.1	20	11	1	0	5-0	10	4.41	81	.303	.352	0-0	—	0		-3	-0.2
Total	3	0	2	.000	22	0	0	0-2	31	52	39	4	0	16-1	16	9.00	42	.377	.439	0-0	—	0		-21	-1.7
SEIBOLD, SOCKS Harry B 4.3.1896 Philadelphia, PA D 9.21.1965 Philadelphia, PA BR/TR 5-8.5/162# d9.18.1915 Mil 1918 ▲																									
1916	Phi A	1	1	.500	3	2	1-1	0	21.2	22	12	0	0	9	5	4.15	69	.272	.344	12-0	.167	-0*	106	-3	-0.2
1917	Phi A	4	16	.200	33	15	9-1	1	160	141	86	1	3	85	55	3.94	70	.243	.343	59-5	.220	2*	84	-16	-1.9
1919	Phi A	2	3	.400	14	4	1	0	45.2	58	34	2	4	26	19	5.32	64	.322	.419	13-2	.154	-1*	34	-9	-1.0
1929	Bos N	12	17	.414	33	27	16-1	1	205.2	228	119	17	2	80	54	4.73	99	.285	.352	70-2	.286	4	84	0	0.5
1930	Bos N	15	16	.484	36	33	20-1	2	251	288	135	16	2	85	70	4.12	120	.290	.348	90-1	.211	0	73	20	2.0
1931	Bos N	10	18	.357	33	29	10-3	0	206.1	226	122	12	3	65	50	4.67	81	.279	.335	70-6	.129	-4	73	-21	-2.8
1932	Bos N	3	10	.231	28	20	6-1	0	136.2	173	91	12	2	41	33	4.68	80	.309	.358	46-2	.152	-2	103	-17	-1.5
1933	Bos N	1	4	.200	11	5	1	1	36.2	43	18	0	0	14	10	3.68	83	.295	.356	9-0	.111	0	87	-3	-0.4
Total	8	48	85	.361	191	135	64-8	5	1063.2	1179	617	60	16	405	296	4.43	91	.284	.350	369-18	.198	-0	81	-49	-5.3
SELE, AARON Aaron Helmer B 6.25.1970 Golden Valley, MN BR/TR 6-5/218# d6.23																									
1993	Bos A	7	2	.778	18	18	0	0-0	111.2	100	42	5	7	48-2	93	2.74	169	.237	.322	0-0	—	0	94	21	1.4
1994	Bos A	8	7	.533	22	22	2	0-0	143.1	140	68	13	9	60-2	105	3.83	131	.261	.342	0-0	—	0	94	18	1.6
1995	Bos A	3	1	.750	6	6	0	0-0	32.1	32	14	3	3	14-0	21	3.06	159	.252	.338	0-0	—	0	102	5	0.6
1996	Bos A	7	11	.389	29	29	1	0-0	157.1	192	110	14	8	67-2	137	5.32	95	.303	.373	0-0	—	0	101	-6	-0.6
1997	Bos A	13	12	.520	33	33	1	0-0	177.1	196	115	25	15	80-4	122	5.38	86	.279	.361	2-0	.000	-0	100	-14	-1.6
1998	†Tex A☆	19	11	.633	33	33	3-2	0-0	212.2	239	116	14	13	84-6	167	4.23	114	.283	.354	4-0	.250	0	121	11	1.3
1999	†Tex A	18	9	.667	33	33	2-2	0-0	205	244	115	21	12	70-3	186	4.79	106	.293	.355	4-1	.000	-0	114	7	0.8
2000	†Sea A★	17	10	.630	34	34	2-2	0-0	211.2	221	110	17	5	74-7	137	4.51	105	.271	.332	3-1	.000	-0	128	7	0.8
2001	†Sea A	15	5	.750	34	33	2-1	0-0	215	216	93	25	7	51-2	114	3.60	115	.261	.306	6-2	.167	0	133	15	1.1
2002	Ana A	8	9	.471	26	26	1-1	0-0	160	190	92	21	7	49-2	82	4.89	91	.299	.351	2-0	.500	0	107	-7	-0.7
2003	Ana A	7	11	.389	25	25	0	0-0	121.2	135	82	17	12	58-1	53	5.77	75	.284	.372	3-0	.333	0	100	-19	-2.3
Total	11	122	88	.581	293	292	14-8	0-0	1748	1905	957	175	98	655-31	1217	4.48	105	.278	.346	24-4	.167	1	110	38	2.4
SELL, EPP Lester Elwood B 4.26.1897 Llewellyn, PA D 2.19.1961 Reading, PA BR/TR 6/175# d9.1																									
1922	StL N	4	2	.667	7	5	0	0	33	47	26	2	2	6	5	6.82	57	.338	.374	12-2	.333	1	139	-10	-1.2
1923	StL N	0	1	.000	5	1	0	0	15	16	10	1	0	8	2	6.00	65	.291	.381	7-0	.000	-1	189	-3	-0.3
Total	2	4	3	.571	12	6	0	0	48	63	36	3	2	14	7	6.56	59	.325	.376	19-2	.211	0	147	-13	-1.5
SELLERS, JEFF Jeffrey Doyle B 5.11.1964 Compton, CA BR/TR 6-1/175# d9.15																									
1985	Bos A	2	0	1.000	4	4	1	0-0	22.1	24	10	1	0	7-1	6	3.63	118	.273	.323	0-0	—	0	122	2	0.1
1986	Bos A	3	7	.300	14	13	1	0-0	82	90	56	13	3	40-1	51	4.94	84	.282	.365	0-0	—	0	90	-10	-1.0
1987	Bos A	7	8	.467	25	22	4-2	0-0	139.2	161	85	10	3	61-0	99	5.28	86	.298	.368	0-0	—	0	100	-9	-0.8
1988	Bos A	1	7	.125	18	12	1	0-0	85.2	89	49	9	3	56-3	70	4.83	85	.268	.379	0-0	—	0	68	-6	-0.5
Total	4	13	22	.371	61	51	7-2	0-0	329.2	364	200	33	9	164-5	226	4.97	87	.285	.367	0-0	—	0	92	-23	-2.2
SELLMAN, FRANK Charles Francis (a.k.a. Frank C. Williams 1871-75) B 1852 Baltimore, MD D 5.6.1907 Baltimore, MD d5.4.1871 ▲																									
1873	Mar NA	0	1	.000	1	1	1	0	9	21	26	0		0	0	8.00	40	.350	.350	3	.333	0	55	-5	-0.3
SELLS, DAVE David Wayne B 9.18.1946 Vacaville, CA BR/TR 5-11/175# d8.2																									
1972	Cal A	2	0	1.000	10	0	0	0-0	16	11	6	0	0	5-1	2	2.81	104	.196	.258	0-0	—	0		0	0.0
1973	Cal A	7	2	.778	51	0	0	10-3	68	72	30	2	5	35-6	25	3.71	96	.277	.368	0-0	—	0		0	-0.1
1974	Cal A	2	3	.400	20	0	0	2-0	39	48	19	3	3	16-0	14	3.69	93	.312	.383	0-0	—	0		-1	-0.2
1975	Cal A	0	0	—	4	0	0	0-1	8.1	9	10	3	0	8-1	7	8.64	41	.250	.386	0-0	—	0		-5	-0.3
	LA N	0	2	.000	5	0	0	0-1	7	6	3	2	0	3-0	1	3.86	88	.222	.300	1-0	1.000	1		0	0.0
Total	4	11	7	.611	90	0	0	12-5	138.1	146	68	10	8	67-8	49	3.90	88	.274	.359	1-0	1.000	1		-6	-0.6
SELMA, DICK Richard Jay B 11.4.1943 Santa Ana, CA D 8.29.2001 Clovis, CA BR/TR 5-11/175# d9.2																									
1965	NY N	2	1	.667	4	4	1-1	0	26.2	22	11	2	1	9-0	26	3.71	95	.229	.302	9-0	.222	0*	105	0	0.1
1966	NY N	4	6	.400	30	7	0	1	80.2	84	47	11	3	39-5	58	4.24	86	.274	.358	14-1	.071	0*	80	-7	-0.7
1967	NY N	2	4	.333	38	4	0	2	81.1	71	29	3	2	36-6	52	2.77	122	.241	.326	22-1	.091	-1*	91	5	0.3
1968	NY N	9	10	.474	33	23	4-3	0	169.2	148	63	11	5	54-5	117	2.76	110	.233	.297	58-4	.207	2*	102	3	0.6
1969	SD N	2	2	.500	4	3	1	0-0	22	19	10	3	0	9-0	20	4.09	87	.229	.304	7-1	.286	0	50	-1	-0.1
	Chi N	10	8	.556	36	25	4-2	1-1	168.2	137	74	13	3	72-7	161	3.63	111	.222	.305	52-7	.154	-0	127	8	0.7
	Year	12	10	.545	40	28	5-2	1-1	190.2	156	80	16	3	81-7	181	3.68	108	.223	.305	59-8	.169	-0	120	7	0.6
1970	Phi N	8	9	.471	73	0	0	22-11	134.1	108	42	8	4	59-9	153	2.75	145	.226	.315	20-1	.150	0		**20**	3.1
1971	Phi N	0	2	.000	17	0	0	1-0	24.2	21	9	2	2	8-0	15	3.28	107	.231	.307	1-0	1.000	0*		1	0.2
1972	Phi N	2	9	.182	46	10	1	3-0	98.2	91	67	13	5	73-9	58	5.56	65	.249	.375	20-1	.200	1*	59	-20	-2.2
1973	Phi N	1	1	.500	6	0	0	0-0	8	6	5	1	0	5-1	4	5.63	68	.240	.355	0-0	—	0		-1	-0.2
1974	Cal A	2	2	.500	18	0	0	1-3	23	22	13	2	1	17-2	15	5.09	68	.272	.404	0-0	—	0		-3	-0.6
	Mil A	0	0	—	2	0	0	0-0	2.1	5	5	0	1	0-0	2	19.29	19	.455	.462	0-0	—	0		-4	-0.2
	Year	2	2	.500	20	0	0	1-3	25.1	27	20	2	2	17-2	17	6.39	54	.293	.411	0-0	—	0		-8	-0.8
Total	10	42	54	.438	307	76	11-6	31-15	840	734	375	69	27	381-44	681	3.62	100	.238	.325	203-16	.172	2	100	1	1.0
SEMBERA, CARROLL Carroll William B 7.26.1941 Shiner, TX BR/TR 6/155# d9.28																									
1965	Hou N	0	1	.000	2	1	0	0	7.1	5	3	0	0	3-0	4	3.68	91	.185	.267	1-1	.000	-0	52	0	0.0
1966	Hou N	1	2	.333	24	0	0	1	33	36	11	3	0	16-0	21	3.00	114	.288	.366	3-0	.000	-0		2	0.2
1967	Hou N	2	6	.250	45	0	0	3	59.2	66	39	7	1	19-4	48	4.83	69	.269	.323	7-1	.143	-0		-11	-1.5
1969	Mon N	0	2	.000	23	0	0	2-1	33	28	14	1	2	24-4	15	3.55	104	.246	.383	4-0	.250	0		1	0.1
1970	Mon N	0	0	—	5	0	0	0-0	6.2	14	14	2	1	11-3	6	18.90	22	.424	.578	0-0	—	0		-10	-0.5

Year	Tm Lg	W	L	Pct	G	GS	CG-Sho	SV-BS	IP	H	R	HR	HB	BB-IB	SO	ERA	AERA	OAV	OOB	AB-SH	AVG	PB	Sup	APR	PW
Total	5	3	11	.214	99	1	0	6-1	139.2	149	81	13	4	73-11	94	4.70	74	.274	.362	15-2	.133	-0	52	-18	-1.7
SEMINARA, FRANK Frank Peter B 5.16.1967 Brooklyn, NY BR/TR 6-2/205# d6.2																									
1992	SD N	9	4	.692	19	18	0	0-0	100.1	98	46	5	3	46-3	61	3.68	97	.257	.340	34-2	.118	-1	128	-2	-0.2
1993	SD N	3	3	.500	18	7	0	0-1	46.1	53	30	5	3	21-3	22	4.47	93	.294	.374	10-1	.200	0	112	-3	-0.4
1994	NY N	0	2	.000	10	1	0	0-0	17	20	12	2	0	8-0	7	5.82	72	.303	.373	3-0	.000	-0	109	-3	-0.4
Total	3	12	9	.571	47	26	0	0-1	163.2	171	88	12	6	75-6	90	4.12	92	.273	.353	47-3	.128	-1	121	-8	-1.0
SEMPROCH, RAY Roman Anthony "Baby" B 1.7.1931 Cleveland, OH BR/TR 5-11/180# d4.15																									
1958	Phi N	13	11	.542	36	30	12-2	0	204.1	211	105	25	6	58-1	92	3.92	101	.264	.318	74-2	.095	-5	116	-1	-0.6
1959	Phi N	3	10	.231	30	18	2	3	111.2	119	76	12	3	59-1	54	5.40	76	.277	.366	34-2	.176	-0	79	-16	-1.7
1960	Det A	3	0	1.000	17	0	0	0	27	29	17	2	0	16-0	9	4.00	99	.269	.363	4-1	.000	-0		-2	-0.1
1961	LA A	0	0	—	2	0	0	0	1	1	2	0	0	3-0	1	9.00	50	.333	.571	0-0	—	0		-1	0.0
Total	4	19	21	.475	85	48	14-2	3	344	360	200	39	9	136-2	156	4.42	91	.269	.338	112-5	.116	-5	101	-20	-2.4
SENTENEY, STEVE Stephen Leonard B 8.7.1955 Indianapolis, IN D 6.18.1989 Colusa, CA BR/TR 6-2/205# d6.6																									
1982	Tor A	0	0	—	11	0	0	0-0	22	23	16	5	0	6-1	20	4.91	91	.247	.290	0-0	—	0		-2	-0.1
SEO, JAE Jae Weong B 5.24.1977 Kwangju, South Korea BR/TR 6-1/215# d7.21																									
2002	NY N	0	0	—	1	0	0	0-0	1	0	0	0	0	0-0	1	0.00	—	.000	.000	0-0	—	0		0	0.0
2003	NY N	9	12	.429	32	31	0	0-0	188.1	193	94	18	6	46-11	110	3.82	109	.260	.307	51-4	.098	-1*	95	3	0.2
Total	2	9	12	.429	33	31	0	0-0	189.1	193	94	18	6	46-11	111	3.80	109	.259	.306	51-4	.098	-1	95	3	0.2
SEOANE, MANNY Manuel Modesto B 6.26.1955 Tampa, FL BR/TR 6-3/187# d9.18																									
1977	Phi N	0	0	—	2	1	0	0-0	6	11	4	0	0	3-0	4	6.00	67	.407	.467	2-0	.500	0	111	-1	0.0
1978	Chi N	1	0	1.000	7	1	0	0-0	8.1	11	6	0	0	6-2	5	5.40	75	.297	.395	0-0	—	0	89	-1	-0.2
Total	2	1	0	1.000	9	2	0	0-0	14.1	22	10	0	0	9-2	9	5.65	71	.344	.425	2-0	.500	0	100	-2	-0.2
SERAD, BILLY William I. B 1863 Philadelphia, PA D 11.1.1925 Chester, PA BR/TR 5-7/156# d5.5																									
1884	Buf N	16	20	.444	37	37	34-2	0	308	373	285	21		111	150	4.27	74	.281	.336	137	.175	-7	105	-38	-4.0
1885	Buf N	7	21	.250	30	29	27	0	241.1	299	194	5		80	90	4.10	73	.293	.344	104	.154	-6	72	-31	-3.5
1887	Cin AA	10	11	.476	22	21	20-2	1	187.1	201	139	7	8	80	34	4.08	106	.266	.343	79	.177	-4	89	4	-0.1
1888	Cin AA	2	3	.400	6	5	5	0	50.2	62	43	1	6	19	4	3.55	89	.291	.366	23	.130	-1	110	-5	-0.5
Total	4	35	55	.389	95	92	86-4	1	787.1	935	661	34	14	290	278	4.13	82	.282	.342	343	.166	-17	92	-70	-8.1
SERAFINI, DAN Daniel Joseph B 1.25.1974 San Francisco, CA BB/TL 6-1/185# d6.25																									
1996	Min A	0	1	.000	1	1	0	0-0	4.1	7	5	1	1	2-0	1	10.38	49	.368	.435	0-0	—	0	36	-2	-0.4
1997	Min A	2	1	.667	6	4	1	0-0	26.1	27	11	1	0	11-0	15	3.42	136	.273	.345	0-0	—	0	138	3	0.3
1998	Min A	7	4	.636	28	9	0	0-0	75	95	58	10	1	29-1	46	6.48	74	.310	.365	1-0	.000	-0	104	-14	-1.7
1999	Chi N	3	2	.600	42	4	0	1-0	62.1	86	51	9	1	32-3	17	6.93	65	.333	.405	12-1	.083	0	137	-16	-1.2
2000	SD N	0	0	—	3	0	0	0-0	3	9	6	2	0	2-0	3	18.00	24	.500	.550	0-0	—	0		-5	-0.2
	Pit N	2	5	.286	11	11	0	0-0	62.1	70	35	9	4	26-1	32	4.91	94	.292	.368	24-3	.083	-2	96	-1	-0.3
	Year	2	5	.286	14	11	0	0-0	65.1	79	40	11	4	28-1	35	5.51	83	.306	.380	24-3	.083	-2	96	-6	-0.5
2003	Cin N	1	3	.250	10	4	0	0-0	30	41	23	5	0	14-1	13	5.40	79	.336	.399	6-1	.000	-1*	55	-5	-0.7
Total	6	15	16	.484	101	33	1	1-0	263.1	335	189	37	7	116-6	127	5.98	77	.315	.382	43-5	.070	-2	102	-40	-4.2
SERRANO, WASCAR Wascar Radames B 6.2.1978 Santo Domingo, D.R. BR/TR 6-2/178# d5.12																									
2001	SD N	3	3	.500	20	5	0	0-0	46.2	60	37	7	2	21-1	39	6.56	61	.313	.382	9-2	.111	-0	152	-14	-1.5
SERUM, GARY Gary Wayne B 10.24.1956 Fargo, ND BR/TR 6-1/180# d7.22																									
1977	Min A	0	0	—	8	0	0	0-0	22.2	22	11	4	2	10-1	14	4.37	92	.268	.362	0-0	—	0		0	0.0
1978	Min A	9	9	.500	34	23	6-1	1-0	184.1	188	88	14	3	44-2	80	4.10	93	.266	.308	0-0	—	0	107	-2	-0.2
1979	Min A	1	3	.250	20	5	0	0-0	64	93	47	10	0	20-2	31	6.61	66	.354	.398	0-0	—	0	103	-13	-0.7
Total	3	10	12	.455	62	28	6-1	1-0	271	303	146	28	5	74-5	125	4.72	84	.288	.335	0-0	—	0	105	-15	-0.9
SERVICE, SCOTT Scott David B 2.26.1967 Cincinnati, OH BR/TR 6-6/226# d9.5																									
1988	Phi N	0	0	—	5	0	0	0-0	5.1	7	1	0	1	1-0	6	1.69	211	.333	.391	0-0	—	0		1	0.1
1992	Mon N	0	0	—	5	0	0	0-0	7	15	11	1	0	5-0	11	14.14	25	.417	.488	2-0	.000	-0		-8	-0.4
1993	Col N	0	0	—	3	0	0	0-0	4.2	8	5	1	1	1-0	3	9.64	50	.400	.417	0-0	—	0		-2	-0.1
	Cin N	2	2	.500	26	0	0	2-0	41.1	36	19	5	1	15-4	40	3.70	109	.235	.304	7-0	.143	-0*		1	0.1
	Year	2	2	.500	29	0	0	2-0	46	44	29	6	2	16-4	43	4.30	95	.254	.318	7-0	.143	-0		-1	0.0
1994	Cin N	1	2	.333	6	0	0	0-0	7.1	8	9	2	0	3-0	5	7.36	56	.267	.333	0-0	—	0		-4	-0.7
1995	SF N	3	1	.750	28	0	0	0-0	31	18	11	4	2	20-4	30	3.19	128	.176	.317	1-0	.000	-0		4	0.4
1996	Cin N	1	0	1.000	34	1	0	0-0	48	51	21	7	6	18-4	46	3.94	108	.277	.359	5-0	.000	-1	106	3	0.1
1997	Cin N	0	0	—	4	0	0	0-0	5.1	11	7	1	0	1-0	3	11.81	36	.458	.480	0-0	—	0		-4	-0.2
	KC A	0	3	.000	12	0	0	0-1	17	17	9	1	0	5-0	19	4.76	99	.274	.324	0-0	—	0		0	0.0
1998	KC A	6	4	.600	73	0	0	4-4	82.2	70	35	7	9	34-4	95	3.48	139	.231	.322	1-0	.000	-0		12	1.4
1999	KC A	5	5	.500	68	0	0	8-7	75.1	87	51	13	3	42-8	68	6.09	82	.294	.379	0-0	—	0		-7	-0.9
2000	Oak A	1	2	.333	20	0	0	1-0	36.2	45	31	5	1	19-1	35	6.38	74	.302	.380	0-0	—	0		-8	-0.6
2003	Ari N	0	2	.000	18	0	0	1-0	18.1	21	10	1	0	2-1	18	4.91	95	.288	.303	0-0	—	0		0	0.0
	Tor A	0	0	—	15	0	0	0-1	16	17	8	3	0	6-0	17	4.50	102	.274	.333	0-0	—	0		1	0.0
Total	11	19	21	.475	317	1	0	16-13	396	411	228	51	24	172-26	396	4.89	93	.271	.350	16-0	.063	-1	106	-11	-0.8
SETTLEMIRE, MERLE Edgar Merle "Lefty" B 1.19.1903 Santa Fe, OH D 6.12.1988 Russells Point, OH BL/TL 5-9/156# d4.13																									
1928	Bos A	0	6	.000	30	9	0	0	82.1	116	62	2	6	34	12	5.47	75	.345	.415	17-3	.176	-1*	78	-14	-0.8
SEVERINSEN, AL Albert Henry B 11.9.1944 Brooklyn, NY BR/TR 6-3/220# d7.1																									
1969	Bal A	1	1	.500	12	0	0	0-0	19.2	14	6	2	0	10-2	13	2.29	156	.206	.304	3-1	.333	0		3	0.3
1971	SD N	2	5	.286	59	0	0	8-6	70	77	30	4	2	30-10	31	3.47	95	.292	.365	1-1	.000	-0		-1	0.0
1972	SD N	0	1	.000	17	0	0	1-0	21.1	13	8	1	2	7-1	9	2.53	130	.173	.259	1-0	.000	-0		1	0.1
Total	3	3	7	.300	88	0	0	9-6	111	104	44	7	4	47-13	53	3.08	109	.256	.335	5-2	.200	0		3	0.4
SEWARD, ED Edward William (b: Edward William Sourhardt) B 6.29.1867 Cleveland, OH D 7.30.1947 Cleveland, OH TR 5-7/175# d9.30 U1																									
1885	Pro N	0	0	—	1	0	0	0	6	2	0	0		0	1	0.00	—	.100	.100	3	.000	-0		2	0.1
1887	Phi AA	25	25	.500	55	52	52-3	0	470.2	445	293	7	24	140	155	4.13	104	.244	.306	266	.188	-4*	88	16	0.8
1888	Phi AA	35	19	.648	57	57	57-**6**	0	518.2	388	203	4	22	127	**272**	2.01	149	.200	.258	225	.142	-4*	107	60	5.1
1889	Phi AA	21	15	.583	39	38	35-3	0	320	353	212	8	13	101	102	3.97	95	.271	.330	143	.217	6*	109	1	0.5
1890	Phi AA	6	12	.333	21	19	15-1	0	154	165	105	4	7	72	55	4.73	82	.266	.349	72	.139	-1*	102	-11	-1.1
1891	Cle N	2	1	.667	3	3	0	0	16.1	16	10	0	0	11	4	3.86	90	.246	.355	19	.211	0*	80	0	0.0
Total	6	89	72	.553	176	169	159-13	0	1485.2	1369	823	23	66	451	589	3.40	108	.237	.300	728	.174	-4	100	68	5.4
SEWARD, FRANK Frank Martin B 4.7.1921 Pennsauken, NJ BR/TR 6-3/200# d9.28																									
1943	NY N	0	1	.000	1	1	1	0	9	12	3	0	0	5	2	3.00	115	.324	.405	4-0	.000	-1	49	1	0.0
1944	NY N	3	2	.600	25	7	2	0	78.1	98	51	8	2	32	16	5.40	68	.306	.373	24-1	.083	-2	128	-13	-1.0
Total	2	3	3	.500	26	8	3	0	87.1	110	54	8	2	37	18	5.15	71	.308	.376	28-1	.071	-2	118	-12	-1.0
SEWELL, RIP Truett Banks B 5.11.1907 Decatur, AL D 9.3.1989 Plant City, FL BL/TR 6-1/180# d6.14 C1																									
1932	Det A	0	0	—	5	0	0	0	10.2	19	15	2	0	8	2	12.66	37	.388	.474	2-0	.500	0		-8	-0.3
1938	Pit N	0	1	.000	17	0	0	1	38.1	41	27	3	2	21	17	4.23	90	.275	.372	12-0	.083	-1		-4	-0.3
1939	Pit N	10	9	.526	52	12	5-1	2	176.1	177	93	10	1	73	69	4.08	94	.265	.339	55-4	.200	1	110	-5	-0.3
1940	Pit N	16	5	.762	33	23	14-2	1	189.2	169	71	6	3	67	60	2.80	136	.238	.307	73-1	.192	2*	144	20	2.5
1941	Pit N	14	17	.452	39	32	18-2	2	249	225	126	18	3	84	76	3.72	97	.235	.299	92-4	.174	0*	109	-4	-0.3
1942	Pit N	17	15	.531	40	33	18-5	2	248	259	117	13	2	72	69	3.41	99	.265	.317	87-1	.149	-2*	102	-4	-0.6
1943	Pit N★	**21**	9	.700	35	31	**25**-2	3	265.1	267	94	6	2	75	65	2.54	137	.260	.312	105-1	.286	6*	121	27	**3.9**
1944	Pit N★	21	12	.636	38	33	24-3	2	286	263	112	15	3	99	87	3.18	117	.240	.304	112-2	.223	3*	109	21	2.6
1945	Pit N❖	11	9	.550	33	24	9-1	1	188	212	116	9	2	91	60	4.07	97	.279	.357	64-1	.313	6*	125	-9	-0.3

Year	Tm Lg	W	L	Pct	G	GS	CG-Sho	SV-BS	IP	H	R	HR	HB	BB-IB	SO	ERA	AERA	OAV	OOB	AB-SH	AVG	PB	Sup	APR	PW
1946	Pit N★	8	12	.400	25	20	11-2	0	149.1	140	68	6	1	53	33	3.68	96	.245	.310	50-2	.180	0*	104	-1	-0.1
1947	Pit N	6	4	.600	24	12	4-1	0	121	121	58	11	3	36	36	3.57	118	.263	.321	40-0	.125	-1	94	7	0.5
1948	Pit N	13	3	.813	21	17	7	0	121.2	126	51	9	1	37	36	3.48	117	.262	.317	42-1	.143	1	105	8	1.1
1949	Pit N	6	1	.857	28	6	2-1	1	76	82	35	8	0	32	26	3.91	108	.280	.351	16-2	.063	-0	84	3	0.2
Total	13	143	97	.596	390	243	137-20	15	2119.1	2101	983	116	23	748	636	3.48	107	.256	.320	750-19	.203	16	112	51	8.6

SEXAUER, ELMER Elmer George B 5.21.1926 St.Louis Co., MO BR/TR 6-4/220# d9.6

Year	Tm Lg	W	L	Pct	G	GS	CG-Sho	SV-BS	IP	H	R	HR	HB	BB-IB	SO	ERA	AERA	OAV	OOB	AB-SH	AVG	PB	Sup	APR	PW
1948	Bro N	0	0	—	2	0	0	0	0.2	0	1	0	0	2	0	13.50	30	.000	.500	0-0	—	0		-1	0.0

SEXTON, FRANK Frank Joseph B 7.8.1872 Brockton, MA D 1.4.1938 Brighton, MA ?/160# d6.21

Year	Tm Lg	W	L	Pct	G	GS	CG-Sho	SV-BS	IP	H	R	HR	HB	BB-IB	SO	ERA	AERA	OAV	OOB	AB-SH	AVG	PB	Sup	APR	PW
1895	Bos N	1	5	.167	7	5	4	0	49	59	39	2	2	22	14	5.69	89	.294	.369	26-1	.269	-1*	45	-1	-0.2

SEYFRIED, GORDON Gordon Clay B 7.4.1937 Long Beach, CA BR/TR 6/185# d9.13

Year	Tm Lg	W	L	Pct	G	GS	CG-Sho	SV-BS	IP	H	R	HR	HB	BB-IB	SO	ERA	AERA	OAV	OOB	AB-SH	AVG	PB	Sup	APR	PW
1963	Cle A	0	1	.000	3	1	0	0	7.1	9	2	0	0	3-1	1	1.23	295	.300	.364	2-0	.000	-0	25	2	0.2
1964	Cle A	0	0	—	2	0	0	0	2.1	4	0	0	0	0-0	0	0.00	—	.444	.400	0-0	—	0		1	0.0
Total	2	0	1	.000	5	1	0	0	9.2	13	2	0	0	3-1	1	0.93	388	.333	.372	2-0	.000	-0	25	3	0.2

SEYMOUR, JAKE Jacob (b: Jacob Semer) B 1854 Pittsburgh, PA D 8.1.1897 Allegheny, PA d9.23

Year	Tm Lg	W	L	Pct	G	GS	CG-Sho	SV-BS	IP	H	R	HR	HB	BB-IB	SO	ERA	AERA	OAV	OOB	AB-SH	AVG	PB	Sup	APR	PW
1882	Pit AA	0	1	.000	1	1	1	0	8	16	13	0		2	2	7.88	33	.390	.419	4	.000	-1	59	-5	-0.4

SEYMOUR, CY James Bentley B 12.9.1872 Albany, NY D 9.20.1919 New York, NY BL/TL 6/200# d4.22 ▲

Year	Tm Lg	W	L	Pct	G	GS	CG-Sho	SV-BS	IP	H	R	HR	HB	BB-IB	SO	ERA	AERA	OAV	OOB	AB-SH	AVG	PB	Sup	APR	PW
1896	NY N	2	4	.333	11	8	4	0	70.1	75	75	8	3	51	33	6.40	66	.271	.390	32-0	.219	-1*	135	-19	-1.3
1897	NY N	18	14	.563	39	34	29-2	1	286.2	257	162	4	22	168	**156**	3.27	127	**.238**	.352	141-1	.241	1*	101	28	2.9
1898	NY N	25	19	.568	45	43	39-4	0	356.2	313	199	4	32	213	**239**	3.18	109	.234	.353	297-2	.276	7*	113	11	2.1
1899	NY N	14	18	.438	32	32	31	0	268.1	247	139	5	20	170	142	3.56	106	.245	.364	159-5	.327	8*	100	10	2.0
1900	NY N	2	1	.667	13	7	2	0	53	58	54	4	10	54	19	6.96	52	.278	.447	40-0	.300	1*	150	-17	-0.6
1902	Cin N	0	0	—	1	0	0	0	3	4	3	0	0	3	2	9.00	33	.308	.438	244-3	.340	0*		-1	-0.1
Total	6	61	56	.521	141	124	105-6	1	1038	954	632	25	87	659	591	3.73	102	.243	.364	913-11	.296	16	110	12	5.0

SHAFFER, JOHN John W. "Cannon Ball" B 2.18.1864 Lock Haven, PA D 11.21.1926 Endicott, NY 5-10/?# d9.13

Year	Tm Lg	W	L	Pct	G	GS	CG-Sho	SV-BS	IP	H	R	HR	HB	BB-IB	SO	ERA	AERA	OAV	OOB	AB-SH	AVG	PB	Sup	APR	PW
1886	NY AA	5	3	.625	8	8	8-1	0	69	40	29	0	1	29	36	1.96	167	.164	.255	25	.240	1	93	9	1.0
1887	NY AA	2	11	.154	13	13	13	0	112	148	119	3	11	53	22	6.19	69	.310	.391	48	.167	-3	78	-24	-2.0
Total	2	7	14	.333	21	21	21-1	0	181	188	148	3	12	82	58	4.57	84	.260	.346	73	.192	-2	83	-15	-1.0

SHALLIX, GUS August (b: August Schallick) B 3.29.1858 Paderborn, Germany D 10.28.1937 Cincinnati, OH BR/TR 5-11/165# d6.22

Year	Tm Lg	W	L	Pct	G	GS	CG-Sho	SV-BS	IP	H	R	HR	HB	BB-IB	SO	ERA	AERA	OAV	OOB	AB-SH	AVG	PB	Sup	APR	PW
1884	Cin AA	11	10	.524	23	23	23	0	199.2	163	113	6	26	53	78	3.70	90	.212	.286	84	.036	-10	110	-7	-1.5
1885	Cin AA	6	4	.600	13	12	7	0	91.1	95	59	1	13	33	15	3.25	100	.265	.349	39	.128	-2	113	-2	-0.3
Total	2	17	14	.548	36	35	30	0	291	258	172	7	39	86	93	3.56	93	.229	.306	123	.065	-12	111	-9	-1.8

SHANAHAN, GREG Paul Gregory B 12.11.1947 Eureka, CA BR/TR 6-2/190# d9.4

Year	Tm Lg	W	L	Pct	G	GS	CG-Sho	SV-BS	IP	H	R	HR	HB	BB-IB	SO	ERA	AERA	OAV	OOB	AB-SH	AVG	PB	Sup	APR	PW
1973	LA N	0	0	—	7	0	0	1-0	15.2	14	6	2	0	4-0	11	3.45	100	.230	.277	1-0	.000	0		0	0.0
1974	LA N	0	0	—	4	0	0	0-0	7	7	3	1	0	5-0	2	3.86	88	.259	.364	0-0	—	0		0	0.0
Total	2	0	0	—	11	0	0	1-0	22.2	21	9	3	0	9-0	13	3.57	96	.239	.306	1-0	.000	0		0	0.0

SHANK, HARVEY Harvey Tillman B 7.29.1946 Toronto, ON, CAN BR/TR 6-4/220# d5.16

Year	Tm Lg	W	L	Pct	G	GS	CG-Sho	SV-BS	IP	H	R	HR	HB	BB-IB	SO	ERA	AERA	OAV	OOB	AB-SH	AVG	PB	Sup	APR	PW
1970	Cal A	0	0	—	1	0	0	0-0	3	2	0	0	0	2-0	1	0.00	—	.182	.308	0-0	—	0		1	0.1

SHANNER, BILL Wilfred William B 11.4.1894 Oakland City, IN D 12.18.1986 Evansville, IN BL/TR d10.1

Year	Tm Lg	W	L	Pct	G	GS	CG-Sho	SV-BS	IP	H	R	HR	HB	BB-IB	SO	ERA	AERA	OAV	OOB	AB-SH	AVG	PB	Sup	APR	PW
1920	Phi A	0	0	—	1	0	0	0	4	6	4	2	0	1	1	6.75	60	.353	.389	1-0	.000	-0		-1	-0.1

SHANTZ, BOBBY Robert Clayton B 9.26.1925 Pottstown, PA BR/TL 5-6/142# d5.1 b-Billy

Year	Tm Lg	W	L	Pct	G	GS	CG-Sho	SV-BS	IP	H	R	HR	HB	BB-IB	SO	ERA	AERA	OAV	OOB	AB-SH	AVG	PB	Sup	APR	PW
1949	Phi A	6	8	.429	33	7	4-1	2	127	100	50	9	3	74	58	3.40	121	.221	.334	37-3	.189	1	121	12	1.5
1950	Phi A	8	14	.364	36	23	6-1	0	214.2	251	122	18	7	85	93	4.61	99	.294	.362	66-6	.167	-0*	68	-1	0.0
1951	Phi A☆	18	10	.643	32	25	13-3	0	205.1	213	96	15	5	70	77	3.94	108	.270	.333	72-8	.250	2*	107	9	1.5
1952	Phi A★	**24**	7	**.774**	33	33	27-5	0	279.2	230	87	21	4	63	152	2.48	160	.225	**.272**	96-13	.198	2*	102	**43**	**5.1**
1953	Phi A	5	9	.357	16	16	6	0	105.2	107	52	10	0	26	58	4.09	105	.263	.307	38-1	.237	1*	78	2	0.5
1954	Phi A	1	0	1.000	2	1	0	0	8	12	7	2	1	3	3	7.88	50	.364	.421	3-0	.333	0*	135	-3	-0.3
1955	KC A	5	10	.333	23	17	4-1	0	125	124	70	8	1	66-11	58	4.54	92	.264	.352	41-2	.146	-2*	86	-5	-0.6
1956	KC A	2	7	.222	45	2	1	9	101.1	95	51	12	3	37-4	67	4.35	99	.248	.319	22-2	.091	-1*	62	1	0.1
1957	†NY A☆	11	5	.688	30	21	9-1	5	173	157	58	15	6	40-1	72	**2.45**	**147**	.248	.296	56-1	.179	2*	116	21	2.7
1958	NY A	7	6	.538	33	13	3	0	126	127	52	8	2	35-7	80	3.36	105	.262	.312	35-1	.229	2	88	4	0.8
1959	NY A	7	3	.700	33	4	2-2	3	94.2	64	33	4	0	33-5	66	2.38	153	.189	.260	23-3	.217	2*	85	12	1.6
1960	†NY A	5	4	.556	42	0	0	11	67.2	57	24	5	2	24-4	54	2.79	128	.235	.302	10-2	.100	-0*		6	1.0
1961	Pit N	6	3	.667	43	6	2-1	2	89.1	91	38	5	4	26-6	61	3.32	120	.271	.328	16-1	.438	3*	137	6	1.0
1962	Hou N	1	1	.500	3	3	1	0	20.2	15	4	1	0	5-0	14	1.31	286	.208	.256	8-0	.000	-1*	133	6	0.5
	StL N	5	3	.625	28	0	0	4	57.2	45	22	7	1	20-2	47	2.18	195	.211	.282	13-0	.154	-0		10	1.5
	Year	6	4	.600	31	3	1	4	78.1	60	32	8	1	25-2	61	1.95	211	.211	.276	21-0	.095	-1	120	15	2.0
1963	StL N	6	4	.600	55	0	0	11	79.1	55	28	6	2	17-5	70	2.61	136	.192	.240	7-1	.143	0		7	1.3
1964	StL N	1	3	.250	16	0	0	0	17.1	14	6	2	0	7-3	12	3.12	122	.226	.300	0-0	—	0		2	0.4
	Chi N	0	1	.000	20	0	0	1	11.1	15	7	2	0	6-2	12	5.56	67	.319	.396	0-0	—	0		-2	-0.2
	Phi N	1	1	.500	14	0	0	0	32	23	10	1	0	6-3	18	2.25	154	.204	.244	5-0	.000	-0		4	0.3
	Year	2	5	.286	50	0	0	1	60.2	52	23	5	0	19-8	42	3.12	116	.234	.293	5-0	.000	0		4	0.5
Total	16	119	99	.546	537	171	78-15	48	1935.2	1795	817	151	41	643-53	1072	3.38	119	.248	.312	548-44	.195	11	97	134	18.7

SHARROTT, GEORGE George Oscar B 11.2.1869 Staten Island, NY D 1.6.1932 Jamaica, NY BL/TL 5-8/164# d7.27

Year	Tm Lg	W	L	Pct	G	GS	CG-Sho	SV-BS	IP	H	R	HR	HB	BB-IB	SO	ERA	AERA	OAV	OOB	AB-SH	AVG	PB	Sup	APR	PW
1893	Bro N	4	6	.400	13	10	10	1	95	114	80	3	8	58	24	5.87	75	.289	.390	39	.231	0	74	-13	-1.0
1894	Bro N	0	1	.000	3	3	2	0	18	25	21	0	5	8	7	9.00	55	.325	.422	7-0	.429	1	43	-7	-0.2
Total	2	4	7	.364	16	13	12	1	113	139	101	3	13	66	31	6.37	71	.294	.396	46-0	.261	1	67	-20	-1.2

SHARROTT, JACK John Henry B 8.13.1869 Bangor, ME D 12.31.1927 Los Angeles, CA BR/TR 5-9/165# d4.22 ▲

Year	Tm Lg	W	L	Pct	G	GS	CG-Sho	SV-BS	IP	H	R	HR	HB	BB-IB	SO	ERA	AERA	OAV	OOB	AB-SH	AVG	PB	Sup	APR	PW
1890	NY N	11	10	.524	25	19	18	0	184	162	107	3	9	88	84	2.89	122	.229	.322	109	.202	-2*	96	11	0.9
1891	NY N	5	5	.500	10	9	6	0	69.1	47	32	2	4	35	41	2.60	123	.185	.294	30	.333	4	89	6	1.1
1892	NY N	0	0	—	1	0	0	0	2	2	1	0	0	1	1	4.50	72	.250	.333	8	.125	-0*		0	0.0
1893	Phi N	4	2	.667	12	4	2	0	56	53	43	1	4	33	11	4.50	102	.242	.352	152	.250	0*	118	-1	-0.1
Total	4	20	17	.541	48	32	26	0	311.1	264	183	6	17	157	137	3.12	116	.222	.321	299	.237	2	96	16	1.9

SHAUTE, JOE Joseph Benjamin "Lefty" B 8.1.1899 Peckville, PA D 2.21.1970 Scranton, PA BL/TL 6/190# d7.6

Year	Tm Lg	W	L	Pct	G	GS	CG-Sho	SV-BS	IP	H	R	HR	HB	BB-IB	SO	ERA	AERA	OAV	OOB	AB-SH	AVG	PB	Sup	APR	PW
1922	Cle A	0	0	—	2	0	0	0	3.2	7	8	2	0	3	3	19.64	20	.389	.476	5-0	.000	-0*		-6	-0.3
1923	Cle A	10	8	.556	33	16	7	0	172	176	93	4	1	53	61	3.51	113	.275	.332	68-1	.162	-4	126	5	0.0
1924	Cle A	20	17	.541	46	34	21-2	2	283	317	138	8	6	83	68	3.75	114	.287	.340	107-3	.318	9	106	19	3.0
1925	Cle A	4	12	.250	26	17	10-1	4	131	160	91	6	1	44	34	5.43	81	.304	.358	53-0	.302	3*	96	-13	-1.2
1926	Cle A	14	10	.583	34	25	15-1	1	206.2	215	92	9	3	65	47	3.53	115	.278	.337	73-7	.274	4	113	13	1.6
1927	Cle A	9	16	.360	45	28	14	2	230.1	255	140	9	2	75	63	4.22	100	.286	.343	83-0	.325	6	77	-5	0.0
1928	Cle A	13	17	.433	36	31	21-1	2	253.2	295	145	9	6	68	81	4.04	102	.299	.348	92-4	.228	3	107	0	0.4
1929	Cle A	8	8	.500	26	24	8	0	162	211	100	6	1	52	43	4.28	104	.320	.370	58-5	.293	3	94	0	0.2
1930	Cle A	0	0	—	4	0	0	0	4.2	8	10	0	0	4	2	15.43	31	.333	.429	0-0	—	0		-5	-0.2
1931	Bro N	11	8	.579	25	19	6	0	128.2	162	87	9	1	32	50	4.83	79	.305	.346	45-1	.178	-0	123	-18	-2.3
1932	Bro N	7	7	.500	34	9	1	4	117	147	67	8	2	21	32	4.54	84	.301	.333	45-1	.200	1*	127	-9	-1.0
1933	Bro N	3	4	.429	41	4	0	2	108.1	125	63	4	1	31	26	3.49	92	.287	.336	27-0	.222	1	52	-9	-0.4
1934	Cin N	0	2	.000	8	1	0	1	17.1	19	9	1	0	3	2	4.15	98	.268	.297	4-0	.250	0	106	0	0.0
Total	13	99	109	.476	360	208	103-5	18	1818.1	2097	1043	75	24	534	512	4.15	99	.293	.345	660-22	.258	25	105	-28	-0.2

SHAVER, JEFF Jeffrey Thomas B 7.30.1963 Beaver, PA BR/TR 6-3/195# d7.6

Year	Tm Lg	W	L	Pct	G	GS	CG-Sho	SV-BS	IP	H	R	HR	HB	BB-IB	SO	ERA	AERA	OAV	OOB	AB-SH	AVG	PB	Sup	APR	PW
1988	Oak A	0	0	—	1	0	0	0-0	1	0	0	0	1	0-0	0	0.00	—	.000	.333	0-0	—	0		0	0.0

SHAW, DON Donald Wellington B 2.23.1944 Pittsburgh, PA BL/TL 6/185# d4.11 Mil 1967

Year	Tm Lg	W	L	Pct	G	GS	CG-Sho	SV-BS	IP	H	R	HR	HB	BB-IB	SO	ERA	AERA	OAV	OOB	AB-SH	AVG	PB	Sup	APR	PW
1967	NY N	4	5	.444	40	0	0	3	51.1	40	19	5	0	23-5	44	2.98	114	.219	.301	3-1	.000	0		2	0.5
1968	NY N	0	0	—	7	0	0	0	12.1	3	1	1	0	5-0	11	0.73	414	.086	.200	0-0	—	0		3	0.2
1969	Mon N	2	5	.286	35	1	0	1-1	65.2	61	43	9	2	37-5	45	5.21	71	.254	.356	10-0	.000	-0	48	-11	-1.1
1971	StL N	7	2	.778	45	0	0	2-2	51	45	19	1	1	31-6	19	2.65	136	.237	.342	1-1	.000	-0		4	0.7
1972	StL N	0	1	.000	8	0	0	0-3	3	5	3	1	0	3-0	0	9.00	38	.417	.500	1-0	.000	-0		-2	-0.4
	Oak A	0	1	.000	3	0	0	0-0	5.1	12	10	2	0	2-0	4	16.88	17	.500	.500	0-0	—	0		-8	-1.2
Total	5	13	14	.481	138	1	0	6-6	188.2	166	95	19	3	101-16	123	4.01	88	.243	.338	15-2	.000	-0	48	-12	-1.3

SHAW, DUPEE Frederick Lander B 5.31.1859 Charlestown, MA D 6.11.1938 Wakefield, MA BL/TL 5-8/165# d6.18

Year	Tm Lg	W	L	Pct	G	GS	CG-Sho	SV-BS	IP	H	R	HR	HB	BB-IB	SO	ERA	AERA	OAV	OOB	AB-SH	AVG	PB	Sup	APR	PW
1883	Det N	10	15	.400	26	25	23-1	0	227	238	135	3		44	73	2.50	124	.256	.290	141	.206	-3*	96	10	0.7
1884	Det N	9	18	.333	28	28	25	0	227.2	219	153	8		72	142	3.04	95	.237	.292	136	.191	-1*	84	-4	-0.4
	Bos U	21	15	.583	39	38	35-5	0	315.2	227	128	1		37	309	1.77	135	.188	.212	153	.242	-5*	93	20	1.3
1885	Pro N	23	26	.469	49	49	47-6	0	399.2	343	209	7		99	194	2.57	105	.209	.254	165	.133	-10	74	5	-0.5
1886	Was N	13	31	.295	45	44	43-1	0	385.2	384	224	12		91	177	3.34	97	.250	.291	148	.088	-10	75	-4	-1.3
1887	Was N	7	13	.350	21	20	20	0	181.1	263	177	8	3	46	47	6.45	62	.328	.366	70	.186	-2	85	-40	-3.3
1888	Was N	0	3	.000	3	3	3	0	25	36	24	2	0	7	8	6.48	43	.333	.374	10	.000	-1	37	-9	-1.0
Total	6	83	121	.407	211	207	196-13	0	1762	1710	1050	41	3	396	950	3.10	96	.239	.279	823	.170	-32	83	-22	-4.5

SHAW, JIM James Aloysius "Grunting Jim" B 8.19.1893 Pittsburgh, PA D 1.27.1962 Washington, DC BR/TR 6/180# d9.15

Year	Tm Lg	W	L	Pct	G	GS	CG-Sho	SV-BS	IP	H	R	HR	HB	BB-IB	SO	ERA	AERA	OAV	OOB	AB-SH	AVG	PB	Sup	APR	PW
1913	Was A	0	1	.000	2	1	0	0	13	8	4	0	1	7	14	2.08	142	.216	.356	2-0	.000	-0	0	1	0.1
1914	Was A	15	17	.469	48	31	15-5	**4**	257	198	99	3	8	137	164	2.70	104	.216	.324	85-3	.118	-3	84	3	0.1
1915	Was A	6	11	.353	25	18	7-1	1	133	102	50	2	2	76	78	2.50	119	.220	.333	43-1	.233	1	68	7	1.0
1916	Was A	3	8	.273	26	9	5-2	1	106.1	86	36	1	2	50	44	2.62	106	.227	.320	32-2	.156	-0	78	3	0.2
1917	Was A	15	14	.517	47	31	15-2	1	266.1	233	118	1	1	123	118	3.21	82	.242	.328	91-3	.154	-2	85	-15	-2.0
1918	Was A	16	12	.571	41	30	14-4	1	241.1	201	88	2	1	90	129	2.42	113	.228	.300	83-3	.133	-5	102	9	0.3
1919	Was A	17	17	.500	**45**	37	23-3	**5**	**306.2**	274	118	5	5	101	128	2.73	118	.244	.309	106-6	.160	-1	100	19	1.6
1920	Was A	11	18	.379	38	32	17	1	236.1	285	127	12	4	87	88	4.27	87	.314	.376	74-3	.189	0	83	-9	-1.1
1921	Was A	1	0	1.000	15	5	0	3	40.1	59	37	2	0	17	4	7.36	56	.345	.404	12-1	.417	2	174	-14	-0.5
Total	9	84	98	.462	287	194	96-17	17	1600.1	1446	677	28	24	688	767	3.07	99	.247	.329	528-22	.163	-8	91	4	-0.3

SHAW, JEFF Jeffrey Lee B 7.7.1966 Washington Court House, OH BR/TR 6-2/200# d4.30

Year	Tm Lg	W	L	Pct	G	GS	CG-Sho	SV-BS	IP	H	R	HR	HB	BB-IB	SO	ERA	AERA	OAV	OOB	AB-SH	AVG	PB	Sup	APR	PW
1990	Cle A	3	4	.429	12	9	0	0-0	48.2	73	38	11	0	20-0	25	6.66	59	.356	.408	0-0	—	0	106	-14	-1.7
1991	Cle A	0	5	.000	29	1	0	1-3	72.1	72	34	6	4	27-5	31	3.36	124	.262	.332	0-0	—	0	0	5	0.3
1992	Cle A	0	1	.000	2	1	0	0-0	7.2	7	7	2	0	4-0	3	8.22	48	.259	.355	0-0	—	0	117	-3	-0.4
1993	Mon N	2	7	.222	55	8	0	0-1	95.2	91	47	12	7	32-2	50	4.14	101	.254	.326	15-0	.067	-1	54	3	0.1
1994	Mon N	5	2	.714	46	0	0	1-1	67.1	67	32	8	2	15-2	47	3.88	109	.254	.295	7-1	.286	1		3	0.4
1995	Mon N	1	6	.143	50	0	0	3-2	62.1	58	35	4	3	26-4	45	4.62	93	.250	.332	6-0	.000	-0		-2	-0.2
	Chi A	0	0	—	9	0	0	0-0	9.2	12	7	2	1	1-0	6	6.52	68	.316	.350	0-0	—	0		-2	-0.1
1996	Cin N	8	6	.571	78	0	0	4-7	104.2	99	34	8	2	29-11	69	2.49	170	.252	.303	5-0	.000	-0		19	2.4
1997	Cin N	4	2	.667	78	0	0	**42-7**	94.2	79	26	7	1	12-3	74	2.38	180	.227	.253	3-1	.000	-0		**20**	2.7
1998	Cin N	2	4	.333	39	0	0	23-5	49.2	40	11	2	1	12-4	29	1.81	236	.231	.282	2-1	.000	-0		13	2.6
	LA N★	1	4	.200	34	0	0	25-4	35.1	35	11	6	0	7-1	26	2.55	156	.252	.288	0-0	—	0		6	1.2
	Year	3	8	.273	73	0	0	48-9	85	75	25	8	1	19-5	55	2.12	196	.240	.284	2-1	.000	-0		19	3.8
1999	LA N	2	4	.333	64	0	0	34-5	68	64	25	6	1	15-1	43	2.78	154	.242	.283	0-0	—	0		11	1.8
2000	LA N	3	4	.429	60	0	0	27-7	57.1	61	29	7	1	16-3	39	4.24	102	.265	.316	0-0	—	0		1	0.3
2001	LA N★	3	5	.375	77	0	0	43-9	74.2	63	32	10	2	18-8	58	3.62	111	.227	.277	0-0	—	0		4	0.8
Total	12	34	54	.386	633	19	0	203-51	848	821	368	91	25	234-44	545	3.54	118	.255	.308	38-3	.079	-1	76	64	10.2

SHAW, BOB Robert John B 6.29.1933 Bronx, NY BR/TR 6-2/195# d8.11 C1

Year	Tm Lg	W	L	Pct	G	GS	CG-Sho	SV-BS	IP	H	R	HR	HB	BB-IB	SO	ERA	AERA	OAV	OOB	AB-SH	AVG	PB	Sup	APR	PW
1957	Det A	0	1	.000	7	0	0	0	9.2	11	9	2	0	7-1	4	7.45	52	.289	.400	2-0	.000	-0		-4	-0.4
1958	Det A	1	2	.333	11	2	0	0	26.2	32	16	2	0	13-1	17	5.06	80	.302	.375	8-0	.375	1*	33	-3	-0.1
	Chi A	4	2	.667	29	3	0	1	64	67	33	8	2	28-3	18	4.64	78	.271	.346	14-0	.000	-1	156	-6	-0.5
	Year	5	4	.556	40	5	0	1	90.2	99	39	10	2	41-4	35	4.76	79	.280	.355	22-0	.136	-0	105	-8	-0.6
1959	†Chi A	18	6	**.750**	47	26	8-3	3	230.2	217	72	15	6	54-5	89	2.69	140	.249	.295	73-10	.123	-2	101	31	2.9
1960	Chi A	13	13	.500	36	32	7-1	0	192.2	221	97	16	3	62-3	46	4.06	93	.292	.345	58-7	.138	-0	101	-6	-0.8
1961	Chi A	3	4	.429	14	10	3	0	71.1	85	40	11	1	20-5	31	3.79	103	.302	.346	18-2	.000	-1	97	-2	-0.3
	KC A	9	10	.474	26	24	6	0	150.1	165	87	14	7	58-2	60	4.31	97	.281	.348	55-1	.200	-1*	93	-4	-0.5
	Year	12	14	.462	40	34	9	0	221.2	250	91	25	8	78-7	91	4.14	99	.288	.347	73-3	.151	-2	95	-7	-0.8
1962	Mil N★	15	9	.625	38	29	12-3	2	225	223	80	20	12	44-10	124	2.80	136	.260	.303	73-1	.137	1	102	26	2.6
1963	Mil N	7	11	.389	48	16	3-3	13	159	144	51	10	4	55-12	105	2.66	121	.243	.310	41-7	.122	0	97	11	1.4
1964	SF N	7	6	.538	61	1	0	11	93.1	105	43	5	5	31-6	57	3.76	95	.286	.348	13-0	.000	-1	74	-2	-0.5
1965	SF N	16	9	.640	42	33	6-1	2	235	213	85	17	3	53-5	148	2.64	136	.236	.280	79-4	.101	-3	99	22	2.0
1966	SF N	1	4	.200	13	6	0	0	31.2	45	23	9	0	7-1	21	6.25	59	.324	.356	6-2	.000	-1	76	-8	-1.2
	NY N	11	10	.524	26	25	7-2	0	167.2	171	85	12	7	42-1	104	3.92	93	.261	.312	50-5	.260	3	86	-6	-0.3
	Year	12	14	.462	39	31	7-2	0	199.1	216	89	21	7	49-2	125	4.29	85	.272	.319	56-7	.232	2	84	-17	-1.5
1967	NY N	3	9	.250	23	13	3-1	0	98.2	105	54	9	2	28-9	49	4.29	79	.273	.325	25-1	.040	-2	70	-10	-1.4
	Chi N	0	2	.000	9	3	0	0	22.1	33	16	0	4	9-4	7	6.04	59	.351	.418	4-0	.250	0	99	-6	-0.5
	Year	3	11	.214	32	16	3-1	0	121	138	20	9	6	37-13	56	4.61	74	.289	.344	29-1	.069	-1	75	-15	-1.9
Total	11	108	98	.524	430	223	55-14	32	1778	1837	791	150	56	511-68	880	3.52	105	.267	.321	519-40	.133	-7	96	33	2.4

SHAW, SAM Samuel E. B 5.1864 Baltimore, MD BR/TR 5-5/140# d5.3

Year	Tm Lg	W	L	Pct	G	GS	CG-Sho	SV-BS	IP	H	R	HR	HB	BB-IB	SO	ERA	AERA	OAV	OOB	AB-SH	AVG	PB	Sup	APR	PW
1888	Bal AA	2	4	.333	6	6	6	0	53	65	37	2	4	15	22	3.40	88	.291	.347	20	.150	-1	110	-5	-0.5
1893	Chi N	1	0	1.000	2	2	1	0	16	12	12	2	9	13	1	5.63	82	.203	.420	7	.286	-0	151	-1	-0.1
Total	2	3	4	.429	8	8	7	0	69	77	49	4	13	28	23	3.91	86	.273	.365	27	.185	-1	123	-6	-0.6

SHAWKEY, BOB James Robert B 12.4.1890 Sigel, PA D 12.31.1980 Syracuse, NY BR/TR 5-11/168# d7.16 Mil 1918 M1 C1

Year	Tm Lg	W	L	Pct	G	GS	CG-Sho	SV-BS	IP	H	R	HR	HB	BB-IB	SO	ERA	AERA	OAV	OOB	AB-SH	AVG	PB	Sup	APR	PW
1913	Phi A	6	5	.545	18	15	8-1	0	111.1	92	41	2	3	50	52	2.34	118	.221	.309	44-2	.136	-2	116	3	0.2
1914	†Phi A	15	8	.652	38	31	18-5	2	237	223	88	4	2	75	89	2.73	96	.262	.323	83-4	.205	2	122	-4	-0.2
1915	Phi A	6	6	.500	17	13	7-1	2	100	103	57	3	1	38	56	4.05	72	.278	.346	31-2	.129	-1	123	-11	-1.2
	NY A	4	7	.364	16	9	5-1	0	85.2	78	38	2	2	35	31	3.26	90	.265	.347	29-0	.241	1	61	-3	-0.2
	Year	10	13	.435	33	22	12-2	2	185.2	181	40	5	3	73	87	3.68	80	.272	.347	60-2	.183	1	97	-13	-1.4
1916	NY A	24	14	.632	53	27	21-4	**8**	276.2	204	78	4	6	81	122	2.21	131	.209	.273	93-4	.183	-1	102	24	3.4
1917	NY A	13	15	.464	32	26	16-2	0	236.1	207	81	2	6	72	97	2.44	110	.243	.306	84-4	.190	-0	99	8	1.2
1918	NY A	1	1	.500	3	2	1-1	0	16	7	2	0	0	10	3	1.13	251	.143	.288	4-1	.750	2	107	3	0.7
1919	NY A	20	11	.645	41	27	22-3	**5**	261.1	218	94	7	5	92	122	2.72	117	.231	.303	94-6	.234	-0	104	16	1.8
1920	NY A	20	13	.606	38	31	20-5	2	267.2	246	88	10	1	85	126	**2.45**	**156**	.248	.308	100-1	.230	-0	98	41	4.6
1921	†NY A	18	12	.600	38	31	18-3	2	245	245	131	15	7	86	126	4.08	104	.263	.329	90-8	.300	4	125	6	0.8
1922	†NY A	20	12	.625	39	34	22-3	1	299.2	286	112	16	0	98	130	2.91	138	.256	.316	115-7	.183	-3	103	37	3.3
1923	†NY A	16	11	.593	36	31	17-1	1	258.2	232	114	17	4	102	125	3.51	112	**.246**	.322	99-3	.202	-3	115	12	0.8
1924	NY A	16	11	.593	38	25	10-1	0	207.2	226	107	11	3	74	114	4.12	101	.286	.350	69-4	.319	8	133	2	0.8
1925	NY A	6	14	.300	33	19	9-1	0	186	209	101	12	5	67	81	4.11	104	.294	.359	68-0	.147	-4	59	2	-0.3
1926	†NY A	8	7	.533	29	10	3-1	3	104.1	102	49	8	2	37	63	3.62	106	.263	.330	35-2	.257	2	125	4	0.6
1927	NY A	2	3	.400	19	2	0	4	43.2	44	19	1	1	16	23	2.89	134	.262	.330	11-0	.091	-1	130	4	0.4
Total	15	195	150	.565	488	333	197-33	28	2937	2722	1200	114	48	1018	1360	3.09	114	.252	.319	1049-48	.214	4	108	144	16.7

SHEA, SPEC Francis Joseph "The Naugatuck Nugget" (b: Francis Joseph O'shea) B 10.2.1920 Naugatuck, CT D 7.19.2002 New Haven, CT BR/TR 6/195# d4.19

Year	Tm Lg	W	L	Pct	G	GS	CG-Sho	SV-BS	IP	H	R	HR	HB	BB-IB	SO	ERA	AERA	OAV	OOB	AB-SH	AVG	PB	Sup	APR	PW
1947	†NY A★	14	5	.737	27	23	13-3	1	178.2	127	63	10	4	89	89	3.07	115	**.200**	.303	56-8	.196	2	128	11	1.2
1948	NY A	9	10	.474	28	22	8-3	1	155.2	117	66	10	2	87	71	3.41	120	**.208**	.316	47-5	.149	1	105	12	1.2
1949	NY A	1	1	.500	20	3	0	1	52.1	48	36	5	0	43	22	5.33	76	.250	.387	12-0	.250	1	81	-8	-0.3
1951	NY A	5	5	.500	25	11	2-2	0	95.2	112	59	11	4	50	38	4.33	88	.300	.389	28-1	.214	1	135	-9	-0.7
1952	Was A	11	7	.611	22	21	12-2	0	169	144	62	6	2	92	65	2.93	121	.231	.331	63-1	.238	2	104	12	1.5
1953	Was A	12	7	.632	23	23	11-1	0	164.2	151	82	11	4	75	38	3.94	99	.244	.329	62-4	.177	-1	120	-1	-0.3

Year	Tm Lg	W	L	Pct	G	GS	CG-Sho	SV-BS	IP	H	R	HR	HB	BB-IB	SO	ERA	AERA	OAV	OOB	AB-SH	AVG	PB	Sup	APR	PW
1954	Was A	2	9	.182	23	11	1	0	71.1	97	54	9	2	34	22	6.18	58	.340	.412	20-0	.050	-2	108	-21	-2.9
1955	Was A	2	2	.500	27	4	1-1	2	56.1	53	31	4	1	27-0	16	3.99	96	.251	.335	10-0	.400	2	93	-2	0.0
Total	8	56	46	.549	195	118	48-12	5	943.2	849	453	66	19	497-0	361	3.80	99	.243	.339	298-19	.195	6	114	-6	-0.3
SHEA, JOHN John Michael Joseph "Lefty" B 12.27.1904 Everett, MA D 11.30.1956 Malden, MA BL/TL 5-10.5/171# d6.30																									
1928	Bos A	0	0	—	1	0	0	0	1	1	2	0	0	1	0	18.00	23	.250	.400	0-0	—	0		-1	-0.1
SHEA, MIKE Michael Joseph B 3.10.1867 New Orleans, LA D 8.22.1927 New Orleans, LA TR 5-10/170# d4.20																									
1887	Cin AA	1	1	.500	2	2	2	0	16.2	26	25	0	0	10	0	7.02	62	.333	.409	8	.250	0	147	-6	-0.5
SHEA, RED Patrick Henry B 11.29.1898 Ware, MA D 11.17.1981 Stafford Springs, CT BR/TR 6/165# d5.6																									
1918	Phi A	0	0	—	3	0	0	0	9	14	8	0	0	2	2	4.00	73	.378	.410	3-0	.000	-0		-2	-0.2
1921	NY N	5	2	.714	9	2	1	0	32	28	13	2	3	2	10	3.09	119	.239	.270	9-0	.111	-1	56	2	0.3
1922	NY N	0	3	.000	11	2	0	0	23	22	14	2	0	11	5	4.70	85	.256	.340	7-0	.000	-1	122	-2	-0.2
Total	3	5	5	.500	23	4	1	0	64	64	35	4	3	15	17	3.80	97	.267	.318	19-0	.053	-2	93	-2	-0.1
SHEA, STEVE Steven Francis B 12.5.1942 Worcester, MA BR/TR 6-3/215# d7.14																									
1968	Hou N	4	4	.500	30	0	0	6	34.2	27	14	0	3	11-0	15	3.38	88	.229	.306	6-0	.000	-1		-1	-0.3
1969	Mon N	0	0	—	10	0	0	0-0	15.2	18	8	2	0	8-2	11	2.87	128	.300	.371	0-0	—	0		0	0.0
Total	2	4	4	.500	40	0	0	6-0	50.1	45	22	2	3	19-2	26	3.22	99	.253	.328	6-0	.000	-1		-1	-0.3
SHEALY, AL Albert Berley B 3.20.1900 Chapin, SC D 3.7.1967 Hagerstown, MD BR/TR 5-11/175# d4.13																									
1928	NY A	8	6	.571	23	12	3	2	96	124	64	4	1	42	39	5.06	74	.308	.375	38-2	.237	2	128	-15	-1.7
1930	Chi N	0	0	—	24	0	0	0	27	37	24	2	0	14	14	8.00	61	.327	.402	5-0	.600	1		-8	-0.2
Total	2	8	6	.571	47	12	3	2	123	161	88	6	1	56	53	5.71	70	.313	.381	43-2	.279	4	128	-23	-1.9
SHEARON, JOHN John M. B 1870 Pittsburgh, PA D 2.1.1923 Bradford, PA d7.28 ▲																									
1891	Cle N	1	3	.250	6	5	4	0	46	57	39	2	1	24	19	3.52	98	.292	.373	124	.242	-0*	79	-2	-0.1
SHEARS, GEORGE George Penfield B 4.13.1890 Marshall, MO D 11.12.1978 Loveland, CO BR/TL 6-3/180# d4.24																									
1912	NY A	0	0	—	4	0	0	0	15	24	18	0	0	11	9	5.40	67	.364	.455	6-0	.167	0		-5	-0.2
SHEEHAN, TOM Thomas Clancy B 3.31.1894 Grand Ridge, IL D 10.29.1982 Chillicothe, OH BR/TR 6-2.5/190# d7.14 M1 C5																									
1915	Phi A	4	9	.308	15	13	8-1	0	102	131	73	1	1	38	22	4.15	71	.335	.395	34-2	.118	-3	82	-17	-2.2
1916	Phi A	1	16	.059	38	17	8	0	188	197	111	2	2	94	54	3.69	78	.287	.374	56-1	.125	-2	70	-21	-1.8
1921	NY A	1	0	1.000	12	1	0	1	33	43	23	1	1	19	7	5.45	78	.326	.414	8-2	.625	2	217	-4	0.0
1924	Cin N	9	11	.450	39	14	8-2	1	166.2	170	72	5	1	54	52	3.24	116	.269	.328	58-0	.310	4*	79	10	1.4
1925	Cin N	1	0	1.000	10	3	1	1	29	37	31	3	0	12	5	8.07	51	.298	.360	5-2	.200	1	123	-13	-0.5
	Pit N	1	1	.500	23	0	0	2	57.1	63	25	2	0	13	13	2.67	167	.286	.326	20-0	.150	-1*		9	0.3
	Year	2	1	.667	33	3	1	3	86.1	100	62	5	0	25	18	4.48	97	.291	.339	25-2	.160	-0	117	-2	-0.2
1926	Pit N	0	2	.000	9	2	1	0	31	36	24	0	2	12	16	6.68	59	.298	.370	9-2	.111	-1	116	-8	-0.5
Total	6	17	39	.304	146	50	26-3	5	607	677	359	14	7	242	169	4.00	86	.294	.362	190-9	.205	0	82	-44	-3.3
SHEETS, BEN Ben M. B 7.18.1978 Baton Rouge, LA BR/TR 6-1/195# d4.5																									
2001	Mil N★	11	10	.524	25	25	1-1	0-0	151.1	166	89	23	5	48-6	94	4.76	90	.283	.340	42-2	.071	-2	105	-9	-1.2
2002	Mil N	11	16	.407	34	34	1	0-0	216.2	237	105	21	10	70-10	170	4.15	99	.281	.343	68-4	.088	-3	81	0	-0.1
2003	Mil N	11	13	.458	34	34	1	0-0	220.2	232	122	29	6	43-2	157	4.45	96	.268	.305	66-5	.076	-4	105	-7	-1.2
Total	3	33	39	.458	93	93	3-1	0-0	588.2	635	316	73	21	161-18	421	4.42	95	.277	.328	176-11	.080	-8	96	-16	-2.5
SHELDON, ROLLIE Roland Frank B 12.17.1936 Putnam, CT BR/TR 6-4/190# d4.23																									
1961	NY A	11	5	.688	35	21	6-2	0	162.2	149	70	17	2	55-2	84	3.60	103	.246	.310	56-2	.125	-2*	112	3	0.1
1962	NY A	7	8	.467	34	16	2	1	118	136	78	12	1	28-3	54	5.49	68	.289	.324	26-6	.077	0	115	-23	-2.6
1964	†NY A	5	2	.714	19	12	3	1	102.1	92	43	18	1	18-2	57	3.61	100	.243	.276	34-2	.088	-2	129	1	-0.1
1965	NY A	0	0	—	3	0	0	0	6.1	5	1	0	0	1-0	7	1.42	240	.238	.261	1-0	.000	-0		1	0.1
	KC A	10	8	.556	32	29	4-1	0	186.2	180	86	22	7	56-3	105	3.95	88	.251	.311	51-7	.078	-3	96	-7	-1.0
	Year	10	8	.556	35	29	4-1	0	193	185	90	22	7	57-3	112	3.87	90	.251	.310	52-7	.077	-3	96	-4	-0.9
1966	KC A	4	7	.364	14	13	1-1	0	69	73	31	3	1	26-3	26	3.13	109	.275	.337	23-2	.087	-1	82	0	-0.1
	Bos A	1	6	.143	23	10	1	0	79.2	106	49	15	2	23-4	38	4.97	77	.320	.367	18-0	.111	-1	76	-9	-0.8
	Year	5	13	.278	37	23	2-1	0	148.2	179	52	18	3	49-7	64	4.12	88	.300	.353	41-2	.098	-2	78	-8	-0.9
Total	5	38	36	.514	160	101	17-4	2	724.2	741	358	87	14	207-17	371	4.09	89	.266	.317	209-19	.096	-9	102	-34	-4.4
SHELLENBACK, FRANK Frank Victor B 12.16.1898 Joplin, MO D 8.17.1969 Newton, MA BR/TR 6-2/192# d5.8 C15																									
1918	Chi A	9	12	.429	28	21	10-2	2	182.2	180	77	1	4	74	47	2.66	103	.262	.338	54-5	.130	-1*	109	-1	-0.5
1919	Chi A	1	3	.250	8	4	2	0	35	40	24	1	0	16	10	5.14	62	.303	.378	11-0	.091	-0	111	-7	-0.8
Total	2	10	15	.400	36	25	12-2	2	217.2	220	101	2	4	90	57	3.06	92	.269	.344	65-5	.123	-1	109	-8	-1.3
SHELLENBACK, JIM James Philip B 11.18.1943 Riverside, CA BL/TL 6-2/200# d9.15 C1																									
1966	Pit N	0	0	—	2	0	0	0	3	3	3	2	0	3-1	0	9.00	40	.300	.462	0-0	—	0		-2	-0.1
1967	Pit N	1	1	.500	6	2	1	0	23.1	23	12	1	1	12-1	11	2.70	125	.250	.343	6-0	.167	-0	65	0	0.0
1969	Pit N	0	0	—	8	0	0	0-0	16.2	14	8	1	0	4-0	7	3.24	108	.233	.277	1-0	.000	-0		0	0.1
	Was A	4	7	.364	30	11	2	1-1	84.2	87	43	8	1	48-3	50	4.04	86	.268	.362	27-0	.185	-0	109	-5	-0.6
1970	Was A	6	7	.462	39	14	2-1	0-0	117.1	107	57	6	0	51-4	57	3.68	97	.246	.322	30-4	.067	-2*	107	-3	-0.5
1971	Was A	3	11	.214	40	15	3-1	0-0	120	123	56	10	3	49-5	47	3.53	94	.267	.338	30-1	.167	0	72	-4	-0.4
1972	Tex A	2	4	.333	22	6	0	1-0	57	46	24	6	2	16-0	30	3.47	87	.221	.283	10-1	.100	-0	59	-2	-0.3
1973	Tex A	0	0	—	2	0	0	0-0	1.2	0	0	0	0	0-0	3	0.00	—	.000	.000	0-0	—	0		1	0.0
1974	Tex A	0	0	—	11	0	0	0-0	24.2	30	18	5	1	12-0	14	5.84	61	.306	.384	0-0	—	0		-6	-0.3
1977	Min A	0	0	—	5	0	0	0-0	5.2	10	7	1	0	5-0	3	7.94	50	.385	.469	0-0	—	0		-3	-0.2
Total	9	16	30	.348	165	48	8-2	2-1	454	443	228	40	8	200-14	222	3.81	89	.258	.335	104-6	.135	-2	89	-24	-2.3
SHEPARD, BERT Bert Robert B 6.28.1920 Dana, IN BL/TL 5-11/185# d8.4 C1																									
1945	Was A	0	0	—	1	0	0	0	5.1	3	1	0	1	1	2	1.69	184	.167	.250	3-0	.000	-0		1	0.0
SHEPHERD, KEITH Keith Wayne B 1.21.1968 Wabash, IN BR/TR 6-2/205# d9.6																									
1992	Phi N	1	1	.500	12	0	0	2-4	22	19	10	0	0	6-1	10	3.27	107	.244	.287	0-0	—	0		0	0.0
1993	Col N	1	3	.250	14	1	0	1-1	19.1	26	16	4	1	4-0	7	6.98	68	.333	.369	2-0	.000	-0	113	-4	-0.7
1995	Bos A	0	0	—	2	0	0	0-0	1	4	4	0	0	2-0	0	36.00	14	.571	.667	0-0	—	0		-3	-0.1
1996	Bal A	0	1	.000	13	0	0	0-0	20.2	31	27	6	0	18-1	17	8.71	57	.341	.445	0-0	—	0		-11	-0.5
Total	4	2	5	.286	41	1	0	3-5	63	80	57	10	1	30-2	34	6.71	65	.315	.383	2-0	.000	-0	113	-18	-1.3
SHERDEL, BILL William Henry "Wee Willie" B 8.15.1896 McSherrystown, PA D 11.14.1968 McSherrystown, PA BL/TL 5-10/160# d4.22																									
1918	StL N	6	12	.333	35	16	9-1	0	182.1	174	78	3	3	49	40	2.71	100	.259	.313	62-2	.242	3	108	-2	0.2
1919	StL N	5	9	.357	36	11	7	1	137.1	137	66	3	2	42	52	3.47	80	.270	.328	48-0	.271	2*	101	-10	-0.7
1920	StL N	11	10	.524	43	7	4	**6**	170	183	72	1	11	40	74	3.28	91	.297	.350	63-2	.222	2*	94	-4	-0.2
1921	StL N	9	8	.529	38	8	5-1	1	144.1	137	62	7	3	38	57	3.18	115	.247	.299	44-0	.114	-2*	118	8	0.7
1922	StL N	17	13	.567	47	31	15-3	2	242	298	132	12	5	62	79	3.87	100	.303	.348	88-2	.193	1*	119	-2	-0.4
1923	StL N	15	13	.536	39	26	14	2	225	270	127	15	6	59	78	4.32	90	.296	.343	83-3	.337	9*	106	-9	-0.3
1924	StL N	8	9	.471	35	10	6	1	168.2	188	77	9	5	38	57	3.42	111	.291	.335	75-1	.200	2*	99	7	0.8
1925	StL N	15	6	**.714**	32	21	17-2	1	200	216	77	8	3	42	53	3.11	139	.277	.316	73-1	.205	2*	112	29	2.8
1926	†StL N	16	12	.571	34	29	17-3	0	234.2	255	103	15	5	49	59	3.49	112	.278	.318	90-3	.244	2*	107	13	1.4
1927	StL N	17	12	.586	39	28	18	**6**	232.1	241	109	17	3	48	59	3.53	112	.269	.308	72-6	.194	1	109	12	1.3
1928	†StL N	21	10	.677	38	27	20	**5**	248.2	251	96	17	2	56	72	2.86	140	.261	.303	84-10	.226	4	112	31	3.9
1929	StL N	10	15	.400	33	22	11-1	0	195.2	278	144	14	2	58	69	5.93	79	.337	.382	70-6	.229	2	85	-26	-2.6
1930	StL N	3	2	.600	13	7	1	0	64	86	34	5	1	13	29	4.64	108	.325	.358	19-6	.105	-1	122	5	0.1
	Bos N	6	5	.545	21	14	7	1	119.1	131	73	10	2	30	26	4.75	104	.283	.329	42-2	.095	-4	105	1	-0.2
	Year	9	7	.563	34	21	8	1	183.1	217	79	15	3	43	55	4.71	105	.298	.340	61-8	.098	-5	110	6	-0.1
1931	Bos N	6	10	.375	27	16	8	0	137.2	163	70	13	1	35	34	4.25	89	.294	.337	46-0	.304	4	66	-5	-0.3

Year	Tm Lg	W	L	Pct	G	GS	CG-Sho	SV-BS	IP	H	R	HR	HB	BB-IB	SO	ERA	AERA	OAV	OOB	AB-SH	AVG	PB	Sup	APR	PW
1932	Bos N	0	0	—	1	0	0	0	1.2	3	3	0	0	1	0	0.00	—	.375	.444	0-0	—	0		-1	0.0
	StL N	0	0	—	3	0	0	0	5.2	7	3	0	0	1	1	4.76	83	.304	.333	1-0	1.000	1		0	0.1
	Year	0	0	—	4	0	0	0	7.1	10	9	0	0	2	1	3.68	106	.323	.364	1-0	1.000	1		-1	0.1
Total	15	165	146	.531	514	273	159-11	26	2709.1	3018	1326	149	54	661	839	3.72	103	.285	.330	960-44	.223	27	107	47	6.6
SHERID, ROY Royden Richard B 1.25.1907 Norristown, PA D 2.28.1982 Parker Ford, PA BR/TR 6-2/185# d5.11																									
1929	NY A	6	6	.500	33	15	9	1	154.2	165	81	6	5	55	51	3.61	107	.277	.343	50-3	.180	-1	120	2	0.0
1930	NY A	12	13	.480	37	21	8	4	184	214	122	13	5	87	59	5.23	82	.289	.368	69-4	.101	-6	131	-17	-2.5
1931	NY A	5	5	.500	17	8	3	2	74.1	94	52	4	3	24	39	5.69	70	.306	.362	30-5	.333	2	149	-15	-1.5
Total	3	23	24	.489	87	44	20	7	413	473	255	23	13	166	149	4.71	87	.288	.358	149-12	.174	-4	131	-30	-4.0
SHERMAN, JOE Joel Powers B 11.4.1890 Yarmouth, MA D 12.21.1987 Cape Coral, FL BR/TR 6/165# d9.24																									
1915	Phi A	1	0	1.000	2	1	1	0	15	15	4	0	2	1	5	2.40	122	.259	.295	6-0	.333	1	100	1	0.1
SHERMAN, DAN Lester Daniel "Babe" B 5.9.1890 Hubbardsville, NY D 9.16.1955 Highland Park, MI BR/TR 5-6/145# d6.4																									
1914	Chi F	0	1	.000	1	1	0	0	0.1	0	2	0	0	2	0	0.00	—	.000	.667	0-0	—	0	103	-1	-0.1
SHERRILL, TIM Timothy Shawn B 9.10.1965 Harrison, AR BL/TL 5-11/170# d8.14																									
1990	StL N	0	0	—	8	0	0	0-0	4.1	10	5	0	0	3-0	3	6.23	61	.476	.542	0-0	—	0		-2	-0.1
1991	StL N	0	0	—	10	0	0	0-0	14.1	20	13	2	2	3-1	4	8.16	46	.339	.379	0-0	—	0		-6	-0.3
Total	2	0	0	—	18	0	0	0-0	18.2	30	18	2	2	6-1	7	7.71	49	.375	.422	0-0	—	0		-8	-0.4
SHERRY, FRED Fred Peter (b: Fred Peter Schuerholz) B 1.13.1889 Honesdale, PA D 7.27.1975 Honesdale, PA BR/TR 6/170# d4.25																									
1911	Was A	0	4	.000	10	3	2	0	52.1	63	40	1	0	19	20	4.30	76	.310	.369	19-0	.158	-1	66	-7	-0.5
SHERRY, LARRY Lawrence B 7.25.1935 Los Angeles, CA BR/TR 6-2/204# d4.17 C4 b-Norm																									
1958	LA N	0	0	—	5	0	0	0	4.1	10	7	0	1	7-1	2	12.46	33	.476	.621	0-0	—	0		-4	-0.2
1959	†LA N	7	2	.778	23	9	1-1	3	94.1	75	27	9	2	43-5	72	2.19	193	.218	.308	32-1	.219	2	101	19	2.1
1960	LA N	14	10	.583	57	3	1	7	142.1	125	65	14	6	82-15	114	3.79	105	.238	.346	37-3	.162	1	89	4	0.7
1961	LA N	4	4	.500	53	1	0	15	94.2	90	48	10	4	39-9	79	3.90	111	.252	.332	13-0	.154	-0	0	4	0.3
1962	LA N	7	3	.700	58	0	0	11	90	81	40	8	6	44-5	71	3.20	113	.241	.335	17-1	.118	-0		3	0.4
1963	LA N	2	6	.250	36	3	0	3	79.2	82	43	8	4	24-4	47	3.73	81	.265	.321	9-1	.111	1	67	-9	-0.8
1964	Det A	7	5	.583	38	0	0	11	66.1	52	29	7	3	37-2	58	3.66	100	.216	.325	14-0	.000	-2		0	-0.1
1965	Det A	3	6	.333	39	0	0	5	78.1	71	30	5	1	40-10	46	3.10	112	.254	.346	10-2	.300	2		3	0.6
1966	Det A	8	5	.615	55	0	0	20	77.2	66	38	8	3	36-2	63	3.82	91	.232	.320	10-0	.400	2		-3	-0.6
1967	Det A	0	1	.000	20	0	0	1	28	35	22	3	1	7-0	20	6.43	51	.289	.328	1-0	.000	-0		-10	-0.5
	Hou N	1	2	.333	29	0	0	6	40.2	53	26	4	1	13-2	32	4.87	68	.327	.374	5-0	.000	-1		-8	-0.8
1968	Cal A	0	0	—	3	0	0	0	3	7	2	2	0	2-0	2	6.00	49	.467	.529	0-0	—	0		-1	-0.1
Total	11	53	44	.546	416	16	2-1	82	799.1	747	377	78	32	374-55	606	3.67	101	.249	.336	148-8	.169	4	92	-2	1.0
SHIELDS, BEN Benjamin Cowan "Big Ben" or "Lefty" B 6.17.1903 Huntersville, NC D 1.24.1982 Woodruff, SC BR/TL 6-1.5/195# d4.17																									
1924	NY A	0	0	—	2	0	0	0	2	6	6	0	0	2	3	27.00	15	.545	.615	0-0	—	0		-5	-0.2
1925	NY A	3	0	1.000	4	2	2	0	24	24	13	2	2	12	5	4.88	87	.267	.365	8-0	.125	-1	128	-1	-0.2
1930	Bos A	0	0	—	3	0	0	0	10	16	11	0	0	6	1	9.00	51	.400	.478	3-0	.000	-1		-5	-0.2
1931	Phi N	1	0	1.000	4	0	0	0	5.1	9	9	1	0	7	0	15.19	28	.391	.533	2-0	.000	-0		-5	-0.8
Total	4	4	0	1.000	13	2	2	0	41.1	55	39	3	2	27	9	8.27	53	.335	.435	13-0	.077	-2	128	-16	-1.4
SHIELDS, CHARLIE Charles Jessamine B 12.10.1879 Jackson, TN D 8.27.1953 Memphis, TN BL/TL d4.23																									
1902	Bal A	4	11	.267	23	15	10-1	1	142.1	201	102	7	2	32	28	4.24	89	.333	.368	48-1	.167	-1*	92	-8	-1.0
	StL A	3	0	1.000	4	4	3	0	30	37	16	1	0	7	6	3.30	107	.303	.341	13-1	.462	2	163	0	0.2
	Year	7	11	.389	27	19	13-1	1	172.1	238	24	8	2	39	34	4.07	92	.328	.364	61-2	.230	1	106	-8	-0.8
1907	StL N	0	2	.000	3	2	0	0	6.2	12	11	0	2	7	1	9.45	26	.444	.583	2-0	.000	-0	100	-5	-1.0
Total	2	7	13	.350	30	21	13-1	1	179	250	129	8	4	46	35	4.27	86	.332	.374	63-2	.222	1	103	-13	-1.8
SHIELDS, SCOT Robert Scot B 7.22.1975 Fort Lauderdale, FL BR/TR 6-1/175# d5.26																									
2001	Ana A	0	0	—	8	0	0	0-0	11	8	1	0	1	7-0	7	0.00	—	.200	.333	0-0	—	0		5	0.2
2002	†Ana A	5	3	.625	29	1	0	0-0	49	31	13	4	1	21-1	30	2.20	201	.188	.283	0-0	—	0	126	12	1.8
2003	Ana A	5	6	.455	44	13	0	1-0	148.1	138	56	12	5	38-6	111	2.85	151	.247	.299	0-0	—	0	75	23	1.6
Total	3	10	9	.526	81	14	0	1-0	208.1	177	70	16	7	66-7	148	2.55	171	.232	.297	0-0	—	0	79	40	3.6
SHIELDS, STEVE Stephen Mack B 11.30.1958 Gadsden, AL BR/TR 6-5/230# d6.1																									
1985	Atl N	1	2	.333	23	6	0	0-0	68	86	46	9	1	32-6	29	5.16	75	.320	.390	18-0	.111	-1	92	-10	-0.6
1986	Atl N	0	0	—	6	0	0	0-0	12.2	13	10	4	0	7-0	6	7.11	56	.271	.364	1-0	.000	-0		-4	-0.2
	KC A	0	0	—	3	0	0	0-1	8.2	3	3	1	0	4-1	2	2.08	205	.111	.212	0-0	—	0		2	0.1
1987	Sea A	2	0	1.000	20	0	0	3-1	30	43	25	7	0	12-1	22	6.60	72	.333	.382	0-0	—	0		-6	-0.5
1988	NY A	5	5	.500	39	0	0	0-2	82.1	96	44	8	2	30-4	55	4.37	90	.298	.360	0-0	—	0		-4	-0.5
1989	Min A	0	1	.000	11	0	0	0-1	17.1	28	18	3	0	6-1	12	7.79	53	.354	.400	0-0	—	0		-7	-0.4
Total	5	8	8	.500	102	6	0	3-5	219	269	146	32	3	91-13	126	5.26	77	.308	.371	19-0	.105	-1	92	-29	-2.1
SHIELDS, VINCE Vincent William B 11.18.1900 Fredericton, NB, CAN D 10.17.1952 Plaster Rock, NB, CAN BL/TR 5-11/185# d9.20																									
1924	StL N	1	1	.500	2	1	0	0	12	10	5	1	3	3	4	3.00	126	.227	.320	5-0	.400	0*	67	1	0.2
SHIELL, JASON Jason Alexander B 10.19.1976 Savannah, GA BR/TR 6/180# d9.8																									
2002	SD N	0	0	—	3	0	0	0-0	1.1	7	4	0	0	3-0	1	27.00	14	.700	.769	0-0	—	0		-4	-0.2
2003	Bos A	2	0	1.000	17	0	0	1-1	23.1	23	13	4	2	17-2	23	4.63	99	.253	.382	0-0	—	0		0	0.0
Total	2	2	0	1.000	20	0	0	1-1	24.2	30	17	4	2	20-2	24	5.84	77	.297	.423	0-0	—	0		-4	-0.2
SHIFFLETT, GARLAND Garland Jessie "Duck" B 3.28.1935 Elkton, VA BR/TR 5-10.5/165# d4.22																									
1957	Was A	0	0	—	6	1	0	0	8	6	9	0	0	10-0	2	10.13	38	.222	.421	0-0	—	0	160	-5	-0.3
1964	Min A	0	2	.000	10	0	0	1	17.2	22	9	1	1	7-0	8	4.58	78	.297	.366	4-0	.000	-0		-1	-0.2
Total	2	0	2	.000	16	1	0	1	25.2	28	18	1	1	17-0	10	6.31	58	.277	.383	4-0	.000	-0	160	-6	-0.5
SHIFFLETT, STEVE Stephen Earl B 1.5.1966 Kansas City, MO BR/TR 6-1/205# d7.3																									
1992	KC A	1	4	.200	34	0	0	0-2	52	55	15	6	2	17-6	25	2.60	156	.279	.341	0-0	—	0		9	0.8
SHINALL, ZAK Zakary Sebastien B 10.14.1968 St.Louis, MO BR/TR 6-3/215# d5.12																									
1993	Sea A	0	0	—	1	0	0	0-0	2.2	4	1	1	0	2-0	0	3.38	131	.333	.429	0-0	—	0		0	0.0
SHIPANOFF, DAVE David Noel B 11.13.1959 Edmonton, AL, CAN BR/TR 6-2/185# d8.9																									
1985	Phi N	1	2	.333	26	0	0	3-0	36.1	33	15	3	1	16-3	26	3.22	115	.231	.309	3-0	.000	-0		2	0.1
SHIPLEY, JOE Joseph Clark "Moses" B 5.9.1935 Morristown, TN BR/TR 6-4/210# d7.14																									
1958	SF N	0	0	—	1	0	0	0	1.1	3	5	0	2	3-0	0	33.75	11	.429	.667	0-0	—	0		-4	-0.2
1959	SF N	0	0	—	10	1	0	0	18	16	11	2	1	17-0	11	4.50	85	.239	.400	3-0	.000	-0	70	-2	-0.1
1960	SF N	0	0	—	15	0	0	0	20	20	13	2	3	9-1	9	5.40	64	.274	.372	0-0	—	0		-4	-0.2
1963	Chi A	0	1	.000	3	0	0	0	4.2	9	7	0	0	6-0	3	5.79	61	.409	.536	2-0	.000	-0		-3	-0.6
Total	4	0	1	.000	29	1	0	0	44	48	36	4	6	35-1	23	5.93	61	.284	.422	5-0	.000	-1	70	-13	-1.1
SHIREY, DUKE Clair Lee B 6.20.1898 Jersey Shore, PA D 9.1.1962 Hagerstown, MD BR/TR 6-1/175# d9.28																									
1920	Was A	0	1	.000	2	1	0	0	4	5	4	0	1	2	0	6.75	55	.313	.421	1-0	.000	-0	128	-1	-0.3
SHIRLEY, TEX Alvis Newman B 4.25.1918 Birthright, TX D 11.7.1993 DeSoto, TX BB/TR 6-1/175# d9.6																									
1941	Phi A	0	1	.000	5	0	0	1	7.1	8	4	1	0	6	1	2.45	171	.286	.412	1-0	.000	-0		1	0.1
1942	Phi A	0	1	.000	15	1	0	1	35.2	37	30	0	2	22	10	5.30	71	.272	.381	9-1	.000	-1	136	-8	-0.5
1944	†StL A	5	4	.556	23	11	2-1	0	80.1	59	45	4	1	64	35	4.15	87	.203	.348	28-0	.143	-2*	101	-5	-0.8
1945	StL A	8	12	.400	32	24	10-2	0	183.2	191	79	8	1	93	77	3.63	97	.274	.360	70-2	.286	2*	98	0	0.2
1946	StL A	6	12	.333	27	18	7	0	139.2	148	89	7	1	105	45	4.96	75	.273	.391	51-1	.196	-0*	119	-18	-2.1
Total	5	19	30	.388	102	54	19-3	2	446.2	443	247	20	5	290	168	4.25	85	.261	.371	159-4	.214	-1	106	-30	-3.1

SHIRLEY, BOB Robert Charles B 6.25.1954 Cushing, OK BR/TL 5-11/185# d4.10

Year	Tm Lg	W	L	Pct	G	GS	CG-Sho	SV-BS	IP	H	R	HR	HB	BB-IB	SO	ERA	AERA	OAV	OOB	AB-SH	AVG	PB	Sup	APR	PW
1977	SD N	12	18	.400	39	35	1	0-0	214	215	107	22	4	100-14	146	3.70	96	.259	.339	74-4	.122	-2	93	-7	-1.0
1978	SD N	8	11	.421	50	20	2	5-2	166	164	75	10	3	61-11	102	3.69	90	.262	.328	40-7	.125	-0	102	-6	-0.5
1979	SD N	8	16	.333	49	25	4-1	0-1	205	196	89	15	6	59-8	117	3.38	105	.257	.313	55-5	.091	-2	106	3	0.2
1980	SD N	11	12	.478	59	12	3	7-3	137	143	58	12	0	54-15	67	3.55	97	.276	.341	30-4	.033	-2	93	-1	-0.3
1981	StL N	6	4	.600	28	11	1	1-0	79.1	78	42	6	1	34-3	36	4.08	87	.260	.335	22-1	.136	-1	113	-6	-0.8
1982	Cin N	8	13	.381	41	20	1	0-0	152.2	138	74	17	3	73-13	89	3.60	103	.248	.335	42-5	.143	-1	63	-1	-0.2
1983	NY A	5	8	.385	25	17	1-1	0-0	108	122	71	10	0	36-3	53	5.08	77	.293	.345	0-0	—	0	107	-16	-1.6
1984	NY A	3	3	.500	41	7	1	0-1	114.1	119	47	8	0	38-2	48	3.38	112	.274	.331	0-0	—	0	78	6	0.3
1985	NY A	5	5	.500	48	8	2	2-2	109	103	34	5	0	26-2	55	2.64	152	.251	.293	0-0	—	0	91	18	1.5
1986	NY A	0	4	.000	39	6	0	3-0	105.1	108	60	13	3	40-1	64	5.04	81	.271	.336	0-0	—	0	48	-9	-0.4
1987	NY A	1	0	1.000	12	1	0	0-0	34	36	20	4	0	16-0	12	4.50	98	.277	.342	0-0	—	0	83	-1	-0.1
	KC A	0	0	—	3	0	0	0-0	7.1	10	12	5	0	6-0	1	14.73	31	.323	.432	0-0	—	0		-7	-0.3
	Year	1	0	1.000	15	1	0	0-0	41.1	46	36	9	0	22-0	13	6.31	70	.286	.360	0-0	—	0	82	-9	-0.4
Total	11	67	94	.416	434	162	16-2	18-9	1432	1432	689	127	20	543-72	790	3.82	96	.264	.331	263-26	.110	-8	91	-27	-3.2

SHIRLEY, STEVE Steven Brian B 10.12.1956 San Francisco, CA BL/TL 6/185# d6.21

Year	Tm Lg	W	L	Pct	G	GS	CG-Sho	SV-BS	IP	H	R	HR	HB	BB-IB	SO	ERA	AERA	OAV	OOB	AB-SH	AVG	PB	Sup	APR	PW
1982	LA N	1	1	.500	11	0	0	0-0	12.2	15	6	0	0	7-2	8	4.26	82	.300	.386	1-0	1.000	0		-1	0.0

SHOCKER, URBAN Urban James (b: Urbain Jacques Shockcor) B 9.22.1892 Cleveland, OH D 9.9.1928 Denver, CO BR/TR 5-10/170# d4.24 Mil 1918

Year	Tm Lg	W	L	Pct	G	GS	CG-Sho	SV-BS	IP	H	R	HR	HB	BB-IB	SO	ERA	AERA	OAV	OOB	AB-SH	AVG	PB	Sup	APR	PW
1916	NY A	4	3	.571	12	9	4-1	0	82.1	67	25	2	6	32	43	2.62	110	.230	.319	21-2	.190	1	102	4	0.5
1917	NY A	8	5	.615	26	13	7	1	145	124	59	5	0	46	68	2.61	103	.241	.303	45-5	.178	-1	109	0	0.0
1918	StL A	6	5	.545	14	9	7	2	94.2	69	26	0	1	40	33	1.81	152	.209	.296	34-0	.324	4	61	10	1.8
1919	StL A	13	11	.542	30	25	14-5	0	211	193	75	6	4	55	86	2.69	123	.244	.296	58-2	.138	-0	83	17	1.7
1920	StL A	20	10	.667	38	28	22-5	**5**	245.2	224	97	10	4	70	107	2.71	145	.248	.305	80-5	.225	2	98	30	3.7
1921	StL A	**27**	12	.692	47	38	30-4	4	326.2	345	151	21	6	86	132	3.55	126	.270	.319	104-7	.260	5	105	33	4.2
1922	StL A	24	17	.585	48	38	29-2	3	348	365	141	22	4	57	**149**	2.97	139	.272	.304	115-6	.191	2	97	44	**4.9**
1923	StL A	20	12	.625	43	35	24-3	5	277.1	292	122	12	3	49	109	3.41	122	.272	**.306**	80-12	.200	2	93	24	2.6
1924	StL A	16	13	.552	40	33	17-4	1	246.1	270	128	11	3	52	88	4.20	107	.277	.315	67-9	.239	5	105	11	1.5
1925	NY A	12	12	.500	41	30	15-2	2	244.1	278	108	17	3	58	74	3.65	117	.294	.336	64-10	.172	5	104	20	2.1
1926	†NY A	19	11	.633	41	32	18	2	258.1	272	113	13	2	71	59	3.38	114	.269	.318	76-20	.171	1	117	16	1.7
1927	NY A	18	6	.750	31	27	13-2	0	200	207	86	8	1	41	35	2.84	136	.268	.306	54-20	.241	3	127	20	2.3
1928	NY A	0	0	—	1	0	0	0	2	3	0	0	0	0	0	0.00	—	.429	.429	0-0	—	0		1	0.0
Total	13	187	117	.615	412	317	200-28	25	2681.2	2709	1131	127	37	657	983	3.17	124	.265	.311	798-98	.209	28	103	230	27.0

SHOFFNER, MILT Milburn James B 11.13.1905 Sherman, TX D 1.19.1978 Madison, OH BL/TL 6-1.5/184# d7.20

Year	Tm Lg	W	L	Pct	G	GS	CG-Sho	SV-BS	IP	H	R	HR	HB	BB-IB	SO	ERA	AERA	OAV	OOB	AB-SH	AVG	PB	Sup	APR	PW
1929	Cle A	2	3	.400	11	3	1	0	44.2	46	28	4	3	22	15	5.04	88	.284	.380	15-0	.000	-2	38	-2	-0.4
1930	Cle A	3	4	.429	24	10	1	0	84.2	129	86	8	1	50	17	7.97	61	.362	.442	33-2	.212	1	114	-26	-1.6
1931	Cle A	2	3	.400	12	4	1	0	41	55	34	4	2	26	12	7.24	64	.320	.415	13-0	.077	-1	96	-9	-1.0
1937	Bos N	3	1	.750	6	5	3-1	1	42.2	38	14	1	1	9	13	2.53	142	.239	.284	16-3	.125	1	144	5	0.6
1938	Bos N	8	7	.533	26	15	9-1	1	139.2	147	60	7	2	36	49	3.54	97	.270	.317	57-0	.211	3*	100	0	0.3
1939	Bos N	4	6	.400	25	11	7	1	132.1	133	56	4	1	42	51	3.13	118	.265	.324	44-2	.159	-0	92	8	0.6
	Cin N	2	2	.500	10	3	0	0	37.2	43	18	3	2	11	6	3.35	115	.289	.346	11-1	.091	-1	99	1	0.0
	Year	6	8	.429	35	14	7	1	170	176	22	7	3	53	57	3.18	117	.271	.329	55-3	.145	-1	94	9	0.6
1940	Cin N	1	0	1.000	20	0	0	0	54.1	56	35	3	0	18	17	5.63	67	.268	.326	16-1	.125	-1		-10	-0.6
Total	7	25	26	.490	134	51	22-2	3	577	647	331	34	12	214	180	4.59	85	.287	.352	205-9	.156	-0	102	-33	-2.1

SHORE, ERNIE Ernest Grady B 3.24.1891 East Bend, NC D 9.24.1980 Winston-Salem, NC BR/TR 6-4/220# d6.20 Mil 1918

Year	Tm Lg	W	L	Pct	G	GS	CG-Sho	SV-BS	IP	H	R	HR	HB	BB-IB	SO	ERA	AERA	OAV	OOB	AB-SH	AVG	PB	Sup	APR	PW
1912	NY N	0	0	—	1	0	0	1	1	8	10	1	0	1	1	27.00	13	.667	.692	0-0	—	0		-5	-0.6
1914	Bos A	10	5	.667	20	16	10-1	1	139.2	103	45	1	5	34	51	2.00	135	.204	.261	49-1	.102	-3	88	10	0.9
1915	†Bos A	19	8	.704	38	32	17-4	0	247	207	75	3	4	66	102	1.64	169	.228	.283	79-5	.101	-3	90	27	2.8
1916	†Bos A	16	10	.615	38	28	10-3	1	225.2	221	83	1	4	49	62	2.63	105	.259	.302	77-4	.091	-5	95	3	0.1
1917	Bos A	13	10	.565	29	27	14-1	1	226.2	201	76	1	12	55	57	2.22	116	.240	.297	78-4	.167	-1	94	8	0.8
1919	NY A	5	8	.385	20	13	3	0	95	105	50	4	1	44	24	4.17	77	.288	.366	28-2	.143	-2	70	-8	-1.2
1920	NY A	2	2	.500	14	5	2	1	44.1	61	31	1	1	21	12	4.87	78	.333	.405	11-2	.182	0	112	-6	-0.4
Total	7	65	43	.602	160	121	56-9	5	979.1	906	370	12	27	270	309	2.47	113	.247	.304	322-18	.121	-14	91	29	2.4

SHORE, RAY Raymond Everett B 6.9.1921 Cincinnati, OH D 8.13.1996 St.Louis, MO BR/TR 6-3/210# d9.21 C5

Year	Tm Lg	W	L	Pct	G	GS	CG-Sho	SV-BS	IP	H	R	HR	HB	BB-IB	SO	ERA	AERA	OAV	OOB	AB-SH	AVG	PB	Sup	APR	PW
1946	StL A	0	0	—	1	0	0	0	1	3	2	0	0	1	1	18.00	21	.500	.571	0-0	—	0		-1	-0.1
1948	StL A	1	2	.333	17	4	0	0	38	40	30	2	4	35	12	6.39	71	.270	.422	9-0	.000	-1	79	-7	-0.6
1949	StL A	0	1	.000	13	0	0	0	23.1	27	30	3	2	31	13	10.80	42	.297	.484	5-0	.000	-1		-14	-0.7
Total	3	1	3	.250	31	4	0	0	62.1	70	62	5	6	67	26	8.23	55	.286	.450	14-0	.000	-2	79	-22	-1.4

SHORES, BILL William David B 5.26.1904 Abilene, TX D 2.19.1984 Purcell, OK BR/TR 6/185# d4.11

Year	Tm Lg	W	L	Pct	G	GS	CG-Sho	SV-BS	IP	H	R	HR	HB	BB-IB	SO	ERA	AERA	OAV	OOB	AB-SH	AVG	PB	Sup	APR	PW
1928	Phi A	1	1	.500	3	2	1	0	14	13	7	0	0	7	5	3.21	125	.250	.339	5-0	.000	-1	53	1	0.0
1929	Phi A	11	6	.647	39	13	5-1	7	152.2	150	71	9	3	59	49	3.60	118	.262	.334	40-6	.125	-2	94	11	1.0
1930	†Phi A	12	4	.750	31	19	7-1	0	159	169	86	11	3	70	48	4.19	112	.276	.353	57-3	.193	-2	120	8	0.4
1931	Phi A	0	3	.000	6	2	0	0	16	26	18	3	0	10	2	5.06	89	.361	.439	3-0	.333	0	66	-4	-0.6
1933	NY N	2	1	.667	8	3	1	0	36.2	41	18	4	0	14	20	3.93	82	.291	.355	11-0	.273	1	121	-2	-0.1
1936	Chi A	0	0	—	9	0	0	0	17	26	18	1	0	8	5	9.53	55	.356	.420	5-0	.200	-0		-7	-0.3
Total	6	26	15	.634	96	39	14-2	7	395.1	425	218	28	6	168	129	4.17	105	.279	.353	121-9	.174	-4	106	7	0.4

SHORT, CHRIS Christopher Joseph B 9.19.1937 Milford, DE D 8.1.1991 Wilmington, DE BR/TL 6-4/205# d4.19

Year	Tm Lg	W	L	Pct	G	GS	CG-Sho	SV-BS	IP	H	R	HR	HB	BB-IB	SO	ERA	AERA	OAV	OOB	AB-SH	AVG	PB	Sup	APR	PW
1959	Phi N	0	0	—	3	2	0	0	14.1	19	13	3	1	10-0	8	8.16	50	.317	.423	6-0	.000	-1	141	-6	-0.3
1960	Phi N	6	9	.400	42	10	2	3	107.1	101	55	8	3	52-5	54	3.94	99	.249	.335	25-0	.000	-3	80	-2	-0.5
1961	Phi N	6	12	.333	39	16	1	1	127.1	157	94	12	3	71-11	80	5.94	69	.304	.390	37-7	.162	-1*	97	-26	-3.3
1962	Phi N	11	9	.550	47	12	4	3	142	149	66	13	8	56-6	91	3.42	113	.272	.347	36-4	.222	1*	70	5	0.8
1963	Phi N	9	12	.429	38	27	6-3	0	198	185	77	12	3	69-6	160	2.95	109	.248	.314	66-4	.106	-2	112	5	0.5
1964	Phi N★	17	9	.654	42	31	12-4	2	220.2	174	63	10	4	51-5	181	2.20	158	.217	.266	65-8	.108	-1*	96	31	3.6
1965	Phi N	18	11	.621	47	40	15-5	2	297.1	260	102	18	5	89-8	237	2.82	123	.235	.294	99-8	.131	-2	92	24	2.0
1966	Phi N	20	10	.667	42	39	19-4	0	272	257	120	28	9	68-2	177	3.54	102	.250	.301	106-1	.208	1	122	1	0.2
1967	Phi N★	9	11	.450	29	26	8-2	1	199.1	163	55	9	4	74-7	142	2.39	142	.225	.300	66-4	.091	-2	90	25	2.4
1968	Phi N	19	13	.594	42	36	9-2	1	269.2	236	99	25	9	81-10	202	2.94	102	.236	.298	79-8	.152	0*	102	3	0.3
1969	Phi N	0	0	—	2	2	0	0-0	10	11	8	2	1	4-0	5	7.20	49	.282	.364	3-0	.000	-0	112	-4	-0.2
1970	Phi N	9	16	.360	36	34	7-2	1-0	199	211	100	13	6	66-3	133	4.30	93	.272	.330	61-7	.049	-5	74	-6	-1.2
1971	Phi N	7	14	.333	31	26	5-2	1-0	173	182	85	22	3	63-2	95	3.85	92	.274	.339	48-6	.083	-1	82	-7	-0.9
1972	Phi N	1	1	.500	19	0	0	1-1	23	24	12	3	0	8-2	20	3.91	92	.267	.320	0-0	—	0		-1	-0.1
1973	Mil A	3	5	.375	42	7	0	2-3	72	86	42	5	2	44-7	44	5.13	73	.299	.394	0-0	—	0	109	-9	-1.0
Total	15	135	132	.506	501	308	88-24	18-4	2325	2215	991	183	61	806-74	1629	3.43	103	.252	.318	697-57	.126	-17	95	33	2.3

SHORT, BILL William Ross B 11.27.1937 Kingston, NY BL/TL 5-9/170# d4.23

Year	Tm Lg	W	L	Pct	G	GS	CG-Sho	SV-BS	IP	H	R	HR	HB	BB-IB	SO	ERA	AERA	OAV	OOB	AB-SH	AVG	PB	Sup	APR	PW
1960	NY A	3	5	.375	10	10	2	0	47	49	25	5	1	30-1	14	4.79	75	.282	.390	15-0	.200	1	103	-5	-0.7
1962	Bal A	0	0	—	5	0	0	0	4	8	7	0	1	6-0	3	15.75	23	.381	.536	1-0	.000	-0		-5	-0.3
1966	Bal A	2	3	.400	6	6	1-1	0	37.2	34	15	2	0	10-0	27	2.87	116	.239	.286	11-0	.091	-1	48	1	0.1
	Bos A	0	0	—	8	0	0	0	8.1	10	6	1	0	2-0	2	4.32	88	.294	.333	1-0	.000	-0		-1	0.0
	Year	2	3	.400	14	6	1-1	0	46	44	23	3	0	12-0	29	3.13	109	.250	.295	12-0	.083	-1	47	0	0.1
1967	Pit N	0	0	—	6	0	0	1	2.1	1	1	0	0	1-0	1	3.86	87	.143	.250	1-0	.000	-0		0	0.0
1968	NY N	0	3	.000	34	0	0	1	30.1	24	17	0	1	14-1	24	4.75	64	.220	.307	2-0	.000	-0		-5	-0.6
1969	Cin N	0	0	—	4	0	0	0-0	2.1	4	4	0	0	1-0	0	15.43	24	.400	.455	1-0	.000	-0		-3	-0.2
Total	6	5	11	.313	73	16	3-1	2-0	132	130	75	8	3	64-2	71	4.70	73	.262	.346	32-0	.125	-1	85	-18	-1.7

SHOUN, CLYDE Clyde Mitchell "Hardrock" B 3.20.1912 Mountain City, TN D 3.20.1968 Mountain Home, TN BL/TL 6-1/188# d8.7 Mil 1945

Year	Tm Lg	W	L	Pct	G	GS	CG-Sho	SV-BS	IP	H	R	HR	HB	BB-IB	SO	ERA	AERA	OAV	OOB	AB-SH	AVG	PB	Sup	APR	PW
1935	Chi N	1	0	1.000	5	1	0	0	12.2	14	4	2	0	5	5	2.84	138	.298	.365	3-0	.000	-0	43	2	0.1

Year	Tm Lg	W	L	Pct	G	GS	CG-Sho	SV-BS	IP	H	R	HR	HB	BB-IB	SO	ERA	AERA	OAV	OOB	AB-SH	AVG	PB	Sup	APR	PW
1936	Chi N	0	0	—	4	0	0	0	4.1	3	6	0	0	6	1	12.46	32	.200	.429	0-0	—	0		-4	-0.2
1937	Chi N	7	7	.500	37	9	2	0	93	118	65	9	0	45	43	5.61	71	.309	.382	29-1	.138	-1	111	-17	-2.3
1938	StL N	6	6	.500	40	12	3	1	117.1	130	58	8	1	43	37	4.14	96	.283	.345	31-2	.258	0	102	1	0.0
1939	StL N	3	1	.750	**53**	2	0	**9**	103	98	51	4	2	42	50	3.76	109	.248	.323	26-2	.115	-1	117	**3**	0.0
1940	StL N	13	11	.542	**54**	19	13-1	5	197.1	193	96	13	2	46	82	3.92	102	.255	.299	63-2	.190	-1	81	3	0.3
1941	StL N	3	5	.375	26	6	0	0	70	98	48	9	0	20	34	5.66	67	.337	.379	22-3	.182	0	116	-13	-1.2
1942	StL N	0	0	—	2	0	0	0	1.2	1	0	0	0	0	0	0.00	—	.167	.167	0-0	—	0		1	0.0
	Cin N	1	3	.250	34	0	0	0	72.2	55	23	2	0	24	32	2.23	147	.216	.283	13-0	.308	1		8	0.6
	Year	1	3	.250	36	0	0	0	74.1	56	28	2	0	24	32	2.18	151	.215	.281	13-0	.308	1		9	0.6
1943	Cin N	14	5	.737	45	5	2	7	147	131	52	5	0	46	61	3.06	108	.241	.300	42-1	.310	4	82	6	1.2
1944	Cin N	13	10	.565	38	21	12-1	2	202.2	193	83	10	3	42	55	3.02	116	.248	.290	67-5	.224	1	88	9	0.9
1946	Cin N	1	6	.143	27	5	0	0	79	87	42	3	1	26	20	4.10	82	.292	.351	21-1	.095	-1	67	-7	-0.8
1947	Cin N	0	0	—	10	0	0	0	14.1	16	8	2	1	5	7	5.02	82	.320	.393	0-0	—	0		-1	0.0
	Bos N	5	3	.625	26	3	1-1	1	73.2	73	41	6	0	21	23	4.40	89	.254	.305	19-1	.158	-1	83	-4	-0.5
	Year	5	3	.625	36	3	1-1	1	88	89	45	8	1	26	30	4.50	87	.264	.319	19-1	.158	-1	82	-5	-0.5
1948	Bos N	5	1	.833	36	2	1	4	74	77	37	7	0	20	25	4.01	96	.267	.315	21-2	.190	0	139	-2	-0.2
1949	Bos N	0	0	—	1	0	0	0	1	1	0	0	0	0	0	0.00	—	.250	.250	0-0	—	0		0	0.0
	Chi A	1	1	.500	16	0	0	0	23.1	37	17	1	0	13	8	5.79	72	.370	.442	5-0	.200	0		-4	-0.3
Total	14	73	59	.553	454	85	34-3	29	1287	1325	631	81	10	404	483	3.91	96	.267	.324	362-20	.202	1	94	-19	-2.4
SHOUSE, BRIAN Brian Douglas B 9.26.1968 Effingham, IL BL/TL 5-11/180# d7.31																									
1993	Pit N	0	0	—	6	0	0	0-0	4	7	4	1	0	2-0	3	9.00	45	.368	.409	0-0	—	0		-2	-0.1
1998	Bos A	0	1	.000	7	0	0	0-0	8	9	5	2	0	4-0	5	5.63	84	.281	.361	0-0	—	0		-1	-0.1
2002	KC A	0	0	—	23	0	0	0-0	14.2	15	10	3	2	9-1	11	6.14	82	.259	.371	0-0	—	0		-1	0.0
2003	Tex A	0	1	.000	62	0	0	1-0	61	62	24	1	4	14-6	40	3.10	160	.267	.320	0-0	—	0		11	0.6
Total	4	0	2	.000	98	0	0	1-0	87.2	93	43	7	6	29-7	59	4.11	120	.273	.339	0-0	—	0		7	0.4
SHOW, ERIC Eric Vaughn B 5.19.1956 Riverside, CA D 3.16.1994 Dulzura, CA BR/TR 6-1/185# d9.2																									
1981	SD N	1	3	.250	15	0	0	3-3	23	17	9	2	1	9-3	22	3.13	104	.213	.300	0-0	—	0		0	0.0
1982	SD N	10	6	.625	47	14	2-2	3-0	150	117	49	10	5	48-3	88	2.64	130	.217	.284	41-2	.146	-1	103	14	1.5
1983	SD N	15	12	.556	35	33	4-2	0-0	200.2	201	97	25	6	74-3	120	4.17	84	.263	.331	64-5	.172	1	107	-13	-1.6
1984	†SD N	15	9	.625	32	32	3-1	0-0	206.2	175	88	18	4	88-4	104	3.40	105	.234	.316	69-6	.246	6	90	4	1.1
1985	SD N	12	11	.522	35	35	5-2	0-0	233	212	95	27	5	87-7	141	3.09	115	.243	.314	79-7	.127	-1	96	10	0.6
1986	SD N	9	5	.643	24	22	2	0-0	136.1	109	47	11	4	69-4	94	2.97	123	.225	.326	43-3	.163	1	92	12	1.2
1987	SD N	8	16	.333	34	34	5-3	0-0	206.1	188	99	26	9	85-7	117	3.84	103	.241	.321	70-7	.071	-4	90	3	-0.2
1988	SD N	16	11	.593	32	32	13-1	0-0	234.2	201	86	22	6	53-5	144	3.26	104	.231	.279	81-5	.148	-0	94	7	0.5
1989	SD N	8	6	.571	16	16	1	0-0	106.1	113	59	9	2	39-3	66	4.23	83	.274	.336	34-4	.235	2*	104	-9	-1.1
1990	SD N	6	8	.429	39	12	0	1-0	106.1	131	74	16	4	41-9	55	5.76	67	.306	.369	25-1	.200	1	96	-21	-2.5
1991	Oak A	1	2	.333	23	5	0	0-0	51.2	62	36	5	0	17-1	20	5.92	65	.298	.345	0-0	—	0	114	-13	-0.7
Total	11	101	89	.532	332	235	35-11	7-3	1655	1526	739	171	46	610-49	971	3.66	98	.247	.317	506-40	.160	3	97	-6	-1.2
SHREVE, LEV Leven Lawrence B 1.14.1869 Louisville, KY D 10.18.1942 Detroit, MI BR/TR 5-11/150# d5.2																									
1887	Bal AA	3	1	.750	5	5	4-1	0	38	33	26	0	1	19	13	3.79	108	.228	.321	24	.167	-1*	143	1	0.0
	Ind N	5	9	.357	14	14	14-1	0	122	141	100	5	4	65	22	4.72	88	.278	.365	49	.265	0	73	-9	-0.7
1888	Ind N	11	24	.314	35	35	34-1	0	297.2	352	208	23	8	93	101	4.63	64	.288	.342	115	.183	-1*	74	-49	-4.8
1889	Ind N	0	3	.000	3	3	1	0	15.2	25	27	3	1	12	5	13.79	30	.352	.452	7	.000	-1	145	-14	-1.6
Total	3	19	37	.339	57	57	53-3	0	473.1	551	361	31	14	189	141	4.89	70	.283	.351	195	.195	-3	85	-71	-7.1
SHRIVER, HARRY Harry Graydon "Pop" B 9.2.1896 Wadestown, WV D 1.21.1970 Morgantown, WV BR/TR 6-2/180# d4.14																									
1922	Bro N	4	6	.400	25	13	4-2	0	108.1	114	49	5	2	48	38	2.99	136	.287	.367	27-3	.037	-3	48	11	0.5
1923	Bro N	0	0	—	1	1	0	0	4	8	3	0	0	0	1	6.75	58	.444	.444	1-0	.000	-0	148	-1	-0.1
Total	2	4	6	.400	26	14	4-2	0	112.1	122	52	5	2	48	39	3.12	130	.294	.370	28-3	.036	-3	54	10	0.4
SHUEY, PAUL Paul Kenneth B 9.16.1970 Lima, OH BR/TR 6-3/215# d5.8																									
1994	Cle A	0	1	.000	14	0	0	5-0	11.2	14	11	1	0	12-1	16	8.49	56	.280	.419	0-0	—	0		-4	-0.6
1995	Cle A	0	2	.000	7	0	0	0-0	6.1	5	4	0	0	5-0	5	4.26	110	.238	.385	0-0	—	0		0	0.0
1996	†Cle A	5	2	.714	42	0	0	4-3	53.2	45	19	6	0	26-3	44	2.85	172	.231	.317	0-0	—	0		12	1.5
1997	Cle A	4	2	.667	40	0	0	2-1	45	52	31	5	1	28-3	46	6.20	76	.294	.389	1-0	.000	-0		-6	-0.7
1998	†Cle A	5	4	.556	43	0	0	2-3	51	44	19	6	3	25-5	58	3.00	159	.229	.327	1-0	.000	-0		9	1.5
1999	†Cle A	8	5	.615	72	0	0	6-6	81.2	68	37	8	1	40-7	103	3.53	143	.223	.314	0-0	—	0		12	1.8
2000	Cle A	4	2	.667	57	0	0	0-5	63.2	51	25	4	3	30-3	69	3.39	147	.219	.312	0-0	—	0		11	0.9
2001	†Cle A	5	3	.625	47	0	0	2-3	54.1	53	25	1	1	26-5	70	2.82	161	.251	.333	0-0	—	0		7	1.0
2002	Cle A	3	0	1.000	39	0	0	0-2	37.1	31	11	1	0	10-1	39	2.41	183	.225	.275	0-0	—	0		8	0.6
	LA N	5	2	.714	28	0	0	1-2	30.2	25	18	2	1	21-1	24	4.40	87	.217	.341	3-0	.333	0		-3	-0.5
2003	LA N	6	4	.600	62	0	0	0-1	69	50	24	6	4	33-3	60	3.00	134	.207	.312	2-0	.000	-0		9	1.2
Total	10	45	27	.625	451	0	0	22-26	504.1	438	224	40	14	256-32	534	3.57	130	.233	.327	7-0	.143	-0		55	6.7
SHULTZ, TOOTS Wallace Luther B 10.10.1888 Homestead, PA D 1.30.1959 McKeesport, PA BR/TR 5-10/175# d5.5																									
1911	Phi N	0	3	.000	5	3	2	0	25	30	28	5	4	15	9	9.36	37	.300	.412	8-1	.250	0	73	-14	-1.3
1912	Phi N	1	4	.200	22	4	1	1	59	75	44	2	3	35	20	4.58	79	.333	.430	21-0	.238	0*	157	-7	-0.5
Total	2	1	7	.125	27	7	3	1	84	105	72	7	7	50	29	6.00	60	.323	.424	29-1	.241	0	121	-21	-1.8
SHUMAKER, ANTHONY Anthony Warren B 5.14.1973 Tucson, AZ BL/TL 6-5/225# d7.23																									
1999	Phi N	0	3	.000	8	4	0	0-0	22.2	23	17	3	1	14-0	17	5.96	79	.261	.369	5-0	.200	0	92	-3	-0.3
SHUMAN, HARRY Harry B 3.5.1915 Philadelphia, PA D 10.25.1996 Philadelphia, PA BR/TR 6-2/195# d9.14																									
1942	Pit N	0	0	—	1	0	0	0	2	0	0	0	0	1	1	0.00	—	.000	.167	0-0	—	0		1	0.0
1943	Pit N	0	0	—	11	0	0	0	22	30	20	0	2	8	5	5.32	65	.337	.404	2-0	.000	-0		-6	-0.3
1944	Phi N	0	0	—	18	0	0	0	26.2	26	15	1	0	11	4	4.05	89	.245	.316	1-0	.000	-0		-2	-0.1
Total	3	0	0	—	30	0	0	0	50.2	56	35	1	2	20	10	4.44	80	.280	.351	3-0	.000	-0		-7	-0.4
SIEBERT, PAUL Paul Edward B 6.5.1953 Minneapolis, MN BL/TL 6-2/205# d9.7 f-Dick																									
1974	Hou N	1	1	.500	5	5	1-1	0-0	25.1	21	12	3	0	11-0	10	3.55	98	.236	.314	6-2	.000	-1	111	-1	-0.1
1975	Hou N	0	2	.000	7	2	0	2-0	18.1	20	7	0	1	6-1	6	2.95	115	.294	.360	3-0	.000	-0	26	1	0.1
1976	Hou N	0	2	.000	19	0	0	0-0	25.2	29	10	0	1	18-7	10	3.16	101	.296	.403	2-0	.000	-0		0	0.0
1977	SD N	0	0	—	4	0	0	0-0	3.2	3	4	1	0	4-1	1	2.45	144	.214	.368	0-0	—	0		-1	-0.1
	NY N	2	1	.667	25	0	0	0-0	28	27	12	0	1	13-4	20	3.86	97	.257	.336	1-0	.000	-0		0	0.0
	Year	2	1	.667	29	0	0	0-0	31.2	30	17	1	1	17-5	21	3.69	101	.252	.340	1-0	.000	-0		-1	-0.1
1978	NY N	0	2	.000	27	0	0	1-1	28	30	16	2	1	21-5	12	5.14	68	.283	.406	1-0	.000	-0		-5	-0.3
Total	5	3	8	.273	87	7	1-1	3-1	129	130	61	6	4	73-18	59	3.77	92	.271	.366	13-2	.000	-2	87	-6	-0.4
SIEBERT, SONNY Wilfred Charles B 1.14.1937 St.Marys, MO BR/TR 6-3/198# d4.26 C2																									
1964	Cle A	7	9	.438	41	14	3-1	3	156	142	61	15	2	57-4	144	3.23	111	.243	.310	49-0	.265	5*	85	7	1.2
1965	Cle A	16	8	.667	39	27	4-1	1	188.2	139	58	14	5	46-2	191	2.43	143	.206	**.259**	66-1	.106	-2*	102	22	2.7
1966	Cle A★	16	8	**.667**	34	32	11-1	1	241	193	89	25	6	62-3	163	2.80	123	.221	.276	85-5	.129	-2	111	15	1.3
1967	Cle A	10	12	.455	34	26	7-1	4	185.1	136	59	17	6	54-2	136	2.38	137	.202	.266	52-5	.135	1	80	17	2.2
1968	Cle A	12	10	.545	31	30	8-4	0	206	145	76	12	8	88-10	146	2.97	100	.198	.288	70-5	.157	1*	114	1	0.3
1969	Cle A	0	1	.000	2	2	0	0-0	14	10	5	1	0	8-0	6	3.21	117	.196	.305	4-0	.250	0	35	1	0.1
	Bos A	14	10	.583	43	22	2	5-3	163.1	151	93	21	4	68-1	127	3.80	100	.245	.321	53-4	.151	1	110	-6	-0.6
	Year	14	11	.560	45	24	2	5-3	177.1	161	98	22	4	76-1	133	3.76	101	.241	.320	57-4	.158	1	104	-5	-0.5
1970	Bos A	15	8	.652	33	33	7-2	0-0	222.2	207	98	29	6	60-2	142	3.44	115	.248	.302	77-4	.130	-2	102	12	1.0
1971	Bos A☆	16	10	.615	32	32	12-4	0-0	235.1	220	84	20	3	60-5	131	2.91	127	.245	.292	79-7	.266	10	104	19	3.2
1972	Bos A	12	12	.500	32	30	7-3	0-0	196.1	204	105	17	7	59-4	123	3.80	85	.264	.321	72-1	.236	6*	130	-16	-1.2
1973	Bos A	0	1	.000	2	0	0	0-1	2.1	5	2	1	0	1-0	5	7.71	52	.417	.462	0-0	—	0		-1	-0.2

Year	Tm Lg	W	L	Pct	G	GS	CG-Sho	SV-BS	IP	H	R	HR	HB	BB-IB	SO	ERA	AERA	OAV	OOB	AB-SH	AVG	PB	Sup	APR	PW
	Tex A	7	11	.389	25	20	1-1	2-0	119.2	120	68	11	3	37-1	76	3.99	93	.258	.314	0-0	—	0	97	-7	-0.8
	Year	7	12	.368	27	20	1-1	2-1	122	125	72	12	3	38-1	81	4.06	92	.262	.318	0-0	—	0	97	-9	-1.0
1974	StL N	8	8	.500	28	20	5-3	0-0	133.2	150	66	8	3	51-14	68	3.84	93	.288	.353	44-2	.114	-2	99	-5	-0.7
1975	SD N	3	2	.600	6	6	0	0-0	26.2	37	15	2	1	10-4	10	4.39	79	.330	.387	8-1	.375	2*	80	-3	-0.2
	Oak A	4	4	.500	17	13	0	0-0	61	60	28	4	0	31-3	44	3.69	99	.252	.335	1-0	.000	-0	97	0	-0.1
Total	12	140	114	.551	399	307	67-21	16-4	2152	1919	907	197	54	692-55	1512	3.21	110	.238	.301	660-35	.173	18	103	56	8.2

SIEBLER, DWIGHT Dwight Leroy B 8.5.1937 Columbus, NE BR/TR 6-2/184# d8.26

Year	Tm Lg	W	L	Pct	G	GS	CG-Sho	SV-BS	IP	H	R	HR	HB	BB-IB	SO	ERA	AERA	OAV	OOB	AB-SH	AVG	PB	Sup	APR	PW
1963	Min A	2	1	.667	7	5	2	0	38.2	25	13	6	1	12-0	22	2.79	130	.182	.253	15-0	.133	-0	112	4	0.2
1964	Min A	0	0	—	9	0	0	0	11	10	6	1	0	6-1	10	4.91	73	.256	.356	0-0	—	0		-1	-0.1
1965	Min A	0	0	—	7	1	0	0	15	11	7	2	0	11-0	15	4.20	85	.193	.324	1-0	.000	-0	49	-1	0.0
1966	Min A	2	2	.500	23	2	0	1	49.2	47	26	6	1	14-2	24	3.44	104	.253	.302	11-0	.000	-1	159	-1	-0.2
1967	Min A	0	0	—	2	0	0	0	3	4	1	0	0	1-0	0	3.00	115	.364	.417	0-0	—	0		0	0.0
Total	5	4	3	.571	48	8	2	1	117.1	97	53	15	2	44-3	71	3.45	104	.226	.298	27-0	.074	-1	116	1	-0.1

SIERRA, CANDY Ulises (Pizarro) B 3.27.1967 Rio Piedras, P.R. BR/TR 6-2/190# d4.6

Year	Tm Lg	W	L	Pct	G	GS	CG-Sho	SV-BS	IP	H	R	HR	HB	BB-IB	SO	ERA	AERA	OAV	OOB	AB-SH	AVG	PB	Sup	APR	PW
1988	SD N	0	1	.000	15	0	0	0-1	23.2	36	15	2	0	11-2	20	5.70	60	.379	.439	3-0	.000	-0		-5	-0.3
	Cin N	0	0	—	1	0	0	0-0	4	5	2	0	0	1-0	4	4.50	80	.294	.333	1-0	.000	-0		0	0.0
	Year	0	1	.000	16	0	0	0-1	27.2	41	22	2	0	12-2	24	5.53	62	.366	.424	4-0	.000	-0		-5	-0.3

SIEVER, ED Edward Tilden B 4.2.1877 Goddard, KS D 2.4.1920 Detroit, MI BL/TL 5-11.5/190# d4.26

Year	Tm Lg	W	L	Pct	G	GS	CG-Sho	SV-BS	IP	H	R	HR	HB	BB-IB	SO	ERA	AERA	OAV	OOB	AB-SH	AVG	PB	Sup	APR	PW
1901	Det A	18	14	.563	38	33	30-2	0	288.2	334	166	9	8	65	85	3.24	119	.286	.328	107-6	.168	-5	102	18	1.2
1902	Det A	8	11	.421	25	23	17-4	1	188.1	166	73	0	2	32	36	**1.91**	**191**	.237	.272	66-4	.152	-4	86	29	2.1
1903	StL A	13	14	.481	31	27	24-1	0	254	245	102	6	5	39	90	2.48	117	.253	.285	93-2	.140	-4	83	11	0.8
1904	StL A	10	15	.400	29	24	19-2	0	217	235	112	3	3	65	77	2.65	93	.277	.330	71-0	.155	-1*	86	-14	-1.7
1906	Det A	14	11	.560	30	25	20-1	0	222.2	240	95	5	10	45	71	2.71	102	.278	.321	77-7	.156	-3	93	-1	-0.6
1907	†Det A	18	11	.621	39	33	22-3	1	274.2	256	89	1	11	52	88	2.16	120	.249	.293	94-3	.160	-3	110	16	1.2
1908	Det A	2	6	.250	11	9	4-1	0	61.2	74	37	0	0	13	23	3.50	69	.302	.337	18-1	.167	-1	97	-8	-1.1
Total	7	83	82	.503	203	174	136-14	2	1507	1550	674	24	39	311	470	2.60	116	.266	.308	526-23	.156	-21	95	51	1.9

SIGNER, WALTER Walter Donald Aloysius B 10.12.1910 New York, NY D 7.23.1974 Greenwich, CT BR/TR 6/185# d9.18

Year	Tm Lg	W	L	Pct	G	GS	CG-Sho	SV-BS	IP	H	R	HR	HB	BB-IB	SO	ERA	AERA	OAV	OOB	AB-SH	AVG	PB	Sup	APR	PW
1943	Chi N	2	1	.667	4	2	1	0	25	24	8	3	0	4	5	2.88	116	.245	.275	8-0	.250	0	38	2	0.3
1945	Chi N	0	0	—	6	0	0	1	8	11	6	1	0	5	0	3.38	108	.256	.333	1-0	.000	-0		-1	-0.1
Total	2	2	1	.667	10	2	1	1	33	35	14	4	0	9	5	3.00	114	.248	.293	9-0	.222	0	38	1	0.2

SIGSBY, SETH Seth De Witt (b: Seth De Witt) B 4.30.1874 Cobleskill, NY D 9.15.1953 Schenectady, NY 6/175# d6.27

Year	Tm Lg	W	L	Pct	G	GS	CG-Sho	SV-BS	IP	H	R	HR	HB	BB-IB	SO	ERA	AERA	OAV	OOB	AB-SH	AVG	PB	Sup	APR	PW
1893	NY N	0	0	—	1	0	0	0	3	1	4	0	1	4	2	9.00	52	.100	.400	1	.000	-0		-1	-0.1

SIKORSKI, BRIAN Brian Patrick B 7.27.1974 Detroit, MI BR/TR 6-1/190# d8.16

Year	Tm Lg	W	L	Pct	G	GS	CG-Sho	SV-BS	IP	H	R	HR	HB	BB-IB	SO	ERA	AERA	OAV	OOB	AB-SH	AVG	PB	Sup	APR	PW
2000	Tex A	1	3	.250	10	5	0	0-0	37.2	46	31	9	1	25-1	32	5.73	87	.287	.385	0-0	—	0	112	-5	-0.4

SILVA, CARLOS Carlos B 4.23.1979 Bolivar, Venezuela BR/TR 6-4/225# d4.1

Year	Tm Lg	W	L	Pct	G	GS	CG-Sho	SV-BS	IP	H	R	HR	HB	BB-IB	SO	ERA	AERA	OAV	OOB	AB-SH	AVG	PB	Sup	APR	PW
2002	Phi N	5	0	1.000	68	0	0	1-4	84	88	34	4	4	22-6	41	3.21	122	.282	.334	2-0	.000	0		6	0.4
2003	Phi N	3	1	.750	62	1	0	1-2	87.1	92	43	7	8	37-5	48	4.43	90	.280	.365	9-1	.222	1	235	-3	-0.1
Total	2	8	1	.889	130	1	0	2-6	171.1	180	77	11	12	59-11	89	3.83	103	.281	.351	11-1	.182	1	235	3	0.3

SILVA, JOSE Jose Leonel B 12.19.1973 Tijuana, Mexico BR/TR 6-5/210# d9.10

Year	Tm Lg	W	L	Pct	G	GS	CG-Sho	SV-BS	IP	H	R	HR	HB	BB-IB	SO	ERA	AERA	OAV	OOB	AB-SH	AVG	PB	Sup	APR	PW
1996	Tor A	0	0	—	2	0	0	0-0	2	5	3	1	0	0-0	0	13.50	37	.455	.455	0-0	—	0		-2	-0.1
1997	Pit N	2	1	.667	11	4	0	0-0	36.1	52	26	4	1	16-3	30	5.94	72	.347	.406	7-3	.143	-0	107	-6	-0.5
1998	Pit N	6	7	.462	18	18	1	0-0	100.1	104	55	7	1	30-2	64	4.40	98	.271	.321	27-5	.037	-1	83	-1	-0.2
1999	Pit N	2	8	.200	34	12	0	4-1	97.1	108	70	10	3	39-0	77	5.73	80	.281	.349	20-2	.100	-1	122	-13	-1.2
2000	Pit N	11	9	.550	51	19	1	0-2	136	178	96	16	5	50-7	98	5.56	83	.317	.375	34-5	.176	0	98	-16	-1.9
2001	Pit N	3	3	.500	26	0	0	0-2	32	35	24	6	0	9-1	23	6.75	67	.271	.319	2-0	.000	-0		-7	-1.1
2002	Cin N	1	0	1.000	12	0	0	0-0	23.1	25	11	3	3	10-3	6	4.24	100	.294	.384	0-1	—	0		1	0.1
Total	7	25	28	.472	154	53	2	4-5	427.1	507	285	47	13	154-16	298	5.41	83	.297	.357	90-16	.111	-3	99	-44	-4.9

SIMA, AL Albert B 10.7.1921 Mahwah, NJ D 8.17.1993 Suffern, NY BR/TL 6/187# d6.28

Year	Tm Lg	W	L	Pct	G	GS	CG-Sho	SV-BS	IP	H	R	HR	HB	BB-IB	SO	ERA	AERA	OAV	OOB	AB-SH	AVG	PB	Sup	APR	PW
1950	Was A	4	5	.444	17	9	1	0	77	89	49	9	1	26	23	4.79	94	.291	.348	26-1	.115	-2	78	-3	-0.6
1951	Was A	3	7	.300	18	8	1	0	77	79	51	5	0	41	26	4.79	85	.261	.349	17-5	.176	1	92	-8	-0.8
1953	Was A	2	3	.400	31	5	1	1	68.1	63	31	7	3	31	25	3.42	114	.249	.338	17-0	.118	-1	82	3	0.1
1954	Chi A	0	1	.000	5	1	0	1	7	11	5	1	0	2	1	5.14	73	.393	.406	2-0	.000	-0	47	-1	-0.2
	Phi A	2	5	.286	29	7	1	2	79.1	101	51	9	0	32	36	5.22	75	.309	.368	20-2	.050	-2	58	-11	-1.2
	Year	2	6	.250	34	8	1	3	86.1	112	54	10	0	34	37	5.21	75	.315	.372	22-2	.045	-2	57	-12	-1.4
Total	4	11	21	.344	100	30	4	4	308.2	343	187	31	4	132	111	4.61	89	.282	.353	82-8	.110	-5	77	-20	-2.7

SIMAS, BILL William Anthony B 11.28.1971 Hanford, CA BL/TR 6-3/220# d8.15

Year	Tm Lg	W	L	Pct	G	GS	CG-Sho	SV-BS	IP	H	R	HR	HB	BB-IB	SO	ERA	AERA	OAV	OOB	AB-SH	AVG	PB	Sup	APR	PW
1995	Chi A	1	1	.500	14	0	0	0-0	14	15	5	1	1	10-2	16	2.57	173	.273	.394	0-0	—	0		3	0.3
1996	Chi A	2	8	.200	64	0	0	2-6	72.2	75	39	5	3	39-6	65	4.58	104	.265	.358	0-0	—	0		2	0.2
1997	Chi A	3	1	.750	40	0	0	1-1	41.1	46	23	6	2	24-3	38	4.14	106	.279	.375	0-0	—	0		0	0.0
1998	Chi A	4	3	.571	60	0	0	18-6	70.2	54	29	12	1	22-4	56	3.57	128	.206	.270	0-0	—	0		9	1.1
1999	Chi A	6	3	.667	70	0	0	2-3	72	73	36	6	6	32-6	41	3.75	130	.263	.347	0-0	—	0		8	0.8
2000	†Chi A	2	3	.400	60	0	0	0-5	67.2	69	27	9	1	22-6	49	3.46	144	.276	.332	0-0	—	0		12	0.7
Total	6	18	19	.486	308	0	0	23-21	338.1	332	159	39	14	149-27	265	3.83	123	.257	.337	0-0	—	0		34	3.1

SIMMONS, CURT Curtis Thomas B 5.19.1929 Egypt, PA BL/TL 6/187# d9.28 Mil 1951

Year	Tm Lg	W	L	Pct	G	GS	CG-Sho	SV-BS	IP	H	R	HR	HB	BB-IB	SO	ERA	AERA	OAV	OOB	AB-SH	AVG	PB	Sup	APR	PW
1947	Phi N	1	0	1.000	1	1	1	0	9	5	1	0	0	6	9	1.00	401	.161	.297	2-1	.500	0	66	3	0.4
1948	Phi N	7	13	.350	31	23	7	0	170	169	110	8	2	108	86	4.87	81	.266	.374	51-3	.137	-1	81	-18	-1.9
1949	Phi N	4	10	.286	38	14	2	1	131.1	133	72	7	1	55	83	4.59	86	.275	.350	41-0	.171	-1*	105	-9	-0.9
1950	Phi N	17	8	.680	31	27	11-2	1	214.2	178	93	19	2	88	146	3.40	119	.223	.302	77-3	.156	-1*	118	16	1.6
1952	Phi N★	14	8	.636	28	28	15-**6**	0	201.1	170	72	11	1	70	141	2.82	130	.227	.294	67-5	.164	2	100	20	2.2
1953	Phi N★	16	13	.552	32	30	19-4	0	238	211	102	17	3	82	138	3.21	131	.236	.302	93-4	.140	-3	110	25	2.3
1954	Phi N	14	15	.483	34	33	21-3	1	253	226	101	14	5	98	125	2.81	144	.239	.312	91-6	.176	-1*	95	29	2.9
1955	Phi N	8	8	.500	25	22	3	0	130	148	76	15	3	50-2	58	4.92	81	.290	.355	46-1	.174	-1*	99	-12	-1.4
1956	Phi N	15	10	.600	33	27	14	0	198	186	95	17	3	65-7	88	3.36	111	.248	.308	72-2	.236	3*	113	4	0.8
1957	Phi N★	12	11	.522	32	29	9-2	0	212	214	92	11	2	50-11	92	3.44	111	.264	.305	71-3	.239	4*	92	8	1.1
1958	Phi N	7	14	.333	29	27	7-1	1	168.1	196	92	11	3	40-4	78	4.38	90	.293	.332	59-3	.203	0*	87	-7	-0.9
1959	Phi N	0	0	—	7	0	0	0	10	16	5	2	1	0-0	4	4.50	91	.400	.415	0-0	—	0*		0	0.0
1960	Phi N	0	0	—	4	2	0	0	4	13	8	3	0	6-0	4	18.00	22	.542	.633	0-0	—	0	114	-6	-0.3
	StL N	7	4	.636	23	17	3-1	0	152	149	50	11	0	31-6	63	2.66	154	.257	.294	47-2	.213	1*	86	22	1.7
	Year	7	4	.636	27	19	3-1	0	156	162	54	14	0	37-6	67	3.06	134	.269	.309	47-2	.213	1	89	18	1.4
1961	StL N	9	10	.474	30	29	6-2	0	195.2	203	91	14	4	64-6	99	3.13	**141**	.269	.326	66-3	.303	5*	107	21	2.5
1962	StL N	10	10	.500	31	22	9-4	0	154	167	78	18	3	32-2	74	3.51	122	.280	.318	50-2	.160	0	112	8	1.0
1963	StL N	15	9	.625	32	32	11-6	0	232.2	209	82	13	6	48-3	127	2.48	143	.239	.281	81-3	.160	0	112	23	2.2
1964	†StL N	18	9	.667	34	34	12-3	0	244	233	106	24	5	49-1	104	3.43	111	.249	.288	94-8	.106	-3	135	11	0.8
1965	StL N	9	15	.375	34	32	5	0	203	229	104	19	4	54-8	96	4.08	94	.283	.330	64-3	.047	-5	82	-6	-1.2
1966	StL N	1	1	.500	10	5	1	0	33.1	35	17	3	0	14-2	14	4.59	78	.269	.338	8-0	.125	0	78	-3	-0.1
	Chi N	4	7	.364	19	10	3-1	0	77.1	79	39	7	1	21-3	24	4.07	90	.268	.317	18-3	.111	-0	77	-3	-0.4
	Year	5	8	.385	29	15	4-1	0	110.2	114	42	10	1	35-5	38	4.23	86	.268	.323	26-3	.115	-0	77	-7	-0.5
1967	Chi N	3	7	.300	17	14	3	0	82	100	54	10	2	23-4	31	4.94	72	.300	.342	28-1	.143	-1	112	-14	-1.6
	Cal A	2	1	.667	14	4	1-1	1	34.2	44	11	1	2	9-3	13	2.60	121	.321	.372	9-1	.222	1	118	2	0.3
Total	20	193	183	.513	569	462	163-36	5	3348.1	3313	1551	255	53	1063-**62**	1697	3.54	111	.259	.317	1135-57	.171	1	102	114	11.1

SIMMONS, PAT Patrick Clement (b: Patrick Clement Simoni) B 11.29.1908 Watervliet, NY D 7.3.1968 Albany, NY BR/TR 5-11/172# d4.18

Year	Tm Lg	W	L	Pct	G	GS	CG-Sho	SV-BS	IP	H	R	HR	HB	BB-IB	SO	ERA	AERA	OAV	OOB	AB-SH	AVG	PB	Sup	APR	PW
1928	Bos A	0	2	.000	31	3	0	1	69	69	38	4	1	38	16	4.04	102	.271	.367	15-0	.133	-1	82	0	-0.1
1929	Bos A	0	0	—	2	0	0	1	7	6	0	0	0	3	2	0.00	—	.231	.310	1-0	.000	-0		3	0.1

Year	Tm Lg	W	L	Pct	G	GS	CG-Sho	SV-BS	IP	H	R	HR	HB	BB-IB	SO	ERA	AERA	OAV	OOB	AB-SH	AVG	PB	Sup	APR	PW
Total	2	0	2	.000	33	3	0	2	76	75	38	4	1	41	18	3.67	112	.267	.362	16-0	.125	-1	82	3	0.0
SIMONS, DOUG Douglas Eugene B 9.15.1966 Bakersfield, CA BL/TL 6/170# d4.9																									
1991	NY N	2	3	.400	42	1	0	1-0	60.2	55	40	5	2	19-5	38	5.19	70	.246	.305	3-1	.000	-0	123	-11	-0.8
1992	Mon N	0	0	—	7	0	0	0-0	5.1	15	14	3	1	2-0	6	23.63	15	.500	.529	0-0	—	0		-11	-0.6
Total	2	2	3	.400	49	1	0	1-0	66	70	54	8	3	21-5	44	6.68	54	.276	.332	3-1	.000	-0	123	-22	-1.4
SIMONTACCHI, JASON Jason William B 11.13.1973 Mountain View, CA BR/TR 6-2/185# d5.4																									
2002	StL N	11	5	.688	24	24	0	0-0	143.1	134	68	18	6	54-4	72	4.02	99	.253	.327	50-4	.240	2*	103	0	0.3
2003	StL N	9	5	.643	46	16	1	1-2	126.1	153	82	21	5	41-0	74	5.56	73	.299	.355	38-0	.132	-1*	153	-22	-2.2
Total	2	20	10	.667	70	40	1	1-2	269.2	287	150	39	11	95-4	146	4.74	85	.276	.340	88-4	.193	1	123	-22	-1.9
SIMPSON, STEVE Steven Edward B 8.30.1948 St.Joseph, MO D 11.2.1989 Omaha, NE BR/TR 6-3/200# d9.10																									
1972	SD N	0	2	.000	9	0	0	2-1	11.1	10	6	0	0	8-1	9	4.76	69	.238	.360	0-0	—	0		-2	-0.3
SIMPSON, DUKE Thomas Leo B 9.15.1927 Columbus, OH BR/TR 6-1.5/190# d5.6																									
1953	Chi N	1	2	.333	30	1	0	0	45	60	47	8	1	25	21	8.00	56	.314	.396	8-0	.250	0	20	-17	-1.0
SIMPSON, WAYNE Wayne Kirby B 12.2.1948 Los Angeles, CA BR/TR 6-3/220# d4.9																									
1970	Cin N☆	14	3	.824	26	26	10-2	0-0	176	125	73	15	9	81-3	119	3.02	134	**.198**	.296	64-5	.094	-4*	134	18	1.3
1971	Cin N	4	7	.364	22	21	1	0-0	117.1	106	66	9	3	77-5	61	4.76	71	.244	.359	32-5	.031	-2	98	-18	-1.7
1972	Cin N	8	5	.615	24	22	1	0-0	130.1	124	63	17	2	49-4	70	4.14	78	.247	.316	48-0	.063	-3	136	-13	-1.6
1973	KC A	3	4	.429	16	10	1	0-0	59.2	66	39	1	1	35-0	29	5.73	72	.284	.375	0-0	—	0	113	-9	-0.9
1975	Phi N	1	0	1.000	7	5	0	0-0	30.2	31	11	1	1	11-0	19	3.23	116	.263	.328	9-0	.222	0	127	2	0.2
1977	Cal A	6	12	.333	27	23	0	0-0	122	154	90	14	7	62-3	55	5.83	67	.308	.389	0-0	—	0	95	-26	-3.3
Total	6	36	31	.537	122	107	13-2	0-0	636	606	342	57	23	315-15	353	4.37	85	.251	.340	153-10	.078	-8	116	-46	-6.0
SIMS, PETE Clarence B 5.24.1891 Crown City, OH D 12.2.1968 Dallas, TX BR/TR 5-11.5/165# d9.16																									
1915	StL A	1	0	1.000	3	2	0	0	8.1	6	4	0	0	6	4	4.32	66	.214	.353	1-1	1.000	1	89	-1	0.0
SINCLAIR, STEVE Steven Scott B 8.2.1971 Victoria, BC, CAN BL/TL 6-2/190# d4.25																									
1998	Tor A	0	2	.000	24	0	0	0-2	15	13	7	0	0	5-0	8	3.60	130	.232	.295	0-0	—	0		2	0.2
1999	Tor A	0	0	—	3	0	0	0-0	5.2	7	8	4	1	4-0	3	12.71	39	.304	.429	0-0	—	0		-4	-0.2
	Sea A	0	1	.000	18	0	0	0-0	13.2	15	8	1	1	10-2	15	3.95	120	.268	.388	0-0	—	0		1	0.0
	Year	0	1	.000	21	0	0	0-0	19.1	22	20	5	2	14-2	18	6.52	74	.278	.400	0-0	—	0		-4	-0.2
Total	2	0	3	.000	45	0	0	0-2	34.1	35	23	5	2	19-2	26	5.24	90	.259	.359	0-0	—	0		-1	0.0
SINCOCK, BERT Herbert Sylvester B 9.8.1887 Barkerville, BC, CAN D 8.1.1946 Houghton, MI BL/TL 5-10.5/165# d6.25																									
1908	Cin N	0	0	—	1	0	0	0	4.2	3	2	0	0	0	1	3.86	60	.176	.176	2-0	.000	-0		0	-0.1
SINGER, BILL William Robert "The Singer Throwing Machine" B 4.24.1944 Los Angeles, CA BR/TR 6-4/200# d9.24																									
1964	LA N	0	1	.000	2	2	0	0	14	11	5	0	0	12-1	3	3.21	101	.216	.365	6-0	.167	0	81	0	0.0
1965	LA N	0	0	—	2	0	0	0	1	2	0	0	0	2-0	1	0.00	—	.400	.571	0-0	—	0		0	0.0
1966	LA N	0	0	—	3	0	0	0	4	4	0	0	0	2-0	4	0.00	—	.286	.375	0-0	—	0		2	0.1
1967	LA N	12	8	.600	32	29	7-3	0	204.1	185	68	5	8	61-11	169	2.64	117	.239	.300	67-4	.090	-3*	92	11	0.8
1968	LA N	13	17	.433	37	36	12-6	0	256.1	227	97	14	5	78-10	227	2.88	96	.237	.295	81-3	.148	3	106	-4	0.0
1969	LA N★	20	12	.625	41	40	16-2	1-0	315.2	244	96	22	10	74-4	247	2.34	142	.210	.261	108-8	.102	-4	101	36	3.0
1970	LA N	8	5	.615	16	16	5-3	0-0	106.1	79	39	10	2	32-3	93	3.13	123	.203	.267	38-1	.132	-0	117	10	1.0
1971	LA N	10	17	.370	31	31	8-1	0-0	203.1	195	103	19	4	71-1	144	4.16	78	.252	.315	58-8	.103	-0	93	-21	-2.7
1972	LA N	6	16	.273	26	25	4-3	0-0	169.1	148	84	8	5	60-4	101	3.67	91	.237	.306	55-6	.073	-3	71	-7	-1.1
1973	Cal A★	20	14	.588	40	40	19-2	0-0	315.2	280	124	15	9	130-5	241	3.22	110	.235	.314	0-0	—	0	103	15	1.4
1974	Cal A	7	4	.636	14	14	8	0-0	108.2	102	48	3	1	43-0	77	2.98	115	.250	.319	0-0	—	0	128	3	0.3
1975	Cal A	7	15	.318	29	27	8	1-0	179	171	107	18	6	81-5	78	4.98	71	.257	.340	0-0	—	0	86	-27	-2.9
1976	Tex A	4	1	.800	10	10	2-1	0-0	64.2	56	31	4	5	27-0	34	3.48	103	.239	.328	0-0	—	0	120	0	0.0
	Min A	9	9	.500	26	26	5-3	0-0	172	177	88	9	6	69-4	63	3.77	95	.274	.345	0-0	—	0	109	-5	-0.6
	Year	13	10	.565	36	36	7-4	0-0	236.2	233	92	13	11	96-4	97	3.69	97	.264	.340	0-0	—	0	112	-7	-0.6
1977	Tor A	2	8	.200	13	12	0	0-0	59.2	71	54	5	2	39-2	33	6.79	62	.296	.392	0-0	—	0	82	-18	-2.4
Total	14	118	127	.482	322	308	94-24	2-0	2174	1952	944	132	63	781-50	1515	3.39	99	.240	.309	413-30	.109	-7	99	-5	-3.1
SINGLETON, ELMER Bert Elmer "Smoky" B 6.26.1918 Ogden, UT D 1.5.1996 Ogden, UT BR/TR 6-2/174# d8.20																									
1945	Bos N	1	4	.200	7	5	1	0	37.1	35	22	1	1	14	14	4.82	79	.248	.321	11-0	.000	-1	53	-4	-0.6
1946	Bos N	0	1	.000	15	2	0	1	33.2	27	20	3	1	21	17	3.74	92	.221	.340	4-1	.000	-1*	162	-3	-0.2
1947	Pit N	2	2	.500	36	3	0	1	67	70	49	9	2	39	24	6.31	67	.267	.366	13-1	.308	1*	104	-13	-0.6
1948	Pit N	4	6	.400	38	5	1	2	92.1	90	52	11	1	40	53	4.97	82	.253	.330	23-1	.087	-2	105	-7	-0.8
1950	Was A	1	2	.333	21	1	0	0	36.1	39	23	4	0	17	19	5.20	86	.291	.371	7-1	.429	1	261	-2	0.0
1957	Chi N	0	1	.000	5	2	0	0	13.1	20	11	3	0	2-0	6	6.75	57	.333	.355	3-1	.000	-0*	91	-4	-0.3
1958	Chi N	1	0	1.000	2	0	0	0	4.2	1	0	0	0	1-1	2	0.00	—	.071	.133	1-0	.000	-0		2	0.4
1959	Chi N	2	1	.667	21	1	0	0	43	40	15	2	0	12-2	25	2.72	145	.252	.304	6-0	.000	-1	23	6	0.3
Total	8	11	17	.393	145	19	2	4	327.2	322	192	33	5	146-3	160	4.83	83	.258	.338	68-5	.132	-3	99	-25	-1.8
SINGLETON, JOHN John Edward "Sheriff" B 11.27.1896 Gallipolis, OH D 10.23.1937 Dayton, OH BR/TR 5-11/171# d6.8																									
1922	Phi N	1	10	.091	22	9	3-1	0	93	127	80	6	5	38	27	5.90	79	.346	.415	36-1	.139	-2	97	-11	-1.4
SIROTKA, MIKE Michael Robert B 5.13.1971 Houston, TX BL/TL 6-1/190# d7.19																									
1995	Chi A	1	2	.333	6	6	0	0-0	34.1	39	16	2	0	17-0	19	4.19	106	.298	.371	0-0	—	0	84	2	0.1
1996	Chi A	1	2	.333	15	4	0	0-0	26.1	34	27	3	0	12-0	11	7.18	66	.315	.377	0-0	—	0	117	-10	-0.9
1997	Chi A	3	0	1.000	7	4	0	0-0	32	36	9	4	1	5-1	24	2.25	195	.290	.323	1-0	.000	-0	120	8	0.6
1998	Chi A	14	15	.483	33	33	5	0-0	211.2	255	137	30	2	47-0	128	5.06	90	.300	.336	4-0	.000	-0	112	-14	-1.6
1999	Chi A	11	13	.458	32	32	3-1	0-0	209	236	108	24	3	57-2	125	4.00	122	.283	.327	8-0	.250	0	85	18	1.7
2000	†Chi A	15	10	.600	32	32	1	0-0	197	203	101	23	1	69-1	128	3.79	132	.269	.330	4-0	.000	-0	110	22	2.3
Total	6	45	42	.517	125	111	9-1	0-0	710.1	803	398	86	7	207-4	435	4.31	111	.286	.334	17-0	.118	0	103	26	2.2
SISK, DOUG Douglas Randall B 9.26.1957 Renton, WA BR/TR 6-2/210# d9.6																									
1982	NY N	0	1	.000	8	0	0	1-0	8.2	5	1	1	1	4-2	4	1.04	350	.172	.294	0-0	—	0		3	0.3
1983	NY N	5	4	.556	67	0	0	11-6	104.1	88	38	1	4	59-7	33	2.24	162	.235	.342	6-1	.500	1		13	1.4
1984	NY N	1	3	.250	50	0	0	15-3	77.2	57	24	1	3	54-5	32	2.09	170	.215	.354	11-2	.091	-0		11	1.0
1985	NY N	4	5	.444	42	0	0	2-2	73	86	48	3	2	40-2	26	5.30	65	.291	.379	12-0	.000	-1		-16	-2.0
1986	†NY N	4	2	.667	41	0	0	1-0	70.2	77	31	0	5	31-5	31	3.06	116	.282	.366	4-0	.000	-0		2	0.1
1987	NY N	3	1	.750	55	0	0	3-3	78	83	38	5	3	22-4	37	3.46	109	.270	.323	5-0	.000	-1		1	0.1
1988	Bal A	3	3	.500	52	0	0	0-2	94.1	109	43	3	2	45-6	26	3.72	105	.306	.385	0-0	—	0		2	0.1
1990	Atl N	0	0	—	3	0	0	0-0	2.1	1	1	0	0	4-0	1	3.86	105	.143	.385	0-0	—	0		0	0.0
1991	Atl N	2	1	.667	14	0	0	0-0	14.1	21	14	1	0	8-2	5	5.02	77	.333	.403	0-0	—	0		-4	-0.7
Total	9	22	20	.524	332	0	0	33-16	523.1	527	238	15	20	267-33	195	3.27	112	.268	.359	38-3	.105	-1		12	0.3
SISK, TOMMIE Tommie Wayne B 4.12.1942 Ardmore, OK BR/TR 6-3/195# d7.19																									
1962	Pit N	0	2	.000	5	3	1	0	17.2	18	9	1	1	8-1	6	4.08	97	.257	.342	5-0	.200	0	74	0	0.0
1963	Pit N	1	3	.250	57	4	1	1	108	85	42	6	1	45-10	73	2.92	113	.222	.303	16-1	.063	-0	78	4	0.2
1964	Pit N	1	4	.200	42	1	0	0	61.1	91	47	4	3	29-5	35	6.16	57	.364	.432	8-0	.000	-1	150	-18	-1.4
1965	Pit N	7	3	.700	38	12	1-1	0	111.1	103	48	6	1	50-7	66	3.40	103	.248	.328	33-1	.061	-2*	93	2	-0.1
1966	Pit N	10	5	.667	34	23	4-1	1	150	146	74	14	4	52-6	60	4.14	86	.256	.321	51-2	.098	-1	138	-8	-0.9
1967	Pit N	13	13	.500	37	31	11-2	1	207.2	196	88	6	3	78-10	85	3.34	101	.253	.321	69-6	.101	-2	107	1	-0.2
1968	Pit N	5	5	.500	33	11	0	1	96	101	40	3	3	35-8	41	3.28	89	.282	.351	24-2	.083	-1	116	-3	-0.4
1969	SD N	2	13	.133	53	13	1	6-1	143	160	81	11	1	48-8	59	4.78	74	.285	.339	25-4	.120	0	71	-18	-1.9
1970	Chi A	1	1	.500	17	1	0	0-1	33.1	37	28	6	0	13-5	16	5.40	72	.276	.338	4-0	.250	0	46	-8	-0.4
Total	9	40	49	.449	316	99	19-4	10-2	928.1	937	457	57	17	358-60	441	3.92	88	.266	.335	235-16	.094	-7	106	-48	-5.1

Year	Tm Lg	W	L	Pct	G	GS	CG-Sho	SV-BS	IP	H	R	HR	HB	BB-IB	SO	ERA	AERA	OAV	OOB	AB-SH	AVG	PB	Sup	APR	PW
SISLER, DAVE David Michael B 10.16.1931 St.Louis, MO BR/TR 6-4/200# d4.21 b-Dick f-George																									
1956	Bos A	9	8	.529	39	14	3	3	142.1	120	81	13	7	72-2	93	4.62	100	.227	.326	42-4	.119	-2	83	2	-0.1
1957	Bos A	7	8	.467	22	19	5	1	122.1	135	68	15	2	61-1	55	4.71	85	.280	.361	42-4	.167	-0	104	-8	-0.9
1958	Bos A	8	9	.471	30	25	4-1	0	149.1	157	94	22	1	79-2	71	4.94	81	.276	.361	46-11	.196	0	102	-14	-1.5
1959	Bos A	0	0	—	3	0	0	0	6.2	9	5	3	0	1-0	3	6.75	60	.310	.333	2-0	.500	0		-2	-0.1
	Det A	1	3	.250	32	0	0	7	51.2	46	28	4	1	36-1	29	4.01	101	.242	.362	5-1	.200	-0		0	-0.1
	Year	1	3	.250	35	0	0	7	58.1	55	38	7	1	37-1	32	4.32	94	.251	.359	7-1	.286	0		-2	-0.2
1960	Det A	7	5	.583	41	0	0	6	80	56	23	3	2	45-1	47	2.47	160	.199	.311	16-1	.125	-0		14	2.2
1961	Was A	2	8	.200	45	1	0	11	60.1	55	34	6	3	48-5	30	4.18	96	.251	.390	6-0	.000	0	22	-2	-0.3
1962	Cin N	4	3	.571	35	0	0	1	43.2	44	19	4	0	26-3	27	3.92	103	.270	.370	0-0	—	0		2	0.2
Total	7	38	44	.463	247	59	12-1	29	656.1	622	352	70	16	368-15	355	4.33	95	.253	.351	159-21	.157	-2	96	-8	-0.6
SISLER, GEORGE George Harold "Georgeous George" B 3.24.1893 Manchester, OH D 3.26.1973 Richmond Heights, MO BL/TL 5-11/170# d6.28 M3 C1 HF1939 s-Dave s-Dick ▲																									
1915	StL A	4	4	.500	15	8	6	0	70	62	26	0	4	38	41	2.83	101	.247	.355	274-12	.285	3*	73	2	0.5
1916	StL A	1	2	.333	3	3	3-1	0	27	18	4	0	1	6	12	1.00	275	.198	.255	580-19	.305	1*	9	5	0.9
1918	StL A	0	0	—	2	1	0	1	8	10	6	0	1	4	4	4.50	61	.286	.375	452-9	.341	1*	165	-2	0.0
1920	StL A	0	0	—	1	0	0	1	1	0	0	0	0	0	2	0.00	—	.000	.000	631-13	.407	1*		0	0.1
1925	StL A	0	0	—	1	0	0	0	2	1	0	0	0	1	1	0.00	—	.167	.286	649-12	.345	0*		1	0.1
1926	StL A	0	0	—	1	0	0	1	2	0	0	0	0	2	3	0.00	—	.000	.286	613-16	.290	0*		1	0.1
1928	Bos N	0	0	—	1	0	0	0	1	0	0	0	0	1	0	0.00	—	.000	.333	491-14	.340	0*		0	0.0
Total	7	5	6	.455	24	12	9-1	3	111	91	36	0	6	52	63	2.35	123	.231	.330	3690-95	.335	7	64	7	1.7
SITTON, CARL Carl Vetter B 9.22.1882 Pendleton, SC D 9.11.1931 Valdosta, GA BR/TR 5-10.5/170# d4.24																									
1909	Cle A	3	2	.600	14	5	3	0	50	50	22	1	2	16	16	2.88	89	.263	.327	13-0	.154	0	88	-1	-0.1
SIVESS, PETE Peter B 9.23.1913 South River, NJ D 6.1.2003 Candler, NC BR/TR 6-3.5/195# d6.13																									
1936	Phi N	3	4	.429	17	6	2	0	65	84	40	6	1	36	22	4.57	99	.310	.393	25-0	.120	-2	65	0	-0.3
1937	Phi N	1	1	.500	6	2	1	0	23	30	18	5	0	11	4	7.04	62	.330	.402	6-0	.000	-1	60	-5	-0.5
1938	Phi N	3	6	.333	39	8	2	3	116	143	78	12	1	69	32	5.51	71	.306	.397	32-1	.188	-1	76	-19	-1.5
Total	3	7	11	.389	62	16	5	3	204	257	136	23	2	116	58	5.38	77	.310	.396	63-1	.143	-4	71	-24	-2.3
SIWY, JIM James Gerard B 9.20.1958 Central Falls, RI BR/TR 6-4/200# d8.20																									
1982	Chi A	0	0	—	2	1	0	0-0	7	10	8	1	0	5-0	3	10.29	39	.385	.469	0-0	—	0	90	-4	-0.2
1984	Chi A	0	0	—	1	0	0	0-0	4.1	3	1	0	0	2-0	1	2.08	201	.231	.313	0-0	—	0		1	0.1
Total	2	0	0	—	3	1	0	0-0	11.1	13	9	1	0	7-0	4	7.15	57	.333	.417	0-0	—	0	90	-3	-0.1
SKALSKI, JOE Joseph Douglas B 9.26.1964 Burnham, IL BR/TR 6-3/190# d4.10																									
1989	Cle A	0	2	.000	2	1	0	0-0	6.2	7	6	0	2	4-0	3	6.75	59	.259	.394	0-0	—	0	46	-2	-0.4
SKAUGSTAD, DAVE David Wendell B 1.10.1940 Algona, IA BL/TL 6-1/179# d9.25																									
1957	Cin N	0	0	—	2	0	0	0	5.2	4	1	0	0	6-0	4	1.59	259	.190	.370	1-0	.000	0		2	0.1
SKEELS, DAVE David B 12.29.1892 Addy, WA D 12.2.1926 Spokane, WA BL/TR 6-1/187# d9.14																									
1910	Det A	0	0	—	1	1	0	0	6	9	8	0	1	4	2	12.00	22	.333	.438	3-0	.000	-0	229	-5	-0.3
SKOK, CRAIG Craig Richard B 9.1.1947 Dobbs Ferry, NY BR/TL 6/190# d5.4																									
1973	Bos A	0	1	.000	11	0	0	1-0	28.2	35	22	2	0	11-2	22	6.28	64	.304	.357	0-0	—	0		-7	-0.4
1976	Tex A	0	1	.000	9	0	0	0-2	5	13	7	2	0	3-0	5	12.60	28	.481	.533	0-0	—	0		-4	-0.8
1978	Atl N	3	2	.600	43	0	0	2-0	62	64	38	8	0	27-8	28	4.35	93	.266	.338	8-0	.250	0		-3	-0.2
1979	Atl N	1	3	.250	44	0	0	2-2	54.1	58	26	7	3	17-2	30	3.98	102	.282	.341	3-0	.000	-0		1	0.1
Total	4	4	7	.364	107	0	0	5-4	150	170	93	19	3	58-12	85	4.86	83	.289	.352	11-0	.182	0		-13	-1.3
SKOPEC, JOHN John S. "Buckshot" B 5.8.1880 Chicago, IL D 10.20.1912 Chicago, IL BR/TL 5-10/190# d4.25																									
1901	Chi A	6	3	.667	9	9	6	0	68.1	62	39	1	8	45	24	3.16	110	.239	.369	30-0	.333	3	136	2	0.6
1903	Det A	2	2	.500	6	5	3	0	39.1	46	22	0	2	13	14	3.43	85	.291	.353	13-2	.154	-0	79	-2	-0.2
Total	2	8	5	.615	15	14	9	0	107.2	108	61	1	10	58	38	3.26	101	.259	.363	43-2	.279	3	118	0	0.4
SKRMETTA, MATT Matthew Leland B 11.6.1972 Biloxi, MS BB/TR 6-3/220# d6.6																									
2000	Mon N	0	0	—	6	0	0	0-0	5.1	6	10	1	0	6-0	4	15.19	32	.273	.414	0-0	—	0		-6	-0.3
	Pit N	2	2	.500	8	0	0	0-0	9.1	13	12	2	1	3-0	7	9.64	48	.333	.395	2-0	.000	-0		-6	-1.0
	Year	2	2	.500	14	0	0	0-0	14.2	19	28	3	1	9-0	11	11.66	40	.311	.403	2-0	.000	-0		-12	-1.3
SLAGLE, JOHN John A. B Lawrence, IN BL/TR ?/175# d4.30																									
1891	Cin AA	0	0	—	1	0	0	1	1.1	3	0	0	0	1	1	0.00	—	.429	.500	1	.000	-0		1	0.1
SLAGLE, ROGER Roger Lee B 11.4.1953 Wichita, KS BR/TR 6-3/190# d9.7																									
1979	NY A	0	0	—	1	0	0	0-0	2	0	0	0	0	0-0	2	0.00	—	.000	.000	0-0	—	0		1	0.0
SLAGLE, WALT Walter Jennings B 12.15.1878 Kenton, OH D 6.14.1974 San Gabriel, CA BB/TR 6/165# d5.4																									
1910	Cin N	0	0	—	1	0	0	0	1	0	1	0	1	3	0	9.00	32	.000	.571	0-0	—	0		-1	0.0
SLAPNICKA, CY Cyril Charles B 3.23.1886 Cedar Rapids, IA D 10.20.1979 Cedar Rapids, IA BB/TR 5-10/165# d9.26																									
1911	Chi N	0	2	.000	3	2	1	0	24	21	12	0	3	7	10	3.38	98	.236	.313	9-0	.222	-0	91	0	0.0
1918	Pit N	1	4	.200	7	6	4	1	49.1	50	34	2	5	22	3	4.74	61	.269	.362	14-2	.071	-1	101	-10	-1.1
Total	2	1	6	.143	10	8	5	1	73.1	71	46	2	8	29	13	4.30	70	.258	.346	23-2	.130	-1	97	-10	-1.1
SLAPPEY, JOHN John Henry B 8.8.1898 Albany, GA D 6.10.1957 Marietta, GA BL/TL 6-4/170# d8.23																									
1920	Phi A	0	1	.000	3	1	0	0	6.1	15	12	0	0	4	1	7.11	57	.441	.500	2-0	.500	1	99	-4	-0.4
SLATON, JIM James Michael B 6.19.1950 Long Beach, CA BR/TR 6/185# d4.14																									
1971	Mil A	10	8	.556	26	23	5-4	0-0	147.2	140	67	16	1	71-9	63	3.78	92	.253	.338	46-4	.109	-1	99	-3	-0.6
1972	Mil A	1	6	.143	9	8	0	0-0	44	50	31	3	1	21-1	17	5.52	55	.287	.362	11-3	.091	-1	80	-13	-1.9
1973	Mil A	13	15	.464	38	38	13-3	0-0	276.1	266	127	30	1	99-4	134	3.71	101	.251	.314	0-0	—	0	96	3	0.1
1974	Mil A	13	16	.448	40	35	10-3	0-0	250	255	117	22	3	102-6	126	3.92	92	.268	.339	0-0	—	0	101	-8	-0.9
1975	Mil A	11	18	.379	37	33	10-3	0-1	217	238	129	28	2	90-6	119	4.52	85	.276	.343	0-0	—	0	83	-18	-2.1
1976	Mil A	14	15	.483	38	38	12-2	0-0	292.2	287	126	14	6	94-12	138	3.44	102	.259	.317	0-0	—	0	100	2	0.2
1977	Mil A☆	10	14	.417	32	31	7-1	0-0	221	223	104	25	11	77-5	104	3.58	114	.266	.333	0-0	—	0	95	9	0.9
1978	Det A	17	11	.607	35	34	11-2	0-0	233.2	235	117	27	8	85-1	92	4.12	94	.263	.329	0-0	—	0	108	-6	-0.7
1979	Mil A	15	9	.625	32	31	12-3	0-0	213	229	95	15	2	54-1	80	3.63	115	.278	.321	0-0	—	0	111	14	1.4
1980	Mil A	1	1	.500	3	3	0	0-0	16.1	17	10	3	0	5-0	4	4.41	88	.270	.324	0-0	—	0	169	-1	-0.2
1981	†Mil A	5	7	.417	24	21	0	0-0	117.1	120	60	10	2	50-2	47	4.37	78	.273	.346	0-0	—	0	112	-13	-1.2
1982	†Mil A	10	6	.625	39	7	0	6-2	117.2	117	48	14	1	41-3	59	3.29	115	.264	.326	0-0	—	0	137	7	0.9
1983	Mil A	14	6	.700	46	0	0	5-6	112.1	112	57	12	3	56-5	38	4.33	87	.272	.356	0-0	—	0		-7	-1.2
1984	Cal A	7	10	.412	32	22	5-1	0-0	163	192	95	22	2	56-5	67	4.97	80	.295	.350	0-0	—	0	101	-17	-1.5
1985	Cal A	6	10	.375	29	24	1	1-0	148.1	162	82	22	2	63-1	60	4.37	94	.284	.355	0-0	—	0	88	-5	-0.5
1986	Cal A	4	6	.400	14	12	0	0-0	73.1	84	52	9	2	29-1	31	5.65	73	.295	.357	0-0	—	0	103	-13	-1.5
	Det A	0	0	—	22	0	0	2-1	40	46	18	5	1	11-3	12	4.05	102	.287	.333	0-0	—	0		1	0.1
	Year	4	6	.400	36	12	0	2-1	113.1	130	75	14	3	40-4	43	5.08	81	.292	.349	0-0	—	0	103	-11	-1.4
Total	16	151	158	.489	496	360	86-22	14-10	2683.2	2773	1335	277	48	1004-65	1191	4.03	94	.270	.334	57-7	.105	-2	100	-68	-8.7
SLATTERY, PHIL Philip Ryan B 2.25.1893 Harper, IA D 3.2.1968 Long Beach, CA BR/TL 5-11/160# d9.16																									
1915	Pit N	0	0	—	3	0	0	0	8	5	0	0	2	1	1	0.00	—	.185	.267	1-0	.000	-0		2	0.1
SLAUGHTER, BARNEY Byron Atkins B 10.6.1884 Smyrna, DE D 5.17.1961 Philadelphia, PA BR/TR 5-11.5/165# d8.9																									
1910	Phi N	0	1	.000	8	1	0	1	18	21	12	0	0	11	7	5.50	57	.318	.416	5-0	.200	0	167	-4	-0.2
SLAUGHTER, STERLING Sterling Feore B 11.18.1941 Danville, IL BR/TR 5-11/165# d4.19																									
1964	Chi N	2	4	.333	20	6	1	0	51.2	64	35	8	0	32-6	32	5.75	65	.305	.393	12-0	.083	-0	55	-10	-1.2

Year	Tm Lg	W	L	Pct	G	GS	CG-Sho	SV-BS	IP	H	R	HR	HB	BB-IB	SO	ERA	AERA	OAV	OOB	AB-SH	AVG	PB	Sup	APR	PW
SLAYBACK, BILL William Grover B 2.21.1948 Hollywood, CA BR/TR 6-4/200# d6.26																									
1972	Det A	5	6	.455	23	13	3-1	0-0	81.2	74	36	4	1	25-1	65	3.20	99	.239	.297	23-2	.174	-0	93	-2	-0.3
1973	Det A	0	0	—	3	0	0	0-0	2	5	4	0	1	0-0	1	4.50	91	.417	.462	0-0	—	0		-1	-0.1
1974	Det A	1	3	.250	16	4	0	0-0	54.2	57	34	1	3	26-2	23	4.77	80	.273	.351	0-0	—	0	58	-6	-0.4
Total	3	6	9	.400	42	17	3-1	0-0	138.1	136	74	5	5	51-3	89	3.84	89	.256	.323	23-2	.174	-0	80	-9	-0.8
SLAYTON, STEVE Foster Herbert B 4.26.1902 Barre, VT D 12.20.1984 Manchester, NH BR/TR 6/163# d7.21																									
1928	Bos A	0	0	—	3	0	0	0	7	6	3	0	0	3	2	3.86	107	.240	.321	2-0	.000	-0		0	0.0
SLEATER, LOU Louis Mortimer B 9.8.1926 St.Louis, MO BL/TL 5-10/185# d4.25																									
1950	StL A	0	0	—	1	0	0	0	1	0	0	0	0	0	1	0.00	—	.000	.000	0-0	—	0		1	0.0
1951	StL A	1	9	.100	20	8	4	1	81	88	53	7	5	53	33	5.11	86	.271	.381	31-0	.226	0*	51	-7	-0.8
1952	StL A	0	1	.000	4	2	0	0	8.2	9	8	1	0	5	1	7.27	54	.265	.359	2-0	.000	-0	111	-3	-0.3
	Was A	4	2	.667	14	9	3-1	0	57	56	29	4	2	30	22	3.63	98	.260	.356	20-1	.050	-2*	106	-2	-0.5
	Year	4	3	.571	18	11	3-1	0	65.2	65	33	5	2	35	23	4.11	88	.261	.357	22-1	.045	-2	108	-5	-0.8
1955	KC A	1	1	.500	16	1	0	0	25.2	33	22	3	0	21-0	11	7.71	54	.324	.429	13-0	.154	-1*	21	-9	-0.7
1956	Mil N	2	2	.500	25	1	0	2	45.2	42	22	6	0	27-9	32	3.15	110	.240	.338	10-0	.500	2	254	0	0.3
1957	Det A	3	3	.500	41	0	0	2	69.1	61	33	9	1	28-7	43	3.76	102	.237	.313	20-1	.250	3		0	0.3
1958	Det A	0	0	—	4	0	0	0	5.1	3	4	2	0	6-0	4	6.75	60	.158	.360	1-0	1.000	1		-1	0.1
	Bal A	1	0	1.000	6	0	0	0	7	14	10	0	0	2-0	5	12.86	28	.438	.471	6-0	.000	-1*		-7	-0.9
	Year	1	0	1.000	10	0	0	0	12.1	17	24	2	0	8-0	9	10.22	37	.333	.424	7-0	.143	0		-8	-0.8
Total	7	12	18	.400	131	21	7-1	5	300.2	306	181	32	8	172-16	152	4.70	83	.263	.360	103-2	.204	3	86	-28	-2.5
SLOAT, LEFTY Dwain Clifford B 12.1.1918 Nokomis, IL D 4.18.2003 St.Paul, MN BR/TL 6/168# d4.24																									
1948	Bro N	0	1	.000	4	1	0	0	7.1	7	5	0	0	8	1	6.14	65	.280	.455	1-1	.000	-0	0	-1	-0.2
1949	Chi N	0	0	—	5	1	0	0	9	14	7	0	0	3	3	7.00	58	.400	.447	0-1	—	0	87	-3	-0.1
Total	2	0	1	.000	9	2	0	0	16.1	21	12	0	0	11	4	6.61	61	.350	.451	1-2	.000	-0	44	-4	-0.3
SLOCUMB, HEATHCLIFF Heath B 6.7.1966 Jamaica, NY BR/TR 6-3/220# d4.11																									
1991	Chi N	2	1	.667	52	0	0	1-2	62.2	53	29	3	3	30-6	34	3.45	113	.231	.321	1-0	.000	-0		2	0.1
1992	Chi N	0	3	.000	30	0	0	1-0	36	52	27	3	1	21-3	27	6.50	56	.351	.430	4-0	.000	-0		-10	-0.9
1993	Chi N	1	0	1.000	10	0	0	0-0	10.2	7	5	0	0	4-0	4	3.38	118	.189	.262	1-0	.000	-0		0	0.0
	Cle A	3	1	.750	20	0	0	0-2	27.1	28	14	3	0	16-2	18	4.28	101	.272	.364	0-0	—	0		0	0.0
1994	Phi N	5	1	.833	52	0	0	0-5	72.1	75	32	0	2	28-4	58	2.86	150	.262	.328	4-1	.250	0		9	0.7
1995	Phi N★	5	6	.455	61	0	0	32-6	65.1	64	26	2	1	35-3	63	2.89	146	.257	.351	1-0	.000	-0		8	1.7
1996	Bos A	5	5	.500	75	0	0	31-8	83.1	68	31	2	3	55-5	88	3.02	168	.222	.343	0-0	—	0		19	3.2
1997	Bos A	0	5	.000	49	0	0	17-5	46.2	58	32	4	3	34-4	36	5.79	80	.312	.422	0-0	—	0		-5	-0.8
	†Sea A	0	4	.000	27	0	0	10-1	28.1	26	13	2	1	15-1	28	4.13	109	.241	.339	0-0	—	0		2	0.3
	Year	0	9	.000	76	0	0	27-6	75	84	47	6	4	49-5	64	5.16	89	.286	.393	0-0	—	0		-4	-0.5
1998	Sea A	2	5	.286	57	0	0	3-1	67.2	72	40	5	1	44-1	51	5.32	87	.275	.379	0-0	—	0		-3	-0.3
1999	Bal A	0	0	—	10	0	0	0-0	8.2	15	12	2	2	9-2	12	12.46	38	.395	.531	0-0	—	0		-7	-0.3
	StL N	3	2	.600	40	0	0	2-1	53.1	49	16	3	1	30-5	48	2.36	194	.243	.342	0-0	—	0		13	1.1
2000	StL N	2	3	.400	43	0	0	1-0	49.2	50	32	9	1	24-1	34	5.44	85	.266	.349	1-0	.000	-0*		-4	-0.4
	SD N	0	1	.000	22	0	0	0-0	19	19	11	0	2	13-3	12	3.79	114	.264	.378	0-0	—	0		0	0.0
	Year	2	4	.333	65	0	0	1-0	68.2	69	43	9	3	37-4	46	4.98	91	.265	.357	1-0	.000	-0		-5	-0.4
Total	10	28	37	.431	548	0	0	98-31	631	636	320	38	21	358-40	513	4.08	109	.263	.360	12-1	.083	-1		24	4.4
SLUSARSKI, JOE Joseph Andrew B 12.19.1966 Indianapolis, IN BR/TR 6-4/195# d4.11																									
1991	Oak A	5	7	.417	20	19	1	0-0	109.1	121	69	14	4	52-1	60	5.27	73	.283	.364	0-0	—	0	124	-19	-1.9
1992	Oak A	5	5	.500	15	14	0	0-0	76	85	52	15	6	27-0	38	5.45	69	.284	.350	0-0	—	0	144	-15	-1.8
1993	Oak A	0	0	—	2	1	0	0-0	8.2	9	5	1	0	11-3	1	5.19	79	.300	.488	0-0	—	0	68	-1	0.0
1995	Mil A	1	1	.500	12	0	0	0-0	15	21	11	3	2	6-1	6	5.40	92	.333	.403	0-0	—	0		-1	-0.1
1999	Hou N	0	0	—	3	0	0	0-0	3.2	1	0	0	0	3-1	3	0.00	—	.083	.267	0-0	—	0		2	0.1
2000	Hou N	2	7	.222	54	0	0	3-1	77	80	36	8	3	22-3	54	4.21	116	.268	.323	9-0	.111	-0		7	0.6
2001	Atl N	0	0	—	4	0	0	0-0	6	9	6	2	0	1-0	5	9.00	49	.346	.370	0-0	—	0		-3	-0.1
	Hou N	0	1	.000	8	0	0	0-0	10	16	10	2	0	3-0	6	9.00	51	.364	.396	0-0	—	0		-4	-0.4
	Year	0	1	.000	12	0	0	0-0	16	25	19	4	0	4-0	11	9.00	50	.357	.387	0-0	—	0		-7	-0.5
Total	7	13	21	.382	118	34	1	3-1	305.2	342	189	45	15	125-9	173	5.18	80	.285	.357	9-0	.111	-0	120	-34	-3.6
SMALL, AARON Aaron James B 11.23.1971 Oxnard, CA BR/TR 6-5/200# d6.11																									
1994	Tor A	0	0	—	1	0	0	0-0	2	5	2	1	0	2-0	0	9.00	54	.500	.538	0-0	—	0		-1	0.0
1995	Fla N	1	0	1.000	7	0	0	0-0	6.1	7	2	1	0	6-0	5	1.42	297	.269	.406	0-0	—	0		2	0.2
1996	Oak A	1	3	.250	12	3	0	0-0	28.2	37	28	3	1	22-1	17	8.16	60	.308	.417	0-0	—	0	88	-11	-1.1
1997	Oak A	9	5	.643	71	0	0	4-2	96.2	109	50	6	3	40-6	57	4.28	106	.294	.362	1-0	.000	-0		2	0.3
1998	Oak A	1	1	.500	24	0	0	0-0	36	51	34	3	3	14-3	19	7.25	63	.333	.398	0-0	—	0		-11	-0.6
	Ari N	3	1	.750	23	0	0	0-2	31.2	32	14	5	1	8-1	14	3.69	114	.269	.320	0-0	—	0		2	0.2
2002	Atl N	0	0	—	1	0	0	0-0	0.1	2	1	0	0	2-0	1	27.00	15	.667	.800	0-0	—	0		-1	0.0
Total	6	15	10	.600	139	3	0	4-4	201.2	243	131	19	8	94-11	113	5.27	86	.303	.378	1-0	.000	-0	88	-18	-1.0
SMALL, MARK Mark Allen B 11.12.1967 Portland, OR BR/TR 6-3/205# d4.5																									
1996	Hou N	0	1	.000	16	0	0	0-0	24.1	33	23	1	1	13-3	16	5.92	65	.308	.388	1-0	.000	-0		-8	-0.4
SMALLWOOD, WALT Walter Clayton B 4.24.1893 Dayton, MD D 4.29.1967 Baltimore, MD BR/TR 6-2/190# d9.19 Mil 1918-19																									
1917	NY A	0	0	—	2	0	0	0	2	1	0	0	0	1	1	0.00	—	.167	.286	0-0	—	0		1	0.0
1919	NY A	0	0	—	6	0	0	0	21.2	20	12	1	2	9	6	4.98	64	.263	.356	5-0	.000	-1		-3	-0.3
Total	2	0	0	—	8	0	0	0	23.2	21	12	1	2	10	7	4.56	69	.256	.351	5-0	.000	-1		-2	-0.3
SMART, J.D. Jon David B 11.12.1973 San Saba, TX BR/TR 6-2/185# d4.6																									
1999	Mon N	0	1	.000	29	0	0	0-0	52	56	30	4	0	17-0	21	5.02	89	.276	.330	3-0	.000	-0		-2	-0.1
2001	Tex A	1	2	.333	15	0	0	0-2	15.1	19	11	3	0	4-0	10	6.46	72	.306	.338	0-0	—	0		-3	-0.5
Total	2	1	3	.250	44	0	0	0-2	67.1	75	41	7	0	21-0	31	5.35	85	.283	.332	3-0	.000	-0		-5	-0.6
SMILEY, JOHN John Patrick B 3.17.1965 Phoenixville, PA BL/TL 6-4/200# d9.1																									
1986	Pit N	1	0	1.000	12	0	0	0-0	11.2	4	6	2	0	4-0	9	3.86	100	.105	.190	0-0	—	0		0	0.0
1987	Pit N	5	5	.500	63	0	0	4-2	75	69	49	7	0	50-8	58	5.76	71	.244	.354	7-0	.143	0		-12	-1.5
1988	Pit N	13	11	.542	34	32	5-1	0-0	205	185	81	15	3	46-4	129	3.25	105	.241	.284	63-7	.079	-2	90	4	0.3
1989	Pit N	12	8	.600	28	28	8-1	0-0	205.1	174	78	22	4	49-5	123	2.81	120	.226	.273	65-7	.138	1	101	11	1.0
1990	†Pit N	9	10	.474	26	25	2	0-0	149.1	161	83	15	2	36-1	86	4.64	78	.275	.317	49-3	.122	-0	93	-16	-1.8
1991	†Pit N★	**20**	8	**.714**	33	32	2-1	0-0	207.2	194	78	17	3	44-0	129	3.08	116	.251	.292	70-6	.100	-2	116	13	1.4
1992	Min A	16	9	.640	34	34	5-2	0-0	241	205	93	17	6	65-0	163	3.21	126	.231	.286	0-0	—	0	92	22	2.3
1993	Cin N	3	9	.250	18	18	2	0-0	105.2	117	69	15	2	31-0	60	5.62	72	.286	.337	32-5	.250	2	101	-17	-1.5
1994	Cin N	11	10	.524	24	24	1-1	0-0	158.2	169	80	18	4	37-3	112	3.86	107	.275	.320	55-5	.200	3	123	3	0.6
1995	†Cin N★	12	5	.706	28	27	1	0-0	176.2	173	72	11	4	39-3	124	3.46	119	.263	.306	55-6	.164	2	112	14	1.5
1996	Cin N	13	14	.481	35	34	2-2	0-1	217.1	207	100	20	4	54-5	171	3.64	116	.256	.304	68-4	.191	2	91	13	1.6
1997	Cin N	9	10	.474	20	20	0	0-0	117	139	76	17	6	31-3	94	5.23	82	.296	.346	40-2	.100	-2	86	-14	-2.1
	Cle A	2	4	.333	6	6	0	0-0	37.1	45	23	9	1	10-0	26	5.54	85	.304	.350	0-0	—	0	72	-3	-0.4
Total	12	126	103	.550	361	280	28-8	4-3	1907.2	1842	888	185	39	496-32	1284	3.80	102	.255	.305	504-45	.145	3	100	18	1.4
SMITH d6.5																									
1884	Bal U	0	0	—	1	1	0	0	6	12	11	0		2	2	9.00	30	.387	.424	5	.200	-1	191	-4	-0.2
SMITH d5.31																									
1886	Cin AA	0	1	.000	1	1	1	0	9	8	8	0	0	10	1	4.00	88	.229	.400	4	.250	-0	202	-1	-0.1

Year	Tm Lg	W	L	Pct	G	GS	CG-Sho	SV-BS	IP	H	R	HR	HB	BB-IB	SO	ERA	AERA	OAV	OOB	AB-SH	AVG	PB	Sup	APR	PW
SMITH, AL Alfred John B 10.12.1907 Belleville, IL D 4.28.1977 Brownsville, TX BL/TL 5-11/180# d5.5 C1																									
1934	NY N	3	5	.375	30	4	0	5	66.2	70	40	2	0	21	27	4.32	90	.266	.320	14-1	.286	1	84	-4	-0.5
1935	NY N	10	8	.556	40	10	4-1	5	124	125	50	6	7	32	44	3.41	113	.263	.319	34-2	.118	-0	101	8	1.0
1936	†NY N	14	13	.519	43	30	9-4	2	209.1	217	116	16	4	69	89	3.78	103	.274	.335	73-4	.137	-1	128	-3	-0.5
1937	†NY N	5	4	.556	33	9	2	0	85.2	91	45	8	2	30	41	4.20	93	.275	.339	25-1	.120	-2	121	-2	-0.4
1938	Phi N	1	4	.200	37	1	0	1	86	115	70	7	0	40	46	6.28	62	.320	.388	21-0	.000	-2	131	-23	-1.4
1939	Phi N	0	0	—	5	0	0	0	9	11	5	1	2	5	2	4.00	100	.314	.429	2-0	.000	-0		0	0.0
1940	Cle A	15	7	.682	31	24	11-1	2	183	187	79	12	6	55	46	3.44	122	.270	.329	62-1	.306	7	99	17	2.6
1941	Cle A	12	13	.480	29	27	13-2	0	206.2	204	95	12	1	75	76	3.83	103	.256	.321	71-1	.155	2*	92	4	0.8
1942	Cle A	10	15	.400	30	24	7-1	0	168.1	163	96	9	5	71	66	3.96	87	.251	.329	60-2	.250	3	94	-14	-1.6
1943	Cle A☆	17	7	.708	29	27	14-3	1	208.1	186	74	7	0	72	72	2.55	122	.239	.303	68-4	.206	3*	111	12	1.8
1944	Cle A	7	13	.350	28	26	7-1	0	181.2	197	83	6	3	69	44	3.42	96	.280	.347	64-1	.156	-1	91	-3	-0.4
1945	Cle A	5	12	.294	21	19	8-3	1	133.2	141	74	8	2	48	34	3.84	85	.275	.340	41-2	.293	4*	84	-13	-1.0
Total	12	99	101	.495	356	201	75-16	17	1662.1	1707	827	94	32	587	587	3.72	99	.267	.332	535-19	.191	14	101	-21	0.4
SMITH, AL Alfred Kendricks B 12.13.1903 Norristown, PA D 8.11.1995 San Diego, CA BR/TR 6/170# d6.18																									
1926	NY N	0	0	—	1	0	0	0	2	4	2	0	0	2	0	9.00	42	.444	.545	0-0	—	0		-1	-0.1
SMITH, ART Arthur Laird B 6.21.1906 Boston, MA D 11.22.1995 Norwalk, CT BR/TR 6/175# d6.9																									
1932	Chi A	0	1	.000	3	2	0	0	7	17	13	1	0	4	1	11.57	37	.500	.553	1-0	.000	-0	118	-7	-0.7
SMITH, BILLY Billy Lavern B 9.13.1954 LaMarque, TX BR/TR 6-7/200# d6.9																									
1981	†Hou N	1	1	.500	10	1	0	1-1	20.2	20	7	3	0	3-1	3	3.05	108	.263	.291	2-0	.000	-0	54	1	0.1
SMITH, BRYN Bryn Nelson B 8.11.1955 Marietta, GA BR/TR 6-2/205# d9.8																									
1981	Mon N	1	0	1.000	7	0	0	0-0	13	14	4	1	0	3-0	9	2.77	126	.280	.321	1-2	.000	-0		1	0.1
1982	Mon N	2	4	.333	47	1	0	3-0	79.1	81	43	5	0	23-5	50	4.20	87	.264	.311	8-1	.000	-0	0	-5	-0.4
1983	Mon N	6	11	.353	49	12	5-3	3-1	155.1	142	51	13	5	43-6	101	2.49	144	.248	.305	30-7	.167	0	84	18	2.0
1984	Mon N	12	13	.480	28	28	4-2	0-0	179	178	72	15	3	51-7	101	3.32	103	.259	.312	53-7	.132	1	94	3	0.6
1985	Mon N	18	5	.783	32	32	4-2	0-0	222.1	193	85	12	1	41-3	127	2.91	117	.232	.268	72-11	.194	3	141	10	1.3
1986	Mon N	10	8	.556	30	30	1	0-0	187.1	182	101	15	6	63-6	105	3.94	94	.251	.315	58-5	.138	1	109	-9	-0.6
1987	Mon N	10	9	.526	26	26	2	0-0	150.1	164	81	16	2	31-4	94	4.37	96	.274	.310	44-7	.136	-0	112	-2	-0.2
1988	Mon N	12	10	.545	32	32	1	0-0	198	179	79	15	10	32-2	122	3.00	120	.243	.282	55-8	.109	-1	104	12	1.0
1989	Mon N	10	11	.476	33	32	3-1	0-0	215.2	177	76	16	4	54-4	129	2.84	125	.223	.274	62-10	.065	-2	110	16	1.5
1990	StL N	9	8	.529	26	25	0	0-0	141.1	160	81	11	4	30-1	78	4.27	90	.286	.324	39-11	.256	3	97	-10	-0.8
1991	StL N	12	9	.571	31	31	3	0-0	198.2	188	95	16	7	45-3	94	3.85	97	.251	.297	65-7	.246	3	113	-3	-0.1
1992	StL N	4	2	.667	13	1	0	0-0	21.1	20	11	3	3	5-1	9	4.64	73	.247	.315	3-1	.000	-0	400	-3	-0.6
1993	Col N	2	4	.333	11	5	0	0-1	29.2	47	29	2	3	11-1	9	8.49	56	.362	.412	6-0	.000	-0	79	-10	-1.6
Total	13	108	94	.535	365	255	23-8	6-2	1791.1	1725	808	140	48	432-43	1028	3.53	104	.253	.300	496-77	.153	7	110	18	2.2
SMITH, CHUCK Charles Edward B 10.21.1969 Memphis, TN BR/TR 6-1/185# d6.13																									
2000	Fla N	6	6	.500	19	19	1	0-0	122.2	111	53	6	3	54-2	118	3.23	137	.248	.330	40-1	.100	-2*	94	15	1.1
2001	Fla N	5	5	.500	15	15	0	0-0	88	89	47	10	6	35-4	71	4.70	90	.265	.341	26-2	.192	1	112	-4	-0.3
Total	2	11	11	.500	34	34	1	0-0	210.2	200	100	16	9	89-6	189	3.84	113	.255	.335	66-3	.136	-2	102	11	0.8
SMITH, CHARLIE Charles Edwin B 4.20.1880 Cleveland, OH D 1.3.1929 Wickliffe, OH BR/TR 6-1/185# d8.6 b-Fred																									
1902	Cle A	2	1	.667	3	3	2-1	0	20	23	9	0	0	5	5	4.05	85	.287	.329	8-0	.125	-0	111	0	0.0
1906	Was A	9	16	.360	33	22	17-2	0	235.1	250	113	2	8	75	105	2.91	91	.275	.336	87-1	.184	-1	86	-10	-1.2
1907	Was A	10	20	.333	36	31	21-3	0	258.2	254	103	0	1	51	119	2.61	93	.259	.297	84-5	.143	-3*	80	-3	-0.5
1908	Was A	9	13	.409	26	23	14-1	1	183	166	76	2	3	60	83	2.41	95	.247	.311	65-5	.123	-2*	92	-4	-0.8
1909	Was A	3	12	.200	23	15	7-1	0	145.2	140	73	4	5	37	72	3.27	74	.250	.303	45-1	.156	-1	60	-13	-1.4
	Bos A	3	0	1.000	3	3	2	0	25	23	6	2	1	2	11	2.16	116	.237	.260	10-0	.300	1	160	2	0.3
	Year	6	12	.333	26	18	9-1	0	170.2	163	12	6	6	39	83	3.11	78	.248	.297	55-1	.182	-0	77	-10	-1.1
1910	Bos A	11	6	.647	24	18	11	1	156.1	141	57	4	2	35	53	2.30	111	.248	.294	44-10	.114	-2	99	5	0.1
1911	Bos A	0	0	—	1	1	0	0	2	2	3	1	0	1	0	9.00	36	.250	.333	0-0	—	0	66	-1	0.0
	Chi N	3	2	.600	7	5	3-1	0	38	31	11	0	1	7	11	1.42	233	.228	.271	13-1	.077	-1	127	7	0.7
1912	Chi N	7	4	.636	20	5	1	1	94	92	56	2	3	31	47	4.21	79	.269	.335	35-2	.257	1*	88	-9	-0.8
1913	Chi N	7	9	.438	20	17	8-1	0	137.2	138	53	2	4	34	47	2.55	125	.274	.325	45-1	.089	-3	61	9	0.6
1914	Chi N	2	4	.333	16	5	1	0	53.2	49	27	3	1	15	17	3.86	72	.251	.308	11-1	.091	-1	57	-4	-0.5
Total	10	66	87	.431	212	148	87-10	3	1349.1	1309	587	22	29	353	570	2.81	94	.259	.311	447-27	.150	-13	84	-21	-3.5
SMITH, POP-BOY Clarence Ossie B 5.23.1892 Newport, TN D 2.16.1924 Sweetwater, TX BR/TR 6-1/176# d4.19																									
1913	Chi A	0	1	.000	15	2	0	0	32	31	15	0	3	11	13	3.38	87	.263	.341	5-0	.000	-1	51	-1	-0.1
1916	Cle A	1	2	.333	5	3	0	1	25.2	25	15	1	1	11	4	3.86	78	.253	.333	7-1	.286	0	101	-2	-0.3
1917	Cle A	0	1	.000	6	0	0	0	8.2	14	11	0	1	4	3	8.31	34	.368	.442	1-0	.000	-0		-5	-0.5
Total	3	1	4	.200	26	5	0	1	66.1	70	41	1	5	26	20	4.21	70	.275	.353	13-1	.154	-1	81	-8	-0.9
SMITH, CLAY Clay Jamieson B 9.11.1914 Cambridge, KS D 3.5.2002 Winfield, KS BR/TR 6-2/190# d9.13																									
1938	Cle A	0	0	—	4	0	0	0	11	18	10	1	0	2	3	6.55	71	.367	.392	4-0	.000	-0		-3	-0.1
1940	†Det A	1	1	.500	14	1	0	0	28.1	32	18	3	1	13	14	5.08	94	.283	.362	7-0	.000	-1	92	-1	-0.1
Total	2	1	1	.500	18	1	0	0	39.1	50	28	4	1	15	17	5.49	86	.309	.371	11-0	.000	-1	92	-4	-0.2
SMITH, DAN Daniel Charles B 9.15.1975 Flemington, NJ BR/TR 6-3/210# d6.8																									
1999	Mon N	4	9	.308	20	17	0	0-1	89.2	104	64	12	4	39-0	72	6.02	75	.293	.368	24-3	.083	-1	105	-14	-1.7
2000	Bos A	0	0	—	2	0	0	0-0	3.1	2	3	0	0	3-0	1	8.10	62	.250	.357	0-0	—	0		-1	0.0
2002	Mon N	1	1	.500	33	0	0	2-0	46.2	34	18	6	1	21-0	34	3.47	129	.210	.301	3-0	.000	-0		6	0.2
2003	Mon N	2	2	.500	32	0	0	0-1	37.2	42	23	11	2	18-2	35	5.26	89	.280	.365	2-0	.000	-0		-2	-0.2
Total	4	7	12	.368	87	17	0	2-2	177.1	182	108	29	7	81-2	142	5.23	87	.270	.351	29-3	.069	-1	105	-11	-1.7
SMITH, DAN Daniel Scott B 4.20.1969 St.Paul, MN BL/TL 6-5/190# d9.12																									
1992	Tex A	0	3	.000	4	2	0	0-0	14.1	18	8	1	0	8-1	5	5.02	76	.321	.400	0-0	—	0	48	-2	-0.3
1994	Tex A	1	2	.333	13	0	0	0-1	14.2	18	11	2	0	12-0	9	4.30	112	.281	.395	0-0	—	0		-1	-0.1
Total	2	1	5	.167	17	2	0	0-1	29	36	19	3	0	20-1	14	4.66	93	.300	.397	0-0	—	0	48	-3	-0.4
SMITH, DARYL Daryl Clinton B 7.29.1960 Baltimore, MD BR/TR 6-4/185# d9.18																									
1990	KC A	0	1	.000	2	1	0	0-0	6.2	5	3	0	0	4-0	6	4.05	95	.238	.333	0-0	—	0	47	0	0.0
SMITH, DAVE David Merwin B 12.17.1914 Sellers, SC D 4.1.1998 Whiteville, NC BR/TR 5-10/170# d6.16																									
1938	Phi A	2	1	.667	21	0	0	0	44.1	50	29	0	1	28	13	5.08	95	.284	.385	12-0	.000	-1		-1	-0.2
1939	Phi A	0	0	—	1	0	0	0	0	1	0	0	0	2	0	—	—	1.000	1.000	0-0	—	0		0	0.0
Total	2	2	1	.667	22	0	0	0	44.1	51	29	0	1	30	13	5.08	95	.288	.394	12-0	.000	-1		-1	-0.2
SMITH, DAVE David Stanley B 1.21.1955 Richmond, CA BR/TR 6-1/195# d4.11 C3																									
1980	†Hou N	7	5	.583	57	0	0	10-5	102.2	90	24	1	4	32-7	85	1.93	171	.237	.303	12-2	.000	-1		18	2.2
1981	†Hou N	5	3	.625	42	0	0	8-3	75	54	26	2	2	23-4	52	2.76	119	.198	.264	8-0	.250	0		5	0.6
1982	Hou N	5	4	.556	49	1	0	11-3	63.1	69	30	4	0	31-4	28	3.84	87	.285	.361	2-0	.000	-0	186	-4	-0.7
1983	Hou N	3	1	.750	42	0	0	6-1	72.2	72	32	2	0	36-4	41	3.10	110	.258	.338	5-1	.000	-1		1	-0.1
1984	Hou N	5	4	.556	53	0	0	5-3	77.1	60	22	5	1	20-3	45	2.21	150	.214	.268	4-1	.000	-0		10	1.3
1985	Hou N	9	5	.643	64	0	0	27-6	79.1	69	26	3	1	17-5	40	2.27	153	.235	.279	3-1	.000	0		10	2.0
1986	†Hou N☆	4	7	.364	54	0	0	33-6	56	39	17	5	1	22-3	46	2.73	132	.200	.283	2-0	.000	-0		7	1.4
1987	Hou N	2	3	.400	50	0	0	24-5	60	39	13	0	1	21-8	73	1.65	238	.182	.257	2-0	.500	1		15	2.3
1988	Hou N	4	5	.444	51	0	0	27-5	57.1	60	26	1	1	19-8	38	2.67	125	.268	.327	2-0	.000	-0		1	0.2
1989	Hou N	3	4	.429	52	0	0	25-4	58	49	20	1	1	19-7	31	2.64	129	.233	.299	1-0	.000	-0		5	0.9
1990	Hou N★	6	6	.500	49	0	0	23-5	60.1	45	18	4	0	20-4	50	2.39	156	.210	.277	2-0	.000	0		9	1.9
1991	Chi N	0	6	.000	35	0	0	17-6	33	39	22	6	1	19-5	16	6.00	65	.302	.396	1-0	.000	-0		-6	-1.3

Year	Tm Lg	W	L	Pct	G	GS	CG-Sho	SV-BS	IP	H	R	HR	HB	BB-IB	SO	ERA	AERA	OAV	OOB	AB-SH	AVG	PB	Sup	APR	PW
1992	Chi N	0	0	—	11	0	0	0-0	14.1	15	4	0	0	4-2	3	2.51	144	.273	.317	0-0	—	0		2	0.1
Total	13	53	53	.500	609	1	0	216-52	809.1	700	280	34	13	283-64	548	2.67	130	.234	.302	44-5	.068	-2	186	73	10.8
SMITH, DAVE David Wayne B 8.30.1957 Tomball, TX BR/TR 6-1/190# d9.18																									
1984	Cal A	0	0	—	1	0	0	0-0	1	4	2	1	0	0-0	0	18.00	22	.571	.571	0-0	—	0		-1	-0.1
1985	Cal A	0	0	—	4	0	0	0-0	5	5	4	1	0	1-0	3	7.20	57	.278	.300	0-0	—	0		-2	-0.1
Total	2	0	0	—	5	0	0	0-0	6	9	6	2	0	1-0	3	9.00	45	.360	.370	0-0	—	0		-3	-0.2
SMITH, DOUG Douglass Weldon B 5.25.1892 Millers Falls, MA D 9.18.1973 Greenfield, MA BL/TL 5-10/168# d7.10																									
1912	Bos A	0	0	—	1	0	0	0	3	4	1	0	0	0	1	3.00	113	.364	.364	0-0	—	0		0	0.0
SMITH, ED Ed d4.18																									
1884	Bal U	3	4	.429	9	8	5	0	62	86	61	2		17	13	3.48	77	.308	.348	34	.147	-4	114	-8	-1.0
SMITH, EDDIE Edgar B 12.14.1913 Mansfield, NJ D 1.2.1994 Willingboro, NJ BB/TL 5-10/174# d9.20 Mil 1944-45																									
1936	Phi A	1	1	.500	2	2	2	0	19	22	10	3	0	8	7	1.89	269	.275	.341	8-0	.125	-1	86	4	0.3
1937	Phi A	4	17	.190	38	23	14-1	5	196.2	178	100	18	4	90	79	3.94	120	.242	.327	73-2	.233	1*	59	17	1.8
1938	Phi A	3	10	.231	43	7	0	4	130.2	151	102	13	4	76	78	5.92	82	.287	.381	42-2	.286	3	89	-16	-1.1
1939	Phi A	1	0	1.000	3	0	0	0	3.2	7	4	0	0	2	3	9.82	48	.412	.474	0-0	—	0		-2	-0.3
	Chi A	9	11	.450	29	22	7-1	0	176.2	161	83	11	4	90	67	3.67	129	.247	.342	52-5	.115	-1	72	19	1.7
	Year	10	11	.476	32	22	7-1	0	180.1	168	87	11	4	92	70	3.79	125	.251	.346	52-5	.115	-1	72	18	1.4
1940	Chi A	14	9	.609	32	28	12	0	207.1	179	92	16	3	95	119	3.21	138	.228	.313	69-8	.217	2	89	25	2.7
1941	Chi A★	13	17	.433	34	33	21-1	1	263.1	243	107	13	5	114	111	3.18	129	.246	.328	88-4	.216	4	74	28	3.4
1942	Chi A☆	7	20	.259	29	28	18-2	1	215	223	112	17	4	86	78	3.98	90	.269	.341	73-3	.123	-2	61	-10	-1.2
1943	Chi A	11	11	.500	25	25	14-2	0	187.2	197	85	2	5	76	66	3.69	90	.277	.351	69-4	.159	-1	102	-4	-0.6
1946	Chi A	8	11	.421	24	21	3-1	1	145.1	135	71	9	4	60	59	2.85	120	.246	.325	45-0	.178	0	84	4	0.5
1947	Chi A	1	3	.250	15	5	0	0	33.1	40	36	1	0	24	12	7.29	50	.299	.405	6-0	.167	-0	82	-15	-1.7
	Bos A	1	3	.250	8	3	0	0	17	18	14	3	0	18	15	7.41	52	.269	.424	6-0	.167	0	167	-6	-1.1
	Year	2	6	.250	23	8	0	0	50.1	58	21	4	0	42	27	7.33	51	.289	.412	12-0	.167	-0	116	-21	-2.8
Total	10	73	113	.392	282	197	91-8	12	1595.2	1554	816	106	33	739	694	3.82	108	.256	.340	531-28	.188	5	77	44	4.4
SMITH, EDGAR Edgar Eugene B 6.12.1862 Providence, RI D 11.3.1892 Providence, RI BR/TR 5-10/160# d5.25 ▲																									
1883	Phi N	0	1	.000	1	1	0	0	7	18	17	0		3	2	15.43	20	.409	.447	4	.750	1	69	-9	-0.7
1884	Was AA	0	2	.000	3	2	2	0	22	27	23	0	1	5	4	4.91	62	.276	.317	57	.088	-1*	60	-5	-0.4
1885	Pro N	1	0	1.000	1	1	1	0	9	9	3	0		0	1	1.00	269	.273	.273	4	.250	0	84	1	0.1
1890	Cle N	1	4	.200	6	6	5	0	44	42	24	1	1	10	11	4.30	84	.243	.288	24	.292	2*	82	-1	0.1
Total	4	2	7	.222	11	10	8	0	82	96	67	1	2	18	18	5.05	65	.276	.315	89	.180	2	78	-14	-0.9
SMITH, ELMER Elmer Ellsworth B 3.23.1868 Pittsburgh, PA D 11.3.1945 Pittsburgh, PA BL/TL 5-11/178# d9.10 ▲																									
1886	Cin AA	4	4	.500	9	9	8	0	72.2	57	54	1	3	44	40	3.72	95	.211	.328	28	.286	4	125	-5	-0.2
1887	Cin AA	34	17	.667	52	52	49-3	0	447.1	400	224	5	9	126	176	**2.94**	**148**	**.230**	**.286**	186	.253	5	89	71	6.3
1888	Cin AA	22	17	.564	40	40	37-5	0	348.1	309	167	1	19	89	154	2.74	116	.229	.286	129	.225	4	93	19	2.0
1889	Cin AA	9	12	.429	29	22	16	0	203	253	171	11	7	101	104	4.88	80	.296	.375	83	.277	6	102	-21	-1.3
1892	Pit N	6	7	.462	17	13	12-1	0	134	140	94	2	1	58	51	3.63	91	.258	.331	511	.274	6*	128	-5	0.0
1894	Pit N	0	0	—	1	0	0	0	4	6	2	0	1	1	0	4.50	117	.333	.400	490-10	.357	0*		1	0.0
1898	Cin N	0	0	—	1	0	0	0	1	2	2	0	0	3	0	18.00	21	.400	.625	486-6	.342	0*		-1	-0.1
Total	7	75	57	.568	149	136	122-9	0	1210.1	1167	714	20	40	422	525	3.35	113	.244	.311	1913-16	.307	25	98	59	6.7
SMITH, FRANK Frank Elmer "Nig" or "Piano Mover" (b: Frank Elmer Schmidt) B 10.28.1879 Pittsburgh, PA D 11.3.1952 Pittsburgh, PA BR/TR 5-10.5/194# d4.22																									
1904	Chi A	16	9	.640	26	23	22-4	0	202.1	157	62	0	12	58	107	2.09	117	.215	.284	72-3	.250	4	115	9	1.6
1905	Chi A	19	13	.594	39	31	27-4	0	291.2	215	97	0	8	107	171	2.13	116	.208	.287	106-1	.226	7*	133	12	2.2
1906	Chi A	5	5	.500	20	13	8-1	1	122	124	58	3	5	37	53	3.39	75	.267	.327	41-2	.293	5	105	-10	-0.2
1907	Chi A	23	10	.697	41	37	29-3	0	310	280	105	3	2	111	139	2.47	97	.243	.311	92-6	.196	5*	119	2	0.9
1908	Chi A	16	17	.485	41	35	24-3	1	297.2	213	92	2	2	73	129	2.03	114	.203	.256	106-6	.189	2*	106	9	1.5
1909	Chi A	25	17	.595	**51**	**40**	**37**-7	1	**365**	278	104	1	6	70	**177**	1.80	130	.214	.257	127-5	.173	6*	90	23	4.1
1910	Chi A	4	9	.308	19	15	9-3	0	128.2	91	43	1	2	40	50	2.03	118	.204	.272	43-2	.186	2*	67	6	1.0
	Bos A	1	2	.333	4	3	2	0	28	22	19	0	1	11	8	4.82	53	.234	.321	9-1	.111	-0	79	-6	-0.6
	Year	5	11	.313	23	18	11-3	0	156.2	113	22	1	3	51	58	2.53	96	.209	.281	52-3	.173	2	69	-1	0.4
1911	Bos A	0	0	—	1	1	0	0	2.1	6	4	0	0	3	1	15.43	21	.500	.600	0-0	—	0	308	-2	-0.1
	Cin N	10	14	.417	34	18	10	1	176.1	198	112	1	3	55	67	3.98	83	.289	.345	56-5	.214	3*	119	-16	-1.4
1912	Cin N	1	1	.500	7	3	1	0	22.2	34	25	1	0	15	5	6.35	53	.370	.458	6-0	.000	-0	167	-9	-0.7
1914	Bal F	10	8	.556	39	22	9-1	2	174.2	180	86	8	0	47	83	2.99	101	.259	.306	59-3	.203	0*	107	-3	-0.2
1915	Bal F	4	4	.500	17	9	2	0	88.2	108	53	5	0	31	37	4.67	61	.312	.369	29-1	.172	0	100	-15	-1.2
	Bro F	5	2	.714	15	5	4-1	0	63	69	31	2	0	18	24	3.14	87	.290	.340	20-1	.200	0	82	-4	-0.3
	Year	9	6	.600	32	14	6-1	0	151.2	177	34	7	0	49	61	4.04	70	.303	.357	49-2	.184	1	94	-18	-1.5
Total	11	139	111	.556	354	255	184-27	6	2273	1975	891	27	41	676	1051	2.59	99	.237	.297	766-36	.204	35	109	-4	6.6
SMITH, FRANK Frank Thomas B 4.4.1928 Pierrepont Manor, NY BR/TR 6-3/200# d4.18																									
1950	Cin N	2	7	.222	38	4	0	3	90.2	73	43	12	8	39	55	3.87	109	.216	.312	21-0	.095	-2	94	4	0.2
1951	Cin N	5	5	.500	50	0	0	11	76	65	33	7	4	22	34	3.20	128	.230	.295	10-1	.000	-1		7	0.9
1952	Cin N	12	11	.522	53	2	1	7	122.1	109	56	13	7	41	77	3.75	101	.242	.315	29-1	.172	0	83	0	-0.1
1953	Cin N	8	1	.889	50	1	0	2	83.2	89	64	15	3	25	42	5.49	79	.272	.330	13-2	.154	-1	144	-13	-1.3
1954	Cin N	5	8	.385	50	0	0	20	81	60	29	15	3	29	51	2.67	157	.211	.286	10-2	.100	1		12	2.6
1955	StL N	3	1	.750	28	0	0	1	39	27	18	3	5	23-3	17	3.23	126	.205	.337	4-1	.000	-1		2	0.2
1956	Cin N	0	0	—	2	0	0	0	3	3	4	2	0	2-0	1	12.00	33	.300	.385	0-0	—	0		-2	-0.1
Total	7	35	33	.515	271	7	1	44	495.2	426	247	67	30	181-3	277	3.81	107	.234	.311	87-7	.115	-3	99	10	2.4
SMITH, FRED Frederick B 11.24.1878 New Diggings, WI D 2.4.1964 Los Angeles, CA BL/TR 6/186# d6.14																									
1907	Cin N	2	7	.222	18	9	5	1	85.1	90	44	3	4	24	19	2.85	91	.274	.331	28-1	.107	-2	88	-4	-0.6
SMITH, FRED Frederick C. B 3.25.1863 Greene, NY D 1.9.1941 Syracuse, NY BL/TR 5-11/156# d4.18																									
1890	Tol AA	19	13	.594	35	34	31-2	0	286	273	155	13	13	90	116	3.27	121	.244	.307	126	.167	-2*	88	21	1.8
SMITH, GEORGE George Allen "Columbia George" B 5.31.1892 Byram, CT D 1.7.1965 Greenwich, CT BR/TR 6-2/163# d8.9																									
1916	NY N	3	0	1.000	9	1	0	0	20.2	14	8	0	1	6	9	2.61	93	.197	.269	2-1	.000	-0	184	-1	-0.1
1917	NY N	0	3	.000	14	1	1	0	38	38	13	1	1	11	16	2.84	90	.270	.327	9-0	.000	-1	30	0	-0.2
1918	Cin N	2	3	.400	10	6	4-1	0	55.1	71	36	3	0	11	19	4.07	66	.329	.361	17-1	.000	-2	76	-10	-1.1
	NY N	2	3	.400	5	2	1	0	26.2	26	12	0	1	6	4	4.05	65	.255	.303	8-1	.250	0	58	-3	-0.6
	Bro N	4	1	.800	8	5	4	0	50	43	14	0	2	5	18	2.34	119	.249	.278	15-1	.200	0	81	4	0.5
	Year	8	7	.533	23	13	9-1	0	132	140	17	3	3	22	41	3.41	79	.285	.320	40-3	.125	-2	75	-10	-1.2
1919	NY N	0	2	.000	3	2	0	0	11	18	8	1	0	4	0	5.73	49	.383	.431	3-0	.000	-0	113	-3	-0.6
	Phi N	5	11	.313	31	19	11-1	0	184.2	194	94	7	3	46	42	3.22	100	.278	.326	60-2	.133	-3	92	-5	-0.8
	Year	5	13	.278	34	21	11-1	0	195.2	212	98	8	3	50	42	3.36	95	.285	.332	63-2	.127	-4	94	-7	-1.4
1920	Phi N	13	18	.419	43	28	10-1	2	250.2	265	115	10	6	51	51	3.45	99	.283	.324	72-8	.097	-6	77	2	-0.4
1921	Phi N	4	20	.167	39	28	12-1	1	221.1	303	166	12	3	52	45	4.76	89	.335	.373	71-1	.056	-8	69	-14	-2.1
1922	Phi N	5	14	.263	42	16	6-1	0	194	250	124	16	6	35	44	4.78	98	.316	.350	66-0	.076	-7	63	1	-0.7
1923	Bro N	3	6	.333	25	7	3	1	91	99	53	4	3	28	15	3.66	106	.278	.336	26-1	.192	-1	103	0	-0.2
Total	8	41	81	.336	229	115	52-5	4	1143.1	1321	643	54	26	255	263	3.89	94	.298	.340	349-16	.097	-29	78	-29	-6.3
SMITH, HEINIE George Henry B 10.24.1871 Pittsburgh, PA D 6.25.1939 Buffalo, NY BR/TR 5-9.5/160# d9.8.1897 M1 ▲																									
1901	NY N	0	1	.000	2	1	1	0	13.1	24	13	0	3	5	5	8.10	41	.387	.457	29-1	.207	0*	86	-6	-0.3
SMITH, GEORGE George Shelby B 10.27.1901 Louisville, KY D 5.26.1981 Richmond, VA BR/TR 6-1/175# d4.21																									
1926	Det A	1	2	.333	23	1	0	0	44	55	37	3	2	33	15	6.95	58	.318	.433	5-1	.000	-0	41	-12	-0.8
1927	Det A	4	1	.800	29	0	0	0	71.1	62	38	3	2	50	32	3.91	108	.240	.368	19-1	.368	3		3	0.4

Year	Tm Lg	W	L	Pct	G	GS	CG-Sho	SV-BS	IP	H	R	HR	HB	BB-IB	SO	ERA	AERA	OAV	OOB	AB-SH	AVG	PB	Sup	APR	PW
1928	Det A	1	1	.500	39	2	0	3	106	103	55	3	0	50	54	4.42	93	.263	.346	27-1	.111	-2	103	0	-0.3
1929	Det A	3	2	.600	14	2	1	0	35.2	42	33	1	0	36	13	5.80	74	.307	.451	12-0	.417	2	128	-8	-0.7
1930	Bos A	1	2	.333	27	2	0	0	73.2	92	62	7	1	49	21	6.60	70	.317	.418	24-0	.333	2*	103	-16	-0.6
Total	5	10	8	.556	132	7	1	3	330.2	354	225	17	5	218	135	5.28	81	.283	.392	87-3	.264	4	102	-33	-2.0
SMITH, HAL Harold Laverne B 6.30.1902 Creston, IA D 9.27.1992 Ft.Lauderdale, FL BR/TR 6-3/195# d9.14																									
1932	Pit N	1	0	1.000	2	1	1-1	0	12	9	1	0	0	2	4	0.75	508	.209	.244	3-1	.000	-0	154	4	0.3
1933	Pit N	8	7	.533	28	19	8-2	1	145	149	66	5	5	31	40	2.86	116	.261	.305	47-2	.128	-2	107	4	0.1
1934	Pit N	3	4	.429	20	5	1	0	50	72	44	3	4	18	15	7.20	57	.343	.405	17-0	.059	-2	109	-16	-2.1
1935	Pit N	0	0	—	1	0	0	0	3	2	1	0	0	1	0	3.00	137	.200	.273	0-0	—	0		0	0.0
Total	4	12	11	.522	51	25	10-3	1	210	232	112	8	9	52	59	3.77	94	.279	.328	67-3	.104	-4	108	-8	-1.7
SMITH, HARRY Harrison Morton B 8.15.1889 Union, NE D 7.26.1964 Dunbar, NE BR/TR 5-9/160# d10.6																									
1912	Chi A	1	0	1.000	1	1	0	0	5	6	1	0	0	0	1	1.80	178	.333	.333	1-1	.000	-0	208	1	0.2
SMITH, JACK Jack Hatfield B 11.15.1935 Pikeville, KY BR/TR 6/185# d9.10																									
1962	LA N	0	0	—	8	0	0	1	10	10	6	0	0	4-1	7	4.50	81	.263	.326	1-0	.000	-0		-1	-0.1
1963	LA N	0	0	—	4	0	0	0	8.1	10	7	2	2	2-0	5	7.56	40	.303	.368	2-0	.000	-0		-4	-0.2
1964	Mil N	2	2	.500	22	0	0	0	31	28	15	3	0	11-5	19	3.77	93	.237	.300	3-0	.333	0		-1	0.0
Total	3	2	2	.500	34	0	0	1	49.1	48	28	5	2	17-6	31	4.56	76	.254	.318	6-0	.167	-0		-6	-0.3
SMITH, JAKE Jacob (b: Jacob Schmidt) B 6.10.1887 Dravosburg, PA D 11.7.1948 E.McKeesport, PA BB/TL 6-5/200# d10.3																									
1911	Phi N	0	0	—	2	0	0	0	5	3	0	0	0	2	1	0.00	—	.176	.263	3-0	.000	-0		2	0.1
SMITH, PHENOMENAL John Francis (b: John Francis Gammon) B 12.12.1864 Philadelphia, PA D 4.3.1952 Manchester, NH BL/TL 5-6.5/161# d8.14																									
1884	Phi AA	0	1	.000	1	1	1	0	9	14	6	0	0	1	3	4.00	85	.368	.385	4	.250	-0	89	-1	-0.1
	Pit AA	0	1	.000	1	1	1	0	8	11	10	0	1	2	4	9.00	37	.306	.359	4	.000	-1	91	-4	-0.4
	Year	0	2	.000	2	2	2	0	17	25	15	0	1	3	7	6.35	53	.338	.372	8	.125	-1	90	-4	-0.5
1885	Bro AA	0	1	.000	1	1	1	0	8	12	18	0	1	6	2	12.38	27	.300	.404	3	.333	0	90	-8	-0.6
	Phi AA	0	1	.000	1	1	0	0	4	7	9	0	1	4	7	9.00	38	.368	.500	2	.000	-0	189	-3	-0.4
	Year	0	2	.000	2	2	1	0	12	19	20	0	2	10	9	11.25	30	.322	.437	5	.200	-0	141	-11	-1.0
1886	Det N	1	1	.500	3	3	3	0	25	16	9	0		8	15	2.16	154	.174	.240	9	.111	-1	37	3	0.1
1887	Bal AA	25	30	.455	58	55	54-1	0	491.1	526	369	7	14	176	206	3.79	108	.261	.325	205	.234	8*	95	8	1.3
1888	Bal AA	14	19	.424	35	32	31	0	292	249	170	5	24	137	152	3.61	83	.222	.320	109	.248	8	94	-18	-1.1
	Phi AA	2	1	.667	3	3	3	0	22	21	15	0	0	10	19	2.86	104	.241	.320	9	.333	1	123	0	0.1
	Year	16	20	.444	38	35	34	0	314	270	21	5	24	147	171	3.55	84	.224	.320	118	.254	9	97	-9	-1.0
1889	Phi AA	2	3	.400	5	5	5	0	43	53	31	2	3	25	12	4.40	86	.294	.389	16	.188	0	62	-2	-0.2
1890	Phi N	8	12	.400	24	20	19-1	0	204	209	125	5	8	89	81	4.28	86	.257	.336	86	.279	4*	93	-5	-0.1
	Pit N	1	3	.250	5	5	5	0	44	39	25	0	1	13	15	3.07	108	.229	.288	17	.412	2	96	1	0.3
	Year	9	15	.375	29	25	24-1	0	248	248	30	5	9	102	96	4.06	89	.252	.328	103	.301	6	93	-6	0.2
1891	Phi N	1	1	.500	3	2	0	0	19	20	15	1	0	8	3	4.26	80	.260	.329	8	.375	1	105	-2	-0.1
Total	8	54	74	.422	140	129	123-2	0	1169.1	1177	802	20	53	479	519	3.89	93	.251	.327	472	.250	23	93	-31	-1.2
SMITH, CHICK John William (b: Jan Smadt) B 12.2.1892 Dayton, KY D 10.11.1935 Dayton, KY BL/TL 5-8/165# d4.12																									
1913	Cin N	0	1	.000	5	1	0	0	17.2	15	8	1	0	11	11	3.57	91	.238	.351	4-1	.000	-1	23	0	-0.1
SMITH, LEE Lee Arthur B 12.4.1957 Shreveport, LA BR/TR 6-6/225# d9.1																									
1980	Chi N	2	0	1.000	18	0	0	0-0	21.2	21	9	0	0	14-5	17	2.91	135	.259	.365	0-0	—	0		2	0.2
1981	Chi N	3	6	.333	40	1	0	1-3	66.2	57	31	2	1	31-8	50	3.51	105	.239	.327	9-1	.000	-1	24	1	0.0
1982	Chi N	2	5	.286	72	5	0	17-1	117	105	38	5	3	37-5	99	2.69	139	.245	.306	16-1	.063	-0	90	14	1.1
1983	Chi N★	4	10	.286	66	0	0	**29-4**	103.1	70	23	5	1	41-14	91	1.65	230	.194	.277	9-1	.111	-0		23	4.2
1984	†Chi N	9	7	.563	69	0	0	33-9	101	98	42	6	0	35-7	86	3.65	107	.255	.314	13-1	.077	-1		4	0.7
1985	Chi N	7	4	.636	65	0	0	33-9	97.2	87	35	9	1	32-6	112	3.04	132	.242	.305	6-0	.000	-0		10	1.7
1986	Chi N	9	9	.500	66	0	0	31-8	90.1	69	32	7	0	42-11	93	3.09	131	.215	.303	5-0	.000	-1		9	1.9
1987	Chi N★	4	10	.286	62	0	0	36-12	83.2	84	30	4	0	32-5	96	3.12	137	.259	.326	2-0	.000	-0*		11	2.2
1988	†Bos A	4	5	.444	64	0	0	29-8	83.2	72	34	7	1	37-6	96	2.80	147	.225	.306	0-0	—	0		9	1.5
1989	Bos A	6	1	.857	64	0	0	25-5	70.2	53	30	6	0	33-6	96	3.57	115	.209	.299	0-0	—	0		5	0.7
1990	Bos A	2	1	.667	11	0	0	4-1	14.1	13	4	0	0	9-2	17	1.88	217	.236	.344	0-0	—	0		3	0.7
	StL N	3	4	.429	53	0	0	27-5	68.2	58	20	3	0	20-5	70	2.10	182	.227	.281	2-0	.000	-0		12	2.0
1991	StL N☆	6	3	.667	67	0	0	**47-6**	73	70	19	5	0	13-5	67	2.34	159	.249	.281	0-0	—	0		12	2.5
1992	StL N☆	4	9	.308	70	0	0	**43-8**	75	62	28	4	0	26-4	60	3.12	109	.221	.286	0-0	—	0		2	0.5
1993	StL N☆	2	4	.333	55	0	0	43-7	50	49	25	11	0	9-1	49	4.50	88	.251	.282	2-0	.000	-0		-2	-0.4
	NY A	0	0	—	8	0	0	3-0	8	4	0	0	0	5-1	11	0.00	—	.148	.273	0-0	—	0		4	0.2
1994	Bal A★	1	4	.200	41	0	0	**33-6**	38.1	34	16	6	0	11-1	42	3.29	153	.239	.290	0-0	—	0		6	1.2
1995	Cal A☆	0	5	.000	52	0	0	37-4	49.1	42	19	3	1	25-4	43	3.47	136	.237	.330	0-0	—	0		7	1.4
1996	Cal A	0	0	—	11	0	0	0-2	11	8	4	0	0	3-0	6	2.45	204	.205	.250	0-0	—	0		3	0.1
	Cin N	3	4	.429	43	0	0	2-4	44.1	49	20	4	1	23-4	35	4.06	104	.277	.363	0-0	—	0		2	0.3
1997	Mon N	0	1	.000	25	0	0	5-1	21.2	28	16	2	1	8-0	15	5.82	72	.308	.370	0-0	—	0		-4	-0.3
Total	18	71	92	.436	1022	6	0	478-103	1289.1	1133	475	89	10	486-100	1251	3.03	132	.237	.306	64-4	.047	-4	75	133	22.4
SMITH, ROY Le Roy Purdy B 9.6.1961 Mt.Vernon, NY BR/TR 6-3/200# d6.23																									
1984	Cle A	5	5	.500	22	14	0	0-0	86.1	91	49	14	1	40-5	55	4.59	89	.270	.346	0-0	—	0	109	-5	-0.6
1985	Cle A	1	4	.200	12	11	1	0-0	62.1	84	40	8	1	17-0	28	5.34	77	.321	.359	0-0	—	0	124	-8	-0.6
1986	Min A	0	2	.000	5	0	0	0-1	10.1	13	8	1	1	5-1	8	6.97	62	.295	.380	0-0	—	0		-3	-0.4
1987	Min A	1	0	1.000	7	1	0	0-1	16.1	20	10	3	2	6-0	8	4.96	93	.290	.359	0-0	—	0	276	-1	0.0
1988	Min A	3	0	1.000	9	4	0	0-0	37	29	12	3	1	12-1	17	2.68	152	.210	.276	0-0	—	0	134	6	0.4
1989	Min A	10	6	.625	32	26	2	1-0	172.1	180	82	22	5	51-5	92	3.92	106	.269	.324	0-0	—	0	125	4	0.2
1990	Min A	5	10	.333	32	23	1-1	0-0	153.1	191	91	20	0	47-4	87	4.81	87	.313	.356	0-0	—	0	105	-11	-1.1
1991	Bal A	5	4	.556	17	14	0	0-0	80.1	99	52	9	1	24-0	25	5.60	71	.311	.358	0-0	—	0	111	-14	-1.4
Total	8	30	31	.492	136	93	4-1	1-2	618.1	707	344	80	12	202-16	320	4.60	90	.289	.343	0-0	—	0	117	-32	-3.5
SMITH, MARK Mark Christopher B 11.23.1955 Arlington, VA BR/TR 6-2/215# d8.12																									
1983	Oak A	1	0	1.000	8	1	0	0-0	14.2	24	11	0	1	6-1	10	6.75	57	.387	.449	0-0	—	0	47	-4	-0.3
SMITH, MIKE Michael Anthony B 2.23.1961 Jackson, MS BR/TR 6-1/195# d4.6																									
1984	Cin N	1	0	1.000	8	0	0	0-0	10.1	12	6	1	0	5-0	7	5.23	72	.286	.362	0-1	—	0		-1	-0.1
1985	Cin N	0	0	—	2	0	0	0-0	3.1	2	2	2	0	1-0	2	5.40	70	.167	.231	0-0	—	0		0	0.0
1986	Cin N	0	0	—	2	1	0	0-0	3.1	7	5	0	0	1-0	1	13.50	29	.412	.444	0-0	—	0	207	-3	-0.2
1988	Mon N	0	0	—	5	0	0	1-0	8.2	6	3	0	0	5-0	4	3.12	116	.207	.324	2-0	.000	-0		1	0.0
1989	Pit N	0	1	.000	16	0	0	0-0	24	28	12	1	0	10-1	12	3.75	90	.301	.362	3-0	.000	-0		-1	-0.1
Total	5	1	1	.500	33	1	0	1-0	49.2	55	28	4	0	22-1	26	4.71	75	.285	.355	5-1	.000	-1	207	-4	-0.4
SMITH, MIKE Michael Anthony B 10.31.1963 San Antonio, TX BR/TR 6-3/180# d6.30																									
1989	Bal A	2	0	1.000	13	1	0	0-0	20	25	19	3	0	14-2	12	7.65	50	.313	.411	0-0	—	0	143	-9	-0.8
1990	Bal A	0	0	—	2	0	0	0-0	3	4	4	2	0	1-0	2	12.00	32	.308	.357	0-0	—	0		-3	-0.1
Total	2	2	0	1.000	15	1	0	0-0	23	29	23	5	0	15-2	14	8.22	46	.312	.404	0-0	—	0	143	-12	-0.9
SMITH, MIKE Michael Anthony B 9.19.1977 Norwood, MA BR/TR 5-11/195# d4.26																									
2002	Tor A	0	3	.000	14	6	0	0-0	35.1	43	28	3	7	20-0	16	6.62	70	.301	.409	0-0	—	0	84	-8	-0.5
SMITH, PETE Peter John B 2.27.1966 Abington, MA BR/TR 6-2/200# d9.8																									
1987	Atl N	1	2	.333	6	6	0	0-0	31.2	39	21	3	0	14-0	11	4.83	90	.307	.371	11-1	.091	-1	90	-2	-0.3
1988	Atl N	7	15	.318	32	32	5-3	0-0	195.1	183	89	15	1	88-3	124	3.69	100	.250	.330	53-8	.113	-1	73	0	-0.3
1989	Atl N	5	14	.263	28	27	1	0-0	142	144	83	13	0	57-2	115	4.75	77	.263	.330	41-5	.098	-0*	74	-16	-2.0
1990	Atl N	5	6	.455	13	13	3	0-0	77	77	45	11	0	24-2	56	4.79	84	.260	.313	23-4	.087	-1	105	-6	-0.9

Year	Tm Lg	W	L	Pct	G	GS	CG-Sho	SV-BS	IP	H	R	HR	HB	BB-IB	SO	ERA	AERA	OAV	OOB	AB-SH	AVG	PB	Sup	APR	PW
1991	Atl N	1	3	.250	14	10	0	0-0	48	48	33	5	0	22-3	29	5.06	77	.262	.335	12-1	.167	0	109	-7	-0.5
1992	†Atl N	7	0	1.000	12	11	2-1	0-0	79	63	19	3	0	28-2	43	2.05	179	.217	.285	26-3	.038	-1	128	14	1.1
1993	Atl N	4	8	.333	20	14	0	0-0	90.2	92	45	15	2	36-3	53	4.37	92	.270	.339	27-3	.222	1	106	-2	-0.1
1994	NY N	4	10	.286	21	21	1	0-0	131.1	145	83	25	2	42-4	62	5.55	75	.285	.338	37-6	.135	0	85	-17	-1.5
1995	Cin N	1	2	.333	11	2	0	0-0	24.1	30	19	8	1	7-1	14	6.66	62	.319	.362	3-0	.000	0	208	-7	-0.7
1997	SD N	7	6	.538	37	15	0	1-0	118	120	66	16	1	52-2	68	4.81	81	.267	.343	30-6	.167	1*	104	-11	-0.9
1998	SD N	3	2	.600	10	8	0	0-0	43.1	45	23	5	3	18-1	36	4.78	82	.266	.344	14-1	.071	-0*	156	-4	-0.4
	Bal A	2	3	.400	27	4	0	0-1	45	57	31	7	0	16-1	29	6.20	74	.311	.363	2-0	.000	-0	87	-8	-0.7
Total	11	47	71	.398	231	163	12-4	1-1	1025.2	1043	557	126	10	404-24	640	4.55	86	.266	.333	279-38	.118	-2	95	-66	-7.2
SMITH, PETE Peter Luke B 3.19.1940 Natick, MA BR/TR 6-2/190# d9.13 Mil 1963																									
1962	Bos A	0	1	.000	1	1	0	0	3.2	7	8	3	0	2-0	1	19.64	21	.438	.474	1-0	.000	-0	130	-6	-0.8
1963	Bos A	0	0	—	6	1	0	0	15	11	6	2	0	6-2	6	3.60	105	.212	.293	2-0	.000	-0	117	1	0.0
Total	2	0	1	.000	7	2	0	0	18.2	18	14	5	0	8-2	7	6.75	57	.265	.338	3-0	.000	-0	127	-5	-0.8
SMITH, BRIAN Randall Brian B 7.19.1972 Salisbury, NC BR/TR 5-11/185# d9.11																									
2000	Pit N	0	0	—	3	0	0	0-0	4.1	6	5	1	0	2-0	3	10.38	44	.375	.421	0-0	—	0		-3	-0.1
SMITH, REX Rex (b: Henry W. Schmidt) B 1864 Louisville, KY D 6.21.1895 Louisville, KY d7.11																									
1886	Phi AA	0	1	.000	1	1	1	0	9	15	13	0	0	5	4	7.00	50	.385	.455	4	.000	-1	68	-4	-0.3
SMITH, ED Rhesa Edward B 2.21.1879 Mentone, IN D 3.20.1955 Tarpon Springs, FL BR/TR 5-11/170# d4.27																									
1906	StL A	8	11	.421	19	18	13	0	154.2	153	90	3	8	53	45	3.72	69	.261	.331	54-2	.204	2	115	-19	-1.9
SMITH, BUD Robert Allan B 10.23.1979 Torrance, CA BL/TL 6/170# d6.10																									
2001	†StL N	6	3	.667	16	14	1-1	0-0	84.2	79	40	12	1	24-5	59	3.83	112	.250	.304	25-2	.160	-0	114	4	0.4
2002	StL N	1	5	.167	11	10	0	0-0	48	67	39	4	3	22-2	22	6.94	57	.338	.405	14-3	.214	1	93	-16	-1.6
Total	2	7	8	.467	27	24	1-1	0-0	132.2	146	79	16	4	46-7	81	4.95	84	.284	.344	39-5	.179	1	106	-12	-1.2
SMITH, BOB Robert Ashley (a.k.a. Robert M. Brown In 1914) B 7.20.1890 Woodbury, VT D 12.27.1965 West Los Angeles, CA BR/TR 5-11/160# d4.19																									
1913	Chi A	0	0	—	1	0	0	0	2	3	3	0	0	3	1	13.50	22	.273	.429	0-0	—	0		-2	-0.1
1914	Buf F	0	0	—	15	1	0	3	36.2	39	16	3	2	16	13	3.44	86	.281	.363	9-0	.222	0	70	-1	0.0
1915	Buf F	0	0	—	1	0	0	0	1	1	2	0	1	2	0	18.00	16	.333	.667	0-0	—	0		-1	-0.1
Total	3	0	0	—	17	1	0	3	39.2	43	21	3	3	21	14	4.31	69	.281	.379	9-0	.222	0	70	-4	-0.2
SMITH, BOB Robert Eldridge B 4.22.1895 Rogersville, TN D 7.19.1987 Waycross, GA BR/TR 5-10/175# d4.19.1923 ▲																									
1925	Bos N	5	3	.625	13	10	6	0	92.2	110	51	6	0	36	19	4.47	90	.304	.367	174-2	.282	3*	97	-3	0.0
1926	Bos N	10	13	.435	33	23	14-4	1	201.1	199	91	10	0	75	44	3.75	94	.269	.336	84-1	.298	7*	95	-1	0.7
1927	Bos N	10	18	.357	41	31	16-1	3	260.2	297	132	9	2	75	81	3.76	99	.301	.351	109-1	.248	4*	106	-3	0.3
1928	Bos N	13	17	.433	38	26	14	2	244.1	274	138	11	2	74	59	3.87	101	.289	.342	92-6	.250	3*	96	-4	0.0
1929	Bos N	11	17	.393	34	29	19-1	3	231	256	135	20	1	71	65	4.68	100	.285	.338	99-3	.172	-1*	78	1	0.1
1930	Bos N	10	14	.417	38	24	14-2	5	219.2	247	115	25	3	85	84	4.26	116	.290	.357	81-3	.235	-1*	61	17	1.6
1931	Chi N	15	12	.556	36	29	18-2	2	240.1	239	101	10	1	62	63	3.22	120	.256	.303	87-5	.218	2	105	16	1.9
1932	†Chi N	4	3	.571	34	11	4-1	2	119	148	64	4	3	36	35	4.61	82	.303	.355	42-0	.238	2*	126	-8	-0.2
1933	Cin N	4	4	.500	16	6	4	0	73.2	75	27	3	0	11	18	2.20	154	.260	.287	25-1	.200	0*	78	8	0.9
	Bos N	4	3	.571	14	4	3-1	1	58.2	68	24	3	0	7	16	3.22	95	.296	.316	20-0	.200	1	88	-1	0.0
	Year	8	7	.533	30	10	7-1	1	132.1	143	27	6	0	18	34	2.65	123	.276	.300	45-1	.200	1	82	6	0.9
1934	Bos N	6	9	.400	39	5	3	5	121.2	133	69	9	0	36	26	4.66	82	.277	.328	36-2	.250	1*	99	-10	-1.1
1935	Bos N	8	18	.308	46	20	8-2	5	203.1	232	105	13	3	61	58	3.94	96	.285	.337	63-6	.270	2*	85	-4	-0.3
1936	Bos N	6	7	.462	35	11	5-2	8	136	142	65	3	1	35	36	3.77	102	.264	.311	45-2	.222	0	80	1	0.2
1937	Bos N	0	1	.000	18	0	0	3	44	52	22	6	2	6	14	4.09	88	.295	.326	10-0	.200	0*		-2	-0.1
Total	13	106	139	.433	435	229	128-16	40	2246.1	2472	1139	132	18	670	618	3.94	100	.283	.335	967-32	.244	23	91	7	4.0
SMITH, BOB Robert Gilchrist B 2.1.1931 Woodsville, NH BR/TL 6-1.5/190# d4.29																									
1955	Bos A	0	0	—	1	0	0	0	1.2	1	0	0	0	1-0	1	0.00	—	.200	.333	0-0	—	0		1	0.0
1957	StL N	0	0	—	6	0	0	1	9.2	12	10	0	1	6-1	11	4.66	85	.267	.365	2-0	.000	-0		-3	-0.2
	Pit N	2	4	.333	20	4	2	0	55	48	22	3	1	25-3	35	3.11	122	.229	.314	13-1	.077	-1	81	4	0.3
	Year	2	4	.333	26	4	2	1	64.2	60	26	3	2	31-4	46	3.34	114	.235	.323	15-1	.067	-1	81	1	0.1
1958	Pit N	2	2	.500	35	4	0	1	61	61	39	6	2	31-7	24	4.43	87	.262	.352	11-0	.091	-1	110	-6	-0.4
1959	Pit N	0	0	—	20	0	0	0	28.1	32	16	1	0	17-0	12	3.49	111	.291	.383	2-0	.000	-0		0	-0.1
	Det A	0	3	.000	9	0	0	0	11	20	15	5	0	3-1	10	8.18	50	.417	.451	1-0	.000	-0		-6	-1.2
Total	4	4	9	.308	91	8	2	2	166.2	174	102	15	4	83-12	93	4.05	95	.267	.353	29-1	.069	-2	95	-10	-1.6
SMITH, BOB Robert Walkup "Riverboat" B 5.13.1927 Clarence, MO D 6.23.2003 Clarence, MO BR/TL 6/185# d4.22																									
1958	Bos A	4	3	.571	17	7	1	0	66.2	61	32	4	0	45-2	43	3.78	106	.248	.362	19-1	.105	-1	109	2	0.1
1959	Chi N	0	0	—	1	0	0	0	0.2	5	6	0	0	2-1	0	81.00	5	.833	.875	0-0	—	0		-5	-0.2
	Cle A	0	1	.000	12	3	0	0	29.1	31	19	2	0	12-0	17	5.22	71	.282	.341	6-0	.000	-1	112	-5	-0.3
Total	2	4	4	.500	30	10	1	0	96.2	97	57	6	0	59-3	60	4.75	82	.268	.365	25-1	.080	-2	110	-8	-0.4
SMITH, RUFUS Rufus Frazier "Shirt" B 1.24.1905 Guilford College, NC D 8.21.1984 Aiken, SC BR/TL 5-8/165# d10.2																									
1927	Det A	0	0	—	1	1	0	0	8	8	4	0	1	3	2	3.38	125	.242	.324	3-0	.000	-1	99	1	0.0
SMITH, SHERRY Sherrod Malone B 2.18.1891 Monticello, GA D 9.12.1949 Reidsville, GA BR/TL 6-1/170# d5.11 Mil 1918																									
1911	Pit N	0	0	—	1	0	0	0	0.2	4	5	0	0	1	0	54.00	6	.667	.714	0-0	—	0		-4	-0.2
1912	Pit N	0	0	—	3	0	0	1	4	6	3	0	0	1	3	6.75	48	.600	.636	0-0	—	0		-1	-0.1
1915	Bro N	14	8	.636	29	20	11-2	2	173.2	169	71	3	5	42	52	2.59	107	.264	.315	57-1	.246	3	74	2	0.6
1916	†Bro N	14	10	.583	36	25	15-4	1	219	193	76	5	3	45	67	2.34	114	.239	.282	77-3	.273	5*	121	9	1.7
1917	Bro N	12	12	.500	38	23	15	3	211.1	210	103	5	2	51	58	3.32	84	.265	.311	77-1	.195	2*	95	-14	-1.1
1919	Bro N	7	12	.368	30	19	13-2	1	173	181	63	3	4	29	40	2.24	133	.278	.313	54-4	.148	-2	103	11	1.2
1920	†Bro N	11	9	.550	33	13	6-2	3	136.1	134	42	1	2	27	33	1.85	173	.264	.304	43-0	.233	2	60	18	3.2
1921	Bro N	7	11	.389	35	17	9	4	175.1	232	95	4	1	34	36	3.90	100	.319	.350	57-1	.228	1	83	-1	0.2
1922	Bro N	4	8	.333	28	8	3-1	2	108.2	128	71	6	7	35	15	4.56	89	.309	.373	35-0	.257	2	93	-8	-0.5
	Cle A	1	0	1.000	2	2	1	0	15.2	18	7	0	0	3	4	3.45	116	.295	.328	6-0	.333	1	106	1	0.1
1923	Cle A	9	6	.600	30	16	10-1	1	124	129	62	4	2	37	23	3.27	121	.269	.324	45-2	.244	1	121	7	1.0
1924	Cle A	12	14	.462	39	27	20-2	1	247.2	267	110	5	7	42	34	3.02	142	.277	.312	89-4	.202	-1*	88	31	2.9
1925	Cle A	11	14	.440	31	30	**22**-1	1	237	296	151	11	5	48	30	4.86	91	.306	.342	92-3	.304	7	120	-11	-0.3
1926	Cle A	11	10	.524	27	24	16-1	0	188.1	214	80	8	4	31	25	3.73	109	.292	.324	65-4	.215	2	85	12	1.5
1927	Cle A	1	4	.200	11	2	1	1	38	53	25	2	0	14	8	5.45	77	.342	.396	12-0	.167	-0	99	-4	-0.5
Total	14	114	118	.491	373	226	142-16	21	2052.2	2234	964	57	42	440	428	3.32	108	.282	.324	709-23	.233	22	97	48	9.7
SMITH, TOM Thomas Edward B 12.5.1871 Boston, MA D 3.2.1929 Dorchester, MA BR/TR 5-7.5/165# d6.6																									
1894	Bos N	0	0	—	2	0	0	1	6	8	14	2	4	6	2	15.00	38	.320	.514	2-0	.000	-0		-6	-0.2
1895	Phi N	2	3	.400	11	7	4	0	68	76	67	1	7	53	21	6.88	70	.278	.408	33-0	.242	-0	123	-15	-0.8
1896	Lou N	2	3	.400	11	5	4	0	55	73	55	2	4	25	14	5.40	80	.316	.392	39-0	.205	-0*	89	-8	-0.5
1898	StL N	0	1	.000	1	1	1	0	9	9	8	0	2	5	1	2.00	189	.257	.381	2-0	.500	1	94	0	0.1
Total	4	4	7	.364	25	13	9	1	138	166	144	5	17	89	38	6.33	72	.294	.406	76-0	.224	-0	107	-29	-1.4
SMITH, TRAVIS Travis William B 11.7.1972 Springfield, OR BR/TR 5-10/170# d6.21																									
1998	Mil N	0	0	—	1	0	0	0-0	2	1	0	0	0	0-0	1	0.00	—	.143	.143	1-0	.000	-0		1	0.0
2002	StL N	4	2	.667	12	10	0	0-0	54	69	44	10	3	20-0	32	7.17	55	.322	.388	18-2	.167	-0	121	-19	-1.8
Total	2	4	2	.667	13	10	0	0-0	56	70	44	10	3	20-0	33	6.91	58	.317	.381	19-2	.158	-0	121	-18	-1.8
SMITH, ROY Walter Roy B 5.18.1976 St.Petersburg, FL BR/TR 6-6/235# d5.26																									
2001	Cle A	0	0	—	9	0	0	0-0	16.1	16	14	3	2	13-1	17	6.06	75	.246	.387	0-0	—	0		-4	-0.2
2002	Cle A	0	0	—	4	1	0	0-0	6	9	4	1	1	5-0	2	3.00	147	.310	.429	0-0	—	0	148	0	0.0
Total	2	0	0	—	13	1	0	0-0	22.1	25	18	4	3	18-1	19	5.24	86	.266	.400	0-0	—	0	148	-4	-0.2

Year	Tm Lg	W	L	Pct	G	GS	CG-Sho	SV-BS	IP	H	R	HR	HB	BB-IB	SO	ERA	AERA	OAV	OOB	AB-SH	AVG	PB	Sup	APR	PW
SMITH, BILL William Garland B 6.8.1934 Washington, DC D 3.30.1997 Clinton, MD BL/TL 6/190# d9.13																									
1958	StL N	0	1	.000	2	1	0	0	9.2	12	7	0	0	4-0	4	6.52	63	.324	.390	2-0	.000	-0	65	-2	-0.2
1959	StL N	0	0	—	6	0	0	1	8.1	11	3	0	0	3-1	4	1.08	393	.333	.389	1-0	.000	-0		2	0.1
1962	Phi N	1	5	.167	24	5	0	0	50.1	59	32	8	1	10-3	26	4.29	90	.295	.329	11-0	.182	1	77	-5	-0.4
Total	3	1	6	.143	32	6	0	1	68.1	82	42	8	1	17-4	34	4.21	94	.304	.345	14-0	.143	0	74	-5	-0.5
SMITH, WILLIE Willie B 2.11.1939 Anniston, AL BL/TL 6/190# d6.18 ▲																									
1963	Det A	1	0	1.000	11	2	0	2	21.2	24	13	2	0	13-2	16	4.57	82	.300	.389	8-0	.125	-0*	142	-2	-0.2
1964	LA A	1	4	.200	15	1	0	0	31.2	34	13	5	1	10-1	20	2.84	116	.293	.344	359-1	.301	6*	81	1	0.4
1968	Cle A	0	0	—	2	0	0	0	5	2	0	0	0	1-0	1	0.00	—	.125	.176	42-0	.143	0*		2	0.1
	Chi N	0	0	—	1	0	0	0	2.2	0	0	0	0	0-0	2	0.00	—	.000	.000	142-1	.275	0*		1	0.1
Total	3	2	4	.333	29	3	0	2	61	60	26	7	1	24-3	39	3.10	110	.273	.339	551-2	.279	6	130	2	0.4
SMITH, WILLIE Willie Everett B 8.27.1967 Savannah, GA BR/TR 6-6/250# d4.25																									
1994	StL N	1	1	.500	8	0	0	0-1	7	9	7	4	0	3-0	7	9.00	46	.300	.364	0-0	—	0		-4	-0.7
SMITH, ZANE Zane William B 12.28.1960 Madison, WI BL/TL 6-2/195# d9.10																									
1984	Atl N	1	0	1.000	3	3	0	0-0	20	16	7	1	0	13-2	16	2.25	172	.219	.337	9-0	.556	2	76	3	0.4
1985	Atl N	9	10	.474	42	18	2-2	0-0	147	135	70	4	3	80-5	85	3.80	102	.254	.354	37-6	.162	-0*	84	1	0.2
1986	Atl N	8	16	.333	38	32	3-1	1-0	204.2	209	109	8	5	105-6	139	4.05	98	.275	.364	59-9	.085	-3*	83	-3	-0.5
1987	Atl N	15	10	.600	36	**36**	9-3	0-0	242	245	130	19	5	91-6	130	4.09	106	.266	.333	76-14	.132	-1*	109	4	0.4
1988	Atl N	5	10	.333	23	22	3	0-0	140.1	159	72	8	3	44-4	59	4.30	86	.292	.347	42-7	.167	0*	73	-8	-0.6
1989	Atl N	1	12	.077	17	17	0	0-0	99	102	65	5	2	33-3	58	4.45	82	.267	.325	28-4	.179	-0*	71	-12	-1.4
	Mon N	0	1	.000	31	0	0	2-1	48	39	11	2	1	19-4	35	1.50	236	.220	.299	4-0	.250	0*		10	0.6
	Year	1	13	.071	48	17	0	2-1	147	141	79	7	3	52-7	93	3.49	104	.252	.317	32-4	.188	0	72	-3	-0.8
1990	Mon N	6	7	.462	22	21	1	0-0	139.1	141	57	11	3	41-3	80	3.23	113	.266	.321	40-7	.175	1*	74	5	0.6
	†Pit N	6	2	.750	11	10	3-2	0-0	76	55	20	4	0	9-1	50	1.30	278	.203	.228	28-1	.143	1	82	17	1.9
	Year	12	9	.571	33	31	4-2	0-0	215.1	196	23	15	3	50-4	130	2.55	143	.245	.291	68-8	.162	2	77	23	2.5
1991	†Pit N	16	10	.615	35	35	6-3	0-0	228	234	95	15	2	29-3	120	3.20	112	.268	.292	71-13	.183	3*	115	8	1.3
1992	Pit N	8	8	.500	23	22	4-3	0-0	141	138	56	8	2	19-3	56	3.06	113	.261	.287	49-3	.122	-0*	100	4	0.5
1993	Pit N	3	7	.300	14	14	1	0-0	83	97	43	5	0	22-3	32	4.55	89	.298	.343	25-4	.080	-2	84	-4	-0.6
1994	Pit N	10	8	.556	25	24	2-1	0-0	157	162	67	18	0	34-7	57	3.27	132	.270	.307	57-2	.211	1*	85	16	2.0
1995	†Bos A	8	8	.500	24	21	0	0-0	110.2	144	78	7	1	23-1	47	5.61	87	.316	.347	0-0	—	0	111	-10	-1.1
1996	Pit N	4	6	.400	16	16	1-1	0-0	83.1	104	53	7	4	21-4	47	5.08	86	.309	.353	26-2	.154	-1	106	-7	-0.8
Total	13	100	115	.465	360	291	35-16	3-1	1919.1	1980	933	122	31	583-55	1011	3.74	105	.271	.326	551-72	.158	0	94	24	2.9
SMITHBERG, ROGER Roger Craig B 3.21.1966 Elgin, IL BR/TR 6-3/205# d9.1																									
1993	Oak A	1	2	.333	13	0	0	3-1	19.2	13	7	2	1	7-2	4	2.75	149	.197	.284	0-0	—	0		3	0.5
1994	Oak A	0	0	—	2	0	0	0-0	2.1	6	4	1	0	1-0	3	15.43	29	.500	.538	0-0	—	0		-3	-0.1
Total	2	1	2	.333	15	0	0	3-1	22	19	11	3	1	8-2	7	4.09	101	.244	.322	0-0	—	0		0	0.4
SMITHSON, MIKE Billy Mike B 1.21.1955 Centerville, TN BL/TR 6-8/215# d8.27																									
1982	Tex A	3	4	.429	8	8	3	0-0	46.2	51	26	5	3	13-2	24	5.01	77	.282	.338	0-0	—	0	73	-5	-0.7
1983	Tex A	10	14	.417	33	33	10	0-0	223.1	233	102	14	8	71-2	135	3.91	103	.269	.327	0-0	—	0	90	6	0.6
1984	Min A	15	13	.536	36	**36**	10-1	0-0	252	246	113	35	8	54-7	144	3.68	114	.252	.296	0-0	—	0	86	14	1.4
1985	Min A	15	14	.517	37	**37**	8-3	0-0	257	264	134	25	15	78-1	127	4.34	102	.270	.331	0-0	—	0	90	3	0.2
1986	Min A	13	14	.481	34	33	8-1	0-0	198	234	123	26	14	57-4	114	4.77	90	.294	.349	0-0	—	0	103	-13	-1.5
1987	Min A	4	7	.364	21	20	0	0-0	109	126	76	17	9	38-3	53	5.94	78	.286	.351	0-0	—	0	118	-14	-1.3
1988	†Bos A	9	6	.600	31	18	1	0-0	126.2	149	87	25	6	37-1	73	5.97	69	.292	.345	0-0	—	0	125	-23	-2.4
1989	Bos A	7	14	.333	40	19	1-1	2-1	143.2	170	84	21	10	35-5	61	4.95	83	.297	.343	0-0	—	0	108	-10	-1.4
Total	8	76	86	.469	240	204	41-6	2-1	1356.1	1473	745	168	73	383-25	731	4.58	93	.277	.331	0-0	—	0	99	-42	-5.1
SMOLL, LEFTY Clyde Hetrick B 4.17.1914 Quakertown, PA D 8.31.1985 Quakertown, PA BB/TL 5-10/175# d4.26																									
1940	Phi N	2	8	.200	33	9	0	0	109	145	77	6	4	36	31	5.37	73	.322	.378	31-0	.161	-1	59	-19	-1.7
SMOLTZ, JOHN John Andrew B 5.15.1967 Detroit, MI BR/TR 6-3/210# d7.23																									
1988	Atl N	2	7	.222	12	12	0	0-0	64	74	40	10	2	33-4	37	5.48	67	.285	.369	17-3	.118	-0	70	-10	-1.4
1989	Atl N★	12	11	.522	29	29	5	0-0	208	160	79	15	2	72-2	168	2.94	124	.212	.280	62-6	.113	1*	79	15	1.8
1990	Atl N	14	11	.560	34	34	6-2	0-0	231.1	206	109	20	1	90-3	170	3.85	105	.240	.310	74-7	.162	1*	102	6	0.8
1991	†Atl N	14	13	.519	36	36	5	0-0	229.2	206	101	16	3	77-1	148	3.80	102	.243	.305	65-8	.108	-1*	102	6	0.6
1992	†Atl N★	15	12	.556	35	**35**	9-3	0-0	246.2	206	90	17	5	80-5	**215**	2.85	129	.224	.287	75-10	.160	2*	99	20	2.4
1993	†Atl N★	15	11	.577	35	35	3-1	0-0	243.2	208	104	23	6	100-12	208	3.62	111	.230	.309	71-11	.183	3	111	13	1.5
1994	Atl N	6	10	.375	21	21	1	0-0	134.2	120	69	15	4	48-4	113	4.14	103	.239	.307	37-6	.162	2	85	1	0.3
1995	†Atl N	12	7	.632	29	29	2-1	0-0	192.2	166	76	15	4	72-8	193	3.18	134	.232	.304	56-6	.107	-1	94	22	1.8
1996	†Atl N★	**24**	8	**.750**	35	35	6-2	0-0	**253.2**	199	93	19	2	55-3	**276**	2.94	150	.216	**.260**	78-15	.218	4	105	40	5.2
1997	†Atl N	15	12	.556	35	**35**	7-2	0-0	**256**	234	97	21	1	63-9	241	3.02	139	.242	.288	79-6	.228	6*	98	33	3.9
1998	†Atl N	17	3	**.850**	26	26	2-2	0-0	167.2	145	58	10	4	44-2	173	2.90	144	.231	.285	51-8	.196	3	122	25	3.2
1999	†Atl N	11	8	.579	29	29	1-1	0-0	186.1	168	70	14	4	40-2	156	3.19	141	.245	.288	62-4	.274	7	103	29	3.5
2001	†Atl N	3	3	.500	36	5	0	10-1	59	53	24	7	2	10-2	57	3.36	131	.238	.274	7-2	.000	-0	117	7	0.8
2002	†Atl N★	3	2	.600	75	0	0	**55-4**	80.1	59	30	4	0	24-1	85	3.25	126	.206	.266	2-0	.000	-0		9	1.5
2003	†Atl N☆	0	2	.000	62	0	0	45-4	64.1	48	9	2	0	8-1	73	1.12	378	.204	.230	1-0	.000	-0		22	3.5
Total	15	163	120	.576	529	361	47-14	110-9	2618	2252	1049	208	40	816-59	2313	3.29	124	.232	.292	737-92	.172	26	100	238	29.4
SMYTH, STEVE Steven Delton B 6.3.1978 Brawley, CA BL/TL 6-1/220# d8.6																									
2002	Chi N	1	3	.250	8	7	0	0-0	26	34	28	9	1	10-0	16	9.35	43	.321	.372	9-1	.222	0	141	-15	-1.8
SMYTHE, HARRY William Henry B 10.24.1904 Augusta, GA D 8.28.1980 Augusta, GA BL/TL 5-10.5/179# d7.21																									
1929	Phi N	4	6	.400	19	9	2	1	68.2	94	47	3	1	15	12	5.24	99	.330	.365	26-0	.192	-1*	106	-1	-0.1
1930	Phi N	0	3	.000	25	3	0	2	49.2	84	60	3	3	31	9	7.79	70	.368	.450	14-1	.286	-0	112	-15	-0.9
1934	NY A	0	2	.000	8	0	0	1	15	24	16	1	0	8	7	7.80	52	.381	.451	5-0	.200	-0		-7	-0.8
	Bro N	1	1	.500	8	0	0	0	21.1	30	19	3	1	8	5	5.91	66	.337	.398	9-1	.333	1*		-6	-0.3
Total	3	5	12	.294	60	12	2	4	154.2	232	142	10	5	62	33	6.40	78	.349	.408	54-2	.241	0	114	-29	-2.1
SNELL, NATE Nathaniel B 9.2.1952 Orangeburg, SC BR/TR 6-4/190# d9.20																									
1984	Bal A	1	1	.500	5	0	0	0-0	7.2	8	2	1	0	1-0	7	2.35	165	.258	.273	0-0	—	0		1	0.3
1985	Bal A	3	2	.600	43	0	0	5-0	100.1	100	44	4	1	30-5	41	2.69	150	.260	.314	0-0	—	0		10	0.6
1986	Bal A	2	1	.667	34	0	0	0-1	72.1	69	36	9	1	22-4	29	3.86	107	.257	.313	0-0	—	0		2	0.1
1987	Det A	1	2	.333	22	2	0	0-0	38.2	39	20	5	0	19-3	19	3.96	107	.267	.349	0-0	—	0	65	1	0.0
Total	4	7	6	.538	104	2	0	5-1	219	216	102	19	2	72-12	96	3.29	125	.260	.319	0-0	—	0	65	14	1.0
SNOOK, FRANK Frank Walter B 3.28.1949 Somerville, NJ BR/TR 6-2/180# d7.13																									
1973	SD N	0	2	.000	18	0	0	1-1	27.1	19	15	4	0	18-0	13	3.62	96	.200	.319	2-0	.000	-0		-1	-0.1
SNOVER, COLONEL Colonel Lester "Bosco" B 5.16.1895 Hallstead, PA D 4.30.1969 Rochester, NY BL/TL 6-0.5/200# d9.18																									
1919	NY N	0	1	.000	2	1	0	0	9	7	5	0	1	3	4	1.00	281	.212	.297	2-0	.000	0	113	0	0.0
SNYDER, BRIAN Brian Robert B 2.20.1958 Flemington, NJ BL/TL 6-3/185# d5.25																									
1985	Sea A	1	2	.333	15	6	0	1-0	35.1	44	28	2	1	19-2	23	6.37	66	.306	.388	0-0	—	0	97	-9	-0.6
1989	Oak A	0	0	—	2	0	0	0-0	0.2	2	2	1	0	2-0	1	27.00	14	.500	.667	0-0	—	0		-2	-0.1
Total	2	1	2	.333	17	6	0	1-0	36	46	30	3	1	21-2	24	6.75	62	.311	.398	0-0	—	0	97	-11	-0.7
SNYDER, GENE Gene Walter B 3.31.1931 York, PA D 6.2.1996 York, PA BR/TL 5-11/175# d4.26																									
1959	LA N	1	1	.500	11	2	0	0	26.1	32	19	1	0	20-2	20	5.47	77	.299	.409	6-1	.000	-0	85	-4	-0.3
SNYDER, GEORGE George T. B 8.1848 Philadelphia, PA D 8.2.1905 Philadelphia, PA d9.30																									
1882	Phi AA	1	0	1.000	1	1	1	0	9	4	3	0		2	0	0.00	—	.125	.176	3	.333	0	110	2	0.2

Year	Tm Lg	W	L	Pct	G	GS	CG-Sho	SV-BS	IP	H	R	HR	HB	BB-IB	SO	ERA	AERA	OAV	OOB	AB-SH	AVG	PB	Sup	APR	PW
SNYDER, JOHN John Michael B 8.16.1974 Southfield, MI BR/TR 6-3/185# d6.30																									
1998	Chi A	7	2	.778	15	14	1	0-0	86.1	96	49	14	2	23-1	52	4.80	95	.286	.332	0-0	—	0	125	-1	-0.1
1999	Chi A	9	12	.429	25	25	1	0-0	129.1	167	103	27	6	49-0	67	6.68	73	.311	.371	0-0	—	0	101	-24	-3.1
2000	Mil N	3	10	.231	23	23	0	0-0	127	147	95	8	9	77-10	69	6.17	74	.296	.395	38-1	.079	-1*	91	-23	-2.0
Total	3	19	24	.442	63	62	2	0-0	342.2	410	247	49	17	149-11	188	6.01	78	.299	.371	38-1	.079	-1	103	-48	-5.2
SNYDER, KYLE Kyle Ehren B 9.9.1977 Houston, TX BB/TR 6-8/220# d5.1																									
2003	KC A	1	6	.143	15	15	0	0-0	85.1	94	52	11	2	21-3	39	5.17	100	.283	.321	2-0	.000	-0	58	0	0.0
SNYDER, BILL William Nicholas B 1.28.1898 Mansfield, OH D 10.8.1934 Vicksburg, MI BR/TR d9.4																									
1919	Was A	0	1	.000	2	1	0	0	8	6	4	0	0	3	5	1.13	285	.200	.273	2-0	.000	-0	73	1	0.1
1920	Was A	2	1	.667	16	4	1	1	54	59	33	1	6	28	17	4.17	90	.280	.380	19-0	.316	1	101	-3	-0.1
Total	2	2	2	.500	18	5	1	1	62	65	37	1	6	31	22	3.77	97	.270	.367	21-0	.286	1	95	-2	0.0
SOBKOWIAK, SCOTT Scott B 10.26.1977 Woodstock, IL BR/TR 6-5/230# d10.7																									
2001	Atl N	0	0	—	1	0	0	0-0	1	2	1	0	0	0-0	0	9.00	49	.400	.400	0-0	—	0		0	0.0
SODERSTROM, STEVE Stephen Andrew B 4.3.1972 Turlock, CA BR/TR 6-3/215# d9.17																									
1996	SF N	2	0	1.000	3	3	0	0-0	13.2	16	11	1	2	6-0	9	5.27	78	.302	.381	5-0	.000	-1	183	-3	-0.4
SODOWSKY, CLINT Clint Rea B 7.13.1972 Ponca City, OK BL/TR 6-3/180# d9.4																									
1995	Det A	2	2	.500	6	6	0	0-0	23.1	24	15	4	0	18-0	14	5.01	95	.258	.378	0-0	—	0	68	-1	-0.2
1996	Det A	1	3	.250	7	7	0	0-0	24.1	40	34	5	3	20-0	9	11.84	43	.370	.481	0-0	—	0	118	-18	-2.1
1997	Pit N	2	2	.500	45	0	0	0-2	52	49	22	6	2	34-7	51	3.63	118	.249	.362	2-0	.500	0		4	0.3
1998	Ari N	3	6	.333	45	6	0	0-3	77.2	86	56	5	7	39-5	42	5.68	74	.283	.375	10-1	.300	1*	131	-14	-1.3
1999	StL N	0	1	.000	3	1	0	0-0	6.1	15	11	1	0	6-0	2	15.63	29	.455	.538	1-0	.000	-0	141	-7	-0.9
Total	5	8	14	.364	106	20	0	0-5	183.2	214	138	21	12	117-12	118	6.17	72	.291	.395	13-1	.308	1	114	-36	-4.2
SOFF, RAY Raymond John B 10.31.1958 Adrian, MI BR/TR 6/185# d7.17																									
1986	StL N	4	2	.667	30	0	0	0-0	38.1	37	17	4	0	13-1	22	3.29	111	.255	.313	2-1	.000	-0		1	0.1
1987	StL N	1	0	1.000	12	0	0	0-0	15.1	18	11	3	1	5-1	9	6.46	64	.295	.353	1-0	.000	-0		-3	-0.2
Total	2	5	2	.714	42	0	0	0-0	53.2	55	28	7	1	18-2	31	4.19	90	.267	.325	3-1	.000	-0		-2	-0.1
SOLANO, JULIO Julio Cesar B 1.8.1960 Agua Blanca, D.R. BR/TR 6-1/160# d4.5																									
1983	Hou N	0	2	.000	4	0	0	0-0	6	5	5	1	0	4-1	3	6.00	57	.217	.333	0-0	—	0		-2	-0.4
1984	Hou N	1	3	.250	31	0	0	0-2	50.2	31	13	3	0	18-1	33	1.95	170	.179	.253	3-0	.333	0		8	0.6
1985	Hou N	2	2	.500	20	0	0	0-0	33.2	34	13	5	0	13-2	17	3.48	100	.262	.329	2-0	.000	-0		1	0.0
1986	Hou N	3	1	.750	16	1	0	0-1	32	39	28	5	3	22-2	21	7.59	47	.310	.421	6-1	.000	-1	25	-14	-1.6
1987	Hou N	0	0	—	11	0	0	0-0	20	25	17	5	0	9-0	12	7.65	51	.298	.366	2-0	.000	-0		-8	-0.4
1988	Sea A	0	0	—	17	0	0	3-1	22	22	13	3	0	12-2	10	4.09	102	.268	.354	0-0	—	0		-1	0.0
1989	Sea A	0	0	—	7	0	0	0-0	9.2	6	8	1	1	4-0	6	5.59	72	.176	.282	0-0	—	0		-2	-0.1
Total	7	6	8	.429	106	1	0	3-4	174	162	97	23	4	82-8	102	4.55	79	.248	.333	13-1	.077	-1	25	-18	-1.9
SOLIS, MARCELINO Marcelino B 7.19.1930 San Luis Potosi, Mexico BL/TL 6-1/185# d7.16																									
1958	Chi N	3	3	.500	15	4	0	0	52	74	41	5	4	20-1	15	6.06	65	.339	.405	20-0	.250	1	86	-13	-1.2
SOLOMON, EDDIE Eddie "Buddy" B 2.9.1951 Perry, GA D 1.12.1986 Macon, GA BR/TR 6-3/190# d9.2																									
1973	LA N	0	0	—	4	0	0	0-0	6.1	10	5	3	1	4-0	6	7.11	48	.357	.455	1-0	.000	-0		-2	-0.1
1974	†LA N	0	0	—	4	0	0	1-0	6	5	1	1	0	2-0	2	1.50	227	.217	.280	0-0	—	0		1	0.1
1975	Chi N	0	0	—	6	0	0	0-0	6.2	7	6	1	0	6-2	3	1.35	286	.269	.406	0-0	—	0		0	0.0
1976	StL N	1	1	.500	26	2	0	0-0	37	45	24	2	1	16-1	19	4.86	73	.306	.369	5-0	.400	1	174	-6	-0.2
1977	Atl N	6	6	.500	18	16	0	0-0	88.2	110	64	10	2	34-2	54	4.57	98	.305	.365	31-1	.129	-1	90	-6	-0.8
1978	Atl N	4	6	.400	37	8	0	2-2	106	98	52	12	2	50-11	64	4.08	99	.247	.334	29-0	.138	-1*	66	1	0.0
1979	Atl N	7	14	.333	31	30	4	0-0	186	184	98	19	6	51-4	96	4.21	96	.254	.307	64-3	.203	1*	88	-1	-0.1
1980	Pit N	7	3	.700	26	12	2	0-0	100.1	96	44	8	4	37-5	35	2.69	136	.253	.322	32-3	.219	1*	98	6	0.6
1981	Pit N	8	6	.571	22	17	2	1-0	127	133	49	10	3	27-3	38	3.12	115	.278	.320	43-5	.163	-1*	120	7	0.6
1982	Pit N	2	6	.250	11	10	0	0-0	46.2	69	38	9	1	18-0	18	6.75	55	.347	.400	15-1	.133	-1*	112	-15	-2.3
	Chi A	1	0	1.000	6	0	0	0-0	7.1	7	5	1	0	2-0	2	3.68	110	.241	.290	0-0	—	0		0	-0.1
Total	10	36	42	.462	191	95	8	4-2	718	764	386	76	20	247-28	337	4.00	98	.274	.335	220-13	.177	-1	98	-15	-2.3
SOMMER, JOE Joseph John B 11.20.1858 Covington, KY D 1.16.1938 Cincinnati, OH BR/TR d7.8.1880 ▲																									
1883	Cin AA	0	0	—	1	0	0	0	5	9	6	0		1	2	5.40	60	.360	.385	413	.278	0*		-1	-0.1
1885	Bal AA	0	0	—	2	0	0	1	3	6	3	0	0	0	0	9.00	36	.429	.429	471	.251	0*		-1	-0.1
1886	Bal AA	0	0	—	1	0	0	0	4	14	12	0	0	3	1	18.00	19	.519	.567	560	.209	-0*		-6	-0.2
1887	Bal AA	0	0	—	1	0	0	0	1	2	1	0	0	1	0	9.00	46	.333	.429	463	.266	0*		0	0.0
1890	Cle N	0	0	—	1	0	0	0	1	2	3	1	0	2	0	0.00	—	.400	.571	35	.229	-0*		-1	0.0
Total	5	0	0	—	6	0	0	1	14	33	25	1	0	7	3	9.64	35	.429	.476	1942	.248	1		-9	-0.4
SOMMERS, RUDY Rudolph B 10.30.1886 Cincinnati, OH D 3.18.1949 Louisville, KY BB/TL 5-11/165# d9.8																									
1912	Chi N	0	1	.000	1	0	0	0	3	4	1	0	0	2	2	3.00	111	.333	.429	1-0	.000	0		0	0.1
1914	Bro F	2	7	.222	23	8	2	2	82	88	54	2	3	34	40	4.06	71	.282	.358	24-0	.250	2	89	-13	-1.2
1926	Bos A	0	0	—	2	0	0	0	2	3	3	0	0	3	0	13.50	30	.333	.500	0-0	—	0		-2	-0.1
1927	Bos A	0	0	—	7	0	0	0	14	18	15	2	0	14	2	8.36	51	.353	.492	2-0	.500	0		-6	-0.2
Total	4	2	8	.200	33	8	2	2	101	113	73	4	3	53	44	4.81	64	.294	.384	27-0	.259	2	89	-21	-1.4
SOMMERVILLE, ANDY Andrew Henry (b: Henry Travers Summersgill) B 2.6.1876 Brooklyn, NY D 6.16.1931 Richmond Hill, NY d8.8																									
1894	Bro N	0	1	.000	1	1	0	0	0.1	1	6	0	0	5	0	162.00	3	.500	.857	0-0	—	0	71	-5	-0.6
SONGER, DON Donald C. B 1.31.1900 Walnut, KS D 10.3.1962 Kansas City, MO BL/TL 6/165# d9.21																									
1924	Pit N	0	0	—	4	1	0	1	9.1	14	7	1	0	3	3	6.75	57	.333	.378	2-0	.000	-0	221	-3	-0.1
1925	Pit N	0	1	.000	8	0	0	0	11.2	14	7	0	0	8	4	2.31	193	.298	.400	2-0	.000	-0		1	0.1
1926	Pit N	7	8	.467	35	15	5-1	2	126.1	118	60	4	11	52	27	3.13	126	.252	.340	38-0	.105	-2	96	9	0.7
1927	Pit N	0	0	—	2	0	0	0	4.2	10	10	0	1	4	1	11.57	36	.526	.625	1-0	.000	-0		-5	-0.2
	NY N	3	5	.375	22	1	0	1	50.1	48	22	4	1	31	9	2.86	135	.261	.370	10-0	.300	1	44	4	0.8
	Year	3	5	.375	24	1	0	1	55	58	24	4	2	35	10	3.60	108	.286	.396	11-0	.273	1	44	-1	0.6
Total	4	10	14	.417	71	17	5-1	4	202.1	204	106	9	13	98	44	3.38	117	.268	.361	53-0	.132	-2	100	6	1.3
SORENSEN, LARY Lary Alan B 10.4.1955 Detroit, MI BR/TR 6-2/210# d6.7																									
1977	Mil A	7	10	.412	23	20	9	0-0	142.1	147	72	10	1	36-4	57	4.36	94	.270	.315	0-0	—	0	86	-2	-0.2
1978	Mil A★	18	12	.600	37	36	17-3	1-0	280.2	277	111	14	5	50-4	78	3.21	118	.259	.291	0-0	—	0	108	18	1.9
1979	Mil A	15	14	.517	34	34	16-2	0-0	235.1	250	113	30	4	42-3	63	3.98	105	.275	.309	0-0	—	0	99	7	0.8
1980	Mil A	12	10	.545	35	29	8-2	1-0	195.2	242	91	13	2	45-6	54	3.68	105	.311	.347	0-0	—	0	119	4	0.5
1981	StL N	7	7	.500	23	23	3-1	0-0	140.1	149	59	3	1	26-2	52	3.27	109	.271	.305	46-5	.065	-3	102	3	0.0
1982	Cle A	10	15	.400	32	30	6-1	0-0	189.1	251	130	19	3	55-6	62	5.61	73	.322	.365	0-0	—	0	103	-31	-3.6
1983	Cle A	12	11	.522	36	34	8-1	0-0	222.2	238	112	21	2	65-9	76	4.24	100	.276	.326	0-0	—	0	93	2	0.2
1984	Oak A	6	13	.316	46	21	2	1-1	183.1	240	117	21	6	44-4	63	4.91	76	.317	.356	0-0	—	0	99	-28	-2.6
1985	Chi N	3	7	.300	45	3	0	0-1	82.1	86	44	8	4	24-10	34	4.26	94	.274	.331	6-4	.000	-0	118	-3	-0.4
1987	Mon N	3	4	.429	23	5	0	1-0	47.2	56	32	7	3	12-1	21	4.72	89	.286	.333	8-2	.000	-1	77	-4	-0.6
1988	SF N	0	0	—	12	0	0	2-1	16.2	24	13	1	0	3-0	9	4.86	67	.329	.346	1-1	.000	-0		-4	-0.3
Total	11	93	103	.474	346	235	69-10	6-3	1736.1	1960	894	147	31	402-49	569	4.15	96	.287	.327	61-12	.049	-4	101	-38	-4.3
SORIANO, RAFAEL Rafael B 12.19.1979 San Jose, D.R. BR/TR 6-1/175# d5.10																									
2002	Sea A	0	3	.000	10	8	0	1-0	47.1	45	25	8	0	16-1	32	4.56	93	.243	.303	4-0	.000	-0*	69	-2	-0.2
2003	Sea A	3	0	1.000	40	0	0	1-1	53	30	9	2	3	12-1	68	1.53	283	.162	.224	0-0	—	0		18	0.9
Total	2	3	3	.500	50	8	0	2-1	100.1	75	34	10	3	28-2	100	2.96	145	.203	.264	4-0	.000	-0	69	16	0.7

SORRELL, VIC Victor Garland B 4.9.1901 Morrisville, NC D 5.4.1972 Raleigh, NC BR/TR 5-10/180# d4.22

Year	Tm Lg	W	L	Pct	G	GS	CG-Sho	SV-BS	IP	H	R	HR	HB	BB-IB	SO	ERA	AERA	OAV	OOB	AB-SH	AVG	PB	Sup	APR	PW
1928	Det A	8	11	.421	29	23	8	0	171	182	106	9	5	83	67	4.79	86	.277	.363	55-6	.109	-5	107	-11	-1.6
1929	Det A	14	15	.483	36	31	13-1	1	226	270	152	15	2	106	81	5.18	83	.302	.377	83-4	.145	-6	109	-20	-2.7
1930	Det A	16	11	.593	35	30	14-2	1	233.1	245	116	13	0	106	97	3.86	124	.274	.351	80-4	.188	-3	101	24	2.0
1931	Det A	13	14	.481	35	32	19-1	1	245	267	131	8	1	114	99	4.15	110	.278	.355	88-4	.159	-4	81	12	0.8
1932	Det A	14	14	.500	32	31	13-1	0	234.1	234	124	11	3	77	84	4.03	117	.259	.319	76-5	.118	-4*	82	18	1.4
1933	Det A	11	15	.423	36	28	13-1	2	232.2	233	112	18	2	78	75	3.79	114	.260	.321	74-4	.149	-2	83	16	1.3
1934	Det A	6	9	.400	28	19	6-1	2	129.2	146	76	13	3	45	46	4.79	92	.283	.345	37-3	.108	-1	110	-5	-0.5
1935	Det A	4	3	.571	12	6	4	0	51.1	65	28	2	2	25	22	4.03	103	.319	.398	18-0	.000	-3	167	0	-0.3
1936	Det A	6	7	.462	30	14	5-1	3	131.1	153	86	9	2	64	37	5.28	94	.294	.373	39-4	.154	1	109	-4	-0.1
1937	Det A	0	2	.000	7	2	0	1	17	25	18	3	0	8	11	9.00	52	.338	.402	3-1	.000	-0	75	-8	-0.8
Total	10	92	101	.477	280	216	95-8	10	1671.2	1820	949	101	20	706	619	4.43	102	.279	.351	553-35	.139	-27	97	22	-0.5

SOSA, ELIAS Elias (Martinez) B 6.10.1950 LaVega, D.R. BR/TR 6-2/190# d9.8

Year	Tm Lg	W	L	Pct	G	GS	CG-Sho	SV-BS	IP	H	R	HR	HB	BB-IB	SO	ERA	AERA	OAV	OOB	AB-SH	AVG	PB	Sup	APR	PW
1972	SF N	0	1	.000	8	0	0	3-0	15.2	10	4	0	0	12-0	10	2.30	152	.189	.338	4-0	.000	-0		2	0.2
1973	SF N	10	4	.714	71	1	0	18-3	107	95	42	7	4	41-8	70	3.28	117	.241	.315	14-1	.071	-0	115	7	1.1
1974	SF N	9	7	.563	68	0	0	6-8	101	94	54	8	1	45-5	48	3.48	110	.252	.329	15-2	.067	-1		1	-0.1
1975	StL N	0	3	.000	14	1	0	0-1	27.1	22	14	3	1	14-2	15	3.95	95	.227	.319	8-0	.125	-0	47	0	-0.1
	Atl N	2	2	.500	43	0	0	2-2	62.1	70	35	3	3	29-7	31	4.48	85	.294	.376	7-1	.143	-0		-4	-0.3
	Year	2	5	.286	57	1	0	2-3	89.2	92	51	6	4	43-9	46	4.32	88	.275	.359	15-1	.133	-1	47	-5	-0.4
1976	Atl N	4	4	.500	21	0	0	3-4	35.1	41	26	3	1	13-2	32	5.35	71	.287	.346	7-0	.143	-0		-7	-1.4
	LA N	2	4	.333	24	0	0	1-0	33.2	30	16	0	0	12-4	20	3.48	97	.242	.304	0-1	—	0		-1	-0.2
	Year	6	8	.429	45	0	0	4-4	69	71	42	3	1	25-6	52	4.43	81	.266	.327	7-1	.143	-0		-8	-1.6
1977	†LA N	2	2	.500	44	0	0	1-0	63.2	42	15	7	1	12-3	47	1.98	193	.189	.233	4-1	.250	0*		14	0.8
1978	Oak A	8	2	.800	68	0	0	14-4	109	106	37	5	1	44-10	61	2.64	138	.264	.337	0-0	—	0		13	1.5
1979	Mon N	8	7	.533	62	0	0	18-7	96.2	77	24	2	2	37-11	59	1.96	188	.219	.297	13-1	.154	0		19	3.5
1980	Mon N	9	6	.600	67	0	0	9-8	93.2	104	33	5	1	19-3	58	3.07	116	.286	.320	11-1	.091	-1		6	1.0
1981	†Mon N	1	2	.333	32	0	0	3-2	39.1	46	16	3	1	8-0	18	3.66	95	.297	.329	2-0	1.000	1		0	0.1
1982	Det A	3	3	.500	38	0	0	4-3	61	64	31	11	2	18-3	24	4.43	92	.270	.327	0-0	—	0		-1	-0.1
1983	SD N	1	4	.200	41	1	0	1-1	72.1	72	41	7	3	30-5	45	4.35	80	.268	.342	7-0	.143	-0	152	-8	-0.6
Total	12	59	51	.536	601	3	0	83-43	918	873	388	64	21	334-63	538	3.32	112	.255	.322	92-8	.130	-3	104	41	5.4

SOSA, JORGE Jorge Bolivar B 4.28.1978 Santo Domingo, D.R. BB/TR 6-2/180# d4.4

Year	Tm Lg	W	L	Pct	G	GS	CG-Sho	SV-BS	IP	H	R	HR	HB	BB-IB	SO	ERA	AERA	OAV	OOB	AB-SH	AVG	PB	Sup	APR	PW
2002	TB A	2	7	.222	31	14	0	0-0	99.1	88	63	16	2	54-0	48	5.53	81	.236	.332	0-0	—	0	94	-10	-0.9
2003	TB A	5	12	.294	29	19	1-1	0-0	128.2	137	71	14	4	60-4	72	4.62	98	.278	.358	0-0	—	0	81	-1	-0.2
Total	2	7	19	.269	60	33	1-1	0-0	228	225	134	30	6	114-4	120	5.01	90	.260	.346	0-0	—	0	86	-11	-1.1

SOSA, JOSE Jose Ynocencio (b: Jose Ynocencio (Sosa)) B 12.28.1952 Santo Domingo, D.R. BR/TR 5-11/158# d7.22

Year	Tm Lg	W	L	Pct	G	GS	CG-Sho	SV-BS	IP	H	R	HR	HB	BB-IB	SO	ERA	AERA	OAV	OOB	AB-SH	AVG	PB	Sup	APR	PW
1975	Hou N	1	3	.250	25	2	0	1-1	47	51	21	5	1	23-4	31	4.02	84	.291	.371	9-0	.333	2*	104	-3	-0.1
1976	Hou N	0	0	—	9	0	0	0-0	11.2	16	9	0	3	6-2	5	6.94	46	.340	.439	0-0	—	0		-5	-0.2
Total	2	1	3	.250	34	2	0	1-1	58.2	67	30	5	4	29-6	36	4.60	73	.302	.386	9-0	.333	2	104	-8	-0.3

SOTHORON, ALLEN Allen Sutton B 4.27.1893 Bradford, OH D 6.17.1939 St.Louis, MO BB/TR 5-11/182# d9.17 M1 C4

Year	Tm Lg	W	L	Pct	G	GS	CG-Sho	SV-BS	IP	H	R	HR	HB	BB-IB	SO	ERA	AERA	OAV	OOB	AB-SH	AVG	PB	Sup	APR	PW
1914	StL A	0	0	—	1	0	0	0	6	6	4	0	0	4	3	6.00	45	.261	.370	2-0	.000	-0		-2	-0.1
1915	StL A	0	1	.000	3	1	0	0	3.2	8	10	0	0	5	2	7.36	39	.400	.520	1-0	.000	-0	0	-4	-0.7
1917	StL A	14	19	.424	48	32	17-3	4	276.2	259	135	2	9	96	85	2.83	92	.251	.320	92-5	.217	3*	100	-13	-1.2
1918	StL A	12	12	.500	29	24	14-2	1	209	152	64	3	3	67	71	1.94	141	**.205**	.274	63-4	.159	-2	96	17	1.6
1919	StL A	20	12	.625	40	30	21-3	3	270	256	101	4	10	87	106	2.20	151	.246	.311	97-3	.175	-2	82	27	2.5
1920	StL A	8	15	.348	36	26	12-1	2	218.1	263	151	6	6	89	81	4.70	83	.307	.376	72-5	.222	-1	96	-22	-2.2
1921	StL A	1	2	.333	5	4	1	0	27.2	33	19	0	1	8	9	5.20	86	.314	.368	9-1	.111	-1	98	-2	-0.3
	Bos A	0	2	.000	2	2	0	0	6	15	10	0	0	5	2	13.50	31	.455	.526	2-0	.500	1	39	-6	-0.9
	Cle A	12	4	.750	22	16	10-2	0	144.2	146	60	0	7	58	61	3.24	132	.279	.358	58-3	.276	2	128	17	1.7
	Year	13	8	.619	29	22	11-2	0	178.1	194	67	0	8	71	72	3.89	111	.293	.368	69-4	.261	2	115	10	0.5
1922	Cle A	1	3	.250	6	4	2	0	25.1	26	22	1	2	14	8	6.39	63	.274	.378	9-0	.444	1	117	-7	-0.8
1924	StL N	10	16	.385	29	28	16-**4**	0	196.2	209	102	9	10	84	62	3.57	106	.275	.354	72-5	.194	-2	111	1	-0.3
1925	StL N	10	10	.500	28	22	8-2	0	155.2	173	86	7	6	63	67	4.05	107	.280	.353	56-2	.196	-1	106	3	0.0
1926	StL N	3	3	.500	15	4	1	0	42.2	37	22	2	0	16	19	4.22	93	.247	.319	13-0	.231	0	128	-1	-0.1
Total	11	91	99	.479	264	193	102-17	9	1582.1	1583	786	34	54	596	576	3.31	105	.264	.336	546-28	.207	-2	102	8	-0.8

SOTO, MARIO Mario Melvin B 7.12.1956 Bani, D.R. BR/TR 6/185# d7.21

Year	Tm Lg	W	L	Pct	G	GS	CG-Sho	SV-BS	IP	H	R	HR	HB	BB-IB	SO	ERA	AERA	OAV	OOB	AB-SH	AVG	PB	Sup	APR	PW
1977	Cin N	2	6	.250	12	10	2-1	0-0	60.2	60	38	12	3	26-4	44	5.34	74	.258	.337	13-1	.077	-0	90	-9	-1.1
1978	Cin N	1	0	1.000	5	1	0	0-0	18	13	5	1	0	13-3	13	2.50	142	.197	.329	2-1	.000	-0	126	2	0.1
1979	†Cin N	3	2	.600	25	0	0	0-0	37.1	33	25	2	1	30-2	32	5.30	71	.243	.381	7-0	.571	2		-7	-0.7
1980	Cin N	10	8	.556	53	12	3-1	4-1	190.1	126	72	11	2	84-10	182	3.07	117	**.187**	.276	46-8	.043	-4*	112	10	0.5
1981	Cin N	12	9	.571	25	**25**	10-3	0-0	175	142	69	13	3	61-3	151	3.29	108	.220	.289	59-6	.068	-4	105	6	0.1
1982	Cin N★	14	13	.519	35	34	13-2	0-0	257.2	202	88	19	4	71-3	274	2.79	133	.215	**.271**	84-11	.167	1*	91	26	2.8
1983	Cin N★	17	13	.567	34	34	**18**-3	0-0	273.2	207	96	28	5	95-6	242	2.70	141	.208	.278	88-11	.125	-2*	83	30	2.9
1984	Cin N★	18	7	.720	33	33	**13**	0-0	237.1	181	102	26	5	87-6	185	3.53	107	.209	.284	87-4	.207	3	106	7	0.9
1985	Cin N	12	15	.444	36	36	9-1	0-0	256.2	196	109	30	2	104-3	214	3.58	106	.211	.290	83-6	.133	-2*	86	8	0.5
1986	Cin N	5	10	.333	19	19	1-1	0-0	105	113	61	15	1	46-6	67	4.71	82	.280	.352	27-6	.111	-1*	83	-9	-1.3
1987	Cin N	3	2	.600	6	6	0	0-0	31.2	34	18	7	0	12-1	11	5.12	83	.279	.343	12-0	.083	-1	142	-2	-0.4
1988	Cin N	3	7	.300	14	14	3-1	0-0	87	88	49	8	2	28-3	34	4.66	77	.267	.326	22-4	.045	-1	95	-10	-1.1
Total	12	100	92	.521	297	224	72-13	4-1	1730.1	1395	732	172	28	657-50	1449	3.47	108	.220	.294	530-58	.132	-10	95	52	3.2

SOUZA, MARK Kenneth Mark B 2.1.1955 Redwood City, CA BL/TL 6/180# d4.22

Year	Tm Lg	W	L	Pct	G	GS	CG-Sho	SV-BS	IP	H	R	HR	HB	BB-IB	SO	ERA	AERA	OAV	OOB	AB-SH	AVG	PB	Sup	APR	PW
1980	Oak A	0	0	—	5	0	0	0-1	7	9	6	1	0	5-0	2	7.71	49	.310	.412	0-0	—	0		-3	-0.2

SOWDERS, JOHN John B 12.10.1866 Louisville, KY D 7.29.1939 Indianapolis, IN BR/TL 6/150# d6.28 b-Len b-Bill

Year	Tm Lg	W	L	Pct	G	GS	CG-Sho	SV-BS	IP	H	R	HR	HB	BB-IB	SO	ERA	AERA	OAV	OOB	AB-SH	AVG	PB	Sup	APR	PW
1887	Ind N	0	0	—	1	0	0	0	3	11	13	0	0	5	0	21.00	20	.500	.593	2	.000	-0		-6	-0.3
1889	KC AA	6	16	.273	25	23	20	1	185	204	181	9	7	105	104	4.82	87	.271	.366	87	.218	-2*	79	-14	-1.4
1890	Bro P	19	16	.543	39	37	28-1	0	309	358	233	3	11	161	91	3.82	117	.278	.363	132	.189	-5*	95	19	1.1
Total	3	25	32	.439	65	60	48-1	1	497	573	427	12	18	271	195	4.29	102	.278	.366	221	.199	-7	89	-1	-0.6

SOWDERS, BILL William Jefferson "Little Bill" B 11.29.1864 Louisville, KY D 2.2.1951 Indianapolis, IN BR/TR 6/155# d4.24 b-John b-Len

Year	Tm Lg	W	L	Pct	G	GS	CG-Sho	SV-BS	IP	H	R	HR	HB	BB-IB	SO	ERA	AERA	OAV	OOB	AB-SH	AVG	PB	Sup	APR	PW
1888	Bos N	19	15	.559	36	35	34-2	0	317	278	155	3	9	73	132	2.07	139	.226	.275	122	.148	-4	85	19	1.5
1889	Bos N	1	2	.333	7	4	3	3	42	53	35	3	2	23	10	5.14	81	.299	.386	17	.235	-0	89	-5	-0.3
	Pit N	6	5	.545	13	11	9	0	52.2	94	55	1	4	29	33	7.35	51	.376	.449	48	.271	2*	96	-20	-2.7
	Year	7	7	.500	20	15	12	**3**	94.2	147	60	4	6	52	43	6.37	62	.344	.423	65	.262	2	92	-23	-3.0
1890	Pit N	3	8	.273	15	11	9	0	106	117	77	1	2	24	30	4.42	75	.271	.312	50	.180	-2*	71	-13	-1.3
Total	3	29	30	.492	71	61	55-2	3	517.2	542	322	8	17	149	205	3.34	95	.260	.314	237	.186	-4	85	-19	-2.8

SPADE, BOB Robert B 1.4.1877 Akron, OH D 9.7.1924 Cincinnati, OH BR/TR 5-10/190# d9.22

Year	Tm Lg	W	L	Pct	G	GS	CG-Sho	SV-BS	IP	H	R	HR	HB	BB-IB	SO	ERA	AERA	OAV	OOB	AB-SH	AVG	PB	Sup	APR	PW
1907	Cin N	1	2	.333	3	3	3-1	0	27	21	5	0	1	9	7	1.00	260	.219	.292	7-0	.286	1	37	4	0.7
1908	Cin N	17	12	.586	35	28	22-2	1	249.1	230	111	2	5	85	74	2.74	84	.250	.317	87-3	.195	1	107	-12	-1.6
1909	Cin N	5	5	.500	14	13	8	0	98	91	38	0	4	39	31	2.85	91	.236	.313	34-0	.294	4	99	0	0.2
1910	Cin N	1	2	.333	3	3	1	0	17.1	35	19	1	1	9	1	6.75	43	.479	.542	5-0	.000	-1	136	-8	-1.1
	StL A	1	3	.250	7	5	2-1	0	34.2	34	24	1	1	17	8	4.41	56	.270	.361	11-0	.273	2	119	-7	-0.6
Total	4	25	24	.510	62	52	36-4	1	426.1	411	197	4	12	159	121	2.96	82	.257	.329	144-3	.222	7	104	-23	-2.4

SPAHN, WARREN Warren Edward B 4.23.1921 Buffalo, NY D 11.24.2003 Broken Arrow, OK BL/TL 6/175# d4.19 Mil 1943-46 C3 HF1973

Year	Tm Lg	W	L	Pct	G	GS	CG-Sho	SV-BS	IP	H	R	HR	HB	BB-IB	SO	ERA	AERA	OAV	OOB	AB-SH	AVG	PB	Sup	APR	PW
1942	Bos N	0	0	—	4	2	1	0	15.2	25	15	0	0	11	7	5.74	58	.368	.456	6-0	.167	-0	126	-6	-0.3
1946	Bos N	8	5	.615	24	16	8	1	125.2	107	46	6	1	36	67	2.94	117	.228	.285	43-2	.163	-1	105	8	0.6
1947	Bos N★	21	10	.677	40	35	22-**7**	3	**289.2**	245	87	15	1	84	123	**2.33**	**167**	.226	**.283**	98-8	.163	1*	91	**52**	**5.3**
1948	†Bos N	15	12	.556	36	35	16-3	1	257	237	115	19	1	77	114	3.71	103	.242	.298	90-7	.167	2*	113	5	0.7

Year	Tm Lg	W	L	Pct	G	GS	CG-Sho	SV-BS	IP	H	R	HR	HB	BB-IB	SO	ERA	AERA	OAV	OOB	AB-SH	AVG	PB	Sup	APR	PW
1949	Bos N★	**21**	14	.600	38	**38**	**25**-4	0	**302.1**	283	125	27	3	86	**151**	3.07	123	.245	.299	111-5	.162	-0*	110	23	2.3
1950	Bos N☆	**21**	17	.553	41	**39**	25-1	1	293	248	123	22	1	111	**191**	3.16	122	.227	.299	106-5	.217	4	108	22	3.1
1951	Bos N☆	22	14	.611	39	36	**26-7**	0	310.2	278	111	20	1	109	**164**	2.98	123	.238	.304	116-4	.190	5*	124	29	3.6
1952	Bos N☆	14	19	.424	40	35	19-5	3	290	263	109	19	6	73	**183**	2.98	121	.240	.291	112-2	.161	2*	94	20	2.6
1953	Mil N★	**23**	7	.767	35	32	24-5	3	265.2	211	75	14	1	70	148	**2.10**	**187**	**.217**	**.270**	105-5	.219	5*	111	57	**7.0**
1954	Mil N★	21	12	.636	39	34	23-1	3	283.1	262	107	24	1	86	136	3.14	118	.245	.300	101-3	.208	6*	103	22	3.2
1955	Mil N	17	14	.548	39	32	16-1	1	245.2	249	99	25	2	65-4	110	3.26	115	.265	.312	81-3	.210	5*	111	15	2.3
1956	Mil N★	20	11	.645	39	35	20-3	3	281.1	249	92	25	3	52-12	128	2.78	124	.238	.275	105-2	.210	6	108	**28**	3.7
1957	†Mil N☆	**21**	11	.656	39	35	**18**-4	3	271	241	94	23	2	78-4	111	2.69	130	.237	.291	94-3	.138	1	124	26	3.1
1958	†Mil N★	**22**	11	**.667**	38	36	**23**-2	1	**290**	257	106	29	2	76-7	150	3.07	115	.237	.287	108-4	.333	18*	113	18	**4.1**
1959	Mil N☆	**21**	15	.583	40	36	**21-4**	0	**292**	282	106	21	1	70-9	143	2.96	120	.253	.297	104-1	.231	7	113	23	3.4
1960	Mil N	**21**	10	.677	40	33	**18**-4	2	267.2	254	114	24	4	74-9	154	3.50	98	.250	.302	95-2	.147	3	122	0	0.4
1961	Mil N★	**21**	13	.618	38	34	**21-4**	0	262.2	236	96	24	4	64-1	115	**3.02**	124	.243	**.291**	94-2	.223	10*	100	23	**4.1**
1962	Mil N☆	18	14	.563	34	34	**22**	0	269.1	248	97	25	3	55-4	118	3.04	125	.246	.284	98-3	.184	4*	93	26	3.5
1963	Mil N☆	23	7	.767	33	33	**22**-7	0	259.2	241	85	23	0	49-4	102	2.60	124	.248	.282	90-4	.178	5	117	18	3.0
1964	Mil N	6	13	.316	38	25	4-1	4	173.2	204	110	23	2	52-4	78	5.29	67	.297	.345	59-1	.186	2*	115	-32	-3.2
1965	NY N	4	12	.250	20	19	5	0	126	140	70	18	2	35-1	56	4.36	81	.281	.329	35-2	.114	1*	76	-12	-1.2
	SF N	3	4	.429	16	11	3	0	71.2	70	34	8	1	21-1	34	3.39	106	.256	.308	21-0	.143	0	115	0	0.1
	Year	7	16	.304	36	30	8	0	197.2	210	39	26	3	56-2	90	4.01	89	.272	.321	56-2	.125	2	90	-12	-1.1
Total	21	363	245	.597	750	665	382-63	29	5243.2	4830	2016	434	42	1434-**60**	2583	3.09	118	.244	.296	1872-68	.194	88	108	365	51.4
SPALDING, AL Albert Goodwill B 9.2.1850 Byron, IL D 9.9.1915 San Diego, CA BR/TR 6-1/170# d5.5 M2 HF1939 ▲																									
1871	Bos NA	**19**	10	.655	31	31	22-**1**	0	257.1	333	272	2		38	23	3.36	124	.268	.290	144	.271	2	123	22	1.6
1872	Bos NA	**38**	8	**.826**	48	48	41-**3**	0	404.2	417	224	0		27	28	1.85	198	.244	.255	237	.354	18	114	**81**	**7.5**
1873	Bos NA	**41**	14	**.745**	**60**	**54**	46-1	3	**496.2**	643	413	5		36	50	2.99	111	.284	.296	323	.328	19	131	26	**3.4**
1874	Bos NA	**52**	16	**.765**	**71**	**69**	**65-4**	0	**617.1**	755	402	1		19	31	1.92	113	.273	.278	362	.329	21	141	17	**2.8**
1875	Bos NA	**54**	5	**.915**	**72**	62	52-**7**	**9**	570.2	573	241	1		18	75	1.59	135	.245	.251	343	.312	22*	165	33	**4.4**
1876	Chi N	**47**	12	**.797**	61	60	53-8	0	528.2	542	226	6		26	39	1.75	139	.247	.256	292	.312	9*	153	39	4.3
1877	Chi N	1	0	1.000	4	1	0	1	11	17	12	0		0	2	3.27	91	.321	.321	254	.256	0*	197	-1	-0.1
Total	5 NA	204	53	.794	282	264	226-16	12	2346.2	2721	1552	9		138	207	2.21	130	.264	.274	1409	.323	83	135	179	19.7
Total	2	48	12	.800	65	61	53-8	1	539.2	559	238	6		26	41	1.78	138	.249	.257	546	.286	9	153	38	4.2
SPANSWICK, BILL William Henry B 7.8.1938 Springfield, MA BL/TL 6-3/195# d4.18																									
1964	Bos A	2	3	.400	29	7	0	0	65.1	75	51	9	3	44-1	55	6.89	56	.306	.412	14-0	.286	1	128	-19	-1.2
SPARKS, JEFF James Jeffrey B 4.4.1972 Houston, TX BR/TR 6-3/220# d9.12																									
1999	TB A	0	0	—	8	0	0	1-0	10	6	6	1	1	12-1	17	5.40	92	.171	.396	0-0	—	0		0	0.0
2000	TB A	0	1	.000	15	0	0	0-0	20.1	13	8	2	2	18-1	24	3.54	140	.186	.367	0-0	—	0		3	0.1
Total	2	0	1	.000	23	0	0	1-0	30.1	19	14	3	3	30-2	41	4.15	119	.181	.377	0-0	—	0		3	0.1
SPARKS, STEVE Stephen Lanier B 3.28.1975 Mobile, AL BR/TR 6-4/210# d7.19																									
2000	Pit N	0	0	—	3	0	0	0-0	4	4	3	0	0	5-0	2	6.75	68	.267	.450	0-0	—	0		-1	0.0
SPARKS, STEVE Steven William B 7.2.1965 Tulsa, OK BR/TR 6/180# d4.28																									
1995	Mil A	9	11	.450	33	27	3	0-0	202	210	111	17	5	86-1	96	4.63	108	.274	.346	0-0	—	0	88	8	0.9
1996	Mil A	4	7	.364	20	13	1	0-0	88.2	103	66	19	3	52-0	21	6.60	79	.297	.392	0-0	—	0	96	-11	-1.0
1998	Ana A	9	4	.692	22	20	0	0-0	128.2	130	66	14	5	58-0	90	4.34	108	.263	.345	1-1	.000	0	97	6	0.7
1999	Ana A	5	11	.313	28	26	0	0-0	147.2	165	101	21	9	82-0	73	5.42	90	.281	.373	3-0	.333	1*	87	-11	-0.8
2000	Det A	7	5	.583	20	15	1-1	1-0	104	108	55	7	4	29-0	53	4.07	119	.263	.317	0-0	—	0	117	7	0.8
2001	Det A	14	9	.609	35	33	**8-1**	0-0	232	244	110	22	6	64-1	116	3.65	119	.271	.321	4-0	.000	-0*	99	16	1.4
2002	Det A	8	16	.333	32	30	3	0-0	189	238	134	23	12	67-3	98	5.52	78	.306	.366	2-0	.000	-0	90	-29	-2.9
2003	Det A	0	6	.000	42	0	0	2-2	89.2	95	57	11	3	34-4	49	4.72	92	.278	.343	0-0	—	0		-7	-0.4
	†Oak A	0	0	—	9	0	0	0-0	17.1	19	11	2	0	3-0	5	5.71	79	.271	.297	0-0	—	0		-2	-0.1
	Year	0	6	.000	51	0	0	2-2	107	114	72	13	3	37-4	54	4.88	89	.277	.336	0-0	—	0		-8	-0.5
Total	8	56	69	.448	241	164	16-2	3-2	1199	1312	711	136	47	475-9	601	4.77	98	.279	.348	10-1	.100	0	95	-23	-1.4
SPARKS, TULLY Thomas Frank B 12.12.1874 Etna, GA D 7.15.1937 Anniston, AL BR/TR 5-10/160# d9.15																									
1897	Phi N	0	1	.000	1	1	1	0	8	12	9	0	0	4	0	10.13	41	.343	.410	3-0	.000	-1	17	-4	-0.4
1899	Pit N	8	6	.571	28	17	8	0	170	180	101	1	10	82	53	3.86	99	.271	.360	62-0	.129	-2	98	-1	-0.2
1901	Mil A	7	17	.292	29	26	18	0	210	228	157	5	14	93	62	3.51	102	.273	.356	71-3	.169	-1	82	-9	-1.0
1902	NY N	4	10	.286	16	14	12	1	123	142	72	2	4	41	42	4.17	67	.289	.348	40-2	.150	-1	78	-14	-1.3
	Bos A	7	9	.438	17	15	15-1	0	142.2	151	83	4	7	40	37	3.47	103	.272	.329	52-1	.154	-1	67	0	-0.1
1903	Phi N	11	15	.423	28	28	27	0	248	248	109	3	8	56	88	2.72	120	.263	.310	92-3	.109	-5	78	13	0.6
1904	Phi N	7	16	.304	26	25	19-3	0	200.2	208	109	1	5	43	67	2.65	101	.260	.302	76-0	.105	-5	89	-5	-1.3
1905	Phi N	14	11	.560	34	26	20-3	1	259.2	217	86	2	9	73	98	2.18	134	.236	.298	94-3	.128	-2	139	22	1.5
1906	Phi N	19	16	.543	42	37	29-6	3	316.2	244	99	4	10	62	114	2.16	121	.211	.257	104-3	.154	0	87	20	2.1
1907	Phi N	22	8	.733	33	31	24-3	1	265	221	78	2	7	51	90	2.00	121	.228	.271	89-4	.034	-8	117	13	0.3
1908	Phi N	16	15	.516	33	31	24-2	2	263.1	251	98	3	8	51	85	2.60	93	.257	.300	77-11	.052	-5	94	-3	-1.1
1909	Phi N	6	11	.353	24	16	6-1	0	121.2	126	54	4	3	32	40	2.96	88	.280	.332	36-1	.139	-1	49	-5	-0.8
1910	Phi N	0	2	.000	3	3	0	0	15	22	12	2	2	2	4	6.00	52	.324	.361	5-0	.000	-1	95	-4	-0.5
Total	12	121	137	.469	314	270	203-19	8	2343.2	2250	1067	33	87	630	780	2.82	104	.254	.310	801-31	.115	-32	90	23	-2.2
SPARMA, JOE Joseph Blase B 2.4.1942 Massillon, OH D 5.14.1986 Columbus, OH BR/TR 6/195# d5.20																									
1964	Det A	5	6	.455	21	11	3-2	0	84	62	33	4	3	45-1	71	3.00	122	.207	.313	25-0	.160	1*	93	5	0.8
1965	Det A	13	8	.619	30	28	6	0	167	142	69	13	3	75-5	127	3.18	109	.228	.312	52-4	.135	-0	96	4	0.4
1966	Det A	2	7	.222	29	13	0	0	91.2	103	57	14	3	52-0	61	5.30	66	.288	.382	23-2	.217	1	109	-17	-1.6
1967	Det A	16	9	.640	37	37	11-5	0	217.2	186	103	20	8	85-2	153	3.76	87	.227	.305	74-13	.054	-5	132	-13	-2.1
1968	†Det A	10	10	.500	34	31	7-1	0	182.1	169	81	14	7	77-3	110	3.70	81	.246	.326	60-6	.133	-1	120	-13	-1.7
1969	Det A	6	8	.429	23	16	3-2	0-0	92.2	78	55	5	1	77-1	41	4.76	79	.231	.373	29-3	.138	-1	84	-10	-1.6
1970	Mon N	0	4	.000	9	6	1	0-0	29.1	34	25	7	2	25-3	23	7.06	58	.296	.421	6-1	.000	-0	47	-9	-1.1
Total	7	52	52	.500	183	142	31-10	0-0	864.2	774	423	77	27	436-15	586	3.94	86	.239	.332	269-29	.119	-6	107	-53	-6.9
SPECK, CLIFF Robert Clifford B 8.8.1956 Portland, OR BR/TR 6-4/195# d7.30																									
1986	Atl N	2	1	.667	13	1	0	0-0	28.1	25	13	2	1	15-0	21	4.13	96	.238	.336	3-1	.000	-0	67	0	0.0
SPEECE, BY Byron Franklin B 1.6.1897 West Baden, IN D 9.29.1974 Elgin, OR BR/TR 5-11/170# d4.21																									
1924	†Was A	2	1	.667	21	1	0	0	54.1	60	30	0	2	27	15	2.65	152	.303	.392	20-0	.150	-1	21	**4**	0.2
1925	Cle A	3	5	.375	28	3	3	1	90.1	106	48	0	3	28	26	4.28	103	.297	.353	31-0	.161	-2	51	3	0.1
1926	Cle A	0	0	—	2	0	0	0	3	1	1	0	0	2	1	0.00	—	.125	.300	0-0	—	0		1	0.1
1930	Phi N	0	0	—	11	0	0	0	19.2	41	30	1	0	4	9	13.27	41	.432	.455	3-0	.333	0		-14	-0.6
Total	4	5	6	.455	62	4	3	1	167.1	208	109	1	5	61	51	4.73	93	.316	.378	54-0	.167	-2	43	-6	-0.2
SPEER, FLOYD Floyd Vernie B 1.27.1913 Booneville, AR D 3.22.1969 Little Rock, AR BR/TR 6/180# d4.25																									
1943	Chi A	0	0	—	1	0	0	0	1	1	1	0	0	2	1	9.00	37	.250	.500	0-0	—	0		-1	0.0
1944	Chi A	0	0	—	2	0	0	0	2	4	2	0	0	0	1	9.00	38	.500	.500	0-0	—	0		-1	-0.1
Total	2	0	0	—	3	0	0	0	3	5	3	0	0	2	2	9.00	38	.417	.500	0-0	—	0		-2	-0.1
SPEER, KID George Nathan B 6.16.1886 Corning, MO D 1.13.1946 Edmonton, AL, CAN BL/TL 5-9/152# d4.24																									
1909	Det A	4	4	.500	12	8	4	1	76.1	88	39	2	4	13	12	2.83	89	.293	.331	25-0	.120	-0*	133	-5	-0.5
SPEIER, JUSTIN Justin James B 11.6.1973 Daly City, CA BR/TR 6-4/200# d5.27 f-Chris																									
1998	Chi N	0	0	—	1	0	0	0-0	1.1	2	2	0	0	1-0	2	13.50	33	.333	.429	0-0	—	0		-1	-0.1
	Fla N	0	3	.000	18	0	0	0-1	19.1	25	18	7	0	12-1	15	8.38	48	.325	.411	0-0	—	0		-9	-1.2
	Year	0	3	.000	19	0	0	0-1	20.2	27	25	7	0	13-1	17	8.71	47	.325	.412	0-0	—	0		-10	-1.3

Year	Tm Lg	W	L	Pct	G	GS	CG-Sho	SV-BS	IP	H	R	HR	HB	BB-IB	SO	ERA	AERA	OAV	OOB	AB-SH	AVG	PB	Sup	APR	PW
1999	Atl N	0	0	—	19	0	0	0-0	28.2	28	18	8	0	13-1	22	5.65	80	.248	.323	3-0	.333	0		-3	-0.1
2000	Cle A	5	2	.714	47	0	0	0-1	68.1	57	27	9	4	28-3	69	3.29	151	.226	.309	2-0	.500	0		12	1.1
2001	Cle A	2	0	1.000	12	0	0	0-0	20.2	24	16	5	3	8-0	15	6.97	65	.293	.365	0-0	—	0		-5	-0.4
	Col N	4	3	.571	42	0	0	0-1	56	47	24	8	5	12-3	47	3.70	144	.229	.283	7-0	.000	-1		9	0.8
2002	Col N	5	1	.833	63	0	0	1-3	62.1	51	31	9	3	19-4	47	4.33	110	.216	.282	3-0	.333	0		3	0.2
2003	Col N	3	1	.750	72	0	0	9-3	73.1	73	37	11	7	23-6	66	4.05	121	.257	.324	1-0	.000	-0		6	0.3
Total	6	19	10	.655	274	0	0	10-9	330	307	173	57	22	116-18	283	4.50	108	.245	.315	16-0	.188	-0		12	0.6

SPENCER, HACK Fred Calvin B 4.25.1885 St.Cloud, MN D 2.5.1969 St.Anthony, MN BR/TR 5-7/172# d4.18

Year	Tm Lg	W	L	Pct	G	GS	CG-Sho	SV-BS	IP	H	R	HR	HB	BB-IB	SO	ERA	AERA	OAV	OOB	AB-SH	AVG	PB	Sup	APR	PW
1912	StL A	0	0	—	1	0	0	0	1.2	2	2	0	0	0	0	0.00	—	.286	.286	0-0	—	0		0	0.0

SPENCER, GEORGE George Elwell B 7.7.1926 Columbus, OH BR/TR 6-1/215# d8.17

Year	Tm Lg	W	L	Pct	G	GS	CG-Sho	SV-BS	IP	H	R	HR	HB	BB-IB	SO	ERA	AERA	OAV	OOB	AB-SH	AVG	PB	Sup	APR	PW
1950	NY N	1	0	1.000	10	1	1	0	25.1	12	7	3	0	7	5	2.49	165	.141	.207	4-0	.000	-1	108	5	0.2
1951	†NY N	10	4	.714	57	4	2	6	132	125	62	21	1	56	36	3.75	104	.254	.332	32-3	.125	-1	135	4	0.3
1952	NY N	3	5	.375	35	4	0	3	60	57	39	13	3	21	27	5.55	67	.251	.323	10-0	.200	0	138	-11	-1.4
1953	NY N	0	0	—	1	0	0	0	2.1	3	2	0	0	2	1	7.71	56	.300	.417	0-0	—	0		-1	0.0
1954	NY N	1	0	1.000	6	0	0	0	12.1	9	5	1	0	8	4	3.65	111	.209	.333	3-0	.000	-0		1	0.1
1955	NY N	0	0	—	1	0	0	0	1.2	1	1	1	0	3-0	0	5.40	75	.167	.444	0-0	—	0		0	0.0
1958	Det A	1	0	1.000	7	0	0	0	10	11	4	0	0	4-0	5	2.70	149	.289	.349	0-0	—	0		1	0.1
1960	Det A	0	1	.000	5	0	0	0	7.2	10	3	1	0	5-1	4	3.52	112	.323	.417	1-0	.000	-0		1	0.0
Total	8	16	10	.615	122	9	3	9	251.1	228	123	40	4	106-1	82	4.05	96	.245	.324	50-3	.120	-2	131	0	-0.7

SPENCER, GLENN Glenn Edward B 9.11.1905 Corning, NY D 12.30.1958 Binghamton, NY BR/TR 5-11/155# d4.11

Year	Tm Lg	W	L	Pct	G	GS	CG-Sho	SV-BS	IP	H	R	HR	HB	BB-IB	SO	ERA	AERA	OAV	OOB	AB-SH	AVG	PB	Sup	APR	PW
1928	Pit N	0	0	—	4	0	0	0	5.2	4	3	0	0	3	2	1.59	256	.200	.304	1-0	.000	-0		1	0.0
1930	Pit N	8	9	.471	41	11	5	4	156.2	185	110	16	2	63	60	5.40	92	.305	.372	53-1	.113	-4	102	-7	-1.1
1931	Pit N	11	12	.478	38	18	11-1	3	186.2	180	83	8	5	65	51	3.42	112	.260	.328	52-10	.096	-3	73	10	0.9
1932	Pit N	4	8	.333	39	13	5-1	1	137.2	167	104	10	3	44	35	4.97	77	.288	.341	37-3	.162	-1	104	-22	-1.8
1933	NY N	0	2	.000	17	3	1	0	47.1	52	33	3	1	26	14	5.13	63	.284	.376	12-0	.167	-0	95	-11	-0.6
Total	5	23	31	.426	139	45	22-2	8	534	588	333	37	11	201	162	4.53	91	.282	.349	155-14	.123	-9	90	-29	-2.6

SPENCER, SEAN Sean James B 5.29.1975 Seattle, WA BL/TL 5-11/185# d5.6

Year	Tm Lg	W	L	Pct	G	GS	CG-Sho	SV-BS	IP	H	R	HR	HB	BB-IB	SO	ERA	AERA	OAV	OOB	AB-SH	AVG	PB	Sup	APR	PW
1999	Sea A	0	0	—	2	0	0	0-0	1.2	5	4	0	0	3-0	2	21.60	22	.556	.667	0-0	—	0		-3	-0.1
2000	Mon N	0	0	—	8	0	0	0-0	6.2	7	4	2	0	3-0	6	5.40	89	.292	.357	0-0	—	0		0	0.0
Total	2	0	0	—	10	0	0	0-0	8.1	12	8	2	0	6-0	8	8.64	55	.364	.450	0-0	—	0		-3	-0.1

SPENCER, STAN Stanley Roger B 8.2.1968 Vancouver, WA BR/TR 6-4/205# d8.27

Year	Tm Lg	W	L	Pct	G	GS	CG-Sho	SV-BS	IP	H	R	HR	HB	BB-IB	SO	ERA	AERA	OAV	OOB	AB-SH	AVG	PB	Sup	APR	PW
1998	SD N	1	0	1.000	6	5	0	0-0	30.2	29	16	5	1	4-0	31	4.70	83	.244	.274	9-3	.111	-0	150	-2	-0.1
1999	SD N	0	7	.000	9	8	0	0-0	38.1	56	44	11	1	11-1	36	9.16	46	.335	.380	10-1	.000	-1	55	-23	-3.1
2000	SD N	2	2	.500	8	8	0	0-0	49.2	44	22	7	2	19-1	40	3.26	133	.239	.316	12-2	.333	1*	82	5	0.5
Total	3	3	9	.250	23	21	0	0-0	118.2	129	82	23	4	34-2	107	5.54	75	.274	.328	31-6	.161	1	87	-20	-2.7

SPICER, BOB Robert Oberton B 4.11.1925 Richmond, VA BL/TR 5-10/173# d4.17

Year	Tm Lg	W	L	Pct	G	GS	CG-Sho	SV-BS	IP	H	R	HR	HB	BB-IB	SO	ERA	AERA	OAV	OOB	AB-SH	AVG	PB	Sup	APR	PW
1955	KC A	0	0	—	2	0	0	0	2.2	9	10	2	1	4-0	2	33.75	12	.529	.636	1-0	.000	-0		-8	-0.4
1956	KC A	0	0	—	2	0	0	0	2.1	6	5	1	1	1-0	0	19.29	22	.545	.615	0-0	—	0		-3	-0.2
Total	2	0	0	—	4	0	0	0	5	15	15	3	2	5-0	2	27.00	16	.536	.629	1-0	.000	-0		-11	-0.6

SPILLNER, DAN Daniel Ray B 11.27.1951 Casper, WY BR/TR 6-1/190# d5.21

Year	Tm Lg	W	L	Pct	G	GS	CG-Sho	SV-BS	IP	H	R	HR	HB	BB-IB	SO	ERA	AERA	OAV	OOB	AB-SH	AVG	PB	Sup	APR	PW
1974	SD N	9	11	.450	30	25	5-2	0-0	148	153	78	15	0	70-4	95	4.01	89	.267	.344	43-5	.023	-4	79	-9	-1.6
1975	SD N	5	13	.278	37	25	3	1-0	166.2	194	93	14	2	63-7	104	4.27	82	.293	.353	45-6	.133	1	83	-14	-1.3
1976	SD N	2	11	.154	32	14	0	0-1	106.2	120	70	11	0	55-8	57	5.06	65	.291	.371	25-0	.040	-1*	79	-23	-2.7
1977	SD N	7	6	.538	76	0	0	6-5	123	130	61	12	1	60-13	74	3.73	95	.280	.359	17-0	.118	1		-4	-0.5
1978	SD N	1	0	1.000	17	0	0	0-1	25.2	32	15	2	0	7-1	16	4.56	73	.317	.358	0-1	—	0		-4	-0.2
	Cle A	3	1	.750	36	0	0	3-2	56.1	54	26	2	1	21-3	48	3.67	102	.254	.323	0-0	—	0		0	0.0
1979	Cle A	9	5	.643	49	13	3	1-2	157.2	153	82	16	3	64-4	97	4.62	92	.256	.327	0-0	—	0	118	-3	-0.3
1980	Cle A	16	11	.593	34	30	7-1	0-0	194.1	225	122	23	3	74-2	100	5.28	77	.288	.350	0-0	—	0	113	-25	-3.1
1981	Cle A	4	4	.500	32	5	1	7-1	97.1	86	41	3	0	39-3	59	3.14	115	.240	.309	0-0	—	0	99	4	0.4
1982	Cle A	12	10	.545	65	0	0	21-10	133.2	117	44	9	0	45-7	90	2.49	164	.235	.295	0-0	—	0		22	4.1
1983	Cle A	2	9	.182	60	0	0	8-5	92.1	117	54	7	2	38-9	48	5.07	84	.315	.376	0-0	—	0		-7	-0.9
1984	Cle A	0	5	.000	14	8	0	1-0	51	70	36	3	0	22-2	23	5.65	73	.332	.385	0-0	—	0	74	-9	-0.8
	Chi A	1	0	1.000	22	0	0	1-1	48.1	51	25	7	1	14-0	26	4.10	102	.276	.328	0-0	—	0*		0	0.0
	Year	1	5	.167	36	8	0	2-1	99.1	121	64	10	1	36-2	49	4.89	84	.306	.359	0-0	—	0	74	-9	-0.8
1985	Chi A	4	3	.571	52	3	0	1-1	91.2	83	39	10	0	33-2	41	3.44	126	.245	.309	0-0	—	0*	112	8	0.5
Total	12	75	89	.457	556	123	19-3	50-29	1492.2	1585	786	134	13	605-65	878	4.21	91	.275	.342	130-12	.077	-3	93	-64	-6.4

SPINKS, SCIPIO Scipio Ronald B 7.12.1947 Chicago, IL BR/TR 6-1/185# d9.16

Year	Tm Lg	W	L	Pct	G	GS	CG-Sho	SV-BS	IP	H	R	HR	HB	BB-IB	SO	ERA	AERA	OAV	OOB	AB-SH	AVG	PB	Sup	APR	PW
1969	Hou N	0	0	—	1	0	0	0-0	2	1	1	0	0	1-0	4	0.00	—	.143	.250	0-0	—	0		0	0.0
1970	Hou N	0	1	.000	5	2	0	0-0	13.2	17	15	5	0	9-0	6	9.88	39	.293	.388	3-0	.000	-0*	127	-9	-0.6
1971	Hou N	1	0	1.000	5	3	1	0-0	29.1	22	12	2	1	13-0	26	3.68	92	.210	.303	9-0	.222	0	132	0	0.0
1972	StL N	5	5	.500	16	16	6	0-0	118	96	39	5	2	59-2	93	2.67	128	.221	.317	42-2	.167	-1*	94	10	0.8
1973	StL N	1	5	.167	8	8	0	0-0	38.2	39	25	4	0	25-2	25	4.89	75	.269	.374	11-1	.182	1	67	-6	-0.7
Total	5	7	11	.389	35	29	7	0-0	201.2	175	92	16	3	107-4	154	3.70	94	.234	.331	65-3	.169	0	93	-5	-0.5

SPLITTORFF, PAUL Paul William B 10.8.1946 Evansville, IN BL/TL 6-3/210# d9.23

Year	Tm Lg	W	L	Pct	G	GS	CG-Sho	SV-BS	IP	H	R	HR	HB	BB-IB	SO	ERA	AERA	OAV	OOB	AB-SH	AVG	PB	Sup	APR	PW
1970	KC A	0	1	.000	2	1	0	0-0	8.2	16	9	1	0	5-0	10	7.27	51	.390	.457	2-0	.500	0	0	-4	-0.3
1971	KC A	8	9	.471	22	22	6-3	0-0	144.1	129	49	4	4	35-1	80	2.68	128	.243	.292	48-1	.104	-1	78	12	1.3
1972	KC A	12	12	.500	35	33	12-2	0-1	216	189	81	11	4	67-2	140	3.13	97	.241	.301	71-7	.225	4	132	-1	0.5
1973	KC A	20	11	.645	38	38	12-3	0-0	262	279	135	19	5	78-7	110	3.98	103	.272	.325	0-0	—	0	123	1	0.2
1974	KC A	13	19	.406	36	36	8-1	0-0	226	252	122	23	1	75-8	90	4.10	93	.285	.338	0-0	—	0*	78	-8	-1.0
1975	KC A	9	10	.474	35	23	6-3	1-0	159	156	75	10	1	56-10	76	3.17	122	.255	.316	0-0	—	0	90	7	1.0
1976	†KC A	11	8	.579	26	23	5-1	0-0	158.2	169	79	11	3	59-0	59	3.97	88	.277	.341	0-0	—	0	106	-7	-0.7
1977	†KC A	16	6	**.727**	37	37	6-2	0-0	229	243	104	11	2	83-2	99	3.69	110	.278	.340	0-0	—	0	121	10	0.9
1978	†KC A	19	13	.594	39	38	13-2	0-0	262	244	113	22	3	60-2	76	3.40	113	.247	.290	0-0	—	0	112	13	1.6
1979	KC A	15	17	.469	36	35	11	0-0	240	248	137	25	5	77-1	77	4.24	101	.268	.324	0-0	—	0	105	-3	-0.4
1980	†KC A	14	11	.560	34	33	4	0-0	204	236	101	17	1	43-1	53	4.15	98	.296	.329	0-0	—	0	103	0	0.0
1981	KC A	5	5	.500	21	15	1	0-0	99	111	48	12	1	23-4	48	4.36	83	.294	.331	0-0	—	0	116	-6	-0.5
1982	KC A	10	10	.500	29	28	0	0-0	162	166	83	14	3	57-1	74	4.28	96	.266	.328	0-0	—	0	111	-2	-0.2
1983	KC A	13	8	.619	27	27	4	0-0	156	159	77	9	1	52-2	61	3.63	113	.262	.319	0-0	—	0	99	5	0.7
1984	KC A	1	3	.250	12	3	0	0-0	28	47	30	3	0	10-0	4	7.71	52	.376	.413	0-0	—	0	75	-13	-1.5
Total	15	166	143	.537	429	392	88-17	1-1	2554.2	2644	1243	192	34	780-41	1057	3.81	101	.270	.323	121-8	.182	3	106	4	1.6

SPOLJARIC, PAUL Paul Nikola B 9.24.1970 Kelowna, BC, CAN BR/TL 6-3/205# d4.6

Year	Tm Lg	W	L	Pct	G	GS	CG-Sho	SV-BS	IP	H	R	HR	HB	BB-IB	SO	ERA	AERA	OAV	OOB	AB-SH	AVG	PB	Sup	APR	PW
1994	Tor A	0	1	.000	2	1	0	0-0	2.1	5	10	3	0	9-1	2	38.57	13	.417	.667	0-0	—	0	76	-8	-1.2
1996	Tor A	2	2	.500	28	0	0	1-0	38	30	17	6	2	19-1	38	3.08	163	.214	.315	0-0	—	0		7	0.7
1997	Tor A	0	3	.000	37	0	0	3-0	48	37	17	3	2	21-4	43	3.19	144	.215	.305	1-0	.000	-0		8	0.6
	†Sea A	0	0	—	20	0	0	0-2	22.2	24	13	1	1	15-2	27	4.76	95	.276	.388	0-0	—	0		-1	0.0
	Year	0	3	.000	57	0	0	3-2	70.2	61	34	4	3	36-6	70	3.69	124	.236	.333	1-0	.000	-0		7	0.6
1998	Sea A	4	6	.400	53	6	0	0-2	83.1	85	67	14	1	55-3	89	6.48	72	.263	.369	0-0	—	0	84	-18	-1.8
1999	Phi N	0	3	.000	5	3	0	0-0	11.1	23	24	1	1	7-0	10	15.09	31	.426	.492	2-2	.000	-0	71	-14	-2.2
	Tor A	2	2	.500	37	2	0	0-1	62	62	41	9	2	32-2	63	4.65	106	.258	.347	0-0	—	0	75	-1	0.0
2000	KC A	0	0	—	13	0	0	0-0	9.2	9	7	4	0	5-0	6	6.52	79	.265	.359	0-0	—	0		-1	0.0
Total	6	8	17	.320	195	12	0	4-5	277.1	275	196	41	9	163-13	278	5.52	86	.259	.359	3-2	.000	-0	78	-28	-3.9

SPONGBERG, CARL Carl Gustav B 5.21.1884 Idaho Falls, ID D 7.21.1938 Los Angeles, CA BR/TR 6-2/208# d8.1

Year	Tm Lg	W	L	Pct	G	GS	CG-Sho	SV-BS	IP	H	R	HR	HB	BB-IB	SO	ERA	AERA	OAV	OOB	AB-SH	AVG	PB	Sup	APR	PW
1908	Chi N	0	0	—	1	0	0	0	7	9	7	1	2	6	4	9.00	26	.321	.472	3-0	.667	1		-4	-0.1

Year	Tm Lg	W	L	Pct	G	GS	CG-Sho	SV-BS	IP	H	R	HR	HB	BB-IB	SO	ERA	AERA	OAV	OOB	AB-SH	AVG	PB	Sup	APR	PW
SPOONER, KARL Karl Benjamin B 6.23.1931 Oriskany Falls, NY D 4.10.1984 Vero Beach, FL BR/TL 6/185# d9.22																									
1954	Bro N	2	0	1.000	2	2	2-2	0	18	7	0	0	0	6	27	0.00	—	.113	.191	6-0	.167	0	44	8	1.1
1955	†Bro N	8	6	.571	29	14	2-1	2	98.2	79	50	8	5	41-1	78	3.65	111	.215	.300	28-2	.286	3	110	3	0.7
Total	2	10	6	.625	31	16	4-3	2	116.2	86	50	8	5	47-1	105	3.09	132	.200	.285	34-2	.265	3	101	11	1.8
SPOONEYBARGER, TIM Timothy Floyd B 10.21.1979 San Diego, CA BR/TR 6-3/190# d9.5																									
2001	Atl N	0	1	.000	4	0	0	0-0	4	5	1	0	0	2-1	3	2.25	196	.313	.368	0-0	—	0		1	0.2
2002	Atl N	1	0	1.000	51	0	0	1-0	51.1	38	16	4	2	26-5	33	2.63	156	.207	.310	1-0	.000	-0		9	0.4
2003	Fla N	1	2	.333	33	0	0	0-1	42	27	21	1	1	11-0	32	4.07	101	.190	.248	3-0	.000	-0		0	0.0
Total	3	2	3	.400	88	0	0	1-1	97.1	70	38	5	3	39-6	68	3.24	127	.205	.288	4-0	.000	-0		10	0.6
SPRADLIN, JERRY Jerry Carl B 6.14.1967 Fullerton, CA BB/TR 6-7/230# d7.2																									
1993	Cin N	2	1	.667	37	0	0	2-1	49	44	20	4	0	9-0	24	3.49	116	.249	.279	2-0	.000	-0		3	0.1
1994	Cin N	0	0	—	6	0	0	0-0	8	12	11	2	0	2-0	4	10.13	41	.353	.368	0-0	—	0		-6	-0.3
1996	Cin N	0	0	—	1	0	0	0-0	0.1	0	0	0	0	0-0	0	0.00	—	.000	.000	0-0	—	0		0	0.0
1997	Phi N	4	8	.333	76	0	0	1-4	81.2	86	45	9	1	27-3	67	4.74	90	.274	.331	1-0	.000	-0		-3	-0.5
1998	Phi N	4	4	.500	69	0	0	1-3	81.2	63	34	9	2	20-1	76	3.53	123	.216	.270	1-0	1.000	1		7	0.7
1999	Cle A	0	0	—	4	0	0	0-0	3	6	6	1	0	3-0	2	18.00	28	.400	.500	0-0	—	0		-4	-0.2
	SF N	3	1	.750	59	0	0	0-1	58	59	31	4	10	29-6	52	4.19	100	.259	.367	1-0	.000	-0		-1	-0.1
2000	KC A	4	4	.500	50	0	0	7-4	75	81	49	9	3	27-2	54	5.52	93	.283	.350	0-0	—	0		-3	-0.4
	Chi N	0	1	.000	8	1	0	0-0	15	20	15	2	1	5-1	13	8.40	54	.328	.377	1-0	.000	-0	81	-7	-0.4
Total	7	17	19	.472	310	1	0	11-13	371.2	371	211	40	17	122-13	292	4.75	93	.264	.327	6-0	.167	0	81	-14	-1.1
SPRAGINS, HOMER Homer Franklin B 11.9.1920 Grenada, MS D 12.10.2002 Minter City, MS BR/TR 6-1/190# d9.13																									
1947	Phi N	0	0	—	4	0	0	0	5.1	3	4	0	0	3	3	6.75	59	.158	.273	0-0	—	0		-1	-0.1
SPRAGUE, CHARLIE Charles Wellington B 10.10.1864 Cleveland, OH D 12.31.1912 Des Moines, IA BL/TL 5-11/150# d9.17 ▲																									
1887	Chi N	1	0	1.000	3	3	2	0	22	24	16	1	4	13	9	4.91	92	.276	.394	13	.154	-1	82	0	-0.1
1889	Cle N	0	2	.000	2	2	2	0	17	27	31	0	2	10	8	8.47	48	.351	.438	7	.143	-0	117	-11	-0.8
1890	Tol AA	9	5	.643	19	12	9	0	122.2	111	83	0	18	78	59	3.89	102	.234	.363	199	.236	3*	145	0	0.1
Total	3	10	7	.588	24	17	13	0	161.2	162	130	1	24	101	76	4.51	89	.254	.376	219	.228	1	130	-11	-0.8
SPRAGUE, ED Edward Nelson Sr. B 9.16.1945 Boston, MA BR/TR 6-4/195# d4.10 s-Ed																									
1968	Oak A	3	4	.429	47	1	0	4	68.2	51	29	5	2	34-5	34	3.28	86	.209	.309	7-0	.000	-1	62	-4	-0.5
1969	Oak A	1	1	.500	27	0	0	2-1	46.1	47	24	4	2	31-6	20	4.47	77	.267	.383	5-2	.200	0		-5	-0.1
1971	Cin N	1	0	1.000	7	0	0	0-1	11	8	2	0	0	1-0	7	0.00	—	.195	.209	1-0	.000	-0		3	0.3
1972	Cin N	3	3	.500	33	1	0	0-0	56.2	55	33	6	3	26-3	25	4.13	78	.261	.347	7-0	.000	-1	83	-8	-1.0
1973	Cin N	1	3	.250	28	0	0	1-0	38.2	35	22	3	2	22-7	19	5.12	67	.246	.353	2-1	.000	-0		-7	-0.7
	StL N	0	0	—	8	0	0	0-1	8	8	2	1	0	4-0	2	2.25	162	.276	.353	0-0	—	0		1	0.1
	Year	1	3	.250	36	0	0	1-1	46.2	43	27	4	2	26-7	21	4.63	75	.251	.353	2-1	.000	-0		-5	-0.6
	Mil A	0	1	.000	7	0	0	1-2	9.2	13	11	0	2	14-5	3	9.31	40	.317	.492	0-0	—	0		-6	-0.7
1974	Mil A	7	2	.778	20	10	3	0-0	94	94	32	3	4	31-0	57	2.39	151	.266	.327	0-0	—	0	161	11	0.9
1975	Mil A	1	7	.125	18	11	0	1-0	67.1	81	46	5	2	40-3	21	4.68	82	.297	.389	0-0	—	0	88	-9	-1.0
1976	Mil A	0	2	.000	3	0	0	0-0	7.2	14	7	0	0	3-1	0	7.04	50	.438	.472	0-0	—	0		-3	-0.6
Total	8	17	23	.425	198	23	3	9-5	408	406	208	27	17	206-30	188	3.84	89	.263	.353	22-3	.045	-1	127	-27	-3.3
SPRING, JACK Jack Russell B 3.11.1933 Spokane, WA BR/TL 6-1/180# d4.16																									
1955	Phi N	0	1	.000	2	0	0	0	2.2	2	2	2	0	1-0	2	6.75	59	.200	.273	1-0	.000	-0		-1	-0.2
1957	Bos A	0	0	—	1	0	0	0	1	0	0	0	0	0-0	2	0.00	—	.000	.000	0-0	—	0		0	0.0
1958	Was A	0	0	—	3	1	0	0	7	16	11	1	0	7-3	1	14.14	27	.457	.535	2-0	.000	-0	259	-8	-0.4
1961	LA A	3	0	1.000	18	4	0	0	38	35	19	4	3	15-2	27	4.26	106	.243	.323	8-3	.000	-1	123	2	0.0
1962	LA A	4	2	.667	57	0	0	6	65	66	32	7	2	30-10	31	4.02	96	.270	.353	11-1	.091	-1		0	-0.1
1963	LA A	3	0	1.000	45	0	0	2	38.1	40	18	3	0	9-0	13	3.05	112	.268	.310	3-0	.333	0		0	0.1
1964	LA A	1	0	1.000	6	0	0	0	3.1	3	1	1	0	3-1	0	2.70	122	.273	.429	0-0	—	0		0	0.1
	Chi N	0	0	—	7	0	0	0	6	4	5	0	0	2-0	1	6.00	62	.200	.261	0-0	—	0		-2	-0.1
	StL N	0	0	—	2	0	0	0	3	8	9	1	0	1-1	0	3.00	127	.471	.500	0-0	—	0		-3	-0.1
	Year	0	0	—	9	0	0	0	9	12	20	1	0	3-1	1	5.00	75	.324	.366	0-0	—	0		-5	-0.2
1965	Cle A	1	2	.333	14	0	0	0	21.2	21	9	2	0	10-1	9	3.74	93	.259	.337	3-1	.333	0		0	0.0
Total	8	12	5	.706	155	5	0	8	186	195	106	21	5	78-18	86	4.26	90	.273	.346	28-5	.107	-1	167	-12	-0.7
SPRINGER, BRAD Bradford Louis B 5.9.1904 Detroit, MI D 1.4.1970 Birmingham, MI BL/TL 6/155# d5.1																									
1925	StL A	0	0	—	2	0	0	0	3	1	2	0	0	7	0	3.00	156	.200	.667	0-0	—	0		0	0.0
1926	Cin N	0	0	—	1	0	0	0	1.1	2	3	0	1	2	1	6.75	55	.286	.500	1-0	.000	-0		-1	-0.1
Total	2	0	0	—	3	0	0	0	4.1	3	5	0	1	9	1	4.15	105	.250	.591	1-0	.000	-0		-1	-0.1
SPRINGER, DENNIS Dennis Leroy B 2.12.1965 Fresno, CA BR/TR 5-10/185# d9.14																									
1995	Phi N	0	3	.000	4	4	0	0-0	22.1	21	15	3	1	9-1	15	4.84	87	.256	.337	8-0	.125	-0	75	-2	-0.3
1996	Cal A	5	6	.455	20	15	2-1	0-0	94.2	91	65	24	6	43-0	64	5.51	91	.251	.339	0-0	—	0	105	-6	-0.6
1997	Ana A	9	9	.500	32	28	3-1	0-0	194.2	199	118	32	10	73-0	75	5.18	88	.267	.335	3-0	.000	-0	98	-11	-1.0
1998	TB A	3	11	.214	29	17	1	0-0	115.2	120	77	21	12	60-1	46	5.45	88	.271	.372	1-0	.000	-0	59	-9	-1.0
1999	Fla N	6	16	.273	38	29	3-2	1-0	196.1	231	121	23	7	64-4	83	4.86	90	.303	.358	50-3	.120	-2	84	-14	-1.5
2000	NY N	0	1	.000	2	2	0	0-0	11.1	20	11	2	1	5-0	5	8.74	50	.377	.441	4-0	.000	-0	83	-5	-0.4
2001	LA N	1	1	.500	4	3	0	0-0	19	19	7	3	3	2-0	7	3.32	121	.275	.324	6-1	.000	-1	123	2	0.1
2002	LA N	0	1	.000	1	0	0	0-0	1.1	1	1	0	0	2-0	1	6.75	57	.200	.429	0-0	—	0		0	-0.1
Total	8	24	48	.333	130	98	9-4	1-0	655.1	702	415	108	40	258-6	296	5.18	88	.278	.351	72-4	.097	-4	88	-45	-4.8
SPRINGER, ED Edward H. B 2.9.1861 , CA D 4.24.1926 Los Angeles Co., CA 6-2/187# d7.12																									
1889	Lou AA	0	1	.000	1	1	1	0	5	8	8	0	2	2	1	9.00	43	.348	.444	2	.000	-0	16	-3	-0.4
SPRINGER, RUSS Russell Paul B 11.7.1968 Alexandria, LA BR/TR 6-4/195# d4.17																									
1992	NY A	0	0	—	14	0	0	0-0	16	18	11	0	1	10-0	12	6.19	63	.281	.387	0-0	—	0		-4	-0.2
1993	Cal A	1	6	.143	14	9	1	0-0	60	73	48	11	3	32-1	31	7.20	63	.303	.390	0-0	—	0	91	-15	-1.5
1994	Cal A	2	2	.500	18	5	0	2-1	45.2	53	28	9	0	14-0	28	5.52	89	.291	.340	0-0	—	0	124	-2	-0.2
1995	Cal A	1	2	.333	19	6	0	1-1	51.2	60	37	11	5	25-1	38	6.10	77	.290	.380	0-0	—	0	116	-8	-0.4
	Phi N	0	0	—	14	0	0	0-0	26.2	22	11	5	2	10-3	32	3.71	114	.227	.306	1-1	.000	-0		2	0.1
1996	Phi N	3	10	.231	51	7	0	0-3	96.2	106	60	12	1	38-6	94	4.66	93	.272	.336	17-2	.059	-1	78	-5	-0.8
1997	†Hou N	3	3	.500	54	0	0	3-4	55.1	48	28	4	4	27-2	74	4.23	95	.232	.329	1-0	.000	-0		-1	-0.1
1998	Ari N	4	3	.571	26	0	0	0-3	32.2	29	16	4	1	14-1	37	4.13	102	.232	.314	1-0	.000	-0		1	0.0
	Atl N	1	1	.500	22	0	0	0-1	20	22	10	0	0	16-3	19	4.05	103	.301	.422	0-0	—	0		0	0.0
	Year	5	4	.556	48	0	0	0-4	52.2	51	30	4	1	30-4	56	4.10	102	.258	.357	1-0	.000	-0		0	0.0
1999	†Atl N	2	1	.667	49	0	0	1-0	47.1	31	20	5	2	22-2	49	3.42	131	.185	.284	0-0	—	0		6	0.3
2000	Ari N	2	4	.333	52	0	0	0-2	62	63	36	11	2	34-6	59	5.08	93	.261	.354	5-0	.200	-0		-2	-0.2
2001	Ari N	0	0	—	18	0	0	1-0	17.2	20	16	5	0	4-0	12	7.13	64	.274	.308	0-0	—	0		-5	-0.3
2003	StL N	1	1	.500	17	0	0	0-1	17.1	19	16	8	1	6-0	11	8.31	49	.271	.338	1-1	.000	-0		-8	-0.8
Total	11	20	33	.377	368	27	1	8-16	549	564	337	85	22	252-25	496	5.18	85	.264	.345	26-4	.077	-2	103	-41	-4.1
SPROULL, CHARLIE Charles William B 1.9.1919 Taylorsville, GA D 1.13.1980 Rockford, IL BR/TR 6-3/185# d4.19																									
1945	Phi N	4	10	.286	34	19	2	1	130.1	158	102	10	0	80	47	5.94	65	.298	.390	35-3	.143	-1	92	-28	-2.8
SPROUT, BOB Robert Samuel B 12.5.1941 Florin, PA BL/TL 6/165# d9.27																									
1961	LA A	0	0	—	1	1	0	0	4	4	3	0	0	3-0	2	4.50	100	.267	.389	0-1	—	0	157	0	0.0
SPROWL, BOBBY Robert John B 4.14.1956 Sandusky, OH BL/TL 6-2/190# d9.5																									
1978	Bos A	0	2	.000	3	3	0	0-0	12.2	12	10	3	0	10-0	10	6.39	65	.245	.373	0-0	—	0	73	-3	-0.4
1979	Hou N	0	0	—	3	0	0	0-0	4	1	0	0	0	2-0	3	0.00	—	.083	.214	0-0	—	0		2	0.1

Year	Tm Lg	W	L	Pct	G	GS	CG-Sho	SV-BS	IP	H	R	HR	HB	BB-IB	SO	ERA	AERA	OAV	OOB	AB-SH	AVG	PB	Sup	APR	PW
1980	Hou N	0	0	—	1	0	0	0-0	1	1	0	0	0	1-0	3	0.00	—	.250	.400	0-0	—	0		0	0.0
1981	Hou N	0	1	.000	15	1	0	0-0	28.2	40	20	1	0	14-1	18	5.97	55	.333	.397	6-0	.167	-0	162	-8	-0.5
Total	4	0	3	.000	22	4	0	0-0	46.1	54	30	4	0	27-1	34	5.44	65	.292	.379	6-0	.167	-0	101	-9	-0.8
SPURGEON, JAY Jay Aaron B 7.5.1976 West Covina, CA BR/TR 6-6/211# d8.15																									
2000	Bal A	1	1	.500	7	4	0	0-0	24	26	16	5	2	15-0	11	6.00	79	.283	.394	0-0	—	0	114	-3	-0.2
SPURLING, CHRIS Christopher Michael B 6.28.1977 Dayton, OH BR/TR 6-6/240# d4.2																									
2003	Det A	1	3	.250	66	0	0	3-3	77	78	42	9	3	22-1	38	4.68	92	.266	.319	0-0	—	0		-2	-0.2
STABLEIN, GEORGE George Charles B 10.29.1957 Inglewood, CA BR/TR 6-4/185# d9.20																									
1980	SD N	0	1	.000	4	2	0	0-0	11.2	16	4	0	0	3-0	4	3.09	111	.340	.380	3-0	.000	-0	65	1	0.0
STACK, EDDIE William Edward B 10.24.1887 Chicago, IL D 8.28.1958 Chicago, IL BR/TR 6/175# d6.7																									
1910	Phi N	6	7	.462	20	16	8-1	0	117	115	61	7	4	34	48	4.00	78	.266	.326	36-2	.083	-3	76	-8	-1.2
1911	Phi N	5	5	.500	13	10	5	0	77.2	67	48	3	6	41	36	3.59	96	.234	.342	24-0	.083	-2	85	-4	-0.6
1912	Bro N	7	5	.583	28	17	4	1	142	139	80	3	9	55	45	3.36	100	.264	.343	52-2	.135	-3	94	-3	-0.6
1913	Bro N	4	4	.500	23	9	4-1	0	87	79	30	0	1	32	34	2.38	138	.250	.321	25-0	.160	-1	97	8	0.5
	Chi N	4	2	.667	11	7	3-1	1	51	56	29	1	2	15	28	4.24	75	.280	.336	16-1	.063	-1	105	-5	-0.7
	Year	8	6	.571	34	16	7-2	1	138	135	33	1	3	47	62	3.07	106	.262	.327	41-1	.122	-2	100	5	-0.2
1914	Chi N	0	1	.000	7	1	0	0	16.1	13	11	0	0	11	9	4.96	56	.220	.343	4-0	.000	-0	0	-3	-0.2
Total	5	26	24	.520	102	60	24-3	2	491	469	259	14	22	188	200	3.52	93	.258	.334	157-5	.108	-10	88	-15	-2.8
STAFFORD, GENERAL James Joseph "Jamsey" B 7.9.1868 Webster, MA D 9.18.1923 Worcester, MA BR/TR 5-8/165# d8.27 b-John ▲																									
1890	Buf P	3	9	.250	12	12	11	0	98	123	89	8	4	43	21	5.14	80	.294	.366	49	.143	-2*	89	-13	-1.2
STAFFORD, JOHN John Henry "Doc" B 4.8.1870 Dudley, MA D 7.3.1940 Worcester, MA BR/TR 5-10/170# d6.15 b-General																									
1893	Cle N	0	1	.000	2	0	0	0	7	12	15	1	0	7	4	14.14	35	.364	.475	4	.000	-1		-6	-0.6
STAFFORD, BILL William Charles B 8.13.1939 Catskill, NY D 9.19.2001 Wayne, MI BR/TR 6-2/193# d4.17																									
1960	†NY A	3	1	.750	11	8	2-1	0	60	50	17	3	1	18-0	36	2.25	159	.226	.286	22-0	.045	-2*	80	10	0.4
1961	†NY A	14	9	.609	36	25	8-3	2	195	168	65	13	5	59-4	101	2.68	139	.232	.294	67-3	.179	2	120	24	2.8
1962	†NY A	14	9	.609	35	33	7-2	0	213.1	188	95	23	4	77-6	109	3.67	102	.233	.301	78-4	.218	3	130	3	0.5
1963	NY A	4	8	.333	28	14	0	3	89.2	104	64	16	3	42-3	52	6.02	58	.287	.363	24-2	.292	3	117	-25	-2.9
1964	NY A	5	0	1.000	31	1	0	4	60.2	50	19	4	2	22-7	39	2.67	136	.231	.308	13-0	.077	-1	270	7	0.6
1965	NY A	3	8	.273	22	15	1	0	111.1	93	45	16	2	31-4	71	3.56	96	.229	.284	29-4	.000	-3	89	0	-0.3
1966	KC A	0	4	.000	9	8	0	0	39.2	42	28	2	2	12-1	31	4.99	68	.273	.327	11-2	.000	-1	68	-8	-0.9
1967	KC A	0	1	.000	14	0	0	0	16	12	4	0	0	9-2	10	1.69	189	.214	.323	1-1	.000	-0		2	0.1
Total	8	43	40	.518	186	104	18-6	9	785.2	707	337	77	19	270-27	449	3.52	103	.240	.306	245-16	.155	0	113	13	0.3
STALEY, GERRY Gerald Lee B 8.21.1920 Brush Prairie, WA BR/TR 6/195# d4.20																									
1947	StL N	1	0	1.000	18	1	1	0	29.1	33	11	2	1	8	14	2.76	150	.287	.339	6-0	.000	-1	64	4	0.2
1948	StL N	4	4	.500	31	3	0	0	52	61	44	5	0	21	23	6.92	59	.288	.352	9-1	.222	1	123	-16	-2.0
1949	StL N	10	10	.500	45	17	5-2	6	171.1	154	65	6	3	41	55	2.73	152	**.238**	.286	41-6	.122	-0	73	24	2.9
1950	StL N	13	13	.500	42	22	7-1	3	169.2	201	101	14	7	61	62	4.99	86	.300	.365	55-4	.145	-1	73	-11	-1.4
1951	StL N	19	13	.594	42	30	10-4	3	227	244	108	14	8	74	67	3.81	104	.275	.337	81-4	.160	-1	81	3	0.3
1952	StL N☆	17	14	.548	35	33	15	0	239.2	238	101	21	7	52	93	3.27	114	.256	.301	85-7	.153	-2	121	11	1.3
1953	StL N☆	18	9	.667	40	32	10-1	4	230	243	118	31	17	54	88	3.99	107	.269	.322	78-7	.103	-5	105	4	0.0
1954	StL N	7	13	.350	48	20	3-1	2	155.2	198	107	21	6	47	50	5.26	78	.308	.357	36-7	.139	-0	126	-21	-2.3
1955	Cin N	5	8	.385	30	18	2	0	119.2	146	72	22	3	28-3	40	4.66	91	.309	.347	36-4	.056	-4	97	-6	-0.9
	NY A	0	0	—	2	0	0	0	2	5	5	1	0	1-0	0	13.50	28	.417	.462	0-0	—	0		-3	-0.1
1956	NY A	0	0	—	1	0	0	0	0.1	4	4	0	0	0-0	1	108.00	4	.800	.800	1-0	.000	-0		-4	-0.2
	Chi A	8	3	.727	26	10	5	0	101.2	98	37	11	6	20-3	25	2.92	140	.251	.297	32-1	.094	-2	122	13	1.0
	Year	8	3	.727	27	10	5	0	102	102	43	11	6	20-3	26	3.26	126	.258	.303	33-1	.091	-3	122	10	0.8
1957	Chi A	5	1	.833	47	0	0	7	105	95	27	7	0	27-9	44	2.06	182	.244	.293	22-4	.045	-1		**19**	1.3
1958	Chi A	4	5	.444	50	0	0	8	85.1	81	36	10	0	24-3	27	3.16	115	.259	.307	11-1	.000	-1		3	0.4
1959	†Chi A	8	5	.615	**67**	0	0	14	116.1	111	39	5	0	25-9	54	2.24	167	.259	.298	13-4	.154	0		**17**	2.3
1960	Chi A★	13	8	.619	64	0	0	10	115.1	94	40	8	3	25-7	52	2.42	156	.227	.271	17-1	.235	1		**15**	**3.2**
1961	Chi A	0	3	.000	16	0	0	0	18	17	10	3	0	5-1	8	5.00	78	.246	.297	0-0	—	0		-2	-0.2
	KC A	1	1	.500	23	0	0	2	30	32	15	4	2	10-1	16	3.60	116	.278	.341	1-0	.000	0		1	0.2
	Det A	1	1	.500	13	0	0	2	13.1	15	6	1	0	6-1	8	3.38	121	.288	.356	1-0	.000	-0		1	0.2
	Year	2	5	.286	52	0	0	4	61.1	64	31	8	2	21-3	32	3.96	103	.271	.332	2-0	.000	0		0	0.2
Total	15	134	111	.547	640	186	58-9	61	1981.2	2070	946	186	63	529-37	727	3.70	108	.270	.321	525-51	.126	-16	101	52	6.2
STALEY, HARRY Henry Eli B 11.3.1866 Jacksonville, IL D 1.12.1910 Battle Creek, MI BR/TR 5-10/175# d6.23																									
1888	Pit N	12	12	.500	25	24	24-2	0	207.1	185	104	6	7	53	89	2.69	98	.235	.289	85	.129	-4	105	-3	-0.7
1889	Pit N	21	26	.447	49	47	46-1	1	420	433	254	11	8	116	159	3.51	107	.258	.309	186	.161	-7*	90	4	-0.1
1890	Pit P	21	25	.457	46	46	44-3	0	387.2	392	246	5	11	74	145	3.23	121	.251	**.290**	164	.207	1*	85	29	2.5
1891	Pit N	4	5	.444	9	7	6	0	71.2	77	49	4	2	11	25	2.89	114	.265	.296	31	.226	1	122	2	0.3
	Bos N	20	8	.714	31	30	26-1	0	252.1	236	111	12	4	69	114	2.50	146	.238	.290	102	.167	-2	99	32	2.8
	Year	24	13	.649	40	37	32-1	0	324	313	117	16	6	80	139	2.58	138	.244	**.292**	133	.180	-1	103	36	3.1
1892	†Bos N	22	10	.688	37	35	31-3	0	299.2	273	144	10	3	97	93	3.03	116	.233	.293	122	.131	-6*	106	18	1.0
1893	Bos N	18	10	.643	36	31	23	0	263	344	224	22	6	81	61	5.13	96	.307	.356	113	.265	3	132	-11	-0.7
1894	Bos N	12	10	.545	27	21	18	1	208.2	305	204	15	5	61	32	6.81	83	.337	.382	85-2	.235	0*	126	-18	-1.4
1895	StL N	6	13	.316	23	16	13	0	158.2	223	136	8	2	39	28	5.22	93	.327	.365	67-2	.134	-6	96	-9	-1.4
Total	8	136	119	.533	283	257	231-10	2	2269	2468	1472	93	48	601	746	3.80	105	.269	.317	955-4	.182	-19	104	44	2.3
STALLARD, TRACY Evan Tracy B 8.31.1937 Coeburn, VA BR/TR 6-5/205# d9.24																									
1960	Bos A	0	0	—	4	0	0	0	4	0	0	0	0	2-0	6	0.00	—	.000	.133	0-0	—	0		2	0.1
1961	Bos A	2	7	.222	43	14	1	2	132.2	110	75	15	1	96-2	109	4.88	85	.229	.354	36-4	.083	-2	91	-7	-0.8
1962	Bos A	0	0	—	1	0	0	0	1	0	0	0	0	0-0	0	0.00	—	.000	.000	0-0	—	0		0	0.0
1963	NY N	6	17	.261	39	23	5	1	154.2	156	89	23	1	77-6	110	4.71	74	.262	.344	48-2	.063	-3	89	-17	-2.8
1964	NY N	10	20	.333	36	34	11-2	0	225.2	213	111	20	6	73-3	118	3.79	94	.252	.314	79-1	.190	2	81	-6	-0.7
1965	StL N	11	8	.579	40	26	4-1	0	194.1	172	83	25	6	70-4	99	3.38	114	.235	.304	68-4	.088	-4	104	8	0.2
1966	StL N	1	5	.167	20	7	0	1	52.1	65	40	9	2	25-4	35	5.68	63	.305	.383	14-0	.000	-2	116	-13	-1.6
Total	7	30	57	.345	183	104	21-3	4	764.2	716	398	92	16	343-19	477	4.17	90	.248	.329	245-11	.110	-9	92	-33	-5.6
STANCEU, CHARLEY Charles B 1.9.1916 Canton, OH D 4.3.1969 Canton, OH BR/TR 6-2/190# d4.16 Mil 1942-45																									
1941	NY A	3	3	.500	22	2	0	0	48	58	41	3	1	35	21	5.63	70	.296	.405	12-0	.000	-2	77	-12	-1.5
1946	NY A	0	0	—	3	0	0	0	4	6	4	0	0	5	3	9.00	38	.316	.458	0-0	—	0		-2	-0.1
	Phi N	2	4	.333	14	11	1	0	70.1	71	35	4	0	39	23	4.22	81	.270	.364	19-1	.000	-2	79	-5	-0.6
Total	2	5	7	.417	39	13	1	0	122.1	135	80	7	1	79	47	4.93	74	.282	.385	31-1	.000	-4	76	-19	-2.2
STANDRIDGE, PETE Alfred Peter B 4.25.1891 Black Diamond, WA D 8.2.1963 San Francisco, CA BR/TR 5-10.5/165# d9.19																									
1911	StL N	0	0	—	2	0	0	0	4.2	10	10	0	1	4	3	9.64	35	.435	.536	1-0	.000	-0		-5	-0.2
1915	Chi N	4	1	.800	29	3	2	0	112.1	120	56	2	2	36	42	3.61	77	.274	.332	40-1	.225	3*	268	-10	-0.3
Total	2	4	1	.800	31	3	2	0	117	130	66	2	3	40	45	3.85	73	.282	.343	41-1	.220	3	268	-15	-0.5
STANDRIDGE, JASON Jason Wayne B 11.9.1978 Birmingham, AL BR/TR 6-4/217# d7.29																									
2001	TB A	0	0	—	9	1	0	0-0	19.1	19	10	5	0	14-1	9	4.66	97	.260	.379	0-0	—	0	62	0	0.0
2002	TB A	0	0	—	1	0	0	0-0	3	7	3	1	0	4-0	1	9.00	50	.500	.611	0-0	—	0		-1	-0.1
2003	TB A	0	5	.000	8	7	1	0-0	35.1	38	25	7	1	16-0	20	6.37	71	.275	.353	0-0	—	0	55	-6	-0.8
Total	3	0	5	.000	18	8	1	0-0	57.2	64	38	13	1	34-1	30	5.93	76	.284	.379	0-0	—	0	56	-7	-0.9
STANEK, AL Albert Wilfred "Lefty" B 12.24.1943 Springfield, MA BL/TL 5-11.5/190# d4.26																									
1963	SF N	0	0	—	11	0	0	0	13.1	10	7	1	0	12-2	5	4.73	68	.217	.379	1-0	.000	-0		-2	-0.1

Year	Tm Lg	W	L	Pct	G	GS	CG-Sho	SV-BS	IP	H	R	HR	HB	BB-IB	SO	ERA	AERA	OAV	OOB	AB-SH	AVG	PB	Sup	APR	PW
STANFIELD, KEVIN Kevin Bruce B 12.19.1955 Huron, SD BL/TL 6/190# d9.14																									
1979	Min A	0	0	—	3	0	0	0-0	3	2	2	0	0	0-0	0	6.00	73	.200	.200	0-0	—	0		0	0.0
STANFORD, JASON Jason John B 1.23.1977 Tucson, AZ BL/TL 6-2/200# d7.6																									
2003	Cle A	1	3	.250	13	8	0	0-0	50	48	20	5	1	16-1	30	3.60	123	.246	.305	0-0	—	0	68	6	0.4
STANGE, LEE Albert Lee B 10.27.1936 Chicago, IL BR/TR 5-10/170# d4.15 C12																									
1961	Min A	1	0	1.000	7	0	0	0	12.1	15	6	1	0	10-1	10	2.92	145	.294	.410	1-0	.000	-0		1	0.1
1962	Min A	4	3	.571	44	6	1	3	95	98	57	14	1	39-3	70	4.45	92	.271	.342	17-2	.059	-1	160	-6	-0.5
1963	Min A	12	5	.706	32	20	7-2	0	164.2	145	53	21	0	43-1	100	2.62	139	.233	.283	52-3	.096	-1	130	19	1.8
1964	Min A	3	6	.333	14	11	2	0	79.2	78	45	13	0	19-3	54	4.74	75	.255	.297	25-0	.040	-1	133	-9	-1.0
	Cle A	4	8	.333	23	14	0	0	91.2	98	47	14	1	31-4	78	4.12	87	.270	.329	25-2	.080	-1*	95	-5	-0.8
	Year	7	14	.333	37	25	2	0	171.1	176	51	27	1	50-7	132	4.41	81	.263	.314	50-2	.060	-2	112	-14	-1.8
1965	Cle A	8	4	.667	41	12	4-2	0	132	122	50	13	1	26-6	80	3.34	104	.247	.284	28-4	.107	1	99	5	0.4
1966	Cle A	1	0	1.000	8	2	1	0	16	17	5	1	1	3-0	8	2.81	122	.279	.318	4-1	.250	0	64	1	0.1
	Bos A	7	9	.438	28	19	8-2	0	153.1	140	65	17	1	43-9	77	3.35	114	.246	.296	48-3	.063	-3	76	7	0.3
	Year	8	9	.471	36	21	9-2	0	169.1	157	68	18	2	46-9	85	3.30	114	.249	.298	52-4	.077	-3	75	9	0.4
1967	†Bos A	8	10	.444	35	24	6-2	1	181.2	171	64	14	2	32-7	101	2.77	126	.246	.281	49-6	.061	-3	99	13	0.9
1968	Bos A	5	5	.500	50	2	1	12	103	89	54	10	1	25-5	53	3.93	80	.237	.280	15-2	.133	0	83	-9	-1.3
1969	Bos A	6	9	.400	41	15	2	3-1	137	137	70	14	6	56-8	59	3.68	104	.256	.332	35-8	.086	-2	96	0	-0.3
1970	Bos A	2	2	.500	20	0	0	2-0	27.1	34	24	5	2	12-3	14	5.60	71	.301	.369	5-1	.000	-0		-6	-1.0
	Chi A	1	0	1.000	16	0	0	0-1	22.1	28	13	5	0	5-1	14	5.24	74	.295	.330	1-0	.000	-0		-2	-0.2
	Year	3	2	.600	36	0	0	2-1	49.2	62	41	10	2	17-4	28	5.44	72	.298	.352	6-1	.000	-0		-9	-1.2
Total	10	62	61	.504	359	125	32-8	21-2	1216	1172	553	142	16	344-51	718	3.56	102	.252	.304	305-32	.079	-11	105	9	-1.5
STANHOUSE, DON Donald Joseph B 2.12.1951 DuQuoin, IL BR/TR 6-2/195# d4.19																									
1972	Tex A	2	9	.182	24	16	1	0-0	104.2	83	48	8	1	73-5	78	3.78	80	.223	.347	31-2	.129	-0*	62	-8	-0.7
1973	Tex A	1	7	.125	21	5	1	1-1	70	70	41	5	2	44-3	42	4.76	78	.262	.368	0-0	—	0*	101	-8	-0.7
1974	Tex A	1	1	.500	18	0	0	0-0	31.1	38	20	4	2	17-0	26	4.88	73	.302	.390	0-0	—	0		-5	-0.3
1975	Mon N	0	0	—	4	3	0	0-0	13	19	12	1	0	11-2	5	8.31	46	.345	.448	3-0	.333	0	107	-5	-0.3
1976	Mon N	9	12	.429	34	26	8-1	1-0	184	182	84	7	4	92-10	79	3.77	99	.263	.351	52-4	.212	2	71	1	0.5
1977	Mon N	10	10	.500	47	16	1-1	10-2	158.1	147	72	12	4	84-9	89	3.41	112	.251	.346	47-4	.191	1	104	5	0.7
1978	Bal A	6	9	.400	56	0	0	24-7	74.2	60	28	0	0	52-6	42	2.89	121	.230	.348	0-0	—	0		5	1.0
1979	†Bal A☆	7	3	.700	52	0	0	21-6	72.2	49	24	4	1	51-7	34	2.85	141	.202	.333	0-0	—	0		11	2.1
1980	LA N	2	2	.500	21	0	0	7-5	25	30	14	4	0	16-3	5	5.04	70	.306	.400	2-0	.000	0		-4	-0.7
1982	Bal A	0	1	.000	17	0	0	0-0	26.2	29	16	3	2	15-1	8	5.40	75	.276	.377	0-0	—	0		-4	-0.2
Total	10	38	54	.413	294	66	11-2	64-21	760.1	707	359	48	16	455-46	408	3.84	95	.252	.355	135-10	.185	4	80	-12	1.4
STANIFER, ROB Robert Wayne B 3.10.1972 Easley, SC BR/TR 6-3/205# d5.3																									
1997	Fla N	1	2	.333	36	0	0	1-1	45	43	23	9	3	16-0	28	4.60	88	.261	.337	3-0	.667	2		-2	0.0
1998	Fla N	2	4	.333	38	0	0	1-2	48	54	33	5	0	22-2	30	5.63	72	.277	.345	5-0	.000	-1		-9	-1.1
2000	Bos A	0	0	—	8	0	0	0-0	13	22	19	3	0	4-1	3	7.62	66	.355	.394	0-0	—	0		-7	-0.3
Total	3	3	6	.333	82	0	0	2-3	106	119	75	17	3	42-3	61	5.43	77	.282	.349	8-0	.250	1		-18	-1.4
STANKA, JOE Joe Donald B 7.23.1931 Hammon, OK BR/TR 6-5/201# d9.2																									
1959	Chi A	1	0	1.000	2	0	0	0	5.1	2	2	1	0	4-1	3	3.38	111	.111	.273	3-0	.333	0		0	0.1
STANLEY, BUCK John Leonard B 11.13.1889 Washington, DC D 8.13.1940 Norfolk, VA BL/TL 5-10/160# d9.12 b-Joe																									
1911	Phi N	0	0	—	4	0	0	0	11.1	14	11	0	0	9	5	6.35	54	.326	.442	4-0	.000	-1		-4	-0.3
STANLEY, BOB Robert William B 11.10.1954 Portland, ME BR/TR 6-4/215# d4.16																									
1977	Bos A	8	7	.533	41	13	3-1	3-2	151	176	74	10	3	43-5	44	3.99	113	.294	.343	0-0	—	0	103	7	0.8
1978	Bos A	15	2	.882	52	3	0	10-5	141.2	142	50	5	1	34-5	38	2.60	158	.266	.308	0-0	—	0	189	21	2.8
1979	Bos A★	16	12	.571	40	30	9-4	1-0	216.2	250	110	14	4	44-4	56	3.99	111	.294	.330	0-0	—	0	96	9	1.1
1980	Bos A	10	8	.556	52	17	5-1	14-3	175	186	75	11	7	52-8	71	3.39	125	.278	.335	0-0	—	0	106	14	1.8
1981	Bos A	10	8	.556	35	1	0	0-3	98.2	110	46	3	6	38-4	28	3.83	101	.294	.365	0-0	—	0	46	1	0.4
1982	Bos A	12	7	.632	48	0	0	14-2	168.1	161	60	11	4	50-6	83	3.10	**139**	.255	.312	0-0	—	0		23	3.1
1983	Bos A★	8	10	.444	64	0	0	33-14	145.1	145	56	7	3	38-12	65	2.85	153	.266	.315	0-0	—	0		21	3.3
1984	Bos A	9	10	.474	57	0	0	22-5	106.2	113	57	9	2	23-9	52	3.54	118	.267	.307	0-0	—	0		3	0.8
1985	Bos A	6	6	.500	48	0	0	10-8	87.2	76	30	7	2	30-10	46	2.87	149	.237	.303	0-0	—	0		14	2.0
1986	†Bos A	6	6	.500	66	1	0	16-5	82.1	109	48	9	0	22-8	54	4.37	95	.322	.360	0-0	—	0	109	-3	-0.5
1987	Bos A	4	15	.211	34	20	4-1	0-2	152.2	198	96	17	1	42-7	67	5.01	91	.321	.363	0-0	—	0	85	-9	-1.0
1988	†Bos A	6	4	.600	57	0	0	5-6	101.2	90	41	6	7	29-7	57	3.19	129	.242	.304	0-0	—	0		9	0.9
1989	Bos A	5	2	.714	43	0	0	4-0	79.1	102	54	4	1	26-2	32	4.88	84	.321	.366	0-0	—	0		-9	-0.7
Total	13	115	97	.542	637	85	21-7	132-55	1707	1858	797	113	41	471-87	693	3.64	118	.282	.331	0-0	—	0	102	101	14.8
STANTON, MIKE Michael Thomas B 9.25.1952 Phenix City, AL BB/TR 6-2/205# d7.9																									
1975	Hou N	0	2	.000	7	2	0	1-0	17.1	20	14	1	0	20-0	16	7.27	46	.290	.449	4-0	.250	0	26	-7	-0.8
1980	Cle A	1	3	.250	51	0	0	5-1	85.2	98	58	5	3	44-1	74	5.46	75	.297	.382	0-0	—	0		-14	-0.7
1981	Cle A	3	3	.500	24	0	0	2-2	43.1	43	21	4	0	18-4	34	4.36	83	.262	.333	0-0	—	0		-3	-0.4
1982	Sea A	2	4	.333	56	1	0	7-3	71.1	70	37	5	0	21-3	49	4.16	102	.260	.312	0-0	—	0	64	1	0.1
1983	Sea A	2	3	.400	50	0	0	7-2	65	65	26	3	1	28-5	47	3.32	129	.273	.349	0-0	—	0		7	0.6
1984	Sea A	4	4	.500	54	0	0	8-5	61	55	28	3	2	22-4	55	3.54	113	.241	.312	0-0	—	0		3	0.3
1985	Sea A	1	2	.333	24	0	0	1-1	29	32	20	4	3	21-3	17	5.28	80	.278	.403	0-0	—	0		-4	-0.4
	Chi A	0	1	.000	11	0	0	0-2	11.2	15	14	2	0	8-0	12	9.26	47	.294	.383	0-0	—	0		-7	-0.5
	Year	1	3	.250	35	0	0	1-3	40.2	47	37	6	3	29-3	29	6.42	66	.283	.397	0-0	—	0		-10	-0.9
Total	7	13	22	.371	277	3	0	31-16	384.1	398	218	27	9	182-20	304	4.61	88	.272	.354	4-0	.250	0	37	-24	-1.8
STANTON, MIKE William Michael B 6.2.1967 Houston, TX BL/TL 6-1/190# d8.24																									
1989	Atl N	0	1	.000	20	0	0	7-1	24	17	4	0	0	8-1	27	1.50	244	.207	.278	0-0	—	0		6	0.5
1990	Atl N	0	3	.000	7	0	0	2-1	7	16	16	1	1	4-2	7	18.00	22	.444	.512	0-0	—	0		-10	-1.8
1991	†Atl N	5	5	.500	74	0	0	7-3	78	62	27	6	1	21-6	54	2.88	135	.217	.273	6-0	.500	2		9	1.5
1992	†Atl N	5	4	.556	65	0	0	8-3	63.2	59	32	6	2	20-2	44	4.10	89	.247	.308	2-0	.500	0		-3	-0.4
1993	†Atl N	4	6	.400	63	0	0	27-6	52	51	35	4	0	29-7	43	4.67	86	.255	.346	0-0	—	0		-6	-1.2
1994	Atl N	3	1	.750	49	0	0	3-1	45.2	41	18	2	3	26-3	35	3.55	120	.248	.359	3-1	.667	1		4	0.5
1995	Atl N	1	1	.500	26	0	0	1-1	19.1	31	14	3	1	6-2	13	5.59	76	.369	.413	0-0	—	0		-3	-0.3
	†Bos A	1	0	1.000	22	0	0	0-1	21	17	9	3	0	8-0	10	3.00	162	.224	.298	0-0	—	0		4	0.2
1996	Bos A	4	3	.571	59	0	0	1-4	56.1	58	24	9	0	23-4	46	3.83	132	.275	.343	0-0	—	0		9	1.0
	†Tex A	0	1	.000	22	0	0	0-1	22.1	20	8	2	0	4-1	14	3.22	163	.241	.276	0-0	—	0		5	0.2
	Year	4	4	.500	81	0	0	1-5	78.2	78	34	11	0	27-5	60	3.66	140	.265	.325	0-0	—	0		14	1.2
1997	†NY A	6	1	.857	64	0	0	3-2	66.2	50	19	3	3	34-2	70	2.57	174	.205	.310	0-0	—	0		15	1.5
1998	†NY A	4	1	.800	67	0	0	6-4	79	71	51	13	4	26-1	69	5.47	80	.239	.307	1-0	.000	-0		-10	-0.7
1999	†NY A	2	2	.500	73	1	0	0-5	62.1	71	30	5	1	18-4	59	4.33	109	.289	.337	1-0	.000	-0	118	4	0.2
2000	†NY A	2	3	.400	69	0	0	0-4	68	68	32	5	2	24-2	75	4.10	118	.263	.325	1-0	1.000	0		6	0.5
2001	†NY A★	9	4	.692	76	0	0	0-1	80.1	80	25	4	4	29-9	78	2.58	175	.263	.332	0-0	—	0		17	2.5
2002	†NY A	7	1	.875	79	0	0	6-3	78	73	29	4	0	28-3	44	3.00	146	.256	.316	2-0	.000	-0		12	1.2
2003	NY N	2	7	.222	50	0	0	5-2	45.1	37	25	6	2	19-4	34	4.57	91	.219	.301	1-0	.000	-0		-2	-0.5
Total	15	55	44	.556	885	1	0	76-43	869	822	398	76	24	327-53	722	3.81	115	.252	.322	17-1	.412	3	118	57	4.9
STAPLETON, DAVE David Earl B 10.16.1961 Miami, AZ BL/TL 6-1/185# d9.14																									
1987	Mil A	2	0	1.000	4	0	0	0-0	14.2	13	3	0	0	3-0	14	1.84	249	.241	.281	0-0	—	0		4	0.6
1988	Mil A	0	0	—	6	0	0	0-0	13.2	20	9	1	1	9-1	6	5.93	67	.339	.435	0-0	—	0		-2	-0.1
Total	2	2	0	1.000	10	0	0	0-0	28.1	33	12	1	1	12-1	20	3.81	113	.292	.365	0-0	—	0		2	0.5

Year	Tm Lg	W	L	Pct	G	GS	CG-Sho	SV-BS	IP	H	R	HR	HB	BB-IB	SO	ERA	AERA	OAV	OOB	AB-SH	AVG	PB	Sup	APR	PW
STARK, DENNY Dennis James B 10.27.1974 Hicksville, OH BR/TR 6-2/210# d9.15																									
1999	Sea A	0	0	—	5	0	0	0-0	6.1	10	8	0	0	4-0	4	9.95	48	.370	.452	0-0	—	0		-4	-0.2
2001	Sea A	1	1	.500	4	3	0	0-0	14.2	21	15	5	0	4-0	12	9.20	45	.333	.368	0-0	—	0	59	-8	-0.9
2002	Col N	11	4	.733	32	20	0	0-1	128.1	108	69	25	5	64-4	64	4.00	120	.225	.321	41-3	.171	0*	121	7	0.7
2003	Col N	3	3	.500	17	13	0	0-0	78.2	98	57	12	3	33-2	30	5.83	84	.305	.368	22-1	.000	-2	125	-8	-0.7
Total	4	15	8	.652	58	36	0	0-1	228	237	149	42	8	105-6	110	5.13	93	.266	.345	63-4	.111	-1	117	-13	-1.1
STARKEL, CON Conrad B 11.16.1880 , Germany D 1.19.1933 Tacoma, WA BR/TR 6/200# d4.19																									
1906	Was A	0	0	—	1	0	0	0	3	7	6	1	0	2	1	18.00	15	.467	.529	0-0	—	0		-4	-0.2
STARR, RAY Raymond Francis "Iron Man" B 4.23.1906 Nowata, OK D 2.9.1963 Baylis, IL BR/TR 6-1/178# d9.11																									
1932	StL N	1	1	.500	3	2	1-1	0	20	19	7	2	1	10	6	2.70	146	.284	.385	4-1	.250	0	43	3	0.3
1933	NY N	0	1	.000	6	2	0	0	13.1	19	11	0	1	10	2	5.40	59	.339	.448	3-0	.000	-0	104	-4	-0.3
	Bos N	0	1	.000	9	1	0	0	28	32	15	4	1	9	15	3.86	79	.296	.356	7-1	.143	0	81	-3	-0.1
	Year	0	2	.000	15	3	0	0	41.1	51	18	4	2	19	17	4.35	71	.311	.389	10-1	.100	-0	98	-8	-0.4
1941	Cin N	3	2	.600	7	4	3-2	0	34	28	10	1	1	6	11	2.65	136	.219	.259	11-4	.182	-0	100	4	0.6
1942	Cin N☆	15	13	.536	37	33	17-4	0	276.2	228	88	10	3	106	83	2.67	123	.226	.301	88-12	.091	-5	78	24	1.9
1943	Cin N	11	10	.524	36	33	9-2	1	217.1	201	93	9	5	91	42	3.64	91	.248	.328	74-6	.122	-4	120	-6	-1.0
1944	Pit N	6	5	.545	27	12	5	3	89.2	116	60	6	1	36	25	5.02	74	.314	.377	22-0	.136	1	135	-12	-1.4
1945	Pit N	0	2	.000	4	0	0	0	6.2	10	7	0	0	4	0	9.45	42	.370	.452	1-0	1.000	1		-3	-0.5
	Chi N	1	0	1.000	9	1	0	0	13.1	17	11	1	0	7	5	7.43	49	.298	.375	2-1	.500	0	255	-5	-0.3
	Year	1	2	.333	13	1	0	0	20	27	22	1	0	11	5	8.10	46	.321	.400	3-1	.667	1	248	-9	-0.8
Total	7	37	35	.514	138	88	35-9	4	699	670	302	33	13	279	189	3.53	96	.255	.329	212-25	.123	-7	105	-2	-0.8
STARR, DICK Richard Eugene B 3.2.1921 Kittanning, PA BR/TR 6-3/190# d9.5																									
1947	NY A	1	0	1.000	4	1	1	0	12.1	12	4	1	0	8	1	1.46	242	.250	.357	3-1	.333	1	200	2	0.2
1948	NY A	0	0	—	1	0	0	0	2	0	1	0	0	2	2	4.50	91	.000	.250	0-0	—	0		0	0.0
1949	StL A	1	7	.125	30	8	1-1	0	83.1	96	46	6	1	48	44	4.32	105	.292	.384	23-0	.087	-1	74	2	0.0
1950	StL A	7	5	.583	32	16	4-1	2	123.2	140	83	11	7	74	30	5.02	99	.287	.389	36-4	.139	-3*	105	-2	-0.5
1951	StL A	2	5	.286	15	9	0	0	62	66	55	10	2	42	26	7.40	59	.273	.385	18-1	.222	0	92	-19	-1.7
	Was A	1	7	.125	11	11	1	0	61.1	76	41	12	0	24	17	5.58	73	.304	.365	17-0	.176	1	104	-9	-1.1
	Year	3	12	.200	26	20	1	0	123.1	142	46	22	2	66	43	6.49	65	.289	.375	35-1	.200	1	98	-28	-2.8
Total	5	12	24	.333	93	45	7-2	2	344.2	390	230	40	10	198	120	5.25	86	.286	.381	97-6	.155	-2	98	-26	-3.1
STARRETTE, HERMAN Herman Paul B 11.20.1938 Statesville, NC BR/TR 6/175# d7.1 C17																									
1963	Bal A	0	1	.000	18	0	0	0	26	26	10	1	2	7-0	13	3.46	100	.271	.327	1-1	.000	0		1	0.1
1964	Bal A	1	0	1.000	5	0	0	0	11	9	3	0	0	6-0	5	1.64	218	.250	.349	3-0	.000	-0		2	0.1
1965	Bal A	0	0	—	4	0	0	0	9	8	3	0	0	3-0	3	1.00	347	.258	.324	1-0	.000	-0		2	0.1
Total	3	1	1	.500	27	0	0	0	46	43	16	1	2	16-0	21	2.54	137	.264	.332	5-1	.000	-0		5	0.3
STAUFFER, ED Charles Edward B 1.10.1898 Emsworth, PA D 7.2.1979 St.Petersburg, FL BR/TR 5-11/185# d4.26																									
1923	Chi N	0	0	—	1	0	0	0	2	5	3	0	0	1	0	13.50	30	.556	.600	0-0	—	0		-2	-0.1
1925	StL A	0	1	.000	20	1	0	0	30.1	34	21	1	0	21	13	5.34	87	.283	.390	4-0	.250	-0	108	-2	-0.1
Total	2	0	1	.000	21	1	0	0	32.1	39	24	1	0	22	13	5.85	79	.302	.404	4-0	.250	-0	108	-4	-0.2
STEARNS, BILL William E. B 3.20.1853 Washington, DC D 12.30.1898 Washington, DC TR d6.26																									
1871	Oly NA	2	0	1.000	2	2	2	0	18	10	11	0		8	0	2.50	167	.149	.240	9	.000	-1	138	3	0.1
1872	Nat NA	0	11	.000	11	11	11	0	99	193	190	2		3	2	6.18	75	.339	.343	45	.244	-3	60	-13	-1.1
1873	Was NA	7	25	.219	32	32	32	0	283	481	395	8		16	5	4.61	73	.332	.340	133	.180	-6	83	-37	-3.0
1874	Har NA	3	14	.176	22	18	14	0	158.2	237	194	0		15	14	2.95	78	.297	.310	132	.159	-5*	70	-12	-1.3
1875	Was NA	1	14	.067	17	16	14	0	141	246	211	3		4	3	4.02	59	.332	.336	78	.256	-0*	52	-25	-2.1
Total	5 NA	13	64	.169	84	79	73	0	699.2	1167	1001	13		46	24	4.28	72	.322	.331	397	.191	-16	73	-84	-7.4
STECHER, WILLIAM William Theodore B 10.20.1869 Riverside, NJ D 12.26.1926 Riverside, NJ d9.6																									
1890	Phi AA	0	10	.000	10	10	9	0	68	111	110	1	14	60	18	10.32	38	.356	.479	29	.241	1	47	-48	-4.4
STECHSCHULTE, GENE Gene Urban B 8.12.1973 Lima, OH BR/TR 6-5/210# d4.20																									
2000	StL N	1	0	1.000	20	0	0	0-1	25.2	24	22	6	0	17-1	12	6.31	73	.247	.353	0-0	—	0		-6	-0.3
2001	†StL N	1	5	.167	67	0	0	6-2	70	71	35	10	4	30-2	51	3.86	111	.273	.354	3-0	.667	2*		2	0.4
2002	StL N	6	2	.750	29	0	0	0-2	32	27	19	4	1	17-1	21	4.78	83	.235	.328	2-0	.000	-0		-3	-0.7
Total	3	8	7	.533	116	0	0	6-5	127.2	122	76	20	5	64-4	84	4.58	93	.258	.347	5-0	.400	2		-7	-0.6
STEELE, ELMER Elmer Rae B 5.17.1886 Poughkeepsie, NY D 3.9.1966 Rhinebeck, NY BB/TR 5-11/200# d9.12																									
1907	Bos A	0	1	.000	4	1	0	0	11.1	11	7	0	0	1	10	1.59	162	.256	.273	4-0	.000	-1	0	0	-0.1
1908	Bos A	5	7	.417	16	13	9-1	0	118	85	34	1	3	13	37	1.83	134	.209	.239	39-1	.051	-4	77	8	0.4
1909	Bos A	4	4	.500	16	8	2	1	75.2	75	37	1	1	15	32	2.85	88	.255	.294	22-1	.227	1	148	-4	-0.3
1910	Pit N	0	3	.000	3	3	2	0	24	19	9	0	0	3	7	2.25	138	.221	.247	7-0	.000	-1	32	2	0.2
1911	Pit N	9	9	.500	31	16	7-2	2	166	153	65	5	4	31	52	2.60	132	.256	.297	61-1	.180	-0	142	14	1.4
	Bro N	0	0	—	5	2	0	0	23	24	10	0	0	5	9	3.13	107	.258	.296	9-0	.000	-1	146	1	0.0
	Year	9	9	.500	36	18	7-2	2	189	177	17	5	4	36	61	2.67	128	.257	.297	70-1	.157	-1	143	15	1.4
Total	5	18	24	.429	75	43	20-3	3	418	367	162	7	8	68	147	2.41	122	.241	.278	142-3	.127	-6	114	21	1.6
STEELE, BOB Robert Wesley B 1.5.1894 Cassburn, ON, CAN D 1.27.1962 Ocala, FL BB/TL 5-10.5/175# d4.17																									
1916	StL N	5	15	.250	29	21	7-1	0	148	156	74	6	3	42	67	3.41	78	.285	.340	51-0	.196	-1	73	-12	-1.9
1917	StL N	1	3	.250	12	6	1	0	42	33	17	1	0	19	23	3.21	84	.223	.311	13-0	.385	2	70	-2	0.0
	Pit N	5	11	.313	27	19	13-1	1	179.2	158	71	0	5	53	82	2.76	103	.237	.298	76-1	.224	1*	73	1	0.0
	Year	6	14	.300	39	25	14-1	1	221.2	191	74	1	5	72	105	2.84	99	.235	.301	89-1	.247	2	72	-1	0.0
1918	Pit N	2	3	.400	10	4	2-1	1	49	44	25	2	2	17	21	3.31	87	.240	.312	16-0	.125	-0	79	-3	-0.3
	NY N	3	5	.375	12	7	5-1	1	66	56	29	1	3	11	24	2.59	101	.226	.267	21-0	.286	2	115	-2	-0.1
	Year	5	8	.385	22	11	7-2	2	115	100	33	3	5	28	45	2.90	94	.232	.287	37-0	.216	2	101	-5	-0.4
1919	NY N	0	1	.000	1	0	0	0	3	3	3	0	0	2	0	6.00	47	.250	.357	1-0	.000	-0		-1	-0.3
Total	4	16	38	.296	91	57	28-4	3	487.2	450	219	10	13	144	217	3.05	90	.249	.310	178-1	.225	3	78	-19	-2.6
STEELE, BILL William Mitchell "Big Bill" B 10.5.1885 Milford, PA D 10.19.1949 Overland, MO BR/TR 5-11/200# d9.10																									
1910	StL N	4	4	.500	9	8	8	1	71.2	71	35	1	6	24	25	3.27	91	.264	.338	31-0	.258	1	119	-3	-0.2
1911	StL N	18	19	.486	43	34	23-1	3	287.1	287	153	8	10	113	115	3.73	91	.269	.345	101-3	.208	4	77	-11	-0.7
1912	StL N	9	13	.409	40	25	7	2	194	245	143	5	7	66	67	4.69	73	.322	.381	61-1	.180	1*	128	-27	-2.3
1913	StL N	4	4	.500	12	9	2	0	54	58	31	3	3	18	10	5.00	65	.286	.353	18-1	.056	-1	98	-9	-1.3
1914	StL N	1	2	.333	17	2	0	0	53.1	55	30	3	3	7	16	2.70	104	.274	.308	17-1	.294	2	90	-2	0.1
	Bro N	1	1	.500	8	1	0	1	16.1	17	16	1	0	7	3	5.51	52	.258	.329	3-1	.333	1	175	-5	-0.6
	Year	2	3	.400	25	3	0	1	69.2	72	23	4	3	14	19	3.36	84	.270	.313	20-2	.300	2	119	-6	-0.5
Total	5	37	43	.463	129	79	40-1	7	676.2	733	408	21	29	235	236	4.02	82	.286	.352	231-7	.203	8	102	-57	-5.0
STEEN, BILL William John B 11.11.1887 Pittsburgh, PA D 3.13.1979 Signal Hill, CA BR/TR 6-0.5/180# d4.15																									
1912	Cle A	9	8	.529	26	16	6-1	0	143.1	163	75	3	1	45	61	3.77	90	.298	.352	48-1	.271	2	102	-3	-0.2
1913	Cle A	4	5	.444	22	13	7-2	2	128.1	113	52	3	4	49	57	2.45	124	.239	.316	41-4	.171	-0	107	6	0.4
1914	Cle A	9	14	.391	30	22	13-1	0	200.2	201	74	0	4	68	97	2.60	111	.272	.337	70-3	.200	1	82	9	1.1
1915	Cle A	1	4	.200	10	7	2	0	45.1	51	30	1	2	15	22	4.96	61	.290	.352	16-0	.188	-0	85	-8	-0.7
	Det A	5	1	.833	20	7	3	4	79.1	83	35	0	1	22	28	2.72	111	.269	.319	28-1	.179	-1	168	1	0.1
	Year	6	5	.545	30	14	5	4	124.2	134	42	1	3	37	50	3.54	86	.276	.331	44-1	.182	-1	127	-7	-0.6
Total	4	28	32	.467	108	65	31-4	6	597	611	266	7	12	199	265	3.05	101	.273	.335	203-9	.207	1	102	5	0.7
STEENGRAFE, MILT Milton Henry B 5.26.1900 San Francisco, CA D 6.2.1977 Oklahoma City, OK BR/TR 6/170# d5.5																									
1924	Chi A	0	0	—	3	0	0	0	5.2	15	8	0	0	4	3	12.71	32	.484	.543	1-0	.000	-0		-5	-0.2
1926	Chi A	1	1	.500	13	1	0	0	38.1	43	22	1	2	19	10	3.99	97	.295	.383	14-1	.000	-2	44	-2	-0.3

Year	Tm Lg	W	L	Pct	G	GS	CG-Sho	SV-BS	IP	H	R	HR	HB	BB-IB	SO	ERA	AERA	OAV	OOB	AB-SH	AVG	PB	Sup	APR	PW
Total	2	1	1	.500	16	1	0	0	44	58	30	1	2	23	13	5.11	76	.328	.411	15-1	.000	-2	44	-7	-0.5
STEENSTRA, KENNIE Kenneth Gregory B 10.13.1970 Springfield, MO BR/TR 6-5/220# d5.21																									
1998	Chi N	0	0	—	4	0	0	0-0	3.1	7	4	2	0	1-0	4	10.80	41	.412	.444	0-0	—	0		-2	-0.1
STEEVENS, MORRIE Morris Dale B 10.7.1940 Salem, IL BL/TL 6-2/175# d4.13																									
1962	Chi N	0	1	.000	12	1	0	0	15	10	4	0	1	11-0	5	2.40	173	.196	.333	1-0	.000	-0	63	3	0.2
1964	Phi N	0	0	—	4	0	0	0	2.2	5	3	0	0	1-0	3	3.38	103	.385	.429	0-0	—	0		-1	0.0
1965	Phi N	0	1	.000	6	0	0	0	2.2	5	5	1	0	4-0	3	16.88	20	.417	.563	0-0	—	0		-4	-0.7
Total	3	0	2	.000	22	1	0	0	20.1	20	12	1	1	16-0	11	4.43	90	.263	.385	1-0	.000	-0	63	-2	-0.5
STEIN, ED Edward F. B 9.5.1869 Detroit, MI D 5.10.1928 Detroit, MI BR/TR 5-11/170# d7.24																									
1890	Chi N	12	6	.667	20	18	14-1	0	160.2	147	100	9	11	83	65	3.81	96	.236	.336	59	.153	-2	99	-1	-0.3
1891	Chi N	7	6	.538	14	10	9-1	0	101	99	68	7	2	57	38	3.74	89	.247	.343	43	.163	-1	104	-6	-0.6
1892	Bro N	27	16	.628	48	42	38-6	1	377.1	310	166	6	15	150	190	2.84	111	.215	.296	144	.215	4	110	16	2.0
1893	Bro N	19	15	.559	37	34	28-1	0	298.1	294	190	4	8	119	81	3.77	117	.250	.323	118	.212	-3	99	20	1.5
1894	Bro N	26	14	.650	44	40	37-2	1	350	388	261	10	14	170	84	4.63	107	.278	.362	143-4	.252	4*	116	11	1.2
1895	Bro N	15	13	.536	32	27	24-1	1	255.1	282	163	8	6	93	55	4.72	93	.276	.340	104-2	.250	2	95	-5	-0.2
1896	Bro N	3	6	.333	17	10	6	0	90.1	130	79	6	2	51	16	4.88	84	.334	.414	39-1	.256	0	105	-12	-0.8
1898	Bro N	0	2	.000	3	2	2	0	23	39	21	0	0	9	6	5.48	65	.371	.421	10-0	.400	1	59	-5	-0.3
Total	8	109	78	.583	215	183	158-12	3	1656	1689	1048	50	58	732	535	3.97	103	.258	.338	660-7	.224	5	105	18	2.5
STEIN, IRV Irvin Michael B 5.21.1911 Madisonville, LA D 1.7.1981 Covington, LA BR/TR 6-2/170# d7.7																									
1932	Phi A	0	0	—	1	0	0	0	3	7	4	2	0	1	0	12.00	38	.500	.533	1-0	.000	-0		-2	-0.1
STEIN, BLAKE William Blake B 8.3.1973 McComb, MS BR/TR 6-7/210# d5.10																									
1998	Oak A	5	9	.357	24	20	1-1	0-0	117.1	117	92	22	5	71-3	89	6.37	72	.255	.359	5-1	.000	-0	104	-23	-2.3
1999	Oak A	0	0	—	1	1	0	0-0	2.2	6	5	1	0	6-0	4	16.88	28	.462	.632	0-0	—	0	220	-4	-0.2
	KC A	1	2	.333	12	11	0	0-0	70.1	59	33	10	7	41-1	43	4.09	123	.230	.350	0-0	—	0	76	8	0.3
	Year	1	2	.333	13	12	0	0-0	73	65	37	11	7	47-1	47	4.56	110	.241	.366	0-0	—	0	87	4	0.1
2000	KC A	8	5	.615	17	17	1	0-0	107.2	98	57	19	3	57-1	78	4.68	110	.247	.343	2-0	.000	-0	110	6	0.6
2001	KC A	7	8	.467	36	15	0	1-1	131	112	73	20	3	79-2	113	4.74	104	.233	.342	2-0	.000	-0	91	4	0.2
2002	KC A	0	4	.000	27	2	0	1-1	46.2	59	41	6	3	27-1	42	7.91	64	.306	.394	0-0	—	0	83	-12	-1.0
Total	5	21	28	.429	117	66	2-1	2-2	475.2	451	301	78	21	281-8	369	5.41	91	.251	.356	9-1	.000	-1	98	-21	-2.4
STEIN, RANDY William Randolph B 3.7.1953 Pomona, CA BR/TR 6-4/210# d4.17																									
1978	Mil A	3	2	.600	31	1	0	1-1	72.2	78	51	5	4	39-1	42	5.33	71	.280	.371	0-0	—	0	48	-14	-0.9
1979	Sea A	2	3	.400	23	1	0	0-3	41.1	48	29	7	1	27-4	39	5.88	74	.291	.390	0-0	—	0	21	-6	-0.7
1981	Sea A	0	1	.000	5	0	0	0-1	9.1	18	12	1	0	8-0	6	10.61	36	.429	.510	0-0	—	0		-7	-0.6
1982	Chi N	0	0	—	6	0	0	0-0	10.1	7	4	2	0	7-2	6	3.48	107	.200	.326	0-0	—	0		0	0.0
Total	4	5	6	.455	65	2	0	1-5	133.2	151	96	15	5	81-7	93	5.72	69	.290	.385	0-0	—	0	34	-27	-2.2
STEINEDER, RAY Raymond J. B 11.13.1895 Salem, NJ D 8.25.1982 Vineland, NJ BR/TR 6-0.5/160# d7.16																									
1923	Pit N	2	0	1.000	15	2	1	0	55	58	30	3	2	18	23	4.75	85	.278	.341	15-1	.467	3	297	-3	0.1
1924	Pit N	0	1	.000	5	0	0	0	2.2	6	6	0	0	5	0	13.50	28	.400	.550	0-0	—	0		-3	-0.6
	Phi N	1	1	.500	9	0	0	0	28.2	31	15	1	0	16	11	4.40	101	.284	.376	10-0	.300	0		1	0.1
	Year	1	2	.333	14	0	0	0	31.1	37	36	1	0	21	11	5.17	85	.298	.400	10-0	.300	0		-2	-0.5
Total	2	3	2	.600	29	2	1	0	86.1	95	51	4	2	39	34	4.90	85	.285	.364	25-1	.400	3	297	-5	-0.4
STEIRER, RICK Ricky Francis B 8.27.1956 Baltimore, MD BR/TR 6-4/200# d8.5																									
1982	Cal A	1	0	1.000	10	1	0	0-1	26.1	25	14	2	1	11-0	14	3.76	108	.243	.322	0-0	—	0	157	0	0.0
1983	Cal A	3	2	.600	19	5	0	0-0	61.2	77	40	3	3	18-4	25	4.82	84	.302	.351	0-0	—	0	122	-7	-0.5
1984	Cal A	0	1	.000	1	1	0	0-0	2.2	6	5	0	0	2-1	2	16.88	24	.500	.571	0-0	—	0	91	-4	-0.5
Total	3	4	3	.571	30	7	0	0-1	90.2	108	59	5	4	31-5	41	4.86	83	.292	.350	0-0	—	0	122	-11	-1.0
STELLBERGER, BILL William F. B 4.22.1865 Detroit, MI D 11.9.1936 Detroit, MI BL/TL d10.1																									
1885	Pro N	0	1	.000	1	1	1	0	8	14	10	0		4	0	7.88	34	.389	.450	4	.000	-1	126	-4	-0.4
STEMBER, JEFF Jeffrey Alan B 3.2.1958 Elizabeth, NJ BR/TR 6-5/220# d8.5																									
1980	SF N	0	0	—	1	1	0	0-0	3	2	3	1	0	2-0	0	3.00	118	.167	.286	1-0	.000	-0	227	-1	-0.1
STEMMEYER, BILL William "Cannon Ball" B 5.6.1865 Cleveland, OH D 5.3.1945 Cleveland, OH BR/TR 6-2/190# d10.3																									
1885	Bos N	1	1	.500	2	2	2-1	0	11	7	7	0		11	8	0.00	—	.194	.383	7	.429	1	200	1	0.4
1886	Bos N	22	18	.550	41	41	41	0	348.2	300	218	11		144	239	3.02	106	.218	.292	148	.277	9	115	5	1.1
1887	Bos N	6	8	.429	15	14	14	1	119.1	138	107	4	2	41	41	5.20	79	.274	.331	47	.255	2	80	-17	-1.4
1888	Cle AA	0	2	.000	2	2	2	0	16	37	42	0	1	9	7	9.00	34	.435	.495	10	.400	1*	94	-14	-1.1
Total	4	29	29	.500	60	59	59-1	1	495	482	374	15	3	205	295	3.67	93	.241	.312	212	.283	14	108	-25	-1.0
STENHOUSE, DAVE David Rotchford B 9.12.1933 Westerly, RI BR/TR 6/195# d4.18 s-Mike																									
1962	Was A★	11	12	.478	34	26	9-2	0	197	169	84	24	2	90-9	123	3.65	110	.234	.319	58-6	.052	-5	89	10	0.7
1963	Was A	3	9	.250	16	16	2-1	0	87	90	46	12	1	45-2	47	4.55	82	.260	.345	25-1	.080	-1	72	-6	-0.9
1964	Was A	2	7	.222	26	14	1	1	88	80	54	12	1	39-1	44	4.81	77	.239	.320	20-3	.300	2	91	-10	-0.8
Total	3	16	28	.364	76	56	12-3	1	372	339	184	48	4	174-12	214	4.14	94	.241	.326	103-10	.107	-4	84	-6	-1.0
STEPHEN, BUZZ Louis Roberts B 7.13.1944 Porterville, CA BR/TR 6-4/205# d9.20																									
1968	Min A	1	1	.500	2	2	0	0	11.1	11	7	0	1	7-0	4	4.76	65	.275	.388	3-1	.000	-0	85	-2	-0.4
STEPHENS, BRYAN Bryan Maris B 7.14.1920 Fayetteville, AR D 11.21.1991 Santa Ana, CA BR/TR 6-4/175# d5.15																									
1947	Cle A	5	10	.333	31	5	1	1	92	79	46	6	2	39	34	4.01	87	.230	.312	27-1	.111	-2	102	-6	-1.2
1948	StL A	3	6	.333	43	12	2	3	122.2	141	94	14	4	67	35	6.02	76	.289	.379	32-2	.125	-1	119	-20	-1.4
Total	2	8	16	.333	74	17	3	4	214.2	220	140	20	6	106	69	5.16	79	.264	.352	59-3	.119	-3	119	-26	-2.6
STEPHENS, CLARENCE Clarence Wright B 8.19.1863 Cincinnati, OH D 2.28.1945 Cincinnati, OH TR d10.8																									
1886	Cin AA	1	0	1.000	1	1	1	0	8	9	8	0	1	5	6	5.63	63	.273	.385	5	.600	1	236	-2	-0.1
1891	Cin N	0	1	.000	1	1	1	0	8	9	9	1	0	3	3	7.88	43	.273	.333	3	.000	-0	0	-3	-0.3
1892	Cin N	0	1	.000	1	1	0	0	7	12	3	0	0	4	1	1.29	254	.364	.432	2	.000	-0	39	1	0.1
Total	3	1	2	.333	3	3	2	0	23	30	20	1	1	12	10	5.09	67	.303	.384	10	.300	0	95	-4	-0.3
STEPHENS, BEN George Benjamin B 9.28.1867 Romeo, MI D 8.5.1896 Armada, MI TR 5-10.5/170# d8.5																									
1892	Bal N	1	1	.500	5	2	2	1	29	37	22	2	1	9	7	2.79	123	.298	.351	13	.000	-2	120	0	-0.2
1893	Was N	0	6	.000	9	6	6	0	63.2	83	58	1	4	31	14	5.80	80	.306	.386	29	.103	-4	50	-8	-0.8
1894	Was N	0	0	—	3	2	1	0	11	19	16	1	1	8	1	4.91	108	.373	.467	4-0	.250	-0	67	-1	-0.1
Total	3	1	7	.125	17	10	9	1	103.2	139	96	4	6	48	22	4.86	90	.312	.386	46-0	.087	-5	67	-9	-1.1
STEPHENS, JOHN John M. B 11.15.1979 Sydney, Australia BR/TR 6-1/200# d7.30																									
2002	Bal A	2	5	.286	12	11	0	0-0	65	68	44	13	3	22-2	56	6.09	70	.271	.332	0-0	—	0	81	-12	-1.1
STEPHENSON, EARL Chester Earl B 7.31.1947 Benson, NC BL/TL 6-3/175# d4.7																									
1971	Chi N	1	0	1.000	16	0	0	1-2	20.1	24	10	1	0	11-0	11	4.43	89	.316	.393	2-0	.000	-0		-1	0.0
1972	Mil A	3	5	.375	35	8	1	0-1	80.1	79	32	5	3	33-5	33	3.25	94	.262	.339	18-0	.000	-2	62	-2	-0.4
1977	Bal A	0	0	—	1	0	0	0-0	3	5	3	1	0	0-0	2	9.00	42	.357	.357	0-0	—	0		-2	-0.1
1978	Bal A	0	0	—	2	0	0	0-0	9.2	10	3	0	0	5-0	4	2.79	126	.294	.375	0-0	—	0		1	0.0
Total	4	4	5	.444	54	8	1	1-3	113.1	118	48	7	3	49-5	50	3.57	91	.277	.353	20-0	.000	-2	62	-4	-0.5
STEPHENSON, GARRETT Garrett Charles B 1.2.1972 Takoma Park, MD BR/TR 6-4/185# d7.25																									
1996	Bal A	0	1	.000	3	0	0	0-0	6.1	13	9	1	1	3-1	3	12.79	39	.433	.500	0-0	—	0		-5	-0.6
1997	Phi N	8	6	.571	20	18	2	0-0	117	104	45	11	3	38-0	81	3.15	135	.244	.307	32-5	.094	-1	80	14	1.4
1998	Phi N	0	2	.000	6	6	0	0-0	23	31	24	3	0	19-0	17	9.00	48	.316	.427	6-1	.167	0	124	-11	-0.8

Year	Tm Lg	W	L	Pct	G	GS	CG-Sho	SV-BS	IP	H	R	HR	HB	BB-IB	SO	ERA	AERA	OAV	OOB	AB-SH	AVG	PB	Sup	APR	PW
1999	StL N	6	3	.667	18	12	0	0-0	85.1	90	43	11	5	29-1	59	4.22	108	.275	.339	27-3	.074	-2	105	4	0.2
2000	†StL N	16	9	.640	32	31	3-2	0-0	200.1	209	105	31	7	63-0	123	4.49	103	.270	.327	59-13	.051	-4	116	5	0.1
2002	StL N	2	5	.286	12	10	0	0-0	45	48	27	4	5	25-0	34	5.40	73	.282	.388	12-2	.000	-1	138	-6	-0.9
2003	StL N	7	13	.350	32	27	1	0-0	174.1	167	94	30	13	60-3	91	4.59	89	.255	.326	44-7	.205	2	98	-11	-1.0
Total	7	39	39	.500	123	104	6-2	0-0	651.1	662	347	91	34	237-5	408	4.55	96	.267	.336	180-31	.100	-5	106	-10	-1.6

STEPHENSON, JERRY Jerry Joseph B 10.6.1943 Detroit, MI BL/TR 6-2/185# d4.14 f-Joe

Year	Tm Lg	W	L	Pct	G	GS	CG-Sho	SV-BS	IP	H	R	HR	HB	BB-IB	SO	ERA	AERA	OAV	OOB	AB-SH	AVG	PB	Sup	APR	PW
1963	Bos A	0	0	—	1	1	0	0	2.1	5	2	0	0	2-0	3	7.71	49	.556	.538	1-0	.000	-0	141	-1	-0.1
1965	Bos A	1	5	.167	15	8	0	0	52	62	41	7	1	33-0	49	6.23	60	.287	.382	13-0	.231	0	74	-13	-1.3
1966	Bos A	2	5	.286	15	11	1	0	66.1	68	51	6	1	44-1	50	5.83	65	.264	.370	17-2	.118	-1	112	-14	-1.5
1967	†Bos A	3	1	.750	8	6	0	1	39.2	32	18	4	1	16-2	24	3.86	90	.227	.308	16-0	.250	0	92	-1	-0.1
1968	Bos A	2	8	.200	23	7	2	0	68.2	81	51	4	2	42-3	51	5.64	56	.295	.387	17-0	.353	2	87	-19	-2.4
1969	Sea A	0	0	—	2	0	0	0-0	2.2	6	4	0	1	3-0	1	10.13	36	.429	.556	0-0	—	0		-2	-0.1
1970	LA N	0	0	—	3	0	0	0-0	6.2	11	7	0	0	5-0	6	9.45	41	.379	.471	1-0	.000	-0		-4	-0.2
Total	7	8	19	.296	67	33	3	1-0	238.1	265	174	21	6	145-6	184	5.70	62	.281	.377	65-2	.231	2	96	-54	-5.7

STERLING, JOHN John A. B Philadelphia, PA 6-1/172# d10.12

Year	Tm Lg	W	L	Pct	G	GS	CG-Sho	SV-BS	IP	H	R	HR	HB	BB-IB	SO	ERA	AERA	OAV	OOB	AB-SH	AVG	PB	Sup	APR	PW
1890	Phi AA	0	1	.000	1	1	1	0	5	16	12	1	1	4	1	21.60	18	.516	.583	2	.000	-0	35	-8	-0.9

STERLING, RANDY Randall Wayne B 4.21.1951 Key West, FL BB/TR 6-2/195# d9.16

Year	Tm Lg	W	L	Pct	G	GS	CG-Sho	SV-BS	IP	H	R	HR	HB	BB-IB	SO	ERA	AERA	OAV	OOB	AB-SH	AVG	PB	Sup	APR	PW
1974	NY N	1	1	.500	3	2	0	0-0	9.1	13	8	0	1	3-0	2	4.82	74	.351	.405	2-0	.000	0	73	-2	-0.4

STEVENS, DAVE David James B 3.4.1970 Fullerton, CA BR/TR 6-3/210# d5.20

Year	Tm Lg	W	L	Pct	G	GS	CG-Sho	SV-BS	IP	H	R	HR	HB	BB-IB	SO	ERA	AERA	OAV	OOB	AB-SH	AVG	PB	Sup	APR	PW
1994	Min A	5	2	.714	24	0	0	0-0	45	55	35	6	1	23-2	24	6.80	72	.302	.383	0-0	—	0		-9	-1.1
1995	Min A	5	4	.556	56	0	0	10-2	65.2	74	40	14	1	32-1	47	5.07	94	.285	.359	0-0	—	0		-2	-0.3
1996	Min A	3	3	.500	49	0	0	11-5	58	58	31	12	0	25-2	29	4.66	110	.264	.335	0-0	—	0		3	0.4
1997	Min A	1	3	.250	6	6	0	0-0	23	41	23	8	0	17-0	16	9.00	52	.383	.468	0-0	—	0	122	-10	-1.3
	Chi N	0	2	.000	10	0	0	0-0	9.1	13	11	0	1	9-0	13	9.64	45	.333	.460	1-0	.000	-0		-6	-1.0
1998	Chi N	1	2	.333	31	0	0	0-0	38	42	20	6	1	17-5	31	4.74	93	.288	.364	4-0	.250	0		-1	-0.1
1999	Cle A	0	0	—	5	0	0	0-0	9	10	10	1	0	8-1	6	10.00	50	.286	.409	0-0	—	0		-4	-0.2
2000	Atl N	0	0	—	2	0	0	0-0	3	5	4	2	0	1-0	4	12.00	38	.357	.400	1-0	.000	-0		-2	-0.1
Total	7	15	16	.484	183	6	0	21-7	251	298	174	49	4	132-11	170	6.02	80	.297	.377	6-0	.167	-0	122	-31	-3.7

STEVENS, JIM James Arthur "Steve" B 8.25.1889 Williamsburg, MD D 9.25.1966 Baltimore, MD BR/TR 5-11/180# d8.24

Year	Tm Lg	W	L	Pct	G	GS	CG-Sho	SV-BS	IP	H	R	HR	HB	BB-IB	SO	ERA	AERA	OAV	OOB	AB-SH	AVG	PB	Sup	APR	PW
1914	Was A	0	0	—	2	0	0	0	3	4	3	0	1	2	0	9.00	31	.364	.500	1-0	.000	-0		-2	-0.1

STEWART, DAVE David Keith B 2.19.1957 Oakland, CA BR/TR 6-2/200# d9.22 C3

Year	Tm Lg	W	L	Pct	G	GS	CG-Sho	SV-BS	IP	H	R	HR	HB	BB-IB	SO	ERA	AERA	OAV	OOB	AB-SH	AVG	PB	Sup	APR	PW
1978	LA N	0	0	—	1	0	0	0-0	2	1	0	0	0	0-0	1	0.00	—	.167	.167	0-0	—	0		1	0.0
1981	†LA N	4	3	.571	32	0	0	6-2	43.1	40	13	3	0	14-5	29	2.49	133	.250	.305	5-0	.400	2		4	1.0
1982	LA N	9	8	.529	45	14	0	1-1	146.1	137	72	14	2	49-11	80	3.81	91	.249	.310	39-5	.179	1	98	-7	-0.7
1983	LA N	5	2	.714	46	1	0	8-4	76	67	28	4	2	33-7	54	2.96	122	.237	.318	7-1	.143	-0	172	6	0.6
	Tex A	5	2	.714	8	8	2	0-0	59	50	15	2	2	17-0	24	2.14	188	.233	.294	0-0	—	0	62	13	1.5
1984	Tex A	7	14	.333	32	27	3	0-1	192.1	193	106	26	4	87-3	119	4.73	88	.258	.337	0-0	—	0	75	-8	-0.8
1985	Tex A	0	6	.000	42	5	0	4-3	81.1	86	53	13	2	37-5	64	5.42	78	.273	.351	0-0	—	0	52	-10	-0.8
	Phi N	0	0	—	4	0	0	0-0	4.1	5	4	0	0	4-0	2	6.23	59	.278	.409	0-0	—	0		-1	-0.1
1986	Phi N	0	0	—	8	0	0	0-0	12.1	15	9	1	0	4-0	9	6.57	59	.306	.339	0-0	—	0		-3	-0.2
	Oak A	9	5	.643	29	17	4-1	0-1	149.1	137	67	15	3	65-0	102	3.74	104	.241	.320	0-0	—	0	96	3	0.3
1987	Oak A	**20**	13	.606	37	37	8-1	0-0	261.1	224	121	24	6	105-2	205	3.68	112	.229	.306	0-0	—	0	104	14	1.4
1988	†Oak A	21	12	.636	37	**37**	**14**-2	0-0	**275.2**	240	111	14	3	110-5	192	3.23	117	.234	.307	0-0	—	0	115	16	1.6
1989	†Oak A★	21	9	.700	36	**36**	8	0-0	257.2	260	105	23	6	69-0	155	3.32	111	.263	.313	0-0	—	0	106	13	1.3
1990	†Oak A	22	11	.667	36	**36**	**11-4**	0-0	**267**	226	84	16	5	83-1	166	2.56	145	.231	.291	0-0	—	0	113	36	4.3
1991	Oak A	11	11	.500	35	**35**	2-1	0-0	226	245	135	24	9	105-1	144	5.18	74	.278	.356	0-0	—	0	134	-35	-3.0
1992	†Oak A	12	10	.545	31	31	2	0-0	199.1	175	96	25	8	79-1	130	3.66	103	.237	.315	0-0	—	0	112	0	-0.2
1993	†Tor A	12	8	.600	26	26	0	0-0	162	146	86	23	4	72-0	96	4.44	97	.242	.325	0-0	—	0	109	-1	-0.2
1994	Tor A	7	8	.467	22	22	1	0-0	133.1	151	89	26	4	62-4	111	5.87	82	.285	.362	0-0	—	0	100	-13	-1.3
1995	Oak A	3	7	.300	16	16	0	0-0	81	101	65	11	2	39-1	58	6.89	65	.305	.379	0-0	—	0	103	-22	-2.1
Total	16	168	129	.566	523	348	55-9	19-12	2629.2	2499	1259	264	62	1034-46	1741	3.95	100	.251	.322	51-6	.196	2	106	6	2.6

STEWART, FRANK Frank "Stewy" B 9.8.1906 Minneapolis, MN D 4.30.2001 Stillwater, MN BR/TR 6-1.5/180# d10.2

Year	Tm Lg	W	L	Pct	G	GS	CG-Sho	SV-BS	IP	H	R	HR	HB	BB-IB	SO	ERA	AERA	OAV	OOB	AB-SH	AVG	PB	Sup	APR	PW
1927	Chi A	0	1	.000	1	1	0	0	4	5	4	0	0	4	0	9.00	45	.357	.500	1-0	.000	-0	62	-2	-0.3

STEWART, JOE Joseph Lawrence "Ace" B 3.11.1879 Monroe, NC D 2.9.1913 Youngstown, OH TR 5-11/175# d6.9

Year	Tm Lg	W	L	Pct	G	GS	CG-Sho	SV-BS	IP	H	R	HR	HB	BB-IB	SO	ERA	AERA	OAV	OOB	AB-SH	AVG	PB	Sup	APR	PW
1904	Bos N	0	0	—	2	0	0	0	9.1	12	11	0	1	4	1	9.64	29	.286	.362	5-0	.200	-0		-6	-0.3

STEWART, JOSH Joshua Craig B 12.5.1978 Paducah, KY BL/TL 6-3/200# d4.6

Year	Tm Lg	W	L	Pct	G	GS	CG-Sho	SV-BS	IP	H	R	HR	HB	BB-IB	SO	ERA	AERA	OAV	OOB	AB-SH	AVG	PB	Sup	APR	PW
2003	Chi A	1	2	.333	5	5	0	0-0	25.2	28	18	4	0	16-0	13	5.96	76	.272	.367	0-0	—	0	125	-4	-0.3

STEWART, SAMMY Samuel Lee B 10.28.1954 Asheville, NC BR/TR 6-3/208# d9.1

Year	Tm Lg	W	L	Pct	G	GS	CG-Sho	SV-BS	IP	H	R	HR	HB	BB-IB	SO	ERA	AERA	OAV	OOB	AB-SH	AVG	PB	Sup	APR	PW
1978	Bal A	1	1	.500	2	2	0	0-0	11.1	10	5	0	0	3-0	11	3.18	110	.238	.289	0-0	—	0	141	0	0.0
1979	†Bal A	8	5	.615	31	3	1	1-1	117.2	96	47	11	5	71-4	71	3.52	114	.232	.349	0-0	—	0	128	9	1.0
1980	Bal A	7	7	.500	33	3	2	3-2	118.2	103	51	9	2	60-8	78	3.56	111	.235	.328	0-0	—	0	68	5	0.6
1981	Bal A	4	8	.333	29	3	0	4-1	112.1	89	33	8	3	57-4	57	2.32	**156**	.225	.325	0-0	—	0	33	16	1.8
1982	Bal A	10	9	.526	38	12	1-1	5-4	139	140	68	9	2	62-3	69	4.14	98	.263	.339	0-0	—	0*	109	-2	-0.2
1983	†Bal A	9	4	.692	58	1	0	7-2	144.1	138	60	7	1	67-4	95	3.62	110	.253	.334	0-0	—	0*	0	8	0.7
1984	Bal A	7	4	.636	60	0	0	13-3	93	81	42	7	1	47-7	56	3.29	118	.241	.332	0-0	—	0		5	0.6
1985	Bal A	5	7	.417	56	1	0	9-1	129.2	117	60	15	1	66-10	77	3.61	112	.246	.336	0-0	—	0	45	5	0.4
1986	Bos A	4	1	.800	27	0	0	0-0	63.2	64	33	7	0	48-2	47	4.38	95	.266	.381	0-0	—	0		-1	-0.1
1987	Cle A	4	2	.667	25	0	0	3-4	27	25	22	4	1	21-1	25	5.67	80	.234	.362	0-0	—	0		-4	-0.8
Total	10	59	48	.551	359	25	4-1	45-18	956.2	863	421	77	16	502-43	586	3.59	110	.245	.338	0-0	—	0	92	41	4.0

STEWART, SCOTT Scott Edward B 8.14.1975 Stoughton, MA BR/TL 6-2/225# d4.5

Year	Tm Lg	W	L	Pct	G	GS	CG-Sho	SV-BS	IP	H	R	HR	HB	BB-IB	SO	ERA	AERA	OAV	OOB	AB-SH	AVG	PB	Sup	APR	PW
2001	Mon N	3	1	.750	62	0	0	3-1	47.2	43	20	5	3	13-0	39	3.78	118	.243	.299	0-0	—	0		4	0.4
2002	Mon N	4	2	.667	67	0	0	17-2	64	49	29	4	1	22-5	67	3.09	144	.207	.275	2-0	.000	-0		7	0.9
2003	Mon N	3	1	.750	51	0	0	0-1	43	52	22	5	1	13-4	29	3.98	118	.306	.357	2-0	.000	-0		3	0.2
Total	3	10	4	.714	180	0	0	20-4	154.2	144	71	14	5	48-9	135	3.55	128	.247	.306	4-0	.000	-0		14	1.5

STEWART, BUNKY Veston Goff B 1.7.1931 Jasper, NC BL/TL 6/155# d5.4

Year	Tm Lg	W	L	Pct	G	GS	CG-Sho	SV-BS	IP	H	R	HR	HB	BB-IB	SO	ERA	AERA	OAV	OOB	AB-SH	AVG	PB	Sup	APR	PW
1952	Was A	0	0	—	1	0	0	0	1	2	2	0	0	1	1	18.00	20	.500	.600	0-0	—	0		-2	-0.1
1953	Was A	0	2	.000	2	2	1	0	15.1	17	9	1	1	11	3	4.70	83	.283	.403	5-0	.200	-0	57	-1	-0.2
1954	Was A	0	2	.000	29	2	0	1	50.2	67	52	3	4	27	27	7.64	47	.324	.410	3-0	.000	0	99	-25	-1.2
1955	Was A	0	0	—	7	1	0	0	15.1	18	7	0	0	6-1	10	4.11	93	.295	.358	2-0	.000	-0	93	0	0.0
1956	Was A	5	7	.417	33	9	1	2	105	111	77	15	5	82-4	36	5.57	78	.276	.402	28-4	.250	-0*	71	-15	-1.5
Total	5	5	11	.313	72	14	2	3	187.1	215	147	19	10	127-5	77	6.01	67	.293	.402	38-4	.211	-0	75	-43	-3.0

STEWART, LEFTY Walter Cleveland B 9.23.1900 Sparta, TN D 9.26.1974 Knoxville, TN BR/TL 5-10/160# d4.20

Year	Tm Lg	W	L	Pct	G	GS	CG-Sho	SV-BS	IP	H	R	HR	HB	BB-IB	SO	ERA	AERA	OAV	OOB	AB-SH	AVG	PB	Sup	APR	PW
1921	Det A	0	0	—	5	0	0	1	9	20	12	0	0	5	4	12.00	36	.455	.510	1-0	.000	-0		-7	-0.3
1927	StL A	8	11	.421	27	19	11	1	155.2	187	83	7	2	43	43	4.28	102	.310	.357	49-4	.306	3*	82	4	0.7
1928	StL A	7	9	.438	29	17	7-1	3	142.2	173	81	5	2	32	25	4.67	90	.310	.350	51-0	.275	3	113	-5	-0.2
1929	StL A	9	6	.600	23	18	8-1	0	149.2	137	67	11	4	49	47	3.25	136	.246	.312	51-6	.118	-4	97	17	1.1
1930	StL A	20	12	.625	35	33	23-1	0	271	281	119	21	1	70	79	3.45	141	.268	.315	90-6	.244	2	87	41	4.4
1931	StL A	14	17	.452	36	33	20-1	0	258	287	155	17	3	85	89	4.40	105	.277	.334	88-3	.250	6	93	5	1.2
1932	StL A	15	19	.441	41	32	18-2	1	259.2	269	148	22	3	99	86	4.61	105	.270	.338	82-6	.146	-2	79	10	0.9
1933	†Was A	15	6	.714	34	31	11-1	1	230.2	227	116	19	1	60	69	3.82	109	.256	.304	77-9	.143	1*	115	7	0.6
1934	Was A	7	11	.389	24	22	7-1	0	152	184	74	8	1	36	36	4.03	107	.303	.343	45-13	.156	-1*	72	6	0.5
1935	Was A	0	1	.000	1	1	0	0	2.2	8	9	1	0	2	1	13.50	32	.533	.588	1-0	.000	-0	0	-5	-0.7

Year	Tm Lg	W	L	Pct	G	GS	CG-Sho	SV-BS	IP	H	R	HR	HB	BB-IB	SO	ERA	AERA	OAV	OOB	AB-SH	AVG	PB	Sup	APR	PW
	Cle A	6	6	.500	24	10	2	2	91	122	68	6	1	17	24	5.44	83	.312	.342	30-2	.200	-1	108	-11	-1.4
	Year	6	7	.462	25	11	2	2	93.2	130	74	7	1	19	25	5.67	79	.320	.352	31-2	.194	-1	98	-17	-2.1
Total	10	101	98	.508	279	216	107-8	8	1722	1895	932	117	18	498	503	4.19	108	.281	.332	565-49	.204	6	92	62	6.8
STEWART, MACK William Macklin B 9.23.1914 Stevenson, AL D 3.21.1960 Macon, GA BR/TR 6/167# d7.7																									
1944	Chi N	0	0	—	8	0	0	0	12.1	11	2	1	0	4	3	1.46	242	.239	.300	1-0	.000	-0		3	0.1
1945	Chi N	0	1	.000	16	1	0	0	28.1	37	16	0	0	14	9	4.76	77	.322	.395	3-0	.333	0	70	-3	-0.1
Total	2	0	1	.000	24	1	0	0	40.2	48	18	1	0	18	12	3.76	96	.298	.369	4-0	.250	0	70	0	0.0
STIDHAM, PHIL Phillip Wayne B 11.18.1968 Tulsa, OK BR/TR 6/180# d6.4																									
1994	Det A	0	0	—	5	0	0	0-0	4.1	12	12	3	0	4-1	4	24.92	19	.571	.615	0-0	—	0		-9	-0.4
STIEB, DAVE David Andrew B 7.22.1957 Santa Ana, CA BR/TR 6-1/195# d6.29																									
1979	Tor A	8	8	.500	18	18	7-1	0-0	129.1	139	70	11	4	48-3	52	4.31	101	.276	.342	0-0	—	0*	95	1	0.2
1980	Tor A★	12	15	.444	34	32	14-4	0-0	242.2	232	108	12	6	83-6	108	3.71	116	.260	.324	1-0	.000	-0*	80	17	2.0
1981	Tor A★	11	10	.524	25	25	11-2	0-0	183.2	148	70	10	11	61-2	89	3.19	124	.223	.296	0-0	—	0*	64	16	1.9
1982	Tor A	17	14	.548	38	38	**19-5**	0-0	**288.1**	271	116	27	5	75-4	141	3.25	138	.248	.298	0-0	—	0	80	**36**	3.9
1983	Tor A★	17	12	.586	36	36	14-4	0-0	278	223	105	21	14	93-6	187	3.04	142	.219	.291	0-0	—	0	95	**36**	3.6
1984	Tor A★	16	8	.667	35	35	11-2	0-0	**267**	215	87	19	11	88-1	198	2.83	**145**	**.221**	.292	0-0	—	0	92	**39**	3.4
1985	†Tor A★	14	13	.519	36	36	8-2	0-0	265	206	89	22	9	96-3	167	**2.48**	**170**	**.213**	.290	0-0	—	0	96	**47**	4.8
1986	Tor A	7	12	.368	37	34	1-1	1-0	205	239	128	29	15	87-1	127	4.74	89	.297	.373	0-0	—	0*	101	-16	-1.2
1987	Tor A	13	9	.591	33	31	3-1	0-0	185	164	92	16	7	87-4	115	4.09	110	.239	.329	0-0	—	0*	121	8	0.9
1988	Tor A★	16	8	.667	32	31	8-4	0-0	207.1	157	76	15	13	79-0	147	3.04	130	.210	.295	0-0	—	0*	109	22	2.4
1989	†Tor A	17	8	.680	33	33	3-2	0-0	206.2	164	83	12	13	76-2	101	3.35	113	.219	.301	0-0	—	0	124	11	1.3
1990	Tor A★	18	6	.750	33	33	2-2	0-0	208.2	179	73	11	10	64-0	125	2.93	135	.230	.296	0-0	—	0	104	23	2.7
1991	Tor A	4	3	.571	9	9	1	0-0	59.2	52	22	4	2	23-0	29	3.17	133	.243	.321	0-0	—	0	80	7	0.8
1992	Tor A	4	6	.400	21	14	1	0-0	96.1	98	58	9	4	43-3	45	5.04	81	.275	.355	0-0	—	0	93	-10	-0.8
1993	Chi A	1	3	.250	4	4	0	0-0	22.1	27	17	1	0	14-0	11	6.04	69	.300	.390	0-0	—	0	99	-5	-0.7
1998	Tor A	1	2	.333	19	3	0	2-0	50.1	58	31	6	5	17-1	27	4.83	97	.284	.351	1-0	.000	-0	139	-1	-0.1
Total	16	176	137	.562	443	412	103-30	3-0	2895.1	2572	1225	225	129	1034-36	1669	3.44	122	.239	.312	2-0	.000	-0	96	231	25.1
STIELY, FRED Fred Warren "Lefty" B 6.1.1901 Pillow, PA D 1.6.1981 Valley View, PA BL/TL 5-8/170# d10.6																									
1929	StL A	1	0	1.000	1	1	1	0	9	11	2	0	1	3	2	0.00	—	.297	.366	3-0	.667	1	76	3	0.6
1930	StL A	0	1	.000	4	2	1	0	19	27	21	4	1	8	5	8.53	57	.346	.414	7-0	.429	1*	115	-8	-0.2
1931	StL A	0	0	—	4	0	0	0	6.2	7	5	0	1	3	2	6.75	69	.269	.367	0-0	—	0		-1	-0.1
Total	3	1	1	.500	9	3	2	0	34.2	45	28	4	3	14	9	5.97	79	.319	.392	10-0	.500	2	103	-6	0.3
STIGMAN, DICK Richard Lewis B 1.24.1936 Nimrod, MN BR/TL 6-3/200# d4.22																									
1960	Cle A☆	5	11	.313	41	18	3	9	133.2	118	78	13	0	87-1	104	4.51	83	.238	.348	36-1	.222	2	79	-13	-1.4
1961	Cle A	2	5	.286	22	6	0	0	64.1	65	35	9	0	25-1	48	4.62	85	.264	.327	16-0	.125	-1	49	-4	-0.4
1962	Min A	12	5	.706	40	15	6	3	142.2	122	60	19	2	64-3	116	3.66	112	.233	.318	45-0	.044	-4	152	9	0.5
1963	Min A	15	15	.500	33	33	15-3	0	241	210	90	32	0	81-2	193	3.25	112	.231	.293	84-5	.107	-2	108	15	1.4
1964	Min A	6	15	.286	32	29	5-1	0	190	160	94	31	5	70-7	159	4.03	89	.225	.298	69-0	.101	-3	81	-8	-1.2
1965	Min A	4	2	.667	33	8	0	4	70	59	34	14	0	33-3	70	4.37	81	.227	.312	15-1	.133	-0	114	-4	-0.4
1966	Bos A	2	1	.667	34	10	1-1	0	81	85	51	15	1	46-5	65	5.44	70	.268	.361	17-2	.118	-1	79	-11	-0.7
Total	7	46	54	.460	235	119	30-5	16	922.2	819	442	133	8	406-22	755	4.03	93	.237	.316	282-9	.113	-8	97	-16	-2.2
STILES, ROLLIE Rolland Mays "Lena" B 11.17.1906 Ratcliff, AR BR/TR 6-1.5/180# d6.19																									
1930	StL A	3	6	.333	20	7	3	0	102	136	77	10	1	41	25	5.91	82	.337	.399	37-0	.270	0	98	-11	-0.8
1931	StL A	3	1	.750	34	2	0	0	81	112	72	2	2	60	32	7.22	64	.352	.458	22-0	.045	-2	100	-19	-1.1
1933	StL A	3	7	.300	31	9	6-1	1	115	154	83	4	2	47	29	5.01	93	.327	.390	33-2	.061	-3	95	-9	-1.0
Total	3	9	14	.391	85	18	9-1	1	298	402	232	16	5	148	86	5.92	80	.337	.412	92-2	.141	-5	97	-39	-2.9
STIMMEL, ARCHIE Archibald May "Lumbago" B 5.30.1873 Woodsboro, MD D 8.18.1958 Frederick, MD BR/TR 6/175# d7.3																									
1900	Cin N	1	1	.500	2	1	1	0	13	18	11	1	0	4	2	6.92	53	.327	.373	5-0	.200	-0	0	-4	-0.5
1901	Cin N	4	14	.222	20	18	14-1	0	153.1	170	96	10	12	44	55	4.11	78	.279	.339	62-2	.081	-5*	66	-16	-2.1
1902	Cin N	0	4	.000	4	3	3	0	26	37	16	1	2	12	7	3.46	87	.333	.408	10-0	.200	-0	53	-1	-0.2
Total	3	5	19	.208	26	22	18-1	0	192.1	225	123	12	14	60	64	4.21	76	.290	.352	77-2	.104	-5	61	-21	-2.8
STIMSON, CARL Carl Remus B 7.18.1894 Hamburg, IA D 11.9.1936 Omaha, NE BB/TR 6-5/190# d6.6																									
1923	Bos A	0	0	—	2	0	0	0	4	12	10	0	1	5	1	22.50	18	.750	.818	2-0	.000	-0		-7	-0.3
STINE, HARRY Harry C. B 2.20.1864 Shenandoah, PA D 6.5.1924 Niagara Falls, NY TL 5-6/150# d7.22																									
1890	Phi AA	0	1	.000	1	1	1	0	8	17	9	0	0	4	1	9.00	43	.415	.467	3	.000	-0	52	-4	-0.3
STINE, LEE Lee Elbert B 11.17.1913 Stillwater, OK BR/TR 5-11/185# d4.17																									
1934	Chi A	0	0	—	4	0	0	0	11	11	10	2	1	10	8	8.18	58	.268	.423	1-0	.000	0		-3	-0.2
1935	Chi A	0	0	—	1	0	0	0	2	2	2	1	0	3	1	9.00	51	.286	.500	0-0	—	0		-1	0.0
1936	Cin N	3	8	.273	40	13	5-1	2	121.2	157	79	6	8	41	26	5.03	76	.318	.379	27-2	.296	3	107	-16	-1.0
1938	NY A	0	0	—	4	0	0	0	8.2	9	1	0	0	1	4	1.04	437	.333	.357	2-0	.500	0		4	0.2
Total	4	3	8	.273	49	13	5-1	2	143.1	179	92	9	9	55	39	5.09	78	.315	.384	30-2	.300	4	107	-16	-1.0
STIVETTS, JACK John Elmer "Happy Jack" B 3.31.1868 Ashland, PA D 4.18.1930 Ashland, PA BR/TR 6-2/185# d6.26 ▲																									
1889	StL AA	12	7	.632	26	20	18-2	2	191.2	153	85	4	5	68	143	**2.25**	**188**	**.212**	**.285**	79	.228	-1*	72	36	2.8
1890	StL AA	27	21	.563	54	46	41-3	0	419.1	399	255	14	17	179	289	3.52	123	.243	.324	226	.288	14*	103	31	4.2
1891	StL AA	33	22	.600	**64**	56	40-3	1	440	357	237	15	18	232	**259**	2.86	147	.214	.317	302	.305	9*	95	**58**	**6.8**
1892	†Bos N	35	16	.686	54	48	45-3	1	415.2	346	223	12	10	171	180	3.03	116	.217	.297	240	.296	15*	109	18	3.3
1893	Bos N	20	12	.625	38	34	29-1	1	283.2	315	194	17	10	115	61	4.41	112	.273	.344	172	.297	7*	115	15	1.7
1894	Bos N	26	14	.650	45	39	30	0	338	429	278	27	13	127	76	4.90	116	.306	.369	244-3	.328	10*	121	22	2.5
1895	Bos N	17	17	.500	38	34	30	0	291	341	219	15	12	89	111	4.64	110	.288	.344	158-2	.190	-7*	86	15	0.5
1896	Bos N	22	14	.611	42	36	31-2	0	329	353	219	19	7	99	71	4.10	111	.272	.327	222-4	.347	12*	111	20	2.6
1897	†Bos N	11	4	.733	18	15	10	0	129.1	147	75	5	5	43	27	3.41	131	.284	.345	199-1	.367	7*	141	12	1.8
1898	Bos N	0	1	.000	2	1	1	0	12	17	12	2	0	7	1	8.25	45	.333	.414	111-4	.252	0*	58	-5	-0.3
1899	Cle N	0	4	.000	7	4	3	0	38	48	39	0	2	25	5	5.68	65	.308	.410	39-0	.205	1*	49	-11	-0.8
Total	11	203	132	.606	388	333	278-14	5	2887.2	2905	1836	130	99	1155	1223	3.74	121	.255	.329	1992-14	.298	65	104	211	25.1
STOBBS, CHUCK Charles Klein B 7.2.1929 Wheeling, WV BL/TL 6-1/185# d9.15																									
1947	Bos A	0	1	.000	4	1	0	0	9	10	6	0	0	10	5	6.00	65	.294	.455	1-0	.000	-0	68	-2	-0.2
1948	Bos A	0	0	—	6	0	0	0	7	9	5	0	0	7	4	6.43	68	.321	.457	1-0	.000	-0		-1	-0.1
1949	Bos A	11	6	.647	26	19	10	0	152	145	72	10	2	75	70	4.03	108	.254	.343	53-6	.208	0	124	7	0.6
1950	Bos A	12	7	.632	32	21	6	1	169.1	158	104	17	5	88	78	5.10	96	.250	.346	57-4	.246	3	151	-3	0.0
1951	Bos A	10	9	.526	34	25	6	0	170	180	100	16	5	74	75	4.76	94	.271	.349	61-5	.180	-2	111	-5	-0.7
1952	Chi A	7	12	.368	38	17	2	1	135	118	54	9	5	72	73	3.13	116	.237	.339	38-4	.079	-1	70	7	0.8
1953	Was A	11	8	.579	27	20	8	0	153	146	64	11	1	44	67	3.29	118	.246	.299	44-10	.227	1	128	10	1.3
1954	Was A	11	11	.500	31	24	10-3	0	182	189	87	6	1	67	67	4.10	87	.270	.330	51-9	.137	0	103	-8	-0.8
1955	Was A	4	14	.222	41	16	2	3	140.1	169	90	13	1	57-8	60	5.00	77	.302	.364	35-1	.171	2	73	-20	-2.0
1956	Was A	15	15	.500	37	33	15-1	1	240	264	115	29	1	54-4	97	3.60	120	.279	.316	84-4	.179	-2*	77	16	1.7
1957	Was A	8	20	.286	42	31	5-2	1	211.2	235	140	28	5	80-10	114	5.36	73	.279	.343	76-4	.211	1	76	-35	-4.1
1958	Was A	2	6	.250	19	8	0	0	56.2	87	44	7	2	16-0	23	6.04	63	.369	.405	12-0	.000	-2	77	-15	-2.0
	StL N	1	3	.250	17	0	0	1	39.2	40	16	4	0	14-1	25	3.63	114	.261	.323	4-1	.250	0		3	0.4
1959	Was A	1	8	.111	41	7	0	7	90.2	82	42	13	2	24-1	50	2.98	131	.238	.290	19-1	.105	-1	74	6	0.5
1960	Was A	12	7	.632	40	13	1-1	2	119.1	115	54	13	3	38-4	72	3.32	117	.252	.311	34-1	.088	-2	92	7	0.8
1961	Min A	2	3	.400	24	3	0	2	44.2	56	37	8	2	15-2	17	7.46	57	.311	.363	8-0	.375	1	49	-13	-1.3
Total	15	107	130	.451	459	238	65-7	19	1920.1	2003	1030	184	35	735-30	897	4.29	95	.269	.336	578-50	.176	-1	99	-46	-5.1

Year	Tm Lg	W	L	Pct	G	GS	CG-Sho	SV-BS	IP	H	R	HR	HB	BB-IB	SO	ERA	AERA	OAV	OOB	AB-SH	AVG	PB	Sup	APR	PW
STOCK, WES Wesley Gay B 4.10.1934 Longview, WA BR/TR 6-2/188# d4.19 C16																									
1959	Bal A	0	0	—	7	0	0	1	12.2	16	6	1	0	2-0	8	3.55	107	.302	.327	2-0	.000	-0		0	0.0
1960	Bal A	2	2	.500	17	0	0	2	34.1	26	11	2	1	14-1	23	2.88	132	.218	.306	6-0	.000	-1		4	0.5
1961	Bal A	5	0	1.000	35	1	0	3	71.2	58	24	3	2	27-2	47	3.01	128	.225	.300	11-0	.000	-1	0	8	0.6
1962	Bal A	3	2	.600	53	0	0	3	65	50	33	7	1	36-6	34	4.43	83	.217	.326	3-0	.000	-0		-4	-0.2
1963	Bal A	7	0	1.000	47	0	0	1	75.1	69	41	11	0	31-7	55	3.94	88	.246	.319	10-0	.000	-1		-6	-0.7
1964	Bal A	2	0	1.000	14	0	0	0	20.2	17	9	5	0	8-1	14	3.92	91	.233	.305	4-0	.000	-0		0	-0.1
	KC A	6	3	.667	50	0	0	5	93	69	21	10	4	34-7	101	1.94	197	.213	.292	15-3	.200	0		19	2.0
	Year	8	3	.727	64	0	0	5	113.2	86	30	15	4	42-8	115	2.30	164	.217	.295	19-3	.158	-0		19	1.9
1965	KC A	0	4	.000	62	2	0	4	99.2	96	62	18	4	40-2	52	5.24	67	.251	.326	6-2	.000	-1	113	-18	-0.9
1966	KC A	2	2	.500	35	0	0	3	44	30	15	3	3	21-3	31	2.66	128	.199	.307	2-0	.000	-0		4	0.3
1967	KC A	0	0	—	1	0	0	0	1	3	2	0	0	2-0	0	18.00	18	.500	.625	0-0	—	0		-2	-0.1
Total	9	27	13	.675	321	3	0	22	517.1	434	224	60	15	215-29	365	3.60	101	.231	.313	59-5	.051	-4	73	5	1.4
STOCKSDALE, OTIS Otis Hinkley "Old Gray Fox" B 8.7.1871 Arcadia, MD D 3.15.1933 Pennsville, NJ BL/TR 5-10.5/180# d7.24																									
1893	Was N	2	8	.200	11	11	7	0	69	111	82	4	5	32	12	8.22	56	.352	.420	40	.300	2*	85	-24	-2.2
1894	Was N	5	9	.357	18	14	11	0	117.1	176	115	10	14	42	10	5.06	104	.342	.407	71-1	.324	1*	95	1	0.2
1895	Was N	6	11	.353	20	17	11	1	136	199	143	7	8	52	23	6.09	79	.336	.397	74-1	.311	2*	99	-18	-1.4
	Bos N	2	2	.500	4	4	1	0	23	31	22	2	0	8	2	5.87	87	.316	.368	15-0	.267	-0*	133	-2	-0.3
	Year	8	13	.381	24	21	12	1	159	230	32	9	8	60	25	6.06	80	.333	.393	89-1	.303	2	106	-25	-1.7
1896	Bal N	0	1	.000	1	0	0	0	1.2	4	4	0	1	2	1	16.20	26	.444	.583	3-0	.333	1*		-2	-0.3
Total	4	15	31	.326	54	46	30	1	347	521	366	23	28	136	48	6.20	80	.341	.405	203-2	.310	5	97	-45	-4.0
STODDARD, BOB Robert Lyle B 3.8.1957 San Jose, CA BR/TR 6-1/200# d9.4																									
1981	Sea A	2	1	.667	5	5	1	0-0	34.2	35	10	3	1	9-0	22	2.60	149	.269	.321	0-0	—	0	98	5	0.4
1982	Sea A	3	3	.500	9	9	2-1	0-0	67.1	48	22	7	3	18-0	24	2.41	177	.205	.267	0-0	—	0	71	12	1.1
1983	Sea A	9	17	.346	35	23	2-1	0-0	175.2	182	95	29	4	58-0	87	4.41	97	.274	.334	0-0	—	0	60	-2	-0.1
1984	Sea A	2	3	.400	27	6	0	0-0	79	86	51	10	2	37-3	39	5.13	78	.278	.357	0-0	—	0	87	-10	-0.6
1985	Det A	0	0	—	8	0	0	1-0	13.1	15	11	3	0	5-0	11	6.75	60	.268	.328	0-0	—	0		-4	-0.2
1986	SD N	1	0	1.000	18	0	0	1-1	23.1	20	7	1	1	11-1	17	2.31	158	.227	.317	1-0	.000	-0		3	0.2
1987	KC A	1	3	.250	17	2	0	1-0	40	51	26	3	3	22-2	23	4.27	107	.313	.402	0-0	—	0	40	-1	0.0
Total	7	18	27	.400	119	45	5-2	3-1	433.1	437	222	56	14	160-6	223	4.03	104	.266	.334	1-0	.000	-0	69	3	0.8
STODDARD, TIM Timothy Paul B 1.24.1953 E.Chicago, IN BR/TR 6-7/250# d9.7																									
1975	Chi A	0	0	—	1	0	0	0-0	1	2	1	1	0	0-0	0	9.00	43	.400	.400	0-0	—	0		-1	0.0
1978	Bal A	0	1	.000	8	0	0	0-0	18	22	17	3	2	8-1	14	6.00	58	.301	.386	0-0	—	0		-7	-0.4
1979	†Bal A	3	1	.750	29	0	0	3-3	58	44	12	3	0	19-2	47	1.71	236	.212	.278	0-0	—	0		16	1.2
1980	Bal A	5	3	.625	64	0	0	26-7	86	72	27	2	1	38-1	64	2.51	158	.233	.317	0-0	—	0		14	2.1
1981	Bal A	4	2	.667	31	0	0	7-4	37.1	38	16	6	2	18-0	32	3.86	94	.268	.358	0-0	—	0		0	0.0
1982	Bal A	3	4	.429	50	0	0	12-3	56	53	26	4	1	29-6	42	4.02	101	.249	.337	0-0	—	0		0	0.0
1983	Bal A	4	3	.571	47	0	0	9-2	57.2	65	39	10	1	29-4	50	6.09	65	.293	.371	0-0	—	0		-12	-1.7
1984	†Chi N	10	6	.625	58	0	0	7-4	92	77	41	9	1	57-11	87	3.82	103	.236	.346	11-1	.091	-1		2	0.2
1985	SD N	1	6	.143	44	0	0	1-0	60	63	35	3	0	37-7	42	4.65	76	.269	.366	5-1	.000	-1		-7	-0.9
1986	SD N	1	3	.250	30	0	0	0-1	45.1	33	20	6	0	34-6	47	3.77	97	.200	.337	4-0	.250	1		0	0.1
	NY A	4	1	.800	24	0	0	0-1	49.1	41	23	6	0	23-3	34	3.83	107	.232	.317	0-0	—	0		2	0.2
1987	NY A	4	3	.571	57	0	0	8-1	92.2	83	38	13	0	30-2	78	3.50	126	.235	.293	0-0	—	0		10	0.8
1988	NY A	2	2	.500	28	0	0	3-0	55	62	41	5	2	27-1	33	6.38	62	.286	.361	0-0	—	0		-14	-1.1
1989	Cle A	0	0	—	14	0	0	0-0	21.1	25	7	1	0	7-1	12	2.95	134	.313	.356	0-0	—	0		3	0.1
Total	13	41	35	.539	485	0	0	76-26	729.2	680	343	72	10	356-45	582	3.95	100	.250	.335	20-2	.100	-0		6	0.6
STOKES, ART Arthur Milton B 9.13.1896 Emmitsburg, MD D 6.3.1962 Titusville, PA BR/TR 5-10.5/155# d5.5																									
1925	Phi A	1	1	.500	12	0	0	0	24.1	24	15	0	2	10	7	4.07	114	.270	.356	4-0	.000	-0		1	0.0
STONE, DICK Charles Richard B 12.5.1911 Oklahoma City, OK D 2.18.1980 Oklahoma City, OK BL/TL 5-9/153# d8.26																									
1945	Was A	0	0	—	3	0	0	0	5	6	0	0	0	2	0	0.00	—	.316	.381	0-0	—	0		2	0.1
STONE, DEAN Darrah Dean B 9.1.1930 Moline, IL BL/TL 6-4/205# d9.13																									
1953	Was A	0	1	.000	3	1	0	0	8.2	13	8	0	0	5	5	8.31	47	.361	.439	2-0	.000	-0	46	-4	-0.4
1954	Was A★	12	10	.545	31	23	10-2	0	178.2	161	76	7	1	69	87	3.22	110	.240	.310	52-6	.096	-0	113	6	0.5
1955	Was A	6	13	.316	43	24	5-1	1	180	180	98	14	3	114-5	84	4.15	92	.267	.371	46-10	.043	-4	80	-8	-1.2
1956	Was A	5	7	.417	41	21	2	3	132	148	107	10	7	93-0	86	6.27	69	.282	.395	34-2	.088	-1*	109	-28	-2.5
1957	Was A	0	0	—	3	0	0	0	3.1	5	3	0	0	2-1	3	8.10	48	.357	.412	0-0	—	0		-1	-0.1
	Bos A	1	3	.250	17	8	0	1	51.1	56	42	5	0	35-0	32	5.08	78	.284	.386	14-1	.000	-1	101	-10	-0.8
	Year	1	3	.250	20	8	0	1	54.2	61	47	5	0	37-1	35	5.27	76	.289	.387	14-1	.000	-1	101	-12	-0.9
1959	StL N	0	1	.000	18	1	0	1	30	30	15	4	0	16-4	17	4.20	101	.273	.357	4-0	.000	-0	0	0	0.0
1962	Hou N	3	2	.600	15	7	2-2	0	52.1	61	31	4	1	20-0	31	4.47	84	.295	.360	16-3	.250	1	107	-5	-0.3
	Chi A	1	0	1.000	27	0	0	5	30.1	28	11	3	1	9-2	23	3.26	120	.255	.306	2-0	.500	1		3	0.2
1963	Bal A	1	2	.333	17	0	0	1	19.1	23	11	0	0	10-2	12	5.12	68	.307	.384	0-0	—	0		-3	-0.5
Total	8	29	39	.426	215	85	19-5	12	686	705	402	47	13	373-14	380	4.47	86	.269	.360	170-22	.088	-6	100	-50	-5.1
STONE, DWIGHT Dwight Ely B 8.2.1886 Holt Co., NE D 6.3.1976 Glendale, CA BR/TR 6-1.5/170# d4.13																									
1913	StL A	2	6	.250	18	7	4-1	0	91	94	45	0	7	46	37	3.56	82	.271	.368	33-0	.273	2	72	-5	-0.2
1914	KC F	8	14	.364	39	22	6	0	186.2	205	110	8	8	77	88	4.34	64	.281	.356	58-2	.121	-4	91	-30	-3.5
Total	2	10	20	.333	57	29	10-1	0	277.2	299	155	8	15	123	125	4.08	69	.278	.360	91-2	.176	-2	86	-35	-3.7
STONE, ARNIE Edwin Arnold B 10.9.1892 North Creek, NY D 7.29.1948 Hudson Falls, NY BR/TL 6/180# d7.30																									
1923	Pit N	0	1	.000	9	0	0	0	12.1	19	12	0	0	4	2	8.03	50	.352	.397	1-0	.000	-0		-5	-0.4
1924	Pit N	4	2	.667	26	2	1	0	64	57	27	0	0	15	7	2.95	130	.259	.306	15-0	.133	-1	155	5	0.3
Total	2	4	3	.571	35	2	1	0	76.1	76	39	0	0	19	9	3.77	102	.277	.324	16-0	.125	-1	155	0	-0.1
STONE, GEORGE George Heard B 7.9.1946 Ruston, LA BL/TL 6-3/205# d9.15																									
1967	Atl N	0	0	—	2	1	0	0	7.1	8	4	0	0	1-0	5	4.91	68	.267	.290	2-0	.000	-0	26	-1	-0.1
1968	Atl N	7	4	.636	17	10	2	0	75	63	27	9	0	19-4	52	2.76	108	.222	.271	27-1	.333	3	142	2	0.5
1969	†Atl N	13	10	.565	36	20	3	3-1	165.1	166	82	20	5	48-5	102	3.65	99	.260	.316	59-5	.186	1	119	-4	-0.4
1970	Atl N	11	11	.500	35	30	9-2	0-0	207.1	218	111	27	6	50-7	131	3.86	111	.267	.312	72-3	.236	4	113	5	1.0
1971	Atl N	6	8	.429	27	24	4-2	0-0	172.2	186	80	19	6	35-4	110	3.60	103	.274	.313	62-3	.177	-0*	89	2	0.1
1972	Atl N	6	11	.353	31	16	2-1	1-0	111	143	72	18	4	44-11	63	5.51	69	.315	.378	25-6	.200	1*	92	-18	-2.3
1973	†NY N	12	3	.800	27	20	2	1-0	148	157	53	16	0	31-3	77	2.80	130	.274	.308	48-3	.271	2*	112	13	1.5
1974	NY N	2	7	.222	15	13	1	0-0	77	103	57	10	0	21-4	29	5.03	71	.322	.362	26-0	.115	-1	94	-16	-1.7
1975	NY N	3	3	.500	13	11	1	0-0	57	75	38	3	0	21-3	21	5.05	69	.323	.378	18-2	.167	0	134	-11	-1.0
Total	9	60	57	.513	203	145	24-5	5-1	1020.2	1119	524	122	21	270-41	590	3.89	96	.278	.325	339-23	.212	10	108	-28	-2.4
STONE, ROCKY John Vernon B 8.23.1918 Redding, CA D 11.12.1986 Fountain Valley, CA BR/TR 6/200# d5.2																									
1943	Cin N	0	1	.000	13	0	0	0	24.2	23	14	0	0	8	11	4.38	76	.237	.295	4-0	.250	0		-3	-0.2
STONE, RICKY Ricky L. B 11.25.1975 Hamilton, OH BR/TR 6-1/168# d9.21																									
2001	Hou N	0	0	—	6	0	0	0-0	7.2	8	3	1	0	2-1	4	2.35	195	.258	.303	0-0	—	0		1	0.1
2002	Hou N	3	3	.500	78	0	0	1-1	77.1	78	36	9	1	34-3	63	3.61	118	.266	.342	4-1	.000	-0		4	0.3
2003	Hou N	6	4	.600	65	0	0	1-0	83	76	36	11	6	31-4	47	3.69	120	.247	.327	3-0	.000	-0		7	0.7
Total	3	9	7	.563	149	0	0	2-1	168	162	75	21	7	67-8	114	3.59	122	.256	.333	7-1	.000	-1		12	1.1
STONE, STEVE Steven Michael B 7.14.1947 Euclid, OH BR/TR 5-10/175# d4.8																									
1971	SF N	5	9	.357	24	19	2-2	0-0	110.2	110	56	9	3	55-4	63	4.15	82	.259	.349	34-3	.000	-2	89	-7	-1.0
1972	SF N	6	8	.429	27	16	4-1	0-1	123.2	97	48	11	2	49-2	85	2.98	117	.218	.297	34-6	.118	-1	95	6	0.6
1973	Chi A	6	11	.353	36	22	3	1-0	176.1	163	87	11	7	82-0	138	4.24	94	.245	.334	0-0	—	0*	64	-2	-0.2

Year	Tm Lg	W	L	Pct	G	GS	CG-Sho	SV-BS	IP	H	R	HR	HB	BB-IB	SO	ERA	AERA	OAV	OOB	AB-SH	AVG	PB	Sup	APR	PW
1974	Chi N	8	6	.571	38	23	1	0-0	169.2	185	92	19	4	64-4	90	4.14	92	.278	.343	58-5	.121	-3*	109	-6	-0.7
1975	Chi N	12	8	.600	33	32	6-1	0-0	214.1	198	103	24	5	80-3	139	3.95	98	.245	.314	72-7	.111	-2*	103	-1	-0.3
1976	Chi N	3	6	.333	17	15	1-1	0-0	75	70	36	6	3	21-1	33	4.08	95	.250	.305	21-1	.143	-1	73	-1	-0.2
1977	Chi A	15	12	.556	31	31	8	0-0	207.1	228	115	25	5	80-3	124	4.51	91	.281	.346	0-0	—	0	109	-8	-1.0
1978	Chi A	12	12	.500	30	30	6-1	0-0	212	196	110	19	3	84-1	118	4.37	87	.247	.319	0-0	—	0	97	-11	-1.2
1979	†Bal A	11	7	.611	32	32	3	0-0	186	173	91	31	1	73-1	96	3.77	107	.248	.320	0-0	—	0	108	4	0.3
1980	Bal A★	**25**	7	**.781**	37	37	9-1	0-0	250.2	224	103	22	6	101-3	149	3.23	123	.240	.318	0-0	—	0*	125	18	2.0
1981	Bal A	4	7	.364	15	12	0	0-0	62.2	63	39	7	1	27-0	30	4.60	79	.266	.342	0-0	—	0	89	-8	-1.3
Total	11	107	93	.535	320	269	43-7	1-1	1788.1	1707	880	184	40	716-22	1065	3.97	97	.253	.326	219-22	.100	-9	100	-16	-3.0
STONEMAN, BILL William Hambly B 4.7.1944 Oak Park, IL BR/TR 5-10/170# d7.16																									
1967	Chi N	2	4	.333	28	2	0	4	63	51	24	7	0	22-4	52	3.29	108	.223	.289	13-3	.000	-1	99	2	0.1
1968	Chi N	0	1	.000	18	0	0	0	29.1	35	19	6	1	14-1	18	5.52	57	.310	.388	4-0	.000	-0		-7	-0.4
1969	Mon N	11	19	.367	42	36	8-5	0-0	235.2	233	133	26	12	123-4	185	4.39	84	.261	.356	73-8	.055	-3	94	-18	-2.5
1970	Mon N	7	15	.318	40	30	5-3	0-0	207.2	209	118	26	14	109-8	176	4.59	90	.263	.360	60-4	.100	-2*	78	-11	-1.3
1971	Mon N	17	16	.515	39	**39**	20-3	0-0	294.2	243	112	20	5	146-11	251	3.15	112	.225	.320	93-8	.129	-1*	95	13	1.4
1972	Mon N★	12	14	.462	36	35	13-4	0-0	250.2	213	93	15	3	102-12	171	2.98	119	.229	.305	75-13	.080	-4*	77	14	1.0
1973	Mon N	4	8	.333	29	17	0	1-0	96.2	120	77	12	6	55-6	48	6.80	56	.310	.400	20-2	.050	-1	110	-27	-3.1
1974	Cal A	1	8	.111	13	11	0	0-0	58.2	78	41	8	2	31-0	33	6.14	56	.322	.401	0-0	—	0	77	-16	-2.1
Total	8	54	85	.388	245	170	46-15	5-0	1236.1	1182	617	120	43	602-46	934	4.08	90	.253	.342	338-38	.086	-13	89	-50	-6.9
STONER, LIL Ulysses Simpson Grant B 2.28.1899 Bowie, TX D 6.26.1966 Enid, OK BR/TR 5-9.5/180# d4.15																									
1922	Det A	4	4	.500	17	7	2	0	62.2	76	53	3	3	35	18	7.04	55	.315	.409	20-1	.100	-1	144	-20	-2.2
1924	Det A	11	11	.500	36	25	10-1	0	215.2	271	130	13	5	65	66	4.72	87	.316	.367	77-1	.195	1*	111	-11	-0.9
1925	Det A	10	9	.526	34	18	8	1	152	166	79	6	9	53	51	4.26	101	.283	.352	55-1	.291	4	132	3	0.6
1926	Det A	7	10	.412	32	22	7	0	159.2	179	115	11	3	63	57	5.47	74	.291	.359	53-0	.170	-2	109	-24	-2.3
1927	Det A	10	13	.435	38	24	13	5	215	251	118	9	3	77	63	3.98	106	.301	.362	74-4	.108	-6	94	6	-0.1
1928	Det A	5	8	.385	36	11	4	4	126.1	151	75	16	3	42	29	4.35	95	.296	.353	39-3	.179	-1	127	-4	-0.5
1929	Det A	3	3	.500	24	3	1	4	53	57	37	2	2	31	12	5.26	82	.288	.390	15-0	.067	-2	98	-5	-0.7
1930	Pit N	0	0	—	5	0	0	0	5.2	7	3	2	0	3	1	4.76	105	.318	.400	0-0	—	0		0	0.0
1931	Phi N	0	0	—	7	1	0	0	13.2	22	13	0	0	5	2	6.59	64	.373	.422	5-0	.000	-1	101	-4	-0.3
Total	9	50	58	.463	229	111	45-1	14	1003.2	1180	623	62	28	374	299	4.76	87	.301	.366	338-10	.172	-7	113	-59	-6.4
STOOPS, JIM James Wellington B 6.30.1972 Edison, NJ BR/TR 6-2/180# d9.9																									
1998	Col N	1	0	1.000	3	0	0	0-0	4	5	1	1	1	3-0	0	2.25	230	.385	.529	0-0	—	0		1	0.2
STOTTLEMYRE, MEL Melvin Leon Jr. B 12.28.1963 Prosser, WA BR/TR 6/190# d7.17 b-Todd f-Mel																									
1990	KC A	0	1	.000	13	2	0	0-0	31.1	35	18	3	0	12-1	14	4.88	79	.280	.343	0-0	—	0	47	-3	-0.2
STOTTLEMYRE, MEL Melvin Leon Sr. B 11.13.1941 Hazleton, MO BR/TR 6-2/190# d8.12 C20 s-Mel s-Todd																									
1964	†NY A	9	3	.750	13	12	5-2	0	96	77	26	3	2	35-3	49	2.06	176	.219	.294	37-1	.243	2*	113	16	2.3
1965	NY A☆	20	9	.690	37	37	**18**-4	0	**291**	250	99	18	7	88-3	155	2.63	129	.233	.294	99-9	.131	1	109	24	2.8
1966	NY A★	12	20	.375	37	35	9-3	1	251	239	116	18	1	82-7	146	3.80	87	.253	.311	80-4	.138	1	98	-12	-1.1
1967	NY A	15	15	.500	36	36	10-4	0	255	235	96	20	2	88-11	151	2.96	105	.248	.311	82-6	.098	-3	96	6	0.6
1968	NY A★	21	12	.636	36	36	19-6	0	278.2	243	86	21	3	65-7	140	2.45	118	.234	.280	91-3	.143	2	108	15	2.3
1969	NY A★	20	14	.588	39	39	**24**-3	0-0	303	267	105	19	6	97-11	113	2.82	123	.239	.301	101-4	.178	5	93	24	3.7
1970	NY A★	15	13	.536	37	37	14	0-0	271	262	110	23	6	84-8	126	3.09	114	.255	.313	85-3	.188	9*	105	12	2.3
1971	NY A	16	12	.571	35	35	19-7	0-0	269.2	234	100	16	4	69-6	132	2.87	113	.233	.284	94-3	.170	2	115	11	1.6
1972	NY A	14	18	.438	36	36	9-7	0-0	260	250	99	13	4	85-13	110	3.22	92	.254	.314	80-9	.200	3*	90	-5	-0.1
1973	NY A	16	16	.500	38	38	19-4	0-0	273	259	112	13	5	79-3	95	3.07	120	.253	.307	0-0	—	0	95	17	1.9
1974	NY A	6	7	.462	16	15	6	0-0	113	119	54	7	4	37-3	40	3.58	98	.272	.333	0-0	—	0*	83	-1	-0.2
Total	11	164	139	.541	360	356	152-40	1-0	2661.1	2435	1003	171	44	809-75	1257	2.97	112	.245	.303	749-42	.160	21	100	107	16.1
STOTTLEMYRE, TODD Todd Vernon B 5.20.1965 Sunnyside, WA BL/TR 6-3/195# d4.6 b-Mel f-Mel																									
1988	Tor A	4	8	.333	28	16	0	0-1	98	109	70	15	4	46-5	67	5.69	69	.283	.363	0-0	—	0	103	-20	-2.1
1989	†Tor A	7	7	.500	27	18	0	0-0	127.2	137	56	11	5	44-4	63	3.88	97	.282	.343	0-0	—	0	80	1	0.0
1990	Tor A	13	17	.433	33	33	4	0-0	203	214	101	18	8	69-4	115	4.34	91	.274	.337	0-0	—	0	116	-7	-0.9
1991	†Tor A	15	8	.652	34	34	1	0-0	219	194	97	21	12	75-3	116	3.78	111	.235	.305	0-0	—	0	93	12	1.1
1992	†Tor A	12	11	.522	28	27	6-2	0-0	174	175	99	20	10	63-4	98	4.50	91	.262	.329	0-0	—	0	118	-10	-1.2
1993	†Tor A	11	12	.478	30	28	1-1	0-0	176.2	204	107	11	3	69-5	98	4.84	89	.292	.353	0-0	—	0	103	-11	-1.3
1994	Tor A	7	7	.500	26	19	3-1	1-2	140.2	149	67	19	7	48-2	105	4.22	114	.275	.339	0-0	—	0	80	11	0.9
1995	Oak A	14	7	.667	31	31	2	0-0	209.2	228	117	26	6	80-7	205	4.55	98	.276	.343	1-0	.000	-0	131	-3	-0.3
1996	†StL N	14	11	.560	34	33	5-2	0-0	223.1	191	100	30	4	93-8	194	3.87	108	.231	.309	66-9	.227	4	103	11	1.5
1997	StL N	12	9	.571	28	28	0	0-0	181	155	86	16	12	65-3	160	3.88	107	.231	.308	55-5	.236	6*	100	6	1.3
1998	StL N	9	9	.500	23	23	3	0-0	161.1	146	74	20	4	51-0	147	3.51	119	.240	.301	53-5	.226	2	96	10	1.4
	†Tex A	5	4	.556	10	10	0	0-0	60.1	68	33	5	0	30-1	57	4.33	112	.282	.358	0-0	—	0	141	3	0.3
1999	†Ari N	6	3	.667	17	17	0	0-0	101.1	106	51	12	6	40-1	74	4.09	112	.268	.343	32-3	.125	1	126	5	0.5
2000	Ari N	9	6	.600	18	18	0	0-0	95.1	98	55	18	2	36-2	76	4.91	96	.268	.336	31-3	.194	2	118	-2	0.0
2002	Ari N	0	2	.000	5	4	0	0-0	20.1	26	17	4	0	7-0	12	7.52	59	.313	.363	4-1	.000	-0	62	-6	-0.5
Total	14	138	121	.533	372	339	25-6	1-3	2191.2	2200	1130	246	83	816-49	1587	4.28	100	.262	.330	242-26	.207	15	107	0	0.7
STOUT, ALLYN Allyn McClelland "Fish Hook" B 10.31.1904 Peoria, IL D 12.22.1974 Sikeston, MO BR/TR 5-10/167# d5.16																									
1931	StL N	6	0	1.000	30	3	1	3	72.2	87	40	2	1	34	40	4.21	93	.305	.381	19-2	.105	-1	189	-2	-0.3
1932	StL N	4	5	.444	36	3	1	1	73.2	87	40	5	4	28	32	4.40	89	.305	.375	20-1	.100	-1	64	-3	-0.4
1933	StL N	0	0	—	1	0	0	0	2	1	0	0	0	1	1	0.00	—	.167	.286	0-0	—	0		1	0.1
	Cin N	2	3	.400	23	5	2	0	71.1	85	36	3	0	26	29	3.79	90	.295	.354	22-1	.182	-0	113	-2	-0.2
	Year	2	3	.400	24	5	2	0	73.1	86	41	3	0	27	30	3.68	92	.293	.352	22-1	.182	-0	113	-3	-0.1
1934	Cin N	6	8	.429	41	16	4	1	140.2	170	85	10	4	47	51	4.86	84	.297	.354	43-2	.186	0	111	-9	-0.8
1935	NY N	1	4	.200	40	2	0	5	88	99	58	7	4	37	29	4.91	79	.289	.365	15-0	.133	0	132	-12	-0.8
1943	Bos N	1	0	1.000	9	0	0	1	9.1	17	12	1	0	4	3	6.75	51	.378	.429	2-0	.000	-0		-5	-0.6
Total	6	20	20	.500	180	29	8	11	457.2	546	271	28	13	177	185	4.54	85	.299	.365	121-6	.149	-3	117	-32	-3.0
STOVALL, JESSE Jesse Cramer "Scout" B 7.24.1875 Leeds, MO D 7.12.1955 San Diego, CA BL/TR 6/175# d8.31 b-George																									
1903	Cle A	5	1	.833	6	6	6-2	0	57	44	17	0	3	21	12	2.05	139	.213	.294	22-0	.045	-2	100	6	0.4
1904	Det A	2	13	.133	22	17	13-1	0	146.2	170	97	3	16	45	41	4.42	58	.291	.358	56-0	.196	0*	69	-29	-2.8
Total	2	7	14	.333	28	23	19-3	0	203.2	214	114	3	19	66	53	3.76	70	.270	.341	78-0	.154	-2	78	-23	-2.4
STOVEY, HARRY Harry Duffield (b: Harry Duffield Stowe) B 12.20.1856 Philadelphia, PA D 9.20.1937 New Bedford, MA BR/TR 5-11.5/175# d5.1 M2 ▲																									
1880	Wor N	0	0	—	2	0	0	0	6	8	4	0		3	3	4.50	58	.308	.379	355	.265	0*		-1	0.0
1883	Phi AA	0	0	—	1	0	0	0	3	5	3	0		0	4	9.00	39	.357	.357	421	.304	0*		-1	0.0
1886	Phi AA	0	0	—	1	0	0	0	0.1	2	2	0	0	0	0	27.00	13	.667	.667	489	.294	0*		-1	0.0
Total	3	0	0	—	4	0	0	0	9.1	15	9	0	0	3	7	6.75	44	.349	.391	1265	.289	1		-3	0.0
STOWE, HAL Harold Rudolph B 8.29.1937 Gastonia, NC BL/TL 6/170# d9.30																									
1960	NY A	0	0	—	1	0	0	0	1	0	1	0	0	1-0	0	9.00	40	.000	.333	0-0	—	0		-1	0.0
STRAHLER, MIKE Michael Wayne B 3.14.1947 Chicago, IL BR/TR 6-4/180# d9.12																									
1970	LA N	1	1	.500	6	0	0	1-0	18.2	13	6	1	0	10-0	11	1.45	265	.194	.299	8-0	.250	0		4	0.5
1971	LA N	0	0	—	6	0	0	0-0	12.2	10	4	1	0	8-0	7	2.84	114	.217	.333	1-0	.000	-0		1	0.0
1972	LA N	1	2	.333	19	2	1	0-0	47	42	25	5	1	22-1	25	3.26	102	.237	.322	11-0	.182	1	106	-1	0.0
1973	Det A	4	5	.444	22	11	1	0-1	80.1	84	45	7	1	39-1	37	4.37	94	.273	.355	0-0	—	0	95	-4	-0.4
Total	4	6	8	.429	53	13	2	1-1	158.2	149	80	14	2	79-2	80	3.57	105	.249	.337	20-0	.200	1	102	0	0.1
STRAHS, DICK Richard Bernard B 12.4.1923 Evanston, IL D 5.26.1988 Las Vegas, NV BL/TR 6/192# d7.24																									
1954	Chi A	0	0	—	9	0	0	1	14.1	16	10	0	0	8	8	5.65	66	.271	.358	1-1	.000	-0		-3	-0.2

Year	Tm Lg	W	L	Pct	G	GS	CG-Sho	SV-BS	IP	H	R	HR	HB	BB-IB	SO	ERA	AERA	OAV	OOB	AB-SH	AVG	PB	Sup	APR	PW
STRAKER, LES Lester Paul (Bolnalda) B 10.10.1959 Ciudad Bolivar, Venezuela BR/TR 6-1/193# d4.11																									
1987	†Min A	8	10	.444	31	26	1	0-0	154.1	150	79	24	2	59-6	76	4.37	106	.257	.325	0-0	—	0	86	5	0.5
1988	Min A	2	5	.286	16	14	1-1	1-0	82.2	86	39	8	0	25-1	23	3.92	104	.276	.326	0-0	—	0	97	1	0.1
Total	2	10	15	.400	47	40	2-1	1-0	237	236	118	32	2	84-7	99	4.22	105	.264	.325	0-0	—	0	90	6	0.6
STRAMPE, BOB Robert Edwin B 6.13.1950 Janesville, WI BB/TR 6-1/185# d5.10																									
1972	Det A	0	0	—	7	0	0	0-0	4.2	6	6	0	0	7-1	4	11.57	27	.300	.481	0-0	—	0		-4	-0.2
STRAND, PAUL Paul Edward B 12.19.1893 Carbonado, WA D 7.2.1974 Salt Lake City, UT BR/TL 6-0.5/190# d5.15 ▲																									
1913	Bos N	0	0	—	7	0	0	0	17	22	9	1	0	12	6	2.12	155	.393	.500	6-0	.167	-0		1	0.0
1914	Bos N	6	2	.750	16	3	1	0	55.1	47	23	1	1	23	33	2.44	113	.235	.317	24-0	.333	2*	164	0	0.3
1915	Bos N	1	1	.500	6	2	2	1	22.2	26	12	0	0	3	13	2.38	109	.295	.319	22-0	.091	-0*	158	-1	-0.2
Total	3	7	3	.700	29	5	3	1	95	95	44	2	1	38	52	2.37	119	.276	.350	52-0	.212	2	156	0	0.1
STRANGE, PAT Patrick Martin B 8.23.1980 Springfield, MA BR/TR 6-5/243# d9.13																									
2002	NY N	0	0	—	5	0	0	0-0	8	6	1	0	0	1-1	4	1.13	353	.207	.233	0-0	—	0		3	0.1
2003	NY N	0	0	—	6	0	0	0-0	9	13	11	4	0	11-0	5	11.00	38	.351	.500	1-0	.000	-0		-7	-0.3
Total	2	0	0	—	11	0	0	0-0	17	19	12	4	0	12-1	9	6.35	64	.288	.397	1-0	.000	-0		-4	-0.2
STRATTON, SCOTT C. Scott B 10.2.1869 Campbellsburg, KY D 3.8.1939 Louisville, KY BL/TR 6/180# d4.21 ▲																									
1888	Lou AA	10	17	.370	33	28	28-2	0	269.2	287	196	7	15	53	97	3.64	85	.263	.306	249	.257	5*	102	-12	-0.5
1889	Lou AA	3	13	.188	19	17	13	1	133.2	157	126	6	7	42	42	3.23	119	.284	.342	229	.288	4*	82	-5	0.0
1890	†Lou AA	34	14	**.708**	50	49	44-4	0	431	398	186	3	13	61	207	**2.36**	**163**	.238	**.270**	189	.323	16*	124	**74**	**8.9**
1891	Pit N	0	2	.000	2	2	2	0	18.1	16	9	0	0	5	5	2.45	134	.225	.276	8	.125	-1	55	2	0.2
	Lou AA	6	13	.316	20	20	20-1	0	172	204	112	10	7	34	52	4.08	90	.285	.324	115	.235	1*	73	-6	-0.3
1892	Lou N	21	19	.525	42	40	39-2	0	351.2	342	188	1	9	70	93	2.92	105	.245	.285	219	.256	10*	90	5	1.6
1893	Lou N	12	23	.343	37	35	34-1	0	314.2	445	253	8	8	100	43	5.43	81	.323	.373	221	.226	3*	92	-39	-2.6
1894	Lou N	1	5	.167	7	5	4	0	43	72	50	3	3	13	3	8.37	61	.367	.415	37-0	.324	2*	58	-13	-1.0
	Chi N	8	5	.615	16	13	12	0	128.1	205	131	5	3	42	24	5.89	96	.357	.403	99-0	.374	7*	123	-6	0.2
	Year	9	10	.474	23	18	16	0	171.1	277	141	8	6	55	27	6.51	84	.359	.406	136-0	.360	9	106	-19	-0.8
1895	Chi N	2	3	.400	5	5	3	0	30	51	42	1	4	14	4	9.60	53	.370	.442	24-1	.292	1*	81	-13	-1.3
Total	8	97	114	.460	231	214	199-10	1	1892.1	2177	1293	44	69	434	570	3.87	99	.280	.323	1390-1	.274	48	99	-13	5.2
STRATTON, MONTY Monty Franklin Pierce "Gander" B 5.21.1912 Celeste, TX D 9.29.1982 Greenville, TX BR/TR 6-5/180# d6.2 C3																									
1934	Chi A	0	0	—	1	0	0	0	3.1	4	2	0	0	1	0	5.40	88	.333	.385	2-0	.000	-0		0	0.0
1935	Chi A	1	2	.333	5	5	2	0	38	40	17	0	2	9	8	4.03	115	.274	.325	14-1	.143	-1	75	3	0.2
1936	Chi A	5	7	.417	16	14	3	0	95	117	66	8	1	46	37	5.21	100	.305	.381	37-0	.216	1	109	-2	0.0
1937	Chi A❖	15	5	.750	22	21	14-5	0	164.2	142	55	6	2	37	69	2.40	**191**	.234	**.280**	60-5	.200	-0	90	39	4.3
1938	Chi A	15	9	.625	26	22	17	2	186.1	186	95	18	7	56	82	4.01	122	.255	.315	79-2	.266	5*	133	19	2.7
Total	5	36	23	.610	70	62	36-5	2	487.1	489	235	32	12	149	196	3.71	130	.261	.319	192-8	.224	5	109	59	7.2
STRATTON, ED William Edward B Baltimore, MD d5.14																									
1873	Mar NA	0	3	.000	3	3	3	0	27	75	75	1		1	0	8.33	39	.412	.415	16	.125	-1*	41	-14	-1.0
STREIT, OSCAR Oscar William B 7.7.1873 Florence, AL D 10.10.1935 Birmingham, AL BL/TL 6-5/190# d4.21																									
1899	Bos N	1	0	1.000	2	1	1	0	14.2	15	17	1	2	15	0	6.75	62	.263	.432	7-0	.000	-1	121	-5	-0.3
1902	Cle A	0	7	.000	8	7	4	0	51.2	72	54	3	3	25	10	5.23	66	.330	.407	19-1	.211	1	81	-14	-1.4
Total	2	1	7	.125	10	8	5	0	66.1	87	71	4	5	40	10	5.56	65	.316	.412	26-1	.154	-0	85	-19	-1.7
STRELECKI, ED Edward Harold B 4.10.1905 Newark, NJ D 1.9.1968 Newark, NJ BR/TR 5-11.5/180# d4.16																									
1928	StL A	0	2	.000	22	2	1	1	50.1	49	27	4	1	17	8	4.29	98	.269	.335	10-2	.200	0	71	0	0.0
1929	StL A	1	1	.500	7	0	0	0	11	12	8	1	1	6	2	4.91	90	.279	.380	2-0	.000	-0		-1	-0.2
1931	Cin N	0	0	—	13	0	0	0	24.1	37	25	2	3	9	3	9.25	40	.394	.462	5-0	.200	0		-13	-0.6
Total	3	1	3	.250	42	2	1	1	85.2	98	60	7	5	32	13	5.78	71	.307	.379	17-2	.176	0	71	-14	-0.8
STREMMEL, PHIL Philip B 4.16.1880 Zanesville, OH D 12.26.1947 Chicago, IL BR/TR 6/175# d9.16																									
1909	StL A	0	2	.000	2	2	2	0	18	20	9	0	1	4	6	4.50	54	.308	.357	6-0	.000	-1	44	-3	-0.4
1910	StL A	0	2	.000	5	2	2	0	29	31	19	0	0	16	7	3.72	66	.287	.379	8-1	.125	-0	54	-4	-0.2
Total	2	0	4	.000	7	4	4	0	47	51	28	0	1	20	13	4.02	61	.295	.371	14-1	.071	-1	49	-7	-0.6
STRICKER, CUB John A. (b: John A. Streaker) B 2.15.1860 Philadelphia, PA D 11.19.1937 Philadelphia, PA BR/TR 5-3/138# d5.2 M1 ▲																									
1882	Phi AA	1	0	1.000	2	0	0	0	7	3	1	0		1	2	1.29	218	.120	.154	272	.217	0*		1	0.2
1884	Phi AA	0	0	—	1	0	0	0	3	6	2	0	0	1	1	6.00	56	.333	.368	399	.231	0*		-1	0.0
1887	Cle AA	0	0	—	3	0	0	1	5.2	5	5	0	0	7	2	3.18	137	.238	.429	534	.264	0*		0	0.0
1888	Cle AA	1	0	1.000	2	0	0	0	12	16	6	0	1	2	5	4.50	69	.308	.345	493	.233	0*		-1	0.0
Total	4	2	0	1.000	8	0	0	1	27.2	30	14	0	1	11	10	3.58	93	.259	.328	1698	.240	1		-1	0.2
STRICKLAND, JIM James Michael B 6.12.1946 Los Angeles, CA BL/TL 6/175# d5.19																									
1971	Min A	1	0	1.000	24	0	0	1-1	31.1	20	14	2	2	18-2	21	1.44	248	.183	.303	1-0	.000	0		4	0.2
1972	Min A	3	1	.750	25	0	0	3-1	36	28	16	7	0	19-2	30	2.50	129	.214	.313	3-0	.333	1		1	0.2
1973	Min A	0	1	.000	7	0	0	0-0	5.1	11	8	0	0	5-0	6	11.81	34	.440	.516	0-0	—	0		-4	-0.7
1975	Cle A	0	0	—	4	0	0	1-0	4.2	4	1	0	1	2-0	3	1.93	197	.222	.333	0-0	—	0		1	0.0
Total	4	4	2	.667	60	0	0	5-2	77.1	63	39	9	3	44-4	60	2.68	129	.223	.329	4-0	.250	1		2	-0.3
STRICKLAND, SCOTT Scott Michael B 4.26.1976 Houston, TX BR/TR 5-11/180# d8.14																									
1999	Mon N	0	1	.000	17	0	0	0-0	18	15	10	3	0	11-0	23	4.50	100	.231	.342	0-0	—	0		0	0.0
2000	Mon N	4	3	.571	49	0	0	9-4	48	38	18	3	1	16-2	48	3.00	160	.215	.279	2-0	.000	-0		9	1.4
2001	Mon N	2	6	.250	77	0	0	9-3	81.1	67	36	9	4	41-5	85	3.21	139	.222	.322	3-0	.000	-0		9	0.9
2002	Mon N	0	0	—	1	0	0	0-0	1	0	0	0	0	0-0	2	0.00	—	.000	.000	0-0	—	0		0	0.0
	NY N	6	9	.400	68	0	0	2-4	67.2	61	29	7	2	33-9	67	3.59	110	.236	.325	0-0	—	0		4	0.7
	Year	6	9	.400	69	0	0	2-4	68.2	61	31	7	2	33-9	69	3.54	112	.234	.322	0-0	—	0		4	0.7
2003	NY N	0	2	.000	19	0	0	0-1	20	16	6	1	1	10-1	16	2.25	185	.219	.321	1-1	.000	-0		4	0.3
Total	5	12	21	.364	231	0	0	20-12	236	197	99	23	8	111-17	241	3.28	133	.224	.315	6-1	.000	-1		26	3.3
STRICKLAND, BILL William Goss B 3.29.1908 Bay City, GA D 1.26.2000 Lakeland, FL BR/TR 6-2/170# d7.16																									
1937	StL A	0	0	—	9	0	0	0	21.1	28	18	2	2	15	6	5.91	82	.341	.455	6-0	.167	-0		-3	-0.2
STRICKLETT, ELMER Elmer Griffin "Spitball" B 8.29.1876 Glasco, KS D 6.7.1964 Santa Cruz, CA BR/TR 5-6/140# d4.22																									
1904	Chi A	0	1	.000	1	1	0	0	7	12	10	0	0	2	3	10.29	24	.375	.412	3-0	.000	-0	58	-6	-0.6
1905	Bro N	9	18	.333	33	28	25-1	1	237.1	259	143	0	14	71	77	3.34	87	.282	.343	88-2	.148	-1	82	-19	-1.6
1906	Bro N	14	18	.438	41	35	28-5	5	291.2	273	128	2	5	77	88	2.72	93	.253	.306	97-3	.206	5	92	-11	-0.1
1907	Bro N	12	14	.462	29	26	25-4	0	229.2	211	85	1	8	65	69	2.27	103	.255	.315	81-1	.148	1*	81	1	0.7
Total	4	35	51	.407	104	90	78-10	6	765.2	755	366	3	27	215	237	2.84	91	.264	.322	269-6	.167	4	85	-35	-1.6
STRIKE, JOHN John B 1865 , PA d9.24																									
1886	Phi N	1	1	.500	2	2	1	0	15	19	10	1		7	11	4.80	69	.311	.382	7	.000	-1	84	-1	-0.2
STRIKER, JAKE Wilbur Scott B 10.23.1933 New Washington, OH BL/TL 6-2/200# d9.25																									
1959	Cle A	1	0	1.000	1	1	0	0	6.2	8	2	0	0	4-0	5	2.70	136	.296	.375	1-0	.000	1	192	1	0.2
1960	Chi A	0	0	—	2	0	0	0	3.2	5	3	1	1	1-0	1	4.91	77	.357	.438	0-0	—	0		-1	0.0
Total	2	1	0	1.000	3	1	0	0	10.1	13	5	1	1	5-0	6	3.48	107	.317	.396	1-0	.000	1	192	0	0.2
STRINCEVICH, NICK Nicholas "Jumbo" B 3.1.1915 Gary, IN BR/TR 6-1/180# d4.23																									
1940	Bos N	4	8	.333	32	14	5	1	128.2	142	89	17	8	63	54	5.53	67	.278	.367	43-2	.116	-2*	99	-27	-2.5
1941	Bos N	0	0	—	3	0	0	0	3.1	7	5	0	1	6	1	10.80	33	.412	.583	0-0	—	0		-3	-0.1
	Pit N	1	2	.333	12	3	0	0	31	35	23	4	1	13	12	5.23	69	.280	.353	7-0	.429	1	141	-6	-0.4
	Year	1	2	.333	15	3	0	0	34.1	42	29	4	2	19	13	5.77	63	.296	.387	7-0	.429	1	141	-9	-0.5

Year	Tm Lg	W	L	Pct	G	GS	CG-Sho	SV-BS	IP	H	R	HR	HB	BB-IB	SO	ERA	AERA	OAV	OOB	AB-SH	AVG	PB	Sup	APR	PW
1942	Pit N	0	0	—	7	1	0	0	22.1	19	7	2	1	9	10	2.82	120	.229	.312	4-1	.000	-1	50	2	0.0
1944	Pit N	14	7	.667	40	26	11	2	190	190	86	5	4	37	47	3.08	121	.257	.296	57-5	.158	-1	109	11	1.3
1945	Pit N	16	10	.615	36	29	18-1	2	228.1	235	94	7	3	49	74	3.31	119	.260	.301	84-6	.202	0	104	18	1.8
1946	Pit N	10	15	.400	32	22	11-3	1	176	185	77	7	4	44	49	3.58	98	.268	.316	52-4	.154	1	78	1	0.1
1947	Pit N	1	6	.143	32	7	1	0	89	111	59	9	2	37	22	5.26	80	.316	.385	21-1	.048	-2	84	-10	-0.8
1948	Pit N	0	0	—	3	0	0	0	4.1	8	4	0	0	2	1	8.31	49	.444	.500	0-0	—	0		-2	-0.1
	Phi N	0	1	.000	6	1	0	0	16.2	26	18	1	0	10	4	9.18	43	.347	.424	4-0	.000	-1	0	-9	-0.5
	Year	0	1	.000	9	1	0	0	21	34	18	1	0	12	5	9.00	44	.366	.438	4-0	.000	-1	0	-11	-0.6
Total	8	46	49	.484	203	103	46-4	6	889.2	958	462	52	24	270	274	4.05	93	.273	.329	272-19	.158	-4	98	-25	-1.2
STROHMAYER, JOHN John Emery B 10.13.1946 Belle Fourche, SD BR/TR 6-1/181# d4.29																									
1970	Mon N	3	1	.750	42	0	0	0-2	76	85	48	7	2	39-3	74	4.86	85	.279	.364	6-1	.167	-0		-7	-0.4
1971	Mon N	7	5	.583	27	14	2	1-0	114	124	63	16	4	31-2	56	4.34	81	.281	.331	35-5	.229	1	142	-11	-1.1
1972	Mon N	1	2	.333	48	0	0	3-0	76.2	73	32	6	1	31-3	50	3.52	101	.256	.328	4-1	.000	-0		1	0.1
1973	Mon N	0	1	.000	17	3	0	0-1	34.2	34	20	4	1	22-2	15	5.19	74	.260	.370	5-0	.200	0	115	-4	-0.2
	NY N	0	0	—	7	0	0	0-0	10	13	10	2	0	4-1	5	8.10	45	.310	.370	0-0	—	0		-5	-0.3
	Year	0	1	.000	24	3	0	0-1	44.2	47	35	6	1	26-3	20	5.84	65	.272	.370	5-0	.200	0	117	-9	-0.5
1974	NY N	0	0	—	1	0	0	0-0	1	0	0	0	0	1-0	0	0.00	—	.000	.250	0-0	—	0		0	0.0
Total	5	11	9	.550	142	17	2	4-3	312.1	329	173	35	8	128-11	200	4.47	83	.272	.344	50-7	.200	1	132	-26	-1.9
STROM, BRENT Brent Terry B 10.14.1948 San Diego, CA BR/TL 6-3/190# d7.31 C3																									
1972	NY N	0	3	.000	11	5	0	0-0	30.1	34	25	7	0	15-1	20	6.82	49	.296	.374	6-1	.000	-1	105	-12	-1.1
1973	Cle A	2	10	.167	27	18	2	0-0	123	134	73	18	3	47-4	91	4.61	85	.278	.344	0-0	—	0	85	-11	-0.9
1975	SD N	8	8	.500	18	16	6-2	0-0	120.1	103	42	6	2	33-2	56	2.54	137	.233	.287	30-6	.100	-1	66	13	1.6
1976	SD N	12	16	.429	36	33	8-1	0-0	210.2	188	100	15	2	73-8	103	3.29	100	.239	.302	63-10	.063	-2*	93	-6	-1.0
1977	SD N	0	2	.000	8	3	0	0-0	16.2	23	25	5	0	12-2	8	12.42	29	.329	.417	3-1	.333	0	109	-17	-1.7
Total	5	22	39	.361	100	75	16-3	0-0	501	482	265	51	7	180-17	278	3.95	88	.254	.318	102-18	.078	-3	86	-33	-3.1
STROMME, FLOYD Floyd Marvin "Rock" B 8.1.1916 Cooperstown, ND D 2.7.1993 Wenatchee, WA BR/TR 5-11/170# d7.5																									
1939	Cle A	0	1	.000	5	0	0	0	13	13	8	1	0	13	4	4.85	91	.265	.419	3-0	.333	0		-1	0.0
STRONG, JOE Joseph Benjamin B 9.9.1962 Fairfield, CA BB/TR 6/200# d5.11																									
2000	Fla N	1	1	.500	18	0	0	1-1	19.2	26	16	3	2	12-1	18	7.32	61	.325	.426	1-0	.000	-0		-6	-0.5
2001	Fla N	0	0	—	5	0	0	0-0	6.2	3	1	1	0	3-0	4	1.35	312	.136	.240	1-0	.000	-0		2	0.1
Total	2	1	1	.500	23	0	0	1-1	26.1	29	17	4	2	15-1	22	5.81	75	.284	.387	2-0	.000	-0		-4	-0.4
STROUD, SAILOR Ralph Vivian B 5.15.1885 Ironia, NJ D 4.11.1970 Stockton, CA BR/TR 6/160# d4.29																									
1910	Det A	5	9	.357	28	15	7-3	1	130.1	123	54	9	7	41	63	3.25	81	.257	.325	39-0	.026	-4	88	-5	-1.2
1915	NY N	12	9	.571	32	22	8	1	184	194	76	3	6	35	62	2.79	92	.281	.321	56-3	.161	-1	157	-6	-0.7
1916	NY N	3	2	.600	10	4	0	1	46.2	47	18	1	1	9	16	2.70	90	.266	.305	14-1	.071	-1	131	-2	-0.3
Total	3	20	20	.500	70	41	15-3	3	361	364	148	13	14	85	141	2.94	88	.271	.321	109-4	.101	-6	128	-13	-2.2
STRUSS, STEAMBOAT Clarence Herbert B 2.24.1909 Riverdale, IL D 9.12.1985 Grand Rapids, MI BR/TR 5-11/163# d9.30																									
1934	Pit N	0	1	.000	1	1	0	0	7	7	6	0	0	6	3	6.43	64	.250	.382	3-0	.333	0	105	-2	-0.2
STRYKER, DUTCH Sterling Alpa B 7.29.1895 Atlantic Highlands, NJ D 11.5.1964 Red Bank, NJ BR/TR 5-11.5/180# d4.16																									
1924	Bos N	3	8	.273	20	10	2	0	73.1	90	56	4	1	22	22	6.01	64	.314	.365	23-0	.217	-0	107	-18	-2.1
1926	Bro N	0	0	—	2	0	0	0	2	8	8	0	0	1	0	27.00	14	.571	.600	0-0	—	0		-5	-0.3
Total	2	3	8	.273	22	10	2	0	75.1	98	64	4	1	23	22	6.57	58	.326	.375	23-0	.217	-0	107	-23	-2.4
STUART, JOHNNY John Davis "Stud" B 4.27.1901 Clinton, TN D 5.13.1970 Charleston, WV BR/TR 5-11/170# d7.27																									
1922	StL N	0	0	—	2	1	0	0	2	2	4	0	1	2	1	9.00	43	.222	.417	0-0	—	0	148	-2	-0.1
1923	StL N	9	5	.643	37	10	7-1	3	149.2	139	82	11	9	70	55	4.27	91	.252	.345	57-0	.246	1	122	-4	-0.4
1924	StL N	9	11	.450	28	22	13	0	159	167	100	12	5	60	54	4.75	80	.273	.343	54-1	.204	-1*	127	-18	-2.1
1925	StL N	2	2	.500	15	1	1	0	47	52	41	6	2	24	14	6.13	71	.278	.366	16-0	.250	1	78	-11	-0.7
Total	4	20	18	.526	82	34	21-1	3	357.2	360	227	29	17	156	124	4.76	82	.265	.348	127-1	.228	1	122	-35	-3.3
STUART, MARLIN Marlin Henry B 8.8.1918 Paragould, AR D 6.16.1994 Paragould, AR BL/TR 6-2/185# d4.26																									
1949	Det A	0	2	.000	14	2	0	0	29.2	39	33	3	0	35	14	9.10	46	.348	.503	6-0	.333	1*	118	-16	-0.9
1950	Det A	3	1	.750	19	1	0	2	43.2	59	32	6	1	22	19	5.56	84	.330	.406	12-1	.083	-1	96	-5	-0.5
1951	Det A	4	6	.400	29	15	5	1	124	119	60	9	7	71	46	3.77	111	.258	.365	43-1	.233	1	84	5	0.5
1952	Det A	3	2	.600	30	9	2	1	91.1	91	60	8	3	48	32	4.93	77	.265	.360	23-3	.087	-1	127	-13	-0.8
	StL A	1	2	.333	12	2	0	1	26	26	18	3	0	9	13	4.15	94	.260	.321	6-0	.000	-1	156	-2	-0.4
	Year	4	4	.500	42	11	2	2	117.1	117	25	11	3	57	45	4.76	81	.264	.352	29-3	.069	-2	132	-14	-1.2
1953	StL A	8	2	.800	60	2	0	7	114.1	136	62	6	1	44	46	3.94	107	.300	.363	26-0	.192	-1	95	1	0.0
1954	Bal A	1	2	.333	22	0	0	2	38.1	46	23	2	2	15	13	4.46	80	.303	.371	3-0	.000	-0		-5	-0.4
	NY A	3	0	1.000	10	0	0	1	18.1	28	12	0	0	12	2	5.40	64	.350	.435	6-0	.333	0		-4	-0.6
	Year	4	2	.667	32	0	0	3	56.2	74	40	2	2	27	15	4.76	74	.319	.393	9-0	.222	0		-9	-1.0
Total	6	23	17	.575	196	31	7	15	485.2	544	300	37	14	256	185	4.65	87	.289	.378	125-5	.176	-1	104	-39	-3.1
STUELAND, GEORGE George Anton B 3.2.1899 Algona, IA D 9.9.1964 Onawa, IA BB/TR 6-1.5/174# d9.15																									
1921	Chi N	0	1	.000	2	1	0	0	11	11	7	0	0	7	4	5.73	67	.282	.391	3-0	.333	0	65	-2	-0.1
1922	Chi N	9	4	.692	35	11	4	0	113	129	81	9	5	49	44	5.81	72	.292	.369	31-1	.129	-2	129	-17	-1.9
1923	Chi N	0	1	.000	6	0	0	0	8	11	7	0	0	5	2	5.63	71	.478	.571	0-0	—	0		-2	-0.2
1925	Chi N	0	0	—	2	0	0	0	3	2	1	0	0	3	2	3.00	144	.182	.357	1-0	1.000	0		1	0.1
Total	4	9	6	.600	45	12	4	0	135	153	96	9	5	64	52	5.73	73	.297	.380	35-1	.171	-1	124	-20	-2.1
STUFFEL, PAUL Paul Harrington "Stu" B 3.22.1927 Canton, OH BR/TR 6-2/185# d9.16																									
1950	Phi N	0	0	—	3	0	0	0	5	4	1	0	1	1	3	1.80	225	.211	.286	0-0	—	0		1	0.1
1952	Phi N	1	0	1.000	2	1	0	0	6	5	3	0	0	7	3	3.00	122	.217	.400	2-0	.000	-0	171	0	0.0
1953	Phi N	0	0	—	2	0	0	0	0	0	4	0	0	4	0	o	—	—	1.000	0-0	—	0		-4	-0.3
Total	3	1	0	1.000	7	1	0	0	11	9	8	0	1	12	6	5.73	67	.214	.400	2-0	.000	-0	171	-3	-0.2
STULL, EVERETT Everett James B 8.24.1971 Fort Riley, KS BR/TR 6-3/200# d4.14																									
1997	Mon N	0	1	.000	3	0	0	0-0	3.1	7	7	1	0	4-0	2	16.20	26	.438	.550	0-1	—	0		-5	-0.8
1999	Atl N	0	0	—	1	0	0	0-0	0.2	2	3	0	0	2-0	0	13.50	33	.500	.571	0-0	—	0		-2	-0.1
2000	Mil N	2	3	.400	20	4	0	0-0	43.1	41	30	7	4	30-3	33	5.82	78	.256	.381	9-0	.000	-1	65	-6	-0.6
2002	Mil N	0	1	.000	2	2	0	0-0	10	15	7	0	1	9-2	7	6.30	65	.357	.481	3-0	.333	0	113	-2	-0.1
Total	4	2	5	.286	26	6	0	0-0	57.1	65	47	8	5	45-5	42	6.59	68	.293	.417	12-1	.083	-0	79	-15	-1.6
STULTZ, GEORGE George Irvin B 6.30.1873 Louisville, KY D 3.19.1955 Louisville, KY 5-10/150# d9.22																									
1894	Bos N	1	0	1.000	1	1	1	0	9	4	2	0	0	5	1	0.00	—	.133	.257	3-0	.333	-0	37	5	0.5
STUMP, JIM James Gilbert B 2.10.1932 Lansing, MI BR/TR 6/188# d8.29																									
1957	Det A	1	0	1.000	6	0	0	0	13.1	11	4	0	0	8-0	2	2.03	190	.220	.328	2-1	.500	0		2	0.2
1959	Det A	0	0	—	5	0	0	0	11.1	12	3	1	0	4-0	6	2.38	170	.279	.340	1-0	1.000	1		2	0.2
Total	2	1	0	1.000	11	0	0	0	24.2	23	7	1	0	12-0	8	2.19	180	.247	.333	3-1	.667	1		4	0.4
STUPER, JOHN John Anton B 5.9.1957 Butler, PA BR/TR 6-2/200# d6.1																									
1982	†StL N	9	7	.563	23	21	2	0-0	136.2	137	55	8	0	55-5	53	3.36	108	.266	.336	42-4	.119	-1	85	5	0.3
1983	StL N	12	11	.522	40	30	6-1	1-0	198	202	95	15	2	71-3	81	3.68	99	.265	.327	59-7	.136	-1	110	-2	-0.4
1984	StL N	3	5	.375	15	12	0	0-0	61.1	73	39	4	2	20-2	19	5.28	66	.297	.351	16-3	.063	-1	87	-12	-1.5
1985	Cin N	8	5	.615	33	13	1	0-0	99	116	60	8	0	37-3	38	4.55	83	.303	.358	17-7	.059	-0	120	-10	-1.2
Total	4	32	28	.533	111	76	9-1	1-0	495	528	249	35	4	183-13	191	3.96	92	.277	.339	134-21	.112	-3	101	-19	-2.8
STURDIVANT, TOM Thomas Virgil "Snake" B 4.28.1930 Gordon, KS BL/TR 6-1/186# d4.14																									
1955	†NY A	1	3	.250	33	1	0	0	68.1	48	24	6	2	42-1	48	3.16	118	.203	.329	12-1	.083	-1	24	6	0.2

Year	Tm Lg	W	L	Pct	G	GS	CG-Sho	SV-BS	IP	H	R	HR	HB	BB-IB	SO	ERA	AERA	OAV	OOB	AB-SH	AVG	PB	Sup	APR	PW
1956	†NY A	16	8	.667	32	17	6-2	5	158.1	134	63	15	4	52-4	110	3.30	117	.224	.291	64-3	.313	4	141	12	2.0
1957	†NY A	16	6	**.727**	28	28	7-2	0	201.2	170	65	14	4	80-2	118	2.54	141	.232	.309	71-4	.183	1	106	25	2.6
1958	NY A	3	6	.333	15	10	0	0	70.2	77	37	6	3	38-0	41	4.20	84	.274	.364	21-1	.190	0	99	-5	-0.6
1959	NY A	0	2	.000	7	3	0	0	25.1	20	16	4	0	9-0	16	4.97	73	.222	.290	6-0	.000	-1	48	-4	-0.3
	KC A	2	6	.250	36	3	0	5	71.2	70	45	9	6	34-4	57	4.65	86	.258	.347	17-1	.059	-2*	95	-6	-0.8
	Year	2	8	.200	43	6	0	5	97	90	49	13	6	43-4	73	4.73	83	.249	.333	23-1	.043	-3	71	-10	-1.1
1960	Bos A	3	3	.500	40	3	0	1	101.1	106	58	16	2	45-5	67	4.97	81	.279	.353	22-1	.182	-1	94	-8	-0.5
1961	Was A	2	6	.250	15	10	1-1	0	80	67	42	6	3	40-3	39	4.61	87	.233	.328	26-4	.077	-1	90	-3	-0.4
	Pit N	5	2	.714	13	11	6-1	1	85.2	81	29	6	1	17-3	45	2.84	141	.249	.288	32-1	.250	1	121	12	0.9
1962	Pit N	9	5	.643	49	12	2-1	2	125.1	120	62	12	3	39-11	76	3.73	105	.260	.318	33-4	.182	0	87	2	0.2
1963	Pit N	0	0	—	3	0	0	0	8.1	8	6	1	0	4-0	6	6.48	51	.267	.353	2-0	.000	-0		-2	-0.1
	Det A	1	2	.333	28	0	0	2	55	43	26	7	1	24-2	36	3.76	99	.221	.304	9-0	.000	-1		0	-0.1
	KC A	1	2	.333	17	3	0	0	53	47	24	3	1	17-2	26	3.74	104	.237	.300	11-2	.000	-1	99	1	-0.1
	Year	2	4	.333	45	3	0	2	108	90	28	10	2	41-4	62	3.75	102	.229	.302	20-2	.000	-2	101	1	-0.2
1964	KC A	0	0	—	3	0	0	0	3.2	4	4	0	2	1-0	1	9.82	39	.308	.438	1-0	1.000	0		-2	-0.1
	NY N	0	0	—	16	0	0	1	28.2	34	20	2	2	7-0	18	5.97	60	.306	.347	1-0	.000	-0		-7	-0.4
Total	10	59	51	.536	335	101	22-7	17	1137	1029	521	107	34	449-37	704	3.74	102	.244	.319	328-22	.183	-1	105	21	2.5
STURTZE, TANYON Tanyon James B 10.12.1970 Worcester, MA BR/TR 6-5/190# d5.3																									
1995	Chi N	0	0	—	2	0	0	0-0	2	2	2	1	0	1-0	0	9.00	46	.250	.333	0-0	—	0		-1	-0.1
1996	Chi N	1	0	1.000	6	0	0	0-0	11	16	11	3	0	5-0	7	9.00	48	.348	.412	1-1	.000	-0		-5	-0.4
1997	Tex A	1	1	.500	9	5	0	0-0	32.2	45	30	6	0	18-0	18	8.27	58	.338	.406	0-0	—	0	119	-11	-0.6
1999	Chi A	0	0	—	1	1	0	0-0	6	4	0	0	0	2-0	2	0.00	—	.200	.273	0-0	—	0	19	3	0.2
2000	Chi A	1	2	.333	10	1	0	0-0	15.2	25	23	4	2	15-0	6	12.06	41	.379	.494	0-0	—	0	38	-12	-1.7
	TB A	4	0	1.000	19	5	0	0-0	52.2	47	16	4	1	14-1	38	2.56	193	.236	.290	0-0	—	0	125	14	0.9
	Year	5	2	.714	29	6	0	0-0	68.1	72	23	8	3	29-1	44	4.74	105	.272	.348	0-0	—	0	110	2	-0.8
2001	TB A	11	12	.478	39	27	0	1-2	195.1	200	98	23	9	79-0	110	4.42	102	.271	.345	8-0	.125	-0	98	6	0.6
2002	TB A	4	18	.182	33	33	4	0-0	224	271	141	33	9	89-2	137	5.18	86	.302	.369	4-1	.000	-0	77	-18	-1.6
2003	Tor A	7	6	.538	40	8	0	0-0	89.1	107	67	14	7	43-3	54	5.94	77	.296	.380	0-0	—	0	113	-14	-1.7
Total	8	29	39	.426	159	80	4	1-2	628.2	717	388	88	28	266-6	372	5.20	88	.291	.363	13-2	.077	-1	92	-38	-4.4
SUCH, DICK Richard Stanley B 10.15.1944 Sanford, NC BL/TR 6-4/190# d4.6 C19																									
1970	Was A	1	5	.167	21	5	0	0-0	50	48	42	8	3	45-5	41	7.56	47	.258	.403	13-0	.231	1*	60	-21	-2.1
SUCHE, CHARLEY Charles Morris B 8.5.1915 Cranes Mill, TX D 2.11.1984 San Antonio, TX BR/TL 6-2/190# d9.18																									
1938	Cle A	0	0	—	1	0	0	0	1.1	4	4	0	0	3	1	27.00	17	.571	.700	1-0	1.000	1		-3	-0.1
SUCHECKI, JIM James Joseph B 8.25.1926 Chicago, IL D 7.20.2000 Crofton, MD BR/TR 5-11/185# d5.20																									
1950	Bos A	0	0	—	4	0	0	0	4	3	2	0	0	4	3	4.50	109	.231	.412	0-0	—	0		0	0.0
1951	StL A	0	6	.000	29	6	0	0	89.2	113	64	8	1	42	47	5.42	81	.299	.371	20-2	.100	-2	74	-11	-0.8
1952	Pit N	0	0	—	5	0	0	0	10	14	7	1	1	4	6	5.40	74	.326	.396	2-0	.000	0		-2	-0.1
Total	3	0	6	.000	38	6	0	0	103.2	130	73	9	2	50	56	5.38	81	.300	.374	22-2	.091	-2	74	-13	-0.9
SUDHOFF, WILLIE John William "Wee Willie" B 9.17.1874 St.Louis, MO D 5.25.1917 St.Louis, MO BR/TR 5-7/165# d8.20																									
1897	StL N	2	7	.222	11	9	9	0	92.2	126	72	8	4	21	19	4.47	98	.321	.362	42-1	.238	-1	86	-3	-0.3
1898	StL N	11	27	.289	41	38	35	1	315	355	205	11	27	102	65	4.34	87	.282	.349	120-5	.158	-6	70	-17	-1.9
1899	Cle N	3	8	.273	11	10	8	0	86.1	131	85	3	7	25	10	6.98	53	.347	.399	31-2	.065	-2	88	-30	-2.8
	StL N	12	10	.545	25	23	16	0	178.1	193	109	6	15	62	29	4.04	99	.276	.347	64-5	.203	-0	97	2	0.4
	Year	15	18	.455	36	33	24	0	264.2	324	114	9	22	87	39	5.00	78	.301	.365	95-7	.158	-2	94	-24	-2.4
1900	StL N	6	8	.429	16	14	13-2	0	127	128	62	3	8	37	29	2.76	132	.261	.323	106-1	.189	-0*	100	11	1.0
1901	StL N	17	11	.607	38	26	25-1	2	276.1	281	142	4	18	92	78	3.52	90	.262	.331	108-2	.176	3	129	-10	-0.5
1902	StL A	12	12	.500	30	25	20	0	220	213	99	6	12	67	42	2.86	123	.254	.319	77-3	.169	-2*	73	14	1.3
1903	StL A	21	15	.583	38	35	30-5	0	293.2	262	100	4	9	56	104	2.27	128	.238	.281	110-3	.182	-1*	88	23	2.7
1904	StL A	8	15	.348	27	24	20-1	0	222.1	232	121	8	10	54	63	3.76	66	.269	.320	85-1	.165	0*	98	-31	-2.7
1905	StL A	10	20	.333	32	30	23-1	0	244	222	121	8	13	78	70	2.99	85	.244	.313	86-0	.186	2	77	-14	-1.3
1906	Was A	0	2	.000	9	5	0	0	19.2	30	25	1	2	9	7	9.15	29	.353	.427	7-0	.429	1	169	-14	-1.1
Total	10	102	135	.430	278	239	199-10	3	2075.1	2173	1141	62	125	603	516	3.60	91	.269	.329	836-23	.178	-7	90	-69	-5.2
SUGGS, GEORGE George Franklin B 7.7.1882 Kinston, NC D 4.4.1949 Kinston, NC BR/TR 5-7.5/168# d4.21																									
1908	Det A	1	1	.500	6	1	1	1	27	32	8	0	0	2	8	1.67	145	.299	.312	10-1	.200	0	57	2	0.2
1909	Det A	1	3	.250	9	4	2	1	44.1	34	12	1	3	10	18	2.03	124	.228	.290	15-1	.067	-1	112	3	0.2
1910	Cin N	20	12	.625	35	30	23-2	3	266	248	96	6	14	48	91	2.40	121	.253	.297	85-2	.165	2	105	18	2.4
1911	Cin N	15	13	.536	36	29	17-1	0	260.2	258	110	3	10	79	91	3.00	110	.268	.330	90-2	.256	6	102	12	2.1
1912	Cin N	19	16	.543	42	36	25-5	3	303	320	132	6	11	56	104	2.94	114	.278	.318	106-5	.160	-1	96	16	1.6
1913	Cin N	8	15	.348	36	22	9-2	2	199	220	110	6	7	35	73	4.03	81	.292	.329	67-2	.254	2	81	-13	-1.1
1914	Bal F	24	14	.632	46	38	26-6	4	319.1	322	118	6	10	57	132	2.90	104	.266	.304	99-7	.212	2	100	10	1.7
1915	Bal F	11	17	.393	35	25	12	3	232.2	288	134	12	7	68	71	4.14	69	.318	.370	77-3	.221	0	90	-31	-3.3
Total	8	99	91	.521	245	185	115-16	17	1652	1722	720	40	62	355	588	3.11	100	.277	.322	549-23	.204	11	97	17	3.8
SUKLA, ED Edward Anthony (b: Edward Anthony Suckla) B 3.3.1943 Long Beach, CA BR/TR 5-11/170# d9.17																									
1964	LA A	0	1	.000	2	0	0	0	2.2	2	2	1	0	1-0	3	6.75	49	.200	.273	0-0	—	0		-1	-0.2
1965	Cal A	2	3	.400	25	0	0	3	32	32	16	3	1	10-2	15	4.50	76	.264	.326	0-0	—	0		-3	-0.5
1966	Cal A	1	1	.500	12	0	0	1	16.2	18	12	4	0	6-0	8	6.48	52	.281	.343	1-0	.000	-0		-5	-0.7
Total	3	3	5	.375	39	0	0	4	51.1	52	30	8	1	17-2	26	5.26	64	.267	.329	1-0	.000	-0		-9	-1.4
SULLIVAN, CHARLIE Charles Edward B 5.23.1903 Yadkin Valley, NC D 5.28.1935 Maiden, NC BL/TR 6-1/185# d4.21																									
1928	Det A	0	2	.000	3	2	0	0	12.1	18	12	1	0	6	2	6.57	63	.360	.429	4-0	.000	-1	72	-4	-0.5
1930	Det A	1	5	.167	40	3	2	5	93.2	112	72	9	1	53	38	6.53	73	.311	.401	24-0	.292	2	24	-14	-0.7
1931	Det A	3	2	.600	31	4	2	0	95	109	60	6	1	46	28	4.93	93	.288	.366	24-0	.167	-1	101	-3	-0.3
Total	3	4	9	.308	74	9	4	5	201	239	144	16	2	105	68	5.78	81	.303	.386	52-0	.212	-0	67	-21	-1.5
SULLIVAN, FLEURY Florence P. B 1862 E.St.Louis, IL D 2.15.1897 E.St.Louis, IL d5.3																									
1884	Pit AA	16	35	.314	51	51	51-2	0	441	496	328	15	20	96	189	4.20	79	.268	.311	189	.153	-9*	65	-44	-4.7
SULLIVAN, FRANK Franklin Leal B 1.23.1930 Hollywood, CA BR/TR 6-6.5/215# d7.31																									
1953	Bos A	1	1	.500	14	0	0	0	25.2	24	16	3	1	11	17	5.61	75	.264	.350	4-0	.250	0		-3	-0.2
1954	Bos A	15	12	.556	36	26	11-3	1	206.1	185	81	19	6	66	124	3.14	131	.240	.304	68-3	.103	-3	106	21	2.5
1955	Bos A★	**18**	13	.581	35	**35**	16-3	0	**260**	235	103	23	7	100-5	129	2.91	147	.241	.313	89-12	.112	-4	101	34	3.4
1956	Bos A☆	14	7	.667	34	33	12-1	0	242	253	112	22	8	82-6	116	3.42	135	.268	.330	85-7	.141	-5	107	27	1.6
1957	Bos A	14	11	.560	31	30	14-3	0	240.2	206	76	16	7	48-4	127	2.73	146	.230	**.273**	79-6	.165	-2	86	**35**	**3.5**
1958	Bos A	13	9	.591	32	29	10-2	3	199.1	216	91	12	3	49-0	103	3.57	112	.278	.322	67-8	.164	-1	104	9	0.8
1959	Bos A	9	11	.450	30	26	5-2	1	177.2	172	86	17	7	67-2	107	3.95	103	.258	.331	60-7	.200	-1	94	2	0.1
1960	Bos A	6	16	.273	40	22	4	1	153.2	164	94	12	6	52-6	98	5.10	79	.269	.331	40-4	.125	-1	92	-16	-2.2
1961	Phi N	3	16	.158	49	18	1-1	6	159.1	161	93	19	5	55-5	114	4.29	95	.262	.326	33-3	.152	0	70	-7	-0.7
1962	Phi N	0	2	.000	19	0	0	0	23	38	21	2	2	12-2	12	6.26	62	.396	.460	0-0	—	0		-8	-0.6
	Min A	4	1	.800	21	0	0	5	33.1	33	17	3	0	13-0	10	3.24	126	.258	.324	4-0	.000	-0		2	0.2
1963	Min A	0	1	.000	10	0	0	1	11	15	7	1	0	4-1	2	5.73	64	.349	.404	0-0	—	0		-2	-0.2
Total	11	97	100	.492	351	219	73-15	18	1732	1702	797	149	52	559-31	959	3.60	116	.257	.319	529-50	.144	-17	97	94	8.2
SULLIVAN, HARRY Harry Andrew B 4.22.1888 Rockford, IL D 9.22.1919 Rockford, IL BL/TL d8.11																									
1909	StL N	0	0	—	2	1	0	0	1	4	6	1	0	2	1	36.00	7	.500	.600	1-0	.000	-0	138	-4	-0.2
SULLIVAN, JIM James E. B 4.25.1869 Charlestown, MA D 11.30.1901 Roxbury, MA BR/TR 5-10/155# d4.22																									
1891	Bos N	0	0	—	1	0	0	0	0.1	2	4	0	0	5	0	81.00	5	.667	.875	0	—	0		-2	-0.1
	Col AA	0	1	.000	1	1	1	0	9	10	9	1	1	5	1	4.00	86	.270	.372	4	.000	-1	90	-2	-0.2

Year	Tm Lg	W	L	Pct	G	GS	CG-Sho	SV-BS	IP	H	R	HR	HB	BB-IB	SO	ERA	AERA	OAV	OOB	AB-SH	AVG	PB	Sup	APR	PW
1895	Bos N	11	9	.550	21	19	16	0	178.1	231	133	10	16	58	45	4.74	107	.309	.371	85-1	.176	-6*	123	8	0.1
1896	Bos N	11	12	.478	31	26	21-1	1	225.1	268	148	13	6	68	33	4.03	113	.293	.346	88-2	.216	-2	97	15	0.8
1897	†Bos N	4	5	.444	13	9	8-1	2	89	91	56	1	2	26	17	3.94	113	.262	.317	33-1	.182	-3	80	4	0.1
Total	4	26	27	.491	67	55	46-2	3	502	602	350	25	25	162	96	4.32	109	.294	.353	210-4	.190	-11	104	23	0.7
SULLIVAN, JIM James Richard B 4.5.1894 Mine Run, VA D 2.12.1972 Burtonsville, MD BR/TR 5-11/165# d9.27																									
1921	Phi A	0	2	.000	2	2	2	0	17	20	13	0	0	7	8	3.18	140	.294	.360	6-0	.000	-1	37	0	-0.1
1922	Phi A	0	2	.000	20	2	1	0	51.1	76	43	3	1	25	15	5.44	78	.373	.443	11-1	.091	-1	30	-9	-0.5
1923	Cle A	0	1	.000	3	0	0	0	5	10	10	0	1	5	4	14.40	28	.476	.593	1-0	.000	-0		-6	-0.9
Total	3	0	5	.000	25	4	3	0	73.1	106	66	3	2	37	27	5.52	78	.362	.437	18-1	.056	-2	35	-15	-1.5
SULLIVAN, JOE Joe B 9.26.1910 Mason City, IL D 4.8.1985 Sequim, WA BL/TL 5-11/175# d4.20																									
1935	Det A	6	6	.500	25	12	5	0	125.2	119	66	4	3	71	53	3.51	119	.244	.344	43-1	.163	-1	106	5	0.3
1936	Det A	2	5	.286	26	4	1	1	79.2	111	70	4	2	40	32	6.78	73	.331	.406	28-1	.179	-1	98	-17	-1.3
1939	Bos N	6	9	.400	31	11	7	2	113.2	114	57	3	2	50	46	3.64	101	.266	.346	40-1	.300	3*	86	-1	0.3
1940	Bos N	10	14	.417	36	22	7	1	177.1	157	89	9	8	89	64	3.55	105	.240	.339	71-3	.197	-0	110	-1	-0.1
1941	Bos N	2	2	.500	16	2	0	0	52.1	60	26	3	2	26	11	4.13	86	.290	.374	15-0	.067	-1	107	-2	-0.2
	Pit N	4	1	.800	16	4	0	1	39.1	40	26	2	0	22	10	2.97	121	.258	.350	11-0	.364	1	100	-1	-0.1
	Year	6	3	.667	32	6	0	1	91.2	100	30	5	2	48	21	3.63	99	.276	.364	26-0	.192	-0	103	-5	-0.3
Total	5	30	37	.448	150	55	20	5	588	601	334	25	17	298	216	4.01	99	.265	.355	208-6	.207	1	101	-17	-1.1
SULLIVAN, JOHN John Jeremiah "Lefty" B 5.31.1894 Chicago, IL D 7.7.1958 Chicago, IL BL/TL 5-11/165# d7.18																									
1919	Chi A	0	1	.000	4	2	1	0	15	24	15	0	1	8	9	4.20	76	.364	.440	3-0	.000	-0	160	-4	-0.3
SULLIVAN, MIKE Michael Joseph "Big Mike" B 10.23.1866 Boston, MA D 6.14.1906 Boston, MA BL 6-1/210# d6.17																									
1889	Was N	0	3	.000	9	3	3	0	41	47	47	2	3	32	15	7.24	54	.280	.404	19	.053	-2	108	-14	-0.9
1890	Chi N	5	6	.455	12	12	10	0	96	108	77	3	4	58	33	4.59	80	.275	.374	40	.125	-3	82	-10	-1.2
1891	Phi AA	0	2	.000	2	2	2	0	18	17	13	2	3	10	7	3.50	108	.239	.357	7	.000	-1	65	0	-0.2
	NY N	1	2	.333	3	3	3	0	24	24	19	0	1	8	11	3.38	95	.250	.314	10	.200	-0	81	-1	-0.2
1892	Cin N	12	4	.750	21	16	15	0	166.1	179	90	8	9	74	56	3.08	106	.264	.344	74	.176	-2	102	2	-0.2
1893	Cin N	8	11	.421	27	18	14	1	183.2	200	146	5	17	103	40	5.05	95	.269	.370	79	.203	-3	89	-7	-0.8
1894	Was N	2	10	.167	20	12	11	1	117.2	166	134	10	8	74	21	6.58	80	.329	.422	57-1	.158	-4	100	-15	-1.4
	Cle N	6	5	.545	13	11	9	0	90.2	128	82	4	3	47	19	6.35	86	.329	.405	44-1	.295	0	105	-5	-0.5
	Year	8	15	.348	33	23	20	1	208.1	294	90	14	11	121	40	6.48	83	.329	.415	101-2	.218	-4	103	-26	-1.9
1895	Cle N	1	2	.333	4	3	2	0	31	42	34	1	1	16	5	8.42	59	.318	.396	15-0	.133	-2	119	-9	-0.7
1896	NY N	10	13	.435	25	22	18	0	185.1	188	131	3	13	71	42	4.66	90	.261	.338	77-2	.208	-3	83	-8	-1.0
1897	NY N	8	7	.533	23	16	11-1	2	148.2	183	113	6	14	71	35	5.09	82	.300	.386	66-0	.273	0	101	-11	-0.9
1898	Bos N	0	1	.000	3	2	0	0	12	19	16	1	1	9	1	12.00	31	.358	.460	3-0	.333	0	77	-9	-0.6
1899	Bos N	1	0	1.000	1	1	1	0	9	10	6	1	1	4	1	5.00	83	.278	.366	3-0	.333	0	121	-1	0.0
Total	11	54	66	.450	163	121	99-1	4	1123.1	1311	908	46	78	577	286	5.11	84	.285	.374	494-4	.196	-21	94	-88	-8.6
SULLIVAN, LEFTY Paul Thomas B 9.7.1916 Nashville, TN D 11.1.1988 Scottsdale, AZ BL/TL 6-3/204# d5.6																									
1939	Cle A	0	1	.000	7	1	0	0	12.2	9	8	0	1	9	4	4.26	103	.214	.365	3-0	.000	-0	20	0	-0.1
SULLIVAN, TOM Thomas B 3.1.1860 New York, NY D 4.12.1947 Cincinnati, OH d9.27																									
1884	Col AA	2	2	.500	4	4	4	0	31	42	22	2	0	3	12	4.06	75	.318	.333	11	.091	-1	70	-4	-0.5
1886	Lou AA	2	7	.222	9	9	8	0	75	94	70	6	2	33	27	3.96	92	.305	.376	27	.111	-2	60	-4	-0.5
1888	KC AA	8	16	.333	24	24	24	0	214.2	227	146	2	24	68	84	3.40	101	.262	.332	92	.109	-6*	67	-3	-0.6
1889	KC AA	2	8	.200	10	10	10	0	87.1	111	88	2	7	48	24	5.67	74	.300	.391	33	.152	-1	87	-11	-1.0
Total	4	14	33	.298	47	47	46	0	408	474	326	12	33	152	147	4.04	89	.282	.354	163	.117	-9	70	-22	-2.6
SULLIVAN, TOM Thomas Augustin B 10.18.1895 Boston, MA D 9.23.1962 Boston, MA BL/TL 5-11/178# d5.15																									
1922	Phi N	0	0	—	3	0	0	0	8	16	11	0	1	5	2	11.25	41	.410	.489	4-0	.250	1		-4	-0.1
SULLIVAN, BILL William F. B 12.1868 Providence, RI D 10.8.1905 Providence, RI BR/TR d4.19																									
1890	Syr AA	1	4	.200	6	6	4	0	42	51	50	2	6	27	13	7.93	45	.291	.404	22	.091	-2	137	-22	-1.9
SULLIVAN, SCOTT William Scott B 3.13.1971 Tuscaloosa, AL BR/TR 6-3/210# d5.6																									
1995	Cin N	0	0	—	3	0	0	0-0	3.2	4	2	0	0	2-0	2	4.91	84	.286	.375	1-0	.000	-0		0	0.0
1996	Cin N	0	0	—	7	0	0	0-0	8	7	2	0	1	5-0	3	2.25	188	.250	.382	1-0	.000	-0		2	0.1
1997	Cin N	5	3	.625	59	0	0	1-1	97.1	79	36	12	7	30-8	96	3.24	132	.220	.291	7-2	.000	-1		12	0.8
1998	Cin N	5	5	.500	67	0	0	1-3	102	98	62	14	9	36-4	86	5.21	82	.253	.327	11-1	.091	-1		-10	-1.0
1999	Cin N	5	4	.556	79	0	0	3-2	113.2	88	41	10	8	47-4	78	3.01	155	.216	.307	15-0	.000	-2		21	1.3
2000	Cin N	3	6	.333	79	0	0	3-3	106.1	87	44	14	9	38-8	96	3.47	136	.226	.307	7-0	.286	0*		15	1.1
2001	Cin N	7	1	.875	79	0	0	0-3	103.1	94	44	10	8	36-8	82	3.31	138	.243	.317	3-0	.000	-0		13	0.8
2002	Cin N	6	5	.545	71	0	0	1-2	78.2	93	60	15	5	31-11	78	6.06	70	.294	.363	3-0	.333	0		-16	-2.0
2003	Cin N	6	0	1.000	50	0	0	0-1	49.2	39	22	4	5	26-4	43	3.62	118	.211	.321	0-0	—	0		3	0.3
	Chi A	0	0	—	15	0	0	0-0	14.1	9	6	2	1	6-0	13	3.77	121	.184	.281	0-0	—	0		1	0.1
Total	9	37	24	.607	509	0	0	9-15	677	598	319	81	53	257-47	577	3.91	114	.237	.318	48-3	.083	-3		41	1.5
SUMMERS, ED Oron Edgar "Kickapoo Ed" or "Chief" B 12.5.1884 Ladoga, IN D 5.12.1953 Indianapolis, IN BB/TR 6-2/180# d4.16																									
1908	†Det A	24	12	.667	40	32	23-5	1	301	271	112	3	20	55	103	1.64	147	.242	.290	113-4	.124	-6	116	15	1.1
1909	†Det A	19	9	.679	35	32	24-3	1	281.2	243	91	4	10	52	107	2.24	113	.227	.269	94-3	.106	-4	109	10	0.6
1910	Det A	13	12	.520	30	25	18-1	0	220.1	211	83	8	5	60	82	2.53	104	.254	.308	76-4	.184	-0	111	2	0.3
1911	Det A	11	11	.500	30	20	13	1	179.1	189	108	3	11	51	65	3.66	95	.274	.334	63-3	.254	1	122	-7	-0.7
1912	Det A	1	1	.500	3	3	1	0	16.2	16	10	1	0	3	5	4.86	67	.250	.284	6-0	.500	1	136	-2	-0.1
Total	5	68	45	.602	138	112	79-9	3	999	930	404	19	46	221	362	2.42	111	.246	.296	352-14	.162	-9	115	18	1.2
SUNDIN, GORDIE Gordon Vincent B 10.10.1937 Minneapolis, MN BR/TR 6-4/215# d9.19																									
1956	Bal A	0	0	—	1	0	0	0	0	0	1	0	0	2-0	0	o	—	—	1.000	0-0	—	0		-1	-0.1
SUNDRA, STEVE Stephen Richard "Smokey" B 3.27.1910 Luxor, PA D 3.23.1952 Cleveland, OH BR/TR 6-2/190# d4.17 Mil 1944-45																									
1936	NY A	0	0	—	1	0	0	0	2	2	0	0	0	2	1	0.00	—	.286	.444	1-0	.000	-0		1	0.0
1938	NY A	6	4	.600	25	8	3	0	93.2	107	61	7	0	43	33	4.80	94	.291	.365	33-2	.182	1	141	-4	-0.2
1939	†NY A	11	1	.917	24	11	8-1	0	120.2	110	43	7	0	56	27	2.76	158	.240	.323	49-2	.265	4	162	22	2.3
1940	NY A	4	6	.400	27	8	2	2	99.1	121	68	11	1	42	26	5.53	73	.299	.366	29-1	.138	-1	101	-17	-1.6
1941	Was A	9	13	.409	28	23	11	0	168.1	203	108	11	1	61	50	5.29	76	.294	.352	60-4	.217	2	105	-20	-2.0
1942	Was A	1	3	.250	6	4	2	0	33.2	43	24	1	1	15	5	5.61	65	.305	.376	12-0	.167	-0	99	-7	-0.7
	StL A	8	3	.727	20	13	6	0	110.2	122	56	2	0	29	26	3.82	97	.275	.319	40-3	.225	3	138	-2	0.1
	Year	9	6	.600	26	17	8	0	144.1	165	62	3	1	44	31	4.24	87	.282	.333	52-3	.212	2	129	-8	-0.6
1943	StL A	15	11	.577	32	29	13-3	0	208	212	89	10	0	66	44	3.25	103	.266	.322	73-4	.219	1	104	1	0.2
1944	StL A	2	0	1.000	3	3	2	0	19	15	3	1	0	4	1	1.42	253	.211	.253	5-0	.000	-0	85	5	0.5
1946	StL A	0	0	—	2	0	0	0	4	9	9	0	0	3	1	11.25	33	.409	.480	0-0	—	0		-4	-0.2
Total	9	56	41	.577	168	99	47-4	2	859.1	944	461	50	3	321	214	4.17	94	.277	.340	302-16	.209	10	116	-25	-1.6
SUNKEL, TOM Thomas Jacob "Lefty" B 8.9.1912 Paris, IL D 4.6.2002 Paris, IL BL/TL 6-1/190# d8.26																									
1937	StL N	0	0	—	9	1	0	1	29.1	24	11	0	0	11	9	2.76	144	.214	.285	9-0	.111	-1	173	4	0.1
1939	StL N	4	4	.500	20	11	2-1	0	85.1	79	47	4	1	56	54	4.22	98	.242	.354	28-1	.321	2	98	-1	0.0
1941	NY N	1	1	.500	2	2	1-1	0	15.1	7	5	0	1	12	14	2.93	126	.140	.317	6-0	.333	0	34	2	0.2
1942	NY N	3	6	.333	19	11	3	0	63.2	65	40	5	0	41	29	4.81	70	.269	.375	19-0	.105	-1	80	-10	-1.5
1943	NY N	0	1	.000	1	1	0	0	2.2	4	3	1	0	3	0	10.13	34	.308	.438	0-0	—	0	0	-2	-0.3
1944	Bro N	1	3	.250	12	3	0	1	24	39	20	1	0	10	6	7.50	47	.368	.422	4-1	.000	-1	79	-9	-1.5
Total	6	9	15	.375	63	29	6-2	2	220.1	218	126	11	2	133	112	4.53	83	.256	.358	66-2	.212	0	84	-16	-3.0
SUPPAN, JEFF Jeffrey Scot B 1.2.1975 Oklahoma City, OK BR/TR 6-1/200# d7.17																									
1995	Bos A	1	2	.333	8	3	0	0-0	22.2	29	15	4	0	5-1	19	5.96	82	.312	.343	0-0	—	0	89	-2	-0.2

Year	Tm Lg	W	L	Pct	G	GS	CG-Sho	SV-BS	IP	H	R	HR	HB	BB-IB	SO	ERA	AERA	OAV	OOB	AB-SH	AVG	PB	Sup	APR	PW
1996	Bos A	1	1	.500	8	4	0	0-0	22.2	29	19	3	1	13-0	13	7.54	67	.330	.406	0-0	—	0	123	-5	-0.4
1997	Bos A	7	3	.700	23	22	0	0-0	112.1	140	75	12	4	36-1	67	5.69	82	.305	.358	2-0	.000	-0	118	-12	-1.0
1998	Ari N	1	7	.125	13	13	1	0-0	66	82	55	12	1	21-1	39	6.68	63	.301	.351	22-1	.273	1	96	-19	-1.7
	KC A	0	0	—	4	1	0	0-0	12.2	9	1	1	0	1-0	12	0.71	680	.200	.217	0-0	—	0	0	6	0.3
1999	KC A	10	12	.455	32	32	4-1	0-0	208.2	222	113	28	3	62-4	103	4.53	111	.274	.326	5-0	.200	0	98	12	1.0
2000	KC A	10	9	.526	35	33	3-1	0-0	217	240	121	36	7	84-3	128	4.94	104	.284	.351	3-0	.000	-0	95	7	0.4
2001	KC A	10	14	.417	34	34	1	0-0	218.1	227	120	26	12	74-3	120	4.37	112	.267	.333	5-0	.400	1	82	11	1.1
2002	KC A	9	16	.360	33	33	3-1	0-0	208	229	134	32	7	68-3	109	5.32	94	.279	.335	1-3	.000	0	83	-7	-0.7
2003	Pit N	10	7	.588	21	21	3-2	0-0	141	147	57	11	6	31-5	78	3.57	123	.268	.313	41-8	.293	3	93	14	1.9
	Bos A	3	4	.429	11	10	0	0-0	63	70	41	12	2	20-0	32	5.57	82	.281	.335	2-1	.000	-0	113	-6	-0.6
Total	9	62	75	.453	222	206	15-5	0-0	1292.1	1424	751	177	43	415-21	720	4.90	99	.280	.337	81-13	.259	5	94	-1	0.1
SURHOFF, RICH Richard Clifford B 10.3.1962 Bronx, NY BR/TR 6-3/210# d9.8 b-B.J.																									
1985	Phi N	1	0	1.000	2	0	0	0-0	1	2	0	0	0	0-0	1	0.00	—	.500	.500	0-0	—	0		0	0.1
	Tex A	0	1	.000	7	0	0	2-1	8.1	12	7	2	0	3-0	8	7.56	56	.343	.395	0-0	—	0		-3	-0.4
Total	1	1	1	.500	9	0	0	2-1	9.1	14	7	2	0	3-0	9	6.75	62	.359	.405	0-0	—	0		-3	-0.3
SURKONT, MAX Matthew Constantine B 6.16.1922 Central Falls, RI D 10.8.1986 Largo, FL BR/TR 6/205# d4.19																									
1949	Chi A	3	5	.375	44	2	0	4	96	92	61	9	3	60	38	4.78	87	.255	.366	22-0	.045	-1	75	-8	-0.8
1950	Bos N	5	2	.714	9	6	2	0	55.2	63	29	5	2	20	21	3.23	119	.285	.350	23-0	.435	5	142	1	0.7
1951	Bos N	12	16	.429	37	33	11-2	1	237	230	119	21	7	89	110	3.99	92	.252	.323	73-8	.151	0	98	-8	-1.0
1952	Bos N	12	13	.480	31	29	12-3	0	215	201	95	19	3	76	125	3.77	96	.245	.311	63-7	.111	-1	86	-2	-0.3
1953	Mil N	11	5	.688	28	24	11-2	0	170	168	82	22	0	64	83	4.18	94	.255	.321	56-5	.286	7	121	-1	0.6
1954	Pit N	9	18	.333	33	29	11	0	208.1	216	124	25	4	78	78	4.41	95	.268	.333	60-9	.167	0	78	-8	-0.8
1955	Pit N	7	14	.333	35	22	5	2	166.1	194	109	23	3	78-4	84	5.57	74	.298	.374	50-4	.140	-1	87	-22	-2.7
1956	Pit N	0	0	—	1	0	0	0	2	2	1	0	0	3-0	1	4.50	84	.333	.500	0-0	—	0		0	0.0
	StL N	0	0	—	5	0	0	0	5.2	10	6	3	0	2-0	5	9.53	40	.417	.462	1-0	.000	-0		-3	-0.2
	NY N	2	2	.500	8	4	1	1	32	24	17	5	0	9-1	18	4.78	79	.202	.256	9-2	.111	-0	93	-3	-0.4
	Year	2	2	.500	14	4	1	1	39.2	36	21	8	0	14-1	24	5.45	69	.242	.303	10-2	.100	-0	93	-6	-0.6
1957	NY N	0	1	.000	5	0	0	0	6.1	9	7	2	0	2-0	8	9.95	40	.321	.367	0-0	—	0		-4	-0.5
Total	9	61	76	.445	236	149	53-7	8	1194.1	1209	650	134	22	481-5	571	4.38	89	.262	.334	357-35	.176	8	94	-58	-5.4
SUSCE, GEORGE George Daniel B 9.13.1931 Pittsburgh, PA BR/TR 6-1/180# d4.15 f-George																									
1955	Bos A	9	7	.563	29	15	6-1	1	144.1	123	54	12	8	49-4	60	3.06	140	.232	.305	49-3	.143	-2	80	19	1.8
1956	Bos A	2	4	.333	21	6	0	0	69.2	71	54	14	4	44-1	26	6.20	74	.262	.371	18-0	.222	1	103	-10	-0.7
1957	Bos A	7	3	.700	29	5	0	1	88.1	93	45	6	3	41-5	40	4.28	93	.274	.354	25-1	.120	-1	85	-2	-0.3
1958	Bos A	0	0	—	2	0	0	0	2	6	4	1	0	1-0	0	18.00	22	.600	.583	0-0	—	0		-3	-0.1
	Det A	4	3	.571	27	10	2	1	90.2	90	45	7	3	26-1	42	3.67	110	.259	.312	24-2	.125	-1	89	2	0.0
	Year	4	3	.571	29	10	2	1	92.2	96	49	8	3	27-1	42	3.98	101	.269	.321	24-2	.125	-1	89	-1	-0.1
1959	Det A	0	0	—	9	0	0	0	14.2	24	22	4	2	9-0	9	12.89	32	.358	.449	1-0	.000	-0		-13	-0.6
Total	5	22	17	.564	117	36	8-1	3	409.2	407	224	44	20	170-11	177	4.42	95	.260	.337	117-6	.145	-2	88	-7	0.1
SUTCLIFFE, RICK Richard Lee B 6.21.1956 Independence, MO BL/TR 6-7/215# d9.29																									
1976	LA N	0	0	—	1	1	0	0-0	5	2	0	0	0	1-0	3	0.00	—	.125	.176	1-0	.000	-0	26	2	0.1
1978	LA N	0	0	—	2	0	0	0-0	1.2	2	0	0	1	1-0	0	0.00	—	.286	.444	0-0	—	0		1	0.0
1979	LA N	17	10	.630	39	30	5-1	0-0	242	217	104	16	2	97-6	117	3.46	105	.243	.316	85-6	.247	5*	131	7	1.1
1980	LA N	3	9	.250	42	10	1-1	5-3	110	122	73	10	1	55-2	59	5.56	63	.285	.366	27-3	.148	-0*	127	-25	-2.8
1981	LA N	2	2	.500	14	6	0	0-0	47	41	24	5	2	20-2	16	4.02	83	.238	.321	11-0	.182	1	71	-5	-0.3
1982	Cle A	14	8	.636	34	27	6-1	1-0	216	174	81	16	4	98-2	142	**2.96**	138	**.226**	.314	0-0	—	0	101	26	2.6
1983	Cle A☆	17	11	.607	36	35	10-2	0-1	243.1	251	131	23	6	102-5	160	4.29	99	.268	.341	0-0	—	0	105	-2	-0.2
1984	Cle A	4	5	.444	15	15	2	0-0	94.1	111	60	7	2	46-3	58	5.15	79	.298	.375	0-0	—	0	116	-11	-0.9
	†Chi N	16	1	**.941**	20	20	7-3	0-0	150.1	123	53	9	1	39-0	155	2.69	145	.220	.271	56-5	.250	3	125	17	2.4
1985	Chi N	8	8	.500	20	20	6-3	0-0	130	119	51	12	3	44-3	102	3.18	126	.240	.304	43-2	.233	2	82	10	1.5
1986	Chi N	5	14	.263	28	27	4-1	0-0	176.2	166	92	18	1	96-8	122	4.64	87	.252	.347	53-4	.208	2*	72	-8	-0.5
1987	Chi N★	**18**	10	.643	34	34	6-1	0-0	237.1	223	106	24	4	106-14	174	3.68	116	.252	.332	81-11	.148	2*	114	16	2.2
1988	Chi N	13	14	.481	32	32	12-2	0-0	226	232	97	18	2	70-9	144	3.86	94	.269	.323	75-4	.160	3*	99	-2	0.2
1989	†Chi N★	16	11	.593	35	34	5-1	0-0	229	202	98	18	2	69-8	153	3.66	103	.240	.296	70-10	.143	1*	104	5	0.8
1990	Chi N	0	2	.000	5	5	0	0-0	21.1	25	14	2	0	12-0	7	5.91	69	.305	.385	5-1	.000	0	89	-3	-0.3
1991	Chi N	6	5	.545	19	18	0	0-0	96.2	96	52	4	0	45-2	52	4.10	95	.264	.338	32-5	.094	-1*	98	-3	-0.5
1992	Bal A	16	15	.516	36	**36**	5-2	0-0	237.1	251	123	20	7	74-4	109	4.47	90	.273	.328	0-0	—	0	92	-10	-1.3
1993	Bal A	10	10	.500	29	28	3	0-0	166	212	112	23	6	74-5	80	5.75	78	.314	.385	0-0	—	0	102	-22	-2.1
1994	StL N	6	4	.600	16	14	0	0-0	67.2	93	53	11	2	32-2	26	6.52	64	.331	.402	23-3	.130	-1	110	-18	-2.2
Total	18	171	139	.552	457	392	72-18	6-4	2697.2	2662	1324	236	46	1081-75	1679	4.08	97	.260	.331	562-54	.181	17	103	-25	-0.2
SUTER, HARRY Harry Richard "Handsome Harry" or "Rube" B 9.15.1887 Independence, MO D 7.24.1971 Topeka, KS BL/TL 5-10/190# d4.16																									
1909	Chi A	2	3	.400	18	7	3-1	1	87.1	72	34	2	4	28	53	2.47	95	.199	.264	32-1	.094	-1	112	-1	-0.3
SUTHERLAND, DARRELL Darrell Wayne B 11.14.1941 Glendale, CA BR/TR 6-4/169# d6.28 b-Gary																									
1964	NY N	0	3	.000	10	4	0	0	26.2	32	26	1	2	12-0	9	7.76	46	.302	.377	5-0	.200	0	111	-12	-1.2
1965	NY N	3	1	.750	18	2	0	0	48	33	16	4	4	17-2	16	2.81	125	.199	.284	13-0	.154	0	111	4	0.5
1966	NY N	2	0	1.000	31	0	0	1	44.1	60	25	6	2	25-8	23	4.87	75	.339	.422	3-0	.667	1		-5	-0.1
1968	Cle A	0	0	—	3	0	0	0	3.1	6	3	0	0	4-1	2	8.10	37	.375	.500	0-0	—	0		-2	-0.1
Total	4	5	4	.556	62	6	0	1	122.1	131	70	11	8	58-11	50	4.78	75	.282	.366	21-0	.238	1	111	-15	-0.9
SUTHERLAND, SUDS Harvey Scott B 2.20.1894 Beaverton, OR D 5.11.1972 Portland, OR BR/TR 6/180# d4.14																									
1921	Det A	6	2	.750	13	8	3	0	58	80	43	1	0	18	18	4.97	86	.328	.374	27-0	.407	2*	156	-6	-0.3
SUTHERLAND, DIZZY Howard Alvin B 4.9.1922 Washington, DC D 8.26.1979 Washington, DC BL/TL 6/200# d9.20																									
1949	Was A	0	1	.000	1	1	0	0	1	2	5	0	0	6	0	45.00	9	.400	.727	0-0	—	0	126	-4	-0.6
SUTTER, BRUCE Howard Bruce B 1.8.1953 Lancaster, PA BR/TR 6-2/190# d5.9																									
1976	Chi N	6	3	.667	52	0	0	10-2	83.1	63	27	4	0	26-8	73	2.70	143	.209	.271	8-0	.000	-1		10	1.3
1977	Chi N❖	7	3	.700	62	0	0	31-9	107.1	69	21	5	1	23-7	129	1.34	327	.183	.231	20-0	.150	-0		31	4.7
1978	Chi N★	8	10	.444	64	0	0	27-14	98.2	82	44	10	1	34-7	106	3.19	126	.220	.285	13-4	.077	-0		6	1.2
1979	Chi N★	6	6	.500	62	0	0	**37-10**	101.1	67	29	3	0	32-5	110	2.22	186	.186	.249	12-2	.250	0		**19**	3.8
1980	Chi N★	5	8	.385	60	0	0	**28-9**	102.1	90	35	5	1	34-8	76	2.64	149	.242	.306	9-1	.111	-1		13	2.3
1981	StL N★	3	5	.375	48	0	0	**25-7**	82.1	64	24	5	1	24-8	57	2.62	136	.218	.276	9-0	.000	-1		9	1.4
1982	†StL N	9	8	.529	70	0	0	**36-9**	102.1	88	38	8	3	34-13	61	2.90	125	.235	.302	8-2	.125	-0		8	1.6
1983	StL N	9	10	.474	60	0	0	21-9	89.1	90	45	8	1	30-14	64	4.23	86	.262	.321	7-1	.000	-1		-5	-1.0
1984	StL N☆	5	7	.417	71	0	0	**45-8**	122.2	109	26	9	1	23-4	77	1.54	226	.245	.281	10-0	.000	-1		**26**	**4.3**
1985	Atl N	7	7	.500	58	0	0	23-12	88.1	91	46	13	3	29-4	52	4.48	86	.267	.328	4-0	.000	-0		-4	-0.9
1986	Atl N	2	0	1.000	16	0	0	3-3	18.2	17	9	3	0	9-2	16	4.34	92	.243	.329	1-0	.000	-0		0	0.0
1988	Atl N	1	4	.200	38	0	0	14-9	45.1	49	26	4	1	11-3	40	4.76	77	.275	.321	1-0	.000	0		-5	-0.8
Total	12	68	71	.489	661	0	0	300-101	1042	879	370	77	13	309-83	861	2.83	136	.230	.288	102-10	.088	-5		108	17.9
SUTTHOFF, JACK John Gerhard "Sunny Jack" B 6.29.1873 Cincinnati, OH D 8.3.1942 Cincinnati, OH BL/TR 5-9/175# d9.15																									
1898	Was N	0	0	—	2	1	0	0	8.1	16	13	1	0	8	3	12.96	28	.400	.500	3-0	.333	0	194	-7	-0.3
1899	StL N	1	2	.333	3	3	3	0	24	29	25	0	0	15	8	4.13	97	.299	.393	10-0	.100	-1	120	-3	-0.4
1901	Cin N	1	6	.143	10	4	4	0	70.1	82	55	2	2	39	12	5.50	58	.289	.378	28-1	.107	-2*	78	-17	-1.6
1903	Cin N	16	9	.640	30	27	21-3	0	224.2	207	104	2	16	79	76	2.80	127	.246	.323	84-2	.143	-3	107	19	1.4
1904	Cin N	5	6	.455	12	10	8	0	90	83	49	1	3	43	27	2.30	127	.255	.348	33-1	.182	-0	120	1	0.0
	Phi N	6	13	.316	19	18	17	0	163.2	172	90	2	9	71	46	3.68	73	.272	.354	61-2	.164	-0	98	-14	-1.6
	Year	11	19	.367	31	28	25	0	253.2	255	94	3	12	114	73	3.19	87	.266	.352	94-3	.170	-1	107	-14	-1.6

Year	Tm Lg	W	L	Pct	G	GS	CG-Sho	SV-BS	IP	H	R	HR	HB	BB-IB	SO	ERA	AERA	OAV	OOB	AB-SH	AVG	PB	Sup	APR	PW
1905	Phi N	3	4	.429	13	6	4-1	0	77.2	82	46	2	4	36	26	3.82	76	.290	.378	25-1	.080	-1	82	-8	-0.7
Total	6	32	40	.444	89	69	57-4	0	658.2	671	382	10	34	291	198	3.54	89	.268	.352	244-7	.143	-7	107	-29	-3.2
SUTTON, DON Donald Howard B 4.2.1945 Clio, AL BR/TR 6-1/185# d4.14 HF1998																									
1966	LA N	12	12	.500	37	35	6-2	0	225.2	192	82	19	3	52-6	209	2.99	110	.228	.274	82-2	.183	1*	95	10	1.2
1967	LA N	11	15	.423	37	34	11-3	1	232.2	223	106	18	6	57-9	169	3.95	79	.250	.299	75-7	.133	-0*	107	-19	-2.2
1968	LA N	11	15	.423	35	27	7-2	1	207.2	179	64	6	2	59-14	162	2.60	106	.232	.287	62-6	.177	1*	87	7	1.0
1969	LA N	17	18	.486	41	41	11-4	0-0	293.1	269	123	25	3	91-6	217	3.47	96	.242	.299	98-9	.153	-1	107	-3	-0.5
1970	LA N	15	13	.536	38	38	10-4	0-0	260.1	251	127	38	10	78-7	201	4.08	94	.249	.308	84-5	.155	3*	111	-6	-0.3
1971	LA N	17	12	.586	38	37	12-4	1-0	265.1	231	85	10	5	55-5	194	2.54	127	.238	.280	88-4	.216	3*	99	22	2.7
1972	LA N★	19	9	.679	33	33	18-**9**	0-0	272.2	186	78	13	4	63-1	207	2.08	160	**.189**	**.240**	91-11	.143	-1	106	39	3.9
1973	LA N★	18	10	.643	33	33	14-3	0-0	256.1	196	78	18	5	56-4	200	2.42	142	.209	.257	84-7	.119	-2	92	31	3.2
1974	†LA N	19	9	.679	40	**40**	10-5	0-0	276	241	111	23	6	80-2	179	3.23	106	.229	.287	98-9	.184	1	138	8	0.7
1975	LA N★	16	13	.552	35	35	11-4	0-0	254.1	202	87	17	3	62-5	175	2.87	119	.213	**.263**	80-12	.138	-1	88	18	1.8
1976	LA N	21	10	.677	35	34	15-4	0-0	267.2	231	98	22	3	82-6	161	3.06	111	.234	.293	84-9	.083	-3	101	11	0.8
1977	†LA N★	14	8	.636	33	33	9-3	0-0	240.1	207	93	23	3	69-2	150	3.18	120	.233	.289	73-10	.151	1	112	18	1.6
1978	†LA N	15	11	.577	34	34	12-2	0-0	238.1	228	109	29	5	54-7	154	3.55	99	.250	.294	72-14	.083	-3	115	-2	-0.6
1979	LA N	12	15	.444	33	32	6-1	1-0	226	201	109	21	1	61-6	146	3.82	95	.239	.288	77-8	.143	-2	106	-4	-0.7
1980	LA N	13	5	.722	32	31	4-2	1-0	212.1	163	56	20	2	47-5	128	**2.20**	159	.211	**.257**	64-8	.078	-4	86	32	2.2
1981	Hou N	11	9	.550	23	23	6-3	0-0	158.2	132	51	6	1	29-3	104	2.61	126	.230	**.265**	51-5	.137	0	104	13	1.8
1982	Hou N	13	8	.619	27	27	4	0-0	195	169	75	10	1	46-2	139	3.00	111	.232	.277	68-4	.162	-0	98	7	0.6
	†Mil A	4	1	.800	7	7	2-1	0-0	54.2	55	21	8	0	18-0	36	3.29	115	.263	.322	0-0	—	0	202	4	0.3
1983	Mil A	8	13	.381	31	31	4	0-0	220.1	209	109	21	5	54-2	134	4.08	92	.246	.292	0-0	—	0	102	-9	-0.8
1984	Mil A	14	12	.538	33	33	1	0-0	212.2	224	103	24	3	51-2	143	3.77	102	.266	.306	0-0	—	0	90	1	0.0
1985	Oak A	13	8	.619	29	29	1-1	0-0	194.1	194	88	19	0	51-0	91	3.89	99	.256	.301	0-0	—	0	111	2	0.1
	Cal A	2	2	.500	5	5	0	0-0	31.2	27	13	6	0	8-0	16	3.69	111	.233	.282	0-0	—	0	97	2	0.2
	Year	15	10	.600	34	34	1-1	0-0	226	221	17	25	0	59-0	107	3.86	101	.253	.298	0-0	—	0	109	4	0.3
1986	†Cal A	15	11	.577	34	34	3-1	0-0	207	192	93	31	3	49-2	116	3.74	110	.242	.287	0-0	—	0	102	10	0.9
1987	Cal A	11	11	.500	35	34	1	0-0	191.2	199	101	38	7	41-0	99	4.70	92	.269	.311	0-0	—	0	104	-3	-0.4
1988	LA N	3	6	.333	16	16	0	0-0	87.1	91	44	7	1	30-6	44	3.92	85	.270	.327	23-6	.087	-1	103	-6	-0.7
Total	23	324	256	.559	774	756	178-58	5-0	5282.1	4692	2104	472	82	1343-102	3574	3.26	108	.236	.286	1354-136	.144	-7	105	183	16.8
SUTTON, JOHN Johnny Ike B 11.13.1952 Dallas, TX BR/TR 5-11/185# d4.7																									
1977	StL N	2	1	.667	14	0	0	0-1	24.1	28	10	1	0	9-1	9	2.59	149	.315	.370	1-0	.000	-0		3	0.3
1978	Min A	0	0	—	17	0	0	0-0	44.1	46	19	3	1	15-3	18	3.45	111	.264	.326	0-0	—	0		2	0.1
Total	2	2	1	.667	31	0	0	0-1	68.2	74	29	4	1	24-4	27	3.15	122	.281	.341	1-0	.000	-0		5	0.4
SUZUKI, MAC Makoto B 5.31.1975 Kobe, Japan BR/TR 6-3/195# d7.7																									
1996	Sea A	0	0	—	1	0	0	0-0	1.1	2	3	0	0	2-1	1	20.25	24	.333	.500	0-0	—	0		-2	-0.1
1998	Sea A	1	2	.333	6	5	0	0-0	26.1	34	23	3	0	15-0	19	7.18	65	.304	.386	0-0	—	0	76	-8	-0.7
1999	Sea A	0	2	.000	16	4	0	0-0	42	47	47	7	4	34-2	32	9.43	50	.283	.411	0-0	—	0	103	-22	-1.0
	KC A	2	3	.400	22	9	0	0-0	68	77	45	9	3	30-1	36	5.16	97	.287	.365	0-0	—	0	81	-2	-0.2
	Year	2	5	.286	38	13	0	0-0	110	124	49	16	7	64-3	68	6.79	72	.286	.384	0-0	—	0	88	-24	-1.2
2000	KC A	8	10	.444	32	29	1-1	0-0	188.2	195	100	26	3	94-6	135	4.34	118	.265	.349	5-1	.200	0	88	14	1.1
2001	KC A	2	5	.286	15	9	0	0-0	56	61	38	12	3	25-1	37	5.30	93	.277	.355	0-0	—	0	92	-3	-0.3
	Col N	0	2	.000	3	1	0	0-0	6.1	9	12	3	1	11-0	5	15.63	34	.333	.538	1-1	.000	-0	52	-6	-1.0
	Mil N	3	5	.375	15	9	0	0-0	56	52	37	5	4	37-3	47	5.30	81	.251	.375	17-2	.000	-2	100	-7	-1.0
	Year	3	7	.300	18	10	0	0-0	62.1	61	42	8	5	48-3	52	6.35	69	.261	.397	18-3	.000	-2	94	-14	-2.0
2002	KC A	0	2	.000	7	1	0	0-0	21	24	21	2	0	17-2	15	9.00	56	.296	.414	2-0	.500	0	55	-8	-0.6
Total	6	16	31	.340	117	67	1-1	0-0	465.2	501	326	67	18	265-16	327	5.72	86	.275	.370	25-4	.080	-1	88	-44	-3.8
SWAGGERTY, BILL William David B 12.5.1956 Sanford, FL BR/TR 6-2/186# d8.13																									
1983	Bal A	1	1	.500	7	2	0	0-0	21.2	23	8	1	0	6-0	7	2.91	136	.267	.315	0-0	—	0	137	3	0.3
1984	Bal A	3	2	.600	23	6	0	0-0	57	68	41	7	0	21-3	18	5.21	74	.302	.356	0-0	—	0*	105	-11	-0.9
1985	Bal A	0	0	—	1	0	0	0-0	1.2	3	1	0	0	2-1	2	5.40	75	.375	.500	0-0	—	0		0	0.0
1986	Bal A	0	0	—	1	0	0	0-0	1	6	2	0	0	1-1	1	18.00	23	.750	.778	0-0	—	0		-1	-0.1
Total	4	4	3	.571	32	8	0	0-0	81.1	100	52	8	0	30-5	28	4.76	82	.306	.360	0-0	—	0	113	-9	-0.7
SWAIM, CY John Hillary B 3.11.1874 Cadwallader, OH D 12.27.1945 Eustis, FL 6-6/180# d5.3																									
1897	Was N	9	11	.450	26	19	14	0	184	219	129	5	10	59	52	4.60	94	.293	.353	71-1	.225	-3	105	0	-0.4
1898	Was N	3	11	.214	16	13	9	1	101.1	119	77	4	4	28	30	4.26	86	.290	.342	35-0	.143	-3	69	-10	-1.4
Total	2	12	22	.353	42	32	23	1	285.1	338	206	9	14	87	82	4.48	92	.292	.349	106-1	.198	-6	91	-10	-1.8
SWAN, CRAIG Craig Steven B 11.30.1950 Van Nuys, CA BR/TR 6-3/215# d9.3																									
1973	NY N	0	1	.000	3	1	0	0-0	8.1	16	9	2	0	2-0	4	8.64	42	.432	.450	2-0	.000	-0	73	-5	-0.5
1974	NY N	1	3	.250	7	5	0	0-1	30.1	28	19	1	0	21-3	10	4.45	80	.255	.366	11-0	.364	1	117	-4	-0.3
1975	NY N	1	3	.250	6	6	0	0-0	31	38	22	4	1	13-2	19	6.39	54	.302	.366	7-2	.000	-1	72	-9	-1.1
1976	NY N	6	9	.400	23	22	2-1	0-0	132.1	129	64	11	5	44-3	89	3.54	93	.254	.316	39-6	.103	-1	102	-6	-0.7
1977	NY N	9	10	.474	26	24	2-1	0-0	146.2	153	76	10	1	56-3	71	4.23	88	.268	.332	48-6	.188	-0	100	-8	-1.1
1978	NY N	9	6	.600	29	28	5-1	0-0	207.1	164	62	12	2	58-8	125	**2.43**	**144**	.219	.275	65-8	.154	-0	97	25	1.8
1979	NY N	14	13	.519	35	35	10-3	0-0	251.1	241	102	20	2	57-9	145	3.29	111	.255	.296	81-4	.123	-1	84	10	0.9
1980	NY N	5	9	.357	21	21	4-1	0-0	128.1	117	59	20	0	30-3	79	3.58	99	.247	.289	32-7	.219	2	74	-1	-0.1
1981	NY N	0	2	.000	5	3	0	0-0	13.2	10	6	0	0	1-0	9	3.29	106	.204	.220	3-0	.000	-0	93	0	0.0
1982	NY N	11	7	.611	37	21	2	1-1	166.1	165	70	13	0	37-4	67	3.35	108	.256	.295	44-3	.182	3	87	6	0.9
1983	NY N	2	8	.200	27	18	0	1-0	96.1	112	63	14	0	42-3	43	5.51	66	.299	.366	26-1	.077	-2	91	-18	-2.0
1984	NY N	1	0	1.000	10	0	0	0-1	18.2	18	17	5	0	7-0	10	8.20	43	.247	.309	0-1	—	0		-9	-0.5
	Cal A	0	1	.000	2	1	0	0-0	5	8	6	3	0	0-0	2	10.80	37	.348	.348	0-0	—	0	114	-4	-0.6
Total	12	59	72	.450	231	185	25-7	2-3	1235.2	1199	575	115	11	368-38	673	3.74	96	.256	.309	358-38	.151	1	91	-23	-3.3
SWAN, DUCKY Harry Gordon B 8.11.1887 Lancaster, PA D 5.8.1946 Pittsburgh, PA BR/TR 5-10/165# d4.28																									
1914	KC F	0	0	—	1	0	0	0	1	0	0	0	0	1	1	0.00	—	.000	.250	0-0	—	0		0	0.0
SWAN, RUSS Russell Howard B 1.3.1964 Fremont, CA BL/TL 6-4/215# d8.3																									
1989	SF N	0	2	.000	2	2	0	0-0	6.2	11	10	4	0	4-0	2	10.80	31	.393	.469	2-0	.000	-0	92	-6	-1.0
1990	SF N	0	1	.000	2	1	0	0-0	2.1	6	4	0	0	4-0	1	3.86	95	.429	.556	1-0	.000	-0	74	-1	-0.3
	Sea A	2	3	.400	11	8	0	0-0	47	42	22	3	0	18-2	15	3.64	109	.244	.311	0-0	—	0	89	2	0.2
1991	Sea A	6	2	.750	63	0	0	2-3	78.2	81	35	8	0	28-7	33	3.43	120	.269	.330	0-0	—	0		5	0.5
1992	Sea A	3	10	.231	55	9	1	9-2	104.1	104	60	8	3	45-7	45	4.74	84	.262	.338	0-0	—	0	61	-9	-1.0
1993	Sea A	3	3	.500	23	0	0	0-0	19.2	25	20	2	2	18-1	10	9.15	48	.316	.455	0-0	—	0		-9	-1.7
1994	Cle A	0	1	.000	12	0	0	0-0	8	13	11	1	0	7-1	2	11.25	42	.382	.488	0-0	—	0		-6	-0.6
Total	6	14	22	.389	168	20	1	11-5	266.2	282	162	26	5	124-18	108	4.83	84	.275	.353	3-0	.000	-0	73	-24	-3.9
SWANSON, RED Arthur Leonard B 10.15.1936 Baton Rouge, LA BR/TR 6-1.5/175# d9.10																									
1955	Pit N	0	0	—	1	0	0	0	2	2	4	1	0	3-0	0	18.00	23	.286	.500	0-0	—	0		-3	-0.1
1956	Pit N	0	0	—	9	0	0	0	11.2	21	13	1	0	8-1	5	10.03	38	.438	.492	0-0	—	0*		-7	-0.3
1957	Pit N	3	3	.500	32	8	1	0	72.2	68	35	9	1	31-3	29	3.72	102	.248	.327	13-0	.000	-1	128	0	-0.1
Total	3	3	3	.500	42	8	1	0	86.1	91	52	11	1	42-4	34	4.90	77	.277	.357	13-0	.000	-1	128	-10	-0.5
SWARBACK, BILL William (b: William Schwappach) B 10.1867 New York, NY D 5.17.1949 Stamford, CT d7.9																									
1887	NY N	0	2	.000	2	2	2	0	16	27	23	1	1	6	6	5.06	74	.346	.400	7	.000	-1	172	-5	-0.5
SWARTZ, BUD Sherwin Merle B 6.13.1929 Tulsa, OK D 6.24.1991 Los Angeles, CA BL/TL 6-2.5/180# d7.12																									
1947	StL A	0	0	—	5	0	0	0	5.1	9	6	1	0	7	1	6.75	57	.360	.500	1-0	1.000	0		-2	-0.1

Year	Tm Lg	W	L	Pct	G	GS	CG-Sho	SV-BS	IP	H	R	HR	HB	BB-IB	SO	ERA	AERA	OAV	OOB	AB-SH	AVG	PB	Sup	APR	PW
SWARTZ, MONTY Vernon Monroe "Dazzy" B 1.1.1897 Farmersville, OH D 1.13.1980 Germantown, OH BR/TR 5-11/182# d10.3																									
1920	Cin N	0	1	.000	1	1	1	0	12	17	6	0	0	2	2	4.50	68	.333	.358	4-0	.500	1	78	-1	0.0
SWARTZBAUGH, DAVE David Theodore B 2.11.1968 Middletown, OH BR/TR 6-2/195# d9.3																									
1995	Chi N	0	0	—	7	0	0	0-0	7.1	5	2	0	0	3-1	5	0.00	—	.208	.296	0-0	—	0		3	0.1
1996	Chi N	0	2	.000	6	5	0	0-0	24	26	17	3	0	14-1	13	6.38	68	.277	.370	6-0	.000	-0	67	-5	-0.3
1997	Chi N	0	1	.000	2	2	0	0-0	8	12	8	1	1	7-0	4	9.00	48	.364	.476	4-0	.000	-0	64	-4	-0.4
Total	3	0	3	.000	15	7	0	0-0	39.1	43	27	4	1	24-2	22	5.72	75	.285	.384	10-0	.000	-1	66	-6	-0.6
SWARTZEL, PARK Park B. B 11.21.1865 Knightstown, IN D 1.3.1940 Los Angeles, CA BR/TR 5-10/?# d4.17																									
1889	KC AA	19	27	.413	48	47	45	1	410.1	481	334	21	23	117	147	4.32	97	.283	.338	174	.144	-9*	90	-2	-0.5
SWEENEY, BRIAN Brian Edward B 6.13.1974 Yonkers, NY BR/TR 6-2/180# d8.16																									
2003	Sea A	0	0	—	5	0	0	0-0	9.1	7	2	0	1	1-0	7	1.93	225	.212	.257	0-0	—	0		3	0.1
SWEENEY, CHARLIE Charles J. B 4.13.1863 San Francisco, CA D 4.4.1902 San Francisco, CA BR/TR 5-10.5/181# d5.11.1882 ▲																									
1883	Pro N	7	7	.500	20	18	14	0	146.2	142	94	3		28	48	3.13	98	.237	.272	87	.218	-1*	108	0	0.0
1884	Pro N	17	8	.680	27	24	22-4	1	221	153	70	4		29	145	1.55	184	**.187**	**.215**	168	.298	8*	95	36	4.4
	StL U	24	7	.774	33	32	31-2	0	271	207	112	2		13	192	1.83	131	.197	.207	171	.316	6*	109	17	2.2
1885	StL N	11	21	.344	35	35	32-2	0	275	276	175	6		50	84	3.93	70	.250	.282	267	.206	-0*	72	-30	-2.8
1886	StL N	5	6	.455	11	11	11	0	93	108	73	9		39	28	4.16	77	.285	.352	64	.250	1*	92	-9	-0.6
1887	Cle AA	0	3	.000	3	3	3	0	24	42	36	0	0	13	8	8.25	53	.372	.437	133	.226	0*	59	-10	-0.7
Total	5	64	52	.552	129	123	113-8	1	1030.2	928	560	24	0	172	505	2.87	98	.228	.260	890	.252	14	93	4	2.5
SWEENEY, BILL William J. B Philadelphia, PA D 8.2.1903 Philadelphia, PA TR 5-11/160# d6.27																									
1882	Phi AA	9	10	.474	20	20	18	0	170	178	119	4		42	48	2.91	96	.252	.294	88	.159	-2*	116	-8	-0.9
1884	Bal U	**40**	21	.656	**62**	**60**	**58**-4	0	**538**	522	294	13		74	374	2.59	103	.238	.263	296	.240	-16*	101	7	-0.6
Total	2	49	31	.613	82	80	76-4	0	708	700	413	17		116	422	2.67	102	.241	.270	384	.221	-18	105	-1	-1.5
SWEETLAND, LES Lester Leo (Born Leo Sweetland) B 8.15.1901 St.Ignace, MI D 3.4.1974 Melbourne, FL BR/TL 5-11.5/155# d7.4																									
1927	Phi N	2	10	.167	21	13	6	0	103.2	147	77	3	3	53	21	6.16	67	.348	.425	38-1	.316	3*	93	-21	-1.5
1928	Phi N	3	15	.167	37	18	5	2	135.1	163	111	15	15	97	23	6.58	65	.306	.426	47-1	.191	1*	86	-32	-3.4
1929	Phi N	13	11	.542	43	26	10-2	2	204.1	255	129	23	9	87	47	5.11	102	.316	.389	89-1	.292	3*	88	2	0.7
1930	Phi N	7	15	.318	34	25	8-1	0	167	271	164	24	5	60	36	7.71	71	.373	.425	57-4	.281	4*	100	-37	-3.2
1931	Chi N	8	7	.533	26	14	9	0	130.1	156	89	3	5	61	32	5.04	77	.297	.375	56-1	.268	5*	144	-19	-1.4
Total	5	33	58	.363	161	96	38-3	4	740.2	992	570	68	37	358	159	6.10	77	.329	.407	287-8	.272	16	100	-107	-8.8
SWETONIC, STEVE Stephen Albert B 8.13.1903 Mt.Pleasant, PA D 4.22.1974 Canonsburg, PA BR/TR 5-11/185# d4.17																									
1929	Pit N	8	10	.444	41	12	3	5	143.2	172	87	6	5	50	35	4.82	99	.299	.360	48-1	.271	3*	107	0	0.4
1930	Pit N	6	6	.500	23	6	3-1	5	96.2	107	53	7	0	27	35	4.47	111	.276	.323	36-0	.111	-3	96	7	0.5
1931	Pit N	0	2	.000	14	0	0	1	27.2	28	12	0	0	16	8	3.90	99	.264	.361	7-0	.143	-0		1	0.0
1932	Pit N	11	6	.647	24	19	11-**4**	0	162.2	134	57	11	0	55	39	2.82	135	**.221**	.286	54-2	.093	-4	92	21	1.6
1933	Pit N	12	12	.500	31	21	8-3	0	164.2	166	78	10	2	64	37	3.50	95	.260	.330	55-6	.200	1	100	-3	-0.4
Total	5	37	36	.507	133	58	25-8	11	595.1	607	287	34	7	212	154	3.81	107	.262	.326	200-9	.170	-3	96	26	2.1
SWIFT, BILL William Charles B 10.27.1961 Portland, ME BR/TR 6/180# d6.7																									
1985	Sea A	6	10	.375	23	21	0	0-0	120.2	131	71	8	5	48-5	55	4.77	88	.279	.350	0-0	—	0	87	-8	-0.9
1986	Sea A	2	9	.182	29	17	1	0-1	115.1	148	85	5	7	55-2	55	5.46	78	.319	.397	0-0	—	0	97	-18	-1.4
1988	Sea A	8	12	.400	38	24	6-1	0-1	174.2	199	99	10	8	65-3	47	4.59	91	.294	.362	0-0	—	0	102	-7	-0.7
1989	Sea A	7	3	.700	37	16	0	1-0	130	140	72	7	2	38-4	45	4.43	91	.278	.329	0-0	—	0	125	-5	-0.1
1990	Sea A	6	4	.600	55	8	0	6-1	128	135	46	4	7	21-6	42	2.39	166	.272	.309	0-0	—	0	109	19	1.5
1991	Sea A	1	2	.333	71	0	0	17-1	90.1	74	22	3	1	26-4	48	1.99	207	.224	.283	0-0	—	0		21	1.4
1992	SF N	10	4	.714	30	22	3-2	1-0	164.2	144	41	6	3	43-3	77	**2.08**	159	.239	.292	51-5	.157	1*	111	24	2.4
1993	SF N	21	8	.724	34	34	1-1	0-0	232.2	195	82	18	6	55-5	157	2.82	139	.226	.277	80-10	.262	6	116	28	4.0
1994	SF N	8	7	.533	17	17	0	0-0	109.1	109	49	10	1	31-6	62	3.38	119	.262	.313	32-5	.188	2*	87	6	1.0
1995	†Col N	9	3	.750	19	19	0	0-0	105.2	122	62	12	1	43-2	68	4.94	109	.296	.363	36-5	.194	0	115	5	0.7
1996	Col N	1	1	.500	7	3	0	2-0	18.1	23	12	1	0	5-0	5	5.40	97	.307	.346	6-0	.333	0	63	0	0.0
1997	Col N	4	6	.400	14	13	0	0-0	65.1	85	57	11	2	26-0	29	6.34	82	.317	.377	19-4	.211	1*	119	-9	-1.0
1998	Sea A	11	9	.550	29	26	0	0-0	144.2	183	103	21	10	51-2	77	5.85	79	.306	.369	5-0	.000	-0	132	-20	-2.2
Total	13	94	78	.547	403	220	11-4	27-4	1599.2	1688	801	116	53	507-42	767	3.95	106	.273	.332	229-29	.210	10	111	36	4.7
SWIFT, BILL William Vincent B 1.10.1908 Elmira, NY D 2.23.1969 Bartow, FL BR/TR 6-1.5/192# d4.12																									
1932	Pit N	14	10	.583	39	23	11	4	214.1	205	97	15	2	26	64	3.61	106	.248	.272	78-3	.192	-1	105	9	0.6
1933	Pit N	14	10	.583	37	29	13-2	0	218.1	214	96	11	4	36	64	3.13	106	.251	.285	82-0	.244	3	124	4	0.6
1934	Pit N	11	13	.458	37	25	13-1	0	212.2	244	107	15	8	46	81	3.98	103	.284	.326	84-1	.214	2	115	4	0.4
1935	Pit N	15	8	.652	39	22	11-3	1	203.2	193	76	6	1	37	74	2.70	152	.247	.282	78-1	.244	3	120	31	3.3
1936	Pit N	16	16	.500	45	31	17	2	262.1	275	132	18	5	63	92	4.01	101	.265	.310	105-1	.295	9	99	4	1.1
1937	Pit N	9	10	.474	36	17	9	3	164	160	79	14	3	34	84	3.95	98	.256	.297	54-2	.167	-1	79	1	-0.1
1938	Pit N	7	5	.583	36	9	2	4	150	155	65	9	4	40	77	3.24	117	.271	.323	50-2	.200	2	69	9	0.8
1939	Pit N	5	7	.417	36	8	2-1	4	129.2	150	60	6	3	28	56	3.89	99	.293	.333	42-2	.238	2	80	1	0.1
1940	Bos N	1	1	.500	4	0	0	1	9.1	12	7	0	0	7	7	2.89	129	.308	.413	3-0	.000	-0		-1	-0.2
1941	Bro N	3	0	1.000	9	0	0	1	22	26	9	4	0	7	9	3.27	112	.289	.340	5-0	.200	-0		1	0.1
1943	Chi A	0	2	.000	18	1	0	0	51.1	48	25	5	6	27	28	4.21	79	.246	.355	10-0	.100	0	25	-3	-0.3
Total	11	95	82	.537	336	165	78-7	20	1637.2	1682	753	103	36	351	636	3.58	108	.263	.305	591-12	.227	18	104	60	6.4
SWIGART, OAD Oadis Vaughn B 2.13.1915 Archie, MO D 8.8.1997 St.Joseph, MO BL/TR 6/175# d9.14 Mil 1941-45																									
1939	Pit N	1	1	.500	3	3	1-1	0	24.1	27	14	1	0	6	8	4.44	87	.293	.337	8-2	.250	0	144	-2	-0.1
1940	Pit N	0	2	.000	7	2	0	0	22.1	27	14	1	0	10	9	4.43	86	.297	.366	5-1	.200	-0	57	-2	-0.2
Total	2	1	3	.250	10	5	1-1	0	46.2	54	28	2	0	16	17	4.44	86	.295	.352	13-3	.231	0	109	-4	-0.3
SWIGLER, AD Adam William "Doc" B 9.21.1895 Philadelphia, PA D 2.5.1975 Philadelphia, PA BR/TR 5-10/180# d9.25																									
1917	NY N	0	1	.000	1	1	0	0	6	7	4	0	0	8	4	6.00	43	.333	.517	2-0	.000	-0	89	-2	-0.3
SWINDELL, GREG Forest Gregory B 1.2.1965 Fort Worth, TX BR/TL 6-3/225# d8.21																									
1986	Cle A	5	2	.714	9	9	1	0-0	61.2	57	35	9	1	15-0	46	4.23	98	.243	.290	0-0	—	0	141	-2	-0.1
1987	Cle A	3	8	.273	16	15	4-1	0-0	102.1	112	62	18	1	37-1	97	5.10	89	.283	.343	0-0	—	0	90	-4	-0.4
1988	Cle A	18	14	.563	33	33	12-4	0-0	242	234	97	18	1	45-3	180	3.20	129	.252	.286	0-0	—	0	89	23	2.9
1989	Cle A★	13	6	.684	28	28	5-2	0-0	184.1	170	71	16	0	51-1	129	3.37	118	.246	.297	0-0	—	0	91	15	1.4
1990	Cle A	12	9	.571	34	34	3	0-0	214.2	245	110	27	1	47-2	135	4.40	89	.288	.324	0-0	—	0	121	-9	-0.9
1991	Cle A	9	16	.360	33	33	7	0-0	238	241	112	21	3	31-1	169	3.48	120	.263	.287	0-0	—	0	75	14	1.3
1992	Cin N	12	8	.600	31	30	5-3	0-0	213.2	210	72	14	2	41-4	138	2.70	134	.260	.295	80-5	.125	-2	110	20	1.7
1993	Hou N	12	13	.480	31	30	1-1	0-0	190.1	215	98	24	1	40-3	124	4.16	93	.283	.318	60-10	.183	0	98	-6	-0.6
1994	Hou N	8	9	.471	24	24	1	0-0	148.1	175	80	20	1	26-2	74	4.37	91	.302	.329	44-12	.250	3	109	-7	-0.5
1995	Hou N	10	9	.526	33	26	1-1	0-2	153	180	86	21	2	39-2	96	4.47	87	.297	.337	50-6	.240	4*	127	-11	-0.7
1996	Hou N	0	3	.000	8	4	0	0-2	23	35	25	5	1	11-0	15	7.83	49	.340	.405	6-0	.333	1	175	-12	-1.2
	Cle A	1	1	.500	13	2	0	0-0	28.2	31	21	8	0	8-0	21	6.59	74	.279	.325	0-0	—	0	227	-5	-0.2
1997	Min A	7	4	.636	65	1	0	1-6	115.2	102	46	12	2	25-3	75	3.58	130	.238	.282	0-0	—	0	79	15	1.3
1998	Min A	3	3	.500	52	0	0	2-2	66.1	67	27	10	3	18-2	45	3.66	130	.263	.317	0-0	—	0		9	0.7
	†Bos A	2	3	.400	29	0	0	0-1	24	25	13	3	0	13-1	18	3.38	140	.278	.369	0-0	—	0		2	0.4
	Year	5	6	.455	81	0	0	2-3	90.1	92	44	13	3	31-3	63	3.59	133	.267	.331	0-0	—	0		11	1.1
1999	†Ari N	4	0	1.000	63	0	0	1-1	64.2	54	19	8	1	21-1	51	2.51	183	.230	.296	4-2	.000	-0		15	0.8
2000	Ari N	2	6	.250	64	0	0	1-0	76	71	29	7	1	20-5	64	3.20	147	.247	.295	1-1	.000	-0		13	1.2
2001	†Ari N	2	6	.250	64	0	0	2-3	53.2	51	27	12	0	8-2	42	4.53	101	.250	.277	0-0	—	0		1	0.1
2002	†Ari N	0	2	.000	34	0	0	0-1	33	38	23	9	0	5-1	23	6.27	71	.279	.301	0-0	—	0		-6	-0.3
Total	17	123	122	.502	664	269	40-12	7-18	2233.1	2313	1053	262	21	501-34	1542	3.86	107	.268	.308	245-36	.188	6	101	65	6.9

Year	Tm Lg	W	L	Pct	G	GS	CG-Sho	SV-BS	IP	H	R	HR	HB	BB-IB	SO	ERA	AERA	OAV	OOB	AB-SH	AVG	PB	Sup	APR	PW
SWINDELL, JOSH Joshua Ernest B 7.5.1883 Rose Hill, KS D 3.19.1969 Fruita, CO BR/TR 6/180# d9.16																									
1911	Cle A	0	1	.000	4	1	1	0	17.1	19	9	0	1	4	6	2.08	164	.257	.304	4-0	.250	-0	21	1	0.0
SWINGLE, PAUL Paul Christopher B 12.21.1966 Inglewood, CA BR/TR 6/185# d9.7																									
1993	Cal A	0	1	.000	9	0	0	0-0	9.2	15	9	2	0	6-0	6	8.38	54	.357	.429	0-0	—	0		-4	-0.3
SWITZER, JON Jon Michael B 8.13.1979 Bowling Green, KY BL/TL 6-3/190# d8.2																									
2003	TB A	0	0	—	5	0	0	0-0	9.2	13	8	2	4	3-0	7	7.45	61	.342	.435	0-0	—	0		-3	-0.1
SWORMSTEDT, LEN Leonard Jordan B 10.6.1878 Cincinnati, OH D 7.19.1964 Salem, MA BR/TR 5-11.5/165# d9.29																									
1901	Cin N	2	1	.667	3	3	3	0	26	19	8	2	2	5	13	1.73	185	.202	.257	9-0	.000	-1	52	4	0.3
1902	Cin N	0	2	.000	2	2	2	0	18	22	11	1	0	5	3	4.00	75	.301	.346	6-0	.000	-1	45	-1	-0.2
1906	Bos A	1	1	.500	3	2	2	0	21	17	6	0	1	0	6	1.29	214	.224	.234	8-0	.125	-1	79	3	0.2
Total	3	3	4	.429	8	7	7	0	65	58	25	3	3	10	22	2.22	136	.239	.277	23-0	.043	-3	57	6	0.3
SYKES, BOB Robert Joseph B 12.11.1954 Neptune, NJ BB/TL 6-2/200# d4.9																									
1977	Det A	5	7	.417	32	20	3	0-1	132.2	141	74	15	2	50-0	58	4.41	98	.271	.334	0-0	—	0	110	-2	-0.2
1978	Det A	6	6	.500	22	10	3-2	2-2	93.2	99	43	14	1	34-0	58	3.94	98	.275	.338	0-0	—	0	104	0	0.0
1979	StL N	4	3	.571	13	11	0	0-0	67	86	49	11	1	34-2	35	6.18	61	.315	.392	21-2	.095	-0	139	-17	-1.6
1980	StL N	6	10	.375	27	19	4-3	0-1	126	134	67	12	0	54-3	50	4.64	80	.277	.348	39-3	.103	-2	120	-10	-1.5
1981	StL N	2	0	1.000	22	1	0	0-1	37.1	37	20	2	1	18-1	14	4.58	78	.266	.354	2-0	.000	0	175	-4	-0.2
Total	5	23	26	.469	116	61	10-5	2-5	456.2	497	253	54	5	190-6	215	4.65	84	.280	.349	62-5	.097	-2	119	-33	-3.5
SYLVESTER, LOU Louis J. B 2.14.1855 Springfield, IL D 5.5.1936 Brooklyn, NY BR/TR 5-6/165# d4.18 ▲																									
1884	Cin U	0	1	.000	6	1	1	1	32.2	32	27	0		6	7	3.58	71	.239	.271	333	.267	-0*	100	-4	-0.2
TABAKA, JEFF Jeffrey Jon B 1.17.1964 Barberton, OH BR/TL 6-2/195# d4.19																									
1994	Pit N	0	0	—	5	0	0	0-0	4	4	8	1	0	8-0	2	18.00	24	.250	.500	0-0	—	0		-6	-0.3
	SD N	3	1	.750	34	0	0	1-0	37	28	21	0	0	19-3	30	3.89	106	.209	.305	1-0	1.000	1		0	0.1
	Year	3	1	.750	39	0	0	1-0	41	32	35	1	0	27-3	32	5.27	78	.213	.331	1-0	1.000	1		-7	-0.2
1995	SD N	0	0	—	10	0	0	0-1	6.1	10	5	1	0	5-1	6	7.11	57	.370	.469	0-0	—	0		-2	-0.1
	Hou N	1	0	1.000	24	0	0	0-0	24.1	17	6	1	0	12-0	19	2.22	174	.202	.302	1-1	.000	-0		5	0.2
	Year	1	0	1.000	34	0	0	0-1	30.2	27	11	2	0	17-1	25	3.23	121	.243	.344	1-1	.000	-0		3	0.1
1996	Hou N	0	2	.000	18	0	0	1-0	20.1	28	18	5	3	14-0	18	6.64	58	.322	.433	1-0	.000	-0		-7	-0.7
1997	Cin N	0	0	—	3	0	0	0-0	2	1	1	1	2	1-0	1	4.50	95	.143	.400	0-0	—	0		0	0.0
1998	Pit N	2	2	.500	37	0	0	0-0	50.2	37	19	6	5	22-4	40	3.02	142	.204	.305	1-0	.000	-0		7	0.5
2001	StL N	0	0	—	8	0	0	0-1	3.2	6	3	1	0	1-0	3	7.36	58	.375	.412	0-0	—	0		-1	0.0
Total	6	6	5	.545	139	0	0	2-2	148.1	131	81	16	10	82-8	119	4.31	95	.237	.345	4-1	.250	1		-4	-0.3
TABER, LEFTY Edward Timothy B 1.11.1900 Rock Island, IL D 11.5.1983 Lincoln, NE BL/TL 6/180# d9.4																									
1926	Phi N	0	0	—	6	0	0	0	8.1	8	7	0	2	5	0	7.56	55	.242	.375	1-0	.000	-0		-2	-0.1
1927	Phi N	0	1	.000	3	1	0	0	3.1	8	9	0	1	5	0	18.90	22	.533	.667	1-0	.000	-0	41	-6	-1.0
Total	2	0	1	.000	9	1	0	0	11.2	16	16	0	3	10	0	10.80	38	.333	.475	2-0	.000	-0	41	-8	-1.1
TABER, JOHN John Pardon B 6.28.1868 Acushnet, MA D 2.21.1940 Boston, MA BR/TR 5-8/?# d4.30																									
1890	Bos N	0	1	.000	2	1	1	1	13	11	8	0	0	8	3	4.15	90	.220	.328	6	.000	-1	118	0	-0.1
TAFF, JOHN John Gallatin B 6.3.1890 Austin, TX D 5.15.1961 Houston, TX BR/TR 6/170# d5.11																									
1913	Phi A	0	1	.000	7	1	0	1	17.2	22	13	0	0	5	9	6.62	42	.306	.351	5-0	.200	-0	54	-7	-0.4
TALBOT, FRED Frederick Lealand "Bubby" B 6.28.1941 Washington, DC BR/TR 6-2/195# d9.28																									
1963	Chi A	0	0	—	1	0	0	0	3	2	1	0	0	4-0	2	3.00	117	.222	.462	1-0	.000	-0		0	0.0
1964	Chi A	4	5	.444	17	12	3-2	0	75.1	83	31	7	4	20-0	34	3.70	93	.288	.340	19-2	.263	3*	99	0	0.2
1965	KC A	10	12	.455	39	33	2-1	0	198	188	96	25	6	86-3	117	4.14	84	.251	.330	70-3	.200	3*	99	-12	-0.9
1966	KC A	4	4	.500	11	11	0	0	67.2	65	39	6	2	28-6	37	4.79	71	.248	.324	20-5	.150	0	78	-10	-1.0
	NY A	7	7	.500	23	19	3	0	124.1	123	59	16	3	45-3	48	4.13	81	.262	.329	35-4	.143	1	117	-9	-0.8
	Year	11	11	.500	34	30	3	0	192	188	63	22	5	73-9	85	4.36	77	.257	.327	55-9	.145	1	103	-18	-1.8
1967	NY A	6	8	.429	29	22	2	0	138.2	132	78	20	6	54-5	61	4.22	74	.252	.325	38-2	.158	3*	111	-18	-1.3
1968	NY A	1	9	.100	29	11	1	0	99	89	47	6	2	42-6	67	3.36	86	.241	.319	17-2	.118	1	63	-7	-0.6
1969	NY A	0	0	—	8	0	0	0-1	12.1	13	9	1	0	6-2	7	5.11	68	.283	.352	1-1	.000	-0		-3	-0.2
	Sea A	5	8	.385	25	16	1-1	0-0	114.2	125	58	12	4	41-6	67	4.16	87	.278	.342	37-2	.162	2*	100	-6	-0.4
	Oak A	1	2	.333	12	2	0	1-0	19	22	11	2	0	7-0	9	5.21	66	.297	.358	3-0	.333	0	141	-3	-0.5
	Year	6	10	.375	45	18	1-1	1-1	146	160	17	15	4	54-8	83	4.38	82	.281	.345	41-3	.171	2	105	-11	-1.1
1970	Oak A	0	1	.000	1	0	0	0-0	1.2	2	2	1	0	1-0	0	10.80	33	.286	.375	0-0	—	0		-1	-0.2
Total	8	38	56	.404	195	126	12-4	1-1	853.2	844	431	96	27	334-31	449	4.12	81	.260	.331	241-21	.174	13	100	-69	-5.7
TALCOTT, ROY Lé Roy Everett B 1.16.1920 Brookline, MA D 12.6.1999 Miami, FL BR/TR 6-1.5/180# d6.24																									
1943	Bos N	0	0	—	1	0	0	0	0.2	1	2	0	0	2	0	27.00	13	.333	.600	0-0	—	0		-2	-0.1
TALLET, BRIAN Brian Curtis B 9.21.1977 Midwest City, OK BL/TL 6-7/208# d9.16																									
2002	Cle A	1	0	1.000	2	2	0	0-0	12	9	3	0	1	4-0	5	1.50	293	.214	.298	0-0	—	0	127	4	0.3
2003	Cle A	0	2	.000	5	3	0	0-0	19	23	14	2	1	8-0	9	4.74	93	.303	.376	2-0	.000	-0	62	-2	-0.2
Total	2	1	2	.333	7	5	0	0-0	31	32	17	2	2	12-0	14	3.48	127	.271	.348	2-0	.000	-0	88	2	0.1
TAM, JEFF Jeffrey Eugene B 8.19.1970 Fullerton, CA BR/TR 6-1/202# d6.30																									
1998	NY N	1	1	.500	15	0	0	0-1	14.1	13	10	2	2	4-1	8	6.28	66	.241	.317	1-0	.000	-0		-3	-0.4
1999	Cle A	0	0	—	1	0	0	0-0	0.1	2	3	0	0	1-1	0	81.00	6	1.000	1.000	0-0	—	0		-3	-0.1
	NY N	0	0	—	9	0	0	0-0	11.1	6	4	3	0	3-0	8	3.18	138	.150	.209	0-0	—	0		2	0.1
2000	†Oak A	3	3	.500	72	0	0	3-3	85.2	86	30	3	1	23-8	46	2.63	181	.268	.315	0-0	—	0		20	1.3
2001	†Oak A	2	4	.333	70	0	0	3-3	74.2	68	27	3	3	29-9	44	3.01	147	.250	.326	0-0	—	0		12	0.9
2002	Oak A	1	2	.333	40	0	0	0-4	40.1	56	26	2	2	13-5	14	5.13	86	.333	.384	0-0	—	0		-4	-0.2
2003	Tor A	0	4	.000	44	0	0	1-1	44.2	58	30	5	1	25-7	26	5.64	81	.314	.396	1-0	1.000	1		-5	-0.3
Total	6	7	14	.333	251	0	0	7-12	271.1	289	130	18	9	98-31	146	3.91	116	.277	.342	2-0	.500	1		19	1.3
TAMULIS, VITO Vitautis Casimirus B 7.11.1911 Cambridge, MA D 5.5.1974 Nashville, TN BL/TL 5-9/170# d9.25																									
1934	NY A	1	0	1.000	1	1	1-1	0	9	7	0	0	0	1	5	0.00	—	.219	.242	4-0	.250	0	107	4	0.6
1935	NY A	10	5	.667	30	19	9-3	1	160.2	178	80	7	2	55	57	4.09	99	.280	.339	57-3	.246	4	129	2	0.5
1938	StL A	0	3	.000	3	2	0	0	15.1	26	15	2	0	10	11	7.63	65	.366	.444	5-0	.400	1	80	-5	-0.6
	Bro N	12	6	.667	38	18	9	2	159.2	181	81	11	2	40	70	3.83	102	.288	.333	55-3	.127	-3*	118	1	-0.2
1939	Bro N	9	8	.529	39	17	8-1	4	158.2	177	81	10	8	45	83	4.37	92	.287	.343	55-3	.182	-1	92	-3	-0.4
1940	Bro N	8	5	.615	41	12	4-1	2	154.1	147	60	5	3	34	55	3.09	129	.244	.288	46-1	.130	-1*	96	15	1.0
1941	Phi N	0	1	.000	6	1	0	0	12	21	13	1	1	7	5	9.00	41	.382	.460	2-0	.000	-0	46	-7	-0.5
	Bro N	0	0	—	12	0	0	1	22	21	10	1	0	10	8	3.68	100	.244	.323	5-0	.000	-1		0	-0.1
	Year	0	1	.000	18	1	0	1	34	42	25	2	1	17	13	5.56	66	.298	.377	7-0	.000	-1	46	-6	-0.6
Total	6	40	28	.588	170	70	31-6	10	691.2	758	340	37	16	202	294	3.97	101	.278	.331	229-10	.175	-1	109	7	0.3
TANANA, FRANK Frank Daryl B 7.3.1953 Detroit, MI BL/TL 6-3/195# d9.9																									
1973	Cal A	2	2	.500	4	4	2-1	0-0	26.1	20	11	2	0	8-0	22	3.08	115	.200	.259	0-0	—	0	76	1	0.2
1974	Cal A	14	19	.424	39	35	12-4	0-1	268.2	262	104	27	8	77-4	180	3.12	111	.255	.311	0-0	—	0	84	12	1.5
1975	Cal A	16	9	.640	34	33	16-5	0-0	257.1	211	80	21	7	73-6	**269**	2.62	136	.226	.286	0-0	—	0	118	31	3.1
1976	Cal A★	19	10	.655	34	34	23-2	0-0	288.1	212	88	24	9	73-5	261	2.43	137	.203	**.261**	0-0	—	0*	100	31	3.3
1977	Cal A✧	15	9	.625	31	31	20-**7**	0-0	241.1	201	72	19	12	61-2	205	**2.54**	**155**	.227	.284	0-0	—	0	110	**42**	4.1
1978	Cal A☆	18	12	.600	33	33	10-4	0-0	239	239	108	26	9	60-7	137	3.65	99	.258	.306	0-0	—	0	117	0	-0.1
1979	†Cal A	7	5	.583	18	17	2-1	0-0	90.1	93	44	9	2	25-0	46	3.89	105	.264	.315	0-0	—	0	108	2	0.2
1980	Cal A	11	12	.478	32	31	7	0-0	204	223	107	18	8	45-0	113	4.15	95	.277	.320	0-0	—	0	110	-6	-0.6
1981	Bos A	4	10	.286	24	23	5-2	0-0	141.1	142	70	17	4	43-4	78	4.01	97	.265	.322	0-0	—	0	98	-1	-0.1

Year	Tm Lg	W	L	Pct	G	GS	CG-Sho	SV-BS	IP	H	R	HR	HB	BB-IB	SO	ERA	AERA	OAV	OOB	AB-SH	AVG	PB	Sup	APR	PW
1982	Tex A	7	18	.280	30	30	7	0-0	194.1	199	102	16	7	55-10	87	4.21	92	.264	.319	0-0	—	0	78	-9	-1.0
1983	Tex A	7	9	.438	29	22	3	0-0	159.1	144	70	14	7	49-5	108	3.16	127	.240	.303	0-0	—	0	80	12	1.3
1984	Tex A	15	15	.500	35	35	9-1	0-0	246.1	234	117	30	6	81-3	141	3.25	128	.245	.306	0-0	—	0	96	17	2.0
1985	Tex A	2	7	.222	13	13	0	0-0	77.2	89	53	15	1	23-2	52	5.91	72	.287	.334	0-0	—	0	74	-13	-1.2
	Det A	10	7	.588	20	20	4	0-0	137.1	131	59	13	2	34-6	107	3.34	122	.250	.296	0-0	—	0	105	11	1.2
	Year	12	14	.462	33	33	4	0-0	215	220	64	28	3	57-8	159	4.27	97	.264	.310	0-0	—	0	93	-3	0.0
1986	Det A	12	9	.571	32	31	3-1	0-0	188.1	196	95	23	3	65-9	119	4.16	99	.268	.328	0-0	—	0	105	0	0.1
1987	†Det A	15	10	.600	34	34	5-3	0-0	218.2	216	106	27	5	56-5	146	3.91	108	.256	.302	0-0	—	0	117	9	1.0
1988	Det A	14	11	.560	32	32	2	0-0	203	213	105	25	4	64-7	127	4.21	91	.267	.323	0-0	—	0	98	-9	-0.9
1989	Det A	10	14	.417	33	33	6-1	0-0	223.2	227	105	21	8	74-8	147	3.58	107	.265	.326	0-0	—	0	87	4	0.6
1990	Det A	9	8	.529	34	29	1	1-0	176.1	190	104	25	9	66-7	114	5.31	75	.280	.349	0-0	—	0	118	-22	-1.9
1991	Det A	13	12	.520	33	33	3-2	0-0	217.1	217	98	26	2	78-9	107	3.77	110	.265	.327	1-0	.000	-0	105	10	1.1
1992	Det A	13	11	.542	32	31	3	0-0	186.2	188	102	22	7	90-9	91	4.39	90	.267	.351	0-0	—	0	106	-11	-1.2
1993	NY N	7	15	.318	29	29	0	0-0	183	198	100	26	9	48-7	104	4.48	90	.278	.330	58-3	.155	0	93	-7	-0.8
	NY A	0	2	.000	3	3	0	0-0	19.2	18	10	2	0	7-1	12	3.20	130	.222	.284	0-0	—	0	96	1	0.1
Total	21	240	236	.504	638	616	143-34	1-1	4188.1	4063	1910	448	129	1255-116	2773	3.66	106	.254	.312	59-3	.153	0	102	105	12.0
TANKERSLEY, DENNIS Dennis Lee B 2.24.1979 Troy, MO BR/TR 6-2/185# d5.10																									
2002	SD N	1	4	.200	17	9	0	0-0	51.1	59	46	10	6	40-3	39	8.06	47	.304	.434	13-0	.308	2	90	-24	-1.8
2003	SD N	0	1	.000	1	1	0	0-0	0	3	7	0	0	4-0	0	o	—	1.000	1.000	0-0	—	0	262	-7	-0.5
Total	2	1	5	.167	18	10	0	0-0	51.1	62	53	10	6	44-3	39	9.29	41	.315	.450	13-0	.308	2	108	-31	-2.3
TANNEHILL, JESSE Jesse Niles "Powder" B 7.14.1874 Dayton, KY D 9.22.1956 Dayton, KY BB/TL 5-8/150# d6.17 C1 b-Lee ▲																									
1894	Cin N	1	1	.500	5	2	1	1	29	37	30	1	1	16	7	7.14	78	.306	.391	11-0	.000	-2	89	-4	-0.4
1897	Pit N	9	9	.500	21	16	11-1	1	142	172	97	1	8	24	40	4.25	98	.297	.333	184-0	.266	3*	68	-3	0.1
1898	Pit N	25	13	.658	43	38	34-5	2	326.2	338	147	2	12	63	93	2.95	121	.265	.306	152-6	.289	7*	102	23	3.4
1899	Pit N	24	14	.632	41	36	33-3	1	322	361	139	4	14	52	65	2.82	135	.283	.318	136-4	.250	4*	114	36	4.3
1900	Pit N	20	6	.769	29	27	23-2	0	234	247	108	3	17	43	50	2.88	126	.271	.316	110-5	.336	8*	118	20	2.7
1901	Pit N	18	10	.643	32	30	25-4	1	252.1	240	94	1	10	36	118	**2.18**	150	.249	.283	135-3	.244	5*	106	30	3.3
1902	Pit N	20	6	.769	26	24	23-2	0	231	203	78	0	10	25	100	1.95	141	.236	.266	148-1	.291	7*	149	17	2.7
1903	NY A	15	15	.500	32	31	22-2	0	239.2	258	123	3	10	34	106	3.27	96	.274	.307	111-1	.234	5*	107	-4	0.2
1904	Bos A	21	11	.656	33	31	30-4	0	281.2	256	89	5	13	33	116	2.04	131	.243	.275	122-2	.197	3*	110	19	2.8
1905	Bos A	22	9	.710	37	32	27-6	0	271.2	238	91	7	13	59	113	2.48	109	.237	.288	93-2	.226	6	122	9	1.9
1906	Bos A	13	11	.542	27	26	18-2	0	196.1	207	91	9	10	39	82	3.16	87	.274	.318	79-1	.278	6*	113	-8	-0.3
1907	Bos A	6	7	.462	18	16	10-2	1	131	131	59	3	5	20	29	2.47	104	.263	.298	51-1	.196	1*	97	-1	0.1
1908	Bos A	0	0	—	1	1	0	0	5	4	2	0	0	3	2	3.60	68	.200	.304	2-0	.500	0	111	0	0.0
	Was A	2	4	.333	10	9	5	0	71.2	77	36	0	6	23	14	3.77	61	.278	.346	43-0	.256	2*	116	-9	-0.5
	Year	2	4	.333	11	10	5	0	76.2	81	40	0	6	26	16	3.76	61	.273	.343	45-0	.267	2	116	-10	-0.5
1909	Was A	1	1	.500	3	2	2-1	0	21	19	8	1	1	5	8	3.43	71	.268	.325	36-0	.167	0*	73	-1	0.0
1911	Cin N	0	0	—	1	0	0	0	4.1	6	7	0	0	3	1	6.23	53	.316	.409	1-0	.000	-0		-3	-0.1
Total	15	197	117	.627	359	321	264-34	7	2759.1	2794	1199	40	130	478	944	2.80	114	.263	.303	1414-26	.255	54	109	121	20.2
TANNER, BRUCE Bruce Matthew B 12.9.1961 New Castle, PA BL/TR 6-3/220# d6.12 C3 f-Chuck																									
1985	Chi A	1	2	.333	10	4	0	0-0	27	34	17	1	2	13-3	9	5.33	81	.309	.389	0-0	—	0	79	-3	-0.2
TAPANI, KEVIN Kevin Ray B 2.18.1964 Des Moines, IA BR/TR 6/187# d7.4																									
1989	NY N	0	0	—	3	0	0	0-0	7.1	5	3	1	0	4-0	2	3.68	89	.192	.290	2-0	.000	-0		0	0.0
	Min A	2	2	.500	5	5	0	0-0	32.2	34	15	2	0	8-1	21	3.86	108	.266	.307	0-0	—	0	79	1	0.1
1990	Min A	12	8	.600	28	28	1-1	0-0	159.1	164	75	12	2	29-2	101	4.07	102	.264	.297	0-0	—	0	90	4	0.4
1991	†Min A	16	9	.640	34	34	4-1	0-0	244	225	84	23	2	40-0	135	2.99	143	.245	.277	0-0	—	0	104	36	3.4
1992	Min A	16	11	.593	34	34	4-1	0-0	220	226	103	17	5	48-2	138	3.97	102	.269	.309	0-0	—	0	120	3	0.4
1993	Min A	12	15	.444	36	35	3-1	0-0	225.2	243	123	21	6	57-1	150	4.43	99	.272	.318	0-0	—	0	86	-2	-0.2
1994	Min A	11	7	.611	24	24	4-1	0-0	156	181	86	13	4	39-0	91	4.62	106	.291	.334	0-0	—	0	95	5	0.5
1995	Min A	6	11	.353	20	20	3-1	0-0	133.2	155	79	21	4	34-2	88	4.92	97	.290	.335	0-0	—	0	90	-2	-0.2
	†LA N	4	2	.667	13	11	0	0-0	57	72	37	8	1	14-2	43	5.05	75	.306	.345	17-3	.176	0	169	-9	-0.7
1996	Chi A	13	10	.565	34	34	1	0-0	225.1	236	123	34	3	76-5	150	4.59	103	.268	.326	0-0	—	0	109	5	0.4
1997	Chi N	9	3	.750	13	13	1-1	0-0	85	77	33	7	2	23-2	55	3.39	127	.242	.296	22-4	.136	-0	104	9	1.2
1998	†Chi N	19	9	.679	35	34	2-2	0-0	219	244	120	30	5	62-4	136	4.85	91	.284	.333	75-5	.133	1	112	-7	-0.8
1999	Chi N	6	12	.333	23	23	1	0-0	136	151	81	12	4	33-2	73	4.83	93	.280	.322	39-5	.051	-2	86	-5	-0.8
2000	Chi N	8	12	.400	30	30	2	0-0	195.2	208	113	35	8	47-1	150	5.01	91	.271	.319	56-9	.179	2	99	-9	-0.7
2001	Chi N	9	14	.391	29	29	0	0-0	168.1	186	93	24	7	40-6	149	4.49	92	.279	.325	50-7	.240	2	91	-8	-0.6
Total	13	143	125	.534	361	354	26-9	0-0	2265	2407	1168	260	53	554-30	1482	4.35	101	.272	.317	261-33	.153	3	101	21	2.4
TATE, RANDY Randall Lee B 10.23.1952 Florence, AL BR/TR 6-3/190# d4.14																									
1975	NY N	5	13	.278	26	23	2	0-0	137.2	121	73	8	5	86-3	99	4.45	78	.240	.355	41-5	.000	-4	85	-14	-2.1
TATE, STU Stuart Douglas B 6.17.1962 Huntsville, AL BR/TR 6-3/205# d9.20																									
1989	SF N	0	0	—	2	0	0	0-0	2.2	3	3	0	0	0-0	4	3.38	100	.250	.250	0-0	—	0		-1	0.0
TATE, AL Walter Alvin B 7.1.1918 Coleman, OK D 5.8.1993 Bountiful, UT BR/TR 6/180# d9.27																									
1946	Pit N	0	1	.000	2	1	1	0	9	8	5	0	0	7	2	5.00	70	.267	.405	3-0	.333	0	49	-1	-0.1
TATIS, RAMON Ramon Francisco (Medrano) B 1.5.1973 Guayubin, D.R. BL/TL 6-2/185# d4.6																									
1997	Chi N	1	1	.500	56	0	0	0-1	55.2	66	36	13	3	29-6	33	5.34	81	.308	.394	3-0	.000	-0		-6	-0.3
1998	TB A	0	0	—	22	0	0	0-0	11.2	23	19	2	1	16-1	5	13.89	35	.418	.556	0-0	—	0		-11	-0.5
Total	2	1	1	.500	78	0	0	0-1	67.1	89	55	15	4	45-7	38	6.82	64	.331	.430	3-0	.000	-0		-17	-0.8
TATUM, KEN Kenneth Ray B 4.25.1944 Alexandria, LA BR/TR 6-2/205# d5.28																									
1969	Cal A	7	2	.778	45	0	0	22-1	86.1	51	13	1	4	39-5	65	1.36	257	.172	.276	21-2	.286	4		**22**	4.1
1970	Cal A	7	4	.636	62	0	0	17-8	88.2	68	35	12	5	26-5	50	2.94	123	.208	.274	11-0	.182	1		6	1.0
1971	Bos A	2	4	.333	36	1	0	9-3	53.2	50	27	3	8	25-7	21	4.19	88	.255	.358	10-0	.300	2	73	-3	-0.2
1972	Bos A	0	2	.000	22	0	0	4-2	29.1	32	12	3	2	15-3	15	3.07	105	.283	.377	2-0	.000	0		0	0.0
1973	Bos A	0	0	—	1	0	0	0-0	4	6	4	2	0	3-0	0	9.00	45	.462	.529	0-0	—	0		-2	-0.1
1974	Chi A	0	0	—	10	1	0	0-0	20.2	23	12	3	0	9-0	5	4.79	78	.274	.340	1-0	.000	-0	260	-2	-0.1
Total	6	16	12	.571	176	2	0	52-14	282.2	230	103	24	19	117-20	156	2.93	122	.224	.311	45-2	.244	7	174	21	4.7
TAUSCHER, WALT Walter Edward B 11.22.1901 LaSalle, IL D 11.27.1992 Winter Park, FL BR/TR 6-1/186# d4.19																									
1928	Pit N	0	0	—	17	0	0	1	29.1	28	20	0	3	12	7	4.91	83	.280	.374	6-0	.167	-0		-3	-0.2
1931	Was A	1	0	1.000	6	0	0	0	12	24	16	2	0	4	5	7.50	57	.429	.467	0-2	—	0		-6	-0.4
Total	2	1	0	1.000	23	0	0	1	41.1	52	36	2	3	16	12	5.66	73	.333	.406	6-2	.167	-0		-9	-0.6
TAVAREZ, JULIAN Julian (Carmen) B 5.22.1973 Santiago, D.R. BL/TR 6-2/165# d8.7																									
1993	Cle A	2	2	.500	8	7	0	0-0	37	53	29	7	2	13-2	19	6.57	66	.340	.395	0-0	—	0	155	-9	-0.8
1994	Cle A	0	1	.000	1	1	0	0-0	1.2	6	8	1	0	1-1	0	21.60	22	.500	.500	0-0	—	0	97	-5	-0.6
1995	†Cle A	10	2	.833	57	0	0	0-4	85	76	36	7	3	21-0	68	2.44	193	.235	.286	0-0	—	0		17	2.0
1996	†Cle A	4	7	.364	51	4	0	0-0	80.2	101	49	9	1	22-5	46	5.36	91	.315	.356	0-0	—	0	85	-3	-0.3
1997	†SF N	6	4	.600	**89**	0	0	0-3	88.1	91	43	6	4	34-5	38	3.87	106	.277	.344	1-0	.000	-0		2	0.2
1998	SF N	5	3	.625	60	0	0	1-5	85.1	96	41	5	8	36-11	52	3.80	105	.298	.379	9-1	.111	-0		1	0.0
1999	SF N	2	0	1.000	47	0	0	0-2	54.2	65	38	7	8	25-3	33	5.93	71	.295	.384	5-0	.200	0		-11	-0.5
2000	Col N	11	5	.688	51	12	1	1-0	120	124	68	11	7	53-9	62	4.43	131	.268	.349	35-3	.086	-3	96	13	1.3
2001	Chi N	10	9	.526	34	28	0	0-0	161.1	172	98	13	11	69-4	107	4.52	92	.277	.358	41-11	.122	-0	113	-12	-1.1
2002	Fla N	10	12	.455	29	27	0	0-1	153.2	188	100	9	15	74-7	67	5.39	73	.308	.395	40-5	.125	-1	93	-26	-3.2
2003	Pit N	3	3	.500	64	0	0	11-3	83.2	75	37	1	5	27-8	39	3.66	120	.244	.314	4-0	.000	-0		6	0.6
Total	11	63	48	.568	491	79	1	13-18	951.1	1047	547	76	64	375-55	531	4.52	98	.284	.358	135-20	.111	-5	104	-27	-2.4

Year	Tm Lg	W	L	Pct	G	GS	CG-Sho	SV-BS	IP	H	R	HR	HB	BB-IB	SO	ERA	AERA	OAV	OOB	AB-SH	AVG	PB	Sup	APR	PW
TAYLOR, AARON Aaron Wade B 8.20.1977 Valdosta, GA BR/TR 6-7/230# d9.9																									
2002	Sea A	0	0	—	5	0	0	0-1	5	8	5	2	0	0-0	6	9.00	47	.348	.348	0-0	—	0		-3	-0.1
2003	Sea A	0	0	—	10	0	0	0-0	12.2	17	12	0	1	6-0	9	8.53	51	.315	.387	0-0	—	0		-6	-0.3
Total	2	0	0	—	15	0	0	0-1	17.2	25	17	2	1	6-0	15	8.66	50	.325	.376	0-0	—	0		-9	-0.4
TAYLOR, ARLAS Arlas Walter "Lefty" or "Foxy" B 3.16.1896 Warrick County, IN D 9.10.1958 Dade City, FL BR/TL 5-11/?# d9.15																									
1921	Phi A	0	1	.000	1	1	0	0	2	7	5	1	0	2	1	22.50	20	.636	.692	0-0	—	0	56	-3	-0.5
TAYLOR, BEN Benjamin Harrison B 4.2.1889 Paoli, IN D 11.3.1946 Martin County, IN BR/TR 5-11/163# d6.28																									
1912	Cin N	0	0	—	2	0	0	0	5.2	9	7	0	1	3	2	3.18	106	.360	.448	2-0	.000	0		-1	-0.1
TAYLOR, BRUCE Bruce Bell B 4.16.1953 Holden, MA BR/TR 6/178# d8.5																									
1977	Det A	1	0	1.000	19	0	0	2-1	29.1	23	11	2	1	10-3	19	3.38	127	.219	.293	0-0	—	0		3	0.2
1978	Det A	0	0	—	1	0	0	0-0	1	0	0	0	0	0-0	0	0.00	—	.000	.000	0-0	—	0		0	0.0
1979	Det A	1	2	.333	10	0	0	0-0	18.2	16	13	1	2	7-2	8	4.82	90	.242	.325	0-0	—	0		-2	-0.3
Total	3	2	2	.500	30	0	0	2-1	49	39	24	3	3	17-5	27	3.86	112	.224	.301	0-0	—	0		1	-0.1
TAYLOR, CHUCK Charles Gilbert B 4.18.1942 Murfreesboro, TN BR/TR 6-2/195# d5.27																									
1969	StL N	7	5	.583	27	13	5-1	0-0	126.2	108	39	8	3	30-5	62	2.56	140	.235	.285	39-2	.179	1	74	15	1.4
1970	StL N	6	7	.462	56	7	1-1	8-3	124.1	116	47	5	2	31-10	64	3.11	132	.256	.303	26-3	.115	-1	84	14	1.5
1971	StL N	3	1	.750	43	1	0	3-2	71.1	72	32	7	1	25-5	46	3.53	102	.267	.327	12-0	.167	0	148	0	0.0
1972	NY N	0	0	—	20	0	0	2-0	31	44	19	2	1	9-3	9	5.52	61	.341	.386	3-0	.000	-0		-7	-0.3
	Mil A	0	0	—	5	0	0	1-0	11.2	8	2	0	1	3-0	5	1.54	197	.200	.273	2-0	.500	0		2	0.2
1973	Mon N	2	0	1.000	8	0	0	0-1	20.1	17	4	3	0	2-1	10	1.77	216	.230	.250	4-2	.000	-0		5	0.4
1974	Mon N	6	2	.750	61	0	0	11-3	107.2	101	27	8	3	25-8	43	2.17	177	.256	.301	10-4	.300	1		20	2.0
1975	Mon N	2	2	.500	54	0	0	6-4	74	72	32	6	1	24-5	29	3.53	109	.264	.321	2-0	.000	-0		3	0.2
1976	Mon N	2	3	.400	31	0	0	0-0	40	38	20	4	0	13-4	14	4.50	83	.273	.333	3-0	.000	-0		-2	-0.3
Total	8	28	20	.583	305	21	6-2	31-13	607	576	222	43	12	162-41	282	3.07	123	.258	.309	101-11	.158	0	81	50	5.1
TAYLOR, DORN Donald Clyde B 8.11.1958 Abington, PA BR/TR 6-2/180# d4.30																									
1987	Pit N	2	3	.400	14	8	0	0-0	53.1	48	35	10	1	28-1	37	5.74	72	.247	.342	18-0	.167	-0*	96	-8	-0.7
1989	Pit N	1	1	.500	9	0	0	0-0	10.2	14	6	0	0	5-2	3	5.06	66	.333	.404	1-0	.000	-0*		-2	-0.3
1990	Bal A	0	1	.000	4	0	0	0-0	3.2	4	3	0	0	2-0	4	2.45	155	.250	.333	0-0	—	0		0	-0.1
Total	3	3	5	.375	27	8	0	0-0	67.2	66	44	10	1	35-3	44	5.45	73	.262	.352	19-0	.158	-0	96	-10	-1.1
TAYLOR, ED Edgar Ruben "Rube" B 3.23.1877 Palestine, TX D 1.31.1912 Dallas, TX TL d8.8																									
1903	StL N	0	0	—	1	0	0	0	3	0	0	0	0	0	1	0.00	—	.000	.000	1-0	.000	-0		1	0.0
TAYLOR, GARY Gary William B 10.19.1945 Detroit, MI BR/TR 6-2/190# d9.2																									
1969	Det A	0	1	.000	7	0	0	0-0	10.1	10	6	2	0	6-0	3	5.23	71	.244	.340	1-0	.000	-0		-1	-0.1
TAYLOR, HARRY Harry Evans B 12.2.1935 San Angelo, TX BR/TR 6/185# d9.17																									
1957	KC A	0	0	—	2	0	0	0	8.2	11	4	0	1	4-0	4	3.12	127	.314	.400	4-0	.250	0		0	0.0
TAYLOR, HARRY James Harry B 5.20.1919 E.Glenn, IN D 11.5.2000 Terre Haute, IN BR/TR 6-1/175# d9.22																									
1946	Bro N	0	0	—	4	0	0	1	4.2	5	2	0	0	1	6	3.86	88	.313	.353	0-0	—	0		0	0.0
1947	†Bro N	10	5	.667	33	20	10-2	1	162	130	63	10	5	83	58	3.11	133	**.225**	.327	62-2	.129	-2	112	19	1.4
1948	Bro N	2	7	.222	17	13	2	0	80.2	90	55	8	3	61	32	5.36	75	.288	.408	22-2	.273	1	130	-12	-1.0
1950	Bos A	2	0	1.000	3	2	2-1	0	19	13	3	0	0	8	8	1.42	345	.197	.284	7-0	.286	0	92	7	0.7
1951	Bos A	4	9	.308	31	8	1	2	81.1	100	59	6	1	42	22	5.75	78	.307	.388	29-1	.103	-3	112	-11	-1.8
1952	Bos A	1	0	1.000	2	1	1	0	10	6	2	1	1	6	1	1.80	219	.176	.317	4-0	.250	0	244	2	0.2
Total	6	19	21	.475	90	44	16-3	4	357.2	344	184	25	10	201	127	4.10	102	.258	.359	124-5	.161	-3	118	5	-0.5
TAYLOR, JACK John Budd "Brewery Jack" B 5.23.1873 Staten Island, NY D 2.7.1900 Staten Island, NY BR/TR 6-1/190# d9.16																									
1891	NY N	0	1	.000	1	1	1	0	8	4	2	1	0	3	3	1.13	285	.143	.226	2	.000	0	37	2	0.2
1892	Phi N	1	0	1.000	3	3	2	0	26	28	19	2	0	10	7	1.38	234	.264	.328	12	.167	-0	169	1	0.0
1893	Phi N	10	9	.526	25	16	14	1	170	187	113	8	10	77	41	4.24	108	.271	.353	93	.215	-2*	100	5	0.3
1894	Phi N	23	13	.639	41	34	31-1	1	298	347	201	13	17	96	76	4.08	126	.288	.349	145-0	.338	9*	105	31	3.5
1895	Phi N	26	14	.650	41	37	33-1	1	335	403	233	7	15	83	93	4.49	107	.293	.340	155-1	.290	7*	111	9	1.5
1896	Phi N	20	21	.488	45	41	35-1	1	359	459	282	17	20	112	97	4.79	90	.308	.365	157-8	.185	-7*	114	-26	-2.6
1897	Phi N	16	20	.444	40	37	35-2	2	317.1	376	204	5	28	76	88	4.23	99	.292	.345	139-2	.252	2*	96	-3	0.0
1898	StL N	15	29	.341	**50**	**47**	**42**	1	**397.1**	465	259	14	25	83	89	3.90	97	.290	.335	157-5	.242	3*	84	-12	-0.3
1899	Cin N	9	10	.474	25	19	16-2	2	180.1	207	110	7	11	43	35	4.09	96	.287	.337	71-3	.239	-1	81	-3	-0.4
Total	9	120	117	.506	271	235	209-7	9	2091	2476	1423	74	126	583	529	4.22	104	.291	.346	931-19	.252	12	100	4	2.2
TAYLOR, JACK John W. B 1.14.1874 New Straitsville, OH D 3.4.1938 Columbus, OH BR/TR 5-10/170# d9.25																									
1898	Chi N	5	0	1.000	5	5	5	0	41	32	12	0	1	10	11	2.20	163	.213	.267	15-0	.200	1	95	8	1.0
1899	Chi N	18	21	.462	41	39	39-1	0	354.2	380	223	6	22	84	67	3.76	100	.274	.325	139-1	.266	10*	120	1	1.0
1900	Chi N	10	17	.370	28	26	25-2	1	222.1	226	130	4	8	58	57	2.55	141	.263	.316	81-3	.235	2	63	18	2.0
1901	Chi N	13	19	.406	33	31	30	0	275.2	341	165	5	8	44	68	3.36	96	.302	.332	106-2	.217	2*	92	-7	-0.4
1902	Chi N	23	11	.676	37	34	34-**8**	1	333.2	273	86	2	12	45	88	**1.29**	**209**	.224	**.258**	189-9	.233	3*	94	**51**	**6.1**
1903	Chi N	21	14	.600	37	33	33-1	1	312.1	277	137	2	5	57	83	2.45	128	.235	.273	126-3	.222	4*	109	23	2.8
1904	StL N	20	19	.513	41	39	**39**-2	1	352	297	133	5	13	82	103	2.22	121	.220	.271	133-1	.211	4*	103	17	2.4
1905	StL N	15	21	.417	37	34	34-3	1	309	302	155	10	11	85	102	3.44	87	.259	.315	121-2	.190	4*	75	-14	-1.2
1906	StL N	8	9	.471	17	17	17-1	0	155	133	50	3	7	47	27	2.15	122	.227	.292	53-2	.208	3	86	8	1.3
	Chi N	12	3	.800	17	16	15-2	0	147.1	116	42	1	6	39	34	1.83	144	.223	.285	53-0	.208	2	121	13	1.6
	Year	20	12	.625	34	33	32-3	0	302.1	249	46	4	13	86	61	1.99	132	.225	.289	106-2	.208	5	103	20	2.9
1907	Chi N	7	5	.583	18	13	8	0	123	127	62	3	1	33	22	3.29	76	.268	.318	47-0	.191	0	101	-9	-0.9
Total	10	152	139	.522	311	287	279-20	5	2626	2504	1195	41	94	584	662	2.65	115	.250	.297	1063-23	.222	34	97	109	15.7
TAYLOR, KERRY Kerry Thomas B 1.25.1971 Bemidji, MN BR/TR 6-3/200# d4.13																									
1993	SD N	0	5	.000	36	7	0	0-0	68.1	72	53	5	4	49-0	45	6.45	64	.277	.396	12-1	.000	-1	81	-16	-1.2
1994	SD N	0	0	—	1	1	0	0-0	4.1	9	4	1	1	1-0	3	8.31	50	.409	.458	2-0	.000	-0	89	-2	-0.1
Total	2	0	5	.000	37	8	0	0-0	72.2	81	57	6	5	50-0	48	6.56	63	.287	.400	14-1	.000	-2	82	-18	-1.3
TAYLOR, DUMMY Luther Haden B 2.21.1875 Oskaloosa, KS D 8.22.1958 Jacksonville, IL BR/TR 6-1/160# d8.27																									
1900	NY N	4	3	.571	11	7	6	0	62.1	74	31	0	5	24	16	2.45	147	.294	.367	22-1	.136	-1	98	7	0.4
1901	NY N	18	27	.400	**45**	**43**	37-4	0	353.1	377	193	8	16	112	136	3.18	104	.271	.333	136-1	.132	-8	70	-1	-0.8
1902	Cle A	1	3	.250	4	4	4-1	0	34	37	17	0	2	8	8	1.59	217	.278	.329	10-0	.100	-0	52	5	0.5
	NY N	7	15	.318	26	25	18	0	200.2	194	98	4	15	55	87	2.29	123	.254	.317	65-2	.092	-5	61	5	-0.1
1903	NY N	13	13	.500	33	31	18-1	0	244.2	306	143	6	4	89	94	4.23	79	.314	.374	82-6	.146	-2	116	-19	-1.9
1904	NY N	21	15	.583	37	36	29-5	0	296.1	231	100	6	9	75	138	2.34	117	.214	.270	102-6	.157	-1*	108	15	1.8
1905	NY N	16	9	.640	32	28	18-4	0	213.1	200	85	5	8	51	91	2.66	110	.247	.298	69-10	.130	-1	125	7	0.7
1906	NY N	17	9	.654	31	27	13-2	0	213	186	81	4	6	57	91	2.20	119	.233	.289	76-2	.184	0	127	6	0.7
1907	NY N	11	7	.611	28	21	11-3	1	171	145	66	1	3	46	56	2.42	102	.232	.288	48-5	.125	-1*	94	0	-0.2
1908	NY N	8	5	.615	27	15	6-1	2	127.2	127	56	5	4	34	50	2.33	104	.253	.306	35-5	.229	2	138	-3	-0.2
Total	9	116	106	.523	274	237	160-21	3	1916.1	1877	870	39	72	551	767	2.75	107	.256	.314	645-38	.144	-17	100	22	0.9
TAYLOR, WILEY Philip Wiley B 3.18.1888 Wamego, KS D 7.8.1954 Westmoreland, KS BR/TR 6-1/175# d9.6																									
1911	Det A	0	2	.000	3	2	1	0	19	18	11	0	1	10	9	3.79	91	.247	.345	6-0	.000	-1	0	-1	-0.2
1912	Chi A	0	1	.000	3	3	0	0	20	21	12	0	0	14	4	4.95	65	.309	.427	5-0	.000	-1	115	-3	-0.2
1913	StL A	0	2	.000	5	4	1	0	31.2	33	19	0	0	16	12	4.83	61	.284	.371	10-0	.000	-1	120	-5	-0.4
1914	StL A	2	5	.286	16	8	2-1	0	50	41	24	0	2	25	20	3.42	79	.209	.305	12-0	.167	-0	74	-3	-0.5
Total	4	2	10	.167	27	17	4-1	0	120.2	113	66	0	3	65	45	4.10	72	.249	.347	33-0	.061	-3	81	-12	-1.3

Year	Tm Lg	W	L	Pct	G	GS	CG-Sho	SV-BS	IP	H	R	HR	HB	BB-IB	SO	ERA	AERA	OAV	OOB	AB-SH	AVG	PB	Sup	APR	PW
TAYLOR, SCOTT Rodney Scott B 8.2.1967 Defiance, OH BL/TL 6-1/185# d9.17																									
1992	Bos A	1	1	.500	4	1	0	0-0	14.2	13	8	4	0	4-0	7	4.91	86	.245	.298	0-0	—	0	65	-1	-0.1
1993	Bos A	0	1	.000	16	0	0	0-0	11	14	10	1	1	12-3	8	8.18	57	.311	.466	0-0	—	0		-4	-0.3
Total	2	1	2	.333	20	1	0	0-0	25.2	27	18	5	1	16-3	15	6.31	70	.276	.383	0-0	—	0	65	-5	-0.4
TAYLOR, RON Ronald Wesley B 12.13.1937 Toronto, ON, CAN BR/TR 6-1/195# d4.11																									
1962	Cle A	2	2	.500	8	4	1	0	33.1	36	23	6	1	13-4	15	5.94	65	.281	.347	11-0	.273	0	98	-7	-0.7
1963	StL N	9	7	.563	54	9	2	11	133.1	119	44	10	4	30-6	91	2.84	125	.243	.289	32-2	.031	-3	67	12	1.2
1964	†StL N	8	4	.667	63	2	0	7	101.1	109	56	15	1	33-7	69	4.62	82	.274	.329	15-0	.133	-0	58	-6	-0.8
1965	StL N	2	1	.667	25	0	0	1	43.2	43	24	6	1	15-4	26	4.53	85	.261	.321	5-0	.400	1		-3	-0.1
	Hou N	1	5	.167	32	1	0	4	57.2	68	42	5	5	16-6	37	6.40	52	.305	.359	13-0	.000	-1	104	-18	-2.2
	Year	3	6	.333	57	1	0	5	101.1	111	46	11	6	31-10	63	5.60	64	.286	.343	18-0	.111	-1	98	-21	-2.3
1966	Hou N	2	3	.400	36	1	0	0	64.2	89	47	5	5	10-4	29	5.71	60	.333	.364	12-0	.167	0	77	-17	-1.3
1967	NY N	4	6	.400	50	0	0	8	73	60	21	1	1	23-14	46	2.34	145	.230	.290	7-1	.000	-1		9	1.3
1968	NY N	1	5	.167	58	0	0	13	76.2	64	24	4	1	18-9	49	2.70	112	.228	.275	9-0	.000	-1		3	0.4
1969	†NY N	9	4	.692	59	0	0	13-4	76	61	23	7	1	24-6	42	2.72	134	.228	.292	4-0	.250	0		9	1.9
1970	NY N	5	4	.556	57	0	0	13-6	66.1	65	31	5	0	16-10	28	3.93	102	.265	.305	4-1	.000	-0		1	0.2
1971	NY N	2	2	.500	45	0	0	2-1	69	71	28	7	1	11-6	32	3.65	93	.269	.300	4-0	.250	0		0	0.0
1972	SD N	0	0	—	4	0	0	0-0	5	9	7	5	0	0-0	0	12.60	26	.375	.375	0-0	—	0		-5	-0.3
Total	11	45	43	.511	491	17	3	72-11	800	794	370	76	21	209-76	464	3.93	91	.264	.312	116-4	.103	-5	78	-22	-0.4
TAYLOR, SCOTT Scott Michael B 10.3.1966 Topeka, KS BR/TR 6-3/200# d7.28																									
1995	Tex A	1	2	.333	3	3	0	0-0	15.1	25	16	6	0	5-0	10	9.39	51	.379	.423	0-0	—	0	58	-7	-1.0
TAYLOR, TERRY Terry Derrell B 7.28.1964 Crestview, FL BR/TR 6-1/180# d8.19																									
1988	Sea A	0	1	.000	5	5	0	0-0	23	26	17	2	0	11-1	9	6.26	67	.295	.370	0-0	—	0	118	-5	-0.3
TAYLOR, PETE Vernon Charles B 11.26.1927 Severn, MD D 11.17.2003 Annapolis, MD BR/TR 6-1/170# d5.2																									
1952	StL A	0	0	—	1	0	0	0	2	4	3	0	0	3	0	13.50	29	.500	.636	0-0	—	0		-2	-0.1
TAYLOR, WADE Wade Eric B 10.19.1965 Mobile, AL BR/TR 6-1/185# d6.2																									
1991	NY A	7	12	.368	23	22	0	0-0	116.1	144	85	13	7	53-0	72	6.27	66	.314	.388	0-0	—	0	91	-26	-3.4
TAYLOR, BILLY William Henry "Bollicky Bill" B 1855 Washington, DC D 5.14.1900 Jacksonville, FL BR/TR 5-11.5/204# d5.21 ▲																									
1881	Wor N	0	1	.000	1	1	1	0	8	15	13	0		6	0	7.88	38	.366	.447	28	.107	-0*	18	-4	-0.4
	Cle N	0	0	—	1	0	0	0	3	0	0	0		1	2	0.00	—	.000	.100	103	.243	-0*		1	0.0
	Year	0	1	.000	2	1	1	0	11	15	14	0		7	2	5.73	51	.300	.386	131	.214	-0	19	-3	-0.4
1882	Pit AA	0	1	.000	1	0	0	0	5	11	10	0		4	1	16.20	16	.407	.484	299	.281	0*		-6	-0.7
1883	Pit AA	4	7	.364	19	9	8	0	127	166	115	4		34	41	5.39	60	.296	.337	369	.260	3*	90	-28	-1.7
1884	StL U	25	4	.862	33	29	29-2	**4**	263	222	97	2		40	154	1.68	143	.213	.243	186	.366	13*	142	21	**2.8**
	Phi AA	18	12	.600	30	30	30-1	0	260	232	118	3	12	44	130	2.53	134	.219	.258	111	.252	3	89	21	2.5
1885	Phi AA	1	5	.167	6	6	6	0	52.1	68	35	0	1	9	11	3.27	105	.343	.375	21	.190	-1	63	1	0.0
1886	Bal AA	1	6	.143	8	8	8	0	72.1	87	63	1	2	20	37	5.72	60	.284	.332	39	.308	1*	113	-15	-1.0
1887	Phi AA	1	0	1.000	1	1	1	0	9	10	5	1	0	7	0	3.00	143	.286	.405	4	.250	-0	89	1	0.1
Total	7	50	36	.581	100	84	83-3	4	799.2	811	456	11	15	165	376	3.17	96	.248	.287	1160	.277	20	107	-8	1.6
TAYLOR, BILLY William Howell B 10.16.1961 Monticello, FL BR/TR 6-8/200# d4.5																									
1994	Oak A	1	3	.250	41	0	0	1-2	46.1	38	24	4	2	18-5	48	3.50	127	.220	.299	0-0	—	0		3	0.2
1996	Oak A	6	3	.667	55	0	0	17-2	60.1	52	30	5	4	25-4	67	4.33	114	.231	.315	0-0	—	0		5	0.8
1997	Oak A	3	4	.429	72	0	0	23-7	73	70	32	3	5	36-9	66	3.82	119	.254	.348	0-0	—	0		6	0.9
1998	Oak A	4	9	.308	70	0	0	33-4	73	71	37	7	3	22-4	58	3.58	128	.255	.312	0-0	—	0		6	1.2
1999	Oak A	1	5	.167	43	0	0	26-7	43	48	23	3	2	14-3	38	3.98	117	.287	.346	0-0	—	0		2	0.5
	NY N	0	1	.000	18	0	0	0-1	13.1	20	12	2	0	9-5	14	8.10	54	.345	.433	0-0	—	0		-6	-0.3
2000	TB A	1	3	.250	17	0	0	0-2	13.2	13	13	2	2	9-2	13	8.56	58	.255	.387	0-0	—	0		-5	-0.9
2001	Pit N	0	0	—	1	0	0	0-0	2	2	1	1	0	0-0	3	4.50	100	.250	.250	0-0	—	0		0	0.0
Total	7	16	28	.364	317	0	0	100-25	324.2	314	172	27	18	133-32	307	4.21	110	.254	.332	0-0	—	0		11	2.4
TEACHOUT, BUD Arthur John B 2.27.1904 Los Angeles, CA D 5.11.1985 Laguna Beach, CA BR/TL 6-2/183# d5.12																									
1930	Chi N	11	4	.733	40	16	6	0	153	178	80	16	0	48	59	4.06	120	.296	.348	63-3	.270	3*	133	14	1.3
1931	Chi N	1	2	.333	27	3	1	0	61.1	79	40	6	1	28	14	5.72	67	.305	.375	21-0	.238	0*	96	-10	-0.5
1932	StL N	0	0	—	1	0	0	0	1	2	1	0	0	0	0	0.00	—	.400	.400	0-0	—	0		0	0.0
Total	3	12	6	.667	68	19	7	0	215.1	259	121	22	1	76	73	4.51	102	.299	.356	84-3	.262	3	131	4	0.8
TEBEAU, GEORGE George E. "White Wings" B 12.26.1861 St.Louis, MO D 2.4.1923 Denver, CO BR/TR 5-9/175# d4.16 b-Patsy ▲																									
1887	Cin AA	0	1	.000	1	1	1	0	8	21	16	0	1	3	1	13.50	32	.488	.532	318	.296	0*	88	-7	-0.5
1890	Tol AA	0	0	—	1	0	0	0	5	9	8	0	0	5	0	9.00	44	.375	.483	381	.268	0*		-3	-0.1
Total	2	0	1	.000	2	1	1	0	13	30	24	0	1	8	1	11.77	36	.448	.513	699	.280	1	88	-10	-0.6
TEDROW, AL Allen Seymour B 12.14.1891 Westerville, OH D 1.23.1958 Westerville, OH BR/TL 6/180# d9.15																									
1914	Cle A	1	2	.333	4	3	1	0	22.1	19	6	0	3	14	4	1.21	239	.235	.367	6-0	.167	0	67	3	0.5
TEJERA, MICHAEL Michael B 10.18.1976 Havana, Cuba BL/TL 5-9/175# d9.8																									
1999	Fla N	0	0	—	3	1	0	0-0	6.1	10	8	1	0	5-0	7	11.37	38	.385	.484	0-0	—	0	105	-5	-0.2
2002	Fla N	8	8	.500	47	18	0	1-2	139.2	144	71	17	6	60-3	95	4.45	89	.269	.347	37-2	.189	2*	83	-6	-0.4
2003	†Fla N	3	4	.429	50	6	0	2-0	81	82	44	6	1	36-3	58	4.67	88	.267	.345	15-1	.067	-1	84	-5	-0.4
Total	3	11	12	.478	100	25	0	3-2	227	236	123	24	7	101-6	160	4.72	85	.272	.350	52-3	.154	1	84	-16	-1.0
TEKULVE, KENT Kenton Charles B 3.5.1947 Cincinnati, OH BR/TR 6-4/180# d5.20																									
1974	Pit N	1	1	.500	8	0	0	0-2	9	12	6	1	1	5-2	6	6.00	58	.343	.419	0-0	—	0		-2	-0.4
1975	†Pit N	1	2	.333	34	0	0	5-0	56	43	20	2	1	23-6	28	2.25	158	.215	.296	11-0	.091	-0		7	0.5
1976	Pit N	5	3	.625	64	0	0	9-3	102.2	91	30	3	0	25-7	68	2.45	142	.241	.287	9-1	.000	-1		13	1.2
1977	Pit N	10	1	.909	72	0	0	7-7	103	89	41	5	1	33-6	59	3.06	130	.236	.296	12-0	.250	0		10	1.3
1978	Pit N	8	7	.533	**91**	0	0	31-9	135.1	115	44	5	2	55-18	77	2.33	159	.228	.304	21-0	.095	-1		19	3.0
1979	†Pit N	10	8	.556	**94**	0	0	31-6	134.1	109	46	5	2	49-20	75	2.75	142	.222	.295	15-1	.133	-0		17	3.0
1980	Pit N☆	8	12	.400	78	0	0	21-11	93	96	39	6	1	40-16	47	3.39	108	.267	.342	9-0	.000	-1		3	0.5
1981	Pit N	5	5	.500	45	0	0	3-5	65	61	19	1	1	17-5	34	2.49	144	.250	.299	2-0	.000	-0		8	1.4
1982	Pit N	12	8	.600	**85**	0	0	20-10	128.2	113	47	7	3	46-23	66	2.87	129	.237	.305	14-1	.071	-1		11	2.0
1983	Pit N	7	5	.583	76	0	0	18-6	99	78	27	1	0	36-12	52	1.64	227	.223	.293	8-1	.000	-1		19	2.9
1984	Pit N	3	9	.250	72	0	0	13-4	88	86	30	4	1	33-12	36	2.66	136	.262	.330	7-0	.000	-1		9	1.4
1985	Pit N	0	0	—	3	0	0	0-0	3.1	7	7	1	0	5-1	4	16.20	22	.467	.600	0-0	—	0		-5	-0.2
	Phi N	4	10	.286	58	0	0	14-8	72.1	67	28	4	2	25-9	36	2.99	124	.246	.312	3-0	.000	-0		5	1.1
	Year	4	10	.286	61	0	0	14-8	75.2	74	39	5	2	30-10	40	3.57	103	.258	.330	3-0	.000	-0		1	0.9
1986	Phi N	11	5	.688	73	0	0	4-2	110	99	35	2	0	25-10	57	2.54	152	.240	.281	5-0	.000	-0		16	2.3
1987	Phi N	6	4	.600	**90**	0	0	3-3	105	96	38	8	0	29-13	60	3.09	138	.243	.293	1-1	.000	0		14	1.3
1988	Phi N	3	7	.300	70	0	0	4-3	80	87	34	3	2	22-11	43	3.60	99	.276	.326	2-0	.000	-0		0	0.1
1989	Cin N	0	3	.000	37	0	0	1-2	52	56	35	5	0	23-8	31	5.02	72	.272	.342	2-0	.500	0		-9	-0.5
Total	16	94	90	.511	1050	0	0	184-81	1436.2	1305	526	63	17	491-179	779	2.85	131	.244	.307	121-5	.083	-6		135	20.9
TELEMACO, AMAURY Amaury (Regalado) B 1.19.1974 Higuey, D.R. BR/TR 6-4/220# d5.16																									
1996	Chi N	5	7	.417	25	17	0	0-0	97.1	108	67	20	3	31-2	64	5.46	80	.281	.336	29-4	.103	-1	114	-13	-1.5
1997	Chi N	0	3	.000	10	5	0	0-0	38	47	26	4	0	11-0	29	6.16	70	.303	.347	9-0	.222	0	68	-7	-0.4
1998	Chi N	1	1	.500	14	0	0	0-0	27.2	23	12	5	0	13-0	18	3.90	113	.219	.305	6-0	.167	-0		2	0.1
	Ari N	6	9	.400	27	18	0	0-0	121	127	63	13	4	33-2	60	3.94	107	.271	.321	29-1	.069	-1	80	2	0.0
	Year	7	10	.412	41	18	0	0-0	148.2	150	67	18	4	46-2	78	3.93	108	.262	.318	35-1	.086	-1	79	3	0.1
1999	Ari N	1	0	1.000	5	0	0	0-0	6	7	5	2	0	6-1	2	7.50	61	.333	.481	0-0	—	0		-2	-0.2

Year	Tm Lg	W	L	Pct	G	GS	CG-Sho	SV-BS	IP	H	R	HR	HB	BB-IB	SO	ERA	AERA	OAV	OOB	AB-SH	AVG	PB	Sup	APR	PW
	Phi N	3	0	1.000	44	0	0	0-1	47	45	29	8	2	20-3	41	5.55	85	.250	.330	0-0	—	0		-3	-0.2
	Year	4	0	1.000	49	0	0	0-1	53	52	34	10	2	26-4	43	5.77	81	.259	.348	0-0	—	0		-5	-0.4
2000	Phi N	1	3	.250	13	2	0	0-1	24.1	25	22	6	0	14-0	22	6.66	70	.275	.364	4-0	.000	-0	49	-6	-0.9
2001	Phi N	5	5	.500	24	14	1	0-0	89.1	93	59	15	9	32-3	59	5.54	77	.274	.350	21-2	.095	-0	115	-13	-1.3
2003	Phi N	1	4	.200	8	8	0	0-0	45.1	41	22	5	7	11-2	29	3.97	101	.238	.309	14-1	.286	2	88	0	0.2
Total	7	23	32	.418	170	64	1	0-2	496	516	305	78	25	171-13	324	5.03	86	.269	.334	112-8	.125	-0	94	-40	-4.2
TELFORD, ANTHONY Anthony Charles B 3.6.1966 San Jose, CA BR/TR 6/175# d8.19																									
1990	Bal A	3	3	.500	8	8	0	0-0	36.1	43	22	4	1	19-0	20	4.95	77	.295	.375	0-0	—	0	99	-5	-0.7
1991	Bal A	0	0	—	9	1	0	0-0	26.2	27	12	3	0	6-1	24	4.05	98	.265	.303	0-0	—	0	116	0	0.0
1993	Bal A	0	0	—	3	0	0	0-0	7.1	11	8	3	1	1-0	6	9.82	46	.344	.382	0-0	—	0		-4	-0.2
1997	Mon N	4	6	.400	65	0	0	1-4	89	77	34	11	5	33-4	61	3.24	130	.236	.315	15-1	.200	0		10	1.2
1998	Mon N	3	6	.333	77	0	0	1-4	91	85	45	9	4	36-1	59	3.86	109	.247	.322	4-0	.250	0		3	0.3
1999	Mon N	5	4	.556	79	0	0	2-7	96	112	52	3	3	38-3	69	3.94	114	.295	.359	2-2	.000	0		4	0.4
2000	Mon N	5	4	.556	64	0	0	3-2	78.1	76	38	10	5	23-1	68	3.79	127	.257	.317	2-1	.000	-0		8	0.8
2001	Mon N	0	1	.000	8	0	0	0-0	7	14	12	2	1	5-1	5	10.29	43	.412	.500	0-0	—	0		-6	-0.7
2002	Tex A	2	1	.667	20	0	0	1-1	23.2	30	18	3	4	15-2	19	6.46	73	.316	.422	0-0	—	0		-4	-0.5
Total	9	22	25	.468	333	9	0	8-18	455.1	475	241	48	24	176-13	331	4.17	104	.271	.342	23-4	.174	0	89	6	0.6
TELGHEDER, DAVE David William B 11.11.1966 Middletown, NY BR/TR 6-3/212# d6.12																									
1993	NY N	6	2	.750	24	7	0	0-0	75.2	82	40	10	4	21-2	35	4.76	84	.276	.331	15-4	.067	-0	128	-4	-0.4
1994	NY N	0	1	.000	6	0	0	0-0	10	11	8	2	0	8-2	4	7.20	58	.282	.404	0-0	—	0		-3	-0.3
1995	NY N	1	2	.333	7	4	0	0-0	25.2	34	18	4	0	7-3	16	5.61	72	.318	.357	6-1	.333	1	95	-5	-0.4
1996	Oak A	4	7	.364	16	14	1-1	0-0	79.1	92	42	12	1	26-1	43	4.65	106	.292	.345	0-0	—	0	87	3	0.4
1997	Oak A	4	6	.400	20	19	0	0-0	101	134	71	15	2	35-1	55	6.06	75	.324	.373	2-0	.000	-0	127	-16	-1.2
1998	Oak A	0	1	.000	8	2	0	0-0	20	19	12	4	2	6-0	5	3.60	127	.235	.303	0-0	—	0	71	1	0.0
Total	6	15	19	.441	81	46	1-1	0-0	311.2	372	191	47	9	103-9	158	5.23	85	.297	.351	23-5	.130	-0	111	-24	-1.9
TELLMANN, TOM Thomas John B 3.29.1954 Warren, PA BR/TR 6-3/195# d6.9																									
1979	SD N	0	0	—	1	0	0	0-0	2.2	7	5	1	0	0-0	1	16.88	21	.467	.467	1-0	.000	-0		-4	-0.2
1980	SD N	3	0	1.000	6	2	2	1-0	22.1	23	5	0	0	8-0	9	1.61	213	.264	.326	8-0	.125	-0	130	4	0.6
1983	Mil A	9	4	.692	44	0	0	8-4	99.2	95	34	7	2	35-4	48	2.80	134	.259	.324	0-0	—	0		11	1.7
1984	Mil A	6	3	.667	50	0	0	4-3	81	82	28	6	1	31-10	28	2.78	139	.272	.338	0-0	—	0		10	1.2
1985	Oak A	0	0	—	11	0	0	0-0	21.1	33	12	3	1	9-1	8	5.06	76	.347	.406	0-0	—	0		-2	-0.1
Total	5	18	7	.720	112	2	2	13-7	227	240	84	17	4	83-15	94	3.05	123	.277	.341	9-0	.111	-0	130	19	3.2
TEMPLETON, CHUCK Charles Sherman B 6.1.1932 Detroit, MI D 10.9.1997 Irving, TX BR/TL 6-3/210# d9.9																									
1955	Bro N	0	1	.000	4	0	0	0	4.2	5	7	2	1	5-0	3	11.57	35	.294	.478	0-0	—	0		-4	-0.7
1956	Bro N	0	1	.000	6	2	0	0	16.1	20	13	2	0	10-0	8	6.61	60	.294	.380	3-1	.000	-0	111	-4	-0.3
Total	2	0	2	.000	10	2	0	0	21	25	20	4	1	15-0	11	7.71	52	.294	.402	3-1	.000	-0	111	-8	-1.0
TENER, JOHN John Kinley B 7.25.1863 County Tyrone, Ireland D 5.19.1946 Pittsburgh, PA BR/TR 6-4/180# d6.8.1885																									
1888	Chi N	7	5	.583	12	12	11-1	0	102	90	59	6	8	25	39	2.74	111	.228	.288	46	.196	-0	101	1	0.1
1889	Chi N	15	15	.500	35	30	28-1	0	287	302	192	16	7	105	105	3.64	114	.262	.328	150	.273	5*	112	14	1.7
1890	Pit P	3	11	.214	14	14	13	0	117	160	147	6	5	70	30	7.31	53	.312	.400	63	.190	2*	122	-43	-3.1
Total	3	25	31	.446	61	56	52-2	0	506	552	398	28	20	200	174	4.30	90	.268	.339	259	.239	6	112	-28	-1.3
TENNANT, JIM James McDonnell B 3.3.1907 Shepherdstown, WV D 4.16.1967 Trumbull, CT BR/TR 6-1/190# d9.28																									
1929	NY N	0	0	—	1	0	0	0	1	1	0	0	0	0	1	0.00	—	.333	.333	0-0	—	0		1	0.0
TENNEY, FRED Fred Clay B 7.9.1859 Marlborough, NH D 6.15.1919 Fall River, MA d4.28 ▲																									
1884	Bos U	3	1	.750	4	4	4	0	35	31	21	0		5	18	2.31	103	.221	.248	17	.118	-3	148	-1	-0.3
	Wil U	0	1	.000	1	1	1	0	8	6	5	0		4	10	1.13	237	.194	.286	3	.000	-1	64	1	0.0
	Year	3	2	.600	5	5	5	0	43	37	9	0		9	28	2.09	116	.216	.256	20	.100	-3	130	0	-0.3
TERLECKI, BOB Robert Joseph B 2.14.1945 Trenton, NJ BR/TR 5-8/185# d8.16																									
1972	Phi N	0	0	—	9	0	0	0-0	13.1	16	9	2	0	10-0	5	4.73	76	.308	.406	0-0	—	0		-2	-0.1
TERLECKY, GREG Gregory John B 3.20.1952 Culver City, CA BR/TR 6-3/200# d6.12																									
1975	StL N	0	1	.000	20	0	0	0-0	30.1	38	16	4	0	12-5	13	4.45	85	.306	.365	3-0	.333	0		-1	-0.1
TERPKO, JEFF Jeffrey Michael B 10.16.1950 Sayre, PA BR/TR 6/180# d9.21																									
1974	Tex A	0	0	—	3	0	0	0-0	7	6	1	0	0	4-0	3	1.29	278	.231	.333	0-0	—	0		2	0.1
1976	Tex A	3	3	.500	32	0	0	0-3	52.2	42	15	3	0	29-1	24	2.39	150	.223	.321	0-0	—	0		7	0.8
1977	Mon N	0	1	.000	13	0	0	0-0	20.2	28	13	2	0	15-1	14	5.66	67	.346	.448	1-0	.000	-0		-4	-0.2
Total	3	3	4	.429	48	0	0	0-3	80.1	76	29	5	0	48-2	41	3.14	116	.258	.357	1-0	.000	-0		5	0.7
TERRELL, WALT Charles Walter B 5.11.1958 Jeffersonville, IN BL/TR 6-2/205# d9.8																									
1982	NY N	0	3	.000	3	3	0	0-0	21	22	12	2	0	14-2	8	3.43	106	.268	.375	5-1	.400	1	32	-1	0.0
1983	NY N	8	8	.500	21	20	4-2	0-0	133.2	123	57	7	2	55-7	59	3.57	102	.251	.326	44-3	.182	3	78	3	0.6
1984	NY N	11	12	.478	33	33	3-1	0-0	215	232	99	16	4	80-1	114	3.52	101	.282	.345	75-1	.080	-4	107	0	-0.4
1985	Det A	15	10	.600	34	34	5-3	0-0	229	221	107	9	4	95-5	130	3.85	106	.255	.329	0-0	—	0	102	7	0.8
1986	Det A	15	12	.556	34	33	9-2	0-0	217.1	199	116	30	3	98-5	93	4.56	91	.245	.328	0-0	—	0	105	-8	-0.8
1987	†Det A	17	10	.630	35	35	10-1	0-0	244.2	254	123	30	3	94-7	143	4.05	105	.268	.333	0-0	—	0	116	6	0.5
1988	Det A	7	16	.304	29	29	11-1	0-0	206.1	199	101	20	2	78-8	84	3.97	96	.258	.326	0-0	—	0	92	-4	-0.4
1989	SD N	5	13	.278	19	19	4-1	0-0	123.1	134	65	14	0	26-1	63	4.01	87	.277	.313	40-1	.100	-0	73	-8	-1.0
	NY A	6	5	.545	13	13	1-1	0-0	83	102	52	9	2	24-0	30	5.20	74	.307	.356	0-0	—	0	122	-12	-1.4
1990	Pit N	2	7	.222	16	16	0	0-0	82.2	98	59	13	4	33-1	34	5.88	62	.295	.364	28-1	.107	-1	118	-21	-2.0
	Det A	6	4	.600	13	12	0	0-0	75.1	86	39	7	8	24-3	30	4.54	87	.290	.358	0-0	—	0	107	-4	-0.5
1991	Det A	12	14	.462	35	33	8-2	0-0	218.2	257	115	16	2	79-10	80	4.24	98	.301	.358	0-0	—	0	104	-3	-0.4
1992	Det A	7	10	.412	36	14	1	0-1	136.2	163	86	14	3	48-10	61	5.20	76	.298	.354	0-0	—	0	117	-19	-2.1
Total	11	111	124	.472	321	294	56-14	0-1	1986.2	2090	1031	187	37	748-60	929	4.22	93	.274	.339	192-7	.120	-1	103	-64	-7.1
TERRY, JOHN John Burchard B 11.1.1879 Waterbury, CT D 4.27.1933 Kansas City, MO d9.17																									
1902	Det A	0	1	.000	1	1	1	0	5	8	3	0	0	1	0	3.60	101	.364	.391	2-0	.000	-0	20	0	-0.1
1903	StL A	1	1	.500	3	1	1	0	17.2	21	6	0	3	4	2	2.55	114	.296	.359	9-0	.000	-1	245	1	0.0
Total	2	1	2	.333	4	2	2	0	22.2	29	9	0	3	5	2	2.78	111	.312	.366	11-0	.000	-2	128	1	-0.1
TERRY, YANK Lancelot Yank B 2.11.1911 Bedford, IN D 11.4.1979 Bloomington, IN BR/TR 6-1/180# d8.3																									
1940	Bos A	1	0	1.000	4	1	0	0	19.1	24	19	2	0	11	9	8.84	51	.304	.389	8-0	.250	0	234	-8	-0.4
1942	Bos A	6	5	.545	20	11	3	1	85	82	48	5	2	43	37	3.92	95	.248	.339	27-1	.111	-1	125	-4	-0.6
1943	Bos A	7	9	.438	30	22	7	1	163.2	147	70	8	1	63	63	3.52	94	.242	.314	45-3	.067	-3	97	-3	-0.6
1944	Bos A	6	10	.375	27	17	3	0	132.2	142	72	10	3	65	30	4.21	81	.276	.361	47-0	.234	1	114	-13	-1.2
1945	Bos A	0	4	.000	12	4	1	0	56.2	68	29	8	0	14	28	4.13	82	.296	.336	18-0	.111	-2	69	-4	-0.4
Total	5	20	28	.417	93	55	14	2	457.1	463	238	33	6	196	167	4.09	85	.263	.339	145-4	.145	-4	109	-32	-3.2
TERRY, RALPH Ralph Willard B 1.9.1936 Big Cabin, OK BR/TR 6-3/195# d8.6																									
1956	NY A	1	2	.333	3	3	0	0	13.1	17	15	2	0	11-0	8	9.45	41	.347	.459	6-0	.167	-0	100	-8	-1.3
1957	NY A	1	1	.500	7	2	1-1	0	20.2	18	7	1	0	8-1	7	3.05	118	.240	.310	4-0	.250	0	100	2	0.2
	KC A	4	11	.267	21	19	3-1	0	130.2	119	63	15	4	47-2	80	3.38	117	.239	.309	42-2	.143	-2*	71	4	0.3
	Year	5	12	.294	28	21	4-2	0	151.1	137	66	16	4	55-3	87	3.33	117	.239	.309	46-2	.152	-2	74	5	0.5
1958	KC A	11	13	.458	40	33	8-3	2	216.2	217	111	29	2	61-4	134	4.24	92	.262	.313	71-3	.197	-0	114	-7	-0.9
1959	KC A	2	4	.333	9	7	2	0	46.1	56	29	9	1	19-1	35	5.24	76	.308	.374	17-1	.176	-1	113	-5	-0.6
	NY A	3	7	.300	24	16	5-1	0	127.1	130	55	7	2	30-5	55	3.39	107	.270	.312	41-2	.098	-3	86	4	0.0
	Year	5	11	.313	33	23	7-1	0	173.2	186	59	16	3	49-6	90	3.89	96	.281	.329	58-3	.121	-3	95	-3	-0.6
1960	†NY A	10	8	.556	35	23	7-3	1	166.2	149	78	15	4	52-3	92	3.40	105	.237	.299	49-7	.122	-2	96	1	-0.1

Year	Tm Lg	W	L	Pct	G	GS	CG-Sho	SV-BS	IP	H	R	HR	HB	BB-IB	SO	ERA	AERA	OAV	OOB	AB-SH	AVG	PB	Sup	APR	PW
1961	†NY A	16	3	.842	31	27	9-2	0	188.1	162	74	19	1	42-0	86	3.15	118	.232	.275	66-5	.227	2	127	12	1.3
1962	†NY A☆	**23**	12	.657	43	**39**	14-3	2	**298.2**	257	123	40	3	57-1	176	3.19	117	.231	.268	106-11	.189	1	127	18	1.8
1963	†NY A	17	15	.531	40	**37**	**18**-3	1	268	246	103	29	4	39-1	114	3.22	109	.242	**.271**	87-9	.080	-6	103	10	0.5
1964	†NY A	7	11	.389	27	14	2-1	4	115	130	60	20	1	31-3	77	4.54	80	.283	.326	35-4	.200	1	103	-10	-1.4
1965	Cle A	11	6	.647	30	26	6-2	0	165.2	154	77	22	1	23-3	84	3.69	94	.242	.268	49-10	.143	2	116	-3	-0.3
1966	KC A	1	5	.167	15	10	0	0	64	65	35	7	1	15-3	33	3.80	89	.263	.305	14-1	.214	1	101	-5	-0.3
	NY N	0	1	.000	11	1	0	1	24.2	27	14	1	0	11-1	14	4.74	77	.293	.369	6-0	.167	-0	121	-3	-0.2
1967	NY N	0	0	—	2	0	0	0	3.1	1	0	0	0	0-0	5	0.00	—	.091	.091	0-0	—	0		1	0.1
Total	12	107	99	.519	338	257	75-20	11	1849.1	1748	844	216	24	446-28	1000	3.62	102	.249	.294	593-55	.160	-6	108	11	-0.9
TERRY, SCOTT Scott Ray B 11.21.1959 Hobbs, NM BR/TR 5-11/195# d4.9																									
1986	Cin N	1	2	.333	28	3	0	0-0	55.2	66	40	8	0	32-3	32	6.14	63	.300	.387	4-1	.250	0*	138	-12	-0.6
1987	StL N	0	0	—	11	0	0	0-0	13.1	13	5	0	0	8-2	9	3.38	123	.260	.362	2-0	.000	-0		1	0.1
1988	StL N	9	6	.600	51	11	1	3-4	129.1	119	48	5	0	34-6	65	2.92	119	.247	.295	28-5	.250	2	111	7	1.1
1989	StL N	8	10	.444	31	24	1	2-0	148.2	142	65	14	3	43-6	69	3.57	102	.253	.308	45-4	.156	2*	93	1	0.4
1990	StL N	2	6	.250	50	2	0	2-1	72	75	45	7	4	27-5	35	4.75	80	.264	.331	11-1	.455	2	83	-8	-0.7
1991	StL N	4	4	.500	65	0	0	1-2	80.1	76	31	1	0	32-14	52	2.80	133	.249	.320	7-0	.143	-0		7	0.7
Total	6	24	28	.462	236	40	2	8-7	499.1	491	234	35	7	176-36	262	3.73	99	.258	.321	97-11	.216	6	100	-4	1.0
TERRY, ADONIS William H B 8.7.1864 Westfield, MA D 2.24.1915 Milwaukee, WI BR/TR 5-11.5/168# d5.1 U1 ▲																									
1884	Bro AA	19	35	.352	56	55	54-2	0	476	486	308	10	8	72	230	3.55	93	.247	.276	236	.233	3*	66	-14	-1.2
1885	Bro AA	6	17	.261	25	23	23	1	209	213	147	9	4	42	96	4.26	77	.262	.301	264	.170	-3*	82	-16	-1.6
1886	Bro AA	18	16	.529	34	34	32-5	0	288.1	263	177	1	16	115	162	3.09	113	.231	.310	299	.237	2*	98	12	1.5
1887	Bro AA	16	16	.500	40	35	35-1	**3**	318	331	230	10	9	99	138	4.02	107	.262	.320	352	.293	7*	100	7	1.2
1888	Bro AA	13	8	.619	23	23	20-2	0	195	145	79	2	9	67	138	2.03	147	**.199**	.275	115	.252	3*	100	21	2.2
1889	†Bro AA	22	15	.595	41	39	35-2	0	326	285	189	6	16	126	186	3.29	113	.228	.307	160	.300	12*	101	10	2.1
1890	†Bro N	26	16	.619	46	44	38-1	0	370	362	200	3	15	133	185	2.94	117	.248	.317	363	.278	15*	102	19	2.9
1891	Bro N	6	16	.273	25	22	18-1	1	194	207	139	5	7	80	65	4.22	78	.263	.336	91	.209	3*	86	-18	-1.3
1892	Bal N	0	1	.000	1	1	1	0	9	7	7	0	0	7	3	4.00	86	.206	.341	4	.000	-1	18	-1	-0.1
	Pit N	18	7	.720	30	26	24-2	1	240	185	106	3	8	106	95	2.51	131	.204	.293	100	.160	1*	111	23	2.2
	Year	18	8	.692	31	27	25-2	1	249	192	112	3	8	113	98	2.57	129	.204	.295	104	.154	1	107	23	2.1
1893	Pit N	12	8	.600	26	19	14	0	170	177	121	5	11	99	52	4.45	102	.260	.363	71	.254	2	112	2	0.4
1894	Pit N	0	1	.000	1	1	0	0	0.2	2	5	0	0	4	0	67.50	8	.500	.750	0-0	—	0	68	-4	-0.5
	Chi N	5	11	.313	23	21	16	0	163.1	232	191	12	16	123	39	5.84	97	.330	.441	95-0	.347	4*	96	-15	-0.7
	Year	5	12	.294	24	22	16	0	164	234	199	12	16	127	39	6.09	93	.331	.444	95-0	.347	4	95	-20	-1.2
1895	Chi N	21	14	.600	38	34	31	0	311.1	346	228	4	17	131	88	4.80	106	.277	.354	137-5	.219	-6*	89	12	0.6
1896	Chi N	15	14	.517	30	28	25-1	0	235.2	273	166	6	10	88	75	4.43	102	.288	.354	99-3	.263	2	112	1	0.3
1897	Chi N	0	1	.000	1	1	1	0	8	11	10	0	2	6	1	10.13	44	.324	.452	3-1	.000	-1	64	-4	-0.3
Total	14	197	196	.501	440	406	367-17	6	3514.1	3525	2303	76	148	1298	1553	3.74	103	.252	.323	2389-9	.249	45	95	35	7.7
TERWILLIGER, DICK Richard Martin B 6.27.1906 Sand Lake, MI D 1.21.1969 Greenville, MI BR/TR 5-11/178# d8.18																									
1932	StL N	0	0	—	1	0	0	0	3	1	0	0	1	2	2	0.00	—	.143	.400	1-0	.000	-0		1	0.1
TESREAU, JEFF Charles Monroe B 3.5.1889 Silver Mine, MO D 9.24.1946 Hanover, NH BR/TR 6-2/218# d4.12 Mil 19D1-18 C1																									
1912	†NY N	17	7	.708	36	28	19-3	1	243	177	90	2	10	106	119	**1.96**	**172**	**.204**	.298	82-2	.146	-2	91	34	2.9
1913	†NY N	22	13	.629	41	**38**	17-1	0	282	222	98	7	7	119	167	2.17	144	**.220**	.306	95-3	.221	2	109	28	3.6
1914	NY N	26	10	.722	42	**41**	26-**8**	1	322.1	238	104	8	7	128	189	2.37	112	**.209**	.293	117-4	.239	6	144	12	1.9
1915	NY N	19	16	.543	43	39	24-8	3	306	235	98	4	5	75	176	2.29	112	.215	.269	103-2	.233	6	113	11	2.0
1916	NY N	14	14	.500	40	32	23-5	2	268.1	249	103	9	6	65	113	2.92	83	.250	.300	94-3	.191	2*	120	-13	-1.3
1917	†NY N	13	8	.619	33	20	11-1	2	183.2	168	71	6	3	58	85	3.09	83	.249	.312	61-3	.230	2	86	-8	-0.7
1918	NY N	4	4	.500	12	9	3-1	0	73.2	61	27	1	0	21	31	2.32	113	.227	.283	22-2	.318	2	106	1	0.4
Total	7	115	72	.615	247	207	123-27	9	1679	1350	591	37	38	572	880	2.43	114	.223	.295	574-19	.216	17	113	65	8.8
TESSMER, JAY Jay Weldon B 12.26.1971 Meadville, PA BR/TR 6-3/190# d8.27																									
1998	NY A	1	0	1.000	7	0	0	0-0	8.2	4	3	1	0	4-0	6	3.12	141	.143	.242	0-0	—	0		1	0.1
1999	NY A	0	0	—	6	0	0	0-0	6.2	16	11	1	1	4-2	3	14.85	32	.444	.512	0-0	—	0		-7	-0.3
2000	NY A	0	0	—	7	0	0	0-0	6.2	9	6	3	0	1-1	5	6.75	72	.300	.323	0-0	—	0		-2	-0.1
2002	NY A	0	0	—	2	0	0	0-0	1.1	0	1	0	0	2-0	0	6.75	65	.000	.333	0-0	—	0		0	0.0
Total	4	1	0	1.000	22	0	0	0-0	23.1	29	21	5	1	11-3	14	7.71	60	.296	.369	0-0	—	0		-8	-0.3
TEUT, NATE Nathan Mark B 3.11.1976 Newton, IA BR/TL 6-7/220# d5.4																									
2002	Fla N	0	1	.000	2	1	0	0-0	7.1	13	8	0	0	3-1	4	9.82	40	.394	.444	2-0	.000	-0	94	-5	-0.5
TEWKSBURY, BOB Robert Alan B 11.30.1960 Concord, NH BR/TR 6-4/200# d4.11																									
1986	NY A	9	5	.643	23	20	2	0-0	130.1	144	58	8	5	31-0	49	3.31	124	.282	.325	0-0	—	0	111	10	1.0
1987	NY A	1	4	.200	8	6	0	0-0	33.1	47	26	5	1	7-0	12	6.75	65	.338	.374	0-0	—	0	93	-8	-1.0
	Chi N	0	4	.000	7	3	0	0-1	18	32	15	1	0	13-3	10	6.50	66	.421	.500	5-0	.000	-1	49	-5	-0.9
1988	Chi N	0	0	—	1	1	0	0-0	3.1	6	5	1	0	2-0	1	8.10	45	.400	.444	2-0	.000	-0	270	-2	-0.1
1989	StL N	1	0	1.000	7	4	1-1	0-0	30	25	12	2	2	10-3	17	3.30	110	.225	.298	9-0	.111	-0	104	1	0.0
1990	StL N	10	9	.526	28	20	3-2	1-0	145.1	151	67	7	3	15-3	50	3.47	110	.267	.286	41-9	.171	1	84	4	0.6
1991	StL N	11	12	.478	30	30	3	0-0	191	206	86	13	5	38-2	75	3.25	114	.281	.317	58-7	.155	1	97	5	0.7
1992	StL N★	16	5	**.762**	33	32	5	0-0	233	217	63	15	3	20-0	91	2.16	157	.248	.265	70-6	.086	-2	108	32	2.7
1993	StL N	17	10	.630	32	32	2	0-0	213.2	258	99	15	6	20-1	97	3.83	104	.301	.318	69-7	.203	2*	110	5	0.9
1994	StL N	12	10	.545	24	24	4-1	0-0	155.2	190	97	19	3	22-1	79	5.32	78	.304	.328	54-4	.185	1	101	-20	-2.2
1995	Tex A	8	7	.533	21	21	4-1	0-0	129.2	169	75	8	3	20-4	53	4.58	105	.319	.346	1-0	.000	-0*	108	2	0.2
1996	SD N	10	10	.500	36	33	1	0-0	206.2	224	116	17	3	43-3	126	4.31	92	.275	.310	65-8	.031	-5	116	-11	-1.2
1997	Min A	8	13	.381	26	26	5-2	0-0	168.2	200	83	12	1	31-1	92	4.22	111	.297	.325	5-0	.200	0	73	9	1.1
1998	Min A	7	13	.350	26	25	1	0-0	148.1	174	82	19	6	20-1	60	4.79	100	.292	.318	1-0	.000	-0	69	1	0.2
Total	13	110	102	.519	302	277	31-7	1-1	1807	2043	884	142	41	292-22	812	3.92	104	.287	.316	380-41	.132	-3	98	23	2.0
THATCHER, GRANT Ulysses Grant B 2.23.1877 Maytown, PA D 3.17.1936 Lancaster, PA TR 5-10.5/180# d9.9																									
1903	Bro N	3	1	.750	4	4	4	0	28	33	12	1	0	7	9	2.89	110	.292	.333	11-0	.182	0	106	1	0.2
1904	Bro N	1	0	1.000	1	0	0	0	9	9	6	0	0	2	4	4.00	69	.281	.324	4-0	.250	0		-1	-0.1
Total	2	4	1	.800	5	4	4	0	37	42	18	1	0	9	13	3.16	98	.290	.331	15-0	.200	0	106	0	0.1
THAYER, GREG Gregory Allen B 10.23.1949 Cedar Rapids, IA BR/TR 5-11/182# d4.7																									
1978	Min A	1	1	.500	20	0	0	0-2	45	40	19	5	3	30-1	30	3.80	101	.258	.380	0-0	—	0		1	0.1
THEIS, JACK John Louis B 7.23.1891 Georgetown, OH D 7.6.1941 Georgetown, OH BR/TR 6/190# d7.5																									
1920	Cin N	0	0	—	1	0	0	0	2	1	0	0	0	3	0	0.00	—	.143	.400	0-0	—	0		1	0.0
THEISS, DUANE Duane Charles B 11.20.1953 Zanesville, OH BR/TR 6-3/185# d8.5																									
1977	Atl N	1	1	.500	17	0	0	0-0	20.2	26	16	1	1	16-5	7	6.53	68	.338	.439	1-1	.000	-0		-4	-0.3
1978	Atl N	0	0	—	3	0	0	0-0	6.1	3	1	0	1	3-0	3	1.42	285	.158	.292	1-0	.000	-0		2	0.1
Total	2	1	1	.500	20	0	0	0-0	27	29	17	1	2	19-5	10	5.33	82	.302	.410	2-1	.000	-0		-2	-0.2
THESENGA, JUG Arnold Joseph B 4.27.1914 Jefferson, SD D 12.3.2002 Wichita, KS BR/TR 6/200# d9.1																									
1944	Was A	0	0	—	5	1	0	0	12.1	18	9	0	0	12	2	5.11	64	.340	.462	2-1	.000	-0	257	-3	-0.2
THIEL, BERT Maynard Bert B 5.4.1926 Marion, WI BR/TR 5-10/185# d4.17																									
1952	Bos N	1	1	.500	4	0	0	0	7	11	7	1	2	4	6	7.71	47	.344	.447	0-0	—	0		-3	-0.7
THIELMAN, HENRY Henry Joseph B 10.3.1880 St.Cloud, MN D 9.2.1942 New York, NY BR/TR 5-11/175# d4.17 b-Jake																									
1902	NY N	0	1	.000	2	2	0	0	6	8	10	0	0	6	5	1.50	187	.320	.452	9-0	.111	-0*	121	-2	-0.3
	Cin N	9	15	.375	25	23	22	1	211	201	111	2	19	78	49	3.24	92	.251	.332	91-2	.132	-4*	90	-4	-0.8
	Year	9	16	.360	27	25	22	1	217	209	115	2	19	84	54	3.19	94	.253	.336	100-2	.130	-4	92	-10	-1.1

Year	Tm Lg	W	L	Pct	G	GS	CG-Sho	SV-BS	IP	H	R	HR	HB	BB-IB	SO	ERA	AERA	OAV	OOB	AB-SH	AVG	PB	Sup	APR	PW
1903	Bro N	0	3	.000	4	3	3	0	29	31	20	3	2	14	10	4.66	69	.330	.427	23-0	.217	1*	35	-4	-0.2
Total	2	9	19	.321	31	28	25	1	246	240	141	5	21	98	64	3.37	90	.261	.346	123-2	.146	-3	85	-10	-1.3
THIELMAN, JAKE John Peter B 5.20.1879 St.Cloud, MN D 1.28.1928 Minneapolis, MN BR/TR 5-11/175# d4.23 b-Henry																									
1905	StL N	15	16	.484	32	29	26	0	242	265	138	4	12	62	87	3.50	85	.281	.333	91-2	.231	8*	94	-18	-1.1
1906	StL N	0	1	.000	1	1	0	0	5	5	6	0	0	2	0	3.60	73	.263	.333	2-0	.500	0	139	-2	-0.3
1907	Cle A	11	8	.579	20	18	18-3	0	166	151	60	2	7	34	56	2.33	107	.245	.292	59-4	.203	1*	96	5	0.5
1908	Cle A	4	3	.571	11	8	5	0	61.2	59	26	2	4	9	15	3.65	65	.260	.300	23-3	.348	4*	125	-5	-0.1
	Bos A	0	0	—	1	0	0	0	0.2	3	4	1	0	0	0	40.50	6	.600	.600	0-0	—	0		-3	-0.1
	Year	4	3	.571	12	8	5	0	62.1	62	34	3	4	9	15	4.04	59	.267	.306	23-3	.348	4	125	-8	-0.2
Total	4	30	28	.517	65	56	49-3	0	475.1	483	234	9	23	107	158	3.16	86	.267	.316	175-9	.240	13	100	-23	-1.1
THIES, DAVE David Robert B 3.21.1937 Minneapolis, MN BR/TR 6-4/205# d4.20																									
1963	KC A	0	1	.000	9	2	0	0	25.1	26	15	2	2	12-0	9	4.62	84	.274	.364	6-0	.333	1	171	-2	0.0
THIES, JAKE Vernon Arthur B 4.1.1926 St.Louis, MO BR/TR 5-11/170# d4.24																									
1954	Pit N	3	9	.250	33	18	3-1	0	130.1	120	70	13	3	49	57	3.87	108	.244	.312	33-2	.030	-2	77	2	0.0
1955	Pit N	0	1	.000	1	1	0	0	3.2	5	5	0	1	3-1	0	4.91	84	.357	.450	0-0	—	0	65	-1	-0.2
Total	2	3	10	.231	34	19	3-1	0	134	125	75	13	4	52-1	57	3.90	107	.248	.317	33-2	.030	-2	76	1	-0.2
THIGPEN, BOBBY Robert Thomas B 7.17.1963 Tallahassee, FL BR/TR 6-3/195# d8.6																									
1986	Chi A	2	0	1.000	20	0	0	7-4	35.2	26	7	1	1	12-0	20	1.77	245	.205	.277	0-0	—	0		10	0.9
1987	Chi A	7	5	.583	51	0	0	16-3	89	86	30	10	3	24-5	52	2.73	168	.256	.311	0-0	—	0		18	2.8
1988	Chi A	5	8	.385	68	0	0	34-9	90	96	38	6	4	33-3	62	3.30	121	.273	.338	0-0	—	0		7	1.4
1989	Chi A	2	6	.250	61	0	0	34-9	79	62	34	10	1	40-3	47	3.76	101	.218	.311	0-0	—	0		2	0.3
1990	Chi A★	4	6	.400	**77**	0	0	**57-8**	88.2	60	20	5	1	32-3	70	1.83	210	.195	.271	0-0	—	0		20	4.2
1991	Chi A	7	5	.583	67	0	0	30-9	69.2	63	32	10	4	38-8	47	3.49	114	.245	.348	0-0	—	0		3	0.6
1992	Chi A	1	3	.250	55	0	0	22-7	55	58	29	4	3	33-5	45	4.75	82	.275	.375	0-0	—	0		-4	-0.5
1993	Chi A	0	0	—	25	0	0	1-1	34.2	51	25	5	5	12-0	19	5.71	73	.349	.410	0-0	—	0		-6	-0.3
	†Phi N	3	1	.750	17	0	0	0-2	19.1	23	13	2	1	9-1	10	6.05	66	.307	.384	1-0	.000	-0		-4	-0.7
1994	Sea A	0	2	.000	7	0	0	0-0	7.2	12	9	3	0	5-0	4	9.39	52	.353	.436	0-0	—	0		-4	-0.7
Total	9	31	36	.463	448	0	0	201-52	568.2	537	237	56	23	238-28	376	3.43	118	.252	.330	1-0	.000	-0		42	8.0
THOBE, J. J. John Joseph B 11.19.1970 Covington, KY BR/TR 6-6/200# d9.18 b-Tom																									
1995	Mon N	0	0	—	4	0	0	0-0	4	6	4	0	0	3-0	0	9.00	48	.333	.429	0-0	—	0		-2	-0.1
THOBE, TOM Thomas Neal B 9.3.1969 Covington, KY BL/TL 6-6/195# d9.12 b-J.J.																									
1995	Atl N	0	0	—	3	0	0	0-0	3.1	7	4	0	0	0-0	2	10.80	40	.412	.412	0-0	—	0		-2	-0.1
1996	Atl N	0	1	.000	4	0	0	0-0	6	5	2	1	0	0-0	1	1.50	294	.217	.208	1-0	.000	-0		1	0.2
Total	2	0	1	.000	7	0	0	0-0	9.1	12	6	1	0	0-0	3	4.82	90	.300	.293	1-0	.000	-0		-1	0.1
THOENEN, DICK Richard Crispin B 1.9.1944 Mexico, MO BR/TR 6-6/215# d9.16																									
1967	Phi N	0	0	—	1	0	0	0	1	2	1	0	0	0-0	0	9.00	38	.500	.500	0-0	—	0		-1	0.0
THOMAS, TOMMY Alphonse B 12.23.1899 Baltimore, MD D 4.27.1988 Dallastown, PA BR/TR 5-10/175# d4.17																									
1926	Chi A	15	12	.556	44	32	13-2	2	249	225	113	7	1	110	127	3.80	102	**.244**	.325	86-3	.186	-1	103	6	0.3
1927	Chi A	19	16	.543	40	**36**	24-3	1	**307.2**	271	110	16	1	94	107	2.98	136	.244	.303	95-19	.147	-3	87	**42**	3.8
1928	Chi A	17	16	.515	36	32	24-3	2	283	277	114	14	4	76	129	3.08	131	.259	.310	96-7	.219	3	93	31	3.5
1929	Chi A	14	18	.438	36	31	**24**-2	1	259.2	270	127	17	0	60	62	3.19	134	.269	.310	98-1	.255	2*	75	24	2.7
1930	Chi A	5	13	.278	34	27	7	0	169	229	125	13	1	44	58	5.22	89	.323	.364	56-4	.125	-4	91	-13	-1.4
1931	Chi A	10	14	.417	43	36	11-2	2	245.1	298	166	17	5	69	72	4.73	90	.292	.340	87-5	.241	1	108	-18	-1.4
1932	Chi A	3	3	.500	12	3	1	0	43.2	55	33	6	1	15	11	6.18	70	.307	.364	13-1	.077	-1	105	-8	-0.9
	Was A	8	7	.533	18	14	7-1	0	117	114	48	5	0	46	36	3.54	122	.255	.325	42-1	.238	1	100	12	1.3
	Year	11	10	.524	30	17	8-1	0	160.2	169	53	11	1	61	47	4.26	101	.270	.336	55-2	.200	0	101	6	0.4
1933	†Was A	7	7	.500	35	14	2	3	135	149	87	9	2	49	35	4.80	87	.273	.336	42-6	.238	1	128	-12	-1.1
1934	Was A	8	9	.471	33	18	7-1	1	133.1	154	87	9	3	58	42	5.47	79	.294	.368	38-7	.184	-0	88	-16	-1.8
1935	Was A	0	0	—	1	0	0	0	0.1	3	2	0	0	0	0	54.00	8	.750	.750	0-0	—	0		-2	-0.1
	Phi N	0	1	.000	4	1	0	0	12	15	9	2	0	5	3	5.25	86	.313	.377	3-0	.000	-0	56	-1	-0.1
1936	StL A	11	9	.550	36	21	8-1	0	179.2	219	132	25	4	72	40	5.26	102	.297	.362	58-7	.138	-3	97	-3	-0.6
1937	StL A	0	1	.000	17	2	0	0	30.2	46	26	2	1	10	10	7.04	69	.348	.399	4-0	.000	-1	117	-7	-0.4
	Bos A	0	2	.000	9	0	0	0	11	16	6	2	1	4	4	4.09	116	.340	.404	4-0	.250	-0		1	0.1
	Year	0	3	.000	26	2	0	0	41.2	62	39	4	2	14	14	6.26	77	.346	.400	8-0	.125	-1	118	-6	-0.3
Total	12	117	128	.478	398	267	128-15	12	2176.1	2341	1185	144	24	712	736	4.11	104	.275	.333	722-61	.195	-5	95	36	3.9
THOMAS, BLAINE Blaine M. "Baldy" B 8.1888 Glendora, CA D 8.21.1915 Glendora, CA BR/TR 5-10/165# d8.25																									
1911	Bos A	0	0	—	2	2	0	0	4.2	3	2	0	1	7	0	0.00	—	.273	.579	2-0	.500	0	99	1	0.1
THOMAS, BRAD Bradley Richard B 10.22.1977 Sydney, Australia BL/TL 6-4/220# d5.26																									
2001	Min A	0	2	.000	5	5	0	0-0	16.1	20	17	6	1	14-0	6	9.37	49	.303	.432	0-0	—	0	80	-8	-0.8
2003	Min A	0	1	.000	3	0	0	0-0	4.2	6	4	1	0	3-1	2	7.71	59	.316	.409	0-0	—	0		-2	-0.3
Total	2	0	3	.000	8	5	0	0-0	21	26	21	7	1	17-1	8	9.00	51	.306	.427	0-0	—	0	80	-10	-1.1
THOMAS, CARL Carl Leslie B 5.28.1932 Minneapolis, MN BR/TR 6-5/245# d4.19																									
1960	Cle A	1	0	1.000	4	0	0	0	9.2	8	8	1	1	10-0	5	7.45	50	.229	.413	3-1	.333	1*		-4	-0.3
THOMAS, LEFTY Clarence Fletcher B 10.4.1903 Glade Spring, VA D 3.21.1952 Charlottesville, VA BL/TL 6/183# d9.26																									
1925	Was A	0	2	.000	2	2	1	0	13	14	8	0	0	7	10	2.08	204	.264	.350	5-0	.000	-1	80	1	0.1
1926	Was A	0	0	—	6	0	0	0	8.2	8	7	0	0	10	3	5.19	74	.267	.450	2-0	.000	0		-2	-0.1
Total	2	0	2	.000	8	2	1	0	21.2	22	15	0	0	17	13	3.32	123	.265	.390	7-0	.000	-1	80	-1	0.0
THOMAS, CLAUDE Claude Alfred "Lefty" B 5.15.1890 Stanberry, MO D 3.6.1946 Sulphur, OK BL/TL 6-1/180# d9.14																									
1916	Was A	1	2	.333	7	4	1-1	0	28.1	27	14	1	2	12	7	4.13	68	.265	.353	10-0	.100	-1	102	-3	-0.4
THOMAS, FAY Fay Wesley "Scow" B 10.10.1903 Holyrood, KS D 8.12.1990 Chatsworth, CA BR/TR 6-2/195# d6.27																									
1927	NY N	0	0	—	9	0	0	0	16.1	19	10	3	1	4	11	3.31	117	.302	.353	2-0	.000	-0		0	-0.1
1931	Cle A	2	4	.333	16	2	1	0	48.2	63	34	2	1	32	25	5.18	89	.323	.421	13-0	.154	-1	64	-3	-0.4
1932	Bro N	0	1	.000	7	2	0	0	17	22	15	0	0	8	9	7.41	51	.306	.375	3-1	.000	-0	88	-6	-0.4
1935	StL A	7	15	.318	49	19	4	1	147	165	95	11	3	89	67	4.78	100	.289	.388	38-4	.105	-3	51	-2	-0.4
Total	4	9	20	.310	81	23	5	1	229	269	154	16	5	133	112	4.95	93	.299	.392	56-5	.107	-4	54	-11	-1.3
THOMAS, FROSTY Forrest B 5.23.1881 Faucett, MO D 3.18.1970 St.Joseph, MO BR/TR 6/185# d5.1																									
1905	Det A	0	1	.000	2	1	0	0	6	10	8	0	1	3	5	7.50	36	.370	.452	2-0	.000	0	104	-3	-0.5
THOMAS, LARRY Larry Wayne B 10.25.1969 Miami, FL BR/TL 6-1/190# d8.11																									
1995	Chi A	0	0	—	17	0	0	0-0	13.2	8	2	1	0	6-1	12	1.32	339	.167	.259	0-0	—	0		5	0.2
1996	Chi A	2	3	.400	57	0	0	0-2	30.2	32	11	1	3	14-2	20	3.23	147	.281	.374	0-0	—	0		6	0.8
1997	Chi A	0	0	—	5	0	0	0-0	3.1	3	3	1	0	2-0	0	8.10	54	.250	.357	0-0	—	0		-1	-0.1
Total	3	2	3	.400	79	0	0	0-2	47.2	43	16	3	3	22-3	32	3.02	154	.247	.342	0-0	—	0		10	0.9
THOMAS, BUD Luther Baxter B 9.9.1910 Faber, VA D 5.20.2001 North Garden, VA BR/TR 6/180# d9.13																									
1932	Was A	0	0	—	2	0	0	0	3	1	0	0	0	2	1	0.00	—	.100	.250	0-0	—	0		1	0.1
1933	Was A	0	0	—	2	0	0	0	4	11	8	1	1	2	1	15.75	27	.550	.609	1-0	.000	-0		-5	-0.2
1937	Phi A	8	15	.348	35	26	6-1	0	169.2	208	108	15	1	52	54	4.99	95	.295	.344	47-7	.128	-1	73	-4	-0.6
1938	Phi A	9	14	.391	42	29	7-1	0	212.1	259	138	23	2	62	48	4.92	98	.299	.347	69-7	.130	-3	87	-2	-0.5
1939	Phi A	0	1	.000	2	2	0	0	4	8	8	2	0	1	0	15.75	30	.421	.450	3-0	.000	-0	150	-5	-0.8
	Was A	0	0	—	4	0	0	0	9	11	7	0	0	2	0	6.00	72	.306	.342	2-0	.000	-0		-2	-0.1
	Det A	7	0	1.000	27	0	0	1	47.1	45	25	7	0	20	14	4.18	117	.254	.330	9-1	.111	-1		4	0.4

Year	Tm Lg	W	L	Pct	G	GS	CG-Sho	SV-BS	IP	H	R	HR	HB	BB-IB	SO	ERA	AERA	OAV	OOB	AB-SH	AVG	PB	Sup	APR	PW
	Year	7	1	.875	33	2	0	1	60.1	64	48	9	0	23	14	5.22	92	.276	.341	14-1	.071	-2	147	-3	-0.5
1940	Det A	0	1	.000	3	0	0	0	4	8	5	1	0	3	0	9.00	53	.421	.500	0-0	—	0		-2	-0.3
1941	Det A	1	3	.250	26	1	0	2	72.2	74	45	4	0	22	17	4.21	108	.260	.313	19-1	.105	-1	57	0	0.0
Total	7	25	34	.424	143	58	13-2	3	526	625	344	53	4	166	135	4.96	96	.292	.345	150-16	.120	-7	83	-15	-2.0
THOMAS, MIKE Michael Steven B 9.2.1969 Sacramento, CA BL/TL 6-2/205# d7.12																									
1995	Mil A	0	0	—	1	0	0	0-0	1.1	2	0	0	0	1-0	0	0.00	—	.333	.429	0-0	—	0		1	0.0
THOMAS, MYLES Myles Lewis B 10.22.1897 State College, PA D 12.12.1963 Toledo, OH BR/TR 5-9.5/170# d4.18																									
1926	†NY A	6	6	.500	33	13	3	0	140.1	140	79	6	3	65	38	4.23	91	.271	.356	43-5	.116	-3	136	-6	-0.7
1927	NY A	7	4	.636	21	9	1	0	88.2	111	58	4	1	43	25	4.87	79	.322	.398	27-3	.333	2	130	-11	-1.0
1928	NY A	1	0	1.000	12	1	0	0	31.2	33	19	3	0	9	10	3.41	110	.277	.328	10-0	.400	1*	135	-1	0.0
1929	NY A	0	2	.000	5	1	0	0	15	27	21	1	0	9	3	10.80	36	.409	.480	7-0	.143	-1	87	-12	-1.2
	Was A	7	8	.467	22	14	7	2	125.1	139	72	3	0	48	33	3.52	121	.288	.352	48-1	.292	2	99	4	0.6
	Year	7	10	.412	27	15	7	2	140.1	166	77	4	0	57	36	4.30	98	.302	.368	55-1	.273	1	99	-7	-0.6
1930	Was A	2	2	.500	12	2	0	0	33.2	49	35	3	0	15	12	8.29	55	.358	.421	11-0	.182	-1*	56	-14	-1.4
Total	5	23	22	.511	105	40	11	2	434.2	499	284	20	4	189	121	4.64	87	.299	.372	146-9	.240	0	116	-40	-3.7
THOMAS, ROY Roy Justin B 6.22.1953 Quantico, VA BR/TR 6-6/200# d9.21																									
1977	Hou N	0	0	—	4	0	0	0-0	6.1	5	2	0	0	3-0	4	2.84	126	.208	.296	0-0	—	0		1	0.0
1978	StL N	1	1	.500	16	1	0	3-0	28.1	21	14	0	0	16-3	16	3.81	92	.216	.316	4-0	.250	0	77	-1	-0.1
1979	StL N	3	4	.429	26	6	0	1-1	77	66	29	9	0	24-3	44	2.92	129	.237	.298	17-1	.059	-1	63	7	0.5
1980	StL N	2	3	.400	24	5	0	0-1	55	59	32	3	3	25-5	22	4.75	78	.274	.352	13-0	.154	-0	126	-6	-0.5
1983	Sea A	3	1	.750	43	0	0	1-3	88.2	95	44	3	2	32-3	77	3.45	124	.275	.337	0-0	—	0		5	0.2
1984	Sea A	3	2	.600	21	1	0	1-0	49.2	52	33	8	4	37-1	42	5.26	76	.280	.399	0-0	—	0	90	-7	-0.7
1985	Sea A	7	0	1.000	40	0	0	1-0	93.2	66	37	8	2	48-12	70	3.36	125	.202	.303	0-0	—	0		9	0.6
1987	Sea A	1	0	1.000	8	0	0	0-0	20.2	23	12	2	1	11-0	14	5.23	91	.299	.380	0-0	—	0		0	0.0
Total	8	20	11	.645	182	13	0	7-5	419.1	387	203	33	12	196-27	289	3.82	105	.250	.334	34-1	.118	-1	85	8	0.0
THOMAS, STAN Stanley Brown B 7.11.1949 Rumford, ME BR/TR 6-2/185# d7.5																									
1974	Tex A	0	0	—	12	0	0	0-0	13.2	22	10	1	0	6-2	8	6.59	54	.379	.431	0-0	—	0		-4	-0.2
1975	Tex A	4	4	.500	46	1	0	3-0	81.1	72	36	2	3	34-6	46	3.10	122	.239	.322	0-0	—	0	23	4	0.5
1976	Cle A	4	4	.500	37	7	2	6-2	105.2	88	33	5	4	41-4	54	2.30	152	.229	.309	0-0	—	0	137	13	1.3
1977	Sea A	2	6	.250	13	9	1	0-1	58.1	74	49	8	3	25-0	14	6.02	69	.310	.378	0-0	—	0	82	-15	-1.7
	NY A	1	0	1.000	3	0	0	0-0	6.1	7	7	0	0	4-0	1	7.11	56	.280	.367	0-0	—	0		-3	-0.4
	Year	3	6	.333	16	9	1	0-1	64.2	81	60	8	3	29-0	15	6.12	67	.307	.377	0-0	—	0	83	-17	-2.1
Total	4	11	14	.440	111	17	3	9-3	265.1	263	135	16	10	110-12	123	3.70	101	.261	.338	0-0	—	0	102	-5	-0.5
THOMAS, TOM Thomas R. "Savage Tom" B 12.27.1873 Shawnee, OH D 9.23.1942 Shawnee, OH BR/TR 6-4/195# d9.20																									
1894	Cle N	0	0	—	1	0	0	1	0.1	0	1	0	0	2	0	27.00	20	.000	.667	0-0	—	0		-1	-0.1
1899	StL N	1	1	.500	4	2	2	0	25	22	14	1	0	4	8	2.52	158	.237	.268	12-0	.250	0	90	3	0.2
1900	StL N	2	2	.500	5	1	1	0	26.1	38	22	2	1	4	7	3.76	97	.336	.364	11-1	.091	-1	171	-2	-0.4
Total	3	3	3	.500	10	3	3	1	51.2	60	37	3	1	10	15	3.31	115	.290	.326	23-1	.174	-1	117	0	-0.3
THOMASON, ERSKINE Melvin Erskine B 8.13.1948 Laurens, SC BR/TR 6-1/190# d9.18																									
1974	Phi N	0	0	—	1	0	0	0-0	1	0	0	0	0	0-0	1	0.00	—	.000	.000	0-0	—	0		0	0.0
THOMPSON, ART Arthur J. d6.17																									
1884	Was U	0	1	.000	1	1	1	0	8	10	11	0		3	8	6.75	36	.286	.342	3	.000	-1	18	-4	-0.4
THOMPSON, FORREST David Forrest B 3.3.1918 Mooresville, NC D 2.26.1979 Charlotte, NC BL/TL 5-11/195# d4.26																									
1948	Was A	6	10	.375	46	7	0	4	131.1	134	71	9	1	54	40	3.84	113	.262	.334	35-0	.286	2	74	4	0.7
1949	Was A	1	3	.250	9	1	1	0	16.1	22	11	1	1	9	8	4.41	97	.328	.416	5-0	.600	2*	21	-1	0.0
Total	2	7	13	.350	55	8	1	4	147.2	156	82	10	2	63	48	3.90	111	.270	.344	40-0	.325	4	68	3	0.7
THOMPSON, JUNIOR Eugene Earl B 6.7.1917 Latham, IL BR/TR 6-1/185# d4.26 Def 1943, Mil 1944-45																									
1939	†Cin N	13	5	.722	42	11	5-3	2	152.1	130	51	6	3	55	87	2.54	151	.236	.309	48-3	.229	0	70	22	2.4
1940	†Cin N	16	9	.640	33	31	17-3	0	225.1	197	90	10	2	96	103	3.32	114	.233	.313	79-8	.228	3	107	13	1.6
1941	Cin N	6	6	.500	27	15	4	1	109	117	65	6	3	57	46	4.87	74	.272	.361	30-7	.233	1	105	-14	-1.2
1942	Cin N	4	7	.364	29	10	1	0	101.2	86	61	5	2	53	35	3.36	98	.226	.324	30-1	.267	2	107	-7	-0.3
1946	NY N	4	6	.400	39	1	0	4	62.2	36	18	5	0	40	31	1.29	266	.190	.332	7-1	.143	0	50	12	2.1
1947	NY N	4	2	.667	15	0	0	0	35.2	36	20	3	1	27	13	4.29	95	.279	.408	6-0	.000	-1		-1	-0.2
Total	6	47	35	.573	185	68	27-6	7	686.2	602	305	35	11	328	315	3.26	113	.239	.329	200-20	.225	6	100	25	4.4
THOMPSON, FULLER Fuller Weidner B 5.1.1889 Los Angeles, CA D 2.19.1972 Los Angeles, CA BR/TR 5-11.5/164# d8.19																									
1911	Bos N	0	0	—	3	0	0	0	4.2	5	4	0	0	2	0	3.86	99	.294	.368	0-0	—	0		0	0.0
THOMPSON, HARRY Harold B 9.9.1889 Nanticoke, PA D 2.14.1951 Reno, NV BL/TL 5-8/150# d4.24																									
1919	Was A	0	3	.000	12	2	0	1	43.1	48	21	0	2	8	10	3.53	91	.293	.333	32-2	.250	1*	37	-1	0.1
	Phi A	0	1	.000	3	0	0	0	12	16	9	4	0	3	1	6.75	51	.327	.365	6-0	.000	-1*		-3	-0.3
	Year	0	4	.000	15	2	0	1	55.1	64	32	4	2	11	11	4.23	77	.300	.341	38-2	.211	0	36	-5	-0.2
THOMPSON, LEE John Dudley "Lefty" B 2.26.1898 Smithfield, UT D 2.17.1963 Santa Barbara, CA BL/TL 6-1/185# d9.4																									
1921	Chi A	0	3	.000	4	4	0	0	20.2	32	21	0	0	6	4	8.27	51	.333	.373	7-1	.286	0	89	-9	-1.0
THOMPSON, GUS John Gustav B 6.22.1877 Humboldt, IA D 3.28.1958 Kalispell, MT 6-2/185# d8.31																									
1903	†Pit N	2	2	.500	5	4	3	0	43	52	30	1	1	16	22	3.56	91	.295	.358	16-0	.250	0	109	-3	-0.2
1906	StL N	2	11	.154	17	12	8	0	103	111	61	2	5	25	36	4.28	61	.285	.336	34-0	.176	-1	60	-18	-2.1
Total	2	4	13	.235	22	16	11	0	146	163	91	3	6	41	58	4.07	69	.288	.343	50-0	.200	-0	74	-21	-2.3
THOMPSON, JOCKO John Samuel B 1.17.1917 Beverly, MA D 2.3.1988 Olney, MD BL/TL 6/185# d9.21																									
1948	Phi N	1	0	1.000	2	2	1	0	13	10	4	0	0	9	7	2.77	142	.233	.365	3-0	.000	0	135	2	0.2
1949	Phi N	1	3	.250	8	5	1	0	31.1	38	24	6	0	11	12	6.89	57	.314	.371	11-0	.182	-0*	67	-9	-1.0
1950	Phi N	0	0	—	2	0	0	0	4	1	1	0	0	4	2	0.00	—	.077	.294	0-0	—	0		1	0.1
1951	Phi N	4	8	.333	29	14	3-2	1	119.1	102	55	12	2	59	60	3.85	100	.231	.325	39-1	.103	-1*	102	1	-0.1
Total	4	6	11	.353	41	21	5-2	1	167.2	151	84	18	2	83	81	4.24	91	.244	.336	53-1	.113	-1	96	-5	-0.8
THOMPSON, JUSTIN Justin Willard B 3.8.1973 San Antonio, TX BL/TL 6-4/215# d5.27																									
1996	Det A	1	6	.143	11	11	0	0-0	59	62	35	7	2	31-2	44	4.58	111	.267	.356	0-0	—	0	58	2	0.3
1997	Det A★	15	11	.577	32	32	4	0-0	223.1	188	82	20	2	66-1	151	3.02	152	.233	.289	2-0	.000	-0	91	38	4.1
1998	Det A	11	15	.423	34	34	5	0-0	222	227	114	20	2	79-4	149	4.05	116	.267	.329	7-0	.143	-0	97	14	1.4
1999	Det A	9	11	.450	24	24	0	0-0	142.2	152	85	24	4	59-1	83	5.11	97	.274	.344	5-0	.000	-1	82	-2	-0.3
Total	4	36	43	.456	101	101	9	0-0	647	629	316	71	10	235-8	427	3.98	120	.257	.322	14-0	.071	-1	87	52	5.5
THOMPSON, MARK Mark Radford B 4.7.1971 Russellville, KY BR/TR 6-2/205# d7.26																									
1994	Col N	1	1	.500	2	2	0	0-0	9	16	9	2	1	8-0	5	9.00	55	.400	.510	4-1	.000	-0	92	-3	-0.6
1995	†Col N	2	3	.400	21	5	0	0-0	51	73	42	7	1	22-2	30	6.53	83	.349	.407	13-1	.385	1	94	-5	-0.4
1996	Col N	9	11	.450	34	28	3-1	0-1	169.2	189	109	25	13	74-1	99	5.30	99	.285	.367	58-5	.138	-2	99	-1	-0.4
1997	Col N	3	3	.500	6	6	0	0-0	29.2	40	27	8	4	13-0	9	7.89	66	.323	.399	11-2	.182	1	116	-7	-1.0
1998	Col N	1	2	.333	6	6	0	0-0	23.1	36	22	8	5	12-0	14	7.71	67	.379	.465	7-0	.143	-0	77	-6	-0.6
1999	StL N	1	3	.250	5	5	0	0-0	29.1	26	12	1	2	17-1	22	2.76	166	.241	.354	8-1	.000	-1	76	5	0.5
2000	StL N	1	1	.500	20	0	0	0-1	25	24	21	4	3	15-0	19	5.04	92	.250	.365	3-0	.000	-0		-4	-0.3
Total	7	18	24	.429	94	52	3-1	0-2	337	404	242	55	29	161-4	198	5.74	90	.303	.386	104-10	.154	-3	96	-21	-2.8
THOMPSON, MIKE Michael Wayne B 9.6.1949 Denver, CO BR/TR 6-3/190# d5.19																									
1971	Was A	1	6	.143	16	12	0	0-0	66.2	53	39	3	3	54-2	41	4.86	68	.222	.370	17-0	.118	0	86	-11	-1.0
1973	StL N	0	0	—	2	2	0	0-0	4	1	0	0	0	5-0	3	0.00	—	.077	.333	1-0	.000	-0	60	2	0.1

Year	Tm Lg	W	L	Pct	G	GS	CG-Sho	SV-BS	IP	H	R	HR	HB	BB-IB	SO	ERA	AERA	OAV	OOB	AB-SH	AVG	PB	Sup	APR	PW
1974	StL N	0	3	.000	19	4	0	0-0	38.1	37	24	1	2	35-4	25	5.63	64	.274	.430	8-0	.000	-1	104	-7	-0.6
	Atl N	0	0	—	1	1	0	0-0	4	7	2	0	0	2-0	2	4.50	84	.412	.474	1-0	1.000	0	115	0	0.0
	Year	0	3	.000	20	5	0	0-0	42.1	44	7	1	2	37-4	27	5.53	65	.289	.435	9-0	.111	-1	107	-7	-0.6
1975	Atl N	0	6	.000	16	10	0	0-0	51.2	60	32	2	0	32-0	42	4.70	80	.305	.397	14-2	.071	-1	81	-5	-0.6
Total	4	1	15	.063	54	29	0	0-0	164.2	158	97	6	5	128-6	113	4.86	73	.263	.394	41-2	.098	-1	86	-21	-2.1
THOMPSON, RICH Richard Neil B 11.1.1958 New York, NY BR/TR 6-3/225# d4.28																									
1985	Cle A	3	8	.273	57	0	0	5-6	80	95	63	8	6	48-6	30	6.30	66	.303	.398	0-0	—	0		-20	-2.7
1989	Mon N	0	2	.000	19	1	0	0-0	33	27	11	2	2	11-2	15	2.18	162	.241	.315	2-0	.000	0	50	4	0.2
1990	Mon N	0	0	—	1	0	0	0-0	1	1	0	0	0	0-0	0	0.00	—	.250	.250	0-0	—	0		0	0.0
Total	3	3	10	.231	77	1	0	5-6	114	123	74	10	8	59-8	45	5.05	78	.286	.376	2-0	.000	0	50	-16	-2.5
THOMPSON, TOMMY Thomas Carl B 11.7.1889 Spring City, TN D 1.16.1963 LaJolla, CA BR/TR 5-9.5/170# d6.5 b-Homer																									
1912	NY A	0	2	.000	7	2	1	0	32.2	43	32	0	3	13	15	6.06	59	.341	.415	10-1	.300	1*	82	-9	-0.4
THOMPSON, WILL Will McLain B 8.30.1870 Pittsburgh, PA D 6.9.1962 Pittsburgh, PA BR/TR 5-11.5/190# d7.9																									
1892	Pit N	0	1	.000	1	1	0	0	3	3	5	0	1	5	0	3.00	110	.250	.500	0	—	0	96	-1	-0.1
THOMSON, JOHN John Carl B 10.1.1973 Vicksburg, MS BR/TR 6-3/175# d5.11																									
1997	Col N	7	9	.438	27	27	2-1	0-0	166.1	193	94	15	5	51-0	106	4.71	110	.296	.350	47-6	.213	-0	82	7	0.6
1998	Col N	8	11	.421	26	26	2	0-0	161	174	86	21	2	49-0	106	4.81	108	.282	.335	50-9	.120	-3	84	8	0.5
1999	Col N	1	10	.091	14	13	1	0-0	62.2	85	62	11	1	36-1	34	8.04	72	.324	.405	18-0	.167	-0	71	-13	-1.8
2001	Col N	4	5	.444	14	14	1-1	0-0	93.2	84	46	15	4	25-3	68	4.04	132	.239	.295	29-6	.241	1	98	11	1.0
2002	Col N	7	8	.467	21	21	0	0-0	127.1	136	77	21	2	27-6	76	4.88	98	.268	.304	34-3	.176	-0	98	-2	-0.2
	NY N	2	6	.250	9	9	0	0-0	54.1	65	39	7	0	17-3	31	4.31	92	.290	.336	18-3	.278	1	101	-7	-0.7
	Year	9	14	.391	30	30	0	0-0	181.2	201	43	28	2	44-9	107	4.71	96	.275	.314	52-6	.212	1	99	-9	-0.9
2003	Tex A	13	14	.481	35	35	3-1	0-0	217	234	125	27	4	49-2	136	4.85	102	.276	.316	1-0	.000	-0	97	3	0.4
Total	6	42	63	.400	146	145	9-3	0-0	882.1	971	529	117	18	254-15	557	4.93	103	.281	.330	197-27	.188	-2	90	7	-0.2
THORMAHLEN, HANK Herbert Ehler "Lefty" B 7.5.1896 Jersey City, NJ D 2.6.1955 Los Angeles, CA BL/TL 6/180# d9.29																									
1917	NY A	0	1	.000	1	1	0	0	8	9	3	0	1	4	5	2.25	119	.281	.378	2-0	.000	-0	27	0	0.0
1918	NY A	7	3	.700	16	12	5-2	0	112.2	85	39	1	6	52	22	2.48	114	.217	.318	39-4	.077	-3	118	4	0.0
1919	NY A	12	8	.600	30	25	13-2	1	188.2	155	69	10	4	61	62	2.62	122	.228	.295	59-3	.186	-0	103	12	1.1
1920	NY A	9	6	.600	29	15	6	1	143.1	178	86	5	2	43	35	4.14	92	.312	.362	45-5	.222	1	116	-7	-0.5
1921	Bos A	1	7	.125	23	9	3	0	96.1	101	56	3	6	34	17	4.48	94	.277	.349	23-1	.174	-1	57	-3	-0.3
1925	Bro N	0	3	.000	5	2	0	0	16	22	14	0	2	9	7	3.94	106	.333	.429	5-0	.200	0	61	-2	-0.2
Total	6	29	28	.509	104	64	27-4	2	565	550	267	19	21	203	148	3.33	105	.261	.332	173-13	.168	-3	98	4	0.1
THORMODSGARD, PAUL Paul Gayton B 11.10.1953 San Francisco, CA BR/TR 6-2/190# d4.10																									
1977	Min A	11	15	.423	37	37	8-1	0-0	218	236	122	25	3	65-1	94	4.62	86	.280	.331	0-0	—	0	111	-15	-1.6
1978	Min A	1	6	.143	12	12	1	0-0	66	81	40	7	1	17-0	23	5.05	76	.308	.347	0-0	—	0	72	-8	-0.8
1979	Min A	0	0	—	1	0	0	0-0	1	3	1	1	0	0-0	1	9.00	49	.500	.500	0-0	—	0		0	0.0
Total	3	12	21	.364	50	49	9-1	0-0	285	320	163	33	4	82-1	118	4.74	84	.288	.336	0-0	—	0	102	-23	-2.4
THORNTON, JOHN John B 1870 Washington, DC BL 5-10.5/175# d8.14																									
1889	Was N	0	1	.000	1	1	1	0	9	8	11	0	0	7	3	5.00	79	.229	.357	4	.000	-1	153	-2	-0.2
1891	Phi N	15	16	.484	37	32	23-1	2	269	268	161	3	10	115	52	3.68	93	.250	.328	123	.138	-7*	91	-6	-1.2
1892	Phi N	0	2	.000	3	2	1	0	12	16	19	1	0	17	2	12.75	25	.308	.478	13	.385	1*	127	-10	-1.1
Total	3	15	19	.441	41	35	25-1	2	290	292	191	4	10	139	57	4.10	83	.252	.337	140	.157	-7	95	-18	-2.5
THORNTON, WALTER Walter Miller B 2.18.1875 Lewiston, ME D 7.14.1960 Los Angeles, CA BL/TL 6-1/180# d7.1 ▲																									
1895	Chi N	2	0	1.000	7	2	2	1	40	58	50	3	5	31	13	6.07	84	.333	.448	22-0	.318	2*	196	-8	-0.2
1896	Chi N	2	1	.667	5	5	2	0	23.2	30	26	1	0	13	10	5.70	80	.306	.387	22-0	.364	2*	144	-5	-0.4
1897	Chi N	6	7	.462	16	16	15	0	130.1	164	91	4	6	51	55	4.70	95	.305	.371	265-4	.321	4*	107	0	0.4
1898	Chi N	13	10	.565	28	25	21-2	0	215.1	226	116	4	18	56	56	3.34	107	.268	.327	210-3	.295	6*	104	10	1.4
Total	4	23	18	.561	56	48	40-2	1	409.1	478	283	12	29	151	134	4.18	97	.289	.359	519-7	.312	13	114	-3	1.2
THORPE, BOB Robert Joseph B 1.12.1935 San Diego, CA D 3.17.1960 San Diego, CA BR/TR 6-1/170# d4.17																									
1955	Chi N	0	0	—	2	0	0	0	3	4	2	0	0	0-0	0	3.00	136	.333	.333	0-0	—	0		0	0.0
THROOP, GEORGE George Lynford B 11.24.1950 Pasadena, CA BR/TR 6-7/205# d9.7																									
1975	KC A	0	0	—	7	0	0	2-0	9	8	5	1	0	2-0	8	4.00	97	.250	.286	0-0	—	0		0	0.0
1977	KC A	0	0	—	4	0	0	1-0	5.1	1	2	1	0	4-0	1	3.38	120	.059	.238	0-0	—	0		1	0.0
1978	KC A	1	0	1.000	1	0	0	0-0	3	2	0	0	0	3-0	2	0.00	—	.222	.417	0-0	—	0		1	0.3
1979	KC A	0	0	—	4	0	0	0-0	2.2	7	4	0	0	5-2	1	13.50	32	.467	.600	0-0	—	0		-2	-0.1
	Hou N	1	0	1.000	14	0	0	0-0	22.1	23	10	4	1	11-0	15	3.22	109	.271	.357	3-0	.000	-0		0	0.0
Total	4	2	0	1.000	30	0	0	3-0	42.1	41	21	6	1	25-2	27	3.83	97	.259	.360	3-0	.000	-0		0	0.2
THUMAN, LOU Louis Charles Frank B 12.13.1916 Baltimore, MD D 12.19.2000 Baltimore, MD BR/TR 6-2/185# d9.8 Mil 1941-45																									
1939	Was A	0	0	—	3	0	0	0	4	5	6	0	0	2	1	9.00	48	.278	.350	0-0	—	0		-3	-0.1
1940	Was A	0	1	.000	2	0	0	0	5	10	11	0	0	7	0	14.40	29	.400	.531	2-0	.000	-0		-7	-0.9
Total	2	0	1	.000	5	0	0	0	9	15	17	0	0	9	1	12.00	35	.349	.462	2-0	.000	-0		-10	-1.0
THURMAN, COREY Corey Lamar B 11.5.1978 Augusta, GA BR/TR 6-1/215# d4.5																									
2002	Tor A	2	3	.400	43	1	0	0-2	68	65	34	11	2	45-2	56	4.37	106	.248	.362	1-1	.000	-0	60	3	0.1
2003	Tor A	1	1	.500	6	3	0	0-0	15.1	21	11	3	0	9-1	11	6.46	71	.313	.395	0-0	—	0	100	-3	-0.3
Total	2	3	4	.429	49	4	0	0-2	83.1	86	45	14	2	54-3	67	4.75	97	.261	.369	1-1	.000	-0	90	0	-0.2
THURMAN, MIKE Michael Richard B 7.22.1973 Corvallis, OR BR/TR 6-4/190# d9.2																									
1997	Mon N	1	0	1.000	5	2	0	0-0	11.2	8	9	3	1	4-0	8	5.40	78	.186	.271	2-1	.500	0	154	-2	-0.1
1998	Mon N	4	5	.444	14	13	0	0-0	67	60	38	7	3	26-2	32	4.70	89	.238	.312	23-2	.000	-2	119	-3	-0.6
1999	Mon N	7	11	.389	29	27	0	0-0	146.2	140	84	17	7	52-4	85	4.05	111	.251	.321	40-4	.025	-3	77	3	-0.1
2000	Mon N	4	9	.308	17	17	0	0-0	88.1	112	69	9	3	46-4	52	6.42	75	.315	.393	24-6	.042	-2	78	-15	-2.0
2001	Mon N	9	11	.450	28	26	0	0-0	147	172	90	21	6	50-7	96	5.33	84	.294	.351	42-3	.024	-3	99	-12	-1.7
2002	NY A	1	0	1.000	12	2	0	0-1	33	45	21	2	1	12-1	23	5.18	84	.328	.387	0-0	—	0	244	-3	-0.1
Total	6	26	36	.419	105	87	0	0-1	493.2	537	311	59	21	190-18	296	5.05	89	.278	.346	131-16	.031	-10	95	-32	-4.6
THURMOND, MARK Mark Anthony B 9.12.1956 Houston, TX BL/TL 6/193# d5.14																									
1983	SD N	7	3	.700	21	18	2	0-0	115.1	104	40	7	2	33-2	49	2.65	132	.248	.304	37-6	.054	-2	114	10	0.7
1984	†SD N	14	8	.636	32	29	1-1	0-0	178.2	174	70	12	0	55-3	57	2.97	120	.256	.310	58-7	.190	1	105	10	1.5
1985	SD N	7	11	.389	36	23	1-1	2-1	138.1	154	70	9	3	44-5	57	3.97	89	.291	.347	34-9	.088	-2	89	-7	-1.0
1986	SD N	3	7	.300	17	15	2-1	0-0	70.2	96	58	7	0	27-5	32	6.50	56	.325	.380	24-2	.250	1*	93	-23	-2.6
	Det A	4	1	.800	25	4	0	3-1	51.2	44	13	7	0	17-2	17	1.92	216	.234	.296	0-0	—	0	93	13	1.2
1987	†Det A	0	1	.000	48	0	0	5-2	61.2	83	32	5	0	24-4	21	4.23	100	.331	.384	0-0	—	0		0	0.0
1988	Bal A	1	8	.111	43	6	0	3-0	74.2	80	43	10	2	27-3	29	4.58	85	.277	.339	0-0	—	0	58	-6	-0.7
1989	Bal A	2	4	.333	49	2	0	4-0	90	102	43	6	1	17-2	34	3.90	97	.288	.322	0-0	—	0	48	-2	-0.2
1990	SF N	2	3	.400	43	0	0	4-3	56.2	53	26	6	0	18-3	24	3.34	109	.257	.309	5-0	.000	-1		1	0.1
Total	8	40	46	.465	314	97	6-3	21-7	837.2	890	395	69	8	262-29	320	3.69	101	.277	.330	158-24	.139	-1	94	-4	-1.0
THURSTON, SLOPPY Hollis John B 6.2.1899 Fremont, NE D 9.14.1973 Los Angeles, CA BR/TR 5-11/165# d4.19																									
1923	StL A	0	0	—	2	1	0	0	4	8	4	0	0	2	0	6.75	62	.421	.476	0-0	—	0	139	-1	-0.1
	Chi A	7	8	.467	44	12	8	4	191.2	223	70	11	1	36	55	3.05	130	.308	.341	79-1	.316	6*	85	22	2.2
	Year	7	8	.467	46	13	8	4	195.2	231	74	11	1	38	55	3.13	127	.310	.345	79-1	.316	6	90	22	2.1
1924	Chi A	20	14	.588	38	36	**28**-1	1	291	330	150	17	6	60	37	3.80	108	.290	.329	122-5	.254	4*	117	9	1.5
1925	Chi A	10	14	.417	36	25	9	1	183	250	140	14	5	47	35	5.95	70	.335	.378	84-3	.286	7*	125	-38	-3.3
1926	Chi A	6	8	.429	31	13	6-1	3	134.1	164	85	10	1	36	35	5.02	77	.311	.356	61-1	.311	6*	99	-17	-1.2

Year	Tm Lg	W	L	Pct	G	GS	CG-Sho	SV-BS	IP	H	R	HR	HB	BB-IB	SO	ERA	AERA	OAV	OOB	AB-SH	AVG	PB	Sup	APR	PW
1927	Was A	13	13	.500	29	28	13-2	0	205.1	254	118	16	2	60	38	4.47	91	.308	.356	92-4	.315	9*	98	-8	-0.1
1930	Bro N	6	4	.600	24	11	5-2	1	106	110	46	4	0	17	26	3.40	145	.266	.295	50-4	.200	-0*	74	19	1.6
1931	Bro N	9	9	.500	24	17	11	0	143	175	72	3	1	39	23	3.97	96	.301	.346	60-2	.217	2	138	-2	0.0
1932	Bro N	12	8	.600	28	19	10-2	0	153	174	81	14	1	38	35	4.06	94	.287	.330	56-2	.304	5*	134	-5	0.0
1933	Bro N	6	8	.429	32	15	5	3	131.1	171	70	4	6	34	22	4.52	71	.319	.366	44-1	.159	-1	100	-16	-1.6
Total	9	89	86	.509	288	177	95-8	13	1542.2	1859	836	93	23	369	306	4.24	94	.304	.346	648-23	.270	38	111	-37	-1.0
TIANT, LUIS Luis Clemente (Vega) B 11.23.1940 Marianao, Cuba BR/TR 5-11/190# d7.19																									
1964	Cle A	10	4	.714	19	16	9-3	1	127	94	41	13	2	47-2	105	2.83	127	.207	.283	45-3	.111	-1	116	13	1.2
1965	Cle A	11	11	.500	41	30	10-2	1	196.1	166	88	20	3	66-3	152	3.53	99	.228	.293	68-4	.088	-2	115	-1	-0.3
1966	Cle A	12	11	.522	46	16	7-**5**	8	155	121	50	16	2	50-4	145	2.79	123	.213	.279	36-8	.111	-1	88	13	1.8
1967	Cle A	12	9	.571	33	29	9-1	2	213.2	177	76	24	1	67-2	219	2.74	119	.221	.282	71-3	.254	5	109	12	1.7
1968	Cle A★	21	9	.700	34	32	19-**9**	0	258.1	152	53	16	4	73-4	264	**1.60**	**185**	**.168**	.233	87-11	.080	-5	97	**39**	**4.4**
1969	Cle A	9	20	.310	38	37	9-1	0-0	249.2	229	123	37	8	129-11	156	3.71	102	.246	.340	81-4	.235	6	87	-1	0.5
1970	†Min A	7	3	.700	18	17	2-1	0-0	92.2	84	36	12	2	41-0	50	3.40	110	.246	.328	32-3	.406	5	131	5	1.2
1971	Bos A	1	7	.125	21	10	1	0-0	72.1	73	42	8	1	32-1	59	4.85	76	.259	.333	19-0	.158	-0	87	-9	-0.9
1972	Bos A	15	6	.714	43	19	12-6	3-4	179	128	45	7	0	65-5	123	**1.91**	**169**	.202	.275	56-3	.107	-2	114	24	2.9
1973	Bos A	20	13	.606	35	35	23	0-0	272	217	105	32	7	78-3	206	3.34	120	.219	**.278**	0-0	—	0	89	22	2.6
1974	Bos A★	22	13	.629	38	38	25-**7**	0-0	311.1	281	106	21	4	82-3	176	2.92	132	.241	.291	0-0	—	0	95	32	3.5
1975	†Bos A	18	14	.563	35	35	18-2	0-0	260	262	126	25	4	72-0	142	4.02	102	.264	.315	1-0	.000	-0	104	3	0.2
1976	Bos A★	21	12	.636	38	38	19-3	0-0	279	274	107	25	3	64-2	131	3.06	128	.260	.303	1-0	.000	-0	108	25	2.8
1977	Bos A	12	8	.600	32	32	3-3	0-0	188.2	210	98	26	2	51-3	124	4.53	99	.279	.325	0-0	—	0	117	1	0.0
1978	Bos A	13	8	.619	32	31	12-5	0-0	212.1	185	80	26	5	57-4	114	3.31	125	.234	.289	0-0	—	0	105	21	1.9
1979	NY A	13	8	.619	30	30	5-1	0-0	195.2	190	94	22	0	53-1	104	3.91	105	.251	.299	0-0	—	0	118	4	0.3
1980	NY A	8	9	.471	25	25	3	0-0	136.1	139	79	10	1	50-3	84	4.89	80	.265	.326	0-0	—	0	109	-13	-1.3
1981	Pit N	2	5	.286	9	9	1	0-0	57.1	54	31	3	0	19-2	32	3.92	92	.243	.303	16-2	.188	1	85	-3	-0.3
1982	Cal A	2	2	.500	6	5	0	0-0	29.2	39	20	3	0	8-0	30	5.76	70	.310	.351	0-0	—	0	121	-5	-0.7
Total	19	229	172	.571	573	484	187-49	15-<u>4</u>	3486.1	3075	1400	346	49	1104-53	2416	3.30	114	.236	.297	513-41	.164	5	105	182	21.5
TIBBS, JAY Jay Lindsey B 1.4.1962 Birmingham, AL BR/TR 6-3/185# d7.15																									
1984	Cin N	6	2	.750	14	14	3-1	0-0	100.2	87	34	4	0	33-1	40	2.86	132	.238	.302	36-1	.139	-1	105	10	0.6
1985	Cin N	10	16	.385	35	34	5-2	0-0	218	216	111	14	0	83-10	98	3.92	97	.262	.326	65-6	.092	-3*	96	-5	-0.9
1986	Mon N	7	9	.438	35	31	3-2	0-0	190.1	181	96	12	3	70-3	117	3.97	93	.256	.324	54-4	.130	-0*	87	-7	-0.6
1987	Mon N	4	5	.444	19	12	0	0-0	83	95	55	10	0	34-2	54	4.99	84	.289	.354	25-0	.120	0	106	-8	-0.8
1988	Bal A	4	15	.211	30	24	1	0-0	158.2	184	103	18	3	63-2	82	5.39	73	.293	.356	0-0	—	0	83	-26	-2.7
1989	Bal A	5	0	1.000	10	8	1	0-0	54.1	62	17	2	0	20-0	30	2.82	135	.287	.345	0-0	—	0	161	7	0.6
1990	Bal A	2	7	.222	10	10	0	0-0	50.2	55	34	8	0	14-1	23	5.68	67	.279	.324	0-0	—	0	74	-11	-1.6
	Pit N	1	0	1.000	5	0	0	0-0	7	7	2	0	0	2-0	4	2.57	141	.259	.310	0-0	—	0		1	0.1
Total	7	39	54	.419	158	133	13-5	0-0	862.2	887	452	68	6	319-19	448	4.20	91	.269	.333	180-11	.117	-4	96	-39	-5.3
TIDROW, DICK Richard William B 5.14.1947 San Francisco, CA BR/TR 6-4/213# d4.18																									
1972	Cle A	14	15	.483	39	34	10-3	0-0	237.1	200	83	21	6	70-13	123	2.77	117	.230	.289	70-13	.100	-3	82	11	0.8
1973	Cle A	14	16	.467	42	40	13-2	0-0	274.2	289	150	31	8	95-10	138	4.42	89	.270	.332	0-0	—	0	96	-15	-1.6
1974	Cle A	1	3	.250	4	4	0	0-0	19	21	17	4	2	13-1	8	7.11	51	.276	.387	0-0	—	0	85	-7	-1.2
	NY A	11	9	.550	33	25	5	1-0	190.2	205	99	14	4	53-7	100	3.87	91	.279	.327	0-0	—	0	118	-9	-1.0
	Year	12	12	.500	37	29	5	1-0	209.2	226	104	18	6	66-8	108	4.16	85	.279	.333	0-0	—	0	113	-20	-2.2
1975	NY A	6	3	.667	37	0	0	5-4	69.1	65	27	5	3	31-6	38	3.12	118	.256	.341	0-0	—	0		5	0.6
1976	†NY A	4	5	.444	47	2	0	10-3	92.1	80	29	5	1	24-1	65	2.63	130	.233	.282	0-0	—	0	218	9	1.0
1977	†NY A	11	4	.733	49	7	0	5-2	151	143	57	20	2	41-11	83	3.16	125	.250	.300	0-0	—	0	162	15	1.4
1978	†NY A	7	11	.389	31	25	4	0-0	185.1	191	87	13	5	53-3	73	3.84	95	.267	.320	0-0	—	0	100	-3	-0.4
1979	NY A	2	1	.667	14	0	0	2-1	22.2	38	20	5	0	4-0	7	7.94	51	.409	.424	0-0	—	0		-9	-1.1
	Chi N	11	5	.688	63	0	0	4-1	102.2	86	35	5	2	42-11	68	2.72	152	.231	.310	10-2	.200	0		15	2.4
1980	Chi N	6	5	.545	**84**	0	0	6-6	116	97	44	10	5	53-16	97	2.79	140	.229	.319	4-0	.000	-0		12	1.2
1981	Chi N	3	10	.231	51	0	0	9-4	74.2	73	45	6	1	30-15	39	5.06	73	.256	.328	5-1	.000	-1		-10	-1.9
1982	Chi N	8	3	.727	65	0	0	6-1	103.2	106	45	6	3	29-10	62	3.39	111	.265	.318	6-0	.000	-1		3	0.2
1983	†Chi A	2	4	.333	50	1	0	7-2	91.2	86	50	13	1	34-8	66	4.22	100	.242	.308	0-0	—	0	108	-1	-0.1
1984	NY N	0	0	—	11	0	0	0-0	15.2	25	19	5	0	7-0	8	9.19	39	.357	.410	0-0	—	0		-10	-0.5
Total	13	100	94	.515	620	138	32-5	55-24	1746.2	1705	807	163	43	579-112	975	3.68	101	.257	.318	95-16	.095	-5	100	6	-0.2
TIEFENAUER, BOBBY Bobby Gene B 10.10.1929 Desloge, MO D 6.13.2000 Desloge, MO BR/TR 6-2/185# d7.14 C1																									
1952	StL N	0	0	—	6	0	0	0	8	12	8	1	0	7	3	7.88	47	.343	.452	1-0	.000	-0		-4	-0.2
1955	StL N	1	4	.200	18	0	0	0	32.2	31	19	6	4	10-4	16	4.41	92	.261	.331	5-1	.000	-0		-2	-0.3
1960	Cle A	0	1	.000	6	0	0	0	9	8	2	0	0	3-0	2	2.00	187	.242	.306	1-0	.000	0		2	0.2
1961	StL N	0	0	—	3	0	0	0	4.1	9	4	0	0	4-0	3	6.23	71	.450	.542	0-0	—	0		-1	-0.1
1962	Hou N	2	4	.333	43	0	0	1	85	91	42	6	2	21-2	60	4.34	86	.277	.320	9-0	.111	0		-3	-0.3
1963	Mil N	1	1	.500	12	0	0	2	29.2	20	4	1	0	4-0	22	1.21	265	.194	.222	5-1	.000	-0		7	0.6
1964	Mil N	4	6	.400	46	0	0	13	73	61	33	6	3	15-2	48	3.21	110	.225	.273	14-1	.000	-1		1	0.0
1965	Mil N	0	1	.000	6	0	0	0	7	8	7	1	1	3-1	7	7.71	46	.286	.364	0-0	—	0		-3	-0.4
	NY A	1	1	.500	10	0	0	2	20.1	19	10	3	1	5-1	15	3.54	96	.253	.301	2-0	.000	0		-1	-0.1
	Cle A	0	5	.000	15	0	0	4	22.1	24	17	3	1	10-3	13	4.84	72	.273	.354	1-0	.000	-0		-5	-1.0
	Year	1	6	.143	25	0	0	6	42.2	43	31	6	2	15-4	28	4.22	82	.264	.330	3-0	.000	-0		-5	-1.1
1967	Cle A	0	1	.000	5	0	0	0	11.1	9	3	0	0	3-1	6	0.79	411	.225	.279	0-0	—	0		2	0.2
1968	Chi N	0	1	.000	9	0	0	1	13.1	20	12	2	0	2-1	9	6.08	52	.351	.367	1-0	.000	-0		-5	-0.5
Total	10	9	25	.265	179	0	0	23	316	312	161	29	12	87-<u>15</u>	204	3.84	94	.260	.314	39-3	.026	-1		-12	-1.9
TIEFENTHALER, VERLE Verle Matthew B 7.11.1937 Breda, IA BL/TR 6-1/190# d4.19																									
1962	Chi A	0	0	—	3	0	0	0	3.2	6	4	1	0	7-0	1	9.82	40	.353	.542	0-0	—	0		-2	-0.1
TIERNAN, MIKE Michael Joseph "Silent Mike" B 1.21.1867 Trenton, NJ D 11.9.1918 New York, NY BL/TL 5-11/165# d4.30 ▲																									
1887	NY N	1	2	.333	5	0	0	**1**	19.2	33	25	2	1	7	3	8.69	43	.398	.451	407	.287	2*		-10	-1.1
TIETJE, LES Leslie William "Toots" B 9.11.1911 Sumner, IA D 10.2.1996 Rochester, MN BR/TR 6-0.5/178# d9.18																									
1933	Chi A	2	0	1.000	3	3	1	0	22.1	16	8	1	0	15	9	2.42	175	.203	.330	8-1	.125	0	100	4	0.4
1934	Chi A	5	14	.263	34	22	6-1	0	176	174	106	20	2	96	81	4.81	98	.257	.351	59-3	.017	-7	65	0	-0.6
1935	Chi A	9	15	.375	30	21	9-1	0	169.2	184	88	14	2	81	64	4.30	108	.277	.357	61-3	.197	-1	75	7	0.7
1936	Chi A	0	0	—	2	0	0	0	2.1	6	7	0	0	5	3	27.00	19	.462	.611	0-0	—	0		-5	-0.2
	StL A	3	5	.375	14	7	2	0	50.1	65	44	2	2	30	16	6.62	81	.310	.401	15-1	.067	-1*	87	-7	-1.0
	Year	3	5	.375	16	7	2	0	52.2	71	49	2	2	35	19	7.52	71	.318	.415	15-1	.067	-1	87	-12	-1.2
1937	StL A	1	2	.333	5	4	2	0	30	32	15	0	0	17	5	4.20	115	.283	.377	10-1	.000	-2	50	2	0.0
1938	StL A	2	5	.286	17	8	2-1	0	62	83	55	8	0	38	15	7.55	66	.327	.414	18-3	.111	-1*	95	-16	-1.5
Total	6	22	41	.349	105	65	22-3	0	512.2	560	323	45	6	282	193	5.11	93	.279	.369	171-12	.099	-12	75	-15	-2.2
TIFT, RAY Raymond Frank B 6.21.1884 Fitchburg, MA D 3.29.1945 Verona, NJ TL d8.7																									
1907	NY A	0	0	—	4	1	0	0	19	33	14	0	0	4	6	4.74	59	.384	.411	5-0	.000	-0	145	-3	-0.3
TILLMAN, JOHNNY John Lawrence "Ducky" B 10.6.1893 Bridgeport, CT D 4.7.1964 Harrisburg, PA BB/TR 5-11/170# d9.20																									
1915	StL A	1	0	1.000	2	1	0	0	10	6	2	0	0	4	6	0.90	318	.176	.263	3-0	.000	-0	76	2	0.2
TILLOTSON, THAD Thaddeus Asa B 12.20.1940 Merced, CA BR/TR 6-2.5/195# d4.14																									
1967	NY A	3	9	.250	43	5	1	2	98.1	99	52	9	2	39-3	62	4.03	78	.261	.331	16-1	.063	-0	56	-10	-1.3
1968	NY A	1	0	1.000	7	0	0	0	10.1	11	6	0	0	7-2	1	4.35	67	.282	.383	1-0	.000	-0		-2	-0.2
Total	2	4	9	.308	50	5	1	2	108.2	110	58	9	2	46-5	63	4.06	77	.263	.336	17-1	.059	-1	56	-12	-1.5

Year	Tm Lg	W	L	Pct	G	GS	CG-Sho	SV-BS	IP	H	R	HR	HB	BB-IB	SO	ERA	AERA	OAV	OOB	AB-SH	AVG	PB	Sup	APR	PW
TIMBERLAKE, GARY Gary Dale B 8.8.1948 Laconia, IN BR/TL 6-2/205# d6.18 Mil 1969																									
1969	Sea A	0	0	—	2	2	0	0-0	6	7	6	0	0	9-0	4	7.50	49	.269	.457	1-1	.000	-0	122	-3	-0.2
TIMLIN, MIKE Michael August B 3.10.1966 Midland, TX BR/TR 6-4/210# d4.8																									
1991	†Tor A	11	6	.647	63	3	0	3-5	108.1	94	43	6	1	50-11	85	3.16	133	.233	.317	0-0	—	0	43	12	1.8
1992	†Tor A	0	2	.000	26	0	0	1-0	43.2	45	23	0	1	20-5	35	4.12	99	.271	.351	0-0	—	0		-1	0.0
1993	†Tor A	4	2	.667	54	0	0	1-3	55.2	63	32	7	1	27-3	49	4.69	92	.284	.360	0-0	—	0		-2	-0.2
1994	Tor A	0	1	.000	34	0	0	2-2	40	41	25	5	2	20-0	38	5.17	93	.261	.352	0-0	—	0		-2	-0.1
1995	Tor A	4	3	.571	31	0	0	5-4	42	38	13	1	2	17-5	36	2.14	220	.242	.324	0-0	—	0		11	1.9
1996	Tor A	1	6	.143	59	0	0	31-7	56.2	47	25	4	2	18-4	52	3.65	137	.229	.294	0-0	—	0		9	1.6
1997	Tor A	3	2	.600	38	0	0	9-4	47	41	17	6	1	15-4	36	2.87	160	.243	.306	0-0	—	0		9	1.1
	†Sea A	3	2	.600	26	0	0	1-4	25.2	28	13	2	0	5-1	9	3.86	117	.280	.314	0-0	—	0		1	0.2
	Year	6	4	.600	64	0	0	10-8	72.2	69	32	8	1	20-5	45	3.22	142	.257	.309	0-0	—	0		10	1.3
1998	Sea A	3	3	.500	70	0	0	19-5	79.1	78	26	5	3	16-2	60	2.95	157	.264	.306	0-0	—	0		16	1.7
1999	Bal A	3	9	.250	62	0	0	27-9	63	51	30	9	5	23-3	50	3.57	132	.221	.304	0-0	—	0		7	1.2
2000	Bal A	2	3	.400	37	0	0	11-4	35	37	22	6	2	15-3	26	4.89	97	.276	.355	0-0	—	0		-1	-0.2
	†StL N	3	1	.750	25	0	0	1-2	29.2	30	11	2	2	20-3	26	3.34	138	.265	.382	0-0	—	0		5	0.6
2001	†StL N	4	5	.444	67	0	0	3-4	72.2	78	35	6	3	19-4	47	4.09	104	.277	.327	1-0	.000	-0*		2	0.3
2002	StL N	1	3	.250	42	1	0	0-2	61	48	19	9	4	7-2	35	2.51	158	.215	.252	6-0	.000	-1	23	10	0.6
	Phi N	3	3	.500	30	0	0	0-2	35.2	27	16	6	1	7-0	15	3.79	103	.206	.250	0-0	—	0		1	0.1
	Year	4	6	.400	72	1	0	0-4	96.2	75	36	15	5	14-2	50	2.98	132	.212	.251	6-0	.000	-1	23	11	0.7
2003	†Bos A	6	4	.600	72	0	0	2-4	83.2	77	37	11	4	9-3	65	3.55	129	.239	.268	0-0	—	0		9	1.0
Total	13	51	55	.481	736	4	0	116-61	879	823	387	85	34	288-53	664	3.56	125	.248	.313	7-0	.000	-1	36	86	11.6
TIMMERMANN, TOM Thomas Henry B 5.12.1940 Breese, IL BR/TR 6-4/215# d6.18																									
1969	Det A	4	3	.571	31	1	1	1-1	55.2	50	22	1	2	26-4	42	2.75	136	.238	.326	9-0	.111	-0	95	5	0.5
1970	Det A	6	7	.462	61	0	0	27-5	85.1	90	44	3	2	34-11	49	4.11	91	.273	.337	16-0	.000	-2		-4	-1.0
1971	Det A	7	6	.538	52	2	0	4-6	84	82	36	6	3	37-3	51	3.86	93	.262	.345	19-2	.053	-1	137	-1	-0.3
1972	Det A	8	10	.444	34	25	3-2	0-0	149.2	121	57	12	5	41-1	88	2.89	109	.216	.276	44-2	.136	-0*	110	3	0.2
1973	Det A	1	1	.500	17	1	0	1-0	39	39	17	4	0	11-1	21	3.69	111	.258	.309	0-0	—	0	0	2	0.1
	Cle A	8	7	.533	29	15	4	2-1	124.1	117	73	15	3	54-7	62	4.92	80	.251	.330	0-0	—	0	111	-12	-1.4
	Year	9	8	.529	46	16	4	3-1	163.1	156	78	19	3	65-8	83	4.63	86	.252	.325	0-0	—	0	103	-10	-1.3
1974	Cle A	1	1	.500	4	0	0	0-0	10	9	6	1	0	5-0	2	5.40	67	.250	.341	0-0	—	0		-2	-0.3
Total	6	35	35	.500	228	44	8-2	35-13	548	508	255	42	15	208-27	315	3.78	96	.246	.317	88-4	.091	-4	104	-9	-2.2
TINCUP, BEN Austin Ben B 12.14.1890 Adair, OK D 7.5.1980 Claremore, OK BL/TR 6-1/180# d5.22 Mil 1918 C1																									
1914	Phi N	8	10	.444	28	17	9-3	2	155	165	71	0	4	62	108	2.61	113	.286	.359	53-2	.170	-1*	92	4	0.4
1915	Phi N	0	0	—	10	0	0	0	31	26	8	1	0	9	10	2.03	135	.263	.324	9-0	.000	-1*		3	0.1
1918	Phi N	0	1	.000	8	1	0	0	16.2	24	20	0	0	6	6	7.56	40	.329	.380	8-0	.125	-0*	50	-9	-0.5
1928	Chi N	0	0	—	2	0	0	0	9	14	7	0	0	1	3	7.00	55	.378	.395	3-0	.000	-0		-3	-0.2
Total	4	8	11	.421	48	18	9-3	2	211.2	229	106	1	4	78	127	3.10	95	.291	.358	73-2	.137	-3	90	-5	-0.2
TINNING, BUD Lyle Forrest B 3.12.1906 Pilger, NE D 1.17.1961 Evansville, IN BB/TR 5-11/198# d4.20																									
1932	†Chi N	5	3	.625	24	7	2	0	93.1	93	34	3	2	24	30	2.80	135	.263	.313	23-0	.087	-1	77	10	0.7
1933	Chi N	13	6	.684	32	21	10-3	1	175.1	169	73	3	4	60	59	3.18	103	.255	.320	67-3	.209	1	135	3	0.2
1934	Chi N	4	6	.400	39	7	1-1	3	129.1	134	59	9	1	46	44	3.34	116	.269	.332	39-2	.179	-1	89	6	0.3
1935	StL N	0	0	—	4	0	0	0	7.2	9	6	1	1	5	2	5.87	70	.300	.417	1-0	.000	-0		-2	-0.1
Total	4	22	15	.595	99	35	13-4	4	405.2	405	172	16	8	135	135	3.19	113	.262	.325	130-5	.177	-1	109	17	1.1
TIPPLE, DAN Daniel E. "Big Dan" or "Rusty" B 2.13.1890 Rockford, IL D 3.26.1960 Omaha, NE BR/TR 6/176# d9.18																									
1915	NY A	1	1	.500	3	2	2	0	19	14	6	1	0	11	14	0.95	310	.203	.313	6-0	.000	-1	99	3	0.1
TISING, JACK Johnnie Joseph B 10.9.1903 High Point, MO D 9.5.1967 Leadville, CO BL/TR 6-2/180# d4.24																									
1936	Pit N	1	3	.250	10	6	1	0	47	52	26	5	0	24	27	4.21	96	.272	.353	11-0	.273	0	77	-1	-0.1
TITCOMB, CANNONBALL Ledell B 8.21.1866 W.Baldwin, ME D 6.8.1950 Kingston, NH BL/TL 5-6/157# d5.5																									
1886	Phi N	0	5	.000	5	5	5	0	41	43	45	1		24	24	3.73	88	.244	.335	16	.063	-2	45	-6	-0.7
1887	Phi AA	1	2	.333	3	3	3	0	24	31	30	1	0	19	16	6.75	64	.298	.407	10	.000	-1	89	-8	-0.8
	NY N	4	3	.571	9	9	9	0	72	68	50	3	1	37	34	3.88	97	.233	.321	29	.069	-4	78	-1	-0.4
1888	†NY N	14	8	.636	23	23	22-4	0	197	149	91	4	5	46	129	2.24	122	.201	.253	82	.122	-4	123	10	0.4
1889	NY N	1	2	.333	3	3	3	0	26	27	26	1	2	16	7	6.58	60	.260	.369	12	.083	-1	74	-6	-0.6
1890	Roc AA	10	9	.526	20	19	19-1	0	168.2	168	123	6	14	97	73	3.74	95	.251	.358	75	.107	-5*	122	-9	-1.4
Total	5	30	29	.508	63	62	61-5	0	528.2	486	365	16	22	239	283	3.47	96	.233	.318	224	.098	-18	104	-20	-3.5
TOBIK, DAVE David Vance B 3.2.1953 Euclid, OH BR/TR 6-1/195# d8.26																									
1978	Det A	0	0	—	5	0	0	0-0	12	12	5	1	0	3-0	11	3.75	103	.261	.306	0-0	—	0		0	0.0
1979	Det A	3	5	.375	37	0	0	3-5	68.2	59	34	12	0	25-5	48	4.33	100	.231	.295	0-0	—	0		1	0.1
1980	Det A	1	0	1.000	17	1	0	0-0	61	61	27	7	0	21-4	34	3.98	103	.266	.325	0-0	—	0	152	2	0.1
1981	Det A	2	2	.500	27	0	0	1-2	60.1	47	19	7	0	33-3	32	2.69	141	.215	.313	0-0	—	0		7	0.4
1982	Det A	4	9	.308	51	1	0	9-3	98.2	86	45	8	1	38-8	63	3.56	114	.241	.312	0-0	—	0	157	5	0.6
1983	Tex A	2	1	.667	27	0	0	9-0	44	36	18	2	0	13-3	30	3.68	109	.222	.278	0-0	—	0		3	0.3
1984	Tex A	1	6	.143	24	0	0	5-3	42.1	44	20	5	1	17-6	30	3.61	115	.265	.337	0-0	—	0		2	0.4
1985	Sea A	1	0	1.000	8	0	0	1-1	9	10	8	2	0	3-0	8	6.00	70	.286	.325	0-0	—	0		-2	-0.3
Total	8	14	23	.378	196	2	0	28-14	396	355	176	44	2	153-29	256	3.70	110	.242	.310	0-0	—	0	155	18	1.6
TOBIN, JIM James Anthony "Abba Dabba" B 12.27.1912 Oakland, CA D 5.19.1969 Oakland, CA BR/TR 6/185# d4.30 b-Johnny																									
1937	Pit N	6	3	.667	20	8	7	1	87	74	38	1	1	28	37	3.00	129	.226	.289	34-0	.441	7*	100	7	1.3
1938	Pit N	14	12	.538	40	33	14-2	0	241.1	254	109	17	6	66	70	3.47	109	.270	.321	103-1	.243	7*	99	9	1.5
1939	Pit N	9	9	.500	25	19	8	0	145.1	194	84	7	2	33	43	4.52	85	.319	.356	74-1	.243	5*	99	-11	-0.8
1940	Bos N	7	3	.700	15	11	9	0	96.1	102	41	8	0	24	29	3.83	97	.264	.307	43-0	.279	3*	132	1	0.4
1941	Bos N	12	12	.500	33	26	20-3	0	238	229	91	12	0	60	61	3.10	115	.253	.300	103-0	.184	3*	93	15	2.1
1942	Bos N	12	21	.364	37	33	**28**-1	0	**287.2**	283	145	20	6	96	71	3.97	84	.257	.320	114-0	.246	14*	86	-19	-0.3
1943	Bos N	14	14	.500	33	30	24-1	0	250	241	96	12	2	69	52	2.66	128	.251	.303	107-0	.280	6*	80	18	3.1
1944	Bos N★	18	19	.486	43	36	**28**-5	3	299.1	271	125	18	3	97	83	3.01	127	.240	.302	116-2	.190	5*	85	23	3.8
1945	Bos N	9	14	.391	27	25	16	0	196.2	220	101	10	5	56	38	3.84	100	.282	.334	77-0	.143	5*	110	-2	0.5
	†Det A	4	5	.444	14	6	2	1	58.1	61	31	2	4	28	14	3.55	99	.274	.365	25-1	.120	0*	69	-1	-0.2
Total	9	105	112	.484	287	227	156-12	5	1900	1929	861	107	29	557	498	3.44	106	.262	.316	796-5	.230	54	94	40	11.4
TOBIN, PAT Marion Brooks B 1.28.1916 Hermitage, AR D 1.21.1975 Shreveport, LA BR/TR 6-1/198# d8.21																									
1941	Phi A	0	0	—	1	0	0	0	1	4	5	0	0	2	0	36.00	12	.571	.667	0-0	—	0		-4	-0.2
TODD, FRANK George Franklin B 10.18.1869 Aberdeen, MD D 8.11.1919 Havre De Grace, MD TL d7.14																									
1898	Lou N	0	2	.000	4	2	0	0	11	23	21	0	2	8	5	13.91	26	.418	.508	5-0	.200	0	49	-12	-1.5
TODD, JACKSON Jackson A B 11.20.1951 Tulsa, OK BR/TR 6-2/180# d5.5																									
1977	NY N	3	6	.333	19	10	0	0-0	71.2	78	41	8	2	20-5	39	4.77	78	.273	.325	17-0	.059	-1	93	-8	-1.0
1979	Tor A	0	1	.000	12	1	0	0-0	32.1	40	26	7	1	7-0	14	5.85	75	.299	.333	0-0	—	0	21	-6	-0.3
1980	Tor A	5	2	.714	12	12	4	0-0	85	90	40	14	2	30-1	44	4.02	107	.276	.340	0-0	—	0	97	4	0.3
1981	Tor A	2	7	.222	21	13	3	0-0	97.2	94	51	10	4	31-2	41	3.96	100	.251	.313	0-0	—	0	63	-1	0.0
Total	4	10	16	.385	64	36	7	0-0	286.2	302	158	39	9	88-8	138	4.40	92	.270	.326	17-0	.059	-1	81	-11	-1.0
TODD, JIM James Richard B 9.21.1947 Lancaster, PA BL/TR 6-2/190# d4.29																									
1974	Chi N	4	2	.667	43	6	0	3-1	88	82	45	7	3	41-3	42	3.89	98	.252	.338	16-0	.063	-1	72	-1	-0.2
1975	†Oak A	8	3	.727	58	0	0	12-2	122	104	40	4	3	33-4	50	2.29	159	.234	.290	0-0	—	0		17	2.0
1976	Oak A	7	8	.467	49	0	0	4-1	82.2	87	43	6	6	34-8	22	3.81	88	.276	.357	0-0	—	0		-6	-1.0

Year	Tm Lg	W	L	Pct	G	GS	CG-Sho	SV-BS	IP	H	R	HR	HB	BB-IB	SO	ERA	AERA	OAV	OOB	AB-SH	AVG	PB	Sup	APR	PW
1977	Chi N	1	1	.500	20	0	0	0-1	30.2	47	37	1	2	19-2	17	9.10	48	.336	.422	1-1	.000	-0		-15	-0.9
1978	Sea A	3	4	.429	49	2	0	3-2	106.2	113	52	4	0	61-4	37	3.88	98	.280	.373	0-0	—	0	71	-1	-0.1
1979	Oak A	2	5	.286	51	0	0	2-3	81	108	66	12	2	51-10	26	6.56	62	.329	.415	0-0	—	0		-23	-1.8
Total	6	25	23	.521	270	8	0	24-10	511	541	283	34	16	239-31	194	4.23	89	.277	.357	17-1	.059	-2	73	-29	-2.0
TOENES, HAL William Harrel B 10.8.1917 Mobile, AL BR/TR 5-11.5/175# d9.17																									
1947	Was A	0	1	.000	3	1	0	0	6.2	11	5	0	0	2	5	6.75	55	.379	.419	1-1	.000	0	48	-2	-0.3
TOLAR, KEVIN Kevin Anthony B 1.28.1971 Panama City, FL BR/TL 6-3/225# d9.11																									
2000	Det A	0	0	—	5	0	0	0-0	3	1	1	0	0	1-0	3	3.00	161	.091	.167	0-0	—	0		1	0.0
2001	Det A	0	0	—	9	0	0	0-0	10.2	7	8	0	0	13-1	11	6.75	64	.189	.400	0-0	—	0		-3	-0.1
2003	Bos A	0	0	—	6	0	0	0-0	4	5	5	1	0	2-0	3	9.00	51	.313	.389	0-0	—	0		-2	-0.1
Total	3	0	0	—	20	0	0	0-0	17.2	13	14	1	0	16-1	17	6.62	68	.203	.363	0-0	—	0		-4	-0.2
TOLIVER, FREDDIE Freddie Lee B 2.3.1961 Natchez, MS BR/TR 6-1/170# d9.15																									
1984	Cin N	0	0	—	3	1	0	0-0	10	7	2	0	0	7-0	4	0.90	420	.206	.341	1-1	.000	-0	47	3	0.1
1985	Phi N	0	4	.000	11	3	0	1-1	25	27	15	2	0	17-1	23	4.68	79	.273	.376	4-0	.500	1	40	-3	-0.4
1986	Phi N	0	2	.000	5	5	0	0-0	25.2	28	14	0	0	11-0	20	3.51	110	.286	.358	6-0	.000	-0	92	0	0.0
1987	Phi N	1	1	.500	10	4	0	0-0	30.1	34	19	2	1	17-3	25	5.64	75	.291	.380	5-2	.000	-1	149	-4	-0.2
1988	Min A	7	6	.538	21	19	0	0-0	114.2	116	57	8	1	52-1	69	4.24	96	.270	.349	0-0	—	0	101	-2	-0.2
1989	Min A	1	3	.250	7	5	0	0-0	29	39	26	2	1	15-0	11	7.76	53	.317	.396	0-0	—	0*	52	-10	-1.1
	SD N	0	0	—	9	0	0	0-0	14	17	14	5	1	9-0	14	7.07	50	.321	.422	0-0	—	0		-6	-0.3
1993	Pit N	1	0	1.000	12	0	0	0-0	21.2	20	10	2	2	8-0	14	3.74	108	.267	.341	2-0	.000	-0		1	0.0
Total	7	10	16	.385	78	37	0	1-1	270.1	288	157	21	6	136-5	180	4.73	85	.280	.365	18-3	.111	-0	93	-21	-2.1
TOLLBERG, BRIAN Brian Patrick B 9.16.1972 Tampa, FL BR/TR 6-3/195# d6.20																									
2000	SD N	4	5	.444	19	19	1	0-0	118	126	58	13	5	35-4	76	3.58	121	.274	.332	32-6	.094	-2	84	8	0.3
2001	SD N	10	4	.714	19	19	0	0-0	117.1	133	58	15	2	25-3	71	4.30	93	.287	.321	40-5	.200	1	131	-2	0.0
2002	SD N	1	5	.167	12	11	0	0-0	61.2	88	47	11	1	19-2	33	6.13	62	.342	.382	19-1	.158	1	96	-18	-1.4
2003	SD N	0	2	.000	3	3	0	0-0	10.1	9	11	1	0	4-0	2	6.97	57	.231	.295	2-1	.000	-0	87	-5	-0.8
Total	4	15	16	.484	53	52	1	0-0	307.1	356	174	40	8	83-9	182	4.48	91	.292	.337	93-13	.151	0	103	-17	-1.9
TOMANEK, DICK Richard Carl "Bones" B 1.6.1931 Avon Lake, OH BL/TL 6-1/175# d9.25																									
1953	Cle A	1	0	1.000	1	1	1	0	9	6	3	1	1	6	6	2.00	188	.176	.317	5-0	.000	-1	284	2	0.1
1954	Cle A	0	0	—	1	0	0	0	1.2	1	1	1	0	1	0	5.40	68	.167	.286	0-0	—	0		0	0.0
1957	Cle A	2	1	.667	34	2	0	0	69.2	67	51	13	1	37-3	55	5.68	65	.248	.341	13-0	.231	0	132	-16	-0.7
1958	Cle A	2	3	.400	18	6	2	0	57.2	61	37	8	2	28-2	42	5.62	65	.276	.361	17-1	.118	0*	111	-12	-0.9
	KC A	5	5	.500	36	2	1	5	72.1	69	34	5	0	28-3	50	3.61	108	.252	.321	13-0	.231	1	103	1	0.3
	Year	7	8	.467	54	8	3	5	130	130	39	13	2	56-5	92	4.50	84	.263	.339	30-1	.167	1	107	-10	-0.6
1959	KC A	0	1	.000	16	0	0	2	20.2	27	15	6	2	12-1	13	6.53	61	.310	.406	2-0	.500	0		-5	-0.2
Total	5	10	10	.500	106	11	4	7	231	231	141	34	6	112-9	166	4.95	77	.259	.345	50-1	.180	1	127	-30	-1.4
TOMASIC, ANDY Andrew John B 12.10.1919 Hokendauqua, PA BR/TR 6/175# d4.28																									
1949	NY N	0	1	.000	2	0	0	0	5	9	10	2	0	5	2	18.00	22	.375	.483	1-0	.000	-0		-7	-1.0
TOMKO, BRETT Brett Daniel B 4.7.1973 Cleveland, OH BR/TR 6-4/215# d5.27																									
1997	Cin N	11	7	.611	22	19	0	0-0	126	106	50	14	4	47-4	95	3.43	125	.233	.305	36-3	.139	-0*	86	12	1.5
1998	Cin N	13	12	.520	34	34	1	0-0	210.2	198	111	22	7	64-3	162	4.44	96	.247	.307	65-9	.108	-2*	99	-4	-0.6
1999	Cin N	5	7	.417	33	26	1	0-0	172	175	103	31	4	60-10	132	4.92	95	.263	.325	47-8	.213	2	102	-5	-0.1
2000	†Sea A	7	5	.583	32	8	0	1-1	92.1	92	53	12	3	40-4	59	4.68	101	.264	.341	0-0	—	0	92	0	-0.1
2001	Sea A	3	1	.750	11	4	0	0-1	34.2	42	24	9	0	15-2	22	5.19	80	.288	.350	0-0	—	0	173	-5	-0.5
2002	SD N	10	10	.500	32	32	3	0-0	204.1	212	107	31	2	60-9	126	4.49	84	.267	.317	66-7	.182	1	103	-15	-1.2
2003	StL N	13	9	.591	33	32	2	0-0	202.2	252	126	35	5	57-2	114	5.28	77	.305	.352	63-11	.286	6*	132	-29	-2.2
Total	7	62	51	.549	197	155	7	1-2	1042.2	1077	574	154	25	343-34	710	4.62	92	.267	.326	277-38	.188	6	106	-46	-3.2
TOMLIN, DAVE David Allen B 6.22.1949 Maysville, KY BL/TL 6-3/185# d9.2																									
1972	Cin N	0	0	—	3	0	0	0-0	4	7	4	2	0	1-0	2	9.00	36	.412	.421	0-0	—	0		-3	-0.1
1973	†Cin N	1	2	.333	16	0	0	1-0	27.2	24	15	5	0	15-3	20	4.88	70	.238	.336	3-0	.000	-0		-4	-0.5
1974	SD N	2	0	1.000	47	0	0	2-0	58	59	29	4	2	30-10	29	4.34	82	.271	.360	4-0	.000	-0		-4	-0.2
1975	SD N	4	2	.667	67	0	0	1-1	83	87	38	5	2	31-9	48	3.25	107	.275	.340	5-2	.200	1		1	0.3
1976	SD N	0	1	.000	49	1	0	0-1	73	62	24	4	1	20-6	43	2.84	116	.235	.289	8-0	.000	-1	188	5	0.3
1977	SD N	4	4	.500	76	0	0	3-4	101.2	98	38	3	2	32-11	55	3.01	118	.259	.317	7-1	.286	0		7	0.7
1978	Cin N	9	1	.900	57	0	0	4-4	62.1	88	54	3	3	30-7	32	5.78	62	.326	.397	5-0	.200	0		-20	-3.2
1979	†Cin N	2	2	.500	53	0	0	1-1	58.1	59	29	3	1	18-5	30	2.62	143	.269	.325	2-0	.500	0		3	0.2
1980	Cin N	3	0	1.000	27	0	0	0-0	26	38	17	2	0	11-5	6	5.54	65	.355	.412	0-0	—	0		-6	-0.5
1982	Mon N	0	0	—	1	0	0	0-0	2	1	1	0	0	1-0	2	4.50	81	.167	.286	0-0	—	0		0	0.0
1983	Pit N	0	0	—	5	0	0	0-0	4	6	4	0	0	1-0	5	6.75	55	.316	.350	0-0	—	0		-2	-0.1
1985	Pit N	0	0	—	1	0	0	0-0	1	1	0	0	0	1-0	0	0.00	—	.333	.500	0-0	—	0		0	0.0
1986	Mon N	0	0	—	7	0	0	0-0	10.1	13	8	1	1	7-2	6	5.23	71	.317	.420	0-0	—	0		-2	-0.1
Total	13	25	12	.676	409	1	0	12-11	511.1	543	261	32	12	198-58	278	3.82	92	.277	.344	34-3	.147	1	188	-25	-3.2
TOMLIN, RANDY Randy Leon B 6.14.1966 Bainbridge, MD BL/TL 5-11/170# d8.6																									
1990	Pit N	4	4	.500	12	12	2	0-0	77.2	62	24	5	1	12-1	42	2.55	142	.221	.254	25-2	.040	-1	98	10	0.9
1991	†Pit N	8	7	.533	31	27	4-2	0-0	175	170	75	9	6	54-4	104	2.98	120	.254	.315	52-13	.192	1*	130	8	0.9
1992	†Pit N	14	9	.609	35	33	1-1	0-0	208.2	226	85	11	5	42-4	90	3.41	101	.282	.320	65-7	.138	-0	111	1	0.3
1993	Pit N	4	8	.333	18	18	1	0-0	98.1	109	57	11	5	15-0	44	4.85	84	.291	.320	33-2	.182	0	85	-9	-0.9
1994	Pit N	0	3	.000	10	4	0	0-1	20.2	23	9	1	0	10-0	17	3.92	110	.291	.371	6-0	.500	1	90	1	0.3
Total	5	30	31	.492	106	94	8-3	0-1	580.1	590	250	37	17	133-9	297	3.43	106	.268	.312	181-24	.160	1	109	11	1.5
TOMPKINS, CHUCK Charles Herbert B 9.1.1889 Prescott, AR D 9.20.1975 Prescott, AR BR/TR 6/185# d6.25																									
1912	Cin N	0	0	—	1	0	0	0	3	5	1	0	0	0	1	0.00	—	.357	.357	1-0	1.000	0		1	0.1
TOMPKINS, RON Ronald Everett "Stretch" B 11.27.1944 San Diego, CA BR/TR 6-4/198# d9.9																									
1965	KC A	0	0	—	5	1	0	0	10.1	9	4	0	1	3-0	4	3.48	100	.237	.310	1-0	.000	-0	50	0	0.0
1971	Chi N	0	2	.000	35	0	0	3-1	39.2	31	18	3	3	21-3	20	4.08	96	.214	.324	0-1	—	0		0	0.1
Total	2	0	2	.000	40	1	0	3-1	50	40	22	3	4	24-3	24	3.96	97	.219	.321	1-1	.000	-0	50	0	0.1
TOMS, TOMMY Thomas Howard B 10.15.1951 Charlottesville, VA BR/TR 6-4/195# d5.4																									
1975	SF N	0	1	.000	7	0	0	0-0	10.1	13	8	1	0	6-5	6	6.10	63	.317	.396	0-0	—	0		-3	-0.2
1976	SF N	0	1	.000	7	0	0	1-0	8.2	13	7	1	0	1-0	4	6.23	58	.351	.359	0-0	—	0		-2	-0.3
1977	SF N	0	1	.000	4	0	0	0-0	4.1	7	5	0	0	2-0	2	2.08	189	.333	.391	0-0	—	0		-1	-0.2
Total	3	0	3	.000	18	0	0	1-0	23.1	33	20	2	0	9-5	12	5.40	70	.333	.382	0-0	—	0		-6	-0.7
TONEY, FRED Fred Alexandra B 12.11.1888 Nashville, TN D 3.11.1953 Nashville, TN BR/TR 6-1/195# d4.15																									
1911	Chi N	1	1	.500	18	4	1	0	67	55	36	2	5	35	27	2.42	137	.229	.339	18-2	.111	-1	91	2	0.0
1912	Chi N	1	2	.333	9	2	0	0	24	21	19	0	1	11	9	5.25	63	.247	.340	4-0	.000	-0	33	-6	-0.7
1913	Chi N	2	2	.500	7	5	2	0	39	52	29	1	1	22	12	6.00	53	.327	.412	12-0	.250	1	95	-10	-0.8
1915	Cin N	17	6	.739	36	23	18-6	2	222.2	160	46	1	3	73	108	1.58	181	.207	.278	74-4	.095	-5	84	32	3.0
1916	Cin N	14	17	.452	41	38	21-3	1	300	247	98	7	8	78	146	2.28	114	.231	.288	99-2	.121	-4	71	10	0.4
1917	Cin N	24	16	.600	43	42	31-7	1	339.2	300	119	4	6	77	123	2.20	119	.238	.286	116-9	.112	-6	110	17	1.1
1918	Cin N	6	10	.375	21	19	9-1	2	136.2	148	61	2	0	31	32	2.90	92	.282	.322	42-3	.214	0	106	-5	-0.5
	NY N	6	2	.750	11	9	7-1	1	85.1	55	19	1	2	7	19	1.69	156	.192	.216	32-0	.188	-1	83	10	0.9
	Year	12	12	.500	32	28	16-2	**3**	222	203	22	3	2	38	51	2.43	109	.250	.285	74-3	.203	-0	99	4	0.4
1919	NY N	13	6	.684	24	20	14-4	1	181	157	47	6	2	35	40	1.84	152	.235	.276	66-5	.227	1	116	20	2.1
1920	NY N	21	11	.656	42	37	17-4	1	278.1	266	101	8	6	57	81	2.65	113	.259	.302	96-2	.240	3	111	11	1.5

Year	Tm Lg	W	L	Pct	G	GS	CG-Sho	SV-BS	IP	H	R	HR	HB	BB-IB	SO	ERA	AERA	OAV	OOB	AB-SH	AVG	PB	Sup	APR	PW
1921	†NY N	18	11	.621	42	32	16-1	3	249.1	274	112	14	4	65	63	3.61	102	.289	.338	86-1	.209	2	110	4	0.5
1922	NY N	5	6	.455	13	12	6	0	86.1	91	44	5	2	31	10	4.17	96	.277	.343	30-0	.067	-3	95	0	-0.3
1923	StL N	11	12	.478	29	28	16-1	0	196.2	211	104	8	6	61	48	3.84	102	.282	.341	69-3	.116	-5	92	1	-0.3
Total	12	139	102	.577	336	271	158-28	12	2206	2037	835	59	46	583	718	2.69	113	.251	.305	744-31	.159	-18	98	86	6.9
TONKIN, DOC Harry Glenville B 8.11.1881 Concord, NH D 5.30.1959 Miami, FL BL/TL 5-9/165# d8.19																									
1907	Was A	0	0	—	1	0	0	0	2.2	6	3	0	0	5	0	6.75	36	.462	.611	2-0	1.000	1		-1	0.1
TOOLE, STEVE Stephen John B 4.9.1859 New Orleans, LA D 3.28.1919 Pittsburgh, PA BR/TL 6/170# d4.20 U1																									
1886	Bro AA	6	6	.500	13	12	11	0	104	100	92	0	8	64	48	4.41	79	.246	.359	57	.351	4*	106	-11	-0.6
1887	Bro AA	14	10	.583	24	24	22-1	0	194	186	133	1	12	106	48	4.31	100	.254	.358	103	.233	-1*	104	3	0.2
1888	KC AA	5	6	.455	12	10	10	0	91.2	124	99	4	5	50	35	6.68	51	.312	.395	48	.208	-0*	122	-26	-2.4
1890	Bro AA	2	4	.333	6	6	6	0	53.1	47	32	0	4	39	10	4.05	96	.229	.363	20	.300	2	66	1	0.3
Total	4	27	26	.509	55	52	49-1	0	443	457	356	5	29	259	141	4.79	81	.262	.367	228	.263	5	104	-33	-2.5
TOPPIN, RUPE Ruperto B 12.7.1941 Panama City, Panama BR/TR 6/185# d7.28																									
1962	KC A	0	0	—	2	0	0	0	2	1	3	0	0	5-0	1	13.50	31	.167	.545	1-0	1.000	0		-2	0.0
TORKELSON, RED Chester Leroy B 3.19.1894 Chicago, IL D 9.22.1964 Chicago, IL BR/TR 6/175# d8.29 Mil 1918																									
1917	Cle A	2	1	.667	4	3	0	0	22.1	33	25	1	2	13	10	7.66	37	.333	.421	9-0	.222	-0	118	-11	-1.2
TORREALBA, PABLO Pablo Arnoldo (Torrealba) B 4.28.1948 Barquisimeto, Venezuela BL/TL 5-9/175# d4.9 s-Steve																									
1975	Atl N	0	1	.000	6	0	0	0-0	6.2	7	2	0	0	3-0	5	1.35	280	.250	.323	1-0	1.000	0		1	0.3
1976	Atl N	0	2	.000	36	0	0	2-1	53	67	25	0	3	22-7	33	3.57	106	.315	.387	4-0	.000	-0		1	0.1
1977	Oak A	4	6	.400	41	10	3	2-0	116.2	127	45	5	2	38-2	51	2.62	154	.279	.335	0-0	—	0	58	16	1.4
1978	Chi A	2	4	.333	25	3	1-1	1-1	57.1	69	37	6	3	39-5	23	4.71	81	.301	.407	0-0	—	0	86	-7	-0.8
1979	Chi A	0	0	—	3	0	0	0-1	5.2	5	1	1	0	2-0	1	1.59	268	.250	.318	0-0	—	0		2	0.1
Total	5	6	13	.316	111	13	4-1	5-3	239.1	275	110	12	8	104-14	113	3.27	120	.291	.364	5-0	.200	-0	65	13	1.1
TORRES, ANGEL Angel Rafael (Ruiz) B 10.24.1952 Las Cienagas, D.R. BL/TL 5-11/168# d9.12																									
1977	Cin N	0	0	—	5	0	0	0-0	8.1	7	2	2	0	8-1	8	2.16	182	.233	.395	0-0	—	0		2	0.1
TORRES, DILSON Dilson Dario B 5.31.1970 Sur Edo Aragua, Venezuela BR/TR 6-3/200# d4.29																									
1995	KC A	1	2	.333	24	2	0	0-0	44.1	56	30	6	1	17-2	28	6.09	79	.311	.374	0-0	—	0	107	-5	-0.2
TORRES, GIL Don Gilberto (Nunez) B 8.23.1915 Regla, Cuba D 1.10.1983 Regla, Cuba BR/TR 6/155# d4.25 f-Ricardo ▲																									
1940	Was A	0	0	—	2	0	0	0	2.2	3	1	0	0	0	1	0.00	—	.273	.273	0-0	—	0		1	0.0
1946	Was A	0	0	—	3	0	0	1	7	9	6	0	0	3	2	7.71	43	.310	.375	185-4	.254	1*		-3	-0.1
Total	2	0	0	—	5	0	0	1	9.2	12	7	0	0	3	3	5.59	64	.300	.349	185-4	.254	1		-2	-0.1
TORRES, SALOMON Salomon (Ramirez) B 3.11.1972 San Pedro De Macoris, D.R. BR/TR 5-11/165# d8.29																									
1993	SF N	3	5	.375	8	8	0	0-0	44.2	37	21	5	1	27-3	23	4.03	97	.231	.344	13-3	.231	0	63	0	0.0
1994	SF N	2	8	.200	16	14	1	0-0	84.1	95	55	10	7	34-2	42	5.44	74	.292	.364	26-3	.154	-0	75	-14	-1.5
1995	SF N	0	1	.000	4	1	0	0-0	8	13	8	4	0	7-0	2	9.00	45	.394	.500	1-0	.000	-0	66	-4	-0.4
	Sea A	3	8	.273	16	13	1	0-0	72	87	53	12	2	42-3	45	6.00	79	.291	.382	0-0	—	0	91	-10	-1.2
1996	Sea A	3	3	.500	10	7	1-1	0-0	49	44	27	5	3	23-2	36	4.59	108	.242	.335	0-0	—	0	120	2	0.2
1997	Sea A	0	0	—	2	0	0	0-0	3.1	7	10	0	1	3-0	0	27.00	17	.412	.524	0-0	—	0		-8	-0.3
	Mon N	0	0	—	12	0	0	0-0	22.1	25	19	2	2	12-0	11	7.25	58	.284	.379	6-0	.000	-1		-7	-0.4
2002	Pit N	2	1	.667	5	5	0	0-0	30	28	10	2	3	13-1	12	2.70	155	.257	.352	13-0	.154	-0	128	5	0.4
2003	Pit N	7	5	.583	41	16	0	2-1	121	128	65	19	7	42-5	84	4.76	92	.276	.344	32-6	.063	-1*	119	-3	-0.4
Total	7	20	31	.392	114	64	3-1	2-1	434.2	464	268	59	26	203-16	255	5.24	83	.277	.361	91-12	.121	-2	97	-39	-3.6
TORREZ, MIKE Michael Augustine B 8.28.1946 Topeka, KS BR/TR 6-5/220# d9.10																									
1967	StL N	0	1	.000	3	1	0	0	5.2	5	2	0	1	1-0	5	3.18	103	.238	.304	1-0	.000	-0	134	0	0.0
1968	StL N	2	1	.667	5	2	0	0	19.1	20	7	1	1	12-0	6	2.79	104	.286	.388	7-0	.286	0	165	0	0.1
1969	StL N	10	4	.714	24	15	3	0-0	107.2	96	47	7	3	62-2	61	3.59	99	.240	.345	41-4	.073	-2	147	1	-0.1
1970	StL N	8	10	.444	30	28	5-1	0-0	179.1	168	96	12	4	103-10	100	4.22	98	.248	.348	63-2	.270	4	90	-3	0.1
1971	StL N	1	2	.333	9	6	0	0-0	36	41	27	2	1	30-3	8	6.00	60	.304	.431	7-1	.143	1	102	-9	-0.6
	Mon N	0	0	—	1	0	0	0-0	3	4	0	0	0	1-0	2	0.00	—	.308	.357	0-0	—	0		1	0.1
	Year	1	2	.333	10	6	0	0-0	39	45	31	2	1	31-3	10	5.54	65	.304	.425	7-1	.143	1	103	-8	-0.5
1972	Mon N	16	12	.571	34	33	13	0-0	243.1	215	97	15	6	103-5	112	3.33	107	.242	.323	85-4	.176	0	93	6	0.9
1973	Mon N	9	12	.429	35	34	3-1	0-0	208	207	116	17	4	115-11	90	4.46	86	.262	.357	69-6	.174	-1*	103	-12	-1.1
1974	Mon N	15	8	.652	32	30	6-1	0-0	186.1	184	90	10	3	84-3	92	3.57	108	.257	.336	64-3	.125	-3*	106	3	0.3
1975	Bal A	20	9	**.690**	36	36	16-2	0-0	270.2	238	103	15	5	133-5	119	3.06	115	.239	.331	0-0	—	0	122	13	1.4
1976	Oak A	16	12	.571	39	39	13-4	0-0	266.1	231	93	15	6	87-2	115	2.50	134	.235	.301	0-0	—	0	106	22	2.3
1977	Oak A	3	1	.750	4	4	2	0-0	26.1	23	14	3	1	11-0	12	4.44	91	.242	.318	0-0	—	0	106	-1	-0.1
	†NY A	14	12	.538	31	31	15-2	0-0	217	212	99	20	6	75-1	90	3.82	104	.259	.324	0-0	—	0	111	5	0.4
	Year	17	13	.567	35	35	17-2	0-0	243.1	235	104	23	7	86-1	102	3.88	102	.257	.323	0-0	—	0	110	5	0.3
1978	Bos A	16	13	.552	36	36	15-2	0-0	250	272	122	19	3	99-10	120	3.96	104	.281	.347	0-0	—	0	116	5	0.5
1979	Bos A	16	13	.552	36	36	12-1	0-0	252.1	254	144	20	5	121-8	125	4.49	99	.264	.346	0-0	—	0	124	-4	-0.4
1980	Bos A	9	16	.360	36	32	6-1	0-0	207.1	256	124	18	1	75-10	97	5.08	83	.313	.367	0-0	—	0	104	-17	-1.8
1981	Bos A	10	3	.769	22	22	2	0-0	127.1	130	61	10	0	51-2	54	3.68	105	.267	.336	0-0	—	0	122	2	0.1
1982	Bos A	9	9	.500	31	31	1	0-0	175.2	196	107	20	6	74-1	84	5.23	83	.282	.353	0-0	—	0	121	-15	-1.5
1983	NY N	10	17	.370	39	34	5	0-0	222.1	227	120	16	1	113-11	94	4.37	83	.271	.356	65-8	.046	-5	81	-16	-2.3
1984	NY N	1	5	.167	9	8	0	0-0	37.2	55	25	3	2	18-0	16	5.02	71	.369	.434	10-0	.300	1	66	-7	-0.8
	Oak A	0	0	—	2	0	0	0-0	2.1	9	7	0	0	3-0	2	27.00	14	.563	.632	0-0	—	0		-6	-0.3
Total	18	185	160	.536	494	458	117-15	0-0	3044	3043	1501	223	59	1371-84	1404	3.96	97	.264	.343	412-28	.155	-4	109	-32	-2.8
TOST, LOU Louis Eugene B 6.1.1911 Cumberland, WA D 2.21.1967 Santa Clara, CA BL/TL 6/175# d4.20 Mil 1944-45																									
1942	Bos N	10	10	.500	35	22	5-1	0	147.2	146	66	12	4	52	43	3.53	94	.256	.322	51-2	.176	0	104	-3	-0.4
1943	Bos N	0	1	.000	3	1	0	0	6.2	10	5	2	0	4	3	5.40	63	.357	.438	1-0	.000	-0	25	-2	-0.2
1947	Pit N	0	0	—	1	0	0	0	1	3	1	0	0	0	0	9.00	47	.600	.600	0-0	—	0		0	0.0
Total	3	10	11	.476	39	23	5-1	0	155.1	159	72	14	4	56	46	3.65	92	.263	.330	52-2	.173	-0	100	-5	-0.6
TOTH, PAUL Paul Louis B 6.30.1935 McRoberts, KY D 3.20.1999 Anaheim, CA BR/TR 6-1/175# d4.22																									
1962	StL N	1	0	1.000	6	1	1	0	16.2	18	10	1	0	4-0	5	5.40	79	.295	.333	5-0	.400	0	144	-1	0.0
	Chi N	3	1	.750	6	4	1	0	34	29	17	2	2	10-1	11	4.24	98	.240	.306	11-1	.182	0	100	0	0.0
	Year	4	1	.800	12	5	2	0	50.2	47	22	3	2	14-1	16	4.62	91	.258	.315	16-1	.250	1	109	-1	0.0
1963	Chi N	5	9	.357	27	14	3-2	0	130.2	115	50	9	2	35-3	66	3.10	113	.240	.291	39-2	.026	-3	75	6	0.3
1964	Chi N	0	2	.000	4	2	0	0	10.2	15	10	2	0	5-0	0	8.44	44	.341	.408	3-0	.333	0	59	-5	-0.7
Total	3	9	12	.429	43	21	5-2	0	192	177	87	14	4	54-4	82	3.80	97	.251	.305	58-3	.103	-2	83	0	-0.4
TOUCHSTONE, CLAY Clayland Maffitt B 1.24.1903 Moores, PA D 4.28.1949 Beaumont, TX BR/TR 5-9/175# d9.4																									
1928	Bos N	0	0	—	5	0	0	0	8	15	8	0	1	2	1	4.50	87	.417	.462	2-0	.000	-0		-2	-0.1
1929	Bos N	0	0	—	1	0	0	0	2.2	6	5	1	0	0	1	16.88	28	.429	.429	1-0	1.000	-0		-3	-0.1
1945	Chi A	0	0	—	6	0	0	0	10	14	10	1	1	6	4	5.40	61	.311	.404	1-0	.000	-0		-4	-0.2
Total	3	0	0	—	12	0	0	0	20.2	35	23	2	2	8	6	6.53	57	.368	.429	4-0	.250	0		-9	-0.4
TOWERS, JOSH Joshua Eric B 2.26.1977 Port Hueneme, CA BR/TR 6-1/165# d5.2																									
2001	Bal A	8	10	.444	24	20	1-1	0-0	140.1	165	74	21	6	16-0	58	4.49	96	.296	.321	2-0	.000	-0	99	-2	-0.2
2002	Bal A	0	3	.000	5	3	0	0-0	27.1	42	24	11	0	5-0	13	7.90	54	.362	.382	0-0	—	0	22	-11	-0.9
2003	Tor A	8	1	.889	14	8	1	1-0	64.1	67	34	15	4	7-1	42	4.48	103	.266	.294	1-0	.000	-0	133	1	0.2
Total	3	16	14	.533	43	31	2-1	1-0	232	274	132	47	10	28-1	113	4.89	90	.296	.321	3-0	.000	-0	101	-12	-0.9
TOWNSEND, IRA Ira Dance "Pat" B 1.9.1894 Weimar, TX D 7.21.1965 Schulenburg, TX BR/TR 6-1/180# d8.25																									
1920	Bos N	0	0	—	4	1	0	0	6.2	10	3	0	1	2	1	1.35	226	.370	.433	2-0	.000	-0	258	1	0.0

Year	Tm Lg	W	L	Pct	G	GS	CG-Sho	SV-BS	IP	H	R	HR	HB	BB-IB	SO	ERA	AERA	OAV	OOB	AB-SH	AVG	PB	Sup	APR	PW
1921	Bos N	0	0	—	4	0	0	0	7.1	11	7	1	2	4	0	6.14	59	.344	.447	2-0	.000	-0		-3	-0.1
Total	2	0	0	—	8	1	0	0	14	21	10	1	3	6	1	3.86	87	.356	.441	4-0	.000	-1	258	-2	-0.1
TOWNSEND, HAPPY John B 4.9.1879 Townsend, DE D 12.21.1963 Wilmington, DE BR/TR 6/190# d4.19																									
1901	Phi N	9	6	.600	19	16	14-2	0	143.2	118	73	3	5	64	72	3.45	99	**.223**	.312	64-0	.109	-4	102	0	-0.5
1902	Was A	8	16	.333	27	26	22	0	220.1	233	157	12	13	89	71	4.45	83	.272	.349	87-3	.264	3	99	-21	-1.6
1903	Was A	2	11	.154	20	13	10	0	126.2	145	85	3	9	48	54	4.76	66	.287	.359	44-0	.045	-4	61	-20	-2.2
1904	Was A	5	26	.161	36	34	31-2	0	291.1	319	163	3	9	100	143	3.58	74	.279	.342	119-0	.168	-2*	61	-31	-3.4
1905	Was A	7	16	.304	34	24	22	0	263	247	117	2	15	84	102	2.63	100	.250	.318	83-4	.181	1	86	-2	-0.2
1906	Cle A	3	7	.300	17	12	8-1	0	92.2	92	45	1	6	31	31	2.91	90	.262	.332	30-1	.133	-1	124	-3	-0.5
Total	6	34	82	.293	153	125	107-5	0	1137.2	1154	640	24	57	416	473	3.59	83	.264	.336	427-8	.166	-8	87	-77	-8.4
TOWNSEND, LEO Leo Alphonse "Lefty" B 1.15.1891 Mobile, AL D 12.3.1976 Mobile, AL BL/TL 5-10/160# d9.8																									
1920	Bos N	2	2	.500	7	1	1	0	24.1	18	4	1	0	2	0	1.48	206	.220	.238	6-1	.167	0	26	5	0.8
1921	Bos N	0	1	.000	1	1	0	0	1.1	2	4	0	0	3	0	27.00	14	.400	.625	0-0	—	0	180	-3	-0.5
Total	2	2	3	.400	8	2	1	0	25.2	20	8	1	0	5	0	2.81	110	.230	.272	6-1	.167	0	115	2	0.3
TOZER, BILL William Louis B 7.3.1882 St.Louis, MO D 2.23.1955 Belmont, CA BR/TR 6/200# d4.16																									
1908	Cin N	0	0	—	4	0	0	0	10.2	11	5	0	1	4	5	1.69	137	.268	.348	2-0	.000	-0		0	0.0
TRABER, BILLY William Henry B 9.18.1979 Torrance, CA BL/TL 6-5/200# d4.4																									
2003	Cle A	6	9	.400	33	18	1-1	0-0	111.2	132	67	15	5	40-4	88	5.24	84	.293	.355	4-0	.000	-0	94	-7	-0.8
TRACHSEL, STEVE Stephen Christopher B 10.31.1970 Oxnard, CA BR/TR 6-4/205# d9.19																									
1993	Chi N	0	2	.000	3	3	0	0-0	19.2	16	10	4	0	3-0	14	4.58	87	.219	.247	6-0	.167	0	75	-1	0.0
1994	Chi N	9	7	.563	22	22	1	0-0	146	133	57	19	3	54-4	108	3.21	130	.242	.312	43-8	.186	1	96	15	1.7
1995	Chi N	7	13	.350	30	29	2	0-0	160.2	174	104	25	0	76-8	117	5.15	80	.277	.352	49-6	.265	3	103	-19	-1.8
1996	Chi N★	13	9	.591	31	31	3-2	0-0	205	181	82	30	8	62-3	132	3.03	143	.235	.298	66-6	.106	-2	91	26	2.4
1997	Chi N	8	12	.400	34	34	0	0-0	201.1	225	110	32	5	69-6	160	4.51	95	.287	.344	60-11	.117	-0	89	-5	-0.4
1998	Chi N	15	8	.652	33	33	1	0-0	208	204	107	27	8	84-5	149	4.46	99	.260	.334	64-9	.266	6	109	0	0.8
1999	Chi N	8	18	.308	34	34	4	0-0	205.2	226	133	32	3	64-4	149	5.56	81	.280	.330	63-7	.111	-2	85	-21	-2.4
2000	TB A	6	10	.375	23	23	3-1	0-0	137.2	160	76	16	6	49-1	78	4.58	108	.294	.356	4-0	.250	0	75	6	0.6
	Tor A	2	5	.286	11	11	0	0-0	63	72	40	10	0	25-1	32	5.29	96	.293	.357	0-0	—	0	102	-1	-0.1
	Year	8	15	.348	34	34	3-1	0-0	200.2	232	46	26	6	74-2	110	4.80	104	.294	.356	4-0	.250	0	84	6	0.5
2001	NY N	11	13	.458	28	28	1-1	0-0	173.2	168	90	28	3	47-7	144	4.46	93	.254	.304	56-5	.161	-0	80	-5	-0.6
2002	NY N	11	11	.500	30	30	1-1	0-0	173.2	170	80	16	0	69-4	105	3.37	118	.258	.327	46-9	.109	-1*	96	9	1.0
2003	NY N	16	10	.615	33	33	2-2	0-0	204.2	204	90	26	3	65-9	111	3.78	110	.264	.320	58-11	.190	1*	101	10	1.3
Total	11	106	118	.473	312	311	18-7	0-0	1899	1933	979	265	39	667-52	1299	4.26	102	.265	.328	515-72	.167	6	93	14	2.5
TRAUTMAN, FRED Frederick Orlando B 3.24.1892 Bucyrus, OH D 2.15.1964 Bucyrus, OH BR/TR 6-1/175# d4.27																									
1915	New F	0	0	—	1	0	0	0	3	4	3	0	1	1	2	6.00	43	.364	.462	1-0	.000	-0		-1	-0.1
TRAUTWEIN, JOHN John Howard B 8.7.1962 Lafayette Hill, PA BR/TR 6-3/205# d4.7																									
1988	Bos A	0	1	.000	9	0	0	0-0	16	26	17	2	1	9-0	8	9.00	46	.382	.462	0-0	—	0		-8	-0.5
TRAVERS, ALLAN Aloysius Joseph "Joe" B 5.7.1892 Philadelphia, PA D 4.19.1968 Philadelphia, PA BR/TR 6-1/180# d5.18																									
1912	Det A	0	1	.000	1	1	1	0	8	26	24	0	0	7	1	15.75	21	.605	.660	3-0	.000	-0	45	-13	-0.9
TRAVERS, BILL William Edward B 10.27.1952 Norwood, MA BL/TL 6-6/200# d5.19																									
1974	Mil A	2	3	.400	23	1	0	0-0	53	59	29	6	1	30-5	31	4.92	74	.296	.386	0-0	—	0	195	-7	-0.6
1975	Mil A	6	11	.353	28	23	5	1-0	136.1	130	78	15	11	60-3	57	4.29	90	.251	.338	0-0	—	0	79	-8	-1.0
1976	Mil A☆	15	16	.484	34	34	15-3	0-0	240	211	92	21	8	95-5	120	2.81	124	.237	.315	0-0	—	0	77	15	1.9
1977	Mil A	4	12	.250	19	19	2-1	0-0	121.2	140	75	13	7	57-5	49	5.25	78	.291	.370	0-0	—	0	63	-14	-1.6
1978	Mil A	12	11	.522	28	28	8-3	0-0	175.2	184	93	20	6	58-1	66	4.41	86	.268	.329	0-0	—	0	132	-11	-1.2
1979	Mil A	14	8	.636	30	27	9-2	0-0	187.1	196	89	33	3	45-0	74	3.89	107	.270	.313	0-1	—	0	99	7	0.6
1980	Mil A	12	6	.667	29	25	7-1	0-0	154.1	147	76	20	6	47-2	62	3.91	99	.249	.309	0-0	—	0	128	-1	-0.1
1981	Cal A	0	1	.000	4	4	0	0-0	9.2	14	11	2	0	4-0	5	8.38	44	.333	.391	0-0	—	0	104	-5	-0.5
1983	Cal A	0	3	.000	10	7	0	0-0	42.2	58	32	4	2	19-1	24	5.91	68	.331	.397	0-0	—	0	81	-10	-0.6
Total	9	65	71	.478	205	168	46-10	1-0	1120.2	1139	575	134	44	415-22	488	4.10	94	.264	.333	0-1	—	0	97	-34	-3.1
TREKELL, HARRY Harry Roy B 11.18.1892 Buda, IL D 11.4.1965 Spokane, WA BR/TR 6-1.5/170# d8.16																									
1913	StL N	0	1	.000	7	1	1	0	30	25	20	2	2	8	15	4.50	72	.221	.285	9-0	.111	-0	47	-5	-0.3
TREMEL, BILL William Leonard "Mumbles" B 7.4.1929 Lilly, PA BR/TR 5-11/180# d6.12																									
1954	Chi N	1	2	.333	33	0	0	4	51.1	45	27	3	0	28	21	4.21	100	.243	.338	8-0	.250	0		0	0.0
1955	Chi N	3	0	1.000	23	0	0	2	38.2	33	18	2	0	18-2	13	3.72	110	.239	.323	7-0	.286	0		1	0.1
1956	Chi N	0	0	—	1	0	0	0	1	3	1	0	0	0-0	0	9.00	42	.600	.600	0-0	—	0		-1	0.0
Total	3	4	2	.667	57	0	0	6	91	81	46	5	0	46-2	34	4.05	102	.247	.335	15-0	.267	1		0	0.1
TRICE, BOB Robert Lee B 8.28.1926 Newton, GA D 9.16.1988 Weirton, WV BR/TR 6-3/190# d9.13																									
1953	Phi A	2	1	.667	3	3	1	0	23	25	14	4	0	6	4	5.48	78	.275	.320	7-0	.143	0	180	-2	-0.2
1954	Phi A	7	8	.467	19	18	8-1	0	119	146	86	14	0	48	22	5.60	70	.305	.362	42-0	.286	4*	103	-23	-2.0
1955	KC A	0	0	—	4	0	0	0	10	14	13	4	0	6-0	2	9.00	46	.326	.400	3-0	.667	1		-6	-0.2
Total	3	9	9	.500	26	21	9-1	0	152	185	113	22	0	60-0	28	5.80	69	.302	.359	52-0	.288	5	114	-31	-2.4
TRIMBLE, JOE Joseph Gerard B 10.12.1930 Providence, RI BR/TR 6-1/190# d4.29																									
1955	Bos A	0	0	—	2	0	0	0	2	0	0	0	0	3-0	1	0.00	—	.000	.375	0-0	—	0		1	0.1
1957	Pit N	0	2	.000	5	4	0	0	19.2	23	19	7	1	13-1	9	8.24	46	.291	.398	7-0	.143	-0	116	-9	-0.8
Total	2	0	2	.000	7	4	0	0	21.2	23	19	7	1	16-1	10	7.48	51	.274	.396	7-0	.143	-0	116	-8	-0.7
TRINKLE, KEN Kenneth Wayne B 12.15.1919 Paoli, IN D 5.10.1976 Paoli, IN BR/TR 6-1.5/175# d4.25 Mil 1944-45																									
1943	NY N	1	5	.167	11	6	1	0	45.2	51	23	3	1	15	10	3.74	92	.276	.333	12-0	.250	1	74	-2	-0.1
1946	NY N	7	14	.333	**48**	13	2	2	151	146	77	8	2	74	49	3.87	89	.253	.340	38-2	.079	-2	124	-8	-1.3
1947	NY N	8	4	.667	**62**	0	0	10	93.2	100	47	3	1	48	37	3.75	109	.278	.364	16-0	.188	-0		2	0.4
1948	NY N	4	5	.444	53	0	0	7	70.2	66	28	6	3	41	20	3.18	124	.244	.350	8-0	.250	0		6	1.0
1949	Phi N	1	1	.500	42	0	0	2	74.1	79	37	3	3	30	14	4.00	99	.299	.377	6-0	.000	-0		-1	0.0
Total	5	21	29	.420	216	19	3	21	435.1	442	212	23	10	208	130	3.74	100	.267	.352	80-2	.138	-2	102	-3	0.0
TRLICEK, RICK Richard Alan B 4.26.1969 Houston, TX BR/TR 6-2/200# d4.8																									
1992	Tor A	0	0	—	2	0	0	0-0	1.2	2	2	0	0	2-0	1	10.80	38	.286	.444	0-0	—	0		-1	-0.1
1993	LA N	1	2	.333	41	0	0	1-0	64	59	32	3	2	21-4	41	4.08	94	.244	.309	4-0	.250	0		-1	0.0
1994	Bos A	1	1	.500	12	1	0	0-1	22.1	32	21	5	0	16-2	7	8.06	62	.330	.425	0-0	—	0	37	-7	-0.5
1996	NY N	0	1	.000	5	0	0	0-0	5.1	3	2	0	1	3-1	3	3.38	119	.214	.389	0-0	—	0		1	0.1
1997	Bos A	3	4	.429	18	0	0	0-0	23.1	26	14	2	1	18-4	10	4.63	100	.289	.409	0-0	—	0		0	-0.1
	NY N	0	0	—	9	0	0	0-1	9	10	9	2	0	5-0	4	8.00	50	.303	.395	0-0	—	0		-4	-0.2
Total	5	5	8	.385	87	1	0	1-2	125.2	132	80	12	4	65-11	66	5.23	80	.273	.363	4-0	.250	0	37	-12	-0.8
TROEDSON, RICH Richard La Monte B 5.1.1950 Palo Alto, CA BL/TL 6-1/170# d4.9																									
1973	SD N	7	9	.438	50	18	2	1-0	152.1	167	77	12	1	59-8	81	4.25	82	.284	.347	40-3	.175	0	79	-11	-0.9
1974	SD N	1	1	.500	15	1	0	1-0	18.2	24	18	6	1	8-1	11	8.68	41	.300	.371	1-0	.000	-0	24	-10	-1.1
Total	2	8	10	.444	65	19	2	2-0	171	191	95	18	2	67-9	92	4.74	74	.286	.350	41-3	.171	-0	76	-21	-2.0
TROMBLEY, MIKE Michael Scott B 4.14.1967 Springfield, MA BR/TR 6-2/208# d8.19																									
1992	Min A	3	2	.600	10	7	0	0-0	46.1	43	20	5	1	17-0	38	3.30	123	.247	.318	0-0	—	0	96	3	0.3
1993	Min A	6	6	.500	44	10	0	2-3	114.1	131	72	15	3	41-4	85	4.88	90	.290	.348	0-0	—	0	95	-8	-0.7
1994	Min A	2	0	1.000	24	0	0	0-1	48.1	56	36	10	3	18-2	32	6.33	77	.287	.353	0-0	—	0		-7	-0.4
1995	Min A	4	8	.333	20	18	0	0-0	97.2	107	68	18	3	42-1	68	5.62	85	.273	.346	0-0	—	0	108	-10	-1.0

Year	Tm Lg	W	L	Pct	G	GS	CG-Sho	SV-BS	IP	H	R	HR	HB	BB-IB	SO	ERA	AERA	OAV	OOB	AB-SH	AVG	PB	Sup	APR	PW
1996	Min A	5	1	.833	43	0	0	6-3	68.2	61	24	2	5	25-8	57	3.01	170	.236	.312	0-0	—	0		16	1.4
1997	Min A	2	3	.400	67	0	0	1-0	82.1	77	43	7	2	31-4	74	4.37	107	.248	.317	1-0	.000	-0		3	0.1
1998	Min A	6	5	.545	77	1	0	1-3	96.2	90	41	16	5	41-3	89	3.63	131	.247	.331	0-0	—	0	78	12	1.2
1999	Min A	2	8	.200	75	0	0	24-6	87.1	93	42	15	2	28-2	82	4.33	118	.272	.328	0-0	—	0		8	1.2
2000	Bal A	4	5	.444	75	0	0	4-7	72	67	34	15	4	38-8	72	4.13	115	.247	.346	1-0	.000	-0		6	0.7
2001	Bal A	3	4	.429	50	0	0	6-3	54.2	38	23	4	2	27-2	45	3.46	124	.200	.302	0-0	—	0		5	0.7
	LA N	0	4	.000	19	0	0	0-0	23.1	27	17	5	0	10-3	27	6.56	61	.290	.356	0-0	—	0		-6	-1.0
2002	Min A	0	1	.000	5	0	0	0-1	4	10	7	2	0	1-0	3	15.75	29	.455	.478	0-0	—	0		-5	-0.8
Total	11	37	47	.440	509	36	0	44-27	795.2	800	427	114	30	319-37	672	4.48	104	.261	.334	2-0	.000	-0	99	17	1.7
TROSKY, HAL Harold Arthur Jr. "Hoot" (b: Harold Arthur Troyavesky Jr.) B 9.29.1936 Cleveland, OH BR/TR 6-3/205# d9.25 f-Hal																									
1958	Chi A	1	0	1.000	2	0	0	0	3	5	3	0	0	2-0	1	6.00	61	.385	.467	0-0	—	0		-1	-0.2
TROTTER, BILL William Felix B 8.10.1908 Cisne, IL D 8.26.1984 Arlington, MA BR/TR 6-2/195# d4.23																									
1937	StL A	2	9	.182	34	12	3	1	122.1	150	88	14	7	50	37	5.81	83	.304	.376	33-2	.030	-3	92	-12	-1.2
1938	StL A	0	1	.000	1	1	1	0	8	8	7	0	0	0	1	5.63	88	.242	.242	2-1	.000	-0	89	-1	-0.1
1939	StL A	6	13	.316	41	13	4	0	156.2	205	120	16	5	54	61	5.34	91	.318	.376	37-7	.108	-1	68	-14	-1.5
1940	StL A	7	6	.538	36	4	1	2	98	117	56	5	1	31	29	3.77	122	.300	.353	22-2	.045	-2	67	4	0.3
1941	StL A	4	2	.667	29	0	0	0	49.2	68	35	2	2	19	17	5.98	72	.332	.394	6-1	.000	-1		-8	-0.8
1942	StL A	0	1	.000	3	0	0	0	2	5	5	0	0	2	0	18.00	21	.385	.467	0-0	—	0		-3	-0.6
	Was A	3	1	.750	17	0	0	0	40.2	52	29	4	0	14	13	5.75	63	.304	.357	8-1	.000	-0		-9	-0.8
	Year	3	2	.600	20	0	0	0	42.2	57	38	4	0	16	13	6.33	58	.310	.365	8-1	.000	-0		-12	-1.4
1944	StL N	0	1	.000	2	1	0	0	6	14	14	5	0	4	0	13.50	26	.467	.529	1-0	.000	-0	119	-8	-1.0
Total	7	22	34	.393	163	31	9	3	483.1	619	354	46	15	174	158	5.40	85	.313	.373	109-14	.055	-7	82	-51	-5.7
TROUT, DIZZY Paul Howard B 6.29.1915 Sandcut, IN D 2.28.1972 Harvey, IL BR/TR 6-2.5/195# d4.25 s-Steve																									
1939	Det A	9	10	.474	33	22	6	2	162	168	82	5	4	74	72	3.61	135	.270	.351	57-2	.211	-0*	91	19	1.9
1940	†Det A	3	7	.300	33	10	1	2	100.2	125	60	4	3	54	64	4.47	106	.307	.392	31-0	.129	-2	100	2	0.1
1941	Det A	9	9	.500	37	18	6-1	2	151.2	144	76	7	2	84	88	3.74	122	.252	.350	50-0	.180	0*	81	11	1.3
1942	Det A	12	18	.400	35	29	13-1	0	223	214	98	15	4	89	91	3.43	115	.249	.322	75-4	.213	2*	82	14	2.2
1943	Det A	**20**	12	.625	44	30	18-**5**	6	246.2	204	83	6	0	101	111	2.48	142	.227	.305	91-4	.220	2*	98	26	4.1
1944	Det A☆	27	14	.659	49	**40**	**33-7**	0	**352.1**	314	104	9	4	83	144	**2.12**	**168**	.237	.284	133-2	.271	12*	96	**53**	**8.2**
1945	†Det A	18	15	.545	41	31	18-4	2	246.1	252	108	8	0	79	97	3.14	112	.267	.324	102-0	.245	4*	127	9	1.7
1946	Det A	17	13	.567	38	32	23-5	3	276.1	244	85	11	3	97	151	2.34	156	.238	.306	103-4	.194	3*	95	37	4.7
1947	Det A☆	10	11	.476	32	26	9-2	2	186.1	186	85	6	3	65	74	3.48	108	.261	.325	68-1	.162	3*	115	5	1.1
1948	Det A	10	14	.417	32	23	11-2	2	183.2	193	87	6	2	73	91	3.43	127	.269	.338	69-2	.217	2	94	16	2.1
1949	Det A	3	6	.333	33	0	0	3	59.1	68	35	2	0	21	19	4.40	95	.292	.350	14-0	.143	0		-3	-0.3
1950	Det A	13	5	.722	34	20	11-1	4	184.2	190	84	13	5	64	88	3.75	125	.267	.332	63-3	.190	1	97	19	1.9
1951	Det A	9	14	.391	42	22	7	5	191.2	172	98	13	1	75	89	4.04	103	.240	.312	52-3	.269	5	85	2	1.0
1952	Det A	1	5	.167	10	2	0	1	27	30	16	4	0	19	20	5.33	71	.286	.395	9-1	.333	1	23	-4	-0.6
	Bos A	9	8	.529	26	17	2	1	133.2	133	62	3	3	68	57	3.64	108	.263	.354	44-0	.136	-1	95	4	0.4
	Year	10	13	.435	36	19	2	2	160.2	163	66	7	3	87	77	3.92	100	.267	.361	53-1	.170	-1	88	1	-0.2
1957	Bal A	0	0	—	2	0	0	0	0.1	4	3	0	0	0-0	0	81.00	4	.800	.800	0-0	—	0		-3	-0.1
Total	15	170	161	.514	521	322	158-28	35	2725.2	2641	1166	112	34	1046-**0**	1256	3.23	124	.255	.325	961-26	.213	31	96	207	29.7
TROUT, STEVE Steven Russell B 7.30.1957 Detroit, MI BL/TL 6-4/195# d7.1 f-Dizzy																									
1978	Chi A	3	0	1.000	4	3	1	0-0	22.1	19	10	0	0	11-0	11	4.03	95	.229	.313	0-0	—	0	157	0	0.0
1979	Chi A	11	8	.579	34	18	6-2	4-3	155	165	77	10	5	59-5	76	3.89	110	.273	.341	0-0	—	0	111	7	0.8
1980	Chi A	9	16	.360	32	30	7-2	0-0	199.2	229	102	14	9	49-5	89	3.70	109	.290	.337	0-0	—	0	85	4	0.6
1981	Chi A	8	7	.533	20	18	3	0-0	124.2	122	53	7	4	38-0	54	3.47	103	.261	.320	0-0	—	0	107	3	0.3
1982	Chi A	6	9	.400	25	19	2	0-0	120.1	130	76	9	2	50-2	62	4.26	95	.273	.342	0-0	—	0	95	-8	-0.8
1983	Chi N	10	14	.417	34	32	1	0-0	180	217	105	13	2	59-5	80	4.65	82	.305	.357	62-8	.194	1	97	-17	-1.9
1984	†Chi N	13	7	.650	32	31	6-2	0-1	190	205	80	7	2	59-7	81	3.41	115	.285	.339	61-5	.131	-1	116	9	1.0
1985	Chi N	9	7	.563	24	24	3-1	0-0	140.2	142	57	8	1	63-7	44	3.39	118	.270	.347	46-9	.109	-2	106	9	0.9
1986	Chi N	5	7	.417	37	25	0	0-0	161	184	88	6	1	78-13	69	4.75	85	.298	.375	43-4	.209	1	115	-10	-0.6
1987	Chi N	6	3	.667	11	11	3-2	0-0	75	72	27	3	1	27-0	32	3.00	143	.260	.326	26-3	.154	-1	106	10	1.2
	NY A	0	4	.000	14	9	0	0-0	46.1	51	36	4	1	37-0	27	6.60	67	.274	.397	0-0	—	0	85	-11	-0.8
1988	Sea A	4	7	.364	15	13	0	0-0	56.1	86	53	6	5	31-2	14	7.83	53	.361	.440	0-0	—	0	89	-21	-3.3
1989	Sea A	4	3	.571	19	3	0	0-2	30	43	27	3	0	17-2	17	6.60	61	.333	.408	0-0	—	0	135	-9	-1.7
Total	12	88	92	.489	301	236	32-9	4-6	1501.1	1665	791	90	33	578-48	656	4.18	96	.286	.351	238-29	.160	-2	103	-34	-4.3
TROWBRIDGE, BOB Robert B 6.27.1930 Hudson, NY D 4.3.1980 Hudson, NY BR/TR 6-1/190# d4.22																									
1956	Mil N	3	2	.600	19	4	1	0	50.2	38	15	4	2	34-2	40	2.66	130	.210	.339	7-1	.000	-1	146	6	0.5
1957	†Mil N	7	5	.583	32	16	3-1	1	126	118	57	9	1	52-5	75	3.64	96	.248	.321	39-1	.103	-2	138	-2	-0.4
1958	Mil N	1	3	.250	27	4	0	1	55	53	26	4	1	26-3	31	3.93	90	.252	.332	9-1	.111	-1	89	-3	-0.3
1959	Mil N	1	0	1.000	16	0	0	1	30.1	45	25	2	0	10-2	22	5.93	60	.344	.387	4-0	.000	-0		-10	-0.6
1960	KC A	1	3	.250	22	1	0	2	68.1	70	41	6	1	34-3	33	4.61	86	.281	.365	18-0	.056	-1	111	-5	-0.4
Total	5	13	13	.500	116	25	4-1	5	330.1	324	164	25	5	156-15	201	3.95	91	.260	.341	77-3	.078	-5	128	-14	-1.2
TROY, BUN Robert B 8.27.1888 Bad Wurzach, Germany D 10.7.1918 Petit Maujouym, France BR/TR 6-4/195# d9.15																									
1912	Det A	0	1	.000	1	1	0	0	6.2	9	4	0	1	3	1	5.40	60	.346	.433	2-0	.000	-0	68	-1	-0.2
TRUCKS, VIRGIL Virgil Oliver "Fire" B 4.26.1917 Birmingham, AL BR/TR 5-11/198# d9.27 Mil 1944-45 C1																									
1941	Det A	0	0	—	1	0	0	0	2	4	2	0	0	0	3	9.00	50	.500	.500	0-0	—	0		-1	0.0
1942	Det A	14	8	.636	28	20	8-2	0	167.2	147	64	3	2	74	91	2.74	144	.231	.314	65-1	.123	-4	96	20	2.1
1943	Det A	16	10	.615	33	25	10-2	2	202.2	170	72	11	1	52	118	2.84	124	.225	.276	72-0	.181	-2	111	16	1.8
1945	†Det A	0	0	—	1	1	0	0	5.1	3	1	0	0	2	3	1.69	208	.176	.263	2-0	.000	-0	145	1	0.1
1946	Det A	14	9	.609	32	29	15-2	0	236.2	217	94	23	3	75	161	3.23	113	.241	.302	95-2	.179	-1	95	12	0.9
1947	Det A	10	12	.455	36	26	8-2	2	180.2	186	105	14	2	79	108	4.53	83	.263	.339	70-0	.271	2	132	-15	-1.5
1948	Det A	14	13	.519	43	26	7	2	211.2	190	97	14	2	85	123	3.78	115	.240	.315	79-2	.165	-3	91	16	1.4
1949	Det A★	19	11	.633	41	32	17-**6**	4	275	209	95	16	4	124	**153**	2.81	148	.211	.301	100-5	.120	-6	82	42	3.5
1950	Det A	3	1	.750	7	7	2-1	0	48.1	45	20	6	1	21	25	3.54	133	.243	.324	20-0	.150	-1	113	6	0.4
1951	Det A	13	8	.619	37	18	6-1	1	153.2	153	81	9	5	75	89	4.33	96	.262	.350	55-2	.236	-0	108	-2	-0.2
1952	Det A	5	19	.208	35	29	8-3	1	197	190	99	12	7	82	129	3.97	96	.251	.330	64-2	.188	-0	62	-4	-0.4
1953	StL A	5	4	.556	16	12	4-2	2	88	83	37	4	4	32	47	3.07	137	.249	.322	25-4	.160	-1	72	9	0.8
	Chi A	15	6	.714	24	21	13-3	1	176.1	151	60	14	3	67	102	2.86	141	.232	.306	63-9	.238	2	133	24	3.0
	Year	20	10	.667	40	33	17-5	3	264.1	234	66	18	7	99	149	2.93	139	.238	.312	88-13	.216	1	110	32	3.8
1954	Chi A★	19	12	.613	40	33	16-**5**	3	264.2	224	87	13	1	95	152	2.79	134	.228	.296	93-9	.183	-1	117	30	3.3
1955	Chi A	13	8	.619	32	26	7-3	0	175	176	78	19	2	61-5	91	3.96	100	.260	.322	64-7	.125	-3	116	2	-0.1
1956	Det A	6	5	.545	22	16	3-1	1	120	104	56	15	6	63-5	43	3.83	108	.239	.342	45-2	.244	1	111	5	0.4
1957	KC A	9	7	.563	48	7	0	7	116	106	45	12	2	62-8	55	3.03	131	.248	.345	28-1	.143	-1	52	11	1.4
1958	KC A	0	1	.000	16	0	0	3	22	18	7	2	0	15-1	15	2.05	191	.222	.340	1-0	.000	-0		4	0.3
	NY A	2	1	.667	25	0	0	1	39.2	40	24	1	2	24-0	26	4.54	78	.265	.359	8-0	.250	0		-5	-0.4
	Year	2	2	.500	41	0	0	4	61.2	58	33	3	2	39-1	41	3.65	100	.250	.352	9-0	.222	0		-1	-0.1
Total	17	177	135	.567	517	328	124-33	30	2682.1	2416	1124	188	47	1088-**19**	1534	3.39	117	.240	.316	949-46	.180	-19	101	171	16.8
TRUJILLO, J.J. John B 10.9.1975 Corpus Christi, TX BR/TR 6/180# d6.11																									
2002	SD N	0	1	.000	4	0	0	0-0	2.2	4	3	1	1	6-0	3	10.13	37	.364	.611	0-0	—	0		-2	-0.4
TRUJILLO, MIKE Michael Andrew B 1.12.1960 Denver, CO BR/TR 6-1/180# d4.14																									
1985	Bos A	4	4	.500	27	7	1	1-0	84	112	55	7	3	23-1	19	4.82	89	.320	.365	0-0	—	0	121	-7	-0.6
1986	Bos A	0	0	—	3	0	0	0-0	5.2	7	6	0	0	6-2	4	9.53	44	.304	.448	0-0	—	0		-3	-0.1
	Sea A	3	2	.600	11	4	1-1	1-0	41.1	32	11	5	0	15-1	19	2.40	178	.215	.285	0-0	—	0	80	9	1.0
	Year	3	2	.600	14	4	1-1	1-0	47	39	15	5	0	21-3	23	3.26	130	.227	.309	0-0	—	0	80	6	0.9

Year	Tm Lg	W	L	Pct	G	GS	CG-Sho	SV-BS	IP	H	R	HR	HB	BB-IB	SO	ERA	AERA	OAV	OOB	AB-SH	AVG	PB	Sup	APR	PW
1987	Sea A	4	4	.500	28	7	0	1-1	65.2	70	46	12	2	26-0	36	6.17	77	.277	.346	0-0	—	0	96	-8	-0.9
1988	Det A	0	0	—	6	0	0	0-0	12.1	11	7	2	0	5-2	5	5.11	75	.234	.308	0-0	—	0		-1	-0.1
1989	Det A	1	2	.333	8	4	1	0-0	25.2	35	17	3	0	13-0	13	5.96	64	.333	.397	0-0	—	0	130	-5	-0.5
Total	5	12	12	.500	83	22	3-1	3-1	234.2	267	142	29	5	88-6	96	5.02	86	.288	.350	0-0	—	0	107	-15	-1.2

TRUMBULL, ED Edward J. (b: Edward J. Trembly) B 11.3.1860 Chicopee, MA D 1.14.1937 Kingston, PA d5.10 ▲

Year	Tm Lg	W	L	Pct	G	GS	CG-Sho	SV-BS	IP	H	R	HR	HB	BB-IB	SO	ERA	AERA	OAV	OOB	AB-SH	AVG	PB	Sup	APR	PW
1884	Was AA	1	9	.100	10	10	10	0	84	108	90	4	1	31	43	4.71	64	.295	.352	86	.116	-2*	88	-18	-1.8

TSAMIS, GEORGE George Alex B 6.14.1967 Campbell, CA BR/TL 6-2/190# d4.26

Year	Tm Lg	W	L	Pct	G	GS	CG-Sho	SV-BS	IP	H	R	HR	HB	BB-IB	SO	ERA	AERA	OAV	OOB	AB-SH	AVG	PB	Sup	APR	PW
1993	Min A	1	2	.333	41	0	0	1-1	68.1	86	51	9	3	27-5	30	6.19	71	.317	.378	0-0	—	0		-14	-0.6

TSAO, CHIN-HUI Chin-Hui B 6.2.1981 Hualien, Taiwan BR/TR 6-2/170# d7.25

Year	Tm Lg	W	L	Pct	G	GS	CG-Sho	SV-BS	IP	H	R	HR	HB	BB-IB	SO	ERA	AERA	OAV	OOB	AB-SH	AVG	PB	Sup	APR	PW
2003	Col N	3	3	.500	9	8	0	0-0	43.1	48	30	11	4	20-1	29	6.02	82	.284	.373	13-2	.154	-0	84	-4	-0.5

TSITOURIS, JOHN John Philip B 5.4.1936 Monroe, NC BR/TR 6/175# d6.13

Year	Tm Lg	W	L	Pct	G	GS	CG-Sho	SV-BS	IP	H	R	HR	HB	BB-IB	SO	ERA	AERA	OAV	OOB	AB-SH	AVG	PB	Sup	APR	PW
1957	Det A	1	0	1.000	2	0	0	0	3.1	8	3	0	0	2-0	2	8.10	48	.500	.556	1-0	.000	-0		-1	-0.3
1958	KC A	0	0	—	1	1	0	0	3	2	1	0	0	2-0	1	3.00	130	.182	.308	1-0	.000	-0	92	0	0.0
1959	KC A	4	3	.571	24	10	0	0	83.1	90	52	3	3	35-3	50	4.97	81	.271	.344	20-3	.150	-1	110	-8	-0.7
1960	KC A	0	2	.000	14	2	0	0	33	38	25	3	8	21-1	12	6.55	61	.297	.421	6-1	.000	-1	111	-8	-0.5
1962	Cin N	1	0	1.000	4	2	1-1	0	21.1	13	2	0	3	7-0	7	0.84	477	.181	.280	5-1	.000	-1	87	7	0.3
1963	Cin N	12	8	.600	30	21	8-3	0	191	167	73	20	11	38-1	113	3.16	106	.232	.280	62-3	.081	-3	83	5	-0.1
1964	Cin N	9	13	.409	37	24	6-1	2	175.1	178	90	20	5	75-6	146	3.80	95	.263	.338	58-2	.190	2	96	-6	-0.6
1965	Cin N	6	9	.400	31	20	3	1	131	134	87	18	9	65-1	91	4.95	76	.265	.354	43-3	.070	-2	120	-19	-2.3
1966	Cin N	0	0	—	1	0	0	0	1	3	2	0	0	1-0	0	18.00	22	.750	.800	0-0	—	0		-1	-0.1
1967	Cin N	1	0	1.000	2	1	0	0	8	4	3	1	0	6-0	4	3.38	111	.154	.313	0-1	—	0	234	0	0.1
1968	Cin N	0	3	.000	3	3	0	0	12.2	16	10	6	1	8-0	6	7.11	44	.302	.403	2-0	.000	0	27	-5	-0.9
Total	11	34	38	.472	149	84	18-5	3	663	653	348	71	40	260-12	432	4.13	88	.257	.333	198-14	.111	-6	100	-36	-5.1

TUCKER, T.J. Thomas John B 8.20.1978 Clearwater, FL BR/TR 6-3/245# d6.3

Year	Tm Lg	W	L	Pct	G	GS	CG-Sho	SV-BS	IP	H	R	HR	HB	BB-IB	SO	ERA	AERA	OAV	OOB	AB-SH	AVG	PB	Sup	APR	PW
2000	Mon N	0	1	.000	2	2	0	0-0	7	11	9	5	0	3-0	2	11.57	41	.344	.400	1-0	1.000	0	96	-5	-0.5
2002	Mon N	6	3	.667	57	0	0	4-3	61.1	69	32	5	0	31-9	42	4.11	109	.290	.369	4-0	.750	1*		2	0.4
2003	Mon N	2	3	.400	45	7	0	0-2	80	90	49	8	4	20-1	47	4.72	99	.278	.327	19-1	.263	1*	100	-1	0.0
Total	3	8	7	.533	104	9	0	4-5	148.1	170	90	18	4	54-10	91	4.79	96	.286	.348	24-1	.375	2	101	-4	-0.1

TUCKEY, TOM Thomas H. "Tabasco Tom" B 10.7.1883 Birmingham, England D 10.17.1950 New York, NY TL 6-3/?# d8.11

Year	Tm Lg	W	L	Pct	G	GS	CG-Sho	SV-BS	IP	H	R	HR	HB	BB-IB	SO	ERA	AERA	OAV	OOB	AB-SH	AVG	PB	Sup	APR	PW
1908	Bos N	3	3	.500	8	8	3-1	0	72	60	21	2	4	20	26	2.50	96	.265	.336	20-1	.050	-2	80	2	0.0
1909	Bos N	0	9	.000	17	10	4	0	90.2	104	59	1	3	22	16	4.27	66	.295	.342	29-2	.138	-1	82	-13	-1.3
Total	2	3	12	.200	25	18	7-1	0	162.2	164	80	3	7	42	42	3.49	76	.284	.340	49-3	.102	-3	81	-11	-1.3

TUDOR, JOHN John Thomas B 2.2.1954 Schenectady, NY BL/TL 6/185# d8.16

Year	Tm Lg	W	L	Pct	G	GS	CG-Sho	SV-BS	IP	H	R	HR	HB	BB-IB	SO	ERA	AERA	OAV	OOB	AB-SH	AVG	PB	Sup	APR	PW
1979	Bos A	1	2	.333	6	6	1	0-0	28	39	23	2	0	9-1	11	6.43	69	.345	.384	0-0	—	0	85	-6	-0.5
1980	Bos A	8	5	.615	16	13	5	0-0	92.1	81	35	4	3	31-1	45	3.02	140	.238	.304	0-0	—	0	99	11	1.6
1981	Bos A	4	3	.571	18	11	2	1-0	78.2	74	44	11	3	28-1	44	4.58	85	.252	.319	0-0	—	0	118	-5	-0.4
1982	Bos A	13	10	.565	32	30	6-1	0-0	195.2	215	90	20	8	59-3	146	3.63	119	.280	.336	0-0	—	0	95	12	1.5
1983	Bos A	13	12	.520	34	34	7-2	0-0	242	236	122	32	4	81-3	136	4.09	107	.255	.316	0-0	—	0	84	7	0.6
1984	Pit N	12	11	.522	32	32	6-1	0-0	212	200	81	19	1	56-2	117	3.27	110	.248	.295	76-4	.211	2*	83	10	1.3
1985	†StL N	21	8	.724	36	36	14-**10**	0-0	275	209	68	14	5	49-4	169	1.93	183	.209	**.249**	94-7	.138	1*	111	49	5.6
1986	StL N	13	7	.650	30	30	3	0-0	219	197	81	22	1	53-5	107	2.92	125	.244	.289	72-13	.153	-0	95	17	1.5
1987	†StL N	10	2	.833	16	16	0	0-0	96	100	43	11	1	32-1	54	3.84	108	.272	.331	35-3	.200	1*	109	4	0.6
1988	StL N	6	5	.545	21	21	4-1	0-0	145.1	131	44	5	1	31-7	55	2.29	152	.247	.287	46-5	.109	-1*	92	18	1.3
	†LA N	4	3	.571	9	9	1	0-0	52.1	58	16	5	0	10-0	32	2.41	139	.284	.318	13-2	.000	-1	95	6	0.6
	Year	10	8	.556	30	30	5-1	0-0	197.2	189	20	10	1	41-7	87	2.32	148	.257	.295	59-7	.085	-2	93	24	1.9
1989	LA N	0	0	—	6	3	0	0-0	14.1	17	5	1	0	6-0	9	3.14	109	.309	.377	2-0	.000	-0	86	1	0.0
1990	StL N	12	4	.750	25	22	1-1	0-0	146.1	120	48	10	2	30-4	63	2.40	159	.225	.268	46-7	.152	0	111	21	2.4
Total	12	117	72	.619	281	263	50-16	1-0	1797	1677	700	156	29	475-32	988	3.12	124	.248	.299	384-41	.154	3	97	145	16.1

TUERO, OSCAR Oscar (Monzon) (b: Oscar Tuero Monzon) B 12.17.1898 , , CAN D 10.21.1960 Houston, TX BR/TR 5-8.5/158# d5.30

Year	Tm Lg	W	L	Pct	G	GS	CG-Sho	SV-BS	IP	H	R	HR	HB	BB-IB	SO	ERA	AERA	OAV	OOB	AB-SH	AVG	PB	Sup	APR	PW
1918	StL N	1	2	.333	11	3	2	0	44.1	32	12	0	3	10	13	1.02	267	.208	.269	12-0	.250	0*	28	7	0.4
1919	StL N	5	7	.417	**45**	16	4	**4**	154.2	137	71	4	10	42	45	3.20	87	.242	.306	39-2	.205	1	100	-8	-0.6
1920	StL N	0	0	—	2	0	0	0	0.2	5	4	0	0	1	0	54.00	6	.833	.857	0-0	—	0		-4	-0.2
Total	3	6	9	.400	58	19	6	4	199.2	174	87	4	13	53	58	2.88	96	.240	.303	51-2	.216	1	88	-5	-0.4

TUFTS, BOB Robert Malcolm B 11.2.1955 Medford, MA BL/TL 6-5/215# d8.10

Year	Tm Lg	W	L	Pct	G	GS	CG-Sho	SV-BS	IP	H	R	HR	HB	BB-IB	SO	ERA	AERA	OAV	OOB	AB-SH	AVG	PB	Sup	APR	PW
1981	SF N	0	0	—	11	0	0	0-1	15.1	20	9	1	1	6-0	12	3.52	97	.308	.370	1-0	.000	-0		-1	0.0
1982	KC A	2	0	1.000	10	0	0	2-1	20	24	10	3	0	3-0	13	4.50	91	.293	.314	0-0	—	0		0	-0.1
1983	KC A	0	0	—	6	0	0	0-0	6.2	16	8	1	1	5-0	3	8.10	50	.444	.524	0-0	—	0		-4	-0.2
Total	3	2	0	1.000	27	0	0	2-2	42	60	27	5	2	14-0	28	4.71	82	.328	.378	1-0	.000	-0		-5	-0.3

TUNNELL, LEE Byron Lee B 10.30.1960 Tyler, TX BR/TR 6-1/180# d9.4

Year	Tm Lg	W	L	Pct	G	GS	CG-Sho	SV-BS	IP	H	R	HR	HB	BB-IB	SO	ERA	AERA	OAV	OOB	AB-SH	AVG	PB	Sup	APR	PW
1982	Pit N	1	1	.500	5	3	0	0-0	18.1	17	8	1	2	5-0	4	3.93	95	.254	.324	4-1	.000	-0	127	0	0.0
1983	Pit N	11	6	.647	35	25	5-3	0-0	177.2	167	81	15	2	58-3	95	3.65	102	.252	.311	58-8	.121	-1	97	1	0.0
1984	Pit N	1	7	.125	26	6	0	1-4	68.1	81	44	6	0	40-6	51	5.27	68	.298	.387	12-3	.083	-1	94	-12	-1.4
1985	Pit N	4	10	.286	24	23	0	0-0	132.1	126	70	11	1	57-4	74	4.01	89	.251	.327	47-0	.085	-2	95	-8	-1.0
1987	†StL N	4	4	.500	32	9	0	0-0	74.1	90	45	5	1	34-7	49	4.84	86	.307	.377	17-3	.235	0*	143	-6	-0.5
1989	Min A	1	0	1.000	10	0	0	0-0	12	18	8	1	0	6-1	7	6.00	69	.340	.407	0-0	—	0		-2	-0.2
Total	6	22	28	.440	132	66	5-3	1-4	483	499	256	39	6	200-21	280	4.23	88	.270	.341	138-15	.116	-4	104	-27	-3.1

TURBEVILLE, GEORGE George Elkins B 8.24.1914 Turbeville, SC D 10.5.1983 Salisbury, NC BR/TL 6-1/175# d7.20

Year	Tm Lg	W	L	Pct	G	GS	CG-Sho	SV-BS	IP	H	R	HR	HB	BB-IB	SO	ERA	AERA	OAV	OOB	AB-SH	AVG	PB	Sup	APR	PW
1935	Phi A	0	3	.000	19	6	2	0	63.2	74	58	2	0	69	20	7.63	60	.312	.467	19-1	.105	-2	51	-20	-1.1
1936	Phi A	2	5	.286	12	6	2	0	43.2	42	36	6	6	32	10	6.39	80	.258	.398	14-1	.143	-1	60	-6	-0.9
1937	Phi A	0	4	.000	31	3	0	0	77.1	80	50	2	0	56	17	4.77	99	.266	.381	26-0	.231	0	117	-1	-0.1
Total	3	2	12	.143	62	15	4	0	184.2	196	144	10	6	157	47	6.14	77	.280	.416	59-2	.169	-2	69	-27	-2.1

TURK, LUCAS Lucas Newton "Harlem" or "Chief" B 5.2.1898 Homer, GA D 1.11.1994 Homer, GA BR/TR 6/165# d6.7

Year	Tm Lg	W	L	Pct	G	GS	CG-Sho	SV-BS	IP	H	R	HR	HB	BB-IB	SO	ERA	AERA	OAV	OOB	AB-SH	AVG	PB	Sup	APR	PW
1922	Was A	0	0	—	5	0	0	0	11.2	16	10	0	0	5	1	6.94	56	.340	.404	4-0	.250	0		-4	-0.2

TURLEY, BOB Robert Lee "Bullet Bob" B 9.19.1930 Troy, IL BR/TR 6-2/215# d9.29 Mil 1952 C1

Year	Tm Lg	W	L	Pct	G	GS	CG-Sho	SV-BS	IP	H	R	HR	HB	BB-IB	SO	ERA	AERA	OAV	OOB	AB-SH	AVG	PB	Sup	APR	PW
1951	StL A	0	1	.000	1	1	0	0	7.1	11	6	0	0	3	5	7.36	60	.355	.412	2-0	.000	-0	61	-2	-0.2
1953	StL A	2	6	.250	10	7	3-1	0	60.1	39	24	4	2	44	61	3.28	128	.184	.329	18-2	.278	1	39	6	0.9
1954	Bal A☆	14	15	.483	35	35	14	0	247.1	178	106	7	7	181	**185**	3.46	104	**.203**	.340	81-6	.136	-3	82	4	0.2
1955	†NY A☆	17	13	.567	36	34	13-6	1	246.2	168	92	16	7	177-4	210	3.06	122	**.193**	.331	82-8	.134	-0	118	22	2.4
1956	†NY A	8	4	.667	27	21	5-1	1	132	138	76	13	4	103-0	91	5.05	77	.273	.398	46-3	.174	-0	152	-15	-1.3
1957	†NY A	13	6	.684	32	23	9-4	3	176.1	120	59	17	9	85-1	152	2.71	133	**.194**	.298	57-2	.088	-2	115	19	1.8
1958	†NY A★	**21**	7	**.750**	33	31	**19**-6	1	245.1	178	82	24	8	128-2	168	2.97	119	**.206**	.311	88-6	.136	-1	128	22	2.2
1959	NY A	8	11	.421	33	22	7-3	0	154.1	141	80	15	3	83-3	111	4.32	84	.245	.338	46-2	.087	-2	90	-10	-1.3
1960	†NY A	9	3	.750	34	24	4-1	5	173.1	138	67	14	5	87-3	87	3.27	110	.222	.319	55-2	.073	-4	139	9	0.2
1961	NY A	3	5	.375	15	12	1	0	72	74	47	11	4	51-0	48	5.75	65	.269	.390	21-3	.095	-1	103	-16	-1.6
1962	NY A	3	3	.500	24	8	0	1	69	68	45	8	4	47-2	42	4.57	82	.263	.379	12-3	.000	-1	110	-9	-0.9
1963	LA A	2	7	.222	19	12	3-2	0	87.1	71	41	5	2	51-6	70	3.30	104	.222	.331	25-0	.160	1	73	0	0.0
	Bos A	1	4	.200	11	7	0	0	41.1	42	28	6	1	28-0	35	6.10	62	.256	.366	14-0	.214	0	77	-9	-1.0
	Year	3	11	.214	30	19	3-2	0	128.2	113	31	11	3	79-6	105	4.20	84	.233	.343	39-0	.179	1	75	-10	-1.0
Total	12	101	85	.543	310	237	78-24	12	1712.2	1366	753	140	56	1068-**21**	1265	3.64	101	.220	.337	547-37	.126	-12	109	21	1.4

TURNBOW, DERRICK Thomas Derrick B 1.25.1978 Union City, TN BR/TR 6-3/195# d4.17

Year	Tm Lg	W	L	Pct	G	GS	CG-Sho	SV-BS	IP	H	R	HR	HB	BB-IB	SO	ERA	AERA	OAV	OOB	AB-SH	AVG	PB	Sup	APR	PW
2000	Ana A	0	0	—	24	1	0	0-0	38	36	21	7	2	36-0	25	4.74	107	.254	.409	0-0	—	0	277	2	0.0
2003	Ana A	2	0	1.000	11	0	0	0-0	15.1	7	1	0	0	3-0	15	0.59	736	.140	.189	0-0	—	0		7	0.8

Year	Tm Lg	W	L	Pct	G	GS	CG-Sho	SV-BS	IP	H	R	HR	HB	BB-IB	SO	ERA	AERA	OAV	OOB	AB-SH	AVG	PB	Sup	APR	PW
Total	2	2	0	1.000	35	1	0	0-0	53.1	43	22	7	2	39-0	40	3.54	137	.224	.359	0-0	—	0	277	9	0.8
TURNER, JIM James Riley "Milkman Jim" B 8.6.1903 Antioch, TN D 11.29.1998 Nashville, TN BL/TR 6/185# d4.30 C24																									
1937	Bos N	20	11	.645	33	30	**24-5**	1	256.2	228	80	13	0	52	69	**2.38**	**150**	.235	**.274**	96-7	.250	4*	100	**36**	**4.8**
1938	Bos N☆	14	18	.438	35	34	22-3	0	268	267	123	21	5	54	71	3.46	99	.259	.299	96-4	.229	4	87	-2	0.5
1939	Bos N	4	11	.267	25	22	9	0	157.2	181	83	10	4	51	50	4.28	86	.293	.351	55-3	.236	2	96	-9	-0.4
1940	†Cin N	14	7	.667	24	23	11	0	187	187	70	9	0	32	53	2.89	131	.264	.296	75-1	.240	3*	95	17	2.1
1941	Cin N	6	4	.600	23	10	3	0	113	120	49	5	1	24	34	3.11	116	.277	.317	41-2	.146	-1	116	5	0.4
1942	Cin N	0	0	—	3	0	0	0	3.1	5	5	1	0	3	0	10.80	30	.333	.444	1-0	.000	-0		-3	-0.1
	†NY A	1	1	.500	5	0	0	1	7	4	1	0	0	1	2	1.29	268	.167	.200	1-0	.000	-0		2	0.4
1943	NY A	3	0	1.000	18	0	0	1	43.1	44	22	1	0	13	15	3.53	91	.260	.313	13-0	.077	-1		-2	-0.3
1944	NY A	4	4	.500	35	0	0	7	41.2	42	23	3	0	22	13	3.46	101	.264	.354	10-0	.200	0		-2	-0.3
1945	NY A	3	4	.429	30	0	0	**10**	54.1	45	26	4	0	31	22	3.64	95	.225	.329	11-0	.091	-1		-1	-0.3
Total	9	69	60	.535	231	119	69-8	20	1132	1123	482	67	10	283	329	3.22	111	.260	.307	399-17	.218	12	96	41	6.8
TURNER, KEN Kenneth Charles B 8.17.1943 Framingham, MA BR/TL 6-2/190# d6.11																									
1967	Cal A	1	2	.333	13	1	0	0	17.1	16	9	4	1	4-0	6	4.15	76	.239	.292	4-0	.000	-0	28	-2	-0.3
TURNER, TED Theodore Holhot B 5.4.1892 Lawrenceburg, KY D 2.4.1958 Lexington, KY BR/TR 6/180# d4.20																									
1920	Chi N	0	0	—	1	0	0	0	1.1	2	2	0	0	1	0	13.50	24	.400	.500	1-0	.000	-0		-1	-0.1
TURNER, TINK Thomas Lovatt B 2.20.1890 Swarthmore, PA D 2.25.1962 Philadelphia, PA BR/TR 6-1/190# d9.24																									
1915	Phi A	0	1	.000	1	1	0	0	2	5	6	1	0	3	0	22.50	13	.500	.615	0-0	—	0	125	-4	-0.6
TURNER, MATT William Matthew B 2.18.1967 Lexington, KY BR/TR 6-5/215# d4.23																									
1993	Fla N	4	5	.444	55	0	0	0-1	68	55	23	7	1	26-9	59	2.91	149	.227	.300	2-0	.000	-0		10	1.2
1994	Cle A	1	0	1.000	9	0	0	1-2	12.2	13	6	0	3	7-0	5	2.13	222	.241	.359	0-0	—	0		3	0.2
Total	2	5	5	.500	64	0	0	1-3	80.2	68	29	7	4	33-9	64	2.79	158	.230	.312	2-0	.000	-0		13	1.4
TUTWILER, ELMER Elmer Strange B 11.19.1905 Carbon Hill, AL D 5.3.1976 Pensacola, FL BR/TR 5-11/158# d8.20																									
1928	Pit N	0	0	—	2	0	0	0	3.2	4	2	0	0	0	1	4.91	83	.267	.267	1-0	.000	-0		0	0.0
TWINING, TWINK Howard Earle "Doc" B 5.30.1894 Horsham, PA D 6.14.1973 Lansdale, PA BR/TR 6/168# d7.9																									
1916	Cin N	0	0	—	1	0	0	0	2	4	3	1	1	1	0	13.50	19	.444	.545	0-0	—	0		-2	-0.1
TWITCHELL, LARRY Lawrence Grant B 2.18.1864 Cleveland, OH D 8.23.1930 Cleveland, OH BR/TR 6/185# d4.30 ▲																									
1886	Det N	0	2	.000	4	4	2	0	25	35	22	1		12	6	6.48	51	.347	.416	16	.063	-2	101	-7	-0.5
1887	†Det N	11	1	.917	15	12	11	**1**	112.1	120	74	3	10	36	24	4.33	94	.268	.336	264	.333	4*	144	-2	0.1
1888	Det N	0	0	—	2	0	0	1	4	6	3	1	0	0	3	6.75	41	.375	.375	524	.244	0*		-1	0.0
1889	Cle N	0	0	—	1	0	0	0	1	0	0	0	0	1	0	0.00	—	.000	.250	549	.275	0*		0	0.0
1890	Buf P	5	7	.417	13	12	12	0	104.1	112	77	3	15	72	29	4.57	90	.262	.387	172	.221	1*	77	-4	-0.1
1891	Col AA	1	1	.500	6	1	1	0	31	29	22	1	3	13	8	4.06	85	.240	.328	224	.277	2*	18	-2	0.0
1894	Lou N	0	0	—	1	0	0	0	3	5	2	1	0	1	0	6.00	85	.357	.400	210-9	.267	0*		0	0.0
Total	7	17	11	.607	42	29	26	2	280.2	307	200	10	28	135	70	4.62	85	.272	.363	1959-9	.267	6	107	-16	-0.5
TWITCHELL, WAYNE Wayne Lee B 3.10.1948 Portland, OR BR/TR 6-6/220# d9.7																									
1970	Mil A	0	0	—	2	0	0	0-0	1.2	3	2	0	0	1-0	5	10.80	35	.333	.400	0-0	—	0		-1	-0.1
1971	Phi N	1	0	1.000	6	1	0	0-0	16	8	4	1	1	10-0	15	0.00	—	.145	.284	3-0	.000	-0	126	4	0.2
1972	Phi N	5	9	.357	49	15	1-1	1-1	139.2	138	72	6	2	56-6	112	4.06	89	.259	.329	28-1	.071	-2	54	-8	-1.0
1973	Phi N★	13	9	.591	34	28	10-5	0-0	223.1	172	71	16	10	99-9	169	2.50	152	.219	.312	72-7	.097	-4	80	30	2.3
1974	Phi N	6	9	.400	25	18	2	0-2	112.1	122	71	11	7	65-7	72	5.21	73	.276	.375	35-2	.171	-1	101	-16	-2.1
1975	Phi N	5	10	.333	36	20	0	0-0	134.1	132	82	10	1	78-3	101	4.42	85	.261	.358	34-3	.088	-2	107	-13	-1.7
1976	Phi N	3	1	.750	26	2	0	1-0	61.2	55	18	3	3	18-1	67	1.75	203	.241	.302	6-0	.167	0	62	10	0.7
1977	Phi N	0	5	.000	12	8	0	0-0	45.2	50	27	3	0	25-1	37	4.53	88	.287	.377	11-0	.091	-0	72	-3	-0.3
	Mon N	6	5	.545	22	22	2	0-0	139	116	71	18	5	49-3	93	4.21	91	.230	.301	39-4	.205	2	98	-6	-0.2
	Year	6	10	.375	34	30	2	0-0	184.2	166	75	21	5	74-4	130	4.29	90	.244	.321	50-4	.180	2	91	-9	-0.5
1978	Mon N	4	12	.250	33	15	0	0-1	112	121	68	16	5	71-5	69	5.38	66	.286	.392	24-2	.083	-1	100	-21	-2.8
1979	NY N	5	3	.625	33	2	0	0-1	63.2	55	44	6	4	55-8	44	5.23	70	.243	.396	8-1	.375	1	97	-13	-1.4
	Sea A	0	2	.000	4	2	0	0-0	13.2	11	11	2	2	10-0	5	5.27	83	.220	.365	0-0	—	0	62	-2	-0.3
Total	10	48	65	.425	282	133	15-6	2-5	1063	983	541	92	40	537-43	789	3.98	94	.250	.343	260-20	.127	-6	89	-39	-6.7
TWITTY, JEFF Jeffrey Dean B 11.10.1957 Lancaster, SC BL/TL 6-2/185# d7.5																									
1980	KC A	2	1	.667	13	0	0	0-0	22.1	33	17	4	0	7-3	9	6.04	67	.351	.392	0-0	—	0		-5	-0.6
TWOMBLY, CY Edwin Parker B 6.15.1897 Groveland, MA D 12.3.1974 Savannah, GA BR/TR 5-10.5/170# d6.25																									
1921	Chi A	1	2	.333	7	4	0	0	27.2	26	21	1	2	25	7	5.86	72	.283	.445	10-0	.000	-2	128	-5	-0.6
TYLER, LEFTY George Albert B 12.14.1889 Derry, NH D 9.29.1953 Lowell, MA BL/TL 6/175# d9.20 b-Fred																									
1910	Bos N	0	0	—	2	0	0	0	11.1	11	3	1	0	6	6	2.38	140	.275	.370	4-0	.500	1		1	0.2
1911	Bos N	7	10	.412	28	20	10-1	0	165.1	150	118	11	10	109	90	5.06	76	.243	.365	61-2	.164	-1	97	-19	-1.6
1912	Bos N	12	22	.353	42	31	15-1	0	256.1	262	150	8	10	126	144	4.18	86	.276	.367	96-1	.198	-1	86	-13	-1.4
1913	Bos N	16	17	.485	39	34	**28**-4	2	290.1	245	131	2	11	108	143	2.79	118	.235	.313	102-5	.206	4*	94	14	2.4
1914	†Bos N	16	13	.552	38	34	21-5	2	271.1	247	113	7	14	101	140	2.69	103	.249	.327	94-6	.202	1	93	-2	-0.3
1915	Bos N	10	9	.526	32	24	15-1	0	204.2	182	87	6	5	84	89	2.86	91	.243	.324	88-3	.261	8*	116	-6	0.3
1916	Bos N	17	9	.654	34	28	21-6	1	249.1	200	79	6	3	58	117	2.02	123	.226	.276	93-4	.204	7*	107	11	2.3
1917	Bos N	14	12	.538	32	28	22-4	1	239	203	81	1	6	86	98	2.52	101	.240	.314	134-7	.231	4*	99	2	1.1
1918	†Chi N	19	8	.704	33	30	22-6	1	269.1	218	72	1	5	67	102	2.00	139	.226	.279	100-3	.210	1*	126	27	3.2
1919	Chi N	2	2	.500	6	5	3	0	30	20	8	0	0	13	9	2.10	137	.196	.287	7-1	.143	1	94	3	0.6
1920	Chi N	11	12	.478	27	27	18-2	0	193	193	83	6	3	57	57	3.31	97	.268	.324	65-2	.262	4*	105	0	0.7
1921	Chi N	3	2	.600	10	6	4	0	50	59	22	2	0	14	8	3.24	118	.294	.340	26-1	.231	1*	115	3	0.3
Total	12	127	116	.523	323	267	179-30	7	2230	1990	947	51	67	829	1003	2.95	101	.245	.320	870-35	.217	30	102	21	7.8
TYNG, JIM James Alexander B 3.27.1856 Philadelphia, PA D 10.30.1931 New York, NY 5-9/155# d9.23																									
1879	Bos N	1	2	.333	3	3	3	0	27	35	25	0		6	7	5.00	50	.292	.325	14	.357	1	106	-7	-0.5
1888	Phi N	0	0	—	1	0	0	1	4	8	4	0	1	2	2	4.50	66	.381	.458	1	.000	-0		-1	0.0
Total	2	1	2	.333	4	3	3	1	31	43	29	0	1	8	9	4.94	52	.305	.347	15	.333	1	106	-8	-0.5
TYRIVER, DAVE David Burton B 10.31.1937 Oshkosh, WI D 10.28.1988 Oshkosh, WI BR/TR 6- /175# d8.21																									
1962	Cle A	0	0	—	4	0	0	0	10.2	10	6	2	1	7-1	7	4.22	92	.250	.375	3-0	.000	-0		-1	-0.1
UCHRINSCKO, JIMMY James Emerson B 10.20.1900 W.Newton, PA D 3.17.1995 Mt.Pleasant, PA BL/TR 6/180# d7.20																									
1926	Was A	0	0	—	3	0	0	0	8	13	9	0	0	8	0	10.13	38	.433	.553	2-0	.000	-0		-5	-0.3
UHL, BOB Robert Ellwood "Lefty" B 9.17.1913 San Francisco, CA D 8.21.1990 Santa Rosa, CA BB/TL 5-11/175# d5.8																									
1938	Chi A	0	0	—	1	0	0	0	2	1	0	0	0	0	0	0.00	—	.167	.167	0-0	—	0		1	0.0
1940	Det A	0	0	—	1	0	0	0	0	4	5	0	0	2	0	o	—	1.000	1.000	0-0	—	0		-4	-0.3
Total	2	0	0	—	2	0	0	0	2	5	5	0	0	2	0	18.00	27	.500	.583	0-0	—	0		-3	-0.3
UHLE, GEORGE George Ernest "The Bull" B 9.18.1898 Cleveland, OH D 2.26.1985 Lakewood, OH BR/TR 6/190# d4.30 C4 ▲																									
1919	Cle A	10	5	.667	26	12	7-1	0	127	129	52	1	7	43	50	2.91	115	.261	.329	43-1	.302	3	127	7	1.0
1920	†Cle A	4	5	.444	27	6	2	1	84.2	98	52	3	8	29	27	5.21	73	.296	.367	32-0	.344	2	94	-10	-0.7
1921	Cle A	16	13	.552	41	28	13-2	2	238	288	132	9	4	63	63	4.01	106	.306	.352	94-1	.245	3*	119	4	0.6
1922	Cle A	22	16	.579	50	**40**	23-**5**	3	287.1	328	147	6	13	89	82	4.07	98	.290	.348	109-3	.266	9*	121	-1	0.5
1923	Cle A	**26**	16	.619	54	**44**	**29**-1	5	**357.2**	378	167	8	12	102	109	3.77	105	.271	.326	144-5	.361	16*	140	16	**3.4**
1924	Cle A	9	15	.375	28	25	15	1	196.1	238	134	6	13	75	57	4.77	90	.306	.376	107-0	.308	7*	92	-13	-0.7
1925	Cle A	13	11	.542	29	26	17-1	0	210.2	218	118	5	8	78	68	4.10	108	.268	.339	101-4	.287	6*	86	6	1.0
1926	Cle A	**27**	11	**.711**	39	**36**	**32**-3	1	**318.1**	300	114	7	13	118	159	2.83	143	.253	.328	132-4	.227	4*	100	**45**	**5.4**

Year	Tm Lg	W	L	Pct	G	GS	CG-Sho	SV-BS	IP	H	R	HR	HB	BB-IB	SO	ERA	AERA	OAV	OOB	AB-SH	AVG	PB	Sup	APR	PW
1927	Cle A	8	9	.471	25	22	10-1	1	153.1	187	88	3	9	59	69	4.34	97	.310	.379	79-2	.266	4*	89	-2	0.1
1928	Cle A	12	17	.414	31	28	18-2	1	214.1	252	121	8	8	48	74	4.07	102	.300	.344	98-6	.286	7*	77	0	0.8
1929	Det A	15	11	.577	32	30	23-1	0	249	283	141	9	2	58	100	4.08	105	.287	.328	108-2	.343	8*	120	4	1.0
1930	Det A	12	12	.500	33	29	18-1	3	239	239	110	18	5	75	117	3.65	131	.264	.323	117-4	.308	8*	106	31	3.4
1931	Det A	11	12	.478	29	18	15-2	2	193	190	88	10	4	49	63	3.50	131	.255	.304	90-1	.244	5*	56	23	2.9
1932	Det A	6	6	.500	33	15	6-1	5	146.2	152	84	15	4	42	51	4.48	105	.266	.320	55-2	.182	1*	103	5	0.4
1933	Det A	0	0	—	1	0	0	0	0.2	2	2	1	0	0	1	27.00	16	.500	.500	0-0	—	0		-2	-0.1
	NY N	1	1	.500	6	1	0	0	13.2	16	12	1	0	6	4	7.90	41	.302	.373	5-0	.000	-0*	26	-6	-0.8
	NY A	6	1	.857	12	6	4	0	61	63	42	4	3	20	26	5.16	75	.257	.321	20-1	.400	4	179	-10	-0.6
1934	NY A	2	4	.333	10	2	0	0	16.1	30	19	3	0	7	10	9.92	41	.400	.451	5-0	.600	2	107	-11	-1.7
1936	Cle A	0	1	.000	7	0	0	0	12.2	26	12	2	0	5	5	8.53	59	.419	.463	21-0	.381	4*		-4	0.0
Total	17	200	166	.546	513	368	232-21	25	3119.2	3417	1635	119	113	966	1135	3.99	105	.281	.340	1360-36	.289	92	106	82	15.9

UJDUR, JERRY Gerald Raymond B 3.5.1957 Duluth, MN BR/TR 6-1/195# d8.17

Year	Tm Lg	W	L	Pct	G	GS	CG-Sho	SV-BS	IP	H	R	HR	HB	BB-IB	SO	ERA	AERA	OAV	OOB	AB-SH	AVG	PB	Sup	APR	PW
1980	Det A	1	0	1.000	9	2	0	0-0	21.1	36	20	5	1	10-2	8	7.59	54	.383	.443	0-0	—	0	141	-8	-0.4
1981	Det A	0	0	—	4	4	0	0-0	14	19	12	2	0	5-0	5	6.43	59	.322	.369	0-0	—	0	113	-5	-0.2
1982	Det A	10	10	.500	25	25	7	0-0	178	150	76	29	3	69-4	86	3.69	110	.230	.304	0-0	—	0	93	10	1.0
1983	Det A	0	4	.000	11	6	0	0-0	34	41	33	6	1	20-1	13	7.15	55	.293	.385	0-0	—	0	81	-14	-1.4
1984	Cle A	1	2	.333	4	3	0	0-0	14.1	22	14	1	2	6-0	6	6.91	59	.355	.423	0-0	—	0	110	-5	-0.9
Total	5	12	16	.429	53	40	7	0-0	261.2	268	155	43	7	110-7	118	4.78	85	.266	.340	0-0	—	0	97	-22	-1.9

ULLRICH, SANDY Carlos Santiago (Castello) B 7.25.1921 Havana, Cuba D 4.21.2001 Miami, FL BR/TR 6-1/180# d5.3

Year	Tm Lg	W	L	Pct	G	GS	CG-Sho	SV-BS	IP	H	R	HR	HB	BB-IB	SO	ERA	AERA	OAV	OOB	AB-SH	AVG	PB	Sup	APR	PW
1944	Was A	0	0	—	3	0	0	0	9.2	17	10	2	1	4	2	9.31	35	.386	.449	3-0	.333	0		-6	-0.3
1945	Was A	3	3	.500	28	6	0	1	81.1	91	45	3	0	34	26	4.54	68	.276	.343	22-1	.273	1	114	-12	-0.6
Total	2	3	3	.500	31	6	0	1	91	108	55	5	1	38	28	5.04	62	.289	.356	25-1	.280	1	114	-18	-0.9

ULRICH, DUTCH Frank W. B 11.18.1899 Baltimore, MD D 2.11.1929 Baltimore, MD BR/TR 6-2/195# d4.18

Year	Tm Lg	W	L	Pct	G	GS	CG-Sho	SV-BS	IP	H	R	HR	HB	BB-IB	SO	ERA	AERA	OAV	OOB	AB-SH	AVG	PB	Sup	APR	PW
1925	Phi N	3	3	.500	21	4	2-1	0	65	73	30	6	1	12	29	3.05	157	.285	.320	16-0	.125	-1	57	10	0.8
1926	Phi N	8	13	.381	45	16	8-1	1	147.2	178	85	9	1	37	52	4.08	101	.304	.347	49-2	.245	1	91	-1	0.1
1927	Phi N	8	11	.421	32	18	14-1	1	193.1	201	82	6	0	40	42	3.17	131	.271	.308	73-3	.123	-6	84	17	0.9
Total	3	19	27	.413	98	38	24-3	2	406	452	197	21	2	89	123	3.48	122	.286	.324	138-5	.167	-5	83	26	1.8

UMBACH, ARNOLD Arnold William B 12.6.1942 Williamsburg, VA BR/TR 6-1/180# d10.3

Year	Tm Lg	W	L	Pct	G	GS	CG-Sho	SV-BS	IP	H	R	HR	HB	BB-IB	SO	ERA	AERA	OAV	OOB	AB-SH	AVG	PB	Sup	APR	PW
1964	Mil N	1	0	1.000	1	1	0	0	8.1	11	5	0	0	4-0	7	3.24	109	.333	.395	3-0	.000	0	275	0	-0.1
1966	Atl N	0	2	.000	22	3	0	0	40.2	40	15	1	2	18-3	23	3.10	117	.256	.339	5-1	.200	0	73	3	0.2
Total	2	1	2	.333	23	4	0	0	49	51	20	1	2	22-3	30	3.12	116	.270	.349	8-1	.125	0	122	3	0.1

UMBARGER, JIM James Harold B 2.17.1953 Burbank, CA BL/TL 6-6/200# d4.8

Year	Tm Lg	W	L	Pct	G	GS	CG-Sho	SV-BS	IP	H	R	HR	HB	BB-IB	SO	ERA	AERA	OAV	OOB	AB-SH	AVG	PB	Sup	APR	PW
1975	Tex A	8	7	.533	56	12	3-2	2-0	131	134	63	11	2	59-9	50	4.12	91	.276	.353	0-0	—	0	72	-2	-0.2
1976	Tex A	10	12	.455	30	30	10-3	0-0	197.1	208	86	12	2	54-4	105	3.15	114	.274	.321	0-0	—	0	107	7	0.7
1977	Oak A	1	5	.167	12	8	1	0-0	44	62	40	3	4	28-2	24	6.55	62	.354	.448	0-0	—	0	67	-14	-1.5
	Tex A	1	1	.500	3	2	0	0-0	13	14	8	2	0	4-0	5	5.54	74	.275	.321	0-0	—	0	176	-2	-0.2
	Year	2	6	.250	15	10	1	0-0	57	76	16	5	4	32-2	29	6.32	64	.336	.421	0-0	—	0	89	-16	-1.7
1978	Tex A	5	8	.385	32	9	1	1-2	97.2	116	58	9	2	36-4	60	4.88	77	.299	.358	0-0	—	0	85	-11	-1.3
Total	4	25	33	.431	133	61	15-5	3-2	483	534	255	37	10	181-19	244	4.14	90	.287	.350	0-0	—	0	94	-22	-2.5

UMBRICHT, JIM James B 9.17.1930 Chicago, IL D 4.8.1964 Houston, TX BR/TR 6-4/215# d9.26

Year	Tm Lg	W	L	Pct	G	GS	CG-Sho	SV-BS	IP	H	R	HR	HB	BB-IB	SO	ERA	AERA	OAV	OOB	AB-SH	AVG	PB	Sup	APR	PW
1959	Pit N	0	0	—	1	1	0	0	7	7	5	3	0	4-0	3	6.43	60	.259	.355	3-0	.000	-0	139	-2	-0.1
1960	Pit N	1	2	.333	17	3	0	1	40.2	40	23	5	0	27-1	26	5.09	74	.270	.374	6-0	.333	0	118	-5	-0.4
1961	Pit N	0	0	—	1	0	0	0	3.1	5	2	0	0	2-1	1	2.70	148	.333	.412	1-0	1.000	0		0	0.0
1962	Hou N	4	0	1.000	34	0	0	2	67	51	19	3	2	17-1	55	2.01	185	.213	.269	9-1	.111	-0		13	0.8
1963	Hou N	4	3	.571	35	3	0	0	76	52	23	6	1	21-2	48	2.61	121	.195	.253	9-3	.111	-0	9	6	0.5
Total	5	9	5	.643	88	7	0	3	194	155	72	17	3	71-5	133	3.06	115	.222	.294	28-4	.179	-0	78	12	0.8

UNDERHILL, WILLIE Willie Vern B 9.6.1904 Yowell, TX D 10.26.1970 Bay City, TX BR/TR 6-2/185# d9.8

Year	Tm Lg	W	L	Pct	G	GS	CG-Sho	SV-BS	IP	H	R	HR	HB	BB-IB	SO	ERA	AERA	OAV	OOB	AB-SH	AVG	PB	Sup	APR	PW
1927	Cle A	0	2	.000	4	1	0	0	8.1	12	11	0	0	11	4	9.72	43	.375	.535	1-1	.000	-0	79	-5	-0.9
1928	Cle A	1	2	.333	11	3	1	0	28	33	23	0	1	20	16	4.50	92	.306	.419	11-0	.364	2	150	-4	-0.2
Total	2	1	4	.200	15	4	1	0	36.1	45	34	0	1	31	20	5.70	73	.321	.448	12-1	.333	1	132	-9	-1.1

UNDERWOOD, FRED Frederick Theodore B 10.14.1868 St.Louis Co., MO D 1.26.1906 Kansas City, MO ?/170# d7.18

Year	Tm Lg	W	L	Pct	G	GS	CG-Sho	SV-BS	IP	H	R	HR	HB	BB-IB	SO	ERA	AERA	OAV	OOB	AB-SH	AVG	PB	Sup	APR	PW
1894	Bro N	2	4	.333	7	6	5	0	47	80	62	1	2	30	10	7.85	63	.372	.453	18-0	.389	2	90	-18	-1.3

UNDERWOOD, PAT Patrick John B 2.9.1957 Kokomo, IN BL/TL 6/175# d5.31 b-Tom

Year	Tm Lg	W	L	Pct	G	GS	CG-Sho	SV-BS	IP	H	R	HR	HB	BB-IB	SO	ERA	AERA	OAV	OOB	AB-SH	AVG	PB	Sup	APR	PW
1979	Det A	6	4	.600	27	15	1	0-0	121.2	126	64	17	2	29-1	83	4.59	95	.269	.312	0-0	—	0	110	-2	-0.2
1980	Det A	3	6	.333	49	7	0	5-0	112.2	121	51	12	2	35-7	60	3.59	115	.277	.333	0-0	—	0	118	6	0.5
1982	Det A	4	8	.333	33	12	2	3-2	99	108	66	17	0	22-2	43	4.73	86	.269	.305	0-0	—	0	97	-11	-1.2
1983	Det A	0	0	—	4	0	0	0-0	10.1	11	10	1	0	6-0	2	8.71	45	.289	.386	0-0	—	0		-5	-0.3
Total	4	13	18	.419	113	34	3	8-2	343.2	366	191	47	4	92-10	188	4.43	94	.272	.319	0-0	—	0	108	-12	-1.2

UNDERWOOD, TOM Thomas Gerald B 12.22.1953 Kokomo, IN BR/TL 5-11/170# d8.19 b-Pat

Year	Tm Lg	W	L	Pct	G	GS	CG-Sho	SV-BS	IP	H	R	HR	HB	BB-IB	SO	ERA	AERA	OAV	OOB	AB-SH	AVG	PB	Sup	APR	PW
1974	Phi N	1	0	1.000	7	0	0	0-0	13	15	8	1	0	5-1	8	4.85	78	.313	.364	1-0	.000	-0		-2	-0.1
1975	Phi N	14	13	.519	35	35	7-2	0-0	219.1	221	110	12	6	84-5	123	4.14	90	.262	.331	74-7	.122	-2	97	-8	-1.3
1976	†Phi N	10	5	.667	33	25	3	2-0	155.2	154	63	9	1	63-0	94	3.53	101	.260	.331	46-3	.109	-1*	100	3	0.0
1977	Phi N	3	2	.600	14	0	0	1-0	33.1	44	21	2	0	18-2	20	5.13	78	.328	.403	3-1	.000	-0		-4	-0.6
	StL N	6	9	.400	19	17	1	0-0	100	104	61	7	1	57-4	66	4.95	78	.278	.372	30-2	.133	-0	86	-12	-1.6
	Year	9	11	.450	33	17	1	1-0	133.1	148	65	9	1	75-6	86	4.99	78	.291	.380	33-3	.121	-0	85	-17	-2.2
1978	Tor A	6	14	.300	31	30	7-1	0-0	197.2	201	105	23	2	87-4	139	4.10	96	.263	.339	0-0	—	0	100	-7	-0.8
1979	Tor A	9	16	.360	33	32	12-1	0-0	227	213	113	23	9	95-3	127	3.69	118	.253	.333	0-0	—	0	72	13	1.3
1980	†NY A	13	9	.591	38	27	2-2	2-1	187	163	85	15	4	66-4	116	3.66	107	.237	.306	0-0	—	0	127	6	0.7
1981	NY A	1	4	.200	9	6	0	0-0	32.2	32	17	2	0	13-1	29	4.41	81	.262	.333	0-0	—	0	88	-3	-0.4
	†Oak A	3	2	.600	16	5	1	1-1	51	37	21	4	2	25-1	46	3.18	110	.202	.305	0-0	—	0	124	1	0.1
	Year	4	6	.400	25	11	1	1-1	83.2	69	26	6	2	38-2	75	3.66	96	.226	.316	0-0	—	0	104	-1	-0.3
1982	Oak A	10	6	.625	56	10	2	7-6	153	136	66	11	1	68-4	79	3.29	119	.241	.321	0-0	—	0	105	9	0.9
1983	Oak A	9	7	.563	51	15	0	4-2	144.2	156	69	13	2	50-4	62	4.04	96	.277	.332	0-0	—	0	106	-1	-0.3
1984	Bal A	1	0	1.000	37	1	0	1-1	71.2	78	33	8	0	31-5	39	3.52	110	.282	.350	0-0	—	0	47	2	0.2
Total	11	86	87	.497	379	203	35-6	18-11	1586	1554	772	130	28	662-38	948	3.89	100	.259	.333	154-13	.117	-4	98	-3	-1.9

UPCHURCH, WOODY Jefferson Woodrow B 4.13.1911 Buies Creek, NC D 10.23.1971 Buies Creek, NC BR/TL 6/180# d9.14

Year	Tm Lg	W	L	Pct	G	GS	CG-Sho	SV-BS	IP	H	R	HR	HB	BB-IB	SO	ERA	AERA	OAV	OOB	AB-SH	AVG	PB	Sup	APR	PW
1935	Phi A	0	2	.000	3	3	1	0	21.1	23	13	3	0	12	2	5.06	90	.271	.361	7-0	.286	0	76	-1	0.0
1936	Phi A	0	2	.000	7	2	1	0	22.1	36	27	7	0	14	6	9.67	53	.353	.431	7-0	.143	-0	86	-11	-0.8
Total	2	0	4	.000	10	5	2	0	43.2	59	40	10	0	26	8	7.42	65	.316	.399	14-0	.214	-0	80	-12	-0.8

UPHAM, BILL William Lawrence B 4.4.1888 Akron, OH D 9.14.1959 Newark, NJ BB/TR 6/178# d4.10

Year	Tm Lg	W	L	Pct	G	GS	CG-Sho	SV-BS	IP	H	R	HR	HB	BB-IB	SO	ERA	AERA	OAV	OOB	AB-SH	AVG	PB	Sup	APR	PW
1915	Bro F	7	8	.467	33	11	4-2	4	121	129	61	0	0	40	46	3.35	81	.274	.331	36-0	.111	-2	94	-9	-1.3
1918	Bos N	1	1	.500	3	2	2	0	20.2	28	14	2	0	1	8	5.23	51	.326	.333	9-0	.222	0	141	-5	-0.4
Total	2	8	9	.471	36	13	6-2	4	141.2	157	75	2	0	41	54	3.62	75	.282	.332	45-0	.133	-2	100	-14	-1.7

UPP, JERRY George Henry B 12.10.1883 Sandusky, OH D 6.30.1937 Sandusky, OH TL d9.2

Year	Tm Lg	W	L	Pct	G	GS	CG-Sho	SV-BS	IP	H	R	HR	HB	BB-IB	SO	ERA	AERA	OAV	OOB	AB-SH	AVG	PB	Sup	APR	PW
1909	Cle A	2	1	.667	7	4	2	0	26.2	26	10	0	0	12	13	1.69	152	.260	.339	9-0	.222	0	90	2	0.3

UPSHAW, CECIL Cecil Lee B 10.22.1942 Spearsville, LA D 2.7.1995 Lawrenceville, GA BR/TR 6-6/205# d10.1

Year	Tm Lg	W	L	Pct	G	GS	CG-Sho	SV-BS	IP	H	R	HR	HB	BB-IB	SO	ERA	AERA	OAV	OOB	AB-SH	AVG	PB	Sup	APR	PW
1966	Atl N	0	0	—	1	0	0	0	3	0	0	0	0	3-0	2	0.00	—	.000	.273	1-0	1.000	0		1	0.1
1967	Atl N	2	3	.400	30	0	0	8	45.1	42	14	4	4	8-4	31	2.58	129	.247	.295	6-2	.167	1		4	0.7
1968	Atl N	8	7	.533	52	0	0	13	116.2	98	41	6	4	24-7	74	2.47	121	.229	.275	23-6	.174	0		5	0.8
1969	†Atl N	6	4	.600	62	0	0	27-5	105.1	102	36	7	1	29-6	57	2.91	124	.259	.309	21-3	.238	2		9	1.6
1971	Atl N	11	6	.647	49	0	0	17-9	82	95	33	5	2	28-12	56	3.51	106	.292	.349	15-2	.000	-2		3	0.5

Year	Tm Lg	W	L	Pct	G	GS	CG-Sho	SV-BS	IP	H	R	HR	HB	BB-IB	SO	ERA	AERA	OAV	OOB	AB-SH	AVG	PB	Sup	APR	PW
1972	Atl N	3	5	.375	42	0	0	13-2	53.2	50	22	5	1	19-9	23	3.69	103	.249	.315	7-1	.143	-0		2	0.3
1973	Atl N	0	1	.000	5	0	0	0-0	3.2	8	5	0	0	2-1	3	9.82	40	.444	.476	0-0	—	0		-2	-0.5
	Hou N	2	3	.400	35	0	0	1-0	38.1	38	21	3	1	15-4	21	4.46	82	.259	.331	2-0	.000	-0		-4	-0.4
	Year	2	4	.333	40	0	0	1-0	42	46	29	3	1	17-5	24	4.93	74	.279	.348	2-0	.000	-0		-6	-0.9
1974	Cle A	0	1	.000	7	0	0	0-1	8	10	4	1	0	4-1	7	3.38	107	.345	.400	0-0	—	0		0	0.0
	NY A	1	5	.167	36	0	0	6-3	59.2	53	25	1	3	24-3	27	3.02	117	.254	.339	0-0	—	0		3	0.4
	Year	1	6	.143	43	0	0	6-4	67.2	63	29	2	3	28-4	34	3.06	116	.265	.347	0-0	—	0		2	0.4
1975	Chi A	1	1	.500	29	0	0	1-2	47.1	49	19	5	4	21-3	22	3.23	120	.271	.359	0-0	—	0		3	0.2
Total	9	34	36	.486	348	0	0	86-22	563	545	220	37	20	177-50	323	3.13	112	.258	.320	75-14	.160	1		24	3.7
UPTON, BILL William Ray B 6.18.1929 Esther, MO D 1.2.1987 San Diego, CA BR/TR 6/167# d4.13 b-Tom																									
1954	Phi A	0	0	—	2	0	0	1	5	6	1	1	0	1	2	1.80	217	.300	.333	0-0	—	0		1	0.1
URBAN, JACK Jack Elmer B 12.5.1928 Omaha, NE BR/TR 5-8/155# d6.13																									
1957	KC A	7	4	.636	31	13	3	0	129.1	111	55	7	1	45-3	55	3.34	118	.237	.300	39-1	.282	2*	97	8	1.0
1958	KC A	8	11	.421	30	24	5-1	1	132	150	92	17	2	51-1	54	5.93	66	.286	.348	46-0	.152	-2*	87	-27	-3.6
1959	StL N	0	0	—	8	0	0	0	10.2	18	11	1	0	7-4	4	9.28	46	.409	.490	1-0	.000	-0		-5	-0.3
Total	3	15	15	.500	69	37	8-1	1	272	279	158	25	3	103-8	113	4.83	82	.269	.333	86-1	.209	0	90	-24	-2.9
URBANI, TOM Thomas James B 1.21.1968 Santa Cruz, CA BL/TL 6-1/190# d4.21																									
1993	StL N	1	3	.250	18	9	0	0-1	62	73	44	4	0	26-2	33	4.65	85	.296	.355	16-2	.188	1	116	-8	-0.4
1994	StL N	3	7	.300	20	10	0	0-0	80.1	98	48	12	3	21-0	43	5.15	81	.302	.348	24-3	.250	1	85	-9	-0.8
1995	StL N	3	5	.375	24	13	0	0-0	82.2	99	40	11	2	21-4	52	3.70	113	.305	.351	19-2	.316	3	66	4	0.8
1996	StL N	1	0	1.000	3	2	0	0-0	11.2	15	10	3	0	4-0	1	7.71	54	.319	.365	6-0	.167	-0*	118	-4	-0.3
	Det A	2	2	.500	16	2	0	0-0	23.2	31	22	8	2	14-0	20	8.37	60	.310	.402	0-0	—	0	128	-8	-1.0
Total	4	10	17	.370	81	36	0	0-1	260.1	316	164	38	7	86-6	149	4.98	84	.303	.357	65-7	.246	6	90	-25	-1.7
URBINA, UGUETH Ugueth Urtain (Villarreal) B 2.15.1974 Caracas, Venezuela BR/TR 6-2/185# d5.9																									
1995	Mon N	2	2	.500	7	4	0	0-0	23.1	26	17	6	0	14-1	15	6.17	70	.280	.374	6-0	.333	0	63	-5	-0.6
1996	Mon N	10	5	.667	33	17	0	0-1	114	102	54	18	1	44-4	108	3.71	117	.234	.304	29-3	.103	-1	80	7	0.6
1997	Mon N	5	8	.385	63	0	0	27-5	64.1	52	29	9	1	29-2	84	3.78	111	.214	.300	5-0	.000	-1		3	0.6
1998	Mon N★	6	3	.667	64	0	0	34-4	69.1	37	11	2	0	33-2	94	1.30	324	.157	.259	6-0	.000	-1		23	4.5
1999	Mon N	6	6	.500	71	0	0	**41-9**	75.2	59	35	6	0	36-6	100	3.69	122	.208	.295	5-0	.000	-1		7	1.2
2000	Mon N	0	1	.000	13	0	0	8-2	13.1	11	6	1	0	5-0	22	4.05	119	.224	.296	1-0	.000	-0		1	0.2
2001	Mon N	2	1	.667	45	0	0	15-3	46.2	42	24	8	0	21-1	57	4.24	105	.236	.315	1-0	.000	-0		1	0.1
	Bos A	0	1	.000	19	0	0	9-1	20	16	5	1	0	3-0	32	2.25	200	.219	.250	0-0	—	0		5	0.6
2002	Bos A★	1	6	.143	61	0	0	40-6	60	44	21	8	0	20-5	71	3.00	150	.202	.266	0-0	—	0		10	2.0
2003	Tex A	0	4	.000	39	0	0	26-4	38.2	33	19	6	0	18-2	41	4.19	119	.232	.313	0-0	—	0		3	0.6
	†Fla N	3	0	1.000	33	0	0	6-2	38.1	23	6	2	0	13-0	37	1.41	291	.174	.245	0-1	—	0		12	1.2
Total	9	35	37	.486	448	21	0	206-37	563.2	445	227	67	2	236-23	661	3.32	132	.214	.292	53-4	.094	-2	77	67	11.0
URREA, JOHN John Godoy B 2.9.1955 Los Angeles, CA BR/TR 6-3/205# d4.10																									
1977	StL N	7	6	.538	41	12	2-1	4-2	139.2	126	56	13	0	35-3	81	3.16	122	.244	.291	29-3	.138	2	102	11	1.2
1978	StL N	4	9	.308	27	12	1	0-1	98.2	108	75	4	7	47-4	61	5.38	65	.284	.369	24-2	.125	-1	89	-24	-2.9
1979	StL N	0	0	—	3	2	0	0-0	11.1	13	7	0	0	9-0	5	3.97	95	.310	.431	4-0	.250	0	153	-1	0.0
1980	StL N	4	1	.800	30	1	0	3-0	64.2	57	28	2	2	41-9	36	3.48	106	.239	.352	13-2	.231	0	217	2	0.1
1981	SD N	2	2	.500	38	0	0	2-1	49	43	14	1	3	28-0	19	2.39	136	.239	.346	4-0	.250	0		5	0.4
Total	5	17	18	.486	139	27	3-1	9-4	363.1	347	180	20	12	160-16	202	3.74	98	.256	.337	74-7	.162	2	106	-7	-1.2
VAIL, BOB Robert Garfield "Doc" B 9.24.1881 Linneus, ME D 3.22.1942 Philadelphia, PA BR/TR 5-10/165# d8.27																									
1908	Pit N	1	2	.333	4	1	0	0	15	15	10	0	1	7	9	6.00	38	.268	.359	3-0	.333	1	0	-5	-0.9
VALDES, ISMAEL Ismael (Alvarez) B 8.21.1973 Victoria, Mexico BR/TR 6-3/185# d6.15																									
1994	LA N	3	1	.750	21	1	0	0-0	28.1	21	10	2	0	10-2	28	3.18	124	.206	.277	2-0	.000	-0	162	3	0.4
1995	†LA N	13	11	.542	33	27	6-2	1-0	197.2	168	76	17	1	51-5	150	3.05	124	.228	.277	62-7	.097	-3	87	19	1.8
1996	†LA N	15	7	.682	33	33	0	0-0	225	219	94	20	3	54-10	173	3.32	116	.251	.294	70-13	.143	-1	107	16	1.3
1997	LA N	10	11	.476	30	30	0	0-0	196.2	171	68	16	3	47-1	140	2.65	145	.234	.282	57-7	.088	-2	82	27	2.5
1998	LA N	11	10	.524	27	27	2-2	0-0	174	171	82	17	2	66-4	122	3.98	100	.256	.323	48-8	.167	1	97	1	0.2
1999	LA N	9	14	.391	32	32	2-1	0-0	203.1	213	97	32	6	58-2	143	3.98	108	.270	.321	58-10	.086	-3	90	8	0.5
2000	Chi N	2	4	.333	12	12	0	0-0	67	71	40	17	2	27-2	45	5.37	85	.273	.344	14-5	.286	2*	83	-5	-0.2
	LA N	0	3	.000	9	8	0	0-0	40	53	29	5	1	13-0	29	6.07	71	.327	.376	11-2	.091	0	127	-8	-0.5
	Year	2	7	.222	21	20	0	0-0	107	124	35	22	3	40-2	74	5.64	79	.294	.356	25-7	.200	2	100	-13	-0.7
2001	Ana A	9	13	.409	27	27	1	0-0	163.2	177	82	20	8	50-3	100	4.45	103	.277	.338	5-0	.200	0	68	5	0.7
2002	Tex A	6	9	.400	23	23	0	0-0	146.2	135	65	19	9	36-1	75	3.93	120	.242	.297	3-1	.000	-0	75	14	1.2
	Sea A	2	3	.400	8	8	1	0-0	49.1	59	29	7	0	11-0	27	4.93	86	.299	.333	0-0	—	0	143	-4	-0.3
	Year	8	12	.400	31	31	1	0-0	196	194	36	26	9	47-1	102	4.18	110	.257	.306	3-1	.000	-0	91	12	0.9
2003	Tex A	8	8	.500	22	22	0	0-0	115	148	83	23	5	29-0	47	6.10	81	.318	.359	4-2	.000	-0	90	-13	-1.5
Total	10	88	94	.484	277	250	12-5	1-0	1606.2	1606	755	195	40	452-30	1079	3.93	107	.260	.312	334-55	.120	-6	91	63	6.1
VALDES, MARC Marc Christopher B 12.20.1971 Dayton, OH BR/TR 6/170# d8.28																									
1995	Fla N	0	0	—	3	3	0	0-0	7	17	13	1	1	9-0	2	14.14	30	.459	.563	2-0	.000	-0	136	-8	-0.4
1996	Fla N	1	3	.250	11	8	0	0-1	48.2	63	32	5	1	23-0	13	4.81	85	.315	.383	14-0	.000	-1	75	-6	-0.6
1997	Mon N	4	4	.500	48	7	0	2-0	95	84	36	2	8	39-5	54	3.13	134	.240	.326	19-0	.105	-1	69	12	0.8
1998	Mon N	1	3	.250	20	4	0	0-0	36.1	41	34	6	1	21-2	28	7.43	57	.285	.375	5-0	.400	1	44	-13	-1.1
2000	Hou N	5	5	.500	53	0	0	2-4	56.2	69	41	3	5	25-1	35	5.08	96	.301	.379	3-0	.000	-0		-4	-0.6
2001	Atl N	1	0	1.000	9	0	0	0-0	7	7	6	4	0	1-1	3	7.71	57	.259	.286	0-0	—	0		-2	-0.3
Total	6	12	15	.444	144	22	0	4-5	250.2	281	162	21	16	118-9	135	4.95	87	.285	.366	43-0	.093	-1	73	-21	-2.2
VALDEZ, CARLOS Carlos Luis (Lorenzo) B 12.26.1971 Nizao Bani, D.R. BR/TR 5-11/165# d7.18																									
1995	SF N	0	1	.000	11	0	0	0-0	14.2	19	10	1	1	8-1	7	6.14	67	.322	.406	1-0	.000	-0		-3	-0.2
1998	Bos A	1	0	1.000	4	0	0	0-0	3.1	1	0	0	0	5-0	4	0.00	—	.100	.375	0-0	—	0		2	0.3
Total	2	1	1	.500	15	0	0	0-0	18	20	10	1	1	13-1	11	5.00	84	.290	.400	1-0	.000	-0		-1	0.1
VALDEZ, EFRAIN Efrain Antonio B 7.11.1966 Nizao Bani, D.R. BL/TL 5-11/180# d8.13																									
1990	Cle A	1	1	.500	13	0	0	0-0	23.2	20	10	2	0	14-3	13	3.04	129	.233	.330	0-0	—	0		2	0.1
1991	Cle A	0	0	—	7	0	0	0-0	6	5	1	0	1	3-1	1	1.50	277	.238	.346	0-0	—	0		2	0.1
1998	Ari N	0	0	—	6	0	0	0-0	4.1	7	2	2	0	1-0	2	4.15	101	.368	.400	0-0	—	0		0	0.0
Total	3	1	1	.500	26	0	0	0-0	34	32	13	4	1	18-4	16	2.91	138	.254	.342	0-0	—	0		4	0.2
VALDEZ, RAFAEL Rafael Emilio (Diaz) B 12.17.1967 Nizao Bani, D.R. BR/TR 5-11/165# d4.18																									
1990	SD N	0	1	.000	3	0	0	0-0	5.2	11	7	4	0	2-0	3	11.12	34	.393	.433	1-0	.000	-0		-4	-0.6
VALDEZ, RENE Rene Gutierrez (b: Rene Gutierrez (Valdez)) B 6.2.1929 Guanabacoa, Cuba BR/TR 6-3/175# d4.21																									
1957	Bro N	1	1	.500	5	1	0	0	13	13	8	1	0	7-1	10	5.54	75	.265	.351	3-0	.000	0	169	-1	-0.2
VALDEZ, SERGIO Sergio Sanchez (b: Sergio Sanchez (Valdez)) B 9.7.1964 Elias Pina, D.R. BR/TR 6-1/190# d9.10																									
1986	Mon N	0	4	.000	5	5	0	0-0	25	39	20	2	1	11-0	20	6.84	54	.361	.425	8-0	.125	-0	53	-8	-1.1
1989	Atl N	1	2	.333	19	1	0	0-0	32.2	31	24	5	0	17-3	26	6.06	60	.246	.336	1-0	1.000	0	48	-8	-0.7
1990	Atl N	0	0	—	6	0	0	0-0	5.1	6	4	0	0	3-0	3	6.75	60	.273	.360	0-0	—	0		-1	-0.1
	Cle A	6	6	.500	24	13	0	0-0	102.1	109	62	17	1	35-2	63	4.75	83	.276	.333	0-0	—	0	123	-11	-1.2
1991	Cle A	1	0	1.000	6	0	0	0-0	16.1	15	11	3	0	5-1	11	5.51	75	.238	.290	0-0	—	0		-2	-0.2
1992	Mon N	0	2	.000	27	0	0	0-1	37.1	25	12	2	0	12-1	32	2.41	144	.185	.252	3-0	.000	-0		4	0.2
1993	Mon N	0	0	—	4	0	0	0-0	3	4	4	1	0	1-0	2	9.00	46	.308	.357	0-0	—	0		-2	-0.1
1994	Bos A	0	1	.000	12	1	0	0-0	14.1	25	14	4	0	8-1	4	8.16	62	.391	.458	0-0	—	0	73	-5	-0.2
1995	SF N	4	5	.444	13	11	1	0-0	66.1	78	43	12	3	17-3	29	4.75	86	.298	.344	21-3	.095	-1	92	-7	-0.9

Year	Tm Lg	W	L	Pct	G	GS	CG-Sho	SV-BS	IP	H	R	HR	HB	BB-IB	SO	ERA	AERA	OAV	OOB	AB-SH	AVG	PB	Sup	APR	PW
Total	8	12	20	.375	116	31	1	0-1	302.2	332	194	46	5	109-11	190	5.06	78	.279	.340	33-3	.121	-1	98	-40	-4.3
VALENTINE, CORKY Harold Lewis B 1.4.1929 Troy, OH BR/TR 6-1/203# d4.17																									
1954	Cin N	12	11	.522	36	28	7-3	1	194.1	211	98	24	4	60	73	4.45	94	.282	.337	65-5	.138	-2	87	-1	-0.4
1955	Cin N	2	1	.667	10	5	0	0	26.2	29	23	5	1	16-2	14	7.43	57	.276	.368	7-0	.000	-1	118	-8	-0.8
Total	2	14	12	.538	46	33	7-3	1	221	240	121	29	5	76-2	87	4.81	87	.282	.341	72-5	.125	-3	92	-9	-1.2
VALENTINE, JOHN John Gill B 11.21.1855 Brooklyn, NY D 10.10.1903 Central Islip, NY d5.3																									
1883	Col AA	2	10	.167	13	12	11	0	102	130	80	0		17	13	3.53	87	.291	.317	60	.283	3*	70	-8	-0.4
VALENTINE, JOE Joseph John B 12.24.1979 Las Vegas, NV BR/TR 6-2/190# d8.24																									
2003	Cin N	0	0	—	2	0	0	0-0	2	5	4	1	0	1-0	1	18.00	24	.455	.500	0-0	—	0		-3	-0.1
VALENTINETTI, VITO Vito John B 9.16.1928 W.New York, NJ BR/TR 6/195# d6.20																									
1954	Chi A	0	0	—	1	0	0	0	1	4	6	1	0	2	1	54.00	7	.571	.667	0-0	—	0		-5	-0.2
1956	Chi N	6	4	.600	42	2	0	1	95.1	84	47	10	1	36-7	26	3.78	100	.243	.313	20-1	.100	-1	128	0	-0.3
1957	Chi N	0	0	—	9	0	0	0	12	12	5	1	0	7-1	8	2.25	172	.255	.352	2-0	.000	0		1	0.1
	Cle A	2	2	.500	11	2	1	0	23.2	26	14	3	1	13-0	9	4.94	75	.289	.381	5-0	.200	-0	96	-3	-0.4
1958	Det A	1	0	1.000	15	0	0	2	18.2	18	7	4	1	5-0	10	3.38	120	.257	.316	0-0	—	0		2	0.1
	Was A	4	6	.400	23	10	2	0	95.2	106	54	16	2	49-7	33	5.08	75	.286	.372	28-2	.321	2	85	-11	-0.8
	Year	5	6	.455	38	10	2	2	114.1	124	58	20	3	54-7	43	4.80	80	.282	.363	28-2	.321	2	84	-9	-0.7
1959	Was A	0	2	.000	7	1	0	0	10.2	16	12	0	1	10-0	7	10.13	39	.356	.482	0-0	—	0	45	-6	-1.0
Total	5	13	14	.481	108	15	3	3	257	266	145	35	6	122-15	94	4.73	81	.273	.356	55-3	.218	1	89	-22	-2.5
VALENZUELA, FERNANDO Fernando (Anguamea) B 11.1.1960 Navojoa, Mexico BL/TL 5-11/195# d9.15																									
1980	LA N	2	0	1.000	10	0	0	1-0	17.2	8	2	0	0	5-0	16	0.00	—	.136	.200	1-0	.000	-0		6	0.8
1981	†LA N★	13	7	.650	25	**25**	**11-8**	0-0	**192.1**	140	55	11	1	61-4	**180**	2.48	134	.205	.270	64-6	.250	3	96	20	2.6
1982	LA N★	19	13	.594	37	37	18-4	0-0	285	247	105	13	2	83-12	199	2.87	121	.236	.292	95-10	.168	1*	100	19	2.4
1983	†LA N☆	15	10	.600	35	35	9-4	0-0	257	245	122	16	3	99-10	189	3.75	96	.255	.325	91-12	.187	2*	119	-1	0.3
1984	LA N★	12	17	.414	34	34	12-2	0-0	261	218	109	14	2	106-4	240	3.03	117	.229	.306	79-9	.190	4*	78	12	2.0
1985	†LA N★	17	10	.630	35	35	14-5	0-0	272.1	211	92	14	1	101-5	208	2.45	142	.214	.286	97-5	.216	4	107	31	3.5
1986	LA N★	**21**	11	.656	34	34	**20**-3	0-0	269.1	226	104	18	1	85-5	242	3.14	110	.226	.287	109-6	.220	5*	121	11	2.0
1987	LA N	14	14	.500	34	34	**12**-1	0-0	251	254	120	25	4	124-4	190	3.98	100	.262	.348	92-8	.141	-1*	92	2	0.3
1988	LA N	5	8	.385	23	22	3	1-0	142.1	142	71	11	0	76-4	64	4.24	79	.268	.357	44-7	.182	1	129	-13	-0.8
1989	LA N	10	13	.435	31	31	3	0-0	196.2	185	89	11	2	98-6	116	3.43	100	.251	.337	66-7	.182	1*	94	-3	-0.1
1990	LA N	13	13	.500	33	33	5-2	0-0	204	223	112	19	0	77-4	115	4.59	80	.276	.337	69-7	.304	8*	124	-19	-1.3
1991	Cal A	0	2	.000	2	2	0	0-0	6.2	14	10	3	0	3-0	5	12.15	34	.452	.486	0-0	—	0	0	-6	-0.9
1993	Bal A	8	10	.444	32	31	5-2	0-0	178.2	179	104	18	4	79-2	78	4.94	91	.266	.343	0-0	—	0	95	-8	-0.6
1994	Phi N	1	2	.333	8	7	0	0-0	45	42	16	8	0	7-1	19	3.00	143	.247	.274	12-4	.250	1	67	7	0.5
1995	SD N	8	3	.727	29	15	0	0-0	90.1	101	53	16	0	34-2	57	4.98	81	.289	.351	32-3	.250	3	109	-8	-0.4
1996	†SD N	13	8	.619	33	31	0	0-0	171.2	177	78	17	0	67-2	95	3.62	110	.269	.334	63-3	.143	-1*	106	6	0.7
1997	SD N	2	8	.200	13	13	1	0-0	66.1	84	42	10	4	32-0	51	4.75	82	.309	.387	17-4	.176	0*	68	-8	-1.0
	StL N	0	4	.000	5	5	0	0-0	22.2	22	19	2	1	14-0	10	5.56	75	.253	.363	5-2	.200	0	93	-5	-0.7
	Year	2	12	.143	18	18	1	0-0	89	106	23	12	5	46-0	61	4.96	80	.295	.381	22-6	.182	0	75	-14	-1.7
Total	17	173	153	.531	453	424	113-31	2-0	2930	2718	1303	226	25	1151-65	2074	3.54	103	.248	.319	936-93	.200	32	103	43	9.3
VALERA, JULIO Julio Enrique (Torres) B 10.13.1968 Aguadilla, P.R. BR/TR 6-2/215# d9.1																									
1990	NY N	1	1	.500	3	3	0	0-0	13	20	11	1	0	7-0	4	6.92	54	.351	.422	5-0	.200	0	137	-5	-0.6
1991	NY N	0	0	—	2	0	0	0-0	2	1	0	0	0	4-1	3	0.00	—	.143	.455	0-0	—	0		1	0.0
1992	Cal A	8	11	.421	30	28	4-2	0-0	188	188	82	15	2	64-5	113	3.73	107	.262	.323	0-0	—	0	84	7	0.5
1993	Cal A	3	6	.333	19	5	0	4-3	53	77	44	8	2	15-2	28	6.62	68	.344	.388	0-0	—	0	134	-12	-1.9
1996	KC A	3	2	.600	31	2	0	1-0	61.1	75	44	7	2	27-3	31	6.46	78	.307	.375	0-0	—	0	83	-8	-0.6
Total	5	15	20	.429	85	38	4-2	5-3	317.1	361	181	31	6	117-11	179	4.85	88	.289	.351	5-0	.200	0	92	-17	-2.6
VALVERDE, JOSE Jose Rafael B 7.24.1979 San Pedro De Macoris, D.R. BR/TR 6-4/220# d6.1																									
2003	Ari N	2	1	.667	54	0	0	10-1	50.1	24	16	4	2	26-2	71	2.15	218	.137	.255	1-0	1.000	1		12	1.1
Van ALSTYNE, CLAY Clayton Emory "Spike" B 5.24.1900 Stuyvesant, NY D 1.5.1960 Hudson, NY BR/TR 5-11/180# d8.20																									
1927	Was A	0	0	—	2	0	0	0	3	3	1	0	0	0	0	3.00	136	.250	.250	0-0	—	0		0	0.0
1928	Was A	0	0	—	4	0	0	0	21.1	26	14	0	1	13	5	5.48	73	.329	.430	8-0	.250	1		-3	0.0
Total	2	0	0	—	6	0	0	0	24.1	29	15	0	1	13	5	5.18	78	.319	.410	8-0	.250	1		-3	0.0
Van ATTA, RUSS Russell "Sheriff" B 6.21.1906 Augusta, NJ D 10.10.1986 Andover, NJ BL/TL 6/184# d4.25																									
1933	NY A	12	4	.750	26	22	10-2	1	157	160	81	8	1	63	76	4.18	93	.262	.332	60-5	.283	4	149	-4	0.0
1934	NY A	3	5	.375	28	9	0	0	88	107	69	3	2	46	39	6.34	64	.307	.390	29-1	.207	1	100	-23	-1.6
1935	NY A	0	0	—	5	0	0	0	4.2	5	5	0	0	4	3	3.86	105	.263	.391	1-0	.000	-0		-1	-0.1
	StL A	9	16	.360	53	17	1	3	170.1	201	116	10	3	87	87	5.34	90	.292	.374	42-6	.214	-1	80	-9	-1.3
	Year	9	16	.360	**58**	17	1	3	175	206	120	10	3	91	90	5.30	90	.291	.375	43-6	.209	-1	80	-11	-1.4
1936	StL A	4	7	.364	**52**	9	2	2	122.2	164	101	9	2	68	59	6.60	81	.320	.401	29-0	.172	-1*	78	-15	-1.1
1937	StL A	1	2	.333	16	6	1	0	58.2	74	41	2	0	32	34	5.52	87	.307	.388	13-0	.462	3	78	-5	0.1
1938	StL A	4	7	.364	25	12	3-1	0	104	118	75	7	1	61	35	6.06	82	.289	.382	30-3	.133	-1	61	-11	-1.0
1939	StL A	0	0	—	2	1	0	0	7	9	10	0	1	7	6	11.57	42	.310	.459	2-0	.000	-0	127	-5	-0.2
Total	7	33	41	.446	207	76	17-3	6	712.1	838	498	39	10	368	339	5.60	82	.293	.376	206-15	.228	5	95	-73	-5.2
Van BRABANT, OZZIE Camille Oscar B 9.28.1926 Kingsville, ON, CAN BR/TR 6-1/165# d4.13																									
1954	Phi A	0	2	.000	9	2	0	0	26.2	35	23	3	1	18	10	7.09	55	.347	.446	5-0	.200	0	34	-9	-0.5
1955	KC A	0	0	—	2	0	0	0	2	4	4	1	0	2-1	1	18.00	23	.400	.462	0-0	—	0		-3	-0.1
Total	2	0	2	.000	11	2	0	0	28.2	39	27	4	1	20-1	11	7.85	50	.351	.448	5-0	.200	0	34	-12	-0.6
VANCE, DAZZY Clarence Arthur B 3.4.1891 Orient, IA D 2.16.1961 Homosassa Springs, FL BR/TR 6-2/200# d4.16 HF1955																									
1915	Pit N	0	1	.000	1	1	0	0	2.2	3	3	0	1	5	0	10.13	27	.375	.643	1-0	.000	-0	54	-2	-0.3
	NY A	0	3	.000	8	3	1	0	28	23	14	1	2	16	18	3.54	83	.232	.350	3-1	.667	2	41	-2	0.0
1918	NY A	0	0	—	2	0	0	0	2.1	9	5	0	0	2	0	15.43	18	.692	.733	0-0	—	0		-3	-0.2
1922	Bro N	18	12	.600	36	31	16-**5**	0	245.2	259	122	9	8	94	**134**	3.70	110	.276	.347	89-6	.225	1	112	10	1.3
1923	Bro N	18	15	.545	37	35	21-3	0	280.1	263	127	10	11	100	**197**	3.50	111	.250	.322	83-7	.084	-3	95	17	1.5
1924	Bro N	**28**	6	.824	35	34	**30**-3	0	308.1	238	89	11	9	77	**262**	**2.16**	**173**	**.213**	**.269**	106-8	.151	-2	114	**57**	**5.9**
1925	Bro N	**22**	9	.710	31	31	26-**4**	0	265.1	247	115	8	10	66	**221**	3.53	118	.250	.304	98-2	.143	-0	115	24	2.5
1926	Bro N	9	10	.474	24	22	12	1	169	172	80	7	1	58	**140**	3.89	98	.271	.333	55-3	.182	-1	84	2	0.2
1927	Bro N	16	15	.516	34	32	**25**-2	1	273.1	242	98	12	6	69	**184**	2.70	147	**.239**	.291	90-6	.167	-2	82	38	3.9
1928	Bro N	22	10	.688	38	32	24-**4**	2	280.1	226	79	11	7	72	**200**	**2.09**	**191**	**.221**	**.277**	96-1	.177	2	85	**60**	**7.2**
1929	Bro N	14	13	.519	31	27	17-1	0	231.1	244	110	15	9	47	126	3.89	119	.274	.316	74-2	.135	-2	76	23	2.1
1930	Bro N	17	15	.531	35	31	20-**4**	0	258.2	241	97	15	5	55	173	**2.61**	**188**	**.246**	**.289**	89-3	.135	-5	83	**64**	**6.4**
1931	Bro N	11	13	.458	30	29	12-2	0	218.2	221	99	12	0	53	150	3.38	113	.261	.304	67-7	.134	-2	79	9	0.7
1932	Bro N	12	11	.522	27	24	9-1	1	175.2	171	90	10	1	57	103	4.20	91	.256	.315	56-5	.089	-4	94	-6	-1.1
1933	StL N	6	2	.750	28	11	2	3	99	105	42	3	1	28	67	3.55	98	.267	.318	28-3	.179	-1	98	1	0.0
1934	Cin N	0	2	.000	6	2	0	0	18	28	21	1	1	11	9	7.50	54	.350	.435	4-0	.250	0	63	-8	-0.7
	†StL N	1	1	.500	19	4	1	1	59	62	26	4	2	14	33	3.66	115	.271	.318	15-1	.133	-0	61	4	0.2
	Year	1	3	.250	25	6	1	1	77	90	29	5	3	25	42	4.56	92	.291	.350	19-1	.158	0	62	-3	-0.5
1935	Bro N	3	2	.600	20	0	0	2	51	55	29	3	3	16	28	4.41	90	.268	.330	17-0	.059	-2		-2	-0.4
Total	16	197	140	.585	442	349	216-29	11	2966.2	2809	1246	132	77	840	2045	3.24	125	.251	.308	971-55	.150	-18	92	286	29.2
VANCE, CORY Cory Wade B 6.20.1979 Dayton, OH BL/TL 6-1/195# d9.21																									
2002	Col N	0	0	—	2	1	0	0-0	4	4	3	2	1	4-0	1	6.75	71	.267	.450	1-0	.000	-0	155	-1	0.0
2003	Col N	1	3	.250	9	3	0	0-1	27.1	31	19	6	1	10-0	12	5.60	88	.287	.347	7-2	.286	0	45	-2	-0.2
Total	2	1	3	.250	11	4	0	0-1	31.1	35	22	8	2	14-0	13	5.74	85	.285	.362	8-2	.250	0	72	-3	-0.2

Year	Tm Lg	W	L	Pct	G	GS	CG-Sho	SV-BS	IP	H	R	HR	HB	BB-IB	SO	ERA	AERA	OAV	OOB	AB-SH	AVG	PB	Sup	APR	PW
VANCE, SANDY Gene Covington B 1.5.1947 Lamar, CO BR/TR 6-2/180# d4.26																									
1970	LA N	7	7	.500	20	18	2	0-0	115	109	47	9	1	37-2	45	3.13	123	.248	.306	37-4	.189	1	101	8	0.8
1971	LA N	2	1	.667	10	3	0	0-1	26	38	21	1	0	9-0	11	6.92	47	.355	.398	5-0	.000	-0	137	-11	-1.2
Total	2	9	8	.529	30	21	2	0-1	141	147	68	10	1	46-2	56	3.83	97	.269	.324	42-4	.167	0	106	-3	-0.4
VANCE, JOE Joseph Albert "Sandy" B 9.16.1905 Devine, TX D 7.4.1978 San Antonio, TX BR/TR 6-1.5/190# d4.18																									
1935	Chi A	2	2	.500	10	0	0	0	31	36	26	1	0	21	12	6.68	69	.295	.399	11-0	.182	-1		-7	-0.7
1937	NY A	1	0	1.000	2	2	0	0	15	11	5	2	0	9	3	3.00	148	.204	.317	5-0	.000	-1	88	3	0.1
1938	NY A	0	0	—	3	1	0	0	11.1	20	9	2	0	4	2	7.15	63	.408	.453	4-0	.750	2*	136	-3	0.1
Total	3	3	2	.600	15	3	0	0	57.1	67	40	5	0	34	17	5.81	79	.298	.390	20-0	.250	1	102	-7	-0.5
Van CUYK, CHRIS Christian Gerald B 1.3.1927 Kimberly, WI D 11.3.1992 Hudson, FL BL/TL 6-6/215# d7.16 b-Johnny																									
1950	Bro N	1	3	.250	12	4	1	0	33.1	33	19	3	1	12	21	4.86	84	.266	.336	10-1	.100	-1	119	-3	-0.4
1951	Bro N	1	2	.333	9	6	0	0	29.1	33	22	4	4	11	16	5.52	71	.295	.378	8-0	.250	0	124	-6	-0.5
1952	Bro N	5	6	.455	23	16	4	1	97.2	104	58	12	5	40	66	5.16	71	.271	.347	33-3	.242	2	144	-15	-1.5
Total	3	7	11	.389	44	26	5	1	160.1	170	99	19	10	63	103	5.16	73	.274	.351	51-4	.216	1	134	-24	-2.4
Van CUYK, JOHNNY John Henry B 7.7.1921 Little Chute, WI BL/TL 6-1/190# d9.18 b-Chris																									
1947	Bro N	0	0	—	2	0	0	0	3.1	5	2	0	0	1	2	5.40	77	.357	.400	0-0	—	0		0	0.0
1948	Bro N	0	0	—	3	0	0	0	5	4	3	1	0	1	1	3.60	111	.200	.238	0-0	—	0		0	0.0
1949	Bro N	0	0	—	2	0	0	0	2	3	2	0	0	1	0	9.00	46	.429	.500	0-0	—	0		-1	-0.1
Total	3	0	0	—	7	0	0	0	10.1	12	7	1	0	3	3	5.23	78	.293	.341	0-0	—	0		-1	-0.1
VANDE BERG, ED Edward John B 10.26.1958 Redlands, CA BR/TL 6-2/180# d4.7																									
1982	Sea A	9	4	.692	**78**	0	0	5-2	76	54	21	5	2	32-7	60	2.37	179	.207	.296	0-0	—	0		16	2.8
1983	Sea A	2	4	.333	68	0	0	5-4	64.1	59	32	6	1	22-6	49	3.36	127	.246	.308	0-0	—	0		4	0.4
1984	Sea A	8	12	.400	50	17	2	7-5	130.1	165	76	18	0	50-4	71	4.76	84	.313	.368	0-0	—	0*	79	-11	-1.6
1985	Sea A	2	1	.667	76	0	0	3-1	67.2	71	30	4	1	31-5	34	3.72	113	.274	.350	0-0	—	0		4	0.2
1986	LA N	1	5	.167	60	0	0	0-2	71.1	83	32	8	1	33-7	42	3.41	102	.290	.364	1-0	.000	-0		0	0.0
1987	Cle A	1	0	1.000	55	0	0	0-1	72.1	96	42	9	0	21-2	40	5.10	89	.325	.364	0-0	—	0		-2	-0.1
1988	Tex A	2	2	.500	26	0	0	2-0	37	44	19	2	0	11-4	18	4.14	99	.308	.353	0-0	—	0		0	0.0
Total	7	25	28	.472	413	17	2	22-15	519	572	252	52	5	200-35	314	3.92	105	.284	.347	1-0	.000	-0	79	11	1.7
VANDENBERG, HY Harold Harris B 3.17.1906 Abilene, KS D 7.31.1994 Bloomington, MN BR/TR 6-4/220# d6.8																									
1935	Bos A	0	0	—	3	0	0	0	5.1	15	12	1	0	4	2	20.25	23	.500	.559	1-0	1.000	0		-8	-0.3
1937	NY N	0	1	.000	1	1	1	0	8	10	7	0	0	6	2	7.88	49	.313	.421	4-0	.000	-1	89	-3	-0.3
1938	NY N	0	1	.000	6	1	0	0	18	28	16	2	0	12	7	7.50	50	.368	.455	4-0	.000	-1	270	-7	-0.3
1939	NY N	0	0	—	2	1	0	0	6.1	10	5	0	0	6	3	5.68	69	.345	.457	2-0	.000	-0	134	-1	-0.1
1940	NY N	1	1	.500	13	3	1	1	32.1	27	15	2	1	16	17	3.90	100	.227	.324	8-1	.125	-0	172	0	0.0
1944	Chi N	7	4	.636	35	9	2	2	126.1	123	67	8	1	51	54	3.63	97	.255	.327	38-3	.237	1	119	-4	-0.3
1945	†Chi N	7	3	.700	30	7	3-1	2	95.1	91	44	4	4	33	35	3.49	105	.259	.330	32-1	.125	-1	99	2	0.1
Total	7	15	10	.600	90	22	7-1	5	291.2	304	166	17	6	128	120	4.32	85	.271	.349	89-5	.169	-1	126	-21	-1.2
VANDER MEER, JOHNNY John Samuel "Double No-Hit" or "The Dutch Master" B 11.2.1914 Prospect Park, NJ D 10.6.1997 Tampa, FL BB/TL 6-1/190# d4.22 Mil 1944-45																									
1937	Cin N	3	5	.375	19	10	4	0	84.1	63	41	0	2	69	52	3.84	97	.209	.359	23-1	.217	1*	92	0	0.2
1938	Cin N★	15	10	.600	32	29	16-3	0	225.1	177	89	12	3	103	125	3.12	117	**.213**	.302	83-5	.181	-2*	104	14	1.2
1939	Cin N☆	5	9	.357	30	21	8	0	129	128	76	7	2	95	102	4.67	82	.264	.387	36-7	.111	-1	110	-11	-1.3
1940	†Cin N	3	1	.750	10	7	2	1	48	38	24	3	1	41	41	3.75	101	.211	.360	20-0	.300	2*	111	-1	0.2
1941	Cin N	16	13	.552	33	32	18-6	0	226.1	172	83	8	1	126	**202**	2.82	127	.214	.321	76-9	.132	-3*	84	19	2.1
1942	Cin N★	18	12	.600	33	33	21-4	0	244	188	78	6	1	102	**186**	2.43	135	.208	.290	75-8	.147	-1*	85	25	3.1
1943	Cin N★	15	16	.484	36	**36**	21-3	0	289	228	102	5	3	162	**174**	2.87	116	.224	.332	95-8	.137	-2*	85	15	1.5
1946	Cin N	10	12	.455	29	25	11-4	0	204.1	175	77	11	0	78	94	3.17	105	.233	.305	73-1	.247	2*	73	7	0.9
1947	Cin N	9	14	.391	30	29	9-3	0	186	186	104	11	3	87	79	4.40	93	.261	.343	57-9	.088	-3*	104	-7	-1.0
1948	Cin N	17	14	.548	33	33	14-3	0	232	204	97	15	1	124	120	3.41	115	.239	.336	78-4	.141	0*	82	14	1.8
1949	Cin N	5	10	.333	28	24	7-3	0	159.2	172	92	12	2	85	76	4.90	85	.281	.370	52-8	.077	-3*	99	-9	-1.0
1950	Chi N	3	4	.429	32	6	0	1	73.2	60	46	10	2	59	41	3.79	111	.221	.363	16-0	.125	-0*	63	-1	-0.1
1951	Cle A	0	1	.000	1	1	0	0	3	8	6	0	0	1	2	18.00	21	.500	.529	1-0	.000	-0	235	-5	-0.7
Total	13	119	121	.496	346	286	131-29	2	2104.2	1799	915	100	21	1132	1294	3.44	107	.232	.332	685-60	.152	-9	92	60	6.9
Van DYKE, BEN Benjamin Harrison B 8.15.1888 Clintonville, PA D 10.22.1973 Sarasota, FL BR/TL 6-1/150# d5.11																									
1909	Phi N	0	0	—	2	0	0	0	7.1	7	3	0	0	4	5	3.68	71	.269	.367	3-0	.000	-0		0	-0.1
1912	Bos A	0	0	—	3	1	0	0	14.1	13	10	0	1	7	8	3.14	108	.245	.344	4-0	.250	-0	325	-1	-0.1
Total	2	0	0	—	5	1	0	0	21.2	20	13	0	1	11	13	3.32	94	.253	.352	7-0	.143	-0	325	-1	-0.2
Van EGMOND, TIM Timothy Layne B 5.31.1969 Shreveport, LA BR/TR 6-2/185# d6.26																									
1994	Bos A	2	3	.400	7	7	1	0-0	38.1	38	27	7	0	21-3	22	6.34	79	.255	.341	0-0	—	0	89	-4	-0.5
1995	Bos A	0	1	.000	4	1	0	0-0	6.2	9	7	2	0	6-0	5	9.45	52	.310	.429	0-0	—	0	57	-3	-0.4
1996	Mil A	3	5	.375	12	9	0	0-0	54.2	58	35	6	1	23-2	33	5.27	99	.274	.343	0-0	—	0	59	-1	-0.1
Total	3	5	9	.357	23	17	1	0-0	99.2	105	69	15	1	50-5	60	5.96	86	.269	.349	0-0	—	0	71	-8	-1.0
VANGILDER, ELAM Elam Russell B 4.23.1896 Cape Girardeau, MO D 4.30.1977 Cape Girardeau, MO BR/TR 6-1/192# d9.18																									
1919	StL A	1	0	1.000	3	1	1	0	13	15	4	0	0	3	6	2.08	160	.306	.346	3-0	.667	1	71	2	0.2
1920	StL A	3	8	.273	24	13	4	0	104.2	131	83	7	3	40	25	5.50	71	.310	.373	30-0	.133	-2	94	-19	-1.9
1921	StL A	11	12	.478	31	21	10-1	0	180.1	196	98	10	2	67	48	3.94	114	.278	.342	65-2	.200	-2	82	9	0.7
1922	StL A	19	13	.594	43	30	19-3	4	245	248	109	13	6	48	63	3.42	121	.270	.310	93-9	.344	13*	141	21	3.8
1923	StL A	16	17	.485	41	35	20-4	1	282.1	276	129	11	6	120	74	3.06	136	.266	.345	110-1	.218	-0*	82	**28**	2.8
1924	StL A	5	10	.333	43	18	5	1	145.1	183	114	10	9	55	49	5.64	80	.317	.385	44-0	.295	3	114	-20	-1.4
1925	StL A	14	8	.636	52	16	4-1	6	193.1	225	127	11	6	92	61	4.70	99	.303	.385	71-3	.183	-3	102	-3	-0.5
1926	StL A	9	11	.450	42	19	8-1	1	181	196	121	12	2	98	40	5.17	83	.285	.376	58-4	.190	1	89	-16	-1.5
1927	StL A	10	12	.455	44	23	12-3	1	203	245	136	13	5	102	62	4.79	91	.310	.392	68-4	.279	2	85	-11	-1.0
1928	Det A	11	10	.524	38	11	7	5	156.1	163	82	4	3	68	43	3.91	105	.273	.350	58-1	.259	2	94	4	0.6
1929	Det A	0	1	.000	6	0	0	0	11.1	16	11	1	0	7	3	6.35	68	.348	.434	1-0	.000	-0		-3	-0.2
Total	11	99	102	.493	367	187	90-13	19	1715.2	1894	1014	92	42	700	474	4.28	100	.288	.360	601-24	.243	15	98	-8	1.6
Van HALTREN, GEORGE George Edward Martin "Rip" B 3.30.1866 St.Louis, MO D 9.29.1945 Oakland, CA BL/TL 5-11/170# d6.27 M1 ▲																									
1887	Chi N	11	7	.611	20	18	18-1	**1**	161	177	113	8	16	66	76	3.86	117	.277	.359	172	.203	-2*	92	10	0.7
1888	Chi N	13	13	.500	30	24	24-4	1	245.2	263	149	15	13	60	139	3.52	86	.267	.318	318	.283	11*	104	-9	0.2
1890	Bro P	15	10	.600	28	25	23	2	223	272	190	8	21	89	48	4.28	104	.288	.362	376	.335	10*	109	2	1.0
1891	Bal AA	0	1	.000	6	1	0	0	23	38	34	1	4	10	7	5.09	73	.358	.433	566	.318	3*	316	-7	-0.2
1892	Bal N	0	0	—	4	0	0	0	14.2	28	17	1	0	7	5	9.20	37	.389	.443	556	.302	2*		-7	-0.2
1895	NY N	0	0	—	1	0	0	0	5	13	12	0	2	2	1	12.60	37	.481	.548	521-6	.340	0*		-5	-0.2
1896	NY N	1	0	1.000	2	0	0	0	8	5	2	1	0	1	3	2.25	187	.179	.207	562-4	.351	1*		2	0.3
1900	NY N	0	0	—	1	0	0	0	3	1	0	0	0	3	0	0.00	—	.100	.308	571-13	.315	0*		1	0.1
1901	NY N	0	0	—	1	0	0	0	6	12	10	0	1	6	2	3.00	110	.414	.528	543-7	.335	0*		-2	-0.1
Total	9	40	31	.563	93	68	65-5	4	689.1	809	527	34	57	244	281	4.05	96	.285	.353	4185-30	.319	25	107	-15	1.6
Van HEKKEN, ANDY Andrew William B 7.31.1979 Holland, MI BR/TL 6-3/175# d9.3																									
2002	Det A	1	3	.250	5	5	1-1	0-0	30	38	13	2	0	6-0	5	3.00	144	.311	.341	0-0	—	0	52	4	0.4
Van LANDINGHAM, WILLIAM William Joseph B 7.16.1970 Columbia, TN BR/TR 6-2/210# d5.21																									
1994	SF N	8	2	.800	16	14	0	0-0	84	70	37	4	2	43-4	56	3.54	113	.223	.319	31-4	.065	-2	122	4	0.2
1995	SF N	6	3	.667	18	18	1	0-0	122.2	124	58	14	2	40-2	95	3.67	111	.264	.321	46-1	.152	0	119	5	0.4
1996	SF N	9	14	.391	32	32	0	0-0	181.2	196	123	17	9	78-6	97	5.40	76	.276	.352	61-6	.131	-1	100	-27	-3.0
1997	SF N	4	7	.364	18	17	0	0-0	89	80	56	11	0	59-3	52	4.96	83	.237	.345	26-2	.115	-0	85	-9	-1.1
Total	4	27	26	.509	84	81	1	0-0	477.1	470	274	46	13	220-15	300	4.54	90	.257	.337	164-13	.122	-3	105	-27	-3.5

Year	Tm Lg	W	L	Pct	G	GS	CG-Sho	SV-BS	IP	H	R	HR	HB	BB-IB	SO	ERA	AERA	OAV	OOB	AB-SH	AVG	PB	Sup	APR	PW
Van POPPEL, TODD Todd Matthew B 12.9.1971 Hinsdale, IL BR/TR 6-5/210# d9.11																									
1991	Oak A	0	0	—	1	1	0	0-0	4.2	7	5	1	0	2-0	6	9.64	40	.368	.429	0-0	—	0	143	-3	-0.1
1993	Oak A	6	6	.500	16	16	0	0-0	84	76	50	10	2	62-0	47	5.04	81	.243	.369	0-0	—	0	127	-9	-1.2
1994	Oak A	7	10	.412	23	23	0	0-0	116.2	108	80	20	3	89-2	83	6.09	73	.250	.379	0-0	—	0	112	-20	-2.4
1995	Oak A	4	8	.333	36	14	1	0-0	138.1	125	77	16	4	56-1	122	4.88	92	.244	.320	0-0	—	0	83	-5	-0.4
1996	Oak A	1	5	.167	28	6	0	1-1	63	86	56	13	2	33-3	37	7.71	64	.333	.406	0-0	—	0	107	-19	-1.6
	Det A	2	4	.333	9	9	1-1	0-0	36.1	53	51	11	1	29-0	16	11.39	44	.338	.439	0-0	—	0	128	-26	-2.9
	Year	3	9	.250	37	15	1-1	1-1	99.1	139	58	24	3	62-3	53	9.06	55	.335	.419	0-0	—	0	120	-45	-4.5
1998	Tex A	1	2	.333	4	4	0	0-0	19.1	26	20	5	1	10-0	10	8.84	55	.313	.389	2-2	.000	-0	96	-8	-1.0
	Pit N	1	2	.333	18	7	0	0-0	47	53	32	4	0	18-3	32	5.36	80	.286	.346	12-1	.250	1	110	-5	-0.3
2000	Chi N	4	5	.444	51	2	0	2-3	86.1	80	38	10	2	48-2	77	3.75	121	.249	.348	9-2	.000	-1	111	8	0.7
2001	Chi N	4	1	.800	59	0	0	0-0	75	63	22	9	0	38-4	90	2.52	164	.223	.316	7-0	.286	0		15	0.9
2002	Tex A	3	2	.600	50	0	0	1-1	72.2	80	44	14	3	29-1	85	5.45	87	.275	.346	1-0	.000	-0		-4	-0.3
2003	Tex A	1	0	1.000	7	1	0	0-0	12.2	20	14	1	0	9-2	9	8.53	58	.345	.433	0-0	—	0	111	-5	-0.3
	Cin N	2	1	.667	9	4	0	0-0	35.2	31	18	7	1	6-0	25	4.54	94	.228	.266	9-1	.111	-0	88	0	-0.1
Total	10	36	46	.439	311	87	2-1	4-5	791.2	808	507	121	19	429-18	639	5.50	82	.265	.357	40-6	.150	-0	110	-81	-9.0
Van RYN, BEN Benjamin Ashley B 8.9.1971 Fort Wayne, IN BL/TL 6-5/185# d5.9																									
1996	Cal A	0	0	—	1	0	0	0-0	1	1	0	0	0	1-0	0	0.00	—	.250	.400	0-0	—	0		1	0.0
1998	Chi N	0	0	—	9	0	0	0-0	8	9	3	0	1	6-0	6	3.38	131	.290	.410	1-0	.000	-0		1	0.0
	SD N	0	1	.000	6	0	0	0-1	2.2	3	3	0	1	4-0	1	10.13	39	.273	.500	0-0	—	0		-2	-0.4
	Year	0	1	.000	15	0	0	0-1	10.2	12	11	0	2	10-0	7	5.06	85	.286	.436	1-0	.000	-0		-1	-0.4
	Tor A	0	1	.000	10	0	0	0-0	4	6	4	0	0	2-0	3	9.00	52	.400	.471	0-0	—	0		-2	-0.3
Total	2	0	2	.000	26	0	0	0-1	15.2	19	10	0	2	13-0	10	5.74	77	.311	.442	1-0	.000	-0		-2	-0.7
Van ZANDT, IKE Charles Isaac B 2.1876 Brooklyn, NY D 9.14.1908 Nashua, NH BL/TL d8.5 ▲																									
1901	NY N	0	0	—	2	0	0	0	12.2	16	15	0	1	8	2	7.11	47	.308	.410	6-0	.167	-0*		-6	-0.3
1905	StL A	0	0	—	1	0	0	0	6.2	2	0	0	1	2	3	0.00	—	.095	.208	322-9	.233	0*		2	0.1
Total	2	0	0	—	3	0	0	0	19.1	18	15	0	2	10	5	4.66	65	.247	.353	328-9	.232	-0		-4	-0.2
VARGA, ANDY Andrew William B 12.11.1930 Chicago, IL D 11.4.1992 Orlando, FL BR/TL 6-4/187# d9.9																									
1950	Chi N	0	0	—	1	0	0	0	1	0	0	0	0	1	0	0.00	—	.000	.333	0-0	—	0		0	0.0
1951	Chi N	0	0	—	2	0	0	0	3	2	1	0	0	6	1	3.00	136	.200	.500	0-0	—	0		0	0.0
Total	2	0	0	—	3	0	0	0	4	2	1	0	0	7	1	2.25	183	.167	.474	0-0	—	0		0	0.0
VARGAS, CLAUDIO Claudio (Almonte) B 5.19.1979 Valderde Mao, D.R. BR/TR 6-3/210# d4.26																									
2003	Mon N	6	8	.429	23	20	0	0-0	114	111	59	16	7	41-5	62	4.34	108	.255	.326	30-4	.000	-3	73	5	0.2
VARGAS, ROBERTO Roberto Enrique (Velez) B 5.29.1929 Santurce, P.R. BL/TL 5-11/170# d4.17																									
1955	Mil N	0	0	—	25	0	0	2	24.2	39	25	4	1	14-2	13	8.76	43	.355	.432	2-0	.500	0		-14	-0.6
VARGUS, BILL William Fay B 11.11.1899 N.Scituate, MA D 2.12.1979 Hyannis, MA BL/TL 6/165# d6.23																									
1925	Bos N	1	1	.500	11	2	1	0	36.1	45	24	1	2	13	5	3.96	101	.302	.366	12-0	.250	0	137	-2	-0.1
1926	Bos N	0	0	—	4	0	0	0	3	4	1	0	0	1	0	3.00	118	.333	.385	0-0	—	0		0	0.0
Total	2	1	1	.500	15	2	1	0	39.1	49	25	1	2	14	5	3.89	102	.304	.367	12-0	.250	0	137	-2	-0.1
VARNEY, DIKE Lawrence Delano (b: Lawrence Delano De Varney) B 8.9.1880 Dover, NH D 4.23.1950 Long Island City, NY BL/TL 6/165# d7.3																									
1902	Cle A	1	1	.500	3	3	0	0	14.2	14	15	0	5	12	7	6.14	56	.250	.425	6-0	.167	-0	174	-4	-0.5
VASBINDER, CAL Moses Calhoun B 7.19.1880 Scio, OH D 12.22.1950 Cadiz, OH BR/TR 6-2/?# d4.27																									
1902	Cle A	0	0	—	2	0	0	0	5	5	5	1	0	8	2	9.00	38	.263	.481	2-0	.500	0		-2	-0.1
VASQUEZ, RAFAEL Rafael B 6.28.1958 LaRomana, D.R. BR/TR 6/160# d4.6																									
1979	Sea A	1	0	1.000	9	0	0	0-0	16	23	9	4	1	6-1	9	5.06	86	.354	.411	0-0	—	0		-1	-0.1
VAUGHAN, PORTER Cecil Porter "Lefty" B 5.11.1919 Stevensville, VA BR/TL 6-1/178# d6.16 Mil 1942-45																									
1940	Phi A	2	9	.182	18	15	5	2	99.1	104	74	9	3	61	46	5.35	83	.264	.367	34-1	.235	0	95	-11	-1.1
1941	Phi A	0	2	.000	5	3	1	0	22.2	32	25	3	0	12	6	7.94	53	.327	.400	7-0	.143	-0	96	-10	-0.8
1946	Phi A	0	0	—	1	0	0	0	0	1	0	0	0	1	0	—	—	1.000	1.000	0-0	—	0		0	0.0
Total	3	2	11	.154	24	18	6	2	122	137	99	12	3	74	52	5.83	75	.278	.375	41-1	.220	-0	95	-21	-1.9
VAUGHAN, CHARLIE Charles Wayne B 10.6.1947 Mercedes, TX BR/TL 6-1.5/185# d9.3																									
1966	Atl N	1	0	1.000	1	1	0	0	7	8	2	0	0	3-0	6	2.57	141	.296	.355	4-0	.250	0	290	1	0.1
1969	Atl N	0	0	—	1	0	0	0-0	1	1	2	0	0	3-0	1	18.00	20	.250	.571	0-0	—	0		-1	-0.1
Total	2	1	0	1.000	2	1	0	0-0	8	9	4	0	0	6-0	7	4.50	81	.290	.395	4-0	.250	0	290	0	0.0
VAUGHN, ROY Clarence Leroy B 9.4.1911 Sedalia, MO D 3.1.1937 Martinsville, VA BB/TR 6-0.5/178# d7.1																									
1934	Phi A	0	0	—	2	0	0	0	4.1	3	2	1	0	3	1	2.08	211	.176	.300	2-0	.000	-0		1	0.0
VAUGHN, DE WAYNE De Wayne Mathew B 7.22.1959 Oklahoma City, OK BR/TR 5-11/180# d4.17																									
1988	Tex A	0	0	—	8	0	0	0-0	15.1	24	15	4	0	4-0	8	7.63	54	.348	.373	0-0	—	0		-6	-0.3
VAUGHN, HIPPO James Leslie B 4.9.1888 Weatherford, TX D 5.29.1966 Chicago, IL BB/TL 6-4/215# d6.19																									
1908	NY A	0	0	—	2	0	0	0	2.1	1	1	0	0	4	2	3.86	64	.167	.500	1-0	.000	-0		0	0.0
1910	NY A	13	11	.542	30	25	18-5	1	221.2	190	76	1	10	58	107	1.83	146	.237	.297	75-0	.133	-2	98	14	1.3
1911	NY A	8	10	.444	26	19	10	0	145.2	158	92	2	7	54	74	4.39	82	.284	.354	49-2	.143	-1	100	-11	-1.2
1912	NY A	2	8	.200	15	10	5-1	0	63	66	48	1	1	37	46	5.14	70	.264	.361	21-0	.095	-2	109	-9	-1.4
	Was A	4	3	.571	12	8	4	0	81	75	33	0	4	43	49	2.89	115	.253	.356	30-0	.200	-1	69	5	0.5
	Year	6	11	.353	27	18	9-1	0	144	141	36	1	5	80	95	3.88	89	.258	.358	51-0	.157	-2	93	-5	-0.9
1913	Chi N	5	1	.833	7	6	5-2	0	56	37	13	0	2	27	36	1.45	220	.182	.284	21-0	.190	-1	114	10	1.1
1914	Chi N	21	13	.618	42	35	23-4	1	293.2	236	119	1	8	109	165	2.05	135	.222	.299	97-4	.144	-0	104	18	2.1
1915	Chi N	20	12	.625	41	34	18-4	1	269.2	240	105	4	11	77	148	2.87	97	.238	.299	86-2	.163	1*	110	-1	0.0
1916	Chi N	17	15	.531	44	35	21-4	1	294	269	94	4	7	67	144	2.20	132	.250	.298	104-5	.135	-4	89	20	1.9
1917	Chi N	23	13	.639	41	38	27-5	0	295.2	255	97	3	9	91	195	2.01	144	.235	.300	100-2	.160	-1	98	25	3.4
1918	†Chi N	**22**	10	.688	35	**33**	27-**8**	0	**290.1**	216	75	4	7	76	**148**	**1.74**	**161**	**.208**	.266	96-4	.240	4	95	**34**	**4.5**
1919	Chi N	21	14	.600	38	**37**	25-4	1	**306.2**	264	83	3	6	62	**141**	1.79	161	.234	.278	98-1	.173	-0	85	**36**	4.3
1920	Chi N	19	16	.543	40	38	24-4	0	301	301	113	8	8	81	131	2.54	126	.264	.318	102-2	.216	4	99	19	2.6
1921	Chi N	3	11	.214	17	14	7	0	109.1	153	90	8	5	31	30	6.01	64	.341	.390	41-1	.244	2	109	-29	-2.8
Total	13	178	137	.565	390	332	214-41	5	2730	2461	1039	39	85	817	1416	2.49	120	.244	.306	921-23	.173	-1	98	131	16.3
VAZQUEZ, JAVIER Javier Carlos B 6.25.1976 Ponce, P.R. BR/TR 6-2/180# d4.3																									
1998	Mon N	5	15	.250	33	32	0	0-0	172.1	196	121	31	11	68-2	139	6.06	69	.292	.364	52-6	.173	1	89	-31	-2.9
1999	Mon N	9	8	.529	26	26	3-1	0-0	154.2	154	98	20	4	52-4	113	5.00	90	.255	.316	42-8	.286	4	99	-9	-0.3
2000	Mon N	11	9	.550	33	33	2-1	0-0	217.2	247	104	24	5	61-10	196	4.05	118	.286	.335	65-13	.231	2	76	19	1.8
2001	Mon N	16	11	.593	32	32	5-**3**	0-0	223.2	197	92	24	3	44-4	208	3.42	131	.235	.274	62-16	.258	4	94	26	3.4
2002	Mon N	10	13	.435	34	34	2	0-0	230.1	243	111	28	4	49-6	179	3.91	114	.271	.310	73-10	.178	-1	92	14	1.2
2003	Mon N	13	12	.520	34	34	4-1	0-0	230.2	198	93	28	4	57-5	241	3.24	145	.229	.278	65-12	.154	-1	75	34	3.4
Total	6	64	68	.485	192	191	16-6	0-0	1229.1	1235	619	155	31	331-31	1076	4.16	109	.260	.311	359-65	.209	10	86	53	6.6
VEACH, AL Alvis Lindel B 8.6.1909 Maylene, AL D 9.6.1990 Charlotte, NC BR/TR 5-11/178# d9.22																									
1935	Phi A	0	2	.000	2	2	1	0	10	20	15	1	0	9	3	11.70	39	.417	.509	4-0	.000	-1	10	-8	-1.1
VEACH, PEEK-A-BOO William Walter B 6.15.1862 Indianapolis, IN D 11.12.1937 Indianapolis, IN 6/175# d8.24 ▲																									
1884	KC U	3	9	.250	12	12	12	0	104	95	57	1		10	62	2.42	92	.227	.245	82	.134	-3*	61	-3	-0.6
1887	Lou AA	0	1	.000	1	1	1	0	9	5	6	1	0	8	2	4.00	110	.172	.351	3	.000	-0	58	1	0.0
Total	2	3	10	.231	13	13	13	0	113	100	63	2	0	18	64	2.55	94	.223	.253	85	.129	-4	60	-2	-0.6

Year	Tm Lg	W	L	Pct	G	GS	CG-Sho	SV-BS	IP	H	R	HR	HB	BB-IB	SO	ERA	AERA	OAV	OOB	AB-SH	AVG	PB	Sup	APR	PW
VEALE, BOB Robert Andrew B 10.28.1935 Birmingham, AL BB/TL 6-6/212# d4.16																									
1962	Pit N	2	2	.500	11	6	2	1	45.2	39	25	2	0	25-1	42	3.74	105	.235	.332	16-0	.250	1	97	0	0.0
1963	Pit N	5	2	.714	34	7	3-2	3	77.2	59	15	1	1	40-2	68	1.04	316	.215	.314	23-0	.087	-0*	93	18	1.8
1964	Pit N	18	12	.600	40	38	14-1	0	279.2	222	100	8	3	124-9	**250**	2.74	128	.217	.302	96-6	.156	-0*	110	22	2.3
1965	Pit N☆	17	12	.586	39	37	14-7	0	266	221	98	5	7	119-7	276	2.84	124	.225	.312	93-8	.086	-4	91	20	1.6
1966	Pit N☆	16	12	.571	38	37	12-3	0	268.1	228	99	18	5	102-6	229	3.02	118	.232	.306	94-3	.138	-2	104	17	1.4
1967	Pit N	16	8	.667	33	31	6-1	0	203	184	90	12	5	119-10	179	3.64	93	.245	.350	69-3	.043	-5	121	-4	-1.0
1968	Pit N	13	14	.481	36	33	13-4	0	245.1	187	67	13	2	94-5	171	2.05	142	.211	.287	82-2	.110	-2	82	24	2.5
1969	Pit N	13	14	.481	34	34	9-1	0-0	225.2	232	93	8	3	91-4	213	3.23	108	.267	.336	79-4	.051	-5	97	6	0.1
1970	Pit N	10	15	.400	34	32	5-1	0-0	202	189	99	15	3	94-11	178	3.92	100	.246	.329	67-1	.164	1	93	-1	0.0
1971	†Pit N	6	0	1.000	37	0	0	2-0	46.1	59	38	5	0	24-2	40	6.99	48	.314	.388	9-1	.333	1		-18	-2.3
1972	Pit N	0	0	—	5	0	0	0-0	9	10	7	0	0	7-2	6	6.00	55	.313	.425	1-0	.000	-0		-3	-0.2
	Bos A	2	0	1.000	6	0	0	2-0	8	2	0	0	0	3-0	10	0.00	—	.083	.185	1-0	.000	-0		3	0.7
1973	Bos A	2	3	.400	32	0	0	11-4	36.1	37	16	2	0	12-2	25	3.47	116	.268	.327	0-0	—	0		2	0.4
1974	Bos A	0	1	.000	18	0	0	2-2	13	15	8	2	0	4-1	16	5.54	69	.283	.328	0-0	—	0		-2	-0.2
Total	13	120	95	.558	397	255	78-20	21-6	1926	1684	755	91	29	858-62	1703	3.07	113	.236	.319	630-28	.114	-17	100	84	7.1
VEDDER, LOU Louis Edward B 4.20.1897 Oakville, MI D 3.9.1990 Lake Placid, FL BR/TR 5-10.5/175# d9.18																									
1920	Det A	0	0	—	1	0	0	0	2	0	0	0	0	0	1	0.00	—	.000	.000	0-0	—	0		1	0.1
VEIGEL, AL Allen Francis B 1.30.1917 Dover, OH BR/TR 6-1/180# d9.21																									
1939	Bos N	0	1	.000	2	2	0	0	2.2	3	6	0	0	5	1	6.75	55	.250	.471	1-0	.000	-0	106	-3	-0.5
VEIL, BUCKY Frederick William B 8.2.1881 Tyrone, PA D 4.16.1931 Altoona, PA BR/TR 5-10/165# d4.19																									
1903	†Pit N	5	3	.625	12	6	4	0	70.2	70	35	1	2	36	20	3.82	85	.269	.362	29-0	.207	-0	97	-1	-0.2
1904	Pit N	0	0	—	1	1	0	0	4.2	4	3	0	1	4	1	5.79	47	.250	.429	1-0	1.000	0	150	-1	0.0
Total	2	5	3	.625	13	7	4	0	75.1	74	38	1	3	40	21	3.94	81	.268	.367	30-0	.233	0	102	-2	-0.2
VELAZQUEZ, CARLOS Carlos (Quinones) B 3.22.1948 Loiza, P.R. BR/TR 5-11/180# d7.20																									
1973	Mil A	2	2	.500	18	0	0	2-1	38.1	46	15	5	0	10-1	12	2.58	146	.297	.337	0-0	—	0		4	0.4
VENAFRO, MIKE Michael Robert B 8.2.1973 Takoma Park, MD BL/TL 5-10/170# d4.24																									
1999	†Tex A	3	2	.600	65	0	0	0-1	68.1	63	29	4	3	22-0	37	3.29	154	.251	.317	0-0	—	0		12	0.8
2000	Tex A	3	1	.750	77	0	0	1-1	56.1	64	27	2	4	21-4	32	3.83	131	.295	.362	0-0	—	0		7	0.5
2001	Tex A	5	5	.500	70	0	0	4-4	60	54	35	2	7	28-4	29	4.80	97	.240	.337	0-0	—	0		-1	-0.2
2002	Oak A	2	2	.500	47	0	0	0-0	37	45	22	5	2	14-2	16	4.62	95	.308	.372	0-0	—	0		-1	-0.1
2003	TB A	1	0	1.000	24	0	0	0-0	19	24	10	1	3	3-0	9	4.74	96	.308	.353	0-0	—	0		0	0.0
Total	5	14	10	.583	283	0	0	5-6	240.2	250	123	14	19	88-10	123	4.11	117	.273	.344	0-0	—	0		17	1.0
VERAS, DARIO Dario Antonio B 3.13.1973 Santiago, D.R. BR/TR 6-2/165# d7.31																									
1996	†SD N	3	1	.750	23	0	0	0-0	29	24	10	3	1	10-4	23	2.79	142	.231	.302	0-0	—	0		4	0.5
1997	SD N	2	1	.667	23	0	0	0-1	24.2	28	18	5	2	12-3	21	5.11	76	.280	.368	0-0	—	0		-5	-0.6
1998	Bos A	0	1	.000	7	0	0	0-0	8	12	9	0	1	7-0	2	10.13	47	.343	.465	0-0	—	0		-4	-0.5
Total	3	5	3	.625	53	0	0	0-1	61.2	64	37	8	4	29-7	46	4.67	86	.268	.355	0-0	—	0		-5	-0.6
VERBANIC, JOE Joseph Michael B 4.24.1943 Washington, PA BR/TR 6/155# d7.22																									
1966	Phi N	1	1	.500	17	0	0	0	14	12	9	2	0	10-3	7	5.14	70	.226	.344	0-0	—	0		-2	-0.3
1967	NY A	4	3	.571	28	6	1-1	2	80.1	74	27	6	2	21-3	39	2.80	112	.249	.300	18-3	.111	-0	79	4	0.4
1968	NY A	6	7	.462	40	11	2-1	4	97	104	36	6	6	41-8	40	3.15	92	.284	.363	25-3	.080	-1	104	-1	-0.2
1970	NY A	1	0	1.000	7	0	0	0-0	15.2	20	9	1	1	12-0	8	4.60	77	.323	.440	3-0	.333	0		-2	0.0
Total	4	12	11	.522	92	17	3-2	6-0	207	210	81	15	9	84-14	94	3.26	95	.270	.345	46-6	.109	-1	92	-1	-0.1
VERDEL, AL Albert Alfred "Stumpy" B 6.10.1921 Punxsutawney, PA D 4.16.1991 Sarasota, FL BR/TR 5-9.5/186# d4.20																									
1944	Phi N	0	0	—	1	0	0	0	1	0	0	0	0	0	0	0.00	—	.000	.000	0-0	—	0		0	0.0
VEREKER, TOMMY John James B 12.2.1893 Baltimore, MD D 4.2.1974 Baltimore, MD 5-10/185# d6.17																									
1915	Bal F	0	0	—	2	0	0	0	3	3	5	1	1	2	1	15.00	19	.273	.429	0-0	—	0		-3	-0.2
VERES, DAVE David Scott B 10.19.1966 Montgomery, AL BR/TR 6-2/195# d5.10																									
1994	Hou N	3	3	.500	32	0	0	1-0	41	39	13	4	1	7-3	28	2.41	164	.247	.280	2-1	.500	1		7	1.0
1995	Hou N	5	1	.833	72	0	0	1-2	103.1	89	29	5	4	30-6	94	2.26	171	.241	.299	5-1	.000	-1		20	1.0
1996	Mon N	6	3	.667	68	0	0	4-2	77.2	85	39	10	6	32-2	81	4.17	104	.277	.353	8-0	.375	1		2	0.3
1997	Mon N	2	3	.400	53	0	0	1-3	62	68	28	5	2	27-3	47	3.48	120	.278	.353	1-0	1.000	0		4	0.3
1998	Col N	3	1	.750	63	0	0	8-5	76.1	67	26	6	2	27-2	74	2.83	183	.233	.301	3-0	.333	0		16	1.1
1999	Col N	4	8	.333	73	0	0	31-8	77	88	46	14	2	37-7	71	5.14	113	.290	.369	1-0	.000	-0		5	0.9
2000	†StL N	3	5	.375	71	0	0	29-7	75.2	65	26	6	6	25-2	67	2.85	162	.239	.315	1-0	.000	-0		15	2.4
2001	†StL N	3	2	.600	71	0	0	15-4	65.2	57	29	12	2	28-1	61	3.70	115	.232	.314	3-1	.000	-0		4	0.4
2002	†StL N	5	8	.385	71	0	0	4-4	82.2	67	34	12	2	39-4	68	3.48	114	.224	.315	3-0	.333	0		5	0.8
2003	†Chi N	2	1	.667	31	0	0	1-1	32.2	36	17	4	1	5-0	26	4.68	90	.290	.313	0-0	—	0		-1	-0.1
Total	10	36	35	.507	605	0	0	95-36	694	661	287	78	28	257-30	617	3.44	130	.253	.323	27-3	.259	2		77	8.1
VERES, RANDY Randolph Ruhland B 11.25.1965 Sacramento, CA BR/TR 6-3/210# d7.1																									
1989	Mil A	0	1	.000	3	1	0	0-0	8.1	9	5	0	0	4-0	8	4.32	89	.290	.361	0-0	—	0	24	-1	-0.1
1990	Mil A	0	3	.000	26	0	0	1-0	41.2	38	17	5	1	16-3	16	3.67	106	.247	.318	0-0	—	0		2	0.2
1994	Chi N	1	1	.500	10	0	0	0-2	9.2	12	6	3	1	2-0	5	5.59	74	.308	.349	1-0	.000	-0		-1	-0.3
1995	Fla N	4	4	.500	47	0	0	1-1	48.2	46	25	6	1	22-7	31	3.88	109	.251	.329	3-0	.000	-0		1	0.1
1996	Det A	0	4	.000	25	0	0	0-2	30.1	38	29	6	2	23-4	28	8.31	61	.306	.414	0-0	—	0		-10	-1.1
1997	KC A	4	0	1.000	24	0	0	1-2	35.1	36	17	4	3	7-1	28	3.31	142	.273	.313	0-0	—	0		4	0.4
Total	6	9	13	.409	135	1	0	3-7	174	179	99	24	8	74-15	116	4.60	95	.270	.343	4-0	.000	-0	24	-5	-0.8
VERHOEVEN, JOHN John C B 7.3.1952 Long Beach, CA BR/TR 6-5/200# d7.6																									
1976	Cal A	0	2	.000	21	0	0	4-3	37.1	35	15	2	0	14-8	23	3.38	99	.252	.320	0-0	—	0		0	0.1
1977	Cal A	0	2	.000	3	0	0	0-1	4.2	4	3	0	1	4-1	3	3.86	102	.222	.391	0-0	—	0		0	0.0
	Chi A	0	0	—	6	0	0	0-0	10.1	9	3	0	0	2-0	6	2.61	157	.231	.268	0-0	—	0		2	0.1
	Year	0	2	.000	9	0	0	0-1	15	13	7	0	1	6-1	9	3.00	135	.228	.313	0-0	—	0		2	0.1
1980	Min A	3	4	.429	44	0	0	0-0	99.2	109	53	10	3	29-5	42	3.97	110	.289	.337	0-0	—	0		3	0.2
1981	Min A	0	0	—	25	0	0	0-1	52	57	27	4	2	14-4	16	3.98	99	.288	.335	0-0	—	0		-1	0.0
Total	4	3	8	.273	99	0	0	4-5	204	214	101	16	6	63-18	90	3.79	107	.278	.332	0-0	—	0		4	0.4
VERNON, JOE Joseph Henry B 11.25.1889 Mansfield, MA D 3.13.1955 Philadelphia, PA BR/TR 5-11/160# d7.20																									
1912	Chi N	0	0	—	1	0	0	0	4	4	6	0	1	6	1	11.25	30	.286	.524	2-0	.000	-0		-3	-0.2
1914	Bro F	0	0	—	1	1	0	0	3.1	4	4	0	0	5	0	10.80	27	.308	.500	1-0	.000	-0	286	-2	-0.1
Total	2	0	0	—	2	1	0	0	7.1	8	10	0	1	11	1	11.05	28	.296	.513	3-0	.000	-0	286	-5	-0.3
VESELIC, BOB Robert Michael B 9.27.1955 Pittsburgh, PA D 12.26.1995 Los Angeles, CA BR/TR 6/175# d9.18																									
1980	Min A	0	0	—	1	0	0	0-0	4	3	2	1	0	1-0	2	4.50	97	.214	.267	0-0	—	0		0	0.0
1981	Min A	1	1	.500	5	0	0	0-1	22.2	22	8	1	0	12-2	13	3.18	124	.250	.337	0-0	—	0		2	0.2
Total	2	1	1	.500	6	0	0	0-1	26.2	25	10	2	0	13-2	15	3.38	119	.245	.328	0-0	—	0		2	0.2
VIAU, LEE Leon A. B 7.5.1866 Corinth, VT D 12.17.1947 Hopewell, NJ BR/TR 5-4/160# d4.22																									
1888	Cin AA	27	14	.659	42	42	42-1	0	387.2	331	192	7	20	110	164	2.65	120	.222	.285	149	.087	-11*	100	21	0.7
1889	Cin AA	22	20	.524	47	42	38-1	1	373	379	224	8	10	136	152	3.79	103	.255	.322	147	.143	-9	92	13	0.2
1890	Cin N	7	5	.583	13	10	7-1	0	90	97	69	8	1	39	41	4.50	79	.266	.339	36	.139	-2	87	-7	-0.9
	Cle N	4	9	.308	13	13	13-1	0	107	101	65	4	5	42	30	3.36	107	.241	.318	43	.163	-2	54	1	-0.1
	Year	11	14	.440	26	23	20-2	0	197	198	68	12	6	81	71	3.88	92	.253	.328	79	.152	-4	68	-8	-1.0
1891	Cle N	18	17	.514	45	38	31	0	343.2	367	239	3	15	138	130	3.01	115	.263	.336	144	.160	-3	105	9	0.5

Year	Tm Lg	W	L	Pct	G	GS	CG-Sho	SV-BS	IP	H	R	HR	HB	BB-IB	SO	ERA	AERA	OAV	OOB	AB-SH	AVG	PB	Sup	APR	PW
1892	Cle N	0	1	.000	1	1	0	0	1	5	5	0	0	1	0	36.00	9	.625	.667	0	—	0	56	-3	-0.4
	Lou N	4	11	.267	16	15	14-1	0	130.2	156	86	7	0	56	36	3.99	77	.285	.351	66	.197	1*	78	-12	-0.9
	Bos N	1	0	1.000	1	1	1	0	9	5	1	0	0	4	1	0.00	—	.156	.250	3	.000	-0	144	3	0.3
	Year	5	12	.294	18	17	15-1	0	140.2	166	9	7	0	61	37	3.97	78	.282	.350	69	.188	1	82	-10	-1.0
Total	5	83	77	.519	178	162	146-5	1	1442	1441	881	37	51	526	554	3.33	105	.251	.320	588	.139	-27	93	25	-0.6
VICKERS, RUBE Harry Porter B 5.17.1878 St.Marys, ON, CAN D 12.9.1958 Belleville, MI BL/TR 6-2/225# d9.21																									
1902	Cin N	0	3	.000	3	3	3	0	21	31	20	0	1	8	6	6.00	50	.341	.400	11-0	.364	1*	60	-6	-0.7
1903	Bro N	0	1	.000	4	1	1	0	14	27	23	0	1	9	5	10.93	29	.415	.493	10-0	.100	-1*	63	-12	-0.7
1907	Phi A	2	2	.500	10	4	3-1	0	50.1	44	27	1	1	12	21	3.40	77	.238	.288	20-1	.150	-1	78	-4	-0.4
1908	Phi A	18	19	.486	53	34	21-6	1	317	264	114	0	11	71	156	2.21	116	.231	.282	106-4	.160	-1	88	10	1.0
1909	Phi A	2	2	.500	18	3	1	1	55.2	60	32	0	2	19	25	3.40	71	.274	.338	16-1	.063	-1	107	-7	-0.8
Total	5	22	27	.449	88	45	29-7	2	458	426	216	1	16	119	213	2.93	88	.250	.305	163-6	.160	-3	86	-19	-1.6
VICKERY, TOM Thomas Gill "Vinegar Tom" B 5.5.1867 Milford, NJ D 3.21.1921 Burlington, NJ TR 6/170# d4.21																									
1890	Phi N	24	22	.522	46	46	41-2	0	382	405	250	8	29	184	162	3.44	106	.263	.353	159	.208	-4	83	4	-0.1
1891	Chi N	6	5	.545	14	12	7	0	79.2	72	55	4	5	44	39	4.07	82	.232	.337	39	.179	-2	124	-6	-0.8
1892	Bal N	8	10	.444	24	21	17	0	176	189	134	3	10	87	49	3.53	97	.264	.351	74	.243	2	106	-8	-0.6
1893	Phi N	4	5	.444	13	11	7	0	80	100	65	1	6	37	15	5.40	85	.297	.376	35	.314	1*	90	-7	-0.4
Total	4	42	42	.500	97	90	72-2	0	717.2	766	504	16	50	352	265	3.75	98	.264	.353	307	.225	-3	94	-17	-1.9
VILLAFUERTE, BRANDON Brandon Paul B 12.17.1975 Hilo, HI BR/TR 5-11/180# d5.23																									
2000	Det A	0	0	—	3	0	0	0-0	4.1	4	5	0	0	4-0	1	10.38	47	.250	.400	0-0	—	0		-3	-0.1
2001	Tex A	0	0	—	6	0	0	0-0	5.2	12	9	3	1	4-0	4	14.29	33	.414	.486	0-0	—	0		-6	-0.3
2002	SD N	1	2	.333	31	0	0	1-0	32	29	5	2	2	12-2	25	1.41	268	.248	.326	0-0	—	0		9	0.9
2003	SD N	0	2	.000	31	0	0	2-3	40.2	39	20	7	3	26-2	34	4.20	94	.252	.368	1-0	.000	-0		-1	0.0
Total	4	1	4	.200	71	0	0	3-3	82.2	84	39	12	6	46-4	64	4.14	96	.265	.366	1-0	.000	-0		-1	0.5
VILLARREAL, OSCAR Oscar Eduardo B 11.22.1981 Monterrey, Mexico BL/TR 6/170# d3.31																									
2003	Ari N	10	7	.588	86	1	0	0-4	98	80	40	6	3	46-10	80	2.57	182	.222	.312	3-0	.000	-0	60	17	2.7
VILLEGAS, ISMAEL Ismael (Diaz) B 8.12.1976 Rio Piedras, P.R. BR/TR 6-1/188# d7.3																									
2000	Atl N	0	0	—	1	0	0	0-0	2.2	4	4	2	1	2-0	2	13.50	34	.333	.467	1-0	.000	-0		-2	-0.1
VILLONE, RON Ronald Thomas B 1.16.1970 Englewood, NJ BL/TL 6-3/230# d4.28																									
1995	Sea A	0	2	.000	19	0	0	0-3	19.1	20	19	6	1	23-0	26	7.91	60	.270	.449	0-0	—	0		-7	-0.6
	SD N	2	1	.667	19	0	0	1-1	25.2	24	12	5	0	11-0	37	4.21	96	.242	.315	1-0	.000	-0		0	0.0
1996	SD N	1	1	.500	21	0	0	0-1	18.1	17	6	2	1	7-0	19	2.95	135	.243	.321	0-0	—	0		3	0.3
	Mil A	0	0	—	23	0	0	2-0	24.2	14	9	4	4	18-0	19	3.28	158	.175	.346	0-0	—	0		5	0.2
1997	Mil A	1	0	1.000	50	0	0	0-2	52.2	54	23	4	1	36-2	40	3.42	135	.271	.386	1-0	.000	-0		7	0.3
1998	Cle A	0	0	—	25	0	0	0-0	27	30	18	3	2	22-0	15	6.00	80	.297	.425	0-0	—	0		-3	-0.1
1999	Cin N	9	7	.563	29	22	0	2-0	142.2	114	70	8	5	73-2	97	4.23	110	.219	.319	43-5	.070	-3	91	8	0.6
2000	Cin N	10	10	.500	35	23	2	0-0	141	154	95	22	9	78-3	77	5.43	87	.286	.381	43-2	.163	-1	109	-12	-1.5
2001	Col N	1	3	.250	22	6	0	0-0	46.2	56	35	6	1	29-4	48	6.36	84	.295	.389	9-2	.000	-1	92	-4	-0.4
	†Hou N	5	7	.417	31	6	0	0-0	68	77	46	12	4	24-1	65	5.56	82	.282	.349	13-2	.077	-1	61	-7	-1.1
	Year	6	10	.375	53	12	0	0-0	114.2	133	49	18	5	53-5	113	5.89	83	.287	.366	22-4	.045	-2	79	-11	-1.5
2002	Pit N	4	6	.400	45	7	0	0-1	93	95	63	8	5	34-3	55	5.81	72	.270	.340	16-0	.250	1	60	-15	-1.3
2003	Hou N	6	6	.500	19	19	0	0-0	106.2	91	51	16	5	48-1	91	4.13	107	.233	.323	42-1	.167	1	121	4	0.6
Total	9	39	43	.476	338	83	2	5-8	765.2	746	447	96	38	403-16	589	4.91	94	.258	.354	168-12	.131	-4	98	-21	-3.0
VINES, BOB Robert Earl B 2.25.1897 Waxahachie, TX D 10.18.1982 Orlando, FL BR/TR 6-4/184# d9.3																									
1924	StL N	0	0	—	2	0	0	0	10.2	23	13	1	0	0	0	9.28	41	.426	.426	4-0	.000	-1		-7	-0.4
1925	Phi N	0	0	—	3	0	0	0	4	9	10	0	0	3	0	11.25	42	.450	.522	0-0	—	0		-4	-0.2
Total	2	0	0	—	5	0	0	0	14.2	32	23	1	0	3	0	9.82	41	.432	.455	4-0	.000	-1		-11	-0.6
VINEYARD, DAVE David Kent B 2.25.1941 Clay, WV BR/TR 6-3/195# d7.18																									
1964	Bal A	2	5	.286	19	6	1	0	54	57	34	5	0	27-2	50	4.17	86	.274	.354	12-2	.167	0	71	-7	-0.8
VINING, KEN Kenneth Edward B 12.5.1974 Decatur, GA BL/TL 6/180# d5.23																									
2001	Chi A	0	0	—	8	0	0	0-0	6.2	15	14	3	1	7-0	3	17.55	26	.441	.548	0-0	—	0		-9	-0.4
VINTON, BILL William Miller B 4.27.1865 Winthrop, MA D 9.3.1893 Pawtucket, RI BR/TR 6-1/160# d7.3																									
1884	Phi N	10	10	.500	21	21	20	0	182	166	131	6		35	105	2.23	134	.220	.255	78	.115	-6	110	4	-0.1
1885	Phi N	3	6	.333	9	9	8	0	77	90	59	0		23	21	3.04	92	.269	.317	30	.067	-3	113	-4	-0.7
	Phi AA	4	3	.571	7	7	6-2	0	55	46	41	1	4	15	34	2.45	140	.200	.261	26	.154	-0	130	3	0.2
Total	2	17	19	.472	37	37	34-2	0	314	302	231	7	4	73	160	2.46	122	.229	.272	134	.112	-10	115	3	-0.6
VIOLA, FRANK Frank John B 4.19.1960 Hempstead, NY BL/TL 6-4/209# d6.6																									
1982	Min A	4	10	.286	22	22	3-1	0-0	126	152	77	22	0	38-2	84	5.21	82	.302	.351	0-0	—	0	91	-12	-1.2
1983	Min A	7	15	.318	35	34	4	0-0	210	242	141	34	8	92-7	127	5.49	78	.287	.362	0-0	—	0	96	-27	-2.5
1984	Min A	18	12	.600	35	35	10-4	0-0	257.2	225	101	28	4	73-1	149	3.21	131	.233	.289	0-0	—	0	89	27	2.9
1985	Min A	18	14	.563	36	36	9	0-0	250.2	262	136	26	2	68-3	135	4.09	108	.268	.315	0-0	—	0	85	4	0.4
1986	Min A	16	13	.552	37	**37**	7-1	0-0	245.2	257	136	37	3	83-0	191	4.51	96	.268	.327	0-0	—	0	103	-5	-0.7
1987	†Min A	17	10	.630	36	36	7-1	0-0	251.2	230	91	29	6	66-1	197	2.90	160	.241	.293	0-0	—	0	85	46	4.5
1988	Min A★	**24**	7	**.774**	35	35	7-2	0-0	255.1	236	80	20	3	54-2	193	2.64	154	.245	.286	0-0	—	0	118	**40**	**4.7**
1989	Min A	8	12	.400	24	24	7-1	0-0	175.2	171	80	17	3	47-1	138	3.79	109	.256	.306	0-0	—	0	86	7	0.7
	NY N	5	5	.500	12	12	2-1	0-0	85.1	75	35	5	1	27-3	73	3.38	97	.236	.296	23-5	.130	-0	111	-1	-0.1
1990	NY N★	20	12	.625	35	**35**	7-3	0-0	**249.2**	227	83	15	2	60-2	182	2.67	141	.242	.288	85-7	.153	-1	104	30	**3.7**
1991	NY N★	13	15	.464	35	35	3	0-0	231.1	259	112	25	1	54-4	132	3.97	92	.286	.325	71-10	.127	-1	84	-7	-0.9
1992	Bos A	13	12	.520	35	35	6-1	0-0	238	214	99	13	7	89-4	121	3.44	123	.242	.313	0-0	—	0	75	21	2.3
1993	Bos A	11	8	.579	29	29	2-1	0-0	183.2	180	76	12	6	72-5	91	3.14	148	.259	.331	0-0	—	0	87	27	2.6
1994	Bos A	1	1	.500	6	6	0	0-0	31	34	17	2	0	17-0	9	4.65	108	.296	.381	0-0	—	0	94	2	0.1
1995	Cin N	0	1	.000	3	3	0	0-0	14.1	20	11	3	0	3-1	4	6.28	66	.333	.359	6-0	.167	0	88	-4	-0.2
1996	Tor A	1	3	.250	6	6	0	0-0	30.1	43	28	6	2	21-3	18	7.71	65	.350	.443	0-0	—	0	99	-9	-0.9
Total	15	176	150	.540	421	420	74-16	0-0	2836.1	2827	1303	294	48	864-39	1844	3.73	112	.260	.316	185-22	.141	-2	93	139	15.4
VITELLI, JOE Antonio Joseph B 4.12.1908 McKees Rocks, PA D 2.7.1967 Pittsburgh, PA BR/TR 6-1/195# d5.30																									
1944	Pit N	0	0	—	4	0	0	0	7	5	6	1	1	7	2	2.57	145	.185	.371	3-0	.000	-0		-1	-0.1
VITKO, JOE Joseph John B 2.1.1970 Somerville, NJ BR/TR 6-8/210# d9.18																									
1992	NY N	0	1	.000	3	1	0	0-0	4.2	12	11	1	0	1-0	6	13.50	26	.444	.448	0-0	—	0	156	-7	-1.1
VIZCAINO, LUIS Luis (Arias) B 6.1.1975 Bani, D.R. BR/TR 6-1/170# d7.23																									
1999	Oak A	0	0	—	1	0	0	0-0	3.1	3	2	1	0	3-0	2	5.40	86	.231	.375	0-0	—	0		0	0.0
2000	Oak A	0	1	.000	12	0	0	0-0	19.1	25	17	2	2	11-0	18	7.45	64	.305	.396	0-0	—	0		-6	-0.2
2001	Oak A	2	1	.667	36	0	0	1-0	36.2	38	19	8	0	12-1	31	4.66	95	.266	.321	0-0	—	0		0	0.0
2002	Mil N	5	3	.625	76	0	0	5-1	81.1	55	27	6	3	30-4	79	2.99	137	.192	.272	2-0	.000	-0		11	1.0
2003	Mil N	4	3	.571	75	0	0	0-6	62	64	45	16	1	25-3	61	6.39	67	.263	.333	0-0	—	0		-14	-1.4
Total	5	11	8	.579	200	0	0	6-7	202.2	185	110	33	6	81-8	191	4.80	89	.241	.316	2-0	.000	-0		-9	-0.6
VOGELSONG, RYAN Ryan Andrew B 7.22.1977 Charlotte, NC BR/TR 6-3/195# d9.2																									
2000	SF N	0	0	—	4	0	0	0-0	6	4	0	0	0	2-0	6	0.00	—	.182	.250	0-0	—	0		3	0.1
2001	SF N	0	3	.000	13	0	0	0-0	28.2	29	21	5	2	14-0	17	5.65	71	.257	.346	8-0	.125	0		-6	-0.5
	Pit N	0	2	.000	2	2	0	0-0	6	10	10	1	0	6-1	7	12.00	37	.357	.471	2-0	.000	-0	103	-5	-0.9
	Year	0	5	.000	15	2	0	0-0	34.2	39	15	6	2	20-1	24	6.75	60	.277	.372	10-0	.100	-0	113	-12	-1.4
2003	Pit N	2	2	.500	6	5	0	0-0	22	30	19	1	2	9-3	15	6.55	67	.323	.390	6-2	.167	-0	111	-6	-0.9

Year	Tm Lg	W	L	Pct	G	GS	CG-Sho	SV-BS	IP	H	R	HR	HB	BB-IB	SO	ERA	AERA	OAV	OOB	AB-SH	AVG	PB	Sup	APR	PW
Total	3	2	7	.222	25	7	0	0-0	62.2	73	50	7	4	31-4	45	6.03	70	.285	.369	16-2	.125	-0	114	-14	-2.2
VOIGT, OLLIE Olen Edward "Ode" B 1.29.1900 Wheaton, IL D 4.7.1970 Scottsdale, AZ BL/TR 6-1/170# d4.19																									
1924	StL A	1	0	1.000	8	1	0	0	16.1	21	13	1	0	13	4	5.51	82	.356	.472	4-0	.250	1	131	-2	0.0
VOISELLE, BILL William Symmes "Big Bill" or "Ninety-Six" B 1.29.1919 Greenwood, SC BR/TR 6-4/200# d9.1																									
1942	NY N	0	1	.000	2	1	0	0	9	6	4	1	0	4	5	2.00	168	.176	.263	2-0	.000	0	50	1	0.1
1943	NY N	1	2	.333	4	4	3	0	31	18	10	1	0	14	19	2.03	170	.154	.244	9-3	.111	-1	62	4	0.3
1944	NY N☆	21	16	.568	43	**41**	25-1	0	**312.2**	276	138	31	4	118	**161**	3.02	121	.232	.303	105-9	.210	3*	103	17	2.0
1945	NY N	14	14	.500	41	**35**	14-4	0	232.1	249	128	15	4	97	115	4.49	87	.273	.345	79-7	.127	-3	105	-13	-1.7
1946	NY N	9	15	.375	36	25	10-2	0	178	171	88	14	0	85	89	3.74	92	.248	.330	55-7	.164	-1	114	-7	-1.0
1947	NY N	1	4	.200	11	5	1	0	42.2	44	26	4	1	22	20	4.64	88	.284	.376	15-0	.133	-1	100	-3	-0.4
	Bos N	8	7	.533	22	20	7	0	131.1	146	66	10	1	51	59	4.32	90	.280	.345	53-3	.170	-1	118	-4	-0.4
	Year	9	11	.450	33	25	8	0	174	190	71	14	2	73	79	4.40	90	.281	.352	68-3	.162	-1	114	-7	-0.8
1948	†Bos N	13	13	.500	37	30	9-2	2	215.2	226	93	18	3	90	89	3.63	106	.272	.345	72-7	.097	-4	89	7	0.3
1949	Bos N	7	8	.467	30	22	5-4	1	169.1	170	84	14	1	78	63	4.04	94	.263	.343	61-0	.115	-2	109	-3	-0.4
1950	Chi N	0	4	.000	19	7	0	0	51.1	64	39	7	1	29	25	5.79	73	.303	.390	13-0	.077	-1	90	-9	-0.7
Total	9	74	84	.468	245	190	74-13	3	1373.1	1370	676	115	15	588	645	3.83	98	.258	.334	464-36	.147	-10	103	-10	-1.9
VOLZ, JAKE Jacob Phillip "Silent Jake" B 4.4.1878 San Antonio, TX D 8.11.1962 San Antonio, TX BR/TR 5-10/175# d9.28																									
1901	Bos A	1	0	1.000	1	1	1	0	7	6	9	2	0	9	5	9.00	39	.231	.429	4-0	.000	-1	191	-4	-0.4
1905	Bos N	0	2	.000	3	2	0	0	8.2	12	11	0	1	8	1	10.38	30	.364	.500	2-0	.000	-0	47	-6	-1.1
1908	Cin N	1	2	.333	7	4	1	0	22.2	16	9	1	2	12	6	3.57	65	.195	.313	4-0	.250	0	76	-2	-0.3
Total	3	2	4	.333	11	7	2	0	38.1	34	29	3	3	29	12	6.10	44	.241	.382	10-0	.100	-1	89	-12	-1.8
Von FRICKEN, TONY Anthony B 5.30.1869 Brooklyn, NY D 3.22.1947 Troy, NY BB/TR 5-11.5/160# d5.9																									
1890	Bos N	0	1	.000	1	1	1	0	8	23	16	0	0	8	2	10.13	37	.489	.564	3	.000	-1	50	-6	-0.5
Von HOFF, BRUCE Bruce Frederick B 11.17.1943 Oakland, CA BR/TR 6/187# d9.28																									
1965	Hou N	0	0	—	3	0	0	0	3	3	3	0	0	2-0	1	9.00	37	.250	.357	0-0	—	0		-2	-0.1
1967	Hou N	0	3	.000	10	10	0	0	50.1	52	29	3	0	28-1	22	4.83	69	.268	.356	15-1	.067	-1	90	-8	-0.6
Total	2	0	3	.000	13	10	0	0	53.1	55	32	3	0	30-1	23	5.06	65	.267	.356	15-1	.067	-1	90	-10	-0.7
Von OHLEN, DAVE David B 10.25.1958 Flushing, NY BL/TL 6-2/200# d5.13																									
1983	StL N	3	2	.600	46	0	0	2-2	68.1	71	27	3	3	25-8	21	3.29	110	.280	.345	7-1	.143	0		3	0.2
1984	StL N	1	0	1.000	27	0	0	1-1	34.2	39	13	0	0	8-3	19	3.12	112	.300	.341	1-0	1.000	0		2	0.2
1985	Cle A	3	2	.600	26	0	0	0-1	43.1	47	20	3	0	20-6	12	2.91	142	.288	.358	0-0	—	0		4	0.4
1986	Oak A	0	3	.000	24	0	0	1-1	15.1	18	7	0	0	7-2	4	3.52	110	.300	.373	0-0	—	0		0	0.1
1987	Oak A	0	0	—	4	0	0	0-0	6	10	5	1	0	1-0	3	7.50	55	.400	.407	0-0	—	0		-2	-0.1
Total	5	7	7	.500	127	0	0	4-5	167.2	185	72	7	3	61-19	59	3.33	113	.293	.353	8-1	.250	1		7	0.8
VORHEES, CY Henry Bert B 9.30.1874 Lodi, OH D 2.8.1910 Perry, OH TR 6-3/200# d4.17																									
1902	Phi N	3	3	.500	10	5	3-1	0	53.2	63	33	1	1	20	24	3.86	73	.292	.354	20-0	.350	2	121	-7	-0.5
	Was A	0	1	.000	1	1	1	0	8	10	6	0	0	2	1	4.50	82	.303	.343	3-0	.667	1	39	-1	0.0
Total	1	3	4	.429	11	6	4-1	0	61.2	73	39	1	1	22	25	3.94	74	.293	.353	23-0	.391	3	103	-8	-0.5
VOSBERG, ED Edward John B 9.28.1961 Tucson, AZ BL/TL 6-1/190# d9.17																									
1986	SD N	0	1	.000	5	3	0	0-0	13.2	17	11	1	0	9-1	8	6.59	56	.304	.400	2-0	.000	-0	106	-4	-0.3
1990	SF N	1	1	.500	18	0	0	0-0	24.1	21	16	3	0	12-2	12	5.55	66	.233	.324	0-0	—	0		-5	-0.4
1994	Oak A	0	2	.000	16	0	0	0-1	13.2	16	7	2	0	5-0	12	3.95	112	.320	.382	0-0	—	0		1	0.1
1995	Tex A	5	5	.500	44	0	0	4-4	36	32	15	3	0	16-1	36	3.00	161	.241	.316	0-0	—	0		6	1.1
1996	†Tex A	1	1	.500	52	0	0	8-1	44	51	17	4	0	21-4	32	3.27	160	.298	.373	0-0	—	0		9	0.7
1997	Tex A	1	2	.333	42	0	0	0-1	41	44	23	3	2	15-6	29	4.61	104	.277	.341	0-0	—	0		1	0.0
	†Fla N	1	1	.500	17	0	0	1-1	12	15	7	0	3	6-0	8	3.75	108	.313	.414	0-0	—	0		0	-0.1
1999	SD N	0	0	—	15	0	0	0-2	8.1	16	11	1	2	3-0	6	9.72	43	.421	.467	0-0	—	0		-6	-0.3
	Ari N	0	1	.000	4	0	0	0-0	2.2	6	1	0	0	0-0	2	3.38	136	.462	.462	0-0	—	0		0	0.1
	Year	0	1	.000	19	0	0	0-2	11	22	16	1	2	3-0	8	8.18	52	.431	.466	0-0	—	0		-6	-0.2
2000	Phi N	1	1	.500	31	0	0	0-0	24	21	11	4	0	18-0	23	4.13	113	.241	.371	0-0	—	0		2	0.2
2001	Phi N	0	0	—	18	0	0	0-0	12.2	8	4	0	0	3-0	11	2.84	150	.186	.239	0-0	—	0		2	0.1
2002	Mon N	0	0	—	4	0	0	0-0	1	3	3	1	0	1-0	0	18.00	25	.429	.500	0-0	—	0		-2	-0.1
Total	10	10	15	.400	266	3	0	13-10	233.1	250	126	22	7	109-14	179	4.32	106	.279	.358	2-0	.000	-0	106	4	1.1
VOSS, ALEX Alexander B 5.16.1858 Roswell, GA D 8.31.1906 Cincinnati, OH BR/TR 6-1/180# d4.17 ▲																									
1884	Was U	5	14	.263	27	20	18	0	186.1	206	136	2		32	112	3.57	67	.262	.291	245	.192	-9*	91	-24	-2.4
	KC U	0	6	.000	7	6	6	0	53	74	45	2		7	17	4.25	53	.310	.329	45	.089	-4*	41	-12	-1.3
	Year	5	20	.200	34	26	24	0	239.1	280	47	4		39	129	3.72	63	.273	.300	290	.176	-13	80	-36	-3.7
VOWINKEL, RIP John Henry B 11.18.1884 Oswego, NY D 7.13.1966 Oswego, NY BR/TR 5-10/195# d9.5																									
1905	Cin N	3	3	.500	6	6	4	0	45.1	52	31	2	1	10	7	4.17	79	.302	.344	14-2	.071	-0	116	-4	-0.6
VOYLES, BRAD Bradley Roy B 12.30.1976 Green Bay, WI BR/TR 6-1/195# d9.8																									
2001	KC A	0	0	—	7	0	0	0-0	9.1	5	4	1	1	8-0	6	3.86	127	.161	.350	0-0	—	0		1	0.0
2002	KC A	0	2	.000	22	0	0	1-1	27.2	31	21	5	2	18-1	26	6.51	77	.284	.395	0-0	—	0		-4	-0.3
2003	KC A	0	2	.000	11	3	0	0-0	31.1	47	29	6	1	18-1	24	7.18	72	.348	.423	1-0	.000	-0	89	-7	-0.4
Total	3	0	4	.000	40	3	0	1-1	68.1	83	54	12	4	44-2	56	6.45	79	.302	.403	1-0	.000	-0	89	-10	-0.7
VUCKOVICH, PETE Peter Dennis B 10.27.1952 Johnstown, PA BR/TR 6-4/220# d8.3 C4																									
1975	Chi A	0	1	.000	4	2	0	0-0	10.1	17	15	0	0	7-1	5	13.06	30	.386	.471	0-0	—	0	193	-10	-0.8
1976	Chi A	7	4	.636	33	7	1	0-0	110.1	122	59	3	4	60-4	62	4.65	77	.287	.375	0-0	—	0	102	-12	-1.1
1977	Tor A	7	7	.500	53	8	3-1	8-4	148	143	64	13	5	59-5	123	3.47	122	.257	.329	0-0	—	0	88	12	1.2
1978	StL N	12	12	.500	45	23	6-2	1-3	198.1	187	65	9	2	59-5	149	2.54	139	.253	.308	58-7	.138	-1	78	22	2.5
1979	StL N	15	10	.600	34	32	9	0-0	233	229	108	22	3	64-4	145	3.59	105	.260	.310	79-8	.152	-2	117	3	0.0
1980	StL N	12	9	.571	32	30	7-3	1-0	222.1	203	96	18	2	68-5	132	3.40	109	.247	.304	71-9	.183	1	107	6	0.7
1981	†Mil A	**14**	4	**.778**	24	23	2-1	0-1	149.2	137	61	9	4	57-1	84	3.55	97	.249	.323	0-0	—	0	131	-1	-0.1
1982	†Mil A	18	6	**.750**	30	30	9-1	0-0	223.2	234	96	14	5	102-1	105	3.34	114	.275	.354	0-0	—	0	126	10	1.0
1983	Mil A	0	2	.000	3	3	0	0-0	14.2	15	9	0	1	10-1	10	4.91	76	.259	.377	0-0	—	0	89	-2	-0.3
1985	Mil A	6	10	.375	22	22	1	0-0	112.2	134	74	16	7	48-2	55	5.51	76	.298	.374	0-0	—	0	100	-15	-1.8
1986	Mil A	2	4	.333	6	6	0	0-0	32.1	33	18	3	2	11-0	12	3.06	142	.273	.336	0-0	—	0	42	2	0.4
Total	11	93	69	.574	286	186	38-8	10-8	1455.1	1454	665	107	35	545-29	882	3.66	103	.264	.332	208-24	.159	-2	107	15	1.7
WACHTEL, PAUL Paul Horine B 4.30.1888 Myersville, MD D 12.15.1964 San Antonio, TX BR/TR 5-11/175# d9.18																									
1917	Bro N	0	0	—	2	0	0	0	6	9	7	0	0	4	3	10.50	27	.375	.464	3-0	.333	0		-4	-0.2
WACKER, CHARLIE Charles James B 12.8.1883 Jeffersonville, IN D 8.7.1948 Evansville, IN BL/TL 5-9/?# d4.28																									
1909	Pit N	0	0	—	1	0	0	0	2	2	2	0	0	1	0	0.00	—	.400	.500	0-0	—	0		0	0.0
WADDELL, RUBE George Edward B 10.13.1876 Bradford, PA D 4.1.1914 San Antonio, TX BR/TL 6-1.5/196# d9.8 HF1946																									
1897	Lou N	0	1	.000	2	1	1	0	14	17	6	0	1	6	5	3.21	133	.298	.375	6-0	.000	-1	17	2	0.0
1899	Lou N	7	2	.778	10	9	9-1	1	79	69	38	4	8	14	44	3.08	125	.235	.288	34-0	.235	-0	89	8	0.7
1900	†Pit N	8	13	.381	29	22	16-2	0	208.2	176	96	3	13	55	130	**2.37**	**153**	**.229**	.291	81-0	.173	-2*	105	24	1.9
1901	Pit N	0	2	.000	2	2	0	0	7.2	10	12	0	1	9	4	9.39	35	.313	.476	3-0	.000	-0	76	-5	-0.9
	Chi N	14	14	.500	29	28	26	0	243.2	239	123	5	9	66	168	2.81	115	.255	.310	98-0	.255	6*	102	9	1.8
	Year	14	16	.467	31	30	26	0	251.1	249	128	5	10	75	172	3.01	108	.257	.317	101-0	.248	6	101	3	0.9
1902	Phi A	24	7	.774	33	27	26-3	0	276.1	224	90	7	10	64	**210**	2.05	179	.222	.276	112-1	.286	7*	95	48	5.8
1903	Phi A	21	16	.568	39	38	**34**-4	0	324	274	109	3	8	85	**302**	2.44	125	.229	.284	115-5	.122	-6	83	23	1.8
1904	Phi A	25	19	.568	46	46	39-8	0	383	307	109	5	14	91	**349**	1.62	**165**	.221	.275	139-1	.122	-7	97	40	4.1

Year	Tm Lg	W	L	Pct	G	GS	CG-Sho	SV-BS	IP	H	R	HR	HB	BB-IB	SO	ERA	AERA	OAV	OOB	AB-SH	AVG	PB	Sup	APR	PW
1905	Phi A	**27**	10	**.730**	**46**	34	27-7	0	328.2	231	86	5	10	90	**287**	**1.48**	**180**	**.200**	.263	116-6	.172	-1	106	**40**	**4.5**
1906	Phi A	15	17	.469	43	34	22-8	0	272.2	221	89	1	10	92	**196**	2.21	123	.225	.297	86-5	.163	-0	74	17	1.9
1907	Phi A	19	13	.594	44	33	20-7	0	284.2	234	115	2	15	73	**232**	2.15	121	.227	.287	101-2	.119	-5	100	8	0.2
1908	StL A	19	14	.576	43	36	25-5	3	285.2	223	93	0	8	90	232	1.89	127	.213	.281	91-3	.110	-1	101	14	1.5
1909	StL A	11	14	.440	31	28	16-5	0	220.1	204	78	1	7	57	141	2.37	102	.267	.323	75-0	.067	-5	78	1	-0.6
1910	StL A	3	1	.750	10	2	0	1	33	31	19	1	1	11	16	3.55	70	.242	.307	9-0	.111	-0	108	-4	-0.5
Total	13	193	143	.574	407	340	261-50	5	2961.1	2460	1063	37	115	803	2316	2.16	135	.228	.288	1066-23	.161	-17	93	225	22.2
WADDELL, TOM Thomas David B 9.17.1958 Dundee, Scotland BR/TR 6-1/185# d4.15																									
1984	Cle A	7	4	.636	58	0	0	6-4	97	68	35	12	1	37-4	59	3.06	134	.202	.276	0-0	—	0		11	1.3
1985	Cle A	8	6	.571	49	9	1	9-4	112.2	104	61	20	1	39-8	53	4.87	85	.246	.309	0-0	—	0	134	-6	-0.8
1987	Cle A	0	1	.000	6	0	0	0-0	5.2	7	10	1	1	7-0	6	14.29	32	.292	.469	0-0	—	0		-6	-0.8
Total	3	15	11	.577	113	9	1	15-8	215.1	179	106	33	3	83-12	118	4.30	96	.229	.300	0-0	—	0	134	-1	-0.3
WADE, BEN Benjamin Styron B 11.26.1922 Morehead City, NC D 12.2.2002 Los Angeles, CA BR/TR 6-3/205# d4.30 b-Jake																									
1948	Chi N	0	1	.000	2	0	0	0	5	4	4	0	0	4	1	7.20	54	.211	.348	2-0	.000	-0		-2	-0.3
1952	Bro N	11	9	.550	37	24	5-1	3	180	166	81	19	2	94	118	3.60	101	.246	.340	60-2	.117	1	100	0	0.0
1953	†Bro N	7	5	.583	32	0	0	3	90.1	79	40	15	4	33	65	3.79	113	.232	.308	24-3	.167	0		6	0.6
1954	Bro N	1	1	.500	23	0	0	3	45	62	46	9	0	21	25	8.20	50	.339	.393	5-1	.000	-1		-21	-1.2
	StL N	0	0	—	13	0	0	0	23	27	15	3	2	15	19	5.48	75	.303	.411	3-0	.000	-0		-3	-0.2
	Year	1	1	.500	36	0	0	3	68	89	65	12	2	36	44	7.28	56	.327	.399	8-1	.000	-1		-24	-1.4
1955	Pit N	0	1	.000	11	1	0	1	28	26	12	3	1	14-4	7	3.21	128	.252	.339	4-0	.000	-0	151	3	0.1
Total	5	19	17	.528	118	25	5-1	10	371.1	364	198	49	9	181-4	235	4.34	90	.259	.344	98-6	.112	-0	96	-17	-1.0
WADE, TERRELL Hawatha Terrell B 1.25.1973 Rembert, SC BL/TL 6-3/205# d9.12																									
1995	Atl N	0	1	.000	3	0	0	0-0	4	3	2	1	0	4-0	3	4.50	95	.214	.389	0-0	—	0		0	0.0
1996	†Atl N	5	0	1.000	44	8	0	1-1	69.2	57	28	9	1	47-6	79	2.97	148	.227	.350	13-2	.154	-0	125	10	0.6
1997	Atl N	2	3	.400	12	9	0	0-0	42	60	31	6	2	16-1	35	5.36	79	.349	.400	12-1	.250	1	112	-7	-0.6
1998	TB A	1	1	.500	2	2	0	0-0	10.2	14	6	3	0	2-0	8	5.06	95	.318	.348	0-0	—	0	87	0	0.0
Total	4	8	5	.615	61	19	0	1-1	126.1	134	67	19	3	69-7	125	3.99	110	.279	.369	25-3	.200	1	114	3	0.0
WADE, JAKE Jacob Fields "Whistling Jake" B 4.1.1912 Morehead City, NC BL/TL 6-2/175# d4.22 Mil 1945 b-Ben																									
1936	Det A	4	5	.444	13	11	4-1	0	78.1	93	60	7	1	52	30	5.29	94	.296	.398	29-0	.172	-0	95	-6	-0.6
1937	Det A	7	10	.412	33	25	7-1	0	165.1	160	106	13	3	107	69	5.39	87	.257	.368	59-1	.186	-1	95	-10	-1.0
1938	Det A	3	2	.600	27	2	0	0	70	73	56	9	0	48	23	6.56	76	.268	.378	21-0	.048	-2	53	-11	-0.9
1939	Bos A	1	4	.200	20	6	1	0	47.2	68	34	1	0	37	21	6.23	76	.358	.463	12-0	.000	-2	81	-6	-0.7
	StL A	0	2	.000	4	2	1	0	16.1	26	25	1	0	19	9	11.02	44	.356	.489	5-0	.000	-1	36	-12	-1.1
	Year	1	6	.143	24	8	2	0	64	94	27	2	0	56	30	7.45	64	.357	.470	17-0	.000	-3	69	-18	-1.8
1942	Chi A	5	5	.500	15	10	3	0	85.2	84	45	2	0	56	32	4.10	88	.255	.363	29-0	.241	1	93	-5	-0.3
1943	Chi A	3	7	.300	21	9	3-1	0	83.2	66	34	3	4	54	41	3.01	111	.222	.349	27-1	.148	-0	62	3	0.3
1944	Chi A	2	4	.333	19	5	1	2	74.2	75	46	3	0	41	35	4.82	71	.261	.354	24-0	.292	1	112	-11	-0.8
1946	NY A	2	1	.667	13	1	0	1	35.1	33	9	2	1	14	22	2.29	151	.250	.327	9-0	.111	-0	0	5	0.5
	Was A	0	0	—	6	0	0	0	11.1	12	6	1	0	12	9	4.76	70	.279	.436	1-0	.000	-0		-1	-0.1
	Year	2	1	.667	19	1	0	1	46.2	45	15	3	1	26	31	2.89	118	.257	.356	10-0	.100	-0	0	4	0.4
Total	8	27	40	.403	171	71	20-3	3	668.1	690	421	42	9	440	291	5.00	84	.269	.378	216-2	.167	-5	89	-54	-4.7
WADSWORTH, JACK John L. B 12.17.1867 Wellington, OH D 7.8.1941 Elyria, OH BL/TR ?/180# d5.1																									
1890	Cle N	2	16	.111	20	19	19	0	169.2	202	139	6	6	81	26	5.20	69	.286	.364	68	.176	-3	68	-27	-2.4
1893	Bal N	0	3	.000	3	3	0	0	16	37	30	0	0	8	2	11.25	42	.440	.489	7	.429	1	118	-12	-1.3
1894	Lou N	4	18	.182	22	22	20	0	173	261	204	10	4	103	57	7.60	67	.344	.425	74-1	.257	0	79	-45	-3.6
1895	Lou N	0	1	.000	2	0	0	0	9	24	20	0	0	7	2	16.00	29	.480	.544	4-1	.250	-0		-10	-0.7
Total	4	6	38	.136	47	44	39	0	367.2	524	393	16	10	199	87	6.85	64	.328	.405	153-2	.229	-2	78	-94	-8.0
WAECHTER, DOUG Douglas Michael B 1.28.1981 St.Petersburg, FL BR/TR 6-4/200# d8.27																									
2003	TB A	3	2	.600	6	5	1-1	0-0	35.1	29	13	4	1	15-0	29	3.31	137	.225	.310	0-0	—	0	110	5	0.6
WAGNER, CHARLIE Charles Thomas "Broadway" B 12.3.1912 Reading, PA BR/TR 5-11/170# d4.19 Mil 1943-45 C1																									
1938	Bos A	1	3	.250	13	6	1	0	36.2	47	36	5	1	24	14	8.35	59	.309	.407	12-0	.167	-1	113	-12	-1.1
1939	Bos A	3	1	.750	9	5	0	0	38.1	49	19	3	0	14	13	4.23	112	.320	.377	14-0	.071	-2*	123	3	0.1
1940	Bos A	1	0	1.000	12	1	0	0	29.1	45	22	5	0	8	13	5.52	81	.344	.381	5-0	.200	-0*	234	-4	-0.2
1941	Bos A	12	8	.600	29	25	12-3	0	187.1	175	76	14	1	85	51	3.07	136	.245	.326	63-10	.159	-1	120	22	2.0
1942	Bos A	14	11	.560	29	26	17-2	0	205.1	184	87	5	5	95	52	3.29	113	.247	.336	65-11	.077	-5	98	9	0.6
1946	Bos A	1	0	1.000	8	4	0	0	30.2	32	21	6	0	19	14	5.87	62	.276	.378	11-2	.091	-1	187	-6	-0.4
Total	6	32	23	.582	100	67	30-5	0	527.2	532	261	38	7	245	157	3.91	104	.264	.346	170-23	.118	-9	117	12	1.0
WAGNER, GARY Gary Edward B 6.28.1940 Bridgeport, IL BR/TR 6-4/191# d4.18																									
1965	Phi N	7	7	.500	59	0	0	7	105	87	43	6	2	49-8	91	3.00	115	.233	.323	13-1	.077	-0		4	0.6
1966	Phi N	0	1	.000	5	1	0	0	6.1	8	6	1	0	5-0	2	8.53	42	.333	.433	0-0	—	0	171	-3	-0.5
1967	Phi N	0	0	—	1	0	0	0	2	1	0	0	0	0-0	1	0.00	—	.167	.167	0-0	—	0		1	0.0
1968	Phi N	4	4	.500	44	0	0	8	78	69	27	0	5	31-6	43	3.00	100	.243	.326	12-0	.083	-1		1	0.1
1969	Phi N	0	3	.000	9	2	0	0-1	19.1	31	22	3	0	7-1	8	7.91	45	.365	.404	3-0	.000	-0	50	-11	-1.5
	Bos A	1	3	.250	6	1	0	0-0	16.1	18	11	1	0	15-0	9	6.06	63	.300	.440	3-1	.000	-0	0	-3	-0.7
1970	Bos A	3	1	.750	38	0	0	7-1	40.1	36	21	3	2	19-1	20	3.35	118	.232	.320	6-0	.167	-0		1	0.1
Total	6	15	19	.441	162	4	0	22-2	267.1	250	130	14	9	126-16	174	3.70	93	.253	.340	37-2	.081	-2	70	-10	-1.9
WAGNER, HECTOR Hector Raul Guerrero (b: Hector Raul Guerrero (Wagner)) B 11.26.1968 San Juan, D.R. BR/TR 6-3/185# d9.10																									
1990	KC A	0	2	.000	5	5	0	0-0	23.1	32	24	4	0	11-1	14	8.10	47	.323	.384	0-0	—	0	109	-11	-0.8
1991	KC A	1	1	.500	2	2	0	0-0	10	16	10	2	0	3-0	5	7.20	57	.348	.388	0-0	—	0	211	-4	-0.6
Total	2	1	3	.250	7	7	0	0-0	33.1	48	34	6	0	14-1	19	7.83	50	.331	.385	0-0	—	0	139	-15	-1.4
WAGNER, MATT Matthew William B 4.4.1972 Cedar Falls, IA BR/TR 6-5/215# d6.5																									
1996	Sea A	3	5	.375	15	14	1	0-0	80	91	62	15	3	38-2	41	6.86	72	.285	.363	0-0	—	0	122	-15	-1.2
WAGNER, PAUL Paul Alan B 11.14.1967 Milwaukee, WI BR/TR 6-1/202# d7.26																									
1992	Pit N	2	0	1.000	6	1	0	0-0	13	9	1	0	0	5-0	5	0.69	498	.191	.269	3-0	.333	0	131	4	0.7
1993	Pit N	8	8	.500	44	17	1-1	2-3	141.1	143	72	15	1	42-2	114	4.27	95	.263	.314	42-4	.190	0	94	-4	-0.4
1994	Pit N	7	8	.467	29	17	1	0-0	119.2	136	69	7	8	50-4	86	4.59	94	.293	.369	37-2	.162	-0	77	-4	-0.4
1995	Pit N	5	16	.238	33	25	3-1	1-0	165	174	96	18	7	72-7	120	4.80	90	.273	.352	42-6	.214	2*	69	-8	-0.7
1996	Pit N	4	8	.333	16	15	1	0-0	81.2	86	49	10	3	39-2	81	5.40	81	.275	.360	25-3	.040	-2*	85	-7	-1.0
1997	Pit N	0	0	—	14	0	0	0-1	16	17	7	3	0	13-3	9	3.94	109	.274	.395	1-0	.000	-0		1	0.0
	Mil A	1	0	1.000	2	0	0	0-0	2	3	2	1	0	0-0	0	9.00	51	.375	.375	0-0	—	0		-1	-0.2
1998	Mil N	1	5	.167	13	9	0	0-0	55.2	67	49	10	1	31-1	37	7.11	60	.302	.387	19-1	.158	-0	67	-18	-1.7
1999	Cle A	1	0	1.000	3	0	0	0-0	4.1	5	4	0	2	3-0	0	4.15	122	.263	.417	0-0	—	0		0	-0.1
Total	8	29	45	.392	160	84	6-2	3-4	598.2	640	349	64	22	255-19	452	4.83	88	.276	.351	169-16	.166	-0	79	-37	-3.8
WAGNER, RYAN Ryan Scott B 7.15.1982 Yoakum, TX BR/TR 6-4/210# d7.19																									
2003	Cin N	2	0	1.000	17	0	0	0-1	21.2	13	4	2	0	12-1	25	1.66	257	.173	.284	0-0	—	0		6	0.5
WAGNER, BILLY William Edward B 7.25.1971 Tannersville, VA BL/TL 5-10/180# d9.13																									
1995	Hou N	0	0	—	1	0	0	0-0	0.1	0	0	0	0	0-0	0	0.00	—	.000	.000	0-0	—	0		0	0.0
1996	Hou N	2	2	.500	37	0	0	9-4	51.2	28	16	6	3	30-2	67	2.44	159	.165	.298	5-0	.000	-1		9	0.8
1997	†Hou N	7	8	.467	62	0	0	23-6	66.1	49	23	5	3	30-1	106	2.85	140	.204	.299	1-0	.000	-0		9	1.8
1998	†Hou N	4	3	.571	58	0	0	30-5	60	46	19	6	0	25-1	97	2.70	150	.211	.292	3-0	.333	0		10	1.9
1999	†Hou N★	4	1	.800	66	0	0	39-3	74.2	35	14	5	1	23-1	124	1.57	282	.135	.208	0-0	—	0		**24**	3.7
2000	Hou N	2	4	.333	28	0	0	6-9	27.2	28	19	6	1	18-0	28	6.18	79	.255	.364	2-0	.000	-0		-3	-0.6

Year	Tm Lg	W	L	Pct	G	GS	CG-Sho	SV-BS	IP	H	R	HR	HB	BB-IB	SO	ERA	AERA	OAV	OOB	AB-SH	AVG	PB	Sup	APR	PW
2001	†Hou N★	2	5	.286	64	0	0	39-2	62.2	44	19	5	5	20-0	79	2.73	168	.198	.278	0-0	—	0		13	2.6
2002	Hou N	4	2	.667	70	0	0	35-6	75	51	21	7	2	22-5	88	2.52	170	.196	.261	2-0	.000	-0		15	2.3
2003	Hou N★	1	4	.200	78	0	0	44-3	86	52	18	8	3	23-5	105	1.78	250	.169	.234	2-0	.000	0		25	3.6
Total	9	26	29	.473	464	0	0	225-38	504.1	333	149	48	18	191-15	694	2.53	169	.186	.270	15-0	.067	-1		102	16.1
WAGNER, BULL William George B 12.25.1887 Lilley, MI D 10.2.1967 Muskegon, MI BR/TR 6-0.5/225# d6.2																									
1913	Bro N	4	2	.667	18	1	0	0	70.2	77	49	5	3	30	11	5.48	60	.285	.363	26-0	.231	0	251	-14	-1.1
1914	Bro N	0	1	.000	6	0	0	0	12.1	14	11	0	1	12	4	6.57	44	.311	.466	1-0	.000	-0		-4	-0.3
Total	2	4	3	.571	24	1	0	0	83	91	60	5	4	42	15	5.64	57	.289	.380	27-0	.222	0	251	-18	-1.4
WAINHOUSE, DAVE David Paul B 11.7.1967 Toronto, ON, CAN BL/TR 6-2/190# d8.3																									
1991	Mon N	0	1	.000	2	0	0	0-0	2.2	2	2	0	0	4-0	1	6.75	54	.222	.429	0-0	—	0		-1	-0.2
1993	Sea A	0	0	—	3	0	0	0-0	2.1	7	7	1	1	5-0	2	27.00	16	.500	.650	0-0	—	0		-6	-0.3
1996	Pit N	1	0	1.000	17	0	0	0-0	23.2	22	16	3	0	10-1	16	5.70	77	.250	.320	1-0	.000	-0		-3	-0.1
1997	Pit N	0	1	.000	25	0	0	0-0	28	34	28	2	3	17-0	21	8.04	53	.301	.403	2-0	.000	-0		-12	-0.6
1998	Col N	1	0	1.000	10	0	0	0-1	11	15	6	1	2	5-0	3	4.91	105	.341	.431	1-0	.000	-0		0	0.1
1999	Col N	0	0	—	19	0	0	0-0	28.2	37	22	6	0	16-0	18	6.91	84	.330	.405	1-0	.000	-0		-2	-0.1
2000	StL N	0	1	.000	9	0	0	0-0	8.2	13	10	2	2	4-1	5	9.35	49	.351	.442	0-0	—	0		-5	-0.4
Total	7	2	3	.400	85	0	0	0-1	105	130	91	15	8	61-2	66	7.37	65	.312	.404	5-0	.000	-1		-29	-1.6
WAITS, RICK Michael Richard B 5.15.1952 Atlanta, GA BL/TL 6-3/195# d9.17 C1																									
1973	Tex A	0	0	—	1	0	0	1-0	1	1	1	0	0	1-0	0	9.00	41	.333	.500	0-0	—	0		-1	-0.1
1975	Cle A	6	2	.750	16	7	3	1-0	70.1	57	25	3	1	25-5	34	2.94	129	.221	.292	0-0	—	0	103	7	0.8
1976	Cle A	7	9	.438	26	22	4-2	0-0	123.2	143	60	7	0	54-1	65	4.00	87	.297	.368	0-0	—	0*	83	-7	-0.8
1977	Cle A	9	7	.563	37	16	1	2-3	135.1	132	67	8	1	64-7	62	3.99	99	.262	.346	0-0	—	0*	99	-1	0.0
1978	Cle A	13	15	.464	34	33	15-2	0-0	230.1	206	97	16	2	86-0	97	3.20	117	.240	.309	0-0	—	0*	97	11	1.5
1979	Cle A	16	13	.552	34	34	8-3	0-0	231	230	123	26	4	91-1	91	4.44	96	.264	.334	0-0	—	0	100	-3	-0.2
1980	Cle A	13	14	.481	33	33	9-2	0-0	224.1	231	118	18	1	82-6	109	4.45	92	.270	.332	0-0	—	0	96	-8	-0.9
1981	Cle A	8	10	.444	22	21	5-1	0-0	126.1	173	74	7	1	44-1	51	4.92	74	.330	.380	0-0	—	0	94	-17	-2.1
1982	Cle A	2	13	.133	25	21	2	0-1	115	128	74	13	1	57-2	44	5.40	76	.290	.370	0-0	—	0	86	-16	-1.7
1983	Cle A	0	1	.000	8	0	0	0-1	19.2	23	13	1	0	9-2	13	4.58	93	.307	.364	0-0	—	0		-2	-0.1
	Mil A	0	2	.000	10	2	0	0-0	30	39	20	1	0	11-1	20	5.10	74	.320	.373	0-0	—	0	133	-6	-0.3
	Year	0	3	.000	18	2	0	0-1	49.2	62	26	2	0	20-3	33	4.89	81	.315	.369	0-0	—	0	127	-7	-0.4
1984	Mil A	2	4	.333	47	1	0	3-1	73	84	32	7	0	24-3	49	3.58	108	.297	.348	0-0	—	0	70	3	0.2
1985	Mil A	3	2	.600	24	0	0	1-1	47	67	37	3	0	20-5	24	6.51	64	.340	.399	1-0	.000	-0		-11	-1.1
Total	12	79	92	.462	317	190	47-10	8-7	1427	1514	741	110	11	568-34	659	4.25	92	.277	.344	1-0	.000	-0	95	-51	-4.8
WAKEFIELD, TIM Timothy Stephen B 8.2.1966 Melbourne, FL BR/TR 6-2/204# d7.31																									
1992	†Pit N	8	1	.889	13	13	4-1	0-0	92	76	26	3	1	35-1	51	2.15	160	.232	.305	28-4	.071	-1*	107	12	1.1
1993	Pit N	6	11	.353	24	20	3-2	0-0	128.1	145	83	14	9	75-2	59	5.61	72	.291	.389	43-4	.163	1	87	-22	-2.4
1995	†Bos A	16	8	.667	27	27	6-1	0-0	195.1	163	76	22	9	68-0	119	2.95	165	.227	.300	0-0	—	0	92	38	4.2
1996	Bos A	14	13	.519	32	32	6	0-0	211.2	238	151	38	12	90-0	140	5.14	99	.280	.353	0-0	—	0	90	-7	-0.9
1997	Bos A	12	15	.444	35	29	4-2	0-0	201.1	193	109	24	16	87-5	151	4.25	109	.256	.343	1-0	.000	-0	96	6	0.7
1998	†Bos A	17	8	.680	36	33	2	0-0	216	211	123	30	14	79-1	146	4.58	103	.252	.324	2-2	.000	0*	130	2	0.1
1999	†Bos A	6	11	.353	49	17	0	15-3	140	146	93	19	5	72-2	104	5.08	98	.266	.352	3-0	.000	-0	88	-3	-0.5
2000	Bos A	6	10	.375	51	17	0	0-1	159.1	170	107	31	4	65-3	102	5.48	92	.272	.340	2-1	.000	-0*	117	-8	-0.8
2001	Bos A	9	12	.429	45	17	0	3-2	168.2	156	84	13	18	73-5	148	3.90	115	.248	.339	3-1	.333	0	90	10	1.1
2002	Bos A	11	5	.688	45	15	0	3-2	163.1	121	57	15	9	51-2	134	2.81	160	.204	.276	0-0	—	0	110	30	2.6
2003	†Bos A	11	7	.611	35	33	0	1-0	202.1	193	106	23	12	71-0	169	4.09	112	.246	.317	0-0	—	0	112	9	0.7
Total	11	116	101	.535	392	253	25-6	22-8	1878.1	1812	1015	232	109	766-21	1323	4.24	110	.253	.331	82-12	.122	-0	102	67	5.9
WAKEFIELD, BILL William Sumner B 5.24.1941 Kansas City, MO BR/TR 6/175# d4.18																									
1964	NY N	3	5	.375	62	4	0	2	119.2	103	57	10	9	61-6	61	3.61	99	.235	.337	24-3	.167	-0	98	-1	-0.1
WALBERG, RUBE George Elvin B 7.27.1896 Pine City, MN D 10.27.1978 Tempe, AZ BL/TL 6-1.5/190# d4.29																									
1923	NY N	0	0	—	2	0	0	0	5	4	2	0	0	1	1	1.80	212	.211	.250	1-0	.000	-0		1	0.0
	Phi A	4	8	.333	26	10	4	0	115	122	77	10	2	60	38	5.32	77	.280	.369	41-3	.317	3	121	-12	-0.8
1924	Phi A	0	0	—	6	2	0	0	7	10	10	0	0	10	3	12.86	33	.345	.513	2-0	.500	0	89	-6	-0.2
1925	Phi A	8	14	.364	53	20	7	7	191.2	197	99	11	2	77	82	3.99	117	.269	.340	64-0	.156	-4	80	14	1.2
1926	Phi A	12	10	.545	40	19	5-2	2	151	168	67	4	6	60	72	2.80	149	.292	.365	46-5	.152	-2	83	19	2.3
1927	Phi A	16	12	.571	46	33	14	4	249.1	257	139	18	4	91	136	3.93	108	.271	.337	87-2	.207	3*	120	5	0.8
1928	Phi A	17	12	.586	38	30	15-3	1	235.2	236	111	19	3	64	112	3.55	113	.265	.317	86-3	.209	1	112	12	1.5
1929	†Phi A	18	11	.621	40	33	20-3	4	267.2	256	115	22	0	99	94	3.60	118	.254	.320	103-6	.223	-0	108	24	2.2
1930	†Phi A	13	12	.520	38	30	12-2	1	205.1	207	121	6	2	85	100	4.69	100	.262	.335	73-3	.164	-3	95	1	-0.3
1931	†Phi A	20	12	.625	44	35	19-1	3	**291**	298	133	16	0	109	106	3.74	120	.266	.331	105-4	.124	-6*	92	28	2.0
1932	Phi A	17	10	.630	41	34	19-3	1	272	305	159	16	0	103	96	4.73	96	.282	.344	94-9	.170	-3	120	-7	-0.9
1933	Phi A	9	13	.409	40	20	10-1	4	201	224	132	12	1	95	68	4.88	88	.278	.354	68-7	.132	-1*	86	-14	-1.5
1934	Bos A	6	7	.462	30	10	2	1	104.2	118	62	5	1	41	38	4.04	119	.284	.350	32-1	.188	-1	98	6	0.6
1935	Bos A	5	9	.357	44	10	4	3	142.2	152	71	10	2	54	44	3.91	121	.273	.340	37-3	.162	-2	64	13	1.0
1936	Bos A	5	4	.556	24	9	5	0	100.1	98	53	7	1	36	49	4.40	121	.257	.323	32-3	.156	-1	72	11	0.7
1937	Bos A	5	7	.417	32	11	3	1	104.2	143	72	7	3	46	46	5.59	85	.332	.400	34-3	.147	-1	85	-9	-1.0
Total	15	155	141	.524	544	306	139-15	32	2644	2795	1423	163	27	1031	1085	4.16	107	.273	.341	905-52	.179	-18	99	86	7.6
WALDBAUER, DOC Albert Charles B 2.22.1892 Richmond, VA D 7.16.1969 Yakima, WA BR/TR 6/172# d9.24																									
1917	Was A	0	0	—	2	0	0	1	5	10	4	0	0	2	2	7.20	36	.476	.522	1-0	.000	-0		-2	-0.1
WALK, BOB Robert Vernon B 11.26.1956 Van Nuys, CA BR/TR 6-4/208# d5.26																									
1980	†Phi N	11	7	.611	27	27	2	0-0	151.2	163	82	8	2	71-2	94	4.57	83	.276	.353	50-7	.140	-0	113	-10	-1.2
1981	Atl N	1	4	.200	12	8	0	0-0	43.1	41	25	6	0	23-0	16	4.57	78	.250	.342	7-3	.143	-0	118	-5	-0.6
1982	†Atl N	11	9	.550	32	27	3-1	0-0	164.1	179	101	19	6	59-2	84	4.87	77	.280	.344	51-6	.196	2	120	-20	-2.2
1983	Atl N	0	0	—	1	1	0	0-0	3.2	7	3	0	0	2-0	4	7.36	53	.412	.474	1-0	.000	-0	136	-1	-0.1
1984	Pit N	1	1	.500	2	2	0	0-0	10.1	8	5	1	0	4-1	10	2.61	138	.200	.273	3-0	.000	-0	98	0	0.0
1985	Pit N	2	3	.400	9	9	1-1	0-0	58.2	60	27	3	0	18-2	40	3.68	97	.265	.318	17-4	.000	-1	115	-1	-0.3
1986	Pit N	7	8	.467	44	15	1-1	2-2	141.2	129	66	14	3	64-7	78	3.75	102	.251	.334	39-1	.154	0	84	1	0.2
1987	Pit N	8	2	.800	39	12	1-1	0-0	117	107	52	11	3	51-2	78	3.31	124	.245	.327	26-1	.231	1	119	8	0.8
1988	Pit N★	12	10	.545	32	32	1-1	0-0	212.2	183	75	6	2	65-5	81	2.71	126	.230	.288	69-3	.087	-2*	94	15	1.3
1989	Pit N	13	10	.565	33	31	2	0-1	196	208	106	15	4	65-1	83	4.41	76	.271	.330	70-5	.186	3	129	-23	-2.2
1990	†Pit N	7	5	.583	26	24	1-1	1-0	129.2	136	59	17	4	36-2	73	3.75	97	.270	.322	37-10	.162	1	123	-1	-0.1
1991	†Pit N	9	2	.818	25	20	0	0-1	115	104	53	10	5	35-2	67	3.60	99	.240	.302	39-2	.205	2	135	-1	0.1
1992	†Pit N	10	6	.625	36	19	1	2-1	135	132	54	10	6	43-5	60	3.20	108	.258	.322	43-1	.093	-2	133	3	0.2
1993	Pit N	13	14	.481	32	32	3	0-0	187	214	121	23	5	70-5	80	5.68	71	.294	.356	58-7	.121	-2	103	-32	-4.1
Total	14	105	81	.565	350	259	16-6	5-5	1666	1671	829	143	40	606-36	848	4.03	91	.263	.329	510-50	.145	1	114	-67	-8.2
WALKER, ED Edward Harrison B 8.11.1874 Cambois, England D 9.29.1947 Akron, OH BL/TL 6-5/242# d9.26																									
1902	Cle A	0	1	.000	1	1	1	0	8	11	4	0	0	3	1	3.38	102	.324	.378	3-0	.333	0	42	0	0.0
1903	Cle A	0	1	.000	3	3	0	0	12	13	12	0	0	10	4	5.25	54	.277	.404	3-0	.000	-0	159	-4	-0.3
Total	2	0	2	.000	4	4	1	0	20	24	16	0	0	13	5	4.50	69	.296	.394	6-0	.167	0	122	-4	-0.3
WALKER, DIXIE Ewart Gladstone B 6.1.1887 Brownsville, PA D 11.14.1965 Leeds, AL BL/TR 6/192# d9.17 b-Ernie s-Dixie s-Harry																									
1909	Was A	3	1	.750	4	4	4	0	36	31	12	0	0	6	25	2.50	97	.217	.248	13-0	.154	-0	138	0	0.0
1910	Was A	11	11	.500	29	26	16-3	0	199.1	177	83	2	8	68	84	3.30	76	.245	.317	69-1	.130	-3	80	-10	-1.4
1911	Was A	8	13	.381	32	24	15-2	0	185.2	205	103	2	8	50	65	3.39	97	.286	.339	66-0	.303	4*	102	-3	0.0
1912	Was A	3	6	.333	9	8	5	0	60	72	40	2	4	18	29	5.25	64	.300	.359	16-0	.125	1	100	-9	-1.1
Total	4	25	31	.446	74	62	40-5	0	481	485	238	6	20	142	203	3.52	82	.266	.326	164-1	.201	2	96	-22	-2.5

Year	Tm Lg	W	L	Pct	G	GS	CG-Sho	SV-BS	IP	H	R	HR	HB	BB-IB	SO	ERA	AERA	OAV	OOB	AB-SH	AVG	PB	Sup	APR	PW
WALKER, MYSTERIOUS Frederick Mitchell B 3.21.1884 Utica, NE D 2.1.1958 Oak Park, IL BR/TR 5-10.5/185# d6.28																									
1910	Cin N	0	0	—	1	0	0	0	3	4	2	0	0	4	1	3.00	97	.333	.500	1-0	.000	-0		0	0.0
1912	Cle A	0	0	—	1	0	0	0	1	0	0	0	0	1	0	0.00	—	.000	.200	0-0	—	0		0	0.0
1913	Bro N	1	3	.250	11	8	3	0	58.1	44	26	3	5	35	35	3.55	93	.233	.367	18-1	.167	-0	80	0	0.1
1914	Pit F	4	16	.200	35	21	12	0	169.1	197	108	3	3	74	79	4.31	67	.294	.367	53-2	.113	-3*	88	-29	-3.2
1915	Bro F	2	4	.333	13	7	2	1	65.2	61	37	3	0	22	28	3.70	73	.242	.303	27-0	.222	0	151	-8	-0.6
Total	5	7	23	.233	61	36	17	1	297.1	306	173	9	8	136	143	4.00	73	.272	.354	99-3	.152	-3	98	-37	-3.7
WALKER, GEORGE George A. B 1863 Hamilton, ON, CAN TR 5-9/184# d8.1																									
1888	Bal AA	1	3	.250	4	4	4-1	0	35	36	31	2	0	14	18	5.91	50	.257	.325	13	.077	-1	68	-10	-1.0
WALKER, LUKE James Luke B 9.2.1943 DeKalb, TX BL/TL 6-1.5/192# d9.7																									
1965	Pit N	0	0	—	2	0	0	0	5	2	0	0	0	1-0	5	0.00	—	.118	.167	0-0	—	0		2	0.1
1966	Pit N	0	1	.000	10	1	0	0	10	8	9	0	1	15-2	7	4.50	79	.205	.436	2-0	.000	-0	98	-3	-0.3
1968	Pit N	0	3	.000	39	2	0	3	61.2	42	18	1	1	39-0	66	2.04	143	.190	.314	8-1	.000	-1	89	5	0.3
1969	Pit N	4	6	.400	31	15	3-1	0-0	118.2	98	51	5	2	57-3	96	3.64	96	.226	.318	32-3	.000	-3	115	-1	-0.3
1970	†Pit N	15	6	.714	42	19	5-3	3-1	163	129	56	6	1	89-8	124	3.04	129	.219	.322	46-8	.130	-1	118	19	2.2
1971	†Pit N	10	8	.556	28	24	4-2	0-0	159.2	157	69	9	2	53-2	86	3.55	95	.262	.321	46-2	.022	-3	117	-2	-0.6
1972	†Pit N	4	6	.400	26	12	2	2-0	92.2	98	41	4	0	34-4	48	3.40	98	.278	.338	24-1	.083	-1	100	-1	-0.3
1973	Pit N	7	12	.368	37	18	2-1	1-1	122	129	75	9	1	66-8	74	4.65	76	.270	.358	30-3	.067	-2	99	-17	-2.7
1974	Det A	5	5	.500	28	9	0	0-0	92	100	56	9	2	54-1	52	4.99	76	.278	.374	0-0	—	0	121	-11	-1.1
Total	9	45	47	.489	243	100	16-7	9-2	824.2	763	375	43	10	408-28	558	3.65	97	.247	.335	188-18	.059	-11	112	-9	-2.7
WALKER, JAMIE James Ross B 7.1.1971 McMinnville, TN BL/TL 6-2/190# d4.2																									
1997	KC A	3	3	.500	50	0	0	0-1	43	46	28	6	3	20-3	24	5.44	87	.271	.354	0-0	—	0		-3	-0.4
1998	KC A	0	1	.000	6	2	0	0-0	17.1	30	20	5	2	3-0	15	9.87	49	.380	.412	0-0	—	0	96	-9	-0.4
2002	Det A	1	1	.500	57	0	0	1-3	43.2	32	19	9	4	9-1	40	3.71	116	.199	.257	0-0	—	0		4	0.1
2003	Det A	4	3	.571	78	0	0	3-4	65	61	30	9	2	17-1	45	3.32	130	.247	.299	0-0	—	0		6	0.6
Total	4	8	8	.500	191	2	0	4-8	169	169	97	29	11	49-5	124	4.63	96	.257	.317	0-0	—	0	96	-2	-0.1
WALKER, ROY James Roy "Dixie" B 4.13.1893 Lawrenceburg, TN D 2.10.1962 New Orleans, LA BR/TR 6-1.5/180# d9.16																									
1912	Cle A	0	0	—	1	0	0	0	2	0	0	0	0	2	1	0.00	—	.000	.250	0-0	—	0		1	0.0
1915	Cle A	4	9	.308	25	15	4	1	131	122	73	1	7	65	57	3.98	77	.261	.360	38-3	.132	-2	86	-10	-1.4
1917	Chi N	0	1	.000	2	1	0	0	7	8	5	0	0	5	4	3.86	75	.286	.394	1-0	.000	-0	26	-1	-0.2
1918	Chi N	1	3	.250	13	7	2	1	43.1	50	27	1	1	15	20	2.70	103	.298	.359	11-1	.000	-1	112	-3	-0.4
1921	StL N	11	12	.478	38	23	11	3	170.2	194	93	10	1	53	52	4.22	87	.293	.347	54-4	.204	-0	100	-9	-1.1
1922	StL N	1	2	.333	12	2	0	0	32	34	20	1	0	15	14	4.78	81	.293	.374	7-1	.143	-0	84	-3	-0.4
Total	6	17	27	.386	91	48	17	5	386	408	218	13	9	155	148	3.99	85	.282	.355	111-9	.153	-4	94	-25	-3.5
WALKER, JERRY Jerry Allen B 2.12.1939 Ada, OK BB/TR 6-1/195# d7.6 C5																									
1957	Bal A	1	0	1.000	13	3	1-1	1	27.2	24	9	1	0	14-1	13	2.93	123	.245	.336	5-0	.000	-1	99	3	0.1
1958	Bal A	0	0	—	6	0	0	0	10.1	16	8	2	0	5-0	6	6.97	52	.340	.404	2-0	.000	-0		-4	-0.2
1959	Bal A★	11	10	.524	30	22	7-2	4	182	160	68	13	3	52-9	100	2.92	130	.240	.295	65-3	.169	-1*	92	17	1.9
1960	Bal A	3	4	.429	29	18	1	5	118	107	53	15	3	56-0	48	3.74	102	.247	.335	38-1	.368	5*	107	2	0.7
1961	KC A	8	14	.364	36	24	4	2	168	161	100	23	10	96-2	56	4.82	87	.253	.356	64-1	.250	3*	90	-10	-0.9
1962	KC A	8	9	.471	31	21	3-1	0	143.1	165	101	27	7	78-4	57	5.90	72	.288	.377	57-2	.263	5*	126	-24	-2.0
1963	Cle A	6	6	.500	39	2	0	1	88	92	53	15	2	36-6	41	4.91	74	.265	.334	19-0	.105	-0	25	-12	-1.6
1964	Cle A	0	1	.000	6	0	0	0	9.2	9	5	1	0	4-0	5	4.66	77	.257	.333	2-0	.000	-0		-1	-0.1
Total	8	37	44	.457	190	90	16-4	13	747	734	397	97	25	341-22	326	4.36	90	.259	.340	252-7	.230	10	103	-29	-2.1
WALKER, KEVIN Kevin Michael B 9.20.1976 Irving, TX BL/TL 6-4/190# d4.14																									
2000	SD N	7	1	.875	70	0	0	0-0	66.2	49	35	5	5	38-6	56	4.18	103	.206	.325	4-0	.250	0		1	0.1
2001	SD N	0	0	—	16	0	0	0-1	12	5	4	0	0	8-2	17	3.00	133	.122	.265	0-0	—	0		2	0.1
2002	SD N	0	1	.000	11	0	0	0-1	8	12	6	2	0	5-1	11	5.63	67	.333	.415	0-0	—	0		-2	-0.2
2003	SD N	0	0	—	11	0	0	0-0	6.2	5	4	1	0	5-0	5	5.40	73	.200	.333	0-0	—	0		-1	0.0
Total	4	7	2	.778	108	0	0	0-2	93.1	71	49	8	5	56-9	89	4.24	99	.209	.328	4-0	.250	0		0	0.0
WALKER, MARTY Martin Van Buren "Buddy" B 3.27.1899 Philadelphia, PA D 4.24.1978 Philadelphia, PA BL/TL 6/170# d9.30																									
1928	Phi N	0	1	.000	1	1	0	0	0	2	4	0	0	3	0	o	—	1.000	1.000	0-0	—	0	20	-3	-0.2
WALKER, MIKE Michael Aaron B 6.23.1965 Houston, TX BR/TR 6-3/205# d6.16																									
1992	Sea A	0	3	.000	5	3	0	0-0	14.2	21	14	4	0	9-3	5	7.36	54	.333	.411	0-0	—	0	77	-6	-1.0
WALKER, MIKE Michael Charles B 10.4.1966 Chicago, IL BR/TR 6-1/195# d9.9																									
1988	Cle A	0	1	.000	3	1	0	0-0	8.2	8	7	0	0	10-0	7	7.27	57	.258	.439	0-0	—	0	0	-3	-0.2
1990	Cle A	2	6	.250	18	11	0	0-0	75.2	82	49	6	6	42-4	34	4.88	81	.277	.376	0-0	—	0	72	-10	-1.0
1991	Cle A	0	1	.000	5	0	0	0-0	4.1	6	1	0	1	2-1	2	2.08	200	.316	.409	0-0	—	0		1	0.2
1995	Chi N	1	3	.250	42	0	0	1-2	44.2	45	22	2	0	24-3	20	3.22	127	.259	.342	3-0	.000	-0		3	0.2
1996	Det A	0	0	—	20	0	0	1-1	27.2	40	26	10	1	17-1	13	8.46	60	.351	.433	0-0	—	0		-9	-0.4
Total	5	3	11	.214	88	12	0	2-3	161	181	105	18	8	95-9	76	5.09	82	.285	.381	3-0	.000	-0	62	-18	-1.2
WALKER, PETE Peter Brian B 4.8.1969 Beverly, MA BR/TR 6-2/195# d6.7																									
1995	NY N	1	0	1.000	13	0	0	0-0	17.2	24	9	3	0	5-0	5	4.58	88	.329	.367	0-0	—	0		-1	0.0
1996	SD N	0	0	—	1	0	0	0-0	0.2	0	0	0	0	3-0	1	0.00	—	.000	.600	0-0	—	0		0	0.0
2000	Col N	0	0	—	3	0	0	0-0	4.2	10	9	1	0	4-0	2	17.36	33	.435	.519	0-0	—	0		-5	-0.2
2001	NY N	0	0	—	2	0	0	0-0	6.2	6	2	0	0	0-0	4	2.70	153	.240	.240	1-1	.000	-0		1	0.0
2002	NY N	0	0	—	1	0	0	0-0	1	2	1	0	0	0-0	0	9.00	44	.400	.400	0-0	—	0		-1	0.0
	Tor A	10	5	.667	37	20	0	1-0	139.1	143	72	18	3	51-5	80	4.33	107	.270	.334	0-0	—	0	103	4	0.5
2003	Tor A	2	2	.500	23	7	0	0-0	55.1	59	31	11	2	24-2	29	4.88	94	.277	.354	0-0	—	0	123	-1	0.0
Total	6	13	7	.650	80	27	0	1-0	225.1	244	124	33	5	87-7	121	4.71	97	.280	.346	1-1	.000	-0	109	-3	0.3
WALKER, TOM Robert Thomas B 11.7.1948 Tampa, FL BR/TR 6-1/188# d4.23																									
1972	Mon N	2	2	.500	46	0	0	2-0	74.2	71	27	4	1	22-2	42	2.89	123	.248	.304	3-0	.000	-0		5	0.2
1973	Mon N	7	5	.583	54	0	0	4-2	91.2	95	52	7	3	42-12	68	3.63	105	.274	.349	7-1	.000	-1		-2	-0.3
1974	Mon N	4	5	.444	33	8	1	2-0	91.2	96	45	7	2	28-5	70	3.83	101	.266	.321	16-1	.188	0	102	0	0.0
1975	Det A	3	8	.273	36	9	1	0-0	115.1	116	69	16	5	40-3	60	4.45	91	.261	.325	0-0	—	0	61	-6	-0.6
1976	StL N	1	2	.333	10	0	0	3-1	19.2	22	10	2	0	3-1	11	4.12	86	.265	.291	5-0	.400	1		-1	-0.2
1977	Mon N	1	1	.500	11	0	0	0-0	19	15	10	2	0	7-0	10	4.74	81	.221	.293	2-2	.000	-0		-1	-0.2
	Cal A	0	0	—	1	0	0	0-0	2	3	2	2	0	0-0	1	9.00	44	.375	.375	0-0	—	0		-1	-0.1
Total	6	18	23	.439	191	17	2	11-3	414	418	215	40	11	142-23	262	3.87	99	.262	.323	33-4	.152	-0	83	-6	-1.2
WALKER, TOM Thomas William B 8.1.1881 Philadelphia, PA D 7.10.1944 Woodbury Heights, NJ BR/TR 5-11/170# d9.27																									
1902	Phi A	0	1	.000	1	1	1	0	8	10	7	0	1	0	2	5.63	65	.303	.324	4-0	.250	-0	98	-2	-0.1
1904	Cin N	15	8	.652	24	24	22-2	0	217	196	76	2	18	53	64	2.24	131	.238	.299	77-2	.117	-4	85	17	1.2
1905	Cin N	9	7	.563	23	19	12-1	0	144.2	171	71	3	6	44	28	3.24	102	.305	.362	51-2	.137	-1	105	3	0.2
Total	3	24	16	.600	48	44	35-3	0	369.2	377	154	5	25	97	94	2.70	114	.266	.325	132-4	.129	-6	94	18	1.3
WALKER, TYLER Tyler Lanier B 5.15.1976 San Francisco, CA BR/TR 6-3/225# d7.2																									
2002	NY N	1	0	1.000	5	1	0	0-0	10.2	11	7	3	0	5-1	7	5.91	67	.250	.327	2-0	.000	-0	116	-2	-0.2
WALKER, BILL William Henry B 10.7.1903 E.St.Louis, IL D 6.14.1966 E.St.Louis, IL BR/TL 6/175# d9.13																									
1927	NY N	0	0	—	3	0	0	0	4	6	6	0	0	5	4	9.00	43	.429	.579	0-0	—	0		-3	-0.1
1928	NY N	3	6	.333	22	8	1	0	76.1	79	43	9	1	31	39	4.72	83	.275	.348	22-2	.091	-2	108	-6	-0.8
1929	NY N	14	7	.667	29	23	13-1	0	177.2	188	71	11	4	57	65	**3.09**	148	.274	.334	61-7	.115	-3	110	30	2.6
1930	NY N	17	15	.531	39	34	13-2	1	245.1	258	133	19	7	88	105	3.93	121	.268	.334	86-5	.186	-1*	96	19	1.9
1931	NY N	16	9	.640	37	28	19-**6**	3	239.1	212	78	6	3	64	121	**2.26**	**164**	.231	.283	77-3	.065	-6	102	**37**	2.9

Year	Tm Lg	W	L	Pct	G	GS	CG-Sho	SV-BS	IP	H	R	HR	HB	BB-IB	SO	ERA	AERA	OAV	OOB	AB-SH	AVG	PB	Sup	APR	PW
1932	NY N	8	12	.400	31	22	9	2	163	177	95	23	3	55	74	4.14	90	.274	.334	52-1	.135	-2	111	-10	-1.2
1933	StL N	9	10	.474	29	20	6-2	0	158	168	71	8	1	67	41	3.42	102	.273	.346	53-3	.132	-2	90	1	-0.1
1934	†StL N	12	4	.750	24	19	10-1	0	153	160	59	11	2	66	76	3.12	136	.270	.345	54-3	.093	-4	90	19	1.3
1935	StL N★	13	8	.619	37	25	8-2	1	193.1	222	93	7	5	78	79	3.82	107	.288	.357	59-7	.102	-4*	95	7	0.2
1936	StL N	5	6	.455	21	13	4-1	1	79.2	106	62	5	2	27	22	5.87	67	.318	.373	25-2	.280	2*	127	-19	-2.0
Total	10	97	77	.557	272	192	83-15	8	1489.2	1576	711	99	28	538	626	3.59	114	.271	.335	489-33	.127	-23	102	75	4.7
WALKUP, JIM James Elton B 12.14.1909 Havana, AR D 2.7.1997 Danville, AR BR/TR 6-1/170# d9.22																									
1934	StL A	0	0	—	3	0	0	0	8.1	6	4	0	0	5	6	2.16	231	.200	.314	3-0	.333	0		2	0.1
1935	StL A	6	9	.400	55	20	4-1	0	181.1	226	139	17	2	104	44	6.25	77	.305	.392	47-4	.128	-3	95	-25	-2.0
1936	StL A	0	3	.000	5	2	0	0	15.2	20	17	0	0	6	5	8.04	67	.308	.366	4-0	.000	-1	41	-5	-0.7
1937	StL A	9	12	.429	27	18	6	0	150.1	218	127	16	0	83	46	7.36	66	.347	.423	58-3	.241	-1	111	-36	-3.8
1938	StL A	1	12	.077	18	13	1	0	94	127	83	13	3	53	28	6.80	73	.329	.414	29-3	.138	-2	67	-20	-2.3
1939	StL A	0	1	.000	1	0	0	0	0.2	2	1	0	0	1	0	0.00	—	.500	.600	0-0	—	0		0	0.0
	Det A	0	1	.000	7	0	0	0	12	15	10	3	0	8	5	7.50	65	.319	.418	2-0	.500	0		-3	-0.2
	Year	0	2	.000	8	0	0	0	12.2	17	15	3	0	9	5	7.11	69	.333	.433	2-0	.500	0		-3	-0.2
Total	6	16	38	.296	116	53	11-1	0	462.1	614	381	49	5	260	134	6.74	72	.323	.406	143-10	.182	-6	91	-87	-8.9
WALKUP, JIM James Huey B 11.3.1895 Havana, AR D 6.12.1990 Duncan, OK BR/TL 5-8/150# d4.30																									
1927	Det A	0	0	—	2	0	0	0	1.2	3	1	0	0	0	0	5.40	78	.429	.429	1-0	.000	-0		0	0.0
WALL, DONNE Donnell Lee B 7.11.1967 Potosi, MO BR/TR 6-1/180# d9.2																									
1995	Hou N	3	1	.750	6	5	0	0-0	24.1	33	19	5	0	5-0	16	5.55	70	.320	.345	5-3	.000	-1	149	-6	-0.9
1996	Hou N	9	8	.529	26	23	2-1	0-0	150	170	84	17	6	34-3	99	4.56	85	.286	.329	44-8	.205	2	106	-12	-1.0
1997	Hou N	2	5	.286	8	8	0	0-0	41.2	53	31	8	2	16-0	25	6.26	64	.315	.382	10-1	.100	-0	72	-10	-1.4
1998	†SD N	5	4	.556	46	1	0	1-3	70.1	50	20	6	1	32-2	56	2.43	161	.202	.293	7-0	.286	0	70	13	1.6
1999	SD N	7	4	.636	55	0	0	0-6	70.1	58	31	11	0	23-3	53	3.07	137	.219	.280	1-0	.000	-0		7	1.0
2000	SD N	5	2	.714	44	0	0	1-4	53.2	36	20	4	0	21-1	29	3.35	129	.193	.274	1-1	.000	-0		7	0.8
2001	NY N	0	4	.000	32	0	0	0-0	42.2	51	24	8	1	17-6	31	4.85	85	.300	.363	0-0	—	0*		-3	-0.2
2002	Ana A	0	0	—	17	0	0	0-0	21	17	15	3	1	7-1	13	6.43	69	.221	.291	0-0	—	0		-4	-0.2
Total	8	31	28	.525	234	37	2-1	2-13	474	468	244	62	11	155-16	322	4.20	96	.258	.318	68-13	.176	1	101	-8	-0.3
WALL, MURRAY Murray Wesley B 9.19.1926 Dallas, TX D 10.8.1971 Lone Oak, TX BR/TR 6-3/185# d7.4																									
1950	Bos N	0	0	—	1	0	0	0	4	6	5	0	0	2	2	9.00	43	.333	.400	1-0	.000	-0		-3	-0.1
1957	Bos A	3	0	1.000	11	0	0	1	24.1	21	11	3	0	2-0	13	3.33	120	.233	.247	6-0	.333	0		1	0.3
1958	Bos A	8	9	.471	52	1	0	10	114.1	109	51	14	5	33-4	53	3.62	111	.255	.313	28-0	.107	-2	67	5	0.8
1959	Bos A	1	4	.200	15	0	0	3	31.2	31	21	5	0	15-2	8	5.40	75	.267	.348	7-0	.000	-1		-5	-0.8
	Was A	0	0	—	1	0	0	0	1.1	3	1	1	0	0-0	0	6.75	58	.600	.600	1-0	.000	-0		0	0.0
	Bos A	1	1	.500	11	0	0	0	17.1	26	11	2	1	11-4	6	5.71	71	.371	.458	3-0	.000	-0		-3	-0.3
	Year	2	5	.286	27	0	0	3	50.1	60	36	8	1	26-6	14	5.54	73	.314	.395	11-0	.000	-1		-7	-1.1
Total	4	13	14	.481	91	1	0	14	193	196	100	25	6	63-10	82	4.20	96	.270	.330	46-0	.109	-3	67	-5	-0.1
WALL, STAN Stanley Arthur B 6.16.1951 Butler, MO BL/TL 6-1/175# d7.19																									
1975	LA N	0	1	.000	10	0	0	0-0	16	12	6	0	1	7-0	6	1.69	202	.222	.308	0-0	—	0		2	0.1
1976	LA N	2	2	.500	31	0	0	1-1	50	50	21	5	2	15-2	27	3.60	94	.269	.325	4-0	.000	-0		-1	-0.1
1977	LA N	2	3	.400	25	0	0	0-0	32	36	20	3	1	13-2	22	5.34	72	.279	.350	1-1	.000	-0		-5	-0.7
Total	3	4	6	.400	66	0	0	1-1	98	98	47	8	4	35-4	55	3.86	92	.266	.331	5-1	.000	-1		-4	-0.7
WALLACE, DAVE David William B 9.7.1947 Waterbury, CT BR/TR 5-10/185# d7.18 C6																									
1973	Phi N	0	0	—	4	0	0	0-0	3.2	13	9	1	0	2-0	2	22.09	17	.591	.625	0-0	—	0		-7	-0.3
1974	Phi N	0	1	.000	3	0	0	0-0	3	4	4	2	0	3-1	3	9.00	42	.308	.438	0-0	—	0		-2	-0.4
1978	Tor A	0	0	—	6	0	0	0-0	14	12	6	1	0	11-0	7	3.86	102	.245	.371	0-0	—	0		0	0.0
Total	3	0	1	.000	13	0	0	0-0	20.2	29	19	4	0	16-1	12	7.84	50	.345	.441	0-0	—	0		-9	-0.7
WALLACE, DEREK Derek Robert B 9.1.1971 Van Nuys, CA BR/TR 6-3/200# d8.13																									
1996	NY N	2	3	.400	19	0	0	3-0	24.2	29	12	2	0	14-2	15	4.01	100	.290	.377	0-0	—	0		0	0.1
1999	KC A	0	1	.000	8	0	0	0-0	8.1	7	4	2	0	5-0	5	3.24	155	.259	.364	0-0	—	0		1	0.1
Total	2	2	4	.333	27	0	0	3-0	33	36	16	4	0	19-2	20	3.82	112	.283	.374	0-0	—	0		1	0.2
WALLACE, HUCK Harry Clinton "Lefty" B 7.27.1882 Richmond, IN D 7.6.1951 Cleveland, OH BL/TL 5-6/160# d6.5																									
1912	Phi N	0	0	—	4	0	0	0	4.2	7	5	0	0	4	4	0.00	—	.350	.458	0-0	—	0		0	0.0
WALLACE, LEFTY James Harold B 8.12.1921 Evansville, IN D 7.28.1982 Evansville, IN BL/TL 5-11/160# d5.5 Mil 1943-44																									
1942	Bos N	1	3	.250	19	3	1	0	49.1	39	21	3	2	24	20	3.83	87	.217	.316	14-0	.143	-0	109	-1	-0.2
1945	Bos N	1	0	1.000	5	3	1	0	20	18	11	1	1	9	4	4.50	85	.240	.329	6-1	.000	-1*	96	-1	-0.1
1946	Bos N	3	3	.500	27	8	2	0	75.1	76	41	5	1	31	27	4.18	82	.253	.325	18-0	.056	-1	94	-6	-0.5
Total	3	5	6	.455	51	14	4	0	144.2	133	73	9	4	64	51	4.11	84	.240	.323	38-1	.079	-2	98	-8	-0.8
WALLACE, JEFF Jeffrey Allen B 4.12.1976 Wheeling, WV BL/TL 6-2/240# d8.21																									
1997	Pit N	0	0	—	11	0	0	0-1	12	8	2	0	0	8-1	14	0.75	572	.200	.327	0-0	—	0		4	0.2
1999	Pit N	1	0	1.000	41	0	0	0-1	39	26	17	2	0	38-1	41	3.69	124	.195	.372	0-0	—	0		4	0.2
2000	Pit N	2	0	1.000	38	0	0	0-0	35.2	42	32	5	4	34-1	27	7.07	65	.290	.432	1-0	.000	-0		-10	-0.5
2001	TB A	0	3	.000	29	1	0	0-0	50.1	43	26	4	1	37-0	38	3.40	132	.232	.363	0-0	—	0	41	4	0.2
Total	4	3	3	.500	119	1	0	0-2	137	119	77	11	5	117-3	120	4.20	108	.237	.383	1-0	.000	0	41	2	0.1
WALLACE, MIKE Michael Sherman B 2.3.1951 Gastonia, NC BL/TL 6-2/204# d6.27																									
1973	Phi N	1	1	.500	20	3	1	1-1	33.1	38	16	1	0	15-4	20	3.78	101	.304	.373	4-0	.000	-0	131	0	0.0
1974	Phi N	1	0	1.000	8	0	0	0-0	8.1	12	6	0	0	2-0	1	5.40	70	.324	.359	0-0	—	0		-2	-0.2
	NY A	6	0	1.000	23	1	0	0-0	52.1	42	18	3	0	35-3	34	2.41	147	.222	.339	0-0	—	0	75	6	0.6
1975	NY A	0	0	—	3	0	0	0-0	4.1	11	7	1	0	1-0	2	14.54	25	.458	.480	0-0	—	0		-5	-0.2
	StL N	0	0	—	9	0	0	0-0	8.2	9	2	0	0	5-2	6	2.08	181	.281	.378	0-0	—	0		2	0.1
1976	StL N	3	2	.600	49	0	0	2-2	66.1	66	34	3	0	39-2	40	4.07	87	.264	.358	3-0	.333	0		-4	-0.2
1977	Tex A	0	0	—	5	0	0	0-0	8.1	10	7	1	0	10-0	2	7.56	54	.323	.488	0-0	—	0		-3	-0.1
Total	5	11	3	.786	117	4	1	3-3	181.2	188	90	9	0	107-11	105	3.91	93	.273	.367	7-0	.143	0	121	-6	0.0
WALLACE, BOBBY Rhoderick John B 11.4.1873 Pittsburgh, PA D 11.3.1960 Torrance, CA BR/TR 5-8/170# d9.15 M3 C1 U1 HF1953 ▲																									
1894	Cle N	2	1	.667	4	3	2	0	26	28	25	1	1	20	10	5.19	106	.272	.395	13-0	.154	-1	103	0	-0.1
1895	Cle N	12	14	.462	30	28	22-1	1	228.2	271	166	3	8	87	63	4.09	122	.290	.356	98-6	.214	-3	112	17	1.3
1896	†Cle N	10	7	.588	22	16	13-2	0	145.1	167	75	2	4	49	46	3.34	136	.286	.345	149-4	.235	0*	93	19	1.8
1902	StL A	0	0	—	1	1	0	0	2	3	2	0	0	0	1	0.00	—	.333	.333	494-6	.285	0*	82	0	0.0
Total	4	24	22	.522	57	48	37-3	1	402	469	268	6	13	156	120	3.87	125	.288	.355	754-16	.264	-3	104	36	3.0
WALLER, RED John Francis B 6.16.1883 Washington, DC D 2.9.1915 Secaucus, NJ BR/TR 6/175# d4.27																									
1909	NY N	0	0	—	1	0	0	0	1	3	2	0	1	0	1	0.00	—	.429	.500	0-0	—	0		0	0.0
WALROND, LES Leslie Dale B 11.7.1976 Muskogee, OK BL/TL 6/190# d6.8																									
2003	KC A	0	2	.000	7	0	0	0-0	8	11	9	2	0	7-1	6	10.13	51	.324	.439	0-0	—	0		-4	-0.6
WALSH, AUGIE August Sothley B 8.17.1904 Wilmington, DE D 11.12.1985 San Rafael, CA BR/TR 6/175# d10.2																									
1927	Phi N	0	1	.000	1	1	1	0	10	12	5	3	0	5	0	4.50	92	.333	.415	4-0	.250	-0	82	0	0.0
1928	Phi N	4	9	.308	38	11	2	2	122.1	160	92	13	5	40	38	6.18	69	.321	.378	39-1	.256	2*	83	-23	-2.0
Total	2	4	10	.286	39	12	3	2	132.1	172	97	16	5	45	38	6.05	70	.322	.380	43-1	.256	2	83	-23	-2.0
WALSH, CONNIE Cornelius R. B 4.23.1882 St.Louis, MO D 4.5.1953 St.Louis, MO TR d9.16																									
1907	Pit N	0	0	—	1	0	0	0	1	1	1	0	0	1	0	9.00	27	.250	.400	0-0	—	0		-1	0.0

Year	Tm Lg	W	L	Pct	G	GS	CG-Sho	SV-BS	IP	H	R	HR	HB	BB-IB	SO	ERA	AERA	OAV	OOB	AB-SH	AVG	PB	Sup	APR	PW
WALSH, DAVE David Peter B 9.25.1960 Arlington, MA BL/TL 6-1/185# d8.13																									
1990	LA N	1	0	1.000	20	0	0	1-1	16.1	15	12	1	0	6-1	15	3.86	95	.242	.304	0-0	—	0		-2	-0.1
WALSH, ED Edward Arthur B 2.11.1905 Meriden, CT D 10.31.1937 Meriden, CT BR/TR 6-1/180# d7.4 f-Ed																									
1928	Chi A	4	7	.364	14	10	3	0	78	86	45	2	5	42	32	4.96	82	.290	.387	27-1	.111	-2	86	-5	-0.8
1929	Chi A	6	11	.353	24	20	7	0	129	156	94	9	4	64	31	5.65	76	.312	.394	43-1	.233	2*	81	-19	-1.8
1930	Chi A	1	4	.200	37	4	0	0	103.2	131	67	8	4	30	37	5.38	86	.316	.367	34-1	.265	1*	93	-5	-0.1
1932	Chi A	0	2	.000	4	4	1	0	20.1	26	22	3	0	13	7	8.41	51	.299	.390	7-0	.286	0	98	-9	-0.7
Total	4	11	24	.314	79	38	11	0	331	399	228	22	13	149	107	5.57	78	.307	.384	111-3	.216	1	84	-38	-3.4
WALSH, ED Edward Augustine "Big Ed" B 5.14.1881 Plains, PA D 5.26.1959 Pompano Beach, FL BR/TR 6-1/193# d5.7 M1 C6 U1 HF1946 s-Ed																									
1904	Chi A	6	3	.667	18	8	6-1	1	110.2	90	45	1	3	32	57	2.60	94	.223	.285	41-1	.220	3	120	-2	0.1
1905	Chi A	8	3	.727	22	13	9-1	0	136.2	121	53	0	3	29	71	2.17	113	.239	.284	58-1	.155	-0*	121	3	0.2
1906	†Chi A	17	13	.567	41	31	24-**10**	2	278.1	215	83	1	7	58	171	1.88	135	.217	.265	99-3	.141	-2*	90	21	2.6
1907	Chi A	24	18	.571	**56**	**46**	**37**-5	**4**	**422.1**	341	120	3	8	87	206	**1.60**	**150**	.223	.269	154-1	.162	-1*	100	**33**	**4.6**
1908	Chi A	**40**	15	**.727**	**66**	**49**	**42-11**	**6**	**464**	343	111	2	9	56	**269**	1.42	163	.203	.232	157-8	.172	2	98	**43**	**6.8**
1909	Chi A	15	11	.577	31	28	20-**8**	2	230.1	166	52	0	4	50	127	1.41	166	.203	**.253**	84-1	.214	4*	111	**25**	**4.1**
1910	Chi A	18	20	.474	**45**	36	33-7	**5**	369.2	242	87	5	4	61	258	**1.27**	**189**	**.187**	**.226**	138-5	.217	4*	71	45	**6.3**
1911	Chi A	27	18	.600	**56**	37	33-5	**4**	**368.2**	327	125	4	7	72	**255**	2.22	145	.239	**.280**	155-3	.219	-1*	117	42	5.5
1912	Chi A	27	17	.614	**62**	**41**	32-6	**10**	**393**	332	125	6	1	94	254	2.15	149	.231	.279	136-4	.243	6	94	49	6.5
1913	Chi A	8	3	.727	16	14	7-1	1	97.2	91	37	1	4	39	34	2.58	113	.245	.324	32-1	.156	-1*	96	5	0.5
1914	Chi A	2	3	.400	8	5	3-1	0	44.2	33	19	0	1	20	15	2.82	95	.212	.305	16-1	.063	-1*	60	0	-0.1
1915	Chi A	3	0	1.000	3	3	3-1	0	27	19	4	0	0	7	12	1.33	223	.202	.257	11-1	.364	1*	147	5	0.7
1916	Chi A	0	1	.000	2	1	0	0	3.1	4	3	0	0	3	3	2.70	102	.286	.412	0-0	—	0	55	-1	-0.1
1917	Bos N	0	1	.000	4	3	1	0	18	22	9	0	1	9	4	3.50	73	.314	.400	4-0	.250	1	108	-2	0.0
Total	14	195	126	.607	430	315	250-57	35	2964.1	2346	873	23	52	617	1736	1.82	145	.218	.264	1085-30	.194	15	99	266	37.7
WALSH, JUNIOR James Gerald B 3.7.1919 Newark, NJ D 11.12.1990 Olyphant, PA BR/TR 5-11/185# d9.14																									
1946	Pit N	0	1	.000	4	2	0	0	10.1	9	6	0	1	10	2	5.23	67	.237	.408	4-0	.000	-1	182	-1	-0.2
1948	Pit N	1	0	1.000	2	0	0	0	4.1	4	5	1	0	5	0	10.38	39	.235	.409	2-0	.000	-0		-3	-0.5
1949	Pit N	1	4	.200	9	7	1-1	0	42.2	40	27	5	0	16	24	5.06	83	.244	.311	12-0	.000	-1	60	-4	-0.6
1950	Pit N	1	1	.500	38	2	0	2	62.1	56	36	6	1	34	33	5.05	87	.246	.346	6-0	.167	1	201	-3	0.0
1951	Pit N	1	4	.200	36	1	0	0	73.1	92	66	9	1	46	32	6.87	61	.304	.397	7-0	.143	0	21	-21	-1.2
Total	5	4	10	.286	89	12	1-1	2	193	201	140	21	3	111	91	5.88	72	.268	.365	31-0	.065	-1	97	-32	-2.5
WALSH, JIM James Thomas B 7.10.1894 Roxbury, MA D 5.13.1967 Boston, MA BL/TL 5-11/175# d8.25																									
1921	Det A	0	0	—	3	0	0	0	4	2	1	0	0	1	3	2.25	190	.125	.176	0-0	—	0		1	0.0
WALTER, GENE Gene Winston B 11.22.1960 Chicago, IL BL/TL 6-4/200# d8.9																									
1985	SD N	0	2	.000	15	0	0	3-0	22	12	6	0	0	8-1	18	2.05	173	.158	.235	1-0	.000	0		4	0.4
1986	SD N	2	2	.500	57	0	0	1-1	98	89	47	7	4	49-7	84	3.86	95	.247	.341	10-2	.200	1		-2	0.0
1987	NY N	1	2	.333	21	0	0	0-2	19.2	18	10	1	1	13-3	11	3.20	118	.243	.360	1-1	.000	0		0	0.1
1988	NY N	0	1	.000	19	0	0	0-0	16.2	21	9	0	0	11-1	14	3.78	85	.309	.400	0-0	—	0		-2	-0.1
	Sea A	1	0	1.000	16	0	0	0-0	26.1	21	16	0	2	15-4	13	5.13	81	.216	.330	0-0	—	0		-2	-0.1
Total	4	4	7	.364	128	0	0	4-3	182.2	161	88	8	7	96-16	140	3.74	99	.238	.336	12-3	.167	1		-2	0.3
WALTER, BERNIE James Bernard B 8.15.1908 Dover, TN D 10.30.1988 Nashville, TN BR/TR 6-1/175# d8.16																									
1930	Pit N	0	0	—	1	0	0	0	1	0	0	0	0	0	1	0.00	—	.000	.000	0-0	—	0		1	0.0
WALTERS, CHARLIE Charles Leonard B 2.21.1947 Minneapolis, MN BR/TR 6-4/190# d4.11																									
1969	Min A	0	0	—	6	0	0	0-0	6.2	6	4	1	1	3-0	2	5.40	68	.240	.345	0-0	—	0		-1	-0.1
WALTERS, MIKE Michael Charles B 10.18.1957 St.Louis, MO BR/TR 6-5/203# d7.8																									
1983	Min A	1	1	.500	23	0	0	2-0	59	52	31	4	2	20-4	21	4.12	104	.243	.311	0-0	—	0		0	0.0
1984	Min A	0	3	.000	23	0	0	2-2	29	31	14	1	1	14-4	10	3.72	113	.287	.368	0-0	—	0		1	0.1
Total	2	1	4	.200	46	0	0	4-2	88	83	45	5	3	34-8	31	3.99	106	.258	.331	0-0	—	0		1	0.1
WALTERS, BUCKY William Henry B 4.19.1909 Philadelphia, PA D 4.20.1991 Abington, PA BR/TR 6-1/180# d9.18.1931 M2 C8 ▲																									
1934	Phi N	0	0	—	2	1	0	0	7	8	3	1	1	2	7	1.29	367	.296	.367	300-3	.260	0*	73	2	0.1
1935	Phi N	9	9	.500	24	22	8-2	0	151	168	86	9	7	68	40	4.17	109	.289	.370	96-2	.250	1*	85	5	0.8
1936	Phi N	11	21	.344	40	33	15-**4**	0	258	284	146	11	5	115	66	4.26	107	.277	.353	121-3	.240	2*	79	9	1.9
1937	Phi N★	14	15	.483	37	**34**	15-3	0	246.1	292	148	14	3	86	87	4.75	91	.295	.353	137-2	.277	4*	101	-11	-0.4
1938	Phi N	4	8	.333	12	12	9-1	0	82.2	91	53	8	3	42	28	5.23	74	.276	.363	35-0	.286	3*	102	-11	-1.0
	Cin N	11	6	.647	27	22	11-2	1	168.1	168	81	5	2	66	65	3.69	99	.255	.324	64-2	.141	-0*	136	-1	0.0
	Year	15	14	.517	39	34	20-3	1	251	259	87	13	5	108	93	4.20	89	.262	.337	99-2	.192	3	124	-11	-1.0
1939	†Cin N☆	**27**	11	.711	39	**36**	**31**-2	0	**319**	250	98	15	6	109	**137**	**2.29**	**168**	**.220**	.291	120-5	.325	13*	110	**54**	**8.2**
1940	†Cin N★	**22**	10	.688	36	36	**29**-3	0	**305**	241	95	19	5	92	115	**2.48**	**153**	**.220**	.283	117-6	.205	2*	117	**44**	4.7
1941	Cin N★	19	15	.559	37	35	**27**-5	2	**302**	292	108	10	2	88	129	2.83	127	.255	.309	106-4	.189	2*	88	27	3.3
1942	Cin N★	15	14	.517	34	32	21-2	0	253.2	223	101	8	5	73	109	2.66	123	.231	.289	99-2	.242	6*	97	14	2.5
1943	Cin N	15	15	.500	34	34	21-5	0	246.1	244	105	8	1	109	80	3.54	94	.264	.342	90-5	.267	8*	88	-5	0.3
1944	Cin N★	**23**	8	.742	34	32	27-6	1	285	233	92	10	4	87	77	2.40	145	**.219**	.281	107-5	.280	8*	97	**34**	**4.7**
1945	Cin N	10	10	.500	22	22	12-3	0	168	166	62	6	2	51	45	2.68	140	.259	.316	61-3	.230	5*	69	18	2.6
1946	Cin N	10	7	.588	22	22	10-2	0	151.1	146	55	9	2	64	60	2.56	131	.258	.336	55-4	.127	-1*	111	12	1.3
1947	Cin N	8	8	.500	20	20	5-2	0	122	137	83	15	3	49	43	5.75	71	.278	.347	45-2	.267	3	109	-20	-2.0
1948	Cin N	0	3	.000	7	5	1	0	35	42	25	6	0	18	19	4.63	84	.316	.397	15-0	.267	0	113	-5	-0.3
1950	Bos N	0	0	—	1	0	0	0	4	5	2	0	0	2	0	4.50	86	.313	.389	2-0	.000	-0		0	0.0
Total	16	198	160	.553	428	398	242-42	4	3104.2	2990	1343	154	51	1121	1107	3.30	115	.253	.321	1570-48	.246	57	99	166	26.7
WALTON, BRUCE Bruce Kenneth B 12.25.1962 Bakersfield, CA BR/TR 6-2/195# d5.11 C1																									
1991	Oak A	1	0	1.000	12	0	0	0-1	13	11	9	3	1	6-0	10	6.23	62	.229	.321	0-0	—	0		-3	-0.3
1992	Oak A	0	0	—	7	0	0	0-0	10	17	11	1	0	3-0	7	9.90	38	.378	.408	0-0	—	0		-7	-0.3
1993	Mon N	0	0	—	4	0	0	0-0	5.2	11	6	1	0	3-0	0	9.53	44	.407	.467	1-0	.000	-0		-3	-0.1
1994	Col N	1	0	1.000	4	0	0	0-0	5.1	6	5	1	0	3-1	1	8.44	59	.273	.360	0-0	—	0		-2	-0.3
Total	4	2	0	1.000	27	0	0	0-1	34	45	31	6	1	15-1	18	8.21	49	.317	.381	1-0	.000	-0		-15	-1.0
WANTZ, DICK Richard Carter B 4.11.1940 South Gate, CA D 5.13.1965 Inglewood, CA BR/TR 6-5/175# d4.13																									
1965	Cal A	0	0	—	1	0	0	0	1	3	2	0	0	0-0	2	18.00	19	.500	.500	0-0	—	0		-2	-0.1
WAPNICK, STEVE Steven Lee B 9.25.1965 Panorama City, CA BR/TR 6-2/200# d4.14																									
1990	Det A	0	0	—	4	0	0	0-0	7	8	5	0	0	10-0	6	6.43	62	.296	.486	0-0	—	0		-2	-0.1
1991	Chi A	0	1	.000	6	0	0	0-0	5	2	1	0	0	4-0	1	1.80	221	.111	.273	0-0	—	0		1	0.2
Total	2	0	1	.000	10	0	0	0-0	12	10	6	0	0	14-0	7	4.50	88	.222	.407	0-0	—	0		-1	0.1
WARD, BRYAN Bryan Matthew B 1.25.1972 Bristol, PA BL/TL 6-2/210# d7.3																									
1998	Chi A	1	2	.333	28	0	0	1-3	27	30	13	4	0	7-0	17	3.33	137	.278	.319	0-0	—	0		3	0.3
1999	Chi A	0	1	.000	40	0	0	0-0	39.1	63	36	10	0	11-1	35	7.55	65	.368	.404	0-0	—	0		-11	-0.5
2000	Phi N	0	0	—	20	0	0	0-0	19.1	14	5	2	0	8-0	11	2.33	200	.206	.282	0-0	—	0		5	0.2
	Ana A	0	0	—	7	0	0	0-0	8	8	6	1	0	2-0	3	5.63	90	.235	.278	0-0	—	0		-1	0.0
Total	3	1	3	.250	95	0	0	1-3	93.2	115	60	17	0	28-1	66	5.09	93	.302	.346	0-0	—	0		-4	0.0
WARD, COLIN Colin Norval B 11.22.1960 Los Angeles, CA BL/TL 6-3/190# d9.21																									
1985	SF N	0	0	—	6	2	0	0-0	12.1	10	6	0	0	7-0	8	4.38	79	.233	.333	2-0	.000	-0	115	-1	-0.1
WARD, JOHNNY John B East St.Louis, IL d9.19																									
1885	Pro N	0	1	.000	1	1	1	0	8	10	7	0		1	3	4.50	60	.286	.306	3	.000	-0	0	-2	-0.2

Year	Tm Lg	W	L	Pct	G	GS	CG-Sho	SV-BS	IP	H	R	HR	HB	BB-IB	SO	ERA	AERA	OAV	OOB	AB-SH	AVG	PB	Sup	APR	PW
WARD, JOHN John Montgomery B 3.3.1860 Bellefonte, PA D 3.4.1925 Augusta, GA BL/TR 5-9/165# d7.15 M7 HF1964 ▲																									
1878	Pro N	22	13	.629	37	37	37-6	0	334	308	151	3		34	116	**1.51**	**146**	.231	.251	138	.196	2	95	22	**2.2**
1879	Pro N	**47**	19	**.712**	70	60	58-2	**1**	587	571	270	5		36	**239**	2.15	110	.239	.250	364	.286	17*	144	13	2.7
1880	Pro N	39	24	.619	70	67	59-**8**	1	595	501	230	5		45	230	1.74	127	.217	.232	356	.228	1*	108	35	3.5
1881	Pro N	18	18	.500	39	35	32-3	0	330	326	183	2		53	119	2.13	125	.242	.271	357	.244	3*	94	16	1.9
1882	Pro N	19	13	.594	34	33	30-4	**1**	286	268	143	6		36	72	2.55	111	.232	.255	355	.245	1*	95	11	1.2
1883	NY N	16	13	.552	34	25	24-1	0	277	278	165	3		31	121	2.70	115	.246	.267	380	.255	6*	97	13	1.7
1884	NY N	3	3	.500	9	5	5	0	60.2	72	43	2		18	23	3.41	87	.280	.327	482	.253	1*	160	-4	-0.2
Total	7	164	103	.614	293	262	245-24	3	2469.2	2324	1185	26		253	920	2.10	118	.234	.254	2432	.249	31	111	106	13.0
WARD, DICK Richard Ole B 5.21.1909 Herrick, SD D 5.30.1966 Freeland, WA BR/TR 6-1/198# d5.3																									
1934	Chi N	0	0	—	3	0	0	0	6	9	6	0	0	2	1	3.00	129	.375	.423	1-0	.000	-0		-1	-0.1
1935	StL N	0	0	—	1	0	0	0	0	0	1	0	0	1	0	—	—	—	1.000	0-0	—	0		0	0.0
Total	2	0	0	—	4	0	0	0	6	9	7	0	0	3	1	3.00	129	.375	.444	1-0	.000	-0		-1	-0.1
WARD, COLBY Robert Colby B 1.2.1964 Lansing, MI BR/TR 6-2/185# d7.27																									
1990	Cle A	1	3	.250	22	0	0	1-1	36	31	17	3	1	21-4	23	4.25	92	.238	.344	0-0	—	0		-1	-0.1
WARD, DUANE Roy Duane B 5.28.1964 Park View, NM BR/TR 6-4/210# d4.12																									
1986	Atl N	0	1	.000	10	0	0	0-0	16	22	13	2	0	8-0	8	7.31	54	.349	.423	1-0	.000	-0		-5	-0.3
	Tor A	0	1	.000	2	1	0	0-0	2	3	4	0	1	4-0	1	13.50	31	.300	.533	0-0	—	0	64	-2	-0.4
1987	Tor A	1	0	1.000	12	1	0	0-0	11.2	14	9	0	0	12-2	10	6.94	65	.326	.464	0-0	—	0	203	-3	-0.2
1988	Tor A	9	3	.750	64	0	0	15-3	111.2	101	46	5	5	60-8	91	3.30	119	.245	.344	0-0	—	0		8	0.9
1989	†Tor A	4	10	.286	66	0	0	15-12	114.2	94	55	4	5	58-11	122	3.77	100	.230	.326	0-0	—	0		-1	0.0
1990	Tor A	2	8	.200	73	0	0	11-7	127.2	101	51	9	1	42-10	112	3.45	114	.221	.287	0-0	—	0		8	0.7
1991	†Tor A	7	6	.538	**81**	0	0	23-4	107.1	80	36	3	2	33-3	132	2.77	152	.207	.271	0-0	—	0		17	2.5
1992	†Tor A	7	4	.636	79	0	0	12-4	101.1	76	27	5	1	39-3	103	1.95	209	.207	.282	0-0	—	0		**22**	2.7
1993	†Tor A★	2	3	.400	71	0	0	**45-6**	71.2	49	17	4	1	25-2	97	2.13	203	.193	.266	0-0	—	0		18	3.1
1995	Tor A	0	1	.000	4	0	0	0-0	2.2	11	10	0	1	5-0	3	27.00	17	.579	.680	0-0	—	0		-7	-1.2
Total	9	32	37	.464	462	2	0	121-36	666.2	551	268	32	17	286-39	679	3.28	123	.228	.310	1-0	.000	-0	147	55	7.8
WARDEN, JON Jonathan Edgar "Warbler" B 10.1.1946 Columbus, OH BB/TL 6/205# d4.11																									
1968	Det A	4	1	.800	28	0	0	3	37.1	30	15	5	0	15-2	25	3.62	83	.217	.294	2-0	.000	-0		-2	-0.4
WARDLE, CURT Curtis Ray B 11.16.1960 Downey, CA BL/TL 6-5/220# d8.30																									
1984	Min A	0	0	—	2	0	0	0-0	4	3	2	2	0	0-0	5	4.50	94	.200	.200	0-0	—	0		0	0.0
1985	Min A	1	3	.250	35	0	0	1-4	49	49	32	9	1	28-0	47	5.51	80	.266	.364	0-0	—	0		-5	-0.3
	Cle A	7	6	.538	15	12	0	0-0	66	78	51	11	1	34-0	37	6.68	62	.297	.373	0-0	—	0	136	-17	-2.8
	Year	8	9	.471	50	12	0	1-4	115	127	57	20	2	62-0	84	6.18	69	.284	.369	0-0	—	0	132	-22	-3.1
Total	2	8	9	.471	52	12	0	1-4	119	130	85	22	2	62-0	89	6.13	69	.281	.365	0-0	—	0	132	-22	-3.1
WARE, JEFF Jeffrey Allan B 11.11.1970 Norfolk, VA BR/TR 6-3/190# d9.2																									
1995	Tor A	2	1	.667	5	5	0	0-0	26.1	28	18	2	1	21-0	18	5.47	86	.277	.407	0-0	—	0	99	-2	-0.2
1996	Tor A	1	5	.167	13	4	0	0-0	32.2	35	34	6	2	31-1	11	9.09	55	.271	.420	0-0	—	0	46	-14	-1.9
Total	2	3	6	.333	18	9	0	0-0	59	63	52	8	3	52-1	29	7.47	65	.274	.414	0-0	—	0	74	-16	-2.1
WARHOP, JACK John Milton "Chief" or "Crab" (b: John Milton Wauhop) B 7.4.1884 Hinton, WV D 10.4.1960 Freeport, IL BR/TR 5-9.5/168# d9.19																									
1908	NY A	1	2	.333	5	4	3	0	36.1	40	19	0	4	8	11	4.46	56	.292	.349	16-0	.063	-1*	62	-5	-0.5
1909	NY A	13	15	.464	36	23	21-3	2	243.1	197	84	2	26	81	95	2.40	105	.233	.319	86-2	.128	-2	101	7	0.6
1910	NY A	14	14	.500	37	27	20	2	243	219	108	1	18	79	75	3.00	89	.246	.320	79-4	.177	-1	104	-8	-1.2
1911	NY A	12	13	.480	31	25	17-1	0	209.2	239	118	6	15	44	71	4.16	86	.286	.333	77-2	.156	-4*	85	-8	-1.3
1912	NY A	10	19	.345	39	22	16	3	258	256	121	3	16	59	110	2.86	126	.266	.319	92-2	.207	-1	64	17	1.6
1913	NY A	4	5	.444	15	7	1	0	62.1	69	42	1	12	33	11	3.75	80	.297	.412	23-0	.130	0	113	-8	-1.1
1914	NY A	8	15	.348	37	23	15	0	216.2	182	75	8	11	44	56	2.37	117	.235	.286	71-2	.141	-1*	83	8	0.7
1915	NY A	7	9	.438	21	19	12	0	143.1	164	74	7	12	52	34	3.96	74	.309	.384	51-0	.137	-2	103	-14	-1.7
Total	8	69	92	.429	221	150	105-4	7	1412.2	1366	641	28	114	400	463	3.12	96	.262	.328	495-12	.156	-12	89	-11	-2.9
WARMOTH, CY Wallace Walter B 2.2.1893 Bone Gap, IL D 6.20.1957 Mt.Carmel, IL BL/TL 5-11/158# d8.31																									
1916	StL N	0	0	—	3	0	0	0	5	12	10	0	1	4	1	14.40	18	.500	.586	2-0	.000	-0		-6	-0.4
1922	Was A	1	0	1.000	5	1	1	0	19	15	6	0	0	9	8	1.42	272	.205	.293	7-0	.143	-0	132	4	0.2
1923	Was A	7	5	.583	21	13	3	0	105	103	64	4	1	76	45	4.29	88	.261	.381	36-2	.222	2	112	-8	-0.5
Total	3	8	5	.615	29	14	4	0	129	130	80	4	2	89	54	4.26	88	.264	.379	45-2	.200	1	114	-10	-0.7
WARNEKE, LON Lonnie "The Arkansas Hummingbird" B 3.28.1909 Mt.Ida, AR D 6.23.1976 Hot Springs, AR BR/TR 6-2/185# d4.18 Mil 1944 U7																									
1930	Chi N	0	0	—	1	0	0	0	1.1	2	5	0	0	5	0	33.75	14	.400	.700	0-0	—	0		-4	-0.2
1931	Chi N	2	4	.333	20	7	3	0	64.1	67	33	1	3	37	27	3.22	120	.269	.370	19-0	.263	1	73	2	0.2
1932	†Chi N	**22**	6	**.786**	35	32	25-**4**	0	277	247	84	12	2	64	106	**2.37**	**159**	.237	.283	99-4	.192	-0	112	**45**	4.3
1933	Chi N★	18	13	.581	36	34	**26**-4	1	287.1	262	83	8	3	75	133	2.00	163	.244	.295	100-3	.300	10*	88	39	5.8
1934	Chi N★	22	10	.688	43	35	23-3	3	291.1	273	116	16	2	66	143	3.21	121	.244	.287	113-2	.195	-1*	115	23	2.2
1935	†Chi N	20	13	.606	42	30	20-1	4	261.2	257	102	19	3	50	120	3.06	128	.257	.294	91-7	.220	1*	111	27	3.3
1936	Chi N★	16	13	.552	40	29	13-**4**	1	240.1	246	108	10	4	76	113	3.45	116	.264	.322	84-10	.202	0	109	12	1.3
1937	StL N	18	11	.621	36	33	18-2	0	238.2	280	139	32	0	69	87	4.53	88	.287	.335	80-6	.262	4	114	-13	-1.0
1938	StL N	13	8	.619	31	26	12-4	0	197	199	102	14	2	64	89	3.97	100	.256	.314	71-3	.324	5	116	1	0.5
1939	StL N☆	13	7	.650	34	21	6-2	2	162	160	73	14	2	49	59	3.78	109	.259	.316	52-6	.192	1	126	8	1.0
1940	StL N	16	10	.615	33	31	17-1	0	232	235	103	17	3	47	85	3.14	127	.257	.296	86-7	.209	2	129	18	2.1
1941	StL N☆	17	9	.654	37	30	12-4	0	246	227	100	19	3	82	83	3.15	120	.249	.313	77-8	.117	-2	101	17	1.4
1942	StL N	6	4	.600	12	12	5	0	82	76	34	8	0	15	31	3.29	104	.238	.272	30-3	.333	3	155	2	0.5
	Chi N	5	7	.417	15	12	8-1	2	99	97	33	2	0	21	28	2.27	141	.259	.298	32-2	.188	-0	88	9	1.1
	Year	11	11	.500	27	24	13-1	2	181	173	36	10	0	36	59	2.73	121	.249	.286	62-5	.258	2	123	11	1.6
1943	Chi N	4	5	.444	21	10	4	0	88.1	82	40	3	0	18	30	3.16	106	.246	.285	26-1	.192	1	107	0	0.2
1945	Chi N	0	1	.000	9	1	0	0	14	16	9	0	0	1	6	3.86	95	.267	.279	2-0	.000	0	116	-1	-0.1
Total	15	192	121	.613	445	343	192-30	13	2782.1	2726	1164	175	27	739	1140	3.18	119	.255	.304	962-62	.223	27	112	185	22.6
WARNER, ED Edward Emory B 6.20.1889 Fitchburg, MA D 2.5.1954 New York, NY BR/TL 5-10.5/165# d7.2																									
1912	Pit N	1	1	.500	11	3	1-1	0	45	40	20	0	3	18	13	3.60	91	.242	.328	15-0	.133	-1	112	-1	-0.1
WARNER, JACK Jack Dyer B 7.12.1940 Brandywine, WV BR/TR 5-11/190# d4.10																									
1962	Chi N	0	0	—	7	0	0	0	7	9	7	3	0	0-0	3	7.71	54	.321	.321	0-0	—	0		-3	-0.1
1963	Chi N	0	1	.000	8	0	0	0	22.2	21	7	1	0	8-2	7	2.78	126	.256	.319	4-0	.250	0		2	0.1
1964	Chi N	0	0	—	7	0	0	0	9.1	12	3	0	0	4-0	6	2.89	128	.333	.390	0-0	—	0		1	0.1
1965	Chi N	0	1	.000	11	0	0	0	15.2	22	16	1	0	9-1	7	8.62	43	.355	.431	1-0	.000	-0		-8	-0.5
Total	4	0	2	.000	33	0	0	0	54.2	64	33	5	0	21-3	23	5.10	72	.308	.366	5-0	.200	0		-8	-0.4
WARREN, MIKE Michael Bruce B 3.26.1961 Inglewood, CA BR/TR 6-1/175# d6.12																									
1983	Oak A	5	3	.625	12	9	3-1	0-0	65.2	51	33	4	1	18-1	30	4.11	94	.215	.269	0-0	—	0	110	-2	-0.2
1984	Oak A	3	6	.333	24	12	0	0-0	90	104	52	11	3	44-1	61	4.90	77	.291	.370	0-0	—	0	104	-11	-1.1
1985	Oak A	1	4	.200	16	6	0	0-0	49	52	42	13	4	38-0	48	6.61	58	.261	.387	0-0	—	0	98	-17	-1.5
Total	3	9	13	.409	52	27	3-1	0-0	204.2	207	127	28	8	100-2	139	5.06	75	.261	.346	0-0	—	0	105	-30	-2.8
WARREN, TOMMY Thomas Gentry B 7.5.1917 Tulsa, OK D 1.2.1968 Tulsa, OK BB/TL 6-1/190# d4.18																									
1944	Bro N	1	4	.200	22	4	2	0	68.2	74	52	4	0	40	18	4.98	71	.270	.363	43-0	.256	2*	100	-14	-0.8
WARTHEN, DAN Daniel Dean B 12.1.1952 Omaha, NE BB/TL 6/200# d5.18 C8																									
1975	Mon N	8	6	.571	40	18	2	3-0	167.2	130	62	8	1	87-4	128	3.11	123	.217	.315	51-4	.118	-2	85	14	1.0
1976	Mon N	2	10	.167	23	16	2-1	0-0	90	76	59	8	2	66-2	67	5.30	70	.232	.361	27-1	.000	-3	83	-14	-2.0

Year	Tm Lg	W	L	Pct	G	GS	CG-Sho	SV-BS	IP	H	R	HR	HB	BB-IB	SO	ERA	AERA	OAV	OOB	AB-SH	AVG	PB	Sup	APR	PW
1977	Mon N	2	3	.400	12	6	1	0-0	35	33	34	7	0	38-1	26	7.97	48	.262	.430	9-1	.111	-0	148	-16	-1.9
	Phi N	0	1	.000	3	0	0	0-0	3.2	4	3	0	0	5-0	1	0.00	—	.267	.450	0-0	—	0		0	0.1
	Year	2	4	.333	15	6	1	0-0	38.2	37	43	7	0	43-1	27	7.22	53	.262	.432	9-1	.111	-0	147	-16	-1.8
1978	Hou N	0	1	.000	5	1	0	0-1	10.2	10	5	3	0	2-0	2	4.22	79	.250	.279	2-0	.000	-0	27	-1	-0.1
Total	4	12	21	.364	83	41	5-1	3-1	307	253	163	26	3	198-7	224	4.31	88	.228	.344	89-6	.079	-6	92	-17	-2.9
WASDIN, JOHN John Truman B 8.5.1972 Fort Belvoir, VA BR/TR 6-2/190# d8.24																									
1995	Oak A	1	1	.500	5	2	0	0-0	17.1	14	9	4	1	3-0	6	4.67	96	.215	.261	0-0	—	0	94	0	0.0
1996	Oak A	8	7	.533	25	21	1	0-1	131.1	145	96	24	4	50-5	75	5.96	83	.283	.348	0-0	—	0	105	-17	-1.6
1997	Bos A	4	6	.400	53	7	0	0-2	124.2	121	68	18	3	38-4	84	4.40	105	.251	.306	0-0	—	0	82	3	0.1
1998	†Bos A	6	4	.600	47	8	0	0-1	96	111	57	14	2	27-8	59	5.25	90	.288	.333	0-0	—	0	96	-4	-0.3
1999	†Bos A	8	3	.727	45	0	0	2-3	74.1	66	38	14	0	18-0	57	4.12	121	.236	.280	0-0	—	0		7	0.9
2000	Bos A	1	3	.250	25	1	0	1-1	44.2	48	25	8	2	15-1	36	5.04	100	.273	.328	0-0	—	0	74	1	0.0
	Col N	0	3	.000	14	3	1	0-0	35.2	42	23	6	3	9-2	35	5.80	100	.302	.353	8-1	.250	-0	37	1	0.0
2001	Col N	2	1	.667	18	0	0	0-3	24.1	32	19	7	1	8-2	17	7.03	76	.320	.373	3-0	.333	0		-3	-0.3
	Bal A	1	1	.500	26	0	0	0-2	49.2	54	25	4	5	16-4	47	4.17	103	.277	.341	0-0	—	0		1	0.0
2003	Tor A	0	1	.000	3	2	0	0-0	5	16	13	2	0	4-0	5	23.40	20	.533	.571	0-0	—	0	90	-10	-1.3
Total	8	31	30	.508	261	44	2	3-13	603	649	373	101	21	188-26	421	5.22	93	.274	.329	11-1	.273	1	93	-21	-2.5
WASHBURN, GEORGE George Edward B 10.6.1914 Solon, ME D 1.5.1979 Baton Rouge, LA BL/TR 6-1/175# d5.4																									
1941	NY A	0	1	.000	1	1	0	0	2	2	4	0	0	5	1	13.50	29	.286	.583	1-0	.000	-0	22	-2	-0.4
WASHBURN, GREG Gregory James B 12.3.1946 Coal City, IL BR/TR 6/190# d6.7																									
1969	Cal A	0	2	.000	8	2	0	0-0	11.1	21	11	0	1	5-0	4	7.94	44	.404	.458	0-0	—	0	38	-6	-0.9
WASHBURN, JARROD Jarrod Michael B 8.13.1974 LaCrosse, WI BL/TL 6-1/190# d6.2																									
1998	Ana A	6	3	.667	15	11	0	0-0	74	70	40	11	3	27-1	48	4.62	102	.248	.317	1-2	.000	-0	148	1	0.1
1999	Ana A	4	5	.444	16	10	0	0-0	61.2	61	36	6	1	26-0	39	5.25	92	.261	.335	0-0	—	0	58	-1	-0.2
2000	Ana A	7	2	.778	14	14	0	0-0	84.1	64	38	16	1	37-0	49	3.74	136	.215	.301	3-2	.333	1	107	12	1.2
2001	Ana A	11	10	.524	30	30	1	0-0	193.1	196	89	25	7	54-4	126	3.77	121	.263	.318	5-0	.600	1	97	16	1.7
2002	†Ana A	18	6	.750	32	32	1	0-0	206	183	75	19	3	59-1	139	3.15	141	.235	.289	5-0	.200	0	96	31	3.2
2003	Ana A	10	15	.400	32	32	2	0-0	207.1	205	106	34	11	54-4	118	4.43	98	.256	.310	5-0	.200	0	89	0	-0.1
Total	6	56	41	.577	139	129	4	0-0	826.2	779	384	111	26	257-10	519	3.96	115	.248	.308	19-4	.316	2	98	59	5.9
WASHBURN, LIBE Libeus B 6.16.1874 Lyme, NH D 3.22.1940 Malone, NY BB/TL 5-10/180# d5.30.1902 ▲																									
1903	Phi N	0	4	.000	4	4	4	0	35	44	23	0	0	11	9	4.37	75	.326	.377	18-0	.167	-0*	62	-4	-0.4
WASHBURN, RAY Ray Clark B 5.31.1938 Pasco, WA BR/TR 6-1/205# d9.20																									
1961	StL N	1	1	.500	3	2	1	0	20.1	10	4	1	1	7-0	12	1.77	248	.152	.243	8-0	.125	-1	131	6	0.5
1962	StL N	12	9	.571	34	25	2-1	0	175.2	187	90	25	3	58-2	109	4.10	104	.273	.331	56-4	.179	1	102	4	0.5
1963	StL N	5	3	.625	11	11	4-2	0	64.1	50	25	5	1	14-0	47	3.08	115	.212	.259	19-4	.053	-1	93	3	0.3
1964	StL N	3	4	.429	15	10	0	2	60	60	29	7	5	17-2	28	4.05	94	.264	.325	15-3	.133	-0	67	0	0.0
1965	StL N	9	11	.450	28	16	1-1	2	119.1	114	57	15	1	28-7	67	3.62	106	.254	.298	33-3	.152	0	77	1	0.1
1966	StL N	11	9	.550	27	26	4-1	0	170	183	75	15	1	44-5	98	3.76	95	.280	.324	54-4	.093	-1	100	-1	-0.2
1967	†StL N	10	7	.588	27	27	3-1	0	186.1	190	78	14	4	42-7	98	3.53	93	.265	.307	66-4	.091	-2	106	-3	-0.4
1968	†StL N	14	8	.636	31	30	8-4	0	215	191	67	9	1	47-7	124	2.26	128	.239	.282	60-11	.083	0	118	14	1.3
1969	StL N	3	8	.273	28	16	2	1-0	132.1	133	59	9	1	49-9	80	3.06	117	.261	.324	37-1	.081	-2	81	4	0.1
1970	†Cin N	4	4	.500	35	3	0	0-0	66.1	90	61	7	0	48-9	37	6.92	58	.324	.421	13-1	.000	-1	81	-22	-2.4
Total	10	72	64	.529	239	166	25-10	5-0	1209.2	1208	545	107	18	354-48	700	3.53	101	.261	.315	361-35	.105	-7	97	6	-0.2
WASHER, BUCK William B 10.11.1882 Akron, OH D 12.8.1955 Akron, OH BR/TR 5-10/175# d4.25																									
1905	Phi N	0	0	—	1	0	0	0	3	4	2	0	0	5	0	6.00	49	.333	.529	1-0	.000	-0		-1	-0.1
WASLEWSKI, GARY Gary Lee B 7.21.1941 Meriden, CT BR/TR 6-4/195# d6.11																									
1967	†Bos A	2	2	.500	12	8	0	0	42	34	18	3	1	20-2	20	3.21	108	.225	.314	11-1	.091	-1	94	1	0.0
1968	Bos A	4	7	.364	34	11	2	2	105.1	108	50	9	6	40-9	59	3.67	86	.269	.341	26-2	.038	-2*	83	-6	-0.8
1969	StL N	0	2	.000	12	0	0	1-0	20.2	19	9	3	1	8-4	16	3.92	91	.244	.318	1-0	.000	-0		0	0.0
	Mon N	3	7	.300	30	14	3-1	1-0	109.1	102	53	5	8	63-5	63	3.29	112	.252	.362	30-0	.033	-2	67	2	0.0
	Year	3	9	.250	42	14	3-1	2-0	130	121	56	8	9	71-9	79	3.39	108	.251	.355	31-0	.032	-2	67	1	0.0
1970	Mon N	0	2	.000	6	4	0	0-1	24.2	23	14	3	0	15-4	19	5.11	81	.247	.352	6-1	.000	-0	60	-2	-0.2
	NY A	2	2	.500	26	5	0	0-0	55	42	20	4	4	27-4	27	3.11	113	.219	.323	10-1	.100	-1	71	4	0.2
1971	NY A	0	1	.000	24	0	0	1-0	35.2	28	15	2	1	16-2	17	3.28	99	.214	.302	1-0	.000	-0		0	0.0
1972	Oak A	0	3	.000	8	0	0	0-0	17.2	12	5	3	0	8-1	8	2.04	140	.190	.282	3-0	.000	-0		1	0.2
Total	6	11	26	.297	152	42	5-1	5-1	410.1	368	184	32	21	197-31	229	3.44	100	.243	.336	88-5	.045	-6	77	0	-0.6
WATERBURY, STEVE Steven Craig B 4.6.1952 Carbondale, IL BR/TR 6-5/190# d9.14																									
1976	StL N	0	0	—	5	0	0	0-0	6	7	4	0	0	3-0	4	6.00	59	.304	.385	0-0	—	0		-1	-0.1
WATERS, FRED Fred Warren B 2.2.1927 Benton, MS D 8.28.1989 Pensacola, FL BL/TL 5-11/185# d9.20																									
1955	Pit N	0	0	—	2	0	0	0	5	7	2	1	0	2-0	0	3.60	114	.318	.375	1-0	.000	-0		0	0.0
1956	Pit N	2	2	.500	23	5	1	0	51	48	18	3	1	30-1	14	2.82	134	.258	.357	20-0	.050	-1	112	5	0.2
Total	2	2	2	.500	25	5	1	0	56	55	20	4	1	32-1	14	2.89	131	.264	.359	21-0	.048	-1	112	5	0.2
WATKINS, BOB Robert Cecil B 3.12.1948 San Francisco, CA BR/TR 6-1/170# d9.6																									
1969	Hou N	0	0	—	5	0	0	0-0	15.2	13	9	1	0	13-0	11	5.17	69	.241	.382	2-0	.000	-0		-2	-0.2
WATKINS, SCOTT Scott Allen B 5.15.1970 Tulsa, OK BL/TL 6-3/180# d8.1																									
1995	Min A	0	0	—	27	0	0	0-2	21.2	22	14	2	0	11-1	11	5.40	88	.278	.355	0-0	—	0		-1	-0.1
WATSON, ALLEN Allen Kenneth B 11.18.1970 Jamaica, NY BL/TL 6-3/190# d7.8																									
1993	StL N	6	7	.462	16	15	0	0-1	86	90	53	11	3	28-2	49	4.60	86	.271	.330	26-1	.231	2	121	-8	-0.8
1994	StL N	6	5	.545	22	22	0	0-0	115.2	130	73	15	8	53-0	74	5.52	75	.286	.370	38-7	.158	1	124	-17	-1.3
1995	StL N	7	9	.438	21	19	0	0-0	114.1	126	68	17	5	41-0	49	4.96	85	.285	.352	36-3	.417	6	79	-8	-0.3
1996	SF N	8	12	.400	29	29	2	0-0	185.2	189	105	28	5	69-2	128	4.61	89	.273	.339	65-2	.231	4*	91	-9	-0.5
1997	Ana A	12	12	.500	35	34	0	0-0	199	220	121	37	8	73-0	141	4.93	93	.279	.344	0-0	—	0	105	-9	-0.9
1998	Ana A	6	7	.462	28	14	1	0-0	92.1	122	67	12	3	34-0	64	6.04	78	.323	.378	0-0	—	0	88	-14	-1.6
1999	NY N	2	2	.500	14	4	0	1-0	39.2	36	18	5	1	22-3	32	4.08	107	.252	.347	10-0	.300	1	84	2	0.2
	Sea A	0	1	.000	3	0	0	0-0	3	6	9	5	0	3-0	2	12.00	40	.400	.474	0-0	—	0		-5	-0.8
	†NY A	4	0	1.000	21	0	0	0-1	34.1	30	8	3	0	10-0	30	2.10	226	.236	.292	0-0	—	0		11	1.1
	Year	4	1	.800	24	0	0	0-1	37.1	36	21	8	0	13-0	32	2.89	164	.254	.314	0-0	—	0		6	0.3
2000	NY A	0	0	—	17	0	0	0-0	22	30	25	6	2	18-0	20	10.23	47	.330	.442	0-0	—	0		-12	-0.6
Total	8	51	55	.481	206	137	3	1-2	892	979	547	139	35	351-7	589	5.03	86	.283	.352	175-13	.257	15	100	-69	-5.5
WATSON, DOC Charles John B 1.30.1885 Kensington, OH D 12.30.1949 San Diego, CA BR/TL 6/170# d9.3																									
1913	Chi N	1	0	1.000	1	1	1	0	9	8	2	0	1	6	1	1.00	318	.242	.375	2-1	.000	0	166	2	0.2
1914	Chi F	9	8	.529	26	18	10-3	1	172	145	50	2	3	49	69	2.04	130	.236	.295	54-6	.093	-5	95	14	0.7
	StL F	3	4	.429	9	7	4-2	0	56	41	18	1	4	24	18	1.93	158	.211	.311	16-1	.125	-1	42	6	0.5
	Year	12	12	.500	35	25	14-5	1	228	186	20	3	7	73	87	2.01	137	.230	.299	70-7	.100	-6	79	20	1.2
1915	StL F	9	9	.500	33	20	6	0	135.2	132	66	1	4	58	45	3.98	72	.273	.355	40-2	.125	-3	77	-13	-2.2
Total	3	22	21	.512	69	46	21-5	1	372.2	326	136	4	12	137	133	2.70	104	.246	.322	112-10	.107	-9	80	9	-0.8
WATSON, MULE John Reeves B 10.15.1896 Homer, LA D 8.25.1949 Shreveport, LA BR/TR 6-1.5/185# d7.4																									
1918	Phi A	7	10	.412	21	19	11-3	0	141.2	139	74	0	2	44	30	3.37	87	.288	.350	47-1	.128	-3	104	-8	-1.4
1919	Phi A	0	1	.000	4	2	0	0	14.1	17	11	2	0	7	6	6.91	50	.309	.387	6-0	.000	-1	103	-4	-0.3
1920	Bos N	0	0	—	1	0	0	0	3	0	0	0	0	0	0	0.00	—	.000	.000	1-0	.000	-0		1	0.0
	Pit N	0	0	—	5	0	0	0	11.1	15	11	2	0	7	1	8.74	37	.326	.415	3-0	.000	-0		-6	-0.3

Year	Tm Lg	W	L	Pct	G	GS	CG-Sho	SV-BS	IP	H	R	HR	HB	BB-IB	SO	ERA	AERA	OAV	OOB	AB-SH	AVG	PB	Sup	APR	PW
	Bos N	5	4	.556	12	10	4-2	0	71.2	79	33	0	1	17	16	3.77	81	.298	.343	23-1	.130	-1	67	-4	-0.7
	Year	5	4	.556	18	10	4-2	0	86	94	36	2	1	24	17	4.29	72	.294	.345	27-1	.111	-2	67	-9	-1.0
1921	Bos N	14	13	.519	44	31	15-1	2	259.1	269	128	11	7	57	48	3.85	95	.270	.314	87-6	.138	-4	105	-6	-1.0
1922	Bos N	8	14	.364	41	27	8-1	1	201	262	140	9	5	59	53	4.70	85	.317	.366	66-3	.197	-0	79	-20	-1.8
1923	Bos N	1	2	.333	11	4	1	1	31.1	42	26	2	0	20	10	5.17	77	.339	.431	8-1	.250	-0	103	-6	-0.5
	†NY N	8	5	.615	17	15	8	0	108.1	117	43	11	1	21	26	3.41	112	.280	.316	46-1	.174	-1	92	7	0.6
	Year	9	7	.563	28	19	9	1	139.2	159	47	13	1	41	36	3.80	101	.293	.344	54-2	.185	-1	94	0	0.1
1924	†NY N	7	4	.636	22	16	6-1	0	99.2	122	54	7	1	24	18	3.79	97	.303	.343	35-0	.257	4	110	-4	-0.1
Total	7	50	53	.485	178	124	53-8	4	941.2	1062	520	44	17	256	208	4.03	89	.293	.342	322-13	.165	-8	95	-50	-5.5
WATSON, MARK Mark Bradford B 1.23.1974 Atlanta, GA BR/TL 6-4/215# d5.19																									
2000	Cle A	0	1	.000	6	0	0	0-0	6.1	12	7	0	1	2-0	4	8.53	58	.400	.455	0-0	—	0		-3	-0.4
2002	Sea A	1	0	1.000	3	0	0	0-0	4	8	8	1	0	4-0	1	18.00	24	.421	.500	0-0	—	0		-6	-1.0
2003	Cin N	0	0	—	2	0	0	0-0	2	2	1	0	0	1-0	2	4.50	95	.250	.333	0-0	—	0		0	0.0
Total	3	1	1	.500	11	0	0	0-0	12.1	22	16	1	1	7-0	7	10.95	42	.386	.455	0-0	—	0		-9	-1.4
WATSON, MILT Milton Wilson "Mule" B 1.10.1890 Flovilla, GA D 4.10.1962 Pine Bluff, AR BR/TR 6-1/180# d7.26																									
1916	StL N	4	6	.400	18	13	5-2	0	103	109	51	3	4	33	27	3.06	86	.283	.346	32-1	.219	0	83	-6	-0.6
1917	StL N	10	13	.435	41	20	5-3	0	161.1	149	74	3	9	51	45	3.51	77	.252	.321	51-0	.098	-4	74	-14	-2.3
1918	Phi N	5	7	.417	23	11	6	0	112.2	126	51	1	2	36	29	3.43	87	.293	.350	40-1	.075	-4	99	-4	-0.9
1919	Phi N	2	4	.333	8	4	3	0	47	51	30	2	2	19	12	5.17	62	.282	.356	16-0	.063	-2	74	-8	-1.1
Total	4	21	30	.412	90	48	19-5	0	424	435	206	9	17	139	113	3.57	79	.274	.339	139-2	.115	-9	82	-32	-4.9
WATSON, MOTHER Walter L. B 1.27.1865 Middleport, OH D 11.23.1898 Middleport, OH 5-9/145# d5.19																									
1887	Cin AA	0	1	.000	2	2	1	0	14	22	18	0	0	6	1	5.79	75	.328	.384	8	.125	-0	139	-3	-0.2
WATT, EDDIE Edward Dean B 4.4.1941 Lamoni, IA BR/TR 5-10/197# d4.12																									
1966	Bal A	9	7	.563	43	13	1	4	145.2	123	67	11	5	44-1	102	3.83	87	.230	.292	46-2	.304	6	126	-7	-0.3
1967	Bal A	3	5	.375	49	0	0	8	103.2	67	26	5	3	37-6	93	2.26	140	.183	.262	22-2	.182	2		12	1.3
1968	Bal A	5	5	.500	59	0	0	11	83.1	63	32	1	2	35-7	72	2.27	129	.209	.293	8-0	.000	-0		3	0.4
1969	†Bal A	5	2	.714	56	0	0	16-5	71	49	18	3	2	26-5	46	1.65	217	.194	.270	8-0	.000	-0		14	2.0
1970	†Bal A	7	7	.500	53	0	0	12-7	55.1	44	20	3	5	29-5	33	3.25	112	.239	.355	8-0	.125	-0		4	0.7
1971	†Bal A	3	1	.750	35	0	0	11-1	39.2	39	12	1	0	8-1	26	1.82	185	.260	.296	5-0	.000	-0		6	0.9
1972	Bal A	2	3	.400	38	0	0	7-3	45.2	30	12	2	2	20-6	23	2.17	142	.191	.286	2-0	.000	-0		5	0.7
1973	†Bal A	3	4	.429	30	0	0	5-2	71	62	26	8	2	21-5	38	3.30	113	.235	.296	0-0	—	0		5	0.5
1974	Phi N	1	1	.500	42	0	0	6-0	38.1	39	20	3	2	26-8	23	3.99	95	.275	.385	1-0	.000	-0		-1	-0.1
1975	Chi N	0	1	.000	6	0	0	0-1	6	14	11	0	1	8-4	6	13.50	29	.452	.575	0-0	—	0		-6	-0.9
Total	10	38	36	.514	411	13	1	80-19	659.2	530	244	37	24	254-48	462	2.91	116	.222	.301	100-4	.190	6	126	35	5.2
WATT, FRANK Frank Marion "Kilo" B 12.15.1902 Washington, DC D 8.31.1956 Washington, DC BR/TR 6-1/205# d4.14 b-Allie																									
1931	Phi N	5	5	.500	38	12	5	2	122.2	147	81	5	3	49	25	4.84	88	.296	.362	39-0	.205	0	101	-8	-0.7
WAUGH, JIM James Elden B 11.25.1933 Lancaster, OH BR/TR 6-3/185# d4.19																									
1952	Pit N	1	6	.143	17	7	1	0	52.1	61	43	4	2	32	18	6.36	63	.285	.383	10-1	.100	-0	86	-13	-1.6
1953	Pit N	4	5	.444	29	11	1	0	90.1	108	70	21	0	56	23	6.48	69	.295	.389	22-1	.227	0	94	-18	-1.5
Total	2	5	11	.313	46	18	2	0	142.2	169	113	25	2	88	41	6.43	67	.291	.387	32-2	.188	0	91	-31	-3.1
WAYENBERG, FRANK Frank B 8.27.1898 Franklin, KS D 4.16.1975 Zanesville, OH BR/TR 6-0.5/172# d8.25																									
1924	Cle A	0	0	—	2	1	0	0	6.2	7	4	0	1	5	3	5.40	79	.259	.394	2-0	.500	0	118	0	0.0
WAYNE, GARY Gary Anthony B 11.30.1962 Dearborn, MI BL/TL 6-3/192# d4.7																									
1989	Min A	3	4	.429	60	0	0	1-2	71	55	28	4	1	36-4	41	3.30	126	.212	.309	0-0	—	0		6	0.6
1990	Min A	1	1	.500	38	0	0	1-1	38.2	38	19	5	1	13-0	28	4.19	99	.255	.315	0-0	—	0		0	0.0
1991	Min A	1	0	1.000	8	0	0	1-0	12.1	11	7	1	1	4-0	7	5.11	84	.244	.314	0-0	—	0		-1	-0.1
1992	Min A	3	3	.500	41	0	0	0-3	48	46	18	2	3	19-5	29	2.63	155	.260	.337	0-0	—	0		6	0.8
1993	Col N	5	3	.625	65	0	0	1-2	62.1	68	40	8	1	26-8	49	5.05	94	.276	.339	1-0	1.000	0		-2	-0.2
1994	LA N	1	3	.250	19	0	0	0-2	17.1	19	13	2	3	6-2	10	4.67	84	.279	.359	1-0	.000	-0		-3	-0.6
Total	6	14	14	.500	231	0	0	4-10	249.2	237	125	22	10	104-19	164	3.93	109	.251	.327	2-0	.500	0		6	0.5
WAYNE, JUSTIN Justin Morgan B 4.16.1979 Honolulu, HI BR/TR 6-3/200# d9.3																									
2002	Fla N	2	3	.400	5	5	0	0-0	23.2	22	16	3	0	13-0	16	5.32	74	.244	.333	7-1	.000	-1	94	-4	-0.8
2003	Fla N	0	2	.000	2	2	0	0-0	5.1	9	7	1	1	5-0	1	11.81	35	.375	.484	2-0	.000	-0	34	-5	-0.7
Total	2	2	5	.286	7	7	0	0-0	29	31	23	4	1	18-0	17	6.52	61	.272	.368	9-1	.000	-1	77	-9	-1.5
WEAFER, KEN Kenneth Albert "Al" B 2.6.1914 Woburn, MA BR/TR 6-0.5/183# d5.29																									
1936	Bos N	0	0	—	1	0	0	0	3	6	4	1	0	3	0	12.00	32	.375	.474	1-0	.000	-0		-3	-0.1
WEATHERS, DAVID John David B 9.25.1969 Lawrenceburg, TN BR/TR 6-3/205# d8.2																									
1991	Tor A	1	0	1.000	15	0	0	0-0	14.2	15	9	1	2	17-3	13	4.91	86	.263	.442	0-0	—	0		-1	-0.1
1992	Tor A	0	0	—	2	0	0	0-0	3.1	5	3	1	0	2-0	3	8.10	50	.385	.467	0-0	—	0		-1	-0.1
1993	Fla N	2	3	.400	14	6	0	0-0	45.2	57	26	3	1	13-1	34	5.12	84	.306	.355	10-3	.100	-1	56	-3	-0.4
1994	Fla N	8	12	.400	24	24	0	0-0	135	166	87	13	4	59-9	72	5.27	83	.306	.376	44-4	.068	-2*	88	-12	-1.8
1995	Fla N	4	5	.444	28	15	0	0-0	90.1	104	68	8	5	52-3	60	5.98	71	.295	.391	26-5	.154	-1	124	-18	-1.7
1996	Fla N	2	2	.500	31	8	0	0-0	71.1	85	41	7	4	28-4	40	4.54	90	.302	.373	19-0	.158	1*	122	-4	-0.1
	†NY A	0	2	.000	11	4	0	0-0	17.1	23	19	1	2	14-1	13	9.35	53	.315	.433	0-0	—	0	155	-9	-0.8
1997	NY A	0	1	.000	10	0	0	0-1	9	15	10	1	0	7-0	4	10.00	45	.375	.468	0-0	—	0		-5	-0.5
	Cle A	1	2	.333	9	1	0	0-0	16.2	23	14	2	1	8-0	14	7.56	62	.343	.416	0-0	—	0	39	-5	-0.7
	Year	1	3	.250	19	1	0	0-1	25.2	38	16	3	1	15-0	18	8.42	55	.355	.435	0-0	—	0	40	-10	-1.2
1998	Cin N	2	4	.333	16	9	0	0-0	62.1	86	47	3	1	27-2	51	6.21	69	.330	.393	15-3	.067	0	117	-14	-1.1
	Mil N	4	1	.800	28	0	0	0-1	47.2	44	22	3	2	14-1	43	3.21	133	.246	.306	8-1	.125	-0		4	0.3
	Year	6	5	.545	44	9	0	0-1	110	130	74	6	3	41-3	94	4.91	87	.295	.358	23-4	.087	0	117	-10	-0.8
1999	Mil N	7	4	.636	63	0	0	2-4	93	102	49	14	2	38-3	74	4.65	98	.279	.346	7-0	.143	0		0	0.1
2000	Mil N	3	5	.375	69	0	0	1-6	76.1	73	29	7	2	32-8	50	3.07	149	.260	.339	1-0	.000	-0		13	1.1
2001	Mil N	3	4	.429	52	0	0	4-3	57.2	37	14	3	2	25-7	46	2.03	212	.188	.284	1-0	.000	0		15	1.8
	Chi N	1	1	.500	28	0	0	0-3	28.1	28	10	3	1	9-1	20	3.18	130	.269	.328	0-0	—	0		4	0.2
	Year	4	5	.444	80	0	0	4-6	86	65	24	6	3	34-8	66	2.41	176	.216	.299	1-0	.000	0		19	2.0
2002	NY N	6	3	.667	71	0	0	0-5	77.1	69	30	6	3	36-7	61	2.91	136	.245	.332	1-0	.000	-0		9	0.9
2003	NY N	1	6	.143	77	0	0	7-2	87.2	87	33	6	6	40-6	75	3.08	135	.264	.354	3-0	.000	-0		10	0.9
Total	13	45	55	.450	548	67	0	14-25	933.2	1019	511	82	38	421-56	673	4.49	96	.282	.361	135-16	.104	-3	106	-17	-2.0
WEAVER, FLOYD David Floyd B 5.12.1941 Ben Franklin, TX BR/TR 6-4/195# d9.30																									
1962	Cle A	1	0	1.000	1	1	0	0	5	3	1	1	0	0-0	8	1.80	215	.167	.167	2-0	.500	0	138	1	0.3
1965	Cle A	2	2	.500	32	1	0	1	61.1	61	40	10	5	24-3	37	5.43	64	.265	.344	11-0	.091	0	277	-12	-0.8
1970	Chi A	1	2	.333	31	3	0	0-0	61.2	52	33	7	2	31-5	51	4.38	89	.233	.328	7-1	.000	-1	114	-3	-0.3
1971	Mil A	0	1	.000	21	0	0	0-0	27.1	33	22	3	1	18-6	12	7.24	48	.320	.416	0-1	—	0		-10	-0.5
Total	4	4	5	.444	85	5	0	1-0	155.1	149	96	21	8	73-14	108	5.21	70	.260	.346	20-2	.100	-0	155	-24	-1.3
WEAVER, HARRY Harry Abraham B 2.26.1892 Clarendon, PA D 5.30.1983 Rochester, NY BR/TR 5-11/160# d9.18 Mil 1918																									
1915	Phi A	0	2	.000	2	2	2	0	18	18	10	1	1	10	1	3.00	98	.290	.397	6-0	.167	0	50	-1	0.0
1916	Phi A	0	0	—	3	0	0	0	8	14	10	0	0	5	2	10.13	28	.424	.500	2-0	.500	0		-6	-0.3
1917	Chi N	1	1	.500	4	2	1-1	0	19.2	17	10	0	0	7	8	2.75	106	.230	.296	5-0	.200	-0	39	0	0.0
1918	Chi N	2	2	.500	8	3	1-1	1	32.2	27	13	1	0	7	9	2.20	126	.227	.270	8-0	.250	-0	90	1	0.2
1919	Chi N	0	1	.000	2	1	0	0	3.1	6	7	0	1	2	1	10.80	27	.375	.474	1-0	.000	-0	28	-4	-0.7
Total	5	3	6	.333	19	8	4-2	1	81.2	82	50	2	2	31	21	3.64	79	.270	.341	22-0	.227	0	59	-10	-0.8

Year	Tm Lg	W	L	Pct	G	GS	CG-Sho	SV-BS	IP	H	R	HR	HB	BB-IB	SO	ERA	AERA	OAV	OOB	AB-SH	AVG	PB	Sup	APR	PW
WEAVER, JIM James Brian "Fluff" B 2.19.1939 Lancaster, PA BL/TL 6/178# d8.13																									
1967	Cal A	3	0	1.000	13	2	0	1	30.1	26	11	2	1	9-2	20	2.67	118	.232	.293	6-1	.000	-1	83	1	0.2
1968	Cal A	0	1	.000	14	0	0	0	22.2	22	7	4	0	10-2	8	2.38	122	.259	.337	1-0	.000	-0		1	0.0
Total 2		3	1	.750	27	2	0	1	53	48	18	6	1	19-4	28	2.55	119	.244	.312	7-1	.000	-1	83	2	0.2
WEAVER, JIM James Dement "Big Jim" B 11.25.1903 Obion County, TN D 12.12.1983 Lakeland, FL BR/TR 6-6/230# d8.27																									
1928	Was A	0	0	—	3	0	0	0	6	2	2	0	1	6	2	1.50	267	.143	.429	1-0	.000	-0		1	0.0
1931	NY A	2	1	.667	17	5	2	0	57.2	66	37	1	1	29	28	5.31	75	.280	.361	20-4	.050	-3	256	-8	-0.6
1934	StL A	2	0	1.000	5	5	2	0	19.2	17	14	3	0	20	11	6.41	78	.236	.402	7-0	.143	-0	122	-2	-0.1
	Chi N	11	9	.550	27	20	8-1	0	159	163	77	5	4	54	98	3.91	99	.263	.326	52-4	.058	-5	94	0	-0.6
1935	Pit N	14	8	.636	33	22	11-**4**	0	176.1	177	85	9	2	58	87	3.42	120	.254	.313	56-7	.071	-4	100	13	1.0
1936	Pit N	14	8	.636	38	31	11-1	0	225.2	239	125	12	1	74	108	4.31	94	.272	.329	79-6	.101	-5	111	-5	-1.0
1937	Pit N	8	5	.615	32	9	2-1	0	109.2	106	49	2	0	31	44	3.20	121	.255	.307	27-2	.148	-0	99	7	0.7
1938	StL A	0	1	.000	1	1	0	0	7	9	7	0	0	9	4	9.00	55	.321	.486	2-0	.000	-0	0	-3	-0.3
	Cin N	6	4	.600	30	15	2	3	129.1	109	58	6	1	54	64	3.13	117	.227	.306	44-4	.205	0	114	5	0.4
1939	Cin N	0	0	—	3	0	0	0	3	3	1	0	0	1	3	3.00	128	.250	.308	1-0	.000	-0		0	0.0
Total 8		57	36	.613	189	108	38-7	3	893.1	891	455	38	10	336	449	3.88	102	.258	.326	289-27	.104	-17	112	8	-0.5
WEAVER, ERIC James Eric B 8.4.1973 Springfield, IL BR/TR 6-5/230# d5.30																									
1998	LA N	2	0	1.000	7	0	0	0-0	9.2	5	1	1	0	6-0	5	0.93	426	.179	.324	1-0	.000	-0		4	0.7
1999	Sea A	0	1	.000	8	0	0	0-1	9.1	14	12	2	0	8-1	14	10.61	45	.318	.423	0-0	—	0		-6	-0.5
2000	Ana A	0	2	.000	17	0	0	0-1	18.1	20	16	5	0	16-1	8	6.87	74	.267	.391	0-0	—	0		-4	-0.3
Total 3		2	3	.400	32	0	0	0-2	37.1	39	29	8	0	30-2	27	6.27	75	.265	.388	1-0	.000	-0		-6	-0.1
WEAVER, JEFF Jeffrey Charles B 8.22.1976 Northridge, CA BR/TR 6-5/200# d4.14																									
1999	Det A	9	12	.429	30	29	0	0-0	163.2	176	104	27	17	56-2	114	5.55	89	.278	.350	4-1	.500	1*	91	-9	-0.9
2000	Det A	11	15	.423	31	30	2	0-0	200	205	102	26	15	52-2	136	4.32	112	.266	.322	3-0	.000	-0	82	13	1.4
2001	Det A	13	16	.448	33	33	5	0-0	229.1	235	116	19	14	68-4	152	4.08	107	.266	.326	5-1	.000	-0	94	6	0.7
2002	Det A	6	8	.429	17	17	3-3	0-0	121.2	112	50	4	8	33-1	75	3.18	136	.243	.304	7-0	.286	0	66	15	1.7
	†NY A	5	3	.625	15	8	0	2-0	78	81	38	12	3	15-3	57	4.04	108	.260	.300	0-0	—	0	133	3	0.3
	Year	11	11	.500	32	25	3-**3**	2-0	199.2	193	44	16	11	48-4	132	3.52	123	.250	.302	7-0	.286	0	87	18	2.0
2003	†NY A	7	9	.438	32	24	0	0-0	159.1	211	113	16	11	47-2	93	5.99	73	.320	.371	0-0	—	0	104	-28	-2.4
Total 5		51	63	.447	158	141	10-3	2-0	952	1020	523	104	68	271-14	627	4.59	99	.274	.332	19-2	.211	1	91	0	0.8
WEAVER, MONTE Montie Morton "Prof" B 6.15.1906 Helton, NC D 6.14.1994 Orlando, FL BL/TR 6/170# d9.20																									
1931	Was A	1	0	1.000	3	1	1	0	10	11	6	0	0	6	6	4.50	95	.268	.362	3-0	.000	-0	118	0	0.0
1932	Was A	22	10	.688	43	30	13-1	2	234	236	126	9	0	112	83	4.08	106	.261	.342	94-2	.287	6*	124	3	0.8
1933	†Was A	10	5	.667	23	21	12-1	0	152.1	147	57	3	1	53	45	3.25	129	.257	.322	56-1	.125	-3	107	18	1.2
1934	Was A	11	15	.423	31	31	11	0	204.2	255	127	16	0	63	51	4.79	90	.306	.355	80-4	.162	-2	103	-13	-1.7
1935	Was A	1	1	.500	5	2	0	0	12	16	8	1	0	6	4	5.25	82	.320	.393	3-0	.333	0	100	-1	-0.2
1936	Was A	6	4	.600	26	5	3	1	91	92	57	3	0	38	15	4.35	110	.262	.334	25-0	.200	1	122	2	0.2
1937	Was A	12	9	.571	30	26	9	0	188.2	197	102	21	0	70	44	4.20	105	.266	.330	68-4	.206	1	89	6	0.6
1938	Was A	7	6	.538	31	18	7	0	139	157	93	9	3	74	43	5.24	86	.282	.370	45-2	.267	4	114	-11	-0.5
1939	Bos A	1	0	1.000	9	1	1	1	20.1	26	15	0	1	13	6	6.64	71	.321	.421	4-0	.000	-1	149	-3	-0.3
Total 9		71	50	.587	201	135	57-2	4	1052	1137	591	62	5	435	297	4.36	101	.276	.345	378-13	.209	5	108	1	0.1
WEAVER, ORLIE Orville Forest B 6.4.1886 Newport, KY D 11.28.1970 New Orleans, LA BR/TR 6/180# d9.14																									
1910	Chi N	1	1	.500	7	2	2	0	32	34	17	2	1	15	22	3.66	79	.270	.352	13-0	.154	-1	90	-3	-0.3
1911	Chi N	2	2	.500	6	3	1-1	0	43.2	29	12	0	4	17	20	2.06	161	.196	.296	17-1	.059	-1	98	7	0.4
	Bos N	3	12	.200	27	17	4	0	121	140	102	9	7	84	50	6.47	59	.303	.418	41-1	.122	-2	84	-28	-3.2
	Year	5	14	.263	33	20	5-1	0	164.2	169	106	9	11	101	70	5.30	70	.277	.389	58-2	.103	-4	88	-23	-2.8
Total 2		6	15	.286	40	22	7-1	0	196.2	203	131	11	12	116	92	5.03	71	.276	.383	71-2	.113	-4	89	-24	-3.1
WEAVER, ROGER Roger Edward B 10.6.1954 Amsterdam, NY BR/TR 6-3/190# d6.6																									
1980	Det A	3	4	.429	19	6	0	0-0	63.2	56	32	5	1	34-3	42	4.10	101	.247	.342	0-0	—	0	87	0	0.0
WEAVER, SAM Samuel H. B 7.10.1855 Philadelphia, PA D 2.1.1914 Philadelphia, PA BR/TR 5-10/175# d10.25																									
1875	Phi NA	1	0	1.000	1	1	1	0	6	6	2	0		2	2	1.50	152	.240	.296	4	.250	0	263	1	0.1
1878	Mil N	12	31	.279	45	43	39-1	0	383	371	214	2		21	95	1.95	135	.237	**.247**	170	.200	-3*	66	**23**	2.1
1882	Phi AA	26	15	.634	42	41	41-2	0	371	374	182	6		35	104	2.74	102	.245	.262	155	.232	2*	96	8	0.9
1883	Lou AA	24	22	.522	46	46	45-4	0	400.2	451	261	3		35	105	3.71	81	.266	.281	193	.192	0*	110	-32	-2.9
1884	Phi U	5	10	.333	17	17	14	0	136	206	146	3		11	40	5.76	40	.328	.339	84	.214	-5*	116	-52	-4.4
1886	Phi AA	0	2	.000	2	2	1	0	11	30	29	0	1	2	2	14.73	24	.423	.446	7	.143	-1	25	-13	-1.4
Total 5		67	80	.456	152	149	140-7	0	1301.2	1432	832	14	1	104	346	3.22	87	.261	.275	609	.207	-6	92	-66	-5.7
WEBB, BRANDON Brandon Tyler B 5.9.1979 Ashland, KY BR/TR 6-3/190# d4.22																									
2003	Ari N	10	9	.526	29	28	1-1	0-0	180.2	140	65	12	13	68-4	172	2.84	165	.212	.298	50-7	.100	-2	93	33	3.1
WEBB, LEFTY Cleon Earl B 3.1.1885 Mt.Gilead, OH D 1.12.1958 Circleville, OH BB/TL 5-11/165# d5.23																									
1910	Pit N	2	1	.667	7	3	2	0	27	29	17	0	2	9	6	5.67	55	.266	.333	10-0	.200	-0	144	-5	-0.6
WEBB, HANK Henry Gaylon Matthew B 5.21.1950 Copiague, NY BR/TR 6-3/175# d9.5																									
1972	NY N	0	0	—	6	2	0	0-0	18.1	18	9	1	0	9-1	15	4.42	76	.261	.342	5-0	.000	-1	105	-2	-0.1
1973	NY N	0	0	—	2	0	0	0-0	1.2	2	2	1	0	2-0	1	10.80	34	.286	.444	0-0	—	0		-1	-0.1
1974	NY N	0	2	.000	3	2	0	0-0	10	15	9	1	1	10-0	8	7.20	50	.341	.473	3-0	.000	-0	85	-4	-0.7
1975	NY N	7	6	.538	29	15	3-1	0-0	115	102	58	12	1	62-4	38	4.07	85	.236	.331	31-0	.258	2*	86	-8	-0.7
1976	NY N	0	1	.000	8	0	0	0-1	16	17	9	2	2	7-0	7	4.50	73	.274	.366	1-0	.000	0		-2	-0.1
1977	LA N	0	0	—	5	0	0	0-0	8	5	2	1	1	1-0	2	2.25	170	.192	.250	0-0	—	0		2	0.1
Total 6		7	9	.438	53	19	3-1	0-1	169	159	89	18	5	91-5	71	4.31	80	.248	.345	40-0	.200	1	88	-15	-1.6
WEBB, RED Samuel Henry B 9.25.1924 Washington, DC D 2.7.1996 Hyattsville, MD BL/TR 6/175# d9.15																									
1948	NY N	2	1	.667	5	3	2	0	28	27	12	2	1	10	9	3.21	122	.248	.317	9-2	.222	0	120	2	0.2
1949	NY N	1	1	.500	20	0	0	0	44.2	41	23	3	0	21	9	4.03	99	.248	.333	10-0	.400	2		0	0.3
Total 2		3	2	.600	25	3	2	0	72.2	68	35	5	1	31	18	3.72	107	.248	.327	19-2	.316	2	120	2	0.5
WEBB, BILL Willie Fred B 12.12.1913 Atlanta, GA D 6.1.1994 Austell, GA BR/TR 6-2/180# d5.15																									
1943	Phi N	0	0	—	1	0	0	0	1	1	1	1	0	1	0	9.00	37	.333	.500	0-0	—	0		-1	0.0
WEBBER, LES Lester Elmer B 5.6.1915 Kelseyville, CA D 11.13.1986 Santa Maria, CA BR/TR 6-0.5/185# d5.17																									
1942	Bro N	3	2	.600	19	3	1	1	51.2	46	17	2	0	22	23	2.96	110	.230	.306	14-2	.071	-1	223	3	0.2
1943	Bro N	2	2	.500	54	0	0	**10**	115.2	112	54	6	5	69	24	3.81	88	.264	.373	25-1	.120	-1		-5	-0.3
1944	Bro N	7	8	.467	48	9	1	3	140.1	157	85	9	1	64	42	4.94	72	.282	.357	39-2	.205	1	89	-20	-1.7
1945	Bro N	7	3	.700	17	7	5	0	75.1	69	37	3	1	25	30	3.58	105	.237	.300	22-6	.091	-1	148	2	0.1
1946	Bro N	3	3	.500	11	4	0	0	43	34	11	5	0	15	16	2.30	147	.225	.295	10-1	.100	-1	63	6	0.7
	Cle A	1	1	.500	4	2	0	0	5.1	13	14	0	0	5	5	23.63	14	.464	.545	1-0	.000	0	91	-12	-1.9
1948	Cle A	0	0	—	1	0	0	0	0.2	3	3	0	0	1	1	40.50	10	.750	.800	0-0	—	0		-3	-0.1
Total 6		23	19	.548	154	25	7	14	432	434	221	25	7	201	141	4.19	83	.262	.345	111-12	.135	-2	119	-29	-3.0
WEBER, BEN Benjamin Edward B 11.17.1969 Port Arthur, TX BR/TR 6-4/185# d4.3																									
2000	SF N	0	1	.000	9	0	0	0-2	8	16	13	0	0	4-0	6	14.63	29	.400	.455	0-0	—	0		-9	-1.0
	Ana A	1	0	1.000	10	0	0	0-0	14.2	12	6	0	0	2-1	8	1.84	276	.214	.237	0-0	—	0		4	0.2
2001	Ana A	6	2	.750	56	0	0	0-1	68.1	66	28	4	5	31-8	40	3.42	133	.251	.341	0-0	—	0		9	0.9
2002	†Ana A	7	2	.778	63	0	0	7-4	78	70	25	4	3	22-3	43	2.54	175	.249	.308	0-0	—	0		16	1.9
2003	Ana A	5	1	.833	62	0	0	0-2	80.1	84	26	7	0	22-7	46	2.69	161	.275	.323	0-0	—	0		15	1.0
Total 4		19	6	.760	200	0	0	7-9	249.1	248	98	15	8	81-19	143	3.18	141	.262	.325	0-0	—	0		35	3.0

Year	Tm	Lg	W	L	Pct	G	GS	CG-Sho	SV-BS	IP	H	R	HR	HB	BB-IB	SO	ERA	AERA	OAV	OOB	AB-SH	AVG	PB	Sup	APR	PW
WEBER, CHARLIE Charles P. "Count" B 10.22.1868 Cincinnati, OH D 6.13.1914 Beaumont, TX TR d7.30																										
1898	Was	N	0	1	.000	1	1	0	0	4	9	9	0	2	1	0	15.75	23	.450	.522	2-0	.000	-0	58	-5	-0.7
WEBER, NEIL Neil Aaron B 12.6.1972 Newport Beach, CA BL/TL 6-5/215# d9.11																										
1998	Ari	N	0	0	—	4	0	0	0-0	2.1	5	3	0	0	3-0	4	11.57	36	.417	.533	0-0	—	0		-2	-0.1
WEGENER, MIKE Michael Denis B 10.8.1946 Denver, CO BR/TR 6-4/215# d4.9																										
1969	Mon	N	5	14	.263	32	26	4-1	0-1	165.2	150	92	10	4	96-6	124	4.40	84	.243	.347	54-3	.241	2	91	-12	-1.0
1970	Mon	N	3	6	.333	25	16	1	0-0	104.1	100	70	16	4	56-3	35	5.26	78	.252	.349	34-1	.118	-2	86	-14	-1.2
Total	2		8	20	.286	57	42	5-1	0-1	270	250	162	26	8	152-9	159	4.73	81	.247	.347	88-4	.193	0	89	-26	-2.2
WEGMAN, BILL William Edward B 12.19.1962 Cincinnati, OH BR/TR 6-5/220# d9.14																										
1985	Mil	A	2	0	1.000	3	3	0	0-0	17.2	17	8	3	0	3-0	6	3.57	117	.246	.274	0-0	—	0	167	1	0.1
1986	Mil	A	5	12	.294	35	32	2	0-0	198.1	217	120	32	7	43-2	82	5.13	85	.279	.321	0-0	—	0*	84	-13	-1.0
1987	Mil	A	12	11	.522	34	33	7	0-1	225	229	113	31	6	53-2	102	4.24	108	.265	.310	0-0	—	0	101	9	0.8
1988	Mil	A	13	13	.500	32	31	4-1	0-0	199	207	104	24	4	50-5	84	4.12	97	.265	.309	0-0	—	0*	92	-4	-0.5
1989	Mil	A	2	6	.250	11	8	0	0-1	51	69	44	6	0	21-2	27	6.71	57	.321	.375	0-0	—	0	97	-17	-2.2
1990	Mil	A	2	2	.500	8	5	1-1	0-0	29.2	37	21	6	0	6-1	20	4.85	80	.298	.328	0-0	—	0	122	-4	-0.5
1991	Mil	A	15	7	.682	28	28	7-2	0-0	193.1	176	76	16	7	40-0	89	2.84	140	.242	.286	0-0	—	0	115	21	2.4
1992	Mil	A	13	14	.481	35	35	7	0-0	261.2	251	104	28	9	55-3	127	3.20	120	.250	.294	0-0	—	0	102	18	1.9
1993	Mil	A	4	14	.222	20	18	5	0-0	120.2	135	70	13	2	34-5	50	4.48	95	.291	.335	0-0	—	0	66	-5	-0.5
1994	Mil	A	8	4	.667	19	19	0	0-0	115.2	140	64	14	2	26-0	59	4.51	112	.303	.339	0-0	—	0	115	6	0.6
1995	Mil	A	5	7	.417	37	4	0	2-1	70.2	89	45	14	3	21-2	50	5.35	93	.312	.363	0-0	—	0*	56	-2	-0.4
Total	11		81	90	.474	262	216	33-4	2-3	1482.2	1567	769	187	40	352-22	696	4.16	102	.271	.315	0-0	—	0	98	10	0.7
WEHDE, BIGGS Wilbur B 11.23.1906 Holstein, IA D 9.21.1970 Sioux Falls, SD BR/TR 5-10.5/180# d9.15																										
1930	Chi	A	0	0	—	4	0	0	0	6.1	7	8	1	1	7	3	9.95	46	.304	.484	1-0	.000	-0		-3	-0.1
1931	Chi	A	1	0	1.000	8	0	0	0	16	19	12	0	2	10	3	6.75	63	.333	.449	3-0	.000	-0		-4	-0.2
Total	2		1	0	1.000	12	0	0	0	22.1	26	20	1	3	17	6	7.66	57	.325	.460	4-0	.000	-1		-7	-0.3
WEHMEIER, HERM Herman Ralph B 2.18.1927 Cincinnati, OH D 5.21.1973 Dallas, TX BR/TR 6-2/200# d9.7																										
1945	Cin	N	0	1	.000	2	2	0	0	5	10	7	0	0	4	0	12.60	30	.435	.519	1-0	.000	-0*	124	-5	-0.7
1947	Cin	N	0	0	—	1	0	0	0	1	0	0	0	0	0	0	0.00	—	.000	.000	0-0	—	0		0	0.0
1948	Cin	N	11	8	.579	33	24	6	0	147.1	179	105	21	2	75	56	5.86	67	.299	.379	55-3	.091	-3*	113	-31	-3.7
1949	Cin	N	11	12	.478	33	29	11-1	0	213.1	202	119	20	7	117	80	4.68	89	.253	.353	78-5	.256	2*	98	-8	-0.7
1950	Cin	N	10	18	.357	41	32	12	4	230	255	157	27	4	135	121	5.67	75	.281	.376	92-1	.152	-3*	97	-33	-3.9
1951	Cin	N	7	10	.412	39	22	10-2	2	184.2	167	82	15	4	89	93	3.70	110	.241	.330	59-2	.288	3*	79	10	1.1
1952	Cin	N	9	11	.450	33	26	6-1	0	190.1	197	115	23	7	103	83	5.15	73	.269	.365	64-2	.188	2*	99	-27	-2.6
1953	Cin	N	1	6	.143	28	10	2	0	81.2	100	71	20	0	47	32	7.16	61	.299	.385	20-0	.200	-0*	82	-24	-1.8
1954	Cin	N	0	3	.000	12	3	0	2	33.2	36	29	6	1	21	13	6.68	63	.271	.372	9-1	.000	-1*	57	-10	-0.9
	Phi	N	10	8	.556	25	17	10-2	0	138	117	61	10	1	51	49	3.85	105	.231	.300	50-5	.120	-2	90	5	0.4
	Year		10	11	.476	37	20	10-2	2	171.2	153	65	16	2	72	62	4.40	92	.239	.316	59-6	.102	-3	84	-5	-0.5
1955	Phi	N	10	12	.455	31	29	10-1	0	193.2	176	101	21	2	67-7	85	4.41	90	.241	.304	72-3	.278	4*	104	-7	-0.4
1956	Phi	N	0	2	.000	3	3	0	0	20	18	9	2	0	11-0	8	4.05	92	.240	.333	8-0	.000	-1	39	0	-0.2
	StL	N	12	9	.571	34	19	7-2	1	170.2	150	80	16	1	71-8	68	3.69	102	.240	.315	58-1	.224	4*	78	2	0.6
	Year		12	11	.522	37	22	7-2	1	190.2	168	83	18	1	82-8	76	3.73	101	.240	.317	66-1	.197	3	73	0	0.4
1957	StL	N	10	7	.588	36	18	5	0	165	165	91	25	2	54-7	91	4.31	92	.253	.311	59-0	.203	0*	125	-7	-0.7
1958	StL	N	0	1	.000	3	3	0	0	6	13	9	2	0	2-0	4	13.50	31	.448	.484	2-0	.500	1	102	-6	-0.7
	Det	A	1	0	1.000	7	3	0	0	22.2	21	8	2	0	5-0	11	2.38	169	.241	.280	6-0	.000	-1	67	3	0.1
Total	13		92	108	.460	361	240	79-9	9	1803	1806	1044	210	31	852-22	794	4.80	84	.260	.343	633-23	.196	5	96	-138	-14.1
WEHRMEISTER, DAVE David Thomas B 11.9.1952 Berwyn, IL BR/TR 6-4/195# d4.16																										
1976	SD	N	0	4	.000	7	4	0	0-0	19.1	27	17	0	0	11-1	10	7.45	44	.333	.409	6-0	.000	-1	74	-9	-1.6
1977	SD	N	1	3	.250	30	6	0	0-0	69.2	81	53	8	3	44-4	32	6.07	58	.293	.393	12-2	.167	0	163	-21	-1.1
1978	SD	N	1	0	1.000	4	0	0	0-0	7.1	8	5	1	0	5-1	2	6.14	54	.276	.382	0-1	—	0		-2	-0.3
1981	NY	A	0	0	—	5	0	0	0-0	7	6	4	0	0	7-2	7	5.14	70	.240	.394	0-0	—	0		-1	0.0
1984	Phi	N	0	0	—	7	0	0	0-0	15	18	12	1	1	7-2	13	7.20	51	.300	.371	2-0	.000	-0		-5	-0.3
1985	Chi	A	2	2	.500	23	0	0	2-2	39.1	35	15	4	3	10-0	32	3.43	126	.241	.304	0-0	—	0		4	0.4
Total	6		4	9	.308	76	10	0	2-2	157.2	175	106	14	7	84-10	96	5.65	65	.284	.373	20-3	.100	-1	121	-34	-2.9
WEIK, DICK Richard Henry "Legs" B 11.17.1927 Waterloo, IA D 4.21.1991 Harvey, IL BR/TR 6-3.5/184# d9.8 Mil 1951																										
1948	Was	A	1	2	.333	3	3	0	0	12.2	14	8	1	0	22	8	5.68	76	.311	.537	4-0	.750	2	69	-1	-0.1
1949	Was	A	3	12	.200	27	14	2-2	1	95.1	78	61	5	0	103	58	5.38	79	.230	.410	28-2	.179	-1*	56	-10	-1.4
1950	Was	A	1	3	.250	14	5	1	0	44	38	27	2	0	47	26	4.30	105	.236	.409	13-0	.154	-1	60	0	-0.1
	Cle	A	1	3	.250	11	2	0	0	26	18	17	1	1	26	16	3.81	114	.205	.391	5-0	.200	0	83	0	0.0
	Year		2	6	.250	25	7	1	0	70	56	21	3	1	73	42	4.11	108	.225	.402	18-0	.167	-1	67	-1	-0.1
1953	Det	A	0	1	.000	12	1	0	0	19.1	32	30	3	0	23	6	13.97	29	.386	.519	2-1	.500	1	218	-19	-0.9
1954	Det	A	0	1	.000	9	1	0	0	16.1	23	14	3	1	16	9	7.16	52	.354	.482	1-0	.000	-0	382	-6	-0.4
Total	5		6	22	.214	76	26	3-2	1	213.2	203	157	15	2	237	123	5.90	72	.260	.433	53-3	.226	1	78	-36	-2.9
WEILAND, ED Edwin Nicholas B 11.26.1914 Evanston, IL D 7.12.1971 Chicago, IL BL/TR 5-11/180# d5.1 Mil 1943-45 b-Bob																										
1940	Chi	A	0	0	—	5	0	0	0	14.1	15	15	5	0	7	3	8.79	50	.263	.344	5-0	.200	-0		-6	-0.3
1942	Chi	A	0	0	—	5	0	0	0	9.2	18	11	0	0	3	4	7.45	48	.383	.420	2-0	.000	-0		-5	-0.3
Total	2		0	0	—	10	0	0	0	24	33	26	5	0	10	7	8.25	50	.317	.377	7-0	.143	-0		-11	-0.6
WEILAND, BOB Robert George "Lefty" B 12.14.1905 Chicago, IL D 11.9.1988 Chicago, IL BL/TL 6-4/215# d9.30 b-Ed																										
1928	Chi	A	1	0	1.000	1	1	1-1	0	9	7	0	0	1	5	9	0.00	—	.212	.333	3-0	.333	0	21	4	0.5
1929	Chi	A	2	4	.333	15	9	1	1	62	62	42	3	3	43	25	5.81	74	.268	.390	18-1	.111	-1	101	-8	-0.8
1930	Chi	A	0	4	.000	14	3	0	0	32.2	38	31	1	2	21	15	6.61	70	.297	.404	8-0	.000	-1	43	-8	-0.9
1931	Chi	A	2	7	.222	15	8	3	0	75	75	55	3	4	46	38	5.16	83	.259	.368	22-0	.182	1	92	-9	-0.7
1932	Bos	A	6	16	.273	43	27	7	1	195.2	231	125	11	6	97	63	4.51	100	.295	.377	61-2	.148	-1	75	-3	-0.2
1933	Bos	A	8	14	.364	39	27	12	3	216.1	197	107	19	5	100	97	3.87	113	.244	.331	65-6	.108	-4	65	13	0.7
1934	Bos	A	1	5	.167	11	7	2	0	55.2	63	41	4	0	27	29	5.50	87	.293	.372	19-0	.105	-1	88	-4	-0.5
	Cle	A	1	5	.167	16	7	2	0	70	71	41	5	0	30	42	4.11	111	.262	.336	24-1	.125	-0	57	2	0.1
	Year		2	10	.167	27	14	4	0	125.2	134	44	9	0	57	71	4.73	99	.276	.352	43-1	.116	-1	73	-4	-0.4
1935	StL	A	0	2	.000	14	4	0	0	32	39	35	6	1	31	11	9.56	50	.298	.436	8-1	.000	-1	100	-14	-0.8
1937	StL	N	15	14	.517	41	**34**	21-2	0	264.1	283	127	14	5	94	105	3.54	112	.276	.339	89-5	.169	0	106	11	1.1
1938	StL	N	16	11	.593	35	29	11-1	1	228.1	248	118	14	4	67	117	3.59	110	.272	.324	80-10	.138	-3	112	6	0.3
1939	StL	N	10	12	.455	32	23	6-3	1	146.1	146	69	4	6	50	63	3.57	115	.264	.331	46-6	.065	-4	103	7	0.5
1940	StL	N	0	0	—	1	0	0	0	1	3	3	1	0	0	0	27.00	15	.600	.600	0-0	—	0		-2	-0.1
Total	12		62	94	.397	277	179	66-7	7	1388.1	1463	794	85	37	611	614	4.24	100	.272	.350	443-32	.129	-16	90	-5	-0.8
WEILMAN, CARL Carl Woolworth "Zeke" (b: Carl Woolworth Weilenmann) B 11.29.1889 Hamilton, OH D 5.25.1924 Hamilton, OH BL/TL 6-5.5/187# d8.24																										
1912	StL	A	2	4	.333	8	6	5-2	1	48.1	42	19	0	0	3	24	2.79	119	.227	.239	17-1	.118	-1*	100	3	0.4
1913	StL	A	10	19	.345	39	28	17-2	0	251.2	262	122	2	4	60	79	3.40	86	.283	.330	82-2	.146	-3	82	-10	-1.4
1914	StL	A	17	12	.586	44	36	20-3	1	299	260	96	1	11	84	119	2.08	130	.237	.298	101-2	.149	-1	92	21	2.0
1915	StL	A	18	19	.486	47	31	19-3	4	295.2	240	110	6	3	83	125	2.34	122	.229	.287	100-3	.230	2	79	17	2.4
1916	StL	A	17	18	.486	46	31	19-1	2	276	237	90	3	8	76	91	2.15	128	.242	.301	91-4	.154	-1	106	17	2.0
1917	StL	A	1	2	.333	5	3	0	0	19	19	9	1	0	6	9	1.89	137	.268	.325	4-0	.000	-1	74	0	0.0
1919	StL	A	10	6	.625	20	20	12-3	0	148	133	51	3	3	45	44	2.07	160	.244	.305	47-4	.191	0	118	17	1.9
1920	StL	A	9	13	.409	30	24	13-1	2	183.1	201	103	6	3	61	45	4.47	88	.291	.351	63-4	.175	-2	109	-7	-0.9
Total	8		84	93	.475	239	179	105-15	10	1521	1394	600	22	32	418	536	2.67	112	.251	.308	505-20	.170	-7	97	58	6.4
WEIMER, JAKE Jacob "Tornado Jake" B 11.29.1873 Ottumwa, IA D 6.19.1928 Chicago, IL BR/TL 5-11/175# d4.17																										
1903	Chi	N	20	8	.714	35	33	27-3	0	282	241	111	4	11	104	128	2.30	136	**.225**	.301	107-1	.196	2	116	28	2.6

Year	Tm Lg	W	L	Pct	G	GS	CG-Sho	SV-BS	IP	H	R	HR	HB	BB-IB	SO	ERA	AERA	OAV	OOB	AB-SH	AVG	PB	Sup	APR	PW
1904	Chi N	20	14	.588	37	37	31-5	0	307	229	96	1	7	97	177	1.91	140	.204	.272	115-2	.183	-1	102	26	2.8
1905	Chi N	18	12	.600	33	30	26-2	1	250.1	212	84	1	12	80	107	2.26	132	.229	.299	92-1	.207	2	130	21	2.5
1906	Cin N	20	14	.588	41	39	31-6	1	304.2	263	105	0	13	99	141	2.22	124	.236	.306	108-2	.269	6	94	18	2.8
1907	Cin N	11	14	.440	29	26	19-3	0	209	165	73	6	23	63	67	2.41	108	.226	.308	72-4	.194	2*	88	6	1.1
1908	Cin N	8	7	.533	15	15	9-2	0	116.2	110	38	2	6	50	36	2.39	96	.255	.341	45-2	.244	2	136	1	0.5
1909	NY N	0	0	—	1	0	0	0	3	7	4	0	1	0	1	9.00	28	.467	.500	1-0	.000	-0		-2	-0.1
Total	7	97	69	.584	191	180	143-21	2	1472.2	1227	511	14	73	493	657	2.23	125	.227	.300	540-12	.213	11	108	98	12.2
WEINERT, LEFTY Phillip Walter B 4.21.1902 Philadelphia, PA D 4.17.1973 Rockledge, FL BL/TL 6-1/195# d9.24																									
1919	Phi N	0	0	—	1	0	0	0	4	11	9	0	0	2	0	18.00	18	.478	.520	2-0	1.000	1		-6	-0.2
1920	Phi N	1	1	.500	10	2	0	0	22	27	17	1	1	19	10	6.14	56	.333	.465	5-0	.000	-1	127	-5	-0.5
1921	Phi N	1	0	1.000	8	0	0	0	12.1	8	6	1	1	5	2	1.46	290	.216	.326	1-0	1.000	0		2	0.2
1922	Phi N	8	11	.421	34	22	10	1	166.2	189	103	10	5	70	58	3.40	137	.289	.362	58-1	.241	-0	82	13	1.3
1923	Phi N	4	17	.190	38	20	8	1	156	207	131	10	8	81	46	5.42	85	.327	.410	59-0	.322	2*	76	-18	-1.9
1924	Phi N	0	1	.000	8	1	0	0	14.2	10	7	0	0	11	7	2.45	182	.204	.350	4-0	.000	-1	38	2	0.1
1927	Chi N	1	1	.500	5	3	1	0	19.2	21	13	2	0	6	5	4.58	84	.259	.310	5-0	.200	0	118	-2	-0.2
1928	Chi N	1	0	1.000	10	1	0	0	17	24	10	0	1	9	8	5.29	73	.393	.479	2-0	.000	-0	154	-2	-0.2
1931	NY A	2	2	.500	17	0	0	0	24.2	31	19	2	5	19	24	6.20	64	.316	.451	6-0	.000	-0		-6	-0.9
Total	9	18	33	.353	131	49	19	2	437	528	315	26	21	222	160	4.59	97	.308	.393	142-1	.261	2	85	-22	-2.3
WEIR, ROY William Franklin "Bill" B 2.25.1911 Portland, ME D 9.30.1989 Anaheim, CA BL/TL 5-8.5/170# d6.25																									
1936	Bos N	4	3	.571	12	7	3-2	0	57.1	53	23	0	0	24	29	2.83	136	.241	.316	18-1	.278	2*	63	6	0.9
1937	Bos N	1	1	.500	10	4	1	0	33	27	18	0	0	19	8	3.82	94	.227	.333	10-0	.000	-1	138	-2	-0.2
1938	Bos N	1	0	1.000	5	0	0	0	13.1	14	10	4	0	6	3	6.75	51	.269	.345	3-0	.333	0		-5	-0.3
1939	Bos N	0	0	—	2	0	0	0	2.2	1	0	0	0	1	2	0.00	—	.125	.222	1-0	.000	-0		1	0.1
Total	4	6	4	.600	29	11	4-2	0	106.1	95	51	4	0	50	42	3.55	104	.238	.323	32-1	.188	1	90	0	0.5
WELCH, TED Floyd John B 10.17.1892 Coyville, KS D 1.7.1943 Great Bend, KS BL/TR 5-9.5/160# d5.15																									
1914	StL F	0	0	—	3	0	0	0	6	6	4	0	3	3	2	6.00	51	.273	.429	1-0	.000	-0		-1	-0.1
WELCH, JOHNNY John Vernon B 12.2.1906 Washington, DC D 9.2.1940 St.Louis, MO BL/TR 6-3/184# d5.22																									
1926	Chi N	0	0	—	3	0	0	0	4.1	5	2	0	0	1	0	2.08	185	.357	.400	1-0	1.000	0		1	0.1
1927	Chi N	0	0	—	1	0	0	0	1	0	1	0	0	3	1	9.00	43	.000	.500	0-0	—	0		-1	0.0
1928	Chi N	0	0	—	3	0	0	0	4	13	7	0	0	0	2	15.75	24	.591	.591	0-0	—	0		-5	-0.2
1931	Chi N	2	1	.667	8	3	1	0	33.2	39	16	2	1	10	7	3.74	103	.291	.345	12-0	.417	2	148	1	0.2
1932	Bos A	4	6	.400	20	8	3-1	0	72.1	93	46	3	3	38	26	5.23	86	.312	.395	36-1	.250	2*	66	-4	-0.3
1933	Bos A	4	9	.308	47	7	1	3	129	142	81	6	2	67	68	4.60	95	.283	.370	37-2	.162	-1	97	-4	-0.5
1934	Bos A	13	15	.464	41	22	8-1	0	206.1	223	112	14	8	76	91	4.49	107	.274	.342	74-6	.203	-1	110	11	1.1
1935	Bos A	10	9	.526	31	19	10-1	2	143	155	82	4	4	53	48	4.47	106	.273	.339	50-2	.180	-0	96	5	0.6
1936	Bos A	2	1	.667	9	3	1	0	32.2	43	24	4	0	8	9	5.51	96	.305	.342	11-0	.273	1	127	-1	0.0
	Pit N	0	0	—	9	1	0	1	22	22	12	3	0	6	5	4.50	90	.265	.315	7-0	.286	1	146	-1	0.0
Total	9	35	41	.461	172	63	24-3	6	648.1	735	383	36	18	262	257	4.66	99	.285	.355	228-11	.219	3	103	2	1.0
WELCH, MICKEY Michael Francis "Smiling Mickey" (b: Michael Francis Walsh) B 7.4.1859 Brooklyn, NY D 7.30.1941 Concord, NH BR/TR 5-8/160# d5.1 HF1973																									
1880	Tro N	34	30	.531	65	64	64-4	0	574	575	321	7		80	123	2.54	99	.249	.274	251	.287	10*	96	-2	0.5
1881	Tro N	21	18	.538	40	40	40-4	0	368	371	186	7		78	104	2.67	111	.255	.293	148	.203	-4	86	10	0.3
1882	Tro N	14	16	.467	33	33	30-5	0	281	334	221	7		62	53	3.46	82	.280	.315	151	.245	1*	96	-22	-1.8
1883	NY N	25	23	.521	54	52	46-4	0	426	431	271	11		66	144	2.73	114	.244	.272	320	.234	3*	97	16	1.4
1884	NY N	39	21	.650	65	65	62-4	0	557.1	528	275	12		146	345	2.50	119	.237	.284	249	.241	9*	106	29	3.2
1885	NY N	44	11	**.800**	56	55	55-7	1	492	372	170	4		131	258	1.66	160	.203	.256	199	.206	5	127	60	6.0
1886	NY N	33	22	.600	59	59	56-1	0	500	514	279	13		163	272	2.99	107	.259	.315	213	.216	1	94	10	0.7
1887	NY N	22	15	.595	41	40	39-2	0	346	339	191	7	5	91	115	3.36	112	.253	.303	148	.243	4	94	23	2.1
1888	†NY N	26	19	.578	47	47	47-5	0	425.1	328	156	12	14	108	167	1.93	142	.207	.263	169	.189	1	97	42	3.9
1889	†NY N	27	12	.692	45	41	39-3	2	375	340	196	14	10	149	125	3.02	130	.234	.310	156	.192	-2	120	41	3.1
1890	NY N	17	14	.548	37	37	33-2	0	292.1	268	145	5	12	122	97	2.99	117	.236	.317	123	.179	-3	85	24	1.6
1891	NY N	5	9	.357	22	15	14	1	160	177	136	7	11	97	46	4.27	75	.270	.373	71	.141	-4	92	-20	-1.9
1892	NY N	0	0	—	1	1	0	0	5	11	9	0	0	4	1	14.40	22	.423	.500	3	.333	0	177	-5	-0.2
Total	13	307	210	.594	565	549	525-41	4	4802	4588	2556	106	52	1297	1850	2.71	113	.242	.292	2201	.224	21	100	206	18.9
WELCH, MIKE Michael Paul B 8.25.1972 Haverhill, MA BL/TR 6-2/210# d7.17																									
1998	Phi N	0	2	.000	10	2	0	0-0	20.2	26	19	7	2	7-0	15	8.27	52	.310	.376	3-0	.000	-0	32	-8	-0.7
WELCH, BOB Robert Lynn B 11.3.1956 Detroit, MI BR/TR 6-3/190# d6.20 C1																									
1978	†LA N	7	4	.636	23	13	4-3	3-0	111.1	92	28	6	1	26-2	66	2.02	174	.229	.274	29-6	.172	0	102	19	1.9
1979	LA N	5	6	.455	25	12	1	5-4	81.1	82	42	7	3	32-4	64	3.98	91	.265	.339	19-3	.158	-0	89	-3	-0.5
1980	LA N★	14	9	.609	32	32	3-2	0-0	213.2	190	85	15	3	79-6	141	3.29	107	.242	.310	70-5	.243	3*	97	6	0.9
1981	†LA N	9	5	.643	23	23	2-1	0-0	141.1	141	56	11	3	41-0	88	3.44	97	.259	.313	45-7	.222	2	130	-1	0.0
1982	LA N	16	11	.593	36	36	9-3	0-0	235.2	199	94	19	5	81-5	176	3.36	103	.229	.297	85-7	.141	-1*	115	6	0.4
1983	†LA N	15	12	.556	31	31	4-3	0-0	204	164	73	13	3	72-4	156	2.65	136	.222	.291	73-3	.096	-2	78	22	2.5
1984	LA N	13	13	.500	31	29	3-1	0-1	178.2	191	86	11	2	58-7	126	3.78	94	.273	.330	51-8	.078	-3*	92	-4	-0.8
1985	†LA N	14	4	.778	23	23	8-3	0-0	167.1	141	49	16	6	35-2	96	2.31	151	.225	.272	50-7	.180	1*	118	23	2.7
1986	LA N	7	13	.350	33	33	7-3	0-0	235.2	227	95	14	7	55-6	183	3.28	105	.251	.297	76-5	.105	-0*	84	5	0.3
1987	LA N	15	9	.625	35	35	6-**4**	0-0	251.2	204	94	21	4	86-6	196	3.22	123	.221	.289	83-8	.157	1*	107	25	2.4
1988	†Oak A	17	9	.654	36	36	4-2	0-0	244.2	237	107	22	10	81-1	158	3.64	104	.257	.321	0-0	—	0	111	5	0.4
1989	†Oak A	17	8	.680	33	33	1	0-0	209.2	191	82	13	6	78-3	137	3.00	123	.241	.312	0-0	—	0	112	16	1.8
1990	†Oak A★	**27**	6	**.818**	35	35	2-2	0-0	238	214	90	26	5	77-4	127	2.95	126	.242	.304	0-0	—	0	123	20	2.6
1991	Oak A	12	13	.480	35	**35**	7-1	0-0	220	220	124	25	11	91-3	101	4.58	84	.263	.341	0-0	—	0*	103	-22	-2.2
1992	†Oak A	11	7	.611	20	20	0	0-0	123.2	114	47	13	2	43-0	47	3.27	115	.247	.312	0-0	—	0	110	9	1.1
1993	Oak A	9	11	.450	30	28	0	0-0	166.2	208	102	25	7	56-5	63	5.29	77	.310	.368	0-0	—	0	85	-22	-2.2
1994	Oak A	3	6	.333	25	8	0	0-1	68.2	79	56	10	1	43-2	44	7.08	63	.290	.384	1-0	.000	-0*	112	-20	-2.2
Total	17	211	146	.591	506	462	61-28	8-6	3092	2894	1310	267	79	1034-60	1969	3.47	106	.249	.312	582-59	.151	2	104	84	9.1
WELCHEL, DON Donald Ray B 2.3.1957 Atlanta, TX BR/TR 6-4/205# d9.15																									
1982	Bal A	1	0	1.000	2	0	0	0-0	4.1	6	6	0	0	2-0	3	8.31	49	.300	.364	0-0	—	0		-3	-0.5
1983	Bal A	0	2	.000	11	0	0	0-0	26.2	33	18	1	0	10-1	16	5.40	73	.297	.352	0-0	—	0		-4	-0.3
Total	2	1	2	.333	13	0	0	0-0	31	39	24	1	0	12-1	19	5.81	69	.298	.354	0-0	—	0		-7	-0.8
WELLEMEYER, TODD Todd Allen B 8.30.1978 Louisville, KY BR/TR 6-3/200# d5.15																									
2003	Chi N	1	1	.500	15	0	0	1-0	27.2	25	22	5	0	19-1	30	6.51	65	.245	.364	1-1	.000	0		-7	-0.5
WELLS, DAVID David Lee "Boomer" B 5.20.1963 Torrance, CA BL/TL 6-4/225# d6.30																									
1987	Tor A	4	3	.571	18	2	0	1-1	29.1	37	14	0	0	12-0	32	3.99	113	.311	.374	0-0	—	0	10	2	0.3
1988	Tor A	3	5	.375	41	0	0	4-2	64.1	65	36	12	2	31-9	56	4.62	85	.269	.354	0-0	—	0		-5	-0.6
1989	†Tor A	7	4	.636	54	0	0	2-7	86.1	66	25	5	0	28-7	78	2.40	158	.207	.269	0-0	—	0		14	1.7
1990	Tor A	11	6	.647	43	25	0	3-0	189	165	72	14	2	45-3	115	3.14	126	.235	.283	0-0	—	0	110	16	1.5
1991	†Tor A	15	10	.600	40	28	2	1-1	198.1	188	88	24	2	49-1	106	3.72	113	.251	.297	0-0	—	0	94	11	1.4
1992	†Tor A	7	9	.438	41	14	0	2-2	120	138	84	16	8	36-6	62	5.40	76	.289	.346	0-0	—	0	101	-19	-2.3
1993	Det A	11	9	.550	32	30	0	0-0	187	183	93	26	7	42-6	139	4.19	103	.254	.300	0-0	—	0	106	4	0.4
1994	Det A	5	7	.417	16	16	5-1	0-0	111.1	113	54	13	2	24-6	71	3.96	122	.260	.302	0-0	—	0	98	11	1.0
1995	Det A★	10	3	.769	18	18	3	0-0	130.1	120	54	17	2	37-5	83	3.04	157	.242	.297	0-0	—	0	95	22	1.9
	†Cin N	6	5	.545	11	11	3	0-0	72.2	74	34	6	0	16-4	50	3.59	115	.265	.304	28-1	.143	-1	104	3	0.3
1996	†Bal A	11	14	.440	34	34	3	0-0	224.1	247	132	32	7	51-7	130	5.14	96	.285	.325	0-0	—	0	100	-3	-0.1
1997	†NY A	16	10	.615	32	32	5-2	0-0	218	239	109	24	6	45-0	156	4.21	106	.278	.317	0-0	—	0	95	7	0.8
1998	†NY A★	18	4	**.818**	30	30	8-**5**	0-0	214.1	195	86	29	1	29-0	163	3.49	126	.239	**.265**	4-0	.250	0	142	24	2.1

Year	Tm Lg	W	L	Pct	G	GS	CG-Sho	SV-BS	IP	H	R	HR	HB	BB-IB	SO	ERA	AERA	OAV	OOB	AB-SH	AVG	PB	Sup	APR	PW
1999	Tor A	17	10	.630	34	34	**7-1**	0-0	**231.2**	246	132	32	6	62-2	169	4.82	103	.271	.320	6-1	.000	-1	112	5	0.4
2000	Tor A★	**20**	8	.714	35	**35**	**9-1**	0-0	229.2	266	115	23	8	31-0	166	4.11	124	.289	.316	6-0	.167	-0	108	24	2.4
2001	Chi A	5	7	.417	16	16	1	0-0	100.2	120	55	12	3	21-1	59	4.47	103	.297	.335	2-0	.000	-0	95	1	0.1
2002	†NY A	19	7	.731	31	31	2-1	0-0	206.1	210	100	21	5	45-2	137	3.75	117	.259	.300	4-1	.000	-0	137	13	1.3
2003	†NY A	15	7	.682	31	30	4-1	0-0	213	242	101	24	8	20-0	101	4.14	106	.286	.306	6-0	.167	0	120	9	0.9
Total	17	200	128	.610	557	386	52-12	13-13	2826.2	2914	1384	330	69	624-59	1873	4.06	111	.266	.307	56-3	.125	-2	110	139	13.5
WELLS, ED Edwin Lee "Satchelfoot" B 6.7.1900 Ashland, OH D 5.1.1986 Montgomery, AL BL/TL 6-1.5/183# d6.16																									
1923	Det A	0	0	—	7	0	0	0	10	11	6	0	0	6	6	5.40	72	.306	.405	1-0	.000	-0		-1	-0.1
1924	Det A	6	8	.429	29	15	5	4	102	117	58	2	1	42	33	4.06	101	.291	.360	33-2	.212	-1	79	0	0.0
1925	Det A	6	9	.400	35	14	5	2	134.1	190	106	8	2	62	45	6.23	69	.345	.413	43-1	.279	3	103	-28	-2.4
1926	Det A	12	10	.545	36	26	9-**4**	0	178	201	101	7	2	76	58	4.15	98	.297	.370	73-0	.205	0	114	-2	-0.4
1927	Det A	0	1	.000	8	1	0	1	20	28	16	3	0	5	5	6.75	62	.333	.371	7-0	.286	0	40	-4	-0.2
1929	NY A	13	9	.591	31	23	10-3	0	193.1	179	102	19	1	81	78	4.33	89	.248	.324	74-3	.230	2	156	-6	-0.7
1930	NY A	12	3	.800	27	21	7	0	150.2	185	101	11	4	49	46	5.20	83	.302	.358	58-2	.259	0*	151	-14	-1.2
1931	NY A	9	5	.643	27	10	6	2	116.2	130	68	7	1	37	34	4.32	92	.286	.341	45-2	.222	1*	194	-7	-0.7
1932	NY A	3	3	.500	22	0	0	2	31.2	38	19	1	0	12	13	4.26	96	.302	.362	6-1	.000	-1*		-1	-0.3
1933	StL A	6	14	.300	36	22	10	1	203.2	230	113	13	1	63	58	4.20	111	.278	.330	71-4	.197	-1*	95	7	0.4
1934	StL A	1	7	.125	33	8	2	1	92	108	60	7	0	35	27	4.79	104	.292	.353	22-1	.045	-2	89	1	0.0
Total	11	68	69	.496	291	140	54-7	13	1232.1	1417	750	78	12	468	403	4.65	91	.291	.355	433-16	.215	1	121	-55	-5.6
WELLS, JOHN John Frederick B 11.25.1922 Junction City, KS D 10.23.1993 Olean, NY BR/TR 5-11.5/180# d9.14																									
1944	Bro N	0	2	.000	4	2	0	0	15	18	9	1	0	11	7	5.40	66	.316	.426	4-0	.250	0	71	-2	-0.3
WELLS, KIP Robert Kip B 4.21.1977 Houston, TX BR/TR 6-3/195# d8.2																									
1999	Chi A	4	1	.800	7	7	0	0-0	35.2	33	17	2	3	15-0	29	4.04	121	.248	.333	0-0	—	0	98	4	0.4
2000	Chi A	6	9	.400	20	20	0	0-0	98.2	126	76	15	2	58-4	71	6.02	83	.312	.398	2-0	.000	-0	108	-12	-1.6
2001	Chi A	10	11	.476	40	20	0	0-2	133.1	145	80	14	12	61-5	99	4.79	96	.281	.366	6-0	.167	-0	85	-4	-0.4
2002	Pit N	12	14	.462	33	33	1-1	0-0	198.1	197	92	21	7	71-11	134	3.58	117	.261	.328	63-13	.190	1*	88	11	1.4
2003	Pit N	10	9	.526	31	31	1	0-0	197.1	171	77	24	7	76-7	147	3.28	134	.233	.310	68-4	.191	2*	88	24	2.3
Total	5	42	44	.488	131	111	2-1	0-2	663.1	672	342	76	31	281-27	480	4.12	109	.264	.342	139-17	.187	3	93	23	2.1
WELLS, BOB Robert Lee B 11.1.1966 Yakima, WA BR/TR 6/180# d5.16																									
1994	Phi N	1	0	1.000	6	0	0	0-0	5	4	1	0	1	3-0	3	1.80	239	.235	.381	0-0	—	0		1	0.2
	Sea A	1	0	1.000	1	0	0	0-0	4	4	1	0	0	1-0	3	2.25	217	.250	.294	0-0	—	0		1	0.2
1995	†Sea A	4	3	.571	30	4	0	0-1	76.2	88	51	11	3	39-3	38	5.75	82	.284	.364	0-0	—	0	69	-7	-0.6
1996	Sea A	12	7	.632	36	16	1-1	0-0	130.2	141	78	25	6	46-5	94	5.30	93	.274	.338	0-0	—	0	122	-3	-0.4
1997	†Sea A	2	0	1.000	46	1	0	2-2	67.1	88	49	11	3	18-1	51	5.75	78	.314	.360	0-0	—	0	204	-11	-0.5
1998	Sea A	2	2	.500	30	0	0	0-1	51.2	54	38	12	2	16-1	29	6.10	76	.261	.319	0-0	—	0		-8	-0.6
1999	Min A	8	3	.727	**76**	0	0	1-4	87.1	79	41	8	5	28-4	44	3.81	134	.245	.312	0-0	—	0		11	1.2
2000	Min A	0	7	.000	76	0	0	10-10	86.1	80	39	14	4	15-2	76	3.65	142	.247	.284	0-0	—	0		13	1.1
2001	Min A	8	5	.615	65	0	0	2-2	68.2	72	39	12	10	18-2	49	5.11	90	.273	.338	0-0	—	0		-3	-0.5
2002	†Min A	2	1	.667	48	0	0	0-0	58	78	41	8	1	16-1	30	5.90	76	.325	.367	0-0	—	0		-9	-0.5
Total	9	40	28	.588	414	21	1-1	15-20	635.2	688	378	101	35	200-19	417	5.03	96	.276	.335	0-0	—	0	118	-15	-0.4
WELLS, TERRY Terry B 9.10.1963 Kankakee, IL BL/TL 6-3/205# d7.3																									
1990	LA N	1	2	.333	5	5	0	0-0	20.2	25	23	4	0	14-0	18	7.84	47	.287	.386	7-0	.000	-1	123	-11	-1.4
WELSH, CHRIS Christopher Charles B 4.14.1955 Wilmington, DE BL/TL 6-2/185# d4.12																									
1981	SD N	6	7	.462	22	19	4-2	0-0	123.2	122	55	9	1	41-4	51	3.78	86	.264	.323	41-3	.146	0	105	-7	-0.6
1982	SD N	8	8	.500	28	20	3-1	0-0	139.1	146	88	16	3	63-2	48	4.91	70	.268	.346	42-5	.262	4	108	-25	-2.1
1983	SD N	0	1	.000	7	1	0	0-0	14.1	13	5	2	0	2-0	5	2.51	139	.236	.263	4-0	.000	-0	25	1	0.0
	Mon N	0	1	.000	16	5	0	0-0	44.2	46	30	5	4	18-1	17	5.04	71	.267	.349	14-0	.286	1	143	-8	-0.2
	Year	0	2	.000	23	6	0	0-0	59	59	36	7	4	20-1	22	4.42	81	.260	.329	18-0	.222	1	124	-7	-0.2
1985	Tex A	2	5	.286	25	6	0	0-0	76.1	101	40	11	4	25-3	31	4.13	103	.316	.371	0-0	—	0	72	0	0.0
1986	Cin N	6	9	.400	24	24	1	0-0	139.1	163	79	9	3	40-4	40	4.78	81	.301	.350	42-4	.119	0	111	-12	-1.1
Total	5	22	31	.415	122	75	8-3	0-0	537.2	591	297	52	15	189-14	192	4.45	82	.282	.344	143-12	.182	5	106	-51	-4.0
WELTEROTH, DICK Richard John B 8.3.1927 Williamsport, PA BR/TR 5-11/165# d5.16																									
1948	Was A	2	1	.667	33	2	0	1	65.1	73	43	6	1	50	16	5.51	79	.286	.405	10-0	.100	-1	135	-7	-0.5
1949	Was A	2	5	.286	52	2	0	2	95.1	107	83	6	1	89	37	7.36	58	.296	.437	17-1	.059	-1	95	-30	-2.1
1950	Was A	0	0	—	5	0	0	0	6	5	5	0	0	6	2	3.00	150	.217	.379	0-0	—	0		0	0.0
Total	3	4	6	.400	90	4	0	3	166.2	185	131	12	2	145	55	6.48	66	.290	.422	27-1	.074	-2	115	-37	-2.6
WELZER, TONY Anton Frank B 4.5.1899 , Germany D 3.18.1971 Milwaukee, WI BR/TR 5-11/160# d4.13																									
1926	Bos A	4	3	.571	39	5	1-1	0	139	167	88	5	3	53	29	4.86	84	.308	.373	38-0	.211	2	83	-12	-0.2
1927	Bos A	6	11	.353	37	19	8	1	171.2	214	109	10	4	71	56	4.72	89	.318	.386	42-7	.095	-2	79	-10	-1.0
Total	2	10	14	.417	76	24	9-1	1	310.2	381	197	15	7	124	85	4.78	87	.313	.380	80-7	.150	-0	81	-22	-1.2
WENDELL, TURK Steven John B 5.19.1967 Pittsfield, MA BB/TR 6-2/190# d6.17																									
1993	Chi N	1	2	.333	7	4	0	0-0	22.2	24	13	0	0	8-1	15	4.37	91	.273	.333	7-0	.143	-0	113	-1	-0.2
1994	Chi N	0	1	.000	6	2	0	0-0	14.1	22	20	3	0	10-1	9	11.93	35	.349	.432	2-0	.000	0	88	-12	-0.7
1995	Chi N	3	1	.750	43	0	0	0-0	60.1	71	35	11	2	24-4	50	4.92	83	.298	.363	7-0	.000	-0		-5	-0.3
1996	Chi N	4	5	.444	70	0	0	18-3	79.1	58	26	8	3	44-4	75	2.84	153	.201	.313	2-1	.500	1		13	2.0
1997	Chi N	3	5	.375	52	0	0	4-1	60	53	32	4	1	39-5	54	4.20	103	.238	.350	3-0	.000	-0		0	0.0
	NY N	0	0	—	13	0	0	1-1	16.1	15	10	3	1	14-1	10	4.96	81	.250	.400	2-0	.000	-0		-2	-0.1
	Year	3	5	.375	65	0	0	5-2	76.1	68	46	7	2	53-6	64	4.36	97	.240	.361	5-0	.000	-0		-2	-0.1
1998	NY N	5	1	.833	66	0	0	4-4	76.2	62	25	4	2	33-9	58	2.93	141	.221	.306	4-0	.000	-0		11	0.8
1999	†NY N	5	4	.556	80	0	0	3-3	85.2	80	31	9	2	37-8	77	3.05	144	.245	.324	6-0	.000	-0		13	1.1
2000	†NY N	8	6	.571	77	0	0	1-4	82.2	60	36	9	5	41-7	73	3.59	123	.206	.312	4-0	.250	0		8	1.2
2001	NY N	4	3	.571	49	0	0	1-2	51.1	42	23	8	3	22-6	41	3.51	118	.223	.310	2-0	.000	-0		3	0.4
	Phi N	0	2	.000	21	0	0	0-0	15.2	21	13	4	1	12-3	15	7.47	57	.323	.430	0-0	—	0		-5	-0.6
	Year	4	5	.444	70	0	0	1-2	67	63	36	12	4	34-9	56	4.43	94	.249	.342	2-0	.000	-0		-2	-0.2
2003	Phi N	3	3	.500	56	0	0	1-4	64	54	24	6	6	28-5	27	3.38	119	.235	.330	2-0	.000	-0		6	0.5
Total	10	36	33	.522	540	6	0	33-22	629	562	288	69	26	312-54	504	3.85	110	.240	.333	41-1	.073	-1	101	29	4.1
WENGERT, DON Donald Paul B 11.6.1969 Sioux City, IA BR/TR 6-2/205# d4.30																									
1995	Oak A	1	1	.500	19	0	0	0-0	29.2	30	14	3	1	12-2	16	3.34	134	.263	.336	0-0	—	0		3	0.1
1996	Oak A	7	11	.389	36	25	1-1	0-0	161.1	200	102	29	6	60-5	75	5.58	88	.307	.368	0-0	—	0	96	-9	-1.0
1997	Oak A	5	11	.313	49	12	1	2-1	134	177	96	21	8	41-4	68	6.04	75	.321	.372	0-0	—	0	85	-22	-2.3
1998	SD N	0	0	—	10	0	0	1-0	13.2	21	9	2	0	5-0	5	5.93	66	.356	.406	3-0	.000	-0		-3	-0.2
	Chi N	1	5	.167	21	6	0	0-0	49.2	55	29	8	3	23-0	41	5.07	87	.279	.363	13-1	.000	-1*	104	-3	-0.5
	Year	1	5	.167	31	6	0	1-0	63.1	76	34	10	3	28-0	46	5.26	82	.297	.373	16-1	.000	-2	107	-6	-0.7
1999	KC A	0	1	.000	11	1	0	0-3	24.1	41	26	6	0	5-0	10	9.25	54	.376	.397	0-0	—	0	93	-11	-0.5
2000	Atl N	0	1	.000	10	0	0	0-0	10	12	9	2	0	5-0	7	7.20	64	.286	.362	0-0	—	0		-3	-0.3
2001	Pit N	0	2	.000	4	4	0	0-0	16	33	22	2	0	6-2	4	12.38	36	.429	.470	3-1	.000	-0	118	-13	-1.2
Total	7	14	32	.304	160	48	2-1	3-4	438.2	569	307	73	18	157-13	226	6.01	78	.316	.374	19-2	.000	-2	97	-61	-5.9
WENSLOFF, BUTCH Charles William B 12.3.1915 Sausalito, CA D 2.18.2001 San Rafael, CA BR/TR 5-11/185# d5.2 Def 1944, Mil 1945-46																									
1943	NY A	13	11	.542	29	27	18-1	1	223.1	179	80	7	1	70	105	2.54	127	.219	.282	79-3	.177	-0	96	15	1.5
1947	†NY A	3	1	.750	11	5	1	0	51.2	41	17	3	0	22	18	2.61	135	.217	.299	19-1	.263	1	155	5	0.4
1948	Cle A	0	1	.000	1	0	0	0	1.2	2	2	1	0	3	2	10.80	38	.286	.500	0-0	—	0		-1	-0.2
Total	3	16	13	.552	41	32	19-1	1	276.2	222	99	11	1	95	125	2.60	126	.219	.287	98-4	.194	0	105	19	1.7

Year	Tm Lg	W	L	Pct	G	GS	CG-Sho	SV-BS	IP	H	R	HR	HB	BB-IB	SO	ERA	AERA	OAV	OOB	AB-SH	AVG	PB	Sup	APR	PW
WENZ, FRED Frederick Charles "Fireball" B 8.26.1941 Bound Brook, NJ BR/TR 6-3/214# d6.4																									
1968	Bos A	0	0	—	1	0	0	0	1	0	0	0	0	2-0	3	0.00	—	.000	.400	0-0	—	0		0	0.0
1969	Bos A	1	0	1.000	8	0	0	0-0	11	9	7	7	0	10-3	11	5.73	66	.225	.380	0-0	—	0		-2	-0.1
1970	Phi N	2	0	1.000	22	0	0	1-0	30.1	27	16	2	1	13-0	24	4.45	90	.237	.313	5-0	.000	-1		-1	-0.2
Total 3		3	0	1.000	31	0	0	1-0	42.1	36	23	9	1	25-3	38	4.68	84	.229	.333	5-0	.000	-0		-3	-0.3
WERDEN, PERRY Percival Wheritt B 7.21.1865 St.Louis, MO D 1.9.1934 Minneapolis, MN BR/TR 6-2/220# d4.24 ▲																									
1884	StL U	12	1	.923	16	16	12-1	0	141.1	113	61	1		22	51	1.97	121	.204	.235	76	.237	-4*	153	7	0.2
WERLE, BILL William George "Bugs" B 12.21.1920 Oakland, CA BL/TL 6-2.5/182# d4.22 C1																									
1949	Pit N	12	13	.480	35	29	10-2	0	221	243	117	23	8	51	106	4.24	99	.278	.324	77-2	.117	-3	93	-2	-0.4
1950	Pit N	8	16	.333	48	22	6	8	215.1	249	127	25	6	65	78	4.60	95	.290	.344	67-2	.194	1	81	-6	-0.3
1951	Pit N	8	6	.571	59	9	2	6	149.2	181	102	20	6	51	57	5.65	75	.304	.364	40-1	.300	3	116	-20	-1.3
1952	Pit N	0	0	—	5	0	0	0	4	9	5	1	0	1	1	9.00	44	.429	.455	0-0	—	0		-2	-0.1
	StL N	1	2	.333	19	0	0	1	39	40	23	6	1	15	23	4.85	77	.268	.339	9-0	.111	-0		-5	-0.3
	Year	1	2	.333	24	0	0	1	43	49	34	7	1	16	24	5.23	71	.288	.353	9-0	.111	-0		-7	-0.4
1953	Bos A	0	1	.000	5	0	0	0	11.2	7	3	1	0	1	4	1.54	273	.179	.200	2-0	.000	-0		3	0.3
1954	Bos A	0	1	.000	14	0	0	0	24.2	41	13	5	2	10	14	4.38	94	.376	.434	4-0	.000	-0		0	0.0
Total 6		29	39	.426	185	60	18-2	15	665.1	770	390	81	23	194	283	4.69	90	.291	.345	199-5	.176	1	92	-32	-2.1
WERLEY, GEORGE George William B 9.8.1938 St.Louis, MO BR/TR 6-2/196# d9.29																									
1956	Bal A	0	0	—	1	0	0	0	1	1	1	0	0	2-0	0	9.00	44	.250	.500	0-0	—	0		-1	0.0
WERTS, JOHNNY Henry Levi B 4.20.1898 Pomaria, SC D 9.24.1990 Newberry, SC BR/TR 5-10/180# d4.14																									
1926	Bos N	11	9	.550	32	23	7-1	0	189.1	212	85	6	10	47	65	3.28	108	.287	.338	64-3	.266	4	82	4	1.0
1927	Bos N	4	10	.286	42	15	4	1	164.1	204	95	5	4	52	39	4.55	82	.315	.369	43-2	.163	-0	84	-15	-1.2
1928	Bos N	0	2	.000	10	2	0	0	18.1	31	22	2	0	8	5	10.31	38	.369	.424	3-0	.333	0	87	-12	-1.1
1929	Bos N	0	0	—	4	0	0	1	6	13	8	1	0	4	2	10.50	45	.433	.500	1-0	1.000	0		-4	-0.1
Total 4		15	21	.417	88	40	11-1	2	378	460	210	14	14	111	111	4.29	85	.307	.360	111-5	.234	4	82	-27	-1.4
WERTZ, BILL William Charles B 1.15.1967 Cleveland, OH BR/TR 6-6/220# d5.22																									
1993	Cle A	2	3	.400	34	0	0	0-2	59.2	54	28	5	1	32-2	53	3.62	120	.238	.333	0-0	—	0		4	0.2
1994	Cle A	0	0	—	1	0	0	0-0	4.1	9	5	0	0	1-0	1	10.38	45	.409	.435	0-0	—	0		-2	-0.1
Total 2		2	3	.400	35	0	0	0-2	64	63	33	5	1	33-2	54	4.08	107	.253	.342	0-0	—	0		2	0.1
WEST, DAVID David Lee B 9.1.1964 Memphis, TN BL/TL 6-6/230# d9.24																									
1988	NY N	1	0	1.000	2	1	0	0-0	6	6	2	0	0	3-0	3	3.00	108	.273	.360	2-0	1.000	1	385	0	0.2
1989	NY N	0	2	.000	11	2	0	0-0	24.1	25	20	4	1	14-2	19	7.40	44	.260	.357	5-0	.200	0	68	-11	-0.8
	Min A	3	2	.600	10	5	0	0-1	39.1	48	29	5	2	19-1	31	6.41	65	.306	.383	0-0	—	0	96	-9	-1.0
1990	Min A	7	9	.438	29	27	2	0-0	146.1	142	88	21	4	78-1	92	5.10	82	.256	.350	0-0	—	0	97	-13	-1.3
1991	†Min A	4	4	.500	15	12	0	0-0	71.1	66	37	13	1	28-0	52	4.54	94	.244	.314	0-0	—	0	91	-1	-0.1
1992	Min A	1	3	.250	9	3	0	0-0	28.1	32	24	3	1	20-0	19	6.99	58	.276	.381	0-0	—	0	30	-9	-1.1
1993	†Phi N	6	4	.600	76	0	0	3-6	86.1	60	37	6	5	51-4	87	2.92	136	.194	.316	5-0	.400	1		8	0.9
1994	Phi N	4	10	.286	31	14	0	0-2	99	74	44	7	1	61-2	83	3.55	121	.205	.320	28-1	.071	-2	73	8	0.8
1995	Phi N	3	2	.600	8	8	0	0-0	38	34	17	5	1	19-0	25	3.79	112	.241	.335	8-6	.125	1	96	2	0.3
1996	Phi N	2	2	.500	7	6	0	0-0	28.1	31	17	0	0	11-0	22	4.76	91	.272	.336	7-2	.286	1	70	-2	-0.1
1998	Bos A	0	0	—	6	0	0	0-0	2	7	6	1	0	7-0	4	27.00	17	.538	.700	0-0	—	0		-5	-0.2
Total 10		31	38	.449	204	78	2	3-9	569.1	525	321	65	16	311-10	437	4.66	89	.244	.341	55-9	.182	2	90	-32	-2.4
WEST, FRANK J. Franklin B 1.1874 Johnstown, PA D 9.6.1932 Wilmerding, PA ?/180# d7.11																									
1894	Bos N	0	0	—	1	0	0	0	3	5	5	0	0	2	1	9.00	63	.357	.438	1-0	.000	-0		-1	-0.1
WEST, HI James Hiram B 8.8.1884 Roseville, IL D 5.24.1963 Los Angeles, CA BR/TR 6/185# d9.8																									
1905	Cle A	2	2	.500	6	4	4-1	0	33	43	23	0	3	10	15	4.09	64	.316	.376	13-0	.077	-1	40	-6	-0.9
1911	Cle A	3	4	.429	13	8	3	1	64.2	84	35	1	3	18	17	3.76	91	.343	.395	23-0	.130	-2	95	-2	-0.4
Total 2		5	6	.455	19	12	7-1	1	97.2	127	58	1	6	28	32	3.87	81	.333	.388	36-0	.111	-3	80	-8	-1.3
WEST, LEFTY Weldon Edison B 9.3.1915 Gibsonville, NC D 7.23.1979 Hendersonville, NC BR/TL 6/165# d4.30																									
1944	StL A	0	0	—	11	0	0	0	24.1	34	18	1	1	19	11	6.29	57	.366	.478	7-0	.143	-0		-6	-0.4
1945	StL A	3	4	.429	24	8	1	0	74.1	71	37	2	0	31	38	3.63	97	.245	.318	27-1	.074	-3	73	-2	-0.6
Total 2		3	4	.429	35	8	1	0	98.2	105	55	3	1	50	49	4.29	83	.274	.359	34-1	.088	-3	73	-8	-1.0
WESTBROOK, JAKE Jacob Cauthen B 9.29.1977 Athens, GA BR/TR 6-3/190# d6.17																									
2000	NY A	0	2	.000	3	2	0	0-0	6.2	15	10	1	0	4-1	1	13.50	36	.469	.500	0-0	—	0	107	-6	-1.0
2001	Cle A	4	4	.500	23	6	0	0-0	64.2	79	43	6	4	22-4	48	5.85	77	.306	.363	1-1	.000	-0	92	-8	-0.8
2002	Cle A	1	3	.250	11	4	0	0-2	41.2	50	30	6	1	12-1	20	5.83	75	.296	.344	0-0	—	0	63	-7	-0.6
2003	Cle A	7	10	.412	34	22	1	0-0	133	142	70	9	12	56-1	58	4.33	102	.281	.365	0-0	—	0	95	3	0.4
Total 4		12	19	.387	71	34	1	0-2	246	286	153	22	17	94-7	127	5.23	85	.297	.366	1-1	.000	0	91	-18	-2.0
WESTERVELT, HUYLER Huyler B 10.1.1869 Tenafly, NJ D 10.14.1949 Pelham Manor, NY TR 5-9/170# d4.21																									
1894	NY N	7	10	.412	23	18	11-1	0	141	170	118	4	5	76	35	5.04	104	.295	.382	56-2	.143	-5	92	4	0.0
WESTON, MICKEY Michael Lee B 3.26.1961 Flint, MI BR/TR 6-1/187# d6.18																									
1989	Bal A	1	0	1.000	7	0	0	1-0	13	18	8	1	1	2-0	7	5.54	69	.346	.382	0-0	—	0		-2	-0.2
1990	Bal A	0	1	.000	9	2	0	0-0	21	28	20	6	0	6-1	9	7.71	49	.322	.366	0-0	—	0	96	-10	-0.5
1991	Tor A	0	0	—	2	0	0	0-0	2	1	0	0	0	1-1	1	0.00	—	.143	.250	0-0	—	0		1	0.0
1992	Phi N	0	1	.000	1	1	0	0-0	3.2	7	5	1	1	1-0	0	12.27	28	.412	.474	2-0	.000	-0	26	-3	-0.5
1993	NY N	0	0	—	4	0	0	0-0	5.2	11	5	0	1	1-0	2	7.94	51	.393	.433	0-0	—	0		-2	-0.1
Total 5		1	2	.333	23	3	0	1-0	45.1	65	38	8	3	11-2	19	7.15	53	.340	.385	2-0	.000	-0	71	-16	-1.3
WETTELAND, JOHN John Karl B 8.21.1966 San Mateo, CA BR/TR 6-2/195# d5.31																									
1989	LA N	5	8	.385	31	12	0	1-0	102.2	81	46	8	0	34-4	96	3.77	91	.218	.283	21-5	.143	-0	95	-3	-0.5
1990	LA N	2	4	.333	22	5	0	0-1	43	44	28	6	4	17-3	36	4.81	76	.263	.344	7-1	.143	1	123	-6	-0.8
1991	LA N	1	0	1.000	6	0	0	0-0	9	5	2	0	1	3-0	9	0.00	—	.161	.250	0-0	—	0		3	0.3
1992	Mon N	4	4	.500	67	0	0	37-9	83.1	64	27	6	4	36-3	99	2.92	119	.213	.304	5-1	.200	0		6	1.1
1993	Mon N	9	3	.750	70	0	0	43-6	85.1	58	17	3	2	28-3	113	1.37	305	.188	.260	4-1	.000	-0		25	5.1
1994	Mon N	4	6	.400	52	0	0	25-10	63.2	46	22	5	3	21-4	68	2.83	149	.202	.273	4-1	.250	0		10	2.0
1995	†NY A	1	5	.167	60	0	0	31-6	61.1	40	22	6	0	14-2	66	2.93	157	.185	.233	0-0	—	0		11	1.9
1996	†NY A☆	2	3	.400	62	0	0	**43-4**	63.2	54	23	9	0	21-4	69	2.83	175	.224	.284	0-0	—	0		14	2.6
1997	Tex A	7	2	.778	61	0	0	31-6	65	43	18	5	0	21-3	63	1.94	247	.182	.248	1-0	1.000	1		19	3.7
1998	†Tex A★	3	1	.750	63	0	0	42-5	62	47	17	6	0	14-1	72	2.03	238	.203	.247	0-0	—	0		18	3.0
1999	†Tex A★	4	4	.500	62	0	0	43-7	66	67	30	9	0	19-1	60	3.68	138	.262	.307	0-0	—	0		9	1.7
2000	Tex A	6	5	.545	62	0	0	34-9	60	67	35	10	2	24-2	53	4.20	119	.285	.351	0-0	—	0		4	0.6
Total 12		48	45	.516	618	17	0	330-63	765	616	287	73	16	252-30	804	2.93	147	.218	.284	42-9	.167	1	86	110	20.7
WETZEL, BUZZ Charles Edward B 8.25.1894 Jay, OK D 3.7.1941 Globe, AZ BR/TR 6-1/162# d7.25																									
1927	Phi A	0	0	—	2	1	0	0	4.2	8	5	0	0	5	0	7.71	55	.400	.520	1-0	1.000	0	117	-2	0.0
WETZEL, SHORTY George William B 1868 Philadelphia, PA D 2.25.1899 Dayton, OH d8.26																									
1885	Bal AA	0	2	.000	2	2	1	0	17	27	26	0	3	9	6	8.47	38	.333	.419	7	.000	-1	45	-10	-0.8
WEVER, STEFAN Stefan Matthew B 4.22.1958 Marburg, W.Germany BR/TR 6-8/245# d9.17																									
1982	NY A	0	1	.000	1	1	0	0-0	2.2	6	9	1	0	3-0	2	27.00	15	.429	.500	0-0	—	0	0	-7	-0.9
WEYHING, GUS August "Cannonball" B 9.29.1866 Louisville, KY D 9.4.1955 Louisville, KY BR/TR 5-10/145# d5.2 b-John																									
1887	Phi AA	26	28	.481	55	55	53-2	0	466.1	465	342	12	37	167	193	4.27	101	.253	.328	209	.201	-9*	94	-5	-1.2
1888	Phi AA	28	18	.609	47	47	45-3	0	404	314	198	4	42	111	204	2.25	133	.207	.279	184	.217	4*	124	30	3.3

Year	Tm Lg	W	L	Pct	G	GS	CG-Sho	SV-BS	IP	H	R	HR	HB	BB-IB	SO	ERA	AERA	OAV	OOB	AB-SH	AVG	PB	Sup	APR	PW
1889	Phi AA	30	21	.588	54	53	50-4	0	449	382	271	15	34	212	213	2.95	128	.223	.321	191	.131	-15	98	35	1.6
1890	Bro P	30	16	.652	49	46	38-3	0	390	419	250	10	17	179	177	3.60	124	.263	.343	165	.164	-6	104	40	2.5
1891	Phi AA	31	20	.608	52	51	51-3	0	450	428	231	12	31	161	219	3.18	119	.242	.316	198	.111	-16*	91	29	1.0
1892	Phi N	32	21	.604	59	49	46-6	**3**	469.2	411	213	9	18	168	202	2.66	122	.226	.298	214	.136	-10*	104	31	1.6
1893	Phi N	23	16	.590	42	40	33-2	0	345.1	399	235	10	20	145	101	4.74	97	.281	.356	147	.150	-9*	117	-2	-1.0
1894	Phi N	16	14	.533	40	36	26-2	1	279	379	224	12	16	120	83	5.71	90	.321	.391	121-8	.174	-9	104	-11	-1.7
1895	Phi N	0	2	.000	2	2	0	0	9	23	22	0	0	13	5	20.00	24	.469	.581	4-0	.000	-1	104	-13	-1.6
	Pit N	1	0	1.000	1	1	1	0	9	10	7	0	0	5	3	1.00	451	.278	.366	4-0	.250	0	158	2	0.2
	Lou N	7	19	.269	28	25	22-1	0	213	285	205	9	8	66	53	5.41	86	.316	.368	89-0	.225	-0	77	-24	-2.1
	Year	8	21	.276	31	28	23-1	0	231	318	210	9	8	84	61	5.81	80	.322	.380	97-0	.216	-1	82	-38	-3.5
1896	Lou N	2	3	.400	5	5	4	0	42	62	46	6	2	15	9	6.64	65	.339	.395	15-0	.133	-1	105	-10	-0.9
1898	Was N	15	26	.366	45	42	39	0	361	428	232	10	16	84	92	4.51	81	.292	.338	141-7	.177	-5*	85	-25	-2.8
1899	Was N	17	21	.447	43	38	34-2	0	334.2	414	223	8	28	76	96	4.54	86	.303	.352	126-6	.206	-1	96	-20	-2.2
1900	StL N	3	2	.600	7	5	3	0	46.2	60	44	2	1	21	6	4.63	79	.311	.381	21-0	.095	-2	118	-8	-0.9
	Bro N	3	4	.429	8	8	3	0	48	66	33	1	2	20	8	4.31	89	.325	.391	18-0	.222	-0	146	-3	-0.4
	Year	6	6	.500	15	13	6	0	94.2	126	41	3	3	41	14	4.47	84	.318	.386	39-0	.154	-3	137	-10	-1.3
1901	Cle A	0	0	—	2	1	0	0	11.1	20	11	0	4	5	0	7.94	45	.377	.468	5-0	.000	-1	228	-4	-0.3
	Cin N	0	1	.000	1	1	1	0	9	11	9	0	2	2	3	3.00	107	.297	.366	3-0	.000	-0	22	-2	-0.2
Total	14	264	232	.532	540	505	449-28	4	4337	4576	2796	120	278	1570	1667	3.88	102	.264	.335	1855-21	.166	-83	102	40	-5.1

WEYHING, JOHN John B 6.24.1869 Louisville, KY D 6.20.1890 Louisville, KY BL/TL 6-2/185# d7.13 b-Gus

1888	Cin AA	3	4	.429	8	8	7	0	65.2	52	26	0	1	17	30	1.23	257	.210	.263	23	.130	-2	66	10	0.8
1889	Col AA	0	0	—	1	0	0	0	1	1	3	0	0	4	0	27.00	13	.250	.625	0	—	0		-2	-0.1
Total	2	3	4	.429	9	8	7	0	66.2	53	29	0	1	21	30	1.62	196	.210	.274	23	.130	-2	66	8	0.7

WHEAT, LEE Leroy William B 9.15.1929 Edwardsville, IL BR/TR 6-4/200# d4.21

1954	Phi A	0	2	.000	8	1	0	0	28.1	38	18	1	1	9	7	5.72	68	.304	.350	8-0	.125	-0	68	-5	-0.4
1955	KC A	0	0	—	3	0	0	0	2	8	7	1	0	3-2	1	22.50	19	.533	.611	0-0	—	0		-4	-0.2
Total	2	0	2	.000	11	1	0	0	30.1	46	25	2	1	12-2	8	6.82	57	.329	.381	8-0	.125	-0	68	-9	-0.6

WHEATLEY, CHARLIE Charles B 6.27.1893 Rosedale, KS D 12.10.1982 Tulsa, OK BR/TR 5-11/174# d9.6

1912	Det A	1	4	.200	5	5	2	0	35	45	27	1	2	17	14	6.17	53	.331	.413	12-0	.000	-2	68	-9	-1.2

WHEATON, WOODY Elwood Pierce B 10.3.1914 Philadelphia, PA D 12.11.1995 Lancaster, PA BL/TL 5-8.5/160# d9.28.1943 ▲

1944	Phi A	0	1	.000	11	1	1	0	38	36	17	1	1	20	15	3.55	98	.255	.352	59-1	.186	0*	0	0	0.0

WHEELER, DAN Daniel Michael B 12.10.1977 Providence, RI BR/TR 6-3/215# d9.1

1999	TB A	0	4	.000	6	6	0	0-0	30.2	35	20	7	0	13-1	32	5.87	85	.287	.356	0-0	—	0	78	-2	-0.2
2000	TB A	1	1	.500	11	2	0	0-1	23	29	14	2	2	11-2	17	5.48	90	.302	.382	0-0	—	0	76	-1	0.0
2001	TB A	1	0	1.000	13	0	0	0-0	17.2	30	17	3	0	5-0	12	8.66	52	.375	.402	0-0	—	0		-7	-0.3
2003	NY N	1	3	.250	35	0	0	2-1	51	49	23	6	1	17-4	35	3.71	112	.253	.312	2-0	.000	-0		2	0.1
Total	4	3	8	.273	65	8	0	2-2	122.1	143	74	18	3	46-7	96	5.30	86	.291	.351	2-0	.000	-0	85	-8	-0.4

WHEELER, RIP Floyd Clark B 3.2.1898 Marion, KY D 9.18.1968 Marion, KY BR/TR 6/180# d9.30

1921	Pit N	0	0	—	1	0	0	0	3	6	4	0	1	1	0	9.00	43	.500	.571	1-0	.000	-0		-2	-0.1
1922	Pit N	0	0	—	1	0	0	0	1	1	0	0	0	2	0	0.00	—	.333	.600	0-0	—	0		0	0.0
1923	Chi N	1	2	.333	3	3	1	0	24	28	14	2	3	5	5	4.88	82	.298	.353	9-0	.111	-1	82	-2	-0.2
1924	Chi N	3	6	.333	29	4	0	0	101.1	103	53	8	0	21	16	3.91	100	.265	.303	32-0	.219	-1	82	0	-0.1
Total	4	4	8	.333	34	7	1	0	129.1	138	71	10	4	29	21	4.18	94	.278	.323	42-0	.190	-2	83	-4	-0.4

WHEELER, GEORGE George Louis (b: George Louis Heroux) B 7.30.1869 Methuen, MA D 3.21.1946 Santa Ana, CA BB/TR 5-9/180# d9.18

1896	Phi N	1	1	.500	3	2	2	0	16.1	18	11	0	2	5	2	3.86	112	.277	.347	9-0	.111	-1	124	0	-0.1
1897	Phi N	11	10	.524	26	19	17	0	191	229	114	3	3	62	35	3.96	106	.295	.349	79-1	.203	-1	91	4	0.4
1898	Phi N	6	8	.429	15	13	10	0	112.1	155	94	1	6	36	20	4.17	82	.325	.380	43-3	.186	-1	98	-16	-1.5
1899	Phi N	3	1	.750	6	5	3	0	39	44	30	1	3	13	3	6.00	61	.284	.351	17-1	.235	1	164	-8	-0.5
Total	4	21	20	.512	50	39	32	0	358.2	446	249	5	14	116	60	4.24	92	.303	.359	148-5	.196	-2	103	-20	-1.7

WHEELER, HARRY Harry Eugene B 3.3.1858 Versailles, IN D 10.9.1900 Cincinnati, OH BR/TR 5-11/165# d6.19 M1 ▲

1878	Pro N	6	1	.857	7	6	6	0	62	70	40	1		25	25	3.48	63	.275	.339	27	.148	-1	191	-6	-0.7
1879	Cin N	0	1	.000	1	1	0	0	1	6	10	0		4	0	81.00	3	.667	.769	3	.000	-0	20	-7	-0.8
1882	Cin AA	1	2	.333	4	1	1	0	21.2	21	17	0		12	10	5.40	49	.239	.330	344	.250	1*	156	-4	-0.5
1883	Col AA	0	1	.000	1	1	0	0	5	13	7	0		2	0	7.20	43	.448	.484	371	.226	0*	56	-2	-0.3
1884	KC U	0	1	.000	1	1	1	0	8	7	6	0		0	6	1.13	198	.219	.219	62	.258	-0*	38	0	0.0
Total	5	7	6	.538	14	10	8	0	97.2	117	80	1		43	41	4.70	50	.283	.351	807	.235	-1	141	-19	-2.3

WHEELOCK, GARY Gary Richard B 11.29.1951 Bakersfield, CA BR/TR 6-3/205# d9.17

1976	Cal A	0	0	—	2	0	0	0-0	2	6	6	0	1	1-0	2	27.00	12	.500	.571	0-0	—	0		-5	-0.3
1977	Sea A	6	9	.400	17	17	2	0-0	88.1	94	58	16	2	26-0	47	4.89	84	.268	.321	0-0	—	0	86	-10	-1.4
1980	Sea A	0	0	—	1	1	0	0-0	3	4	2	0	0	1-0	1	6.00	69	.333	.385	0-0	—	0	65	-1	0.0
Total	3	6	9	.400	20	18	2	0-0	93.1	104	66	16	3	28-0	50	5.40	76	.277	.332	0-0	—	0	85	-16	-1.7

WHILLOCK, JACK Jack Franklin B 11.4.1942 Clinton, AR BR/TR 6-3/195# d8.29

1971	Det A	0	2	.000	7	0	0	1-1	8	10	5	0	0	2-0	6	5.63	64	.323	.364	1-0	.000	-0		-2	-0.3

WHISENANT, MATT Matthew Michael B 6.8.1971 Los Angeles, CA BR/TL 6-3/215# d7.4

1997	Fla N	0	0	—	4	0	0	0-0	2.2	4	6	0	0	6-0	4	16.88	24	.333	.556	0-0	—	0*		-4	-0.2
	KC A	1	0	1.000	24	0	0	0-0	19	15	7	0	3	12-0	16	2.84	166	.211	.349	0-0	—	0		4	0.2
1998	KC A	2	1	.667	70	0	0	2-3	60.2	61	37	3	3	33-2	45	4.90	99	.271	.365	0-0	—	0		-1	0.0
1999	KC A	4	4	.500	48	0	0	1-3	39.2	40	28	4	7	26-1	27	6.35	79	.267	.399	0-0	—	0		-5	-0.8
	SD N	0	1	.000	19	0	0	0-1	14.2	10	6	0	0	10-1	10	3.68	114	.200	.333	0-0	—	0		1	0.1
2000	SD N	2	2	.500	24	0	0	0-3	21.1	16	12	1	0	17-1	12	3.80	114	.213	.351	0-0	—	0		0	0.1
Total	4	9	8	.529	189	0	0	3-10	158	146	96	8	13	104-5	114	4.96	95	.250	.372	0-0	—	0		-5	-0.6

WHITAKER, PAT William H. B 11.1864 St.Louis, MO D 7.15.1902 St.Louis, MO TR d10.11

1888	Bal AA	1	1	.500	2	2	2	0	14	13	12	0	2	6	5	5.14	58	.236	.333	6	.000	-1	68	-3	-0.4
1889	Bal AA	1	0	1.000	1	1	1	0	9	10	4	0	0	4	1	2.00	197	.270	.341	4	.250	-0	126	2	0.2
Total	2	2	1	.667	3	3	3	0	23	23	16	0	2	10	6	3.91	86	.250	.337	10	.100	-1	89	-1	-0.2

WHITBY, BILL William Edward B 7.29.1943 Crewe, VA BR/TR 6-1/190# d6.17

1964	Min A	0	0	—	4	0	0	0	6.1	8	6	3	0	1-0	2	8.53	42	.308	.333	1-0	.000	-0		-3	-0.2

WHITCHER, BOB Robert Arthur B 4.29.1917 Berlin, NH D 5.8.1997 Akron, OH BL/TL 5-8/165# d8.20

1945	Bos N	0	2	.000	6	3	0	0	15.2	12	6	1	0	12	6	2.87	133	.235	.381	3-0	.333	0*	37	2	0.2

WHITE, ABE Adel B 5.16.1904 Winder, GA D 10.1.1978 Atlanta, GA BR/TL 6/185# d7.10

1937	StL N	0	1	.000	5	0	0	0	9.1	14	7	1	0	3	2	6.75	59	.341	.386	1-0	1.000	0		-2	-0.2

WHITE, ERNIE Ernest Daniel B 9.5.1916 Pacolet Mills, SC D 5.22.1974 Augusta, GA BR/TL 5-11.5/175# d5.9 Mil 1944-45 C3

1940	StL N	1	1	.500	8	1	0	0	21.2	29	13	0	1	14	15	4.15	96	.315	.411	7-0	.429	1*	0	-1	0.1
1941	StL N	17	7	.708	32	25	12-3	2	210	169	72	12	6	70	117	2.40	157	.217	.287	79-3	.190	0*	113	28	3.0
1942	†StL N	7	5	.583	26	19	7-1	2	128.1	113	57	11	2	41	67	2.52	136	.232	.294	41-5	.195	0*	123	7	0.5
1943	†StL N	5	5	.500	14	10	5-1	0	78.2	78	38	4	1	33	28	3.78	89	.257	.332	28-2	.214	0*	124	-3	-0.5
1946	Bos N	0	1	.000	12	1	0	0	23.2	22	11	1	0	12	8	4.18	82	.256	.347	4-0	.250	0*	150	-1	-0.1
1947	Bos N	0	0	—	1	1	0	0	4	1	0	0	0	1	1	0.00	—	.083	.154	1-0	1.000	0	68	2	0.1
1948	Bos N	0	2	.000	15	0	0	2	23	13	7	0	0	17	8	1.96	196	.167	.316	3-0	.000	-0*		4	0.3
Total	7	30	21	.588	108	57	24-5	6	489.1	425	198	28	10	188	244	2.78	130	.231	.306	163-10	.209	2	115	36	3.4

Year	Tm Lg	W	L	Pct	G	GS	CG-Sho	SV-BS	IP	H	R	HR	HB	BB-IB	SO	ERA	AERA	OAV	OOB	AB-SH	AVG	PB	Sup	APR	PW
WHITE, GABE Gabriel Allen B 11.20.1971 Sebring, FL BL/TL 6-2/200# d5.27																									
1994	Mon N	1	1	.500	7	5	0	1-0	23.2	24	16	4	1	11-0	17	6.08	69	.261	.343	4-1	.000	-0	108	-4	-0.4
1995	Mon N	1	2	.333	19	1	0	0-0	25.2	26	21	7	1	9-0	25	7.01	61	.260	.319	3-1	.000	-0	63	-7	-0.8
1997	Cin N	2	2	.500	12	6	0	1-0	41	39	20	6	1	8-1	25	4.39	97	.253	.291	9-2	.111	-0	108	0	-0.1
1998	Cin N	5	5	.500	69	3	0	9-4	98.2	86	46	17	1	27-6	83	4.01	107	.231	.284	6-4	.167	-0	50	3	0.3
1999	Cin N	1	2	.333	50	0	0	0-1	61	68	31	13	2	14-1	61	4.43	105	.281	.324	0-0	—	0		2	0.1
2000	Cin N	0	0	—	1	0	0	0-0	1	2	2	1	0	1-0	2	18.00	26	.400	.500	0-0	—	0		-1	-0.1
	Col N	11	2	.846	67	0	0	5-4	83	62	21	5	3	14-2	82	2.17	268	.208	.246	9-1	.222	1		27	4.0
	Year	11	2	.846	68	0	0	5-4	84	64	25	6	3	15-2	84	2.36	246	.211	.251	9-1	.222	1		**26**	3.9
2001	Col N	1	7	.125	69	0	0	0-2	67.2	70	47	18	1	26-5	47	6.25	85	.270	.337	3-0	.000	-0		-4	-0.5
2002	Cin N	6	1	.857	62	0	0	0-1	54.1	49	19	3	2	10-2	41	2.98	143	.238	.280	2-1	.000	-0		8	0.9
2003	Cin N	3	0	1.000	34	0	0	0-1	34.1	36	15	5	1	6-3	23	3.93	109	.275	.307	2-0	.000	-0		2	0.1
	†NY A	2	1	.667	12	0	0	0-1	12.1	8	7	2	1	2-1	6	4.38	100	.182	.229	0-0	—	0		0	0.0
Total	9	33	23	.589	402	15	0	16-14	502.2	470	245	81	14	128-21	412	4.26	110	.247	.296	38-10	.105	-1	85	26	3.5
WHITE, DEKE George Frederick B 9.8.1872 Albany, NY D 11.5.1957 Ilion, NY BB/TL d9.14																									
1895	Phi N	1	0	1.000	3	1	1	1	17.1	17	23	1	2	13	6	9.87	48	.254	.390	8-1	.125	-1	134	-9	-0.5
WHITE, DOC Guy Harris B 4.9.1879 Washington, DC D 2.19.1969 Silver Spring, MD BL/TL 6-1/150# d4.22 ▲																									
1901	Phi N	14	13	.519	31	27	22	0	236.2	241	122	2	14	56	132	3.19	106	.262	.314	98-7	.276	5	118	3	0.9
1902	Phi N	16	20	.444	36	35	34-3	1	306	277	126	3	13	72	185	2.53	111	.241	.294	179-9	.263	4*	78	7	1.5
1903	Chi A	17	16	.515	37	36	29-3	0	300	258	119	4	14	69	114	2.13	132	.232	.285	99-2	.202	6*	95	19	2.8
1904	Chi A	16	12	.571	30	30	23-7	0	228	201	82	6	9	68	115	1.78	138	.238	.301	76-2	.158	0*	94	10	1.4
1905	Chi A	17	13	.567	36	33	25-4	0	260.1	204	67	2	9	58	120	1.76	140	.218	.270	90-4	.167	0*	86	24	2.9
1906	†Chi A	18	6	.750	28	24	20-7	0	219.1	160	47	2	5	38	95	**1.52**	**167**	.207	**.249**	65-7	.185	4*	120	28	**3.9**
1907	Chi A	**27**	13	.675	46	35	24-6	1	291	270	93	3	6	38	141	2.26	106	.248	.278	90-12	.222	4*	118	7	1.7
1908	Chi A	18	13	.581	41	37	24-5	0	296	262	94	3	9	69	126	2.55	91	.240	.291	109-9	.229	4*	104	-1	0.8
1909	Chi A	11	9	.550	24	21	14-3	0	177.2	149	56	1	7	31	77	1.72	136	.226	.269	192-13	.234	6*	80	10	1.9
1910	Chi A	15	13	.536	33	29	20-2	1	236.2	219	84	2	12	50	111	2.66	90	.243	.291	126-12	.198	2*	106	0	0.4
1911	Chi A	10	14	.417	34	29	16-4	2	214.1	219	91	2	9	35	72	2.98	108	.271	.309	78-4	.256	3*	109	8	1.1
1912	Chi A	8	10	.444	32	19	9-1	0	172	172	81	1	8	47	57	3.24	99	.267	.325	56-2	.125	-1	91	1	-0.2
1913	Chi A	2	4	.333	19	8	2	0	103	106	56	2	5	39	39	3.50	84	.281	.356	25-2	.120	-1*	73	-6	-0.3
Total	13	189	156	.548	427	363	262-45	5	3041	2738	1118	33	120	670	1384	2.39	112	.242	.292	1283-85	.217	37	100	110	18.8
WHITE, HAL Harold George B 3.18.1919 Utica, NY D 4.21.2001 Venice, FL BR/TR 5-10/170# d4.22 Mil 1944-45																									
1941	Det A	0	0	—	4	0	0	0	9	11	6	0	0	6	2	6.00	76	.306	.405	2-0	.000	-0		-1	-0.1
1942	Det A	12	12	.500	34	25	12-4	1	216.2	212	80	6	5	82	93	2.91	136	.252	.323	77-3	.169	-1	109	25	2.5
1943	Det A	7	12	.368	32	24	7-2	2	177.2	150	84	6	1	71	58	3.39	104	.228	.304	57-2	.140	-1	105	1	0.0
1946	Det A	1	1	.500	11	1	1	0	27.1	34	20	5	0	15	12	5.60	65	.312	.395	7-2	.000	-1	164	-6	-0.5
1947	Det A	4	5	.444	35	5	0	2	84.2	91	43	5	2	47	33	3.61	104	.279	.373	18-1	.167	0	61	0	0.1
1948	Det A	2	1	.667	27	0	0	1	42.2	46	31	2	1	26	17	6.12	71	.272	.372	13-0	.154	0		-7	-0.5
1949	Det A	1	0	1.000	9	0	0	2	12	5	0	0	0	4	4	0.00	—	.125	.205	3-0	.333	0*		6	0.7
1950	Det A	9	6	.600	42	8	3-1	1	111	96	59	7	1	65	53	4.54	103	.239	.347	33-2	.121	-2	103	3	0.2
1951	Det A	3	4	.429	38	4	0	4	76	74	45	7	2	49	23	4.74	88	.264	.378	16-0	.250	0	48	-5	-0.4
1952	Det A	1	8	.111	41	0	0	5	63.1	53	29	1	0	39	18	3.69	103	.237	.350	11-0	.182	-0		1	0.2
1953	StL A	0	0	—	10	0	0	0	10.1	8	3	1	1	3	2	2.61	161	.205	.279	1-0	.000	0		2	0.1
	StL N	6	5	.545	49	0	0	7	84.2	84	32	5	0	39	32	2.98	143	.272	.353	16-0	.000	-2		12	1.4
1954	StL N	0	0	—	4	0	0	0	5	11	11	2	1	4	2	19.80	21	.440	.533	1-0	.000	-0		-8	-0.4
Total	12	46	54	.460	336	67	23-7	25	920.1	875	443	47	14	450	349	3.78	106	.253	.342	255-10	.145	-7	99	23	3.3
WHITE, DEACON James Laurie B 12.7.1847 Caton, NY D 7.7.1939 Aurora, IL BL/TR 5-11/175# d5.4.1871 M2 b-Will ▲																									
1876	Chi N	0	0	—	1	0	0	1	2	1	0	0		0	3	0.00	—	.143	.143	303	.343	0*		1	0.1
1890	Buf P	0	0	—	1	0	0	0	8	18	15	0	0	2	0	9.00	46	.429	.455	439	.260	0*		-5	-0.2
Total	2	0	0	—	2	0	0	1	10	19	15	0	0	2	3	7.20	53	.388	.412	742	.294	1		-4	-0.1
WHITE, LARRY Larry David B 9.25.1958 San Fernando, CA BR/TR 6-5/190# d9.20																									
1983	LA N	0	0	—	4	0	0	0-0	7	4	1	0	0	3-0	5	1.29	280	.174	.269	0-0	—	0		2	0.1
1984	LA N	0	1	.000	7	1	0	0-0	12	9	5	2	0	6-2	10	3.00	118	.209	.300	1-0	.000	-0	100	1	0.0
Total	2	0	1	.000	11	1	0	0-0	19	13	6	2	0	9-2	15	2.37	150	.197	.289	1-0	.000	-0	100	3	0.1
WHITE, MATT Matthew J. B 8.19.1977 Pittsfield, MA BR/TL 6/205# d5.27																									
2003	Bos A	0	1	.000	3	0	0	0-0	3.2	10	11	1	0	3-0	0	27.00	17	.526	.565	0-0	—	0		-9	-1.3
	Sea A	0	0	—	3	0	0	0-0	2	3	3	2	0	2-0	0	13.50	32	.375	.500	0-0	—	0		-2	-0.1
	Year	0	1	.000	6	0	0	0-0	5.2	13	18	3	0	5-0	0	22.24	20	.481	.545	0-0	—	0		-11	-1.4
WHITE, KIRBY Oliver Kirby "Red" or "Buck" B 1.3.1884 Hillsboro, OH D 4.22.1943 Hillsboro, OH BL/TR 6/190# d5.4																									
1909	Bos N	6	13	.316	23	19	11-1	0	148.1	134	73	5	1	80	53	3.22	88	.245	.343	50-3	.160	-1	69	-6	-0.9
1910	Bos N	1	2	.333	3	3	3	0	26	15	7	2	3	12	6	1.38	240	.188	.316	6-1	.333	1	45	5	0.7
	Pit N	10	9	.526	30	21	7-3	2	153.1	142	73	2	5	75	42	3.46	90	.258	.352	46-2	.261	3	106	-4	-0.3
	Year	11	11	.500	33	24	10-3	2	179.1	157	77	4	8	87	48	3.16	99	.249	.347	52-3	.269	4	98	0	0.4
1911	Pit N	0	1	.000	2	1	0	0	3	3	4	1	0	1	1	9.00	38	.250	.308	1-0	.000	-0	0	-2	-0.4
Total	3	17	25	.405	58	44	21-4	2	330.2	294	157	10	9	168	102	3.24	93	.247	.345	103-6	.214	3	83	-7	-0.9
WHITE, RICK Richard Allen B 12.23.1968 Springfield, OH BR/TR 6-4/215# d4.6																									
1994	Pit N	4	5	.444	43	5	0	6-3	75.1	79	35	9	6	17-3	38	3.82	113	.280	.329	13-0	.077	-1	105	4	0.4
1995	Pit N	2	3	.400	15	9	0	0-0	55	66	33	3	2	18-0	29	4.75	91	.299	.352	15-2	.067	-1	105	-3	-0.3
1998	TB A	2	6	.250	38	3	0	0-0	68.2	66	32	8	2	23-2	39	3.80	126	.253	.315	3-0	.333	0	65	7	0.7
1999	TB A	5	3	.625	63	1	0	0-2	108	132	56	8	1	38-5	81	4.08	122	.304	.358	0-0	—	0	75	10	0.7
2000	TB A	3	6	.333	44	0	0	2-3	71.1	57	30	7	5	26-3	47	3.41	145	.220	.301	0-0	—	0		12	1.3
	†NY N	2	3	.400	22	0	0	1-1	28.1	26	14	2	2	12-2	20	3.81	116	.232	.315	5-0	.200	0*		2	0.2
2001	NY N	4	5	.444	55	0	0	2-2	69.2	71	38	7	2	17-4	51	3.88	107	.257	.303	3-0	.000	-0		0	-0.1
2002	Col N	2	6	.250	41	0	0	0-1	40.2	49	30	4	1	18-4	27	6.20	77	.310	.376	0-0	—	0		-5	-0.9
	†StL N	3	1	.750	20	0	0	0-0	22	13	3	0	0	3-1	14	0.82	484	.169	.200	1-0	.000	-0		8	1.3
	Year	5	7	.417	61	0	0	0-1	62.2	62	37	4	1	21-5	41	4.31	104	.264	.322	1-0	.000	-0		1	0.4
2003	Chi A	1	2	.333	34	0	0	1-0	47.2	56	39	11	1	13-2	37	6.61	69	.295	.340	0-0	—	0		-11	-0.6
	Hou N	0	0	—	15	0	0	0-0	19.1	18	9	2	3	8-0	17	3.72	119	.243	.341	0-0	—	0		1	0.0
Total	8	28	40	.412	390	18	0	12-12	606	633	319	61	25	193-26	400	4.17	110	.270	.329	40-2	.100	-2	94	25	2.7
WHITE, STEVE Stephen Vincent B 12.21.1884 Dorchester, MA D 1.29.1975 Braintree, MA BR/TR 5-10/160# d5.29																									
1912	Was A	0	0	—	1	0	0	0	0.2	2	2	1	0	0	1	0.00	—	.667	.667	0-0	—	0		0	0.0
	Bos N	0	0	—	3	0	0	0	6	9	5	0	1	5	2	6.00	60	.429	.556	3-0	.000	-0		-1	-0.1
Total	1	0	0	—	4	0	0	0	6.2	11	7	1	1	5	3	5.40	66	.458	.567	3-0	.000	-0		-1	-0.1
WHITE, WILL William Henry "Whoop-La" B 10.11.1854 Caton, NY D 8.31.1911 Port Carling, ON, CAN BB/TR 5-9.5/175# d7.20 M1 b-Deacon																									
1877	Bos N	2	1	.667	3	3	3-1	0	27	27	15	0		2	7	3.00	94	.243	.257	15	.200	-1	197	0	-0.1
1878	Cin N	30	21	.588	52	52	52-5	0	468	477	249	1		45	169	1.79	119	.252	.269	197	.142	-8	111	16	0.6
1879	Cin N	43	31	.581	**76**	**75**	**75**-4	0	**680**	676	404	10		68	232	1.99	117	.238	.256	294	.136	-17	122	22	0.1
1880	Cin N	18	42	.300	62	62	58-3	0	517.1	550	323	9		56	161	2.14	116	.255	.273	207	.169	-9	73	14	0.3
1881	Det N	0	2	.000	2	2	2	0	18	24	18	0		2	5	5.00	58	.296	.313	7	.000	-1	46	-4	-0.4
1882	Cin AA	**40**	12	**.769**	54	54	**52-8**	0	**480**	411	164	3		71	122	1.54	172	.216	.244	207	.266	6	117	**60**	**6.7**
1883	Cin AA	**43**	22	.662	65	64	64-**6**	0	577	473	255	16		104	141	**2.09**	155	.209	.244	240	.225	3	119	**75**	**6.9**
1884	Cin AA	34	18	.654	52	52	52-**7**	0	456	479	224	16	35	74	118	3.32	101	.255	.296	184	.190	-2	116	5	-0.1
1885	Cin AA	18	15	.545	34	34	33-2	0	293.1	295	169	9	27	64	80	3.53	92	.255	.309	118	.169	-3	97	-5	-0.8
1886	Cin AA	1	2	.333	3	3	3	0	26	28	23	1	6	10	6	4.15	85	.280	.379	9	.111	-1	107	-3	-0.4

Year	Tm Lg	W	L	Pct	G	GS	CG-Sho	SV-BS	IP	H	R	HR	HB	BB-IB	SO	ERA	AERA	OAV	OOB	AB-SH	AVG	PB	Sup	APR	PW
Total	10	229	166	.580	403	401	394-36	0	3542.2	3440	1844	65	68	496	1041	2.28	120	.239	.268	1478	.183	-33	109	180	12.8

WHITEHEAD, JOHN John Henderson "Silent John" B 4.27.1909 Coleman, TX D 10.20.1964 Bonham, TX BR/TR 6-2/195# d4.19

Year	Tm Lg	W	L	Pct	G	GS	CG-Sho	SV-BS	IP	H	R	HR	HB	BB-IB	SO	ERA	AERA	OAV	OOB	AB-SH	AVG	PB	Sup	APR	PW
1935	Chi A	13	13	.500	28	27	18-1	0	222.1	209	101	17	2	101	72	3.72	124	.250	.332	82-4	.146	-5	90	23	1.9
1936	Chi A	13	13	.500	34	32	15-1	1	230.2	254	137	9	5	98	70	4.64	112	.276	.349	87-7	.241	1	104	13	1.4
1937	Chi A	11	8	.579	26	24	8-4	0	165.2	191	84	14	5	56	45	4.07	113	.294	.354	58-4	.224	1	104	11	1.1
1938	Chi A	10	11	.476	32	24	10-2	2	183.1	218	108	12	3	80	38	4.76	103	.299	.370	60-5	.100	-4	71	5	0.1
1939	Chi A	0	3	.000	7	4	0	0	32	60	30	4	0	5	9	8.16	58	.408	.428	9-0	.000	-1	70	-11	-0.9
	StL A	1	3	.250	26	4	0	1	66	88	49	10	2	17	9	5.86	83	.321	.365	17-0	.059	-1	118	-7	-0.5
	Year	1	6	.143	33	8	0	1	98	148	56	14	2	22	18	6.61	73	.352	.387	26-0	.038	-3	94	-18	-1.4
1940	StL A	1	3	.250	15	4	1-1	0	40	46	25	3	0	14	11	5.40	85	.286	.343	12-0	.167	-1	72	-3	-0.3
1942	StL A	0	0	—	4	0	0	0	4	8	3	0	1	1	0	6.75	55	.421	.476	0-0	—	0		-1	0.0
Total	7	49	54	.476	172	119	52-9	4	944	1074	537	69	18	372	254	4.60	105	.287	.355	325-20	.169	-11	93	30	2.8

WHITEHILL, EARL Earl Oliver B 2.7.1900 Cedar Rapids, IA D 10.22.1954 Omaha, NE BL/TL 5-9.5/174# d9.15 C2

Year	Tm Lg	W	L	Pct	G	GS	CG-Sho	SV-BS	IP	H	R	HR	HB	BB-IB	SO	ERA	AERA	OAV	OOB	AB-SH	AVG	PB	Sup	APR	PW
1923	Det A	2	0	1.000	8	3	1	0	33	22	14	2	3	15	19	2.73	142	.188	.296	11-1	.364	1	143	3	0.3
1924	Det A	17	9	.654	35	32	16-2	0	233	260	125	8	13	79	65	3.86	106	.288	.353	89-1	.213	1*	130	6	0.6
1925	Det A	11	11	.500	35	**33**	15-1	2	239.1	267	135	13	10	88	83	4.66	92	.293	.361	87-3	.218	0*	105	-5	-0.5
1926	Det A	16	13	.552	36	34	13	0	252.1	271	136	7	8	79	109	3.99	102	.277	.336	91-3	.253	4	98	2	0.5
1927	Det A	16	14	.533	41	31	17-3	3	236	238	110	4	9	105	95	3.36	125	.267	.350	78-6	.205	-0	93	22	2.4
1928	Det A	11	16	.407	31	30	12-1	0	196.1	214	131	8	1	78	93	4.31	95	.277	.344	67-3	.194	-1	95	-11	-1.4
1929	Det A	14	15	.483	38	28	18-1	1	245.1	267	147	16	3	96	103	4.62	93	.280	.348	90-4	.256	5	114	-7	-0.2
1930	Det A	17	13	.567	34	31	16	1	220.2	248	139	8	8	80	109	4.24	113	.285	.351	83-1	.193	-4	83	6	0.3
1931	Det A	13	16	.448	34	34	22	0	271.1	287	152	22	5	118	81	4.08	112	.274	.351	97-4	.155	-5	82	12	0.7
1932	Det A	16	12	.571	33	31	17-3	0	244	255	136	17	5	93	81	4.54	104	.269	.337	90-5	.244	1	112	9	1.0
1933	†Was A	22	8	.733	39	**37**	19-2	1	270	271	112	9	4	100	96	3.33	125	.262	.329	108-5	.222	2*	119	26	2.7
1934	Was A	14	11	.560	32	31	15	0	235	269	129	10	3	94	96	4.52	96	.290	.357	85-6	.200	4*	108	-4	0.0
1935	Was A	14	13	.519	34	34	19-1	0	279.1	318	149	16	7	104	102	4.29	101	.289	.354	104-4	.183	-1	113	1	0.1
1936	Was A	14	11	.560	28	28	14	0	212.1	252	124	17	2	89	63	4.87	98	.294	.362	77-5	.169	-0	101	2	0.2
1937	Cle A	8	8	.500	33	22	6-1	2	147	189	111	9	6	80	53	6.49	71	.322	.409	49-6	.224	1	120	-26	-2.2
1938	Cle A	9	8	.529	26	23	4	0	160.1	187	109	18	9	83	60	5.56	83	.289	.378	56-0	.125	-2	105	-15	-1.5
1939	Chi N	4	7	.364	24	11	2-1	1	89.1	102	59	8	5	50	42	5.14	77	.292	.389	29-0	.103	-2	83	-12	-1.5
Total	17	218	185	.541	541	473	226-16	11	3564.2	3917	2018	192	101	1431	1350	4.36	100	.282	.353	1291-57	.204	4	105	9	1.5

WHITEHOUSE, CHARLIE Charles Evis "Lefty" B 1.25.1894 Charleston, IL D 7.19.1960 Indianapolis, IN BB/TL 6/152# d8.29

Year	Tm Lg	W	L	Pct	G	GS	CG-Sho	SV-BS	IP	H	R	HR	HB	BB-IB	SO	ERA	AERA	OAV	OOB	AB-SH	AVG	PB	Sup	APR	PW
1914	Ind F	2	0	1.000	8	2	2	0	26	34	14	0	1	5	10	4.85	64	.324	.360	8-0	.000	-1	143	-3	-0.4
1915	New F	2	2	.500	11	3	1	0	39.2	46	29	0	5	17	18	4.31	59	.299	.386	10-1	.000	-1	127	-9	-1.0
1919	Was A	0	1	.000	6	1	0	0	12	13	7	1	0	6	5	4.50	71	.283	.365	1-0	.000	-0	98	-1	-0.1
Total	3	4	3	.571	25	6	3	0	77.2	93	50	1	6	28	33	4.52	63	.305	.375	19-1	.000	-2	129	-13	-1.5

WHITEHOUSE, LEN Leonard Joseph B 9.10.1957 Burlington, VT BL/TL 5-11/175# d9.1

Year	Tm Lg	W	L	Pct	G	GS	CG-Sho	SV-BS	IP	H	R	HR	HB	BB-IB	SO	ERA	AERA	OAV	OOB	AB-SH	AVG	PB	Sup	APR	PW
1981	Tex A	0	1	.000	2	1	0	0-0	3.1	8	7	1	0	2-0	2	16.20	21	.500	.526	0-0	—	0	52	-5	-0.9
1983	Min A	7	1	.875	60	0	0	2-1	73.2	70	34	6	2	44-11	44	4.15	103	.261	.365	0-0	—	0		2	0.2
1984	Min A	2	2	.500	30	0	0	1-3	31.1	29	11	3	2	17-3	18	3.16	133	.254	.361	0-0	—	0		4	0.5
1985	Min A	0	0	—	5	0	0	1-0	7.1	12	9	4	0	2-0	4	11.05	40	.353	.389	0-0	—	0		-5	-0.2
Total	4	9	4	.692	97	1	0	4-4	115.2	119	61	14	4	65-14	68	4.67	91	.275	.372	0-0	—	0	52	-4	-0.4

WHITEHURST, WALLY Walter Richard B 4.11.1964 Shreveport, LA BR/TR 6-3/195# d7.17

Year	Tm Lg	W	L	Pct	G	GS	CG-Sho	SV-BS	IP	H	R	HR	HB	BB-IB	SO	ERA	AERA	OAV	OOB	AB-SH	AVG	PB	Sup	APR	PW
1989	NY N	0	1	.000	9	1	0	0-0	14	17	7	2	0	5-0	9	4.50	73	.293	.344	1-1	.000	0	81	-2	-0.1
1990	NY N	1	0	1.000	38	0	0	2-0	65.2	63	27	5	0	9-2	46	3.29	114	.251	.277	8-1	.250	0		3	0.2
1991	NY N	7	12	.368	36	20	0	1-0	133.1	142	67	12	4	25-3	87	4.18	87	.274	.311	33-5	.182	1	95	-7	-0.7
1992	NY N	3	9	.250	44	11	0	0-3	97	99	45	4	4	33-5	70	3.62	96	.264	.328	22-1	.182	1	88	-2	-0.2
1993	SD N	4	7	.364	21	19	0	0-0	105.2	109	47	11	3	30-5	57	3.83	108	.276	.326	24-10	.083	-2	79	5	0.4
1994	SD N	4	7	.364	13	13	0	0-0	64	84	37	8	1	26-4	43	4.92	84	.319	.383	19-0	.105	0	80	-5	-0.7
1996	NY A	1	1	.500	2	2	0	0-0	8	11	6	1	0	2-0	1	6.75	73	.324	.361	0-0	—	0	75	-1	-0.3
Total	7	20	37	.351	163	66	0	3-3	487.2	525	236	43	12	130-19	313	4.02	95	.277	.325	107-18	.150	1	87	-9	-1.4

WHITESIDE, SEAN David Sean B 4.19.1971 Lakeland, FL BL/TL 6-4/190# d4.29

Year	Tm Lg	W	L	Pct	G	GS	CG-Sho	SV-BS	IP	H	R	HR	HB	BB-IB	SO	ERA	AERA	OAV	OOB	AB-SH	AVG	PB	Sup	APR	PW
1995	Det A	0	0	—	2	0	0	0-0	3.2	7	6	1	0	4-1	2	14.73	32	.438	.500	0-0	—	0		-4	-0.2

WHITESIDE, MATT Matthew Christopher B 8.8.1967 Charleston, MO BR/TR 6/205# d8.5

Year	Tm Lg	W	L	Pct	G	GS	CG-Sho	SV-BS	IP	H	R	HR	HB	BB-IB	SO	ERA	AERA	OAV	OOB	AB-SH	AVG	PB	Sup	APR	PW
1992	Tex A	1	1	.500	20	0	0	4-0	28	26	8	1	0	11-2	13	1.93	197	.245	.314	0-0	—	0		6	0.5
1993	Tex A	2	1	.667	60	0	0	1-4	73	78	37	7	1	23-6	39	4.32	96	.281	.337	0-0	—	0		-1	-0.1
1994	Tex A	2	2	.500	47	0	0	1-2	61	68	40	6	1	28-3	37	5.02	96	.286	.361	0-0	—	0		-2	-0.1
1995	Tex A	5	4	.556	40	0	0	3-1	53	48	24	5	1	19-2	46	4.08	119	.242	.308	0-0	—	0		5	0.8
1996	Tex A	0	1	.000	14	0	0	0-0	32.1	43	24	8	0	11-1	15	6.68	78	.321	.367	0-0	—	0		-4	-0.2
1997	Tex A	4	1	.800	42	1	0	0-4	72.2	85	45	4	3	26-3	44	5.08	94	.296	.355	0-0	—	0	134	-2	0.0
1998	Phi N	1	1	.500	10	0	0	0-0	18	27	18	6	0	5-0	14	8.50	51	.338	.376	2-0	.000	-0		-8	-0.8
1999	SD N	1	0	1.000	10	0	0	0-0	11	19	17	1	0	5-0	9	13.91	30	.396	.444	0-0	—	0		-12	-0.9
2000	SD N	2	3	.400	28	0	0	0-0	37	32	21	6	1	17-3	27	4.14	105	.232	.318	0-0	—	0		0	0.0
2001	Atl N	0	1	.000	13	0	0	0-0	16.1	23	14	5	1	7-1	10	7.16	62	.319	.383	0-0	—	0		-5	-0.3
Total	10	18	15	.545	284	1	0	9-11	402.1	449	248	49	8	152-21	254	5.10	89	.284	.347	2-0	.000	-0	134	-23	-1.1

WHITING, JESSE Jesse W. B 5.30.1879 Philadelphia, PA D 10.28.1937 Philadelphia, PA TR 5-10/154# d9.27

Year	Tm Lg	W	L	Pct	G	GS	CG-Sho	SV-BS	IP	H	R	HR	HB	BB-IB	SO	ERA	AERA	OAV	OOB	AB-SH	AVG	PB	Sup	APR	PW
1902	Phi N	0	1	.000	1	1	1	0	9	13	8	0	0	6	0	5.00	56	.333	.422	3-0	.333	0	48	-3	-0.2
1906	Bro N	1	1	.500	3	2	2-1	0	24.2	26	10	0	1	6	7	2.92	86	.286	.337	10-0	.300	1	72	-1	0.0
1907	Bro N	0	0	—	1	0	0	0	3	3	4	0	0	3	2	12.00	20	.273	.429	2-0	.000	-0*		-3	-0.2
Total	3	1	2	.333	5	3	3-1	0	36.2	42	22	0	1	15	9	4.17	62	.298	.369	15-0	.267	0	65	-7	-0.4

WHITNEY, ART Arthur Wilson B 1.16.1858 Brockton, MA D 8.15.1943 Lowell, MA BR/TR 5-8/155# d5.1.1880 b-Frank ▲

Year	Tm Lg	W	L	Pct	G	GS	CG-Sho	SV-BS	IP	H	R	HR	HB	BB-IB	SO	ERA	AERA	OAV	OOB	AB-SH	AVG	PB	Sup	APR	PW
1882	Det N	0	1	.000	3	2	1	0	18	31	17	1		8	11	6.00	49	.373	.429	115	.183	-1*	99	-5	-0.3
1886	Pit AA	0	0	—	1	0	0	0	6	7	4	0	0	3	2	3.00	113	.304	.385	511	.239	0*		0	0.0
1889	†NY N	0	0	—	1	0	0	0	4.1	1	3	0	0	4	3	2.08	190	.071	.278	473	.218	0*		0	0.0
Total	3	0	1	.000	5	2	1	0	28.1	39	24	1	0	15	16	4.76	67	.325	.400	1099	.224	-1	99	-5	-0.3

WHITNEY, JIM James Evans "Grasshopper Jim" B 11.10.1857 Conklin, NY D 5.21.1891 Binghamton, NY BL/TR 6-2/172# d5.2

Year	Tm Lg	W	L	Pct	G	GS	CG-Sho	SV-BS	IP	H	R	HR	HB	BB-IB	SO	ERA	AERA	OAV	OOB	AB-SH	AVG	PB	Sup	APR	PW
1881	Bos N	**31**	33	.484	**66**	**63**	**57**-6	0	**552.1**	548	284	6		90	162	2.48	107	.248	.277	282	.255	11*	86	11	2.1
1882	Bos N	24	21	.533	49	48	46-3	0	420	404	229	3		41	180	2.64	109	.237	.255	251	.323	23*	110	7	2.8
1883	Bos N	37	21	.638	62	56	54-1	**2**	514	492	258	7		35	**345**	2.24	138	.238	.251	409	.281	20*	106	44	5.6
1884	Bos N	23	14	.622	38	37	35-6	0	336	272	140	12		27	270	2.09	138	.207	.223	270	.259	10*	100	27	3.6
1885	Bos N	18	32	.360	51	50	50-2	0	441.1	503	286	14		37	200	2.98	90	.272	.286	290	.234	7*	95	-23	-1.3
1886	KC N	12	32	.273	46	44	42-3	0	393	465	292	9		55	167	4.49	84	.284	.308	247	.239	5*	64	-27	-1.4
1887	Was N	24	21	.533	47	47	46-2	0	404.2	430	253	16	16	42	146	3.22	125	.259	.284	201	.264	10*	85	30	3.9
1888	Was N	18	21	.462	39	39	37-3	0	325	317	184	7	9	54	79	3.05	91	.245	.280	141	.170	-1*	92	-14	-1.6
1889	Ind N	2	7	.222	9	8	7	0	70	106	73	4	2	19	16	6.81	61	.339	.380	32	.375	5*	107	-19	-1.4
1890	Phi AA	2	2	.500	6	4	3	0	40	61	27	1	1	11	6	5.17	75	.341	.382	21	.238	-0*	109	-4	-0.3
Total	10	191	204	.484	413	396	377-26	2	3496.1	3598	2026	79	28	411	1571	2.97	104	.253	.275	2144	.261	89	93	32	12.0

WHITROCK, BILL William Franklin B 3.4.1870 Cincinnati, OH D 7.26.1935 Derby, CT TR 5-7.5/170# d5.3

Year	Tm Lg	W	L	Pct	G	GS	CG-Sho	SV-BS	IP	H	R	HR	HB	BB-IB	SO	ERA	AERA	OAV	OOB	AB-SH	AVG	PB	Sup	APR	PW
1890	StL AA	5	6	.455	16	11	10	1	105	104	62	2	7	40	39	3.51	123	.251	.327	48	.146	-3	68	8	0.5
1893	Lou N	2	5	.286	8	8	5	0	46.2	64	53	3	4	19	8	8.10	54	.317	.387	21	.286	1	88	-19	-1.8
1894	Lou N	0	1	.000	1	1	0	0	4	8	8	0	0	2	0	9.00	57	.400	.455	2-0	.000	-0	97	-2	-0.4
	Cin N	2	6	.250	11	9	9	0	79.1	121	88	7	9	46	10	6.24	89	.347	.436	65-0	.231	-2*	67	-9	-0.7
	Year	2	7	.222	12	10	9	0	83.1	129	93	7	9	48	10	6.37	87	.350	.437	67-0	.224	-3	69	-11	-1.1
1896	Phi N	0	1	.000	2	1	1	0	9	10	5	0	0	3	1	3.00	144	.278	.333	3-0	.000	-0	33	1	0.1

Year	Tm Lg	W	L	Pct	G	GS	CG-Sho	SV-BS	IP	H	R	HR	HB	BB-IB	SO	ERA	AERA	OAV	OOB	AB-SH	AVG	PB	Sup	APR	PW
Total	4	9	19	.321	38	30	25	1	244	307	216	12	20	110	58	5.35	89	.300	.379	139-0	.201	-4	72	-21	-2.3
WHITSON, ED Eddie Lee B 5.19.1955 Johnson City, TN BR/TR 6-3/195# d9.4																									
1977	Pit N	1	0	1.000	5	2	0	0-0	15.2	11	6	0	0	9-1	10	3.45	116	.204	.308	4-0	.000	-0	67	1	0.0
1978	Pit N	5	6	.455	43	0	0	4-3	74	66	31	5	2	37-5	64	3.28	113	.243	.333	11-1	.182	-0		3	0.5
1979	Pit N	2	3	.400	19	7	0	1-0	57.2	53	36	6	1	36-3	31	4.37	89	.238	.346	13-4	.000	-1	143	-5	-0.6
	SF N	5	8	.385	18	17	2	0-0	100.1	98	47	5	4	39-6	62	3.95	89	.254	.326	32-5	.156	-1	92	-4	-0.5
	Year	7	11	.389	37	24	2	1-0	158	151	51	11	5	75-9	93	4.10	89	.248	.334	45-9	.111	-2	107	-10	-1.1
1980	SF N☆	11	13	.458	34	34	6-2	0-0	211.2	222	88	7	4	56-7	90	3.10	114	.271	.318	66-9	.091	-4	79	8	0.4
1981	SF N	6	9	.400	22	22	2-1	0-0	123	130	61	10	2	47-5	65	4.02	85	.273	.339	33-9	.091	-1	95	-8	-1.1
1982	Cle A	4	2	.667	40	9	1-1	2-0	107.2	91	43	6	0	58-3	61	3.26	125	.231	.324	0-0	—	0	72	10	0.5
1983	SD N	5	7	.417	31	21	2	1-0	144.1	143	73	23	1	50-1	81	4.30	81	.256	.316	44-2	.182	1	101	-12	-1.1
1984	†SD N	14	8	.636	31	31	1	0-0	189	181	72	16	3	42-1	103	3.24	110	.255	.296	61-6	.049	-5*	105	9	0.6
1985	NY A	10	8	.556	30	30	2-2	0-0	158.2	201	100	19	2	43-0	89	4.88	82	.309	.350	0-0	—	0	135	-18	-1.8
1986	NY A	5	2	.714	14	4	0	0-0	37	54	37	5	0	23-1	27	7.54	54	.335	.412	0-0	—	0	155	-15	-2.4
	SD N	1	7	.125	17	12	0	0-0	75.2	85	48	8	0	37-0	46	5.59	66	.287	.364	18-2	.167	-0	91	-14	-1.3
1987	SD N	10	13	.435	36	34	3-1	0-0	205.2	197	113	36	3	64-3	135	4.73	84	.251	.309	65-10	.123	-1	101	-14	-1.7
1988	SD N	13	11	.542	34	33	3-1	0-0	205.1	202	93	17	1	45-1	118	3.77	90	.259	.298	66-9	.167	1	98	-8	-0.8
1989	SD N	16	11	.593	33	33	5-1	0-0	227	198	77	22	5	48-6	117	2.66	132	.235	.278	72-7	.139	1*	100	21	2.5
1990	SD N	14	9	.609	32	32	6-3	0-0	228.2	215	73	13	1	47-8	127	2.60	147	.251	.289	67-13	.149	1*	105	**32**	3.3
1991	SD N	4	6	.400	13	12	2	0-0	78.2	93	47	13	0	17-3	40	5.03	76	.299	.332	24-2	.125	-1	87	-10	-1.2
Total	15	126	123	.506	452	333	35-12	8-3	2240	2240	1045	211	29	698-54	1266	3.79	97	.261	.316	576-79	.125	-11	101	-24	-4.7
WHITTAKER, WALT Walter Elton "Doc" B 6.11.1894 Chelsea, MA D 8.7.1965 Pembroke, MA BL/TR 5-9.5/165# d7.6																									
1916	Phi A	0	0	—	1	0	0	0	2	3	1	0	0	2	0	4.50	63	.375	.500	0-0	—	0		0	0.0
WICKANDER, KEVIN Kevin Dean B 1.4.1965 Fort Dodge, IA BL/TL 6-2/202# d8.10																									
1989	Cle A	0	0	—	2	0	0	0-0	2.2	6	1	0	0	2-1	0	3.38	118	.462	.533	0-0	—	0		0	0.0
1990	Cle A	0	1	.000	10	0	0	0-1	12.1	14	6	0	1	4-0	10	3.65	108	.304	.358	0-0	—	0		0	0.0
1992	Cle A	2	0	1.000	44	0	0	1-2	41	39	14	1	4	28-3	38	3.07	127	.258	.384	0-0	—	0		5	0.2
1993	Cle A	0	0	—	11	0	0	0-0	8.2	15	7	3	0	3-0	3	4.15	104	.366	.409	0-0	—	0		-1	-0.1
	Cin N	1	0	1.000	33	0	0	0-1	25.1	32	20	5	2	19-1	20	6.75	60	.308	.424	2-0	.000	-0		-7	-0.4
1995	Det A	0	0	—	21	0	0	1-2	17.1	18	6	1	1	9-4	9	2.60	183	.273	.364	0-0	—	0		4	0.2
	Mil A	0	0	—	8	0	0	0-0	6	1	0	0	0	3-1	2	0.00	—	.059	.190	0-0	—	0		3	0.1
	Year	0	0	—	29	0	0	1-2	23.1	19	10	1	1	12-5	11	1.93	250	.229	.327	0-0	—	0		7	0.3
1996	Mil A	2	0	1.000	21	0	0	0-2	25.1	26	16	2	0	17-2	19	4.97	104	.265	.368	0-0	—	0		0	0.0
Total	6	5	1	.833	150	0	0	2-8	138.2	151	70	12	8	85-12	101	4.02	108	.282	.383	2-0	.000	-0		4	-0.0
WICKER, KEMP Kemp Caswell (b: Kemp Caswell Whicker) B 8.13.1906 Kernersville, NC D 6.11.1973 Kernersville, NC BR/TL 5-11/182# d8.14																									
1936	NY A	1	2	.333	7	0	0	0	20	31	18	2	0	11	5	7.65	61	.356	.429	7-0	.143	-0		-7	-0.8
1937	†NY A	7	3	.700	16	10	6-1	0	88	107	52	8	0	26	14	4.40	101	.296	.343	35-1	.114	-3	153	0	-0.4
1938	NY A	1	0	1.000	1	0	0	0	1	0	0	0	0	1	0	0.00	—	.000	.250	0-0	—	0		1	0.1
1941	Bro N	1	2	.333	16	2	0	1	32	30	14	3	0	14	8	3.66	100	.252	.331	4-3	.250	0	81	1	0.1
Total	4	10	7	.588	40	12	6-1	1	141	168	84	13	0	52	27	4.66	92	.294	.353	46-4	.130	-2	143	-5	-1.0
WICKER, BOB Robert Kitridge B 5.25.1877 Bono, IN D 1.22.1955 Evanston, IL BL/TR 5-11/210# d8.11																									
1901	StL N	0	0	—	1	0	0	0	3	4	3	0	0	1	2	0.00	—	.308	.357	3-0	.333	0*		0	0.0
1902	StL N	5	12	.294	22	16	14-1	0	152.1	159	82	1	2	45	78	3.19	86	.269	.322	77-2	.234	1*	67	-9	-0.6
1903	StL N	0	0	—	1	0	0	0	5	4	1	0	0	3	3	0.00	—	.174	.269	2-0	.000	-0		2	0.1
	Chi N	20	9	.690	32	27	24-1	1	247	236	114	3	3	74	110	3.02	104	.253	.311	98-1	.245	6	119	8	1.2
	Year	20	9	.690	33	27	24-1	1	252	240	120	3	3	77	113	2.96	106	.252	.309	100-1	.240	6	119	5	1.3
1904	Chi N	17	9	.654	30	27	23-4	0	229	201	92	6	3	58	99	2.67	100	.232	.282	155-3	.219	1*	112	2	0.0
1905	Chi N	13	6	.684	22	22	17-4	0	178	139	46	3	1	47	86	2.02	147	.221	.276	72-3	.139	-2*	99	22	1.9
1906	Chi N	3	5	.375	10	8	5	0	72.1	70	36	0	0	19	25	2.99	88	.257	.306	20-0	.100	-1	97	-4	-0.6
	Cin N	6	11	.353	20	17	14	0	150	150	69	3	1	46	69	2.70	102	.263	.319	50-1	.180	2	76	-1	-0.1
	Year	9	16	.360	30	25	19	0	222.1	220	72	3	1	65	94	2.79	97	.261	.315	70-1	.157	1	83	-7	-0.7
Total	6	64	52	.552	138	117	97-10	1	1036.2	963	443	16	10	293	472	2.73	105	.247	.301	477-10	.205	6	99	20	1.9
WICKERSHAM, DAVE David Clifford B 9.27.1935 Erie, PA BR/TR 6-3/190# d9.18																									
1960	KC A	0	0	—	5	0	0	2	8.1	4	1	0	0	1-0	3	1.08	369	.148	.179	1-0	.000	-0		3	0.1
1961	KC A	2	1	.667	17	0	0	2	21	25	12	0	2	5-1	10	5.14	81	.309	.360	3-0	.667	1		-1	-0.1
1962	KC A	11	4	.733	30	9	3	1	110	105	53	13	8	43-1	61	4.17	101	.257	.337	35-2	.057	-3	106	2	0.0
1963	KC A	12	15	.444	38	34	4-1	1	237.2	244	116	21	9	79-2	118	4.09	95	.268	.330	80-4	.138	-3	86	-3	-0.6
1964	Det A	19	12	.613	40	36	11-1	1	254	224	108	28	12	81-3	164	3.44	106	.232	.299	82-12	.073	-5	96	5	0.0
1965	Det A	9	14	.391	34	27	8-3	0	195.1	179	91	12	11	61-6	109	3.78	92	.241	.307	58-7	.069	-4	87	-6	-1.1
1966	Det A	8	3	.727	38	14	3	1	140.2	139	64	14	8	54-4	93	3.20	109	.261	.336	45-1	.044	-3	125	1	-0.2
1967	Det A	4	5	.444	36	4	0	4	85.1	72	30	6	4	33-2	44	2.74	119	.235	.315	15-1	.000	-2	60	4	0.4
1968	Pit N	1	0	1.000	11	0	0	1	20.2	21	12	0	0	13-3	9	3.48	84	.276	.362	3-1	.333	0		-2	-0.1
1969	KC A	2	3	.400	34	0	0	5-2	50	58	27	6	2	14-2	27	3.96	93	.294	.346	2-0	.000	0		-2	-0.3
Total	10	68	57	.544	283	124	29-5	18-2	1123	1071	514	100	56	384-24	638	3.66	100	.252	.320	324-28	.086	-18	94	1	-1.9
WICKMAN, BOB Robert Joe B 2.6.1969 Green Bay, WI BR/TR 6-1/212# d8.24																									
1992	NY A	6	1	.857	8	8	0	0-0	50.1	51	25	2	2	20-0	21	4.11	95	.273	.344	0-0	—	0	145	-1	-0.1
1993	NY A	14	4	.778	41	19	1-1	4-4	140	156	82	13	5	69-7	70	4.63	90	.284	.368	0-0	—	0	161	-9	-1.1
1994	NY A	5	4	.556	**53**	0	0	6-4	70	54	26	3	1	27-3	56	3.09	148	.213	.287	0-0	—	0		12	1.5
1995	†NY A	2	4	.333	63	1	0	1-9	80	77	38	6	5	33-3	51	4.05	114	.253	.335	0-0	—	0	81	5	0.4
1996	NY A	4	1	.800	58	0	0	0-3	79	94	41	7	5	34-1	61	4.67	106	.299	.373	0-0	—	0		4	0.3
	Mil A	3	0	1.000	12	0	0	0-1	16.2	12	9	3	0	10-2	14	3.24	160	.200	.314	0-0	—	0		2	0.3
	Year	7	1	.875	70	0	0	0-4	95.2	106	54	10	5	44-3	75	4.42	113	.283	.363	0-0	—	0		6	0.6
1997	Mil A	7	6	.538	74	0	0	1-4	95.2	89	32	8	3	41-7	78	2.73	169	.252	.333	0-0	—	0		20	2.4
1998	Mil N	6	9	.400	72	0	0	25-7	82.1	79	38	5	4	39-2	71	3.72	115	.262	.352	1-0	.000	-0		5	0.9
1999	Mil N	3	8	.273	71	0	0	37-8	74.1	75	31	6	2	38-6	60	3.39	134	.262	.351	1-0	.000	-0		9	1.8
2000	Mil N★	2	2	.500	43	0	0	16-4	46	37	18	1	1	20-2	44	2.93	155	.215	.299	0-0	—	0		8	1.1
	Cle A	1	3	.250	26	0	0	14-3	26.2	27	12	0	0	12-3	11	3.38	147	.270	.348	0-0	—	0		4	0.8
2001	†Cle A	5	0	1.000	70	0	0	32-3	67.2	61	18	4	2	14-2	66	2.39	189	.240	.285	0-0	—	0		17	2.4
2002	Cle A	1	3	.250	36	0	0	20-2	34.1	42	22	3	1	10-0	36	4.46	99	.284	.333	0-0	—	0		-2	-0.4
Total	11	59	45	.567	627	28	1-1	156-52	863	854	392	61	31	367-38	639	3.68	122	.260	.338	2-0	.000	-0	141	74	10.3
WIDMAR, AL Albert Joseph B 3.20.1925 Cleveland, OH BR/TR 6-3/185# d4.25 C17																									
1947	Bos A	0	0	—	2	0	0	0	1.1	1	2	1	0	2	1	13.50	29	.200	.429	0-0	—	0		-1	-0.1
1948	StL A	2	6	.250	49	0	0	1	82.2	88	42	4	0	48	34	4.46	102	.275	.370	10-0	.300	1		2	0.4
1950	StL A	7	15	.318	36	26	8-1	4	194.2	211	115	16	3	74	78	4.76	104	.271	.337	67-2	.149	-3	72	6	0.3
1951	StL A	4	9	.308	26	16	4	0	107.2	157	84	19	2	52	28	6.52	67	.344	.414	30-6	.167	-1	92	-22	-2.3
1952	Chi A	0	0	—	1	0	0	0	2	4	1	1	0	0	2	4.50	81	.444	.444	0-0	—	0		0	0.0
Total	5	13	30	.302	114	42	12-1	5	388.1	461	244	41	5	176	143	5.21	90	.294	.367	107-8	.168	-4	80	-15	-1.7
WIDNER, WILD BILL William Waterfield B 6.3.1867 Cincinnati, OH D 12.10.1908 Cincinnati, OH BR/TR 6/180# d6.8																									
1887	Cin AA	1	0	1.000	1	1	1	0	9	11	8	2	1	2	0	5.00	87	.275	.326	4	.250	-0	132	-1	-0.1
1888	Was N	5	7	.417	13	13	13	0	115	111	69	7	6	22	33	2.82	99	.247	.291	60	.200	-1*	89	-5	-0.5
1889	Col AA	12	20	.375	41	34	25-2	1	294	368	241	11	18	85	63	5.20	70	.297	.351	133	.211	-2	113	-46	-3.8
1890	Col AA	4	8	.333	13	10	8-1	0	96	103	52	3	3	24	14	3.28	109	.266	.314	41	.195	-1	86	4	0.4
1891	Cin AA	0	1	.000	1	1	1	0	8	13	7	0	2	4	0	7.88	52	.351	.442	4	.250	-0	61	-2	-0.2
Total	5	22	36	.379	69	59	48-3	1	522	606	377	23	30	137	110	4.36	79	.281	.333	242	.207	-3	104	-50	-4.2

Year	Tm Lg	W	L	Pct	G	GS	CG-Sho	SV-BS	IP	H	R	HR	HB	BB-IB	SO	ERA	AERA	OAV	OOB	AB-SH	AVG	PB	Sup	APR	PW
WIEAND, TED Franklin Delano Roosevelt B 4.4.1933 Walnutport, PA BR/TR 6-2/195# d9.27																									
1958	Cin N	0	0	—	1	0	0	0	2	4	2	1	0	0-0	2	9.00	46	.400	.400	0-0	—	0		-1	0.0
1960	Cin N	0	1	.000	5	0	0	0	4.1	4	5	2	0	5-1	3	10.38	37	.250	.429	0-0	—	0		-3	-0.5
Total	2	0	1	.000	6	0	0	0	6.1	8	7	3	0	5-1	5	9.95	39	.308	.419	0-0	—	0		-4	-0.5
WIEDEMEYER, CHARLIE Charles John "Chick" B 1.31.1914 Chicago, IL D 10.27.1979 Lake Geneva, FL BL/TL 6-3/180# d9.9																									
1934	Chi N	0	0	—	4	1	0	0	8.1	16	10	0	1	4	2	9.72	40	.432	.500	1-0	.000	-0	156	-6	-0.3
WIEDMAN, STUMP George Edward B 2.17.1861 Rochester, NY D 3.2.1905 New York, NY BR/TR 5-7.5/165# d8.26 U1 ▲																									
1880	Buf N	0	9	.000	17	13	9	0	113.2	141	77	1		9	25	3.40	72	.291	.304	78	.103	-5*	57	-10	-1.1
1881	Det N	8	5	.615	13	13	13-1	0	115	108	48	1		12	26	**1.80**	**162**	.238	**.258**	47	.255	0	101	13	1.2
1882	Det N	25	20	.556	46	45	43-4	0	411	391	204	10		39	161	2.63	112	.236	.253	193	.218	-5*	86	18	1.2
1883	Det N	20	24	.455	52	47	41-3	**2**	402.1	435	265	8		72	183	3.53	88	.257	.288	313	.185	-8*	90	-13	-1.6
1884	Det N	4	21	.160	26	26	24	0	212.2	257	179	9		57	96	3.72	78	.273	.314	300	.163	-4*	55	-21	-2.2
1885	Det N	14	24	.368	38	38	37-3	0	330	343	198	7		63	149	3.14	91	.252	.286	153	.157	-4*	90	-5	-1.0
1886	KC N	12	36	.250	51	51	48-1	0	427.2	549	323	11		112	168	4.52	83	.303	.344	179	.168	-10	63	-31	-3.4
1887	Det N	13	7	.650	21	21	20	0	183	221	132	9	9	60	56	5.36	76	.296	.356	82	.207	-2	117	-18	-1.6
	NY AA	4	8	.333	12	12	11-1	0	97	122	84	3	1	25	37	4.64	92	.292	.333	46	.152	-2*	60	-6	-0.6
	NY N	0	1	.000	1	1	1	0	8	10	6	0	0	2	4	1.13	335	.286	.324	3	.333	0	52	1	0.1
1888	NY N	1	1	.500	2	2	2	0	18	17	20	2	2	8	5	3.50	78	.230	.321	7	.000	-0	179	-4	-0.4
Total	9	101	156	.393	279	269	249-13	2	2318.1	2594	1536	61	12	459	910	3.61	89	.268	.302	1401	.177	-41	81	-76	-9.4
WIENEKE, JACK John B 3.10.1894 Saltsburg, PA D 3.16.1933 Pleasant Ridge, MI BR/TL 6/182# d7.4																									
1921	Chi A	0	1	.000	10	3	0	0	25.1	39	24	4	1	17	10	8.17	52	.351	.442	9-0	.111	-1	66	-10	-0.5
WIESLER, BOB Robert George B 8.13.1930 St.Louis, MO BB/TL 6-2/195# d8.3 Mil 1951																									
1951	NY A	0	2	.000	4	3	0	0	9.1	13	15	0	0	11	3	13.50	28	.361	.511	3-0	.000	-1	54	-10	-1.6
1954	NY A	3	2	.600	6	5	0	0	30.1	28	15	0	0	30	25	4.15	83	.259	.420	11-1	.273	1	97	-2	-0.3
1955	NY A	0	2	.000	16	7	0	0	53	39	27	1	1	49-0	22	3.91	96	.212	.380	14-0	.143	-1	105	-1	-0.1
1956	Was A	3	12	.200	37	21	3	0	123	141	98	11	3	112-1	49	6.44	67	.300	.435	33-4	.091	-3*	88	-27	-3.0
1957	Was A	1	1	.500	3	2	1	0	16.1	15	8	2	1	11-0	9	4.41	88	.250	.375	6-0	.167	0	126	-1	0.0
1958	Was A	0	0	—	4	0	0	0	9.1	14	8	2	1	5-0	5	6.75	56	.359	.435	2-0	.000	-0		-3	-0.2
Total	6	7	19	.269	70	38	4	0	241.1	250	171	16	6	218-1	113	5.74	70	.279	.421	69-5	.130	-3	92	-44	-5.2
WIGGINS, SCOTT Scott Joseph B 3.24.1976 Fort Thomas, KY BL/TL 6-3/205# d9.11																									
2002	Tor A	0	0	—	3	0	0	0-0	2.2	5	1	1	0	1-0	3	3.38	137	.417	.462	0-0	—	0		0	0.0
WIGGS, JIMMY James Alvin "Big Jim" B 9.1.1876 Trondheim, Norway D 1.20.1963 Xenia, OH BB/TR 6-4/200# d4.23																									
1903	Cin N	0	1	.000	2	1	0	0	5	12	7	0	1	2	2	5.40	66	.500	.556	1-0	.000	-0	57	-2	-0.3
1905	Det A	3	3	.500	7	7	4	0	41.1	30	25	0	1	29	37	3.27	84	.205	.341	15-0	.133	-0	78	-4	-0.5
1906	Det A	0	0	—	4	1	0	0	10.1	11	9	1	2	7	7	5.23	53	.275	.408	3-0	.333	0	182	-3	-0.1
Total	3	3	4	.429	13	9	4	0	56.2	53	41	1	4	38	46	3.81	74	.252	.377	19-0	.158	-0	87	-9	-0.9
WIGHT, BILL William Robert "Lefty" B 4.12.1922 Rio Vista, CA BL/TL 6-1/180# d4.17																									
1946	NY A	2	2	.500	14	4	1	0	40.1	44	22	1	1	30	11	4.46	77	.289	.410	9-2	.000	-1	124	-4	-0.5
1947	NY A	1	0	1.000	1	1	1	0	9	8	3	0	0	2	3	1.00	353	.242	.286	2-1	.000	0	125	2	0.2
1948	Chi A	9	20	.310	34	32	7-1	1	223.1	238	132	9	1	135	68	4.80	89	.278	.377	73-3	.082	-7	62	-13	-2.1
1949	Chi A	15	13	.536	35	33	14-3	1	245	254	106	9	0	96	78	3.31	126	.275	.343	85-9	.165	-1	96	22	2.2
1950	Chi A	10	16	.385	30	28	13-3	0	206	213	89	10	0	79	62	3.58	125	.270	.336	61-10	.000	-9	63	22	1.7
1951	Bos A	7	7	.500	34	17	4-2	0	118.1	128	77	5	0	63	38	5.10	88	.282	.369	41-0	.073	-4	95	-8	-1.2
1952	Bos A	2	1	.667	10	2	0	0	24.1	14	11	3	1	14	5	2.96	133	.169	.296	7-0	.143	-0	122	2	0.2
	Det A	5	9	.357	23	19	8-3	0	143.2	167	71	7	0	55	65	3.88	98	.291	.354	50-2	.220	1	93	-2	0.1
	Year	7	10	.412	33	21	8-3	0	168	181	75	10	1	69	70	3.75	102	.276	.346	57-2	.211	1	96	1	0.3
1953	Det A	0	3	.000	13	4	0	0	25.1	35	33	4	0	14	10	8.88	46	.333	.412	7-0	.429	1	126	-16	-1.5
	Cle A	2	1	.667	20	0	0	1	26.2	29	12	1	0	16	14	3.71	101	.282	.378	5-0	.000	-1		0	0.0
	Year	2	4	.333	33	4	0	1	52	64	51	5	0	30	24	6.23	63	.308	.395	12-0	.250	0	131	-16	-1.5
1955	Cle A	0	0	—	17	0	0	1	24	24	8	0	0	9-1	9	2.63	152	.261	.327	0-1	—	0		4	0.3
	Bal A	6	8	.429	19	14	8-2	2	117.1	111	43	6	1	39-1	54	2.45	155	.252	.311	36-5	.083	-2	60	16	1.7
	Year	6	8	.429	36	14	8-2	3	141.1	135	46	6	1	48-2	63	2.48	155	.254	.313	36-6	.083	-2	59	19	2.0
1956	Bal A	9	12	.429	35	26	7-1	0	174.2	198	92	7	6	72-3	84	4.02	98	.289	.361	60-2	.200	-1	92	-5	-0.6
1957	Bal A	6	6	.500	27	17	2	0	121	122	53	4	4	54-1	50	3.64	99	.271	.351	34-4	.029	-3	92	-1	-0.4
1958	Cin N	0	1	.000	7	0	0	0	6.2	7	4	1	0	4-0	5	4.05	102	.292	.393	0-0	—	0		0	0.0
	StL N	3	0	1.000	28	1	1	2	57.1	64	35	7	0	32-1	18	5.02	82	.290	.375	10-1	.100	-0	109	-5	-0.3
	Year	3	1	.750	35	1	1	2	64	71	40	8	0	36-1	23	4.92	84	.290	.377	10-1	.100	-0	109	-5	-0.3
Total	12	77	99	.438	347	198	66-15	8	1563	1656	791	74	14	714-7	574	3.95	103	.277	.354	480-40	.115	-28	84	14	-0.2
WIGINGTON, FRED Fred Thomas B 12.16.1897 Rogers, NE D 5.8.1980 Mesa, AZ BR/TR 5-10/168# d4.20																									
1923	StL N	0	0	—	4	0	0	0	8.1	11	4	0	0	5	2	3.24	121	.367	.457	1-0	.000	-0		0	0.0
WIHTOL, SANDY Alexander Ames B 6.1.1955 Palo Alto, CA BR/TR 6-1/195# d9.7																									
1979	Cle A	0	0	—	5	0	0	0-0	10.2	10	4	0	0	3-0	6	3.38	126	.238	.289	0-0	—	0		1	0.1
1980	Cle A	1	0	1.000	17	0	0	1-1	35.1	35	18	2	2	14-2	20	3.57	114	.257	.333	0-0	—	0		1	0.0
1982	Cle A	0	0	—	6	0	0	0-0	11.2	9	6	1	1	7-0	8	4.63	88	.220	.340	0-0	—	0		0	0.0
Total	3	1	0	1.000	28	0	0	1-1	57.2	54	28	3	3	24-2	34	3.75	110	.247	.327	0-0	—	0		2	0.1
WILCOX, MILT Milton Edward B 4.20.1950 Honolulu, HI BR/TR 6-2/185# d9.5																									
1970	†Cin N	3	1	.750	5	2	1-1	1-0	22.1	19	6	2	1	7-0	13	2.42	167	.229	.297	5-1	.200	0	133	4	0.8
1971	Cin N	2	2	.500	18	3	0	1-0	43.1	43	22	2	2	17-2	21	3.32	101	.269	.343	9-0	.000	-1	62	-2	-0.3
1972	Cle A	7	14	.333	32	27	4-2	0-0	156	145	67	18	5	72-11	90	3.40	95	.251	.336	45-4	.200	1	74	-3	-0.5
1973	Cle A	8	10	.444	26	19	4	0-0	134.1	143	90	14	8	68-9	82	5.83	67	.275	.366	0-0	—	0*	105	-25	-2.8
1974	Cle A	2	2	.500	41	2	1	4-1	71.1	74	42	10	5	24-4	33	4.67	78	.271	.339	0-0	—	0	134	-8	-0.5
1975	Chi N	0	1	.000	25	0	0	0-0	38.1	50	27	4	1	17-2	21	5.63	68	.323	.389	3-0	.333	0		-7	-0.3
1977	Det A	6	2	.750	20	13	1	0-0	106.1	96	46	13	1	37-1	82	3.64	118	.241	.305	0-0	—	0	103	8	0.5
1978	Det A	13	12	.520	29	27	16-2	0-0	215.1	208	94	22	8	68-2	132	3.76	103	.255	.317	0-0	—	0	100	5	0.6
1979	Det A	12	10	.545	33	29	7	0-0	196.1	201	105	18	11	73-8	109	4.35	100	.267	.338	0-0	—	0	90	-1	0.0
1980	Det A	13	11	.542	32	31	13-1	0-1	198.2	201	112	24	6	68-5	97	4.48	92	.262	.325	0-0	—	0*	130	-10	-1.0
1981	Det A	12	9	.571	24	24	8-1	0-0	166.1	152	61	10	6	52-3	79	3.03	125	.247	.310	0-0	—	0	81	13	1.6
1982	Det A	12	10	.545	29	29	9-1	0-0	193.2	187	91	18	7	85-5	112	3.62	112	.257	.338	0-0	—	0*	111	8	0.9
1983	Det A	11	10	.524	26	26	9-2	0-0	186	164	89	19	4	74-6	101	3.97	99	.237	.313	0-0	—	0	110	0	0.1
1984	†Det A	17	8	.680	33	33	0	0-0	193.2	183	99	13	8	66-5	119	4.00	98	.252	.318	0-0	—	0	138	-2	-0.2
1985	Det A	1	3	.250	8	8	0	0-0	39	51	24	6	0	14-2	20	4.85	84	.315	.369	0-0	—	0	100	-4	-0.3
1986	Sea A	0	8	.000	13	10	0	0-0	55.2	74	38	11	1	28-1	26	5.50	77	.327	.399	0-0	—	0	58	-8	-0.9
Total	16	119	113	.513	394	283	73-10	6-2	2016.2	1991	1013	204	74	770-66	1137	4.07	97	.260	.331	62-5	.177	0	104	-32	-2.3
WILES, RANDY Randall E B 9.10.1951 Fort Belvoir, VA BL/TL 6-1/185# d8.7																									
1977	Chi A	1	1	.500	5	0	0	0-0	2.2	5	3	1	0	3-1	0	10.13	40	.417	.533	0-0	—	0		-2	-0.3
WILEY, MARK Mark Eugene B 2.28.1948 National City, CA BR/TR 6-1/200# d6.17 C13																									
1975	Min A	1	3	.250	15	3	1	2-1	38.2	50	30	4	1	13-1	15	6.05	63	.325	.374	0-0	—	0	115	-10	-1.0
1978	SD N	1	0	1.000	4	1	0	0-0	7.2	11	6	1	0	1-0	1	5.87	57	.324	.343	2-0	.000	-0	243	-2	-0.3
	Tor A	0	0	—	2	0	0	0-0	2.2	3	2	0	0	1-0	2	6.75	58	.273	.333	0-0	—	0		-1	0.0
Total	2	2	3	.400	21	4	1	2-1	49	64	38	5	1	15-1	18	6.06	62	.322	.367	2-0	.000	-0	141	-13	-1.3
WILHELM, HARRY Harry Lester B 4.7.1874 Uniontown, PA D 2.20.1944 Republic, PA BR/TR 5-7/155# d8.12																									
1899	Lou N	1	0	1.000	5	3	2	0	25	36	22	1	1	3	6	6.12	63	.336	.360	12-0	.250	2	131	-5	-0.1

Year	Tm Lg	W	L	Pct	G	GS	CG-Sho	SV-BS	IP	H	R	HR	HB	BB-IB	SO	ERA	AERA	OAV	OOB	AB-SH	AVG	PB	Sup	APR	PW
WILHELM, KAISER Irvin Key B 1.26.1874 Wooster, OH D 5.22.1936 Rochester, NY BR/TR 6/162# d4.18 M2 C1 U1																									
1903	Pit N	5	3	.625	12	9	7-1	0	86	88	51	0	3	25	20	3.24	100	.264	.321	34-0	.088	-2*	106	-2	-0.3
1904	Bos N	14	20	.412	39	36	30-3	0	288	316	150	8	7	74	73	3.69	75	.285	.333	100-5	.070	-8	88	-22	-3.2
1905	Bos N	3	23	.115	34	28	23	0	242.1	287	166	7	5	75	76	4.53	68	.295	.349	100-3	.160	-2*	64	-38	-3.7
1908	Bro N	16	22	.421	42	36	33-6	0	332	266	105	3	6	83	99	1.87	125	.217	.271	111-5	.108	-4	67	13	1.3
1909	Bro N	3	13	.188	22	17	14-1	0	163	176	92	3	2	59	45	3.26	80	.289	.353	57-2	.228	2	49	-18	-1.4
1910	Bro N	3	7	.300	15	5	0	0	68.1	88	45	3	1	18	17	4.74	64	.314	.358	19-2	.316	2	59	-13	-1.4
1914	Bal F	12	17	.414	47	27	11-1	5	243.2	263	141	10	0	81	113	4.03	75	.291	.349	84-4	.250	1*	82	-25	-2.6
1915	Bal F	0	0	—	1	0	0	0	1	0	0	0	0	0	0	0.00	—	.000	.000	0-0	—	0		0	0.0
1921	Phi N	0	0	—	4	0	0	0	8	11	3	0	0	3	1	3.38	125	.393	.452	2-0	.000	-0		1	0.0
Total	9	56	105	.348	216	158	118-12	5	1432.1	1495	753	34	24	418	444	3.44	81	.274	.328	507-21	.154	-12	75	-104	-11.3
WILHELM, HOYT James Hoyt B 7.26.1922 Huntersville, NC D 8.23.2002 Sarasota, FL BR/TR 6/195# d4.18 HF1985																									
1952	NY N	15	3	**.833**	**71**	0	0	11	159.1	127	60	12	5	57	108	**2.43**	**152**	.220	.296	38-3	.158	0		19	2.3
1953	NY N☆	7	8	.467	**68**	0	0	15	145	127	61	13	4	77	71	3.04	141	.238	.339	33-5	.152	1		**18**	2.1
1954	†NY N	12	4	.750	57	0	0	7	111.1	77	32	5	5	52	64	2.10	192	.198	.298	21-1	.048	-2		**23**	3.2
1955	NY N	4	1	.800	59	0	0	0	103	104	53	10	2	40-5	71	3.93	102	.266	.333	19-1	.158	-1		1	0.1
1956	NY N	4	9	.308	64	0	0	8	89.1	97	45	7	2	43-10	71	3.83	99	.280	.361	9-0	.222	0		-1	-0.1
1957	StL N	1	4	.200	40	0	0	11	55	52	28	7	3	21-1	29	4.25	93	.254	.332	6-0	.000	-1		-1	-0.3
	Cle A	1	0	1.000	2	0	0	1	3.2	2	1	1	1	1-0	0	2.45	151	.154	.267	0-0	—	0		1	0.1
1958	Cle A	2	7	.222	30	6	1	5	90.1	70	32	4	1	35-2	57	2.49	146	.215	.291	21-3	.095	-1	82	10	1.0
	Bal A	1	3	.250	9	4	3-1	0	40.2	25	9	2	1	10-2	35	1.99	180	.179	.238	11-1	.091	-1	44	8	0.7
	Year	3	10	.231	39	10	4-1	5	131	95	11	6	2	45-4	92	2.34	155	.204	.276	32-4	.094	-2	67	18	1.7
1959	Bal A★	15	11	.577	32	27	13-3	0	226	178	64	13	10	77-3	139	**2.19**	**173**	.224	.299	76-4	.053	-6	82	**40**	3.7
1960	Bal A	11	8	.579	41	11	3-1	7	147	125	69	13	1	39-0	107	3.31	115	.228	.279	42-3	.071	-3	74	5	0.3
1961	Bal A★	9	7	.563	51	1	0	18	109.2	89	35	5	4	41-5	87	2.30	167	.219	.296	20-2	.050	-1	92	18	3.0
1962	Bal A✧	7	10	.412	52	0	0	15	93	64	28	5	3	34-2	90	1.94	191	.197	.276	16-0	.125	-0		17	3.5
1963	Chi A	5	8	.385	55	3	0	21	136.1	106	47	8	4	30-1	111	2.64	133	.215	.263	29-3	.069	-1	68	13	1.5
1964	Chi A	12	9	.571	73	0	0	27	131.1	94	35	7	2	30-1	95	1.99	174	.202	.252	21-2	.143	-0		21	4.2
1965	Chi A	7	7	.500	66	0	0	20	144	88	34	11	2	32-7	106	1.81	176	.177	.227	22-4	.000	-2		**23**	2.7
1966	Chi A	5	2	.714	46	0	0	6	81.1	50	21	6	1	17-2	61	1.66	191	.178	.226	8-0	.125	0		13	1.3
1967	Chi A	8	3	.727	49	0	0	12	89	58	21	2	4	34-4	76	1.31	236	.183	.270	13-0	.077	-1		**16**	2.4
1968	Chi A	4	4	.500	72	0	0	12	93.2	69	20	4	2	24-5	72	1.73	175	.205	.261	3-1	.000	-0		14	1.6
1969	Cal A	5	7	.417	44	0	0	10-3	65.2	45	21	4	3	18-4	53	2.47	141	.194	.260	8-0	.000	-1		8	1.5
	Atl N	2	0	1.000	8	0	0	4-1	12.1	5	1	0	1	4-0	14	0.73	494	.119	.213	1-0	.000	-0		4	0.9
1970	Atl N☆	6	4	.600	50	0	0	13-4	78.1	69	29	7	1	39-7	67	3.10	138	.234	.323	11-0	.091	-0		10	1.6
	Chi N	0	1	.000	3	0	0	0-0	3.2	4	4	1	0	3-0	1	9.82	46	.286	.412	0-0	—	0		-2	-0.3
	Year	6	5	.545	53	0	0	13-4	82	73	36	8	1	42-7	68	3.40	127	.236	.328	11-0	.091	-0		9	1.3
1971	Atl N	0	0	—	3	0	0	0-1	2.1	6	5	2	0	1-0	1	15.43	24	.500	.538	0-0	—	0		-3	-0.1
	LA N	0	1	.000	9	0	0	3-0	17.2	6	2	1	0	4-0	15	1.02	318	.111	.169	3-0	.000	-0		5	0.4
	Year	0	1	.000	12	0	0	3-1	20	12	7	3	0	5-0	16	2.70	122	.182	.236	3-0	.000	-0		1	0.3
1972	LA N	0	1	.000	16	0	0	1-0	25.1	20	16	0	0	15-0	9	4.62	72	.217	.315	1-1	.000	-0		-4	-0.2
Total	21	143	122	.540	1070	52	20-5	227-9	2254.1	1757	773	150	62	778-61	1610	2.52	146	.216	.288	432-34	.088	-21	78	276	37.1
WILKIE, LEFTY Aldon Jay B 10.30.1914 Zealandia, SK, CAN D 8.5.1992 Tualatin, OR BL/TL 5-11.5/175# d4.22 Mil 1943-45																									
1941	Pit N	2	4	.333	26	6	2-1	2	79	90	42	1	1	40	16	4.56	79	.289	.372	24-0	.292	1	98	-6	-0.3
1942	Pit N	6	7	.462	35	6	3	1	107.1	112	53	4	1	37	18	4.19	81	.269	.330	38-0	.263	2*	99	-7	-0.5
1946	Pit N	0	0	—	7	0	0	0	7.2	13	9	0	0	3	3	10.57	33	.382	.432	0-0	—	0		-5	-0.3
Total	3	8	11	.421	68	12	5-1	3	194	215	104	5	2	80	37	4.59	76	.283	.352	62-0	.274	3	99	-18	-1.1
WILKINS, DEAN Dean Allan B 8.24.1966 Blue Island, IL BR/TR 6-1/170# d8.21																									
1989	Chi N	1	0	1.000	11	0	0	0-0	15.2	13	9	2	0	9-2	14	4.60	82	.228	.333	1-1	.000	-0		-1	-0.1
1990	Chi N	0	0	—	7	0	0	1-0	7.1	11	8	1	1	7-0	3	9.82	42	.333	.463	0-0	—	0		-4	-0.2
1991	Hou N	2	1	.667	7	0	0	1-1	8	16	14	0	0	10-2	4	11.25	31	.410	.531	1-0	.000	-0		-9	-1.6
Total	3	3	1	.750	25	0	0	2-1	31	40	31	3	1	26-4	21	7.55	50	.310	.429	2-1	.000	-0		-14	-1.9
WILKINS, ERIC Eric Lamoine B 12.9.1956 St.Louis, MO BR/TR 6-1/190# d4.11																									
1979	Cle A	2	4	.333	16	14	0	0-0	69.2	77	41	4	4	38-1	52	4.39	97	.289	.384	0-0	—	0	90	-2	-0.2
WILKINS, MARC Marc Allen B 10.21.1970 Mansfield, OH BR/TR 5-11/200# d5.11																									
1996	Pit N	4	3	.571	47	2	0	1-4	75	75	36	6	6	36-6	62	3.84	114	.266	.357	9-0	.222	0	124	4	0.4
1997	Pit N	9	5	.643	70	0	0	2-2	75.2	65	33	7	4	33-2	47	3.69	116	.242	.333	4-1	.000	-0		6	0.9
1998	Pit N	0	0	—	16	0	0	0-1	15.1	13	6	1	2	9-2	17	3.52	122	.236	.358	0-0	—	0		2	0.1
1999	Pit N	2	3	.400	46	0	0	0-0	51	49	28	3	4	26-1	44	4.24	108	.257	.354	1-0	.000	-0		2	0.2
2000	Pit N	4	2	.667	52	0	0	0-0	60.1	54	34	4	6	43-3	37	5.07	91	.248	.376	6-0	.167	-0		-1	-0.1
2001	Pit N	0	1	.000	14	0	0	0-0	17.1	22	13	2	1	8-1	11	6.75	67	.319	.397	0-0	—	0		-4	-0.2
Total	6	19	14	.576	245	2	0	3-7	294.2	278	150	23	23	155-15	218	4.28	104	.256	.357	20-1	.150	0	124	9	1.3
WILKINSON, ROY Roy Hamilton B 5.8.1893 Canandaigua, NY D 7.2.1956 Louisville, KY BR/TR 6-1/170# d4.29 ggf-Jim Bluejacket																									
1918	Cle A	0	0	—	1	0	0	0	1	0	0	0	0	0	0	0.00	—	.000	.000	0-0	—	0		0	0.0
1919	†Chi A	1	1	.500	4	1	1-1	0	22	21	9	0	0	10	5	2.05	156	.266	.348	8-0	.375	2	172	2	0.4
1920	Chi A	7	9	.438	34	12	8	2	145	162	75	6	2	48	30	4.03	93	.297	.356	48-1	.146	-3	83	-3	-0.7
1921	Chi A	4	20	.167	36	23	11	3	198.1	259	135	4	4	78	50	5.13	83	.334	.397	65-0	.123	-4	57	-22	-2.4
1922	Chi A	0	1	.000	4	1	0	1	14.1	24	15	1	1	6	3	8.79	46	.393	.456	3-0	.000	-0	0	-7	-0.6
Total	5	12	31	.279	79	37	20-1	6	380.2	466	234	11	7	142	88	4.66	86	.318	.381	124-1	.145	-5	67	-30	-3.3
WILKINSON, BILL William Carl B 8.10.1964 Greybull, WY BR/TL 5-10/160# d6.13																									
1985	Sea A	0	2	.000	2	2	0	0-0	6	8	9	2	0	6-1	5	13.50	31	.333	.467	0-0	—	0	86	-6	-0.9
1987	Sea A	3	4	.429	56	0	0	10-2	76.1	61	33	8	0	21-1	73	3.66	130	.223	.272	0-0	—	0		9	0.9
1988	Sea A	2	2	.500	30	0	0	2-1	31	28	14	3	0	15-0	25	3.48	120	.233	.316	0-0	—	0		2	0.2
Total	3	5	8	.385	88	2	0	12-3	113.1	97	56	13	0	42-2	103	4.13	110	.232	.298	0-0	—	0	86	5	0.2
WILKS, TED Theodore "Cork" B 11.13.1915 Fulton, NY D 8.21.1989 Houston, TX BR/TR 5-9.5/178# d4.25 C2																									
1944	†StL N	17	4	**.810**	36	21	16-4	0	207.2	173	61	12	1	49	70	2.64	133	.227	**.275**	64-6	.141	-1	141	25	2.1
1945	StL N	4	7	.364	18	16	4-1	0	98.1	103	39	9	1	29	28	2.93	128	.270	.324	30-1	.133	-0	76	8	0.7
1946	†StL N	8	0	1.000	40	4	0	1	95	88	41	13	2	38	40	3.41	101	.248	.324	24-0	.208	0	112	1	0.0
1947	StL N	4	0	1.000	37	0	0	5	50.1	57	33	10	2	11	28	5.01	83	.279	.323	6-0	.167	0		-5	-0.5
1948	StL N	6	6	.500	57	2	1	13	130.2	113	40	5	0	39	71	2.62	156	.235	.293	30-3	.167	0	163	**21**	2.3
1949	StL N	10	3	.769	**59**	0	0	**9**	118.1	105	52	8	0	38	71	3.73	112	.240	.301	27-1	.037	-3		7	0.4
1950	StL N	2	0	1.000	18	0	0	0	24.1	27	18	4	0	9	15	6.66	65	.287	.356	4-0	.000	-0		-5	-0.4
1951	StL N	0	0	—	17	0	0	1	18	19	7	1	0	5	5	3.00	132	.279	.329	1-0	.000	-0		2	0.0
	Pit N	3	5	.375	48	1	1	12	82.2	69	31	6	2	24	43	2.83	149	.231	.292	12-1	.083	-1	84	12	1.4
	Year	3	5	.375	**65**	1	1	**13**	100.2	88	35	7	2	29	48	2.86	146	.240	.299	13-1	.077	-1	85	**14**	1.4
1952	Pit N	5	5	.500	44	0	0	4	72.1	65	32	9	2	31	24	3.61	111	.245	.329	8-1	.125	-0		3	0.4
	Cle A	0	0	—	7	0	0	1	11.2	8	6	0	0	7	6	3.86	87	.186	.300	0-0	—	0		-1	0.0
1953	Cle A	0	0	—	4	0	0	0	3.2	5	4	0	0	3	2	7.36	51	.278	.381	0-0	—	0		-2	-0.1
Total	10	59	30	.663	385	44	22-5	46	913	832	364	77	11	283	403	3.26	118	.244	.304	206-13	.131	-5	110	66	6.3
WILLETT, ED Robert Edgar B 3.7.1884 Norfolk, VA D 5.10.1934 Wellington, KS BR/TR 6/183# d9.5																									
1906	Det A	0	3	.000	3	3	3	0	25	24	12	0	2	8	16	3.96	70	.255	.327	9-0	.000	-1	17	-2	-0.4
1907	Det A	1	5	.167	10	6	1	0	48.2	47	31	0	2	20	27	3.70	70	.255	.335	13-0	.077	-1	52	-6	-0.8
1908	Det A	15	8	.652	30	23	18-2	1	197.1	186	67	2	14	60	77	2.28	106	.261	.331	67-2	.164	-2	127	5	0.7
1909	†Det A	21	10	.677	41	34	25-3	1	292.2	239	112	5	15	76	89	2.34	108	.221	.281	112-3	.196	3*	134	3	0.6

Year	Tm Lg	W	L	Pct	G	GS	CG-Sho	SV-BS	IP	H	R	HR	HB	BB-IB	SO	ERA	AERA	OAV	OOB	AB-SH	AVG	PB	Sup	APR	PW
1910	Det A	16	11	.593	37	25	18-4	0	224.1	175	85	2	17	74	65	2.37	111	.217	.296	83-2	.133	-2*	96	4	0.6
1911	Det A	13	14	.481	38	27	15-2	1	231.1	261	136	5	14	80	86	3.66	95	.295	.363	82-4	.268	7*	117	-8	-0.1
1912	Det A	17	15	.531	37	31	28-1	0	284.1	281	144	3	17	84	89	3.29	99	.262	.326	115-3	.165	-2	112	-2	-0.1
1913	Det A	13	14	.481	34	30	19	0	242	237	117	0	11	89	59	3.09	95	.263	.336	92-6	.283	7*	115	-5	0.4
1914	StL F	4	17	.190	27	22	14	0	175	208	102	5	10	56	73	4.27	71	.295	.355	64-2	.234	2*	73	-21	-1.9
1915	StL F	2	3	.400	17	2	1	2	52.2	61	36	2	3	18	19	4.61	62	.295	.360	15-1	.200	0	170	-11	-1.0
Total	10	102	100	.505	274	203	142-12	5	1773.1	1719	842	24	105	565	600	3.08	94	.259	.326	652-23	.199	11	109	-43	-2.0
WILLEY, CARL Carlton Francis B 6.6.1931 Cherryfield, ME BR/TR 6/175# d4.30																									
1958	†Mil N	9	7	.563	23	19	9-**4**	0	140	110	44	14	2	53-4	74	2.70	130	.215	.289	48-5	.104	-2	110	15	1.3
1959	Mil N	5	9	.357	26	15	5-2	0	117	126	60	12	2	31-4	51	4.15	85	.273	.319	39-1	.103	-1	103	-8	-1.0
1960	Mil N	6	7	.462	28	21	2-1	0	144.2	136	78	19	7	65-5	109	4.35	79	.248	.333	48-5	.146	1	104	-16	-1.2
1961	Mil N	6	12	.333	35	22	4	0	159.2	147	71	20	2	65-9	91	3.83	98	.247	.322	54-3	.019	-6	85	0	-0.5
1962	Mil N	2	5	.286	30	6	0	1	73.1	95	49	9	1	20-3	40	5.40	70	.319	.361	11-1	.273	1	96	-13	-1.0
1963	NY N	9	14	.391	30	28	7-4	0	183	149	74	24	4	69-2	101	3.10	113	.220	.294	54-6	.111	-1	82	8	0.9
1964	NY N	0	2	.000	14	3	0	0	30	37	19	5	1	8-2	14	3.60	99	.301	.343	4-1	.000	-0	65	-2	-0.3
1965	NY N	1	2	.333	13	3	1	0	28	30	13	2	2	15-1	13	4.18	84	.270	.364	5-2	.000	-1	58	-1	-0.2
Total	8	38	58	.396	199	117	28-11	1	875.2	830	408	105	21	326-30	493	3.76	95	.250	.318	263-24	.099	-9	93	-17	-2.0
WILLHITE, NICK Jon Nicholas B 1.27.1941 Tulsa, OK BL/TL 6-2/195# d6.16																									
1963	LA N	2	3	.400	8	8	1-1	0	38	44	19	5	0	10-2	28	3.79	80	.286	.329	10-1	.300	1	89	-4	-0.4
1964	LA N	2	4	.333	10	7	2	0	43.2	43	19	4	0	13-2	24	3.71	87	.264	.315	11-1	.000	-0	81	-2	-0.2
1965	Was A	0	0	—	5	0	0	0	6.1	10	11	2	0	4-0	3	7.11	49	.345	.424	0-0	—	0		-5	-0.3
	LA N	2	2	.500	15	6	0	1	42	47	26	7	2	22-1	28	5.36	61	.288	.380	10-0	.400	3	103	-10	-0.6
1966	LA N	0	0	—	6	0	0	0	4.1	3	1	0	0	5-0	4	2.08	159	.214	.421	0-0	—	0		1	0.1
1967	Cal A	0	2	.000	10	7	0	0	39.1	39	20	8	0	16-0	22	4.35	72	.258	.329	10-0	.000	-1	55	-5	-0.4
	NY N	0	1	.000	4	1	0	0	8.1	9	8	1	0	5-0	9	8.64	39	.257	.350	2-0	.000	-0	259	-4	-0.5
Total	5	6	12	.333	58	29	3-1	1	182	195	104	27	2	75-5	118	4.55	70	.275	.345	43-2	.163	2	88	-29	-2.3
WILLIAMS, ALBERT Albert Hamilton (De Souza) B 5.6.1954 Laguna De Perlas, Nicaragua BR/TR 6-4/190# d5.7																									
1980	Min A	6	2	.750	18	9	3	1-0	77	73	33	9	0	30-1	35	3.51	125	.253	.323	0-0	—	0	125	7	0.7
1981	Min A	6	10	.375	23	22	4	0-0	150	160	72	11	1	52-4	76	4.08	97	.276	.334	0-0	—	0	97	0	-0.1
1982	Min A	9	7	.563	26	26	3	0-0	153.2	166	74	18	0	55-5	61	4.22	101	.276	.333	0-0	—	0	99	2	0.2
1983	Min A	11	14	.440	36	29	4-1	1-1	193.1	196	105	21	4	68-6	68	4.14	103	.262	.325	0-0	—	0	95	-1	-0.2
1984	Min A	3	5	.375	17	11	1	0-0	68.2	75	46	9	7	22-1	22	5.77	73	.284	.351	0-0	—	0	82	-10	-1.1
Total	5	35	38	.479	120	97	15-1	2-1	642.2	670	330	68	12	227-17	262	4.24	99	.270	.332	0-0	—	0	98	-2	-0.5
WILLIAMS, AL Almon Edward B 5.11.1914 Valhermoso Springs, AL D 7.19.1969 Groves, TX BR/TR 6-3/200# d4.19																									
1937	Phi A	4	1	.800	16	8	2	1	75.1	88	51	0	1	49	27	5.38	88	.300	.402	24-3	.083	-2	132	-4	-0.4
1938	Phi A	0	7	.000	30	8	1	0	93.1	128	93	6	1	54	25	6.94	70	.324	.407	25-1	.040	-3	71	-25	-1.7
Total	2	4	8	.333	46	16	3	1	168.2	216	144	6	2	103	52	6.24	77	.314	.405	49-4	.061	-5	101	-29	-2.1
WILLIAMS, GUS Augustine H. B 1870 New York, NY D 10.14.1890 New York, NY 5-11/170# d4.18																									
1890	Bro AA	0	1	.000	2	2	1	0	12	13	15	0	0	12	2	7.50	52	.265	.410	4	.500	1	207	-4	-0.3
WILLIAMS, BRIAN Brian O'Neal B 2.15.1969 Lancaster, SC BR/TR 6-2/195# d9.16																									
1991	Hou N	0	1	.000	2	2	0	0-0	12	11	5	2	1	4-0	4	3.75	94	.250	.327	3-2	.000	-0	102	0	0.0
1992	Hou N	7	6	.538	16	16	0	0-0	96.1	92	44	10	0	42-1	54	3.92	86	.255	.330	30-5	.133	-0*	109	-5	-0.7
1993	Hou N	4	4	.500	42	5	0	3-3	82	76	48	7	4	38-4	56	4.83	80	.248	.335	10-3	.200	0	116	-8	-0.6
1994	Hou N	6	5	.545	20	13	0	0-0	78.1	112	64	9	4	41-4	49	5.74	69	.343	.416	23-5	.261	1	138	-21	-2.3
1995	SD N	3	10	.231	44	6	0	0-2	72	79	54	3	8	38-4	75	6.00	67	.279	.379	14-0	.071	-1	127	-16	-2.5
1996	Det A	3	10	.231	40	17	2-1	2-2	121	145	107	21	6	85-2	72	6.77	75	.304	.411	0-0	—	0	88	-26	-2.3
1997	Bal A	0	0	—	13	0	0	0-1	24	20	8	0	0	18-0	14	3.00	147	.220	.345	0-0	—	0		4	0.2
1999	Hou N	2	1	.667	50	0	0	0-2	67.1	69	35	4	5	35-2	53	4.41	100	.272	.366	3-0	.333	0		0	0.1
2000	Chi N	1	1	.500	22	0	0	1-1	24.1	28	27	4	3	23-2	14	9.62	47	.304	.454	2-0	.500	1		-14	-1.0
	Cle A	0	0	—	7	0	0	0-0	18	23	9	2	1	8-1	6	4.00	124	.324	.395	0-0	—	0		2	0.1
Total	9	26	38	.406	256	59	2-1	6-11	595.1	655	401	62	32	332-20	397	5.37	78	.284	.378	85-15	.176	1	108	-84	-9.0
WILLIAMS, CHARLIE Charles Prosek B 10.11.1947 Flushing, NY BR/TR 6-2/200# d4.23																									
1971	NY N	5	6	.455	31	9	1	0-0	90.1	92	53	7	2	41-8	53	4.78	71	.267	.343	23-4	.087	-1	118	-14	-1.7
1972	SF N	0	2	.000	3	2	0	0-0	9.1	14	10	3	0	3-0	3	8.68	40	.333	.378	2-0	.000	-0	38	-5	-0.9
1973	SF N	3	0	1.000	12	2	0	0-0	23	32	19	2	0	7-2	11	6.65	58	.330	.371	3-1	.333	0	231	-7	-0.8
1974	SF N	1	3	.250	39	7	0	0-1	100.1	93	38	6	2	31-6	48	2.78	137	.250	.308	22-2	.136	-1	85	10	0.6
1975	SF N	5	3	.625	55	2	0	3-2	98	94	41	2	4	66-14	45	3.49	109	.261	.378	16-0	.125	0	69	4	0.4
1976	SF N	2	0	1.000	48	2	0	1-1	85	80	33	4	2	39-2	34	2.96	123	.256	.340	8-0	.125	-0	158	6	0.4
1977	SF N	6	5	.545	55	8	1	0-0	119.1	116	62	9	3	60-16	41	4.00	98	.262	.352	18-1	.222	0	102	-1	-0.1
1978	SF N	1	3	.250	25	1	0	0-1	48	60	31	5	1	28-6	22	5.44	64	.314	.401	5-0	.000	-1	26	-10	-0.9
Total	8	23	22	.511	268	33	2	4-5	573.1	581	287	38	14	275-54	257	3.97	93	.269	.352	97-8	.134	-2	105	-17	-3.0
WILLIAMS, LEFTY Claude Preston B 3.9.1893 Aurora, MO D 11.4.1959 Laguna Beach, CA BR/TL 5-9/160# d9.17 Mil 19D1-18																									
1913	Det A	1	3	.250	5	4	3	1	29	34	18	0	1	4	9	4.97	59	.286	.315	10-0	.100	-0	82	-5	-0.8
1914	Det A	0	1	.000	1	1	0	0	1	3	5	0	0	2	0	0.00	—	.429	.556	0-0	—	0*	156	-1	-0.3
1916	Chi A	13	7	.650	43	26	10-2	1	224.1	220	99	5	8	65	138	2.89	96	.267	.327	74-0	.135	-0	124	-4	-0.7
1917	†Chi A	17	8	.680	45	29	8-1	1	230	221	94	3	9	81	85	2.97	89	.252	.321	67-6	.090	-3	121	-5	-1.1
1918	Chi A	6	4	.600	15	14	7-2	1	105.2	76	32	0	5	47	30	2.73	100	.209	.308	38-3	.132	-2	126	4	0.0
1919	†Chi A	23	11	.676	41	**40**	27-5	1	297	265	104	7	11	58	125	2.64	121	.244	.289	94-12	.181	1	127	20	2.0
1920	Chi A	22	14	.611	39	38	25	0	299	302	145	15	12	90	128	3.91	96	.271	.332	101-8	.218	0	95	0	-0.2
Total	7	82	48	.631	189	152	80-10	5	1186	1121	497	30	46	347	515	3.13	99	.255	.316	384-29	.159	-4	116	9	-1.1
WILLIAMS, DAVE David Aaron B 3.12.1979 Anchorage, AK BL/TL 6-2/205# d6.6																									
2001	Pit N	3	7	.300	22	18	0	0-0	114	100	53	15	7	45-4	57	3.71	121	.244	.324	34-3	.118	-1	79	9	0.6
2002	Pit N	2	5	.286	9	9	0	0-0	43.1	38	26	9	4	24-2	33	4.98	84	.232	.342	16-0	.125	0*	52	-4	-0.4
Total	2	5	12	.294	31	27	0	0-0	157.1	138	79	24	11	69-6	90	4.06	108	.241	.329	50-3	.120	-1	70	5	0.2
WILLIAMS, MUTT David Carter B 7.31.1891 Ozark, AR D 3.30.1962 Fayetteville, AR BR/TR 6-3.5/195# d10.4																									
1913	Was A	1	0	1.000	1	1	0	0	4	4	3	1	0	2	1	4.50	66	.308	.400	2-0	.500	0*	251	-1	-0.1
1914	Was A	0	0	—	5	0	0	1	7	5	5	0	0	4	3	5.14	55	.227	.346	0-0	—	0		-2	-0.1
Total	2	1	0	1.000	6	1	0	1	11	9	8	1	0	6	4	4.91	58	.257	.366	2-0	.500	0	251	-3	-0.2
WILLIAMS, DAVE David Owen B 2.7.1881 Scranton, PA D 4.25.1918 Hot Springs, AR BR/TL 5-11.5/167# d7.2																									
1902	Bos A	0	0	—	3	0	0	0	18.2	22	18	0	1	11	7	5.30	67	.293	.391	9-0	.333	1		-4	-0.2
WILLIAMS, DON Donald Fred B 9.14.1931 Floyd, VA BR/TR 6-2/180# d9.12																									
1958	Pit N	0	0	—	2	0	0	0	4	6	3	1	0	1-0	3	6.75	57	.375	.412	0-0	—	0		-1	-0.1
1959	Pit N	0	0	—	6	0	0	0	12	17	9	1	0	3-1	3	6.75	57	.362	.377	3-0	.333	1		-3	-0.1
1962	KC A	0	0	—	3	0	0	0	4	6	4	0	1	0-0	1	9.00	47	.353	.389	1-0	.000	-0		-2	-0.1
Total	3	0	0	—	11	0	0	0	20	29	16	2	1	4-1	7	7.20	55	.363	.386	4-0	.250	1		-6	-0.3
WILLIAMS, DON Donald Reid "Dino" B 9.2.1935 Los Angeles, CA D 12.20.1991 LaJolla, CA BR/TR 6-5/218# d8.4																									
1963	Min A	0	0	—	3	0	0	0	4.1	8	5	1	0	6-0	2	10.38	35	.381	.519	0-0	—	0		-3	-0.1
WILLIAMS, DALE Elisha Alphonso B 10.6.1855 Ludlow, KY D 10.22.1939 Covington, KY BR/TR 5-9/175# d8.12																									
1876	Cin N	1	8	.111	9	9	9	0	83	123	75	1		4	9	4.23	52	.339	.346	35	.200	-2	43	-15	-1.4
WILLIAMS, FRANK Frank Lee B 2.13.1958 Seattle, WA BR/TR 6-1/190# d4.5																									
1984	SF N	9	4	.692	61	1	1-1	3-4	106.1	88	49	2	3	51-6	91	3.55	99	.226	.319	18-0	.222	1	176	-1	0.2

Year	Tm Lg	W	L	Pct	G	GS	CG-Sho	SV-BS	IP	H	R	HR	HB	BB-IB	SO	ERA	AERA	OAV	OOB	AB-SH	AVG	PB	Sup	APR	PW
1985	SF N	2	4	.333	49	0	0	0-1	73	65	39	5	6	35-7	54	4.19	82	.242	.338	3-1	.000	-0		-6	-0.5
1986	SF N	3	1	.750	36	0	0	1-2	52.1	35	8	0	4	21-4	33	1.20	293	.212	.314	2-1	.500	0		14	1.2
1987	Cin N	4	0	1.000	85	0	0	2-5	105.2	101	37	5	2	39-9	60	2.30	185	.254	.322	5-1	.000	-1		19	0.9
1988	Cin N	3	2	.600	60	0	0	1-1	62.2	59	24	6	2	35-4	43	2.59	139	.252	.354	1-0	.000	-0		5	0.4
1989	Det A	3	3	.500	42	0	0	1-1	71.2	70	37	5	3	46-10	33	3.64	105	.254	.362	0-0	—	0		0	-0.1
Total	6	24	14	.632	333	1	1-1	8-14	471.2	418	194	23	20	227-40	314	3.00	124	.242	.334	29-3	.172	1	176	31	2.1
WILLIAMS, WOODY Gregory Scott B 8.19.1966 Houston, TX BR/TR 6/190# d5.14																									
1993	Tor A	3	1	.750	30	0	0	0-2	37	40	18	2	1	22-3	24	4.38	99	.274	.371	0-0	—	0		1	0.1
1994	Tor A	1	3	.250	38	0	0	0-0	59.1	44	24	5	2	33-1	56	3.64	133	.205	.313	0-0	—	0		9	0.5
1995	Tor A	1	2	.333	23	3	0	0-1	53.2	44	23	6	2	28-1	41	3.69	128	.220	.322	0-0	—	0	132	7	0.3
1996	Tor A	4	5	.444	12	10	1	0-0	59	64	33	8	1	21-1	43	4.73	106	.278	.340	0-0	—	0	89	2	0.3
1997	Tor A	9	14	.391	31	31	0	0-0	194.2	201	98	31	5	66-3	124	4.35	106	.269	.329	2-0	.500	0	59	8	0.7
1998	Tor A	10	9	.526	32	32	1-1	0-0	209.2	196	112	36	2	81-3	151	4.46	105	.245	.314	6-0	.333	1	96	6	0.4
1999	SD N	12	12	.500	33	33	0	0-0	208.1	213	106	33	2	73-5	137	4.41	95	.268	.328	73-4	.178	2*	95	-2	-0.1
2000	SD N	10	8	.556	23	23	4	0-0	168	152	74	23	3	54-2	111	3.75	115	.239	.300	58-1	.259	7*	87	13	1.8
2001	SD N	8	8	.500	23	23	0	0-0	145	170	88	28	5	37-4	102	4.97	81	.296	.340	55-1	.164	2*	138	-16	-1.4
	†StL N	7	1	.875	11	11	3-1	0-0	75	54	22	7	3	19-1	52	2.28	187	.205	.267	27-1	.259	2	104	16	1.9
	Year	15	9	.625	34	34	3-1	0-0	220	224	27	35	8	56-5	154	4.05	101	.268	.317	82-2	.195	4	127	0	0.5
2002	†StL N	9	4	.692	17	17	1	0-0	103.1	84	30	10	4	25-2	76	2.53	157	.222	.276	29-5	.207	3*	95	18	2.6
2003	StL N★	18	9	.667	34	33	0	0-1	220.2	220	101	20	11	55-2	153	3.87	105	.256	.307	70-9	.243	8	143	5	1.3
Total	11	92	76	.548	307	216	10-2	0-4	1533.2	1482	729	209	41	514-28	1070	4.04	108	.254	.316	320-21	.219	24	100	67	8.4
WILLIAMS, JEFF Jeffrey F. B 6.6.1972 Canberra, Australia BR/TL 6/180# d9.12																									
1999	LA N	2	0	1.000	5	3	0	0-0	17.2	12	10	2	0	9-0	7	4.08	105	.190	.292	5-1	.200	0	200	0	0.0
2000	LA N	0	0	—	7	0	0	0-1	5.2	12	11	1	0	8-0	3	15.88	27	.462	.571	0-0	—	0		-8	-0.4
2001	LA N	2	1	.667	15	1	0	0-0	24.1	26	18	5	1	17-1	9	6.29	64	.295	.407	4-0	.000	-0	46	-6	-0.7
2002	LA N	0	0	—	10	0	0	0-0	10	15	13	2	1	7-0	11	11.70	33	.333	.426	2-0	.500	0		-9	-0.4
Total	4	4	1	.800	37	4	0	0-1	57.2	65	52	10	2	41-1	30	7.49	55	.293	.401	11-1	.182	0	169	-23	-1.5
WILLIAMS, JEROME Jerome Lee B 12.4.1981 Honolulu, HI BR/TR 6-3/180# d4.26																									
2003	†SF N	7	5	.583	21	21	2-1	0-0	131	116	54	10	7	49-3	88	3.30	125	.242	.319	37-6	.108	-1	89	11	0.7
WILLIAMS, JOHNNIE John Brodie "Honolulu Johnnie" B 7.16.1889 Honolulu, HI D 9.8.1963 Long Beach, CA BR/TR 6/180# d4.21																									
1914	Det A	0	2	.000	4	3	1	0	11.1	17	12	0	0	5	4	6.35	44	.378	.440	3-0	.000	-0	95	-5	-0.8
WILLIAMS, LEON Leon Theo "Lefty" B 12.2.1905 Macon, GA D 11.20.1984 Atlanta, GA BL/TL 5-10.5/154# d6.2																									
1926	Bro N	0	0	—	8	0	0	0	8.1	16	6	0	0	2	3	5.40	71	.421	.450	5-0	.200	0*		-1	0.0
WILLIAMS, MARSH Marshall McDiarmid "Cap" B 2.21.1893 Faison, NC D 2.22.1935 Tucson, AZ BR/TR 6/180# d7.7																									
1916	Phi A	0	6	.000	10	4	3	0	51.1	71	53	4	0	31	17	7.89	36	.350	.436	19-0	.105	-1	60	-26	-2.7
WILLIAMS, MATT Matthew Evan B 7.25.1959 Houston, TX BR/TR 6-1/200# d8.2																									
1983	Tor A	1	1	.500	4	3	0	0-0	8	13	13	5	1	7-0	5	14.63	30	.361	.467	0-0	—	0	175	-8	-1.3
1985	Tex A	2	1	.667	6	3	0	0-0	26	20	7	3	0	10-0	22	2.42	175	.211	.286	0-0	—	0	79	5	0.6
Total	2	3	2	.600	10	6	0	0-0	34	33	20	8	1	17-0	27	5.29	80	.252	.340	0-0	—	0	128	-3	-0.7
WILLIAMS, MATT Matthew Taylor B 4.12.1971 Virginia Beach, VA BB/TL 6/185# d4.5																									
2000	Mil N	0	0	—	11	0	0	0-0	9	7	7	2	1	13-0	7	7.00	65	.219	.457	1-0	.000	-0		-2	-0.1
WILLIAMS, MIKE Michael Darren B 7.29.1968 Radford, VA BR/TR 6-2/199# d6.30																									
1992	Phi N	1	1	.500	5	5	1	0-0	28.2	29	20	3	0	7-0	5	5.34	66	.259	.300	10-1	.400	1	155	-7	-0.3
1993	Phi N	1	3	.250	17	4	0	0-0	51	50	32	5	0	22-2	33	5.29	75	.253	.327	12-3	.083	-1	130	-7	-0.6
1994	Phi N	2	4	.333	12	8	0	0-0	50.1	61	31	7	0	20-3	29	5.01	86	.310	.368	12-5	.167	0	93	-4	-0.4
1995	Phi N	3	3	.500	33	8	0	0-0	87.2	78	37	10	3	29-2	57	3.29	129	.239	.304	16-7	.125	-0	69	8	0.5
1996	Phi N	6	14	.300	32	29	0	0-0	167	188	107	25	6	67-6	103	5.44	79	.290	.360	51-6	.157	-1*	89	-18	-1.8
1997	KC A	0	2	.000	10	0	0	1-0	14	20	11	1	1	8-1	10	6.43	73	.333	.414	0-0	—	0		-3	-0.4
1998	Pit N	4	2	.667	37	1	0	0-1	51	39	12	1	0	16-4	59	1.94	221	.211	.271	3-2	.000	-0	107	13	1.4
1999	Pit N	3	4	.429	58	0	0	23-5	58.1	63	36	9	1	37-7	76	5.09	90	.276	.378	2-0	.000	-0		-3	-0.5
2000	Pit N	3	4	.429	72	0	0	24-5	72	56	34	8	4	40-3	71	3.50	131	.218	.328	1-0	.000	-0		8	1.1
2001	Pit N	2	4	.333	40	0	0	22-2	41.2	39	18	6	0	21-2	43	3.67	122	.244	.331	0-0	—	0		4	0.8
	†Hou N	4	0	1.000	25	0	0	0-1	22.1	21	10	3	0	14-1	16	4.03	114	.244	.347	0-0	—	0		2	0.3
	Year	6	4	.600	65	0	0	22-3	64	60	33	9	0	35-3	59	3.80	119	.244	.337	0-0	—	0		6	1.1
2002	Pit N★	2	6	.250	59	0	0	46-4	61.1	54	24	6	1	21-3	43	2.93	142	.233	.299	1-0	.000	0		7	1.6
2003	Pit N☆	1	3	.250	40	0	0	25-5	37.1	42	26	5	1	22-1	20	6.27	70	.282	.374	0-0	—	0		-7	-1.3
	Phi N	0	4	.000	28	0	0	3-2	25.2	24	18	0	3	19-5	19	5.96	67	.247	.387	0-0	—	0		-6	-0.9
	Year	1	7	.125	68	0	0	28-7	63	66	44	5	4	41-6	39	6.14	69	.268	.379	0-0	—	0		-13	-2.2
Total	12	32	54	.372	468	55	1	144-25	768.1	764	416	89	20	343-40	584	4.45	97	.260	.339	108-24	.157	-1	94	-13	-0.5
WILLIAMS, MITCH Mitchell Steven "Wild Thing" B 11.17.1964 Santa Ana, CA BL/TL 6-4/205# d4.9																									
1986	Tex A	8	6	.571	**80**	0	0	8-7	98	69	39	8	11	79-8	90	3.58	120	.202	.366	0-0	—	0		10	1.4
1987	Tex A	8	6	.571	85	1	0	6-1	108.2	63	47	9	7	94-7	129	3.23	139	.175	.353	0-0	—	0	122	14	1.8
1988	Tex A	2	7	.222	67	0	0	18-8	68	48	38	4	6	47-3	61	4.63	88	.203	.345	0-0	—	0		-3	-0.5
1989	†Chi N★	4	4	.500	**76**	0	0	36-11	81.2	71	27	6	8	52-4	67	2.76	137	.238	.361	5-0	.200	1		9	1.7
1990	Chi N	1	8	.111	59	2	0	16-4	66.1	60	38	4	1	50-6	55	3.93	104	.239	.364	5-0	.000	-1	66	-1	-0.3
1991	Phi N	12	5	.706	69	0	0	30-9	88.1	56	24	4	8	62-5	84	2.34	157	.182	.330	1-0	.000	0		13	2.8
1992	Phi N	5	8	.385	66	0	0	29-7	81	69	39	4	6	64-2	74	3.78	93	.240	.386	4-0	.250	0		-3	-0.7
1993	†Phi N	3	7	.300	65	0	0	43-6	62	56	30	3	2	44-1	60	3.34	119	.245	.368	1-0	1.000	0		3	0.5
1994	Hou N	1	4	.200	25	0	0	6-2	20	21	17	4	1	24-2	21	7.65	52	.269	.442	0-0	—	0		-8	-1.5
1995	Cal A	1	2	.333	20	0	0	0-1	10.2	13	10	1	2	21-0	9	6.75	70	.317	.554	0-0	—	0		-3	-0.6
1997	KC A	0	1	.000	7	0	0	0-0	6.2	11	8	2	0	7-1	10	10.80	44	.367	.474	0-0	—	0		-4	-0.5
Total	11	45	58	.437	619	3	0	192-56	691.1	537	317	49	52	544-39	660	3.65	110	.218	.367	16-0	.188	1	90	27	4.1
WILLIAMS, STEAMBOAT Rees Gephardt B 1.31.1892 Cascade, MT D 6.29.1979 Deer River, MN BL/TR 5-11/170# d7.12																									
1914	StL N	0	1	.000	5	1	0	0	11	13	8	1	0	6	2	6.55	43	.295	.380	1-0	.000	-0	77	-3	-0.3
1916	StL N	6	7	.462	36	8	5	1	105	121	63	6	1	27	25	4.20	63	.291	.336	24-0	.208	1	92	-17	-2.0
Total	2	6	8	.429	41	9	5	1	116	134	71	7	1	33	27	4.42	60	.291	.340	25-0	.200	1	90	-20	-2.3
WILLIAMS, RICK Richard Allen B 11.9.1952 Merced, CA BR/TR 6-1/180# d6.12																									
1978	Hou N	1	2	.333	17	1	0	0-0	34.2	43	19	2	0	10-2	17	4.67	71	.301	.342	5-0	.000	-1	54	-5	-0.5
1979	Hou N	4	7	.364	31	16	2-2	0-0	121.1	122	45	6	2	30-1	37	3.26	108	.261	.306	31-2	.258	3	58	6	0.8
Total	2	5	9	.357	48	17	2-2	0-0	156	165	64	8	2	40-3	54	3.58	97	.270	.315	36-2	.222	2	59	1	0.3
WILLIAMS, ACE Robert Fulton B 3.18.1917 Montclair, NJ D 9.16.1999 Fort Myers, FL BR/TL 6-2/174# d7.15 Mil 1943-45																									
1940	Bos N	0	0	—	5	0	0	0	9	21	17	0	1	12	5	16.00	23	.375	.493	2-0	.000	-0		-12	-0.6
1946	Bos N	0	0	—	1	0	0	0	0	1	0	0	0	1	0	—	—	1.000	1.000	0-0	—	0		0	0.0
Total	2	0	0	—	6	0	0	0	9	22	17	0	1	13	5	16.00	23	.386	.507	2-0	.000	-0		-12	-0.6
WILLIAMS, SHAD Shad Clayton B 3.10.1971 Fresno, CA BR/TR 6/198# d5.18																									
1996	Cal A	0	2	.000	13	2	0	0-0	28.1	42	34	7	2	21-4	26	8.89	56	.341	.442	0-0	—	0	56	-14	-0.8
1997	Ana A	0	0	—	1	0	0	0-0	1	1	0	0	0	1-0	0	0.00	—	.250	.400	0-0	—	0		1	0.0
Total	2	0	2	.000	14	2	0	0-0	29.1	43	34	7	2	22-4	26	8.59	58	.339	.441	0-0	—	0	56	-13	-0.8
WILLIAMS, STAN Stanley Wilson B 9.14.1936 Enfield, NH BR/TR 6-5/230# d5.17 C14																									
1958	LA N	9	7	.563	27	21	3-2	0	119	99	58	10	7	65-1	80	4.01	102	.228	.336	40-3	.050	-3	92	2	-0.1
1959	†LA N	5	5	.500	35	15	2	0	124.2	102	64	12	9	86-7	89	3.97	106	.228	.359	36-1	.194	1	99	2	0.2

Year	Tm Lg	W	L	Pct	G	GS	CG-Sho	SV-BS	IP	H	R	HR	HB	BB-IB	SO	ERA	AERA	OAV	OOB	AB-SH	AVG	PB	Sup	APR	PW
1960	LA N★	14	10	.583	38	30	9-2	1	207.1	162	84	26	5	72-1	175	3.00	133	.210	.280	64-7	.141	0	109	19	2.1
1961	LA N	15	12	.556	41	35	6-2	0	235.1	213	114	21	6	108-9	205	3.90	111	.242	.327	78-6	.167	-1	90	11	1.1
1962	LA N	14	12	.538	40	28	4-1	1	185.2	184	104	16	0	98-11	108	4.46	81	.253	.338	66-1	.076	-2	118	-17	-2.4
1963	†NY A	9	8	.529	29	21	6-1	0	146	137	59	7	6	57-1	98	3.21	110	.249	.325	49-1	.102	-1	126	4	0.4
1964	NY A	1	5	.167	21	10	1	0	82	76	39	7	0	38-2	54	3.84	94	.248	.329	21-1	.143	-0*	91	-2	-0.2
1965	Cle A	0	0	—	3	0	0	0	4.1	6	4	1	0	3-1	1	6.23	56	.353	.450	0-0	—	0		-2	-0.1
1967	Cle A	6	4	.600	16	8	2-1	1	79	64	26	6	1	24-2	75	2.62	125	.218	.277	22-0	.091	-1	73	6	0.5
1968	Cle A	13	11	.542	44	24	6-2	9	194.1	163	64	14	10	51-7	147	2.50	118	.225	.284	56-4	.161	1	81	10	1.4
1969	Cle A	6	14	.300	61	15	3	12-5	178.1	155	86	25	12	67-6	139	3.94	96	.235	.312	40-4	.100	-1	95	-2	-0.3
1970	†Min A	10	1	.909	68	0	0	15-4	113.1	85	34	8	5	32-6	76	1.99	188	.208	.272	19-0	.000	-2		20	2.0
1971	Min A	4	5	.444	46	1	0	4-3	78	63	44	7	8	44-7	47	4.15	86	.220	.336	10-1	.000	-1	126	-7	-1.0
	StL N	3	0	1.000	10	0	0	0-1	12.2	13	2	0	2	2-1	8	1.42	254	.265	.315	1-0	.000	-0		3	0.7
1972	Bos A	0	0	—	3	0	0	0-0	4.1	5	3	0	0	1-0	3	6.23	52	.294	.333	0-0	—	0		-1	-0.1
Total	14	109	94	.537	482	208	42-11	43-13	1764.1	1527	785	160	71	748-62	1305	3.48	108	.232	.315	502-29	.118	-10	101	46	4.2

WILLIAMS, TOM Thomas C. B 8.19.1870 Minersville, OH D 7.27.1940 Columbus, OH d5.1

1892	Cle N	1	0	1.000	2	1	1	0	9	9	4	1	0	1	3	3.00	113	.250	.270	10	.100	-1*	205	1	0.0
1893	Cle N	1	1	.500	5	2	2	0	24	33	18	1	1	10	6	4.88	100	.317	.383	18	.278	0*	79	1	0.1
Total	2	2	1	.667	7	3	3	0	33	42	22	2	1	11	9	4.36	102	.300	.355	28	.214	-0	112	2	0.1

WILLIAMS, TODD Todd Michael B 2.13.1971 Syracuse, NY BR/TR 6-3/185# d4.29

1995	LA N	2	2	.500	16	0	0	0-1	19.1	19	11	3	0	7-2	8	5.12	74	.264	.325	2-0	.500	0		-2	-0.4
1998	Cin N	0	1	.000	6	0	0	0-0	9.1	15	8	1	0	6-0	4	7.71	56	.341	.420	2-0	.000	-0		-3	-0.3
1999	Sea A	0	0	—	13	0	0	0-0	9.2	11	5	1	1	7-0	7	4.66	102	.289	.413	0-0	—	0		0	0.0
2001	NY A	1	0	1.000	15	0	0	0-0	15.1	22	9	1	2	9-2	13	4.70	96	.324	.402	0-0	—	0		0	0.0
Total	4	3	3	.500	50	0	0	0-1	53.2	67	33	6	3	29-4	32	5.37	79	.302	.384	4-0	.250	0		-5	-0.7

WILLIAMS, POP Walter Merrill B 5.19.1874 Bowdoinham, ME D 8.4.1959 Topsham, ME BL/TR 5-11/190# d9.14

1898	Was N	0	2	.000	2	2	2	0	17	32	18	0	0	7	3	8.47	43	.395	.443	8-0	.375	1	106	-7	-0.5
1902	Chi N	11	16	.407	32	32	27-1	0	263.1	267	112	1	10	63	99	2.49	108	.263	.312	120-3	.208	3*	100	8	1.3
1903	Chi N	0	1	.000	1	1	1	0	5	9	3	0	0	0	2	5.40	58	.409	.409	2-0	.000	0*	0	-1	-0.1
	Phi N	1	1	.500	2	2	2	0	18	21	11	0	1	6	8	3.00	109	.304	.368	7-0	.286	0	103	0	0.0
	Bos N	4	5	.444	10	10	9-1	0	83	97	60	3	9	37	20	4.12	78	.295	.381	42-1	.238	-0*	97	-9	-0.9
	Year	5	7	.417	13	13	12-1	0	106	127	65	3	10	43	30	3.99	81	.302	.381	51-1	.235	0	90	-13	-1.0
Total	3	16	25	.390	47	47	41-2	0	386.1	426	204	4	20	113	132	3.17	91	.281	.339	179-4	.223	5	97	-9	-0.2

WILLIAMSON, ED Edward Nagle B 10.24.1857 Philadelphia, PA D 3.3.1894 Mountain Valley Springs, AR BR/TR 5-11/210# d5.1.1878 ▲

1881	Chi N	1	1	.500	3	1	1	0	18	14	9	0		0	2	2.00	137	.209	.209	343	.268	1*	118	1	0.1
1882	Chi N	0	0	—	1	0	0	0	3	9	8	1		1	0	6.00	48	.500	.526	348	.282	0*		-2	-0.1
1883	Chi N	0	0	—	1	0	0	0	1	1	2	0		1	1	9.00	37	.167	.286	402	.276	0*		-1	0.0
1884	Chi N	0	0	—	2	0	0	0	2	8	8	0		2	0	18.00	17	.500	.556	417	.278	1*		-3	-0.1
1885	†Chi N	0	0	—	2	0	0	**2**	6	2	0	0		0	3	0.00	—	.080	.080	407	.238	0*		2	0.2
1886	†Chi N	0	0	—	2	0	0	1	3	2	2	0		0	1	0.00	—	.143	.143	430	.216	0*		1	0.0
1887	Chi N	0	0	—	1	0	0	0	2	2	2	0	0	1	0	9.00	50	.222	.300	439	.267	0*		-1	0.0
Total	7	1	1	.500	12	1	1	3	35	38	31	1	0	5	7	3.34	90	.245	.269	2786	.260	3	118	-3	0.1

WILLIAMSON, MARK Mark Alan B 7.21.1959 Corpus Christi, TX BR/TR 6/172# d4.8

1987	Bal A	8	9	.471	61	2	0	3-7	125	122	59	12	3	41-15	73	4.03	109	.261	.322	0-0	—	0	103	7	0.8
1988	Bal A	5	8	.385	37	10	2	2-1	117.2	125	70	14	2	40-8	69	4.90	80	.272	.332	0-0	—	0	65	-13	-1.3
1989	Bal A	10	5	.667	65	0	0	9-6	107.1	105	35	4	2	30-9	55	2.93	130	.261	.313	0-0	—	0		12	1.6
1990	Bal A	8	2	.800	49	0	0	1-4	85.1	65	25	8	0	28-2	60	2.21	172	.215	.276	0-0	—	0		14	1.7
1991	Bal A	5	5	.500	65	0	0	4-3	80.1	87	42	9	0	35-7	53	4.48	88	.275	.343	0-0	—	0		-4	-0.5
1992	Bal A	0	0	—	12	0	0	1-0	18.2	16	3	1	0	10-1	14	0.96	418	.239	.338	0-0	—	0		6	0.3
1993	Bal A	7	5	.583	48	1	0	0-2	88	106	54	5	0	25-8	45	4.91	91	.304	.345	0-0	—	0	62	-5	-0.6
1994	Bal A	3	1	.750	28	2	0	1-1	67.1	75	33	9	2	17-1	28	4.01	125	.278	.323	0-0	—	0	92	6	0.3
Total	8	46	35	.568	365	15	2	21-24	689.2	701	321	62	9	226-51	397	3.86	108	.266	.323	0-0	—	0	75	23	2.3

WILLIAMSON, SCOTT Scott Ryan B 2.17.1976 Fort Polk, LA BR/TR 6/185# d4.5

1999	Cin N☆	12	7	.632	62	0	0	19-7	93.1	54	29	8	1	43-6	107	2.41	193	.171	.271	7-3	.000	-1		22	4.2
2000	Cin N	5	8	.385	48	10	0	6-2	112	92	45	7	3	75-7	136	3.29	143	.224	.346	16-4	.063	-1	78	17	1.8
2001	Cin N	0	0	—	2	0	0	0-0	0.2	1	0	0	1	2-0	0	0.00	—	.333	.667	0-0	—	0		0	0.0
2002	Cin N	3	4	.429	63	0	0	8-4	74	46	27	5	2	36-5	84	2.92	146	.181	.286	0-0	—	0		11	1.1
2003	Cin N	5	3	.625	42	0	0	21-5	42.1	34	15	6	1	25-4	53	3.19	134	.214	.324	0-0	—	0		6	1.1
	†Bos A	0	1	.000	24	0	0	0-2	20.1	20	15	1	0	9-2	21	6.20	74	.253	.326	0-0	—	0		-3	-0.2
Total	5	25	23	.521	241	10	0	54-20	342.2	247	131	27	8	190-24	401	3.13	145	.202	.312	23-7	.043	-1	78	53	8.0

WILLIAMSON, AL Silas Albert B 2.20.1900 Buckville, AR D 11.29.1978 Hot Springs, AR BR/TR 5-11/160# d4.27

1928	Chi A	0	0	—	1	0	0	0	2	1	0	0	0	0	0	0.00	—	.167	.167	0-0	—	0		1	0.0

WILLIS, CARL Carl Blake B 12.28.1960 Danville, VA BL/TR 6-4/213# d6.9 C1

1984	Det A	0	2	.000	10	2	0	0-0	16	25	13	1	0	5-2	4	7.31	54	.362	.405	0-0	—	0	104	-5	-0.6
	Cin N	0	1	.000	7	0	0	1-0	9.2	8	4	1	0	2-0	3	3.72	102	.222	.263	0-0	—	0		0	0.0
1985	Cin N	1	0	1.000	11	0	0	1-0	13.2	21	18	3	0	5-0	6	9.22	41	.344	.382	1-1	.000	0		-9	-0.7
1986	Cin N	1	3	.250	29	0	0	0-1	52.1	54	29	4	1	32-9	24	4.47	87	.278	.382	3-1	.333	0		-3	-0.2
1988	Chi A	0	0	—	6	0	0	0-0	12	17	12	3	0	7-1	6	8.25	48	.362	.436	0-0	—	0		-5	-0.3
1991	†Min A	8	3	.727	40	0	0	2-1	89	76	31	4	1	19-1	53	2.63	163	.232	.273	0-0	—	0		15	1.6
1992	Min A	7	3	.700	59	0	0	1-2	79.1	73	25	4	0	11-1	45	2.72	149	.246	.270	0-0	—	0		12	1.4
1993	Min A	3	0	1.000	53	0	0	5-4	58	56	23	2	0	17-5	44	3.10	141	.259	.312	0-0	—	0		8	0.4
1994	Min A	2	4	.333	49	0	0	3-4	59.1	89	48	6	0	12-5	37	5.92	82	.335	.359	0-0	—	0		-9	-0.9
1995	Min A	0	0	—	3	0	0	0-0	0.2	5	7	0	0	5-0	0	94.50	5	.833	.909	0-0	—	0		-6	-0.3
Total	9	22	16	.579	267	2	0	13-12	390	424	210	28	2	115-24	222	4.25	100	.279	.327	4-2	.250	0	104	-2	0.4

WILLIS, LEFTY Charles William B 11.4.1905 Leetown, WV D 5.10.1962 Bethesda, MD BL/TL 6-1/175# d10.3

1925	Phi A	0	0	—	1	1	0	0	5	9	7	2	0	2	3	10.80	43	.409	.458	3-0	.000	-1	145	-3	-0.2
1926	Phi A	0	0	—	13	1	0	1	32.1	31	9	0	1	12	13	1.39	300	.270	.344	9-0	.222	-0	81	9	0.4
1927	Phi A	3	1	.750	15	2	1	0	27	32	18	2	0	11	7	5.67	75	.308	.374	6-0	.000	-1	88	-3	-0.4
Total	3	3	1	.750	29	4	1	1	64.1	72	34	4	1	25	23	3.92	108	.299	.367	18-0	.111	-1	104	3	-0.2

WILLIS, DALE Dale Jerome B 5.29.1938 Calhoun, GA BR/TR 5-11/165# d4.14

1963	KC A	0	2	.000	25	0	0	1	44.2	46	28	3	4	25-3	47	5.04	77	.266	.369	6-0	.167	-0*		-5	-0.3

WILLIS, DONTRELLE Dontrelle Wayne B 1.12.1982 Oakland, CA BL/TL 6-4/200# d5.9

2003	†Fla N☆	14	6	.700	27	27	2-2	0-0	160.2	148	61	13	3	58-0	142	3.30	124	.245	.314	58-2	.241	5	104	16	2.2

WILLIS, JIM James Gladden B 3.20.1927 Doyline, LA BL/TR 6-3/175# d4.22

1953	Chi N	2	1	.667	13	3	2	0	43.1	37	15	1	3	17	15	3.12	143	.228	.313	9-1	.000	-1	94	7	0.4
1954	Chi N	0	1	.000	14	1	0	0	23	22	10	1	3	18	5	3.91	107	.256	.402	5-0	.000	-1	21	1	0.0
Total	2	2	2	.500	27	4	2	0	66.1	59	25	2	6	35	20	3.39	129	.238	.346	14-1	.000	-2	77	8	0.4

WILLIS, JOE Joseph Denk B 4.9.1890 Coal Grove, OH D 12.4.1966 Ironton, OH BR/TL 6-1/185# d5.3

1911	StL A	0	1	.000	1	1	0	0	7	8	5	0	0	3	0	5.14	66	.308	.379	2-0	.000	0	43	-1	-0.1
	StL N	0	1	.000	2	2	1	0	15	13	9	0	0	4	5	4.20	80	.232	.283	5-0	.000	-1	56	-1	-0.1
1912	StL N	4	9	.308	31	17	4	2	129.2	143	83	3	5	62	55	4.44	77	.288	.372	38-1	.158	-2	107	-12	-1.2
1913	StL N	0	0	—	7	0	0	1	9.2	9	9	0	0	11	6	7.45	43	.257	.435	3-0	.000	-0		-4	-0.3
Total	3	4	11	.267	41	20	5	3	161.1	173	106	3	5	80	66	4.63	74	.282	.369	48-1	.125	-2	99	-18	-1.7

Year	Tm Lg	W	L	Pct	G	GS	CG-Sho	SV-BS	IP	H	R	HR	HB	BB-IB	SO	ERA	AERA	OAV	OOB	AB-SH	AVG	PB	Sup	APR	PW
WILLIS, LES Lester Evans "Wimpy" or "Lefty" B 1.17.1908 Nacogdoches, TX D 1.22.1982 Jasper, TX BL/TL 5-9.5/195# d4.28																									
1947	Cle A	0	2	.000	22	2	0	1	44	58	26	3	0	24	10	3.48	100	.324	.404	11-1	.091	-1	89	-4	-0.3
WILLIS, MIKE Michael Henry B 12.26.1950 Oklahoma City, OK BL/TL 6-2/210# d4.13																									
1977	Tor A	2	6	.250	43	3	0	5-4	107.1	105	48	15	0	38-6	59	3.94	107	.260	.321	0-0	—	0	78	5	0.4
1978	Tor A	3	7	.300	44	2	1	7-2	100.2	104	55	11	0	39-2	52	4.56	86	.271	.336	0-0	—	0	103	-7	-0.7
1979	Tor A	0	3	.000	17	1	0	0-0	26.2	35	27	1	1	16-2	8	8.44	52	.333	.419	0-0	—	0	42	-11	-1.1
1980	Tor A	2	1	.667	20	0	0	3-1	26.1	25	6	3	1	11-4	14	1.71	252	.248	.325	0-0	—	0		7	0.9
1981	Tor A	0	4	.000	20	0	0	0-1	35	43	25	6	1	20-1	16	5.91	67	.301	.386	0-0	—	0		-6	-0.7
Total	5	7	21	.250	144	6	1	15-8	296	312	161	36	3	124-15	149	4.59	90	.274	.344	0-0	—	0	80	-12	-1.2
WILLIS, RON Ronald Earl B 7.12.1943 Willisville, TN D 11.21.1977 Memphis, TN BR/TR 6-2/195# d9.20																									
1966	StL N	0	0	—	4	0	0	1	3	1	0	0	0	1-1	2	0.00	—	.100	.182	0-0	—	0		1	0.1
1967	†StL N	6	5	.545	65	0	0	10	81	76	27	3	3	43-20	42	2.67	123	.257	.354	8-0	.375	1		6	1.2
1968	†StL N	2	3	.400	48	0	0	4	63.2	50	25	4	1	28-11	39	3.39	85	.213	.299	11-0	.000	-1		-2	-0.3
1969	StL N	1	2	.333	26	0	0	0-0	32.1	26	16	4	1	19-3	23	4.18	86	.224	.331	1-0	1.000	0		-2	-0.1
	Hou N	0	0	—	3	0	0	0-0	2.1	3	0	0	0	0-0	2	0.00	—	.300	.273	0-0	—	0		1	0.0
	Year	1	2	.333	29	0	0	0-0	34.2	29	20	4	1	19-3	25	3.89	92	.230	.327	1-0	1.000	0		-1	-0.1
1970	SD N	2	2	.500	42	0	0	4-2	56	53	33	4	4	28-5	20	4.02	99	.247	.340	5-0	.000	-1		-2	-0.2
Total	5	11	12	.478	188	0	0	19-2	238.1	209	101	15	9	119-40	128	3.32	102	.237	.330	25-0	.160	0		2	0.7
WILLIS, VIC Victor Gazaway B 4.12.1876 Cecil Co., MD D 8.3.1947 Elkton, MD BR/TR 6-2/185# d4.20 HF1995																									
1898	Bos N	25	13	.658	41	38	29-1	0	311	264	143	5	29	148	160	2.84	130	.228	.331	117-2	.145	-6	100	26	2.2
1899	Bos N	27	8	.771	41	38	35-**5**	2	342.2	277	126	6	30	117	120	2.50	**167**	**.221**	.303	134-3	.216	-4	102	**58**	4.8
1900	Bos N	10	17	.370	32	29	22-2	0	236	258	157	11	12	106	53	4.19	98	.277	.359	88-3	.136	-6	94	-1	-0.7
1901	Bos N	20	17	.541	38	35	33-**6**	0	305.1	262	111	6	11	78	133	2.36	**153**	.230	.286	107-3	.187	-1	78	**39**	4.2
1902	Bos N	27	20	.574	**51**	**46**	**45**-4	**3**	**410**	372	142	6	14	101	**225**	2.20	129	.242	.295	150-1	.153	-6*	93	28	2.8
1903	Bos N	12	18	.400	33	32	29-2	0	278	256	121	3	10	88	125	2.98	108	.251	.317	128-2	.188	-1*	72	14	1.3
1904	Bos N	18	25	.419	43	43	**39**-2	0	350	357	174	7	14	109	196	2.85	97	.266	.327	148-3	.182	1*	82	-8	-0.4
1905	Bos N	12	29	.293	41	41	36-4	0	342	340	174	7	13	107	149	3.21	97	.265	.328	131-2	.153	-3*	76	-8	-0.8
1906	Pit N	23	13	.639	41	36	32-6	1	322	295	84	0	5	76	124	1.73	154	.250	.298	115-3	.174	-1	111	34	4.3
1907	Pit N	21	11	.656	39	37	27-6	1	292.2	234	96	4	7	69	107	2.34	104	.219	.271	103-5	.136	-2	137	8	0.7
1908	Pit N	23	11	.676	41	38	25-7	0	304.2	239	95	2	6	69	97	2.07	111	.213	.262	103-4	.165	-1	122	9	0.9
1909	†Pit N	22	11	.667	39	**35**	24-4	1	289.2	243	84	3	4	83	95	2.24	122	.231	.289	103-6	.136	-2	120	20	2.1
1910	StL N	9	12	.429	33	23	12-1	3	212	224	113	6	1	61	67	3.35	89	.275	.326	66-4	.167	-2	84	-14	-1.4
Total	13	249	205	.548	513	471	388-50	11	3996	3621	1620	66	156	1212	1651	2.63	118	.243	.307	1493-41	.166	-33	97	205	20.0
WILLOUGHBY, CLAUDE Claude William "Flunky" or "Weeping Willie" B 11.14.1898 Buffalo, KS D 8.14.1973 McPherson, KS BR/TR 5-9.5/165# d9.18																									
1925	Phi N	2	1	.667	3	3	1	0	23	26	7	0	1	11	6	1.96	244	.295	.380	8-0	.000	-1	71	6	0.6
1926	Phi N	8	12	.400	47	19	6	1	168	218	125	7	5	71	37	5.95	70	.327	.396	52-3	.212	-1	113	-28	-2.8
1927	Phi N	3	7	.300	35	6	1-1	2	97.2	126	83	7	2	53	14	6.54	63	.321	.404	26-1	.077	-2	106	-26	-2.6
1928	Phi N	6	5	.545	35	13	5-1	1	130.2	180	92	6	3	83	26	5.30	81	.340	.432	40-1	.150	-1	81	-16	-1.3
1929	Phi N	15	14	.517	49	35	14-1	4	243.1	288	156	15	5	108	50	4.99	104	.296	.370	91-1	.143	-5	99	3	0.1
1930	Phi N	4	17	.190	41	24	5-1	1	153	241	147	17	2	68	38	7.59	72	.369	.430	48-0	.104	-4	103	-31	-3.6
1931	Pit N	0	2	.000	9	2	1	0	25.2	32	21	4	0	12	4	6.31	61	.305	.376	7-0	.286	0	178	-7	-0.4
Total	7	38	58	.396	219	102	33-4	9	841.1	1111	631	56	18	406	175	5.84	81	.326	.401	272-6	.143	-14	104	-99	-10.0
WILLOUGHBY, JIM James Arthur B 1.31.1949 Salinas, CA BR/TR 6-2/185# d9.5																									
1971	SF N	0	1	.000	2	1	0	0-0	4	8	4	0	0	1-0	3	9.00	38	.400	.429	1-0	.000	-0	78	-2	-0.4
1972	SF N	6	4	.600	11	11	7	0-0	87.2	72	25	8	2	14-4	40	2.36	148	.222	.257	27-5	.185	0	97	11	1.4
1973	SF N	4	5	.444	39	12	1-1	1-0	123	138	74	21	3	37-4	60	4.68	82	.295	.347	28-3	.143	1*	106	-11	-0.8
1974	SF N	1	4	.200	18	4	0	0-0	40.2	51	27	7	0	9-1	12	4.65	82	.304	.339	10-0	.100	-0*	69	-4	-0.5
1975	†Bos A	5	2	.714	24	0	0	8-1	48.1	46	25	6	2	16-3	29	3.54	115	.247	.311	0-0	—	0		1	0.2
1976	Bos A	3	12	.200	54	0	0	10-3	99	94	38	4	8	31-12	37	2.82	139	.256	.324	1-0	.000	-0		10	1.8
1977	Bos A	6	2	.750	31	0	0	2-2	54.2	54	32	5	2	18-3	33	4.94	91	.258	.320	0-0	—	0		-2	-0.3
1978	Chi A	1	6	.143	59	0	0	13-2	93.1	95	41	6	4	19-2	36	3.86	99	.275	.319	0-0	—	0		1	0.2
Total	8	26	36	.419	238	28	8-1	34-8	550.2	558	266	57	21	145-29	250	3.79	102	.267	.319	67-8	.149	1	92	4	1.6
WILLS, FRANK Frank Lee B 10.26.1958 New Orleans, LA BR/TR 6-2/202# d7.31																									
1983	KC A	2	1	.667	6	4	0	0-0	34.2	35	17	2	0	15-0	23	4.15	98	.259	.329	0-0	—	0	106	0	0.0
1984	KC A	2	3	.400	10	5	0	0-0	37	39	21	3	0	13-0	21	5.11	79	.271	.323	0-0	—	0	90	-4	-0.5
1985	Sea A	5	11	.313	24	18	1	1-0	123	122	85	18	3	68-3	67	6.00	70	.266	.359	0-0	—	0	94	-22	-2.4
1986	Cle A	4	4	.500	26	0	0	4-2	40.1	43	23	6	0	16-4	32	4.91	85	.272	.335	0-0	—	0		-3	-0.5
1987	Cle A	0	1	.000	6	0	0	1-0	5.1	3	3	0	0	7-0	4	5.06	90	.176	.400	0-0	—	0		0	0.0
1988	Tor A	0	0	—	10	0	0	0-0	20.2	22	12	2	0	6-2	19	5.23	75	.272	.318	0-0	—	0		-2	-0.1
1989	Tor A	3	1	.750	24	4	0	0-0	71.1	65	31	4	1	30-2	41	3.66	103	.242	.319	0-0	—	0	120	2	0.1
1990	Tor A	6	4	.600	44	4	0	0-0	99	101	54	13	1	38-7	72	4.73	84	.266	.333	0-0	—	0	98	-8	-0.7
1991	Tor A	0	1	.000	4	0	0	0-0	4.1	8	8	2	1	5-0	2	16.62	25	.421	.560	0-0	—	0		-5	-1.0
Total	9	22	26	.458	154	35	1	6-2	435.2	438	254	50	6	198-18	281	5.06	80	.264	.341	0-0	—	0	99	-42	-5.1
WILLS, TED Theodore Carl B 2.9.1934 Fresno, CA BL/TL 6-2/200# d5.24																									
1959	Bos A	2	6	.250	9	8	2	0	56.1	68	35	9	1	24-2	24	5.27	77	.302	.369	16-2	.250	1	65	-7	-0.7
1960	Bos A	1	1	.500	15	0	0	1	30.1	38	26	4	3	16-1	28	7.42	55	.317	.404	8-0	.250	1*		-10	-0.6
1961	Bos A	3	2	.600	17	0	0	0	19.2	24	17	2	0	19-0	11	5.95	70	.304	.434	2-0	.000	-0		-5	-0.9
1962	Bos A	0	0	—	1	0	0	0	0	2	1	0	0	1-0	0	o	—	1.000	1.000	0-0	—	0		-1	-0.1
	Cin N	0	2	.000	26	5	0	3	61	61	36	12	5	23-0	58	5.31	76	.266	.346	16-0	.313	1	148	-7	-0.2
1965	Chi A	2	0	1.000	15	0	0	1	19	17	8	2	1	14-2	12	2.84	112	.258	.386	2-0	.000	0		0	0.1
Total	5	8	11	.421	83	13	2	5	186.1	210	123	29	10	97-5	133	5.51	72	.291	.380	44-2	.250	3	99	-30	-2.4
WILMET, PAUL Paul Richard B 11.8.1958 Green Bay, WI BR/TR 5-11/170# d7.25																									
1989	Tex A	0	0	—	3	0	0	0-0	2.1	5	4	0	0	2-1	1	15.43	26	.417	.500	0-0	—	0		-3	-0.1
WILSHERE, WHITEY Vernon Sprague B 8.3.1912 Poplar Ridge, NY D 5.23.1985 Cooperstown, NY BL/TL 6/180# d6.24																									
1934	Phi A	0	1	.000	9	2	0	0	21.2	39	30	0	1	15	19	12.05	36	.394	.478	3-0	.000	-0	119	-18	-0.9
1935	Phi A	9	9	.500	27	18	7-3	1	142.1	136	69	8	10	78	80	4.05	112	.253	.358	43-5	.093	-4	90	10	0.7
1936	Phi A	1	2	.333	5	3	0	0	18.1	21	17	1	0	19	4	6.87	74	.288	.435	4-0	.000	-0	52	-4	-0.5
Total	3	10	12	.455	41	23	7-3	1	182.1	196	116	9	11	112	103	5.28	87	.276	.383	50-5	.080	-4	87	-12	-0.7
WILSHUSEN, TERRY Terry Wayne B 3.22.1949 Atascadero, CA D 12.1.2000 Lomita, CA BR/TR 6-2/210# d4.7																									
1973	Cal A	0	0	—	1	0	0	0-0	0.1	0	3	0	1	2-0	0	81.00	4	.000	.750	0-0	—	0		-3	-0.1
WILSON, DON Donald Edward B 2.12.1945 Monroe, LA D 1.5.1975 Houston, TX BR/TR 6-3/205# d9.29																									
1966	Hou N	1	0	1.000	1	0	0	0	6	5	2	1	0	1-0	7	3.00	114	.238	.273	2-0	.500	1		0	0.2
1967	Hou N	10	9	.526	31	28	7-3	0	184	141	67	10	7	69-2	159	2.79	119	.209	.288	66-2	.091	-2	100	10	0.7
1968	Hou N	13	16	.448	33	30	9-3	0	208.2	187	85	9	4	70-5	175	3.28	90	.236	.300	70-6	.214	4*	89	-7	-0.7
1969	Hou N	16	12	.571	34	34	13-1	0-0	225	210	119	16	9	97-8	235	4.00	89	.245	.326	81-2	.099	-1	134	-13	-1.6
1970	Hou N	11	6	.647	29	27	3	0-0	184.1	188	92	15	7	66-4	94	3.91	99	.259	.325	69-3	.116	-2*	120	-2	-0.5
1971	Hou N★	16	10	.615	35	34	18-3	0-0	268	195	80	15	7	79-3	180	2.45	137	**.202**	.266	91-6	.154	-1	92	29	2.5
1972	Hou N	15	10	.600	33	33	13-3	0-0	228.1	196	79	16	2	66-2	172	2.68	126	.233	.289	76-8	.105	-2	116	16	1.5
1973	Hou N	11	16	.407	37	32	10-3	2-0	239.1	187	94	21	7	92-6	149	3.20	114	.213	.291	79-6	.177	1	77	11	1.2
1974	Hou N	11	13	.458	33	27	5-4	0-1	204.2	170	80	16	4	100-2	112	3.08	113	.227	.318	63-9	.206	2	81	9	1.1
Total	9	104	92	.531	266	245	78-20	2-1	1748.1	1479	698	119	47	640-32	1283	3.15	109	.228	.299	597-42	.146	-1	102	53	4.4
WILSON, DUANE Duane Lewis B 6.29.1934 Wichita, KS BL/TL 6-1/185# d7.3																									
1958	Bos A	0	0	—	2	2	0	0	6.1	10	5	0	0	7-1	3	5.68	70	.400	.515	1-1	.000	-0	112	-1	-0.1

Year	Tm Lg	W	L	Pct	G	GS	CG-Sho	SV-BS	IP	H	R	HR	HB	BB-IB	SO	ERA	AERA	OAV	OOB	AB-SH	AVG	PB	Sup	APR	PW
WILSON, FIN Finis Elbert B 12.9.1889 East Fork, KY D 3.9.1959 Coral Gables, FL BL/TL 6-1/194# d9.26																									
1914	Bro F	0	1	.000	2	1	1	0	7	7	7	0	0	11	4	7.71	37	.269	.486	2-0	.500	1	72	-3	-0.4
1915	Bro F	1	8	.111	18	11	5	0	102.1	85	56	2	4	53	47	3.78	72	.249	.356	35-1	.314	2*	87	-12	-0.7
Total	2	1	9	.100	20	12	6	0	109.1	92	63	2	4	64	51	4.03	68	.250	.367	37-1	.324	3	85	-15	-1.1
WILSON, ZEKE Frank Ealton B 12.24.1869 Benton, AL D 4.26.1928 Montgomery, AL BR/TR 5-10/165# d4.23																									
1895	Bos N	2	4	.333	6	6	4	0	45	54	48	1	0	27	5	5.20	98	.293	.384	19-0	.316	1	65	-4	-0.3
	Cle N	3	1	.750	9	8	4	0	52.2	75	38	4	4	24	20	4.27	117	.329	.402	22-2	.136	-3	87	3	0.0
	Year	5	5	.500	15	14	8	0	97.2	129	44	5	4	51	25	4.70	107	.313	.394	41-2	.220	-2	78	-1	-0.3
1896	Cle N	17	9	.654	33	29	20-1	1	240	265	150	9	8	81	56	4.01	113	.278	.339	100-2	.270	2	114	14	1.5
1897	Cle N	16	11	.593	34	30	26-1	0	263.2	323	171	9	9	83	69	4.16	108	.299	.354	116-3	.224	-3*	94	8	0.4
1898	Cle N	13	18	.419	33	31	28-1	0	254.2	307	141	4	7	51	45	3.60	100	.296	.333	118-7	.178	-3*	83	2	0.1
1899	StL N	1	1	.500	5	2	2	0	26	30	18	0	2	4	3	4.50	88	.288	.327	10-0	.000	-1	99	-1	-0.1
Total	5	52	44	.542	120	106	84-3	1	882	1054	566	27	30	270	198	4.03	106	.294	.348	385-14	.216	-8	95	22	1.6
WILSON, GARY Gary Morris B 1.1.1970 Arcata, CA BR/TR 6-3/190# d4.28																									
1995	Pit N	0	1	.000	10	0	0	0-0	14.1	13	8	2	2	5-0	8	5.02	86	.241	.328	0-1	—	0		-1	-0.1
WILSON, GARY Gary Steven B 11.21.1954 Camden, AR BR/TR 6-2/185# d4.13																									
1979	Hou N	0	0	—	6	0	0	0-0	7.1	15	11	2	0	6-0	6	12.27	29	.441	.500	0-0	—	0		-7	-0.4
WILSON, TEX Gomer Russell B 7.8.1901 Trenton, TX D 9.15.1946 Sulphur Springs, TX BR/TL 5-10/170# d9.2																									
1924	Bro N	0	0	—	2	0	0	0	3.2	7	6	0	0	1	1	14.73	25	.412	.444	1-0	.000	-0		-4	-0.2
WILSON, HIGHBALL Howard Paul B 8.9.1878 Philadelphia, PA D 10.16.1934 Havre De Grace, MD TR 5-9/164# d9.13																									
1899	Cle N	0	1	.000	1	1	1	0	8	12	8	0	0	5	1	9.00	41	.343	.425	3-0	.333	0	39	-4	-0.3
1902	Phi A	7	4	.636	13	10	8	0	96.1	103	44	1	9	19	18	2.43	151	.274	.324	35-1	.171	-1	108	11	0.9
1903	Was A	7	18	.280	30	28	25-1	0	242.1	269	123	7	10	43	56	3.31	95	.280	.318	85-2	.200	2*	70	-6	-0.5
1904	Was A	0	3	.000	3	3	3	0	25	33	17	0	2	4	11	4.68	57	.317	.355	9-1	.222	1*	36	-5	-0.5
Total	4	14	26	.350	47	42	37-1	0	371.2	417	192	8	21	71	86	3.29	99	.283	.325	132-4	.197	2	77	-4	-0.4
WILSON, JIM James Alger B 2.20.1922 San Diego, CA D 9.2.1986 Newport Beach, CA BR/TR 6-1.5/200# d4.18																									
1945	Bos A	6	8	.429	23	21	8-2	0	144.1	121	61	7	1	88	50	3.30	103	.228	.339	53-2	.245	2*	89	2	0.2
1946	Bos A	0	0	—	1	0	0	0	0.2	2	2	1	0	0	0	27.00	14	.500	.500	0-0	—	0		-2	-0.1
1948	StL A	0	0	—	4	0	0	0	2.2	5	4	0	0	5	1	13.50	34	.417	.588	0-0	—	0		-2	-0.1
1949	Phi A	0	0	—	2	0	0	0	5	7	8	2	0	5	2	14.40	29	.350	.480	3-0	.000	-0		-5	-0.3
1951	Bos N	7	7	.500	20	15	5	1	110	131	67	14	4	40	33	5.40	68	.294	.357	39-3	.179	0	152	-19	-2.1
1952	Bos N	12	14	.462	33	33	14	0	234	234	114	19	4	90	104	4.23	85	.262	.333	86-3	.163	-0	101	-13	-1.4
1953	Mil N	4	9	.308	20	18	5	0	114	107	59	16	3	43	71	4.34	90	.243	.315	36-2	.167	1	94	-4	-0.2
1954	Mil N☆	8	2	.800	27	19	6-4	0	127.2	129	55	12	5	36	52	3.52	106	.266	.321	44-2	.159	0	150	4	0.4
1955	Bal A☆	12	18	.400	34	31	14-4	0	235.1	200	104	17	4	87-5	96	3.44	111	.228	.297	89-2	.169	-2	78	10	1.0
1956	Bal A	4	2	.667	7	7	1	0	48.1	49	27	5	2	16-1	31	5.03	78	.268	.332	15-0	.267	2	91	-5	-0.3
	Chi A★	9	12	.429	28	21	6-3	0	159.2	149	82	15	2	70-5	82	4.06	101	.248	.328	62-2	.306	4	105	0	0.3
	Year	13	14	.481	35	28	7-3	0	208	198	87	20	4	86-6	113	4.28	95	.253	.329	77-2	.299	6	102	-5	0.0
1957	Chi A	15	8	.652	30	29	12-**5**	0	201.2	189	85	22	3	65-8	100	3.48	107	.249	.309	68-4	.147	-0*	115	6	0.5
1958	Chi A	9	9	.500	28	23	4-1	1	155.2	156	75	21	1	63-8	70	4.10	89	.268	.337	51-4	.078	-3	125	-7	-1.1
Total	12	86	89	.491	257	217	75-19	2	1539	1479	743	151	29	608-27	692	4.01	93	.254	.326	546-24	.181	4	108	-35	-3.2
WILSON, JACK John Francis "Black Jack" B 4.12.1912 Portland, OR D 4.19.1995 Edmonds, WA BR/TR 5-11/210# d9.9																									
1934	Phi A	0	1	.000	2	2	1	0	9	15	12	1	0	9	2	12.00	37	.405	.522	3-1	.000	-0	119	-7	-0.6
1935	Bos A	3	4	.429	23	6	2	1	64	72	35	0	2	36	19	4.22	112	.290	.385	16-1	.313	2	70	4	0.6
1936	Bos A	6	8	.429	43	9	2	3	136.1	152	83	4	1	86	74	4.42	120	.284	.384	50-1	.220	-0*	63	10	0.8
1937	Bos A	16	10	.615	51	21	14-1	7	221.1	209	111	13	3	119	137	3.70	128	.248	.343	85-2	.165	-3	118	22	2.1
1938	Bos A	15	15	.500	37	27	11-3	1	194.2	200	108	16	2	91	96	4.30	115	.262	.342	68-6	.221	0	81	13	1.6
1939	Bos A	11	11	.500	36	22	6	2	177.1	198	109	10	1	75	80	4.67	101	.281	.351	63-5	.159	-4*	103	0	-0.4
1940	Bos A	12	6	.667	41	16	9	5	157.2	170	104	17	3	87	102	5.08	89	.270	.362	66-0	.273	4	144	-13	-1.0
1941	Bos A	4	13	.235	27	12	4-1	1	116.1	140	82	7	5	70	55	5.03	83	.300	.397	44-2	.159	-1	90	-13	-1.7
1942	Was A	1	4	.200	12	6	1	0	42	57	34	2	1	23	18	6.64	55	.322	.403	17-1	.118	-1	125	-13	-1.4
	Det A	0	0	—	9	0	0	0	13	20	8	3	0	5	7	4.85	81	.351	.403	1-0	.000	-0		-1	-0.1
	Year	1	4	.200	21	6	1	0	55	77	47	5	1	28	25	6.22	60	.329	.403	18-1	.111	-1	122	-14	-1.5
Total	9	68	72	.486	281	121	50-5	20	1131.2	1233	686	73	18	601	590	4.59	102	.276	.364	413-19	.199	-3	100	2	-0.1
WILSON, JOHN John Nicodemus B 6.15.1890 Boonsboro, MD D 9.23.1954 Annapolis, MD BR/TL 6-1/185# d6.11																									
1913	Was A	0	0	—	3	0	0	0	4	4	2	0	0	3	1	4.50	66	.286	.412	0-0	—	0		0	0.0
WILSON, JOHN John Samuel B 4.25.1903 Coal City, AL D 8.27.1980 Chattanooga, TN BR/TR 6-2/164# d5.9																									
1927	Bos A	0	2	.000	5	2	2	0	25.1	31	19	1	0	13	8	3.55	119	.326	.407	9-0	.111	-1	30	-1	-0.2
1928	Bos A	0	0	—	2	0	0	0	5	6	5	0	0	6	1	9.00	46	.333	.500	1-0	.000	-0		-2	-0.1
Total	2	0	2	.000	7	2	2	0	30.1	37	24	1	0	19	9	4.45	94	.327	.424	10-0	.100	-1	30	-3	-0.3
WILSON, KRIS Kristopher Kyle B 8.6.1976 Washington, DC BR/TR 6-4/225# d7.28																									
2000	KC A	0	1	.000	20	0	0	0-1	34.1	38	16	3	0	11-3	17	4.19	122	.288	.340	0-0	—	0		4	0.2
2001	KC A	6	5	.545	29	15	0	1-0	109.1	132	78	26	7	32-0	67	5.19	95	.297	.352	3-0	.333	0	88	-7	-0.6
2002	KC A	2	0	1.000	12	0	0	0-2	18.2	29	18	7	2	5-0	10	8.20	61	.354	.396	0-0	—	0		-6	-0.5
2003	KC A	6	3	.667	29	4	0	0-1	72.2	92	49	13	6	16-3	42	5.33	97	.305	.348	0-0	—	0	76	-2	-0.2
Total	4	14	9	.609	90	19	0	1-4	235	291	161	49	15	64-6	136	5.32	95	.303	.353	3-0	.333	0	84	-11	-1.1
WILSON, MAX Max B 6.3.1916 Haw River, NC D 1.2.1977 Greensboro, NC BL/TL 5-7/160# d9.10 Mil 1942-45																									
1940	Phi N	0	0	—	3	0	0	0	7	16	13	1	0	2	3	12.86	30	.444	.474	2-0	.000	-0		-8	-0.4
1946	Was A	0	1	.000	9	0	0	0	12.2	16	12	1	0	9	8	7.11	47	.320	.424	2-0	.000	0		-5	-0.4
Total	2	0	1	.000	12	0	0	0	19.2	32	25	2	0	11	11	9.15	39	.372	.443	4-0	.000	-0		-13	-0.8
WILSON, PAUL Paul Anthony B 3.28.1973 Orlando, FL BR/TR 6-5/235# d4.4																									
1996	NY N	5	12	.294	26	26	1	0-0	149	157	102	15	10	71-11	109	5.38	75	.268	.355	50-4	.080	-2	99	-23	-2.5
2000	TB A	1	4	.200	11	7	0	0-0	51	38	20	1	4	16-2	40	3.35	148	.209	.284	0-0	—	0	41	9	0.8
2001	TB A	8	9	.471	37	24	0	0-1	151.1	165	94	21	13	52-2	119	4.88	92	.278	.343	0-0	—	0	95	-7	-0.7
2002	TB A	6	12	.333	30	30	1	0-0	193.2	219	113	29	13	67-2	111	4.83	92	.287	.352	5-1	.000	-1	90	-8	-0.7
2003	Cin N	8	10	.444	28	28	0	0-0	166.2	190	97	24	7	50-5	93	4.64	92	.285	.342	52-4	.115	-1*	99	-9	-1.0
Total	5	28	47	.373	132	115	2	0-1	711.2	769	426	90	47	256-22	472	4.81	91	.276	.344	107-9	.093	-3	92	-38	-4.1
WILSON, PETE Peter Alex B 10.9.1885 Springfield, MA D 6.5.1957 St.Petersburg, FL TL d9.15																									
1908	NY A	3	3	.500	6	6	4-1	0	39	27	16	0	1	33	28	3.46	72	.191	.349	14-1	.071	-1*	55	-2	-0.4
1909	NY A	6	5	.545	14	13	7-1	0	93.2	82	55	2	4	43	44	3.17	80	.230	.320	34-1	.118	-1	114	-9	-1.1
Total	2	9	8	.529	20	19	11-2	0	132.2	109	71	2	5	76	72	3.26	77	.219	.329	48-2	.104	-2	94	-11	-1.5
WILSON, EARL Robert Earl (Name Changed From Wilson, Earl Lawrence) B 10.2.1934 Ponchatoula, LA BR/TR 6-3/216# d7.28																									
1959	Bos A	1	1	.500	9	4	0	0	23.2	21	17	2	0	31-0	17	6.08	67	.241	.441	8-0	.500	2	201	-5	-0.2
1960	Bos A	3	2	.600	13	9	2	0	65	61	36	4	0	48-1	40	4.71	86	.247	.367	23-0	.174	-0*	109	-4	-0.3
1962	Bos A	12	8	.600	31	28	4-1	0	191.1	163	86	21	6	111-2	137	3.90	106	.231	.338	69-1	.174	3*	107	8	1.0
1963	Bos A	11	16	.407	37	34	6-3	0	210.2	184	99	18	1	105-4	123	3.76	101	.234	.323	72-2	.208	5*	89	0	0.5
1964	Bos A	11	12	.478	33	31	5	0	202.1	213	121	37	2	73-3	166	4.49	86	.269	.328	73-1	.205	8*	117	-17	-0.9
1965	Bos A	13	14	.481	36	36	8-1	0	230.2	221	119	27	4	77-4	164	3.98	94	.250	.311	79-3	.177	8*	108	-6	0.2
1966	Bos A	5	5	.500	15	14	5-1	0	100.2	88	45	14	2	36-2	67	3.84	99	.235	.303	32-2	.250	3*	106	1	0.5
	Det A	13	6	.684	23	23	8-2	0	163.1	126	49	16	4	38-1	133	2.59	134	.213	.265	64-4	.234	9*	123	18	3.2
	Year	18	11	.621	38	37	13-3	0	264	214	54	30	6	74-3	200	3.07	117	.222	.280	96-6	.240	12	116	19	3.7
1967	Det A	**22**	11	.667	39	38	12	0	264	216	103	34	3	92-7	184	3.27	100	.224	.291	108-4	.185	7*	126	1	1.0

Year	Tm Lg	W	L	Pct	G	GS	CG-Sho	SV-BS	IP	H	R	HR	HB	BB-IB	SO	ERA	AERA	OAV	OOB	AB-SH	AVG	PB	Sup	APR	PW
1968	†Det A	13	12	.520	34	33	10-3	0	224.1	192	77	20	0	65-4	168	2.85	106	.231	.287	88-1	.227	10*	97	4	1.7
1969	Det A	12	10	.545	35	35	5-1	0-0	214.2	209	93	23	4	69-4	150	3.31	113	.256	.315	76-2	.132	-0*	102	8	0.8
1970	Det A	4	6	.400	18	16	4-1	0-0	96	87	53	15	2	32-1	74	4.41	85	.238	.303	31-2	.194	2	94	-8	-0.5
	SD N	1	6	.143	15	9	0	0-0	65	82	36	5	2	19-2	29	4.85	82	.309	.356	17-0	.059	0	100	-5	-0.5
Total	11	121	109	.526	338	310	69-13	0-0	2051.2	1863	934	236	30	796-35	1452	3.69	99	.242	.313	740-22	.195	57	109	-5	6.5
WILSON, ROY Roy Edward "Lefty" B 9.13.1896 Foster, IA D 12.3.1969 Clarion, IA BL/TL 6/175# d4.18																									
1928	Chi A	0	0	—	1	0	0	0	3.1	2	0	0	0	3	2	0.00	—	.167	.333	1-0	.000	-0		1	0.1
WILSON, STEVE Stephen Douglas B 12.13.1964 Victoria, BC, CAN BL/TL 6-4/195# d9.16																									
1988	Tex A	0	0	—	3	0	0	0-0	7.2	7	5	1	0	4-1	1	5.87	70	.259	.355	0-0	—	0		-1	-0.1
1989	†Chi N	6	4	.600	53	8	0	2-1	85.2	83	43	6	1	31-5	65	4.20	90	.257	.320	16-1	.063	-1	97	-3	-0.4
1990	Chi N	4	9	.308	45	15	1	1-1	139	140	77	17	2	43-6	95	4.79	85	.259	.315	37-5	.162	0	97	-8	-0.7
1991	Chi N	0	0	—	8	0	0	0-0	12.1	13	7	1	0	5-1	9	4.38	89	.277	.340	1-0	.000	-0*		-1	-0.1
	LA N	0	0	—	11	0	0	2-0	8.1	1	0	0	0	4-0	5	0.00	—	.042	.179	1-0	.000	-0		3	0.2
	Year	0	0	—	19	0	0	2-0	20.2	14	11	1	0	9-1	14	2.61	144	.197	.284	2-0	.000	-0		2	0.1
1992	LA N	2	5	.286	60	0	0	0-4	66.2	74	37	6	1	29-7	54	4.18	82	.282	.351	3-0	.333	0		-6	-0.6
1993	LA N	1	0	1.000	25	0	0	1-0	25.2	30	13	2	1	14-4	23	4.56	84	.288	.378	2-0	.000	-0		-1	-0.1
Total	6	13	18	.419	205	23	1	6-6	345.1	348	182	33	5	130-24	252	4.40	87	.262	.328	60-6	.133	-1	101	-17	-1.8
WILSON, TREVOR Trevor Kirk B 6.7.1966 Torrance, CA BL/TL 6/195# d9.5																									
1988	SF N	0	2	.000	4	4	0	0-0	22	25	14	1	0	8-0	15	4.09	80	.298	.355	7-1	.286	1	88	-3	-0.3
1989	SF N	2	3	.400	14	4	0	0-0	39.1	28	20	2	4	24-0	22	4.35	78	.207	.341	8-0	.250	1	138	-4	-0.3
1990	SF N	8	7	.533	27	17	3-2	0-0	110.1	87	52	11	1	49-3	66	4.00	91	.218	.304	29-5	.138	0	89	-4	-0.4
1991	SF N	13	11	.542	44	29	2-1	0-1	202	173	87	13	5	77-4	139	3.56	101	.234	.308	51-8	.235	5*	98	0	0.7
1992	SF N	8	14	.364	26	26	1-1	0-0	154	152	82	18	6	64-5	88	4.21	79	.265	.342	39-7	.077	-1*	84	-18	-2.3
1993	SF N	7	5	.583	22	18	1	0-0	110	110	45	8	6	40-3	57	3.60	109	.275	.347	29-8	.138	1	84	5	0.6
1995	SF N	3	4	.429	17	17	0	0-0	82.2	82	42	8	4	38-1	38	3.92	104	.269	.355	30-3	.233	1*	92	1	0.2
1998	Ana A	0	0	—	15	0	0	0-2	7.2	8	4	0	1	5-2	6	3.52	133	.267	.378	0-0	—	0		1	0.0
Total	8	41	46	.471	169	115	7-4	0-3	728	665	346	61	27	305-18	431	3.87	94	.249	.330	193-32	.176	7	92	-22	-1.8
WILSON, WALTER Walter Wood B 11.24.1913 Glenn, GA D 4.17.1994 Bremen, GA BL/TR 6-4/190# d4.17																									
1945	Det A	1	3	.250	25	4	1	0	70.1	76	40	4	3	35	28	4.61	76	.284	.373	19-2	.053	-2	79	-7	-0.5
WILSON, WILLY William B 1.7.1884 Columbus, OH D 10.28.1925 Seattle, WA BR/TR d10.3																									
1906	Was A	0	1	.000	1	1	1	0	7	3	2	0	1	2	1	2.57	102	.130	.231	2-0	.000	-0	27	0	0.0
WILSON, MUTT William Clarence "Lank" B 7.20.1896 Keyser, NC D 8.31.1962 Leesburg, FL BR/TR 6-3/167# d9.11																									
1920	Det A	1	1	.500	3	2	1	0	13	12	10	0	0	5	4	3.46	108	.240	.309	4-1	.250	-0	96	-1	-0.2
WILSON, BILL William Harlan B 9.21.1942 Pomeroy, OH D 8.11.1993 Broken Arrow, OK BR/TR 6-2/200# d4.8																									
1969	Phi N	2	5	.286	37	0	0	6-3	62.1	53	26	6	1	36-8	48	3.32	107	.231	.336	6-0	.000	-0		2	0.1
1970	Phi N	1	0	1.000	37	0	0	0-1	58.1	57	35	5	0	33-0	41	4.78	84	.263	.357	4-0	.250	0		-6	-0.3
1971	Phi N	4	6	.400	38	0	0	7-2	58.2	39	20	4	1	22-4	40	3.07	115	.188	.266	10-0	.100	-1		4	0.8
1972	Phi N	1	1	.500	23	0	0	0-2	30	26	13	1	0	11-3	18	3.30	109	.234	.301	0-0	—	0		1	0.0
1973	Phi N	1	3	.250	44	0	0	4-2	48.2	54	39	7	0	29-7	24	6.66	57	.293	.388	4-0	.000	-0		-14	-1.4
Total	5	9	15	.375	179	0	0	17-10	258	229	133	23	2	131-22	171	4.22	88	.241	.332	24-0	.083	-1		-13	-0.8
WILTSE, HOOKS George Leroy B 9.7.1880 Hamilton, NY D 1.21.1959 Long Beach, NY BR/TL 6/185# d4.21 C1 b-Snake																									
1904	NY N	13	3	.813	24	16	14-2	3	164.2	150	66	8	5	61	105	2.84	96	.240	.313	67-2	.224	3*	169	0	0.5
1905	NY N	15	6	.714	32	19	18-1	3	197	158	71	5	4	61	120	2.47	119	.219	.284	72-2	.278	7*	114	12	2.3
1906	NY N	16	11	.593	38	26	21-4	6	249.1	227	92	3	3	58	125	2.27	115	.241	.288	94-4	.191	2*	102	7	1.0
1907	NY N	13	12	.520	33	21	14-3	2	190.1	171	63	3	5	48	79	2.18	114	.241	.294	67-1	.134	0*	114	6	0.9
1908	NY N	23	14	.622	44	38	30-7	2	330	266	95	4	9	73	118	2.24	108	.224	.274	110-7	.236	6*	126	12	2.1
1909	NY N	20	11	.645	37	30	22-4	3	269.1	228	91	9	6	51	119	2.00	128	.233	.275	95-2	.200	2	133	16	2.0
1910	NY N	14	12	.538	36	30	18-2	2	235.1	232	96	4	2	52	88	2.72	109	.261	.303	74-5	.176	0	110	7	0.6
1911	†NY N	12	9	.571	30	24	11-4	0	187.1	177	83	7	2	39	92	3.27	103	.251	.292	69-2	.188	-1*	107	5	0.3
1912	NY N	9	6	.600	28	17	5	3	134	140	63	7	1	28	58	3.16	107	.273	.312	46-1	.326	4	129	5	0.9
1913	†NY N	0	0	—	17	2	0	3	57.2	53	24	1	1	8	25	1.56	200	.237	.266	24-0	.208	0*	133	6	0.4
1914	NY N	1	1	.500	20	0	0	1	38	41	21	2	0	12	19	2.84	93	.289	.344	3-0	.667	2*		-3	0.0
1915	Bro F	3	5	.375	18	3	1	5	59.1	49	22	1	2	7	17	2.28	120	.226	.257	22-0	.045	-3*	26	2	0.0
Total	12	139	90	.607	357	226	154-27	33	2112.1	1892	787	54	40	498	965	2.47	112	.241	.290	743-26	.210	22	120	75	11.0
WILTSE, HAL Harold James "Whitey" B 8.6.1903 Clay City, IL D 11.2.1983 Bunkie, LA BL/TL 5-9/168# d4.13																									
1926	Bos A	8	15	.348	37	29	9-1	0	196.1	201	112	6	6	99	59	4.22	97	.273	.363	59-4	.085	-5	79	-5	-0.9
1927	Bos A	10	18	.357	36	29	13-1	1	219	276	146	5	4	76	47	5.10	83	.321	.379	77-2	.208	-2	72	-20	-2.2
1928	Bos A	0	2	.000	2	2	1	0	12	16	12	1	3	1	5	9.00	46	.314	.364	4-0	.000	-1	62	-6	-0.7
	StL A	2	5	.286	26	5	0	0	72	93	49	4	3	35	23	5.25	80	.316	.395	22-1	.227	0	93	-8	-0.6
	Year	2	7	.222	28	7	1	0	84	109	54	5	6	36	28	5.79	72	.316	.390	26-1	.192	-1	84	-13	-1.3
1931	Phi N	0	0	—	1	0	0	0	1	3	1	0	0	0	0	9.00	47	.600	.600	0-0	—	0		0	0.0
Total	4	20	40	.333	102	65	23-2	1	500.1	589	320	16	16	211	134	4.87	85	.303	.375	162-7	.160	-7	76	-39	-4.4
WILTSE, SNAKE Lewis De Witt B 12.5.1871 Bouckville, NY D 8.25.1928 Harrisburg, PA BR/TL d5.5 b-Hooks																									
1901	Pit N	1	4	.200	7	5	3	0	44.1	57	28	2	5	13	10	4.26	77	.310	.371	19-1	.158	-1	82	-4	-0.4
	Phi A	13	5	.722	19	19	18-2	0	166	185	91	1	7	35	40	3.58	105	.279	.322	67-2	.373	8	122	4	1.2
1902	Phi A	8	8	.500	19	17	13	1	138	182	99	7	5	41	28	5.15	71	.318	.368	57-0	.175	-0*	113	-17	-1.8
	Bal A	7	11	.389	19	18	18	0	164	215	127	4	8	51	37	5.10	74	.316	.371	132-2	.295	6*	122	-20	-1.3
	Year	15	19	.441	38	35	31	1	302	397	133	11	13	92	65	5.13	73	.317	.370	189-2	.259	5	118	-38	-3.1
1903	NY A	0	3	.000	4	3	2	1	25	35	17	1	1	6	6	5.40	58	.330	.372	9-0	.222	0	46	-5	-0.5
Total	3	29	31	.483	68	62	54-2	2	537.1	674	362	15	26	146	121	4.59	80	.305	.356	284-5	.278	13	113	-42	-2.8
WINCHELL, FRED Frederick Russell (b: Frederick Cook) B 1.23.1882 Arlington, MA D 8.8.1958 Toronto, ON, CAN TR 5-8/?# d9.16																									
1909	Cle A	0	3	.000	4	3	0	1	14.1	16	11	0	0	2	7	6.28	41	.296	.321	5-0	.200	0	74	-5	-0.9
WINCHESTER, SCOTT Scott Joseph B 4.20.1973 Midland, MI BR/TR 6-2/210# d9.8																									
1997	Cin N	0	0	—	5	0	0	0-0	6	9	5	1	1	2-0	3	6.00	71	.360	.429	0-0	—	0		-1	-0.1
1998	Cin N	3	6	.333	16	16	1	0-0	79	101	56	12	4	27-2	40	5.81	74	.312	.370	23-2	.130	-1	81	-14	-1.4
2000	Cin N	0	0	—	5	0	0	0-0	7.1	10	4	1	0	2-0	3	3.68	128	.313	.343	0-0	—	0		0	0.0
2001	Cin N	0	2	.000	12	1	0	0-0	24	29	19	7	3	4-3	9	4.50	101	.315	.353	3-0	.000	-0	81	-2	-0.2
Total	4	3	8	.273	38	17	1	0-0	116.1	149	84	21	8	35-5	55	5.42	81	.315	.368	26-2	.115	-1	79	-17	-1.7
WINEAPPLE, ED Edward "Lefty" B 8.10.1905 Boston, MA D 7.23.1996 Delray Beach, FL BL/TL 6/210# d9.15																									
1929	Was A	0	0	—	1	0	0	0	4	7	4	0	0	3	1	4.50	94	.467	.556	2-0	.000	-0		-1	-0.1
WINEGARNER, RALPH Ralph Lee B 10.29.1909 Benton, KS D 4.14.1988 Wichita, KS BR/TR 6/182# d9.20.1930 C4																									
1932	Cle A	1	0	1.000	5	1	1	0	17.1	7	4	0	0	13	5	1.04	457	.123	.286	7-0	.143	-0*	108	6	0.2
1934	Cle A	5	4	.556	22	6	4	0	78.1	91	55	1	2	39	32	5.51	82	.289	.371	51-0	.196	1*	108	-8	-0.6
1935	Cle A	2	2	.500	25	4	2	0	67.1	89	51	10	1	29	41	5.75	78	.313	.379	84-1	.310	4*	135	-10	0.0
1936	Cle A	0	0	—	9	0	0	0	14.2	18	9	0	0	6	3	4.91	103	.295	.358	16-0	.125	-1*		0	-0.1
1949	StL A	0	0	—	9	0	0	0	16.2	24	16	2	0	2	8	7.56	60	.329	.347	5-0	.400	2		-5	-0.1
Total	5	8	6	.571	70	11	7	0	194.1	229	135	13	3	89	89	5.33	86	.290	.364	163-1	.252	5	117	-17	-0.6
WINFORD, JIM James Head "Cowboy" B 10.9.1909 Shelbyville, TN D 12.16.1970 Miami, OK BR/TR 6-1/180# d9.10																									
1932	StL N	1	1	.500	4	1	0	0	8.1	9	7	0	0	5	4	6.48	61	.273	.368	3-0	.667	1	86	-2	-0.3
1934	StL N	0	2	.000	5	1	0	0	12.2	17	13	0	2	6	3	7.82	54	.327	.417	1-0	.000	0	41	-5	-0.6
1935	StL N	0	0	—	2	1	0	0	11.1	13	5	1	0	5	7	3.97	103	.283	.353	2-1	.000	-0	145	0	0.0

Year	Tm Lg	W	L	Pct	G	GS	CG-Sho	SV-BS	IP	H	R	HR	HB	BB-IB	SO	ERA	AERA	OAV	OOB	AB-SH	AVG	PB	Sup	APR	PW
1936	StL N	11	10	.524	39	23	10-1	3	192	203	90	10	5	68	72	3.80	104	.269	.333	59-0	.085	-4	90	4	-0.2
1937	StL N	2	4	.333	16	4	0	0	46.1	56	31	2	0	27	17	5.83	68	.311	.401	8-0	.125	-1	70	-7	-0.9
1938	Bro N	0	1	.000	2	1	0	0	5.2	9	10	1	0	4	4	11.12	35	.346	.433	1-0	.000	0	87	-5	-0.7
Total	6	14	18	.438	68	31	10-1	3	276.1	307	156	14	7	115	107	4.56	87	.281	.353	74-1	.108	-3	87	-15	-2.7
WINGARD, ERNIE Ernest James "Jim" B 10.17.1900 Prattville, AL D 1.17.1977 Prattville, AL BL/TL 6-2/176# d5.1																									
1924	StL A	13	12	.520	36	26	14	1	218	215	103	6	3	85	23	3.51	129	.262	.334	77-4	.234	2*	76	22	2.2
1925	StL A	9	10	.474	32	18	8	0	145	183	111	10	3	77	20	5.52	85	.319	.403	52-4	.288	3*	114	-15	-1.1
1926	StL A	5	8	.385	39	16	7	3	169	188	86	9	5	76	30	3.57	120	.290	.369	61-1	.230	1*	93	10	1.0
1927	StL A	2	13	.133	38	17	7	0	156.1	213	132	7	2	79	28	6.56	66	.340	.415	56-0	.179	2*	90	-34	-2.5
Total	4	29	43	.403	145	77	36	4	688.1	799	432	32	13	317	101	4.64	96	.299	.377	246-9	.232	7	92	-17	-0.4
WINGFIELD, TED Frederick Davis B 8.7.1899 Bedford, VA D 7.18.1975 Johnson City, TN BR/TR 5-11/168# d9.23																									
1923	Was A	0	0	—	1	0	0	0	1	0	0	0	0	0	1	0.00	—	.000	.000	0-0	—	0		0	0.0
1924	Was A	0	0	—	4	0	0	0	7	9	2	0	0	4	2	2.57	157	.300	.382	2-0	.000	-0		1	0.0
	Bos A	0	2	.000	4	3	2	0	25.2	23	12	0	0	8	4	2.45	178	.240	.298	9-0	.333	1	64	4	0.3
	Year	0	2	.000	8	3	2	0	32.2	32	15	0	0	12	6	2.48	173	.254	.319	11-0	.273	0	65	5	0.3
1925	Bos A	12	19	.387	41	27	18-2	2	254.1	267	149	11	8	92	30	3.96	115	.278	.346	94-5	.245	1	77	13	1.8
1926	Bos A	11	16	.407	43	20	9-1	3	190.2	220	119	11	2	50	30	4.44	92	.298	.344	69-0	.217	-0	64	-12	-1.4
1927	Bos A	1	7	.125	20	8	2	0	74.2	105	60	2	3	27	1	5.06	83	.357	.417	18-0	.222	0*	57	-11	-0.8
Total	5	24	44	.353	113	58	31-3	5	553.1	624	342	24	13	181	68	4.18	103	.294	.353	192-5	.234	1	70	-5	-0.1
WINHAM, LAVE Lafayette Sharkey "Lefty" B 10.23.1881 Brooklyn, NY D 9.12.1951 Brooklyn, NY BL/TL 5-11/200# d4.21																									
1902	Bro N	0	0	—	1	0	0	0	3	4	2	0	0	2	1	0.00	—	.308	.400	2-0	.000	-0		0	0.0
1903	Pit N	3	1	.750	5	4	3-1	0	36	33	20	0	0	21	22	2.25	144	.231	.329	14-0	.071	-1	120	2	0.0
Total	2	3	1	.750	6	4	3-1	0	39	37	22	0	0	23	23	2.08	154	.237	.335	16-0	.063	-2	120	2	0.0
WINKELSAS, JOE Joseph B 9.14.1973 Buffalo, NY BR/TR 6-3/188# d4.10																									
1999	Atl N	0	0	—	1	0	0	0-0	0.1	4	2	0	0	1-1	0	54.00	8	1.000	1.000	0-0	—	0		-2	-0.1
WINN, GEORGE George Benjamin "Breezy" or "Lefty" B 10.26.1897 Perry, GA D 11.1.1969 Roberta, GA BL/TL 5-11/170# d4.29																									
1919	Bos A	0	0	—	3	0	0	0	4.2	6	4	0	0	1	0	7.71	39	.353	.389	1-0	.000	-0		-2	-0.1
1922	Cle A	1	2	.333	8	3	1	0	33.2	44	20	2	0	5	7	4.54	88	.317	.340	9-0	.333	1	78	-2	-0.1
1923	Cle A	0	0	—	1	0	0	0	2	0	0	0	0	1	0	0.00	—	.000	.143	0-0	—	0		1	0.0
Total	3	1	2	.333	12	3	1	0	40.1	50	24	2	0	7	7	4.69	83	.309	.337	10-0	.300	1	78	-3	-0.2
WINN, JIM James Francis B 9.23.1959 Stockton, CA BR/TR 6-3/210# d4.10																									
1983	Pit N	0	0	—	7	0	0	0-0	11	12	9	2	0	6-0	3	7.36	50	.267	.353	0-0	—	0		-4	-0.2
1984	Pit N	1	0	1.000	9	0	0	1-0	18.2	19	8	2	0	9-1	11	3.86	93	.264	.346	1-0	.000	-0		0	0.0
1985	Pit N	3	6	.333	30	7	0	0-1	75.2	77	45	4	2	31-2	22	5.23	69	.266	.340	18-2	.111	-0	67	-12	-1.3
1986	Pit N	3	5	.375	50	3	0	3-4	88	85	44	9	2	38-7	70	3.58	107	.258	.335	16-1	.063	-1	70	0	0.0
1987	Chi A	4	6	.400	56	0	0	6-6	94	95	54	10	6	62-5	44	4.79	96	.271	.390	0-0	—	0		-2	-0.1
1988	Min A	1	0	1.000	9	0	0	0-0	21	33	15	4	0	10-1	9	6.00	68	.355	.417	0-0	—	0		-4	-0.2
Total	6	12	17	.414	161	10	0	10-11	308.1	321	175	31	10	156-16	159	4.67	86	.272	.361	35-3	.086	-1	63	-22	-1.8
WINSTON, DARRIN Darrin Alexander B 7.6.1966 Passaic, NJ BR/TL 6/195# d9.10																									
1997	Phi N	2	0	1.000	7	1	0	0-0	12	8	8	4	2	3-1	8	5.25	81	.178	.260	2-0	.500	1	43	-1	-0.2
1998	Phi N	2	2	.500	27	0	0	1-1	25	31	18	7	2	6-0	11	6.12	71	.298	.348	1-0	.000	-0		-5	-0.7
Total	2	4	2	.667	34	1	0	1-1	37	39	26	11	4	9-1	19	5.84	74	.262	.321	3-0	.333	1	43	-6	-0.9
WINSTON, HANK Henry Rudolph B 6.15.1904 Youngsville, NC D 2.4.1974 Jacksonville, FL BL/TR 6-3.5/226# d9.30																									
1933	Phi A	0	0	—	1	0	0	0	6.2	7	5	0	0	6	2	6.75	63	.280	.419	3-0	.000	-0		-1	-0.1
1936	Bro N	1	3	.250	14	0	0	0	32.1	40	27	2	1	16	8	6.12	67	.301	.380	11-0	.091	-1		-7	-0.8
Total	2	1	3	.250	15	0	0	0	39	47	32	2	1	22	10	6.23	67	.297	.387	14-0	.071	-1		-8	-0.9
WINTER, GEORGE George Lovington "Sassafras" B 4.27.1878 New Providence, PA D 5.26.1951 Franklin Lakes, NJ TR 5-8/155# d6.15																									
1901	Bos A	16	12	.571	28	28	26-1	0	241	234	127	4	4	66	63	2.80	126	.252	.304	100-0	.190	-4	101	15	1.0
1902	Bos A	11	9	.550	20	20	18	0	168.1	149	77	2	7	53	51	2.99	119	.238	.305	61-0	.164	-2	84	12	1.0
1903	Bos A	9	8	.529	24	19	14	0	178.1	182	92	4	7	37	64	3.08	99	.263	.307	66-2	.106	-4	117	-3	-0.8
1904	Bos A	8	4	.667	20	16	12-1	0	135.2	126	47	4	6	27	31	2.32	115	.247	.293	43-4	.116	-2*	133	6	0.2
1905	Bos A	16	17	.485	35	27	24-2	0	264.1	249	118	5	5	54	119	2.96	91	.251	.293	92-0	.261	3	100	-9	-0.7
1906	Bos A	6	18	.250	29	22	18-1	2	207.2	215	118	8	5	38	72	4.12	67	.270	.308	69-2	.246	2	94	-27	-2.8
1907	Bos A	12	15	.444	35	27	21-4	1	256.2	198	91	2	3	61	88	2.07	124	.215	.267	94-1	.223	1	90	12	1.4
1908	Bos A	4	14	.222	22	17	8	0	147.2	150	71	3	4	34	55	3.05	81	.274	.321	49-0	.184	-1	72	-9	-1.2
	†Det A	1	5	.167	7	6	5	1	56.1	49	19	0	3	7	25	1.60	151	.240	.276	18-2	.111	-1	57	4	0.3
	Year	5	19	.208	29	23	13	1	204	199	21	3	7	41	80	2.65	93	.265	.309	67-2	.164	-2	68	-5	-0.9
Total	8	83	102	.449	220	182	146-9	4	1656	1552	760	32	44	377	568	2.87	101	.250	.297	592-11	.193	-8	97	1	-1.6
WINTERS, CLARENCE Clarence John B 9.7.1898 Detroit, MI D 6.29.1945 Detroit, MI TR d8.28																									
1924	Bos A	0	1	.000	4	2	0	0	7	22	16	0	0	4	3	20.57	21	.512	.553	3-0	.333	0	145	-11	-1.1
WINTERS, JESSE Jesse Franklin "Buck" or "T-Bone" B 12.22.1893 Stephenville, TX D 6.5.1986 Abilene, TX BR/TR 6-1/165# d5.3																									
1919	NY N	1	2	.333	16	2	0	3	28	39	18	1	3	13	6	5.46	51	.339	.420	3-0	.000	-0	128	-7	-1.0
1920	NY N	0	0	—	21	0	0	0	46.1	37	19	1	4	28	14	3.50	86	.233	.361	7-0	.000	-1		-1	-0.1
1921	Phi N	5	10	.333	18	14	10	0	114	142	73	4	4	28	22	3.63	116	.310	.355	39-1	.128	-3	78	3	0.2
1922	Phi N	6	6	.500	34	9	4	2	138.1	176	100	8	4	56	29	5.33	87	.319	.386	43-2	.256	0	85	-7	-0.5
1923	Phi N	1	6	.143	21	6	1	1	78.1	116	76	7	4	39	23	7.35	63	.348	.423	25-1	.160	-1	80	-20	-1.6
Total	5	13	24	.351	110	31	15	6	405	510	286	21	19	164	94	5.04	83	.316	.385	117-4	.171	-5	85	-32	-3.0
WIRTH, ALAN Alan Lee B 12.8.1956 Mesa, AZ BR/TR 6-4/190# d4.9																									
1978	Oak A	5	6	.455	16	14	2-1	0-0	81.1	72	39	6	3	34-0	31	3.43	106	.252	.333	0-0	—	0	61	1	0.1
1979	Oak A	1	0	1.000	5	1	0	0-0	12	14	8	2	1	8-0	7	6.00	68	.298	.404	0-0	—	0	112	-2	-0.2
1980	Oak A	0	0	—	2	0	0	0-0	2	3	1	0	0	0-0	1	4.50	84	.333	.333	0-0	—	0		0	0.0
Total	3	6	6	.500	23	15	2-1	0-0	95.1	89	48	8	4	42-0	39	3.78	98	.260	.344	0-0	—	0	65	-1	-0.1
WISE, ARCHIE Archibald Edwin B 7.31.1912 Waxahachie, TX D 2.2.1978 Dallas, TX BR/TR 6/165# d7.24																									
1932	Chi A	0	0	—	2	0	0	0	7.1	8	5	1	1	5	2	4.91	88	.258	.378	4-0	.000	-1*		-1	-0.1
WISE, MATT Matthew John B 11.18.1975 Montclair, CA BR/TR 6-4/190# d8.2																									
2000	Ana A	3	3	.500	8	6	0	0-0	37.1	40	23	7	1	13-1	20	5.54	92	.272	.331	0-0	—	0	80	-1	-0.1
2001	Ana A	1	4	.200	11	9	0	0-0	49.1	47	27	11	2	18-1	50	4.38	104	.250	.321	0-0	—	0	72	1	0.0
2002	Ana A	0	0	—	7	0	0	0-0	8.1	7	3	0	1	1-0	6	3.24	137	.233	.281	0-0	—	0		1	0.0
Total	3	4	7	.364	26	15	0	0-0	95	94	53	18	4	32-2	76	4.74	100	.258	.322	0-0	—	0	76	1	-0.1
WISE, RICK Richard Charles B 9.13.1945 Jackson, MI BR/TR 6-2/195# d4.18																									
1964	Phi N	5	3	.625	25	8	0	0	69	78	41	7	3	25-2	39	4.04	86	.277	.341	17-2	.294	2	136	-7	-0.6
1966	Phi N	5	6	.455	22	13	3	0	99.1	100	50	5	3	24-3	58	3.71	97	.262	.308	30-1	.000	-4*	100	-3	-0.8
1967	Phi N	11	11	.500	36	25	6-3	0	181.1	177	69	8	4	45-5	111	3.28	104	.259	.307	53-2	.208	3	79	6	1.0
1968	Phi N	9	15	.375	30	30	7-1	0	182	210	100	12	6	37-3	97	4.55	66	.292	.330	58-2	.241	7	79	-29	-2.9
1969	Phi N	15	13	.536	33	31	14-4	0-0	220	215	100	17	2	61-3	144	3.23	110	.257	.307	74-6	.270	7	114	3	1.2
1970	Phi N	13	14	.481	35	34	5-1	0-0	220.1	253	115	15	3	65-7	113	4.17	96	.287	.337	75-6	.200	5*	88	-7	-0.2
1971	Phi N☆	17	14	.548	38	37	17-4	0-0	272.1	261	110	20	4	70-5	155	2.88	123	.254	.301	97-4	.237	10*	78	15	2.8
1972	StL N	16	16	.500	35	35	20-2	0-0	269	250	98	16	1	71-13	142	3.11	109	.251	.299	93-6	.172	1	96	12	1.6
1973	StL N★	16	12	.571	35	34	14-5	0-0	259	259	113	18	3	59-12	144	3.37	108	.257	.300	88-6	.193	6	100	7	1.4
1974	Bos A	3	4	.429	9	9	1	0-0	49	47	23	2	1	16-1	25	3.86	100	.251	.308	0-0	—	0	97	0	0.0
1975	†Bos A	19	12	.613	35	35	17-1	0-0	255.1	262	126	34	4	72-1	141	3.95	103	.263	.313	0-0	—	0	116	3	0.3

Year	Tm Lg	W	L	Pct	G	GS	CG-Sho	SV-BS	IP	H	R	HR	HB	BB-IB	SO	ERA	AERA	OAV	OOB	AB-SH	AVG	PB	Sup	APR	PW
1976	Bos A	14	11	.560	34	34	11-4	0-0	224.1	218	100	18	2	48-1	93	3.53	111	.255	.294	0-0	—	0	96	9	1.1
1977	Bos A	11	5	.688	26	20	4-2	0-0	128.1	151	68	19	4	28-1	85	4.77	94	.291	.332	0-0	—	0	107	-1	-0.1
1978	Cle A	9	19	.321	33	31	9-1	0-0	211.2	226	116	22	3	59-3	106	4.34	86	.275	.322	0-0	—	0	85	-15	-1.8
1979	Cle A	15	10	.600	34	34	9-2	0-0	231.2	229	111	24	1	68-9	108	3.73	114	.256	.307	0-0	—	0	94	12	1.3
1980	SD N	6	8	.429	27	27	1	0-0	154.1	172	69	14	0	37-10	59	3.67	94	.285	.325	58-2	.138	-1*	92	-4	-0.5
1981	SD N	4	8	.333	18	18	0	0-0	98	116	44	10	0	19-4	27	3.77	87	.296	.327	25-3	.040	-2	67	-5	-0.8
1982	SD N	0	0	—	1	0	0	0-0	2	3	2	0	0	0-0	0	9.00	38	.333	.333	0-0	—	0		-1	-0.1
Total	18	188	181	.509	506	455	138-30	0-0	3127	3227	1455	261	44	804-83	1647	3.69	100	.267	.313	668-40	.195	34	95	-5	2.9
WISE, OGDEN Roy Ogden B 11.18.1925 Springfield, IL BB/TR 6-2/170# d5.12																									
1944	Pit N	0	0	—	2	0	0	0	3	4	3	0	0	3	1	9.00	41	.333	.467	0-0	—	0		-1	-0.1
WISE, BILL William E. B 3.15.1861 Washington, DC D 5.5.1940 Washington, DC d5.2																									
1882	Bal AA	1	2	.333	3	3	3	0	26	30	14	1		4	9	2.77	99	.270	.296	20	.100	-1*	50	0	-0.1
1884	Was U	23	18	.561	50	41	34-4	0	364.1	383	219	5		60	268	3.04	79	.252	.281	339	.233	-8*	94	-24	-2.4
1886	Was N	0	1	.000	1	1	0	0	3	6	6	0		2	0	9.00	36	.400	.471	3	.000	-0	19	-2	-0.4
Total	3	24	21	.533	54	45	37-4	0	393.1	419	239	6		66	277	3.07	79	.255	.284	362	.224	-9	90	-26	-2.9
WISNER, JACK John Henry B 11.5.1899 Grand Rapids, MI D 12.15.1981 Jackson, MI BR/TR 6-3/195# d9.12																									
1919	Pit N	1	0	1.000	4	1	1	0	18.2	12	3	0	1	7	4	0.96	313	.185	.274	7-0	.000	-1	158	4	0.1
1920	Pit N	1	3	.250	17	2	1	0	44.2	46	19	1	1	10	13	3.43	94	.274	.318	7-0	.000	-1	49	0	-0.1
1925	NY N	0	0	—	25	0	0	0	40.1	33	19	4	2	14	13	3.79	106	.228	.304	7-0	.000	-1		2	0.0
1926	NY N	2	2	.500	5	3	2	0	28	21	12	4	0	10	5	3.54	106	.208	.279	10-0	.200	-0	148	1	0.1
Total	4	4	5	.444	51	6	4	0	131.2	112	53	9	4	41	35	3.21	111	.234	.300	31-0	.065	-3	114	7	0.1
WISTERT, WHITEY Francis Michael B 2.20.1912 Chicago, IL D 4.23.1985 Painesville, OH BR/TR 6-4/210# d9.11																									
1934	Cin N	0	1	.000	2	1	0	0	8	5	1	1	0	5	1	1.13	363	.185	.313	3-0	.000	-0*	0	3	0.3
WITASICK, JAY Gerald Alphonse B 8.28.1972 Baltimore, MD BR/TR 6-4/205# d7.7																									
1996	Oak A	1	1	.500	12	0	0	0-1	13	12	9	5	0	5-0	12	6.23	79	.245	.309	0-0	—	0		-2	-0.2
1997	Oak A	0	0	—	8	0	0	0-0	11	14	7	2	0	6-0	8	5.73	79	.304	.385	0-0	—	0		-1	-0.1
1998	Oak A	1	3	.250	7	3	0	0-0	27	36	24	9	0	15-1	29	6.33	72	.310	.389	0-0	—	0	81	-7	-0.8
1999	KC A	9	12	.429	32	28	1-1	0-0	158.1	191	108	23	8	83-1	102	5.57	90	.304	.387	5-0	.000	-1	100	-10	-1.2
2000	KC A	3	8	.273	22	14	2	0-0	89.1	109	65	15	4	38-0	67	5.94	86	.301	.371	4-0	.000	-0	120	-9	-1.0
	SD N	3	2	.600	11	11	0	0-0	60.2	69	42	9	3	35-5	54	5.64	77	.284	.379	22-2	.136	-0	102	-9	-0.6
2001	SD N	5	2	.714	31	0	0	1-2	38.2	31	14	3	4	15-3	53	1.86	215	.218	.311	1-0	.000	-0		8	1.3
	†NY A	3	0	1.000	32	0	0	0-1	40.1	47	27	5	2	18-1	53	4.69	96	.283	.356	0-0	—	0		-3	-0.2
2002	†SF N	1	0	1.000	44	0	0	0-0	68.1	58	19	3	4	21-3	54	2.37	164	.234	.303	5-0	.000	-1		12	0.5
2003	SD N	3	7	.300	46	0	0	2-5	45.2	42	24	6	1	25-4	42	4.53	87	.244	.342	0-0	—	0		-3	-0.6
Total	8	29	35	.453	245	56	3-1	3-9	552.1	609	339	80	26	261-18	474	4.89	94	.280	.362	37-2	.081	-2	112	-24	-2.9
WITHEM, SHANNON Shannon Bolt B 9.21.1972 Ann Arbor, MI BR/TR 6-3/185# d9.18																									
1998	Tor A	0	0	—	1	0	0	0-0	3	3	1	0	0	2-0	2	3.00	156	.250	.357	0-0	—	0		1	0.0
WITHEROW, CHARLES Charles Lafayette B 4.1852 Washington, DC D 7.3.1948 Washington, DC d7.1																									
1875	Was NA	0	1	.000	1	1	0	0	1	4	5	0		0	0	18.00	13	.444	.444	1	.000	-0	30	-1	-0.2
WITHERUP, ROY Foster Leroy B 7.26.1886 N.Washington, PA D 12.23.1941 New Bethlehem, PA BR/TR 6/185# d5.14																									
1906	Bos N	0	3	.000	8	3	3	0	46	59	37	2	1	19	14	6.26	43	.322	.389	15-0	.133	-1	63	-15	-1.0
1908	Was A	2	4	.333	6	6	4	0	48.1	51	21	0	1	8	31	2.98	77	.264	.297	18-0	.167	-1	115	-3	-0.4
1909	Was A	1	5	.167	12	8	5	0	68	79	41	1	0	20	26	4.24	57	.306	.356	19-1	.053	-2	65	-12	-1.3
Total	3	3	12	.200	26	17	12	0	162.1	189	99	3	2	47	71	4.44	55	.298	.348	52-1	.115	-3	81	-30	-2.7
WITT, GEORGE George Adrian "Red" B 11.9.1933 Long Beach, CA BR/TR 6-3/200# d9.21																									
1957	Pit N	0	1	.000	1	1	0	0	1.1	4	6	1	0	5-0	1	40.50	9	.500	.692	0-0	—	0	116	-5	-0.7
1958	Pit N	9	2	.818	18	15	5-3	0	106	78	22	2	2	59-3	81	1.61	240	.209	.318	39-1	.154	-1	93	27	2.5
1959	Pit N	0	7	.000	15	11	0	0	50.2	58	43	7	1	32-2	30	6.93	56	.293	.394	12-2	.000	-1	78	-17	-2.1
1960	†Pit N	1	2	.333	10	6	0	0	30	33	18	3	0	12-0	15	4.20	89	.300	.363	9-0	.000	-1	110	-3	-0.4
1961	Pit N	0	1	.000	9	1	0	0	15.2	17	12	5	0	5-0	9	6.32	63	.274	.328	2-1	.500	1	44	-4	-0.2
1962	LA A	1	1	.500	5	2	0	0	10	15	12	4	0	5-0	10	8.10	48	.349	.408	3-0	.333	0	139	-5	-0.9
	Hou N	0	2	.000	8	2	0	0	15.1	20	14	2	1	9-0	10	7.04	53	.339	.423	4-0	.250	0	23	-6	-0.6
Total	6	11	16	.407	66	38	5-3	0	229	225	127	24	4	127-5	156	4.32	89	.263	.359	69-4	.130	-2	89	-13	-2.4
WITT, MIKE Michael Atwater B 7.20.1960 Fullerton, CA BR/TR 6-7/192# d4.11																									
1981	Cal A	8	9	.471	22	21	7-1	0-0	129	123	60	9	11	47-4	75	3.28	111	.251	.328	0-0	—	0	111	2	0.2
1982	†Cal A	8	6	.571	33	26	5-1	0-0	179.2	177	77	8	7	47-2	85	3.51	116	.260	.312	0-0	—	0	106	10	0.7
1983	Cal A	7	14	.333	43	19	2	5-3	154	173	90	14	6	75-7	77	4.91	82	.293	.375	0-0	—	0	102	-14	-1.8
1984	Cal A	15	11	.577	34	34	9-2	0-0	246.2	227	103	17	5	84-3	196	3.47	115	.244	.308	0-0	—	0	94	14	1.3
1985	Cal A	15	9	.625	35	35	6-1	0-0	250	228	115	22	4	98-6	180	3.56	115	.243	.316	0-0	—	0	91	13	1.1
1986	†Cal A☆	18	10	.643	34	34	14-3	0-0	269	218	95	22	3	73-2	208	2.84	145	.221	.275	0-0	—	0	115	38	3.8
1987	Cal A☆	16	14	.533	36	36	10	0-0	247	252	128	34	4	84-4	192	4.01	108	.261	.321	0-0	—	0	93	7	0.7
1988	Cal A	13	16	.448	34	34	12-2	0-0	249.2	263	130	14	5	87-7	133	4.15	93	.272	.332	0-0	—	0	92	-9	-1.0
1989	Cal A	9	15	.375	33	33	5	0-0	220	252	119	26	2	48-1	123	4.54	84	.292	.326	0-0	—	0	99	-17	-1.5
1990	Cal A	0	3	.000	10	0	0	1-2	20.1	19	9	1	1	13-2	14	1.77	216	.250	.363	0-0	—	0		3	0.4
	NY A	5	6	.455	16	16	2-1	0-0	96.2	87	53	8	4	34-2	60	4.47	89	.240	.308	0-0	—	0	87	-5	-0.5
	Year	5	9	.357	26	16	2-1	1-2	117	106	57	9	5	47-4	74	4.00	99	.241	.318	0-0	—	0	88	-2	-0.1
1991	NY A	0	1	.000	2	2	0	0-0	5.1	8	7	1	0	1-0	0	10.13	41	.320	.346	0-0	—	0	88	-4	-0.5
1993	NY A	3	2	.600	9	9	0	0-0	41	39	26	7	3	22-0	30	5.27	79	.248	.352	0-0	—	0	123	-5	-0.5
Total	12	117	116	.502	341	299	72-11	6-5	2108.1	2066	1012	183	55	713-40	1373	3.83	105	.257	.320	0-0	—	0	99	33	2.4
WITT, BOBBY Robert Andrew B 5.11.1964 Arlington, MA BR/TR 6-2/205# d4.10																									
1986	Tex A	11	9	.550	31	31	0	0-0	157.2	130	104	18	3	143-2	174	5.48	79	.223	.374	0-0	—	0	106	-18	-2.0
1987	Tex A	8	10	.444	26	25	1	0-0	143	114	82	10	3	140-1	160	4.91	91	.219	.385	1-0	.000	-0*	89	-4	-0.4
1988	Tex A	8	10	.444	22	22	13-2	0-0	174.1	134	83	13	1	101-2	148	3.92	104	.216	.324	0-0	—	0	83	4	0.4
1989	Tex A	12	13	.480	31	31	5-1	0-0	194.1	182	123	14	2	114-3	166	5.14	77	.248	.347	0-0	—	0	106	-23	-2.6
1990	Tex A	17	10	.630	33	32	7-1	0-0	222	197	98	12	4	110-3	221	3.36	117	.238	.328	0-0	—	0*	99	12	1.3
1991	Tex A	3	7	.300	17	16	1-1	0-0	88.2	84	66	4	1	74-1	82	6.09	66	.254	.388	0-0	—	0	120	-20	-2.0
1992	Tex A	9	13	.409	25	25	0	0-0	161.1	152	87	14	2	95-1	100	4.46	85	.254	.354	0-0	—	0	93	-11	-1.3
	†Oak A	1	1	.500	6	6	0	0-0	31.2	31	12	2	0	19-1	25	3.41	110	.265	.362	0-0	—	0	93	2	0.1
	Year	10	14	.417	31	31	0	0-0	193	183	16	16	2	114-2	125	4.29	88	.256	.356	0-0	—	0	93	-8	-1.2
1993	Oak A	14	13	.519	35	33	5-1	0-0	220	226	112	16	3	91-5	131	4.21	97	.269	.340	0-0	—	0	87	-4	-0.4
1994	Oak A	8	10	.444	24	24	5-3	0-0	135.2	151	88	22	5	70-4	111	5.04	88	.283	.367	0-0	—	0*	103	-12	-1.4
1995	Fla N	2	7	.222	19	19	1	0-0	110.2	104	52	8	2	47-1	95	3.90	108	.251	.328	32-4	.063	-2*	76	4	0.1
	Tex A	3	4	.429	10	10	1	0-0	61.1	81	35	4	1	21-1	46	4.55	106	.324	.376	0-0	—	0	67	1	0.1
1996	†Tex A	16	12	.571	33	32	2	0-0	199.2	235	129	28	2	96-3	157	5.41	97	.295	.370	0-0	—	0	94	-4	-0.4
1997	Tex A	12	12	.500	34	32	3	0-0	209	245	118	33	2	74-4	121	4.82	99	.294	.350	6-0	.333	2*	95	2	0.3
1998	Tex A	5	4	.556	14	13	0	0-0	69.1	95	62	14	0	33-1	30	7.66	63	.328	.391	1-0	.000	-0*	144	-20	-2.1
	StL N	2	5	.286	17	5	0	0-0	47.1	55	32	7	2	20-1	28	4.94	85	.289	.362	10-1	.200	1	61	-5	-0.6
1999	TB A	7	15	.318	32	32	3-2	0-0	180.1	213	130	23	3	96-1	123	5.84	85	.304	.386	2-0	.000	-0	80	-16	-1.5
2000	Cle A	0	1	.000	7	2	0	0-0	15.1	28	13	4	0	6-1	6	7.63	65	.394	.442	0-0	—	0	113	-4	-0.2
2001	Ari N	4	1	.800	14	7	0	0-0	43.1	36	23	6	3	25-1	31	4.78	96	.222	.333	12-1	.250	0	109	0	0.0
Total	16	142	157	.475	430	397	47-11	0-0	2465	2493	1449	252	39	1375-37	1955	4.83	90	.265	.358	64-6	.141	0	96	-116	-12.6
WITTIG, JOHNNIE John Carl "Hans" B 6.16.1914 Baltimore, MD D 2.24.1999 Nassawadox, VA BR/TR 6/180# d8.4 Mil 1944-45																									
1938	NY N	2	3	.400	13	6	2	0	39.1	41	22	4	0	26	14	4.81	78	.263	.368	10-1	.000	-1	90	-3	-0.6

Year	Tm Lg	W	L	Pct	G	GS	CG-Sho	SV-BS	IP	H	R	HR	HB	BB-IB	SO	ERA	AERA	OAV	OOB	AB-SH	AVG	PB	Sup	APR	PW
1939	NY N	0	2	.000	5	2	1	0	16.2	18	15	0	1	14	4	7.56	52	.281	.418	5-0	.000	-1	56	-6	-0.7
1941	NY N	3	5	.375	25	9	0	0	85.1	111	57	5	1	45	47	5.59	66	.319	.398	25-1	.200	-0	61	-16	-1.4
1943	NY N	5	15	.250	40	22	4-1	4	164	172	85	14	0	76	56	4.23	82	.273	.352	51-2	.098	-3	81	-13	-2.1
1949	Bos A	0	0	—	1	0	0	0	2	2	2	0	0	2	0	9.00	48	.286	.444	0-0	—	0		-1	0.0
Total	5	10	25	.286	84	39	7-1	4	307.1	344	181	23	2	163	121	4.89	73	.286	.372	91-4	.110	-6	76	-39	-4.8
WOHLERS, MARK Mark Edward B 1.23.1970 Holyoke, MA BR/TR 6-4/207# d8.17																									
1991	†Atl N	3	1	.750	17	0	0	2-2	19.2	17	7	1	2	13-3	13	3.20	121	.239	.368	1-0	.000	-0		2	0.4
1992	†Atl N	1	2	.333	32	0	0	4-2	35.1	28	11	0	1	14-4	17	2.55	144	.235	.319	2-0	.000	-0		4	0.4
1993	†Atl N	6	2	.750	46	0	0	0-0	48	37	25	2	1	22-3	45	4.50	89	.218	.309	0-0	—	0		-2	-0.3
1994	Atl N	7	2	.778	51	0	0	1-1	51	51	35	1	0	33-9	58	4.59	93	.264	.362	1-1	1.000	0		-5	-0.7
1995	†Atl N	7	3	.700	65	0	0	25-4	64.2	51	16	2	1	24-3	90	2.09	204	.211	.285	3-0	.000	-0		16	3.1
1996	†Atl N★	2	4	.333	77	0	0	39-5	77.1	71	30	8	2	21-3	100	3.03	146	.240	.293	3-0	.000	-0		11	1.6
1997	†Atl N	5	7	.417	71	0	0	33-7	69.1	57	29	4	0	38-0	92	3.50	120	.224	.321	2-0	.000	-0		6	1.1
1998	Atl N	0	1	.000	27	0	0	8-0	20.1	18	23	2	1	33-0	22	10.18	41	.231	.464	0-0	—	0		-13	-1.4
1999	Atl N	0	0	—	2	0	0	0-0	0.2	1	2	0	0	6-0	0	27.00	17	.333	.778	0-0	—	0		-2	-0.1
2000	Cin N	1	2	.333	20	0	0	0-0	28	19	14	3	0	17-0	20	4.50	105	.192	.308	0-0	—	0		1	0.1
2001	Cin N	3	1	.750	30	0	0	0-1	32	36	20	5	1	7-2	21	3.94	116	.286	.326	0-0	—	0		0	0.0
	†NY A	1	0	1.000	31	0	0	0-0	35.2	33	20	3	1	18-0	33	4.54	99	.241	.329	0-0	—	0		0	0.0
2002	Cle A	3	4	.429	64	0	0	7-4	71.1	71	41	6	3	26-3	46	4.79	92	.261	.330	0-0	—	0		-3	-0.3
Total	12	39	29	.574	533	0	0	119-26	553.1	490	273	37	13	227-30	557	3.97	108	.238	.328	12-1	.083	-1		15	3.9
WOJCIECHOWSKI, STEVE Steven Joseph B 7.29.1970 Blue Island, IL BL/TL 6-2/185# d7.18																									
1995	Oak A	2	3	.400	14	7	0	0-0	48.2	51	28	7	1	28-1	13	5.18	86	.273	.367	0-0	—	0	107	-3	-0.3
1996	Oak A	5	5	.500	16	15	0	0-0	79.2	97	57	10	2	28-0	30	5.65	87	.300	.358	0-0	—	0*	118	-8	-0.8
1997	Oak A	0	2	.000	2	2	0	0-0	10.1	17	9	2	0	1-0	5	7.84	58	.386	.400	0-0	—	0	51	-4	-0.5
Total	3	7	10	.412	32	24	0	0-0	138.2	165	94	19	3	57-1	48	5.65	84	.298	.364	0-0	—	0	110	-15	-1.6
WOJEY, PETE Peter Paul B 12.1.1919 Stowe, PA D 4.23.1991 Mobile, AL BR/TR 5-11/185# d7.2																									
1954	Bro N	1	1	.500	14	1	0	1	27.2	24	13	3	2	14	21	3.25	126	.242	.348	3-1	.000	-0	131	2	0.1
1956	Det A	0	0	—	2	0	0	0	4	2	1	0	0	1-0	1	2.25	183	.167	.231	0-0	—	0		1	0.1
1957	Det A	0	0	—	2	0	0	0	1.1	1	0	0	0	0-0	0	0.00	—	.200	.200	0-0	—	0		1	0.0
Total	3	1	1	.500	18	1	0	1	33	27	14	3	2	15-0	22	3.00	136	.233	.331	3-1	.000	-0	131	4	0.2
WOJNA, ED Edward David B 8.20.1960 Bridgeport, CT BR/TR 6-1/185# d6.16																									
1985	SD N	2	4	.333	15	7	0	0-0	42	53	35	6	3	19-0	18	5.79	61	.312	.385	12-0	.167	-0	111	-13	-1.6
1986	SD N	2	2	.500	7	7	1	0-0	39	42	19	2	1	16-3	19	3.23	113	.268	.339	14-2	.143	-0	118	0	0.0
1987	SD N	0	3	.000	5	3	0	0-0	18.1	25	12	2	1	6-0	13	5.89	67	.333	.386	5-0	.000	-1	23	-3	-0.5
1989	Cle A	0	1	.000	9	3	0	0-0	33	31	17	0	0	14-1	10	4.09	97	.254	.328	0-0	—	0	99	-1	0.0
Total	4	4	10	.286	36	20	1	0-0	132.1	151	83	10	5	55-4	60	4.62	81	.288	.358	31-2	.129	-1	97	-17	-2.1
WOLCOTT, BOB Robert William B 9.8.1973 Huntington Beach, CA BR/TR 6/190# d8.18																									
1995	†Sea A	3	2	.600	7	6	0	0-0	36.2	43	18	6	2	14-0	19	4.42	107	.297	.360	0-0	—	0	108	2	0.2
1996	Sea A	7	10	.412	30	28	1	0-0	149.1	179	101	26	7	54-5	78	5.73	87	.297	.360	0-0	—	0	110	-12	-1.1
1997	Sea A	5	6	.455	19	18	0	0-0	100	129	71	22	5	29-2	58	6.03	75	.314	.365	1-0	.000	-0	126	-17	-1.5
1998	Ari N	1	3	.250	6	6	0	0-0	33	32	27	7	0	13-1	21	7.09	59	.252	.321	9-0	.222	0	73	-10	-1.0
1999	Bos A	0	0	—	4	0	0	0-0	6.2	8	6	1	1	3-0	2	8.10	61	.333	.414	0-0	—	0		-2	-0.1
Total	5	16	21	.432	66	58	1	0-0	325.2	391	223	62	15	113-8	178	5.86	81	.298	.359	10-0	.200	0	111	-39	-3.5
WOLF, ERNIE Ernest Adolph B 2.2.1889 Newark, NJ D 5.23.1964 Atlantic Highlands, NJ BR/TR 5-11/174# d9.10																									
1912	Cle A	0	0	—	1	0	0	0	5.2	8	6	0	0	4	1	6.35	54	.348	.444	2-0	.000	-0		-2	-0.1
WOLF, RANDY Randall Christopher B 8.22.1976 Canoga Park, CA BL/TL 6/190# d6.11																									
1999	Phi N	6	9	.400	22	21	0	0-0	121.2	126	78	20	5	67-0	116	5.55	85	.266	.362	30-7	.233	1	98	-10	-0.9
2000	Phi N	11	9	.550	32	32	1	0-0	206.1	210	107	25	8	83-2	160	4.36	107	.269	.342	57-10	.193	1	85	8	0.8
2001	Phi N	10	11	.476	28	25	4-2	0-0	163	150	74	15	10	51-4	152	3.70	115	.248	.314	45-5	.178	1	88	9	1.1
2002	Phi N	11	9	.550	31	31	3-2	0-0	210.2	172	77	23	7	63-5	172	3.20	122	.223	.285	59-12	.136	2*	85	19	1.9
2003	Phi N★	16	10	.615	33	33	2-2	0-0	200	176	101	27	6	78-4	177	4.23	95	.233	.309	70-6	.200	5	129	-6	-0.2
Total	5	54	48	.529	146	142	10-6	0-0	901.2	834	437	110	36	342-15	777	4.10	104	.246	.320	261-40	.184	10	97	20	2.7
WOLF, WALLY Walter Beck B 1.5.1942 Los Angeles, CA BR/TR 6-0.5/191# d9.27																									
1969	Cal A	0	0	—	2	0	0	0-0	2.1	3	3	1	0	3-0	2	11.57	30	.333	.500	0-0	—	0		-2	-0.1
1970	Cal A	0	0	—	4	0	0	0-0	5.1	3	3	1	0	4-0	5	5.06	71	.176	.333	0-0	—	0		-1	0.0
Total	2	0	0	—	6	0	0	0-0	7.2	6	6	2	0	7-0	7	7.04	51	.231	.394	0-0	—	0		-3	-0.1
WOLF, LEFTY Walter Francis B 6.10.1900 Hartford, CT D 9.25.1971 New Orleans, LA BR/TL 5-10/163# d7.4																									
1921	Phi A	0	0	—	8	0	0	0	15	15	15	0	2	16	11	7.20	62	.273	.452	4-0	.250	-0		-4	-0.2
WOLF, JIMMY William Van Winkle "Chicken" B 5.12.1862 Louisville, KY D 5.16.1903 Louisville, KY BR/TR 5-9/190# d5.2 M1 ▲																									
1882	Lou AA	0	0	—	1	0	0	0	6	11	11	0		3	1	9.00	28	.367	.424	318	.299	0*		-4	-0.2
1885	Lou AA	0	0	—	1	0	0	0	1	1	2	0	0	0	1	9.00	36	.200	.200	483	.292	0*		-1	0.0
1886	Lou AA	0	0	—	1	0	0	0	3	7	8	0	0	0	0	15.00	24	.350	.350	545	.272	0*		-3	-0.1
Total	3	0	0	—	3	0	0	0	10	19	21	0	0	3	2	10.80	27	.345	.379	1346	.285	1		-8	-0.3
WOLFE, CHUCK Charles Hunt B 2.15.1897 Wolfsburg, PA D 11.27.1957 Schellsburg, PA BL/TR 5-7/175# d8.2																									
1923	Phi A	0	0	—	3	0	0	0	9.2	6	4	1	0	8	1	3.72	110	.194	.359	3-0	.333	0		1	0.0
WOLFE, ED Edward Anthony B 1.2.1928 Los Angeles, CA BR/TR 6-3/185# d4.19																									
1952	Pit N	0	0	—	3	0	0	0	3.2	7	3	1	1	5	1	7.36	54	.467	.619	0-0	—	0		-1	0.0
WOLFE, BARNEY Wilbert Otto B 1.9.1876 Independence, PA D 2.27.1953 N.Charleroi, PA BR/TR 6-1/?# d4.24																									
1903	NY A	6	9	.400	20	16	12-1	0	148.1	143	66	1	6	26	48	2.97	105	.253	.293	53-1	.075	-4	89	3	-0.2
1904	NY A	0	3	.000	7	3	2	0	33.2	31	18	1	2	4	8	3.21	85	.246	.280	10-1	.000	-1	44	-2	-0.3
	Was A	6	10	.375	17	16	13-2	0	126.2	131	64	0	11	22	44	3.27	81	.268	.314	42-2	.119	-2	82	-9	-1.3
	Year	6	13	.316	24	19	15-2	0	160.1	162	67	1	13	26	52	3.26	82	.263	.307	52-3	.096	-3	76	-10	-1.6
1905	Was A	9	14	.391	28	23	17-1	1	182	162	76	1	8	37	52	2.57	103	.240	.287	63-0	.127	-1	66	1	-0.2
1906	Was A	0	3	.000	4	3	2	0	20	17	11	0	2	10	8	4.05	65	.233	.341	7-0	.286	0	55	-3	-0.3
Total	4	21	39	.350	76	61	46-4	1	510.2	484	235	3	29	99	160	2.96	94	.251	.298	175-4	.109	-8	75	-10	-2.3
WOLFE, BILL William B Jersey City, NJ d9.10																									
1902	Phi N	0	1	.000	1	1	1	0	9	11	5	0	1	4	3	4.00	70	.297	.381	3-0	.333	0	24	-1	-0.1
WOLFF, ROGER Roger Francis B 4.10.1911 Evansville, IL D 3.23.1994 Chester, IL BR/TR 6-0.5/208# d9.20																									
1941	Phi A	0	2	.000	2	2	2	0	17	15	6	0	0	4	2	3.18	132	.231	.275	5-0	.200	-0	10	2	0.2
1942	Phi A	12	15	.444	32	25	15-2	3	214.1	206	99	16	3	69	94	3.32	114	.249	.309	68-4	.088	-3	72	8	0.7
1943	Phi A	10	15	.400	41	26	13-2	6	221	232	97	11	4	72	91	3.54	96	.274	.334	74-3	.122	-4	78	-2	-0.8
1944	Was A	4	15	.211	33	21	5	2	155	186	107	9	6	60	73	4.99	65	.295	.362	55-1	.218	1	101	-32	-3.4
1945	Was A	20	10	.667	33	29	21-4	2	250	200	68	7	1	53	108	2.12	146	.215	**.258**	84-5	.107	-5	101	31	3.3
1946	Was A	5	8	.385	21	17	6	0	122	115	51	8	5	30	50	2.58	130	.249	.302	39-2	.103	-1	113	7	0.6
1947	Cle A	0	0	—	7	2	0	0	16	15	7	1	2	10	5	3.94	88	.259	.386	3-2	.000	-0	102	-1	0.0
	Pit N	1	4	.200	13	6	1	0	30	49	33	4	1	18	7	8.70	49	.368	.447	9-0	.000	-1	129	-14	-2.0
Total	7	52	69	.430	182	128	63-8	13	1025.1	1018	468	56	22	316	430	3.41	100	.258	.316	337-17	.122	-13	92	-1	-1.4
WOLFGANG, MELLIE Meldon John "Red" B 3.20.1890 Albany, NY D 6.30.1947 Albany, NY BR/TR 5-9/160# d4.18																									
1914	Chi A	9	5	.643	24	11	9-2	0	119.1	96	42	0	0	32	50	1.89	142	.219	.272	40-2	.175	-0	79	9	1.3
1915	Chi A	2	2	.500	17	2	0	0	53.2	39	18	0	1	12	21	1.84	161	.211	.263	17-1	.118	-1	98	5	0.2
1916	Chi A	4	6	.400	27	14	6-1	0	127	103	39	2	2	42	36	1.98	139	.228	.296	40-2	.225	0*	90	11	0.9

Year	Tm Lg	W	L	Pct	G	GS	CG-Sho	SV-BS	IP	H	R	HR	HB	BB-IB	SO	ERA	AERA	OAV	OOB	AB-SH	AVG	PB	Sup	APR	PW
1917	Chi A	0	0	—	5	0	0	0	17.2	18	10	1	1	6	3	5.09	52	.305	.379	4-0	.000	-1		-3	-0.3
1918	Chi A	0	1	.000	4	0	0	0	8.1	12	6	0	0	3	1	5.40	51	.333	.385	2-0	.500	0*		-2	-0.2
Total	5	15	14	.517	77	27	15-3	0	326	268	115	3	4	95	111	2.18	127	.229	.289	103-5	.184	-1	85	20	1.9
WOLTER, HARRY Harry Meigs B 7.11.1884 Monterey, CA D 7.6.1970 Palo Alto, CA BL/TL 5-10/175# d5.14 ▲																									
1907	Pit N	0	0	—	1	0	0	0	2	3	2	0	0	2	0	4.50	54	.333	.455	1-0	.000	-0		-1	-0.1
	StL N	0	2	.000	3	3	1	0	23	27	13	1	2	18	8	4.30	58	.318	.448	47-0	.340	1*	104	-3	-0.2
	Year	0	2	.000	4	3	1	0	25	30	17	1	2	20	8	4.32	58	.319	.448	48-0	.333	1	105	0	-0.3
1909	Bos A	4	4	.500	11	6	0	0	59	66	33	0	4	30	21	3.51	71	.303	.397	121-5	.240	2*	94	-7	-0.8
Total	2	4	6	.400	15	9	1	0	84	96	48	1	6	50	29	3.75	67	.308	.413	169-5	.266	3	97	-11	-1.1
WOLTERS, RYNIE Reinder Albertus B 3.17.1842 Schantz, Netherlands D 1.3.1917 Newark, NJ TR 6/165# d5.18																									
1871	Mut NA	16	16	.500	**32**	**32**	**31-1**	0	**283**	345	283	7		39	22	3.43	110	**.263**	.285	138	.370	20	97	12	2.0
1872	Cle NA	3	6	.333	12	8	5	0	75.1	115	106	3		7	4	6.09	58	.304	.317	69	.232	-0*	89	-23	-1.7
1873	Res NA	0	1	.000	1	1	1	0	9	13	23	0		1	1	0.00	—	.220	.233	4	.000	-1	53	1	0.0
Total	3 NA	19	23	.452	45	41	37-1	0	367.1	473	412	10		47	27	3.90	96	.271	.290	211	.318	19	94	-10	0.3
WOMACK, DOOLEY Horace Guy B 8.25.1939 Columbia, SC BL/TR 6/170# d4.14																									
1966	NY A	7	3	.700	42	1	0	4	75	52	25	6	3	23-3	50	2.64	126	.198	.270	5-0	.200	0	53	6	1.0
1967	NY A	5	6	.455	65	0	0	18	97	80	33	6	3	35-14	57	2.41	130	.230	.300	14-0	.286	1		7	1.4
1968	NY A	3	7	.300	45	0	0	2	61.2	53	23	6	1	29-9	27	3.21	90	.244	.335	5-0	.200	0		-1	0.0
1969	Hou N	2	1	.667	30	0	0	0-1	51.1	49	21	1	3	20-5	32	3.51	101	.259	.338	6-1	.167	-0		1	0.2
	Sea A	2	1	.667	9	0	0	0-0	14.1	15	4	0	0	3-2	8	2.51	145	.273	.310	1-0	.000	-0		2	0.4
1970	Oak A	0	0	—	2	0	0	0-0	3	4	5	2	0	1-0	3	15.00	24	.308	.357	0-0	—	0		-4	-0.2
Total	5	19	18	.514	193	1	0	24-1	302.1	253	111	21	10	111-33	177	2.95	110	.233	.308	31-1	.226	1	53	11	2.8
WOOD, SPADES Charles Asher B 1.13.1909 Spartanburg, SC D 5.18.1986 Wichita, KS BL/TL 5-10.5/150# d8.16																									
1930	Pit N	4	3	.571	9	7	4-2	0	58	61	34	4	0	32	23	5.12	97	.270	.360	20-2	.250	1	105	1	0.1
1931	Pit N	2	6	.250	15	10	2	0	64	69	45	2	1	46	33	6.05	64	.273	.387	22-1	.227	1	96	-13	-1.3
Total	2	6	9	.400	24	17	6-2	0	122	130	79	6	1	78	56	5.61	78	.271	.375	42-3	.238	1	99	-12	-1.2
WOOD, GEORGE George A. "Dandy" B 11.9.1858 Boston, MA D 4.4.1924 Harrisburg, PA BL/TR 5-10.5/175# d5.1.1880 M1 U1 ▲																									
1883	Det N	0	0	—	1	0	0	0	5	8	9	0		3	0	7.20	43	.348	.423	441	.302	0*		-3	-0.1
1885	Det N	0	0	—	1	0	0	0	4	5	2	0		1	1	0.00	—	.333	.375	362	.290	0*		1	0.0
1888	Phi N	0	0	—	2	0	0	**2**	2	3	3	0	0	1	0	4.50	66	.300	.364	433	.229	0*		-1	-0.1
1889	Phi N	0	0	—	1	0	0	0	1	2	2	0	0	0	2	18.00	24	.400	.400	422	.251	0*		-1	0.0
Total	4	0	0	—	5	0	0	2	12	18	16	0	0	5	3	5.25	59	.340	.397	1658	.267	1		-4	-0.2
WOOD, JOE Joe "Smokey Joe" (b: Howard Ellsworth Wood) B 10.25.1889 Kansas City, MO D 7.27.1985 West Haven, CT BR/TR 5-11/180# d8.24 s-Joe ▲																									
1908	Bos A	1	1	.500	6	2	1-1	0	22.2	14	12	0	1	16	11	2.38	103	.161	.298	7-0	.000	-1	125	-1	-0.2
1909	Bos A	11	7	.611	24	19	13-4	0	160.2	121	51	1	6	43	88	2.18	114	.209	.270	55-1	.164	-0	93	7	0.5
1910	Bos A	12	13	.480	35	17	14-3	0	196.2	155	81	3	10	56	145	1.69	151	.220	.287	69-3	.261	5	93	9	1.9
1911	Bos A	23	17	.575	44	33	25-5	3	275.2	226	113	2	11	76	231	2.02	162	.223	.284	88-6	.261	9	105	34	**5.7**
1912	†Bos A	**34**	5	**.872**	43	38	**35-10**	1	344	267	104	2	12	82	258	1.91	178	.216	.272	124-6	.290	11	122	53	7.6
1913	Bos A	11	5	.688	23	18	12-1	2	145.2	120	54	0	8	61	123	2.29	129	.232	.323	56-1	.268	4*	148	9	1.8
1914	Bos A	10	3	.769	18	14	11-1	1	113.1	94	38	1	0	34	67	2.62	103	.229	.288	43-1	.140	-0*	110	3	0.4
1915	Bos A	15	5	**.750**	25	16	10-3	2	157.1	120	32	1	1	44	63	**1.49**	187	.216	.275	54-5	.259	4*	116	25	3.9
1917	Cle A	0	1	.000	5	1	0	1	15.2	17	7	0	0	7	2	3.45	82	.309	.387	6-0	.000	-1*	76	-1	-0.1
1919	Cle A	0	0	—	1	0	0	1	0.2	0	0	0	0	0	0	0.00	—	.000	.000	192-9	.255	0*		0	0.1
1920	†Cle A	0	0	—	1	0	0	1	2	4	5	0	0	2	1	22.50	17	.444	.545	137-12	.270	0*		-4	-0.2
Total	11	117	57	.672	225	158	121-28	10	1434.1	1138	497	10	49	421	989	2.03	146	.220	.285	831-44	.249	31	114	134	21.4
WOOD, JOHN John B. B 1871 Philadelphia, PA D 1.30.1929 Philadelphia, PA 5-7/142# d5.9																									
1896	StL N	0	0	—	1	0	0	0	0	1	1	0	1	2	0	o	—	1.000	1.000	0-0	—	0		-1	-0.1
WOOD, JOE Joseph Frank B 5.20.1916 Shohola, PA D 10.10.2002 Old Saybrook, CT BR/TR 6/190# d5.1 f-Joe																									
1944	Bos A	0	1	.000	3	1	0	0	9.2	13	9	0	0	3	5	6.52	52	.317	.364	2-0	.000	-0	25	-4	-0.4
WOOD, KERRY Kerry Lee B 6.16.1977 Irving, TX BR/TR 6-5/225# d4.12																									
1998	†Chi N	13	6	.684	26	26	1-1	0-0	166.2	117	69	14	11	85-1	233	3.40	129	**.196**	.306	54-8	.130	-0	111	17	1.7
2000	Chi N	8	7	.533	23	23	1	0-0	137	112	77	17	9	87-0	132	4.80	95	.226	.349	40-4	.250	3*	97	-4	-0.1
2001	Chi N	12	6	.667	28	28	1-1	0-0	174.1	127	70	16	10	92-3	217	3.36	123	**.202**	.311	48-13	.188	1*	93	16	1.7
2002	Chi N	12	11	.522	33	33	4-1	0-0	213.2	169	92	22	16	97-5	217	3.66	110	.221	.320	72-6	.167	1	114	10	1.1
2003	†Chi N★	14	11	.560	32	32	4-2	0-0	211	152	77	24	21	100-2	**266**	3.20	132	.203	.312	61-8	.164	2	101	27	3.1
Total	5	59	41	.590	142	142	11-5	0-0	902.2	677	385	93	67	461-11	1065	3.62	117	.209	.318	275-39	.175	6	104	66	7.5
WOOD, MIKE Michael Burton B 4.26.1980 West Palm Beach, FL BR/TR 6-3/190# d8.21																									
2003	Oak A	2	1	.667	7	1	0	0-0	13.2	24	17	1	2	7-2	15	10.54	43	.387	.465	0-0	—	0	61	-9	-1.5
WOOD, PETE Peter Burke B 2.1.1857 Hamilton, ON, CAN D 3.15.1923 Chicago, IL TR 5-7/185# d7.15 b-Fred																									
1885	Buf N	8	15	.348	24	22	21	0	198.2	235	170	8		66	38	4.44	67	.280	.332	104	.221	-1*	102	-32	-3.1
1889	Phi N	1	1	.500	3	2	2	0	19	28	15	0	0	3	8	5.21	83	.333	.356	8	.000	-1	147	-1	-0.2
Total	2	9	16	.360	27	24	23	0	217.2	263	185	8	0	69	46	4.51	69	.285	.334	112	.205	-2	106	-33	-3.3
WOOD, WILBUR Wilbur Forrester B 10.22.1941 Cambridge, MA BR/TL 6/180# d6.30																									
1961	Bos A	0	0	—	6	1	0	0	13	14	8	2	0	7-0	7	5.54	75	.269	.350	3-0	.000	-0	170	-1	-0.1
1962	Bos A	0	0	—	1	1	0	0	7.2	6	3	0	0	3-0	3	3.52	117	.214	.290	3-0	.000	-0	65	1	0.0
1963	Bos A	0	5	.000	25	6	0	0	64.2	67	35	10	3	13-1	28	3.76	101	.270	.311	12-1	.000	-1	78	-2	-0.3
1964	Bos A	0	0	—	4	0	0	0	5.2	13	11	1	0	3-2	5	17.47	22	.433	.485	1-0	.000	-0		-8	-0.4
	Pit N	0	2	.000	3	2	1	0	17.1	16	8	0	2	11-3	7	3.63	97	.246	.367	5-1	.000	-0	50	0	-0.1
1965	Pit N	1	1	.500	34	1	0	0	51.1	44	21	3	1	16-3	29	3.16	111	.237	.298	6-0	.000	-1	50	2	0.0
1967	Chi A	4	2	.667	51	8	0	4	95.1	95	34	2	1	28-4	47	2.45	126	.260	.312	16-0	.063	-0	91	6	0.4
1968	Chi A	13	12	.520	**88**	2	0	16	159	127	39	8	3	33-12	74	1.87	162	.222	.266	22-2	.091	-1	173	**20**	3.8
1969	Chi A	10	11	.476	**76**	0	0	15-7	119.2	113	48	13	3	40-15	73	3.01	128	.248	.311	15-2	.000	-1		9	1.6
1970	Chi A	9	13	.409	**77**	0	0	21-6	121.2	118	50	7	2	36-7	85	2.81	139	.258	.312	18-2	.111	-1		11	2.4
1971	Chi A☆	22	13	.629	44	42	22-7	1-0	334	272	95	21	7	62-2	210	1.91	**188**	.222	.263	96-17	.052	-5	91	**56**	**5.8**
1972	Chi A★	**24**	17	.585	49	**49**	20-8	0-0	**376.2**	325	119	28	7	74-5	193	2.51	125	.235	.276	125-13	.136	-2	103	25	2.8
1973	Chi A	**24**	20	.545	49	**48**	21-4	0-0	**359.1**	381	166	25	7	91-3	199	3.46	115	.270	.315	0-0	—	0	99	15	1.8
1974	Chi A☆	20	19	.513	42	**42**	22-1	0-0	320.1	305	143	27	9	80-8	169	3.60	104	.254	.303	0-0	—	0	105	5	0.8
1975	Chi A	16	20	.444	43	**43**	14-2	0-0	291.1	309	148	26	5	92-5	140	4.11	95	.272	.328	0-0	—	0	98	-7	-0.8
1976	Chi A	4	3	.571	7	7	5-1	0-0	56.1	51	24	3	0	11-0	31	2.24	160	.242	.278	0-0	—	0	91	4	0.6
1977	Chi A	7	8	.467	24	18	5-1	0-0	122.2	139	75	10	10	50-0	42	4.99	82	.293	.371	0-0	—	0	82	-11	-1.1
1978	Chi A	10	10	.500	28	27	4	0-0	168	187	103	23	3	74-1	69	5.20	73	.285	.357	0-0	—	0	106	-24	-2.4
Total	17	164	156	.512	651	297	114-24	57-13	2684	2582	1130	209	63	724-71	1411	3.24	113	.254	.306	322-38	.084	-14	99	101	14.8
WOODALL, BRAD David Bradley B 6.25.1969 Atlanta, GA BB/TL 6/175# d7.22																									
1994	Atl N	0	1	.000	1	1	0	0-0	6	5	3	2	0	2-0	2	4.50	94	.227	.292	2-0	.500	0	43	0	0.1
1995	Atl N	1	1	.500	9	0	0	0-0	10.1	13	10	1	0	8-1	5	6.10	70	.310	.412	1-0	1.000	0		-3	-0.5
1996	Atl N	2	2	.500	8	3	0	0-0	19.2	28	19	4	0	4-0	20	7.32	60	.333	.356	5-0	.200	0	130	-7	-1.1
1998	Mil N	7	9	.438	31	20	0	0-0	138	145	81	25	6	47-4	85	4.96	86	.273	.337	38-5	.237	3*	116	-10	-0.6
1999	Chi N	0	1	.000	6	3	0	0-0	16	17	12	5	1	6-0	7	5.63	80	.270	.338	2-0	.500	1	115	-2	0.0
Total	5	10	14	.417	55	27	0	0-0	190	208	125	37	7	67-5	119	5.31	81	.280	.343	48-5	.271	5	115	-22	-2.1
WOODARD, STEVE Steven Larry B 5.15.1975 Hartselle, AL BL/TR 6-4/225# d7.28																									
1997	Mil A	3	3	.500	7	7	0	0-0	36.2	39	25	5	2	6-0	32	5.15	90	.269	.307	0-0	—	0	60	-3	-0.4

Year	Tm Lg	W	L	Pct	G	GS	CG-Sho	SV-BS	IP	H	R	HR	HB	BB-IB	SO	ERA	AERA	OAV	OOB	AB-SH	AVG	PB	Sup	APR	PW
1998	Mil N	10	12	.455	34	26	0	0-0	165.2	170	83	19	9	33-4	135	4.18	102	.264	.307	50-2	.140	-1	65	2	0.0
1999	Mil N	11	8	.579	31	29	2	0-0	185	219	101	23	6	36-7	119	4.52	100	.294	.330	53-10	.132	0	104	0	0.0
2000	Mil N	1	7	.125	27	11	1	0-0	93.2	125	70	16	4	33-4	65	5.96	77	.325	.381	22-2	.045	-1	92	-16	-1.2
	Cle A	3	3	.500	13	11	0	0-0	54	57	35	10	2	11-1	35	5.67	88	.269	.310	0-0	—	0	127	-4	-0.3
2001	Cle A	3	3	.500	29	10	0	0-0	97	129	60	10	5	17-1	52	5.20	87	.325	.358	1-0	.000	-0	100	-6	-0.3
2002	Tex A	0	0	—	14	0	0	0-1	17.2	20	13	4	2	8-1	14	6.62	71	.274	.361	0-0	—	0		-3	-0.1
2003	Bos A	1	0	1.000	7	0	0	0-0	17.2	23	10	3	1	5-2	12	5.09	90	.311	.358	0-0	—	0		-1	0.0
Total	7	32	36	.471	162	94	3	0-1	667.1	782	397	90	31	149-20	464	4.94	92	.292	.335	126-14	.119	-2	91	-31	-2.3
WOODBURN, GENE Eugene Stewart B 8.20.1886 Bellaire, OH D 1.18.1961 Sandusky, OH BR/TR 6/175# d7.27																									
1911	StL N	1	5	.167	11	6	1	0	38.1	22	32	0	6	40	23	5.40	63	.167	.382	6-1	.167	1	82	-10	-1.1
1912	StL N	1	4	.200	20	5	1	0	48.1	60	48	0	4	42	25	5.59	61	.306	.438	13-0	.000	-2	68	-13	-1.4
Total	2	2	9	.182	31	11	2	0	86.2	82	80	0	10	82	48	5.50	62	.250	.414	19-1	.053	-0	75	-23	-2.5
WOODCOCK, FRED Fred Wayland B 5.17.1868 Winchendon, MA D 8.11.1943 Ashburnham, MA BL/TL 6-2/190# d5.17																									
1892	Pit N	1	2	.333	5	4	3	0	33	42	28	1	2	17	8	3.55	93	.298	.381	15	.200	0	110	-3	-0.2
WOODEND, GEORGE George Anthony B 12.9.1917 Hartford, CT D 2.6.1980 Hartford, CT BR/TR 6/200# d4.22																									
1944	Bos N	0	0	—	3	0	0	0	2	5	4	0	0	5	0	13.50	28	.556	.714	0-0	—	0		-2	-0.1
WOODESHICK, HAL Harold Joseph B 8.24.1932 Wilkes-Barre, PA BR/TL 6-3/200# d9.14																									
1956	Det A	0	2	.000	2	2	0	0	5.1	12	8	1	0	3-0	1	13.50	30	.444	.500	0-0	—	0	130	-5	-0.8
1958	Cle A	6	6	.500	14	9	3	0	71.2	71	32	4	6	25-0	27	3.64	100	.265	.341	24-0	.167	-1	99	0	0.1
1959	Was A	2	4	.333	31	3	0	0	61	58	39	2	1	36-8	30	3.69	106	.253	.352	8-0	.000	-1*	38	-3	-0.3
1960	Was A	4	5	.444	41	14	1	4	115	131	67	7	3	60-3	46	4.70	83	.289	.375	29-6	.069	-2	126	-9	-0.8
1961	Was A	3	2	.600	7	6	1	0	40.1	38	19	3	3	24-0	24	4.02	100	.257	.369	16-0	.125	-1	99	1	0.1
	Det A	1	1	.500	12	2	0	0	18.1	25	17	3	0	17-1	13	7.85	52	.316	.438	4-0	.000	-1	65	-7	-0.6
	Year	4	3	.571	19	8	1	0	58.2	63	20	6	3	41-1	37	5.22	77	.278	.393	20-0	.100	-1	90	-7	-0.5
1962	Hou N	5	16	.238	31	26	2-1	0	139.1	161	84	3	3	54-1	82	4.39	85	.290	.352	37-3	.081	-1	72	-13	-1.8
1963	Hou N★	11	9	.550	55	0	0	10	114	75	29	3	6	42-6	94	1.97	160	.186	.269	23-0	.130	-0		16	3.2
1964	Hou N	2	9	.182	61	0	0	**23**	78.1	73	32	3	7	32-11	58	2.76	124	.249	.336	10-1	.000	-0		4	0.9
1965	Hou N	3	4	.429	27	0	0	3	32.1	27	13	3	0	18-5	22	3.06	110	.227	.328	6-1	.167	-0		1	0.2
	StL N	3	2	.600	51	0	0	15	59.2	47	14	1	2	27-11	37	1.81	212	.221	.314	8-0	.000	-1		12	1.8
	Year	6	6	.500	78	0	0	18	92	74	30	4	2	45-16	59	2.25	163	.223	.319	14-1	.071	-1		13	2.0
1966	StL N	2	1	.667	59	0	0	4	70.1	57	17	5	1	23-6	30	1.92	187	.224	.289	5-0	.200	0		13	0.9
1967	†StL N	2	1	.667	36	0	0	2	41.2	41	29	2	3	28-9	20	5.18	63	.252	.367	4-0	.000	-0		-10	-0.8
Total	11	44	62	.415	427	62	7-1	61	847.1	816	400	40	35	389-61	484	3.56	102	.254	.339	174-11	.092	-7	95	0	2.1
WOODMAN, DAN Daniel Courtenay "Cocoa" B 7.8.1893 Danvers, MA D 12.14.1962 Danvers, MA BR/TR 5-8/160# d7.10																									
1914	Buf F	0	0	—	13	0	0	1	33.2	30	16	0	1	11	13	2.41	123	.246	.313	7-0	.143	-1		0	-0.1
1915	Buf F	0	0	—	5	1	0	0	15.1	14	9	0	0	9	1	4.11	68	.246	.348	4-0	.250	-0*	125	-2	-0.1
Total	2	0	0	—	18	1	0	1	49	44	25	0	1	20	14	2.94	99	.246	.325	11-0	.182	-1	125	-2	-0.2
WOODS, CLARENCE Clarence Cofield B 6.11.1892 Woods Ridge, IN D 7.2.1969 Rising Sun, IN BR/TR 6-5/230# d8.8																									
1914	Ind F	0	0	—	2	0	0	1	2	1	1	0	0	2	1	4.50	69	.167	.375	0-0	—	0		0	0.0
WOODS, PINKY George Rowland B 5.22.1915 Waterbury, CT D 10.29.1982 Los Angeles, CA BR/TR 6-5/225# d6.20																									
1943	Bos A	5	6	.455	23	12	2	1	100.2	109	61	6	1	55	32	4.92	67	.284	.375	36-0	.222	-0	102	-18	-1.9
1944	Bos A	4	8	.333	38	20	5-1	0	170.2	171	73	4	6	88	56	3.27	104	.266	.360	48-4	.146	-1	88	2	0.0
1945	Bos A	4	7	.364	24	12	3	2	107.1	108	56	3	1	63	36	4.19	81	.268	.368	42-1	.214	1	100	-9	-0.7
Total	3	13	21	.382	85	44	10-1	3	378.2	388	190	13	8	206	124	3.97	85	.272	.366	126-5	.190	-1	95	-25	-2.6
WOODS, JOHN John Fulton "Abe" B 1.18.1898 Princeton, WV D 10.4.1946 Norfolk, VA BR/TR 6/175# d9.16																									
1924	Bos A	0	0	—	1	0	0	0	1	0	0	0	0	3	0	0.00	—	.000	.500	0-0	—	0		0	0.0
WOODS, WALT Walter Sydney B 4.28.1875 Rye, NH D 10.30.1951 Portsmouth, NH BR/TR 5-9.5/165# d4.20																									
1898	Chi N	9	13	.409	27	22	18-3	0	215	224	128	7	10	59	26	3.14	114	.266	.322	154-3	.175	-4*	98	8	0.3
1899	Lou N	9	13	.409	26	21	17	0	186.1	216	100	9	7	37	21	3.28	117	.290	.329	126-6	.151	-3*	119	12	1.1
1900	Pit N	0	0	—	1	0	0	0	3	9	7	0	0	1	1	21.00	17	.500	.526	1-0	.000	-0		-5	-0.2
Total	3	18	26	.409	54	43	35-3	0	404.1	449	235	16	17	97	48	3.34	111	.280	.328	281-9	.164	-7	109	15	1.2
WOODSON, DICK Richard Lee B 3.30.1945 Oelwein, IA BR/TR 6-5/207# d4.8																									
1969	†Min A	7	5	.583	44	10	2	1-1	110.1	99	49	11	3	49-3	66	3.67	100	.237	.322	27-0	.074	-1	145	1	0.0
1970	†Min A	1	2	.333	21	0	0	1-1	30.2	29	18	2	0	19-0	22	3.82	98	.244	.345	2-0	.000	-0		-2	-0.2
1972	Min A	14	14	.500	36	36	9-3	0-0	251.2	193	93	19	2	101-5	150	2.72	118	.211	.290	88-8	.080	-5	86	13	0.9
1973	Min A	10	8	.556	23	23	4-2	0-0	141.1	137	68	12	2	68-0	53	3.95	100	.254	.338	0-0	—	0	105	1	0.1
1974	Min A	1	1	.500	5	4	0	0-0	27	30	16	5	1	4-0	12	4.33	86	.273	.304	0-0	—	0	89	-2	-0.1
	NY A	1	2	.333	8	3	0	0-0	28	34	19	6	1	12-2	12	5.79	61	.301	.370	0-0	—	0	75	-6	-0.6
	Year	2	3	.400	13	7	0	0-0	55	64	22	11	2	16-2	24	5.07	72	.287	.339	0-0	—	0	83	-9	-0.7
Total	5	34	32	.515	137	76	15-5	2-2	589	522	263	55	9	253-10	315	3.47	102	.236	.316	117-8	.077	-7	100	5	0.1
WOODSON, KERRY Walter Browne B 5.18.1969 Jacksonville, FL BR/TR 6-2/190# d7.19																									
1992	Sea A	0	1	.000	8	1	0	0-0	13.2	12	7	0	2	11-0	6	3.29	121	.245	.403	0-0	—	0	69	0	0.0
WOODWARD, FRANK Frank Russell B 5.17.1894 New Haven, CT D 6.11.1961 New Haven, CT BR/TR 5-10/175# d4.17 Mil 1918																									
1918	Phi N	0	0	—	2	0	0	0	6	6	4	0	0	4	4	6.00	50	.250	.357	3-0	.333	0		-1	-0.1
1919	Phi N	6	9	.400	17	12	6	0	100.2	109	63	5	5	35	27	4.74	68	.291	.359	29-4	.207	1	111	-15	-2.1
	StL N	3	5	.375	17	7	2	1	72	65	27	1	1	28	18	2.63	106	.248	.323	21-1	.048	-2	65	1	-0.1
	Year	9	14	.391	34	19	8	1	172.2	174	29	6	6	63	45	3.86	79	.273	.344	50-5	.140	-1	96	-14	-2.2
1921	Was A	0	0	—	3	1	0	0	10.2	11	7	0	0	3	4	5.91	70	.282	.333	3-0	.333	0	142	-2	-0.1
1922	Was A	0	0	—	1	0	0	0	2.1	3	3	0	0	3	2	11.57	33	.375	.545	1-0	.000	-0		-2	-0.1
1923	Chi A	0	1	.000	2	1	0	0	2	5	3	0	0	1	0	13.50	29	.500	.545	0-0	—	0	63	-2	-0.3
Total	5	9	15	.375	42	21	8	1	193.2	199	107	6	6	74	55	4.23	74	.277	.350	57-5	.158	-1	97	-21	-2.8
WOODWARD, ROB Robert John B 9.28.1962 Hanover, NH BR/TR 6-3/185# d9.5																									
1985	Bos A	1	0	1.000	5	2	0	0-0	26.2	17	8	0	2	9-0	16	1.69	254	.168	.250	0-0	—	0	159	6	0.3
1986	Bos A	2	3	.400	9	6	0	0-0	35.2	46	26	4	1	11-0	14	5.30	79	.313	.360	0-0	—	0	80	-6	-0.7
1987	Bos A	1	1	.500	9	6	0	0-0	37	53	33	6	1	15-0	15	7.05	65	.338	.394	0-0	—	0	127	-11	-0.5
1988	Bos A	0	0	—	1	0	0	0-0	0.2	2	1	0	0	1-0	0	13.50	31	.500	.600	0-0	—	0		-1	0.0
Total	4	4	4	.500	24	14	0	0-0	100	118	68	10	4	36-0	45	5.04	86	.289	.349	0-0	—	0	112	-12	-0.9
WOOLDRIDGE, FLOYD Floyd Lewis B 8.25.1928 Jerico Springs, MO BR/TR 6-1/185# d5.1																									
1955	StL N	2	4	.333	18	8	2	0	57.2	64	36	9	1	27-4	14	4.84	84	.281	.355	18-1	.222	0	110	-6	-0.6
WORDEN, FRED Frederick Bamford B 9.4.1894 St.Louis, MO D 11.9.1941 St.Louis, MO BR/TR d9.28																									
1914	Phi A	0	0	—	1	0	0	0	2	8	5	0	0	0	1	18.00	15	.615	.615	1-0	.000	-0		-4	-0.2
WORKMAN, HOGE Harry Hall B 9.25.1899 Huntington, WV D 5.20.1972 Ft.Myers, FL BR/TR 5-11/170# d6.27																									
1924	Bos A	0	0	—	11	0	0	0	18	25	19	2	2	11	7	8.50	51	.325	.422	2-0	.000	-0		-7	-0.4
WORKS, RALPH Ralph Talmadge "Judge" B 3.16.1888 Payson, IL D 8.8.1941 Pasadena, CA BL/TR 6-2.5/185# d5.1																									
1909	†Det A	4	1	.800	16	4	4	2	64	62	19	0	1	17	31	1.97	128	.261	.313	17-0	.059	-2	140	4	0.1
1910	Det A	3	6	.333	18	10	5	1	85.2	73	47	1	4	39	36	3.57	74	.235	.328	30-1	.267	1	115	-9	-0.9
1911	Det A	11	5	.688	30	15	9-3	0	167.1	173	93	3	6	67	68	3.87	89	.268	.342	61-0	.148	-3	94	-6	-1.0
1912	Det A	5	10	.333	27	16	9-1	1	157	185	101	1	7	66	64	4.24	77	.308	.383	56-3	.143	-3	120	-17	-1.8
	Cin N	1	1	.500	3	1	1	0	9.2	4	5	0	1	5	5	2.79	120	.133	.278	5-0	.200	-0	262	0	0.0
1913	Cin N	0	1	.000	5	2	0	0	15	15	14	0	3	8	4	7.80	42	.242	.356	6-0	.167	-0	116	-6	-0.4

Year	Tm Lg	W	L	Pct	G	GS	CG-Sho	SV-BS	IP	H	R	HR	HB	BB-IB	SO	ERA	AERA	OAV	OOB	AB-SH	AVG	PB	Sup	APR	PW
Total	5	24	24	.500	99	48	28-4	4	498.2	512	279	5	22	202	208	3.79	83	.271	.348	175-4	.160	-8	115	-34	-4.0
WORRELL, TIM Timothy Howard B 7.5.1967 Pasadena, CA BR/TR 6-4/220# d6.25 b-Todd																									
1993	SD N	2	7	.222	21	16	0	0-0	100.2	104	63	11	0	43-5	52	4.92	84	.269	.338	31-2	.032	-3	109	-9	-1.0
1994	SD N	0	1	.000	3	3	0	0-0	14.2	9	7	0	0	5-0	14	3.68	112	.170	.237	2-1	.500	1	118	1	0.1
1995	SD N	1	0	1.000	9	0	0	0-0	13.1	16	7	2	1	6-0	13	4.73	85	.291	.371	1-0	.000	-0		-1	-0.1
1996	†SD N	9	7	.563	50	11	0	1-1	121	109	45	9	6	39-1	99	3.05	130	.236	.304	20-6	.150	-0	74	13	1.5
1997	SD N	4	8	.333	60	10	0	3-4	106.1	116	67	14	7	50-2	81	5.16	75	.280	.363	15-0	.200	1	123	-16	-1.5
1998	Det A	2	6	.250	15	9	0	0-1	61.2	66	42	11	1	19-2	47	5.98	79	.270	.325	0-0	—	0	105	-7	-0.8
	Cle A	0	0	—	3	0	0	0-0	5.1	6	3	0	0	2-0	2	5.06	94	.300	.333	0-0	—	0		0	0.0
	Oak A	0	1	.000	25	0	0	0-2	36	34	17	5	0	8-1	33	4.00	114	.241	.282	0-0	—	0		3	0.1
	Year	2	7	.222	43	9	0	0-3	103	106	67	16	1	29-3	82	5.24	89	.262	.311	0-0	—	0	106	-5	-0.7
1999	Oak A	2	2	.500	53	0	0	0-5	69.1	69	38	6	3	34-1	62	4.15	112	.256	.344	0-0	—	0		3	0.1
2000	Bal A	2	2	.500	5	0	0	0-0	7.1	12	6	3	0	5-3	5	7.36	64	.353	.436	0-0	—	0		-2	-0.4
	Chi N	3	4	.429	54	0	0	3-3	62	60	20	7	1	24-8	52	2.47	184	.252	.322	2-0	.000	-0		14	1.4
2001	SF N	2	5	.286	73	0	0	0-3	78.1	71	33	4	3	33-4	63	3.45	116	.240	.318	2-1	.000	-0		5	0.4
2002	†SF N	8	2	.800	80	0	0	0-1	72	55	21	3	0	30-2	55	2.25	173	.212	.290	3-0	.000	-0		13	1.6
2003	†SF N	4	4	.500	76	0	0	38-7	78.1	74	35	5	0	28-6	65	2.87	143	.246	.307	3-0	.000	-0		7	1.2
Total	11	39	49	.443	527	49	0	45-27	826.1	801	404	80	22	326-35	643	3.90	107	.252	.324	79-10	.101	-2	104	24	2.6
WORRELL, TODD Todd Roland B 9.28.1959 Arcadia, CA BR/TR 6-5/222# d8.28 b-Tim																									
1985	†StL N	3	0	1.000	17	0	0	5-2	21.2	17	7	2	0	7-2	17	2.91	122	.215	.273	1-0	.000	-0		2	0.3
1986	StL N	9	10	.474	74	0	0	**36-10**	103.2	86	29	9	1	41-16	73	2.08	175	.229	.303	7-0	.143	0		**17**	3.6
1987	†StL N	8	6	.571	75	0	0	33-10	94.2	86	29	8	0	34-11	92	2.66	156	.242	.307	10-1	.100	-0		16	3.1
1988	StL N★	5	9	.357	68	0	0	32-9	90	69	32	7	1	34-14	78	3.00	116	.214	.287	6-0	.000	-0		5	1.1
1989	StL N	3	5	.375	47	0	0	20-3	51.2	42	21	4	0	26-13	41	2.96	123	.222	.315	1-1	.000	-0		3	0.6
1992	StL N	5	3	.625	67	0	0	3-4	64	45	15	4	1	25-5	64	2.11	161	.198	.281	0-0	—	0		10	1.2
1993	LA N	1	1	.500	35	0	0	5-3	38.2	46	28	6	0	11-1	31	6.05	63	.313	.348	0-0	—	0		-9	-0.6
1994	LA N	6	5	.545	38	0	0	11-8	42	37	21	4	1	12-1	44	4.29	92	.236	.291	0-0	—	0		-1	-0.3
1995	LA N✣	4	1	.800	59	0	0	32-4	62.1	50	15	4	1	19-2	61	2.02	188	.221	.282	2-0	.000	-0		14	2.3
1996	†LA N★	4	6	.400	72	0	0	**44-9**	65.1	70	29	5	2	15-1	66	3.03	128	.265	.307	0-0	—	0		5	0.9
1997	LA N	2	6	.250	65	0	0	35-9	59.2	60	38	12	0	23-1	61	5.28	73	.250	.316	0-0	—	0		-10	-1.9
Total	11	50	52	.490	617	0	0	256-71	693.2	608	264	65	7	247-67	628	3.09	122	.235	.301	27-2	.074	-1		52	10.3
WORTHAM, RICH Richard Cooper B 10.22.1953 Odessa, TX BR/TL 6/185# d5.3																									
1978	Chi A	3	2	.600	8	8	2	0-0	59	59	24	1	0	23-0	25	3.05	125	.267	.333	0-0	—	0	100	4	0.3
1979	Chi A	14	14	.500	34	33	5	0-0	204	195	126	21	3	100-3	119	4.90	87	.255	.339	0-0	—	0	96	-13	-1.6
1980	Chi A	4	7	.364	41	10	0	1-2	92	102	73	4	3	58-5	45	5.97	68	.285	.383	0-0	—	0	84	-21	-2.2
1983	Oak A	0	0	—	1	0	0	0-0	0	3	1	0	0	1-0	0	o	—	1.000	1.000	0-0	—	0		-1	-0.1
Total	4	21	23	.477	84	51	7	1-2	355	359	224	26	6	182-8	189	4.89	84	.266	.352	0-0	—	0	95	-31	-3.6
WORTHINGTON, AL Allan Fulton "Red" B 2.5.1929 Birmingham, AL BR/TR 6-2/205# d7.6 C2																									
1953	NY N	4	8	.333	20	17	5-2	0	102	103	55	6	2	54	52	3.44	125	.258	.349	31-4	.065	-2	97	5	0.4
1954	NY N	0	2	.000	10	1	0	0	18	21	7	0	0	15	8	3.50	115	.333	.456	4-0	.000	-1	155	2	0.1
1956	NY N	7	14	.333	28	24	4	0	165.2	158	82	20	4	74-6	95	3.97	95	.254	.335	51-6	.235	2	75	-3	-0.1
1957	NY N	8	11	.421	55	12	1-1	4	157.2	140	75	19	5	56-7	90	4.22	93	.237	.306	40-1	.100	-2	103	-1	-0.4
1958	SF N	11	7	.611	54	12	1	6	151.1	152	72	17	2	57-6	76	3.63	105	.255	.320	44-3	.182	0	110	2	0.3
1959	SF N	2	3	.400	42	3	0	2	73.1	68	34	8	5	37-4	45	3.68	103	.253	.347	13-0	.077	-1	133	1	0.0
1960	Bos A	0	1	.000	6	0	0	0	11.2	17	12	1	0	11-3	7	7.71	52	.340	.459	1-0	.000	-0		-5	-0.4
	Chi A	1	1	.500	4	0	0	0	5.1	3	2	0	0	4-0	1	3.38	112	.176	.318	2-0	1.000	1		0	0.2
	Year	1	2	.333	10	0	0	0	17	20	20	1	0	15-3	8	6.35	62	.299	.422	3-0	.667	1		-5	-0.2
1963	Cin N	4	4	.500	50	0	0	10	81.1	75	34	6	3	31-3	55	2.99	112	.248	.321	12-2	.083	-0		2	0.3
1964	Cin N	1	0	1.000	6	0	0	0	7	14	11	0	1	2-0	6	10.29	35	.400	.436	0-0	—	0		-6	-0.8
	Min A	5	6	.455	41	0	0	14	72.1	47	18	4	0	28-6	59	1.37	261	.183	.262	16-4	.063	-1		16	2.9
1965	†Min A	10	7	.588	62	0	0	21	80.1	57	25	4	3	41-2	59	2.13	167	.207	.312	10-2	.100	0		11	2.6
1966	Min A	6	3	.667	65	0	0	16	91.1	66	26	6	1	27-3	93	2.46	146	.199	.260	11-0	.273	1		12	1.8
1967	Min A	8	9	.471	59	0	0	16	92	77	36	6	1	38-10	80	2.84	122	.229	.307	8-0	.000	-1		5	1.0
1968	Min A	4	5	.444	54	0	0	**18**	76.1	67	26	1	0	32-9	57	2.71	114	.238	.311	7-2	.000	-1		4	0.6
1969	†Min A	4	1	.800	46	0	0	3-1	61	65	31	7	0	20-2	51	4.57	80	.278	.333	5-1	.000	-1		-4	-0.5
Total	14	75	82	.478	602	69	11-3	110-1	1246.2	1130	546	105	27	527-61	834	3.39	110	.243	.320	255-25	.137	-5	100	41	8.0
WRIGHT, GENE Clarence Eugene "Big Gene" B 12.11.1878 Cleveland, OH D 10.29.1930 Barberton, OH BR/TR 6-2/185# d10.5																									
1901	Bro N	1	0	1.000	1	1	1	0	9	6	2	0	0	1	6	1.00	335	.188	.212	3-0	.333	0	85	2	0.2
1902	Cle A	7	10	.412	21	18	15-1	1	148	150	94	6	8	75	52	3.95	87	.263	.357	70-1	.143	-2*	132	-7	-1.0
1903	Cle A	3	10	.231	15	12	8	0	101.2	122	94	1	4	58	42	5.75	50	.296	.388	43-1	.209	2	115	-32	-3.1
	StL A	3	5	.375	8	8	7-1	0	61	73	29	2	4	16	37	3.69	79	.296	.348	21-0	.143	-1	86	-3	-0.4
	Year	6	15	.286	23	20	15-1	0	162.2	195	33	3	8	74	79	4.98	58	.296	.374	64-1	.188	2	103	-38	-3.5
1904	StL A	0	1	.000	1	1	0	0	4	10	6	0	0	2	3	13.50	18	.476	.522	1-0	.000	-0	115	-4	-0.6
Total	4	14	26	.350	46	40	31-2	1	323.2	361	225	9	16	152	140	4.50	70	.282	.365	138-2	.167	-1	117	-44	-4.9
WRIGHT, CLYDE Clyde B 2.20.1941 Jefferson City, TN BR/TL 6-1/185# d6.15 s-Jaret																									
1966	Cal A	4	7	.364	20	13	3-1	0	91.1	92	39	11	1	25-4	37	3.74	90	.265	.314	29-3	.103	-1*	93	-2	-0.4
1967	Cal A	5	5	.500	20	11	1	0	77.1	76	33	5	1	24-2	35	3.26	96	.260	.316	22-3	.273	2*	78	-1	0.1
1968	Cal A	10	6	.625	41	13	2-1	3	125.2	123	58	13	2	44-6	71	3.94	74	.256	.319	37-2	.216	2*	92	-13	-1.5
1969	Cal A	1	8	.111	37	5	0	0-2	63.2	66	33	4	1	30-5	31	4.10	85	.278	.361	11-0	.182	0*	30	-4	-0.5
1970	Cal A★	22	12	.647	39	39	7-2	0-0	260.2	226	97	24	7	88-4	110	2.83	128	.232	.298	105-4	.171	3*	122	21	2.9
1971	Cal A	16	17	.485	37	37	10-2	0-0	276.2	225	105	17	3	82-10	135	2.99	108	.226	.283	91-9	.154	2*	79	8	1.4
1972	Cal A	18	11	.621	35	35	15-2	0-0	251	229	101	14	4	80-6	87	2.98	98	.246	.307	83-6	.217	7	119	-5	0.5
1973	Cal A	11	19	.367	37	36	13-1	0-0	257	273	120	26	3	76-0	65	3.68	97	.273	.324	0-0	—	0	96	-4	-0.2
1974	Mil A	9	20	.310	38	32	15	0-0	232	264	122	22	0	54-4	64	4.42	82	.284	.322	0-0	—	0	89	-20	-2.2
1975	Tex A	4	6	.400	25	14	1	0-0	93.1	105	56	7	1	47-3	32	4.44	85	.294	.370	0-0	—	0	110	-8	-0.7
Total	10	100	111	.474	329	235	67-9	3-2	1728.2	1679	764	143	23	550-44	667	3.50	96	.256	.314	378-27	.183	14	99	-28	-0.6
WRIGHT, DAVE David William B 8.27.1875 Dennison, OH D 1.18.1946 Dennison, OH BR/TR 6/185# d7.22																									
1895	Pit N	0	0	—	1	0	0	0	2	6	6	0	0	1	0	27.00	17	.500	.538	1-0	.000	-0		-4	-0.2
1897	Chi N	1	0	1.000	1	1	1	0	7	17	14	1	2	2	4	15.43	29	.459	.512	3-0	.333	0	224	-7	-0.6
Total	2	1	0	1.000	2	1	1	0	9	23	20	1	2	3	4	18.00	25	.469	.519	4-0	.250	0	224	-11	-0.8
WRIGHT, ED Henderson Edward B 5.15.1919 Dyersburg, TN D 11.19.1995 Dyersburg, TN BR/TR 6-1/180# d7.29																									
1945	Bos N	8	3	.727	15	12	7-1	0	111.1	104	35	7	0	33	24	2.51	153	.254	.310	39-2	.128	-2	107	17	1.3
1946	Bos N	12	9	.571	36	21	9-2	0	176.1	164	82	8	2	71	44	3.52	97	.250	.325	59-4	.305	6	114	-3	0.3
1947	Bos N	3	3	.500	23	6	1	0	64.2	80	52	9	2	35	14	6.40	61	.305	.391	23-0	.130	-0	113	-19	-1.5
1948	Bos N	0	0	—	3	0	0	0	4.2	9	3	0	0	2	2	1.93	199	.474	.524	0-0	—	0		0	0.0
1952	Phi A	2	1	.667	24	0	0	1	41.1	55	36	6	3	20	9	6.53	61	.320	.400	7-0	.143	-0		-12	-0.9
Total	5	25	16	.610	101	39	17-3	1	398.1	412	208	30	7	161	93	4.00	92	.271	.344	128-6	.211	3	110	-17	-0.8
WRIGHT, JIM James "Jiggs" B 9.19.1900 Hyde, England D 4.11.1963 Oakland, CA BR/TR 6-2.5/195# d9.14																									
1927	StL A	1	0	1.000	2	1	1	0	12	8	6	0	0	4	4	4.50	97	.182	.250	4-0	.000	-0	172	0	0.0
1928	StL A	0	0	—	2	0	0	0	2	3	3	0	0	2	2	13.50	31	.375	.500	0-0	—	0		-2	-0.1
Total	2	1	0	1.000	4	1	1	0	14	11	9	0	0	6	6	5.79	75	.212	.293	4-0	.000	-0	172	-2	-0.1
WRIGHT, JIM James Clifton B 12.21.1950 Reed City, MI BR/TR 6-1/165# d4.15																									
1978	Bos A	8	4	.667	24	16	5-3	0-0	116	122	51	8	7	24-2	56	3.57	116	.276	.321	0-0	—	0	86	7	0.6
1979	Bos A	1	0	1.000	11	1	0	0-0	23	19	13	5	3	7-1	15	5.09	87	.226	.302	0-0	—	0	82	-1	-0.1

Year	Tm Lg	W	L	Pct	G	GS	CG-Sho	SV-BS	IP	H	R	HR	HB	BB-IB	SO	ERA	AERA	OAV	OOB	AB-SH	AVG	PB	Sup	APR	PW
Total	2	9	4	.692	35	17	5-3	0-0	139	141	64	13	10	31-3	71	3.82	109	.268	.318	0-0	—	0	85	6	0.5
WRIGHT, JIM James Leon B 3.3.1955 St.Joseph, MO BR/TR 6-5/205# d4.22 C2																									
1981	KC A	2	3	.400	17	4	0	0-0	52	57	21	5	2	21-7	27	3.46	104	.277	.348	0-0	—	0	75	1	0.1
1982	KC A	0	0	—	7	0	0	0-0	23.2	32	18	3	0	6-0	9	5.32	77	.320	.358	0-0	—	0		-4	-0.2
Total	2	2	3	.400	24	4	0	0-0	75.2	89	39	8	2	27-7	36	4.04	93	.291	.351	0-0	—	0	75	-3	-0.1
WRIGHT, RICKY James Richard B 11.22.1958 Paris, TX BL/TL 6-3/175# d7.28																									
1982	LA N	2	1	.667	14	5	0	0-0	32.2	28	12	1	0	20-6	24	3.03	115	.233	.340	8-0	.125	0	137	2	0.2
1983	LA N	0	0	—	6	0	0	0-0	6.1	5	2	0	0	2-1	5	2.84	127	.227	.280	0-0	—	0		1	0.0
	Tex A	0	0	—	1	0	0	0-0	2	0	0	0	0	1-0	2	0.00	—	.000	.167	0-0	—	0		1	0.0
1984	Tex A	0	2	.000	8	1	0	0-1	14.2	20	10	3	0	11-0	6	6.14	68	.357	.463	0-0	—	0	44	-3	-0.3
1985	Tex A	0	0	—	5	0	0	0-0	7.2	5	4	0	0	5-1	7	4.70	90	.185	.313	0-0	—	0		0	0.0
1986	Tex A	1	0	1.000	21	1	0	0-0	39.1	44	22	1	0	21-0	23	5.03	86	.284	.369	0-0	—	0*	42	-2	-0.1
Total	5	3	3	.500	55	7	0	0-1	102.2	102	50	5	0	60-8	67	4.30	92	.265	.362	8-0	.125	0	100	-1	-0.2
WRIGHT, JAMEY Jamey Alan B 12.24.1974 Oklahoma City, OK BR/TR 6-6/205# d7.3																									
1996	Col N	4	4	.500	16	15	0	0-0	91.1	105	60	8	7	41-1	45	4.93	106	.298	.381	26-5	.077	-1	100	0	0.0
1997	Col N	8	12	.400	26	26	1	0-0	149.2	198	113	19	11	71-3	59	6.25	83	.327	.406	48-3	.125	-2	90	-15	-1.8
1998	Col N	9	14	.391	34	34	1	0-0	206.1	235	143	24	11	95-3	86	5.67	91	.294	.374	57-8	.175	0	92	-11	-0.9
1999	Col N	4	3	.571	16	16	0	0-0	94.1	110	52	10	4	54-3	49	4.87	119	.307	.400	32-3	.125	-2	96	9	0.5
2000	Mil N	7	9	.438	26	25	0	0-0	164.2	157	81	12	18	88-5	96	4.10	111	.261	.368	46-4	.065	-3	82	9	0.4
2001	Mil N	11	12	.478	33	33	1-1	0-0	194.2	201	115	26	20	98-10	129	4.90	88	.272	.370	67-4	.194	2*	102	-13	-1.1
2002	Mil N	5	13	.278	19	19	1-1	0-0	114.1	115	72	15	11	63-8	69	5.35	77	.270	.374	33-6	.152	0	66	-15	-2.0
	StL N	2	0	1.000	4	3	0	0-0	15	15	8	2	0	12-1	8	4.80	83	.259	.386	5-1	.000	-1	225	-1	-0.2
	Year	7	13	.350	23	22	1-1	0-0	129.1	130	18	17	11	75-9	77	5.29	77	.269	.375	38-7	.132	-0	87	-16	-2.2
2003	KC A	1	2	.333	4	4	2-1	0-0	25.1	23	14	1	1	11-0	19	4.26	121	.245	.330	0-0	—	0	71	2	0.2
Total	8	51	69	.425	178	175	6-3	0-0	1055.2	1159	658	117	83	533-34	560	5.15	94	.287	.379	314-34	.137	-6	92	-35	-4.9
WRIGHT, JARET Jaret Samuel B 12.29.1975 Anaheim, CA BR/TR 6-2/220# d6.24 f-Clyde																									
1997	†Cle A	8	3	.727	16	16	0	0-0	90.1	81	45	9	5	35-0	63	4.38	107	.238	.314	3-2	.000	-0	125	4	0.4
1998	†Cle A	12	10	.545	32	32	1-1	0-0	192.2	207	109	22	11	87-4	140	4.72	101	.277	.358	7-0	.429	1	108	1	0.2
1999	†Cle A	8	10	.444	26	26	0	0-0	133.2	144	99	18	7	77-1	91	6.06	83	.277	.376	1-0	.000	-0	97	-15	-1.7
2000	Cle A	3	4	.429	9	9	1-1	0-0	51.2	44	27	6	1	28-0	36	4.70	106	.235	.336	1-1	.000	-0	121	2	0.2
2001	Cle A	2	2	.500	7	7	0	0-0	29	36	22	2	0	22-0	18	6.52	69	.313	.420	2-0	.500	0	114	-6	-0.6
2002	Cle A	2	3	.400	8	6	0	0-0	18.1	40	34	3	2	19-0	12	15.71	28	.435	.526	0-0	—	0	141	-23	-3.5
2003	SD N	1	5	.167	39	0	0	2-2	47.1	69	44	9	2	28-2	41	8.37	47	.348	.427	4-1	.250	1		-24	-2.6
	†Atl N	1	0	1.000	11	0	0	0-1	9	7	2	0	1	3-0	9	2.00	211	.226	.314	0-0	—	0		2	0.2
	Year	2	5	.286	50	0	0	2-3	56.1	76	53	9	3	31-2	50	7.35	54	.332	.412	4-1	.250	1		-21	-2.4
Total	7	37	37	.500	148	96	2-2	2-3	572	628	382	69	29	299-7	410	5.68	83	.282	.371	18-4	.278	1	113	-59	-7.4
WRIGHT, DAN Jonathan Daniel B 12.14.1977 Longview, TX BR/TR 6-5/225# d7.27																									
2001	Chi A	5	3	.625	13	12	0	0-0	66.1	78	45	12	2	39-1	36	5.70	81	.300	.389	0-0	—	0	130	-7	-0.7
2002	Chi A	14	12	.538	33	33	1-1	0-0	196.1	200	124	32	6	71-1	136	5.18	87	.263	.327	4-0	.000	-0	110	-14	-1.6
2003	Chi A	1	7	.125	20	15	0	1-0	86.1	91	63	16	3	46-2	47	6.15	74	.277	.366	2-0	.000	-0	86	-15	-1.2
Total	3	20	22	.476	66	60	1-1	1-0	349	369	232	60	11	156-4	219	5.52	82	.273	.349	6-0	.000	-1	108	-36	-3.5
WRIGHT, KEN Kenneth Warren B 9.4.1946 Pensacola, FL BR/TR 6-2/210# d4.10																									
1970	KC A	1	2	.333	47	0	0	3-1	53.1	49	33	2	7	29-0	30	5.23	71	.261	.374	4-0	.000	-0		-8	-0.6
1971	KC A	3	6	.333	21	12	1-1	1-0	78	66	34	6	3	47-0	56	3.69	93	.230	.344	22-1	.091	-1	83	-2	-0.3
1972	KC A	1	2	.333	17	0	0	4-1	18.1	15	10	0	1	15-1	18	4.91	62	.231	.378	2-0	.000	-0		-3	-0.8
1973	KC A	6	5	.545	25	12	1	0-1	80.2	60	48	6	0	82-0	75	4.91	84	.210	.383	0-0	—	0	81	-6	-0.8
1974	NY A	0	0	—	3	0	0	0-0	5.2	5	2	0	0	7-0	2	3.18	111	.227	.414	0-0	—	0		0	0.0
Total	5	11	15	.423	113	24	2-1	8-3	236	195	127	14	11	180-1	181	4.54	82	.230	.369	28-1	.071	-2	83	-19	-2.5
WRIGHT, MEL Melvin James B 5.11.1928 Manila, AR D 5.16.1983 Houston, TX BR/TR 6-3/210# d4.17 C13																									
1954	StL N	0	0	—	9	0	0	0	10.1	16	15	2	2	11	4	10.45	39	.348	.492	1-0	.000	-0		-8	-0.4
1955	StL N	2	2	.500	29	0	0	1	36.1	44	26	4	1	9-2	18	6.19	66	.308	.351	6-0	.000	-1		-8	-0.9
1960	Chi N	0	1	.000	9	0	0	2	16.1	17	9	1	0	3-1	8	4.96	76	.279	.299	2-0	.000	-0		-2	-0.2
1961	Chi N	0	1	.000	11	0	0	0	21	42	26	3	0	4-0	6	10.71	39	.416	.438	2-0	.000	-0		-13	-0.6
Total	4	2	4	.333	58	0	0	3	84	119	76	10	3	27-3	36	7.61	53	.339	.387	11-0	.000	-2		-31	-2.1
WRIGHT, BOB Robert Cassius B 12.13.1891 Decatur Co., IN D 7.30.1993 Carmichael, CA BR/TR 6-1.5/175# d9.21																									
1915	Chi N	0	0	—	2	0	0	0	4	6	4	0	0	0	3	2.25	123	.353	.353	0-0	—	0		-1	0.0
WRIGHT, ROY Roy Earl B 9.26.1933 Buchtel, OH BR/TR 6-2/170# d9.30																									
1956	NY N	0	1	.000	1	1	0	0	2.2	8	5	1	0	2-0	0	16.88	22	.533	.588	1-0	.000	-0	47	-4	-0.6
WRIGHT, RASTY Wayne Bromley B 11.5.1895 Ceredo, WV D 6.12.1948 Columbus, OH BR/TR 5-11/160# d6.22																									
1917	StL A	0	1	.000	16	1	0	0	39.2	48	31	0	1	10	5	5.45	48	.300	.345	10-1	.200	0	111	-12	-0.6
1918	StL A	8	2	.800	18	13	6-1	0	111.1	99	39	1	5	18	25	2.51	109	.244	.285	34-2	.294	3	106	4	0.6
1919	StL A	0	5	.000	24	5	2	0	63.1	79	44	1	1	20	14	5.54	60	.315	.368	12-0	.083	-1	66	-13	-1.0
1922	StL A	9	7	.563	31	16	5	5	154	148	64	7	8	50	44	2.92	142	.262	.331	50-4	.140	-2	113	19	1.8
1923	StL A	7	4	.636	20	8	4	0	82.2	107	64	6	5	34	26	6.42	65	.317	.387	27-3	.222	0	134	-17	-1.9
Total	5	24	19	.558	109	43	17-1	5	451	481	242	15	20	132	114	4.05	87	.280	.338	133-10	.195	1	111	-19	-1.1
WRIGHT, HARRY William Henry B 1.10.1835 Sheffield, England D 10.3.1895 Atlantic City, NJ BR/TR 5-9.5/157# d5.5 M23 HF1953 b-George b-Sam ▲																									
1871	Bos NA	1	0	1.000	9	0	0	**3**	18.2	34	31	0		4	0	6.27	66	.337	.362	147	.299	1*		-4	-0.2
1872	Bos NA	1	0	1.000	7	0	0	**4**	25.2	26	12	0		0	1	2.10	173	.239	.239	208	.255	0*		**5**	0.3
1873	Bos NA	2	2	.500	14	6	0	**4**	39.1	65	47	0		6	5	4.12	81	.328	.348	263	.259	2*	153	-3	-0.2
1874	Bos NA	0	2	.000	6	2	0	**3**	16.2	24	13	0		4	0	2.16	100	.324	.359	184	.315	2*	88	0	0.1
Total	4 NA	4	4	.500	36	8	0	14	100.1	149	103	0		14	6	3.68	92	.309	.329	802	.278	5	132	-2	0.0
WRIGHT, LUCKY William Simmons "William The Red" or "Deacon" B 2.21.1880 Waterville, OH D 7.7.1941 Tontogany, OH BR/TR 6/178# d4.18																									
1909	Cle A	0	4	.000	5	4	3	0	28	21	16	0	0	7	5	3.21	80	.223	.277	7-0	.000	-1	55	-2	-0.4
WUNSCH, KELLY Kelly Douglas B 7.12.1972 Houston, TX BL/TL 6-5/192# d4.3																									
2000	†Chi A	6	3	.667	**83**	0	0	1-4	61.1	50	22	4	2	29-1	51	2.93	170	.221	.313	0-0	—	0		14	1.8
2001	Chi A	2	1	.667	33	0	0	0-2	22.1	21	19	4	6	9-1	16	7.66	60	.247	.353	0-0	—	0		-7	-0.7
2002	Chi A	2	1	.667	50	0	0	0-1	31.2	26	12	3	5	19-1	22	3.41	132	.230	.365	0-0	—	0		4	0.4
2003	Chi A	0	0	—	43	0	0	0-0	36	17	13	1	7	25-4	33	2.75	165	.139	.308	0-0	—	0		7	0.3
Total	4	10	5	.667	209	0	0	1-7	151.1	114	66	12	20	82-7	122	3.69	128	.209	.329	0-0	—	0		18	1.8
WURM, FRANK Frank James B 4.27.1924 Cambridge, NY D 9.19.1993 Glens Falls, NY BB/TL 6-1/175# d9.4																									
1944	Bro N	0	0	—	1	1	0	0	0.1	1	4	0	0	5	1	108.00	3	.500	.857	0-0	—	0	142	-4	-0.2
WYATT, JOHN John Thomas B 4.19.1935 Chicago, IL D 4.6.1998 Omaha, NE BR/TR 5-11.5/200# d9.8																									
1961	KC A	0	0	—	5	0	0	1	7.1	8	3	0	1	4-0	6	2.45	170	.296	.394	0-0	—	0		1	0.1
1962	KC A	10	7	.588	59	9	0	11	125	121	66	12	5	80-5	106	4.46	95	.253	.363	29-0	.103	-2	101	-2	-0.5
1963	KC A	6	4	.600	63	0	0	21	92	83	37	12	0	43-2	81	3.13	125	.239	.321	9-0	.000	-1		7	0.9
1964	KC A★	9	8	.529	**81**	0	0	20	128	111	53	23	1	52-5	74	3.59	106	.236	.311	14-4	.000	-1		4	0.5
1965	KC A	2	6	.250	65	0	0	18	88.2	78	36	8	4	53-12	70	3.25	107	.241	.350	4-1	.000	-0		2	0.3
1966	KC A	0	3	.000	19	0	0	2	23.2	19	14	3	2	16-4	25	5.32	64	.213	.346	0-0	—	0		-4	-0.6
	Bos A	3	4	.429	42	0	0	8	71.2	59	27	3	4	27-3	63	3.14	121	.229	.308	11-0	.000	-1		5	0.4
	Year	3	7	.300	61	0	0	10	95.1	78	46	6	6	43-7	88	3.68	101	.225	.318	11-0	.000	-1		2	-0.2
1967	†Bos A	10	7	.588	60	0	0	20	93.1	71	30	6	2	39-5	68	2.60	134	.217	.303	12-0	.083	-0		9	1.9

Year	Tm Lg	W	L	Pct	G	GS	CG-Sho	SV-BS	IP	H	R	HR	HB	BB-IB	SO	ERA	AERA	OAV	OOB	AB-SH	AVG	PB	Sup	APR	PW
1968	Bos A	1	2	.333	8	0	0	0	10.2	9	7	2	1	6-0	11	4.22	75	.231	.348	0-0	—	0		-2	-0.4
	NY A	0	2	.000	7	0	0	0	8.1	7	3	1	0	9-0	6	2.16	134	.219	.381	1-0	.000	-0		0	0.1
	Det A	1	0	1.000	22	0	0	2	30.1	26	9	2	1	11-2	25	2.37	127	.236	.311	2-0	.000	-0		2	0.1
	Year	2	4	.333	37	0	0	2	49.1	42	19	5	2	26-2	42	2.74	110	.232	.333	3-0	.000	-0		1	-0.2
1969	Oak A	0	1	.000	4	0	0	0-0	8.1	8	5	0	2	6-1	5	5.40	64	.250	.400	1-0	.000	-0		-2	-0.2
Total	9	42	44	.488	435	9	0	103-0	687.1	600	290	72	23	346-39	540	3.47	108	.237	.331	83-5	.048	-6	101	20	2.6
WYATT, WHIT John Whitlow B 9.27.1907 Kensington, GA D 7.16.1999 Carrollton, GA BR/TR 6-1/185# d9.16 Mil 1944 C13																									
1929	Det A	0	1	.000	4	4	1	0	25.1	30	22	1	1	18	14	6.75	64	.309	.422	10-0	.100	-1	128	-6	-0.4
1930	Det A	4	5	.444	21	7	2	2	85.2	76	41	6	3	35	68	3.57	134	.239	.320	34-1	.353	3*	105	11	1.3
1931	Det A	0	2	.000	4	1	1	0	20.1	30	23	2	1	12	8	8.85	52	.361	.448	7-0	.286	0	18	-9	-0.7
1932	Det A	9	13	.409	43	22	10	1	205.2	228	136	12	3	102	82	5.03	93	.286	.369	78-1	.192	-0	100	-6	-0.6
1933	Det A	0	1	.000	10	0	0	0	17	20	9	1	2	9	9	4.24	102	.299	.397	2-0	.000	-0		0	0.0
	Chi A	3	4	.429	26	7	2	1	87.2	91	51	7	2	45	31	4.62	92	.266	.355	28-1	.214	0	106	-2	-0.1
	Year	3	5	.375	36	7	2	1	104.2	111	56	8	4	54	40	4.56	93	.271	.362	30-1	.200	-0	106	-2	-0.1
1934	Chi A	4	11	.267	23	6	2	2	67.2	83	59	10	1	37	36	7.18	66	.303	.388	26-1	.231	0	86	-16	-2.8
1935	Chi A	4	3	.571	30	1	0	5	52	65	41	6	2	25	22	6.75	68	.308	.387	13-0	.231	1	94	-11	-1.2
1936	Chi A	0	0	—	3	0	0	1	3	3	0	0	0	0	0	0.00	—	.273	.273	0-0	—	0		2	0.1
1937	Cle A	2	3	.400	29	4	2	0	73	67	38	3	0	40	52	4.44	104	.244	.340	18-1	.389	3	80	3	0.4
1939	Bro N☆	8	3	.727	16	14	6-2	0	109	88	34	3	2	39	52	2.31	174	.224	.297	36-0	.167	-0	91	19	1.9
1940	Bro N★	15	14	.517	37	34	16-**5**	0	239.1	233	105	19	5	62	124	3.46	116	.254	.304	80-8	.175	-0	97	13	1.3
1941	†Bro N★	**22**	10	.688	38	35	23-**7**	1	288.1	223	89	10	2	82	176	2.34	157	**.212**	**.270**	109-8	.239	7*	114	**42**	**5.3**
1942	Bro N☆	19	7	.731	31	30	16	0	217.1	185	82	9	7	63	104	2.73	119	.225	.286	77-6	.182	1	121	11	1.2
1943	Bro N	14	5	.737	26	26	13-3	0	180.2	139	55	5	0	43	80	2.49	135	**.207**	**.255**	60-6	.283	4*	117	18	2.3
1944	Bro N	2	6	.250	9	9	1	0	37.2	51	37	1	2	16	4	7.17	50	.311	.379	13-1	.154	-0*	97	-16	-2.7
1945	Phi N	0	7	.000	10	10	2	0	51.1	72	38	3	0	14	10	5.26	73	.330	.371	16-0	.125	0	80	-8	-0.9
Total	16	106	95	.527	360	210	97-17	13	1761	1684	860	98	33	642	872	3.79	105	.251	.319	607-34	.219	18	102	45	4.4
WYCKOFF, WELDON John Weldon B 2.19.1892 Williamsport, PA D 5.8.1961 Sheboygan Falls, WI BR/TR 6-1/175# d4.19																									
1913	Phi A	2	4	.333	17	7	4	0	61.2	56	44	1	3	46	31	4.38	63	.262	.399	21-0	.190	-0	134	-15	-1.3
1914	†Phi A	11	7	.611	32	20	11	2	185	153	82	2	4	103	86	3.02	87	.228	.334	75-1	.147	-0*	133	-12	-1.4
1915	Phi A	10	22	.313	43	34	20-1	0	276	238	139	1	5	165	157	3.52	83	.246	.359	96-3	.125	-4*	77	-15	-1.9
1916	Phi A	0	1	.000	7	2	1	0	21.1	20	16	1	1	20	4	5.48	52	.247	.402	8-0	.375	1*	172	-6	-0.2
	Bos A	0	0	—	8	0	0	1	22.2	19	13	0	0	18	18	4.76	58	.232	.370	6-0	.167	-0		-4	-0.3
	Year	0	1	.000	15	2	1	1	44	39	36	1	1	38	22	5.11	55	.239	.386	14-0	.286	1	175	-10	-0.5
1917	Bos A	0	0	—	1	0	0	0	5	4	3	0	1	4	1	1.80	143	.222	.391	1-0	.000	-0		0	0.0
1918	Bos A	0	0	—	1	0	0	0	2	4	1	0	0	1	2	0.00	—	.400	.455	1-0	.000	-0		0	0.0
Total	6	23	34	.404	109	63	36-1	3	573.2	494	298	5	14	357	299	3.55	79	.242	.358	208-4	.149	-4	103	-52	-5.1
WYMAN, FRANK Frank H. B 5.10.1862 Haverhill, MA D 2.4.1916 Everett, MA d6.10 ▲																									
1884	KC U	0	1	.000	3	1	1	0	21	37	29	0		3	9	6.86	33	.363	.381	124	.218	-1*	96	-11	-0.5
WYNN, EARLY Early "Gus" B 1.6.1920 Hartford, AL D 4.4.1999 Venice, FL BB/TR 6/200# d9.13 Mil 1944-46 C6 HF1972																									
1939	Was A	0	2	.000	3	3	1	0	20.1	26	15	0	0	10	1	5.75	76	.313	.387	6-1	.167	0	108	-3	-0.3
1941	Was A	3	1	.750	5	5	4	0	40	35	14	1	0	10	15	1.57	257	.226	.273	15-1	.133	-0	111	9	0.8
1942	Was A	10	16	.385	30	28	10-1	0	190	246	129	6	3	73	58	5.12	71	.314	.374	69-2	.217	2	103	-31	-3.5
1943	Was A	18	12	.600	37	**33**	12-3	0	256.2	232	97	15	1	83	89	2.91	110	.240	.301	98-1	.296	7*	108	10	1.9
1944	Was A	8	17	.320	33	25	19-2	2	207.2	221	97	3	2	67	65	3.38	96	.277	.334	92-0	.207	2*	85	-3	-0.3
1946	Was A	8	5	.615	17	12	9	0	107	112	45	8	3	33	36	3.11	108	.267	.325	47-0	.319	7*	81	3	1.1
1947	Was A☆	17	15	.531	33	31	22-2	0	247	251	114	13	5	90	73	3.64	102	.262	.329	120-0	.275	7*	91	1	0.9
1948	Was A	8	19	.296	33	31	15-1	0	198	236	144	18	1	94	49	5.82	75	.295	.370	106-0	.217	3*	80	-31	-3.3
1949	Cle A	11	7	.611	26	23	6	0	164.2	186	84	8	1	57	62	4.15	96	.282	.340	70-2	.143	-2*	109	-3	-0.4
1950	Cle A	18	8	.692	32	28	14-2	0	213.2	166	88	20	4	101	143	**3.20**	135	**.212**	**.305**	77-4	.234	7*	118	28	3.7
1951	Cle A	20	13	.606	37	**34**	21-3	1	**274.1**	227	102	18	3	107	133	3.02	126	.225	.301	108-3	.185	2*	103	27	3.1
1952	Cle A	23	12	.657	42	33	19-4	3	285.2	239	103	23	1	132	153	2.90	115	.231	.318	99-4	.222	5*	121	18	2.6
1953	Cle A	17	12	.586	36	34	16-1	0	251.2	234	121	19	4	107	138	3.93	95	.245	.324	91-6	.275	9*	118	-4	0.4
1954	†Cle A	**23**	11	.676	40	**36**	20-3	2	**270.2**	225	93	21	0	83	155	2.73	135	.225	.283	93-5	.183	1	109	29	3.6
1955	Cle A★	17	11	.607	32	31	16-6	0	230	207	86	19	3	80-3	122	2.82	142	.240	.304	84-2	.179	1*	91	28	3.3
1956	Cle A★	20	9	.690	38	35	18-4	2	277.2	233	93	19	5	91-7	158	2.72	154	.228	.291	101-5	.228	3	105	**46**	**5.1**
1957	Cle A★	14	17	.452	40	**37**	13-1	1	263	270	139	32	5	104-7	**184**	4.31	86	.265	.335	86-3	.116	-2	107	-15	-1.8
1958	Chi A★	14	16	.467	40	34	11-4	2	239.2	214	115	27	6	104-3	**179**	4.13	88	.242	.323	75-2	.200	3	105	-11	-1.1
1959	†Chi A★	**22**	10	.688	37	**37**	14-5	0	**255.2**	202	106	20	9	119-5	179	3.17	119	.216	.308	90-2	.244	9	122	15	2.7
1960	Chi A★	13	12	.520	36	35	13-**4**	1	237.1	220	105	20	4	112-2	158	3.49	108	.247	.332	75-6	.200	7	125	7	1.2
1961	Chi A	8	2	.800	17	16	5	0	110.1	88	43	11	1	47-0	64	3.51	112	.220	.302	37-1	.162	-0	127	7	0.5
1962	Chi A	7	15	.318	27	26	11-3	0	167.2	171	90	15	3	56-6	91	4.46	88	.264	.325	54-2	.130	0	81	-10	-1.3
1963	Cle A	1	2	.333	20	5	1	1	55.1	50	14	2	0	15-3	29	2.28	159	.250	.300	11-0	.273	1	88	9	0.6
Total	23	300	244	.551	691	612	290-49	15	4564	4291	2037	338	64	1775-**36**	2334	3.54	106	.248	.320	1704-52	.214	72	105	126	19.5
WYNNE, BILLY Billy Vernon B 7.31.1943 Williamston, NC BL/TR 6-5/206# d8.6																									
1967	NY N	0	0	—	6	1	0	0	8.2	12	4	0	0	2-0	4	3.12	109	.324	.350	1-0	.000	-0	130	0	0.0
1968	Chi A	0	0	—	1	0	0	0	2	2	2	0	0	2-0	1	4.50	67	.250	.400	0-0	—	0		-1	0.0
1969	Chi A	7	7	.500	20	20	6-1	0-0	128.2	143	63	14	3	50-8	67	4.06	95	.283	.350	41-7	.122	-1	80	-3	-0.4
1970	Chi A	1	4	.200	12	9	0	0-0	44	54	30	8	1	22-2	19	5.32	73	.298	.374	13-0	.077	-1	104	-7	-0.7
1971	Cal A	0	0	—	3	0	0	0-0	3.2	6	2	0	0	2-0	6	4.91	66	.375	.444	0-0	—	0		-1	0.0
Total	5	8	11	.421	42	30	6-1	0-0	187	217	101	22	4	78-10	97	4.33	88	.290	.359	55-7	.109	-2	90	-12	-1.1
WYNNE, BILL William Andrew B 3.27.1869 Neuse, NC D 8.7.1951 Raleigh, NC BR/TR 5-11.5/161# d8.31																									
1894	Was N	0	1	.000	1	1	1	0	8	10	11	0	2	8	2	6.75	78	.303	.465	3-0	.000	-0	67	-2	-0.2
WYSE, HANK Henry Washington "Hooks" B 3.1.1918 Lunsford, AR D 10.22.2000 Pryor, OK BR/TR 5-11.5/185# d9.7																									
1942	Chi N	2	1	.667	4	4	1-1	0	28	33	10	1	0	6	8	1.93	166	.287	.322	8-2	.125	-0	171	3	0.3
1943	Chi N	9	7	.563	38	15	8-2	5	156	159	57	4	2	34	45	2.94	113	.264	.306	50-5	.080	-4*	117	8	0.7
1944	Chi N	16	15	.516	41	34	14-3	1	257.1	277	113	9	2	57	86	3.15	112	.278	.318	90-6	.178	-1	116	9	0.9
1945	†Chi N❖	22	10	.688	38	34	23-2	0	278.1	272	95	17	5	55	77	2.68	136	.256	.296	101-8	.168	-2	102	32	3.3
1946	Chi N	14	12	.538	40	27	12-2	1	201.1	206	73	7	3	52	52	2.68	124	.265	.313	74-4	.243	1	107	13	1.9
1947	Chi N	6	9	.400	37	19	5-1	1	142	158	84	12	3	64	53	4.31	92	.286	.363	45-4	.111	-1	73	-8	-0.8
1950	Phi A	9	14	.391	41	23	4	0	170.2	192	121	16	8	87	33	5.85	78	.287	.376	59-3	.153	-3	97	-24	-2.9
1951	Phi A	1	2	.333	9	1	0	0	14.2	24	14	0	0	8	5	7.98	54	.381	.451	4-0	.250	-0	83	-6	-1.0
	Was A	0	0	—	3	2	0	0	9.1	17	14	0	1	10	3	9.64	42	.378	.500	4-0	.000	-1	130	-7	-0.4
	Year	1	2	.333	12	3	0	0	24	41	20	0	1	18	8	8.63	49	.380	.472	8-0	.125	-1	113	-12	-1.4
Total	8	79	70	.530	251	159	67-11	8	1257.2	1338	581	66	24	373	362	3.52	105	.274	.329	435-32	.163	-11	104	20	2.0
WYSONG, BIFF Harlan B 4.13.1905 Clarksville, OH D 8.8.1951 Xenia, OH BL/TL 6-3/195# d8.10																									
1930	Cin N	0	1	.000	1	1	0	0	2.1	6	5	0	0	3	1	19.29	25	.545	.643	0-0	—	0	0	-4	-0.5
1931	Cin N	0	2	.000	12	2	0	0	21.2	25	22	2	0	23	5	7.89	47	.298	.449	4-0	.250	0	115	-10	-0.8
1932	Cin N	1	0	1.000	7	0	0	0	12.1	13	7	0	0	8	5	3.65	106	.277	.382	2-0	.000	-0		0	0.0
Total	3	1	3	.250	20	3	0	0	36.1	44	34	2	0	34	11	7.18	54	.310	.443	6-0	.167	-0	74	-14	-1.3
YAN, ESTEBAN Esteban Luis B 6.22.1975 Campina, D.R. BR/TR 6-4/230# d5.20																									
1996	Bal A	0	0	—	4	0	0	0-0	9.1	13	7	3	0	3-1	7	5.79	85	.333	.381	0-0	—	0		-1	-0.1
1997	Bal A	0	1	.000	3	2	0	0-0	9.2	20	18	3	2	7-0	4	15.83	28	.417	.500	0-0	—	0	83	-13	-1.0
1998	TB A	5	4	.556	64	0	0	1-4	88.2	78	41	11	5	41-2	77	3.86	124	.236	.326	0-0	—	0		9	0.8
1999	TB A	3	4	.429	50	1	0	0-3	61	77	41	8	9	32-4	46	5.90	84	.326	.421	0-0	—	0	131	-4	-0.4

Year	Tm Lg	W	L	Pct	G	GS	CG-Sho	SV-BS	IP	H	R	HR	HB	BB-IB	SO	ERA	AERA	OAV	OOB	AB-SH	AVG	PB	Sup	APR	PW
2000	TB A	7	8	.467	43	20	0	0-2	137.2	158	98	26	11	42-0	111	6.21	80	.285	.344	1-1	1.000	1	110	-17	-1.4
2001	TB A	4	6	.400	54	0	0	22-9	62.1	64	34	7	5	11-1	64	3.90	115	.262	.307	0-0	—	0		3	0.5
2002	TB A	7	8	.467	55	0	0	19-8	69	70	35	10	3	29-1	53	4.30	104	.259	.337	0-0	—	0		2	0.3
2003	Tex A	0	1	.000	15	0	0	0-0	23.1	31	19	5	2	7-1	25	6.94	72	.307	.364	0-0	—	0		-5	-0.2
	StL N	2	0	1.000	39	0	0	1-0	43.1	53	29	8	5	16-4	28	6.02	68	.308	.376	1-0	1.000	1		-9	-0.4
Total 8		28	32	.467	327	23	0	43-26	504.1	564	322	81	42	188-14	415	5.41	87	.283	.354	2-1	1.000	2	113	-35	-1.9
YARNALL, ED Harvey Edward B 12.4.1975 Lima, PA BL/TL 6-3/234# d7.15																									
1999	NY A	1	0	1.000	5	2	0	0-0	17	17	8	1	0	10-0	13	3.71	128	.254	.351	0-0	—	0	167	2	0.1
2000	NY A	0	0	—	2	1	0	0-0	3	5	5	1	1	3-0	1	15.00	32	.417	.563	0-0	—	0	252	-3	-0.1
Total 2		1	0	1.000	7	3	0	0-0	20	22	13	2	1	13-0	14	5.40	88	.278	.387	0-0	—	0	196	-1	0.0
YARNALL, RUSTY Waldo Ward B 10.22.1902 Chicago, IL D 10.9.1985 Lowell, MA BR/TR 6/175# d6.30																									
1926	Phi N	0	1	.000	1	0	0	0	1	3	2	0	0	1	0	18.00	23	.500	.571	1-0	.000	-0		-1	-0.2
YARRISON, RUBE Byron Wardsworth B 3.9.1896 Montgomery, PA D 4.22.1977 Williamsport, PA BR/TR 5-11/165# d4.13																									
1922	Phi A	1	2	.333	18	1	0	0	33.2	50	32	4	2	12	10	8.29	51	.362	.421	6-0	.167	-0	40	-12	-0.9
1924	Bro N	0	2	.000	3	2	0	0	11	12	10	0	1	3	2	6.55	57	.267	.327	2-0	.000	-0	79	-4	-0.6
Total 2		1	4	.200	21	3	0	0	44.2	62	42	4	3	15	12	7.86	53	.339	.398	8-0	.125	-0	62	-16	-1.5
YDE, EMIL Emil Ogden B 1.28.1900 Great Lakes, IL D 12.4.1968 Leesburg, FL BB/TL 5-11/165# d4.21																									
1924	Pit N	16	3	**.842**	33	22	14-**4**	0	194	171	70	3	6	62	53	2.83	136	.244	.311	88-4	.239	2*	114	22	2.2
1925	†Pit N	17	9	.654	33	28	13	0	207	254	125	11	2	75	41	4.13	108	.309	.369	89-2	.191	-2*	109	4	0.2
1926	Pit N	8	7	.533	37	22	12-1	0	187.1	181	97	3	2	81	34	3.65	108	.260	.339	74-2	.230	3*	110	4	0.5
1927	†Pit N	1	3	.250	9	2	0	0	29.2	45	35	1	2	15	9	9.71	42	.375	.453	18-0	.167	-0*	73	-17	-1.8
1929	Det A	7	3	.700	29	6	4-1	0	86.2	100	60	8	0	63	23	5.30	81	.296	.406	48-1	.333	2*	183	-9	-0.5
Total 5		49	25	.662	141	80	43-6	0	704.2	751	387	26	12	296	160	4.02	102	.281	.355	317-9	.233	5	116	4	0.6
YEAGER, JOE Joseph F. "Little Joe" B 8.28.1875 Philadelphia, PA D 7.2.1937 Detroit, MI BR/TR 5-10/160# d4.22 ▲																									
1898	Bro N	12	22	.353	36	33	32	0	291.1	333	177	4	6	80	70	3.65	98	.285	.334	134-3	.172	-3*	84	-6	-0.7
1899	Bro N	2	2	.500	10	4	2-1	1	47.2	56	29	1	2	16	6	4.72	83	.292	.352	47-2	.191	1*	142	-2	-0.1
1900	Bro N	1	1	.500	2	2	2	0	17	21	13	1	0	5	2	6.88	56	.304	.351	9-0	.333	0*	90	-4	-0.3
1901	Det A	12	11	.522	26	25	22-2	1	199.2	209	105	4	8	46	38	2.61	147	.266	.313	125-2	.296	5*	85	22	2.9
1902	Det A	6	12	.333	19	15	14	0	140	171	90	5	5	41	28	4.82	76	.301	.353	161-1	.242	3*	95	-13	-1.0
1903	Det A	0	1	.000	1	1	1	0	9	15	7	0	0	0	1	4.00	73	.366	.366	402-9	.256	0*	74	-1	-0.1
Total 6		33	49	.402	94	80	73-3	2	704.2	805	421	15	21	188	145	3.74	99	.285	.334	878-17	.244	6	90	-4	0.7
YEARGIN, AL James Almond B 10.16.1901 Mauldin, SC D 5.8.1937 Greenville, SC BR/TR 5-11/170# d10.1																									
1922	Bos N	0	1	.000	1	1	1	0	7	5	3	1	0	2	1	1.29	311	.192	.250	3-0	.000	-0	0	1	0.1
1924	Bos N	1	11	.083	32	12	6	0	141.1	162	90	7	3	42	34	5.09	75	.293	.346	42-2	.143	-2	65	-19	-1.4
Total 2		1	12	.077	33	13	7	0	148.1	167	93	8	3	44	35	4.91	78	.288	.342	45-2	.133	-2	60	-18	-1.3
YELLEN, LARRY Lawrence Alan B 1.4.1943 Brooklyn, NY BR/TR 5-11/190# d9.26																									
1963	Hou N	0	0	—	1	1	0	0	5	7	4	0	0	1-0	3	3.60	88	.280	.296	2-0	.000	-0	137	-1	-0.1
1964	Hou N	0	0	—	13	1	0	0	21	27	19	4	0	10-1	9	6.86	50	.297	.363	3-0	.000	-0	129	-9	-0.5
Total 2		0	0	—	14	2	0	0	26	34	23	4	0	11-1	12	6.23	54	.293	.349	5-0	.000	-0	130	-10	-0.6
YELLOWHORSE, CHIEF Moses J. B 1.28.1898 Pawnee, OK D 4.10.1964 Pawnee, OK BR/TR 5-10/180# d4.15																									
1921	Pit N	5	3	.625	10	4	1	1	48.1	45	17	1	0	13	19	2.98	129	.254	.305	17-0	.000	-2	75	5	0.5
1922	Pit N	3	1	.750	28	4	2	0	77.2	92	48	0	2	20	24	4.52	90	.305	.352	19-2	.316	1	120	-4	-0.2
Total 2		8	4	.667	38	8	3	1	126	137	65	1	2	33	43	3.93	101	.286	.335	36-2	.167	-2	97	1	0.3
YERKES, CARROLL Charles Carroll "Lefty" B 6.13.1903 McSherrystown, PA D 12.20.1950 Oakland, CA BR/TL 5-11/180# d5.31																									
1927	Phi A	0	0	—	1	0	0	0	1	0	0	0	0	1	0	0.00	—	.000	.333	0-0	—	0		0	0.0
1928	Phi A	0	1	.000	2	1	1	0	8.2	7	2	0	0	2	1	2.08	193	.233	.281	3-0	.000	-0	0	2	0.2
1929	Phi A	1	0	1.000	19	2	0	1	37.1	47	20	0	1	13	11	4.58	92	.329	.389	10-0	.000	-2	179	0	-0.1
1932	Chi N	0	0	—	2	0	0	0	9	5	3	2	0	3	4	3.00	126	.167	.242	3-0	.333	0		1	0.1
1933	Chi N	0	0	—	1	0	0	0	2	2	1	0	0	1	0	4.50	73	.286	.375	0-0	—	0		0	0.0
Total 5		1	1	.500	25	3	1	1	58	61	26	2	1	20	16	3.88	106	.288	.352	16-0	.063	-2	124	3	0.2
YERKES, STAN Stanley Lewis "Yank" B 11.28.1874 Cheltenham, PA D 7.28.1940 Boston, MA BR/TR 5-10/165# d5.3																									
1901	Bal A	0	1	.000	1	1	1	0	8	12	9	0	0	2	4	6.75	57	.343	.378	3-0	.333	0	70	-2	-0.2
	StL N	3	1	.750	4	4	4	0	34	35	14	2	1	6	15	3.18	100	.265	.302	12-1	.083	-1	117	1	0.0
1902	StL N	12	21	.364	39	37	27-1	0	272.2	341	160	1	2	79	81	3.66	75	.306	.353	91-0	.132	-3	93	-28	-3.4
1903	StL N	0	1	.000	1	1	0	0	5	8	6	0	0	0	3	1.80	181	.333	.333	2-0	.000	-0	124	-1	-0.1
Total 3		15	24	.385	45	43	32-1	0	319.2	396	189	3	3	87	103	3.66	77	.303	.348	108-1	.130	-4	95	-30	-3.7
YETT, RICH Richard Martin B 10.6.1962 Pomona, CA BR/TR 6-2/187# d4.13																									
1985	Min A	0	0	—	1	1	0	0-0	0.1	1	1	0	0	2-0	0	27.00	16	.333	.600	0-0	—	0	144	-1	0.0
1986	Cle A	5	3	.625	39	3	1-1	1-3	78.2	84	48	10	1	37-4	50	5.15	81	.275	.351	0-0	—	0	146	-7	-0.7
1987	Cle A	3	9	.250	37	11	2	1-2	97.2	96	63	21	3	49-3	59	5.25	86	.257	.346	0-0	—	0	99	-7	-0.8
1988	Cle A	9	6	.600	23	22	0	0-0	134.1	146	72	11	1	55-1	71	4.62	89	.275	.344	0-0	—	0	93	-6	-0.7
1989	Cle A	5	6	.455	32	12	1	0-0	99	111	56	10	2	47-1	47	5.00	79	.283	.360	0-0	—	0	110	-9	-1.0
1990	Min A	0	0	—	4	0	0	0-0	4.1	6	2	1	0	1-1	2	2.08	201	.353	.389	0-0	—	0		1	0.0
Total 6		22	24	.478	136	49	4-1	2-5	414.1	444	242	53	7	191-10	229	4.95	85	.274	.351	0-0	—	0	102	-29	-3.2
YINGLING, EARL Earl Hershey "Chink" B 10.29.1888 Chillicothe, OH D 10.2.1962 Columbus, OH BL/TL 5-11.5/180# d4.12 Mil 1918																									
1911	Cle A	1	0	1.000	4	3	1	0	22.1	30	17	1	1	9	6	4.43	77	.326	.392	11-0	.273	0*	127	-3	-0.1
1912	Bro N	6	11	.353	25	16	12	0	163	186	90	10	1	56	51	3.59	93	.293	.351	64-1	.250	3	89	-5	-0.2
1913	Bro N	8	8	.500	26	13	8-2	0	146.2	158	56	2	2	10	40	2.58	128	.280	.295	60-2	.383	8*	97	10	2.0
1914	Cin N	9	13	.409	34	27	8-3	0	198	207	102	6	6	54	80	3.45	85	.274	.328	120-1	.192	1*	98	-9	-0.8
1918	Was A	1	2	.333	5	2	2	0	38	30	15	0	0	12	15	2.13	128	.238	.304	15-0	.467	3*	69	2	0.6
Total 5		25	34	.424	94	61	31-5	0	568	611	280	19	10	141	192	3.22	98	.281	.328	270-4	.267	16	96	-5	1.5
YINGLING, JOE Joseph Granville B 7.23.1866 Westminster, MD D 10.24.1946 Manchester, MD BR/TL 5-7.5/145# d5.28																									
1886	Was N	0	0	—	1	0	0	0	3	7	6	1		1	1	12.00	27	.412	.444	2	.000	-0		-3	-0.1
YOCHIM, LEN Leonard Joseph B 10.16.1928 New Orleans, LA BL/TL 6-2/200# d9.18 b-Ray																									
1951	Pit N	1	1	.500	2	2	0	0	8.2	10	9	0	1	11	5	8.31	51	.278	.458	3-1	.000	-0	94	-4	-0.6
1954	Pit N	0	1	.000	10	1	0	0	19.2	30	17	2	0	8	7	7.32	57	.361	.409	2-0	.500	0	0	-6	-0.2
Total 2		1	2	.333	12	3	0	0	28.1	40	26	2	1	19	12	7.62	55	.336	.426	5-1	.200	-0	63	-10	-0.8
YOCHIM, RAY Raymond Austin Aloysius B 7.19.1922 New Orleans, LA D 1.26.2002 New Orleans, LA BR/TR 6-1/170# d5.2 b-Len																									
1948	StL N	0	0	—	1	0	0	0	1	0	0	0	0	3	1	0.00	—	.000	.500	0-0	—	0		0	0.0
1949	StL N	0	0	—	3	0	0	0	2.1	3	4	1	0	4	3	15.43	27	.273	.467	0-0	—	0		-3	-0.1
Total 2		0	0	—	4	0	0	0	3.1	3	4	1	0	7	4	10.80	38	.214	.476	0-0	—	0		-3	-0.1
YORK, LEFTY James Edward B 11.1.1892 West Fork, AR D 4.9.1961 York, PA BL/TL 5-10/185# d9.12																									
1919	Phi A	0	2	.000	2	2	0	0	4.1	13	13	0	0	5	2	24.92	14	.500	.581	1-0	.000	-0	114	-9	-1.3
1921	Chi N	5	9	.357	40	11	4-1	1	139	170	82	5	5	63	57	4.73	81	.308	.384	39-3	.128	-2	67	-13	-1.5
Total 2		5	11	.313	42	13	4-1	1	143.1	183	95	5	5	68	59	5.34	71	.317	.393	40-3	.125	-2	73	-22	-2.8
YORK, JIM James Harlan B 8.27.1947 Maywood, CA BR/TR 6-3/200# d9.21																									
1970	KC A	1	1	.500	4	0	0	0-1	8	5	3	2	0	2-0	6	3.38	111	.179	.226	2-0	.000	-0		1	0.1
1971	KC A	5	5	.500	53	0	0	3-2	93.1	70	32	7	3	44-7	103	2.89	119	.203	.297	17-0	.118	1		6	0.8
1972	Hou N	0	1	.000	26	0	0	0-0	36	45	21	3	1	18-3	25	5.25	64	.321	.398	1-0	.000	-0		-7	-0.4
1973	Hou N	3	4	.429	41	0	0	6-3	53	65	26	4	1	20-5	22	4.42	82	.305	.364	5-1	.000	-0		-3	-0.5

Year	Tm Lg	W	L	Pct	G	GS	CG-Sho	SV-BS	IP	H	R	HR	HB	BB-IB	SO	ERA	AERA	OAV	OOB	AB-SH	AVG	PB	Sup	APR	PW
1974	Hou N	2	2	.500	28	0	0	1-0	38.1	48	20	1	1	19-6	15	3.29	106	.298	.374	4-0	.000	-1		-1	-0.2
1975	Hou N	4	4	.500	19	4	0	0-0	46.2	43	22	1	5	25-3	17	3.86	88	.251	.358	11-0	.091	-0	156	-3	-0.5
1976	NY A	1	0	1.000	3	0	0	0-0	9.2	14	7	1	1	4-0	6	5.59	61	.333	.404	0-0	—	0		-3	-0.2
Total	7	16	17	.485	174	4	0	10-6	285	290	131	19	12	132-24	194	3.79	92	.264	.346	40-1	.075	-1	156	-10	-0.9
YORK, MIKE Michael David B 9.6.1964 Oak Park, IL BR/TR 6-1/187# d8.17																									
1990	Pit N	1	1	.500	4	1	0	0-0	12.2	13	5	0	1	5-0	4	2.84	127	.277	.352	3-0	.333	0	175	1	0.2
1991	Cle A	1	4	.200	14	4	0	0-0	34.2	45	29	2	2	19-3	19	6.75	62	.333	.412	0-0	—	0	148	-10	-1.2
Total	2	2	5	.286	18	5	0	0-0	47.1	58	34	2	3	24-3	23	5.70	70	.319	.397	3-0	.333	0	155	-9	-1.0
YOSHII, MASATO Masato B 4.20.1965 Osaka, Japan BR/TR 6-2/210# d4.5																									
1998	NY N	6	8	.429	29	29	1	0-0	171.2	166	79	22	6	53-5	117	3.93	105	.255	.315	48-8	.063	-2	85	4	0.0
1999	†NY N	12	8	.600	31	29	1	0-0	174	168	86	25	6	58-3	105	4.40	100	.260	.324	55-6	.164	-1	111	0	-0.2
2000	Col N	6	15	.286	29	29	0	0-0	167.1	201	112	32	2	53-6	88	5.86	99	.306	.357	50-12	.180	-1	82	1	0.0
2001	Mon N	4	7	.364	42	11	0	0-0	113	127	65	18	5	26-2	63	4.78	93	.279	.323	16-2	.125	-0	98	-4	-0.4
2002	Mon N	4	9	.308	31	20	1	0-0	131.1	143	66	15	4	32-2	74	4.11	109	.281	.326	35-5	.057	-2	98	5	0.3
Total	5	32	47	.405	162	118	3	0-0	757.1	805	408	112	23	222-18	447	4.62	101	.276	.329	204-33	.123	-6	94	6	-0.3
YOST, GUS August 6-5/?# d6.12																									
1893	Chi N	0	1	.000	1	1	0	0	2.2	3	4	0	0	8	1	13.50	34	.273	.579	1	.000	-0	91	-2	-0.3
YOUMANS, FLOYD Floyd Everett B 5.11.1964 Tampa, FL BR/TR 6-1/190# d7.1																									
1985	Mon N	4	3	.571	14	12	0	0-0	77	57	27	3	1	49-1	54	2.45	138	.206	.325	19-3	.053	-0	98	7	0.4
1986	Mon N	13	12	.520	33	32	6-2	0-0	219	145	93	14	4	118-4	202	3.53	105	.188	.297	75-2	.160	2	97	5	0.6
1987	Mon N	9	8	.529	23	23	3-3	0-0	116.1	112	63	13	1	47-2	94	4.64	91	.251	.321	40-1	.150	1	83	-3	-0.4
1988	Mon N	3	6	.333	14	13	1-1	0-0	84	64	35	8	2	41-1	54	3.21	112	.213	.307	26-0	.154	-0	89	3	0.3
1989	Phi N	1	5	.167	10	10	0	0-0	42.2	50	31	7	2	25-3	20	5.70	62	.299	.391	13-1	.077	-1	87	-10	-1.4
Total	5	30	34	.469	94	90	10-6	0-0	539	428	249	45	10	280-11	424	3.74	100	.218	.316	173-7	.139	1	92	2	-0.5
YOUNG, ANTHONY Anthony Wayne B 1.19.1966 Houston, TX BR/TR 6-2/210# d8.5																									
1991	NY N	2	5	.286	10	8	0	0-0	49.1	48	20	4	1	12-1	20	3.10	117	.257	.303	14-1	.143	0	74	3	0.3
1992	NY N	2	14	.125	52	13	1	15-5	121	134	66	8	1	31-5	64	4.17	84	.285	.328	27-2	.111	-1	96	-11	-1.8
1993	NY N	1	16	.059	39	10	1	3-2	100.1	103	62	8	1	42-9	62	3.77	107	.265	.336	14-2	.143	-0	45	-3	-0.5
1994	Chi N	4	6	.400	20	19	0	0-0	114.2	103	57	12	0	46-2	65	3.92	106	.246	.318	34-5	.176	0	105	2	0.2
1995	Chi N	3	4	.429	32	1	0	2-0	41.1	47	20	5	3	14-2	15	3.70	111	.288	.356	3-0	.667	1	110	1	0.3
1996	Hou N	3	3	.500	28	0	0	0-1	33.1	36	18	4	4	22-4	19	4.59	84	.279	.397	2-0	.000	-0		-2	-0.4
Total	6	15	48	.238	181	51	2	20-8	460	471	243	41	10	167-23	245	3.89	99	.268	.333	94-10	.160	-0	86	-10	-1.9
YOUNG, PETE Bryan Owen B 3.19.1968 Meadville, MS BR/TR 6/225# d6.5																									
1992	Mon N	0	0	—	13	0	0	0-0	20.1	18	9	0	1	9-2	11	3.98	87	.247	.329	0-0	—	0		-1	-0.1
1993	Mon N	1	0	1.000	4	0	0	0-0	5.1	4	2	1	0	0-0	3	3.38	124	.211	.211	1-0	.000	-0		1	0.1
Total	2	1	0	1.000	17	0	0	0-0	25.2	22	11	1	1	9-2	14	3.86	94	.239	.308	1-0	.000	-0		0	0.0
YOUNG, CHARLIE Charles "Cy" B 1.12.1893 Philadelphia, PA D 5.12.1952 Riverside, NJ BB/TR 5-10.5/155# d9.5																									
1915	Bal F	2	3	.400	9	5	1	0	35	39	32	0	4	21	13	5.91	49	.289	.400	9-1	.222	0	49	-12	-1.5
YOUNG, CLIFF Clifford Raphael B 8.2.1964 Willis, TX D 11.4.1993 Montgomery Co., TX BL/TL 6-4/200# d7.14																									
1990	Cal A	1	1	.500	17	0	0	0-2	30.2	40	14	2	1	7-1	19	3.52	109	.325	.356	0-0	—	0		1	0.1
1991	Cal A	1	0	1.000	11	0	0	0-0	12.2	12	6	3	0	3-1	6	4.26	96	.261	.306	0-0	—	0		0	0.0
1993	Cle A	3	3	.500	21	7	0	1-1	60.1	74	35	9	3	18-1	31	4.62	94	.298	.352	0-0	—	0	82	-2	-0.2
Total	3	5	4	.556	49	7	0	1-3	103.2	126	55	14	4	28-3	56	4.25	98	.302	.348	0-0	—	0	82	-1	-0.1
YOUNG, CURT Curtis Allen B 4.16.1960 Saginaw, MI BR/TL 6-1/180# d6.24																									
1983	Oak A	0	1	.000	8	2	0	0-0	9	17	17	1	1	5-0	5	16.00	24	.386	.460	0-0	—	0	153	-12	-1.2
1984	Oak A	9	4	.692	20	17	2-1	0-0	108.2	118	53	9	8	31-0	41	4.06	92	.274	.331	0-0	—	0	126	-3	-0.4
1985	Oak A	0	4	.000	19	7	0	0-0	46	57	38	15	1	22-0	19	7.24	53	.300	.374	0-0	—	0	115	-17	-1.3
1986	Oak A	13	9	.591	29	27	5-2	0-0	198	176	88	19	7	57-1	116	3.45	112	.236	.293	0-0	—	0	99	8	0.8
1987	Oak A	13	7	.650	31	31	6	0-0	203	194	102	38	3	44-0	124	4.08	102	.252	.293	1-0	.000	-0	122	2	0.2
1988	†Oak A	11	8	.579	26	26	1	0-0	156.1	162	77	23	4	50-3	69	4.14	91	.275	.333	0-0	—	0	104	-6	-0.7
1989	Oak A	5	9	.357	25	20	1	0-0	111	117	56	10	3	47-2	55	3.73	99	.264	.338	0-0	—	0	88	-2	-0.3
1990	†Oak A	9	6	.600	26	21	0	0-0	124.1	124	70	17	2	53-1	56	4.85	77	.266	.342	0-0	—	0*	120	-14	-1.4
1991	Oak A	4	2	.667	41	1	0	0-0	68.1	74	38	8	2	34-2	27	5.00	77	.278	.363	0-0	—	0	71	-8	-0.6
1992	KC A	1	2	.333	10	2	0	0-1	24.1	29	14	1	0	7-1	7	5.18	78	.293	.336	0-0	—	0	90	-2	-0.3
	NY A	3	0	1.000	13	5	0	0-1	43.1	51	21	1	2	10-1	13	3.32	118	.298	.341	0-0	—	0	135	1	0.1
	Year	4	2	.667	23	7	0	0-2	67.2	80	27	2	2	17-2	20	3.99	100	.296	.339	0-0	—	0	121	0	-0.2
1993	Oak A	1	1	.500	3	3	0	0-0	14.2	14	7	5	0	6-0	4	4.30	95	.241	.313	0-0	—	0	98	0	0.0
Total	11	69	53	.566	251	162	15-3	0-2	1107	1133	581	147	33	366-11	536	4.31	90	.265	.326	1-0	.000	-0	110	-53	-5.1
YOUNG, DANNY Daniel Bracy B 11.3.1971 Smyrna, TN BR/TL 6-4/210# d3.30																									
2000	Chi N	0	1	.000	4	0	0	0-0	3	5	7	1	0	6-0	0	21.00	22	.357	.550	0-0	—	0		-5	-0.9
YOUNG, CY Denton True B 3.29.1867 Gilmore, OH D 11.4.1955 Newcomerstown, OH BR/TR 6-2/210# d8.6 M1 HF1937																									
1890	Cle N	9	7	.563	17	16	16	0	147.2	145	87	6	8	30	39	3.47	103	.249	.295	65	.123	-6	78	2	-0.3
1891	Cle N	27	22	.551	55	46	43	2	423.2	431	244	4	10	140	147	2.85	122	.254	.314	174	.167	-3	104	28	2.3
1892	†Cle N	**36**	12	**.750**	53	49	48-**9**	0	453	363	158	8	11	118	168	**1.93**	**176**	.211	**.266**	196	.158	-8	108	**74**	**6.4**
1893	Cle N	34	16	.680	53	46	42-1	1	422.2	442	230	10	10	103	102	3.36	145	.261	**.307**	187	.235	-6	102	74	6.5
1894	Cle N	26	21	.553	52	47	44-2	1	408.2	488	265	19	5	106	108	3.94	139	.293	.337	186-0	.215	-8	92	65	5.0
1895	†Cle N	**35**	10	.778	47	40	36-**4**	0	369.2	363	177	10	8	75	121	3.26	153	.253	**.294**	140-2	.214	-4	84	**73**	6.9
1896	†Cle N	28	15	.651	51	46	42-**5**	**3**	414.1	477	214	7	11	62	**140**	3.24	140	.286	.316	180-2	.289	7*	96	56	**5.7**
1897	Cle N	21	19	.525	46	38	35-2	0	335.2	391	189	7	9	49	88	3.78	119	.289	.318	153-3	.222	-4*	89	27	2.3
1898	Cle N	25	13	.658	46	41	40-1	0	377.2	387	167	6	9	41	101	2.53	143	.263	.287	154-5	.253	5*	100	40	4.4
1899	StL N	26	16	.619	44	42	**40**-4	1	369.1	368	173	10	6	44	111	2.58	154	.260	**.285**	148-6	.216	-1	101	50	**5.1**
1900	StL N	19	19	.500	41	35	32-**4**	0	321.1	337	144	7	3	36	115	3.00	121	.269	.291	124-1	.177	-2	86	28	2.6
1901	Bos A	**33**	10	.767	43	41	38-**5**	0	371.1	324	112	6	7	37	**158**	**1.62**	**217**	**.232**	**.256**	153-3	.209	0*	110	**77**	**7.9**
1902	Bos A	**32**	11	.744	**45**	**43**	**41**-3	0	**384.2**	350	136	6	13	53	160	2.15	166	.243	.276	148-1	.230	2	107	**59**	**6.0**
1903	†Bos A	**28**	9	**.757**	40	35	**34-7**	**2**	**341.2**	294	115	6	9	37	176	2.08	146	.232	.259	137-5	.321	12*	136	**34**	**4.8**
1904	Bos A	26	16	.619	43	41	40-**10**	1	380	327	104	6	4	29	200	1.97	136	.233	**.251**	148-1	.223	2	94	33	3.8
1905	Bos A	18	19	.486	38	33	31-4	0	320.2	248	99	3	8	30	210	1.82	148	.215	**.241**	120-2	.150	-2	77	25	2.7
1906	Bos A	13	21	.382	39	34	28	2	287.2	288	137	3	8	25	140	3.19	86	.263	.285	104-2	.154	-2*	74	-14	-1.9
1907	Bos A	21	15	.583	43	37	33-6	2	343.1	286	101	3	7	51	147	1.99	129	.229	**.263**	125-1	.216	0*	86	25	2.4
1908	Bos A	21	11	.656	36	33	30-3	2	299	230	68	1	1	37	150	1.26	195	.213	.240	115-2	.226	1	110	36	4.1
1909	Cle A	19	15	.559	35	34	30-3	0	294.1	267	110	4	8	59	109	2.26	113	.250	.294	107-6	.196	-0	110	9	0.9
1910	Cle A	7	10	.412	21	20	14-1	0	163.1	149	62	0	4	27	58	2.53	102	.252	.289	55-3	.145	-0	74	2	0.2
1911	Cle A	3	4	.429	7	7	4	0	46.1	54	28	2	1	13	20	3.88	88	.298	.349	16-0	.063	-2	60	-3	-0.5
	Bos N	4	5	.444	11	11	8-2	0	80	83	47	4	3	15	35	3.71	103	.268	.308	25-5	.080	-2	66	0	-0.3
Total	22	511	316	.618	906	815	749-76	17	7356	7092	3167	138	163	1217	2803	2.63	138	.252	.287	2960-50	.210	-22	97	800	77.0
YOUNG, HARLEY Harlan Edward "Cy The Third" B 9.28.1883 Portland, IN D 3.26.1975 Jacksonville, FL BR/TR 6-2/?# d4.21																									
1908	Pit N	0	2	.000	8	3	0	0	48.1	40	21	0	5	10	17	2.23	103	.234	.296	12-1	.083	-1	61	-1	-0.1
	Bos N	0	1	.000	6	2	1	0	27.1	29	19	0	3	4	12	3.29	73	.269	.313	10-1	.200	0	117	-4	-0.2
	Year	0	3	.000	14	5	1	0	75.2	69	23	0	8	14	29	2.62	89	.247	.302	22-2	.136	-0	84	-6	-0.3
YOUNG, IRV Irving Melrose "Young Cy" or "Cy The Second" B 7.21.1877 Columbia Falls, ME D 1.14.1935 Brewer, ME BL/TL 5-10/170# d4.14																									
1905	Bos N	20	21	.488	43	**42**	**41**-7	0	**378**	337	146	6	8	71	156	2.90	107	.241	.282	136-1	.103	-8	59	14	0.9
1906	Bos N	16	25	.390	43	**41**	**37**-4	0	**358.1**	349	157	7	6	83	151	2.91	92	.263	.309	125-2	.096	-7	72	-7	-1.5

Year	Tm Lg	W	L	Pct	G	GS	CG-Sho	SV-BS	IP	H	R	HR	HB	BB-IB	SO	ERA	AERA	OAV	OOB	AB-SH	AVG	PB	Sup	APR	PW
1907	Bos N	10	23	.303	40	32	22-3	1	245.1	287	131	5	13	58	86	3.96	64	.306	.354	80-1	.162	-1	74	-33	-4.4
1908	Bos N	4	9	.308	16	11	7-1	0	85	94	49	2	2	19	32	2.86	84	.289	.332	32-1	.156	-1	101	-8	-1.4
	Pit N	4	3	.571	16	7	3-1	1	89.2	73	33	1	5	21	31	2.01	115	.225	.283	30-0	.200	1	100	1	0.2
	Year	8	12	.400	32	18	10-2	1	174.2	167	36	3	7	40	63	2.42	97	.257	.307	62-1	.177	0	101	-9	-1.2
1910	Chi A	4	8	.333	27	17	7-4	0	135.2	122	52	0	3	39	64	2.72	88	.247	.306	44-3	.114	-2	74	-2	-0.4
1911	Chi A	5	6	.455	24	11	3-1	2	92.2	99	61	2	0	25	40	4.37	74	.229	.271	28-1	.179	-0	85	-12	-1.3
Total	6	63	95	.399	209	161	120-21	4	1384.2	1361	629	23	37	316	560	3.11	88	.260	.307	475-9	.126	-18	73	-47	-7.9
YOUNG, J. B. J. B. B Mt.Carmel, PA d6.10																									
1892	StL N	0	0	—	1	0	0	0	2	9	13	0	0	2	1	22.50	14	.600	.647	1	.000	-0		-6	-0.3
YOUNG, JASON Jason Kariya B 9.28.1979 Oakland, CA BR/TR 6-5/210# d5.12																									
2003	Col N	0	2	.000	8	3	0	0-0	21.1	34	22	8	1	9-0	18	8.44	58	.354	.411	7-0	.286	1	102	-7	-0.5
YOUNG, KIP Kip Lane B 10.29.1954 Georgetown, OH BR/TR 5-11/175# d7.21																									
1978	Det A	6	7	.462	14	13	7	0-0	105.2	94	34	9	2	30-1	49	2.81	138	.246	.303	0-0	—	0	93	13	1.5
1979	Det A	2	2	.500	13	7	0	0-0	43.2	60	32	11	1	11-0	22	6.39	68	.323	.362	0-0	—	0	128	-9	-0.7
Total	2	8	9	.471	27	20	7	0-0	149.1	154	66	20	3	41-1	71	3.86	104	.271	.322	0-0	—	0	107	4	0.8
YOUNG, MATT Matthew John B 8.9.1958 Pasadena, CA BL/TL 6-3/205# d4.6																									
1983	Sea A★	11	15	.423	33	32	5-2	0-0	203.2	178	86	17	7	79-2	130	3.27	131	.236	.312	0-0	—	0	67	20	2.5
1984	Sea A	6	8	.429	22	22	1	0-0	113.1	141	81	11	1	57-3	73	5.72	70	.307	.380	0-0	—	0	125	-22	-2.3
1985	Sea A	12	19	.387	37	35	5-2	1-0	218.1	242	135	23	7	76-3	136	4.91	86	.282	.344	0-0	—	0	96	-18	-2.3
1986	Sea A	8	6	.571	65	5	1	13-12	103.2	108	50	9	8	46-2	82	3.82	111	.272	.357	0-0	—	0	107	5	0.6
1987	LA N	5	8	.385	47	0	0	11-4	54.1	62	30	3	0	17-5	42	4.47	89	.288	.339	3-0	.000	-0		-3	-0.7
1989	†Oak A	1	4	.200	26	4	0	0-1	37.1	42	31	2	0	31-2	27	6.75	55	.286	.408	0-0	—	0	61	-13	-1.5
1990	Sea A	8	18	.308	34	33	7-1	0-0	225.1	198	106	15	6	107-7	176	3.51	113	.237	.325	0-0	—	0	85	9	0.9
1991	Bos A	3	7	.300	19	16	0	0-0	88.2	92	55	4	2	53-2	69	5.18	83	.266	.365	0-0	—	0	84	-8	-0.8
1992	Bos A	0	4	.000	28	8	1	0-0	70.2	69	42	7	3	42-2	57	4.58	92	.257	.360	0-0	—	0	73	-3	-0.2
1993	Cle A	1	6	.143	22	8	0	0-0	74.1	75	45	8	3	57-0	65	5.21	83	.266	.394	0-0	—	0	82	-6	-0.5
Total	10	55	95	.367	333	163	20-5	25-17	1189.2	1207	661	99	37	565-28	857	4.40	94	.265	.348	3-0	.000	-0	88	-39	-4.3
YOUNG, TIM Timothy R. B 10.15.1973 Gulfport, MS BL/TL 5-9/170# d9.5																									
1998	Mon N	0	0	—	10	0	0	0-0	6	6	4	0	0	4-0	7	6.00	70	.250	.357	0-0	—	0		-1	0.0
2000	Bos A	0	0	—	8	0	0	0-0	7	7	5	3	1	2-0	6	6.43	79	.269	.345	0-0	—	0		-1	0.0
Total	2	0	0	—	18	0	0	0-0	13	13	9	3	1	6-0	13	6.23	75	.260	.351	0-0	—	0		-2	0.0
YOUNGBLOOD, CHIEF Albert Clyde B 6.13.1900 Hillsboro, TX D 7.6.1968 Amarillo, TX BL/TR 6-3/202# d7.16																									
1922	Was A	0	0	—	2	0	0	0	4.1	9	9	0	2	7	0	14.54	27	.429	.600	2-0	.000	-0		-6	-0.3
YOUNT, DUCKY Herbert Macon "Hub" B 12.7.1885 Iredell Co., NC D 5.9.1970 Winston-Salem, NC BR/TR 6-2/178# d5.20																									
1914	Bal F	1	1	.500	13	1	1	0	41.1	44	28	2	2	19	19	4.14	73	.280	.365	12-1	.083	-1*	0	-6	-0.4
YOUNT, LARRY Lawrence King B 2.15.1950 Houston, TX BR/TR 6-2/185# d9.15 b-Robin																									
1971	Hou N	0	0	—	1	0	0	0-0	0	0	0	0	0	0-0	0	—	—	—	—	0-0	—	0		0	0.0
YOWELL, CARL Carl Columbus "Sundown" B 12.20.1902 Madison, VA D 7.27.1985 Jacksonville, TX BL/TL 6-4/180# d9.5																									
1924	Cle A	1	1	.500	4	2	2	0	27	37	21	1	0	13	8	6.67	64	.343	.413	11-0	.182	-1	148	-6	-0.4
1925	Cle A	2	3	.400	12	4	1	0	36.1	40	21	1	1	17	12	4.46	99	.310	.395	8-1	.125	-1	57	0	-0.1
Total	2	3	4	.429	16	6	3	0	63.1	77	42	2	1	30	20	5.40	81	.325	.403	19-1	.158	-1	87	-6	-0.5
YUHAS, EDDIE John Edward B 8.5.1924 Youngstown, OH D 7.6.1986 Winston-Salem, NC BR/TR 6-1/180# d4.17																									
1952	StL N	12	2	.857	54	2	0	6	99.1	90	35	5	2	35	39	2.72	137	.243	.312	21-2	.190	1	72	11	1.6
1953	StL N	0	0	—	2	0	0	0	1	3	2	0	0	0	0	18.00	24	.500	.500	0-0	—	0		-1	-0.1
Total	2	12	2	.857	56	2	0	6	100.1	93	37	5	2	35	39	2.87	130	.247	.315	21-2	.190	1	72	10	1.5
ZABALA, ADRIAN Adrian (Rodriguez) B 8.26.1916 San Antonio De Los Banos, Cuba D 1.4.2002 Jacksonville, FL BL/TL 5-11/165# d8.11																									
1945	NY N	2	4	.333	11	5	1	0	43.1	46	25	2	0	14	4.78		82	.284	.363	13-0	.231	1	69	-4	-0.4
1949	NY N	2	3	.400	15	4	2-1	1	41	44	28	5	1	10	13	5.27	76	.278	.325	13-0	.077	-1	122	-6	-0.8
Total	2	4	7	.364	26	9	3-1	1	84.1	90	53	7	1	30	27	5.02	79	.281	.345	26-0	.154	-0	92	-10	-1.2
ZABEL, ZIP George Washington B 2.18.1891 Wetmore, KS D 5.31.1970 Beloit, WI BR/TR 6-1.5/185# d10.5																									
1913	Chi N	1	0	1.000	1	1	0	0	5	3	0	0	0	1	0	0.00	—	.167	.211	2-0	.000	0	118	2	0.4
1914	Chi N	4	4	.500	29	7	2	3	128	104	45	5	2	45	50	2.18	128	.235	.309	38-2	.184	-1	114	9	0.5
1915	Chi N	7	10	.412	36	17	8-3	0	163	124	80	3	4	84	60	3.20	87	.218	.323	54-2	.074	-4*	105	-10	-1.2
Total	3	12	14	.462	66	25	10-3	3	296	231	125	8	6	130	110	2.71	103	.224	.315	94-4	.117	-4	108	1	-0.3
ZACHARY, CHINK Albert Myron (b: Albert Myron Zarski) B 10.19.1917 Brooklyn, NY BR/TR 5-11/182# d4.30																									
1944	Bro N	0	2	.000	4	2	0	0	10.1	10	11	2	1	7	3	9.58	37	.238	.360	3-0	.000	-0	94	-6	-1.0
ZACHARY, TOM Jonathan Thompson Walton (a.k.a. Zach Walton In 1918) B 5.7.1896 Graham, NC D 1.24.1969 Burlington, NC BL/TL 6-1/187# d7.11 Mil 1918-19																									
1918	Phi A	2	0	1.000	2	2	0	0	8	9	5	0	0	7	1	5.63	52	.321	.457	4-0	.500	1	231	-2	-0.3
1919	Was A	1	5	.167	17	7	0	0	61.2	68	29	0	1	20	9	2.92	110	.292	.350	15-0	.333	2	77	1	0.3
1920	Was A	15	16	.484	44	31	19-3	2	262.2	289	141	7	4	78	53	3.77	99	.285	.339	111-0	.261	6*	106	-2	0.3
1921	Was A	18	16	.529	39	30	17-2	1	250	314	130	10	6	59	53	3.96	104	.319	.361	90-3	.256	3	96	6	0.9
1922	Was A	15	10	.600	32	25	13-1	1	184.2	190	74	6	3	43	37	3.12	124	.275	.321	71-2	.296	5	106	18	2.8
1923	Was A	10	16	.385	35	29	10	0	204.1	270	117	9	4	63	40	4.49	84	.321	.372	78-4	.192	-0	95	-14	-1.6
1924	†Was A	15	9	.625	33	27	13-1	2	202.2	198	74	5	3	53	45	2.75	147	.264	.315	72-4	.306	4	104	30	3.7
1925	†Was A	12	15	.444	38	**33**	11-1	2	217.2	247	112	10	2	74	58	3.85	110	.296	.355	69-7	.174	-2	84	9	0.8
1926	StL A	14	15	.483	34	31	18-3	0	247.1	264	126	14	6	97	53	3.60	119	.288	.359	86-2	.267	4	81	14	2.1
1927	StL A	4	6	.400	13	12	6	0	78.1	110	48	4	0	27	13	4.37	100	.345	.396	28-2	.107	-2	94	-1	-0.3
	Was A	4	7	.364	15	14	5-1	0	102.2	116	54	2	2	30	13	3.94	103	.290	.343	36-2	.139	-2	95	1	-0.2
	Year	8	13	.381	28	26	11-1	0	181	226	59	6	2	57	26	4.13	102	.314	.366	64-4	.125	-4	95	0	-0.5
1928	Was A	6	9	.400	20	14	5-1	0	102.2	130	72	5	1	40	19	5.44	74	.322	.384	33-5	.303	1	92	-16	-1.8
	†NY A	3	3	.500	7	6	3	1	45.2	54	26	1	0	15	7	3.94	95	.320	.375	15-1	.133	-0	109	-2	-0.2
	Year	9	12	.429	27	20	8-1	1	148.1	184	31	6	1	55	26	4.98	79	.321	.382	48-6	.250	1	97	-18	-2.0
1929	NY A	12	0	1.000	26	11	7-2	2	119.2	131	43	5	2	30	35	2.48	155	.277	.323	42-5	.238	1	135	19	1.7
1930	NY A	1	1	.500	3	3	0	0	16.2	18	16	0	0	9	1	6.48	66	.269	.355	8-0	.250	1	126	-5	-0.4
	Bos N	11	5	.688	24	22	10-1	0	151.1	192	90	9	0	50	57	4.58	108	.317	.369	54-4	.241	2*	110	5	0.5
1931	Bos N	11	15	.423	33	28	16-3	2	229	243	87	8	1	53	64	3.10	122	.272	.314	84-0	.167	-1	82	19	2.0
1932	Bos N	12	11	.522	32	24	12-1	0	212	231	83	5	2	55	67	3.10	121	.280	.326	77-0	.273	5*	84	17	2.2
1933	Bos N	7	9	.438	26	20	6-2	2	125	134	64	1	0	35	22	3.53	87	.276	.325	42-3	.119	-2*	94	-11	-1.5
1934	Bos N	1	2	.333	5	4	2-1	0	24	27	9	1	0	8	4	3.38	113	.278	.333	8-0	.000	-1	34	2	0.1
	Bro N	5	6	.455	22	12	4	2	101.2	122	53	5	2	21	28	4.43	88	.301	.339	38-0	.184	1*	101	-4	-0.3
	Year	6	8	.429	27	16	6-1	2	125.2	149	58	6	2	29	32	4.23	92	.297	.338	46-0	.152	-0	85	-2	-0.2
1935	Bro N	7	12	.368	25	21	9-1	4	158	193	76	10	2	35	33	3.59	111	.297	.335	52-2	.135	-1	82	7	0.6
1936	Bro N	0	0	—	1	0	0	0	0.1	2	2	0	0	1	0	54.00	8	1.000	1.000	0-0	—	0		-2	-0.1
	Phi N	0	3	.000	7	2	0	1	20.1	28	20	2	0	11	8	7.97	57	.329	.406	9-0	.333	1*	112	-6	-0.7
	Year	0	3	.000	8	2	0	1	20.2	30	26	2	0	12	8	8.71	52	.345	.424	9-0	.333	1	112	-7	-0.8
Total	19	186	191	.493	533	408	186-24	22	3126.1	3580	1551	119	41	914	720	3.73	106	.294	.345	1122-46	.226	25	95	83	10.6
ZACHARY, CHRIS William Christopher B 2.19.1944 Knoxville, TN D 4.19.2003 Knoxville, TN BL/TR 6-2/200# d4.11																									
1963	Hou N	2	2	.500	22	7	0	0	57	62	38	5	3	22-0	42	4.89	64	.272	.340	13-1	.000	-1	125	-12	-0.9
1964	Hou N	0	1	.000	1	1	0	0	4	6	5	1	0	1-0	2	9.00	38	.333	.368	1-0	.000	-0	77	-3	-0.4
1965	Hou N	0	2	.000	4	2	0	0	10.2	12	6	0	0	6-1	4	4.22	80	.273	.360	2-0	.000	-0	13	-1	-0.2
1966	Hou N	3	5	.375	10	8	0	0	55	44	22	1	1	32-2	37	3.44	100	.221	.330	18-0	.222	1	90	1	0.2

Year	Tm Lg	W	L	Pct	G	GS	CG-Sho	SV-BS	IP	H	R	HR	HB	BB-IB	SO	ERA	AERA	OAV	OOB	AB-SH	AVG	PB	Sup	APR	PW
1967	Hou N	1	6	.143	9	7	0	0	36.1	42	27	5	2	12-1	18	5.70	58	.290	.352	10-0	.100	-0*	49	-10	-1.7
1969	KC A	0	1	.000	8	2	0	0-0	18.1	27	17	4	0	7-0	6	7.85	47	.346	.395	2-0	.500	0	60	-8	-0.4
1971	StL N	3	10	.231	23	12	1-1	0-1	89.2	114	58	3	4	26-7	48	5.32	68	.316	.364	33-0	.242	1*	117	-16	-2.1
1972	†Det A	1	1	.500	25	1	0	1-1	38.1	27	6	2	1	15-2	21	1.41	224	.201	.283	2-0	.500	1	56	8	0.5
1973	Pit N	0	1	.000	6	0	0	1-0	12	10	4	1	0	1-0	6	3.00	118	.222	.234	2-0	.000	-0		1	0.1
Total	9	10	29	.256	108	40	1-1	2-2	321.1	344	183	22	11	122-13	184	4.57	74	.275	.341	83-1	.181	1	91	-40	-4.9

ZACHRY, PAT Patrick Paul B 4.24.1952 Richmond, TX BR/TR 6-5/180# d4.11

Year	Tm Lg	W	L	Pct	G	GS	CG-Sho	SV-BS	IP	H	R	HR	HB	BB-IB	SO	ERA	AERA	OAV	OOB	AB-SH	AVG	PB	Sup	APR	PW
1976	†Cin N	14	7	.667	38	28	6-1	0-0	204	170	70	8	2	83-4	143	2.74	128	.228	.305	62-12	.113	-2	123	17	1.4
1977	Cin N	3	7	.300	12	12	3	0-0	75	78	45	7	1	29-1	36	5.04	78	.273	.338	22-4	.136	-1	87	-9	-1.1
	NY N	7	6	.538	19	19	2-1	0-0	119.2	129	59	14	3	48-4	63	3.76	100	.278	.347	42-1	.143	-1	84	-2	-0.4
	Year	10	13	.435	31	31	5-1	0-0	194.2	207	63	21	4	77-5	99	4.25	90	.276	.344	64-5	.141	-2	85	-11	-1.5
1978	NY N☆	10	6	.625	21	21	5-2	0-0	138	120	57	9	1	60-4	78	3.33	105	.236	.316	43-5	.070	-2	96	2	0.1
1979	NY N	5	1	.833	7	7	1	0-0	42.2	44	19	3	2	21-2	17	3.59	102	.267	.356	16-0	.125	-1	125	0	0.0
1980	NY N	6	10	.375	28	26	7-3	0-0	164.2	145	65	16	5	58-5	88	3.01	118	.240	.310	46-5	.043	-4	91	9	0.3
1981	NY N	7	14	.333	24	24	3	0-0	139	151	78	13	4	56-1	76	4.14	84	.282	.349	38-4	.158	0	80	-11	-1.5
1982	NY N	6	9	.400	36	16	2	1-2	137.2	149	69	10	0	57-5	69	4.05	90	.279	.346	38-2	.079	-2	99	-5	-0.8
1983	†LA N	6	1	.857	40	1	0	0-0	61.1	63	22	4	1	21-6	36	2.49	144	.278	.337	4-0	.500	1	49	7	0.8
1984	LA N	5	6	.455	58	0	0	2-2	82.2	84	38	3	2	51-13	55	3.81	93	.267	.367	6-0	.333	1		-1	-0.1
1985	Phi N	0	0	—	10	0	0	0-0	12.2	14	7	1	0	11-1	8	4.26	87	.280	.410	1-0	.000	-0		-1	0.0
Total	10	69	67	.507	293	154	29-7	3-4	1177.1	1147	529	88	21	495-46	669	3.52	102	.259	.333	318-33	.113	-11	96	6	-1.3

ZACKERT, GEORGE George Carl "Zeke" B 12.24.1884 Horton, VT D 2.18.1977 Burlington, IA BL/TL 6/177# d9.22

Year	Tm Lg	W	L	Pct	G	GS	CG-Sho	SV-BS	IP	H	R	HR	HB	BB-IB	SO	ERA	AERA	OAV	OOB	AB-SH	AVG	PB	Sup	APR	PW
1911	StL N	0	2	.000	4	1	0	0	7.1	17	13	0	0	6	6	11.05	31	.486	.561	1-0	.000	-0	89	-7	-1.2
1912	StL N	0	0	—	1	0	0	0	1	2	2	0	1	1	0	18.00	19	.667	.800	0-0	—	0*		-1	-0.1
Total	2	0	2	.000	5	1	0	0	8.1	19	15	0	1	7	6	11.88	28	.500	.587	1-0	.000	-0	89	-8	-1.3

ZAHN, GEOFF Geoffrey Clayton B 12.19.1945 Baltimore, MD BL/TL 6-1/180# d9.2

Year	Tm Lg	W	L	Pct	G	GS	CG-Sho	SV-BS	IP	H	R	HR	HB	BB-IB	SO	ERA	AERA	OAV	OOB	AB-SH	AVG	PB	Sup	APR	PW
1973	LA N	1	0	1.000	6	1	0	0-0	13.1	5	2	2	0	2-0	9	1.35	255	.116	.156	2-0	.000	-0	77	3	0.2
1974	LA N	3	5	.375	21	10	1	0-0	79.2	78	28	3	2	16-1	33	2.03	168	.254	.295	23-3	.174	-0	97	10	0.9
1975	LA N	0	1	.000	2	0	0	0-0	3	2	3	0	0	5-1	1	9.00	38	.222	.500	0-0	—	0		-2	-0.3
	Chi N	2	7	.222	16	10	0	1-0	62.2	67	37	2	0	26-3	21	4.45	87	.282	.348	15-7	.133	-1	71	-5	-0.6
	Year	2	8	.200	18	10	0	1-0	65.2	69	40	2	0	31-4	22	4.66	82	.279	.356	15-7	.133	-1	71	-6	-0.9
1976	Chi N	0	1	.000	3	2	0	0-0	8.1	16	10	0	1	2-0	4	10.80	36	.410	.452	3-0	.000	-0	160	-5	-0.6
1977	Min A	12	14	.462	34	32	7-1	0-0	198	234	116	20	5	66-4	88	4.68	85	.299	.355	0-0	—	0	108	-16	-1.7
1978	Min A	14	14	.500	35	35	12-1	0-0	252.1	260	101	18	4	81-2	106	3.03	126	.274	.331	0-0	—	0	94	20	2.1
1979	Min A	13	7	.650	26	24	4	0-0	169	181	74	13	0	41-1	58	3.57	123	.279	.319	0-0	—	0	101	14	1.6
1980	Min A	14	18	.438	38	35	13-5	0-0	232.2	273	138	17	2	66-3	96	4.41	99	.302	.347	0-0	—	0	92	-4	-0.5
1981	Cal A	10	11	.476	25	25	9	0-0	161.1	181	93	18	0	43-2	52	4.41	83	.285	.329	0-0	—	0	137	-15	-1.8
1982	†Cal A	18	8	.692	34	34	12-4	0-0	229.1	225	100	18	4	65-5	81	3.73	109	.259	.313	0-0	—	0	125	10	1.0
1983	Cal A	9	11	.450	29	28	11-3	0-0	203	212	90	22	0	51-2	81	3.33	121	.269	.311	0-0	—	0	97	13	1.1
1984	Cal A	13	10	.565	28	27	9-5	0-0	199.1	200	78	11	1	48-4	61	3.12	128	.263	.306	0-0	—	0	104	18	2.0
1985	Cal A	2	2	.500	7	7	1-1	0-0	37	44	19	5	0	14-0	14	4.38	94	.299	.358	0-0	—	0	111	-1	0.0
Total	13	111	109	.505	304	270	79-20	1-0	1849	1978	889	149	19	526-28	705	3.74	107	.278	.327	43-10	.140	-2	105	40	3.4

ZAHNISER, PAUL Paul Vernon B 9.6.1896 Sac City, IA D 9.26.1964 Klamath Falls, OR BR/TR 5-10.5/170# d5.18

Year	Tm Lg	W	L	Pct	G	GS	CG-Sho	SV-BS	IP	H	R	HR	HB	BB-IB	SO	ERA	AERA	OAV	OOB	AB-SH	AVG	PB	Sup	APR	PW
1923	Was A	9	10	.474	33	21	10-1	0	177	201	103	7	3	76	52	3.86	97	.291	.364	52-3	.096	-1	121	-6	-0.8
1924	Was A	5	7	.417	24	14	5-1	0	92	98	52	2	4	49	28	4.40	92	.283	.378	31-1	.129	-2	90	-3	-0.6
1925	Bos A	5	12	.294	37	21	7-1	1	176.2	232	124	6	1	89	30	5.15	88	.327	.403	58-1	.138	-4	63	-10	-1.3
1926	Bos A	6	18	.250	30	24	7-1	0	172	213	106	5	3	69	35	4.97	82	.321	.387	49-0	.163	-1	59	-15	-1.7
1929	Cin N	0	0	—	1	0	0	0	1	2	3	1	0	1	0	27.00	17	.400	.500	0-0	—	0		-2	-0.1
Total	5	25	47	.347	125	80	29-4	1	618.2	746	388	21	11	284	145	4.66	88	.309	.384	190-5	.132	-8	80	-36	-4.5

ZAMBRANO, CARLOS Carlos Alberto B 6.1.1981 Carabobo, Venezuela BB/TR 6-4/250# d8.20

Year	Tm Lg	W	L	Pct	G	GS	CG-Sho	SV-BS	IP	H	R	HR	HB	BB-IB	SO	ERA	AERA	OAV	OOB	AB-SH	AVG	PB	Sup	APR	PW
2001	Chi N	1	2	.333	6	1	0	0-1	7.2	11	13	2	1	8-0	4	15.26	27	.355	.488	2-0	.000	-0	45	-9	-1.6
2002	Chi N	4	8	.333	32	16	0	0-0	108.1	94	53	9	4	63-2	93	3.66	110	.235	.344	30-2	.033	-2	80	2	0.1
2003	†Chi N	13	11	.542	32	32	3-1	0-0	214	188	88	9	10	94-12	168	3.11	135	.239	.326	75-4	.240	6	101	24	3.3
Total	3	18	21	.462	70	49	3-1	0-1	330	293	154	20	15	165-14	265	3.57	116	.241	.337	107-6	.178	3	93	17	1.8

ZAMBRANO, VICTOR Victor Manuel B 8.6.1975 Los Teques, Venezuela BR/TR 6/190# d6.21

Year	Tm Lg	W	L	Pct	G	GS	CG-Sho	SV-BS	IP	H	R	HR	HB	BB-IB	SO	ERA	AERA	OAV	OOB	AB-SH	AVG	PB	Sup	APR	PW
2001	TB A	6	2	.750	36	0	0	2-4	51.1	38	21	6	3	18-0	58	3.16	142	.201	.281	0-0	—	0		7	1.1
2002	TB A	8	8	.500	42	11	0	1-2	114	120	77	15	4	68-5	73	5.53	81	.278	.375	1-0	.000	-0	96	-14	-1.7
2003	TB A	12	10	.545	34	28	1	0-0	188.1	165	97	21	20	106-2	132	4.21	108	.237	.349	3-2	.000	-0	104	6	0.5
Total	3	26	20	.565	112	39	1	3-6	353.2	323	195	42	27	192-7	263	4.48	101	.245	.349	4-2	.000	-0	103	-1	-0.1

ZAMLOCH, CARL Carl Eugene B 10.6.1889 Oakland, CA D 8.19.1963 Santa Barbara, CA BR/TR 6-1/176# d5.7

Year	Tm Lg	W	L	Pct	G	GS	CG-Sho	SV-BS	IP	H	R	HR	HB	BB-IB	SO	ERA	AERA	OAV	OOB	AB-SH	AVG	PB	Sup	APR	PW
1913	Det A	1	6	.143	17	5	3	1	69.2	66	31	1	3	23	28	2.45	119	.260	.329	22-0	.182	-1	76	2	0.1

ZAMORA, OSCAR Oscar Jose (Sosa) B 9.23.1944 Camaguey, Cuba BR/TR 5-10/178# d6.18

Year	Tm Lg	W	L	Pct	G	GS	CG-Sho	SV-BS	IP	H	R	HR	HB	BB-IB	SO	ERA	AERA	OAV	OOB	AB-SH	AVG	PB	Sup	APR	PW
1974	Chi N	3	9	.250	56	0	0	10-3	83.2	82	33	6	0	19-7	38	3.12	123	.264	.301	11-3	.182	-0		7	1.1
1975	Chi N	5	2	.714	52	0	0	10-1	71	84	42	17	0	15-5	28	5.07	76	.298	.326	6-4	.167	-0		-8	-1.0
1976	Chi N	5	3	.625	40	2	0	3-2	55	70	34	8	1	17-6	27	5.24	74	.317	.365	9-0	.000	-1	91	-7	-1.2
1978	Hou N	0	0	—	10	0	0	0-0	15	20	12	2	0	7-3	6	7.20	46	.328	.391	2-0	.000	-0		-6	-0.4
Total	4	13	14	.481	158	2	0	23-6	224.2	256	121	33	1	58-21	99	4.53	84	.293	.332	28-7	.107	-2	91	-14	-1.5

ZANNI, DOM Dominick Thomas B 3.1.1932 Bronx, NY BR/TR 5-11/180# d9.28

Year	Tm Lg	W	L	Pct	G	GS	CG-Sho	SV-BS	IP	H	R	HR	HB	BB-IB	SO	ERA	AERA	OAV	OOB	AB-SH	AVG	PB	Sup	APR	PW
1958	SF N	1	0	1.000	1	0	0	0	4	7	1	1	0	1-0	3	2.25	169	.412	.444	2-0	.000	-0		1	0.1
1959	SF N	0	0	—	9	0	0	0	11	12	10	2	1	8-0	11	6.55	58	.273	.389	0-0	—	0		-4	-0.1
1961	SF N	1	0	1.000	8	0	0	0	13.2	13	7	1	0	12-2	11	3.95	96	.277	.417	0-0	—	0		0	0.0
1962	Chi A	6	5	.545	44	2	0	5	86.1	67	42	12	1	31-3	66	3.75	104	.214	.285	18-2	.278	2	57	0	0.3
1963	Chi A	0	0	—	5	0	0	0	4.1	5	4	1	0	4-0	2	8.31	42	.294	.429	0-0	—	0		-2	-0.1
	Cin N	1	1	.500	31	1	0	5	43	39	22	2	4	21-3	40	4.19	80	.247	.346	3-0	.333	0	206	-4	-0.2
1965	Cin N	0	0	—	8	0	0	0	13.1	7	2	1	0	5-0	10	1.35	278	.159	.240	1-0	.000	-0		3	0.2
1966	Cin N	0	0	—	5	0	0	0	7.1	5	1	0	1	3-1	5	0.00	—	.192	.300	1-0	1.000	0		3	0.2
Total	7	9	6	.600	111	3	0	10	183	155	89	20	7	85-9	148	3.79	99	.233	.323	25-2	.280	2	102	-3	0.4

ZASKE, JEFF Lloyd Jeffrey B 10.6.1960 Seattle, WA BR/TR 6-5/180# d7.21

Year	Tm Lg	W	L	Pct	G	GS	CG-Sho	SV-BS	IP	H	R	HR	HB	BB-IB	SO	ERA	AERA	OAV	OOB	AB-SH	AVG	PB	Sup	APR	PW
1984	Pit N	0	0	—	3	0	0	0-0	5	4	0	0	0	1-0	2	0.00	—	.211	.250	0-0	—	0		2	0.1

ZAVARAS, CLINT Clinton Wayne B 1.4.1967 Denver, CO BR/TR 6-1/175# d6.3

Year	Tm Lg	W	L	Pct	G	GS	CG-Sho	SV-BS	IP	H	R	HR	HB	BB-IB	SO	ERA	AERA	OAV	OOB	AB-SH	AVG	PB	Sup	APR	PW
1989	Sea A	1	6	.143	10	10	0	0-0	52	49	33	4	2	30-1	31	5.19	78	.253	.357	0-0	—	0	70	-6	-0.7

ZAY d10.7

Year	Tm Lg	W	L	Pct	G	GS	CG-Sho	SV-BS	IP	H	R	HR	HB	BB-IB	SO	ERA	AERA	OAV	OOB	AB-SH	AVG	PB	Sup	APR	PW
1886	Bal AA	0	1	.000	1	1	0	0	2	4	4	0	0	4	2	9.00	38	.333	.500	1	.000	-0	121	-1	-0.2

ZEISER, MATT Matthew J. B 9.25.1888 Chicago, IL D 6.10.1942 Chicago, IL BR/TR 5-10/170# d4.27

Year	Tm Lg	W	L	Pct	G	GS	CG-Sho	SV-BS	IP	H	R	HR	HB	BB-IB	SO	ERA	AERA	OAV	OOB	AB-SH	AVG	PB	Sup	APR	PW
1914	Bos A	0	0	—	2	0	0	0	10	9	4	0	1	8	0	1.80	150	.281	.439	3-0	.000	-0		1	0.0

ZEPP, BILL William Clinton B 7.22.1946 Detroit, MI BR/TR 6-2/185# d8.12

Year	Tm Lg	W	L	Pct	G	GS	CG-Sho	SV-BS	IP	H	R	HR	HB	BB-IB	SO	ERA	AERA	OAV	OOB	AB-SH	AVG	PB	Sup	APR	PW
1969	Min A	0	0	—	4	0	0	0-1	5.1	6	7	1	0	4-1	2	6.75	54	.286	.385	1-0	.000	-0		-3	-0.2
1970	†Min A	9	4	.692	43	20	1-1	2-2	151	154	63	9	9	51-4	64	3.22	116	.266	.334	44-2	.136	-1	102	8	0,5
1971	Det A	1	1	.500	16	4	0	2-1	31.2	41	20	2	3	17-3	15	5.12	70	.328	.412	4-0	.000	-0	94	-5	-0.4
Total	3	10	5	.667	63	24	1-1	4-4	188	201	90	12	12	72-8	81	3.64	102	.278	.350	49-2	.122	-2	100	0	-0.1

ZERBE, CHAD William Chad B 4.27.1972 Findlay, OH BL/TL 6/190# d9.18

Year	Tm Lg	W	L	Pct	G	GS	CG-Sho	SV-BS	IP	H	R	HR	HB	BB-IB	SO	ERA	AERA	OAV	OOB	AB-SH	AVG	PB	Sup	APR	PW
2000	SF N	0	0	—	4	0	0	0-0	6	6	3	1	0	1-0	5	4.50	94	.273	.304	0-0	—	0		0	0.0

Year	Tm Lg	W	L	Pct	G	GS	CG-Sho	SV-BS	IP	H	R	HR	HB	BB-IB	SO	ERA	AERA	OAV	OOB	AB-SH	AVG	PB	Sup	APR	PW
2001	SF N	3	0	1.000	27	1	0	0-0	39	41	21	3	1	10-0	22	3.92	102	.281	.327	9-2	.222	0	139	-1	0.0
2002	†SF N	2	0	1.000	50	0	0	0-1	56.1	52	22	3	4	21-2	26	3.04	128	.248	.326	6-1	.167	-0		5	0.2
2003	SF N	1	1	.500	33	1	0	0-1	49.2	60	26	3	1	14-2	17	4.71	87	.311	.349	5-1	.000	-1	69	-3	-0.1
Total	4	6	1	.857	114	2	0	0-2	151	159	72	10	6	46-4	70	3.87	103	.278	.333	20-4	.150	-0	104	1	0.1
ZETTLEIN, GEORGE George "Charmer" B 7.18.1844 Brooklyn, NY D 5.23.1905 Patchogue, NY BR/TR 5-9/162# d5.8																									
1871	Chi NA	18	9	.667	28	28	25	0	240.2	298	233	6		25	22	**2.73**	**168**	.267	**.283**	128	.250	-7	93	**45**	**2.6**
1872	Tro NA	14	8	.636	25	22	17-2	1	187.2	207	132	2		8	17	2.16	168	.250	.257	114	.254	0	118	31	2.4
	Eck NA	1	8	.111	9	9	8	0	75.1	106	62	1		6	8	3.58	95	.299	.311	34	.088	-4	56	2	-0.1
	Year	15	16	.484	34	31	25-2	1	263	313	67	3		14	25	2.57	139	.265	.273	148	.216	-4	101	30	2.3
1873	Phi NA	36	15	.706	51	51	49	0	460	594	368	3		41	29	2.86	115	.284	.298	241	.207	-8	108	30	1.7
1874	Chi NA	27	30	.474	57	57	57-3	0	515.2	640	439	3		43	26	2.43	92	.273	.286	244	.193	-9	94	-13	-1.7
1875	Chi NA	17	14	.548	31	31	29-6	0	282	266	142	0		6	18	1.28	178	.230	.234	133	.218	-3*	84	31	2.5
	Phi NA	12	8	.600	21	21	20-1	0	181.1	209	121	0		10	13	2.08	109	.264	.273	83	.181	-4	113	1	-0.3
	Year	29	22	.569	52	52	49-**7**	0	463.1	475	128	0		16	31	1.59	143	.244	.250	216	.204	-7	96	24	2.2
1876	Phi N	4	20	.167	28	25	23-1	2	234	358	212	2		6	10	3.88	62	.331	.334	128	.211	-5*	73	-25	-2.4
Total	5 NA	125	92	.576	222	219	205-12	1	1942.2	2320	1497	15		139	133	2.39	124	.267	.279	977	.210	-36	99	127	7.1
ZICK, BOB Robert George B 4.26.1927 Chicago, IL BL/TR 6/168# d5.2																									
1954	Chi N	0	0	—	8	0	0	0	16.1	23	15	1	0	7	9	8.27	51	.343	.405	4-0	.250	0*		-6	-0.3
ZIEGLER, GEORGE George J. B 1872 Chicago, IL D 7.22.1916 Kankakee, IL 5-8/150# d6.19																									
1890	Pit N	0	1	.000	1	1	0	0	6	12	7	0	0	0	1	10.50	31	.400	.400	2	.000	-0	19	-4	-0.4
ZIEM, STEVE Stephen Graeling B 10.24.1961 Milwaukee, WI BR/TR 6-2/210# d4.30																									
1987	Atl N	0	1	.000	2	0	0	0-0	2.1	4	3	0	0	1-0	0	7.71	56	.364	.417	0-0	—	0		-1	-0.2
ZIMMERMAN, JEFF Jeffrey Ross B 8.9.1972 Kelowna, BC, CAN BR/TR 6-1/200# d4.13 b-Jordan																									
1999	†Tex A★	9	3	.750	65	0	0	3-4	87.2	50	24	9	2	23-1	67	2.36	215	.166	.225	0-0	—	0		26	3.1
2000	Tex A	4	5	.444	65	0	0	1-2	69.2	80	45	10	2	34-3	74	5.30	95	.286	.361	0-0	—	0		-2	-0.2
2001	Tex A	4	4	.500	66	0	0	28-3	71.1	48	19	10	4	16-1	72	2.40	195	.192	.251	0-0	—	0		18	2.9
Total	3	17	12	.586	196	0	0	32-9	228.2	178	88	29	8	73-5	213	3.27	151	.214	.280	0-0	—	0		42	5.8
ZIMMERMAN, JORDAN Jordan William B 4.28.1975 Kelowna, BC, CAN BR/TL 6/200# d5.17 b-Jeff																									
1999	Sea A	0	0	—	12	0	0	0-0	8	14	8	0	1	4-0	3	7.88	60	.389	.463	0-0	—	0		-3	-0.1
ZINK, WALTER Walter Noble B 11.21.1898 Pittsfield, MA D 6.12.1964 Quincy, MA BR/TR 6/165# d7.6																									
1921	NY N	0	0	—	2	0	0	0	4	4	3	0	0	3	1	2.25	163	.235	.350	1-0	.000	-0		0	0.0
ZINN, JIMMY James Edward B 1.21.1895 Benton, AR D 2.26.1991 Memphis, TN BL/TR 6-0.5/195# d9.4																									
1919	Phi A	1	3	.250	5	3	2	0	25.2	38	20	1	1	10	9	6.31	54	.365	.426	13-0	.308	2*	61	-7	-0.7
1920	Pit N	1	1	.500	6	3	2	0	31	32	14	2	1	5	18	3.48	92	.260	.295	15-0	.200	0*	98	-1	0.0
1921	Pit N	7	6	.538	32	9	5-1	4	127.1	159	63	3	2	30	49	3.68	104	.318	.359	49-0	.224	0*	112	2	0.1
1922	Pit N	0	0	—	5	0	0	1	9.2	11	4	1	0	2	3	1.86	219	.297	.333	1-0	.000	-0		2	0.1
1929	Cle A	4	6	.400	18	11	6-1	2	105.1	150	75	8	3	33	29	5.04	88	.340	.390	42-3	.381	7*	119	-8	0.0
Total	5	13	16	.448	66	26	15-2	7	299	390	176	15	7	80	108	4.30	92	.324	.369	120-3	.283	9	109	-12	-0.5
ZINSER, BILL William Francis B 1.6.1918 Astoria, NY D 2.16.1993 Englewood, FL BR/TR 6-1/185# d8.19																									
1944	Was A	0	0	—	2	0	0	0	0.2	1	2	0	0	5	1	27.00	12	.333	.750	0-0	—	0		-2	-0.1
ZITO, BARRY Barry William B 5.13.1978 Las Vegas, NV BL/TL 6-4/205# d7.22																									
2000	†Oak A	7	4	.636	14	14	1-1	0-0	92.2	64	30	6	2	45-2	78	2.72	175	.195	.296	0-0	—	0	148	22	2.4
2001	†Oak A	17	8	.680	35	**35**	3-2	0-0	214.1	184	92	18	13	80-0	205	3.49	127	.230	.309	5-0	.000	-0	121	23	2.3
2002	†Oak A★	**23**	5	.821	35	**35**	1	0-0	229.1	182	79	24	9	78-2	182	2.75	160	.218	.289	4-2	.000	-0	122	42	4.8
2003	†Oak A✣	14	12	.538	35	35	4-1	0-0	231.2	186	98	19	6	88-3	146	3.30	137	.219	.295	6-0	.000	-1	83	30	2.9
Total	4	61	29	.678	119	119	9-4	0-0	768	616	299	67	30	291-7	611	3.12	144	.219	.297	15-2	.000	-1	113	117	12.4
ZMICH, ED Edward Albert B 10.1.1884 Cleveland, OH D 8.20.1950 Cleveland, OH BL/TL 6/180# d7.23																									
1910	StL N	0	5	.000	9	6	2	0	36	38	27	0	3	29	19	6.25	48	.304	.446	13-0	.077	-1	67	-11	-1.5
1911	StL N	1	0	1.000	4	0	0	0	12.2	8	5	0	1	8	4	2.13	158	.182	.321	4-0	.000	-1		1	0.0
Total	2	1	5	.167	13	6	2	0	48.2	46	32	0	4	37	23	5.18	60	.272	.414	17-0	.059	-2	67	-10	-1.5
ZOLDAK, SAM Samuel Walter "Sad Sam" B 12.8.1918 Brooklyn, NY D 8.25.1966 New Hyde Park, NY BL/TL 5-11.5/185# d5.13																									
1944	StL A	0	0	—	18	0	0	0	38.2	49	22	1	0	19	15	3.72	97	.310	.384	6-0	.333	0		-2	0.0
1945	StL A	3	2	.600	26	1	1	0	69.2	74	32	3	0	18	19	3.36	105	.267	.312	20-0	.050	-2*	48	0	-0.3
1946	StL A	9	11	.450	35	21	9-2	2	170.1	166	71	11	1	57	51	3.43	109	.256	.317	52-3	.173	-0	72	7	0.8
1947	StL A	9	10	.474	35	19	6-1	1	171	162	76	7	0	76	36	3.47	112	.254	.334	58-1	.172	-1	90	7	0.8
1948	StL A	2	4	.333	11	9	0	0	54	64	30	4	1	19	13	4.67	98	.296	.356	22-1	.273	0	77	0	0.1
	Cle A	9	6	.600	23	12	4-1	0	105.2	104	37	6	0	24	17	2.81	144	.261	.303	36-2	.139	-2	95	16	1.9
	Year	11	10	.524	34	21	4-1	0	159.2	168	41	10	1	43	30	3.44	123	.274	.322	58-3	.190	-2	88	15	2.0
1949	Cle A	1	2	.333	27	0	0	0	53	60	30	4	0	18	11	4.25	94	.291	.348	8-0	.375	1		-3	0.1
1950	Cle A	4	2	.667	33	3	0	4	63.2	64	33	6	1	21	15	3.96	109	.259	.320	16-0	.188	0	97	2	0.2
1951	Phi A	6	10	.375	26	18	8-1	0	128	127	51	9	0	24	18	3.16	135	.257	.292	45-1	.156	-3	83	15	1.3
1952	Phi A	0	6	.000	16	10	2	1	75.1	86	41	3	0	25	12	4.06	97	.290	.345	23-1	.174	-1	68	-2	-0.1
Total	9	43	53	.448	250	93	30-5	8	929.1	956	423	54	3	301	207	3.54	112	.267	.325	286-9	.175	-7	82	40	4.8
ZUBER, BILL William Henry "Goober" B 3.26.1913 Middle Amana, IA D 11.2.1982 Cedar Rapids, IA BR/TR 6-2/195# d9.16																									
1936	Cle A	1	1	.500	2	2	1	0	13.2	14	11	0	0	15	5	6.59	76	.269	.433	5-0	.200	-0	131	-2	-0.2
1938	Cle A	0	3	.000	15	0	0	1	28.2	33	18	0	0	20	14	5.02	92	.295	.402	7-1	.000	-1		-1	-0.2
1939	Cle A	2	0	1.000	16	1	0	0	31.2	41	24	2	1	19	16	5.97	74	.323	.415	5-0	.200	1	160	-6	-0.2
1940	Cle A	1	1	.500	17	0	0	0	24	25	17	3	0	14	12	5.63	75	.260	.355	3-0	.333	0		-4	-0.3
1941	Was A	6	4	.600	36	7	1	2	96.1	110	63	5	2	61	51	5.42	75	.291	.392	26-2	.000	-3	95	-13	-1.5
1942	Was A	9	9	.500	37	7	3-1	1	126.2	115	66	5	0	82	64	3.84	95	.243	.355	39-3	.154	0	74	-3	-0.5
1943	NY A	8	4	.667	20	13	7	1	118	100	54	3	0	74	57	3.89	83	.234	.347	38-5	.184	2	167	-6	-0.5
1944	NY A	5	7	.417	22	13	2-1	0	107	101	54	5	1	54	59	4.21	83	.255	.346	31-4	.129	-2	92	-6	-0.9
1945	NY A	5	11	.313	21	14	7	1	127	121	50	2	0	56	50	3.19	109	.259	.338	42-2	.167	-1	56	5	0.4
1946	NY A	0	1	.000	3	0	0	0	5.2	10	9	2	0	3	3	12.71	27	.385	.448	2-0	.000	-0		-6	-0.9
	†Bos A	5	1	.833	15	7	2-1	0	56.2	37	20	4	0	39	29	2.54	144	.187	.321	18-1	.111	-1	150	6	0.5
	Year	5	2	.714	18	7	2-1	0	62.1	47	26	6	0	42	32	3.47	105	.210	.335	20-1	.100	-1	151	0	-0.4
1947	Bos A	1	0	1.000	20	1	0	0	50.2	60	32	4	0	31	23	5.33	73	.311	.406	13-2	.154	-0	114	-7	-0.4
Total	11	43	42	.506	224	65	23-3	6	786	767	418	35	4	468	383	4.28	87	.260	.362	229-20	.135	-6	103	-43	-4.7
ZUVERINK, GEORGE George B 8.20.1924 Holland, MI BR/TR 6-4/200# d4.21																									
1951	Cle A	0	0	—	16	0	0	0	25.1	24	17	2	1	13	14	5.33	71	.253	.349	0-0	—	0		-5	-0.2
1952	Cle A	0	0	—	1	0	0	0	1.1	1	0	0	0	0	1	0.00	—	.200	.200	0-0	—	0*		1	0.0
1954	Cin N	0	0	—	2	0	0	0	6	10	6	1	0	1	2	9.00	47	.385	.407	2-0	.500	0		-3	-0.1
	Det A	9	13	.409	35	25	9-2	4	203	201	93	22	8	62	70	3.59	103	.257	.317	64-9	.125	-3	75	2	0.0
1955	Det A	0	5	.000	14	1	0	0	28.1	38	27	6	1	14-3	13	6.99	55	.309	.384	4-0	.000	-1	116	-11	-1.7
	Bal A	4	3	.571	28	5	0	4	86.1	80	28	5	4	17-1	31	2.19	174	.264	.309	23-1	.217	1	107	15	1.4
	Year	4	8	.333	42	6	0	4	114.2	118	33	11	5	31-4	44	3.38	113	.277	.331	27-1	.185	0	109	4	-0.3
1956	Bal A	7	6	.538	**62**	0	0	**16**	97.1	112	52	6	3	34-9	33	4.16	94	.294	.352	17-4	.118	-1		-4	-0.6
1957	Bal A	10	6	.625	**56**	0	0	9	112.2	105	37	9	4	39-13	36	2.48	145	.257	.325	23-2	.130	-0		13	2.0
1958	Bal A	2	2	.500	45	0	0	7	69	74	29	4	6	17-3	22	3.39	106	.286	.340	9-0	.222	1		2	0.3
1959	Bal A	0	1	.000	6	0	0	0	13	15	7	1	0	6-0	1	4.15	91	.306	.382	0-0	—	1		-1	0.0
Total	8	32	36	.471	265	31	9-2	40	642.1	660	296	56	27	203-29	223	3.54	105	.271	.332	142-16	.148	-2	82	9	1.1

THE MEN IN THE DUGOUT: THE MANAGERS

Vin Scully, on the flap of the dust jacket for Leonard Koppett's 1993 book *The Man in the Dugout,* praised the author by saying, "If there would be a degree in baseball, Leonard Koppett would be a professor."

True enough. The late, great Koppett was certainly a professor of the National Pastime, and he was writing about men who had hard-earned Ph.D.'s in the game. The men in the dugout are perhaps the least understood of the important "players" in the game today. Manager's roles have changed greatly in recent decades; partly because of the prominence of millionaire superstars, but mostly due to the increasingly visible intrusion of the business of baseball into the game on the field.

In the early days, baseball was not nearly as studied a tactical game as it would later become and, when players did get "scientific," it was usually in the heat of battle rather than in any planned fashion. At this time, a manager's job involved mostly keeping his players under contract, on-time, on the train, and out of the bars. Players generally knew their roles, particularly in the days where regulars, including pitchers, played nearly every game.

Many of the great early managers—such as Cap Anson, Harry Wright, Monty Ward, and Charlie Comiskey—were thought of not only leaders of men but also as particularly brainy players and sharp businessmen.

As baseball became more specialized in the 1890s, different managerial skills came into vogue. Managers began to make more of the decisions to bunt, steal, and the like, instead of letting the players play as they thought best. Furthermore, while teams always had a need to find and evaluate talent, the reserve clause now forced clubs to look into the "minor" leagues for new players. Well-traveled players and former players, who knew many different leagues, became especially valuable. Many of them—such as Hughie Jennings, John McGraw, and Wilbert Robinson—ended up as longtime managers.

In the 1890s, approximately half of managers were playing managers. Their experience on the field also helped these men manage ballplayers. Even at this time, rarely could a skipper become "one of the boys." Managers have long been expected to keep a fair distance from their players, because—as Sparky Anderson would comment many years later—"You take a guy out for a pinch hitter, he ain't gonna be your friend."

Most of the best managers—Joe McCarthy, Casey Stengel, Ned Hanlon, Frank Selee, Connie Mack, John McGraw, Earl Weaver, Walter Alston, Bill McKechnie, and others—respected their players and tried to treat them fairly, even if they weren't necessarily nice people to be around. Many of the greatest managers, especially in the early days, were also great teachers who showed younger men how to play the game as well as how to conduct their lives.

True renegades (e.g., Leo Durocher, Billy Martin, and Paul Richards) were impetuous, conniving, and often devious or deceitful. While many of their players didn't like them, the results were often positive—at least in the short term.

By the 1910s, managers were required to be better tacticians, not just shepherds of hard-bitten players. Relief pitchers, pinch hitters, and even platooning had come into use. As managing became more involved, fewer players were thought to be able to simultaneously handle the increased responsibility.

When the power era began in the 1920s, many a manager found himself less able to influence the game through tactical decisions and instead had to configure his lineup and rotation to provide the best offense and the most reliable pitching. Moreover, most managers were no longer the locus of player procurement. Clubs were now using general managers and, as a result, much of the personnel decisions were now out of the field manager's hands. The field manager also didn't necessarily control the salaries or the contracts of his players, taking away much of his power.

Managers ever since have had to deal with open revolt, dissension, and disobedience while maintaining order amidst changing social mores. Player salaries began to rise in the 1930s, and star players soon made as much as or more money than the manager. How, then, to keep the respect of the players? The more successful and famous managers of the 1940s—Lou Boudreau, Leo Durocher, and Billy Southworth, for example—would have expressed very different opinions.

Increasing expectations of success during the postwar boom also meant that managers were being fired more often. Some of the most successful managers of the 1950s—Casey Stengel, Chuck Dressen, Charlie Grimm, and Fred Haney—lost their jobs when things got rocky.

Stengel, Al Lopez, and Walter Alston were tremendous managers, and all had different ways of winning. Lopez was largely focused on power and starting pitching, while Stengel kept the entire roster involved and always had strong defensive teams. The unflappable Alston used one-run offensive strategies and depended heavily on pitching and defense to keep opponents from scoring.

The success of the quiet, dignified Lopez and Alston was not lost among managers of the 1960s, who generally became less confrontational (with exceptions like Durocher and Alvin Dark). Most of the top managers of that time—Alston, Red Schoendienst, Ralph Houk, Gil Hodges—met this standard. However, highly qualified "Nervous Nellies"—tough, involved guys like Gene Mauch, Harry Walker, Dick Williams, and Dave Bristol—also enjoyed success, usually when brought in to turn around underachieving teams with fire and brimstone.

Free agency in the late 1970s meant even more challenges for managers trying to keep their highly paid and mobile stars in line. The kindly old man in the dugout was largely a character of the past. Instead, tough little guys—firebrands like Williams, Sparky Anderson, Earl Weaver, Billy Martin, and Whitey Herzog—became the game's top skippers in the 1970s and early 1980s. Much of their success came from a lack of fear of using untested players. The successful skippers of the era were never big stars; some had never even reached the majors. Therefore, they knew—as did Joe McCarthy, John McGraw, and Connie Mack before them—that plenty of talent was trapped in the minor leagues, just waiting to be given a chance.

By the 1980s and 1990s, the best managers had learned that lesson as a new type of manager evolved. True; there were some tough guys, like in the 1970s, but they were also more "nice guys." The *personalities* of winners like Tony La Russa, Tommy Lasorda, Bobby Cox, Jim Leyland, and Davey Johnson were very different. What they had in common, though, was an ability to keep a lid on the clubhouse full of millionaire players and big egos.

Keeping dissension and "private matters" out of the public eye became an important mark of most successful teams. Baseball people now saw the media as even more of an enemy, largely because the rise in salaries had caused a rift between the press and the players, and because the media was working harder to break juicy stories rather than just report the games. Modern managers were able to get their players to buy into the team concept. Different managers did this in various ways, either through enthusiastic positive reinforcement, a caring demeanor, or simply excellent personnel management. Many teams continued to hire the older "pepperpot" type of manager, though few of them were now successful.

Today's managers must balance the skills and egos of their players, the omnipresence of the media, and their relationship with the front office to succeed on the field—but they have to do it with a decreasing amount of perceived authority. The contemporary game's ever-changing finances mean that few managers can count on a consistently high payroll. It's a tough job to do, and the most successful managers of today—such as Cox, La Russa, Dusty Baker, Lou Piniella, and Joe Torre—do it through by earning respect and building consensus.

This Manager Register includes everyone who has ever managed a major league baseball team, from 1871 to the present, from the National Association to the Federal League to the American League, from Bill Adair to Ted Turner to Don Zimmer. Identifying managers, however, has not always been so obvious as it would seem, so there are some important things to note about this section.

First, a quick tongue-twister: A manager has to have managed to be listed as a manager, but he doesn't have to have been called a manager to have managed. In the early days of baseball history, the term "team manager" did not mean what it does now. Then, the person called the manager was what would now be called a general manager or a vice president. If those official team manager's duties did not include traveling with the club, making out the lineups, deciding when to change pitchers, arguing with the umpires, and the like, then this register does not include him. The "real" field manager of the team back then may have been the team captain; if so, this register will show him as the manager regardless of his title. This is a record of those who did the job of a baseball manager, not those who had the title of manager.

Sometimes baseball managers have been referred to as coaches, as they are in other sports. The most famous recent example comes from P.K. Wrigley's rotating "College of Coaches" that ran the Cubs for five seasons during the 1960s. In that case, the coach referred to as head coach by the team is listed herein as the Cubs' manager for the period he was head coach.

Managers do not necessarily manage every single game in a season, of course. Managers are human beings, and they do occasionally miss a few games when they fall ill, get suspended, or attend to their families. In those cases, the coach left in charge does not become the manager in any real sense. Though the coach may make the moves, he is in most cases simply carrying out the manager's wishes.

When a long absence occurs, however, the situation gets muddier. This section uses a reasonable, though admittedly arbitrary, requirement of 30 consecutive days of managing the team in these cases for a substitute to qualify as the *de facto* manager.

When a manager is fired, however, the situation requires a different standard. When the manager's position is left vacant for any reason, the interim manager *is* definitely in charge. Thus, even if his managerial career lasts but one day, he is considered to have been a manager.

This register lists the following information for each manager:

Date of birth for all managers, plus full biographical information for managers who were not major leaguer players (and are, therefore, not listed in the batter or pitcher registers). Managers who never played professional baseball are shown with a "DNP" code.

The team(s) he managed in each season, along with that team's won-lost record and winning percentage during when he was manager. A lowercase e, w, or c after the league code indicates the team's division (East, West, or Central, respectively) from 1969–present. Player-managers are indicated by boldface years in the first column. Further information is available under the following headings:

The **Mgr/Yr** column gives results for clubs with multiple managers in a single season. If the team had more than one manager in the season listed, two numbers are shown, separated by a slash. In these cases, the second number indicates how many managers the team employed that season, and the first number indicating which of these the listed manager was. For example, Jack McKeon is listed in 2003 as 2/2, because he was the second of two managers for the Florida Marlins.

The **Finish** column indicates how the team did under that manager. For managers who guided the team all season, the number gives the team's standing at year's end. If manager B took over from manager A *during* the season, the first number indicates the team's standing when manager B took over, and the second number the team's standing at the end of the season. Three or more managers in one season for a team would produce a three-number entry for the manager(s) in the middle: the team's standing before, during, and after said manager was running the club.

Symbols after the finish show if the team that finished first won any postseason series. A solid star (★) indicates the team won the World Series (including the NL-AA World Series in the nineteenth century). A solid diamond (◆) indicates the team won their LCS but lost the World Series (1969–present). A (●) solid bullet indicates a team won the NL championship in the 1890s (i.e., the 1892 series between the first- and second-place teams, the 1894–97 Temple Cup, or the 1900 *Chronicle-Telegraph Cup*). A hollow star (☆) indicates the team won a Division Series but lost in their LCS (1995–present). A cross (✣) indicates a Wild Card team. A solid triangle (▲) indicates the team was tied at the end of the regular season for first place or the Wild Card and played a one-game or three-game playoff. A (*t*) after the finish indicates a tie in the standings below first place (e.g., *4t* means the team tied for fourth place that year).

The column marked **Yr+/-** indicates how many games the team won compared to how many the team was projected to win based on its run production. In other words, a manager with a ranking of 6.6 for a season did much better than could have been expected. A rating below zero indicates a disappointing performance, worse than expected given the team's runs scored and allowed.

On the career line, the manager's lifetime won-lost record and winning percentage are shown along with the number of seasons he managed and how many games his teams won compared to their projections.

Year	Tm/Lg	W	L	Pct	Finish	Mgr/Yr	+/-
ADAIR, BILL B2.10.1913 Mobile, AL Marion Danne Adair, D6.17.2002 Bay Minette, AL BR/TR, 5-8/190# (2B)							
1970	Chi A w	4	6	.400	6-6-6	2/3	0.2
ADCOCK, JOE B 10.30.1927							
1967	Cle A	75	87	.463	8		0.0
ADDY, BOB B 2.1845							
1875	Phi NA	3	4	.429	4-5	2/2	-1.3
1877	Cin N	5	19	.208	6-6-6	2/3	-0.3
2		8	23	.258			-1.6
ALLEN, BOB B 7.10.1867							
1890	Phi N	25	10	.714	3-2-3	4/5	4.8
1900	Cin N	62	77	.446	7		-3.5
2		87	87	.500			1.3
ALLISON, ANDY B 1848							
1872	Eck NA	0	11	.000	10-9	1/3	1.2
ALLISON, DOUG B 7.1845							
1873	Res NA	2	21	.087	8		5.0
ALOU, FELIPE B 5.12.1935							
1992	Mon N e	70	55	.560	4-2	2/2	1.9
1993	Mon N e	94	68	.580	2		7.9
1994	Mon N e	74	40	.649	1		4.0
1995	Mon N e	66	78	.458	5		-4.3
1996	Mon N e	88	74	.543	2		-0.4
1997	Mon N e	78	84	.481	4		1.9
1998	Mon N e	65	97	.401	4		-1.9
1999	Mon N e	68	94	.420	4		0.0
2000	Mon N e	67	95	.414	4		1.5
2001	Mon N e	21	33	.389	5-5	1/2	-1.3
2003	SF N w	100	61	.621	1		7.6
11		791	779	.504			16.8
ALSTON, WALTER B 12.1.1911							
1954	Bro N	92	62	.597	2		11.4
1955	Bro N	98	55	.641	1★		1.6
1956	Bro N	93	61	.604	1		3.8
1957	Bro N	84	70	.545	3		-3.3
1958	LA N	71	83	.461	7		3.2
1959	LA N	88	68	.564	1▲★		6.5
1960	LA N	82	72	.532	4		-2.3
1961	LA N	89	65	.578	2		8.3
1962	LA N	102	63	.618	2▲		5.3
1963	LA N	99	63	.611	1★		8.0
1964	LA N	80	82	.494	6t		-5.7
1965	LA N	97	65	.599	1★		6.1
1966	LA N	95	67	.586	1		0.6
1967	LA N	73	89	.451	8		0.7
1968	LA N	76	86	.469	7t		-0.2
1969	LA N w	85	77	.525	4		-5.2
1970	LA N w	87	74	.540	2		-0.0
1971	LA N w	89	73	.549	2		-0.2
1972	LA N w	85	70	.548	3		1.1
1973	LA N w	95	66	.590	2		2.6
1974	LA N w	102	60	.630	1◆		-3.6
1975	LA N w	88	74	.543	2		-5.7
1976	LA N w	90	68	.570	2-2	1/2	3.9
23		2040	1613	.558			36.8
ALTOBELLI, JOE B 5.26.1932							
1977	SF N w	75	87	.463	4		-2.1
1978	SF N w	89	73	.549	3		5.9
1979	SF N w	61	79	.436	4-4	1/2	-2.1
1983	Bal A e	98	64	.605	1★		2.3
1984	Bal A e	85	77	.525	5		2.5
1985	Bal A e	29	26	.527	4-4	1/3	-0.3
1991	Chi N e	0	1	.000	4-5-4	2/3	-0.5
7		437	407	.518			5.8
AMALFITANO, JOEY B 1.23.1934							
1979	Chi N e	2	5	.286	5-5	2/2	-1.5
1980	Chi N e	26	46	.361	6-6	2/2	-4.7
1981-1	Chi N e	15	37	.288	6		-1.5
-2	Chi N e	23	28	.451	5		-1.5
3		66	116	.363			-9.3
ANDERSON, SPARKY B 2.22.1934							
1970	Cin N w	102	60	.630	1◆		11.6
1971	Cin N w	79	83	.488	4t		-2.6
1972	Cin N w	95	59	.617	1◆		2.3
1973	Cin N w	99	63	.611	1		5.6
1974	Cin N w	98	64	.605	2		2.2
1975	Cin N w	108	54	.667	1★		1.3
1976	Cin N w	102	60	.630	1★		-1.2
1977	Cin N w	88	74	.543	2		-0.5
1978	Cin N w	92	69	.571	2		9.3
1979	Det A e	56	50	.528	5-5	3/3	0.9
1980	Det A e	84	78	.519	5		-4.0
1981-1	Det A e	31	26	.544	4		3.0
-2	Det A e	29	23	.558	2t		3.0
1982	Det A e	83	79	.512	4		-2.5
1983	Det A e	92	70	.568	2		0.0
1984	Det A e	104	58	.642	1★		4.5
1985	Det A e	84	77	.522	3		-0.6
1986	Det A e	87	75	.537	3		-2.2
1987	Det A e	98	64	.605	1		1.8
1988	Det A e	88	74	.543	2		2.3
1989	Det A e	59	103	.364	7		-1.9
1990	Det A e	79	83	.488	3		-1.6
1991	Det A e	84	78	.519	2t		0.8
1992	Det A e	75	87	.463	6		-5.7
1993	Det A e	85	77	.525	3t		-1.7
1994	Det A e	53	62	.461	5		-2.8
1995	Det A e	60	84	.417	4		5.7
26		2194	1834	.545			26.9
ANSON, CAP B 4.17.1852							
1875	Ath NA	4	2	.667	2-2	2/2	-0.9
1879	Chi N	41	21	.661	2-4	1/2	8.1
1880	Chi N	67	17	.798	1		4.0
1881	Chi N	56	28	.667	1		-1.3
1882	Chi N	55	29	.655	1		-9.3
1883	Chi N	59	39	.602	2		-1.8
1884	Chi N	62	50	.554	4t		-9.5
1885	Chi N	87	25	.777	1★		-1.1
1886	Chi N	90	34	.726	1		-2.5
1887	Chi N	71	50	.587	3		2.1
1888	Chi N	77	58	.570	2		2.5
1889	Chi N	67	65	.508	3		-3.5
1890	Chi N	84	53	.613	2		1.5
1891	Chi N	82	53	.607	2		5.4
1892-1	Chi N	31	39	.443	8		6.8
-2	Chi N	39	37	.513	7		6.8
1893	Chi N	56	71	.441	9		-3.8
1894	Chi N	57	75	.432	8		-7.2
1895	Chi N	72	58	.554	4		6.0
1896	Chi N	71	57	.555	5		6.1
1897	Chi N	59	73	.447	9		-1.7
1898	NY N	9	13	.409	6-7-7	2/3	-2.5
21		1296	947	.578			4.1
APPLING, LUKE B 4.2.1907							
1967	KC A	10	30	.250	10-10	2/2	-6.5
ARMOUR, BILL B9.3.1869 Homestead, PA Armour, William Clark D12.2.1922 Minneapolis, MN (DNP)							
1902	Cle A	69	67	.507	5		-0.8
1903	Cle A	77	63	.550	3		0.9
1904	Cle A	86	65	.570	4		-7.8
1905	Det A	79	74	.516	3		12.8
1906	Det A	71	78	.477	6		5.3
5		382	347	.524			10.4
ASPROMONTE, KEN B 9.22.1931							
1972	Cle A e	72	84	.462	5		-0.4
1973	Cle A e	71	91	.438	6		4.4
1974	Cle A e	77	85	.475	4		-0.7
3		220	260	.458			3.3
AUSTIN, JIMMY B 12.8.1879							
1913	StL A	2	6	.250	7-7-8	2/3	-1.3
1918	StL A	7	9	.438	6-6-5	2/3	-0.7
1923	StL A	22	29	.431	3-5	2/2	-2.4
3		31	44	.413			-4.5
BAKER, DEL B 5.3.1892							
1933	Det A	2	0	1.000	5-5	2/2	1.0
1936	Det A	18	16	.529	3-4-2	2/3	0.0
1937	Det A	34	20	.630	3-3-2	2/5	4.1
	Det A	7	3	.700	2-2-2	4/5	1.5
1938	Det A	37	19	.661	5-4	2/2	6.8
1939	Det A	81	73	.526	5		-4.1
1940	Det A	90	64	.584	1		-2.9
1941	Det A	75	79	.487	4t		3.6
1942	Det A	73	81	.474	5		-4.2
1960	Bos A	2	5	.286	8-8-7	2/3	-1.0
9		419	360	.538			4.7
BAKER, DUSTY B 6.15.1949							
1993	SF N w	103	59	.636	2		4.7
1994	SF N w	55	60	.478	2		-2.9
1995	SF N w	67	77	.465	4		6.8
1996	SF N w	68	94	.420	4		-2.5
1997	SF N w	90	72	.556	1		9.9
1998	SF N w	89	74	.546	2▲		-2.7
1999	SF N w	86	76	.531	2		1.2
2000	SF N w	97	65	.599	1		-0.6
2001	SF N w	90	72	.556	2		4.0
2002	SF N w	95	66	.590	2◆✥		-2.6
2003	Chi N c	88	74	.543	1☆		2.8
11		928	789	.540			18.1
BAMBERGER, GEORGE B 8.1.1925							
1978	Mil A e	93	69	.574	3		-3.4
1979	Mil A e	95	66	.590	2		6.2
1980	Mil A e	47	45	.511	2-4-3	2/3	-6.2
1982	NY N e	65	97	.401	6		-4.1
1983	NY N e	16	30	.348	6-6	1/2	-3.8
1985	Mil A e	71	90	.441	6		1.5
1986	Mil A e	71	81	.467	6-6	1/2	1.4
7		458	478	.489			-8.3
BANCROFT, DAVE B 4.20.1891							
1924	Bos N	27	38	.415	6-8	1/3	6.6
	Bos N	15	35	.300	8-8	3/3	-0.7
1925	Bos N	70	83	.458	5		2.5
1926	Bos N	66	86	.434	7		-0.4
1927	Bos N	60	94	.390	7		-5.1
4		238	336	.415			2.9
BANCROFT, FRANK B 5.9.1846 Lancaster, MA Bancroft, Frank Carter D 3.30.1921 Cincinnati, OH (DNP)							
1880	Wor N	40	43	.482	5		-5.7
1881	Det N	41	43	.488	4		-2.0
1882	Det N	42	41	.506	6		8.0
1883	Cle N	55	42	.567	4		3.2
1884	Pro N	84	28	.750	1★		0.7
1885	Pro N	53	57	.482	4		7.0
1887	Phi AA	26	29	.473	6-5	1/2	-1.6
1889	Ind N	25	43	.368	7-7	1/2	-5.8
1902	Cin N	9	7	.563	6-6-4	2/3	0.2
9		375	333	.530			4.0
BARKLEY, SAM B 5.24.1858							
1888	KC AA	21	36	.368	8-8-8	2/3	4.8
BARNIE, BILLY B 1.26.1853							
1883	Bal AA	28	68	.292	8		2.9
1884	Bal AA	63	43	.594	6		-1.1
1885	Bal AA	41	68	.376	8		-0.7
1886	Bal AA	48	83	.366	8		5.6
1887	Bal AA	77	58	.570	3		0.0
1888	Bal AA	57	80	.416	5		0.2
1889	Bal AA	70	65	.519	5		2.9
1890	Bal AA	15	19	.441	8		-1.0
1891	Bal AA	71	64	.526	3		-1.0
1892-1	Was N	0	2	.000	11t-7	1/2	-0.8
1893	Lou N	50	75	.400	11		2.4
1894	Lou N	36	94	.277	12		-2.4
1897	Bro N	61	71	.462	6t		-1.3
1898	Bro N	15	20	.429	9-10	1/3	1.5
14		632	810	.438			7.0
BARROW, ED B5.10.1868 Springfield, IL Barrow, Edward Grant "Cousin Ed" D12.15.1953 Port Chester, NY (DNP)							
1903	Det A	65	71	.478	5		-6.0
1904	Det A	32	46	.410	7-7	1/2	0.1
1918	Bos A	75	51	.595	1★		1.2
1919	Bos A	66	71	.482	6		-3.8
1920	Bos A	72	81	.471	5		0.4
5		310	320	.492			-8.1
BARRY, JACK B 4.26.1887							
1917	Bos A	90	62	.592	2		2.2
BATTIN, JOE B 11.11.1851							
1883	Pit AA	2	11	.154	7-7	3/3	-2.2
1884	Pit AA	6	7	.462	11-10-10	3/5	3.1
	CP U	1	5	.167	5-5	2/3	-1.7
2		9	23	.281			-0.9
BAUER, HANK B 7.31.1922							
1961	KC A	35	67	.343	8-9t	2/2	-4.9
1962	KC A	72	90	.444	9		-0.2
1964	Bal A	97	65	.599	3		3.8
1965	Bal A	94	68	.580	3		6.1
1966	Bal A	97	63	.606	1★		1.1
1967	Bal A	76	85	.472	6t		-11.2
1968	Bal A	43	37	.538	3-2	1/2	-1.7
1969	Oak A w	80	69	.537	2-2	1/2	-0.3
8		594	544	.522			-7.2
BAYLOR, DON B 6.28.1949							
1993	Col N w	67	95	.414	6		5.2
1994	Col N w	53	64	.453	3		0.6
1995	Col N w	77	67	.535	2✥	4.8	
1996	Col N w	82	79	.509	3		2.3
1997	Col N w	83	79	.512	3		0.7
1998	Col N w	77	85	.475	4		-1.3
2000	Chi N c	65	97	.401	6		-2.9
2001	Chi N c	88	74	.543	3		-0.5
2002	Chi N c	39	49	.443	5-4	1/2	-2.1
9		631	689	.478			6.6
BELL, BUDDY B 8.27.1951							
1996	Det A e	53	109	.327	5		0.1
1997	Det A e	79	83	.488	3		-1.4
1998	Det A c	52	85	.380	5-5	1/2	-5.1
2000	Col N w	82	80	.506	4		-5.3
2001	Col N w	73	89	.451	5		-9.5
2002	Col N w	6	16	.273	5-4	1/2	-3.5
6		345	462	.428			-24.6

Year	Tm/Lg	W	L	Pct	Finish	Mgr/Yr	+/-
BENSON, VERN B 9.19.1924							
1977	Atl N w	1	0	1.000	6-6-6	3/4	0.6
BERRA, YOGI B 5.12.1925							
1964	NY A	99	63	.611	1		1.7
1972	NY N e	83	73	.532	3		10.6
1973	NY N e	82	79	.509	1◆		-0.7
1974	NY N e	71	91	.438	5		-1.9
1975	NY N e	56	53	.514	3-3*t*	1/2	-0.0
1984	NY A e	87	75	.537	3		-2.0
1985	NY A e	6	10	.375	7-2	1/2	-3.7
7		484	444	.522			4.0
BEVINGTON, TERRY B 7.7.1956 Akron, OH Bevington, Terry Paul BR/TR, 6-2/190# (C)							
1995	Chi A c	57	56	.504	4-3	2/2	0.7
1996	Chi A c	85	77	.525	2		-5.7
1997	Chi A c	80	81	.497	2		4.6
3		222	214	.509			-0.3
BEZDEK, HUGO B4.1.1884 Prague, Czechoslovakia Bezdek, Hugo Frank D9.19.1952 Atlantic City, NJ (DNP)							
1917	Pit N	30	59	.337	8-8	3/3	-5.8
1918	Pit N	65	60	.520	4		-3.6
1919	Pit N	71	68	.511	4		0.8
3		166	187	.470			-8.6
BICKERSON (DNP)							
1884	Was AA	0	1	.000	12-12	2/2	-0.2
BIRMINGHAM, JOE B 8.6.1884							
1912	Cle A	21	7	.750	6-5	2/2	7.1
1913	Cle A	86	66	.566	3		-0.6
1914	Cle A	51	102	.333	8		-7.3
1915	Cle A	12	16	.429	6-7	1/2	0.6
4		170	191	.471			-0.2
BISSONETTE, DEL B 9.6.1899							
1945	Bos N	25	34	.424	7-6	2/2	-4.2
BLACKBURNE, LENA B 10.23.1886							
1928	Chi A	40	40	.500	6-5	2/2	3.6
1929	Chi A	59	93	.388	7		-0.8
2		99	133	.427			2.8
BLADES, RAY B 8.6.1896							
1939	StL N	92	61	.601	2		1.0
1940	StL N	14	24	.368	6-3	1/3	-6.2
1948	Bro N	1	0	1.000	5-5-3	2/3	0.5
3		107	85	.557			-4.7
BLAIR, WALTER B 10.13.1883							
1915	Buf F	1	1	.500	8-8-6	2/3	0.1
BLUEGE, OSSIE B 10.24.1900							
1943	Was A	84	69	.549	2		0.1
1944	Was A	64	90	.416	8		-5.4
1945	Was A	87	67	.565	2		3.5
1946	Was A	76	78	.494	4		9.1
1947	Was A	64	90	.416	7		6.5
5		375	394	.488			13.7
BOCHY, BRUCE B 4.16.1955							
1995	SD N w	70	74	.486	3		-1.6
1996	SD N w	91	71	.562	1		1.1
1997	SD N w	76	86	.469	4		3.9
1998	SD N w	98	64	.605	1◆		5.3
1999	SD N w	74	88	.457	4		0.0
2000	SD N w	76	86	.469	5		1.1
2001	SD N w	79	83	.488	4		0.2
2002	SD N w	66	96	.407	5		0.2
2003	SD N w	64	98	.395	5		-2.0
9		694	746	.482			8.2
BOLES, JOHN B8.19.1948 Chicago, IL Boles, John BL/TR, 5-10/165# (OF)							
1996	Fla N e	40	35	.533	4-3	3/3	3.2
1999	Fla N e	64	98	.395	5		-1.3
2000	Fla N e	79	82	.491	3		4.9
2001	Fla N e	22	26	.458	3-4	1/2	-1.9
4		205	241	.460			4.8
BOND, TOMMY B 4.2.1856							
1882	Wor N	2	4	.333	8-8-8	2/3	0.7
BOONE, BOB B 11.19.1947							
1995	KC A c	70	74	.486	2		4.1
1996	KC A c	75	86	.466	5		-1.6
1997	KC A c	36	46	.439	4-5	1/2	-1.4
2001	Cin N c	66	96	.407	5		-4.0
2002	Cin N c	78	84	.481	3		3.4
2003	Cin N c	46	58	.442	5-5	1/3	5.8
6		371	444	.455			6.4
BOROS, STEVE B 9.3.1936							
1983	Oak A w	74	88	.457	4		0.3
1984	Oak A w	20	24	.455	5-4	1/2	-0.5
1986	SD N w	74	88	.457	4		-0.1
3		168	200	.457			-0.3

Year	Tm/Lg	W	L	Pct	Finish	Mgr/Yr	+/-
BOTTOMLEY, JIM B 4.23.1900							
1937	StL A	21	56	.273	7-8	2/2	-3.7
BOUDREAU, LOU B 7.17.1917							
1942	Cle A	75	79	.487	4		5.3
1943	Cle A	82	71	.536	3		3.0
1944	Cle A	72	82	.468	5*t*		-1.5
1945	Cle A	73	72	.503	5		-0.5
1946	Cle A	68	86	.442	6		2.0
1947	Cle A	80	74	.519	4		-7.4
1948	Cle A	97	58	.626	1▲★		-7.7
1949	Cle A	89	65	.578	3		1.4
1950	Cle A	92	62	.597	4		0.1
1952	Bos A	76	78	.494	6		-2.0
1953	Bos A	84	69	.549	4		5.0
1954	Bos A	69	85	.448	4		-5.2
1955	KC A	63	91	.409	6		11.9
1956	KC A	52	102	.338	8		-4.3
1957	KC A	36	67	.350	8-7	1/2	-5.2
1960	Chi N	54	83	.394	7-7	2/2	-1.9
16		1162	1224	.487			-6.9
BOWA, LARRY B 12.6.1945							
1987	SD N w	65	97	.401	6		-6.4
1988	SD N w	16	30	.348	5-3	1/2	-7.3
2001	Phi N e	86	76	.531	2		2.3
2002	Phi N e	80	81	.497	3		0.9
2003	Phi N e	86	76	.531	3		-4.3
5		333	360	.481			-14.9
BOWERMAN, FRANK B 12.5.1868							
1909	Bos N	22	54	.289	8-8	1/2	-2.2
BOYD, BILL B 12.22.1852							
1875	Atl NA	0	2	.000	12-12	2/2	0.2
BOYER, KEN B 5.20.1931							
1978	StL N e	62	81	.434	6-5	3/3	-4.1
1979	StL N e	86	76	.531	3		1.1
1980	StL N e	18	33	.353	6-4	1/4	-8.4
3		166	190	.466			-11.3
BRADLEY, BILL B 2.13.1878							
1905	Cle A	20	21	.488	1*t*-2-5	2/3	0.2
1914	Bro F	77	77	.500	5		1.5
2		97	98	.497			1.7
BRAGAN, BOBBY B 10.30.1917							
1956	Pit N	66	88	.429	7		-4.1
1957	Pit N	36	67	.350	7-7*t*	1/2	-7.8
1958	Cle A	31	36	.463	6-4	1/2	-5.1
1963	Mil N	84	78	.519	6		-4.9
1964	Mil N	88	74	.543	5		1.3
1965	Mil N	86	76	.531	5		-2.8
1966	Atl N	52	59	.468	7-5	1/2	-10.3
7		443	478	.481			-33.8
BRENLY, BOB B 2.25.1954							
2001	Ari N w	92	70	.568	1★		-2.9
2002	Ari N w	98	64	.605	1		2.7
2003	Ari N w	84	78	.519	3		-0.3
3		274	212	.564			-0.5
BRESNAHAN, ROGER B 6.11.1879							
1909	StL N	54	98	.355	7		-6.8
1910	StL N	63	90	.412	7		-5.5
1911	StL N	75	74	.503	5		7.9
1912	StL N	63	90	.412	6		2.9
1915	Chi N	73	80	.477	4		1.9
5		328	432	.432			0.5
BRISTOL, DAVE B 6.23.1933 Macon, GA Bristol, James David BR/TR, 5-11/175# (2B)							
1966	Cin N	39	38	.506	8-7	2/2	1.0
1967	Cin N	87	75	.537	4		1.4
1968	Cin N	83	79	.512	4		0.2
1969	Cin N w	89	73	.549	3		5.1
1970	Mil A w	65	97	.401	4*t*		-1.7
1971	Mil A w	69	92	.429	6		-3.1
1972	Mil A e	10	20	.333	6-6	1/3	-2.8
1976	Atl N w	70	92	.432	6		-2.6
1977	Atl N w	8	21	.276	6-6	1/4	-2.8
	Atl N w	52	79	.397	6-6	4/4	3.4
1979	SF N w	10	12	.455	4-4	2/2	0.1
1980	SF N w	75	86	.466	5		1.2
11		657	764	.462			-0.5
BROWN, FREEMAN B1.31.1845 Hubbardston, MA Brown, Freeman D 12.27.1916 Worcester, MA (DNP)							
1882	Wor N	9	32	.220	8-8	1/3	-0.1
BROWN, MORDECAI B 10.19.1876							
1914	StL F	50	63	.442	7-8	1/2	3.9
BROWN, TOM B 9.21.1860							
1897	Was N	52	46	.531	11-6*t*	2/2	3.8
1898	Was N	12	26	.316	11-11	1/4	-1.6
2		64	72	.471			2.2

Year	Tm/Lg	W	L	Pct	Finish	Mgr/Yr	+/-
BRUCKER, EARLE B 5.6.1901							
1952	Cin N	3	2	.600	7-7-6	2/3	0.6
BUCKENBERGER, AL B1.31.1861 Detroit, MI Buckenberger, Albert C. D7.1.1917 Syracuse, NY (DNP)							
1889	Col AA	60	78	.435	6		3.5
1890	Col AA	39	41	.488	5-2	1/3	-12.9
1892-1	Pit N	15	14	.517	7-6	1/2	0.4
-2	Pit N	38	27	.585	10-4	2/2	5.3
1893	Pit N	81	48	.628	2		-0.3
1894	Pit N	53	55	.491	7-7	1/2	0.0
1895	StL N	16	34	.320	11-11	1/4	-0.0
1902	Bos N	73	64	.533	3		-1.6
1903	Bos N	58	80	.420	6		1.0
1904	Bos N	55	98	.359	7		5.9
9		488	539	.475			1.2
BUFFINTON, CHARLIE B 6.14.1861							
1890	Phi P	61	54	.530	5-5	2/2	-2.6
BURDOCK, JACK B 4.1852							
1883	Bos N	30	24	.556	4-1	1/2	-7.4
BURKE, JIMMY B 10.12.1874							
1905	StL N	34	56	.378	7-6-6	2/3	1.2
1918	StL A	29	31	.483	6-5	3/3	0.2
1919	StL A	67	72	.482	5		1.1
1920	StL A	76	77	.497	4		-3.4
4		206	236	.466			-0.9
BURNHAM, GEORGE B5.20.1860 Albion, MI Burnham, George Walter "Watch" D11.18.1902 Detroit, MI (DNP)							
1887	Ind N	6	22	.214	8-8	1/3	-1.7
BURNS, TOM B 3.30.1857							
1892-1	Pit N	22	25	.468	7-6	2/2	-1.7
-2	Pit N	5	7	.417	10-4	1/2	-1.0
1898	Chi N	85	65	.567	4		-4.2
1899	Chi N	75	73	.507	8		-3.6
3		187	170	.524			-10.5
BURWELL, BILL B 3.27.1895							
1947	Pit N	1	0	1.000	8-7*t*	2/2	0.5
BUSH, DONIE B 10.8.1887							
1923	Was A	75	78	.490	4		1.1
1927	Pit N	94	60	.610	1		1.6
1928	Pit N	85	67	.559	4		-3.5
1929	Pit N	67	51	.568	2-2	1/2	-0.7
1930	Chi A	62	92	.403	7		-0.6
1931	Chi A	56	97	.366	8		1.2
1933	Cin N	58	94	.382	8		-1.8
7		497	539	.480			-2.7
BUTLER, ORMOND B 11.1854 , WV Butler, Ormond Hook D 9.12.1915 Mt.Hope, MD (DNP)							
1883	Pit AA	17	36	.321	6-6-7	2/3	-0.3
BYRNE, CHARLIE B 9.1843 New York, NY Byrne, Charles H. D 1.4.1898 New York, NY (DNP)							
1885	Bro AA	38	37	.507	7-5*t*	2/2	2.0
1886	Bro AA	76	61	.555	3		7.5
1887	Bro AA	60	74	.448	6		-5.8
3		174	172	.503			3.7
CALLAHAN, NIXEY B 3.18.1874							
1903	Chi A	60	77	.438	7		1.7
1904	Chi A	23	18	.561	4-3	1/2	-1.1
1912	Chi A	78	76	.506	4		1.9
1913	Chi A	78	74	.513	5		3.2
1914	Chi A	70	84	.455	6*t*		1.5
1916	Pit N	65	89	.422	6		-0.3
1917	Pit N	20	40	.333	8-8	1/3	-4.1
7		394	458	.462			2.8
CAMPAU, COUNT B 10.17.1863							
1890	StL AA	27	14	.659	5-2-3	4/6	2.9
CANTILLON, JOE B8.19.1861 Janesville, WI Cantillon, Joseph D. "Pongo Joe" D1.31.1930 Hickman, KY (DNP)							
1907	Was A	49	102	.325	8		-6.4
1908	Was A	67	85	.441	7		-2.0
1909	Was A	42	110	.276	8		-1.9
3		158	297	.347			-10.2
CAREY, MAX B 1.11.1890							
1932	Bro N	81	73	.526	3		3.5
1933	Bro N	65	88	.425	6		-3.4
2		146	161	.476			0.1
CAREY, TOM B 1849							
1873	Bal NA	14	9	.609	3-3	2/2	-2.9
1874	Mut NA	13	12	.520	3-2	1/2	-3.4
2		27	21	.563			-6.3
CARRIGAN, BILL B 10.22.1883							
1913	Bos A	40	30	.571	5-4	2/2	4.0
1914	Bos A	91	62	.595	2		5.5
1915	Bos A	101	50	.669	1★		6.9

Year	Tm/Lg	W	L	Pct	Finish	Mgr/Yr	+/-
1916	Bos A	91	63	.591	1★		5.8
1927	Bos A	51	103	.331	8		-0.7
1928	Bos A	57	96	.373	8		-1.2
1929	Bos A	58	96	.377	8		0.7
	7	489	500	.494			21.0
CARUTHERS, BOB B 1.5.1864							
1892-2	StL N	16	32	.333	12-11	3/3	-1.5
CAVARRETTA, PHIL B 7.19.1916							
1951	Chi N	27	47	.365	7-8	2/2	-3.4
1952	Chi N	77	77	.500	5		0.3
1953	Chi N	65	89	.422	7		7.7
	3	169	213	.442			4.6
CAYLOR, O.P. B 12.17.1849 Near Dayton, OH Caylor, Oliver Perry D 10.19.1897 Winona, MN (DNP)							
1885	Cin AA	63	49	.563	2		0.9
1886	Cin AA	65	73	.471	5		-5.5
1887	NY AA	35	60	.368	7-7	3/3	7.4
	3	163	182	.472			2.7
CHANCE, FRANK B 9.9.1877							
1905	Chi N	55	33	.625	4-3	2/2	-3.5
1906	Chi N	116	36	.763	1		3.4
1907	Chi N	107	45	.704	1★		8.9
1908	Chi N	99	55	.643	1★		3.3
1909	Chi N	104	49	.680	2		-1.1
1910	Chi N	104	50	.675	1		4.2
1911	Chi N	92	62	.597	2		-0.3
1912	Chi N	91	59	.607	3		7.4
1913	NY A	57	94	.377	7		-3.6
1914	NY A	60	74	.448	7-6t	1/2	-5.7
1923	Bos A	61	91	.401	8		7.4
	11	946	648	.593			20.4
CHAPMAN, JACK B 5.8.1843							
1876	Lou N	30	36	.455	5		3.4
1877	Lou N	35	25	.583	2		0.2
1878	Mil N	15	45	.250	6		-3.0
1882	Wor N	7	30	.189	8-8	3/3	-1.2
1883	Det N	40	58	.408	7		2.1
1884	Det N	28	84	.250	8		-0.9
1885	Buf N	31	57	.352	7-7	2/2	5.7
1889	Lou AA	1	6	.143	8-8	4/4	-0.5
1890	Lou AA	88	44	.667	1		0.5
1891	Lou AA	54	83	.394	7		1.1
1892-1	Lou N	21	33	.389	10-11	1/2	-0.6
	11	350	501	.411			6.8
CHAPMAN, BEN B 12.25.1908							
1945	Phi N	28	57	.329	8-8	2/2	2.8
1946	Phi N	69	85	.448	5		7.2
1947	Phi N	62	92	.403	7t		-4.8
1948	Phi N	37	42	.468	7-6	1/3	4.7
	4	196	276	.415			10.0
CHASE, HAL B 2.13.1883							
1910	NY A	10	4	.714	3-2	2/2	2.3
1911	NY A	76	76	.500	6		3.9
	2	86	80	.518			6.2
CLAPP, JOHN B 7.17.1851							
1872	Man NA	5	19	.208	8		0.9
1878	Ind N	24	36	.400	5		-2.7
1879	Buf N	46	32	.590	3		4.2
1880	Cin N	21	59	.262	8		-1.6
1881	Cle N	32	41	.438	6-7	2/2	-2.6
1883	NY N	46	50	.479	6		2.2
	6	174	237	.423			0.3
CLARKE, FRED B 10.3.1872							
1897	Lou N	35	54	.393	9-11	2/2	2.3
1898	Lou N	70	81	.464	9		4.4
1899	Lou N	75	76	.497	9		-5.3
1900	Pit N	79	60	.568	2		-2.2
1901	Pit N	90	49	.647	1		-3.2
1902	Pit N	103	36	.741	1		-0.9
1903	Pit N	91	49	.650	1		3.9
1904	Pit N	87	66	.569	4		1.8
1905	Pit N	96	57	.627	2		6.7
1906	Pit N	93	60	.608	3		-0.7
1907	Pit N	91	63	.591	2		0.2
1908	Pit N	98	56	.636	2t		7.5
1909	Pit N	110	42	.724	1★		6.3
1910	Pit N	86	67	.562	3		1.1
1911	Pit N	85	69	.552	3		-11.4
1912	Pit N	93	58	.616	2		-1.5
1913	Pit N	78	71	.523	4		-5.8
1914	Pit N	69	85	.448	7		-3.7
1915	Pit N	73	81	.474	5		-8.2
	19	1602	1180	.576			-8.6
CLEMENTS, JACK B 7.24.1864							
1890	Phi N	13	6	.684	1-2-3	2/5	2.0

Year	Tm/Lg	W	L	Pct	Finish	Mgr/Yr	+/-
COBB, TY B 12.18.1886							
1921	Det A	71	82	.464	6		-8.3
1922	Det A	79	75	.513	3		-1.4
1923	Det A	83	71	.539	2		-2.5
1924	Det A	86	68	.558	3		4.1
1925	Det A	81	73	.526	4		-2.7
1926	Det A	79	75	.513	6		5.5
	6	479	444	.519			-5.3
COCHRANE, MICKEY B 4.6.1903							
1934	Det A	101	53	.656	1		1.2
1935	Det A	93	58	.616	1★		-6.1
1936	Det A	29	24	.547	3-2	1/3	1.0
	Det A	36	31	.537	4-2	3/3	0.6
1937	Det A	16	13	.552	3-2	1/5	-0.1
	Det A	26	20	.565	3-2-2	3/5	0.5
1938	Det A	47	51	.480	5-4	1/2	-5.9
	5	348	250	.582			-8.8
COHEN, ANDY B 10.25.1904							
1960	Phi N	1	0	1.000	6t-4t-8	2/3	0.6
COLEMAN, JERRY B 9.14.1924							
1980	SD N w	73	89	.451	6		-1.2
COLEMAN, BOB B 9.26.1890							
1943	Bos N	21	25	.457	6-6	1/2	3.0
1944	Bos N	65	89	.422	6		-3.5
1945	Bos N	42	51	.452	7-6	1/2	-4.1
	3	128	165	.437			-4.6
COLLINS, EDDIE B 5.2.1887							
1924	Chi A	14	13	.519	6	3/4	1.6
1925	Chi A	79	75	.513	5		-1.8
1926	Chi A	81	72	.529	5		-2.0
	3	174	160	.521			-2.3
COLLINS, JIMMY B 1.16.1870							
1901	Bos A	79	57	.581	2		-3.4
1902	Bos A	77	60	.562	3		2.2
1903	Bos A	91	47	.659	1★		1.1
1904	Bos A	95	59	.617	1		1.7
1905	Bos A	78	74	.513	4		0.5
1906	Bos A	35	79	.307	8-8	1/2	-2.3
	6	455	376	.548			-0.3
COLLINS, SHANO B 12.4.1885							
1931	Bos A	62	90	.408	6		3.2
1932	Bos A	11	44	.200	8-8	1/2	-4.4
	2	73	134	.353			-1.2
COLLINS, TERRY B 5.27.1949 Midland, MI Collins, Terry Lee BL/TR, 5-8/160# (2B)							
1994	Hou N c	66	49	.574	2		-1.1
1995	Hou N c	76	68	.528	2		-3.0
1996	Hou N c	82	80	.506	2		4.8
1997	Ana A w	84	78	.519	2		-0.3
1998	Ana A w	85	77	.525	2		3.6
1999	Ana A w	51	82	.383	4-4	1/2	-6.3
	6	444	434	.506			-2.3
COMISKEY, CHARLIE B 8.15.1859							
1883	StL AA	12	7	.632	2-2	2/2	-0.1
1884	StL AA	16	7	.696	5-4	2/2	2.2
1885	StL AA	79	33	.705	1		2.7
1886	StL AA	93	46	.669	1★		-8.3
1887	StL AA	95	40	.704	1		-2.5
1888	StL AA	92	43	.681	1		-3.7
1889	StL AA	89	46	.659	2		-1.9
1890	Chi P	75	62	.547	4		-3.5
1891	StL AA	85	51	.625	2		-2.0
1892-1	Cin N	44	31	.587	4		3.6
-2	Cin N	38	37	.507	8		3.6
1893	Cin N	65	63	.508	6t		5.8
1894	Cin N	55	75	.423	10		3.2
	12	838	541	.608			-0.9
CONNOR, ROGER B 7.1.1857							
1896	StL N	8	37	.178	11-11-11	4/5	-4.3
COOKE, DUSTY B 6.23.1907							
1948	Phi N	6	6	.500	7-6-6	2/3	1.1
COOMBS, JACK B 11.18.1882							
1919	Phi N	18	44	.290	8-8	1/2	-4.3
COONEY, JOHNNY B 3.18.1901							
1949	Bos N	20	25	.444	4-4	2/2	-2.1
CORRALES, PAT B 3.20.1941							
1978	Tex A w	1	0	1.000	2t-2t	2/2	0.5
1979	Tex A w	83	79	.512	3		-3.2
1980	Tex A w	76	85	.472	4		-4.9
1982	Phi N e	89	73	.549	2		6.9
1983	Phi N e	43	42	.506	1-1◆	1/2	-2.9
	Cle A e	30	32	.484	7-7	2/2	2.1
1984	Cle A e	75	87	.463	6		-5.5
1985	Cle A e	60	102	.370	7		-8.4
1986	Cle A e	84	78	.519	5		3.9

Year	Tm/Lg	W	L	Pct	Finish	Mgr/Yr	+/-
1987	Cle A e	31	56	.356	7-7	1/2	-1.8
	9	572	634	.474			-13.2
CORRIDEN, RED B 9.4.1887							
1950	Chi A	52	72	.419	8-6	2/2	0.1
COTTIER, CHUCK B 1.8.1936							
1984	Sea A w	15	12	.556	7-5t	2/2	3.0
1985	Sea A w	74	88	.457	6		2.6
1986	Sea A w	9	19	.321	6-7	1/3	-3.0
	3	98	119	.452			2.6
COX, BOBBY B 5.21.1941							
1978	Atl N w	69	93	.426	6		3.6
1979	Atl N w	66	94	.412	6		-4.6
1980	Atl N w	81	80	.503	4		3.7
1981-1	Atl N w	25	29	.463	4		-0.7
-2	Atl N w	25	27	.481	5		-0.7
1982	Tor A e	78	84	.481	6t		2.2
1983	Tor A e	89	73	.549	4		1.2
1984	Tor A e	89	73	.549	2		2.6
1985	Tor A e	99	62	.615	1		0.8
1990	Atl N w	40	57	.412	6-6	2/2	-0.3
1991	Atl N w	94	68	.580	1◆		2.3
1992	Atl N w	98	64	.605	1◆		4.8
1993	Atl N w	104	58	.642	1		1.2
1994	Atl N e	68	46	.596	2		1.4
1995	Atl N e	90	54	.625	1★		7.0
1996	Atl N e	96	66	.593	1◆		2.3
1997	Atl N e	101	61	.623	1☆		-1.7
1998	Atl N e	106	56	.654	1☆		0.1
1999	Atl N e	103	59	.636	1◆		4.4
2000	Atl N e	95	67	.586	1		4.6
2001	Atl N e	88	74	.543	1☆		-1.9
2002	Atl N e	101	59	.631	1		5.7
2003	Atl N e	101	61	.623	1		4.3
	22	1906	1465	.565			42.3
CRAFT, HARRY B 4.19.1915							
1957	KC A	23	27	.460	8-7	2/2	3.0
1958	KC A	73	81	.474	7		3.2
1959	KC A	66	88	.429	7		-3.3
1961	Chi N	4	8	.333	6t-7-7	2/9	-1.2
	Chi N	3	1	.750	7-7-7	5/9	1.3
1962	Hou N	64	96	.400	8		-2.8
1963	Hou N	66	96	.407	9		5.2
1964	Hou N	61	88	.409	9-9	1/2	0.4
	7	360	485	.426			6.0
CRAIG, ROGER B 2.17.1930							
1978	SD N w	84	78	.519	4		3.8
1979	SD N w	68	93	.422	5		-4.2
1985	SF N w	6	12	.333	6-6	2/2	-1.6
1986	SF N w	83	79	.512	3		-6.4
1987	SF N w	90	72	.556	1		-2.4
1988	SF N w	83	79	.512	4		-2.7
1989	SF N w	92	70	.568	1◆		0.5
1990	SF N w	85	77	.525	3		3.1
1991	SF N w	75	87	.463	4		-1.0
1992	SF N w	72	90	.444	5		-1.0
	10	738	737	.500			-11.9
CRANDALL, DEL B 3.5.1930							
1972	Mil A e	54	70	.435	6-6	3/3	1.2
1973	Mil A e	74	88	.457	5		-4.7
1974	Mil A e	76	86	.469	5		-3.6
1975	Mil A e	67	94	.416	5-5	1/2	-1.9
1983	Sea A w	34	55	.382	7-7	2/2	0.1
1984	Sea A w	59	76	.437	7-5t	1/2	-0.8
	6	364	469	.437			-9.7
CRANE, SAM B 1.2.1854							
1880	Buf N	24	58	.293	7		-0.6
1884	Cin U	49	21	.700	5-3	2/2	-0.2
	2	73	79	.480			-0.8
CRAVATH, GAVY B 3.23.1881							
1919	Phi N	29	46	.387	8-8	2/2	2.0
1920	Phi N	62	91	.405	8		1.0
	2	91	137	.399			2.9
CRAVER, BILL B 6.1844							
1871	Tro NA	12	12	.500	7-6	2/2	0.6
1872	Bal NA	27	13	.675	2-2	1/2	-2.6
1875	Cen NA	2	12	.143	11		0.3
1876	NY N	21	35	.375	6		6.3
	4	62	72	.463			4.6
CREAMER, GEORGE B 1855							
1884	Pit AA	0	8	.000	10-10-10	4/5	-1.8
CRONIN, JOE B 10.12.1906							
1933	Was A	99	53	.651	1		5.4
1934	Was A	66	86	.434	7		-2.7
1935	Bos A	78	75	.510	4		2.9
1936	Bos A	74	80	.481	6		-4.0
1937	Bos A	80	72	.526	5		-0.3

Year	Tm/Lg	W	L	Pct	Finish	Mgr/Yr	+/-
1938	Bos A	88	61	.591	2		-0.1
1939	Bos A	89	62	.589	2		4.9
1940	Bos A	82	72	.532	4t		0.8
1941	Bos A	84	70	.545	2		-3.7
1942	Bos A	93	59	.612	2		0.2
1943	Bos A	68	84	.447	7		-3.2
1944	Bos A	77	77	.500	4		-6.3
1945	Bos A	71	83	.461	7		1.9
1946	Bos A	104	50	.675	1		7.1
1947	Bos A	83	71	.539	3		0.9
	15	1236	1055	.540			3.7
CROOKS, JACK B 11.9.1865							
1892-1	StL N	24	22	.522	11-9	3/3	7.2
-2	StL N	3	11	.214	12-11	1/3	-2.1
CROSS, LAVE B 5.12.1866							
1899	Cle N	8	30	.211	12-12	1/2	4.7
CUBBAGE, MIKE B 7.21.1950							
1991	NY N e	3	4	.429	3-5	2/2	-0.5
CURTIS, ED Curtis, Edwin R. (DNP)							
1884	Alt U	6	19	.240	6		4.3
CUSHMAN, CHARLIE B5.25.1850 New York, NY Cushman, Charles H. D6.29.1909 Milwaukee, WI (DNP)							
1891	Mil AA	21	15	.583	5		-3.5
CUTHBERT, NED B 6.20.1845							
1882	StL AA	37	43	.463	5		5.7
DAHLEN, BILL B 1.5.1870							
1910	Bro N	64	90	.416	6		1.1
1911	Bro N	64	86	.427	7		1.9
1912	Bro N	58	95	.379	7		-9.3
1913	Bro N	65	84	.436	6		-7.6
	4	251	355	.414			-13.8
DARK, ALVIN B 1.7.1922							
1961	SF N	85	69	.552	3		-3.7
1962	SF N	103	62	.624	1▲		2.2
1963	SF N	88	74	.543	3		-1.7
1964	SF N	90	72	.556	4		1.5
1966	KC A	74	86	.463	7		3.2
1967	KC A	52	69	.430	10-10	1/2	2.0
1968	Cle A	86	75	.534	3		4.1
1969	Cle A e	62	99	.385	6		-3.2
1970	Cle A e	76	86	.469	5		-2.3
1971	Cle A e	42	61	.408	6-6	1/2	4.3
1974	Oak A w	90	72	.556	1★		-6.0
1975	Oak A w	98	64	.605	1		1.3
1977	SD N w	48	65	.425	4-5	3/3	1.2
	13	994	954	.510			2.9
DAVENPORT, JIM B 8.17.1933							
1985	SF N w	56	88	.389	6-6	1/2	-4.6
DAVIDSON, MORDECAI B11.30.1846 Port Washington, OH Davidson, Mordecai H. D 9.6.1940 Louisville, KY (DNP)							
1888	Lou AA	1	2	.333	8-8-7	2/4	-0.1
	Lou AA	34	52	.395	8-7	4/4	1.3
DAVIS, GEORGE B 8.23.1870							
1895	NY N	16	17	.485	8-9	1/3	-0.9
1900	NY N	39	37	.513	8-8	2/2	6.5
1901	NY N	52	85	.380	7		4.4
	3	107	139	.435			10.0
DAVIS, HARRY B 7.19.1873							
1912	Cle A	54	71	.432	6-5	1/2	-8.2
DAVIS, SPUD B 12.20.1904							
1946	Pit N	1	2	.333	7-7	2/2	-0.3
DAY, JOHN B 9.23.1847 Colchester, CT Day, John B. D 1.25.1925 Cliffside, NJ (DNP)							
1899	NY N	29	35	.453	9-10	1/2	2.0
DEANE, HARRY B 5.6.1846							
1871	Kek NA	2	3	.400	7-8	2/2	1.4
DENT, BUCKY B 11.25.1951							
1989	NY A e	18	22	.450	6-5	2/2	0.3
1990	NY A e	18	31	.367	7-7	1/2	-1.9
	2	36	53	.404			-1.6
DICKEY, BILL B 6.6.1907							
1946	NY A	57	48	.543	2-3-3	2/3	-5.4
DIDDLEBOCK, HARRY B6.27.1854 Philadelphia, PA Diddlebock, Henry H. D2.5.1900 Philadelphia, PA (DNP)							
1896	StL N	7	10	.412	10-11	1/5	2.4
DIERKER, LARRY B 9.22.1946							
1997	Hou N c	84	78	.519	1		-8.8
1998	Hou N c	102	60	.630	1		-4.1
1999	Hou N c	37	23	.617	1-1	1/3	1.6
	Hou N c	47	28	.627	1t-1	3/3	2.7
2000	Hou N c	72	90	.444	4		-8.5
2001	Hou N c	93	69	.574	1		4.6
	5	435	348	.556			-12.4

Year	Tm/Lg	W	L	Pct	Finish	Mgr/Yr	+/-
DOBY, LARRY B 12.13.1923							
1978	Chi A w	37	50	.425	5-5	2/2	-1.1
DONOVAN, PATSY B 3.16.1865							
1897	Pit N	60	71	.458	8		8.8
1899	Pit N	69	58	.543	10-7	2/2	-0.1
1901	StL N	76	64	.543	4		-3.6
1902	StL N	56	78	.418	6		7.2
1903	StL N	43	94	.314	8		3.0
1904	Was A	37	97	.276	8-8	2/2	-0.3
1906	Bro N	66	86	.434	5		4.3
1907	Bro N	65	83	.439	5		0.1
1908	Bro N	53	101	.344	7		-6.4
1910	Bos A	81	72	.529	4		-3.9
1911	Bos A	78	75	.510	5		-2.3
	11	684	879	.438			6.8
DONOVAN, BILL B 10.13.1876							
1915	NY A	69	83	.454	5		-6.6
1916	NY A	80	74	.519	4		1.2
1917	NY A	71	82	.464	6		-1.6
1921	Phi N	25	62	.287	8-8	1/2	-2.3
	4	245	301	.449			-9.3
DOOIN, RED B 6.12.1879							
1910	Phi N	78	75	.510	4		-2.1
1911	Phi N	79	73	.520	4		4.1
1912	Phi N	73	79	.480	5		-1.2
1913	Phi N	88	63	.583	2		6.6
1914	Phi N	74	80	.481	6		0.7
	5	392	370	.514			8.0
DORGAN, MIKE B 10.2.1853							
1879	Syr N	17	26	.395	6-7	1/3	6.1
1880	Pro N	26	12	.684	3-2	3/3	1.3
1881	Wor N	24	32	.429	7-8	1/2	1.1
	3	67	70	.489			8.6
DOWD, TOMMY B 4.20.1869							
1896	StL N	25	38	.397	11-11	5/5	7.8
1897	StL N	6	22	.214	12-12	1/4	0.9
	2	31	60	.341			8.8
DOYLE, JACK B 10.25.1869							
1895	NY N	32	31	.508	8-9-9	2/3	-0.2
1898	Was N	8	9	.471	11-10-11	2/4	1.9
	2	40	40	.500			1.7
DRESSEN, CHUCK B 9.20.1898							
1934	Cin N	21	39	.350	8-8	3/3	-0.7
1935	Cin N	68	85	.444	6		4.0
1936	Cin N	74	80	.481	5		0.7
1937	Cin N	51	78	.395	8-8	1/2	-5.4
1951	Bro N	97	60	.618	2▲		0.8
1952	Bro N	96	57	.627	1		2.2
1953	Bro N	105	49	.682	1		3.5
1955	Was A	53	101	.344	8		-4.9
1956	Was A	59	95	.383	7		7.6
1957	Was A	4	16	.200	8-8	1/2	-3.4
1960	Mil N	88	66	.571	2		4.4
1961	Mil N	71	58	.550	3-4	1/2	1.8
1963	Det A	55	47	.539	9-5t	2/2	4.2
1964	Det A	85	77	.525	4		1.8
1965	Det A	65	55	.542	3-4	2/2	-1.2
1966	Det A	16	10	.615	3-3	1/3	2.7
	16	1008	973	.509			18.1
DUFFY, HUGH B 11.26.1866							
1901	Mil A	48	89	.350	8		-3.2
1904	Phi N	52	100	.342	8		-2.4
1905	Phi N	83	69	.546	4		-3.8
1906	Phi N	71	82	.464	4		-1.4
1910	Chi A	68	85	.444	6		-5.8
1911	Chi A	77	74	.510	4		-8.1
1921	Bos A	75	79	.487	5		0.8
1922	Bos A	61	93	.396	8		1.2
	8	535	671	.444			-22.7
DUNLAP, FRED B 5.21.1859							
1882	Cle N	42	36	.538	8-5	2/2	3.8
1884	StL U	66	16	.805	1-1	2/2	-4.3
1885	StL N	21	29	.420	5-8	1/3	5.5
	StL N	9	11	.450	8-8	3/3	2.8
1889	Pit N	7	10	.412	6-7-5	2/3	-0.6
	4	145	102	.587			7.1
DUROCHER, LEO B 7.27.1905							
1939	Bro N	84	69	.549	3		1.1
1940	Bro N	88	65	.575	2		3.7
1941	Bro N	100	54	.649	1		0.8
1942	Bro N	104	50	.675	2		2.7
1943	Bro N	81	72	.529	3		0.4
1944	Bro N	63	91	.409	7		-0.4
1945	Bro N	87	67	.565	3		3.2
1946	Bro N	96	60	.615	2▲		4.2
1948	Bro N	35	37	.486	5-3	1/3	-4.5

Year	Tm/Lg	W	L	Pct	Finish	Mgr/Yr	+/-
	NY N	41	38	.519	4-5	2/2	-2.3
1949	NY N	73	81	.474	5		-8.3
1950	NY N	86	68	.558	3		-0.2
1951	NY N	98	59	.624	1▲		5.5
1952	NY N	92	62	.597	2		6.6
1953	NY N	70	84	.455	5		-9.0
1954	NY N	97	57	.630	1★		1.1
1955	NY N	80	74	.519	3		0.1
1966	Chi N	59	103	.364	10		-5.5
1967	Chi N	87	74	.540	3		-1.7
1968	Chi N	84	78	.519	3		2.9
1969	Chi N e	92	70	.568	2		-0.4
1970	Chi N e	84	78	.519	2		-9.6
1971	Chi N e	83	79	.512	3t		3.2
1972	Chi N e	46	44	.511	4-2	1/2	-6.3
	Hou N w	16	15	.516	2-2	3/3	-1.0
1973	Hou N w	82	80	.506	4		0.1
	24	2008	1709	.540			-13.6
DWYER, FRANK B 3.25.1868							
1902	Det A	52	83	.385	7		-6.4
DYER, EDDIE B 10.11.1900							
1946	StL N	98	58	.628	1▲★		2.3
1947	StL N	89	65	.578	2		-2.5
1948	StL N	85	69	.552	2		-1.6
1949	StL N	96	58	.623	2		3.8
1950	StL N	78	75	.510	5		-0.8
	5	446	325	.578			1.2
DYKES, JIMMY B 11.10.1896							
1934	Chi A	49	88	.358	8-8	2/2	0.4
1935	Chi A	74	78	.487	5		-0.8
1936	Chi A	81	70	.536	3		1.4
1937	Chi A	86	68	.558	3		4.2
1938	Chi A	65	83	.439	6		-4.9
1939	Chi A	85	69	.552	4		6.3
1940	Chi A	82	72	.532	4t		-1.3
1941	Chi A	77	77	.500	3		1.1
1942	Chi A	66	82	.446	6		-0.3
1943	Chi A	82	72	.532	4		7.3
1944	Chi A	71	83	.461	7		6.8
1945	Chi A	71	78	.477	6		0.4
1946	Chi A	10	20	.333	7-5	1/2	-4.3
1951	Phi A	70	84	.455	6		-6.1
1952	Phi A	79	75	.513	4		7.9
1953	Phi A	59	95	.383	7		-1.4
1954	Bal A	54	100	.351	7		-2.7
1958	Cin N	24	17	.585	8-4	2/2	1.5
1959	Det A	74	63	.540	8-4	2/2	7.2
1960	Det A	44	52	.458	6-6	1/3	-3.3
	Cle A	26	32	.448	4-4	3/3	-2.0
1961	Cle A	77	83	.481	5-5	1/2	-1.5
	21	1406	1541	.477			15.7
EBBETS, CHARLIE B10.29.1859 New York, NY Ebbets, Charles Hercules D4.18.1925 New York, NY (DNP)							
1898	Bro N	38	68	.358	9-10	3/3	-2.8
EDWARDS, DOC B 12.10.1936							
1987	Cle A e	30	45	.400	7-7	2/2	1.7
1988	Cle A e	78	84	.481	6		3.6
1989	Cle A e	65	78	.455	6-6	1/2	-1.7
	3	173	207	.455			3.6
ELBERFELD, KID B 4.13.1875							
1908	NY A	27	71	.276	6-8	2/2	-4.4
ELIA, LEE B 7.16.1937							
1982	Chi N e	73	89	.451	5		-4.6
1983	Chi N e	54	69	.439	5-5	1/2	-6.1
1987	Phi N e	51	50	.505	5-4t	2/2	3.4
1988	Phi N e	60	92	.395	6-6	1/2	-2.5
	4	238	300	.442			-9.8
ELLICK, JOE B 4.3.1854							
1884	CP U	6	6	.500	5-5	3/3	0.6
ELLIOTT, BOB B 11.26.1916							
1960	KC A	58	96	.377	8		-4.8
ENS, JEWEL B 8.24.1889							
1929	Pit N	21	14	.600	2-2	2/2	0.9
1930	Pit N	80	74	.519	5		6.2
1931	Pit N	75	79	.487	5		3.6
	3	176	167	.513			10.8
ERMER, CAL B 11.10.1923							
1967	Min A	66	46	.589	6-2t	2/2	3.9
1968	Min A	79	83	.488	7		-3.8
	2	145	129	.529			0.1
ESSIAN, JIM B 1.2.1951							
1991	Chi N e	59	63	.484	5-4	3/3	1.0
ESTERBROOK, DUDE B 6.20.1857							
1889	Lou AA	2	8	.200	7-8	1/4	-0.2

Year	Tm/Lg	W	L	Pct	Finish	Mgr/Yr	+/-
EVERS, JOHNNY	B 7.21.1881						
1913	Chi N	88	65	.575	3		2.4
1921	Chi N	41	55	.427	6-7	.1/2	-0.6
1924	Chi A	10	11	.476	6	1/4	0.3
	Chi A	41	61	.402	8	4/4	-6.0
	3	180	192	.484			-3.9
EWING, BUCK	B 10.17.1859						
1890	NY P	74	57	.565	3		-2.8
1895	Cin N	66	64	.508	8		-3.0
1896	Cin N	77	50	.606	3		-1.3
1897	Cin N	76	56	.576	4		4.7
1898	Cin N	92	60	.605	3		7.4
1899	Cin N	83	67	.553	6		0.2
1900	NY N	21	41	.339	8-8	1/2	-5.5
	7	489	395	.553			-0.3
FAATZ, JAY	B 10.24.1860						
1890	Buf P	9	24	.273	8-8-8	2/3	0.4
FALK, BIBB	B 1.27.1899						
1933	Cle A	1	0	1.000	5-5-4	2/3	0.5
FANNING, JIM	B 9.14.1927						
1981-2	Mon N e	16	11	.593	2-1☆	2/2	1.2
1982	Mon N e	86	76	.531	3		-3.5
1984	Mon N e	14	16	.467	5-5	2/2	-1.2
	3	116	103	.530			-3.5
FARRELL, JACK	B 7.5.1857						
1881	Pro N	24	27	.471	4-2	1/2	-2.7
FARRELL, KERBY	B 9.3.1913						
1957	Cle A	76	77	.497	6		3.5
FELSKE, JOHN	B 5.30.1942						
1985	Phi N e	75	87	.463	5		-5.4
1986	Phi N e	86	75	.534	2		2.9
1987	Phi N e	29	32	.475	5-4t	1/2	0.3
	3	190	194	.495			-2.2
FERGUSON, BOB	B 1.31.1845						
1871	Mut NA	16	17	.485	4		0.3
1872	Atl NA	9	28	.243	6		6.7
1873	Atl NA	17	37	.315	6		3.5
1874	Atl NA	22	33	.400	6		6.7
1875	Har NA	54	28	.659	3		-6.8
1876	Har N	47	21	.691	3		-2.9
1877	Har N	31	27	.534	3		-0.7
1878	Chi N	30	30	.500	4		-3.5
1879	Tro N	7	22	.241	8-8	2/2	0.2
1880	Tro N	41	42	.494	4		3.9
1881	Tro N	39	45	.464	5		-0.3
1882	Tro N	35	48	.422	7		1.7
1883	Phi N	4	13	.235	8-8	1/2	1.9
1884	Pit AA	11	31	.262	9-11-10	2/5	1.6
1886	NY AA	48	70	.407	8-7	2/2	0.3
1887	NY AA	6	24	.200	8-7	1/3	-2.7
	16	417	516	.447			9.7
FERRARO, MIKE	B 8.18.1944						
1983	Cle A e	40	60	.400	7-7	1/2	-5.1
1986	KC A w	36	38	.486	4-3t	2/2	-0.1
	2	76	98	.437			-5.1
FESSENDEN, WALLACE	B 10.5.1860 Windham, NH						
Fessenden, Wallace Clifton D5.16.1935 Brooklyn, NY (DNP)							
1890	Syr AA	4	7	.364	7-7-6	2/3	-0.5
FITZSIMMONS, FREDDIE	B 7.28.1901						
1943	Phi N	26	38	.406	7-7	2/2	-1.4
1944	Phi N	61	92	.399	8		-2.7
1945	Phi N	18	51	.261	8-8	1/2	-2.4
	3	105	181	.367			-6.5
FLETCHER, ART	B 1.5.1885						
1923	Phi N	50	104	.325	8		-3.8
1924	Phi N	55	96	.364	7		-4.1
1925	Phi N	68	85	.444	6t		2.0
1926	Phi N	58	93	.384	8		2.3
1929	NY A	6	5	.545	2-2	2/2	-0.3
	5	237	383	.382			-4.0
FLINT, SILVER	B 8.3.1855						
1879	Chi N	5	12	.294	2-4	2/2	-4.0
FOGARTY, JIM	B 2.12.1864						
1890	Phi P	7	9	.438	5-5	1/2	-1.9
FOGEL, HORACE	B 3.2.1861 Macungie, PA Fogel,						
Horace S. D 11.15.1928 Philadelphia, PA (DNP)							
1887	Ind N	20	49	.290	8-8	3/3	1.1
1902	NY N	18	23	.439	4-8	1/3	4.2
	2	38	72	.345			5.4
FOHL, LEE	B 11.28.1876						
1915	Cle A	45	79	.363	6-7	2/2	-5.6
1916	Cle A	77	77	.500	6		-3.0
1917	Cle A	88	66	.571	3		6.4
1918	Cle A	73	54	.575	2		3.2

Year	Tm/Lg	W	L	Pct	Finish	Mgr/Yr	+/-
1919	Cle A	44	34	.564	3-2	1/2	-0.7
1921	StL A	81	73	.526	3		4.9
1922	StL A	93	61	.604	2		-5.5
1923	StL A	52	49	.515	3-5	1/2	3.6
1924	Bos A	67	87	.435	7		-3.2
1925	Bos A	47	105	.309	8		-2.5
1926	Bos A	46	107	.301	8		-3.3
	11	713	792	.474			-5.6
FONSECA, LEW	B 1.21.1899						
1932	Chi A	49	102	.325	7		-5.0
1933	Chi A	67	83	.447	6		4.5
1934	Chi A	4	11	.267	8-8	1/2	-1.3
	3	120	196	.380			-1.8
FOUTZ, DAVE	B 9.7.1856						
1893	Bro N	65	63	.508	6t		6.9
1894	Bro N	70	61	.534	5		4.2
1895	Bro N	71	60	.542	5t		2.1
1896	Bro N	58	73	.443	9t		-1.0
	4	264	257	.507			12.2
FOX, CHARLIE	B 10.7.1921						
1970	SF N w	67	53	.558	4-3	2/2	6.7
1971	SF N w	90	72	.556	1		2.6
1972	SF N w	69	86	.445	5		-9.8
1973	SF N w	88	74	.543	3		3.3
1974	SF N w	34	42	.447	5-5	1/2	0.3
1976	Mon N e	12	22	.353	6-6	2/2	-0.4
1983	Chi N e	17	22	.436	5-5	2/2	-2.1
	7	377	371	.504			0.5
FRANCONA, TERRY	B 4.22.1959						
1997	Phi N e	68	94	.420	5		3.9
1998	Phi N e	75	87	.463	3		3.3
1999	Phi N e	77	85	.475	3		-3.5
2000	Phi N e	65	97	.401	5		-4.1
	4	285	363	.440			-0.4
FRANKS, HERMAN	B 1.4.1914						
1965	SF N	95	67	.586	2		4.5
1966	SF N	93	68	.578	2		7.3
1967	SF N	91	71	.562	2		-1.1
1968	SF N	88	74	.543	2		-1.0
1977	Chi N e	81	81	.500	4		4.7
1978	Chi N e	79	83	.488	3		4.2
1979	Chi N e	78	77	.503	5-5	1/2	0.6
	7	605	521	.537			19.2
FRAZER, GEORGE	B1.7.1861 Syracuse, NY Frazer,						
George Kasson D2.5.1913 Philadelphia, PA (DNP)							
1890	Syr AA	31	40	.437	7-6	1/3	2.0
	Syr AA	20	25	.444	7-6	3/3	1.6
FRAZIER, JOE	B 10.6.1922						
1976	NY N e	86	76	.531	3		-3.7
1977	NY N e	15	30	.333	6-6	1/2	-5.2
	2	101	106	.488			-8.9
FREGOSI, JIM	B 4.4.1942						
1978	Cal A w	62	54	.534	3-2t	2/2	2.1
1979	Cal A w	88	74	.543	1		-2.3
1980	Cal A w	65	95	.406	6		-5.3
1981-1	Cal A w	22	25	.468	4-4	1/2	-2.5
1986	Chi A w	45	51	.469	5-5	3/3	0.4
1987	Chi A w	77	85	.475	5		-4.2
1988	Chi A w	71	90	.441	5		3.4
1991	Phi N e	74	75	.497	6-3	2/2	4.5
1992	Phi N e	70	92	.432	6		-7.8
1993	Phi N e	97	65	.599	1◆		3.0
1994	Phi N e	54	61	.470	4		-5.9
1995	Phi N e	69	75	.479	2t		1.3
1996	Phi N e	67	95	.414	5		0.1
1999	Tor A e	84	78	.519	3		1.1
2000	Tor A e	83	79	.512	3		6.3
	15	1028	1094	.484			-5.9
FREY, JIM	B 5.26.1931 Cleveland, OH Frey, James						
Gottfried BL/TL, 5-9/170# (OF)							
1980	KC A w	97	65	.599	1◆		4.7
1981-1	KC A w	20	30	.400	5		-0.6
-2	KC A w	10	10	.500	2t-1	1/2	0.2
1984	Chi N e	96	65	.596	1		5.0
1985	Chi N e	77	84	.478	4		0.9
1986	Chi N e	23	33	.411	5-5	1/3	-1.5
	5	323	287	.530			8.6
FRISCH, FRANKIE	B 9.9.1898						
1933	StL N	36	26	.581	5-5	2/2	1.7
1934	StL N	95	58	.621	1★		4.5
1935	StL N	96	58	.623	2		-0.9
1936	StL N	87	67	.565	2t		9.9
1937	StL N	81	73	.526	4		-1.4
1938	StL N	63	72	.467	6-6	1/2	-4.8
1940	Pit N	78	76	.506	4		-1.4
1941	Pit N	81	73	.526	4		-0.8

Year	Tm/Lg	W	L	Pct	Finish	Mgr/Yr	+/-
1942	Pit N	66	81	.449	5		-2.6
1943	Pit N	80	74	.519	4		-3.7
1944	Pit N	90	63	.588	2		5.3
1945	Pit N	82	72	.532	4		-1.6
1946	Pit N	62	89	.411	7-7	1/2	-1.3
1949	Chi N	42	62	.404	7-8	2/2	2.2
1950	Chi N	64	89	.418	7		0.3
1951	Chi N	35	45	.438	7-8	1/2	2.1
	16	1138	1078	.514			7.4
FUCHS, JUDGE	B 4.17.1878 Hamburg, Germany						
Fuchs, Emil Edwin D 12.5.1961 Boston, MA (DNP)							
1929	Bos N	56	98	.364	8		-0.2
GAFFNEY, JOHN	B 6.29.1855 Roxbury, MA						
Gaffney, John H. D 8.8.1913 New York, NY (DNP)							
1886	Was N	15	25	.375	8	2/2	6.0
1887	Was N	46	76	.377	7		5.0
	2	61	101	.377			11.0
GALANTE, MATT	B 3.22.1944 Brooklyn, NY						
Galante, Matthew Joseph BR/TR, 5-6/175# (2B)							
1999	Hou N c	13	14	.481	1t-1	2/3	-2.9
GALVIN, JIM	B 12.25.1856						
1885	Buf N	7	17	.292	7-7	1/2	0.1
GANZEL, JOHN	B 4.7.1874						
1908	Cin N	73	81	.474	5		2.4
1915	Bro F	17	18	.486	7-7	2/2	0.1
	2	90	99	.476			2.5
GARCIA, DAVE	B 9.15.1920 E.St.Louis, IL Garcia,						
David BR/TR, 6/180# (2B)							
1977	Cal A w	35	46	.432	5-5	2/2	-4.5
1978	Cal A w	25	21	.543	3-2t	1/2	1.3
1979	Cle A e	38	28	.576	6-6	2/2	6.8
1980	Cle A e	79	81	.494	6		5.7
1981-1	Cle A e	26	24	.520	6		1.6
-2	Cle A e	26	27	.491	5		1.6
1982	Cle A e	78	84	.481	6t		3.6
	6	307	311	.497			16.1
GARDENHIRE, RON	B 10.24.1957						
2002	Min A c	94	67	.584	1☆		8.0
2003	Min A c	90	72	.556	1		4.8
	2	184	139	.570			12.8
GARDNER, BILLY	B 7.19.1927						
1981-1	Min A w	6	14	.300	6-7	2/2	-1.9
-2	Min A w	24	29	.453	4		-1.9
1982	Min A w	60	102	.370	7		-4.9
1983	Min A w	70	92	.432	5		0.0
1984	Min A w	81	81	.500	2		0.2
1985	Min A w	27	35	.435	6-4	1/2	-1.1
1987	KC A w	62	64	.492	4-2	1/2	-2.9
	6	330	417	.442			-12.5
GARNER, PHIL	B 4.30.1949						
1992	Mil A e	92	70	.568	2		-3.2
1993	Mil A e	69	93	.426	7		-6.2
1994	Mil A c	53	62	.461	5		-0.8
1995	Mil A c	65	79	.451	4		-6.3
1996	Mil A c	80	82	.494	3		-0.5
1997	Mil A c	78	83	.484	3		3.7
1998	Mil N c	74	88	.457	5		3.3
1999	Mil N c	52	60	.464	5-5	1/2	0.6
2000	Det A c	79	83	.488	3		-1.6
2001	Det A c	66	96	.407	4		-0.5
2002	Det A c	0	6	.000	5-5	1/2	-1.9
	11	708	802	.469			-13.6
GASTON, CITO	B 3.17.1944						
1989	Tor A e	77	49	.611	6-1	2/2	7.6
1990	Tor A e	86	76	.531	2		-5.7
1991	Tor A e	66	54	.550	1-1	1/3	1.1
	Tor A e	6	3	.667	1-1	3/3	1.1
1992	Tor A e	96	66	.593	1★		5.2
1993	Tor A e	95	67	.586	1★		3.9
1994	Tor A e	55	60	.478	3		-1.3
1995	Tor A e	56	88	.389	5		-3.1
1996	Tor A e	74	88	.457	4		-2.9
1997	Tor A e	72	85	.459	5-5	1/2	-2.5
	9	683	636	.518			3.6
GERHARDT, JOE	B 2.14.1855						
1883	Lou AA	52	45	.536	5		3.3
1890	StL AA	20	16	.556	2-3	6/6	-1.1
	2	72	61	.541			2.2
GESSLER, DOC	B 12.23.1880						
1914	Pit F	3	8	.273	8-7	1/2	-1.8
GIBSON, GEORGE	B 7.22.1880						
1920	Pit N	79	75	.513	4		4.5
1921	Pit N	90	63	.588	2		3.4
1922	Pit N	32	33	.492	5-3t	1/2	-5.6
1925	Chi N	12	14	.462	7-8	3/3	-0.2

Year	Tm/Lg	W	L	Pct	Finish	Mgr/Yr	+/-
1932	Pit N	86	68	.558	2		10.0
1933	Pit N	87	67	.565	2		5.0
1934	Pit N	27	24	.529	4-5	1/2	0.8
7		413	344	.546			17.9

GIFFORD, JIM B 10.18.1845 Warren, NY Gifford, James H. D 12.19.1901 Columbus, OH (DNP)

Year	Tm/Lg	W	L	Pct	Finish	Mgr/Yr	+/-
1884	Ind AA	25	60	.294	10-11	1/2	3.5
1885	NY AA	44	64	.407	7		4.5
1886	NY AA	5	12	.294	8-7	1/2	-1.9
3		74	136	.352			6.1

GLASSCOCK, JACK B 7.22.1859

Year	Tm/Lg	W	L	Pct	Finish	Mgr/Yr	+/-
1889	Ind N	34	32	.515	7-7	2/2	4.1
1892-1	StL N	1	3	.250	10-9	1/3	-0.5
2		35	35	.500			3.7

GLEASON, KID B 10.26.1866

Year	Tm/Lg	W	L	Pct	Finish	Mgr/Yr	+/-
1919	Chi A	88	52	.629	1		4.4
1920	Chi A	96	58	.623	2		6.4
1921	Chi A	62	92	.403	7		1.6
1922	Chi A	77	77	.500	5		0.0
1923	Chi A	69	85	.448	7		-3.1
5		392	364	.519			9.3

GOMEZ, PRESTON B 4.20.1923

Year	Tm/Lg	W	L	Pct	Finish	Mgr/Yr	+/-
1969	SD N w	52	110	.321	6		1.5
1970	SD N w	63	99	.389	6		-7.3
1971	SD N w	61	100	.379	6		-5.2
1972	SD N w	4	7	.364	4-6	1/2	-0.1
1974	Hou N w	81	81	.500	4		-2.2
1975	Hou N w	47	80	.370	6-6	1/2	-12.7
1980	Chi N e	38	52	.422	6-6	1/2	-0.4
7		346	529	.395			-26.5

GONZALEZ, MIKE B 9.24.1890

Year	Tm/Lg	W	L	Pct	Finish	Mgr/Yr	+/-
1938	StL N	8	8	.500	6-6	2/2	-0.0
1940	StL N	1	5	.167	6-7-3	2/3	-2.2
2		9	13	.409			-2.2

GORDON, JOE B 2.18.1915

Year	Tm/Lg	W	L	Pct	Finish	Mgr/Yr	+/-
1958	Cle A	46	40	.535	6-4	2/2	-0.4
1959	Cle A	89	65	.578	2		2.1
1960	Cle A	49	46	.516	4-4	1/3	3.1
	Det A	26	31	.456	6-6	3/3	-2.1
1961	KC A	26	33	.441	8-9t	1/2	2.9
1969	KC A w	69	93	.426	4		-1.1
5		305	308	.498			4.6

GORE, GEORGE B 5.3.1857

Year	Tm/Lg	W	L	Pct	Finish	Mgr/Yr	+/-
1892-2	StL N	6	9	.400	12-12-11	2/3	0.5

GORYL, JOHNNY B 10.21.1933

Year	Tm/Lg	W	L	Pct	Finish	Mgr/Yr	+/-
1980	Min A w	23	13	.639	4-3	2/2	6.2
1981-1	Min A w	11	25	.306	6-7	1/2	-3.2
2		34	38	.472			3.0

GOULD, CHARLIE B 8.21.1847

Year	Tm/Lg	W	L	Pct	Finish	Mgr/Yr	+/-
1875	NH NA	2	21	.087	11-8	1/3	0.1
1876	Cin N	9	56	.138	8		5.4
2		11	77	.125			5.5

GOWDY, HANK B 8.24.1889

Year	Tm/Lg	W	L	Pct	Finish	Mgr/Yr	+/-
1946	Cin N	3	1	.750	6-6	2/2	1.1

GRAFFEN, MASE B 1845 Philadelphia, PA Graffen, Samuel Mason D 11.18.1883 Silver City, NM (DNP)

Year	Tm/Lg	W	L	Pct	Finish	Mgr/Yr	+/-
1876	StL N	39	17	.696	2-2	1/2	-2.3

GRAMMAS, ALEX B 4.3.1926

Year	Tm/Lg	W	L	Pct	Finish	Mgr/Yr	+/-
1969	Pit N e	4	1	.800	3-3	2/2	1.3
1976	Mil A e	66	95	.410	6		-5.3
1977	Mil A e	67	95	.414	6		-1.2
3		137	191	.418			-5.1

GREEN, DALLAS B 8.4.1934

Year	Tm/Lg	W	L	Pct	Finish	Mgr/Yr	+/-
1979	Phi N e	19	11	.633	5-4	2/2	4.7
1980	Phi N e	91	71	.562	1★		0.8
1981-1	Phi N e	34	21	.618	1		3.6
-2	Phi N e	25	27	.481	3		3.6
1989	NY A e	56	65	.463	6-5	1/2	2.5
1993	NY N e	46	78	.371	7-7	2/2	-10.4
1994	NY N e	55	58	.487	3		0.5
1995	NY N e	69	75	.479	2t		-6.9
1996	NY N e	59	72	.450	4-4	1/2	-3.9
8		454	478	.487			-5.6

GRIFFIN, MIKE B 3.20.1865

Year	Tm/Lg	W	L	Pct	Finish	Mgr/Yr	+/-
1898	Bro N	1	3	.250	9-9-10	2/3	-0.5

GRIFFIN, SANDY B 10.24.1858

Year	Tm/Lg	W	L	Pct	Finish	Mgr/Yr	+/-
1891	Was AA	2	4	.333	8-8	4/4	0.4

GRIFFITH, CLARK B 11.20.1869

Year	Tm/Lg	W	L	Pct	Finish	Mgr/Yr	+/-
1901	Chi A	83	53	.610	1		-2.3
1902	Chi A	74	60	.552	4		-0.2
1903	NY A	72	62	.537	4		4.4
1904	NY A	92	59	.609	2		8.5
1905	NY A	71	78	.477	6		0.2
1906	NY A	90	61	.596	2		4.0
1907	NY A	70	78	.473	5		2.4
1908	NY A	24	32	.429	6-8	1/2	6.0
1909	Cin N	77	76	.503	4		-0.3
1910	Cin N	75	79	.487	5		4.6
1911	Cin N	70	83	.458	6		-4.1
1912	Was A	91	61	.599	2		2.7
1913	Was A	90	64	.584	2		9.3
1914	Was A	81	73	.526	3		-2.1
1915	Was A	85	68	.556	4		-0.4
1916	Was A	76	77	.497	7		0.3
1917	Was A	74	79	.484	5		-0.0
1918	Was A	72	56	.563	3		2.3
1919	Was A	56	84	.400	7		-10.0
1920	Was A	68	84	.447	6		-0.5
20		1491	1367	.522			24.9

GRIMES, BURLEIGH B 8.18.1893

Year	Tm/Lg	W	L	Pct	Finish	Mgr/Yr	+/-
1937	Bro N	62	91	.405	6		1.1
1938	Bro N	69	80	.463	7		-4.9
2		131	171	.434			-3.8

GRIMM, CHARLIE B 8.28.1898

Year	Tm/Lg	W	L	Pct	Finish	Mgr/Yr	+/-
1932	Chi N	37	18	.673	2-1	2/2	6.4
1933	Chi N	86	68	.558	3		-2.9
1934	Chi N	86	65	.570	3		3.8
1935	Chi N	100	54	.649	1		-1.5
1936	Chi N	87	67	.565	2t		-5.4
1937	Chi N	93	61	.604	2		3.6
1938	Chi N	45	36	.556	3-1	1/2	-1.9
1944	Chi N	74	69	.517	8-4	3/3	-0.6
1945	Chi N	98	56	.636	1		-0.3
1946	Chi N	82	71	.536	3		0.7
1947	Chi N	69	85	.448	6		7.9
1948	Chi N	64	90	.416	8		-1.8
1949	Chi N	19	31	.380	7-8	1/2	-0.1
1952	Bos N	51	67	.432	7-7	2/2	-1.2
1953	Mil N	92	62	.597	2		-0.4
1954	Mil N	89	65	.578	3		-0.1
1955	Mil N	85	69	.552	2		0.6
1956	Mil N	24	22	.522	5-2	1/2	-3.4
1960	Chi N	6	11	.353	7-7	1/2	-0.9
19		1287	1067	.547			2.4

GROH, HEINIE B 9.18.1889

Year	Tm/Lg	W	L	Pct	Finish	Mgr/Yr	+/-
1918	Cin N	7	3	.700	4-3	2/2	1.7

GUTTERIDGE, DON B 6.19.1912

Year	Tm/Lg	W	L	Pct	Finish	Mgr/Yr	+/-
1969	Chi A w	60	85	.414	4-5	2/2	-3.4
1970	Chi A w	49	87	.360	6-6	1/3	-3.1
2		109	172	.388			-6.5

HAAS, EDDIE B 5.26.1935

Year	Tm/Lg	W	L	Pct	Finish	Mgr/Yr	+/-
1985	Atl N w	50	71	.413	5-5	1/2	0.8

HACK, STAN B 12.6.1909

Year	Tm/Lg	W	L	Pct	Finish	Mgr/Yr	+/-
1954	Chi N	64	90	.416	7		-6.6
1955	Chi N	72	81	.471	6		4.4
1956	Chi N	60	94	.390	8		-5.4
1958	StL N	3	7	.300	5-5t	2/2	-1.4
4		199	272	.423			-9.1

HACKETT, CHARLIE B 1855 Lee, MA Hackett, Charles M. D 8.1.1898 Holyoke, MA (DNP)

Year	Tm/Lg	W	L	Pct	Finish	Mgr/Yr	+/-
1884	Cle N	35	77	.313	7		3.0
1885	Bro AA	15	22	.405	7-5t	1/2	-2.7
2		50	99	.336			0.3

HALLMAN, BILL B 3.31.1867

Year	Tm/Lg	W	L	Pct	Finish	Mgr/Yr	+/-
1897	StL N	13	36	.265	12-12-12	3/4	4.2

HANEY, FRED B 4.25.1898

Year	Tm/Lg	W	L	Pct	Finish	Mgr/Yr	+/-
1939	StL A	43	111	.279	8		-7.1
1940	StL A	67	87	.435	6		1.6
1941	StL A	15	29	.341	7-6t	1/2	-5.4
1953	Pit N	50	104	.325	8		-1.6
1954	Pit N	53	101	.344	8		4.6
1955	Pit N	60	94	.390	8		4.2
1956	Mil N	68	40	.630	5-2	2/2	3.7
1957	Mil N	95	59	.617	1★		2.0
1958	Mil N	92	62	.597	1		0.7
1959	Mil N	86	70	.551	2▲		-2.3
10		629	757	.454			0.4

HANLON, NED B 8.22.1857

Year	Tm/Lg	W	L	Pct	Finish	Mgr/Yr	+/-
1889	Pit N	26	18	.591	7-5	3/3	6.2
1890	Pit P	60	68	.469	6		0.7
1891	Pit N	31	47	.397	8-8	1/2	-4.5
1892-1	Bal N	17	39	.304	12-12	3/3	-3.0
-2	Bal N	26	46	.361	10		-6.5
1893	Bal N	60	70	.462	8		1.0
1894	Bal N	89	39	.695	1		-1.9
1895	Bal N	87	43	.669	1		-8.8
1896	Bal N	90	39	.698	1●		-2.7
1897	Bal N	90	40	.692	2●		-0.1
1898	Bal N	96	53	.644	2		-7.8
1899	Bro N	100	47	.680	1		4.7
1900	Bro N	82	54	.603	1●		5.4
1901	Bro N	79	57	.581	3		-2.8
1902	Bro N	75	63	.543	2		1.1
1903	Bro N	70	66	.515	5		3.4
1904	Bro N	56	97	.366	6		-7.4
1905	Bro N	48	104	.316	8		3.0
1906	Cin N	64	87	.424	6		-6.0
1907	Cin N	66	87	.431	6		-11.3
19		1312	1164	.530			-37.1

HARDER, MEL B 10.15.1909

Year	Tm/Lg	W	L	Pct	Finish	Mgr/Yr	+/-
1961	Cle A	1	0	1.000	5-5	2/2	0.5
1962	Cle A	2	0	1.000	6-6	2/2	1.1
2		3	0	1.000			1.6

HARGROVE, MIKE B 10.26.1949

Year	Tm/Lg	W	L	Pct	Finish	Mgr/Yr	+/-
1991	Cle A e	32	53	.376	7-7	2/2	-0.5
1992	Cle A e	76	86	.469	4t		2.3
1993	Cle A e	76	86	.469	6		-2.8
1994	Cle A c	66	47	.584	2		-1.1
1995	Cle A c	100	44	.694	1◆		5.9
1996	Cle A c	99	62	.615	1		1.7
1997	Cle A c	86	75	.534	1◆		0.6
1998	Cle A c	89	73	.549	1☆		1.3
1999	Cle A c	97	65	.599	1		2.8
2000	Bal A e	74	88	.457	4		4.0
2001	Bal A e	63	98	.391	4		-3.6
2002	Bal A e	67	95	.414	4		-3.3
2003	Bal A e	71	91	.438	4		-2.5
13		996	963	.508			4.8

HARRAH, TOBY B 10.26.1948

Year	Tm/Lg	W	L	Pct	Finish	Mgr/Yr	+/-
1992	Tex A w	32	44	.421	3-4	2/2	-2.6

HARRELSON, BUD B 6.6.1944

Year	Tm/Lg	W	L	Pct	Finish	Mgr/Yr	+/-
1990	NY N e	71	49	.592	4-2	2/2	-1.3
1991	NY N e	74	80	.481	3-5	1/2	-2.4
2		145	129	.529			-3.7

HARRIS, LUM B 1.17.1915

Year	Tm/Lg	W	L	Pct	Finish	Mgr/Yr	+/-
1961	Bal A	17	10	.630	3-3	2/2	1.7
1964	Hou N	5	8	.385	9-9	2/2	-0.3
1965	Hou N	65	97	.401	9		-0.8
1968	Atl N	81	81	.500	5		4.1
1969	Atl N w	93	69	.574	1		5.7
1970	Atl N w	76	86	.469	5		-1.5
1971	Atl N w	82	80	.506	3		6.8
1972	Atl N w	47	57	.452	4-4	1/2	2.0
8		466	488	.488			17.7

HARRIS, BUCKY B 11.8.1896

Year	Tm/Lg	W	L	Pct	Finish	Mgr/Yr	+/-
1924	Was A	92	62	.597	1★		0.6
1925	Was A	96	55	.636	1		5.3
1926	Was A	81	69	.540	4		2.2
1927	Was A	85	69	.552	3		3.0
1928	Was A	75	79	.487	4		-3.3
1929	Det A	70	84	.455	6		-6.8
1930	Det A	75	79	.487	5		2.6
1931	Det A	61	93	.396	7		1.9
1932	Det A	76	75	.503	5		-0.6
1933	Det A	73	79	.480	5-5	1/2	-1.9
1934	Bos A	76	76	.500	4		-4.2
1935	Was A	67	86	.438	6		-2.3
1936	Was A	82	71	.536	4		-2.6
1937	Was A	73	80	.477	6		4.4
1938	Was A	75	76	.497	5		4.8
1939	Was A	65	87	.428	6		-1.9
1940	Was A	64	90	.416	7		1.1
1941	Was A	70	84	.455	6t		-0.3
1942	Was A	62	89	.411	7		2.3
1943	Phi N	38	52	.422	7-7	1/2	-0.5
1947	NY A	97	57	.630	1★		-2.9
1948	NY A	94	60	.610	3		-4.6
1950	Was A	67	87	.435	5		1.9
1951	Was A	62	92	.403	7		-6.0
1952	Was A	78	76	.506	5		2.1
1953	Was A	76	76	.500	5		-7.5
1954	Was A	66	88	.429	6		-6.1
1955	Det A	79	75	.513	5		-9.5
1956	Det A	82	72	.532	5		-3.7
29		2157	2218	.493			-32.5

HART, JIM B 7.10.1855 Fairview, PA Hart, James Aristotle D 7.18.1919 Chicago, IL (DNP)

Year	Tm/Lg	W	L	Pct	Finish	Mgr/Yr	+/-
1885	Lou AA	53	59	.473	5t		0.2
1886	Lou AA	66	70	.485	4		-4.4
1889	Bos N	83	45	.648	2		0.8
3		202	174	.537			-3.4

HART, JOHN B 7.21.1948 Tampa, FL Hart, John Henry (born John Henry Reen) BR/TR, 6-1/180# (C)

Year	Tm/Lg	W	L	Pct	Finish	Mgr/Yr	+/-
1989	Cle A e	8	11	.421	6-6	2/2	-0.9

HARTNETT, GABBY B 12.20.1900

Year	Tm/Lg	W	L	Pct	Finish	Mgr/Yr	+/-
1938	Chi N	44	27	.620	3-1	2/2	2.9
1939	Chi N	84	70	.545	4		2.4

Year	Tm/Lg	W	L	Pct	Finish	Mgr/Yr	+/-
1940	Chi N	75	79	.487	5		-6.6
	3	203	176	.536			-1.3
HARTSFIELD, ROY B 10.25.1925							
1977	Tor A e	54	107	.335	7		-4.6
1978	Tor A e	59	102	.366	7		-2.4
1979	Tor A e	53	109	.327	7		-3.2
	3	166	318	.343			-10.3
HASTINGS, SCOTT B 8.10.1847							
1871	Rok NA	4	21	.160	9		-4.8
1872	Cle NA	6	14	.300	6-7	1/2	0.9
	2	10	35	.222			-3.9
HATFIELD, JOHN B 7.20.1847							
1872	Mut NA	24	14	.632	4-3	2/2	-3.6
1873	Mut NA	11	17	.393	5-4	1/2	-4.6
	2	35	31	.530			-8.1
HATTON, GRADY B 10.7.1922							
1966	Hou N	72	90	.444	8		-0.2
1967	Hou N	69	93	.426	9		-0.0
1968	Hou N	23	38	.377	10-10	1/2	-4.1
	3	164	221	.426			-4.3
HECKER, GUY B 4.3.1856							
1890	Pit N	23	113	.169	8		7.5
HEFFNER, DON B 2.8.1911							
1966	Cin N	37	46	.446	8-7	1/2	-4.0
HEILBRONER, LOUIE B7.4.1861 Ft.Wayne, IN Heilbroner, Louis Wilbur D12.21.1933 Ft.Wayne, IN (DNP)							
1900	StL N	23	25	.479	7-5*t*	2/2	-0.9
HELMS, TOMMY B 5.5.1941							
1988	Cin N w	12	15	.444	4-4-2	2/3	-2.3
1989	Cin N w	16	21	.432	4*t*-5	2/2	-1.1
	2	28	36	.438			-3.4
HEMUS, SOLLY B 4.17.1923							
1959	StL N	71	83	.461	7		2.5
1960	StL N	86	68	.558	3		6.6
1961	StL N	33	41	.446	6-5	1/2	-5.7
	3	190	192	.497			3.3
HENDERSON, BILL Henderson, William C. (DNP)							
1884	Bal U	58	47	.552	4		-2.5
HENDRICKS, JACK B 4.9.1875							
1918	StL N	51	78	.395	8		-5.5
1924	Cin N	83	70	.542	4		-0.9
1925	Cin N	80	73	.523	3		-1.3
1926	Cin N	87	67	.565	2		0.3
1927	Cin N	75	78	.490	5		-0.5
1928	Cin N	78	74	.513	5		5.9
1929	Cin N	66	88	.429	7		-3.7
	7	520	528	.496			-5.7
HENGLE, ED B Chicago, IL Hengle, Edward Siegfried D 11.4.1927 Norwich, England (DNP)							
1884	CP U	34	39	.466	5	1/3	0.9
HERMAN, BILLY B 7.7.1909							
1947	Pit N	61	92	.399	8-7*t*	1/2	-8.7
1964	Bos A	2	0	1.000	8-8	2/2	1.1
1965	Bos A	62	100	.383	9		-6.8
1966	Bos A	64	82	.438	9-9	1/2	-2.0
	4	189	274	.408			-16.4
HERZOG, BUCK B 7.9.1885							
1914	Cin N	60	94	.390	8		-3.8
1915	Cin N	71	83	.461	7		1.9
1916	Cin N	34	49	.410	8-7*t*	1/3	-0.7
	3	165	226	.422			-2.6
HERZOG, WHITEY B 11.9.1931							
1973	Tex A w	47	91	.341	6-6	1/3	-2.9
1974	Cal A w	2	2	.500	6-6-6	2/3	0.1
1975	KC A w	41	25	.621	2-2	2/2	5.4
1976	KC A w	90	72	.556	1		-1.7
1977	KC A w	102	60	.630	1		4.0
1978	KC A w	92	70	.568	1		-0.2
1979	KC A w	85	77	.525	2		0.7
1980	StL N e	38	35	.521	6-5-4	3/4	0.2
1981-1	StL N e	30	20	.600	2		3.2
-2	StL N e	29	23	.558	2		3.2
1982	StL N e	92	70	.568	1★		2.9
1983	StL N e	79	83	.488	4		1.2
1984	StL N e	84	78	.519	3		2.3
1985	StL N e	101	61	.623	1◆		1.6
1986	StL N e	79	82	.491	3		-0.4
1987	StL N e	95	67	.586	1◆		3.6
1988	StL N e	76	86	.469	5		1.0
1989	StL N e	86	76	.531	3		2.4
1990	StL N e	33	47	.412	6-6	1/3	-1.8
	18	1281	1125	.532			24.8

Year	Tm/Lg	W	L	Pct	Finish	Mgr/Yr	+/-
HEWETT, WALTER B 1861 Washington, DC Hewett, Walter F. D 10.7.1944 Washington, DC (DNP)							
1888	Was N	10	29	.256	8-8	1/2	-2.2
HICKS, NAT B 4.19.1845							
1874	Phi NA	29	29	.500	4		-3.6
1875	Mut NA	30	38	.441	7		4.9
	2	59	67	.468			1.3
HIGGINS, PINKY B 5.27.1909							
1955	Bos A	84	70	.545	4		-3.2
1956	Bos A	84	70	.545	4		4.2
1957	Bos A	82	72	.532	3		-0.3
1958	Bos A	79	75	.513	3		1.4
1959	Bos A	31	42	.425	8-8	1/3	-6.9
1960	Bos A	48	57	.457	8-7	3/3	3.3
1961	Bos A	76	86	.469	6		1.2
1962	Bos A	76	84	.475	8		0.9
	8	560	556	.502			0.6
HIGHAM, DICK B 7.24.1851							
1874	Mut NA	29	11	.725	3-2	2/2	2.8
HIMSL, VEDIE B 4.2.1917 Plevna, MT Himsl, Avitus Bernard BR/TR, 6-1/200# (P)							
1961	Chi N	5	6	.455	6-6*t*	1/9	0.3
	Chi N	5	12	.294	7-7-7	3/9	-2.3
	Chi N	0	3	.000	7-7-7	6/9	-1.3
HITCHCOCK, BILLY B 7.31.1916							
1960	Det A	1	0	1.000	6-6-6	2/3	0.5
1962	Bal A	77	85	.475	7		-1.1
1963	Bal A	86	76	.531	4		2.5
1966	Atl N	33	18	.647	7-5	2/2	4.4
1967	Atl N	77	82	.484	7-7	1/2	-1.6
	5	274	261	.512			4.8
HOBSON, BUTCH B 8.17.1951							
1992	Bos A e	73	89	.451	7		-0.5
1993	Bos A e	80	82	.494	5		0.2
1994	Bos A e	54	61	.470	4		3.0
	3	207	232	.472			2.7
HODGES, GIL B 4.4.1924							
1963	Was A	42	79	.347	10-10	3/3	-0.6
1964	Was A	62	100	.383	9		-2.7
1965	Was A	70	92	.432	8		2.7
1966	Was A	71	88	.447	8		2.6
1967	Was A	76	85	.472	6*t*		5.1
1968	NY N	73	89	.451	9		-4.8
1969	NY N e	100	62	.617	1★		8.9
1970	NY N e	83	79	.512	3		-4.8
1971	NY N e	83	79	.512	3*t*		-2.3
	9	660	753	.467			4.1
HOEY, FRED B 1866 New York, NY Hoey, Frederick Chamberlain D 12.7.1933 Paris, France (DNP)							
1899	NY N	31	55	.360	9-10	2/2	-5.3
HOFFMAN, GLENN B 7.7.1958							
1998	LA N w	47	41	.534	3-3	2/2	3.5
HOLBERT, BILL B 3.14.1855							
1879	Syr N	0	1	.000	6-6-7	2/3	-0.3
HOLLINGSHEAD, HOLLY B 1.17.1853							
1875	Was NA	4	16	.200	8-10	1/2	6.4
1884	Was AA	12	50	.194	12-12	1/2	1.2
	2	16	66	.195			7.6
HOLMES, TOMMY B 3.29.1917							
1951	Bos N	48	47	.505	5-4	2/2	-3.3
1952	Bos N	13	22	.371	7-7	1/2	-2.5
	2	61	69	.469			-5.8
HORNSBY, ROGERS B 4.27.1896							
1925	StL N	64	51	.557	8-4	2/2	2.0
1926	StL N	89	65	.578	1★		-1.5
1927	NY N	22	10	.688	4-3	2/2	4.1
1928	Bos N	39	83	.320	7-7	2/2	-3.2
1930	Chi N	4	0	1.000	2-2	2/2	1.7
1931	Chi N	84	70	.545	3		-4.3
1932	Chi N	53	46	.535	2-1	1/2	-2.2
1933	StL A	19	33	.365	8-8	3/3	-2.0
1934	StL A	67	85	.441	6		3.2
1935	StL A	65	87	.428	7		8.5
1936	StL A	57	95	.375	7		3.5
1937	StL A	25	52	.325	7-8	1/2	0.3
1952	StL A	22	29	.431	8-7	1/2	0.9
	Cin N	27	24	.529	7-6	3/3	3.0
1953	Cin N	64	82	.438	6-6	1/2	-2.2
	14	701	812	.463			11.9
HOUK, RALPH B 8.9.1919							
1961	NY A	109	53	.673	1★		6.3
1962	NY A	96	66	.593	1★		1.5
1963	NY A	104	57	.646	1		5.6
1966	NY A	66	73	.475	10-10	2/2	-3.4
1967	NY A	72	90	.444	9		2.2

Year	Tm/Lg	W	L	Pct	Finish	Mgr/Yr	+/-
1968	NY A	83	79	.512	5		1.4
1969	NY A e	80	81	.497	5		2.3
1970	NY A e	93	69	.574	2		4.8
1971	NY A e	82	80	.506	4		0.3
1972	NY A e	79	76	.510	4		-1.9
1973	NY A e	80	82	.494	4		-4.3
1974	Det A e	72	90	.444	6		6.2
1975	Det A e	57	102	.358	6		-0.3
1976	Det A e	74	87	.460	5		4.0
1977	Det A e	74	88	.457	4		-3.3
1978	Det A e	86	76	.531	5		-1.3
1981-1	Bos A e	30	26	.536	5		1.3
-2	Bos A e	29	23	.558	2*t*		1.3
1982	Bos A e	89	73	.549	3		4.0
1983	Bos A e	78	84	.481	6		2.0
1984	Bos A e	86	76	.531	4		0.6
	20	1619	1531	.514			29.0
HOWARD, FRANK B 8.8.1936							
1981-1	SD N w	23	33	.411	6		-6.1
-2	SD N w	18	36	.333	6		-6.1
1983	NY N e	52	64	.448	6-6	2/2	2.1
	2	93	133	.412			-10.0
HOWE, ART B 12.15.1946							
1989	Hou N w	86	76	.531	3		7.3
1990	Hou N w	75	87	.463	4*t*		3.0
1991	Hou N w	65	97	.401	6		-4.2
1992	Hou N w	81	81	.500	4		6.4
1993	Hou N w	85	77	.525	3		-5.0
1996	Oak A w	78	84	.481	3		0.5
1997	Oak A w	65	97	.401	4		0.8
1998	Oak A w	74	88	.457	4		-1.2
1999	Oak A w	87	75	.537	2		1.7
2000	Oak A w	91	70	.565	1		-1.7
2001	Oak A w	102	60	.630	2■		-2.3
2002	Oak A w	103	59	.636	1		7.4
2003	NY N e	66	95	.410	5		-3.1
	13	1058	1046	.503			9.7
HOWLEY, DAN B 10.16.1885							
1927	StL A	59	94	.386	7		-0.8
1928	StL A	82	72	.532	3		2.1
1929	StL A	79	73	.520	4		1.0
1930	Cin N	59	95	.383	7		0.3
1931	Cin N	58	96	.377	8		-3.7
1932	Cin N	60	94	.390	8		-2.4
	6	397	524	.431			-3.5
HOWSER, DICK B 5.14.1936							
1978	NY A e	0	1	.000	3-4-1★▲	2/3	-0.6
1980	NY A e	103	59	.636	1		6.3
1981-2	KC A w	20	13	.606	2*t*-1	2/2	3.8
1982	KC A w	90	72	.556	2		2.4
1983	KC A w	79	83	.488	2		5.1
1984	KC A w	84	78	.519	1		4.3
1985	KC A w	91	71	.562	1★		5.0
1986	KC A w	40	48	.455	4-3*t*	1/2	-2.9
	8	507	425	.544			23.4
HUFF, GEORGE B 6.11.1872 Champaign, IL Huff, George A. "Gee" D 10.1.1936 Champaign, IL (DNP)							
1907	Bos A	2	6	.250	4*t*-6-7	2/4	-1.4
HUGGINS, MILLER B 3.27.1879							
1913	StL N	51	99	.340	8		-0.5
1914	StL N	81	72	.529	3		2.5
1915	StL N	72	81	.471	6		-3.3
1916	StL N	60	93	.392	7*t*		0.6
1917	StL N	82	70	.539	3		10.0
1918	NY A	60	63	.488	4		-3.4
1919	NY A	80	59	.576	3		2.7
1920	NY A	95	59	.617	3		-2.3
1921	NY A	98	55	.641	1		-0.4
1922	NY A	94	60	.610	1		2.9
1923	NY A	98	54	.645	1★		2.4
1924	NY A	89	63	.586	2		0.3
1925	NY A	69	85	.448	7		-1.4
1926	NY A	91	63	.591	1		1.3
1927	NY A	110	44	.714	1★		-2.4
1928	NY A	101	53	.656	1★		4.4
1929	NY A	82	61	.573	2-2	1/2	0.0
	17	1413	1134	.555			13.5
HUNTER, BILLY B 6.4.1928							
1977	Tex A w	60	33	.645	5-2	4/4	7.1
1978	Tex A w	86	75	.534	2*t*-2*t*	1/2	-0.8
	2	146	108	.575			6.4
HURDLE, CLINT B 7.30.1957							
2002	Col N w	67	73	.479	5-4	2/2	6.7
2003	Col N w	74	88	.457	4		-3.4
	2	141	161	.467			3.2

Year	Tm/Lg	W	L	Pct	Finish	Mgr/Yr	+/-
HURST, TIM B 6.30.1865 Ashland, PA Hurst, Timothy Carroll D 6.4.1915 Pottsville, PA 5-5/(DNP)							
1898	StL N	39	111	.260	12		-1.6
HUTCHINSON, FRED B 8.12.1919							
1952	Det A	27	55	.329	8-8	2/2	-4.0
1953	Det A	60	94	.390	6		4.4
1954	Det A	68	86	.442	5		-0.5
1956	StL N	76	78	.494	4		1.0
1957	StL N	87	67	.565	2		2.9
1958	StL N	69	75	.479	5-5*t*	1/2	5.1
1959	Cin N	39	35	.527	7-5*t*	2/2	0.8
1960	Cin N	67	87	.435	6		-4.7
1961	Cin N	93	61	.604	1		10.3
1962	Cin N	98	64	.605	3		5.4
1963	Cin N	86	76	.531	5		-0.9
1964	Cin N	54	45	.545	3-2*t*	1/4	-1.8
	Cin N	6	4	.600	4-3-2*t*	3/4	0.4
12		830	827	.501			18.5
IRWIN, ARTHUR B 2.14.1858							
1889	Was N	28	45	.384	8-8	2/2	4.8
1891	Bos AA	93	42	.689	1		-4.8
1892-1	Was N	35	39	.473	11*t*-7	2/2	4.3
-2	Was N	11	21	.344	11-12	1/2	-2.3
1894	Phi N	71	57	.555	4		-6.6
1895	Phi N	78	53	.595	3		4.0
1896	NY N	36	53	.404	10-7	1/2	-9.0
1898	Was N	10	19	.345	11-11	4/4	-0.4
1899	Was N	54	98	.355	11		-0.4
8		416	427	.493			-10.4
JENNINGS, HUGHIE B 4.2.1869							
1907	Det A	92	58	.613	1		-0.2
1908	Det A	90	63	.588	1		2.7
1909	Det A	98	54	.645	1		2.8
1910	Det A	86	68	.558	3		-1.0
1911	Det A	89	65	.578	2		7.0
1912	Det A	69	84	.451	6		-2.0
1913	Det A	66	87	.431	6		-1.3
1914	Det A	80	73	.523	4		3.8
1915	Det A	100	54	.649	2		4.7
1916	Det A	87	67	.565	3		2.1
1917	Det A	78	75	.510	4		-5.1
1918	Det A	55	71	.437	7		0.6
1919	Det A	80	60	.571	4		5.9
1920	Det A	61	93	.396	7		1.5
1924	NY N	32	12	.727	3-1-1	2/3	4.0
1925	NY N	21	11	.656	1-1-2	2/3	4.3
16		1184	995	.543			29.9
JOHNSON, DARRELL B 8.25.1928							
1974	Bos A e	84	78	.519	3		-0.6
1975	Bos A e	95	65	.594	1◆		6.5
1976	Bos A e	41	45	.477	5-3	1/2	-5.1
1977	Sea A w	64	98	.395	6		5.9
1978	Sea A w	56	104	.350	7		-2.1
1979	Sea A w	67	95	.414	6		-3.4
1980	Sea A w	39	65	.375	6-7	1/2	-1.0
1982	Tex A w	26	40	.394	6-6	2/2	-0.2
8		472	590	.444			0.1
JOHNSON, DAVEY B 1.30.1943							
1984	NY N e	90	72	.556	2		11.5
1985	NY N e	98	64	.605	2		3.4
1986	NY N e	108	54	.667	1★		5.8
1987	NY N e	92	70	.568	2		-1.2
1988	NY N e	100	60	.625	1		1.5
1989	NY N e	87	75	.537	2		-3.4
1990	NY N e	20	22	.476	4-2	1/2	-5.3
1993	Cin N w	53	65	.449	5-5	2/2	-1.5
1994	Cin N c	66	48	.579	1		-2.5
1995	Cin N c	85	59	.590	1☆		0.9
1996	Bal A e	88	74	.543	2☆✜		2.9
1997	Bal A e	98	64	.605	1☆		4.1
1999	LA N w	77	85	.475	3		-4.6
2000	LA N w	86	76	.531	2		-1.7
14		1148	888	.564			9.8
JOHNSON, ROY B 10.1.1895							
1944	Chi N	0	1	.000	8-8-4	2/3	-0.5
JOHNSON, TIM B 7.22.1949							
1998	Tor A e	88	74	.543	3		2.4
JOHNSON, WALTER B 11.6.1887							
1929	Was A	71	81	.467	5		-0.6
1930	Was A	94	60	.610	2		-2.0
1931	Was A	92	62	.597	3		0.4
1932	Was A	93	61	.604	3		4.3
1933	Cle A	48	51	.485	5-4	3/3	-0.5
1934	Cle A	85	69	.552	3		3.2
1935	Cle A	46	48	.489	5-3	1/2	-3.2
7		529	432	.550			1.6
JONES, FIELDER B 8.13.1871							
1904	Chi A	66	47	.584	4-3	2/2	-0.4
1905	Chi A	92	60	.605	2		-2.6
1906	Chi A	93	58	.616	1★		4.7
1907	Chi A	87	64	.576	3		-1.7
1908	Chi A	88	64	.579	3		4.1
1914	StL F	12	26	.316	7-8	2/2	-3.5
1915	StL F	87	67	.565	2		-1.9
1916	StL A	79	75	.513	5		-2.8
1917	StL A	57	97	.370	7		-0.9
1918	StL A	22	24	.478	6-5	1/3	-0.1
10		683	582	.540			-5.0
JOOST, EDDIE B 6.5.1916							
1954	Phi A	51	103	.331	8		7.2
JORGENSEN, MIKE B 8.16.1948							
1995	StL N c	42	54	.438	4-4	2/2	0.5
JOYCE, BILL B 9.21.1865							
1896	NY N	28	14	.667	10-7	2/2	6.8
1897	NY N	83	48	.634	3		-0.6
1898	NY N	22	21	.512	6-7	1/3	-0.5
	NY N	46	39	.541	7-7	3/3	1.6
3		179	122	.595			7.3
JURGES, BILLY B 5.9.1908							
1959	Bos A	44	36	.550	8-5	3/3	2.5
1960	Bos A	15	27	.357	8-7	1/3	-2.9
2		59	63	.484			-0.4
KASKO, EDDIE B 6.27.1932							
1970	Bos A e	87	75	.537	3		-0.3
1971	Bos A e	85	77	.525	3		1.5
1972	Bos A e	85	70	.548	2		5.4
1973	Bos A e	88	73	.547	2-2	1/2	-1.8
4		345	295	.539			4.8
KEANE, JOHNNY B11.3.1911 St.Louis, MO Keane, John Joseph D1.6.1967 Houston, TX BR/TR, 5-10/165# (SS)							
1961	StL N	47	33	.587	6-5	2/2	5.2
1962	StL N	84	78	.519	6		-8.1
1963	StL N	93	69	.574	2		-0.3
1964	StL N	93	69	.574	1★		5.5
1965	NY A	77	85	.475	6		-4.8
1966	NY A	4	16	.200	10-10	1/2	-6.0
6		398	350	.532			-8.5
KELLEY, JOE B 12.9.1871							
1902	Cin N	34	26	.567	6-4	3/3	1.0
1903	Cin N	74	65	.532	4		-5.8
1904	Cin N	88	65	.575	3		-4.3
1905	Cin N	79	74	.516	5		-1.2
1908	Bos N	63	91	.409	6		-4.6
5		338	321	.513			-14.9
KELLY, TOM B 8.15.1950							
1986	Min A w	12	11	.522	7-6	2/2	1.8
1987	Min A w	85	77	.525	1★		5.9
1988	Min A w	91	71	.562	2		1.2
1989	Min A w	80	82	.494	5		-1.2
1990	Min A w	74	88	.457	7		-0.6
1991	Min A w	95	67	.586	1★		1.5
1992	Min A w	90	72	.556	2		-0.6
1993	Min A w	71	91	.438	5*t*		3.4
1994	Min A c	53	60	.469	4		4.9
1995	Min A c	56	88	.389	5		0.8
1996	Min A c	78	84	.481	4		-0.9
1997	Min A c	68	94	.420	4		-4.6
1998	Min A c	70	92	.432	4		-2.9
1999	Min A c	63	97	.394	5		-1.5
2000	Min A c	69	93	.426	5		0.5
2001	Min A c	85	77	.525	2		3.5
16		1140	1244	.478			11.3
KELLY, KICK B 10.31.1856							
1887	Lou AA	76	60	.559	4		-0.5
1888	Lou AA	10	29	.256	8-7	1/4	-4.8
2		86	89	.491			-5.3
KELLY, KING B 12.31.1857							
1887	Bos N	49	43	.533	5-5	1/2	0.3
1890	Bos P	81	48	.628	1		-1.9
1891	Cin AA	43	57	.430	6		1.3
3		173	148	.539			-0.3
KENNEDY, JIM B 1867 New York, NY Kennedy, James C. D 4.20.1904 Brighton Beach, NY (DNP)							
1890	Bro AA	26	73	.263	8		-2.8
KENNEDY, KEVIN B 9.26.1954 Los Angeles, CA Kennedy, Kevin Curtis BR/TR, 6-3/220# (C)							
1993	Tex A w	86	76	.531	2		-3.1
1994	Tex A w	52	62	.456	1		2.4
1995	Bos A e	86	58	.597	1		5.3
1996	Bos A e	85	77	.525	3		3.4
4		309	273	.531			8.1
KENNEDY, BOB B 8.18.1920							
1963	Chi N	82	80	.506	7		1.9
1964	Chi N	76	86	.469	8		2.7
1965	Chi N	24	32	.429	9-8	1/2	-0.8
1968	Oak A	82	80	.506	6		-1.9
4		264	278	.487			1.9
KERINS, JOHN B 7.15.1858							
1888	Lou AA	3	4	.429	8-8-7	3/4	0.3
1890	StL AA	9	8	.529	4-4-3	2/6	-1.0
2		12	12	.500			-0.6
KERRIGAN, JOE B 11.30.1954							
2001	Bos A e	17	26	.395	2-2	2/2	-5.2
KESSINGER, DON B 7.17.1942							
1979	Chi A w	46	60	.434	5-5	1/2	-5.8
KILLEFER, BILL B 10.10.1887							
1921	Chi N	23	34	.404	6-7	2/2	-1.7
1922	Chi N	80	74	.519	5		6.5
1923	Chi N	83	71	.539	4		0.9
1924	Chi N	81	72	.529	5		4.6
1925	Chi N	33	42	.440	7-8	1/3	-2.2
1930	StL A	64	90	.416	6		-0.6
1931	StL A	63	91	.409	5		-0.1
1932	StL A	63	91	.409	6		0.9
1933	StL A	34	57	.374	8-8	1/3	-2.7
9		524	622	.457			5.7
KIMM, BRUCE B 6.29.1951							
2002	Chi N c	28	46	.378	3-4	2/2	-6.6
KING, CLYDE B 5.23.1924							
1969	SF N w	90	72	.556	2		1.0
1970	SF N w	19	23	.452	4-3	1/2	-2.1
1974	Atl N w	38	25	.603	4-3	2/2	2.3
1975	Atl N w	58	76	.433	5-5	1/2	4.6
1982	NY A e	29	33	.468	5*t*-5	3/3	-1.7
5		234	229	.505			4.1
KITTRIDGE, MALACHI B 10.12.1869							
1904	Was A	1	16	.059	8-8	1/2	-3.7
KLEIN, LOU B 10.22.1918							
1961	Chi N	5	6	.455	7-7-7	8/9	0.3
1962	Chi N	12	18	.400	9-9-9	2/3	0.6
1965	Chi N	48	58	.453	9-8	2/2	1.0
3		65	82	.442			1.9
KLING, JOHNNY B 2.25.1875							
1912	Bos N	52	101	.340	8		-7.7
KNABE, OTTO B 6.12.1884							
1914	Bal F	84	70	.545	3		5.2
1915	Bal F	47	107	.305	8		-8.4
2		131	177	.425			-3.2
KNIGHT, LON B 6.16.1853							
1883	Phi AA	66	32	.673	1		2.6
1884	Phi AA	61	46	.570	7		-6.1
2		127	78	.620			-3.5
KNIGHT, RAY B 12.28.1952							
1996	Cin N c	81	81	.500	3		-0.5
1997	Cin N c	43	56	.434	4-3	1/2	0.5
2003	Cin N c	1	0	1.000	5-5-5	2/3	0.6
3		125	137	.477			0.6
KNOOP, BOBBY B 10.18.1938							
1994	Cal A w	1	1	.500	3-2-4	2/3	0.2
KROL, JACK B7.5.1936 Chicago, IL Krol, John Thomas D5.30.1994 Winston-Salem, NC BR/TR, 5-11/175# (2B)							
1978	StL N e	1	1	.500	6-6-5	2/3	0.1
1980	StL N e	0	1	.000	6-6-4	2/4	-0.5
2		1	2	.333			-0.4
KUEHL, KARL B 9.5.1937 Monterey Park, CA Kuehl, Karl Otto BL/TL, 5-11/175# (1B)							
1976	Mon N e	43	85	.336	6-6	1/2	-3.8
KUENN, HARVEY B 12.4.1930							
1975	Mil A e	1	0	1.000	5-5	2/2	0.6
1982	Mil A e	72	43	.626	5-1◆	2/2	2.7
1983	Mil A e	87	75	.537	5		0.4
3		160	118	.576			3.7
KUHEL, JOE B 6.25.1906							
1948	Was A	56	97	.366	7		1.4
1949	Was A	50	104	.325	8		0.7
2		106	201	.345			2.1
LACHEMANN, MARCEL B 6.13.1941							
1994	Cal A w	30	44	.405	2-4	3/3	-0.0
1995	Cal A w	78	67	.538	2▲		-4.2
1996	Cal A w	52	59	.468	4	1/2	8.0
3		160	170	.485			3.8
LACHEMANN, RENE B 5.4.1945							
1981-1	Sea A w	15	18	.455	7-6	2/2	1.4
-2	Sea A w	23	29	.442	5		-0.8

Year	Tm/Lg	W	L	Pct	Finish	Mgr/Yr	+/-
1982	Sea A w	76	86	.469	4		1.3
1983	Sea A w	26	47	.356	7-7	1/2	-1.8
1984	Mil A e	67	94	.416	7		-4.0
1993	Fla N e	64	98	.395	6		-1.9
1994	Fla N e	51	54	.486	5		4.3
1995	Fla N e	67	76	.469	4		-4.5
1996	Fla N e	39	47	.453	4-3	1/3	-3.2
	8	428	549	.438			-9.1

LAJOIE, NAP B 9.5.1874

Year	Tm/Lg	W	L	Pct	Finish	Mgr/Yr	+/-
1905	Cle A	37	21	.638	1*t*-5	1/3	9.0
	Cle A	19	36	.345	2-5	3/3	-7.6
1906	Cle A	89	64	.582	3		-7.7
1907	Cle A	85	67	.559	4		8.3
1908	Cle A	90	64	.584	2		0.1
1909	Cle A	57	57	.500	4-6	1/2	3.4
	5	377	309	.550			5.4

LAKE, FRED B 10.16.1866

Year	Tm/Lg	W	L	Pct	Finish	Mgr/Yr	+/-
1908	Bos A	22	17	.564	6-5	2/2	1.0
1909	Bos A	88	63	.583	3		6.8
1910	Bos N	53	100	.346	8		-1.1
	3	163	180	.475			6.8

LAMONT, GENE B 12.25.1946

Year	Tm/Lg	W	L	Pct	Finish	Mgr/Yr	+/-
1992	Chi A w	86	76	.531	3		0.1
1993	Chi A w	94	68	.580	1		1.7
1994	Chi A c	67	46	.593	1		-2.3
1995	Chi A c	11	20	.355	4-3	1/2	-4.4
1997	Pit N c	79	83	.488	2		1.5
1998	Pit N c	69	93	.426	6		-5.0
1999	Pit N c	78	83	.484	3		-1.8
2000	Pit N c	69	93	.426	5		-3.2
	8	553	562	.496			-13.3

LANIER, HAL B 7.4.1942

Year	Tm/Lg	W	L	Pct	Finish	Mgr/Yr	+/-
1986	Hou N w	96	66	.593	1		5.7
1987	Hou N w	76	86	.469	3		-1.9
1988	Hou N w	82	80	.506	5		2.5
	3	254	232	.523			6.4

LARKIN, HENRY B 1.12.1860

Year	Tm/Lg	W	L	Pct	Finish	Mgr/Yr	+/-
1890	Cle P	34	45	.430	7-7	1/2	3.1

LaRUSSA, TONY B 10.4.1944

Year	Tm/Lg	W	L	Pct	Finish	Mgr/Yr	+/-
1979	Chi A w	27	27	.500	5-5	2/2	0.6
1980	Chi A w	70	90	.438	5		4.2
1981-1	Chi A w	31	22	.585	3		-4.5
-2	Chi A w	23	30	.434	6		-4.5
1982	Chi A w	87	75	.537	3		-1.5
1983	Chi A w	99	63	.611	1		3.0
1984	Chi A w	74	88	.457	5*t*		-1.2
1985	Chi A w	85	77	.525	3		2.4
1986	Chi A w	26	38	.406	6-5	1/3	-3.7
	Oak A w	45	34	.570	7-3*t*	3/3	6.9
1987	Oak A w	81	81	.500	3		-1.6
1988	Oak A w	104	58	.642	1◆		4.8
1989	Oak A w	99	63	.611	1★		3.5
1990	Oak A w	103	59	.636	1◆		4.8
1991	Oak A w	84	78	.519	4		4.6
1992	Oak A w	96	66	.593	1		7.6
1993	Oak A w	68	94	.420	7		-0.3
1994	Oak A w	51	63	.447	2		-2.2
1995	Oak A w	67	77	.465	4		-2.1
1996	StL N c	88	74	.543	1☆		1.7
1997	StL N c	73	89	.451	4		-6.1
1998	StL N c	83	79	.512	3		-0.7
1999	StL N c	75	86	.466	4		-2.8
2000	StL N c	95	67	.586	1☆		3.1
2001	StL N c	93	69	.574	2✤	-0.8	
2002	StL N c	97	65	.599	1☆		2.0
2003	StL N c	85	77	.525	3		-3.5
	25	2009	1789	.529			13.6

LASORDA, TOM B 9.22.1927

Year	Tm/Lg	W	L	Pct	Finish	Mgr/Yr	+/-
1976	LA N w	2	2	.500	2-2	2/2	-0.2
1977	LA N w	98	64	.605	1◆		-2.4
1978	LA N w	95	67	.586	1◆		-2.3
1979	LA N w	79	83	.488	3		-4.2
1980	LA N w	92	71	.564	2▲		2.7
1981-1	LA N w	36	21	.632	1★		-2.4
-2	LA N w	27	26	.509	4		-2.4
1982	LA N w	88	74	.543	2		-1.4
1983	LA N w	91	71	.562	1		5.1
1984	LA N w	79	83	.488	4		0.2
1985	LA N w	95	67	.586	1		2.9
1986	LA N w	73	89	.451	5		-3.7
1987	LA N w	73	89	.451	4		-3.8
1988	LA N w	94	67	.584	1★		4.1
1989	LA N w	77	83	.481	4		-5.1
1990	LA N w	86	76	.531	2		0.6
1991	LA N w	93	69	.574	2		1.1
1992	LA N w	63	99	.389	6		-8.2
1993	LA N w	81	81	.500	4		-1.4
1994	LA N w	58	56	.509	1		-1.3
1995	LA N w	78	66	.542	1		3.4
1996	LA N w	41	35	.539	1-2	1/2	0.5
	21	1599	1439	.526			-17.9

LATHAM, JUICE B 9.6.1852

Year	Tm/Lg	W	L	Pct	Finish	Mgr/Yr	+/-
1875	NH NA	4	14	.222	11-8-8	2/3	2.5
1882	Phi AA	41	34	.547	2		1.9
	2	45	48	.484			4.4

LATHAM, ARLIE B 3.15.1860

Year	Tm/Lg	W	L	Pct	Finish	Mgr/Yr	+/-
1896	StL N	0	3	.000	10-10-11	2/5	-0.8

LAVAGETTO, COOKIE B 12.1.1912

Year	Tm/Lg	W	L	Pct	Finish	Mgr/Yr	+/-
1957	Was A	51	83	.381	8-8	2/2	1.7
1958	Was A	61	93	.396	8		4.2
1959	Was A	63	91	.409	8		-5.6
1960	Was A	73	81	.474	5		-1.6
1961	Min A	19	30	.388	8-7	1/4	-3.4
	Min A	4	6	.400	9-9-7	3/4	-0.6
	5	271	384	.414			-5.3

LEADLEY, BOB B 11.11.1858 Brooklyn, NY Leadley, Robert H. D 5.19.1936 Los Angeles, CA (DNP)

Year	Tm/Lg	W	L	Pct	Finish	Mgr/Yr	+/-
1888	Det N	19	19	.500	3-5	2/2	-2.5
1890	Cle N	23	33	.411	7-7	2/2	2.8
1891	Cle N	34	34	.500	4-5	1/2	2.2
	3	76	86	.469			2.5

LEFEBVRE, JIM B 1.7.1942

Year	Tm/Lg	W	L	Pct	Finish	Mgr/Yr	+/-
1989	Sea A w	73	89	.451	6		-4.6
1990	Sea A w	77	85	.475	5		0.2
1991	Sea A w	83	79	.512	5		-0.9
1992	Chi N e	78	84	.481	4		0.4
1993	Chi N e	84	78	.519	4		3.1
1999	Mil N c	22	27	.449	5-5	2/2	-0.5
	6	417	442	.485			-2.2

LEMON, JIM B 3.23.1928

Year	Tm/Lg	W	L	Pct	Finish	Mgr/Yr	+/-
1968	Was A	65	96	.404	10		0.1

LEMON, BOB B 9.22.1920

Year	Tm/Lg	W	L	Pct	Finish	Mgr/Yr	+/-
1970	KC A w	46	64	.418	5-4*t*	2/2	-2.3
1971	KC A w	85	76	.528	2		0.4
1972	KC A w	76	78	.494	4		-4.9
1977	Chi A w	90	72	.556	3		2.1
1978	Chi A w	34	40	.459	5-5	1/2	1.6
	NY A e	48	20	.706	4-1★▲	3/3	7.3
1979	NY A e	34	31	.523	4-4	1/2	-1.0
	NY A e	11	14	.440	4-6	2/2	-3.5
1982	NY A e	6	8	.429	4*t*-5	1/3	-0.9
	8	430	403	.516			-1.4

LENNON, BILL B 1848

Year	Tm/Lg	W	L	Pct	Finish	Mgr/Yr	+/-
1871	Kek NA	5	9	.357	7-8	1/2	3.2

LEYLAND, JIM B 12.15.1944 Toledo, OH Leyland, James Richard BR/TR, 5-11/170# (P)

Year	Tm/Lg	W	L	Pct	Finish	Mgr/Yr	+/-
1986	Pit N e	64	98	.395	6		-13.2
1987	Pit N e	80	82	.494	4*t*		1.1
1988	Pit N e	85	75	.531	2		1.3
1989	Pit N e	74	88	.457	5		-2.4
1990	Pit N e	95	67	.586	1		2.2
1991	Pit N e	98	64	.605	1		3.1
1992	Pit N e	96	66	.593	1		4.6
1993	Pit N e	75	87	.463	5		3.7
1994	Pit N c	53	61	.465	3*t*		7.3
1995	Pit N c	58	86	.403	5		-3.6
1996	Pit N c	73	89	.451	5		-2.6
1997	Fla N e	92	70	.568	2★✤	3.8	
1998	Fla N e	54	108	.333	5		-2.5
1999	Col N w	72	90	.444	5		1.6
	14	1069	1131	.486			4.3

LEYVA, NICK B 8.16.1953 Ontario, CA Leyva, Nicholas Tomas BR/TR, 5-11/165# (3B)

Year	Tm/Lg	W	L	Pct	Finish	Mgr/Yr	+/-
1989	Phi N e	67	95	.414	6		-3.0
1990	Phi N e	77	85	.475	4*t*		4.5
1991	Phi N e	4	9	.308	6-3	1/2	-2.1
	3	148	189	.439			-0.5

LILLIS, BOB B 6.2.1930

Year	Tm/Lg	W	L	Pct	Finish	Mgr/Yr	+/-
1982	Hou N w	28	23	.549	5-5	2/2	4.3
1983	Hou N w	85	77	.525	3		4.3
1984	Hou N w	80	82	.494	2*t*		-7.6
1985	Hou N w	83	79	.512	3*t*		0.5
	4	276	261	.514			1.5

LIPON, JOHNNY B 11.10.1922

Year	Tm/Lg	W	L	Pct	Finish	Mgr/Yr	+/-
1971	Cle A e	18	41	.305	6-6	2/2	-3.6

LITTLE, GRADY B 3.30.1950 Abilene, TX Little, William Grady BR/TR, 5-11/190# (C)

Year	Tm/Lg	W	L	Pct	Finish	Mgr/Yr	+/-
2002	Bos A e	93	69	.574	2		-7.0
2003	Bos A e	95	67	.586	2☆✤	0.2	
	2	188	136	.580			-6.8

LOBERT, HANS B 10.18.1881

Year	Tm/Lg	W	L	Pct	Finish	Mgr/Yr	+/-
1938	Phi N	0	2	.000	8-8	2/2	-0.6
1942	Phi N	42	109	.278	8		1.2
	2	42	111	.275			0.6

LOCKMAN, WHITEY B 7.25.1926

Year	Tm/Lg	W	L	Pct	Finish	Mgr/Yr	+/-
1972	Chi N e	39	26	.600	4-2	2/2	1.3
1973	Chi N e	77	84	.478	5		0.9
1974	Chi N e	41	52	.441	5-6	1/2	3.4
	3	157	162	.492			5.5

LOFTUS, TOM B 11.15.1856

Year	Tm/Lg	W	L	Pct	Finish	Mgr/Yr	+/-
1884	Mil U	8	4	.667	2		-0.1
1888	Cle AA	30	38	.441	8-6	2/2	4.7
1889	Cle N	61	72	.459	6		0.5
1890	Cin N	77	55	.583	4		-0.2
1891	Cin N	56	81	.409	7		0.9
1900	Chi N	65	75	.464	5*t*		6.3
1901	Chi N	53	86	.381	6		-4.5
1902	Was A	61	75	.449	6		0.6
1903	Was A	43	94	.314	8		1.3
	9	454	580	.439			9.6

LOPAT, ED B 6.21.1918

Year	Tm/Lg	W	L	Pct	Finish	Mgr/Yr	+/-
1963	KC A	73	89	.451	8		1.4
1964	KC A	17	35	.327	10-10	1/2	-2.1
	2	90	124	.421			-0.7

LOPES, DAVEY B 5.3.1945

Year	Tm/Lg	W	L	Pct	Finish	Mgr/Yr	+/-
2000	Mil N c	73	89	.451	3		0.3
2001	Mil N c	68	94	.420	4		-6.6
2002	Mil N c	3	12	.200	6-6	1/2	-2.7
	3	144	195	.425			-9.0

LOPEZ, AL B 8.20.1908

Year	Tm/Lg	W	L	Pct	Finish	Mgr/Yr	+/-
1951	Cle A	93	61	.604	2		5.4
1952	Cle A	93	61	.604	2		0.2
1953	Cle A	92	62	.597	2		0.7
1954	Cle A	111	43	.721	1		8.3
1955	Cle A	93	61	.604	2		6.0
1956	Cle A	88	66	.571	2		-2.6
1957	Chi A	90	64	.584	2		-1.8
1958	Chi A	82	72	.532	2		3.0
1959	Chi A	94	60	.610	1		8.4
1960	Chi A	87	67	.565	3		-2.5
1961	Chi A	86	76	.531	4		1.1
1962	Chi A	85	77	.525	5		-1.1
1963	Chi A	94	68	.580	2		-2.2
1964	Chi A	98	64	.605	2		1.1
1965	Chi A	95	67	.586	2		3.9
1968	Chi A	6	5	.545	9-9-8*t*	3/5	1.0
	Chi A	15	21	.417	9-8*t*	5/5	-1.3
1969	Chi A w	8	9	.471	4-5	1/2	0.6
	17	1410	1004	.584			28.3

LORD, HARRY B 3.8.1882

Year	Tm/Lg	W	L	Pct	Finish	Mgr/Yr	+/-
1915	Buf F	60	49	.550	8-6	3/3	10.1

LOWE, BOBBY B 7.10.1865

Year	Tm/Lg	W	L	Pct	Finish	Mgr/Yr	+/-
1904	Det A	30	44	.405	7-7	2/2	-0.3

LUCCHESI, FRANK B 4.24.1927 San Francisco, CA Lucchesi, Frank Joseph BR/TR, 5-8/175# (OF)

Year	Tm/Lg	W	L	Pct	Finish	Mgr/Yr	+/-
1970	Phi N e	73	88	.453	5		6.7
1971	Phi N e	67	95	.414	6		0.1
1972	Phi N e	26	50	.342	6-6	1/2	-4.9
1975	Tex A w	35	32	.522	4-3	2/2	2.3
1976	Tex A w	76	86	.469	4*t*		-1.1
1977	Tex A w	31	31	.500	3*t*-2	1/4	-4.3
1987	Chi N e	8	17	.320	5-6	2/2	-3.3
	7	316	399	.442			-4.4

LUMLEY, HARRY B 9.29.1880

Year	Tm/Lg	W	L	Pct	Finish	Mgr/Yr	+/-
1909	Bro N	55	98	.359	6		-0.6

LYONS, TED B 12.28.1900

Year	Tm/Lg	W	L	Pct	Finish	Mgr/Yr	+/-
1946	Chi A	64	60	.516	7-5	2/2	4.9
1947	Chi A	70	84	.455	6		4.6
1948	Chi A	51	101	.336	8		0.6
	3	185	245	.430			10.1

MACHA, KEN B 9.29.1950

Year	Tm/Lg	W	L	Pct	Finish	Mgr/Yr	+/-
2003	Oak A w	96	66	.593	1		2.3

MACK, CONNIE B 12.22.1862

Year	Tm/Lg	W	L	Pct	Finish	Mgr/Yr	+/-
1894	Pit N	12	10	.545	7-7	2/2	1.2
1895	Pit N	71	61	.538	7		3.6
1896	Pit N	66	63	.512	6		-2.5
1901	Phi A	74	62	.544	4		2.0
1902	Phi A	83	53	.610	1		2.0
1903	Phi A	75	60	.556	2		-0.7
1904	Phi A	81	70	.536	5		-0.7
1905	Phi A	92	56	.622	1		3.0
1906	Phi A	78	67	.538	4		3.1
1907	Phi A	88	57	.607	2		7.4
1908	Phi A	68	85	.444	6		0.3
1909	Phi A	95	58	.621	2		-4.1
1910	Phi A	102	48	.680	1★		1.1
1911	Phi A	101	50	.669	1★		0.5
1912	Phi A	90	62	.592	3		2.2
1913	Phi A	96	57	.627	1★		-0.6

Year	Tm/Lg	W	L	Pct	Finish	Mgr/Yr	+/-
1914	Phi A	99	53	.651	1		-0.2
1915	Phi A	43	109	.283	8		0.8
1916	Phi A	36	117	.235	8		-5.5
1917	Phi A	55	98	.359	8		-4.2
1918	Phi A	52	76	.406	8		2.0
1919	Phi A	36	104	.257	8		-4.8
1920	Phi A	48	106	.312	8		-1.3
1921	Phi A	53	100	.346	8		-1.0
1922	Phi A	65	89	.422	7		-0.1
1923	Phi A	69	83	.454	6		2.8
1924	Phi A	71	81	.467	5		4.0
1925	Phi A	88	64	.579	2		0.9
1926	Phi A	83	67	.553	3		-3.1
1927	Phi A	91	63	.591	2		3.1
1928	Phi A	98	55	.641	2		0.6
1929	Phi A	104	46	.693	1★		1.9
1930	Phi A	102	52	.662	1★		7.0
1931	Phi A	107	45	.704	1		8.6
1932	Phi A	94	60	.610	2		-3.5
1933	Phi A	79	72	.523	3		1.5
1934	Phi A	68	82	.453	5		-0.1
1935	Phi A	58	91	.389	8		-1.8
1936	Phi A	53	100	.346	8		5.9
1937	Phi A	39	80	.328	7-7	1/2	-9.0
1938	Phi A	53	99	.349	8		-2.1
1939	Phi A	25	37	.403	6-7	1/2	5.3
1940	Phi A	54	100	.351	8		-1.9
1941	Phi A	64	90	.416	8		-1.0
1942	Phi A	55	99	.357	8		3.5
1943	Phi A	49	105	.318	8		-4.4
1944	Phi A	72	82	.468	5*t*		2.7
1945	Phi A	52	98	.347	8		-7.1
1946	Phi A	49	105	.318	8		-11.8
1947	Phi A	78	76	.506	5		-1.0
1948	Phi A	84	70	.545	4		7.6
1949	Phi A	81	73	.526	5		3.9
1950	Phi A	52	102	.338	8		-2.3
	53	3731	3948	.486			13.6

MACK, DENNY B 1851

Year	Tm/Lg	W	L	Pct	Finish	Mgr/Yr	+/-
1882	Lou AA	42	38	.525	3		-6.7

MACK, EARLE B 2.1.1890

Year	Tm/Lg	W	L	Pct	Finish	Mgr/Yr	+/-
1937	Phi A	15	17	.469	7-7	2/2	2.1
1939	Phi A	30	60	.333	6-7	2/2	1.4
	2	45	77	.369			3.5

MACULLAR, JIMMY B 1.16.1855

Year	Tm/Lg	W	L	Pct	Finish	Mgr/Yr	+/-
1879	Syr N	5	21	.192	6-7	3/3	-1.6

MADDON, JOE B 2.8.1954 Hazleton, PA Maddon, Joseph John BR/TR, 5-11/190# (C)

Year	Tm/Lg	W	L	Pct	Finish	Mgr/Yr	+/-
1999	Ana A w	19	10	.655	4-4	2/2	6.5

MAGEE, LEE B 6.4.1889

Year	Tm/Lg	W	L	Pct	Finish	Mgr/Yr	+/-
1915	Bro F	53	64	.453	7-7	1/2	-3.5

MALONE, FERGY B 1842

Year	Tm/Lg	W	L	Pct	Finish	Mgr/Yr	+/-
1873	Phi NA	36	27	.571	2		0.1
1874	Chi NA	18	18	.500	4-5	1/2	2.9
1884	Phi U	21	46	.313	7		-2.1
	3	75	91	.452			0.9

MANNING, JIMMY B 1.31.1862

Year	Tm/Lg	W	L	Pct	Finish	Mgr/Yr	+/-
1901	Was A	61	72	.459	6		2.7

MANNING, JACK B 12.20.1853

Year	Tm/Lg	W	L	Pct	Finish	Mgr/Yr	+/-
1877	Cin N	7	12	.368	6-6	3/3	2.8

MANUEL, CHARLIE B 1.4.1944

Year	Tm/Lg	W	L	Pct	Finish	Mgr/Yr	+/-
2000	Cle A c	90	72	.556	2		-3.2
2001	Cle A c	91	71	.562	1		3.0
2002	Cle A c	39	48	.448	3-3	1/2	0.6
	3	220	191	.535			0.4

MANUEL, JERRY B 12.23.1953

Year	Tm/Lg	W	L	Pct	Finish	Mgr/Yr	+/-
1998	Chi A c	80	82	.494	2		5.3
1999	Chi A c	75	86	.466	2		3.3
2000	Chi A c	95	67	.586	1		1.5
2001	Chi A c	83	79	.512	3		1.7
2002	Chi A c	81	81	.500	2		-5.4
2003	Chi A c	86	76	.531	2		-2.5
	6	500	471	.515			3.9

MARANVILLE, RABBIT B 11.11.1891

Year	Tm/Lg	W	L	Pct	Finish	Mgr/Yr	+/-
1925	Chi N	23	30	.434	7-7-8	2/3	-1.8

MARION, MARTY B 12.1.1917

Year	Tm/Lg	W	L	Pct	Finish	Mgr/Yr	+/-
1951	StL N	81	73	.526	3		2.8
1952	StL A	42	61	.408	8-7	2/2	-0.7
1953	StL A	54	100	.351	8		-0.3
1954	Chi A	3	6	.333	3-3	2/2	-2.7
1955	Chi A	91	63	.591	3		-3.5
1956	Chi A	85	69	.552	3		-6.1
	6	356	372	.489			-10.5

MARSHALL, JIM B 5.25.1931

Year	Tm/Lg	W	L	Pct	Finish	Mgr/Yr	+/-
1974	Chi N e	25	44	.362	5-6	2/2	-2.9
1975	Chi N e	75	87	.463	5*t*		5.2
1976	Chi N e	75	87	.463	4		6.2
1979	Oak A w	54	108	.333	7		2.0
	4	229	326	.413			10.5

MARTIN, BILLY B 5.16.1928

Year	Tm/Lg	W	L	Pct	Finish	Mgr/Yr	+/-
1969	Min A w	97	65	.599	1		-1.5
1971	Det A e	91	71	.562	2		4.2
1972	Det A e	86	70	.551	1		3.0
1973	Det A e	71	63	.530	3-3	1/2	6.8
	Tex A w	9	14	.391	6-6	3/3	0.7
1974	Tex A w	84	76	.525	2		4.8
1975	Tex A w	44	51	.463	4-3	1/2	-2.4
	NY A e	30	26	.536	3-3	2/2	-1.5
1976	NY A e	97	62	.610	1◆		1.3
1977	NY A e	100	62	.617	1★		1.1
1978	NY A e	52	42	.553	3-1★▲	1/3	-4.3
1979	NY A e	55	40	.579	4-4	2/2	3.8
1980	Oak A w	83	79	.512	2		-2.6
1981-1	Oak A w	37	23	.617	1☆		3.6
-2	Oak A w	27	22	.551	2		3.6
1982	Oak A w	68	94	.420	5		-0.4
1983	NY A e	91	71	.562	3		3.3
1985	NY A e	91	54	.628	7-2	2/2	2.6
1988	NY A e	40	28	.588	2-5	1/2	5.0
	16	1253	1013	.553			31.2

MARTIN, PHONNEY B 8.4.1845

Year	Tm/Lg	W	L	Pct	Finish	Mgr/Yr	+/-
1872	Eck NA	1	8	.111	10-9	3/3	2.0

MARTINEZ, BUCK B 11.7.1948

Year	Tm/Lg	W	L	Pct	Finish	Mgr/Yr	+/-
2001	Tor A e	80	82	.494	3		-2.4
2002	Tor A e	20	33	.377	4-3	1/2	-6.0
	2	100	115	.465			-8.4

MARTINEZ, MARTY B 8.23.1941

Year	Tm/Lg	W	L	Pct	Finish	Mgr/Yr	+/-
1986	Sea A w	0	1	.000	6-6-7	2/3	-0.4

MASON, CHARLIE B 6.25.1853

Year	Tm/Lg	W	L	Pct	Finish	Mgr/Yr	+/-
1887	Phi AA	38	40	.487	6-5	2/2	-1.1

MATHEWS, EDDIE B 10.13.1931

Year	Tm/Lg	W	L	Pct	Finish	Mgr/Yr	+/-
1972	Atl N w	23	27	.460	4-4	2/2	1.4
1973	Atl N w	76	85	.472	5		-6.9
1974	Atl N w	50	49	.505	4-3	1/2	-6.1
	3	149	161	.481			-11.6

MATHEWSON, CHRISTY B 8.12.1880

Year	Tm/Lg	W	L	Pct	Finish	Mgr/Yr	+/-
1916	Cin N	25	43	.368	8-7*t*	3/3	-3.4
1917	Cin N	78	76	.506	4		2.1
1918	Cin N	61	57	.517	4-3	1/2	-1.3
	3	164	176	.482			-2.7

MATTICK, BOBBY B 12.5.1915

Year	Tm/Lg	W	L	Pct	Finish	Mgr/Yr	+/-
1980	Tor A e	67	95	.414	7		0.2
1981-1	Tor A e	16	42	.276	7		-1.0
-2	Tor A e	21	27	.438	7		-1.0
	2	104	164	.388			-1.8

MAUCH, GENE B 11.18.1925

Year	Tm/Lg	W	L	Pct	Finish	Mgr/Yr	+/-
1960	Phi N	58	94	.382	4*t*-8	3/3	-2.8
1961	Phi N	47	107	.305	8		-8.7
1962	Phi N	81	80	.503	7		5.9
1963	Phi N	87	75	.537	4		-1.0
1964	Phi N	92	70	.568	2*t*		4.6
1965	Phi N	85	76	.528	6		5.9
1966	Phi N	87	75	.537	4		0.1
1967	Phi N	82	80	.506	5		-2.4
1968	Phi N	27	27	.500	6*t*-7*t*	1/3	2.7
1969	Mon N e	52	110	.321	6		-7.5
1970	Mon N e	73	89	.451	6		3.9
1971	Mon N e	71	90	.441	5		1.6
1972	Mon N e	70	86	.449	5		2.7
1973	Mon N e	79	83	.488	4		1.5
1974	Mon N e	79	82	.491	4		-2.0
1975	Mon N e	75	87	.463	5*t*		3.5
1976	Min A w	85	77	.525	3		0.1
1977	Min A w	84	77	.522	4		-5.0
1978	Min A w	73	89	.451	4		-6.8
1979	Min A w	82	80	.506	4		-2.9
1980	Min A w	54	71	.432	4-3	1/2	-4.2
1981-1	Cal A w	9	4	.692	4-4	2/2	2.2
-2	Cal A w	20	30	.400	7		-6.4
1982	Cal A w	93	69	.574	1		-2.3
1985	Cal A w	90	72	.556	2		6.1
1986	Cal A w	92	70	.568	1		0.8
1987	Cal A w	75	87	.463	6*t*		-2.8
	26	1902	2037	.483			-13.2

McALEER, JIMMY B 7.10.1864

Year	Tm/Lg	W	L	Pct	Finish	Mgr/Yr	+/-
1901	Cle A	54	82	.397	7		1.0
1902	StL A	78	58	.574	2		8.8
1903	StL A	65	74	.468	6		-1.7
1904	StL A	65	87	.428	6		3.0
1905	StL A	54	99	.353	8		-11.8
1906	StL A	76	73	.510	5		-5.5
1907	StL A	69	83	.454	6		-5.4
1908	StL A	83	69	.546	4		-0.1
1909	StL A	61	89	.407	7		1.7
1910	Was A	66	85	.437	7		-3.7
1911	Was A	64	90	.416	7		1.1
	11	735	889	.453			-12.7

McBRIDE, GEORGE B 11.20.1880

Year	Tm/Lg	W	L	Pct	Finish	Mgr/Yr	+/-
1921	Was A	80	73	.523	4		6.8

McBRIDE, DICK B 1845

Year	Tm/Lg	W	L	Pct	Finish	Mgr/Yr	+/-
1871	Ath NA	21	7	.750	1		0.1
1872	Ath NA	30	14	.682	4		-5.1
1873	Ath NA	28	23	.549	5		-2.7
1874	Ath NA	33	23	.589	3		-2.2
1875	Ath NA	49	18	.731	2-2	1/2	-6.1
	5	161	85	.654			-16.0

McCALLISTER, JACK B 1.19.1879 Marietta, OH McCallister, John D 10.18.1946 Columbus, OH (DNP)

Year	Tm/Lg	W	L	Pct	Finish	Mgr/Yr	+/-
1927	Cle A	66	87	.431	6		-0.9

McCARTHY, JOE B4.21.1887 Philadelphia, PA McCarthy, Joseph Vincent "Marse Joe" D1.13.1978 Buffalo, NY BR/TR, 5-8.5/190# (2B)

Year	Tm/Lg	W	L	Pct	Finish	Mgr/Yr	+/-
1926	Chi N	82	72	.532	4		-3.3
1927	Chi N	85	68	.556	4		-0.3
1928	Chi N	91	63	.591	3		3.9
1929	Chi N	98	54	.645	1		1.9
1930	Chi N	86	64	.573	2-2	1/2	0.2
1931	NY A	94	59	.614	2		-9.3
1932	NY A	107	47	.695	1★		4.9
1933	NY A	91	59	.607	2		1.7
1934	NY A	94	60	.610	2		0.4
1935	NY A	89	60	.597	2		-3.4
1936	NY A	102	51	.667	1★		-3.9
1937	NY A	102	52	.662	1★		-3.5
1938	NY A	99	53	.651	1★		-0.5
1939	NY A	106	45	.702	1★		-8.5
1940	NY A	88	66	.571	3		-3.1
1941	NY A	101	53	.656	1★		4.5
1942	NY A	103	51	.669	1		-4.3
1943	NY A	98	56	.636	1★		7.4
1944	NY A	83	71	.539	3		0.1
1945	NY A	81	71	.533	4		-2.2
1946	NY A	22	13	.629	2-3	1/3	1.2
1948	Bos A	96	59	.619	2▲		1.2
1949	Bos A	96	58	.623	2		-2.6
1950	Bos A	31	28	.525	4-3	1/2	-5.9
	24	2125	1333	.615			-23.6

McCARTHY, TOMMY B 7.24.1863

Year	Tm/Lg	W	L	Pct	Finish	Mgr/Yr	+/-
1890	StL AA	11	11	.500	4-3	1/6	-1.9
	StL AA	4	1	.800	2-2-3	5/6	1.1

McCLENDON, LLOYD B 1.11.1959

Year	Tm/Lg	W	L	Pct	Finish	Mgr/Yr	+/-
2001	Pit N c	62	100	.383	6		0.7
2002	Pit N c	72	89	.447	4		0.7
2003	Pit N c	75	87	.463	4		-1.4
	3	209	276	.431			0.0

McCLOSKEY, JOHN B4.4.1862 Louisville, KY McCloskey, John Joseph "Honest John" D11.17.1940 Louisville, KY (DNP)

Year	Tm/Lg	W	L	Pct	Finish	Mgr/Yr	+/-
1895	Lou N	35	96	.267	12		1.6
1896	Lou N	2	17	.105	12-12	1/2	-3.2
1906	StL N	52	98	.347	7		-7.5
1907	StL N	52	101	.340	8		-2.3
1908	StL N	49	105	.318	8		1.9
	5	190	417	.313			-9.4

McCORMICK, JIM B 11.3.1856

Year	Tm/Lg	W	L	Pct	Finish	Mgr/Yr	+/-
1879	Cle N	27	55	.329	6		-0.5
1880	Cle N	47	37	.560	3		-0.1
1882	Cle N	0	4	.000	8-5	1/2	-2.0
	3	74	96	.435			-2.6

McGAHA, MEL B9.26.1926 Bastrop, LA McGaha, Fred Melvin D2.3.2002 Tulsa, OK BR/TR, 6-2/210# (OF)

Year	Tm/Lg	W	L	Pct	Finish	Mgr/Yr	+/-
1962	Cle A	78	82	.488	6-6	1/2	4.3
1964	KC A	40	70	.364	10-10	2/2	-0.3
1965	KC A	5	21	.192	10-10	1/2	-5.2
	3	123	173	.416			-1.2

McGEARY, MIKE B 1851

Year	Tm/Lg	W	L	Pct	Finish	Mgr/Yr	+/-
1875	Phi NA	34	27	.557	4-5	1/2	-3.8
1880	Pro N	8	7	.533	4-2	1/3	-1.7
1881	Cle N	4	7	.364	6-7	1/2	-1.2
	3	46	41	.529			-6.7

McGRAW, JOHN B 4.7.1873

Year	Tm/Lg	W	L	Pct	Finish	Mgr/Yr	+/-
1899	Bal N	86	62	.581	4		-0.9
1901	Bal A	68	65	.511	5		0.6
1902	Bal A	26	31	.456	7-8	1/2	2.5
	NY N	25	38	.397	8-8	3/3	3.8
1903	NY N	84	55	.604	2		-1.6
1904	NY N	106	47	.693	1		0.3
1905	NY N	105	48	.686	1★		-0.2
1906	NY N	96	56	.632	2		7.2

Year	Tm/Lg	W	L	Pct	Finish	Mgr/Yr	+/-
1907	NY N	82	71	.536	4		-1.8
1908	NY N	98	56	.636	2t		-1.2
1909	NY N	92	61	.601	3		7.0
1910	NY N	91	63	.591	2		-1.4
1911	NY N	99	54	.647	1		0.4
1912	NY N	103	48	.682	1		2.4
1913	NY N	101	51	.664	1		6.7
1914	NY N	84	70	.545	2		-3.2
1915	NY N	69	83	.454	8		-2.1
1916	NY N	86	66	.566	4		-0.5
1917	NY N	98	56	.636	1		0.7
1918	NY N	71	53	.573	2		1.7
1919	NY N	87	53	.621	2		2.4
1920	NY N	86	68	.558	2		-5.8
1921	NY N	94	59	.614	1★		-2.1
1922	NY N	93	61	.604	1★		-2.7
1923	NY N	95	58	.621	1		1.9
1924	NY N	16	13	.552	3-1	1/3	-2.4
	NY N	45	35	.563	1-1	3/3	-5.9
1925	NY N	10	4	.714	1-2	1/3	2.7
	NY N	55	51	.519	1-2	3/3	-0.3
1926	NY N	74	77	.490	5		-1.0
1927	NY N	70	52	.574	4-3	1/2	1.7
1928	NY N	93	61	.604	2		0.9
1929	NY N	84	67	.556	3		-8.9
1930	NY N	87	67	.565	3		-2.8
1931	NY N	87	65	.572	2		-6.0
1932	NY N	17	23	.425	8-6t	1/2	-4.2
	33	2763	1948	.586			-11.9

McGUIRE, DEACON B 11.18.1863

Year	Tm/Lg	W	L	Pct	Finish	Mgr/Yr	+/-
1898	Was N	21	47	.309	10-11-11	3/4	-3.3
1907	Bos A	45	61	.425	8-7	4/4	-0.4
1908	Bos A	53	62	.461	6-5	1/2	-8.8
1909	Cle A	14	25	.359	4-6	2/2	-4.3
1910	Cle A	71	81	.467	5		7.0
1911	Cle A	6	11	.353	7-3	1/2	-2.3
	6	210	287	.423			-12.2

McGUNNIGLE, BILL B 1.1.1855

Year	Tm/Lg	W	L	Pct	Finish	Mgr/Yr	+/-
1888	Bro AA	88	52	.629	2		1.0
1889	Bro AA	93	44	.679	1		-0.4
1890	Bro N	86	43	.667	1★		-1.7
1891	Pit N	24	33	.421	8-8	2/2	-1.9
1896	Lou N	36	76	.321	12-12	2/2	5.1
	5	327	248	.569			2.1

McINNIS, STUFFY B 9.19.1890

Year	Tm/Lg	W	L	Pct	Finish	Mgr/Yr	+/-
1927	Phi N	51	103	.331	8		-4.9

McKECHNIE, BILL B 8.7.1886

Year	Tm/Lg	W	L	Pct	Finish	Mgr/Yr	+/-
1915	New F	54	45	.545	6-5	2/2	2.8
1922	Pit N	53	36	.596	5-3t	2/2	1.5
1923	Pit N	87	67	.565	3		1.3
1924	Pit N	90	63	.588	3		-0.6
1925	Pit N	95	58	.621	1★		0.4
1926	Pit N	84	69	.549	3		-0.4
1928	StL N	95	59	.617	1		1.2
1929	StL N	34	29	.540	4-4	3/3	1.5
1930	Bos N	70	84	.455	6		6.5
1931	Bos N	64	90	.416	7		2.8
1932	Bos N	77	77	.500	5		0.6
1933	Bos N	83	71	.539	4		3.6
1934	Bos N	78	73	.517	4		5.6
1935	Bos N	38	115	.248	8		-11.3
1936	Bos N	71	83	.461	6		2.6
1937	Bos N	79	73	.520	5		0.5
1938	Cin N	82	68	.547	4		-1.9
1939	Cin N	97	57	.630	1		2.5
1940	Cin N	100	53	.654	1★		4.5
1941	Cin N	88	66	.571	3		5.4
1942	Cin N	76	76	.500	4		2.0
1943	Cin N	87	67	.565	2		2.8
1944	Cin N	89	65	.578	3		8.0
1945	Cin N	61	93	.396	7		0.8
1946	Cin N	64	86	.427	6-6	1/2	-5.8
	25	1896	1723	.524			37.0

McKEON, JACK B 11.23.1930 South Amboy, NJ
McKeon, John Aloysius BR/TR, 5-8/205# (C)

Year	Tm/Lg	W	L	Pct	Finish	Mgr/Yr	+/-
1973	KC A w	88	74	.543	2		6.7
1974	KC A w	77	85	.475	5		-4.5
1975	KC A w	50	46	.521	2-2	1/2	-1.7
1977	Oak A w	26	27	.491	5t-7	1/2	4.4
1978	Oak A w	45	78	.366	1-6	2/2	-3.4
1988	SD N w	67	48	.583	5-3	2/2	8.6
1989	SD N w	89	73	.549	2		6.3
1990	SD N w	37	43	.463	4-5	1/2	-3.0
1997	Cin N c	33	30	.524	4-3	2/2	6.0
1998	Cin N c	77	85	.475	4		-3.0
1999	Cin N c	96	67	.589	2▲		-0.4
2000	Cin N c	85	77	.525	2		-1.8
2003	Fla N e	74	49	.602	4-2✣★	2/2	8.0
	13	844	782	.519			22.2

McKINNON, ALEX B 8.14.1856

Year	Tm/Lg	W	L	Pct	Finish	Mgr/Yr	+/-
1885	StL N	6	32	.158	5-8-8	2/3	-5.8

McKNIGHT, DENNY B1847 Pittsburgh, PA
McKnight, Dennis Hamar D5.5.1900 Pittsburgh, PA (DNP)

Year	Tm/Lg	W	L	Pct	Finish	Mgr/Yr	+/-
1884	Pit AA	4	8	.333	9-10	1/5	1.3

McMANUS, GEORGE B 6.28.1846 Ireland
McManus, George D 10.2.1918 New York, NY (DNP)

Year	Tm/Lg	W	L	Pct	Finish	Mgr/Yr	+/-
1876	StL N	6	2	.750	2-2	2/2	0.1
1877	StL N	28	32	.467	4		1.2
	2	34	34	.500			1.3

McMANUS, MARTY B 3.14.1900

Year	Tm/Lg	W	L	Pct	Finish	Mgr/Yr	+/-
1932	Bos A	32	67	.323	8-8	2/2	4.2
1933	Bos A	63	86	.423	7		-5.9
	2	95	153	.383			-1.7

McMILLAN, ROY B 7.17.1929

Year	Tm/Lg	W	L	Pct	Finish	Mgr/Yr	+/-
1972	Mil A e	1	1	.500	6-6-6	2/3	0.1
1975	NY N e	26	27	.491	3-3t	2/2	-1.2
	2	27	28	.491			-1.1

McNAMARA, JOHN B 6.4.1932 Sacramento, CA
McNamara, John Francis BR/TR, 5-10/175# (C)

Year	Tm/Lg	W	L	Pct	Finish	Mgr/Yr	+/-
1969	Oak A w	8	5	.615	2-2	2/2	1.0
1970	Oak A w	89	73	.549	2		-1.1
1974	SD N w	60	102	.370	6		8.8
1975	SD N w	71	91	.438	4		4.2
1976	SD N w	73	89	.451	5		2.0
1977	SD N w	20	28	.417	4-5	1/3	0.1
1979	Cin N w	90	71	.559	1		0.6
1980	Cin N w	89	73	.549	3		4.2
1981-1	Cin N w	35	21	.625	2		9.5
-2	Cin N w	31	21	.596	2		9.5
1982	Cin N w	34	58	.370	6-6	1/2	-4.8
1983	Cal A w	70	92	.432	5t		-5.4
1984	Cal A w	81	81	.500	2t		0.1
1985	Bos A e	81	81	.500	5		-7.9
1986	Bos A e	95	66	.590	1◆		4.8
1987	Bos A e	78	84	.481	5		-4.6
1988	Bos A e	43	42	.506	4-1	1/2	-5.9
1990	Cle A e	77	85	.475	4		-3.5
1991	Cle A e	25	52	.325	7-7	1/2	-4.4
1996	Cal A w	18	32	.360	4	2/2	-1.8
	19	1168	1247	.484			5.5

McPHEE, BID B 11.1.1859

Year	Tm/Lg	W	L	Pct	Finish	Mgr/Yr	+/-
1901	Cin N	52	87	.374	8		7.2
1902	Cin N	27	37	.422	6-4	1/3	-8.2
	2	79	124	.389			-0.9

McRAE, HAL B 7.10.1945

Year	Tm/Lg	W	L	Pct	Finish	Mgr/Yr	+/-
1991	KC A w	66	58	.532	7-6	3/3	3.6
1992	KC A w	72	90	.444	5t		-2.9
1993	KC A w	84	78	.519	3		5.0
1994	KC A c	64	51	.557	3		2.4
2001	TB A e	58	90	.392	5-5	2/2	3.0
2002	TB A e	55	106	.342	5		-2.1
	6	399	473	.458			9.0

McVEY, CAL B 8.30.1850

Year	Tm/Lg	W	L	Pct	Finish	Mgr/Yr	+/-
1873	Bal NA	20	13	.606	3-3	1/2	-4.3
1878	Cin N	37	23	.617	2		2.1
1879	Cin N	34	28	.548	4-5	2/2	1.6
	3	91	64	.587			-0.6

MELE, SAM B 1.21.1923

Year	Tm/Lg	W	L	Pct	Finish	Mgr/Yr	+/-
1961	Min A	2	5	.286	8-9-7	2/4	-1.2
	Min A	45	49	.479	9-7	4/4	2.1
1962	Min A	91	71	.562	2		1.6
1963	Min A	91	70	.565	3		-6.5
1964	Min A	79	83	.488	6t		-8.0
1965	Min A	102	60	.630	1		3.1
1966	Min A	89	73	.549	2		-0.9
1967	Min A	25	25	.500	6-2t	1/2	-2.7
	7	524	436	.546			-12.4

MELILLO, SKI B 8.4.1899

Year	Tm/Lg	W	L	Pct	Finish	Mgr/Yr	+/-
1938	StL A	2	7	.222	7-7	2/2	-1.4

MELVIN, BOB B 10.28.1961

Year	Tm/Lg	W	L	Pct	Finish	Mgr/Yr	+/-
2003	Sea A w	93	69	.574	2		-3.9

MERRILL, STUMP B 2.25.1944 Brunswick, ME
Merrill, Carl Harrison BL/TR, 5-8/190# (C)

Year	Tm/Lg	W	L	Pct	Finish	Mgr/Yr	+/-
1990	NY A e	49	64	.434	7-7	2/2	3.1
1991	NY A e	71	91	.438	5		0.3
	2	120	155	.436			3.4

METRO, CHARLIE B 4.28.1919

Year	Tm/Lg	W	L	Pct	Finish	Mgr/Yr	+/-
1962	Chi N	43	69	.384	9-9	3/3	0.5
1970	KC A w	19	33	.365	5-4t	1/2	-3.8
	2	62	102	.378			-3.3

MEYER, BILLY B 1.14.1892

Year	Tm/Lg	W	L	Pct	Finish	Mgr/Yr	+/-
1948	Pit N	83	71	.539	4		5.5
1949	Pit N	71	83	.461	6		1.7
1950	Pit N	57	96	.373	8		-2.8
1951	Pit N	64	90	.416	7		1.9
1952	Pit N	42	112	.273	8		-6.3
	5	317	452	.412			0.0

MICHAEL, GENE B 6.2.1938

Year	Tm/Lg	W	L	Pct	Finish	Mgr/Yr	+/-
1981-1	NY A e	34	22	.607	1◆		-3.3
-2	NY A e	14	12	.538	4-6	1/2	-1.1
1982	NY A e	44	42	.512	4t-5t-5	2/3	1.4
1986	Chi N e	46	56	.451	5-5	3/3	1.4
1987	Chi N e	68	68	.500	5-6	1/2	6.7
	4	206	200	.507			5.1

MILAN, CLYDE B 3.25.1887

Year	Tm/Lg	W	L	Pct	Finish	Mgr/Yr	+/-
1922	Was A	69	85	.448	6		-2.3

MILEY, DAVE B 4.3.1962 Tampa, FL Miley, David Allen BL/TR, 6-3/220# (C)

Year	Tm/Lg	W	L	Pct	Finish	Mgr/Yr	+/-
2003	Cin N c	22	35	.386	5-5	3/3	-0.0

MILLER, DOGGIE B 8.15.1864

Year	Tm/Lg	W	L	Pct	Finish	Mgr/Yr	+/-
1894	StL N	56	76	.424	9		5.2

MILLER, RAY B 4.30.1945 Takoma Park, MD Miller, Raymond Roger BR/TR, 6-3/215# (P)

Year	Tm/Lg	W	L	Pct	Finish	Mgr/Yr	+/-
1985	Min A w	50	50	.500	6-4	2/2	4.7
1986	Min A w	59	80	.424	7-6	1/2	-2.4
1998	Bal A e	79	83	.488	4		-5.1
1999	Bal A e	78	84	.481	4		-6.4
	4	266	297	.472			-9.1

MILLS, BUSTER B 9.16.1908

Year	Tm/Lg	W	L	Pct	Finish	Mgr/Yr	+/-
1953	Cin N	4	4	.500	6-6	2/2	0.4

MILLS, EVERETT B 1.20.1845

Year	Tm/Lg	W	L	Pct	Finish	Mgr/Yr	+/-
1872	Bal NA	8	6	.571	2-2	2/2	-2.3

MITCHELL, FRED B 6.5.1878

Year	Tm/Lg	W	L	Pct	Finish	Mgr/Yr	+/-
1917	Chi N	74	80	.481	5		-1.3
1918	Chi N	84	45	.651	1		3.2
1919	Chi N	75	65	.536	3		-0.7
1920	Chi N	75	79	.487	5t		-0.3
1921	Bos N	79	74	.516	4		0.1
1922	Bos N	53	100	.346	8		-1.2
1923	Bos N	54	100	.351	7		-7.0
	7	494	543	.476			-7.2

MIZEROCK, JOHN B 12.8.1960

Year	Tm/Lg	W	L	Pct	Finish	Mgr/Yr	+/-
2002	KC A c	5	8	.385	4-4-4	2/3	-0.3

MOORE, JACKIE B 2.19.1939

Year	Tm/Lg	W	L	Pct	Finish	Mgr/Yr	+/-
1984	Oak A w	57	61	.483	5-4	2/2	2.1
1985	Oak A w	77	85	.475	4t		-1.1
1986	Oak A w	29	44	.397	6t-3t	1/3	-6.2
	3	163	190	.462			-5.2

MOORE, TERRY B 5.27.1912

Year	Tm/Lg	W	L	Pct	Finish	Mgr/Yr	+/-
1954	Phi N	35	42	.455	3-4	2/2	-5.8

MORAN, PAT B 2.7.1876

Year	Tm/Lg	W	L	Pct	Finish	Mgr/Yr	+/-
1915	Phi N	90	62	.592	1		-0.4
1916	Phi N	91	62	.595	2		4.0
1917	Phi N	87	65	.572	2		2.2
1918	Phi N	55	68	.447	6		1.9
1919	Cin N	96	44	.686	1★		6.0
1920	Cin N	82	71	.536	3		-2.0
1921	Cin N	70	83	.458	6		-3.3
1922	Cin N	86	68	.558	2		0.2
1923	Cin N	91	63	.591	2		6.0
	9	748	586	.561			14.6

MORGAN, JOE B 11.19.1930

Year	Tm/Lg	W	L	Pct	Finish	Mgr/Yr	+/-
1988	Bos A e	46	31	.597	4-1	2/2	1.7
1989	Bos A e	83	79	.512	3		-1.8
1990	Bos A e	88	74	.543	1		3.4
1991	Bos A e	84	78	.519	2t		1.1
	4	301	262	.535			4.3

MORIARTY, GEORGE B 6.7.1884

Year	Tm/Lg	W	L	Pct	Finish	Mgr/Yr	+/-
1927	Det A	82	71	.536	4		1.8
1928	Det A	68	86	.442	6		-3.3
	2	150	157	.489			-1.5

MORRILL, JOHN B 2.19.1855

Year	Tm/Lg	W	L	Pct	Finish	Mgr/Yr	+/-
1882	Bos N	45	39	.536	3t		-2.4
1883	Bos N	33	11	.750	4-1	2/2	2.5
1884	Bos N	73	38	.658	2		-3.1
1885	Bos N	46	66	.411	5		-4.2
1886	Bos N	56	61	.479	5		-2.1
1887	Bos N	12	17	.414	5-5	2/2	-3.3
1888	Bos N	70	64	.522	4		-1.9
1889	Was N	13	38	.255	8-8	1/2	-3.2
	8	348	334	.510			-17.7

MORTON, CHARLIE B 10.12.1854

Year	Tm/Lg	W	L	Pct	Finish	Mgr/Yr	+/-
1884	Tol AA	46	58	.442	8		4.6
1885	Det N	7	31	.184	8-6	1/2	-9.7
1890	Tol AA	68	64	.515	4		-2.6
	3	121	153	.442			-7.8

Year	Tm/Lg	W	L	Pct	Finish	Mgr/Yr	+/-
MOSES, FELIX B 5.13.1853 Charleston, SC Moses, Felix Inglesby D 5.5.1888 Sheffield, AL (DNP)							
1884	Ric AA	12	30	.286	12		0.2
MOSS, LES B 5.14.1925							
1968	Chi A	0	2	.000	9-9-8*t*	2/5	-0.9
	Chi A	12	22	.353	9-9-8*t*	4/5	-3.4
1979	Det A e	27	26	.509	5-5	1/3	-0.5
2		39	50	.438			-4.8
MURNANE, TIM B 6.4.1852							
1884	Bos U	58	51	.532	5		-3.6
MURRAY, BILLY B 4.13.1864 Peabody, MA Murray, William Jeremiah D 3.25.1937 Youngstown, OH (DNP)							
1907	Phi N	83	64	.565	3		5.1
1908	Phi N	83	71	.539	4		-1.2
1909	Phi N	74	79	.484	5		-2.3
3		240	214	.529			1.7
MURTAUGH, DANNY B 10.8.1917							
1957	Pit N	26	25	.510	7-7*t*	2/2	4.3
1958	Pit N	84	70	.545	2		1.3
1959	Pit N	78	76	.506	4		4.0
1960	Pit N	95	59	.617	1★		3.5
1961	Pit N	75	79	.487	6		-3.9
1962	Pit N	93	68	.578	4		4.2
1963	Pit N	74	88	.457	8		-3.9
1964	Pit N	80	82	.494	6*t*		-3.9
1967	Pit N	39	39	.500	6-6	2/2	0.7
1970	Pit N e	89	73	.549	1		1.3
1971	Pit N e	97	65	.599	1★		-3.4
1973	Pit N e	13	13	.500	2-3	2/2	-0.2
1974	Pit N e	88	74	.543	1		-2.6
1975	Pit N e	92	69	.571	1		-4.2
1976	Pit N e	92	70	.568	2		2.9
15		1115	950	.540			0.2
MUSER, TONY B 8.1.1947							
1997	KC A c	31	48	.392	4-5	2/2	-5.1
1998	KC A c	72	89	.447	3		9.0
1999	KC A c	64	97	.398	4		-10.6
2000	KC A c	77	85	.475	4		0.6
2001	KC A c	65	97	.401	5		-3.6
2002	KC A c	8	15	.348	4-4	1/3	-1.4
6		317	431	.424			-11.1
MUTRIE, JIM B6.13.1851 Chelsea, MA Mutrie, James J. "Truthful Jim" D1.24.1938 New York, NY (DNP)							
1883	NY AA	54	42	.563	4		-3.1
1884	NY AA	75	32	.701	1		-7.5
1885	NY N	85	27	.759	2		-2.3
1886	NY N	75	44	.630	3		2.8
1887	NY N	68	55	.553	4		-1.6
1888	NY N	84	47	.641	1★		-0.3
1889	NY N	83	43	.659	1★		0.8
1890	NY N	63	68	.481	6		-3.9
1891	NY N	71	61	.538	3		1.1
9		658	419	.611			-14.1
MYATT, GEORGE B 6.14.1914							
1968	Phi N	1	0	1.000	6*t*-5-7*t*	2/3	0.5
1969	Phi N e	19	35	.352	5-5	2/2	-4.6
2		20	35	.364			-4.0
MYERS, HENRY B 5.1858							
1882	Bal AA	19	54	.260	6		4.8
NARRON, JERRY B 1.15.1956							
2001	Tex A w	62	72	.463	4-4	2/2	0.7
2002	Tex A w	72	90	.444	4-4		-5.4
2		134	162	.453			-4.7
NASH, BILLY B 6.24.1865							
1896	Phi N	62	68	.477	8		-2.9
NEUN, JOHNNY B 10.28.1900							
1946	NY A	8	6	.571	3-3	3/3	-0.3
1947	Cin N	73	81	.474	5		3.3
1948	Cin N	44	56	.440	7-7	1/2	4.8
3		125	143	.466			7.8
NEWMAN, JEFF B 9.11.1948							
1986	Oak A w	2	8	.200	6*t*-7-3*t*	2/3	-2.8
NICHOLS, KID B 9.14.1869							
1904	StL N	75	79	.487	5		-2.8
1905	StL N	5	9	.357	7-6	1/3	-0.1
2		80	88	.476			-2.9
NICOL, HUGH B 1.1.1858							
1897	StL N	8	32	.200	12-12-12	2/4	0.8
NIXON, RUSS B 2.19.1935							
1982	Cin N w	27	43	.386	6-6	2/2	-2.5
1983	Cin N w	74	88	.457	6		2.1
1988	Atl N w	42	79	.347	6-6	2/2	-3.7
1989	Atl N w	63	97	.394	6		-6.7
1990	Atl N w	25	40	.385	6-6	1/2	-2.0

Year	Tm/Lg	W	L	Pct	Finish	Mgr/Yr	+/-
5		231	347	.400			-12.8
NORMAN, BILL B 7.16.1910							
1958	Det A	56	49	.533	8-5	2/2	-0.3
1959	Det A	2	15	.118	8-4	1/2	-6.3
2		58	64	.475			-6.6
OAKES, REBEL B 12.17.1883							
1914	Pit F	61	78	.439	8-7	2/2	0.4
1915	Pit F	86	67	.562	3		1.9
2		147	145	.503			2.3
OATES, JOHNNY B 1.21.1946							
1991	Bal A e	54	71	.432	7-6	2/2	-0.1
1992	Bal A e	89	73	.549	3		2.9
1993	Bal A e	85	77	.525	3*t*		-0.0
1994	Bal A e	63	49	.563	2		-1.9
1995	Tex A w	74	70	.514	3		4.8
1996	Tex A w	90	72	.556	1		-2.9
1997	Tex A w	77	85	.475	3		-2.5
1998	Tex A w	88	74	.543	1		0.8
1999	Tex A w	95	67	.586	1		6.3
2000	Tex A w	71	91	.438	4		1.3
2001	Tex A w	11	17	.393	4	1/2	-1.8
11		797	746	.517			6.9
O'CONNOR, JACK B 6.2.1869							
1910	StL A	47	107	.305	8		1.9
O'DAY, HANK B 7.8.1862							
1912	Cin N	75	78	.490	4		5.1
1914	Chi N	78	76	.506	4		4.5
2		153	154	.498			9.6
O'FARRELL, BOB B 10.19.1896							
1927	StL N	92	61	.601	2		6.7
1934	Cin N	30	60	.333	8-8	1/3	-2.5
2		122	121	.502			4.2
O'LEARY, DAN B 10.22.1856							
1884	Cin U	20	15	.571	5-3	1/2	-4.6
O'NEILL, STEVE B 7.6.1891							
1935	Cle A	36	23	.610	5-3	2/2	5.1
1936	Cle A	80	74	.519	5		-2.3
1937	Cle A	83	71	.539	4		1.4
1943	Det A	78	76	.506	5		-6.8
1944	Det A	88	66	.571	2		2.8
1945	Det A	88	65	.575	1★		4.2
1946	Det A	92	62	.597	2		0.6
1947	Det A	85	69	.552	2		0.6
1948	Det A	78	76	.506	5		3.6
1950	Bos A	63	32	.663	4-3	2/2	3.5
1951	Bos A	87	67	.565	3		2.5
1952	Phi N	59	32	.648	6-4	2/2	6.9
1953	Phi N	83	71	.539	3*t*		1.0
1954	Phi N	40	37	.519	3-4	1/2	-0.8
14		1040	821	.559			22.2
ONSLOW, JACK B 10.13.1888							
1949	Chi A	63	91	.409	6		-5.1
1950	Chi A	8	22	.267	8-6	1/2	-4.6
2		71	113	.386			-9.7
O'ROURKE, JIM B 9.1.1850							
1881	Buf N	45	38	.542	3		4.1
1882	Buf N	45	39	.536	3*t*		-0.5
1883	Buf N	52	45	.536	5		0.2
1884	Buf N	64	47	.577	3		2.0
1893	Was N	40	89	.310	12		0.8
5		246	258	.488			6.7
ORR, DAVE B 9.29.1859							
1887	NY AA	3	5	.375	8-7-7	2/3	0.7
OTT, MEL B 3.2.1909							
1942	NY N	85	67	.559	3		1.2
1943	NY N	55	98	.359	8		-5.2
1944	NY N	67	87	.435	5		-1.1
1945	NY N	78	74	.513	5		5.3
1946	NY N	61	93	.396	8		-8.5
1947	NY N	81	73	.526	4		-2.5
1948	NY N	37	38	.493	4-5	1/2	-4.1
7		464	530	.467			-14.8
OWENS, PAUL B2.7.1924 Salamanca, NY Owens, Paul Francis D12.26.2003 Woodbury, NJ BR/TR, 6-3/185# (1B)							
1972	Phi N e	33	47	.412	6-6	2/2	0.5
1983	Phi N e	47	30	.610	1-1◆	2/2	5.5
1984	Phi N e	81	81	.500	4		-3.1
3		161	158	.505			2.9
OZARK, DANNY B11.26.1923 Buffalo, NY Ozark, Daniel Leonard (b. Daniel Leonard Orzechowski) BR/TR, 6-3/210# (1B)							
1973	Phi N e	71	91	.438	6		-2.2
1974	Phi N e	80	82	.494	3		1.6
1975	Phi N e	86	76	.531	2		0.9
1976	Phi N e	101	61	.623	1		-2.3
1977	Phi N e	101	61	.623	1		2.4

Year	Tm/Lg	W	L	Pct	Finish	Mgr/Yr	+/-
1978	Phi N e	90	72	.556	1		-4.0
1979	Phi N e	65	67	.492	5-4	1/2	1.9
1984	SF N w	24	32	.429	6-6	2/2	0.3
8		618	542	.533			-1.4
PABOR, CHARLIE B 9.24.1846							
1871	Cle NA	10	19	.345	7		1.6
1875	Atl NA	2	40	.048	12-12	1/2	5.3
	NH NA	1	5	.167	8-8	3/3	0.5
2		13	64	.169			7.5
PARKER, SALTY B 7.8.1913							
1967	NY N	4	7	.364	10-10	2/2	-0.2
1972	Hou N w	1	0	1.000	2-2	2/3	0.5
2		5	7	.417			0.3
PARKS, BILL B 6.4.1849							
1875	Was NA	1	7	.125	8-10	2/2	2.0
PARRISH, LARRY B 11.10.1953							
1998	Det A c	13	12	.520	5-5	2/2	2.6
1999	Det A c	69	92	.429	3		1.2
2		82	104	.441			3.8
PEARCE, DICKEY B 2.29.1836							
1872	Mut NA	10	6	.625	4-3	1/2	-1.6
1875	StL NA	39	29	.574	4		3.4
2		49	35	.583			1.8
PECKINPAUGH, ROGER B 2.5.1891							
1914	NY A	10	10	.500	7-6*t*	2/2	0.2
1928	Cle A	62	92	.403	7		0.0
1929	Cle A	81	71	.533	3		6.8
1930	Cle A	81	73	.526	4		6.2
1931	Cle A	78	76	.506	4		-3.7
1932	Cle A	87	65	.572	4		1.9
1933	Cle A	26	25	.510	5-4	1/3	1.0
1941	Cle A	75	79	.487	4*t*		-2.9
8		500	491	.505			9.5
PENA, TONY B 6.4.1957							
2002	KC A c	49	77	.389	4-4	3/3	-2.7
2003	KC A c	83	79	.512	3		4.9
2		132	156	.458			2.2
PEREZ, TONY B 5.14.1942							
1993	Cin N w	20	24	.455	5-5	1/2	-0.3
2001	Fla N e	54	60	.474	3-4	2/2	-2.9
2		74	84	.468			-3.2
PERKINS, CY B 2.27.1896							
1937	Det A	6	9	.400	2-2	5/5	-2.3
PESKY, JOHNNY B 9.27.1919							
1963	Bos A	76	85	.472	7		-0.6
1964	Bos A	70	90	.438	8-8	1/2	0.3
1980	Bos A e	1	4	.200	3-4	2/2	-1.5
3		147	179	.451			-1.8
PFEFFER, FRED B 3.17.1860							
1892-1	Lou N	9	14	.391	10-11	2/2	-0.2
-2	Lou N	33	42	.440	9		2.1
PHELAN, LEW Phelan, Lewis G. (DNP)							
1895	StL N	11	30	.268	11-11	4/4	-2.1
PHILLIPS, LEFTY B6.16.1919 Los Angeles, CA Phillips, Harold Ross D6.12.1972 Fullerton, CA BL/TL, 5-11/192# (P)							
1969	Cal A w	60	63	.488	6-3	2/2	9.0
1970	Cal A w	86	76	.531	3		4.9
1971	Cal A w	76	86	.469	4		2.5
3		222	225	.497			16.4
PHILLIPS, HORACE B 5.14.1853 Salem, OH Phillips, Horace B. (DNP)							
1879	Tro N	12	34	.261	8-8	1/2	1.2
1883	Col AA	32	65	.330	6		-0.4
1884	Pit AA	9	24	.273	10-10	5/5	1.6
1885	Pit AA	56	55	.505	3		-0.3
1886	Pit AA	80	57	.584	2		-3.7
1887	Pit N	55	69	.444	6		4.7
1888	Pit N	66	68	.493	6		3.9
1889	Pit N	28	43	.394	6-5	1/3	-3.9
8		338	415	.449			3.1
PHILLIPS, BILL B 11.9.1868							
1914	Ind F	88	65	.575	1		-2.6
1915	New F	26	27	.491	6-5	1/2	-1.4
2		114	92	.553			-4.0
PIKE, LIP B 5.25.1845							
1871	Tro NA	1	3	.250	7-6	1/2	-0.9
1874	Har NA	16	37	.302	7		-3.0
1877	Cin N	3	11	.214	6-6	1/3	-0.1
3		20	51	.282			-4.0
PINIELLA, LOU B 8.28.1943							
1986	NY A e	90	72	.556	2		3.2
1987	NY A e	89	73	.549	4		5.1
1988	NY A e	45	48	.484	2-5	2/2	-2.9
1990	Cin N w	91	71	.562	1★		-0.2

Year	Tm/Lg	W	L	Pct	Finish	Mgr/Yr	+/-
1991	Cin N w	74	88	.457	5		-6.8
1992	Cin N w	90	72	.556	2		3.5
1993	Sea A w	82	80	.506	4		0.7
1994	Sea A w	49	63	.438	3		-2.7
1995	Sea A w	79	66	.545	1☆▲		-1.7
1996	Sea A w	85	76	.528	2		-4.1
1997	Sea A w	90	72	.556	1		0.6
1998	Sea A w	76	85	.472	3		-4.9
1999	Sea A w	79	83	.488	3		2.2
2000	Sea A w	91	71	.562	2☆❖	-1.8	
2001	Sea A w	116	46	.716	1☆		5.9
2002	Sea A w	93	69	.574	3		0.7
2003	TB A e	63	99	.389	5		-4.8
	17	1382	1234	.528			-7.7

PLUMMER, BILL B 3.21.1947

1992	Sea A w	64	98	.395	7		-5.1

POPOWSKI, EDDIE B 8.20.1913 Sayreville, NJ Popowski, Edward Joseph D 12.4.2001 Sayreville, NJ BR/TR, 5-4.5/145# (2B)

1969	Bos A e	5	4	.556	3-3	2/2	0.5
1973	Bos A e	1	0	1.000	2-2	2/2	0.4
	2	6	4	.600			0.9

PORTER, MATTHEW B

1884	KC U	3	13	.188	8-8-8	2/3	0.5

POWERS, PAT B 6.27.1860 Trenton, NJ Powers, Patrick Thomas D 8.29.1925 Belmar, NJ (DNP)

1890	Roc AA	63	63	.500	5		0.2
1892-1	NY N	31	43	.419	10		-3.1
-2	NY N	40	37	.519	6		-3.1
	2	134	143	.484			-6.1

PRATT, AL B 11.19.1848

1882	Pit AA	39	39	.500	4		-0.9
1883	Pit AA	12	20	.375	6-7	1/3	1.6
	2	51	59	.464			0.6

PRICE, JIM B 1847 New York, NY Price, James L. D 10.6.1931 Chicago, IL (DNP)

1884	NY N	56	42	.571	4-4t	1/2	1.5

PROTHRO, DOC B 7.16.1893

1939	Phi N	45	106	.298	8		-0.6
1940	Phi N	50	103	.327	8		0.4
1941	Phi N	43	111	.279	8		-3.7
	3	138	320	.301			-3.9

PUJOLS, LUIS B 11.18.1955

2002	Det A c	55	100	.355	5-5	2/2	5.4

PURCELL, BLONDIE B

1883	Phi N	13	68	.160	8-8	2/2	3.0

QUEEN, MEL B 3.26.1942

1997	Tor A e	4	1	.800	5-5	2/2	1.6

QUILICI, FRANK B 5.11.1939

1972	Min A w	41	43	.488	3-3	2/2	-1.1
1973	Min A w	81	81	.500	3		-4.6
1974	Min A w	82	80	.506	3		0.6
1975	Min A w	76	83	.478	4		-2.3
	4	280	287	.494			-7.5

QUINN, JOE B 12.25.1864

1895	StL N	11	28	.282	11-11-11	3/4	-1.5
1899	Cle N	12	104	.103	12-12	2/2	2.0
	2	23	132	.148			0.5

RADER, DOUG B 7.30.1944

1983	Tex A w	77	85	.475	3		-7.3
1984	Tex A w	69	92	.429	7		-5.5
1985	Tex A w	9	23	.281	7-7	1/2	-3.6
1986	Chi A w	1	1	.500	6-5-5	2/3	0.1
1989	Cal A w	91	71	.562	3		0.2
1990	Cal A w	80	82	.494	4		0.6
1991	Cal A w	61	63	.492	7-7	1/2	-1.3
	7	388	417	.482			-16.9

RAPP, VERN B 5.11.1928 St.Louis, MO Rapp, Vernon Fred BR/TR, 6/195# (C)

1977	StL N e	83	79	.512	3		-3.0
1978	StL N e	6	11	.353	6-5	1/3	-1.9
1984	Cin N w	51	70	.421	5-5	1/2	-0.3
	3	140	160	.467			-5.1

REACH, AL B 5.25.1840

1890	Phi N	4	7	.364	2-3-3	3/5	-2.4

REGAN, PHIL B 4.6.1937

1995	Bal A e	71	73	.493	3		-7.3

RICE, DEL B 10.27.1922

1972	Cal A w	75	80	.484	5		6.9

RICHARDS, PAUL B 11.21.1908

1951	Chi A	81	73	.526	4		-3.1
1952	Chi A	81	73	.526	3		-0.6
1953	Chi A	89	65	.578	3		-0.8
1954	Chi A	91	54	.628	3-3	1/2	-0.5
1955	Bal A	57	97	.370	7		2.3
1956	Bal A	69	85	.448	6		6.0
1957	Bal A	76	76	.500	5		-1.0
1958	Bal A	74	79	.484	6		3.6
1959	Bal A	74	80	.481	6		4.6
1960	Bal A	89	65	.578	2		4.1
1961	Bal A	78	57	.578	3-3	1/2	1.3
1976	Chi A w	64	97	.398	6		0.1
	12	923	901	.506			15.9

RICHARDSON, DANNY B 1.25.1863

1892-2	Was N	12	31	.279	11-12	2/2	-5.9

RICKEY, BRANCH B 12.20.1881

1913	StL A	5	6	.455	7-8	3/3	0.4
1914	StL A	71	82	.464	5		4.8
1915	StL A	63	91	.409	6		3.2
1919	StL N	54	83	.394	7		-4.7
1920	StL N	75	79	.487	5t		-1.3
1921	StL N	87	66	.569	3		-1.8
1922	StL N	85	69	.552	3t		4.0
1923	StL N	79	74	.516	5		1.1
1924	StL N	65	89	.422	6		-11.0
1925	StL N	13	25	.342	8-4	1/2	-7.5
	10	597	664	.473			-12.7

RIDDOCH, GREG B 7.17.1945 Greeley, CO Riddoch, Gregory Lee BR/TR, 5-11/175# (SS)

1990	SD N w	38	44	.463	4-5	2/2	-3.0
1991	SD N w	84	78	.519	3		4.1
1992	SD N w	78	72	.520	3-3	1/2	4.9
	3	200	194	.508			6.0

RIGGLEMAN, JIM B 11.9.1952 Fort Dix, NJ Riggleman, James David BR/TR, 5-11/175# (3B)

1992	SD N w	4	8	.333	3-3	2/2	-1.8
1993	SD N w	61	101	.377	7		-10.7
1994	SD N w	47	70	.402	4		-6.2
1995	Chi N c	73	71	.507	3		-1.1
1996	Chi N c	76	86	.469	4		-5.1
1997	Chi N c	68	94	.420	5		-5.8
1998	Chi N c	90	73	.552	2❖▲		4.8
1999	Chi N c	67	95	.414	6		2.2
	8	486	598	.448			-23.8

RIGNEY, BILL B 1.29.1918

1956	NY N	67	87	.435	6		1.9
1957	NY N	69	85	.448	6		-2.1
1958	SF N	80	74	.519	3		0.1
1959	SF N	83	71	.539	3		-3.4
1960	SF N	33	25	.569	2-5	1/2	2.4
1961	LA A	70	91	.435	8		-6.6
1962	LA A	86	76	.531	3		3.8
1963	LA A	70	91	.435	9		-3.7
1964	LA A	82	80	.506	5		1.8
1965	Cal A	75	87	.463	7		-1.2
1966	Cal A	80	82	.494	6		3.2
1967	Cal A	84	77	.522	5		5.7
1968	Cal A	67	95	.414	8		-0.6
1969	Cal A w	11	28	.282	6-3	1/2	-5.2
1970	Min A w	98	64	.605	1		2.5
1971	Min A w	74	86	.463	5		-4.3
1972	Min A w	36	34	.514	3-3	1/2	0.9
1976	SF N w	74	88	.457	4		2.7
	18	1239	1321	.484			-2.0

RIPKEN, CAL B 12.17.1935 Aberdeen, MD Ripken, Calvin Edwin Sr. D 3.25.1999 Baltimore, MD BR/TR, 6/175# (C)

1985	Bal A e	1	0	1.000	4-4-4	2/3	0.5
1987	Bal A e	67	95	.414	6		0.4
1988	Bal A e	0	6	.000	7-7	1/2	-2.1
	3	68	101	.402			-1.2

ROBINSON, FRANK B 8.31.1935

1975	Cle A e	79	80	.497	4		1.0
1976	Cle A e	81	78	.509	4		1.5
1977	Cle A e	26	31	.456	5-5	1/2	-0.2
1981-1	SF N w	27	32	.458	5		-0.9
-2	SF N w	29	23	.558	3		-0.9
1982	SF N w	87	75	.537	3		7.4
1983	SF N w	79	83	.488	5		-1.0
1984	SF N w	42	64	.396	6-6	1/2	-2.9
1988	Bal A e	54	101	.348	7-7	2/2	0.4
1989	Bal A e	87	75	.537	2		3.7
1990	Bal A e	76	85	.472	5		-1.5
1991	Bal A e	13	24	.351	7-6	1/2	-3.0
2002	Mon N e	83	79	.512	2		0.3
2003	Mon N e	83	79	.512	4		2.5
	13	846	909	.482			6.5

ROBINSON, WILBERT B 6.29.1863

1902	Bal A	24	57	.296	7-8	2/2	-9.5
1914	Bro N	75	79	.487	5		-2.4
1915	Bro N	80	72	.526	3		6.7
1916	Bro N	94	60	.610	1		3.9
1917	Bro N	70	81	.464	7		-0.0
1918	Bro N	57	69	.452	5		6.1
1919	Bro N	69	71	.493	5		-2.3
1920	Bro N	93	61	.604	1		1.7
1921	Bro N	77	75	.507	5		2.4
1922	Bro N	76	78	.494	6		0.1
1923	Bro N	76	78	.494	6		-2.2
1924	Bro N	92	62	.597	2		11.2
1925	Bro N	68	85	.444	6t		-1.2
1926	Bro N	71	82	.464	6		2.9
1927	Bro N	65	88	.425	6		-3.0
1928	Bro N	77	76	.503	6		-2.1
1929	Bro N	70	83	.458	6		5.7
1930	Bro N	86	68	.558	4		-3.3
1931	Bro N	79	73	.520	4		2.2
	19	1399	1398	.500			16.8

ROBISON, STAN B 3.30.1859 Pittsburgh, PA Robison, Matthew Stanley D 3.24.1911 Cleveland, OH (DNP)

1905	StL N	19	31	.380	6-6	3/3	0.8

RODGERS, BUCK B 8.16.1938

1980	Mil A e	26	21	.553	2-3	1/3	-1.2
	Mil A e	13	10	.565	4-3	3/3	-0.3
1981-1	Mil A e	31	25	.554	3		4.0
-2	Mil A e	31	22	.585	1		4.0
1982	Mil A e	23	24	.489	5-1❖	1/2	-5.3
1985	Mon N e	84	77	.522	3		3.8
1986	Mon N e	78	83	.484	4		2.8
1987	Mon N e	91	71	.562	3		7.9
1988	Mon N e	81	81	.500	3		-3.9
1989	Mon N e	81	81	.500	4		-0.2
1990	Mon N e	85	77	.525	3		-2.9
1991	Mon N e	20	29	.408	6-6	1/2	-2.0
	Cal A w	20	18	.526	7-7	2/2	0.7
1992	Cal A w	19	20	.487	5-5t	1/3	1.9
	Cal A w	14	20	.412	5-5t	3/3	-0.9
1993	Cal A w	71	91	.438	5t		-1.4
1994	Cal A w	16	23	.410	3-4	1/3	0.2
	13	784	773	.504			7.5

ROGERS, JIM B 4.9.1872

1897	Lou N	17	24	.415	9-11	1/2	1.9

ROJAS, COOKIE B 3.6.1939

1988	Cal A w	75	79	.487	4-4	1/2	3.4
1996	Fla N e	1	0	1.000	4-4-3	2/3	0.5
	2	76	79	.490			3.9

ROLFE, RED B 10.17.1908

1949	Det A	87	67	.565	4		0.4
1950	Det A	95	59	.617	2		6.2
1951	Det A	73	81	.474	5		1.5
1952	Det A	23	49	.319	8-8	1/2	-4.2
	4	278	256	.521			3.9

ROSE, PETE B 4.14.1941

1984	Cin N w	19	22	.463	5-5	2/2	1.6
1985	Cin N w	89	72	.553	2		7.4
1986	Cin N w	86	76	.531	2		3.5
1987	Cin N w	84	78	.519	2		-0.0
1988	Cin N w	11	12	.478	4-2	1/3	-1.2
	Cin N w	64	47	.577	4-2	3/3	5.1
1989	Cin N w	59	66	.472	4t-5	1/2	1.3
	6	412	373	.525			17.7

ROSEMAN, CHIEF B 1856

1890	StL AA	7	8	.467	4-5-3	3/6	-1.8

ROTHSCHILD, LARRY B 3.12.1954

1998	TB A e	63	99	.389	5		-4.5
1999	TB A e	69	93	.426	5		1.1
2000	TB A e	69	92	.429	5		-1.0
2001	TB A e	4	10	.286	5-5	1/2	-1.2
	4	205	294	.411			-5.6

ROWE, DAVE B 10.9.1854

1886	KC N	30	91	.248	7		3.9
1888	KC AA	14	36	.280	8-8	1/3	-0.2
	2	44	127	.257			3.7

ROWE, JACK B 12.8.1856

1890	Buf P	22	58	.275	8-8	1/3	1.1
	Buf P	5	14	.263	8-8	3/3	0.0

ROWLAND, PANTS B 2.12.1879 Platteville, WI Rowland, Clarence Henry D 5.17.1969 Chicago, IL BR/TR, 5-9/168# (C)

1915	Chi A	93	61	.604	3		-6.2
1916	Chi A	89	65	.578	2		0.3
1917	Chi A	100	54	.649	1★		1.5
1918	Chi A	57	67	.460	6		-6.2
	4	339	247	.578			-10.7

ROYSTER, JERRY B 10.18.1952

2002	Mil N c	53	94	.361	6-6	2/2	-2.8

RUDOLPH, DICK B 8.25.1887

1924	Bos N	11	27	.289	6-8-8	2/3	-0.9

Year	Tm/Lg	W	L	Pct	Finish	Mgr/Yr	+/-
RUEL, MUDDY B 2.20.1896							
1947	StL A	59	95	.383	8		0.5
RUNNELLS, TOM B 4.17.1955							
1991	Mon N e	51	61	.455	6-6	2/2	0.7
1992	Mon N e	17	20	.459	4-2	1/2	-3.2
2		68	81	.456			-2.4
RUNNELS, PETE B 1.28.1928							
1966	Bos A	8	8	.500	9-9	2/2	0.8
RUSSELL, BILL B 10.21.1948							
1996	LA N w	49	37	.570	1-2✣	2/2	3.2
1997	LA N w	88	74	.543	2		-2.9
1998	LA N w	36	38	.486	3-3	1/2	-0.6
3		173	149	.537			-0.3
RYAN, CONNIE B 2.27.1920							
1975	Atl N w	9	18	.333	5-5	2/2	-1.8
1977	Tex A w	2	4	.333	3-5-2	3/4	-1.4
2		11	22	.333			-3.2
SAWYER, EDDIE B9.10.1910 Westerly, RI Sawyer, Edwin Milb D9.22.1997 Phoenixville, PA BR/TR, 6/210# (OF)							
1948	Phi N	23	40	.365	6-6	3/3	-2.7
1949	Phi N	81	73	.526	3		4.6
1950	Phi N	91	63	.591	1		4.0
1951	Phi N	73	81	.474	5		-4.4
1952	Phi N	28	35	.444	6-4	1/2	-8.1
1958	Phi N	30	40	.429	8-8	2/2	-0.6
1959	Phi N	64	90	.416	8		-0.1
1960	Phi N	0	1	.000	6t-8	1/3	-0.4
8		390	423	.480			-7.8
SCANLON, MIKE B 11.1843 Cork, Ireland Scanlon, Michael B. D 1.18.1929 Washington, DC (DNP)							
1884	Was U	47	65	.420	6		0.7
1886	Was N	13	67	.162	8-8	1/2	-5.0
2		60	132	.313			-4.3
SCHAEFER, BOB B 5.22.1944 Putnam, CT Schaefer, Robert Walden BL/TR, 5-11/180# (SS)							
1991	KC A w	1	0	1.000	7-7-6	2/3	0.5
SCHALK, RAY B 8.12.1892							
1927	Chi A	70	83	.458	5		-1.9
1928	Chi A	32	42	.432	6-5	1/2	-1.7
2		102	125	.449			-3.6
SCHEFFING, BOB B 8.11.1913							
1957	Chi N	62	92	.403	7t		-5.4
1958	Chi N	72	82	.468	5t		-3.4
1959	Chi N	74	80	.481	5t		-1.5
1961	Det A	101	61	.623	2		3.3
1962	Det A	85	76	.528	4		-2.1
1963	Det A	24	36	.400	9-5t	1/2	-5.9
6		418	427	.495			-15.1
SCHLAFLY, LARRY B 9.20.1878							
1914	Buf F	80	71	.530	4		2.6
1915	Buf F	13	28	.317	8-6	1/3	-5.8
2		93	99	.484			-3.2
SCHMELZ, GUS B9.26.1850 Columbus, OH Schmelz, Gustavius Heinrich D10.13.1925 Columbus, OH (DNP)							
1884	Col AA	69	39	.639	2		2.7
1886	StL N	43	79	.352	6		-2.3
1887	Cin AA	81	54	.600	2		0.8
1888	Cin AA	80	54	.597	4		1.9
1889	Cin AA	76	63	.547	4		-4.7
1890	Cle N	21	55	.276	7-7	1/2	-6.4
	Col AA	38	13	.745	5-2	2/3	4.9
1891	Col AA	61	76	.445	6		-0.6
1894	Was N	45	87	.341	11		-2.5
1895	Was N	43	85	.336	10		-4.1
1896	Was N	58	73	.443	9t		1.0
1897	Was N	9	25	.265	11-6t	1/2	-7.7
11		624	703	.470			-17.1
SCHOENDIENST, RED B 2.2.1923							
1965	StL N	80	81	.497	7		-3.9
1966	StL N	83	79	.512	6		2.7
1967	StL N	101	60	.627	1★		5.7
1968	StL N	97	65	.599	1		2.9
1969	StL N e	87	75	.537	4		-0.2
1970	StL N e	76	86	.469	4		-4.7
1971	StL N e	90	72	.556	2		5.0
1972	StL N e	75	81	.481	4		0.5
1973	StL N e	81	81	.500	2		-4.3
1974	StL N e	86	75	.534	2		1.9
1975	StL N e	82	80	.506	3t		3.8
1976	StL N e	72	90	.444	5		-4.6
1980	StL N e	18	19	.486	5-4	4/4	-1.1
1990	StL N e	13	11	.542	6-6-6	2/3	2.6
14		1041	955	.522			6.2
SCHULTZ, JOE B 8.29.1918							
1969	Sea A w	64	98	.395	6		-0.8

Year	Tm/Lg	W	L	Pct	Finish	Mgr/Yr	+/-
1973	Det A e	14	14	.500	3-3	2/2	0.6
2		78	112	.411			-0.3
SCIOSCIA, MIKE B 11.27.1958							
2000	Ana A w	82	80	.506	3		1.5
2001	Ana A w	75	87	.463	3		-2.0
2002	Ana A w	99	63	.611	2★✣		-2.4
2003	Ana A w	77	85	.475	3		-3.3
4		333	315	.514			-6.3
SELEE, FRANK B 10.26.1859 Amherst, NY Selee, Frank Gibson D 7.5.1909 Denver, CO (DNP)							
1890	Bos N	76	57	.571	5		-6.5
1891	Bos N	87	51	.630	1		0.7
1892-1	Bos N	52	22	.703	1		6.7
-2	Bos N	50	26	.658	2●		6.7
1893	Bos N	86	43	.667	1		4.3
1894	Bos N	83	49	.629	3		1.0
1895	Bos N	71	60	.542	5t		-1.3
1896	Bos N	74	57	.565	4		-0.4
1897	Bos N	93	39	.705	1		-3.5
1898	Bos N	102	47	.685	1		2.7
1899	Bos N	95	57	.625	2		-1.4
1900	Bos N	66	72	.478	4		-6.6
1901	Bos N	69	69	.500	5		2.7
1902	Chi N	68	69	.496	5		-4.8
1903	Chi N	82	56	.594	3		3.6
1904	Chi N	93	60	.608	2		7.5
1905	Chi N	37	28	.569	4-3	1/2	-6.2
16		1284	862	.598			5.2
SEWELL, LUKE B 1.5.1901							
1941	StL A	55	55	.500	7-6t	2/2	3.9
1942	StL A	82	69	.543	3		-2.8
1943	StL A	72	80	.474	6		-3.1
1944	StL A	89	65	.578	1		1.9
1945	StL A	81	70	.536	3		0.1
1946	StL A	53	71	.427	7-7	1/2	-1.6
1949	Cin N	1	2	.333	7-7	2/2	-0.2
1950	Cin N	66	87	.431	6		-2.5
1951	Cin N	68	86	.442	6		2.5
1952	Cin N	39	59	.398	7-6	1/3	-7.1
10		606	644	.485			-9.0
SHANNON, DAN B 3.23.1865							
1889	Lou AA	10	46	.179	8-8-8	3/4	-2.1
1891	Was AA	15	34	.306	7-8-8	3/4	2.0
2		25	80	.238			-0.1
SHARSIG, BILL B 1855 Philadelphia, PA Sharsig, William A. D 2.1.1902 Philadelphia, PA (DNP)							
1886	Phi AA	22	17	.564	6-6	2/2	6.7
1888	Phi AA	81	52	.609	3		-7.1
1889	Phi AA	75	58	.564	3		0.5
1890	Phi AA	54	78	.409	7		8.6
1891	Phi AA	6	11	.353	7-4	1/2	-2.8
5		238	216	.524			5.9
SHAWKEY, BOB B 12.4.1890							
1930	NY A	86	68	.558	3		-4.8
SHEEHAN, TOM B 3.31.1894							
1960	SF N	46	50	.479	2-5	2/2	-4.6
SHEPARD, LARRY B 4.3.1919 Lakewood, OH Shepard, Lawrence William BR/TR, 5-11/180# (P)							
1968	Pit N	80	82	.494	6		-6.9
1969	Pit N e	84	73	.535	3-3	1/2	-1.8
2		164	155	.514			-8.6
SHERRY, NORM B 7.16.1931							
1976	Cal A w	37	29	.561	6-4t	2/2	7.7
1977	Cal A w	39	42	.481	5-5	1/2	-0.5
2		76	71	.517			7.2
SHETTSLINE, BILL B10.25.1863 Philadelphia, PA Shettsline, William Joseph D2.22.1933 Philadelphia, PA (DNP)							
1898	Phi N	59	44	.573	8t-6	2/2	5.0
1899	Phi N	94	58	.618	3		2.2
1900	Phi N	75	63	.543	3		4.4
1901	Phi N	83	57	.593	2		0.2
1902	Phi N	56	81	.409	7		4.8
5		367	303	.548			16.6
SHOTTON, BURT B 10.18.1884							
1928	Phi N	43	109	.283	8		-5.7
1929	Phi N	71	82	.464	5		5.9
1930	Phi N	52	102	.338	8		-4.4
1931	Phi N	66	88	.429	6		2.8
1932	Phi N	78	76	.506	4		-3.4
1933	Phi N	60	92	.395	7		-0.7
1934	Cin N	1	0	1.000	8-8-8	2/3	0.6
1947	Bro N	92	60	.605	1t-1	2/2	5.6
1948	Bro N	48	33	.593	5-3	3/3	3.6
1949	Bro N	97	57	.630	1		-1.8
1950	Bro N	89	65	.578	2		0.4
11		697	764	.477			3.0

Year	Tm/Lg	W	L	Pct	Finish	Mgr/Yr	+/-
SHOWALTER, BUCK B5.23.1956 DeFuniak Springs, FL Showalter, William Nathaniel BL/TL, 5-9/195# (1B)							
1992	NY A e	76	86	.469	4t		-3.7
1993	NY A e	88	74	.543	2		1.2
1994	NY A e	70	43	.619	1		1.0
1995	NY A e	79	65	.549	2✣		1.2
1998	Ari N w	65	97	.401	5		-1.4
1999	Ari N w	100	62	.617	1		-3.3
2000	Ari N w	85	77	.525	3		0.3
2003	Tex A w	71	91	.438	4		2.9
8		634	595	.516			-1.7
SILVESTRI, KEN B 5.3.1916							
1967	Atl N	0	3	.000	7-7	2/2	-1.5
SIMMONS, JOE B 6.13.1845							
1875	Wes NA	1	12	.077	13		-1.5
1884	Wil U	2	16	.111	8		1.2
2		3	28	.097			-0.2
SIMMONS, LEW B 8.27.1838 New Castle, PA Simmons, Lewis D 9.2.1911 Jamestown, PA (DNP)							
1886	Phi AA	41	55	.427	6-6	1/2	3.3
SISLER, GEORGE B 3.24.1893							
1924	StL A	74	78	.487	4		1.6
1925	StL A	82	71	.536	3		6.0
1926	StL A	62	92	.403	7		0.6
3		218	241	.475			8.2
SISLER, DICK B 11.2.1920							
1964	Cin N	3	3	.500	3-4-2t	2/4	-0.4
	Cin N	29	18	.617	3-2t	4/4	2.5
1965	Cin N	89	73	.549	4		-3.8
2		121	94	.563			-1.7
SKAFF, FRANK B 9.30.1910							
1966	Det A	40	39	.506	2-3	3/3	-0.5
SKINNER, JOEL B 2.21.1961							
2002	Cle A c	35	40	.467	3-3	2/2	1.9
SKINNER, BOB B 10.3.1931							
1968	Phi N	48	59	.449	5-7t	3/3	-0.2
1969	Phi N e	44	64	.407	5-5	1/2	-3.2
1977	SD N w	1	0	1.000	4-4-5	2/3	0.6
3		93	123	.431			-2.7
SLATTERY, JACK B 1.6.1878							
1928	Bos N	11	20	.355	7-7	1/2	0.3
SMITH, MAYO B 1.17.1915							
1955	Phi N	77	77	.500	4		-0.9
1956	Phi N	71	83	.461	5		1.0
1957	Phi N	77	77	.500	5		3.5
1958	Phi N	39	45	.464	8-8	1/2	2.3
1959	Cin N	35	45	.438	7-5t	1/2	-6.3
1967	Det A	91	71	.562	2t		-0.3
1968	Det A	103	59	.636	1★		1.8
1969	Det A e	90	72	.556	2		-1.6
1970	Det A e	79	83	.488	4		4.6
9		662	612	.520			4.0
SMITH, HEINIE B 10.24.1871							
1902	NY N	5	27	.156	4-8-8	2/3	-5.7
SMITH, HARRY B 10.31.1874							
1909	Bos N	23	54	.299	8-8	2/2	-1.6
SMITH, BILL B							
1873	Mar NA	0	6	.000	9		3.9
SNYDER, POP B 10.6.1854							
1882	Cin AA	55	25	.688	1		-6.6
1883	Cin AA	61	37	.622	3		-10.6
1884	Cin AA	24	14	.632	5-5	2/2	-2.5
1891	Was AA	23	46	.333	6-7-8	2/4	4.7
4		163	122	.572			-14.9
SNYDER, JIM B 8.15.1932							
1988	Sea A w	45	60	.429	6-7	2/2	-2.2
SOTHORON, ALLEN B 4.27.1893							
1933	StL A	2	6	.250	8-8-8	2/3	-1.2
SOUTHWORTH, BILLY B 3.9.1893							
1929	StL N	43	45	.489	4-4	1/3	-2.3
1940	StL N	69	40	.633	7-3	3/3	11.1
1941	StL N	97	56	.634	2		5.6
1942	StL N	106	48	.688	1★		-0.3
1943	StL N	105	49	.682	1		5.4
1944	StL N	105	49	.682	1★		-1.8
1945	StL N	95	59	.617	2		0.2
1946	Bos N	81	72	.529	4		0.5
1947	Bos N	86	68	.558	3		1.3
1948	Bos N	91	62	.595	1		-1.4
1949	Bos N	55	54	.505	4-4	1/2	1.4
1950	Bos N	83	71	.539	4		1.3
1951	Bos N	28	31	.475	5-4	1/2	-3.8
13		1044	704	.597			17.2

Year	Tm/Lg	W	L	Pct	Finish	Mgr/Yr	+/-
SPALDING, AL B 9.2.1850							
1876	Chi N	52	14	.788	1		-11.1
1877	Chi N	26	33	.441	5		-2.7
2		78	47	.624			-13.9
SPEAKER, TRIS B 4.4.1888							
1919	Cle A	40	21	.656	3-2	2/2	5.0
1920	Cle A	98	56	.636	1★		0.3
1921	Cle A	94	60	.610	2		-2.6
1922	Cle A	78	76	.506	4		5.6
1923	Cle A	82	71	.536	3		-7.5
1924	Cle A	67	86	.438	6		-4.0
1925	Cle A	70	84	.455	6		-3.7
1926	Cle A	88	66	.571	2		-1.8
8		617	520	.543			-8.7
SPENCE, HARRY B 2.2.1856 New York, NY Spence, Harrison L. D 5.17.1908 Chicago, IL (DNP)							
1888	Ind N	50	85	.370	7		-5.2
STAHL, CHICK B 1.10.1873							
1906	Bos A	14	26	.350	8-8	2/2	0.9
STAHL, JAKE B 4.13.1879							
1905	Was A	64	87	.424	7		-4.6
1906	Was A	55	95	.367	7		-4.4
1912	Bos A	105	47	.691	1★		3.1
1913	Bos A	39	41	.488	5-4	1/2	-2.2
4		263	270	.493			-8.0
STALLINGS, GEORGE B 11.17.1867							
1897	Phi N	55	77	.417	10		-7.5
1898	Phi N	19	27	.413	8t-6	1/2	-5.1
1901	Det A	74	61	.548	3		2.2
1909	NY A	74	77	.490	5		-1.7
1910	NY A	78	59	.569	3-2	1/2	2.7
1913	Bos N	69	82	.457	5		-1.5
1914	Bos N	94	59	.614	1★		5.7
1915	Bos N	83	69	.546	2		2.9
1916	Bos N	89	63	.586	3		2.4
1917	Bos N	72	81	.471	6		-2.7
1918	Bos N	53	71	.427	7		-4.0
1919	Bos N	57	82	.410	6		-1.6
1920	Bos N	62	90	.408	7		1.8
13		879	898	.495			-6.6
STANKY, EDDIE B 9.3.1916							
1952	StL N	88	66	.571	3		6.2
1953	StL N	83	71	.539	3t		0.6
1954	StL N	72	82	.468	6		-5.8
1955	StL N	17	19	.472	5-7	1/2	1.4
1966	Chi A	83	79	.512	4		-4.6
1967	Chi A	89	73	.549	4		3.2
1968	Chi A	34	45	.430	9-8	1/5	-1.7
1977	Tex A w	1	0	1.000	3t-3-2	2/4	0.4
8		467	435	.518			-0.3
START, JOE B 10.14.1842							
1873	Mut NA	18	7	.720	5-4	2/2	4.1
STENGEL, CASEY B 7.30.1890							
1934	Bro N	71	81	.467	6		-0.6
1935	Bro N	70	83	.458	5		-1.1
1936	Bro N	67	87	.435	7		-1.0
1938	Bos N	77	75	.507	5		7.2
1939	Bos N	63	88	.417	7		-3.3
1940	Bos N	65	87	.428	7		1.2
1941	Bos N	62	92	.403	7		-1.8
1942	Bos N	59	89	.399	7		-1.0
1943	Bos N	47	60	.439	6-6	2/2	5.1
1949	NY A	97	57	.630	1★		1.3
1950	NY A	98	56	.636	1★		0.2
1951	NY A	98	56	.636	1★		3.5
1952	NY A	95	59	.617	1★		0.3
1953	NY A	99	52	.656	1★		-2.0
1954	NY A	103	51	.669	2		1.6
1955	NY A	96	58	.623	1		-0.7
1956	NY A	97	57	.630	1★		-1.8
1957	NY A	98	56	.636	1		1.2
1958	NY A	92	62	.597	1★		-3.6
1959	NY A	79	75	.513	3		-2.1
1960	NY A	97	57	.630	1		8.0
1962	NY N	40	120	.250	10		-8.1
1963	NY N	51	111	.315	10		-0.8
1964	NY N	53	109	.327	10		-6.4
1965	NY N	31	64	.326	10-10	1/2	-0.1
25		1905	1842	.508			-4.8
STOVALL, GEORGE B 11.23.1877							
1911	Cle A	74	62	.544	7-3	2/2	7.7
1912	StL A	41	74	.357	8-7	2/2	-0.1
1913	StL A	50	84	.373	7-8	1/3	-6.1
1914	KC F	67	84	.444	6		-4.5
1915	KC F	81	72	.529	4		4.9
5		313	376	.454			1.9

Year	Tm/Lg	W	L	Pct	Finish	Mgr/Yr	+/-
STOVEY, HARRY B 12.20.1856							
1881	Wor N	8	18	.308	7-8	2/2	-2.6
1885	Phi AA	55	57	.491	4		-7.1
2		63	75	.457			-9.7
STREET, GABBY B 9.30.1882							
1929	StL N	1	0	1.000	4-4-4	2/3	0.5
1930	StL N	92	62	.597	1		-4.4
1931	StL N	101	53	.656	1★		4.2
1932	StL N	72	82	.468	6t		-1.7
1933	StL N	46	45	.505	5-5	1/2	-4.3
1938	StL A	53	90	.371	7-7	1/2	-0.9
6		365	332	.524			-6.6
STRICKER, CUB B 2.15.1860							
1892-1	StL N	6	17	.261	10-11-9	2/3	-2.4
STRICKLAND, GEORGE B 1.10.1926							
1964	Cle A	33	39	.458	8-6t	1/2	-2.8
1966	Cle A	15	24	.385	3-5	2/2	-4.2
2		48	63	.432			-7.0
STUBING, MOOSE B 3.31.1938							
1988	Cal A w	0	8	.000	4-4	2/2	-3.7
SUKEFORTH, CLYDE B 11.30.1901							
1947	Bro N	2	0	1.000	1t-1	1/2	0.9
SULLIVAN, HAYWOOD B 12.15.1930							
1965	KC A	54	82	.397	10-10	2/2	0.9
SULLIVAN, PAT Sullivan, James Patrick D5.22.1898 (DNP)							
1890	Col AA	2	1	.667	5-5-2	3/3	0.1
SULLIVAN, TED B 1851							
1883	StL AA	53	26	.671	2-2	1/2	2.7
1884	StL U	28	3	.903	1-1	1/2	1.4
	KC U	13	46	.220	8-8	3/3	3.9
1888	Was N	38	57	.400	8-8	2/2	8.2
3		132	132	.500			16.2
SULLIVAN, BILLY B 2.1.1875							
1909	Chi A	78	74	.513	4		-1.4
SWEASY, CHARLIE B 11.2.1847							
1875	RS NA	4	15	.211	9		3.4
SWIFT, BOB B 3.6.1915							
1965	Det A	24	18	.571	3-4	1/2	0.8
1966	Det A	32	25	.561	3-2-3	2/3	2.8
2		56	43	.566			3.6
TANNER, CHUCK B 7.4.1929							
1970	Chi A w	3	13	.188	6-6	3/3	-3.1
1971	Chi A w	79	83	.488	3		-4.2
1972	Chi A w	87	67	.565	2		6.9
1973	Chi A w	77	85	.475	5		1.5
1974	Chi A w	80	80	.500	4		3.8
1975	Chi A w	75	86	.466	5		-0.5
1976	Oak A w	87	74	.540	2		-2.8
1977	Pit N e	96	66	.593	2		8.0
1978	Pit N e	88	73	.547	2		2.6
1979	Pit N e	98	64	.605	1★		3.6
1980	Pit N e	83	79	.512	3		-0.1
1981-1	Pit N e	25	23	.521	4		-3.1
-2	Pit N e	21	33	.389	6		-3.1
1982	Pit N e	84	78	.519	4		0.2
1983	Pit N e	84	78	.519	2		1.8
1984	Pit N e	75	87	.463	6		-11.3
1985	Pit N e	57	104	.354	6		-8.6
1986	Atl N w	72	89	.447	6		2.3
1987	Atl N w	69	92	.429	5		-3.6
1988	Atl N w	12	27	.308	6-6	1/2	-2.7
19		1352	1381	.495			-12.7
TAPPE, EL B 5.21.1927							
1961	Chi N	2	0	1.000	7-7-7	4/9	1.1
	Chi N	35	43	.449	7-7-7	7/9	1.5
	Chi N	5	11	.313	7-7	9/9	-1.9
1962	Chi N	4	16	.200	9-9	1/3	-3.6
2		46	70	.397			-2.9
TAYLOR, GEORGE B 11.22.1852 , NY Taylor, George J. D 10.28.1911 New York, NY (DNP)							
1884	Bro AA	40	64	.385	9		3.7
TAYLOR, ZACK B 7.27.1898							
1946	StL A	13	17	.433	7-7	2/2	-0.2
1948	StL A	59	94	.386	6		-0.4
1949	StL A	53	101	.344	7		-0.9
1950	StL A	58	96	.377	7		2.6
1951	StL A	52	102	.338	8		1.1
5		235	410	.364			2.2
TEBBETTS, BIRDIE B 11.10.1912							
1954	Cin N	74	80	.481	5		0.3
1955	Cin N	75	79	.487	5		-9.5
1956	Cin N	91	63	.591	3		2.5
1957	Cin N	80	74	.519	4		6.2

Year	Tm/Lg	W	L	Pct	Finish	Mgr/Yr	+/-
1958	Cin N	52	61	.460	8-4	1/2	-10.1
1961	Mil N	12	13	.480	3-4	2/2	-1.4
1962	Mil N	86	76	.531	5		-1.6
1963	Cle A	79	83	.488	5t		5.0
1964	Cle A	46	44	.511	8-6t	2/2	1.2
1965	Cle A	87	75	.537	5		0.7
1966	Cle A	66	57	.537	3-5	1/2	5.5
11		748	705	.515			-1.3
TEBEAU, PATSY B 12.5.1864							
1890	Cle P	21	30	.412	7-7	2/2	1.0
1891	Cle N	31	40	.437	4-5	2/2	-2.2
1892-1	Cle N	40	33	.548	5		-4.9
-2	Cle N	53	23	.697	1		-4.9
1893	Cle N	73	55	.570	3		-2.0
1894	Cle N	68	61	.527	6		0.6
1895	Cle N	84	46	.646	2●		2.3
1896	Cle N	80	48	.625	2		-1.2
1897	Cle N	69	62	.527	5		-4.9
1898	Cle N	81	68	.544	5		1.8
1899	StL N	84	67	.556	5		0.9
1900	StL N	42	50	.457	7-5t	1/2	-3.8
11		726	583	.555			-17.1
TENACE, GENE B 10.10.1946							
1991	Tor A e	19	14	.576	1-1-1	2/3	1.2
TENNEY, FRED B 11.26.1871							
1905	Bos N	51	103	.331	7		2.7
1906	Bos N	49	102	.325	8		0.9
1907	Bos N	58	90	.392	7		0.3
1911	Bos N	44	107	.291	8		-2.4
4		202	402	.334			1.5
TERRY, BILL B 10.30.1898							
1932	NY N	55	59	.482	8-6t	2/2	-5.5
1933	NY N	91	61	.599	1★		1.6
1934	NY N	93	60	.608	2		-1.4
1935	NY N	91	62	.595	3		5.1
1936	NY N	92	62	.597	1		2.8
1937	NY N	95	57	.625	1		5.8
1938	NY N	83	67	.553	3		1.1
1939	NY N	77	74	.510	5		-0.3
1940	NY N	72	80	.474	6		-4.4
1941	NY N	74	79	.484	5		1.4
10		823	661	.555			6.3
THOMAS, FRED B , IN Thomas, Frederick L. (DNP)							
1887	Ind N	11	18	.379	8-8-8	2/3	3.1
THOMPSON, ANDREW B11.9.1845 Seward, IL Thompson, Andrew M. D2.17.1895 Pecatonica, IL (DNP)							
1884	Stp U	2	6	.250	7		1.3
TIGHE, JACK B8.9.1913 Kearny, NJ Tighe, John Thomas D8.1.2002 Pompano Beach, FL BR/TR, 5-8/170# (C)							
1957	Det A	78	76	.506	4		1.0
1958	Det A	21	28	.429	8-5	1/2	-5.3
2		99	104	.488			-4.3
TINKER, JOE B 7.27.1880							
1913	Cin N	64	89	.418	7		-1.2
1914	Chi F	87	67	.565	2		-1.6
1915	Chi F	86	66	.566	1		-1.1
1916	Chi N	67	86	.438	5		-7.1
4		304	308	.497			-10.9
TORBORG, JEFF B 11.26.1941							
1977	Cle A e	45	59	.433	5-5	2/2	-2.9
1978	Cle A e	69	90	.434	6		-4.8
1979	Cle A e	43	52	.453	6-6	1/2	-1.9
1989	Chi A w	69	92	.429	7		-5.8
1990	Chi A w	94	68	.580	2		7.8
1991	Chi A w	87	75	.537	2		-1.8
1992	NY N e	72	90	.444	5		-3.2
1993	NY N e	13	25	.342	7-7	1/2	-4.3
2001	Mon N e	47	61	.435	5-5	2/2	2.4
2002	Fla N e	79	83	.488	4		4.4
2003	Fla N e	17	22	.436	4-2✜1/2	-3.9	
11		635	717	.470			-13.9
TORRE, JOE B 7.18.1940							
1977	NY N e	49	68	.419	6-6	2/2	-3.6
1978	NY N e	66	96	.407	6		-6.2
1979	NY N e	63	99	.389	6		-6.0
1980	NY N e	67	95	.414	5		-4.4
1981-1	NY N e	17	34	.333	5		-1.3
-2	NY N e	24	28	.462	4		-1.3
1982	Atl N w	89	73	.549	1		4.3
1983	Atl N w	88	74	.543	2		-3.9
1984	Atl N w	80	82	.494	2t		1.4
1990	StL N e	24	34	.414	6-6	3/3	-1.2
1991	StL N e	84	78	.519	2		2.7
1992	StL N e	83	79	.512	3		-0.9
1993	StL N e	87	75	.537	3		4.6

Year	Tm/Lg	W	L	Pct	Finish	Mgr/Yr	+/-
1994	StL N c	53	61	.465	3t		4.1
1995	StL N c	20	27	.426	4-4	1/2	-0.3
1996	NY A e	92	70	.568	1★		3.1
1997	NY A e	96	66	.593	2✣	-4.5	
1998	NY A e	114	48	.704	1★		3.7
1999	NY A e	77	49	.611	1-1★	2/2	1.6
2000	NY A e	87	74	.540	1★		1.2
2001	NY A e	95	65	.594	1◆		6.1
2002	NY A e	103	58	.640	1		3.4
2003	NY A e	101	61	.623	1		4.5
	22	1659	1494	.526			7.3

TOSCA, CARLOS B 9.29.1953 Pinar Del Rio, Cuba Tosca, Carlos 5-7/158# (DNP)

Year	Tm/Lg	W	L	Pct	Finish	Mgr/Yr	+/-
2002	Tor A e	58	51	.532	4-3	2/2	4.5
2003	Tor A e	86	76	.531	3		-1.3
	2	144	127	.531			3.2

TRACEWSKI, DICK B 2.3.1935

Year	Tm/Lg	W	L	Pct	Finish	Mgr/Yr	+/-
1979	Det A e	2	0	1.000	5-5-5	2/3	1.0

TRACY, JIM B 12.31.1955

Year	Tm/Lg	W	L	Pct	Finish	Mgr/Yr	+/-
2001	LA N w	86	76	.531	3		3.6
2002	LA N w	92	70	.568	3		3.7
2003	LA N w	85	77	.525	2		2.0
	3	263	223	.541			9.3

TRAMMELL, ALAN B 2.21.1958

Year	Tm/Lg	W	L	Pct	Finish	Mgr/Yr	+/-
2003	Det A c	43	119	.265	5		-5.0

TRAYNOR, PIE B 11.11.1899

Year	Tm/Lg	W	L	Pct	Finish	Mgr/Yr	+/-
1934	Pit N	47	52	.475	4-5	2/2	-3.9
1935	Pit N	86	67	.562	4		-0.1
1936	Pit N	84	70	.545	4		-1.3
1937	Pit N	86	68	.558	3		3.2
1938	Pit N	86	64	.573	2		3.2
1939	Pit N	68	85	.444	6		-3.0
	6	457	406	.530			-1.8

TREBELHORN, TOM B 1.27.1948 Portland, OR Trebelhorn, Thomas Lynn BL/TR, 5-11/178# (C)

Year	Tm/Lg	W	L	Pct	Finish	Mgr/Yr	+/-
1986	Mil A e	6	3	.667	6-6	2/2	1.9
1987	Mil A e	91	71	.562	3		5.8
1988	Mil A e	87	75	.537	3t		-1.0
1989	Mil A e	81	81	.500	4		-2.9
1990	Mil A e	74	88	.457	6		-4.2
1991	Mil A e	83	79	.512	3		-3.3
1994	Chi N c	49	64	.434	5		-2.7
	7	471	461	.505			-6.4

TROTT, SAM B 3.1859

Year	Tm/Lg	W	L	Pct	Finish	Mgr/Yr	+/-
1891	Was AA	4	7	.364	6-9	1/4	1.1

TURNER, TED B 11.19.1938 Cincinnati, OH Turner, Robert Edward (DNP)

Year	Tm/Lg	W	L	Pct	Finish	Mgr/Yr	+/-
1977	Atl N w	0	1	.000	6-6-6	2/4	-0.4

UNGLAUB, BOB B 7.31.1881

Year	Tm/Lg	W	L	Pct	Finish	Mgr/Yr	+/-
1907	Bos A	9	20	.310	6-8-7	3/4	-3.4

VALENTINE, BOBBY B 5.13.1950

Year	Tm/Lg	W	L	Pct	Finish	Mgr/Yr	+/-
1985	Tex A w	53	76	.411	7-7	2/2	2.2
1986	Tex A w	87	75	.537	2		3.3
1987	Tex A w	75	87	.463	6t		-3.6
1988	Tex A w	70	91	.435	6		-0.4
1989	Tex A w	83	79	.512	4		3.9
1990	Tex A w	83	79	.512	3		4.1
1991	Tex A w	85	77	.525	3		2.6
1992	Tex A w	45	41	.523	3-4	1/2	5.8
1996	NY N e	12	19	.387	4-4	2/2	-2.9
1997	NY N e	88	74	.543	3		0.3
1998	NY N e	88	74	.543	2		0.7
1999	NY N e	97	66	.595	2☆▲✣		1.7
2000	NY N e	94	68	.580	2◆✣		6.3
2001	NY N e	82	80	.506	3		8.4
2002	NY N e	75	86	.466	5		-4.2
	15	1117	1072	.510			28.1

VanHALTREN, GEORGE B 3.30.1866

Year	Tm/Lg	W	L	Pct	Finish	Mgr/Yr	+/-
1892-1	Bal N	1	10	.091	12-12	1/3	-2.9

VERNON, MICKEY B 4.22.1918

Year	Tm/Lg	W	L	Pct	Finish	Mgr/Yr	+/-
1961	Was A	61	100	.379	9t		-3.4
1962	Was A	60	101	.373	10		-8.2
1963	Was A	14	26	.350	10-10	1/3	-0.1
	3	135	227	.373			-11.7

VIRDON, BILL B 6.9.1931

Year	Tm/Lg	W	L	Pct	Finish	Mgr/Yr	+/-
1972	Pit N e	96	59	.619	1		-0.8
1973	Pit N e	67	69	.493	2-3	1/2	-1.9
1974	NY A e	89	73	.549	2		2.9
1975	NY A e	53	51	.510	3-3	1/2	-5.4
	Hou N w	17	17	.500	6-6	2/2	1.0
1976	Hou N w	80	82	.494	3		2.4
1977	Hou N w	81	81	.500	3		-3.1
1978	Hou N w	74	88	.457	5		-3.9
1979	Hou N w	89	73	.549	2		7.9
1980	Hou N w	93	70	.571	1▲		6.2

Year	Tm/Lg	W	L	Pct	Finish	Mgr/Yr	+/-
1981-1	Hou N w	28	29	.491	3		-1.4
-2	Hou N w	33	20	.623	1		-1.4
1982	Hou N w	49	62	.441	5-5	1/2	-2.6
1983	Mon N e	82	80	.506	3		-2.3
1984	Mon N e	64	67	.489	5-5	1/2	-2.2
	13	995	921	.519			-4.5

VITT, OSSIE B 1.4.1890

Year	Tm/Lg	W	L	Pct	Finish	Mgr/Yr	+/-
1938	Cle A	86	66	.566	3		4.0
1939	Cle A	87	67	.565	3		0.7
1940	Cle A	89	65	.578	2		4.6
	3	262	198	.570			9.3

VonDER AHE, CHRIS B10.7.1851 Hille, Prussia Von Der Ahe, Christian Frederick Wilhelm D6.5.1913 St.Louis, MO (DNP)

Year	Tm/Lg	W	L	Pct	Finish	Mgr/Yr	+/-
1895	StL N	1	0	1.000	11-11-11	2/4	0.7
1896	StL N	0	2	.000	10-11-11	3/5	-0.5
1897	StL N	2	12	.143	12-12	4/4	-0.5
	3	3	14	.176			-0.4

VUKOVICH, JOHN B 7.31.1947

Year	Tm/Lg	W	L	Pct	Finish	Mgr/Yr	+/-
1986	Chi N e	1	1	.500	5-5-5	2/3	0.1
1988	Phi N e	5	4	.556	6-6	2/2	1.3
	2	6	5	.545			1.4

WAGNER, HEINIE B 9.23.1880

Year	Tm/Lg	W	L	Pct	Finish	Mgr/Yr	+/-
1930	Bos A	52	102	.338	8		-5.1

WAGNER, HONUS B 2.24.1874

Year	Tm/Lg	W	L	Pct	Finish	Mgr/Yr	+/-
1917	Pit N	1	4	.200	8-8-8	2/3	-1.0

WALKER, HARRY B 10.22.1916

Year	Tm/Lg	W	L	Pct	Finish	Mgr/Yr	+/-
1955	StL N	51	67	.432	5-7	2/2	-0.2
1965	Pit N	90	72	.556	3		-1.3
1966	Pit N	92	70	.568	3		-1.0
1967	Pit N	42	42	.500	6-6	1/2	0.8
1968	Hou N	49	52	.485	10-10	2/2	4.1
1969	Hou N w	81	81	.500	5		-0.8
1970	Hou N w	79	83	.488	4		-0.1
1971	Hou N w	79	83	.488	4t		-4.0
1972	Hou N w	67	54	.554	2-2	1/3	0.7
	9	630	604	.511			-1.9

WALLACE, BOBBY B 11.4.1873

Year	Tm/Lg	W	L	Pct	Finish	Mgr/Yr	+/-
1911	StL A	45	107	.296	8		-6.6
1912	StL A	12	27	.308	8-7	1/2	-1.9
1937	Cin N	5	20	.200	8-8	2/2	-5.9
	3	62	154	.287			-14.5

WALSH, ED B 5.14.1881

Year	Tm/Lg	W	L	Pct	Finish	Mgr/Yr	+/-
1924	Chi A	1	2	.333	6	2/4	-0.4

WALSH, MIKE B 4.29.1850 Ireland Walsh, Michael John D 2.2.1929 Louisville, KY (DNP)

Year	Tm/Lg	W	L	Pct	Finish	Mgr/Yr	+/-
1884	Lou AA	68	40	.630	3		-0.7

WALTERS, BUCKY B 4.19.1909

Year	Tm/Lg	W	L	Pct	Finish	Mgr/Yr	+/-
1948	Cin N	20	33	.377	7-7	2/2	-0.8
1949	Cin N	61	90	.404	7-7	1/2	-0.4
	2	81	123	.397			-1.2

WALTZ, JAMES B 1.12.1860 , MD Waltz, James Wilson D 4.27.1931 Baltimore, MD (DNP)

Year	Tm/Lg	W	L	Pct	Finish	Mgr/Yr	+/-
1892-1	Bal N	2	6	.250	12-12-12	2/3	-0.9

WARD, JOHN B 3.3.1860

Year	Tm/Lg	W	L	Pct	Finish	Mgr/Yr	+/-
1880	Pro N	18	13	.581	4-3-2	2/3	-2.1
1884	NY N	6	8	.429	4-4t	2/2	-1.8
1890	Bro P	76	56	.576	2		4.3
1891	Bro N	61	76	.445	6		-2.6
1892-1	Bro N	51	26	.662	2		-0.7
-2	Bro N	44	33	.571	3		-0.7
1893	NY N	68	64	.515	5		-5.9
1894	NY N	88	44	.667	2●		8.4
	7	412	320	.563			-1.1

WATERMAN, FRED B 12.1845

Year	Tm/Lg	W	L	Pct	Finish	Mgr/Yr	+/-
1872	Oly NA	2	7	.222	10		3.1

WATHAN, JOHN B 10.4.1949

Year	Tm/Lg	W	L	Pct	Finish	Mgr/Yr	+/-
1987	KC A w	21	15	.583	4-2	2/2	2.5
1988	KC A w	84	77	.522	3		-2.3
1989	KC A w	92	70	.568	2		5.2
1990	KC A w	75	86	.466	6		-5.3
1991	KC A w	15	22	.405	7-6	1/3	-3.6
1992	Cal A w	39	50	.438	5-5-5t	2/3	-0.0
	6	326	320	.505			-3.6

WATKINS, HARVEY Watkins, Harvey L. (DNP)

Year	Tm/Lg	W	L	Pct	Finish	Mgr/Yr	+/-
1895	NY N	18	17	.514	9-9	3/3	0.1

WATKINS, BILL B 5.5.1858

Year	Tm/Lg	W	L	Pct	Finish	Mgr/Yr	+/-
1884	Ind AA	4	18	.182	10-11	2/2	-1.6
1885	Det N	34	36	.486	8-6	2/2	3.2
1886	Det N	87	36	.707	2		-1.0
1887	Det N	79	45	.637	1★		-4.4
1888	Det N	49	44	.527	3-5	1/2	-3.7
	KC AA	8	17	.320	8-8	3/3	0.9
1889	KC AA	55	82	.401	7		1.1
1893	StL N	57	75	.432	10		-1.6

Year	Tm/Lg	W	L	Pct	Finish	Mgr/Yr	+/-
1898	Pit N	72	76	.486	8		4.1
1899	Pit N	7	15	.318	10-7	1/2	-5.0
	9	452	444	.504			-8.0

WEAVER, EARL B 8.14.1930 St.Louis, MO Weaver, Earl Sidney BR/TR, 5-7/180# (2B)

Year	Tm/Lg	W	L	Pct	Finish	Mgr/Yr	+/-
1968	Bal A	48	34	.585	3-2	2/2	2.2
1969	Bal A e	109	53	.673	1◆		0.2
1970	Bal A e	108	54	.667	1★		4.5
1971	Bal A e	101	57	.639	1◆		-0.4
1972	Bal A e	80	74	.519	3		-7.8
1973	Bal A e	97	65	.599	1		-4.3
1974	Bal A e	91	71	.562	1		5.0
1975	Bal A e	90	69	.566	2		-3.4
1976	Bal A e	88	74	.543	2		4.7
1977	Bal A e	97	64	.602	2t		9.7
1978	Bal A e	90	71	.559	4		6.7
1979	Bal A e	102	57	.642	1◆		4.4
1980	Bal A e	100	62	.617	2		2.4
1981-1	Bal A e	31	23	.574	2		7.3
-2	Bal A e	28	23	.549	4		7.3
1982	Bal A e	94	68	.580	2		4.3
1985	Bal A e	53	52	.505	4-4	3/3	-2.9
1986	Bal A e	73	89	.451	7		-2.8
	17	1480	1060	.583			37.2

WEDGE, ERIC B 1.27.1968

Year	Tm/Lg	W	L	Pct	Finish	Mgr/Yr	+/-
2003	Cle A c	68	94	.420	4		-5.2

WESTRUM, WES B 11.28.1922

Year	Tm/Lg	W	L	Pct	Finish	Mgr/Yr	+/-
1965	NY N	19	48	.284	10-10	2/2	-2.9
1966	NY N	66	95	.410	9		3.5
1967	NY N	57	94	.377	10-10	1/2	-0.4
1974	SF N w	38	48	.442	5-5	2/2	-0.1
1975	SF N w	80	81	.497	3		0.8
	5	260	366	.415			0.9

WHEELER, HARRY B 3.3.1858

Year	Tm/Lg	W	L	Pct	Finish	Mgr/Yr	+/-
1884	KC U	0	4	.000	8-8	1/3	-0.6

WHITE, DEACON B 12.7.1847

Year	Tm/Lg	W	L	Pct	Finish	Mgr/Yr	+/-
1872	Cle NA	0	2	.000	6-7	2/2	-0.5
1879	Cin N	9	9	.500	4-5	1/2	-0.4
	2	9	11	.450			-0.9

WHITE, JO-JO B 6.1.1909

Year	Tm/Lg	W	L	Pct	Finish	Mgr/Yr	+/-
1960	Cle A	1	0	1.000	4-4-4	2/3	0.5

WHITE, WILL B 10.11.1854

Year	Tm/Lg	W	L	Pct	Finish	Mgr/Yr	+/-
1884	Cin AA	44	27	.620	5	1/2	-5.6

WHITE, WARREN B 1844

Year	Tm/Lg	W	L	Pct	Finish	Mgr/Yr	+/-
1872	Nat NA	0	11	.000	11		1.2
1874	Bal NA	9	38	.191	8		6.6
	2	9	49	.155			7.8

WILBER, DEL B 2.24.1919

Year	Tm/Lg	W	L	Pct	Finish	Mgr/Yr	+/-
1973	Tex A w	1	0	1.000	6-6-6	2/3	0.6

WILHELM, KAISER B 1.26.1874

Year	Tm/Lg	W	L	Pct	Finish	Mgr/Yr	+/-
1921	Phi N	26	41	.388	8-8	2/2	5.0
1922	Phi N	57	96	.373	7		-2.9
	2	83	137	.377			2.1

WILLIAMS, JIMMY B1.4.1847 Catawba, OH Williams, James Andrews D10.23.1918 Westbury, NY (DNP)

Year	Tm/Lg	W	L	Pct	Finish	Mgr/Yr	+/-
1884	StL AA	51	33	.607	5-4	1/2	0.5
1887	Cle AA	39	92	.298	8		4.4
1888	Cle AA	20	44	.313	8-6	1/2	-3.8
	3	110	169	.394			1.1

WILLIAMS, JIMY B 10.4.1943

Year	Tm/Lg	W	L	Pct	Finish	Mgr/Yr	+/-
1986	Tor A e	86	76	.531	4		-2.4
1987	Tor A e	96	66	.593	2		-3.7
1988	Tor A e	87	75	.537	3t		-2.3
1989	Tor A e	12	24	.333	6-1	1/2	-7.8
1997	Bos A e	78	84	.481	4		-2.4
1998	Bos A e	92	70	.568	2✣	-3.0	
1999	Bos A e	94	68	.580	2☆✣	1.6	
2000	Bos A e	85	77	.525	2		-0.6
2001	Bos A e	65	53	.551	2-2	1/2	4.1
2002	Hou N c	84	78	.519	2		-2.4
2003	Hou N c	87	75	.537	2		-6.7
	11	866	746	.537			-25.8

WILLIAMS, DICK B 5.7.1929

Year	Tm/Lg	W	L	Pct	Finish	Mgr/Yr	+/-
1967	Bos A	92	70	.568	1		-0.3
1968	Bos A	86	76	.531	4		4.7
1969	Bos A e	82	71	.536	3-3	1/2	4.8
1971	Oak A w	101	60	.627	1		6.9
1972	Oak A w	93	62	.600	1★		-1.4
1973	Oak A w	94	68	.580	1★		-1.7
1974	Cal A w	36	48	.429	6-6	3/3	-3.8
1975	Cal A w	72	89	.447	6		1.3
1976	Cal A w	39	57	.406	6-4t	1/2	-3.7
1977	Mon N e	75	87	.463	5		1.2
1978	Mon N e	76	86	.469	4		-7.4
1979	Mon N e	95	65	.594	2		2.3

Year	Tm/Lg	W	L	Pct	Finish	Mgr/Yr	+/-
1980	Mon N e	90	72	.556	2		2.2
1981-1	Mon N e	30	25	.545	3		0.7
-2	Mon N e	14	12	.538	2-1☆	1/2	-0.3
1982	SD N w	81	81	.500	4		-1.8
1983	SD N w	81	81	.500	4		0.0
1984	SD N w	92	70	.568	1◆		5.5
1985	SD N w	83	79	.512	3*t*		-1.0
1986	Sea A w	58	75	.436	6-7	3/3	0.8
1987	Sea A w	78	84	.481	4		1.0
1988	Sea A w	23	33	.411	6-7	1/2	-2.2
	21	1571	1451	.520			8.0
WILLIAMS, TED B 8.30.1918							
1969	Was A e	86	76	.531	4		-0.2
1970	Was A e	70	92	.432	6		-4.4
1971	Was A e	63	96	.396	5		-3.1
1972	Tex A w	54	100	.351	6		-4.2
	4	273	364	.429			-11.8
WILLS, MAURY B 10.2.1932							
1980	Sea A w	20	38	.345	6-7	2/2	-2.3
1981-1	Sea A w	6	18	.250	7-6	1/2	-3.9
	2	26	56	.317			-6.2
WILSON, JIMMIE B 7.23.1900							
1934	Phi N	56	93	.376	7		-7.1
1935	Phi N	64	89	.418	7		5.2
1936	Phi N	54	100	.351	8		-9.2
1937	Phi N	61	92	.399	7		-1.9
1938	Phi N	45	103	.304	8-8	1/2	-0.7
1941	Chi N	70	84	.455	6		-6.6
1942	Chi N	68	86	.442	6		-1.2
1943	Chi N	74	79	.484	5		-6.0
1944	Chi N	1	9	.100	8-4	1/3	-4.2
	9	493	735	.401			-31.8
WINE, BOBBY B 9.17.1938							
1985	Atl N w	16	25	.390	5-5	2/2	-0.7
WINGO, IVEY B 7.8.1890							
1916	Cin N	1	1	.500	8-8-7*t*	2/3	0.2
WINKLES, BOBBY B 3.11.1930 Tuckerman, AR Winkles, Bobby Brooks BR/TR, 5-9/170# (SS)							
1973	Cal A w	79	83	.488	4		1.0
1974	Cal A w	30	44	.405	6-6	1/3	-5.1
1977	Oak A w	37	71	.343	5*t*-7	2/2	-7.0
1978	Oak A w	24	15	.615	1-6	1/2	8.7
	4	170	213	.444			-2.5

Year	Tm/Lg	W	L	Pct	Finish	Mgr/Yr	+/-
WOLF, JIMMY B 5.12.1862							
1889	Lou AA	14	51	.215	8-8-8	2/4	-0.0
WOLVERTON, HARRY B 12.6.1873							
1912	NY A	50	102	.329	8		-5.5
WOOD, GEORGE B 11.9.1858							
1891	Phi AA	67	55	.549	7-4	2/2	4.2
WOOD, JIMMY B 12.1.1844							
1871	Chi NA	19	9	.679	2		0.8
1872	Tro NA	15	10	.600	5		-3.2
	Eck NA	2	7	.222	10-10-9	2/3	3.0
1874	Chi NA	10	13	.435	4-5	2/2	0.4
1875	Chi NA	30	37	.448	6		-0.2
	4	76	76	.500			0.8
WRIGHT, AL B 3.30.1842 Cedar Grove, NJ Wright, Alfred Hector D 4.20.1905 New York, NY (DNP)							
1876	Phi N	14	45	.237	7		-3.5
WRIGHT, GEORGE B 1.28.1847							
1879	Pro N	59	25	.702	1		-5.9
WRIGHT, HARRY B 1.10.1835							
1871	Bos NA	20	10	.667	3		-1.2
1872	Bos NA	39	8	.830	1		-6.0
1873	Bos NA	43	16	.729	1		-5.2
1874	Bos NA	52	18	.743	1		-6.9
1875	Bos NA	71	8	.899	1		-7.2
1876	Bos N	39	31	.557	4		2.3
1877	Bos N	42	18	.700	1		-2.0
1878	Bos N	41	19	.683	1		5.3
1879	Bos N	54	30	.643	2		-7.5
1880	Bos N	40	44	.476	6		1.8
1881	Bos N	38	45	.458	6		2.8
1882	Pro N	52	32	.619	2		-0.3
1883	Pro N	58	40	.592	3		-9.1
1884	Phi N	39	73	.348	6		6.7
1885	Phi N	56	54	.509	3		0.8
1886	Phi N	71	43	.623	4		2.0
1887	Phi N	75	48	.610	2		-3.4
1888	Phi N	69	61	.531	3		1.2
1889	Phi N	63	64	.496	3		0.0
1890	Phi N	14	8	.636	1-3	1/5	1.3
	Phi N	22	23	.489	2-3	5/5	-4.0
1891	Phi N	68	69	.496	4		1.0
1892-1	Phi N	46	30	.605	3		-5.6
-2	Phi N	41	36	.532	5		-5.6

Year	Tm/Lg	W	L	Pct	Finish	Mgr/Yr	+/-
1893	Phi N	72	57	.558	4		-6.2
	23	1225	885	.581			-45.1
YORK, RUDY B 8.17.1913							
1959	Bos A	0	1	.000	8-8-5	2/3	-0.5
YORK, TOM B 7.13.1851							
1878	Pro N	33	27	.550	3		1.6
1881	Pro N	23	10	.697	4-2	2/2	5.7
	2	56	37	.602			7.3
YOST, NED B 8.19.1954							
2003	Mil N c	68	94	.420	6		2.2
YOST, EDDIE B 10.13.1926							
1963	Was A	0	1	.000	10-10-10	2/3	-0.4
YOUNG, CY B 3.29.1867							
1907	Bos A	3	3	.500	4*t*-7	1/4	0.4
YOUNG, NICK B9.12.1840 Fort Johnson, NY Young, Nicholas Ephraim D10.31.1916 Washington, DC (OF)							
1871	Oly NA	15	15	.500	5		-0.5
1873	Was NA	8	31	.205	7		2.2
	2	23	46	.333			1.7
ZIMMER, CHIEF B 11.23.1860							
1903	Phi N	49	86	.363	7		-6.9
ZIMMER, DON B 1.17.1931							
1972	SD N w	54	88	.380	4-6	2/2	1.0
1973	SD N w	60	102	.370	6		2.4
1976	Bos A e	42	34	.553	5-3	2/2	1.3
1977	Bos A e	97	64	.602	2*t*		2.4
1978	Bos A e	99	64	.607	2▲		3.5
1979	Bos A e	91	69	.569	3		-1.5
1980	Bos A e	82	73	.529	3-4	1/2	5.4
1981-1	Tex A w	33	22	.600	2		-2.2
-2	Tex A w	24	26	.480	3		-2.2
1982	Tex A w	38	58	.396	6-6	1/2	-0.2
1988	Chi N e	77	85	.475	4		-0.5
1989	Chi N e	93	69	.574	1		3.7
1990	Chi N e	77	85	.475	4*t*		4.4
1991	Chi N e	18	19	.486	4-4	1/3	0.4
1999	NY A e	21	15	.583	1-1	1/2	-0.6
	14	906	873	.509			17.4

HOMETOWN HEROES: TEAM ROSTERS

Nineteenth century baseball writers often referred to their local clubs as the "hometown nine." That was both accurate and appropriate in an era when teams had very few extra players, when top pitchers started half or more of their team's games (and played in the field when they weren't pitching), and when most managers were player-managers. Moreover, baseball had little competition for the hearts of the fans from other team sports back then.

Today, with twenty-five-player active rosters, plus well-used disabled lists, plus shuttles operating almost daily between top farm teams and their parent clubs, calling a major league team the "hometown thirty-five" would be more accurate, if hardly as appealing.

Almost all players who don the uniform of a major league team, however, are truly hometown heroes—a phrase with a double meaning: Big league ballplayers are heroes where they play—their team's hometown—as well as in their individual hometowns, whether they came from large cities or from small towns.

One of the foremost goals of any encyclopedia is to present information in an accessible manner. The player registers show year-by-year information for each player's career, and the Historical Record presents detailed annual information for each league. Another important component is this Team Rosters section, which features a chronological record of all regular players and pitchers plus important reserves on each team, season-by-season, for the whole 133-year span of professional baseball history.

Roster format. In this section rosters are grouped by league for each year, with the teams in each league shown in alphabetical order. This enables quick comparisons of the various teams in a pennant race without constantly flipping from page to page. Mortal enemies like the 1951 Giants and Dodgers will be found cheek-by-jowl; and all four teams that engaged in the down-to-the-wire 1967 AL pennant race will be at most a column or two away from each other.

These team rosters provide much more complete information than typical rosters do about how each team was put together and how it utilized its players in a given season. This is especially true in the past two decades, when teams have become much more reluctant to let young pitchers learn the ropes or to let struggling players work their way out of slumps. The increasing frequency of serious injuries has also resulted in less stable lineups.

The plethora of televised games and the omnipresent and instantaneous nature of the electronic media today put tremendous pressure on major league team owners, general managers, and managers to solve problems *right now*. Of course, the enormous amount of money at stake is also a huge factor in the decreasing amount of patience exhibited by teams at every level. Big league teams, managers, and players have lived under the microscope of the media throughout baseball history, but now that media microscope broadcasts full-color video accompanied by unabashedly critical commentary, 24–7.

This intense pressure has resulted in managers using scores of different lineups and having far fewer "set" positions than in the past. This roster-coding scheme may seem complex, but it gives a much more detailed understanding of whatever team is being examined. From 1990–2003, these rosters show 8,067 player-seasons, with 78 percent of the entries using the familiar single-position codes. Because of the way these codes are defined, however, even the standard codes like *SS* and *RF* now convey more information than in other sources.

Simpler rosters that showed pitching staffs composed simply of *SPs* and *RPs* would be far less useful than rosters showing that many pitchers spent part of the season in the rotation as well as the bullpen. Rosters that showed position players only by their primary positions, or that labeled all reserves simply as utility players, would also omit much useful information. The most common combination codes are, not surprisingly, *RS* and *SR*, followed by several codes for utility players. Two-position combination codes normally show up only a few times for each team.

From top to bottom, rosters list starting pitchers first, then relief pitchers, then regular position players, then reserves. Non-playing managers are shown last. Regular players who are traded during the season will normally show up on the team where they spent the bulk of the year, though some will fail to play at least half of either team's games and, thus, not qualify for either team's roster.

Pitchers. The rosters list as many as five starting pitchers and four relief pitchers for each team. Pitcher codes are:

- *SP* – starting pitcher;
- *RP* – relief pitcher;
- *SR* – starter-reliever;
- *RS* – reliever-starter;
- *CL* – closer.

Starting pitchers qualify if they are among the top five pitchers on the team in innings pitched, provided that they have pitched at least 0.6 innings for each of their team's games played. Relief pitchers make the roster if they are among the top four pitchers on the team in innings pitched plus saves, provided that they pitched at least 0.3 innings per team game.

Pitchers are assigned codes according to the following rules:

If a starting pitcher has 0–9 games in relief, he is labeled as *SP.*

If a pitcher has 10 or more games in relief, and if at least one third of his appearances are games started, then he is labeled as *SR.*

If the pitcher has started at least 5 games and has 10 or more games in relief, he is labeled as *RS*—provided he started less than one third of the time.

If a relief pitcher has from 0–4 games started, he is labeled as *RP.*

If a relief pitcher's saves total is equal to at least one third of his relief appearances, than he is labeled as *CL.*

Position Players. In order to include as clear a picture as possible of each team, every player who played in at least 50 percent of his team's games is shown, so no one who made a major impact during the regular season is missing. Position players who played in fewer than 60 percent of their team's games are marked by a dash after their position code.

Regular players are always listed in the order shown below. If a player played at least 75 percent of his team's games at one position, he is shown as the regular with the following codes:

- *C* – catcher
- *1B* – first base (*1* when combined with other positions)
- *2B* – second base (*2* when combined)
- *3B* – third base (*3* when combined)

- *SS* – shortstop (*S* when combined)
- *LF*– left fielder (*L* when combined)
- *CF*– center fielder (*M* when combined)
- *RF* – right fielder (*R* when combined)
- *DH* – designated hitter (*D* when combined)

If no one played at least 75 percent of a team's games at one position, the regular shown will be the player who played the most games at that position—unless a player happened to have played the most games at two positions. If so, that player will be shown where he played the most, and the player with the second-most games at the other position will be shown as the regular. For example, for Oakland in 2001, Johnny Damon played 67 games in left and 86 in center out of a total of 154 games in the outfield. He led the team in games at both positions. Terrence Long played 62 games in left, 74 in center, and 28 in right (162 total). Damon was listed as *ML*, since he played more than 50 percent of his games in center and more than 25 percent in left. Long was listed as the regular center fielder with an *UO* code because he did not play 50 percent of his games at any one position, but he did play all three outfield spots.

In the overwhelming majority of circumstances, the regular at each position will have the standard position code or a combination code that starts with the first letter of that position (e.g., *3S* for third base/shortstop; *L1* for left field/first base). However, when a team has several players shifting among different positions during the season, the regular shown at a particular position might not have the expected code. (This usually happens on bad teams that have no set lineup.) The lineups that "fit the best" with the players who played the most are always shown.

In these rare circumstances, the "regular" third baseman might be someone who played only 40 games there, but who still played third more than anyone else on that team who wasn't a regular at another position. For example, in 1918 Fred Thomas played only 41 games at third base for the pennant-winning Red Sox, but that was still more than anyone else, so Thomas is shown as the regular.

Aside from the position codes shown above, four other codes are used for players who have played less than 75 percent of their games at one position. Details on these codes are found below:

- *OF* – outfield (*O* when used in combination);
- *IF* – infield (*I* when used in combination);
- *UT* – utility player (*U* when used in combination);
- *P* – Pitcher (when used in combination with position codes).

Combination Position Codes. If a player played between 50 percent and 75 percent of his games at one position, his primary position will be signified by the *first* letter of the above codes. (Exception: To avoid confusion with catcher, we have revived the old newspaper box score code *M*—for "middle outfielder"—to indicate center field).

Players with at least half their games at one position, but less than three quarters of their games at that position, are also given a secondary position code. The secondary code assigned depends on how many games they played at other positions, of course, as well as the number of other positions they played. The rules for secondary position codes are:

If a player played at least 25 percent of his other games at a position other than his primary position, the secondary position will be shown as the second letter of his position code.

If the player did not play 25 percent of his other games at any single position, but he did play at least 25 percent of his additional (i.e., non-primary position) games in the infield, the second letter of his position code will be *I*. In 2003 Desi Relaford played 141 games for Kansas City: 89 at second base, 33 at third base, 20 in the outfield, and 6 at shortstop. His 89 games at second put him in 50–75 percent range for a two-character code, with *2* as the first character. His next highest position was less than 25 percent of his total games, so his secondary code is a utility code. With 39 games at third and short combined, his second character becomes *I* and his position code becomes *2I*.

If the player did not play 25 percent of his other games at a single position, but he did play at least 25 percent of his additional games in the outfield, the second letter of his position code will be *O*. In 2003 Dustan Mohr of Minnesota had 30 games in left, 11 in center, and 70 in right out of a total of 121 games. Thus he qualifies for an *RO* code, with 50–75 percent of his games in right, less than 25 percent at any other position, but a total of 41 in left and center.

If a player's games are scattered among so many positions that none of these conditions apply, his secondary code will be *U*.

If the player's secondary position was pitcher and he pitched in at least 10 games, his second letter will be *P*. Only a few position players since 1901—the most famous being Babe Ruth, of course—have pitched in 10 games in one year while also playing in half their team's games.

If the position player has 100 innings pitched in a season and a *P* wouldn't appear as his secondary position code under the preceding rules, the *P* will take precedence. This occurs exclusively in the nineteenth century. A lowercase *p* will be used to distinguish, for example, between a right fielder who also pitched (*Rp*) from a relief pitcher (*RP*), though the location of such players on the roster will usually make this clear.

Utility Codes. No two-letter coding scheme can account for all the ways that managers can use players during a season. Therefore, a few utility codes are used to cover versatile players who didn't play 50 percent of their games at any position. (Of course, complete data on games at position for every player can be found in the player registers.) Utility codes indicating specific positions are used only for catchers and those who also pitched a substantial amount (see paragraphs immediately above). Otherwise, utility codes are assigned by the following rules:

If the player played all three outfield positions but never played the infield, he will be labeled *UO* (utility outfielder). Quinton McCracken had 115 games in 2003: 10 in left, 16 in center, and 34 in right. Since he did not have 50 percent of his games at any one position, but did play all three outfield positions, he is labeled *UO*.

If the player played two outfield positions but never played the infield, he will be labeled *OF* (outfield). In 2003 Troy O'Leary of the Chicago Cubs had 28 games in left and 24 in right out of 93 games. He is an *OF*.

If the player played three or four infield positions but never played the outfield, he will be labeled as *UI* (utility infielder). In 2003 Carlos Baerga of Arizona had 19 games at first base, 15 at second base, and 5 at third base out of 105 games total, making him a *UI*.

If the player played two infield positions but never played the outfield, he will be labeled as *IF* (infielder). In 2001 Keith Lockhart of Atlanta had 47 games at second base and 4 games at third base out of 104 total. Since he played only two infield positions with no games in the outfield and no position with at least 50 percent of his games, he qualifies as an *IF*.

If the player played two or more Outfield positions as well as at least one infield position, and he played more games in the outfield than in the Infield, he will be labeled as *OI* (outfielder-infielder). In 2003 Brian Banks had 92 games total for Florida: 23 games in left, 12 at first, and 10 in right, qualifying him as *OI*.

If the player played two or more infield positions and at least one outfield position, and he played more games in the infield than in the outfield, he will be labeled as *IO* (infielder-outfielder). In 2003 Greg Norton of Colorado had 34 games at third, 9 at first, and 3 in right field (114 games total), giving him an *IO* code.

If a player's first or second position (in terms of number of games) is catcher, but he played less than 50 percent of his games there or at any other position, he will be labeled as *IC* (infielder/catcher) or *OC* (outfielder/catcher) depending on whether he played primarily in the infield or the outfield. If he played more games at catcher than elsewhere, and he did not play another defensive position in most of his other games (i.e., he was a DH or a pinch hitter), he will be labeled as *UC* (utility catcher). In 2001 Shawn Wooten played 79 games for Anaheim: 27 at DH, 25 at catcher, 21 at first, and 1 at third. Since his second position was catcher, but he played more there than in the infield or outfield, he is listed as *UC*.

If a player doesn't fit into any of these categories, he will be labeled as *UT* (utility). Matt Franco, who was mainly a pinch hitter for Atlanta in 2003, played 112 games: 3 games at first base, 2 in right, and 1 in left. Since he played the same number of games in the infield and outfield, he gets a *UT* code.

Managers. Managers are indicated by the code *M;* see the Manager Register introduction for an explanation of who qualifies as a manager. If a team had multiple managers in a season, the order in which these managers served is shown by the number after the *M* (i.e., the first manager will be *M1,* the second *M2,* etc.). Managers' names are italicized in the rosters. Player-managers are shown with standard position code(s) and located as a player; their italicization indicates managerial status. Non-playing managers are shown at the end of the team roster.

Most of the above rules apply only to a small fraction of the players and pitchers listed in the team rosters. More than three quarters of the 40,989 player and pitcher seasons in this section are shown with a primary position code. Most of the remaining players are shown with two-position codes.

BOS 1871 NA
SP A Spalding
C C McVey
1B C Gould
2S R Barnes
SS- G Wright
3B H Schafer
LF F Cone
CF H Wright
RF D Birdsall
LU- F Barrows
2B- S Jackson

CHI 1871 NA
SP G Zettlein
C3 C Hodes
1B B McAtee
2B J Wood
SS E Duffy
3B E Pinkham
LF F Treacey
MR T Foley
RM J Simmons
MC M King

CLE 1871 NA
SP A Pratt
C D White
1B J Carleton
2I G Kimball
SS J Bass
3B E Sutton
LF C Pabor
CF A Allison
RF- E White
2R- C Johnson

KEK 1871 NA
SP B Mathews
C B Lennon
1B J Foran
2B T Carey
S3 W Goldsmith
3B F Sellman
LF- E Mincher
CF B Armstrong
RF B Kelly
M2 H Deane

MUT 1871 NA
SP R Wolters
C C Mills
1B J Start
2R D Higham
SS D Pearce
32 B Ferguson
LI J Hatfield
CF D Eggler
RL D Patterson
3B- C Smith

ATH 1871 NA
SP D McBride
C F Malone
1B W Fisler
2B A Reach
SS J Radcliff
3B L Meyerle
LF N Cuthbert
CF C Sensenderfer
RF G Heubel
RU G Bechtel

ROK 1871 NA
SP C Fisher
C S Hastings
1B D Mack
2B B Addy
SS C Fulmer
3B C Anson
LF R Ham
CF G Bird
RF G Stires

TRO 1871 NA
SP J McMullin
C M McGeary
1R C Flynn
2U B Craver
SS D Flowers
3B S Bellan
LF S King
CF T York
R2 L Pike

OLY 1871 NA
SP A Brainard
C D Allison
1B E Mills
2L A Leonard
SS D Force
3B F Waterman
L2- H Berthrong
CF G Hall
RF J Glenn
M N Young

BAL 1872 NA
SP B Mathews
SP C Fisher
C B Craver
1B E Mills
2I T Carey
SS J Radcliff
3B- D Force
LF T York
CF G Hall
UT L Pike
CR D Higham

BOS 1872 NA
SP A Spalding
C C McVey
1B C Gould
2B R Barnes
SS G Wright
3B H Schafer
LF A Leonard
CF H Wright
RF F Rogers

ECK 1872 NA
SP P Martin
SP G Zettlein
SP J McDermott
C D Allison
1B A Allison
IO C Nelson
SS J Snyder
3B- F Fleet
LF C Gedney
CF- D Patterson
UT J Clinton
M2 J Wood

ATL 1872 NA
SP J Britt
C T Barlow
1B H Dehlman
2B- J Hall
SS J Burdock
3B B Ferguson
LF- A Thake
CF J Remsen
RF- J McDonald

CLE 1872 NA
SP A Pratt
SP R Wolters
C2 D White
1B J Simmons
2B- C Sweasy
SS J Holdsworth
3B E Sutton
LF C Pabor
CF A Allison
RF R Wolters
C2 S Hastings

MAN 1872 NA
SP C Bentley
SP F Buttery
C J Clapp
1B T Murnane
2B E Booth
SC J O'Rourke
3O G Fields
LF J Tipper
CF F McCarton
RF C Bentley
S3 H Allen

MUT 1872 NA
SP C Cummings
C N Hicks
1B J Start
2B J Hatfield
SS D Pearce
3B B Boyd
LF J McMullin
CF D Eggler
RL G Bechtel
3S C Fulmer

ATH 1872 NA
SP D McBride
C1 F Malone
1S D Mack
2B W Fisler
IC M McGeary
3B C Anson
LF N Cuthbert
CF F Treacey
RF- L Meyerle
RF- A Reach

TRO 1872 NA
SP G Zettlein
C D Allison
1B B McAtee
2B J Wood
IO S Bellan
3S D Force
LF S King
CF- C Gedney
RF P Martin

OLY 1872 NA
SP A Brainard
C F Sellman
1B C Flynn
2U T Beals
S2 W Goldsmith
3B F Waterman
LF J Glenn
CF- G Heubel
RF V Robinson

NAT 1872 NA
SP B Stearns
C B Lennon
1B P Hines
2B H Hollingshead
SS J Doyle
3B W White
LF E Mincher
CF- S Studley
RF O Bielaski
MI D Coughlin

MAR 1873 NA
SP E Stratton
SP Mc Doolan
SP F Sellman
MC B Smith
1B B Lennon
2B M Simpson
SR- L Say
3B H Kohler
LC- M Hooper
SL J Smith
IO B French

BAL 1873 NA
SP C Cummings
SP A Brainard
CI C McVey
1B E Mills
2B T Carey
3S J Radcliff
3S D Force
LF T York
CF G Hall
RF L Pike
CS B Craver
CM-S Hastings

BOS 1873 NA
SP A Spalding
C D White
1R J O'Rourke
2B R Barnes
SS G Wright
3B H Schafer
LF A Leonard
CF H Wright
RF- B Addy
1B- J Manning

ATL 1873 NA
SP J Britt
C T Barlow
1B H Dehlman
2B J Burdock
SS D Pearce
3B B Ferguson
LF C Pabor
CF J Remsen
RF B Boyd

RES 1873 NA
SP H Campbell
C D Allison
1B M Campbell
2B- B Laughlin
SS- F Wordsworth
3B- A Nevin
LF E Booth
OI A Allison
MR H Austin
UI F Fleet

MUT 1873 NA
SP B Mathews
C - N Hicks
1B J Start
2B C Nelson
SS J Holdsworth
3B J Hatfield
LF C Gedney
CF D Eggler
RF- P Martin
OI D Higham

PHI 1873 NA
SP G Zettlein
C F Malone
1B D Mack
2B J Wood
SS C Fulmer
3B L Meyerle
LF N Cuthbert
CF F Treacey
RF G Bechtel
13- J Devlin

ATH 1873 NA
SP D McBride
C J Clapp
1I C Anson
2B W Fisler
SS M McGeary
3B E Sutton
LF J McMullin
MI T Murnane
RF C Fisher

WAS 1873 NA
SP B Stearns
SP J Greason
C P Snyder
1B J Glenn
2C T Beals
SS- J Gerhardt
3B W White
LF P Hines
CF H Hollingshead
RF O Bielaski
IO J Donnelly
M N Young

BAL 1874 NA
SP A Brainard
SP J Manning
C P Snyder
1B C Gould
2B J Manning
SS- L Say
3B W White
LF J Ryan
CF- H Deane
RF O Bielaski

BOS 1874 NA
SP A Spalding
C D White
1B J O'Rourke
2B R Barnes
SS G Wright
3B H Schafer
LI A Leonard
UO G Hall
RC C McVey
CF- H Wright

ATL 1874 NA
SP T Bond
C - J Knowdell
1B H Dehlman
C2- J Farrow
SS D Pearce
3B B Ferguson
LF E Booth
CF- B Clack
RF J Chapman

CHI 1874 NA
SP G Zettlein
C F Malone
1R J Glenn
23 L Meyerle
S2 J Peters
3S D Force
LF N Cuthbert
CF P Hines
RM-F Treacey
1R J Devlin
M2 J Wood

HAR 1874 NA
SP C Fisher
SP B Stearns
C S Hastings
1B E Mills
2B B Addy
SS T Barlow
3B- B Boyd
LF J Tipper
MS L Pike
CR B Barnie

MUT 1874 NA
SP B Mathews
CR D Higham
1B J Start
2B C Nelson
SS J Holdsworth
3B J Burdock
LF J Hatfield
CF J Remsen
RC D Allison

PHI 1874 NA
SP C Cummings
C N Hicks
1B D Mack
2B B Craver
S3 C Fulmer
3S J Holdsworth
LF T York
CF D Eggler
RF- G Bechtel

ATH 1874 NA
SP D McBride
CS M McGeary
1B W Fisler
2B J Battin
3S E Sutton
IO C Anson
LF C Gedney
CF J McMullin
CR J Clapp

BOS 1875 NA
SR A Spalding
C D White
1O C McVey
2B R Barnes
SS G Wright
3B H Schafer
LF A Leonard
M3 J O'Rourke
Rp J Manning
MO-T Beals
M H Wright

ATL 1875 NA
SP J Cassidy
SP J Clinton
SP J O'Neill
C J Knowdell
1B- F Crane
IC- F Fleet
SO- H Kessler
3B A Nichols
LF C Pabor
CF- B Clack
IO B Boyd

CHI 1875 NA
SP G Zettlein
SP M Golden
CO S Hastings
1p J Devlin
2B- J Miller
SS J Peters
3B W White
L1 J Glenn
M2 P Hines
RF O Bielaski
C2 D Higham
M J Wood

HAR 1875 NA
SP C Cummings
SP T Bond
C D Allison
1B E Mills
2B J Burdock
SS T Carey
3B B Ferguson
LF T York
CF J Remsen
RF- A Allison
CI B Harbridge

WES 1875 NA
SP M Golden
C P Quinn
1B J Carbine
2B J Miller
SS J Hallinan
3B W Goldsmith
LF C Jones
MU J Simmons
RF B Riley
OC B Barnie

NH 1875 NA
SP T Nichols
C T McGinley
1B- C Gould
2B E Somerville
SS S Wright
3B H Luff
LF J Ryan
CF J Tipper
RF J McKelvey
UT B Geer
M2 J Latham
M3 C Pabor

MUT 1875 NA
SP B Mathews
C N Hicks
1B J Start
23 C Nelson
SS J Hallinan
3B J Gerhardt
LF C Gedney
MS J Holdsworth
RF E Booth

CEN 1875 NA
SP G Bechtel
C T McGinley
1B J Abadie
2B E Somerville
S3 B Craver
3B G Trenwith
LF F Treacey
CF F Warner
RL C Mason

PHI 1875 NA
SP C Fisher
SP G Zettlein
SP J Borden
C P Snyder
UT T Murnane
23 L Meyerle
SS C Fulmer
UT M McGeary
LF F Treacey
ML J McMullin
RF B Addy
1B- F Malone

ATH 1875 NA
SP D McBride
SP L Knight
C J Clapp
1B W Fisler
2B B Craver
SS D Force
3B E Sutton
LF G Hall
CF D Eggler
RF- G Bechtel
UT C Anson
2O- J Richmond

STL 1875 NA
SP G Bradley
SP J Galvin
C T Miller
1B H Dehlman
2B J Battin
SS D Pearce
3B B Hague
LF N Cuthbert
CF L Pike
RF J Chapman
RF- C Waitt

RS 1875 NA
SP J Blong
C S Flint
1B C Hautz
2B C Sweasy
SS B Redmon
3L T McSorley
LM A Croft
OP D Morgan
RF T Oran

WAS 1875 NA
SP B Stearns
C - A Thompson
1B A Allison
2B S Brady
SI J Dailey
3B H Doscher
Lp B Parks
MO H Hollingshead
R2 L Ressler

BOS 1876 NL
SP J Borden
SP F Bradley
C L Brown
1B T Murnane
2C J Morrill
SS G Wright
3B H Schafer
L2 A Leonard
CF J O'Rourke
Rp J Manning
LR- F Whitney
M H Wright

CHI 1876 NL
SP A Spalding
C D White
1B C McVey
2B R Barnes
SS J Peters
3B C Anson
LF J Glenn
CF P Hines
RF- O Bielaski

CIN 1876 NL
SP D Dean
SP C Fisher
SP D Williams
IC A Booth
1B C Gould
2B C Sweasy
SS H Kessler
3B W Foley
LF R Snyder
CF C Jones
CR D Pierson

HAR 1876 NL
SP T Bond
SP C Cummings
C D Allison
1B E Mills
2B J Burdock
SS T Carey
3B B Ferguson
LF T York
CF J Remsen
RF D Higham

LOU 1876 NL
SP J Devlin
C P Snyder
1B J Gerhardt
2B E Somerville
SS C Fulmer
3B B Hague
LF J Ryan
CF S Hastings
R1- A Allison
M J Chapman

NY 1876 NL
SP B Mathews
C N Hicks
1B J Start
2B B Craver
SS J Hallinan
3B A Nichols
LF F Treacey
CF J Holdsworth
RF E Booth

PHI 1876 NL
SP L Knight
SP G Zettlein
C - F Malone
12 E Sutton
UT W Fisler
SS D Force
3B L Meyerle
LF G Hall
CF D Eggler
RC W Coon
M A Wright

STL 1876 NL
SP G Bradley
C J Clapp
1B H Dehlman
2B M McGeary
SS D Mack
3B J Battin
LF N Cuthbert
CF L Pike
RF J Blong
M1 M Graffen
M2 G McManus

BOS 1877 NL
SP T Bond
C L Brown
1R D White
2B G Wright
S3 E Sutton
IO J Morrill
LS A Leonard
ML J O'Rourke
R3- H Schafer
MU-T Murnane
M H Wright

CHI 1877 NL
SP G Bradley
C3 C McVey
1B A Spalding
2B- R Barnes
SS J Peters
3C C Anson
L1 J Glenn
CF- D Eggler
OI P Hines

CIN 1877 NL
SP C Cummings
SP B Mathews
SP B Mitchell
C - S Hastings
1B- C Gould
2B- J Hallinan
UT J Manning
3B W Foley
1L- C Jones
M2 L Pike
RF B Addy
IC A Booth
LF C Jones

HAR 1877 NL
SP T Larkin
C B Harbridge
1B J Start
2B J Burdock
SS T Carey
3B B Ferguson
LF T York
CF J Holdsworth
RF J Cassidy

LOU 1877 NL
SP J Devlin
C P Snyder
1B J Latham
2B J Gerhardt
SS B Craver
3B B Hague
LF G Hall
CF B Crowley
RF O Shafer
M J Chapman

STL 1877 NL
SP T Nichols
C J Clapp
1B- H Dehlman
23 M McGeary
SS D Force
32 J Battin
OP J Blong
CF- J Remsen
UT M Dorgan
1L A Croft
M G McManus

BOS 1878 NL
SP T Bond
C P Snyder
1B J Morrill
2B J Burdock
SS G Wright
3B E Sutton
LF A Leonard
CF J O'Rourke
RF J Manning
M H Wright

CHI 1878 NL
SP T Larkin
C B Harbridge
1B J Start
2B B McClellan
SS B Ferguson
3B F Hankinson
LF C Anson
CF J Remsen
RF J Cassidy

CIN 1878 NL
SP W White
SP B Mitchell
C D White
1B C Sullivan
2B J Gerhardt
SS B Geer
3B C McVey
LF C Jones
CF- L Pike
RF K Kelly

IND 1878 NL
SP T Nolan
SP J McCormick
SP T Healey
C S Flint
1B A Croft
2B J Quest
SS F Warner
3B E Williamson
LI J Clapp
CF R McKelvy
RF O Shafer

MIL 1878 NL
SP S Weaver
CM C Bennett
1B J Goodman
2S J Peters
SS B Redmon
3B W Foley
LF A Dalrymple
Mp M Golden
RC B Holbert
2M G Creamer
M J Chapman

PRO 1878 NL
SP J Ward
SP T Nichols
SP H Wheeler
C L Brown
1B T Murnane
2B C Sweasy
SS T Carey
3B B Hague
LF T York
CF P Hines
RF D Higham

BOS 1879 NL
SP T Bond
SP C Foley
C P Snyder
1B- E Cogswell
2B J Burdock

S3 E Sutton
31 J Morrill
LF C Jones
CF J O'Rourke
RS S Houck
M H Wright

BUF 1879 NL
SP J Galvin
SP B McGunnigle
C J Clapp
1B O Walker
2B C Fulmer
SS D Force
3B H Richardson
LF J Hornung
CF D Eggler
RU B Crowley

CHI 1879 NL
SP T Larkin
SP F Hankinson
C S Flint
1B C Anson
2B J Quest
SS J Peters
3B E Williamson
LF A Dalrymple
CF G Gore
RF O Shafer
M1- J Remsen

CIN 1879 NL
SP W White
C D White
1B C McVey
2I J Gerhardt
SS R Barnes
3R W Foley
LF B Dickerson
CF P Hotaling
UT K Kelly

CLE 1879 NL
SP J McCormick
SP B Mitchell
C - D Kennedy
1B B Phillips
2B J Glasscock
SS T Carey
3O F Warner
LF- B Riley
CF G Strief
RF C Eden
CL B Gilligan

PRO 1879 NL
SR J Ward
SP B Mathews
C L Brown
1B J Start
2B M McGeary
SS G Wright
3B- B Hague
LF T York
CF P Hines
RI J O'Rourke

SYR 1879 NL
SP H McCormick
C B Holbert
13 H Carpenter
2B J Farrell
SM J Macullar
3B- R Woodhead
LF M Mansell
OI J Richmond
Rp B Purcell
IO M Dorgan

TRO 1879 NL
SP G Bradley
SP H Salisbury
SP F Goldsmith
C C Reilley
1B- D Brouthers
2B T Hawkes
SC E Caskin
3B H Doscher
LF- T Mansell
CF A Hall
RF J Evans
M1 H Phillips
M2 B Ferguson

BOS 1880 NL
SP T Bond
SP C Foley
C - P Powers
1B C Foley
2B J Burdock
S3 E Sutton
13 J Morrill
LF C Jones
CF Jo O'Rourke
UT Ji O'Rourke
M H Wright

BUF 1880 NL
SP J Galvin
SP S Wiedman
SP T Poorman
C J Rowe
1U D Esterbrook
2S D Force
SS- M Moynahan
3B H Richardson
LF J Hornung
RC B Crowley
RC- E Stearns
M S Crane

CHI 1880 NL
SP L Corcoran
SP F Goldsmith
C S Flint
1B C Anson
2B J Quest
SS T Burns
3B E Williamson
LF A Dalrymple
CF G Gore
RF K Kelly

CIN 1880 NL
SP W White
C J Clapp
1B J Reilly
2B P Smith
SS- L Say
3B H Carpenter
LF M Mansell
Mp B Purcell
RF- J Manning

CLE 1880 NL
SP J McCormick
SP G Gardner
C D Kennedy
1B B Phillips
2B F Dunlap
SS J Glasscock
3B F Hankinson
LF N Hanlon
CF P Hotaling
RF O Shafer

PRO 1880 NL
SP J Ward
C E Gross
1B J Start
2B J Farrell
SS J Peters
3p G Bradley
LF T York
CF P Hines
RF M Dorgan
LF- S Houck
M1 M McGeary
M2 M Ward

TRO 1880 NL
SP M Welch
SP T Keefe
C B Holbert
1B- E Cogswell
2B B Ferguson
SS E Caskin
3B R Connor
LF P Gillespie
MR J Cassidy
RF- J Evans

WOR 1880 NL
SP L Richmond
SP F Corey
C - C Bennett
1B- C Sullivan
2B G Creamer
SS A Irwin
3B A Whitney
LF G Wood
M1 H Stovey
RF- L Knight
M F Bancroft

BOS 1881 NL
SP J Whitney
SP J Fox
C P Snyder
1B J Morrill
2B J Burdock
SS R Barnes
3B E Sutton
LF J Hornung
MR B Crowley
RF- F Lewis
CU- P Deasley
M H Wright

BUF 1881 NL
SP J Galvin
SP J Lynch
CU J Rowe
L1 D Brouthers
2S D Force
SS J Peters
3U J O'Rourke
LF- B Purcell
CF H Richardson
R1 C Foley
UT D White

CHI 1881 NL
SP L Corcoran
SP F Goldsmith
C S Flint
1B C Anson
2B J Quest
SS T Burns
3B E Williamson
LF A Dalrymple
CF G Gore
RF K Kelly

CLE 1881 NL
SP J McCormick
SP T Nolan
CO J Clapp
1B B Phillips
2B F Dunlap
SS J Glasscock
3B G Bradley
LF- M Moynahan
CF- J Remsen
RF O Shafer
M1 M McGeary

DET 1881 NL
SP G Derby
SP S Wiedman
SP F Mountain
C C Bennett
1B M Powell
2B J Gerhardt
SS S Houck
3B A Whitney
LF G Wood
CF N Hanlon
RF L Knight
M F Bancroft

PRO 1881 NL
SP C Radbourn
SP B Mathews
C - E Gross
1B J Start
2B J Farrell
SO B McClellan
3B J Denny
LF T York
CF P Hines
OP J Ward
C - B Gilligan

TRO 1881 NL
SP T Keefe
SP M Welch
CS B Ewing
1B R Connor
2B B Ferguson
SS E Caskin
3B F Hankinson
LF P Gillespie
CF J Cassidy
RF J Evans
C - B Holbert

WOR 1881 NL
SP L Richmond
SP H McCormick
C D Bushong
1B H Stovey
2B G Creamer
SS A Irwin
3B H Carpenter
LF B Dickerson
CF P Hotaling
Rp F Corey
1R M Dorgan

BOS 1882 NL
SP J Whitney
SP B Mathews
C P Deasley
1B J Morrill
2B J Burdock
SS S Wise
3B E Sutton
LF J Hornung
CF P Hotaling
RC E Rowen

BUF 1882 NL
SP J Galvin
SP H Daily
CS J Rowe
1B D Brouthers
2B H Richardson
SS D Force
3B D White
LF B Purcell
CF J O'Rourke
RF C Foley

CHI 1882 NL
SP F Goldsmith
SP L Corcoran
C S Flint
1B C Anson
2S T Burns
SR K Kelly
3B E Williamson
LF A Dalrymple
CF G Gore
RF- H Nicol
2B- J Quest

CLE 1882 NL
SP J McCormick
SP G Bradley
C F Briody
1B B Phillips
2B F Dunlap
SS J Glasscock
3L M Muldoon
LF- D Esterbrook
CF- J Richmond
RF O Shafer

DET 1882 NL
SP S Wiedman
SP G Derby
C C Bennett
1B M Powell
2B- D Troy
SS- M McGeary
32 J Farrell
LF G Wood
CF N Hanlon
RF L Knight
M F Bancroft

PRO 1882 NL
SP C Radbourn
C B Gilligan
1B J Start
2B J Farrell
SS- G Wright
3B J Denny
LF T York
CF P Hines
Rp J Ward
M H Wright

TRO 1882 NL
SP T Keefe
SP M Welch
SP J Egan
C B Holbert
1B- J Smith
2B B Ferguson
SS F Pfeffer
3C B Ewing
LF P Gillespie
1O R Connor
RF C Roseman

WOR 1882 NL
SP L Richmond
SP F Mountain
C D Bushong
1L H Stovey
2B G Creamer
3S A Irwin
3B- F Mann
LF- J Clinton
MU J Hayes
RF J Evans
Sp F Corey
M1 F Brown
M2 T Bond
M3 J Chapman

BAL 1882 AA
SP D Landis
SP T Nichols
SP E Geis
C E Whiting
1B C Householder
2B- G Pierce
SS H Myers
32 J Shetzline
LF C Waitt
CF- M Cline
RF T Brown

CIN 1882 AA
SP W White
SP H McCormick
C P Snyder
1U E Stearns
2B B McPhee
SS C Fulmer
3B H Carpenter
LF J Sommer
CF J Macullar
RF H Wheeler

LOU 1882 AA
SP T Mullane
C D Sullivan
1p G Hecker
2S P Browning
S2 D Mack
3B B Schenck
LF L Maskrey
MU J Reccius
RF J Wolf

PHI 1882 AA
SP S Weaver
SP B Sweeney
SP F Mountain
CO J O'Brien
1B J Latham
2B C Stricker
SS L Say
3B- F Mann
LF J Birchall
CF- J Mansell
UT B Blakiston
CR- J Dorgan

PIT 1882 AA
SP H Salisbury
SP D Driscoll
SP H Arundel
IC B Taylor
1B C Lane
2B G Strief
SS J Peters
3B- J Battin
LF M Mansell
RM E Swartwood
3R J Leary
M A Pratt

STL 1882 AA
SP J McGinnis
SP J Schappert
SP B Dorr
C S Sullivan
1B C Comiskey
2B B Smiley
SS B Gleason
3B J Gleason
LF N Cuthbert
CF O Walker
RU- G Seward

BOS 1883 NL
SP J Whitney
C M Hines
1B J Morrill
2B J Burdock
SS S Wise
3B E Sutton
LF J Hornung
CF- E Smith
RM P Radford
PR C Buffinton

BUF 1883 NL
SP J Galvin
SP G Derby
CL J Rowe
1B D Brouthers
2B H Richardson
SS D Force
3B D White
LC J O'Rourke
MO-J Lillie
RF O Shafer

CHI 1883 NL
SP L Corcoran
SP F Goldsmith
C S Flint
1B C Anson
2B F Pfeffer
SS T Burns
3B E Williamson
LF A Dalrymple
CF G Gore
RF K Kelly

CLE 1883 NL
SP H Daily
SP J McCormick
SP W Sawyer
C D Bushong
1B B Phillips
2B F Dunlap
SS J Glasscock
3B M Muldoon
LF T York
CF P Hotaling
RF J Evans
M F Bancroft

DET 1883 NL
SP S Wiedman
SP D Shaw
SP D Burns
SP J Jones
C C Bennett
1B M Powell
2C S Trott
SS S Houck
3B J Farrell
LF G Wood
CF N Hanlon
RF S Wiedman
M J Chapman

NY 1883 NL
SP M Welch
SP T O'Neill
CU B Ewing
1B R Connor
2B D Troy
SS E Caskin
3B F Hankinson
LF P Gillespie
Mp J Ward
RF M Dorgan
M J Clapp

PHI 1883 NL
SP J Coleman
SP A Hagan
SP J Neagle
C - E Gross
1B S Farrar
2B B Ferguson
SS B McClellan
3B- F Warner
UT B Purcell
UT B Harbridge
RF J Manning
CU F Ringo

PRO 1883 NL
SP C Radbourn
SP C Sweeney
SP L Richmond
C B Gilligan
1B J Start
2B J Farrell
SS A Irwin
3B J Denny
LF- C Carroll
CF P Hines
RF J Cassidy
M H Wright

BAL 1883 AA
SP H Henderson
SP B Emslie
SP J Fox
C - J Kelly
1B E Stearns
2B- T Manning
SS L Say
3B J McCormick
LF J Clinton
CF- D Eggler
RF D Rowe
M B Barnie

CIN 1883 AA
SP W White
SP R Deagle
SP H McCormick
C - P Snyder
1B J Reilly
2B B McPhee
SS C Fulmer
3B H Carpenter
LF J Sommer
CF C Jones
RF P Corkhill

COL 1883 AA
SP F Mountain
SP E Dundon
SP J Valentine
C R Kemmler
1B J Field
2B P Smith
SS J Richmond
3I B Kuehne
LF H Wheeler
CF F Mann
RF T Brown
M H Phillips

LOU 1883 AA
SP G Hecker
SP S Weaver
C - E Whiting
1B J Latham
2B J Gerhardt
SS- J Leary
3B J Gleason
UT P Browning
OI L Maskrey
RF J Wolf

NY 1883 AA
SP T Keefe
SP J Lynch
C B Holbert
1B S Brady
2B S Crane
SS C Nelson
3B D Esterbrook
LF E Kennedy
CF J O'Rourke
RF C Roseman
M J Mutrie

PHI 1883 AA
SP B Mathews
SP J Jones
SP J Bakely
CM J O'Brien
1B H Stovey
2B C Stricker
SS M Moynahan
3p G Bradley
LF J Birchall
CF- B Blakiston
RF L Knight
3p F Corey
C - E Rowen

PIT 1883 AA
SP D Driscoll
SP B Barr
SP J Neagle
CU J Hayes
1M E Swartwood
2B G Creamer
S1 D Mack
3B J Battin
LF M Mansell
RM B Dickerson
Cp B Taylor
M1 A Pratt
M2 O Butler

STL 1883 AA
SP T Mullane
SP J McGinnis
C - P Deasley
1B C Comiskey
2B G Strief
SS B Gleason
3B A Latham
CO T Dolan
CF- F Lewis
RF H Nicol
M1 T Sullivan

BOS 1884 NL
SP C Buffinton
SP J Whitney
C M Hackett
1B J Morrill
2B J Burdock
SS S Wise
3B E Sutton
LF J Hornung
CF J Manning
RF B Crowley

BUF 1884 NL
SP J Galvin
SP B Serad
CO J Rowe
1B D Brouthers
2U H Richardson
SS D Force
3B D White
LF J O'Rourke
CF- D Eggler
RF J Lillie
CO G Myers

CHI 1884 NL
SP L Corcoran
SP F Goldsmith
SP J Clarkson
C S Flint
1B C Anson
2B F Pfeffer
SS T Burns
3B E Williamson
LF A Dalrymple
CF G Gore
RC K Kelly

CLE 1884 NL
SP J Harkins
SP J McCormick
SP S Moffett
C - D Bushong
1B B Phillips
2S G Smith
SS J Glasscock
3B M Muldoon
LF- W Murphy
CF P Hotaling
RL J Evans
M C Hackett

DET 1884 NL
SP D Shaw
SP C Getzien
SP F Brill
C C Bennett
1B M Scott
2B B Geis
Sp F Meinke
3B J Farrell
LF G Wood
CF N Hanlon
Rp S Wiedman
M J Chapman

NY 1884 NL
SP M Welch
SP E Begley
C B Ewing
1B A McKinnon
2M R Connor
SS E Caskin
3B F Hankinson
LF P Gillespie
M2 J Ward
Rp M Dorgan
RS D Richardson
M1 J Price
M2 M Ward

PHI 1884 NL
SP C Ferguson
SP B Vinton
SP J Coleman
SP J McElroy
C - J Crowley
1B S Farrar
2B E Andrews
SS B McClellan
3B J Mulvey
LF B Purcell
MU J Fogarty
RF J Manning
M H Wright

PRO 1884 NL
SP C Radbourn
SP C Sweeney
SP E Conley
C B Gilligan
1B J Start
2B J Farrell
SS A Irwin
3B J Denny
LF C Carroll
CF P Hines
RF P Radford
M F Bancroft

BAL 1884 AA
SP B Emslie
SP H Henderson
C S Trott
1B E Stearns
2B T Manning
SS J Macullar
3B J Sommer
LF T York
ML J Clinton
RF- G Gardner
C - B Traffley
M B Barnie

BRO 1884 AA
SP A Terry
SP S Kimber
SP J Conway
CU- J Corcoran
1C C Householder
2B B Greenwood
SS B Geer
3B F Warner
LF- I Benners
ML J Remsen
RF J Cassidy
OI O Walker
M G Taylor

CIN 1884 AA
SP W White
SP B Mountjoy
SP G Shallix
C - P Snyder
1B J Reilly
2B B McPhee
SU J Peoples
3B H Carpenter
LM- T Mansell
LM C Jones
RF P Corkhill

COL 1884 AA
SP E Morris
SP F Mountain
SP E Dundon
C - R Kemmler
1B J Field
2B P Smith
SS J Richmond
3B B Kuehne
LF- J Cahill
CF F Mann
RF T Brown
C F Carroll
M G Schmelz

IND 1884 AA
SP L McKeon

SP B Barr
SP J Aydelott
SP A McCauley
C J Keenan
1B J Kerins
2B- E Merrill
SS M Phillips
3B- P Callaghan
LF J Peltz
CF- J Morrison
RM- P Weihe
M1 J Gifford
M2 B Watkins

LOU 1884 AA
SP G Hecker
SP D Driscoll
SP R Deagle
C - D Sullivan
1B J Latham
2B J Gerhardt
SS T McLaughlin
3I P Browning
LF L Maskrey
CF M Cline
RF J Wolf
3p P Reccius
M M Walsh

NY 1884 AA
SP J Lynch
SP T Keefe
C - B Holbert
1B D Orr
2B D Troy
SS C Nelson
3B D Esterbrook
LF E Kennedy
CF C Roseman
RF S Brady
C - C Reipschlager
M J Mutrie

PHI 1884 AA
SP B Mathews
SP B Taylor
SP A Atkinson
C J Milligan
1B H Stovey
2B C Stricker
SS S Houck
3B F Corey
LF- J Birchall
ML H Larkin
RF L Knight

PIT 1884 AA
SP F Sullivan
SP J Neagle
C - E Colgan
1B- J Knowles
2B G Creamer
SS B White
3B- J Battin
LC D Miller
CF- L Taylor
RF E Swartwood
M1 D McKnight
M2 B Ferguson
M5 H Phillips

RIC 1884 AA
SP P Meegan
SP E Dugan
C - J Hanna
1B J Powell
2B T Larkin
SS B Schenck
3B B Nash
LF E Glenn
CF D Johnston
RF M Mansell
M F Moses

STL 1884 AA
SP J McGinnis
SP D Foutz
SP D Davis
SP B Caruthers
C P Deasley
1B C Comiskey
2B J Quest
SS B Gleason
3B A Latham
Lp T O'Neill
CF F Lewis
RF H Nicol
M1 J Williams

TOL 1884 AA
SP T Mullane
SP H O'Day
C - F Walker
1B- C Lane
2B S Barkley
SS J Miller
3B- E Brown
LF- F Olin
CF C Welch
RF T Poorman
1I- J Moffett
M C Morton

WAS 1884 AA
SP B Barr
SP J Hamill
CU J Humphries
1B W Prince
2B T Hawkes
SS F Fennelly
3B B Gladman
UT B Morgan
CF- H Mullin
OP- E Trumbull
M1 H Hollingshead
M2 Bickerson

ALT 1884 UA
SP J Murphy
SP J Leary
CR J Moore
1O F Harris
2O C Dougherty
SS G Smith
3B H Koons
LF J Murphy
OI T Shafer
PR J Brown
M E Curtis

BAL 1884 UA
SP B Sweeney
SP T Lee
SP A Atkinson
C E Fusselback
1B C Levis
2B D Phelan
SS L Say
3U Y Robinson
LF E Seery
CF- N Cuthbert
MR- B Graham
CO- R Sweeney
M B Henderson

BOS 1884 UA
SP J Burke
SP D Shaw
SP T Bond
C1 L Brown
1B T Murnane
2B T O'Brien
SS W Hackett
3B J Irwin
LI K Butler
CF M Slattery
OC E Crane

CP 1884 UA
SP H Daily
SP A Atkinson
SP J Horan
CO B Krieg
1B J Schoeneck
2B- M Hengle
SS- S Matthias
3B- W Foley
IO C Householder
CF- H Wheeler
RS J Ellick
MI- C Briggs
UT- G Gardner
CS- T Suck
M1 E Hengle
M2 J Battin

CIN 1884 UA
SP G Bradley
SP J McCormick
C - J Kelly
1B- M Powell
2B S Crane
S2 J Jones
3B- C Barber
LR L Sylvester
MR B Harbridge
OI B Hawes
PM D Burns
SS- J Glasscock
1B- M McQuery
M1 D O'Leary

KC 1884 UA
SP E Hickman
SP B Black
SP P Veach
SP A Voss
C K Baldwin
1B- J Sweeney
2B- C Berry
SS- C Cross
3M- P Sullivan
UT- F Wyman
UT- B McLaughlin
RF- T Shafer
M1 H Wheeler
M2 M Porter
M3 T Sullivan

MIL 1884 UA
SP H Porter
SP E Cushman
CM C Broughton
1B T Griffin
2B A Myers
SS T Sexton
3B T Morrissey
LF S Behel
MP- L Baldwin
RF E Hogan
M T Loftus

PHI 1884 UA
SP J Bakely
SP S Weaver
SP Fisher
C - T Gillen
1B J McGuinness
2B E Peak
SS- H Easterday
3B J McCormick
LI B Hoover
CF B Kienzle
RF J Flynn
OC J Clements
M F Malone

STL 1884 UA
SP C Sweeney
SP B Taylor
SP P Werden
SP C Hodnett
C G Baker
1B J Quinn
2B F Dunlap
SS M Whitehead
3B J Gleason
Lp- H Boyle
CF D Rowe
RF O Shafer
CO- J Brennan
LF- B Dickerson
M1 T Sullivan

STP 1884 UA
SP J Brown
SP L Galvin
C C Ganzel
1B S Dunn
2B M Hengle
SS J Werrick
3B B O'Brien
LF J Tilley
CF B Barnes
RF S Carroll
M A Thompson

WAS 1884 UA
SP B Wise
SP A Voss
SP C Gagus
SP A Powell
CO- C Fulmer
1B- P Joy
2B T Evers
SS- J Halpin
3B- J McCormick
LF H Moore
UT P Baker
RF B Wise
CO- J Gunson
M M Scanlon

WIL 1884 UA
SP J Murphy
SP T Nolan
SP D Casey
SP J Bakely
CS T Cusick
1B R Snyder
2B C Bastian
SS- H Myers
3B J Say
CL T Lynch
CF- G Fisher
RF- J Munce
M J Simmons

BOS 1885 NL
SP J Whitney
SP C Buffinton
SP D Davis
C - T Gunning
1B J Morrill
2B- J Burdock
SU S Wise
3B E Sutton
LF- T McCarthy
CF J Manning
RF- T Poorman

BUF 1885 NL
SP J Galvin
SP B Serad
SP P Conway
SP P Wood
C G Myers
1B D Brouthers
2S D Force
SU J Rowe
3B D White
LF B Crowley
2M H Richardson
RF J Lillie
M2 J Chapman

CHI 1885 NL
SP J Clarkson
SP J McCormick
SP T Kennedy
C S Flint
1B C Anson
2B F Pfeffer
SS T Burns
3B E Williamson
LF A Dalrymple
CF G Gore
RC K Kelly

DET 1885 NL
SP C Getzien
SP S Wiedman
SP L Baldwin
SP D Casey
CU C Bennett
1B M McQuery
2B S Crane
SS- M Phillips
3B- J Donnelly
LF G Wood
CF N Hanlon
RF- S Thompson
M1 C Morton
M2 B Watkins

NY 1885 NL
SP M Welch
SP T Keefe
SP D Richardson
C B Ewing
1B R Connor
2B J Gerhardt
SS J Ward
3B D Esterbrook
LF P Gillespie
CF J O'Rourke
RF M Dorgan
M J Mutrie

PHI 1885 NL
SP E Daily
SP C Ferguson
SP B Vinton
C - J Clements
1B S Farrar
2B A Myers
SS C Bastian
3B J Mulvey
LF E Andrews
CF J Fogarty
RF J Manning
M H Wright

PRO 1885 NL
SP C Radbourn
SP D Shaw
C B Gilligan
1B J Start
2B J Farrell
SS- A Irwin
3B J Denny
LF C Carroll
CF P Hines
RF P Radford
UI C Bassett
C - C Daily
M F Bancroft

STL 1885 NL
SP H Boyle
SP J Kirby
SP H Daily
C - F Briody
1B A McKinnon
2B F Dunlap
SS J Glasscock
3B E Caskin
LF- E Seery
CF- F Lewis
RF O Shafer
OP C Sweeney
UT J Quinn
M3 F Dunlap

BAL 1885 AA
SP H Henderson
SP B Emslie
SP J Henry
C B Traffley
1B E Stearns
2B- T Manning
SS J Macullar
3B M Muldoon
LF J Sommer
CF- D Casey
Rp T Burns
MU- E Greer
M B Barnie

BRO 1885 AA
SP H Porter
SP J Harkins
C - J Hayes
1B B Phillips
23 G Pinkney
SS G Smith
32 B McClellan
UT E Swartwood
CF P Hotaling
RF- J Cassidy
Lp A Terry
M1 C Hackett
M2 C Byrne

CIN 1885 AA
SP W White
SP L McKeon
SP B Mountjoy
SP G Pechiney
SP G Shallix
C - P Snyder
1B J Reilly
2B B McPhee
SS F Fennelly
3B H Carpenter
LF C Jones
CF J Clinton
RF P Corkhill
M O Caylor

LOU 1885 AA
SP G Hecker
SP N Baker
SP A Mays
SP T Ramsey
C - J Crotty
1B J Kerins
2B T McLaughlin
SS J Miller
3B P Reccius
LF L Maskrey
CF P Browning
RF J Wolf
M J Hart

NY 1885 AA
SP J Lynch
SP E Cushman
SP D Crothers
SP E Begley
SP B Becannon
C C Reipschlager
1B D Orr
2B- T Forster
SS C Nelson
3B F Hankinson
LF E Kennedy
CF C Roseman
RF S Brady
CU- B Holbert
M J Gifford

PHI 1885 AA
SP B Mathews
SP T Lovett
SP E Knouff
SP E Cushman
C - J Milligan
1M H Stovey
2B C Stricker
SS S Houck
3B F Corey
LF- B Purcell
ML H Larkin
RF J Coleman
CI- J O'Brien

PIT 1885 AA
SP E Morris
SP P Meegan
SP H O'Day
SP J Galvin
C F Carroll
1B- J Field
2B P Smith
SS A Whitney
3B B Kuehne
LF C Eden
CF F Mann
RF T Brown
M H Phillips

STL 1885 AA
SP B Caruthers
SP D Foutz
SP J McGinnis
C D Bushong
1B C Comiskey
2B S Barkley
SS B Gleason
3B A Latham
LI Y Robinson
CF C Welch
RF H Nicol

BOS 1886 NL
SP C Radbourn
SP B Stemmeyer
SP C Buffinton
C - C Daily
1I S Wise
2B- J Burdock
UI J Morrill
3B B Nash
LF J Hornung
CF D Johnston
RF T Poorman
UT E Sutton

CHI 1886 NL
SP J Clarkson
SP J McCormick
SP J Flynn
C - S Flint
1B C Anson
2B F Pfeffer
SS E Williamson
3B T Burns
LF A Dalrymple
CF G Gore
OC K Kelly
UT J Ryan

DET 1886 NL
SP L Baldwin
SP C Getzien
SP P Conway
SP B Schmidt
C - C Bennett
1B D Brouthers
2B- F Dunlap
SS J Rowe
3B D White
L2 H Richardson
CF N Hanlon
RF S Thompson
M B Watkins

KC 1886 NL
SP S Wiedman
SP J Whitney
SP P Conway
C - F Briody
1B M McQuery
2B A Myers
SS C Bassett
3B J Donnelly
LF J Lillie
CF D Rowe
RF P Radford
C - M Hackett

NY 1886 NL
SP T Keefe
SP M Welch
CO- B Ewing
1B R Connor
2B J Gerhardt
SS J Ward
3B D Esterbrook
LF P Gillespie
ML- D Richardson
RF M Dorgan
MC J O'Rourke
M J Mutrie

PHI 1886 NL
SP C Ferguson
SP D Casey
C - D McGuire
1B S Farrar
2B C Bastian
SS A Irwin
3B J Mulvey
LF G Wood
CF E Andrews
RF J Fogarty
Rp E Daily
M H Wright

STL 1886 NL
SP J Healy
SP J Kirby
SP H Boyle
SP C Sweeney
C G Myers
1B A McKinnon
2B- F Dunlap
SS J Glasscock
3B J Denny
LF E Seery
CF- J McGeachy
RF J Cahill
MI- J Quinn
M G Schmelz

WAS 1886 NL
SP D Shaw
SP B Barr
SP T Madigan
SP F Gilmore
C B Gilligan
1O P Baker
2B- J Farrell
SS- D Force
23 J Knowles
LF C Carroll
CF P Hines
RU E Crane
M1 M Scanlon
M2 J Gaffney

BAL 1886 AA
SP M Kilroy
SP J McGinnis
SP H Henderson
C - C Fulmer
1B M Scott
23 M Muldoon
SS J Macullar
3B- J Davis
LI J Sommer
CF- P O'Connell
RF J Manning
23- J Farrell
M B Barnie

BRO 1886 AA
SP H Porter
SP J Harkins
SP A Terry
SP H Henderson
SP S Toole
C J Peoples
1B B Phillips
2B B McClellan
SS G Smith
3B G Pinkney
LF E Burch
CF J McTamany
RF E Swartwood
CO- B Clark
M C Byrne

CIN 1886 AA
SP T Mullane
SP G Pechiney
SP L McKeon
C K Baldwin
1B J Reilly
2B B McPhee
SS F Fennelly
3B H Carpenter
LF C Jones
CF- F Lewis
RF P Corkhill
M O Caylor

LOU 1886 AA
SP T Ramsey
SP G Hecker
C1- A Cross
C1 J Kerins
2B R Mack
SS B White
3B J Werrick
LF- J Strauss
ML P Browning
RF J Wolf
M J Hart

NY 1886 AA
SP J Lynch
SP A Mays
SP E Cushman
C - C Reipschlager
1B D Orr
2B- T Forster
SM C Nelson
3B F Hankinson
LM C Roseman
ML- S Behel
RF S Brady
SS- T McLaughlin
M1 J Gifford
M2 B Ferguson

PHI 1886 AA
SP A Atkinson
SP B Mathews
SP B Hart
SP T Kennedy
SP C Miller
C1 W Robinson
1M H Stovey
2B L Bierbauer
SS- C McGarr
3B- J Gleason
LF H Larkin
CF- E Greer
RF J Coleman
IC J O'Brien
C1- J Milligan
M1 L Simmons
M2 B Sharsig

PIT 1886 AA
SP E Morris
SP J Galvin
SP J Handiboe
CU F Carroll
1B- O Schomberg
2B S Barkley
SS P Smith
3S A Whitney
LF- E Glenn
CF F Mann
RF T Brown
UT B Kuehne
CO- D Miller
M H Phillips

STL 1886 AA
SP D Foutz
SP B Caruthers
SP N Hudson
SP J McGinnis
C D Bushong
1B C Comiskey
2B Y Robinson
SS B Gleason
3B A Latham
LF T O'Neill
CF C Welch
RF- H Nicol

BOS 1887 NL
SP C Radbourn
SP K Madden
SP D Conway
SP B Stemmeyer
C - P Tate
1B J Morrill
2B- J Burdock
SU S Wise
3B B Nash
LF J Hornung
CF D Johnston
R2 K Kelly
UT E Sutton

CHI 1887 NL
SP J Clarkson
SP M Baldwin
SP G Van Haltren
C - T Daly
1B C Anson
2B F Pfeffer
SS E Williamson
3B T Burns
LF M Sullivan
CF J Ryan
RM- B Sunday

DET 1887 NL
SP C Getzien
SP L Baldwin
SP S Wiedman
SP P Conway
SP L Twitchell
C - C Ganzel
1B D Brouthers
2B- F Dunlap
SS J Rowe
3B D White
2L H Richardson
CF N Hanlon
RF S Thompson
M B Watkins

IND 1887 NL
SP J Healy
SP H Boyle
SP L Shreve
CU- G Myers
1B O Schomberg
2B C Bassett
SS J Glasscock
3B J Denny
LF E Seery
CF J McGeachy
RF- J Cahill
M1 W Burnham
M2 F Thomas
M3 H Fogel

NY 1887 NL
SP T Keefe
SP M Welch
SP B George
C - W Brown
1B R Connor
2B D Richardson
SS J Ward
3U- B Ewing
LF- P Gillespie

CF G Gore
RL M Tiernan
IC J O'Rourke
RF- M Dorgan
M J Mutrie

PHI 1887 NL
SP D Casey
SP C Buffinton
SP C Ferguson
C - J Clements
1B S Farrar
2B- B McLaughlin
SS A Irwin
3B J Mulvey
LF G Wood
CF E Andrews
RF J Fogarty
M H Wright

PIT 1887 NL
SP J Galvin
SP J McCormick
SP E Morris
C D Miller
12 S Barkley
2S P Smith
SS B Kuehne
3B A Whitney
LF A Dalrymple
CF- T Brown
RF J Coleman
OC F Carroll
M H Phillips

WAS 1887 NL
SP J Whitney
SP H O'Day
SP F Gilmore
SP D Shaw
C C Mack
1B B O'Brien
2S A Myers
S2 J Farrell
3B J Donnelly
LF C Carroll
CF P Hines
RF E Daily
RU- G Shoch
M J Gaffney

BAL 1887 AA
SP M Kilroy
SP P Smith
C S Trott
1B T Tucker
2B B Greenwood
S3 T Burns
3S J Davis
LF J Sommer
CF M Griffin
RF B Purcell
M B Barnie

BRO 1887 AA
SP H Porter
SP J Harkins
SP S Toole
SP H Henderson
C - J Peoples
1B B Phillips
2B B McClellan
SS G Smith
3B G Pinkney
LF E Greer
CF J McTamany
RF E Swartwood
OP A Terry
M C Byrne

CIN 1887 AA
SP E Smith
SP T Mullane
SP B Serad
C K Baldwin
1B J Reilly
2B B McPhee
SS F Fennelly
3B H Carpenter
LF G Tebeau
CF P Corkhill
RF H Nicol
M G Schmelz

CLE 1887 AA
SP B Crowell
SP M Morrison
SP H Daily
SP B Gilks
SP G Pechiney
C - P Snyder
1B J Toy
2B C Stricker
SS E McKean
3B- P Reccius
LR- F Mann
CF P Hotaling
LR M Allen
M J Williams

LOU 1887 AA
SP T Ramsey
SP E Chamberlain
C - P Cook
1C J Kerins
2B R Mack
SS B White
3B J Werrick
LF H Collins
CF P Browning
RF J Wolf
1p G Hecker
M J Kelly

NY 1887 AA
SP A Mays
SP E Cushman
SP J Lynch
SP J Shaffer
SP S Wiedman
C - B Holbert
1B D Orr
2B J Gerhardt
SR P Radford
3B F Hankinson
LF D O'Brien
CF- C Jones
MO-C Roseman
M1 B Ferguson
M3 O Caylor

PHI 1887 AA
SP E Seward
SP G Weyhing
SP A Atkinson
C - W Robinson
1C J Milligan
2B L Bierbauer
SS C McGarr
3B D Lyons
LI H Larkin
OI H Stovey
RF T Poorman
M1 F Bancroft
M2 C Mason

STL 1887 AA
SP S King
C J Boyle
1B C Comiskey
2B Y Robinson
SS B Gleason
3B A Latham
LF T O'Neill
CF C Welch
Rp B Caruthers
Rp D Foutz

BOS 1888 NL
SP J Clarkson
SP B Sowders
SP C Radbourn
SP K Madden
CR K Kelly
1B J Morrill
2B- J Quinn
SS S Wise
3B B Nash
LF J Hornung
CF D Johnston
RF T Brown

CHI 1888 NL
SP G Krock
SP M Baldwin
SP G Van Haltren
SP J Tener
C - T Daly
1B C Anson
2B F Pfeffer
SS E Williamson
3B T Burns
LF- M Sullivan
CF J Ryan
RF- H Duffy

DET 1888 NL
SP C Getzien
SP P Conway
SP H Gruber
SP E Beatin
C - C Bennett
1B D Brouthers
2B- H Richardson
SS J Rowe
3B D White
LF L Twitchell
CF N Hanlon
RF- C Campau
2C C Ganzel
M1 B Watkins
M2 B Leadley

IND 1888 NL
SP H Boyle
SP J Healy
SP L Shreve
SP B Burdick
C3- D Buckley
1B- D Esterbrook
2B C Bassett
SS J Glasscock
3B J Denny
LF E Seery
CF P Hines
RF J McGeachy
M H Spence

NY 1888 NL
SP T Keefe
SP M Welch
SP C Titcomb
SP E Crane
C B Ewing
1B R Connor
2B D Richardson
SS J Ward
3B A Whitney
LU J O'Rourke
CF M Slattery
RF M Tiernan
M J Mutrie

PHI 1888 NL
SP C Buffinton
SP D Casey
SP B Sanders
SP K Gleason
C J Clements
1B S Farrar
2B C Bastian
SS A Irwin
3B J Mulvey
LF G Wood
CF E Andrews
RF J Fogarty
2B- E Delahanty
M H Wright

PIT 1888 NL
SP E Morris
SP J Galvin
SP H Staley
CO D Miller
1B- J Beckley
2B- F Dunlap
S2 P Smith
3S B Kuehne
LF- A Dalrymple
CF B Sunday
RF J Coleman
CL F Carroll
1R- A Maul
M H Phillips

WAS 1888 NL
SP H O'Day
SP J Whitney
SP W Widner
SP G Keefe
SP F Gilmore
C C Mack
1B B O'Brien
2B A Myers
SR G Shoch
3B J Donnelly
LF W Wilmot
CF D Hoy
RF E Daily
M1 W Hewett
M2 T Sullivan

BAL 1888 AA
SP B Cunningham
SP M Kilroy
SP P Smith
C - C Fulmer
1B T Tucker
2U B Greenwood
S2 J Farrell
3B B Shindle
LS- T Burns
CF M Griffin
RF B Purcell
UT- J Sommer
M B Barnie

BRO 1888 AA
SP M Hughes
SP A Terry
SP A Mays
C - D Bushong
1B D Orr
2B- J Burdock
SS G Smith
3B G Pinkney
LF D O'Brien
CF P Radford
Rp D Foutz
OP B Caruthers
2B- B McClellan
M B McGunnigle

CIN 1888 AA
SP L Viau
SP T Mullane
SP E Smith
C J Keenan
1B J Reilly
2B B McPhee
SS F Fennelly
3B H Carpenter
LF G Tebeau
CF P Corkhill
RF H Nicol
M G Schmelz

CLE 1888 AA
SP J Bakely
SP D O'Brien
SP B Crowell
C - C Zimmer
1B J Faatz
2B C Stricker
SL E McKean
S3 G Alberts
UT B Gilks
CF P Hotaling
RL- E Hogan
M1 J Williams
M2 T Loftus

KC 1888 AA
SP H Porter
SP T Sullivan
SP B Fagan
SP F Hoffman
SP S Toole
C J Donahue
1B B Phillips
2B S Barkley
SS H Easterday
3B J Davis
RL- M Cline
MR J McTamany
RF- B Hamilton
M1 D Rowe
M3 B Watkins

LOU 1888 AA
SP T Ramsey
SP S Stratton
SP G Hecker
SP E Chamberlain
SP J Ewing
C - P Cook
1B- S Smith
2B R Mack
SS- B White
3B J Werrick
UT H Collins
CF P Browning
RS J Wolf
OC- J Kerins
M1 J Kelly
M2 M Davidson
M4 M Davidson

PHI 1888 AA
SP E Seward
SP G Weyhing
SP M Mattimore
C - W Robinson
1B H Larkin
2B L Bierbauer
SS B Gleason
3B D Lyons
LF H Stovey
CF C Welch
RF T Poorman
M B Sharsig

STL 1888 AA
SP S King
SP N Hudson
SP E Chamberlain
SP J Devlin
C - J Boyle
1B C Comiskey
2B Y Robinson
SS- B White
3B A Latham
LF T O'Neill
CF H Lyons
RF T McCarthy

BOS 1889 NL
SP J Clarkson
SP C Radbourn
SP K Madden
C C Bennett
1B D Brouthers
2L H Richardson
S2 J Quinn
3B B Nash
LF T Brown
CF D Johnston
RF K Kelly
CR- C Ganzel
M J Hart

CHI 1889 NL
SP B Hutchison
SP J Tener
SP F Dwyer
SP A Gumbert
C D Farrell
1B C Anson
2B F Pfeffer
SS- E Williamson
3B T Burns
LF G Van Haltren
CF J Ryan
RF H Duffy

CLE 1889 NL
SP D O'Brien
SP E Beatin
SP J Bakely
SP H Gruber
C C Zimmer
1B J Faatz
2B C Stricker
SS E McKean
3B P Tebeau
LF L Twitchell
CF J McAleer
RF P Radford
M T Loftus

IND 1889 NL
SP H Boyle
SP C Getzien
SR A Rusie
C - D Buckley
1B P Hines
2B C Bassett
SS J Glasscock
3B J Denny
LF E Seery
CF- M Sullivan
RF J McGeachy
M1 F Bancroft

NY 1889 NL
SP M Welch
SP T Keefe
SP E Crane
C B Ewing
1B R Connor
2B D Richardson
SS J Ward
3B A Whitney
LF J O'Rourke
CF G Gore
RF M Tiernan
M J Mutrie

PHI 1889 NL
SP C Buffinton
SP B Sanders
SP K Gleason
SP D Casey
C J Clements
1B S Farrar
2B- A Myers
SS B Hallman
3B J Mulvey
LF G Wood
CF J Fogarty
RF S Thompson
M H Wright

PIT 1889 NL
SP H Staley
SP J Galvin
SP E Morris
CO D Miller
1B J Beckley
2B F Dunlap
SS- J Rowe
3B B Kuehne
LR- A Maul
CF N Hanlon
RF B Sunday
OC F Carroll
LU- J Fields
SS- P Smith
M1 H Phillips

WAS 1889 NL
SP A Ferson
SP G Haddock
SP G Keefe
SP H O'Day
SP J Healy
C - T Daly
1B- J Carney
2I S Wise
SS A Irwin
3B- J Irwin
LF W Wilmot
CF D Hoy
RF- E Beecher
OC C Mack
M1 J Morrill

BAL 1889 AA
SP M Kilroy
SP F Foreman
SP B Cunningham
C - P Tate
1B T Tucker
2B R Mack
SS- J Farrell
3B B Shindle
LF J Hornung
CF M Griffin
RF J Sommer
M B Barnie

BRO 1889 AA
SP B Caruthers
SP A Terry
SP T Lovett
SP M Hughes
CR- J Visner
1B D Foutz
2B H Collins
SS G Smith
3B G Pinkney
LF D O'Brien
CF P Corkhill
RF T Burns
M B McGunnigle

CIN 1889 AA
SP J Duryea
SP L Viau
SP T Mullane
SP E Smith
C J Keenan
1B J Reilly
2B B McPhee
SS O Beard
3B H Carpenter
LF G Tebeau
CF B Holliday
RF H Nicol
M G Schmelz

COL 1889 AA
SP M Baldwin
SP W Widner
SP H Gastright
SP A Mays
C J O'Connor
1B D Orr
2B B Greenwood
SS H Easterday
UT L Marr
LF E Daily
CF J McTamany
R3 S Johnson
M A Buckenberger

KC 1889 AA
SP P Swartzel
SP J Conway
SP J Sowders
SP J McCarty
SP T Sullivan
C - C Hoover
1B E Stearns
2B- S Barkley
SS H Long
3B- J Davis
L2 J Manning
CF J Burns
RF B Hamilton
M B Watkins

LOU 1889 AA
SP R Ehret
SP J Ewing
SP T Ramsey
SP S Stratton
C - P Cook
1p- G Hecker
2B D Shannon
SS P Tomney
3B H Raymond
LF- P Browning
CF F Weaver
RI J Wolf
CU F Vaughn
M1 D Esterbrook
M2 C Wolf
M4 J Chapman

PHI 1889 AA
SP G Weyhing
SP E Seward
SP S McMahon
C - W Robinson
1B H Larkin
2B L Bierbauer
SS F Fennelly
3B D Lyons
LF H Stovey
CF C Welch
RF B Purcell
M B Sharsig

STL 1889 AA
SP S King
SP E Chamberlain
SP J Stivetts
C J Boyle
1B C Comiskey
2B Y Robinson
SS S Fuller
3B A Latham
LF T O'Neill
CF C Duffee
RF T McCarthy
C - J Milligan

BOS 1890 NL
SP K Nichols
SP J Clarkson
SP C Getzien
C C Bennett
1B T Tucker
2B P Smith
SS H Long
3B C McGarr
LF M Sullivan
CF- P Hines
RF S Brodie
M F Selee

BRO 1890 NL
SP T Lovett
SP B Caruthers
C T Daly
1B D Foutz
2B H Collins
SS G Smith
3B G Pinkney
OP A Terry
LM D O'Brien
RF T Burns
M B McGunnigle

CHI 1890 NL
SP B Hutchison
SP P Luby
SP E Stein
SP M Sullivan
SP R Coughlin
C M Kittridge
1B C Anson
2B- B Glenalvin
SS J Cooney
3B T Burns
LF C Carroll
CF W Wilmot
RF- J Andrews
R2 H Earl

CIN 1890 NL
SP B Rhines
SP J Duryea
SP T Mullane
SP F Foreman
SP L Viau
C - J Harrington
1B J Reilly
2B B McPhee
SS O Beard
IO L Marr
LF J Knight
CF B Holliday
RF- H Nicol
M T Loftus

CLE 1890 NL
SP E Beatin
SP J Wadsworth
SP C Young
SP E Lincoln
SP L Viau
C C Zimmer
1B- P Veach
2B J Ardner
SS E McKean
3B W Smalley
LF B Gilks
CF G Davis
RF- V Dailey
M1 G Schmelz
M2 B Leadley

NY 1890 NL
SP A Rusie
SP M Welch
SP J Sharrott
C - D Buckley
1B- L Whistler
2B C Bassett
SS J Glasscock
3B J Denny
L1 J Hornung
CF M Tiernan
Rp J Burkett
OC A Clarke
M J Mutrie

PHI 1890 NL
SP K Gleason
SP T Vickery
SP P Smith
C J Clements
1B A McCauley
2B A Myers
SS B Allen
3B E Mayer
LF B Hamilton
CF E Burke
RF S Thompson
M1 H Wright
M3 A Reach
M5 H Wright

PIT 1890 NL
SP K Baker
SP D Anderson
SP B Sowders
SP C Schmit
C H Decker
1p G Hecker
2S S LaRoque
SS- E Sales
3U D Miller
LF- J Kelty
MR B Sunday
UT T Berger
OC B Wilson

BAL 1890 AA
SP L German
SP S McMahon
SP M O'Rourke
SP M Morrison
C - G Townsend
12 T Power
2B R Mack
SS I Ray
3B P Gilbert
LF J Sommer
CF- D Long
RF B Johnson
M B Barnie

BRO 1890 AA
SP C McCullough
SP M Mattimore
SP B Murphy
C - J Toy
1B B O'Brien
2B J Gerhardt
SS- C Nelson
3B- J Davis
LF H Simon
CF J Peltz
Rp E Daily
OC F Bowes
C3 H Pitz
M J Kennedy

COL 1890 AA
SP H Gastright
SP F Knauss
SP J Easton
SP E Chamberlain
SP W Widner
C J O'Connor
1B M Lehane
2B J Crooks
SS- H Easterday
3B C Reilly
LR S Johnson
CF J McTamany
RF J Sneed
IC- J Doyle
M1 A Buckenberger
M2 G Schmelz
M3 J Sullivan

LOU 1890 AA
SP S Stratton
SP R Ehret
SP G Meakim
SP H Goodall
SP E Daily
C J Ryan
1B H Taylor
2B T Shinnick
SS P Tomney
3B H Raymond
LF C Hamburg
CF F Weaver
RF J Wolf
M J Chapman

PHI 1890 AA
SP S McMahon
SP E Green
SP E Seward
SP D Esper
C W Robinson
1B J O'Brien
2B- T Shafer
S2 B Conroy
3B D Lyons
LF B Purcell
CF C Welch

RF O Shafer
M B Sharsig

ROC 1890 AA
SP B Barr
SP W Calihan
SP C Titcomb
SP B Miller
C D McGuire
1B- T O'Brien
2B B Greenwood
SS- M Phillips
3B J Knowles
LF H Lyons
CF S Griffin
RF T Scheffler
C - D McKeough
M P Powers

STL 1890 AA
SP J Stivetts
SP T Ramsey
SP B Hart
SP B Whitrock
C J Munyan
1B- E Cartwright
2B- B Higgins
SS S Fuller
M3 C Duffee
LR- C Campau
M1- C Roseman
RF T McCarthy
M2 J Kerins
M5 T McCarthy
M6 J Gerhardt

SYR 1890 AA
SP D Casey
SP J Keefe
SP M Morrison
SP E Mars
CM G Briggs
1B M McQuery
2B C Childs
SS B McLaughlin
C - T O'Rourke
LS B Ely
CF R Wright
RF- P Friel
3B T O'Rourke
M1 G Frazer
M2 W Fessenden
M3 G Frazer

TOL 1890 AA
SP J Healy
SP E Cushman
SP F Smith
SP C Sprague
C H Sage
1B P Werden
2B P Nicholson
SS F Scheibeck
3B B Alvord
LF B Van Dyke
CF G Tebeau
RF E Swartwood
M C Morton

BOS 1890 PL
SP C Radbourn
SP A Gumbert
SP B Daley
SP M Kilroy
C - M Murphy
1B D Brouthers
2B J Quinn
SS A Irwin
3B B Nash
LF H Richardson
CF T Brown
RF H Stovey
CS K Kelly

BRO 1890 PL
SP G Weyhing
SP J Sowders
SP C Murphy
SP G Hemming
C - T Kinslow
1B D Orr
2B L Bierbauer
SS J Ward
3B B Joyce
LF E Seery
CF E Andrews
RM J McGeachy
Rp G Van Haltren
M M Ward

BUF 1890 PL
SP G Haddock
SP B Cunningham
SP G Keefe
SP L Twitchell
SP G Stafford
C C Mack
31 D White
2B S Wise
SS J Rowe
3B- J Irwin
LF E Beecher
CF D Hoy
RC- J Halligan
OC- S Clark
M2 J Faatz
M3 J Rowe

CHI 1890 PL
SP M Baldwin
SP S King
SP C Bartson
C D Farrell
1B C Comiskey
2B F Pfeffer
SS- C Bastian
3S- E Williamson
LF T O'Neill
CF J Ryan
RF H Duffy
C3 J Boyle

CLE 1890 PL
SP H Gruber
SP J Bakely
SP D O'Brien
SP W McGill
C S Sutcliffe
1B H Larkin
2B C Stricker
SU E Delahanty
3B P Tebeau
LF P Browning
CF J McAleer
UT P Radford
M1 T Larkin

NY 1890 PL
SP H O'Day
SP E Crane
SP J Ewing
SP T Keefe
C B Ewing
1B R Connor
2B D Shannon
S2 D Richardson
3S A Whitney
LM G Gore
LM M Slattery
RF J O'Rourke
3S- G Hatfield
CF- D Johnston

PHI 1890 PL
SP B Sanders
SP P Knell
SP C Buffinton
SP B Husted
SP B Cunningham
C - J Milligan
1B S Farrar
2B J Pickett
SS B Shindle
3B J Mulvey
LF G Wood
CF M Griffin
RM J Fogarty
OC B Hallman

PIT 1890 PL
SP H Staley
SP A Maul
SP J Galvin
SP E Morris
SP J Tener
CL F Carroll
1B J Beckley
2B Y Robinson
SS T Corcoran
3B B Kuehne
LI J Fields
CF N Hanlon
RF J Visner

BOS 1891 NL
SP J Clarkson
SP K Nichols
SP H Staley
SP C Getzien
C - C Bennett
1B T Tucker
2B J Quinn
SS H Long
3B B Nash
LM B Lowe
CF S Brodie
RL H Stovey
C - C Ganzel
M F Selee

BRO 1891 NL
SP T Lovett
SP B Caruthers
SP G Hemming
SP A Terry
SP B Inks
C - T Kinslow
1B D Foutz
2L H Collins
SS J Ward
3B G Pinkney
LF D O'Brien
CF M Griffin
RF T Burns
M M Ward

CHI 1891 NL
SP B Hutchison
SP A Gumbert
SP P Luby
SP E Stein
C - M Kittridge
1B C Anson
2B F Pfeffer
SS J Cooney
3O B Dahlen
LM W Wilmot
ML J Ryan
RF C Carroll

CIN 1891 NL
SP T Mullane
SP B Rhines
SP C Radbourn
SP E Crane
C J Harrington
1O J Reilly
2B B McPhee
SS G Smith
3B A Latham
LF- P Browning
ML B Holliday
RF- L Marr
1C- J Keenan
M T Loftus

CLE 1891 NL
SP C Young
SP H Gruber
SP L Viau
C C Zimmer
1B J Virtue
2B C Childs
SS E McKean
3B- P Tebeau
LF J McAleer
CF G Davis
RF- S Johnson
OC- J Doyle
M1 B Leadley

NY 1891 NL
SP A Rusie
SP J Ewing
SP M Welch
C - D Buckley
1B R Connor
2B D Richardson
SS J Glasscock
3B C Bassett
LF J O'Rourke
CF G Gore
RF M Tiernan
UT- L Whistler
M J Mutrie

PHI 1891 NL
SP K Gleason
SP D Esper
SP J Thornton
C J Clements
1B W Brown
2B A Myers
SS B Allen
3B B Shindle
LF B Hamilton
MU E Delahanty
RF S Thompson
M H Wright

PIT 1891 NL
SP M Baldwin
SP S King
SP J Galvin
C - C Mack
1B J Beckley
2B L Bierbauer
SS- F Shugart
3B C Reilly
LF- P Browning
ML N Hanlon
RF F Carroll
IC D Miller
M2 B McGunnigle

BAL 1891 AA
SP S McMahon
SP B Cunningham
SP K Madden
SP J Healy
C W Robinson
1B P Werden
2B S Wise
LS G Van Haltren
3B P Gilbert
UO B Johnson
CF C Welch
RS I Ray
M B Barnie

BOS 1891 AA
SP G Haddock
SP C Buffinton
SR D O'Brien
SP B Daley
C M Murphy
1B D Brouthers
2B C Stricker
SS P Radford
3C D Farrell
LF- H Richardson
CF T Brown
RF H Duffy
3B- B Joyce
M A Irwin

CIN 1891 AA
SP F Dwyer
SP E Crane
SP W Mains
SP W McGill
C K Kelly
1B J Carney
2B Y Robinson
SS J Canavan
3B A Whitney
LF E Andrews
CF D Johnston
RF E Seery

COL 1891 AA
SP P Knell
SP H Gastright
SP J Dolan
SP J Easton
C - J Donahue
1B M Lehane
2B J Crooks
SS B Wheelock
3B- B Kuehne
LM C Duffee
CF- J McTamany
RF J Sneed
M G Schmelz

LOU 1891 AA
SP W Fitzgerald
SP R Ehret
SP J Meekin
SP S Stratton
SP J Doran
RP E Daily
CI- J Ryan
1B H Taylor
2B T Shinnick
SS H Jennings
3B- O Beard
LF P Donovan
CF F Weaver
RF J Wolf
IC T Cahill
M J Chapman

MIL 1891 AA
SP G Davies
SP F Killen
SP F Dwyer
C F Vaughn
1B J Carney
2S J Canavan
S3 G Shoch
3B- G Alberts
LF A Dalrymple
CF E Burke
RF H Earl
C3 J Grim
M C Cushman

PHI 1891 AA
SP G Weyhing
SP E Chamberlain
SP B Sanders
SP W Calihan
C1 J Milligan
1B H Larkin
2B B Hallman
SS T Corcoran
3B J Mulvey
LF G Wood
CF- P Corkhill
OC L Cross
M1 B Sharsig

STL 1891 AA
SP J Stivetts
SP W McGill
SR C Griffith
SP J Neale
SP G Rettger
C J Boyle
1B C Comiskey
2B- B Eagan
SS S Fuller
3B D Lyons
LF T O'Neill
CF D Hoy
RF T McCarthy

WAS 1891 AA
SP K Carsey
SP F Foreman
SP J Bakely
C D McGuire
1B- M McQuery
2B T Dowd
SS G Hatfield
3B- B Alvord
LF- E Beecher
CF- P Hines
LR L Murphy
M1 S Trott
M2 P Snyder
M3 D Shannon
M4 S Griffin

BAL 1892 NL
SP S McMahon
SP G Cobb
SP T Vickery
SP C Buffinton
C - W Robinson
1B- S Sutcliffe
2B- C Stricker
SS- T O'Rourke
3B B Shindle
LF- H Stovey
CF- C Welch
UT G Van Haltren
C - J Gunson
UT- J McGraw
M2 J Waltz
M3 N Hanlon

BOS 1892 NL
SP K Nichols
SP J Stivetts
SP H Staley
SP J Clarkson
C - K Kelly
1B T Tucker
2B J Quinn
SS H Long
3B B Nash
LI B Lowe
CF H Duffy
RF T McCarthy
M F Selee

BRO 1892 NL
SP G Haddock
SP E Stein
SP D Foutz
SP B Hart
SP B Kennedy
C - C Daily
1B D Brouthers
2B J Ward
SS T Corcoran
3B B Joyce
LF D O'Brien
CF M Griffin
RF T Burns
IC T Daly
M M Ward

CHI 1892 NL
SP B Hutchison
SP A Gumbert
SP P Luby
C P Schriver
1B C Anson
2B J Canavan
S3 B Dahlen
3B- J Parrott
LF W Wilmot
CF J Ryan
RL S Dungan
RF- G Decker

CIN 1892 NL
SP E Chamberlain
SP T Mullane
SP F Dwyer
SP M Sullivan
C - M Murphy
1B C Comiskey
2B B McPhee
SS G Smith
3B A Latham
LF T O'Neill
ML- P Browning
MR B Holliday
CU- F Vaughn

CLE 1892 NL
SP C Young
SP N Cuppy
SP J Clarkson
SP G Davies
C C Zimmer
1B J Virtue
2B C Childs
SS E McKean
3R G Davis
LF J Burkett
CF J McAleer
RU J O'Connor
3B- P Tebeau

LOU 1892 NL
SP S Stratton
SP B Sanders
SP F Clausen
SP J Meekin
SP A Jones
RP L Viau
CU J Grim
1B- L Whistler
2B F Pfeffer
SS H Jennings
3B- B Kuehne
LF F Weaver
CF T Brown
UT H Taylor
3B- C Bassett
M1 J Chapman

NY 1892 NL
SP A Rusie
SP S King
SP E Crane
C1 J Boyle
1C B Ewing
2L- E Burke
SS S Fuller
3B D Lyons
LF J O'Rourke
CF H Lyons
RF M Tiernan
IC- J Doyle
M P Powers

PHI 1892 NL
SR G Weyhing
SP K Carsey
SP T Keefe
SP D Esper
C J Clements
1B R Connor
2B B Hallman
SS B Allen
3B- C Reilly
LF B Hamilton
CF E Delahanty
RF S Thompson
IC L Cross
M H Wright

PIT 1892 NL
SP M Baldwin
SP R Ehret
SP A Terry
SP J Galvin
C C Mack
1B J Beckley
2B L Bierbauer
SS F Shugart
3B D Farrell
Lp E Smith
OC D Miller
RF- P Donovan
M1 A Buckenberger
M2 T Burns
M3 A Buckenberger

STL 1892 NL
SP K Gleason
SP T Breitenstein
SP P Hawley
SP C Getzien
SP B Hawke
C D Buckley
1B P Werden
2B J Crooks
SS J Glasscock
3B- G Pinkney
LF C Carroll
CF S Brodie
Rp B Caruthers
M2 C Stricker
M4 G Gore

WAS 1892 NL
SP F Killen
SP B Abbey
SP P Knell
SP J Duryea
SP J Meekin
C D McGuire
1B H Larkin
2U T Dowd
S2 D Richardson
3B- Y Robinson
LR C Duffee
CF D Hoy
UT P Radford
C1- J Milligan
M1 B Barnie
M2 A Irwin

BAL 1893 NL
SP S McMahon
SP T Mullane
SP B Hawke
SP E McNabb
SP K Baker
C W Robinson
1B H Taylor
2B H Reitz
SS J McGraw
3B B Shindle
LF- J Long
CF J Kelley
RF G Treadway
M N Hanlon

BOS 1893 NL
SP K Nichols
SP J Stivetts
SP H Staley
SP H Gastright
C - C Bennett
1B T Tucker
2B B Lowe
SS H Long
3B B Nash
LF T McCarthy
CF H Duffy
RL C Carroll
CO- C Ganzel
M F Selee

BRO 1893 NL
SP B Kennedy
SP E Stein
SP G Haddock
SP D Daub
SP T Lovett
RP G Sharrott
C T Kinslow
1B- D Brouthers
2B- D Richardson
SS T Corcoran
23 T Daly
L1 D Foutz
CF M Griffin
RF T Burns
UT G Shoch

CHI 1893 NL
SP B Hutchison
SP W McGill
SP H Mauck
C - M Kittridge
1B C Anson
UT B Lange
SS B Dahlen
3B J Parrott
LF W Wilmot
CF J Ryan
RF S Dungan
UT G Decker

CIN 1893 NL
SP F Dwyer
SP E Chamberlain
SP M Sullivan
SP T Parrott
SP T Mullane
RP S King
CU F Vaughn
1B- C Comiskey
2B B McPhee
SS G Smith
3B A Latham
LF J Canavan
CF B Holliday
RF- J McCarthy

CLE 1893 NL
SP C Young
SP J Clarkson
SP N Cuppy
SP C Hastings
C - C Zimmer
1B J Virtue
2B C Childs
SS E McKean
3B- C McGarr
LF J Burkett
CF J McAleer
RF B Ewing
CM J O'Connor
UI P Tebeau

LOU 1893 NL
SP G Hemming
SP S Stratton
SP B Rhodes
SP J Menefee
C J Grim
1B W Brown
2B F Pfeffer
SO T O'Rourke
3B G Pinkney
LF- P Browning
CF T Brown
RU F Weaver
M B Barnie

NY 1893 NL
SP A Rusie
SP M Baldwin
SP L German
CM J Doyle
1B R Connor
2B J Ward
SS S Fuller
3B G Davis
LF E Burke
CF- G Stafford
RF M Tiernan
M M Ward

PHI 1893 NL
SP G Weyhing
SP K Carsey
SP T Keefe
SP J Taylor
C J Clements
1B J Boyle
2B B Hallman
SS B Allen
3B C Reilly
LF E Delahanty
CF B Hamilton
RF S Thompson
IC L Cross
M H Wright

PIT 1893 NL
SP F Killen
SP R Ehret
SP A Terry
SP A Gumbert
C - D Miller
1B J Beckley
2B L Bierbauer
SS- J Glasscock
3B D Lyons
LF E Smith
CF G Van Haltren
RF P Donovan
M A Buckenberger

STL 1893 NL
SP T Breitenstein
SP K Gleason
SP P Hawley
SP D Clarkson
C H Peitz
1B P Werden
2B J Quinn
SS- J Glasscock
3B J Crooks
LF- C Frank
CF S Brodie
OI T Dowd
M B Watkins

WAS 1893 NL
SP D Esper
SP A Maul
SP J Meekin
SP J Duryea
C3 D Farrell
1B H Larkin
23 S Wise
SS J Sullivan
3B- J Mulvey
L1 J O'Rourke
CF D Hoy
RF P Radford

BAL 1894 NL
SP S McMahon
SP B Hawke
SP K Gleason
SP B Inks
SP T Mullane
RP D Esper
C W Robinson
1B D Brouthers
2B H Reitz
SS H Jennings
3B J McGraw
LF J Kelley
CF S Brodie
RF W Keeler
M N Hanlon

BOS 1894 NL
SP K Nichols
SP J Stivetts
SP H Staley

SP T Lovett
C - C Ganzel
1B T Tucker
2B B Lowe
SS H Long
3B B Nash
LF T McCarthy
CF H Duffy
RF J Bannon
M F Selee

BRO 1894 NL
SP B Kennedy
SP E Stein
SP D Daub
SP H Gastright
C - T Kinslow
1B- D Foutz
2B T Daly
SS T Corcoran
3B B Shindle
LF G Treadway
CF M Griffin
RF T Burns
C - C Daily
1B- C LaChance

CHI 1894 NL
SP B Hutchison
SP C Griffith
SP W McGill
SP A Terry
SP S Stratton
RP B Abbey
C P Schriver
1B C Anson
2B J Parrott
S3 B Dahlen
3S C Irwin
LF W Wilmot
CF B Lange
RF J Ryan
1O G Decker

CIN 1894 NL
SP F Dwyer
SP T Parrott
SP E Chamberlain
SP C Fisher
C - M Murphy
1B- C Comiskey
2B B McPhee
SS G Smith
3B A Latham
LF B Holliday
CF D Hoy
RF J Canavan
C1- F Vaughn

CLE 1894 NL
SP C Young
SR N Cuppy
SP J Clarkson
SP M Sullivan
C C Zimmer
1B P Tebeau
2B C Childs
SS E McKean
3B C McGarr
LF J Burkett
CF- J McAleer
RF- H Blake
CM J O'Connor

LOU 1894 NL
SP G Hemming
SP P Knell
SP J Menefee
SP J Wadsworth
CI J Grim
1B- L Lutenberg
2B F Pfeffer
SS D Richardson
3B- J Denny
LF- F Clarke
CF T Brown
RF- O Smith
M B Barnie

NY 1894 NL
SP A Rusie
SP J Meekin
SP L German
SP H Westervelt
C D Farrell
1B J Doyle
2B J Ward
SS S Fuller
3B G Davis
LF E Burke
CF G Van Haltren
RF M Tiernan
SR- Y Murphy
M M Ward

PHI 1894 NL
SP J Taylor
SP K Carsey
SP G Weyhing
SP G Harper
C - J Clements
1B J Boyle
2B B Hallman
SS- J Sullivan
3B L Cross
LI E Delahanty
CF B Hamilton
RF S Thompson
LR T Turner
M A Irwin

PIT 1894 NL
SP R Ehret
SP A Gumbert
SP F Killen
SP T Colcolough
SP J Menefee
C - C Mack
1B J Beckley
2B L Bierbauer
SS J Glasscock
3B- D Lyons
LF E Smith
CF J Stenzel
RF P Donovan
M1 A Buckenberger

STL 1894 NL
SP T Breitenstein
SP P Hawley
SP D Clarkson
IC D Miller
1B R Connor
2B J Quinn
SS B Ely
IC H Peitz
LF C Frank
CF F Shugart
RL T Dowd
M G Miller

WAS 1894 NL
SR W Mercer
SP A Maul
SP M Sullivan
SP O Stocksdale
SP D Esper
RP C Petty
C D McGuire
1B E Cartwright
2B P Ward
SS- F Scheibeck
3B B Joyce
OI K Selbach
ML C Abbey
R3 B Hassamaer
UT P Radford
M G Schmelz

BAL 1895 NL
SP B Hoffer
SP G Hemming
SP D Esper
SP D Clarkson
SP S McMahon
C - W Robinson
1B S Carey
2B K Gleason
SS H Jennings
3B J McGraw
LF J Kelley
CF S Brodie
RF W Keeler
C - B Clarke
23- H Reitz
M N Hanlon

BOS 1895 NL
SP K Nichols
SP J Stivetts
SP C Dolan
SP J Sullivan
C C Ganzel
1B T Tucker
2B B Lowe
SS H Long
3B B Nash
LF T McCarthy
CF H Duffy
RF J Bannon
M F Selee

BRO 1895 NL
SP B Kennedy
SP E Stein
SP A Gumbert
SP D Daub
SP C Lucid
C J Grim
1B C LaChance
2B T Daly
SS T Corcoran
3B B Shindle
LF J Anderson
CF M Griffin
RF G Treadway
M D Foutz

CHI 1895 NL
SP C Griffith
SP A Terry
SP B Hutchison
C - T Donahue
1B C Anson
2B A Stewart
SS B Dahlen
3B B Everitt
LF W Wilmot
CF B Lange
RF J Ryan
UT- G Decker

CIN 1895 NL
SP F Dwyer
SP B Rhines
SR T Parrott
SP F Foreman
SP B Phillips
C F Vaughn
1B B Ewing
2B B McPhee
SS G Smith
3B A Latham
LM D Hoy
MO-G Hogriever
RF D Miller

CLE 1895 NL
SP C Young
SP N Cuppy
SP B Wallace
SP P Knell
C C Zimmer
RF- P Tebeau
2B C Childs
SS E McKean
3B C McGarr
LF J Burkett
CF J McAleer
RF H Blake
C1 J O'Connor
R1 G Tebeau

LOU 1895 NL
SP B Cunningham
SP G Weyhing
SP M McDermott
SP B Inks
C - J Warner
1C- H Spies
2B J O'Brien
SS F Shugart
3B J Collins
LF F Clarke
MR-J Wright
MR-T Gettinger
M J McCloskey

NY 1895 NL
SP A Rusie
SP D Clarke
SP J Meekin
SP L German
C3 D Farrell
1U J Doyle
2B G Stafford
SS S Fuller
3U G Davis
LF- E Burke
CF G Van Haltren
RF M Tiernan
C - P Wilson
M3 H Watkins

PHI 1895 NL
SP K Carsey
SP J Taylor
SP W McGill
SP A Orth
C J Clements
1B J Boyle
2B B Hallman
SS J Sullivan
3B L Cross
LF E Delahanty
CF B Hamilton
RF S Thompson
M A Irwin

PIT 1895 NL
SP P Hawley
SP B Hart
SP B Foreman
SP F Killen
SP J Gardner
C - B Merritt
1B J Beckley
2B L Bierbauer
SS M Cross
3B B Clingman
LF E Smith
CF J Stenzel
RF P Donovan
UT- F Genins
M C Mack

STL 1895 NL
SP T Breitenstein
SP R Ehret
SP H Staley
SR B Kissinger
SP D McDougal
C H Peitz
1B R Connor
2B J Quinn
SS B Ely
IC D Miller
LF D Cooley
CF T Brown
RM T Dowd
M1 A Buckenberger
M2 C Von Der Ahe
M4 L Phelan

WAS 1895 NL
SP W Mercer
SP V Anderson
SP O Stocksdale
SP A Maul
SR J Malarkey
RP J Boyd
C D McGuire
1B E Cartwright
2B J Crooks
SS- F Scheibeck
3B B Joyce
LF K Selbach
MO C Abbey
RF B Hassamaer
M G Schmelz

BAL 1896 NL
SP B Hoffer
SP A Pond
SP G Hemming
SP S McMahon
SP D Esper
C - W Robinson
1B J Doyle
2B H Reitz
SS H Jennings
3B J McGraw
LF J Kelley
CF S Brodie
RF W Keeler
C B Clarke
M N Hanlon

BOS 1896 NL
SP K Nichols
SP J Stivetts
SP J Sullivan
SP F Klobedanz
C - M Bergen
1B T Tucker
2B- B Lowe
SS H Long
3B J Collins
LF H Duffy
CF B Hamilton
RF J Bannon
RC F Tenney
M F Selee

BRO 1896 NL
SP B Kennedy
SP H Payne
SP D Daub
SP B Abbey
SP E Stein
RP G Harper
C J Grim
1B C LaChance
2B- T Daly
SS T Corcoran
3B B Shindle
LF T McCarthy
CF M Griffin
RF F Jones
OI J Anderson
2B- G Shoch
M D Foutz

CHI 1896 NL
SP C Griffith
SP D Friend
SP A Terry
SP B Briggs
C - M Kittridge
1B C Anson
2B F Pfeffer
SS B Dahlen
3O B Everitt
L1 G Decker
CF B Lange
RF J Ryan

CIN 1896 NL
SP F Dwyer
SP R Ehret
SP F Foreman
SR C Fisher
SP B Rhines
C - H Peitz
1B- B Ewing
2B B McPhee
SS G Smith
3B C Irwin
LF E Burke
CF D Hoy
RF D Miller
1C F Vaughn

CLE 1896 NL
SP C Young
SP N Cuppy
SP Z Wilson
SP B Wallace
C C Zimmer
1B P Tebeau
2B C Childs
SS E McKean
3B C McGarr
LF J Burkett
CF J McAleer
RF H Blake
C1- J O'Connor

LOU 1896 NL
SP C Fraser
SP B Hill
SP B Cunningham
SP A Herman
IC D Miller
1B- J Rogers
2B- J O'Brien
SS- J Dolan
3B B Clingman
LF F Clarke
CM C Dexter
RF T McCreery
M1 J McCloskey
M2 B McGunnigle

NY 1896 NL
SP D Clarke
SP J Meekin
SP M Sullivan
SP E Doheny
C - P Wilson
1B- W Clark
2B K Gleason
SL F Connaughton
3S G Davis
LF- G Stafford
CF G Van Haltren
RF M Tiernan
M1 A Irwin
M2 B Joyce

PHI 1896 NL
SP J Taylor
SP A Orth
SP K Carsey
SP H Keener
SP W McGill
C - M Grady
1B- D Brouthers
2B B Hallman
SS B Hulen
3B- B Nash
LF E Delahanty
ML- D Cooley
RF S Thompson
3S L Cross

PIT 1896 NL
SP F Killen
SP P Hawley
SR J Hughey
SP C Hastings
C J Sugden
1B- J Beckley
2B- D Padden
SS B Ely
3B D Lyons
LF E Smith
CF J Stenzel
RF P Donovan
C - B Merritt
M C Mack

STL 1896 NL
SP T Breitenstein
SP B Hart
SP R Donahue
SP B Kissinger
C E McFarland
1B R Connor
2M T Dowd
SS M Cross
3B B Myers
LF- J Sullivan
MO T Parrott
RL K Douglass
M1 H Diddlebock
M2 A Latham
M3 C Von Der Ahe

WAS 1896 NL
SP W Mercer
SP D McJames
SP L German
SP S King
C D McGuire
1B E Cartwright
2B- J O'Brien
SS De Montreville
32 B Joyce
LF K Selbach
CF T Brown
RU B Lush
RF- C Abbey
M G Schmelz

BAL 1897 NL
SP J Corbett
SP B Hoffer
SP A Pond
SP J Nops
C - B Clarke
1B J Doyle
2B H Reitz
SS H Jennings
3B J McGraw
LF J Kelley
CF J Stenzel
RF W Keeler
UT- J Quinn
M N Hanlon

BOS 1897 NL
SP K Nichols
SP F Klobedanz
SP T Lewis
SP J Stivetts
SP J Sullivan
C M Bergen
1B F Tenney
2B B Lowe
SS H Long
3B J Collins
LF H Duffy
CF B Hamilton
RF C Stahl
M F Selee

BRO 1897 NL
SP B Kennedy
SP H Payne
SP J Dunn
SP C Fisher
SP D Daub
C - J Grim
1B C LaChance
2B G Shoch
SS G Smith
3B B Shindle
LF J Anderson
CF M Griffin
RF F Jones
M B Barnie

CHI 1897 NL
SP C Griffith
SP D Friend
SP B Briggs
SP W Thornton
SP R Denzer
C - M Kittridge
1B C Anson
2B- J Connor
SS- B Dahlen
3B B Everitt
L1 G Decker
CF B Lange
RF J Ryan
2p N Callahan
3S B McCormick

CIN 1897 NL
SP T Breitenstein
SP B Rhines
SP F Dwyer
SR R Ehret
SP B Dammann
C - H Peitz
1B J Beckley
2B B McPhee
SU C Ritchey
3B C Irwin
LF E Burke
CF D Hoy
RF D Miller
S2 T Corcoran
M B Ewing

CLE 1897 NL
SP C Young
SP Z Wilson
SP J Powell
SP N Cuppy
C C Zimmer
1B P Tebeau
2B C Childs
SS E McKean
3B B Wallace
LF J Burkett
OI J O'Connor
RF- C Sockalexis

LOU 1897 NL
SP C Fraser
SP B Cunningham
SP B Hill
SP B Magee
C B Wilson
1B P Werden
2B- J Rogers
SS G Stafford
3B B Clingman
LF F Clarke
CF- O Pickering
RF T McCreery
OC- C Dexter

NY 1897 NL
SP A Rusie
SP J Meekin
SP C Seymour
SP M Sullivan
SP E Doheny
C J Warner
1B W Clark
2B K Gleason
SS G Davis
3B B Joyce
LF- D Holmes
CF G Van Haltren
RL M Tiernan

PHI 1897 NL
SP J Taylor
SP A Orth
SP J Fifield
SP G Wheeler
C1- J Boyle
1B N Lajoie
32 L Cross
SS- S Gillen
3B B Nash
LF E Delahanty
CF D Cooley
RM T Dowd
UT P Geier
M G Stallings

PIT 1897 NL
SP F Killen
SP P Hawley
SP J Hughey
SP J Tannehill
SP C Hastings
RP J Gardner
C J Sugden
13 H Davis
2B D Padden
SS B Ely
3B- J Hoffmeister
LF E Smith
CF S Brodie
RF P Donovan

STL 1897 NL
SP R Donahue
SP B Hart
SP K Carsey
SP W Sudhoff
OC K Douglass
1B M Grady
2B B Hallman
SS M Cross
3B F Hartman
LF D Lally
CF D Harley
RF T Turner
2O J Houseman
M1 T Dowd
M2 H Nicol
M4 C Von Der Ahe

WAS 1897 NL
SP W Mercer
SP D McJames
SP C Swaim
SP S King
RS L German
C D McGuire
1B T Tucker
2B J O'Brien
SU De Montreville
3B C Reilly
LF K Selbach
CF T Brown
RF C Abbey
UT Z Wrigley
C - D Farrell
M1 G Schmelz

BAL 1898 NL
SP D McJames
SP J Hughes
SP A Maul
SP J Nops
SP F Kitson
C - W Robinson
1B D McGann
2B De Montreville
SS H Jennings
3B J McGraw
LF D Holmes
ML J Kelley
RF W Keeler
C - B Clarke
M N Hanlon

BOS 1898 NL
SP K Nichols
SP T Lewis
SP V Willis
SP F Klobedanz
C M Bergen
1B F Tenney
2B B Lowe
SS H Long
3B J Collins
LF H Duffy
CF B Hamilton
RF C Stahl
M F Selee

BRO 1898 NL
SP B Kennedy
SP J Dunn
SP J Yeager
SP R Miller
SP K McKenna
C - J Ryan
1S C LaChance
2B B Hallman
SS G Magoon
3B B Shindle
LF J Sheckard
CF M Griffin
RF F Jones
M1 B Barnie
M3 C Ebbets

CHI 1898 NL
SP C Griffith
SP N Callahan
SP W Thornton
SP W Woods
SP M Kilroy
C T Donahue
1B B Everitt
2B J Connor
SS B Dahlen
3B B McCormick
LF J Ryan
CF B Lange
RU- S Mertes
M T Burns

CIN 1898 NL
SP P Hawley
SP T Breitenstein
SP B Hill
SP F Dwyer
SR B Dammann
C H Peitz
1B J Beckley
2B B McPhee
SS T Corcoran
3B C Irwin
LF E Smith
CF A McBride
RF D Miller
UT- H Steinfeldt
1C- F Vaughn
M B Ewing

CLE 1898 NL
SP C Young
SP J Powell
SP Z Wilson
SP N Cuppy
C - L Criger
12 P Tebeau
2B C Childs
SS E McKean
3B B Wallace
LF J Burkett
CF J McAleer
RF H Blake
1C J O'Connor

LOU 1898 NL
SP B Cunningham
SP B Magee
SP P Dowling
SP C Fraser
C - M Kittridge
UI H Wagner
2B- H Smith
S2 C Ritchey

3S B Clingman
LF F Clarke
CF D Hoy
RF C Dexter

NY 1898 NL
SP C Seymour
SP J Meekin
SP A Rusie
SP E Doheny
SP C Gettig
C J Warner
1B B Joyce
2B K Gleason
SS G Davis
3B F Hartman
LF M Tiernan
CF G Van Haltren
UT- J Doyle
CO- M Grady
M2 C Anson
M3 B Joyce

PHI 1898 NL
SP W Piatt
SP R Donahue
SP A Orth
SP J Fifield
SP G Wheeler
C E McFarland
1B K Douglass
2B N Lajoie
SS M Cross
3B B Lauder
LF E Delahanty
CF D Cooley
RF E Flick
M1 G Stallings
M2 B Shettsline

PIT 1898 NL
SP J Tannehill
SP B Rhines
SP J Gardner
SP F Killen
SP C Hastings
RP B Hart
C P Schriver
1B- W Clark
2B D Padden
SS B Ely
3B B Gray
LF J McCarthy
MI T O'Brien
RF P Donovan
M B Watkins

STL 1898 NL
SP J Taylor
SP W Sudhoff
SP J Hughey
SP K Carsey
C J Clements
1B- G Decker
2B- J Crooks
SS- G Smith
3B L Cross
LF D Harley
CF J Stenzel
RM T Dowd
2S J Quinn
CU- J Sugden
M T Hurst

WAS 1898 NL
SP G Weyhing
SP W Mercer
SP B Dinneen
SP F Killen
SP C Swaim
C1 D McGuire
1B- J Doyle
2B H Reitz
SS Z Wrigley
3I- J Smith
LF K Selbach
MU J Anderson
RF J Gettman
C1 D Farrell
M1 T Brown
M4 A Irwin

BAL 1899 NL
SP J McGinnity
SP F Kitson
SP J Nops
SP H Howell
C W Robinson
1B C LaChance
2B- De Montreville
S2 B Keister
3B J McGraw
LF D Holmes
CF S Brodie
RF J Sheckard

BOS 1899 NL
SP V Willis
SP K Nichols
SP T Lewis
SP J Meekin
SP F Killen
C - M Bergen
1B F Tenney
2B B Lowe
SS H Long
3B J Collins
LF H Duffy
CF- B Hamilton
RF C Stahl
M F Selee

BRO 1899 NL
SP J Dunn
SP J Hughes
SP B Kennedy
SP D McJames
C - D Farrell
1B- D McGann
2B T Daly
SS B Dahlen
3B D Casey
LF J Kelley
CF F Jones
RF W Keeler
M1 J Anderson
M N Hanlon

CHI 1899 NL
SP J Taylor
SP C Griffith
SP N Callahan
SP N Garvin
C T Donahue
1B B Everitt
2B B McCormick
SS- De Montreville
3B H Wolverton
LF J Ryan
UT S Mertes
RF D Green
CF B Lange
M T Burns

CIN 1899 NL
SP N Hahn
SP P Hawley
SP B Phillips
SP T Breitenstein
SP J Taylor
C - H Peitz
1B J Beckley
2B B McPhee
SS T Corcoran
3B- C Irwin
UO- E Smith
LM K Selbach
RF- D Miller
32 H Steinfeldt
M B Ewing

CLE 1899 NL
SP J Hughey
SP C Knepper
SP F Bates
SP C Schmit
SP H Colliflower
C - J Sugden
1B T Tucker
2B J Quinn
SS H Lochhead
3B S Sullivan
LF D Harley
CF T Dowd
RU S McAllister
M1 L Cross

LOU 1899 NL
SP B Cunningham
SP D Phillippe
SP P Dowling
SP W Woods
C - C Zimmer
1B- M Kelley
2B C Ritchey
SS B Clingman
3B T Leach
LF F Clarke
CF D Hoy
RF- C Dexter
3R H Wagner

NY 1899 NL
SP B Carrick
SP E Doheny
SP C Seymour
SP J Meekin
SP C Gettig
C - J Warner
1B J Doyle
2B K Gleason
SS G Davis
3B- F Hartman
LF T O'Brien
CF G Van Haltren
RF- P Foster
IC P Wilson
C3- M Grady
M1 J Day
M2 F Hoey

PHI 1899 NL
SP W Piatt
SP R Donahue
SP C Fraser
SP A Orth
SP B Bernhard
RP J Fifield
C E McFarland
1B D Cooley
2B- N Lajoie
SS M Cross
3B B Lauder
LF E Delahanty
CF R Thomas
RF E Flick
UT P Chiles
C - K Douglass
M B Shettsline

PIT 1899 NL
SR S Leever
SP J Tannehill
SR T Sparks
SP B Hoffer
SP J Chesbro
C1 F Bowerman
1B- W Clark
2B- J O'Brien
SS B Ely
3B J Williams
LF J McCarthy
CF G Beaumont
RF P Donovan
UT T McCreery
C - P Schriver
M1 B Watkins

STL 1899 NL
SP J Powell
SP C Young
SP W Sudhoff
SP N Cuppy
C - L Criger
1B- P Tebeau
2B C Childs
S3 B Wallace
3B L Cross
LF J Burkett
MU H Blake
RF E Heidrick
C1- J O'Connor

WAS 1899 NL
SP G Weyhing
SP B Dinneen
SP D McFarlan
C - D McGuire
1B- D McGann
2B- F Bonner
S2 D Padden
3B- C Atherton
LF J O'Brien
CF J Slagle
RF B Freeman
3p W Mercer
UT- S Barry
M A Irwin

BOS 1900 NL
SP B Dinneen
SP V Willis
SP K Nichols
SP T Lewis
SP T Pittinger
RP N Cuppy
C - B Clarke
1B F Tenney
2B B Lowe
SS H Long
3B J Collins
RL C Stahl
CF B Hamilton
RU B Freeman
UT- S Barry
C - B Sullivan
M F Selee

BRO 1900 NL
SP J McGinnity
SP B Kennedy
SR F Kitson
SR H Howell
C- D Farrell
1B H Jennings
2B T Daly
SS B Dahlen
3B L Cross
LF J Sheckard
CF F Jones
RF W Keeler
L1 J Kelley
C - D McGuire
M N Hanlon

CHI 1900 NL
SP N Callahan
SP C Griffith
SP N Garvin
SP J Taylor
SP J Menefee
C - T Donahue
1B- J Ganzel
2B C Childs
SS B McCormick
3B B Bradley
LF J McCarthy
MR D Green
RL J Ryan
M1 S Mertes
M T Loftus

CIN 1900 NL
SP E Scott
SP N Hahn
SP D Newton
SP B Phillips
SP T Breitenstein
C H Peitz
1B J Beckley
2B- J Quinn
SS T Corcoran
32 H Steinfeldt
LU S Crawford
CF J Barrett
RF A McBride
3U C Irwin
M B Allen

NY 1900 NL
SP B Carrick
SP P Hawley
SP W Mercer
SP E Doheny
C - F Bowerman
1B J Doyle
2B K Gleason
SS G Davis
3B C Hickman
LF K Selbach
CF G Van Haltren
RF E Smith
IC- M Grady
M1 B Ewing

PHI 1900 NL
SP A Orth
SP R Donahue
SP C Fraser
SP B Bernhard
SP W Piatt
C E McFarland
1B E Delahanty
2B N Lajoie
SS M Cross
3B H Wolverton
LF J Slagle
CF R Thomas
RF E Flick
UI- J Dolan
M B Shettsline

PIT 1900 NL
SP D Phillippe
SP J Tannehill
SP S Leever
SP J Chesbro
SP R Waddell
C - C Zimmer
1B- D Cooley
2B C Ritchey
SS B Ely
3B J Williams
LF F Clarke
CF G Beaumont
RF H Wagner
1U T O'Brien

STL 1900 NL
SP C Young
SP C Jones
SP J Powell
SP W Sudhoff
SP J Hughey
C - L Criger
1B D McGann
2B B Keister
SS B Wallace
3B J McGraw
LF J Burkett
CF E Heidrick
RF P Donovan
OI- M Donlin
M1 P Tebeau
M2 L Heilbroner

BOS 1901 NL
SP K Nichols
SP B Dinneen
SP V Willis
SP T Pittinger
C M Kittridge
1B F Tenney
2B De Montreville
SS H Long
3B B Lowe
OI- D Cooley
CF B Hamilton
RF- J Slagle
M F Selee

BRO 1901 NL
SP B Donovan
SP F Kitson
SP J Hughes
SP D Newton
SP D McJames
RP B Kennedy
C D McGuire
1B J Kelley
2B T Daly
SS B Dahlen
3B- C Irwin
LF J Sheckard
CF T McCreery
RF W Keeler
CU- D Farrell
M N Hanlon

CHI 1901 NL
SP T Hughes
SP J Taylor
SP R Waddell
SP M Eason
SP J Menefee
C - J Kling
1B- J Doyle
2B- C Childs
SS B McCormick
3I F Raymer
LF T Hartsel
CF D Green
RU- F Chance
UT C Dexter
M T Loftus

CIN 1901 NL
SP N Hahn
SP B Phillips
SP D Newton
SP A Stimmel
C B Bergen
1B J Beckley
32 H Steinfeldt
SS G Magoon
3B- C Irwin
LF D Harley
CF J Dobbs
RF S Crawford
C2- H Peitz
M B McPhee

NY 1901 NL
SP D Taylor
SP C Mathewson
SP B Phyle
C J Warner
1B J Ganzel
2B- R Nelson
SS G Davis
32 S Strang
LF K Selbach
CF G Van Haltren
RF- A McBride
UT C Hickman

PHI 1901 NL
SP R Donahue
SP B Duggleby
SP A Orth
SP D White
SP H Townsend
C - E McFarland
1B- H Jennings
23 B Hallman
SS M Cross
3B H Wolverton
L1 E Delahanty
CF R Thomas
RF E Flick
M B Shettsline

PIT 1901 NL
SP D Phillippe
SP J Chesbro
SP J Tannehill
SP S Leever
C - C Zimmer
1B K Bransfield
2B C Ritchey
SS- B Ely
3B T Leach
LF F Clarke
CF G Beaumont
RF L Davis
UT H Wagner

STL 1901 NL
SP J Powell
SP J Harper
SR W Sudhoff
SP E Murphy
C - J Ryan
1B D McGann
2B D Padden
SS B Wallace
3B O Krueger
LF J Burkett
CF E Heidrick
RF P Donovan
CM A Nichols

BAL 1901 AL
SP J McGinnity
SP H Howell
SP F Foreman
SP J Nops
C R Bresnahan
1B- B Hart
2B J Williams
SS B Keister
3B- J McGraw
ML J Jackson
CF S Brodie
RF C Seymour
L1 M Donlin
3U J Dunn

BOS 1901 AL
SP C Young
SP T Lewis
SP G Winter
SP F Mitchell
SP N Cuppy
C O
Schreckengost
1B B Freeman
2B H Ferris
SS F Parent
3B J Collins
LF T Dowd
CF C Stahl
RF C Hemphill
C - L Criger

CHI 1901 AL
SP R Patterson
SP C Griffith
SP N Callahan
SP J Katoll
SP Z Harvey
C B Sullivan
1B F Isbell
2B S Mertes
SS F Shugart
3B F Hartman
LF H McFarland
CF D Hoy
RF F Jones

CLE 1901 AL
SP P Dowling
SP E Moore
SP B Hart
SP E Scott
SP B Hoffer
RP J Bracken
RP H McNeal
C B Wood
1B C LaChance
2B E Beck
SS F Scheibeck
3B B Bradley
LF J McCarthy
CF O Pickering
RL J O'Brien
M J McAleer

DET 1901 AL
SP R Miller
SP E Siever
SP J Cronin
SP J Yeager
C - F Buelow
1B- P Dillon
2B K Gleason
SS K Elberfeld
3B D Casey
LF D Nance
CF J Barrett
RF D Holmes
IC S McAllister
M G Stallings

MIL 1901 AL
SP B Reidy
SR N Garvin
SP B Husting
SP T Sparks
SP P Hawley
C B Maloney
1B J Anderson
2B B Gilbert
SS W Conroy
3B- J Burke
RL B Hallman
CF- H Duffy
RF- I Waldron
3O B Friel

PHI 1901 AL
SP C Fraser
SP E Plank
SP B Bernhard
SP S Wiltse
SP W Piatt
C D Powers
1B H Davis
2B N Lajoie
S3 J Dolan
3B L Cross
LF- M McIntyre
MU D Fultz
RU S Seybold
M C Mack

WAS 1901 AL
SP B Carrick
SP W Lee
SP C Patten
SP W Mercer
SP D Gear
C B Clarke
1C M Grady
2M J Farrell
SS B Clingman
3B B Coughlin
LF P Foster
CF- I Waldron
R1 S Dungan
M J Manning

BOS 1902 NL
SP V Willis
SP T Pittinger
SP M Eason
SP J Malarkey
C - M Kittridge
1B F Tenney
2B De Montreville
SS H Long
3B E Gremminger
LU D Cooley
CF B Lush
RF P Carney
C - P Moran
M A Buckenberger

BRO 1902 NL
SP B Donovan
SP F Kitson
SP D Newton
SP J Hughes
SP R Evans
C - H Hearne
1B T McCreery
2B T Flood
SS B Dahlen
3B C Irwin
LF J Sheckard
CF C Dolan
RF W Keeler
C1- D Farrell
M N Hanlon

CHI 1902 NL
SP J Taylor
SP P Williams
SP J Menefee
SP C Lundgren
SP B Rhoads
RP J St.Vrain
C J Kling
1C- F Chance
2B B Lowe
SS J Tinker
3B- G Schaefer
LF J Slagle
CF- J Dobbs
MR- D Jones
31- C Dexter
M F Selee

CIN 1902 NL
SP N Hahn
SP B Phillips
SP H Thielman
SP E Poole
SP B Ewing
C B Bergen
1B J Beckley
IC H Peitz
SS T Corcoran
3B H Steinfeldt
LF- J Dobbs
CF- D Hoy
RF S Crawford
M1 B McPhee
M2 F Bancroft
M3 J Kelley

NY 1902 NL
SP C Mathewson
SP D Taylor
SP R Evans
SP J McGinnity
SP T Sparks
RP J Cronin
C F Bowerman
1B- D McGann
2B H Smith
SS- J Bean
3B B Lauder
LO- J Jones
CF S Brodie
UT J Dunn
LF- G Browne
M1 H Fogel
M3 J McGraw

PHI 1902 NL
SP D White
SP B Duggleby
SP H Iburg
SP C Fraser
C R Dooin
1B- H Jennings
2B P Childs
SS R Hulswitt
3B- B Hallman
LF- G Browne
CF R Thomas
RF S Barry
1C K Douglass
M B Shettsline

PIT 1902 NL
SP J Chesbro
SP D Phillippe
SP J Tannehill
SP S Leever
SP E Doheny
C - H Smith
1B K Bransfield
2B C Ritchey
SS W Conroy
3B T Leach
LF F Clarke
CF G Beaumont
UT H Wagner

STL 1902 NL
SP M O'Neill
SP S Yerkes
SP E Murphy
SP B Wicker
SP C Currie
C - J Ryan
1U R Brashear
2B J Farrell
SS O Krueger
3B F Hartman
LF G Barclay
CF H Smoot
RF P Donovan
1B- A Nichols

BAL 1902 AL
SP J McGinnity
SP H Howell
SP S Wiltse
SP C Shields
SP J Katoll
RP I Butler
RP T Hughes
C W Robinson
1B- D McGann
2B J Williams
SS B Gilbert
IC- R Bresnahan
LF K Selbach
CF- H McFarland
RF- C Seymour
M1 J McGraw

BOS 1902 AL
SP C Young
SP B Dinneen
SP G Winter
SP T Sparks
C L Criger
1B C LaChance
2B H Ferris
SS F Parent
3B J Collins
LF P Dougherty
CF C Stahl
RF B Freeman
UT- H Gleason

CHI 1902 AL
SP N Callahan
SP R Patterson
SP W Piatt

SP C Griffith
SP N Garvin
C - B Sullivan
1B F Isbell
2B T Daly
SS G Davis
3B S Strang
LF S Mertes
CF F Jones
RF D Green
C - E McFarland

CLE 1902 AL
SP E Moore
SP A Joss
SP B Bernhard
SP G Wright
C H Bemis
1B C Hickman
2B N Lajoie
SS J Gochnauer
3B B Bradley
LF J McCarthy
MO H Bay
RF E Flick
CF- O Pickering
CU- B Wood
M B Armour

DET 1902 AL
SP W Mercer
SP G Mullin
SP E Siever
SP R Miller
SP J Yeager
C - D McGuire
1B- P Dillon
2B K Gleason
SS K Elberfeld
3B D Casey
LF D Harley
CF J Barrett
RF D Holmes
M F Dwyer

PHI 1902 AL
SP E Plank
SP R Waddell
SP B Husting
SP S Wiltse
SP F Mitchell
RP H Wilson
C - O
Schreckengost
1B H Davis
2B- D Murphy
SS M Cross
3B L Cross
LF T Hartsel
CF D Fultz
RF S Seybold
C - D Powers
M C Mack

STL 1902 AL
SP J Powell
SP R Donahue
SP J Harper
SP W Sudhoff
SP B Reidy
C - J Sugden
1B J Anderson
2B D Padden
SS B Wallace
3B B McCormick
LF J Burkett
CF E Heidrick
RM C Hemphill
UT- B Friel
M J McAleer

WAS 1902 AL
SP A Orth
SP C Patten
SP B Carrick
SP H Townsend
C B Clarke
1B S Carey
2B- J Doyle
SS B Ely
3S B Coughlin
LF E Delahanty
CF J Ryan
UO W Lee
UT B Keister
M T Loftus

BOS 1903 NL
SP T Pittinger
SP V Willis
SP J Malarkey
SP W Piatt
C P Moran
1B F Tenney
2B E Abbaticchio
SS H Aubrey
3B E Gremminger
LF D Cooley
MU C Dexter
RF P Carney
OI J Stanley
M A Buckenberger

BRO 1903 NL
SP O Jones
SP H Schmidt
SP N Garvin
SP R Evans
SP B Reidy
C - L Ritter
1B J Doyle
2B T Flood
SS B Dahlen
3B S Strang
LF J Sheckard
CF J Dobbs
RF- W McCredie
2U- D Jordan
M N Hanlon

CHI 1903 NL
SP J Taylor
SP J Weimer
SP B Wicker
SP C Lundgren
SP J Menefee
C J Kling
1B F Chance
2B J Evers
SS J Tinker
3B D Casey
LF J Slagle
MR D Jones
RF D Harley
M F Selee

CIN 1903 NL
SP N Hahn
SP B Ewing
SP J Sutthoff
SP E Poole
SP J Harper
RP B Phillips
CU H Peitz
1B J Beckley
2B- T Daly
SS T Corcoran
3B H Steinfeldt
LR M Donlin
CF C Seymour
RF C Dolan
LI J Kelley

NY 1903 NL
SP J McGinnity
SP C Mathewson
SP D Taylor
SP J Cronin
C J Warner
1B D McGann
2B B Gilbert
SS C Babb
3B B Lauder
LF S Mertes
MU R Bresnahan
RF G Browne
IO- J Dunn
CF- G Van Haltren
M J McGraw

PHI 1903 NL
SP B Duggleby
SP C Fraser
SP T Sparks
SP F Mitchell
SP J McFetridge
C - F Roth
1B K Douglass
2B K Gleason
SS R Hulswitt
3B H Wolverton
LF S Barry
CF R Thomas
RF B Keister
RL- J Titus
M C Zimmer

PIT 1903 NL
SP D Phillippe
SP S Leever
SP E Doheny
SP B Kennedy
SP K Wilhelm
C - E Phelps
1B K Bransfield
2B C Ritchey
SS H Wagner
3B T Leach
LF F Clarke
CF G Beaumont
RF J Sebring
IO- O Krueger

STL 1903 NL
SP C McFarland
SP M Brown
SP C Currie
SP M O'Neill
SP B Rhoads
RP E Murphy
RP J Dunleavy
C - J O'Neill
1B J Hackett
2B J Farrell
S3 D Brain
3B J Burke
LF G Barclay
CF H Smoot
RF P Donovan

BOS 1903 AL
SP C Young
SP B Dinneen
SP T Hughes
SP N Gibson
SP G Winter
C L Criger
1B C LaChance
2B H Ferris
SS F Parent
3B J Collins
LF P Dougherty
CF- C Stahl
RF B Freeman
MU J O'Brien

CHI 1903 AL
SP D White
SP P Flaherty
SP R Patterson
SP F Owen
C - J Slattery
1B F Isbell
2B G Magoon
SS L Tannehill
3B N Callahan
LF D Holmes
CF F Jones
RF D Green
M J Callahan

CLE 1903 AL
SP A Joss
SP E Moore
SP B Bernhard
SP R Donahue
SP G Wright
C H Bemis
1B C Hickman
2B N Lajoie
SS J Gochnauer
3B B Bradley
LF J McCarthy
CF H Bay
RF E Flick
C - F Abbott
M B Armour

DET 1903 AL
SP G Mullin
SP B Donovan
SP F Kitson
SP R Kisinger
C - D McGuire
1B C Carr
2B H Smith
SU- S McAllister
3B J Yeager
LU B Lush
CF J Barrett
RL S Crawford
S2- H Long
M E Barrow

NY 1903 AL
SP J Chesbro
SP J Tannehill
SP C Griffith
SR H Howell
SP B Wolfe
C M Beville
1B J Ganzel
2B J Williams
SS K Elberfeld
3B W Conroy
LF L Davis
ML H McFarland
RF W Keeler
CF- D Fultz

PHI 1903 AL
SP E Plank
SP R Waddell
SP C Bender
SP W Henley
C O
Schreckengost
1B H Davis
2B D Murphy
SS M Cross
3B L Cross
LF T Hartsel
CF O Pickering
RF S Seybold
LR- D Hoffman
C - D Powers
M C Mack

STL 1903 AL
SP J Powell
SP W Sudhoff
SP E Siever
SP R Donahue
C - M Kahoe
1B J Anderson
2U B Friel
SS B Wallace
3B H Hill
LF J Burkett
CF E Heidrick
RF C Hemphill
C - J Sugden
M J McAleer

WAS 1903 AL
SP C Patten
SP A Orth
SP H Wilson
SP H Townsend
SP D Dunkle
C - M Kittridge
1C B Clarke
2B- B McCormick
SS C Moran
3B B Coughlin
LF K Selbach
CF J Ryan
Rp- W Lee
UT R Robinson
M T Loftus

BOS 1904 NL
SP V Willis
SP T Pittinger
SP K Wilhelm
SR T Fisher
SP E McNichol
C - T Needham
1B F Tenney
2B F Raymer
SS E Abbaticchio
3B J Delahanty
LF D Cooley
CF P Geier
RO R Cannell
C3 P Moran
RF- P Carney
M A Buckenberger

BRO 1904 NL
SP O Jones
SP J Cronin
SP N Garvin
SP E Poole
SP D Scanlan
C B Bergen
1B P Dillon
2B- D Jordan
SS C Babb
3B M McCormick
LF J Sheckard
CF J Dobbs
RF H Lumley
MU D Gessler
M N Hanlon

CHI 1904 NL
SP J Weimer
SP B Briggs
SP C Lundgren
SP B Wicker
SP M Brown
RP F Corridon
C J Kling
1B F Chance
2B J Evers
SS J Tinker
3B D Casey
LF J Slagle
CF J McCarthy
RF D Jones
M F Selee

CIN 1904 NL
SP N Hahn
SP J Harper
SP W Kellum
SP T Walker
SP B Ewing
C A Schlei
1B J Kelley
2B M Huggins
SS T Corcoran
3B H Steinfeldt
LF F Odwell
CF C Seymour
RU C Dolan
C - H Peitz
3I- S Woodruff

NY 1904 NL
SP J McGinnity
SP C Mathewson
SP D Taylor
SP H Wiltse
SP R Ames
C - J Warner
1B D McGann
2B B Gilbert
SS B Dahlen
3B A Devlin
LF S Mertes
MU R Bresnahan
RF G Browne
C - F Bowerman
M J McGraw

PHI 1904 NL
SP C Fraser
SP B Duggleby
SP T Sparks
SP J Sutthoff
SP J McPherson
RP F Mitchell
C R Dooin
1B- J Doyle
2B K Gleason
SS R Hulswitt
3B H Wolverton
LU J Titus
CF R Thomas
RF S Magee
1R J Lush
C - F Roth
M H Duffy

PIT 1904 NL
SP S Leever
SP P Flaherty
SP M Lynch
SP D Phillippe
SP C Case
RP R Miller
C E Phelps
1B K Bransfield
2B C Ritchey
SS H Wagner
3B T Leach
LF- F Clarke
CF G Beaumont
RF- J Sebring
UT- O Krueger

STL 1904 NL
SP J Taylor
SP K Nichols
SP C McFarland
SP M O'Neill
SP J Corbett
C M Grady
1B J Beckley
2B J Farrell
SS D Shay
3B J Burke
LF G Barclay
CF H Smoot
RF S Shannon
UT D Brain

BOS 1904 AL
SP C Young
SP B Dinneen
SP J Tannehill
SP N Gibson
SP G Winter
C L Criger
1B C LaChance
2B H Ferris
SS F Parent
3B J Collins
LF K Selbach
CF C Stahl
RF B Freeman

CHI 1904 AL
SP F Owen
SP N Altrock
SP D White
SP F Smith
SP R Patterson
RS E Walsh
C B Sullivan
1B J Donahue
2B G Dundon
SS G Davis
3B L Tannehill
LF N Callahan
CF F Jones
RF D Green
12 F Isbell
M1 J Callahan

CLE 1904 AL
SP B Bernhard
SP R Donahue
SP E Moore
SP A Joss
SP B Rhoads
RP O Hess
C H Bemis
21- C Hickman
2S N Lajoie
SS T Turner
3B B Bradley
LF B Lush
CF H Bay
RF E Flick
M B Armour

DET 1904 AL
SP G Mullin
SP E Killian
SP B Donovan
SP F Kitson
SP J Stovall
C - L Drill
1B- C Carr
2B B Lowe
SS C O'Leary
3B- E Gremminger
LF M McIntyre
CF J Barrett
RF S Crawford
UT R Robinson
M1 E Barrow

NY 1904 AL
SP J Chesbro
SP J Powell
SP A Orth
SP T Hughes
SP C Griffith
C D McGuire
1B J Ganzel
2B J Williams
SS K Elberfeld
3B W Conroy
LF P Dougherty
OI J Anderson
RF W Keeler
CF D Fultz

PHI 1904 AL
SP R Waddell
SP E Plank
SP W Henley
SP C Bender
C O
Schreckengost
1B H Davis
2B D Murphy
SS M Cross
3B L Cross
LF T Hartsel
CF O Pickering
RF S Seybold
M C Mack

STL 1904 AL
SP B Pelty
SP H Howell
SP F Glade
SP W Sudhoff
SP E Siever
C J Sugden
1B T Jones
2B D Padden
SS B Wallace
3B- C Moran
LF J Burkett
CF E Heidrick
RO C Hemphill
M J McAleer

WAS 1904 AL
SP C Patten
SP H Townsend
SP B Jacobson
SP B Wolfe
SP T Hughes
C - M Kittridge
1B J Stahl
2B B McCormick
SU J Cassidy
3B- H Hill
LF- F Huelsman
CF B O'Neill
RF P Donovan
C1- B Clarke

BOS 1905 NL
SP I Young
SP V Willis
SP C Fraser
SP K Wilhelm
C - P Moran
1B F Tenney
2B F Raymer
SS E Abbaticchio
3B H Wolverton
LF J Delahanty
CF R Cannell
RF C Dolan
C - T Needham

BRO 1905 NL
SP H McIntire
SP D Scanlan
SP E Stricklett
SP M Eason
SP O Jones
RP F Mitchell
C - L Ritter
1B D Gessler
2U C Malay
SS P Lewis
3B E Batch
LF J Sheckard
CF J Dobbs
RF H Lumley
C - B Bergen
M N Hanlon

CHI 1905 NL
SP E Reulbach
SP J Weimer
SP M Brown
SP B Wicker
SP C Lundgren
RP B Briggs
RP B Pfeffer
C J Kling
1B F Chance
2B J Evers
SS J Tinker
3B D Casey
LF F Schulte
CF J Slagle
RF B Maloney
2U- S Hofman
M1 F Selee

CIN 1905 NL
SP O Overall
SP B Ewing
SR C Chech
SP J Harper
SP T Walker
C A Schlei
1B S Barry
2B M Huggins
SS T Corcoran
3B H Steinfeldt
LF- J Kelley
CF C Seymour
RL F Odwell
3U- A Bridwell

NY 1905 NL
SP C Mathewson
SP J McGinnity
SP R Ames
SP D Taylor
SR H Wiltse
C R Bresnahan
1B D McGann
2B B Gilbert
SS B Dahlen
3B A Devlin
LF S Mertes
CF M Donlin
RF G Browne
CU F Bowerman
UT S Strang
M J McGraw

PHI 1905 NL
SP T Pittinger
SP B Duggleby
SP T Sparks
SP F Corridon
SP K Nichols
C R Dooin
1B K Bransfield
2B K Gleason
SS M Doolan
3B E Courtney
LF S Magee
CF R Thomas
RF J Titus
M H Duffy

PIT 1905 NL
SP D Phillippe
SP S Leever
SP C Case
SR M Lynch
SP P Flaherty
RP C Robitaille
C - H Peitz
1U D Howard
2B C Ritchey
SS H Wagner
3B- D Brain
LF F Clarke
CF G Beaumont
RF O Clymer
UT T Leach

STL 1905 NL
SP J Taylor
SP C McFarland
SP J Thielman
SP B Brown
SP W Egan
CU M Grady
1B J Beckley
2B H Arndt
SS- G McBride
3B J Burke
LF S Shannon
CF H Smoot
RF J Dunleavy
2S- D Shay
M1 K Nichols
M3 S Robison

BOS 1905 AL
SP C Young
SP J Tannehill
SP G Winter
SP B Dinneen
SP N Gibson
C L Criger
1B- M Grimshaw
2B H Ferris
SS F Parent
3B J Collins
LF J Burkett
CF C Stahl
RF K Selbach
1R B Freeman

CHI 1905 AL
SP F Owen
SP N Altrock
SP F Smith
SP D White
SP E Walsh
C B Sullivan
1B J Donahue
2B G Dundon
SS G Davis
3B L Tannehill
LU N Callahan
CF F Jones
RF D Green
LF- D Holmes
UT- F Isbell
C - E McFarland

CLE 1905 AL
SP A Joss
SP E Moore
SP B Rhoads
SP O Hess
SP B Bernhard
RP R Donahue
C - F Buelow
1B- C Carr
2B- N Lajoie
SS T Turner
3B B Bradley
LF J Jackson
CF H Bay
RF E Flick
12 G Stovall
M3 N Lajoie

DET 1905 AL
SP G Mullin
SP E Killian
SP B Donovan
SP F Kitson
C - L Drill
1B- C Lindsay
2B G Schaefer
SS C O'Leary
3B B Coughlin
LF M McIntyre
CF D Cooley
R1 S Crawford
M B Armour

NY 1905 AL
SP A Orth
SP J Chesbro
SR B Hogg
SR J Powell
RS C Griffith
C - R Kleinow
1B H Chase
2B J Williams
SS K Elberfeld
3B J Yeager
LF P Dougherty
CF D Fultz
RF W Keeler
UT W Conroy

PHI 1905 AL
SP E Plank
SR R Waddell
SP A Coakley
SR C Bender
SP W Henley

C O
Schreckengost
1B H Davis
2B D Murphy
SS- J Knight
3B L Cross
LF T Hartsel
CF D Hoffman
RF S Seybold
SS- M Cross
M C Mack

STL 1905 AL
SP H Howell
SP F Glade
SP B Pelty
SP W Sudhoff
SP J Buchanan
C - J Sugden
1B T Jones
2B I Rockenfield
SS B Wallace
3B H Gleason
LF G Stone
CF B Koehler
RF E Frisk
OI I Van Zandt
M J McAleer

WAS 1905 AL
SP C Patten
SP T Hughes
SR H Townsend
SP B Wolfe
SP B Jacobson
C - M Heydon
1B J Stahl
2B- C Hickman
SS J Cassidy
3B H Hill
LF F Huelsman
CF C Jones
RF J Anderson
32 R Nill
C - M Kittridge
RU- P Knoll

BOS 1906 NL
SP I Young
SP V Lindaman
SP B Pfeffer
SP G Dorner
C - T Needham
1B F Tenney
2B A Strobel
SS A Bridwell
3B D Brain
L2 D Howard
CF J Bates
RF C Dolan

BRO 1906 NL
SP E Stricklett
SP D Scanlan
SP H McIntire
SP M Eason
SP J Pastorius
C B Bergen
1B T Jordan
2B W Alperman
SS P Lewis
3B D Casey
LF- J McCarthy
CF B Maloney
RF H Lumley
2U J Hummel
M P Donovan

CHI 1906 NL
SP M Brown
SP J Pfiester
SP E Reulbach
SP C Lundgren
SP J Taylor
RP O Overall
C J Kling
1B F Chance
2B J Evers
SS J Tinker
3B H Steinfeldt
LF J Sheckard
CF J Slagle
RF F Schulte

CIN 1906 NL
SP J Weimer
SP B Ewing
SP C Fraser
SP B Wicker
SP C Hall
C A Schlei
1B- S Deal
2B M Huggins
SS T Corcoran
3B J Delahanty
LF J Kelley
CF- C Seymour
RF- F Jude
IO- H Lobert
M N Hanlon

NY 1906 NL
SP J McGinnity
SP C Mathewson
SR H Wiltse
SP D Taylor
SP R Ames
RP G Ferguson
CM R Bresnahan
1B D McGann
2B B Gilbert
SS B Dahlen
3B A Devlin
LF- S Shannon
CF- C Seymour
RF G Browne
CU F Bowerman
2O S Strang
M J McGraw

PHI 1906 NL
SP T Sparks
SR B Duggleby
SP J Lush
SR L Richie
SP T Pittinger
C R Dooin
1B K Bransfield
2B K Gleason
SS M Doolan
3B E Courtney
LF S Magee
CF R Thomas
RF J Titus
M H Duffy

PIT 1906 NL
SP V Willis
SP S Leever
SP L Leifield
SP D Phillippe
SP M Lynch
C - G Gibson
1B J Nealon
2B C Ritchey
SS H Wagner
3B T Sheehan
LF F Clarke
CF- G Beaumont
RF B Ganley
UT T Leach
OI- D Meier

STL 1906 NL
SP B Brown
SP E Karger
SP F Beebe
SP J Taylor
SP C Druhot
RP G Thompson
C1 M Grady
1B- J Beckley
2B P Bennett
SS- G McBride
3B- H Arndt
LF- S Shannon
MR-H Smoot
MR-A Burch
3U A Hoelskoetter
M J McCloskey

BOS 1906 AL
SP C Young
SP J Harris
SP B Dinneen
SP G Winter
SP J Tannehill
RP R Glaze
C - C Armbruster
1B M Grimshaw
2B H Ferris
SS F Parent
3B- R Morgan
LF J Hoey
CF C Stahl
RF- J Hayden
R1 B Freeman
M1 J Collins

CHI 1906 AL
SP F Owen
SP N Altrock
SR E Walsh
SP D White
SP R Patterson
RP F Smith
C B Sullivan
1B J Donahue
2B F Isbell
SS G Davis
3B L Tannehill
RL E Hahn
CF F Jones
RF B O'Neill
3U- G Rohe

CLE 1906 AL
SP O Hess
SP B Rhoads
SP A Joss
SP B Bernhard
C - H Bemis
1B C Rossman
2B N Lajoie
SS T Turner
3B- B Bradley
LF J Jackson
MR E Flick
RF B Congalton
UI G Stovall

DET 1906 AL
SP G Mullin
SP R Donahue
SP E Siever
SP B Donovan
SP E Killian
RS J Eubank
C - B Schmidt
1B C Lindsay
2B G Schaefer
SS C O'Leary
3B B Coughlin
LF M McIntyre
MO T Cobb
RF S Crawford
CF- D Jones
M B Armour

NY 1906 AL
SP A Orth
SP J Chesbro
SP B Hogg
SR W Clarkson
SP D Newton
C R Kleinow
1B H Chase
2B J Williams
SS K Elberfeld
3B F LaPorte
UT W Conroy
CF D Hoffman
RF W Keeler
LF- F Delahanty
M C Griffith

PHI 1906 AL
SP R Waddell
SP C Bender
SR J Dygert
SP E Plank
SP J Coombs
RP A Coakley
C O
Schreckengost
1B H Davis
2B D Murphy
SS M Cross
3B- J Knight
LF T Hartsel
CF B Lord
RF S Seybold
OF H Armbruster
M C Mack

STL 1906 AL
SP H Howell
SP F Glade
SP B Pelty
SP J Powell
SP B Jacobson
RP E Smith
C - B Rickey
1B T Jones
2B P O'Brien
SS B Wallace
3B R Hartzell
LF G Stone
MR C Hemphill
RU H Niles
M J McAleer

WAS 1906 AL
SP C Falkenberg
SP C Patten
SR C Smith
SP T Hughes
SP F Kitson
C - H Wakefield
1B J Stahl
2B L Schlafly
SS D Altizer
3B L Cross
LF J Anderson
CF C Jones
RF C Hickman
IO- R Nill

BOS 1907 NL
SP G Dorner
SP V Lindaman
SP I Young
SP P Flaherty
SP B Pfeffer
RS J Boultes
C - T Needham
1B F Tenney
2B C Ritchey
SS A Bridwell
3B D Brain
LF- N Randall
CF G Beaumont
RF J Bates

BRO 1907 NL
SP N Rucker
SP G Bell
SP E Stricklett
SP J Pastorius
SP H McIntire
RP D Scanlan
C L Ritter
1B T Jordan
2B W Alperman
SS P Lewis
3B D Casey
LU E Batch
CF B Maloney
RF H Lumley
UT J Hummel
M P Donovan

CHI 1907 NL
SP O Overall
SP M Brown
SP C Lundgren
SP J Pfiester
SP E Reulbach
RP C Fraser
RP J Taylor
C J Kling
1B F Chance
2B J Evers
SS J Tinker
3B H Steinfeldt
LF J Sheckard
CF J Slagle
RF F Schulte
UT S Hofman

CIN 1907 NL
SP B Ewing
SP A Coakley
SP J Weimer
SP R Hitt
SP D Mason
C L McLean
1B J Ganzel
2B M Huggins
SS H Lobert
3B M Mowrey
LF F Odwell
ML A Kruger
RF M Mitchell
UT- J Kane
C - A Schlei
M N Hanlon

NY 1907 NL
SP C Mathewson
SR J McGinnity
SR R Ames
SR H Wiltse
SP D Taylor
C R Bresnahan
1B- D McGann
2B- L Doyle
SS B Dahlen
3B A Devlin
LF S Shannon
CF C Seymour
RF G Browne
C1 F Bowerman
UT S Strang
M J McGraw

PHI 1907 NL
SP F Corridon
SP T Sparks
SP L Moren
SP B Brown
SR L Richie
RP T Pittinger
C R Dooin
1B K Bransfield
2B O Knabe
SS M Doolan
31 E Courtney
LF S Magee
CF R Thomas
RF J Titus
M B Murray

PIT 1907 NL
SP V Willis
SP L Leifield
SP S Leever
SP D Phillippe
SR H Camnitz
C G Gibson
1B J Nealon
2B E Abbaticchio
SS H Wagner
3I A Storke
LF F Clarke
MI T Leach
RU G Anderson
UO- B Hallman

STL 1907 NL
SP S McGlynn
SP E Karger
SP F Beebe
SP A Fromme
SP J Lush
C - D Marshall
1B- E Konetchy
2B- P Bennett
SS E Holly
3B B Byrne
LF R Murray
CF- J Burnett
RF- S Barry
2U A Hoelskoetter
M J McCloskey

BOS 1907 AL
SP C Young
SP G Winter
SR R Glaze
SR T Pruiett
SP J Tannehill
RP C Morgan
C - L Criger
1B B Unglaub
2B H Ferris
SS H Wagner
3B J Knight
LF J Barrett
CF D Sullivan
RF B Congalton
UT F Parent
M2 G Huff
M4 D McGuire

CHI 1907 AL
SR E Walsh
SP F Smith
SR D White
SP N Altrock
SP R Patterson
C B Sullivan
1B J Donahue
2B F Isbell
SS G Davis
32 G Rohe
LF P Dougherty
CF F Jones
RF E Hahn

CLE 1907 AL
SP A Joss
SP G Liebhardt
SP B Rhoads
SP J Thielman
C N Clarke
1B G Stovall
2B N Lajoie
SS T Turner
3B B Bradley
LF B Hinchman
MU J Birmingham
RF E Flick

DET 1907 AL
SP G Mullin
SP E Killian
SP E Siever
SP B Donovan
C B Schmidt
1B C Rossman
2B R Downs
SS C O'Leary
3B B Coughlin
LF D Jones
CF S Crawford
RF T Cobb
2I G Schaefer
M H Jennings

NY 1907 AL
SP A Orth
SP J Chesbro
SP S Doyle
SP B Hogg
SP D Newton
C - R Kleinow
1B H Chase
2B J Williams
SS K Elberfeld
3U G Moriarty
LS W Conroy
CF D Hoffman
RF W Keeler
UT F LaPorte
C - I Thomas
M C Griffith

PHI 1907 AL
SP E Plank
SR R Waddell
SR J Dygert
SP C Bender
SP J Coombs
C O
Schreckengost
1B H Davis
2B D Murphy
SI S Nicholls
3B J Collins
LF T Hartsel
CF R Oldring
RF S Seybold
SS- M Cross
M C Mack

STL 1907 AL
SP H Howell
SP B Pelty
SP J Powell
SP F Glade
SP B Dinneen
C - T Spencer
1B T Jones
2B H Niles
SS B Wallace
3U J Yeager
LF G Stone
CF C Hemphill
RF O Pickering
M J McAleer

WAS 1907 AL
SP C Smith
SP C Patten
SP C Falkenberg
SR T Hughes
SP W Johnson
RP O Graham
C - J Warner
1L- J Anderson
23 J Delahanty
S1 D Altizer
3B- B Shipke
OI- O Clymer
MU C Jones
RL B Ganley
M J Cantillon

BOS 1908 NL
SR V Lindaman
SP P Flaherty
SR G Dorner
SR G Ferguson
CU- F Bowerman
1B D McGann
2B C Ritchey
SS B Dahlen
3B B Sweeney
LF J Bates
CF G Beaumont
RF G Browne
UT- J Hannifin
M J Kelley

BRO 1908 NL
SP N Rucker
SP K Wilhelm
SP H McIntire
SP J Pastorius
SR G Bell
C B Bergen
1B T Jordan
2B- H Pattee
SS P Lewis
3B T Sheehan
UO A Burch
CF B Maloney
RF H Lumley
L2 J Hummel
M P Donovan

CHI 1908 NL
SR M Brown
SR E Reulbach
SP J Pfiester
SR O Overall
SP C Fraser
RP C Lundgren
C J Kling
1B F Chance
2B J Evers
SS J Tinker
3B H Steinfeldt
LF J Sheckard
ML J Slagle
RF F Schulte
UT S Hofman
RM D Howard

CIN 1908 NL
SP B Ewing
SP B Spade
SP A Coakley
SR B Campbell
SP J Weimer
C - A Schlei
1B J Ganzel
2B M Huggins
SS R Hulswitt
3U H Lobert
LM D Paskert
CF J Kane
RF M Mitchell
CU L McLean

NY 1908 NL
SR C Mathewson
SR H Wiltse
SP D Crandall
SR J McGinnity
SR D Taylor
RP R Ames
C R Bresnahan
1B F Tenney
2B L Doyle
SS A Bridwell
3B A Devlin
LF- S Shannon
CF C Seymour
RF M Donlin
M J McGraw

PHI 1908 NL
SP G McQuillan
SP T Sparks
SP F Corridon
SR L Richie
SR L Moren
RP B Foxen
C R Dooin
1B K Bransfield
2B O Knabe
SS M Doolan
3B E Grant
LF S Magee
CF F Osborn
RF J Titus
M B Murray

PIT 1908 NL
SP V Willis
SP N Maddox
SR H Camnitz
SP L Leifield
SR S Leever
C G Gibson
1B- H Swacina
2B E Abbaticchio
SS H Wagner
3B T Leach
LF F Clarke
CF R Thomas
RF C Wilson

STL 1908 NL
SR B Raymond
SP J Lush
SR F Beebe
SR E Karger
SR S Sallee
RP A Fromme
RP I Higginbotham
C - B Ludwig
1B E Konetchy
2B- B Gilbert
SS- P O'Rourke
3B B Byrne
LF J Delahanty
MU A Shaw
MR R Murray
2S C Charles
M J McCloskey

BOS 1908 AL
SP C Young
SR E Cicotte
SP C Morgan
SR F Burchell
SP G Winter
RP E Steele
C - L Criger
1B- J Stahl
2B A McConnell
SS H Wagner
3B H Lord
LF J Thoney
CF D Sullivan
RF D Gessler
LU G Cravath
M1 D McGuire
M2 F Lake

CHI 1908 AL
SR E Walsh
SP F Smith
SP D White
SR F Owen
SR N Altrock
C B Sullivan
1B- J Donahue
2U G Davis
SS F Parent
3B L Tannehill
LF P Dougherty
CF F Jones
RO E Hahn
RU J Anderson
2U- J Atz
1B- F Isbell

CLE 1908 AL
SP A Joss
SP B Rhoads
SR G Liebhardt
SP H Berger
SP C Chech
C N Clarke
1B G Stovall
2B N Lajoie
S3- G Perring
3B B Bradley
LF J Clarke
CF J Birmingham
UT B Hinchman
C - H Bemis

DET 1908 AL
SP E Summers
SP G Mullin
SP B Donovan
SP E Willett
SP E Killian
C B Schmidt
1B C Rossman
2B- R Downs
UI G Schaefer
3B B Coughlin
LF M McIntyre
CF S Crawford
RF T Cobb
M H Jennings

NY 1908 AL
SR J Chesbro
SR J Lake
SR R Manning
SP B Hogg
SP A Orth
C R Kleinow
1B H Chase
2B H Niles
SS N Ball
3B W Conroy
LF- J Stahl
CF C Hemphill
RF- W Keeler
13 G Moriarty
M1 C Griffith
M2 K Elberfeld

PHI 1908 AL
SR R Vickers
SP E Plank
SR J Dygert
SP J Coombs
SP C Bender
RP B Schlitzer
C - O
Schreckengost
1B H Davis
UT E Collins
SS S Nicholls
3B J Collins
LF T Hartsel
CF R Oldring
UT D Murphy
M C Mack

STL 1908 AL
SP H Howell
SP R Waddell
SP J Powell
SR B Dinneen
SP B Pelty
RP B Grahame
RS B Bailey
C - T Spencer
1B T Jones
2B J Williams
SS B Wallace
3B H Ferris
LF G Stone
UO D Hoffman
RI R Hartzell
M J McAleer

WAS 1908 AL
SR T Hughes
SP W Johnson
SP C Smith
SR B Keeley
SP B Burns
RP E Cates
C G Street
1B J Freeman

2B- J Delahanty
SS G McBride
3B B Shipke
LF B Ganley
CF C Milan
RU O Pickering
RU O Clymer
M J Cantillon

BOS 1909 NL
SR A Mattern
SP G Ferguson
SP K White
SP L Richie
SP B Brown
C - P Graham
1B- F Stem
2B- D Shean
SS- J Coffey
3B B Sweeney
LF- R Thomas
CF G Beaumont
RF B Becker
OI F Beck
M1 F Bowerman
M2 H Smith

BRO 1909 NL
SP N Rucker
SP G Bell
SP H McIntire
SP K Wilhelm
SP D Scanlan
RP G Hunter
C B Bergen
1B T Jordan
2B W Alperman
SS T McMillan
3B E Lennox
LF- W Clement
ML A Burch
RF- H Lumley
UT J Hummel
UT- P McElveen

CHI 1909 NL
SR M Brown
SP O Overall
SP E Reulbach
SP J Pfiester
SP R Kroh
C - J Archer
1B F Chance
2B J Evers
SS J Tinker
3B H Steinfeldt
LF J Sheckard
CF S Hofman
RF F Schulte

CIN 1909 NL
SP A Fromme
SR H Gaspar
SR J Rowan
SP B Ewing
SR B Campbell
RP B Spade
C L McLean
1B D Hoblitzel
2B D Egan
SS T Downey
3B H Lobert
LF B Bescher
CF R Oakes
RF M Mitchell
OI D Paskert
M C Griffith

NY 1909 NL
SP C Mathewson
SP H Wiltse
SP B Raymond
SP R Ames
SP R Marquard
RS D Crandall
C - A Schlei
1B F Tenney
2B L Doyle
SS A Bridwell
3B A Devlin
LF M McCormick
CF B O'Hara
RF R Murray
1B- F Merkle
CU- C Meyers
CF- C Seymour
M J McGraw

PHI 1909 NL
SP E Moore
SP L Moren
SR G McQuillan
SP F Corridon
SP H Coveleski
RP T Sparks
C R Dooin
1B K Bransfield
2B O Knabe
SS M Doolan
3B E Grant
LF S Magee
CF- J Bates
RF J Titus
M B Murray

PIT 1909 NL
SP V Willis
SR H Camnitz
SP N Maddox
SP L Leifield
SR B Adams
RP D Phillippe
C G Gibson
1B B Abstein
2B D Miller
SS H Wagner
3B- J Barbeau
LF F Clarke
CF T Leach
RF C Wilson

STL 1909 NL
SR F Beebe
SP J Lush
SR S Sallee
SP B Harmon
SP L Backman
RP S Melter
C E Phelps
1B E Konetchy
2S C Charles
SS- R Hulswitt
3B B Byrne
LF R Ellis
CF A Shaw
RF S Evans
OI J Delahanty
M R Bresnahan

BOS 1909 AL
SR F Arellanes
SR E Cicotte
SP J Wood
SP C Chech
C B Carrigan
1B J Stahl
2B A McConnell
SS H Wagner
3B H Lord
LO H Niles
CF T Speaker
RF D Gessler
LF- H Hooper
M F Lake

CHI 1909 AL
SR F Smith
SP J Scott
SP E Walsh
SP D White
SP B Burns
C B Sullivan
1B F Isbell
2B J Atz
SO F Parent
3S L Tannehill
LF P Dougherty
OI D Altizer
RF- E Hahn
32 B Purtell

CLE 1909 AL
SP C Young
SP H Berger
SP A Joss
SP C Falkenberg
SP B Rhoads
C T Easterly
1B G Stovall
2B N Lajoie
SS N Ball
3B B Bradley
LM B Hinchman
CF J Birmingham
RF W Good
3B- G Perring
M2 D McGuire

DET 1909 AL
SP G Mullin
SP E Willett
SP E Summers
SP E Killian
SP B Donovan
C - B Schmidt
1B- C Rossman
2B- G Schaefer
SS D Bush
3B G Moriarty
LF M McIntyre
CF S Crawford
RF T Cobb
M H Jennings

NY 1909 AL
SR J Warhop
SP J Lake
SP R Manning
SP L Brockett
SP S Doyle
RP T Hughes
RS J Quinn
RP P Wilson
C - R Kleinow
1B H Chase
2B- F LaPorte
SI J Knight
3B J Austin
LF C Engle
MR R Demmitt
RF W Keeler
UT B Cree
S3 K Elberfeld
M G Stallings

PHI 1909 AL
SP E Plank
SP C Bender
SP C Morgan
SR H Krause
SP J Coombs
RS J Dygert
C - I Thomas
1B H Davis
2B E Collins
SS J Barry
3B F Baker
LF- T Hartsel
ML- R Oldring
RF D Murphy
CF- B Ganley
M C Mack

STL 1909 AL
SP J Powell
SP R Waddell
SP B Pelty
SR B Bailey
SR B Grahame
RP B Dinneen
C - L Criger
1B T Jones
2B J Williams
SS B Wallace
3B H Ferris
LF- G Stone
CF D Hoffman
RS R Hartzell
UT A Griggs
OI- J McAleese
C - J Stephens
M J McAleer

WAS 1909 AL
SP W Johnson
SR B Groom
SR D Gray
SP C Smith
SP T Hughes
C G Street
1B- J Donahue
2B- J Delahanty
SS G McBride
3B W Conroy
UO- J Lelivelt
MU C Milan
LR G Browne
UT B Unglaub
M J Cantillon

BOS 1910 NL
SR A Mattern
SR B Brown
SR S Frock
SP C Curtis
SR G Ferguson
C P Graham
1B B Sharpe
2B D Shean
SI B Sweeney
3B B Herzog
LF B Collins
CF F Beck
RF D Miller
M F Lake

BRO 1910 NL
SP N Rucker
SP G Bell
SP C Barger
SP D Scanlan
SP E Knetzer
RP R Dessau
C - B Bergen
1B J Daubert
2B J Hummel
SS T Smith
3B E Lennox
LF Z Wheat
CF B Davidson
RF- J Dalton
OI A Burch
C - T Erwin
M B Dahlen

CHI 1910 NL
SR M Brown
SR K Cole
SP H McIntire
SP E Reulbach
SP O Overall
RS L Richie
RP J Pfiester
C - J Kling
1B- F Chance
2B J Evers
SS J Tinker
3B H Steinfeldt
LF J Sheckard
CF S Hofman
RF F Schulte
C1 J Archer
IO H Zimmerman

CIN 1910 NL
SR H Gaspar
SP G Suggs
SR J Rowan
SP F Beebe
SR B Burns
C L McLean
1B D Hoblitzel
2B D Egan
SS- T McMillan
3B- H Lobert
LF B Bescher
CF D Paskert
RF M Mitchell
S3 T Downey
OF- W Miller
M C Griffith

NY 1910 NL
SP C Mathewson
SP H Wiltse
SP L Drucke
SR D Crandall
SR R Ames
RP B Raymond
C C Meyers
1B F Merkle
2B L Doyle
SS A Bridwell
3B A Devlin
LF J Devore
ML F Snodgrass
RF R Murray
OI- B Becker
CF- C Seymour
M J McGraw

PHI 1910 NL
SR E Moore
SP B Ewing
SP L Moren
SP G McQuillan
SP E Stack
RS L Schettler
C R Dooin
1B K Bransfield
2B O Knabe
SS M Doolan
3B E Grant
LF S Magee
CF J Bates
RF J Titus
UT- J Walsh

PIT 1910 NL
SP H Camnitz
SP B Adams
SR L Leifield
SP K White
RS D Phillippe
RS S Leever
C G Gibson
1B J Flynn
2B D Miller
SS H Wagner
3B B Byrne
LF F Clarke
CF T Leach
RF C Wilson
UO V Campbell

STL 1910 NL
SR B Harmon
SR J Lush
SR V Willis
SR F Corridon
SR L Backman
RP S Sallee
C E Phelps
1B E Konetchy
2B M Huggins
SS A Hauser
3B M Mowrey
LF R Ellis
CF R Oakes
RF S Evans
C - R Bresnahan

BOS 1910 AL
SP E Cicotte
SP R Collins
SR J Wood
SR C Hall
SP E Karger
RP C Smith
RP F Arellanes
C B Carrigan
1B J Stahl
2B L Gardner
SS H Wagner
3B- H Lord
LF D Lewis
CF T Speaker
RF H Hooper
UT C Engle
M P Donovan

CHI 1910 AL
SP E Walsh
SP D White
SR J Scott
SR F Olmstead
SR I Young
RP F Lange
RP F Smith
C - F Payne
1B- C Gandil
2S R Zeider
SS- L Blackburne
3B B Purtell
LF P Dougherty
MU- F Parent
OI S Collins
M H Duffy

CLE 1910 AL
SP C Falkenberg
SR W Mitchell
SP C Young
SR E Koestner
SR S Harkness
RP F Link
RP A Joss
CR T Easterly
1B G Stovall
2B N Lajoie
S3 T Turner
3B- B Bradley
UO J Graney
CF J Birmingham
RL- B Lord
M D McGuire

DET 1910 AL
SP G Mullin
SR E Willett
SP E Summers
SP B Donovan
SR S Stroud
C - O Stanage
1B T Jones
2B J Delahanty
SS D Bush
3B G Moriarty
LF D Jones
CF T Cobb
RF S Crawford
LU- M McIntyre
M H Jennings

NY 1910 AL
SP R Ford
SR J Warhop
SP J Quinn
SP H Vaughn
SP T Hughes
C - E Sweeney
1B H Chase
2U F LaPorte
SI J Knight
3B J Austin
ML B Cree
MR C Hemphill
RF H Wolter
LF B Daniels
2B- E Gardner
M1 G Stallings

PHI 1910 AL
SP J Coombs
SP C Morgan
SP E Plank
SP C Bender
SP H Krause
RS J Dygert
C - J Lapp
1B H Davis
2B E Collins
SS J Barry
3B F Baker
LF- T Hartsel
CF R Oldring
RF D Murphy
M C Mack

STL 1910 AL
SP J Lake
SR B Bailey
SP B Pelty
SP F Ray
SP J Powell
C J Stephens
1B P Newnam
2B F Truesdale
S3 B Wallace
3S R Hartzell
LF G Stone
CF D Hoffman
RM A Schweitzer
UT A Griggs
M J O'Connor

WAS 1910 AL
SP W Johnson
SP B Groom
SP D Gray
SP D Walker
SR D Reisling
C - G Street
1B B Unglaub
2B R Killefer
SS G McBride
3B K Elberfeld
LU J Lelivelt
CF C Milan
RF D Gessler
UT W Conroy
M J McAleer

BOS 1911 NL
SR B Brown
SR A Mattern
SP L Tyler
SP H Perdue
SR O Weaver
RS B Pfeffer
C - J Kling
1B F Tenney
2B B Sweeney
SS- B Herzog
UT S Ingerton
LM- A Kaiser
CF- M Donlin
RF D Miller

BRO 1911 NL
SR N Rucker
SP C Barger
SR E Knetzer
SR B Schardt
SP D Scanlan
RP G Bell
RS P Ragan
C - B Bergen
1B J Daubert
2B J Hummel
SS B Tooley
3B E Zimmerman
LF Z Wheat
CF- B Davidson
RF B Coulson
C - T Erwin
M B Dahlen

CHI 1911 NL
SR M Brown
SP L Richie
SP E Reulbach
SP K Cole
SP H McIntire
RS R Richter
C J Archer
1B- V Saier
2B H Zimmerman
SS J Tinker
3B J Doyle
LF J Sheckard
M1 S Hofman
RF F Schulte
M F Chance

CIN 1911 NL
SP G Suggs
SR H Gaspar
SR B Keefe
SR A Fromme
SR F Smith
C L McLean
1B D Hoblitzel
2B D Egan
SS T Downey
3B E Grant
LF B Bescher
CF J Bates
RF M Mitchell
C - T Clarke
M C Griffith

NY 1911 NL
SP C Mathewson
SR R Marquard
SR R Ames
SR D Crandall
SP H Wiltse
C C Meyers
1B F Merkle
2B L Doyle
SS- A Bridwell
3B A Devlin
LR J Devore
CF F Snodgrass
RL R Murray
SI A Fletcher
UO- B Becker
M J McGraw

PHI 1911 NL
SR G Alexander
SP E Moore
SR G Chalmers
SP B Burns
C - R Dooin
1B F Luderus
2B O Knabe
SS M Doolan
3B H Lobert
LF S Magee
CF D Paskert
RF- F Beck
UT J Walsh

PIT 1911 NL
SP L Leifield
SP B Adams
SP H Camnitz
SR E Steele
SR C Hendrix
C G Gibson
1B- N Hunter
2B D Miller
SS H Wagner
3B B Byrne
LF F Clarke
ML M Carey
RF C Wilson
CF T Leach
1I B McKechnie

STL 1911 NL
SR B Harmon
SR B Steele
SP S Sallee
SR R Geyer
SP R Golden
C J Bliss
1B E Konetchy
2B M Huggins
SS A Hauser
3B M Mowrey
LF R Ellis
CF R Oakes
RF S Evans
C - R Bresnahan
IO- W Smith

BOS 1911 AL
SR J Wood
SR E Cicotte
SP R Collins
SP L Pape
SP E Karger
RS C Hall
C - B Carrigan
UT C Engle
2S- H Wagner
SS S Yerkes
32 L Gardner
LF D Lewis
CF T Speaker
RF H Hooper
1C R Williams
M P Donovan

CHI 1911 AL
SR E Walsh
SR J Scott
SP D White
SP F Lange
RS F Olmstead
RS I Young
RS J Baker
C - B Sullivan
1B S Collins
2B A McConnell
SI L Tannehill
3B H Lord
LF N Callahan
MU P Bodie
RF M McIntyre
M H Duffy

CLE 1911 AL
SP V Gregg
SP G Krapp
SR F Blanding
SP W Mitchell
SR G Kahler
RP C Falkenberg
C - G Fisher
1B G Stovall
2B N Ball
SS I Olson
3B T Turner
LF J Graney
CF J Birmingham
RM J Jackson
RU T Easterly
IF- N Lajoie
M1 D McGuire

DET 1911 AL
SP G Mullin
SR E Willett
SR E Summers
SP E Lafitte
SP B Donovan
RS R Works
RP J Lively
C O Stanage
UI J Delahanty
2B- C O'Leary
SS D Bush
3B G Moriarty
LF D Jones
CF T Cobb
RF S Crawford
LF D Drake
M H Jennings

NY 1911 AL
SP R Ford
SR R Caldwell
SP J Warhop
SR J Quinn
SP R Fisher
RP H Vaughn
C - W Blair
1B H Chase
2B E Gardner
SI J Knight
3B R Hartzell
LF B Cree
MO B Daniels
RF H Wolter
C - E Sweeney

PHI 1911 AL
SP J Coombs
SR E Plank
SP C Morgan
SP C Bender
SP H Krause
C I Thomas
1B S McInnis
2B E Collins
SS J Barry
3B F Baker
LF B Lord
CF R Oldring
RF D Murphy
M C Mack

STL 1911 AL
SP J Lake
SP J Powell
SP B Pelty
SR E Hamilton
SR R Mitchell
RS L George
C - N Clarke
1B- J Black
2B F LaPorte
SS B Wallace
3B J Austin
LF W Hogan
CF B Shotton
RU- A Schweitzer

WAS 1911 AL
SP W Johnson
SP B Groom
SP T Hughes
SP D Walker
SR D Gray
C - G Street
1B G Schaefer
2B B Cunningham
SS G McBride
3B W Conroy
LF T Walker
CF C Milan
RF D Gessler
23 K Elberfeld
C1- J Henry
M J McAleer

BOS 1912 NL
SR L Tyler
SP O Hess
SP H Perdue
SR W Dickson
SR E Donnelly

RS B Brown
C - J Kling
1B B Houser
2B B Sweeney
SS- F O'Rourke
3B E McDonald
LF G Jackson
CF V Campbell
RF J Titus
1I A Devlin
LU J Kirke
C - B Rariden

BRO 1912 NL
SR N Rucker
SR P Ragan
SP E Yingling
SR E Stack
SR E Knetzer
RP F Allen
RP C Barger
RS M Kent
C O Miller
1B J Daubert
2B G Cutshaw
SS- B Tooley
3B R Smith
LF Z Wheat
MR H Moran
UO H Northen
IO J Hummel
SS- B Fisher
M B Dahlen

CHI 1912 NL
SP L Cheney
SR J Lavender
SR L Richie
SR E Reulbach
RS C Smith
C J Archer
1B V Saier
2B J Evers
SS J Tinker
3B H Zimmerman
LF J Sheckard
CF- T Leach
RF F Schulte
UO- W Miller
M F Chance

CIN 1912 NL
SP G Suggs
SR R Benton
SP A Fromme
SR B Humphries
C L McLean
1B D Hoblitzel
2B D Egan
SS- J Esmond
3B A Phelan
LF B Bescher
MU A Marsans
RF M Mitchell
SU E Grant
CF- J Bates
M H O'Day

NY 1912 NL
SP C Mathewson
SP R Marquard
SP J Tesreau
SR R Ames
SR H Wiltse
RS D Crandall
C C Meyers
1B F Merkle
2B L Doyle
SS A Fletcher
3B B Herzog
UT F Snodgrass
MU B Becker
RF R Murray
LU J Devore
UI- T Shafer
M J McGraw

PHI 1912 NL
SR G Alexander
SR T Seaton
SP E Moore
SP A Brennan
SP E Rixey
RP T Shultz
C - B Killefer
1B F Luderus
2B O Knabe
SS M Doolan
3B- H Lobert
LF S Magee
CF D Paskert
RO G Cravath
M R Dooin

PIT 1912 NL
SP C Hendrix
SP H Camnitz
SP M O'Toole
SR H Robinson
SP B Adams
C G Gibson
1B D Miller
2B A McCarthy
SS H Wagner
3B B Byrne
LF M Carey
MR C Wilson
RU- M Donlin
M F Clarke

STL 1912 NL
SR S Sallee
SP B Harmon
SR B Steele
SR R Geyer
SR J Willis
RS G Woodburn
C I Wingo
1B E Konetchy
2B M Huggins
SS A Hauser
3B M Mowrey
LU L Magee
CF R Oakes
RF S Evans
LU R Ellis
M R Bresnahan

BOS 1912 AL
SP J Wood
SP B O'Brien
SR H Bedient
SP R Collins
SR C Hall
C - B Carrigan
1B J Stahl
2B S Yerkes
SS H Wagner
3B L Gardner
LF D Lewis
CF T Speaker
RF H Hooper

CHI 1912 AL
SR E Walsh
SR J Benz
SR D White
SR F Lange
SP E Cicotte
RS R Peters
C - W Kuhn
13 R Zeider
2B M Rath
SS B Weaver
3O H Lord
LF N Callahan
MR P Bodie
R1 S Collins
MU- W Mattick
M J Callahan

CLE 1912 AL
SP V Gregg
SP F Blanding
SP G Kahler
SR W Mitchell
SR B Steen
RS J Baskette
C - S O'Neill
1B- A Griggs
2B N Lajoie
SS- R Peckinpaugh
3B T Turner
LR B Ryan
CF J Birmingham
RF J Jackson
IO I Olson
LF- J Graney
M1 H Davis

DET 1912 AL
SP E Willett
SR J Dubuc
SP G Mullin
SR J Lake
SR R Works
C O Stanage
13 G Moriarty
2I B Louden
SS D Bush
3B- C Deal
LU D Jones
CF T Cobb
RF S Crawford
2L- J Delahanty
M H Jennings

NY 1912 AL
SP R Ford
SR J Warhop
SP R Caldwell
SP G McConnell
SP J Quinn
C E Sweeney
1B H Chase
2B H Simmons
SS- J Martin
UT R Hartzell
LR B Daniels
UT- D Sterrett
RM G Zinn
M H Wolverton

PHI 1912 AL
SP J Coombs
SP E Plank
SR B Brown
SR B Houck
SP C Bender
RP C Morgan
RP H Pennock
C - J Lapp
1B S McInnis
2B E Collins
SS J Barry
3B F Baker
LM A Strunk
CF R Oldring
RF B Lord
M C Mack

STL 1912 AL
SR E Hamilton
SP J Powell
SP G Baumgardner
SR M Allison
SR E Brown
C - J Stephens
1B G Stovall
2B D Pratt
SS B Wallace
3B J Austin
LF W Hogan
CF B Shotton
RF- G Williams
OF P Compton
UT- F LaPorte

WAS 1912 AL
SR W Johnson
SP B Groom
SP T Hughes
SP C Cashion
C - J Henry
1B C Gandil
2B- R Morgan
SS G McBride
3B E Foster
LF H Shanks
CF C Milan
RF D Moeller
M C Griffith

BOS 1913 NL
SP L Tyler
SR D Rudolph
SP O Hess
SP H Perdue
SR B James
RP W Dickson
C B Rariden
1B H Myers
2B B Sweeney
SS R Maranville
3B- A Devlin
LF J Connolly
CF L Mann
RF- J Titus
3I- F Smith
C - B Whaling
M G Stallings

BRO 1913 NL
SR P Ragan
SP N Rucker
SP F Allen
SR C Curtis
SR E Yingling
RP E Reulbach
C O Miller
1B J Daubert
2B G Cutshaw
SS B Fisher
3B R Smith
LF Z Wheat
CF C Stengel
RF H Moran
M B Dahlen

CHI 1913 NL
SR L Cheney
SR J Lavender
SP B Humphries
SP G Pierce
SP C Smith
C J Archer
1B V Saier
2B J Evers
SS A Bridwell
3B H Zimmerman
LF- M Mitchell
CF T Leach
RF F Schulte
LU- W Miller
23- A Phelan

CIN 1913 NL
SR C Johnson
SR G Suggs
SR G Packard
SP R Ames
SR M Brown
RP R Benton
RP F Harter
C T Clarke
1B D Hoblitzel
2B H Groh
SS J Tinker
3B J Dodge
LF B Bescher
UT A Marsans
RU J Bates
C - J Kling

NY 1913 NL
SP C Mathewson
SP R Marquard
SP J Tesreau
SP A Demaree
SR A Fromme
RP D Crandall
C C Meyers
1B F Merkle
2B L Doyle
SS A Fletcher
3B B Herzog
LF G Burns
CF F Snodgrass
RF R Murray
3I T Shafer
M J McGraw

PHI 1913 NL
SR T Seaton
SR G Alexander
SR A Brennan
SR E Mayer
SR E Rixey
RS G Chalmers
C B Killefer
1B F Luderus
2B O Knabe
SS M Doolan
3B H Lobert
LF S Magee
CF D Paskert
RF G Cravath
OI- B Becker
M R Dooin

PIT 1913 NL
SP B Adams
SR C Hendrix
SR H Robinson
SR H Camnitz
SR M O'Toole
RP G McQuillan
C - M Simon
1B D Miller
2B J Viox
SS H Wagner
3B B Byrne
LF M Carey
CF- M Mitchell
RF C Wilson
IO- A Butler
M F Clarke

STL 1913 NL
SR S Sallee
SR B Harmon
SP D Griner
SR P Perritt
SP B Doak
RP R Geyer
C I Wingo
1B E Konetchy
2B M Huggins
SS C O'Leary
3B M Mowrey
LF L Magee
CF R Oakes
RU S Evans
UT P Whitted

BOS 1913 AL
SR H Bedient
SR D Leonard
SP R Collins
SP J Wood
SP E Moseley
RP C Hall
C - B Carrigan
1B C Engle
2B S Yerkes
SS H Wagner
3B L Gardner
LF D Lewis
CF T Speaker
RF H Hooper
SI- H Janvrin
M1 J Stahl

CHI 1913 AL
SR R Russell
SR J Scott
SR E Cicotte
SR J Benz
SR D White
RP E Walsh
C R Schalk
1B H Chase
2B M Rath
SS B Weaver
3B H Lord
ML P Bodie
CF- W Mattick
RF S Collins
2B- J Berger
M J Callahan

CLE 1913 AL
SR V Gregg
SP C Falkenberg
SR W Mitchell
SR F Blanding
SP B Steen
RP G Kahler
RS N Cullop
C - S O'Neill
1B D Johnston
2B N Lajoie
SS R Chapman
3U I Olson
LF J Graney
MU N Leibold
RF J Jackson
3I T Turner
C - F Carisch
M J Birmingham

DET 1913 AL
SP J Dubuc
SP E Willett
SP H Dauss
SP M Hall
SR J Lake
RP F House
C - O Stanage
1B D Gainer
2B O Vitt
SS D Bush
3B G Moriarty
LF B Veach
CF T Cobb
RF S Crawford
UO- H High
M H Jennings

NY 1913 AL
SR R Fisher
SP R Ford
SR A Schulz
SR G McConnell
SR R Caldwell
RP R Keating
C E Sweeney
12- J Knight
2U R Hartzell
SS R Peckinpaugh
3B- E Midkiff
LF B Cree
CF H Wolter
RF B Daniels
M F Chance

PHI 1913 AL
SR C Bender
SR E Plank
SP B Brown
SR J Bush
SR B Houck
RP B Shawkey
C - J Lapp
1B S McInnis
2B E Collins
SS J Barry
3B F Baker
LF R Oldring
UO J Walsh
RF E Murphy
CF A Strunk
C - W Schang
M C Mack

STL 1913 AL
SP G Baumgardner
SR C Weilman
SR R Mitchell
SP E Hamilton
SP W Leverenz
C S Agnew
1B- G Stovall
2B D Pratt
SS- M Balenti
3B J Austin
LF J Johnston
CF B Shotton
RF G Williams
1U- B Brief
M3 B Rickey

WAS 1913 AL
SR W Johnson
SP B Groom
SR J Boehling
SR J Engel
RS T Hughes
RP B Gallia
C J Henry
1B C Gandil
2B R Morgan
SS G McBride
3B E Foster
LF H Shanks
CF C Milan
RF D Moeller
C - E Ainsmith
3U- F LaPorte
M C Griffith

BOS 1914 NL
SP D Rudolph
SP B James
SP L Tyler
SR D Crutcher
C H Gowdy
1B B Schmidt
2B J Evers
SS R Maranville
3B- C Deal
LF J Connolly
CF L Mann
RU- L Gilbert
M G Stallings

BRO 1914 NL
SP J Pfeffer
SR E Reulbach
SR P Ragan
SP R Aitchison
SR F Allen
RP N Rucker
C - L McCarty
1B J Daubert
2B G Cutshaw
SS D Egan
3B- R Smith
LF Z Wheat
CF J Dalton
RF C Stengel
M W Robinson

CHI 1914 NL
SR L Cheney
SP H Vaughn
SP J Lavender
SR B Humphries
SR G Pierce
RS Z Zabel
RP C Hageman
C R Bresnahan
1B V Saier
2B B Sweeney
SS R Corriden
3B H Zimmerman
LF F Schulte
CF T Leach
RF W Good
C - J Archer
M H O'Day

CIN 1914 NL
SR R Ames
SP R Benton
SR P Douglas
SP E Yingling
SR P Schneider
C T Clarke
1B- D Hoblitzel
2B H Groh
SS B Herzog
3B B Niehoff
LF- G Twombly
RM- B Daniels
RF H Moran
C M Gonzalez
UO- D Miller

NY 1914 NL
SP J Tesreau
SP C Mathewson
SP R Marquard
SP A Demaree
RS A Fromme
C C Meyers
1B F Merkle
2B L Doyle
SS A Fletcher
3B M Stock
LR G Burns
CF B Bescher
UT F Snodgrass
3I- E Grant
C - L McLean
OF- R Murray
RU- D Robertson
M J McGraw

PHI 1914 NL
SP G Alexander
SR E Mayer
SR B Tincup
SR R Marshall
SR J Oeschger
RP E Rixey
C B Killefer
1B F Luderus
2B B Byrne
SS- J Martin
3B H Lobert
LO B Becker
CF D Paskert
RF G Cravath
IO S Magee
M R Dooin

PIT 1914 NL
SP B Adams
SP W Cooper
SR G McQuillan
SP B Harmon
RS J Conzelman
C G Gibson
1B E Konetchy
2B J Viox
SS H Wagner
3B- M Mowrey
LF M Carey
OF- J Kelly
RF- M Mitchell
CF J Kelly
M F Clarke

STL 1914 NL
SR S Sallee
SP P Perritt
SP B Doak
SR D Griner
SP H Perdue
RS H Robinson
C F Snyder
1S D Miller
2B M Huggins
SS- A Butler
3B Z Beck
LU C Dolan
M1 L Magee
RF C Wilson
OF W Cruise
C - I Wingo

BOS 1914 AL
SP R Collins
SR D Leonard
SP R Foster
SR H Bedient
SP E Shore
RP J Wood
RP R Johnson
C - B Carrigan
1B- D Hoblitzel
2B- S Yerkes
SS E Scott
3B L Gardner
LF D Lewis
CF T Speaker
RF H Hooper
UI H Janvrin
OF- W Rehg

CHI 1914 AL
SR J Benz
SR E Cicotte
SR J Scott
SR R Faber
SR R Russell
RS M Wolfgang
RP B Lathrop
C R Schalk
1B J Fournier
2B L Blackburne
SS B Weaver
3B- J Breton
LF R Demmitt
CF P Bodie
RM S Collins
M J Callahan

CLE 1914 AL
SP W Mitchell
SP B Steen
SR R Hagerman
SR G Morton
SR F Blanding
RS A Collamore
RP V Gregg
C - S O'Neill
1B D Johnston
21 N Lajoie
S2 R Chapman
3B T Turner
LF J Graney
CF N Leibold
RM J Jackson
UT- I Olson
M J Birmingham

DET 1914 AL
SP H Coveleski
SR H Dauss
SP J Dubuc
SR P Cavet
SR A Main
RS R Reynolds
C O Stanage
1B G Burns
2B M Kavanagh
SS D Bush
3B G Moriarty
LF B Veach
CF T Cobb
RF S Crawford
UO- H High
M H Jennings

NY 1914 AL
SR J Warhop
SR R Caldwell
SP R Fisher
SP R Keating
SP M McHale
RS K Cole
RP B Brown
C - E Sweeney
1B- C Mullen
2B L Boone
SS R Peckinpaugh
3B F Maisel
LO R Hartzell
CF- B Cree
RF D Cook
C - L Nunamaker
M1 F Chance

PHI 1914 AL
SP B Shawkey
SR J Bush
SR E Plank
SR W Wyckoff
SP C Bender
RS H Pennock
RS R Bressler
C W Schang
1B S McInnis
2B E Collins
SS J Barry
3B F Baker
LF R Oldring
CF A Strunk
RF E Murphy
M C Mack

STL 1914 AL
SP E Hamilton
SP C Weilman
SP B James
SR G Baumgardner
SR W Leverenz
RS R Mitchell
C S Agnew
1B J Leary
2B D Pratt
SS- D Lavan
3B J Austin
LF T Walker
CF B Shotton
RF G Williams
UT- I Howard
SS- B Wares
M B Rickey

WAS 1914 AL
SR W Johnson
SR D Ayers
SR J Shaw
SP J Boehling
SR J Bentley
RS J Engel
RP H Harper
C - J Henry
1B C Gandil
2B R Morgan
SS G McBride
3B E Foster
LM H Shanks
CF C Milan
RF D Moeller
CU- R Williams
M C Griffith

BAL 1914 FL
SP J Quinn
SP G Suggs
SR K Wilhelm
SR F Smith

SP B Bailey
RS S Conley
C F Jacklitsch
1B H Swacina
2B O Knabe
SS M Doolan
3B J Walsh
LI H Simmons
MO V Duncan
RF B Meyer
CU- H Russell

BRO 1914 FL
SP T Seaton
SP E Lafitte
SP H Finneran
C G Land
1B- H Myers
2U S Hofman
SS- E Gagnier
3B T Wisterzil
UO C Cooper
CF A Shaw
RO S Evans
LU G Anderson
SS- A Halt
M B Bradley

BUF 1914 FL
SP F Anderson
SP R Ford
SP G Krapp
SP E Moore
SP A Schulz
RS H Moran
C W Blair
1L J Agler
2B T Downey
SS B Louden
3B F Smith
LF- F Delahanty
CF C Hanford
RF- T McDonald
UO- D Young
M L Schlafly

CHI 1914 FL
SR C Hendrix
SR M Fiske
SR E Lange
SP D Watson
SR M Prendergast
RS T McGuire
RP R Johnson
C A Wilson
1B F Beck
2B J Farrell
SS J Tinker
3B R Zeider
LF M Flack
CF D Zwilling
RF A Wickland

IND 1914 FL
SP C Falkenberg
SP E Moseley
SP G Kaiserling
SR G Mullin
SR H Billiard
C B Rariden
1B C Carr
2B F LaPorte
SS J Esmond
3B B McKechnie
UT A Scheer
MR V Campbell
UO B Kauff
M B Phillips

KC 1914 FL
SP G Packard
SP N Cullop
SR D Stone
SR B Harris
SR P Henning
RS D Adams
RP C Johnson
C T Easterly
1B G Stovall
2B B Kenworthy
S3 P Goodwin
31 G Perring
LF C Chadbourne
CF A Kruger
RF G Gilmore
OI- C Coles

PIT 1914 FL
SP E Knetzer
SP H Camnitz
SP W Dickson
SP C Barger
SR M Walker
RS G LeClair
C C Berry
1B H Bradley
2B J Lewis
SS E Holly
3B E Lennox
LF D Jones
CF R Oakes
RI J Savage
M1 D Gessler

STL 1914 FL
SP B Groom
SP D Davenport
SR H Keupper
SP M Brown
SP E Willett
RP E Herbert
C M Simon
1B H Miller
2p D Crandall
SS A Bridwell
3B A Boucher
LM W Miller
LM D Drake
RF J Tobin
2S J Misse
IC- G Hartley
M2 F Jones

BOS 1915 NL
SP D Rudolph
SR T Hughes
SP P Ragan
SP L Tyler
C H Gowdy
1B B Schmidt
2B- J Evers
SS R Maranville
3B R Smith
LF J Connolly
MU S Magee
RF H Moran
2O E Fitzpatrick
UT- D Egan
M G Stallings

BRO 1915 NL
SP J Pfeffer
SR W Dell
SP J Coombs
SP S Smith
SP N Rucker
RS E Appleton
RP P Douglas
C - O Miller
1B J Daubert
2B G Cutshaw
SS O O'Mara
3B G Getz
LF Z Wheat
CF H Myers
RF C Stengel
C - L McCarty
M W Robinson

CHI 1915 NL
SP H Vaughn
SR J Lavender
SR G Pierce
SP B Humphries
SR Z Zabel
RP L Cheney
RP P Standridge
RS K Adams
C J Archer
1B V Saier
23 H Zimmerman
SS B Fisher
3B A Phelan
LF F Schulte
CF C Williams
RF W Good
M R Bresnahan

CIN 1915 NL
SR G Dale
SR P Schneider
SR F Toney
SR R Benton
SR K Lear
RS L McKenry
C I Wingo
1B F Mollwitz
2B- B Rodgers
SS B Herzog
3B H Groh
LM R Killefer
CF T Leach
RF T Griffith
C T Clarke

NY 1915 NL
SP J Tesreau
SP P Perritt
SP C Mathewson
SR S Stroud
SP R Marquard
RS R Schauer
RP H Ritter
RP F Schupp
C C Meyers
1B F Merkle
2B L Doyle
SS A Fletcher
3B H Lobert
LF G Burns
CF- F Snodgrass
RF D Robertson
IO- F Brainerd
UI- E Grant
M J McGraw

PHI 1915 NL
SP G Alexander
SR E Mayer
SP A Demaree
SP E Rixey
SP G Chalmers
RP S Baumgartner
C B Killefer
1B F Luderus
2B B Niehoff
SS D Bancroft
3B B Byrne
LF B Becker
ML P Whitted
RF G Cravath
MU D Paskert
M P Moran

PIT 1915 NL
SP B Harmon
SP A Mamaux
SR B Adams
SR W Cooper
SR E Kantlehner
RS G McQuillan
RP J Conzelman
C G Gibson
1B D Johnston
2B J Viox
SS H Wagner
3B D Baird
LF M Carey
CF Z Collins
RF B Hinchman
M F Clarke

STL 1915 NL
SR S Sallee
SP B Doak
SR L Meadows
SR D Griner
SR H Robinson
RS H Perdue
RP R Ames
C F Snyder
12 D Miller
2B M Huggins
SS A Butler
3B B Betzel
LF B Bescher
MR C Wilson
RM T Long
UO C Dolan
1O H Hyatt

BOS 1915 AL
SP R Foster
SP E Shore
SP B Ruth
SR D Leonard
SP J Wood
RS C Mays
RS R Collins
C - P Thomas
1B D Hoblitzel
2B- H Wagner
SS E Scott
3B L Gardner
LF D Lewis
CF T Speaker
RF H Hooper
SI H Janvrin
2B- J Barry
C - H Cady
1U- D Gainer
M B Carrigan

CHI 1915 AL
SP R Faber
SR J Scott
SR J Benz
SR R Russell
SR E Cicotte
C R Schalk
1L J Fournier
2B E Collins
SS B Weaver
3B L Blackburne
OI S Collins
ML H Felsch
RF- E Murphy
M P Rowland

CLE 1915 AL
SP G Morton
SP W Mitchell
SP R Hagerman
SR R Walker
SP F Coumbe
RS S Jones
RS O Harstad
C S O'Neill
1B- J Kirke
23 B Wambsganss
SS R Chapman
3B- W Barbare
LF J Graney
CF- N Leibold
RU E Smith
R1- J Jackson
M1 J Birmingham
M2 L Fohl

DET 1915 AL
SR H Coveleski
SR H Dauss
SP J Dubuc
SR B Boland
C O Stanage
1B G Burns
2B R Young
SS D Bush
3B O Vitt
LF B Veach
CF T Cobb
RF S Crawford
IO M Kavanagh
M H Jennings

NY 1915 AL
SP R Caldwell
SP R Fisher
SP J Warhop
SP B Brown
SR C Pieh
C - L Nunamaker
1B W Pipp
2B L Boone
SS R Peckinpaugh
3B F Maisel
LF R Hartzell
ML H High
RF D Cook
M B Donovan

PHI 1915 AL
SP W Wyckoff
SR R Bressler
SP J Bush
SP T Sheehan
SP T Knowlson
RP B Shawkey
C J Lapp
1B S McInnis
2B N Lajoie
S3 L Kopf
IC W Schang
LF R Oldring
UT J Walsh
OI A Strunk
M C Mack

STL 1915 AL
SR C Weilman
SP G Lowdermilk
SP E Hamilton
SR B James
SR E Koob
RP P Perryman
C S Agnew
1U- J Leary
2B D Pratt
SS D Lavan
3B J Austin
LF B Shotton
CF T Walker
UT- D Walsh
UT I Howard
C - H Severeid
M B Rickey

WAS 1915 AL
SP W Johnson
SR B Gallia
SP J Boehling
SR D Ayers
SP J Shaw
C J Henry
1B C Gandil
2B- R Morgan
SS G McBride
32 E Foster
L3 H Shanks
CF C Milan
RF D Moeller
IC- R Williams
M C Griffith

BAL 1915 FL
SR J Quinn
SR G Suggs
SR B Bailey
SP C Bender
SP R Johnson
C F Owens
1B- H Swacina
2B O Knabe
SS M Doolan
3B J Walsh
UT V Duncan
UO J McCandless
RF- S Evans
LU G Zinn

BRO 1915 FL
SR H Finneran
SR D Marion
SP T Seaton
SP J Bluejacket
SP E Lafitte
RS B Upham
RP F Wilson
C G Land
1B H Myers
2B L Magee
SS F Smith
3S A Halt
LU C Cooper
CF B Kauff
RL G Anderson
M2 J Ganzel

BUF 1915 FL
SP A Schulz
SR H Bedient
SP F Anderson
SP G Krapp
SP R Ford
RP R Marshall
RP H Ehmke
C W Blair
1B H Chase
2I B Louden
SS R Roach
3B H Lord
LF B Meyer
MI C Engle
UO J Dalton
UT S Hofman
C - N Allen
23 T Downey
RU- T McDonald
M1 L Schlafly

CHI 1915 FL
SP G McConnell
SP C Hendrix
SR M Prendergast
SR M Brown
SR D Black
RP A Brennan
C A Wilson
1B F Beck
2I R Zeider
SS J Smith
3B- H Fritz
LO L Mann
CF D Zwilling
RL M Flack
C W Fischer
UO- C Hanford
M J Tinker

KC 1915 FL
SP N Cullop
SR G Packard
SR C Johnson
SP A Main
SR P Henning
C T Easterly
1B G Stovall
2B B Kenworthy
SS J Rawlings
3I G Perring
LF A Shaw
CF C Chadbourne
RF G Gilmore
C - D Brown
S2- P Goodwin
UO- A Kruger

NEW 1915 FL
SP E Reulbach
SP E Moseley
SR G Kaiserling
SR H Moran
SP C Falkenberg
C B Rariden
1B E Huhn
2B F LaPorte
SS J Esmond
3B B McKechnie
LF A Scheer
CF E Roush
RF V Campbell
M1 B Phillips

PIT 1915 FL
SP F Allen
SP E Knetzer
SP C Rogge
SR B Hearn
SR C Barger
RS W Dickson
C C Berry
1B E Konetchy
2B S Yerkes
SS M Berghammer
3B M Mowrey
LF A Wickland
CF R Oakes
RF J Kelly
2U- J Lewis

STL 1915 FL
SP D Davenport
SP D Crandall
SR E Plank
SR B Groom
SR D Watson
C G Hartley
1B B Borton
2B B Vaughn
SS E Johnson
3B- C Deal
LF W Miller
MR D Drake
RF J Tobin
M F Jones

BOS 1916 NL
SP D Rudolph
SP L Tyler
SP P Ragan
SR J Barnes
SR A Nehf
RS T Hughes
RP F Allen
RS E Reulbach
C H Gowdy
1B E Konetchy
2B- J Evers
SS R Maranville
3B R Smith
LF S Magee
CF F Snodgrass
RF J Wilhoit
UO- Z Collins
2U- D Egan
2R- E Fitzpatrick
M G Stallings

BRO 1916 NL
SP J Pfeffer
SP L Cheney
SR S Smith
SR R Marquard
SP J Coombs
RS W Dell
C - C Meyers
1B J Daubert
2B G Cutshaw
SS I Olson
3B M Mowrey
LF Z Wheat
CF H Myers
RF C Stengel
UO J Johnston
M W Robinson

CHI 1916 NL
SP H Vaughn
SR C Hendrix
SR J Lavender
SP G McConnell
SR G Packard
RS M Prendergast
RS T Seaton
C - J Archer
1B V Saier
2B- O Knabe
SS- C Wortman
3B H Zimmerman
LO L Mann
CF C Williams
RF M Flack
32 R Zeider
M J Tinker

CIN 1916 NL
SP F Toney
SR P Schneider
SR A Schulz
SP C Mitchell
SR E Knetzer
RS E Moseley
C I Wingo
1U H Chase
2B B Louden
SS- B Herzog
3I H Groh
LM G Neale
CF- E Roush
RF T Griffith
CU- T Clarke
M3 C Mathewson

NY 1916 NL
SP J Tesreau
SR P Perritt
SP R Benton
SR F Anderson
SR F Schupp
RP S Sallee
C B Rariden
1B F Merkle
2B L Doyle
SS A Fletcher
3B- B McKechnie
LF G Burns
CF B Kauff
RF D Robertson
M J McGraw

PHI 1916 NL
SP G Alexander
SP E Rixey
SP A Demaree
SR E Mayer
SR C Bender
RP G McQuillan
C B Killefer
1B F Luderus
2B B Niehoff
SS D Bancroft
3B M Stock
LF P Whitted
CF D Paskert
RF G Cravath
C - E Burns
M P Moran

PIT 1916 NL
SP A Mamaux
SR W Cooper
SR F Miller
SR B Harmon
SR E Kantlehner
RS E Jacobs
C - W Schmidt
1B D Johnston
2O- J Farmer
SU H Wagner
3U D Baird
RL- F Schulte
CF M Carey
RU B Hinchman
M J Callahan

STL 1916 NL
SR L Meadows
SR R Ames
SP B Doak
SP B Steele
SR H Jasper
RS S Williams
RP M Watson
C M Gonzalez
12 D Miller
2B B Betzel
SS R Corhan
3S R Hornsby
LF B Bescher
CF J Smith
RM C Wilson
RF T Long
C1 F Snyder
UT- A Butler
M M Huggins

BOS 1916 AL
SP B Ruth
SR D Leonard
SR C Mays
SR E Shore
SR R Foster
C P Thomas
1B D Hoblitzel
2B J Barry
SS E Scott
3B L Gardner
LF D Lewis
CF T Walker
RF H Hooper
S2 H Janvrin
C - H Cady
IO- M McNally
M B Carrigan

CHI 1916 AL
SR R Russell
SR L Williams
SR R Faber
SR E Cicotte
SR J Scott
RS J Benz
RS M Wolfgang
C R Schalk
1B J Fournier
2B E Collins
SS Z Terry
3S B Weaver
LF J Jackson
CF H Felsch
RF S Collins
M P Rowland

CLE 1916 AL
SR J Bagby
SR S Coveleski
SP G Morton
SR E Klepfer
SR F Coumbe
RS A Gould
RP F Beebe
C S O'Neill
1B C Gandil
2B- I Howard
SS B Wambsganss
32 T Turner
LF J Graney
CF T Speaker
RF B Roth
UI R Chapman
RU- E Smith
M L Fohl

DET 1916 AL
SP H Coveleski
SR H Dauss
SR J Dubuc
SR B James
SR G Cunningham
RS B Boland
RP W Mitchell
C O Stanage
1B G Burns
2B R Young
SS D Bush
3B O Vitt
LF B Veach
CF T Cobb
RF S Crawford
UT H Heilmann
M H Jennings

NY 1916 AL
SR B Shawkey
SP G Mogridge
SR R Fisher
SR A Russell
SP N Cullop
RP R Caldwell
RP S Love
C - L Nunamaker
1B W Pipp
2B J Gedeon
SS R Peckinpaugh
3B F Baker
LF H High
CF L Magee
RF- F Gilhooley
UT- P Baumann
M B Donovan

PHI 1916 AL
SP E Myers
SP J Bush
SR J Nabors
SR T Sheehan
C - B Meyer
1B S McInnis
2B N Lajoie
SS W Witt
3B C Pick
LC W Schang
CF A Strunk
RF J Walsh
M C Mack

STL 1916 AL
SR D Davenport
SR C Weilman
SR E Plank
SR B Groom
SR E Koob
C H Severeid
1B G Sisler
2B D Pratt
SS D Lavan
3B J Austin
LF B Shotton
CF A Marsans
RF W Miller
C - G Hartley
M F Jones

WAS 1916 AL
SR W Johnson
SR B Gallia
SP H Harper
SR D Ayers
SP J Boehling
RS J Shaw
C J Henry
1B J Judge
2B R Morgan
SS G McBride
32 E Foster

LI H Shanks
CF C Milan
RL- D Moeller
M C Griffith

BOS 1917 NL
SR J Barnes
SP D Rudolph
SP L Tyler
SR A Nehf
SR P Ragan
RS F Allen
C W Tragesser
1B E Konetchy
2B J Rawlings
SS R Maranville
3B R Smith
LF J Kelly
CF- R Powell
RF- W Rehg
M G Stallings

BRO 1917 NL
SP L Cadore
SP J Pfeffer
SP R Marquard
SR S Smith
SR L Cheney
RS J Coombs
C - O Miller
1B J Daubert
2B G Cutshaw
SS I Olson
3B- M Mowrey
LF Z Wheat
MO J Hickman
RF C Stengel
UT J Johnston
MI H Myers
M W Robinson

CHI 1917 NL
SP H Vaughn
SR P Douglas
SR C Hendrix
SP A Demaree
SR P Carter
RS V Aldridge
RS M Prendergast
C - A Wilson
1B F Merkle
2B L Doyle
SS- C Wortman
3B C Deal
LF L Mann
CF C Williams
RL M Flack
RF H Wolter
IO R Zeider
C - R Elliott
M F Mitchell

CIN 1917 NL
SP F Toney
SP P Schneider
SP M Regan
SR C Mitchell
RS H Eller
C I Wingo
1B H Chase
2B D Shean
SS L Kopf
3B H Groh
LO G Neale
CF E Roush
RF T Griffith
M C Mathewson

NY 1917 NL
SP F Schupp
SR S Sallee
SR R Benton
SP P Perritt
SR J Tesreau
RS F Anderson
C B Rariden
1B W Holke
2B B Herzog
SS A Fletcher
3B H Zimmerman
LF G Burns
CF B Kauff
RF D Robertson
M J McGraw

PHI 1917 NL
SP G Alexander
SP E Rixey
SR J Oeschger
SR E Mayer
SR J Lavender
RS C Bender
C B Killefer
1B F Luderus
2B B Niehoff
SS D Bancroft
3B M Stock
LF P Whitted
CF D Paskert
RF G Cravath
M P Moran

PIT 1917 NL
SP W Cooper
SR E Jacobs
SR F Miller
SR B Grimes
SP B Steele
RS H Carlson
CU W Fischer
1I- H Wagner
2B J Pitler
SS C Ward
3B- T Boeckel
LU C Bigbee
CF M Carey
RF L King
M1 J Callahan
M3 H Bezdek

STL 1917 NL
SP B Doak
SP L Meadows
SR R Ames
SR M Watson
RS G Packard
RS O Horstmann
C F Snyder
1B G Paulette
21 D Miller
SR R Hornsby
3B D Baird
ML W Cruise
UO J Smith
RF T Long
2U B Betzel
CU M Gonzalez
M M Huggins

BOS 1917 AL
SP B Ruth
SP D Leonard
SP C Mays
SP E Shore
SP R Foster
RS H Pennock
C - S Agnew
1B D Hoblitzel
2B J Barry
SS E Scott
3B L Gardner
LF D Lewis
CF T Walker
RF H Hooper
C - P Thomas

CHI 1917 AL
SR E Cicotte
SR R Faber
SR L Williams
SR R Russell
SP J Scott
RS D Danforth
RP J Benz
C R Schalk
1B C Gandil
2B E Collins
SS S Risberg
3B B Weaver
LF J Jackson
CF H Felsch
RF N Leibold
RF- S Collins
M P Rowland

CLE 1917 AL
SR J Bagby
SP S Coveleski
SR E Klepfer
SR G Morton
SR O Lambeth
RS F Coumbe
C S O'Neill
1B J Harris
2B B Wambsganss
SS R Chapman
3B J Evans
LF J Graney
CF T Speaker
RF B Roth
M L Fohl

DET 1917 AL
SP H Dauss
SR B Boland
SR H Ehmke
SR B James
SP W Mitchell
RS G Cunningham
C O Stanage
1B G Burns
2B R Young
SS D Bush
3B O Vitt
LF B Veach
CF T Cobb
RU H Heilmann
M H Jennings

NY 1917 AL
SP B Shawkey
SP R Caldwell
SP G Mogridge
SR N Cullop
SR U Shocker
RP R Fisher
RS S Love
RS A Russell
C L Nunamaker
1B W Pipp
2B F Maisel
SS R Peckinpaugh
3B F Baker
LF H High
UO E Miller
RU T Hendryx
M B Donovan

PHI 1917 AL
SP J Bush
SR R Schauer
SR E Myers
SR J Johnson
SP W Noyes
RS S Seibold
CU W Schang
1B S McInnis
2B R Grover
SS W Witt
3B R Bates
LF P Bodie
CF A Strunk
RF- C Jamieson
M C Mack

STL 1917 AL
SP D Davenport
SR A Sothoron
SR B Groom
SR E Koob
SP E Plank
RS T Rogers
C H Severeid
1B G Sisler
2B D Pratt
SS D Lavan
3B J Austin
LF B Shotton
RM B Jacobson
RU T Sloan
UI- E Johnson
OF- W Rumler
M F Jones

WAS 1917 AL
SR W Johnson
SR J Shaw
SR D Ayers
SR B Gallia
SP G Dumont
RP H Harper
C E Ainsmith
1B J Judge
2B R Morgan
SU H Shanks
32 E Foster
LF M Menosky
CF C Milan
RF S Rice
3U J Leonard
M C Griffith

BOS 1918 NL
SP A Nehf
SP P Ragan
SP D Rudolph
SP B Hearn
SP D Fillingim
C A Wilson
1B E Konetchy
2B B Herzog
SU J Rawlings
3B R Smith
UT- R Massey
CF- R Powell
RF A Wickland
M G Stallings

BRO 1918 NL
SR B Grimes
SP R Marquard
SR L Cheney
SR J Coombs
SP D Robertson
C - O Miller
1B J Daubert
2B M Doolan
SS I Olson
3B O O'Mara
LF Z Wheat
CF H Myers
RU J Johnston
M W Robinson

CHI 1918 NL
SP H Vaughn
SP L Tyler
SP C Hendrix
SP P Douglas
C B Killefer
1B F Merkle
2B R Zeider
SS C Hollocher
3B C Deal
LF L Mann
CF D Paskert
RF M Flack
M F Mitchell

CIN 1918 NL
SR H Eller
SP P Schneider
SP J Ring
SP F Toney
SP R Bressler
RP D Luque
RS M Regan
C I Wingo
1B- H Chase
2B L Magee
SS L Blackburne
3B H Groh
LU G Neale
CF E Roush
RF T Griffith
1L S Magee
M1 C Mathewson

NY 1918 NL
SP P Perritt
SR R Causey
SR A Demaree
SP S Sallee
SP F Toney
C L McCarty
1B W Holke
2B L Doyle
SS A Fletcher
3B H Zimmerman
LF G Burns
CF- B Kauff
RF R Youngs
C - B Rariden
MO-J Wilhoit
M J McGraw

PHI 1918 NL
SP M Prendergast
SP B Hogg
SP J Oeschger
SP E Jacobs
SR M Watson
RP E Mayer
RP D Davis
C B Adams
1B F Luderus
2B- P McGaffigan
SS D Bancroft
3B M Stock
LM I Meusel
CF C Williams
RF G Cravath
C - E Burns
LR- J Fitzgerald
M P Moran

PIT 1918 NL
SP W Cooper
SP F Miller
SR R Sanders
SP E Mayer
SP B Harmon
RP R Comstock
C W Schmidt
1B F Mollwitz
2B G Cutshaw
SS H Caton
3B B McKechnie
LF C Bigbee
CF M Carey
RF- B Southworth
M H Bezdek

STL 1918 NL
SP B Doak
SR R Ames
SP G Packard
SR B Sherdel
SP L Meadows
RS J May
C M Gonzalez
1B G Paulette
2B- B Fisher
SS R Hornsby
3B D Baird
LF A McHenry
CF C Heathcote
LU- W Cruise
UT- B Betzel
M J Hendricks

BOS 1918 AL
SP C Mays
SP J Bush
SP S Jones
SP D Leonard
C - S Agnew
1B S McInnis
2B D Shean
SS E Scott
3B- F Thomas
LF- G Whiteman
CF A Strunk
RF H Hooper
Lp B Ruth
CU W Schang
M E Barrow

CHI 1918 AL
SP E Cicotte
SP F Shellenback
SR J Benz
SP R Russell
SP L Williams
RS D Danforth
RP R Faber
C R Schalk
1B C Gandil
2B E Collins
SS B Weaver
3B- F McMullin
LF N Leibold
OI S Collins
RU E Murphy
IO S Risberg
M P Rowland

CLE 1918 AL
SP S Coveleski
SR J Bagby
SP G Morton
SR F Coumbe
SR J Enzmann
C S O'Neill
1B- D Johnston
2B B Wambsganss
SS R Chapman
3B J Evans
LU J Wood
CF T Speaker
RF B Roth
LU- J Graney
32- T Turner
M L Fohl

DET 1918 AL
SP H Dauss
SP B Boland
SP R Kallio
SR G Cunningham
SP B James
RP E Erickson
C - A Yelle
R1 H Heilmann
2B R Young
SS D Bush
3B O Vitt
LF B Veach
CF T Cobb
RF- G Harper
3B- B Jones
CU- T Spencer
M H Jennings

NY 1918 AL
SR G Mogridge
SP S Love
SP R Caldwell
SP A Russell
SR H Finneran
RP H Thormahlen
C T Hannah
1B W Pipp
2B D Pratt
SS R Peckinpaugh
3B F Baker
LF P Bodie
CF- E Miller
RF F Gilhooley
C - R Walters
M M Huggins

PHI 1918 AL
SP S Perry
SP V Gregg
SR W Adams
SP M Watson
SP E Myers
RP B Geary
C W McAvoy
1B G Burns
2B- J Dykes
S2 J Dugan
3B L Gardner
LF M Kopp
CF T Walker
RF C Jamieson
C - C Perkins
S2- R Shannon
M C Mack

STL 1918 AL
SP A Sothoron
SP D Davenport
SR T Rogers
SP B Gallia
SP R Wright
RP U Shocker
RP G Lowdermilk
RP B Houck
C L Nunamaker
1B G Sisler
2B J Gedeon
S3 J Austin
3B F Maisel
LM E Smith
ML J Tobin
RF R Demmitt
UO T Hendryx
M1 F Jones
M3 J Burke

WAS 1918 AL
SR W Johnson
SP H Harper
SR J Shaw
SR D Ayers
C E Ainsmith
1B J Judge
2B R Morgan
SS D Lavan
3B E Foster
LR B Shotton
CF C Milan
RU F Schulte
UT H Shanks
M C Griffith

BOS 1919 NL
SP D Rudolph
SR D Fillingim
SP A Nehf
SP R Keating
SR A Demaree
RP J Scott
C - H Gowdy
1B W Holke
2B- B Herzog
SS R Maranville
3B T Boeckel
UO- W Cruise
CF- J Riggert
RF R Powell
OI R Smith
2B- J Rawlings
C - A Wilson
M G Stallings

BRO 1919 NL
SP J Pfeffer
SP L Cadore
SP A Mamaux
SP B Grimes
SR S Smith
RS C Mitchell
C - E Krueger
1B E Konetchy
2U J Johnston
SS I Olson
3B- L Malone
LF Z Wheat
CF H Myers
RF T Griffith
M W Robinson

CHI 1919 NL
SP H Vaughn
SP G Alexander
SP C Hendrix
SR S Martin
SP P Douglas
RS P Carter
C B Killefer
1B F Merkle
2B- C Pick
SS C Hollocher
3B C Deal
LF- L Mann
CF D Paskert
RF M Flack
LU- T Barber
UT- L Magee
M F Mitchell

CIN 1919 NL
SP H Eller
SP D Ruether
SP S Sallee
SR J Ring
SP R Fisher
RS D Luque
C - I Wingo
1B J Daubert
2B M Rath
SS L Kopf
3B H Groh
LU- R Bressler
CF E Roush
RF G Neale
C - B Rariden
M P Moran

NY 1919 NL
SP J Barnes
SP R Benton
SP F Toney
SP R Causey
SP A Nehf
RS J Dubuc
CU L McCarty
1B H Chase
2B L Doyle
SS A Fletcher
3B H Zimmerman
LF G Burns
CF B Kauff
RF R Youngs
M J McGraw

PHI 1919 NL
SR G Smith
SP L Meadows
SP E Rixey
SP B Hogg
SP G Packard
RP E Jacobs
RP F Woodward
C - B Adams
1B F Luderus
2B- G Paulette
SS D Bancroft
3B- L Blackburne
UO I Meusel
CF C Williams
UO- L Callahan
RU G Cravath
L2- P Whitted
M1 J Coombs

PIT 1919 NL
SP W Cooper
SP B Adams
SP F Miller
SP E Hamilton
SP H Carlson
RP E Mayer
C W Schmidt
1B- F Mollwitz
2B G Cutshaw
SS Z Terry
3B W Barbare
LR B Southworth
ML C Bigbee
RF C Stengel
M H Bezdek

STL 1919 NL
SP B Doak
SR M Goodwin
SR O Tuero
SP J May
SR L Meadows
RS B Sherdel
RP E Jacobs
C V Clemons
12 D Miller
23 M Stock
SS D Lavan
3S R Hornsby
LO A McHenry
MU C Heathcote
RM J Smith
RU J Schultz
LF B Shotton
M B Rickey

BOS 1919 AL
SP S Jones
SP H Pennock
SP C Mays
SR A Russell
SR W Hoyt
RP R Caldwell
C W Schang
1B S McInnis
2B- R Shannon
SS E Scott
3B O Vitt
Lp B Ruth
CF- B Roth
RF H Hooper
M E Barrow

CHI 1919 AL
SP E Cicotte
SP L Williams
SR D Kerr
SP R Faber
SP G Lowdermilk
RP D Danforth
C R Schalk
1B C Gandil
2B E Collins
SS S Risberg
3S B Weaver
LF J Jackson
CF H Felsch
RF N Leibold
M K Gleason

CLE 1919 AL
SP S Coveleski
SP J Bagby
SP G Morton
SP E Myers
SR G Uhle
RP T Phillips
C S O'Neill
1B D Johnston
2B B Wambsganss
SS R Chapman
3B L Gardner
LF J Graney
CF T Speaker
RF E Smith
RO- J Wood
M1 L Fohl

DET 1919 AL
SP H Dauss
SP H Ehmke
SP B Boland
SP D Leonard
SR S Love
RS D Ayers
RP G Cunningham
C E Ainsmith
1B H Heilmann
2B R Young
SS D Bush
3B B Jones
LF B Veach
CF T Cobb
RF I Flagstead
RU C Shorten
M H Jennings

NY 1919 AL
SP J Quinn
SR B Shawkey
SP H Thormahlen
SR G Mogridge
SP C Mays
RP E Shore
RS A Russell
C - M Ruel
1B W Pipp
2B D Pratt
SS R Peckinpaugh
3B F Baker
LF D Lewis
CF P Bodie
RF S Vick
UT- C Fewster
C - T Hannah
M M Huggins

PHI 1919 AL
SP R Naylor
SR W Kinney
SP J Johnson
SP S Perry
SP T Rogers
C C Perkins
1R G Burns
UT W Witt
SS J Dugan
3B F Thomas
LF- M Kopp
MU T Walker
RU- A Strunk
1U- D Burrus
M C Mack

STL 1919 AL
SR A Sothoron
SP B Gallia
SP U Shocker
SP C Weilman
SP D Davenport
RS L Leifield
RP E Koob
RS R Wright
C H Severeid
1B G Sisler
2B J Gedeon
SS W Gerber
3B J Austin
LF J Tobin
MO B Jacobson
RU E Smith
RU- R Demmitt
M J Burke

WAS 1919 AL
SP J Shaw

SR W Johnson
SP H Harper
SP E Erickson
C - V Picinich
1B J Judge
2B- H Janvrin
S2 H Shanks
3B E Foster
LF M Menosky
CF C Milan
RF S Rice
CL P Gharrity
IO- J Leonard
MU-B Murphy
M C Griffith

BOS 1920 NL
SP J Oeschger
SR J Scott
SP D Fillingim
SR H McQuillan
C M O'Neil
1B W Holke
2B C Pick
SS R Maranville
3B T Boeckel
LF L Mann
CF R Powell
RF- W Cruise
UO-E Eayrs
2I- H Ford
C - H Gowdy
RO-J Sullivan
M G Stallings

BRO 1920 NL
SP B Grimes
SP L Cadore
SP J Pfeffer
SR A Mamaux
SP R Marquard
RS S Smith
C - O Miller
1B E Konetchy
2B P Kilduff
SS I Olson
3B J Johnston
LF Z Wheat
CF H Myers
RF T Griffith
RU B Neis
M W Robinson

CHI 1920 NL
SP G Alexander
SP H Vaughn
SP C Hendrix
SP L Tyler
SR S Martin
RS P Carter
C B O'Farrell
1B- F Merkle
S2 Z Terry
SS- C Hollocher
3B C Deal
LF D Robertson
CF D Paskert
RF M Flack
1U T Barber
23- B Herzog
OI- B Twombly
M F Mitchell

CIN 1920 NL
SP D Ruether
SP J Ring
SR H Eller
SR D Luque
SR R Fisher
RP S Sallee
C I Wingo
1B J Daubert
2B M Rath
SS L Kopf
3B H Groh
LF P Duncan
CF E Roush
RF G Neale
M P Moran

NY 1920 NL
SP J Barnes
SP A Nehf
SP F Toney
SR P Douglas
SP R Benton
C - F Snyder
1B G Kelly
2B L Doyle
SS D Bancroft
3B F Frisch
LF G Burns
CF L King
RF R Youngs
C - E Smith
M J McGraw

PHI 1920 NL
SP E Rixey
SR G Smith
SP L Meadows
SP R Causey
SP B Hubbell
C - M Wheat
1B G Paulette
2B J Rawlings
SS A Fletcher
3B R Miller
LR I Meusel
CF C Williams
RF C Stengel
2I D Miller
LO- B LeBourveau
M G Cravath

PIT 1920 NL
SP W Cooper
SP B Adams
SP H Carlson
SR E Hamilton
SR E Ponder
C W Schmidt
1B C Grimm
2B G Cutshaw
SS H Caton
3B P Whitted
LF C Bigbee
CF M Carey
RF B Southworth
UO F Nicholson
M M Gibson

STL 1920 NL
SR J Haines
SP B Doak
SP F Schupp
SR M Goodwin
RS B Sherdel
C V Clemons
1B J Fournier
2B R Hornsby
SS D Lavan
3B M Stock
LM A McHenry
MO-J Smith
MR C Heathcote
RF J Schultz
UT- H Janvrin
M B Rickey

BOS 1920 AL
SP S Jones
SP J Bush
SP H Pennock
SP H Harper
SR W Hoyt
RP A Russell
RP E Myers
C - R Walters
1B S McInnis
2B M McNally
SS E Scott
3B E Foster
LF M Menosky
CF T Hendryx
RF H Hooper
CM W Schang
3U- O Vitt
M E Barrow

CHI 1920 AL
SP R Faber
SP E Cicotte
SP L Williams
SR D Kerr
SR R Wilkinson
C R Schalk
1B S Collins
2B E Collins
SS S Risberg
3B B Weaver
LF J Jackson
CF H Felsch
RF N Leibold
M K Gleason

CLE 1920 AL
SR J Bagby
SP S Coveleski
SP R Caldwell
SR G Morton
C S O'Neill
1B D Johnston
2B B Wambsganss
SS R Chapman
3B L Gardner
LF C Jamieson
CF T Speaker
RF E Smith

DET 1920 AL
SP H Ehmke
SP H Dauss
SR R Oldham
SR D Ayers
SP D Leonard
C - O Stanage
1B H Heilmann
2B R Young
SS D Bush
3U B Pinelli
LF B Veach
CF T Cobb
RM C Shorten
RU I Flagstead
3B- B Jones
M H Jennings

NY 1920 AL
SP C Mays
SP B Shawkey
SP J Quinn
SR R Collins
SR H Thormahlen
RS G Mogridge
C - M Ruel
1B W Pipp
2B D Pratt
SS R Peckinpaugh
3B A Ward
LF D Lewis
CF P Bodie
RL B Ruth
UT B Meusel
C - T Hannah
M M Huggins

PHI 1920 AL
SP S Perry
SP R Naylor
SP S Harriss
SR E Rommel
SR R Moore
RS D Keefe
C C Perkins
1B I Griffin
2B J Dykes
SS C Galloway
3B- F Thomas
LF T Walker
CF F Welch
RO- A Strunk
UI J Dugan
M C Mack

STL 1920 AL
SP D Davis
SR U Shocker
SR A Sothoron
SP C Weilman
SR E Vangilder
RP B Burwell
RP B Bayne
C H Severeid
1B G Sisler
2B J Gedeon
SS W Gerber
3B- J Austin
LU K Williams
CF B Jacobson
RF J Tobin
3U E Smith
M J Burke

WAS 1920 AL
SR T Zachary
SR E Erickson
SP J Shaw
SR H Courtney
SP W Johnson
RS A Schacht
C P Gharrity
1B J Judge
2B B Harris
SS- J O'Neill
3U F Ellerbe
LF C Milan
CF S Rice
RF B Roth
UT H Shanks
M C Griffith

BOS 1921 NL
SR J Oeschger
SR M Watson
SR H McQuillan
SR D Fillingim
SR J Scott
C M O'Neil
1B W Holke
2B H Ford
SS W Barbare
3B T Boeckel
LF W Cruise
CF R Powell
RF B Southworth
LU- F Nicholson
M F Mitchell

BRO 1921 NL
SP B Grimes
SP D Ruether
SP L Cadore
SR C Mitchell
SR S Smith
RS J Miljus
C - O Miller
1B R Schmandt
2B P Kilduff
SS I Olson
3B J Johnston
LF Z Wheat
CF H Myers
RF T Griffith
OI B Neis
M W Robinson

CHI 1921 NL
SP G Alexander
SP S Martin
SR B Freeman
SR V Cheeves
SP H Vaughn
RS L York
RP P Jones
C B O'Farrell
1B R Grimes
2B Z Terry
SS C Hollocher
3B C Deal
LO T Barber
CF G Maisel
RF M Flack
IO J Kelleher
UO-B Twombly
M1 J Evers
M2 B Killefer

CIN 1921 NL
SP D Luque
SP E Rixey
SR R Marquard
SP R Donohue
RS B Napier
C I Wingo
1B J Daubert
23 S Bohne
SS L Kopf
3B H Groh
LF P Duncan
CF E Roush
RU R Bressler
2U- L Fonseca
C B Hargrave
M P Moran

NY 1921 NL
SR J Barnes
SP A Nehf
SR F Toney
SR P Douglas
SR R Ryan
RP S Sallee
C F Snyder
1B G Kelly
2B- J Rawlings
SS D Bancroft
32 F Frisch
LF- I Meusel
LM G Burns
RF R Youngs
C - E Smith
M J McGraw

PHI 1921 NL
SP J Ring
SP B Hubbell
SR G Smith
SP L Meadows
SP J Winters
RP H Betts
C F Bruggy
1B- E Konetchy
2B- J Smith
SS F Parkinson
UT R Wrightstone
RL- I Meusel
CF C Williams
RL B LeBourveau
1R- C Lee
UI- D Miller
M1 B Donovan
M2 K Wilhelm

PIT 1921 NL
SP W Cooper
SR W Glazner
SP E Hamilton
SP B Adams
SP J Morrison
RS J Zinn
RS H Carlson
C W Schmidt
1B C Grimm
2B G Cutshaw
SS R Maranville
3B C Barnhart
LF C Bigbee
CF M Carey
RF P Whitted
23 C Tierney
M M Gibson

STL 1921 NL
SP J Haines
SP B Doak
SP B Pertica
SR R Walker
SP J Pfeffer
RS B Sherdel
RP L North
C V Clemons
1B J Fournier
2B R Hornsby
SS D Lavan
3B M Stock
LF A McHenry
MU L Mann
RU J Smith
RU- J Schultz
M B Rickey

BOS 1921 AL
SP S Jones
SP J Bush
SP H Pennock
SR A Russell
SR E Myers
RS B Karr
RS H Thormahlen
C M Ruel
1B S McInnis
2B D Pratt
SS E Scott
3B E Foster
LF M Menosky
CF N Leibold
RM S Collins
3B- O Vitt
M H Duffy

CHI 1921 AL
SP R Faber
SP D Kerr
SR R Wilkinson
RS S Hodge
RS D McWeeny
C R Schalk
1B E Sheely
2B E Collins
SS E Johnson
3B E Mulligan
LF B Falk
MR A Strunk
RF H Hooper
CF J Mostil
M K Gleason

CLE 1921 AL
SP S Coveleski
SR G Uhle
SR D Mails
SR J Bagby
SP A Sothoron
RS R Caldwell
RS G Morton
C S O'Neill
1B D Johnston
2B B Wambsganss
SS J Sewell
3B L Gardner
LF C Jamieson
CF T Speaker
RF E Smith
1B- G Burns

DET 1921 AL
SP D Leonard
SP H Dauss
SR R Oldham
SP H Ehmke
SP B Cole
RS C Holling
RS J Middleton
C J Bassler
1B L Blue
2B R Young
SS D Bush
3B B Jones
LF B Veach
CF T Cobb
RF H Heilmann
SU- I Flagstead
UO- C Shorten

NY 1921 AL
SR C Mays
SR W Hoyt
SP B Shawkey
SR R Collins
SR J Quinn
C W Schang
1B W Pipp
2B A Ward
SS R Peckinpaugh
3B F Baker
LF B Ruth
CF- E Miller
RF B Meusel
M M Huggins

PHI 1921 AL
SR E Rommel
SR S Harriss
SP R Moore
SP B Hasty
SR R Naylor
RS D Keefe
RP H Freeman
C C Perkins
1B J Walker
2B J Dykes
SS C Galloway
3B J Dugan
LF T Walker
CF F Welch
RF W Witt
M C Mack

STL 1921 AL
SP U Shocker
SP D Davis
SR E Vangilder
SR R Kolp
RS B Bayne
RP B Burwell
C H Severeid
1B G Sisler
2B M McManus
SS W Gerber
3B F Ellerbe
LF K Williams
CF B Jacobson
RF J Tobin
M L Fohl

WAS 1921 AL
SP G Mogridge
SP W Johnson
SP T Zachary
SR E Erickson
SR H Courtney
RS J Acosta
RS A Schacht
C P Gharrity
1B J Judge
2B B Harris
SS F O'Rourke
3B H Shanks
LF B Miller
CF S Rice
UO C Milan
RU- F Brower
M G McBride

BOS 1922 NL
SR M Watson
SP F Miller
SR R Marquard
SR J Oeschger
SR H McQuillan
RS D Fillingim
RS T McNamara
RS G Braxton
C - M O'Neil
1B W Holke
2S L Kopf
SS H Ford
3B T Boeckel
LM- A Nixon
CF R Powell
RL W Cruise
UI W Barbare
C - H Gowdy
RL- F Nicholson
M F Mitchell

BRO 1922 NL
SP D Ruether
SP B Grimes
SP D Vance
SP L Cadore
SR H Shriver
RS S Smith
RS A Mamaux
C - H DeBerry
1B R Schmandt
UI J Johnston
2S I Olson
3B A High
LF Z Wheat
CF H Myers
RF T Griffith
RU B Griffith
M W Robinson

CHI 1922 NL
SP V Aldridge
SP G Alexander
SR T Osborne
SR V Cheeves
SR P Jones
RS T Kaufmann
RS G Stueland
C B O'Farrell
1B R Grimes
2B Z Terry
SS C Hollocher
3B M Krug
LF H Miller
CF J Statz
RU B Friberg
OI- T Barber
M B Killefer

CIN 1922 NL
SP E Rixey
SR J Couch
SP D Luque
SP P Donohue
SR C Keck
RP D Gillespie
C B Hargrave
1B J Daubert
2B S Bohne
SS I Caveney
3B B Pinelli
LF P Duncan
MR G Burns
RF G Harper
2B- L Fonseca
C - I Wingo
M P Moran

NY 1922 NL
SP A Nehf
SP J Barnes
SR R Ryan
SP P Douglas
RP C Jonnard
RP R Causey
RP V Barnes
C F Snyder
1B G Kelly
23 F Frisch
SS D Bancroft
3B H Groh
LF I Meusel
CF- C Stengel
RF R Youngs
CF- B Cunningham
2B- J Rawlings
C - E Smith
M J McGraw

PHI 1922 NL
SP J Ring
SP L Meadows
SR G Smith
SP B Hubbell
SR L Weinert
RS J Winters
RS J Singleton
C B Henline
1B R Leslie
2B F Parkinson
SS A Fletcher
3B G Rapp
LU C Lee
CF C Williams
RF C Walker
UI R Wrightstone
M K Wilhelm

PIT 1922 NL
SP W Cooper
SR J Morrison
SP W Glazner
SP B Adams
SR E Hamilton
RS H Carlson
RP C Yellowhorse
C J Gooch
1B C Grimm
2B C Tierney
SS R Maranville
3B P Traynor
LF C Bigbee
CF M Carey
RF- R Russell
M1 M Gibson
M2 B McKechnie

STL 1922 NL
SR J Pfeffer
SR B Sherdel
SP J Haines
SP B Doak
SR B Pertica
RS L North
RP C Barfoot
C E Ainsmith
1B J Fournier
2B R Hornsby
SS S Toporcer
3B M Stock
UO J Schultz
MR J Smith
RF- M Flack
SS- D Lavan
MU-L Mann
M B Rickey

BOS 1922 AL
SP J Quinn
SP R Collins
SP H Pennock
SR A Ferguson
SR B Piercy
RS B Karr
RS A Russell
RP C Fullerton
C M Ruel
1B G Burns
2B D Pratt
SS- J Mitchell
3B- J Dugan
LU M Menosky
CF- N Leibold
OI S Collins
LU J Harris
M H Duffy

CHI 1922 AL
SP R Faber
SP C Robertson
SP D Leverett
SP T Blankenship
RS S Hodge
C R Schalk
1B E Sheely
2B E Collins
SS E Johnson
3B E Mulligan
LF B Falk
CF J Mostil
RF H Hooper
3B- H McClellan
MU-A Strunk
M K Gleason

CLE 1922 AL
SR G Uhle
SP S Coveleski
SR G Morton
SR D Mails
SR J Bagby
RS J Lindsey
C S O'Neill
1B S McInnis
2B B Wambsganss
SS J Sewell
3B L Gardner
LF C Jamieson
CF T Speaker
RF J Wood
UT- R Stephenson

DET 1922 AL
SR H Ehmke
SP H Pillette
SR H Dauss
SR R Oldham
SR O Olsen
RS S Johnson
C J Bassler
1B L Blue
2B G Cutshaw
SS T Rigney
3B B Jones
LF B Veach
CF T Cobb
RF H Heilmann
IO- D Clark
3U- F Haney

NY 1922 AL
SP B Shawkey
SR S Jones
SP W Hoyt
SP J Bush
SP C Mays
RP G Murray
C W Schang
1B W Pipp
2B A Ward
SS E Scott
3B- J Dugan
LR B Ruth
CF W Witt
RL B Meusel
M M Huggins

PHI 1922 AL
SR E Rommel
SR S Harriss
SP B Hasty
SR F Heimach
SP R Naylor
RP J Sullivan
RP C Eckert
C C Perkins
1B J Hauser
2B R Young

SS C Galloway
3B J Dykes
LF T Walker
MR B Miller
RF F Welch
MR B McGowan
M C Mack

STL 1922 AL
SR U Shocker
SR E Vangilder
SP D Davis
SR R Kolp
SR R Wright
RS H Pruett
RS B Bayne
C H Severeid
1B G Sisler
2B M McManus
SS W Gerber
3B- F Ellerbe
LF K Williams
CF B Jacobson
RF J Tobin
M L Fohl

WAS 1922 AL
SR W Johnson
SP G Mogridge
SR R Francis
SP T Zachary
SR E Erickson
RS J Brillheart
C P Gharrity
1B J Judge
2B B Harris
SS R Peckinpaugh
3B- B LaMotte
LF G Goslin
CF S Rice
RF F Brower
3L- H Shanks
M C Milan

BOS 1923 NL
SP R Marquard
SR J Genewich
SP J Barnes
SR J Oeschger
SR T McNamara
RS L Benton
RS D Fillingim
RS J Cooney
C M O'Neil
1B S McInnis
2B H Ford
SS B Smith
3B T Boeckel
LF G Felix
CF R Powell
RF B Southworth
MU-A Nixon
M F Mitchell

BRO 1923 NL
SP B Grimes
SP D Vance
SP D Ruether
SR L Dickerman
RS A Decatur
C Z Taylor
1B J Fournier
2B- I Olson
2S J Johnston
3S A High
LF Z Wheat
MU B Neis
RF T Griffith
OI G Bailey
C - H DeBerry
LU- B Griffith
M W Robinson

CHI 1923 NL
SP G Alexander
SP V Aldridge
SP T Kaufmann
SR T Osborne
SR V Keen
RS N Dumovich
RP F Fussell
C B O'Farrell
1B- R Grimes
2B G Grantham
SS S Adams
3B B Friberg
LF H Miller
CF J Statz
RF C Heathcote
IC- G Hartnett
M B Killefer

CIN 1923 NL
SP D Luque
SP E Rixey
SP P Donohue
SP R Benton
RS C Keck
C B Hargrave
1B J Daubert
23 S Bohne
SS I Caveney
3B B Pinelli
LF P Duncan
CF E Roush
RF G Burns
M P Moran

NY 1923 NL
SP H McQuillan
SR J Scott
SP A Nehf
SP J Bentley
SP M Watson
RS R Ryan
RP C Jonnard
RP V Barnes
C F Snyder
1B G Kelly
2B F Frisch
SS D Bancroft
3B H Groh
LF I Meusel
MU-B Cunningham
RF R Youngs
S3 T Jackson
MU-J O'Connell
M J McGraw

PHI 1923 NL
SP J Ring
SP W Glazner
SR L Weinert
SR C Mitchell
SR P Behan
RS R Head
RS B Hubbell
C B Henline
1B W Holke
2B C Tierney
SS H Sand
3I R Wrightstone
LU J Mokan
CF C Williams
RF C Walker
LR C Lee
C - J Wilson
M A Fletcher

PIT 1923 NL
SP J Morrison
SP W Cooper
SP L Meadows
SP B Adams
SR E Hamilton
C W Schmidt
1B C Grimm
2B J Rawlings
SS R Maranville
3B P Traynor
LF C Bigbee
CF M Carey
RF C Barnhart
RF R Russell
M B McKechnie

STL 1923 NL
SP J Haines
SR B Sherdel
SP F Toney
SP B Doak
SP J Pfeffer
RS J Stuart
RP C Barfoot
RP L North
C - E Ainsmith
1B J Bottomley
2B R Hornsby
SS H Freigau
3B M Stock
LO J Smith
CF H Myers
RF M Flack
LF R Blades
2S S Toporcer
CF- H Mueller
M B Rickey

BOS 1923 AL
SP H Ehmke
SR J Quinn
SP A Ferguson
SP B Piercy
SR G Murray
RS C Fullerton
RP L O'Doul
C - V Picinich
1B G Burns
2S- C Fewster
SS- J Mitchell
32 H Shanks
LF J Harris
MU D Reichle
RF I Flagstead
MR S Collins
32 N McMillan
UO- M Menosky
M F Chance

CHI 1923 AL
SP C Robertson
SP R Faber
SR M Cvengros
SR T Blankenship
SR D Leverett
RS S Thurston
C R Schalk
1B E Sheely
2B E Collins
SS H McClellan
3B W Kamm
LF- B Falk
CF J Mostil
RF H Hooper
LU- R Elsh
M K Gleason

CLE 1923 AL
SR G Uhle
SP S Coveleski
SR J Edwards
SR J Shaute
SR G Morton
RS S Smith
RS D Metivier
RP D Boone
C S O'Neill
1B F Brower
2B B Wambsganss
SS J Sewell
3B R Lutzke
LF C Jamieson
CF T Speaker
RF H Summa
C G Myatt
2U- R Stephenson

DET 1923 AL
SR H Dauss
SR H Pillette
SR K Holloway
SR S Johnson
RS B Cole
RS R Francis
C J Bassler
1B L Blue
UI F Haney
SS T Rigney
3B B Jones
UO B Veach
CF T Cobb
RF H Heilmann
UO B Fothergill
LU H Manush
2I D Pratt

NY 1923 AL
SP J Bush
SP B Shawkey
SR S Jones
SP H Pennock
SP W Hoyt
C - W Schang
1B W Pipp
2B A Ward
SS E Scott
3B J Dugan
LR B Meusel
CF W Witt
OI B Ruth
M M Huggins

PHI 1923 AL
SR E Rommel
SP B Hasty
SR S Harriss
SR F Heimach
SP R Naylor
RS R Walberg
RP C Ogden
C C Perkins
1B J Hauser
2B J Dykes
SS C Galloway
3B S Hale
LF B Miller
CF W Matthews
RF F Welch
UO B McGowan
M C Mack

STL 1923 AL
SP E Vangilder
SP U Shocker
SP D Danforth
SR R Kolp
SP D Davis
RS H Pruett
RP C Root
C H Severeid
1B D Schliebner
2B M McManus
SS W Gerber
3B- G Robertson
LF K Williams
CF B Jacobson
RF J Tobin
CU- P Collins
3B- H Ezzell
M1 L Fohl
M2 J Austin

WAS 1923 AL
SP W Johnson
SP G Mogridge
SP T Zachary
SR P Zahniser
SP C Warmoth
RS A Russell
C M Ruel
1B J Judge
2B B Harris
SS R Peckinpaugh
3B O Bluege
LF G Goslin
CF N Leibold
RF S Rice
MU J Evans
IC P Gharrity
M D Bush

BOS 1924 NL
SP J Barnes
SP J Genewich
SR J Cooney
SR T McNamara
SR A Yeargin
RS L Benton
C M O'Neil
1B S McInnis
2B C Tierney
SS B Smith
3B E Padgett
LF B Cunningham
MU- G Felix
RF C Stengel
SS- D Bancroft
CU- F Gibson
M2 R Rudolph
M3 D Bancroft

BRO 1924 NL
SP B Grimes
SP D Vance
SP D Ruether
SP B Doak
SP T Osborne
RS A Decatur
C Z Taylor
1B J Fournier
2B A High
SS- J Mitchell
3B M Stock
LF Z Wheat
CF E Brown
RF T Griffith
C - H DeBerry
SU- J Johnston
UO- B Neis
M W Robinson

CHI 1924 NL
SP V Aldridge
SR V Keen
SP T Kaufmann
SR E Jacobs
SP G Alexander
RS S Blake
RP R Wheeler
C G Hartnett
1B H Cotter
2B G Grantham
SS S Adams
3B B Friberg
LF D Grigsby
CF J Statz
RF C Heathcote
M B Killefer

CIN 1924 NL
SP E Rixey
SR C Mays
SP P Donohue
SP D Luque
SR T Sheehan
RS R Benton
RP J May
C B Hargrave
1B J Daubert
2B H Critz
SS I Caveney
3B B Pinelli
LF P Duncan
CF E Roush
RF C Walker
UI S Bohne
UT R Bressler
RF G Burns
M J Hendricks

NY 1924 NL
SP V Barnes
SP J Bentley
SP H McQuillan
SR A Nehf
SP W Dean
RS R Ryan
RP M Watson
RP C Jonnard
C F Snyder
1B G Kelly
2B F Frisch
SS T Jackson
3B H Groh
LF I Meusel
CF H Wilson
RF R Youngs
MU B Southworth
C - H Gowdy
UM- B Terry
M1 J McGraw
M2 H Jennings
M3 J McGraw

PHI 1924 NL
SP J Ring
SR H Carlson
SR B Hubbell
SP C Mitchell
SR W Glazner
RS H Betts
RS J Couch
CU B Henline
1B W Holke
2B H Ford
SS H Sand
3B R Wrightstone
LF J Mokan
CF C Williams
RF G Harper
C J Wilson
LR- J Schultz
M A Fletcher

PIT 1924 NL
SP W Cooper
SR R Kremer
SR J Morrison
SP L Meadows
SR E Yde
RP A Stone
C - J Gooch
1B C Grimm
2B R Maranville
SS G Wright
3B P Traynor
LR K Cuyler
CF M Carey
RF C Barnhart
LF- C Bigbee
M B McKechnie

STL 1924 NL
SP J Haines
SP A Sothoron
SP J Stuart
SR E Dyer
SP L Dickerman
RS B Sherdel
RS H Bell
C M Gonzalez
1B J Bottomley
2B R Hornsby
SS J Cooney
3B H Freigau
LF R Blades
CF- W Holm
RO J Smith
OI- H Mueller
M B Rickey

BOS 1924 AL
SP H Ehmke
SP A Ferguson
SP J Quinn
SR C Fullerton
SP B Piercy
RS G Murray
C S O'Neill
1B J Harris
2B B Wambsganss
SS- D Lee
3B D Clark
LF B Veach
CF I Flagstead
RF I Boone
OI- S Collins
3U- H Ezzell
M L Fohl

CHI 1924 AL
SP S Thurston
SR T Lyons
SP R Faber
SR T Blankenship
SR M Cvengros
RS S Connally
RS D Leverett
RP C Robertson
C B Crouse
1B E Sheely
2B E Collins
SU B Barrett
3B W Kamm
LF B Falk
CF J Mostil
RF H Hooper
CF M Archdeacon
M1 J Evers
M2 E Walsh
M3 Collins
M4 J Evers

CLE 1924 AL
SR J Shaute
SR S Smith
SR S Coveleski
SP G Uhle
RS D Metivier
C G Myatt
1B G Burns
2B C Fewster
SS J Sewell
3B R Lutzke
LF C Jamieson
CF T Speaker
RF H Summa
UO P McNulty

DET 1924 AL
SP E Whitehill
SP R Collins
SR L Stoner
SR B Cole
SR E Wells
RS K Holloway
RS H Dauss
RS S Johnson
C J Bassler
1B L Blue
21 D Pratt
SS T Rigney
3B B Jones
LF H Manush
CF T Cobb
RF H Heilmann
3U- F Haney
UO- A Wingo

NY 1924 AL
SP H Pennock
SP J Bush
SR W Hoyt
SR B Shawkey
SR S Jones
RP M Gaston
C W Schang
1B W Pipp
2B A Ward
SS E Scott
3B J Dugan
LR B Meusel
CF W Witt
RL B Ruth
M M Huggins

PHI 1924 AL
SP E Rommel
SR F Heimach
SR S Baumgartner
SR D Burns
SR D Gray
RS R Meeker
RS S Harriss
RP B Hasty
C C Perkins
1B J Hauser
2B- M Bishop
SS C Galloway
3B- H Riconda
LF- B Lamar
ML A Simmons
RU B Miller
2I J Dykes
RF F Welch
3U- S Hale
M C Mack

STL 1924 AL
SP U Shocker
SR D Danforth
SR E Wingard
SP D Davis
SR E Vangilder
RS R Kolp
RS G Lyons
RP H Pruett
RP B Bayne
C H Severeid
1B G Sisler
2B M McManus
SS W Gerber
3B G Robertson
LF K Williams
CF B Jacobson
RF J Tobin
UO- J Evans

WAS 1924 AL
SP W Johnson
SP G Mogridge
SP T Zachary
SR J Martina
SP C Ogden
RS F Marberry
RP A Russell
RP B Speece
C M Ruel
1B J Judge
2B B Harris
SS R Peckinpaugh
3B O Bluege
LF G Goslin
MU- N Leibold
RF S Rice

BOS 1925 NL
SP J Cooney
SP J Barnes
SR L Benton
SR J Genewich
SR S Graham
RS R Ryan
RP B Smith
RS R Marquard
RP I Kamp
C F Gibson
1B D Burrus
2B- D Gautreau
SS D Bancroft
3B W Marriott
LF D Harris
ML G Felix
RF J Welsh
MU B Neis
2I- E Padgett

BRO 1925 NL
SP D Vance
SP B Grimes
SR R Ehrhardt
SR T Osborne
SP J Petty
RS B Hubbell
C Z Taylor
1B J Fournier
2B M Stock
SS J Mitchell
3U J Johnston
LF Z Wheat
CF E Brown
RF D Cox
3U C Tierney
M W Robinson

CHI 1925 NL
SP G Alexander
SP S Blake
SP W Cooper
SP T Kaufmann
SR G Bush
RS P Jones
RS V Keen
C G Hartnett
1B C Grimm
2B S Adams
SS- R Maranville
3B H Freigau
LF- A Jahn
CF- M Brooks
RF C Heathcote
M1 B Killefer
M3 M Gibson

CIN 1925 NL
SP P Donohue
SP D Luque
SP E Rixey
SR R Benton
RS J May
RP H Biemiller
C - B Hargrave
1B- W Holke
2B H Critz
SS I Caveney
3B B Pinelli
LF B Zitzmann
CF E Roush
RF C Walker
1L R Bressler
LR E Smith
M J Hendricks

NY 1925 NL
SP J Scott
SP V Barnes
SP K Greenfield
SP J Bentley
SP A Nehf
RS W Dean
RP W Huntzinger
C F Snyder
1B B Terry
2U G Kelly
SS T Jackson
3B F Lindstrom
LF I Meusel
CF B Southworth
RF R Youngs
UI F Frisch
M1 J McGraw
M2 H Jennings
M3 J McGraw

PHI 1925 NL
SP J Ring
SP H Carlson
SP C Mitchell
SR A Decatur
SR J Knight
RS H Betts
RS J Couch
C J Wilson
1B C Hawks
2B- B Friberg
SS H Sand
3B C Huber
LF- G Burns
UO G Harper
RF C Williams
21 L Fonseca
CU B Henline
UT R Wrightstone
M A Fletcher

PIT 1925 NL
SP L Meadows
SR R Kremer
SR J Morrison
SP V Aldridge
SP E Yde
RS B Adams
RP T Sheehan
C E Smith
1B G Grantham
2B E Moore
SS G Wright
3B P Traynor
LF C Barnhart
CF M Carey
RF K Cuyler
C - J Gooch
M B McKechnie

STL 1925 NL
SP J Haines
SR B Sherdel
SP F Rhem
SP A Sothoron
SP A Reinhart
RS L Dickerman
RP D Mails
C B O'Farrell
1B J Bottomley
2B R Hornsby
SS- S Toporcer
3B L Bell
LF R Blades
MU- H Mueller
RL C Hafey
RU- M Flack
UO- J Smith
M1 B Rickey

BOS 1925 AL
SP H Ehmke
SR T Wingfield
SR R Ruffing
SR P Zahniser
SP J Quinn
RS B Ross
RS O Fuhr
C - V Picinich
1B P Todt
2B B Wambsganss
SS- D Lee
3B D Prothro
OF R Carlyle
CF I Flagstead
RF I Boone
OF T Vache
M L Fohl

CHI 1925 AL
SR T Lyons
SP R Faber
SR T Blankenship
SR S Thurston
SP C Robertson
RP S Connally
RS M Cvengros
C R Schalk

1B E Sheely
2B E Collins
SS I Davis
3B W Kamm
LF B Falk
CF J Mostil
RF H Hooper
2R- B Barrett
M Collins

CLE 1925 AL

SP S Smith
SP G Uhle
SP B Karr
SR J Miller
SR G Buckeye
RP J Shaute
C G Myatt
1B G Burns
2B C Fewster
SS J Sewell
3B- R Lutzke
LF C Jamieson
CF T Speaker
RO P McNulty
32 F Spurgeon
RU- C Lee

DET 1925 AL

SP E Whitehill
SP H Dauss
SR K Holloway
SR L Stoner
SP R Collins
RS E Wells
RP D Leonard
RP J Doyle
C J Bassler
1B L Blue
2B F O'Rourke
SS J Tavener
3B F Haney
LF A Wingo
CF T Cobb
RF H Heilmann
MU H Manush
2U- L Burke

NY 1925 AL

SR H Pennock
SR W Hoyt
SR S Jones
SR U Shocker
SR B Shawkey
RP H Johnson
RS A Ferguson
C B Bengough
1B L Gehrig
2B A Ward
SS P Wanninger
3B J Dugan
LR B Meusel
CF E Combs
RL B Ruth
UO- B Paschal
M M Huggins

PHI 1925 AL

SR E Rommel
SR S Harriss
SP D Gray
SR R Walberg
SR L Grove
RS S Baumgartner
RP J Quinn
C M Cochrane
1B J Poole
2B M Bishop
SS C Galloway
3B S Hale
LF B Lamar
CF A Simmons
RF B Miller
32 J Dykes
RU- F Welch
M C Mack

STL 1925 AL

SR M Gaston
SP J Bush
SR D Davis
SR D Danforth
SP J Giard
RS E Vangilder
RS E Wingard
C - L Dixon
1B G Sisler
2B M McManus
SS B LaMotte
3B G Robertson
LF K Williams
CF B Jacobson
RU H Rice
UO H Bennett
OI- J Tobin

WAS 1925 AL

SP S Coveleski
SP W Johnson
SP D Ruether
SP T Zachary
RP F Marberry
RS V Gregg
RP A Russell
C M Ruel
1B J Judge
2B B Harris
SS R Peckinpaugh
3B O Bluege
LF G Goslin
CF E McNeely
RF S Rice
1R J Harris

BOS 1926 NL

SR L Benton
SR J Genewich
SR B Smith
SP J Werts
SR B Hearn
RS G Mogridge
RP H Goldsmith
C Z Taylor
1B D Burrus
2B- D Gautreau
SS D Bancroft
32 A High
ML E Brown
MO J Smith
RF J Welsh
3S E Taylor
LU- F Wilson

BRO 1926 NL

SP J Petty
SP B Grimes
SR D McWeeny
SR B McGraw
SP D Vance
RP J Barnes
RP R Ehrhardt
C - M O'Neil
1O B Herman
2B C Fewster
S3 J Butler
3B W Marriott
LF Z Wheat
ML G Felix
RF D Cox
UO M Jacobson
1U- J Fournier
C - C Hargreaves
SS- R Maranville
M W Robinson

CHI 1926 NL

SR C Root
SR S Blake
SP T Kaufmann
SR P Jones
SR G Bush
RS B Osborn
C G Hartnett
1B C Grimm
2B S Adams
SS J Cooney
3B H Freigau
LF- R Stephenson
CF H Wilson
RF C Heathcote
C - M Gonzalez
OI- P Scott
M J McCarthy

CIN 1926 NL

SR P Donohue
SP C Mays
SP D Luque
SP E Rixey
RS J May
RS R Lucas
C B Hargrave
1B W Pipp
2B H Critz
SS- F Emmer
3B C Dressen
LU C Christensen
CF E Roush
RF C Walker
LF- R Bressler
C - V Picinich
M J Hendricks

NY 1926 NL

SR J Scott
SR K Greenfield
SR F Fitzsimmons
SP V Barnes
SR J Ring
RS H McQuillan
RP C Davies
C - P Florence
1B G Kelly
2B F Frisch
SS T Jackson
3B F Lindstrom
LF I Meusel
CF T Tyson
RF R Youngs
UT B Terry
UO- H Mueller
M J McGraw

PHI 1926 NL

SP H Carlson
SP W Dean
SP C Mitchell
SR C Willoughby
SR D Ulrich
RS J Knight
RS R Pierce
RP E Baecht
C - J Wilson
1U- J Bentley
2B B Friberg
SS H Sand
3B C Huber
LR J Mokan
ML F Leach
RF C Williams
C B Henline
CF A Nixon
IO R Wrightstone
M A Fletcher

PIT 1926 NL

SR R Kremer
SP L Meadows
SP V Aldridge
SR E Yde
SR D Songer
RS J Morrison
RP J Bush
C E Smith
1B G Grantham
2S H Rhyne
SS G Wright
3B P Traynor
ML K Cuyler
CF- M Carey
RF P Waner
C - J Gooch
M B McKechnie

STL 1926 NL

SP F Rhem
SP B Sherdel
SR J Haines
SP V Keen
SP G Alexander
RS A Reinhart
RP B Hallahan
RS S Johnson
C B O'Farrell
1B J Bottomley
2B R Hornsby
SS T Thevenow
3B L Bell
LF R Blades
CF T Douthit
RF B Southworth
OF- C Hafey

BOS 1926 AL

SP H Wiltse
SR T Wingfield
SP P Zahniser
SR R Ruffing
SP S Harriss
RS T Welzer
RP F Heimach
RS J Russell
RP H Ehmke
C A Gaston
1B P Todt
2B B Regan
SS T Rigney
3B F Haney
OF S Rosenthal
CF I Flagstead
MR B Jacobson
M L Fohl

CHI 1926 AL

SP T Lyons
SR T Thomas
SP T Blankenship
SP R Faber
SR J Edwards
RS S Thurston
RS S Connally
C - R Schalk
1B E Sheely
2B E Collins
SU B Hunnefield
3B W Kamm
LF B Falk
CF J Mostil
RF B Barrett
RU- S Harris
M Collins

CLE 1926 AL

SP G Uhle
SP D Levsen
SP J Shaute
SP S Smith
SR G Buckeye
RS B Karr
C L Sewell
1B G Burns
2B F Spurgeon
SS J Sewell
3B R Lutzke
LF C Jamieson
CF T Speaker
RF H Summa

DET 1926 AL

SP E Whitehill
SR S Gibson
SR E Wells
SR L Stoner
SR R Collins
RS K Holloway
RS H Dauss
RS A Johns
C - C Manion
1B L Blue
2B C Gehringer
SS J Tavener
3B J Warner
LO B Fothergill
CF H Manush
RF H Heilmann
1U J Neun
32 F O'Rourke
LU A Wingo
UO- T Cobb

NY 1926 AL

SP H Pennock
SP U Shocker
SR W Hoyt
SR S Jones
SR M Thomas
RS B Shawkey
RP G Braxton
C P Collins
1B L Gehrig
2B T Lazzeri
SS M Koenig
3B J Dugan
LR B Meusel
CF E Combs
LR B Ruth
UO B Paschal
M M Huggins

PHI 1926 AL

SR L Grove
SR E Rommel
SR J Quinn
SR R Walberg
SR D Gray
RP H Ehmke
RP J Pate
C M Cochrane
1B J Poole
2B M Bishop
SS C Galloway
32 J Dykes
LF B Lamar
CF A Simmons
RF W French
3U S Hale
1U J Hauser
M C Mack

STL 1926 AL

SP T Zachary
SP M Gaston
SR E Vangilder
SR E Wingard
RS W Ballou
C W Schang
1B G Sisler
2B S Melillo
SS W Gerber
32 M McManus
LF K Williams
RM H Rice
RL B Miller
UO- H Bennett
MU- C Durst
CU- P Hargrave
3U- G Robertson

WAS 1926 AL

SP W Johnson
SP S Coveleski
SP D Ruether
SP A Crowder
SR C Ogden
RS F Marberry
RP B Morrell
RP A Ferguson
C M Ruel
1B J Judge
2B B Harris
SS B Myer
3B O Bluege
LM E McNeely
LM G Goslin
RF S Rice
UT J Harris

BOS 1927 NL

SR B Smith
SP K Greenfield
SR J Genewich
SR J Werts
SP C Robertson
RP G Mogridge
C - S Hogan
1B J Fournier
2U- D Gautreau
SS D Bancroft
3B A High
LF E Brown
CF J Welsh
RF L Richbourg
S2 D Farrell
UT E Moore
UO- J Smith

BRO 1927 NL

SP D Vance
SP J Petty
SP J Elliott
SR D McWeeny
SP B Doak
RP R Ehrhardt
RP W Clark
C - H DeBerry
1B B Herman
2B J Partridge
S3 J Butler
3B B Barrett
LF G Felix
CF J Statz
RF M Carey
R1 H Hendrick
M W Robinson

CHI 1927 NL

SR C Root
SP S Blake
SR G Bush
SP H Carlson
SR J Brillheart
RS P Jones
RS B Osborn
C G Hartnett
1B C Grimm
2B C Beck
SS- W English
UI S Adams
LF R Stephenson
CF H Wilson
RF E Webb
RU- C Heathcote
M J McCarthy

CIN 1927 NL

SR R Lucas
SR J May
SP D Luque
SP E Rixey
SP P Donohue
C B Hargrave
1B W Pipp
2B H Critz
SS H Ford
3B C Dressen
LF R Bressler
MU E Allen
RF C Walker
UT- B Zitzmann
M J Hendricks

NY 1927 NL

SP B Grimes
SR F Fitzsimmons
SP V Barnes
SP L Benton
RS D Henry
RP D Songer
C - Z Taylor
1B B Terry
2B R Hornsby
SS T Jackson
3L F Lindstrom
LU- H Mueller
CF E Roush
RF G Harper
3U R Reese
OF- M Ott
M1 J McGraw

PHI 1927 NL

SR J Scott
SP A Ferguson
SR D Ulrich
SP H Pruett
SP L Sweetland
RS C Willoughby
RP C Mitchell
RP A Decatur
C J Wilson
1B R Wrightstone
2B F Thompson
S3 H Sand
3B B Friberg
LF D Spalding
CF F Leach
RF C Williams
M S McInnis

PIT 1927 NL

SP L Meadows
SR C Hill
SP V Aldridge
SP R Kremer
RP J Morrison
RP M Cvengros
C J Gooch
1B J Harris
2B G Grantham
SS G Wright
3B P Traynor
LF C Barnhart
ML L Waner
RF P Waner
MO- K Cuyler
M D Bush

STL 1927 NL

SP J Haines
SP G Alexander
SR B Sherdel
SP F Rhem
SP B McGraw
RP H Bell
C - F Snyder
1B J Bottomley
2B F Frisch
SS- H Schuble
3B L Bell
LU C Hafey
CF T Douthit
RF B Southworth
LO W Holm
3S- S Toporcer
M B O'Farrell

BOS 1927 AL

SP H Wiltse
SR S Harriss
SR T Welzer
SR D Mac Fayden
SP R Ruffing
RS J Russell
RS D Lundgren
C G Hartley
1B P Todt
2B B Regan
SS B Myer
3U- B Rogell
LO W Shaner
CF I Flagstead
RF J Tobin
RL C Carlyle
UI J Rothrock
C - F Hofmann
3U- R Rollings
M B Carrigan

CHI 1927 AL

SP T Lyons
SP T Thomas
SP T Blankenship
SR S Connally
SP R Faber
RS E Jacobs
RP B Cole
C - H McCurdy
1B B Clancy
2B A Ward
SU B Hunnefield
3B W Kamm
LF B Falk
CF A Metzler
RF B Barrett
C - B Crouse
M R Schalk

CLE 1927 AL

SR W Hudlin
SR J Shaute
SR G Buckeye
SR J Miller
SP G Uhle
RP G Grant
C L Sewell
1B G Burns
2B L Fonseca
SS J Sewell
3B R Lutzke
LF C Jamieson
CF- I Eichrodt
RF H Summa
3B- J Hodapp
M J McCallister

DET 1927 AL

SR E Whitehill
SR L Stoner
SR K Holloway
SP S Gibson
SP R Collins
RS O Carroll
RP G Smith
C - L Woodall
1B L Blue
2B C Gehringer
SS J Tavener
3B J Warner
LF B Fothergill
CF H Manush
RF H Heilmann
UI M McManus
C - J Bassler
1U- J Neun
M G Moriarty

NY 1927 AL

SP W Hoyt
SP H Pennock
SP U Shocker
SP D Ruether
SP G Pipgras
RS W Moore
C - P Collins
1B L Gehrig
2I T Lazzeri
SS M Koenig
3B J Dugan
LR B Meusel
CF E Combs
RL B Ruth
M M Huggins

PHI 1927 AL

SR L Grove
SR R Walberg
SP J Quinn
SP H Ehmke
SR E Rommel
RS D Gray
RP J Pate
C M Cochrane
1I J Dykes
2B M Bishop
SS J Boley
3B S Hale
LF- B Lamar
CF A Simmons
RM T Cobb
2U E Collins
RU W French
SS- C Galloway
LU- Z Wheat
M C Mack

STL 1927 AL

SP M Gaston
SR E Vangilder
SP S Jones
SP L Stewart
SR E Wingard
RS E Nevers
C W Schang
1B G Sisler
2B S Melillo
SS W Gerber
3B F O'Rourke
LF K Williams
UO B Miller
RM H Rice
23- S Adams
UO H Bennett
M D Howley

WAS 1927 AL

SP H Lisenbee
SP S Thurston
SP B Hadley
SP W Johnson
SP T Zachary
RP G Braxton
RS F Marberry
RS B Burke
C M Ruel
1B J Judge
2B B Harris
SS B Reeves
3B O Bluege
LF G Goslin
CF T Speaker
RF S Rice

BOS 1928 NL

SR B Smith
SP E Brandt
SR A Delaney
SR K Greenfield
RP F Edwards
C Z Taylor
1B G Sisler
2B R Hornsby
SS D Farrell
3B L Bell
LM E Brown
UO J Smith
RF L Richbourg
M1 J Slattery

BRO 1928 NL

SP D Vance
SR D McWeeny
SP J Petty
SP W Clark
SR J Elliott
RS B Doak
RS R Moss
RP R Ehrhardt
C - H DeBerry
1B D Bissonette
2B J Flowers
SS D Bancroft
3U H Hendrick
LF R Bressler
MR M Carey
RF B Herman
2I- H Riconda
MU- J Statz
M W Robinson

CHI 1928 NL

SR P Malone
SP S Blake
SR C Root
SR G Bush
SR A Nehf
RS P Jones
RP H Carlson
C G Hartnett
1B C Grimm
2B F Maguire
SS W English
3S C Beck
LF R Stephenson
CF H Wilson
RF K Cuyler
M J McCarthy

CIN 1928 NL

SP E Rixey
SP D Luque
SR R Kolp
SP R Lucas
SP P Donohue
RP P Appleton
C V Picinich
1B G Kelly
2B H Critz
SS H Ford
3B C Dressen
OI B Zitzmann
CF E Allen
RF C Walker
1B W Pipp
LM- M Callaghan
M J Hendricks

NY 1928 NL

SP L Benton
SP F Fitzsimmons
SP J Genewich
SP C Hubbell
SP V Aldridge
RS J Faulkner
C S Hogan
1B B Terry
2B A Cohen
SS T Jackson
3B F Lindstrom
LF L O'Doul
CF J Welsh
RF M Ott
LI R Reese
RF- L Mann
M J McGraw

PHI 1928 NL

SR R Benge
SR J Ring
SR A Ferguson
SR L Sweetland
SR C Willoughby
RS A Walsh
RP B McGraw
RS R Miller
C W Lerian
1B D Hurst
2B F Thompson
SS H Sand
3B P Whitney
LU F Leach
CF D Sothern

UO C Williams
M B Shotton

PIT 1928 NL
SR B Grimes
SP C Hill
SP R Kremer
SP F Fussell
SR E Brame
RS J Dawson
C - C Hargreaves
1B G Grantham
2B S Adams
SS G Wright
3B P Traynor
LU- F Brickell
CF L Waner
RF P Waner
M D Bush

STL 1928 NL
SR B Sherdel
SP G Alexander
SP J Haines
SP F Rhem
SP C Mitchell
RS S Johnson
RP H Haid
C J Wilson
1B J Bottomley
2B F Frisch
SS R Maranville
3B W Holm
LF C Hafey
CF T Douthit
RF G Harper
3U A High
M B McKechnie

BOS 1928 AL
SP R Ruffing
SR E Morris
SP J Russell
SP D Mac Fayden
SR S Harriss
RS M Settlemire
RP P Simmons
C - F Hofmann
1B P Todt
2B B Regan
SS W Gerber
3B B Myer
LF K Williams
CF I Flagstead
RF D Taitt
SU B Rogell
UT J Rothrock
C - C Berry
C - J Heving
M B Carrigan

CHI 1928 AL
SP T Thomas
SR T Lyons
SP G Adkins
SP R Faber
SP T Blankenship
RS S Connally
C - B Crouse
1B B Clancy
2B B Hunnefield
SS B Cissell
3B W Kamm
LF B Falk
CF J Mostil
UO A Metzler
2S- B Redfern
RU- C Reynolds
M1 R Schalk
M2 L Blackburne

CLE 1928 AL
SP J Shaute
SR W Hudlin
SP G Uhle
SP J Miller
SR G Grant
RS B Bayne
RP M Harder
C L Sewell
1I- L Fonseca
2B C Lind
SS J Sewell
3B J Hodapp
LF C Jamieson
ML S Langford
RF H Summa
1U- G Burns
M R Peckinpaugh

DET 1928 AL
SP O Carroll
SP E Whitehill
SP V Sorrell
SR K Holloway
SP S Gibson
RS E Vangilder
RS L Stoner
RP J Billings
RP G Smith
CU P Hargrave
1B- B Sweeney
2B C Gehringer
SS J Tavener
31 M McManus
LU B Fothergill
CF H Rice
RF H Heilmann
UO- A Wingo
M G Moriarty

NY 1928 AL
SP G Pipgras
SR W Hoyt
SP H Pennock
SP H Johnson
SR A Shealy
RP W Moore
C - J Grabowski
1B L Gehrig
2B T Lazzeri
SS M Koenig
3B J Dugan
LR B Meusel
CF E Combs
RL B Ruth
2S L Durocher
3B- G Robertson
M M Huggins

PHI 1928 AL
SP L Grove
SP R Walberg
SP J Quinn
SP G Earnshaw
SP H Ehmke
RS E Rommel
RS O Orwoll
C M Cochrane
1B J Hauser
2B M Bishop
SS J Boley
3B- S Hale
LF A Simmons
UO B Miller
RF T Cobb
31 J Foxx
IO- J Dykes
CF- M Haas
M C Mack

STL 1928 AL
SP D Gray
SR A Crowder
SP J Ogden
SR G Blaeholder
SR L Stewart
RS D Coffman
RS H Wiltse
RP E Strelecki
C - W Schang
1B L Blue
2B O Brannan
SS R Kress
3B F O'Rourke
LF H Manush
CF F Schulte
RF E McNeely
M D Howley

WAS 1928 AL
SP B Hadley
SP S Jones
SR G Braxton
SP M Gaston
SR L Brown
RS F Marberry
RP T Zachary
C M Ruel
1B J Judge
2B B Harris
SI B Reeves
3B O Bluege
LF G Goslin
UO S West
RF S Rice
CF R Barnes

BOS 1929 NL
SP B Smith
SP S Seibold
SR P Jones
SP E Brandt
SP B Cantwell
RS D Leverett
C A Spohrer
1B G Sisler
2B F Maguire
SS R Maranville
3B L Bell
LF G Harper
CF- E Clark
RF L Richbourg
M J Fuchs

BRO 1929 NL
SP W Clark
SP D Vance
SR R Moss
SR C Dudley
SR D McWeeny
RS J Morrison
RP C Moore
RP W Ballou
C V Picinich
1B D Bissonette
2S E Moore
SS D Bancroft
3B W Gilbert
LF R Bressler
CF J Frederick
RF B Herman
UT H Hendrick
M W Robinson

CHI 1929 NL
SR G Bush
SR C Root
SR P Malone
SP S Blake
SR A Nehf
RS H Carlson
RP M Cvengros
C - Z Taylor
1B C Grimm
2B R Hornsby
SS W English
3B N McMillan
LF R Stephenson
CF H Wilson
RF K Cuyler
RU- C Heathcote
M J McCarthy

CIN 1929 NL
SP R Lucas
SR E Rixey
SR J May
SP P Donohue
SR D Luque
RS R Kolp
RS K Ash
RP R Ehrhardt
C - J Gooch
1B G Kelly
2B H Critz
S2 H Ford
3B C Dressen
LM E Swanson
CF E Allen
RF C Walker
SU- P Pittinger
OF- P Purdy
C - C Sukeforth
M J Hendricks

NY 1929 NL
SP C Hubbell
SP L Benton
SP F Fitzsimmons
SP B Walker
RS C Mays
RS D Henry
RP R Judd
C S Hogan
1B B Terry
2B A Cohen
SS T Jackson
3B F Lindstrom
LF F Leach
CF E Roush
RF M Ott
C - B O'Farrell
ML- C Fullis
M J McGraw

PHI 1929 NL
SR C Willoughby
SR L Sweetland
SR R Benge
RS P Collins
RS H Elliott
RP B McGraw
RF S Dailey
C W Lerian
1B D Hurst
2B F Thompson
SS- T Thevenow
3B P Whitney
LF L O'Doul
CF- D Sothern
RF C Klein
C S Davis
SO B Friberg
M B Shotton

PIT 1929 NL
SP B Grimes
SP E Brame
SP R Kremer
SR J Petty
SR L French
RS S Swetonic
RP H Meine
RP C Hill
C C Hargreaves
1B E Sheely
2U G Grantham
S2 D Bartell
3B P Traynor
LF A Comorosky
CF L Waner
RF P Waner
C - R Hemsley
M1 D Bush
M2 J Ens

STL 1929 NL
SR B Sherdel
SR S Johnson
SP J Haines
SP C Mitchell
SR H Haid
RS F Frankhouse
RP G Alexander
RP B Hallahan
C J Wilson
1B J Bottomley
2B F Frisch
SS C Gelbert
3B A High
LF C Hafey
CF T Douthit
RU E Orsatti
RF- W Roettger
M1 B Southworth
M2 G Street
M3 B McKechnie

BOS 1929 AL
SR M Gaston
SP R Ruffing
SP J Russell
SP D Mac Fayden
SP E Morris
RP E Carroll
C - C Berry
1B P Todt
2B B Regan
SS H Rhyne
3B B Reeves
LF R Scarritt
CF J Rothrock
3U- B Barrett
RU E Bigelow
S2 B Narleski
RF B Barrett
M B Carrigan

CHI 1929 AL
SP T Thomas
SP T Lyons
SP R Faber
SR G Adkins
SP E Walsh
RS H McKain
C M Berg
1B A Shires
2B J Kerr
SS B Cissell
3B W Kamm
LF A Metzler
MU D Hoffman
RO C Reynolds
1B B Clancy
MR- J Watwood
M L Blackburne

CLE 1929 AL
SP W Hudlin
SR W Ferrell
SP J Miller
SP J Shaute
SR J Miljus
RS K Holloway
RP J Zinn
C L Sewell
1B L Fonseca
2B- J Hodapp
SS J Tavener
3B J Sewell
LF C Jamieson
CF E Averill
OF B Falk
RF E Morgan
SS- R Gardner
M R Peckinpaugh

DET 1929 AL
SP G Uhle
SR E Whitehill
SP V Sorrell
SP O Carroll
RS A Prudhomme
RS E Yde
RP L Stoner
C - E Phillips
1B D Alexander
2B C Gehringer
SS- H Schuble
3B M McManus
LM R Johnson
CF H Rice
RF H Heilmann
OF B Fothergill
M B Harris

NY 1929 AL
SP G Pipgras
SP W Hoyt
SP E Wells
SP H Pennock
SR R Sherid
RS F Heimach
RS T Zachary
RP W Moore
C B Dickey
1B L Gehrig
2B T Lazzeri
SS L Durocher
3B- G Robertson
LR B Meusel
CF E Combs
RL B Ruth
S3 M Koenig
LO- C Durst
3U- L Lary
M1 M Huggins
M2 A Fletcher

PHI 1929 AL
SP L Grove
SP R Walberg
SR G Earnshaw
SR J Quinn
RS B Shores
RS E Rommel
C M Cochrane
1B J Foxx
2B M Bishop
SS J Boley
3B S Hale
LF A Simmons
CF M Haas
RF B Miller
S3 J Dykes
M C Mack

STL 1929 AL
SP D Gray
SP A Crowder
SR G Blaeholder
SP R Collins
SP L Stewart
RS J Ogden
RP C Kimsey
RP D Coffman
C W Schang
1B L Blue
2B S Melillo
SS R Kress
3B F O'Rourke
LF H Manush
CF F Schulte
RM B McGowan
M D Howley

WAS 1929 AL
SR F Marberry
SR B Hadley
SR G Braxton
SR L Brown
SP S Jones
RS B Burke
RP M Thomas
RS A Liska
C - B Tate
1B J Judge
23 B Myer
SS J Cronin
32 J Hayes
LF G Goslin
CF S West
RF S Rice
M W Johnson

BOS 1930 NL
SP S Seibold
SR B Smith
SR B Cantwell
SP T Zachary
SP B Sherdel
RS E Brandt
RS F Frankhouse
RS B Cunningham
C A Spohrer
1B G Sisler
2B F Maguire
SS R Maranville
3B B Chatham
LF W Berger
CF J Welsh
RF L Richbourg
UO- E Clark
OI- R Moore
1U- J Neun
M B McKechnie

BRO 1930 NL
SP D Vance
SR W Clark
SP D Luque
SR J Elliott
SR R Phelps
RS R Moss
RS S Thurston
C A Lopez
1B D Bissonette
2B- N Finn
SS G Wright
3B W Gilbert
LF R Bressler
CF J Frederick
RF B Herman
2U- J Flowers
M W Robinson

CHI 1930 NL
SR P Malone
SR G Bush
SP C Root
SR S Blake
SR B Teachout
RS B Osborn
RP L Nelson
C G Hartnett
1B C Grimm
2B F Blair
3S W English
3B- L Bell
LU R Stephenson
CF H Wilson
RF K Cuyler
S2- C Beck
M1 J McCarthy
M2 R Hornsby

CIN 1930 NL
SR B Frey
SP R Lucas
SR L Benton
SR R Kolp
SR E Rixey
RP J May
RP S Johnson
RP A Campbell
C C Sukeforth
13 J Stripp
S2 H Ford
SS L Durocher
3B T Cuccinello
LR C Walker
LM B Meusel
RU H Heilmann
MU E Swanson
OF- M Callaghan
C - J Gooch
M D Howley

NY 1930 NL
SP B Walker
SP C Hubbell
SR F Fitzsimmons
SP C Mitchell
RS H Pruett
RP J Heving
C S Hogan
1B B Terry
2B H Critz
SS T Jackson
3B F Lindstrom
LF F Leach
MO W Roettger
RF M Ott
CU B O'Farrell
SI- D Marshall
M J McGraw

PHI 1930 NL
SR P Collins
SP R Benge
SP L Sweetland
SR C Willoughby
SR H Collard
RS H Elliott
RP H Smythe
C S Davis
1B D Hurst
2B F Thompson
SS T Thevenow
3B P Whitney
LF L O'Doul
CF- D Sothern
RF C Klein
UT B Friberg
CU- H McCurdy
1B- M Sherlock
M B Shotton

PIT 1930 NL
SP L French
SP R Kremer
SP E Brame
SP H Meine
RS G Spencer
RS S Swetonic
C R Hemsley
1B G Suhr
2B G Grantham
SS D Bartell
3B P Traynor
LF A Comorosky
CF- L Waner
RF P Waner
C - A Bool
M J Ens

STL 1930 NL
SP B Hallahan
SP S Johnson
SP J Haines
SP B Grimes
SP F Rhem
RS H Bell
RS J Lindsey
RS A Grabowski
C J Wilson
1B J Bottomley
2B F Frisch
SS C Gelbert
3B S Adams
LF C Hafey
CF T Douthit
RU G Watkins
OF- S Fisher
M G Street

BOS 1930 AL
SP M Gaston
SP D Mac Fayden
SP H Lisenbee
SP J Russell
SR E Durham
RP G Smith
C - C Berry
1B P Todt
2B B Regan
SS H Rhyne
3U O Miller
LF R Scarritt
CF T Oliver
RF E Webb
OF C Durst
3I- B Reeves
1U- B Sweeney
M H Wagner

CHI 1930 AL
SP T Lyons
SR P Caraway
SP R Faber
SP T Thomas
SR D Henry
RP E Walsh
RS H McKain
C - B Tate
UT J Watwood
2B B Cissell
SS- G Mulleavy
3B W Kamm
RL S Jolley
CF- R Barnes
UO C Reynolds
M D Bush

CLE 1930 AL
SP W Ferrell
SP W Hudlin
SP C Brown
SR M Harder
RS P Appleton
C - L Sewell
1B E Morgan
2B J Hodapp
SS J Goldman
3B J Sewell
LF C Jamieson
CF E Averill
RF D Porter
OF- B Falk
C - G Myatt
LO- B Seeds
M R Peckinpaugh

DET 1930 AL
SP G Uhle
SP V Sorrell
SP E Whitehill
SR C Hogsett
SP W Hoyt
RP C Sullivan
C - R Hayworth
1B D Alexander
2B C Gehringer
SS- M Koenig
3B M McManus
LU J Stone
CF L Funk
RF R Johnson
S3- B Akers
M B Harris

NY 1930 AL
SR G Pipgras
SP R Ruffing
SR R Sherid
SR H Johnson
SP H Pennock
RP E Wells
RP L McEvoy
C B Dickey
1B L Gehrig
23 T Lazzeri
SS L Lary
32 B Chapman
UO E Combs
CF H Rice
RL B Ruth
LR- S Byrd
UO- D Cooke
2U- J Reese
M B Shawkey

PHI 1930 AL
SR L Grove
SR G Earnshaw
SP R Walberg
SR B Shores
SR R Mahaffey
RS E Rommel
RS J Quinn
C M Cochrane
1B J Foxx
2B M Bishop
SS J Boley
3B J Dykes
LF A Simmons
CF M Haas
RF B Miller
IO- E McNair
M C Mack

STL 1930 AL
SP L Stewart
SP D Coffman
SR G Blaeholder
SR R Collins
SP D Gray
RP C Kimsey
RS R Stiles
RP H Holshouser
C R Ferrell
1B L Blue
2B S Melillo
SS R Kress
3U F O'Rourke
LF G Goslin
CF F Schulte
RF- T Gullic
UO- R Badgro
M B Killefer

WAS 1930 AL
SP B Hadley
SP A Crowder
SR L Brown
SR F Marberry
SP S Jones
RS A Liska
C R Spencer
1B J Judge
2B B Myer
SS J Cronin
3B O Bluege
LF- H Manush
CF S West
RF S Rice
M W Johnson

BOS 1931 NL
SP E Brandt
SP T Zachary
SP S Seibold
SR B Cantwell
SR B Sherdel
RS B Cunningham
RS F Frankhouse
RP H Haid
C A Spohrer
1B E Sheely
2B F Maguire
SS R Maranville
3B- B Urbanski
LF R Worthington
CF W Berger
RF W Schulmerich
RU L Richbourg
UT- R Moore
UL- J Neun
M B McKechnie

BRO 1931 NL
SP W Clark
SP D Vance
SP R Phelps
SP S Thurston
SP J Shaute
RS F Heimach
RP D Luque
CL J Quinn
RP C Moore
C A Lopez
1B D Bissonette
2B N Finn
SS- G Slade
3B W Gilbert
LF L O'Doul
CF J Frederick
RF B Herman
SS- G Wright
M W Robinson

CHI 1931 NL
SP C Root
SP B Smith
SP P Malone
SR G Bush
SR L Sweetland
RP J May
RP B Teachout
C G Hartnett
1B C Grimm
23 R Hornsby
SS W English
3B- L Bell
UO- D Taylor
ML H Wilson
RM K Cuyler
21- F Blair
32- B Jurges
LF- R Stephenson

CIN 1931 NL
SP S Johnson
SP R Lucas
SR L Benton
SR B Frey
SP E Rixey
RS R Kolp
RS O Carroll
C C Sukeforth
1B H Hendrick
2B T Cuccinello
SS L Durocher
3B J Stripp
OF E Roush
CF T Douthit
RU E Crabtree
LF N Cullop
SS- H Ford
RU- C Heathcote
M D Howley

NY 1931 NL
SP F Fitzsimmons
SP C Hubbell
SP B Walker
SP C Mitchell
SR J Berly
C S Hogan
1B B Terry
2B- B Hunnefield
SS T Jackson
3B J Vergez
LF F Leach
UO E Allen
MR M Ott
MU- C Fullis
RF- F Lindstrom
C - B O'Farrell
M J McGraw

PHI 1931 NL
SR J Elliott
SP R Benge
SR P Collins
SP C Dudley
SR S Bolen
RS F Watt
C S Davis
1B D Hurst
2B L Mallon
SS D Bartell
3B P Whitney
LR C Klein
CF F Brickell
RF B Arlett
2I B Friberg
M B Shotton

PIT 1931 NL
SP H Meine
SP L French
SP R Kremer
SR G Spencer
SP E Brame
RP B Osborn
C E Phillips
1B- G Suhr
12 G Grantham
SS T Thevenow
3B P Traynor
LF A Comorosky
CF L Waner
RF P Waner
M J Ens

STL 1931 NL
SP B Hallahan
SR P Derringer
SP B Grimes
SP F Rhem
SP S Johnson
RP J Haines
RP J Lindsey
RP A Stout
C J Wilson
1B J Bottomley
2B F Frisch
SS C Gelbert
3B S Adams
LF C Hafey
CF P Martin
RF G Watkins
1B- R Collins
M G Street

BOS 1931 AL
SP J Russell
SP D Mac Fayden
SR E Durham
SR H Lisenbee
SR E Morris
RS W Moore
RP M Gaston
RS B Kline
C C Berry
1B B Sweeney
2S- R Warstler
SS H Rhyne
3U O Miller
LI J Rothrock
CF T Oliver
RF E Webb
3U U Pickering
LU A Van Camp
M S Collins

CHI 1931 AL
SR V Frasier
SP T Thomas
SR P Caraway
SR R Faber
SR T Lyons
RS H McKain
RP J Moore
RP G Braxton
C - B Tate
1B L Blue
2B J Kerr
SS B Cissell
3B- B Sullivan
LU L Fonseca
MU J Watwood
RF C Reynolds
SS L Appling
OF B Fothergill
C - F Grube
3B- I Jeffries
M D Bush

CLE 1931 AL
SP W Ferrell
SR W Hudlin
SP C Brown
SR M Harder
RP P Appleton
C L Sewell
1B E Morgan
2B J Hodapp
SS- E Montague
3B W Kamm
LF J Vosmik
CF E Averill
RF D Porter
S2 J Burnett
OF- B Falk
M R Peckinpaugh

DET 1931 AL
SP E Whitehill
SP V Sorrell
SR G Uhle
SR T Bridges
SR A Herring
RS C Hogsett
RP C Sullivan
C - R Hayworth
1B D Alexander
2B C Gehringer
SS- B Rogell
3U M McManus
LF J Stone
MU- H Walker
RF R Johnson
2S M Koenig
UI M Owen
M B Harris

NY 1931 AL
SR L Gomez
SP R Ruffing
SR H Johnson
SP H Pennock
SR G Pipgras
RS E Wells
C B Dickey
1B L Gehrig
23 T Lazzeri
SS L Lary
3B J Sewell
LR B Chapman
CF E Combs
RL B Ruth
UO S Byrd
M J McCarthy

PHI 1931 AL
SR L Grove
SP R Walberg
SR G Earnshaw
SR R Mahaffey
SR E Rommel
RP W Hoyt
C M Cochrane
1B J Foxx
2B M Bishop
SS- D Williams
3B J Dykes
LF A Simmons
CF M Haas
RF B Miller
3I- E McNair
M C Mack

STL 1931 AL
SP D Gray
SP L Stewart
SP G Blaeholder
SR D Coffman
SP R Collins
RS W Hebert
RP C Kimsey
RP R Stiles
C R Ferrell
1B J Burns
2B S Melillo
SS J Levey
3R R Kress
LF G Goslin
CF F Schulte
RU- T Jenkins
3B- L Storti
M B Killefer

WAS 1931 AL
SR L Brown
SR A Crowder
SR F Marberry
SR C Fischer
SP S Jones
RS B Hadley
RS B Burke
C R Spencer
1B J Kuhel
2B B Myer
SS J Cronin
3B O Bluege
LF H Manush
CF S West
RU S Rice
RU- D Harris
M W Johnson

BOS 1932 NL
SP E Brandt
SP H Betts
SP B Brown
SP T Zachary
SP S Seibold
RS B Cantwell
RS F Frankhouse
RP B Cunningham
C A Spohrer
1B- A Shires
2B R Maranville
SS B Urbanski
3B- F Knothe
LF R Worthington
CF W Berger
RF W Schulmerich
IO R Moore
C - P Hargrave
UO- F Leach
M B McKechnie

BRO 1932 NL
SP W Clark
SP V Mungo
SP D Vance
SR F Heimach
SP S Thurston
RS J Shaute
RP J Quinn
RP C Moore
C A Lopez
1B- G Kelly
2B T Cuccinello
SS G Wright
31 J Stripp
LF L O'Doul
CF D Taylor
RF H Wilson
UO J Frederick
S3- G Slade
M M Carey

CHI 1932 NL
SP L Warneke
SR G Bush
SP P Malone
SR C Root
SR B Grimes
RS B Smith
RS B Tinning
RP J May
C G Hartnett
1B C Grimm
2B B Herman
SS B Jurges
3S W English
LF R Stephenson
CF J Moore
RM K Cuyler
M1 R Hornsby

CIN 1932 NL
SP R Lucas
SR S Johnson
SP O Carroll
SR L Benton
SR R Kolp
RS B Frey
RS E Rixey
RP J Ogden
C E Lombardi
1B H Hendrick
2B G Grantham
SS L Durocher
3B W Gilbert
LF W Roettger
MU E Crabtree
RF B Herman
CF T Douthit
LF- C Hafey
3U- A High
S2- J Morrissey
M D Howley

NY 1932 NL
SP C Hubbell
SP F Fitzsimmons
SP B Walker
SR J Mooney
SR H Schumacher
RS H Bell
RS D Luque
RP W Hoyt
RS S Gibson
C S Hogan
1B B Terry
2B H Critz
SS- D Marshall
3B J Vergez
LF- J Moore
CF F Lindstrom
RF M Ott
OI C Fullis
U3- S Leslie
M1 J McGraw

PHI 1932 NL
SP E Holley
SR R Benge
SR S Hansen
SR P Collins
SP F Rhem
RS J Elliott
C S Davis
1B D Hurst
2B L Mallon
SS D Bartell
3B P Whitney
LF H Lee
CF K Davis
RF C Klein
M B Shotton

PIT 1932 NL
SR L French
SR B Swift
SP H Meine
SR B Harris
SP S Swetonic
RS G Spencer
RS L Chagnon
RP E Brame
C E Grace
1B G Suhr
2B T Piet
SS A Vaughan
3B P Traynor
LU A Comorosky
CF L Waner
RF P Waner
LF D Barbee
M M Gibson

STL 1932 NL
SR D Dean
SP P Derringer
SR T Carleton
SP B Hallahan
SR S Johnson
RS J Lindsey
RP A Stout
C G Mancuso
1R R Collins
2B- J Reese
SS C Gelbert
3B- J Flowers
ML E Orsatti
CF- P Martin
UO G Watkins
23 F Frisch
RU- R Blades
1B- J Bottomley
C - J Wilson
M G Street

BOS 1932 AL
SR B Weiland
SR E Durham
SR B Kline
SP I Andrews
RP W Moore
RS J Michaels
RS L Boerner
C - B Tate
1B D Alexander
2B M Olson
SS R Warstler
3B U Pickering
LF S Jolley
CF T Oliver
RO R Johnson
OI J Watwood
23 M McManus
UO- G Stumpf
M1 S Collins

CHI 1932 AL
SP T Lyons
SP S Jones
SP M Gaston
SP V Frasier
RS P Gregory
RS R Faber
C F Grube
1B L Blue
2B J Hayes
SI L Appling
3U C Selph
OF B Fothergill
CF L Funk
UO B Seeds
UT R Kress
1U B Sullivan
M L Fonseca

CLE 1932 AL
SP W Ferrell
SP C Brown
SP M Harder
SR W Hudlin
SR O Hildebrand
RS S Connally
RP J Russell
C - L Sewell
1B E Morgan
2B B Cissell
SS J Burnett
3B W Kamm
LF J Vosmik
CF E Averill
RF D Porter
C - G Myatt
M R Peckinpaugh

DET 1932 AL
SP E Whitehill
SP V Sorrell
SR W Wyatt
SP T Bridges
SR G Uhle
RS C Hogsett
C R Hayworth
1B H Davis
2B C Gehringer
SS B Rogell
3U H Schuble
LM J Stone
ML G Walker
RF- E Webb
IO- B Rhiel
UO- J White
M B Harris

NY 1932 AL
SP L Gomez
SP R Ruffing
SP G Pipgras
SR J Allen
SP H Pennock
RP D Mac Fayden
RP J Brown
C B Dickey
1B L Gehrig
2B T Lazzeri
S3 F Crosetti
3B J Sewell
RL B Chapman
CF E Combs
RL B Ruth
MU S Byrd
SS- L Lary
M J McCarthy

PHI 1932 AL
SR L Grove
SP R Walberg
SP G Earnshaw
SP R Mahaffey
SP T Freitas
RP E Rommel
RP L Krausse
C M Cochrane
1B J Foxx
2B M Bishop
SS E McNair
3B J Dykes
LF A Simmons
CF M Haas
OF- D Cramer
RF B Miller
M C Mack

STL 1932 AL
SP L Stewart
SP G Blaeholder
SP B Hadley
SR D Gray
SR W Hebert
RS C Fischer
RP C Kimsey
C R Ferrell
1B J Burns
2B S Melillo
SS J Levey
3B- A Scharein
LF G Goslin
CF F Schulte
RF B Campbell
M B Killefer

WAS 1932 AL
SR A Crowder
SR M Weaver
SR L Brown
SP T Thomas
RS F Marberry
C R Spencer
1B J Kuhel
2B B Myer
SS J Cronin
3B O Bluege
LF H Manush
CF S West
RF C Reynolds
UO S Rice
UO- D Harris
1B- J Judge
M W Johnson

BOS 1933 NL
SP E Brandt
SR B Cantwell
SR F Frankhouse
SP H Betts
SP T Zachary
C S Hogan
1B B Jordan
2B R Maranville
SS B Urbanski
3B P Whitney
LF- H Lee
CF W Berger
RF R Moore
LU- J Mowry
M B McKechnie

BRO 1933 NL
SP B Beck
SR V Mungo
SP R Benge
SP O Carroll
SR S Thurston
RP J Shaute
RP R Ryan
C A Lopez
1B S Leslie
2B T Cuccinello
SU- G Wright
3B J Stripp
LU H Wilson
CF D Taylor
RU J Frederick
UO- B Boyle
IO- J Flowers
CU- C Outen
M M Carey

CHI 1933 NL
SP L Warneke
SP G Bush
SP C Root
SP P Malone
SR B Tinning
C G Hartnett
1B C Grimm
2B Bi Herman
SS B Jurges
3B W English
LF R Stephenson
CF F Demaree
RF Ba Herman
UI- M Koenig

CIN 1933 NL
SP P Derringer
SP R Lucas
SP S Johnson
SR L Benton
SR R Kolp
RS B Frey
RP E Rixey
C E Lombardi
1B J Bottomley
2S J Morrissey
SS O Bluege
3B S Adams
LM J Moore
ML C Hafey
RF H Rice
2B- G Grantham
UO- W Roettger
M D Bush

NY 1933 NL
SR C Hubbell
SP H Schumacher
SP F Fitzsimmons
SP R Parmelee
RS H Bell
RP D Luque
RP G Spencer
C G Mancuso
1B B Terry
2B H Critz
SS B Ryan
3B J Vergez
LF J Moore
CF K Davis
RF M Ott
OF- L O'Doul
UO- H Peel

PHI 1933 NL
SP E Holley
SR S Hansen
SR J Elliott
SR C Moore
SP F Rhem
RS P Collins
RP A Liska
C S Davis
1B D Hurst
23 J Warner
SS D Bartell
3B- J McLeod
LF W Schulmerich
CF C Fullis
RF C Klein
M B Shotton

PIT 1933 NL
SR L French
SR B Swift
SP H Meine
SR S Swetonic
SP H Smith
RS W Hoyt
RS L Chagnon
RP B Harris
C E Grace
1B G Suhr
2B T Piet
SS A Vaughan
3B P Traynor
LM L Waner
CF F Lindstrom
RF P Waner
M M Gibson

STL 1933 NL
SR D Dean
SR T Carleton
SP B Hallahan
SP B Walker
SR D Vance
RS J Haines
RP S Johnson
C J Wilson
1B R Collins
2B F Frisch
SS L Durocher
3B P Martin
LF J Medwick
CF E Orsatti
RF G Watkins
MU- E Allen
UI- P Crawford
M1 G Street

BOS 1933 AL
SP G Rhodes
SR B Weiland
SR L Brown
SP H Johnson
SR I Andrews
RS J Welch
RS B Kline
RP G Pipgras
C R Ferrell
1B D Alexander
2B J Hodapp
SS R Warstler
3I M McManus
LU S Jolley
ML D Cooke
RO R Johnson
S3 B Werber
CF T Oliver
1O- B Seeds

CHI 1933 AL
SP T Lyons
SP S Jones
SP M Gaston
SP E Durham
SR J Miller
RS J Heving
RP P Gregory
RP C Kimsey
RP R Faber
C - F Grube
1B R Kress
2B J Hayes
SS L Appling
3B J Dykes
LF A Simmons
CF M Haas
RF E Swanson
C - C Berry
M L Fonseca

CLE 1933 AL
SR M Harder
SP O Hildebrand
SP W Ferrell
SR C Brown
SR W Hudlin
RP M Pearson
RP S Connally
RP B Bean
C - R Spencer
1B H Boss
2U O Hale
SS- B Knickerbocker
3B W Kamm
LF J Vosmik
CF E Averill
RF D Porter
2S B Cissell
UI- J Burnett
C - F Pytlak
M1 R Peckinpaugh
M2 B Falk
M3 W Johnson

DET 1933 AL
SP F Marberry
SP T Bridges
SP V Sorrell
SR C Fischer
SP S Rowe
RP C Hogsett
RP V Frasier
RP A Herring
C R Hayworth
1B H Greenberg
2B C Gehringer
SS B Rogell
3B M Owen
LU G Walker
CF P Fox
RF J Stone
UO- J White
M1 B Harris
M2 D Baker

NY 1933 AL
SP R Ruffing
SP L Gomez
SP J Allen
SP R Van Atta
RP W Moore
RS H Pennock
C B Dickey
1B L Gehrig
2B T Lazzeri
SS F Crosetti
3B J Sewell
RL B Chapman
MU E Combs
RL B Ruth
MU D Walker
UO- S Byrd
M J McCarthy

PHI 1933 AL
SR L Grove
SP S Cain
SR R Walberg
SR R Mahaffey
SP G Earnshaw
RS J Peterson
C M Cochrane
1B J Foxx
2B M Bishop
S2 D Williams
3B P Higgins
LF B Johnson
CF D Cramer
RF E Coleman
S2- E McNair
M C Mack

STL 1933 AL
SP B Hadley
SP G Blaeholder
SR E Wells
RS D Gray
RS R Stiles
RS W Hebert
RS H McDonald
C M Shea
1B J Burns
2B S Melillo
SS J Levey
3B A Scharein
LF C Reynolds
CF S West
RF B Campbell
UT T Gullic
UO- D Garms
M1 B Killefer
M2 A Sothoron
M3 R Hornsby

WAS 1933 AL
SR A Crowder
SP E Whitehill
SP L Stewart
SP M Weaver
SR T Thomas
RP J Russell
RS B Burke
RP B McAfee
C L Sewell
1B J Kuhel
2B B Myer
SS J Cronin
3B O Bluege
LF H Manush
CF F Schulte
RF G Goslin
UT- D Harris

BOS 1934 NL
SR E Brandt
SP F Frankhouse
SR H Betts
SP F Rhem
SP B Cantwell
RS B Smith
RP L Mangum
C A Spohrer
1B B Jordan
23 M McManus
SS B Urbanski
3B P Whitney
LF H Lee
CF W Berger
RU T Thompson
C S Hogan
OI R Moore
M B McKechnie

BRO 1934 NL
SP V Mungo
SP R Benge
SR D Leonard
SP J Babich
SR T Zachary
RS L Munns
RS O Carroll
C A Lopez
1B S Leslie
23 T Cuccinello
SS L Frey
3B J Stripp
LU D Taylor
CF L Koenecke
RO B Boyle
RU J Frederick
S2 J Jordan
M C Stengel

CHI 1934 NL
SP L Warneke
SP B Lee
SR G Bush
SR P Malone
SP J Weaver
RS B Tinning
RS C Root
C G Hartnett
1B- C Grimm
2B Bi Herman
SS B Jurges
3B S Hack
LF C Klein
CF K Cuyler
RF Ba Herman
S3 W English
LO T Stainback

CIN 1934 NL
SR P Derringer
SP B Frey
SR S Johnson
SR T Freitas
SR A Stout
RS D Brennan
RP R Kolp
C E Lombardi
1B J Bottomley
IF T Piet
S2 G Slade
UI M Koenig
LF H Pool
CF C Hafey
RL A Comorosky
IF- S Adams
M1 B O'Farrell
M2 B Shotton
M3 C Dressen

NY 1934 NL
SR C Hubbell
SP H Schumacher
SP F Fitzsimmons
SP R Parmelee
RS J Bowman
RP A Smith
RP H Bell
C G Mancuso
1B B Terry
2B H Critz
SS T Jackson
3B J Vergez
LF J Moore
MU G Watkins
RF M Ott
3S B Ryan
OF- L O'Doul

PHI 1934 NL
SR C Davis
SR P Collins
SR C Moore
SP E Moore
RS S Hansen
RS S Johnson
RS R Grabowski
C A Todd
1B D Camilli
2U L Chiozza
SS D Bartell
3B- B Walters
LM E Allen
CF K Davis
RF J Moore
C J Wilson

PIT 1934 NL
SR L French
SR B Swift
SR R Birkofer
SR W Hoyt
SP R Lucas
RS H Meine
RP L Chagnon
RS H Smith
C E Grace
1B G Suhr
2B- C Lavagetto
SS A Vaughan
3B P Traynor
LF F Lindstrom
CF L Waner
RF P Waner
23 T Thevenow
LU- W Jensen
C - T Padden
M1 M Gibson

STL 1934 NL
SR D Dean
SP T Carleton
SR P Dean
SP B Hallahan
SP B Walker
RS J Haines
RS J Mooney
C S Davis
1B R Collins
2B F Frisch
SS L Durocher
3B P Martin
LF J Medwick
CF E Orsatti
RF J Rothrock
UI B Whitehead
C B DeLancey

BOS 1934 AL
SR G Rhodes
SR J Welch
SR F Ostermueller
SP W Ferrell
SR H Johnson
RS L Grove
RS R Walberg
RP H Pennock
C R Ferrell
1B E Morgan
2B B Cissell
SS L Lary
3B B Werber
LF R Johnson
MR C Reynolds
RF- D Porter
2U M Bishop
MR M Solters
M B Harris

CHI 1934 AL
SP G Earnshaw
SP T Lyons
SP M Gaston
SP S Jones
SR L Tietje
RS P Gallivan
RP J Heving
RS W Wyatt
C - E Madjeski
1B Z Bonura
2B- J Hayes
SS L Appling
3I J Dykes
LF A Simmons
CF M Haas
RF E Swanson
2S- B Boken
M1 L Fonseca

CLE 1934 AL
SR M Harder
SP M Pearson
SP O Hildebrand
SR W Hudlin
SR L Brown
RP B Bean
RP C Brown
C - F Pytlak
1B H Trosky
2B O Hale
SS B Knickerbocker
3B W Kamm
LF J Vosmik
CF E Averill
RU S Rice
M W Johnson

DET 1934 AL
SP T Bridges
SR S Rowe
SR E Auker
SR F Marberry
SP V Sorrell
RP C Fischer
RP C Hogsett
C M Cochrane
1B H Greenberg
2B C Gehringer
SS B Rogell
3B M Owen
LF G Goslin
CF J White
RF P Fox
UO G Walker

NY 1934 AL
SP L Gomez
SP R Ruffing
SR J Murphy
SP J Broaca
SR J DeShong
RS D Mac Fayden
C B Dickey
1B L Gehrig
2U T Lazzeri
SS F Crosetti
3B J Saltzgaver
RL M Hoag
ML B Chapman
RL B Ruth
RL S Byrd
S3- R Rolfe
M J McCarthy

PHI 1934 AL
SP J Marcum
SP S Cain
SP B Dietrich
SR J Cascarella
SR A Benton
RS R Mahaffey
C C Berry
1B J Foxx
2B R Warstler
SS E McNair
3B P Higgins
LF B Johnson
CF D Cramer
RF E Coleman
OI L Finney
C F Hayes
RU- B Miller
M C Mack

STL 1934 AL
SR B Newsom
SP G Blaeholder
SP B Hadley
SR D Coffman
RS I Andrews
SR J Knott
RS E Wells
RP B McAfee
C R Hemsley
1B J Burns
2B S Melillo
SS A Strange
3B H Clift
LM R Pepper
CF S West
RF B Campbell
IO O Bejma
UO- D Garms
M R Hornsby

WAS 1934 AL
SP E Whitehill
SP M Weaver
SR B Burke
SP L Stewart
SR T Thomas
RS J Russell
RP A McColl
RS A Crowder
C - E Phillips
1B- J Kuhel
2B B Myer
SS J Cronin
3B C Travis
LF H Manush
CF F Schulte
RF J Stone
IO O Bluege
RU D Harris

BOS 1935 NL
SR F Frankhouse
SR B Cantwell
SR B Smith
SP E Brandt
SR H Betts
RP D Mac Fayden
RP L Benton
C A Spohrer
1U B Jordan
23 L Mallon
SS B Urbanski
32 P Whitney
LF H Lee
CF W Berger
RU T Thompson
RU R Moore
UI- J Coscarart
UO- J Mowry
M B McKechnie

BRO 1935 NL
SR V Mungo
SP W Clark
SP G Earnshaw
SP T Zachary
SR J Babich
RS D Leonard
RP R Benge
RS L Munns
RP D Vance
C A Lopez
1B S Leslie
23 T Cuccinello
SS L Frey
3B J Stripp
LF D Taylor
MO F Bordagaray
RF B Boyle
UT J Bucher
UI J Jordan
MU L Koenecke
M C Stengel

CHI 1935 NL
SR L Warneke
SP B Lee
SR L French
SR C Root
SP T Carleton
RS R Henshaw
RP F Kowalik
C G Hartnett
1B P Cavarretta
2B B Herman
SS B Jurges
3B S Hack
LF A Galan
MR F Demaree
RF C Klein
M3- F Lindstrom
M C Grimm

CIN 1935 NL
SR P Derringer
SR A Hollingsworth
SR G Schott
SR T Freitas
SR S Johnson
RS D Brennan
RS B Frey
RS L Herrmann
CU E Lombardi
1B J Bottomley
2B A Kampouris
SS B Myers
3B L Riggs
LF- B Herman
ML S Byrd
RF I Goodman
C - G Campbell
UI- B Sullivan
M C Dressen

NY 1935 NL
SP C Hubbell
SP H Schumacher
SP R Parmelee
SP S Castleman
RS A Smith
RP A Stout
RP F Gabler
C G Mancuso
1B B Terry
2I M Koenig
SS D Bartell
3B T Jackson
LF J Moore
CF H Leiber
RF M Ott

PHI 1935 NL
SR C Davis
SR O Jorgens
SR S Johnson
SP B Walters
SR J Bowman
RS J Bivin
RS P Pezzullo
RS R Prim
RS H Mulcahy
C A Todd
1B D Camilli
2B L Chiozza
SS M Haslin
3B J Vergez
LF G Watkins
CF E Allen
RF J Moore
C - J Wilson

PIT 1935 NL
SP C Blanton
SR G Bush
SR B Swift
SR J Weaver
SR R Birkofer
RS W Hoyt
RP R Lucas
C T Padden
1B G Suhr
2B P Young
SS A Vaughan
3U T Thevenow
LF W Jensen
CF L Waner
RF P Waner
C - E Grace
2U- C Lavagetto
M P Traynor

STL 1935 NL
SR D Dean
SR P Dean
SR B Walker
SR B Hallahan
SR J Haines
RS E Heusser
C B DeLancey
1B R Collins
2B F Frisch
SS L Durocher
3B P Martin
LF J Medwick
CF T Moore
RF J Rothrock
C S Davis
2U B Whitehead
UO- E Orsatti

BOS 1935 AL
SP W Ferrell
SP L Grove
SR G Rhodes
SR J Welch
SP F Ostermueller
RS R Walberg
RS J Wilson
RP G Hockette
C R Ferrell
1B B Dahlgren
2B S Melillo
SS J Cronin
3B B Werber
LF R Johnson
CF M Almada
UO D Cooke
OF- B Miller
RF- C Reynolds

CHI 1935 AL
SP J Whitehead
SP V Kennedy
SP T Lyons
SP L Tietje
SP S Jones
RS R Phelps
RP W Wyatt
C L Sewell
1B Z Bonura
2B- J Hayes
SS L Appling
3B J Dykes
LF R Radcliff
CF A Simmons
RU M Haas
RU G Washington
2B- T Piet

CLE 1935 AL
SP M Harder
SP W Hudlin
SR T Lee
SP M Pearson
SR O Hildebrand
RS L Brown
RP R Winegarner
RS C Brown
C - E Phillips
1B H Trosky
2B B Berger
SS B Knickerbocker
3B O Hale
LF J Vosmik
CF E Averill
RO- M Galatzer
RF- B Campbell
UI- R Hughes
M1 W Johnson
M2 S O'Neill

DET 1935 AL
SP S Rowe
SP T Bridges
SP A Crowder
SR E Auker
SR J Sullivan
RP C Hogsett
C M Cochrane
1B H Greenberg
2B C Gehringer
SS B Rogell
3B M Owen
LF G Goslin
CF J White
RF P Fox
UO G Walker

NY 1935 AL
SP L Gomez
SP R Ruffing
SP J Broaca
SP J Allen
SR V Tamulis
RS J Murphy
RP J DeShong
RP P Malone
C B Dickey
1B L Gehrig
2B T Lazzeri
SS- F Crosetti
3B R Rolfe
LF J Hill
CF B Chapman
RF G Selkirk
LU- E Combs
M J McCarthy

PHI 1935 AL
SR J Marcum
SR B Dietrich
SP G Blaeholder
SP W Wilshere
SR R Mahaffey
RP G Caster
RP D Lieber
C - P Richards
1B J Foxx
2B R Warstler
SS E McNair
3B P Higgins
LF B Johnson
CF D Cramer
RF- W Moses
RU L Finney
M C Mack

STL 1935 AL
SR I Andrews
SR J Knott
SR J Walkup
SP S Cain
SR F Thomas
RS R Van Atta
RS D Coffman
C R Hemsley
1B J Burns
2B- T Carey
SS L Lary
3B H Clift
LF M Solters
CF S West
RF E Coleman
UT- B Bell
UO- R Pepper
M R Hornsby

WAS 1935 AL
SP E Whitehill
SP B Hadley
SP B Newsom
SR E Linke
RS J Russell
RS L Pettit
C C Bolton
1B J Kuhel
2B B Myer
S3 O Bluege
3B C Travis
LF H Manush
CF J Powell
RU J Stone
SU- R Kress
UO- F Schulte
M B Harris

BOS 1936 NL
SP D Mac Fayden
SP T Chaplin
SP J Lanning
SR B Cantwell
SP R Benge
RS B Smith
RS B Reis
C A Lopez
1B B Jordan
2B T Cuccinello
S3 B Urbanski
3B J Coscarart
LF H Lee
CF W Berger
RF G Moore
OI T Thompson
M B McKechnie

BRO 1936 NL
SP V Mungo
SP E Brandt
SR F Frankhouse
SR M Butcher
SR W Clark
RS G Jeffcoat
RS T Baker
C R Berres
1B B Hassett
2B J Jordan
SS L Frey
3B J Stripp
LU G Watkins
CF J Cooney
UT F Bordagaray
UT J Bucher
C B Phelps
M C Stengel

CHI 1936 NL
SR B Lee
SR L French
SR L Warneke
SP T Carleton
SP C Davis
RS R Henshaw
RP C Root
RP C Bryant
C G Hartnett
1B P Cavarretta
2B B Herman
SS B Jurges
3B S Hack
LF- E Allen
CF A Galan
RF F Demaree
CU- K O'Dea
M C Grimm

CIN 1936 NL
SR P Derringer
SP A Hollingsworth
SP G Schott
SP B Hallahan
SP P Davis
RS B Frey
RS L Stine
RP D Brennan
C E Lombardi
1B L Scarsella
2B A Kampouris
SS B Myers
3B L Riggs
LF B Herman
MO K Cuyler
RF I Goodman
UT C Chapman
S2 T Thevenow
C - G Campbell
ML- H Walker
M C Dressen

NY 1936 NL
SP C Hubbell
SP H Schumacher
SR A Smith
SR F Fitzsimmons
SR H Gumbert
RS F Gabler
RS S Castleman
RP D Coffman
C G Mancuso
1B S Leslie
2B B Whitehead
SS D Bartell
3B T Jackson
LF J Moore
CF H Leiber
RF M Ott
CF J Ripple
1U- B Terry

PHI 1936 NL
SP B Walters
SR C Passeau
SR J Bowman
SR O Jorgens
RS S Johnson
RS E Moore
C - E Grace
1B D Camilli
2S C Gomez
SS L Norris
3B P Whitney
LR J Moore
ML E Sulik
RF C Klein
MI L Chiozza
CU- J Wilson

PIT 1936 NL
SR B Swift
SR C Blanton
SP J Weaver
SP R Lucas
SR W Hoyt
RS M Brown
RS R Birkofer
C - T Padden
1B G Suhr
2B P Young
SS A Vaughan
3B B Brubaker
LF W Jensen
CF L Waner
RF P Waner
M P Traynor

STL 1936 NL
SR D Dean
SP R Parmelee
SR J Winford

SR J Haines
RP E Heusser
RS G Earnshaw
C S Davis
1B J Mize
2B- S Martin
SS L Durocher
3S C Gelbert
LF J Medwick
CF T Moore
RF P Martin
1U R Collins
C B Ogrodowski
2U F Frisch
UO- L King

BOS 1936 AL
SP W Ferrell
SP L Grove
SR F Ostermueller
SP J Marcum
SR R Walberg
RS J Wilson
C R Ferrell
1B J Foxx
2B S Melillo
S2 E McNair
3L B Werber
LF- H Manush
CF D Cramer
RU D Cooke
RU M Almada
S3- J Cronin
IO- J Kroner

CHI 1936 AL
SP V Kennedy
SP J Whitehead
SP S Cain
SP T Lyons
SP M Stratton
RP C Brown
RP R Evans
C L Sewell
1B Z Bonura
2B J Hayes
SS L Appling
3B J Dykes
LF R Radcliff
UO M Kreevich
RF M Haas
23 T Piet
CF- L Rosenthal

CLE 1936 AL
SP J Allen
SP M Harder
SR O Hildebrand
SR D Galehouse
SP L Brown
RS G Blaeholder
RS T Lee
RS W Hudlin
C - B Sullivan
1B H Trosky
2B R Hughes
SS B Knickerbocker
3B O Hale
LF J Vosmik
CF E Averill
RF- R Weatherly
M S O'Neill

DET 1936 AL
SP T Bridges
SP S Rowe
SP E Auker
SR V Sorrell
RS R Lawson
RP C Kimsey
C - R Hayworth
1B J Burns
2B C Gehringer
SS B Rogell
3B M Owen
LF G Goslin
CF A Simmons
RF G Walker
M1 M Cochrane
M2 D Baker
M3 M Cochrane

NY 1936 AL
SP R Ruffing
SP M Pearson
SR J Broaca
SP L Gomez
SR B Hadley
RS P Malone
C B Dickey
1B L Gehrig
2B T Lazzeri
SS F Crosetti
3B R Rolfe
UO J DiMaggio
OF- J Powell
RF G Selkirk
M J McCarthy

PHI 1936 AL
SP H Kelley
SP G Rhodes
SP B Ross
SR H Fink
RP R Gumpert
C F Hayes
1O L Finney
2B- R Warstler
SS S Newsome
3B P Higgins
LF B Johnson
CF W Moses
RF G Puccinelli
1U C Dean
M C Mack

STL 1936 AL
SR C Hogsett
SR J Knott
SR I Andrews
SR E Caldwell
SR T Thomas
RS R Van Atta
RP G Liebhardt
C R Hemsley
1B J Bottomley
2B T Carey
SS L Lary
3B H Clift
LF M Solters
CF S West
RF B Bell
U2- E Coleman
M R Hornsby

WAS 1936 AL
SP B Newsom
SP J DeShong
SP E Whitehill
SR P Appleton
SP J Cascarella
RS J Russell
C - C Bolton
1B J Kuhel
2S- O Bluege
SR C Travis
3B B Lewis
LF J Stone
CF B Chapman
RF- C Reynolds
S2 R Kress
LU- J Hill
M B Harris

BOS 1937 NL
SP L Fette
SP J Turner
SP D Mac Fayden
SR G Bush
SR J Lanning
RS I Hutchinson
C A Lopez
1B E Fletcher
2B T Cuccinello
SS R Warstler
3B- G English
L3 D Garms
CF V DiMaggio
RF G Moore
LU- R Johnson
M B McKechnie

BRO 1937 NL
SR M Butcher
SR L Hamlin
SP F Frankhouse
SP W Hoyt
SP V Mungo
RS R Henshaw
RP G Jeffcoat
C B Phelps
1B B Hassett
23 C Lavagetto
SS W English
3U- J Stripp
LF T Winsett
CF J Cooney
RF H Manush
UO G Brack
UT J Bucher
M B Grimes

CHI 1937 NL
SP B Lee
SP T Carleton
SR L French
SR C Root
SR R Parmelee
RS C Bryant
RS C Davis
RS C Shoun
C G Hartnett
1B R Collins
2B B Herman
SS B Jurges
3B S Hack
LF A Galan
CF- J Marty
RF F Demaree
OI P Cavarretta
UT- L Frey
C - K O'Dea
M C Grimm

CIN 1937 NL
SR L Grissom
SR P Derringer
SR P Davis
SR A Hollingsworth
SR G Schott
C E Lombardi
1B B Jordan
2B A Kampouris
SS B Myers
3B L Riggs
UO K Cuyler
OF- C Hafey
RF I Goodman
1U L Scarsella
MU- H Walker
M1 C Dressen
M2 B Wallace

NY 1937 NL
SP C Hubbell
SR C Melton
SP H Schumacher
SR H Gumbert
SP S Castleman
RS A Smith
RP D Coffman
C H Danning
1B J McCarthy
2B B Whitehead
SS D Bartell
3B L Chiozza
LF J Moore
OF J Ripple
R3 M Ott
C - G Mancuso
M B Terry

PHI 1937 NL
SR C Passeau
SP B Walters
SR W LaMaster
SR H Mulcahy
SR S Johnson
RS O Jorgens
RP H Kelleher
C - B Atwood
1B D Camilli
2B D Young
SS G Scharein
3B P Whitney
LF M Arnovich
CF H Martin
RL C Klein
OI E Browne
UO J Moore
2I L Norris
C - E Grace
M J Wilson

PIT 1937 NL
SP C Blanton
SR R Bauers
SP E Brandt
SR B Swift
SR J Bowman
RP R Lucas
RP M Brown
RS J Weaver
C A Todd
1B G Suhr
2B L Handley
SS A Vaughan
3B B Brubaker
LM W Jensen
CF L Waner
RF P Waner
UI P Young
LU- J Dickshot
M P Traynor

STL 1937 NL
SP B Weiland
SP L Warneke
SP D Dean
SR S Johnson
SR R Harrell
RS M Ryba
C - B Ogrodowski
1B J Mize
2B J Brown
SS L Durocher
3B D Gutteridge
LF J Medwick
CF T Moore
RF D Padgett
3O F Bordagaray
OI P Martin
2U- S Martin
C - M Owen
M F Frisch

BOS 1937 AL
SP L Grove
SR J Wilson
SP B Newsom
SR J Marcum
SR A McKain
RS R Walberg
C G Desautels
1B J Foxx
2B E McNair
SS J Cronin
3B P Higgins
LF B Mills
CF D Cramer
RF B Chapman

CHI 1937 AL
SP V Kennedy
SP T Lee
SP T Lyons
SP J Whitehead
SP M Stratton
RP B Dietrich
RP C Brown
C L Sewell
1B Z Bonura
2B J Hayes
SS L Appling
3B T Piet
LF R Radcliff
CF M Kreevich
RF D Walker
M J Dykes

CLE 1937 AL
SP M Harder
SP D Galehouse
SR W Hudlin
SP J Allen
SP B Feller
RS E Whitehill
RP J Heving
RS L Brown
RP W Wyatt
C F Pytlak
1B H Trosky
2U- J Kroner
SS L Lary
32 O Hale
LF M Solters
CF E Averill
RF B Campbell
32 R Hughes
M S O'Neill

DET 1937 AL
SP E Auker
SP T Bridges
SP R Lawson
SP J Wade
SR B Poffenberger
RS G Gill
RS S Coffman
C3 R York
1B H Greenberg
2B C Gehringer
SS B Rogell
3B M Owen
LR G Walker
CF J White
RO P Fox
OI- G Goslin
M1 M Cochrane
M2 D Baker
M3 M Cochrane
M4 D Baker
M5 C Perkins

NY 1937 AL
SP L Gomez
SP R Ruffing
SP B Hadley
SP M Pearson
RP J Murphy
RP F Makosky
C B Dickey
1B L Gehrig
2B T Lazzeri
SS F Crosetti
3B R Rolfe
LF J Powell
CF J DiMaggio
RO M Hoag
RF- G Selkirk
M J McCarthy

PHI 1937 AL
SP G Caster
SR H Kelley
SR E Smith
SP B Thomas
SP B Ross
RP L Nelson
RP H Fink
RP G Turbeville
C E Brucker
1B C Dean
23 R Peters
SS S Newsome
3B B Werber
LF B Johnson
CF- J Hill
RF W Moses
1M- L Finney
MU- J Rothrock
M1 C Mack
M2 E Mack

STL 1937 AL
SP O Hildebrand
SR J Knott
SR C Hogsett
SP J Walkup
SR J Bonetti
RS B Trotter
RS L Koupal
C R Hemsley
1B H Davis
2S T Carey
SS B Knickerbocker
3B H Clift
LF J Vosmik
CF S West
RF B Bell
MO E Allen
M1 R Hornsby
M2 J Bottomley

WAS 1937 AL
SP J DeShong
SP W Ferrell
SP M Weaver
SR P Appleton
RS E Linke
RP S Cohen
C - R Ferrell
1B J Kuhel
2B B Myer
SS C Travis
3B B Lewis
LF A Simmons
CF M Almada
RL J Stone
RU- F Sington
M B Harris

BOS 1938 NL
SP J Turner
SP L Fette
SP D Mac Fayden
SR M Shoffner
SR J Lanning
RS I Hutchinson
RS D Errickson
C - R Mueller
1B E Fletcher
2B T Cuccinello
SS R Warstler
3B- J Stripp
LR M West
CF V DiMaggio
RO J Cooney
UT D Garms
M C Stengel

BRO 1938 NL
SR L Hamlin
SP F Fitzsimmons
SR T Pressnell
SR V Tamulis
SR B Posedel
RP V Mungo
RS F Frankhouse
C - B Phelps
1B D Camilli
2B J Hudson
SS L Durocher
3B C Lavagetto
LU B Hassett
OI E Koy
UO G Rosen
RO- K Cuyler
M B Grimes

CHI 1938 NL
SP B Lee
SR C Bryant
SR L French
SP T Carleton
RS C Root
RP J Russell
C - G Hartnett
1B R Collins
2B B Herman
SS B Jurges
3B S Hack
LF A Galan
ML C Reynolds
RF F Demaree
OI- P Cavarretta
CF- J Marty
C - K O'Dea
M1 C Grimm

CIN 1938 NL
SP P Derringer
SP J Vander Meer
SR P Davis
SP B Walters
SR J Weaver
RP G Schott
RP J Cascarella
C E Lombardi
1B F McCormick
2B L Frey
SS B Myers
3B L Riggs
LF W Berger
CF H Craft
RF I Goodman
LU- D Cooke
M B McKechnie

NY 1938 NL
SP C Melton
SP H Gumbert
SP H Schumacher
SP C Hubbell
SR B Lohrman
RP D Coffman
RP J Brown
C H Danning
1B J McCarthy
2B- A Kampouris
SS D Bartell
3B M Ott
LF J Moore
CF H Leiber
RF J Ripple
U3- S Leslie
UO- B Seeds
M B Terry

PHI 1938 NL
SR H Mulcahy
SR C Passeau
SP A Hollingsworth
SP M Butcher
RS P Sivess
RP A Smith
C B Atwood
1B P Weintraub
2B H Mueller
SS D Young
3U P Whitney
LF M Arnovich
CF H Martin
RF C Klein
S2 G Scharein
3U- B Jordan
M1 J Wilson
M2 H Lobert

PIT 1938 NL
SP R Bauers
SP J Tobin
SP C Blanton
SP B Klinger
SR E Brandt
RS B Swift
RP M Brown
C A Todd
1B G Suhr
2B P Young
SS A Vaughan
3B L Handley
LF J Rizzo
CF L Waner
RF P Waner
M P Traynor

STL 1938 NL
SP B Weiland
SR B McGee
SP L Warneke
SR C Davis
SR R Henshaw
RS M Macon
RS C Shoun
RP R Harrell
C M Owen
1B J Mize
2B S Martin
SS- L Myers
3S D Gutteridge
LF J Medwick
CF T Moore
RU E Slaughter
UI J Brown
RU D Padgett
OI- F Bordagaray
OI- P Martin
M1 F Frisch
M2 M Gonzalez

BOS 1938 AL
SR J Bagby
SR J Wilson
SR F Ostermueller
SP L Grove
SR E Dickman
RS A McKain
RP J Marcum
C G Desautels
1B J Foxx
2B B Doerr
SS J Cronin
3B P Higgins
LF J Vosmik
CF D Cramer
RF B Chapman
OI- R Nonnenkamp

CHI 1938 AL
SP T Lee
SP T Lyons
SP M Stratton
SP J Whitehead
SP J Knott
RS J Rigney
C - L Sewell
1B J Kuhel
2B- J Hayes
SS- L Appling
3B M Owen
OF G Walker
CF M Kreevich
RF H Steinbacher
S2 B Berger
LF R Radcliff
M J Dykes

CLE 1938 AL
SP B Feller
SP M Harder
SP J Allen
SP E Whitehill
SR W Hudlin
RS D Galehouse
RS J Humphries
RS A Milnar
C F Pytlak
1B H Trosky
2B O Hale
SS L Lary
3B K Keltner
LF J Heath
CF E Averill
RF B Campbell
UO- R Weatherly
M O Vitt

DET 1938 AL
SP V Kennedy
SP G Gill
SP E Auker
SP T Bridges
SR R Lawson
RS H Eisenstat
RS B Poffenberger
RS S Coffman
RP A Benton
C R York
1B H Greenberg
2B C Gehringer
SS B Rogell
3B- D Ross
LU D Walker
CF- C Morgan
RF P Fox
3U M Christman
UO- J White
M1 M Cochrane
M2 D Baker

NY 1938 AL
SP R Ruffing
SP L Gomez
SP M Pearson
SP S Chandler
SR B Hadley
CL J Murphy
RP I Andrews
C B Dickey
1B L Gehrig
2B J Gordon
SS F Crosetti
3B R Rolfe
LF G Selkirk
CF J DiMaggio
RF T Henrich
UO- M Hoag
M J McCarthy

PHI 1938 AL
SP G Caster
SR B Thomas
SP L Nelson
SP B Ross
RS E Smith
RS N Potter
RS A Williams
C F Hayes
1O L Finney
2B D Lodigiani
SS W Ambler
3B B Werber
LF S Chapman
CF B Johnson
RF W Moses
M C Mack

STL 1938 AL
SP B Newsom
SP L Mills
SP O Hildebrand
SR R Van Atta
RS E Cole
RS B Cox
C B Sullivan
1B G McQuinn
2B D Heffner
SS R Kress
3B H Clift
LF B Mills
CF M Almada
RF B Bell
UO- M Mazzera
M1 G Street
M2 S Melillo

WAS 1938 AL
SP D Leonard
SR K Chase
SP W Ferrell
SR H Kelley
SR M Weaver
RS P Appleton
RS J DeShong
RS J Krakauskas
RS C Hogsett
C R Ferrell
1B Z Bonura
2B B Myer
SS C Travis
3B B Lewis
LF A Simmons
CF S West
RF G Case
UO T Wright
M B Harris

BOS 1939 NL
SP B Posedel
SP D Mac Fayden
SP J Turner
SP L Fette
SR M Shoffner
RS J Lanning
RS D Errickson
RS J Sullivan
C A Lopez
1B B Hassett
2B- T Cuccinello
SS- E Miller
3B H Majeski
UO M West
CF J Cooney
R3 D Garms
LF A Simmons
UI R Warstler
M C Stengel

BRO 1939 NL
SP L Hamlin
SR H Casey
SR V Tamulis
SR T Pressnell
SP F Fitzsimmons
RP W Wyatt
RP I Hutchinson
RS R Evans
C B Phelps
1B D Camilli
2B P Coscarart
SS L Durocher
3B C Lavagetto
LF E Koy
CF- D Walker
RF G Moore
UI J Hudson
C - A Todd

CHI 1939 NL
SP B Lee
SP C Passeau
SR L French
SR C Root
SR V Page
RP D Dean
RP J Russell
C G Hartnett
1B R Russell
2B B Herman
SS D Bartell

3B S Hack
LF A Galan
CF H Leiber
RU J Gleeson
C - G Mancuso
MU-C Reynolds

CIN 1939 NL
SP B Walters
SP P Derringer
SR W Moore
SR L Grissom
SP J Vander Meer
RS J Thompson
C E Lombardi
1B F McCormick
2B L Frey
SS B Myers
3B B Werber
LM W Berger
CF H Craft
RF I Goodman
M B McKechnie

NY 1939 NL
SP H Gumbert
SR C Melton
SR B Lohrman
SP H Schumacher
SR C Hubbell
RS M Salvo
RP J Brown
RP R Lynn
C H Danning
1B Z Bonura
2B B Whitehead
SS B Jurges
3B- T Hafey
LF J Moore
CF F Demaree
RF M Ott
M B Terry

PHI 1939 NL
SP H Mulcahy
SP K Higbe
SR B Beck
SR I Pearson
SP S Johnson
RP M Butcher
RS R Harrell
RP B Kerksieck
C - S Davis
1B- G Suhr
2B- R Hughes
SS G Scharein
3B P May
LF M Arnovich
MU H Martin
RU- L Scott
OI- G Brack
UT H Mueller
MO-J Marty
C - W Millies
SU- D Young
M D Prothro

PIT 1939 NL
SP B Klinger
SR M Brown
SR J Bowman
SP J Tobin
RS R Sewell
RS B Swift
C - R Mueller
1B E Fletcher
2B- P Young
SS A Vaughan
3B L Handley
LF J Rizzo
CF L Waner
RF P Waner
23 B Brubaker
MO-F Bell
C - R Berres
OF- C Klein
M P Traynor

STL 1939 NL
SR C Davis
SR M Cooper
SR L Warneke
SR B McGee
SP B Weiland
RS B Bowman
RP C Shoun
C M Owen
1B J Mize
2B S Martin
S2 J Brown
3B D Gutteridge
LF J Medwick
CF T Moore
RF E Slaughter
UO-L King
OI- P Martin
CU- D Padgett
M R Blades

BOS 1939 AL
SP L Grove
SR J Wilson
SR F Ostermueller
SP E Auker
SR D Galehouse
RP E Dickman
RS J Heving
RS J Wade
C J Peacock
1B J Foxx
2B B Doerr
SS J Cronin
3B J Tabor
LF J Vosmik
CF D Cramer
RF T Williams
UT L Finney

CHI 1939 AL
SP T Lee
SP J Rigney
SP E Smith
SP T Lyons
SP J Knott
RP C Brown
RP B Dietrich
C M Tresh
1B J Kuhel
2B- O Bejma
SS L Appling
3B E McNair
LF G Walker
CF M Kreevich
RU L Rosenthal
RU R Radcliff
M J Dykes

CLE 1939 AL
SP B Feller
SR A Milnar
SP M Harder
SP J Allen
SP W Hudlin
RS H Eisenstat
RP J Dobson
C R Hemsley
1B H Trosky
2U O Hale
SS- S Webb
3B K Keltner
LF J Heath
CF B Chapman
RF B Campbell
UI O Grimes
UO R Weatherly
M O Vitt

DET 1939 AL
SP B Newsom
SP T Bridges
SR D Trout
SP S Rowe
SR A Benton
RS A McKain
RP B Thomas
C B Tebbetts
1B H Greenberg
2B C Gehringer
SS F Croucher
3B P Higgins
LF- E Averill
CF B McCosky
RF P Fox
CU R York
M D Baker

NY 1939 AL
SP R Ruffing
SP L Gomez
SP B Hadley
SP A Donald
SP M Pearson
RP O Hildebrand
RS S Sundra
RS M Russo
CL J Murphy
C B Dickey
1B B Dahlgren
2B J Gordon
SS F Crosetti
3B R Rolfe
LR G Selkirk
CF J DiMaggio
RL C Keller
RM T Henrich
M J McCarthy

PHI 1939 AL
SR L Nelson
SR N Potter
SP B Ross
SP B Beckmann
SR G Caster
RP C Dean
RP C Pippen
RS B Joyce
C F Hayes
1B D Siebert
2U J Gantenbein
SS S Newsome
3U D Lodigiani
LF B Johnson
CF S Chapman
RF W Moses
SS W Ambler
RU D Miles
23 B Nagel
M1 C Mack
M2 E Mack

STL 1939 AL
SP J Kramer
SP V Kennedy
SR R Lawson
SR L Mills
SR B Harris
RS B Trotter
RS G Gill
RP J Whitehead
C - J Glenn
1B G McQuinn
2B J Berardino
S2 D Heffner
3B H Clift
LF- J Gallagher
MU C Laabs
UO M Hoag
OI B Sullivan
SS- M Christman
M F Haney

WAS 1939 AL
SP D Leonard
SP K Chase
SR J Krakauskas
SP J Haynes
SR A Carrasquel
RP P Appleton
RS W Masterson
C - R Ferrell
1B- M Vernon
2B- J Bloodworth
SS C Travis
3B B Lewis
RL T Wright
OI S West
MR G Case
LF- B Estalella
2B- B Myer
M B Harris

BOS 1940 NL
SP D Errickson
SP B Posedel
SR J Sullivan
SP M Salvo
SR N Strincevich
RP J Tobin
RP A Javery
RP D Coffman
C - R Berres
1B B Hassett
2B B Rowell
SS E Miller
3B S Sisti
LF C Ross
CF J Cooney
OI M West
RF G Moore
M C Stengel

BRO 1940 NL
SP W Wyatt
SP L Hamlin
SR T Carleton
SP C Davis
SP F Fitzsimmons
RS V Tamulis
RS H Casey
RP T Pressnell
C B Phelps
1B D Camilli
2B P Coscarart
SS- P Reese
3B C Lavagetto
LF J Medwick
CF D Walker
UO J Vosmik
UI- J Hudson
RU- J Wasdell
M L Durocher

CHI 1940 NL
SR C Passeau
SP L French
SP B Lee
SR V Olsen
SP J Mooty
RS K Raffensberger
RS C Root
RP V Page
C A Todd
1B- P Cavarretta
2B B Herman
SS B Mattick
3B S Hack
RL B Nicholson
MO J Gleeson
OI H Leiber
LU D Dallessandro
M G Hartnett

CIN 1940 NL
SP B Walters
SP P Derringer
SP J Thompson
SP J Turner
SR W Moore
RP J Beggs
RP J Hutchings
RP M Shoffner
C E Lombardi
1B F McCormick
2B L Frey
SS- B Myers
3B B Werber
UO M McCormick
CF H Craft
RF I Goodman
SS- E Joost
M B McKechnie

NY 1940 NL
SP H Gumbert
SP H Schumacher
SP C Hubbell
SP B Lohrman
SR C Melton
RS P Dean
RP J Brown
RP R Joiner
C H Danning
1B B Young
23- T Cuccinello
S2 M Witek
32 B Whitehead
LF J Moore
MR F Demaree
R3 M Ott
MU-J Rucker
M B Terry

PHI 1940 NL
SP K Higbe
SP H Mulcahy
SP I Pearson
SR S Johnson
SR B Beck
RS L Smoll
C B Warren
1B A Mahan
2B H Schulte
SS B Bragan
3B P May
LO J Rizzo
CF J Marty
RF C Klein
UT H Mueller
C - B Atwood
M D Prothro

PIT 1940 NL
SR R Sewell
SP J Bowman
SR M Brown
SR K Heintzelman
SR B Klinger
RS M Butcher
RS J Lanning
RS D Lanahan
RS D Mac Fayden
C S Davis
1B E Fletcher
2B F Gustine
SS A Vaughan
3B L Handley
LF M Van Robays
CF V DiMaggio
RF B Elliott
3U D Garms
RU- P Waner
M F Frisch

STL 1940 NL
SP M Cooper
SP L Warneke
SP B McGee
SR C Shoun
SR B Bowman
RS M Lanier
RP J Russell
C M Owen
1B J Mize
23 J Orengo
SS M Marion
32 S Martin
LF- E Koy
CF T Moore
RF E Slaughter
UI J Brown
OI- J Hopp
OI- P Martin
C - D Padgett
M1 R Blades
M2 M Gonzalez
M3 B Southworth

BOS 1940 AL
SR J Bagby
SR J Wilson
SP L Grove
SR F Ostermueller
SR H Hash
RS J Heving
RP D Galehouse
RS E Dickman
C - G Desautels
1C J Foxx
2B B Doerr
SS J Cronin
3B J Tabor
LF T Williams
MO D DiMaggio
MO D Cramer
R1 L Finney

CHI 1940 AL
SP J Rigney
SP T Lee
SP E Smith
SP T Lyons
SP J Knott
RP B Dietrich
RP C Brown
RP P Appleton
C M Tresh
1B J Kuhel
2B- S Webb
SS L Appling
3B B Kennedy
LF M Solters
CF M Kreevich
RF T Wright
LU L Rosenthal
M J Dykes

CLE 1940 AL
SP B Feller
SP A Milnar
SP M Harder
SP A Smith
SR J Allen
RS J Dobson
RP H Eisenstat
C R Hemsley
1B H Trosky
2B R Mack
SS L Boudreau
3B K Keltner
UO B Chapman
CF R Weatherly
RF B Bell
LF J Heath
M O Vitt

DET 1940 AL
SP B Newsom
SP T Bridges
SP S Rowe
SP J Gorsica
SP H Newhouser
RS D Trout
CL A Benton
RP T Seats
RP A McKain
C B Tebbetts
1B R York
2B C Gehringer
SS D Bartell
3B P Higgins
LF H Greenberg
CF B McCosky
RF P Fox
RU B Campbell
CU- B Sullivan
M D Baker

NY 1940 AL
SP R Ruffing
SP M Russo
SP S Chandler
SP M Breuer
SR A Donald
RP M Pearson
RS S Sundra
RP T Bonham
RP J Murphy
C B Dickey
1B B Dahlgren
2B J Gordon
SS F Crosetti
3B R Rolfe
LR G Selkirk
CF J DiMaggio
RL C Keller
RM-T Henrich
M J McCarthy

PHI 1940 AL
SP J Babich
SP N Potter
SR G Caster
SR C Dean
SP B Ross
RS B Beckmann
RS E Heusser
RP P Vaughan
C F Hayes
1B D Siebert
2B B McCoy
SU A Brancato
3B A Rubeling
LF B Johnson
CF S Chapman
RF W Moses
UO- D Miles
M C Mack

STL 1940 AL
SP E Auker
SP V Kennedy
SP B Harris
SP J Niggeling
SR E Bildilli
RP B Trotter
RP R Lawson
RP S Coffman
RS L Mills
C B Swift
1B G McQuinn
2B D Heffner
SS J Berardino
3B H Clift
LF R Radcliff
CF W Judnich
RU- R Cullenbine
UO C Laabs
RU- J Grace
M F Haney

WAS 1940 AL
SP D Leonard
SP K Chase
SP S Hudson
SR W Masterson
RS J Krakauskas
RS R Monteagudo
RS J Haynes
RP A Carrasquel
C R Ferrell
1B- Z Bonura
2B J Bloodworth
SS J Pofahl
3B C Travis
LF G Walker
CF G Case
RF B Lewis
CU- J Early
UO- J Welaj
M B Harris

BOS 1941 NL
SP J Tobin
SP M Salvo
SR A Johnson
SR D Errickson
SR A Javery
RS T Earley
RS J Hutchings
RP F LaManna
C R Berres
1B B Hassett
2B B Rowell
SS E Miller
3B S Sisti
LF M West
CF J Cooney
RU G Moore
RU P Waner
C - P Masi
M C Stengel

BRO 1941 NL
SP K Higbe
SP W Wyatt
SR H Casey
SR C Davis
SR L Hamlin
C M Owen
1B D Camilli
2B B Herman
SS P Reese
3B C Lavagetto
LF J Medwick
CF P Reiser
RO D Walker
OI- J Wasdell
M L Durocher

CHI 1941 NL
SP C Passeau
SR V Olsen
SP B Lee
SR J Mooty
SR P Erickson
RP L French
RP C Root
RP T Pressnell
RP V Page
C C McCullough
1B B Dahlgren
2B L Stringer
SS B Sturgeon
3B S Hack
OF D Dallessandro
OI P Cavarretta
RF B Nicholson
M J Wilson

CIN 1941 NL
SP B Walters
SP P Derringer
SP J Vander Meer
SR E Riddle
SR J Turner
RS J Thompson
RP J Beggs
RP W Moore
C E Lombardi
1B F McCormick
2B L Frey
SS E Joost
3B B Werber
LU M McCormick
CF H Craft
UO J Gleeson
M B McKechnie

NY 1941 NL
SP H Schumacher
SR C Melton
SP C Hubbell
SR B Lohrman
SR B Carpenter
RP B McGee
RS B Bowman
RP A Adams
RP J Brown
C H Danning
1B B Young
2B B Whitehead
SS B Jurges
3B D Bartell
LF J Moore
CF J Rucker
RF M Ott
LU- M Arnovich
M B Terry

PHI 1941 NL
SR J Podgajny
SR T Hughes
SR S Johnson
SP C Blanton
SR L Grissom
RS I Pearson
RS L Hoerst
RS B Beck
RS B Crouch
C B Warren
1B N Etten
2B- D Murtaugh
SS B Bragan
3B P May
LF D Litwhiler
CF J Marty
RU S Benjamin
CU M Livingston
RU J Rizzo
UT H Mueller
M D Prothro

PIT 1941 NL
SP R Sewell
SP M Butcher
SR K Heintzelman
SR J Lanning
RS B Klinger
RS D Dietz
C A Lopez
1B E Fletcher
2B F Gustine
SS A Vaughan
3B L Handley
LF M Van Robays
CF V DiMaggio
RF B Elliott
UT- D Garms
2U- S Martin
M F Frisch

STL 1941 NL
SP L Warneke
SP E White
SP M Cooper
SR M Lanier
SR H Gumbert
RS H Krist
RS C Shoun
RP I Hutchinson
C G Mancuso
1B J Mize
2B C Crespi
SS M Marion
3B J Brown
OI J Hopp
CF T Moore
RF E Slaughter
LU D Padgett
M B Southworth

BOS 1941 AL
SP D Newsome
SR M Harris
SP C Wagner
SP L Grove
SP J Dobson
RP M Ryba
RS J Wilson
C F Pytlak
1B J Foxx
2B B Doerr
SS J Cronin
3B J Tabor
LF T Williams
CF D DiMaggio
RU L Finney
SU S Newsome
C - J Peacock
OI- S Spence

CHI 1941 AL
SP T Lee
SP E Smith
SP J Rigney
SP T Lyons
SP B Dietrich
RP B Ross
C M Tresh
1B J Kuhel
2B- B Knickerbocker
SS L Appling
3B- D Lodigiani
LU M Hoag
CF M Kreevich
RF T Wright
M J Dykes

CLE 1941 AL
SP B Feller
SP A Milnar
SP A Smith
SP J Bagby
RP C Brown
RP J Heving
C R Hemsley
1B- H Trosky
2B R Mack
SS L Boudreau
3B K Keltner
LF G Walker
CF R Weatherly
RF J Heath
MU S Campbell
M R Peckinpaugh

DET 1941 AL
SP B Newsom
SR J Gorsica
SP H Newhouser
SR A Benton
SR D Trout
RP T Bridges
RS S Rowe
RP B Thomas
C B Tebbetts
1B R York
2B C Gehringer
SS F Croucher
3B P Higgins
LF R Radcliff
CF B McCosky
RF B Campbell
UO T Stainback
CU- B Sullivan
M D Baker

NY 1941 AL
SP M Russo
SP R Ruffing
SP S Chandler
SP A Donald
SP L Gomez
RP M Breuer
RP T Bonham
CL J Murphy
RP N Branch
C B Dickey
1B J Sturm
2B J Gordon

SS P Rizzuto
3B R Rolfe
LF C Keller
CF J DiMaggio
RF T Henrich
M J McCarthy

PHI 1941 AL
SP P Marchildon
SP J Knott
SP L McCrabb
SP B Beckmann
SR B Hadley
RS L Harris
RP T Ferrick
C F Hayes
1B D Siebert
2B B McCoy
SS A Brancato
3B P Suder
LF B Johnson
CF S Chapman
RF W Moses
UO- E Collins
UO- D Miles
M C Mack

STL 1941 AL
SP E Auker
SR B Muncrief
SP D Galehouse
SP B Harris
SP J Niggeling
RS G Caster
RP J Kramer
RP B Trotter
C R Ferrell
1B G McQuinn
2B D Heffner
SS J Berardino
3B H Clift
LU R Cullenbine
CF W Judnich
RO C Laabs
RF J Grace
2U J Lucadello
M1 F Haney
M2 L Sewell

WAS 1941 AL
SP D Leonard
SP S Hudson
SP K Chase
SP S Sundra
RS R Anderson
RS A Carrasquel
RS B Zuber
RS W Masterson
C J Early
1B M Vernon
2B J Bloodworth
SS C Travis
3U G Archie
LF G Case
CF D Cramer
R3 B Lewis
M B Harris

BOS 1942 NL
SP J Tobin
SP A Javery
SR L Tost
SR M Salvo
SP T Earley
RP J Sain
RS B Donovan
RP D Errickson
RP L Wallace
C E Lombardi
1L M West
2B S Sisti
SS E Miller
3L N Fernandez
LU- C Ross
CF T Holmes
RF P Waner
M C Stengel

BRO 1942 NL
SP K Higbe
SP W Wyatt
SP C Davis
SR L French
SR E Head
RP H Casey
RS J Allen
RP L Webber
C M Owen
1B D Camilli
2B B Herman
SS P Reese
3B A Vaughan
LF J Medwick
CF P Reiser
RF D Walker
RF- J Rizzo
M L Durocher

CHI 1942 NL
SP C Passeau
SP B Lee
SR H Bithorn
SR V Olsen
SR B Fleming
RP L Warneke
C C McCullough
OI P Cavarretta
2B L Stringer
SS L Merullo
3B S Hack
LF L Novikoff
UO D Dallessandro
RF B Nicholson
IO R Russell
M J Wilson

CIN 1942 NL
SP R Starr
SP B Walters
SP J Vander Meer
SP P Derringer
SR E Riddle
RS J Thompson
RP J Beggs
RP C Shoun
C R Lamanno
1B F McCormick
2B L Frey
SS E Joost
3B B Haas
LM- E Tipton
MO G Walker
RL M Marshall
RU- I Goodman
M B McKechnie

NY 1942 NL
SP H Schumacher
SP B Carpenter
SP B Lohrman
SP C Hubbell
SP C Melton
RS H Feldman
RS B McGee
RP A Adams
C H Danning
1B J Mize
2B M Witek
SS B Jurges
3B B Werber
LF B Barna
LM W Marshall
RF M Ott
MU B Young
3S- D Bartell
MU-B Maynard

PHI 1942 NL
SP T Hughes
SR R Melton
SR S Johnson
SR J Podgajny
SR L Hoerst
RS I Pearson
RP S Nahem
RP E Naylor
RP B Beck
C - B Warren
1B N Etten
2B A Glossop
SU B Bragan
3B P May
LF D Litwhiler
ML E Koy
RF R Northey
UI D Murtaugh
MU L Waner
OI- S Benjamin
C - M Livingston
M H Lobert

PIT 1942 NL
SP R Sewell
SR B Klinger
SP M Butcher
SP K Heintzelman
SR H Gornicki
RS D Dietz
RS J Lanning
RP L Hamlin
RS L Wilkie
C A Lopez
1B E Fletcher
2B F Gustine
SS P Coscarart
3B B Elliott
RL J Wasdell
CF V DiMaggio
RU J Barrett
C B Phelps
LF M Van Robays
UT- B Stewart
M F Frisch

STL 1942 NL
SP M Cooper
SR J Beazley
SR H Gumbert
SR M Lanier
SP E White
RS M Dickson
RS H Krist
RS H Pollet
C W Cooper
1B J Hopp
2B- C Crespi
SS M Marion
3B W Kurowski
LF S Musial
CF T Moore
RF E Slaughter
23 J Brown
1B R Sanders
M B Southworth

BOS 1942 AL
SP T Hughson
SP C Wagner
SP J Dobson
SP D Newsome
SR O Judd
RS B Butland
RP M Brown
C - B Conroy
1B T Lupien
2B B Doerr
SS J Pesky
3B J Tabor
LF T Williams
CF D DiMaggio
RF L Finney
RF- P Fox
C - J Peacock
M J Cronin

CHI 1942 AL
SP J Humphries
SP E Smith
SP T Lyons
SP B Dietrich
SP B Ross
RP J Haynes
C - M Tresh
1B J Kuhel
2B D Kolloway
SS L Appling
3B B Kennedy
LF- T Wright
ML M Hoag
RF W Moses
M J Dykes

CLE 1942 AL
SP J Bagby
SP M Harder
SP C Dean
SP A Smith
SP A Milnar
RS V Kennedy
RP T Ferrick
RP H Eisenstat
C - O Denning
1B L Fleming
2B R Mack
SS L Boudreau
3B K Keltner
LF J Heath
CF R Weatherly
RF O Hockett
UO- B Mills

DET 1942 AL
SP A Benton
SP D Trout
SP H White
SR H Newhouser
SP T Bridges
RP V Trucks
RP R Henshaw
RP J Gorsica
C B Tebbetts
1B R York
2B J Bloodworth
SS- B Hitchcock
3B P Higgins
LF B McCosky
CF D Cramer
RF N Harris
OI- D Ross
M D Baker

NY 1942 AL
SP T Bonham
SP S Chandler
SP R Ruffing
SP H Borowy
SP M Breuer
RP A Donald
CL J Murphy
RP J Lindell
C - B Dickey
1B B Hassett
2B J Gordon
SS P Rizzuto
3B- F Crosetti
LF C Keller
CF J DiMaggio
RF T Henrich
M J McCarthy

PHI 1942 AL
SP P Marchildon
SP R Wolff
SP L Harris
SR R Christopher
SR D Fowler
RS H Besse
RP J Knott
C H Wagner
1B D Siebert
2B- B Knickerbocker
S3 P Suder
3B B Blair
LF B Johnson
CF M Kreevich
RF E Valo
UO D Miles
2S- C Davis
M C Mack

STL 1942 AL
SP E Auker
SP J Niggeling
SP D Galehouse
SR A Hollingsworth
SP B Muncrief
RP S Sundra
RP G Caster
C R Ferrell
1B G McQuinn
2B D Gutteridge
SS V Stephens
3B H Clift
LU G McQuillen
CF W Judnich
RL C Laabs
UO T Criscola
M L Sewell

WAS 1942 AL
SP S Hudson
SP B Newsom
SP E Wynn
SR A Carrasquel
SR W Masterson
RS B Zuber
C J Early
1B M Vernon
2B- E Clary
SS J Sullivan
3O B Estalella
LR G Case
CF S Spence
RU B Campbell
SI- J Pofahl
UI- B Repass
M B Harris

BOS 1943 NL
SP A Javery
SP N Andrews
SP R Barrett
SP J Tobin
SP M Salvo
RP D Odom
C - P Masi
1B- J McCarthy
2B C Ryan
SS W Wietelmann
32 E Joost
LF B Nieman
CF T Holmes
RF C Workman
LF C Ross
1B- K Farrell
M1 B Coleman
M2 C Stengel

BRO 1943 NL
SP K Higbe
SP W Wyatt
SR E Head
SR C Davis
SR B Newsom
RP L Webber
RS R Melton
C M Owen
1B D Camilli
2B B Herman
IO- A Glossop
S3 A Vaughan
RL D Walker
MU A Galan
RU- P Waner
OI- F Bordagaray
M L Durocher

CHI 1943 NL
SP C Passeau
SP H Bithorn
SR P Derringer
SR H Wyse
SR E Hanyzewski
RS R Prim
C - C McCullough
1B P Cavarretta
2B E Stanky
SS L Merullo
3B S Hack
LF- L Novikoff
CF P Lowrey
RF B Nicholson
OF- D Dallessandro
LU- I Goodman
M J Wilson

CIN 1943 NL
SP J Vander Meer
SP E Riddle
SP B Walters
SP R Starr
RS C Shoun
RP J Beggs
C R Mueller
1B F McCormick
2B L Frey
SS E Miller
3B S Mesner
LF E Tipton
MO G Walker
RF M Marshall
UO E Crabtree
IO B Haas
M B McKechnie

NY 1943 NL
SP C Melton
SR J Wittig
SP R Fischer
SP K Chase
RS V Mungo
RP A Adams
RS H Feldman
RP B Sayles
C G Mancuso
1B- J Orengo
2B M Witek
SU B Jurges
3S D Bartell
LF- J Medwick
CF J Rucker
RF M Ott
IO S Gordon
CU E Lombardi
OI B Maynard

PHI 1943 NL
SP A Gerheauser
SP J Kraus
SP S Rowe
SP D Barrett
SP S Johnson
RS N Kimball
C - M Livingston
1L J Wasdell
2B D Murtaugh
SU G Stewart
3B P May
LF C Triplett
CF B Adams
RF R Northey
13 B Dahlgren
M1 B Harris
M2 F Fitzsimmons

PIT 1943 NL
SP R Sewell
SR M Butcher
SP B Klinger
SR W Hebert
SR H Gornicki
RS X Rescigno
RP B Brandt
C A Lopez
1B E Fletcher
2S P Coscarart
S2 F Gustine
3B B Elliott
LF J Russell
CF V DiMaggio
RU J Barrett
OI- T O'Brien
M F Frisch

STL 1943 NL
SP M Cooper
SP M Lanier
SR H Krist
SR H Brecheen
SP H Gumbert
RP H Pollet
RS M Dickson
RS R Munger
C W Cooper
1B R Sanders
2B L Klein
SS M Marion
3B W Kurowski
LF- D Litwhiler
CF H Walker
RO S Musial
UT- D Garms
OI- J Hopp
M B Southworth

BOS 1943 AL
SP T Hughson
SP Y Terry
SP J Dobson
SP O Judd
SP D Newsome
RS M Ryba
RP M Brown
RS P Woods
C R Partee
1B T Lupien
2B B Doerr
SS S Newsome
3B J Tabor
ML- L Culberson
MR- C Metkovich
RF P Fox
LU- J Lazor
M J Cronin

CHI 1943 AL
SP O Grove
SP J Humphries
SP E Smith
SP B Dietrich
SP B Ross
RP T Lee
RP G Maltzberger
RP J Haynes
RP B Swift
C - M Tresh
1B J Kuhel
2B- D Kolloway
SS L Appling
UT R Hodgin
LF G Curtright
CF T Tucker
RF W Moses
M J Dykes

CLE 1943 AL
SP J Bagby
SP A Smith
SR A Reynolds
SR V Kennedy
SP M Harder
RP J Heving
RP M Naymick
C B Rosar
1B M Rocco
2B R Mack
SS L Boudreau
3B K Keltner
LF J Heath
MO O Hockett
RF R Cullenbine
CF H Edwards
3I- R Peters

DET 1943 AL
SR D Trout
SP V Trucks
SR H Newhouser
SP T Bridges
SP H White
RS S Overmire
RP J Gorsica
RP R Henshaw
C P Richards
1B R York
2B J Bloodworth
SS J Hoover
3B P Higgins
LF D Wakefield
CF D Cramer
RF N Harris
UT- D Ross
M S O'Neill

NY 1943 AL
SP S Chandler
SP T Bonham
SP B Wensloff
SP H Borowy
SP B Zuber
RP A Donald
RS M Russo
RP J Murphy
C - B Dickey
1B N Etten
2B J Gordon
SS F Crosetti
3B B Johnson
LF C Keller
RM J Lindell
RF B Metheny
SS- S Stirnweiss
CF- R Weatherly
M J McCarthy

PHI 1943 AL
SP J Flores
SR R Wolff
SP L Harris
SP D Black
SR O Arntzen
RP R Christopher
C H Wagner
1B D Siebert
2I P Suder
SS I Hall
3B E Mayo
LF B Estalella
CF J White
UO J Welaj
C - B Swift
RU- E Valo
M C Mack

STL 1943 AL
SP D Galehouse
SP S Sundra
SP B Muncrief
SR N Potter
SR A Hollingsworth
RP J Niggeling
RP G Caster
C - F Hayes
1B G McQuinn
2B D Gutteridge
SS V Stephens
3B H Clift
LF C Laabs
MO M Byrnes
RU M Chartak
UI M Christman
M L Sewell

WAS 1943 AL
SP E Wynn
SP D Leonard
SR M Haefner
SP M Candini
RS A Carrasquel
RS J Mertz
C J Early
1B M Vernon
2B J Priddy
SS J Sullivan
3B- E Clary
LF B Johnson
CF S Spence
RF G Case
OI G Moore
M O Bluege

BOS 1944 NL
SP J Tobin
SP N Andrews
SP A Javery
SR R Barrett
RS I Hutchinson
CU- P Masi
1B B Etchison
2B- C Ryan
SS W Wietelmann
3S D Phillips
LR B Nieman
CF T Holmes
RU C Workman
1U M Macon
CU- C Kluttz
M B Coleman

BRO 1944 NL
SP H Gregg
SP C Davis
SR R Melton
RS L Webber
C M Owen
1B H Schultz
2S- E Stanky
SC B Bragan
3B F Bordagaray
LF A Galan
MU- G Rosen
RF D Walker
UT L Olmo
OF- P Waner
M L Durocher

CHI 1944 NL
SP H Wyse
SP C Passeau
SR P Derringer
SR B Fleming
SP B Chipman
RS H Vandenberg
RS P Erickson
C - D Williams
1B P Cavarretta
2B D Johnson
SS- L Merullo
3B S Hack
LF D Dallessandro
CF A Pafko
RF B Nicholson
3S R Hughes
M1 J Wilson
M2 R Johnson
M3 C Grimm

CIN 1944 NL
SP B Walters
SR C Shoun
SP E Heusser
SR T DeLa Cruz
SP H Gumbert
RS A Carter
RP J Konstanty
C R Mueller
1B F McCormick
2B W Williams
SS E Miller
3B S Mesner
LF E Tipton
CF D Clay
RM G Walker
M B McKechnie

NY 1944 NL
SP B Voiselle
SR H Feldman
SR E Pyle
SR R Fischer
RP A Adams
RP A Hansen
C E Lombardi
1B P Weintraub
2B G Hausmann
SS B Kerr
32 H Luby
LF J Medwick
CF J Rucker
RF M Ott
13 N Reyes
3U- B Jurges
C - G Mancuso

PHI 1944 NL
SP K Raffensberger
SR C Schanz
SP D Barrett
SP B Lee
SP A Gerheauser
RP A Karl
C B Finley
1B T Lupien
2B M Mullen
SS- R Hamrick
3S G Stewart
LF J Wasdell
CF B Adams
RF R Northey
UI C Letchas
3U- T Cieslak
C - J Peacock
UO- C Triplett
M F Fitzsimmons

PIT 1944 NL
SP R Sewell
SP F Ostermueller
SP M Butcher
SR N Strincevich
SR P Roe
RS X Rescigno
RP C Cuccurullo
C A Lopez
1B B Dahlgren
2B P Coscarart
SS F Gustine
3B B Elliott
LF J Russell
CF V DiMaggio
RM J Barrett
RU F Colman
OI- T O'Brien
UT- A Rubeling
SS- F Zak
M F Frisch

STL 1944 NL
SP M Cooper
SP M Lanier
SR T Wilks
SP H Brecheen
SR A Jurisich
RP R Munger
RS F Schmidt
RP B Donnelly
C W Cooper
1B R Sanders
2B E Verban
SS M Marion
3B W Kurowski

LF D Litwhiler
CF J Hopp
RF S Musial
OI- A Bergamo
C - K O'Dea
M B Southworth

BOS 1944 AL
SP T Hughson
SR P Woods
SP J Bowman
SP E O'Neill
SR C Hausmann
RS M Ryba
RS Y Terry
RP F Barrett
C - R Partee
1B- L Finney
2B B Doerr
SS S Newsome
3B J Tabor
LF B Johnson
M1 C Metkovich
RF P Fox
32- J Bucher
M J Cronin

CHI 1944 AL
SP B Dietrich
SP O Grove
SP E Lopat
SR J Humphries
SR J Haynes
RP T Lee
RP G Maltzberger
C M Tresh
1B H Trosky
2B R Schalk
SS S Webb
3L R Hodgin
OI E Carnett
CF T Tucker
RF W Moses
M J Dykes

CLE 1944 AL
SR S Gromek
SP M Harder
SR E Klieman
SP A Smith
SP A Reynolds
RP J Heving
RS R Poat
RP P Calvert
C B Rosar
1B M Rocco
2B- R Mack
SS L Boudreau
3B K Keltner
LU P Seerey
ML O Hockett
RF R Cullenbine
2U- R Peters

DET 1944 AL
SP D Trout
SR H Newhouser
SP R Gentry
SP S Overmire
SR J Gorsica
RP B Beck
C P Richards
1B R York
2B E Mayo
SS J Hoover
3B P Higgins
LF- D Wakefield
CF D Cramer
LR J Outlaw
RU- C Hostetler
C - B Swift
M S O'Neill

NY 1944 AL
SP H Borowy
SP M Dubiel
SP T Bonham
SR A Donald
SP B Zuber
RP J Page
C - M Garbark
1B N Etten
2B S Stirnweiss
SS M Milosevich
3B O Grimes
LF- H Martin
CF J Lindell
RF B Metheny
C - R Hemsley
M J McCarthy

PHI 1944 AL
SP B Newsom
SR R Christopher
SP L Hamlin
SP J Flores
SP D Black
RP L Harris
RP J Berry
C F Hayes
1B- B McGhee
2S I Hall
SS E Busch
3B G Kell
LF F Garrison
MU B Estalella
RU- J White
1L D Siebert
M C Mack

STL 1944 AL
SP J Kramer
SP N Potter
SP B Muncrief
SR S Jakucki
SP D Galehouse
RS A Hollingsworth
RP G Caster
C - F Mancuso
1B G McQuinn
2B D Gutteridge
SS V Stephens
3B M Christman
UO M Byrnes
CF M Kreevich
RF G Moore
LU A Zarilla
C - R Hayworth
M L Sewell

WAS 1944 AL
SP M Haefner
SP D Leonard
SP E Wynn
SP J Niggeling
SR R Wolff
RS A Carrasquel
RS M Candini
RP B Lefebvre
C R Ferrell
1B J Kuhel
2B G Myatt
SS J Sullivan
3B G Torres
LO G Case
CF S Spence
RF- R Ortiz
LR J Powell
M O Bluege

BOS 1945 NL
SP J Tobin
SP B Logan
SP N Andrews
SP E Wright
SP B Lee
RS J Hutchings
RP D Hendrickson
C P Masi
1B- V Shupe
2S W Wietelmann
SS D Culler
3B C Workman
OF B Nieman
CF C Gillenwater
RF T Holmes
OF- B Ramsey
M1 B Coleman
M2 D Bissonette

BRO 1945 NL
SP H Gregg
SR V Lombardi
SP C Davis
SP A Herring
SR T Seats
RP C King
RP R Branca
RP C Buker
CS- M Sandlock
IO A Galan
2B E Stanky
SS E Basinski
3U F Bordagaray
LU L Olmo
CF G Rosen
RF D Walker
M L Durocher

CHI 1945 NL
SP H Wyse
SP C Passeau
SP P Derringer
SR R Prim
SP H Borowy
RS P Erickson
RS H Vandenberg
C - M Livingston
1B P Cavarretta
2B D Johnson
SS L Merullo
3B S Hack
LF P Lowrey
CF A Pafko
RF B Nicholson
M C Grimm

CIN 1945 NL
SP E Heusser
SP J Bowman
SP B Walters
SP V Kennedy
SP F Dasso
RS H Fox
RP H Lisenbee
C - A Lakeman
1B F McCormick
2B W Williams
SS E Miller
3B S Mesner
LF E Tipton
CF D Clay
RU A Libke
RU G Walker
OF- D Sipek
M B McKechnie

NY 1945 NL
SP B Voiselle
SP H Feldman
SP V Mungo
SP J Brewer
SR A Hansen
RP A Adams
RS S Emmerich
RP R Fischer
C E Lombardi
1B- P Weintraub
2B G Hausmann
SS B Kerr
3B N Reyes
LU D Gardella
CF J Rucker
RF M Ott
UO- R Treadway

PHI 1945 NL
SP D Barrett
SR C Schanz
SR C Sproull
SP D Mauney
RP A Karl
C - A Seminick
OI J Wasdell
2B- T Daniels
S2- B Mott
3B J Antonelli
LF C Triplett
CF V DiMaggio
OI V Dinges
OP R Monteagudo
UT- G Crawford
IF- J Foxx
M1 F Fitzsimmons
M2 B Chapman

PIT 1945 NL
SP P Roe
SP N Strincevich
SP R Sewell
SP M Butcher
SR A Gerheauser
RS K Gables
RP X Rescigno
RP C Cuccurullo
C - A Lopez
1B B Dahlgren
2B P Coscarart
SS F Gustine
3R B Elliott
LF J Russell
MU A Gionfriddo
MR J Barrett
3B L Handley
C B Salkeld
UT- F Colman
M F Frisch

STL 1945 NL
SP R Barrett
SR K Burkhart
SP B Donnelly
SP H Brecheen
SR G Dockins
RP T Wilks
RS B Byerly
RS A Jurisich
C K O'Dea
1B R Sanders
2B E Verban
SS M Marion
3B W Kurowski
LF R Schoendienst
CF B Adams
RU J Hopp
RU A Bergamo
C - D Rice
M B Southworth

BOS 1945 AL
SP D Ferriss
SP J Wilson
SP E O'Neill
SR C Hausmann
SR P Woods
RS M Ryba
RP R Heflin
RP F Barrett
C - B Garbark
1O C Metkovich
2S S Newsome
SS E Lake
3B- J Tobin
LF B Johnson
CF L Culberson
RU J Lazor
MO T McBride
2B- B Steiner
M J Cronin

CHI 1945 AL
SP T Lee
SP O Grove
SP E Lopat
SP J Humphries
SP B Dietrich
RS E Caldwell
RP J Haynes
RP J Johnson
C M Tresh
1B K Farrell
2B R Schalk
SS C Michaels
3B T Cuccinello
LF J Dickshot
CF O Hockett
RF W Moses
UO G Curtright
3U- F Baker
M J Dykes

CLE 1945 AL
SP S Gromek
SR A Reynolds
SP J Bagby
SP A Smith
RS E Klieman
RS P Center
RP J Salveson
C F Hayes
1B M Rocco
2B D Meyer
SS L Boudreau
3B D Ross
LF J Heath
CF F Mackiewicz
RL P Seerey
UI A Cihocki
RU- P O'Dea

DET 1945 AL
SP H Newhouser
SR D Trout
SP A Benton
SP S Overmire
SP L Mueller
RP W Wilson
RP G Caster
C B Swift
1B R York
2B E Mayo
SS S Webb
3B B Maier
LU J Outlaw
CF D Cramer
RF R Cullenbine
LF- H Greenberg
C - P Richards
M S O'Neill

NY 1945 AL
SP B Bevens
SP T Bonham
SR A Gettel
SP M Dubiel
SP H Borowy
RP B Zuber
RS J Page
RP J Turner
RP K Holcombe
C - M Garbark
1B N Etten
2B S Stirnweiss
SS F Crosetti
3B O Grimes
LF H Martin
CF T Stainback
RF B Metheny
MO-R Derry
M J McCarthy

PHI 1945 AL
SP B Newsom
SP R Christopher
SP J Flores
SR L Knerr
SP D Black
RP J Berry
RS C Gassaway
RP S Gerkin
C B Rosar
1B D Siebert
2B I Hall
SS E Busch
3B G Kell
UO- M Smith
CF B Estalella
RF H Peck
OI B McGhee
M C Mack

STL 1945 AL
SP N Potter
SP J Kramer
SP S Jakucki
SP T Shirley
SP A Hollingsworth
RS B Muncrief
RP S Zoldak
C F Mancuso
1B G McQuinn
2B D Gutteridge
SS V Stephens
3B- M Christman
OI M Byrnes
CF- M Kreevich
RF G Moore
32 L Schulte
OF- P Gray
M L Sewell

WAS 1945 AL
SP R Wolff
SP M Haefner
SR M Pieretti
SP D Leonard
SP J Niggeling
RS A Carrasquel
RS S Ullrich
C - R Ferrell
1B J Kuhel
2U G Myatt
SS G Torres
3B H Clift
LO G Case
MO G Binks
RF- B Lewis
2B- F Vaughn
M O Bluege

BOS 1946 NL
SP J Sain
SP M Cooper
SR E Wright
SP B Lee
SR S Johnson
RP W Spahn
RS L Wallace
C P Masi
1B- R Sanders
2B C Ryan
SS D Culler
3U N Fernandez
LU B Rowell
MU C Gillenwater
RF T Holmes
1M J Hopp
LF- D Litwhiler
M B Southworth

BRO 1946 NL
SR J Hatten
SR K Higbe
SR V Lombardi
SR H Gregg
SR R Melton
RS H Behrman
RP H Casey
RP A Herring
C - B Edwards
1B E Stevens
2B E Stanky
SS P Reese
3B- C Lavagetto
LU P Reiser
CF C Furillo
RF D Walker
LI A Galan
ML D Whitman
C - F Anderson
1B- H Schultz
M L Durocher

CHI 1946 NL
SR J Schmitz
SR H Wyse
SP H Borowy
SP P Erickson
SP C Passeau
RS E Kush
RS B Chipman
C C McCullough
1B E Waitkus
2B- D Johnson
SS- B Jurges
3B- S Hack
LO M Rickert
LM P Lowrey
R1 P Cavarretta
RF B Nicholson
SU B Sturgeon
2B- L Stringer
M C Grimm

CIN 1946 NL
SP J Vander Meer
SP E Blackwell
SP J Beggs
SP E Heusser
SP B Walters
RS J Hetki
RS H Gumbert
RS C Shoun
RP B Malloy
C R Mueller
1B B Haas
2B B Adams
SS- E Miller
3B G Hatton
LU E Lukon
CF D Clay
RF A Libke
2O L Frey
SS- C Corbitt
CU- R Lamanno
OI- B Usher
23- B Zientara
M1 B McKechnie
M2 H Gowdy

NY 1946 NL
SP D Koslo
SR M Kennedy
SR B Voiselle
SR H Schumacher
RS K Trinkle
RS M Budnick
RP J Thompson
C - W Cooper
1B J Mize
2B B Blattner
SS B Kerr
3S B Rigney
LU S Gordon
UO W Marshall
RM G Rosen
RU J Graham
MU J Rucker
UT B Young
CU- E Lombardi
23- M Witek
M M Ott

PHI 1946 NL
SR K Raffensberger
SP O Judd
SP S Rowe
SR C Schanz
SR T Hughes
RP A Karl
RS D Mulligan
C A Seminick
1B F McCormick
2B E Verban
SS S Newsome
3B J Tabor
LF D Ennis
CF J Wyrostek
RF R Northey
RO- C Gilbert
UI- R Hughes
M B Chapman

PIT 1946 NL
SP F Ostermueller
SR N Strincevich
SP K Heintzelman
SP R Sewell
SR E Bahr
RS J Hallett
RS K Gables
RP A Gerheauser
C - A Lopez
1B E Fletcher
2B F Gustine
SS B Cox
3B L Handley
OI J Russell
ML R Kiner
R3 B Elliott
UI- J Brown
M1 F Frisch
M2 S Davis

STL 1946 NL
SP H Pollet
SP H Brecheen
SR M Dickson
SR A Brazle
SP J Beazley
RS K Burkhart
RP T Wilks
C - J Garagiola
1L S Musial
2B R Schoendienst
SS M Marion
3B W Kurowski
LU E Dusak
MU H Walker
RF E Slaughter
OF- B Adams
MU- T Moore
UT- D Sisler
M E Dyer

BOS 1946 AL
SP T Hughson
SP D Ferriss
SP M Harris
SP J Dobson
SR J Bagby
RS E Johnson
RP B Klinger
RP C Dreisewerd
C H Wagner
1B R York
2B B Doerr
SS J Pesky
3B- R Russell
LF T Williams
CF D DiMaggio
RF- C Metkovich
M J Cronin

CHI 1946 AL
SP E Lopat
SP O Grove
SP J Haynes
SP E Smith
SR F Papish
RP E Caldwell
RS R Hamner
RP A Hollingsworth
C - M Tresh
1B- H Trosky
23 D Kolloway
SS L Appling
3B- D Lodigiani
L3 B Kennedy
CF T Tucker
RF T Wright
LU- R Hodgin
2U- C Michaels
UO- W Platt
M1 J Dykes
M2 T Lyons

CLE 1946 AL
SP B Feller
SP R Embree
SP A Reynolds
SP S Gromek
RS B Lemon
RS J Krakauskas
C - J Hegan
1B L Fleming
2B- D Meyer
SS L Boudreau
3B K Keltner
LF G Case
UO P Seerey
RF H Edwards
CF- F Mackiewicz

DET 1946 AL
SP H Newhouser
SP D Trout
SP V Trucks
SP F Hutchinson
SR A Benton
RS S Overmire
C - B Tebbetts
1B H Greenberg
2B- J Bloodworth
SS E Lake
3B G Kell
LF D Wakefield
CF- H Evers
RU R Cullenbine
RF P Mullin
OI- J Outlaw
M S O'Neill

NY 1946 AL
SP S Chandler
SP B Bevens
SR J Page
SR R Gumpert
SP T Bonham
RS A Gettel
C A Robinson
1B N Etten
2B J Gordon
SS P Rizzuto
32 S Stirnweiss
LF C Keller
CF J DiMaggio
R1 T Henrich
OI J Lindell
3B- B Johnson
M1 J McCarthy
M2 B Dickey
M3 J Neun

PHI 1946 AL
SP P Marchildon
SP D Fowler
SR B Savage
SR J Flores
SP L Knerr
RS L Harris
RS R Christopher
C B Rosar
1B G McQuinn
2B- G Handley
S3 P Suder
3B- H Majeski
LM S Chapman
CF- B McCosky
RF E Valo
UO- T Stainback
M C Mack

STL 1946 AL
SP J Kramer
SP D Galehouse
SR S Zoldak
SP N Potter
SP T Shirley
RS B Muncrief
RS E Kinder
RS S Ferens
C - F Mancuso
1B C Stevens
2B J Berardino
SS V Stephens
3S M Christman
LF- J Heath
CF W Judnich
UO A Zarilla
3U- B Dillinger
RF- C Laabs
IF- J Lucadello
M1 L Sewell
M2 Z Taylor

WAS 1946 AL
SP M Haefner
SP B Newsom
SP D Leonard
SR R Scarborough
SR S Hudson
RP R Wolff
RP E Wynn
RP M Pieretti
C - A Evans
1B M Vernon
2B J Priddy
S3 B Hitchcock
S3 C Travis
LF- J Grace
CF S Spence
RF B Lewis
M O Bluege

BOS 1947 NL
SP W Spahn
SP J Sain
SP R Barrett
SP B Voiselle
RS S Johnson
RP C Shoun
RP W Lanfranconi
RS E Wright
C P Masi
1B E Torgeson
2B C Ryan
SS- D Culler
3B B Elliott
LF B Rowell
CF J Hopp
RF T Holmes
SU- N Fernandez
LU- D Litwhiler
1U- F McCormick
ML- M McCormick
M B Southworth

BRO 1947 NL
SP R Branca
SR J Hatten
SR V Lombardi
SR H Taylor
SR H Gregg
RS H Behrman
CL H Casey
RS R Barney
C B Edwards
1B J Robinson

2B E Stanky
SS P Reese
3B S Jorgensen
ML P Reiser
CF C Furillo
RF D Walker
LF- G Hermanski
M1 C Sukeforth
M2 B Shotton

CHI 1947 NL
SR J Schmitz
SP D Lade
SR H Borowy
SR P Erickson
SR H Wyse
RS B Chipman
RP E Kush
RP R Meers
C B Scheffing
1B E Waitkus
2B D Johnson
SS L Merullo
3B P Lowrey
LO P Cavarretta
CF A Pafko
RF B Nicholson
CU- C McCullough
S2- B Sturgeon
M C Grimm

CIN 1947 NL
SP E Blackwell
SP J Vander Meer
SR K Peterson
SR B Lively
SP B Walters
RS E Erautt
RP K Raffensberger
RP H Gumbert
RS J Hetki
C R Lamanno
1B B Young
2B B Zientara
SS E Miller
3B G Hatton
LF A Galan
OI B Haas
RF F Baumholtz
2B- B Adams
OF- E Lukon
MU- C Vollmer
M J Neun

NY 1947 NL
SR L Jansen
SP D Koslo
SR M Kennedy
SP C Hartung
RP K Trinkle
RP J Beggs
C W Cooper
1B J Mize
23 B Rigney
SS B Kerr
3B J Lohrke
LF S Gordon
CF B Thomson
RF W Marshall
M M Ott

PHI 1947 NL
SP D Leonard
SP S Rowe
SR O Judd
SP K Heintzelman
SR T Hughes
RS B Donnelly
RS A Jurisich
RS C Schanz
RS F Schmidt
C A Seminick
1B H Schultz
2B E Verban
SS S Newsome
3B L Handley
LF D Ennis
CF H Walker
RF J Wyrostek
UO- C Gilbert
M B Chapman

PIT 1947 NL
SR K Higbe
SP F Ostermueller
SR T Bonham
SP R Roe
SR R Sewell
RS J Bagby
RS N Strincevich
RP E Singleton
C - D Howell
1B H Greenberg
2B- J Bloodworth
SS B Cox
3B F Gustine
LF R Kiner
CF J Russell
RF W Westlake
UO C Rikard
M1 Herman
M2 B Burwell

STL 1947 NL
SR M Dickson
SP R Munger
SP H Brecheen
SR H Pollet
SR A Brazle
RS J Hearn
RS K Burkhart
RP T Wilks
C D Rice
1B S Musial
2B R Schoendienst
SS M Marion
3B W Kurowski
LU E Slaughter
CF T Moore
RU R Northey
UO C Diering
OI E Dusak
M E Dyer

BOS 1947 AL
SP J Dobson
SP D Ferriss
SP T Hughson
SR E Johnson
SP D Galehouse
RS H Dorish
RP J Murphy
RP B Zuber
C - B Tebbetts
1B J Jones
2B B Doerr
SS J Pesky
3B- S Dente
LF T Williams
CF D DiMaggio
RO S Mele
RU- W Moses
M J Cronin

CHI 1947 AL
SP E Lopat
SR F Papish
SP J Haynes
SP O Grove
SP B Gillespie
RP E Harrist
RP P Gebrian
RP G Maltzberger
RP E Caldwell
C - M Tresh
1B R York
2B D Kolloway
SS L Appling
3B F Baker
RL T Wright
ML D Philley
RF B Kennedy
23 C Michaels
C - G Dickey
MU- T Tucker
IO- J Wallaesa
M T Lyons

CLE 1947 AL
SP B Feller
SP D Black
SR B Lemon
SP R Embree
SR A Gettel
RP E Klieman
RS B Stephens
RS S Gromek
C J Hegan
1B E Robinson
2B J Gordon
SS L Boudreau
3B K Keltner
LM D Mitchell
CF C Metkovich
RL H Edwards
1U L Fleming
RF H Peck
LU- P Seerey

DET 1947 AL
SP H Newhouser
SP F Hutchinson
SP D Trout
SR V Trucks
SR S Overmire
RS A Benton
RS A Houtteman
RS H White
RP J Gorsica
C B Swift
1B R Cullenbine
2B E Mayo
SS E Lake
3B G Kell
LF D Wakefield
CF H Evers
RF P Mullin
UO V Wertz
M S O'Neill

NY 1947 AL
SP A Reynolds
SP S Shea
SP B Bevens
SP S Chandler
SP B Newsom
RP J Page
RP V Raschi
RS R Gumpert
C - A Robinson
1B G McQuinn
2B S Stirnweiss
SS P Rizzuto
3B B Johnson
LF J Lindell
CF J DiMaggio
RF T Henrich
CO- Y Berra
M B Harris

PHI 1947 AL
SP P Marchildon
SP D Fowler
SR B McCahan
SR J Coleman
SP J Flores
RS B Savage
RP C Scheib
RP R Christopher
C B Rosar
1B F Fain
2B P Suder
SS E Joost
3B H Majeski
LF B McCosky
CF S Chapman
RF E Valo
OI G Binks
M C Mack

STL 1947 AL
SP J Kramer
SP E Kinder
SR F Sanford
SP B Muncrief
SR S Zoldak
RP C Fannin
RS N Potter
RP G Moulder
C L Moss
1B W Judnich
2B- J Berardino
SS V Stephens
3B B Dillinger
LF J Heath
CF P Lehner
RO A Zarilla
RU R Coleman
C - J Early
2I- B Hitchcock
M M Ruel

WAS 1947 AL
SP W Masterson
SP E Wynn
SP M Haefner
SR R Scarborough
SP S Hudson
RP M Candini
RP T Ferrick
RP S Cary
C A Evans
1B M Vernon
2B J Priddy
SS M Christman
3B E Yost
LU- J Grace
CF S Spence
RF B Lewis
LU S Robertson
M O Bluege

BOS 1948 NL
SP J Sain
SP W Spahn
SP B Voiselle
SR V Bickford
SR R Barrett
RP B Hogue
RP C Shoun
C P Masi
1B E Torgeson
2B- E Stanky
SS A Dark
3B B Elliott
LF J Heath
CF- J Russell
RF T Holmes
UO M McCormick
ML- C Conatser
C - B Salkeld
2S- S Sisti
M B Southworth

BRO 1948 NL
SR R Barney
SP R Branca
SR J Hatten
SR P Roe
RS E Palica
RP H Behrman
RP P Minner
RP W Ramsdell
C - R Campanella
1C G Hodges
2B J Robinson
SS P Reese
3B- B Cox
UO- M Rackley
CF C Furillo
RF G Hermanski
CU B Edwards
23- E Miksis
M1 L Durocher
M2 R Blades
M3 B Shotton

CHI 1948 NL
SP J Schmitz
SP R Meyer
SR D McCall
SR B Rush
SR H Borowy
RS R Hamner
RS C Chambers
RP J Dobernic
RP E Kush
C B Scheffing
1B E Waitkus
2B H Schenz
SS R Smalley
3B A Pafko
UT P Lowrey
CF H Jeffcoat
RF B Nicholson
UT P Cavarretta
LU- C Maddern
CU- R Walker
M C Grimm

CIN 1948 NL
SP J Vander Meer
SR K Raffensberger
SR H Fox
SP H Wehmeier
SP E Blackwell
RS K Peterson
RP H Gumbert
RP W Cress
C R Lamanno
1B T Kluszewski
2U- B Adams
SS V Stallcup
3B G Hatton
LF H Sauer
CF J Wyrostek
RO F Baumholtz
RU D Litwhiler
2I- C Corbitt
M1 J Neun
M2 B Walters

NY 1948 NL
SP L Jansen
SR S Jones
SR R Poat
SR C Hartung
SR D Koslo
RP M Kennedy
RS A Hansen
RP K Trinkle
C - W Cooper
1B J Mize
2B B Rigney
SS B Kerr
3B S Gordon
UO B Thomson
ML W Lockman
RF W Marshall
32 J Lohrke
M1 M Ott
M2 L Durocher

PHI 1948 NL
SP D Leonard
SP C Simmons
SR M Dubiel
SR S Rowe
SP R Roberts
RP B Donnelly
RS K Heintzelman
RP E Heusser
RP S Nahem
C A Seminick
1B D Sisler
2S G Hamner
SS E Miller
3U P Caballero
LF J Blatnik
CF R Ashburn
RF D Ennis
31 B Haas
MU H Walker
UT- B Rowell
M1 B Chapman
M2 D Cooke
M3 E Sawyer

PIT 1948 NL
SP B Chesnes
SP E Riddle
SR V Lombardi
SP T Bonham
SP F Ostermueller
RS K Higbe
RP R Sewell
RS E Singleton
RS M Queen
C E Fitz Gerald
1B E Stevens
2B D Murtaugh
SS S Rojek
3B F Gustine
LF R Kiner
MR W Westlake
RF D Walker
MU J Hopp
C C Kluttz
UT- M West
M B Meyer

STL 1948 NL
SR M Dickson
SP H Brecheen
SR H Pollet
SR R Munger
SR A Brazle
RP T Wilks
RP G Staley
C D Rice
1B N Jones
2B R Schoendienst
SS M Marion
3B D Lang
LR E Slaughter
CF- T Moore
OI S Musial
UT E Dusak
RU R Northey
3B- W Kurowski
2S- R LaPointe
M E Dyer

BOS 1948 AL
SP J Dobson
SP M Parnell
SP J Kramer
SP E Kinder
SR D Galehouse
RS D Ferriss
RP M Harris
RP E Johnson
C B Tebbetts
1B B Goodman
2B B Doerr
SS V Stephens
3B J Pesky
LF T Williams
CF D DiMaggio
RU S Spence
RU- W Moses
M J McCarthy

CHI 1948 AL
SP B Wight
SP J Haynes
SP A Gettel
SP M Pieretti
SR F Papish
RS H Judson
RP R Gumpert
RS G Moulder
RS B Gillespie
C A Robinson
1B T Lupien
2U D Kolloway
S2 C Michaels
3S L Appling
LF P Seerey
CF D Philley
RF T Wright
3U F Baker
UO R Hodgin
M T Lyons

CLE 1948 AL
SP B Lemon
SP B Feller
SP G Bearden
SR S Zoldak
RS S Gromek
RP E Klieman
CL R Christopher
C J Hegan
1B E Robinson
2B J Gordon
SS L Boudreau
3B K Keltner
LF D Mitchell
CF- T Tucker
MR L Doby
RL- A Clark
OI- W Judnich

DET 1948 AL
SP H Newhouser
SP F Hutchinson
SR V Trucks
SP D Trout
SR A Houtteman
RP S Overmire
RS B Pierce
C B Swift
1B G Vico
2B E Mayo
SS J Lipon
3B- G Kell
LR V Wertz
CF H Evers
RF P Mullin
LF D Wakefield
IF- N Berry
M S O'Neill

NY 1948 AL
SP A Reynolds
SP E Lopat
SP V Raschi
SP S Shea
SR T Byrne
RP J Page
RS F Hiller
C - G Niarhos
1B G McQuinn
2B S Stirnweiss
SS P Rizzuto
3B B Johnson
LF- J Lindell
CF J DiMaggio
R1 T Henrich
CR Y Berra
UT B Brown
LF- C Keller
M B Harris

PHI 1948 AL
SP P Marchildon
SP J Coleman
SP D Fowler
SP C Scheib
SR L Brissie
RP B Harris
RP B Savage
C - B Rosar
1B F Fain
2B P Suder
SS E Joost
3B H Majeski
LF B McCosky
CF S Chapman
RF E Valo
OI- D White
M C Mack

STL 1948 AL
SP F Sanford
SP C Fannin
SR N Garver
SP B Kennedy
RS B Stephens
RP F Biscan
RP A Widmar
C L Moss
1B- C Stevens
2B J Priddy
SS E Pellagrini
3B B Dillinger
LF W Platt
CF P Lehner
UO A Zarilla
SS S Dente
C - R Partee
M Z Taylor

WAS 1948 AL
SP E Wynn
SP W Masterson
SP R Scarborough
SR S Hudson
SP M Haefner
RS F Thompson
RP M Candini
RP T Ferrick
RP D Welteroth
C J Early
1B M Vernon
2B A Kozar
SS M Christman
3B E Yost
LF G Coan
MR- J Wooten
RM B Stewart
C A Evans
CF- C Gillenwater
OF- T McBride
SU- J Sullivan
M J Kuhel

BOS 1949 NL
SP W Spahn
SP J Sain
SP V Bickford
SR J Antonelli
RP N Potter
RP B Hogue
RS B Hall
C - B Salkeld
1B E Fletcher
2B E Stanky
SS A Dark
3B B Elliott
LR M Rickert
MU J Russell
RF T Holmes
UT S Sisti
OI- P Reiser
UI- C Ryan
UO- E Sauer
M1 B Southworth
M2 J Cooney

BRO 1949 NL
SP D Newcombe
SP P Roe
SP J Hatten
SP R Branca
SR R Barney
RS J Banta
RP E Palica
RP P Minner
C R Campanella
1B G Hodges
2B J Robinson
SS P Reese
3B B Cox
LU- G Hermanski
CF D Snider
RF C Furillo
M B Shotton

CHI 1949 NL
SP J Schmitz
SP B Rush
SP D Leonard
SR M Dubiel
SR D Lade
RS W Hacker
RS B Chipman
RS D Adkins
RP B Muncrief
C - M Owen
1B H Reich
2B E Verban
SS R Smalley
3U F Gustine
LF H Sauer
M3 A Pafko
MR H Jeffcoat
1U P Cavarretta
M1 C Grimm
M2 F Frisch

CIN 1949 NL
SP K Raffensberger
SP H Fox
SP H Wehmeier
SP J Vander Meer
RS E Erautt
RS B Lively
RP E Blackwell
RS K Peterson
C - W Cooper
1B T Kluszewski
2U J Bloodworth
SS V Stallcup
3B G Hatton
LF- P Lowrey
CF L Merriman
RM J Wyrostek
2U B Adams
RU D Litwhiler
OI- H Walker
M1 B Walters
M2 L Sewell

NY 1949 NL
SP L Jansen
SP M Kennedy
SR D Koslo
SR S Jones
SP C Hartung
RP K Higbe
RP H Behrman
RP A Hansen
C - W Westrum
1B J Mize
2B- H Thompson
SS- B Kerr
3B S Gordon
LF W Lockman
CF B Thomson
RF W Marshall
SI B Rigney
M L Durocher

PHI 1949 NL
SP K Heintzelman
SR R Roberts
SP R Meyer
SP H Borowy
SR C Simmons
RP J Konstanty
RP K Trinkle
RS S Rowe
C A Seminick
1B D Sisler
2B- E Miller
SS G Hamner
3B W Jones
LF D Ennis
CF R Ashburn
RF B Nicholson
RF- S Hollmig
CU- S Lopata
M E Sawyer

PIT 1949 NL
SR M Dickson
SP B Werle
SR C Chambers
SP B Chesnes
SR V Lombardi
RS R Sewell
C - C McCullough
OI- J Hopp
2B M Basgall
SS S Rojek
3B P Castiglione
LF R Kiner
MU- D Restelli
RM W Westlake
3B- E Bockman
1B- J Hopp
UT- D Walker
M B Meyer

STL 1949 NL
SR H Pollet
SP H Brecheen
SR A Brazle
SP R Munger
SR G Staley
RP T Wilks
C - D Rice
1B N Jones
2B R Schoendienst
SS M Marion
3B- E Kazak
LF E Slaughter
CF C Diering
RM S Musial
C - J Garagiola
3B- T Glaviano
1B- R Nelson
RF- R Northey
M E Dyer

BOS 1949 AL
SP M Parnell
SR E Kinder
SP J Dobson
SP C Stobbs
SP J Kramer
RP T Hughson
RP E Johnson
C B Tebbetts
1B B Goodman
2B B Doerr
SS V Stephens
3B J Pesky
LF T Williams
CF D DiMaggio
RF A Zarilla
M J McCarthy

CHI 1949 AL
SP B Wight
SP R Gumpert
SP B Pierce
SR B Kuzava
SR H Judson
RS M Pieretti
RP M Surkont
C - D Wheeler
1B C Kress
2B C Michaels
SS L Appling

3B F Baker
LU- G Zernial
CF C Metkovich
RF D Philley
UT- S Souchock
M J Onslow

CLE 1949 AL
SP B Lemon
SP B Feller
SR M Garcia
SP E Wynn
SR G Bearden
RS A Benton
RS S Paige
RP F Papish
RP S Zoldak
C J Hegan
1B M Vernon
2B J Gordon
S3 L Boudreau
3B- K Keltner
LF D Mitchell
CF L Doby
RF B Kennedy
SS- R Boone
OF- T Tucker

DET 1949 AL
SP H Newhouser
SP V Trucks
SP A Houtteman
SP T Gray
SR F Hutchinson
RP D Trout
C A Robinson
1B- P Campbell
2B N Berry
SS J Lipon
3B G Kell
LM H Evers
CF J Groth
RF V Wertz
UI D Kolloway
UI E Lake
LU P Mullin
M R Rolfe

NY 1949 AL
SP V Raschi
SP E Lopat
SP A Reynolds
SP T Byrne
SR F Sanford
RP J Page
RP S Shea
RP C Marshall
C Y Berra
R1 T Henrich
2B J Coleman
SS P Rizzuto
3B B Brown
LU G Woodling
MR C Mapes
RO H Bauer
3U B Johnson
LF- J Lindell
M C Stengel

PHI 1949 AL
SR A Kellner
SP J Coleman
SP L Brissie
SP D Fowler
SR C Scheib
RS B Shantz
RP B Harris
C M Guerra
1B F Fain
2B P Suder
SS E Joost
3B H Majeski
LF E Valo
CF S Chapman
RF W Moses
2B- N Fox
M C Mack

STL 1949 AL
SP N Garver
SR A Papai
SP C Fannin
SP K Drews
SR R Embree
RS B Kennedy
RS J Ostrowski
RP T Ferrick
RS D Starr
C S Lollar
1B J Graham
2B J Priddy
SS- E Pellagrini
3B B Dillinger
ML R Sievers
OI S Spence
RF D Kokos
OI P Lehner
C L Moss
LU W Platt
SI J Sullivan
M Z Taylor

WAS 1949 AL
SR S Hudson
SP R Scarborough
SR P Calvert
SP M Harris
SR D Weik
RS L Hittle
RS J Haynes
RP D Welteroth
C A Evans
1B E Robinson
2B A Kozar
SS S Dente
3B E Yost
LO B Stewart
CF C Vollmer
RU B Lewis
LM G Coan
2U S Robertson
RM- S Mele
M J Kuhel

BOS 1950 NL
SP V Bickford
SP W Spahn
SP J Sain
SR B Chipman
RP B Hogue
RS J Antonelli
RP B Hall
C W Cooper
1B E Torgeson
2B R Hartsfield
SS B Kerr
3B B Elliott
LF S Gordon
CF S Jethroe
RF T Holmes
RU W Marshall
C - D Crandall
M B Southworth

BRO 1950 NL
SP D Newcombe
SP P Roe
SR E Palica
SR R Branca
SP C Erskine
RS D Bankhead
C R Campanella
1B G Hodges
2B J Robinson
SS P Reese
3B B Cox
LF G Hermanski
CF D Snider
RF C Furillo
LU- J Russell
M B Shotton

CHI 1950 NL
SP B Rush
SP P Minner
SR J Schmitz
SR F Hiller
SR D Lade
RS M Dubiel
RS J Klippstein
RP D Leonard
RS J Vander Meer
C - M Owen
1B- P Ward
2B W Terwilliger
SS R Smalley
3B B Serena
LF H Sauer
CF A Pafko
OI- B Borkowski
1B- P Cavarretta
M F Frisch

CIN 1950 NL
SP E Blackwell
SP K Raffensberger
SP H Wehmeier
SR H Fox
SP W Ramsdell
RP F Smith
RP E Erautt
RP J Hetki
C - D Howell
1B T Kluszewski
2B C Ryan
SS V Stallcup
3B G Hatton
LU J Adcock
CF B Usher
RF J Wyrostek
IF B Adams
CF L Merriman
LU- P Lowrey
M L Sewell

NY 1950 NL
SP L Jansen
SR S Maglie
SR S Jones
SR D Koslo
SP J Hearn
RS M Kennedy
RS J Kramer
RP A Hansen
C W Westrum
1B T Gilbert
2B E Stanky
SS A Dark
3B H Thompson
LF W Lockman
CF B Thomson
RF D Mueller
1R M Irvin
M L Durocher

PHI 1950 NL
SP R Roberts
SP C Simmons
SR B Miller
SP R Meyer
SR B Church
RP J Konstanty
RP K Heintzelman
C A Seminick
1B E Waitkus
2B M Goliat
SS G Hamner
3B W Jones
LF D Sisler
CF R Ashburn
RF D Ennis
M E Sawyer

PIT 1950 NL
SP C Chambers
SR M Dickson
SR B Werle
SR B Macdonald
SR V Law
RS M Queen
RP V Lombardi
RP J Walsh
C C McCullough
1U J Hopp
2B D Murtaugh
SS- S Rojek
3B- N Fernandez
LF R Kiner
MU W Westlake
RF G Bell
UI P Castiglione
SS- D O'Connell
M B Meyer

STL 1950 NL
SP H Pollet
SP M Lanier
SR G Staley
SP H Brecheen
SR R Munger
RS A Brazle
RS C Boyer
RP F Martin
C D Rice
1B- R Nelson
2B R Schoendienst
SS M Marion
3B T Glaviano
OI S Musial
UO B Howerton
RF E Slaughter
CF- C Diering
3U E Kazak
M E Dyer

BOS 1950 AL
SP M Parnell
SR E Kinder
SR J Dobson
SR C Stobbs
SR M McDermott
RS W Masterson
RP W Nixon
C - B Tebbetts
1B W Dropo
2B B Doerr
SS V Stephens
3B J Pesky
LF- T Williams
CF D DiMaggio
RF A Zarilla
IO B Goodman
M1 J McCarthy
M2 S O'Neill

CHI 1950 AL
SP B Pierce
SP B Wight
SR B Cain
SR R Gumpert
SP R Scarborough
RP H Judson
RP K Holcombe
RP L Aloma
C P Masi
1B E Robinson
2B N Fox
SS C Carrasquel
3B H Majeski
LF G Zernial
RM D Philley
RF- M Rickert
3U- F Baker
UT- G Goldsberry
M1 J Onslow
M2 R Corriden

CLE 1950 AL
SP B Lemon
SP B Feller
SP E Wynn
SP M Garcia
SR S Gromek
RP S Zoldak
RP A Benton
RP J Flores
RP M Pieretti
C J Hegan
1B L Easter
2B J Gordon
SS R Boone
3B A Rosen
LF D Mitchell
CF L Doby
RF B Kennedy
2B- B Avila
SS- L Boudreau

DET 1950 AL
SP A Houtteman
SR F Hutchinson
SP H Newhouser
SR D Trout
SP T Gray
RS H White
RP P Calvert
C A Robinson
1B D Kolloway
2B J Priddy
SS J Lipon
3B G Kell
LF H Evers
CF J Groth
RF V Wertz
M R Rolfe

NY 1950 AL
SP V Raschi
SP A Reynolds
SP E Lopat
SP T Byrne
SP W Ford
RS F Sanford
CL J Page
RP T Ferrick
C Y Berra
1B J Collins
2B J Coleman
SS P Rizzuto
3B B Johnson
LF G Woodling
CF J DiMaggio
RL H Bauer
3B B Brown
RU C Mapes
1B- J Mize
M C Stengel

PHI 1950 AL
SR L Brissie
SP A Kellner
SR B Shantz
SR B Hooper
SR H Wyse
RS C Scheib
C - M Guerra
1B F Fain
2B B Hitchcock
SS E Joost
3B- B Dillinger
LU P Lehner
CF S Chapman
RL E Valo
RU- W Moses
3U- K Wahl
M C Mack

STL 1950 AL
SP N Garver
SR A Widmar
SR S Overmire
SR D Starr
SR H Dorish
RP C Fannin
RS D Johnson
RP C Marshall
C S Lollar
1L D Lenhardt
2B O Friend
SS T Upton
32- B Sommers
LR D Kokos
UO R Coleman
RU K Wood
1B H Arft
MU R Sievers
CU- L Moss
23 S Stirnweiss
M Z Taylor

WAS 1950 AL
SP S Hudson
SP B Kuzava
SP C Marrero
SP S Consuegra
SR J Haynes
RP M Harris
RP J Pearce
C - A Evans
1B- M Vernon
2B C Michaels
SS S Dente
3B E Yost
RL B Stewart
CF I Noren
RO S Mele
LF G Coan
M B Harris

BOS 1951 NL
SP W Spahn
SP M Surkont
SP V Bickford
SP J Sain
SR C Nichols
RP J Wilson
RS D Cole
RP G Estock
RP B Chipman
C W Cooper
1B E Torgeson
2B R Hartsfield
SS- B Kerr
3B B Elliott
LU S Gordon
CF S Jethroe
RF W Marshall
IO S Sisti
UO- B Addis
M1 B Southworth
M2 T Holmes

BRO 1951 NL
SP D Newcombe
SP P Roe
SR R Branca
SR C Erskine
RP C King
RS B Podbielan
C R Campanella
1B G Hodges
2B J Robinson
SS P Reese
3B B Cox
LF- A Pafko
CF D Snider
RF C Furillo
LU- D Thompson
M C Dressen

CHI 1951 NL
SP B Rush
SP P Minner
SR C McLish
SP F Hiller
SR T Lown
RS J Klippstein
RS B Kelly
RP D Leonard
RP M Dubiel
CU S Burgess
1B- C Connors
2B E Miksis
SS- R Smalley
3B R Jackson
LF H Sauer
UO H Jeffcoat
UO F Baumholtz
1U- P Cavarretta
M1 F Frisch

CIN 1951 NL
SP K Raffensberger
SP E Blackwell
SR H Fox
SP W Ramsdell
SR H Wehmeier
RS H Perkowski
RP F Smith
RP B Byerly
C - D Howell
1B T Kluszewski
2B C Ryan
SS V Stallcup
3B G Hatton
LF J Adcock
ML L Merriman
RF J Wyrostek
IO B Adams
MU B Usher
SU- R McMillan
M L Sewell

NY 1951 NL
SP S Maglie
SP L Jansen
SP J Hearn
SR D Koslo
RP G Spencer
RS S Jones
RS M Kennedy
RP A Gettel
C W Westrum
1B W Lockman
2B E Stanky
SS A Dark
3B- H Thompson
L1 M Irvin
CF W Mays
RF D Mueller
OI B Thomson
M L Durocher

PHI 1951 NL
SP R Roberts
SP B Church
SP R Meyer
SR J Thompson
SR K Heintzelman
RP J Konstanty
RP K Johnson
C A Seminick
1B E Waitkus
2U- P Caballero
SS G Hamner
3B W Jones
LF D Sisler
CF R Ashburn
RF D Ennis
UT- T Brown
UL- B Nicholson
2U- E Pellagrini
C - D Wilber
M E Sawyer

PIT 1951 NL
SR M Dickson
SR M Queen
SR B Friend
SP H Pollet
SR V Law
RS B Werle
RP T Wilks
RP J Walsh
C - C McCullough
1B- J Phillips
2B- D Murtaugh
SS G Strickland
3B P Castiglione
L1 R Kiner
M1 C Metkovich
RF G Bell
OI- B Howerton
M B Meyer

STL 1951 NL
SR G Staley
SR T Poholsky
SP M Lanier
SR H Brecheen
SP C Chambers
RS A Brazle
RS R Munger
RP D Bokelmann
C D Rice
1B- N Jones
2B R Schoendienst
SS S Hemus
3B B Johnson
L1 S Musial
MU P Lowrey
RF E Slaughter
M M Marion

BOS 1951 AL
SP M Parnell
SR R Scarborough
SR M McDermott
SP C Stobbs
SR W Nixon
RP E Kinder
RS B Wight
RP L Kiely
RS H Taylor
C - L Moss
1B W Dropo
2B B Doerr
SS J Pesky
3B V Stephens
LF T Williams
CF D DiMaggio
RF C Vollmer
UT B Goodman
SU- L Boudreau
3U- F Hatfield
M S O'Neill

CHI 1951 AL
SP B Pierce
SP S Rogovin
SP K Holcombe
SP J Dobson
SR R Gumpert
RP L Kretlow
RS H Judson
RP H Dorish
RP L Aloma
C - P Masi
1B E Robinson
2B N Fox
SS C Carrasquel
3B- B Dillinger
UT M Minoso
CF J Busby
RF A Zarilla
LU B Stewart
3U- F Baker
M P Richards

CLE 1951 AL
SP E Wynn
SP B Lemon
SR M Garcia
SP B Feller
RP L Brissie
RS S Gromek
C J Hegan
1B L Easter
2B B Avila
SS R Boone
3B A Rosen
LF D Mitchell
CF L Doby
RF B Kennedy
OI S Chapman
OI H Simpson
M A Lopez

DET 1951 AL
SP T Gray
SR D Trout
SR F Hutchinson
SR V Trucks
SR B Cain
RS M Stuart
RP G Bearden
RP H Newhouser
RP H White
C J Ginsberg
1B D Kryhoski
2B J Priddy
SS J Lipon
3B G Kell
LM H Evers
CF J Groth
RF V Wertz
LU P Mullin
1B- D Kolloway
UT- S Souchock
M R Rolfe

NY 1951 AL
SP V Raschi
SP E Lopat
SR A Reynolds
SR T Morgan
SR S Shea
RP J Ostrowski
C Y Berra
1B J Collins
2B J Coleman
SS P Rizzuto
3B B Brown
LF G Woodling
CF J DiMaggio
RL H Bauer
RF M Mantle
32 G McDougald
1B J Mize
M C Stengel

PHI 1951 AL
SP A Kellner
SP B Shantz
SR B Hooper
SR M Martin
SP S Zoldak
RS C Scheib
RP D Fowler
RS J Coleman
RP J Kucab
C - J Tipton
1B F Fain
2B P Suder
SS E Joost
3B- H Majeski
LF G Zernial
CF D Philley
RF E Valo
1U L Limmer
32- B Hitchcock
M J Dykes

STL 1951 AL
SP N Garver
SR D Pillette
SP T Byrne
SR A Widmar
RP B Mahoney
RP S Paige
RS B Kennedy
C S Lollar
1B H Arft
2B B Young
SS- B Jennings
3B F Marsh
LR- R Coleman
CF J Delsing
RL K Wood
C - M Batts
M Z Taylor

WAS 1951 AL
SP C Marrero
SP D Johnson
SP S Hudson
SR J Moreno
SP B Porterfield
RS S Consuegra
RP M Harris
RP J Haynes
C - M Guerra
1B M Vernon
2B C Michaels
SS- P Runnels
3B E Yost
LF G Coan
CF I Noren
RU S Mele
SU- S Dente
UO- M McCormick
M B Harris

BOS 1952 NL
SP W Spahn
SP J Wilson
SP M Surkont
SP V Bickford
RS L Burdette
RP S Jones
C W Cooper
1B E Torgeson
2B J Dittmer
SS J Logan
3B E Mathews
LF S Gordon
CF S Jethroe
RU J Daniels
UT- S Sisti
RF- B Thorpe
M1 T Holmes
M2 C Grimm

BRO 1952 NL
SP C Erskine
SR B Loes
SR B Wade
SP P Roe
SR J Rutherford
RP J Black
RP C Van Cuyk
C R Campanella
1B G Hodges
2B J Robinson
SS P Reese
3B B Cox
LR A Pafko
CF D Snider
RF C Furillo
LU G Shuba
M C Dressen

CHI 1952 NL
SP B Rush
SR J Klippstein
SR W Hacker
SP P Minner
SR T Lown
RS B Kelly
RP D Leonard
RS B Schultz
C T Atwell
1B D Fondy
2S E Miksis
SS- R Smalley
3B R Jackson
LF H Sauer
CF H Jeffcoat
RM F Baumholtz

RU G Hermanski
IF B Serena
UO B Addis
M P Cavarretta

CIN 1952 NL
SP K Raffensberger
SP H Perkowski
SP H Wehmeier
SP B Church
SR F Hiller
RP F Smith
RP E Blackwell
RS J Nuxhall
C A Seminick
1B T Kluszewski
2B G Hatton
SS R McMillan
3B B Adams
LU J Adcock
MO B Borkowski
RF W Marshall
M1 L Sewell
M2 E Brucker
M3 R Hornsby

NY 1952 NL
SP J Hearn
SP S Maglie
SR D Koslo
SP L Jansen
SR M Lanier
RP H Wilhelm
RS M Kennedy
RP G Spencer
C W Westrum
1B W Lockman
2B D Williams
SS A Dark
3M B Thomson
LU B Elliott
UT H Thompson
RF D Mueller
M L Durocher

PHI 1952 NL
SP R Roberts
SP R Meyer
SP K Drews
SP C Simmons
SR S Ridzik
RP J Konstanty
RP A Hansen
C S Burgess
1B E Waitkus
2B C Ryan
SS G Hamner
3B W Jones
LF D Ennis
CF R Ashburn
RF J Wyrostek
M1 E Sawyer
M2 S O'Neill

PIT 1952 NL
SP M Dickson
SP H Pollet
SR B Friend
RS W Main
RP T Wilks
RP P LaPalme
C J Garagiola
1B T Bartirome
2U J Merson
SS D Groat
3B- P Castiglione
LF R Kiner
CF B Del Greco
RF G Bell
UI C Koshorek
1O C Metkovich
M B Meyer

STL 1952 NL
SP G Staley
SP V Mizell
SR J Presko
SP C Boyer
SR H Brecheen
RS A Brazle
RP E Yuhas
RS C Chambers
C D Rice
1B D Sisler
2B R Schoendienst
SS S Hemus
3B B Johnson
OI P Lowrey
MU S Musial
RF E Slaughter
LF H Rice
3U- T Glaviano
M E Stanky

BOS 1952 AL
SP M Parnell
SP M McDermott
SP D Trout
SP S Hudson
SP D Brodowski
RS W Nixon
RS E Kinder
RS I Delock
RS R Scarborough
C S White
1B D Gernert
2U B Goodman
SS- J Lipon
3B- G Kell
LF H Evers
CF D DiMaggio
RU F Throneberry
23- T Lepcio
S3- V Stephens
UO- C Vollmer
M L Boudreau

CHI 1952 AL
SP B Pierce
SP S Rogovin
SP J Dobson
SP M Grissom
SR C Stobbs
RP H Dorish
RP B Kennedy
C S Lollar
1B E Robinson
2B N Fox
SS C Carrasquel
3B H Rodriguez
UT M Minoso
UO- R Coleman
RF S Mele
LU- B Stewart
M P Richards

CLE 1952 AL
SP B Lemon
SR M Garcia
SP E Wynn
SP B Feller
SR S Gromek
RP L Brissie
RP M Harris
C J Hegan
1B L Easter
2B B Avila
SS R Boone
3B A Rosen
LF D Mitchell
CF L Doby
RF H Simpson
M A Lopez

DET 1952 AL
SP T Gray
SP A Houtteman
SP V Trucks
SP H Newhouser
SP B Wight
RS B Hoeft
RP H White
RP D Littlefield
C J Ginsberg
1B W Dropo
2B- J Priddy
SS- N Berry
3B F Hatfield
LU P Mullin
CF J Groth
RF- V Wertz
RO- C Mapes
UT- S Souchock
M1 R Rolfe
M2 F Hutchinson

NY 1952 AL
SP A Reynolds
SP V Raschi
SR J Sain
SP E Lopat
SR B Kuzava
RP T Morgan
RS J McDonald
RP B Hogue
C Y Berra
1B J Collins
2B B Martin
SS P Rizzuto
3B G McDougald
LF G Woodling
CF M Mantle
RF H Bauer
UR- J Mize
OI I Noren
M C Stengel

PHI 1952 AL
SP B Shantz
SP A Kellner
SP H Byrd
SR C Scheib
RS B Hooper
RP J Kucab
C J Astroth
1B F Fain
2B- S Kell
SS E Joost
3B B Hitchcock
LF G Zernial
CF D Philley
RF E Valo
M J Dykes

STL 1952 AL
SP D Pillette
SP T Byrne
SP B Cain
SR G Bearden
SP N Garver
RS S Paige
RS E Harrist
RP D Madison
C C Courtney
1B D Kryhoski
2B B Young
SS- J DeMaestri
3L J Dyck
UO J Delsing
CF J Rivera
RU B Nieman
1B- G Goldsberry
M1 R Hornsby
M2 M Marion

WAS 1952 AL
SP B Porterfield
SP C Marrero
SP S Shea
SP W Masterson
SP J Moreno
RP R Gumpert
RP S Consuegra
RS D Johnson
RP J Haynes
C M Grasso
1B M Vernon
2B F Baker
SS P Runnels
3B E Yost
LF G Coan
CF J Busby
RF J Jensen
M B Harris

BRO 1953 NL
SP C Erskine
SR R Meyer
SP B Loes
SP P Roe
SR J Podres
RS B Milliken
RS C Labine
RP J Hughes
RP B Wade
C R Campanella
1B G Hodges
2B J Gilliam
SS P Reese
3B B Cox
LR D Thompson
CF D Snider
RF C Furillo
L3 J Robinson
M C Dressen

CHI 1953 NL
SP W Hacker
SP P Minner
SR J Klippstein
SP B Rush
SP H Pollet
RS T Lown
SR B Church
RP D Leonard
C- C McCullough
1B D Fondy
2S E Miksis
SS- R Smalley
3B R Jackson
LF R Kiner
MR F Baumholtz
RL H Sauer
CF H Jeffcoat
23 B Serena
M P Cavarretta

CIN 1953 NL
SP H Perkowski
SR B Podbielan
SP K Raffensberger
SR J Nuxhall
SP F Baczewski
RS J Collum
RP F Smith
RP C King
RS B Kelly
C A Seminick
1B T Kluszewski
2B R Bridges
SS R McMillan
3B B Adams
LF J Greengrass
CF G Bell
RF W Marshall
RU B Borkowski
UI- G Hatton
M1 R Hornsby
M2 B Mills

MIL 1953 NL
SP W Spahn
SP J Antonelli
SP M Surkont
SR B Buhl
SR D Liddle
RS L Burdette
RP J Wilson
RP E Johnson
C D Crandall
1B J Adcock
2B J Dittmer
SS J Logan
3B E Mathews
LF S Gordon
CF B Bruton
RF A Pafko
LO J Pendleton
M C Grimm

NY 1953 NL
SP R Gomez
SP J Hearn
SR L Jansen
SP S Maglie
SP A Worthington
RP H Wilhelm
RS D Koslo
RS A Corwin
C W Westrum
1B W Lockman
2B D Williams
SU A Dark
3B H Thompson
LF M Irvin
CF B Thomson
RF D Mueller
UI D Spencer
M L Durocher

PHI 1953 NL
SP R Roberts
SP C Simmons
SR K Drews
SR J Konstanty
SR B Miller
RS S Ridzik
RP A Hansen
C S Burgess
1B E Torgeson
2S G Hamner
SS T Kazanski
3B W Jones
LF D Ennis
CF R Ashburn
RF J Wyrostek
C- S Lopata
2U- C Ryan
1U- E Waitkus
M S O'Neill

PIT 1953 NL
SR M Dickson
SR P LaPalme
SP J Lindell
SP B Friend
SR B Hall
RP J Hetki
RS R Face
RP R Bowman
C- M Sandlock
1B- P Ward
2B- J O'Brien
SS- E O'Brien
32 D O'Connell
LF- H Rice
CF F Thomas
RF C Abrams
SS D Cole
1U P Smith
MO C Bernier
UI- E Pellagrini
M F Haney

STL 1953 NL
SP H Haddix
SP G Staley
SP V Mizell
SP J Presko
SR S Miller
RP A Brazle
RP H White
RS C Chambers
C D Rice
1B S Bilko
2B R Schoendienst
SS S Hemus
3B R Jablonski
LF S Musial
CF R Repulski
RF E Slaughter
UT P Lowrey
M E Stanky

BOS 1953 AL
SP M Parnell
SP M McDermott
SP H Brown
SR S Hudson
SP W Nixon
RP E Kinder
RS B Flowers
RP I Delock
C S White
1B D Gernert
2B B Goodman
SS M Bolling
3B G Kell
LF H Evers
CF T Umphlett
RF J Piersall
IF- F Baker
LF- G Stephens
M L Boudreau

CHI 1953 AL
SP B Pierce
SP V Trucks
SR M Fornieles
SP S Rogovin
SR S Consuegra
RS H Dorish
RP J Dobson
RS B Keegan
RP G Bearden
C S Lollar
1B F Fain
2B N Fox
SS C Carrasquel
3B- B Elliott
LF M Minoso
CF J Rivera
RF S Mele
OF- T Wright
M P Richards

CLE 1953 AL
SP B Lemon
SP M Garcia
SP E Wynn
SP B Feller
SP A Houtteman
RS D Hoskins
RP B Hooper
C J Hegan
1B B Glynn
2B B Avila
SS G Strickland
3B A Rosen
LF D Mitchell
CF L Doby
RL B Kennedy
RF- H Simpson
UO- W Westlake
M A Lopez

DET 1953 AL
SP B Hoeft
SP N Garver
SP T Gray
SP S Gromek
SP R Branca
RS D Marlowe
RP R Herbert
RP D Madison
C M Batts
1B W Dropo
2U J Pesky
SS H Kuenn
3B R Boone
LR B Nieman
CF J Delsing
RL D Lund
UI F Hatfield
OF- P Mullin
OI- S Souchock
M F Hutchinson

NY 1953 AL
SP W Ford
SR J Sain
SP V Raschi
SP E Lopat
SR A Reynolds
RP J McDonald
RS B Kuzava
RP T Gorman
RP R Scarborough
C Y Berra
1B J Collins
2B B Martin
SS P Rizzuto
3B G McDougald
LF G Woodling
CF M Mantle
RF H Bauer
UO I Noren
UR- J Mize
M C Stengel

PHI 1953 AL
SP H Byrd
SR M Fricano
SP A Kellner
SR C Bishop
SP B Shantz
RS M Martin
RS C Scheib
RP F Fanovich
C- J Astroth
1B E Robinson
2B C Michaels
SS J DeMaestri
3B L Babe
LF G Zernial
CF E McGhee
RF D Philley
32 P Suder
C- R Murray
M J Dykes

STL 1953 AL
SR D Larsen
SP D Pillette
SR D Littlefield
SR H Brecheen
SR B Cain
RP S Paige
RP M Stuart
RS M Blyzka
C C Courtney
1B D Kryhoski
2B B Young
SS B Hunter
OI J Dyck
LU D Kokos
CF J Groth
RF V Wertz
LU D Lenhardt
C- L Moss
1B- R Sievers
M M Marion

WAS 1953 AL
SP B Porterfield
SP W Masterson
SP S Shea
SP C Stobbs
SP C Marrero
RS S Dixon
RS J Schmitz
RS A Sima
RP J Lane
C- E Fitz Gerald
1B M Vernon
2B W Terwilliger
SS P Runnels
3B E Yost
LF C Vollmer
CF J Busby
RF J Jensen
M B Harris

BRO 1954 NL
SP C Erskine
SP R Meyer
SP J Podres
SP B Loes
SP D Newcombe
RP C Labine
CL J Hughes
RP E Palica
RP B Milliken
C R Campanella
1B G Hodges
2B J Gilliam
SS P Reese
3B- D Hoak
L3 J Robinson
CF D Snider
RF C Furillo
LF- S Amoros
3B- B Cox
M W Alston

CHI 1954 NL
SP B Rush
SP P Minner
SR W Hacker
SR J Klippstein
SP H Pollet
RS J Davis
RP H Jeffcoat
RP B Tremel
C- J Garagiola
1B D Fondy
2B G Baker
SS E Banks
3B R Jackson
LF R Kiner
CF B Talbot
RF H Sauer
MO-F Baumholtz
M S Hack

CIN 1954 NL
SR A Fowler
SP C Valentine
SR J Nuxhall
SP B Podbielan
SP F Baczewski
CL F Smith
RS H Judson
RS H Perkowski
RP J Collum
C- A Seminick
1B T Kluszewski
2B J Temple
SS R McMillan
3B B Adams
LF J Greengrass
CF G Bell
RF W Post
3U C Harmon
M B Tebbetts

MIL 1954 NL
SP W Spahn
SP L Burdette
SP G Conley
SP J Wilson
SR C Nichols
RP D Jolly
RS B Buhl
RP E Johnson
RP R Crone
C D Crandall
1B J Adcock
2I D O'Connell
SS J Logan
3B E Mathews
LF H Aaron
CF B Bruton
RF A Pafko
M C Grimm

NY 1954 NL
SP J Antonelli
SP R Gomez
SP S Maglie
SP J Hearn
SP D Liddle
RP M Grissom
RP H Wilhelm
RP W McCall
C W Westrum
1B W Lockman
2B D Williams
SS A Dark
3B H Thompson
LF M Irvin
CF W Mays
RF D Mueller
C- R Katt
UO- D Rhodes
M L Durocher

PHI 1954 NL
SP R Roberts
SP C Simmons
SP M Dickson
SR B Miller
SP H Wehmeier
RS S Ridzik
RP J Konstanty
C S Burgess
1B E Torgeson
2B G Hamner
SS B Morgan
3B W Jones
LU D Schell
CF R Ashburn
OI D Ennis
RL- M Clark
C- S Lopata
RU J Wyrostek
M1 S O'Neill
M2 T Moore

PIT 1954 NL
SP M Surkont
SR B Friend
SR V Law
SP D Littlefield
SR J Thies
RS B Purkey
RS P LaPalme
RP J Hetki
C T Atwell
1B B Skinner
2B C Roberts
SS G Allie
UI D Cole
UO D Hall
ML F Thomas
R3 S Gordon
UO J Lynch
IO P Ward
C- J Shepard
M F Haney

STL 1954 NL
SP H Haddix
SP V Raschi
SR B Lawrence
SR G Staley
SR T Poholsky
RP A Brazle
RP C Deal
RS J Presko
RP R Lint
C B Sarni
1B- J Cunningham
2B R Schoendienst
SS A Grammas
3B R Jablonski
LF R Repulski
CF W Moon
RF S Musial
SI S Hemus
OI- J Frazier
M E Stanky

BAL 1954 AL
SP B Turley
SP J Coleman
SP D Larsen
SP D Pillette
SR L Kretlow
RS B Chakales
RP M Blyzka
RP H Fox
C C Courtney
1B E Waitkus
2B B Young
SS B Hunter
3B V Stephens
LF- J Fridley
CF C Diering
RF C Abrams
OF G Coan
3U B Kennedy
1U D Kryhoski
M J Dykes

BOS 1954 AL
SR F Sullivan
SP W Nixon
SR T Brewer
SP L Kiely
SR B Henry
RP E Kinder
RS H Brown
RS S Hudson
C S White
1B H Agganis
2I T Lepcio
SS M Bolling
3B G Hatton
LF T Williams
MR J Jensen
RU J Piersall
2I B Goodman
UO K Olson
SI- B Consolo
M L Boudreau

CHI 1954 AL
SP V Trucks
SP B Keegan
SR B Pierce
SR J Harshman
SR S Consuegra
RS D Johnson
RS H Dorish
RP M Martin
C S Lollar
1B- F Fain
2B N Fox
SS C Carrasquel
3B C Michaels
LF M Minoso
CF J Groth
RF J Rivera
M1 P Richards
M2 M Marion

CLE 1954 AL
SP E Wynn
SR M Garcia
SP B Lemon
SP A Houtteman
SP B Feller
RP R Narleski
RS D Mossi
RP H Newhouser
C J Hegan
1B B Glynn
2B B Avila

SS G Strickland
31 A Rosen
LU A Smith
CF L Doby
RF D Philley
1B V Wertz
LO- W Westlake
M A Lopez

DET 1954 AL
SP S Gromek
SP N Garver
SR G Zuverink
SP B Hoeft
SR A Aber
RP D Marlowe
RP R Herbert
RP B Miller
C F House
1B W Dropo
2B F Bolling
SS H Kuenn
3B R Boone
LU J Delsing
CF B Tuttle
RF A Kaline
1B- W Belardi
2U- F Hatfield
LU- B Nieman
M F Hutchinson

NY 1954 AL
SP W Ford
SR B Grim
SP E Lopat
SR A Reynolds
SR T Morgan
RP H Byrd
CL J Sain
C Y Berra
1B J Collins
23 G McDougald
SS P Rizzuto
3B A Carey
OI I Noren
CF M Mantle
RF H Bauer
2S J Coleman
LF G Woodling
SS- W Miranda
UR- E Robinson
1U- B Skowron
M C Stengel

PHI 1954 AL
SP A Portocarrero
SP A Kellner
SR M Fricano
SP B Trice
SP J Gray
RS S Dixon
RP M Burtschy
RP C Bishop
RS A Sima
C - J Astroth
1U L Limmer
2B S Jacobs
SS J DeMaestri
3B J Finigan
LF G Zernial
UT V Power
RF B Renna
1U D Bollweg
OF E Valo
CF B Wilson
M E Joost

WAS 1954 AL
SP B Porterfield
SP M McDermott
SP J Schmitz
SP C Stobbs
SP D Stone
RP C Pascual
RP G Keriazakos
RP B Stewart
C E Fitz Gerald
1B M Vernon
2B W Terwilliger
SS P Runnels
3B E Yost
LF R Sievers
CF J Busby
RF T Umphlett
M B Harris

BRO 1955 NL
SP D Newcombe
SP C Erskine
SP J Podres
SP B Loes
SR K Spooner
RS C Labine
RP E Roebuck
RP D Bessent
C R Campanella
1B G Hodges
2L J Gilliam
SS P Reese
3B J Robinson
LF S Amoros
CF D Snider
RF C Furillo
3B D Hoak
2I- D Zimmer
M W Alston

CHI 1955 NL
SP S Jones
SP B Rush
SP W Hacker
SP P Minner
SR J Davis
RP H Jeffcoat
RS H Pollet
RP D Hillman
RP H Perkowski
C H Chiti
1B D Fondy
2B G Baker
SS E Banks
3B R Jackson
LF- H Sauer
MR E Miksis
RU J King
OF F Baumholtz
LU B Speake
M S Hack

CIN 1955 NL
SR J Nuxhall
SR A Fowler
SR J Klippstein
SR J Collum
SR G Staley
RS R Minarcin
RS J Black
RP H Freeman
C S Burgess
1B T Kluszewski
2B J Temple
SS R McMillan
3S R Bridges
LU- S Palys
CF G Bell
RF W Post
UT C Harmon
UL- B Thurman
M B Tebbetts

MIL 1955 NL
SP W Spahn
SP L Burdette
SR B Buhl
SP G Conley
SR C Nichols
RS R Crone
SR E Johnson
RP D Jolly
C D Crandall
1B G Crowe
2B D O'Connell
SS J Logan
3B E Mathews
LF B Thomson
CF B Bruton
RU H Aaron
LU C Tanner
1B- J Adcock
RU- A Pafko
M C Grimm

NY 1955 NL
SP J Antonelli
SP J Hearn
SP R Gomez
SP S Maglie
SR D Liddle
RP H Wilhelm
RS W McCall
RP M Grissom
RS R Monzant
C R Katt
1B- G Harris
2B- W Terwilliger
SS A Dark
3B H Thompson
L1 W Lockman
CF W Mays
RF D Mueller
IC B Hofman
UL D Rhodes
2B- D Williams
M L Durocher

PHI 1955 NL
SP R Roberts
SP M Dickson
SP H Wehmeier
SP C Simmons
RS J Meyer
RP B Miller
C A Seminick
1U M Blaylock
2S B Morgan
SS- R Smalley
3B W Jones
LF D Ennis
CF R Ashburn
RF J Greengrass
2B G Hamner
CU S Lopata
RU- G Gorbous
M M Smith

PIT 1955 NL
SR B Friend
SR V Law
SR M Surkont
SR R Kline
SR D Littlefield
RS R Face
RS L Donoso
RP D Hall
C J Shepard
1B D Long
2B- J O'Brien
SS D Groat
IF G Freese
OF- J Lynch
LM F Thomas
RF R Clemente
UI- D Cole
1U- P Ward
M F Haney

STL 1955 NL
SP H Haddix
SR L Jackson
SR L Arroyo
SP T Poholsky
SP W Schmidt
RS B Lawrence
RP P LaPalme
C B Sarni
1O S Musial
2B R Schoendienst
SS A Grammas
3B K Boyer
LU R Repulski
CF B Virdon
OI W Moon
UI S Hemus
M1 E Stanky
M2 H Walker

BAL 1955 AL
SP J Wilson
SP E Palica
SP B Wight
RS R Moore
RS A Schallock
RP H Dorish
RS D Johnson
C H Smith
1C G Triandos
2B- F Marsh
SS W Miranda
3B- W Causey
RL- D Philley
CF C Diering
OI C Abrams
UO- D Pope
M P Richards

BOS 1955 AL
SP F Sullivan
SP W Nixon
SP T Brewer
SR I Delock
SR G Susce
RP L Kiely
RP T Hurd
CL E Kinder
C S White
1B N Zauchin
2B B Goodman
SS B Klaus
3B G Hatton
LF T Williams
CF J Piersall
RF J Jensen
LU G Stephens
M P Higgins

CHI 1955 AL
SP B Pierce
SP D Donovan
SP J Harshman
SP V Trucks
SP C Johnson
RS S Consuegra
RP D Howell
RP M Martin
C S Lollar
1B W Dropo
2B N Fox
SS C Carrasquel
3B G Kell
LF M Minoso
CF J Busby
RF J Rivera
RL B Nieman
3U- B Kennedy
M M Marion

CLE 1955 AL
SP E Wynn
SP H Score
SP M Garcia
SP B Lemon
SR A Houtteman
RP R Narleski
RP D Mossi
C J Hegan
1B- V Wertz
2B B Avila
SS G Strickland
3B A Rosen
LF R Kiner
CF L Doby
R3 A Smith
LF- G Woodling
M A Lopez

DET 1955 AL
SP F Lary
SP N Garver
SP B Hoeft
SP S Gromek
RP A Aber
RP B Birrer
RP P Foytack
C F House
1B- E Torgeson
2B F Hatfield
SS H Kuenn
3B R Boone
LF J Delsing
CF B Tuttle
RF A Kaline
LU B Phillips
C - R Wilson
M B Harris

KC 1955 AL
SR A Ditmar
SP A Kellner
SP B Shantz
SR A Ceccarelli
SP A Portocarrero
RP T Gorman
RP V Raschi
RS C Boyer
RP B Harrington
C J Astroth
1B V Power
23 J Finigan
SS J DeMaestri
32 H Lopez
LF G Zernial
CF H Simpson
RU E Slaughter
RU B Renna
MO B Wilson
UO E Valo
C - B Shantz
M L Boudreau

NY 1955 AL
SP W Ford
SP B Turley
SP T Byrne
SR J Kucks
SP D Larsen
RP J Konstanty
RP T Morgan
RP T Sturdivant
C Y Berra
1U B Skowron
2B G McDougald
SS B Hunter
3B A Carey
LF I Noren
CF M Mantle
RF H Bauer
1R J Collins
LU E Howard
SS- P Rizzuto
1U- E Robinson
M C Stengel

WAS 1955 AL
SR D Stone
SP B Porterfield
SR J Schmitz
SR M McDermott
SR C Stobbs
RS P Ramos
RS C Pascual
RS T Abernathy
RP S Shea
C - E Fitz Gerald
1B M Vernon
2B P Runnels
SS J Valdivielso
3B E Yost
LF R Sievers
MO T Umphlett
RU C Paula
OF E Oravetz
SS- B Kline
M C Dressen

BRO 1956 NL
SP D Newcombe
SP R Craig
SP S Maglie
SP C Erskine
SR D Drysdale
RP C Labine
RP E Roebuck
RP D Bessent
RP K Lehman
C R Campanella
1B G Hodges
2L J Gilliam
SS P Reese
3B R Jackson
LU S Amoros
CF D Snider
RF C Furillo
3I J Robinson
M W Alston

CHI 1956 NL
SP B Rush
SP S Jones
SR W Hacker
SP D Kaiser
RP T Lown
RS J Davis
RP V Valentinetti
RS J Brosnan
C H Landrith
1B D Fondy
2B G Baker
SS E Banks
3B D Hoak
LF M Irvin
CF P Whisenant
RF W Moryn
LU J King
UT E Miksis
M S Hack

CIN 1956 NL
SR B Lawrence
SP J Klippstein
SR J Nuxhall
SR A Fowler
SR H Jeffcoat
RP H Freeman
RS T Acker
RP J Black
C E Bailey
1B T Kluszewski
2B J Temple
SS R McMillan
3B R Jablonski
LF F Robinson
CF G Bell
RF W Post
CU- S Burgess
OF- B Thurman
M B Tebbetts

MIL 1956 NL
SP W Spahn
SP L Burdette
SP B Buhl
SR R Crone
SR G Conley
RP E Johnson
RP B Trowbridge
C D Crandall
1B J Adcock
2B D O'Connell
SS J Logan
3B E Mathews
LF B Thomson
CF B Bruton
RF H Aaron
1B F Torre
M1 C Grimm
M2 F Haney

NY 1956 NL
SP J Antonelli
SP R Gomez
SP A Worthington
SR J Hearn
RS D Littlefield
RP H Wilhelm
RS S Ridzik
RP M Grissom
C - B Sarni
1B B White
2B- R Schoendienst
UI D Spencer
3B F Castleman
LF J Brandt
CF W Mays
RF D Mueller
LU D Rhodes
3U- H Thompson
M B Rigney

PHI 1956 NL
SP R Roberts
SP H Haddix
SP C Simmons
SP S Rogovin
SP S Miller
RS B Miller
RS J Meyer
RP R Negray
C1 S Lopata
1B M Blaylock
2B T Kazanski
SS G Hamner
3B W Jones
LF D Ennis
CF R Ashburn
RF E Valo
RU- J Greengrass
2U- S Hemus
M M Smith

PIT 1956 NL
SP B Friend
SP R Kline
SP V Law
SR R Munger
RP R Face
RP N King
RS F Waters
C J Shepard
1B D Long
2B- B Mazeroski
SS D Groat
3L F Thomas
LR L Walls
CF B Virdon
RO R Clemente
UT B Skinner
C - H Foiles
M B Bragan

STL 1956 NL
SP V Mizell
SP T Poholsky
SP M Dickson
SR H Wehmeier
SR W Schmidt
RS L McDaniel
RP L Jackson
RP J Collum
C - H Smith
1R S Musial
2S D Blasingame
SS A Dark
3B K Boyer
LF R Repulski
CF B Del Greco
R1 W Moon
M F Hutchinson

BAL 1956 AL
SP R Moore
SP C Johnson
SP B Wight
SR H Brown
SR E Palica
RP G Zuverink
RS M Fornieles
RS D Ferrarese
RS B Loes
C1 G Triandos
1B- B Boyd
2B B Gardner
SS W Miranda
3B G Kell
LF B Nieman
CF- D Williams
RM T Francona
1U- B Hale
CF- J Pyburn
C - H Smith
M P Richards

BOS 1956 AL
SP T Brewer
SP F Sullivan
SP W Nixon
SR D Sisler
SP M Parnell
RS I Delock
RP B Porterfield
RP T Hurd
C S White
1B M Vernon
2B B Goodman
SS D Buddin
3B B Klaus
LF T Williams
CF J Piersall
RF J Jensen
UT D Gernert
LU G Stephens
23- T Lepcio
M P Higgins

CHI 1956 AL
SP B Pierce
SP D Donovan
SP J Harshman
SP J Wilson
SP B Keegan
RS G Staley
RP D Howell
C S Lollar
1B W Dropo
2B N Fox
SS L Aparicio
3B F Hatfield
LF M Minoso
CF L Doby
RF J Rivera
3B- S Esposito
1O- D Philley
M M Marion

CLE 1956 AL
SP E Wynn
SP B Lemon
SP H Score
SP M Garcia
RP D Mossi
RP R Narleski
RP C McLish
RP A Houtteman
C J Hegan
1B V Wertz
2B B Avila
SS C Carrasquel
3B A Rosen
UT A Smith
CF J Busby
RF R Colavito
LF G Woodling
UI- G Strickland
1U- P Ward
M A Lopez

DET 1956 AL
SP F Lary
SR P Foytack
SP B Hoeft
SP V Trucks
RS S Gromek
RP A Aber
RS D Maas
RP W Masterson
C F House
1U E Torgeson
2B F Bolling
SS H Kuenn
3B R Boone
LF C Maxwell
CF B Tuttle
RF A Kaline
UT- W Belardi
C - R Wilson
M B Harris

KC 1956 AL
SR A Ditmar
SP W Burnette
SP L Kretlow
SR T Herriage
RS T Gorman
RS J Crimian
RP B Shantz
CU- T Thompson
12 V Power
23- J Finigan
SS J DeMaestri
3B H Lopez
LU- L Skizas
MO J Groth
RU H Simpson
LU G Zernial
UO- E Slaughter
M L Boudreau

NY 1956 AL
SP W Ford
SP J Kucks
SR D Larsen
SR T Sturdivant
SP B Turley
RS T Byrne
RP T Morgan
RS B Grim
C Y Berra
1B B Skowron
2B B Martin
SS G McDougald
3B A Carey
LC E Howard
CF M Mantle
RF H Bauer
OI J Collins
2S- J Coleman
M C Stengel

WAS 1956 AL
SP C Stobbs
SR C Pascual
SR P Ramos
SR D Stone
SR B Wiesler
RS B Stewart
RP B Chakales
RS H Griggs
RP C Grob
C C Courtney
12 P Runnels
2U- H Plews
SS- J Valdivielso
3B E Yost
L1 R Sievers
MU W Herzog
RF J Lemon
CU L Berberet
CF K Olson
UO- E Oravetz
M C Dressen

BRO 1957 NL
SP D Drysdale
SP D Newcombe
SP J Podres
SP D McDevitt
SR R Craig
RP C Labine
RS S Koufax
RP E Roebuck
RP S Maglie
C R Campanella
1B G Hodges
2B J Gilliam
SS C Neal
3U P Reese
LR G Cimoli
CF D Snider
RF C Furillo
LU S Amoros
OF- E Valo
UI- D Zimmer
M W Alston

CHI 1957 NL
SP M Drabowsky
SP D Drott
SP B Rush
SR D Elston
SR D Hillman
RP T Lown
RS J Brosnan
RP D Littlefield
C C Neeman
1B D Long
2B B Morgan
SS- J Littrell
S3 E Banks
LO L Walls
OI B Speake
RF W Moryn
OI J Bolger
LM C Tanner
M B Scheffing

CIN 1957 NL
SR B Lawrence
SP H Jeffcoat
SR J Nuxhall
SR D Gross
SR J Klippstein
RS T Acker
RP H Freeman
RS A Fowler
RP R Sanchez
C E Bailey
1B G Crowe
2B J Temple
SS R McMillan
3B D Hoak
LU F Robinson
CF G Bell
RF W Post
CU- S Burgess
M B Tebbetts

MIL 1957 NL
SP W Spahn
SP L Burdette
SP B Buhl
SR G Conley
SR B Trowbridge
RS J Pizarro
RS T Phillips
RP E Johnson
RP D McMahon
C D Crandall
1B F Torre
2B R Schoendienst

SS J Logan
3B E Mathews
LF W Covington
CF- B Bruton
RM H Aaron
UO- A Pafko
M F Haney

NY 1957 NL
SP R Gomez
SR J Antonelli
SP C Barclay
SR S Miller
SP R Crone
RS A Worthington
RP M Grissom
RP R Monzant
C - V Thomas
1B W Lockman
23 D O'Connell
SI D Spencer
3U R Jablonski
LF H Sauer
CF W Mays
RF D Mueller
3O O Virgil
1U- G Harris
OF- D Rhodes
LU- B Thomson
M B Rigney

PHI 1957 NL
SP R Roberts
SP J Sanford
SP C Simmons
SP H Haddix
SR D Cardwell
RP T Farrell
RP J Hearn
RP B Miller
RP S Morehead
C S Lopata
1B E Bouchee
2B G Hamner
SS C Fernandez
3B W Jones
LF H Anderson
CF R Ashburn
RL R Repulski
RF B Bowman
M M Smith

PIT 1957 NL
SP B Friend
SP R Kline
SR B Purkey
SP V Law
RS L Arroyo
RP R Face
SR R Swanson
RP B Smith
C H Foiles
1B D Fondy
2B B Mazeroski
SS D Groat
3U G Freese
LU B Skinner
CF B Virdon
RF R Clemente
3S G Baker
UT F Thomas
OI- P Smith
M1 B Bragan
M2 D Murtaugh

STL 1957 NL
SR L Jackson
SP L McDaniel
SP S Jones
SR H Wehmeier
SR V Mizell
RS W Schmidt
RP L Merritt
RP H Wilhelm
C H Smith
1B S Musial
2B D Blasingame
SS A Dark
3B E Kasko
LR W Moon
M3 K Boyer
LR D Ennis
UT J Cunningham
MU B Smith
M F Hutchinson

BAL 1957 AL
SP C Johnson
SP R Moore
SR B Loes
SP H Brown
SR B O'Dell
RP G Zuverink
RS B Wight
RP K Lehman
C G Triandos
1B B Boyd
2B B Gardner
SS W Miranda
3B G Kell
LF B Nieman
CF- J Busby
RM A Pilarcik
RL T Francona
SS- J Brideweser
UO- J Durham
C - J Ginsberg
M P Richards

BOS 1957 AL
SP F Sullivan
SP T Brewer
SP W Nixon
SP M Fornieles
SP D Sisler
RP I Delock
RS B Porterfield
C S White
1U D Gernert
2B- T Lepcio
SS B Klaus
3B F Malzone
LF T Williams
CF J Piersall
RF J Jensen
LU G Stephens
1U M Vernon
C - P Daley
M P Higgins

CHI 1957 AL
SP B Pierce
SP D Donovan
SP J Wilson
SP J Harshman
SR B Keegan
RS B Fischer
RP G Staley
RP D Howell
C S Lollar
1B- E Torgeson
2B N Fox
SS L Aparicio
3B B Phillips
LF M Minoso
CF L Doby
UO J Landis
3I S Esposito
RU J Rivera
1U W Dropo
M A Lopez

CLE 1957 AL
SP E Wynn
SR M Garcia
SR D Mossi
SP B Lemon
RS R Narleski
RS C McLish
RS B Daley
RP D Tomanek
C - J Hegan
1B V Wertz
2B B Avila
SS C Carrasquel
3M A Smith
LF G Woodling
CF R Maris
RF R Colavito
IO L Raines
1U- J Altobelli
2S- G Strickland
M K Farrell

DET 1957 AL
SR J Bunning
SP F Lary
SR D Maas
SR P Foytack
SP B Hoeft
RP L Sleater
RP H Byrd
C F House
1B R Boone
2B F Bolling
SS H Kuenn
3B R Bertoia
LF C Maxwell
CF B Tuttle
RF A Kaline
M J Tighe

KC 1957 AL
SP N Garver
SP A Kellner
SP R Terry
SR J Urban
SR A Portocarrero
RS T Morgan
RS T Gorman
RS V Trucks
RS W Burnette
C H Smith
1B V Power
2S B Hunter
SS J DeMaestri
3B H Lopez
LF G Zernial
CF- W Held
R3 L Skizas
UO B Cerv
UT- I Noren
C - T Thompson
M1 L Boudreau
M2 H Craft

NY 1957 AL
SP T Sturdivant
SR J Kucks
SP B Turley
SP B Shantz
SP D Larsen
RS A Ditmar
RP W Ford
CL B Grim
RP T Byrne
C Y Berra
1B B Skowron
2B B Richardson
SS G McDougald
3B- A Carey
LC E Howard
CF M Mantle
RF H Bauer
UT T Kubek
LU E Slaughter
UT- J Collins
M C Stengel

WAS 1957 AL
SR P Ramos
SR C Stobbs
SP C Pascual
SR R Kemmerer
RS T Clevenger
RP D Hyde
RP B Byerly
C L Berberet
1I P Runnels
2B H Plews
SS R Bridges
3B E Yost
LF R Sievers
CF B Usher
RF J Lemon
U1 J Becquer
2S- M Bolling
CU- C Courtney
UT- A Schult
M1 C Dressen
M2 C Lavagetto

CHI 1958 NL
SR T Phillips
SP D Drott
SR D Hillman
SP M Drabowsky
SP J Briggs
RS G Hobbie
RP D Elston
RP B Henry
C S Taylor
1B D Long
2B T Taylor
SS E Banks
3B A Dark
LF W Moryn
CF B Thomson
RF L Walls
UO- J Bolger
32- J Goryl
M B Scheffing

CIN 1958 NL
SP B Purkey
SR B Lawrence
SP H Haddix
SR J Nuxhall
SP D Newcombe
RS T Acker
RP H Jeffcoat
RP W Schmidt
C E Bailey
1B G Crowe
2B J Temple
SS R McMillan
3B D Hoak
LM F Robinson
CF G Bell
RF J Lynch
CU S Burgess
S3 A Grammas
OF B Thurman
UT- D Fondy
OI- P Whisenant
M1 B Tebbetts
M2 J Dykes

LA 1958 NL
SR D Drysdale
SP J Podres
SR S Koufax
SP S Williams
RP C Labine
RS F Kipp
RP J Klippstein
RS C Erskine
C J Roseboro
1B G Hodges
2B C Neal
SS D Zimmer
3B- D Gray
UT J Gilliam
ML G Cimoli
RF C Furillo
MU D Snider
OI N Larker
M W Alston

MIL 1958 NL
SP W Spahn
SP L Burdette
SP B Rush
SP C Willey
SP J Pizarro
RP J Jay
RS G Conley
RP D McMahon
RP B Trowbridge
C D Crandall
1B F Torre
2B R Schoendienst
SS J Logan
3B E Mathews
LF A Pafko
CF B Bruton
RF H Aaron
1U J Adcock
LF- W Covington
UT- F Mantilla
M F Haney

PHI 1958 NL
SP R Roberts
SP R Semproch
SR J Sanford
SP C Simmons
SP D Cardwell
RP T Farrell
RS J Meyer
RP J Hearn
C - S Lopata
1B- E Bouchee
2B S Hemus
SS C Fernandez
3B W Jones
L1 H Anderson
CF R Ashburn
RF W Post
2I T Kazanski
UO- B Bowman
UT- D Philley
OF- R Repulski
M1 M Smith
M2 E Sawyer

PIT 1958 NL
SP B Friend
SP R Kline
SP V Law
SR C Raydon
SP G Witt
CL R Face
RS B Porterfield
RP D Gross
RP R Blackburn
C H Foiles
1U T Kluszewski
2B B Mazeroski
SS D Groat
3B F Thomas
LF B Skinner
CF B Virdon
RF R Clemente
M D Murtaugh

STL 1958 NL
SP S Jones
SR L Jackson
SP V Mizell
SR J Brosnan
SR B Mabe
RP L McDaniel
RS B Muffett
RP P Paine
RP B Wight
C - H Smith
1B S Musial
2B D Blasingame
SU E Kasko
3B K Boyer
LF D Ennis
CF C Flood
RL W Moon
1R J Cunningham
RC G Green
LU I Noren
M1 F Hutchinson
M2 S Hack

SF 1958 NL
SP J Antonelli
SR R Gomez
SR S Miller
SR M McCormick
SR R Monzant
RS A Worthington
RP M Grissom
C B Schmidt
1B O Cepeda
2B D O'Connell
SS D Spencer
3B J Davenport
LF- H Sauer
CF W Mays
RF W Kirkland
3U- R Jablonski
UT- W Lockman
M B Rigney

BAL 1958 AL
SP J Harshman
SR B O'Dell
SP A Portocarrero
SR M Pappas
SP C Johnson
RS B Loes
RP H Brown
RP G Zuverink
RP K Lehman
C G Triandos
1B B Boyd
2B B Gardner
SS W Miranda
3B B Robinson
RL G Woodling
CF J Busby
RO A Pilarcik
SS F Castleman
LF B Nieman
UT D Williams
1U- J Marshall
M P Richards

BOS 1958 AL
SP T Brewer
SP F Sullivan
SR I Delock
SP D Sisler
RP M Wall
RS M Fornieles
RP L Kiely
C S White
1B D Gernert
21 P Runnels
SS D Buddin
3B F Malzone
LF T Williams
CF J Piersall
RF J Jensen
LU G Stephens
M P Higgins

CHI 1958 AL
SP D Donovan
SP B Pierce
SP E Wynn
SP J Wilson
SR R Moore
RP G Staley
RP B Shaw
C S Lollar
1B E Torgeson
2B N Fox
SS L Aparicio
3B B Goodman
UO J Rivera
CF J Landis
LR A Smith
3U S Esposito
1B- R Boone
3O- B Phillips
M A Lopez

CLE 1958 AL
SP C McLish
SR M Grant
SR R Narleski
SR G Bell
SR D Ferrarese
RS D Mossi
RS H Wilhelm
C R Nixon
1B M Vernon
23 B Avila
SS- B Hunter
IO B Harrell
LF M Minoso
MU- L Doby
RF R Colavito
2S B Moran
OI- G Geiger
IO V Power
M1 B Bragan
M2 J Gordon

DET 1958 AL
SP F Lary
SP P Foytack
SP J Bunning
SR B Hoeft
SR H Moford
RP H Aguirre
RP T Morgan
C R Wilson
1B G Harris
2B F Bolling
S3 B Martin
3B- R Bertoia
LF C Maxwell
CF H Kuenn
RF A Kaline
LO- J Groth
M1 J Tighe
M2 B Norman

KC 1958 AL
SP R Terry
SP N Garver
SR R Herbert
SP J Urban
SR B Grim
RS M Dickson
RP T Gorman
RP D Tomanek
RS B Daley
C H Chiti
1B- V Power
2B- M Baxes
SS J DeMaestri
23 H Lopez
LF B Cerv
MR B Tuttle
RF R Maris
UO B Martyn
IC H Smith
OI- W Herzog
1U- H Simpson
IO- P Ward
M H Craft

NY 1958 AL
SP B Turley
SP W Ford
SR A Ditmar
SR J Kucks
SR B Shantz
RP D Larsen
RP D Maas
CL R Duren
RS Z Monroe
CU Y Berra
1B B Skowron
2B G McDougald
SS T Kubek
3B A Carey
LF N Siebern
CF M Mantle
RF H Bauer
CU E Howard
3B- J Lumpe
OF- E Slaughter
M C Stengel

WAS 1958 AL
SP P Ramos
SR R Kemmerer
SP C Pascual
SR H Griggs
SR V Valentinetti
RP T Clevenger
RP D Hyde
C C Courtney
1B N Zauchin
2B- K Aspromonte
SS R Bridges
3B E Yost
LF R Sievers
CF A Pearson
RF J Lemon
OI N Chrisley
23 H Plews
SU- O Alvarez
UT- J Becquer
M C Lavagetto

CHI 1959 NL
SP B Anderson
SR G Hobbie
SR D Hillman
SP M Drabowsky
SP A Ceccarelli
RP B Henry
RP D Elston
RS J Buzhardt
C S Taylor
1B D Long
2B T Taylor
SS E Banks
3B A Dark
LM B Thomson
CF G Altman
RF L Walls
1U J Marshall
LF W Moryn
M B Scheffing

CIN 1959 NL
SP D Newcombe
SP B Purkey
SP J Nuxhall
SP J O'Toole
RS O Pena
RS B Lawrence
RP W Schmidt
RP T Acker
C E Bailey
1B F Robinson
2B J Temple
S3 E Kasko
3B- W Jones
LF J Lynch
CF V Pinson
RF G Bell
3L F Thomas
SS- R McMillan
M1 M Smith
M2 F Hutchinson

LA 1959 NL
SP D Drysdale
SP J Podres
SR S Koufax
SR R Craig
SR D McDevitt
RS S Williams
RP C Labine
RP A Fowler
C J Roseboro
1B G Hodges
2B C Neal
SS D Zimmer
3B J Gilliam
LF W Moon
CF D Demeter
RM D Snider
RO R Fairly
1O N Larker
SS- M Wills
M W Alston

MIL 1959 NL
SP W Spahn
SP L Burdette
SP B Buhl
SR J Jay
SR J Pizarro
RS C Willey
RS B Rush
RP D McMahon
C D Crandall
1B J Adcock
2I F Mantilla
SS J Logan
3B E Mathews
LF W Covington
CF B Bruton
RF H Aaron
1B F Torre
M F Haney

PHI 1959 NL
SP R Roberts
SP J Owens
SP G Conley
SP D Cardwell
SR R Semproch
RP J Meyer
RP H Robinson
RP T Phillips
RP T Farrell
C - C Sawatski
1B E Bouchee
2B S Anderson
SS J Koppe
3B G Freese
LF H Anderson
CF R Ashburn
RF W Post
UT D Philley
M E Sawyer

PIT 1959 NL
SP V Law
SP B Friend
SP H Haddix
SP R Kline
SR B Daniels
RP R Face
C S Burgess
1B D Stuart
2B B Mazeroski
SS D Groat
3B D Hoak
LF B Skinner
CF B Virdon
RF R Clemente
RO R Mejias
1U R Nelson
IO- D Schofield
M D Murtaugh

STL 1959 NL
SP L Jackson
SP V Mizell
SR E Broglio
SR G Blaylock
RS L McDaniel
RP M Bridges
C H Smith
1B S Musial
2B D Blasingame
SS A Grammas
3B K Boyer
UO G Cimoli
CF C Flood
RF J Cunningham
L1 B White
M S Hemus

SF 1959 NL
SP J Antonelli
SR S Jones
SR M McCormick
SP J Sanford
RS S Miller
RP A Worthington
C H Landrith
1B O Cepeda
2B D Spencer
SS E Bressoud
3B J Davenport
LF J Brandt
CF W Mays
RF W Kirkland
RU F Alou
UL- L Wagner
M B Rigney

BAL 1959 AL
SP H Wilhelm
SP M Pappas
SR B O'Dell
SP J Walker
SR H Brown
CL B Loes
RP E Johnson
C G Triandos
1B B Boyd
2B B Gardner
SS C Carrasquel
3B- B Robinson
LR G Woodling
CF W Tasby
RF A Pilarcik
S3 B Klaus
LF B Nieman
UO- A Pearson
M P Richards

BOS 1959 AL
SP T Brewer
SP J Casale
SP F Sullivan
SR B Monbouquette
SR I Delock
RS F Baumann
RP M Fornieles
RP L Kiely
C S White
1U D Gernert
21 P Runnels
SS D Buddin
3B F Malzone
LO- G Stephens
ML G Geiger
RF J Jensen
MU M Keough
1U V Wertz
LU T Williams
M1 P Higgins
M2 R York
M3 B Jurges

CHI 1959 AL
SP E Wynn
SR B Shaw
SP B Pierce
SP D Donovan
SR B Latman
RP G Staley
RP T Lown
C S Lollar
1B E Torgeson
2B N Fox
SS L Aparicio
3B B Phillips
LR A Smith

CF J Landis
RL- J Rivera
3U B Goodman
M A Lopez

CLE 1959 AL
SR G Bell
SP C McLish
SR M Grant
SP H Score
RS J Perry
RS M Garcia
C - R Nixon
1B V Power
2B- B Martin
S3 W Held
3S G Strickland
LF M Minoso
CF J Piersall
RF R Colavito
M1 T Francona
23- J Baxes
M J Gordon

DET 1959 AL
SP J Bunning
SP P Foytack
SP D Mossi
SP F Lary
RS R Narleski
RP T Morgan
RP P Burnside
RP D Sisler
C L Berberet
1B G Harris
2B F Bolling
SS R Bridges
3B E Yost
LF C Maxwell
CF A Kaline
RF H Kuenn
1U- B Osborne
SS- C Veal
M1 B Norman
M2 J Dykes

KC 1959 AL
SR B Daley
SP N Garver
SR R Herbert
SR J Kucks
RS B Grim
RP T Sturdivant
RP M Dickson
C F House
1B K Hadley
2B- W Terwilliger
SS J DeMaestri
3I D Williams
LF B Cerv
CF B Tuttle
RF R Maris
2S J Lumpe
3U H Smith
M H Craft

NY 1959 AL
SP W Ford
SR A Ditmar
SR B Turley
SR D Maas
SP R Terry
RP D Larsen
RP J Coates
RP B Shantz
CL R Duren
C Y Berra
1B- B Skowron
2B B Richardson
SO T Kubek
3L H Lopez
LU N Siebern
CF M Mantle
RF H Bauer
IC E Howard
UI G McDougald
1U- M Throneberry
M C Stengel

WAS 1959 AL
SP C Pascual
SP P Ramos
SP R Kemmerer
SP B Fischer
RS T Clevenger
RS H Griggs
RS C Stobbs
RP H Woodeshick
C - H Naragon
1B R Sievers
2B- R Bertoia
SS- B Consolo
3B H Killebrew
LF J Lemon
CF B Allison
RU F Throneberry
U2 J Becquer
UO- L Green
S2- R Samford
M C Lavagetto

CHI 1960 NL
SR G Hobbie
SP B Anderson
SP D Cardwell
SP D Ellsworth
RP D Elston
RS S Morehead
RS M Freeman
RP J Schaffernoth
C - M Thacker
1B E Bouchee
2B- J Kindall
SS E Banks
3B R Santo
ML R Ashburn
OI G Altman
RF B Will
UT F Thomas
23 D Zimmer
M1 C Grimm
M2 L Boudreau

CIN 1960 NL
SP B Purkey
SP J Hook
SP J O'Toole
SR C McLish
RS J Nuxhall
RP J Brosnan
RP B Henry
RP C Osteen
C E Bailey
1L F Robinson
2B B Martin
SS R McMillan
32 E Kasko
LR- W Post
CF V Pinson
RL G Bell
OF J Lynch
3U- W Jones
M F Hutchinson

LA 1960 NL
SP D Drysdale
SP J Podres
SP S Williams
SR S Koufax
SP R Craig
RP L Sherry
RP E Roebuck
RS D McDevitt
C J Roseboro
1B N Larker
2B C Neal
SS M Wills
3B J Gilliam
LF W Moon
MO T Davis
RF F Howard
1B G Hodges
OF D Snider
M W Alston

MIL 1960 NL
SR L Burdette
SP W Spahn
SP B Buhl
SP C Willey
SR J Jay
RP J Pizarro
RP D McMahon
RP R Piche
C D Crandall
1B J Adcock
2B C Cottier
SS J Logan
3B E Mathews
LF A Spangler
CF B Bruton
RF H Aaron
LF W Covington
M C Dressen

PHI 1960 NL
SP R Roberts
SP J Buzhardt
SP G Conley
SP J Owens
SR D Green
RP T Farrell
RS C Short
RP A Mahaffey
RP R Gomez
C - J Coker
1B P Herrera
2B T Taylor
SS- R Amaro
3B- A Dark
LU B Smith
CF B Del Greco
RF K Walters
LU T Curry
UO J Callison
CU- C Dalrymple
CF- T Gonzalez
UI- B Malkmus
M1 E Sawyer
M2 A Cohen
M3 G Mauch

PIT 1960 NL
SP B Friend
SP V Law
SP H Haddix
SP V Mizell
RP R Face
RP F Green
C S Burgess
1B D Stuart
2B B Mazeroski
SS D Groat
3B D Hoak
LF B Skinner
CF B Virdon
RF R Clemente
ML G Cimoli
1B R Nelson
C - H Smith
M D Murtaugh

STL 1960 NL
SP L Jackson
SR E Broglio
SP R Sadecki
SP C Simmons
SR R Kline
RP L McDaniel
C H Smith
1B B White
2B J Javier
SS D Spencer
3B K Boyer
OI S Musial
CF C Flood
RF J Cunningham
UI A Grammas
RL- W Moryn
LU- B Nieman
C - C Sawatski
M S Hemus

SF 1960 NL
SP M McCormick
SP S Jones
SP J Sanford
SR B O'Dell
RS J Antonelli
RP S Miller
RP G Maranda
C B Schmidt
1U W McCovey
2B D Blasingame
SS E Bressoud
3B J Davenport
LO F Alou
CF W Mays
RF W Kirkland
32 J Amalfitano
L1 O Cepeda
S3- A Rodgers
M1 B Rigney
M2 T Sheehan

BAL 1960 AL
SR C Estrada
SP M Pappas
SR J Fisher
SP S Barber
SR H Brown
RS H Wilhelm
RS J Walker
RP G Jones
C G Triandos
1B J Gentile
2B M Breeding
SS R Hansen
3B B Robinson
LF G Woodling
MR J Brandt
RL- G Stephens
RU A Pilarcik
CF- J Busby
CU- C Courtney
1B- W Dropo
M P Richards

BOS 1960 AL
SP B Monbouquette
SP T Brewer
SR F Sullivan
SP I Delock
SP B Muffett
RP M Fornieles
RP T Sturdivant
RS J Casale
RP T Borland
C - R Nixon
1B V Wertz
2B P Runnels
SS D Buddin
3B F Malzone
LF T Williams
CF W Tasby
RF L Clinton
2S P Green
RF- G Geiger
M1 B Jurges
M2 D Baker
M3 P Higgins

CHI 1960 AL
SP E Wynn
SP B Pierce
SP B Shaw
SR F Baumann
SP H Score
RP G Staley
RS R Kemmerer
RS D Donovan
RP T Lown
C S Lollar
1B R Sievers
2B N Fox
SS L Aparicio
3B G Freese
LF M Minoso
CF J Landis
RF A Smith
U1- T Kluszewski
M A Lopez

CLE 1960 AL
SP J Perry
SR M Grant
SP G Bell
SR B Latman
SR D Stigman
RS B Locke
RP J Klippstein
RP D Newcombe
C J Romano
1B V Power
23 K Aspromonte
SS W Held
3B B Phillips
LF T Francona
CF J Piersall
RF H Kuenn
2B J Temple
M1 J Gordon
M2 J White
M3 J Dykes

DET 1960 AL
SP F Lary
SP J Bunning
SP D Mossi
SR B Bruce
SR P Burnside
RS H Aguirre
RS P Foytack
RP D Sisler
RS B Fischer
C - L Berberet
1B N Cash
2B F Bolling
SS C Fernandez
3B E Yost
LF C Maxwell
CF A Kaline
RF R Colavito
OI N Chrisley
1B- S Bilko
M1 J Dykes
M2 B Hitchcock
M3 J Gordon

KC 1960 AL
SR R Herbert
SP B Daley
SP D Hall
SR N Garver
SR J Kucks
RS K Johnson
RP M Kutyna
C - P Daley
1U M Throneberry
2B J Lumpe
SS K Hamlin
3B A Carey
L1 N Siebern
CF B Tuttle
UO R Snyder
RU H Bauer
IO D Williams
RL- W Herzog
M B Elliott

NY 1960 AL
SP A Ditmar
SP W Ford
SR B Turley
SR R Terry
SR J Coates
RP B Shantz
RP D Maas
RP R Duren
RP J Gabler
C E Howard
1B B Skowron
2B B Richardson
SS T Kubek
3B C Boyer
LU H Lopez
CF M Mantle
RF R Maris
CO Y Berra
32 G McDougald
LU- B Cerv
M C Stengel

WAS 1960 AL
SP P Ramos
SR D Lee
SP C Pascual
SR J Kralick
SR H Woodeshick
RS T Clevenger
RS C Stobbs
CL R Moore
C E Battey
1U J Becquer
2B B Gardner
SS J Valdivielso
3B R Bertoia
LF J Lemon
MU L Green
RF B Allison
SS B Consolo
MO D Dobbek
13 H Killebrew
UO- F Throneberry
M C Lavagetto

CHI 1961 NL
SP D Cardwell
SP G Hobbie
SP D Ellsworth
SP J Curtis
RS B Anderson
RP D Elston
RS D Drott
RS J Brewer
C - D Bertell
1B E Bouchee
2B D Zimmer
SS E Banks
3B R Santo
LF B Williams
CF A Heist
RF G Altman
MU R Ashburn
2S J Kindall
C - S Taylor
OI- B Will
M1 V Himsl
M2 H Craft
M3 V Himsl
M4 E Tappe
M5 H Craft
M6 V Himsl
M7 E Tappe
M8 L Klein
M9 E Tappe

CIN 1961 NL
SP J O'Toole
SP J Jay
SP B Purkey
SP K Hunt
SR J Maloney
RP J Brosnan
CL B Henry
RS J Hook
RP S Jones
C - J Zimmerman
1B G Coleman
2B D Blasingame
SS E Kasko
3B G Freese
OF W Post
CF V Pinson
RL F Robinson
UO G Bell
OF J Lynch
M F Hutchinson

LA 1961 NL
SP S Koufax
SP D Drysdale
SP S Williams
SP J Podres
SR R Craig
RP L Sherry
RP T Farrell
RP R Perranoski
C J Roseboro
1B G Hodges
2B C Neal
SS M Wills
32 J Gilliam
LF W Moon
CF W Davis
OI T Davis
OI R Fairly
1B N Larker
RU- F Howard
RM- D Snider
M W Alston

MIL 1961 NL
SP L Burdette
SP W Spahn
SP B Buhl
SR C Willey
SP B Hendley
RS D Nottebart
RP D McMahon
C J Torre
1B J Adcock
2B F Bolling
SS R McMillan
3B E Mathews
LF F Thomas
RM H Aaron
RU L Maye
M1 C Dressen
M2 B Tebbetts

PHI 1961 NL
SP A Mahaffey
SR J Buzhardt
SR F Sullivan
SR C Short
SP R Roberts
RS D Ferrarese
RS D Green
RP J Owens
RP J Baldschun
C C Dalrymple
1B P Herrera
2B T Taylor
SS R Amaro
3B C Smith
LR J Callison
MR T Gonzalez
RU- K Walters
UI B Malkmus
OI D Demeter
UO- B Smith
UT- L Walls
M G Mauch

PIT 1961 NL
SP B Friend
SP J Gibbon
SP H Haddix
SP E Francis
SP V Mizell
RP R Face
RP C Labine
RS B Shantz
RP A McBean
C S Burgess
1B D Stuart
2B B Mazeroski
SS D Groat
3B D Hoak
LF B Skinner
CF B Virdon
RF R Clemente
M D Murtaugh

STL 1961 NL
SP R Sadecki
SP B Gibson
SP L Jackson
SP C Simmons
SP E Broglio
RP L McDaniel
RS B Miller
RS A Cicotte
C - J Schaffer
1B B White
2B J Javier
SU- A Grammas
3B K Boyer
LF S Musial
CF C Flood
RL C James
RF J Cunningham
UO D Taussig
S2- B Lillis
CU- C Sawatski
M1 S Hemus
M2 J Keane

SF 1961 NL
SP M McCormick
SP J Sanford
SP J Marichal
SR S Jones
SP B Loes
RP S Miller
RS B O'Dell
RP J Duffalo
RP B Bolin
C E Bailey
1B W McCovey
2B J Amalfitano
SS J Pagan
3B J Davenport
LI H Kuenn
CF W Mays
RL F Alou
1L O Cepeda
UO- M Alou
M A Dark

BAL 1961 AL
SP S Barber
SP C Estrada
SR J Fisher
SP M Pappas
SP H Brown
RS B Hoeft
RP H Wilhelm
RS D Hall
RP W Stock
C G Triandos
1B J Gentile
2B J Adair
SS R Hansen
3B B Robinson
LO R Snyder
CF J Brandt
RU W Herzog
LU D Williams
2B- M Breeding
OI D Philley
RF- E Robinson
M1 P Richards
M2 L Harris

BOS 1961 AL
SP B Monbouquette
SP G Conley
SP D Schwall
SP I Delock
RS T Stallard
RP M Fornieles
RS B Muffett
RP D Hillman
C J Pagliaroni
1B P Runnels
2B C Schilling
SS D Buddin
3B F Malzone
LF C Yastrzemski
CF G Geiger
RF J Jensen
SU- P Green
UO- C Hardy
C - R Nixon
1B V Wertz
M P Higgins

CHI 1961 AL
SR J Pizarro
SR F Baumann
SR B Pierce
SP C McLish
SP R Herbert
RP T Lown
RP E Wynn
RP R Kemmerer
RP D Larsen
C S Lollar
1B R Sievers
2B N Fox
SS L Aparicio
3R A Smith
LF M Minoso
CF J Landis
RF F Robinson
13 J Martin
M A Lopez

CLE 1961 AL
SP M Grant
SP G Bell
SP J Perry
SR B Latman
SP W Hawkins
RP F Funk
RP B Locke
RP B Allen
RS D Stigman
C J Romano
1B V Power
2B J Temple
SS W Held
3B B Phillips
LF T Francona
CF J Piersall
RF W Kirkland
M1 J Dykes
M2 M Harder

DET 1961 AL
SP F Lary
SP J Bunning
SP D Mossi
SR P Foytack
SR P Regan
RP T Fox
RP H Aguirre
C - D Brown
1B N Cash
2B J Wood
SS C Fernandez
3B S Boros
LF R Colavito
CF B Bruton
RF A Kaline
C - M Roarke
M B Scheffing

KC 1961 AL
SR J Archer
SR N Bass
SR J Walker
SP B Shaw
SR J Nuxhall
RS E Rakow
RP B Kunkel
RS A Ditmar
C H Sullivan
1L N Siebern
2B J Lumpe
SS D Howser
3B W Causey
LR L Posada
CF- B Del Greco
UT- D Johnson
C - J Pignatano
M1 J Gordon
M2 H Bauer

LA 1961 AL
SP K McBride
SR E Grba
SR T Bowsfield
SR R Moeller
SR R Kline
RS J Donohue
RP T Morgan
RS R Duren
RP A Fowler
C E Averill
1B S Bilko
2B- K Aspromonte
SS- J Koppe
3B- E Yost
LF L Wagner
MU K Hunt
RM A Pearson
1U T Kluszewski
R1 L Thomas
2S- R Bridges
M B Rigney

MIN 1961 AL
SP P Ramos
SP C Pascual
SP J Kralick
SP J Kaat
RS D Lee
RP R Moore
RP B Pleis
C E Battey
1B H Killebrew
2B B Martin
SS Z Versalles
3B B Tuttle
LF J Lemon
CF L Green
RF B Allison
M1 C Lavagetto
M2 S Mele
M3 C Lavagetto
M4 S Mele

NY 1961 AL
SP W Ford
SR B Stafford
SP R Terry
SR R Sheldon
SP B Daley
RP L Arroyo
RS J Coates
C E Howard
1B B Skowron
2B B Richardson
SS T Kubek
3B C Boyer
LU Y Berra
CF M Mantle
RF R Maris
CU- J Blanchard
LU- H Lopez
M R Houk

WAS 1961 AL
SP J McClain

SP B Daniels
SP D Donovan
SP E Hobaugh
SR P Burnside
RS M Kutyna
RP J Klippstein
RP D Sisler
CU G Green
1B D Long
2B C Cottier
SS- C Veal
32 D O'Connell
OI M Keough
CF W Tasby
RU G Woodling
RU J King
LU C Hinton
3U- B Klaus
M M Vernon

CHI 1962 NL

SP B Buhl
SP D Ellsworth
SR D Cardwell
SP C Koonce
SR G Hobbie
RP B Anderson
RP B Schultz
RP D Elston
RP D Gerard
C - D Bertell
1B E Banks
2B K Hubbs
SS A Rodgers
3B R Santo
LF B Williams
CF L Brock
RF G Altman
UO- D Landrum
U1- B Will
M1 E Tappe
M2 L Klein
M3 C Metro

CIN 1962 NL

SP B Purkey
SP J Jay
SP J O'Toole
SP J Maloney
RS J Klippstein
RP J Brosnan
RS T Wills
C J Edwards
1B G Coleman
2B D Blasingame
SS L Cardenas
3B E Kasko
LF W Post
CF V Pinson
RF F Robinson
OI M Keough
LU J Lynch
M F Hutchinson

HOU 1962 NL

SR T Farrell
SP K Johnson
SP B Bruce
SR J Golden
SP H Woodeshick
RP B Tiefenauer
RP D McMahon
RP R Kemmerer
RP J Umbricht
C H Smith
1B N Larker
2B J Amalfitano
SS B Lillis
3B B Aspromonte
LU A Spangler
CF C Warwick
RF R Mejias
LU J Pendleton
UI- B Goodman
M H Craft

LA 1962 NL

SP D Drysdale
SP J Podres
SR S Williams
SP S Koufax
RP E Roebuck
RP R Perranoski
RP L Sherry
RP P Ortega
C J Roseboro
1B R Fairly
2B L Burright
SS M Wills
23 J Gilliam
LF T Davis
CF W Davis
RF F Howard
1U- T Harkness
OI- W Moon
M W Alston

MIL 1962 NL

SP W Spahn
SP B Shaw
SP B Hendley
SR L Burdette
SP T Cloninger
RS J Curtis
RS C Willey
RP D Nottebart
C D Crandall
1B J Adcock
2B F Bolling
SS R McMillan
3B E Mathews
ML L Maye
MR H Aaron
RF- M Jones
1B T Aaron
M B Tebbetts

NY 1962 NL

SP R Craig
SP A Jackson
SP J Hook
SR B Miller
RS C Anderson
RS B Moorhead
RP R Daviault
RP K Mac Kenzie
C - C Cannizzaro
1B M Throneberry
2S C Neal
SS E Chacon
3I F Mantilla
LF F Thomas
MO J Hickman
OI R Ashburn
UO J Christopher
UT R Kanehl
OF- G Woodling
M C Stengel

PHI 1962 NL

SP A Mahaffey
SR J Hamilton
SP D Bennett
SP C McLish
RS C Short
RS D Green
RP J Baldschun
RS B Smith
C C Dalrymple
1B R Sievers
2B T Taylor
SS B Wine
3M D Demeter
LU T Savage
CF T Gonzalez
RF J Callison
LF W Covington
3S B Klaus
1U F Torre
M G Mauch

PIT 1962 NL

SP B Friend
SP A McBean
SR E Francis
SP H Haddix
SP V Law
RS T Sturdivant
CL R Face
RP D Olivo
RP J Lamabe
C S Burgess
1B D Stuart
2B B Mazeroski
SS D Groat
3B D Hoak
LF B Skinner
CF B Virdon
RF R Clemente
LO- H Goss
M D Murtaugh

STL 1962 NL

SP L Jackson
SP B Gibson
SP E Broglio
SP R Washburn
SP C Simmons
RP L McDaniel
RP R Sadecki
RP B Shantz
RP D Ferrarese
C G Oliver
1B B White
2B J Javier
SS J Gotay
3B K Boyer
LU S Musial
CF C Flood
RF C James
C - C Sawatski
IF R Schoendienst
LU- B Smith
M J Keane

SF 1962 NL

SP B O'Dell
SP J Sanford
SP J Marichal
SP B Pierce
RP S Miller
RS B Bolin
RP D Larsen
C - T Haller
1B O Cepeda
2B C Hiller
SS J Pagan
3B J Davenport
LF H Kuenn
CF W Mays
RF F Alou
C - E Bailey
OI- W McCovey
M A Dark

BAL 1962 AL

SP C Estrada
SP M Pappas
SP R Roberts
SP J Fisher
SS S Barber
RS D Hall
RP B Hoeft
RP H Wilhelm
RP W Stock
C - G Triandos
1B J Gentile
2B- M Breeding
SS J Adair
3B B Robinson
LF B Powell
CF J Brandt
UO R Snyder
RU W Herzog
UO- D Nicholson
CU- C Lau
UT- D Williams
M B Hitchcock

BOS 1962 AL

SP G Conley
SP B Monbouquette
SP E Wilson
SP D Schwall
RP D Radatz
RP M Fornieles
RP A Earley
RP H Kolstad
C - J Pagliaroni
1B P Runnels
2B C Schilling
SS E Bressoud
3B F Malzone
LF C Yastrzemski
CF G Geiger
RM C Hardy
RF L Clinton
C - B Tillman
M P Higgins

CHI 1962 AL

SP R Herbert
SP J Pizarro
SP E Wynn
SP J Buzhardt
SP J Horlen
RS E Fisher
RS F Baumann
RP D Zanni
RP T Lown
C C Carreon
1B J Cunningham
2B N Fox
SS L Aparicio
3L A Smith
LR F Robinson
CF J Landis
RM M Hershberger
C - S Lollar
M A Lopez

CLE 1962 AL

SP D Donovan
SR P Ramos
SP J Perry
SR B Latman
SP M Grant
RS G Bell
RP F Funk
C J Romano
1B T Francona
2B J Kindall
SS W Held
3B B Phillips
LF C Essegian
CF T Cline
RF W Kirkland
LU- A Luplow
UO- D Dillard
M1 M McGaha
M2 M Harder

DET 1962 AL

SP J Bunning
SR H Aguirre
SP D Mossi
SR P Regan
SP P Foytack
RS S Jones
RP R Kline
CL T Fox
RP R Nischwitz
C D Brown
1B N Cash
2B J Wood
SS C Fernandez
3B S Boros
LF R Colavito
CF B Bruton
RF A Kaline
23 D McAuliffe
OI- B Morton
M B Scheffing

KC 1962 AL

SP E Rakow
SR D Pfister
SR J Walker
SR B Fischer
SR D Segui
RS J Wyatt
RS D Wickersham
RP D McDevitt
C - H Sullivan
1B N Siebern
2B J Lumpe
SS- D Howser
3B E Charles
LF M Jimenez
ML B Del Greco
RF G Cimoli
UI W Causey
CF J Tartabull
OI- G Alusik
M H Bauer

LA 1962 AL

SR D Chance
SP B Belinsky
SR E Grba
SP D Lee
SP K McBride
RP T Bowsfield
RP A Fowler
RP R Duren
RP J Spring
C B Rodgers
1R L Thomas
2B B Moran
SS J Koppe
3B F Torres
LR L Wagner
CF A Pearson
RF- G Thomas
LU- E Averill
UT- T Burgess
M B Rigney

MIN 1962 AL

SP J Kaat
SP C Pascual
SP J Kralick
SR D Stigman
SR J Bonikowski
RS L Stange
RP R Moore
RP G Maranda
C E Battey
1B V Power
2B B Allen
SS Z Versalles
3B R Rollins
LF B Killebrew
CF L Green
RF B Allison
CF B Tuttle
U2- D Mincher
M S Mele

NY 1962 AL

SP R Terry
SP W Ford
SP B Stafford
SR J Bouton
SR R Sheldon
RS J Coates
RS B Daley
CL M Bridges
C E Howard
1B B Skowron
2B B Richardson
SL T Tresh
3B C Boyer
LU H Lopez
CF M Mantle
RM R Maris
OC- Y Berra
OC- J Blanchard
UO- J Reed
M R Houk

WAS 1962 AL

SP D Stenhouse
SR D Rudolph
SR T Cheney
SR B Daniels
SR P Burnside
RP C Osteen
RS S Hamilton
RP M Kutyna
RP J Hannan
C K Retzer
1B H Bright
2B C Cottier
SS K Hamlin
3S B Johnson
UT C Hinton
CF J Piersall
RU J King
UO J Hicks
IF- D O'Connell
3U- J Schaive
C - B Schmidt
M M Vernon

CHI 1963 NL

SP D Ellsworth
SP L Jackson
SP B Buhl
SR G Hobbie
SR P Toth
CL L McDaniel
RP D Elston
RP J Brewer
C D Bertell
1B E Banks
2B K Hubbs
SS A Rodgers
3B R Santo
LF B Williams
CF- E Burton
RF L Brock
MU- D Landrum
M B Kennedy

CIN 1963 NL

SP J Maloney
SP J O'Toole
SP J Nuxhall
SP J Tsitouris
SP J Jay
RP B Purkey
RP A Worthington
RP B Henry
C J Edwards
1B G Coleman
2B P Rose
SS L Cardenas
3B- G Freese
LF F Robinson
CF V Pinson
RU T Harper
UT- M Keough
M F Hutchinson

HOU 1963 NL

SP K Johnson
SP T Farrell
SP D Nottebart
SP B Bruce
SP H Brown
RP H Woodeshick
RP D McMahon
RP J Umbricht
RS C Zachary
C J Bateman
1R R Staub
2B E Fazio
SS B Lillis
3B B Aspromonte
LM A Spangler
CF H Goss
RF C Warwick
12 P Runnels
23 J Temple
M H Craft

LA 1963 NL

SP D Drysdale
SP S Koufax
SP J Podres
SR B Miller
RP R Perranoski
RP L Sherry
C J Roseboro
1B R Fairly
2B J Gilliam
SS M Wills
3B- K McMullen
LF T Davis
CF W Davis
RF F Howard
UO W Moon
SS D Tracewski
1U- B Skowron
M W Alston

MIL 1963 NL

SP W Spahn
SR D Lemaster
SR B Hendley
SR T Cloninger
SP B Sadowski
RS B Shaw
RS H Fischer
RP C Raymond
RP R Piche
C1 J Torre
1L- G Oliver
2B F Bolling
SS R McMillan
3B E Mathews
ML L Maye
MU- M Jones
RF H Aaron
S3 D Menke
C - D Crandall
M B Bragan

NY 1963 NL

SR R Craig
SP A Jackson
SP C Willey
SR T Stallard
SR J Hook
RS G Cisco
RP L Bearnarth
RP K Mac Kenzie
RP D Rowe
C C Coleman
1B T Harkness
2B R Hunt
SS A Moran
3B- C Neal
LF F Thomas
OI J Hickman
UO D Snider
UT R Kanehl
RU- E Kranepool
M C Stengel

PHI 1963 NL

SP C McLish
SP R Culp
SR C Short
SP A Mahaffey
SR D Green
RP J Baldschun
RP D Bennett
RP J Klippstein
RS R Duren
C C Dalrymple
1B R Sievers
2B T Taylor
SS B Wine
3B D Hoak
ML T Gonzalez
M3 D Demeter
RF J Callison
S3 R Amaro
LF W Covington
1U- F Torre
M G Mauch

PIT 1963 NL

SP B Friend
SP D Cardwell
SP D Schwall
SR J Gibbon
RS A McBean
RP T Sisk
RP R Face
RS B Veale
C - J Pagliaroni
1B D Clendenon
2B B Mazeroski
SS D Schofield
3B B Bailey
OI W Stargell
CF B Virdon
RF R Clemente
C - S Burgess
SU- J Logan
LU- J Lynch
UO- T Savage
M D Murtaugh

STL 1963 NL

SP B Gibson
SP E Broglio
SP C Simmons
SP R Sadecki
RS R Taylor
RP B Shantz
RP E Bauta
C T McCarver
1B B White
2B J Javier
SS D Groat
3B K Boyer
LU C James
CF C Flood
RF G Altman
LF S Musial
M J Keane

SF 1963 NL

SP J Marichal
SP J Sanford
SP B O'Dell
SR B Pierce
RS B Bolin
RS J Fisher
RP G Perry
RS J Duffalo
C E Bailey
1B O Cepeda
2B C Hiller
SS J Pagan
3B J Davenport
LF W McCovey
CF W Mays
RF F Alou
C T Haller
OI H Kuenn
UI- E Bowman
M A Dark

BAL 1963 AL

SP S Barber
SP R Roberts
SP M Pappas
SP M McCormick
SP D McNally
RP S Miller
RP D Hall
RP W Stock
C J Orsino
1B J Gentile
2B J Adair
SS L Aparicio
3B B Robinson
LF B Powell
MR J Brandt
MR R Snyder
MI B Saverine
RF A Smith
2U- B Johnson
M B Hitchcock

BOS 1963 AL

SP B Monbouquette
SP E Wilson
SP D Morehead
SP B Heffner
RP J Lamabe
RP D Radatz
RP A Earley
RS W Wood
C - B Tillman
1B D Stuart
2B C Schilling
SS E Bressoud
3B F Malzone
LF C Yastrzemski
MU G Geiger
RF L Clinton
MU R Mejias
C R Nixon
M J Pesky

CHI 1963 AL

SR G Peters
SP R Herbert
SP J Pizarro
SP J Buzhardt
SR J Horlen
RP H Wilhelm
RS E Fisher
RP J Brosnan
RP F Baumann
C J Martin
1B T McCraw
2B N Fox
SS R Hansen
3B P Ward
LF D Nicholson
CF J Landis
RF F Robinson
C C Carreon
MR M Hershberger
UI A Weis
M A Lopez

CLE 1963 AL

SP M Grant
SP D Donovan
SP J Kralick
SR P Ramos
SR B Latman
RS G Bell
RP J Walker
RP T Abernathy
RP B Allen
C - J Azcue
1B F Whitfield
2O W Held
S2- J Kindall
3B M Alvis
LF T Francona
CF- V Davalillo
MR W Kirkland
1B- J Adcock
RU A Luplow
C - J Romano
M B Tebbetts

DET 1963 AL

SP J Bunning
SP H Aguirre
SR P Regan
SR M Lolich
SP D Mossi
RP F Lary
RP T Fox
RP B Anderson
RP T Sturdivant
C G Triandos
1B N Cash
2B- J Wood
SS D McAuliffe
3B B Phillips
LF R Colavito
CF B Bruton
RF A Kaline
CU B Freehan
M1 B Scheffing
M2 C Dressen

KC 1963 AL

SP D Wickersham
SP O Pena
SP M Drabowsky
SP E Rakow
SR D Segui
RS T Bowsfield
RP J Wyatt
RP B Fischer
C - D Edwards
1B N Siebern
2B J Lumpe
SS W Causey
3B E Charles
MU B Del Greco
CF- J Tartabull
RF G Cimoli
LU C Essegian
UO- G Alusik
M E Lopat

LA 1963 AL

SR D Chance
SP K McBride
SR D Osinski
SR D Lee
RP J Navarro
RP A Fowler
RS P Foytack
RP M Nelson
C B Rodgers
1R L Thomas
2B B Moran
SS J Fregosi
3B F Torres
LF L Wagner
CF A Pearson
UO- B Perry
UT- B Sadowski
M B Rigney

MIN 1963 AL

SP C Pascual
SP D Stigman
SP J Kaat
SR J Perry
SR L Stange
RP B Dailey
RP B Pleis
RP G Roggenburk
C E Battey
1B V Power
2B B Allen
SS Z Versalles
3B R Rollins
LF H Killebrew
ML J Hall
RF B Allison
CF L Green
1U- D Mincher
M S Mele

NY 1963 AL

SP W Ford
SP R Terry
SR J Bouton
SP A Downing
SP S Williams
CL H Reniff
RP S Hamilton

C E Howard
1B J Pepitone
2B B Richardson
SS T Kubek
3B C Boyer
LF H Lopez
ML T Tresh
UO J Reed
RF- R Maris
M R Houk

WAS 1963 AL
SR C Osteen
SR D Rudolph
SR B Daniels
SP T Cheney
SR J Duckworth
RP R Kline
RP P Burnside
RP E Roebuck
RP J Bronstad
C - K Retzer
1U B Osborne
2B C Cottier
SS E Brinkman
3B- D Zimmer
LR C Hinton
CF D Lock
RF J King
LU M Minoso
1U D Phillips
M1 M Vernon
M2 E Yost
M3 G Hodges

CHI 1964 NL
SP L Jackson
SP D Ellsworth
SP B Buhl
SR L Burdette
SP E Broglio
RP L McDaniel
RP D Elston
RS S Slaughter
C D Bertell
1B E Banks
2B J Amalfitano
SS A Rodgers
3B R Santo
LF B Williams
CF B Cowan
RU- L Gabrielson
IO J Stewart
M B Kennedy

CIN 1964 NL
SP J O'Toole
SP J Maloney
SP B Purkey
SR J Jay
SR J Tsitouris
RS J Nuxhall
RS S Ellis
RP B McCool
RP B Henry
C J Edwards
1B D Johnson
2B P Rose
SS L Cardenas
3B S Boros
LF T Harper
CF V Pinson
RL F Robinson
RU M Keough
1U- G Coleman
M1 F Hutchinson
M2 D Sisler
M3 F Hutchinson
M4 D Sisler

HOU 1964 NL
SP K Johnson
SP B Bruce
SP T Farrell
SP D Nottebart
SP H Brown
RS J Owens
RS D Larsen
CL H Woodeshick
RP C Raymond
C J Grote
1R W Bond
2B N Fox
SS E Kasko
3B B Aspromonte
LF A Spangler
MU- M White
RF- J Gaines
UI B Lillis
1R- R Staub
M1 H Craft
M2 L Harris

LA 1964 NL
SP D Drysdale
SP S Koufax
SP P Ortega
SP J Moeller
RP B Miller
RP R Perranoski
RS J Brewer
C J Roseboro
1B R Fairly
2B N Oliver
SS M Wills
3U J Gilliam
LF T Davis
CF W Davis
RF F Howard
OI W Parker
23 D Tracewski
M W Alston

MIL 1964 NL
SP T Cloninger
SP D Lemaster
SR W Spahn
SR B Sadowski
SP H Fischer
RS W Blasingame
RP B Tiefenauer
RP B Hoeft
RP C Olivo
C1 J Torre
1B- G Oliver
2B F Bolling
SS D Menke
3B E Mathews
LF R Carty
ML L Maye
RF H Aaron
OI F Alou
OI T Cline
C - E Bailey
M B Bragan

NY 1964 NL
SP J Fisher
SP T Stallard
SP A Jackson
SR G Cisco
RP B Wakefield
RP L Bearnarth
RP B Hunter
CU J Gonder
1B E Kranepool
2B R Hunt
SS R McMillan
3S C Smith
LF G Altman
ML J Hickman
RF J Christopher
UT R Kanehl
OC- H Taylor
M C Stengel

PHI 1964 NL
SP J Bunning
SR C Short
SP D Bennett
SP A Mahaffey
SR R Culp
RP J Baldschun
RP E Roebuck
RS R Wise
RP J Boozer
C C Dalrymple
1L J Herrnstein
2B T Taylor
SS B Wine
3B D Allen
LF W Covington
CF T Gonzalez
RF J Callison
S1 R Amaro
UT C Rojas
M G Mauch

PIT 1964 NL
SP B Veale
SP B Friend
SP V Law
SP J Gibbon
SR S Blass
CL A McBean
RP R Face
RP T Butters
RP T Sisk
C - J Pagliaroni
1B D Clendenon
2B B Mazeroski
SS D Schofield
3O B Bailey
OI M Mota
CF B Virdon
RF R Clemente
3U G Freese
LU J Lynch
OI W Stargell
SS- G Alley
M D Murtaugh

STL 1964 NL
SP B Gibson
SP C Simmons
SP R Sadecki
SR R Craig
RP R Taylor
RS M Cuellar
CL B Schultz
C T McCarver
1B B White
2B J Javier
SS D Groat
3B K Boyer
LF L Brock
CF C Flood
RF- M Shannon
LU- C James
OF- C Warwick
M J Keane

SF 1964 NL
SP J Marichal
SR G Perry
SR B Bolin
SP B Hendley
SR R Herbel
RP J Sanford
RP B Shaw
RS B O'Dell
RP J Duffalo
C T Haller
1B O Cepeda
2B H Lanier
SS J Pagan
3B J Hart
LR H Kuenn
CF W Mays
RF J Alou
UO M Alou
S3 J Davenport
LU W McCovey
OF- D Snider
M A Dark

BAL 1964 AL
SP M Pappas
SP W Bunker
SP R Roberts
SP D McNally
SR S Barber
CL S Miller
RP H Haddix
RP D Hall
RS D Vineyard
C - D Brown
1B N Siebern
2B J Adair
SS L Aparicio
3B B Robinson
LF B Powell
CF J Brandt
RF S Bowens
IO- B Johnson
C - J Orsino
M H Bauer

BOS 1964 AL
SP B Monbouquette
SP E Wilson
SR J Lamabe
SP D Morehead
RP D Radatz
RS B Heffner
RS P Charton
RS B Spanswick
C B Tillman
1B D Stuart
2U D Jones
SS E Bressoud
3B F Malzone
LU T Conigliaro
CF C Yastrzemski
RF L Thomas
UT F Mantilla
CU- R Nixon
M1 J Pesky
M2 Herman

CHI 1964 AL
SP G Peters
SP J Pizarro
SP J Horlen
SP J Buzhardt
SP R Herbert
RP H Wilhelm
RP E Fisher
C J Martin
1L T McCraw
2B A Weis
SS R Hansen
3B P Ward
RF F Robinson
CF J Landis
RM M Hershberger
23 D Buford
LF- D Nicholson
UO- G Stephens
M A Lopez

CLE 1964 AL
SP J Kralick
SP S McDowell
SP D Donovan
SR S Siebert
SR P Ramos
RP L Tiant
RP D McMahon
RP G Bell
RP T Abernathy
C J Romano
1R B Chance
2B L Brown
SS D Howser
3B M Alvis
LF L Wagner
CF V Davalillo
RU T Francona
UT W Held
1B F Whitfield
C - J Azcue
R2- C Salmon
M1 G Strickland
M2 B Tebbetts

DET 1964 AL
SP D Wickersham
SR M Lolich
SP H Aguirre
SR P Regan
SP D McLain
RS E Rakow
RP L Sherry
RP F Gladding
RP T Fox
C B Freehan
1B N Cash
2B J Lumpe
SS D McAuliffe
3B D Wert
LF G Brown
MO G Thomas
RF A Kaline
MU B Bruton
OI D Demeter
M C Dressen

KC 1964 AL
SP O Pena
SP D Segui
SP J O'Donoghue
SR M Drabowsky
RP J Wyatt
RS T Bowsfield
RP W Stock
RS J Santiago
C - D Edwards
1B J Gentile
2B D Green
SS W Causey
3B E Charles
UO J Tartabull
CF N Mathews
RF R Colavito
OI G Alusik
CU- B Bryan
OF- M Jimenez
M1 E Lopat
M2 M McGaha

LA 1964 AL
SR D Chance
SP F Newman
SR B Latman
SP B Belinsky
SP K McBride
RS B Lee
RP D Osinski
RS D Lee
RP B Duliba
C B Rodgers
1B J Adcock
2B B Knoop
SS J Fregosi
3U F Torres
UO W Smith
LM- J Piersall
RF- L Clinton
UO A Pearson
UI T Satriano
M B Rigney

MIN 1964 AL
SP C Pascual
SP J Kaat
SP D Stigman
SP M Grant
RS G Arrigo
CL A Worthington
RP J Perry
RP B Pleis
C E Battey
1O B Allison
2B- B Allen
SS Z Versalles
3B R Rollins
LF H Killebrew
CF J Hall
RF T Oliva
1U D Mincher
M S Mele

NY 1964 AL
SP J Bouton
SP A Downing
SP W Ford
SR R Terry
SP R Sheldon
RP P Mikkelsen
RP H Reniff
RP B Stafford
RP S Hamilton
C E Howard
1B J Pepitone
2B B Richardson
SS T Kubek
3B C Boyer
LM T Tresh
MU M Mantle
RU R Maris
UT P Linz
LO H Lopez
M Y Berra

WAS 1964 AL
SP C Osteen
SP B Narum
SP B Daniels
SR A Koch
RP S Ridzik
RS J Hannan
RP R Kline
RS D Rudolph
C M Brumley
1B- B Skowron
2B D Blasingame
SS E Brinkman
3S J Kennedy
LF C Hinton
CF D Lock
RF J King
1U D Phillips
UO F Valentine
3U D Zimmer
M G Hodges

CHI 1965 NL
SP L Jackson
SP D Ellsworth
SP B Buhl
SR C Koonce
RP T Abernathy
RP L McDaniel
RP B Humphreys
RP B Hoeft
C - V Roznovsky
1B E Banks
2B G Beckert
SS D Kessinger
3B R Santo
UO D Clemens
CF D Landrum
RO B Williams
OI J Stewart
OI- G Altman
M1 B Kennedy
M2 L Klein

CIN 1965 NL
SP S Ellis
SP J Maloney
SR J Jay
SR J Nuxhall
SR J Tsitouris
RP J O'Toole
RP B McCool
RP T Davidson
RP R Craig
C J Edwards
1B T Perez
2B P Rose
SS L Cardenas
3B D Johnson
LF T Harper
CF V Pinson
RF F Robinson
1B G Coleman
M D Sisler

HOU 1965 NL
SP B Bruce
SP T Farrell
SP D Nottebart
SP L Dierker
SR D Giusti
RS C Raymond
RP J Owens
RP R Taylor
RP M Cuellar
C R Brand
1O W Bond
2B J Morgan
SS B Lillis
3B B Aspromonte
LF L Maye
CF J Wynn
RF R Staub
OF J Gaines
1B- J Gentile
M L Harris

LA 1965 NL
SP S Koufax
SP D Drysdale
SP C Osteen
SP J Podres
RP R Perranoski
RP B Miller
RS H Reed
RP J Brewer
C J Roseboro
1B W Parker
2B J Lefebvre
SS M Wills
3B J Kennedy
LF L Johnson
CF W Davis
RF R Fairly
3U J Gilliam
M W Alston

MIL 1965 NL
SP T Cloninger
SP W Blasingame
SP K Johnson
SP D Lemaster
SR B Sadowski
RP B O'Dell
RS H Fischer
RP D Osinski
RP P Niekro
C1 J Torre
UT F Alou
2B F Bolling
SS W Woodward
3B E Mathews
LF- R Carty
CF M Jones
RF H Aaron
C1 G Oliver
OI T Cline
S3- M DeLa Hoz
M B Bragan

NY 1965 NL
SP J Fisher
SP A Jackson
SP W Spahn
SR G Cisco
RS T McGraw
RS T Parsons
RP L Bearnarth
RS L Miller
C C Cannizzaro
1B E Kranepool
2B C Hiller
SS R McMillan
3B C Smith
LO R Swoboda
UT J Hickman
RM J Lewis
OF J Christopher
2I B Klaus
MU- B Cowan
M1 C Stengel
M2 W Westrum

PHI 1965 NL
SP C Short
SP J Bunning
SP R Culp
SP R Herbert
SR B Belinsky
RP G Wagner
RP J Baldschun
RP E Roebuck
C C Dalrymple
1B D Stuart
2B T Taylor
SS B Wine
3B D Allen
LF- A Johnson
ML T Gonzalez
RF J Callison
1S R Amaro
LU W Covington
2M C Rojas
MU- J Briggs
M G Mauch

PIT 1965 NL
SP B Veale
SP D Cardwell
SP B Friend
SP V Law
SR J Gibbon
RP A McBean
RS T Sisk
RP D Schwall
RP W Wood
C J Pagliaroni
1B D Clendenon
2B B Mazeroski
S2 G Alley
3B B Bailey
LF W Stargell
CF B Virdon
RF R Clemente
UO M Mota
M H Walker

STL 1965 NL
SP B Gibson
SP C Simmons
SR T Stallard
SP R Sadecki
SR B Purkey
RS R Washburn
RP N Briles
RP H Woodeshick
RP D Dennis
C T McCarver
1B B White
2B- J Javier
SS D Groat
3B K Boyer
LF L Brock
CF C Flood
RU M Shannon
UT P Gagliano
OI- T Francona
M R Schoendienst

SF 1965 NL
SP J Marichal
SP B Shaw
SR G Perry
SR R Herbel
RS B Bolin
CL F Linzy
RP M Murakami
C T Haller
1B W McCovey
2B H Lanier
SS D Schofield
3B J Hart
LO M Alou
CF W Mays
RF J Alou
UI J Davenport
LF- L Gabrielson
M H Franks

BAL 1965 AL
SP S Barber
SP M Pappas
SP D McNally
SP W Bunker
SP R Roberts
RP S Miller
RP D Hall
RP D Larsen
C - D Brown
1L B Powell
2B J Adair
SS L Aparicio
3B B Robinson
RL C Blefary
CF P Blair
UO R Snyder
1U N Siebern
RU- S Bowens
UO- J Brandt
UI- B Johnson
M H Bauer

BOS 1965 AL
SP E Wilson
SP B Monbouquette
SP D Morehead
SP J Lonborg
SR D Bennett
RP D Radatz
RP A Earley
RP J Ritchie
RP B Duliba
C B Tillman
1B L Thomas
2B F Mantilla
SS R Petrocelli
3B F Malzone
LF C Yastrzemski
MU L Green
RF T Conigliaro
SS E Bressoud
3U D Jones
CF- J Gosger
M Herman

CAL 1965 AL
SP F Newman
SP D Chance
SP M Lopez
SR G Brunet
SR R May
RP B Lee
RP A Gatewood
C B Rodgers
1B V Power
2B B Knoop
SS J Fregosi
3B P Schaal
LF W Smith
CF J Cardenal
RU A Pearson
1B J Adcock
RF- L Clinton
M B Rigney

CHI 1965 AL
SP J Horlen
SP J Buzhardt
SR T John
SP G Peters
SP B Howard
RP E Fisher
RP H Wilhelm
RP B Locker
C J Martin
1B B Skowron
2B D Buford
SS R Hansen
3B P Ward
LF D Cater
CF K Berry
RF F Robinson
1L T McCraw
C J Romano
2U A Weis
M A Lopez

CLE 1965 AL
SP S McDowell
SR L Tiant
SR S Siebert
SP R Terry
RS L Stange
RP G Bell
RP D McMahon
RP F Weaver
C J Azcue
1B F Whitfield
2B P Gonzalez
LS L Brown
3B M Alvis
LF L Wagner
CF V Davalillo
RF R Colavito
UT C Hinton
SU D Howser
M B Tebbetts

DET 1965 AL
SP M Lolich
SP D McLain
SP H Aguirre
SP D Wickersham
SP J Sparma
RP T Fox
RP L Sherry
RP F Gladding
RP O Pena
C B Freehan
1B N Cash
2B J Lumpe
SS D McAuliffe
3B D Wert
LF W Horton
OI D Demeter
OI A Kaline
LU- G Brown
SU- R Oyler
M1 B Swift
M2 C Dressen

KC 1965 AL
SP F Talbot
SP R Sheldon
SP J O'Donoghue
SR D Segui
SR C Hunter
RP J Wyatt
RP W Stock
RP J Dickson
RP D Mossi
C B Bryan
1B K Harrelson
2B D Green
SS B Campaneris
3B E Charles
LF- T Reynolds
CF J Landis
RF M Hershberger
UI W Causey
C - R Lachemann
UT- S Rosario
M1 M McGaha

M2 H Sullivan

MIN 1965 AL
SP M Grant
SP J Kaat
SR J Perry
SP C Pascual
SR D Boswell
CL A Worthington
RP J Klippstein
RS D Stigman
RP M Nelson
C E Battey
1B D Mincher
2B J Kindall
SS Z Versalles
3B R Rollins
LF B Allison
CF J Hall
RF T Oliva
13 H Killebrew
OF S Valdespino
MU-J Nossek
C - J Zimmerman
M S Mele

NY 1965 AL
SP M Stottlemyre
SP W Ford
SP A Downing
SP J Bouton
SP B Stafford
RP P Ramos
RP H Reniff
RP P Mikkelsen
RP S Hamilton
C E Howard
1B J Pepitone
2B B Richardson
SS T Kubek
3B C Boyer
LF M Mantle
ML T Tresh
OI H Lopez
1U R Barker
SU P Linz
MR-R Moschitto
M J Keane

WAS 1965 AL
SP P Richert
SP P Ortega
SP B Narum
SR M McCormick
SR B Daniels
RP R Kline
RP S Ridzik
RS H Koplitz
RP M Bridges
C - M Brumley
1B- D Nen
2B D Blasingame
SS E Brinkman
3B K McMullen
LF F Howard
CF D Lock
UT W Held
2S K Hamlin
RU J King
RL W Kirkland
1U- J Cunningham
IC- D Zimmer
M G Hodges

ATL 1966 NL
SP T Cloninger
SP K Johnson
SP D Lemaster
RP C Carroll
RP C Olivo
RP T Abernathy
RP P Niekro
C J Torre
1L F Alou
2S W Woodward
SS D Menke
3B E Mathews
LF R Carty
CF M Jones
RF H Aaron
M1 B Bragan
M2 B Hitchcock

CHI 1966 NL
SP D Ellsworth
SP K Holtzman
SR B Hands
RS F Jenkins
RS C Koonce
RS B Hendley
C R Hundley
1B E Banks
2B G Beckert
SS D Kessinger
3B R Santo
LM B Browne
CF A Phillips
RF B Williams
OI- G Altman
M L Durocher

CIN 1966 NL
SP J Maloney
SP S Ellis
SP M Pappas
SP J O'Toole
SR J Nuxhall
RP B McCool
RP D Nottebart
RP T Davidson
RP J Baldschun
C J Edwards
1B T Perez
2B P Rose
SS L Cardenas
3B T Helms
L1 D Johnson
CF V Pinson
RL T Harper
1U- G Coleman
CU- D Pavletich
UT- C Ruiz
OF A Shamsky
RU- D Simpson
M1 D Heffner
M2 D Bristol

HOU 1966 NL
SR M Cuellar
SP D Giusti
SP L Dierker
SR T Farrell
SP B Bruce
RP C Raymond
RS B Latman
RP R Taylor
RP J Owens
C J Bateman
1B C Harrison
2B J Morgan
SS S Jackson
3B B Aspromonte
LF L Maye
CF J Wynn
RL R Staub
RU D Nicholson
M G Hatton

LA 1966 NL
SP S Koufax
SP D Drysdale
SP C Osteen
SP D Sutton
RP P Regan
RP B Miller
RP R Perranoski
RS J Moeller
C J Roseboro
1B W Parker
2B J Lefebvre
SS M Wills
3I J Kennedy
LR L Johnson
CF W Davis
RF R Fairly
LF T Davis
3B- J Gilliam
M W Alston

NY 1966 NL
SP J Fisher
SR D Ribant
SP B Shaw
SR R Gardner
RS J Hamilton
RS D Selma
RP B Hepler
RP L Bearnarth
C J Grote
1B E Kranepool
2B R Hunt
SI E Bressoud
3B K Boyer
LF R Swoboda
CF C Jones
RO A Luplow
IO C Hiller
MU-B Murphy
M W Westrum

PHI 1966 NL
SP J Bunning
SP C Short
SP L Jackson
SR B Buhl
SR R Culp
RP D Knowles
RP R Wise
RP R Herbert
C C Dalrymple
1B B White
2O C Rojas
SS D Groat
3L D Allen
LM T Gonzalez
CF- J Briggs
RF J Callison
23 T Taylor
MO-J Brandt
UT- H Kuenn
M G Mauch

PIT 1966 NL
SP B Veale
SP W Fryman
SP V Law
SP S Blass
SR T Sisk
RP P Mikkelsen
RS D Cardwell
RP A McBean
RP R Face
C J Pagliaroni
1B D Clendenon
2B B Mazeroski
SS G Alley
3B B Bailey
LF W Stargell
CF M Alou
RF R Clemente
OI M Mota
3B J Pagan
M H Walker

STL 1966 NL
SP B Gibson
SP A Jackson
SP R Washburn
SR N Briles
SP L Jaster
RP J Hoerner
RP H Woodeshick
RP D Dennis
C T McCarver
1B O Cepeda
2B J Javier
SS D Maxvill
3B C Smith
LF L Brock
CF C Flood
RF M Shannon
UI J Buchek
UT- T Francona
IO- P Gagliano
M R Schoendienst

SF 1966 NL
SP J Marichal
SP G Perry
SP B Bolin
SR R Herbel
SP R Sadecki
RP L McDaniel
RP F Linzy
RP B Priddy
RS J Gibbon
C T Haller
1B W McCovey
2B H Lanier
S2 T Fuentes
3B J Hart
LF J Alou
CF W Mays
RF O Brown
S3 J Davenport
LU- L Gabrielson
LU- C Peterson
M H Franks

BAL 1966 AL
SP D McNally
SP J Palmer
SP W Bunker
SP S Barber
SP J Miller
RS E Watt
CL S Miller
RP M Drabowsky
RP E Fisher
C A Etchebarren
1B B Powell
2B D Johnson
SS L Aparicio
3B B Robinson
LF C Blefary
CF P Blair
RF F Robinson
ML R Snyder
UO-S Bowens
M H Bauer

BOS 1966 AL
SR J Lonborg
SP J Santiago
SR B Brandon
SP L Stange
SP E Wilson
RP D McMahon
RS D Stigman
RP J Wyatt
RP D Osinski
C M Ryan
1B G Scott
2B G Smith
SS R Petrocelli
3B J Foy
LF C Yastrzemski
CF- D Demeter
RF T Conigliaro
2U D Jones
OF- L Green
M1 Herman
M2 P Runnels

CAL 1966 AL
SP D Chance
SP G Brunet
SP M Lopez
SP F Newman
RP B Lee
RS J Sanford
RP M Rojas
RP L Burdette
C B Rodgers
1B N Siebern
2B B Knoop
SS J Fregosi
3B P Schaal
LF- R Reichardt
CF J Cardenal
RU E Kirkpatrick
IC T Satriano
1B- J Adcock
UR- F Malzone
OF- W Smith
M B Rigney

CHI 1966 AL
SP T John
SP J Horlen
SP G Peters
SR J Buzhardt
SP B Howard
RS J Lamabe
RP B Locker
RP D Higgins
RS J Pizarro
C J Romano
1B T McCraw
2U A Weis
SS- L Elia
3B D Buford
LR K Berry
CF T Agee
RF F Robinson
S2 J Adair
1B B Skowron
LI- P Ward
M E Stanky

CLE 1966 AL
SP G Bell
SP S Siebert
SP S McDowell
SR S Hargan
SR L Tiant
RS J O'Donoghue
RP J Kralick
RP D Radatz
RP B Allen
C J Azcue
1B F Whitfield
2B P Gonzalez
SS L Brown
3B M Alvis
LF L Wagner
CF V Davalillo
RF R Colavito
UT C Hinton
UT C Salmon
UO-J Landis
M1 B Tebbetts
M2 G Strickland

DET 1966 AL
SP D McLain
SP M Lolich
SP E Wilson
SR D Wickersham
SR J Podres
RP O Pena
RS H Aguirre
RS B Monbouquette
CL L Sherry
C B Freehan
1B N Cash
2B J Lumpe
SS D McAuliffe
3B D Wert
LF W Horton
MR A Kaline
RF J Northrup
2U J Wood
U3- G Brown
CF- M Stanley
2B- D Tracewski
M1 C Dressen
M2 B Swift
M3 F Skaff

KC 1966 AL
SR L Krausse
SP C Hunter
SP J Nash
SR P Lindblad
RP J Aker
RP K Sanders
C P Roof
1B- K Harrelson
2B D Green
SS B Campaneris
3B E Charles
LU L Stahl
MU-J Nossek
RF M Hershberger
UT D Cater
OI R Repoz
UT- O Chavarria
LM- J Gosger
M A Dark

MIN 1966 AL
SP J Kaat
SP M Grant
SP J Perry
SP D Boswell
SR J Merritt
RP A Worthington
RP C Pascual
RP P Cimino
RP D Siebler
C E Battey
1B D Mincher
2B B Allen
SS Z Versalles
31 H Killebrew
LO J Hall
CF T Uhlaender
RF T Oliva
2U C Tovar
3U- R Rollins
M S Mele

NY 1966 AL
SP M Stottlemyre
SP F Peterson
SP A Downing
SP F Talbot
SP J Bouton
RP H Reniff
RP P Ramos
RP S Hamilton
RP D Womack
C E Howard
1B J Pepitone
2B B Richardson
SU H Clarke
3S C Boyer
OI T Tresh
CF M Mantle
RF R Maris
LU R White
M1 J Keane
M2 R Houk

WAS 1966 AL
SP P Richert
SP M McCormick
SP P Ortega
SP J Hannan
RP C Cox
RP B Humphreys
CL R Kline
RP D Lines
C P Casanova
1B- D Nen
2I B Saverine
SS E Brinkman
3B K McMullen
LF F Howard
CF D Lock
OI F Valentine
RU J King
OF W Kirkland
M G Hodges

ATL 1967 NL
SR P Niekro
SP D Lemaster
SP K Johnson
SP P Jarvis
RS D Kelley
RS C Carroll
RP J Ritchie
RP R Hernandez
C J Torre
1O F Alou
2B W Woodward
SS D Menke
3B C Boyer
LU R Carty
MU M Jones
RF H Aaron
1U- T Francona
M1 B Hitchcock
M2 K Silvestri

CHI 1967 NL
SP F Jenkins
SP R Nye
SR J Niekro
SP R Culp
RS B Hands
RP C Hartenstein
RP B Stoneman
RP C Koonce
C R Hundley
1B E Banks
2B G Beckert
SS D Kessinger
3B R Santo
LF B Williams
CF A Phillips
RU- T Savage
M L Durocher

CIN 1967 NL
SP G Nolan
SP M Pappas
SP J Maloney
SP M Queen
SP S Ellis
RP T Abernathy
RP D Nottebart
RS G Arrigo
RP B Lee
C - J Edwards
1L L May
2S T Helms
SS L Cardenas
3B T Perez
LF P Rose
CF V Pinson
RF T Harper
1B D Johnson
2U C Ruiz
M D Bristol

HOU 1967 NL
SP M Cuellar
SP D Giusti
SP D Wilson
SP B Belinsky
SP L Dierker
RP B Latman
RP C Sembera
RP D Eilers
RP D Schneider
C - J Bateman
1B E Mathews
2B J Morgan
SS S Jackson
3B B Aspromonte
LU- R Davis
CF J Wynn
RF R Staub
C - R Brand
M G Hatton

LA 1967 NL
SP C Osteen
SP D Drysdale
SP D Sutton
SP B Singer
SR J Brewer
RP R Perranoski
RP P Regan
RP B Miller
C J Roseboro
1B W Parker
2B R Hunt
SS G Michael
32 J Lefebvre
LF L Johnson
CF W Davis
R1 R Fairly
3U B Bailey
RU A Ferrara
LR- L Gabrielson
SS- D Schofield
M W Alston

NY 1967 NL
SP T Seaver
SP J Fisher
SR D Cardwell
SR B Shaw
RP D Selma
RP R Taylor
RP D Shaw
C J Grote
1B E Kranepool
2B J Buchek
SS B Harrelson
3B E Charles
LF T Davis
MO C Jones
RF R Swoboda
OI T Reynolds
UI- B Johnson
M1 W Westrum
M2 S Parker

PHI 1967 NL
SP J Bunning
SP L Jackson
SP C Short
SR R Wise
SR D Ellsworth
RP T Farrell
RP D Hall
RP G Jackson
RS J Boozer
C C Dalrymple
1B B White
2B C Rojas
SS B Wine
3B D Allen
LO T Gonzalez
ML J Briggs
RF J Callison
CF D Lock
SU G Sutherland
UI T Taylor
C - G Oliver
M G Mauch

PIT 1967 NL
SP T Sisk
SP B Veale
SR D Ribant
SR S Blass
SR W Fryman
RS A McBean
RS J Pizarro
RP R Face
RP P Mikkelsen
C J May
1B D Clendenon
2B B Mazeroski
SS G Alley
3B M Wills
L1 W Stargell
CF M Alou
RF R Clemente
OI M Mota
IO- J Pagan
M1 H Walker
M2 D Murtaugh

STL 1967 NL
SR D Hughes
SP S Carlton
SP R Washburn
SP B Gibson
SR L Jaster
RS N Briles
RS A Jackson
RP R Willis
RP J Hoerner
C T McCarver
1B O Cepeda
2B J Javier
SS D Maxvill
3B M Shannon
LF L Brock
CF C Flood
RF R Maris
OI B Tolan
RU- A Johnson
M R Schoendienst

SF 1967 NL
SP G Perry
SP M McCormick
SP J Marichal
SR R Sadecki
SR B Bolin
RS R Herbel
RP F Linzy
RP L McDaniel
C T Haller
1B W McCovey
2B T Fuentes
SS H Lanier
3B J Hart
LR J Alou
CF W Mays
RF O Brown
3I J Davenport
M H Franks

BAL 1967 AL
SP T Phoebus
SP P Richert
SR B Dillman
SP D McNally
SP J Hardin
RP E Watt
RP M Drabowsky
RP E Fisher
RP S Miller
C A Etchebarren
1B B Powell
2B D Johnson
SS L Aparicio
3B B Robinson
L1 C Blefary
CF P Blair
RU F Robinson
UO R Snyder
M H Bauer

BOS 1967 AL
SP J Lonborg
SR L Stange
SP G Bell
SR B Brandon
RS J Santiago
RP J Wyatt
RP D Osinski
C - M Ryan
1B G Scott
2B M Andrews
SS R Petrocelli
3B J Foy
LF C Yastrzemski
CF R Smith
RF- T Conigliaro
UO J Tartabull
UI- J Adair
UI- D Jones
M D Williams

CAL 1967 AL
SP G Brunet
SP J McGlothlin
SP R Clark
SP J Hamilton
RP M Rojas
RP B Kelso
RP P Cimino
RP J Coates
C B Rodgers
1B D Mincher
2B B Knoop
SS J Fregosi
3B P Schaal
LF R Reichardt
ML J Cardenal
RF J Hall
IC- T Satriano
M B Rigney

CHI 1967 AL
SP G Peters
SP J Horlen
SP T John
SR B Howard
RP B Locker
RP H Wilhelm
RS W Wood
RP D McMahon
C J Martin
1B T McCraw
2B W Causey
SS R Hansen
3B D Buford
L1 P Ward
CF T Agee
RL K Berry
LU W Williams
M E Stanky

CLE 1967 AL
SP S McDowell
SP S Hargan
SP L Tiant
SP S Siebert
SR J O'Donoghue
RP O Pena
RP G Culver
RP S Bailey
RP B Allen
C - J Azcue
1B T Horton
2B- P Gonzalez
SS L Brown
3B M Alvis
LF L Wagner
CF V Davalillo
RM C Hinton
OI L Maye
1U F Whitfield
UT- C Salmon
C - D Sims
M J Adcock

DET 1967 AL
SP E Wilson
SP D McLain
SP J Sparma
SP M Lolich
RP F Gladding
RP D Wickersham
RP M Marshall
RS J Hiller
C B Freehan

1B N Cash
2B D McAuliffe
SS R Oyler
3B D Wert
ML J Northrup
CF M Stanley
RF A Kaline
LF W Horton
2U- J Lumpe
M M Smith

KC 1967 AL
SP C Hunter
SP J Nash
SP C Dobson
SR L Krausse
SR B Odom
RS P Lindblad
RS T Pierce
RP J Aker
RP D Segui
C P Roof
1U R Webster
2B J Donaldson
SS B Campaneris
UI D Green
UO J Gosger
CF R Monday
RF M Hershberger
IO D Cater
OF- J Nossek
M1 A Dark
M2 L Appling

MIN 1967 AL
SP D Chance
SP J Kaat
SP J Merritt
SP D Boswell
RS J Perry
RP A Worthington
RP R Kline
C J Zimmerman
1B H Killebrew
2B R Carew
SS Z Versalles
3B R Rollins
LF B Allison
CF T Uhlaender
RF T Oliva
UT C Tovar
UT- R Reese
LU S Valdespino
M1 S Mele
M2 C Ermer

NY 1967 AL
SP M Stottlemyre
SP A Downing
SP F Peterson
SP F Talbot
RS B Monbouquette
RP D Womack
RS T Tillotson
RS J Verbanic
C J Gibbs
1B M Mantle
2B H Clarke
SS R Amaro
3B C Smith
LF T Tresh
CF J Pepitone
RO S Whitaker
UO B Robinson
M R Houk

WAS 1967 AL
SP P Ortega
SP C Pascual
SP B Moore
SP J Coleman
RP D Knowles
RS B Priddy
RP B Humphreys
RP D Lines
C P Casanova
1B- M Epstein
2B- B Allen
SS E Brinkman
3B K McMullen
LF F Howard
UO F Valentine
RU C Peterson
ML H Allen
S2 T Cullen
1U D Nen
2U- B Saverine
CF- E Stroud
M G Hodges

ATL 1968 NL
SP P Niekro
SP P Jarvis
SP R Reed
SR K Johnson
SP M Pappas
RP C Upshaw
RS J Britton
RP C Raymond
C J Torre
1B D Johnson
2B F Millan
SS S Jackson
3B- C Boyer
LU M Lum
CF F Alou
RF H Aaron
L1 T Francona
UI M Martinez
L1 T Aaron
C - B Tillman
M L Harris

CHI 1968 NL
SP F Jenkins
SP B Hands
SP K Holtzman
SP J Niekro
SP R Nye
RP P Regan
RP J Lamabe
C R Hundley
1B E Banks
2B G Beckert
SS D Kessinger
3B R Santo
LF B Williams
CF A Phillips
RM- J Hickman
1U- D Nen
UO- A Spangler
M L Durocher

CIN 1968 NL
SP G Culver
SP J Maloney
SP G Arrigo
SP G Nolan
RP T Abernathy
RP C Carroll
RP B Lee
RP J Ritchie
C J Bench
1B L May
2B T Helms
SS L Cardenas
3B T Perez
LF A Johnson
CF V Pinson
RF P Rose
UO M Jones
UI- C Ruiz
US- F Whitfield
M D Bristol

HOU 1968 NL
SP D Giusti
SP L Dierker
SP D Lemaster
SP D Wilson
SP M Cuellar
RP J Buzhardt
RP J Ray
RP T Dukes
C J Bateman
1B R Staub
2B D Menke
SS H Torres
3B D Rader
ML J Wynn
CF- R Davis
RF- N Miller
3L B Aspromonte
OI- L Thomas
M1 G Hatton
M2 H Walker

LA 1968 NL
SP B Singer
SP C Osteen
SP D Drysdale
SP D Sutton
SP M Kekich
RP M Grant
RP J Brewer
RP J Billingham
RP J Purdin
C T Haller
1B W Parker
2S P Popovich
SS Z Versalles
3B B Bailey
LR L Gabrielson
CF W Davis
R1 R Fairly
UO J Fairey
IF- K Boyer
2U- J Lefebvre
M W Alston

NY 1968 NL
SP T Seaver
SP J Koosman
SP D Cardwell
SR D Selma
SP N Ryan
RP C Koonce
RP R Taylor
RP D Frisella
C J Grote
1B E Kranepool
2B- P Linz
SS B Harrelson
3B E Charles
LF C Jones
CF T Agee
RF R Swoboda
LU A Shamsky
S2- A Weis
M G Hodges

PHI 1968 NL
SP C Short
SP L Jackson
SP W Fryman
SP R Wise
SR J James
RP T Farrell
RP G Wagner
RP J Boozer
RS G Jackson
C - M Ryan
1B B White
2B C Rojas
SS R Pena
3B T Taylor
LF D Allen
CF T Gonzalez
RF J Callison
OI J Briggs
UO D Lock
C - C Dalrymple
M1 G Mauch
M2 G Myatt
M3 B Skinner

PIT 1968 NL
SP B Veale
SP S Blass
SP A McBean
SR B Moose
SP J Bunning
RP R Kline
RS D Ellis
RP R Face
RP L Walker
C J May
1B D Clendenon
2B B Mazeroski
SS G Alley
3B M Wills
LF W Stargell
CF M Alou
RF R Clemente
UT M Mota
M L Shepard

STL 1968 NL
SP B Gibson
SP N Briles
SP S Carlton
SP R Washburn
SR L Jaster
RS D Hughes
RP R Willis
CL J Hoerner
RP M Nelson
C T McCarver
1B O Cepeda
2B J Javier
SS D Maxvill
3B M Shannon
LF L Brock
CF C Flood
RF R Maris
CU- J Edwards
RU- B Tolan
M R Schoendienst

SF 1968 NL
SP J Marichal
SP G Perry
SP R Sadecki
SR M McCormick
SR B Bolin
RP F Linzy
C D Dietz
1B W McCovey
2B R Hunt
SS H Lanier
3U J Davenport
RL J Alou
CF W Mays
RF- B Bonds
OI T Cline
3L J Hart
CU- J Hiatt
M H Franks

BAL 1968 AL
SP D McNally
SP J Hardin
SP T Phoebus
SR G Brabender
SR D Leonhard
RP E Watt
RP M Drabowsky
RP P Richert
C - A Etchebarren
1B B Powell
2B D Johnson
SS M Belanger
3B B Robinson
OI C Blefary
CF P Blair
RL F Robinson
UT D Buford
RU- D May
LU- C Motton
M1 H Bauer
M2 E Weaver

BOS 1968 AL
SP R Culp
SP G Bell
SP D Ellsworth
SP J Santiago
SP J Lonborg
RP L Stange
RP J Pizarro
RS G Waslewski
RP S Lyle
C - R Gibson
1B G Scott
2B M Andrews
SS R Petrocelli
3B J Foy
LF C Yastrzemski
CF R Smith
RF K Harrelson
1I D Jones
M D Williams

CAL 1968 AL
SP G Brunet
SP J McGlothlin
SR S Ellis
SP T Murphy
RS C Wright
RP M Pattin
RS A Messersmith
RP T Burgmeier
C - B Rodgers
1B D Mincher
2B B Knoop
SS J Fregosi
3B- A Rodriguez
LF R Reichardt
CF- V Davalillo
MR R Repoz
UT C Hinton
C T Satriano
OI- E Kirkpatrick
RU- B Morton
M B Rigney

CHI 1968 AL
SP J Horlen
SP J Fisher
SP T John
SP G Peters
SP C Carlos
RP W Wood
RS B Priddy
RP H Wilhelm
RP B Locker
C D Josephson
1B T McCraw
2I S Alomar
SS L Aparicio
3U P Ward
LF T Davis
CF K Berry
RL B Bradford
M1 E Stanky
M2 L Moss
M3 A Lopez
M4 L Moss
M5 A Lopez

CLE 1968 AL
SP S McDowell
SP L Tiant
SP S Siebert
SR S Williams
SP S Hargan
RP E Fisher
RS M Paul
RP V Romo
C J Azcue
1B T Horton
2B- V Fuller
SS L Brown
3B M Alvis
LU L Maye
CF J Cardenal
LR T Harper
UT C Salmon
C1 D Sims
2U- D Nelson
M A Dark

DET 1968 AL
SP D McLain
SP E Wilson
SP M Lolich
SP J Sparma
RS P Dobson
RS J Hiller
RP D Patterson
C B Freehan
1B N Cash
2B D McAuliffe
SS R Oyler
3B D Wert
LF W Horton
CF M Stanley
RM J Northrup
RU A Kaline
SI- D Tracewski
M M Smith

MIN 1968 AL
SP D Chance
SP J Merritt
SP J Kaat
SP D Boswell
SR J Perry
RP A Worthington
RP R Perranoski
RP B Miller
RP J Roland
C J Roseboro
1U R Reese
2B R Carew
SS- J Hernandez
UT C Tovar
LF B Allison
CF T Uhlaender
RF T Oliva
3S R Clark
1B H Killebrew
UI- F Quilici
3U- R Rollins
M C Ermer

NY 1968 AL
SP M Stottlemyre
SP S Bahnsen
SP F Peterson
SP S Barber
SR F Talbot
RS J Verbanic
RP D Womack
RP S Hamilton
CL L McDaniel
C J Gibbs
1B M Mantle
2B H Clarke
SS T Tresh
3B B Cox
LU R White
UO B Robinson
RU A Kosco
CF J Pepitone
UI- D Howser
M R Houk

OAK 1968 AL
SP C Hunter
SP B Odom
SP J Nash
SP C Dobson
SR L Krausse
RP D Segui
RP J Aker
RP E Sprague
RP P Lindblad
C - D Duncan
1B D Cater
2B J Donaldson
SS B Campaneris
3B S Bando
LR M Hershberger
CF R Monday
RF R Jackson
UO- J Gosger
M B Kennedy

WAS 1968 AL
SP J Coleman
SP C Pascual
SP J Hannan
SP F Bertaina
SR B Moore
RS D Bosman
RS P Ortega
RP D Higgins
RP B Humphreys
C - P Casanova
1B M Epstein
2B B Allen
SS- R Hansen
3B K McMullen
L1 F Howard
CF D Unser
RO E Stroud
OF- C Peterson
M J Lemon

ATL 1969 NL
SP P Niekro
SP R Reed
SP P Jarvis
SR G Stone
SP M Pappas
RP C Upshaw
RP G Neibauer
C B Didier
1B O Cepeda
2B F Millan
SS S Jackson
3B C Boyer
ML- T Gonzalez
CF F Alou
RF H Aaron
LF R Carty
UO M Lum
IO- B Aspromonte
SS- G Garrido
M L Harris

CHI 1969 NL
SP F Jenkins
SP B Hands
SP K Holtzman
SR D Selma
RP P Regan
RP T Abernathy
RS R Nye
C R Hundley
1B E Banks
2B G Beckert
SS D Kessinger
3B R Santo
LF- B Williams
CF D Young
RF J Hickman
OI W Smith
RU- A Spangler
M L Durocher

CIN 1969 NL
SP J Merritt
SP T Cloninger
SP J Maloney
SR J Fisher
SP G Nolan
RP W Granger
RP C Carroll
RS G Culver
RP P Ramos
C J Bench
1B L May
2B T Helms
SS- W Woodward
3B T Perez
LF A Johnson
MR B Tolan
RM P Rose
UT J Stewart
SS- D Chaney
IO- C Ruiz
M D Bristol

HOU 1969 NL
SP L Dierker
SP D Lemaster
SP D Wilson
SP T Griffin
RS J Ray
CL F Gladding
RP J Billingham
RS W Blasingame
C J Edwards
1B C Blefary
2B J Morgan
SS D Menke
3B D Rader
LR J Alou
CF J Wynn
RF N Miller
LU- G Geiger
M H Walker

LA 1969 NL
SP C Osteen
SP B Singer
SP D Sutton
SP A Foster
CL J Brewer
RP P Mikkelsen
RP J Moeller
C T Haller
1B W Parker
2S T Sizemore
SS M Wills
3B B Sudakis
UO W Crawford
CF W Davis
RL A Kosco
RO B Russell
OI- L Gabrielson
UI- J Lefebvre
LF- M Mota
M W Alston

MON 1969 NL
SP B Stoneman
SR J Robertson
SP M Wegener
SR G Waslewski
SR H Reed
RP D McGinn
RP S Renko
RP D Shaw
RP R Face
C R Brand
1B B Bailey
2B G Sutherland
SS B Wine
3B C Laboy
LF M Jones
CF- A Phillips
RF R Staub
OI T Cline
M G Mauch

NY 1969 NL
SP T Seaver
SP J Koosman
SP G Gentry
SP D Cardwell
SP J McAndrew
RP T McGraw
RP C Koonce
RP R Taylor
RP J DiLauro
C J Grote
1B E Kranepool
2B K Boswell
SS B Harrelson
32 W Garrett
LF C Jones
CF T Agee
RU R Swoboda
RO R Gaspar
RU A Shamsky
S2 A Weis
M G Hodges

PHI 1969 NL
SP G Jackson
SP W Fryman
SP R Wise
SR J Johnson
SP B Champion
RP J Boozer
RP T Farrell
RP A Raffo
RP B Wilson
C M Ryan
1B D Allen
2B C Rojas
SS D Money
32 T Taylor
LM J Briggs
CF L Hisle
RF J Callison
L3 D Johnson
3U R Joseph
UO R Stone
UI- T Harmon
M1 B Skinner
M2 G Myatt

PIT 1969 NL
SP B Veale
SP D Ellis
SP S Blass
SR B Moose
SP J Bunning
RS L Walker
RP C Hartenstein
RP B Dal Canton
RP J Gibbon
C M Sanguillen
1B A Oliver
2B- B Mazeroski
SS F Patek
3B R Hebner
LF W Stargell
CF M Alou
RF R Clemente
UT J Pagan
OI C Taylor
2S- G Alley
M1 L Shepard
M2 A Grammas

STL 1969 NL
SP B Gibson
SP S Carlton
SP N Briles
SR R Washburn
SR C Taylor
RP M Torrez
RS D Giusti
RP M Grant
RP J Hoerner
C T McCarver
1B J Torre
2B J Javier
SS D Maxvill
3B M Shannon
LF L Brock
CF C Flood
RF V Pinson
M R Schoendienst

SD 1969 NL
SP C Kirby
SP J Niekro
SP A Santorini
SP D Kelley
RS T Sisk
RS G Ross
RP F Reberger
RP J Baldschun
C C Cannizzaro
1B N Colbert
2S J Arcia
SS T Dean
3B E Spiezio
LU A Ferrara
CF C Gaston
RF O Brown
OI I Murrell
UI R Pena
OI- L Stahl
M P Gomez

SF 1969 NL
SP G Perry
SP J Marichal
SP M McCormick
SP B Bolin
SR R Sadecki
RP F Linzy
RP R Herbel
C - D Dietz
1B W McCovey
2B R Hunt
SS H Lanier
3B J Davenport
LR K Henderson
CF W Mays
RM B Bonds
UT- B Burda
LU D Marshall
UI D Mason
LU- J Hart
M C King

BAL 1969 AL
SP M Cuellar
SP D McNally
SP T Phoebus
SP J Palmer
SR J Hardin
RP D Leonhard
RP E Watt
RP D Hall
RP M Lopez
C E Hendricks
1B B Powell
2B D Johnson
SS M Belanger
3B B Robinson
LF D Buford
CF P Blair
RF F Robinson
UO- M Rettenmund
M E Weaver

BOS 1969 AL
SP R Culp
SP M Nagy
SR S Siebert
SP J Lonborg
SR L Stange
RS V Romo
RP S Lyle
RS R Jarvis
RS B Landis
C - R Gibson
1U D Jones
2B M Andrews
SS R Petrocelli
31 G Scott
LF C Yastrzemski
CF R Smith
RF T Conigliaro
OI J Lahoud
3I S O'Brien
UT- D Schofield
M1 D Williams
M2 E Popowski

CAL 1969 AL
SP A Messersmith
SP T Murphy
SP J McGlothlin
SR R May
SP G Brunet
CL K Tatum
RP E Fisher
RP H Wilhelm
RS C Wright
C - J Azcue
1B J Spencer
2B S Alomar
SS J Fregosi
3B A Rodriguez
LF R Reichardt
CF J Johnstone
RF B Voss
OI R Repoz
OI- B Morton
M1 B Rigney
M2 L Phillips

CHI 1969 AL
SP J Horlen
SP T John
SP G Peters
SP B Wynne
RP W Wood
RP D Osinski
RP C Carlos
C E Herrmann
1B G Hopkins
2B B Knoop
SS L Aparicio
3B B Melton
LF C May
CF K Berry
RL W Williams
UT P Ward
RM-B Bradford
UI- R Hansen
UT- T McCraw
M1 A Lopez
M2 D Gutteridge

CLE 1969 AL
SP S McDowell
SP L Tiant
SP S Hargan
SR D Ellsworth
RS S Williams
RS M Paul
RP J Pizarro
RP R Law
C D Sims
1B T Horton
2B V Fuller
SS L Brown
3B- M Alvis
UO R Snyder
CF J Cardenal
RF K Harrelson
UO R Scheinblum
OI- C Hinton
3U- L Klimchock
M A Dark

DET 1969 AL
SP D McLain
SP M Lolich
SP E Wilson
SR M Kilkenny
RS P Dobson
RS J Hiller
RP T Timmermann
C B Freehan
1B N Cash
2B- D McAuliffe
SS- T Tresh
3B D Wert
LF W Horton
MR J Northrup
RF A Kaline
MS M Stanley
23- T Matchick
M M Smith

KC 1969 AL
SP W Bunker
SR D Drago
SP B Butler
SP R Nelson
SP J Rooker
RS M Hedlund
RP M Drabowsky
RP D Wickersham
RP T Burgmeier
C - E Rodriguez
1B M Fiore
2B J Adair
SS J Hernandez
3B J Foy
LF L Piniella
UT B Oliver
RM P Kelly
UT E Kirkpatrick
2S- J Rios
M J Gordon

MIN 1969 AL
SR J Perry
SP D Boswell
SP J Kaat
SR T Hall
RP R Perranoski
RS B Miller
RS D Woodson
RP A Worthington
C J Roseboro
1B R Reese
2B R Carew
SS L Cardenas
31 H Killebrew
ML T Uhlaender
UT C Tovar
RF T Oliva
32 F Quilici
LU- B Allison
UO- C Manuel
LU- G Nettles
M B Martin

NY 1969 AL
SP M Stottlemyre
SP F Peterson
SP S Bahnsen
SP B Burbach
SR A Downing
RS M Kekich
RP L McDaniel
RP J Aker
RP S Hamilton
C - J Gibbs
1B J Pepitone
2B H Clarke
SS G Michael
3U J Kenney
LF R White
CF- R Woods
RU B Murcer
3U- B Cox
CU- F Fernandez
OI- B Robinson
M R Houk

OAK 1969 AL
SP C Hunter
SP C Dobson
SP B Odom
SR L Krausse
SP J Nash
RS R Fingers
RP P Lindblad
RP J Roland
C P Roof
1B D Cater
2B D Green
SS B Campaneris
3B S Bando
LF T Reynolds
CF R Monday
RF R Jackson
IF- T Kubiak
M1 H Bauer
M2 J McNamara

SEA 1969 AL
SR G Brabender
SP M Pattin
SP F Talbot
RS D Segui
RS J Gelnar
RP J Bouton
RP B Locker
C J McNertney
1B D Mincher
2B- J Donaldson
SS R Oyler
UT T Harper
LF T Davis
MR W Comer
RM-S Hovley
UI- G Gil
RU- M Hegan
M J Schultz

WAS 1969 AL
SP J Coleman
SP D Bosman
SP J Hannan
SP B Moore
RS C Cox
RP D Higgins
RP D Knowles
RP B Humphreys
C P Casanova
1B M Epstein
2B B Allen
SS E Brinkman
3B K McMullen
L1 F Howard
CF D Unser
UT H Allen
OI B Alyea
2B T Cullen
UO E Stroud
M T Williams

ATL 1970 NL
SP P Jarvis
SP P Niekro
SP J Nash
SP G Stone
SP R Reed
RP H Wilhelm
RP B Priddy
C - B Tillman
1B O Cepeda
2B F Millan
SS S Jackson
3B C Boyer
LF R Carty
CF T Gonzalez
RF H Aaron
SS G Garrido
UO M Lum
CU- H King
M L Harris

CHI 1970 NL
SP F Jenkins
SP K Holtzman
SP B Hands
SP M Pappas
SP J Decker
RP P Regan
RS J Colborn
C - R Hundley
1B- E Banks
2B G Beckert
SS D Kessinger
3B R Santo
LF B Williams
OI J Hickman
RF J Callison
CF C James
UT- W Smith
M L Durocher

CIN 1970 NL
SP G Nolan
SP J Merritt
SP J McGlothlin
SP W Simpson
SR T Cloninger
RP C Carroll
CL W Granger
RP D Gullett
RP R Washburn
C J Bench
1B L May
2B T Helms
SS D Concepcion
3B T Perez
LF B Carbo
CF B Tolan
RF P Rose
UT J Stewart
SS W Woodward
M S Anderson

HOU 1970 NL
SP L Dierker
SR J Billingham
SP D Wilson
SR D Lemaster
SP T Griffin
RP J Ray
RP F Gladding
RS R Cook
RS J Bouton
C J Edwards
1B- B Watson
2B J Morgan
SS D Menke
3B D Rader
ML J Wynn
CF- C Cedeno
RF J Alou
RF- N Miller
M H Walker

LA 1970 NL
SP D Sutton
SP C Osteen
SP A Foster
SR J Moeller
SP S Vance
CL J Brewer
RP B Singer
RP P Mikkelsen
RP F Norman
C T Haller
1B W Parker
2B- T Sizemore
SS M Wills
3S B Grabarkewitz
LF M Mota
CF W Davis
RL W Crawford
2U J Lefebvre
RM-B Russell
IC- B Sudakis
M W Alston

MON 1970 NL
SP C Morton
SP S Renko
SR B Stoneman
SR D McGinn
SP M Wegener
CL C Raymond
RP H Reed
RP J Strohmayer
RS M Marshall
C J Bateman
1B R Fairly
2B G Sutherland
SS B Wine
3B C Laboy
LF M Jones
CF- A Phillips
RF R Staub
IO B Bailey
2B M Staehle
UO- J Fairey
MO- J Gosger
LO- D Hahn
M G Mauch

NY 1970 NL
SP T Seaver
SP J Koosman
SP G Gentry
SP J McAndrew
SP R Sadecki
RP N Ryan
RP T McGraw
RP R Taylor
RP D Frisella
C J Grote
1B D Clendenon
2B K Boswell
SS B Harrelson
3B J Foy
LF C Jones
CF T Agee
RF R Swoboda
32 W Garrett
OI A Shamsky
OF- D Marshall
M G Hodges

PHI 1970 NL
SP R Wise
SP J Bunning
SP C Short
SP G Jackson
SP W Fryman
RP D Selma
RS B Lersch
RS L Palmer
RP J Hoerner
C - M Ryan
1B D Johnson
2B D Doyle
SS L Bowa
3B D Money
LU J Briggs
MR L Hisle
OI R Stone
RO B Browne
IO T Taylor
MR-O Gamble
M F Lucchesi

PIT 1970 NL
SP D Ellis
SP B Veale
SP S Blass
SP B Moose
SR L Walker
RP D Giusti
RS B Dal Canton
C M Sanguillen
1B B Robertson
2B B Mazeroski
SS G Alley
3B R Hebner
LF W Stargell
CF M Alou
RF R Clemente
1R A Oliver
UO- J Jeter
3U- J Pagan
SS- F Patek
M D Murtaugh

STL 1970 NL
SP B Gibson
SP S Carlton
SP M Torrez
SP J Reuss
SR N Briles
RS Ch Taylor
RP F Linzy
RP S Campisi
C - T Simmons
1R J Hague
2B J Javier
SS D Maxvill
C3 J Torre
LF L Brock
CF J Cardenal
RU L Lee
13 D Allen
UO V Davalillo
UT Ca Taylor
M R Schoendienst

SD 1970 NL
SP P Dobson
SP C Kirby
SP D Coombs
SR D Roberts
SP M Corkins
RP R Herbel
RP T Dukes
RP G Ross
RP R Willis
C C Cannizzaro
1B N Colbert
2B D Campbell
SI J Arcia
3B E Spiezio
LU A Ferrara
CF C Gaston
RF O Brown
OI I Murrell
S3 S Huntz
UT- R Webster
M P Gomez

SF 1970 NL
SP G Perry
SP J Marichal
SR R Robertson
SR F Reberger
RP D McMahon
RS R Bryant
RP J Johnson
C D Dietz
1B W McCovey
2U R Hunt
SS H Lanier
3B A Gallagher
LF K Henderson
CF W Mays
RF B Bonds
2S T Fuentes
M1 C King
M2 C Fox

BAL 1970 AL
SP J Palmer
SP M Cuellar
SP D McNally
SR J Hardin
SP T Phoebus
RP P Richert
RP E Watt
RP D Hall
RP M Lopez
C E Hendricks
1B B Powell
2B D Johnson
SS M Belanger
3B B Robinson
LF D Buford
CF P Blair
RF F Robinson
UO M Rettenmund
OI- T Crowley
M E Weaver

BOS 1970 AL
SP R Culp
SP S Siebert
SP G Peters
SR K Brett
SR M Nagy
RS V Romo
RP S Lyle
C - J Moses
1L C Yastrzemski
2B M Andrews
SS R Petrocelli
31 G Scott
LO B Conigliaro
CF R Smith
RF T Conigliaro
M E Kasko

CAL 1970 AL
SP C Wright
SP T Murphy
SP R May
SR A Messersmith
RP E Fisher
RP K Tatum
RS G Garrett
RP M Queen
C J Azcue
1B J Spencer
2B S Alomar
SS J Fregosi
3B K McMullen
LF A Johnson
MU J Johnstone
OI R Repoz
M L Phillips

CHI 1970 AL
SP T John
SP J Janeski
SP J Horlen
RP W Wood
RS J Crider
RP D Murphy
RS B Moore
C - E Herrmann
1U G Hopkins
2B B Knoop
SS L Aparicio
R3 B Melton
LF C May
CF K Berry
RU W Williams
UT T McCraw
32 S O'Brien
C - D Josephson
M1 D Gutteridge
M2 B Adair
M3 C Tanner

CLE 1970 AL
SP S McDowell
SR R Hand
SR D Chance
SP S Hargan
RP D Higgins
RP P Hennigan
RS R Austin
RP F Lasher
C R Fosse
1B T Horton
2B E Leon
SS J Heidemann
3B G Nettles
LF R Foster
CF T Uhlaender
RF V Pinson
UT C Hinton
OC D Sims
M A Dark

DET 1970 AL
SP M Lolich
SP J Niekro
SP L Cain
SR M Kilkenny
CL T Timmermann
RS J Hiller
RP D Patterson
RP F Scherman
C B Freehan
1B N Cash
2B D McAuliffe
SS C Gutierrez
3B D Wert
LF- W Horton
CF M Stanley
RM J Northrup
R1 A Kaline
UT E Maddox
UL- G Brown
UI- D Jones
M M Smith

KC 1970 AL
SP D Drago
SR B Johnson
SP J Rooker
SP B Butler
SR D Morehead
RP W Bunker
RS A Fitzmorris
RP T Burgmeier
RP T Abernathy
CU E Kirkpatrick
13 B Oliver
2B C Rojas
SS- J Hernandez
3B P Schaal
LF L Piniella
CF A Otis
RF P Kelly
M1 C Metro
M2 B Lemon

MIL 1970 AL
SP M Pattin
SP L Krausse
SP S Lockwood
SR B Bolin
SP G Brabender
RP K Sanders
RP J Gelnar
C P Roof
1B M Hegan
2S T Kubiak
SS R Pena
3B T Harper
LF D Walton
CF D May
UO R Snyder
C J McNertney
OI T Savage
M D Bristol

MIN 1970 AL
SP J Perry
SR J Kaat
SP B Blyleven
SR B Zepp
RS T Hall
RP R Perranoski
RP S Williams
C G Mitterwald
1B R Reese
2B- D Thompson
SS L Cardenas
3B H Killebrew
LM J Holt
CF C Tovar
RF T Oliva
2I F Quilici
LF- B Alyea
UT- R Renick
M B Rigney

NY 1970 AL
SP M Stottlemyre
SP F Peterson
SP S Bahnsen
SP S Kline
SR M Kekich
RP L McDaniel
RP R Klimkowski
CL J Aker
RS G Waslewski
C T Munson
1B D Cater
2B H Clarke
SS G Michael
3B J Kenney
LF R White
CF B Murcer
RF C Blefary
RU- J Lyttle
RU- R Woods
M R Houk

OAK 1970 AL
SP C Dobson
SP C Hunter
SR D Segui
SP B Odom
SR R Fingers
RP M Grant
RP P Lindblad
RP M Lachemann
RP B Locker
C - F Fernandez
1B D Mincher
2B D Green
SS B Campaneris
3B S Bando
LR F Alou
CF R Monday
RF R Jackson
L1 J Rudi
C - D Duncan
M J McNamara

WAS 1970 AL
SP D Bosman
SR J Coleman
SP C Cox
SR J Hannan
SP G Brunet
RP D Knowles
RS J Shellenback
RP J Grzenda
RP H Pina
C P Casanova
1B M Epstein
2B T Cullen
SS E Brinkman
3B A Rodriguez
L1 F Howard
CF E Stroud
UO D Unser
2B B Allen
OI R Reichardt
RU- L Maye
M T Williams

ATL 1971 NL
SP P Niekro
SP R Reed
SP G Stone
SR P Jarvis
SP T Kelley
RS J Nash
CL C Upshaw
RP S Barber
RP B Priddy
IC E Williams
1R H Aaron
2B F Millan
SS M Perez
3B- D Evans
LF R Garr
CF S Jackson
RU M Lum
CU- H King
M L Harris

CHI 1971 NL
SP F Jenkins
SP M Pappas
SP B Hands
SP K Holtzman
SP J Pizarro
RP P Regan
RP B Bonham
C - C Cannizzaro
1B J Pepitone
2B G Beckert
SS D Kessinger
3B R Santo
LF B Williams
CF B Davis
RF J Callison
R1 J Hickman
UI- P Popovich
M L Durocher

CIN 1971 NL
SP G Nolan
SP D Gullett
SP J McGlothlin
SP R Grimsley
SP W Simpson
RP W Granger
RP C Carroll
RS J Merritt
RP J Gibbon
C J Bench
1B L May
2B T Helms
SS D Concepcion
3B T Perez
LM H McRae
CF G Foster
RF P Rose
LF B Carbo
S3 W Woodward
M S Anderson

HOU 1971 NL
SP D Wilson
SP J Billingham
SR K Forsch
SP L Dierker
SP W Blasingame
RP G Culver
RP J Ray
RP F Gladding
RP D Lemaster
C J Edwards
1I D Menke
2B J Morgan
SS R Metzger
3B D Rader
RL J Alou
CF C Cedeno
RM J Wynn
L1 B Watson
LU- C Geronimo
M H Walker

LA 1971 NL
SP D Sutton
SP A Downing
SP C Osteen
SP B Singer
CL J Brewer
RP P Mikkelsen
RP J Moeller
C - D Sims
1B W Parker
2B J Lefebvre
SS M Wills
3B- S Garvey
IO D Allen
CF W Davis
RF B Buckner
LR W Crawford
UT B Valentine
C - T Haller
LR- M Mota
UT- B Russell
M W Alston

MON 1971 NL
SP B Stoneman
SP S Renko
SP C Morton
SP E McAnally
SR J Strohmayer
RP M Marshall
RS D McGinn
RP H Reed
RP C Raymond
C J Bateman
1B R Fairly
2B R Hunt
SS B Wine
3B B Bailey
LU- J Fairey
CF B Day
RF R Staub
2S G Sutherland
M G Mauch

NY 1971 NL
SP T Seaver
SP G Gentry
SP J Koosman
SR R Sadecki
SP N Ryan
RP T McGraw
RP D Frisella
RS C Williams
RP R Taylor
C J Grote
1B E Kranepool
2B K Boswell
SS B Harrelson
3B B Aspromonte
LF C Jones
CF T Agee
RU K Singleton
23- T Foli
CF D Hahn
OF D Marshall
1B- D Clendenon
M G Hodges

PHI 1971 NL
SP R Wise
SP B Lersch
SP C Short
SR K Reynolds
SR W Fryman
RS J Bunning
RS B Champion
RP B Brandon
RP J Hoerner
C T McCarver
1B D Johnson
2B- D Doyle
SS L Bowa
3B- J Vukovich
LR- O Gamble
CF W Montanez
RF R Freed
3L D Money
OI- R Stone
M F Lucchesi

PIT 1971 NL
SP S Blass
SP D Ellis
SP B Johnson
SP L Walker
SR B Moose
RS N Briles
CL D Giusti
RP M Grant
C M Sanguillen
1B B Robertson
2B D Cash
SS G Alley
3B R Hebner
LF W Stargell
CF A Oliver
RF R Clemente
UO- G Clines
OI V Davalillo
SS- J Hernandez
M D Murtaugh

STL 1971 NL
SP S Carlton
SP B Gibson
SP R Cleveland
SP J Reuss
RP C Taylor
RP M Drabowsky
RP F Linzy
RP D Shaw
C T Simmons
1R J Hague
2S T Sizemore
SS D Maxvill
3B J Torre
LF L Brock
OI M Alou
RF- J Cardenal
CF- J Cruz
2B- J Javier
RO- L Melendez
M R Schoendienst

SD 1971 NL
SP D Roberts
SP C Kirby
SP S Arlin
SP T Phoebus
SP F Norman
RP A Severinsen
RP B Miller
RP D Kelley
C B Barton
1B N Colbert
2B D Mason
SS E Hernandez
3B E Spiezio
OI L Stahl
CF C Gaston
RF O Brown
23 D Campbell
LU I Murrell
M P Gomez

SF 1971 NL
SP G Perry
SP J Marichal
SR J Cumberland
SP R Bryant
SP S Stone
RP J Johnson
RP D McMahon
RS R Robertson
C D Dietz
1B W McCovey
2B T Fuentes
SS C Speier
3B A Gallagher
LF K Henderson
M1 W Mays
RF B Bonds
3B H Lanier
MU- J Rosario
M C Fox

BAL 1971 AL
SP M Cuellar
SP P Dobson
SP J Palmer
SP D McNally
RS G Jackson
C E Hendricks
1B B Powell
2B D Johnson
SS M Belanger
3B B Robinson
LF D Buford
CF P Blair
RL M Rettenmund
R1 F Robinson
M E Weaver

BOS 1971 AL
SP R Culp
SP S Siebert
SP G Peters
SP J Lonborg
RP B Lee
RP B Bolin
RP S Lyle
RP K Tatum
C - D Josephson
1B G Scott
2B D Griffin
SS L Aparicio
3B R Petrocelli
LF C Yastrzemski
CF B Conigliaro
MR R Smith
RU J Lahoud
M E Kasko

CAL 1971 AL
SP A Messersmith
SP C Wright
SP T Murphy
SP R May
RP E Fisher
RP L Allen
RP D LaRoche
RP M Queen
C J Stephenson
1B J Spencer
2B S Alomar
SU J Fregosi
3B K McMullen
LU T Gonzalez
CF K Berry
RO R Repoz
SU- S O'Brien
M L Phillips

CHI 1971 AL
SP W Wood
SP T Bradley
SP T John
SR J Horlen
RS B Johnson
RP S Kealey
RP V Romo
RP T Forster
C E Herrmann
1B C May
2U M Andrews
SU L Alvarado
3B B Melton
LF R Reichardt
MO J Johnstone
RL W Williams
2U R McKinney
C - T Egan
SI- R Morales
SS- L Richard
M C Tanner

CLE 1971 AL
SP S McDowell
SP S Dunning
SR A Foster
SR R Lamb
SR S Hargan
RS V Colbert
RP P Hennigan
RP E Farmer
RP S Mingori
C R Fosse
1B C Chambliss
2B E Leon
SS- J Heidemann
3B G Nettles
LO T Uhlaender
MR V Pinson
RL R Foster
UT- C Hinton
M1 A Dark
M2 J Lipon

DET 1971 AL
SP M Lolich
SP J Coleman
SP L Cain
SR J Niekro
RP F Scherman
RP T Timmermann
RP B Denehy
C B Freehan
1B N Cash
2B D McAuliffe
SS E Brinkman
3B A Rodriguez
LF W Horton
CF M Stanley
RF A Kaline
ML J Northrup
LU- G Brown
UT- D Jones
M B Martin

KC 1971 AL
SP D Drago
SP M Hedlund
SP P Splittorff
SP B Dal Canton
SR A Fitzmorris
RP T Burgmeier
CL T Abernathy
RP J York
C - J May
1B G Hopkins
2B C Rojas
SS F Patek
3B P Schaal
LF L Piniella
CF A Otis
RF J Keough
OC E Kirkpatrick
1R B Oliver
M B Lemon

MIL 1971 AL
SP M Pattin
SP B Parsons
SP S Lockwood
SR L Krausse
SP J Slaton
RP K Sanders
RP J Morris
C E Rodriguez
OI J Briggs
2B R Theobald
SS- R Auerbach
3B- T Matchick
L3 T Harper
MR D May
RU B Voss
UT A Kosco
UI R Pena
2S- T Kubiak
M D Bristol

MIN 1971 AL
SP B Blyleven
SP J Perry
SP J Kaat
RS R Corbin
RS T Hall
RP S Williams
C G Mitterwald
1B R Reese
2B R Carew
SS L Cardenas
3I S Braun
LR C Tovar
MU J Holt
RF T Oliva
13 H Killebrew
M B Rigney

NY 1971 AL
SP F Peterson
SP M Stottlemyre
SP S Bahnsen
SP S Kline
SR M Kekich
RP L McDaniel
RP J Aker
C T Munson
13 D Cater
2B H Clarke
SS G Michael
3B J Kenney
LF R White
CF B Murcer
OI F Alou
1B- J Ellis
M R Houk

OAK 1971 AL
SP V Blue
SP C Hunter
SP C Dobson
SP D Segui
SP B Odom
RS R Fingers
RP B Locker
RP D Knowles
C D Duncan
1B M Epstein
2B D Green
SS B Campaneris
3B S Bando
LF J Rudi
CF R Monday
RF R Jackson
MO- A Mangual
M D Williams

WAS 1971 AL
SP D Bosman
SP D McLain
SP P Broberg
SR B Gogolewski
SR J Shellenback
RS C Cox
RP P Lindblad
RP J Grzenda
RP D Riddleberger
C - P Casanova
1B D Mincher
2S T Cullen
SS T Harrah
3B- D Nelson
L1 F Howard
MU E Maddox
MR D Unser
IF B Allen
CO D Billings
OI T McCraw
M T Williams

ATL 1972 NL
SP P Niekro
SP R Reed
SR R Schueler
SR T Kelley
SR G Stone
RS P Jarvis
RP C Upshaw
C E Williams
1B H Aaron
2B F Millan
SS M Perez
3B D Evans
LF- R Carty
CF D Baker
LR R Garr
RO M Lum
M1 L Harris
M2 E Mathews

CHI 1972 NL
SP F Jenkins
SP B Hooton
SP M Pappas
SP B Hands
SP R Reuschel
RP T Phoebus
CL J Aker
RP D McGinn
C R Hundley
1U J Hickman
2B G Beckert
SS D Kessinger
3B R Santo
LF B Williams
CF R Monday
RF J Cardenal
IO- C Fanzone
M1 L Durocher
M2 W Lockman

CIN 1972 NL
SP J Billingham
SP R Grimsley
SP G Nolan
SR J McGlothlin
SR D Gullett
RP P Borbon
RP C Carroll
RS T Hall
RP W Simpson
C J Bench
1B T Perez
2B J Morgan
SS D Concepcion
3B D Menke
LF P Rose
CF B Tolan
RF C Geronimo
SS- D Chaney
M S Anderson

HOU 1972 NL
SP D Wilson
SP L Dierker
SP D Roberts
SP J Reuss
SP K Forsch
RP G Culver
RP J Ray
RS T Griffin
RP F Gladding
C J Edwards
1B L May
2B T Helms
SS R Metzger
3B D Rader
LF B Watson
CF C Cedeno
RF J Wynn
M1 H Walker
M2 S Parker
M3 L Durocher

LA 1972 NL
SP D Sutton
SP C Osteen
SP A Downing
SP T John
SP B Singer
RP J Brewer
RP P Mikkelsen
RP P Richert
RP M Strahler
C - C Cannizzaro
1B W Parker
2B- L Lacy
SS B Russell
3B S Garvey
LF M Mota
CF W Davis
RF F Robinson
OI B Buckner
LR W Crawford
UT B Valentine
M W Alston

MON 1972 NL
SP B Stoneman
SP M Torrez
SP C Morton
SP E McAnally
SP B Moore
RP M Marshall
RS S Renko
RP J Strohmayer
RP T Walker
C - J Boccabella
1U M Jorgensen
2B R Hunt
SS T Foli
3B B Bailey
LF K Singleton
CF B Day
UO- C Mashore
R1 R Fairly
MU R Woods
UO- J Fairey
2U- H Torres
M G Mauch

NY 1972 NL
SP T Seaver
SP J Matlack
SP G Gentry
SR J Koosman
SP J McAndrew
RP T McGraw
RP D Frisella
RP R Sadecki
C D Dyer
1B E Kranepool
2B K Boswell
SS B Harrelson
3B J Fregosi
LF J Milner
CF T Agee
RF- R Staub
3U W Garrett
UT T Martinez
LU C Jones
M Y Berra

PHI 1972 NL
SP S Carlton
SR K Reynolds
SP B Champion
SP W Fryman
RS W Twitchell
RS B Brandon
RS D Selma
RS B Lersch
C - J Bateman
1R T Hutton
2B D Doyle
SS L Bowa
3B D Money
LF G Luzinski
CF W Montanez
UO- B Robinson
1U D Johnson
M1 F Lucchesi
M2 P Owens

PIT 1972 NL
SP S Blass
SP B Moose
SP N Briles
SP D Ellis
SR B Kison
RS B Johnson
CL D Giusti
RP R Hernandez
RP B Miller
C M Sanguillen
1U W Stargell
2B D Cash
SS G Alley
3B R Hebner
LO V Davalillo
CF A Oliver
RF R Clemente
UO G Clines
1B B Robertson
UT R Stennett
M B Virdon

STL 1972 NL
SP B Gibson
SP R Wise
SP R Cleveland
SR A Santorini
SP S Spinks
RP D Segui
C T Simmons
1R M Alou
2B T Sizemore
SS D Maxvill
3B J Torre
LF L Brock
MU J Cruz
MR L Melendez
RF B Carbo
UI E Crosby
M R Schoendienst

SD 1972 NL
SP S Arlin
SP C Kirby
SR F Norman
SR M Caldwell
SR B Greif
RS M Corkins
RP G Ross
RP E Acosta
C - F Kendall
1B N Colbert
2S D Thomas
SS E Hernandez
3B D Roberts
LF L Lee
CF J Jeter
RU C Gaston
OI J Morales
OI L Stahl
23 G Jestadt
M1 P Gomez
M2 D Zimmer

SF 1972 NL
SP R Bryant
SR J Barr
SP J Marichal
SP S McDowell
SR S Stone
RP F Reberger
RP J Johnson
RP R Moffitt
RP D McMahon
C D Rader
1B- W McCovey
2B T Fuentes
SS C Speier
3B- A Gallagher
LU K Henderson
CF G Maddox
RF B Bonds
IO D Kingman
M C Fox

BAL 1972 AL
SP J Palmer
SP P Dobson
SP M Cuellar
SP D McNally
RS D Alexander
RP R Harrison
C - J Oates
1B B Powell
2B D Johnson
SS M Belanger
3B B Robinson
LF D Buford
CF P Blair
RF M Rettenmund
OI D Baylor
RU T Crowley
S2 B Grich
M E Weaver

BOS 1972 AL
SP M Pattin
SP S Siebert
SR L Tiant
SP J Curtis
SP L McGlothen
RP R Culp
RP B Lee
RP G Peters
RS L Krausse
C C Fisk
1B- D Cater
2B D Griffin
SS L Aparicio
3B R Petrocelli
L1 C Yastrzemski
CF T Harper
RF R Smith
OF B Oglivie
ML- R Miller
M E Kasko

CAL 1972 AL
SP N Ryan
SP C Wright
SP R May
SP A Messersmith
SR R Clark
RS L Allen
RP E Fisher
RP S Barber
C - A Kusnyer
1B B Oliver
2B S Alomar
SS L Cardenas
3B K McMullen
LF V Pinson
CF K Berry
RF L Stanton
UT- J Spencer
M D Rice

CHI 1972 AL
SP W Wood
SP T Bradley
SP S Bahnsen
SR D Lemonds
RP T Forster
RP R Gossage
RP S Kealey
RP V Romo
C E Herrmann
1B D Allen
2B M Andrews
SS R Morales
3B- E Spiezio
LF C May
CF J Johnstone
RF P Kelly
SS L Alvarado
CF R Reichardt
RU- W Williams
M C Tanner

CLE 1972 AL
SP G Perry
SP D Tidrow
SP M Wilcox
SP S Dunning
RS R Lamb
RP P Hennigan
RP E Farmer
RP S Mingori
C R Fosse
1B C Chambliss
2B J Brohamer
SS F Duffy
3B G Nettles
LF A Johnson
MO D Unser
OI B Bell
OI T McCraw
IF- E Leon
M K Aspromonte

DET 1972 AL
SP M Lolich
SP J Coleman
SP T Timmermann
SP W Fryman
RP C Seelbach
RP F Scherman
C B Freehan
1B N Cash
2B D McAuliffe
SS E Brinkman
3B A Rodriguez
LF W Horton
CF M Stanley
RL J Northrup
LU G Brown
RF A Kaline
2B- T Taylor
M B Martin

KC 1972 AL
SP D Drago
SP P Splittorff
SR R Nelson
SR B Dal Canton
SR M Hedlund
RP A Fitzmorris
RP T Burgmeier
RP T Abernathy
C E Kirkpatrick
1B J Mayberry
2B C Rojas
SS F Patek
3B P Schaal
LF L Piniella
CF A Otis
RF R Scheinblum
UO S Hovley
M B Lemon

MIL 1972 AL
SP J Lonborg
SP B Parsons
SP S Lockwood
SP K Brett
SP G Ryerson
RS J Colborn
RP K Sanders
RP F Linzy
RS E Stephenson
C E Rodriguez
1B G Scott
2B R Theobald
SS R Auerbach
3B M Ferraro
LU J Briggs
CF D May
RL J Lahoud
23 B Heise
UO- B Davis
M1 D Bristol
M2 R McMillan
M3 D Crandall

MIN 1972 AL
SP B Blyleven
SP D Woodson
SP J Perry
SR R Corbin
SP J Kaat
RP W Granger
RP D LaRoche
C - P Roof
1B H Killebrew
2B R Carew
SS D Thompson
3B E Soderholm
LU S Brye
MR B Darwin
RL C Tovar
3I S Braun
MU J Nettles
1U R Reese
M1 B Rigney
M2 F Quilici

NY 1972 AL
SP M Stottlemyre
SP F Peterson
SP S Kline
SP M Kekich
SP R Gardner
RP S Lyle
RP L McDaniel
RP F Beene
C T Munson
1B R Blomberg
2B H Clarke
SS G Michael
3B- C Sanchez
LF R White
CF B Murcer
RF- J Callison
1B F Alou
3U- B Allen
RF- R Torres
M R Houk

OAK 1972 AL
SP C Hunter
SP K Holtzman
SP B Odom
SP V Blue
SR D Hamilton
RP R Fingers
RP B Locker
RS J Horlen
RP D Knowles
C D Duncan
1B M Epstein
2B- T Cullen
SS B Campaneris
3B S Bando
LF J Rudi
MR R Jackson
RO- A Mangual
1U M Hegan
CU- G Tenace
M D Williams

TEX 1972 AL
SR P Broberg
SP D Bosman
SP R Hand
SR M Paul
SR B Gogolewski
RP P Lindblad
RP D Stanhouse
RP J Panther
RP H Pina
CL D Billings
1U F Howard
2B- L Randle
SS T Harrah
3B D Nelson
OI L Biittner
MO J Lovitto
RF T Ford
MO E Maddox
M T Williams

ATL 1973 NL
SP C Morton
SR P Niekro
SR R Schueler
SR R Harrison
SP R Reed
RP T House
C - J Oates
1L M Lum
2B D Johnson
SS M Perez
3B D Evans
LU H Aaron
CF D Baker
RF R Garr
OI S Jackson
C - P Casanova
IC- D Dietz
M E Mathews

CHI 1973 NL
SP F Jenkins
SP B Hooton
SP R Reuschel
SP M Pappas
SR B Bonham
RP B Locker
RP J Aker
RP R Burris
RP D LaRoche
C R Hundley
1U- J Hickman
2B G Beckert
SS D Kessinger
3B R Santo
LF B Williams
CF R Monday
RF J Cardenal
UO G Hiser
2B P Popovich
M W Lockman

CIN 1973 NL
SP J Billingham
SP R Grimsley
SR D Gullett
SP F Norman
RP P Borbon
RS T Hall
RS C Carroll
C J Bench
1B T Perez
2B J Morgan
SS- D Concepcion
3B D Menke
LF P Rose
MU C Geronimo
MR B Tolan
SU D Chaney
3B D Driessen
M S Anderson

HOU 1973 NL
SP J Reuss
SP D Roberts
SP D Wilson
SR K Forsch
SR T Griffin
RP J Crawford
RP J Ray
RP J York
C - S Jutze
1B L May
2B T Helms
SS R Metzger
3B D Rader
LF B Watson
CF C Cedeno
RF J Wynn
UO- T Agee
M L Durocher

LA 1973 NL
SP D Sutton
SP A Messersmith
SP C Osteen
SP T John
SP A Downing
CL J Brewer
RP C Hough
RP D Rau
RP P Richert
C J Ferguson
1L B Buckner
2B D Lopes
SS B Russell
3B R Cey
LF- M Mota
CF W Davis
RF W Crawford
1U S Garvey
OI- T Paciorek
M W Alston

MON 1973 NL
SP S Renko
SP M Torrez
SP B Moore
SP E McAnally
SP S Rogers
RP M Marshall
RP T Walker
C J Boccabella
1B M Jorgensen
2B R Hunt
SS T Foli
3B B Bailey
LF R Fairly
MU R Woods
RF K Singleton
1U H Breeden
UO B Day
IO P Frias
M G Mauch

NY 1973 NL
SP T Seaver
SP J Koosman
SP J Matlack
SP G Stone
SR R Sadecki
RP T McGraw
RS H Parker
C - J Grote
1U J Milner
2B F Millan
SS B Harrelson
3B W Garrett
LF- C Jones
CF- D Hahn
RF R Staub
1L E Kranepool
UT- T Martinez
M Y Berra

PHI 1973 NL
SP S Carlton
SP W Twitchell
SP K Brett
SP J Lonborg
SP D Ruthven
RP B Lersch
RP M Scarce
RP B Brandon
RP B Wilson
C B Boone
1R W Montanez
2B D Doyle
SS L Bowa
3B M Schmidt
LF G Luzinski
CF D Unser
RM B Robinson
1U T Hutton
UT- C Tovar
RU- M Anderson
M D Ozark

PIT 1973 NL
SP N Briles
SP B Moose
SP D Ellis
SR J Rooker
SR L Walker
RP D Giusti
RP R Hernandez
RP B Johnson
CR M Sanguillen
1B B Robertson
2B D Cash
SS- D Maxvill
3B R Hebner
LF W Stargell
M1 A Oliver
RU R Zisk
UO G Clines
C M May
2S R Stennett
M1 B Virdon
M2 D Murtaugh

STL 1973 NL
SP R Wise
SP R Cleveland
SP A Foster
SP B Gibson
RP D Segui
RS R Folkers
RP O Pena
RP A Hrabosky
C T Simmons
1B J Torre
2B T Sizemore
SS M Tyson
3B K Reitz
LF L Brock
MO L Melendez
MR J Cruz
RF B Carbo
1U T McCarver
M R Schoendienst

SD 1973 NL
SP B Greif
SP C Kirby
SP S Arlin
SR R Troedson
SP R Jones
RS M Caldwell
RS M Corkins
RP V Romo
RP G Ross
C F Kendall
1B N Colbert
2B- R Morales
S2 D Thomas
3B D Roberts
LU L Lee
CF J Grubb
RF C Gaston
UO J Morales
OI- I Murrell
M D Zimmer

SF 1973 NL
SP R Bryant
SP J Barr
SP T Bradley
SP J Marichal
RP E Sosa
RS J Willoughby
RP R Moffitt
RP D Carrithers
C D Rader
1B W McCovey
2B T Fuentes
SS C Speier
3B E Goodson
LF G Matthews
CF G Maddox
RF B Bonds
31 D Kingman
UT G Thomasson
M C Fox

BAL 1973 AL
SP J Palmer
SP M Cuellar
SP D McNally
SP D Alexander
SP J Jefferson
RP B Reynolds
RP G Jackson
RP E Watt
C1 E Williams
1B B Powell
2B B Grich
SS M Belanger
3B B Robinson
LF D Baylor
CF P Blair
RM R Coggins
DH T Davis
LR A Bumbry
RF- M Rettenmund
M E Weaver

BOS 1973 AL
SP B Lee
SP L Tiant
SP J Curtis
SP M Pattin
SR R Moret
CL B Bolin
C C Fisk
1U C Yastrzemski
2B D Griffin
SS L Aparicio
3B R Petrocelli
LF T Harper
UO R Miller
RF D Evans
DH O Cepeda
CF R Smith
M1 E Kasko
M2 E Popowski

CAL 1973 AL
SP N Ryan
SP B Singer
SP C Wright
SP R May
RP S Barber
RP D Sells
C J Torborg
1B- M Epstein
2B S Alomar
SS R Meoli
3B A Gallagher
LM V Pinson
CF K Berry
RL L Stanton
DH F Robinson
OI T McCraw
IO B Oliver
M B Winkles

CHI 1973 AL
SP W Wood
SP S Bahnsen
SR S Stone
SR E Fisher
RS T Forster
CL C Acosta
RP R Gossage
C E Herrmann
1B T Muser
2B J Orta
SS E Leon
3B B Melton
DL C May
UO- J Jeter
RF P Kelly
OF- K Henderson
M C Tanner

CLE 1973 AL
SP G Perry
SP D Tidrow
SP M Wilcox
SR T Timmermann
SP B Strom
RP T Hilgendorf
RP R Lamb
RP J Johnson
C - D Duncan
1B C Chambliss
2B J Brohamer
SS F Duffy
3B B Bell
LU C Spikes
CF G Hendrick
RM R Torres
DR O Gamble
CD J Ellis
UT J Lowenstein
LD W Williams
M K Aspromonte

DET 1973 AL
SP M Lolich
SP J Coleman
SP J Perry
SP W Fryman
SP J Hiller
RP F Scherman
RP L LaGrow
C B Freehan
1B N Cash
2B D McAuliffe
SS E Brinkman
3B A Rodriguez
LF W Horton
CF M Stanley
RL J Northrup
DH G Brown
DH- F Howard
R1- A Kaline
RF- D Sharon
2B- T Taylor
M1 B Martin
M2 J Schultz

KC 1973 AL
SP P Splittorff
SP S Busby
SP D Drago
RS G Garber
RP D Bird
RP S Mingori
C - F Healy
1B J Mayberry
2B C Rojas
SS F Patek
3B P Schaal
LF L Piniella
CF A Otis
RO E Kirkpatrick
RD H McRae
UT K Bevacqua
RO S Hovley
M J McKeon

MIL 1973 AL
SP J Colborn
SP J Slaton
SP J Bell
SR S Lockwood
RS B Champion
RS E Rodriguez
RP F Linzy
RS C Short
C D Porter
1B G Scott
2B P Garcia
SS T Johnson
3B D Money
LF J Briggs
CF D May
RO B Coluccio
DH- O Brown
OF- J Lahoud
C - E Rodriguez
M D Crandall

MIN 1973 AL
SP B Blyleven
SP J Kaat
SP J Decker
SR B Hands
SP D Woodson
RS R Corbin
RS D Goltz
RS E Bane
RP B Campbell
C G Mitterwald
1B J Lis
2B R Carew
SS D Thompson
3B S Braun
L1 J Holt
ML L Hisle
RF B Darwin
DH T Oliva
SI J Terrell
CF- S Brye
M F Quilici

NY 1973 AL
SP M Stottlemyre
SP D Medich
SP F Peterson
SP P Dobson
RP L McDaniel
CL S Lyle
C T Munson
1U- F Alou
2B H Clarke
SS G Michael
3B G Nettles
LF R White
CF B Murcer
R1 M Alou
DH J Hart
D1 R Blomberg
M R Houk

OAK 1973 AL
SP K Holtzman
SP V Blue
SP C Hunter
SP B Odom
RP R Fingers
RS D Knowles
RP H Pina
RP P Lindblad
C R Fosse
1B G Tenace
2B D Green
SS B Campaneris
3B S Bando
LF J Rudi
CF B North
RF R Jackson
DH D Johnson
2B T Kubiak
M D Williams

TEX 1973 AL
SP J Bibby
SR J Merritt
SP S Siebert
SP P Broberg
RP B Gogolewski
RS M Paul
RP J Brown
RP S Foucault
C - K Suarez
1B J Spencer
2B D Nelson
SS- J Mason
S3 T Harrah
LD- R Carty
MI V Harris
RL J Burroughs
DL A Johnson
MO E Maddox
OI- L Biittner
C - D Billings
IO- B Sudakis
M1 W Herzog
M2 D Wilber
M3 B Martin

ATL 1974 NL
SP P Niekro
SP C Morton
SR B Capra
SP R Reed
SP R Harrison
RP T House
RP M Leon
RP L Krausse
C J Oates
12 D Johnson
2B M Perez
SS C Robinson
3B D Evans
LF H Aaron
RF D Baker
LR R Garr
CF R Office
1O M Lum
M1 E Mathews
M2 C King

CHI 1974 NL
SP B Bonham
SP R Reuschel
SR B Hooton
SR S Stone
RS K Frailing
RP D LaRoche
RP O Zamora
RS J Todd
C - S Swisher
1B A Thornton
2B- V Harris
SS D Kessinger
3B B Madlock
LR J Morales
CF R Monday
RF J Cardenal
1L B Williams
OI- C Ward
M1 W Lockman
M2 J Marshall

CIN 1974 NL
SP D Gullett
SP C Kirby
SP J Billingham
SP F Norman
RP P Borbon
RP C Carroll
RP T Hall
C J Bench
1B T Perez
2B J Morgan
SS D Concepcion
3B D Driessen
LF P Rose
CF C Geronimo
RM G Foster
32 D Chaney
OI- T Crowley
RF- K Griffey
M S Anderson

HOU 1974 NL
SP L Dierker
SP T Griffin
SP D Roberts
SP D Wilson
SP C Osteen
RP K Forsch
RP M Cosgrove
RP F Scherman
C M May
1B L May
2B T Helms
SS R Metzger
3B D Rader
LF B Watson
CF C Cedeno
RF G Gross
RU B Gallagher
2B L Milbourne
IC- C Johnson
M P Gomez

LA 1974 NL
SP A Messersmith
SP D Sutton
SP D Rau
SP T John
RP M Marshall
RP C Hough
C - S Yeager
1B S Garvey
2B D Lopes
SS B Russell
3B R Cey
LF B Buckner
CF J Wynn
RF W Crawford
CR J Ferguson
UO- V Joshua
LM- T Paciorek
M W Alston

MON 1974 NL
SP S Rogers
SP S Renko
SP M Torrez
SP D Blair
SP E McAnally
RP C Taylor
RS T Walker
RP J Montague
RP D Murray
C B Foote
1U M Jorgensen
2B- J Cox
SS T Foli
32 R Hunt
L3 B Bailey
CF W Davis
RF K Singleton
1U R Fairly
2S L Lintz
UO- R Woods
M G Mauch

NY 1974 NL
SP J Koosman
SP J Matlack
SP T Seaver
SR H Parker
RS B Apodaca
RS R Sadecki
RP T McGraw
RP B Miller
C - J Grote
1B J Milner
2B F Millan
SS B Harrelson
3B W Garrett
LF C Jones
CF D Hahn
RF R Staub
SU T Martinez
UT- K Boswell
OI- E Kranepool
MO- D Schneck
M Y Berra

PHI 1974 NL
SP S Carlton
SP J Lonborg
SP D Ruthven
SR R Schueler
SP W Twitchell
RP M Scarce
C B Boone
1B W Montanez
2B D Cash
SS L Bowa
3B M Schmidt
LF- G Luzinski
CF D Unser
RF M Anderson
UO B Robinson
UT- T Hutton
M D Ozark

PIT 1974 NL
SP J Rooker
SP J Reuss
SP K Brett
SP D Ellis
SR B Kison
RP D Giusti
RP R Hernandez
RP J Morlan
C M Sanguillen
1U- B Robertson
2B R Stennett
SS F Taveras
3B R Hebner
LF W Stargell
M1 A Oliver
RF R Zisk
UO G Clines
1U E Kirkpatrick
SS- M Mendoza
M D Murtaugh

STL 1974 NL
SP B Gibson
SP L McGlothen
SP J Curtis
SP A Foster
SP S Siebert
RP B Forsch
RP A Hrabosky
RP R Folkers
RP M Garman
C T Simmons
1B J Torre
2B T Sizemore
SS M Tyson
3B K Reitz
LF L Brock
CF B McBride
RF R Smith
OI J Cruz
OI- L Melendez
M R Schoendienst

SD 1974 NL
SP B Greif
SP D Freisleben
SP R Jones
SP D Spillner
RP L Hardy
RP V Romo
RP D Tomlin
RP M Corkins
C F Kendall
1B W McCovey
2U D Thomas
SS E Hernandez
3B D Roberts
LO D Winfield
CF J Grubb
RF- B Tolan
1L N Colbert
OF C Gaston
M J McNamara

SF 1974 NL
SR J Barr
SP J D'Acquisto
SP M Caldwell
SP T Bradley
SR R Bryant
RP R Moffitt
RP E Sosa
RS C Williams
C D Rader
1B D Kingman
2B T Fuentes
SS C Speier
3U S Ontiveros
LF G Matthews
CF G Maddox
RF B Bonds
1U E Goodson
UI M Phillips
OI G Thomasson
M1 C Fox
M2 W Westrum

BAL 1974 AL
SP R Grimsley
SP M Cuellar
SP D McNally
SP J Palmer
SR D Alexander
RP G Jackson
RP B Reynolds
RP D Hood
RP J Jefferson
C1 E Williams

1B B Powell
2B B Grich
SS M Belanger
3B B Robinson
LF D Baylor
CF P Blair
RF R Coggins
DH T Davis
LU- A Bumbry
M E Weaver

BOS 1974 AL
SP L Tiant
SP B Lee
SR R Cleveland
SR D Drago
SR R Moret
RP D Segui
C - B Montgomery
1L C Yastrzemski
2B- D Griffin
SS- M Guerrero
3B R Petrocelli
OF B Carbo
CF J Beniquez
RF D Evans
LD T Harper
SS R Burleson
MU R Miller
1D C Cooper
23 D McAuliffe
M D Johnson

CAL 1974 AL
SP N Ryan
SP F Tanana
SP A Hassler
SP D Lange
SP B Singer
RS E Figueroa
RP S Lockwood
C E Rodriguez
1B- J Doherty
2B D Doyle
S3 D Chalk
3B- P Schaal
LR J Lahoud
CF M Rivers
RF L Stanton
DH F Robinson
13 B Oliver
LS B Valentine
M1 B Winkles
M2 W Herzog
M3 D Williams

CHI 1974 AL
SP W Wood
SP J Kaat
SP S Bahnsen
SP B Johnson
RP T Forster
RS S Pitlock
RP R Gossage
C E Herrmann
1B D Allen
2B J Orta
SS B Dent
3B B Melton
LF C May
CF K Henderson
RF B Sharp
DR P Kelly
CR B Downing
1B T Muser
UI R Santo
M C Tanner

CLE 1974 AL
SP G Perry
SP J Perry
SP F Peterson
SP D Bosman
RP T Buskey
RP F Beene
RP M Wilcox
C D Duncan
1C J Ellis
2B J Brohamer
SS F Duffy
3B B Bell
LI J Lowenstein
CF G Hendrick
RF C Spikes
DH O Gamble
UO R Torres
M K Aspromonte

DET 1974 AL
SP M Lolich
SP J Coleman
SP L LaGrow
SP W Fryman
RP J Hiller
RP J Ray
C - J Moses

1C B Freehan
2B G Sutherland
SS E Brinkman
3B A Rodriguez
LF- W Horton
CF M Stanley
RF- J Northrup
DH A Kaline
LU- B Oglivie
M R Houk

KC 1974 AL
SP S Busby
SP P Splittorff
SP A Fitzmorris
SP B Dal Canton
SR M Pattin
RS L McDaniel
RP N Briles
RP D Bird
RP S Mingori
C F Healy
1B J Mayberry
2B C Rojas
SS F Patek
3B G Brett
LF J Wohlford
CF A Otis
RF V Pinson
DL H McRae
RO A Cowens
2S F White
1U- T Solaita
M J McKeon

MIL 1974 AL
SP J Slaton
SP C Wright
SP J Colborn
SR K Kobel
SP B Champion
RP T Murphy
RS E Rodriguez
RP B Travers
C D Porter
1B G Scott
2B P Garcia
SS R Yount
3B D Money
LF J Briggs
MO B Coluccio
RF D May
DO- B Mitchell
CF K Berry
UT- M Hegan
S2- T Johnson
M D Crandall

MIN 1974 AL
SP B Blyleven
SP J Decker
SP D Goltz
SR V Albury
SR R Corbin
RP B Campbell
RS B Hands
RS B Butler
RP T Burgmeier
C G Borgmann
1B- C Kusick
2B R Carew
SS- D Thompson
3B E Soderholm
LM L Hisle
CF S Brye
RF B Darwin
DH T Oliva
LF S Braun
UT H Killebrew
IO J Terrell
SS- L Gomez
M F Quilici

NY 1974 AL
SP P Dobson
SP D Medich
SP D Tidrow
SP R May
SP M Stottlemyre
RP S Lyle
RP C Upshaw
RP M Wallace
C T Munson
1B C Chambliss
2B- S Alomar
SS J Mason
3B G Nettles
LU L Piniella
CF E Maddox
RM B Murcer
DU- R Blomberg
UT R White
2S- G Michael
IF- B Sudakis
M B Virdon

OAK 1974 AL
SP C Hunter
SP V Blue
SP K Holtzman
SR D Hamilton
RP R Fingers
RP P Lindblad
RS B Odom
RP D Knowles
C - L Haney
1C G Tenace
2B D Green
SS B Campaneris
3B S Bando
LF J Rudi
CF B North
RF R Jackson
OF- J Alou
2I T Kubiak
OI A Mangual
LS- H Washington
M A Dark

TEX 1974 AL
SP F Jenkins
SP J Bibby
SP J Brown
SR S Hargan
SP D Clyde
RP S Foucault
C J Sundberg
1U M Hargrove
2B D Nelson
SS T Harrah
32 L Randle
ML C Tovar
CF J Lovitto
RF J Burroughs
1D J Spencer
LD A Johnson
OI- T Grieve
M B Martin

ATL 1975 NL
SP C Morton
SP P Niekro
RP M Leon
RP T House
RP M Beard
RS R Sadecki
C V Correll
1B E Williams
2B M Perez
SS L Blanks
3B D Evans
LF R Garr
CF R Office
RF D Baker
UT M Lum
2U- R Gilbreath
UO- D May
M1 C King
M2 C Ryan

CHI 1975 NL
SP R Burris
SP R Reuschel
SP B Bonham
SP S Stone
RP D Knowles
RS T Dettore
RP O Zamora
RP K Frailing
C - S Swisher
1B A Thornton
2B M Trillo
SS D Kessinger
3B B Madlock
LF J Cardenal
CF R Monday
RF J Morales
1U P LaCock
CU- G Mitterwald
M J Marshall

CIN 1975 NL
SP G Nolan
SP J Billingham
SP F Norman
SP D Gullett
SP P Darcy
RP P Borbon
CL R Eastwick
RP C Kirby
RP W McEnaney
C J Bench
1B T Perez
2B J Morgan
SS D Concepcion
3B P Rose
LO G Foster
CF C Geronimo
RF K Griffey
UT- D Driessen
UI- D Flynn
OI- M Rettenmund

M S Anderson

HOU 1975 NL
SP L Dierker
SP J Richard
SP D Roberts
SP D Konieczny
RS K Forsch
RP J Niekro
RP J Crawford
RP W Granger
C M May
1B B Watson
2B R Andrews
SS R Metzger
3B D Rader
UO W Howard
CF C Cedeno
OF G Gross
UT E Cabell
RU J Cruz
IC C Johnson
IF- K Boswell
M1 P Gomez
M2 B Virdon

LA 1975 NL
SP A Messersmith
SP D Rau
SP D Sutton
SP B Hooton
SR R Rhoden
RP M Marshall
RP C Hough
C S Yeager
1B S Garvey
2B D Lopes
SS- B Russell
3B R Cey
LF- B Buckner
CF J Wynn
RF W Crawford
UT L Lacy
SS- R Auerbach
M W Alston

MON 1975 NL
SP S Rogers
SP S Renko
SP D Warthen
SR D Blair
SR W Fryman
RP D Murray
RP D Carrithers
RP D DeMola
RP C Taylor
C B Foote
1B M Jorgensen
2B P Mackanin
SS T Foli
3B L Parrish
UO L Biittner
CF P Mangual
RC G Carter
LU B Bailey
UT- J Morales
UO- T Scott
M G Mauch

NY 1975 NL
SP T Seaver
SP J Koosman
SP J Matlack
SP R Tate
SR H Webb
RP R Baldwin
RP B Apodaca
RP T Hall
C J Grote
1B E Kranepool
2B F Millan
SS M Phillips
3B W Garrett
L1 D Kingman
CF D Unser
RF R Staub
3U J Torre
UO- G Clines
OI- J Milner
M1 Y Berra
M2 R McMillan

PHI 1975 NL
SP S Carlton
SP T Underwood
SP L Christenson
SP J Lonborg
SR W Twitchell
RP G Garber
RP T McGraw
RP T Hilgendorf
RS R Schueler
C - B Boone
1B D Allen
2B D Cash
SS L Bowa

3B M Schmidt
LF G Luzinski
CF G Maddox
RF M Anderson
1U T Hutton
RF J Johnstone
RL- O Brown
C - J Oates
M D Ozark

PIT 1975 NL
SP J Reuss
SP J Rooker
SP B Kison
SP D Ellis
SP J Candelaria
RS L Demery
RP K Brett
RP D Giusti
RP R Hernandez
C M Sanguillen
1B W Stargell
2B R Stennett
SS F Taveras
3B R Hebner
LF R Zisk
CF A Oliver
RF D Parker
UT- E Kirkpatrick
UO- B Robinson
M D Murtaugh

STL 1975 NL
SP L McGlothen
SP B Forsch
SP R Reed
SR J Curtis
SP J Denny
CL A Hrabosky
RP B Gibson
RP M Garman
C T Simmons
R1 R Smith
2B T Sizemore
SS M Tyson
3B K Reitz
LF L Brock
CF B McBride
RU W Davis
1U R Fairly
UO L Melendez
M R Schoendienst

SD 1975 NL
SP R Jones
SP J McIntosh
SP D Freisleben
SR D Spillner
SP B Strom
RS R Folkers
RP D Frisella
RP D Tomlin
RP B Greif
C F Kendall
1B W McCovey
2B T Fuentes
SS E Hernandez
3U- T Kubiak
LU B Tolan
CF J Grubb
RF D Winfield
13 M Ivie
LU G Locklear
S3 H Torres
UO- D Sharon
M J McNamara

SF 1975 NL
SP J Barr
SP J Montefusco
SP P Falcone
SR M Caldwell
SP E Halicki
RP C Williams
RP G Lavelle
RP R Moffitt
RP D Heaverlo
C D Rader
1B W Montanez
2B D Thomas
SS C Speier
3B S Ontiveros
LF G Matthews
CF V Joshua
RF B Murcer
3I B Miller
OI G Thomasson
M W Westrum

BAL 1975 AL
SP J Palmer
SP M Torrez
SP M Cuellar
SP R Grimsley
SR D Alexander
RP W Garland

RP G Jackson
C D Duncan
1B L May
2B B Grich
SS M Belanger
3B B Robinson
LF D Baylor
CF P Blair
RF K Singleton
DH T Davis
OI A Bumbry
C - E Hendricks
1B- T Muser
MU- J Northrup
M E Weaver

BOS 1975 AL
SP B Lee
SP L Tiant
SP R Wise
SR R Cleveland
SR R Moret
CL D Drago
RP D Segui
RP J Willoughby
RP J Burton
C - C Fisk
1B C Yastrzemski
2B D Griffin
SS R Burleson
3B R Petrocelli
OF B Carbo
CF F Lynn
RF D Evans
LD J Rice
D1 C Cooper
2B- D Doyle
M D Johnson

CAL 1975 AL
SP F Tanana
SP E Figueroa
SP N Ryan
SP B Singer
SR A Hassler
RS D Lange
RP D Kirkwood
RP M Scott
C - E Rodriguez
1B B Bochte
2B J Remy
SS- M Miley
3B D Chalk
UO M Nettles
CF M Rivers
RF L Stanton
DU- T Harper
LF- D Collins
M D Williams

CHI 1975 AL
SP J Kaat
SP W Wood
SP C Osteen
SP J Jefferson
RP R Gossage
RP D Hamilton
RP O Osborn
RP B Gogolewski
C B Downing
UT C May
2B J Orta
SS B Dent
3B B Melton
LO N Nyman
CF K Henderson
RF P Kelly
D1 D Johnson
M C Tanner

CLE 1975 AL
SR D Eckersley
SP F Peterson
SR D Hood
SP R Harrison
SP G Perry
RS J Bibby
RP D LaRoche
RP T Buskey
RP J Brown
C - A Ashby
1B B Powell
2B- D Kuiper
SS F Duffy
3B B Bell
LU O Gamble
MR R Manning
MR G Hendrick
DU R Carty
RL C Spikes
C - J Ellis
UT- J Lowenstein
M F Robinson

DET 1975 AL
SP M Lolich

SP J Coleman
SP V Ruhle
SP L LaGrow
SP R Bare
RS T Walker
RS D Lemanczyk
CL J Hiller
C B Freehan
1B- J Pierce
2B G Sutherland
SS T Veryzer
3B A Rodriguez
LF B Oglivie
CF R LeFlore
RF L Roberts
DH W Horton
L1 D Meyer
M R Houk

KC 1975 AL
SP S Busby
SP A Fitzmorris
SP D Leonard
SR M Pattin
SR P Splittorff
RP D Bird
RP N Briles
RP L McDaniel
RP S Mingori
C - B Martinez
1B J Mayberry
2B C Rojas
SS F Patek
3B G Brett
LF H McRae
CF A Otis
RM A Cowens
DH H Killebrew
RU V Pinson
2S F White
RL J Wohlford
UT- T Solaita
M1 J McKeon
M2 W Herzog

MIL 1975 AL
SP P Broberg
SP J Slaton
SP J Colborn
SP B Travers
SR B Champion
RS T Hausman
RP E Rodriguez
CL T Murphy
C D Porter
1B G Scott
2B P Garcia
SS R Yount
3B D Money
ML B Sharp
CF G Thomas
RF S Lezcano
DH H Aaron
32 K Bevacqua
OI- M Hegan
LF- B Mitchell
M1 D Crandall
M2 H Kuenn

MIN 1975 AL
SP B Blyleven
SP J Hughes
SP D Goltz
SR V Albury
RS B Campbell
RP T Burgmeier
C G Borgmann
1B- C Kusick
2B R Carew
SS D Thompson
3B E Soderholm
LF S Braun
CF D Ford
RM L Bostock
DH T Oliva
IO J Terrell
1O- J Briggs
RO- S Brye
SS- L Gomez
UO- L Hisle
M F Quilici

NY 1975 AL
SP C Hunter
SP D Medich
SP R May
SP P Dobson
SP L Gura
RP S Lyle
RP D Tidrow
C T Munson
1B C Chambliss
2B S Alomar
SS- J Mason
3B G Nettles
LF R White

CF- E Maddox
RM B Bonds
UC- E Herrmann
S2 F Stanley
OI- W Williams
M1 B Virdon
M2 B Martin

OAK 1975 AL
SP V Blue
SP K Holtzman
SP D Bosman
SR G Abbott
SP S Bahnsen
RP R Fingers
RP J Todd
RP P Lindblad
C G Tenace
1L J Rudi
2B P Garner
SS B Campaneris
3B S Bando
LF C Washington
CF B North
RF R Jackson
DH B Williams
1U J Holt
C - R Fosse
UO- D Hopkins
S2- T Martinez
M A Dark

TEX 1975 AL
SP F Jenkins
SP S Hargan
SP G Perry
SP B Hands
RS J Umbarger
RP S Foucault
RP S Thomas
C J Sundberg
1B J Spencer
2M L Randle
SS T Harrah
3B R Howell
L1 M Hargrove
CF- D Moates
RF J Burroughs
DO C Tovar
UO T Grieve
M1 B Martin
M2 F Lucchesi

ATL 1976 NL
SP P Niekro
SP D Ruthven
SP A Messersmith
SP C Morton
SP F LaCorte
RP A Devine
RP B Dal Canton
RP P Torrealba
C - V Correll
1B W Montanez
2B R Gilbreath
SS D Chaney
3B J Royster
LM J Wynn
CF R Office
RF K Henderson
OF D May
UT T Paciorek
M D Bristol

CHI 1976 NL
SP R Reuschel
SP R Burris
SP B Bonham
SP S Renko
RP B Sutter
RP P Reuschel
RP J Coleman
RP D Knowles
C S Swisher
1U P LaCock
2B M Trillo
SS M Kelleher
3B B Madlock
LF J Cardenal
MU R Monday
RF J Morales
CU G Mitterwald
MU J Wallis
SS- D Rosello
OI- C Summers
M J Marshall

CIN 1976 NL
SP G Nolan
SR P Zachry
SP F Norman
SP J Billingham
SP S Alcala
RP R Eastwick
RP P Borbon
RP D Gullett

RP W McEnaney
C J Bench
1B T Perez
2B J Morgan
SS D Concepcion
3B P Rose
LF G Foster
CF C Geronimo
RF K Griffey
UT D Driessen
2I- D Flynn
UO- M Lum
M S Anderson

HOU 1976 NL
SP J Richard
SP L Dierker
SP J Andujar
SR J Niekro
CL K Forsch
RP G Pentz
RP J Sambito
C - E Herrmann
1B B Watson
2B R Andrews
SS R Metzger
3B E Cabell
LO J Cruz
CF C Cedeno
RF G Gross
CU C Johnson
IO- K Boswell
OI- W Howard
LU- L Roberts
M B Virdon

LA 1976 NL
SP D Sutton
SP D Rau
SP B Hooton
SP T John
SP R Rhoden
RP C Hough
RP M Marshall
RP S Wall
C S Yeager
1B S Garvey
2B D Lopes
SS B Russell
3B R Cey
LF B Buckner
MU D Baker
RF- R Smith
IO- E Goodson
2B- T Sizemore
M1 W Alston
M2 T Lasorda

MON 1976 NL
SP S Rogers
SP W Fryman
SP D Stanhouse
SR D Carrithers
RP D Murray
RS S Dunning
RP C Lang
RP J Kerrigan
C B Foote
1O M Jorgensen
2B P Mackanin
SS T Foli
3B L Parrish
UO- D Unser
MU J White
MR- E Valentine
IC J Morales
CR- G Carter
M1 K Kuehl
M2 C Fox

NY 1976 NL
SP T Seaver
SP J Matlack
SP J Koosman
SP M Lolich
SP C Swan
CL S Lockwood
RP B Apodaca
C J Grote
1O E Kranepool
2B F Millan
SS B Harrelson
3B- R Staiger
LF J Milner
CF- D Unser
RF D Kingman
1U J Torre
UO B Boisclair
SI- M Phillips
M J Frazier

PHI 1976 NL
SP S Carlton
SP J Kaat
SP J Lonborg
SP L Christenson
SP T Underwood
RP R Reed
RP T McGraw
RP G Garber
RP W Twitchell
C B Boone
1B- D Allen
2B D Cash
SS L Bowa
3B M Schmidt
LF G Luzinski
CF G Maddox
RF J Johnstone
LO J Martin
UT B Tolan
RF- O Brown
1B- T Hutton
IC- T McCarver
M D Ozark

PIT 1976 NL
SP J Candelaria
SP J Reuss
SP J Rooker
SP B Kison
SP D Medich
RS L Demery
RP K Tekulve
RP B Moose
RP D Giusti
C M Sanguillen
1B W Stargell
2B R Stennett
SS F Taveras
3B R Hebner
LF R Zisk
CF A Oliver
RF D Parker
UT B Robinson
UT- E Kirkpatrick
M D Murtaugh

STL 1976 NL
SP P Falcone
SP J Denny
SP L McGlothen
SP B Forsch
SR E Rasmussen
RS J Curtis
RP A Hrabosky
RP M Wallace
RP B Greif
C T Simmons
1B K Hernandez
2B- M Tyson
SS D Kessinger
3B H Cruz
LF L Brock
MU J Mumphrey
RF W Crawford
UT- V Harris
OI- M Anderson
M R Schoendienst

SD 1976 NL
SP R Jones
SP B Strom
SR D Freisleben
SR D Spillner
RP B Metzger
RP D Tomlin
RP R Folkers
C F Kendall
1B M Ivie
2B T Fuentes
SS E Hernandez
3B D Rader
LR J Grubb
CF W Davis
RF D Winfield
LU J Turner
UI- T Kubiak
UO- M Rettenmund
M J McNamara

SF 1976 NL
SP J Montefusco
SP J Barr
SP E Halicki
SP R Dressler
SP J D'Acquisto
RP G Lavelle
RP R Moffitt
RS M Caldwell
RP C Williams
C - D Rader
1B- D Evans
2B- M Perez
SS C Speier
3B K Reitz
LF G Matthews
CF L Herndon
RF B Murcer
OI G Thomasson
2B- D Thomas
M B Rigney

BAL 1976 AL
SP J Palmer
SR W Garland
SP R May
SP R Grimsley
SP M Cuellar
RP D Miller
C - D Duncan
1B T Muser
2B B Grich
SS M Belanger
3B D DeCinces
LR K Singleton
CF P Blair
RF R Jackson
1D L May
LM A Bumbry
M E Weaver

BOS 1976 AL
SP L Tiant
SP R Wise
SP F Jenkins
SR R Cleveland
SR D Pole
RP J Willoughby
RS R Jones
RP T Murphy
C C Fisk
1L C Yastrzemski
2B D Doyle
SS R Burleson
3B- B Hobson
LD J Rice
CF F Lynn
RF D Evans
1D C Cooper
UO R Miller
3B- R Petrocelli
M1 D Johnson
M2 D Zimmer

CAL 1976 AL
SP F Tanana
SP N Ryan
SP G Ross
SR P Hartzell
SP D Kirkwood
RS S Monge
RP D Drago
C A Etchebarren
OI B Bochte
2B J Remy
S3 D Chalk
3B R Jackson
UO- L Stanton
CF R Torres
RF B Bonds
DH- T Davis
LU D Collins
IF B Melton
IF- M Guerrero
M1 D Williams
M2 N Sherry

CHI 1976 AL
SP R Gossage
SP B Johnson
SP K Brett
SR F Barrios
SR T Forster
RS P Vuckovich
RP D Hamilton
RP C Carroll
C B Downing
1B J Spencer
2B J Brohamer
SS B Dent
3B- K Bell
OI J Orta
CF C Lemon
UO R Garr
DU P Kelly
IO B Stein
UT- L Johnson
M P Richards

CLE 1976 AL
SP P Dobson
SP D Eckersley
SP J Brown
SR J Bibby
SP R Waits
RP J Kern
RP D LaRoche
RS S Thomas
RP T Buskey
C - A Ashby
1B- B Powell
2B D Kuiper
SS F Duffy
3B B Bell
LF G Hendrick
CF R Manning
RF C Spikes
DH R Carty
S2 L Blanks
C - R Fosse
OI- J Lowenstein
M F Robinson

DET 1976 AL
SP D Roberts
SP M Fidrych
SP V Ruhle
SP R Bare
RP J Hiller
RS J Crawford
RP S Grilli
C - B Kimm
1B J Thompson
2B- P Garcia
SS T Veryzer
3B A Rodriguez
LU A Johnson
CF R LeFlore
RF R Staub
DH W Horton
UT D Meyer
OI B Oglivie
UT- M Stanley
M R Houk

KC 1976 AL
SP D Leonard
SP A Fitzmorris
SR D Bird
SP P Splittorff
SR M Pattin
RP M Littell
RP A Hassler
RP S Mingori
C - B Martinez
1B J Mayberry
2B F White
SS F Patek
3B G Brett
LF T Poquette
CF A Otis
RF A Cowens
DH H McRae
LF J Wohlford
M W Herzog

MIL 1976 AL
SP J Slaton
SP B Travers
SP J Colborn
SR J Augustine
RS E Rodriguez
RP B Castro
RP D Frisella
C D Porter
1B G Scott
2B T Johnson
SS R Yount
3B D Money
UO S Lezcano
CF V Joshua
MR G Thomas
DH- H Aaron
CL- C Moore
M A Grammas

MIN 1976 AL
SP D Goltz
SR J Hughes
SP B Singer
SP P Redfern
RP B Campbell
RS S Luebber
RP T Burgmeier
RP V Albury
C B Wynegar
1B R Carew
2B B Randall
SS R Smalley
3B M Cubbage
LF L Hisle
CF L Bostock
RF D Ford
DU C Kusick
DO S Braun
MO- S Brye
UT- J Terrell
M G Mauch

NY 1976 AL
SP C Hunter
SP E Figueroa
SP D Ellis
SP K Holtzman
SP D Alexander
RP S Lyle
RP D Tidrow
RP G Jackson
C T Munson
1B C Chambliss
2B W Randolph
SS F Stanley
3B G Nettles
LF R White
CF M Rivers
RF O Gamble
DH- C May
OF L Piniella
SS- J Mason
M B Martin

OAK 1976 AL
SP V Blue
SP M Torrez
SR S Bahnsen
SP P Mitchell
SR D Bosman
RP R Fingers
RP P Lindblad
RP J Todd
C - L Haney
1C G Tenace
2B P Garner
SS B Campaneris
3B S Bando
LF J Rudi
CF B North
RF C Washington
DH B Williams
OI D Baylor
IO K McMullen
M C Tanner

TEX 1976 AL
SP G Perry
SP N Briles
SP B Blyleven
SP J Umbarger
RS S Hargan
RP S Foucault
RP M Bacsik
RP J Terpko
C J Sundberg
1B M Hargrove
2B L Randle
SS T Harrah
3B R Howell
LF G Clines
CF J Beniquez
RF J Burroughs
DL T Grieve
UO- D Moates
M F Lucchesi

ATL 1977 NL
SP P Niekro
SP D Ruthven
SR B Capra
SP A Messersmith
RP D Campbell
RP R Camp
RS M Leon
RS D Collins
C B Pocoroba
1B W Montanez
2B R Gilbreath
SS- P Rockett
3B J Moore
LF G Matthews
CF R Office
RF J Burroughs
M3 B Bonnell
IO J Royster
UO- B Asselstine
M1 D Bristol
M2 T Turner
M3 V Benson
M4 D Bristol

CHI 1977 NL
SP R Reuschel
SP R Burris
SP B Bonham
SP M Krukow
RP B Sutter
RP W Hernandez
RP P Reuschel
RP D Moore
C G Mitterwald
1B B Buckner
2B M Trillo
SS I DeJesus
3B S Ontiveros
LU J Cardenal
CF J Morales
RF B Murcer
1L L Biittner
UO G Gross
UO G Clines
M H Franks

CIN 1977 NL
SP F Norman
SP T Seaver
SR J Billingham
SP P Moskau
SP D Capilla
RP P Borbon
RP D Murray
C J Bench
1B D Driessen
2B J Morgan
SS D Concepcion
3B P Rose
LF G Foster
CF C Geronimo
RF K Griffey
OI- M Lum
M S Anderson

HOU 1977 NL
SP J Richard
SP M Lemongello
SP J Andujar
SP F Bannister
RS J Niekro
RP J Sambito
RS K Forsch
RS B McLaughlin
C J Ferguson
1B B Watson
2B A Howe
SS- R Metzger
3B E Cabell
LF- T Puhl
CF C Cedeno
RF J Cruz
S2 J Gonzalez
LU- W Howard
M B Virdon

LA 1977 NL
SP D Sutton
SP B Hooton
SP T John
SP R Rhoden
SP D Rau
RP C Hough
RP M Garman
RP E Sosa
C S Yeager
1B S Garvey
2B D Lopes
SS B Russell
3B R Cey
LF D Baker
CF R Monday
RF R Smith
CF- G Burke
M T Lasorda

MON 1977 NL
SP S Rogers
SR J Brown
SR D Stanhouse
SP W Twitchell
SP S Bahnsen
RS S Alcala
RP J Kerrigan
RP B Atkinson
RP W McEnaney
C G Carter
1B T Perez
2B D Cash
SS C Speier
3B L Parrish
LF W Cromartie
CF A Dawson
RF E Valentine
OI D Unser
M D Williams

NY 1977 NL
SP J Koosman
SP N Espinosa
SP J Matlack
SP C Swan
SP P Zachry
RP S Lockwood
RP B Apodaca
RP B Myrick
RP R Baldwin
C J Stearns
1U J Milner
2B- F Millan
SS B Harrelson
3B L Randle
LF S Henderson
CF L Mazzilli
RF M Vail
OI E Kranepool
OI B Boisclair
S2- D Flynn
M1 J Frazier
M2 J Torre

PHI 1977 NL
SP S Carlton
SP L Christenson
SP R Lerch
SP J Kaat
SP J Lonborg
RP R Reed
RP G Garber
RP T McGraw
RP W Brusstar
C B Boone
1B R Hebner
2B T Sizemore
SS L Bowa
3B M Schmidt
LF G Luzinski
CF G Maddox
RF J Johnstone
1U T Hutton
OI J Martin
RU- B McBride
IC- T McCarver
M D Ozark

PIT 1977 NL
SP J Candelaria
SP J Reuss
SP J Rooker
SP B Kison
SR O Jones
RP R Gossage
RP K Tekulve
RP G Jackson
RS L Demery
C - D Dyer
1L B Robinson
2B R Stennett
SS F Taveras
32 P Garner
LF A Oliver
CF O Moreno
RF D Parker
C E Ott
M C Tanner

STL 1977 NL
SP E Rasmussen
SP B Forsch
SP J Denny
SP P Falcone
SP T Underwood
RS J Urrea
RP B Metzger
RP A Hrabosky
RP C Carroll
C T Simmons
1B K Hernandez
2B M Tyson
SS G Templeton
3B K Reitz
LF L Brock
UO J Mumphrey
RU H Cruz
RF- M Anderson
CF- T Scott
M V Rapp

SD 1977 NL
SP B Shirley
SP B Owchinko
SR T Griffin
SP R Jones
SR D Freisleben
RP R Fingers
RP D Spillner
RS R Sawyer
RP D Tomlin
CI G Tenace
1B M Ivie
2B M Champion
SS B Almon
3B- T Ashford
OI G Richards
CF G Hendrick
RF D Winfield
OI M Rettenmund
LU J Turner
C - D Roberts
M1 J McNamara
M2 B Skinner
M3 A Dark

SF 1977 NL
SP E Halicki
SP J Barr
SP B Knepper
SP J Montefusco
RP G Lavelle
RS C Williams
RP D Heaverlo
RP R Moffitt
C M Hill
1B W McCovey
2B R Andrews
SS T Foli
3B B Madlock
OI G Thomasson
MI D Thomas
RF J Clark
L1 D Evans
UO T Whitfield
M J Altobelli

BAL 1977 AL
SP J Palmer
SP R May
SP M Flanagan
SP R Grimsley
RS D Martinez
RS S McGregor
RP T Martinez
C - R Dempsey
1D L May
2B B Smith
SS M Belanger
3B D DeCinces
LF P Kelly
CF A Bumbry
RF K Singleton
D1 E Murray
1U T Muser
2B- R Dauer
M E Weaver

BOS 1977 AL
SP F Jenkins
SP R Cleveland
SP L Tiant
SR B Lee
SP R Wise
RP B Campbell
RS B Stanley
RS M Paxton
RP J Willoughby
C C Fisk
1B G Scott
2B D Doyle
SS R Burleson
3B B Hobson
LF C Yastrzemski
CF F Lynn
RM- R Miller
DO J Rice
RU- B Carbo
M D Zimmer

CAL 1977 AL
SP N Ryan
SP F Tanana
SR P Hartzell
SP K Brett
SP W Simpson
RP D Miller
RP D LaRoche
RP M Barlow
C T Humphrey
1B T Solaita
2B J Remy
SS- R Mulliniks
3B D Chalk
LF- J Rudi
UO G Flores
RF B Bonds
OI D Baylor
IO R Jackson
IF- M Guerrero
M1 N Sherry
M2 D Garcia

CHI 1977 AL
SP F Barrios
SP S Stone
SP K Kravec
SP C Knapp
SP W Wood
RP L LaGrow
RP D Hamilton
C J Essian
1B J Spencer
2B J Orta
SS A Bannister
3B E Soderholm
LF R Garr
CF C Lemon
RU R Zisk
DR O Gamble
D1 L Johnson
M B Lemon

CLE 1977 AL
SP W Garland
SP D Eckersley
SP J Bibby
SR R Waits
SR P Dobson
RP A Fitzmorris
RP J Kern
RS D Hood
C F Kendall
1B A Thornton
2B D Kuiper
SS F Duffy
3B B Bell
L1 B Bochte
MR J Norris
UT P Dade
DH R Carty
SI L Blanks
OI- J Lowenstein
M1 F Robinson
M2 J Torborg

DET 1977 AL
SP D Rozema
SR F Arroyo
SR B Sykes
SP D Roberts
SP M Wilcox
RS J Hiller
RS J Crawford
RP S Foucault
RP S Grilli
C M May
1B J Thompson
2B T Fuentes
SS T Veryzer
3B- A Rodriguez
LF S Kemp
CF R LeFlore
RF B Oglivie
DH R Staub
3B- P Mankowski
M R Houk

KC 1977 AL
SP D Leonard
SP J Colborn
SP P Splittorff
SP A Hassler
RS D Bird
RS M Pattin
RS M Littell
RS L Gura
C D Porter
1B J Mayberry
2B F White
SS F Patek
3B G Brett
LR T Poquette
CF A Otis
RF A Cowens
DL H McRae
LF J Zdeb
UT- P LaCock
M W Herzog

MIL 1977 AL
SP J Slaton
SP J Augustine
SP M Haas
SP L Sorensen
SP B Travers
RS E Rodriguez
RP B Castro
RP B McClure
RP S Hinds
C C Moore
1B C Cooper
2B D Money
SS R Yount
3B S Bando
LF J Wohlford
CF V Joshua
RF S Lezcano
DU- J Quirk
UO- S Brye
M A Grammas

MIN 1977 AL
SP D Goltz
SP P Thormodsgard
SP G Zahn
SP P Redfern
RP T Johnson
RS R Schueler
RP T Burgmeier
RS D Johnson
C B Wynegar
1B R Carew
2B B Randall
SS R Smalley
3B M Cubbage
UO L Hisle
ML L Bostock
RF D Ford
DU C Kusick
DU R Chiles
OF- G Adams
3U- J Terrell
M G Mauch

NY 1977 AL
SP E Figueroa
SP M Torrez
SP R Guidry
SP D Gullett
SP C Hunter
RP S Lyle
RS D Tidrow
RP K Clay
C T Munson
1B C Chambliss
2B W Randolph
SS B Dent
3B G Nettles
LF R White
CF M Rivers
RF R Jackson
DH- C May
OI L Piniella
MR- P Blair
M B Martin

OAK 1977 AL
SP V Blue
SP R Langford
SP D Medich
RS J Coleman
RP B Lacey
RS P Torrealba
RP D Bair
C - J Newman
1B- D Allen
2B M Perez
SS R Picciolo
3B W Gross
LF M Page
MR T Armas
RU- J Tyrone
CD M Sanguillen
2S R Scott
UC E Williams
UT- M Alexander
UT- R McKinney
OI- L Murray
M1 J McKeon
M2 B Winkles

SEA 1977 AL
SP G Abbott
SP D Pole
RS J Montague
RP E Romo
RS D Segui
RP M Kekich
C B Stinson
1B D Meyer
2B- J Baez
SS C Reynolds
3B B Stein
LU S Braun
CF R Jones
RU L Stanton
DI- J Bernhardt
LD D Collins
RF C Lopez
UI- L Milbourne
M D Johnson

TEX 1977 AL
SP G Perry
SP D Alexander
SP B Blyleven
SP D Ellis
SR N Briles
RP A Devine
RP P Lindblad
RP D Knowles
C J Sundberg
1B M Hargrove
2B B Wills
SS B Campaneris
3B T Harrah
LM C Washington
CF J Beniquez
RF D May
DH W Horton
M1 F Lucchesi
M2 E Stanky
M3 C Ryan
M4 B Hunter

TOR 1977 AL
SP D Lemanczyk
SP J Garvin
SP J Jefferson
RS P Vuckovich
RP M Willis
RP J Johnson
RP T Murphy
C A Ashby
1B D Ault
2B- S Staggs
S2- H Torres
3B- R Howell
LF A Woods
OI B Bailor
RU O Velez
UT R Fairly
OI S Ewing
RM- S Bowling
UI- D McKay
IO- D Rader
M R Hartsfield

ATL 1978 NL
SP P Niekro
SP P Hanna
SR M Mahler
SP L McWilliams
RS E Solomon
CL G Garber
RS J Easterly
RP R Camp
C - B Pocoroba
1B D Murphy
2S J Royster
SS- D Chaney
3B- B Horner
LF J Burroughs
CF R Office
RF G Matthews
UT B Beall
OI B Bonnell
32 R Gilbreath
CU- J Nolan
M B Cox

CHI 1978 NL
SP R Reuschel
SP D Lamp
SP R Burris
SR D Roberts
SP M Krukow
RP B Sutter
RP D Moore
RP L McGlothen
RP W Hernandez
C D Rader
1B B Buckner
2B M Trillo
SS I DeJesus
3B- S Ontiveros
LF D Kingman
ML G Gross
RF B Murcer
1U L Biittner
UO G Clines
M H Franks

CIN 1978 NL
SP T Seaver
SP F Norman
SR T Hume
SP P Moskau
SP B Bonham
RP M Sarmiento
RP D Bair
RP P Borbon
RP D Tomlin
C J Bench
1B D Driessen
2B J Morgan
SS D Concepcion
3B P Rose
LF G Foster
CF C Geronimo
RF K Griffey
UO D Collins
2B- J Kennedy
3U- R Knight
OI- M Lum
M S Anderson

HOU 1978 NL
SP J Richard
SP M Lemongello
SP J Niekro
SR T Dixon
SP J Andujar
RS K Forsch
RS F Bannister
RP J Sambito
C - L Pujols
1B B Watson
2B A Howe
SU- J Sexton
3B E Cabell
LU D Walling
ML T Puhl
RF J Cruz
1L D Bergman
OI- W Howard
M B Virdon

LA 1978 NL
SP D Sutton
SP B Hooton
SP T John
SP D Rau
SP R Rhoden
RS B Welch
RP C Hough
CL T Forster
RP L Rautzhan
C - S Yeager
1B S Garvey
2B D Lopes
SS B Russell
3B R Cey
LF D Baker
CF B North
RF R Smith
UT L Lacy
MR R Monday
M T Lasorda

MON 1978 NL
SP R Grimsley
SP S Rogers
SP R May
SR D Schatzeder
SR W Twitchell
RS H Dues
RP S Bahnsen
RP D Knowles
RP M Garman
C G Carter
1B T Perez
2B D Cash
SS C Speier
3B L Parrish
LF W Cromartie
CF A Dawson
RF E Valentine
UT D Unser
M D Williams

NY 1978 NL
SP J Koosman
SP C Swan
SP N Espinosa
SP P Zachry
SP M Bruhert
RS K Kobel
RS S Lockwood
RP D Murray
C J Stearns
1B W Montanez
2B D Flynn
SS T Foli
3B L Randle
LF S Henderson
CF L Mazzilli
R3 E Maddox
RU B Boisclair
UT J Youngblood
M J Torre

PHI 1978 NL
SP S Carlton
SP L Christenson
SP R Lerch
SP D Ruthven
SP J Kaat
RP R Reed
RP J Lonborg
RP T McGraw
RP W Brusstar
C B Boone
1B R Hebner
2B T Sizemore
SS L Bowa
3B M Schmidt
LF G Luzinski
CF G Maddox
RF B McBride
UO J Martin
1U- J Cardenal
IC- T McCarver
M D Ozark

PIT 1978 NL
SP B Blyleven
SP D Robinson
SP J Candelaria
SP J Rooker
SR J Bibby
RP K Tekulve
RP G Jackson
RP E Whitson
C E Ott
1B W Stargell
2B R Stennett
SS F Taveras
23 P Garner
LF B Robinson
CF O Moreno
RF D Parker
L1 J Milner
IC- M Sanguillen
M C Tanner

STL 1978 NL
SP J Denny
SP B Forsch
SR P Vuckovich
SP S Martinez
SR J Urrea
RP M Littell
RP B Schultz
RP A Lopez
RP T Bruno
C T Simmons
1B K Hernandez
2B M Tyson
SS G Templeton
3B K Reitz
LF- L Brock
CF G Hendrick
RM J Morales
UO J Mumphrey
UO- T Scott
M1 V Rapp
M2 J Krol
M3 K Boyer

SD 1978 NL
SP G Perry
SP R Jones
SP B Owchinko
SR B Shirley
SP E Rasmussen
RP R Fingers
RP J D'Acquisto
RP M Lee
C - R Sweet
1C G Tenace
2B F Gonzalez
SS O Smith
3B B Almon
LU G Richards
RM D Winfield
RL O Gamble
M2 D Thomas
UO J Turner
M R Craig

SF 1978 NL
SP B Knepper
SP V Blue
SP J Montefusco
SP E Halicki
SP J Barr
RP G Lavelle
RP R Moffitt
RP J Curtis
C M Hill
1B W McCovey
2B B Madlock
SS J LeMaster
3B D Evans
LF T Whitfield
CF L Herndon
RF J Clark
1U M Ivie
M J Altobelli

BAL 1978 AL
SP J Palmer
SP M Flanagan
SP D Martinez
SP S McGregor
CL D Stanhouse
RP J Kerrigan
RP T Martinez
C R Dempsey
1B E Murray
23 R Dauer
SS M Belanger
3B D DeCinces
LU P Kelly
CF L Harlow
RF K Singleton
DH L May
RM C Lopez
2B- B Smith
M E Weaver

BOS 1978 AL
SP D Eckersley
SP M Torrez
SP L Tiant
SP B Lee
SP J Wright
RP B Stanley
RP D Drago
RP T Burgmeier
RP B Campbell
C C Fisk
1B G Scott
2B J Remy
SS R Burleson
3B B Hobson
OI C Yastrzemski
CF F Lynn
RF D Evans
LD J Rice
IF- J Brohamer
M D Zimmer

CAL 1978 AL
SP F Tanana
SP N Ryan
SP C Knapp
SP D Aase
RS P Hartzell
CL D LaRoche
RS K Brett
RP D Miller
C B Downing
1B- R Fairly
2B B Grich
SI D Chalk
3B C Lansford
LF J Rudi
MR R Miller
RM L Bostock
DU D Baylor
13 R Jackson
UO- K Landreaux
M1 D Garcia
M2 J Fregosi

CHI 1978 AL
SP S Stone
SP K Kravec
SP F Barrios
SP W Wood
RP J Willoughby
RP L LaGrow
RP R Hinton
RS R Schueler
C B Nahorodny
1B- M Squires
2B J Orta
SS D Kessinger
3B E Soderholm
LF R Garr
CF C Lemon
RO- C Washington
1U L Johnson
UO B Molinaro
UI- G Pryor
M1 B Lemon
M2 L Doby

CLE 1978 AL
SP R Waits
SP R Wise
SP M Paxton
SR D Hood
SP D Clyde
RP J Kern
RP S Monge
RP D Spillner
CD- G Alexander
1B A Thornton
2B D Kuiper
SS T Veryzer
3B B Bell
LF J Grubb
CF R Manning
RF- P Dade
DH- B Carbo
OI J Norris
UT- T Cox
M J Torborg

DET 1978 AL
SP J Slaton
SP M Wilcox
SP D Rozema
SP J Billingham
SP K Young
RP J Hiller
RS J Morris
C M May
1B J Thompson
2B L Whitaker
SS A Trammell
3B A Rodriguez
LF S Kemp
CF R LeFlore
RF T Corcoran
DH R Staub
3B- P Mankowski
C - L Parrish
M R Houk

KC 1978 AL
SP D Leonard
SP P Splittorff
SP L Gura
SP R Gale
RS D Bird
CL A Hrabosky
RS M Pattin
RP S Mingori
C D Porter
1B P LaCock
2B F White
SS F Patek
3B G Brett
LM W Wilson
CF A Otis
RF A Cowens
DH H McRae
UT C Hurdle
M W Herzog

MIL 1978 AL
SP M Caldwell
SP L Sorensen
SP J Augustine
SP B Travers
SR A Replogle
RS E Rodriguez
RP B McClure
RP R Stein
RP B Castro
C - C Moore
1B C Cooper
2I P Molitor
SS R Yount
3B S Bando
LU B Oglivie
CF G Thomas
RF S Lezcano
UO L Hisle
UI D Money
C - B Martinez
M G Bamberger

MIN 1978 AL
SP R Erickson
SP G Zahn
SP D Goltz
SR G Serum
RP M Marshall
C B Wynegar
1B R Carew
2B B Randall
SS R Smalley
3B M Cubbage
LF W Norwood
CF D Ford
RF H Powell
DH G Adams
DH J Morales
RL B Rivera
LU- R Chiles
2B- R Wilfong
3B- L Wolfe
M G Mauch

NY 1978 AL
SP R Guidry
SP E Figueroa
SP D Tidrow
SP J Beattie
SP C Hunter
RP R Gossage
RP S Lyle
RS K Clay
C T Munson
1B C Chambliss
2B W Randolph
SS B Dent
3B G Nettles
LU L Piniella
CF M Rivers
RD R Jackson
DC- C Johnson
LU R White
SS- F Stanley
M1 B Martin
M2 D Howser
M3 B Lemon

OAK 1978 AL
SP M Keough
SP J Johnson
SR J Langford
SP P Broberg
SP S Renko
RP D Heaverlo
RP B Lacey
RP E Sosa
C J Essian
1B D Revering
2B M Edwards
SS M Guerrero
3B W Gross
LF M Page
OI M Dilone
RM- T Armas
DH- G Alexander
3B T Duncan
C1 J Newman
MR- J Wallis
M1 B Winkles
M2 J McKeon

SEA 1978 AL
SP P Mitchell
SP G Abbott
SP R Honeycutt
SP J Colborn
SP B McLaughlin
RP E Romo
RS T House
RP S Rawley
RP J Todd
C B Stinson
1B D Meyer
2B J Cruz
SS C Reynolds
3B B Stein
LD B Bochte
CF R Jones
RF L Roberts
UO J Hale
UI- L Milbourne
DL- L Stanton
M D Johnson

TEX 1978 AL
SP J Matlack
SP F Jenkins
SP D Alexander
SP D Medich
SP D Ellis
RS S Comer
RP R Cleveland
RP L Barker
C J Sundberg
1B M Hargrove
2B B Wills
SS B Campaneris
3S T Harrah
LF A Oliver
CF J Beniquez
RF B Bonds
OF R Zisk
3U- K Bevacqua
1B- M Jorgensen
M1 B Hunter
M2 P Corrales

TOR 1978 AL
SP J Jefferson
SP T Underwood
SP J Clancy
SP J Garvin
SR B Moore
RP D Lemanczyk
RP M Willis
RP T Murphy
RP J Coleman
C - R Cerone
1B J Mayberry
2B D McKay
SS L Gomez
3B R Howell
OI- O Velez
CF R Bosetti
RU B Bailor
DH R Carty
C - A Ashby
OI- W Upshaw
M R Hartsfield

ATL 1979 NL
SP P Niekro
SP E Solomon
SP R Matula
SP T Brizzolara
SP M Mahler
RP G Garber
RP J McLaughlin
RP A Devine
RP C Skok
C - B Benedict
1C D Murphy
2B G Hubbard
SS P Frias
31 B Horner
LF J Burroughs
CF R Office
RF G Matthews
UT M Lum
LM B Bonnell
32 J Royster
C - J Nolan
M B Cox

CHI 1979 NL
SP R Reuschel
SR L McGlothen
SP D Lamp
SP M Krukow
SP K Holtzman
RP B Sutter
RP D Tidrow
RP W Hernandez
RP D Moore
C B Foote
1B B Buckner
2B T Sizemore
SS I DeJesus
3B S Ontiveros
LF D Kingman
CF J Martin
RO S Thompson
OI L Biittner
2U- S Dillard
OI- M Vail
M1 H Franks
M2 J Amalfitano

CIN 1979 NL
SP T Seaver
SP M LaCoss
SP F Norman
SP B Bonham
SP P Moskau
RS T Hume
RP D Bair
RP D Tomlin
C J Bench
1B D Driessen
2B J Morgan
SS D Concepcion
3B R Knight
LF G Foster
CF C Geronimo
RF- K Griffey
OI D Collins

2U- J Kennedy
M J McNamara

HOU 1979 NL
SP J Richard
SP J Niekro
SR J Andujar
SP K Forsch
SR R Williams
CL J Sambito
RS R Niemann
C A Ashby
1M C Cedeno
2B R Landestoy
SS C Reynolds
3B E Cabell
LF J Cruz
MR T Puhl
RU J Leonard
23 A Howe
OF- D Walling
M B Virdon

LA 1979 NL
SP R Sutcliffe
SP D Sutton
SP B Hooton
SR J Reuss
RS C Hough
RP D Patterson
C S Yeager
1B S Garvey
2B D Lopes
SS B Russell
3B R Cey
LF D Baker
CF D Thomas
MR G Thomasson
CR J Ferguson
UO- V Joshua
UI- T Martinez
M T Lasorda

MON 1979 NL
SP S Rogers
SP B Lee
SR S Sanderson
SR D Schatzeder
SP R Grimsley
RS D Palmer
RP E Sosa
RP S Bahnsen
RS R May
C G Carter
1B T Perez
2S R Scott
SS C Speier
3B L Parrish
LF W Cromartie
CF A Dawson
RF E Valentine
UT- T Hutton
UO- J White
M D Williams

NY 1979 NL
SP C Swan
SP P Falcone
SP K Kobel
RS N Allen
RP D Murray
RS A Hassler
RP E Glynn
C J Stearns
1B W Montanez
2B D Flynn
SS F Taveras
3B R Hebner
LF S Henderson
CF L Mazzilli
RL J Youngblood
UT- E Kranepool
OI- E Maddox
M J Torre

PHI 1979 NL
SP S Carlton
SP R Lerch
SP N Espinosa
SP D Ruthven
SP L Christenson
RP R Reed
RP T McGraw
RP R Eastwick
RP K Saucier
C B Boone
1B P Rose
2B M Trillo
SS L Bowa
3B M Schmidt
LF G Luzinski
CF G Maddox
RF B McBride
UO G Gross
OI- D Unser
M1 D Ozark
M2 D Green

PIT 1979 NL
SP B Blyleven
SP J Candelaria
SP B Kison
SP D Robinson
SR J Bibby
RP K Tekulve
RP E Romo
RP J Rooker
RP G Jackson
C E Ott
1B W Stargell
2B R Stennett
SS T Foli
3B- B Madlock
LF B Robinson
CF O Moreno
RF D Parker
23 P Garner
L1 J Milner
UT- L Lacy
M C Tanner

STL 1979 NL
SP P Vuckovich
SP B Forsch
SP S Martinez
SP J Denny
SP J Fulgham
RP M Littell
RS R Thomas
RP W McEnaney
RP D Knowles
C T Simmons
1B K Hernandez
2B K Oberkfell
SS G Templeton
3B K Reitz
LF L Brock
CF T Scott
RF G Hendrick
LO J Mumphrey
M K Boyer

SD 1979 NL
SP R Jones
SP G Perry
SR B Shirley
SR E Rasmussen
SR B Owchinko
RS J D'Acquisto
RP R Fingers
RS S Mura
RP M Lee
C - B Fahey
C1 G Tenace
2B F Gonzalez
SS O Smith
3B- P Dade
LF J Turner
MU G Richards
RF D Winfield
2S B Almon
3U K Bevacqua
UT D Briggs
M R Craig

SF 1979 NL
SP V Blue
SP B Knepper
SP J Montefusco
SR E Halicki
SP J Curtis
RP G Lavelle
RS P Nastu
RP E Whitson
RP T Griffin
C - D Littlejohn
1U M Ivie
2B- J Strain
SS J LeMaster
3B D Evans
ML L Herndon
CF B North
RF J Clark
1B W McCovey
LF T Whitfield
SS- R Metzger
M1 J Altobelli
M2 D Bristol

BAL 1979 AL
SP D Martinez
SP M Flanagan
SP S Stone
SP S McGregor
SP J Palmer
RP S Stewart
CL D Stanhouse
RP T Martinez
RP T Stoddard
C R Dempsey
1B E Murray
23 R Dauer
SS K Garcia
3B D DeCinces
LF G Roenicke
CF A Bumbry
RF K Singleton
DH L May
SS M Belanger
UT J Lowenstein
M E Weaver

BOS 1979 AL
SP M Torrez
SP D Eckersley
SR B Stanley
SP S Renko
SP C Rainey
RP D Drago
RP T Burgmeier
RP B Campbell
C G Allenson
1D- B Watson
2B- J Remy
SS R Burleson
3B B Hobson
LF J Rice
CF F Lynn
RF D Evans
UT C Yastrzemski
UC- C Fisk
M D Zimmer

CAL 1979 AL
SP D Frost
SP N Ryan
SR J Barr
SP D Aase
RP M Clear
RP D LaRoche
RP M Barlow
C B Downing
1B R Carew
2B B Grich
SS- B Campaneris
3B C Lansford
LF- J Rudi
CF R Miller
RF D Ford
OI D Baylor
UT W Aikens
SS- J Anderson
M J Fregosi

CHI 1979 AL
SP K Kravec
SP R Wortham
SP R Baumgarten
SR S Trout
RS R Scarbery
RS M Proly
CL E Farmer
RS F Howard
C - M May
1B M Squires
UT A Bannister
SS G Pryor
3B- K Bell
UO- R Torres
CF C Lemon
RF C Washington
D2 J Orta
LU R Garr
1D L Johnson
LU- J Moore
M1 D Kessinger
M2 T LaRussa

CLE 1979 AL
SP R Wise
SP R Waits
SP M Paxton
SR L Barker
RS D Spillner
RP S Monge
RP V Cruz
C G Alexander
1B A Thornton
2B D Kuiper
SS T Veryzer
3B T Harrah
UO J Norris
CF R Manning
RF B Bonds
DH- C Johnson
L1 M Hargrove
M1 J Torborg
M2 D Garcia

DET 1979 AL
SP J Morris
SP M Wilcox
SR J Billingham
SR P Underwood
SP D Petry
RP A Lopez
RP D Rozema
RP J Hiller
RP D Tobik
C L Parrish
1B J Thompson
2B L Whitaker
SS A Trammell
3B A Rodriguez
LF S Kemp
CF R LeFlore
RO J Morales
DH- R Staub
UO- L Jones
RU- C Summers
IC- J Wockenfuss
M1 L Moss
M2 D Tracewski
M3 S Anderson

KC 1979 AL
SP P Splittorff
SP D Leonard
SP L Gura
SP R Gale
RP A Hrabosky
RP E Rodriguez
C D Porter
1B P LaCock
2B F White
SS F Patek
3B G Brett
LF W Wilson
CF A Otis
RF A Cowens
DH H McRae
UI U Washington
1C- J Wathan
M W Herzog

MIL 1979 AL
SP M Caldwell
SP L Sorensen
SP J Slaton
SP B Travers
SP M Haas
RP J Augustine
RP R Cleveland
RP B McClure
RP B Galasso
C C Moore
1B C Cooper
2B P Molitor
SS R Yount
3B S Bando
LU B Oglivie
CF G Thomas
RF S Lezcano
DL- D Davis
UI- D Money
M G Bamberger

MIN 1979 AL
SP J Koosman
SP D Goltz
SP G Zahn
SP P Hartzell
SP R Erickson
RP M Marshall
RS P Redfern
RP M Bacsik
C B Wynegar
1B R Jackson
2B R Wilfong
SS R Smalley
3B J Castino
LR B Rivera
ML K Landreaux
RF H Powell
DH- J Morales
OF G Adams
3U- M Cubbage
UO- D Edwards
OF- W Norwood
M G Mauch

NY 1979 AL
SP T John
SP R Guidry
SP L Tiant
SP E Figueroa
SP C Hunter
RP R Davis
RS K Clay
CL R Gossage
RS D Hood
C T Munson
1B C Chambliss
2B W Randolph
SS B Dent
3B G Nettles
LU L Piniella
CF- B Murcer
RF R Jackson
DU J Spencer
UT- R White
M1 B Lemon
M2 B Martin

OAK 1979 AL
SP R Langford
SP S McCatty
SP M Keough
SR M Norris
SR C Minetto
RP B Kingman
RP D Heaverlo
RS D Hamilton
RP J Todd
C1 J Newman
1B D Revering
2B M Edwards
SS R Picciolo
3B W Gross
LM- R Henderson
CF D Murphy
RO L Murray
DH M Page
CU J Essian
M J Marshall

SEA 1979 AL
SP M Parrott
SP R Honeycutt
SP F Bannister
SP O Jones
SP G Abbott
RS B McLaughlin
RP J Montague
RS R Dressler
RP S Rawley
C L Cox
1B B Bochte
2B J Cruz
SS M Mendoza
3U D Meyer
OF L Roberts
CF R Jones
RO J Simpson
DH W Horton
S2 L Milbourne
OI T Paciorek
3B- B Stein
C - B Stinson
M D Johnson

TEX 1979 AL
SP F Jenkins
SP S Comer
SR D Medich
SP D Alexander
RP J Kern
RP S Lyle
RP D Rajsich
C J Sundberg
1U P Putnam
2B B Wills
SS N Norman
3B B Bell
LU B Sample
ML A Oliver
RF R Zisk
D1 J Ellis
UO J Grubb
1U- M Jorgensen
M P Corrales

TOR 1979 AL
SP T Underwood
SP P Huffman
SP D Lemanczyk
SR B Moore
SP D Stieb
RS J Jefferson
RP D Freisleben
RP T Buskey
C R Cerone
1B J Mayberry
2B- D Ainge
SS A Griffin
3B R Howell
LF A Woods
CF R Bosetti
RF B Bailor
DH R Carty
OI O Velez
M R Hartsfield

ATL 1980 NL
SP P Niekro
SP D Alexander
SP T Boggs
SP R Matula
SP L McWilliams
RP R Camp
RP G Garber
RP P Hanna
RP A Hrabosky
C B Benedict
1B C Chambliss
2B G Hubbard
SS L Gomez
3B B Horner
LU J Burroughs
CF D Murphy
RF G Matthews
IO J Royster
UO- B Asselstine
S3- L Blanks
UT- M Lum
M B Cox

CHI 1980 NL
SP R Reuschel
SP M Krukow
SP D Lamp
SR L McGlothen
RP B Sutter
RP B Caudill
RP D Tidrow
RS W Hernandez
C T Blackwell
1L B Buckner
2B M Tyson
SS I DeJesus
3B L Randle
LF- D Kingman
MR J Martin
RU M Vail
UT L Biittner
32 S Dillard
UO J Figueroa
23 M Kelleher
RU S Thompson
M1 P Gomez
M2 J Amalfitano

CIN 1980 NL
SP F Pastore
SP C Leibrandt
SP M LaCoss
SP T Seaver
SR P Moskau
RS M Soto
RP T Hume
RS J Price
RP D Bair
C J Bench
1B D Driessen
2B J Kennedy
SS D Concepcion
3B R Knight
LF G Foster
CF D Collins
RF K Griffey
CF C Geronimo
2B R Oester
M J McNamara

HOU 1980 NL
SP J Niekro
SP N Ryan
SP K Forsch
SP V Ruhle
SR J Andujar
RP J Richard
RP D Smith
RP J Sambito
RP F LaCorte
C A Ashby
1I A Howe
2B J Morgan
SS C Reynolds
3B E Cabell
LF J Cruz
CF C Cedeno
RF T Puhl
2S R Landestoy
1U D Walling
1U- D Bergman
RU- J Leonard
M B Virdon

LA 1980 NL
SP J Reuss
SP B Welch
SP D Sutton
SP B Hooton
SP D Goltz
RS R Sutcliffe
RP B Castillo
RP S Howe
RP J Beckwith
C - S Yeager
1B S Garvey
2B D Lopes
SS B Russell
3B R Cey
LF D Baker
CF R Law
RF- R Smith
RU J Johnstone
UT D Thomas
UO- R Monday
M T Lasorda

MON 1980 NL
SP S Rogers
SP S Sanderson
SP B Gullickson
SP D Palmer
SP B Lee
RP C Lea
RP E Sosa
RS F Norman
RP W Fryman
C G Carter
1B W Cromartie
2B R Scott
SS C Speier
3B L Parrish
LF R LeFlore
CF A Dawson
RO R Office
LU J White
IF- T Bernazard
RF- E Valentine
M D Williams

NY 1980 NL
SP R Burris
SP P Zachry
SR M Bomback
SR P Falcone
SP C Swan
RP T Hausman
CL N Allen
RP J Reardon
RP E Glynn
C A Trevino
1M L Mazzilli
2B D Flynn
SS F Taveras
3B E Maddox
LF S Henderson
RM J Youngblood
RL- C Washington
1O M Jorgensen
MU- J Morales
C - J Stearns
M J Torre

PHI 1980 NL
SP S Carlton
SP D Ruthven
SP B Walk
SP R Lerch
CL T McGraw
RP R Reed
RP D Noles
RP K Saucier
C B Boone
1B P Rose
2B M Trillo
SS L Bowa
3B M Schmidt
LF G Luzinski
CF G Maddox
RF B McBride
OI G Gross
LO L Smith
UT- D Unser
M D Green

PIT 1980 NL
SP J Bibby
SP J Candelaria
SP B Blyleven
SP D Robinson
SP R Rhoden
RP E Romo
RP K Tekulve
RS E Solomon
RP G Jackson
C E Ott
1U J Milner
2B P Garner
SS T Foli
3B B Madlock
LR M Easler
CF O Moreno
RF D Parker
LF L Lacy
UT B Robinson
3S- D Berra
M C Tanner

STL 1980 NL
SP P Vuckovich
SP B Forsch
SP B Sykes
SP S Martinez
RS J Kaat
RS D Hood
RP J Littlefield
RP J Urrea
C T Simmons
1B K Hernandez
2B K Oberkfell
SS G Templeton
3B K Reitz
LU- B Bonds
CF T Scott
RF G Hendrick
UT D Iorg
OI- L Durham
OC- T Kennedy
M1 K Boyer
M2 J Krol
M3 W Herzog
M4 R Schoendienst

SD 1980 NL
SP J Curtis
SR S Mura
SP R Jones
SP R Wise
SR G Lucas
RS B Shirley
RP R Fingers
RS E Rasmussen
RP D Kinney
C G Tenace
1B W Montanez
2B D Cash
SS O Smith
3B- A Rodriguez
LF G Richards
CF J Mumphrey
RF D Winfield
C - B Fahey
23- T Flannery
OF- J Turner
M J Coleman

SF 1980 NL
SP V Blue
SP B Knepper
SP E Whitson
SP J Montefusco
SP A Ripley
RP G Minton
RP G Lavelle
RP T Griffin
RP A Holland
C M May
1B- M Ivie
2B R Stennett
SS J LeMaster
3B D Evans
UO L Herndon
CF B North
RF J Clark
LF T Whitfield
OI- J Wohlford
M D Bristol

BAL 1980 AL
SP S McGregor
SP M Flanagan
SP S Stone
SP J Palmer
SR D Martinez
RP S Stewart
CL T Stoddard
RP T Martinez
RP D Ford
C R Dempsey
1B E Murray
2B R Dauer
SS M Belanger
3B D DeCinces
LR G Roenicke
CF A Bumbry
RF K Singleton
DU- T Crowley
SS K Garcia
LF J Lowenstein
C - D Graham
OF- P Kelly
M E Weaver

BOS 1980 AL
SP M Torrez
SP D Eckersley
SP S Renko
RS B Stanley
RS D Drago
RP T Burgmeier
C C Fisk
1B T Perez
2B D Stapleton
SS R Burleson
3B G Hoffman
LF J Rice
CF F Lynn
RF D Evans
OI C Yastrzemski
OI- J Dwyer
3D- B Hobson
M1 D Zimmer
M2 J Pesky

CAL 1980 AL
SP F Tanana
SR D Aase
SP A Martinez
SR C Knapp
RS D LaRoche
RP M Clear
RP A Hassler
RP J Montague
C - T Donohue

1U R Carew
2B B Grich
SS- F Patek
3B C Lansford
LF J Rudi
CF R Miller
RM L Harlow
UT J Thompson
OF- D Baylor
M J Fregosi

CHI 1980 AL
SP B Burns
SP S Trout
SP R Dotson
SP R Baumgarten
SR L Hoyt
RP M Proly
RP E Farmer
RS R Wortham
C B Kimm
1B M Squires
2B J Morrison
SS- T Cruz
3B- K Bell
OF W Nordhagen
CF C Lemon
RF H Baines
1D L Johnson
UT B Molinaro
S3 G Pryor
M T LaRussa

CLE 1980 AL
SP L Barker
SP R Waits
SP D Spillner
SP W Garland
SR B Owchinko
RP J Denny
RP S Monge
RP V Cruz
RP M Stanton
C R Hassey
1B M Hargrove
2B- J Brohamer
SS T Veryzer
3B T Harrah
LO M Dilone
CF R Manning
RF J Orta
LD J Charboneau
S2 J Dybzinski
2R- A Bannister
M D Garcia

DET 1980 AL
SP J Morris
SP M Wilcox
SP D Schatzeder
SP D Petry
RS D Rozema
RP A Lopez
RS P Underwood
C L Parrish
13 R Hebner
2B L Whitaker
SS A Trammell
3B T Brookens
LD S Kemp
MU R Peters
RF A Cowens
DO C Summers
UT J Wockenfuss
1U- T Corcoran
M S Anderson

KC 1980 AL
SP L Gura
SP D Leonard
SP P Splittorff
SP R Gale
SR R Martin
RP D Quisenberry
RP M Pattin
CD D Porter
1B W Aikens
2B F White
SS U Washington
3B G Brett
LM W Wilson
CF A Otis
RF C Hurdle
DH H McRae
1B P LaCock
CO J Wathan
M J Frey

MIL 1980 AL
SP M Haas
SP M Caldwell
SP L Sorensen
SP B Travers
RS R Cleveland
RS B McClure
RP B Castro
RP J Augustine
C C Moore
1B C Cooper
2B P Molitor
SS R Yount
32 J Gantner
LF B Oglivie
CF G Thomas
RF S Lezcano
DR D Davis
3U- D Money
M1 B Rodgers
M2 G Bamberger
M3 B Rodgers

MIN 1980 AL
SP J Koosman
SP G Zahn
SP R Erickson
SP D Jackson
SP P Redfern
RP D Corbett
RP J Verhoeven
C B Wynegar
1B R Jackson
2B R Wilfong
SS R Smalley
3B J Castino
LM R Sofield
ML K Landreaux
RF H Powell
DH J Morales
DH G Adams
13 M Cubbage
2S P Mackanin
ML- D Edwards
M1 G Mauch
M2 J Goryl

NY 1980 AL
SP T John
SP R Guidry
SR T Underwood
SR R May
SP L Tiant
RP R Davis
RP R Gossage
RP D Bird
C R Cerone
1B B Watson
2B W Randolph
SS B Dent
3B- G Nettles
LF L Piniella
MO B Brown
RD R Jackson
D3- E Soderholm
OF B Murcer
1B- J Spencer
CF- R Jones
M D Howser

OAK 1980 AL
SP R Langford
SP M Norris
SP M Keough
SP S McCatty
SP B Kingman
RP B Lacey
C - J Essian
1B D Revering
23 D McKay
SS M Guerrero
3B W Gross
LF R Henderson
CF D Murphy
RF T Armas
DH M Page
IC J Newman
CD- M Heath
S2- R Picciolo
M B Martin

SEA 1980 AL
SP F Bannister
SP G Abbott
SP R Honeycutt
SP J Beattie
SR R Dressler
RP S Rawley
RP B McLaughlin
RP D Heaverlo
RP D Roberts
C L Cox
1B B Bochte
2B J Cruz
SS M Mendoza
3B- T Cox
LF D Meyer
OI J Simpson
RO L Roberts
DH- W Horton
S3 J Anderson
UI L Milbourne
OI T Paciorek
M1 D Johnson
M2 M Wills

TEX 1980 AL
SP J Matlack
SP D Medich
SP F Jenkins
SP G Perry
RP D Darwin
RP S Lyle
RP J Kern
C J Sundberg
1B P Putnam
2B B Wills
SS P Frias
3B B Bell
LF A Oliver
CF M Rivers
OI J Norris
DR R Zisk
RU J Grubb
IO D Roberts
D1 R Staub
SS- B Harrelson
UO B Sample
M P Corrales

TOR 1980 AL
SP J Clancy
SP D Stieb
SR P Mirabella
SR J Jefferson
RS J McLaughlin
RP J Garvin
RP T Buskey
RP B Moore
C E Whitt
1B J Mayberry
2B D Garcia
SS A Griffin
3B R Howell
UT B Bailor
UO B Bonnell
RF L Moseby
DH O Velez
LF A Woods
C - B Davis
M B Mattick

ATL 1981 NL
SP G Perry
SP T Boggs
SP P Niekro
SR R Mahler
SR J Montefusco
RP R Camp
RP G Garber
RP P Hanna
RP A Hrabosky
C B Benedict
1B C Chambliss
2B G Hubbard
SS R Ramirez
3B B Horner
LF R Linares
CF D Murphy
RF C Washington
IF- J Royster
OF- B Asselstine
IC- B Pocoroba
M B Cox

CHI 1981 NL
SP M Krukow
SR R Martz
SP R Reuschel
SR K Kravec
SP D Bird
RP D Tidrow
RS B Caudill
RP L Smith
RS L McGlothen
C - J Davis
1B B Buckner
2U- M Tyson
SS I DeJesus
3B K Reitz
LF S Henderson
MO J Morales
RF L Durham
C - T Blackwell
OI- S Thompson
M J Amalfitano

CIN 1981 NL
SP M Soto
SP T Seaver
SP F Pastore
SP B Berenyi
SP M LaCoss
RP T Hume
RP J Price
RP P Moskau
RP D Bair
C J Nolan
1B D Driessen
2B R Oester
SS D Concepcion
3B R Knight
LF G Foster
CF K Griffey
RF D Collins
RU S Mejias
C - M O'Berry
M J McNamara

HOU 1981 NL
SP J Niekro
SP D Sutton
SP B Knepper
SP N Ryan
SP V Ruhle
RP D Smith
RP J Sambito
RP F LaCorte
C A Ashby
1M C Cedeno
2U- J Pittman
SS C Reynolds
3B A Howe
LF J Cruz
CF- T Scott
RU T Puhl
UT- D Walling
RU- G Woods
M B Virdon

LA 1981 NL
SP F Valenzuela
SP J Reuss
SP B Hooton
SP B Welch
RS D Goltz
RP S Howe
RP B Castillo
RP D Stewart
C M Scioscia
1B S Garvey
2B- D Lopes
SS B Russell
3B R Cey
LF D Baker
CF K Landreaux
RU P Guerrero
UT D Thomas
OI- J Johnstone
RU R Monday
M T Lasorda

MON 1981 NL
SP S Rogers
SP B Gullickson
SP S Sanderson
SP R Burris
RS B Lee
RP S Bahnsen
RP W Fryman
RP J Reardon
C G Carter
1R W Cromartie
2B R Scott
SS C Speier
3B L Parrish
LF T Raines
CF A Dawson
UO- J White
UT T Wallach
M1 D Williams
M2 J Fanning

NY 1981 NL
SP P Zachry
SP M Scott
SP E Lynch
SP G Harris
RS P Falcone
RP N Allen
RP D Miller
RP R Searage
C J Stearns
1L D Kingman
2B D Flynn
SS F Taveras
3B H Brooks
LM L Mazzilli
MU M Wilson
RF- E Valentine
U1 M Cubbage
UT M Jorgensen
1U R Staub
C - A Trevino
M J Torre

PHI 1981 NL
SP S Carlton
SP D Ruthven
SP L Christenson
SP N Espinosa
RP S Lyle
RP R Reed
RP M Proly
RP T McGraw
C B Boone
1B P Rose
2B M Trillo
SS L Bowa
3B M Schmidt
LF G Matthews
CF G Maddox
RF- B McBride
UO G Gross
C - K Moreland
UO- L Smith
UT- D Unser
M D Green

PIT 1981 NL
SP R Rhoden
SP E Solomon
SP J Bibby
SP P Perez
RS R Scurry
RP K Tekulve
RP E Romo
RP D Robinson
C T Pena
1B J Thompson
2B- P Garner
SS T Foli
3B B Madlock
LF M Easler
CF O Moreno
RF D Parker
3S D Berra
OI L Lacy
C - S Nicosia
M C Tanner

STL 1981 NL
SP L Sorensen
SP B Forsch
SP J Martin
SP S Martinez
SR B Shirley
RP B Sutter
RP J Kaat
RP M Littell
RP B Sykes
C - D Porter
1B K Hernandez
2B T Herr
SS G Templeton
3B K Oberkfell
LU D Iorg
RM G Hendrick
OF S Lezcano
LR T Landrum
CU- G Tenace
M W Herzog

SD 1981 NL
SP J Eichelberger
SP S Mura
SP C Welsh
SP R Wise
SR T Lollar
RP G Lucas
RS J Curtis
RP J Littlefield
RP D Boone
C T Kennedy
1B B Perkins
2B J Bonilla
SS O Smith
3B L Salazar
LF G Richards
CF R Jones
RF J Lefebvre
1U R Bass
RU- D Edwards
UI- B Evans
M F Howard

SF 1981 NL
SP D Alexander
SP T Griffin
SP V Blue
SP E Whitson
SP A Ripley
RP A Holland
RP G Minton
RP F Breining
RP G Lavelle
C M May
1U E Cabell
2B J Morgan
SS J LeMaster
3B D Evans
LF L Herndon
CF J Martin
RF J Clark
1U- D Bergman
M F Robinson

BAL 1981 AL
SP D Martinez
SP S McGregor
SP J Palmer
SP M Flanagan
RP S Stewart
RP T Martinez
RP T Stoddard
RP D Ford
C R Dempsey
1B E Murray
2B R Dauer
SS M Belanger
3B D DeCinces
LF J Lowenstein
CF A Bumbry
RL G Roenicke
DU T Crowley
LR J Dwyer
RD K Singleton
CU- D Graham
S2- L Sakata
M E Weaver

BOS 1981 AL
SP D Eckersley
SP F Tanana
SP M Torrez
SP J Tudor
SP B Ojeda
RP B Stanley
RP M Clear
RP T Burgmeier
RP B Campbell
C - R Gedman
1D T Perez
2B J Remy
SS G Hoffman
3B C Lansford
LF J Rice
CF R Miller
RF D Evans
D1 C Yastrzemski
UI D Stapleton
M R Houk

CAL 1981 AL
SP G Zahn
SP K Forsch
SP M Witt
SP S Renko
RP A Hassler
RS J Jefferson
RP D Aase
RP L Sanchez
C E Ott
1B R Carew
2B B Grich
SS R Burleson
3B B Hobson
LC B Downing
CF F Lynn
RF D Ford
DH D Baylor
ML- J Beniquez
3B- B Campaneris
M1 J Fregosi
M2 G Mauch

CHI 1981 AL
SP B Burns
SP R Dotson
SR D Lamp
SP S Trout
SP R Baumgarten
RP L Hoyt
RP E Farmer
RP K Hickey
C C Fisk
1B M Squires
2B T Bernazard
SS B Almon
3B J Morrison
LF R LeFlore
CF C Lemon
RF H Baines
DH G Luzinski
UO R Kuntz
RL W Nordhagen
M T LaRussa

CLE 1981 AL
SP B Blyleven
SP L Barker
SP J Denny
SP R Waits
RS D Spillner
RP S Monge
RP M Stanton
C - R Hassey
1B M Hargrove
2B D Kuiper
SS T Veryzer
3B T Harrah
LF M Dilone
CF R Manning
RF J Orta
DH A Thornton
UT A Bannister
C B Diaz
M D Garcia

DET 1981 AL
SP J Morris
SP M Wilcox
SP D Petry
SP D Schatzeder
RS D Rozema
RP A Lopez
CL K Saucier
RP D Tobik
C L Parrish
1B R Hebner
2B L Whitaker
SS A Trammell
3B T Brookens
LF S Kemp
CF A Cowens
UO K Gibson
D1 J Wockenfuss
RU L Jones
3I- M Kelleher
1R- R Leach
MD- R Peters
DR- C Summers
M S Anderson

KC 1981 AL
SP D Leonard
SP L Gura
SP R Gale
SP P Splittorff
SP M Jones
RP D Quisenberry
RP R Martin
RP K Brett
C J Wathan
1B W Aikens
2B F White
SS U Washington
3B G Brett
LF W Wilson
CF A Otis
RF- C Geronimo
DH H McRae
M1 J Frey
M2 D Howser

MIL 1981 AL
SP P Vuckovich
SP M Caldwell
SP M Haas
SP J Slaton
SP R Lerch
RP R Fingers
RP R Cleveland
RP J Easterly
RP J Augustine
C T Simmons
1B C Cooper
2B J Gantner
SS R Yount
3B- D Money
LF B Oglivie
OF G Thomas
RF- M Brouhard
DH- L Hisle
3U R Howell
MD- P Molitor
M B Rodgers

MIN 1981 AL
SP A Williams
SP P Redfern
SP F Arroyo
SP J Koosman
SP R Erickson
RP D Corbett
RP B Havens
RP D Cooper
RP J Verhoeven
C - S Butera
1U- D Goodwin
2B R Wilfong
SD- R Smalley
3B J Castino
LU G Ward
CF M Hatcher
RF D Engle
DH G Adams
UI P Mackanin
RU H Powell
1U- R Jackson
M1 J Goryl
M2 B Gardner

NY 1981 AL
SP R May
SP T John
SP R Guidry
SP D Righetti
SP R Reuschel
RP R Davis
CL R Gossage
RP D LaRoche
C R Cerone
1B- B Watson
2B W Randolph
SS B Dent
3B G Nettles
LF D Winfield
CF J Mumphrey
RD R Jackson
DU- B Murcer
OF O Gamble
SI- L Milbourne
OF- L Piniella
M1 G Michael
M2 B Lemon

OAK 1981 AL
SP R Langford
SP S McCatty
SP M Norris
SP M Keough
SP B Kingman
RP J Jones
RP B Owchinko
C M Heath
1B- J Spencer
2B- S Babitt
SS R Picciolo
3B W Gross
LF R Henderson
CF D Murphy
RF T Armas
DH C Johnson
32 D McKay
C1 J Newman
SS F Stanley
M B Martin

SEA 1981 AL
SP G Abbott
SP F Bannister
SP K Clay
SR M Parrott
SP J Gleaton
RS B Clark
SP S Rawley
RP L Andersen
RP J Beattie
C J Narron
1B B Bochte
2B J Cruz
SS J Anderson
32 L Randle
LF T Paciorek
CF J Simpson
RF J Burroughs
DH R Zisk
UT G Gray
3U D Meyer
C - B Bulling
MR- D Henderson
M1 M Wills
M2 R Lachemann

TEX 1981 AL
SP D Darwin
SP D Medich
SP R Honeycutt
SP F Jenkins
SP J Matlack
RP S Comer
RS C Hough
RP D Schmidt
C J Sundberg
1B P Putnam
2B B Wills
SS M Mendoza
3B B Bell
LF B Sample
CF M Rivers
RL L Roberts
DH A Oliver
RF J Grubb
M D Zimmer

TOR 1981 AL
SP D Stieb
SR L Leal
SP J Clancy
SP J Todd
SP M Bomback
RP J Berenguer
RP J McLaughlin
RP R Jackson
RP J Garvin
C E Whitt
1B J Mayberry
2B D Garcia
SS A Griffin
3B D Ainge
LF A Woods
CF L Moseby
RM B Bonnell
DH O Velez
2I G Iorg
OF- G Bell
UT- W Upshaw
M B Mattick

ATL 1982 NL
SP P Niekro
SP R Mahler
SR R Camp
SP B Walk
RP S Bedrosian
RP G Garber
C B Benedict
1B C Chambliss
2B G Hubbard
SS R Ramirez
3B B Horner
LU- R Linares
ML D Murphy
RF C Washington
3U J Royster
CF- B Butler
OF- L Whisenton
M J Torre

CHI 1982 NL
SP F Jenkins
SP D Bird
SP D Noles
SP R Martz
SP A Ripley
RS L Smith
RP D Tidrow
RP B Campbell
RP W Hernandez
C J Davis
1B B Buckner
2B B Wills
SS L Bowa
3B R Sandberg
OC K Moreland
ML G Woods
RM L Durham
RL J Johnstone
2S J Kennedy
LF- S Henderson
M L Elia

CIN 1982 NL
SP M Soto
SP B Berenyi
SP F Pastore
SR B Shirley
SP T Seaver
RS C Leibrandt
RS G Harris
CL T Hume
RP J Kern
C A Trevino
1B D Driessen
2B R Oester
SS D Concepcion
3B J Bench
LR E Milner
CF C Cedeno
RF P Householder
OI- L Biittner
3U- W Krenchicki
UO- D Walker
M1 J McNamara
M2 R Nixon

HOU 1982 NL
SP J Niekro
SP N Ryan
SP D Sutton
SP B Knepper
SR V Ruhle
RS M LaCoss
RP F LaCorte
RP D Smith
C A Ashby
13 R Knight
2B P Garner
SS D Thon
31 A Howe
LF J Cruz
CF T Scott
RF T Puhl
OI- D Heep
OI- D Walling
M1 B Virdon
M2 B Lillis

LA 1982 NL
SP F Valenzuela
SP J Reuss
SP B Welch
SP B Hooton
RS D Stewart
RP S Howe
RP T Forster
RP T Niedenfuer
C M Scioscia
1B S Garvey
2B S Sax
SS B Russell
3B R Cey
LF D Baker
CF K Landreaux
RM P Guerrero
OI R Monday
UO R Roenicke
OF- J Orta
C - S Yeager
M T Lasorda

MON 1982 NL
SP S Rogers
SP B Gullickson
SP S Sanderson
SP C Lea
SR R Burris
RP J Reardon
RP W Fryman
RP B Smith
C G Carter
1B A Oliver
2B- D Flynn
SS C Speier
3B T Wallach
LF T Raines
CF A Dawson
RF W Cromartie
M J Fanning

NY 1982 NL
SR P Falcone
SR C Puleo
SR C Swan
SR M Scott
SR P Zachry
RS E Lynch
RP J Orosco
RP R Jones
CL N Allen
C J Stearns
1B D Kingman
2B- W Backman
SS R Gardenhire
3B H Brooks
LF G Foster
CF M Wilson
RU E Valentine
S2 B Bailor
UT M Jorgensen
OI R Staub
M G Bamberger

PHI 1982 NL
SP S Carlton
SP L Christenson
SP M Krukow
SP D Ruthven
RP R Reed
RP E Farmer
RP S Monge
C B Diaz
1B P Rose
2B M Trillo
SS I DeJesus
3B M Schmidt
LF G Matthews
CF G Maddox
RF G Vukovich
UO G Gross
MR B Dernier
M P Corrales

PIT 1982 NL
SP R Rhoden
SP D Robinson
SP J Candelaria
SR M Sarmiento
SP L McWilliams
RP K Tekulve
RP R Scurry
RP E Romo
C T Pena
1B J Thompson
2B J Ray
SS D Berra
3B B Madlock
LF M Easler
CF O Moreno
RL L Lacy
M C Tanner

STL 1982 NL
SP J Andujar
SP B Forsch
SP S Mura
SR D LaPoint
SP J Stuper
RP B Sutter
RP D Bair
RP J Kaat
RS J Martin
C D Porter
1B K Hernandez
2B T Herr
SS O Smith
3B K Oberkfell
LF L Smith
CF W McGee
RF G Hendrick
UT D Iorg
IO M Ramsey
M W Herzog

SD 1982 NL
SP T Lollar
SP J Montefusco
SP J Eichelberger
SP C Welsh
SP J Curtis
RS E Show
RP L DeLeon
RP G Lucas
RS D Dravecky
C T Kennedy
1B B Perkins
2B T Flannery
SS G Templeton
3B L Salazar
LF G Richards
CF R Jones
RF S Lezcano
UT J Lefebvre
M D Williams

SF 1982 NL
SP B Laskey
SP A Hammaker
SP R Gale
SP R Martin
RP G Minton
RS F Breining
RS A Holland
RS J Barr
C M May
1B R Smith
2B J Morgan
SS J LeMaster
31 D Evans
LU- J Leonard
CF C Davis
RF J Clark
1U D Bergman
U3 D Kuiper
LU- J Wohlford
3B- T O'Malley
M F Robinson

BAL 1982 AL
SP D Martinez
SP M Flanagan
SP J Palmer
SP S McGregor
RS S Stewart
RP T Martinez
RS S Davis
RP T Stoddard
C R Dempsey
1B E Murray
2B R Dauer
2S L Sakata
S3 C Ripken
LR G Roenicke
CF A Bumbry
RF D Ford
DH K Singleton
LF J Lowenstein
M E Weaver

BOS 1982 AL
SP D Eckersley
SP J Tudor
SP M Torrez
SP C Rainey
SP B Hurst
RP B Stanley
RP M Clear
RP T Burgmeier
RP L Aponte
C - G Allenson
1I D Stapleton
2B J Remy
SS G Hoffman
3B C Lansford
LF J Rice
CF R Miller
RF D Evans
DH C Yastrzemski
IO W Boggs
C - R Gedman
ML- R Nichols
M R Houk

CAL 1982 AL
SP G Zahn
SP K Forsch
SP M Witt
SP S Renko
SR B Kison
RP L Sanchez
RP A Hassler
RP D Corbett
RP D Aase
C B Boone
1B R Carew
2B B Grich
SS T Foli
3B D DeCinces
LF B Downing
CF F Lynn
RF R Jackson
DH D Baylor
UO J Beniquez
RO B Clark
M G Mauch

CHI 1982 AL
SP L Hoyt
SP R Dotson
SR D Lamp
SR J Koosman
SP B Burns
RP S Barojas
RP S Trout
RP K Hickey
RP C Escarrega
C C Fisk
1B M Squires
2B T Bernazard
SS B Almon
3B A Rodriguez
LF S Kemp
MU R Law
RF H Baines
DH G Luzinski
S3 V Law
1B T Paciorek
UO- J Hairston
CF- R LeFlore
M T LaRussa

CLE 1982 AL
SP L Barker
SP R Sutcliffe
SP L Sorensen
SP J Denny
SP R Waits
RP D Spillner
RS E Whitson
RP E Glynn
C R Hassey
1B M Hargrove
2B- J Perconte
SS M Fischlin
3B T Harrah
LF M Dilone
CF R Manning
RF V Hayes
DH A Thornton
UT A Bannister
2B- L Milbourne
M D Garcia

DET 1982 AL
SP J Morris
SP D Petry
SP M Wilcox
SP J Ujdur
SR P Underwood
RP D Tobik
RP E Sosa
RP D Rucker
C L Parrish
13 E Cabell
2B L Whitaker
SS A Trammell
3B T Brookens
LF L Herndon
CF- G Wilson
RU C Lemon
DH- M Ivie
1U- R Leach
DU- J Turner
M S Anderson

KC 1982 AL
SP L Gura
SP V Blue
SP P Splittorff
SP D Leonard
RP D Quisenberry
RP M Armstrong
RP D Hood
C J Wathan
1B W Aikens
2B F White
SS U Washington
3B G Brett
LF W Wilson
CF A Otis
RF J Martin
DH H McRae
M D Howser

MIL 1982 AL
SP M Caldwell
SP P Vuckovich
SP M Haas
SP B McClure
SP R Lerch
RS J Slaton
CL R Fingers
RP D Bernard
C T Simmons
1B C Cooper
2B J Gantner
SS R Yount
3B P Molitor
LF B Oglivie
CF G Thomas
RF C Moore
DH R Howell
DI- D Money
M1 B Rodgers
M2 H Kuenn

MIN 1982 AL
SR B Castillo
SP B Havens
SP A Williams
SP J O'Connor
SP F Viola
RP R Davis
RS T Felton
RP J Pacella
RP P Boris
C - T Laudner
1B K Hrbek
2B J Castino
SS R Washington
3B G Gaetti
LF G Ward
CF B Mitchell
RF T Brunansky
DH- R Johnson
SS- L Faedo
OI- M Hatcher
M B Gardner

NY 1982 AL
SP R Guidry
SP T John
SP D Righetti
SR S Rawley
SP M Morgan
CL R Gossage
RP G Frazier
RS R May
RP D LaRoche
C - R Cerone
1B- J Mayberry
2B W Randolph
S3 R Smalley
3B G Nettles
LF D Winfield
CF J Mumphrey
RF K Griffey
DR O Gamble
OI D Collins
DR L Piniella
M1 B Lemon
M2 G Michael
M3 C King

OAK 1982 AL
SP R Langford
SP M Keough
SP M Norris
SP S McCatty
SP B Kingman
RS T Underwood
RP B Owchinko
RP D Beard
C M Heath
UT D Meyer
2B D Lopes
SS F Stanley
3B W Gross
LF R Henderson
CF D Murphy
RF T Armas
DU- C Johnson
OF J Burroughs
M B Martin

SEA 1982 AL
SP F Bannister
SP G Perry
SP J Beattie
SP M Moore
SP G Nelson
CL B Caudill
RS B Clark
RP L Andersen
RP E Vande Berg
C - R Sweet
1B- G Gray
2B J Cruz
SS T Cruz
3B M Castillo
LU B Bochte
CF D Henderson
RF A Cowens
DH R Zisk
ML J Simpson
M R Lachemann

TEX 1982 AL
SP C Hough
SP F Tanana
SP R Honeycutt
SR J Matlack
SP D Medich
RS D Schmidt
RP S Comer
RP D Darwin
RP P Mirabella
C J Sundberg
1B D Hostetler
2B M Richardt
SS- M Wagner
3B B Bell
LF- B Sample
CF G Wright
RF L Parrish
DU L Johnson
OF J Grubb
2S- D Flynn
IO- B Stein
M1 D Zimmer
M2 D Johnson

TOR 1982 AL
SP D Stieb
SP J Clancy
SP L Leal
SP J Gott
RP D Murray
RP R Jackson
RP J McLaughlin
RP J Garvin
C E Whitt
1B W Upshaw
2B D Garcia
SS A Griffin
3B R Mulliniks
LM B Bonnell
CF L Moseby
RF J Barfield
DH- D Revering
3B G Iorg
RU H Powell
C - B Martinez
LF- A Woods
M B Cox

ATL 1983 NL
SP C McMurtry
SP P Perez
SP P Niekro
SR R Camp
SR P Falcone
RP S Bedrosian
RP K Dayley
RP T Forster
RP D Moore
C B Benedict
1B C Chambliss
2B G Hubbard
SS R Ramirez
3B B Horner
LM B Butler
CF D Murphy
RF C Washington
3U- R Johnson
32- J Royster
M J Torre

CHI 1983 NL
SP C Rainey
SP S Trout
SP F Jenkins
SP D Ruthven
SP D Noles
RP L Smith
RP B Campbell
RS C Lefferts
RP M Proly
C J Davis
1B B Buckner
2B R Sandberg
SS L Bowa
3B R Cey
LM L Durham
CF M Hall
RF K Moreland
OF- J Johnstone
OI- G Woods
M1 L Elia
M2 C Fox

CIN 1983 NL
SP M Soto
SP B Berenyi
SP F Pastore
SP J Price
SP C Puleo
RS T Power
RP B Scherrer
RS R Gale
RP B Hayes
C D Bilardello
1B D Driessen
2B R Oester
SS D Concepcion
3B- N Esasky
LF G Redus
CF E Milner
RM P Householder
IO J Bench
RU C Cedeno
OF D Walker
M R Nixon

HOU 1983 NL
SP J Niekro
SP B Knepper
SP N Ryan
SP M Scott
SR M LaCoss
RS V Ruhle
RP B Dawley
CL F DiPino
RP D Smith
C - A Ashby
1B R Knight
2B B Doran
SS D Thon
3B P Garner
LF J Cruz
CF- O Moreno
RF T Puhl
UT D Walling
RU- K Bass
M B Lillis

LA 1983 NL
SP F Valenzuela
SP J Reuss
SP B Welch
SP A Pena
SP B Hooton
RP T Niedenfuer
CL S Howe
RP D Stewart
RP J Beckwith
C S Yeager
1B G Brock
2B S Sax
SS B Russell
3B P Guerrero
LF D Baker
CF K Landreaux
RF M Marshall
UT D Thomas
OI R Monday
RO- R Roenicke
M T Lasorda

MON 1983 NL
SP S Rogers
SP B Gullickson
SP C Lea
SR R Burris
RS B Smith
RP J Reardon
RP D Schatzeder
RP B James
C G Carter
1B A Oliver
2S D Flynn
SS- C Speier
3B T Wallach
LF T Raines
CF A Dawson
RF W Cromartie
OI T Francona
S2 B Little
RU- J Wohlford
M B Virdon

NY 1983 NL
SP T Seaver
SP M Torrez
SP E Lynch
SP W Terrell
RP J Orosco
RP D Sisk
RS S Holman
RP C Diaz
C R Hodges
1B- K Hernandez
2B B Giles
SS J Oquendo
3B H Brooks
LF G Foster
CF M Wilson
RF D Strawberry
S2 B Bailor
OI D Heep
1U D Kingman
UT R Staub
M1 G Bamberger
M2 F Howard

PHI 1983 NL
SP S Carlton
SP J Denny
SP C Hudson
SP M Bystrom
CL A Holland
RP R Reed
RP W Hernandez
RP T McGraw
C B Diaz
1U P Rose
2B J Morgan
SS I DeJesus
3B M Schmidt
LF G Matthews
CF- G Maddox
RM V Hayes
LO G Gross
RU J Lefebvre
MR B Dernier
2S- K Garcia
1B- T Perez
M1 P Corrales
M2 P Owens

PIT 1983 NL
SP R Rhoden
SP L McWilliams
SP J Candelaria
SR L Tunnell
SP J DeLeon
RP K Tekulve
RP C Guante
RP M Sarmiento
RP R Scurry
C T Pena
1B J Thompson
2B J Ray
SS D Berra
3B B Madlock
LF M Easler
CF M Wynne
RF D Parker
LR L Lacy
OI L Mazzilli
M C Tanner

STL 1983 NL
SP J Andujar
SR J Stuper
SP D LaPoint
SP B Forsch
SP N Allen
CL B Sutter
RP J Lahti
RP D Von Ohlen
RS J Martin
C D Porter
1R G Hendrick
2B- T Herr
SS O Smith
3B K Oberkfell
LF L Smith
CF W McGee
RO D Green
2I- M Ramsey
UT A Van Slyke
M W Herzog

SD 1983 NL
SP E Show
SP D Dravecky
SP T Lollar
SR E Whitson
SP A Hawkins
RP L DeLeon
RP M Thurmond
RP G Lucas
RP S Monge
C T Kennedy
1B S Garvey
2B J Bonilla
SS G Templeton
3B L Salazar
OI A Wiggins
CF R Jones
RF- S Lezcano
3I- T Flannery
RL- T Gwynn
LU- G Richards
M D Williams

SF 1983 NL
SP F Breining
SP M Krukow
SP A Hammaker
SP B Laskey
SR A McGaffigan
RP G Minton
RP M Davis
CL G Lavelle
RP J Barr
C B Brenly
1B D Evans
2B- B Wellman
SS J LeMaster
3B T O'Malley
LF J Leonard
CF C Davis
RF J Clark
2U J Youngblood
1U- D Bergman

UO- M Venable
M F Robinson

BAL 1983 AL
SP S McGregor
SP S Davis
SP M Boddicker
SP D Martinez
SP M Flanagan
RP S Stewart
RP T Martinez
RP T Stoddard
C R Dempsey
1B E Murray
2B R Dauer
SS C Ripken
3B- T Cruz
LF J Lowenstein
CF J Shelby
RF D Ford
OI J Dwyer
CF A Bumbry
LO G Roenicke
DH K Singleton
M J Altobelli

BOS 1983 AL
SP J Tudor
SP B Hurst
SP D Eckersley
SP B Ojeda
SP M Brown
RP B Stanley
RP M Clear
RP O Boyd
RP L Aponte
C - G Allenson
1B D Stapleton
2B J Remy
SS G Hoffman
3B W Boggs
LF J Rice
CF T Armas
RF D Evans
DH C Yastrzemski
OI R Miller
OI R Nichols
C - R Gedman
M R Houk

CAL 1983 AL
SP T John
SP K Forsch
SP G Zahn
SR M Witt
SP B Kison
RP L Sanchez
RP J Curtis
C B Boone
1U R Carew
2B B Grich
SS- T Foli
3B- D DeCinces
LU B Downing
CF F Lynn
RF- E Valentine
DR Re Jackson
UT Ro Jackson
1D D Sconiers
UO- J Beniquez
M J McNamara

CHI 1983 AL
SP L Hoyt
SP R Dotson
SP F Bannister
SP B Burns
SR J Koosman
RS D Lamp
RP S Barojas
RP D Tidrow
C C Fisk
1B M Squires
2B J Cruz
SS J Dybzinski
3B V Law
LF R Kittle
CF R Law
RF H Baines
DH G Luzinski
SS S Fletcher
UO J Hairston
1L T Paciorek
1U G Walker
M T LaRussa

CLE 1983 AL
SP R Sutcliffe
SP L Sorensen
SP B Blyleven
SR N Heaton
SP L Barker
RS J Eichelberger
RP D Spillner
RP B Anderson
RP J Easterly
C R Hassey
1B M Hargrove
2B- M Trillo
SS J Franco
3B T Harrah
UT A Bannister
CF G Thomas
RF G Vukovich
DH A Thornton
LU P Tabler
2U- M Fischlin
M1 M Ferraro
M2 P Corrales

DET 1983 AL
SP J Morris
SP D Petry
SP M Wilcox
SR J Berenguer
SR D Rozema
RP A Lopez
RP H Bailey
RP D Bair
C L Parrish
1B E Cabell
2B L Whitaker
SS A Trammell
3I T Brookens
LF L Herndon
CF C Lemon
RF G Wilson
DO K Gibson
1U R Leach
UC- J Wockenfuss
M S Anderson

KC 1983 AL
SP L Gura
SP B Black
SP P Splittorff
SP S Renko
RP D Quisenberry
RP M Armstrong
C1 J Wathan
1B W Aikens
2B F White
SS U Washington
3B G Brett
ML W Wilson
MR A Otis
UO P Sheridan
DH H McRae
UO- L Roberts
1O- J Simpson
C - D Slaught
M D Howser

MIL 1983 AL
SP M Caldwell
SP D Sutton
SP M Haas
SP B McClure
SP C Porter
RP J Slaton
RP T Tellmann
RS B Gibson
CL P Ladd
C - N Yost
1B C Cooper
2B J Gantner
SS R Yount
3B P Molitor
LF B Oglivie
CF R Manning
RF C Moore
CD T Simmons
M H Kuenn

MIN 1983 AL
SP F Viola
SP K Schrom
SP A Williams
SP B Castillo
RP R Lysander
CL R Davis
RP L Whitehouse
RP M Walters
CU D Engle
1B K Hrbek
2B J Castino
SS R Washington
3B G Gaetti
LF G Ward
CF- D Brown
RF T Brunansky
DH R Bush
UT M Hatcher
M B Gardner

NY 1983 AL
SP R Guidry
SP S Rawley
SP D Righetti
SP B Shirley
RP G Frazier
CL R Gossage
RP D Murray
C - B Wynegar
1B K Griffey
2B W Randolph
SI R Smalley
3B G Nettles
LF D Winfield
CF- J Mumphrey
RF S Kemp
DH D Baylor
SS A Robertson
UT- D Mattingly
M B Martin

OAK 1983 AL
SP C Codiroli
SR S McCatty
SR T Conroy
SP B Krueger
RS T Underwood
RP T Burgmeier
RP K Atherton
RP D Beard
C B Kearney
13 W Gross
2B D Lopes
S2 T Phillips
3B- C Lansford
LF R Henderson
CF D Murphy
RF M Davis
DH J Burroughs
UT B Almon
OI G Hancock
C - M Heath
M S Boros

SEA 1983 AL
SP M Young
SP J Beattie
SR B Stoddard
SR B Clark
SP M Moore
RP G Perry
CL B Caudill
RP R Thomas
RP M Stanton
C - R Sweet
1B P Putnam
2B- T Bernazard
SS- S Owen
3B- J Allen
LF S Henderson
MR D Henderson
RD A Cowens
DH- R Zisk
3U- M Castillo
UO- J Moses
RL R Nelson
M1 R Lachemann
M2 D Crandall

TEX 1983 AL
SP C Hough
SP M Smithson
SP D Darwin
SP R Honeycutt
SP F Tanana
RS J Butcher
RP O Jones
C J Sundberg
1B P O'Brien
2B W Tolleson
SS B Dent
3B B Bell
LF B Sample
CF G Wright
RF L Parrish
DH- D Hostetler
DU- M Rivers
M D Rader

TOR 1983 AL
SP D Stieb
SP J Clancy
SP L Leal
SP J Gott
SP D Alexander
RS J Acker
RP R Jackson
RP J McLaughlin
RP R Moffitt
C E Whitt
1B W Upshaw
2B D Garcia
SS A Griffin
3B R Mulliniks
LR B Bonnell
CF L Moseby
RF J Barfield
DH C Johnson
LF D Collins
32 G Iorg
DU J Orta
C - B Martinez
M B Cox

ATL 1984 NL
SP R Mahler
SP P Perez
SP C McMurtry
SR R Camp
SP L Barker
RS P Falcone
RP G Garber
RP S Bedrosian
RP J Dedmon
C - B Benedict
1B C Chambliss
2B G Hubbard
SS R Ramirez
3B- R Johnson
RL- B Komminsk
CF D Murphy
RF C Washington
1L G Perry
LU- A Hall
IO- J Royster
M J Torre

CHI 1984 NL
SP S Trout
SP D Eckersley
SP R Sutcliffe
SP S Sanderson
SP D Ruthven
RP L Smith
RP T Stoddard
RS R Bordi
RP W Brusstar
C J Davis
1B L Durham
2B R Sandberg
SS L Bowa
3B R Cey
LF G Matthews
CF B Dernier
RI K Moreland
UO H Cotto
OI- G Woods
M J Frey

CIN 1984 NL
SP M Soto
SP J Russell
SP J Price
SP J Tibbs
RP T Power
RS T Hume
RP B Owchinko
RP J Franco
C B Gulden
1B- D Driessen
2B R Oester
S3 D Concepcion
3U N Esasky
LF G Redus
CF E Milner
RF D Parker
OI C Cedeno
SS T Foley
3U- W Krenchicki
LO- D Walker
M1 V Rapp
M2 P Rose

HOU 1984 NL
SP J Niekro
SP B Knepper
SP N Ryan
SP M Scott
SR M LaCoss
RP B Dawley
RS V Ruhle
RP F DiPino
RP D Smith
C M Bailey
1B E Cabell
2B B Doran
SS C Reynolds
32 P Garner
LF J Cruz
CF J Mumphrey
RF T Puhl
OF K Bass
31- R Knight
3U- D Walling
M B Lillis

LA 1984 NL
SP F Valenzuela
SP A Pena
SR O Hershiser
SP R Honeycutt
SP B Welch
RS B Hooton
RS J Reuss
RP P Zachry
RP K Howell
C M Scioscia
1B- G Brock
2B S Sax
SS D Anderson
3B- G Rivera
LF M Marshall
CF K Landreaux
RM C Maldonado
3R P Guerrero
SU- B Russell
1O- F Stubbs
UO- T Whitfield
M T Lasorda

MON 1984 NL
SP B Gullickson
SP C Lea
SP B Smith
SP S Rogers
SR D Schatzeder
CL J Reardon
RP B James
RP D Palmer
RP G Lucas
C G Carter
1B- T Francona
2S D Flynn
SS- A Salazar
3B T Wallach
OI- J Wohlford
CF T Raines
RF A Dawson
SL D Thomas
U1- M Dilone
2B- B Little
UT- P Rose
M1 B Virdon
M2 J Fanning

NY 1984 NL
SP D Gooden
SP W Terrell
SP R Darling
SP B Berenyi
RS E Lynch
CL J Orosco
RP D Sisk
RP B Gaff
C M Fitzgerald
1B K Hernandez
2B W Backman
SS- J Oquendo
3B H Brooks
LF G Foster
CF M Wilson
RF D Strawberry
OI D Heep
M D Johnson

PHI 1984 NL
SP S Carlton
SP J Koosman
SP C Hudson
SP J Denny
SP S Rawley
RS K Gross
RP A Holland
RP L Andersen
RP B Campbell
C O Virgil
1B L Matuszek
2B J Samuel
SS I DeJesus
3B M Schmidt
LU G Wilson
CF V Hayes
RF S Lezcano
1U T Corcoran
OI G Gross
IC- J Wockenfuss
M P Owens

PIT 1984 NL
SP R Rhoden
SP L McWilliams
SP J Tudor
SP J DeLeon
SP J Candelaria
RP D Robinson
RP K Tekulve
RS L Tunnell
C T Pena
1B J Thompson
2B J Ray
SS D Berra
3B B Madlock
RL L Lacy
CF M Wynne
RF D Frobel
LU L Mazzilli
32 J Morrison
M C Tanner

STL 1984 NL
SP J Andujar
SP D LaPoint
SP D Cox
SR R Horton
SP K Kepshire
RP B Sutter
RP N Allen
RP J Lahti
RP D Rucker
C D Porter
1B D Green
2B T Herr
SS O Smith
3B- T Pendleton
LF L Smith
CF W McGee
RF G Hendrick
LO T Landrum
UT A Van Slyke
OI- S Braun
3I- A Howe
M W Herzog

SD 1984 NL
SP E Show
SP T Lollar
SP E Whitson
SP M Thurmond
SR A Hawkins
RS D Dravecky
RP R Gossage
RP C Lefferts
RP G Booker
C T Kennedy
1B S Garvey
2B A Wiggins
SS G Templeton
3B G Nettles
LF C Martinez
CF K McReynolds
RF T Gwynn
UO- B Brown
UI- T Flannery
3O- L Salazar
M D Williams

SF 1984 NL
SP B Laskey
SP M Krukow
SR M Davis
SP J Robinson
RP G Minton
RP G Lavelle
RP F Williams
RP R Lerch
C B Brenly
1U S Thompson
2B M Trillo
SS J LeMaster
3B J Youngblood
LF J Leonard
CF- D Gladden
UO C Davis
OF D Baker
IF- D Kuiper
1B- A Oliver
UO- G Richards
2S- B Wellman
M1 F Robinson
M2 D Ozark

BAL 1984 AL
SP M Boddicker
SP M Flanagan
SP S Davis
SP S McGregor
SR D Martinez
RP T Martinez
RP S Stewart
RP T Underwood
RS B Swaggerty
C R Dempsey
1B E Murray
2B R Dauer
SS C Ripken
3B W Gross
LR G Roenicke
CF J Shelby
RL M Young
DH K Singleton
MU A Bumbry
LU J Lowenstein
3B- T Cruz
C - F Rayford
2B- L Sakata
M J Altobelli

BOS 1984 AL
SP B Hurst
SP B Ojeda
SP O Boyd
SP A Nipper
SP R Clemens
RP B Stanley
RP M Clear
RP J Johnson
RP S Crawford
C R Gedman
1B B Buckner
2B M Barrett
SS J Gutierrez
3B W Boggs
LF J Rice
CF T Armas
RF D Evans
DH M Easler
OI- R Miller
M R Houk

CAL 1984 AL
SP M Witt
SP R Romanick
SP G Zahn
SP T John
SR J Slaton
RP L Sanchez
RP D Corbett
RP C Kaufman
C B Boone
1B- R Carew
2B R Wilfong
SS D Schofield
3B D DeCinces
LF B Downing
CF G Pettis
RF F Lynn
DH R Jackson
LR J Beniquez
2B B Grich
SS- R Picciolo
M J McNamara

CHI 1984 AL
SP R Dotson
SP T Seaver
SP L Hoyt
SP F Bannister
SR B Burns
RP R Reed
RP J Agosto
C C Fisk
1U G Walker
2B J Cruz
SS S Fletcher
3B V Law
LF R Kittle
CF R Law
RF H Baines
DH G Luzinski
UO J Hairston
1O T Paciorek
1U M Squires
SS- J Dybzinski
M T LaRussa

CLE 1984 AL
SP B Blyleven
SP N Heaton
SP S Comer
SR S Farr
RP E Camacho
RP T Waddell
RP M Jeffcoat
RP J Easterly
C - J Willard
1B M Hargrove
2B T Bernazard
SS J Franco
3B B Jacoby
LF- M Hall
CF B Butler
RF G Vukovich
DH A Thornton
IO P Tabler
RF- C Castillo
2I- M Fischlin
M P Corrales

DET 1984 AL
SP J Morris
SP D Petry
SP M Wilcox
SP J Berenguer
SR D Rozema
RP W Hernandez
RP A Lopez
RP D Bair
C L Parrish
1B D Bergman
2B L Whitaker
SS A Trammell
3B H Johnson
LF L Herndon
CF C Lemon
RF K Gibson
IF D Evans
3I T Brookens
1U B Garbey
OF- J Grubb
UO- R Kuntz
M S Anderson

KC 1984 AL
SP B Black
SP M Gubicza
SP L Gura
SR B Saberhagen
SP C Leibrandt
RP D Quisenberry
RP J Beckwith
RP M Huismann
C D Slaught
1B S Balboni
2B F White
SS- O Concepcion
3B G Pryor
LR D Motley
CF W Wilson
RM P Sheridan
DH H McRae
3B G Brett
DU J Orta
C1- J Wathan
M D Howser

MIL 1984 AL
SP D Sutton
SP M Haas
SP J Cocanower
SR B McClure
SP M Caldwell
RP P Ladd
RP T Tellmann
RP R Waits
C J Sundberg
1B C Cooper
2B J Gantner
SS R Yount
3S E Romero
LF B Oglivie
CF R Manning
RO D James
D1 T Simmons
M R Lachemann

MIN 1984 AL
SP F Viola
SP M Smithson
SP J Butcher
SP K Schrom
SR E Hodge
RS P Filson
CL R Davis
RP R Lysander
C D Engle
1B K Hrbek
2B T Teufel
SS H Jimenez
3B G Gaetti
LU M Hatcher
CF K Puckett
RF T Brunansky
DH R Bush
OF- D Brown
C - T Laudner
SS- R Washington
M B Gardner

NY 1984 AL
SP P Niekro
SP R Guidry
SR R Fontenot
SP D Rasmussen
CL D Righetti
RS B Shirley
RP J Howell
RS J Rijo
C B Wynegar
1B D Mattingly
2B W Randolph
SS B Meacham
3B- T Harrah
OI K Griffey
CF O Moreno
RF D Winfield
DH D Baylor
LF- S Kemp
M Y Berra

OAK 1984 AL
SP R Burris
SR L Sorensen
SP S McCatty
SP B Krueger
SP C Young
CL B Caudill
RP K Atherton
C M Heath
1B B Bochte
2B J Morgan
S2 T Phillips
3B C Lansford
LF R Henderson
CF D Murphy
RF M Davis
DH D Kingman
UT B Almon
SI- M Wagner
M1 S Boros
M2 J Moore

SEA 1984 AL
SP M Langston
SP M Moore

SP J Beattie
SR E Vande Berg
SP M Young
RP D Beard
RS B Stoddard
RP E Nunez
RP P Mirabella
C B Kearney
1B A Davis
2B J Perconte
SS S Owen
3B- J Presley
ML P Bradley
CF D Henderson
RF A Cowens
DH K Phelps
LO B Bonnell
UT S Henderson
M1 D Crandall
M2 C Cottier

TEX 1984 AL

SP C Hough
SP F Tanana
SP D Darwin
SP D Stewart
SR M Mason
RP D Schmidt
RP O Jones
C - D Scott
1B P O'Brien
2B W Tolleson
SS C Wilkerson
3B B Bell
LM B Sample
MR G Wright
UO G Ward
RD L Parrish
UO M Rivers
M D Rader

TOR 1984 AL

SP D Stieb
SP D Alexander
SP L Leal
SP J Clancy
SR J Gott
RP R Jackson
RP D Lamp
RP J Acker
RP J Key
C E Whitt
1B W Upshaw
2B D Garcia
SS A Griffin
3B R Mulliniks
LF D Collins
CF L Moseby
RL G Bell
DH C Johnson
RU J Barfield
3B G Iorg
C B Martinez
DH- W Aikens
SS- T Fernandez
M B Cox

ATL 1985 NL

SP R Mahler
SP S Bedrosian
SR Z Smith
RP R Camp
CL B Sutter
RP G Garber
RP J Dedmon
C - R Cerone
13 B Horner
2B G Hubbard
SS R Ramirez
3B K Oberkfell
LF T Harper
CF D Murphy
RF C Washington
UL C Chambliss
RL B Komminsk
1U G Perry
2S- P Zuvella
M1 E Haas
M2 B Wine

CHI 1985 NL

SP D Eckersley
SR R Fontenot
SP S Trout
SP R Sutcliffe
SP S Sanderson
RP L Smith
RP L Sorensen
RP W Brusstar
RP G Frazier
C J Davis
1B L Durham
2B R Sandberg
SS- S Dunston
3B R Cey
LF- G Matthews
CF B Dernier
RF K Moreland
UO T Bosley
UT D Lopes
S3 C Speier
IO- R Hebner
LU- G Woods
M J Frey

CIN 1985 NL

SP T Browning
SP M Soto
SP J Tibbs
SR R Robinson
SR J Stuper
RP J Franco
CL T Power
RP T Hume
RS J Price
C - D Van Gorder
1B P Rose
2B R Oester
SS D Concepcion
3B- B Bell
LM G Redus
CF E Milner
RF D Parker
IO N Esasky
L1- C Cedeno
3U- W Krenchicki

HOU 1985 NL

SP B Knepper
SP N Ryan
SP M Scott
SP J Niekro
CL D Smith
RP B Dawley
RP F DiPino
RP J Calhoun
C M Bailey
1B G Davis
2B B Doran
SS C Reynolds
3B P Garner
LF J Cruz
MR K Bass
RM J Mumphrey
UT D Walling
SS- D Thon
M B Lillis

LA 1985 NL

SP F Valenzuela
SP O Hershiser
SP J Reuss
SP B Welch
SP R Honeycutt
RP T Niedenfuer
RP K Howell
RP C Diaz
RS B Castillo
C M Scioscia
1B G Brock
2B S Sax
SS M Duncan
3S- D Anderson
UO C Maldonado
CF K Landreaux
RF M Marshall
L3 P Guerrero
M T Lasorda

MON 1985 NL

SP B Smith
SP B Gullickson
SP J Hesketh
SP D Palmer
SP D Schatzeder
CL J Reardon
RP T Burke
RP B Roberge
RP G Lucas
C M Fitzgerald
1B- D Driessen
2B V Law
SS H Brooks
3B T Wallach
LF T Raines
CF H Winningham
RF A Dawson
1O T Francona
M B Rodgers

NY 1985 NL

SP D Gooden
SP R Darling
SP E Lynch
SP S Fernandez
SP R Aguilera
RP R McDowell
RP J Orosco
RP D Sisk
RP T Leach
C G Carter
1B K Hernandez
2B W Backman
SS R Santana
3B H Johnson
LF G Foster
CF- M Wilson
RF D Strawberry
CF- L Dykstra
OI- D Heep
3B- R Knight
M D Johnson

PHI 1985 NL

SP J Denny
SP K Gross
SP S Rawley
SR C Hudson
SP J Koosman
RP D Carman
RP K Tekulve
RP D Rucker
RP L Andersen
C O Virgil
13 M Schmidt
2B J Samuel
SS- S Jeltz
3B R Schu
CF V Hayes
CF G Maddox
RF G Wilson
1U T Corcoran
SI- L Aguayo
OI- G Gross
LU- J Russell
LF- J Stone
M J Felske

PIT 1985 NL

SP R Rhoden
SP R Reuschel
SP J DeLeon
SP L Tunnell
SR L McWilliams
RP C Guante
RS D Robinson
RS J Winn
RP J Candelaria
C T Pena
1B J Thompson
2B J Ray
SS- S Khalifa
3B B Madlock
ML J Orsulak
CF M Wynne
RF- G Hendrick
UT- B Almon
LU- S Kemp
UT- L Mazzilli
3U- J Morrison
M C Tanner

STL 1985 NL

SP J Tudor
SP J Andujar
SP D Cox
SP K Kepshire
SR B Forsch
RP R Horton
CL J Lahti
RP K Dayley
RP B Campbell
C - T Nieto
1B J Clark
2B T Herr
SS O Smith
3B T Pendleton
LF V Coleman
CF W McGee
RF A Van Slyke
RF- T Landrum
C - D Porter
M W Herzog

SD 1985 NL

SP E Show
SP A Hawkins
SP D Dravecky
SP L Hoyt
SR M Thurmond
CL R Gossage
RP C Lefferts
RP T Stoddard
C T Kennedy
1B S Garvey
2B T Flannery
SS G Templeton
3B G Nettles
LF C Martinez
CF K McReynolds
RF T Gwynn
23- J Royster
M D Williams

SF 1985 NL

SP D LaPoint
SP M Krukow
SP A Hammaker
SP J Gott
SR V Blue
RP M Davis
RP S Garrelts
RP B Laskey
RP G Minton
C B Brenly
1U D Green
2B M Trillo
SS J Uribe
3B C Brown
LF J Leonard
CF D Gladden
RM C Davis
OI- J Youngblood
M1 J Davenport
M2 R Craig

BAL 1985 AL

SP S McGregor
SP M Boddicker
SP D Martinez
SP S Davis
SR K Dixon
RP S Stewart
RP N Snell
RP D Aase
RP T Martinez
C R Dempsey
1B E Murray
2B- A Wiggins
SS C Ripken
3C F Rayford
LD M Young
CF F Lynn
RF L Lacy
DH L Sheets
OF J Dwyer
3U W Gross
LU G Roenicke
2B- R Dauer
M1 J Altobelli
M3 E Weaver

BOS 1985 AL

SP O Boyd
SP B Hurst
SP A Nipper
SR B Ojeda
RP S Crawford
RP B Stanley
RP M Clear
C R Gedman
1B B Buckner
2B M Barrett
SS J Gutierrez
3B W Boggs
LF J Rice
CF S Lyons
RF D Evans
DH M Easler
MU T Armas
SS- G Hoffman
M J McNamara

CAL 1985 AL

SP M Witt
SP R Romanick
SP K McCaskill
SP J Slaton
RP D Moore
RP S Cliburn
RP P Clements
RP L Sanchez
C B Boone
1B R Carew
2B B Grich
SS D Schofield
3B D DeCinces
LF B Downing
CF G Pettis
UO R Jones
RD R Jackson
UT J Beniquez
2B- R Wilfong
M G Mauch

CHI 1985 AL

SP T Seaver
SP B Burns
SP F Bannister
SR G Nelson
RP B James
RP D Spillner
RP J Agosto
C C Fisk
1B G Walker
2B- J Cruz
SS O Guillen
3B T Hulett
LF R Law
CF- D Boston
RF H Baines
UT R Kittle
UI S Fletcher
M3 L Salazar
UT- J Hairston
M T LaRussa

CLE 1985 AL

SP N Heaton
SP B Blyleven
SR V Ruhle
RS T Waddell
RS J Easterly
RP R Thompson
RS J Reed
C J Willard
1B P Tabler
2B T Bernazard
SS J Franco
3B B Jacoby
LF J Carter
CF B Butler
RF G Vukovich
DH A Thornton
1B M Hargrove
LM O Nixon
M P Corrales

DET 1985 AL

SP J Morris
SP D Petry
SP W Terrell
SP F Tanana
RP W Hernandez
RP A Lopez
RP B Scherrer
RP D Bair
C L Parrish
1U D Evans
2B L Whitaker
SS A Trammell
3B T Brookens
LF L Herndon
CF C Lemon
RF K Gibson
OF- J Grubb
UT- B Garbey
M S Anderson

KC 1985 AL

SP C Leibrandt
SP B Saberhagen
SP D Jackson
SP B Black
SP M Gubicza
RP D Quisenberry
RP J Beckwith
RP M Jones
C J Sundberg
1B S Balboni
2B F White
SS O Concepcion
3B G Brett
LF L Smith
CF W Wilson
RL D Motley
DH H McRae
LR L Jones
DH J Orta
SS- B Biancalana
M D Howser

MIL 1985 AL

SR D Darwin
SP T Higuera
SP R Burris
SP M Haas
SP J Cocanower
RP P Vuckovich
RP B Gibson
RP B McClure
CL R Fingers
C C Moore
1B C Cooper
2B J Gantner
SS E Riles
3B P Molitor
RL B Oglivie
LM R Yount
RM- P Householder
DU T Simmons
UT- E Romero
M G Bamberger

MIN 1985 AL

SP M Smithson
SP F Viola
SP J Butcher
SP K Schrom
SP B Blyleven
RS P Filson
CL R Davis
RP F Eufemia
RP R Lysander
C M Salas
1B K Hrbek
2B T Teufel
SS G Gagne
3B G Gaetti
LF M Hatcher
CF K Puckett
RF T Brunansky
UI R Smalley
OI- R Bush
OI- M Stenhouse
M1 B Gardner
M2 R Miller

NY 1985 AL

SP R Guidry
SP P Niekro
SP J Cowley
SP E Whitson
SP D Rasmussen
RP D Righetti
RP B Fisher
RS B Shirley
RP R Bordi
C B Wynegar
1B D Mattingly
2B W Randolph
SS B Meacham
3B M Pagliarulo
LF K Griffey
CF R Henderson
RF D Winfield
DH D Baylor
C - R Hassey
M1 Y Berra
M2 B Martin

OAK 1985 AL

SP C Codiroli
SP D Sutton
SP B Krueger
SP T Birtsas
RP J Howell
RP K Atherton
RS S McCatty
RP S Ontiveros
C M Heath
1B B Bochte
2B D Hill
SS A Griffin
3B C Lansford
LF D Collins
CF D Murphy
RF M Davis
DH D Kingman
1L D Baker
LU- S Henderson
M J Moore

SEA 1985 AL

SP M Moore
SP M Young
SP M Langston
SP F Wills
SP B Swift
RP E Nunez
RP R Thomas
RP E Vande Berg
C B Kearney
1B A Davis
2B J Perconte
SS S Owen
3B J Presley
LF P Bradley
CF D Henderson
RF A Cowens
DH G Thomas
M C Cottier

TEX 1985 AL

SP C Hough
SP M Mason
SP B Hooton
SR D Noles
RP G Harris
RP D Rozema
RP D Schmidt
RS D Stewart
C D Slaught
1B P O'Brien
2B T Harrah
SS C Wilkerson
3B- B Bell
LF G Ward
CF O McDowell
RM G Wright
DH- C Johnson
SI W Tolleson
OI- B Jones
RU- L Parrish
M1 D Rader
M2 B Valentine

TOR 1985 AL

SP D Stieb
SP D Alexander
SP J Key
SP J Clancy
RP D Lamp
RP J Acker
RP B Caudill
RP G Lavelle
C E Whitt
1B W Upshaw
2B D Garcia
SS T Fernandez
3B R Mulliniks
LF G Bell
CF L Moseby
RF J Barfield
DH- J Burroughs
3B G Iorg
M B Cox

ATL 1986 NL

SP R Mahler
SP D Palmer
SP Z Smith
SP D Alexander
RP J Dedmon
CL G Garber
RS C McMurtry
RP P Assenmacher
C O Virgil
1B B Horner
2B G Hubbard
SS A Thomas
3B K Oberkfell
LU T Harper
CF D Murphy
RO O Moreno
U1 C Chambliss
S3 R Ramirez
RU- B Sample
M C Tanner

CHI 1986 NL

SP D Eckersley
SP R Sutcliffe
SP S Sanderson
SR S Trout
SR E Lynch
CL L Smith
RS G Hoffman
RP D Gumpert
RP J Baller
C J Davis
1B L Durham
2B R Sandberg
SS S Dunston
3B R Cey
LF G Matthews
CF B Dernier
RF K Moreland
ML J Mumphrey
UO- T Bosley
OI- T Francona
3I- C Speier
3U- M Trillo
M1 J Frey
M2 J Vukovich
M3 G Michael

CIN 1986 NL

SP B Gullickson
SP T Browning
SP J Denny
SP C Welsh
SP M Soto
RP R Robinson
RP J Franco
RS T Power
RP S Terry
C B Diaz
1L N Esasky
2B R Oester
SS K Stillwell
3B B Bell
LM E Davis
CF E Milner
RF D Parker
UO M Venable
SI- D Concepcion
M P Rose

HOU 1986 NL

SP M Scott
SP B Knepper
SP N Ryan
SP J Deshaies
RP C Kerfeld
CL D Smith
RP A Lopez
RP L Andersen
C A Ashby
1B G Davis
2B B Doran
SS D Thon
3B D Walling
LF J Cruz
ML B Hatcher
RF K Bass
3B P Garner
SS C Reynolds
RU- T Puhl
CF- T Walker
M H Lanier

LA 1986 NL

SP F Valenzuela
SP B Welch
SP O Hershiser
SP R Honeycutt
RP K Howell
RP T Niedenfuer
RP E Vande Berg
RS D Powell
C M Scioscia
1B G Brock
2B S Sax
SS M Duncan
3B B Madlock
LF F Stubbs
MR R Williams
RF M Marshall
1U E Cabell
MU K Landreaux
UT B Russell
3S- D Anderson
OI- L Matuszek
CU- A Trevino
M T Lasorda

MON 1986 NL

SP F Youmans
SP J Tibbs
SP B Smith
SP D Martinez
RS A McGaffigan
CL J Reardon
RP T Burke
RP B McClure
C - D Bilardello
1B A Galarraga
2B V Law
SS- H Brooks
3B T Wallach
LF T Raines
CF M Webster
RF A Dawson
IO W Krenchicki
2U- A Newman
MU- H Winningham
M B Rodgers

NY 1986 NL

SP D Gooden
SP R Darling
SP B Ojeda
SP S Fernandez
SP R Aguilera
RP R McDowell
CL J Orosco
RP D Sisk
C G Carter
1B K Hernandez
2B W Backman
SS R Santana
3B R Knight
LM M Wilson
CF L Dykstra
RF D Strawberry
UT K Mitchell
LU- D Heep
3S- H Johnson
2B- T Teufel
M D Johnson

PHI 1986 NL

SP K Gross
SP S Rawley
SP B Ruffin
SR C Hudson
RS D Carman
CL S Bedrosian
RP K Tekulve
RP T Hume
C - J Russell
1B V Hayes
2B J Samuel
SS S Jeltz
3B M Schmidt
LF- G Redus
CF- M Thompson
RF G Wilson
MO R Roenicke
OI- G Gross
3U- R Schu
OF- J Stone
M J Felske

PIT 1986 NL

SP R Rhoden
SP R Reuschel
SP M Bielecki
SR B Walk
SP B Kipper
RS L McWilliams
RP J Winn
RP D Robinson
RP C Guante
C T Pena
1B S Bream
2B J Ray

SS R Belliard
3B J Morrison
LR R Reynolds
CF B Bonds
RM J Orsulak
L3 B Almon
UT- M Diaz
RF- M Brown
M J Leyland

STL 1986 NL
SP B Forsch
SP D Cox
SP J Tudor
SP G Mathews
SP T Conroy
RP T Worrell
RS R Horton
RP P Perry
C M LaValliere
1B- J Clark
2B T Herr
SS O Smith
3B T Pendleton
LF V Coleman
CF W McGee
R1 A Van Slyke
OF- C Ford
RU- T Landrum
M W Herzog

SD 1986 NL
SP A Hawkins
SP D Dravecky
SR L Hoyt
SP E Show
RS L McCullers
RP C Lefferts
RP G Walter
CL R Gossage
C T Kennedy
1B S Garvey
2B T Flannery
SS G Templeton
3B G Nettles
ML K McReynolds
CF M Wynne
RF T Gwynn
LU J Kruk
LU C Martinez
2B B Roberts
3I J Royster
IO- D Iorg
M S Boros

SF 1986 NL
SP M Krukow
SP M LaCoss
SR S Garrelts
SP V Blue
RP J Robinson
RP M Davis
RP J Berenguer
RP G Minton
C3 B Brenly
1B W Clark
2B R Thompson
SS J Uribe
3B C Brown
OI C Maldonado
CF D Gladden
RF C Davis
UT- J Youngblood
UT- M Aldrete
LF- J Leonard
C - B Melvin
M R Craig

BAL 1986 AL
SP M Boddicker
SP S McGregor
SP K Dixon
SP M Flanagan
SP S Davis
CL D Aase
RP R Bordi
RP B Havens
RP N Snell
C R Dempsey
1B E Murray
23 J Bonilla
SS C Ripken
3B- F Rayford
UO J Shelby
CF F Lynn
RF L Lacy
DO L Sheets
UT J Beniquez
LD M Young
OI- J Dwyer
M E Weaver

BOS 1986 AL
SP R Clemens
SP O Boyd
SP B Hurst
SP A Nipper
SP T Seaver
RP B Stanley
RP S Stewart
RP S Crawford
CL C Schiraldi
C R Gedman
1B B Buckner
2B M Barrett
SS E Romero
3B W Boggs
LF J Rice
CF T Armas
RF D Evans
DH D Baylor
M J McNamara

CAL 1986 AL
SP M Witt
SP K McCaskill
SP D Sutton
SP R Romanick
CL D Moore
RP D Corbett
C B Boone
1B W Joyner
2B- R Wilfong
SS D Schofield
3B D DeCinces
LF B Downing
CF G Pettis
RF R Jones
DH R Jackson
2B B Grich
RF G Hendrick
UI- R Burleson
M G Mauch

CHI 1986 AL
SP R Dotson
SP F Bannister
SP J Cowley
SP N Allen
SP J Davis
RP G Nelson
RP B Dawley
RP D Schmidt
RP B James
CU C Fisk
1B- G Walker
2B- J Cruz
SS O Guillen
32 T Hulett
OI- R Nichols
MU J Cangelosi
RF H Baines
DU- R Kittle
UT J Hairston
3B- W Tolleson
M1 T LaRussa
M2 D Rader
M3 J Fregosi

CLE 1986 AL
SP T Candiotti
SP P Niekro
SP K Schrom
RS S Bailes
RP R Yett
CL E Camacho
RP B Oelkers
C A Allanson
1B P Tabler
2B T Bernazard
SS J Franco
3B B Jacoby
LF M Hall
CF B Butler
OI J Carter
DH A Thornton
LF O Nixon
RS C Snyder
C - C Bando
UT- C Castillo
M P Corrales

DET 1986 AL
SP J Morris
SP W Terrell
SP F Tanana
SR E King
SP D Petry
RS R O'Neal
CL W Hernandez
RP B Campbell
RP M Thurmond
C - L Parrish
1D D Evans
2B L Whitaker
SS A Trammell
3B D Coles
LU D Collins
CF C Lemon
RF K Gibson
DU- J Grubb
UT T Brookens
LF L Herndon
MR P Sheridan
M S Anderson

KC 1986 AL
SP C Leibrandt
SP D Leonard
SP D Jackson
SR M Gubicza
SP B Saberhagen
RP B Black
RP S Bankhead
RP S Farr
RP D Quisenberry
C J Sundberg
1B S Balboni
2B F White
SS A Salazar
3B G Brett
LF L Smith
CF W Wilson
LR- R Law
DH J Orta
SS B Biancalana
DU H McRae
M1 D Howser
M2 M Ferraro

MIL 1986 AL
SP T Higuera
SP B Wegman
SP T Leary
SP J Nieves
SR D Darwin
RP D Plesac
RP M Clear
RP B Clutterbuck
C - C Moore
1B- B Robidoux
2B J Gantner
SS E Riles
3B P Molitor
UO- R Manning
CF R Yount
RF R Deer
1D C Cooper
OF B Oglivie
3I- D Sveum
M1 G Bamberger
M2 T Trebelhorn

MIN 1986 AL
SP B Blyleven
SP F Viola
SP M Smithson
SP N Heaton
SR M Portugal
RP K Atherton
RP R Jackson
RP F Pastore
C - M Salas
1B K Hrbek
2B S Lombardozzi
SS G Gagne
3B G Gaetti
LU R Bush
CF K Puckett
RF T Brunansky
DH R Smalley
UT M Hatcher
M1 R Miller
M2 T Kelly

NY 1986 AL
SP D Rasmussen
SP R Guidry
SP D Drabek
SP B Tewksbury
SP J Niekro
RP D Righetti
RS B Shirley
RP B Fisher
RP T Stoddard
C - B Wynegar
1B D Mattingly
2B W Randolph
SS- W Tolleson
3B M Pagliarulo
LU D Pasqua
CF R Henderson
RF D Winfield
DH M Easler
M L Piniella

OAK 1986 AL
SP C Young
SR J Rijo
SP J Andujar
SR D Stewart
SR E Plunk
RS B Mooneyham
RP S Ontiveros
CL J Howell
C - M Tettleton
1B B Bochte
23 T Phillips
SS A Griffin
31 C Lansford
LF J Canseco
CF D Murphy
RF M Davis
DH D Kingman
2B D Hill
OI- D Baker
M1 J Moore
M2 J Newman
M3 T LaRussa

SEA 1986 AL
SP M Moore
SP M Langston
SP M Morgan
SR B Swift
RS M Young
RP M Huismann
RP P Ladd
RP L Guetterman
C - B Kearney
1U A Davis
2B H Reynolds
SS S Owen
3B J Presley
LF P Bradley
CF J Moses
RU D Tartabull
DH- G Thomas
OF D Henderson
UT K Phelps
M1 C Cottier
M2 M Martinez
M3 D Williams

TEX 1986 AL
SP C Hough
SP E Correa
SP J Guzman
SP B Witt
SP M Mason
RP G Harris
RP M Williams
RP D Mohorcic
RP J Russell
C - D Slaught
1B P O'Brien
2B- T Harrah
SS S Fletcher
3B S Buechele
RL R Sierra
CF O McDowell
RU P Incaviglia
DH L Parrish
LF G Ward
2S C Wilkerson
UT- T Paciorek
M B Valentine

TOR 1986 AL
SP J Key
SP J Clancy
SP D Stieb
SR J Cerutti
SP D Alexander
RP M Eichhorn
CL T Henke
RP D Lamp
RS J Acker
C E Whitt
1B W Upshaw
2B D Garcia
SS T Fernandez
3B R Mulliniks
LF G Bell
CF L Moseby
RF J Barfield
DH C Johnson
32 G Iorg
OI R Leach
UT- K Gruber
C - B Martinez
M J Williams

ATL 1987 NL
SP Z Smith
SR R Mahler
SP D Palmer
SR C Puleo
SP D Alexander
RP J Acker
RP J Dedmon
RP G Garber
RP P Assenmacher
C O Virgil
1B G Perry
2B G Hubbard
SS- A Thomas
3B K Oberkfell
LF K Griffey
MU D James
RF D Murphy
IF G Nettles
MU- A Hall
M C Tanner

CHI 1987 NL
SP R Sutcliffe
SP J Moyer
SP G Maddux
SR S Sanderson
SP L Lancaster
CL L Smith
RS E Lynch
RP F DiPino
RP D Noles
C J Davis
1B L Durham
2B R Sandberg
SS- S Dunston
3B K Moreland
LU J Mumphrey
CF D Martinez
RF A Dawson
LU B Dayett
UI M Trillo
CF- B Dernier
LU- R Palmeiro
M1 G Michael
M2 F Lucchesi

CIN 1987 NL
SP T Power
SP T Browning
SP B Gullickson
SR G Hoffman
SR R Robinson
CL J Franco
RP F Williams
RP R Murphy
RP B Landrum
C B Diaz
1B N Esasky
2B- R Oester
SS B Larkin
3B B Bell
UO T Jones
CF E Davis
RF D Parker
21 D Concepcion
LF K Daniels
1U T Francona
UI K Stillwell
OI- P O'Neill
M P Rose

HOU 1987 NL
SP M Scott
SP N Ryan
SP D Darwin
SP B Knepper
SP J Deshaies
RP L Andersen
CL D Smith
RP D Meads
C A Ashby
1B G Davis
2B B Doran
SS C Reynolds
3U D Walling
LF J Cruz
ML B Hatcher
RF K Bass
UO- T Puhl
M H Lanier

LA 1987 NL
SP O Hershiser
SP B Welch
SP F Valenzuela
SP R Honeycutt
RS T Leary
CL A Pena
RP B Holton
RP M Young
C M Scioscia
1B F Stubbs
2B S Sax
SS- M Duncan
UT M Hatcher
L1 P Guerrero
CF J Shelby
RF M Marshall
S3 D Anderson
UO K Landreaux
M T Lasorda

MON 1987 NL
SP N Heaton
SP B Sebra
SP B Smith
SP D Martinez
SP F Youmans
RP A McGaffigan
RP T Burke
RP R St.Claire
RP J Parrett
C M Fitzgerald
1B A Galarraga
2B V Law
SS H Brooks
3B T Wallach
LF T Raines
CF H Winningham
RF M Webster
UT C Candaele
UI T Foley
M B Rodgers

NY 1987 NL
SP R Darling
SP D Gooden
SP S Fernandez
SP R Aguilera
SP J Mitchell
RS T Leach
CL R McDowell
RP D Cone
RP J Orosco
C G Carter
1B K Hernandez
2B- T Teufel
SS R Santana
3B H Johnson
LF K McReynolds
CF L Dykstra
RF D Strawberry
MO M Wilson
2B- W Backman
3U- D Magadan
OI- L Mazzilli
M D Johnson

PHI 1987 NL
SP S Rawley
SP D Carman
SP B Ruffin
SP K Gross
CL S Bedrosian
RS M Jackson
RP K Tekulve
RS T Hume
C L Parrish
1B V Hayes
2B J Samuel
SS S Jeltz
3B M Schmidt
LF C James
CF M Thompson
RF G Wilson
OI G Gross
SS- L Aguayo
IF- R Schu
M1 J Felske
M2 L Elia

PIT 1987 NL
SR B Fisher
SP R Reuschel
SP D Drabek
SP M Dunne
SP B Kipper
RS B Walk
RP J Smiley
RP D Robinson
C M LaValliere
1B S Bream
2B J Ray
SS- A Pedrique
3O B Bonilla
LM B Bonds
MU A Van Slyke
RU R Reynolds
UO J Cangelosi
OI M Diaz
SS- R Belliard
3B- J Morrison
M J Leyland

STL 1987 NL
SP D Cox
SP G Mathews
SP B Forsch
SP J Magrane
RS R Horton
CL T Worrell
RP B Dawley
RS L Tunnell
C T Pena
1B J Clark
2B T Herr
SS O Smith
3B T Pendleton
LF V Coleman
CF W McGee
RU- C Ford
RU J Morris
UT J Oquendo
M W Herzog

SD 1987 NL
SP E Show
SP E Whitson
SP J Jones
SP A Hawkins
SP M Grant
RP L McCullers
RP G Booker
RP M Davis
RP R Gossage
C B Santiago
1U J Kruk
2B T Flannery
SS G Templeton
IO R Ready
ML S Jefferson
CF S Mack
RF T Gwynn
L1 C Martinez
UO M Wynne
UT- L Salazar
M L Bowa

SF 1987 NL
SR K Downs
SR M LaCoss
SP A Hammaker
SP M Krukow
SP D Dravecky
RP S Garrelts
RP J Robinson
RP J Gott
C B Brenly
1B W Clark
2B R Thompson
SS- J Uribe
3B- K Mitchell
LF J Leonard
CF C Davis
RF C Maldonado
OI M Aldrete
CF E Milner
UI C Speier
C - B Melvin
IF- H Spilman
SS- M Williams
M R Craig

BAL 1987 AL
SP M Boddicker
SP E Bell
SR D Schmidt
SR J Habyan
SR K Dixon
RP M Williamson
RP T Niedenfuer
RP T Arnold
C T Kennedy
1B E Murray
2B- B Ripken
SS C Ripken
3B R Knight
LM- K Gerhart
CF F Lynn
LR L Sheets
OF M Young
OF- J Dwyer
RF- L Lacy
D2- A Wiggins

BOS 1987 AL
SP R Clemens
SP B Hurst
SP A Nipper
SR B Stanley
SP J Sellers
RP W Gardner
RP C Schiraldi
RP S Crawford
RP T Bolton
C - M Sullivan
1R D Evans
2B M Barrett
SS S Owen
3B W Boggs
LF J Rice
CF E Burks
LU M Greenwell
DH D Baylor
UI- E Romero
M J McNamara

CAL 1987 AL
SP M Witt
SP D Sutton
SR W Fraser
SR J Lazorko
SP J Candelaria
RP D Buice
RP C Finley
RP G Minton
RP G Lucas
C B Boone
1B W Joyner
2B M McLemore
SS D Schofield
3B D DeCinces
L3 J Howell
CF G Pettis
RF D White
DH B Downing
LO- R Jones
M G Mauch

CHI 1987 AL
SP F Bannister
SP R Dotson
SP J DeLeon
SP B Long
RP B Thigpen
RP J Winn
RP B James
RP R Searage
C C Fisk
1B G Walker
2B F Manrique
SS O Guillen
3B- T Hulett
LO G Redus
CF K Williams
RF I Calderon
DH H Baines
OF D Boston
2B D Hill
M J Fregosi

CLE 1987 AL
SP T Candiotti
SP K Schrom
SR S Bailes
SP P Niekro
SP S Carlton
RP G Swindell
RP D Jones
RS R Yett
RP E Vande Berg
C - C Bando
1L J Carter
2B- T Bernazard
SS J Franco
3B B Jacoby
LF M Hall
CF B Butler
RF C Snyder
1D P Tabler
OF- C Castillo
M1 P Corrales
M2 D Edwards

DET 1987 AL
SP J Morris
SP W Terrell
SP F Tanana
SP D Petry
SP J Robinson
RP E King
RP M Henneman
RP M Thurmond
RP W Hernandez
C M Nokes
1D D Evans
2B L Whitaker
SS A Trammell
3B T Brookens
LF K Gibson
CF C Lemon
RF P Sheridan
D1- B Madlock
1U- D Bergman
CO- M Heath
OF- L Herndon
M S Anderson

KC 1987 AL
SP B Saberhagen
SP M Gubicza
SP C Leibrandt
SP D Jackson
SR B Black
RP S Farr
RP D Quisenberry
RP J Gleaton
C J Quirk
1U G Brett
2B F White
SS A Salazar
3B K Seitzer
LF B Jackson
CF W Wilson
RF D Tartabull
UT S Balboni
M1 B Gardner
M2 J Wathan

MIL 1987 AL
SP T Higuera
SP B Wegman
SP J Nieves
SR C Bosio
RS C Crim
CL D Plesac
RP M Clear
RP J Aldrich
C B Surhoff
1B G Brock
2B J Castillo
SS D Sveum
3B- E Riles
LU R Deer
CF R Yount

RF G Braggs
DH- C Cooper
LU M Felder
RO- R Manning
IF P Molitor
23- J Gantner
M T Trebelhorn

MIN 1987 AL
SP B Blyleven
SP F Viola
SP L Straker
SP M Smithson
RS J Berenguer
CL J Reardon
RP G Frazier
RP K Atherton
C T Laudner
1B K Hrbek
2B S Lombardozzi
SS G Gagne
3B G Gaetti
LF D Gladden
CF K Puckett
RL T Brunansky
DU R Smalley
RU R Bush
UO M Davidson
S2 A Newman
UT- G Larkin
M T Kelly

NY 1987 AL
SP T John
SP R Rhoden
SR C Hudson
SP D Rasmussen
SP R Guidry
CL D Righetti
RP T Stoddard
RP P Clements
C R Cerone
1B D Mattingly
2B W Randolph
SS W Tolleson
3B M Pagliarulo
OI G Ward
MU C Washington
RF D Winfield
LU D Pasqua
OF- R Henderson
M L Piniella

OAK 1987 AL
SP D Stewart
SP C Young
SR S Ontiveros
RP D Eckersley
RS G Nelson
RS D Lamp
RP D Leiper
C T Steinbach
1B M McGwire
2B T Phillips
SS A Griffin
3B C Lansford
LF J Canseco
ML L Polonia
RF M Davis
DU R Jackson
MO- S Javier
CF- D Murphy
C - M Tettleton
M T LaRussa

SEA 1987 AL
SP M Langston
SP M Moore
SP M Morgan
SP S Bankhead
SP L Guetterman
RP J Reed
RP B Wilkinson
RS M Trujillo
C S Bradley
1B A Davis
2B H Reynolds
SS R Quinones
3B J Presley
LF P Bradley
CF J Moses
RF M Kingery
DH K Phelps
MR- M Brantley
C - D Valle
M D Williams

TEX 1987 AL
SP C Hough
SP J Guzman
SP B Witt
SR G Harris
RP D Mohorcic
RP M Williams
RP J Russell
RS M Loynd
C - D Slaught
1B P O'Brien
2B J Browne
SS S Fletcher
3B S Buechele
LF P Incaviglia
CF O McDowell
RF R Sierra
DH L Parrish
ML B Brower
CI G Petralli
UC- D Porter
UI- C Wilkerson
M B Valentine

TOR 1987 AL
SP J Key
SP J Clancy
SP D Stieb
SR J Cerutti
RP M Eichhorn
CL T Henke
RS J Nunez
RP J Musselman
C E Whitt
1B W Upshaw
2U G Iorg
SS T Fernandez
3B K Gruber
LF G Bell
CF L Moseby
RF J Barfield
DH F McGriff
OI R Leach
3B R Mulliniks
DU- C Fielder
M J Williams

ATL 1988 NL
SP R Mahler
SP T Glavine
SP P Smith
SP Z Smith
RP C Puleo
RP J Alvarez
RP P Assenmacher
C O Virgil
1B G Perry
2B R Gant
SS A Thomas
3B K Oberkfell
LM D James
MU- A Hall
RF D Murphy
C - B Benedict
M1 C Tanner
M2 R Nixon

CHI 1988 NL
SP G Maddux
SP R Sutcliffe
SP J Moyer
SP C Schiraldi
SR J Pico
RP F DiPino
RP L Lancaster
C - D Berryhill
1B M Grace
2B R Sandberg
SS S Dunston
3B V Law
LF R Palmeiro
UO D Jackson
RF A Dawson
C - J Davis
M D Zimmer

CIN 1988 NL
SP D Jackson
SP T Browning
SR J Rijo
CL J Franco
RP R Murphy
RP T Birtsas
RP F Williams
C - B Diaz
1B N Esasky
2B J Treadway
SS B Larkin
3B C Sabo
LF K Daniels
CF E Davis
RF P O'Neill
OI D Collins
2I- D Concepcion
M1 P Rose
M2 T Helms
M3 P Rose

HOU 1988 NL
SP N Ryan
SP M Scott
SP J Deshaies
SR D Darwin
SP B Knepper
RP J Agosto
RP L Andersen
CL D Smith
C - A Trevino
1B G Davis
2B B Doran
SS R Ramirez
3B- B Bell
LF B Hatcher
CF G Young
RF K Bass
UO T Puhl
M H Lanier

LA 1988 NL
SP O Hershiser
SP T Leary
SP T Belcher
SP F Valenzuela
RP A Pena
RP B Holton
CL J Howell
RP T Crews
C M Scioscia
1U F Stubbs
2B S Sax
SS- A Griffin
3B J Hamilton
LF K Gibson
CF J Shelby
R1 M Marshall
SU D Anderson
RU M Davis
UT- M Hatcher
OI- D Heep
M T Lasorda

MON 1988 NL
SP D Martinez
SP B Smith
SP P Perez
SP J Dopson
SP B Holman
RP T Burke
RP J Parrett
RP A McGaffigan
RP J Hesketh
C - N Santovenia
1B A Galarraga
2S T Foley
SS L Rivera
3B T Wallach
LF T Raines
ML- O Nixon
RF H Brooks
IF- W Johnson
MO- M Webster
M B Rodgers

NY 1988 NL
SP D Gooden
SP R Darling
SP D Cone
SP B Ojeda
SP S Fernandez
RP R McDowell
RP T Leach
CL R Myers
C G Carter
1B- K Hernandez
2B W Backman
SS K Elster
3B H Johnson
LF K McReynolds
CF L Dykstra
RF D Strawberry
13 D Magadan
MO M Wilson
2B- T Teufel
M D Johnson

PHI 1988 NL
SP K Gross
SP D Carman
SP S Rawley
SP D Palmer
RS B Ruffin
RP G Harris
CL S Bedrosian
RP K Tekulve
C L Parrish
1B V Hayes
2B J Samuel
SS S Jeltz
3B M Schmidt
LF P Bradley
CF M Thompson
RU C James
OI G Gross
M1 L Elia
M2 J Vukovich

PIT 1988 NL
SP D Drabek
SP B Walk
SP J Smiley
SP M Dunne
SR B Fisher
RP J Robinson
CL J Gott
RP B Kipper
RP B Jones
C M LaValliere
1B S Bream
2B J Lind
SS R Belliard
3B B Bonilla
LF B Bonds
CF A Van Slyke
RU R Reynolds
M J Leyland

STL 1988 NL
SP J DeLeon
SP J Magrane
SP J Tudor
SR L McWilliams
SR B Forsch
RS S Terry
CL T Worrell
RP K Dayley
RP J Costello
C T Pena
1B- B Horner
2B- L Alicea
SS O Smith
3B T Pendleton
LF V Coleman
CF W McGee
RF T Brunansky
UT J Oquendo
OI- C Ford
IC- T Pagnozzi
M W Herzog

SD 1988 NL
SP E Show
SP A Hawkins
SP E Whitson
SP J Jones
SP D Rasmussen
RP M Davis
RP L McCullers
RS M Grant
RP G Booker
C B Santiago
1L K Moreland
2B R Alomar
SS G Templeton
3B- C Brown
OI C Martinez
ML M Wynne
RF T Gwynn
1O J Kruk
3U R Ready
SU- D Thon
M1 L Bowa
M2 J McKeon

SF 1988 NL
SP R Reuschel
SR D Robinson
SP K Downs
SR A Hammaker
SP M Krukow
RP M LaCoss
RP S Garrelts
RP C Lefferts
RP J Price
C - B Melvin
1B W Clark
2B R Thompson
SS J Uribe
3L K Mitchell
LR M Aldrete
CF B Butler
RF C Maldonado
23- C Speier
UO- J Youngblood
M R Craig

BAL 1988 AL
SP J Bautista
SP J Tibbs
SP J Ballard
SP M Boddicker
RS D Schmidt
RS M Williamson
RP D Sisk
RS M Thurmond
C - M Tettleton
1D J Traber
2B B Ripken
SS C Ripken
3B- R Gonzales
LF- P Stanicek
MU- F Lynn
RL J Orsulak
1D E Murray
OI L Sheets
ML K Gerhart
C - T Kennedy
3B- R Schu
M2 F Robinson

BOS 1988 AL
SP R Clemens
SP B Hurst
SR W Gardner
SP O Boyd
SR M Smithson
CL L Smith
RP B Stanley
RP D Lamp
C - R Gedman
1R T Benzinger
2B M Barrett
SS J Reed
3B W Boggs
LF M Greenwell
CF E Burks
R1 D Evans
DH J Rice
C - R Cerone
SS- S Owen
M1 J McNamara
M2 J Morgan

CAL 1988 AL
SP M Witt
SP W Fraser
SP C Finley
SP K McCaskill
SP D Petry
CL B Harvey
RP G Minton
RP S Cliburn
C B Boone
1B W Joyner
2L J Ray
SS D Schofield
3B J Howell
LM T Armas
CF D White
RF C Davis
DH B Downing
M1 C Rojas
M2 M Stubing

CHI 1988 AL
SP M Perez
SP J Reuss
SR B Long
SP D LaPoint
SP J McDowell
CL B Thigpen
RS R Horton
RP J Davis
RS J Bittiger
C - C Fisk
1B G Walker
2B F Manrique
SS O Guillen
3B S Lyons
UO D Boston
CF D Gallagher
LR D Pasqua
DH H Baines
2U- D Hill
M J Fregosi

CLE 1988 AL
SP G Swindell
SP T Candiotti
SP J Farrell
SR S Bailes
SP R Yett
CL D Jones
RP D Gordon
RP B Havens
C A Allanson
1B W Upshaw
2B J Franco
SS- J Bell
3B B Jacoby
LF M Hall
CF J Carter
RF C Snyder
DH- R Kittle
M D Edwards

DET 1988 AL
SP J Morris
SP D Alexander
SP W Terrell
SP F Tanana
SP J Robinson
CL M Henneman
RP P Gibson
RP W Hernandez
RS E King
C M Nokes
1U R Knight
2B L Whitaker
SS A Trammell
3B T Brookens
LU P Sheridan
CF G Pettis
RF C Lemon
D1 D Evans
1D D Bergman
UT L Salazar
C - M Heath
2U- J Walewander
M S Anderson

KC 1988 AL
SP M Gubicza
SP B Saberhagen
SP C Leibrandt
SP F Bannister
RP S Farr
RP J Montgomery
C - J Quirk
1B G Brett
2B F White
SS K Stillwell
3B K Seitzer
LF B Jackson
CF W Wilson
RF D Tartabull
UT- B Buckner
UO- J Eisenreich
UT- B Pecota
UT- P Tabler
M J Wathan

MIL 1988 AL
SP T Higuera
SP B Wegman
SR C Bosio
SP D August
SP M Birkbeck
RP C Crim
RS J Nieves
RP T Filer
RP O Jones
C B Surhoff
1B G Brock
2B J Gantner
SS D Sveum
3D P Molitor
LF- J Leonard
CF R Yount
RL R Deer
D1 J Meyer
M T Trebelhorn

MIN 1988 AL
SP F Viola
SP B Blyleven
SP A Anderson
SP C Lea
SP F Toliver
CL J Reardon
RP J Berenguer
RP K Atherton
RP M Portugal
C T Laudner
1D K Hrbek
2B S Lombardozzi
SS G Gagne
3B G Gaetti
LF D Gladden
CF K Puckett
RF R Bush
D1 G Larkin
RF M Davidson
UO J Moses
3S A Newman
2B- T Herr
M T Kelly

NY 1988 AL
SP R Rhoden
SP T John
SP R Dotson
SP J Candelaria
SR C Hudson
RP N Allen
CL D Righetti
RP C Guante
RP S Shields
C D Slaught
1B D Mattingly
2B W Randolph
SS R Santana
3B M Pagliarulo
LF R Henderson
CF C Washington
RF D Winfield
DU J Clark
C - J Skinner
UT- G Ward
M1 B Martin
M2 L Piniella

OAK 1988 AL
SP D Stewart
SP B Welch
SP S Davis
SP C Young
SP T Burns
CL D Eckersley
RP G Nelson
RP R Honeycutt
RP E Plunk
C R Hassey
1B M McGwire
2B G Hubbard
SS W Weiss
3B C Lansford
LM S Javier
CF D Henderson
RF J Canseco
DH- D Baylor
2S M Gallego
DL D Parker
C T Steinbach
LF- L Polonia
M T LaRussa

SEA 1988 AL
SP M Langston
SP M Moore
SR B Swift
SP S Bankhead
SP M Campbell
RP M Jackson
RP J Reed
CL M Schooler
C S Bradley
1B A Davis
2B H Reynolds
SS R Quinones
3B J Presley
LF M Brantley
CF H Cotto
RF- G Wilson
DH- K Phelps
D1 S Balboni
C - D Valle
M1 D Williams
M2 J Snyder

TEX 1988 AL
SP C Hough
SP J Guzman
SP P Kilgus
SR J Russell
SP B Witt
RP M Williams
RP C McMurtry
RP D Mohorcic
CU G Petralli
1B P O'Brien
2I C Wilkerson
SS S Fletcher
3B S Buechele
UT C Espy
CF O McDowell
RF R Sierra
DH- L Parrish
LF P Incaviglia
UO- B Brower
CU- M Stanley
M B Valentine

TOR 1988 AL
SP M Flanagan
SP D Stieb
SP J Clancy
SP J Key
RP D Ward
RS J Cerutti
CL T Henke
RP M Eichhorn
C E Whitt
1B F McGriff
2B M Lee
SS T Fernandez
3B K Gruber
LF G Bell
CF L Moseby
RF J Barfield
DH R Mulliniks
2B N Liriano
OI- R Leach
M J Williams

ATL 1989 NL
SP J Smoltz
SP T Glavine
SP D Lilliquist
SP P Smith
SP M Clary
RP J Boever
RP J Acker
RP Z Smith
RP M Eichhorn
C - J Davis
1B- G Perry
2B J Treadway
SS A Thomas
32 J Blauser
LF L Smith
CF- O McDowell
MR D Murphy
IF D Evans
OI T Gregg
OF- G Berroa
M R Nixon

CHI 1989 NL
SP G Maddux
SP R Sutcliffe
SP M Bielecki
SR P Kilgus
SR S Sanderson
CL M Williams
RS J Pico
RS S Wilson
RP C Schiraldi
C - D Berryhill
1B M Grace
2B R Sandberg
SS S Dunston
3B V Law
LR D Smith
CF J Walton
RF A Dawson
LO M Webster
UT- L McClendon
IF- D Ramos
M D Zimmer

CIN 1989 NL
SP T Browning
SP R Mahler
SP D Jackson
SP J Rijo
SP S Scudder
CL J Franco
RP R Dibble
RP N Charlton
RP T Birtsas
C J Reed
1B T Benzinger
2B R Oester
SS- B Larkin
3B- C Sabo
UO R Roomes
CF E Davis
RF P O'Neill
LU K Griffey
23- L Quinones
UO H Winningham
M1 P Rose
M2 T Helms

HOU 1989 NL
SP M Scott
SP J Deshaies
SP J Clancy
SP B Knepper
SR B Forsch
RP D Darwin
RP M Portugal
RP L Andersen
RP J Agosto
C C Biggio
1B G Davis
2B B Doran
SS R Ramirez
3B K Caminiti
LF B Hatcher
CF G Young
RL T Puhl
IO C Reynolds
RL- K Bass
M A Howe

LA 1989 NL
SP O Hershiser
SP T Belcher
SP F Valenzuela
SR M Morgan
SP T Leary
CL J Howell
RS J Wetteland
RP R Martinez
RP A Pena
C M Scioscia
1B E Murray
2B W Randolph
SS A Griffin
3B J Hamilton
LF- K Gibson
CF J Shelby
RF M Marshall
UI- D Anderson
MR- J Gonzalez
UT- M Hatcher
M T Lasorda

MON 1989 NL
SP De Martinez
SP B Smith
SP K Gross
SP P Perez
SP M Langston
CL T Burke
RP A McGaffigan
C - N Santovenia
1B A Galarraga
2B T Foley
SS S Owen

3B T Wallach
LF T Raines
CF Da Martinez
RF H Brooks
C M Fitzgerald
MU O Nixon
UT- R Hudler
US- W Johnson
M B Rodgers

NY 1989 NL
SP D Cone
SP S Fernandez
SP R Darling
SP B Ojeda
SP D Gooden
CL R Myers
RP R Aguilera
RP D Aase
C - B Lyons
1U D Magadan
2B G Jefferies
SS K Elster
3B H Johnson
LF K McReynolds
CF- J Samuel
RF D Strawberry
IF- T Teufel
M D Johnson

PHI 1989 NL
SP K Howell
SR D Carman
SP B Ruffin
SR L McWilliams
SP D Cook
RP J Parrett
RP T Mulholland
RP G Harris
CL R McDowell
C D Daulton
1B R Jordan
2B T Herr
SS D Thon
3B- C Hayes
LF- J Kruk
CF- L Dykstra
RF V Hayes
UT C Ford
S3 S Jeltz
UO B Dernier
UO D Murphy
M N Leyva

PIT 1989 NL
SP D Drabek
SP J Smiley
SP B Walk
SR N Heaton
SR J Robinson
RS R Kramer
CL B Landrum
RP B Kipper
RP D Bair
C - J Ortiz
1U- G Redus
2B J Lind
SS- J Bell
3B B Bonilla
LF B Bonds
CF A Van Slyke
RO R Reynolds
UO J Cangelosi
RF G Wilson
1U- B Distefano
M J Leyland

STL 1989 NL
SP J DeLeon
SP J Magrane
SP K Hill
SP S Terry
RP F DiPino
RP K Dayley
RP D Quisenberry
CL T Worrell
C T Pena
1B P Guerrero
2B J Oquendo
SS O Smith
3B T Pendleton
LF V Coleman
CF M Thompson
RF T Brunansky
UO- J Morris
M W Herzog

SD 1989 NL
SP B Hurst
SP E Whitson
SP D Rasmussen
SP W Terrell
SP E Show
RS G Harris
CL M Davis
RP M Grant
C B Santiago
1B J Clark
2B R Alomar
SS G Templeton
3B- L Salazar
LR- C James
UO M Wynne
MR T Gwynn
L1 C Martinez
UT B Roberts
M J McKeon

SF 1989 NL
SP R Reuschel
SP D Robinson
SP S Garrelts
SR M LaCoss
RP C Lefferts
RP J Brantley
RS A Hammaker
CL S Bedrosian
C T Kennedy
1B W Clark
2B R Thompson
SS J Uribe
3U E Riles
LF K Mitchell
CF B Butler
RF C Maldonado
C - K Manwaring
UO- D Nixon
UI- K Oberkfell
3B- M Williams
M R Craig

BAL 1989 AL
SP B Milacki
SP J Ballard
SR D Schmidt
SP P Harnisch
RS B Holton
RP M Williamson
CL G Olson
RP M Thurmond
CD M Tettleton
1B R Milligan
2B B Ripken
SS C Ripken
3B C Worthington
LF P Bradley
MR M Devereaux
RU J Orsulak
DH L Sheets
CF- B Anderson
RM- S Finley
C - B Melvin
1B- J Traber
M F Robinson

BOS 1989 AL
SP R Clemens
SP M Boddicker
SP J Dopson
SR M Smithson
RP D Lamp
RP R Murphy
CL L Smith
RP B Stanley
C R Cerone
1B N Esasky
2B- M Barrett
SS- L Rivera
3B W Boggs
LF M Greenwell
CF- E Burks
MR- K Romine
RD D Evans
RU D Heep
S2 J Reed
C - R Gedman
M J Morgan

CAL 1989 AL
SP B Blyleven
SP M Witt
SP K McCaskill
SP C Finley
SP J Abbott
RP G Minton
RP W Fraser
CL B Harvey
RP B McClure
C L Parrish
1B W Joyner
2B J Ray
SS- D Schofield
3B J Howell
LF C Davis
CF D White
RF C Washington
DH B Downing
SS- K Anderson
M D Rader

CHI 1989 AL
SP M Perez
SP E King
SR S Rosenberg
SP G Hibbard
SP J Reuss
RS S Hillegas
CL B Thigpen
RS B Long
RP R Dotson
C C Fisk
1D- G Walker
21 S Lyons
SS O Guillen
31 C Martinez
LU D Boston
CF D Gallagher
RU I Calderon
DR- H Baines
M J Torborg

CLE 1989 AL
SP B Black
SP J Farrell
SP T Candiotti
SP G Swindell
SR R Yett
RS S Bailes
CL D Jones
RP J Orosco
C A Allanson
1B P O'Brien
2B J Browne
SS F Fermin
3B B Jacoby
ML J Carter
CF- B Komminsk
RF C Snyder
DU D Clark
M1 D Edwards
M2 J Hart

DET 1989 AL
SP F Tanana
SP D Alexander
SP J Morris
RS P Gibson
RP M Henneman
RP F Williams
RP E Nunez
C M Heath
1B D Bergman
2B L Whitaker
SS A Trammell
3B R Schu
LD F Lynn
CF G Pettis
RF C Lemon
D1- K Moreland
OI G Ward
UT- M Brumley
CD- M Nokes
OI- K Williams
M S Anderson

KC 1989 AL
SP B Saberhagen
SP M Gubicza
SP C Leibrandt
SR L Aquino
RS T Gordon
RP J Montgomery
CL S Farr
RP T Leach
C B Boone
1B G Brett
2B F White
SS K Stillwell
3B K Seitzer
LF B Jackson
CF W Wilson
MR J Eisenreich
RD D Tartabull
UT P Tabler
2S B Wellman
M J Wathan

MIL 1989 AL
SP C Bosio
SP D August
SP T Higuera
SP J Navarro
RP C Crim
RS M Knudson
RS B Krueger
CL D Plesac
C B Surhoff
1B G Brock
2B J Gantner
SS B Spiers
3U P Molitor
LF G Braggs
CF R Yount
RF R Deer
D1- J Meyer
OI M Felder
1D- T Francona
SU- G Sheffield
M T Trebelhorn

MIN 1989 AL
SP A Anderson
SP F Viola
SP R Smith
SP S Rawley
RP J Berenguer
CL J Reardon
RP G Wayne
C B Harper
1B K Hrbek
23 A Newman
SS G Gagne
3B G Gaetti
LF D Gladden
CF K Puckett
RU R Bush
DH- J Dwyer
UT G Larkin
CU T Laudner
OI J Moses
2B- W Backman
RU- C Castillo
M T Kelly

NY 1989 AL
SP A Hawkins
SP C Parker
SP D LaPoint
SR C Cary
RP L Guetterman
CL D Righetti
RP L McCullers
RS E Plunk
C D Slaught
1B D Mattingly
2B S Sax
SS A Espinoza
3B- M Pagliarulo
OF M Hall
CF R Kelly
RF J Barfield
DU S Balboni
DU- K Phelps
M1 D Green
M2 B Dent

OAK 1989 AL
SP D Stewart
SP M Moore
SP B Welch
SP S Davis
SP C Young
RP T Burns
CL D Eckersley
RP R Honeycutt
RP G Nelson
C T Steinbach
1B M McGwire
23 T Phillips
S2 M Gallego
3B C Lansford
LF- R Henderson
CF D Henderson
RM S Javier
DH D Parker
C - R Hassey
SS- W Weiss
M T LaRussa

SEA 1989 AL
SP S Bankhead
SP B Holman
SP R Johnson
SR B Swift
SP E Hanson
CL M Schooler
RP M Jackson
RP J Reed
C - D Valle
1B A Davis
2B H Reynolds
SS O Vizquel
3B J Presley
LF G Briley
CF K Griffey
RI D Coles
CU S Bradley
LM H Cotto
DH J Leonard
M J Lefebvre

TEX 1989 AL
SP N Ryan
SP B Witt
SP K Brown
SP C Hough
SP M Jeffcoat
CL J Russell
RP K Rogers
RP C Guante
RP D Hall
C - C Kreuter
1B R Palmeiro
2B J Franco
SS- S Fletcher
3B S Buechele
LF P Incaviglia
CF C Espy
RF R Sierra
DH- H Baines
SO J Kunkel
OI R Leach
M B Valentine

TOR 1989 AL
SP J Key
SP D Stieb
SP J Cerutti
SP M Flanagan
SP T Stottlemyre
RP D Ward
RP T Henke
RP D Wells
RP F Wills
C E Whitt
1B F McGriff
2B N Liriano
SS T Fernandez
3B K Gruber
LF G Bell
CF L Moseby
RF J Felix
D3 R Mulliniks
IO M Lee
CU- P Borders
M1 J Williams
M2 C Gaston

ATL 1990 NL
SP J Smoltz
SP T Glavine
SP C Leibrandt
SR M Clary
SP S Avery
RP T Castillo
RP M Grant
RP R Luecken
C G Olson
1R D Justice
2B J Treadway
SS J Blauser
3B J Presley
LF L Smith
ML R Gant
RF- D Murphy
UT T Gregg
UI M Lemke
MU O McDowell
SS- A Thomas
M1 R Nixon
M2 B Cox

CHI 1990 NL
SP G Maddux
SP M Harkey
SP M Bielecki
RS S Wilson
RS L Lancaster
RP P Assenmacher
RS J Pico
C J Girardi
1B M Grace
2B R Sandberg
SS S Dunston
3B L Salazar
LM D Dascenzo
CF J Walton
RF A Dawson
3U D Ramos
LU D Smith
UM- D Clark
MU- M Wynne
M D Zimmer

CIN 1990 NL
SP T Browning
SP J Rijo
SP J Armstrong
SR R Mahler
SP D Jackson
RS N Charlton
CL R Myers
RP R Dibble
RP T Layana
C J Oliver
1B T Benzinger
2B M Duncan
SS B Larkin
3B C Sabo
LM B Hatcher
ML E Davis
RF P O'Neill
1U H Morris
UI- L Quinones
MU- H Winningham
M L Piniella

HOU 1990 NL
SP J Deshaies
SP M Scott
SP M Portugal
SP B Gullickson
SR D Darwin
RP J Agosto
CL D Smith
RP L Andersen
RS J Clancy
C C Biggio
1B- G Davis
2B B Doran
SS R Ramirez
3B K Caminiti
UT F Stubbs
MS E Yelding
RF G Wilson
UT C Candaele
RU- E Anthony
M A Howe

LA 1990 NL
SP R Martinez
SP M Morgan
SP F Valenzuela
SP T Belcher
RP T Crews
CL J Howell
RS M Hartley
RP J Gott
C M Scioscia
1B E Murray
2B J Samuel
SS A Griffin
3B M Sharperson
LF K Daniels
MU S Javier
RF H Brooks
UO J Gonzalez
UO C Gwynn
32 L Harris
CF- K Gibson
IO- M Hatcher
M T Lasorda

MON 1990 NL
SP De Martinez
SP O Boyd
SP K Gross
SP M Gardner
SP Z Smith
CL T Burke
RP B Sampen
RP S Frey
RP D Hall
C M Fitzgerald
1B A Galarraga
2B D DeShields
SS S Owen
3B T Wallach
LF T Raines
CF Da Martinez
RF L Walker
UO M Grissom
MU O Nixon
OI- M Aldrete
UT- J Noboa
M B Rodgers

NY 1990 NL
SP F Viola
SP D Gooden
SP D Cone
SP S Fernandez
SR R Darling
RS B Ojeda
CL J Franco
RP A Pena
RP W Whitehurst
C M Sasser
1B D Magadan
2B G Jefferies
SS- K Elster
3S H Johnson
LF K McReynolds
CF D Boston
RF D Strawberry
UO- M Carreon
MU- K Miller
IF- T O'Malley
M1 D Johnson
M2 B Harrelson

PHI 1990 NL
SP P Combs
SP T Mulholland
SP B Ruffin
SP J DeJesus
SP K Howell
RS D Cook
RP R McDowell
RP D Akerfelds
RP D Carman
C D Daulton
1B- R Jordan
2B T Herr
SS D Thon
3B C Hayes
OI J Kruk
CF L Dykstra
RL V Hayes
UT R Ready
M N Leyva

PIT 1990 NL
SP D Drabek
SP J Smiley
SP N Heaton
SP B Walk
RS B Patterson
RP B Landrum
RP S Belinda
RP B Kipper
C - M LaValliere
1B S Bream
2B J Lind
SS J Bell
3B J King
LF B Bonds
CF A Van Slyke
RF B Bonilla
3U W Backman
1B- G Redus
UO- R Reynolds
C - D Slaught
M J Leyland

STL 1990 NL
SP J Magrane
SP J DeLeon
SP B Tewksbury
SP J Tudor
SP B Smith
CL L Smith
RP F DiPino
RP K Dayley
RP S Terry
CU T Zeile
1B P Guerrero
2B J Oquendo
SS O Smith
3B T Pendleton
LF V Coleman
CF W McGee
RU M Thompson
UT D Collins
UT- R Hudler
M1 W Herzog
M2 R Schoendienst
M3 J Torre

SD 1990 NL
SP E Whitson
SP B Hurst
SP A Benes
SP D Rasmussen
RP G Harris
RS E Show
RS C Schiraldi
CL C Lefferts
C B Santiago
1B J Clark
2B R Alomar
SS G Templeton
3B M Pagliarulo
L3 B Roberts
ML J Carter
RF T Gwynn
1U P Stephenson
UO- S Abner
UO- F Lynn
M1 J McKeon
M2 G Riddoch

SF 1990 NL
SP J Burkett
SP S Garrelts
SP D Robinson
SR T Wilson
CL J Brantley
RP S Bedrosian
RS A Hammaker
RP M Thurmond
C T Kennedy
1B W Clark
2B R Thompson
SS J Uribe
3B M Williams
LF K Mitchell
CF B Butler
RU M Kingery
C - G Carter
UT- G Litton
UI- E Riles
M R Craig

BAL 1990 AL
SP P Harnisch
SP D Johnson
SP B Milacki
SR J Ballard
SP B McDonald
RP J Mitchell
CL G Olson
RP M Williamson
RP J Price
CD M Tettleton
1B R Milligan
2B B Ripken
SS C Ripken
3B C Worthington
LF- P Bradley
CF M Devereaux
RM S Finley
DH- S Horn
RU J Orsulak
UO- B Anderson
C - B Melvin
M F Robinson

BOS 1990 AL
SP M Boddicker
SP R Clemens
SP G Harris
SP D Kiecker
SP T Bolton
SP D Lamp
RS W Gardner
CL J Reardon
RP R Murphy
C T Pena
1B C Quintana
2B J Reed
SS L Rivera
3B W Boggs
LF M Greenwell
CF E Burks
RF T Brunansky
DH D Evans
M J Morgan

CAL 1990 AL
SP C Finley
SP M Langston
SP J Abbott
SP K McCaskill
SP B Blyleven
RP M Eichhorn
CL B Harvey
RP W Fraser
RP M Fetters
C L Parrish
1B- W Joyner
2B J Ray
SS D Schofield
3B J Howell
UO D Bichette
CF D White
RF D Winfield
DH- B Downing
DL C Davis
2I D Hill
LU L Polonia
UO- M Venable
M D Rader

CHI 1990 AL
SP G Hibbard
SP J McDowell
SP M Perez
SP E King
CL B Thigpen
RS W Edwards
RP D Pall
RP B Jones
C C Fisk
1B- C Martinez
2B S Fletcher
SS O Guillen
3B R Ventura
LF I Calderon
CF L Johnson
RF S Sosa
DO D Pasqua
D1- R Kittle
1U- S Lyons
M J Torborg

CLE 1990 AL
SP G Swindell
SP T Candiotti
SP B Black
SR S Valdez
CL D Jones
RP S Olin
RP J Orosco
C S Alomar
31 B Jacoby
2B J Browne
SS F Fermin
UI C Baerga
LR C Maldonado
MU M Webster
RF C Snyder
DH C James
UT- D James
M J McNamara

DET 1990 AL
SP J Morris

SP F Tanana
SP D Petry
SP J Robinson
RP M Henneman
RP P Gibson
RP J Gleaton
RP E Nunez
C M Heath
1B C Fielder
2B L Whitaker
SS A Trammell
32 T Phillips
LU G Ward
CF L Moseby
RF C Lemon
D1 D Bergman
OF L Sheets
M S Anderson

KC 1990 AL

SP T Gordon
SP K Appier
SP B Saberhagen
SP S Davis
RS S Farr
RP J Montgomery
RP S Crawford
RP M Davis
C M Macfarlane
1U G Brett
2B- F White
SS K Stillwell
3B K Seitzer
UO W Wilson
ML B Jackson
RL J Eisenreich
D1 G Perry
2I- B Pecota
RD- D Tartabull
M J Wathan

MIL 1990 AL

SP T Higuera
SP M Knudson
SR J Navarro
SP R Robinson
SP C Bosio
RS B Krueger
RP C Crim
CL D Plesac
RS T Edens
C B Surhoff
1B G Brock
2B- J Gantner
SS B Spiers
3B G Sheffield
LR M Felder
CF R Yount
RF R Deer
DH D Parker
21 P Molitor
LF G Vaughn
SS- E Diaz
UO- D Hamilton
M T Trebelhorn

MIN 1990 AL

SP A Anderson
SP K Tapani
SP R Smith
SP D West
SP M Guthrie
RP S Erickson
RP J Berenguer
CL R Aguilera
RP T Drummond
C B Harper
1B K Hrbek
2S A Newman
SS G Gagne
3B G Gaetti
LF D Gladden
CF K Puckett
UO S Mack
UT G Larkin
OI J Moses
M T Kelly

NY 1990 AL

SP T Leary
SP A Hawkins
SP D LaPoint
SP C Cary
RS G Cadaret
RP L Guetterman
CL D Righetti
RP J Robinson
C B Geren
1B D Mattingly
2B S Sax
SS A Espinoza
3B- R Velarde
LU- O Azocar
CF R Kelly
RF J Barfield
DU S Balboni
OF M Hall
3B- J Leyritz
CD- M Nokes
M1 B Dent
M2 S Merrill

OAK 1990 AL

SP D Stewart
SP B Welch
SP S Sanderson
SP M Moore
SP C Young
CL D Eckersley
RP T Burns
RP G Nelson
RP R Honeycutt
CU T Steinbach
1B M McGwire
2B- W Randolph
SS W Weiss
3B C Lansford
LF R Henderson
CF D Henderson
RL F Jose
RD J Canseco
2S M Gallego
UT- L Blankenship
CU- R Hassey
M T LaRussa

SEA 1990 AL

SP E Hanson
SP M Young
SP R Johnson
SP B Holman
RS B Swift
CL M Schooler
RP M Jackson
RP K Comstock
C D Valle
1B P O'Brien
2B H Reynolds
SS- O Vizquel
3B E Martinez
RL G Briley
CF K Griffey
RL H Cotto
D1 A Davis
CU S Bradley
LD J Leonard
M J Lefebvre

TEX 1990 AL

SP B Witt
SP C Hough
SP N Ryan
SP K Brown
RS M Jeffcoat
RP K Rogers
RS J Moyer
RP B Arnsberg
C G Petralli
1B R Palmeiro
2B J Franco
SS J Huson
3B- S Buechele
LF P Incaviglia
CF G Pettis
RF R Sierra
DH H Baines
OI J Daugherty
SI J Kunkel
CU M Stanley
M B Valentine

TOR 1990 AL

SP D Stieb
SP T Stottlemyre
SR D Wells
SP J Key
SP J Cerutti
RP D Ward
CL T Henke
RP F Wills
RP J Acker
C P Borders
1B F McGriff
2B M Lee
SS T Fernandez
3B K Gruber
LD G Bell
CF M Wilson
RF J Felix
DH J Olerud
UO- G Hill
C- G Myers
M C Gaston

ATL 1991 NL

SP T Glavine
SP C Leibrandt
SP J Smoltz
SP S Avery
RP M Stanton
CL J Berenguer
RP K Mercker
C G Olson
1B- B Hunter
2B M Lemke
SS R Belliard
3B T Pendleton
UO O Nixon
CF R Gant
RF D Justice
SI J Blauser
LF L Smith
2B J Treadway
1B- S Bream
M B Cox

CHI 1991 NL

SP G Maddux
SR M Bielecki
SP S Boskie
SP F Castillo
SP R Sutcliffe
RS L Lancaster
RP P Assenmacher
RS B Scanlan
RP C McElroy
C- R Wilkins
1B M Grace
2B R Sandberg
SS S Dunston
3B L Salazar
LF G Bell
CF J Walton
RF A Dawson
ML D Dascenzo
UT C Walker
UO- D Smith
3S- J Vizcaino
M1 D Zimmer
M2 J Altobelli
M3 J Essian

CIN 1991 NL

SP T Browning
SP J Rijo
SP J Armstrong
SR S Scudder
SP C Hammond
RS R Myers
CL R Dibble
RS N Charlton
RP T Power
C- J Oliver
1B H Morris
2B B Doran
SS B Larkin
3B C Sabo
LM B Hatcher
CF- E Davis
RF P O'Neill
2S M Duncan
UI- L Quinones
MU H Winningham
LR- G Braggs
C- J Reed
M L Piniella

HOU 1991 NL

SP P Harnisch
SP M Portugal
SP J Deshaies
SR D Kile
SP J Jones
RP A Osuna
RP C Schilling
RP J Corsi
RP D Henry
C C Biggio
1B J Bagwell
2U C Candaele
SS- E Yelding
3B K Caminiti
LF L Gonzalez
MU G Young
CF S Finley
UI R Ramirez
UO- M Davidson
M A Howe

LA 1991 NL

SP M Morgan
SP R Martinez
SP T Belcher
SP B Ojeda
SP O Hershiser
RS K Gross
RP T Crews
RP J Gott
CL J Howell
C M Scioscia
1B E Murray
2B J Samuel
SS A Griffin
3B L Harris
LF K Daniels
CF B Butler
RF D Strawberry
CU G Carter
OI S Javier
3I M Sharperson
UO- C Gwynn
M T Lasorda

MON 1991 NL

SP De Martinez
SP M Gardner
SP B Barnes
SP C Nabholz
SP O Boyd
RP B Jones
RS B Sampen
RP S Ruskin
RP J Fassero
C- G Reyes
1B A Galarraga
2B D DeShields
SS S Owen
3B T Wallach
LF I Calderon
CF M Grissom
UO Da Martinez
R1 L Walker
S1- T Foley
M1 B Rodgers
M2 T Runnells

NY 1991 NL

SP D Cone
SP F Viola
SP D Gooden
SR W Whitehurst
SP R Darling
RS P Schourek
CL J Franco
RP J Innis
RP A Pena
C- R Cerone
1B D Magadan
23 G Jefferies
SS K Elster
3U H Johnson
LF K McReynolds
MR D Boston
RF H Brooks
UO M Carreon
2O K Miller
OC- M Sasser
M1 B Harrelson
M2 M Cubbage

PHI 1991 NL

SP T Mulholland
SP T Greene
SP J DeJesus
SR B Ruffin
SP D Cox
CL M Williams
RP J Boever
RP R McDowell
RP D Akerfelds
C- D Daulton
1O J Kruk
2B M Morandini
SS D Thon
3B C Hayes
LF W Chamberlain
ML- V Hayes
RF D Murphy
1U R Jordan
IF- W Backman
UO- J Morris
M1 N Leyva
M2 J Fregosi

PIT 1991 NL

SP D Drabek
SP Z Smith
SP J Smiley
SP R Tomlin
SP B Walk
RP S Belinda
RP B Landrum
RS V Palacios
RP N Heaton
C M LaValliere
1B O Merced
2B J Lind
SS J Bell
R3 B Bonilla
LF B Bonds
CF A Van Slyke
OI G Varsho
UT G Redus
OI- L McClendon
UI- C Wilkerson
M J Leyland

STL 1991 NL

SP B Smith
SP B Tewksbury
SP K Hill
SP O Olivares
SP J DeLeon
CL L Smith
RP J Agosto
RP S Terry
RP C Carpenter
C T Pagnozzi
1B P Guerrero
2B J Oquendo
SS O Smith
3B T Zeile
LU M Thompson
CF R Lankford
RF F Jose
UT R Hudler
2B G Pena
1U G Perry
LF- B Gilkey
M J Torre

SD 1991 NL

SP A Benes
SP B Hurst
SP D Rasmussen
SP G Harris
RP M Maddux
CL C Lefferts
RP R Rodriguez
C B Santiago
1B F McGriff
2O B Roberts
SS T Fernandez
3B- J Howell
LU J Clark
MU D Jackson
RF T Gwynn
UO T Howard
23- T Teufel
M G Riddoch

SF 1991 NL

SP B Black
SP J Burkett
SR T Wilson
SR D Robinson
RS K Downs
RP J Brantley
CL D Righetti
RP F Oliveras
C- S Decker
1B W Clark
2B R Thompson
SS- J Uribe
3B M Williams
UT M Felder
MR W McGee
RU K Bass
SI D Anderson
LF K Mitchell
OI- M Kingery
M R Craig

BAL 1991 AL

SP B Milacki
SP B McDonald
SP J Ballard
SP J Mesa
SP J Robinson
CL G Olson
RP M Flanagan
RP T Frohwirth
RP M Williamson
C C Hoiles
1B R Milligan
2B B Ripken
SS C Ripken
3B L Gomez
LO B Anderson
CF M Devereaux
LR J Orsulak
DH S Horn
2B J Bell
RU D Evans
UT- D Segui
M1 F Robinson
M2 J Oates

BOS 1991 AL

SP R Clemens
SR G Harris
SR J Hesketh
SP M Gardiner
SP T Bolton
CL J Reardon
RP D Lamp
RP J Gray
RP T Fossas
C T Pena
1B C Quintana
2B J Reed
SS L Rivera
3B W Boggs
LF M Greenwell
CF E Burks
RF T Brunansky
DH J Clark
UT- S Lyons
M J Morgan

CAL 1991 AL

SP M Langston
SP J Abbott
SP C Finley
SP K McCaskill
CL B Harvey
RP M Eichhorn
RP J Robinson
RP S Bailes
C L Parrish
1B W Joyner
2B L Sojo
SS D Schofield
3B G Gaetti
LF L Polonia
MR- D Gallagher
RF D Winfield
DH D Parker
UO- M Venable
M1 D Rader
M2 B Rodgers

CHI 1991 AL

SP J McDowell
SP C Hough
SP G Hibbard
SP A Fernandez
RS M Perez
CL B Thigpen
RP S Radinsky
RP D Pall
C C Fisk
1R D Pasqua
2B- S Fletcher
SS O Guillen
3B R Ventura
LF T Raines
CF L Johnson
RF S Sosa
D1 F Thomas
2B J Cora
UI C Grebeck
M J Torborg

CLE 1991 AL

SP G Swindell
SP C Nagy
SP E King
SR R Nichols
SP T Candiotti
RP D Otto
RP S Hillegas
CL S Olin
RP J Shaw
C J Skinner
1B- B Jacoby
2S- M Lewis
SS F Fermin
32 C Baerga
LD A Belle
CF A Cole
RF- M Whiten
DO C James
IO J Browne
1U- M Aldrete
M1 J McNamara
M2 M Hargrove

DET 1991 AL

SP B Gullickson
SP W Terrell
SP F Tanana
SR M Leiter
CL M Henneman
RP P Gibson
RS J Cerutti
RP J Gleaton
C M Tettleton
1U- D Bergman
2B L Whitaker
SS A Trammell
3S T Fryman
LF- L Moseby
CF M Cuyler
RF R Deer
1B C Fielder
LD- P Incaviglia
UT T Phillips
M S Anderson

KC 1991 AL

SP K Appier
SP B Saberhagen
SP M Boddicker
SR L Aquino
SP M Gubicza
RS T Gordon
CL J Montgomery
RS S Davis
RS M Davis
C- B Mayne
1B- T Benzinger
2B T Shumpert
SS K Stillwell
3B B Pecota
OI J Eisenreich
CF B McRae
RF D Tartabull
DH G Brett
LU K Gibson
S2- D Howard
C- M Macfarlane
3B- K Seitzer
M1 J Wathan
M2 B Schaefer
M3 H McRae

MIL 1991 AL

SP J Navarro
SP C Bosio
SP B Wegman
SP D August
RS D Plesac
RP C Crim
RP J Machado
RP D Holmes
C B Surhoff
1B F Stubbs
2B W Randolph
SS B Spiers
32 J Gantner
LF G Vaughn
CF R Yount
RF D Bichette
D1 P Molitor
UO D Hamilton
S3- D Sveum
M T Trebelhorn

MIN 1991 AL

SP J Morris
SP K Tapani
SP S Erickson
SP A Anderson
CL R Aguilera
RS M Guthrie
RP C Willis
RP S Bedrosian
C B Harper
1B K Hrbek
2B C Knoblauch
SS G Gagne
3B M Pagliarulo
LF D Gladden
CF K Puckett
RL S Mack
DH C Davis
UT G Larkin
3U S Leius
IO A Newman
OI- R Bush
M T Kelly

NY 1991 AL

SP S Sanderson
SP J Johnson
SR T Leary
SP W Taylor
RS G Cadaret
RS E Plunk
RP L Guetterman
CL S Farr
C M Nokes
1B D Mattingly
2B S Sax
SS A Espinoza
3B- P Kelly
ML R Kelly
CF- B Williams
UO M Hall
DU K Maas
RF- J Barfield
LU- H Meulens
M S Merrill

OAK 1991 AL

SP D Stewart
SP B Welch
SP M Moore
SP J Slusarski
CL D Eckersley
RP C Young
RP S Chitren
RP J Klink
C T Steinbach
1B M McGwire
2B M Gallego
SS- M Bordick
3I E Riles
LF R Henderson
CF D Henderson
RF J Canseco
DH H Baines
UO W Wilson
2O- L Blankenship
M T LaRussa

SEA 1991 AL

SP R Johnson
SP B Holman
SP R DeLucia
SP E Hanson
SR B Krueger
RP B Swift
RP M Jackson
RP R Swan
C D Valle
1B P O'Brien
2B H Reynolds
SS O Vizquel
3B E Martinez
LR G Briley
CF K Griffey
RF J Buhner
DH A Davis
C- S Bradley
S3- J Schaefer
M J Lefebvre

TEX 1991 AL

SP K Brown
SP N Ryan
SP J Guzman
RS K Rogers
CL J Russell
RS G Alexander
RS J Barfield
C- I Rodriguez
1B R Palmeiro
2B J Franco
SS J Huson
3B S Buechele
ML J Gonzalez
CF G Pettis
RF R Sierra
DH B Downing
OF K Reimer
SI- M Diaz
3L- D Palmer
C- G Petralli
CU- M Stanley
M B Valentine

TOR 1991 AL

SP T Stottlemyre
SP J Key
SR D Wells
SP J Guzman
SP T Candiotti
RP D Ward
RP M Timlin
RP J Acker
CL T Henke
C G Myers
1B J Olerud
2B R Alomar
SS M Lee
3B K Gruber
LF- C Maldonado
CF D White
RL J Carter
DH- R Mulliniks
C P Borders
DU- P Tabler
OF- M Wilson
M1 C Gaston
M2 G Tenace
M3 C Gaston

ATL 1992 NL

SP J Smoltz
SP S Avery
SP T Glavine
SP C Leibrandt
RP K Mercker
RP M Stanton
RP M Freeman
C- G Olson
1B S Bream
2B M Lemke
SS R Belliard
3B T Pendleton
LF R Gant
CF O Nixon
RF D Justice
C D Berryhill
SS J Blauser
1B B Hunter
MU- D Sanders
UM- L Smith
M B Cox

CHI 1992 NL

SP G Maddux
SP M Morgan
SP F Castillo
SP D Jackson
RP B Scanlan
RS J Bullinger
RP C McElroy
RS J Robinson
C- J Girardi
1B M Grace
2B R Sandberg
SS- R Sanchez
3B- S Buechele
LF D May
MO D Dascenzo

RF A Dawson
UT L Salazar
UO D Smith
S3- J Vizcaino
C - R Wilkins
M J Lefebvre

CIN 1992 NL

SP T Belcher
SP G Swindell
SP J Rijo
SP C Hammond
CL N Charlton
CL R Dibble
RP D Henry
RP S Bankhead
C J Oliver
1B H Morris
2B B Doran
SS B Larkin
3B- C Sabo
ML R Sanders
CF D Martinez
RF P O'Neill
UT B Roberts
LR- G Braggs
M L Piniella

HOU 1992 NL

SP P Harnisch
SP B Henry
SP J Jones
SP D Kile
SP M Portugal
RP D Jones
RP X Hernandez
RP J Boever
RS W Blair
C E Taubensee
1B J Bagwell
2B C Biggio
SS- A Cedeno
3B K Caminiti
LF L Gonzalez
CF S Finley
RF E Anthony
UT C Candaele
LR P Incaviglia
M A Howe

LA 1992 NL

SP O Hershiser
SP K Gross
SP T Candiotti
SP B Ojeda
SP R Martinez
RP R McDowell
RP J Gott
RP T Crews
RP S Wilson
C M Scioscia
1B E Karros
2I L Harris
SS J Offerman
3B D Hansen
LF- E Davis
CF B Butler
UO M Webster
OI T Benzinger
UI M Sharperson
M T Lasorda

MON 1992 NL

SP D Martinez
SP K Hill
SP C Nabholz
SP M Gardner
SP B Barnes
CL J Wetteland
RP M Rojas
RP J Fassero
RP B Sampen
C - G Carter
31 T Wallach
2B D DeShields
SS S Owen
3U B Barberie
LU M Alou
CF M Grissom
RF L Walker
LU J Vander Wal
1U- A Cianfrocco
C - D Fletcher
M1 T Runnells
M2 F Alou

NY 1992 NL

SP S Fernandez
SP D Gooden
SP D Cone
SP P Schourek
RS A Young
RS W Whitehurst
RP J Innis
RP P Gibson
C T Hundley
1B E Murray
2B- W Randolph
SS D Schofield
3B D Magadan
LU D Boston
CF H Johnson
RF B Bonilla
UO D Gallagher
UI B Pecota
UT C Walker
IC- M Sasser
M J Torborg

PHI 1992 NL

SP T Mulholland
SR C Schilling
SR K Abbott
SP B Rivera
CL M Williams
RS C Brantley
RP M Hartley
RP B Jones
C D Daulton
1B J Kruk
2B M Morandini
SS- J Bell
3B D Hollins
IO M Duncan
CF- L Dykstra
RO R Amaro
ML- S Javier
1U- R Jordan
M J Fregosi

PIT 1992 NL

SP D Drabek
SP R Tomlin
SP Z Smith
SR B Walk
RP R Mason
RP S Belinda
RS D Neagle
RP B Patterson
C - M LaValliere
1B O Merced
2B J Lind
SS J Bell
3B- S Buechele
LF B Bonds
CF A Van Slyke
RO C Espy
3I J King
UO G Varsho
RU- L McClendon
C - D Slaught
M J Leyland

STL 1992 NL

SP B Tewksbury
SP O Olivares
SP R Cormier
SP D Osborne
SP M Clark
CL L Smith
RS J DeLeon
RP M Perez
RP C Carpenter
C T Pagnozzi
1B- A Galarraga
2B- L Alicea
SS O Smith
3B T Zeile
LF B Gilkey
CF R Lankford
RF F Jose
UO M Thompson
UR- G Perry
M J Torre

SD 1992 NL

SP A Benes
SP B Hurst
SP C Lefferts
SP G Harris
SP F Seminara
CL R Myers
RP R Rodriguez
RP J Melendez
RP M Maddux
C B Santiago
1B F McGriff
2B K Stillwell
SS T Fernandez
3B G Sheffield
LF J Clark
CF D Jackson
RF T Gwynn
OF O Azocar
23 T Teufel
UO- K Ward
M1 G Riddoch
M2 J Riggleman

SF 1992 NL

SP J Burkett
SP B Black
SP B Swift
SP T Wilson
RP R Beck
RP J Brantley
RP B Hickerson
RP M Jackson
C K Manwaring
1B W Clark
2B R Thompson
SS R Clayton
3B M Williams
OI M Felder
CF D Lewis
RU W McGee
LU C James
UT C Snyder
LU- K Bass
M R Craig

BAL 1992 AL

SP M Mussina
SP R Sutcliffe
SP B McDonald
SP B Milacki
RP T Frohwirth
RP A Mills
CL G Olson
RP S Davis
C - C Hoiles
1B R Milligan
2B B Ripken
SS C Ripken
3B L Gomez
LF B Anderson
CF M Devereaux
RF J Orsulak
DH G Davis
2U M McLemore
1B D Segui
RU- C Martinez
M J Oates

BOS 1992 AL

SP R Clemens
SP F Viola
SP J Hesketh
SP J Dopson
SR M Gardiner
RS D Darwin
RP G Harris
RS M Young
RP P Quantrill
C T Pena
1B M Vaughn
2B J Reed
SS L Rivera
3B W Boggs
LF- B Hatcher
ML B Zupcic
RU T Brunansky
DH- J Clark
13 S Cooper
OF H Winningham
RU P Plantier
M B Hobson

CAL 1992 AL

SP M Langston
SP J Abbott
SP C Finley
SP J Valera
SP B Blyleven
CL J Grahe
RP C Crim
RP M Eichhorn
C - M Fitzgerald
1B L Stevens
2B L Sojo
SS G DiSarcina
31 G Gaetti
LD L Polonia
CF J Felix
UO C Curtis
DH- H Brooks
32 R Gonzales
RF- V Hayes
M1 B Rodgers
M2 J Wathan
M3 B Rodgers

CHI 1992 AL

SP J McDowell
SP K McCaskill
SP A Fernandez
SP G Hibbard
SP C Hough
RS W Alvarez
RP R Hernandez
CL B Thigpen
RP T Leach
C R Karkovice
1B F Thomas
2B S Sax
SS- C Grebeck
3B R Ventura
LF T Raines
CF L Johnson
RF- S Abner
DH G Bell
RF- D Pasqua
M G Lamont

CLE 1992 AL

SP C Nagy
SR J Armstrong
SP D Cook
SP S Scudder
CL S Olin
RS R Nichols
RP T Power
RP E Plunk
C - S Alomar
1B P Sorrento
2B C Baerga
SS M Lewis
3B B Jacoby
LO T Howard
CF K Lofton
RF M Whiten
DL A Belle
UO G Hill
C - J Ortiz
M M Hargrove

DET 1992 AL

SP B Gullickson
SP F Tanana
SR W Terrell
SR M Leiter
RS J Doherty
CL M Henneman
RP L Lancaster
RP K Knudsen
CD M Tettleton
1U- D Bergman
2B L Whitaker
SS T Fryman
3B S Livingstone
LF D Gladden
CF- M Cuyler
RF R Deer
1D C Fielder
LU M Carreon
UT T Phillips
UT- S Barnes
M S Anderson

KC 1992 AL

SP K Appier
SP H Pichardo
SP M Gubicza
SP R Reed
CL J Montgomery
RS T Gordon
RP R Meacham
RS M Boddicker
C M Macfarlane
1B W Joyner
2B K Miller
SS- D Howard
3B G Jefferies
LF K McReynolds
CF B McRae
RU J Eisenreich
DH G Brett
S2 C Wilkerson
C - B Mayne
RU- G Thurman
M H McRae

MIL 1992 AL

SP B Wegman
SP J Navarro
SP C Bosio
SP R Bones
SP C Eldred
CL D Henry
RP D Plesac
RP M Fetters
RP J Austin
C B Surhoff
1U- F Stubbs
2B S Fletcher
SS P Listach
3B K Seitzer
LF G Vaughn
CF R Yount
RM D Hamilton
D1 P Molitor
RF D Bichette
23 J Gantner
M P Garner

MIN 1992 AL

SP J Smiley
SP K Tapani
SP S Erickson
SP B Krueger
CL R Aguilera
RP M Guthrie
RP C Willis
RP T Edens
C B Harper
1B K Hrbek
2B C Knoblauch
SS G Gagne
3B S Leius
LF S Mack
CF K Puckett
RF P Munoz
DH C Davis
OI R Bush
UT G Larkin
M T Kelly

NY 1992 AL

SP M Perez
SP S Sanderson
SP S Kamieniecki
RS G Cadaret
RP R Monteleone
CL S Farr
RP J Habyan
C M Nokes
1B D Mattingly
2B P Kelly
S2 A Stankiewicz
3B C Hayes
LU M Hall
ML R Kelly
RD D Tartabull
DU K Maas
SU R Velarde
M B Showalter

OAK 1992 AL

SP M Moore
SP R Darling
SP D Stewart
SP B Welch
CL D Eckersley
RP J Parrett
RS K Campbell
RP G Nelson
C T Steinbach
1B M McGwire
2S M Bordick
SS W Weiss
3B C Lansford
LF R Henderson
CF W Wilson
RF- J Canseco
DH H Baines
2O L Blankenship
3O J Browne
M T LaRussa

SEA 1992 AL

SP D Fleming
SP R Johnson
SP E Hanson
RS R Swan
RS J Nelson
RP M Schooler
RP C Jones
C D Valle
1D P O'Brien
2B H Reynolds
SS O Vizquel
3B E Martinez
LM H Cotto
CF K Griffey
RF J Buhner
1D T Martinez
LD K Mitchell
UT- G Briley
M B Plummer

TEX 1992 AL

SP K Brown
SP J Guzman
SP B Witt
SP N Ryan
RS T Burns
RP K Rogers
CL J Russell
C I Rodriguez
1B R Palmeiro
2I A Newman
SS- D Thon
3B D Palmer
LU K Reimer
CF J Gonzalez
RF R Sierra
DH B Downing
S2 J Huson
CU- G Petralli
M1 B Valentine
M2 T Harrah

TOR 1992 AL

SP J Morris
SP J Key
SP J Guzman
SP T Stottlemyre
SR D Wells
RP D Ward
CL T Henke
RP P Hentgen
C P Borders
1B J Olerud
2B R Alomar
SS M Lee
3B K Gruber
LF C Maldonado
CF D White
RF J Carter
DH D Winfield
M C Gaston

ATL 1993 NL

SP G Maddux
SP J Smoltz
SP T Glavine
SP S Avery
RP G McMichael
CL M Stanton
RS K Mercker
RP J Howell
C D Berryhill
1B S Bream
2B M Lemke
SS J Blauser
3B T Pendleton
LF R Gant
CF O Nixon
RF D Justice
S2- R Belliard
C - G Olson
MU- D Sanders
M B Cox

CHI 1993 NL

SP M Morgan
SP J Guzman
SP G Hibbard
SP M Harkey
SP F Castillo
CL R Myers
RS J Bautista
RP B Scanlan
RP S Boskie
C R Wilkins
1B M Grace
2B R Sandberg
SS R Sanchez
3B S Buechele
LF D May
UO D Smith
RM S Sosa
S3 J Vizcaino
CF W Wilson
M J Lefebvre

CIN 1993 NL

SP J Rijo
SP T Pugh
SP T Belcher
SP T Browning
SP J Smiley
RS B Ayala
RP J Reardon
RP J Spradlin
C J Oliver
1B H Morris
2U J Samuel
SS B Larkin
3B C Sabo
LF- K Mitchell
MO J Brumfield
RF R Sanders
UI J Branson
1U- R Milligan
2B- B Roberts
M1 T Perez
M2 D Johnson

COL 1993 NL

SP A Reynoso
SR W Blair
RS B Ruffin
CL D Holmes
RP S Reed
RS J Parrett
C - J Girardi
1B A Galarraga
2L E Young
SS V Castilla
3B C Hayes
L1 J Clark
MU A Cole
RF D Bichette
UO D Boston
MU- C Jones
C - D Sheaffer
UT- J Tatum
M D Baylor

FLA 1993 NL

SP C Hough
SP J Armstrong
SP C Hammond
SP R Bowen
SR L Aquino
CL B Harvey
RP R Lewis
RP M Turner
C B Santiago
1B O Destrade
2B B Barberie
SS W Weiss
3B- G Sheffield
LF J Conine
CF C Carr
RF- D Whitmore
UO G Briley
IO R Renteria
UI- A Arias
M R Lachemann

HOU 1993 NL

SP D Drabek
SP P Harnisch
SP M Portugal
SP G Swindell
SP D Kile
CL D Jones
RP X Hernandez
RS B Williams
RP T Edens
C - E Taubensee
1B J Bagwell
2B C Biggio
SS A Cedeno
3B K Caminiti
LF L Gonzalez
CF S Finley
RF E Anthony
UO K Bass
UI- C Donnels
C - S Servais
M A Howe

LA 1993 NL

SP O Hershiser
SP T Candiotti
SP R Martinez
SP K Gross
SP P Astacio
RP P Martinez
CL J Gott
RP R McDowell
RP R Trlicek
C M Piazza
1B E Karros
2B J Reed
SS J Offerman
3B T Wallach
LF E Davis
CF B Butler
RF C Snyder
IO L Harris
U2- D Hansen
UO- M Webster
M T Lasorda

MON 1993 NL

SP D Martinez
SP K Hill
SP C Nabholz
RS J Fassero
CL J Wetteland
RP B Barnes
RP M Rojas
C D Fletcher
1B- G Colbrunn
2B D DeShields
SS W Cordero
3B S Berry
LF M Alou
CF M Grissom
RF L Walker
UT L Frazier
3S M Lansing
UT J Vander Wal
13- F Bolick
M F Alou

NY 1993 NL

SP D Gooden
SP F Tanana
SP E Hillman
SP B Saberhagen
SR P Schourek
RP S Fernandez
RS A Young
RP J Innis
RP M Maddux
C T Hundley
1B E Murray
2B J Kent
SS- T Bogar
3B- H Johnson
LF- V Coleman
OI J Orsulak
R3 B Bonilla
OI D Gallagher
UI J McKnight
UT C Walker
RU- J Burnitz
M1 J Torborg
M2 D Green

PHI 1993 NL

SP C Schilling
SP D Jackson
SP T Greene
SP T Mulholland
SP B Rivera
CL M Williams
RP D West
RP L Andersen
RP M Williams
C D Daulton
1B J Kruk
2B M Morandini
SS- K Stocker
3B D Hollins
LF M Thompson
CF L Dykstra
RF J Eisenreich
2S M Duncan
LF P Incaviglia
RF- W Chamberlain
UM- R Jordan
M J Fregosi

PIT 1993 NL

SP S Cooke
SP B Walk
SR P Wagner
SP T Wakefield
RP B Minor
RS D Neagle
RS D Otto
RP J Johnston
C D Slaught
1B K Young
2B C Garcia
SS J Bell
3B J King
LM A Martin
CF- A Van Slyke
RF O Merced
OF D Clark
UI- T Foley
RU- L McClendon
LU- L Smith
M J Leyland

STL 1993 NL

SP B Tewksbury
SP R Arocha
SP D Osborne
SR R Cormier
SP J Magrane
RS O Olivares
CL L Smith
RP M Perez
RP R Murphy
C - T Pagnozzi
1B G Jefferies
2B L Alicea
SS O Smith
3B T Zeile
LF B Gilkey
CF R Lankford
RF M Whiten
OI R Brewer
C - E Pappas
UT- G Perry
M J Torre

SD 1993 NL

SP A Benes
SP Gr Harris
SP D Brocail
SP W Whitehurst
SP T Worrell
CL Ge Harris
RS K Taylor
RP T Hoffman
RP R Mason
C - K Higgins
1B- F McGriff
2B J Gardner
SS R Gutierrez
3B- G Sheffield
LF P Plantier
CF D Bell
RF T Gwynn
UT P Clark
UT C Shipley
OI- B Bean
3B- A Cianfrocco
2U- T Teufel
M J Riggleman

SF 1993 NL

SP B Swift
SP J Burkett
SP T Wilson
CL R Beck
RS B Hickerson
RS J Brantley
RS D Burba

C K Manwaring
1B W Clark
2B R Thompson
SS R Clayton
3B M Williams
LF B Bonds
CF D Lewis
RF W McGee
IO- T Benzinger
UO- D Martinez
M D Baker

BAL 1993 AL
SP B McDonald
SP F Valenzuela
SP M Mussina
SP R Sutcliffe
SP J Moyer
RP A Mills
RP T Frohwirth
RP M Williamson
RP J Poole
C C Hoiles
1B D Segui
2B H Reynolds
SS C Ripken
3B- T Hulett
LF B Anderson
CF M Devereaux
RF M McLemore
DH H Baines
M J Oates

BOS 1993 AL
SP D Darwin
SP R Clemens
SP F Viola
SP J Dopson
SP A Sele
RS P Quantrill
RP G Harris
RP S Bankhead
RS J Hesketh
C T Pena
1B M Vaughn
2B S Fletcher
SS J Valentin
3B S Cooper
LF M Greenwell
CF B Hatcher
UO B Zupcic
DH A Dawson
1R C Quintana
UI- E Riles
M B Hobson

CAL 1993 AL
SP M Langston
SP C Finley
SP S Sanderson
RP J Grahe
RP K Patterson
RS J Valera
RP G Nelson
C G Myers
1B J Snow
2B T Lovullo
SS G DiSarcina
31 R Gonzales
LF L Polonia
CF C Curtis
RF T Salmon
DH C Davis
UT- S Javier
M B Rodgers

CHI 1993 AL
SP J McDowell
SP A Fernandez
SP W Alvarez
SP J Bere
SR K McCaskill
CL R Hernandez
RP D Pall
RP S Radinsky
RP J Schwarz
C R Karkovice
1B F Thomas
2B J Cora
SS O Guillen
3B R Ventura
LF T Raines
CF L Johnson
RF E Burks
DH G Bell
OF- B Jackson
M G Lamont

CLE 1993 AL
SP J Mesa
SR T Kramer
SR M Clark
RP E Plunk
RP J Hernandez
RP D Lilliquist
RP J Dipoto
C - J Ortiz
1B P Sorrento
2B C Baerga
SS F Fermin
3B A Espinoza
LF A Belle
CF K Lofton
RF W Kirby
DH R Jefferson
IF- J Treadway
M M Hargrove

DET 1993 AL
SP M Moore
SP D Wells
SP J Doherty
SP B Gullickson
SR M Leiter
RS T Bolton
CL M Henneman
RS B Krueger
RP R Mac Donald
C C Kreuter
1B C Fielder
2B L Whitaker
S3 A Trammell
S3 T Fryman
UT T Phillips
CF- M Cuyler
RF- R Deer
DM K Gibson
3D S Livingstone
IC M Tettleton
UT- S Barnes
LF- D Gladden
M S Anderson

KC 1993 AL
SP D Cone
SP K Appier
SP H Pichardo
SP C Haney
RS T Gordon
CL J Montgomery
RS M Gubicza
C M Macfarlane
1B W Joyner
2B J Lind
SS G Gagne
3B- G Gaetti
LF K McReynolds
CF B McRae
RF F Jose
DH G Brett
LU C Gwynn
3B- P Hiatt
M H McRae

MIL 1993 AL
SP C Eldred
SP J Navarro
SP R Bones
SP B Wegman
SP A Miranda
RP D Henry
RP J Orosco
RP G Lloyd
RP M Fetters
C D Nilsson
1B J Jaha
2B B Spiers
SS P Listach
3B B Surhoff
LD G Vaughn
CF R Yount
RM D Hamilton
DO K Reimer
2S- J Bell
UI- D Thon
M P Garner

MIN 1993 AL
SP K Tapani
SP S Erickson
SP W Banks
SP J Deshaies
RS M Trombley
CL R Aguilera
RP M Hartley
RP G Tsamis
C B Harper
1B K Hrbek
2B C Knoblauch
SS P Meares
3B- M Pagliarulo
LR P Munoz
ML S Mack
MR K Puckett
DU D Winfield
OI D McCarty
S3 J Reboulet
M T Kelly

NY 1993 AL
SP J Key
SP J Abbott
SP M Perez
SR S Kamieniecki
SR B Wickman
RP R Monteleone
RP S Howe
C M Stanley
1B D Mattingly
2B P Kelly
SS S Owen
3B W Boggs
LF D James
CF B Williams
RL P O'Neill
DR D Tartabull
UI M Gallego
UT- J Leyritz
LS- R Velarde
M B Showalter

OAK 1993 AL
SP B Witt
SP R Darling
SP B Welch
RS K Downs
CL D Eckersley
RP J Boever
RP E Nunez
C T Steinbach
1U- M Aldrete
2B B Gates
SS M Bordick
3B C Paquette
LF- R Henderson
MD D Henderson
RF R Sierra
D1 T Neel
MI- L Blankenship
C - S Hemond
M T LaRussa

SEA 1993 AL
SP R Johnson
SP E Hanson
SP T Leary
SP D Fleming
SP C Bosio
RP J Nelson
RP D Henry
C D Valle
1B T Martinez
2I R Amaral
SS O Vizquel
3B M Blowers
LF M Felder
CF K Griffey
RF J Buhner
DU- P O'Brien
OI- M Sasser
M L Piniella

TEX 1993 AL
SP K Brown
SP K Rogers
SP R Pavlik
SP C Leibrandt
CL T Henke
RS B Bohanon
RS C Lefferts
RP M Whiteside
C I Rodriguez
1B R Palmeiro
2B D Strange
SS- M Lee
3B D Palmer
LF J Gonzalez
CF D Hulse
RF- J Canseco
DH J Franco
M K Kennedy

TOR 1993 AL
SP J Guzman
SP P Hentgen
SP T Stottlemyre
SP D Stewart
SP J Morris
CL D Ward
RS A Leiter
RP D Cox
RP M Eichhorn
C P Borders
1B J Olerud
2B R Alomar
SS- T Fernandez
3B E Sprague
OI- T Ward
CF D White
RL J Carter
DH P Molitor
M C Gaston

ATL 1994 NL
SP G Maddux
SP T Glavine
SP S Avery
SP J Smoltz
SP K Mercker
CL G McMichael
RP M Wohlers
RP M Stanton
RP S Bedrosian
C J Lopez
1B F McGriff
2B M Lemke
SS J Blauser
3B T Pendleton
LF R Klesko
CF- R Kelly
RF D Justice
OF T Tarasco
LF D Gallagher
IO- B Pecota
M B Cox

CHI 1994 NL
SP S Trachsel
SP W Banks
SP A Young
SP K Foster
SP M Morgan
RS J Bullinger
RP J Bautista
RP C Crim
CL R Myers
C R Wilkins
1B M Grace
2B- R Sandberg
SS S Dunston
3B S Buechele
LF D May
UO G Hill
RF S Sosa
MU K Rhodes
2S R Sanchez
UT- E Zambrano
M T Trebelhorn

CIN 1994 NL
SP J Rijo
SP J Smiley
SP E Hanson
SP J Roper
SR P Schourek
RP J Brantley
RP J Ruffin
RP C McElroy
RP H Carrasco
C B Dorsett
1B H Morris
2B B Boone
SS B Larkin
3B T Fernandez
LF K Mitchell
CF- D Sanders
RF R Sanders
UI- J Branson
UO- J Brumfield
IO- L Harris
UO T Howard
C - E Taubensee
M D Johnson

COL 1994 NL
SR G Harris
SP D Nied
SP M Freeman
SR M Harkey
SP L Painter
RP W Blair
RP K Ritz
RP B Ruffin
RP S Reed
C J Girardi
1B A Galarraga
2B N Liriano
SS W Weiss
3B C Hayes
LU H Johnson
MU M Kingery
RF D Bichette
UT J Vander Wal
LU E Young
M D Baylor

FLA 1994 NL
SP D Weathers
SP P Rapp
SP C Hough
SP M Gardner
SP C Hammond
CL R Nen
RP R Lewis
RP L Aquino
RP T Mathews
C B Santiago
1B- G Colbrunn
2B B Barberie
SS K Abbott
3O J Browne
LF J Conine
CF C Carr
RF G Sheffield
UO M Carrillo
3U D Magadan
IF- A Arias
M R Lachemann

HOU 1994 NL
SP D Drabek
SP D Kile
SP G Swindell
SR S Reynolds
SP P Harnisch
RP T Jones
RP B Williams
CL J Hudek
RP T Edens
C S Servais
1B J Bagwell
2B C Biggio
SS A Cedeno
3B K Caminiti
LF L Gonzalez
CF S Finley
RF J Mouton
RU K Bass
UO- M Felder
M T Collins

LA 1994 NL
SP R Martinez
SP K Gross
SP T Candiotti
SP P Astacio
SP O Hershiser
RP T Worrell
RP R McDowell
RP J Gott
C M Piazza
1B E Karros
2B D DeShields
SS J Offerman
3B T Wallach
LF H Rodriguez
CF B Butler
RF R Mondesi
LI C Snyder
LU M Webster
OF- C Gwynn
M T Lasorda

MON 1994 NL
SP K Hill
SP P Martinez
SP J Fassero
SP B Henry
SP K Rueter
RP M Rojas
CL J Wetteland
RP G Heredia
RP J Shaw
C D Fletcher
1B C Floyd
2B M Lansing
SS W Cordero
3B S Berry
LR M Alou
CF M Grissom
R1 L Walker
UT L Frazier
C - L Webster
M F Alou

NY 1994 NL
SP B Saberhagen
SP B Jones
SP P Smith
SR M Gozzo
CL J Franco
RP R Mason
RP D Linton
RP J Manzanillo
C T Hundley
1B D Segui
2B J Kent
SS J Vizcaino
3B B Bonilla
UO- J Cangelosi
CF R Thompson
RO J Orsulak
IO F Vina
M D Green

PHI 1994 NL
SP D Jackson
SP B Munoz
SR D West
SP S Boskie
SP C Schilling
CL D Jones
RP H Slocumb
C D Daulton
1B J Kruk
2B M Morandini
SS K Stocker
3B- D Hollins
LF M Thompson
CF L Dykstra
RF J Eisenreich
UI M Duncan
LF P Incaviglia
1U R Jordan
3S- K Batiste
OF T Longmire
M J Fregosi

PIT 1994 NL
SP Z Smith
SP D Neagle
SP S Cooke
SR P Wagner
SP J Lieber
RS R White
RP M Dewey
RP R Manzanillo
C D Slaught
1B B Hunter
2B C Garcia
SS J Bell
3B J King
LF A Martin
CF A Van Slyke
R1 O Merced
RU D Clark
UI- T Foley
OI- G Varsho
13- K Young
M J Leyland

STL 1994 NL
SP B Tewksbury
SR V Palacios
SP A Watson
SR T Urbani
SP O Olivares
RS R Arocha
RP B Eversgerd
RP R Rodriguez
RP J Habyan
C T Pagnozzi
1B G Jefferies
2U G Pena
SS O Smith
3B T Zeile
LF B Gilkey
CF R Lankford
RF M Whiten
2U L Alicea
U2- G Perry
M J Torre

SD 1994 NL
SP A Benes
SP A Ashby
SP S Sanders
SP J Hamilton
CL T Hoffman
RP P Martinez
RP T Mauser
RP A Sager
C B Ausmus
1B- E Williams
2B B Roberts
SS R Gutierrez
3I C Shipley
LF P Plantier
CF D Bell
RF T Gwynn
OI B Bean
S2 L Lopez
31- A Cianfrocco
UT- P Clark
3B- S Livingstone
M J Riggleman

SF 1994 NL
SP J Burkett
SP M Portugal
SP B Swift
SR B Hickerson
SP S Torres
RP Van
Landingham
CL R Beck
RP D Burba
RP M Jackson
C K Manwaring
1B T Benzinger
2U J Patterson
SS R Clayton
3B M Williams
LF B Bonds
CF D Lewis
R1 D Martinez
M D Baker

BAL 1994 AL
SP M Mussina
SP B McDonald
SP J Moyer
SP S Fernandez
RP M Eichhorn
CL L Smith
RP M Williamson
RP A Mills
C C Hoiles
1B R Palmeiro
2B M McLemore
SS C Ripken
3B L Gomez
LM B Anderson
CF M Devereaux
RF J Hammonds
DH H Baines
3O C Sabo
RL- J Voigt
M J Oates

BOS 1994 AL
SP R Clemens
SP A Sele
SP J Hesketh
SP D Darwin
RP K Ryan
RP G Harris
RP C Howard
RP S Bankhead
C D Berryhill
1B M Vaughn
2B- S Fletcher
SS J Valentin
3B S Cooper
LF M Greenwell
CF O Nixon
RL- T Brunansky
DH A Dawson
2I T Naehring
S2- C Rodriguez
UO L Tinsley
M B Hobson

CAL 1994 AL
SP C Finley
SP M Langston
SP P Leftwich
SP B Anderson
SP J Magrane
RS M Leiter
RS J Dopson
RP J Grahe
RS R Springer
C - C Turner
1B- J Snow
2B H Reynolds
SS G DiSarcina
3B S Owen
LO J Edmonds
CF C Curtis
RF T Salmon
DH C Davis
32 D Easley
LU B Jackson
M1 B Rodgers
M2 B Knoop
M3 M Lachemann

CHI 1994 AL
SP J McDowell
SP A Fernandez
SP W Alvarez
SP J Bere
SP S Sanderson
RP J DeLeon
RP R Hernandez
RP K McCaskill
C R Karkovice
1B F Thomas
2B J Cora
SS O Guillen
3B R Ventura
LF T Raines
CF L Johnson
RF D Jackson
DH J Franco
C - M LaValliere
OF- W Newson
M G Lamont

CLE 1994 AL
SP D Martinez
SP C Nagy
SP J Morris
SP M Clark
SP J Grimsley
RP J Mesa
RP E Plunk
C S Alomar
1B P Sorrento
2B C Baerga
SS O Vizquel
3B J Thome
LF A Belle
CF K Lofton
RF M Ramirez
DH E Murray
UI A Espinoza
RU W Kirby
M M Hargrove

DET 1994 AL
SP T Belcher
SP M Moore
SP B Gullickson
SP D Wells
SP J Doherty
RP J Boever
RP M Gardiner
RP S Davis
RP M Henneman
C - C Kreuter
1B C Fielder
2B L Whitaker
SS A Trammell
3B T Fryman
LF T Phillips
ML- M Cuyler
RF J Felix
DO K Gibson
S2 C Gomez
IC M Tettleton
UT- J Samuel
M S Anderson

KC 1994 AL
SP D Cone
SP K Appier
SP T Gordon
SP M Gubicza
CL J Montgomery
RP H Pichardo
RP R Meacham
RP S Belinda
C M Macfarlane
1B W Joyner
2B J Lind
SS G Gagne
3B G Gaetti
LF V Coleman
CF B McRae
RF F Jose
DU B Hamelin
23- T Shumpert
M H McRae

MIL 1994 AL
SP C Eldred
SP R Bones
SP B Wegman
SR B Scanlan
SR J Navarro
CL M Fetters
RP G Lloyd
RS M Ignasiak
RP J Orosco
CD D Nilsson
1B J Jaha
2B J Reed
SS J Valentin
31 K Seitzer
LF G Vaughn
ML T Ward
RF M Mieske
DC- B Harper
MR A Diaz
IO B Spiers
M P Garner

MIN 1994 AL
SP K Tapani
SP S Erickson
SP J Deshaies
SP P Mahomes
SP C Pulido
CL R Aguilera
RP C Willis
RP M Guthrie
RP M Trombley
C M Walbeck
1B K Hrbek
2B C Knoblauch
SS P Meares
3B S Leius
LF S Mack
CF A Cole
RF K Puckett
DH D Winfield
LR P Munoz
SI J Reboulet
IO- C Hale
M T Kelly

NY 1994 AL
SP J Key
SP J Abbott
SP M Perez
SP T Mulholland
SP S Kamieniecki
RP B Wickman
CL S Howe
RS S Hitchcock
RP X Hernandez
C M Stanley
1B D Mattingly
2B P Kelly
SS M Gallego

3B W Boggs
LF L Polonia
CF B Williams
RF P O'Neill
DH D Tartabull
IC J Leyritz
S3 R Velarde
UO-G Williams
M B Showalter

OAK 1994 AL
SP R Darling
SP B Witt
SP T Van Poppel
SR S Ontiveros
RS C Reyes
RS B Welch
CL D Eckersley
RP J Briscoe
C T Steinbach
1D T Neel
2B- B Gates
SS M Bordick
3B S Brosius
LF R Henderson
CF S Javier
RF R Sierra
OI G Berroa
OI M Aldrete
IC S Hemond
M T LaRussa

SEA 1994 AL
SP R Johnson
SP C Bosio
SP D Fleming
SP G Hibbard
CL B Ayala
RP B Risley
RP T Davis
RP R Gossage
C D Wilson
1B T Martinez
2U R Amaral
SS F Fermin
3D E Martinez
LF E Anthony
CF K Griffey
RF J Buhner
DU- R Jefferson
3U M Blowers
2S- L Sojo
M L Piniella

TEX 1994 AL
SP K Brown
SP K Rogers
SP H Fajardo
RP C Carpenter
RP M Whiteside
CL T Henke
RP D Oliver
C I Rodriguez
1B W Clark
2B- J Frye
SS M Lee
3B D Palmer
LF J Gonzalez
CF D Hulse
RM R Greer
DH J Canseco
2U D Strange
MR-O McDowell
M K Kennedy

TOR 1994 AL
SP P Hentgen
SP J Guzman
SP T Stottlemyre
SP D Stewart
SP A Leiter
RP T Castillo
RP W Williams
RP M Timlin
C P Borders
1B J Olerud
2B R Alomar
SS D Schofield
3B E Sprague
LO M Huff
CF D White
RF J Carter
DH P Molitor
M C Gaston

ATL 1995 NL
SP G Maddux
SP T Glavine
SP J Smoltz
SP S Avery
SP K Mercker
CL M Wohlers
RP G McMichael
RP B Clontz
C J Lopez
1B F McGriff
2B M Lemke
SS J Blauser
3B C Jones
LF R Klesko
CF M Grissom
RF D Justice
LO M Kelly
OF D Smith
S2- R Belliard
M B Cox

CHI 1995 NL
SP J Navarro
SP F Castillo
SP K Foster
SP S Trachsel
SP J Bullinger
CL R Myers
RP M Perez
RP T Wendell
RP M Walker
C - S Servais
1B M Grace
2B R Sanchez
SS S Dunston
3B- T Zeile
LF- L Gonzalez
CF B McRae
RF S Sosa
LU S Bullett
UI J Hernandez
IO H Johnson
LU- O Timmons
M J Riggleman

CIN 1995 NL
SP P Schourek
SP J Smiley
SR T Pugh
CL J Brantley
RP X Hernandez
RP H Carrasco
RP M Jackson
C - B Santiago
1B H Morris
2B B Boone
SS B Larkin
3B J Branson
LF R Gant
OI J Walton
RF R Sanders
UT L Harris
UO T Howard
3B- M Lewis
C - E Taubensee
M D Johnson

COL 1995 NL
SP K Ritz
SP B Swift
SP M Freeman
SP A Reynoso
RP C Leskanic
RP S Reed
RS R Bailey
RP D Holmes
C J Girardi
1B A Galarraga
2I J Bates
SS W Weiss
3B V Castilla
LF D Bichette
CF M Kingery
RF L Walker
MU E Burks
UT J Vander Wal
2U E Young
M D Baylor

FLA 1995 NL
SP J Burkett
SP P Rapp
SP C Hammond
SP B Witt
SR D Weathers
RS M Gardner
CL R Nen
RP T Mathews
RP R Veres
C C Johnson
1B G Colbrunn
2B Q Veras
SS K Abbott
3B T Pendleton
LF J Conine
CF C Carr
RF- G Sheffield
UI A Arias
UT- J Browne
RU- A Dawson
OI- T Gregg
M R Lachemann

HOU 1995 NL
SP S Reynolds
SP D Drabek
SP G Swindell
SP M Hampton
SP D Kile
RP T Jones
RP D Veres
RS D Brocail
RP J Dougherty
C T Eusebio
1B J Bagwell
2B C Biggio
SS O Miller
3B D Magadan
UO J Mouton
CF- B Hunter
RM D Bell
UO J Cangelosi
3U C Shipley
UO M Thompson
LU- D May
M T Collins

LA 1995 NL
SP R Martinez
SP I Valdes
SP H Nomo
SP T Candiotti
RS P Astacio
CL T Worrell
RP A Osuna
C M Piazza
1B E Karros
2B D DeShields
SS J Offerman
3B T Wallach
LF- B Ashley
LM R Kelly
RF R Mondesi
UT C Fonville
3U D Hansen
M T Lasorda

MON 1995 NL
SP P Martinez
SP J Fassero
SP C Perez
SP B Henry
SR G Heredia
CL M Rojas
RP T Scott
RP J Shaw
RP G Harris
C D Fletcher
1B D Segui
2B M Lansing
SS W Cordero
3B S Berry
LR M Alou
CF R White
RF T Tarasco
31- S Andrews
UI- M Grudzielanek
M F Alou

NY 1995 NL
SP B Jones
SP D Mlicki
SP B Pulsipher
SP P Harnisch
SP B Saberhagen
RP J Isringhausen
RP J Dipoto
CL J Franco
RP D Henry
C T Hundley
1B R Brogna
2B J Kent
SS J Vizcaino
32 E Alfonzo
LR J Orsulak
CF B Butler
RF- C Everett
IO- T Bogar
3L- B Bonilla
OI- C Jones
C - K Stinnett
MR-R Thompson
M D Green

PHI 1995 NL
SP P Quantrill
SP T Green
SR M Mimbs
SP C Schilling
CL H Slocumb
RP R Bottalico
RS M Williams
RP T Borland
C D Daulton
1B- D Hollins
2B M Morandini
SS K Stocker
3B C Hayes
CF- A Van Slyke
CF- L Dykstra
RL J Eisenreich
1L G Jefferies
OF- G Varsho
M J Fregosi

PIT 1995 NL
SP D Neagle
SP E Loaiza
SP P Wagner
SP J Ericks
CL D Miceli
RP M Dyer
RP D Plesac
RP J McCurry
C - M Parent
1B- M Johnson
2B C Garcia
SS J Bell
31 J King
LF A Martin
CF J Brumfield
RF O Merced
2U N Liriano
OF- D Clark
UO- S Pegues
M J Leyland

STL 1995 NL
SP M Petkovsek
SP A Watson
SP D Osborne
SP K Hill
SP M Morgan
RP D Jackson
CL T Henke
RP R DeLucia
RP J Parrett
C - D Sheaffer
1O J Mabry
2S J Oquendo
SS T Cromer
3B S Cooper
LF B Gilkey
CF R Lankford
RF B Jordan
M1 J Torre
M2 M Jorgensen

SD 1995 NL
SP J Hamilton
SP A Ashby
SP A Benes
SP G Dishman
SP S Sanders
RS W Blair
RS F Valenzuela
CL T Hoffman
RS B Williams
C B Ausmus
1B E Williams
2B J Reed
SS A Cedeno
3B K Caminiti
LU M Nieves
CF S Finley
RF T Gwynn
UI S Livingstone
1U R Petagine
OI- P Clark
L2- B Roberts
M B Bochy

SF 1995 NL
SP M Leiter
SP T Mulholland
SP Van
Landingham
SP M Portugal
RS J Bautista
CL R Beck
RP C Hook
RP S Barton
C K Manwaring
1U M Carreon
2B R Thompson
SS R Clayton
3B- M Williams
LF B Bonds
CF- D Lewis
RF G Hill
2U J Patterson
1B J Phillips
3I- S Scarsone
M D Baker

BAL 1995 AL
SP M Mussina
SP K Brown
SP J Moyer
SP S Erickson
CL D Jones
RP M Oquist
RP J Orosco
RP A Benitez
C C Hoiles
1B R Palmeiro
2B M Alexander
SS C Ripken
3B J Manto
LF B Anderson
CF C Goodwin
OF K Bass
DH H Baines
2B B Barberie
M P Regan

BOS 1995 AL
SP T Wakefield
SP E Hanson
SP R Clemens
SP Z Smith
RS R Cormier
RP M Maddux
RP S Belinda
RP J Hudson
C M Macfarlane
1B M Vaughn
2B L Alicea
SS J Valentin
3B T Naehring
LF M Greenwell
CF L Tinsley
RF T O'Leary
DH J Canseco
M K Kennedy

CAL 1995 AL
SP C Finley
SP M Langston
SP S Boskie
SP B Anderson
CL L Smith
RP T Percival
RP M James
RP B Patterson
C - J Fabregas
1B J Snow
2B D Easley
SS G DiSarcina
3L T Phillips
LF G Anderson
CF J Edmonds
RF T Salmon
DH C Davis
2O- R Hudler
CU- G Myers
UI- S Owen
M M Lachemann

CHI 1995 AL
SP A Fernandez
SP W Alvarez
SP J Bere
SP J Abbott
SR B Keyser
CL R Hernandez
RP K McCaskill
RP J DeLeon
C R Karkovice
OI D Martinez
2B R Durham
SS O Guillen
3B R Ventura
LF T Raines
CF L Johnson
RF M Devereaux
1D F Thomas
UT- N Martin
M1 G Lamont
M2 T Bevington

CLE 1995 AL
SP D Martinez
SP C Nagy
SP O Hershiser
SP M Clark
SP C Ogea
CL J Mesa
RP J Tavarez
RP E Plunk
RP J Poole
C T Pena
1B P Sorrento
2B C Baerga
SS O Vizquel
3B J Thome
LF A Belle
CF K Lofton
RF M Ramirez
DH E Murray
UO W Kirby
M M Hargrove

DET 1995 AL
SR F Lira
SP S Bergman
SP M Moore
SP D Wells
RP J Doherty
RS B Bohanon
RP J Boever
RP M Christopher
C J Flaherty
1D C Fielder
2B- L Whitaker
SS C Gomez
3B T Fryman
RL B Higginson
CF C Curtis
RF D Bautista
DH- K Gibson
IO- J Samuel
SS- A Trammell
M S Anderson

KC 1995 AL
SP M Gubicza
SP K Appier
SP T Gordon
CL J Montgomery
RP H Pichardo
RP R Meacham
RP B Brewer
C B Mayne
1B W Joyner
2U K Lockhart
SS G Gagne
3B G Gaetti
LF- V Coleman
ML T Goodwin
RF J Nunnally
DH- B Hamelin
UT D Howard
M B Boone

MIL 1995 AL
SP S Sparks
SP R Bones
SP S Karl
SP B Givens
RP B Wegman
RP M Kiefer
C J Oliver
1B J Jaha
2B F Vina
SS J Valentin
3B J Cirillo
LM D Hulse
CF D Hamilton
RF M Mieske
DH G Vaughn
2S P Listach
31 K Seitzer
OI B Surhoff
C - M Matheny
RU- D Nilsson
M P Garner

MIN 1995 AL
SP B Radke
SP K Tapani
SP M Trombley
SP F Rodriguez
SP S Erickson
RS P Mahomes
RS E Guardado
RP D Stevens
RP R Robertson
C M Walbeck
1U S Stahoviak
2B C Knoblauch
SS P Meares
3B S Leius
LF M Cordova
CF R Becker
RF K Puckett
DU P Munoz
CU- M Merullo
UI J Reboulet
M T Kelly

NY 1995 AL
SP J McDowell
SP A Pettitte
SP S Hitchcock
SP D Cone
SP S Kamieniecki
CL J Wetteland
RP B Wickman
RP S Howe
RP R Mac Donald
C M Stanley
1B D Mattingly
2B P Kelly
SS T Fernandez
3B W Boggs
LR G Williams
CF B Williams
RF P O'Neill
DH- R Sierra
2S R Velarde
OI- D James
CU- J Leyritz
M B Showalter

OAK 1995 AL
SP T Stottlemyre
SR T Van Poppel
SP S Ontiveros
SP R Darling
CL D Eckersley
RP C Reyes
RP M Acre
RP J Corsi
C T Steinbach
1B M McGwire
2B B Gates
SS M Bordick
3U C Paquette
LF R Henderson
CF S Javier
RF- R Sierra
DR G Berroa
UT S Brosius
M T LaRussa

SEA 1995 AL
SP R Johnson
SP T Belcher
SP C Bosio
RP B Ayala
RP J Nelson
RP B Wells
CL N Charlton
C D Wilson
1B T Martinez
2B J Cora
SS L Sojo
3B M Blowers
LM R Amaral
MU A Diaz
RF J Buhner
DH E Martinez
S2- F Fermin
CF- K Griffey
3U- D Strange
M L Piniella

TEX 1995 AL
SP K Rogers
SP R Pavlik
SP K Gross
SP B Tewksbury
RP R McDowell
RP M Whiteside
RP D Cook
RP T Burrows
C I Rodriguez
1B W Clark
2B J Frye
SS B Gil
3B- M Pagliarulo
L2 M McLemore
CF O Nixon
RF R Greer
DH J Gonzalez
OI M Tettleton
M J Oates

TOR 1995 AL
SP P Hentgen
SP A Leiter
SP J Guzman
SP D Cone
RP T Castillo
RP W Williams
RP D Cox
C - L Parrish
1B J Olerud
2B R Alomar
SS A Gonzalez
3B E Sprague
LF J Carter
CF D White
RF S Green
DH P Molitor
M C Gaston

ATL 1996 NL
SP J Smoltz
SP G Maddux
SP T Glavine
SP S Avery
CL M Wohlers
RP G McMichael
RP B Clontz
RS M Bielecki
C J Lopez
1B F McGriff
2B M Lemke
SS- J Blauser
3B C Jones
LF R Klesko
CF M Grissom
RL J Dye
OF D Smith
SU- R Belliard
M B Cox

CHI 1996 NL
SP J Navarro
SP S Trachsel
SP F Castillo
SR J Bullinger
RP T Adams
RP T Wendell
RP R Myers
RP K Bottenfield
C S Servais
1B M Grace
2B R Sandberg
SS- R Sanchez
3B L Gomez
LF L Gonzalez
CF B McRae
RF S Sosa
UO S Bullett
S3 J Hernandez
M J Riggleman

CIN 1996 NL
SP J Smiley
SP D Burba
SP M Portugal
SP K Jarvis
SR R Salkeld
CL J Brantley
RP J Shaw
RP H Carrasco
RP J Ruffin
C J Oliver
1B H Morris
2B B Boone
SS B Larkin
3U W Greene
UO T Howard
CF E Davis
RF- R Sanders
UI J Branson
UT L Harris
C E Taubensee
LU- E Owens
M R Knight

COL 1996 NL
SP K Ritz
SP M Thompson
SP A Reynoso
SP M Freeman
CL B Ruffin
RP C Leskanic
RP D Holmes
RP S Reed
C J Reed
1B A Galarraga
2B E Young
SS W Weiss
3B V Castilla
LF E Burks
MU Q McCracken
RF D Bichette
OI J Vander Wal
UI- J Bates
MR- L Walker
M D Baylor

FLA 1996 NL
SP K Brown
SP A Leiter
SP P Rapp
SP J Burkett
CL R Nen
RS C Hammond
RP J Powell
RS D Weathers
C C Johnson
1B G Colbrunn
2B- Q Veras
SS E Renteria
3B T Pendleton
LF J Conine
CF D White
RF G Sheffield
UI K Abbott
3U A Arias
OI J Orsulak
UO J Tavarez
M1 R Lachemann
M2 C Rojas
M3 J Boles

HOU 1996 NL
SP S Reynolds
SP D Kile
SP D Drabek
SP M Hampton
SP D Wall
RP X Hernandez
RP T Jones
RP B Wagner
RP D Brocail
C - R Wilkins
1B J Bagwell
2B C Biggio
SS O Miller
3B S Berry
LO J Mouton
CF B Hunter
RF D Bell
OF J Cangelosi
LU D May
3U B Spiers

SS- R Gutierrez
M T Collins

LA 1996 NL
SP H Nomo
SP I Valdes
SP P Astacio
SP R Martinez
SP T Candiotti
RS C Park
CL T Worrell
RP A Osuna
RP M Guthrie
C M Piazza
1B E Karros
2B D DeShields
SS G Gagne
3B- M Blowers
LF T Hollandsworth
MO-R Cedeno
RF R Mondesi
UT C Fonville
M1 T Lasorda
M2 B Russell

MON 1996 NL
SP J Fassero
SP P Martinez
SP R Cormier
SR U Urbina
CL M Rojas
RS O Daal
RP B Manuel
RP D Veres
C D Fletcher
1B D Segui
2B M Lansing
SS M Grudzielanek
3B S Andrews
L1 H Rodriguez
MO F Santangelo
RF M Alou
LU C Floyd
RU- S Obando
3U- D Silvestri
CF- R White
M F Alou

NY 1996 NL
SP M Clark
SP B Jones
SP P Harnisch
SP J Isringhausen
SP P Wilson
RP D Mlicki
RP D Henry
CL J Franco
RP J Dipoto
C T Hundley
1R B Huskey
2B- J Vizcaino
SS R Ordonez
3B- J Kent
LF B Gilkey
CF L Johnson
RF- A Ochoa
23 E Alfonzo
UO C Everett
UI- T Bogar
OI- C Jones
M1 D Green
M2 B Valentine

PHI 1996 NL
SP C Schilling
SP M Williams
SP T Mulholland
SP M Mimbs
CL R Bottalico
RP K Ryan
RS R Springer
RP T Borland
C B Santiago
1L G Jefferies
2B M Morandini
SS K Stocker
3B T Zeile
LU P Incaviglia
CF R Otero
UO J Eisenreich
M J Fregosi

PIT 1996 NL
SP D Neagle
SP D Darwin
RS J Lieber
RS F Cordova
RS D Miceli
RP D Plesac
C J Kendall
1B M Johnson
2B C Garcia
SS J Bell
3B C Hayes
LF A Martin
MU M Kingery
RF O Merced
12 J King
UI N Liriano
OF- D Clark
UT- J Wehner
M J Leyland

STL 1996 NL
SP An Benes
SP T Stottlemyre
SP D Osborne
SP Al Benes
SP M Morgan
CL D Eckersley
RP T Mathews
RS M Petkovsek
RP C Bailey
C T Pagnozzi
1B J Mabry
2B L Alicea
SS R Clayton
3B G Gaetti
LF R Gant
CF R Lankford
RF B Jordan
OI W McGee
OI M Sweeney
SU- O Smith
M T LaRussa

SD 1996 NL
SP J Hamilton
SP B Tewksbury
SP F Valenzuela
SP A Ashby
SR S Sanders
CL T Hoffman
RS T Worrell
RS S Bergman
RP W Blair
C - J Flaherty
1B W Joyner
2B J Reed
SS- C Gomez
3B K Caminiti
LF R Henderson
CF S Finley
RF T Gwynn
IF S Livingstone
OI- C Gwynn
C - B Johnson
OI- M Newfield
M B Bochy

SF 1996 NL
SP A Watson
SP Van
Landingham
SP M Gardner
SP O Fernandez
SP M Leiter
CL R Beck
RP M Dewey
RP J Bautista
RP R DeLucia
C - T Lampkin
1B- M Carreon
2U S Scarsone
SS R Aurilia
3B M Williams
LF B Bonds
CF M Benard
RF G Hill
SS- S Dunston
1U- D McCarty
M D Baker

BAL 1996 AL
SP M Mussina
SP D Wells
SP S Erickson
SP R Coppinger
CL R Myers
RP R McDowell
RP A Mills
RP J Orosco
C C Hoiles
1B R Palmeiro
2B R Alomar
SS C Ripken
3U B Surhoff
UO M Devereaux
CF B Anderson
RD B Bonilla
DH- E Murray
M D Johnson

BOS 1996 AL
SP R Clemens
SP T Gordon
SP T Wakefield
SP A Sele
CL H Slocumb
RS V Eshelman
RS M Maddux
RP M Stanton
C M Stanley
1B M Vaughn
2B J Frye
SS J Valentin
3B T Naehring
LF- M Greenwell
CF- L Tinsley
RL T O'Leary
DH- J Canseco
UT R Jefferson
M K Kennedy

CAL 1996 AL
SP C Finley
SP S Boskie
SP J Abbott
SR J Grimsley
SP M Langston
CL T Percival
RP M James
C - J Fabregas
1B J Snow
2B R Velarde
SS G DiSarcina
3B- G Arias
LF G Anderson
CF J Edmonds
RF T Salmon
DH C Davis
2U- R Hudler
M1 M Lachemann
M2 J McNamara

CHI 1996 AL
SP A Fernandez
SP K Tapani
SP W Alvarez
SP J Baldwin
CL R Hernandez
RP B Simas
RP B Keyser
RP M Karchner
C R Karkovice
1B F Thomas
2B R Durham
SS O Guillen
3B R Ventura
LF T Phillips
CF D Lewis
RF D Tartabull
DH H Baines
MR D Martinez
OF- L Mouton
M T Bevington

CLE 1996 AL
SP C Nagy
SP O Hershiser
SP J McDowell
SP C Ogea
SP D Martinez
CL J Mesa
RP J Tavarez
RP E Plunk
RP P Shuey
C S Alomar
1B J Franco
2B C Baerga
SS O Vizquel
3B J Thome
LF A Belle
CF K Lofton
RF M Ramirez
DH- E Murray
M M Hargrove

DET 1996 AL
SP F Lira
SP O Olivares
SR B Williams
RP R Lewis
RP J Lima
RP M Myers
C - B Ausmus
1B T Clark
2B M Lewis
SS- A Cedeno
3B T Fryman
UO B Higginson
CF C Curtis
RU M Nieves
DU- E Williams
CF K Bartee
1D C Fielder
OF- C Pride
M B Bell

KC 1996 AL
SP T Belcher
SP C Haney
SP K Appier
SP M Gubicza
SP J Rosado
RP D Linton
CL J Montgomery
RP H Pichardo
RP J Valera
C M Macfarlane
12 J Offerman
23 K Lockhart
SS D Howard
3B J Randa
ML T Goodwin
MR J Damon
RL M Tucker
DH- J Vitiello
IO C Paquette
D1- B Hamelin
2U- B Roberts
M B Boone

MIL 1996 AL
SP B McDonald
SP S Karl
SP R Bones
RS A Miranda
CL M Fetters
RP R Garcia
RP G Lloyd
C M Matheny
IF K Seitzer
2B F Vina
SS J Valentin
3B J Cirillo
LF G Vaughn
CF- P Listach
RF M Mieske
1D J Jaha
C J Levis
OI D Nilsson
UO- D Hulse
M P Garner

MIN 1996 AL
SP B Radke
SP F Rodriguez
SP R Robertson
SP S Aldred
SP R Aguilera
RP E Guardado
RP G Hansell
RP M Trombley
RS J Parra
C - G Myers
1B S Stahoviak
2B C Knoblauch
SS P Meares
3B D Hollins
LF M Cordova
CF R Becker
RM R Kelly
DH P Molitor
UT J Reboulet
1U- R Coomer
IO- C Hale
M T Kelly

NY 1996 AL
SP A Pettitte
SP K Rogers
SP D Gooden
SP J Key
RP M Rivera
CL J Wetteland
RP B Wickman
RP J Nelson
C J Girardi
1B T Martinez
2B M Duncan
SS D Jeter
3B W Boggs
LU G Williams
CF B Williams
RF P O'Neill
DL- R Sierra
23 A Fox
CU- J Leyritz
M J Torre

OAK 1996 AL
SR D Wengert
SR D Johns
SP J Wasdin
SP A Prieto
RS C Reyes
RP M Mohler
RP B Groom
RP J Corsi
C T Steinbach
1B M McGwire
2S- R Bournigal
SS M Bordick
3B S Brosius
LF- P Plantier
CF E Young
RF J Herrera
DR G Berroa
UT J Giambi
M A Howe

SEA 1996 AL
SP S Hitchcock
SP B Wolcott
SR B Wells
RP N Charlton
RP R Carmona
RP M Jackson
RP B Ayala
C D Wilson
1B P Sorrento
2B J Cora
SS A Rodriguez
3B- R Davis
LO R Amaral
CF K Griffey
RF J Buhner
DH E Martinez
UT- D Strange
M L Piniella

TEX 1996 AL
SP K Hill
SP R Pavlik
SP B Witt
SP D Oliver
SP K Gross
RP G Heredia
RP D Cook
RP J Russell
C I Rodriguez
1B W Clark
2B M McLemore
SS K Elster
3B D Palmer
LF R Greer
CF D Hamilton
RF J Gonzalez
DH M Tettleton
UO- D Buford
RU- W Newson
M J Oates

TOR 1996 AL
SP P Hentgen
SP E Hanson
SP J Guzman
SR P Quantrill
CL M Timlin
RP T Castillo
RP T Crabtree
C C O'Brien
1B J Olerud
2B- T Perez
SS A Gonzalez
3B E Sprague
L1 J Carter
CF O Nixon
RF S Green
DH C Delgado
UO- J Brumfield
LR- R Perez
M C Gaston

ATL 1997 NL
SP J Smoltz
SP T Glavine
SP G Maddux
SP D Neagle
CL M Wohlers
RP M Bielecki
RP P Byrd
C J Lopez
1B F McGriff
2B M Lemke
SS J Blauser
3B C Jones
LF R Klesko
RM A Jones
RL M Tucker
2U T Graffanino
CF K Lofton
IF- K Lockhart
M B Cox

CHI 1997 NL
SP S Trachsel
SP T Mulholland
SP K Foster
SP J Gonzalez
RP T Adams
RP K Bottenfield
RP M Rojas
RP T Wendell
C S Servais
1B M Grace
2B R Sandberg
SS S Dunston
3B K Orie
LF D Glanville
CF B McRae
RF S Sosa
OF D Clark
IO J Hernandez
S2- R Sanchez
3U- D Hansen
M J Riggleman

CIN 1997 NL
SP M Morgan
SP D Burba
SP K Mercker
SP B Tomko
SP J Smiley
CL J Shaw
RS M Remlinger
RP S Belinda
RP S Sullivan
C J Oliver
1B- H Morris
2B B Boone
SS P Reese
3O W Greene
UO- C Goodwin
ML D Sanders
RF- R Sanders
UT L Harris
1U E Perez
CU E Taubensee
M1 R Knight
M2 J McKeon

COL 1997 NL
SP R Bailey
SP J Thomson
SP J Wright
SP K Ritz
RP J Dipoto
RS D Holmes
RP M DeJean
RP S Reed
C K Manwaring
1B A Galarraga
2B E Young
SS W Weiss
3B V Castilla
LF D Bichette
CF Q McCracken
RF L Walker
ML E Burks
S2- N Perez
C - J Reed
M D Baylor

FLA 1997 NL
SP K Brown
SP A Fernandez
SP A Leiter
SP T Saunders
SP P Rapp
CL R Nen
RP J Powell
RS R Helling
RP D Cook
C C Johnson
1B J Conine
2B- L Castillo
SS E Renteria
3B B Bonilla
LM M Alou
CF- D White
RF G Sheffield
UO J Cangelosi
OI J Eisenreich
2U- K Abbott
M J Leyland

HOU 1997 NL
SP D Kile
SP M Hampton
SP C Holt
SP S Reynolds
SR R Garcia
CL B Wagner
RP J Lima
RP T Martin
RP R Springer
C B Ausmus
1B J Bagwell
2B C Biggio
SS- T Bogar
3B- S Berry
LF L Gonzalez
UO T Howard
RM D Bell
SI R Gutierrez
3I B Spiers
UO- J Mouton
M L Dierker

LA 1997 NL
SP H Nomo
SP I Valdes
SP C Park
SP P Astacio
SR T Candiotti
RP R Martinez
CL T Worrell
RP M Guthrie
RP D Dreifort
C M Piazza
1B E Karros
2B W Guerrero
SS G Gagne
3B T Zeile
LF T Hollandsworth
OF B Butler
RF R Mondesi
M B Russell

MON 1997 NL
SP P Martinez
SP C Perez
SP D Hermanson
SR J Bullinger
SP J Juden
RS M Valdes
CL U Urbina
RP A Telford
RP D Veres
C - C Widger
1B D Segui
2B M Lansing
SS M Grudzielanek
3B D Strange
LF H Rodriguez
CF R White
UT F Santangelo
OI J Orsulak
C - D Fletcher
RF- V Guerrero
OI- R McGuire
M F Alou

NY 1997 NL
SP R Reed
SP D Mlicki
SP B Jones
SP M Clark
CL J Franco
RP G McMichael
RP C Lidle
C T Hundley
1B J Olerud
2B C Baerga
SS R Ordonez
3B E Alfonzo
LF B Gilkey
MR C Everett
RI B Huskey
IO M Franco
RU A Ochoa
M B Valentine

PHI 1997 NL
SP C Schilling
SP M Leiter
SP M Beech
SP G Stephenson
CL R Bottalico
RP J Spradlin
RP R Blazier
RP R Harris
C M Lieberthal
1B R Brogna
2B M Morandini
SS K Stocker
3B S Rolen
LF G Jefferies
OI R Amaro
RF- D Daulton
UI- K Jordan
RU- D May
M T Francona

PIT 1997 NL
SP E Loaiza
SP J Lieber
SP J Schmidt
SP F Cordova
SP S Cooke
CL R Loiselle
RP M Wilkins
RP R Rincon
RP M Ruebel
C J Kendall
1B- K Young
2B T Womack
SS- K Polcovich
3B J Randa
LF A Martin
CF J Allensworth
RF J Guillen
UI D Sveum
M G Lamont

STL 1997 NL
SP M Morris
SP T Stottlemyre
SP An Benes
SP Al Benes
RP M Petkovsek
CL D Eckersley
RP J Frascatore
RP R Beltran
C - M Difelice
1U D Young
2B D DeShields
SS R Clayton
3B G Gaetti
LF R Gant
CF R Lankford
UO W McGee
C T Lampkin
R1 J Mabry
M T LaRussa

SD 1997 NL
SP A Ashby
SP J Hamilton
SP S Hitchcock
SR P Smith
CL T Hoffman
RS T Worrell
RS S Bergman
RS W Cunnane
C J Flaherty
1B W Joyner
2B Q Veras
SS C Gomez
3B K Caminiti
LF G Vaughn
CF S Finley
RF T Gwynn
IO- A Cianfrocco
LO- R Henderson
UO- C Jones
M B Bochy

SF 1997 NL
SP S Estes
SP K Rueter
SP M Gardner
CL R Beck
RP J Tavarez
RP D Henry
RP J Roa
C - R Wilkins
1B J Snow
2B J Kent
SS J Vizcaino
3B B Mueller
LF B Bonds
CF D Hamilton
RM S Javier
RF G Hill
3U M Lewis
UO- M Benard
M D Baker

ANA 1997 AL
SP J Dickson
SP A Watson
SP D Springer
SP C Finley
RS S Hasegawa
RP P Harris
CL T Percival
RP M James
C - C Kreuter
1B D Erstad
2B L Alicea
SS G DiSarcina
3B D Hollins
LF G Anderson
CF J Edmonds
RF T Salmon
DH- E Murray
UT T Phillips
CU- J Leyritz
M T Collins

BAL 1997 AL
SP M Mussina
SP S Erickson
SP J Key
SP S Kamieniecki
CL R Myers
RP A Rhodes
RP A Benitez
RS S Boskie
C L Webster
1B R Palmeiro
2B R Alomar
SS M Bordick
3B C Ripken
LF B Surhoff
CF B Anderson
UO J Hammonds
DR- G Berroa
C C Hoiles
2I J Reboulet
RU T Tarasco
M D Johnson

BOS 1997 AL
SP T Wakefield
SR T Gordon
SP A Sele
SP J Suppan
RS J Wasdin
RS B Henry
RS C Hammond
RP J Corsi
C S Hatteberg
1B M Vaughn

2U J Frye
SS N Garciaparra
3B- T Naehring
LF W Cordero
CF D Bragg
RF T O'Leary
DH R Jefferson
D1- M Stanley
23 J Valentin
M J Williams

CHI 1997 AL

SP J Navarro
SP J Baldwin
SP D Drabek
SP W Alvarez
SP D Darwin
RP M Karchner
RP C Castillo
RP T Castillo
RP C McElroy
C J Fabregas
1D F Thomas
2B R Durham
SS O Guillen
3B- C Snopek
LF A Belle
CF M Cameron
R1 D Martinez
DH- H Baines
CF- D Lewis
RU- L Mouton
M T Bevington

CLE 1997 AL

SP C Nagy
SP O Hershiser
SP C Ogea
RP J Mesa
RP M Jackson
RS A Lopez
RP E Plunk
C S Alomar
1B J Thome
2B T Fernandez
SS O Vizquel
3B M Williams
LO B Giles
CF M Grissom
RF M Ramirez
LD D Justice
M M Hargrove

DET 1997 AL

SP J Thompson
SP W Blair
SP B Moehler
SP O Olivares
CL T Jones
RP A Sager
RP D Miceli
RP D Brocail
C R Casanova
1B T Clark
2B D Easley
SS D Cruz
3B T Fryman
LR B Higginson
CF B Hunter
RF M Nieves
DH B Hamelin
UT- P Nevin
M B Bell

KC 1997 AL

SP K Appier
SP T Belcher
SP J Rosado
SP G Rusch
SP J Pittsley
RP J Montgomery
RP H Pichardo
C - M Macfarlane
1B J King
2B J Offerman
SS J Bell
3B- C Paquette
LF B Roberts
CF T Goodwin
UO J Damon
DH C Davis
C - M Sweeney
M1 B Boone
M2 T Muser

MIL 1997 AL

SP C Eldred
SP S Karl
SP J Mercedes
SP J D'Amico
SP B McDonald
CL D Jones
RP B Wickman
RS J Adamson
RP M Fetters
C M Matheny
UT D Nilsson
2B- F Vina
SS J Valentin
3B J Cirillo
RL- M Mieske
CF G Williams
RF J Burnitz
D1- J Franco
C J Levis
UI M Loretta
UT- J Huson
M P Garner

MIN 1997 AL

SP B Radke
SP B Tewksbury
SP R Robertson
SR F Rodriguez
SP L Hawkins
RP G Swindell
CL R Aguilera
RP M Trombley
RP T Ritchie
C T Steinbach
1B- S Stahoviak
2B C Knoblauch
SS P Meares
3B R Coomer
LF M Cordova
CF R Becker
UO M Lawton
DH P Molitor
UT D Hocking
M T Kelly

NY 1997 AL

SP A Pettitte
SP D Wells
SP D Cone
SP K Rogers
SR R Mendoza
CL M Rivera
RP D Gooden
RP J Nelson
RP M Stanton
C J Girardi
1B T Martinez
2B- L Sojo
SS D Jeter
3B C Hayes
LM- C Curtis
CF B Williams
RF P O'Neill
DH C Fielder
3U W Boggs
M J Torre

OAK 1997 AL

SP S Karsay
SP A Prieto
SP M Oquist
SP D Telgheder
RS D Wengert
RS M Mohler
RP A Small
RP B Taylor
C - B Mayne
1B M McGwire
2B S Spiezio
SS- R Bournigal
3B S Brosius
UT J Giambi
CF- D Mashore
OI M Stairs
CF- J McDonald
IF D Magadan
DR J Canseco
M A Howe

SEA 1997 AL

SP J Fassero
SP R Johnson
SP J Moyer
SP B Wolcott
RP B Ayala
RP N Charlton
RP B Wells
RS S Sanders
C D Wilson
1B P Sorrento
2B J Cora
SS A Rodriguez
3B R Davis
LR- R Ducey
CF K Griffey
RF J Buhner
DH E Martinez
UT- R Amaral
M L Piniella

TEX 1997 AL

SP B Witt
SP D Oliver
SP J Burkett
SP K Hill
SR J Santana
CL J Wetteland
RP M Whiteside
RP D Patterson
RP E Gunderson
C I Rodriguez
1B W Clark
2B- M McLemore
SS B Gil
3B- D Palmer
LF R Greer
CF D Buford
RU- W Newson
DR J Gonzalez
2S D Cedeno
UT L Stevens
M J Oates

TOR 1997 AL

SP R Clemens
SP P Hentgen
SP W Williams
SP R Person
RP P Quantrill
RP D Plesac
C - B Santiago
1B C Delgado
2B C Garcia
SS A Gonzalez
3B E Sprague
OF S Green
CF O Nixon
RF O Merced
OI J Carter
M1 C Gaston
M2 M Queen

ARI 1998 NL

SP A Benes
SP B Anderson
SR O Daal
SP W Blair
SP A Telemaco
CL G Olson
RS C Sodowsky
C - K Stinnett
1B T Lee
2B- A Stankiewicz
SS J Bell
3B M Williams
LF D Dellucci
CF D White
RF K Garcia
UI T Batista
OI B Brede
UT A Fox
LU- Y Benitez
M B Showalter

ATL 1998 NL

SP G Maddux
SP T Glavine
SP D Neagle
SP K Millwood
SP J Smoltz
CL K Ligtenberg
RS D Martinez
C J Lopez
1B A Galarraga
2B K Lockhart
SS- W Weiss
3B C Jones
LF R Klesko
CF A Jones
UO G Williams
2B T Graffanino
RF M Tucker
LU- D Bautista
SS- O Guillen
M B Cox

CHI 1998 NL

SP K Tapani
SP M Clark
SP S Trachsel
SP K Wood
SP J Gonzalez
CL R Beck
RS T Mulholland
RP T Adams
RS D Wengert
C S Servais
1B M Grace
2B M Morandini
SS J Blauser
UT J Hernandez
LF H Rodriguez
ML B Brown
RF S Sosa
IO M Alexander
CU- T Houston
CF- L Johnson
M J Riggleman

CIN 1998 NL

SP B Tomko
SP P Harnisch
SP M Remlinger
SP S Parris
RP G White
RP S Sullivan
RP D Graves
CL J Shaw
C E Taubensee
1B- S Casey
2B B Boone
SS B Larkin
3O W Greene
L1 D Young
MR R Sanders
RM- J Nunnally
LI C Stynes
OF- M Nieves
1U- E Perez
UO- P Watkins
M J McKeon

COL 1998 NL

SP D Kile
SP P Astacio
SP J Wright
SP J Thomson
SR B Jones
RP J Dipoto
RP D Veres
RP C Leskanic
RP M DeJean
C K Manwaring
1B T Helton
2B M Lansing
SS N Perez
3B V Castilla
LF D Bichette
CF E Burks
RF L Walker
MU C Goodwin
C J Reed
OI- J Vander Wal
M D Baylor

FLA 1998 NL

SP L Hernandez
SP B Meadows
SP J Sanchez
RS K Ojala
RP A Alfonseca
RP V Darensbourg
RP M Mantei
C G Zaun
1B D Lee
2B C Counsell
SS E Renteria
3B- T Zeile
LF C Floyd
CF T Dunwoody
RM M Kotsay
UO J Cangelosi
UT R Jackson
UI- D Berg
M J Leyland

HOU 1998 NL

SP J Lima
SP S Reynolds
SP M Hampton
SP S Bergman
CL B Wagner
RP D Henry
RP C Nitkowski
RP S Elarton
C B Ausmus
1B J Bagwell
2B C Biggio
SS R Gutierrez
3B B Spiers
LF M Alou
CF C Everett
RF D Bell
3B S Berry
OF- D Clark
M L Dierker

LA 1998 NL

SP C Park
SP D Dreifort
SP I Valdes
SP D Mlicki
SP R Martinez
RP S Radinsky
RP A Osuna
RP M Guthrie
C C Johnson
1B E Karros
2B E Young
SS- J Vizcaino
3B- A Beltre
OI- T Hubbard
MR R Mondesi
RF- G Sheffield
UO R Cedeno
S2- J Castro
M1 B Russell
M2 G Hoffman

MIL 1998 NL

SP S Karl
SP S Woodard
SP J Juden
SR B Woodall
SP C Eldred
CL B Wickman
RP B Patrick
RP D Jones
RP C Fox
C M Matheny
1S M Loretta
2B F Vina
SS J Valentin
3B J Cirillo
UO D Jackson
CF M Grissom
RF J Burnitz
UT B Hamelin
UT D Nilsson
C - B Hughes
LF- G Jenkins
LU- M Newfield
M P Garner

MON 1998 NL

SP D Hermanson
SP J Vazquez
SP C Perez
SP C Pavano
RS M Batista
CL U Urbina
RP S Bennett
RP A Telford
C C Widger
1B B Fullmer
2U- J Vidro
SS M Grudzielanek
3B S Andrews
L2 F Santangelo
CF- R White
RF V Guerrero
1L R McGuire
LU- D May
M F Alou

NY 1998 NL

SP R Reed
SP B Jones
SP A Leiter
SP M Yoshii
CL J Franco
RP T Wendell
RP D Cook
RP M Rojas
C M Piazza
1B J Olerud
2B C Baerga
SS R Ordonez
3B E Alfonzo
LF- B Gilkey
CF B McRae
RF B Huskey
UT M Franco
UT L Lopez
M B Valentine

PHI 1998 NL

SP C Schilling
SP M Portugal
SP T Green
SP C Loewer
SP M Beech
RP M Leiter
RP W Gomes
RP J Spradlin
RP Y Perez
C - M Lieberthal
1B R Brogna
2B M Lewis
SS D Relaford
3B S Rolen
LF G Jefferies
CF D Glanville
RF B Abreu
UI K Jordan
UT K Sefcik
UO- R Amaro
M T Francona

PIT 1998 NL

SP F Cordova
SP J Schmidt
SP J Lieber
SR C Peters
SP J Silva
RP R Rincon
RS E Dessens
CL R Loiselle
RP J Christiansen
C J Kendall
1B K Young
2B T Womack
SS L Collier
3B- A Ramirez
LF A Martin
UO T Ward
RF J Guillen
SI- K Polcovich
UI- D Strange
M G Lamont

STL 1998 NL

SP K Mercker
SP T Stottlemyre
SR K Bottenfield
SP M Morris
RS J Acevedo
RS M Petkovsek
RP J Frascatore
RP J Brantley
C - E Marrero
1B M McGwire
2B D DeShields
SS- R Clayton
3B- G Gaetti
LF R Gant
CF R Lankford
RF B Jordan
UT J Mabry
OI W McGee
CU- T Lampkin
M T LaRussa

SD 1998 NL

SP K Brown
SP A Ashby
SP J Hamilton
SR S Hitchcock
CL T Hoffman
RP B Boehringer
RP D Miceli
RP D Wall
C C Hernandez
1B W Joyner
2B Q Veras
SS C Gomez
3B K Caminiti
LF G Vaughn
CF S Finley
RF T Gwynn
OI M Sweeney
UI- E Giovanola
RF- R Rivera
UI- A Sheets
M B Bochy

SF 1998 NL

SP M Gardner
SP O Hershiser
SP K Rueter
SP D Darwin
SP S Estes
CL R Nen
RP J Johnstone
RP J Tavarez
RP R Rodriguez
C B Johnson
1B J Snow
2B J Kent
SS R Aurilia
3B B Mueller
LF B Bonds
CF- D Hamilton
RO S Javier
RU M Benard
IF C Hayes
S2 R Sanchez
C - B Mayne
M D Baker

ANA 1998 AL

SP C Finley
SR O Olivares
SP S Sparks
SP J Dickson
SP K Hill
CL T Percival
RP S Hasegawa
RP R DeLucia
RP P Harris
C M Walbeck
1D C Fielder
2B- J Baughman
SS G DiSarcina
3B D Hollins
1L D Erstad
CF J Edmonds
RF G Anderson
DH T Salmon
M T Collins

BAL 1998 AL

SP S Erickson
SP M Mussina
SR S Ponson
SP D Drabek
RP A Benitez
RS D Johns
RP A Rhodes
RP A Mills
C L Webster
1B R Palmeiro
2B R Alomar
SS M Bordick
3B C Ripken
LF B Surhoff
CF B Anderson
OF E Davis
DH H Baines
C - C Hoiles
RD- J Carter
M R Miller

BOS 1998 AL

SP P Martinez
SP T Wakefield
SP B Saberhagen
SR S Avery
RS D Lowe
CL T Gordon
RS J Wasdin
RP J Corsi
C S Hatteberg
1B M Vaughn
2I M Benjamin
SS N Garciaparra
3B J Valentin
LF T O'Leary
MR D Lewis
RF D Bragg
DH- R Jefferson
CF- D Buford
C - J Varitek
M J Williams

CHI 1998 AL

SP M Sirotka
SR J Navarro
SP J Baldwin
SP J Parque
SR S Eyre
RP C Castillo
RP B Simas
RP K Foulke
RP B Howry
C - C Kreuter
1B- W Cordero
2B R Durham
SS M Caruso
3B R Ventura
LF A Belle
CF M Cameron
RF M Ordonez
DH F Thomas
1B G Norton
UO- J Abbott
M J Manuel

CLE 1998 AL

SP C Nagy
SP D Burba
SP B Colon
SP J Wright
SP D Gooden
CL M Jackson
RP J Mesa
RP P Shuey
C S Alomar
1B J Thome
2B D Bell
SS O Vizquel
3B T Fryman
LF B Giles
CF K Lofton
RF M Ramirez
DH D Justice
UO- M Whiten
M M Hargrove

DET 1998 AL

SP J Thompson
SP B Moehler
SR B Florie
SP S Greisinger
SP F Castillo
CL T Jones
RP D Bochtler
RP D Brocail
RP A Sager
C - P Bako
1B T Clark
2B D Easley
SS D Cruz
3B J Randa
LF L Gonzalez
CF B Hunter
RF B Higginson
DU- G Berroa
UI- F Catalanotto
M1 B Bell
M2 L Parrish

KC 1998 AL

SP T Belcher
SP P Rapp
SR J Rosado
SP G Rusch
SP H Pichardo
RS C Haney
CL J Montgomery
RP S Service
RP J Pittsley
C - M Sweeney
1B J King
2B J Offerman
SS- M Lopez
3B D Palmer
LR- J Conine
CF J Damon
OI L Sutton
D3- T Pendleton
UT H Morris
SS- S Halter
M T Muser

MIN 1998 AL

SP B Radke
SP L Hawkins
SP E Milton
SP B Tewksbury
CL R Aguilera
RP M Trombley
RS D Serafini
RP G Swindell
C T Steinbach
1B- D Ortiz
2B T Walker
SS P Meares
3U B Gates
LF M Cordova
CF O Nixon
RM M Lawton
DH P Molitor
31 R Coomer
UT D Hocking
RO- A Ochoa
M T Kelly

NY 1998 AL

SP A Pettitte
SP D Wells
SP D Cone
SP H Irabu
SP O Hernandez
RS R Mendoza
CL M Rivera
RP M Stanton
RP D Holmes
C J Posada
1B T Martinez
2B C Knoblauch
SS D Jeter
3B S Brosius
LM C Curtis
CF B Williams
RF P O'Neill
DH D Strawberry
DL T Raines
M J Torre

OAK 1998 AL

SP K Rogers
SP T Candiotti
SP J Haynes
SP M Oquist
SP B Stein
CL B Taylor
RP T Mathews
RP M Mohler
RP B Groom
C A Hinch
1B J Giambi
2B S Spiezio
SS M Tejada
3B M Blowers
LF R Henderson
CF R Christenson
RF B Grieve
DH M Stairs
2S- R Bournigal
M A Howe

SEA 1998 AL

SP J Moyer
SP J Fassero
SP R Johnson
SP K Cloude
SP B Swift
RP M Timlin
RP B Ayala
RS P Spoljaric
RP H Slocumb
C - D Wilson
1B D Segui
2B J Cora
SS A Rodriguez
3B R Davis
LF- G Hill
CF K Griffey
RO R Ducey
DH E Martinez
M L Piniella

TB 1998 AL
SP R Arrojo
SP T Saunders
SP W Alvarez
SR J Santana
SR D Springer
CL R Hernandez
RP E Yan
RP J Mecir
RP A Lopez
C - J Flaherty
1B F McGriff
2B M Cairo
SS K Stocker
3B B Smith
ML Q McCracken
MO R Winn
OF M Kelly
DU P Sorrento
3D W Boggs
C - M Difelice
SI- A Ledesma
RF- D Martinez
M L Rothschild

TEX 1998 AL
SP R Helling
SP A Sele
SP J Burkett
SP D Oliver
CL J Wetteland
RP T Crabtree
RP E Gunderson
RP D Patterson
C I Rodriguez
1B W Clark
2B M McLemore
SS- K Elster
3B- F Tatis
LF R Greer
CF T Goodwin
RF J Gonzalez
D1 L Stevens
IO L Alicea
OI- M Simms
M J Oates

TOR 1998 AL
SP R Clemens
SP W Williams
SP P Hentgen
SP C Carpenter
SP J Guzman
RP P Quantrill
RP B Risley
RP D Plesac
RP D Stieb
C D Fletcher
1B C Delgado
2B C Grebeck
SS A Gonzalez
3B E Sprague
LF S Stewart
CF J Cruz
RF S Green
DL J Canseco
23 T Fernandez
DU M Stanley
M T Johnson

ARI 1999 NL
SP R Johnson
SP O Daal
SP A Benes
SP A Reynoso
SR B Anderson
RP T Stottlemyre
RP G Olson
RP G Swindell
RP D Holmes
C - K Stinnett
1B T Lee
2B J Bell
SS A Fox
3B M Williams
LF L Gonzalez
CF S Finley
RF T Womack
OF- B Gilkey
C - D Miller
M B Showalter

ATL 1999 NL
SP T Glavine
SP K Millwood
SP G Maddux
SP J Smoltz
CL J Rocker
RP M Remlinger
RP K McGlinchy
RP R Seanez
C E Perez
1B B Hunter
2B B Boone
SS W Weiss
3B C Jones
LF G Williams
CF A Jones
RF B Jordan
1L R Klesko
IF K Lockhart
SU- O Guillen
LU- O Nixon
1B- R Simon
M B Cox

CHI 1999 NL
SP S Trachsel
SP J Lieber
SP K Tapani
SP K Farnsworth
SR T Mulholland
RS S Sanders
RP T Adams
RP R Myers
RP D Serafini
C B Santiago
1B M Grace
2B M Morandini
SS J Hernandez
3U G Gaetti
LF H Rodriguez
CF- L Johnson
RF S Sosa
IO J Blauser
OF G Hill
3U T Houston
IO- M Alexander
OF- C Goodwin
M J Riggleman

CIN 1999 NL
SP P Harnisch
SP B Tomko
SP R Villone
SP S Parris
SP D Neagle
RP D Graves
RP S Sullivan
RP S Williamson
RP D Reyes
C E Taubensee
1B S Casey
2B P Reese
SS B Larkin
3B A Boone
LF G Vaughn
CF M Cameron
RF M Tucker
UO J Hammonds
RU D Young
3U- M Lewis
M J McKeon

COL 1999 NL
SP P Astacio
SP B Bohanon
SP D Kile
SR B Jones
CL D Veres
RP J Dipoto
RP C Leskanic
RP M DeJean
C - H Blanco
1B T Helton
2U- K Abbott
SS N Perez
3B V Castilla
LF D Bichette
CF- D Hamilton
RF L Walker
OI A Echevarria
UT- L Harris
2U- T Shumpert
M J Leyland

FLA 1999 NL
SP D Springer
SP B Meadows
SP R Dempster
SP A Fernandez
SP L Hernandez
RP A Alfonseca
RP B Edmondson
RP B Looper
RS J Sanchez
C - M Redmond
1B K Millar
2B L Castillo
SS A Gonzalez
3B- M Lowell
LU B Aven
MO P Wilson
RF M Kotsay
IO D Berg
C - J Fabregas
M J Boles

HOU 1999 NL
SP J Lima
SP M Hampton
SP S Reynolds
SP C Holt
SR S Elarton
CL B Wagner
SR S Bergman
RP J Powell
RP B Williams
C T Eusebio
1B J Bagwell
2B C Biggio
SS T Bogar
3B- K Caminiti
LF R Hidalgo
CF C Everett
RF D Bell
3O B Spiers
MU- G Barker
SS- R Gutierrez
UI- R Johnson
M1 L Dierker
M2 M Galante
M3 L Dierker

LA 1999 NL
SP K Brown
SP I Valdes
SP C Park
SP D Dreifort
CL J Shaw
RP A Mills
RP J Arnold
RP O Masaoka
C T Hundley
1B E Karros
2B E Young
SS M Grudzielanek
3B A Beltre
LF G Sheffield
CF D White
RF R Mondesi
IO D Hansen
OI- T Hollandsworth
OI- T Hubbard
IO- J Vizcaino
M D Johnson

MIL 1999 NL
SP S Karl
SP S Woodard
SP H Nomo
CL B Wickman
RP D Weathers
RS R Roque
RP E Plunk
C D Nilsson
UI M Loretta
2B R Belliard
SS- J Valentin
3B J Cirillo
LF G Jenkins
CF M Grissom
RF J Burnitz
IC B Banks
1U S Berry
UO A Ochoa
UO- R Becker
M1 P Garner
M2 J Lefebvre

MON 1999 NL
SP D Hermanson
SP J Vazquez
SP M Thurman
SR M Batista
SP C Pavano
CL U Urbina
RP A Telford
RP S Kline
RP B Ayala
C C Widger
1B B Fullmer
2B J Vidro
SS O Cabrera
3B S Andrews
LM R White
CF M Martinez
RF V Guerrero
3C M Barrett
UT W Guerrero
UI M Mordecai
1O- R McGuire
UT- O Merced
UO- J Mouton
M F Alou

NY 1999 NL
SP A Leiter
SP O Hershiser
SP M Yoshii
SP R Reed
RP A Benitez
RP T Wendell
RP D Cook
RP P Mahomes
C M Piazza
1B J Olerud
2B E Alfonzo
SS R Ordonez
3B R Ventura
LF R Henderson
CF- B McRae
RF R Cedeno
UO B Agbayani
UT M Franco
M B Valentine

PHI 1999 NL
SP P Byrd
SP C Schilling
SP C Ogea
SP R Person
SP R Wolf
RP W Gomes
RP S Montgomery
RS M Grace
RP S Schrenk
C M Lieberthal
1B R Brogna
2B M Anderson
SS A Arias
3B S Rolen
LF R Gant
CF D Glanville
RF B Abreu
2B D Doster
UO R Ducey
32 K Jordan
OI K Sefcik
M T Francona

PIT 1999 NL
SP J Schmidt
SP K Benson
SP T Ritchie
SP F Cordova
SR P Schourek
RS J Silva
CL M Williams
RP S Sauerbeck
RP B Clontz
C - J Kendall
1B K Young
2B W Morris
SS M Benjamin
3B E Sprague
LF A Martin
CF B Giles
RM A Brown
OI B Brown
SU- A Nunez
M G Lamont

STL 1999 NL
SP D Oliver
SP K Bottenfield
SP J Jimenez
SP K Mercker
RS J Acevedo
RP M Aybar
RP R Bottalico
RP R Croushore
C E Marrero
1B M McGwire
2O J McEwing
SS E Renteria
3B F Tatis
LF R Lankford
CF J Drew
OI W McGee
OF T Howard
UO- D Bragg
C - A Castillo
2B- P Polanco
M T LaRussa

SD 1999 NL
SP W Williams
SP A Ashby
SP S Hitchcock
SP M Clement
CL T Hoffman
RP C Reyes
RP D Miceli
RP D Wall
C - B Davis
1B W Joyner
2B Q Veras
SS D Jackson
3U P Nevin
UT E Owens
CF R Rivera
LR R Sanders
RF T Gwynn
IF D Magadan
OI J Vander Wal
M B Bochy

SF 1999 NL
SP R Ortiz
SP S Estes
SP K Rueter
SP M Gardner
SP C Brock
CL R Nen
RP J Johnstone
RP F Rodriguez
RP A Embree
C B Mayne
1B J Snow
2B J Kent
SS R Aurilia
3B B Mueller
LF B Bonds
CF M Benard
RF E Burks
UO S Javier
UT F Santangelo
3U- C Hayes
M D Baker

ANA 1999 AL
SP C Finley
SP S Sparks
SP T Belcher
SP O Olivares
SP K Hill
CL T Percival
RP A Levine
RP M Petkovsek
RP S Hasegawa
C M Walbeck
1L D Erstad
2B- R Velarde
SS- G DiSarcina
3B T Glaus
LR O Palmeiro
MU G Anderson
RF T Salmon
1D M Vaughn
OF- T Greene
IO- J Huson
SS- A Sheets
M1 T Collins
M2 J Maddon

BAL 1999 AL
SP S Erickson
SP S Ponson
SP M Mussina
SP J Guzman
SP J Johnson
CL M Timlin
RS D Johns
RP S Kamieniecki
RP A Rhodes
C C Johnson
1U J Conine
2B- D DeShields
SS M Bordick
3B- C Ripken
LF B Surhoff
CF B Anderson
RF A Belle
DH H Baines
32 J Reboulet
UT- R Amaral
M R Miller

BOS 1999 AL
SP P Martinez
SR T Wakefield
SP M Portugal
SP P Rapp
SP B Saberhagen
RP D Lowe
RP J Wasdin
RP R Cormier
C J Varitek
1B M Stanley
2B J Offerman
SS N Garciaparra
3B J Valentin
LF T O'Leary
MR D Lewis
RF T Nixon
DU- R Jefferson
1D B Daubach
CF- D Buford
M J Williams

CHI 1999 AL
SP M Sirotka
SP J Baldwin
SP J Parque
SP J Navarro
SP J Snyder
RP K Foulke
CL B Howry
RP S Lowe
RP B Simas
C B Fordyce
1D P Konerko
2B R Durham
SS M Caruso
3B G Norton
LF C Lee
CF C Singleton
RF M Ordonez
D1 F Thomas
3I C Wilson
M J Manuel

CLE 1999 AL
SP D Burba
SP B Colon
SP C Nagy
SP J Wright
SP D Gooden
CL M Jackson
RP P Shuey
RP S Karsay
RS M Langston
C E Diaz
UT R Sexson
2B R Alomar
SS O Vizquel
3B- T Fryman
LD D Justice
CF K Lofton
RF M Ramirez
1B J Thome
3S E Wilson
M M Hargrove

DET 1999 AL
SP B Moehler
SP D Mlicki
SP J Weaver
SP J Thompson
SR W Blair
CL T Jones
RP D Brocail
RS C Nitkowski
RS N Cruz
C B Ausmus
1B T Clark
2B D Easley
SS D Cruz
3B D Palmer
LF J Encarnacion
CF G Kapler
RF B Higginson
OF- L Polonia
UI F Catalanotto
RL- K Garcia
M L Parrish

KC 1999 AL
SP J Suppan
SP J Rosado
SP J Witasick
SP K Appier
RP S Service
RP J Montgomery
RP A Morman
C C Kreuter
UT M Sweeney
2B C Febles
SS R Sanchez
3B J Randa
LF J Damon
CF C Beltran
RF J Dye
D1- J Giambi
UO- S Pose
M T Muser

MIN 1999 AL
SP B Radke
SP E Milton
SP L Hawkins
SR J Mays
RP M Trombley
RP B Wells
RP B Sampson
RP H Carrasco
C T Steinbach
1B D Mientkiewicz
2U T Walker
SS C Guzman
3U C Koskie
LF C Allen
CF T Hunter
RF M Lawton
DO M Cordova
13 R Coomer
32 B Gates
UT D Hocking
CF- J Jones
M T Kelly

NY 1999 AL
SP O Hernandez
SP D Cone
SP A Pettitte
SP R Clemens
SP H Irabu
RS R Mendoza
CL M Rivera
RP J Grimsley
RP M Stanton
C J Posada
1B T Martinez
2B C Knoblauch
SS D Jeter
3B S Brosius
LF- C Curtis
CF B Williams
RF P O'Neill
DH C Davis
LF- R Ledee
M1 D Zimmer
M2 J Torre

OAK 1999 AL
SP G Heredia
SP J Haynes
SP M Oquist
SP T Hudson
SP K Rogers
RP D Jones
RP T Worrell
RP T Mathews
RP B Rigby
C - M Macfarlane
1B J Giambi
2M T Phillips
SS M Tejada
3B E Chavez
LF B Grieve
CF R Christenson
RF M Stairs
DH J Jaha
ML J McDonald
31- O Saenz
UI- S Spiezio
M A Howe

SEA 1999 AL
SP J Moyer
SP F Garcia
SR J Halama
SP J Fassero
CL J Mesa
RP J Paniagua
RS F Rodriguez
RS P Abbott
C D Wilson
1B- D Segui
2B D Bell
SS A Rodriguez
3B R Davis
LF B Hunter
CF K Griffey
RF- J Buhner
DH E Martinez
OI- R Ibanez
UT- J Mabry
M L Piniella

TB 1999 AL
SP B Witt
SP W Alvarez
SP R Rupe
SP R Arrojo
CL R Hernandez
RP R White
RP A Lopez
RP E Yan
C J Flaherty
1B F McGriff
2B M Cairo
SS- K Stocker
3B- W Boggs
LU- B Trammell
CF- R Winn
RM D Martinez
DH J Canseco
L1 P Sorrento
S3- A Ledesma
M L Rothschild

TEX 1999 AL
SP R Helling
SP A Sele
SP J Burkett
SP M Morgan
SR E Loaiza
CL J Wetteland
RP J Zimmerman
RP M Venafro
RP T Crabtree
C I Rodriguez
1B L Stevens
2B M McLemore
SS R Clayton
3B T Zeile
LF R Greer
CF T Goodwin
RF J Gonzalez
DH R Palmeiro
UO- R Kelly
M J Oates

TOR 1999 AL
SP D Wells
SP P Hentgen
SP K Escobar
SP C Carpenter
SR R Halladay
CL B Koch
RP G Lloyd
RP P Spoljaric
RP P Munro
C D Fletcher
1B C Delgado
2B H Bush
SS T Batista
3B T Fernandez
LF S Stewart
CF J Cruz
RF S Green
DU- W Greene
M J Fregosi

ARI 2000 NL
SP R Johnson
SP B Anderson
SP A Reynoso
RP M Morgan
RP B Kim
RP G Swindell
RP R Springer
C D Miller
1B G Colbrunn
2B J Bell
SS T Womack
3B- M Williams
LF L Gonzalez
CF S Finley
RF- D Bautista
M B Showalter

ATL 2000 NL
SP G Maddux
SP T Glavine
SP K Millwood
SR T Mulholland
SP J Burkett
RP M Remlinger
CL J Rocker
RP K Ligtenberg
C J Lopez
1B A Galarraga
2B- Q Veras
SS R Furcal
3B C Jones
LR R Sanders
CF A Jones
RF B Jordan
LU B Bonilla
UT W Joyner
2U K Lockhart
M B Cox

CHI 2000 NL
SP J Lieber
SP K Tapani
SP K Wood
RP T Van Poppel
RS K Farnsworth
RS D Garibay
RP T Worrell
C J Girardi
1B M Grace
2B E Young
SS R Gutierrez
3B W Greene
LF- H Rodriguez
CF D Buford
RF S Sosa
UI- J Nieves
C - J Reed
M D Baylor

CIN 2000 NL
SP S Parris
SR E Dessens
SR R Villone
SP R Bell
SP P Harnisch
CL D Graves
RP D Neagle
RS S Williamson
RP S Sullivan
C - B Santiago
1B S Casey
2B P Reese
SS B Larkin
3B- A Boone
OI M Tucker
CF K Griffey
RF D Bichette
LR A Ochoa
3U C Stynes
LU D Young
S2- J Castro
C - E Taubensee
M J McKeon

COL 2000 NL
SP P Astacio
SP B Bohanon
SP M Yoshii
SP K Jarvis
SP R Arrojo
RS J Tavarez

RP J Jimenez
RP G White
RP M DeJean
C B Mayne
1B T Helton
2B- M Lansing
SS N Perez
3B J Cirillo
RL- L Walker
CF- T Goodwin
RL J Hammonds
IO T Shumpert
M B Bell

FLA 2000 NL
SP R Dempster
SP J Sanchez
SP R Cornelius
SP C Smith
SP B Penny
CL A Alfonseca
RP R Bones
RP B Looper
RP V Darensbourg
C - M Redmond
1B D Lee
2B L Castillo
SS A Gonzalez
3B M Lowell
LF C Floyd
CF P Wilson
RF M Kotsay
UT K Millar
OF M Smith
SI- D Berg
M J Boles

HOU 2000 NL
SP C Holt
SP J Lima
SP S Elarton
SP S Reynolds
SP W Miller
RS O Dotel
RP J Slusarski
RP J Cabrera
RP M Valdes
C M Meluskey
1B J Bagwell
2B C Biggio
SS T Bogar
3B- C Truby
RL M Alou
CF R Hidalgo
RL L Berkman
S2 J Lugo
UT B Spiers
OI D Ward
CF- G Barker
M L Dierker

LA 2000 NL
SP K Brown
SP C Park
SP D Dreifort
SP C Perez
SP E Gagne
RP M Herges
RP T Adams
CL J Shaw
RP A Osuna
C - T Hundley
1B E Karros
2B M Grudzielanek
SS A Cora
3B A Beltre
LF G Sheffield
CF- T Hollandsworth
RF S Green
IO D Hansen
OI- F Santangelo
M D Johnson

MIL 2000 NL
SP J Haynes
SP J Wright
SP J D'Amico
SP J Snyder
SP J Bere
RP C Leskanic
RP J Acevedo
RP D Weathers
RP V DeLos Santos
C - H Blanco
1B- R Sexson
2B R Belliard
SS- M Loretta
3B J Hernandez
LF G Jenkins
CF M Grissom
RF J Burnitz
IF C Hayes
IF T Houston
C - R Casanova
UO- J Mouton
M D Lopes

MON 2000 NL
SP J Vazquez
SP D Hermanson
RS F Lira
RS M Johnson
RP S Kline
RP A Telford
C - C Widger
1B L Stevens
2B J Vidro
SS O Cabrera
3I- M Mordecai
LO T Jones
CF P Bergeron
RF V Guerrero
UI G Blum
OI W Guerrero
3C- M Barrett
IF- A Tracy
M F Alou

NY 2000 NL
SP M Hampton
SP A Leiter
SP G Rusch
SP R Reed
SP B Jones
CL A Benitez
RS P Mahomes
RP T Wendell
RP D Cook
C M Piazza
1B T Zeile
2B E Alfonzo
SS- M Bordick
3B R Ventura
LF B Agbayani
CF J Payton
RF D Bell
IO M Franco
UT- J McEwing
M B Valentine

PHI 2000 NL
SP R Wolf
SP R Person
SP C Schilling
SP A Ashby
RS C Brock
RP W Gomes
CL J Brantley
C M Lieberthal
1L P Burrell
2B- M Morandini
SS- D Relaford
3B S Rolen
LF- R Gant
CF D Glanville
RF B Abreu
UI K Jordan
UO K Sefcik
UT- B Hunter
M T Francona

PIT 2000 NL
SP K Benson
SP T Ritchie
SP J Anderson
SR J Silva
RP M Williams
RP S Sauerbeck
RP M Wilkins
RP J Manzanillo
C J Kendall
1B K Young
2B W Morris
SS P Meares
RU- A Ramirez
LF- W Cordero
MU A Brown
UO B Giles
OI J Vander Wal
UI- M Benjamin
M G Lamont

STL 2000 NL
SP D Kile
SP G Stephenson
SP P Hentgen
SP R Ankiel
SP A Benes
CL D Veres
RP M Morris
RP M James
RP H Slocumb
C M Matheny
1B- M McGwire
2B F Vina
SS E Renteria
3B- F Tatis
LF R Lankford
CF J Edmonds
RO J Drew
UT S Dunston
3I C Paquette
UI P Polanco
RF- E Davis
OI- T Howard
M T LaRussa

SD 2000 NL
SP M Clement
SP W Williams
SP A Eaton
SP B Meadows
SP B Tollberg
CL T Hoffman
RP C Almanzar
RP K Walker
RP D Wall
C - W Gonzalez
1B R Klesko
2B B Boone
S2 D Jackson
3B P Nevin
LF- A Martin
CF R Rivera
OI E Owens
RU- K DeHaan
UI- D Magadan
M B Bochy

SF 2000 NL
SP L Hernandez
SP R Ortiz
SP S Estes
SP K Rueter
SR M Gardner
CL R Nen
RP F Rodriguez
RP A Fultz
RP A Embree
C B Estalella
1B J Snow
2B J Kent
SS R Aurilia
3B B Mueller
LF B Bonds
CF M Benard
RF E Burks
CF C Murray
RU A Rios
UT- F Crespo
S2- R Martinez
C - D Mirabelli
M D Baker

ANA 2000 AL
SP S Schoeneweis
SP K Bottenfield
SP R Ortiz
RP S Hasegawa
RS A Levine
RP M Petkovsek
CL T Percival
C B Molina
1B M Vaughn
2B A Kennedy
SS B Gil
3B T Glaus
LU D Erstad
CF G Anderson
RF T Salmon
UT S Spiezio
UO O Palmeiro
M M Scioscia

BAL 2000 AL
SP M Mussina
SP S Ponson
SP P Rapp
SR J Mercedes
SR J Johnson
RP M Trombley
RP B Groom
RP C McElroy
C - C Johnson
1B- W Clark
2L D DeShields
SS M Bordick
3B- C Ripken
LF B Surhoff
MO B Anderson
RF A Belle
DH- H Baines
UT J Conine
M M Hargrove

BOS 2000 AL
SP P Martinez
SR J Fassero
SP R Martinez
SP P Schourek
RS T Wakefield
CL D Lowe
RP R Garces
RP R Cormier
C J Varitek
1D- M Stanley
21 J Offerman
SS N Garciaparra
3I M Alexander
LF T O'Leary
CF C Everett
RF T Nixon
1D B Daubach
UO- D Lewis
CU- S Hatteberg
M J Williams

CHI 2000 AL
SP M Sirotka
SP J Parque
SP J Baldwin
SP C Eldred
SP K Wells
CL K Foulke
RP B Howry
RS S Lowe
RP B Simas
C - M Johnson
1B P Konerko
2B R Durham
SS J Valentin
3B H Perry
LF C Lee
CF C Singleton
RF M Ordonez
DH F Thomas
M J Manuel

CLE 2000 AL
SP C Finley
SP D Burba
SP B Colon
RP S Karsay
RP J Speier
RP P Shuey
RP S Reed
C - S Alomar
1D- D Segui
2B R Alomar
SS O Vizquel
3B T Fryman
L1- R Sexson
CF K Lofton
RF M Ramirez
1D J Thome
UT J Cabrera
M C Manuel

DET 2000 AL
SP J Weaver
SP H Nomo
SP B Moehler
SR W Blair
SP D Mlicki
RS C Nitkowski
CL T Jones
RP S Sparks
RP M Anderson
C B Ausmus
1B- T Clark
2B D Easley
SS D Cruz
3B D Palmer
LF B Higginson
CF J Encarnacion
RM- R Becker
RD J Gonzalez
31 S Halter
RO- W Magee
M P Garner

KC 2000 AL
SP J Suppan
SP M Suzuki
SR D Reichert
SR B Stein
RP R Bottalico
RP J Spradlin
RP J Santiago
C - G Zaun
1D M Sweeney
2B C Febles
SS R Sanchez
3B J Randa
OF J Damon
CF C Beltran
RF J Dye
LD M Quinn
1U D McCarty
M T Muser

MIN 2000 AL
SP B Radke
SP E Milton
SP J Mays
SP M Redman
RP L Hawkins
RP B Wells
RS J Santana
RP H Carrasco
C - M LeCroy
1B R Coomer
2B J Canizaro
SS C Guzman
3B C Koskie
LM J Jones
CF T Hunter
RL M Lawton
DU D Ortiz
UT D Hocking
M T Kelly

NY 2000 AL
SP A Pettitte
SP R Clemens
SP O Hernandez
SP D Cone
CL M Rivera
RP J Grimsley
RP J Nelson
RP M Stanton
C J Posada
1B T Martinez
2B C Knoblauch
SS D Jeter
3B S Brosius
LR- D Justice
CF B Williams
RF P O'Neill
OF- S Spencer
UT C Bellinger
M J Torre

OAK 2000 AL
SP T Hudson
SP G Heredia
SP K Appier
SP M Mulder
SP O Olivares
CL J Isringhausen
RP J Tam
RP D Jones
RP T Mathews
C R Hernandez
1B Ja Giambi
2B R Velarde
SS M Tejada
3B E Chavez
LF B Grieve
CF T Long
RD M Stairs
OI Je Giambi
LO R Christenson
M A Howe

SEA 2000 AL
SP A Sele
SP P Abbott
SP J Halama
SP J Moyer
SP F Garcia
CL K Sasaki
RS B Tomko
RP J Paniagua
RP J Mesa
C - D Wilson
1B J Olerud
2B M McLemore
SS A Rodriguez
32 D Bell
OI S Javier
CF M Cameron
RF J Buhner
DH E Martinez
3B- C Guillen
LF- R Henderson
OI- R Ibanez
M L Piniella

TB 2000 AL
SR A Lopez
SP B Rekar
SR E Yan
SP S Trachsel
SR C Lidle
CL R Hernandez
RP R White
RP D Creek
RS T Sturtze
C J Flaherty
1B F McGriff
2B M Cairo
SS F Martinez
3B- V Castilla
LD G Vaughn
CF G Williams
RF J Guillen
DH- J Canseco
OI S Cox
M L Rothschild

TEX 2000 AL
SP K Rogers
SP R Helling
SP D Oliver
SP E Loaiza
SR M Perisho
RS D Davis
CL J Wetteland
RP T Crabtree
RP F Cordero
C - I Rodriguez
1D R Palmeiro
2B L Alicea
SS R Clayton
3B M Lamb
LF R Greer
MR G Kapler
OF C Curtis
D1- D Segui
IO F Catalanotto
M J Oates

TOR 2000 AL
SP D Wells
SR K Escobar
SP C Carpenter
SP F Castillo
CL B Koch
RP P Quantrill
RP J Frascatore
RP L Painter
C D Fletcher
1B C Delgado
2B- H Bush
SS A Gonzalez
3B T Batista
LF S Stewart
CF J Cruz
RF- R Mondesi
DH B Fullmer
M J Fregosi

ARI 2001 NL
SP C Schilling
SP R Johnson
SR M Batista
SP B Anderson
RP B Kim
RP G Swindell
RP E Sabel
RP T Brohawn
C D Miller
1B M Grace
23 J Bell
SS T Womack
3B M Williams
LF L Gonzalez
CF S Finley
RF R Sanders
UO D Bautista
UI C Counsell
UO D Dellucci
UT- E Durazo
M B Brenly

ATL 2001 NL
SP G Maddux
SP J Burkett
SP T Glavine
SR J Marquis
SP K Millwood
RP M Remlinger
RS J Smoltz
RP J Cabrera
RP K Ligtenberg
C J Lopez
1B W Helms
2B- Q Veras
SS- R Furcal
3B C Jones
LF B Surhoff
CF A Jones
RF B Jordan
IF K Lockhart
OI D Martinez
M B Cox

CHI 2001 NL
SP J Lieber
SP J Bere
SP K Wood
SP K Tapani
SP J Tavarez
RP J Fassero
RP K Farnsworth
RP T Van Poppel
C - J Girardi
1U M Stairs
2B E Young
SS R Gutierrez
31 R Coomer
LF- R White
CF G Matthews
RF S Sosa
M D Baylor

CIN 2001 NL
SP E Dessens
SP C Reitsma
SP L Davis
RS J Brower
CL D Graves
RP S Sullivan
RP H Mercado
C J LaRue
1B S Casey
2B- T Walker
S2 P Reese
3B A Boone
L1- D Young
CF K Griffey
RF- A Ochoa
MO R Rivera
UI- J Castro
UO- B Clark
UO- M Tucker
M B Boone

COL 2001 NL
SP M Hampton
SP D Neagle
SP S Chacon
SP P Astacio
RP J Jimenez
RP K Davis
RP G White
RP J Speier
C - B Petrick
1B T Helton
2B- T Walker
SS- N Perez
3B J Cirillo
LR- A Ochoa
CF J Pierre
RF L Walker
UT G Norton
IO T Shumpert
M B Bell

FLA 2001 NL
SP R Dempster
SP B Penny
SP A Burnett
SP M Clement
RP V Nunez
CL A Alfonseca
RP B Looper
RP R Bones
C C Johnson
1B D Lee
2B L Castillo
SS A Gonzalez
3B M Lowell
LF C Floyd
CF P Wilson
RM E Owens
UT K Millar
UI- D Berg
OI- J Mabry
M1 J Boles
M2 T Perez

HOU 2001 NL
SP W Miller
SP S Reynolds
SP R Oswalt
SP S Elarton
RP O Dotel
CL B Wagner
RP N Cruz
RP M Jackson
C B Ausmus
1B J Bagwell
2B C Biggio
SS J Lugo
3B V Castilla
LF L Berkman
CF R Hidalgo
RF M Alou
UI J Vizcaino
UT- O Merced
OI- D Ward
M L Dierker

LA 2001 NL
SP C Park
SR T Adams
SP E Gagne
SP L Prokopec
SP K Brown
CL J Shaw
RP M Herges
RP G Carrara
C P LoDuca
1B E Karros
2B M Grudzielanek
SS A Cora
3B A Beltre
LF G Sheffield
MU M Grissom
RF S Green
MU T Goodwin
IF- D Hansen
SI- J Reboulet
M J Tracy

MIL 2001 NL
SP J Wright
SP J Haynes
SP B Sheets
SR A Levrault
RP M DeJean
RP C Leskanic
RP C Fox
RP D Weathers
C H Blanco
1B R Sexson
2B R Belliard
SS J Hernandez
3B- T Houston
LF G Jenkins
MU D White
RF J Burnitz
23 M Loretta
3I- L Lopez
M D Lopes

MON 2001 NL
SP J Vazquez
SP T Armas
SP M Thurman
RS M Yoshii
RS B Reames
RP S Strickland
RP G Lloyd
C M Barrett
1B L Stevens
2B J Vidro
SS O Cabrera
IO G Blum
LU- M Smith
CF P Bergeron
RF V Guerrero
IO- M Mordecai
M1 F Alou
M2 J Torborg

NY 2001 NL
SP K Appier
SP A Leiter
SP G Rusch
SP S Trachsel
SP R Reed
CL A Benitez
RP R White
RP J Franco
RP T Wendell
C M Piazza
1B T Zeile
2B E Alfonzo
SS R Ordonez
3B R Ventura
LF- B Agbayani
CF J Payton
UO T Shinjo
UT L Harris
UT J McEwing
UI D Relaford
RU- T Perez
M B Valentine

PHI 2001 NL
SP R Person
SP O Daal
SP R Wolf
CL J Mesa
RP R Bottalico
RP J Santiago
RP R Cormier
C - J Estrada
1B T Lee
2B M Anderson
SS J Rollins
3B S Rolen
LF P Burrell
CF D Glanville
RF B Abreu
UO- B Hunter
M L Bowa

PIT 2001 NL
SP T Ritchie
SP J Anderson
SR J Beimel
SP D Williams
RS O Olivares
RP J Manzanillo
RP S Sauerbeck
C J Kendall
1B K Young
2B- P Meares
SS J Wilson
3B A Ramirez
LF B Giles
CF- E Brown
RU- J Vander Wal
IO A Nunez
UT- R Mackowiak
UT- C Wilson
M L McClendon

STL 2001 NL
SP D Kile
SP M Morris
SP D Hermanson
SP A Benes
RS M Matthews
RP S Kline

RP D Veres
RP G Stechschulte
C M Matheny
1B- M McGwire
2B F Vina
SS E Renteria
3S P Polanco
LF- R Lankford
CF J Edmonds
RF J Drew
UT C Paquette
UT A Pujols
UO K Robinson
UT- B Bonilla
C - E Marrero
M T LaRussa

SD 2001 NL

SP B Jones
SP K Jarvis
SP W Williams
SP A Eaton
SP B Tollberg
RS B Lawrence
CL T Hoffman
RP J Nunez
RP D Lee
C B Davis
1B R Klesko
2B D Jackson
SS- D Jimenez
3B P Nevin
LF R Henderson
CF M Kotsay
RU B Trammell
RM M Darr
UI- D Magadan
M B Bochy

SF 2001 NL

SP L Hernandez
SP R Ortiz
SP K Rueter
SP S Estes
CL R Nen
RP F Rodriguez
RP T Worrell
RP A Fultz
C B Santiago
1B J Snow
2B J Kent
SS R Aurilia
3B- P Feliz
LF B Bonds
CF C Murray
MR M Benard
32 R Martinez
OI- S Dunston
RF- A Rios
M D Baker

ANA 2001 AL

SP R Ortiz
SP S Schoeneweis
SP J Washburn
SP P Rapp
SP I Valdes
CL T Percival
RP L Pote
RP A Levine
RP B Weber
C - B Molina
1B S Spiezio
2B A Kennedy
SS D Eckstein
3B T Glaus
LF G Anderson
CF D Erstad
RF T Salmon
UC- S Wooten
IO B Gil
UO O Palmeiro
M M Scioscia

BAL 2001 AL

SP J Johnson
SP J Mercedes
SP J Towers
SP S Ponson
SR W Roberts
RP B Groom
RP M Trombley
RP B Ryan
RP J Wasdin
C - B Fordyce
1O J Conine
2B J Hairston
SS- M Bordick
3B C Ripken
RL B Anderson
MS M Mora
RM C Richard
IF- T Batista
1B- D Segui
M M Hargrove

BOS 2001 AL

SP H Nomo
SR T Wakefield
SP F Castillo
SP D Cone
SP P Martinez
CL D Lowe
RS R Arrojo
RP R Beck
RP R Garces
C - S Hatteberg
1B B Daubach
21 J Offerman
S2 M Lansing
3B S Hillenbrand
LR T O'Leary
CF C Everett
RM T Nixon
DL M Ramirez
OF D Bichette
UO- D Lewis
IO- C Stynes
M1 J Williams
M2 J Kerrigan

CHI 2001 AL

SP M Buehrle
SR K Wells
SP R Biddle
SR J Garland
SP D Wells
RS S Lowe
CL K Foulke
RS G Glover
RP B Howry
C - S Alomar
1B P Konerko
2B R Durham
SS R Clayton
3U- H Perry
LF C Lee
CF C Singleton
RF M Ordonez
DH- J Canseco
3S J Valentin
UT- J Liefer
M J Manuel

CLE 2001 AL

SP B Colon
SP C Sabathia
SP D Burba
SP C Finley
CL B Wickman
RS J Westbrook
RP R Rincon
RP P Shuey
C E Diaz
1B J Thome
2B R Alomar
SS O Vizquel
3B T Fryman
LO M Cordova
CF K Lofton
RF J Gonzalez
DH E Burks
3L R Branyan
UT J Cabrera
LU- W Cordero
M C Manuel

DET 2001 AL

SP S Sparks
SP J Weaver
SP C Holt
SP J Lima
CL M Anderson
RS V Santos
RP D Patterson
RP H Murray
C - B Inge
1D T Clark
2B D Easley
SS D Cruz
3U J Macias
LF B Higginson
MR R Cedeno
RM J Encarnacion
DH- D Palmer
CU R Fick
3S S Halter
UO- W Magee
1D- R Simon
M P Garner

KC 2001 AL

SP J Suppan
SP C Durbin
SR B Stein
SP D Reichert
SR K Wilson
CL R Hernandez
RP J Grimsley
RP D Henry
RP C Bailey
C - H Ortiz
1U D McCarty
2B- C Febles
SS R Sanchez
3B J Randa
OF M Quinn
CF C Beltran
RF- J Dye
1D M Sweeney
2U L Alicea
LU D Brown
UT R Ibanez
M T Muser

MIN 2001 AL

SP J Mays
SP B Radke
SP E Milton
RP E Guardado
CL L Hawkins
RP H Carrasco
RP B Wells
C A Pierzynski
1B D Mientkiewicz
2B L Rivas
SS C Guzman
3B C Koskie
LF J Jones
CF T Hunter
RF M Lawton
DH- D Ortiz
UT D Hocking
M T Kelly

NY 2001 AL

SP M Mussina
SP R Clemens
SP A Pettitte
SP T Lilly
CL M Rivera
RP R Mendoza
RP M Stanton
C J Posada
1B T Martinez
2B A Soriano
SS D Jeter
3B S Brosius
LF C Knoblauch
CF B Williams
RF P O'Neill
DH D Justice
M J Torre

OAK 2001 AL

SP T Hudson
SP M Mulder
SP B Zito
SP C Lidle
SP G Heredia
CL J Isringhausen
RP J Tam
RP J Mecir
RP M Magnante
C R Hernandez
1B J Giambi
2B F Menechino
SS M Tejada
3B E Chavez
ML J Damon
UO T Long
RF- J Dye
1B J Giambi
D1 O Saenz
OI J Giambi
M A Howe

SEA 2001 AL

SP F Garcia
SP A Sele
SP J Moyer
SP P Abbott
SR J Halama
CL K Sasaki
RP R Franklin
RP A Rhodes
RP J Nelson
C D Wilson
1B J Olerud
2B B Boone
SS C Guillen
3B D Bell
LO- S Javier
CF M Cameron
RF I Suzuki
DH E Martinez
LU A Martin
L3 M McLemore
UT- C Gipson
M L Piniella

TB 2001 AL

SR T Sturtze
SR P Wilson
SP R Rupe
SP B Rekar
SP A Lopez
RP J Kennedy
CL E Yan
RP T Phelps
RP D Creek
C - J Flaherty
1U S Cox
2B- B Abernathy
SS- F Martinez
3U A Huff
LM J Tyner
UO R Winn
OF B Grieve
DL G Vaughn
1B- F McGriff
UI- R Johnson
2O- D Rolls
M1 L Rothschild
M2 H McRae

TEX 2001 AL

SP R Helling
SP D Davis
SP D Oliver
SP K Rogers
SP R Bell
RP P Mahomes
CL J Zimmerman
RP M Petkovsek
RP M Venafro
C I Rodriguez
1D R Palmeiro
2B M Young
SS A Rodriguez
3B- M Lamb
LU F Catalanotto
CF G Kapler
RF- R Ledee
DR- R Sierra
M1 J Oates
M2 J Narron

TOR 2001 AL

SP C Carpenter
SP E Loaiza
SP J Hamilton
SP C Michalak
SP S Parris
RS K Escobar
RP R Halladay
CL B Koch
RP P Quantrill
C D Fletcher
1B C Delgado
2B- H Bush
SS A Gonzalez
3B- T Batista
LF S Stewart
CF J Cruz
RF R Mondesi
DH B Fullmer
M B Martinez

ARI 2002 NL

SP R Johnson
SP C Schilling
SP M Batista
SP R Helling
SR B Anderson
CL B Kim
RP M Koplove
C D Miller
1B M Grace
2B J Spivey
SS T Womack
3B C Counsell
LF L Gonzalez
CF S Finley
RM Q McCracken
UO- D Dellucci
M B Brenly

ATL 2002 NL

SP T Glavine
SP K Millwood
SP G Maddux
SP D Moss
SP J Marquis
CL J Smoltz
RP C Hammond
RP M Remlinger
RP K Ligtenberg
C J Lopez
1B J Franco
2U K Lockhart
SS R Furcal
3B V Castilla
LF C Jones
CF A Jones
RF G Sheffield
UO D Bragg
C - H Blanco
1U- M Franco
13- W Helms
M B Cox

CHI 2002 NL

SP K Wood
SP M Clement
SP J Lieber
SP M Prior
SR C Zambrano
RP J Borowski
RS J Cruz
RP A Alfonseca
RP J Fassero
C - J Girardi
1B F McGriff
2I M Bellhorn
SS A Gonzalez
3B B Mueller
LF M Alou
CF C Patterson
RF S Sosa
UO R Brown
IF C Stynes
C - T Hundley
M1 D Baylor
M2 B Kimm

CIN 2002 NL

SP J Haynes
SP E Dessens
SR C Reitsma
SR J Hamilton
RP D Graves
RP S Williamson
RP S Sullivan
RS J Rijo
C J LaRue
1B S Casey
2B T Walker
SS B Larkin
3B A Boone
L1 A Dunn
ML R Taylor
RF A Kearns
IO- R Branyan
MR- J Encarnacion
M B Boone

COL 2002 NL

SP J Jennings
SP M Hampton
SP D Neagle
SR D Stark
SP J Thomson
RP S Chacon
CL J Jimenez
RP T Jones
RP J Speier
C - G Bennett
1B T Helton
23 B Butler
SS J Uribe
3B T Zeile
LF- T Hollandsworth
CF J Pierre
RF L Walker
IO G Norton
2U T Shumpert
M1 B Bell
M2 C Hurdle

FLA 2002 NL

SP A Burnett
SP J Tavarez
SR M Tejera
SP B Penny
SP R Dempster
RP V Nunez
RP J Beckett
RP B Looper
C - C Johnson
1B D Lee
2B L Castillo
SS A Fox
3B M Lowell
LU K Millar
CF P Wilson
LR E Owens
UT T Raines
RU- C Floyd
C - M Redmond
M J Torborg

HOU 2002 NL

SP R Oswalt
SP W Miller
SP C Hernandez
CL B Wagner
RP O Dotel
RS N Cruz
RP R Stone
C B Ausmus
1B J Bagwell
2B C Biggio
SS- J Lugo
3B G Blum
LF D Ward
CF L Berkman
RF R Hidalgo
CF B Hunter
UT O Merced
UI J Vizcaino
M J Williams

LA 2002 NL

SP O Perez
SP H Nomo
SP A Ashby
SR O Daal
SP K Ishii
CL E Gagne
RP G Carrara
RP P Quantrill
RP G Mota
C P LoDuca
1B E Karros
2B M Grudzielanek
SS C Izturis
3B A Beltre
LF B Jordan
CF D Roberts
RF S Green
S2 A Cora
ML M Grissom
IF- D Hansen
M J Tracy

MIL 2002 NL

SP B Sheets
SP G Rusch
SP R Quevedo
SP J Wright
RS J Cabrera
CL M DeJean
RP L Vizcaino
RP R King
C - P Bako
1B R Sexson
2B E Young
SS J Hernandez
3B- T Houston
LF- G Jenkins
CF A Sanchez
MR J Hammonds
IF R Belliard
IO L Harris
OF M Stairs
3U- M Loretta
RU- A Ochoa
M1 D Lopes
M2 J Royster

MON 2002 NL

SP J Vazquez
SP T Ohka
SP T Armas
SR M Yoshii
SP B Colon
RP S Stewart
RP M Herges
RS B Reames
RP T Tucker
C M Barrett
1B A Galarraga
2B J Vidro
SS O Cabrera
3B F Tatis
LU- T O'Leary
OI B Wilkerson
RF V Guerrero
MI- J Macias
M F Robinson

NY 2002 NL

SP A Leiter
SP P Astacio
SP S Trachsel
SP J D'Amico
SP S Estes
CL A Benitez
RP D Weathers
RP S Strickland
C M Piazza
1B M Vaughn
2B R Alomar
SS R Ordonez
3B E Alfonzo
LF R Cedeno
MO T Perez
RF J Burnitz
UT J McEwing
UI J Valentin
CF- J Payton
M B Valentine

PHI 2002 NL

SP R Wolf
SP V Padilla
SP B Duckworth
SR T Adams
CL J Mesa
RP C Silva
RS D Coggin
RP R Cormier
C M Lieberthal
1B T Lee
2B M Anderson
SS J Rollins
3B S Rolen
LF P Burrell
CF D Glanville
RF B Abreu
UT- J Giambi
UO- R Ledee
OI- J Michaels
2I- T Perez
M L Bowa

PIT 2002 NL

SP K Wells
SP J Fogg
SP J Anderson
SP K Benson
CL M Williams
RS R Villone
RS J Beimel
RP B Boehringer
C J Kendall
1B K Young
2B P Reese
SS J Wilson
3B A Ramirez
LF B Giles
RM R Mackowiak
R1 C Wilson
3I M Benjamin
IF A Nunez
MU- A Brown
M L McClendon

STL 2002 NL

SP M Morris
SP J Simontacchi
SP W Williams
CL J Isringhausen
RP D Veres
RS L Hackman
RP S Kline
C M Matheny
1B T Martinez
2B F Vina
SS E Renteria
3B- P Polanco
L3 A Pujols
CF J Edmonds
RF J Drew
UT M Cairo
OC E Marrero
UO K Robinson
UT- E Perez
M T LaRussa

SD 2002 NL

SP B Lawrence
SP B Tomko
SP B Jones
CL T Hoffman
RP J Fikac
C T Lampkin
1B R Klesko
2S R Vazquez
SS D Cruz
31 P Nevin
LF R Gant
CF M Kotsay
RF B Trammell
LF R Gant
UT- T Hubbard
23- D Jimenez
RL- E Kingsale
LU- R Lankford
M B Bochy

SF 2002 NL

SP L Hernandez
SP R Ortiz
SP K Rueter
SP J Schmidt
SP R Jensen
CL R Nen
RP T Worrell
RP F Rodriguez
RP J Witasick
C B Santiago
1B J Snow
2B J Kent
SS R Aurilia
3B D Bell
LF B Bonds
CF T Shinjo
RF R Sanders
1U- D Minor
M D Baker

ANA 2002 AL

SP R Ortiz
SP J Washburn
SP K Appier
SP A Sele
SP J Lackey
RS S Schoeneweis
CL T Percival
RP B Weber
RP A Levine
C B Molina
1B S Spiezio
2B A Kennedy
SS D Eckstein
3B T Glaus
LF G Anderson
CF D Erstad
RF T Salmon
DU B Fullmer
UO O Palmeiro
M M Scioscia

BAL 2002 AL

SP R Lopez
SP S Ponson
SP S Erickson
SR T Driskill
SP J Johnson
CL J Julio
RP R Bauer
RP W Roberts
RP B Groom
C G Gil
1B J Conine
2B J Hairston
SS M Bordick
3B T Batista
UT M Mora
CF C Singleton
RO G Matthews
LD M Cordova
RU J Gibbons
M M Hargrove

BOS 2002 AL

SP D Lowe
SP P Martinez
SP J Burkett
SR F Castillo
RS T Wakefield
RS C Fossum
CL U Urbina
RS R Arrojo
C J Varitek
1B- T Clark
2B R Sanchez
SS N Garciaparra
3B S Hillenbrand
LU- R Henderson
CF J Damon
RF T Nixon
LD M Ramirez
UT B Daubach
2B- L Merloni
M G Little

CHI 2002 AL

SP M Buehrle
SP D Wright
SP J Garland
SR G Glover
SP T Ritchie
RP K Foulke
RS R Biddle
RP A Osuna
RP D Marte
C - M Johnson
1B P Konerko
2B- R Durham
SS R Clayton
3S J Valentin
LF C Lee
ML A Rowand
RF M Ordonez
DH F Thomas
CF- K Lofton
M J Manuel

CLE 2002 AL

SP C Sabathia
SR D Baez
SP R Drese
SP B Colon
SP C Finley
RP M Wohlers
RP D Riske
C E Diaz
1B J Thome
2B- R Gutierrez
SS O Vizquel
3B T Fryman
LR- C Magruder
CF M Bradley
RU M Lawton
DH E Burks
2I- J McDonald
M1 C Manuel
M2 J Skinner

DET 2002 AL

SP M Redman
SP S Sparks
SP M Maroth
SP J Weaver
SR A Bernero

CL J Acevedo
RP J Farnsworth
RP J Santana
C - B Inge
1B- C Pena
2B- D Easley
SI S Halter
3B- C Truby
LF B Higginson
CF W Magee
RF R Fick
D1 R Simon
2U- D Jackson
M1 P Garner
M2 L Pujols

KC 2002 AL

SP P Byrd
SP J Suppan
SP D May
SR M Asencio
RS J Affeldt
CL R Hernandez
RP J Grimsley
RS D Reichert
C B Mayne
1B M Sweeney
2B C Febles
SS N Perez
3B J Randa
LF- C Knoblauch
CF C Beltran
UT M Tucker
OI R Ibanez
IO- L Alicea
M1 T Muser
M2 J Mizerock
M3 T Pena

MIN 2002 AL

SP R Reed
SP K Lohse
SP E Milton
SP B Radke
SR J Santana
CL E Guardado
RP T Fiore
RP J Romero
RP L Hawkins
C A Pierzynski
1B D Mientkiewicz
2B- L Rivas
SS C Guzman
3B C Koskie
LF J Jones
CF T Hunter
RF D Mohr
DH D Ortiz
2I D Hocking
OI B Kielty
M R Gardenhire

NY 2002 AL

SP M Mussina
SP D Wells
SP R Clemens
SP O Hernandez
SP A Pettitte
RP S Karsay
RP R Mendoza
RP M Stanton
C J Posada
1D N Johnson
2B A Soriano
SS D Jeter
3B R Ventura
LF R White
CF B Williams
RL- S Spencer
1D J Giambi
RU- J Vander Wal
M J Torre

OAK 2002 AL

SP T Hudson
SP B Zito
SP M Mulder
SP C Lidle
CL B Koch
RP C Bradford
RP J Mecir
C R Hernandez
1D S Hatteberg
2B M Ellis
SS M Tejada
3B E Chavez
LO- E Byrnes
CF T Long
RF J Dye
DH- R Durham
OF D Justice
1L- J Mabry
M A Howe

SEA 2002 AL

SP J Moyer
SP F Garcia
SP J Pineiro
SP J Baldwin
RS R Franklin
RS J Halama
CL K Sasaki
RP A Rhodes
C D Wilson
1B J Olerud
2B B Boone
SS C Guillen
3B J Cirillo
LF M McLemore
CF M Cameron
RF I Suzuki
DH- E Martinez
UT D Relaford
OF R Sierra
M L Piniella

TB 2002 AL

SP T Sturtze
SP J Kennedy
SP P Wilson
SR J Sosa
RS V Zambrano
CL E Yan
RS T Harper
RP S Kent
C - T Hall
1U S Cox
2B B Abernathy
SS C Gomez
3B J Sandberg
LF- C Crawford
CF R Winn
RF B Grieve
IF A Huff
M H McRae

TEX 2002 AL

SP K Rogers
SP I Valdes
SP C Park
SP D Burba
RP T Van Poppel
RP J Powell
C I Rodriguez
UT M Lamb
2B M Young
SS A Rodriguez
3B H Perry
RL K Mench
CF- R Rivera
UO C Everett
1D R Palmeiro
M J Narron

TOR 2002 AL

SP R Halladay
SP E Loaiza
SR P Walker
SP J Miller
CL K Escobar
RP C Thurman
RP S Cassidy
RP S Eyre
C - K Huckaby
1B C Delgado
2B- O Hudson
SS- C Woodward
3B E Hinske
LD S Stewart
CF V Wells
UO J Cruz
DH- J Phelps
UT D Berg
SS- F Lopez
CU- T Wilson
M1 B Martinez
M2 C Tosca

ARI 2003 NL

SP M Batista
SP B Webb
SP E Dessens
SP C Schilling
SP R Johnson
RP O Villarreal
CL M Mantei
RP S Randolph
RP J Valverde
C - R Barajas
1B- L Overbay
2B J Spivey
SS A Cintron
3S- C Counsell
LF L Gonzalez
CF S Finley
RU- D Bautista
UI C Baerga
UO Q McCracken
13- S Hillenbrand
M B Brenly

ATL 2003 NL

SP G Maddux
SP R Ortiz
SP M Hampton
SP H Ramirez
SP S Reynolds
CL J Smoltz
RP T Hodges
RP R Hernandez
RP R King
C J Lopez
1B R Fick
2B M Giles
SS R Furcal
3B V Castilla
LF C Jones
CF A Jones
RF G Sheffield
UO D Bragg
IO M DeRosa
1U J Franco
UT M Franco
M B Cox

CHI 2003 NL

SP C Zambrano
SP M Prior
SP K Wood
SP M Clement
SP S Estes
CL J Borowski
RP K Farnsworth
RP M Remlinger
RP A Alfonseca
C D Miller
1B E Karros
2B M Grudzielanek
SS A Gonzalez
3B- A Ramirez
LF M Alou
CF- C Patterson
RF S Sosa
UI R Martinez
UO- T Goodwin
OF- T O'Leary
M D Baker

CIN 2003 NL

SP D Graves
SP P Wilson
SP R Dempster
RS J Riedling
RP C Reitsma
RP F Heredia
RP B Reith
C J LaRue
1B S Casey
2B- D Jimenez
SS- B Larkin
3B A Boone
LF A Dunn
RM- A Kearns
RO- J Guillen
UI J Castro
UO R Taylor
M1 B Boone
M2 R Knight
M3 D Miley

COL 2003 NL

SP J Jennings
SP D Oliver
SP S Chacon
SR A Cook
RS J Jimenez
RP J Speier
RP B Fuentes
RP S Reed
C C Johnson
1B T Helton
2B R Belliard
SS- J Uribe
3B C Stynes
LF J Payton
CF P Wilson
RF L Walker
IO G Norton
M C Hurdle

FLA 2003 NL

SP C Pavano
SP B Penny
SP M Redman
SP D Willis
SP J Beckett
CL B Looper
RS M Tejera
RS T Phelps
RP A Almanza
C I Rodriguez
1B D Lee
2B L Castillo
SS A Gonzalez
3B M Lowell
LU- T Hollandsworth
CF J Pierre
RF J Encarnacion
OI- B Banks
L3- M Cabrera
M1 J Torborg
M2 J McKeon

HOU 2003 NL

SP W Miller
SP T Redding
SP J Robertson
SP R Oswalt
SP R Villone
CL B Wagner
RP O Dotel
RP B Lidge
RP R Stone
C B Ausmus
1B J Bagwell
2B J Kent
SS A Everett
3B M Ensberg
LF L Berkman
CF C Biggio
RF R Hidalgo
3I G Blum
UT O Merced
UI- J Vizcaino
M J Williams

LA 2003 NL

SP H Nomo
SP K Brown
SP O Perez
SP K Ishii
CL E Gagne
RP G Mota
RP P Quantrill
RP P Shuey
C P LoDuca
1B- F McGriff
2B A Cora
SS C Izturis
3B A Beltre
LF- B Jordan
CF D Roberts
RF S Green
UT J Cabrera
UT- M Kinkade
M J Tracy

MIL 2003 NL

SP B Sheets
SP W Franklin
SP M Kinney
SR G Rusch
RP M DeJean
RP L Estrella
RP L Vizcaino
RP B Kieschnick
C E Perez
1B R Sexson
2B E Young
SS R Clayton
3B W Helms
LF G Jenkins
CF S Podsednik
RU B Clark
IO K Ginter
RU J Vander Wal
M N Yost

MON 2003 NL

SP L Hernandez
SP J Vazquez
SP T Ohka
SP Z Day
SP C Vargas
CL R Biddle
RS T Tucker
RP L Ayala
RP J Eischen
C B Schneider
1B W Cordero
2B J Vidro
SS O Cabrera
3U J Carroll
LM B Wilkerson
CF E Chavez
RF V Guerrero
UO R Calloway
UT J Macias
UT H Mateo
M F Robinson

NY 2003 NL

SP S Trachsel
SP J Seo
SP T Glavine
SP A Leiter
RP D Weathers
CL A Benitez
RP D Wheeler
C - V Wilson
1U J Phillips
2B- R Alomar
SS- J Reyes
3B T Wigginton
LF C Floyd
UO T Perez
RF R Cedeno
1U T Clark
UO R Gonzalez
UT J McEwing
M A Howe

PHI 2003 NL

SP K Millwood
SP V Padilla
SP R Wolf
SP B Myers
RP C Silva
RP R Cormier
CL J Mesa
RP T Adams
C M Lieberthal
1B J Thome
2B P Polanco
SS J Rollins
3B- D Bell
LF P Burrell
CF M Byrd
RF B Abreu
UO R Ledee
UI T Perez
M L Bowa

PIT 2003 NL

SP K Wells
SP J D'Amico
SP J Fogg
SP J Suppan
SR S Torres
RP K Benson
RP J Tavarez
RS B Meadows
RP J Beimel
C J Kendall
1B- R Simon
2B- J Reboulet
SS J Wilson
3B- A Ramirez
LF B Giles
CF- K Lofton
RL R Sanders
2U A Nunez
OI M Stairs
OI C Wilson
M L McClendon

STL 2003 NL

SP W Williams
SP B Tomko
SP G Stephenson
SP M Morris
SR J Simontacchi
RS J Fassero
RP C Eldred
RP S Kline
C M Matheny
1B T Martinez
2B- B Hart
SS E Renteria
3B S Rolen
L1 A Pujols
CF J Edmonds
UO O Palmeiro
RM J Drew
RU E Perez
UO K Robinson
UT- M Cairo
M T LaRussa

SD 2003 NL

SP B Lawrence
SP J Peavy
SP A Eaton
SP O Perez
RP L Hackman
RP M Matthews
RP S Linebrink
C - G Bennett
1B R Klesko
2B M Loretta
SS R Vazquez
3B S Burroughs
LF R White
CF M Kotsay
RF X Nady
OI B Buchanan
UI D Hansen
UO G Matthews
M B Bochy

SF 2003 NL

SP J Schmidt
SP K Rueter
SP J Williams
SP D Moss
SP J Foppert
CL T Worrell
RS J Brower
RP J Nathan
RP F Rodriguez
C B Santiago
1B J Snow
2B R Durham
SS R Aurilia
3B E Alfonzo
LF B Bonds
CF M Grissom
RF J Cruz
1U A Galarraga
UI N Perez
3U- P Feliz
M F Alou

ANA 2003 AL

SP J Washburn
SP J Lackey
SP R Ortiz
SP A Sele
RS S Shields
RP F Rodriguez
CL T Percival
RP B Weber
C B Molina
13 S Spiezio
2B A Kennedy
SS D Eckstein
3B- T Glaus
LF G Anderson
UO E Owens
RM J DaVanon
RD T Salmon
IF S Wooten
M M Scioscia

BAL 2003 AL

SP J Johnson
SP P Hentgen
SP S Ponson
SP R Lopez
RP R Helling
CL J Julio
RP R Bauer
RP K Ligtenberg
RP B Ryan
C B Fordyce
1B J Conine
2B B Roberts
SS D Cruz
3B T Batista
LF- L Bigbie
CF L Matos
RF J Gibbons
DH- D Segui
LO- M Mora
OI- B Surhoff
M M Hargrove

BOS 2003 AL

SP D Lowe
SP T Wakefield
SP P Martinez
SP J Burkett
CL B Kim
RP M Timlin
RP B Lyon
RS R Mendoza
C J Varitek
1U K Millar
2B T Walker
SS N Garciaparra
3B B Mueller
LF M Ramirez
CF J Damon
RF T Nixon
D1 D Ortiz
UT D Jackson
M G Little

CHI 2003 AL

SP B Colon
SP M Buehrle
SP E Loaiza
SP J Garland
RP D Marte
RP T Gordon
RP B Koch
C M Olivo
1B P Konerko
2B- D Jimenez
SS J Valentin
3B J Crede
LF C Lee
ML- A Rowand
RF M Ordonez
DH F Thomas
UT- B Daubach
UI- T Graffanino
M J Manuel

CLE 2003 AL

SP C Sabathia
SP J Davis
SP B Anderson
SR J Westbrook
SR B Traber
CL D Baez
RP T Mulholland
RP D Riske
RP J Boyd
C - J Bard
1B B Broussard
2B B Phillips
SS- J Peralta
3B C Blake
ML C Crisp
CF M Bradley
UO J Gerut
DH- E Burks
LU M Lawton
UT- T Hafner
UI- J McDonald
M E Wedge

DET 2003 AL

SP N Cornejo
SP M Maroth
SP J Bonderman
SP A Bernero
RS M Roney
RS S Sparks
RS W Ledezma
RP C Spurling
C B Inge
1B C Pena
2B- W Morris
S2 R Santiago
3B E Munson
LR C Monroe
CF A Sanchez
RF B Higginson
UT D Young
IO S Halter
IO- K Witt
M A Trammell

KC 2003 AL

SP D May
SR J Affeldt
CL M Mac Dougal
RP D Carrasco
RP J Grimsley
RP K Wilson
C B Mayne
1U K Harvey
2I D Relaford
SS A Berroa
3B J Randa
LF R Ibanez
CF C Beltran
RF A Guiel
D1 M Sweeney
UO M Tucker
M T Pena

MIN 2003 AL

SP B Radke
SP K Lohse
SP K Rogers
SR J Santana
SP R Reed
RS J Mays
CL E Guardado
RP J Rincon
RP L Hawkins
C A Pierzynski
1B D Mientkiewicz
2B L Rivas
SS C Guzman
3B C Koskie
LU J Jones
CF T Hunter
RO D Mohr
DU M LeCroy
UT- D Hocking
M R Gardenhire

NY 2003 AL

SP M Mussina
SP D Wells
SP R Clemens
SP A Pettitte
SP J Weaver
CL M Rivera
RP C Hammond
RP A Osuna
RP S Hitchcock
C J Posada
1D- N Johnson
2B A Soriano
SS D Jeter
3B- R Ventura
LM H Matsui
CF B Williams
RF R Mondesi
1D J Giambi
M J Torre

OAK 2003 AL

SP T Hudson
SP B Zito
SP M Mulder
SP T Lilly
SR J Halama
CL K Foulke
RP C Bradford
RP R Rincon
C R Hernandez
1B S Hatteberg
2B M Ellis
SS M Tejada
3B E Chavez
ML E Byrnes
CF C Singleton
LR T Long
DH E Durazo
M K Macha

SEA 2003 AL

SP J Moyer
SP R Franklin
SP J Pineiro
SP F Garcia
SP G Meche
RP S Hasegawa
RP J Mateo
RP A Rhodes
RP R Soriano
C - D Wilson
1B J Olerud
2B B Boone
S3 C Guillen
3B- J Cirillo
LF R Winn
CF M Cameron
RF I Suzuki
DH E Martinez
IO M McLemore
UT- W Bloomquist
M B Melvin

TB 2003 AL

SP V Zambrano
SP J Gonzalez
SR J Kennedy
SR J Sosa
SP R Bell
CL L Carter
RP T Harper
RP J Colome
RP A Levine
C T Hall
1B T Lee
2B M Anderson
SS J Lugo
3R D Rolls
LF C Crawford
CF R Baldelli
RU A Huff
DU A Martin
M L Piniella

TEX 2003 AL

SP J Thomson
SP C Lewis
SR R Dickey
SP I Valdes
SP J Benoit
RP F Cordero
RP A Fultz
RP B Shouse
RP J Powell
C E Diaz
1B M Teixeira
2B M Young
SS A Rodriguez
3B H Blalock
LR- C Everett
CF- R Christenson
RD- J Gonzalez
D1 R Palmeiro
M B Showalter

TOR 2003 AL

SP R Halladay
SP C Lidle
SR K Escobar
SP M Hendrickson
RS T Sturtze
RP A Lopez
RP C Politte
RP T Miller
CU G Myers
1B C Delgado
2B O Hudson
SS C Woodward
3B E Hinske
OI F Catalanotto
CF V Wells
RL R Johnson
DH J Phelps
SI M Bordick
C- T Wilson
M C Tosca

THE LONG SEASON: THE HISTORICAL RECORD

Part of what makes baseball special is its long season. It's been said that baseball isn't a sprint, but a marathon, and the historical record bears this out. Having to play nearly every day for six months or more affects *everything* about the game. A manager's strategy can change completely between March to October, given injuries, trades, predictable and not-so-predictable changes in player performance, and the capricious nature of rookies. A season that, at times, seems endless works its charms and wreaks havoc concurrently in many different ways. The best teams of all time still lose series during the season, and even the worst teams fashion together some form of a winning streak.

The long season is a player's chance to make or break his career. It gives a manager the option of sticking with a declining veteran until he rebounds—or until his poor performance sinks the team. After more than 100 games and four months of play, a team can sometimes pull a pennant out of its cap by promoting an untested but promising rookie. The guy who hits .375 in April may hit .130 in May and end up back in the minors, or a Hurricane Hazle can hit .403 down the stretch to win a pennant—and never be seen again.

When pitcher Jim Brosnan penned his 1959 diary, *The Long Season*, one thing he communicated expertly was the way baseball's fortunes could turn 360 degrees within those six months: from despair to ecstasy, with a whole lot of excitement and some stultifying ennui in between. That's how baseball has been for every one of its long seasons dating back to the nineteenth century: a roller-coaster ride of great stories buried inside a simple yet puzzling game that seems, to outsiders and other unfortunates, almost impenetrable.

For those of us who don't get to play the game for half a year at a time, baseball's long season provides artistic, scientific, emotional, and even spiritual fulfillment, and its memories keep us warm through many a long winter. A distillation of more than a century of baseball seasons is presented in this section—to learn about, argue about, and to savor—from team records to top individual performances, using both traditional statistics and new methods of measurement.

Below are the abbreviations employed in this section, but it does not include those that are defined adequately elsewhere. To learn about the formulas and computation, see the Glossary.

Team and League Batting and Basestealing

W	Wins
L	Losses
T	Ties (Ties only happen if the game has completed 5 or more full innings, the game was tied after the last completed inning, and no further runs have been scored unless the home team has gone ahead in the bottom of the current inning.)
PCT	Winning Percentage (calculated by dividing the number of wins by the number of wins and losses)
GB	Games Behind (The number of games behind first place. If the team in question finished 83–79 and the team in first place finished 95–66, the team in question finished 12.5 games behind.)
HW	Home Wins
HL	Home Losses
R	Runs
OR	Opponent Runs
PA	Plate Appearances
H	Hits
2B	Doubles
3B	Triples
HR	Home Runs
BB	Bases on Balls (generally referred to today as walks)
SO	Strikeouts
HB	Hit Batsmen
SH	Sacrifice Hits (sacrifice flies were counted as sacrifice hits from 1908–1930 and in 1939)
AVG	Batting Average (hits divided by at bats)
OBP	On-Base Percentage (Hits plus walks plus hit-by-pitch divided by at-bats plus walks plus hit-by-pitch plus sacrifice flies: H+BB+HB/AB+BB+HB+SF. Sacrifice flies (SF) were not used in the OBP calculation for 1908–30 and 1939 since they were combined with sacrifice bunts in the official stats.)
SLG	Slugging Average (total bases divided by at bats)
OPS	On-Base Percentage plus Slugging Average (the figure is multiplied by 1000, so .320 plus .500 would be 820)
AOPS	Adjusted On-Base plus Slugging (on-base percentage and slugging average are added and normalized for the context of the offensive level of the league and the team's home park(s) and then converted to a scale in which 100 is average)
BR	Batting Runs (the number of runs the team should have scored compared to the average team based on the team's offensive production)
ABR	Adjusted Batting Runs (Batting runs adjusted for the home park and the league average offensive level but ignoring the offensive contributions of pitchers. The entire league average batting stats are used for teams, since teams either have pitcher batting or they don't, depending on the league rules. For individual batters, BR, ABR, and AOPS are calculated using league figures with pitcher batting subtracted. Thus the team definition is slightly different from the player definition.)
PF	Hitters' Park Factor (This measure of how the team's home park affects offense is used to adjust the team's raw offensive performance in a way that takes into account the context of the team's home

park. This also includes a correction for not having to face your own pitchers, which ends up being used in AOPS and ABR.)

SB Stolen Bases (Totals are available for all seasons in all leagues from 1886 on, as well as for all the seasons of the National Association.)

CS Caught Stealing (These totals are available for all American League teams in 1914–15 and from 1920 on; caught stealing totals are available for all National League teams in 1913, 1915, from 1920–26, and from 1951 on.)

BSA Basestealing Average (stolen bases divided by stolen bases plus caught stealing; not possible unless caught stealing totals are available)

BSR Basestealing Runs (the number of runs added by a team's basestealing attempts)

Team and League Pitching and Fielding

CG Complete Games

SHO Shutouts

GR Games in Relief (the total number of relief appearances made by the team's pitchers)

SV Saves (Saves became an official statistic in 1969. Saves are calculated based on the official definition of saves at the time. Saves before 1969 are based on how many times a relief pitcher finished pitching a victory for his team without getting a win.)

IP Innings Pitched

H Hits Allowed

HR Home Runs Allowed

BB Bases on Balls Allowed

SO Strikeouts

BR/9 Baserunners Allowed Per 9 Innings

ERA Earned Run Average (calculated by dividing earned runs by innings pitched and multiplying by 9)

AERA Adjusted Earned Run Average (calculated by normalizing ERA for the context of the offensive level of the league and the team's home park(s) and converting to a scale in which 100 is average)

OAV Opponents' Batting Average (hits allowed divided by opponent at bats)

OOB Opponents' On-Base Percentage

PR Pitching Runs (indicates how many runs the team's pitcher allowed to score compared to the average pitcher)

APR Adjusted Pitching Runs (indicates how many runs the team's pitcher allowed to score compared to the average pitcher in the context of the team's home park(s) and the offensive level of the league)

PF Pitchers' Park Factor (This measures how the team's home park affects pitching. It is used to adjust the team's raw pitching performance in a way that takes the context of the team's home park into account. Again, there is a correction for pitchers not having to face their own batters. Park factor is used in the APR and AERA calculation.)

OSB Opponents' Stolen Bases

OCS Opponents' Caught Stealing

FA Fielding Average (assists plus putouts divided by assists plus putouts plus errors: A+PO/A+PO+E)

E Errors

WPB Wild Pitches plus Passed Balls

DP Double Plays

FW Fielding Wins (total number of wins the team achieved through its fielding compared to the average team in the context of the offensive level of the league and the team's home park(s))

PW Pitching Wins (total number of wins the team achieved through its pitching compared to the average team in the context of the offensive level of the league and the team's home park(s))

BW Batting Wins (the total number of wins the team achieved through its hitting compared to the average team in the context of the offensive level of the league and the team's home park(s))

BSW Basestealing Wins (total number of wins the team achieved through its basestealing compared to the average team in the context of the offensive level of the league and the team's home park(s))

DIF Differential (This measures the difference between how many games the team was projected to win based on its hitting, pitching, fielding, and baserunning, and how many games the team actually won. It is measured in the same way as teams measure how many games in the standings they are behind another.)

The leaderboards below are not listed among the team statistics:

BFW Batter-Fielder Wins (the sum of a player's batting wins, basestealing wins, and fielding wins, this figure indicates how many games the player won or lost for his team compared to an average player)

Total Bases (calculated by adding singles plus 2* doubles plus 3* triples plus 4* home runs)

RBI Runs Batted In

Fielding Runs Infield and Outfield (Fielding Runs measures how many runs the player saves or loses for his team in the field compared to an average fielder. The formula takes into account assists, putouts, errors, and double plays. All of these defensive statistics are adjusted for the context in several different ways. Defensive innings are based on play-play from 1969 forward; they are estimated for previous years.)

Fewest Bases on Balls Per Game

Games

Adjusted Relief Runs (Adjusted Relief Runs indicates how many runs the pitcher allowed to score compared to the average pitcher in the context of the offensive level of the league and the pitcher's home park(s). Relief pitchers are identified as pitchers who averaged less than 3 innings per appearance.)

Relief Ranking (calculated by putting Adjusted Relief Runs into the context of the importance of the relief innings thrown by the relief pitcher while taking into account the number of saves and decisions assigned to the pitcher)

Adjusted Starter Runs (This indicates how many runs the pitcher allowed to score compared to the average pitcher in the context of the offensive level of the league and the pitcher's home park(s). Starting pitchers are identified as pitchers who average at least 3 innings per appearance.)

Pitcher Wins (Individual pitcher wins are calculated by adding up pitching, batting, fielding, and basestealing wins for individual pitchers; different from team pitching wins.)

1871 National Association

TEAM	W	L	T	PCT	GB	HW	HL	R	OR	PA	H	2B	3B	HR	BB	SO	HB	SH	AVG	OBP	SLG	OPS	AOPS	BR	ABR	PF	SB	CS	BSA	BSR
ATH	21	7	0	.750		12	3	376	266	1327	410	66	27	9	46	23			**.320**	**.344**	**.435**	**779**	**125**	**39**	**43**	99	56	12	**82**	8
BOS	20	10	1	.667	2	12	5	**401**	303	1432	**426**	**70**	**37**	3	**60**	19			.310	.339	.422	761	115	34	22	103	**73**	16	**82**	**10**
CHI	19	9	0	.679	2	**13**	3	302	**241**	1256	323	52	21	**10**	**60**	22			.270	.305	.374	679	86	-6	-34	111	69	21	77	8
MUT	16	17	0	.485	7.5	12	7	302	313	1437	403	43	21	1	33	**15**			.287	.303	.350	653	97	-21	10	91	46	15	75	5
OLY	15	15	2	.500	7	8	5	310	303	1401	375	54	26	6	48	13			.277	.302	.369	671	98	-12	5	95	48	13	79	6
TRO	13	15	1	.464	8	7	9	351	362	1297	384	51	34	6	49	19			.308	.334	.417	751	114	25	20	101	62	24	72	5
CLE	10	19	0	.345	11.5	3	10	249	341	1212	328	35	40	7	26	25			.277	.292	.391	683	102	-10	6	95	18	8	69	1
KEK	7	12	0	.368	9.5	5	4	137	243	779	178	19	8	2	33	9			.239	.271	.294	565	63	-34	-37	102	16	4	80	2
ROK	4	21	0	.160	15.5	3	4	231	287	1074	274	44	25	3	38	30			.264	.291	.364	655	92	-16	-5	96	53	10	84	8
TOT	127					75	50	2659		11215	3101	434	239	47	393	175			.287	.312	.384	695					441	123	78	54

TEAM	CG	SHO	GR	SV	IP	H	HR	BB	SO	BR/9	ERA	AERA	OAV	OOB	PR	APR	PF	OSB	OCS	FA	E	WPB	DP	FW	PW	BW	BSW	DIF
ATH	27	0	1	0	249.0	329	3	53	16	13.8	4.95	81	.284	.315	-20	-27	95			.845	**194**	**28**	13	1.1	-1.8	**2.8**	.1	4.7
BOS	22	**1**	**9**	**3**	276.0	367	**2**	42	23	13.3	3.55	117	.273	.296	20	19	99			.834	243	38	**24**	-.3	1.2	1.4	**.3**	2.3
CHI	25	0	3	1	251.0	**308**	6	**28**	22	**12.0**	**2.76**	**166**	**.264**	**.281**	**41**	**47**	109			.829	229	83	16	-.8	**3.1**	-2.2	.1	4.8
MUT	**32**	**1**	1	0	293.0	373	7	42	22	12.7	3.72	102	.271	.292	16	3	90			.840	235	98	14	1.0	.2	.7	-.0	-2.3
OLY	**32**	0	0	0	282.0	371	4	45	13	13.3	4.37	95	.281	.305	-5	-6	99			**.850**	218	49	20	**1.5**	-.4	.3	.0	-1.4
TRO	28	0	1	0	250.0	431	4	75	12	18.2	5.51	76	.342	.378	-36	-36	100			.845	198	96	22	1.3	-2.3	1.3	-.0	-1.2
CLE	23	0	6	0	254.0	346	13	53	**34**	14.1	4.11	100	.283	.312	3	0	98			.818	234	175	15	-.6	.0	.4	-.3	-3.9
KEK	19	**1**	0	0	169.0	261	5	21	17	15.0	5.17	88	.305	.322	-18	-10	108			.803	163	55	8	-.9	-.7	-2.4	-.3	1.7
ROK	23	**1**	2	0	226.0	315	3	34	16	13.9	4.30	95	.282	.303	-2	-6	97			.821	220	76	14	-1.5	-.4	-.3	.1	-6.4
TOT	231	4	23	4	2250.0					14.0	4.22		.287	.312						.833	1934	698	146					

Batter-Fielder Wins	Batting Average	On-Base Percentage	Slugging Average	On-Base Plus Slugging	Adjusted OPS	Adjusted Batter Runs
Barnes-Bos 1.8	Meyerle-Ath 492	Meyerle-Ath 500	Meyerle-Ath 700	Meyerle-Ath 1200	Meyerle-Ath 243	Meyerle-Ath........23.5
Wood-Chi 1.2	McVey-Bos 431	G.Wright-Bos 453	Pike-Tro 654	G.Wright-Bos......1078	G.Wright-Bos 200	Wolters-Mut 17.2
Force-Oly 1.2	Barnes-Bos...........401	Barnes-Bos 447	Bass-Cle...............640	Pike-Tro 1054	Pike-Tro 194	Barnes-Bos 17.1
Pike-Tro 1.1	King-Tro 396	McVey-Bos..................435	Barnes-Bos...........580	Barnes-Bos 1027	Wolters-Mut 189	Pike-Tro 15.0
McVey-Bos 1.1	Wood-Chi 378	Wood-Chi....................425	Treacey-Chi 573	McVey-Bos 991	Barnes-Bos 186	McVey-Bos 14.0

Runs	Hits	Doubles	Triples	Home Runs	Total Bases	Runs Batted In
Barnes-Bos 66	McVey-Bos 66	Anson-Rok 11	Bass-Cle 10	Treacey-Chi 4	Meyerle-Ath 91	Wolters-Mut 44
Birdsall-Bos 51	Meyerle-Ath 64		Wolters-Mut 9	Pike-Tro 4	Barnes-Bos 91	McVey-Bos 43
Radcliff-Ath 47	Barnes-Bos 63		Barnes-Bos 9	Meyerle-Ath 4	Pike-Tro 85	Meyerle-Ath 40
Cuthbert-Ath 47	Start-Mut 58		Pratt-Cle 8		McVey-Bos 85	Pike-Tro 39
Waterman-Oly 46	King-Tro 57				King-Tro 79	

Stolen Bases	Base Stealing Runs	Fielding Runs-Infield	Fielding Runs-Outfield	Wins	Winning Pct.	Complete Games
McGeary-Tro 20	Wood-Chi 3.3	Force-Oly 17.8	Treacey-Chi 6.6	Spalding-Bos 19	McBride-Ath 783	Wolters-Mut 31
Wood-Chi.................18	McGeary-Tro..........3.0	Barnes-Bos 12.3	Hall-Oly..................5.5	Zettlein-Chi 18	Zettlein-Chi 667	Brainard-Oly 30
Cuthbert-Ath 16	Cuthbert-Ath..........2.8	Wood-Chi.......................8.3	Eggler-Mut 4.5	McBride-Ath............18	Spalding-Bos 655	McMullin-Tro..........28
Leonard-Oly............14	Mack-Rok 2.6	Pinkham-Chi 8.3	Cuthbert-Ath..........3.3	Wolters-Mut 16	Wolters-Mut 500	Zettlein-Chi.............25
Eggler-Mut..............14	Cone-Bos 2.3	Craver-Tro 6.4	King-Tro 3.0			McBride-Ath 25

Strikeouts	Fewest BB/Game	Games	Saves	Base Runners/9	Adjusted Relief Runs	Relief Ranking
Pratt-Cle 34	Zettlein-Chi.............93	Wolters-Mut 32	H.Wright-Bos 3	Zettlein-Chi 12.08	Pinkham-Chi..........1.8	Pinkham-Chi 2.0
Spalding-Bos 23	Mathews-Kek 1.12	Spalding-Bos 31	Pinkham-Chi 1	Wolters-Mut 12.21		
Zettlein-Chi 22	Wolters-Mut 1.24	Brainard-Oly 30		Spalding-Bos 12.98		
Wolters-Mut 22	Brainard-Oly 1.26	McMullin-Tro 29		McBride-Ath 13.18		
Mathews-Kek..........17	Fisher-Rok 1.31			Brainard-Oly 13.57		

Innings Pitched	Opponents' Avg.	Opponents' OBP	Earned Run Average	Adjusted ERA	Adjusted Starter Runs	Pitcher Wins
Wolters-Mut 283.0	Wolters-Mut 263	Zettlein-Chi 283	Zettlein-Chi..........2.73	Zettlein-Chi 168	Zettlein-Chi..........45.0	**Zettlein-Chi**........2.6
Brainard-Oly 264.0	Zettlein-Chi...........267	Wolters-Mut 285	Spalding-Bos 3.36	Spalding-Bos........124	Spalding-Bos 22.3	**Wolters-Mut** 2.0
Spalding-Bos 257.1	Spalding-Bos 268	Spalding-Bos 290	Wolters-Mut 3.43	Wolters-Mut.........110	Wolters-Mut 11.6	**Spalding-Bos** 1.6
McMullin-Tro......249.0	Pratt-Cle 277	Fisher-Rok 302	Pratt-Cle 3.77	Pratt-Cle 110	Pratt-Cle 7.2	**Pratt-Cle** 8
Zettlein-Chi........240.2	McBride-Ath 280	McBride-Ath..................307	Fisher-Rok 4.35	Fisher-Rok.............94	Stearns-Oly 3.4	**Stearns-Oly**...........1

Up in Smoke

The Kekiongas of Fort Wayne won the first National Association game ever played as Bobby Mathews shut out Forest City of Cleveland, 2–0, on May 4, 1871. James "Deacon" White of Cleveland doubled for the first hit in the first professional baseball league. The Kekiongas lasted only 19 games into the season and drew just 3,500 fans. It was the start of a disaster-prone pattern that pervaded the NA's tenure: teams open with great fanfare, teams fare poorly, teams draw poorly, teams fold.

The NA had no set schedule, per se; clubs made their own arrangements. They were supposed to play five series of three games each, with the champion being declared based on winning percentage. Of course, not everyone played all the requisite series. Teams with little to gain and longer to travel didn't make every road trip—and the NA wasn't big on discipline for those who strayed. Clubs were often more interested in lucrative non-scheduled "exhibition games" than in fulfilling their league schedule. It was not uncommon for clubs to play twice as many nonleague contests as NA games.

The NA drew 266,500 in its inaugural season; the White Stockings' 69,000 led the circuit even though the Great Chicago Fire wiped out their ballpark and uniforms late in the season. The White Stockings (ancestors of today's Cubs) gamely continued their schedule on the road, wearing an odd assortment of uniforms and finishing a close second. Chicago did not return to the league for two seasons.

The Philadelphia Athletics won the first pennant, thanks in part to two forfeits by Rockford, which left the league after just one year. Rockford's 19-year-old third baseman, Cap Anson, would shift to the Athletics in 1872.

Philadelphia's Levi Meyerle, a notoriously horrendous fielder during a time of rough fields and rougher scorekeepers, began a long tradition of hapless defenders who played every day for a simple reason: they could hit. Numbers calculated years later confirmed eyewitness accounts: His 1871 fielding average was an incomprehensible .642, but he slugged .700 for his hometown Athletics. The brief NA season may have afforded Meyerle just 26 games, but his .492 batting average has never been approached by any batsman in the 132 years following.

1872 National Association

TEAM	W	L	T	PCT	GB	HW	HL	R	OR	PA	H	2B	3B	HR	BB	SO	HB	SH	AVG	OBP	SLG	OPS	AOPS	BR	ABR	PF	SB	CS	BSA	BSR
BOS	39	8	1	.830		20	1	521	**236**	2155	673	**107**	30	7	29	**26**			**.317**	.326	**.405**	**731**	120	**62**	36	105	48	14	**77**	**6**
BAL	35	19	4	.648	7.5	20	7	**617**	434	2600	**753**	106	**31**	**14**	29	28			.293	.301	.375	676	104	25	0	105	53	18	75	5
MUT	34	20	2	.630	8.5	20	8	523	362	2484	670	87	14	4	58	52			.276	.293	.329	622	99	-17	18	94	**59**	22	73	5
ATH	30	14	3	.682	7.5	**22**	4	539	349	2211	679	79	25	4	**69**	47			**.317**	**.338**	.383	721	**124**	60	**58**	100	58	31	65	2
TRO	15	10	0	.600	13	6	6	273	191	1108	330	58	8	5	9	14			.300	.306	.381	687	111	16	13	101	6	7	46	-1
ATL	9	28	0	.243	25	6	12	237	473	1476	377	35	10	1	19	25			.259	.268	.299	567	65	-40	-80	117	19	16	54	-1
CLE	6	16	0	.273	20.5	2	5	174	254	960	272	28	5	0	17	13			.288	.301	.329	630	102	-4	8	95	12	3	80	2
MAN	5	19	0	.208	22.5	4	7	220	348	1023	275	36	9	2	10	13			.271	.279	.331	610	94	-13	0	94	6	7	46	-1
ECK	3	26	0	.103	27	3	11	152	413	1090	248	29	9	0	18	40			.231	.244	.275	519	72	-47	-14	85	8	13	38	-3
OLY	2	7	0	.222	18	1	6	54	140	369	91	10	3	0	4	4			.249	.257	.293	550	75	-12	-8	95	0	3	0	-1
NAT	0	11	0	.000	21	0	7	80	190	452	99	6	1	0	1	3			.220	.221	.237	458	37	-30	-39	117	0	0	0	0
TOT	183					104	74	3390		15928	4467	581	145	37	263	265			.285	.297	.348	645					269	134	67	12

TEAM	CG	SHO	GR	SV	IP	H	HR	BB	SO	BR/9	ERA	AERA	OAV	OOB	PR	APR	PF	OSB	OCS	FA	E	WPB	DP	FW	PW	BW	BSW	DIF
BOS	41	**4**	7	**4**	430.1	**443**	**0**	27	29	**9.8**	**1.86**	**197**	**.243**	**.254**	**86**	**86**	100			**.875**	**280**	53	**44**	4.3	**6.0**	2.5	**.3**	2.3
BAL	48	1	**10**	1	516.0	573	3	63	**77**	11.1	2.90	127	.245	.265	43	45	101			.830	432	93	22	.4	3.1	.0	**.3**	4.2
MUT	**54**	3	2	1	512.0	622	2	33	46	11.5	3.02	112	.271	.282	36	22	93			.868	323	54	33	**5.2**	1.5	1.3	**.3**	-1.3
ATH	47	1	0	0	419.1	508	3	26	44	11.5	2.85	125	.265	.275	37	34	98			.858	298	**28**	20	3.0	2.4	**4.0**	.0	-1.5
TRO	17	2	8	1	225.0	277	2	10	19	11.5	2.60	140	.269	.276	26	26	100			.861	151	18	9	2.0	1.8	.9	-.1	-2.1
ATL	37	0	0	0	336.0	568	6	**21**	13	15.8	4.53	100	.326	.334	-33	0	124			.810	357	66	15	-4.0	.0	-5.6	-.1	.2
CLE	15	0	7	0	199.0	285	6	24	11	14.0	5.70	63	.290	.307	-45	-48	98			.816	184	53	17	-.9	-3.3	.6	.0	-1.4
MAN	20	0	4	0	211.0	366	6	15	10	16.3	5.55	65	.326	.335	-44	-46	99			.804	231	18	11	-2.6	-3.2	.0	-.1	-1.1
ECK	28	0	1	0	259.1	484	7	36	13	18.0	5.55	61	.345	.361	-55	-66	93			.803	274	71	9	-2.8	-4.6	-1.0	-.3	-2.8
OLY	9	0	0	0	79.0	148	**0**	5	1	17.4	6.38	57	.333	.341	-24	-25	99			.786	96	30	7	-1.5	-1.7	-.6	-.1	1.4
NAT	11	0	0	0	99.0	193	2	3	2	17.8	6.18	75	.339	.343	-28	-13	127			.774	120	7	2	-1.9	-.9	-2.7	-.0	.1
TOT	327	11	39	7	3286.0					13.0	3.65		.285	.297						.837	2746	491	189					

Batter-Fielder Wins	Batting Average	On-Base Percentage	Slugging Average	On-Base Plus Slugging	Adjusted OPS	Adjusted Batter Runs
Barnes-Bos 3.5	Barnes-Bos...........430	Anson-Ath 455	Barnes-Bos...........583	Barnes-Bos 1034	Barnes-Bos 205	Barnes-Bos 28.0
Eggler-Mut 2.2	Force-Tro-Bal 418	Barnes-Bos 452	Anson-Ath............525	Anson-Ath 980	Anson-Ath 200	Anson-Ath 25.8
G.Wright-Bos 2.2	Anson-Ath............415	Force-Tro-Bal 423	Wood-Tro-Eck.......500	Force-Tro-Bal........916	Force-Tro-Bal........176	Force-Tro-Bal......19.0
Force-Tro-Bal......1.8	Hastings-Cle-Bal .362	Hastings-Cle-Bal 376	Force-Tro-Bal 493	Wood-Tro-Eck 833	Wood-Tro-Eck 156	Eggler-Mut..........16.8
Ferguson-Atl 1.7	McGeary-Ath 360	McGeary-Ath 366	Meyerle-Ath 486	G.Wright-Bos 816	Meyerle-Ath 147	Hatfield-Mut........14.7

Runs	Hits	Doubles	Triples	Home Runs	Total Bases	Runs Batted In
Eggler-Mut.............94	Barnes-Bos 99	Barnes-Bos...................28	Gould-Bos 8	Pike-Bal 7	Barnes-Bos 134	Pike-Bal 60
G.Wright-Bos 87	Eggler-Mut.............97	Eggler-Mut 20	Anson-Ath 7	Gedney-Tro-Eck 3	Pike-Bal 131	Start-Mut 48
Cuthbert-Ath 83	Force-Tro-Bal..........94	Hall-Bal 17	G.Wright-Bos 6		G.Wright-Bos 120	Fisler-Ath 48
Barnes-Bos 81	Hatfield-Mut............93	G.Wright-Bos 16	Hall-Bal 6		Eggler-Mut............117	Anson-Ath 48
Hatfield-Mut...........76	Anson-Ath 90				Hall-Bal 116	

Stolen Bases	Base Stealing Runs	Fielding Runs-Infield	Fielding Runs-Outfield	Wins	Winning Pct.	Complete Games
Eggler-Mut.............18	Barnes-Bos............1.9	Ferguson-Atl 34.5	Eggler-Mut 14.1	Spalding-Bos 38	Spalding-Bos 826	Cummings-Mut......53
G.Wright-Bos 14	Eggler-Mut 1.9	Barnes-Bos 25.5	York-Bal 9.9	Cummings-Mut 33	McBride-Ath 682	McBride-Ath 47
Cuthbert-Ath 14	Pike-Bal 1.9	G.Wright-Bos 21.6	Reach-Ath...............4.4	McBride-Ath............30	Cummings-Mut.....623	Spalding-Bos 41
McGeary-Ath 13	G.Wright-Bos 1.7	Fisler-Ath 7.3	Meyerle-Ath 3.0	Mathews-Bal 25	Mathews-Bal.........581	Mathews-Bal 39
	Cuthbert-Ath..........1.7	Force-Tro-Bal 7.2	McMullin-Mut 2.9	Zettlein-Tro-Eck 15	Zettlein-Tro-Eck ...484	Britt-Atl 37

Strikeouts	Fewest BB/Game	Games	Saves	Base Runners/9	Adjusted Relief Runs	Relief Ranking
Mathews-Bal 57	Stearns-Nat 27	Cummings-Mut 55	H.Wright-Bos 4	Fisher-Bal 8.51	H.Wright-Bos 5.2	H.Wright-Bos 3.6
Cummings-Mut 45	Buttery-Man 46	Mathews-Bal.................49	Zettlein-Tro-Eck 1	Spalding-Bos 9.87		
McBride-Ath............44	Zettlein-Tro-Eck 48	Spalding-Bos 48	McMullin-Mut 1	Zettlein-Tro-Eck 11.19		
Spalding-Bos 28	Brainard-Oly-Man ..52	McBride-Ath 47	Fisher-Bal 1	McBride-Ath 11.46		
Zettlein-Tro-Eck 25	McBride-Ath 56	Britt-Atl 37		Cummings-Mut..11.50		

Innings Pitched	Opponents' Avg.	Opponents' OBP	Earned Run Average	Adjusted ERA	Adjusted Starter Runs	Pitcher Wins
Cummings-Mut ..497.0	Fisher-Bal 197	Fisher-Bal 216	Fisher-Bal 1.80	Fisher-Bal 205	Spalding-Bos 80.9	**Spalding-Bos** 7.5
McBride-Ath 419.1	Spalding-Bos 244	Spalding-Bos 255	Spalding-Bos 1.85	Spalding-Bos 199	McBride-Ath 34.0	**McBride-Ath** 2.6
Mathews-Bal......406.0	Mathews-Bal...........257	Zettlein-Tro-Eck...........273	Zettlein-Tro-Eck ..2.57	Zettlein-Tro-Eck 139	Zettlein-Tro-Eck ..30.2	**Zettlein-Tro-Eck**2.1
Spalding-Bos 404.2	Zettlein-Tro-Eck ...265	McBride-Ath.................275	McBride-Ath 2.85	McBride-Ath..........125	Mathews-Bal........26.0	**Fisher-Bal** 1.2
Britt-Atl 336.0	McBride-Ath 265	Mathews-Bal 277	Cummings-Mut 3.01	Mathews-Bal 115	Cummings-Mut 23.3	**Cummings-Mut**..1.1

More Is Less

The NA increased to eleven teams in its second year, but several of the new clubs proved to be poor draws. Troy, Cleveland, the Brooklyn Eckfords, the Washington Olympics, and Mansfield of Middletown, Connecticut, wouldn't live to see 1873. Together they drew just 37,000; the six clubs that stuck it out had a combined attendance of 200,000. The Lord Baltimores, however, proved an inspired addition as they drew 40,500 fans and placed second to runaway winner Boston.

Harry Wright's Red Stockings were all business. In a league with questionable organization, officiating, and, in some cases, honesty of its participants, British-born Harry Wright was the pillar of class and professionalism. He had assembled the unbeatable Cincinnati Red Stockings of 1869, and he was hired to do the same thing in Boston in 1871. He brought several of his old Cincinnati players to Boston, including Cal McVey and Charlie Gould, but most important was Harry's brother, George. The Red Stockings finished 2 games back in 1871, but that failure would not happen again.

From 1872–75 Boston went 205–50 for an .804 winning percentage. Wright not only brought holdovers from Cincinnati, he also lured some of the best young talent to Boston. Al Spalding, who pitched in every one of Boston's games in 1872, and Ross Barnes, who averaged more than 2 hits per game during his NA career, both came from the Rockford club. Each was just 21.

Barnes and George Wright ranked 1-2 in runs, hits, doubles, total bases, and slugging. Defensively, second baseman Barnes and shortstop Wright were unmatched. Wright had superb hands and perfected the method of bending his elbows when catching the ball to cushion the shock. Barnes' .904 fielding average on the choppy NA fields was as impressive as his .430 batting average. Boston led the NA in double plays and fielding average as the Red Stockings lost just once in 21 tries at South End Grounds.

Baby-faced Candy Cummings, accused of signing contracts with three different teams before the season, dominated on the mound for the Mutuals. The reputed inventor of the curveball pitched in all but one of New York's games, completing 53. Cummings tossed more innings than every *team* except Baltimore.

1873 National Association

TEAM	W	L	T	PCT	GB	HW	HL	R	OR	PA	H	2B	3B	HR	BB	SO	HB	SH	AVG	OBP	SLG	OPS	AOPS	BR	ABR	PF	SB	CS	BSA	BSR
BOS	43	16	1	.729		**24**	8	**739**	460	2816	**933**	**144**	**44**	**13**	**68**	36			**.340**	**.355**	**.438**	**793**	**128**	**129**	**74**	108	**145**	48	75	**15**
PHI	36	17	0	.679	4	22	5	526	**396**	2388	645	83	20	8	62	41			.277	.296	.340	636	89	-18	-35	104	54	14	**79**	7
BAL	34	22	1	.607	7.5	19	6	644	451	2603	810	109	40	9	43	**30**			.316	.328	.401	729	121	59	62	100	28	13	68	2
MUT	29	24	0	.547	11	22	9	424	385	2254	622	51	36	5	43	22			.281	.295	.344	639	94	-20	-17	99	16	7	70	1
ATH	28	23	1	.549	11	21	6	474	403	2302	683	71	21	4	35	33			.301	.312	.356	668	95	6	-28	108	36	24	60	0
ATL	17	37	1	.315	23.5	14	14	366	549	2262	588	46	23	6	55	47			.266	.284	.316	600	92	-47	3	89	20	13	61	0
WAS	8	31	0	.205	25	6	12	283	485	1580	408	40	19	2	20	36			.262	.271	.315	586	80	-42	-33	97	11	8	58	0
RES	2	21	0	.087	23	0	8	98	299	878	204	25	8	0	9	**30**			.235	.243	.282	525	64	-42	-30	92	4	4	50	-1
MAR	0	6	0	.000	16.5	0	1	26	152	211	33	1	0	0	0	3			.156	.156	.161	317	-5	-26	-21	77	0	0	0	0
TOT	199					128	69	3580		17294	4926	570	211	47	335	278			.290	.304	.357	661					314	131	71	23

TEAM	CG	SHO	GR	SV	IP	H	HR	BB	SO	BR/9	ERA	AERA	OAV	OOB	PR	APR	PF	OSB	OCS	FA	E	WPB	DP	FW	PW	BW	BSW	DIF
BOS	46	1	**14**	**7**	536.0	708	5	**42**	55	12.6	3.07	113	.288	.300	19	23	102			.836	472	99	**54**	.6	1.6	**5.2**	**.9**	5.2
PHI	50	0	3	0	481.0	628	**3**	44	29	12.6	2.92	118	.285	.299	26	28	101			.849	378	**51**	43	2.4	2.0	-2.5	.3	7.3
BAL	**55**	1	2	0	508.2	680	4	43	37	12.8	3.08	110	.285	.298	18	18	100			**.862**	**345**	53	32	**5.6**	1.3	4.4	-.0	-5.3
MUT	48	2	5	0	477.0	**539**	5	68	**80**	**11.5**	**2.64**	**125**	**.255**	.278	**40**	**36**	97			.819	425	91	29	.1	**2.5**	-1.2	-.1	1.2
ATH	44	**3**	8	2	475.0	553	4	58	41	11.6	3.05	117	.257	**.276**	18	26	105			.840	390	84	30	1.4	1.8	-2.0	-.2	1.4
ATL	52	1	3	0	500.0	737	8	43	16	14.0	4.14	77	.305	.317	-41	-58	93			.817	515	53	34	-3.5	-4.1	.2	-.2	-2.4
WAS	39	0	0	0	346.0	594	11	26	10	16.1	4.84	72	.337	.347	-55	-50	103			.812	348	80	27	-1.7	-3.5	-2.3	-.2	-3.8
RES	22	0	1	0	207.0	343	6	10	10	15.3	3.26	107	.312	.318	3	5	103			.789	244	22	14	-2.9	.4	-2.1	-.3	-4.6
MAR	6	0	0	0	54.0	144	1	1	0	24.2	8.00	42	.393	.395	-28	-28	100			.761	74	5	0	-1.3	-2.0	-1.5	-.2	1.9
TOT	362	8	36	9	3584.2					13.2	3.40		.290	.304						.830	3191	538	263					

Batter-Fielder Wins	Batting Average	On-Base Percentage	Slugging Average	On-Base Plus Slugging	Adjusted OPS	Adjusted Batter Runs
Barnes-Bos 4.2	Barnes-Bos...........431	Barnes-Bos 465	Barnes-Bos...........616	Barnes-Bos 1080	Barnes-Bos 200	Barnes-Bos 38.2
G.Wright-Bos 2.6	Anson-Ath............398	Anson-Ath 409	G.Wright-Bos 511	G.Wright-Bos........914	McVey-Bal 159	G.Wright-Bos......19.6
Ferguson-Atl 1.6	White-Bos.............392	G.Wright-Bos 404	White-Bos............508	White-Bos 900	G.Wright-Bos 156	Pabor-Atl 17.3
White-Bos...........1.4	G.Wright-Bos 387	White-Bos 392	McVey-Bal 490	McVey-Bal 879	Pabor-Atl 153	White-Bos 16.7
Force-Bal 1.2	McVey-Bal 380	McVey-Bal 390	Meyerle-Phi 479	Anson-Ath 858	White-Bos 152	McVey-Bal 13.3

Runs	Hits	Doubles	Triples	Home Runs	Total Bases	Runs Batted In
Barnes-Bos 125	Barnes-Bos 138	Barnes-Bos....................31	Barnes-Bos 11	Pike-Bal 4	Barnes-Bos 197	White-Bos.............77
G.Wright-Bos 99	G.Wright-Bos 125	O'Rourke-Bos 21	Mills-Bal 9	G.Wright-Bos 3	G.Wright-Bos 165	Spalding-Bos 71
Spalding-Bos 83	White-Bos 122	Mills-Bal 20	White-Bos 8	Meyerle-Phi 3	White-Bos 158	Leonard-Bos...........60
Eggler-Mut..............82	Spalding-Bos 106	Carey-Bal 18	Pike-Bal 8		Pike-Bal 133	Barnes-Bos 60
Leonard-Bos 81	Anson-Ath 101		Holdsworth-Mut 8			Meyerle-Phi 59

Stolen Bases	Base Stealing Runs	Fielding Runs-Infield	Fielding Runs-Outfield	Wins	Winning Pct.	Complete Games
Barnes-Bos 43	Barnes-Bos............7.4	Ferguson-Atl 27.4	Gedney-Mut 14.2	Spalding-Bos 41	Spalding-Bos 745	Britt-Atl 51
Leonard-Bos 27	White-Bos.............3.1	G.Wright-Bos 19.9	York-Bal 11.2	Zettlein-Phi 36	Zettlein-Phi 706	Zettlein-Phi 49
White-Bos 19	Leonard-Bos 2.8	Barnes-Bos 19.3	Bechtel-Phi 5.9	Mathews-Mut..........29	Cummings-Bal 667	Mathews-Mut 47
Schafer-Bos............14	Cuthbert-Phi 2.4	Fulmer-Phi 18.0	Fisher-Ath 5.8	Cummings-Bal........28	McBride-Ath 558	Spalding-Bos 46
Cuthbert-Phi 14	Spalding-Bos 2.0	Beals-Was 9.0	Eggler-Mut 3.9	McBride-Ath............24	Mathews-Mut 558	Cummings-Bal 42

Strikeouts	Fewest BB/Game	Games	Saves	Base Runners/9	Adjusted Relief Runs	Relief Ranking
Mathews-Mut..........79	H.Campbell-Res 44	Spalding-Bos 60	H.Wright-Bos 4	Fisher-Ath..........10.67		
Spalding-Bos 50	Stearns-Was...........51	Britt-Atl 54	Spalding-Bos 3	Mathews-Mut 11.19		
Cummings-Bal........34	Spalding-Bos 65	Mathews-Mut 52	Fisher-Ath 2	McBride-Ath 11.76		
Zettlein-Phi 29	Brainard-Bal 75	Zettlein-Phi 51		Cummings-Bal ..11.97		
McBride-Ath............25	Britt-Atl 77	McBride-Ath 46		Spalding-Bos 12.30		

Innings Pitched	Opponents' Avg.	Opponents' OBP	Earned Run Average	Adjusted ERA	Adjusted Starter Runs	Pitcher Wins
Spalding-Bos 496.2	Fisher-Ath.............231	Fisher-Ath 250	Fisher-Ath 1.81	Fisher-Ath 197	Mathews-Mut 36.8	**Spalding-Bos** 3.4
Britt-Atl 480.2	Mathews-Mut 251	Mathews-Mut...............274	Mathews-Mut 2.58	Mathews-Mut.........128	Zettlein-Phi 30.1	**Mathews-Mut** 2.5
Zettlein-Phi 460.0	McBride-Ath 262	McBride-Ath.................281	Cummings-Bal 2.80	Cummings-Bal......121	Cummings-Bal 28.4	**Cummings-Bal** ..2.1
Mathews-Mut 443.0	Cummings-Bal 274	Cummings-Bal.............287	Zettlein-Phi 2.86	Zettlein-Phi 121	Spalding-Bos 26.0	**Zettlein-Phi**........1.7
McBride-Ath 382.2	Zettlein-Phi 284	Spalding-Bos 296	H.Campbell-Res ..2.95	H.Campbell-Res ..119	McBride-Ath 15.0	**McBride-Ath** 1.2

Not Much of a Horse Race

Nine teams started 1873, but the Baltimore Marylands called it quits after going 0–6—the briefest of any team in the NA. The Resolutes of Elizabeth, New Jersey, stuck it out until August before quitting (although one of their two wins came against the powerhouse Red Stockings). League attendance was down 16 percent from 1871.

Lip Pike of the Lord Baltimores won his third successive home run crown in 1873. Although Pike homered just once more over the next two NA seasons, his 16 career long balls topped the circuit. Pike was also pretty fast, fast enough to beat a horse, outrunning a trotter in a 100-yard dash at Baltimore's Newington Park in August; "Clarence" had a 25-yard head start, but Pike took the race in 10 seconds flat.

Nearly 100 games into their existence, the Red Stockings were finally shut out. Unfazed, Boston marched to the pennant again, averaging almost 12 runs per game. The Red Stockings dominated every offensive category. Al Spalding not only won 41 times for Boston, he also drove in 71 runs in 60 games.

Cherokee Fisher had an interesting perspective on the NA. He pitched all five seasons in the league for a different team each year. In 1873, as an Athletic, he allowed the fewest runs per game for the second straight year, but he didn't pitch much because of the presence of veteran moundsman Dick McBride, the man who had finally shut out the mighty Red Stockings. Fisher played right field mostly and batted a career-best .262. The Athletics finished just 4 games behind Boston, the closest any NA team would ever get to the Red Stockings again.

Dick McBride managed every game the Athletics ever played as an NA club until October 9, 1875, when he had the rare distinction of being stripped of his job in the middle of a game against Boston. Following an on-field meeting by the club's board of directors, 23-year-old Adrian (not yet Cap) Anson made his managerial debut in the fifth inning.

1874 National Association

TEAM	W	L	T	PCT	GB	HW	HL	R	OR	PA	H	2B	3B	HR	BB	SO	HB	SH	AVG	OBP	SLG	OPS	AOPS	BR	ABR	PF	SB	CS	BSA	BSR
BOS	52	18	1	.743		**27**	9	**735**	415	3163	**977**	**121**	**61**	**17**	34	**28**			**.312**	**.320**	**.406**	**726**	**128**	**113**	**77**	106	**45**	19	70	3
MUT	42	23	0	.646	7.5	**27**	8	501	**377**	2766	714	89	28	7	**36**	40			.262	.271	.322	593	90	-21	-35	103	36	4	**90**	**7**
ATH	33	22	0	.600	11.5	21	8	441	344	2283	647	83	18	6	24	51			.286	.294	.347	641	99	20	-14	109	36	14	72	3
PHI	29	29	0	.500	17	16	9	476	428	2463	677	78	50	2	28	33			.278	.286	.354	640	104	17	1	104	27	18	60	0
CHI	28	31	0	.475	18.5	18	10	418	480	2494	685	87	4	4	32	54			.278	.287	.322	609	97	-2	-6	101	32	12	73	3
ATL	22	33	1	.400	22.5	15	13	301	450	2200	498	45	8	1	31	51			.230	.240	.259	499	71	-85	-44	88	12	4	75	1
HAR	16	37	0	.302	27.5	13	17	371	471	2175	591	86	18	2	31	63			.276	.286	.335	621	97	6	-13	105	42	21	67	2
BAL	9	38	0	.191	31.5	7	13	227	505	1798	435	45	7	1	22	37			.245	.254	.280	534	75	-48	-46	99	12	5	71	1
TOT	232					144	87	3470		19342	5224	634	194	40	238	357			.273	.282	.333	616					242	97	71	19

TEAM	CG	SHO	GR	SV	IP	H	HR	BB	SO	BR/9	ERA	AERA	OAV	OOB	PR	APR	PF	OSB	OCS	FA	E	WPB	DP	FW	PW	BW	BSW	DIF
BOS	**65**	**4**	6	**3**	634.0	779	**1**	23	31	11.4	1.93	112	.274	.280	18	17	99			**.850**	489	50	**53**	4.5	1.3	**6.0**	.0	5.2
MUT	62	**4**	3	0	586.0	663	3	41	**101**	10.8	1.90	118	.261	.273	19	22	103			.847	438	91	22	**4.6**	1.7	-2.7	**.4**	5.6
ATH	55	0	0	0	487.0	**514**	6	32	37	**10.1**	**1.64**	**141**	**.240**	**.251**	**30**	**34**	106			.839	**396**	38	34	2.6	**2.6**	-1.1	.0	1.3
PHI	56	3	2	0	522.0	673	4	19	61	11.9	1.93	115	.278	.284	15	17	101			.809	518	**32**	38	-2.3	1.3	.0	-.2	1.1
CHI	58	3	1	0	533.2	684	7	45	26	12.3	2.65	84	.279	.292	-27	-24	102			.829	477	57	27	.2	-1.9	-.5	.0	.6
ATL	56	1	0	0	506.0	618	15	**11**	42	11.2	2.06	100	.266	.269	7	0	94			.822	500	79	15	-2.2	.0	-3.4	-.1	.3
HAR	45	0	**8**	0	481.0	653	**1**	28	39	12.7	2.53	91	.284	.293	-18	-11	105			.797	521	85	17	-4.5	-.9	-1.0	-.0	-4.1
BAL	42	0	6	0	420.0	640	3	39	20	14.5	3.13	71	.305	.318	-44	-41	102			.812	436	54	15	-2.7	-3.2	-3.6	-.1	-4.9
TOT	439	15	26	3	4169.2					11.8	2.19		.273	.282						.827	3775	486	221					

Batter-Fielder Wins
Barnes-Bos 1.9
Pike-Har 1.8
McVey-Bos 1.7
Craver-Phi 1.5
G.Wright-Bos 1.5

Batting Average
Meyerle-Chi 394
McVey-Bos 359
Pike-Har 355
Manning-Bal-Har .346
McMullin-Ath.........346

On-Base Percentage
Meyerle-Chi 401
Pike-Har......................368
McMullin-Ath 366
McVey-Bos...................360
Barnes-Bos 360

Slugging Average
Pike-Har 504
Craver-Phi............498
Meyerle-Chi 488
McVey-Bos 481
G.Wright-Bos 476

On-Base Plus Slugging
Meyerle-Chi 889
Pike-Har................872
Craver-Phi 851
McVey-Bos 842
G.Wright-Bos 816

Adjusted OPS
Meyerle-Chi 182
Pike-Har................168
Craver-Phi 164
McVey-Bos 158
G.Wright-Bos 150

Adjusted Batter Runs
Meyerle-Chi 22.9
McVey-Bos 20.3
Craver-Phi 17.6
Pike-Har 17.2
G.Wright-Bos......14.7

Runs
McVey-Bos 91
O'Rourke-Bos 82
Spalding-Bos 80
G.Wright-Bos 76
White-Bos 75

Hits
McVey-Bos 123
Spalding-Bos 119
White-Bos 106
Leonard-Bos 106
O'Rourke-Bos 104

Doubles
Pike-Har 22
McVey-Bos 21
Meyerle-Chi 19
Craver-Phi......................19
Leonard-Bos 18

Triples
G.Wright-Bos 15
Craver-Phi 11
Holdsworth-Phi 9

Home Runs
O'Rourke-Bos 5
White-Bos 3
McVey-Bos 3
Clapp-Ath 3

Total Bases
McVey-Bos 165
O'Rourke-Bos 150
G.Wright-Bos 149
White-Bos 134
Spalding-Bos 134

Runs Batted In
McVey-Bos 71
O'Rourke-Bos........61
Craver-Phi 56
Spalding-Bos 54
White-Bos.............52

Stolen Bases
Barlow-Har 17
O'Rourke-Bos 11
Leonard-Bos 11
Craver-Phi 11

Base Stealing Runs
Barlow-Har 2.3
Cuthbert-Chi..........1.8
O'Rourke-Bos........1.7
McGeary-Ath 1.5

Fielding Runs-Infield
White-Bal 27.3
Barnes-Bos 18.8
Burdock-Mut 10.1
Force-Chi 8.9
Pearce-Atl 7.8

Fielding Runs-Outfield
Ryan-Bal..............13.1
York-Phi 7.7
Eggler-Phi..............6.8
Hines-Chi 6.1
Hatfield-Mut 5.5

Wins
Spalding-Bos 52
Mathews-Mut 42
McBride-Ath............33
Cummings-Phi........28
Zettlein-Chi 27

Winning Pct.
Spalding-Bos 765
Mathews-Mut 656
McBride-Ath 600
Cummings-Phi 519
Zettlein-Chi 474

Complete Games
Spalding-Bos 65
Mathews-Mut 62
Zettlein-Chi 57
McBride-Ath 55
Bond-Atl 55

Strikeouts
Mathews-Mut........101
Cummings-Phi........61
Bond-Atl..................42
McBride-Ath............37
Spalding-Bos..........31

Fewest BB/Game
Bond-Atl 14
Spalding-Bos 28
Cummings-Phi 34
Fisher-Har...............36
McBride-Ath 59

Games
Spalding-Bos 71
Mathews-Mut 65
Zettlein-Chi 57
McBride-Ath 55
Bond-Atl 55

Saves
H.Wright-Bos 3

Base Runners/9
McBride-Ath 10.09
Mathews-Mut 10.79
Bond-Atl 11.12
Spalding-Bos 11.28
Cummings-Phi ..11.81

Adjusted Relief Runs

Relief Ranking

Innings Pitched
Spalding-Bos 617.1
Mathews-Mut 578.0
Zettlein-Chi 515.2
Bond-Atl 497.0
McBride-Ath 487.0

Opponents' Avg.
McBride-Ath 240
Mathews-Mut 261
Bond-Atl 266
Spalding-Bos 273
Zettlein-Chi 273

Opponents' OBP
McBride-Ath................251
Bond-Atl......................268
Mathews-Mut...............273
Spalding-Bos 278
Cummings-Phi 282

Earned Run Average
McBride-Ath 1.64
Mathews-Mut 1.90
Spalding-Bos 1.92
Cummings-Phi 1.96
Bond-Atl 2.03

Adjusted ERA
McBride-Ath..........141
Mathews-Mut........118
Cummings-Phi......113
Spalding-Bos........113
Bond-Atl................102

Adjusted Starter Runs
McBride-Ath 34.3
Mathews-Mut 21.7
Spalding-Bos 16.9
Cummings-Phi 15.9
Fisher-Har.............1.4

Pitcher Wins
Spalding-Bos 2.8
McBride-Ath 1.9
Mathews-Mut 1.5
Cummings-Phi 7
Bond-Atl 6

White Stockings to the Rescue, Sort Of

Gambling was officially made against the rules in 1874. Players were threatened with expulsion if they bet on games they were playing in—this at least made gambling more covert. Athletics outfielder John Radcliffe was expelled during the season for offering an umpire $175 to help Chicago win a game (he played 5 games in 1875 for the Centennials).

The batter's box was first introduced in 1874. Walks were awarded on three "wide balls" or nine balls too high or low. A proposal by Henry Chadwick for ten men and ten innings was defeated at the annual league meeting in Boston.

Chicago returned after two years, and, no coincidence, the NA finally surpassed its overall attendance mark set in 1871. The White Stockings outdrew the Red Stockings at the gate but could not compete with them on the diamond; in a 38–1 loss to the Mutuals in June, Chicago committed 36 errors.

In midseason, Boston and the Athletics set sail for Great Britain. Harry Wright planned this tour to his native country, sending Red Stockings star Al Spalding to England to make arrangements. Wright, a professional cricketer less than a decade earlier, was embarrassed that Spalding had led his hosts to believe the American ballplayers were also fine cricketers—they weren't. The tour lost $3,000.

That was about all the Red Stockings lost. Boston did not miss a beat after six weeks away: Cal McVey led an attack that featured teammates in the top five spots in runs, hits, and total bases. (Boston swept the top five in these categories again in 1875.) For good measure, Boston's "Orator" Jim O'Rourke led the NA in home runs in 1874–75.

Boston took the title by 7½ games over New York, but it was only that close because their 9–1 mark against the Lord Baltimores was thrown out when that club did not complete its schedule. Despite the return of the White Stockings, only one midseason team failure, steps to limit gambling, and international press (some of it good), the NA was at a critical juncture. The decision to allow six more teams for 1875 was the fuel that caused the league to explode.

1875 National Association

TEAM	W	L	T	PCT	GB	HW	HL	R	OR	PA	H	2B	3B	HR	BB	SO	HB	SH	AVG	OBP	SLG	OPS	AOPS	BR	ABR	PF	SB	CS	BSA	BSR
BOS	71	8	3	.899		37	0	831	343	3548	1128	167	51	15	33	52			.321	.327	.410	737	153	195	169	104	93	37	72	8
HAR	54	28	4	.659	18.5	26	11	557	343	3390	871	92	35	2	34	64			.260	.267	.310	577	97	6	-20	105	65	33	66	3
ATH	53	20	4	.726	15	28	7	699	402	3288	941	124	57	7	38	55			.290	.298	.369	667	120	103	41	111	75	46	62	0
STL	39	29	2	.574	26.5	21	12	386	369	2706	643	85	29	0	32	102			.240	.249	.294	543	99	-23	17	91	108	36	75	11
PHI	37	31	2	.544	28.5	16	16	470	376	2742	683	67	27	5	21	58			.251	.257	.301	558	92	-13	-29	104	105	51	67	5
MUT	30	38	3	.441	35.5	13	21	328	425	2704	633	82	21	7	19	47			.236	.241	.290	531	82	-35	-55	105	20	24	45	-4
CHI	30	37	2	.448	35	16	16	379	416	2706	699	83	16	0	21	65			.260	.266	.303	569	99	0	-4	101	69	50	58	-2
NH	7	40	0	.149	48	3	24	170	397	1728	373	41	13	2	14	62			.218	.224	.260	484	80	-49	-17	87	35	16	69	2
WAS	5	23	0	.179	40.5	2	10	107	338	1010	194	14	8	0	6	42			.193	.198	.223	421	50	-50	-46	96	23	7	77	3
RS	4	15	0	.211	37	3	11	60	161	700	137	20	1	0	12	45			.199	.213	.231	444	62	-28	-19	90	27	9	75	3
CEN	2	12	0	.143	36.5	0	7	70	138	540	125	22	3	0	10	25			.236	.250	.289	539	97	-5	2	92	4	0	0	1
ATL	2	42	0	.045	51.5	1	26	132	438	1570	304	33	6	2	8	36			.195	.199	.227	426	57	-75	-50	87	1	5	17	-2
WES	1	12	0	.077	37	1	7	45	88	450	81	9	6	0	1	22			.180	.182	.227	409	41	-25	-27	105	4	6	40	-1
TOT	345					167	168	4234		27082	6812	839	273	40	249	675			.254	.261	.310	571					629	320	66	26

TEAM	CG	SHO	GR	SV	IP	H	HR	BB	SO	BR/9	ERA	AERA	OAV	OOB	PR	APR	PF	OSB	OCS	FA	E	WPB	DP	FW	PW	BW	BSW	DIF
BOS	60	10	24	17	732.0	751	2	33	110	9.6	1.87	115	.248	.256	29	23	96			.870	483	113	56	4.3	2.0	14.4	.5	10.3
HAR	83	13	3	0	770.0	708	4	11	152	8.4	1.57	150	.228	.231	56	63	105			.881	438	98	47	7.8	5.4	-1.7	.0	1.5
ATH	75	6	2	0	687.0	776	4	39	45	10.7	2.40	100	.268	.278	-13	0	107			.876	419	83	51	5.7	.0	3.5	-.2	7.5
STL	67	5	3	1	630.0	636	3	21	71	9.4	2.10	96	.241	.247	9	-7	90			.869	425	94	36	3.0	-.6	1.5	.8	.4
PHI	64	5	6	0	628.0	652	6	30	42	9.8	2.12	107	.243	.251	7	11	102			.848	477	78	32	.5	.9	-2.5	.3	3.8
MUT	70	3	1	0	636.2	718	4	21	77	10.4	2.46	95	.258	.264	-17	-9	105			.838	526	100	30	-1.5	-.8	-4.7	-.5	3.5
CHI	65	7	4	0	625.0	649	0	26	55	9.7	1.63	139	.243	.250	42	44	102			.853	478	147	30	.1	3.8	-.3	-.3	-6.7
NH	40	0	8	0	425.0	501	5	21	54	11.1	2.65	78	.254	.262	-20	-29	93			.814	447	103	24	-5.7	-2.5	-1.5	.0	-6.8
WAS	23	0	5	0	250.2	397	6	10	6	14.6	3.77	63	.311	.317	-43	-37	107			.791	285	69	8	-4.3	-3.2	-3.9	.0	2.3
RS	16	2	3	0	171.0	209	0	3	21	11.2	2.63	83	.267	.269	-8	-9	98			.833	150	69	6	-.8	-.8	-1.6	.0	-2.3
CEN	14	0	0	0	126.0	169	0	5	6	12.4	2.71	80	.274	.280	-7	-8	98			.769	164	36	5	-3.2	-.7	.2	-.0	-1.2
ATL	31	0	14	0	396.0	535	6	17	16	12.5	3.16	66	.285	.291	-41	-51	94			.801	432	110	20	-6.0	-4.4	-4.3	-.3	-5.0
WES	13	0	0	0	113.0	111	0	12	20	9.8	1.83	133	.225	.243	5	7	110			.860	78	46	5	.6	.6	-2.3	-.3	-4.1
TOT	621	51	73	18	6190.1					10.3	2.23		.254	.261						.849	4802	1146	350					

Batter-Fielder Wins
Barnes-Bos 4.2
White-Bos 3.9
McVey-Bos 3.7
Pike-StL 2.8
G.Wright-Bos 2.1

Batting Average
White-Bos............367
Barnes-Bos...........364
McVey-Bos 355
Pike-StL 346
G.Wright-Bos 333

On-Base Percentage
Barnes-Bos 375
White-Bos 372
McVey-Bos...................356
Pike-StL 352
G.Wright-Bos 337

Slugging Average
McVey-Bos 517
Pike-StL 494
Craver-Cen-Ath.....455
White-Bos.............453
Barnes-Bos...........443

On-Base Plus Slugging
McVey-Bos 873
Pike-StL 846
White-Bos 824
Barnes-Bos 818
Craver-Cen-Ath 779

Adjusted OPS
Pike-StL 210
McVey-Bos 193
White-Bos 178
Barnes-Bos 177
G.Wright-Bos 159

Adjusted Batter Runs
Pike-StL...............35.1
McVey-Bos 34.8
Barnes-Bos 28.8
White-Bos 27.8
G.Wright-Bos......22.4

Runs
Barnes-Bos 115
G.Wright-Bos........106
O'Rourke-Bos 97
McVey-Bos 89
Leonard-Bos 87

Hits
Barnes-Bos 143
McVey-Bos 138
G.Wright-Bos 136
White-Bos 136
Leonard-Bos 127

Doubles
McVey-Bos 36
White-Bos 23
Pike-StL 22
Force-Ath 22

Triples
Craver-Cen-Ath 13
Pike-StL 12
Hall-Ath 12
McVey-Bos 9
Meyerle-Phi 8

Home Runs
O'Rourke-Bos 6
Start-Mut 4
Hall-Ath 4
Hallinan-Wes-Mut 3
McVey-Bos 3

Total Bases
McVey-Bos 201
G.Wright-Bos 176
Barnes-Bos 174
White-Bos 168
Leonard-Bos 156

Runs Batted In
McVey-Bos 87
Leonard-Bos..........74
O'Rourke-Bos........72
Hall-Ath 62
G.Wright-Bos 61

Stolen Bases
Murnane-Phi 30
Barnes-Bos 29
Pike-StL 25
Dehlman-StL 23
Burdock-Har 20

Base Stealing Runs
Barnes-Bos............4.3
Cuthbert-StL..........3.6
Murnane-Phi...........3.5
McGeary-Phi 2.8
Battin-StL 2.3

Fielding Runs-Infield
Barnes-Bos 23.0
Battin-StL.....................15.4
Sutton-Ath 13.2
Pearce-StL..................11.3
Force-Ath 10.8

Fielding Runs-Outfield
Gedney-Mut 10.9
Anson-Ath.............7.3
A.Allison-Was-Har 5.0
York-Har 4.0
Eggler-Ath.............3.8

Wins
Spalding-Bos 54
McBride-Ath............44
Cummings-Har 35
Bradley-StL 33

Winning Pct.
Spalding-Bos 915
Manning-Bos 889
McBride-Ath 759
Cummings-Har 745
Zettlein-Chi-Phi.....569

Complete Games
Mathews-Mut 69
McBride-Ath 59
Bradley-StL............57
Spalding-Bos 52
Zettlein-Chi-Phi 49

Strikeouts
Cummings-Har 82
Spalding-Bos..........75
Mathews-Mut..........75
Bond-Har...............70
Bradley-StL 60

Fewest BB/Game
Cummings-Har 09
Blong-RS 14
Galvin-StL..............15
Bond-Har 18
Fisher-Phi 23

Games
Spalding-Bos 72
Mathews-Mut 70
McBride-Ath 60
Bradley-StL....................60
Zettlein-Chi-Phi.............52

Saves
Spalding-Bos 9
Manning-Bos 6
McVey-Bos 1
Heifer-Bos 1
Galvin-StL 1

Base Runners/9
Borden-Phi 7.36
Galvin-StL............7.84
Bond-Har 7.90
Cummings-Har 8.68
Fisher-Phi 8.90

Adjusted Relief Runs

Relief Ranking

Innings Pitched
Mathews-Mut 625.2
Spalding-Bos 570.2
McBride-Ath 538.0
Bradley-StL........535.2
Zettlein-Chi-Phi..463.1

Opponents' Avg.
Borden-Phi 181
Galvin-StL.............209
Bond-Har 216
Fisher-Phi 229
Cummings-Har 235

Opponents' OBP
Borden-Phi..................203
Galvin-StL 212
Bond-Har 219
Fisher-Phi 233
Cummings-Har 236

Earned Run Average
Galvin-StL...........1.16
Bond-Har 1.41
Borden-Phi 1.50
Zettlein-Chi-Phi....1.59
Spalding-Bos 1.59

Adjusted ERA
Galvin-StL 173
Bond-Har..............167
Borden-Phi 152
Cummings-Har 146
Zettlein-Chi-Phi 143

Adjusted Starter Runs
Cummings-Har 33.6
Spalding-Bos 33.2
Bond-Har 32.7
Zettlein-Chi-Phi....23.7
Fisher-Phi 13.5

Pitcher Wins
Spalding-Bos 4.4
Bond-Har............3.1
Cummings-Har..2.7
Zettlein-Chi-Phi 1.4
Devlin-Chi 1.2

Windup

Why did the National Association last only five seasons? There were several factors, including gambling, revolving players, and the inability of most clubs to turn a profit. Many of these problems stemmed from the league's big issue—the lack of competition. Harry Wright's Boston Red Stockings won the final 24 games of 1875 after starting the year without a loss in their first 22. On the other end of the standings was Brooklyn, which finished with an unfathomable .045 winning percentage.

The coming and going of franchises severely hurt the league's credibility. Twenty-three different teams played in the NA over five seasons. Only the Red Stockings, Atlantics, and Mutuals were around for the whole show. Because the franchise fee was just $10, there were always teams seemingly guaranteed to fail.

Just seven of 13 teams finished the 1875 season. The Westerns of Keokuk, Iowa, played on a former cornfield bounded by a lake known to swallow up outfielders; it was no surprise that the Westerns disbanded after 13 games. The Washington Nationals, back in the league after a two-year absence, learned one afternoon in St. Louis that the team could not pay their players' way back home. The St. Louis Brown Stockings, who drew a league record 78,000 fans in their only season in the NA, covered their fares back to Washington.

While Boston killed competition in the league, it was the breaking up of that club by Chicago owner William Hulbert (even as the Red Stockings continued drubbing his team) that spelled doom for the NA. Hulbert induced Al Spalding, still under contract to Boston, to join his club. With Spalding's help, Hulbert signed three of Boston's best hitters—Cal McVey, Ross Barnes, and James "Deacon" White—while also luring Cap Anson from the Athletics.

Hulbert had undercut the NA's lax organization and, seeking greater professionalism and profit, made his own arrangements with the owners of other clubs that winter. Six cities that had fielded NA ballclubs in 1875 played ball in an eight-team confederation the next spring. This was the birth of the National League.

1876 National League

TEAM	W	L	T	PCT	GB	HW	HL	R	OR	PA	H	2B	3B	HR	BB	SO	HB	SH	AVG	OBP	SLG	OPS	AOPS	BR	ABR	PF	SB	CS	BSA	BSR
CHI	52	14	0	.788		**25**	6	**624**	257	2818	**926**	**131**	**32**	8	**70**	**45**			**.337**	**.353**	**.417**	**770**	**140**	**164**	**102**	112				
STL	45	19	0	.703	6	24	6	386	**229**	2537	642	73	27	2	59	63			.259	.276	.313	589	102	-7	14	95				
HAR	47	21	1	.691	6	23	9	429	261	2703	711	96	22	2	39	78			.267	.277	.322	599	92	2	-29	108				
BOS	39	31	0	.557	15	19	17	471	450	2780	723	96	24	**9**	58	98			.266	.281	.328	609	102	12	5	102				
LOU	30	36	3	.455	22	15	16	280	344	2594	641	68	14	6	24	98			.249	.256	.294	550	71	-43	-95	118				
NY	21	35	1	.375	26	13	20	260	412	2198	494	39	15	2	18	35			.227	.233	.261	494	75	-79	-42	87				
PHI	14	45	1	.237	34.5	10	24	378	534	2414	646	79	35	7	27	36			.271	.279	.342	621	108	15	18	99				
CIN	9	56	0	.138	42.5	6	24	238	579	2413	555	51	12	4	41	136			.234	.247	.271	518	86	-64	-14	86				
TOT	260					135	122	3066		20457	5338	633	181	40	336	589			.265	.277	.321	598								

TEAM	CG	SHO	GR	SV	IP	H	HR	BB	SO	BR/9	ERA	AERA	OAV	OOB	PR	APR	PF	OSB	OCS	FA	E	WPB	DP	FW	PW	BW	BSW	DIF
CHI	58	9	9	4	592.1	608	6	29	51	9.7	1.76	139	.247	.256	36	42	106			.899	282	**34**	33	6.0	3.7	**9.0**		.4
STL	63	**16**	1	0	577.0	**472**	3	39	103	**8.0**	**1.22**	**175**	**.210**	**.224**	**70**	**64**	93			**.902**	**268**	91	33	**6.1**	**5.6**	1.2		.0
HAR	**69**	11	0	0	624.0	570	**2**	27	114	8.6	1.67	142	.227	.235	44	47	103			.888	337	46	27	4.0	4.1	-2.5		7.4
BOS	49	3	**21**	**7**	632.0	732	7	104	77	11.9	2.51	90	.268	.295	-14	-18	98			.860	442	108	42	-1.1	-1.6	.4		6.3
LOU	67	5	2	0	643.0	605	3	38	**125**	9.0	1.69	160	.229	.240	44	62	118			.875	397	70	44	.9	5.5	-8.4		-1.0
NY	56	2	1	0	530.0	718	8	**24**	37	12.6	2.94	73	.302	.309	-37	-50	93			.825	473	40	18	-6.8	-4.4	-3.7		7.9
PHI	53	1	7	2	550.0	783	**2**	41	22	13.5	3.22	75	.310	.321	-56	-46	105			.839	456	143	32	-5.0	-4.0	1.6		-8.1
CIN	57	0	9	0	591.0	850	9	34	60	13.5	3.62	61	.313	.322	-86	-99	95			.841	469	109	**45**	-4.1	-8.7	-1.2		-9.5
TOT	472	47	50	13	4739.1					10.8	2.31		.265	.277						.866	3124	641	274					

Batter-Fielder Wins
Barnes-Chi 4.2
Anson-Chi 2.8
G.Wright-Bos 2.5
Battin-StL 2.3
Hall-Phi 2.0

Batting Average
Barnes-Chi .429
Hall-Phi .366
Anson-Chi .356
Peters-Chi .351
McVey-Chi .347

On-Base Percentage
Barnes-Chi .462
Hall-Phi .384
Anson-Chi .380
White-Chi .358
O'Rourke-Bos .358

Slugging Average
Barnes-Chi .590
Hall-Phi .545
Pike-StL .472
Anson-Chi .450
Meyerle-Phi .449

On-Base Plus Slugging
Barnes-Chi 1052
Hall-Phi 929
Anson-Chi 830
Pike-StL 813
Meyerle-Phi 797

Adjusted OPS
Barnes-Chi 222
Hall-Phi 208
Pike-StL 178
Meyerle-Phi 165
Jones-Cin 162

Adjusted Batter Runs
Barnes-Chi 39.7
Hall-Phi 29.0
Pike-StL 23.5
Jones-Cin 20.6
O'Rourke-Bos 18.8

Runs
Barnes-Chi 126
G.Wright-Bos 72
Peters-Chi 70
White-Chi 66
Burdock-Har 66

Hits
Barnes-Chi 138
Peters-Chi 111
Anson-Chi 110
McVey-Chi 107
White-Chi 104

Doubles
Hines-Chi 21
Higham-Har 21
Barnes-Chi 21
Pike-StL 19

Triples
Barnes-Chi 14
Hall-Phi 13
Pike-StL 10
Meyerle-Phi 8

Home Runs
Hall-Phi 5
Jones-Cin 4

Total Bases
Barnes-Chi 190
Hall-Phi 146
Anson-Chi 139
Hines-Chi 134

Runs Batted In
White-Chi 60
Hines-Chi 59
Barnes-Chi 59
Anson-Chi 59
McVey-Chi 53

Stolen Bases

Base Stealing Runs

Fielding Runs-Infield
Somerville-Lou 27.6
Force-Phi-NY 19.8
Battin-StL 14.5
G.Wright-Bos 14.1
Anson-Chi 13.7

Fielding Runs-Outfield
F.Treacey-NY 9.1
Remsen-Har 7.0
Pierson-Cin 4.5
Hines-Chi 4.4
Snyder-Cin 3.8

Wins
Spalding-Chi 47
Bradley-StL 45
Bond-Har 31
Devlin-Lou 30
Mathews-NY 21

Winning Pct.
Spalding-Chi .797
Manning-Bos .783
Bond-Har .705
Bradley-StL .703
Cummings-Har .667

Complete Games
Devlin-Lou 66
Bradley-StL 63
Mathews-NY 55
Spalding-Chi 53
Bond-Har 45

Strikeouts
Devlin-Lou 122
Bradley-StL 103
Bond-Har 88
Spalding-Chi 39
Mathews-NY 37

Fewest BB/Game
Zettlein-Phi 23
Fisher-Cin 24
Bond-Har 29
Mathews-NY 42
Williams-Cin 43

Games
Devlin-Lou 68
Bradley-StL 64
Spalding-Chi 61
Mathews-NY 56
Bond-Har 45

Saves
Manning-Bos 5
Zettlein-Phi 2
McVey-Chi 2

Base Runners/9
Bradley-StL 7.98
Bond-Har 8.12
Devlin-Lou 8.73
Cummings-Har 9.54
Spalding-Chi 9.67

Adjusted Relief Runs

Relief Ranking

Innings Pitched
Devlin-Lou 622.0
Bradley-StL 573.0
Spalding-Chi 528.2
Mathews-NY 516.0
Bond-Har 408.0

Opponents' Avg.
Bradley-StL .211
Bond-Har .220
Devlin-Lou .224
Cummings-Har .239
Spalding-Chi .247

Opponents' OBP
Bradley-StL .224
Bond-Har .227
Devlin-Lou .235
Cummings-Har .251
Spalding-Chi .256

Earned Run Average
Bradley-StL 1.23
Devlin-Lou 1.56
Cummings-Har 1.67
Bond-Har 1.68
Spalding-Chi 1.75

Adjusted ERA
Bradley-StL 174
Devlin-Lou 174
Cummings-Har 142
Bond-Har 141
Spalding-Chi 139

Adjusted Starter Runs
Devlin-Lou 67.5
Bradley-StL 62.6
Spalding-Chi 38.7
Bond-Har 32.2
Cummings-Har 15.0

Pitcher Wins
Devlin-Lou 6.2
Bradley-StL 6.2
Spalding-Chi 4.3
Bond-Har 3.1
McVey-Chi .7

Get This Party Started

William Hulbert, owner of Chicago's National Association club, created a new league with the power and profits resting with the owners, rather than players. The National League began play on April 22, Boston beating Philadelphia, 6–5, with Jim O'Rourke connecting for the first hit. Boston (Atlanta Braves) and Chicago (Cubs), both former NA clubs, continue NL affiliations to this day.

Since 1870s baseball was about action, batters called for pitches where they wanted them (high, low, or "fair"). Nine balls were required for a batter to earn a walk. Home plate was square, rather than five-sided, and catchers stood straight up. Nobody used gloves.

Four strikes were required for a strikeout; after two strikes, a hitter ignoring a good ball was given a warning. Though the pitcher's box was just 45 feet away, pitchers were still required to throw underhand or sidearm, and didn't get much speed on the ball. In addition, batted balls bouncing foul before crossing first or third base were counted as fair in 1876. Many, including batting champ Ross Barnes, specialized in such trick hits, and scoring was the highest until 1887 and strikeouts at an all-time nadir.

Barnes was the league's dominant player, scoring 54 more runs than his nearest rival, George Wright. Barnes' lone home run in 1876 was the NL's first long ball, although he also led the league in doubles and triples. His White Stockings teammates were a nineteenth century "Who's Who of Baseball": Cap Anson, Paul Hines, Cal McVey, Deacon White, and pitcher Al Spalding. Pitcher George Bradley of St. Louis threw the NL's first no-hitter and led in ERA; he was also one of a handful of pitchers to exceed a strikeout per game.

Chicago ran away with the championship and, not surprisingly, led in attendance, despite 50-cent admissions (double the old rate), no alcohol, and no Sunday games—Hulbert strategies, adopted league-wide, to attract classier fans. And only the White Stockings made a profit, due to a runaway pennant race. New York and Philadelphia, finishing sixth and seventh, didn't make their final westward road trips, and Hulbert expelled them from the NL. Hulbert made his point clearly: This was not the National Association.

1877 National League

TEAM	W	L	T	PCT	GB	HW	HL	R	OR	PA	H	2B	3B	HR	BB	SO	HB	SH	AVG	OBP	SLG	OPS	AOPS	BR	ABR	PF	SB	CS	BSA	BSR
BOS	42	18	1	.700		**27**	5	**419**	**263**	2433	**700**	**91**	**37**	4	**65**	**121**			**.296**	**.314**	**.370**	**684**	**114**	**49**	**35**	104				
LOU	35	25	1	.583	7	21	9	339	288	2413	659	75	36	**9**	58	140			.280	.297	.354	651	92	19	-37	118				
HAR	31	27	2	.534	10	19	8	341	311	2388	637	63	31	4	30	97			.270	.279	.328	607	105	-18	22	89				
STL	28	32	0	.467	14	20	10	284	318	2235	531	51	36	1	57	147			.244	.263	.302	565	84	-48	-32	95				
CHI	26	33	1	.441	15.5	17	12	366	375	2330	633	79	30	0	57	111			.278	.296	.340	636	92	8	-29	112				
CIN	15	42	1	.263	25.5	12	17	291	485	2213	545	72	34	6	78	110			.255	.282	.329	611	107	-10	29	89				
TOT	180					116	61	2040		14012	3705	431	204	24	345	726			.271	.289	.338	627								

TEAM	CG	SHO	GR	SV	IP	H	HR	BB	SO	BR/9	ERA	AERA	OAV	OOB	PR	APR	PF	OSB	OCS	FA	E	WPB	DP	FW	PW	BW	BSW	DIF
BOS	**61**	**7**	0	0	548.0	**557**	5	**38**	**177**	**9.8**	**2.15**	130	**.249**	**.261**	**40**	40	100			.889	290	68	36	1.2	3.6	**3.1**		4.1
LOU	**61**	4	0	0	559.0	617	4	41	141	10.6	2.25	**147**	.270	.283	34	**56**	118			**.904**	**267**	80	37	**2.4**	**5.0**	-3.3		.9
HAR	59	4	1	0	544.0	572	**2**	56	99	10.4	2.32	105	.253	.271	30	8	87			.885	313	**56**	32	-.2	.7	2.0		-.5
STL	52	1	8	0	541.0	582	**2**	92	132	11.2	2.66	98	.262	.291	9	-4	93			.892	281	110	29	1.4	-.4	-2.9		-.2
CHI	45	3	**16**	**3**	534.0	630	7	58	92	11.6	3.37	88	.274	.292	-33	-22	106			.883	313	119	**43**	-.2	-2.0	-2.6		1.2
CIN	48	1	10	1	515.0	747	4	61	85	14.1	4.19	63	.318	.335	-79	-94	94			.851	394	128	33	-4.7	-8.4	2.6		-3.0
TOT	326	20	35	4	3241.0					11.2	2.81		.271	.289						.884	1858	561	210					

Batter-Fielder Wins	Batting Average	On-Base Percentage	Slugging Average	On-Base Plus Slugging	Adjusted OPS	Adjusted Batter Runs
Jones-Cin-Chi-Cin....2.6	D.White-Bos 387	O'Rourke-Bos 407	D.White-Bos 545	D.White-Bos..........950	D.White-Bos..........190	D.White-Bos 25.9
D.White-Bos........2.2	Cassidy-Har 378	D.White-Bos................405	Jones-Cin-Chi-Cin ...471	O'Rourke-Bos 852	Cassidy-Har..........184	Cassidy-Har........24.2
Peters-Chi............2.0	McVey-Chi 368	McVey-Chi 387	Cassidy-Har 458	Cassidy-Har..........844	Jones-Cin-Chi-Cin....175	Jones-Cin-Chi-Cin..21.7
Gerhardt-Lou......1.7	O'Rourke-Bos.......362	Cassidy-Har.................386	McVey-Chi 455	McVey-Chi 842	O'Rourke-Bos 162	O'Rourke-Bos 19.6
Cassidy-Har........1.6	Anson-Chi.............337	Anson-Chi 360	O'Rourke-Bos.......445	Jones-Cin-Chi-Cin....824	Manning-Cin 157	Manning-Cin 17.2

Runs	Hits	Doubles	Triples	Home Runs	Total Bases	Runs Batted In
O'Rourke-Bos 68	D.White-Bos..........103	Anson-Chi......................19	D.White-Bos............11	Pike-Cin....................4	D.White-Bos..........145	D.White-Bos 49
G.Wright-Bos...........58	McVey-Chi 98	York-Har 16	Jones-Cin-Chi-Cin......10	Shafer-Lou................3	McVey-Chi 121	Peters-Chi 41
McVey-Chi 58	O'Rourke-Bos 96	Manning-Cin 16	Hall-Lou 8	Jones-Cin-Chi-Cin.......2	O'Rourke-Bos 118	Sutton-Bos 39
Start-Har 55	Cassidy-Har............95	G.Wright-Bos 15	Brown-Bos................8	D.White-Bos.............2	Hall-Lou 118	Jones-Cin-Chi-Cin 38
	Start-Har 90	Hall-Lou 15		Snyder-Lou 2	Cassidy-Har..........115	York-Har 37

Stolen Bases	Base Stealing Runs	Fielding Runs-Infield	Fielding Runs-Outfield	Wins	Winning Pct.	Complete Games
		Peters-Chi 20.0	Jones-Cin-Chi-Cin ..12.8	Bond-Bos................40	Bond-Bos 702	Devlin-Lou 61
		Gerhardt-Lou 18.6	Shafer-Lou 12.7	Devlin-Lou 35	Devlin-Lou 583	Bond-Bos 58
		Ferguson-Har..............17.3	Crowley-Lou 7.5	Larkin-Har 29	Larkin-Har.............537	Larkin-Har 55
		G.Wright-Bos 9.7	Addy-Cin................4.9	Nichols-StL 18	Nichols-StL 439	Nichols-StL............35
		Foley-Cin 6.7	Pike-Cin 2.5	Bradley-Chi 18	Bradley-Chi...........439	Bradley-Chi............35

Strikeouts	Fewest BB/Game	Games	Saves	Base Runners/9	Adjusted Relief Runs	Relief Ranking
Bond-Bos.............170	Bond-Bos 62	Devlin-Lou......................61	McVey-Chi 2	Bond-Bos 9.78		
Devlin-Lou 141	Devlin-Lou 66	Bond-Bos 58	Spalding-Chi 1	Larkin-Har..........10.11		
Larkin-Har 96	Cummings-Cin 75	Larkin-Har......................56	Manning-Cin 1	Devlin-Lou 10.59		
Nichols-StL 80	Bradley-Chi............89	Bradley-Chi....................50		Nichols-StL........11.03		
Bradley-Chi 59	Larkin-Har..............95	Nichols-StL 42		Bradley-Chi........11.22		

Innings Pitched	Opponents' Avg.	Opponents' OBP	Earned Run Average	Adjusted ERA	Adjusted Starter Runs	Pitcher Wins
Devlin-Lou 559.0	Larkin-Har.............245	Bond-Bos....................261	Bond-Bos 2.11	Devlin-Lou 147	Devlin-Lou 55.5	**Devlin-Lou**..........5.0
Bond-Bos 521.0	Bond-Bos 249	Larkin-Har 264	Larkin-Har............2.14	Bond-Bos..............133	Bond-Bos 39.8	**Bond-Bos**............3.3
Larkin-Har..........501.0	Blong-StL 262	Devlin-Lou 283	Devlin-Lou 2.25	Larkin-Har 114	Larkin-Har............13.5	**Larkin-Har**..........1.6
Bradley-Chi........394.0	Nichols-StL 263	Bradley-Chi 286	Nichols-StL 2.60	Nichols-StL 100	Reis-Chi 7.8	**Reis-Chi**.................6
Nichols-StL 350.0	Bradley-Chi...........269	Nichols-StL 289	Blong-StL 2.74	Blong-StL................95	Nichols-StL 1.6	

Ramblin' Gamblin' Man

Jim Devlin was one of the finest pitchers in baseball during the 1870s. His great mound work—and the bat of outfielder George Hall—led the Louisville Grays to a big lead in the 1877 NL race. But an inexplicable late-season slump gave Boston the crown. An investigation of the Grays' desultory stretch performance led William Hulbert to ban, for life, four Louisville players—Devlin, Hall, Bill Craver, and Al Nichols—for throwing games. The troubled Devlin died six years later, still begging for reinstatement.

Boston, under Harry Wright, won a tainted title but had the league's top hitters in Deacon White and Jim O'Rourke. Chicago fell to fifth, becoming the only big league team ever to go an entire season without a homer. St. Louis barely missed joining the White Stockings in ignominy, but the Brown Stockings were spared by Jim Battin's lone career NL long ball.

The catcher's mask was first worn this year, and Chicago's Al Spalding, losing his mound skill, began wearing a glove on his catching hand when he played first base. Spalding retired after a final game in 1878 to sell sporting goods. Candy Cummings, purported inventor of the curveball, threw his last major league pitch for Cincinnati. Cummings was a success in the National Association—winning at least 28 games each season—but he was a flop in the new circuit.

The modified strike zone had a "low" pitch ranging from belt to knee and a "high" pitch above the belt and up to the shoulder. Runs declined, although batting average and OPS rose. Strikeouts increased as well. Other rules changes included the abolition of the "fair-foul rule," which helped end Ross Barnes' career, and the placement of home plate in fair territory. In 1877 the home team was allowed to bat first, and no substitutions were allowed, except for injury, after the start of the second inning.

Following the traumatic season, Louisville—along with Hartford and St. Louis—dropped out of the league, which therefore had to scramble for new clubs prior to the 1878 season.

1878 National League

TEAM	W	L	T	PCT	GB	HW	HL	R	OR	PA	H	2B	3B	HR	BB	SO	HB	SH	AVG	OBP	SLG	OPS	AOPS	BR	ABR	PF	SB	CS	BSA	BSR
BOS	41	19	0	.683		23	7	298	**241**	2255	535	75	25	2	35	154			.241	.253	.300	553	79	-36	-55	108				
CIN	37	23	1	.617	4	**25**	8	333	281	2339	**629**	67	22	5	**58**	**141**			**.276**	**.294**	.331	**625**	**120**	**20**	**55**	91				
PRO	33	27	2	.550	8	17	13	**353**	337	2348	604	**107**	**30**	**8**	50	218			.263	.279	**.346**	**625**	109	**20**	21	100				
CHI	30	30	1	.500	11	17	18	371	331	2421	677	91	20	3	88	157			.290	.316	.350	666	115	58	34	107				
IND	24	36	3	.400	17	10	17	293	328	2364	542	76	15	3	64	197			.236	.256	.286	542	95	-43	0	87				
MIL	15	45	1	.250	26	7	18	256	386	2281	552	65	20	2	69	214			.250	.272	.300	572	86	-19	-37	107				
TOT	184					99	81	1904		14008	3539	481	132	23	364	1081			.259	.279	.319	598								

TEAM	CG	SHO	GR	SV	IP	H	HR	BB	SO	BR/9	ERA	AERA	OAV	OOB	PR	APR	PF	OSB	OCS	FA	E	WPB	DP	FW	PW	BW	BSW	DIF
BOS	58	**9**	2	0	544.0	595	6	38	184	10.5	2.32	102	.272	.284	-1	2	102			**.914**	**228**	**62**	**48**	**3.5**	.2	-5.1		12.4
CIN	**61**	6	0	0	548.0	**546**	**2**	63	**220**	**10.0**	**1.84**	**116**	**.248**	.269	**28**	**19**	92			.900	269	99	37	1.5	**1.8**	**5.1**		-1.4
PRO	59	6	4	0	556.0	609	5	86	173	11.3	2.38	93	.265	.291	-5	-12	96			.892	311	133	42	-.5	-1.1	2.0		2.7
CHI	**61**	1	0	0	551.0	577	4	**35**	175	**10.0**	2.37	102	.253	**.265**	-4	3	105			.891	304	141	37	-.4	.3	3.2		-3.0
IND	59	2	4	**1**	578.0	621	3	87	182	11.0	2.32	87	.262	.288	-1	-22	88			.898	290	95	37	.9	-2.1	.0		-4.8
MIL	54	1	**7**	0	547.0	589	3	55	147	10.6	2.60	101	.255	.272	-18	1	114			.866	376	149	32	-4.4	.0	-3.5		-7.2
TOT	352	25	17	1	3324.0					10.6	2.30		.259	.279						.893	1778	679	233					

Batter-Fielder Wins	Batting Average	On-Base Percentage	Slugging Average	On-Base Plus Slugging	Adjusted OPS	Adjusted Batter Runs
Shafer-Ind 3.3	Dalrymple-Mil 354	Ferguson-Chi 375	Hines-Pro 486	Hines-Pro 849	Shafer-Ind 196	Shafer-Ind 29.3
Ferguson-Chi 2.8	Hines-Pro 358	Anson-Chi 372	York-Pro 465	Shafer-Ind 824	Hines-Pro 177	Hines-Pro 20.4
Burdock-Bos 2.0	Ferguson-Chi 351	Shafer-Ind 369	Shafer-Ind............455	Start-Chi 794	Jones-Cin 163	Jones-Cin 17.5
Hines-Pro 1.7	Start-Chi 351	Dalrymple-Mil..............368	Brown-Pro 453	York-Pro................793	York-Pro................159	York-Pro 16.5
Jones-Cin 1.7	Anson-Chi.............341	Hines-Pro....................363	Jones-Cin 441	Dalrymple-Mil 789	Brown-Pro 153	Clapp-Ind............15.6

Runs	Hits	Doubles	Triples	Home Runs	Total Bases	Runs Batted In
Higham-Pro 60	Start-Chi 100	Higham-Pro 22	York-Pro..................10	Hines-Pro 4	York-Pro................125	Hines-Pro 50
Start-Chi 58	Dalrymple-Mil 96	Brown-Pro......................21	O'Rourke-Bos 7	Jones-Cin 3	Start-Chi 125	Brown-Pro 43
York-Pro..................56	Hines-Pro 92	York-Pro 19	Jones-Cin 7	McVey-Cin 2	Hines-Pro 125	Anson-Chi 40
Anson-Chi 55	Ferguson-Chi..........91	Shafer-Ind.......................19		McKelvy-Ind.............2	Shafer-Ind 121	Jones-Cin 39
Dalrymple-Mil 52		O'Rourke-Bos 17			Higham-Pro 117	Ferguson-Chi 39

Stolen Bases	Base Stealing Runs	Fielding Runs-Infield	Fielding Runs-Outfield	Wins	Winning Pct.	Complete Games
		Burdock-Bos 21.2	Shafer-Ind..............7.6	Bond-Bos................40	Bond-Bos 678	Bond-Bos 57
		Hague-Pro 19.1	Cassidy-Chi 7.3	W.White-Cin............30	Ward-Pro 629	Larkin-Chi..............56
		Ferguson-Chi 16.6	Dalrymple-Mil 6.8	Larkin-Chi 29	W.White-Cin 588	W.White-Cin 52
		Wright-Bos..................10.3	Jones-Cin 4.4	Ward-Pro 22	Larkin-Chi.............527	Weaver-Mil 39
		Hankinson-Chi..............7.9	Remsen-Chi 4.2	Nolan-Ind................13		

Strikeouts	Fewest BB/Game	Games	Saves	Base Runners/9	Adjusted Relief Runs	Relief Ranking
Bond-Bos..............182	Weaver-Mil 49	Bond-Bos 59	Healey-Pro-Ind 1	Weaver-Mil 9.21		
W.White-Cin..........169	Larkin-Chi................55	Larkin-Chi.......................56		Ward-Pro 9.22		
Larkin-Chi 163	Bond-Bos 56	W.White-Cin 52		Larkin-Chi............9.64		
Nolan-Ind..............125	Nichols-Pro.............73	Weaver-Mil 45		Mitchell-Cin..........9.79		
Ward-Pro 116	W.White-Cin 87	Nolan-Ind 38		W.White-Cin 10.04		

Innings Pitched	Opponents' Avg.	Opponents' OBP	Earned Run Average	Adjusted ERA	Adjusted Starter Runs	Pitcher Wins
Bond-Bos 532.2	Mitchell-Cin...........223	Weaver-Mil..................247	Ward-Pro 1.51	Ward-Pro 146	Weaver-Mil 23.1	**Ward-Pro** 2.2
Larkin-Chi...........506.0	Ward-Pro 231	Ward-Pro 251	McCormick-Ind 1.69	Weaver-Mil.............134	Ward-Pro 21.8	**Weaver-Mil** 2.1
W.White-Cin 468.0	Weaver-Mil 237	Larkin-Chi 257	W.White-Cin 1.79	McCormick-Ind 120	W.White-Cin 15.7	**Larkin-Chi** 1.9
Weaver-Mil 383.0	Larkin-Chi.............246	Mitchell-Cin 265	Weaver-Mil 1.95	W.White-Cin..........119	Bond-Bos 13.8	**Bond-Bos**..............9
Nolan-Ind 347.0	W.White-Cin 252	W.White-Cin.................269	Bond-Bos 2.06	Bond-Bos..............114	Larkin-Chi..............9.6	**W.White-Cin** 6

A Good Defense

With new franchises in Providence, Indianapolis, and Milwaukee, the six-team National League took on an increasingly Midwestern look. (Newly organized "minor" leagues, chiefly the International Association, had started up to fill the need for organized baseball in the East.) Beginning in 1878 clubs used turnstiles to figure attendance, and team captains mutually determined which team would hit first. Batting orders were also required to remain consistent during the game.

Fortified by free agents Cal McVey, who managed and played third base, and Deacon White, the Cincinnati Red Stockings rose from last to second. Pitcher Will White, Deacon's brother, was outstanding in his first full year, helping the club post the league's best ERA. Paul Hines of third-place Providence won the league's first Triple Crown, but abysmal second-line pitching and poor defense scuttled his club's chances.

Boston won the flag by 4 games under legendary skipper Harry Wright. The starting lineup played nearly every inning—the team's substitute, Harry Schaefer, appeared in only 2 games. Boston's pitcher, Tommy Bond, was the NL's workhorse. He pitched in all but 1 Red Stockings game and won 40 times, 10 more than runner-up White in Cincinnati. Outstanding fielding helped the Red Stockings survive their mediocre offense. The club's .914 fielding percentage was a new record, shattering the old mark by 10 points. At this point, only a few players used gloves—Boston simply had great fielders.

Some top players made their debuts in 1878, including Milwaukee's catcher Charlie Bennett and outfielder Abner Dalrymple, Cincinnati outfielder King Kelly, Indianapolis third baseman Ed Williamson, and Providence pitcher John Montgomery Ward, who led the league with a 1.51 ERA.

Perhaps the greatest achievement from 1878 was that the NL became the first league to complete its entire schedule. It did not mean that everyone would be back on the '79 schedule, though. Indianapolis and Milwaukee, which brought up the rear of the loop in wins and attendance, were both dropped from the league after the season. NL President William Hulbert was in dire straits; despite being a Midwest chauvinist, he was forced to reach back to the East for new clubs to invite to his party.

1879 National League

TEAM	W	L	T	PCT	GB	HW	HL	R	OR	PA	H	2B	3B	HR	BB	SO	HB	SH	AVG	OBP	SLG	OPS	AOPS	BR	ABR	PF	SB	CS	BSA	BSR
PRO	59	25	1	.702		**34**	8	**612**	355	3483	**1003**	142	**55**	12	**91**	**172**			**.296**	**.314**	**.381**	**695**	**134**	**111**	**121**	98				
BOS	54	30	0	.643	5	29	13	562	**348**	3307	883	138	51	**20**	90	222			.274	.294	.368	662	118	69	58	102				
BUF	46	32	1	.590	10	23	16	394	365	2984	733	105	54	2	78	314			.252	.272	.328	600	98	-1	-11	102				
CHI	46	33	4	.582	10.5	29	13	437	411	3189	808	**167**	32	3	73	294			.259	.276	.336	612	98	18	-8	106				
CIN	43	37	1	.538	14	21	16	485	464	3151	813	127	53	8	66	207			.264	.279	.347	626	115	26	50	95				
CLE	27	55	0	.329	31	15	27	322	461	3024	666	116	29	4	37	214			.223	.232	.285	517	73	-83	-80	99				
SYR	22	48	1	.314	30	11	22	276	462	2639	592	61	19	5	28	238			.227	.235	.270	505	78	-85	-50	89				
TRO	19	56	2	.253	35.5	12	27	321	543	2886	673	102	24	4	45	182			.237	.249	.294	543	87	-54	-29	93				
TOT	321					174	142	3409		24663	6171	958	317	58	508	1843			.255	.271	.329	599								

TEAM	CG	SHO	GR	SV	IP	H	HR	BB	SO	BR/9	ERA	AERA	OAV	OOB	PR	APR	PF	OSB	OCS	FA	E	WPB	DP	FW	PW	BW	BSW	DIF
PRO	73	3	**12**	**2**	776.0	765	9	62	**329**	9.6	**2.18**	108	.243	.258	**27**	16	94			.902	382	128	41	1.8	1.5	**11.2**		2.6
BOS	79	**13**	5	0	753.0	757	9	**46**	230	9.6	2.19	**114**	.251	.262	26	**25**	100			**.913**	**319**	108	58	**4.9**	**2.3**	5.3		-.5
BUF	78	8	1	0	713.0	**698**	**3**	47	198	**9.4**	2.34	112	**.242**	**.254**	13	21	105			.906	331	99	**62**	2.9	1.9	-1.0		3.2
CHI	**82**	6	1	0	744.0	762	5	57	211	9.9	2.46	105	.244	.258	3	9	103			.900	381	**93**	52	1.3	.8	-.7		5.1
CIN	79	4	3	0	726.0	756	11	81	246	10.4	2.29	102	.248	.267	16	4	93			.878	450	166	48	-2.9	.4	4.6		.9
CLE	79	3	3	0	741.0	818	4	116	287	11.3	2.65	95	.265	.292	-12	-12	100			.889	406	178	42	-.3	-1.1	-7.4		-5.2
SYR	64	5	7	0	649.0	775	4	52	132	11.5	3.19	74	.277	.290	-50	-62	95			.873	398	150	37	-2.7	-5.7	-4.6		.0
TRO	75	3	2	0	695.0	840	13	47	210	11.5	2.80	89	.275	.286	-23	-22	100			.875	460	217	44	-4.4	-2.0	-2.7		-9.3
TOT	609	45	34	2	5797.0					10.4	2.50		.255	.271						.892	3127	1139	384					

Batter-Fielder Wins	Batting Average	On-Base Percentage	Slugging Average	On-Base Plus Slugging	Adjusted OPS	Adjusted Batter Runs
Kelly-Cin 3.9	Anson-Chi.............317	O'Rourke-Pro...............371	O'Rourke-Bos.......521	O'Rourke-Bos 877	Kelly-Cin 188	Hines-Pro 34.7
Jones-Bos 3.6	Hines-Pro 357	Hines-Pro.....................369	Jones-Bos.............510	Jones-Bos 877	Jones-Bos 182	Kelly-Cin 32.2
Williamson-Chi ..3.3	O'Rourke-Pro 348	Jones-Bos 367	Kelly-Cin 493	Kelly-Cin 855	O'Rourke-Bos 181	Jones-Bos 31.9
Hines-Pro 3.2	Kelly-Cin 348	Kelly-Cin 363	Hines-Pro 482	Hines-Pro 851	Hines-Pro 181	O'Rourke-Pro 28.7
Wright-Pro 2.9	O'Rourke-Bos 34,1	O'Rourke-Bos 357	O'Rourke-Pro 459	O'Rourke-Pro........829	O'Rourke-Pro........174	O'Rourke-Bos 26.3

Runs	Hits	Doubles	Triples	Home Runs	Total Bases	Runs Batted In
Jones-Bos 85	Hines-Pro 146	Eden-Cle........................31	Dickerson-Cin 14	Jones-Bos 9	Hines-Pro 197	O'Rourke-Bos........62
Hines-Pro 81	O'Rourke-Pro........126	York-Pro 25	Williamson-Chi 13	O'Rourke-Bos 6	Jones-Bos 181	Jones-Bos 62
Wright-Pro 79	Kelly-Cin 120	Hines-Pro 25	Kelly-Cin 12	Brouthers-Tro............4	Kelly-Cin 170	Dickerson-Cin........57
Kelly-Cin 78	Jones-Bos 112	Dalrymple-Chi................25	O'Rourke-Bos 11	Eden-Cle 3	O'Rourke-Pro........166	McVey-Cin 55
Dickerson-Cin 73	D.White-Cin 110	Houck-Bos 24			O'Rourke-Bos 165	

Stolen Bases	Base Stealing Runs	Fielding Runs-Infield	Fielding Runs-Outfield	Wins	Winning Pct.	Complete Games
		Wright-Pro 19.6	Shafer-Chi 19.2	Ward-Pro 47	Ward-Pro 712	W.White-Cin 75
		Williamson-Chi............18.9	Evans-Tro 17.6	W.White-Cin............43	Bond-Bos 694	Galvin-Buf 65
		Fulmer-Buf..................18.2	M.Mansell-Syr 14.9	Bond-Bos................43	Hankinson-Chi 600	McCormick-Cle......59
		Quest-Chi 16.0	Jones-Bos............13.0	Galvin-Buf 37	W.White-Cin 581	Bond-Bos 59
		Hawkes-Tro 14.5	Hines-Pro 4.7	Larkin-Chi 31	Galvin-Buf............578	Ward-Pro 58

Strikeouts	Fewest BB/Game	Games	Saves	Base Runners/9	Adjusted Relief Runs	Relief Ranking
Ward-Pro 239	Bond-Bos 39	W.White-Cin 76	Ward-Pro 1	Goldsmith-Tro 8.86		
W.White-Cin...........232	Galvin-Buf...............47	Ward-Pro 70	Mathews-Pro 1	Bond-Bos 9.19		
McCormick-Cle 197	Bradley-Tro 48	Galvin-Buf......................66		Ward-Pro 9.31		
Bond-Bos..............155	Larkin-Chi 53	Bond-Bos 64		Galvin-Buf............9.35		
Larkin-Chi 142	Ward-Pro 55	McCormick-Cle..............62		Larkin-Chi 9.54		

Innings Pitched	Opponents' Avg.	Opponents' OBP	Earned Run Average	Adjusted ERA	Adjusted Starter Runs	Pitcher Wins
W.White-Cin 680.0	McGunnigle-Buf ...235	Larkin-Chi 250	Bond-Bos 1.96	Bond-Bos..............127	Bond-Bos 38.8	**Bond-Bos**............4.1
Galvin-Buf..........593.0	W.White-Cin 238	Ward-Pro 250	W.White-Cin 1.99	W.White-Cin...........117	W.White-Cin 22.1	**Ward-Pro** 2.7
Ward-Pro 587.0	Ward-Pro 239	Galvin-Buf 253	Ward-Pro 2.15	Galvin-Buf 115	Galvin-Buf............20.5	**Galvin-Buf** 2.5
Bond-Bos 555.1	Larkin-Chi.............240	W.White-Cin..................256	Salisbury-Tro 2.22	Salisbury-Tro 112	Ward-Pro 12.9	**McCormick-Cle** ...6
McCormick-Cle..546.1	Galvin-Buf.............243	Bond-Bos......................259	Galvin-Buf...........2.28	Ward-Pro 110	Larkin-Chi 8.2	**Larkin-Chi** 5

The Last Free Season

To increase revenues, the NL expanded its schedule to 84 games and brought in four new teams: Troy, Cleveland, and two top International Association clubs, Buffalo and Syracuse. Despite these changes, however, league attendance was only a little higher for eight teams than it was for six clubs in 1878. Syracuse and Troy were abject failures on the field and at the gate, while Cincinnati's attendance fell dramatically.

Chicago once again had first-rate talent, including Cap Anson and Ned Williamson, and a maniacal fan base, but their pennant hopes evaporated when player-manager Anson went down in midsummer with a liver infection. Hard-charging Providence held off a late Boston rally to claim their first flag. George Wright, in his only season as a manager, bested his brother Harry, whose Boston clubs had won six titles in the last seven years in both the NA and NL. (After a salary dispute with Providence, George would return to play sparingly for Harry's Red Stockings.) Paul Hines and Jim O'Rourke provided most of the big hits for the Grays, while Monty Ward topped the league in wins and strikeouts.

Ward spent the year tossing a Spalding baseball. Former star hurler Al Spalding had retired to sell sporting goods, and he used his ties to get his ball named the official spheroid for all NL contests. Spalding also remained part owner of the Chicago White Stockings. The league adopted several new rules. A foul, hitherto an out if caught on a bounce, now had to be caught on the fly. Rules governing batting orders were established, and pitchers found to be intentionally hitting batters were fined, although batters were not yet allowed to take first base.

Boston's John O'Rourke, brother of Jim, was the league's top rookie, leading in RBIs and slugging (both calculated retroactively). Another freshman, Buffalo third baseman Hardy Richardson, eventually was the bigger star. Cincinnati pitcher Will White set the all-time record with 680 innings pitched, completing each of his 75 starts.

Only Syracuse was judged unfit for the NL. Worcester joined for 1880, giving Massachusetts, New York, and Ohio two teams apiece. Hulbert and his fellow owners had a new surprise up their sleeves: the reserve clause.

1880 National League

TEAM	W	L	T	PCT	GB	HW	HL	R	OR	PA	H	2B	3B	HR	BB	SO	HB	SH	AVG	OBP	SLG	OPS	AOPS	BR	ABR	PF	SB	CS	BSA	BSR
CHI	67	17	2	.798		**37**	5	**538**	317	3239	**876**	**164**	**39**	4	**104**	217			**.279**	**.303**	**.360**	**663**	**119**	**84**	**55**	106				
PRO	52	32	3	.619	15	31	12	419	**299**	3285	793	114	34	**8**	89	**186**			.248	.268	.313	581	101	-6	8	97				
CLE	47	37	1	.560	20	23	19	387	337	3078	726	130	52	7	76	237			.242	.261	.327	588	102	-2	6	98				
TRO	41	42	0	.494	25.5	20	21	392	438	3127	755	114	37	5	120	260			.251	.280	.319	599	100	15	-5	105				
WOR	40	43	2	.482	26.5	24	17	412	370	3105	699	129	52	**8**	81	278			.231	.251	.316	567	86	-22	-52	109				
BOS	40	44	2	.476	27	25	17	416	456	3185	779	134	41	20	105	221			.253	.278	.343	621	115	35	50	97				
BUF	24	58	3	.293	42	13	29	331	502	3052	669	104	37	3	90	327			.226	.249	.289	538	82	-49	-55	102				
CIN	21	59	3	.263	44	14	25	296	472	2970	649	91	36	7	75	267			.224	.244	.288	532	82	-56	-52	99				
TOT	340					187	145	3191		25041	5946	980	328	62	740	1993			.245	.267	.320	587								

TEAM	CG	SHO	GR	SV	IP	H	HR	BB	SO	BR/9	ERA	AERA	OAV	OOB	PR	APR	PF	OSB	OCS	FA	E	WPB	DP	FW	PW	BW	BSW	DIF
CHI	80	8	8	3	775.0	**622**	8	129	**367**	8.7	1.93	126	**.209**	.242	38	42	102			**.913**	**329**	141	41	**2.3**	4.1	**5.3**		13.3
PRO	75	**13**	12	3	799.0	663	7	**51**	286	**8.0**	**1.64**	**134**	.215	**.228**	**65**	**53**	93			.910	357	99	53	1.1	**5.2**	.8		3.0
CLE	**83**	7	2	1	759.2	685	4	98	289	9.3	1.90	124	.228	.253	40	39	99			.910	330	117	52	2.0	3.8	.6		-1.4
TRO	81	4	2	0	738.0	760	8	112	169	10.6	2.74	92	.255	.282	-30	-17	106			.900	366	160	**58**	-.3	-1.7	-.5		2.0
WOR	68	7	**18**	**5**	762.2	709	13	97	297	9.5	2.27	115	.233	.257	9	26	109			.906	355	**94**	49	.7	2.5	-5.1		.3
BOS	70	4	17	0	744.2	840	**2**	86	187	11.2	3.08	74	.276	.296	-59	-70	96			.901	367	132	54	.3	-6.8	4.9		-.4
BUF	72	6	13	1	739.0	879	10	78	186	11.7	3.09	79	.279	.297	-59	-50	104			.891	408	185	55	-2.1	-4.9	-5.3		-4.7
CIN	79	3	4	0	713.1	785	10	88	208	11.0	2.44	102	.259	.280	-5	5	105			.877	437	119	49	-4.1	.5	-5.1		-10.4
TOT	608	52	76	13	6031.1					10.0	2.37		.245	.267						.901	2949	1047	411					

Batter-Fielder Wins	Batting Average	On-Base Percentage	Slugging Average	On-Base Plus Slugging	Adjusted OPS	Adjusted Batter Runs
Clapp-Cin 3.2	Gore-Chi .360	Gore-Chi .399	Gore-Chi .463	Gore-Chi .862	Gore-Chi 180	Gore-Chi 27.3
Irwin-Wor 3.2	Anson-Chi .337	Anson-Chi .362	Connor-Tro .459	Connor-Tro .816	Connor-Tro 166	J.O'Rourke-Bos 22.4
Dunlap-Cle 2.6	Connor-Tro .332	Connor-Tro .357	Dalrymple-Chi .458	Dalrymple-Chi .793	Jones-Bos 159	Connor-Tro 22.2
Gore-Chi 2.5	Dalrymple-Chi .330	Dalrymple-Chi .335	Stovey-Wor .454	Anson-Chi .781	J.O'Rourke-Bos 158	Dalrymple-Chi 20.4
Shafer-Cle 2.3	Burns-Chi .309	Burns-Chi .333	J.O'Rourke-Bos .441	J.O'Rourke-Bos .756	Dalrymple-Chi 156	Anson-Chi 19.9

Runs	Hits	Doubles	Triples	Home Runs	Total Bases	Runs Batted In
Dalrymple-Chi 91	Dalrymple-Chi 126	Dunlap-Cle 27	Stovey-Wor 14	Stovey-Wor 6	Dalrymple-Chi 175	Anson-Chi 74
Stovey-Wor 76	Anson-Chi 120	Dalrymple-Chi 25	Dalrymple-Chi 12	J.O'Rourke-Bos 6	Stovey-Wor 161	Kelly-Chi 60
Kelly-Chi 72	Gore-Chi 116	Anson-Chi 24	J.O'Rourke-Bos 11	Jones-Bos 5	J.O'Rourke-Bos 160	Gore-Chi 47
J.O'Rourke-Bos 71	Hines-Pro 115	Gore-Chi 23	Hornung-Buf 11	Dunlap-Cle 4	Dunlap-Cle 160	Connor-Tro 47
Gore-Chi 70	Connor-Tro 113	J.O'Rourke-Bos 22	Phillips-Cle 10		Connor-Tro 156	J.O'Rourke-Bos 45

Stolen Bases	Base Stealing Runs	Fielding Runs-Infield	Fielding Runs-Outfield	Wins	Winning Pct.	Complete Games
		Irwin-Wor 29.8	Shafer-Cle 14.9	McCormick-Cle 45	Goldsmith-Chi .875	McCormick-Cle 72
		Force-Buf 26.4	Gillespie-Tro 6.3	Corcoran-Chi 43	Corcoran-Chi .754	Welch-Tro 64
		Bradley-Pro 18.4	Bond-Bos 4.8	Ward-Pro 39	Ward-Pro .619	Ward-Pro 59
		Burdock-Bos 15.1	J.O'Rourke-Bos 4.0	Welch-Tro 34	McCormick-Cle .616	W.White-Cin 58
		Williamson-Chi 10.2	Dalrymple-Chi 3.9	Richmond-Wor 32	Welch-Tro .531	

Strikeouts	Fewest BB/Game	Games	Saves	Base Runners/9	Adjusted Relief Runs	Relief Ranking
Corcoran-Chi 268	Bradley-Pro .28	Richmond-Wor 74	Richmond-Wor 3	Keefe-Tro 7.20		
McCormick-Cle 260	Galvin-Buf .63	McCormick-Cle 74	Corey-Wor 2	Bradley-Pro 7.53		
Richmond-Wor 243	Ward-Pro .68	Ward-Pro 70	Corcoran-Chi 2	Ward-Pro 8.26		
Ward-Pro 230	Wiedman-Buf .71	Welch-Tro 65	Bradley-Pro 2	Corcoran-Chi 8.44		
W.White-Cin 161	Goldsmith-Chi .77			Goldsmith-Chi 8.86		

Innings Pitched	Opponents' Avg.	Opponents' OBP	Earned Run Average	Adjusted ERA	Adjusted Starter Runs	Pitcher Wins
McCormick-Cle 657.2	Keefe-Tro .178	Keefe-Tro .212	Keefe-Tro .86	Keefe-Tro 294	McCormick-Cle 39.5	**McCormick-Cle** 4.2
Ward-Pro 595.0	Corcoran-Chi .199	Bradley-Pro .217	Bradley-Pro 1.38	Bradley-Pro 160	Ward-Pro 34.6	**Ward-Pro** 3.5
Richmond-Wor 590.2	Bradley-Pro .210	Ward-Pro .232	Ward-Pro 1.74	Goldsmith-Chi 138	Corcoran-Chi 28.8	**Corcoran-Chi** 2.9
Welch-Tro 574.0	Ward-Pro .217	Corcoran-Chi .236	Goldsmith-Chi 1.75	McCormick-Cle 127	Richmond-Wor 25.4	**Bradley-Pro** 1.9
Corcoran-Chi 536.1	Corey-Wor .219	Corey-Wor .239	McCormick-Cle 1.85	Ward-Pro 127	Bradley-Pro 18.2	**Keefe-Tro** 1.8

Bound for Good

Owners unilaterally instituted a reserve clause after the 1879 season, which allowed each team to protect five players from other offers. This tactic neutralized player mobility and put a drain on salaries. William Hulbert also shoehorned through a provision prohibiting alcohol sales on the grounds of any league club. While these two policies made sense, given Hulbert's love of high class and high profit, they eventually helped give birth to the American Association. Empowered, some owners began fining players for non-existent infractions and, in the case of Boston, blacklisted slugger Charlie Jones in a financial dispute.

Despite the league's machinations, five clubs finished under .500 and pennant-winner Chicago—the NL's only good draw—ran away from the competition. With an offense sporting Cap Anson, King Kelly, Abner Dalrymple, and George Gore, the team topped the league in runs by more than 100. Their pitching permitted the fewest hits, and rookie Larry Corcoran led in strikeouts. Chicago's defense committed 3.82 errors per game, the best in the NL.

Debut players included slugger Roger Connor (the pre-Ruth career home run record holder), pitchers Hoss Radbourn and Tim Keefe, who, as a rookie, set an all-time mark with an 0.86 ERA, outfielder Ned Hanlon, third baseman Arlie Latham, and catcher Buck Ewing, considered by many the greatest player of the nineteenth century.

The league ruled that fouls could be caught on one bounce for an out. In addition, it now took just eight balls for a walk. The league batting average dropped to .245, and scoring fell dramatically. On June 12 Worcester's Lee Richmond threw the first perfect game in major league annals; Providence's Monty Ward tossed the second just five days later. The NL would not attain perfection again until 1964.

After the season Hulbert marshaled a 7–1 vote to expel Cincinnati from the league. The club's owners, unable to compete financially otherwise, had rented their park to other local teams and allowed them to play on Sundays and sell beer.

1881 National League

TEAM	W	L	T	PCT	GB	HW	HL	R	OR	PA	H	2B	3B	HR	BB	SO	HB	SH	AVG	OBP	SLG	OPS	AOPS	BR	ABR	PF	SB	CS	BSA	BSR
CHI	56	28	0	.667		**32**	10	**550**	**380**	3254	**918**	**157**	36	**12**	140	224			**.295**	**.325**	**.380**	**705**	**119**	**88**	**63**	105				
PRO	47	37	1	.560	9	23	20	447	426	3223	780	144	37	11	**146**	**214**			.253	.287	.335	622	100	-3	5	98				
BUF	45	38	0	.542	10.5	25	16	440	447	3127	797	**157**	**50**	**12**	108	270			.264	.289	.361	650	109	22	28	99				
DET	41	43	0	.488	15	23	19	440	429	3131	780	131	53	17	136	250			.260	.293	.357	650	103	21	4	104				
TRO	39	45	1	.464	17	24	18	399	427	3186	754	124	31	5	140	240			.248	.281	.314	595	86	-32	-52	105				
BOS	38	45	0	.458	17.5	19	22	347	410	3026	733	121	27	5	110	193			.251	.279	.317	596	94	-32	-14	95				
CLE	36	48	1	.429	20	20	22	392	414	3249	796	120	39	7	132	224			.255	.286	.326	612	100	-17	7	95				
WOR	32	50	1	.390	23	19	22	410	492	3214	781	114	31	7	121	169			.253	.281	.316	597	86	-32	-54	106				
TOT	336					185	149	3425		25410	6339	1068	304	76	1033	1784			.260	.290	.338	628								

TEAM	CG	SHO	GR	SV	IP	H	HR	BB	SO	BR/9	ERA	AERA	OAV	OOB	PR	APR	PF	OSB	OCS	FA	E	WPB	DP	FW	PW	BW	BSW	DIF
CHI	81	9	3	0	744.2	**722**	14	122	228	**10.2**	2.43	**113**	**.243**	**.273**	29	**26**	99			.916	**309**	105	54	2.1	**2.4**	**5.9**		3.6
PRO	76	7	9	0	757.2	756	**5**	138	264	10.6	**2.40**	111	**.243**	.275	**32**	22	96			.896	390	139	66	-2.0	2.1	.5		4.5
BUF	72	5	**12**	0	742.1	881	9	**89**	185	11.8	2.84	98	.281	.301	-5	-5	100			.892	408	150	48	-3.4	-.5	2.6		4.8
DET	83	**10**	1	0	744.2	785	8	137	**265**	11.1	2.65	110	.257	.289	11	21	105			.906	338	**83**	**80**	.5	2.0	.4		-3.9
TRO	**85**	8	0	0	771.0	805	11	161	207	11.3	2.96	99	.263	.299	-16	-2	106			**.917**	311	85	70	**2.2**	-.2	-4.9		-.1
BOS	72	6	11	**3**	730.2	763	9	143	199	11.2	2.71	98	.258	.292	5	-4	96			.909	325	204	54	1.0	-.4	-1.3		-2.8
CLE	82	2	3	0	760.0	737	9	126	240	**10.2**	2.68	98	.244	.274	8	-5	94			.904	348	129	68	.2	-.5	.7		-6.4
WOR	80	5	3	0	737.1	882	11	120	196	12.2	3.54	85	.288	.315	-63	-39	109			.903	353	113	50	-.5	-3.6	-5.0		.2
TOT	631	52	42	3	5988.1					11.1	2.77		.260	.290						.905	2782	1008	490					

Batter-Fielder Wins	Batting Average	On-Base Percentage	Slugging Average	On-Base Plus Slugging	Adjusted OPS	Adjusted Batter Runs
Anson-Chi 3.6	Anson-Chi .399	Anson-Chi .442	Brouthers-Buf .541	Anson-Chi .952	Anson-Chi 189	Anson-Chi 35.4
Dunlap-Cle 3.2	Powell-Det .338	York-Pro .362	Anson-Chi .510	Brouthers-Buf .902	Brouthers-Buf 182	Brouthers-Buf 25.2
Bennett-Det 3.2	Rowe-Buf .333	Brouthers-Buf .361	Rowe-Buf .480	Bennett-Det .819	Dunlap-Cle 159	Dunlap-Cle 24.8
Richardson-Buf 2.8	Start-Pro .328	Dunlap-Cle .358	Bennett-Det .478	Dunlap-Cle .802	York-Pro 150	York-Pro 19.9
Williamson-Chi 2.1	Dunlap-Cle .325	Gore-Chi .354	Dunlap-Cle .444	York-Pro .790	Bennett-Det 149	O'Rourke-Buf 16.5

Runs	Hits	Doubles	Triples	Home Runs	Total Bases	Runs Batted In
Gore-Chi 86	Anson-Chi 137	Kelly-Chi 27	Rowe-Buf 11	Brouthers-Buf 8	Anson-Chi 175	Anson-Chi 82
Kelly-Chi 84	Dalrymple-Chi 117	Hines-Pro 27	Phillips-Cle 10	Bennett-Det 7	Dunlap-Cle 156	Bennett-Det 64
Dalrymple-Chi 72	Dickerson-Wor 116	Stovey-Wor 25		Farrell-Pro 5	Kelly-Chi 153	Kelly-Chi 55
O'Rourke-Buf 71		Dunlap-Cle 25		Burns-Chi 4	Dalrymple-Chi 150	
Farrell-Pro 69		White-Buf 24			Dickerson-Wor 149	

Stolen Bases	Base Stealing Runs	Fielding Runs-Infield	Fielding Runs-Outfield	Wins	Winning Pct.	Complete Games
		Force-Buf 24.5	Richardson-Buf 22.3	Whitney-Bos 31	Radbourn-Pro .694	Whitney-Bos 57
		Williamson-Chi 21.3	Hornung-Bos 11.8	Corcoran-Chi 31	Corcoran-Chi .689	McCormick-Cle 57
		Glasscock-Cle 9.4	Evans-Tro 11.4	Derby-Det 29	Goldsmith-Chi .649	Derby-Det 55
		Morrill-Bos 7.7	Dickerson-Wor 9.2	Galvin-Buf 28	Welch-Tro .538	Richmond-Wor 50
		Quest-Chi 7.6	Kelly-Chi 5.5	McCormick-Cle 26	Galvin-Buf .538	Galvin-Buf 48

Strikeouts	Fewest BB/Game	Games	Saves	Base Runners/9	Adjusted Relief Runs	Relief Ranking
Derby-Det 212	Galvin-Buf .87	Whitney-Bos 66	Mathews-Pro-Bos 2	Wiedman-Det 9.39		
McCormick-Cle 178	Wiedman-Det .94	McCormick-Cle 59	Morrill-Bos 1	McCormick-Cle 9.72		
Whitney-Bos 162	Goldsmith-Chi 1.20	Galvin-Buf 56		Goldsmith-Chi 10.15		
Richmond-Wor 156	Richmond-Wor 1.32	Derby-Det 56		Radbourn-Pro 10.32		
Corcoran-Chi 150	McCormick-Cle 1.44	Richmond-Wor 53		Ward-Pro 10.34		

Innings Pitched	Opponents' Avg.	Opponents' OBP	Earned Run Average	Adjusted ERA	Adjusted Starter Runs	Pitcher Wins
Whitney-Bos 552.1	Radbourn-Pro .235	Wiedman-Det .258	Wiedman-Det 1.80	Wiedman-Det 162	Derby-Det 33.7	**Derby-Det** 2.3
McCormick-Cle 526.0	McCormick-Cle .235	McCormick-Cle .265	Ward-Pro 2.13	Derby-Det 132	Galvin-Buf 18.3	**Whitney-Bos** 2.1
Derby-Det 494.2	Wiedman-Det .238	Radbourn-Pro .270	Derby-Det 2.20	Ward-Pro 125	Corcoran-Chi 15.8	**Galvin-Buf** 2.0
Galvin-Buf 474.0	Corcoran-Chi .242	Goldsmith-Chi .271	Corcoran-Chi 2.31	Corcoran-Chi 118	Ward-Pro 15.6	**Ward-Pro** 1.9
Richmond-Wor 462.1	Ward-Pro .242	Ward-Pro .271	Galvin-Buf 2.37	Galvin-Buf 117	Radbourn-Pro 14.2	**Radbourn-Pro** 1.4

The Last Solo Flight

The season's most significant change was the decision to move the pitcher's box back 5 feet to a distance of 50 feet from home plate. As a result of this change, league batting average rose 15 points, and scoring increased by nearly half a run. In addition, only seven balls were now required for a walk, and bases on balls shot up 40 percent. Oddly, although the number of strikes for a whiff was also reduced to the present-day three, strikeouts actually decreased.

Much to the delight of William Hulbert, Chicago won again, breaking the race open late in the summer. They led the league in runs and fewest allowed, also making the league's fewest errors. The White Stockings' dominant lineup, held over from 1880, included the top three in runs: George Gore, King Kelly, and Abner Dalrymple. Cap Anson's .399 average topped the loop by 61 points.

Detroit, replacing Cincinnati, finished a surprising fourth, largely due to catcher Charlie Bennett's power hitting. Meanwhile, outfielder Dan Brouthers broke through for Buffalo after two trials with Troy, helping the Bisons rise from seventh to third. Despite great pitching from Monty Ward and Hoss Radbourn, Providence finished second because of several dead spots in the lineup. Overall, the league was much stronger and more balanced; for once, each team was competitive.

With greater competition came bigger crowds, and Detroit's admittance provided an unexpected attendance windfall. Chicago still led the NL in spectators for the fifth time in six seasons. League attendance surpassed 300,000 for the first time, although Troy and Worcester lagged far behind the rest.

Big changes were on the horizon. Several large cities were clamoring for big league ball, and in response, club owners from Philadelphia and Cincinnati founded the American Association in fall 1881. Not around to deal with this new threat was Hulbert, since 1876 the guiding force behind the National League, who died in spring 1882.

1882 National League

TEAM	W	L	T	PCT	GB	HW	HL	R	OR	PA	H	2B	3B	HR	BB	SO	HB	SH	AVG	OBP	SLG	OPS	AOPS	BR	ABR	PF	SB	CS	BSA	BSR
CHI	55	29	0	.655		**35**	10	**604**	**353**	3367	**892**	**209**	**54**	15	**142**	262			**.277**	**.307**	**.389**	**696**	**118**	**87**	**61**	105				
PRO	52	32	0	.619	3	30	12	463	356	3206	776	121	53	11	102	255			.250	.274	.334	608	96	-17	-16	100				
BUF	45	39	0	.536	10	26	13	500	461	3244	858	146	47	18	116	**228**			.274	.300	.368	668	113	51	42	102				
BOS	45	39	1	.536	10	27	15	472	414	3252	823	114	50	15	134	244			.264	.294	.347	641	107	22	21	100				
CLE	42	40	2	.512	12	21	19	402	411	3131	716	139	40	**20**	122	261			.238	.268	.331	599	96	-23	-8	97				
DET	42	41	3	.506	12.5	24	18	407	488	3266	724	117	44	19	122	308			.230	.259	.314	573	84	-54	-53	100				
TRO	35	48	2	.422	19.5	22	20	430	522	3166	747	116	59	12	109	298			.244	.270	.333	603	99	-22	0	95				
WOR	18	66	0	.214	37	12	30	379	652	3097	689	109	57	16	113	303			.231	.259	.322	581	85	-45	-54	102				
TOT	338					197	137	3657		25729	6225	1071	404	126	960	2159			.251	.279	.342	622								

TEAM	CG	SHO	GR	SV	IP	H	HR	BB	SO	BR/9	ERA	AERA	OAV	OOB	PR	APR	PF	OSB	OCS	FA	E	WPB	DP	FW	PW	BW	BSW	DIF
CHI	**83**	7	1	0	763.2	**667**	13	102	279	**9.1**	**2.22**	**129**	**.221**	**.246**	**57**	**52**	99			.898	376	98	54	.1	**4.7**	**5.5**		2.6
PRO	80	**10**	4	**1**	752.0	690	12	87	273	9.3	2.27	123	.228	.250	51	48	97			.901	371	114	67	.4	4.4	-1.5		6.7
BUF	79	3	5	0	737.0	778	16	114	287	10.9	3.25	90	.254	.280	-30	-30	101			**.910**	315	136	42	3.3	-2.7	3.8		-1.4
BOS	81	4	4	0	749.0	738	**10**	**77**	352	9.8	2.80	102	.239	.258	7	4	99			**.910**	**314**	121	37	**3.6**	.4	1.9		-2.8
CLE	81	4	3	0	751.2	743	22	132	232	10.5	2.75	101	.249	.280	11	1	97			.905	358	163	**71**	1.1	.0	-.7		.6
DET	82	7	4	0	793.0	808	19	129	**354**	10.6	2.98	98	.248	.277	-9	-8	101			.893	396	**88**	44	-.4	-.7	-4.8		6.5
TRO	81	6	4	0	758.0	836	13	165	184	11.9	3.08	91	.267	.304	-16	-24	98			.887	432	106	70	-2.5	-2.2	.0		-1.8
WOR	75	0	**9**	0	738.1	964	21	151	195	13.6	3.75	82	.294	.325	-71	-51	107			.878	468	165	66	-4.6	-4.6	-4.9		-9.9
TOT	642	41	34	1	6042.2					10.7	2.88		.251	.279						.897	3030	991	451					

Batter-Fielder Wins	Batting Average	On-Base Percentage	Slugging Average	On-Base Plus Slugging	Adjusted OPS	Adjusted Batter Runs
Glasscock-Cle 4.1	Brouthers-Buf 368	Brouthers-Buf 403	Brouthers-Buf 547	Brouthers-Buf 950	Brouthers-Buf 198	Brouthers-Buf 37.9
Brouthers-Buf 2.8	Anson-Chi............362	Anson-Chi 397	Connor-Tro 530	Anson-Chi 897	Connor-Tro...........188	Connor-Tro 33.4
Dunlap-Cle 2.8	Connor-Tro 330	Whitney-Bos 382	Whitney-Bos 510	Whitney-Bos 892	Whitney-Bos 182	Anson-Chi 29.9
Bennett-Det 2.8	Start-Pro..............329	Gore-Chi 369	Anson-Chi.............500	Connor-Tro...........884	Anson-Chi 177	Whitney-Bos 24.1
Williamson-Chi ..2.6	Whitney-Bos 323	Connor-Tro..................354	Hines-Pro 467	Hines-Pro 793	Hines-Pro 151	Hines-Pro 21.3

Runs	Hits	Doubles	Triples	Home Runs	Total Bases	Runs Batted In
Gore-Chi 99	Brouthers-Buf 129	Kelly-Chi 37	Connor-Tro.............18	Wood-Det 7	Brouthers-Buf 192	Anson-Chi 83
Dalrymple-Chi 96	Anson-Chi 126	Anson-Chi......................29	Wood-Det 12	Muldoon-Cle 6	Connor-Tro............185	Brouthers-Buf.........63
Stovey-Wor 90		Hines-Pro 28	Corey-Wor 12	Brouthers-Buf 6	Hines-Pro 177	Williamson-Chi 60
Kelly-Chi 81		Williamson-Chi 27			Anson-Chi 174	Richardson-Buf 57
Purcell-Buf.............79		Glasscock-Cle 27			Dalrymple-Chi 167	Kelly-Chi 55

Stolen Bases	Base Stealing Runs	Fielding Runs-Infield	Fielding Runs-Outfield	Wins	Winning Pct.	Complete Games
		Glasscock-Cle 24.2	Evans-Wor 14.6	McCormick-Cle 36	Corcoran-Chi 692	McCormick-Cle.....65
		Richardson-Buf 19.3	Hornung-Bos 11.4	Radbourn-Pro 33	Radbourn-Pro.......635	Radbourn-Pro........50
		Dunlap-Cle.................17.9	Hanlon-Det 10.1	Goldsmith-Chi 28	Goldsmith-Chi.......622	Galvin-Buf 48
		A.Irwin-Wor 16.7	Kelly-Chi 8.2	Galvin-Buf 28	Ward-Pro 594	Whitney-Bos..........46
		Williamson-Chi...........15.4	Stovey-Wor 3.2	Corcoran-Chi 27	Mathews-Bos 559	Goldsmith-Chi 45

Strikeouts	Fewest BB/Game	Games	Saves	Base Runners/9	Adjusted Relief Runs	Relief Ranking
Radbourn-Pro 201	Mathews-Bos 69	McCormick-Cle.............68	Ward-Pro 1	Corcoran-Chi 8.70		
McCormick-Cle 200	Galvin-Buf..............81	Radbourn-Pro...............54		Radbourn-Pro......9.14		
Derby-Det 182	Goldsmith-Chi.........84	Galvin-Buf.....................52		Goldsmith-Chi......9.22		
Whitney-Bos 180	Wiedman-Det 85	Whitney-Bos 49		Wiedman-Det 9.42		
Corcoran-Chi 170	Whitney-Bos 88	Richmond-Wor 48		Mathews-Bos 9.47		

Innings Pitched	Opponents' Avg.	Opponents' OBP	Earned Run Average	Adjusted ERA	Adjusted Starter Runs	Pitcher Wins
McCormick-Cle..595.2	Corcoran-Chi 200	Corcoran-Chi 234	Corcoran-Chi 1.95	Corcoran-Chi 147	Radbourn-Pro......34.7	**Radbourn-Pro**....3.2
Radbourn-Pro....466.0	Radbourn-Pro.........226	Mathews-Bos...............246	Radbourn-Pro.......2.11	Radbourn-Pro 133	Corcoran-Chi 34.0	**Corcoran-Chi** 2.9
Galvin-Buf..........445.1	Ward-Pro 232	Radbourn-Pro 247	McCormick-Cle....2.37	Goldsmith-Chi 118	McCormick-Cle.....30.3	**Whitney-Bos** 2.8
Whitney-Bos 420.0	Mathews-Bos 232	Wiedman-Det...............253	Goldsmith-Chi......2.42	McCormick-Cle 117	Goldsmith-Chi......23.2	**McCormick-Cle** 2.3
....	Daily-Buf...............234	Goldsmith-Chi 254	Keefe-Tro 2.49	Keefe-Tro.............113	Wiedman-Det 18.3	**Goldsmith-Chi** ..1.8

The War Is On

In 1882, for the first time, the NL had no franchise shifts or new clubs. However, the ground was still quaking under the Senior Circuit. On William Hulbert's death in April, the league elected Boston owner Arthur Soden as president. Soden took office just as the new American Association, formed the previous winter and setting up shop in six cities forsaken by the NL, prepared for play.

For the third straight season, Chicago defeated Providence to win the NL title, but this time by a small margin. The White Stockings again had a murderous attack, with George Gore, Abner Dalrymple, and King Kelly rating 1-2-4 in runs, and pitchers Fred Goldsmith and Larry Corcoran were every bit the equal of Providence's Hoss Radbourn and Monty Ward. Dan Brouthers of third-place Buffalo led the NL in batting average, slugging percentage, on-base percentage, total bases, and hits.

Even though 1882 saw the first padded glove (worn by Providence shortstop Art Irwin, and later popularized by teammate Monty Ward), the NL's fielding percentage decreased by nearly 10 points. Chicago was last NL pennant winner to have a fielding average below .900.

Six NL clubs finished over .500. Only Worcester was a disaster, compiling a .214 winning percentage. Worcester drew just 11,000 fans all year, and on September 28 the club drew the smallest crowd in major league history: 6, that's right, 6. Worcester, and seventh-place Troy, were bounced from the NL for 1883 as Soden and the other league owners awarded franchises to magnates in Philadelphia and New York.

After a late-season schedule change appeared to give Chicago an unfair advantage, the White Stockings and Grays met in a nine-game series to determine the league champ. Cap Anson's White Stockings appeared to tank the first three games to increase interest in the remaining six, and the series indeed lasted nine games, with the White Stockings triumphing. Prior to their ill-advised postseason skirmish with Providence, the White Stockings split a two-game series with Association champion Cincinnati. The relevant parties duly noted the interest in this matchup.

1882 American Association

TEAM	W	L	T	PCT	GB	HW	HL	R	OR	PA	H	2B	3B	HR	BB	SO	HB	SH	AVG	OBP	SLG	OPS	AOPS	BR	ABR	PF	SB	CS	BSA	BSR
CIN	55	25	0	.688		**31**	11	**489**	**268**	3109	**795**	95	**47**	5	102	204			**.264**	.289	**.332**	**621**	107	37	12	106				
PHI	41	34	0	.547	11.5	21	18	406	389	2832	660	89	21	5	125	164			.244	.277	.298	575	92	-3	-27	107				
LOU	42	38	0	.525	13	26	13	443	352	2934	728	**110**	28	**9**	**128**	**193**			.259	**.292**	.328	620	**120**	**40**	**66**	95				
PIT	39	39	1	.500	15	17	18	428	418	2994	730	**110**	59	18	90	183			.251	.274	.348	622	118	35	57	95				
STL	37	43	0	.463	18	24	20	399	496	2977	663	87	41	11	112	226			.231	.260	.302	562	90	-20	-35	104				
BAL	19	54	1	.260	32.5	9	25	273	515	2655	535	60	24	4	72	215			.207	.229	.254	483	72	-89	-66	92				
TOT	234					128	105	2438		17501	4111	551	220	52	629	1185			.244	.271	.312	582								

TEAM	CG	SHO	GR	SV	IP	H	HR	BB	SO	BR/9	ERA	AERA	OAV	OOB	PR	APR	PF	OSB	OCS	FA	E	WPB	DP	FW	PW	BW	BSW	DIF
CIN	**77**	**11**	3	0	721.1	**609**	7	125	165	**9.2**	**1.65**	**160**	**.214**	**.247**	**83**	**80**	98			**.907**	**332**	**102**	41	**3.7**	**7.3**	1.1		2.9
PHI	72	2	3	0	663.0	682	13	99	190	10.6	2.97	94	.249	.275	-21	-12	105			.895	361	119	36	1.2	-1.1	-2.5		5.9
LOU	73	6	7	0	693.1	637	6	112	240	9.7	2.03	122	.229	.259	51	37	92			.893	385	161	**57**	1.3	3.4	**6.1**		-8.7
PIT	**77**	2	2	0	696.2	694	**4**	**82**	**252**	10.0	2.79	93	.243	.264	-8	-15	97			.889	397	115	40	.5	-1.4	5.2		-4.3
STL	75	3	5	**1**	688.1	729	7	103	225	10.9	2.92	96	.254	.280	-18	-8	105			.875	446	205	41	-1.6	-.7	-3.2		2.5
BAL	64	1	**12**	0	646.1	760	15	108	113	12.1	3.88	71	.275	.302	-86	-80	102			.859	490	183	41	-5.0	-7.3	-6.1		.9
TOT	438	25	32	1	4109.0					10.4	2.68		.244	.271						.886	2411	885	256					

Batter-Fielder Wins	Batting Average	On-Base Percentage	Slugging Average	On-Base Plus Slugging	Adjusted OPS	Adjusted Batter Runs
Browning-Lou 4.6	Browning-Lou 378	Browning-Lou 430	Browning-Lou 510	Browning-Lou 940	Browning-Lou 228	Browning-Lou 40.9
Snyder-Cin 2.6	Carpenter-Cin.......342	Swartwood-Pit 370	Swartwood-Pit 489	Swartwood-Pit......859	Swartwood-Pit......197	Swartwood-Pit....33.4
O'Brien-Phi..........2.2	Swartwood-Pit 329	Carpenter-Cin 360	Taylor-Pit..............452	Carpenter-Cin 782	Taylor-Pit 157	Carpenter-Cin 18.5
Swartwood-Pit....1.8	O'Brien-Phi 303	O'Brien-Phi 339	Mansell-Pit 438	O'Brien-Phi 758	Carpenter-Cin 154	Mansell-Pit 17.1
Mansell-Pit 1.6	Wolf-Lou 299	Sommer-Cin.................333	Carpenter-Cin.......422	Taylor-Pit 749	Mansell-Pit............150	Taylor-Pit 16.9

Runs	Hits	Doubles	Triples	Home Runs	Total Bases	Runs Batted In
Swartwood-Pit........86	Carpenter-Cin 120	Swartwood-Pit 18	Mansell-Pit.............16	Walker-StL 7	Swartwood-Pit......159	
Sommer-Cin 82	Browning-Lou 109	Mansell-Pit 18	Taylor-Pit 13	Browning-Lou 5	Mansell-Pit............152	
Carpenter-Cin 78	Swartwood-Pit......107	Browning-Lou 17	Wheeler-Cin............11	Swartwood-Pit..........4	Carpenter-Cin 148	
Browning-Lou 67	Sommer-Cin 102	Taylor-Pit.........................16	Swartwood-Pit 11		Browning-Lou 147	
Birchall-Phi 65	B.Gleason-StL 100	Cuthbert-StL 16	Wolf-Lou 8		Taylor-Pit 135	

Stolen Bases	Base Stealing Runs	Fielding Runs-Infield	Fielding Runs-Outfield	Wins	Winning Pct.	Complete Games
		Stricker-Phi 22.8	Walker-StL 5.7	White-Cin................40	White-Cin 769	White-Cin 52
		B.Gleason-StL 10.3	O'Brien-Phi 4.6	Mullane-Lou............30	Weaver-Phi 634	Mullane-Lou 51
		Browning-Lou 8.8	Sommer-Cin 3.4	Weaver-Phi 26	McGinnis-StL 581	McGinnis-StL 43
		Peters-Pit 5.7	Blakiston-Phi 3.2	McGinnis-StL...........25	Mullane-Lou 556	Weaver-Phi............41
		Shetzline-Bal 4.1	Mansell-Pit 2.8	Salisbury-Pit 20	Salisbury-Pit.........526	Salisbury-Pit..........38

Strikeouts	Fewest BB/Game	Games	Saves	Base Runners/9	Adjusted Relief Runs	Relief Ranking
Mullane-Lou..........170	Hecker-Lou 43	Mullane-Lou 55	Fusselback-StL 1	Hecker-Lou 6.92		
Salisbury-Pit 135	Driscoll-Pit 54	White-Cin 54		Dorr-StL 7.36		
McGinnis-StL........134	Weaver-Phi.............85	McGinnis-StL..................45		Driscoll-Pit 7.79		
White-Cin..............122	Salisbury-Pit 99	Landis-Phi-Bal 44		McCormick-Cin....8.97		
Weaver-Phi 104	Landis-Phi-Bal 1.17	Weaver-Phi 42		White-Cin 9.04		

Innings Pitched	Opponents' Avg.	Opponents' OBP	Earned Run Average	Adjusted ERA	Adjusted Starter Runs	Pitcher Wins
White-Cin 480.0	Hecker-Lou...........188	Hecker-Lou 199	Driscoll-Pit 1.21	Driscoll-Pit 216	White-Cin 60.3	**White-Cin**............6.7
Mullane-Lou 460.1	McCormick-Cin......206	Driscoll-Pit 218	Hecker-Lou..........1.30	Hecker-Lou 191	Mullane-Lou 34.3	**Mullane-Lou** 5.0
McGinnis-StL 388.1	Driscoll-Pit 206	McCormick-Cin 243	McCormick-Cin....1.52	McCormick-Cin 174	Driscoll-Pit 26.6	**Driscoll-Pit** 2.1
Weaver-Phi 371.0	White-Cin 216	White-Cin......................244	White-Cin 1.54	White-Cin..............172	McCormick-Cin....24.9	**McCormick-Cin** 1.8
Landis-Phi-Bal ..360.0	Geis-Bal 220	Salisbury-Pit 253	Mullane-Lou 1.88	Mullane-Lou..........132	Hecker-Lou 11.1	**Hecker-Lou**........1.6

Association Baseball

The new American Association, in direct contrast to the NL, voted to allow Sunday ball and sale of alcohol at their parks, and allowed clubs to charge just a quarter for admission (the Senior Circuit's ticket prices were 50 cents). These attractions helped the new AA essentially match the NL in attendance for its premier season, even though the new league fielded just six clubs. Three original AA clubs—Cincinnati, Pittsburgh, and St. Louis—remain in operation today as National League franchises.

There were other differences between the leagues. The American Association did not fine pitchers who hit batters intentionally, but they did institute the practice of league-employed umpires, which the NL soon followed. Disdaining the NL's Spalding baseball, the AA used the Mahn ball.

Many of the new league's clubs had local flavors. The Cincinnati club had three regulars (Will White, Joe Sommer, and Hick Carpenter) who had played on the city's final NL entry back in 1880. Rather than go whole-hog to steal away "reserved" NL players, the AA instead used players who had enjoyed success in the minor leagues of the time or had previously washed out of the majors.

Nobody argued that the AA's talent was on an equal level to that of the major leagues, but several future stars got their start in the new loop. Among players making their major league debuts in the 1882 American Association were Louisville's Pete Browning (the league's top offensive player), St. Louis' Charlie Comiskey, and Bid McPhee of Cincinnati.

The Cincinnati Red Stockings ran away with the marbles, zooming out to a quick lead. The first-year league was fairly balanced, with four teams playing .500 ball or better, and St. Louis a respectable 18 games behind in fifth place; Baltimore was the league doormat. White was the AA's dominant pitcher, though he had competition from Tony Mullane of third-place Louisville. Hick Carpenter led the league in hits, while top defender McPhee anchored the infield.

1883 National League

TEAM	W	L	T	PCT	GB	HW	HL	R	OR	PA	H	2B	3B	HR	BB	SO	HB	SH	AVG	OBP	SLG	OPS	AOPS	BR	ABR	PF	SB	CS	BSA	BSR
BOS	63	35	0	.643		**41**	8	669	456	3780	1010	209	**86**	**34**	123	423			.276	.300	**.408**	**708**	**114**	**68**	**53**	102				
CHI	59	39	0	.602	4	36	13	**679**	540	3787	1000	**277**	61	13	129	399			.273	.298	.393	691	104	55	7	108				
PRO	58	40	0	.592	5	34	15	636	**436**	3834	1001	189	59	21	**149**	**309**			.272	.300	.372	672	104	29	13	103				
CLE	55	42	3	.567	7.5	31	18	476	443	3596	852	184	38	8	139	374			.246	.276	.329	605	88	-52	-46	99				
BUF	52	45	1	.536	10.5	36	13	614	576	3876	**1058**	184	59	8	147	342			**.284**	**.311**	.371	682	108	44	30	102				
NY	46	50	2	.479	16	28	19	530	577	3651	900	139	69	24	127	297			.255	.281	.354	635	96	-23	-17	99				
DET	40	58	3	.408	23	23	26	524	650	3892	931	164	48	13	166	378			.250	.282	.330	612	93	-47	-21	95				
PHI	17	81	1	.173	46	9	40	437	887	3717	859	181	48	3	141	355			.240	.269	.320	589	90	-74	-27	91				
TOT	395					238	152	4565		30133	7611	1527	468	124	1121	2877			.262	.290	.360	650								

TEAM	CG	SHO	GR	SV	IP	H	HR	BB	SO	BR/9	ERA	AERA	OAV	OOB	PR	APR	PF	OSB	OCS	FA	E	WPB	DP	FW	PW	BW	BSW	DIF
BOS	89	**6**	9	**3**	860.0	853	11	**90**	**538**	9.9	2.55	121	.245	.264	56	53	99			.901	409	222	58	3.2	4.6	**4.6**		1.6
CHI	91	5	8	1	862.0	942	21	123	299	11.1	2.78	119	.260	.284	34	45	105			.879	543	137	76	-3.5	3.9	.6		8.9
PRO	88	4	10	1	871.0	827	12	111	376	**9.7**	2.37	130	.238	**.262**	74	69	98			.903	419	156	75	2.7	6.0	1.1		-.8
CLE	**92**	5	8	2	879.0	**818**	**7**	217	402	10.6	**2.22**	**142**	**.237**	.282	**89**	**92**	100			**.909**	**389**	135	69	**4.6**	**8.0**	-4.0		-2.1
BUF	90	5	9	2	859.1	971	12	101	362	11.2	3.32	96	.268	.288	-18	-9	101			.896	445	171	52	1.4	-.8	2.6		.3
NY	87	5	11	0	866.0	907	19	170	323	11.2	2.94	105	.253	.287	19	11	99			.889	468	181	52	.2	1.0	-1.5		-1.7
DET	89	5	**12**	2	894.1	1026	22	184	324	12.2	3.56	87	.270	.303	-42	-47	99			.893	470	**132**	**77**	.9	-4.1	-1.8		-3.9
PHI	91	3	9	0	864.2	1267	20	125	253	14.5	5.34	58	.318	.338	-212	-219	98			.858	639	179	62	-8.0	-19.1	-2.4		-2.5
TOT	717	38	76	11	6956.1					11.3	3.13		.262	.290						.891	3782	1313	521					

Batter-Fielder Wins
- **Farrell-Pro** 3.5
- **Richardson-Buf** ..3.1
- **Brouthers-Buf** 3.0
- **Bennett-Det** 3.0
- **Dunlap-Cle** 2.9

Batting Average
- Brouthers-Buf 374
- Connor-NY 357
- Gore-Chi 334
- Burdock-Bos 330
- O'Rourke-Buf 328

On-Base Percentage
- Brouthers-Buf 397
- Connor-NY...................394
- Gore-Chi 377
- Dunlap-Cle...................361
- Burdock-Bos 353

Slugging Average
- Brouthers-Buf 572
- Morrill-Bos 525
- Connor-NY 506
- Sutton-Bos 486
- Ewing-NY 481

On-Base Plus Slugging
- Brouthers-Buf 969
- Connor-NY............900
- Morrill-Bos 868
- Gore-Chi 849
- Sutton-Bos............836

Adjusted OPS
- Brouthers-Buf 186
- Connor-NY............173
- Morrill-Bos 155
- Bennett-Det 155
- Sutton-Bos............147

Adjusted Batter Runs
- Brouthers-Buf 42.7
- Connor-NY 35.9
- Bennett-Det........26.3
- Morrill-Bos..........25.6
- Dunlap-Cle 23.8

Runs
- Hornung-Bos 107
- Gore-Chi 105
- O'Rourke-Buf........102
- Sutton-Bos............101
- Hines-Pro 94

Hits
- Brouthers-Buf 159
- Connor-NY............146
- O'Rourke-Buf.......143
- Sutton-Bos...........134
- Wood-Det 133

Doubles
- Williamson-Chi 49
- Brouthers-Buf 41
- Burns-Chi 37
- Anson-Chi......................36
- ....

Triples
- Brouthers-Buf 17
- Morrill-Bos 16
- Sutton-Bos.............15
- Connor-NY.............15
- ....

Home Runs
- Ewing-NY 10
- Hornung-Bos 8
- Denny-Pro 8
- Ward-NY 7
- Morrill-Bos 6

Total Bases
- Brouthers-Buf 243
- Morrill-Bos 212
- Connor-NY............207
- Sutton-Bos............201
- Hornung-Bos 199

Runs Batted In
- Brouthers-Buf........97
- Burdock-Bos..........88
- Sutton-Bos 73
- Morrill-Bos 68
- Anson-Chi 68

Stolen Bases

Base Stealing Runs

Fielding Runs-Infield
- Farrell-Pro 24.7
- Williamson-Chi............17.7
- Glasscock-Cle 17.7
- Pfeffer-Chi 16.3
- Richardson-Buf 16.0

Fielding Runs-Outfield
- Shafer-Buf 16.2
- Ward-NY 11.0
- Gore-Chi 8.5
- Kelly-Chi 8.3
- Manning-Phi 7.1

Wins
- Radbourn-Pro 48
- Galvin-Buf 46
- Whitney-Bos 37
- Corcoran-Chi 34
- McCormick-Cle 28

Winning Pct.
- McCormick-Cle.....700
- Radbourn-Pro.......658
- Buffinton-Bos 641
- Whitney-Bos 638
- Corcoran-Chi 630

Complete Games
- Galvin-Buf 72
- Radbourn-Pro........66
- Coleman-Phi 59
- Whitney-Bos 54
- Corcoran-Chi 51

Strikeouts
- Whitney-Bos 345
- Radbourn-Pro 315
- Galvin-Buf 279
- Corcoran-Chi 216
- Buffinton-Bos........188

Fewest BB/Game
- Whitney-Bos 61
- Galvin-Buf...............69
- Radbourn-Pro.........80
- Coleman-Phi...........80
- Goldsmith-Chi.........92

Games
- Radbourn-Pro 76
- Galvin-Buf.......................76
- Coleman-Phi..................65
- Whitney-Bos 62
- Corcoran-Chi 56

Saves
- Wiedman-Det 2
- Whitney-Bos 2

Base Runners/9
- Radbourn-Pro......8.81
- Whitney-Bos 9.23
- Galvin-Buf.............9.96
- McCormick-Cle..10.03
- Ward-NY............10.04

Adjusted Relief Runs

Relief Ranking

Innings Pitched
- Galvin-Buf..........656.1
- Radbourn-Pro....632.1
- Coleman-Phi......538.1
- Whitney-Bos 514.0
- Corcoran-Chi 473.2

Opponents' Avg.
- Sawyer-Cle 217
- Radbourn-Pro.......227
- McCormick-Cle.....233
- Sweeney-Pro 237
- Whitney-Bos 238

Opponents' OBP
- Radbourn-Pro 244
- Whitney-Bos 251
- Galvin-Buf 265
- Ward-NY 267
- McCormick-Cle 268

Earned Run Average
- McCormick-Cle....1.84
- Radbourn-Pro......2.05
- Whitney-Bos 2.24
- Sawyer-Cle 2.36
- Daily-Cle 2.42

Adjusted ERA
- McCormick-Cle 171
- Radbourn-Pro 150
- Whitney-Bos 138
- Sawyer-Cle 133
- Corcoran-Chi 132

Adjusted Starter Runs
- Radbourn-Pro......73.5
- McCormick-Cle....47.4
- Whitney-Bos 44.4
- Corcoran-Chi 36.8
- Daily-Cle.............34.0

Pitcher Wins
- **Radbourn-Pro** 8.3
- **Whitney-Bos** 5.6
- **McCormick-Cle** 4.8
- **Corcoran-Chi** 3.2
- **Galvin-Buf** 2.4

Tiny Steps

After a reasonably successful 1882 campaign, the NL awarded franchises to Philadelphia and New York, each competing with AA franchises in the same cities. Both NL teams survive to this day. Prior to 1883 New York had not had any major league team since 1876. A meeting between NL and AA delegates in New York resulted in a peace agreement between the two warring leagues. Each club would now be able to reserve 11 players, rather than 10, and league contracts would be respected.

Abraham Mills was voted the league's new president, to be replaced in 1885 by Nicholas Young. The NL rules committee stated that pitches must not be delivered above the line of the shoulder. Any exception to this would result in a base-advancing "balk." In addition, the league ruled once and for all that a foul must be caught on the fly to register as an out. The AA retained the one-bounce exception.

Chicago again finished just ahead of Providence, but a September rush by the surprising Boston Beaneaters shoved both clubs aside. Boston, with a slugging offense led by Joe Hornung and John Morrill, featured a terrific pitcher in Jim Whitney. Although the White Stockings still led the league in runs, King Kelly and Fred Pfeffer had poor seasons, and Fred Goldsmith lost some of his touch on the hill. Perhaps 1883's most interesting debut came in Chicago, where outfielder and future evangelist Billy Sunday showed off legs that moved almost as quickly as his mouth—Cap Anson signed the 20-year-old outfielder because he "ran like a scared deer."

With two new clubs in large cities, NL attendance increased, but lagged far behind that of the AA. More than twice as many fans came out to see the AA's Philadelphia franchise than to see any NL club. Philadelphia's NL entry, which used an unheard-of 29 players, was allowed to cut its admission to 25 cents to match the AA's price. The last-place club drew 75,000, but that was still just one quarter of the Athletics' business.

1883 American Association

TEAM	W	L	T	PCT	GB	HW	HL	R	OR	PA	H	2B	3B	HR	BB	SO	HB	SH	AVG	OBP	SLG	OPS	AOPS	BR	ABR	PF	SB	CS	BSA	BSR
PHI	66	32	0	.673		37	14	**720**	547	3912	**974**	**149**	50	20	**200**	268			**.262**	**.300**	.346	646	102	**49**	-4	109				
STL	65	33	0	.663	1	35	14	549	409	3619	891	118	46	7	124	**240**			.255	.280	.321	601	91	-13	-41	106				
CIN	61	37	0	.622	5	**38**	13	662	413	3808	961	122	**74**	**34**	139	261			**.262**	.289	**.363**	**652**	106	45	13	106				
NY	54	42	1	.563	11	29	17	498	**405**	3676	883	111	58	6	142	259			.250	.279	.319	598	91	-18	-40	104				
LOU	52	45	1	.536	13.5	29	18	564	562	3694	892	114	64	14	141	304			.251	.280	.331	611	**107**	-4	**40**	93				
COL	32	65	0	.330	33.5	18	29	476	659	3687	854	101	79	15	134	409			.240	.268	.326	594	102	-28	18	92				
PIT	31	67	0	.316	35	18	31	525	728	3771	892	120	58	13	164	345			.247	.280	.324	604	101	-10	14	96				
BAL	28	68	0	.292	37	18	31	471	742	3696	870	125	49	5	164	331			.246	.280	.314	594	91	-19	-35	103				
TOT	390					222	167	4465		29863	7217	960	478	114	1208	2417			.252	.282	.331	613								

TEAM	CG	SHO	GR	SV	IP	H	HR	BB	SO	BR/9	ERA	AERA	OAV	OOB	PR	APR	PF	OSB	OCS	FA	E	WPB	DP	FW	PW	BW	BSW	DIF
PHI	92	1	6	0	873.0	921	22	**95**	347	10.5	2.88	123	.254	.273	41	59	107			.865	584	168	40	-4.1	5.2	-.4		16.2
STL	93	**9**	5	**1**	879.1	**729**	**7**	150	325	**9.0**	**2.23**	**156**	**.211**	**.244**	**104**	**115**	106			**.909**	388	126	62	4.5	**10.1**	-3.6		5.0
CIN	96	8	2	0	866.2	766	17	168	215	9.7	2.26	143	.222	.258	100	95	98			.905	**383**	131	57	**4.7**	8.4	1.1		-2.2
NY	**97**	6	0	0	874.0	751	12	133	**478**	9.1	2.90	115	.218	.247	38	41	101			.905	391	**117**	45	4.1	3.6	-3.5		1.8
LOU	96	7	2	0	873.2	987	**7**	110	269	11.3	3.50	85	.267	.288	-20	-56	91			.886	478	156	67	.6	-4.9	**3.5**		4.3
COL	90	4	7	0	840.1	980	16	211	222	12.8	3.96	78	.274	.314	-62	-89	93			.874	535	170	**69**	-2.1	-7.8	1.6		-8.1
PIT	82	1	**18**	**1**	867.2	1140	21	151	271	13.4	4.62	70	.298	.325	-127	-135	99			.884	504	232	55	-.6	-11.9	1.2		-6.8
BAL	86	1	11	0	844.2	943	12	190	290	12.1	4.08	85	.265	.303	-74	-55	105			.855	624	277	44	-6.3	-4.8	-3.1		-5.8
TOT	732	37	51	2	6919.1					11.0	3.30		.252	.282						.885	3887	1377	439					

Batter-Fielder Wins	Batting Average	On-Base Percentage	Slugging Average	On-Base Plus Slugging	Adjusted OPS	Adjusted Batter Runs
Richmond-Col 3.8	Swartwood-Pit 357	Swartwood-Pit 394	Stovey-Phi 506	Swartwood-Pit 869	Swartwood-Pit 186	Swartwood-Pit 40.9
Smith-Col 3.4	Browning-Lou 338	Browning-Lou 378	Reilly-Cin 485	Stovey-Phi 852	Browning-Lou 183	Browning-Lou 34.4
Swartwood-Pit....2.8	Clinton-Bal 313	Moynahan-Phi 360	Swartwood-Pit 476	Browning-Lou 842	Stovey-Phi 156	Stovey-Phi 25.4
Gerhardt-Lou 2.4	Rowe-Bal 313	Clinton-Bal 357	Jones-Cin 471	Reilly-Cin 810	Reilly-Cin 149	Reilly-Cin 21.1
Holbert-NY 2.2	Reilly-Cin 311	Nelson-NY 353	Browning-Lou 464	Jones-Cin 799	Jones-Cin 146	Jones-Cin 18.2

Runs	Hits	Doubles	Triples	Home Runs	Total Bases	Runs Batted In
Stovey-Phi 110	Swartwood-Pit 147	Stovey-Phi.....................31	Smith-Col................17	Stovey-Phi 14	Stovey-Phi 213	
Reilly-Cin 103	Reilly-Cin 136	Swartwood-Pit 24	Reilly-Cin 14	Jones-Cin 10	Reilly-Cin 212	
Carpenter-Cin 99	Carpenter-Cin 130	Knight-Phi 23	Kuehne-Col 14	Reilly-Cin 9	Swartwood-Pit 196	
Knight-Phi 98	Stovey-Phi 128	Hayes-Pit 23	Mansell-Pit.............13	Fulmer-Cin................5	Jones-Cin 184	
	Nelson-NY 127	....	Mann-Col................13	Brown-Col 5	B.Gleason-StL 167	

Stolen Bases	Base Stealing Runs	Fielding Runs-Infield	Fielding Runs-Outfield	Wins	Winning Pct.	Complete Games
		Battin-Pit 28.8	Wolf-Lou 16.2	White-Cin................43	Mullane-StL 700	Keefe-NY 68
		Richmond-Col 26.9	Nicol-StL.................11.3	Keefe-NY 41	Mathews-Phi.........698	White-Cin 64
		Latham-StL 21.3	Maskrey-Lou..........9.9	Mullane-StL 35	Bradley-Phi...........696	Mountain-Col 57
		Smith-Col....................19.5	Birchall-Phi 5.0	Mathews-Phi 30	White-Cin 662	Hecker-Lou............51
		Gerhardt-Lou 18.4	Clinton-Bal 4.8	....	McGinnis-StL 636	Mullane-StL 49

Strikeouts	Fewest BB/Game	Games	Saves	Base Runners/9	Adjusted Relief Runs	Relief Ranking
Keefe-NY..............359	Mathews-Phi...........73	Keefe-NY 68	Mullane-StL 1	Keefe-NY 8.67		
Mathews-Phi 203	Weaver-Lou 79	White-Cin 65	Barr-Pit 1	Mullane-StL 8.71		
Mullane-StL 191	Lynch-NY 88	Mountain-Col 59		Jones-Phi 8.86		
Hecker-Lou 164	Bradley-Phi.............92	Mullane-StL 53		White-Cin 9.00		
Mountain-Col 159	Driscoll-Pit 1.04	Hecker-Lou 53		McGinnis-StL 9.27		

Innings Pitched	Opponents' Avg.	Opponents' OBP	Earned Run Average	Adjusted ERA	Adjusted Starter Runs	Pitcher Wins
Keefe-NY 619.0	Keefe-NY 203	Keefe-NY 237	White-Cin 2.09	Mullane-StL 159	White-Cin 74.8	**White-Cin**............6.9
White-Cin 577.0	Mullane-StL 207	Mullane-StL 238	Mullane-StL 2.19	White-Cin..............155	Keefe-NY 60.8	**Keefe-NY**..............6.0
Mountain-Col 503.0	White-Cin 209	White-Cin......................244	Deagle-Cin 2.31	McGinnis-StL........149	Mullane-StL 59.6	**Mullane-StL**.........5.5
Hecker-Lou........469.0	McGinnis-StL 215	McGinnis-StL...............249	McGinnis-StL 2.33	Mathews-Phi 144	McGinnis-StL 49.3	**McGinnis-StL** 4.2
Mullane-StL 460.2	Deagle-Cin 229	Bradley-Phi 263	Keefe-NY 2.41	Deagle-Cin 140	Mathews-Phi........37.8	**Mathews-Phi**......2.8

Calm before the Storm

After changing to the Reach baseball, the AA took the field for its second season with new clubs in New York City and Columbus, Ohio. The AA, like the NL, expanded its schedule to 98 games. Most clubs were going to larger rosters and deeper pitching staffs. The Athletics, Reds, and Baltimore used three pitchers for at least 16 starts, though New York (led by Tim Keefe, who completed all 68 of his starts) and Louisville made do with just two. Will White of Cincinnati was again the league's top hurler, but his club—despite leading the league in homers and batting average—was just 24–24 on the road, and finished third.

Philadelphia replaced first baseman Arlie Latham with Harry Stovey, and the new guy led the AA in runs, doubles, homers, and slugging. With fine pitching and an offense that led the league in walks and runs, the Athletics held off St. Louis by 1 game. The Browns, using fine pitching from Tony Mullane and solid defense, came close for garrulous owner Chris Von der Ahe and a fanatical fan base. The rough-and-tumble character of the team gained shape with the acquisition of Latham.

After eking out the league title, the Athletics were to meet the NL champion Boston Red Stockings in a postseason series, but suddenly reversed their decision after faring poorly in an October exhibition series against the NL's pathetic Philadelphia entry. Following this chain of events, the NL and AA met in New York that December and hammered out a "permanent" peace agreement with provisions for an annual postseason series between league champions.

The results of the AA's second season spoke loudly. The eight clubs combined to draw more than 1,000,000, with three clubs, (one of which was last-place Baltimore) pulling in more than 100,000 each. The entire NL drew just over 600,000—a nifty 35 percent increase—but not in the same league as the AA's 251 percent explosion.

1884 National League

TEAM	W	L	T	PCT	GB	HW	HL	R	OR	PA	H	2B	3B	HR	BB	SO	HB	SH	AVG	OBP	SLG	OPS	AOPS	BR	ABR	PF	SB	CS	BSA	BSR
PRO	84	28	2	.750		**45**	11	665	**388**	4393	987	153	43	21	**300**	469			.241	.293	.315	608	97	-16	-5	98				
BOS	73	38	5	.658	10.5	40	16	684	468	4396	1063	**179**	60	36	207	660			.254	.289	.351	640	105	18	21	100				
BUF	64	47	4	.577	19.5	37	18	**700**	626	4412	**1099**	163	**69**	**39**	215	**458**			**.262**	**.298**	**.361**	**659**	**106**	**45**	**22**	103				
NY	62	50	4	.554	22	34	22	693	623	4373	1053	149	68	22	249	492			.255	**.298**	.340	638	102	19	4	102				
CHI	62	50	1	.554	22	39	17	834	647	4446	1176	162	50	142	264	469			.281	.324	.446	770	133	203	139	108				
PHI	39	73	1	.348	45	19	37	549	824	4207	934	149	39	14	209	512			.234	.272	.301	573	88	-72	-45	95				
CLE	35	77	1	.313	49	22	34	458	716	4104	934	147	49	16	170	576			.237	.269	.312	581	83	-64	-82	103				
DET	28	84	2	.250	56	18	38	445	736	4177	825	114	47	31	207	699			.208	.247	.284	531	74	-134	-104	94				
TOT	457					254	193	5028		34508	8071	1216	425	321	1821	4335			.247	.287	.340	626								

TEAM	CG	SHO	GR	SV	IP	H	HR	BB	SO	BR/9	ERA	AERA	OAV	OOB	PR	APR	PF	OSB	OCS	FA	E	WPB	DP	FW	PW	BW	BSW	DIF
PRO	107	**16**	8	**2**	1036.1	**825**	**26**	172	639	**8.7**	**1.61**	**177**	**.209**	**.242**	**158**	**150**	96			.918	398	145	50	5.1	**13.4**	-.4		9.9
BOS	109	14	7	**2**	1037.0	932	30	**135**	**742**	9.3	2.47	117	.226	.250	58	51	97			**.922**	**384**	**138**	46	**6.3**	4.6	1.9		4.7
BUF	108	14	6	1	1001.0	1041	46	189	534	11.1	2.95	107	.254	.286	3	20	106			.905	462	167	71	1.9	1.8	2.0		2.8
NY	**111**	4	5	0	1014.0	1011	28	326	567	11.9	3.12	95	.245	.300	-16	-19	100			.895	514	200	69	-.6	-1.7	.4		8.0
CHI	106	9	**9**	0	997.1	1028	83	231	472	11.4	3.03	103	.250	.290	-6	10	105			.886	595	198	**107**	-5.6	.9	**12.4**		-1.7
PHI	106	3	7	1	981.0	1090	37	254	411	12.3	3.93	76	.261	.304	-103	-105	100			.888	536	326	67	-2.5	-9.4	-4.0		-1.1
CLE	107	7	6	0	994.2	1046	35	269	482	11.9	3.43	92	.256	.302	-50	-30	106			.897	512	230	75	-1.2	-2.7	-7.3		-9.8
DET	109	3	5	0	984.2	1097	36	245	488	12.3	3.38	86	.262	.302	-44	-55	97			.886	550	159	60	-3.0	-4.9	-9.3		-10.8
TOT	863	70	53	6	8046.0					11.1	2.98		.247	.287						.899	3951	1563	545					

Batter-Fielder Wins	Batting Average	On-Base Percentage	Slugging Average	On-Base Plus Slugging	Adjusted OPS	Adjusted Batter Runs
Pfeffer-Chi 6.0	O'Rourke-Buf 347	Kelly-Chi 414	Brouthers-Buf 563	Brouthers-Buf 941	Brouthers-Buf 186	Kelly-Chi 40.9
Williamson-Chi ..4.7	Kelly-Chi 354	Gore-Chi 404	Williamson-Chi 554	Kelly-Chi 938	Kelly-Chi 178	Brouthers-Buf 38.0
Kelly-Chi.............3.3	Sutton-Bos 346	O'Rourke-Buf..............392	Anson-Chi.............543	Anson-Chi 916	Anson-Chi 170	Anson-Chi 36.8
Ewing-NY 3.1	Anson-Chi.............335	Sutton-Bos..................384	Kelly-Chi 524	Williamson-Chi 898	O'Rourke-Buf........167	O'Rourke-Buf......36.4
Sutton-Bos 2.8	Brouthers-Buf 327	Brouthers-Buf 378	Pfeffer-Chi 514	O'Rourke-Buf........872	Williamson-Chi 164	Sutton-Bos 34.7

Runs	Hits	Doubles	Triples	Home Runs	Total Bases	Runs Batted In
Kelly-Chi 120	Sutton-Bos............162	Hines-Pro 36	Ewing-NY 20	Williamson-Chi 27	Dalrymple-Chi 263	Anson-Chi 102
O'Rourke-Buf........119	O'Rourke-Buf........162	O'Rourke-Buf 33	Brouthers-Buf 15	Pfeffer-Chi 25	Anson-Chi 258	Pfeffer-Chi 101
Hornung-Bos 119	Dalrymple-Chi 161	Anson-Chi......................30	Rowe-Buf................14	Dalrymple-Chi 22	Pfeffer-Chi 240	Kelly-Chi................95
Dalrymple-Chi 111	Kelly-Chi 160	Manning-Phi 29	McKinnon-NY 13	Anson-Chi 21	Kelly-Chi 237	Williamson-Chi 84
Anson-Chi 108	Anson-Chi 159		Phillips-Cle 12	Brouthers-Buf 14	Williamson-Chi 231	Connor-NY 82

Stolen Bases	Base Stealing Runs	Fielding Runs-Infield	Fielding Runs-Outfield	Wins	Winning Pct.	Complete Games
		Pfeffer-Chi 43.3	Lillie-Buf 15.8	Radbourn-Pro 59	Radbourn-Pro.......831	Radbourn-Pro........73
		Williamson-Chi...........21.7	Hanlon-Det 12.3	Buffinton-Bos.........48	Buffinton-Bos 750	Galvin-Buf 71
		Mulvey-Phi 12.9	Evans-Cle..............8.2	Galvin-Buf 46	Sweeney-Pro 680	Buffinton-Bos 63
		Ward-NY 10.6	Fogarty-Phi...........6.9	Welch-NY 39	Galvin-Buf............676	Welch-NY 62
		Richardson-Buf 5.2	G.Wood-Det 4.0	L.Corcoran-Chi 35	Welch-NY 650	L.Corcoran-Chi......57

Strikeouts	Fewest BB/Game	Games	Saves	Base Runners/9	Adjusted Relief Runs	Relief Ranking
Radbourn-Pro 441	Whitney-Bos 72	Radbourn-Pro 75	Morrill-Bos 2	Sweeney-Pro 7.41		
Buffinton-Bos.......417	Galvin-Buf...............89	Galvin-Buf......................72	Sweeney-Pro 1	Whitney-Bos 8.01		
Galvin-Buf 369	Buffinton-Bos 1.17	Buffinton-Bos 67	Radbourn-Pro 1	Radbourn-Pro.......8.30		
Welch-NY 345	Sweeney-Pro 1.18	Welch-NY 65	O'Rourke-Buf............1	Getzien-Det 8.74		
L.Corcoran-Chi 272	Coleman-Phi........1.28	L.Corcoran-Chi 60	Ferguson-Phi 1	Galvin-Buf...........8.90		

Innings Pitched	Opponents' Avg.	Opponents' OBP	Earned Run Average	Adjusted ERA	Adjusted Starter Runs	Pitcher Wins
Radbourn-Pro....678.2	Sweeney-Pro 187	Sweeney-Pro 215	Radbourn-Pro......1.38	Radbourn-Pro 206	Radbourn-Pro....116.2	**Radbourn-Pro**..10.7
Galvin-Buf..........636.1	Getzien-Det 204	Whitney-Bos 223	Sweeney-Pro 1.55	Sweeney-Pro.........184	Galvin-Buf............80.9	**Galvin-Buf**..........6.3
Buffinton-Bos 587.0	Radbourn-Pro.......205	Radbourn-Pro 234	Getzien-Det 1.95	Galvin-Buf 158	Buffinton-Bos 51.3	**Buffinton-Bos**.....5.8
Welch-NY 557.1	Whitney-Bos 207	Getzien-Det 237	Galvin-Buf............1.99	Getzien-Det 148	Sweeney-Pro 35.7	**Sweeney-Pro** 4.4
L.Corcoran-Chi ..516.2	Clarkson-Chi.........208	Buffinton-Bos...............244	Whitney-Bos 2.09	Clarkson-Chi 147	L.Corcoran-Chi....34.6	**Whitney-Bos** 3.6

Ride That Hoss

The National League expanded to 112 games, hoping to fight the new Union Association by garnering increased newspaper coverage. There were no franchise shifts. The league also first allowed its pitchers to throw overhand, although the Union and American Associations declined to make this change. Additionally, the NL cut the number of balls needed for a walk to six, while the other leagues held at seven.

The biggest story of the year was in Providence, which began the season with two star pitchers: Hoss Radbourn and Charlie Sweeney. When manager Frank Bancroft said that the two would share mound duties, an offended Radbourn loafed and earned a suspension.

Sweeney, receiving an offer from the wealthy St. Louis Union club, malingered and finagled a suspension as well. He then jumped to the outlaws, and Radbourn had the Grays where he wanted them. Radbourn pledged to pitch the rest of the season for Providence if the team would then allow him to depart via free agency. Radbourn went on to win 59 games, an all-time record. Unfortunately for Old Hoss, his arm was never quite the same, though he remained effective and had five 20-win seasons for Providence (he stayed through 1885) and Boston teams in two different leagues.

The '84 Grays had Paul Hines' big bat in center field, but offense wasn't their forte; four of the league's eight teams scored more runs. They still won by 10½ games, courtesy of Old Hoss. Providence then met American Association champs New York in a three-game tourney. Despite playing at New York's Polo Grounds and under Association rules, Radbourn won three straight—6–0, 3–1, and 11–2—to take what can legitimately be called the first World Series. The gate certainly wasn't great. Total attendance was less than 3,800, and just 300 people showed up for the inconsequential third game. Attendance for the whole NL season rose by just 5,000, despite the extra contests, and dropped precipitously in Detroit, Cleveland, and Chicago.

1884 American Association

TEAM	W	L	T	PCT	GB	HW	HL	R	OR	PA	H	2B	3B	HR	BB	SO	HB	SH	AVG	OBP	SLG	OPS	AOPS	BR	ABR	PF	SB	CS	BSA	BSR
NY	75	32	5	.701		**42**	9	734	**423**	4250	1052	155	64	22	203	**315**		35	.262	**.304**	.349	653	120	73	90	98				
COL	69	39	2	.639	6.5	38	16	585	459	4014	901	107	96	**40**	196	629		59	.240	.288	.351	639	**121**	45	**98**	92				
LOU	68	40	2	.630	7.5	41	14	573	425	4137	1004	152	69	17	146	408		34	.254	.286	.340	626	112	29	58	96				
STL	67	40	3	.626	8	38	14	658	539	4163	987	151	60	11	172	339		39	.250	.288	.327	615	100	18	-3	104				
CIN	68	41	3	.624	8	40	16	**754**	512	4296	1037	109	96	36	154	409		52	.254	.289	.354	643	108	49	19	105				
BAL	63	43	2	.594	11.5	**42**	13	636	515	4120	896	133	84	32	**211**	545		**64**	.233	.284	.336	620	101	26	3	104				
PHI	61	46	1	.570	14	38	16	700	546	4152	**1057**	**167**	**100**	26	153	434		40	**.267**	.301	**.379**	**680**	117	**100**	59	106				
TOL	46	58	6	.442	27.5	28	25	463	571	3895	859	153	48	8	157	545		26	.231	.268	.305	573	87	-36	-53	104				
BRO	40	64	5	.385	33.5	23	26	476	644	3958	845	112	47	16	179	417		16	.225	.263	.292	555	83	-61	-64	101				
RIC	12	30	4	.286	30.5	5	15	194	294	1546	326	40	33	7	53	282		24	.222	.261	.308	569	89	-19	-17	99				
PIT	30	78	2	.278	45.5	18	37	406	725	3873	777	105	50	2	143	411		41	.211	.248	.268	516	73	-110	-105	99				
IND	29	78	3	.271	46	17	39	462	755	3960	890	129	62	20	125	561		22	.233	.262	.315	577	93	-39	-25	97				
WAS	12	51	0	.190	41	10	20	248	481	2282	434	61	24	6	100	377		16	.200	.241	.259	500	75	-76	-44	88				
TOT	659					380	260	6889		48646	11065	1574	833	243	1992	5672	468		.240	.278	.326	604								

TEAM	CG	SHO	GR	SV	IP	H	HR	BB	SO	BR/9	ERA	AERA	OAV	OOB	PR	APR	PF	OSB	OCS	FA	E	WPB	DP	FW	PW	BW	BSW	DIF
NY	110	9	2	0	985.0	**802**	15	115	628	**8.6**	2.46	127	**.209**	**.237**	86	75	96			.907	441	**137**	42	2.3	6.9	8.2		4.1
COL	102	8	8	**1**	962.1	815	22	172	526	9.5	2.68	113	.217	.256	60	38	93			.908	433	191	74	2.3	3.5	**9.0**		.3
LOU	101	6	9	0	989.2	837	**9**	**97**	470	8.8	**2.17**	**142**	.216	.241	**118**	**105**	95			**.912**	**426**	190	**84**	2.6	**9.6**	5.3		-3.5
STL	99	8	**11**	0	987.0	881	16	172	477	10.0	2.67	122	.226	.266	63	63	100			.900	490	174	65	-.2	5.8	-.3		8.2
CIN	**111**	**11**	1	0	983.2	955	27	181	308	11.1	3.33	100	.243	.289	-10	-1	103			.909	430	164	82	**2.8**	-.0	1.7		9.0
BAL	105	8	3	**1**	955.2	869	16	219	**635**	10.5	2.71	128	.224	.271	56	74	107			.899	461	210	61	.7	6.8	.3		2.3
PHI	105	5	3	0	948.2	920	16	127	530	10.3	3.42	99	.237	.269	-18	-4	104			.901	457	199	63	.9	-.4	5.4		1.6
TOL	103	9	6	**1**	946.0	885	12	169	501	10.5	3.06	111	.233	.275	19	34	105			.900	469	294	67	.7	3.1	-4.8		-5.0
BRO	105	6	4	0	948.2	996	20	163	378	11.2	3.79	87	.254	.288	-58	-50	102			.889	520	266	68	-1.6	-4.6	-5.8		.0
RIC	45	1	0	0	370.1	402	14	52	167	11.4	4.52	73	.257	.288	-53	-49	102			.874	239	82	27	-1.5	-4.5	-1.6		-1.4
PIT	108	4	2	0	943.1	1059	25	216	338	12.7	4.35	76	.265	.312	-116	-109	102			.889	523	218	71	-1.6	-10.0	-9.6		-2.9
IND	107	2	3	0	937.2	1000	30	199	479	11.8	4.20	78	.254	.295	-100	-96	101			.889	515	250	45	-1.2	-8.8	-2.3		-12.2
WAS	62	3	1	0	543.2	644	21	110	235	12.8	4.01	76	.273	.311	-46	-64	93			.858	400	165	40	-5.3	-5.8	-4.0		-4.4
TOT	1263	80	53	3	11501.2					10.6	3.24		.240	.278						.897	5804	2540	789					

Batter-Fielder Wins	Batting Average	On-Base Percentage	Slugging Average	On-Base Plus Slugging	Adjusted OPS	Adjusted Batter Runs
Barkley-Tol..........4.8	Orr-NY 354	Jones-Cin.....................376	Reilly-Cin 551	Reilly-Cin 918	Orr-NY 195	Orr-NY................45.5
Fennelly-Was-Cin4.2	Reilly-Cin 339	Nelson-NY 375	Stovey-Phi 545	Stovey-Phi 913	Reilly-Cin 186	Reilly-Cin 39.4
Smith-Col 4.1	Browning-Lou 336	Stovey-Phi 368	Orr-NY 539	Orr-NY...................901	Fennelly-Was-Cin 186	Stovey-Phi 37.7
Latham-StL 4.1	Stovey-Phi 326	Fennelly-Was-Cin 367	Fennelly-Was-Cin .480	Fennelly-Was-Cin 847	Stovey-Phi 182	Browning-Lou 37.4
Esterbrook-NY....3.5	Lewis-StL 323	Reilly-Cin 366	Browning-Lou 472	Jones-Cin 846	Browning-Lou 176	Fennelly-Was-Cin37.3

Runs	Hits	Doubles	Triples	Home Runs	Total Bases	Runs Batted In
Stovey-Phi 124	Orr-NY 162	Barkley-Tol 39	Stovey-Phi 23	Reilly-Cin 11	Reilly-Cin 247	
Jones-Cin 117	Reilly-Cin 152	Browning-Lou 33	Reilly-Cin 19	Stovey-Phi 10	Orr-NY 247	
Latham-StL 115	Esterbrook-NY......150	Orr-NY 32	Mann-Col.................18	Orr-NY.......................9	Stovey-Phi 244	
Reilly-Cin 114	Browning-Lou 150	Esterbrook-NY 29	Peltz-Ind 17	Mann-Col...................7	Jones-Cin 222	
Nelson-NY 114	Jones-Cin 148	Lewis-StL 25	Jones-Cin 17	Jones-Cin 7	Browning-Lou 211	

Stolen Bases	Base Stealing Runs	Fielding Runs-Infield	Fielding Runs-Outfield	Wins	Winning Pct.	Complete Games
		Latham-StL 37.2	Nicol-StL 18.4	Hecker-Lou 52	Morris-Col .723	Hecker-Lou 72
		Smith-Col 29.8	Welch-Tol 14.0	Lynch-NY 37	Hecker-Lou .722	Mullane-Tol 64
		Barkley-Tol 27.3	Knight-Phi 11.0	Keefe-NY 37	Foutz-StL .714	McKeon-Ind 59
		Gerhardt-Lou22.5	Corkhill-Cin 10.3	Mullane-Tol 36	Lynch-NY .712	Keefe-NY 56
		Houck-Phi 22.0	Cline-Lou 6.1		Keefe-NY .685	Terry-Bro 54

Strikeouts	Fewest BB/Game	Games	Saves	Base Runners/9	Adjusted Relief Runs	Relief Ranking
Hecker-Lou 385	Driscoll-Lou 62	Hecker-Lou 75	O'Day-Tol..................1	Hecker-Lou..........8.02		
Henderson-Bal 346	Hecker-Lou.............75	Mullane-Tol 67	Mountain-Col............1	Morris-Col............8.36		
Keefe-NY..............334	Lynch-NY 76	McKeon-Ind 61	T.Burns-Bal 1	Lynch-NY 8.56		
Mullane-Tol 325	E.Dugan-Ric...........81	Keefe-NY 58		Caruthers-StL......8.60		
McKeon-Ind 308	McGinnis-StL 89	Terry-Bro........................56		Keefe-NY 8.68		

Innings Pitched	Opponents' Avg.	Opponents' OBP	Earned Run Average	Adjusted ERA	Adjusted Starter Runs	Pitcher Wins
Hecker-Lou........670.2	Keefe-NY 204	Hecker-Lou 226	Hecker-Lou..........1.80	Hecker-Lou 171	Hecker-Lou........103.0	**Hecker-Lou**......12.9
Mullane-Tol........567.0	Hecker-Lou...........204	Morris-Col 234	Foutz-StL 2.18	Foutz-StL 149	Mullane-Tol 54.6	**Mullane-Tol**........7.1
McKeon-Ind 512.0	Morris-Col.............204	Lynch-NY......................236	Morris-Col............2.18	Morris-Col 139	Keefe-NY 46.2	**Keefe-NY**............5.5
Lynch-NY 496.0	Mountain-Col 209	Keefe-NY 239	Keefe-NY 2.25	Keefe-NY..............138	Morris-Col............45.7	**Morris-Col** 4.5
Keefe-NY 483.0	Foutz-StL 212	Foutz-StL 255	Mountain-Col 2.45	Mullane-Tol 135	Henderson-Bal 36.7	**Henderson-Bal** ..3.9

Mets Win New York's First Flag

While the National League believed it could live with the threat of the American Association, the threat from the new Union Association, whose owners did not respect the reserve clause, was another thing entirely. The NL supported Association expansion into four cities that the Unions might possibly inhabit: Brooklyn (which remains in the NL today as the Los Angeles Dodgers), Washington, Indianapolis, and Toledo.

While scrambling to keep their players from Union Association clutches, the AA debuted St. Louis pitchers Bob Caruthers and Dave Foutz , and Toledo outfielder Curt Welch and catcher Deacon McGuire. Brothers Moses and Welday Walker of Toledo became the first blacks ever to play major league baseball—and the last, thanks to various regressive thinkers, until 1947.

A five-team pennant race produced New York's first major league flag. Jim Mutrie's Metropolitans sported batting titlist Dave Orr and infielder Candy Nelson, whose 74 walks were *twice* the previous major league record. The Mets distributed the load equally on the mound. Tim Keefe and Jack Lynch each won 37 games, the first time in major league history two teammates ranked so high in this category. Columbus and Louisville, with Guy Hecker winning 52 times, finished 2-3 in pitching. St. Louis finished fourth, but when Charlie Comiskey took over the reins late in the year, the team immediately sparked. Cincinnati had slugger John Reilly but little else.

Washington defaulted in August, replaced by Richmond, a club from the Eastern League. About the only positive thing Richmond brought was 19-year-old third baseman Billy Nash, who went on to a long NL career. Following the 1883 season, Richmond, Indianapolis, and Toledo were asked to leave the league, and Columbus merged with Pittsburgh.

Despite increasing the schedule to more than 100 games, and adding extra teams, AA attendance rose by just 75,000. Philadelphia's attendance, the league's best in 1883, dipped by around 60 percent, even though the city's Union club defaulted in early August. Crowds were smaller but there was still plenty of life in them. On August 13 Baltimore management surrounded its field with barbed wire the day after fans surged out of the stands and roughed up the umpire.

1884 Union Association

TEAM	W	L	T	PCT	GB	HW	HL	R	OR	PA	H	2B	3B	HR	BB	SO	HB	SH	AVG	OBP	SLG	OPS	AOPS	BR	ABR	PF	SB	CS	BSA	BSR
STL	94	19	1	.832		**50**	6	**887**	**429**	4466	**1251**	**259**	**41**	**32**	**181**	**542**			**.292**	**.321**	**.394**	**715**	**113**	**-31**	**-53**	104				
MIL	8	4	0	.667	35.5	8	4	53	34	415	88	25	0	0	20	70			.223	.260	.286	546	124	-26	6	54				
CIN	69	36	0	.657	21	35	17	703	466	3933	1027	118	63	26	147	482			.271	.298	.356	654	92	-119	-154	108				
BAL	58	47	1	.552	32	29	21	662	627	4027	952	150	26	17	144	652			.245	.272	.310	582	71	-219	-256	110				
BOS	58	51	2	.532	34	34	23	636	558	4068	928	168	32	19	128	787			.236	.260	.309	569	74	-245	-239	98				
CP	41	50	2	.451	42	21	18	438	482	3331	742	127	26	10	119	505			.231	.258	.296	554	69	-215	-213	99				
WAS	47	65	2	.420	46.5	36	27	572	679	4044	931	120	26	4	118	558			.237	.259	.284	543	68	-278	-266	97				
PHI	21	46	0	.313	50	13	21	414	545	2621	618	108	35	7	103	405			.245	.275	.324	599	89	-128	-106	93				
STP	2	6	1	.250	39.5	0	0	24	57	279	49	13	1	0	7	47			.180	.201	.235	436	61	-30	-19	54				
ALT	6	19	0	.240	44	6	12	90	216	921	223	30	6	2	22	130			.248	.266	.301	567	72	-56	-57	101				
KC	16	63	3	.203	61	11	23	311	618	2925	557	104	15	6	123	529			.199	.232	.253	485	55	-258	-230	87				
WIL	2	16	0	.111	44.5	1	6	35	114	543	91	8	8	2	22	123			.175	.208	.232	440	33	-58	-59	103				
TOT	428					244	178	4825		31573	7457	1230	279	125	1134	4830			.245	.272	.316	588								

TEAM	CG	SHO	GR	SV	IP	H	HR	BB	SO	BR/9	ERA	AERA	OAV	OOB	PR	APR	PF	OSB	OCS	FA	E	WPB	DP	FW	PW	BW	BSW	DIF
STL	**104**	8	9	**6**	993.0	838	**9**	110	550	**8.6**	**1.96**	**152**	**.214**	**.235**	**120**	**115**	98			**.888**	554	**159**	**79**	**3.7**	**10.1**	**-4.6**		28.3
MIL	12	3	0	0	104.0	49	1	13	139	5.4	2.25	73	.132	.161	9	-13	54			.892	53	32	4	.6	-1.1	.5		2.0
CIN	95	**11**	8	1	914.1	831	17	**90**	503	9.1	2.38	134	.226	.245	67	78	105			.882	532	169	45	2.5	6.8	-13.5		20.6
BAL	92	4	14	0	946.2	1002	24	177	628	11.2	3.01	111	.254	.286	3	31	110			.872	616	259	53	-.8	2.7	-22.4		26.0
BOS	100	5	9	1	953.1	885	17	110	**753**	9.4	2.70	110	.231	.252	36	28	98			.868	633	277	39	-.3	2.5	-20.9		22.3
CP	86	6	6	0	803.2	**743**	12	137	679	9.9	2.72	112	.230	.261	29	28	100			.882	**459**	191	38	2.8	2.5	-18.6		8.9
WAS	94	5	**20**	0	953.2	992	16	168	684	10.9	3.43	87	.251	.282	-41	-47	98			.869	625	284	55	.7	-4.1	-23.3		17.7
PHI	64	1	3	0	593.1	726	7	105	310	12.6	4.63	63	.283	.311	-104	-120	95			.841	501	268	36	-5.2	-10.5	-9.3		12.5
STP	7	1	2	0	71.0	72	1	27	44	12.5	3.17	52	.248	.312	-1	-22	54			.872	47	12	6	.2	-1.9	-1.7		1.4
ALT	20	0	5	0	219.2	292	3	52	93	14.1	4.67	71	.300	.335	-40	-31	109			.862	156	63	4	-.6	-2.7	-5.0		1.8
KC	70	0	12	0	702.2	862	14	127	334	12.7	4.05	69	.283	.312	-78	-108	92			.861	520	209	51	-2.5	-9.5	-20.1		8.6
WIL	15	0	2	0	142.0	165	4	18	113	11.6	3.04	109	.273	.294	0	4	109			.860	104	62	10	-.1	.4	-5.2		-2.1
TOT	759	44	90	8	7397.1					10.5	3.04		.245	.272						.872	4800	1985	420					

Batter-Fielder Wins	Batting Average	On-Base Percentage	Slugging Average	On-Base Plus Slugging	Adjusted OPS	Adjusted Batter Runs
Dunlap-StL 7.1	Dunlap-StL 412	Dunlap-StL..................448	Dunlap-StL 621	Dunlap-StL 1069	Dunlap-StL 213	Dunlap-StL 50.5
Shafer-StL 1.9	Taylor-StL 366	Shafer-StL 398	Taylor-StL 548	Shafer-StL 899	Hoover-Phi............180	Shafer-StL 25.2
Hoover-Phi 1.6	Dickerson-StL.......365	Hoover-Phi..................390	Shafer-StL 501	Hoover-Phi............885	Shafer-StL 165	Hoover-Phi..........19.2
Glasscock-Cin....1.4	Hoover-Phi 364	Moore-Was 363	Hoover-Phi 495	Gleason-StL 802	Moore-Was 139	Glasscock-Cin 13.6
Briody-Cin 1.1	Shafer-StL 360	Gleason-StL................361	Burns-Cin 457	Moore-Was 777	Gleason-StL 137	Taylor-StL 12.2

Runs	Hits	Doubles	Triples	Home Runs	Total Bases	Runs Batted In
Dunlap-StL 160	Dunlap-StL 185	Shafer-StL......................40	Burns-Cin 12	Dunlap-StL 13	Dunlap-StL 279	
Shafer-StL 130	Shafer-StL 168	Dunlap-StL 39	Rowe-StL................11	Crane-Bos 12	Shafer-StL 234	
Seery-Bal-KC........115	Moore-Was 155	Rowe-StL 32	Shafer-StL 10	Levis-Bal-Was 5	Rowe-StL...............208	
Robinson-Bal........101	Seery-Bal-KC.........146	O'Brien-Bos 31			Crane-Bos 193	
Rowe-StL................95	Rowe-StL..............142	Gleason-StL 30			Seery-Bal-KC........192	

Stolen Bases	Base Stealing Runs	Fielding Runs-Infield	Fielding Runs-Outfield	Wins	Winning Pct.	Complete Games
		Dunlap-StL..................28.4	Wise-Was 8.2	B.Sweeney-Bal 40	McCormick-Cin.....875	B.Sweeney-Bal 58
		Evers-Was 14.5	Boyle-StL 5.3	Daily-CP-Was 28	Taylor-StL 862	Daily-CP-Was..........56
		Robinson-Bal 12.7	Harbridge-Cin 4.3	Taylor-StL 25	Boyle-StL 833	Bakely-Phi-Wil-KC 43
		Hackett-Bos 11.6	Crane-Bos 4.0	Bradley-Cin 25	Sweeney-StL 774	Bradley-Cin............36
		McCormick-Phi-Was 9.8	B.Sweeney-Bal 3.7	Sweeney-StL 24	B.Sweeney-Bal 656	Shaw-Bos 35

Strikeouts	Fewest BB/Game	Games	Saves	Base Runners/9	Adjusted Relief Runs	Relief Ranking
Daily-CP-Was 483	Sweeney-StL 43	B.Sweeney-Bal 62	Taylor-StL 4	McCormick-Cin....7.07		
B.Sweeney-Bal 374	McCormick-Cin.......60	Daily-CP-Was 58	Sylvester-Cin 1	Sweeney-StL 7.31		
Shaw-Bos 309	Boyle-StL 60	Wise-Was 50	Dunlap-StL 1	Shaw-Bos 7.53		
Wise-Was 268	Bradley-Cin.............61	Bakely-Phi-Wil-KC 46	Brown-Bos 1	Boyle-StL 7.68		
Burke-Bos 255	Murphy-Alt-Wil 62	Bradley-Cin....................41	Boyle-StL..................1	Werden-StL 8.60		

Innings Pitched	Opponents' Avg.	Opponents' OBP	Earned Run Average	Adjusted ERA	Adjusted Starter Runs	Pitcher Wins
B.Sweeney-Bal ..538.0	McCormick-Cin.....188	McCormick-Cin 202	McCormick-Cin....1.54	McCormick-Cin 166	McCormick-Cin....25.5	**Taylor-StL** 2.8
Daily-CP-Was 500.2	Shaw-Bos 188	Sweeney-StL 207	Taylor-StL 1.68	Taylor-StL 142	Taylor-StL 21.3	**Sweeney-StL**......2.2
Bakely-Phi-Wil-KC 394.2	Sweeney-StL 197	Shaw-Bos 212	Boyle-StL 1.74	Boyle-StL..............137	Shaw-Bos 19.9	**McCormick-Cin** 1.9
Wise-Was 364.1	Boyle-StL 202	Boyle-StL 215	Shaw-Bos 1.77	Shaw-Bos 134	Sweeney-StL 16.5	**Shaw-Bos** 1.3
Bradley-Cin........342.0	Werden-StL 205	Werden-StL 235	Sweeney-StL 1.83	Sweeney-StL 131	Boyle-StL 9.6	**Boyle-StL**...............8

One-Shot Deal

The Union Association, set up ostensibly to challenge the reserve clause, sprang from the mind of St. Louis magnate Henry Lucas, who wanted to force his way into the big picture. It's no coincidence, then, that the St. Louis club was the class of the league, winning by 21 games. Several clubs, including Altoona, Philadelphia, and Chicago (which moved to Pittsburgh, *then* disbanded) weren't even around at the finish.

The Union owners went after low-level NL and AA players and the occasional regular, but almost immediately, contract-jumping and charges of game-throwing plagued the new league. Three good young players debuted in the Union Association before catching on elsewhere: shortstop Germany Smith and outfielders Tommy McCarthy and Oyster Burns. But the level of play was not high; journeyman pitcher Hugh "One Arm" Daily fanned 483 hitters, the third highest total ever. St. Louis' Fred Dunlap, the UA's star batter, hit .412 with 13 homers; he was a good hitter in the NL, but no superstar.

Much has been said about the league's thin qualifications as a major league. But the UA *operated* as a major league, raiding NL and AA rosters. It also played more games in 1884 than did clubs in any established minor league. The UA did, however, feature minor league teams. Wilmington, the champions of the Eastern League, jumped to the UA in August to replace Philadelphia. St. Paul joined the Union at the end of the Northwestern League season to finish out the season when Wilmington disbanded. The Milwaukee Grays, also of the Northwestern League, were the league's most successful replacement, going 8–4 in Pittsburgh's stead. Kansas City formed a team to replace Altoona, going 16–63. Only five teams were functioning at season's end.

The fragile league crumbled as soon as the NL accepted the St. Louis club for 1885 to provide competition for Chris Von der Ahe's successful AA franchise. Maroons dominated almost every UA statistical category and drew 116,000 of the league's 411,000 fans.

Vested-interest parties such as Al Spalding and Al Reach had nothing good to say about the Union Association. But many people hated the reserve clause, and it was only a few years until a more powerful league rose to combat it.

1885 National League

TEAM	W	L	T	PCT	GB	HW	HL	R	OR	PA	H	2B	3B	HR	BB	SO	HB	SH	AVG	OBP	SLG	OPS	AOPS	BR	ABR	PF	SB	CS	BSA	BSR
CHI	87	25	1	.777		42	14	**834**	470	4433	1079	**184**	75	**54**	**340**	429			.264	**.320**	**.385**	**705**	116	**146**	56	114				
NY	85	27	0	.759	2	**45**	10	691	**370**	4250	**1085**	150	**82**	16	221	**312**			**.269**	.307	.359	666	**122**	80	**89**	99				
PHI	56	54	1	.509	30	29	26	513	511	4113	891	156	35	20	220	401			.229	.270	.302	572	91	-44	-34	98				
PRO	53	57	0	.482	33	30	24	442	531	3992	820	114	30	6	265	430			.220	.272	.272	544	82	-74	-60	97				
BOS	46	66	1	.411	41	22	35	528	589	4140	915	144	53	22	190	522			.232	.267	.312	579	94	-42	-23	96				
DET	41	67	0	.380	44	29	23	514	582	3989	917	149	66	25	216	451			.243	.284	.337	621	105	17	16	100				
BUF	38	74	0	.339	49	19	38	495	761	4079	980	149	50	23	179	380			.251	.284	.333	617	100	10	-8	103				
STL	36	72	3	.333	49	23	33	390	593	3972	829	121	21	8	214	412			.221	.263	.270	533	81	-92	-62	94				
TOT	445					239	203	4407		32968	7516	1167	412	174	1845	3337			.241	.284	.322	606								

TEAM	CG	SHO	GR	SV	IP	H	HR	BB	SO	BR/9	ERA	AERA	OAV	OOB	PR	APR	PF	OSB	OCS	FA	E	WPB	DP	FW	PW	BW	BSW	DIF
CHI	108	14	**5**	**4**	1015.2	868	37	202	458	9.5	2.23	134	.221	.259	66	80	107			.903	496	133	80	-2.4	7.5	5.3		20.6
NY	109	**16**	3	1	994.0	**758**	**11**	265	**516**	**9.3**	**1.72**	**155**	**.205**	**.258**	**121**	**112**	95			**.929**	**331**	168	**85**	**6.0**	**10.5**	**8.4**		4.1
PHI	108	10	3	0	976.0	860	18	218	378	9.9	2.39	117	.224	.266	46	41	99			.905	447	167	66	-.3	3.9	-3.2		.6
PRO	108	8	3	0	960.2	912	18	235	371	10.7	2.71	99	.235	.278	12	-4	95			.903	459	165	70	-1.1	-.4	-5.6		5.1
BOS	**111**	10	2	0	981.0	1045	26	**188**	480	11.3	3.03	89	.261	.294	-23	-40	95			.901	478	184	79	-1.5	-3.8	-2.2		-2.6
DET	105	6	3	1	954.1	966	18	224	475	11.2	2.88	99	.249	.290	-6	-5	101			.901	462	**115**	61	-1.7	-.5	1.5		-12.4
BUF	107	4	**5**	1	956.0	1175	31	234	320	13.3	4.29	69	.289	.328	-157	-132	106			.901	464	196	65	-.9	-12.4	-.8		-3.9
STL	107	4	4	0	965.1	935	15	278	337	11.3	3.37	82	.245	.296	-59	-69	97			.916	398	178	67	2.3	-6.5	-5.8		-8.0
TOT	863	72	28	7	7803.0					10.8	2.82		.241	.284						.908	3535	1306	573					

Batter-Fielder Wins	Batting Average	On-Base Percentage	Slugging Average	On-Base Plus Slugging	Adjusted OPS	Adjusted Batter Runs
Connor-NY 4.3	Connor-NY 371	Connor-NY...................435	Brouthers-Buf 543	Brouthers-Buf 951	Connor-NY............203	Connor-NY 53.8
Dunlap-StL 4.1	Brouthers-Buf 359	Brouthers-Buf 408	Connor-NY 495	Connor-NY............929	Brouthers-Buf 199	Brouthers-Buf 44.4
Glasscock-StL....3.5	Dorgan-NY 326	Gore-Chi 405	Ewing-NY 471	Gore-Chi 858	Bennett-Det 161	O'Rourke-NY......30.7
Bennett-Det 3.3	Richardson-Buf.....319	Hanlon-Det 372	Anson-Chi.............461	Anson-Chi 819	Ewing-NY 159	Gore-Chi 28.0
Brouthers-Buf 3.1	Gore-Chi...............313	Anson-Chi 357	Richardson-Buf.....458	Bennett-Det 812	O'Rourke-NY 158	Bennett-Det........25.1

Runs	Hits	Doubles	Triples	Home Runs	Total Bases	Runs Batted In
Kelly-Chi 124	Connor-NY............169	Anson-Chi......................35	O'Rourke-NY..........16	Dalrymple-Chi 11	Connor-NY............225	Anson-Chi 108
O'Rourke-NY........119	Brouthers-Buf 146	Brouthers-Buf 32	Connor-NY.............15	Kelly-Chi 9	Brouthers-Buf 221	Kelly-Chi................75
Gore-Chi 115	Anson-Chi 144	Rowe-Buf 28	Gore-Chi 13		Dalrymple-Chi 219	Pfeffer-Chi 73
Dalrymple-Chi 109	Sutton-Bos............143	Dalrymple-Chi................27	Bennett-Det 13		Anson-Chi 214	Burns-Chi 71
Connor-NY............102	O'Rourke-NY 143	Mulvey-Phi 25			O'Rourke-NY 211	

Stolen Bases	Base Stealing Runs	Fielding Runs-Infield	Fielding Runs-Outfield	Wins	Winning Pct.	Complete Games
		Dunlap-StL..................26.5	Fogarty-Phi..........19.5	Clarkson-Chi 53	Welch-NY 800	Clarkson-Chi 68
		Pfeffer-Chi 22.3	Manning-Bos-Det ..7.1	Welch-NY 44	Clarkson-Chi.........768	Welch-NY 55
		Glasscock-StL 21.1	Kelly-Chi 6.1	Keefe-NY 32	McCormick-Pro-Chi .750	Whitney-Bos..........50
		Williamson-Chi..............9.1	Radford-Pro 5.0	Radbourn-Pro 28	Keefe-NY 711	
		Gerhardt-NY 8.8	Carroll-Pro 3.7		Radbourn-Pro.......571	

Strikeouts	Fewest BB/Game	Games	Saves	Base Runners/9	Adjusted Relief Runs	Relief Ranking
Clarkson-Chi 308	Whitney-Bos 75	Clarkson-Chi..................70	Williamson-Chi 2	Baldwin-Det 8.28		
Welch-NY 258	Galvin-Buf.............1.17	Welch-NY 56	Pfeffer-Chi 2	Clarkson-Chi........8.58		
Buffinton-Bos........242	Clarkson-Chi........1.40	Whitney-Bos 51	Welch-NY 1	Keefe-NY 9.05		
Keefe-NY 227	Baldwin-Det 1.41	Buffinton-Bos 51	Galvin-Buf 1	Richardson-NY 9.12		
Whitney-Bos 200	C.Sweeney-StL....1.64	Daily-Phi 50	Baldwin-Det..............1	Welch-NY 9.20		

Innings Pitched	Opponents' Avg.	Opponents' OBP	Earned Run Average	Adjusted ERA	Adjusted Starter Runs	Pitcher Wins
Clarkson-Chi......623.0	Baldwin-Det 197	Baldwin-Det 228	Keefe-NY 1.58	Keefe-NY..............169	Clarkson-Chi........70.8	**Clarkson-Chi**......7.3
Welch-NY 492.0	Welch-NY 203	Clarkson-Chi 239	Welch-NY 1.66	Clarkson-Chi 162	Welch-NY 59.7	**Welch-NY** 6.0
Radbourn-Pro....445.2	Keefe-NY 203	Shaw-Pro.....................254	Clarkson-Chi........1.85	Welch-NY 160	Keefe-NY 46.4	**Keefe-NY**............4.5
Whitney-Bos 441.1	Clarkson-Chi.........208	Keefe-NY 255	Baldwin-Det 1.86	Baldwin-Det..........153	Daily-Phi..............28.8	**Ferguson-Phi** 4.3
Daily-Phi 440.0	Shaw-Pro 209	Daily-Phi 256	Radbourn-Pro......2.20	Daily-Phi 126	Ferguson-Phi 25.7	**Radbourn-Pro**....3.4

Back to Normal

The National League got sneaky, violating the National Agreement by adding the Union Association's St. Louis franchise (in place of Cleveland) to compete with the AA's popular Browns club. The AA laughed last, though, as the dreadful Maroons survived just two years in the NL and drew half the patrons of the Browns.

Syndicate ownership also reared its malformed head. The owner of both the AA and NL New York clubs transferred manager Jim Mutrie and top players Tim Keefe and Dude Esterbrook to the NL's Giants, ostensibly to field a better team for his 50-cent ticket prices. As a result, the Giants improved 23 games in the NL and the Mets fell 32 games in the AA standings.

For this season NL pitchers were constrained by an unusual rule—possibly instituted to balance their new permission to throw overhand—requiring moundsmen to keep both feet on the ground while delivering the ball. Catchers first wore chest protectors in 1885, and the new equipment allowed the receiver to play closer to the batter. Players were required to use round bats, though one section could be flat.

The NL also addressed Chicago infielder Ned Williamson's 27 homers in 1884, which doubled the previous mark. Since 25 of those homers were hit at a small home park, the NL ruled that, as had been common before 1884, fair balls clearing fences 210 feet or less from home plate were doubles.

The NL returned to its earlier form, with two outstanding contenders battling to the finish. New York had two spectacular hitters, Roger Connor and Buck Ewing, and strong pitching in Keefe and Mickey Welch, but couldn't quite match Chicago, who had ironman John Clarkson on the hill and powerful hitters at nearly every position. Unfortunately, the two best teams from the two biggest cities were followed by six also-rans; third-place Philadelphia finished 30 out. Sixth-place Detroit welcomed rookie outfielder Sam Thompson. Buffalo was seventh despite the best efforts of Dan Brouthers, Hardy Richardson, and pitcher Jim "Pud" Galvin. League attendance rose, led by increases in Chicago, New York, and Philadelphia.

1885 American Association

TEAM	W	L	T	PCT	GB	HW	HL	R	OR	PA	H	2B	3B	HR	BB	SO	HB	SH	AVG	OBP	SLG	OPS	AOPS	BR	ABR	PF	SB	CS	BSA	BSR
STL	79	33	0	.705		**44**	11	**677**	**461**	4255	979	**132**	57	17	**234**	**282**		49	.246	**.297**	.321	618	96	2	-25	105				
CIN	63	49	0	.563	16	35	21	642	575	4254	**1046**	108	**77**	**26**	153	420		**51**	**.258**	.294	**.342**	**636**	**103**	**16**	**4**	102				
PIT	56	55	0	.505	22.5	37	20	547	539	4208	955	123	79	5	189	537		44	.240	.282	.315	597	94	-34	-26	99				
PHI	55	57	1	.491	24	33	23	764	691	4410	1099	169	76	30	223	410		45	.265	.310	.365	675	111	80	39	106				
LOU	53	59	0	.473	26	37	19	564	598	4146	986	126	83	19	152	448		25	.248	.281	.336	617	99	-13	-12	100				
BRO	53	59	0	.473	26	36	22	624	650	4223	966	121	65	14	238	324		42	.245	.295	.319	614	97	-4	-8	101				
NY	44	64	0	.407	33	28	24	526	688	3983	921	123	57	21	217	428		35	.247	.295	.327	622	105	5	30	96				
BAL	41	68	1	.376	36.5	29	25	541	683	4141	837	124	59	17	279	529		42	.219	.280	.296	576	87	-51	-43	99				
TOT	445					279	165	4885		33620	7789	1026	553	149	1685	3378	333		.246	.292	.328	620								

TEAM	CG	SHO	GR	SV	IP	H	HR	BB	SO	BR/9	ERA	AERA	OAV	OOB	PR	APR	PF	OSB	OCS	FA	E	WPB	DP	FW	PW	BW	BSW	DIF
STL	**111**	**11**	1	0	1002.0	**879**	12	**168**	378	**9.8**	**2.44**	**134**	**.228**	**.268**	**89**	**91**	101			**.920**	**381**	190	64	**3.0**	**8.2**	-2.3		14.1
CIN	102	7	**10**	1	999.1	998	24	250	330	11.9	3.26	100	.253	.309	-2	-1	100			.911	423	**172**	**86**	.8	-.0	.4		5.9
PIT	104	8	7	0	1011.0	918	14	201	454	10.3	2.92	110	.232	.275	36	33	99			.912	422	213	77	.6	3.0	-2.3		-.8
PHI	105	5	8	0	1003.1	1038	**11**	212	**506**	11.6	3.23	106	.255	.299	2	21	106			.901	483	242	79	-2.2	1.9	**3.5**		-4.2
LOU	109	3	4	1	1002.0	927	13	217	462	10.6	2.68	120	.232	.278	63	61	99			.905	460	248	75	-1.1	5.5	-1.1		-6.3
BRO	110	3	2	1	991.2	955	27	211	436	10.8	3.46	95	.240	.283	-24	-18	102			.910	434	219	56	.2	-1.6	-.7		-.9
NY	103	2	6	0	937.0	1015	36	204	408	11.9	4.15	75	.262	.303	-94	-113	96			.901	452	202	62	-1.6	-10.2	2.7		-1.0
BAL	103	2	7	**4**	971.0	1059	12	222	395	12.3	3.90	83	.269	.316	-71	-70	100			.909	419	272	71	.6	-6.3	-3.9		-3.9
TOT	847	41	45	7	7917.1					11.1	3.24		.246	.292						.909	3474	1758	570					

Batter-Fielder Wins	Batting Average	On-Base Percentage	Slugging Average	On-Base Plus Slugging	Adjusted OPS	Adjusted Batter Runs
Browning-Lou 4.2	Browning-Lou 362	Browning-Lou 393	Orr-NY 543	Browning-Lou 923	Browning-Lou 190	Browning-Lou 48.5
G.Smith-Bro 3.9	Orr-NY 342	Larkin-Phi 373	Browning-Lou 530	Orr-NY 901	Orr-NY 189	Orr-NY 42.4
Larkin-Phi............3.7	Larkin-Phi 329	Stovey-Phi 371	Larkin-Phi 525	Larkin-Phi 899	Larkin-Phi 171	Larkin-Phi 35.5
Jones-Cin 3.3	Jones-Cin 322	Brown-Pit 366	Stovey-Phi 488	Stovey-Phi 858	Stovey-Phi 160	Stovey-Phi 32.4
Nelson-NY 2.9	Stovey-Phi 315	Phillips-Bro 364	Jones-Cin 462	Jones-Cin 824	Jones-Cin 156	Jones-Cin 29.2

Runs	Hits	Doubles	Triples	Home Runs	Total Bases	Runs Batted In
Stovey-Phi 130	Browning-Lou 174	Larkin-Phi 37	Orr-NY 21	Stovey-Phi 13	Browning-Lou 255	Fennelly-Cin 89
Larkin-Phi 114	Jones-Cin 157	Browning-Lou 34	Kuehne-Pit..............19	Fennelly-Cin 10	Orr-NY 241	Larkin-Phi 88
Jones-Cin 108	Stovey-Phi 153	Orr-NY 29	Wolf-Lou 17	Browning-Lou 9	Larkin-Phi 238	Orr-NY 77
Nelson-NY..............98	Orr-NY 152	Stovey-Phi......................27	Jones-Cin 17	Larkin-Phi 8	Stovey-Phi 237	Stovey-Phi 75
Browning-Lou 98	Larkin-Phi 149		Fennelly-Cin 17	Orr-NY.......................6	Jones-Cin 225	Browning-Lou........73

Stolen Bases	Base Stealing Runs	Fielding Runs-Infield	Fielding Runs-Outfield	Wins	Winning Pct.	Complete Games
		G.Smith-Bro 40.3	Corkhill-Cin 15.9	Caruthers-StL 40	Caruthers-StL 755	Morris-Pit 63
		Smith-Pit 28.7	Sommer-Bal 12.5	Morris-Pit 39	Foutz-StL 702	Henderson-Bal 59
		Hankinson-NY 20.9	Welch-StL 12.0	Porter-Bro 33	Mathews-Phi.........638	Porter-Bro..............53
		Houck-Phi 18.6	Nicol-StL 11.4	Foutz-StL 33	Morris-Pit 619	Caruthers-StL........53
		Nelson-NY 16.8	Jones-Cin 11.2		Porter-Bro 611	Hecker-Lou 51

Strikeouts	Fewest BB/Game	Games	Saves	Base Runners/9	Adjusted Relief Runs	Relief Ranking
Morris-Pit..............298	Lynch-NY 1.00	Morris-Pit 63	Burns-Bal..................3	Ramsey-Lou 8.32		
Mathews-Phi 286	Hecker-Lou 1.01	Henderson-Bal 61	Terry-Bro 1	Morris-Pit 8.89		
Henderson-Bal 263	Caruthers-StL 1.06	Porter-Bro 54	Sommer-Bal..............1	Caruthers-StL 9.44		
Hecker-Lou 209	Mathews-Phi........1.21	Hecker-Lou 53	Reccius-Lou..............1	Hecker-Lou 9.86		
Porter-Bro 197	McGinnis-StL 1.53	Caruthers-StL 53	Corkhill-Cin 1	McGinnis-StL 9.88		

Innings Pitched	Opponents' Avg.	Opponents' OBP	Earned Run Average	Adjusted ERA	Adjusted Starter Runs	Pitcher Wins
Morris-Pit 581.0	Morris-Pit 208	Morris-Pit 247	Caruthers-StL.......2.07	Caruthers-StL 158	Caruthers-StL.......61.3	**Caruthers-StL**....6.3
Henderson-Bal ..539.1	Mays-Lou 219	Caruthers-StL 260	Hecker-Lou 2.17	Hecker-Lou 148	Morris-Pit 57.5	**Hecker-Lou** 6.0
Caruthers-StL....482.1	Porter-Bro.............223	Hecker-Lou 265	Morris-Pit 2.35	Mathews-Phi 141	Hecker-Lou..........51.4	**Morris-Pit** 4.7
Porter-Bro..........481.2	McGinnis-StL 225	Cushman-Phi-NY.........266	Mathews-Phi........2.43	Morris-Pit..............137	Mathews-Phi........42.1	**Foutz-StL**............3.5
Hecker-Lou 480.0	Foutz-StL 227	Mathews-Phi 267	Foutz-StL 2.63	Foutz-StL 124	Foutz-StL 29.3	**Mathews-Phi**......3.3

Gloves Off

With the Union Association dead, the two surviving leagues got dirty. The NL manipulated the rules and violated the National Agreement, then placated some aggrieved AA owners with cash payments, while the Association engaged in contract-breaking scams of its own. A midseason meeting resulted in the AA's sudden reversal on overhand pitching, which would now be permitted. This pushed the balance of power toward clubs with pitching and speed.

Therefore, the AA crowned a new champ: Charlie Comiskey's St. Louis Browns, a great defensive club sparked by aggressive baserunning and solid pitching. St. Louis moundsmen Bob Caruthers and Dave Foutz permitted the league's fewest hits, walks, and runs to breeze past Cincinnati by 16 games. Stripped by player transfers to the NL New York club, the defending champion Metropolitans sank to seventh.

The postseason "World Series" caused endless controversy and declared no champion. Game 1, in Chicago, was called by darkness shortly after the White Stockings tied the game in the eighth. The next contest in St. Louis was forfeited to the NL champion White Stockings when Comiskey pulled his team off the field in protest of a call. The Browns, however, won the next two in St. Louis. The teams then went to Pittsburgh for Game 5, which Chicago won, and Cincinnati the next day, resulting in another victory for the White Stockings by the same 9–2 score. The Browns won Game 7, also in Cincy, 13–4. The White Stockings ragged the umpiring, the games' locations, and the rules—all of which Chicago player-manager Cap Anson had agreed to beforehand.

Rival owners Chris Von der Ahe and Al Spalding benefited from the controversy—with no clear winner, the $1,000 purse was returned to them and never paid to the players. NL petulance provided a hearty laugh for AA supporters, but the ledgers supplied only indigestion. League attendance fell by 126,000, spiked by large dips in St. Louis and Baltimore.

1886 National League

TEAM	W	L	T	PCT	GB	HW	HL	R	OR	PA	H	2B	3B	HR	BB	SO	HB	SH	AVG	OBP	SLG	OPS	AOPS	BR	ABR	PF	SB	CS	BSA	BSR
CHI	90	34	2	.726		**52**	10	**900**	555	4838	1223	**198**	**87**	**53**	**460**	513			.279	**.348**	**.401**	**749**	116	**180**	69	115	213			
DET	87	36	3	.707	2.5	48	12	829	538	4875	**1260**	176	81	**53**	374	426			**.280**	.335	.390	725	**122**	137	**108**	104	194			
NY	75	44	5	.630	12.5	47	12	692	558	4535	1156	175	68	21	237	**410**			.269	.307	.356	663	106	29	22	101	155			
PHI	71	43	5	.623	14	45	14	621	**498**	4354	976	145	66	26	282	516			.240	.289	.327	616	91	-39	-44	101	**226**			
BOS	56	61	1	.479	30.5	32	25	657	661	4430	1085	151	59	24	250	537			.260	.301	.341	642	103	-1	16	97	156			
STL	43	79	4	.352	46	27	34	547	712	4485	1001	183	46	30	235	656			.236	.276	.321	597	92	-70	-31	94	156			
KC	30	91	5	.248	58.5	19	42	494	872	4505	967	177	48	19	269	608			.228	.274	.306	580	76	-91	-124	106	96			
WAS	28	92	5	.233	60	19	42	445	791	4347	856	135	51	23	265	582			.210	.258	.285	543	75	-145	-107	93	143			
TOT	495					289	191	5185		36369	8524	1340	506	249	2372	4248			.251	.300	.342	641					1339			

TEAM	CG	SHO	GR	SV	IP	H	HR	BB	SO	BR/9	ERA	AERA	OAV	OOB	PR	APR	PF	OSB	OCS	FA	E	WPB	DP	FW	PW	BW	BSW	DIF
CHI	116	8	**10**	**3**	1097.2	988	49	262	**647**	**10.2**	2.54	**142**	.232	.277	91	**118**	110			.912	475	197	82	-1.8	**10.7**	6.3		12.8
DET	**122**	8	4	0	1103.2	995	**20**	270	592	10.3	2.85	116	.231	.276	53	55	101			.928	373	**138**	82	3.8	5.0	**9.8**		6.9
NY	119	3	5	1	1062.0	1029	23	280	588	11.1	2.86	111	.247	.294	50	39	97			**.929**	**359**	222	70	**4.2**	3.5	2.0		5.8
PHI	110	**10**	9	2	1045.2	**923**	29	264	540	**10.2**	**2.45**	134	**.224**	**.271**	**97**	95	100			.921	393	155	46	1.4	8.6	-4.0		8.0
BOS	116	3	2	0	1029.0	1049	33	298	511	11.8	3.24	99	.252	.302	5	-4	97			.905	465	217	63	-2.7	-.4	1.5		-.8
STL	118	6	8	0	1077.1	1050	34	392	501	12.0	3.24	99	.246	.309	6	-7	97			.914	452	293	**92**	-.5	-.6	-2.8		-14.0
KC	117	4	6	0	1066.2	1345	27	**246**	442	13.4	4.85	77	.295	.331	-185	-117	114			.910	482	230	79	-2.1	-10.6	-11.2		-6.5
WAS	115	4	7	0	1041.0	1147	34	379	500	13.2	4.30	75	.271	.331	-117	-132	98			.910	458	211	69	-1.0	-12.0	-9.7		-9.3
TOT	933	46	51	6	8523.0					11.5	3.29		.251	.300						.916	3457	1663	583					

Batter-Fielder Wins	Batting Average	On-Base Percentage	Slugging Average	On-Base Plus Slugging	Adjusted OPS	Adjusted Batter Runs
Kelly-Chi 5.2	Kelly-Chi .388	Kelly-Chi .483	Brouthers-Det .581	Brouthers-Det 1026	Brouthers-Det 203	Brouthers-Det 62.6
Glasscock-StL 4.6	Anson-Chi .371	Brouthers-Det .445	Anson-Chi .544	Kelly-Chi 1018	Connor-NY 183	Kelly-Chi 48.1
Richardson-Det 4.5	Brouthers-Det .370	Gore-Chi .434	Connor-NY .540	Anson-Chi 977	Kelly-Chi 182	Connor-NY 47.6
Connor-NY 4.2	Connor-NY .355	Anson-Chi .433	Kelly-Chi .534	Connor-NY 945	Anson-Chi 170	Richardson-Det 43.4
Brouthers-Det 3.9	Richardson-Det .351	Connor-NY .405	Richardson-Det .504	Richardson-Det 906	Richardson-Det 168	Anson-Chi 41.9

Runs	Hits	Doubles	Triples	Home Runs	Total Bases	Runs Batted In
Kelly-Chi 155	Richardson-Det 189	Brouthers-Det 40	Connor-NY 20	Richardson-Det 11	Brouthers-Det 284	Anson-Chi 147
Gore-Chi 150	Anson-Chi 187	Anson-Chi 35	Wood-Phi 15	Brouthers-Det 11	Anson-Chi 274	Pfeffer-Chi 95
Brouthers-Det 139	Brouthers-Det 181	Kelly-Chi 32	Brouthers-Det 15	Anson-Chi 10	Richardson-Det 271	Thompson-Det 89
Richardson-Det 125	Kelly-Chi 175	Hines-Was 30	Thompson-Det 13	Hines-Was 9	Connor-NY 262	Rowe-Det 87
Anson-Chi 117	Connor-NY 172			Denny-StL 9	Kelly-Chi 241	Ward-NY 81

Stolen Bases	Base Stealing Runs	Fielding Runs-Infield	Fielding Runs-Outfield	Wins	Winning Pct.	Complete Games
Andrews-Phi 56		Denny-StL 25.2	Johnston-Bos 13.5	Keefe-NY 42	Flynn-Chi 793	Keefe-NY 62
Kelly-Chi 53		Knowles-Was 21.3	Lillie-KC 10.6	Baldwin-Det 42	Ferguson-Phi 769	Radbourn-Bos 57
Hanlon-Det 50		Dunlap-StL-Det 17.4	Thompson-Det 8.2	Clarkson-Chi 36	Baldwin-Det 764	Welch-NY 56
Richardson-Det 42		Glasscock-StL 14.9	Richardson-Det 5.3	Welch-NY 33	McCormick-Chi 738	Baldwin-Det 55
Radford-KC 39		Burns-Chi 11.1	Hornung-Bos 5.1	McCormick-Chi 31	Getzien-Det 732	Clarkson-Chi 50

Strikeouts	Fewest BB/Game	Games	Saves	Base Runners/9	Adjusted Relief Runs	Relief Ranking
Baldwin-Det 323	Whitney-KC 1.26	Keefe-NY 64	Ferguson-Phi 2	Baldwin-Det 8.70		
Clarkson-Chi 313	Ferguson-Phi 1.57	Welch-NY 59	Williamson-Chi 1	Ferguson-Phi 8.78		
Keefe-NY 297	Clarkson-Chi 1.66	Radbourn-Bos 58	Ryan-Chi 1	Flynn-Chi 9.46		
Welch-NY 272	Keefe-NY 1.72	Baldwin-Det 56	Flynn-Chi 1	Gilmore-Was 9.48		
Stemmeyer-Bos 239	Baldwin-Det 1.85	Clarkson-Chi 55	Devlin-NY 1	Clarkson-Chi 9.74		

Innings Pitched	Opponents' Avg.	Opponents' OBP	Earned Run Average	Adjusted ERA	Adjusted Starter Runs	Pitcher Wins
Keefe-NY 535.0	Baldwin-Det .202	Baldwin-Det .243	Boyle-StL 1.76	Boyle-StL 182	Ferguson-Phi 59.3	**Ferguson-Phi** 6.5
Radbourn-Bos 509.1	Ferguson-Phi .210	Ferguson-Phi .244	Ferguson-Phi 1.98	Ferguson-Phi 166	Baldwin-Det 55.4	**Baldwin-Det** 5.7
Welch-NY 500.0	Flynn-Chi .210	Flynn-Chi .257	Baldwin-Det 2.24	Flynn-Chi 161	Clarkson-Chi 50.2	**Clarkson-Chi** 5.0
Baldwin-Det 487.0	Stemmeyer-Bos .218	Boyle-StL .261	Flynn-Chi 2.24	Clarkson-Chi 149	Keefe-NY 39.1	**McCormick-Chi** 3.8
Clarkson-Chi 466.2	Boyle-StL .220	Clarkson-Chi .264	Clarkson-Chi 2.41	Baldwin-Det 148	Casey-Phi 36.7	**Keefe-NY** 3.8

The Brotherhood of Man

When Providence and Buffalo folded following the 1885 season, the NL replaced them with Washington and Kansas City. They weren't inspired choices. The Kansas City Cowboys lasted one miserable year and the Washington Senators didn't see the next decade. The Senators, the first team to use that name, did provide 23-year-old catcher Connie Mack a start for his major league playing career. Finishing their careers, for the same poor club, were famous contract-jumper Davy Force and 43-year-old first baseman Joe Start, an original National Association player.

With salaries depressed by the end of the Union Association, the reserve clause in full effect, and owners ruling players with iron fists, New York Giants Monty Ward, Buck Ewing, and Tim Keefe were instrumental in establishing the Brotherhood of Professional Baseball Players, the game's first union.

The NL returned to the seven-ball walk, and also helped pitchers by allowing them to lift one foot when delivering the ball. This, and the lengthening of the pitcher's box, gave certain hard throwers an extra advantage, because they could get a running start to their delivery. While strikeouts increased, league ERA leapt by nearly half a run, mainly due to the incompetence of the expansion teams' pitching staffs.

The White Stockings won another close race, this one over Detroit. The Wolverines featured the bats of Dan Brouthers, Sam Thompson, and Hardy Richardson, as well as Lady Baldwin's pitching, but the club stalled in August. Cap Anson, King Kelly, and George Gore did the bat work for Chicago, while John Clarkson, Jim McCormick, and one-year wonder Jocko Flynn provided a top mound trio.

Kelly was one of the loop's dominant offensive performers, leading in runs, batting average, and on-base percentage. The charismatic, hard-living Kelly also finished second in the newly tabulated category of stolen bases, inspiring the popular song "Slide! Kelly! Slide!" However, Kelly and his Chicago teammates dropped a six-game World Series to the American Association champion St. Louis Browns.

1886 American Association

TEAM	W	L	T	PCT	GB	HW	HL	R	OR	PA	H	2B	3B	HR	BB	SO	HB	SH	AVG	OBP	SLG	OPS	AOPS	BR	ABR	PF	SB	CS	BSA	BSR
STL	93	46	0	.669		**52**	18	**944**	**592**	5461	**1365**	**206**	85	**20**	400	**425**		**52**	**.273**	**.333**	**.360**	**693**	**116**	**117**	**75**	105	**336**			
PIT	80	57	3	.584	12	46	29	810	647	5370	1171	186	**96**	16	**478**	713		38	.241	.314	.329	643	106	33	37	100	260			
BRO	76	61	4	.555	16	43	25	832	832	5504	1261	196	80	16	433	523		18	.250	.311	.330	641	103	24	16	101	248			
LOU	66	70	2	.485	25.5	37	30	833	805	5357	1294	182	88	**20**	410	558		26	.263	.323	.348	671	108	75	28	106	202			
CIN	65	73	3	.471	27.5	40	31	883	865	5354	1225	145	95	45	374	633		65	.249	.311	.345	656	106	42	16	103	185			
PHI	63	72	4	.467	28	37	32	772	942	5275	1142	192	82	21	378	697		41	.235	.296	.321	617	95	-20	-28	101	284			
NY	53	82	2	.393	38	30	33	628	766	5046	1047	108	72	18	330	578		33	.224	.279	.289	568	88	-106	-47	92	120			
BAL	48	83	8	.366	41	30	31	625	878	5054	945	124	51	8	379	603		36	.204	.269	.258	527	70	-165	-150	98	269			
TOT	557					315	229	6327		42421	9450	1339	649	164	3182	4730	309		.243	.305	.323	628					1904			

TEAM	CG	SHO	GR	SV	IP	H	HR	BB	SO	BR/9	ERA	AERA	OAV	OOB	PR	APR	PF	OSB	OCS	FA	E	WPB	DP	FW	PW	BW	BSW	DIF
STL	134	14	5	**2**	1229.1	**1087**	13	329	583	**10.6**	**2.49**	**138**	**.227**	**.281**	**130**	**128**	100	188		.915	494	**163**	96	3.3	**11.2**	**6.6**		2.4
PIT	137	**15**	3	1	1226.0	1130	**10**	**299**	515	10.7	2.83	120	.235	.285	84	76	98	**140**		**.917**	**487**	220	90	**3.9**	6.7	3.2		-2.3
BRO	**138**	6	3	0	1234.2	1202	17	464	540	12.4	3.42	102	.243	.312	3	8	101	229		.900	610	232	87	-2.2	.7	1.4		7.6
LOU	131	5	7	**2**	1209.2	1109	16	432	720	11.7	3.07	118	.230	.297	51	71	106	229		.901	593	289	89	-2.0	6.2	2.5		-8.7
CIN	129	3	**14**	0	1247.2	1267	25	481	495	13.0	4.18	84	.255	.327	-103	-92	102	224		.905	582	247	**122**	-.8	-8.1	1.4		3.4
PHI	134	4	6	0	1218.2	1309	35	388	513	13.0	3.97	88	.259	.319	-72	-65	102	303		.894	637	317	99	-4.0	-5.7	-2.5		7.7
NY	134	5	3	0	1186.1	1148	23	386	559	11.8	3.50	93	.243	.304	-8	-36	95	271		.907	544	262	81	.3	-3.2	-4.1		-7.6
BAL	134	5	7	0	1206.2	1197	25	403	**805**	12.3	4.08	84	.244	.308	-85	-91	99	319		.910	523	367	59	1.8	-8.0	-13.2		1.8
TOT	1071	57	48	5	9759.0					11.9	3.44		.243	.305						.906	4470	2097	723					

Batter-Fielder Wins	Batting Average	On-Base Percentage	Slugging Average	On-Base Plus Slugging	Adjusted OPS	Adjusted Batter Runs
McPhee-Cin 4.2	Hecker-Lou 341	Larkin-Phi 390	Orr-NY 527	Orr-NY 890	Orr-NY 193	Orr-NY...............56.4
Orr-NY 3.8	Browning-Lou 340	Browning-Lou 389	Caruthers-StL 527	Larkin-Phi 839	Larkin-Phi 161	Larkin-Phi 41.1
Kerins-Lou 3.7	Orr-NY 338	O'Neill-StL 385	Larkin-Phi 450	Browning-Lou 830	Stovey-Phi 154	Caruthers-StL 37.8
Larkin-Phi.............3.7	Caruthers-StL 334	Stovey-Phi 377	Hecker-Lou 446	O'Neill-StL 826	O'Neill-StL 151	O'Neill-StL 33.1
O'Neill-StL 3.2	O'Neill-StL 328	Swartwood-Bro 377	Browning-Lou 441	Stovey-Phi 817	Browning-Lou 151	Stovey-Phi 32.1

Runs	Hits	Doubles	Triples	Home Runs	Total Bases	Runs Batted In
Latham-StL 152	Orr-NY 193	Larkin-Phi 36	Orr-NY 31	McPhee-Cin..............8	Orr-NY 301	O'Neill-StL 107
McPhee-Cin..........139	O'Neill-StL 190	McClellan-Bro 33	Coleman-Phi-Pit 17	Stovey-Phi 7	O'Neill-StL 255	Corkhill-Cin............97
Larkin-Phi 133	Larkin-Phi 180	Welch-StL 31	Kuehne-Pit..............17	Orr-NY 7	Larkin-Phi 254	Welch-StL...............95
McClellan-Bro 131	Latham-StL 174	Barkley-Pit 31	Fennelly-Cin 17		Welch-StL 221	Orr-NY 91
Pinkney-Bro..........119	Phillips-Bro 160	Browning-Lou 29	Larkin-Phi 16		McPhee-Cin..........221	Reilly-Cin 79

Stolen Bases	Base Stealing Runs	Fielding Runs-Infield	Fielding Runs-Outfield	Wins	Winning Pct.	Complete Games
Stovey-Phi 68		McPhee-Cin................26.9	McTamany-Bro 11.3	Morris-Pit................41	Foutz-StL 719	Ramsey-Lou..........66
Latham-StL 60		Hankinson-NY 26.8	Welch-StL 11.1	Foutz-StL 41	Caruthers-StL........682	Kilroy-Bal 66
Welch-StL 59		Smith-Pit 17.7	Wolf-Lou 9.3	Ramsey-Lou 38	Morris-Pit 672	Morris-Pit 63
Robinson-StL..........51		White-Lou 16.7	O'Neill-StL 7.7	Mullane-Cin 33	Hudson-StL 615	Mullane-Cin 55
McClellan-Bro 43		Smith-Bro...................12.8	Sommer-Bal 7.2	Caruthers-StL 30	Atkinson-Phi 595	Foutz-StL 55

Strikeouts	Fewest BB/Game	Games	Saves	Base Runners/9	Adjusted Relief Runs	Relief Ranking
Kilroy-Bal 513	Galvin-Pit 1.55	Kilroy-Bal 68	Morris-Pit.................1	Shaffer-NY 9.13		
Ramsey-Lou 499	Morris-Pit 1.91	Ramsey-Lou 67	Hudson-StL 1	Morris-Pit 9.40		
Morris-Pit.............326	Caruthers-StL......2.00	Morris-Pit 64	Foutz-StL 1	Caruthers-StL 9.67		
Foutz-StL 283	McGinnis-StL-Bal 2.27	Mullane-Cin 63	Ely-Lou 1	Handiboe-Pit......10.03		
Mullane-Cin 250	Atkinson-Phi 2.29	Foutz-StL 59		Ramsey-Lou 10.18		

Innings Pitched	Opponents' Avg.	Opponents' OBP	Earned Run Average	Adjusted ERA	Adjusted Starter Runs	Pitcher Wins
Ramsey-Lou 588.2	Ramsey-Lou 198	Morris-Pit.....................258	Foutz-StL 2.11	Foutz-StL 163	Ramsey-Lou 77.3	**Foutz-StL**............7.6
Kilroy-Bal 583.0	Kilroy-Bal 210	Caruthers-StL 263	Caruthers-StL......2.32	Ramsey-Lou 148	Foutz-StL 71.4	**Caruthers-StL**....7.2
Morris-Pit 555.1	Morris-Pit 214	Ramsey-Lou 269	Ramsey-Lou 2.45	Caruthers-StL 148	Morris-Pit 61.6	**Ramsey-Lou** 6.7
Mullane-Cin 529.2	Foutz-StL 216	Foutz-StL 274	Morris-Pit 2.45	Morris-Pit...............138	Caruthers-StL......50.8	**Morris-Pit** 4.8
Foutz-StL 504.0	Caruthers-StL.......217	Kilroy-Bal 274	Galvin-Pit 2.67	Hecker-Lou 127	Galvin-Pit 31.2	**Hecker-Lou**........4.8

"The $15,000 Slide"

As the National League returned to the seven-ball walk, the AA reduced the free pass requirement to six. Walks nearly doubled. With the league also lengthening the pitching box and allowing hurlers to get running starts and deliver the ball with one foot off the ground, strikeouts soared as well.

The Baltimore Orioles finished last, but rookie pitcher Matt Kilroy set an all-time record by fanning 513 batters. Toad Ramsey of fourth-place Louisville came close to Kilroy, and his 499 is also second on the single-season list.

Rowdy, hard-bitten St. Louis cruised to an easy title. Pitchers Dave Foutz and Bob Caruthers won 71 games between themselves, better than all but two other teams. Arlie Latham scored 152 runs and was one of three Browns among the top four in stolen bases—an official statistic for the first time. Second-place Pittsburgh didn't have much offense, but pitchers Ed Morris and Jim Galvin carried the load.

The Browns took on the Chicago White Stockings in the World Series. Behind John Clarkson, Chicago won two of the first three at home. Then in St. Louis, the Browns whipped the White Stockings twice behind Foutz and third hurler Nat Hudson. Games 4 and 5 were plagued by charges that the White Stockings were "laying down" to extend the Series' gate receipts.

In Game 6, with the Browns up three games to two, the confident White Stockings had Clarkson on the hill and led 3–0 in the eighth. However, poor Chicago fielding and timely Browns hitting tied the game. St. Louis' Curt Welch and Foutz singled in the 10th, and then moved up a base on a sacrifice. On either a wild pitch or passed ball (sources differ), catcher King Kelly couldn't handle Clarkson's pitch and Welch scored the winning run. Some newspapers referred to Welch's plate-crossing as "The $15,000 Slide," referring to the Series' prize money, but it is still not certain whether Welch slid or scored standing up. Either way, the Association was vindicated yet again.

1887 National League

TEAM	W	L	T	PCT	GB	HW	HL	R	OR	PA	H	2B	3B	HR	BB	SO	HB	SH	AVG	OBP	SLG	OPS	AOPS	BR	ABR	PF	SB	CS	BSA	BSR
DET	79	45	3	.637		43	17	**969**	710	5079	**1404**	**213**	**126**	55	352	**258**		38	**.299**	**.353**	**.434**	**787**	**117**	**133**	**98**	104	267			
PHI	75	48	5	.610	3.5	38	23	901	**702**	5067	1269	**213**	89	47	385	346		**52**	.274	.337	.389	726	99	38	-10	106	355			
CHI	71	50	6	.587	6.5	**44**	18	813	716	4777	1177	178	98	**80**	**407**	400		20	.271	.336	.412	748	98	63	-32	113	382			
NY	68	55	6	.553	10.5	36	26	816	723	4924	1259	167	93	48	361	326		47	.279	.339	.389	728	111	36	76	95	**415**			
BOS	61	60	6	.504	16.5	38	21	834	792	4908	1255	185	94	53	340	392		37	.277	.333	.394	727	105	31	22	101	373			
PIT	55	69	1	.444	24	31	34	621	750	4771	1141	183	78	20	319	381		38	.258	.314	.349	663	95	-68	-14	93	221			
WAS	46	76	4	.377	32	27	33	601	825	4624	1039	149	63	47	269	339		41	.241	.292	.337	629	83	-128	-87	94	334			
IND	37	89	1	.294	43	24	39	628	965	4712	1080	162	70	33	300	379		44	.247	.302	.339	641	85	-105	-82	97	334			
TOT	508					281	211	6183		38862	9624	1450	711	383	2733	2821	317		.269	.326	.381	707					2681			

TEAM	CG	SHO	GR	SV	IP	H	HR	BB	SO	BR/9	ERA	AERA	OAV	OOB	PR	APR	PF	OSB	OCS	FA	E	WPB	DP	FW	PW	BW	BSW	DIF
DET	122	3	5	1	1116.1	1172	52	344	337	12.5	3.95	103	.264	.322	12	0	100			**.925**	**394**	**95**	92	**3.3**	.0	**8.3**		5.4
PHI	119	**7**	10	1	1132.2	1173	48	305	435	**12.0**	3.47	121	.259	**.311**	72	87	104			.912	471	152	76	-.4	7.4	-.8		7.4
CHI	117	4	**12**	**3**	1126.0	1156	55	338	**510**	12.4	**3.46**	**129**	.257	.317	**73**	**110**	110			.914	472	201	99	-.6	**9.3**	-2.7		4.5
NY	123	5	7	1	1111.2	**1096**	**27**	373	415	12.2	3.58	105	**.250**	.314	58	19	93			.920	431	196	83	1.8	1.6	6.4		-3.4
BOS	123	4	4	1	1100.2	1226	55	396	254	13.6	4.41	92	.273	.338	-44	-41	101			.905	522	154	94	-3.2	-3.5	1.9		5.3
PIT	123	4	2	0	1108.2	1287	39	**246**	248	12.7	4.12	93	.281	.322	-9	-40	94			.921	425	140	70	1.4	-3.4	-1.2		-3.8
WAS	**124**	3	2	0	1090.1	1216	47	299	396	12.9	4.19	95	.272	.323	-18	-26	99			.909	483	194	77	-1.4	-2.2	-7.4		-4.1
IND	118	4	10	1	1088.0	1289	60	431	245	14.6	5.24	79	.284	.352	-145	-135	102			.912	479	223	**105**	-1.0	-11.4	-6.9		-6.6
TOT	969	34	52	8	8874.1					12.8	4.05		.269	.326						.915	3677	1355	696					

Batter-Fielder Wins	Batting Average	On-Base Percentage	Slugging Average	On-Base Plus Slugging	Adjusted OPS	Adjusted Batter Runs
Ward-NY 4.3	Anson-Chi............347	Brouthers-Det 426	Thompson-Det 565	Brouthers-Det 988	Brouthers-Det 166	Brouthers-Det 46.3
Thompson-Det....4.2	Thompson-Det 372	Anson-Chi 422	Brouthers-Det.......562	Thompson-Det......982	Connor-NY............164	Thompson-Det ..44.6
Glasscock-Ind 4.0	Brouthers-Det.......338	Thompson-Det............416	Connor-NY 541	Anson-Chi 939	Thompson-Det......164	Connor-NY 43.8
Denny-Ind............3.9	Ward-NY...............338	Schomberg-Ind 397	Wise-Bos 522	Connor-NY............933	Carroll-Pit 154	Carroll-Pit 31.9
Richardson-Det..3.3	Wise-Bos 334	Kelly-Bos 393	Anson-Chi............517	Wise-Bos 913	Wise-Bos..............150	Wise-Bos............30.6

Runs	Hits	Doubles	Triples	Home Runs	Total Bases	Runs Batted In
Brouthers-Det 153	Thompson-Det......203	Brouthers-Det 36	Thompson-Det........23	B.O'Brien-Was........19	Thompson-Det......308	Thompson-Det 166
Rowe-Det..............135	Ward-NY 184	Kelly-Bos........................34	Connor-NY..............22	Connor-NY..............17	Brouthers-Det 281	Connor-NY 104
Richardson-Det 131	Richardson-Det 178	Denny-Ind......................34	Johnston-Bos..........20	Pfeffer-Chi 16	Richardson-Det 263	Anson-Chi 102
Kelly-Bos 120	Rowe-Det..............171	Anson-Chi......................33	Brouthers-Det 20	Wood-Phi................14	Denny-Ind 256	Brouthers-Det......101
	Brouthers-Det 169		Wood-Phi................19		Connor-NY............255	Denny-Ind.............97

Stolen Bases	Base Stealing Runs	Fielding Runs-Infield	Fielding Runs-Outfield	Wins	Winning Pct.	Complete Games
Ward-NY 111		Glasscock-Ind 38.7	Fogarty-Phi..........30.1	Clarkson-Chi 38	Getzien-Det 690	Clarkson-Chi 56
Fogarty-Phi 102		Ward-NY 32.4	Johnston-Bos 22.5	Keefe-NY 35	Ferguson-Phi 688	Keefe-NY 54
Kelly-Bos 84		Pfeffer-Chi 22.9	Hornung-Bos 11.5	Getzien-Det 29	Casey-Phi............683	Radbourn-Bos 48
Hanlon-Det 69		Denny-Ind 21.8	Seery-Ind 6.8	Galvin-Pit................28	Keefe-NY 648	Galvin-Pit 47
Glasscock-Ind 62		Bassett-Ind 18.4	Thompson-Det 6.4	Casey-Phi 28	Clarkson-Chi.........644	Whitney-Was 46

Strikeouts	Fewest BB/Game	Games	Saves	Base Runners/9	Adjusted Relief Runs	Relief Ranking
Clarkson-Chi 237	Whitney-Was 93	Clarkson-Chi.................60	VanHaltren-Chi 1	Keefe-NY 10.33		
Keefe-NY 189	Galvin-Pit 1.37	Keefe-NY 56	Twitchell-Det 1	Clarkson-Chi.......10.55		
Baldwin-Chi 164	Ferguson-Phi 1.42	Radbourn-Bos 50	Tiernan-NY 1	Ferguson-Phi 10.75		
Buffinton-Phi 160	Clarkson-Chi........1.58	Galvin-Pit 49	Stemmeyer-Bos........1	Whitney-Was 10.85		
Whitney-Was 146	Boyle-Ind 1.89	Whitney-Was 47	Pettit-Chi 1	Welch-NY 11.32		
			Ferguson-Phi 1			
			Fast-Ind 1			
			Baldwin-Chi 1			

Innings Pitched	Opponents' Avg.	Opponents' OBP	Earned Run Average	Adjusted ERA	Adjusted Starter Runs	Pitcher Wins
Clarkson-Chi......523.0	Keefe-NY 230	Keefe-NY......................276	Casey-Phi............2.86	Casey-Phi 147	Clarkson-Chi........76.4	**Clarkson-Chi**......7.5
Keefe-NY 476.2	Conway-Det 235	Clarkson-Chi 281	Conway-Det 2.90	Clarkson-Chi 145	Casey-Phi............56.6	**Ferguson-Phi** 4.7
Galvin-Pit 440.2	Casey-Phi.............246	Whitney-Was 284	Ferguson-Phi 3.00	Ferguson-Phi.........141	Ferguson-Phi 40.2	**Keefe-NY** 4.2
Radbourn-Bos ..425.0	Clarkson-Chi.........246	Ferguson-Phi 289	Clarkson-Chi.......3.08	Conway-Det..........140	Keefe-NY 39.2	**Whitney-Was**......3.9
Whitney-Was 404.2	Baldwin-Chi 248	Galvin-Pit.....................299	Keefe-NY 3.12	Baldwin-Chi 131	Baldwin-Chi 33.3	**Casey-Phi** 3.6

The Long October

Despite another National Agreement meeting in 1886, the gloves came off. For 1887 the NL lured over the AA's Pittsburgh franchise to replace bankrupt Kansas City. Both the NL and the AA used the same set of playing rules beginning in 1887, which at least helped in planning the World Series.

It was a year of rule changes. First of all, pitchers were prohibited from hiding the ball during their delivery or taking a running start before delivering. It once again took *four* strikes for a strikeout, while the number of balls needed for a walk was lowered to five.

Batters could no longer call for pitches in certain locations, and the strike zone was defined as ranging from the knee to the shoulder. For the first time NL batters hit by pitched balls were awarded first base—provided they at least tried to get out of the way.

For this year only, a walk truly was as good as a hit. Batters were given credits for hits if they drew bases on balls, leading to some stratospheric averages. Modern figures have Sam Thompson of pennant-winning Detroit taking the bat crown (after walks were removed from hit totals) and establishing a nineteenth century mark with 166 RBIs.

Thompson, Dan Brouthers, and Hardy Richardson supplied Detroit's offense, and the deep pitching staff did its best in what appears to have been a strong hitter's park. Second-place Philadelphia allowed the league's fewest runs.

Chicago owner Al Spalding jettisoned King Kelly, his most outspoken, and—not coincidentally—marketable talent. The outspoken, hard-drinking Kelly was sold to Boston for an unheard of $10,000. The White Stockings immediately slumped to third; Boston, with Kelly's 84 steals and 120 runs, did not budge from fifth. After the season, Spalding also dumped pitcher John Clarkson.

Detroit and AA champ St. Louis played a 15-game World Series, including stops at almost every major league city—one day the touring teams played a morning game in Washington and an afternoon tilt in Baltimore. Detroit won 10 to give the NL the crown. By the end of the interminable series, hardly anyone was watching.

1887 American Association

TEAM	W	L	T	PCT	GB	HW	HL	R	OR	PA	H	2B	3B	HR	BB	SO	HB	SH	AVG	OBP	SLG	OPS	AOPS	BR	ABR	PF	SB	CS	BSA	BSR
STL	95	40	3	.704		**58**	15	**1131**	761	5557	**1550**	**261**	78	**39**	442	340		67	**.307**	**.371**	**.413**	**784**	111	**157**	52	111	**581**			
CIN	81	54	1	.600	14	46	27	892	**745**	5235	1285	179	**102**	37	382	366		56	.268	.329	.371	700	97	-15	-35	102	527			
BAL	77	58	6	.570	18	42	21	975	861	5362	1337	202	100	31	**469**	**334**		**68**	.277	.349	.380	729	**114**	51	**110**	94	545			
LOU	76	60	3	.559	19.5	45	23	956	854	5392	1420	194	98	27	436	356		40	.289	.352	.385	737	107	60	41	102	466			
PHI	64	69	4	.481	30	41	27	893	890	5326	1370	231	84	29	321	388		51	.277	.327	.375	702	99	-13	-14	100	476			
BRO	60	74	4	.448	34.5	36	38	904	918	5420	1281	200	82	25	456	365		51	.261	.330	.350	680	92	-40	-50	101	409			
NY	44	89	5	.331	50	25	34	754	1093	5310	1197	193	66	21	439	463		50	.248	.318	.329	647	88	-98	-61	96	305			
CLE	39	92	2	.298	54	22	36	729	1112	5070	1170	178	77	14	375	463		46	.252	.314	.332	646	87	-101	-78	97	355			
TOT	550					315	221	7234		42672	10610	1638	687	223	3320	3075	429		.273	.336	.367	704					3664			

TEAM	CG	SHO	GR	SV	IP	H	HR	BB	SO	BR/9	ERA	AERA	OAV	OOB	PR	APR	PF	OSB	OCS	FA	E	WPB	DP	FW	PW	BW	BSW	DIF
STL	132	6	5	2	1199.1	1254	19	**323**	334	**12.2**	3.77	120	.258	**.311**	69	94	106	**335**		**.916**	**481**	**171**	86	**3.6**	7.6	4.2		12.1
CIN	129	**11**	6	1	1182.2	**1202**	28	396	330	12.6	**3.58**	**121**	**.257**	.322	**93**	**98**	101	358		**.916**	484	203	**106**	3.0	**7.9**	-2.8		5.4
BAL	132	8	**9**	0	1220.0	1288	**16**	418	470	13.0	3.87	106	.262	.326	58	31	95	482		.907	549	229	66	.8	2.5	**8.9**		-2.7
LOU	**133**	3	4	1	1205.2	1274	31	357	**544**	12.5	3.82	115	.260	.316	63	73	102	462		.903	574	221	83	-.9	5.9	3.3		-.3
PHI	131	5	6	1	1186.1	1227	29	433	417	13.1	4.59	93	.259	.331	-39	-41	100	476		.907	528	300	95	1.0	-3.3	-1.1		.9
BRO	132	3	6	**3**	1185.1	1348	27	454	332	14.0	4.47	96	.281	.348	-24	-24	100	520		.905	562	202	88	-.5	-1.9	-4.1		-.5
NY	132	1	**9**	0	1180.1	1545	39	406	316	15.3	5.28	80	.308	.365	-130	-139	99	508		.894	632	194	102	-4.0	-11.3	-4.9		-2.3
CLE	127	2	6	1	1136.0	1472	34	533	332	16.4	4.99	87	.308	.384	-88	-83	101	523		.898	576	245	97	-2.2	-6.7	-6.3		-11.3
TOT	1048	39	51	9	9495.2					13.6	4.29		.273	.336						.906	4386	1765	723					

Batter-Fielder Wins	Batting Average	On-Base Percentage	Slugging Average	On-Base Plus Slugging	Adjusted OPS	Adjusted Batter Runs
O'Neill-StL 4.8	O'Neill-StL 435	O'Neill-StL 490	O'Neill-StL 691	O'Neill-StL 1180	O'Neill-StL 205	O'Neill-StL 70.6
Browning-Lou 3.8	Browning-Lou 402	Browning-Lou 464	Caruthers-StL.......547	Browning-Lou 1011	Browning-Lou 178	Browning-Lou 58.5
Lyons-Phi 3.6	Orr-NY 368	Caruthers-StL 463	Browning-Lou 547	Caruthers-StL 1010	Burns-Bal.............169	Burns-Bal 53.4
Burns-Bal 3.2	Lyons-Phi 367	Robinson-StL..............445	Lyons-Phi 523	Lyons-Phi.............943	Caruthers-StL 164	Lyons-Phi 47.8
McPhee-Cin 2.8	Caruthers-StL.......357	Lyons-Phi.....................421	Burns-Bal 519	Burns-Bal.............933	Lyons-Phi..............162	Caruthers-StL 32.6

Runs	Hits	Doubles	Triples	Home Runs	Total Bases	Runs Batted In
O'Neill-StL 167	O'Neill-StL 225	O'Neill-StL 52	Poorman-Phi 19	O'Neill-StL 14	O'Neill-StL 357	O'Neill-StL 123
Latham-StL 163	Browning-Lou 220	Lyons-Phi 43	O'Neill-StL 19	Reilly-Cin 10	Browning-Lou 299	Browning-Lou......118
Griffin-Bal 142	Lyons-Phi..............209	Reilly-Cin 35	McPhee-Cin.............19	Burns-Bal..................9	Lyons-Phi..............298	Davis-Bal 109
Poorman-Phi 140	Latham-StL 198	Latham-StL 35	Kerins-Lou 19		Burns-Bal..............286	Welch-StL............108
Comiskey-StL 139	Burns-Bal.............188	Browning-Lou 35	Davis-Bal 19		Reilly-Cin 263	Foutz-StL 108
			Burns-Bal................19			

Stolen Bases	Base Stealing Runs	Fielding Runs-Infield	Fielding Runs-Outfield	Wins	Winning Pct.	Complete Games
Nicol-Cin 138		Smith-Bro...................30.1	Welch-StL............17.2	Kilroy-Bal 46	Caruthers-StL.......763	Kilroy-Bal 66
Latham-StL 129		McPhee-Cin...............23.3	Corkhill-Cin..........12.1	Ramsey-Lou 37	King-StL 727	Ramsey-Lou..........61
Comiskey-StL 117		White-Lou 17.5	Wolf-Lou 8.8	Smith-Cin.................34	Kilroy-Bal 708	Smith-Bal 54
Browning-Lou 103		Pinkney-Bro 14.8	D.O'Brien-NY 7.1	King-StL...................32	Foutz-StL 676	Weyhing-Phi..........53
McPhee-Cin...........95		Stricker-Cle 11.1	Allen-Cle.................6.2	Mullane-Cin 31	Smith-Cin 667	Seward-Phi............52

Strikeouts	Fewest BB/Game	Games	Saves	Base Runners/9	Adjusted Relief Runs	Relief Ranking
Ramsey-Lou 355	Hecker-Lou..........1.58	Kilroy-Bal 69	Terry-Bro 3	Smith-Cin 10.76		
Kilroy-Bal 217	Caruthers-StL......1.61	Ramsey-Lou 65		Caruthers-StL....10.93		
Smith-Bal..............206	Lynch-NY 1.73	Smith-Bal 58		Kilroy-Bal 11.64		
Weyhing-Phi 193	Foutz-StL 2.39	Weyhing-Phi 55		Seward-Phi.......11.65		
Smith-Cin..............176	Kilroy-Bal 2.40	Seward-Phi 55		Ramsey-Lou 11.66		

Innings Pitched	Opponents' Avg.	Opponents' OBP	Earned Run Average	Adjusted ERA	Adjusted Starter Runs	Pitcher Wins
Kilroy-Bal 589.1	Smith-Cin 230	Smith-Cin.......................286	Smith-Cin 2.94	Smith-Cin..............148	Kilroy-Bal 71.6	**Kilroy-Bal** 7.2
Ramsey-Lou 561.0	Ramsey-Lou 242	Caruthers-StL 287	Kilroy-Bal 3.07	Caruthers-StL 137	Smith-Cin 71.0	**Smith-Cin** 6.3
Smith-Bal 491.1	Seward-Phi...........244	Ramsey-Lou 299	Mullane-Cin 3.24	Mullane-Cin 134	Ramsey-Lou........57.8	**Caruthers-StL**....5.9
Seward-Phi........470.2	Caruthers-StL.......247	Kilroy-Bal 306	Caruthers-StL......3.30	Kilroy-Bal 133	Mullane-Cin 51.1	**Mullane-Cin**.......4.6
Weyhing-Phi 466.1	Kilroy-Bal 253	Foutz-StL 306	Ramsey-Lou........3.43	Ramsey-Lou 128	Caruthers-StL......45.5	**Ramsey-Lou** 3.7

Sitting in Coach

In agreeing to rewrite their rule book to match the NL's, owners of the American Association took a subordinate position. When the NL stole the AA's Pittsburgh franchise, it was war again. A Cleveland club was added to bring the Americans' total to eight teams.

Various rule changes served to elevate offense; the league's best pitching staff, second-place Cincinnati, had an ERA that would have ranked a poor fifth in the AA the previous season. The days of the one-pitcher team were long gone; all teams now had at least two pitchers (in Brooklyn's case, four) winning in double figures. To address charges that St. Louis' Arlie Latham was disgracing the game with his "coaching" routines, which involved running up and down the baselines shouting at the pitcher, coaches' boxes were installed. From this point, coaches were allowed only to address their own baserunners.

The loss of shouting privileges didn't seem to bother the Browns, who won again by a wide margin over Cincinnati. The Reds had one of the league's top hurlers, Elmer Smith, plus outfielder Hugh Nicol, who stole an all-time record 138 bases. But St. Louis was a juggernaut. The Browns plated a record 1,131 runs, and left fielder Tip O'Neill paced the league in nearly every significant offensive category. An unsung hero for the Browns? Bob Caruthers, who won 29 games on the hill and as a right fielder hit .357, fifth best in the AA.

While last-place Cleveland didn't have much talent, they could boast first baseman Jim Toy, the major leagues' first Native American player. Paul Radford of seventh-place New York became the first player in big league history to draw 100 walks in a season. Buoyed by gains in nearly every city, AA attendance rose to its all-time high, but the NL had caught up and passed its rival. The NL broke the one million mark for the first time and surpassed the AA's overall total for the first time since the Association's inaugural season in 1882.

1888 National League

TEAM	W	L	T	PCT	GB	HW	HL	R	OR	PA	H	2B	3B	HR	BB	SO	HB	SH	AVG	OBP	SLG	OPS	AOPS	BR	ABR	PF	SB	CS	BSA	BSR
NY	84	47	7	.641		**44**	23	659	**479**	5046	1149	130	76	55	270	456		29	.242	.287	.336	623	105	18	26	99	**314**			
CHI	77	58	1	.570	9	43	27	**734**	659	4934	1201	147	**95**	**77**	290	563		28	.260	.308	**.383**	**691**	117	**125**	75	107	287			
PHI	69	61	2	.531	14.5	37	29	535	509	4847	1021	151	46	16	268	485		**51**	.225	.276	.290	566	82	-61	-89	105	246			
BOS	70	64	3	.522	15.5	36	30	669	619	5148	1183	167	89	56	282	524		32	.245	.291	.351	642	107	50	33	103	293			
DET	68	63	3	.519	16	40	26	721	629	5202	**1275**	**177**	72	51	**307**	**396**		46	**.263**	**.313**	.361	674	**120**	112	**104**	101	193			
PIT	66	68	5	.493	19.5	37	30	534	580	4953	1070	150	49	14	194	583		46	.227	.264	.289	553	90	-93	-44	91	287			
IND	50	85	1	.370	36	31	35	603	731	4902	1100	180	33	34	236	492		43	.238	.281	.313	594	93	-20	-31	102	350			
WAS	48	86	2	.358	37.5	26	38	482	731	4835	944	98	49	30	246	499		43	.208	.255	.271	526	78	-132	-99	93	331			
TOT	544					294	238	4937		39867	8943	1200	509	333	2093	3998	318		.239	.285	.325	609					2301			

TEAM	CG	SHO	GR	SV	IP	H	HR	BB	SO	BR/9	ERA	AERA	OAV	OOB	PR	APR	PF	OSB	OCS	FA	E	WPB	DP	FW	PW	BW	BSW	DIF
NY	133	**20**	4	1	1208.0	**907**	27	307	**726**	**9.3**	**1.96**	**139**	**.199**	**.255**	**117**	**107**	96			.924	432	193	76	1.2	**10.5**	2.6		4.2
CHI	123	13	**12**	1	1186.1	1139	63	308	588	11.4	2.96	102	.246	.301	-17	6	106			**.927**	417	186	**112**	1.7	.6	7.4		-.1
PHI	125	16	6	**3**	1167.0	1072	26	196	519	10.0	2.38	124	.236	.271	58	67	104			.923	424	128	70	.6	6.6	-8.8		5.6
BOS	134	7	3	0	1225.1	1104	36	269	484	10.4	2.61	110	.232	.280	30	30	101			.917	494	155	91	-2.2	3.0	3.2		-1.0
DET	130	10	4	1	1199.0	1115	44	**183**	522	10.0	2.74	101	.234	.266	12	2	98			.919	463	**101**	83	-1.1	.2	**10.2**		-6.8
PIT	**135**	13	3	0	1203.1	1190	**23**	223	367	10.8	2.67	98	.249	.287	22	-8	93			**.927**	**416**	141	88	**2.3**	-.8	-4.3		1.9
IND	132	6	5	0	1187.2	1260	64	308	388	12.2	3.81	77	.263	.313	-129	-113	104			.921	449	183	84	-.0	-11.1	-3.0		-3.3
WAS	133	6	3	0	1179.1	1157	50	298	406	11.5	3.54	78	.248	.300	-93	-110	97			.912	494	152	69	-2.4	-10.8	-9.7		4.0
TOT	1045	91	40	6	9556.0					10.7	2.83		.239	.285						.921	3589	1239	673					

Batter-Fielder Wins
Pfeffer-Chi 4.4
Nash-Bos 4.1
Ryan-Chi..............3.9
Ewing-NY 3.8
Anson-Chi............3.8

Batting Average
Anson-Chi.............344
Ryan-Chi...............332
Kelly-Bos 318
Brouthers-Det.......307
Ewing-NY 306

On-Base Percentage
Anson-Chi 400
Brouthers-Det 399
Connor-NY...................389
Ryan-Chi 377
Hoy-Was 374

Slugging Average
Ryan-Chi...............515
Anson-Chi.............499
Connor-NY 480
Kelly-Bos 480
Johnston-Bos 472

On-Base Plus Slugging
Anson-Chi 899
Ryan-Chi 892
Connor-NY............869
Brouthers-Det 862
Kelly-Bos 848

Adjusted OPS
Connor-NY............178
Anson-Chi 172
Brouthers-Det 172
Ryan-Chi 170
Kelly-Bos 164

Adjusted Batter Runs
Brouthers-Det 47.2
Connor-NY 45.2
Ryan-Chi 42.1
Anson-Chi 41.5
Kelly-Bos 31.4

Runs
Brouthers-Det 118
Ryan-Chi 115
Johnston-Bos........102
Anson-Chi 101
Connor-NY..............98

Hits
Ryan-Chi 182
Anson-Chi 177
Johnston-Bos........173
Brouthers-Det 160
White-Det 157

Doubles
Ryan-Chi.........................33
Brouthers-Det 33
Johnston-Bos 31
Denny-Ind 27
Hines-Ind 26

Triples
Johnston-Bos..........18
Connor-NY.............17
Nash-Bos...............15
Ewing-NY 15

Home Runs
Ryan-Chi 16
Connor-NY.............14
Johnston-Bos.........12
Denny-Ind 12
Anson-Chi 12

Total Bases
Ryan-Chi 283
Johnston-Bos........276
Anson-Chi 257
Brouthers-Det 242
Connor-NY............231

Runs Batted In
Anson-Chi 84
Nash-Bos 75
Rowe-Det 74
Williamson-Chi 73

Stolen Bases
Hoy-Was 82
Seery-Ind................80
Sunday-Pit..............71
Pfeffer-Chi 64
Ryan-Chi 60

Base Stealing Runs

Fielding Runs-Infield
Pfeffer-Chi 37.7
Nash-Bos.....................18.3
Burns-Chi.....................17.4
Denny-Ind 15.8
Glasscock-Ind 13.9

Fielding Runs-Outfield
Sunday-Pit 15.1
Fogarty-Phi..........14.1
Wilmot-Was 11.7
Seery-Ind 9.6
Hoy-Was................6.9

Wins
Keefe-NY 35
Clarkson-Bos..........33
Conway-Det...........30
Morris-Pit................29
Buffinton-Phi 28

Winning Pct.
Keefe-NY 745
Conway-Det 682
Sanders-Phi 655
Krock-Chi 641
Clarkson-Bos 623

Complete Games
Morris-Pit 54
Clarkson-Bos 53
Galvin-Pit 49
Keefe-NY 48
Welch-NY 47

Strikeouts
Keefe-NY..............335
Clarkson-Bos........223
Getzien-Det 202
Buffinton-Phi 199
O'Day-Was 186

Fewest BB/Game
Sanders-Phi 1.08
Galvin-Pit 1.09
Krock-Chi 1.19
Getzien-Det 1.20
Madden-Bos 1.31

Games
Morris-Pit 55
Clarkson-Bos 54
Keefe-NY 51
Galvin-Pit 50
Welch-NY 47

Saves
Wood-Phi..................2
VanHaltren-Chi 1
Tyng-Phi 1
Twitchell-Det 1
Crane-NY..................1

Base Runners/9
Keefe-NY 8.68
Buffinton-Phi........8.70
Conway-Det 8.86
Sanders-Phi 9.02
Gruber-Det 9.04

Adjusted Relief Runs

Relief Ranking

Innings Pitched
Clarkson-Bos 483.1
Morris-Pit 480.0
Galvin-Pit 437.1
Keefe-NY 434.1
Welch-NY 425.1

Opponents' Avg.
Keefe-NY 196
Titcomb-NY 201
Welch-NY 207
Conway-Det 208
Buffinton-Phi.........213

Opponents' OBP
Conway-Det................243
Keefe-NY 243
Buffinton-Phi 244
Gruber-Det...................249
Titcomb-NY 253

Earned Run Average
Keefe-NY 1.74
Sanders-Phi 1.90
Buffinton-Phi........1.91
Welch-NY 1.93
Sowders-Bos 2.07

Adjusted ERA
Keefe-NY..............156
Sanders-Phi..........156
Buffinton-Phi 155
Welch-NY 141
Sowders-Bos........138

Adjusted Starter Runs
Keefe-NY 52.9
Buffinton-Phi........44.8
Welch-NY 41.9
Sanders-Phi 29.8
Krock-Chi 23.8

Pitcher Wins
Buffinton-Phi 5.1
Keefe-NY...........4.7
Welch-NY 3.9
Conway-Det 3.9
Sanders-Phi 3.7

Casey Debuts in Mudville

The NL went back to the three-strikes-and-you're-out rule. The new ruling rule helped pitchers dominate. As the NL's batting average dropped by nearly 30 points, scoring fell dramatically in 1888. Whiffs skyrocketed and walks, which still took five balls, dipped.

In this pitcher's year, only Chicago's Jimmy Ryan slugged over .500, and last-place Washington had seven regulars bat .225 or worse. By 1888 nearly all catchers were using a mitt; the 1884 ruling allowing pitchers to throw overhand made the mitt a necessity. And as new ways came in, old ones went out: Ezra Sutton, 38, one of the last remaining active players from the 1871 National Association, retired.

Washington became the first team to do its spring training in Florida. The warm setting might have helped rookie outfielder Dummy Hoy loosen up—he led the NL in stolen bases. Other important first-year men included future Hall of Famers Hugh Duffy of Chicago, Pittsburgh first baseman Jake Beckley, and Philadelphia's Ed Delahanty. Also debuting in Philadelphia was pitcher Kid Gleason, who later became a solid second baseman but is remembered as the blameless manager of the 1919 Black Sox.

The debut with the most lasting impact, though, belonged to a fictional batsman. Ernest Lawrence Thayer's epic baseball poem "Casey at the Bat" was an immediate success, with actors all over the land performing dramatic readings and spreading Casey's name.

Cap Anson won his second batting title, and once again Chicago had the league's top attack. But thanks to pitching Triple Crown winner Tim Keefe and his second, Mickey Welch, New York's mound work was outstanding. Roger Connor and Buck Ewing provided the Giants with enough offense to win easily.

Keefe was dominating in the World Series as the Giants easily breezed by AA champ St. Louis in a 10-game set. The Giants won six of the first seven, defusing any tension that the final games might have otherwise had. Keefe threw 4 complete-game victories, allowing just 2 earned runs in 35 innings.

1888 American Association

TEAM	W	L	T	PCT	GB	HW	HL	R	OR	PA	H	2B	3B	HR	BB	SO	HB	SH	AVG	OBP	SLG	OPS	AOPS	BR	ABR	PF	SB	CS	BSA	BSR
STL	92	43	2	.681		**60**	21	789	**501**	5215	1189	149	47	**36**	**410**	521		50	**.250**	**.316**	.324	640	98	57	-20	111	468			
BRO	88	52	3	.629	6.5	53	20	758	584	5280	1177	172	70	25	353	**439**		56	.242	.300	.321	621	103	18	20	100	334			
PHI	81	52	3	.609	10	54	20	**827**	594	5208	**1209**	**183**	**89**	31	303	473		**77**	**.250**	.305	**.344**	**649**	**113**	**60**	**66**	99	434			
CIN	80	54	3	.597	11.5	56	25	745	628	5206	1161	132	82	32	345	555		60	.242	.301	.323	624	99	19	-18	105	**469**			
BAL	57	80	0	.416	36	30	26	653	779	5012	1068	162	70	19	298	479		58	.229	.284	.306	590	96	-37	-19	97	326			
CLE	50	82	3	.379	40.5	33	28	651	839	4997	1076	128	59	12	315	559		79	.234	.294	.295	589	96	-33	-13	97	353			
LOU	48	87	4	.356	44	27	29	689	870	5272	1177	**183**	67	14	322	604		69	.241	.297	.315	612	102	2	18	98	318			
KC	43	89	0	.326	47.5	23	34	579	896	4933	1000	142	61	19	288	604		57	.218	.273	.288	561	78	-85	-120	106	257			
TOT	548					336	203	5691		41123	9057	1251	545	188	2634	4234	506		.238	.297	.315	612					2959			

TEAM	CG	SHO	GR	SV	IP	H	HR	BB	SO	BR/9	ERA	AERA	OAV	OOB	PR	APR	PF	OSB	OCS	FA	E	WPB	DP	FW	PW	BW	BSW	DIF
STL	132	12	5	0	1212.2	**939**	19	**225**	517	**9.1**	**2.09**	**156**	**.206**	**.254**	**130**	**147**	107	**254**		**.924**	**430**	**167**	73	**3.4**	**13.6**	-1.8		9.3
BRO	**138**	9	5	0	1286.1	1059	15	285	577	9.7	2.33	128	.217	.266	104	94	97	345		.918	502	172	88	.6	8.7	1.8		6.9
PHI	133	**13**	3	0	1208.2	988	**14**	324	596	10.4	2.41	124	.216	.279	87	78	98	353		.919	475	267	73	.7	7.2	**6.1**		.5
CIN	132	10	5	**2**	1237.2	1103	19	310	539	10.8	2.73	116	.230	.288	46	58	104	289		.923	456	178	**100**	2.0	5.4	-1.7		7.3
BAL	130	3	**9**	0	1200.1	1162	23	419	525	12.5	3.78	79	.245	.318	-96	-111	97	434		.920	461	247	88	1.7	-10.3	-1.8		-1.2
CLE	131	6	4	1	1171.0	1235	38	389	500	12.9	3.72	83	.261	.324	-86	-82	101	388		.915	488	249	87	-.2	-7.6	-1.2		-7.0
LOU	133	6	6	0	1231.1	1265	28	281	**599**	11.7	3.25	95	.256	.304	-26	-24	100	384		.900	609	233	75	-6.2	-2.2	1.7		-12.7
KC	128	4	4	0	1157.2	1306	32	401	381	13.8	4.29	80	.275	.340	-159	-100	112	512		.914	507	222	95	-1.9	-9.2	-11.1		-.8
TOT	1057	63	41	3	9705.2					11.3	3.06		.238	.297						.917	3928	1735	679					

Batter-Fielder Wins	Batting Average	On-Base Percentage	Slugging Average	On-Base Plus Slugging	Adjusted OPS	Adjusted Batter Runs
Stovey-Phi 3.5	O'Neill-StL 335	Robinson-StL 400	Reilly-Cin 501	Reilly-Cin 864	Reilly-Cin 167	Stovey-Phi 38.8
Collins-Lou-Bro ..3.2	Reilly-Cin 321	O'Neill-StL 390	Stovey-Phi 460	O'Neill-StL 836	Stovey-Phi 165	Reilly-Cin 36.0
McKean-Cle 3.1	Browning-Lou 313	Browning-Lou 380	O'Neill-StL 446	Stovey-Phi 825	Browning-Lou 164	Collins-Lou-Bro ..35.8
Davis-KC 2.9	Collins-Lou-Bro.....307	Collins-Lou-Bro 373	Browning-Lou 436	Browning-Lou 816	Collins-Lou-Bro 158	Burns-Bal-Bro 29.8
McPhee-Cin 2.8	Orr-Bro 305	Stovey-Phi 365	Burns-Bal-Bro.......435	Collins-Lou-Bro 796	Burns-Bal-Bro 152	Browning-Lou 29.0

Runs	Hits	Doubles	Triples	Home Runs	Total Bases	Runs Batted In
Pinkney-Bro 134	O'Neill-StL 177	Collins-Lou-Bro.............31	Stovey-Phi 20	Reilly-Cin 13	Reilly-Cin 264	Reilly-Cin 103
Collins-Lou-Bro 133	Reilly-Cin 169	Wolf-Lou 28	Burns-Bal-Bro 15	Stovey-Phi 9	Stovey-Phi 244	Larkin-Phi 101
Stovey-Phi 127	McKean-Cle.........164	Reilly-Cin 28	McKean-Cle...........15	Larkin-Phi 7	O'Neill-StL 236	Foutz-Bro 99
Welch-Phi 125	Collins-Lou-Bro 162	Larkin-Phi 28	Reilly-Cin 14		McKean-Cle...........233	O'Neill-StL 98
Latham-StL 119	Corkhill-Cin-Bro 160		Foutz-Bro 13		Burns-Bal-Bro 230	Corkhill-Cin-Bro 93

Stolen Bases	Base Stealing Runs	Fielding Runs-Infield	Fielding Runs-Outfield	Wins	Winning Pct.	Complete Games
Latham-StL 109		Shindle-Bal 38.1	McCarthy-StL 25.5	King-StL..................45	Hudson-StL 714	King-StL 64
Nicol-Cin 103		Davis-KC 28.5	Lyons-StL 6.2	Seward-Phi 35	Chamberlain-Lou-SL.694	Bakely-Cle 60
Welch-Phi 95		Easterday-KC.............26.0	Collins-Lou-Bro......6.1	Caruthers-Bro 29	King-StL 692	Seward-Phi............57
McCarthy-StL 93		McPhee-Cin 25.5	Griffin-Bal 4.9	Weyhing-Phi 28	Caruthers-Bro.......659	Porter-KC 53
Stovey-Phi 87		Stricker-Cle 23.1	Stovey-Phi 3.3	Viau-Cin..................27	Viau-Cin 659	Cunningham-Bal ..50

Strikeouts	Fewest BB/Game	Games	Saves	Base Runners/9	Adjusted Relief Runs	Relief Ranking
Seward-Phi 272	King-StL 1.17	King-StL 66	Mullane-Cin 1	King-StL 8.33		
King-StL................258	Caruthers-Bro......1.22	Bakely-Cle 61	Gilks-Cle 1	Caruthers-Bro......9.19		
Ramsey-Lou 228	Hudson-StL 1.59	Seward-Phi....................57		Seward-Phi.........9.32		
Bakely-Cle 212	Ewing-Lou 1.60	Porter-KC 55		Foutz-Bro 9.51		
Weyhing-Phi 204	Hecker-Lou 1.73	Cunningham-Bal............51		Hughes-Bro 9.55		

Innings Pitched	Opponents' Avg.	Opponents' OBP	Earned Run Average	Adjusted ERA	Adjusted Starter Runs	Pitcher Wins
King-StL 584.2	Terry-Bro 200	King-StL.......................237	King-StL 1.63	King-StL................200	King-StL 95.3	**King-StL** 10.2
Bakely-Cle 532.2	King-StL 200	Caruthers-Bro 255	Seward-Phi..........2.01	Seward-Phi 148	Seward-Phi..........60.1	**Seward-Phi** 5.1
Seward-Phi........518.2	Seward-Phi...........201	Seward-Phi 258	Terry-Bro 2.03	Terry-Bro 147	Hughes-Bro 31.5	**Caruthers-Bro** ...3.7
Porter-KC 474.0	Hughes-Bro 206	Foutz-Bro 262	Hughes-Bro 2.13	Chamberlain-Lou-SL 143	Weyhing-Phi 30.2	**Weyhing-Phi** 3.3
Cunningham-Bal453.1	Chamberlain-Lou-SL.207	Hughes-Bro 262	Chamberlain-Lou-SL2.19	Hughes-Bro 140	Caruthers-Bro......28.2	**Hudson-StL**........2.9

A Less Offensive League

Having lost the battle to the NL's Giants, the New York Metropolitans left the Association, replaced by Kansas City. The Blues duly finished last despite the debut of perhaps the greatest leadoff man of the century: "Sliding Billy" Hamilton. New rules, also adopted by the NL, increased strikeouts, chopped walks, and decreased scoring. Runs per team were down 1.5 per game in 1888 than the previous season. The top run-scoring team recorded 304 fewer runs than the in '87.

After dumping most of his high-salaried club over the winter, St. Louis owner Chris Von der Ahe was as surprised as anyone when his club took over the league lead in August and cruised to the title. Sporting the league's best pitching and second-best attack, the Browns were a complete club. Left fielder Tip O'Neill won his second straight batting title (although his average dropped an amazing 100 points), and unheralded Yank Robinson led the league in on-base percentage and garnered 116 bases on balls, the most walks in a season to that point. Arlie Latham, who paced in steals, was one of four Browns to score more than 100 runs. Silver King, given a bigger share of the load due to the sale of Dave Foutz and Bob Caruthers to Brooklyn, proved the league's top pitcher, posting the league's only ERA under 2.00.

George Pinkney of second-place Brooklyn played in 143 games, a new all-time record, and he led the league in runs. Foutz, when not pitching, was the right fielder for the Bridegrooms; his 99 RBIs were third-best in the league. Brooklyn didn't get much offense from anywhere else and couldn't hold the league lead.

Storm clouds were gathering. Perhaps aided by the decrease in hitting, league attendance dropped by more than 300,000 fans, and even in St. Louis, the crowds fell precipitously. For the first time AA attendance was significantly lower than that of the NL.

1889 National League

TEAM	W	L	T	PCT	GB	HW	HL	R	OR	PA	H	2B	3B	HR	BB	SO	HB	SH	AVG	OBP	SLG	OPS	AOPS	BR	ABR	PF	SB	CS	BSA	BSR
NY	83	43	5	.659		47	15	**935**	708	5236	1319	208	**77**	52	**538**	386		27	**.282**	**.360**	**.393**	**753**	**116**	**105**	**103**	100	292			
BOS	83	45	5	.648	1	**48**	17	826	**626**	5140	1251	196	54	42	471	450		**41**	.270	.343	.363	706	97	22	-23	106	**331**			
CHI	67	65	4	.508	19	37	30	867	814	5397	**1338**	184	66	**79**	518	516		30	.276	.349	.390	739	107	76	34	105	243			
PHI	63	64	3	.496	20.5	43	24	742	748	5123	1248	**215**	52	44	393	**353**		35	.266	.327	.362	689	90	-17	-77	109	269			
PIT	61	71	2	.462	25	40	28	726	801	5212	1202	209	65	42	420	467		44	.253	.320	.351	671	103	-50	28	90	231			
CLE	61	72	3	.459	25.5	33	35	656	720	5140	1167	131	59	25	429	417		38	.250	.318	.319	637	85	-104	-91	98	237			
IND	59	75	1	.440	28	32	36	819	894	5300	1356	228	35	62	377	447		44	.278	.335	.377	712	102	24	9	102	252			
WAS	41	83	3	.331	41	24	29	632	892	4904	1105	151	57	25	466	456		43	.251	.329	.329	658	95	-56	-12	94	232			
TOT	531					304	214	6203		41452	9986	1522	465	371	3612	3492	302		.266	.335	.361	696					2087			

TEAM	CG	SHO	GR	SV	IP	H	HR	BB	SO	BR/9	ERA	AERA	OAV	OOB	PR	APR	PF	OSB	OCS	FA	E	WPB	DP	FW	PW	BW	BSW	DIF
NY	119	6	13	3	1150.0	**1067**	38	524	**558**	12.8	3.47	114	**.240**	.327	70	57	98	193		.919	437	102	90	-.3	4.9	**8.9**		6.5
BOS	121	**10**	12	**5**	1166.0	1152	41	413	497	**12.4**	**3.36**	**124**	.250	**.318**	**86**	**102**	104	**186**		.926	413	**77**	105	1.2	**8.8**	-2.0		10.9
CHI	123	6	13	2	1237.0	1313	71	408	434	12.8	3.73	112	.263	.324	41	62	104	301		.923	463	142	91	-.8	5.4	2.9		-6.5
PHI	106	4	27	2	1153.1	1288	**33**	428	443	13.6	4.00	109	.275	.339	3	39	108	229		.915	466	106	92	-2.0	3.4	-6.7		4.8
PIT	125	5	9	1	1130.2	1296	42	**374**	345	13.5	4.51	83	.272	.329	-60	-84	93	276		.931	385	140	94	2.8	-7.3	2.4		-3.0
CLE	**132**	6	5	1	1191.2	1182	36	519	435	13.2	3.66	110	.252	.332	48	47	100	271		**.936**	**365**	163	**108**	**4.2**	4.1	-7.9		-5.9
IND	109	3	**29**	2	1174.1	1365	73	420	408	14.0	4.85	86	.282	.345	-108	-85	104	297		.926	420	117	102	1.2	-7.4	.8		-2.6
WAS	113	1	16	0	1103.0	1261	37	527	388	14.9	4.68	85	.279	.360	-80	-92	98	334		.904	519	109	91	-5.2	-8.0	-1.0		-6.8
TOT	948	41	124	16	9306.0					13.4	4.02		.266	.335						.923	3468	956	773					

Batter-Fielder Wins
Glasscock-Ind 5.8
Carroll-Pit 3.7
Ewing-NY 3.7
Tiernan-NY 3.7
Wilmot-Was 3.1

Batting Average
Brouthers-Bos 373
Glasscock-Ind.......352
Anson-Chi.............342
Tiernan-NY...........335
Carroll-Pit 330

On-Base Percentage
Carroll-Pit.....................486
Brouthers-Bos 462
Tiernan-NY 447
Anson-Chi 440
Connor-NY...................426

Slugging Average
Connor-NY 528
Ryan-Chi...............516
Brouthers-Bos 507
Tiernan-NY...........497
Thompson-Phi 492

On-Base Plus Slugging
Carroll-Pit 970
Brouthers-Bos 969
Connor-NY............955
Tiernan-NY 944
Ryan-Chi 919

Adjusted OPS
Carroll-Pit 188
Connor-NY............164
Tiernan-NY 162
Brouthers-Bos 160
Ryan-Chi 147

Adjusted Batter Runs
Carroll-Pit 49.6
Tiernan-NY 46.9
Connor-NY 46.1
Brouthers-Bos 42.4
Anson-Chi 36.5

Runs
Tiernan-NY 147
Duffy-Chi 144
Ryan-Chi 140
Gore-NY 132
Glasscock-Ind 128

Hits
Glasscock-Ind 205
Ryan-Chi 187
Duffy-Chi 182
Brouthers-Bos 181
Anson-Chi 177

Doubles
Kelly-Bos........................41
Glasscock-Ind................40
Thompson-Phi 36
O'Rourke-NY 36
Richardson-Bos 33

Triples
Wilmot-Was 19
Fogarty-Phi 17
Connor-NY..............17
Tiernan-NY 14
Ryan-Chi 14

Home Runs
Thompson-Phi........20
Denny-Ind 18
Ryan-Chi.................17
Connor-NY..............13
Duffy-Chi 12

Total Bases
Ryan-Chi 297
Glasscock-Ind 272
Thompson-Phi......262
Connor-NY.........262
Duffy-Chi 253

Runs Batted In
Connor-NY 130
Brouthers-Bos 118
Anson-Chi 117
Denny-Ind............112
Thompson-Phi 111

Stolen Bases
Fogarty-Phi 99
Kelly-Bos 68
Brown-Bos..............63
Ward-NY 62
Glasscock-Ind 57

Base Stealing Runs

Fielding Runs-Infield
Glasscock-Ind 38.1
Richardson-NY 14.9
Denny-Ind 12.7
Bassett-Ind 12.5
Nash-Bos....................11.4

Fielding Runs-Outfield
Fogarty-Phi..........18.3
Wilmot-Was 14.3
Ryan-Chi...............8.5
McGeachy-Ind 7.8
McAleer-Cle 7.5

Wins
Clarkson-Bos..........49
Keefe-NY................28
Buffinton-Phi 28
Welch-NY 27
Galvin-Pit................23

Winning Pct.
Clarkson-Bos 721
Welch-NY 692
Keefe-NY 683
Radbourn-Bos 645
Buffinton-Phi.........636

Complete Games
Clarkson-Bos 68
Staley-Pit 46
Welch-NY 39
O'Brien-Cle............39
Keefe-NY 39

Strikeouts
Clarkson-Bos........284
Keefe-NY..............225
Staley-Pit..............159
Buffinton-Phi 153
Getzien-Ind 139

Fewest BB/Game
Galvin-Pit 2.06
Boyle-Ind 2.26
Radbourn-Bos 2.34
Dwyer-Chi............2.35
Sanders-Phi 2.47

Games
Clarkson-Bos 73
Staley-Pit 49
Keefe-NY 47
Buffinton-Phi..................47
Boyle-Ind........................46

Saves
Sowders-Bos-Pit 3
Welch-NY 2
Bishop-Chi...............2

Base Runners/9
Clarkson-Bos 11.74
Radbourn-Bos ..11.76
Staley-Pit 11.94
Welch-NY 11.98
Keefe-NY 12.07

Adjusted Relief Runs

Relief Ranking

Innings Pitched
Clarkson-Bos 620.0
Staley-Pit 420.0
Buffinton-Phi......380.0
Boyle-Ind 378.2
Welch-NY 375.0

Opponents' Avg.
Keefe-NY 228
Welch-NY 234
Clarkson-Bos 243
Crane-NY 244
Hutchison-Chi.......245

Opponents' OBP
Clarkson-Bos..............306
Radbourn-Bos 306
Staley-Pit 309
Welch-NY......................310
Keefe-NY 312

Earned Run Average
Clarkson-Bos 2.73
Bakely-Cle 2.96
Welch-NY 3.02
Buffinton-Phi........3.24
Keefe-NY 3.36

Adjusted ERA
Clarkson-Bos........153
Bakely-Cle 136
Buffinton-Phi 134
Welch-NY 131
Sanders-Phi..........123

Adjusted Starter Runs
Clarkson-Bos 92.8
Buffinton-Phi........44.6
Welch-NY 40.8
Bakely-Cle 29.5
Keefe-NY 24.4

Pitcher Wins
Clarkson-Bos 8.9
Buffinton-Phi 4.0
Welch-NY 3.1
Bakely-Cle..........2.6
Sanders-Phi 2.4

Land of the Giants

The Detroit club left the NL, and Cleveland jumped from the American Association to fill the space. The new club finished sixth. The game itself underwent significant changes in 1889. First and forevermore, it now took four balls to draw a walk, which helped scoring increase by about 25 percent. In addition, the use of substitutes gained speed as teams were now allowed to change one player per game for any reason—not just injuries—at the end of any complete inning. Also, the owners' decision to institute a salary classification scheme infuriated players, who organized in secret.

New York won its second straight league title, edging out the Boston Beaneaters by 1 game. Tim Keefe's win on the season's last day clinched matters for the Giants, who sported the bats of Roger Connor, Mike Tiernan, and George Gore, and a great second starter in Mickey Welch. Boston contended largely on the arm of John Clarkson, who enjoyed one of the great ironman seasons by any pitcher. He led the league by huge margins in games, innings, wins, strikeouts, and ERA. His 68 complete games weren't quite a record, but no one has surpassed it since; the same can be said of his 49 wins, which still didn't match his career-high 53 victories in '85. Beaneaters teammate Dan Brouthers won his third batting title, but King Kelly, beginning to feel the effects of his dissipated lifestyle, fell off dramatically for Boston.

Future ace Amos Rusie debuted as a third starter for seventh-place Indianapolis. Sam Thompson led the league in homers and Jim Fogarty paced the NL in steals for Harry Wright's fourth-place Phillies.

The Giants took a hotly contested World Series from AA champ Brooklyn—New York's first "Subway Series," so to speak, even though the subway system did not open until 1904. The Bridegrooms, borrowing a tactic from AA St. Louis, won three times by stalling for darkness, but New York responded by outhitting Brooklyn, 102–67. Neither Keefe nor Welch had the strength to win a single contest—second-line hurlers Ed "Cannonball" Crane and Hank O'Day took over and saved the NL's bacon.

1889 American Association

TEAM	W	L	T	PCT	GB	HW	HL	R	OR	PA	H	2B	3B	HR	BB	SO	HB	SH	AVG	OBP	SLG	OPS	AOPS	BR	ABR	PF	SB	CS	BSA	BSR
BRO	93	44	3	.679		50	18	**995**	706	5414	1265	188	79	47	**550**	**401**		49	.263	.344	.364	708	106	44	41	100	389			
STL	90	45	6	.667	2	**51**	18	957	**680**	5487	1312	211	64	**58**	493	477		55	.266	.339	.370	709	94	41	-63	113	336			
PHI	75	58	5	.564	16	46	22	880	787	5464	**1339**	**239**	65	43	534	496		62	**.275**	**.354**	.377	**731**	**114**	**92**	**105**	99	252			
CIN	76	63	2	.547	18	47	26	897	769	5356	1307	197	**96**	52	452	511		60	.270	.340	**.382**	722	107	56	30	103	**462**			
BAL	70	65	4	.519	22	41	23	791	795	5256	1209	155	68	20	418	536		**82**	.254	.325	.328	653	88	-58	-71	102	311			
COL	60	78	2	.435	33.5	36	33	779	924	5365	1247	171	95	36	507	609		42	.259	.335	.356	691	106	7	52	95	304			
KC	55	82	2	.401	38	35	35	852	1031	5443	1256	162	76	18	430	626		66	.254	.322	.328	650	84	-68	-111	106	472			
LOU	27	111	2	.196	66.5	18	47	632	1091	5316	1249	170	75	22	320	521		41	.252	.303	.330	633	86	-114	-100	98	203			
TOT	559					324	222	6783		43101	10184	1493	618	296	3704	4177	457		.262	.333	.354	687					2729			

TEAM	CG	SHO	GR	SV	IP	H	HR	BB	SO	BR/9	ERA	AERA	OAV	OOB	PR	APR	PF	OSB	OCS	FA	E	WPB	DP	FW	PW	BW	BSW	DIF
BRO	120	**10**	20	1	1212.2	1205	33	**400**	471	12.2	3.61	103	.251	.315	31	15	97	361		**.928**	**421**	**142**	92	**4.6**	1.3	3.5		15.2
STL	121	7	20	4	1237.2	**1166**	39	413	**617**	**11.9**	**3.00**	**141**	**.242**	**.309**	**116**	**152**	110	326		.925	438	196	100	3.8	**12.9**	-5.3		11.2
PHI	**130**	9	8	1	1199.1	1199	35	509	479	13.4	3.53	107	.253	.335	42	34	98	**280**		.920	465	152	120	1.7	2.9	**8.9**		-5.0
CIN	114	3	**27**	**8**	1243.0	1270	35	475	562	13.0	3.50	111	.257	.328	47	53	102	294		.926	440	187	**121**	3.7	4.5	2.5		-4.2
BAL	128	**10**	12	1	1192.0	1168	**27**	424	540	12.6	3.56	111	.249	.322	38	48	103	305		.907	536	195	104	-2.1	4.1	-6.0		6.5
COL	114	9	**27**	4	1199.0	1274	33	551	610	14.1	4.39	82	.264	.346	-73	-110	94	431		.915	497	275	92	.3	-9.3	4.4		-4.4
KC	128	0	11	2	1204.1	1373	51	457	447	14.1	4.36	96	.278	.347	-69	-23	109	363		.899	611	201	109	-6.3	-1.9	-9.4		4.1
LOU	127	2	13	1	1226.1	1529	43	475	451	15.1	4.81	80	.297	.362	-132	-133	100	369		.906	584	234	117	-4.5	-11.3	-8.5		-17.7
TOT	982	50	138	22	9714.1					13.3	3.84		.262	.333						.916	3992	1582	855					

Batter-Fielder Wins	Batting Average	On-Base Percentage	Slugging Average	On-Base Plus Slugging	Adjusted OPS	Adjusted Batter Runs
Stovey-Phi 5.0	Tucker-Bal............372	Tucker-Bal 450	Stovey-Phi 525	Tucker-Bal 934	Tucker-Bal 163	Tucker-Bal 46.3
Lyons-Phi 4.5	O'Neill-StL 335	Larkin-Phi 428	Holliday-Cin 497	Stovey-Phi 918	Stovey-Phi 162	Stovey-Phi..........45.8
Bierbauer-Phi 4.3	Lyons-Phi 329	Lyons-Phi....................426	Tucker-Bal............484	O'Neill-StL 897	Lyons-Phi.............157	Lyons-Phi 43.3
Marr-Col 3.6	Orr-Col 327	O'Neill-StL 419	O'Neill-StL 478	Lyons-Phi...............895	Larkin-Phi 145	Larkin-Phi 36.9
McPhee-Cin 3.6	Holliday-Cin 321	Hamilton-KC................413	Lyons-Phi 469	Holliday-Cin 869	Holliday-Cin 142	Marr-Col 35.2

Runs	Hits	Doubles	Triples	Home Runs	Total Bases	Runs Batted In
Stovey-Phi 152	Tucker-Bal 196	Welch-Phi 39	Marr-Col 15	Stovey-Phi 19	Stovey-Phi 292	Stovey-Phi 119
Griffin-Bal 152	Orr-Col..................183	Stovey-Phi......................38	Griffin-Bal 14	Holliday-Cin 19	Holliday-Cin 280	Foutz-Bro 113
O'Brien-Bro 146	Holliday-Cin 181	Lyons-Phi 36	Beard-Cin 14	Duffee-StL 16	Tucker-Bal 255	O'Neill-StL 110
Hamilton-KC 144	O'Neill-StL 179	O'Neill-StL 33		Milligan-StL 12	O'Neill-StL 255	Bierbauer-Phi 105
Collins-Bro............139	Shindle-Bal 178	Long-KC 32			Orr-Col..................250	Holliday-Cin 104

Stolen Bases	Base Stealing Runs	Fielding Runs-Infield	Fielding Runs-Outfield	Wins	Winning Pct.	Complete Games
Hamilton-KC 111		McPhee-Cin................37.3	Stovey-Phi 17.7	Caruthers-Bro 40	Caruthers-Bro.......784	Kilroy-Bal 55
O'Brien-Bro 91		Bierbauer-Phi.............36.4	Duffee-StL 15.7	King-StL..................35	King-StL 686	Baldwin-Col 54
Long-KC..................89		Long-KC.......................31.2	McCarthy-StL 13.0	Duryea-Cin 32	Chamberlain-StL .681	Weyhing-Phi..........50
Nicol-Cin 80		Shindle-Bal 22.6	Hornung-Bal 12.3	Chamberlain-StL 32	Lovett-Bro 630	King-StL 47
Latham-StL 69		Tomney-Lou 21.6	Sommer-Bal 9.1	Weyhing-Phi 30	Duryea-Cin 627	Caruthers-Bro........46

Strikeouts	Fewest BB/Game	Games	Saves	Base Runners/9	Adjusted Relief Runs	Relief Ranking
Baldwin-Col 368	Caruthers-Bro......2.10	Baldwin-Col 63	Mullane-Cin 5	Stivetts-StL 10.61		
Kilroy-Bal 217	Conway-KC..........2.42	Kilroy-Bal 59	Stivetts-StL 2	Caruthers-Bro....11.35		
Weyhing-Phi 213	King-StL 2.46	King-StL 56		Duryea-Cin 11.56		
Chamberlain-StL ..202	Lovett-Bro 2.55	Caruthers-Bro 56		Foreman-Bal 11.76		
King-StL................188	Swartzel-KC 2.57	Weyhing-Phi 54		Conway-KC........11.77		

Innings Pitched	Opponents' Avg.	Opponents' OBP	Earned Run Average	Adjusted ERA	Adjusted Starter Runs	Pitcher Wins
Baldwin-Col 513.2	Stivetts-StL 212	Stivetts-StL 285	Stivetts-StL 2.25	Stivetts-StL 187	Chamberlain-StL 56.0	**Duryea-Cin** 5.7
Kilroy-Bal 480.2	Weyhing-Phi 223	Caruthers-Bro 299	Duryea-Cin 2.56	Duryea-Cin 152	King-StL 51.7	**Kilroy-Bal** 5.7
King-StL 458.0	Terry-Bro 228	Duryea-Cin 303	Kilroy-Bal 2.85	Chamberlain-StL ..142	Duryea-Cin 50.6	**Chamberlain-StL**4.6
Weyhing-Phi 449.0	Foreman-Bal.........229	Foreman-Bal 306	Weyhing-Phi 2.95	Kilroy-Bal 138	Kilroy-Bal 49.4	**Caruthers-Bro** ..4.6
Caruthers-Bro....445.0	Baldwin-Col 231	Conway-KC 306	Chamberlain-StL 2.97	King-StL................134	Stivetts-StL 36.5	**King-StL** 4.4

Forfeiting a Title

Cleveland, a perennial doormat, left the league for the NL and was replaced by Columbus, which finished sixth. The big news in the AA was a dethroning of perennial champion St. Louis. The Browns' questionable on-field ethics, which included the tactic of stalling while ahead until darkness came and ended games, led to several forfeits. Brooklyn, white-hot down the stretch, grabbed the flag in the closet AA race since 1883.

The Bridegrooms led the league in runs despite lacking a single marquee star. Brooklyn moundsman Bob Caruthers paced the league in wins. St. Louis second baseman Yank Robinson broke his own record for walks and put together a .378 on-base percentage, but he hit just .208. Arlie Latham also disappointed at bat. Pitchers Silver King and Icebox Chamberlain were good, if unspectacular, though third arm Jack Stivetts paced the AA in ERA.

Once again, third-place Philadelphia had the AA's top power producer (this time Harry Stovey) as well as other bats in Curt Welch and Henry Larkin. Although the Athletics seem to have played in a good hitter's park, their offensive numbers, and their W-L record, were inadequate on the road.

With four balls once again required for a walk, Columbus pitcher Mark Baldwin set a record by passing 274 hitters. He also paced the league in games, strikeouts, and losses.

Baltimore improved 14 games, largely due to a great season from first baseman Tommy Tucker, who was the AA's surprise batting and on-base titlist in 1889. Seventh-place Kansas City installed rookie Herman Long at shortstop, and next to Billy Hamilton, Long was the team's best player. Meanwhile, last-place Louisville was almost unbelievably bad, finishing 66½ games out and running through four managers and five pitchers who made 18 or more starts.

League attendance rose by nearly 300,000, due to increases in Baltimore, Brooklyn, and Philadelphia. The Bridgerooms' tally of 353,690 was the highest attendance by any major league team to that point; it would not be surpassed for five years.

1890 National League

TEAM	W	L	T	PCT	GB	HW	HL	R	OR	PA	H	2B	3B	HR	BB	SO	HB	SH	AVG	OBP	SLG	OPS	AOPS	BR	ABR	PF	SB	CS	BSA	BSR
BRO	86	43	0	.667		**58**	16	**884**	620	4977	1166	184	75	43	517	**361**		41	.264	.346	**.369**	**715**	**113**	77	**74**	100	**349**			
CHI	84	53	2	.613	6	48	24	847	692	5453	**1271**	147	60	**67**	516	514		46	.260	.336	.356	692	102	37	5	104	329			
PHI	78	54	1	.591	9.5	54	22	823	707	5293	1267	**220**	78	23	522	403		64	**.269**	**.350**	.364	714	110	**84**	63	103	335			
CIN	77	55	2	.583	10.5	50	23	753	633	5128	1203	150	**120**	27	433	377		51	.259	.329	.360	689	106	20	24	100	312			
BOS	76	57	1	.571	12	43	23	763	**593**	5321	1220	175	62	31	**530**	515		**69**	.258	.342	.341	683	96	32	-27	108	285			
NY	63	68	4	.481	24	37	27	713	698	5232	1250	208	89	25	350	479		50	.259	.315	.354	669	99	-17	-18	100	289			
CLE	44	88	4	.333	43.5	30	37	630	832	5172	1073	132	59	21	497	474		42	.232	.312	.299	611	84	-98	-85	98	152			
PIT	23	113	2	.169	66.5	14	25	597	1235	5213	1088	160	43	20	408	458		66	.230	.300	.294	594	87	-134	-53	88	208			
TOT	539					334	197	6010		41789	9538	1376	586	257	3773	3581	429		.254	.329	.342	671					2259			

TEAM	CG	SHO	GR	SV	IP	H	HR	BB	SO	BR/9	ERA	AERA	OAV	OOB	PR	APR	PF	OSB	OCS	FA	E	WPB	DP	FW	PW	BW	BSW	DIF
BRO	115	6	14	2	1145.0	1102	27	401	403	12.2	3.06	112	.246	.315	64	49	96	304	*118*	**.940**	**320**	114	92	4.4	4.4	**6.6**		6.2
CHI	126	6	13	**3**	1237.1	1103	41	481	504	11.9	3.24	113	.234	.311	44	48	103	257	*145*	**.940**	344	138	89	**4.8**	4.3	.4		6.0
PHI	122	9	12	2	1194.2	1210	22	486	507	13.2	3.32	110	.255	.331	32	42	102	266	*139*	.929	398	102	**122**	.4	3.7	5.6		2.3
CIN	124	9	10	1	1190.2	1097	41	407	488	11.8	**2.79**	127	.238	.307	**102**	**100**	100	226	*162*	.932	382	116	106	1.5	**8.9**	2.1		-1.6
BOS	**132**	**13**	2	1	1187.0	1132	27	**354**	506	**11.5**	2.93	**128**	.245	**.303**	83	99	105	**220**	*150*	.935	359	**94**	77	2.9	8.8	-2.4		.2
NY	115	6	**20**	1	1177.0	**1029**	**14**	607	**612**	13.0	3.06	114	**.230**	.331	66	53	98	283	***209***	.922	440	164	104	-1.9	4.7	-1.6		-3.8
CLE	129	2	8	0	1184.1	1322	33	462	306	14.0	4.13	86	.275	.346	-75	-77	100	256	*198*	.929	405	108	108	.5	-6.8	-7.6		-8.1
PIT	119	3	**20**	0	1176.1	1520	52	573	381	16.6	5.97	55	.304	.384	-315	-379	92	447	*200*	.897	607	192	94	-11.6	-33.7	-4.7		5.0
TOT	982	54	99	10	9492.1					13.0	3.56		.254	.329						.928	3255	1028	792					

Batter-Fielder Wins	Batting Average	On-Base Percentage	Slugging Average	On-Base Plus Slugging	Adjusted OPS	Adjusted Batter Runs
Glasscock-NY 4.8	Glasscock-NY.......336	Anson-Chi 443	Tiernan-NY 495	Tiernan-NY 880	Tiernan-NY 156	Tiernan-NY 37.4
McPhee-Cin 3.9	Hamilton-Phi.........325	Hamilton-Phi 430	Clements-Phi 472	Clements-Phi........864	Clements-Phi........148	Anson-Chi 33.9
Allen-Phi..............3.2	Clements-Phi 315	Pinkney-Bro 411	Reilly-Cin 472	Anson-Chi 844	Pinkney-Bro...........145	McKean-Cle........31.3
Clements-Phi......3.0	O'Brien-Bro...........314	McKean-Cle 401	Burns-Bro 464	Pinkney-Bro..........842	Glasscock-NY 143	Pinkney-Bro........31.1
Hamilton-Phi 2.6	Thompson-Phi 313	Glasscock-NY 395	Burkett-NY 461	Glasscock-NY 834	McKean-Cle..........141	Hamilton-Phi 29.2

Runs	Hits	Doubles	Triples	Home Runs	Total Bases	Runs Batted In
Collins-Bro............148	Thompson-Phi.......172	Thompson-Phi 41	Reilly-Cin 26	Wilmot-Chi..............13	Tiernan-NY 274	Burns-Bro............128
Carroll-Chi 134	Glasscock-NY 172	Glasscock-NY................32	McPhee-Cin............22	Tiernan-NY 13	Reilly-Cin 261	Anson-Chi 107
Hamilton-Phi 133	Tiernan-NY 168	Collins-Bro 32	Tiernan-NY 21	Burns-Bro 13	Thompson-Phi......243	Thompson-Phi 102
Tiernan-NY 132	Reilly-Cin 166	Myers-Phi 29	Beard-Cin 15	Long-Bos 8	Wilmot-Chi............239	Wilmot-Chi 99
McPhee-Cin..........125	Carroll-Chi 166	O'Brien-Bro....................28			Glasscock-NY 225	Foutz-Bro 98

Stolen Bases	Base Stealing Runs	Fielding Runs-Infield	Fielding Runs-Outfield	Wins	Winning Pct.	Complete Games
Hamilton-Phi 102		Allen-Phi 32.3	Davis-Cle 12.3	Hutchison-Chi 42	Lovett-Bro.............732	Hutchison-Chi........65
Collins-Bro.............85		McPhee-Cin...............26.4	Wilmot-Chi 10.9	Gleason-Phi............38	Gleason-Phi 691	Rusie-NY 56
Sunday-Pit-Phi........84		Glasscock-NY 23.3	Carroll-Chi 10.9	Lovett-Bro 30	Luby-Chi 690	Gleason-Phi 54
Wilmot-Chi..............76		Smalley-Cle 20.2	Sunday-Pit-Phi 10.3	Rusie-NY 29	Caruthers-Bro.......676	Beatin-Cle 53
Tiernan-NY 56		Bassett-NY 18.7	Gilks-Cle................5.3	Rhines-Cin..............28	Hutchison-Chi.......627	Nichols-Bos 47

Strikeouts	Fewest BB/Game	Games	Saves	Base Runners/9	Adjusted Relief Runs	Relief Ranking
Rusie-NY 341	Young-Cle............1.83	Hutchison-Chi................71	Hutchison-Chi 2	Rhines-Cin 10.43		
Hutchison-Chi 289	Duryea-Cin 1.97	Rusie-NY 67	Gleason-Phi.............2	Nichols-Bos 10.55		
Nichols-Bos 222	Getzien-Bos 2.11	Gleason-Phi 60	Foutz-Bro..................2	Hutchison-Chi....10.70		
Gleason-Phi..........222	Nichols-Bos 2.38	Beatin-Cle.......................54		Getzien-Bos 10.98		
Terry-Bro 185	Rhines-Cin 2.53	Nichols-Bos 48		Duryea-Cin 11.10		

Innings Pitched	Opponents' Avg.	Opponents' OBP	Earned Run Average	Adjusted ERA	Adjusted Starter Runs	Pitcher Wins
Hutchison-Chi....603.0	Rusie-NY 212	Rhines-Cin...................282	Rhines-Cin 1.95	Rhines-Cin............182	Rhines-Cin 67.5	**Rhines-Cin** 6.0
Rusie-NY 548.2	Mullane-Cin 221	Nichols-Bos 284	Nichols-Bos 2.23	Nichols-Bos 168	Nichols-Bos 63.5	**Nichols-Bos** 5.9
Gleason-Phi 506.0	Hutchison-Chi........221	Hutchison-Chi 287	Mullane-Cin 2.24	Mullane-Cin 159	Hutchison-Chi......51.3	**Rusie-NY** 5.9
Beatin-Cle..........474.1	Rhines-Cin 221	Getzien-Bos..................292	Rusie-NY 2.56	Gleason-Phi..........139	Gleason-Phi 50.9	**Hutchison-Chi** ..4.5
Nichols-Bos 424.0	Luby-Chi 222	Duryea-Cin 295	Gleason-Phi 2.63	Rusie-NY 137	Rusie-NY 50.0	**Gleason-Phi** 4.0

Ball of Confusion

The Players' League rocked the NL and AA in 1890, but the Senior Circuit had its own share of intrigue, snaring two more Association franchises, Brooklyn and Cincinnati. The two new teams helped the NL survive; Cincinnati led in the early going and Brooklyn ended up on top at the end.

The Bridegrooms won despite significant injuries. Right fielder Oyster Burns and second baseman Hub Collins were the key offensive contributors, and Bob Caruthers, Tom Lovett, and Adonis Terry provided strong pitching. Second-place Chicago was weak in spots, though 42-game winner Bill Hutchinson certainly helped. Third-place Philadelphia got excellent pitching from Kid Gleason and big hitting from Sam Thompson and new recruit Billy Hamilton. Cincinnati received excellent pitching from rookie Billy Rhines, the only pitcher in the three major leagues to have an ERA below 2.00 in 1890.

Amos Rusie of New York set a new major league record by walking 293 hitters and led the league in losses, but he also paced the NL in strikeouts. His Giants finished sixth even with batting champ Jack Glasscock. Last-place Pittsburgh was so awful that 21 different pitchers started games, none more than 21 times. Billy Gumbert led with 4 wins. The club averaged just over 400 fans per game and soon became a traveling team.

Though the NL and AA had outlawed the pitcher's practice of intentionally defacing the ball with dirt, dilution of talent among the leagues allowed NL pitchers to lower their collective ERA by half a point. The loss of manpower to the PL pushed a great crop of rookies to debut: George Davis, Jesse Burkett, Bobby Lowe, Kid Nichols, and Cy Young.

The postseason, originally expected to be a cakewalk for Brooklyn, instead ended with each team winning three times before rain and low attendance caused the rest of the games to be cancelled. In truth, fans would have been more interested in the World Series had the Players' League champion Boston Reds been involved. Unsurprisingly, given the PL's competition, NL attendance fell by nearly half.

1890 American Association

TEAM	W	L	T	PCT	GB	HW	HL	R	OR	PA	H	2B	3B	HR	BB	SO	HB	SH	AVG	OBP	SLG	OPS	AOPS	BR	ABR	PF	SB	CS	BSA	BSR
LOU	88	44	4	.667		**57**	13	819	**588**	5150	**1310**	156	65	15	410	**460**		53	**.279**	.344	.350	694	**112**	53	71	98	341			
COL	79	55	6	.590	10	47	22	831	617	5332	1225	159	77	16	**545**	557		46	.258	.341	.335	676	**112**	30	**90**	93	353			
STL	78	58	3	.574	12	45	25	**870**	736	5369	1308	**178**	73	**48**	474	490		**95**	.273	**.350**	**.370**	**720**	103	**102**	-8	114	307			
TOL	68	64	2	.515	20	40	27	739	689	5132	1152	152	**108**	24	486	558		71	.252	.333	.348	681	103	29	8	103	**421**			
ROC	63	63	7	.500	22	40	22	709	711	5056	1088	131	64	31	446	538		57	.239	.315	.316	631	98	-55	1	93	310			
BAL	15	19	4	.441	24	8	11	182	192	1366	278	34	16	2	125	152		28	.229	.316	.289	605	79	-24	-32	105	101			
SYR	55	72	1	.433	30.5	30	30	698	831	4961	1158	151	59	14	457	482		35	.259	.333	.329	662	**112**	1	85	90	292			
PHI	54	78	0	.409	34	36	36	702	945	5052	1057	181	51	24	475	540		87	.235	.320	.314	634	93	-37	-33	99	305			
BRO	26	73	1	.263	45.5	15	22	492	733	3834	769	116	47	13	328	456		31	.221	.294	.293	587	80	-99	-83	97	182			
TOT	540					318	208	6042		41252	9345	1258	560	187	3746	4233	503		.253	.330	.332	662					2612			

TEAM	CG	SHO	GR	SV	IP	H	HR	BB	SO	BR/9	ERA	AERA	OAV	OOB	PR	APR	PF	OSB	OCS	FA	E	WPB	DP	FW	PW	BW	BSW	DIF
LOU	114	13	20	**7**	1206.0	1120	18	**293**	587	**10.9**	**2.57**	**149**	.239	**.291**	**173**	**171**	100	**247**	*198*	**.934**	**380**	131	79	**2.8**	**15.0**	6.2		-2.1
COL	120	**14**	**22**	3	1214.2	**976**	20	471	624	11.2	2.99	120	**.214**	.297	118	87	93	321	*205*	.932	396	174	**101**	2.6	7.7	**7.9**		-6.2
STL	118	4	20	1	1195.1	1127	38	447	**733**	12.3	3.67	117	.242	.316	25	74	112	338	*205*	.916	478	158	93	-1.8	6.5	-.7		6.0
TOL	**122**	4	14	2	1159.1	1122	23	429	533	12.6	3.56	111	.247	.321	39	48	102	270	***221***	.925	419	173	75	.4	4.2	.7		-3.4
ROC	**122**	5	12	2	1161.2	1115	19	530	477	13.2	3.56	100	.246	.331	39	-2	92	284	*184*	.926	416	**125**	95	.4	-.2	.0		-.3
BAL	36	1	2	0	315.1	307	3	123	134	13.0	4.00	101	.248	.328	-5	2	105	75	*59*	.928	109	30	21	.6	.2	-2.8		.0
SYR	115	5	12	0	1089.2	1158	28	518	454	14.4	4.98	71	.265	.351	-135	-193	91	390	*170*	.925	391	142	90	.9	-17.0	7.5		.1
PHI	119	3	14	2	1132.0	1405	**17**	514	461	15.8	5.22	74	.296	.373	-171	-170	100	379	*169*	.918	452	145	93	-1.6	-15.0	-2.9		7.5
BRO	96	0	4	0	879.0	1011	21	421	230	15.2	4.71	83	.281	.365	-83	-80	101	308	*163*	.909	404	121	92	-4.4	-7.0	-7.3		-4.8
TOT	962	49	120	17	9353.0					13.1	3.86		.253	.330						.923	3445	1199	739					

Batter-Fielder Wins	Batting Average	On-Base Percentage	Slugging Average	On-Base Plus Slugging	Adjusted OPS	Adjusted Batter Runs
Childs-Syr............6.8	Wolf-Lou 363	Lyons-Phi....................461	Lyons-Phi 531	Lyons-Phi.............992	Lyons-Phi.............193	Childs-Syr 61.0
Lyons-Phi 4.7	Lyons-Phi 354	Swartwood-Tol............444	Campau-StL 513	Childs-Syr 915	Childs-Syr 189	Wolf-Lou 46.8
Swartwood-Tol ..3.8	McCarthy-StL 350	Childs-Syr 434	Childs-Syr............481	Wolf-Lou 900	Wolf-Lou 169	Johnson-Col 46.2
O'Connor-Col......3.7	Johnson-Col 346	McCarthy-StL..............430	Wolf-Lou 479	McCarthy-StL 898	Johnson-Col 168	Lyons-Phi 43.9
Wolf-Lou 3.6	Childs-Syr.............345	Wright-Syr 428	McCarthy-StL 467	Swartwood-Tol......887	Swartwood-Tol......157	Swartwood-Tol....38.4

Runs	Hits	Doubles	Triples	Home Runs	Total Bases	Runs Batted In
McTamany-Col......140	Wolf-Lou 197	Childs-Syr.....................33	Werden-Tol 20	Campau-StL 9	Wolf-Lou 260	Johnson-Col 113
McCarthy-StL 137	McCarthy-StL 192	Wolf-Lou 29	Johnson-Col 18	Cartwright-StL 8	McCarthy-StL 256	Wolf-Lou 98
Fuller-StL..............118	Johnson-Col 186	Lyons-Phi 29	Alvord-Tol...............16	Stivetts-StL 7	Johnson-Col 248	Childs-Syr.............89
Sneed-Tol-Col 117	Childs-Syr 170		Sneed-Tol-Col 15	Lyons-Phi.................7	Childs-Syr 237	Knowles-Roc 84
Welch-Phi-Bal 116	Taylor-Lou 169				Werden-Tol 227	Shinnick-Lou 82

Stolen Bases	Base Stealing Runs	Fielding Runs-Infield	Fielding Runs-Outfield	Wins	Winning Pct.	Complete Games
McCarthy-StL 83		Gerhardt-Bro-StL 38.2	Welch-Phi-Bal......11.9	McMahon-Phi-Bal ..36	Stratton-Lou 708	McMahon-Phi-Bal..55
Scheffler-Roc..........77		Reilly-Col 29.1	Lyons-Roc...........10.9	Stratton-Lou...........34	Chamberlain-SL-Col.682	Barr-Roc.................52
VanDyke-Tol 73		Tomney-Lou 15.0	Scheffler-Roc 8.1	Gastright-Col 30	Gastright-Col 682	Stratton-Lou 44
Welch-Phi-Bal 72		Childs-Syr 14.4	Duffee-StL 7.0	Barr-Roc 28	Ehret-Lou 641	Healy-Tol 44
		Lehane-Col 9.9	Swartwood-Tol 6.5	Stivetts-StL 27	McMahon-Phi-Bal.632	

Strikeouts	Fewest BB/Game	Games	Saves	Base Runners/9	Adjusted Relief Runs	Relief Ranking
McMahon-Phi-Bal 291	Stratton-Lou 1.27	McMahon-Phi-Bal 60	Goodall-Lou..............4	Neale-StL 9.39		
Stivetts-StL 289	Ehret-Lou 1.98	Barr-Roc 57	Knauss-Col 2	Stratton-Lou 9.86		
Ramsey-StL..........257	Ramsey-StL 2.63	Stivetts-StL 54	Ehret-Lou..................2	Gastright-Col 10.43		
Healy-Tol 225	Smith-Tol..............2.83	Stratton-Lou 50		Knauss-Col..........10.87		
Barr-Roc 209	McMahon-Phi-Bal 2.94	Gastright-Col 48		Healy-Tol...........11.04		

Innings Pitched	Opponents' Avg.	Opponents' OBP	Earned Run Average	Adjusted ERA	Adjusted Starter Runs	Pitcher Wins
McMahon-Phi-Bal509.0	Knauss-Col...........202	Stratton-Lou.................270	Stratton-Lou 2.36	Stratton-Lou..........163	Stratton-Lou 73.5	**Stratton-Lou** 8.9
Barr-Roc............493.1	Gastright-Col 208	Gastright-Col 282	Ehret-Lou 2.53	Ehret-Lou..............152	Ehret-Lou 49.8	**Healy-Tol** 4.3
Stratton-Lou 431.0	Easton-Col 220	Knauss-Col....................290	Knauss-Col............2.81	Healy-Tol 136	Healy-Tol.............40.2	**Stivetts-StL**.........4.2
Stivetts-StL 419.1	Chamberlain-SL-Col.220	Healy-Tol 293	Chamberlain-SL-Col 2.83	Meakim-Lou...........132	Stivetts-StL 30.6	**Ehret-Lou** 4.1
Gastright-Col 401.1	Healy-Tol..............221	Ehret-Lou.......................296	Healy-Tol..............2.89	Chamberlain-SL-Col 131	Gastright-Col 29.9	**Gastright-Col** 2.7

Barely There

Buffeted by defections and increased competition from the new Players' League, the AA struggled just to make it through 1890. Two top clubs, Brooklyn and Cincinnati, jumped to the NL, and Kansas City and Baltimore simply quit the league. New clubs in Toledo, Syracuse, and Rochester failed to garner much interest, and an expansion Brooklyn team lost its last 14 before disbanding in August. The Baltimore Orioles, who had deserted the American Association for the Atlantic Association, rejoined in order to help the AA finish the season.

Philadelphia ran out of money in August, and most of the club quit, forcing the recruitment of below-average substitutes. The dismal Athletics lost their final 22 games yet still had twice as many wins as miserable Brooklyn.

Many former Association players jumped to the NL and PL, including St. Louis' Charlie Comiskey, Arlie Latham, Tip O'Neill, and Silver King, Philadelphia slugger Harry Stovey, Kansas City shortstop Herman Long, and Louisville outfielder Pete Browning. The disemboweled Browns fell to third.

Perhaps the best indicator of the AA's quality is that the league champion, Louisville, had finished dead last the previous season with a .196 winning percentage and was the most games back of any team in league history. For 1890 the Colonels made few player changes and improved 67 games. Chicken Wolf, who had hit .300 just once in eight seasons, won the batting title at .363; pitcher Scott Stratton, 3–13 in 1889, went 34–14 and led the league in ERA. Columbus, leaping to second, couldn't provide enough of a challenge despite deep pitching and Jim McTamany's league-leading 140 runs.

Louisville was by far the league's top draw; St. Louis' attendance fell by 70,000, while Brooklyn's new club drew just 1,000 fans per game. Overall AA attendance sank to its lowest since its inaugural season in 1882. A postseason World Series between Louisville and turncoat Brooklyn was closer than expected, but rain postponed several contests. The games did not draw enough interest to continue play into November and the Series was called after six games.

1890 Player's League

TEAM	W	L	T	PCT	GB	HW	HL	R	OR	PA	H	2B	3B	HR	BB	SO	HB	SH	AVG	OBP	SLG	OPS	AOPS	BR	ABR	PF	SB	CS	BSA	BSR
BOS	81	48	1	.628		**48**	21	992	**767**	5321	1306	**223**	76	54	**652**	435		43	.282	**.376**	.398	**774**	**105**	**97**	**34**	107	**412**			
BRO	76	56	1	.576	6.5	46	19	964	893	5431	1352	186	93	34	502	369		42	.277	.349	.374	723	92	-14	-66	106	272			
NY	74	57	1	.565	8	47	19	**1018**	875	5430	**1393**	204	97	**66**	486	364		31	**.284**	.352	**.405**	757	98	39	-38	109	231			
CHI	75	62	1	.547	10	46	23	886	770	5503	1311	200	95	31	492	410		43	.264	.335	.361	696	87	-67	-101	104	276			
PHI	68	63	1	.519	14	35	30	941	855	5337	1350	187	**113**	49	431	**321**		**51**	.278	.343	.393	736	100	-2	-22	102	203			
PIT	60	68	0	.469	20.5	37	28	835	892	5200	1192	168	**113**	35	569	375		54	.260	.349	.369	718	106	-17	60	92	249			
CLE	55	75	1	.423	26.5	31	30	849	1027	5362	1370	213	94	27	509	345		49	.285	.360	.386	746	114	31	115	92	180			
BUF	36	96	2	.273	46.5	23	42	793	1199	5432	1249	180	64	20	541	367		96	.260	.347	.337	684	96	-66	11	92	160			
TOT	529					313	212	7278		43016	10523	1561	745	316	4182	2986	409		.274	.351	.378	729					1983			

TEAM	CG	SHO	GR	SV	IP	H	HR	BB	SO	BR/9	ERA	AERA	OAV	OOB	PR	APR	PF	OSB	OCS	FA	E	WPB	DP	FW	PW	BW	BSW	DIF
BOS	105	6	**26**	4	1137.1	1291	49	467	345	14.3	3.79	116	.274	.346	55	73	104	**143**	*110*	.918	460	97	109	1.7	5.8	2.7		6.2
BRO	111	4	22	**7**	1184.0	1334	**26**	570	377	14.9	3.95	113	.273	.356	37	62	105	195	*142*	.909	531	110	114	-1.8	4.9	-5.3		12.1
NY	111	3	23	6	1172.1	**1216**	37	569	449	14.1	4.17	109	.257	.343	8	44	107	254	*152*	**.921**	**450**	147	94	**2.8**	3.5	-3.0		5.2
CHI	124	5	14	2	1219.1	1238	27	503	**460**	**13.2**	**3.39**	**128**	**.252**	**.327**	**114**	**125**	103	224	***179***	.918	492	**91**	107	1.6	**10.0**	-8.1		2.9
PHI	118	4	14	2	1154.1	1292	33	495	361	14.4	4.05	105	.271	.347	22	27	101	258	*151*	.910	510	106	**118**	-.7	2.2	-1.8		2.8
PIT	121	**7**	7	0	1116.2	1267	32	**334**	318	**13.2**	4.22	93	.274	.328	2	-43	92	231	*103*	.907	512	104	80	-1.7	-3.4	4.8		-3.6
CLE	115	1	16	0	1143.2	1386	45	571	325	15.8	4.23	94	.287	.369	0	-35	94	361	*172*	.907	533	171	103	-2.3	-2.8	**9.2**		-14.1
BUF	**125**	2	9	0	1141.0	1499	67	673	351	17.5	6.11	67	.304	.393	-239	-265	97	317	*160*	.914	491	141	116	.8	-21.1	.9		-10.5
TOT	930	32	131	21	9268.2					14.7	4.23		.274	.351						.913	3979	967	841					

Batter-Fielder Wins
- **Browning-Cle**......4.9
- **Connor-NY** 2.8
- **Radford-Cle** 2.7
- **Farrell-Chi** 2.6
- **B.Ewing-NY** 2.5

Batting Average
- Browning-Cle 373
- Orr-Bro 371
- O'Rourke-NY 360
- Connor-NY 349
- Ryan-Chi...............340

On-Base Percentage
- Brouthers-Bos 466
- Browning-Cle 459
- Connor-NY....................450
- Robinson-Pit 434
- Gore-NY 432

Slugging Average
- Connor-NY 548
- B.Ewing-NY 545
- Beckley-Pit 535
- Orr-Bro 534
- Browning-Cle 517

On-Base Plus Slugging
- Connor-NY............998
- Browning-Cle........976
- Orr-Bro 948
- Gore-NY 931
- O'Rourke-NY 925

Adjusted OPS
- Browning-Cle........175
- Beckley-Pit............156
- Larkin-Cle 153
- Connor-NY............152
- Orr-Bro 144

Adjusted Batter Runs
- Browning-Cle......60.1
- Larkin-Cle 42.7
- Beckley-Pit 39.6
- Connor-NY 36.5
- Brouthers-Bos 32.0

Runs
- Duffy-Chi 161
- Brown-Bos............146
- Stovey-Bos 142
- Ward-Bro 134
- Connor-NY............133

Hits
- Duffy-Chi 191
- Shindle-Phi 189
- Ward-Bro 188
- Browning-Cle........184
- Richardson-Bos....181

Doubles
- Browning-Cle 40
- Beckley-Pit 38
- O'Rourke-NY 37
- Duffy-Chi.......................36
- Brouthers-Bos................36

Triples
- Visner-Pit................22
- Beckley-Pit...............22
- Shindle-Phi 21
- Fields-Pit 20
- Joyce-Bro.................18

Home Runs
- Connor-NY.............14
- Richardson-Bos.......13
- Stovey-Bos 12
- Shindle-Phi 10
- Gore-NY 10

Total Bases
- Shindle-Phi 282
- Duffy-Chi 280
- Beckley-Pit............276
- Richardson-Bos....274
- Connor-NY............265

Runs Batted In
- Richardson-Bos ..146
- Orr-Bro 124
- Beckley-Pit 120
- O'Rourke-NY 115
- Larkin-Cle............112

Stolen Bases
- Stovey-Bos 97
- Brown-Bos..............79
- Duffy-Chi 78
- Hanlon-Pit 65
- Ward-Bro 63

Base Stealing Runs

Fielding Runs-Infield
- Bierbauer-Bro 20.8
- Pfeffer-Chi 20.0
- Nash-Bos....................18.5
- White-Buf....................18.0
- Ward-Bro 16.8

Fielding Runs-Outfield
- Wood-Phi 14.2
- Griffin-Phi 13.1
- Duffy-Chi 9.4
- Seery-Bro 5.9
- Fields-Pit 5.5

Wins
- Baldwin-Chi 33
- Weyhing-Bro 30
- King-Chi..................30
- Radbourn-Bos 27
- Gumbert-Bos..........23

Winning Pct.
- Daley-Bos.............720
- Radbourn-Bos 692
- Knell-Phi 667
- Gumbert-Bos 657
- Weyhing-Bro.........652

Complete Games
- Baldwin-Chi 53
- King-Chi 48
- Staley-Pit 44
- Gruber-Cle 39
- Weyhing-Bro..........38

Strikeouts
- Baldwin-Chi 206
- King-Chi................185
- Weyhing-Bro 177
- Staley-Pit 145
- J.Ewing-NY 145

Fewest BB/Game
- Staley-Pit 1.72
- Sanders-Phi 1.79
- Galvin-Pit 2.03
- Morris-Pit 2.18
- Radbourn-Bos 2.62

Games
- Baldwin-Chi 58
- King-Chi 56
- Weyhing-Bro 49
- Gruber-Cle 48
- Staley-Pit 46

Saves
- Hemming-Cle-Bro 3
- O'Day-NY 3

Base Runners/9
- Staley-Pit 11.07
- King-Chi 11.67
- Radbourn-Bos ..12.15
- Keefe-NY 12.66
- Sanders-Phi 12.75

Adjusted Relief Runs

Relief Ranking

Innings Pitched
- Baldwin-Chi 492.0
- King-Chi 461.0
- Weyhing-Bro......390.0
- Staley-Pit 387.2
- Gruber-Cle 383.1

Opponents' Avg.
- King-Chi 232
- Crane-NY 245
- Keefe-NY 246
- Hemming-Cle-Bro.247
- Knell-Phi...............250

Opponents' OBP
- Staley-Pit 290
- King-Chi........................301
- Radbourn-Bos 310
- Keefe-NY 318
- Sanders-Phi.................320

Earned Run Average
- King-Chi 2.69
- Staley-Pit 3.23
- Radbourn-Bos 3.31
- Baldwin-Chi 3.35
- Keefe-NY 3.38

Adjusted ERA
- King-Chi...............161
- Keefe-NY..............134
- Radbourn-Bos 133
- Baldwin-Chi 130
- Weyhing-Bro 124

Adjusted Starter Runs
- King-Chi 81.7
- Baldwin-Chi 48.7
- Radbourn-Bos 45.5
- Weyhing-Bro........40.2
- Staley-Pit 28.7

Pitcher Wins
- **King-Chi**..............6.6
- **Baldwin-Chi** 4.1
- **Radbourn-Bos** ..3.9
- **Weyhing-Bro** 2.5
- **Staley-Pit**...........2.5

A Short-Lived Brotherhood

When Monty Ward and his associates broke away to form the Players' League, the magnates showed foresight. Their laudable and well-reasoned efforts to break the reserve clause, the use of two, rather than one, umpire to ensure fair play, and the decision to allow two free substitutes, rather than just one, foreshadowed future changes in the game. However, the league also used a substandard and much livelier ball, would not employ black players, did not sell alcohol in the parks, and refused to play ball on Sundays—ensuring that many working fans couldn't come to the games.

The Players' League went directly at the National League, setting up teams in seven NL cities—only Cincinnati was spared direct competition. Brooklyn and Philadelphia, also American Association cities, had three different major league teams simultaneously.

Hugh Duffy, formerly of the Chicago NL club, jumped to the PL's Chicago Pirates and led the new league in runs and hits. Pete Browning of Cleveland won his third big league batting title. Respected veterans like Ward, Ned Hanlon, Charlie Comiskey, and Buck Ewing served as PL managers.

But the league champ was Boston, featuring an all-time cast of characters: player-manager King Kelly, first baseman Dan Brouthers, slugging outfielders Hardy Richardson and outfielder Harry Stovey, plus 36-year-old pitcher Hoss Radbourn, enjoying his last hurrah despite a damaged wing. Brooklyn's club, Ward's Wonders, finished second. Despite Duffy's exploits and the fine pitching of Mark Baldwin and Silver King, Chicago ended up fourth. Veteran shortstop Jack Rowe and 43-year-old infielder Deacon White played their last seasons, for Buffalo. Former NL home run king Ned Williamson also ended his career in the PL, falling prey to the alcoholism that would end his life four years later.

Despite being shut out of any postseason play, the PL finished its first season as the people's choice, leading the three leagues in attendance. However, the costs of instituting a new league that paid players fairly proved daunting, and the league capitulated the following January. Some historians claim that the threat of the Players' League—coming at a cost of more than $250,000 for the National League—was the closest the NL ever came to toppling.

1891 National League

TEAM	W	L	T	PCT	GB	HW	HL	R	OR	PA	H	2B	3B	HR	BB	SO	HB	SH	AVG	OBP	SLG	OPS	AOPS	BR	ABR	PF	SB	CS	BSA	BSR
BOS	87	51	2	.630		**51**	20	**847**	**658**	5571	1264	181	81	53	**533**	537		**82**	.255	**.337**	.356	**693**	97	**54**	-35	112	**289**			
CHI	82	53	2	.607	3.5	43	22	832	730	5449	1231	159	**88**	**60**	526	457		50	.253	.332	.358	690	107	40	41	100	238			
NY	71	61	4	.538	13	39	28	754	711	5307	**1271**	**189**	72	46	438	**394**		36	**.263**	.329	**.360**	689	**111**	34	**68**	96	224			
PHI	68	69	1	.496	18.5	35	34	756	773	5469	1244	180	51	21	482	412		58	.252	.326	.322	648	92	-25	-43	103	232			
CLE	65	74	2	.468	22.5	40	28	835	888	5639	1295	183	**88**	22	519	464		46	.255	.330	.339	669	97	7	-25	104	242			
BRO	61	76	0	.445	25.5	41	31	765	820	5249	1233	200	69	23	465	435		36	.260	.330	.345	675	103	18	23	99	337			
CIN	56	81	1	.409	30.5	26	41	646	790	5249	1158	148	90	40	414	439		44	.242	.308	.335	643	92	-53	-58	101	244			
PIT	55	80	2	.407	30.5	32	34	679	744	5271	1148	148	71	29	427	503		50	.239	.308	.318	626	90	-75	-58	98	205			
TOT	552					307	238	6114		43204	9844	1388	610	294	3804	3641	402		.252	.325	.342	667					2011			

TEAM	CG	SHO	GR	SV	IP	H	HR	BB	SO	BR/9	ERA	AERA	OAV	OOB	PR	APR	PF	OSB	OCS	FA	E	WPB	DP	FW	PW	BW	BSW	DIF
BOS	**126**	9	15	**6**	1241.2	1223	51	**364**	525	**11.8**	**2.76**	**132**	.248	**.305**	**80**	**112**	109	197	*130*	**.938**	**358**	**79**	96	**4.7**	**10.0**	-3.1		6.5
CHI	114	6	24	3	1220.2	1207	53	475	477	12.7	3.47	96	.249	.322	-17	-21	100	**190**	*137*	.932	397	126	**119**	1.5	-1.9	3.7		11.2
NY	117	**11**	21	2	1204.0	**1098**	26	593	**651**	13.1	2.99	107	**.234**	.327	47	29	96	306	*174*	.933	384	136	104	2.2	2.6	**6.1**		-5.8
PHI	105	3	**34**	5	1229.1	1279	30	507	342	13.4	3.73	91	.259	.333	-53	-46	102	275	*128*	.925	443	102	108	-1.3	-4.1	-3.8		8.8
CLE	118	1	25	3	1244.0	1371	**24**	476	400	13.7	3.50	99	.270	.337	-22	-6	103	279	***203***	.920	485	111	86	-3.5	-.5	-2.2		1.7
BRO	121	8	16	3	1204.2	1272	40	459	407	13.4	3.86	86	.261	.332	-68	-76	99	244	*116*	.924	432	95	73	-.8	-6.8	2.1		-2.0
CIN	125	6	13	1	1218.2	1234	40	465	393	13.0	3.55	95	.253	.326	-28	-25	101	279	*134*	.931	409	120	101	.9	-2.2	-5.2		-6.0
PIT	122	7	16	3	1197.2	1160	30	465	446	12.7	2.89	114	.245	.320	61	52	98	241	*151*	.917	475	119	76	-3.6	4.6	-5.2		-8.3
TOT	948	51	164	26	9760.2					13.0	3.34		.252	.325						.928	3383	888	763					

Batter-Fielder Wins	Batting Average	On-Base Percentage	Slugging Average	On-Base Plus Slugging	Adjusted OPS	Adjusted Batter Runs
Hamilton-Phi 4.0	Hamilton-Phi.........340	Hamilton-Phi 453	Stovey-Bos 498	Tiernan-NY 882	Tiernan-NY 163	Tiernan-NY 44.0
Richardson-NY ..4.0	Holliday-Cin 319	Connor-NY..................399	Tiernan-NY..........494	Hamilton-Phi 874	Connor-NY...........153	Hamilton-Phi 42.3
Latham-Cin 3.4	Browning-Pit-Cin .317	Childs-Cle 395	Holliday-Cin 473	Stovey-Bos 871	Hamilton-Phi 151	Connor-NY 36.6
Tiernan-NY..........3.0	Clements-Phi 310	Browning-Pit-Cin 395	Connor-NY 449	Holliday-Cin 848	Holliday-Cin 145	Holliday-Cin........23.8
Pfeffer-Chi 3.0	Tiernan-NY...........306	Tiernan-NY 388	Ryan-Chi..............434	Connor-NY............848	Browning-Pit-Cin ..139	Browning-Pit-Cin 23.0

Runs	Hits	Doubles	Triples	Home Runs	Total Bases	Runs Batted In
Hamilton-Phi 141	Hamilton-Phi 179	Griffin-Bro 36	Stovey-Bos 20	Tiernan-NY 16	Stovey-Bos 271	Anson-Chi 120
Long-Bos 129	McKean-Cle..........170	Davis-Cle 35	Beckley-Pit.............19	Stovey-Bos 16	Tiernan-NY 268	Stovey-Bos 95
Childs-Cle 120	Tiernan-NY 166	Stovey-Bos 31	McPhee-Cin............16	Wilmot-Chi..............11	Long-Bos 235	O'Rourke-NY 95
Latham-Cin 119	Davis-Cle..............165	Tiernan-NY 30	Ryan-Chi 15		Davis-Cle..............233	Nash-Bos 95
Stovey-Bos 118	O'Rourke-NY 164		Virtue-Cle 14		Beckley-Pit............232	Connor-NY 94

Stolen Bases	Base Stealing Runs	Fielding Runs-Infield	Fielding Runs-Outfield	Wins	Winning Pct.	Complete Games
Hamilton-Phi 111		Richardson-NY 44.6	Griffin-Bro 20.0	Hutchison-Chi 44	J.Ewing-NY...........724	Hutchison-Chi........56
Latham-Cin 87		Pfeffer-Chi 23.6	Thompson-Phi 17.7	Rusie-NY 33	Hutchison-Chi.......698	Rusie-NY 52
Griffin-Bro 65		McPhee-Cin.................23.5	Brodie-Bos 7.8	Clarkson-Bos..........33	Staley-Pit-Bos.......649	Baldwin-Pit 48
Long-Bos 60		Latham-Cin 21.3	Davis-Cle 7.8	Nichols-Bos 30	Nichols-Bos 638	Clarkson-Bos 47
		Long-Bos 15.0	Stovey-Bos 6.6	Young-Cle 27	Clarkson-Bos 635	Nichols-Bos 45

Strikeouts	Fewest BB/Game	Games	Saves	Base Runners/9	Adjusted Relief Runs	Relief Ranking
Rusie-NY 337	Nichols-Bos 2.18	Hutchison-Chi 66	Nichols-Bos 3	Staley-Pit-Bos....11.08		
Hutchison-Chi 261	Staley-Pit-Bos......2.22	Rusie-NY 61	Clarkson-Bos...........3	Hutchison-Chi....11.12		
Nichols-Bos 240	Galvin-Pit 2.26	Young-Cle 55	Young-Cle 2	Sharrott-NY 11.16		
Baldwin-Pit 197	Radbourn-Cin 2.56	Clarkson-Bos 55	Thornton-Phi 2	Nichols-Bos 11.28		
King-Pit 160	Hutchison-Chi......2.86			J.Ewing-NY........11.80		

Innings Pitched	Opponents' Avg.	Opponents' OBP	Earned Run Average	Adjusted ERA	Adjusted Starter Runs	Pitcher Wins
Hutchison-Chi....561.0	Rusie-NY 207	Staley-Pit-Bos 292	J.Ewing-NY.........2.27	Nichols-Bos 153	Nichols-Bos 48.2	**Nichols-Bos** 4.5
Rusie-NY 500.1	Baldwin-Pit 228	Hutchison-Chi 293	Nichols-Bos 2.39	J.Ewing-NY 141	Clarkson-Bos 41.0	**Clarkson-Bos** 4.4
Clarkson-Bos 460.2	J.Ewing-NY...........228	Nichols-Bos 296	Rusie-NY 2.55	Staley-Pit-Bos 138	Rusie-NY 39.9	**Rusie-NY** 3.9
Baldwin-Pit 437.2	Hutchison-Chi.......233	J.Ewing-NY 305	Staley-Pit-Bos......2.58	Clarkson-Bos........131	Staley-Pit-Bos......36.0	**Staley-Pit-Bos**....3.3
Mullane-Cin 426.1	Mullane-Cin 234	Clarkson-Bos 305	Baldwin-Pit 2.76	Rusie-NY 125	J.Ewing-NY..........29.8	**J.Ewing-NY** 2.5

Winning the War

With the Players' League dissolved, the NL absorbed most of the players from the defunct loop's New York, Pittsburgh, Chicago, and Brooklyn clubs (including Monty Ward, who served as Brooklyn's player-manager). Boston claimed Harry Stovey from the Philadelphia AA team, citing a waiver error, and a committee ruled Boston did have such a right. The AA angrily responded by withdrawing from the National Agreement—the leagues were now officially at war. The AA's withdrawal from the agreement precluded even a financially rewarding postseason competition. The NL was happy with this decision, as it felt itself to be already winning the attendance war.

And this decision played itself out in the pennant race. Chicago led the NL hunt for most of the year, but an 18-game winning streak gave Boston the flag. Some sources now believe that Cap Anson's Chicago club, rumored despite the NL's objections to be willing to play AA champ Boston in a World Series, was jobbed out of the pennant by league-enforced umpire decisions.

Managed by Frank Selee, the Boston Beaneaters got power from Stovey, excellent all-around play from Herman Long, and top mound work from John Clarkson and Kid Nichols. Chicago, despite big seasons from Anson, rookie Bill Dahlen, and Bill Hutchinson, settled for an angry second. Philadelphia had Billy Hamilton, probably the NL's top player, but the Phillies lacked other offense and finished fourth. Despite the returning talent (at a much lower cost) to the NL, future stars Joe Kelley and Dahlen debuted. Hoss Radbourn pitched his last major league ball for seventh-place Cincinnati.

Following the end of the controversial season, the NL absorbed four AA franchises, and until 1901 there would be but one major league. The decade-long Association war yielded far-reaching spoils. Four NL teams that still exist today—Pittsburgh Pirates, Cincinnati Reds, St. Louis Cardinals, and Los Angeles Dodgers—came from the American Association. Two others current NL teams originated from the National Association (Atlanta Braves and Chicago Cubs), seven more resulted from expansion since 1962, and an eighth originated in the American League. The Philadelphia Phillies and San Francisco Giants, organized in 1883, are the lone nineteenth century teams to play their first games as NL franchises and continue to do so.

1891 American Association

TEAM	W	L	T	PCT	GB	HW	HL	R	OR	PA	H	2B	3B	HR	BB	SO	HB	SH	AVG	OBP	SLG	OPS	AOPS	BR	ABR	PF	SB	CS	BSA	BSR
BOS	93	42	4	.689		51	17	**1028**	**675**	5606	**1341**	163	100	52	**651**	499		66	**.274**	**.367**	**.380**	**747**	**121**	**129**	**144**	99	**447**			
STL	85	51	3	.625	8.5	**52**	21	959	738	5640	1311	165	51	**57**	612	**436**		86	.265	.356	.354	710	94	66	-53	115	279			
MIL	21	15	0	.583	22.5	16	5	227	156	1407	332	58	15	13	107	114		29	.261	.333	.361	694	86	4	-32	120	47			
BAL	71	64	4	.526	22	44	24	850	798	5433	1217	142	99	30	551	553		**111**	.255	.346	.345	691	102	22	13	101	342			
PHI	73	66	4	.525	22	43	26	817	794	5560	1301	**182**	**123**	55	447	548		74	.258	.328	.376	704	106	20	17	100	149			
COL	61	76	1	.445	33	34	29	702	777	5263	1113	154	61	20	529	530		37	.237	.319	.308	627	89	-92	-50	94	280			
CIN	43	57	2	.430	32.5	24	20	549	643	4038	838	105	58	28	428	385		36	.234	.322	.320	642	81	-52	-95	108	164			
LOU	54	83	2	.394	40	39	32	698	873	5270	1229	127	68	17	438	465		68	.258	.329	.324	653	93	-54	-46	99	227			
WAS	44	91	4	.326	49	28	40	691	1067	5259	1183	147	84	19	468	485		76	.251	.328	.330	658	97	-44	-8	95	219			
TOT	557					331	214	6521		43476	9865	1243	659	291	4231	4015	583		.255	.338	.344	682					2154			

TEAM	CG	SHO	GR	SV	IP	H	HR	BB	SO	BR/9	ERA	AERA	OAV	OOB	PR	APR	PF	OSB	OCS	FA	E	WPB	DP	FW	PW	BW	BSW	DIF
BOS	108	**9**	34	7	1219.2	1158	42	497	524	**12.6**	**3.03**	115	.242	**.321**	**92**	64	94	**176**	*173*	.934	392	133	115	4.1	5.5	**12.4**		3.5
STL	101	8	**38**	**10**	1206.2	**1088**	50	571	**613**	12.9	3.23	**130**	**.233**	.325	64	**113**	113	230	*134*	.920	459	155	91	.1	**9.7**	-4.6		11.7
MIL	35	3	1	0	309.2	291	6	120	137	12.2	2.50	175	.241	.314	42	54	118	58	*30*	.922	116	23	20	.2	4.7	-2.8		.9
BAL	118	6	21	2	1217.0	1238	33	472	408	13.1	3.43	108	.255	.329	37	39	100	185	*122*	.915	503	**123**	103	-2.5	3.4	1.1		1.5
PHI	**135**	3	7	0	1233.2	1274	35	520	533	13.6	4.01	94	.258	.338	-42	-31	102	270	*131*	.933	389	129	109	**5.1**	-2.7	1.5		-.3
COL	118	6	21	0	1213.1	1141	**29**	588	502	13.5	3.75	92	.241	.336	-5	-44	93	364	*172*	**.935**	**379**	132	**126**	4.7	-3.8	-4.3		-4.1
CIN	86	2	18	1	902.0	921	20	446	331	14.2	3.43	119	.256	.347	28	59	110	231	*163*	.913	389	84	68	-3.0	5.1	-8.2		-.9
LOU	126	**9**	12	1	1210.0	1334	32	**451**	481	13.8	4.22	87	.271	.340	-69	-79	98	332	***202***	.922	454	168	112	.4	-6.8	-4.0		-4.1
WAS	123	2	17	2	1181.0	1420	44	566	486	15.9	4.83	77	.288	.374	-147	-145	101	308	*184*	.900	589	159	95	-7.6	-12.5	-.7		-2.7
TOT	950	48	169	23	9693.0					13.6	3.71		.255	.338						.922	3670	1106	839					

Batter-Fielder Wins	Batting Average	On-Base Percentage	Slugging Average	On-Base Plus Slugging	Adjusted OPS	Adjusted Batter Runs
Farrell-Bos 4.4	Brouthers-Bos 350	Brouthers-Bos 471	Brouthers-Bos 512	Brouthers-Bos 983	Brouthers-Bos 184	Brouthers-Bos 60.4
Brouthers-Bos 3.5	Duffy-Bos 336	Lyons-StL.....................445	Milligan-Phi...........505	Milligan-Phi 903	Milligan-Phi 158	Brown-Bos..........37.4
Milligan-Phi 3.2	O'Neill-StL 323	Hoy-StL 424	Farrell-Bos 474	Lyons-StL 900	Brown-Bos............150	Duffy-Bos 34.4
Crooks-Col 3.2	Brown-Bos 321	Seery-Cin.....................423	Brown-Bos 469	Brown-Bos............865	Duffy-Bos.............149	Milligan-Phi 34.4
Duffy-Bos 2.7	VanHaltren-Bal 318	Duffy-Bos.....................408	Cross-Phi 458	Duffy-Bos..............861	Farrell-Bos 148	Joyce-Bos 29.0

Runs	Hits	Doubles	Triples	Home Runs	Total Bases	Runs Batted In
Brown-Bos............177	Brown-Bos............189	Milligan-Phi 35	Brown-Bos...............21	Farrell-Bos.............12	Brown-Bos............276	Farrell-Bos 110
VanHaltren-Bal 136	VanHaltren-Bal 180	Brown-Bos 30	Brouthers-Bos 19	Milligan-Phi 11	VanHaltren-Bal 251	Duffy-Bos 110
Hoy-StL 134	Duffy-Bos.............180	O'Neill-StL 28	Canavan-Cin-Mil 18	Lyons-StL 11	Brouthers-Bos 249	Brouthers-Bos 109
Duffy-Bos..............134	McCarthy-StL 176	Duffee-Col 28	Werden-Bal 18		Duffy-Bos..............243	Milligan-Phi..........106
	Brouthers-Bos 170	Larkin-Phi 27			Werden-Bal 234	Werden-Bal 104

Stolen Bases	Base Stealing Runs	Fielding Runs-Infield	Fielding Runs-Outfield	Wins	Winning Pct.	Complete Games
Brown-Bos............106		Stricker-Bos 23.6	Andrews-Cin........15.1	McMahon-Bal 35	Buffinton-Bos 763	McMahon-Bal 53
Duffy-Bos................85		Crooks-Col...................18.2	Weaver-Lou 13.8	Haddock-Bos..........34	Haddock-Bos 756	Weyhing-Phi 51
VanHaltren-Bal 75		Eagan-StL 17.9	Wood-Phi 9.9	Stivetts-StL 33	Weyhing-Phi 608	Knell-Col................47
Hoy-StL 59		Radford-Bos.................17.3	Welch-Bal 7.0	Weyhing-Phi 31	Stivetts-StL 600	Carsey-Was 46
Radford-Bos 55		Wheelock-Col 16.3	Duffee-Col 6.3	Buffinton-Bos..........29	McMahon-Bal 593	Chamberlain-Phi ..44

Strikeouts	Fewest BB/Game	Games	Saves	Base Runners/9	Adjusted Relief Runs	Relief Ranking
Stivetts-StL 259	Stratton-Lou 1.78	Stivetts-StL 64	Neale-StL 3	Buffinton-Bos 10.64		
Knell-Col 228	Sanders-Phi 2.30	McMahon-Bal 61	Griffith-StL-Bos 2	Haddock-Bos 11.40		
Weyhing-Phi 219	McMahon-Bal 2.67	Knell-Col 58	O'Brien-Bos 2	Davies-Mil..........11.65		
McMahon-Bal 219	Ehret-Lou 2.85	Carsey-Was 54	Daley-Bos 2	McMahon-Bal 11.79		
Chamberlain-Phi ..204	Griffith-StL-Bos.....2.90	Weyhing-Phi 52		Killen-Mil...........11.82		

Innings Pitched	Opponents' Avg.	Opponents' OBP	Earned Run Average	Adjusted ERA	Adjusted Starter Runs	Pitcher Wins
McMahon-Bal 503.0	Knell-Col...............209	Buffinton-Bos...............285	Crane-Cin 2.45	Crane-Cin 167	Stivetts-StL 57.8	**Stivetts-StL**........6.8
Knell-Col............462.0	Stivetts-StL 215	Haddock-Bos 299	Haddock-Bos 2.49	Stivetts-StL 146	McMahon-Bal 54.0	**Haddock-Bos** 5.3
Weyhing-Phi 450.0	Buffinton-Bos 219	McMahon-Bal 306	Buffinton-Bos 2.55	Haddock-Bos........140	Buffinton-Bos 45.3	**McMahon-Bal** 4.9
Stivetts-StL 440.0	Crane-Cin 225	Fitzgerald-Lou 316	McMahon-Bal 2.81	Buffinton-Bos........136	Haddock-Bos 44.6	**Buffinton-Bos** 4.0
Carsey-Was 415.0	Haddock-Bos 226	Weyhing-Phi..................317	Stivetts-StL 2.86	Mains-Cin-Mil 134	Crane-Cin 35.5	**Crane-Cin** 2.6

Disassociation

Following the Players' League's dissolution, the AA coaxed the PL's Boston and Philadelphia franchises to join, despite the NL's best efforts to prevent this. As a result, the NL and AA engaged in cataclysmic season-long battles and machinations to destroy each other. There would be no final postseason meeting between the leagues on the field.

Boston was the AA's best club, featuring such stars as Hugh Duffy, Tom Brown, and batting champ Dan Brouthers. Pitchers George Haddock and Charlie Buffinton provided the league's top hill work and just held off St. Louis' strong team. With Charlie Comiskey back in the fold, the Browns—buoyed by Jack Stivetts' pitching, Dummy Hoy and Tommy McCarthy's on-base ability, and Denny Lyons' power—wound up second.

Three future stars debuted in the AA's final season: Clark Griffith, Hugh Jennings, and John McGraw. Veterans Paul Hines—who dated back to the National Association of 1872—and Abner Dalrymple ended their major league careers.

With the PL out of the way, AA attendance rose by more than 300,000, seeing gains in most league cities, but the NL outdrew the Association. Consistent financial woes from the league's worst clubs led league management to seek a truce.

Therefore, postseason meetings between NL and AA moguls ended the Association for good. Four of the league's clubs were absorbed into the National League: St. Louis, Baltimore, Washington, and Louisville. The remaining teams (Boston, Milwaukee—who had replaced defunct Cincinnati in August—Columbus, and Philadelphia, which had replaced the AA's original Philadelphia Athletics) were hung out to dry. The Beer and Whiskey League, as NL supporters had mockingly called the AA because three of the original owners were liquor and beer barons, survived a decade as a major league, drawing practically 10 million fans (outdrawing the NL over the same span).

Though the American Association was history, several of its tenets were adopted by the new 12-team NL-AA amalgam, including Sunday ball, alcohol sales, a permanent core of umpires, and the option to sell tickets cheaply. Unfortunately, the logistics of a 12-team league would pose plenty of problems for the National League in the years ahead.

1892 National League

TEAM	W	L	T	PCT	GB	HW	HL	R	OR	PA	H	2B	3B	HR	BB	SO	HB	SH	AVG	OBP	SLG	OPS	AOPS	BR	ABR	PF	SB	CS	BSA	BSR
BOS	102	48	2	.680		54	21	862	649	5889	1325	203	51	34	526	492		**62**	.250	.325	.327	652	93	24	-43	109	338			
CLE	93	56	4	.624	8.5	54	24	855	**613**	6004	1376	196	96	26	552	538		40	.254	.328	.340	668	103	49	16	104	225			
BRO	95	59	4	.617	9	51	24	**935**	733	6168	**1439**	183	105	30	**629**	508		54	**.262**	**.344**	.350	694	**119**	**111**	**147**	96	**409**			
PHI	87	66	2	.569	16.5	**55**	26	860	690	5995	1420	**225**	95	**50**	528	515		54	**.262**	.334	**.367**	**701**	117	110	113	100	216			
CIN	82	68	5	.547	20	45	32	766	731	5890	1291	155	75	44	503	476		38	.241	.311	.323	634	98	-23	-12	99	270			
PIT	80	73	2	.523	23.5	52	34	802	796	5948	1288	143	**108**	38	435	**453**		44	.236	.297	.322	619	92	-65	-68	100	222			
CHI	70	76	1	.479	30	36	31	635	735	5526	1189	149	92	26	427	482		36	.235	.299	.316	615	90	-63	-70	101	233			
NY	71	80	2	.470	31.5	42	36	811	826	5835	1329	173	85	39	510	474		34	.251	.321	.338	659	106	26	39	98	301			
LOU	63	89	2	.414	40	37	31	649	804	5813	1209	133	61	18	433	508		46	.227	.290	.285	575	86	-138	-83	92	275			
WAS	58	93	2	.384	44.5	34	36	731	869	5772	1246	149	78	37	529	555		39	.239	.314	.319	633	99	-19	3	97	276			
STL	56	94	5	.373	46	37	36	703	922	5918	1188	138	53	45	607	492		52	.226	.312	.298	610	94	-53	-15	95	209			
BAL	46	101	5	.313	54.5	29	46	779	1020	5857	1343	160	111	30	499	480		**62**	.254	.325	.343	668	104	41	19	103	227			
TOT	921					526	377	9388		70615	15643	2007	1010	417	6178	5973	561		.245	.317	.328	644					3201			

TEAM	CG	SHO	GR	SV	IP	H	HR	BB	SO	BR/9	ERA	AERA	OAV	OOB	PR	APR	PF	OSB	OCS	FA	E	WPB	DP	FW	PW	BW	BSW	DIF
BOS	142	**15**	11	1	1336.0	**1156**	41	460	514	11.1	2.86	123	**.224**	.292	64	90	107	**196**	*142*	.929	454	106	128	.5	8.3	-4.0		22.2
CLE	140	11	12	2	1336.0	1178	28	**413**	472	**10.9**	**2.41**	**140**	.228	**.289**	**130**	**139**	103	205	*131*	.935	407	**65**	95	3.4	**12.9**	1.5		.8
BRO	132	12	**26**	**5**	1405.2	1285	26	600	597	12.4	3.25	97	.234	.315	6	-14	96	258	*175*	**.940**	398	130	98	**4.8**	-1.3	**13.6**		.9
PHI	131	10	24	**5**	1379.0	1309	**24**	492	511	12.1	2.93	111	.241	.310	54	48	99	207	*108*	.939	**393**	84	128	4.5	4.4	10.5		-9.0
CIN	130	8	25	2	1377.1	1327	39	535	437	12.5	3.17	103	.243	.317	18	15	99	233	*119*	.939	402	111	**140**	4.0	1.4	-1.1		2.7
PIT	130	3	22	1	1347.1	1300	28	537	455	12.7	3.10	106	.244	.320	28	27	100	240	*201*	.927	483	108	113	-.7	2.5	-6.3		8.0
CHI	133	6	13	1	1298.0	1269	35	424	518	12.0	3.16	105	.246	.308	18	22	101	247	*152*	.932	424	81	85	1.3	2.0	-6.5		.1
NY	139	5	13	1	1322.2	1165	32	635	**650**	12.6	3.29	98	.227	.318	-1	-12	98	371	***223***	.912	565	216	97	-5.8	-1.1	3.6		-1.2
LOU	**147**	9	7	0	1346.0	1358	26	447	430	12.3	3.34	92	.252	.313	-8	-44	93	297	*164*	.928	471	112	133	-.2	-4.1	-7.7		-1.1
WAS	129	5	**26**	3	1315.1	1293	40	556	479	13.1	3.46	94	.247	.327	-26	-32	99	386	*178*	.916	547	120	122	-4.8	-3.0	.3		-10.0
STL	139	4	22	1	1344.2	1466	47	543	478	13.8	4.20	76	.267	.339	-137	-156	97	287	*138*	.929	452	102	100	1.1	-14.4	-1.4		-4.3
BAL	131	2	22	2	1298.2	1537	51	536	437	14.7	4.28	80	.284	.353	-144	-119	104	274	*145*	.910	584	115	100	-7.1	-11.0	1.8		-11.1
TOT	1623	90	223	24	16106.2					12.5	3.28		.245	.317						.928	5580	1350	1339					

Split Season: First-half Winner BOS (52-22); Second-half Winner CLE (53-23)

Batter-Fielder Wins	Batting Average	On-Base Percentage	Slugging Average	On-Base Plus Slugging	Adjusted OPS	Adjusted Batter Runs
Brouthers-Bro 6.8	Brouthers-Bro.......335	Childs-Cle 443	Delahanty-Phi.......495	Brouthers-Bro 911	Brouthers-Bro 182	Brouthers-Bro 63.5
McPhee-Cin 4.7	Hamilton-Phi.........330	Brouthers-Bro 432	Brouthers-Bro.......480	Connor-Phi 883	Connor-Phi 167	Connor-Phi 53.4
Connor-Phi 4.2	Childs-Cle.............317	Hamilton-Phi 423	Ewing-NY 473	Delahanty-Phi 855	Burns-Bro 162	Burns-Bro 42.3
Childs-Cle...........3.9	Burns-Bro 315	Connor-Phi..................420	Connor-Phi 463	Burns-Bro 849	Delahanty-Phi 158	Childs-Cle 41.2
Hamilton-Phi 3.7	Ewing-NY 310	Crooks-StL..................400	Burns-Bro 454	Childs-Cle 841	Hamilton-Phi 152	Hamilton-Phi 40.4

Runs	Hits	Doubles	Triples	Home Runs	Total Bases	Runs Batted In
Childs-Cle 136	Brouthers-Bro 197	Connor-Phi 37	Delahanty-Phi 21	Holliday-Cin 13	Brouthers-Bro 282	Brouthers-Bro......124
Hamilton-Phi 132	Thompson-Phi......186	Long-Bos 33	Virtue-Cle 20	Connor-Phi 12	Holliday-Cin 271	Thompson-Phi 104
Duffy-Bos..............125	Duffy-Bos.............184	Delahanty-Phi 30	Brouthers-Bro 20	Ryan-Chi 10	Thompson-Phi......263	Larkin-Was 96
Connor-Phi 123	Hamilton-Phi 183	Brouthers-Bro 30	Dahlen-Chi 19	Beckley-Pit..............10	Connor-Phi 261	Burns-Bro.............96
Brouthers-Bro 121	Long-Bos 181	Zimmer-Cle 29	Beckley-Pit.............19	Thompson-Phi..........9	Duffy-Bos..............251	Beckley-Pit 96

Stolen Bases	Base Stealing Runs	Fielding Runs-Infield	Fielding Runs-Outfield	Wins	Winning Pct.	Complete Games
Ward-Bro 88		D.Richardson-Was......44.8	Hoy-Was..............20.9	Young-Cle 36	Young-Cle............750	Hutchison-Chi........67
Brown-Lou 78		Shindle-Bal 36.5	Duffee-Was..........17.5	Hutchison-Chi 36	Terry-Bal-Pit 692	Rusie-NY 59
Latham-Cin 66		Bierbauer-Pit 29.1	Brown-Lou 12.4	Stivetts-Bos 35	Haddock-Bro 690	Nichols-Bos 49
Hoy-Was 60		Nash-Bos...................25.1	Hamilton-Phi.........12.2	Nichols-Bos 35	Staley-Bos 688	Young-Cle..............48
Dahlen-Chi 60		Smith-Cin...................23.3	Lowe-Bos 7.8			

Strikeouts	Fewest BB/Game	Games	Saves	Base Runners/9	Adjusted Relief Runs	Relief Ranking
Hutchison-Chi 314	Stratton-Lou 1.79	Hutchison-Chi 75	Weyhing-Phi 3	Young-Cle............9.77		
Rusie-NY 304	Dwyer-StL-Cin 1.98	Rusie-NY 65	Duryea-Cin-Was 2	Nichols-Bos 10.63		
Weyhing-Phi 202	Sanders-Lou.........2.08	Killen-Was......................60		Stratton-Lou 10.77		
Nichols-Bos 192	Young-Cle.............2.34	Weyhing-Phi 59		Mullane-Cin 11.01		
Stein-Bro 190	Ehret-Pit 2.36	Baldwin-Pit 56		Duryea-Cin-Was 11.08		

Innings Pitched	Opponents' Avg.	Opponents' OBP	Earned Run Average	Adjusted ERA	Adjusted Starter Runs	Pitcher Wins
Hutchison-Chi....622.0	Mullane-Cin 201	Young-Cle 266	Young-Cle............1.93	Young-Cle 176	Young-Cle............73.5	**Young-Cle** 6.4
Rusie-NY 541.0	Rusie-NY 202	Nichols-Bos 283	Keefe-Phi 2.36	J.Clarkson-Bos-Cle ..139	Cuppy-Cle............36.7	**Hutchison-Chi** ..4.0
Weyhing-Phi 469.2	Terry-Bal-Pit 205	Stratton-Lou 286	J.Clarkson-Bos-Cle..2.48	Keefe-Phi..............138	J.Clarkson-Bos-Cle..35.7	**Cuppy-Cle** 3.7
Killen-Was 459.2	Young-Cle.............211	Mullane-Cin 290	Cuppy-Cle.............2.51	Cuppy-Cle 135	Hutchison-Chi......35.6	**Stivetts-Bos** 3.3
	Duryea-Cin-Was...212	Duryea-Cin-Was 291	Terry-Bal-Pit 2.57	Davies-Cle............131	Nichols-Bos 33.8	**Nichols-Bos** 3.3

Growing Overnight

The NL expanded to 12 teams by taking on former American Association franchises Baltimore, Louisville, St. Louis, and Washington. As the only "major league," League owners could now theoretically sit back, await the crowds, and print money. It didn't quite work out that way. First of all, the four "new" clubs were bad, already stripped of their best players. (Only St. Louis survived the century intact; Louisville merged with Pittsburgh in 1900.) In addition, the NL game soon became more violent and more crooked, as syndicate ownership reared its misshapen head. Five teams, mostly terrible ones, went through multiple managers.

In 1892 most NL clubs adopted old Association policies of Sunday ball, selling alcohol, and charging as little as 25 cents for tickets. The league also expanded its schedule and played a "split season" in order to create a postseason tournament. Hitters could not attempt to be hit by pitches, and any pitches striking the hands or forearm were ruled strikes. In addition, fair balls hit over fences 235 or fewer feet away were doubles.

Boston, a solid two-way squad, rode its pitching to squeeze by Brooklyn for the first-half title. The Cleveland Spiders, featuring suddenly dominant hurler Cy Young and on-base machine Cupid Childs, barely won the second half. Boston easily took the postseason series. Slugging Roger Connor of Philadelphia set an all-time mark by playing in 155 games. St. Louis infielder Jack Crooks established a record of 136 walks that lasted until 1911. Fittingly, Crooks was also a stolen base threat, even though his club's 209 steals represented the lowest figure in the league—200 fewer than NL-leader Brooklyn.

With no AA, there were fewer major league jobs (and lower salaries). Ending their big league tenures were Jim Galvin, George Gore, Ned Hanlon, Hardy Richardson, and Mickey Welch. Future star "Wee Willie" Keeler debuted in New York. The addition of the new teams swelled league attendance totals, though crowds dwindled in Chicago, Boston, New York, and Philadelphia. The split season may have had something to do with this.

1893 National League

TEAM	W	L	T	PCT	GB	HW	HL	R	OR	PA	H	2B	3B	HR	BB	SO	HB	SH	AVG	OBP	SLG	OPS	AOPS	BR	ABR	PF	SB	CS	BSA	BSR
BOS	86	43	2	.667		49	15	1008	795	5285	1358	178	50	65	**561**	292		46	.290	.372	.391	763	99	58	-9	108	243			
PIT	81	48	2	.628	5	**54**	19	970	**766**	5433	1447	176	**127**	37	537	274		62	.299	**.377**	.411	788	116	94	**114**	98	210			
CLE	73	55	1	.570	12.5	47	22	976	839	5309	1425	222	98	32	532	**229**		30	.300	.374	.408	782	106	87	33	106	252			
PHI	72	57	4	.558	14	43	22	**1011**	841	5690	**1553**	**246**	90	**80**	468	335		**71**	**.301**	.368	**.431**	**799**	**117**	**111**	112	100	202			
NY	68	64	4	.515	19.5	49	20	941	845	5418	1424	182	101	61	504	281		56	.293	.366	.410	776	110	67	62	101	**299**			
CIN	65	63	3	.508	20.5	37	27	759	814	5196	1195	161	65	29	531	257		48	.259	.341	.341	682	84	-88	-106	102	238			
BRO	65	63	2	.508	20.5	43	24	775	845	5024	1200	173	83	45	473	296		40	.266	.341	.371	712	97	-47	-10	95	213			
BAL	60	70	0	.462	26.5	36	24	820	893	5260	1281	164	86	27	539	323		70	.275	.359	.365	724	95	-12	-25	102	233			
CHI	56	71	1	.441	29	38	34	829	874	5166	1299	186	93	32	466	261		36	.279	.349	.379	728	99	-21	-9	99	255			
STL	57	75	3	.432	30.5	40	30	745	829	5466	1288	152	98	10	524	251		63	.264	.343	.341	684	86	-92	-94	100	250			
LOU	50	75	1	.400	34	24	28	759	942	5105	1185	177	73	19	485	306		54	.260	.338	.343	681	92	-93	-30	92	203			
WAS	40	89	1	.310	46	21	27	722	1032	5328	1258	180	83	23	523	237		63	.265	.346	.353	699	92	-62	-40	97	154			
TOT	785					481	292	10315		63680	15913	2197	1047	460	6143	3342	639		.280	.356	.379	736					2752			

TEAM	CG	SHO	GR	SV	IP	H	HR	BB	SO	BR/9	ERA	AERA	OAV	OOB	PR	APR	PF	OSB	OCS	FA	E	WPB	DP	FW	PW	BW	BSW	DIF
BOS	**114**	2	20	2	1163.2	1314	66	402	253	**13.6**	4.43	111	.277	**.339**	30	60	106	**176**	*91*	.936	353	62	118	1.8	4.9	-.7		15.5
PIT	104	**8**	29	2	1167.0	**1232**	29	504	280	13.8	4.08	111	.263	.342	75	61	98	237	*133*	.938	347	77	112	2.1	5.0	**9.3**		.0
CLE	110	2	21	2	1140.1	1361	35	**356**	242	13.8	4.20	**116**	.288	.342	59	82	105	199	*151*	.929	395	98	92	-.9	6.7	2.7		.5
PHI	107	4	28	2	1189.0	1357	30	522	286	14.8	4.68	98	.279	.357	-2	-13	98	186	*108*	**.944**	**318**	**60**	121	**4.1**	-1.1	9.2		-4.7
NY	111	6	26	4	1211.1	1271	36	581	**395**	14.2	4.29	108	**.262**	.347	49	48	100	238	*174*	.927	432	137	95	-1.8	3.9	5.1		-5.2
CIN	97	4	**34**	**5**	1172.0	1305	38	549	258	14.8	4.55	105	.274	.357	15	29	103	211	*109*	.943	321	89	**138**	3.6	2.4	-8.7		3.7
BRO	109	3	23	3	1154.0	1262	41	547	297	14.4	4.55	97	.270	.352	15	-17	95	233	*118*	.930	385	83	88	-.2	-1.4	-.8		3.4
BAL	104	1	26	2	1123.2	1325	29	534	275	15.2	4.97	95	.285	.364	-39	-29	102	248	*100*	.929	384	111	95	-.1	-2.4	-2.0		-.4
CHI	101	4	31	**5**	1117.1	1278	**26**	553	273	15.3	4.81	96	.279	.365	-18	-24	99	242	*148*	.922	421	79	92	-2.5	-2.0	-.7		-2.3
STL	**114**	3	22	4	1207.0	1292	38	542	301	14.1	**4.06**	**116**	.266	.346	**80**	**87**	101	276	*152*	.930	398	107	110	-.0	**7.1**	-7.7		-8.3
LOU	113	4	13	1	1080.0	1431	38	479	190	16.3	5.90	74	.310	.380	-149	-194	94	206	*138*	.937	330	69	111	2.2	-15.9	-2.5		3.6
WAS	110	2	20	0	1139.0	1485	54	574	292	16.7	5.56	83	.306	.387	-114	-121	99	300	***192***	.912	497	85	96	-6.5	-9.9	-3.3		-4.8
TOT	1294	43	293	32	13864.1					14.7	4.66		.280	.356						.931	4581	1057	1268					

Batter-Fielder Wins	Batting Average	On-Base Percentage	Slugging Average	On-Base Plus Slugging	Adjusted OPS	Adjusted Batter Runs
Delahanty-Phi 5.4	Thompson-Phi 370	Hamilton-Phi 490	Delahanty-Phi.......583	Hamilton-Phi 1014	Hamilton-Phi 169	Delahanty-Phi 53.1
McPhee-Cin 3.6	Hamilton-Phi.........380	Childs-Cle 463	Davis-NY 554	Delahanty-Phi 1007	Delahanty-Phi 166	Smith-Pit 44.2
Childs-Cle............3.4	Delahanty-Phi.......368	Burkett-Cle...................459	Thompson-Phi 530	Davis-NY 964	Smith-Pit 158	Thompson-Phi....44.2
Davis-NY..............3.2	Duffy-Bos 363	McGraw-Bal.................454	Smith-Pit...............525	Smith-Pit 960	Davis-NY 154	Hamilton-Phi 41.4
Hamilton-Phi 3.0	Davis-NY 355	Smith-Pit 435	Hamilton-Phi.........524	Thompson-Phi......954	Thompson-Phi......153	Davis-NY 38.0

Runs	Hits	Doubles	Triples	Home Runs	Total Bases	Runs Batted In
Long-Bos..............149	Thompson-Phi......222	Thompson-Phi 37	Werden-StL 29	Delahanty-Phi 19	Delahanty-Phi 347	Delahanty-Phi......146
Duffy-Bos..............147	Delahanty-Phi 219	Delahanty-Phi................35	Davis-NY 27	Clements-Phi..........17	Thompson-Phi......318	McKean-Cle 133
Delahanty-Phi 145	Duffy-Bos.............203	Tebeau-Cle 32	McKean-Cle............24	Tiernan-NY 14	Davis-NY 304	Thompson-Phi 126
Childs-Cle 145	Davis-NY 195	Beckley-Pit 32	Smith-Pit 23	Lowe-Bos...............14	Smith-Pit 272	Nash-Bos 123
Burkett-Cle............145	Ward-NY 193		Beckley-Pit.............19			Ewing-Cle............122

Stolen Bases	Base Stealing Runs	Fielding Runs-Infield	Fielding Runs-Outfield	Wins	Winning Pct.	Complete Games
T.Brown-Lou............66		McPhee-Cin................31.4	T.Brown-Lou 25.7	Killen-Pit 36	Gastright-Pit-Bos.....750	Rusie-NY 50
Dowd-StL.................59		G.Smith-Cin 16.4	Delahanty-Phi......23.7	Young-Cle 34	Killen-Pit 720	Nichols-Bos 43
Latham-Cin 57		Long-Bos 15.8	Treadway-Bal 7.8	Nichols-Bos 34	Nichols-Bos 708	Young-Cle..............42
Burke-NY.................54		Wise-Was 15.5	Griffin-Bro 7.3	Rusie-NY 33	Young-Cle.............680	Kennedy-Bro 40
Brodie-StL-Bal 49		Allen-Phi 15.3	Radford-Was..........6.5	Kennedy-Bro 25	Staley-Bos 643	

Strikeouts	Fewest BB/Game	Games	Saves	Base Runners/9	Adjusted Relief Runs	Relief Ranking
Rusie-NY 208	Young-Cle............2.19	Rusie-NY 56	Mullane-Cin-Bal........2	Young-Cle..........11.82		
Kennedy-Bro 107	Nichols-Bos 2.50	Killen-Pit 55	Baldwin-Pit-NY 2	Nichols-Bos 11.84		
Young-Cle 102	Cuppy-Cle............2.77	Young-Cle.......................53	Dwyer-Cin 2	Killen-Pit 12.06		
Breitenstein-StL....102	Staley-Bos 2.77	Nichols-Bos 52	Donnelly-Chi 2	Breitenstein-StL 12.30		
Weyhing-Phi 101	Stratton-Lou 2.86	Mullane-Cin-Bal 49	Colcolough-Pit..........2	Stein-Bro 12.70		

Innings Pitched	Opponents' Avg.	Opponents' OBP	Earned Run Average	Adjusted ERA	Adjusted Starter Runs	Pitcher Wins
Rusie-NY 482.0	Rusie-NY 240	Young-Cle 308	Breitenstein-StL ..3.18	Breitenstein-StL....149	Rusie-NY 74.0	**Rusie-NY** 6.8
Nichols-Bos 425.0	Breitenstein-StL ...241	Nichols-Bos 308	Rusie-NY 3.23	Young-Cle 145	Young-Cle............73.8	**Young-Cle** 6.5
Young-Cle..........422.2	Killen-Pit 246	Killen-Pit 312	Young-Cle...........3.36	Rusie-NY 144	Breitenstein-StL ..67.7	**Breitenstein-StL**5.6
Killen-Pit 415.0	Kennedy-Bro.........249	Breitenstein-StL...........316	Ehret-Pit 3.44	Nichols-Bos 140	Nichols-Bos 66.0	**Killen-Pit** 5.5
	Stein-Bro 250	Stein-Bro 323	Clarkson-StL........3.48	Clarkson-StL 136	Killen-Pit 45.5	**Nichols-Bos** 5.5

Going Batty

League moguls decided to increase offense for 1893, and moved the mound 5 feet from the plate to its current distance of 60 feet, 6 inches. Pitchers were also now required to keep one foot on a rubber plate while delivering, effectively limiting them to just one stride. Some pitchers couldn't handle the new rules, including former mound stalwarts Gus Weyhing, Bill Hutchinson, and Silver King. On the other hand, Amos Rusie of New York made 52 starts, threw 482 innings, and walked 218 men. No hurler has matched these totals since.

Despite the league making flat-sided bats illegal, scoring duly increased 22 percent to 6.57 runs per game, a new high, with the loop average rising to an unprecedented .280. Five NL players scored 145 or more runs and two teams plated at least 1,000. St. Louis, which had the league's worst ERA in 1892 at 4.20, had the NL's best a year later at 4.06. (It translated into just one extra win for the Browns because of a mediocre offense.)

The Phillies, in a small park, were the league's top scoring club, and had the top three batting title contenders (Billy Hamilton, Sam Thompson, and Ed Delahanty). Philadelphia, though, finished a distant fourth because the team couldn't win on the road. Aside from the three big guns, the Phillies' offense was actually quite poor, and the team's pitching was below the necessary standard.

Although they lacked the big-name marquee stars of other clubs, Frank Selee's Boston Beaneaters took the prize, squeezing past Pittsburgh. Hugh Duffy, Bobby Lowe, and Herman Long provided offense and defense up the middle, and Kid Nichols adapted well to the new mound conditions. Three celebrated careers ended as Tim Keefe, King Kelly, and Curt Welch played their final games.

With more offense, no split season, and a shorter schedule, fans had more interest in the league and attendance duly rose by 400,000, doubling in Chicago and New York. It marked the first time three teams attracted 300,000 fans, and the first time the league reached more than two million. There was no postseason tournament, however. The Temple Cup series, featuring the 1-2 teams in each league that started in 1894, never caught the public imagination.

1894 National League

TEAM	W	L	T	PCT	GB	HW	HL	R	OR	PA	H	2B	3B	HR	BB	SO	HB	SH	AVG	OBP	SLG	OPS	AOPS	BR	ABR	PF	SB	CS	BSA	BSR
BAL	89	39	1	.695		**52**	15	1171	819	5564	1647	271	**150**	33	516	**200**	**151**	**98**	.343	**.418**	.483	**901**	116	**174**	124	104	324			
NY	88	44	7	.667	3	49	17	962	**801**	5480	1469	199	96	45	489	219	80	32	.301	.369	.409	778	92	-69	-63	99	**326**			
BOS	83	49	1	.629	8	44	19	**1220**	1002	5657	1658	**272**	94	**103**	**535**	261	64	47	.331	.401	**.484**	885	109	138	54	108	241			
PHI	71	57	4	.555	18	48	20	1179	995	5779	**1780**	259	137	40	508	254	122	60	**.350**	.415	.478	893	**122**	166	**195**	98	285			
BRO	70	61	4	.534	20.5	42	24	1024	1020	5452	1514	231	130	42	467	295	100	34	.312	.376	.439	815	108	-3	71	93	282			
CLE	68	61	1	.527	21.5	35	24	932	896	5336	1442	241	90	37	471	301	77	24	.303	.368	.414	782	89	-57	-91	104	220			
PIT	65	65	3	.500	25	46	28	965	981	5376	1465	223	125	48	444	210	163	69	.312	.379	.443	822	103	10	21	99	257			
CHI	57	75	5	.432	34	35	30	1056	1080	5643	1574	268	87	65	507	306	76	38	.313	.381	.440	821	97	15	-40	106	332			
STL	56	76	1	.424	35	34	32	771	953	5204	1320	171	113	54	442	289	112	40	.286	.354	.408	762	87	-107	-107	100	190			
CIN	55	75	4	.423	35	38	28	936	1108	5375	1407	228	71	61	517	255	62	43	.296	.370	.412	782	89	-53	-83	103	223			
WAS	45	87	0	.341	46	32	30	882	1122	5325	1317	218	118	59	617	375	56	71	.287	.381	.425	806	101	-6	24	97	249			
LOU	36	94	1	.277	54	24	37	698	1019	5021	1216	173	89	42	355	368	93	54	.269	.330	.375	705	78	-207	-155	93	219			
TOT	799					479	304	11796		65212	17809	2754	1300	629	5868	3333	610	1156	.309	.379	.435	814					3148			

TEAM	CG	SHO	GR	SV	IP	H	HR	BB	SO	BR/9	ERA	AERA	OAV	OOB	PR	APR	PF	OSB	OCS	FA	E	WPB	DP	FW	PW	BW	BSW	DIF
BAL	97	1	**36**	**11**	1116.1	1371	**31**	472	275	15.2	5.00	109	.299	.371	41	56	103	202	*115*	**.944**	**293**	60	105	**5.7**	4.3	9.5		5.6
NY	113	5	30	5	1230.0	**1310**	37	546	**403**	**13.8**	**3.82**	**138**	**.271**	**.349**	**206**	**197**	99	256	***187***	.923	454	102	103	-1.8	**15.1**	-4.8		13.5
BOS	108	3	25	2	1166.0	1529	89	**411**	262	15.3	5.41	105	.314	.372	-11	31	107	223	*146*	.925	415	76	120	-.6	2.4	4.1		11.1
PHI	103	3	35	4	1151.2	1522	62	479	266	16.2	5.63	91	.315	.385	-38	-68	96	285	*118*	.934	351	82	114	2.9	-5.2	**14.9**		-5.6
BRO	106	3	30	5	1171.1	1465	41	558	290	16.0	5.56	89	.303	.383	-30	-85	93	294	*145*	.928	393	103	85	1.0	-6.5	5.4		4.6
CLE	106	**6**	28	2	1124.1	1390	54	435	254	14.9	4.97	110	.301	.366	45	60	103	**161**	*150*	.935	344	71	107	2.9	4.6	-7.0		3.0
PIT	106	2	31	0	1170.2	1563	39	466	308	15.9	5.62	93	.318	.381	-38	-52	98	261	*158*	.936	355	63	106	2.8	-4.0	1.6		-.4
CHI	**118**	0	20	0	1163.0	1575	43	569	284	17.1	5.72	98	.321	.398	-51	-12	106	323	*144*	.918	458	68	115	-2.4	-.9	-3.1		-2.7
STL	114	2	24	0	1161.0	1418	48	500	319	15.2	5.29	102	.299	.371	5	15	102	257	*173*	.923	426	79	109	-1.2	1.1	-8.2		-1.7
CIN	112	4	22	3	1165.1	1615	85	500	223	16.8	5.99	92	.326	.394	-85	-57	104	273	*155*	.925	430	**54**	122	-1.3	-4.4	-6.4		2.0
WAS	102	0	35	4	1107.0	1573	59	446	190	16.9	5.51	96	.331	.396	-23	-30	99	355	*163*	.908	499	82	81	-5.6	-2.3	1.8		-15.0
LOU	114	2	17	1	1104.2	1478	41	486	259	16.4	5.50	93	.318	.387	-21	-52	96	258	***187***	.919	435	67	**131**	-2.1	-4.0	-11.9		-11.1
TOT	1299	31	333	37	13831.1					15.8	5.33		.309	.379						.927	4853	907	1298					

Batter-Fielder Wins
Hamilton-Phi 4.5
Duffy-Bos 4.5
Dahlen-Chi 4.5
Joyce-Was 4.3
E.Delahanty-Phi 4.2

Batting Average
Duffy-Bos 440
Turner-Phi 418
Thompson-Phi 415
E.Delahanty-Phi ...404
Hamilton-Phi.........403

On-Base Percentage
Hamilton-Phi 522
Kelley-Bal....................502
Duffy-Bos....................502
Joyce-Was 496
Childs-Cle 475

Slugging Average
Thompson-Phi 696
Duffy-Bos 694
Joyce-Was 648
Kelley-Bal 602
E.Delahanty-Phi ...584

On-Base Plus Slugging
Duffy-Bos...........1196
Thompson-Phi 1161
Joyce-Was 1143
Kelley-Bal 1104
E.Delahanty-Phi 1059

Adjusted OPS
Thompson-Phi 181
Joyce-Was 179
Duffy-Bos.............172
Kelley-Bal 158
E.Delahanty-Phi ..158

Adjusted Batter Runs
Hamilton-Phi 65.9
Duffy-Bos 63.8
Thompson-Phi....56.6
Kelley-Bal 54.9
Joyce-Was..........52.4

Runs
Hamilton-Phi 198
Kelley-Bal 165
Keeler-Bal 165
Duffy-Bos.............160
Lowe-Bos.............158

Hits
Duffy-Bos..............237
Hamilton-Phi 225
Keeler-Bal 219
Lowe-Bos.............212

Doubles
Duffy-Bos 51
Kelley-Bal 48
Wilmot-Chi 45

Triples
Reitz-Bal 31
Thompson-Phi........28
Treadway-Bro 26
Connor-NY-StL 25
Brouthers-Bal 23

Home Runs
Duffy-Bos................18
Lowe-Bos.................17
Joyce-Was 17
Dahlen-Chi 15

Total Bases
Duffy-Bos.............374
Lowe-Bos.............319
Thompson-Phi......314
Kelley-Bal 305
Keeler-Bal 305

Runs Batted In
Thompson-Phi 147
Duffy-Bos 145
E.Delahanty-Phi ..133
Cross-Phi 132
Wilmot-Chi 130

Stolen Bases
Hamilton-Phi 100
McGraw-Bal............78
Wilmot-Chi..............76
Lange-Chi 66
T.Brown-Lou............66

Base Stealing Runs

Fielding Runs-Infield
Jennings-Bal 33.0
McPhee-Cin 30.0
Dahlen-Chi.................25.7
Cross-Phi...................25.0
Reitz-Bal 20.5

Fielding Runs-Outfield
Bannon-Bos 16.7
E.Delahanty-Phi ..12.5
McCarthy-Bos........9.4
Abbey-Was 7.7
Lange-Chi.............6.7

Wins
Rusie-NY 36
Meekin-NY...............33
Nichols-Bos 32
Breitenstein-StL......27

Winning Pct.
Meekin-NY 786
McMahon-Bal 758
Rusie-NY 735
Nichols-Bos 711

Complete Games
Breitenstein-StL 46
Rusie-NY 45
Young-Cle..............44
Meekin-NY 41
Nichols-Bos 40

Strikeouts
Rusie-NY..............195
Breitenstein-StL....140
Meekin-NY............137
Hawley-StL 120
Nichols-Bos 113

Fewest BB/Game
Young-Cle............2.33
Menefee-Lou-Pit..2.48
Gleason-StL-Bal ..2.54
Staley-Bos 2.63
Nichols-Bos 2.68

Games
Breitenstein-StL 56
Rusie-NY 54
Meekin-NY 53
Hawley-StL 53
Young-Cle 52

Saves
Mullane-Bal-Cle........4
Mercer-Was..............3
Hawke-Bal 3

Base Runners/9
Rusie-NY 12.79
Meekin-NY 12.94
Clarkson-Cle......13.08
Young-Cle..........13.19
Nichols-Bos 13.67

Adjusted Relief Runs

Relief Ranking

Innings Pitched
Breitenstein-StL 447.1
Rusie-NY 444.0
Meekin-NY 418.0
Young-Cle..........408.2
Nichols-Bos 407.0

Opponents' Avg.
Rusie-NY 250
Meekin-NY............256
Stein-Bro 278
Breitenstein-StL ...279
Clarkson-Cle.........285

Opponents' OBP
Rusie-NY 331
Meekin-NY....................333
Clarkson-Cle 336
Young-Cle 338
Nichols-Bos 346

Earned Run Average
Rusie-NY 2.78
Meekin-NY 3.70
Mercer-Was 3.85
Young-Cle............3.94
Taylor-Phi 4.08

Adjusted ERA
Rusie-NY.............189
Meekin-NY...........142
Young-Cle 139
Mercer-Was..........137
McMahon-Bal 130

Adjusted Starter Runs
Rusie-NY 118.0
Meekin-NY 80.9
Young-Cle............65.3
Mercer-Was 40.8
Nichols-Bos 38.8

Pitcher Wins
Rusie-NY 10.2
Meekin-NY 6.2
Young-Cle 5.0
Mercer-Was........3.8
Taylor-Phi 3.5

Bird-Brained Baseball

Offense continued to rise. The league average went to a stratospheric .309, and clubs scored 7.38 runs per game, a mark that has never been bettered. Philadelphia's Billy Hamilton scored the most runs in history—198—and his .522 on-base percentage set a new standard. Boston's Hugh Duffy hit .440, an all-time high, and his record .694 slugging percentage lasted until 1921. Heinie Reitz smacked 31 triples to tie Dave Orr's 1886 mark, and that record wasn't broken until 1912. Bobby Lowe of Boston became the first player in history to homer four times in one game. The 629 home runs hit during the season would not be surpassed until 1925.

The move toward increased offense came partially due to (or in spite of) a rule change; as of 1894, foul bunts were counted as strikes. Meanwhile, pity the pitchers. St. Louis' Ted Breitenstein was tagged for 497 hits and 320 runs, figures of terror that no moundsman has been unlucky enough to match. (Breitenstein still managed to win 27 times.) New York's Amos Rusie was the only pitcher with an ERA under 3.00.

Fans responded to the offense—the NL set another attendance record—but the game was changing for the worse. Greedy owners paid lower salaries, and as payoffs got lower, competition got tougher. Rule-breaking, fistfights, and umpire intimidation (and sometimes outright assault) became the rule.

The kings of this new era were the 1894 champion Baltimore Orioles, who were not above tripping or spiking opponents or stomping on an umpire's toes. Manager Ned Hanlon brought together a talented, smart, and tough club, including Joe Kelley, Hughie Jennings, Willie Keeler, Reitz, and John McGraw; these players would do anything, legal or not, to win. And as the Birds succeeded, other clubs followed. New York was a close second, with an ERA that was a full run better than any other team, led by strikeout pitchers Rusie and Joe Meekin. Boston was third, leading the league with 1,220 runs, but the club's pitchers allowed more than 1,000.

While alcohol disease killed Ned Williamson and King Kelly, other players ended their careers: Pete Browning, John Clarkson, Charlie Comiskey, and Monty Ward. Future stars Fred Clarke and Bobby Wallace debuted.

1895 National League

TEAM	W	L	T	PCT	GB	HW	HL	R	OR	PA	H	2B	3B	HR	BB	SO	HB	SH	AVG	OBP	SLG	OPS	AOPS	BR	ABR	PF	SB	CS	BSA	BSR
BAL	87	43	2	.669		**54**	12	1009	**646**	5311	1530	235	89	25	355	243	125	**106**	.324	.384	.427	811	110	94	68	103	310			
CLE	84	46	2	.646	3	47	13	921	725	5304	1433	194	69	29	476	365	87	49	.305	.375	.395	770	97	28	-22	106	188			
PHI	78	53	2	.595	9.5	51	21	**1068**	957	5689	**1664**	**272**	73	**61**	463	262	120	69	**.330**	**.394**	**.450**	**844**	**122**	**167**	**163**	100	276			
CHI	72	58	3	.554	15	43	26	866	854	5252	1401	171	85	55	422	344	80	42	.298	.361	.405	766	95	3	-50	107	260			
BRO	71	60	3	.542	16.5	43	22	879	838	5284	1346	191	78	41	397	319	67	63	.283	.346	.382	728	99	-64	6	92	184			
BOS	71	60	2	.542	16.5	48	19	911	829	5434	1377	198	57	54	**505**	**239**	**127**	52	.290	.364	.390	754	91	-3	-67	108	200			
PIT	71	61	3	.538	17	44	21	815	799	5226	1355	192	89	27	378	301	106	65	.290	.351	.386	737	99	-46	2	95	257			
CIN	66	64	2	.508	21	42	22	903	854	5190	1395	235	**105**	36	414	249	56	36	.298	.359	.416	775	99	18	-15	104	**326**			
NY	66	65	1	.504	21.5	40	27	852	834	5127	1324	191	90	32	454	292	38	30	.288	.355	.389	744	98	-30	-11	98	292			
WAS	43	85	5	.336	43	31	34	840	1052	5258	1326	209	101	55	522	403	69	52	.287	.366	.412	778	105	33	44	99	238			
STL	39	92	5	.298	48.5	25	41	752	1036	5296	1356	155	88	39	388	283	64	30	.282	.339	.375	714	89	-97	-86	99	208			
LOU	35	96	2	.267	52.5	19	38	698	1090	5205	1320	171	73	34	346	323	58	77	.279	.339	.368	707	92	-103	-51	94	156			
TOT	799					487	296	10514		63576	16827	2414	997	488	5120	3623	671	997	.296	.361	.400	761					2895			

TEAM	CG	SHO	GR	SV	IP	H	HR	BB	SO	BR/9	ERA	AERA	OAV	OOB	PR	APR	PF	OSB	OCS	FA	E	WPB	DP	FW	PW	BW	BSW	DIF
BAL	104	**10**	30	4	1134.1	**1216**	31	430	244	13.4	**3.80**	125	**.271**	.340	**123**	119	100	**155**	*149*	**.946**	**288**	**43**	108	**5.3**	9.6	5.5		1.6
CLE	109	6	25	3	1151.2	1284	34	**350**	330	**13.0**	3.92	**127**	.278	**.334**	110	**130**	104	207	*130*	.936	351	84	77	1.7	**10.5**	-1.8		8.5
PHI	106	2	29	**7**	1161.0	1467	36	485	330	15.6	5.47	87	.304	.375	-89	-89	100	256	*110*	.933	369	68	93	.9	-7.2	**13.2**		5.6
CHI	**119**	3	14	1	1150.2	1422	38	432	297	15.0	4.67	109	.300	.366	13	49	107	254	*114*	.928	401	72	**113**	-.9	4.0	-4.1		8.0
BRO	104	5	29	6	1159.2	1366	42	397	218	14.0	4.93	89	.289	.350	-20	-75	92	188	*143*	.941	326	56	97	3.5	-6.1	.5		7.6
BOS	117	4	18	4	1185.1	1376	56	367	377	13.6	4.25	120	.287	.343	69	102	107	196	*140*	.935	365	76	106	1.1	8.3	-5.4		1.5
PIT	107	4	29	6	1179.2	1279	**19**	500	383	14.2	4.10	110	.273	.353	89	55	94	280	*144*	.930	394	83	95	-.2	4.5	.2		.6
CIN	97	2	35	6	1147.1	1451	39	362	245	14.7	4.81	103	.304	.361	-5	16	104	227	*145*	.931	377	54	112	.3	1.3	-1.2		.6
NY	115	6	18	1	1147.1	1359	34	415	**409**	14.3	4.51	103	.291	.354	33	16	97	247	*157*	.922	438	76	106	-3.1	1.3	-.9		3.2
WAS	99	0	**38**	5	1111.1	1515	55	470	261	16.6	5.26	91	.321	.390	-60	-58	101	299	***191***	.917	450	53	97	-3.6	-4.7	3.6		-16.2
STL	106	1	30	1	1161.1	1572	64	443	284	16.0	5.73	84	.319	.381	-123	-116	101	320	*149*	.930	383	45	94	.6	-9.4	-7.0		-10.7
LOU	104	3	34	1	1117.1	1520	40	469	245	16.5	5.90	78	.320	.388	-139	-164	97	266	*126*	.913	477	79	104	-5.2	-13.3	-4.1		-7.9
TOT	1287	46	329	45	13807.0					14.7	4.77		.296	.361						.930	4619	789	1202					

Batter-Fielder Wins	Batting Average	On-Base Percentage	Slugging Average	On-Base Plus Slugging	Adjusted OPS	Adjusted Batter Runs
Jennings-Bal 6.3	Burkett-Cle 405	Delahanty-Phi 500	Thompson-Phi 654	Delahanty-Phi 1117	Delahanty-Phi 186	Delahanty-Phi 68.7
Thompson-Phi 5.0	Delahanty-Phi.......404	Hamilton-Phi 490	Delahanty-Phi.......617	Thompson-Phi 1085	Thompson-Phi......177	Thompson-Phi....56.9
Delahanty-Phi 4.6	Clements-Phi 394	Burkett-Cle...................482	Clements-Phi 612	Lange-Chi 1032	Stenzel-Pit............160	Hamilton-Phi 50.4
Griffin-Bro 3.8	Thompson-Phi 392	McGraw-Bal.................459	Lange-Chi.............575	Kelley-Bal 1003	Lange-Chi 155	Stenzel-Pit 50.3
G.Davis-NY..........3.2	Lange-Chi.............389	Lange-Chi 456	Kelley-Bal 546	Burkett-Cle..........1001	Hamilton-Phi 154	Burkett-Cle 44.2

Runs	Hits	Doubles	Triples	Home Runs	Total Bases	Runs Batted In
Hamilton-Phi 166	Burkett-Cle............225	Delahanty-Phi................49	Selbach-Was 22	Thompson-Phi........18	Thompson-Phi......352	Thompson-Phi 165
Keeler-Bal 162	Keeler-Bal 213	Thompson-Phi 45	Tiernan-NY 21	Joyce-Was..............17	Delahanty-Phi 296	Kelley-Bal 134
Jennings-Bal 159	Thompson-Phi......211	Jennings-Bal.................41	Thompson-Phi........21	Clements-Phi..........13	Burkett-Cle............288	Brodie-Bal 134
Burkett-Cle............153	Jennings-Bal 204	Stenzel-Pit 38	Cooley-StL..............20	Delahanty-Phi 11	McKean-Cle...........284	Jennings-Bal........125
Delahanty-Phi 149	Hamilton-Phi 201	Griffin-Bro......................38			Kelley-Bal 283	McKean-Cle 119

Stolen Bases	Base Stealing Runs	Fielding Runs-Infield	Fielding Runs-Outfield	Wins	Winning Pct.	Complete Games
Hamilton-Phi 97		Jennings-Bal 37.4	Selbach-Was 14.6	Young-Cle 35	Hoffer-Bal 838	Breitenstein-StL 47
Lange-Chi 67		Dahlen-Chi.................34.7	Clarke-Lou 13.2	Hoffer-Bal 31	Young-Cle............778	Hawley-Pit 44
McGraw-Bal..............61		Fuller-NY 33.1	Thompson-Phi 12.0	Hawley-Pit 31	Rhines-Cin 655	Nichols-Bos 43
Kelley-Bal 54		Cross-Phi....................32.4	Griffin-Bro 11.8			Rusie-NY 42
....	....	Collins-Bos-Lou 19.3	Miller-Cin 10.4		....	Griffith-Chi 39

Strikeouts	Fewest BB/Game	Games	Saves	Base Runners/9	Adjusted Relief Runs	Relief Ranking
Rusie-NY 201	Young-Cle 1.83	Hawley-Pit......................56	Parrott-Cin 3	McMahon-Bal 10.74		
Nichols-Bos 148	Clarke-NY 1.92	Breitenstein-StL 55	Nichols-Bos 3	Young-Cle..........10.86		
Hawley-Pit 142	Nichols-Bos 2.07	Rusie-NY 49	Beam-Phi...................3	Maul-Was 11.68		
Breitenstein-StL 131	Staley-StL............2.21	Nichols-Bos 48		Nichols-Bos 12.19		
Young-Cle 121	Taylor-Phi 2.23			Hawley-Pit 12.23		

Innings Pitched	Opponents' Avg.	Opponents' OBP	Earned Run Average	Adjusted ERA	Adjusted Starter Runs	Pitcher Wins
Hawley-Pit 444.1	Foreman-Pit 245	Young-Cle 294	Maul-Was 2.45	Maul-Was 195	Young-Cle............73.3	**Hawley-Pit**..........7.4
Breitenstein-StL 438.2	Hoffer-Bal 246	Maul-Was......................310	McMahon-Bal 2.94	Young-Cle 153	Nichols-Bos 67.4	**Young-Cle** 6.9
Rusie-NY 393.1	Rusie-NY 252	Nichols-Bos 319	Hawley-Pit 3.18	Nichols-Bos 149	Hawley-Pit 66.2	**Cuppy-Cle** 5.2
Nichols-Bos 390.2	Young-Cle.............253	Hawley-Pit 320	Hoffer-Bal 3.21	Hoffer-Bal 148	Hoffer-Bal 55.9	**Nichols-Bos** 5.2
Young-Cle..........369.2	Maul-Was 257	Cuppy-Cle 323	Foreman-Pit 3.22	Hawley-Pit 142	Cuppy-Cle............51.1	**Hoffer-Bal** 4.6

Refinement of the Formula

Pitchers got some relief in 1895, as scoring per game dipped nearly a run per team. The tight defense and strong teamwork of Baltimore led to as many imitators, as did their umpire-baiting and violence. For the first time the NL regulated the size and weight of fielders' gloves, except for those worn by catchers and first basemen. The league also inaugurated the infield fly rule to keep clubs from intentionally dropping popups. Those rules still couldn't keep the game from getting dirtier, though. The two most unscrupulous clubs, the Orioles and Cleveland Spiders, finished 1-2 in the league. Both clubs also had great talent, not just hard-scrabble rowdies.

Despite injuries to many key players, the Orioles sported the best pitching (led by Bill Hoffer) and the second-most productive hitters; Willie Keeler and Hugh Jennings finished 2-3 in runs. Cleveland was carried by batting champ Jesse Burkett, shortstop Ed McKean, and hurlers Cy Young and Nig Cuppy. Spiders pitching overcame Baltimore bats to win the Temple Cup.

Boston fell to fifth but debuted future third base star Jimmy Collins, while shortstop Jack Glasscock, the 1890 batting champ, tumbled out of the league at age 36. First baseman Harry Davis, who would later win four straight AL home run titles, also made his first appearance.

Nine teams finished over .500, with three former American Association members, who barely drew flies, bringing up the rear. Parity and a decent pennant race raised league attendance 16 percent, due to huge gains in Boston, Chicago, Cincinnati, and especially Philadelphia. The Phillies were the NL's biggest draw—becoming the first team to pass 400,000 fans—and once again featured the league's highest-scoring offense.

Several clubs had by now adopted the monikers by which we know still them, including the Cincinnati Reds, Pittsburgh Pirates, New York Giants, and Philadelphia Phillies—although the league still had its Boston Beaneaters, Chicago Colts, and Brooklyn Bridegrooms (or Superbas, take your pick). Two NL clubs also carried names that their AL successors would adopt: the Orioles and the St. Louis Browns.

1896 National League

TEAM	W	L	T	PCT	GB	HW	HL	R	OR	PA	H	2B	3B	HR	BB	SO	HB	SH	AVG	OBP	SLG	OPS	AOPS	BR	ABR	PF	SB	CS	BSA	BSR
BAL	90	39	3	.698		49	16	**995**	662	5323	**1548**	**207**	**100**	23	386	**201**	98	**120**	**.328**	**.393**	**.429**	**822**	**120**	**153**	**140**	101	**441**			
CLE	80	48	7	.625	9.5	43	19	840	650	5435	1463	**207**	72	28	**436**	316	106	37	.301	.363	.391	754	97	29	-18	106	175			
CIN	77	50	1	.606	12	**51**	15	783	**620**	4911	1283	204	73	20	382	226	**127**	42	.294	.357	.388	745	95	9	-38	107	350			
BOS	74	57	1	.565	17	42	24	865	761	5306	1421	175	75	**36**	414	275	118	51	.301	.364	.393	757	98	29	-17	106	243			
CHI	71	57	4	.555	18.5	42	24	815	804	5118	1311	182	97	34	409	290	92	35	.286	.349	.390	739	95	-8	-37	104	332			
PIT	66	63	2	.512	24	35	31	787	741	5254	1371	169	94	27	387	286	108	58	.292	.353	.385	738	103	-9	25	96	217			
NY	64	67	2	.489	27	39	26	829	821	5225	1383	159	87	40	439	271	72	53	.297	.364	.394	758	107	31	56	97	274			
PHI	62	68	0	.477	28.5	42	27	890	891	5273	1382	234	84	49	438	297	95	60	.295	.363	.413	776	110	62	73	99	191			
WAS	58	73	2	.443	33	38	29	818	920	5315	1328	179	79	45	516	365	99	61	.286	.365	.388	753	103	32	32	100	258			
BRO	58	73	2	.443	33	35	28	692	764	5025	1292	174	87	28	344	269	94	39	.284	.340	.379	719	100	-47	-4	94	198			
STL	40	90	1	.308	50.5	27	34	593	929	4988	1162	134	78	37	332	300	101	35	.257	.313	.346	659	81	-154	-128	96	185			
LOU	38	93	3	.290	53	25	37	653	997	5057	1197	142	80	37	371	427	53	45	.261	.322	.351	673	85	-126	-101	96	195			
TOT	792					468	310	9560		62230	16141	2166	1006	404	4854	3523	636	1163	.290	.354	.387	742					3059			

TEAM	CG	SHO	GR	SV	IP	H	HR	BB	SO	BR/9	ERA	AERA	OAV	OOB	PR	APR	PF	OSB	OCS	FA	E	WPB	DP	FW	PW	BW	BSW	DIF
BAL	115	9	17	1	1168.1	1281	22	339	302	12.7	3.67	116	.277	.331	89	79	98	218	*118*	.945	296	58	114	2.7	6.7	**11.9**		4.3
CLE	113	9	24	**5**	1195.2	1363	27	**280**	336	**12.6**	**3.46**	**131**	.285	**.329**	**119**	**136**	104	183	*133*	.949	288	52	**117**	3.6	**11.5**	-1.5		2.4
CIN	105	**12**	26	4	1108.0	**1240**	27	310	219	13.0	3.67	125	.281	.335	85	.108	106	**167**	*114*	**.951**	**252**	**42**	107	**4.7**	9.2	-3.2		2.9
BOS	110	6	24	3	1155.2	1254	57	397	277	13.1	3.78	120	**.275**	.337	75	93	104	228	*175*	.934	368	76	94	-1.7	7.9	-1.4		3.7
CHI	**118**	2	15	1	1161.1	1307	30	467	354	14.4	4.44	102	.282	.358	-11	11	104	271	*146*	.933	367	59	115	-1.6	.9	-3.1		10.8
PIT	108	8	26	1	1159.1	1286	**18**	439	**362**	13.9	4.30	97	.280	.351	7	-16	96	310	*168*	.941	317	68	103	1.2	-1.4	2.1		-.5
NY	104	1	30	2	1136.2	1303	33	403	312	14.0	4.54	92	.286	.352	-24	-46	96	265	*142*	.933	365	93	90	-1.3	-3.9	4.8		-1.0
PHI	107	3	25	2	1117.0	1473	39	387	243	15.4	5.20	83	.316	.375	-104	-113	99	245	*148*	.941	313	48	112	1.3	-9.6	6.2		-.9
WAS	106	2	29	3	1136.2	1435	24	435	292	15.2	4.61	96	.306	.372	-32	-27	101	289	*152*	.927	398	79	99	-3.3	-2.3	2.7		-4.6
BRO	97	3	**38**	1	1144.0	1353	39	400	259	14.1	4.25	97	.292	.354	14	-18	95	248	*140*	.945	297	52	104	2.7	-1.5	-.3		-8.4
STL	115	1	18	1	1130.2	1448	40	456	279	15.5	5.33	82	.309	.376	-121	-125	100	303	***192***	.936	345	57	73	-.5	-10.6	-10.9		-3.1
LOU	108	1	29	4	1148.2	1398	48	541	288	15.9	5.12	84	.298	.381	-98	-103	99	332	*182*	.916	475	82	110	-7.8	-8.7	-8.6		-2.4
TOT	1306	57	301	28	13762.0					14.1	4.36		.290	.354						.938	4081	766	1238					

Batter-Fielder Wins	Batting Average	On-Base Percentage	Slugging Average	On-Base Plus Slugging	Adjusted OPS	Adjusted Batter Runs
Jennings-Bal 6.7	Burkett-Cle 410	Hamilton-Bos 478	Delahanty-Phi.......631	Delahanty-Phi 1103	Delahanty-Phi 192	Delahanty-Phi 68.4
Childs-Cle............6.3	Jennings-Bal.........401	Jennings-Bal 472	Dahlen-Chi 553	Kelley-Bal 1013	Kelley-Bal 164	Kelley-Bal 53.7
Delahanty-Phi 5.8	Delahanty-Phi.......397	Delahanty-Phi 472	McCreery-Lou.......546	Burkett-Cle..........1002	Joyce-Was-NY......162	Joyce-Was-NY....51.8
Burkett-Cle..........5.7	Keeler-Bal 386	Joyce-Was-NY 470	Kelley-Bal 543	Dahlen-Chi 990	Tiernan-NY 159	Tiernan-NY 48.5
Dahlen-Chi 5.5	Tiernan-NY 369	Kelley-Bal.....................469	Burkett-Cle 541	Joyce-Was-NY......988	E.Smith-Pit 158	Burkett-Cle 46.3

Runs	Hits	Doubles	Triples	Home Runs	Total Bases	Runs Batted In
Burkett-Cle............160	Burkett-Cle............240	Delahanty-Phi 44	VanHaltren-NY........21	Joyce-Was-NY........13	Burkett-Cle............317	Delahanty-Phi.......126
Keeler-Bal 153	Keeler-Bal 210	Miller-Cin.......................38	McCreery-Lou 21	Delahanty-Phi 13	Delahanty-Phi 315	Jennings-Bal.......121
Hamilton-Bos..........153	Jennings-Bal 209	Kelley-Bal 31	Kelley-Bal 19	Thompson-Phi 12	Kelley-Bal 282	Duffy-Bos 113
Kelley-Bal 148	Delahanty-Phi 198	Dahlen-Chi 30	Dahlen-Chi 19	Connor-StL 11	VanHaltren-NY......272	McKean-Cle 112
Dahlen-Chi 137	VanHaltren-NY......197		Clarke-Lou..............18		Keeler-Bal 270	

Stolen Bases	Base Stealing Runs	Fielding Runs-Infield	Fielding Runs-Outfield	Wins	Winning Pct.	Complete Games
Kelley-Bal 87		Childs-Cle 38.9	Burkett-Cle 28.6	Nichols-Bos 30	Hoffer-Bal 781	Killen-Pit 44
Lange-Chi 84		Jennings-Bal 31.2	Thompson-Phi 17.5	Killen-Pit 30	Hemming-Bal 714	Young-Cle..............42
Hamilton-Bos..........83		Corcoran-Bro 25.9	Delahanty-Phi......12.4	Young-Cle 28	Dwyer-Cin.............686	Mercer-Was 38
Miller-Cin 76		Clingman-Lou 23.7	Parrott-StL 7.0	Meekin-NY..............26	Nichols-Bos 682	
Doyle-Bal................73		Dahlen-Chi..................21.8	Brodie-Bal.............6.7		Griffith-Chi 676	

Strikeouts	Fewest BB/Game	Games	Saves	Base Runners/9	Adjusted Relief Runs	Relief Ranking
Young-Cle 140	Young-Cle............1.35	Killen-Pit 52	Young-Cle 3	Rhines-Cin 11.64		
Hawley-Pit 137	Clarke-NY............1.54	Young-Cle 51	Hill-Lou 2	Cuppy-Cle.........11.82		
Killen-Pit 134	Dwyer-Cin............1.87	Nichols-Bos 49	Fisher-Cin 2	Klobedanz-Bos ..11.94		
Breitenstein-StL....114	Cuppy-Cle............1.89	Hawley-Pit......................49		Young-Cle.........11.95		
Meekin-NY............110	Griffith-Chi 1.98	Clarke-NY 48		Nichols-Bos 11.97		

Innings Pitched	Opponents' Avg.	Opponents' OBP	Earned Run Average	Adjusted ERA	Adjusted Starter Runs	Pitcher Wins
Killen-Pit 432.1	Rhines-Cin 238	Rhines-Cin...................311	Rhines-Cin 2.45	Rhines-Cin............188	Nichols-Bos 59.4	**Young-Cle** 5.7
Young-Cle............414.1	Hawley-Pit 261	Cuppy-Cle 314	Nichols-Bos 2.83	Nichols-Bos 160	Young-Cle...........56.4	**Cuppy-Cle** 5.5
Hawley-Pit 378.0	Sullivan-NY...........261	Young-Cle 317	Cuppy-Cle............3.12	Dwyer-Cin 146	Cuppy-Cle............55.0	**Nichols-Bos** 5.4
Nichols-Bos 372.1	Friend-Chi.............264	Nichols-Bos 317	Dwyer-Cin............3.15	Cuppy-Cle 146	Dwyer-Cin...........42.4	**Dwyer-Cin** 4.4
Mercer-Was 366.1	Hoffer-Bal 264	Esper-Bal.....................319	Young-Cle.............3.24	Young-Cle 140	Hoffer-Bal 35.1	**Hoffer-Bal** 3.9

Another Bird Victory

To aid the league's pitchers, the NL passed a rule allowing them to hide the baseball before or during their delivery. At least partially as a result, scoring decreased again, this time by half a run per game per team. The decrease in offense didn't stop everyone. Jesse Burkett's 240 hits set a mark that stood until 1911. Meanwhile, Hughie Jennings got hit by 51 pitches, an all-time high; he broke Curt Welch's 1891 record by 15. (Welch died in 1896, beset by the ravages of the bottle.)

The last player to hold out against wearing a fielder's glove, top shortstop Bid McPhee, finally gave in for 1896. The new innovation made him an even better shortstop. Meanwhile, two men who would go on to greater fame five years later, in the new American League, debuted: Fielder Jones, for Brooklyn, and Nap Lajoie, with Philadelphia.

Baltimore won its third straight league title. The club's offensive prowess put some distance between them and second-place Cleveland. Shortstop Jennings was an offensive and defensive force for the Orioles, and with the help of Willie Keeler, Joe Kelley, and Jack Doyle, the club batted .328, which was 27 points higher than the nearest rival. The Orioles scored 105 more runs and stole 91 more bases than anyone else. (Baltimore's 441 steals have never been surpassed, but there is a reason: through 1897 scorers also credited a stolen base if a runner advanced on a flyball or went two bases on a hit or infield out, as long as a palpable attempt was made to retire him.)

Cleveland again had Cy Young and Nig Cuppy on the hill, but the Spiders had little offense beyond the big three of Burkett, Ed McKean, and Cupid Childs. Surprising Cincinnati, under Buck Ewing, finished third, with Billy Rhines and Frank Dwyer finishing first and fourth in ERA. New York didn't contend, because mound mainstay Amos Rusie sat out the year rather than take a less-than-deserved pay cut.

Last-place Louisville increased its attendance by 30,000, but still drew barely 2,000 per game. The league's overall gate rose just 11,000, but the 2,900,973 tickets sold ranked as the highest total for any one league until 1904.

1897 National League

TEAM	W	L	T	PCT	GB	HW	HL	R	OR	PA	H	2B	3B	HR	BB	SO	HB	SH	AVG	OBP	SLG	OPS	AOPS	BR	ABR	PF	SB	CS	BSA	BSR
BOS	93	39	3	.705		**54**	12	**1025**	**665**	5521	1574	230	83	**45**	423	262	114	47	.319	.378	**.426**	804	110	121	65	106	233			
BAL	90	40	6	.692	2	51	15	964	674	5496	**1584**	**243**	66	19	**437**	256	72	**115**	**.325**	**.394**	.414	**808**	**119**	**145**	**145**	100	**401**			
NY	83	48	7	.634	9.5	51	19	901	696	5395	1452	188	**84**	31	412	327	45	67	.298	.361	.390	751	106	22	46	97	332			
CIN	76	56	2	.576	17	49	18	763	705	5104	1311	219	69	22	380	**218**	**135**	65	.290	.353	.383	736	93	-2	-50	107	194			
CLE	69	62	1	.527	23.5	49	16	773	680	5175	1374	192	88	16	435	344	98	38	.298	.364	.389	753	99	27	-14	105	181			
WAS	61	71	3	.462	32	40	26	781	793	5141	1376	194	77	36	374	348	72	59	.297	.357	.395	752	104	19	23	100	208			
BRO	61	71	4	.462	32	38	29	802	845	5334	1343	202	72	24	351	255	115	58	.279	.336	.366	702	95	-74	-32	95	187			
PIT	60	71	4	.458	32.5	38	27	676	835	5114	1266	140	108	25	359	334	98	67	.276	.337	.370	707	95	-67	-39	96	170			
CHI	59	73	6	.447	34	36	30	832	894	5385	1356	189	97	38	430	317	103	49	.282	.347	.386	733	94	-17	-46	104	264			
PHI	55	77	2	.417	38	32	34	752	792	5294	1392	213	83	40	399	299	97	42	.293	.353	.398	751	106	14	36	97	163			
LOU	52	78	6	.400	40	34	31	675	869	5131	1209	161	70	40	375	460	101	68	.264	.328	.355	683	88	-102	-79	97	200			
STL	29	102	2	.221	63.5	18	41	592	1088	5183	1285	151	67	32	354	314	80	76	.275	.336	.357	693	89	-86	-72	98	172			
TOT	811					490	298	9536		63273	16522	2322	964	368	4729	3734	751	1130	.292	.354	.386	740					2705			

TEAM	CG	SHO	GR	SV	IP	H	HR	BB	SO	BR/9	ERA	AERA	OAV	OOB	PR	APR	PF	OSB	OCS	FA	E	WPB	DP	FW	PW	BW	BSW	DIF
BOS	115	**8**	21	**7**	1194.1	1273	39	393	329	**12.9**	3.65	**122**	.271	**.333**	86	**102**	104	150	*104*	**.951**	272	56	80	3.9	**8.7**	5.6		8.8
BAL	118	3	20	0	1197.2	1296	**18**	382	361	13.2	3.55	117	.274	.338	99	83	97	211	*88*	**.951**	277	67	110	3.7	7.1	**12.4**		1.8
NY	119	**8**	19	3	1196.1	**1217**	26	490	**463**	13.3	**3.45**	120	**.262**	.341	**114**	95	96	**131**	*138*	.930	399	89	109	-3.4	8.1	3.9		8.8
CIN	100	4	**38**	2	1156.2	1375	**18**	329	270	13.7	4.09	111	.294	.347	28	54	106	145	*112*	.948	273	**30**	100	3.6	4.6	-4.3		6.0
CLE	111	6	20	0	1119.1	1297	32	**289**	277	13.1	3.95	114	.288	.337	44	63	104	194	*118*	.950	**261**	46	74	**4.1**	5.4	-1.2		-4.8
WAS	102	7	34	6	1148.0	1383	27	400	348	14.6	4.01	108	.296	.362	37	39	101	278	***175***	.933	369	68	103	-2.0	3.3	2.0		-8.3
BRO	114	4	22	2	1194.2	1417	34	410	256	14.2	4.60	89	.293	.354	-40	-73	95	264	*164*	.936	364	50	99	-1.6	-6.3	-2.7		5.6
PIT	112	2	24	2	1153.1	1397	22	318	342	13.9	4.67	89	.297	.350	-48	-69	97	274	*116*	.936	346	54	70	-.6	-5.9	-3.3		4.4
CHI	**131**	2	7	1	1197.0	1485	30	433	361	14.9	4.53	98	.303	.367	-31	-12	104	261	*146*	.932	393	61	**112**	-3.0	-1.0	-3.9		1.0
PHI	115	4	19	2	1155.1	1415	28	364	253	14.3	4.60	91	.300	.356	-39	-55	97	222	*119*	.944	296	58	72	2.3	-4.7	3.1		-11.6
LOU	115	2	20	0	1155.0	1374	40	467	267	15.0	4.41	97	.294	.368	-14	-21	99	245	*145*	.930	399	91	87	-3.7	-1.8	-6.8		-.8
STL	110	1	25	1	1136.1	1594	54	454	207	16.8	6.17	71	.329	.394	-236	-221	102	330	*154*	.932	380	63	86	-3.0	-18.9	-6.2		-8.4
TOT	1362	51	269	26	14004.0					14.1	4.30		.292	.354						.939	4029	733	1102					

Batter-Fielder Wins	Batting Average	On-Base Percentage	Slugging Average	On-Base Plus Slugging	Adjusted OPS	Adjusted Batter Runs
Jennings-Bal 5.5	Keeler-Bal............424	McGraw-Bal................471	Lajoie-Phi 569	Keeler-Bal 1003	F.Clarke-Lou..........167	F.Clarke-Lou 54.5
Davis-NY.............5.1	F.Clarke-Lou 390	Burkett-Cle..................468	Keeler-Bal............539	F.Clarke-Lou..........992	Keeler-Bal 164	Keeler-Bal 51.9
F.Clarke-Lou........4.1	Burkett-Cle 383	Keeler-Bal 464	Delahanty-Phi.......538	Delahanty-Phi 981	Delahanty-Phi 163	Delahanty-Phi 50.1
Delahanty-Phi 4.0	Delahanty-Phi.......377	Jennings-Bal 463	F.Clarke-Lou 530	Lajoie-Phi 960	Lajoie-Phi 156	Lajoie-Phi 39.3
Keeler-Bal 3.7	Kelley-Bal 362	F.Clarke-Lou................461	Davis-NY 509	Burkett-Cle............944	Kelley-Bal 147	Kelley-Bal 38.7

Runs	Hits	Doubles	Triples	Home Runs	Total Bases	Runs Batted In
Hamilton-Bos........152	Keeler-Bal 239	Stenzel-Bal 43	Davis-Pit 28	Duffy-Bos.................11	Lajoie-Phi 310	Davis-NY 135
Keeler-Bal............145	F.Clarke-Lou...........205	Lajoie-Phi 40	Lajoie-Phi 23	Davis-NY 10	Keeler-Bal 304	Collins-Bos 132
Griffin-Bro 136	Delahanty-Phi 200	Delahanty-Phi 40	Wallace-Cle 21	Lajoie-Phi 9	Delahanty-Phi 285	Duffy-Bos 129
Jones-Bro 134	Burkett-Cle............198	Wallace-Cle 33	Keeler-Bal 19	Grady-Phi-StL 8	F.Clarke-Lou..........279	Lajoie-Phi 127
Jennings-Bal 133	Lajoie-Phi 197	Ryan-Chi.......................33		Beckley-NY-Cin 8		Kelley-Bal 118

Stolen Bases	Base Stealing Runs	Fielding Runs-Infield	Fielding Runs-Outfield	Wins	Winning Pct.	Complete Games
Lange-Chi 73		Clingman-Lou 30.3	Selbach-Was 12.3	Nichols-Bos 31	Klobedanz-Bos 788	Killen-Pit 38
Stenzel-Bal 69		Cross-StL...................29.9	Delahanty-Phi........8.8	Rusie-NY 28	Nops-Bal...............769	Griffith-Chi 38
Hamilton-Bos..........66		Jennings-Bal 23.0	Ryan-Chi................7.4	Klobedanz-Bos 26	Corbett-Bal 750	Donahue-StL 38
Davis-NY 65		Davis-NY 19.9	VanHaltren-NY 6.7	Corbett-Bal 24	Nichols-Bos 738	Nichols-Bos 37
Keeler-Bal 64		Werden-Lou 19.3	Hoy-Cin..................5.1	Breitenstein-Cin......23	Rusie-NY 737	Kennedy-Bro 36

Strikeouts	Fewest BB/Game	Games	Saves	Base Runners/9	Adjusted Relief Runs	Relief Ranking
Seymour-NY 156	Young-Cle............1.31	Mercer-Was 47	Nichols-Bos 3	Nichols-Bos 10.59		
McJames-Was.......156	Tannehill-Pit 1.52	Young-Cle 46	Mercer-Was 3	Rusie-NY 11.48		
Corbett-Bal 149	Nichols-Bos 1.66	Nichols-Bos 46		Amole-Bal..........11.57		
Rusie-NY 135	Cuppy-Cle............1.70	Donahue-StL 46		Cuppy-Cle...........11.80		
Nichols-Bos 127	Killen-Pit 2.03			Sullivan-Bos 12.03		

Innings Pitched	Opponents' Avg.	Opponents' OBP	Earned Run Average	Adjusted ERA	Adjusted Starter Runs	Pitcher Wins
Nichols-Bos 368.0	Seymour-NY.........238	Nichols-Bos 291	Rusie-NY 2.54	Nichols-Bos 169	Nichols-Bos 70.4	**Nichols-Bos** 6.9
Donahue-StL 348.0	Rusie-NY 254	Rusie-NY 308	Nichols-Bos 2.64	Rusie-NY 163	Rusie-NY 57.9	**Rusie-NY** 5.9
Griffith-Chi 343.2	Nichols-Bos 255	Cuppy-Cle 314	Nops-Bal..............2.81	Nops-Bal 148	Mercer-Was 33.2	**Mercer-Was**........3.9
Kennedy-Bro......343.1	Hill-Lou 268	Young-Cle 318	Corbett-Bal 3.11	Powell-Cle 142	Breitenstein-Cin ..31.4	**Breitenstein-Cin**2.9
Mercer-Was 342.0	Corbett-Bal 269	Nops-Bal 319	Powell-Cle............3.16	Cuppy-Cle 140	Corbett-Bal 31.0	**Seymour-NY** 2.9

Clean Beaneaters

The league ruled before the season that pitchers could at no time intentionally deface the baseball, and that runners had to retouch bases when returning—ending the popular practice of simply cutting across the infield. These tactics were meant to clean up the game, but the best move toward making baseball more acceptable to the public was for "clean" teams to win.

This was accomplished when Frank Selee's Boston Beaneaters held off the Orioles to take the NL crown. Kid Nichols led the league in innings and wins, while Hugh Duffy, Fred Tenney, Jimmy Collins, and Billy Hamilton provided good defense as well as overpowering offensive punch—Boston was the last team to surpass 1,000 runs until 1930. Selee expertly combined youth and experience, and Beaneaters owner Arthur Soden challenged his club at midseason by forcing any player fined by an umpire to pay the tariff himself.

Baltimore didn't win despite runaway batting champ Willie Keeler's 44-game hitting streak and big years from Hughie Jennings and John McGraw. The Giants took third, with Amos Rusie returned from his holdout (other club owners, hip to Andrew Freedman's penury, kicked in to raise Rusie's salary). Eleventh-place Louisville didn't have much, but they did have .390-hitting Fred Clarke and versatile rookie Honus Wagner. Other 1897 rookies included Roger Bresnahan, Rube Waddell, and Jimmy Sheckard.

Prior to the season Brooklyn suffered the death of manager Dave Foutz, a 147-win pitcher and solid everyday hitter; he three times led his league in games played. Under replacement skipper Billy Barnie, the Bridegrooms improved three spots, to seventh.

The last original National Association player in the NL, Chicago's Cap Anson, retired at age 45. Anson left the club at the conclusion of a ten-year contract; Pop had been with the club for nineteen seasons as manager, and twenty-two years as a player. The sympathetic public dubbed the club the Orphans in his absence. He went to New York in 1898, but he lasted just two months at the helm.

As the nineteenth century hurtled to its conclusion, several other of the era's biggest stars, like Roger Connor, Buck Ewing, Silver King, Denny Lyons, and Fred Pfeffer took part in their last major league action.

1898 National League

TEAM	W	L	T	PCT	GB	HW	HL	R	OR	PA	H	2B	3B	HR	BB	SO	HB	SH	AVG	OBP	SLG	OPS	AOPS	BR	ABR	PF	SB	CS	BSA	BSR
BOS	102	47	3	.685		**62**	15	872	**614**	5847	1531	190	55	**53**	405	303	134	32	.290	.344	**.377**	721	106	73	31	105	172			
BAL	96	53	5	.644	6	58	15	**933**	623	6000	**1584**	154	77	12	519	316	79	**160**	**.302**	**.382**	.368	**750**	**118**	**160**	**143**	102	**250**			
CIN	92	60	5	.605	11.5	58	28	831	740	5984	1448	207	**101**	19	455	**300**	**136**	59	.271	.335	.359	694	97	24	-28	107	165			
CHI	85	65	2	.567	17.5	58	31	828	679	5879	1431	175	84	18	476	394	113	71	.274	.343	.350	693	104	29	31	100	220			
CLE	81	68	7	.544	21	36	19	730	683	5962	1379	162	56	18	**545**	306	125	46	.263	.338	.325	663	96	-21	-10	99	93			
PHI	78	71	1	.523	24	49	31	823	784	5779	1431	**238**	81	33	472	382	120	69	.280	.348	**.377**	725	**118**	89	127	96	182			
NY	77	73	7	.513	25.5	45	28	837	800	5907	1422	190	86	34	428	372	61	69	.266	.328	.353	681	103	-5	20	97	214			
PIT	72	76	4	.486	29.5	39	35	634	694	5638	1313	140	88	14	336	343	141	74	.258	.313	.328	641	90	-83	-70	98	107			
LOU	70	81	3	.464	33	43	34	728	833	5775	1389	150	71	32	375	429	141	66	.267	.325	.342	667	97	-33	-22	99	235			
BRO	54	91	4	.372	46	30	41	638	811	5610	1314	156	66	17	328	314	91	65	.256	.309	.322	631	85	-101	-98	100	130			
WAS	51	101	3	.336	52.5	34	44	704	939	5785	1423	177	80	36	370	386	88	70	.271	.327	.355	682	100	-6	-4	100	197			
STL	39	111	4	.260	63.5	20	44	571	929	5798	1290	149	55	13	383	402	117	84	.247	.309	.305	614	78	-128	-142	102	104			
TOT	921					532	365	9129		69964	16955	2088	900	299	5092	4247	865	1346	.271	.334	.347	681					2069			

TEAM	CG	SHO	GR	SV	IP	H	HR	BB	SO	BR/9	ERA	AERA	OAV	OOB	PR	APR	PF	OSB	OCS	FA	E	WPB	DP	FW	PW	BW	BSW	DIF
BOS	127	9	26	**8**	1340.0	**1186**	37	470	432	11.6	2.98	124	**.236**	**.310**	93	103	102	149	*125*	.950	310	87	102	3.1	9.6	2.9		11.9
BAL	138	12	15	0	1323.0	1236	17	400	422	**11.5**	2.90	123	.246	**.310**	104	99	99	146	*128*	.947	326	65	105	2.5	9.3	**13.4**		-3.6
CIN	131	10	**27**	2	1385.1	1484	16	449	294	13.0	3.50	109	.272	.336	17	47	106	**109**	*121*	.950	325	44	128	2.9	4.4	-2.6		11.3
CHI	137	**13**	15	0	1342.2	1357	17	364	323	12.1	**2.83**	**126**	.261	.319	**115**	**112**	99	111	*116*	.936	412	51	**149**	-2.9	**10.5**	2.9		-.5
CLE	**142**	9	15	0	1334.0	1429	26	**309**	339	12.1	3.20	113	.272	.320	59	60	100	159	*140*	**.952**	**301**	46	95	**4.2**	5.6	-.9		-2.4
PHI	129	10	22	0	1288.1	1440	23	399	325	13.4	3.72	92	.281	.342	-17	-45	95	151	*136*	.937	379	54	102	-1.2	-4.2	11.9		-3.0
NY	141	9	15	1	1353.2	1359	21	587	**558**	13.5	3.44	101	.260	.344	25	5	96	188	*156*	.932	447	119	113	-4.2	.5	1.9		3.9
PIT	131	10	22	3	1323.2	1400	**14**	346	330	12.3	3.41	104	.270	.323	29	22	99	170	*139*	.946	340	**42**	105	1.4	2.1	-6.5		1.1
LOU	137	4	19	0	1334.0	1457	33	470	271	13.6	4.24	84	.276	.346	-95	-100	99	205	*140*	.939	382	54	114	-.8	-9.3	-2.1		6.7
BRO	134	1	17	0	1298.2	1446	34	476	294	13.7	4.01	89	.280	.348	-59	-64	99	184	*140*	.947	334	56	125	1.3	-6.0	-9.2		-4.6
WAS	129	0	**27**	1	1307.0	1577	29	450	371	14.5	4.52	81	.297	.360	-134	-125	102	256	***161***	.929	443	56	119	-4.2	-11.7	-.4		-8.7
STL	133	0	26	2	1324.1	1584	32	372	288	13.9	4.53	83	.295	.350	-137	-106	105	241	*158*	.939	388	56	97	-1.2	-9.9	-13.3		-11.6
TOT	1609	87	246	17	15954.2					12.9	3.60		.271	.334						.942	4387	730	1354					

Batter-Fielder Wins	Batting Average	On-Base Percentage	Slugging Average	On-Base Plus Slugging	Adjusted OPS	Adjusted Batter Runs
Jennings-Bal 4.9	Keeler-Bal 385	Hamilton-Bos 480	Anderson-Br-Ws-Br .494	Hamilton-Bos........933	Hamilton-Bos........159	Delahanty-Phi 47.8
Dahlen-Chi 4.3	Hamilton-Bos 369	McGraw-Bal................475	Collins-Bos 479	Delahanty-Phi 880	Delahanty-Phi 159	McGraw-Bal........43.7
Davis-NY.............4.0	McGraw-Bal 342	Jennings-Bal 454	Lajoie-Phi 461	Flick-Phi...............878	Flick-Phi...............158	Jennings-Bal 43.7
Delahanty-Phi 3.9	Smith-Cin 342	Flick-Phi......................430	Delahanty-Phi.......454	Jennings-Bal 876	Jennings-Bal 149	Flick-Phi.............40.9
Collins-Bos..........3.9	Burkett-Cle 341	Delahanty-Phi 426	Hamilton-Bos 453	McGraw-Bal..........871	McGraw-Bal..........148	Hamilton-Bos......39.2

Runs	Hits	Doubles	Triples	Home Runs	Total Bases	Runs Batted In
McGraw-Bal..........143	Keeler-Bal 216	Lajoie-Phi 43	Anderson-Br-Ws-Br ..22	Collins-Bos 15	Collins-Bos 286	Lajoie-Phi 127
Jennings-Bal 135	Burkett-Cle............213	Delahanty-Phi 36	VanHaltren-NY........16	Wagner-Lou...........10	Lajoie-Phi 280	Collins-Bos 111
VanHaltren-NY......129	VanHaltren-NY......204	Dahlen-Chi 35	Hoy-Lou 16	Joyce-NY 10	VanHaltren-NY......270	Kelley-Bal 110
Keeler-Bal 126	Lajoie-Phi 197	Collins-Bos 35		Anderson-Br-Ws-Br 9	Anderson-Br-Ws-Br 257	Duffy-Bos 108
Cooley-Phi............123		Anderson-Br-Ws-Br 33		McKean-Cle..............9	Cooley-Phi............256	McGann-Bal 106

Stolen Bases	Base Stealing Runs	Fielding Runs-Infield	Fielding Runs-Outfield	Wins	Winning Pct.	Complete Games
Delahanty-Phi 58		Davis-NY 29.5	Selbach-Was 19.4	Nichols-Bos 31	Lewis-Bos.............765	Taylor-StL 42
Hamilton-Bos..........54		Cross-StL...................20.4	Harley-StL 8.3	Cunningham-Lou....28	Maul-Bal 741	Cunningham-Lou ..41
DeMontreville-Bal 49		Dahlen-Chi..................20.1	Anderson-Br-Ws-Br ..7.4	McJames-Bal..........27	Nichols-Bos 721	Young-Cle..............40
Dexter-Lou.............44		Wallace-Cle 18.3	Delahanty-Phi........7.0	Hawley-Cin 27	Hawley-Cin 711	Nichols-Bos 40
McGraw-Bal...........43		Gleason-NY 17.6	F.Clarke-Lou 6.5	Lewis-Bos 26	Griffith-Chi 706	McJames-Bal 40

Strikeouts	Fewest BB/Game	Games	Saves	Base Runners/9	Adjusted Relief Runs	Relief Ranking
Seymour-NY 239	Young-Cle..............98	Taylor-StL 50	Nichols-Bos 4	Nichols-Bos 9.63		
McJames-Bal........178	Dwyer-Cin.............1.58	Nichols-Bos 50	Tannehill-Pit.............2	Maul-Bal 9.76		
Willis-Bos.............160	Cunningham-Lou 1.62	Young-Cle.......................46	Lewis-Bos 2	Young-Cle..........10.41		
Nichols-Bos 138	Tannehill-Pit 1.74		Hickman-Bos 2	Griffith-Chi 10.75		
Piatt-Phi................121	Griffith-Chi 1.77		Dammann-Cin 2	McJames-Bal 10.88		

Innings Pitched	Opponents' Avg.	Opponents' OBP	Earned Run Average	Adjusted ERA	Adjusted Starter Runs	Pitcher Wins
Taylor-StL 397.1	Nichols-Bos 221	Nichols-Bos 272	Griffith-Chi 1.88	Griffith-Chi 190	Griffith-Chi 63.3	**Nichols-Bos** 6.4
Nichols-Bos 388.0	Willis-Bos 229	Maul-Bal 275	Maul-Bal 2.10	Nichols-Bos 173	Nichols-Bos 62.5	**Griffith-Chi** 5.9
Young-Cle..........377.2	Lewis-Bos 229	Young-Cle 288	Nichols-Bos 2.13	Maul-Bal 170	McJames-Bal 49.2	**Maul-Bal** 4.4
McJames-Bal 374.0	Maul-Bal 232	Griffith-Chi 294	McJames-Bal 2.36	McJames-Bal........151	Maul-Bal 42.2	**Young-Cle** 4.4
Cunningham-Lou362.0	McJames-Bal 234	McJames-Bal..............297	Callahan-Chi........2.46	Callahan-Chi 145	Young-Cle............40.4	**McJames-Bal** 4.3

Beans in My Ears

In another move geared to make the game cleaner and more orderly, the NL voted to allow two umpires to be assigned to cover any game. The league also instituted a rule to prevent balks and began approaching the modern standard of what constitutes a stolen base.

Pitching continued to have the upper hand, as scoring per team dipped to 4.96 runs per game, the lowest mark in a decade. Clark Griffith's 1.88 ERA for Chicago was the game's best since the 1880s. Griffith was a fine pitcher—although a better manager and executive in the next century—and his '98 performance was by far the best of his career.

Helping to spell ace Kid Nichols, rookie hurler Vic Willis won 25 for Boston. The Beaneaters took their second straight flag by holding off a great Baltimore club. Boston's Jimmy Collins, the finest defensive third baseman of his day, also led in homers, and Hugh Duffy and Billy Hamilton were outstanding.

The Orioles led the league in scoring, with John McGraw, Willie Keeler, Hugh Jennings, and Joe Kelley providing the punch. A five-man pitching staff of obscurities and unexpected heroes kept Baltimore in the race until the end.

Giants outfielder George Van Haltren played 156 games, a mark that stood until 1904. Attendance fell, due in part to the Spanish-American War, and also because the twelve-team format hurt interest in many cities. Several clubs were so bad that their chances to win were finished by May. Crowds in Chicago rose dramatically as the Colts hosted more games than usual. The Cleveland Spiders, unpopular despite a winning record and the excellent pitching of Cy Young, were a traveling team much of the season.

Rookies included hurler Sam Leever, future Chicago standouts Harry Steinfeldt and Frank Chance, and two other up-and-comers, Elmer Flick and Tommy Leach. In his first full season, Honus Wagner led Louisville in homers and RBIs.

There was no Temple Cup in 1898—or ever again. Dwindling interest by fans and players alike led to the dissolution of the postseason series after four years.

1899 National League

TEAM	W	L	T	PCT	GB	HW	HL	R	OR	PA	H	2B	3B	HR	BB	SO	HB	SH	AVG	OBP	SLG	OPS	AOPS	BR	ABR	PF	SB	CS	BSA	BSR
BRO	100	47	3	.680		**60**	16	892	658	5614	1436	178	97	27	477	263	75	**125**	.291	**.368**	.383	751	110	89	70	102	271			
BOS	95	57	1	.625	7.5	53	26	858	**645**	5897	1517	178	90	39	431	269	133	43	.287	.345	.377	722	94	20	-53	110	185			
PHI	94	58	2	.618	8.5	58	25	**916**	743	5986	**1613**	**241**	83	31	441	341	117	75	**.301**	.363	**.395**	**758**	**118**	**100**	**134**	97	212			
BAL	86	62	4	.581	14.5	51	24	827	691	5707	1509	204	71	17	418	383	94	122	.297	.365	.376	741	104	73	30	105	**364**			
STL	84	67	4	.556	18	50	33	819	739	5913	1514	172	88	**47**	468	**262**	108	33	.285	.347	.378	725	102	27	8	102	210			
CIN	83	67	7	.553	18.5	57	29	861	777	5946	1448	195	106	13	**487**	300	133	67	.275	.344	.360	704	96	-5	-19	102	228			
PIT	76	73	6	.510	25	49	34	841	771	6079	1582	196	**121**	29	386	346	144	63	.288	.342	.384	726	104	22	25	100	179			
CHI	75	73	4	.507	25.5	44	39	812	763	5766	1428	173	82	27	406	342	148	64	.277	.338	.359	697	99	-26	-5	97	247			
LOU	75	76	5	.497	27	33	28	833	782	6014	1491	195	70	40	437	379	**163**	78	.279	.343	.365	708	100	-1	1	100	234			
NY	60	90	3	.400	41.5	35	38	741	868	5621	1441	165	66	23	389	361	61	46	.281	.337	.353	690	98	-38	-11	97	235			
WAS	54	98	3	.355	48.5	35	43	743	983	5783	1429	162	87	**47**	350	341	90	87	.272	.328	.363	691	96	-48	-40	99	176			
CLE	20	134	0	.130	83.5	9	33	529	1252	5690	1333	142	50	12	289	280	57	65	.253	.299	.305	604	76	-213	-168	93	127			
TOT	923					534	368	9672		70016	17741	2201	1011	352	4979	3867	868	1323	.282	.343	.366	710					2668			

TEAM	CG	SHO	GR	SV	IP	H	HR	BB	SO	BR/9	ERA	AERA	OAV	OOB	PR	APR	PF	OSB	OCS	FA	E	WPB	DP	FW	PW	BW	BSW	DIF
BRO	121	9	30	**9**	1269.1	1320	32	463	331	13.0	**3.25**	120	.268	.337	85	91	102	229	*178*	.948	314	52	125	2.9	8.2	6.3		9.0
BOS	138	13	17	4	1348.0	**1273**	44	432	385	**11.8**	3.26	**127**	**.250**	**.317**	**87**	**123**	108	193	*169*	**.952**	**303**	58	124	**4.0**	**11.1**	-4.8		8.7
PHI	129	**15**	26	2	1333.1	1398	17	370	281	12.5	3.47	106	.270	.329	56	31	96	206	*178*	.940	379	85	110	-.3	2.8	**12.1**		3.3
BAL	132	9	20	5	1304.1	1403	**13**	349	294	12.6	3.31	119	.275	.330	78	90	103	**176**	*127*	.949	308	59	96	3.6	8.2	2.7		-2.4
STL	134	7	23	1	1340.2	1476	41	**321**	331	12.4	3.36	118	.280	.328	73	88	103	180	*173*	.939	397	48	117	-1.2	8.0	.7		1.0
CIN	131	8	28	5	1373.0	1494	26	372	361	12.7	3.70	106	.278	.334	23	30	102	177	*161*	.947	341	43	113	2.3	2.7	-1.7		4.7
PIT	118	9	**39**	4	1373.0	1471	27	438	338	13.0	3.61	105	.274	.337	36	30	99	195	*185*	.945	363	53	100	.8	2.7	2.3		-4.3
CHI	**147**	8	5	1	1331.1	1433	20	330	313	12.5	3.37	111	.275	.328	71	56	97	206	*171*	.935	428	33	**145**	-3.5	5.1	-.5		-.2
LOU	135	5	22	2	1360.1	1517	35	325	288	12.6	3.43	112	.282	.331	63	62	100	197	*171*	.939	399	**30**	103	-1.2	5.6	.0		-5.0
NY	139	4	14	0	1290.2	1463	19	630	**402**	15.3	4.27	88	.286	.375	-61	-80	97	249	*192*	.932	434	97	142	-3.7	-7.3	-1.0		-3.1
WAS	131	3	28	0	1300.1	1649	35	422	328	14.9	4.93	79	.309	.368	-157	-147	102	288	*197*	.935	403	60	99	-1.6	-13.3	-3.6		-3.5
CLE	138	0	18	0	1264.0	1844	43	527	215	17.7	6.37	58	.340	.409	-354	-396	96	372	***218***	.937	388	66	121	-.8	-35.9	-15.2		-5.1
TOT	1593	90	270	33	15888.1					13.4	3.85		.282	.343						.942	4457	684	1395					

Batter-Fielder Wins	Batting Average	On-Base Percentage	Slugging Average	On-Base Plus Slugging	Adjusted OPS	Adjusted Batter Runs
G.Davis-NY 6.1	Delahanty-Phi .410	McGraw-Bal .547	Delahanty-Phi .582	Delahanty-Phi 1046	Delahanty-Phi 193	Delahanty-Phi 76.5
Delahanty-Phi 5.9	Burkett-StL .396	Delahanty-Phi .464	Freeman-Was .563	McGraw-Bal 994	McGraw-Bal 165	McGraw-Bal 52.6
McGraw-Bal 4.9	McGraw-Bal .391	Burkett-StL .463	Williams-Pit .530	Burkett-StL 963	Burkett-StL 160	Burkett-StL 49.2
Williams-Pit 4.7	Keeler-Bro .379	Thomas-Phi .457	Wagner-Lou .501	Williams-Pit 946	Williams-Pit 159	Williams-Pit 48.7
Wallace-StL 4.4	Williams-Pit .354	Stahl-Bos .426	Burkett-StL .500	Freeman-Was 925	Freeman-Was 154	Thomas-Phi 36.6

Runs	Hits	Doubles	Triples	Home Runs	Total Bases	Runs Batted In
McGraw-Bal 140	Delahanty-Phi 238	Delahanty-Phi 55	Williams-Pit 27	Freeman-Was 25	Delahanty-Phi 338	Delahanty-Phi 137
Keeler-Bro 140	Burkett-StL 221	Wagner-Lou 45	Freeman-Was 25	Wallace-StL 12	Freeman-Was 331	Freeman-Was 122
Thomas-Phi 137	Williams-Pit 220	Holmes-Bal 31	Stahl-Bos 19	Williams-Pit 9	Williams-Pit 329	Williams-Pit 116
Delahanty-Phi 135	Keeler-Bro 216	Long-Bos 30	Tenney-Bos 17	Mertes-Chi 9	Wagner-Lou 288	Wagner-Lou 114
Williams-Pit 126	Tenney-Bos 209	Duffy-Bos 29	McCarthy-Pit 17	Delahanty-Phi 9	Stahl-Bos 284	Wallace-StL 108

Stolen Bases	Base Stealing Runs	Fielding Runs-Infield	Fielding Runs-Outfield	Wins	Winning Pct.	Complete Games
Sheckard-Bal 77		G.Davis-NY 46.3	Sheckard-Bal 19.4	McGinnity-Bal 28	Hughes-Bro .824	Young-StL 40
McGraw-Bal 73		Cross-Cle-StL 35.6	Slagle-Was 18.2	Hughes-Bro 28	Willis-Bos .771	Powell-StL 40
Heidrick-StL 55		Wallace-StL 30.3	Selbach-Cin 10.9	Willis-Bos 27	Hahn-Cin .742	Carrick-NY 40
Holmes-Bal 50		Gleason-NY 28.6	Kelley-Bro 9.8	Young-StL 26	Donahue-Phi .724	Taylor-Chi 39
Clarke-Lou 49		Collins-Bos 17.8	Lange-Chi 8.5	Tannehill-Pit 24	Kennedy-Bro .710	McGinnity-Bal 38

Strikeouts	Fewest BB/Game	Games	Saves	Base Runners/9	Adjusted Relief Runs	Relief Ranking
Hahn-Cin 145	Young-StL 1.07	Leever-Pit 51	Leever-Pit 3	Young-StL 10.19		
Seymour-NY 142	Cuppy-StL 1.36	Powell-StL 48		Waddell-Lou 10.37		
Leever-Pit 121	Tannehill-Pit 1.45	McGinnity-Bal 48		Hahn-Cin 10.43		
Willis-Bos 120	Woods-Lou 1.79	Young-StL 44		Orth-Phi 10.64		
Doheny-NY 120	Kitson-Bal 1.79	Carrick-NY 44		Nichols-Bos 10.85		

Innings Pitched	Opponents' Avg.	Opponents' OBP	Earned Run Average	Adjusted ERA	Adjusted Starter Runs	Pitcher Wins
Leever-Pit 379.0	Willis-Bos .222	Young-StL .285	Orth-Phi 2.49	Willis-Bos 166	Willis-Bos 58.2	**Young-StL** 5.1
Powell-StL 373.0	Hughes-Bro .232	Hahn-Cin .290	Willis-Bos 2.50	Young-StL 154	Young-StL 49.9	**Willis-Bos** 4.8
Young-StL 369.1	Hahn-Cin .242	Nichols-Bos .298	Young-StL 2.58	McGinnity-Bal 148	McGinnity-Bal 48.2	**Hughes-Bro** 4.6
McGinnity-Bal 366.1	Seymour-NY .245	Kitson-Bal .303	Bernhard-Phi 2.65	Hahn-Cin 146	Kitson-Bal 41.9	**McGinnity-Bal** 4.5
Carrick-NY 361.2	Leever-Pit .247	Willis-Bos .304	McGinnity-Bal 2.68	Hughes-Bro 145	Hahn-Cin 41.1	**Tannehill-Pit** 4.3

Syndicate Bosses

It was a year destroyed by syndicate ownership. The Robison brothers, detested owners of the Cleveland Spiders, decided to also buy the St. Louis Browns, and siphoned off Cleveland players to contribute to the Browns' effort. Public anger at this sham forced the Spiders, already a traveling team for much of 1898, back to the road. The horrible club finished 84 games out and lost 134 times, both all-time lows. The 6,088 who paid to see the club in Cleveland (the average crowd was 145), was the smallest turnstile count in NL history. It was only right that the Browns finished fifth, although they were second in attendance.

Baltimore suffered through a similar debacle. Orioles stars Ned Hanlon, Willie Keeler, Hughie Jennings, and Joe Kelley were transferred to Brooklyn. John McGraw, however, stayed behind, and took over as player-manager. Wilbert Robinson, who happened to be Mugsy's partner in a Baltimore billiard parlor and bowling alley, also stayed put and batted .284 as the club's regular catcher. McGraw posted a .547 on-base percentage—the highest in the majors until 1941—for his beloved Orioles, who played surprisingly well.

The Bridegrooms used their mother lode to win the crown. Keeler tied for the league lead (with McGraw) in runs, and pitcher Jim Hughes paced in wins. It was a team effort—Hanlon's club had few weaknesses. Boston finished second as Vic Willis became arguably the league's top starter, and Ed Delahanty's bat crown and 55 doubles (the most until 1923) powered the third-place Phillies.

To eliminate unnecessary trickery, catchers were required to stay in their box when pitches were delivered. And from this point on all players' uniforms on the same team had to conform. Several big names debuted, including Joe McGinnity, Deacon Phillippe, Jack Chesbro, Turkey Mike Donlin, and Sam Crawford.

Realizing the inevitable—that twelve teams made no sense, economically or otherwise—the NL contracted Louisville (owned by Barney Dreyfus, who also controlled Pittsburgh), Washington, Baltimore, and Cleveland for 1900. Such wisdom came too late, especially for the Spiders and their remaining fans. National League owners would reap the fruits of their poor stewardship of the game about a year later.

1900 National League

TEAM	W	L	T	PCT	GB	HW	HL	R	OR	PA	H	2B	3B	HR	BB	SO	HB	SH	AVG	OBP	SLG	OPS	AOPS	BR	ABR	PF	SB	CS	BSA	BSR
BRO	82	54	6	.603		43	26	**816**	722	5440	1423	199	81	26	421	**272**	78	**81**	**.293**	**.359**	**.383**	**742**	104	**75**	29	106	**274**			
PIT	79	60	1	.568	4.5	42	28	733	**612**	5317	1312	185	**100**	26	327	321	110	63	.272	.327	.368	695	96	-27	-32	101	174			
PHI	75	63	3	.543	8	**45**	23	810	792	5594	**1439**	187	82	29	**440**	374	113	72	.290	.356	.378	734	**109**	60	**67**	99	205			
BOS	66	72	4	.478	17	42	29	778	739	5499	1403	163	68	**48**	395	278	107	45	.283	.342	.373	715	92	15	-69	112	182			
STL	65	75	2	.464	19	40	31	744	748	5444	1420	141	81	36	406	318	80	**81**	.291	.356	.375	731	108	50	56	99	243			
CHI	65	75	6	.464	19	**45**	30	635	751	5445	1276	**202**	51	33	343	383	**130**	65	.260	.317	.342	659	90	-85	-60	96	189			
CIN	62	77	5	.446	21.5	27	34	703	745	5517	1335	178	83	33	333	408	108	50	.266	.318	.354	672	92	-73	-56	98	183			
NY	60	78	3	.435	23	38	31	713	823	5229	1317	177	61	23	369	343	80	56	.279	.338	.357	695	102	-15	19	95	236			
TOT	569					322	232	5932		43485	10925	1432	607	254	3034	2697	513	806	.279	.339	.366	705					1686			

TEAM	CG	SHO	GR	SV	IP	H	HR	BB	SO	BR/9	ERA	AERA	OAV	OOB	PR	APR	PF	OSB	OCS	FA	E	WPB	DP	FW	PW	BW	BSW	DIF
BRO	104	8	**40**	**4**	1225.2	1370	30	405	300	13.6	3.89	98	.282	.346	-27	-9	104	213	*156*	.948	303	**51**	102	2.6	-.8	2.7		9.6
PIT	114	11	30	1	1229.0	**1232**	24	**295**	**415**	**11.7**	**3.06**	**119**	**.261**	**.313**	**87**	**79**	98	**166**	*151*	.945	322	71	106	1.1	**7.2**	-2.9		4.1
PHI	116	7	28	3	1248.2	1506	29	402	284	14.2	4.12	88	.298	.357	-59	-73	98	272	***185***	.945	330	80	**125**	.8	-6.7	**6.1**		5.8
BOS	116	8	29	2	1240.1	1263	59	463	340	12.9	3.72	111	.264	.335	-4	49	112	213	*165*	**.953**	**273**	85	86	**4.4**	4.5	-6.3		-5.6
STL	117	**12**	26	0	1217.1	1373	37	299	325	12.7	3.75	97	.284	.331	-7	-17	98	216	*167*	.943	331	55	73	.8	-1.6	5.1		-9.4
CHI	**137**	9	9	1	1271.0	1375	**21**	324	357	12.6	3.23	112	.276	.330	66	53	98	234	*172*	.933	418	63	98	-3.9	4.8	-5.5		-.4
CIN	118	9	27	1	1274.2	1383	28	404	399	13.0	3.83	96	.276	.338	-20	-24	99	190	*177*	.945	341	77	120	.5	-2.2	-5.1		-.7
NY	113	4	31	0	1207.1	1423	26	442	277	14.6	3.96	91	.293	.363	-35	-49	98	182	*177*	.928	439	69	124	-6.0	-4.5	1.7		-.3
TOT	935	68	220	12	9914.0					13.2	3.69		.279	.339						.942	2757	551	834					

Batter-Fielder Wins
- **Flick-Phi** 4.5
- **Lajoie-Phi** 4.4
- **Davis-NY** 4.3
- **Wagner-Pit** 4.1
- **Selbach-NY** 3.7

Batting Average
- Wagner-Pit 381
- Flick-Phi 367
- Burkett-StL 363
- Keeler-Bro 362
- McGraw-StL 344

On-Base Percentage
- McGraw-StL................505
- Thomas-Phi 451
- Hamilton-Bos 449
- Flick-Phi......................441
- Wagner-Pit...................434

Slugging Average
- Wagner-Pit 573
- Flick-Phi 545
- Lajoie-Phi 510
- Kelley-Bro 485
- Hickman-NY 482

On-Base Plus Slugging
- Wagner-Pit.........1007
- Flick-Phi...............986
- McGraw-StL..........921
- Burkett-StL...........904
- Selbach-NY 885

Adjusted OPS
- Wagner-Pit...........175
- Flick-Phi...............172
- McGraw-StL..........157
- Selbach-NY 151
- Burkett-StL............150

Adjusted Batter Runs
- Flick-Phi..............55.6
- Wagner-Pit 53.3
- Selbach-NY 41.1
- Burkett-StL 39.3
- McGraw-StL 38.4

Runs
- Thomas-Phi..........132
- Slagle-Phi 115
- VanHaltren-NY......114
- Barrett-Cin............114
- Wagner-Pit...........107

Hits
- Keeler-Bro 204
- Burkett-StL............203
- Wagner-Pit...........201
- Flick-Phi...............200
- Beckley-Cin 190

Doubles
- Wagner-Pit 45
- Lajoie-Phi 33
- Flick-Phi 32
- Delahanty-Phi 32
- VanHaltren-NY 30

Triples
- Wagner-Pit.............22
- Kelley-Bro 17
- Hickman-NY 17
- Stahl-Bos 16
- Flick-Phi.................16

Home Runs
- Long-Bos 12
- Flick-Phi.................11
- Donlin-StL 10
- Hickman-NY 9
- Sullivan-Bos.............8

Total Bases
- Wagner-Pit...........302
- Flick-Phi...............297
- Burkett-StL...........265
- Keeler-Bro 253
- Beckley-Cin 242

Runs Batted In
- Flick-Phi 110
- Delahanty-Phi......109
- Wagner-Pit 100
- Collins-Bos 95
- Beckley-Cin 94

Stolen Bases
- VanHaltren-NY........45
- Donovan-StL 45
- Barrett-Cin.............44
- Keeler-Bro 41

Base Stealing Runs

Fielding Runs-Infield
- Davis-NY 28.7
- Lajoie-Phi...................22.4
- Dahlen-Bro 21.2
- Steinfeldt-Cin 16.1
- Childs-Chi 14.5

Fielding Runs-Outfield
- Selbach-NY 12.4
- VanHaltren-NY 8.5
- Keeler-Bro 5.7
- Burkett-StL 5.6
- Stahl-Bos 4.5

Wins
- McGinnity-Bro 28
- Tannehill-Pit............20
- Phillippe-Pit 20
- Kennedy-Bro 20
- Dinneen-Bos 20

Winning Pct.
- McGinnity-Bro.......778
- Tannehill-Pit 769
- Fraser-Phi............625
- Phillippe-Pit 606
- Kennedy-Bro.........606

Complete Games
- Hawley-NY 34
- Dinneen-Bos 33

Strikeouts
- Hahn-Cin 132
- Waddell-Pit 130
- Young-StL 115
- Garvin-Chi 107
- Dinneen-Bos 107

Fewest BB/Game
- Young-StL............1.01
- Phillippe-Pit 1.35
- Tannehill-Pit 1.65
- Griffith-Chi 1.85
- Leever-Pit 1.86

Games
- Carrick-NY 45
- McGinnity-Bro................44
- Scott-Cin.......................42
- Kennedy-Bro..................42

Saves
- Kitson-Bro 4
- Bernhard-Phi 2

Base Runners/9
- Phillippe-Pit 10.42
- Waddell-Pit 10.52
- Young-StL..........10.53
- Garvin-Chi 11.18
- Leever-Pit..........11.30

Adjusted Relief Runs

Relief Ranking

Innings Pitched
- McGinnity-Bro....343.0
- Carrick-NY 341.2
- Hawley-NY 329.1
- Young-StL..........321.1
- Dinneen-Bos......320.2

Opponents' Avg.
- Waddell-Pit 229
- Garvin-Chi 243
- Nichols-Bos 246
- Dinneen-Bos.........250
- Phillippe-Pit 257

Opponents' OBP
- Phillippe-Pit 289
- Waddell-Pit 291
- Young-StL 291
- Garvin-Chi 304
- Leever-Pit.....................306

Earned Run Average
- Waddell-Pit 2.37
- Garvin-Chi 2.41
- Taylor-Chi 2.55
- Leever-Pit 2.71
- Sudhoff-StL 2.76

Adjusted ERA
- Waddell-Pit 153
- Garvin-Chi 149
- Taylor-Chi 141
- Nichols-Bos 134
- Leever-Pit 134

Adjusted Starter Runs
- Dinneen-Bos........31.8
- Garvin-Chi 28.0
- Young-StL............27.8
- Phillippe-Pit 25.7
- Leever-Pit 24.8

Pitcher Wins
- **Dinneen-Bos**......3.1
- **Tannehill-Pit** 2.7
- **Young-StL** 2.6
- **Leever-Pit** 2.5
- **Garvin-Chi**..........2.4

The Last One-Horse Town

In January 1900 Boston Beaneaters catcher Marty Bergen, injured the previous season and possibly despondent over finances, killed himself and his entire family. The horrific crime was the beginning of the end of a once-great Boston franchise.

The new century saw a streamlined, eight-club NL, free of syndicate ownership and with no team finishing more than 23 games out of first place. The rules committee changed home plate from a 12-inch square to a five-sided shape 17 inches wide, largely for the benefit of umpires.

Brooklyn, now named the Superbas, won the flag again, leading the league in scoring and benefiting from the strong arm of former Oriole "Iron Man" Joe McGinnity, who led the league in wins, but also in walks and hit batsmen (40, the most ever). Second-place Pittsburgh, fortified with stars Honus Wagner, who won his first bat crown, Deacon Phillippe, Rube Waddell, and Fred Clarke from Louisville, made it a close race and positioned themselves as an up-and-coming club.

In the last postseason series between NL clubs until 1969, the Superbas took on the Pirates. Like the Temple Cup this trophy originated in Pittsburgh, and it was even less popular than the first try earlier in the decade. Brooklyn won three of four games from the Pirates for the Chronicle-Telegram Cup. Only one crowd of more than 2,500 came out to see the series.

St. Louis, having changed its name to the Cardinals, purchased John McGraw and Wilbert Robinson, who again refused the call to join Brooklyn after the Orioles disbanded. McGraw once more led the league in on-base percentage, but the Cards ended tied for fifth. A young pitcher with last-place New York went 0–3, but this was just the start for Christy Mathewson.

It was also the beginning of the American League, formerly the minor Western League. President Ban Johnson declared the AL a major for 1900 and fielded eight clubs, one in Chicago and seven in former National League or American Association cities. The new loop counted George Stallings, Connie Mack, and Charlie Comiskey among its skippers, and would soon enter into a fierce battle for talent with the NL—and help save baseball in the process.

1901 National League

TEAM	W	L	T	PCT	GB	HW	HL	R	OR	PA	H	2B	3B	HR	BB	SO	HB	SH	AVG	OBP	SLG	OPS	AOPS	BR	ABR	PF	SB	CS	BSA	BSR
PIT	90	49	1	.647		45	24	776	**534**	5468	1407	182	92	29	386	493	117	52	.286	**.345**	.379	**724**	113	**99**	77	103	**203**			
PHI	83	57	0	.593	7.5	**46**	23	668	543	5411	1275	194	58	24	**430**	549	126	62	.266	.334	.346	680	101	33	20	102	199			
BRO	79	57	1	.581	9.5	43	25	744	600	5312	1399	**206**	93	32	312	**449**	80	41	**.287**	.335	**.387**	722	112	86	67	103	178			
STL	76	64	2	.543	14.5	40	31	**792**	689	5565	**1430**	187	**94**	**39**	314	540	122	**90**	.284	.337	.381	718	**120**	86	**126**	95	190			
BOS	69	69	2	.500	20.5	41	29	531	556	5218	1180	135	36	28	303	519	**135**	34	.249	.298	.310	608	75	-105	-149	109	158			
CHI	53	86	1	.381	37	30	39	578	699	5277	1250	153	61	18	314	532	67	52	.258	.310	.326	636	93	-58	-36	96	204			
NY	52	85	4	.380	37	30	38	544	755	5260	1225	167	46	19	303	575	73	45	.253	.303	.318	621	90	-83	-60	96	133			
CIN	52	87	3	.374	38	27	43	561	818	5392	1232	173	70	38	323	584	113	42	.251	.303	.338	641	97	-57	-15	93	137			
TOT	561					302	252	5194		42903	10398	1397	550	227	2685	4241	418	833	.267	.321	.348	669					1402			

TEAM	CG	SHO	GR	SV	IP	H	HR	BB	SO	BR/9	ERA	AERA	OAV	OOB	PR	APR	PF	OSB	OCS	FA	E	WPB	DP	FW	PW	BW	BSW	DIF
PIT	119	**15**	21	4	1244.2	1198	20	**244**	505	**10.9**	**2.58**	**126**	.252	**.297**	**102**	**95**	98	**133**	*124*	.950	287	**44**	97	1.2	**9.3**	7.5		2.4
PHI	125	**15**	16	2	1246.2	1221	19	259	480	11.0	2.87	119	.255	.300	63	71	102	171	*135*	**.954**	**262**	61	65	**2.7**	7.0	2.0		1.4
BRO	111	7	26	**5**	1213.2	1244	**18**	435	583	12.8	3.14	107	.264	.333	24	27	101	213	*151*	.950	281	59	99	1.2	2.6	6.6		.6
STL	118	5	**29**	**5**	1269.2	1333	39	332	445	12.2	3.68	86	.268	.321	-51	-74	96	186	*146*	.949	305	63	**108**	.4	-7.3	**12.3**		.5
BOS	128	11	13	0	1263.0	**1196**	29	349	558	11.3	2.90	125	**.249**	.305	59	91	109	139	*128*	.952	282	45	89	1.5	8.9	-14.6		4.2
CHI	**131**	2	9	0	1241.2	1348	27	324	**586**	12.5	3.33	97	.275	.327	-2	-14	98	189	*143*	.943	336	61	87	-1.8	-1.4	-3.5		-9.8
NY	118	11	24	1	1232.0	1389	24	377	542	13.4	3.87	85	.283	.342	-75	-79	99	205	***154***	.941	348	97	81	-2.3	-7.7	-5.9		-.5
CIN	126	4	18	0	1265.2	1469	51	365	542	13.5	4.17	77	.289	.345	-120	-143	96	166	*143*	.940	355	**44**	102	-2.6	-14.0	-1.5		.6
TOT	976	70	156	17	9977.0					12.2	3.32		.267	.321						.947	2456	474	728					

Batter-Fielder Wins	Batting Average	On-Base Percentage	Slugging Average	On-Base Plus Slugging	Adjusted OPS	Adjusted Batter Runs
Burkett-StL 5.5	Burkett-StL .376	Burkett-StL .440	Sheckard-Bro .534	Delahanty-Phi .955	Burkett-StL 184	Burkett-StL 66.1
Wallace-StL 5.4	Delahanty-Phi .354	Thomas-Phi .437	Delahanty-Phi .528	Burkett-StL .949	Delahanty-Phi 173	Delahanty-Phi 52.1
Davis-NY 4.6	Sheckard-Bro .354	Delahanty-Phi .427	Crawford-Cin .524	Sheckard-Bro .944	Crawford-Cin 172	Hartsel-Chi 47.7
Flick-Phi 4.5	Wagner-Pit .353	Wagner-Pit .417	Burkett-StL .509	Wagner-Pit .911	Sheckard-Bro 168	Sheckard-Bro 46.7
Wagner-Pit 4.4	Keeler-Bro .339	Hartsel-Chi .414	Flick-Phi .500	Crawford-Cin .903	Hartsel-Chi 163	Crawford-Cin 44.0

Runs	Hits	Doubles	Triples	Home Runs	Total Bases	Runs Batted In
Burkett-StL 142	Burkett-StL 226	Delahanty-Phi 38	Sheckard-Bro 19	Crawford-Cin 16	Burkett-StL 306	Wagner-Pit 126
Keeler-Bro 123	Keeler-Bro 202	Daly-Bro 38	Flick-Phi 17	Sheckard-Bro 11	Sheckard-Bro 296	Delahanty-Phi 108
Beaumont-Pit 120	Sheckard-Bro 196	Wagner-Pit 37		Burkett-StL 10	Delahanty-Phi 286	Sheckard-Bro 104
Clarke-Pit 118	Wagner-Pit 194	Beckley-Cin 36			Wagner-Pit 271	Crawford-Cin 104
Sheckard-Bro 116	Delahanty-Phi 192	Wallace-StL 34				

Stolen Bases	Base Stealing Runs	Fielding Runs-Infield	Fielding Runs-Outfield	Wins	Winning Pct.	Complete Games
Wagner-Pit 49		Wallace-StL 27.2	Flick-Phi 13.9	Donovan-Bro 25	Chesbro-Pit .677	Hahn-Cin 41
Hartsel-Chi 41		Davis-NY 24.3	Sheckard-Bro 9.2	Harper-StL 23	Phillippe-Pit .647	Taylor-NY 37
Strang-NY 40		Dahlen-Bro 13.6	Green-Chi 6.6	Phillippe-Pit 22	Tannehill-Pit .643	Mathewson-NY 36
Harley-Cin 37		Daly-Bro 10.3	VanHaltren-NY 4.1	Hahn-Cin 22	Harper-StL .639	Donovan-Bro 36
Beaumont-Pit 36		Leach-Pit 10.1	Nichols-StL 4.0	Chesbro-Pit 21	Kitson-Bro .633	

Strikeouts	Fewest BB/Game	Games	Saves	Base Runners/9	Adjusted Relief Runs	Relief Ranking
Hahn-Cin 239	Orth-Phi 1.02	Taylor-NY 45	Powell-StL 3	Orth-Phi 9.27		
Donovan-Bro 226	Phillippe-Pit 1.16	Powell-StL 45	Donovan-Bro 3	Phillippe-Pit 9.79		
Hughes-Chi 225	Tannehill-Pit 1.28	Donovan-Bro 45	Sudhoff-StL 2	Tannehill-Pit 10.20		
Mathewson-NY 221	Duggleby-Phi 1.30	Hahn-Cin 42	Phillippe-Pit 2	Chesbro-Pit 10.23		
Waddell-Pit-Chi 172	Powell-StL 1.33	Mathewson-NY 40	Kitson-Bro 2	Willis-Bos 10.35		

Innings Pitched	Opponents' Avg.	Opponents' OBP	Earned Run Average	Adjusted ERA	Adjusted Starter Runs	Pitcher Wins
Hahn-Cin 375.1	Townsend-Phi .223	Orth-Phi .264	Tannehill-Pit 2.18	Willis-Bos 153	Willis-Bos 38.5	**Orth-Phi** 4.4
Taylor-NY 353.1	Mathewson-NY .230	Phillippe-Pit .275	Phillippe-Pit 2.22	Tannehill-Pit 150	Orth-Phi 33.1	**Willis-Bos** 4.2
Donovan-Bro 351.0	Willis-Bos .231	Tannehill-Pit .284	Orth-Phi 2.27	Orth-Phi 150	Phillippe-Pit 33.0	**Phillippe-Pit** 4.1
Powell-StL 338.1	Orth-Phi .237	Chesbro-Pit .284	Willis-Bos 2.36	Phillippe-Pit 147	Mathewson-NY 32.4	**Mathewson-NY** 3.6
Mathewson-NY 336.0	Chesbro-Pit .241	Willis-Bos .286	Chesbro-Pit 2.38	Chesbro-Pit 137	Chesbro-Pit 32.1	**Tannehill-Pit** 3.3

Contraction Leads to Competition as Scoring Drops

While the upstart AL's player raids damaged the Senior Circuit, the eight NL franchises were stable and remained in place until 1953. Their ballparks were not so durable. In-season fires damaged Cincinnati's League Park and St. Louis' Robison Field. Robison was repaired, but the Reds built a new ballpark—The Palace of the Fans—in the same location for 1902.

Contenders Brooklyn and Philadelphia were severely affected by the raiding: the Phillies lost Nap Lajoie, while Brooklyn did without Joe McGinnity and Lave Cross. Pittsburgh, though, came out relatively unscathed and passed New York in mid-June, cruising to the league crown. The Bucs had excellent pitching and a multidimensional offense. Future superstar Honus Wagner spent the year as a utility player yet still led the league in RBIs. In 1902, he'd take over fulltime at shortstop.

Two active players died in 1901. Tom O'Brien, Pittsburgh's first baseman in 1900, died February 4 from intestinal problems first suffered on a baseball trip to Cuba. Brooklyn pitcher Doc McJames, who lost the 1900 season to malaria, was 5-6 in 1901. Sent to South Carolina for rest, he fell from a moving carriage and died.

Two nineteenth century immortals ended their careers. "Sliding" Billy Hamilton, the previous century's top leadoff hitter, paced the NL four times in runs. Amos Rusie, a five-time strikeout champ who won 246 games from 1889–98, was traded at the end of 1900 to Cincinnati for young Christy Mathewson. Rusie's wing, however, was gone. During the season, two outstanding defensive catchers debuted. Pat Moran would later win a World Series as a manager, while Bill Bergen hit just .170 in his 947 big-league games.

NL teams scored only 4.63 runs per game, down more than 12 percent due to adoption of a rule counting foul balls as strikes. The league hit its most homers until 1911, with Sam Crawford's 16 the highest individual total for more than a decade.

1901 American League

TEAM	W	L	T	PCT	GB	HW	HL	R	OR	PA	H	2B	3B	HR	BB	SO	HB	SH	AVG	OBP	SLG	OPS	AOPS	BR	ABR	PF	SB	CS	BSA	BSR
CHI	83	53	1	.610		**49**	21	**819**	631	5397	1303	173	89	32	**475**	337	**135**	**62**	.276	.350	.370	720	**108**	42	**64**	97	**280**			
BOS	79	57	2	.581	4	**49**	20	759	**608**	5349	1353	183	104	**37**	331	**282**	105	47	.278	.330	.381	711	104	6	20	98	157			
DET	74	61	1	.548	8.5	42	27	741	694	5245	1303	180	80	29	380	346	**135**	54	.279	.340	.370	710	98	16	-16	105	204			
PHI	74	62	1	.544	9	42	24	805	760	5320	**1409**	**239**	87	35	301	344	85	52	.289	.337	.395	732	103	45	12	104	173			
BAL	68	65	2	.511	13.5	40	25	760	750	5111	1348	179	**111**	24	369	377	101	52	**.294**	**.353**	**.397**	**750**	**108**	**79**	46	104	207			
WAS	61	72	5	.459	20.5	31	35	682	771	5259	1282	191	83	33	356	340	80	51	.269	.326	.364	690	97	-24	-13	99	127			
CLE	54	82	2	.397	29	28	39	666	831	5200	1311	197	68	12	243	326	76	48	.271	.313	.348	661	92	-83	-56	96	125			
MIL	48	89	2	.350	35.5	32	37	641	828	5288	1250	192	66	26	325	384	122	46	.261	.314	.345	659	91	-81	-47	95	176			
TOT	549					313	228	5873		42169	10559	1534	688	228	2780	2736	412	839	.277	.333	.371	704					1449			

TEAM	CG	SHO	GR	SV	IP	H	HR	BB	SO	BR/9	ERA	AERA	OAV	OOB	PR	APR	PF	OSB	OCS	FA	E	WPB	DP	FW	PW	BW	BSW	DIF
CHI	110	**11**	28	2	1218.1	1250	27	312	394	11.9	**2.98**	**117**	.263	.315	**93**	**71**	95	**153**	*135*	.941	345	55	100	.9	**6.4**	**5.8**		1.9
BOS	123	7	15	1	1217.0	**1178**	33	294	**396**	**11.2**	3.04	116	**.251**	**.301**	84	68	96	173	*157*	**.943**	337	35	104	1.6	6.1	1.8		1.5
DET	118	8	20	2	1188.2	1328	22	313	307	12.8	3.30	116	.280	.330	48	68	105	**153**	*141*	.930	410	38	**127**	-3.3	6.1	-1.4		5.1
PHI	**124**	6	14	1	1200.2	1346	**20**	374	350	13.3	4.00	94	.280	.339	-45	-31	103	187	*148*	.942	337	63	93	1.4	-2.8	1.1		6.3
BAL	115	4	21	3	1158.0	1313	21	344	271	13.3	3.73	104	.282	.338	-9	16	106	167	*112*	.926	401	49	76	-2.9	1.4	4.2		-1.2
WAS	118	8	20	2	1183.0	1396	51	**284**	308	13.3	4.09	89	.291	.339	-57	-58	100	170	*134*	**.943**	**323**	**28**	97	**2.4**	-5.2	-1.2		-1.5
CLE	122	7	19	**4**	1182.1	1365	22	464	334	14.5	4.12	86	.286	.358	-60	-78	97	199	*152*	.942	329	77	99	2.1	-7.0	-5.1		-4.0
MIL	107	3	**34**	3	1218.0	1383	32	395	376	13.6	4.06	89	.283	.344	-53	-65	98	247	***171***	.934	393	64	106	-1.8	-5.9	-4.2		-8.6
TOT	937	54	171	18	9566.					13.0	3.66		.277	.333						.938	2875	409	802					

Batter-Fielder Wins	Batting Average	On-Base Percentage	Slugging Average	On-Base Plus Slugging	Adjusted OPS	Adjusted Batter Runs
Lajoie-Phi 8.1	Lajoie-Phi 426	Lajoie-Phi....................463	Lajoie-Phi 643	Lajoie-Phi 1106	Lajoie-Phi 196	Lajoie-Phi 69.2
Collins-Bos..........4.2	Donlin-Bal 340	Jones-Chi....................412	Freeman-Bos 520	Freeman-Bos........920	Freeman-Bos........157	Freeman-Bos......37.0
Elberfeld-Det 3.5	Freeman-Bos 339	Donlin-Bal 409	Seybold-Phi 503	Seybold-Phi 901	Seybold-Phi 142	Collins-Bos 31.2
Freeman-Bos 2.7	Seybold-Phi 334	Hoy-Chi 407	Williams-Bal 495	Donlin-Bal 883	Collins-Bos 142	McGraw-Bal........29.1
Anderson-Mil 2.5	Collins-Bos 332	Freeman-Bos 400	Collins-Bos 495	Williams-Bal..........883	Donlin-Bal 138	Anderson-Mil 28.0

Runs	Hits	Doubles	Triples	Home Runs	Total Bases	Runs Batted In
Lajoie-Phi 145	Lajoie-Phi 232	Lajoie-Phi 48	Williams-Bal............21	Lajoie-Phi 14	Lajoie-Phi 350	Lajoie-Phi 125
Jones-Chi 120	Anderson-Mil 190	Anderson-Mil 46	Keister-Bal..............21	Freeman-Bos..........12	Collins-Bos 279	Freeman-Bos 114
Williams-Bal.........113	Collins-Bos 187	Collins-Bos 42	Mertes-Chi..............17	Grady-Was................9	Anderson-Mil 274	Anderson-Mil 99
Hoy-Chi 112	Waldron-Mil-Was ..186	Farrell-Was 32	Stahl-Bos................16		Freeman-Bos........255	Mertes-Chi 98
Barrett-Det............110	Dungan-Was 179		Collins-Bos 16		Williams-Bal..........248	Williams-Bal 96

Stolen Bases	Base Stealing Runs	Fielding Runs-Infield	Fielding Runs-Outfield	Wins	Winning Pct.	Complete Games
Isbell-Chi 52		Clingman-Was 22.1	Seymour-Bal........13.9	Young-Bos 33	Griffith-Chi 774	McGinnity-Bal.........39
Mertes-Chi.............46		Lajoie-Phi...................22.0	Pickering-Cle 12.5	McGinnity-Bal 26	Young-Bos 767	Young-Bos 38
Seymour-Bal 38		Elberfeld-Det 19.4	Barrett-Det 11.4	Griffith-Chi 24	Callahan-Chi.........652	Miller-Det 35
Jones-Chi 38		Conroy-Mil 16.9	Donlin-Bal.............6.9	Miller-Det 23	Patten-Was...........643	Fraser-Phi..............35
		Collins-Bos 12.8	Farrell-Was 5.6	Fraser-Phi 22	Miller-Det 639	Carrick-Was 34

Strikeouts	Fewest BB/Game	Games	Saves	Base Runners/9	Adjusted Relief Runs	Relief Ranking
Young-Bos 158	Young-Bos 90	McGinnity-Bal 48	Hoffer-Cle 3	Young-Bos 8.92		
Patterson-Chi........127	Gear-Was 1.21	Dowling-Mil-Cle 43		Callahan-Chi......10.62		
Dowling-Mil-Cle 124	Lee-Was 1.55	Young-Bos 43		Griffith-Chi 11.10		
Garvin-Mil 122	Griffith-Chi 1.69	Carrick-Was 42		Lewis-Bos..........11.32		
Fraser-Phi 110	Cronin-Det 1.72	Patterson-Chi 41		Winter-Bos 11.35		

Innings Pitched	Opponents' Avg.	Opponents' OBP	Earned Run Average	Adjusted ERA	Adjusted Starter Runs	Pitcher Wins
McGinnity-Bal 382.0	Young-Bos 232	Young-Bos 256	Young-Bos 1.62	Young-Bos 217	Young-Bos 77.0	**Young-Bos**..........7.9
Young-Bos 371.1	Callahan-Chi.........239	Callahan-Chi 290	Callahan-Chi........2.42	Yeager-Det............147	Miller-Det 32.9	**Griffith-Chi** 4.2
Miller-Det 332.0	Moore-Cle.............244	Griffith-Chi 300	Yeager-Det 2.61	Callahan-Chi 143	Griffith-Chi 28.6	**Callahan-Chi**........3.7
Fraser-Phi..........331.0	Lewis-Bos.............247	Lewis-Bos 304	Griffith-Chi 2.67	Griffith-Chi 130	Callahan-Chi........25.5	**Miller-Det**............3.3
Carrick-Was 324.0	Winter-Bos 252	Winter-Bos...................304	Winter-Bos 2.80	Miller-Det 130	Yeager-Det 22.2	**Yeager-Det** 2.9

Impressive Instant

Declaring itself a major league, and announcing the fact by recruiting top stars from NL clubs, the American League—formerly a minor league known as the Western League—broke in with a bang. The Philadelphia Athletics lured second baseman Nap Lajoie from the crosstown NL club and were rewarded when Lajoie won the AL's Triple Crown, taking the batting title by nearly 100 points. Others, including the Baltimore Orioles and their hard-boiled player-manager John McGraw, weren't happy with the high salaries paid by the Athletics.

Lajoie alone couldn't carry his team to victory; the Athletics came in fourth. Boston's Cy Young was the league's top pitcher, finishing with an ERA 0.80 lower than his nearest rival, but Boston's fellow moundsmen weren't worthy. The Red Sox finished second behind the White Sox, who had the league's best offense. Chicago's hitters led the league in walks and steals; 39-year-old Dummy Hoy paced the AL with 86 bases on balls and tallied a third-best 113 runs.

The prowess of Hoy, the overwhelming dominance of Young and Lajoie, and other factors reveal that the American League was a bit behind the talent curve in 1901. Runs per game were at 5.35, the loop's highest total until 1930, and fielding average was just .938, a figure that the NL had passed back in 1897. In 1902, however, the talent began to even out as stubborn and penurious NL owners failed to match the salaries offered by their new rivals. The Junior Circuit could soon call itself a peer—maybe even superior.

Several youngsters made their first major league appearances in 1901 due to the AL's need for players. Future Tigers outfielders Davy Jones and Matty McIntyre debuted at age 21, while lefty Eddie Plank finally got a chance to shine with Philadelphia, going 17–13 as a 26-year-old rookie. He would win 309 more games in the majors before retiring, all but 42 with Philadelphia.

1902 National League

TEAM	W	L	T	PCT	GB	HW	HL	R	OR	PA	H	2B	3B	HR	BB	SO	HB	SH	AVG	OBP	SLG	OPS	AOPS	BR	ABR	PF	SB	CS	BSA	BSR
PIT	103	36	3	.741		**56**	15	**775**	**440**	5480	**1410**	**189**	**95**	**18**	**372**	**446**	**118**	**64**	**.286**	**.344**	**.374**	**718**	**124**	**154**	**129**	104	**222**			
BRO	75	63	3	.543	27.5	45	23	564	519	5344	1242	147	49	19	319	489	**118**	62	.256	.311	.319	630	99	-4	-8	101	145			
BOS	73	64	5	.533	29	42	27	572	516	5298	1178	142	39	14	398	481	131	43	.249	.313	.305	618	95	-13	-18	101	189			
CIN	70	70	1	.500	33.5	35	35	633	566	5342	1383	188	77	**18**	297	465	98	39	.282	.328	.362	690	109	96	38	110	131			
CHI	68	69	6	.496	34	31	38	544	505	5428	1224	133	40	6	358	572	156	44	.251	.308	.299	607	95	-37	-21	97	229			
STL	56	78	6	.418	44.5	28	38	517	695	5183	1226	116	37	10	273	438	107	52	.258	.306	.304	610	97	-39	-18	96	158			
PHI	56	81	1	.409	46	29	39	484	649	5125	1139	110	43	5	356	481	122	32	.247	.305	.293	598	90	-51	-51	100	108			
NY	48	88	5	.353	53.5	24	44	405	604	5034	1097	147	34	6	254	540	108	40	.237	.282	.287	569	81	-105	-101	99	187			
TOT	564					290	259	4494		42234	9899	1172	414	96	2627	3912	376	958	.259	.313	.318	631					1369			

TEAM	CG	SHO	GR	SV	IP	H	HR	BB	SO	BR/9	ERA	AERA	OAV	OOB	PR	APR	PF	OSB	OCS	FA	E	WPB	DP	FW	PW	BW	BSW	DIF
PIT	131	**21**	10	3	1264.2	1142	**4**	**250**	**564**	**10.3**	2.30	119	.241	**.288**	68	62	98	**117**	*116*	.958	247	39	87	3.4	6.5	**13.6**		10.0
BRO	131	14	10	3	1256.0	**1113**	10	363	536	10.8	2.69	103	**.238**	.298	12	9	99	217	*.142*	.952	275	47	79	1.5	.9	-.8		4.4
BOS	124	14	18	**4**	1259.2	1233	16	372	523	11.8	2.61	108	.257	.316	24	29	102	156	*134*	**.959**	**240**	42	90	**3.8**	3.1	-1.9		-.5
CIN	130	9	13	1	1239.0	1228	15	352	430	11.9	2.67	112	.259	.318	15	41	108	143	*141*	.945	322	50	**118**	-1.4	4.3	4.0		-6.9
CHI	**134**	17	9	2	1293.1	1244	7	281	447	10.9	**2.19**	**123**	.253	.300	**85**	**75**	97	158	*138*	.946	331	48	113	-1.7	**7.9**	-2.2		-4.5
STL	112	7	**29**	**4**	1227.2	1399	16	338	400	13.0	3.47	79	.287	.338	-95	-103	99	188	*141*	.944	336	**35**	107	-2.4	-10.9	-1.9		4.2
PHI	118	8	21	3	1211.0	1323	12	334	504	12.7	3.50	80	.278	.333	-97	-92	101	217	*143*	.946	305	47	81	-.8	-9.7	-5.4		3.3
NY	120	11	21	1	1242.1	1217	16	337	508	11.6	2.86	98	.257	.313	-11	-9	101	173	***144***	.943	337	60	107	-2.3	-.9	-10.7		-6.1
TOT	1000	101	131	21	9993.2					11.6	2.78		.259	.313						.949	2393	368	782					

Batter-Fielder Wins
Tenney-Bos 4.0
Wagner-Pit 3.8
Leach-Pit 3.4
Kling-Chi..............2.7
Farrell-StL 2.7

Batting Average
Beaumont-Pit 357
Crawford-Cin 333
Keeler-Bro 333
Wagner-Pit 330
Beckley-Cin 330

On-Base Percentage
R.Thomas-Phi 414
Tenney-Bos 409
Beaumont-Pit..............404
Clarke-Pit....................401
Wagner-Pit...................394

Slugging Average
Wagner-Pit 463
Crawford-Cin 461
Clarke-Pit 449
Beckley-Cin 427
Leach-Pit 426

On-Base Plus Slugging
Wagner-Pit............857
Clarke-Pit..............850
Crawford-Cin 848
Beaumont-Pit.........822
Beckley-Cin 804

Adjusted OPS
Wagner-Pit............159
Clarke-Pit..............157
Beaumont-Pit.........148
Crawford-Cin 147
Tenney-Bos 141

Adjusted Batter Runs
Wagner-Pit 37.1
Clarke-Pit............32.7
Beaumont-Pit 31.3
Tenney-Bos 29.0
Crawford-Cin 28.9

Runs
Wagner-Pit............105
Clarke-Pit.............103
Beaumont-Pit........100
Leach-Pit 97
Crawford-Cin 92

Hits
Beaumont-Pit........193
Keeler-Bro 186
Crawford-Cin 185
Wagner-Pit............176
Beckley-Cin 175

Doubles
Wagner-Pit 30
Clarke-Pit 27
Cooley-Bos 26
Dahlen-Bro 25
Beckley-Cin....................23

Triples
Leach-Pit 22
Crawford-Cin 22
Wagner-Pit..............16
Clarke-Pit.................14
Gremminger-Bos 12

Home Runs
Leach-Pit 6
Beckley-Cin 5
Sheckard-Bro 4
McCreery-Bro 4

Total Bases
Crawford-Cin 256
Wagner-Pit............247
Beckley-Cin 227
Beaumont-Pit........226
Leach-Pit 219

Runs Batted In
Wagner-Pit 91
Leach-Pit 85
Crawford-Cin 78
Dahlen-Bro............74

Stolen Bases
Wagner-Pit.............42
Slagle-Chi 41
Donovan-StL 34
Beaumont-Pit..........33
Smith-NY 32

Base Stealing Runs

Fielding Runs-Infield
Farrell-StL 31.8
Steinfeldt-Cin 21.9
H.Long-Bos 19.8
Lowe-Chi 17.6
Leach-Pit 12.4

Fielding Runs-Outfield
Donovan-StL..........8.9
Lush-Bos 8.6
Sheckard-Bro 8.5
Dobbs-Cin-Chi 7.8
Brodie-NY.............7.3

Wins
Chesbro-Pit 28
Willis-Bos................27
Pittinger-Bos 27
Taylor-Chi 23
Hahn-Cin 23

Winning Pct.
Chesbro-Pit 824
Doheny-Pit 800
Tannehill-Pit 769
Phillippe-Pit 690
Leever-Pit.............682

Complete Games
Willis-Bos 45
Pittinger-Bos..........36
Hahn-Cin 35
White-Phi 34
Taylor-Chi 34

Strikeouts
Willis-Bos..............225
White-Phi..............185
Pittinger-Bos 174
Donovan-Bro 170
Mathewson-NY 164

Fewest BB/Game
Phillippe-Pit 86
Tannehill-Pit 97
Menefee-Chi........1.19
Taylor-Chi 1.21
Leever-Pit 1.26

Games
Willis-Bos 51
Pittinger-Bos 46
Yerkes-StL 39
Taylor-Chi 37

Saves
Willis-Bos..................3
M.O'Neill-StL 2
Newton-Bro 2
Leever-Pit 2

Base Runners/9
Taylor-Chi 8.90
Tannehill-Pit 9.27
McGinnity-NY 9.59
Hahn-Cin 9.70
Cronin-NY............9.71

Adjusted Relief Runs

Relief Ranking

Innings Pitched
Willis-Bos 410.0
Pittinger-Bos......389.1
Taylor-Chi 333.2
Hahn-Cin 321.0
White-Phi 306.0

Opponents' Avg.
Newton-Bro 217
McGinnity-NY 219
Taylor-Chi 224
Donovan-Bro 228
Chesbro-Pit 229

Opponents' OBP
Taylor-Chi......................258
Tannehill-Pit.................266
McGinnity-NY 273
Hahn-Cin 275
Phillippe-Pit 276

Earned Run Average
Taylor-Chi 1.29
Hahn-Cin 1.77
Tannehill-Pit 1.95
Lundgren-Chi 1.97
Phillippe-Pit 2.05

Adjusted ERA
Taylor-Chi 209
Hahn-Cin 170
Poole-Pit-Cin 142
Tannehill-Pit..........140
Lundgren-Chi........137

Adjusted Starter Runs
Taylor-Chi 50.8
Hahn-Cin 40.6
Willis-Bos 27.9
Chesbro-Pit 23.2
Phillippe-Pit 18.9

Pitcher Wins
Taylor-Chi 6.1
Hahn-Cin 4.4
Willis-Bos 2.8
Tannehill-Pit 2.7
Phillips-Cin 2.6

Change is Gonna Come

By 1902 the old days were clearly gone. Jim "Pud" Galvin, a great nineteenth century hurler who once threw 72 complete games in a season, died at 46. Boston's Vic Willis topped the NL with 45 complete games as old-timers bemoaned pitchers' lack of stamina. Forty-year-old center fielder Dummy Hoy, who lived nearly sixty more years, played his final game.

The Reds opened The Palace of the Fans, which sported a 450-foot right-field line. Scoring decreased another 14 percent as foul bunts were also now counted as strikes. Homers dropped 58 percent as NL ERA dipped 51 points.

The already great Pirates further improved, taking the pennant by an amazing 27½ games. Leading from start to finish, Pittsburgh was 10 games up in mid-May. One of the dominant clubs of all time, the '02 Bucs led the league in runs by 142 and in runs allowed by 65. Competition would soon come from Chicago and New York as two pieces of a growing Cubs powerhouse, infielders Joe Tinker and Johnny Evers, debuted in 1902. In New York, young right-hander Christy Mathewson had his second spectacular season for a terrible team, going 14-17 with 8 shutouts for the Giants.

The most significant news occurred with the AL's Baltimore Orioles. As a result of a complicated conspiracy that included John McGraw, Reds owner John Brush, and Giants owner Andrew Freedman, the Orioles were stripped of their best players by nefarious means. Several Orioles—John McGraw, Roger Bresnahan, and pitcher Joe McGinnity among them—ended up in New York. Others wound up in Cincinnati. Brush purchased the Giants after the season, reaping the benefits as the moribund franchise was transformed overnight into a contender. The story did not end perfectly for masterminds Brush and McGraw, though. Infuriated, AL President Ban Johnson engineered the sale of what was left of the Orioles to New York investors the following year, bringing major league competition into the NL's biggest market.

1902 American League

TEAM	W	L	T	PCT	GB	HW	HL	R	OR	PA	H	2B	3B	HR	BB	SO	HB	SH	AVG	OBP	SLG	OPS	AOPS	BR	ABR	PF	SB	CS	BSA	BSR
PHI	83	53	1	.610		**56**	17	**775**	636	5261	1369	235	67	38	343	**293**	118	38	.287	**.340**	**.389**	**729**	104	**52**	23	104	201			
STL	78	58	4	.574	5	49	21	619	607	5251	1254	208	61	29	373	327	104	38	.265	.323	.353	676	94	-37	-28	99	137			
BOS	77	60	1	.562	6.5	43	27	664	**600**	5292	1356	195	**95**	**42**	275	375	100	**42**	.278	.322	.383	705	98	-4	-22	103	132			
CHI	74	60	4	.552	8	48	19	675	602	5255	1248	170	50	14	**411**	381	**154**	36	.268	.332	.335	667	95	-43	-14	96	**265**			
CLE	69	67	1	.507	14	40	25	686	667	5303	**1401**	**248**	68	33	308	356	120	35	**.289**	.336	**.389**	725	**111**	43	**73**	96	140			
WAS	61	75	2	.449	22	40	28	707	790	5188	1338	261	66	47	329	296	81	44	.283	.335	.395	730	107	**52**	46	101	121			
DET	52	83	2	.385	30.5	35	33	566	657	5139	1167	141	55	22	359	287	83	53	.251	.312	.320	632	79	-112	-122	102	130			
BAL	50	88	3	.362	34	32	31	715	848	5348	1318	202	107	33	417	429	117	54	.277	.342	.385	727	103	50	19	104	189			
TOT	553					343	201	5407		42037	10451	1660	569	258	2815	2744	340	877	.275	.331	.369	700					1315			

TEAM	CG	SHO	GR	SV	IP	H	HR	BB	SO	BR/9	ERA	AERA	OAV	OOB	PR	APR	PF	OSB	OCS	FA	E	WPB	DP	FW	PW	BW	BSW	DIF
PHI	114	5	**25**	2	1216.1	1292	33	368	**455**	12.7	3.29	111	.273	.334	39	49	103	157	*147*	.953	270	41	75	1.4	4.6	2.2		6.8
STL	120	7	22	2	1244.0	1273	36	343	348	12.0	3.34	106	.266	.321	32	26	99	154	*124*	.953	274	45	122	1.5	2.5	-2.7		8.6
BOS	123	6	16	1	1238.0	1217	27	326	431	**11.5**	**3.02**	**118**	**.258**	**.311**	**75**	**75**	100	132	*135*	**.955**	263	**40**	101	2.0	**7.1**	-2.1		1.5
CHI	116	11	22	0	1221.2	1269	30	331	346	12.1	3.41	99	.269	.323	22	-5	95	**121**	*118*	**.955**	**257**	54	**125**	**2.3**	-.5	-1.3		6.5
CLE	116	**16**	23	**3**	1204.1	**1199**	26	411	361	12.4	3.28	105	.260	.327	39	21	96	183	*136*	.950	287	66	96	.3	2.0	**6.9**		-8.3
WAS	**130**	2	8	0	1207.2	1403	56	**312**	300	13.2	4.36	85	.291	.341	-106	-85	104	173	*128*	.945	316	42	70	-1.3	-8.1	4.4		-2.0
DET	116	9	22	**3**	1190.2	1267	**20**	370	245	12.7	3.56	102	.274	.333	1	10	102	198	*136*	.943	332	44	111	-2.5	.9	-11.6		-2.4
BAL	119	3	22	1	1210.1	1531	30	354	258	14.3	4.33	87	.309	.360	-102	-73	106	197	*119*	.938	357	52	109	-3.5	-6.9	1.8		-10.4
TOT	954	59	160	12	9733.0					12.6	3.57		.275	.331						.949	2356	384	809					

Batter-Fielder Wins
Lajoie-Phi-Cle 5.6
Delahanty-Was ..5.0
Bradley-Cle 4.8
Hickman-Bos-Cle2.6
L.Cross-Phi..........2.3

Batting Average
Delahanty-Was.....376
Lajoie-Phi-Cle.......378
Hickman-Bos-Cle .361
Dougherty-Bos 342
L.Cross-Phi...........342

On-Base Percentage
Delahanty-Was 453
Dougherty-Bos 407
Barrett-Det...................397
Selbach-Bal 393
Jones-Chi.....................390

Slugging Average
Delahanty-Was.....590
Lajoie-Phi-Cle.......565
Hickman-Bos-Cle .539
Bradley-Cle...........515
Seybold-Phi 506

On-Base Plus Slugging
Delahanty-Was ..1043
Hickman-Bos-Cle 926
Bradley-Cle 890
Seybold-Phi 881
Williams-Bal..........861

Adjusted OPS
Delahanty-Was 186
Hickman-Bos-Cle 159
Bradley-Cle 151
Seybold-Phi 137
Freeman-Bos........131

Adjusted Batter Runs
Delahanty-Was ..57.7
Hickman-Bos-Cle39.4
Lajoie-Phi-Cle 37.3
Bradley-Cle 35.8
Seybold-Phi........24.5

Runs
Hartsel-Phi 109
Fultz-Phi 109
Strang-Chi 108
Bradley-Cle 104
Delahanty-Was 103

Hits
Hickman-Bos-Cle 193
L.Cross-Phi 191
Bradley-Cle 187
Delahanty-Was 178
Freeman-Bos........174

Doubles
Delahanty-Was 43
Davis-Phi 43
L.Cross-Phi....................39
Bradley-Cle....................39
Freeman-Bos 38

Triples
Williams-Bal............21
Freeman-Bos..........19
Ferris-Bos 14
Delahanty-Was 14
Hickman-Bos-Cle ..13

Home Runs
Seybold-Phi 16
Hickman-Bos-Cle ..11
Freeman-Bos..........11
Bradley-Cle 11
Delahanty-Was 10

Total Bases
Hickman-Bos-Cle 288
Freeman-Bos........283
Bradley-Cle 283
Delahanty-Was 279
Seybold-Phi 264

Runs Batted In
Freeman-Bos 121
Hickman-Bos-Cle 110
L.Cross-Phi 108
Seybold-Phi 97

Stolen Bases
Hartsel-Phi 47
Mertes-Chi..............46
Fultz-Phi 44

Base Stealing Runs

Fielding Runs-Infield
Ferris-Bos 23.8
Padden-StL 12.3
Bradley-Cle 12.0
Elberfeld-Det 11.6
M.Cross-Phi..................9.3

Fielding Runs-Outfield
Selbach-Bal 10.4
Jones-Chi 9.8
Barrett-Det 5.7
Mertes-Chi 5.4
Burkett-StL 5.2

Wins
Young-Bos 32
Waddell-Phi 24
Powell-StL 22
R.Donahue-StL 22
Dinneen-Bos 21

Winning Pct.
Bernhard-Phi-Cle .783
Waddell-Phi 774
Young-Bos 744
R.Donahue-StL.....667
Griffith-Chi 625

Complete Games
Young-Bos 41
Dinneen-Bos 39
Powell-StL 36
Orth-Was 36

Strikeouts
Waddell-Phi 210
Young-Bos.............160
Powell-StL 137
Dinneen-Bos 136
Plank-Phi..............107

Fewest BB/Game
Orth-Was 1.11
Young-Bos............1.24
Bernhard-Phi-Cle 1.47
Siever-Det............1.53
Plank-Phi 1.83

Games
Young-Bos 45
Powell-StL......................42
Dinneen-Bos..................42
Wiltse-Phi-Bal 38
Orth-Was 38

Saves
Powell-StL 2

Base Runners/9
Bernhard-Phi-Cle 8.68
Siever-Det...........9.56
Waddell-Phi 9.71
Young-Bos 9.73
Joss-Cle 10.46

Adjusted Relief Runs

Relief Ranking

Innings Pitched
Young-Bos 384.2
Dinneen-Bos......371.1
Powell-StL..........328.1
Orth-Was 324.0
R.Donahue-StL..316.1

Opponents' Avg.
Bernhard-Phi-Cle .216
Waddell-Phi 223
Joss-Cle 228
Siever-Det............237
Winter-Bos 238

Opponents' OBP
Bernhard-Phi-Cle.........254
Siever-Det 273
Waddell-Phi 276
Young-Bos 276
Joss-Cle.......................291

Earned Run Average
Siever-Det...........1.91
Waddell-Phi 2.05
Bernhard-Phi-Cle 2.15
Young-Bos 2.15
Garvin-Chi 2.21

Adjusted ERA
Siever-Det 191
Waddell-Phi 179
Young-Bos............166
Bernhard-Phi-Cle..160
Garvin-Chi 153

Adjusted Starter Runs
Young-Bos 59.4
Waddell-Phi 48.3
Bernhard-Phi-Cle 33.3
Dinneen-Bos........33.1
Siever-Det...........29.4

Pitcher Wins
Young-Bos..........6.0
Waddell-Phi.........5.8
Bernhard-Phi-Cle....3.0
Dinneen-Bos......2.3
Plank-Phi............2.3

Growing Pains

Prior to 1902 the poorly attended and unsuccessful Milwaukee franchise shifted to St. Louis to become the Browns. The fledgling AL's other sticky spot was Baltimore, a franchise that was ultimately ripped apart by its manager, John McGraw, as part of his blood feud with AL President Ban Johnson. The Orioles finished last, despite topping the loop in on-base percentage and triples, losing their best players—as well as McGraw—to the NL. Orioles catcher Wilbert Robinson retired, later to manage in Brooklyn for 18 years.

Boston outfielder Patsy Dougherty hit .342 in his first season, and Cleveland hurler Addie Joss was equally impressive (17–13 with a league-best 5 shutouts) as a rookie. Joss, just 22, was an exception to the rule—few regulars or starting pitchers of the time were younger than 25.

The defending champion White Sox led in July by as much as 5½ games but fell apart in August as a four-team scramble developed. Out of the chaos came the Philadelphia Athletics, who pulled away from St. Louis and Boston in September. The Browns' surprising second-place finish was the only time the franchise ended above fourth place until 1921.

Philadelphia's league-best offense was powered by slugger Socks Seybold, on-base threat Topsy Hartsel, and third baseman Lave Cross, who batted in 108 runs without a single homer. Pitcher Rube Waddell, a man-child who wore out welcomes with the Pirates and the Cubs, found a home under Connie Mack's wing. He went 24–7, leading the AL in strikeouts.

Although runs fell by 8 percent, home runs skyrocketed to 258, the AL's highest total until 1920. Seybold's 16 taters were two more than hit by the entire White Sox team, and his total stood as the league record until Babe Ruth broke it in 1919. Cleveland and Philadelphia saw their attendance rise more than 100 percent as, overall, the league saw a healthy sales increase of 31 percent in its second campaign.

1903 National League

TEAM	W	L	T	PCT	GB	HW	HL	R	OR	PA	H	2B	3B	HR	BB	SO	HB	SH	AVG	OBP	SLG	OPS	AOPS	BR	ABR	PF	SB	CS	BSA	BSR
PIT	91	49	1	.650		**46**	24	**793**	613	5511	**1429**	208	**110**	**34**	364		109	50	.286	.341	**.393**	734	**113**	87	**64**	103	172			
NY	84	55	3	.604	6.5	41	27	729	**567**	5397	1290	181	49	20	379		**185**	**92**	.272	.338	.344	682	97	11	-13	104	264			
CHI	82	56	1	.594	8	45	28	695	599	5323	1300	191	62	9	422		118	50	.275	.340	.347	687	105	21	39	97	259			
CIN	74	65	2	.532	16.5	41	35	765	656	5379	1399	**228**	92	28	403		89	30	**.288**	.346	.390	**736**	104	**97**	20	111	151			
BRO	70	66	3	.515	19	40	33	667	682	5233	1201	177	56	15	**522**		124	53	.265	**.348**	.339	687	105	31	52	97	**273**			
BOS	58	80	2	.420	32	31	35	578	699	5240	1145	176	47	25	398		101	59	.245	.312	.318	630	90	-82	-58	96	159			
PHI	49	86	4	.363	39.5	25	33	617	738	5313	1283	186	62	12	338		155	39	.268	.322	.341	663	98	-34	-12	97	120			
STL	43	94	2	.314	46.5	22	45	505	795	5096	1176	138	65	8	277		96	34	.251	.297	.313	610	83	-130	-113	97	171			
TOT	560					291	260	5349		42492	10223	1485	543	151	3103	3767	407	977	.269	.331	.349	679					1569			

TEAM	CG	SHO	GR	SV	IP	H	HR	BB	SO	BR/9	ERA	AERA	OAV	OOB	PR	APR	PF	OSB	OCS	FA	E	WPB	DP	FW	PW	BW	BSW	DIF
PIT	117	**16**	26	5	1251.1	1215	**9**	384	454	11.8	2.91	111	.255	.316	48	44	99	**151**	*143*	**.951**	295	54	100	1.6	4.2	**6.1**		9.0
NY	115	8	**29**	**8**	1262.2	1257	20	371	**628**	11.9	2.95	113	.258	.316	43	54	102	163	*155*	**.951**	287	47	87	**2.3**	5.2	-1.2		8.3
CHI	117	6	24	6	1240.1	**1182**	14	**354**	451	**11.4**	**2.77**	113	**.250**	**.307**	**67**	48	96	161	*156*	.942	338	**32**	78	-1.6	4.6	3.7		6.3
CIN	**126**	11	16	1	1230.0	1277	14	378	480	12.6	3.07	**116**	.268	.331	26	**60**	109	166	*150*	.946	312	55	84	.4	**5.8**	1.9		-3.6
BRO	118	11	23	4	1221.1	1276	18	377	438	12.7	3.44	92	.275	.339	-25	-39	98	270	*154*	**.951**	**284**	46	98	2.0	-3.7	5.0		-1.3
BOS	125	8	15	1	1228.2	1310	30	460	516	13.4	3.34	96	.278	.348	-11	-21	98	206	***184***	.939	361	71	89	-3.0	-2.0	-5.6		-.4
PHI	**126**	5	13	3	1212.1	1347	21	425	381	13.6	3.96	82	.285	.352	-95	-97	100	235	*169*	.947	300	58	76	1.0	-9.3	-1.2		-9.0
STL	111	4	**29**	2	1212.1	1353	25	430	419	13.6	3.67	89	.284	.350	-55	-56	100	217	*178*	.940	354	51	**111**	-2.7	-5.4	-10.8		-6.6
TOT	955	69	175	30	9859.0					12.6	3.26		.269	.331						.946	2531	414	723					

Batter-Fielder Wins	Batting Average	On-Base Percentage	Slugging Average	On-Base Plus Slugging	Adjusted OPS	Adjusted Batter Runs
Sheckard-Bro 5.8	Wagner-Pit 355	Thomas-Phi 453	Clarke-Pit 532	Clarke-Pit..............946	Clarke-Pit..............164	Sheckard-Bro 44.6
Wagner-Pit 5.6	Clarke-Pit 351	Bresnahan-NY 443	Wagner-Pit 518	Donlin-Cin 936	Bresnahan-NY......161	Wagner-Pit 38.8
Thomas-Phi 3.9	Donlin-Cin.............351	Chance-Chi 439	Donlin-Cin.............516	Bresnahan-NY......936	Sheckard-Bro 160	Chance-Chi 37.9
Tenney-Bos 3.2	Bresnahan-NY 350	Sheckard-Bro..............423	Bresnahan-NY 493	Wagner-Pit............931	Wagner-Pit............160	Bresnahan-NY....35.9
Chance-Chi 3.1	Seymour-Cin.........342	Donlin-Cin 420	Steinfeldt-Cin 481	Sheckard-Bro 899	Chance-Chi 155	Thomas-Phi........35.2

Runs	Hits	Doubles	Triples	Home Runs	Total Bases	Runs Batted In
Beaumont-Pit........137	Beaumont-Pit........209	Steinfeldt-Cin 32	Wagner-Pit..............19	Sheckard-Bro 9	Beaumont-Pit........272	Mertes-NY 104
Donlin-Cin 110	Seymour-Cin 191	Mertes-NY 32	Donlin-Cin 18		Seymour-Cin 267	Wagner-Pit 101
Browne-NY 105	Browne-NY 185	Clarke-Pit 32	Leach-Pit 17		Wagner-Pit...........265	Doyle-Bro 91
Slagle-Chi 104	Wagner-Pit............182				Donlin-Cin 256	Leach-Pit 87
Strang-Bro 101	Donlin-Cin 174				Sheckard-Bro 245	Steinfeldt-Cin 83

Stolen Bases	Base Stealing Runs	Fielding Runs-Infield	Fielding Runs-Outfield	Wins	Winning Pct.	Complete Games
Sheckard-Bro 67		Farrell-StL 21.1	Sheckard-Bro 25.2	McGinnity-NY 31	Leever-Pit 781	McGinnity-NY........44
Chance-Chi 67		Dahlen-Bro 19.3	Thomas-Phi 12.0	Mathewson-NY 30	Phillippe-Pit 735	Mathewson-NY......37
Wagner-Pit.............46		Wagner-Pit..................17.9	Mertes-NY 8.7	Phillippe-Pit 25	Weimer-Chi............714	Pittinger-Bos...........35
Strang-Bro 46		Ritchey-Pit 16.5	Sebring-Pit 4.9	Leever-Pit 25	Mathewson-NY.....698	Hahn-Cin 34
Mertes-NY 45		Gremminger-Bos 16.3	Keister-Phi 4.8	....	Wicker-StL-Chi 690	Taylor-Chi 33

Strikeouts	Fewest BB/Game	Games	Saves	Base Runners/9	Adjusted Relief Runs	Relief Ranking
Mathewson-NY 267	Phillippe-Pit 90	McGinnity-NY 55	Miller-NY 3	Phillippe-Pit 9.39		
McGinnity-NY 171	Hahn-Cin 1.43	Mathewson-NY 45	Lundgren-Chi............3	Taylor-Chi 9.77		
Garvin-Bro............154	Taylor-Chi 1.64	Pittinger-Bos 44		Leever-Pit 10.13		
Pittinger-Bos 140	McFarland-StL 1.89	Schmidt-Bro 40		Mathewson-NY..10.59		
Weimer-Chi 128	Leever-Pit 1.90			Hahn-Cin 10.70		

Innings Pitched	Opponents' Avg.	Opponents' OBP	Earned Run Average	Adjusted ERA	Adjusted Starter Runs	Pitcher Wins
McGinnity-NY 434.0	Weimer-Chi...........225	Phillippe-Pit 263	Leever-Pit 2.06	Leever-Pit 157	McGinnity-NY 42.2	**Mathewson-NY** ..4.6
Mathewson-NY..366.1	Mathewson-NY.....231	Taylor-Chi.....................273	Mathewson-NY....2.26	Mathewson-NY 148	Mathewson-NY.....39.2	**McGinnity-NY** 4.0
Pittinger-Bos......351.2	Taylor-Chi 235	Leever-Pit......................282	Weimer-Chi..........2.30	Hahn-Cin 141	Leever-Pit 37.5	**Leever-Pit** 3.4
Jones-Bro 324.1	McGinnity-NY 236	Mathewson-NY 287	Phillippe-Pit 2.43	McGinnity-NY 137	Hahn-Cin 32.4	**Hahn-Cin** 3.1
Taylor-Chi 312.1	Leever-Pit 238	McGinnity-NY 291	McGinnity-NY 2.43	Weimer-Chi 136	Weimer-Chi..........27.7	**Phillippe-Pit** 2.9

The Makings of a Struggle

Largely on the strength of Honus Wagner, who captured the first of his eight batting titles, the Pirates were the class of the Senior Circuit for the third straight year. The Bucs, whose pitching staff had nearly twice as many shutouts as home runs allowed, emerged from a tangle with the Cubs and Giants in June. Despite playing just 104 games, Pittsburgh player-manager Fred Clarke paced the league in doubles.

The Giants finished 47 games closer to first place than in 1902, edging out the much-improved Cubs for second place. New York's metamorphosis led to a 91 percent rise in crowds at the Polo Grounds in 1903 as league attendance jumped 42 percent.

Mordecai "Three-Finger Brown," a 27-year-old rookie righty with two fingers missing from his pitching hand, entered the league with St. Louis. The Cubs would acquire him over the winter, fortifying an already excellent pitching staff and setting up one of the great pitching rivalries: "Three Fingers" against "The Big Six," New York's Christy Mathewson. Matty, still just 23, struck out 267 batters, 96 more than his nearest rival.

One of the least remembered nineteenth-century stars, outfielder Jimmy Ryan, retired with 2,513 hits under his belt, most of them collected with Chicago. Another little-recalled veteran outfielder, George Van Haltren, called it quits at age 37 with 2,544 hits.

Following the two-year slump in offense, NL hitters got well and team runs boomed to 4.78 per contest. Homers were way up, and stolen bases rose to 1.40 per game, the highest in NL history. Also at a peak was the interest level in a postseason AL-NL series, as the AL and NL champions agreed to a best-of-nine competition. Before it started, the Pirates lost 16-game winner Ed Doheny to a mental breakdown. His loss, and an injury to Sam Leever, stretched the Bucs' pitching staff to its breaking point as Boston won the first modern World Series in eight games.

1903 American League

TEAM	W	L	T	PCT	GB	HW	HL	R	OR	PA	H	2B	3B	HR	BB	SO	HB	SH	AVG	OBP	SLG	OPS	AOPS	BR	ABR	PF	SB	CS	BSA	BSR
BOS	91	47	3	.659		**49**	20	**708**	**504**	5365	**1336**	222	**113**	**48**	262	561	148	36	**.272**	**.313**	**.392**	**705**	111	**89**	55	105	141			
PHI	75	60	2	.556	14.5	44	21	597	519	5074	1236	227	68	32	268	513	101	32	.264	.309	.363	672	102	39	13	105	157			
CLE	77	63	0	.550	15	**49**	25	639	579	5225	1265	**231**	95	31	259	595	**153**	40	.265	.308	.373	681	**112**	51	**63**	98	**175**			
NY	72	62	2	.537	17	41	26	579	573	5091	1136	193	62	18	**332**	**465**	129	**65**	.249	.309	.330	639	92	-3	-36	106	160			
DET	65	71	1	.478	25	37	28	567	539	5090	1229	162	91	12	292	526	170	46	.268	.318	.351	669	110	37	55	97	128			
STL	65	74	0	.468	26.5	38	32	500	525	5047	1133	166	68	12	271	539	111	26	.244	.290	.317	607	90	-68	-54	97	101			
CHI	60	77	1	.438	30.5	41	28	516	613	5175	1152	176	49	14	325	537	142	38	.247	.301	.314	615	94	-45	-21	96	180			
WAS	43	94	3	.314	47.5	29	40	437	691	4990	1066	172	72	17	257	463	81	39	.231	.277	.311	588	80	-100	-109	102	131			
TOT	554					328	220	4543		41057	9553	1549	618	184	2266	4199	322	1035	.255	.303	.344	648					1173			

TEAM	CG	SHO	GR	SV	IP	H	HR	BB	SO	BR/9	ERA	AERA	OAV	OOB	PR	APR	PF	OSB	OCS	FA	E	WPB	DP	FW	PW	BW	BSW	DIF
BOS	123	**20**	18	**4**	1255.0	1142	23	269	579	**10.4**	**2.57**	**118**	**.242**	**.288**	**55**	**63**	102	**123**	*130*	.959	239	44	86	2.3	**6.5**	5.7		7.5
PHI	112	10	**28**	1	1207.0	**1124**	20	315	**728**	11.3	2.98	103	.246	.305	-2	10	103	140	*122*	**.960**	**217**	58	66	**3.2**	1.0	1.3		1.9
CLE	**125**	**20**	15	0	1243.2	1161	**16**	271	521	10.6	2.73	105	.247	.293	32	18	96	135	*120*	.946	322	51	**99**	-3.2	1.9	**6.5**		1.8
NY	111	7	26	2	1201.1	1171	19	245	463	10.9	3.08	101	.255	.299	-16	5	105	133	*89*	.953	264	43	87	.0	.5	-3.7		8.2
DET	123	15	15	2	1196.0	1169	19	336	554	11.5	2.75	106	.256	.310	28	21	98	185	*126*	.950	281	40	82	-.9	2.2	5.7		-10.0
STL	124	12	16	3	1222.1	1220	26	**237**	511	11.0	2.77	105	.260	.300	26	19	98	127	*108*	.953	268	**34**	94	.2	2.0	-5.6		-1.0
CHI	114	9	26	**4**	1235.0	1233	23	287	391	11.5	3.02	93	.260	.309	-8	-30	95	131	*107*	.949	297	52	85	-1.8	-3.1	-2.2		-1.4
WAS	122	6	18	3	1223.2	1333	38	306	452	12.4	3.82	82	.277	.325	-116	-89	106	199	*127*	.954	260	37	86	.8	-9.2	-11.3		-5.7
TOT	954	99	162	19	9784.0					11.2	2.96		.255	.303						.953	2148	359	685					

Batter-Fielder Wins	Batting Average	On-Base Percentage	Slugging Average	On-Base Plus Slugging	Adjusted OPS	Adjusted Batter Runs
Lajoie-Cle 8.1	Lajoie-Cle 344	Barrett-Det 407	Lajoie-Cle 518	Lajoie-Cle 896	Lajoie-Cle 170	Lajoie-Cle 40.6
Bradley-Cle 4.8	Crawford-Det 335	Hartsel-Phi..................391	Bradley-Cle...........496	Hartsel-Phi 868	Crawford-Det........159	Crawford-Det......36.3
Crawford-Det......3.6	Dougherty-Bos 331	Lajoie-Cle 379	Freeman-Bos 496	Crawford-Det........855	Bradley-Cle 154	Barrett-Det..........32.8
Barrett-Det..........3.4	Barrett-Det 315	Lush-Det 379	Crawford-Det 489	Bradley-Cle 844	Hartsel-Phi 152	Bradley-Cle 32.5
Collins-Bos..........2.9	Bradley-Cle...........313	Green-Chi 375	Hartsel-Phi 477	Freeman-Bos........823	Green-Chi 146	Green-Chi 30.0

Runs	Hits	Doubles	Triples	Home Runs	Total Bases	Runs Batted In
Dougherty-Bos 107	Dougherty-Bos 195	Seybold-Phi 45	Crawford-Det..........25	Freeman-Bos..........13	Freeman-Bos........281	Freeman-Bos 104
Bradley-Cle 101	Crawford-Det........184	Lajoie-Cle 41	Bradley-Cle 22	Hickman-Cle 12	Crawford-Det.........269	Hickman-Cle...........97
Keeler-NY 95	Parent-Bos............170	Freeman-Bos 39	Freeman-Bos..........20	Ferris-Bos 9	Bradley-Cle 266	Lajoie-Cle 93
Barrett-Det.............95	Bay-Cle 169	Bradley-Cle.....................36	Parent-Bos.............17	Seybold-Phi 8	Lajoie-Cle 251	L.Cross-Phi 90
Bay-Cle 94	Bradley-Cle 168	Anderson-StL 34	Collins-Bos 17		Dougherty-Bos 250	Crawford-Det 89

Stolen Bases	Base Stealing Runs	Fielding Runs-Infield	Fielding Runs-Outfield	Wins	Winning Pct.	Complete Games
Bay-Cle 45		Lajoie-Cle 39.1	Lush-Det.............12.8	Young-Bos 28	Young-Bos 757	Young-Bos 34
Pickering-Phi 40		Wallace-StL 18.4	Barrett-Det 6.7	Plank-Phi 23	Hughes-Bos 741	Waddell-Phi 34
Holmes-Was-Chi 35		Williams-NY 15.5	Holmes-Was-Chi ..6.4		Moore-Cle.............714	Donovan-Det 34
Dougherty-Bos 35		Ferris-Bos 14.3	Crawford-Det 5.2		Dinneen-Bos.........618	
Conroy-NY..............33		Carr-Det......................12.7	Robinson-Was 4.3		Plank-Phi 590	

Strikeouts	Fewest BB/Game	Games	Saves	Base Runners/9	Adjusted Relief Runs	Relief Ranking
Waddell-Phi 302	Young-Bos 97	Plank-Phi 43	Young-Bos 2	Joss-Cle 8.82		
Donovan-Det 187	Bernhard-Cle 1.14	Mullin-Det 41	Powell-StL 2	Young-Bos 8.96		
Young-Bos 176	Donahue-StL-Cle 1.14	Young-Bos 40	Orth-Was 2	Bernhard-Cle 9.34		
Plank-Phi 176	Joss-Cle 1.17	Flaherty-Chi 40	Mullin-Det 2	Moore-Cle.............9.56		
Mullin-Det 170	Tannehill-NY........1.28	Chesbro-NY 40	Dinneen-Bos 2	Dinneen-Bos........9.78		

Innings Pitched	Opponents' Avg.	Opponents' OBP	Earned Run Average	Adjusted ERA	Adjusted Starter Runs	Pitcher Wins
Young-Bos 341.2	Moore-Cle.............217	Joss-Cle........................256	Moore-Cle............1.74	Moore-Cle 164	Young-Bos 34.0	**Young-Bos**..........4.8
Plank-Phi 336.0	Donovan-Det 220	Young-Bos 259	Young-Bos 2.08	Young-Bos 146	Dinneen-Bos........27.8	**Mullin-Det** 3.5
Chesbro-NY 324.2	Joss-Cle 223	Bernhard-Cle 267	Bernhard-Cle 2.12	Bernhard-Cle........135	Moore-Cle............26.8	**Donovan-Det**.......3.0
Waddell-Phi 324.0	Waddell-Phi 229	Moore-Cle 271	White-Chi 2.13	Dinneen-Bos 134	Donovan-Det 25.4	**Dinneen-Bos**.......2.9
Mullin-Det 320.2	Dinneen-Bos.........230	Dinneen-Bos 276	Joss-Cle 2.19	White-Chi..............132	Waddell-Phi 23.2	**White-Chi**............2.8

Upstart Champions

Prior to the season, the NL weighed its options. After first proposing a merger with the AL, the Senior Circuit settled for a truce, and the two leagues agreed to respect each other's player contracts and to end their war. With the sale of the rubble of the Baltimore franchise to New York investors, the AL was now set with eight signature clubs, which remained in the same cities until 1953.

Two noteworthy players died. Tigers pitcher Win Mercer, apparently despondent at gambling losses, turned on the gas in a hotel room on January 13 and died at 28. He had recently been named Detroit's manager. In the year's oddest tragedy, slugging outfielder Ed Delahanty of Washington fell into the Niagara River on July 2 and was apparently swept over Niagara Falls to his death after being ejected from a train due to drunkenness. He was just 34.

On the field, the biggest story was the strikeout and the resulting huge 16 percent drop in scoring. The league's adoption of the foul-strike rule led, predictably, to K's rising by a whopping 58 percent. Rube Waddell of the Athletics shattered the big-league strikeout record by 63.

By the end of July, the AL race was essentially over. Boston, the league leader in runs and ERA, emerged from the pack and cruised to the pennant. Philadelphia's already good pitching was bolstered by rookie Chief Bender, but Boston had the league's best mound staff (ed by Cy Young) plus two first-rate hitters in Buck Freeman and Patsy Dougherty.

The first interleague championship since 1890 and the first modern World Series pitted the Boston Americans against NL champion Pittsburgh Pirates, with the newly "recognized" Junior Circuit winning the best-of-nine series, five games to three, after losing three of the first four games. Americans starter Bill Dinneen won thrice as Young took two more, besting the efforts of Pirates ace Deacon Phillippe, who pitched five complete games.

1904 National League

TEAM	W	L	T	PCT	GB	HW	HL	R	OR	PA	H	2B	3B	HR	BB	SO	HB	SH	AVG	OBP	SLG	OPS	AOPS	BR	ABR	PF	SB	CS	BSA	BSR
NY	106	47	5	.693		**56**	26	**744**	**474**	5829	**1347**	**202**	65	**31**	**434**		**166**	**79**	**.262**	**.328**	**.344**	**672**	**109**	**92**	**62**	104	**283**			
CHI	93	60	3	.608	13	49	27	597	517	5697	1294	157	62	22	298		141	48	.248	.295	.315	610	94	-41	-42	100	227			
CIN	88	65	4	.575	18	49	27	695	547	5814	1332	189	92	21	399		135	49	.255	.313	.338	651	98	42	-12	109	180			
PIT	87	66	3	.569	19	48	30	675	592	5722	1333	164	**102**	15	391		124	47	.258	.316	.338	654	105	46	29	103	178			
STL	75	79	1	.487	31.5	39	36	602	595	5622	1292	175	66	24	343		129	46	.253	.306	.327	633	106	7	36	96	199			
BRO	56	97	1	.366	50	31	44	497	614	5499	1142	159	53	15	411		129	42	.232	.297	.295	592	91	-56	-42	98	205			
BOS	55	98	2	.359	51	34	45	491	749	5594	1217	153	50	24	316		101	42	.237	.287	.300	587	90	-80	-61	96	143			
PHI	52	100	3	.342	53.5	28	43	571	784	5639	1268	170	54	23	377		119	40	.248	.305	.316	621	102	-10	12	96	159			
TOT	623					334	278	4872		45416	10225	1369	544	175	2969	4277	393	104	4.249	.306	.322	628					1574			

TEAM	CG	SHO	GR	SV	IP	H	HR	BB	SO	BR/9	ERA	AERA	OAV	OOB	PR	APR	PF	OSB	OCS	FA	E	WPB	DP	FW	PW	BW	BSW	DIF
NY	127	**21**	**29**	**15**	1396.2	1151	36	349	**707**	**9.9**	**2.17**	**125**	**.222**	**.276**	**86**	**83**	100	**134**	*167*	**.956**	294	43	**93**	**2.3**	**8.8**	**6.6**		11.9
CHI	139	18	17	6	1383.2	**1150**	16	402	618	10.3	2.30	115	.224	.285	65	55	97	160	*164*	.954	298	49	89	1.8	5.8	-4.4		13.3
CIN	142	12	15	2	1392.2	1256	**13**	343	502	10.7	2.34	**125**	.241	.295	60	82	107	192	*176*	.954	301	60	81	1.7	8.7	-1.3		2.4
PIT	133	15	25	1	1348.1	1273	**13**	379	455	11.4	2.89	95	.248	.306	-24	-24	100	187	*160*	.955	**291**	49	**93**	2.2	-2.5	3.1		7.7
STL	**146**	7	8	2	1368.0	1286	23	**319**	529	10.8	2.64	102	.239	.286	13	5	99	235	*109*	.952	307	42	83	1.1	.5	3.8		-7.4
BRO	135	12	20	2	1337.1	1281	27	414	453	11.8	2.70	101	.255	.319	4	4	100	193	*180*	.945	343	**41**	87	-1.4	.4	-4.4		-15.1
BOS	136	13	20	0	1348.1	1405	25	500	544	13.1	3.43	80	.272	.343	-105	-104	101	230	***199***	.945	353	77	91	-1.9	-11.0	-6.5		-2.2
PHI	131	10	25	2	1339.1	1418	22	425	469	12.9	3.39	79	.270	.332	-99	-112	98	243	*183*	.937	403	50	**93**	-5.1	-11.9	1.3		-8.3
TOT	1089	108	159	30	10914.1					11.3	2.73		.249	.306						.950	2590	411	710					

Batter-Fielder Wins
- **Wagner-Pit** 5.3
- **Thomas-Phi** 4.1
- **Leach-Pit** 4.0
- **Chance-Chi** 3.8
- **Dahlen-NY** 3.2

Batting Average
- Wagner-Pit 349
- Donlin-Cin-NY 329
- Beckley-StL 325
- Grady-StL 313
- Seymour-Cin.........313

On-Base Percentage
- Wagner-Pit..................423
- Thomas-Phi 416
- Chance-Chi 382
- Huggins-Cin................377
- Beckley-StL 375

Slugging Average
- Wagner-Pit 520
- Grady-StL 474
- Donlin-Cin-NY 457
- Seymour-Cin.........439
- Chance-Chi 430

On-Base Plus Slugging
- Wagner-Pit............944
- Chance-Chi 812
- Seymour-Cin 790
- Beckley-StL 778
- Thomas-Phi 761

Adjusted OPS
- Wagner-Pit............186
- Chance-Chi 150
- Beckley-StL 147
- Thomas-Phi 141
- Lumley-Bro 137

Adjusted Batter Runs
- Wagner-Pit 51.7
- Thomas-Phi........32.5
- Beckley-StL.........30.2
- Chance-Chi 27.3
- Grady-StL 25.7

Runs
- Browne-NY 99
- Wagner-Pit.............97
- Beaumont-Pit...........97
- Huggins-Cin............96

Hits
- Beaumont-Pit........185
- Beckley-StL 179
- Wagner-Pit............171
- Browne-NY 169
- Seymour-Cin 166

Doubles
- Wagner-Pit 44
- Mertes-NY 28
- Delahanty-Bos 27
- Seymour-Cin..................26
- Dahlen-NY 26

Triples
- Lumley-Bro 18
- Wagner-Pit.............14
- Tinker-Chi 13
- Seymour-Cin 13
- Kelley-Cin 13

Home Runs
- Lumley-Bro 9
- Brain-StL 7

Total Bases
- Wagner-Pit............255
- Lumley-Bro 247
- Seymour-Cin 233
- Beaumont-Pit........230
- Beckley-StL 222

Runs Batted In
- Dahlen-NY 80
- Mertes-NY 78
- Lumley-Bro............78
- Wagner-Pit 75
- Corcoran-Cin 74

Stolen Bases
- Wagner-Pit.............53
- Mertes-NY 47
- Dahlen-NY..............47
- McGann-NY............42
- Chance-Chi 42

Base Stealing Runs

Fielding Runs-Infield
- Leach-Pit 35.8
- Evers-Chi 28.2
- Dahlen-NY 25.0
- Tinker-Chi 15.6
- Farrell-StL 14.5

Fielding Runs-Outfield
- Thomas-Phi 12.9
- Odwell-Cin 12.3
- Sheckard-Bro 10.5
- Sebring-Pit-Cin 9.8
- Titus-Phi 9.7

Wins
- McGinnity-NY 35
- Mathewson-NY 33
- Harper-Cin..............23
- Taylor-NY................21
- Nichols-StL 21

Winning Pct.
- McGinnity-NY 814
- Mathewson-NY.....733
- Harper-Cin 719
- Flaherty-Pit...........679

Complete Games
- Willis-Bos 39
- Taylor-StL 39
- McGinnity-NY........38
- Jones-Bro..............38

Strikeouts
- Mathewson-NY 212
- Willis-Bos..............196
- Weimer-Chi 177
- Pittinger-Bos 146
- McGinnity-NY 144

Fewest BB/Game
- Hahn-Cin 1.06
- Phillippe-Pit 1.40
- Nichols-StL..........1.42
- Kellum-Cin 1.84
- McFarland-StL 1.87

Games
- McGinnity-NY 51
- Mathewson-NY..............48
- Jones-Bro 46
- Willis-Bos 43
- Fraser-Phi 42

Saves
- McGinnity-NY 5
- Wiltse-NY 3
- Briggs-Chi 3
- Ames-NY 3

Base Runners/9
- Brown-Chi............8.94
- McGinnity-NY 8.96
- Robitaille-Pit 9.00
- Hahn-Cin 9.07
- Nichols-StL..........9.17

Adjusted Relief Runs

Relief Ranking

Innings Pitched
- McGinnity-NY 408.0
- Jones-Bro 377.0
- Mathewson-NY..367.2
- Taylor-StL 352.0
- Willis-Bos 350.0

Opponents' Avg.
- Brown-Chi............199
- Weimer-Chi...........204
- McGinnity-NY 206
- Taylor-NY 214
- Garvin-Bro 218

Opponents' OBP
- Brown-Chi 253
- Nichols-StL 256
- McGinnity-NY 256
- Hahn-Cin 262
- Mathewson-NY 270

Earned Run Average
- McGinnity-NY 1.61
- Garvin-Bro 1.68
- Brown-Chi............1.86
- Weimer-Chi..........1.91
- Nichols-StL 2.02

Adjusted ERA
- McGinnity-NY 169
- Garvin-Bro............162
- Brown-Chi 142
- Hahn-Cin 142
- Weimer-Chi 139

Adjusted Starter Runs
- McGinnity-NY 50.2
- Hahn-Cin 27.2
- Mathewson-NY.....26.9
- Nichols-StL 26.8
- Weimer-Chi..........25.9

Pitcher Wins
- **McGinnity-NY**....5.4
- **Mathewson-NY**..4.2
- **Hahn-Cin** 3.2
- **Weimer-Chi** 2.8
- **Nichols-StL**.........2.8

Take a Giant Step

National League teams were first required to play a 154-game schedule in 1904, an arrangement that lasted for 58 years through 1961 (except for wartime changes). In addition, home teams were now required to provide more than one baseball for each game, and clubs had to wear different uniforms for home and road contests. Finally, outfield fences had to be at least 235 feet from home plate, and the distance from home plate to the backstop was first regulated.

The league's fielding average reached .950, and skyrocketed in the next two years. Oddly enough, shortstop Herman Long, a great defender in the nineteenth century, hung 'em up in 1904 at age 38. The Giants, meanwhile, brought back two popular 1880s stars for limited engagements. "Orator Jim" O'Rourke, who collected 2,304 hits in his 19-year career, was 1-for-4 in one game as a catcher at age 54, while 46-year-old outfielder Dan Brouthers, a five-time batting champ, went hitless in five tries. Two star outfielders, neither of whom was born when Brouthers won his first home run title, debuted in 1904. Frank Schulte became a key component of the Cubs' success, while Philadelphia's Sherry Magee led the NL four times in RBIs.

Team runs decreased to 3.91 per game (batters clubbed more homers, but batting average fell 20 points to .249). George Browne of the Giants topped the NL with 99 runs; no league leader had fewer until 1915. The Giants won 18 straight at one point, moving into first for good in June. Skipper John McGraw had world-class pitching with Christy Mathewson, Iron Joe McGinnity, Dummy Taylor, and rookie Hooks Wiltse. Offensively, New York led in runs, hits, doubles, homers, and walks.

Nevertheless, the proud Giants refused to play a World Series. Calling the Junior Circuit "bush," McGraw and Giants owner John Brush invited a hailstorm of criticism as the Giants refused to accept the AL, and defending world champion Boston, as a peer.

1904 American League

TEAM	W	L	T	PCT	GB	HW	HL	R	OR	PA	H	2B	3B	HR	BB	SO	HB	SH	AVG	OBP	SLG	OPS	AOPS	BR	ABR	PF	SB	CS	BSA	BSR
BOS	95	59	3	.617		49	30	608	**466**	5784	1294	194	**105**	26	347	570	155	51	.247	.301	.340	641	102	41	9	106	101			
NY	92	59	4	.609	1.5	46	29	598	526	5724	**1354**	195	91	27	312	**548**	135	**57**	.259	**.308**	.347	655	107	69	41	105	163			
CHI	89	65	2	.578	6	**50**	27	600	482	5638	1217	193	68	14	**373**	586	**197**	41	.242	.300	.316	616	104	6	29	96	**216**			
CLE	86	65	3	.570	7.5	44	31	**647**	482	5669	1340	**225**	90	27	307	714	164	46	**.260**	**.308**	**.354**	**662**	**116**	**80**	**86**	99	178			
PHI	81	70	4	.536	12.5	47	31	557	503	5578	1266	197	77	**31**	313	605	137	40	.249	.298	.336	634	101	29	1	105	137			
STL	65	87	4	.428	29	32	43	481	604	5817	1266	153	53	10	332	609	138	56	.239	.291	.294	585	96	-53	-19	94	150			
DET	62	90	10	.408	32	34	40	505	627	5853	1231	154	69	11	344	635	154	34	.231	.282	.292	574	90	-77	-61	97	112			
WAS	38	113	6	.252	55.5	23	52	437	743	5606	1170	171	57	10	283	759	115	59	.227	.275	.288	563	84	-95	-88	98	150			
TOT	626					325	283	4433		45669	10138	1482	610	156	2611	5026	384	1195	.244	.295	.321	616					1207			

TEAM	CG	SHO	GR	SV	IP	H	HR	BB	SO	BR/9	ERA	AERA	OAV	OOB	PR	APR	PF	OSB	OCS	FA	E	WPB	DP	FW	PW	BW	BSW	DIF
BOS	**148**	21	9	1	1406.0	1208	31	**233**	612	**9.4**	**2.12**	**126**	.233	**.270**	**75**	**84**	103	118	*114*	.962	242	**41**	83	1.6	**9.4**	1.0		6.0
NY	123	15	**33**	1	1380.2	1180	29	311	684	10.0	2.57	106	.232	.282	4	21	104	161	*125*	.958	275	58	90	-.8	2.3	4.6		10.4
CHI	134	**26**	22	**3**	1380.0	1161	13	303	550	9.8	2.30	107	**.229**	.279	45	24	95	**112**	*111*	**.964**	**238**	57	95	**1.7**	2.7	3.2		4.4
CLE	141	20	15	0	1356.2	1273	**10**	285	627	10.6	2.22	114	.249	.294	56	48	98	121	*110*	.959	255	50	86	.4	5.4	**9.6**		-4.9
PHI	136	**26**	20	0	1361.1	**1149**	13	366	**887**	10.4	2.35	114	.230	.291	38	48	103	141	*104*	.959	250	44	67	.8	5.4	.1		-.8
STL	135	13	22	1	1410.0	1335	25	333	577	11.0	2.83	88	.251	.303	-36	-58	96	164	*128*	.960	267	44	78	-.2	-6.5	-2.1		-2.2
DET	143	15	21	0	1430.0	1345	16	433	556	11.6	2.77	92	.250	.314	-27	-36	98	188	*135*	.959	273	58	92	.0	-4.0	-6.8		-3.2
WAS	137	7	20	**3**	1359.2	1487	19	347	533	12.5	3.62	73	.279	.330	-155	-142	102	202	***139***	.951	314	52	**97**	-3.1	-15.9	-9.8		-8.6
TOT	1097	143	162	9	11084.1					10.7	2.60		.244	.295						.959	2114	404	688					

Batter-Fielder Wins
Lajoie-Cle 7.4
Flick-Cle 4.5
Bradley-Cle 4.0
Murphy-Phi..........3.7
Davis-Chi 3.7

Batting Average
Lajoie-Cle 376
Keeler-NY 343
Davis-Phi 309
Flick-Cle 306
Bradley-Cle 300

On-Base Percentage
Lajoie-Cle 413
Keeler-NY 390
Flick-Cle.......................371
Stahl-Bos.....................366
Burkett-StL...................363

Slugging Average
Lajoie-Cle 546
Davis-Phi 490
Flick-Cle 449
Murphy-Phi 440
Hickman-Cle-Det .437

On-Base Plus Slugging
Lajoie-Cle 959
Flick-Cle................820
Keeler-NY 799
Stahl-Bos..............782
Murphy-Phi 760

Adjusted OPS
Lajoie-Cle 204
Flick-Cle................160
Keeler-NY 146
Stahl-Bos..............139
Hickman-Cle-Det ..137

Adjusted Batter Runs
Lajoie-Cle 64.3
Flick-Cle 40.2
Keeler-NY 28.4
Stahl-Bos............27.8
Burkett-StL 25.0

Runs
Dougherty-Bos-NY113
Flick-Cle..................97
Bradley-Cle 94
Lajoie-Cle 92

Hits
Lajoie-Cle 208
Keeler-NY 186
Bradley-Cle 183
Dougherty-Bos-NY181
Flick-Cle................177

Doubles
Lajoie-Cle 49
Collins-Bos 33
Bradley-Cle....................32

Triples
Stahl-Bos................19
Freeman-Bos..........19
Cassidy-Was 19
Murphy-Phi 17
Flick-Cle..................17

Home Runs
Davis-Phi 10
Murphy-Phi 7
Freeman-Bos............7

Total Bases
Lajoie-Cle 302
Flick-Cle................260
Bradley-Cle 249
Freeman-Bos........246

Runs Batted In
Lajoie-Cle............102
Freeman-Bos 84
Bradley-Cle.............83
Anderson-NY 82

Stolen Bases
Flick-Cle..................38
Bay-Cle 38
Heidrick-StL............35
Davis-Chi................32
Conroy-NY..............30

Base Stealing Runs

Fielding Runs-Infield
Tannehill-Chi 27.3
Davis-Chi 18.1
Carr-Det-Cle 15.7
Williams-NY 14.5
Murphy-Phi 14.2

Fielding Runs-Outfield
McIntyre-Det........11.9
Barrett-Det 9.0
Donovan-Was........8.8
Heidrick-StL 6.7
Bay-Cle..................6.3

Wins
Chesbro-NY............41
Young-Bos..............26
Plank-Phi 26
Waddell-Phi 25

Winning Pct.
Chesbro-NY 774
Tannehill-Bos 656
Smith-Chi 640
Bernhard-Cle 639
Dinneen-Bos.........622

Complete Games
Chesbro-NY 48
Mullin-Det.............42
Young-Bos 40
Waddell-Phi 39
Powell-NY..............38

Strikeouts
Waddell-Phi 349
Chesbro-NY..........239
Powell-NY 202
Plank-Phi 201
Young-Bos 200

Fewest BB/Game
Young-Bos 69
Tannehill-Bos 1.05
Patterson-Chi 1.31
Joss-Cle 1.40
Altrock-Chi 1.41

Games
Chesbro-NY 55
Powell-NY 47
Waddell-Phi 46
Patten-Was....................45
Mullin-Det 45

Saves
Patten-Was 3

Base Runners/9
Young-Bos 8.53
Chesbro-NY 8.57
Owen-Chi 9.00
Joss-Cle 9.22
Dinneen-Bos........9.33

Adjusted Relief Runs

Relief Ranking

Innings Pitched
Chesbro-NY 454.2
Powell-NY..........390.1
Waddell-Phi 383.0
Mullin-Det 382.1
Young-Bos 380.0

Opponents' Avg.
Chesbro-NY 208
Owen-Chi 214
Smith-Chi 215
Gibson-Bos...........219
Waddell-Phi 221

Opponents' OBP
Young-Bos 251
Chesbro-NY.................252
Owen-Chi......................261
Joss-Cle.......................266
Dinneen-Bos 268

Earned Run Average
Joss-Cle 1.59
Waddell-Phi 1.62
Hess-Cle..............1.67
White-Chi 1.78
Chesbro-NY 1.82

Adjusted ERA
Waddell-Phi 165
Joss-Cle...............159
Chesbro-NY..........149
White-Chi..............138
Young-Bos 136

Adjusted Starter Runs
Chesbro-NY 41.2
Waddell-Phi 39.7
Young-Bos 33.4
Plank-Phi 23.4
Joss-Cle 19.9

Pitcher Wins
Chesbro-NY 6.1
Waddell-Phi........4.1
Young-Bos..........3.8
Plank-Phi............3.2
Owen-Chi............3.2

Pilgrims' Progress

AL offense continued to plummet in 1904, as scoring decreased another 14 percent due to substantial drops in both homers (almost 30 percent) and steals (which fell to less than one per game for the only time until 1918). Concomitantly, strikeouts continued to increase as Rube Waddell broke his own record by fanning 349, a major league mark that would last until 1965. Another top hurler, Ed Walsh of the White Sox, debuted at 23; he would eventually win 195 games.

The "First in War, First in Peace, Last in the American League" Washington Senators moved into a new stadium. However, there was nothing to celebrate about the move, as the club's .252 winning percentage was the majors' worst until 1916. The Tigers played 162 games, 10 of them ties; outfielder Jimmy Barrett took part in *all* of them, setting a games-played record that stood until 1961 (when the AL expanded and increased the schedule from 154 to 162 games).

The young but successful American League posted another huge attendance increase. Chicago, New York, and Boston—the league's three top performers—enjoyed large crowds as the new league's first real pennant race set the sporting world abuzz.

Jack Chesbro won 41 games, the most by anyone who played after the nineteenth century, but "Happy Jack" would be remembered more for a wild pitch that cost his team, the New York Highlanders, the pennant. New York and Boston, clinging together at the top of the standings for the final two months, met for a season-ending series at New York. With the Pilgrims up by 1½ and just two games remaining, Chesbro's ninth-inning wild pitch allowed the winning run—and resulted in a title—for Boston. Unfortunately, the obstinate New York Giants, perhaps afraid of losing, refused to agree to play in a World Series. This would be the only season without postseason baseball until 1994.

1905 National League

TEAM	W	L	T	PCT	GB	HW	HL	R	OR	PA	H	2B	3B	HR	BB	SO	HB	SH	AVG	OBP	SLG	OPS	AOPS	BR	ABR	PF	SB	CS	BSA	BSR
NY	105	48	2	.686		**54**	21	**780**	505	5839	1392	**191**	88	**39**	**517**		138	**90**	**.273**	**.351**	**.368**	**719**	**119**	**148**	**132**	102	**291**			
PIT	96	57	2	.627	9	49	28	692	570	5790	1385	190	91	22	382		159	36	.266	.320	.350	670	104	38	21	103	202			
CHI	92	61	2	.601	13	**54**	25	667	**442**	5810	1249	157	82	12	448		**193**	61	.245	.313	.314	627	90	-30	-53	104	267			
PHI	83	69	3	.546	21.5	39	36	708	603	5867	1362	187	82	16	406		174	44	.260	.318	.336	654	106	14	39	96	180			
CIN	79	74	2	.516	26	50	28	736	698	5865	**1401**	160	**101**	27	434		174	52	.269	.332	.354	686	101	73	3	111	181			
STL	58	96	0	.377	47.5	32	45	535	734	5609	1254	140	85	20	391		109	43	.248	.307	.321	628	97	-38	-19	97	162			
BOS	51	103	2	.331	54.5	29	46	468	733	5631	1217	148	52	17	302		85	54	.234	.284	.293	577	80	-137	-126	98	132			
BRO	48	104	3	.316	56.5	29	47	506	807	5604	1255	154	60	29	327		136	41	.246	.297	.317	614	97	-68	-23	93	186			
TOT	620					336	276	5092		46015	10515	1327	641	182	3207	4462	421	1168	.255	.315	.332	647					1601			

TEAM	CG	SHO	GR	SV	IP	H	HR	BB	SO	BR/9	ERA	AERA	OAV	OOB	PR	APR	PF	OSB	OCS	FA	E	WPB	DP	FW	PW	BW	BSW	DIF
NY	117	18	42	**15**	1370.0	1160	25	**364**	**760**	10.2	2.39	122	.229	**.284**	91	82	98	**123**	*138*	.960	258	82	93	2.3	8.5	**13.7**		4.0
PIT	113	12	**47**	6	1382.2	1270	**12**	389	512	11.2	2.86	104	.248	.308	20	16	100	164	*152*	.961	255	61	112	2.5	1.7	2.2		13.2
CHI	133	**23**	22	2	1407.1	**1135**	14	385	627	**10.0**	**2.04**	**146**	**.224**	.286	**149**	**145**	99	168	*150*	**.962**	**248**	45	99	**2.9**	**15.1**	-5.5		3.0
PHI	119	12	42	5	1398.2	1303	21	411	516	11.5	2.81	104	.252	.316	28	13	97	173	*160*	.957	275	**40**	99	1.2	1.4	4.1		.4
CIN	119	10	39	2	1365.2	1409	22	439	547	12.5	3.01	109	.272	.335	-3	38	110	203	*176*	.953	310	68	**122**	-1.0	3.9	.3		-.8
STL	135	10	19	2	1347.2	1431	28	367	411	12.3	3.59	83	.276	.329	-89	-93	99	238	*161*	.957	274	48	83	1.2	-9.7	-2.0		-8.5
BOS	**139**	14	18	0	1383.0	1390	36	433	533	12.1	3.52	88	.265	.326	-81	-66	103	278	***191***	.951	325	85	89	-1.8	-6.9	-13.1		-4.2
BRO	125	7	33	3	1347.0	1416	24	476	556	13.1	3.76	77	.274	.343	-114	-137	96	252	*182*	.937	408	**40**	101	-7.2	-14.2	-2.4		-4.2
TOT	1000	106	262	35	11002.0					11.6	2.99		.255	.315						.954	2353	469	798					

Batter-Fielder Wins
- **Wagner-Pit** 7.5
- **Seymour-Cin** 5.6
- **Huggins-Cin** 4.7
- **Titus-Phi** 4.1
- **Thomas-Phi** 4.1

Batting Average
- Seymour-Cin......... 377
- Wagner-Pit 363
- Donlin-NY 356
- Beaumont-Pit 328
- Thomas-Phi 317

On-Base Percentage
- Chance-Chi 450
- Seymour-Cin 429
- Wagner-Pit................... 427
- Thomas-Phi 417
- Donlin-NY 413

Slugging Average
- Seymour-Cin......... 559
- Wagner-Pit 505
- Donlin-NY 495
- Titus-Phi 436
- Grady-StL 434

On-Base Plus Slugging
- Seymour-Cin 988
- Wagner-Pit............ 932
- Donlin-NY 908
- Chance-Chi 883
- Titus-Phi 834

Adjusted OPS
- Seymour-Cin 175
- Wagner-Pit............ 173
- Donlin-NY 166
- Chance-Chi 157
- Titus-Phi 154

Adjusted Batter Runs
- Seymour-Cin 52.3
- Wagner-Pit 50.4
- Donlin-NY 49.3
- Titus-Phi 40.4
- Chance-Chi 34.8

Runs
- Donlin-NY 124
- Thomas-Phi 118
- Huggins-Cin.......... 117
- Wagner-Pit............ 114
- ....

Hits
- Seymour-Cin 219
- Donlin-NY 216
- Wagner-Pit............ 199
- Barry-Chi-Cin 182
- Magee-Phi 180

Doubles
- Seymour-Cin................. 40
- Titus-Phi 36
- Wagner-Pit 32
- Donlin-NY 31
- Ritchey-Pit 29

Triples
- Seymour-Cin 21
- Mertes-NY 17
- Magee-Phi 17
- Smoot-StL 16
- Donlin-NY 16

Home Runs
- Odwell-Cin................ 9
- Seymour-Cin 8
- Lumley-Bro 7
- Donlin-NY 7
- Dahlen-NY................ 7

Total Bases
- Seymour-Cin 325
- Donlin-NY 300
- Wagner-Pit............ 277
- Magee-Phi 253
- Titus-Phi 239

Runs Batted In
- Seymour-Cin 121
- Mertes-NY 108
- Wagner-Pit 101
- Magee-Phi 98
- Titus-Phi 89

Stolen Bases
- Maloney-Chi 59
- Devlin-NY 59
- Wagner-Pit.............. 57
- Mertes-NY 52
- Magee-Phi 48

Base Stealing Runs

Fielding Runs-Infield
- Huggins-Cin................ 36.8
- Tenney-Bos 22.1
- Gilbert-NY 20.3
- Corcoran-Cin 20.1
- Dahlen-NY 19.8

Fielding Runs-Outfield
- Sheckard-Bro 16.6
- Thomas-Phi 14.8
- Seymour-Cin.......... 9.8
- Magee-Phi 9.7
- Dunleavy-StL 6.9

Wins
- Mathewson-NY 31
- Pittinger-Phi 23
- Ames-NY 22
- McGinnity-NY 21

Winning Pct.
- Leever-Pit 800
- Mathewson-NY..... 775
- Ames-NY 733
- Wiltse-NY 714
- Lynch-Pit............... 680

Complete Games
- Young-Bos 41
- Willis-Bos 36
- Fraser-Bos 35
- Taylor-StL 34

Strikeouts
- Mathewson-NY 206
- Ames-NY 198
- Overall-Cin............ 173
- Ewing-Cin 164
- Young-Bos 156

Fewest BB/Game
- Phillippe-Pit 1.55
- Brown-Chi............ 1.59
- Young-Bos 1.69
- Mathewson-NY.... 1.70
- McGinnity-NY 1.99

Games
- Pittinger-Phi 46
- McGinnity-NY 46
- Young-Bos 43
- Mathewson-NY 43
- Overall-Cin 42

Saves
- Elliott-NY 6
- Wiltse-NY 3
- McGinnity-NY 3
- Mathewson-NY 3

Base Runners/9
- Mathewson-NY.... 8.42
- Reulbach-Chi 9.23
- Phillippe-Pit 9.45
- Wicker-Chi 9.46
- Hillebrand-Pit 9.49

Adjusted Relief Runs

Relief Ranking

Innings Pitched
- Young-Bos 378.0
- Willis-Bos 342.0
- Mathewson-NY.. 338.2
- Pittinger-Phi 337.1
- Fraser-Bos 334.1

Opponents' Avg.
- Reulbach-Chi 201
- Mathewson-NY..... 205
- Wiltse-NY 219
- Lundgren-Chi 220
- Wicker-Chi 221

Opponents' OBP
- Mathewson-NY 245
- Reulbach-Chi............... 266
- Brown-Chi 271
- Phillippe-Pit 274
- Wicker-Chi 276

Earned Run Average
- Mathewson-NY.... 1.28
- Reulbach-Chi 1.42
- Wicker-Chi 2.02
- Briggs-Chi............ 2.14
- Brown-Chi............ 2.17

Adjusted ERA
- Mathewson-NY 229
- Reulbach-Chi........ 209
- Wicker-Chi 147
- Briggs-Chi 139
- Brown-Chi 137

Adjusted Starter Runs
- Mathewson-NY.... 56.6
- Reulbach-Chi 48.0
- Ewing-Cin 26.9
- Wicker-Chi 22.3
- Phillippe-Pit 22.1

Pitcher Wins
- **Mathewson-NY** .. 8.5
- **Reulbach-Chi** 4.6
- **Ewing-Cin** 2.9
- **Weimer-Chi** 2.5
- **Wiltse-NY** 2.3

Christy Blanks A's

Four-time batting champion Pete Browning died at 44 from complications of mastoiditis, a disease that plagued him throughout his career. Outfielder Jesse "The Crab" Burkett and first baseman Dirty Jack Doyle played their final major league games, bringing to an end two great careers as well as two great nicknames. More were coming.

The Mahatma entered the major leagues on June 16, as the St. Louis Browns inserted 24-year-old catcher Branch Rickey into a game. Rickey's tenure as a player was brief, but he remained a fixture in the game for sixty years. Two weeks after Rickey's debut, New York Giants outfielder Moonlight Graham played his only game; he would languish in obscurity until revived nearly eighty years later by author W.P. Kinsella.

The suddenly unstoppable Giants again blew away the league, pacing the field wire to wire and surviving their only challenge, a brief August initiative from the Pirates. The Cubs, however, won 17 of their last 20, forecasting their great 1906 performance to come.

The Giants boasted few offensive leaders, but their lineup did everything well. Using the stolen base, the base on balls, and even the home run, New York led the league in runs by more than 40. Pittsburgh finished second; Honus Wagner failed to lead the league in a major offensive category for the only time between 1900 and 1912, but he was still the league's best hitter. Christy Mathewson was its best pitcher. New York's star captured 31 victories to lead the league by a margin of eight. On the other side, Vic Willis of seventh-place Boston dropped 29, the highest total of the twentieth century.

While the AL champion Philadelphia Athletics were an excellent club, they were clearly no match for the Giants in the World Series. Philadelphia won Game 2 with a shutout, as were all five games. However, Mathewson threw three of New York's four whitewashes in one of the greatest performances in postseason history.

1905 American League

TEAM	W	L	T	PCT	GB	HW	HL	R	OR	PA	H	2B	3B	HR	BB	SO	HB	SH	AVG	OBP	SLG	OPS	AOPS	BR	ABR	PF	SB	CS	BSA	BSR
PHI	92	56	4	.622		**51**	22	**623**	488	5721	1310	**256**	51	24	376	644	165	34	**.255**	**.310**	**.338**	**648**	**109**	**65**	**54**	102	190			
CHI	92	60	6	.605	2	50	29	612	**451**	5852	1213	200	55	11	439	613	**241**	58	.237	.305	.304	609	103	3	28	96	194			
DET	79	74	1	.516	15.5	45	30	512	604	5566	1209	190	54	13	375	583	180	40	.243	.302	.311	613	99	1	-3	101	129			
BOS	78	74	1	.513	16	44	32	579	565	5711	1179	165	69	**29**	**486**	553	139	37	.234	.305	.311	616	100	13	7	101	131			
CLE	76	78	1	.494	19	41	36	564	587	5655	**1318**	211	**72**	18	286	712	148	55	**.255**	.301	.334	635	106	32	24	101	188			
NY	71	78	3	.477	21.5	40	35	586	621	5535	1228	163	61	23	360	**537**	151	**67**	.248	.307	.319	626	93	24	-35	111	**200**			
WAS	64	87	3	.424	29.5	33	42	559	623	5528	1121	193	68	22	298	824	161	54	.224	.274	.302	576	92	-72	-52	96	169			
STL	54	99	3	.353	40.5	34	42	512	608	5768	1205	153	49	16	362	639	150	52	.232	.288	.289	577	93	-66	-37	95	144			
TOT	617					338	268	4547		45336	9783	1531	479	156	2982	5105	397	1335	.241	.299	.314	613					1345			

TEAM	CG	SHO	GR	SV	IP	H	HR	BB	SO	BR/9	ERA	AERA	OAV	OOB	PR	APR	PF	OSB	OCS	FA	E	WPB	DP	FW	PW	BW	BSW	DIF
PHI	117	**19**	37	0	1383.1	**1137**	21	409	**895**	10.5	2.19	121	.227	.294	70	68	100	144	*124*	.957	265	61	64	.3	7.5	**5.9**		4.3
CHI	131	16	32	0	1427.0	1163	**11**	329	613	**9.6**	**1.99**	**124**	**.226**	**.277**	**105**	**78**	93	**132**	*126*	**.967**	**218**	58	**95**	**4.1**	**8.6**	3.1		.2
DET	124	17	31	1	1348.0	1226	**11**	474	578	11.7	2.83	96	.246	.318	-27	-18	103	232	*142*	.957	267	**38**	80	.4	-2.0	-.3		4.4
BOS	124	15	30	1	1356.1	1198	33	**292**	652	10.2	2.84	95	.238	.286	-29	-20	102	135	*132*	.953	296	51	75	-1.6	-2.2	.8		5.1
CLE	**140**	16	15	0	1363.1	1251	23	334	555	10.9	2.85	92	.245	.299	-30	-32	99	162	*125*	.963	233	56	84	2.8	-3.5	2.6		-2.9
NY	88	**19**	**76**	**4**	1353.2	1235	26	396	642	11.1	2.93	100	.246	.307	-42	-2	111	142	*120*	.952	293	69	88	-1.5	-.2	-3.8		2.1
WAS	118	12	40	1	1362.1	1250	12	385	539	11.2	2.87	92	.247	.308	-33	-36	100	168	*150*	.951	318	43	76	-3.0	-4.0	-5.7		1.1
STL	134	11	22	2	1384.2	1245	19	389	633	11.0	2.74	93	.243	.304	-14	-34	96	225	***157***	.955	296	61	78	-1.3	-3.7	-4.1		-13.4
TOT	976	125	283	9	10978.2					10.8	2.65		.241	.299						.957	2186	437	640					

Batter-Fielder Wins
Davis-Chi 4.4
Crawford-Det 4.2
Wallace-StL 4.2
Flick-Cle 3.3
Stone-StL 2.8

Batting Average
Flick-Cle 308
Keeler-NY 302
Bay-Cle 301
Crawford-Det 297
Isbell-Chi 296

On-Base Percentage
Hartsel-Phi..................409
Flick-Cle.......................383
Keeler-NY 357
Crawford-Det 357
Selbach-Bos 355

Slugging Average
Flick-Cle 462
Isbell-Chi 440
Crawford-Det 430
Davis-Phi 422
Stone-StL 410

On-Base Plus Slugging
Flick-Cle................845
Crawford-Det 786
Stone-StL 756
Davis-Phi 756
Hartsel-Phi 755

Adjusted OPS
Flick-Cle................165
Crawford-Det 148
Stone-StL 147
Hartsel-Phi 138
Davis-Phi 137

Adjusted Batter Runs
Flick-Cle 37.7
Hartsel-Phi 32.7
Stone-StL 32.0
Crawford-Det......31.4
Davis-Phi 25.1

Runs
Davis-Phi 93
Jones-Chi 91
Bay-Cle 90
Hartsel-Phi 88
Keeler-NY 81

Hits
Stone-StL 187
Davis-Phi 173
Crawford-Det 171
Keeler-NY 169
Bay-Cle 166

Doubles
Davis-Phi 47
Crawford-Det 38
Hickman-Det-Was..........37
Seybold-Phi 37

Triples
Flick-Cle..................18
Ferris-Bos 16
Turner-Cle 14
Stone-StL 13
Burkett-Bos 13

Home Runs
Davis-Phi 8
Stone-StL 7

Total Bases
Stone-StL 259
Davis-Phi 256
Crawford-Det 247
Hickman-Det-Was 232
Flick-Cle................231

Runs Batted In
Davis-Phi 83
L.Cross-Phi 77
Donahue-Chi 76
Crawford-Det 75
Turner-Cle 72

Stolen Bases
Hoffman-Phi 46
Fultz-NY 44
Stahl-Was 41
Hartsel-Phi 37

Base Stealing Runs

Fielding Runs-Infield
Cassidy-Was 34.8
Tannehill-Chi 25.3
Wallace-StL 20.7
Davis-Chi 16.4
Ferris-Bos 14.6

Fielding Runs-Outfield
McIntyre-Det........17.8
Jones-Was 13.5
Crawford-Det 10.0
Seybold-Phi 7.9
Jones-Chi 7.1

Wins
Waddell-Phi 27
Plank-Phi 24
Killian-Det 23
Altrock-Chi..............23
Tannehill-Bos..........22

Winning Pct.
Waddell-Phi 730
Tannehill-Bos 710
Coakley-Phi 692
Plank-Phi 667
Altrock-Chi 657

Complete Games
Plank-Phi 35
Mullin-Det..............35
Howell-StL 35
Killian-Det..............33
Owen-Chi 32

Strikeouts
Waddell-Phi 287
Young-Bos............210
Plank-Phi 210
Howell-StL 198
Smith-Chi..............171

Fewest BB/Game
Young-Bos 84
Joss-Cle 1.45
Owen-Chi 1.51
Bernhard-Cle 1.76
Altrock-Chi 1.80

Games
Waddell-Phi 46
Mullin-Det 44
Patten-Was 42
Owen-Chi 42

Saves
Buchanan-StL 2

Base Runners/9
Young-Bos 8.03
Griffith-NY............8.68
Patterson-Chi 9.03
Waddell-Phi 9.06
Owen-Chi 9.19

Adjusted Relief Runs

Relief Ranking

Innings Pitched
Mullin-Det..........347.2
Plank-Phi 346.2
Owen-Chi 334.0
Waddell-Phi 328.2
Howell-StL 323.0

Opponents' Avg.
Waddell-Phi 200
Smith-Chi.............208
Young-Bos 216
Howell-StL 217
White-Chi 218

Opponents' OBP
Young-Bos 241
Waddell-Phi 264
Owen-Chi......................267
White-Chi......................270
Joss-Cle........................274

Earned Run Average
Waddell-Phi 1.48
White-Chi 1.76
Young-Bos 1.82
Coakley-Phi 1.84
Altrock-Chi 1.88

Adjusted ERA
Waddell-Phi..........179
Young-Bos 147
Coakley-Phi 144
White-Chi..............140
Chesbro-NY..........133

Adjusted Starter Runs
Waddell-Phi 40.1
Young-Bos 25.4
White-Chi 24.0
Altrock-Chi 23.9
Plank-Phi 19.6

Pitcher Wins
Waddell-Phi........4.5
Howell-StL..........3.6
White-Chi............2.9
Altrock-Chi 2.7
Young-Bos..........2.7

Goose Eggs and Tough Guys

The Boston Americans and New York Highlanders sank from contention in 1905, falling to fourth and sixth places. After an early foray by Cleveland, the race settled into a battle between Philadelphia and Chicago. While both teams were hot down the stretch, the Athletics never trailed after early August.

The White Sox, finishing just 2 games out, were the first team since 1888 to post an ERA under 2.00. Of their six pitchers, the highest ERA belonged to Ed Walsh at 2.17. The White Sox hitters, an underrated bunch, were productive, with player-manager Fielder Jones scoring 91 runs—second in the league—despite hitting only .245.

Three influential players of great skill but questionable ethics made their debuts in 1905. On August 30, a Georgia freshman named Ty Cobb saw his first major league action for the Tigers. Two others with abundant talent but character even more dubious than that of Cobb made their first appearances: slick-fielding Hal Chase took over at first for New York, while 21-year-old pitcher Eddie Cicotte was 1–1 for Detroit. These two men would help to nearly destroy baseball in the next decade.

Enjoying another spectacular season in 1905, Philadelphia's Rube Waddell won the pitching "Triple Crown"; he also allowed just 6.33 hits per game, lowest in the AL until 1968. Eddie Plank, Andy Coakley, and Chief Bender rounded out one of the top rotations in history. However, the A's attack was equally strong; Topsy Hartsel led the league in walks for the second of five times as first sacker Harry Davis provided the punch, pacing the AL in doubles, homers, RBIs, and runs. In a year where just three AL regulars hit over .300, Philadelphia—the league's best offense—scored 4.06 runs per game. However, the A's tallied just three in a five-game World Series loss to the Giants.

1906 National League

TEAM	W	L	T	PCT	GB	HW	HL	R	OR	PA	H	2B	3B	HR	BB	SO	HB	SH	AVG	OBP	SLG	OPS	AOPS	BR	ABR	PF	SB	CS	BSA	BSR
CHI	116	36	3	.763		**56**	21	**704**	**381**	5742	**1316**	**181**	**71**	**20**	448		**231**	45	**.262**	.328	**.339**	**667**	109	85	49	106	283			
NY	96	56	1	.632	20	51	24	625	509	5556	1217	162	53	15	**563**		154	**71**	.255	**.343**	.321	664	**112**	**97**	**83**	102	**288**			
PIT	93	60	1	.608	23.5	49	27	623	470	5686	1313	164	67	12	424		190	42	.261	.324	.327	651	105	55	29	104	162			
PHI	71	82	1	.464	45.5	37	40	528	564	5524	1183	197	47	12	432		145	36	.241	.307	.307	614	98	-6	-7	100	180			
BRO	66	86	1	.434	50	31	44	496	625	5483	1156	141	68	25	388		162	36	.236	.297	.308	605	103	-34	9	92	176			
CIN	64	87	4	.424	51.5	36	40	533	582	5642	1198	140	**71**	16	395		164	58	.238	.301	.304	605	91	-31	-53	104	170			
STL	52	98	4	.347	63	28	48	470	607	5613	1195	137	69	10	361		139	38	.235	.291	.296	587	93	-69	-48	96	110			
BOS	49	102	1	.325	66.5	28	47	408	649	5452	1115	136	43	16	356		119	52	.226	.286	.281	567	85	-98	-86	97	93			
TOT	615					316	291	4387		44698	9693	1258	489	126	3367	4537	378	1304	.244	.310	.310	620					1462			

TEAM	CG	SHO	GR	SV	IP	H	HR	BB	SO	BR/9	ERA	AERA	OAV	OOB	PR	APR	PF	OSB	OCS	FA	E	WPB	DP	FW	PW	BW	BSW	DIF
CHI	125	**30**	33	10	1388.1	**1018**	**12**	446	**702**	**9.8**	**1.75**	**150**	**.207**	**.280**	**135**	**135**	100	**107**	*143*	**.969**	**194**	**34**	100	**4.5**	**15.0**	5.4		15.0
NY	105	19	**55**	**18**	1334.1	1207	13	394	639	11.0	2.49	105	.241	.300	20	15	99	144	*154*	.963	233	50	84	1.8	1.7	**9.2**		7.3
PIT	116	27	42	2	1358.0	1234	13	**309**	532	10.5	2.21	120	.245	.294	62	69	102	157	*133*	.964	228	52	**109**	2.2	7.7	3.2		3.4
PHI	108	21	52	5	1354.1	1201	18	436	500	11.3	2.58	101	.235	.304	7	0	99	203	*119*	.956	271	46	83	-.6	.0	-.8		-4.1
BRO	119	22	36	11	1348.2	1255	15	453	476	11.7	3.13	80	.249	.316	-76	-97	96	192	*151*	.955	283	**34**	73	-1.5	-10.8	1.0		1.3
CIN	126	12	31	5	1369.2	1248	14	470	567	11.6	2.69	102	.250	.320	-10	5	105	184	*161*	.959	262	55	97	.0	.6	-5.9		-6.3
STL	118	4	37	2	1354.0	1246	17	479	559	11.9	3.04	86	.246	.318	-63	-65	100	250	*164*	.957	272	75	92	-.7	-7.2	-5.3		-9.8
BOS	**137**	10	16	0	1334.1	1291	24	436	562	12.0	3.14	85	.261	.328	-76	-69	102	225	***181***	.947	337	49	102	-5.2	-7.7	-9.6		-4.1
TOT	954	145	302	53	10841.2					11.2	2.62		.244	.310						.959	2080	395	740					

Batter-Fielder Wins	Batting Average	On-Base Percentage	Slugging Average	On-Base Plus Slugging	Adjusted OPS	Adjusted Batter Runs
Wagner-Pit 7.2	Wagner-Pit .339	Bresnahan-NY .419	Lumley-Bro .477	Wagner-Pit .875	Lumley-Bro 184	Lumley-Bro 45.3
Devlin-NY 6.6	Steinfeldt-Chi .327	Chance-Chi .419	Wagner-Pit .459	Lumley-Bro .864	Wagner-Pit 166	Wagner-Pit 42.1
Lumley-Bro 4.5	Lumley-Bro .324	Wagner-Pit .416	Strang-NY .435	Chance-Chi .849	Chance-Chi 156	Chance-Chi 34.9
Bresnahan-NY 4.2	Strang-NY .319	Devlin-NY .396	Steinfeldt-Chi .430	Steinfeldt-Chi .825	Jordan-Bro 153	Steinfeldt-Chi 31.5
Huggins-Cin 4.0	Chance-Chi .319	Steinfeldt-Chi .395	Chance-Chi .430	Devlin-NY .786	Steinfeldt-Chi 149	Devlin-NY 28.3

Runs	Hits	Doubles	Triples	Home Runs	Total Bases	Runs Batted In
Wagner-Pit 103	Steinfeldt-Chi 176	Wagner-Pit 38	Schulte-Chi 13	Jordan-Bro 12	Wagner-Pit 237	Steinfeldt-Chi 83
Chance-Chi 103	Wagner-Pit 175	Magee-Phi 36	Clarke-Pit 13	Lumley-Bro 9	Steinfeldt-Chi 232	Nealon-Pit 83
Sheckard-Chi 90	Seymour-Cin-NY 165	Bransfield-Phi 28	Nealon-Pit 12	Seymour-Cin-NY 8	Lumley-Bro 231	Seymour-Cin-NY 80
Nealon-Pit 82	Magee-Phi 159	Steinfeldt-Chi 27	Lumley-Bro 12	Schulte-Chi 7	Magee-Phi 229	Jordan-Bro 78
	Huggins-Cin 159	Sheckard-Chi 27			Schulte-Chi 223	

Stolen Bases	Base Stealing Runs	Fielding Runs-Infield	Fielding Runs-Outfield	Wins	Winning Pct.	Complete Games
Chance-Chi 57		Devlin-NY 28.8	Magee-Phi 11.9	McGinnity-NY 27	Reulbach-Chi .826	Young-Bos 37
Magee-Phi 55		Brain-Bos 25.0	Maloney-Bro 9.1	Brown-Chi 26	Brown-Chi .813	Pfeffer-Bos 33
Devlin-NY 54		Gilbert-NY 21.9	Thomas-Phi 8.4	Willis-Pit 23	Leever-Pit .759	
Wagner-Pit 53		Huggins-Cin 21.9	Titus-Phi 6.8	Mathewson-NY 22	Lundgren-Chi .739	
Evers-Chi 49		Wagner-Pit 20.0	Clarke-Pit 4.9	Leever-Pit 22	Pfiester-Chi .714	

Strikeouts	Fewest BB/Game	Games	Saves	Base Runners/9	Adjusted Relief Runs	Relief Ranking
Beebe-Chi-StL 171	Phillippe-Pit 1.07	McGinnity-NY 45	Ferguson-NY 7	Brown-Chi 8.53		
Pfeffer-Bos 158	Leever-Pit 1.66	Young-Bos 43	Wiltse-NY 6	Pfiester-Chi 8.94		
Ames-NY 156	Sparks-Phi 1.76	Sparks-Phi 42	Stricklett-Bro 5	Sparks-Phi 8.98		
Pfiester-Chi 153	Ewing-Cin 1.88	Duggleby-Phi 42		Reulbach-Chi 9.66		
	McGinnity-NY 1.88			Ewing-Cin 9.70		

Innings Pitched	Opponents' Avg.	Opponents' OBP	Earned Run Average	Adjusted ERA	Adjusted Starter Runs	Pitcher Wins
Young-Bos 358.1	Reulbach-Chi .175	Brown-Chi .252	Brown-Chi 1.04	Brown-Chi 253	Brown-Chi 45.1	**Brown-Chi** 6.1
McGinnity-NY 339.2	Pfiester-Chi .194	Sparks-Phi .257	Pfiester-Chi 1.51	Pfiester-Chi 174	Willis-Pit 34.0	**Willis-Pit** 4.3
Willis-Pit 322.0	Brown-Chi .202	Pfiester-Chi .258	Reulbach-Chi 1.65	Reulbach-Chi 159	Pfiester-Chi 29.9	**Reulbach-Chi** 2.8
Sparks-Phi 316.2	Beebe-Chi-StL .209	Phillippe-Pit .276	Willis-Pit 1.73	Willis-Pit 154	Reulbach-Chi 25.6	**Taylor-StL-Chi** 2.8
Lindaman-Bos 307.1	Sparks-Phi .211	Reulbach-Chi .278	Leifield-Pit 1.87	Leifield-Pit 143	Taylor-StL-Chi 20.0	**Weimer-Cin** 2.8

A Chicago Revival

Staking their claim as the team of the decade, the Chicago Cubs walloped the rest of the league, going 116–36 to post the NL's best record ever while capturing the franchise's first flag since 1886. Chicago went 26–3 in August and easily held off a good New York team that won 96 games. Three Finger Brown had a 1.04 ERA, the best in modern NL history, and Ed Reulbach allowed just 5.33 hits per game, a record that would stand until 1968. The Cubs staff ERA was a spectacular 1.76.

The Cubs also had a productive offense headed by first baseman-manager Frank Chance and third sacker Harry Steinfeldt, one of baseball's first great offensive-minded third basemen. On the other hand, Boston (known as both the Doves and Beaneaters) lost 19 in a row and finished 66½ games out, an all-time National League record for team futility. The Cubs had seven players score more often than Boston's runs leader, Fred Tenney.

Pitcher Babe Adams made his debut with the Cardinals. Purchased by Pittsburgh the next year, Adams remained with the club until 1926 and won 194 games. Hugh Duffy, who batted .440 in 1894, saw his last at bat at age 39, and John McGraw ended his playing days to concentrate fully on managing from the dugout. Kid Nichols, a 361-game winner who starred for Boston from 1980–1901, and who was arguably the greatest pitcher of the nineteenth century, retired. Buck Ewing, a pre-eminent star of nineteenth century ball, died at age 47.

Offense again dropped significantly in 1906. Small-ball techniques like the sacrifice bunt and the steal were at their apex. The orthodox little man's game became relevant in October's intra-city World Series, where the "Hitless Wonder" White Sox pulled off a surprise upset of the Cubs.

1906 American League

TEAM	W	L	T	PCT	GB	HW	HL	R	OR	PA	H	2B	3B	HR	BB	SO	HB	SH	AVG	OBP	SLG	OPS	AOPS	BR	ABR	PF	SB	CS	BSA	BSR
CHI	93	58	3	.616		**54**	23	570	**460**	5654	1133	152	52	7	**453**		**226**	**50**	.230	.301	.286	587	91	-45	-31	97	216			
NY	90	61	4	.596	3	53	23	640	543	5661	1354	166	**77**	17	331		189	46	.266	.316	.339	655	101	57	-1	110	192			
CLE	89	64	4	.582	5	47	30	**663**	481	5987	**1514**	**240**	73	12	330		191	41	**.279**	**.325**	**.357**	**682**	**121**	**114**	**124**	99	203			
PHI	78	67	4	.538	12	48	23	561	539	5475	1206	213	49	**32**	385		164	43	.247	.308	.330	638	102	35	17	103	165			
STL	76	73	5	.510	16	40	34	560	499	5614	1244	145	60	20	366		171	47	.247	.304	.312	616	102	-7	18	96	**221**			
DET	71	78	2	.477	21	42	34	518	598	5474	1195	154	64	10	333		178	33	.242	.295	.306	601	91	-38	-51	103	206			
WAS	55	95	1	.367	37.5	33	41	519	665	5455	1180	144	65	26	306		144	49	.238	.289	.309	598	97	-46	-21	95	233			
BOS	49	105	1	.318	45.5	22	54	463	706	5645	1223	160	75	13	298		138	41	.237	.284	.304	588	89	-69	-68	100	99			
TOT	613					339	262	4494		44965	10049	1374	515	137	2802	4561	350	1401	.249	.303	.318	621					1535			

TEAM	CG	SHO	GR	SV	IP	H	HR	BB	SO	BR/9	ERA	AERA	OAV	OOB	PR	APR	PF	OSB	OCS	FA	E	WPB	DP	FW	PW	BW	BSW	DIF
CHI	117	**32**	43	4	1375.1	1212	11	**255**	543	**9.8**	2.13	119	.239	**.280**	85	66	94	**133**	*133*	.963	243	52	80	1.8	7.3	-3.4		11.8
NY	99	18	**68**	5	1357.2	1236	21	351	605	10.8	2.78	107	.246	.301	-13	25	110	184	*144*	.957	272	54	69	.1	2.7	-.1		11.7
CLE	**133**	27	27	4	1412.2	1197	16	365	530	10.3	**2.09**	**125**	.232	.289	**94**	**87**	97	170	*140*	**.967**	**217**	45	**111**	**3.8**	**9.6**	**13.6**		-14.5
PHI	107	19	51	4	1322.0	1135	**9**	425	**749**	11.0	2.60	105	.236	.305	13	16	101	192	*159*	.956	267	47	86	-.2	1.8	1.9		2.1
STL	**133**	17	21	5	1357.2	**1132**	14	314	558	10.0	2.23	116	**.230**	.284	70	56	96	211	*151*	.954	290	58	80	-1.1	6.2	2.0		-5.5
DET	128	7	25	4	1334.1	1398	14	389	469	12.4	3.06	90	.272	.330	-55	-42	103	171	*161*	.959	260	**34**	86	.4	-4.6	-5.6		6.3
WAS	115	13	47	1	1322.2	1331	15	451	558	12.4	3.25	81	.265	.331	-83	-93	98	229	*161*	.955	279	54	78	-.8	-10.2	-2.3		-6.7
BOS	124	6	35	**6**	1382.0	1360	37	285	549	11.0	3.41	81	.262	.306	-111	-103	102	245	***182***	.949	335	57	84	-3.9	-11.3	-7.5		-5.3
TOT	956	139	317	33	10864.1					11.0	2.69		.249	.303						.958	2163	401	674					

Batter-Fielder Wins	Batting Average	On-Base Percentage	Slugging Average	On-Base Plus Slugging	Adjusted OPS	Adjusted Batter Runs
Lajoie-Cle 7.6	Stone-StL 358	Stone-StL....................417	Stone-StL 501	Stone-StL 918	Stone-StL 195	Stone-StL 63.3
Stone-StL 5.9	Lajoie-Cle 355	Lajoie-Cle 392	Lajoie-Cle 465	Lajoie-Cle 857	Lajoie-Cle 170	Lajoie-Cle 48.2
Turner-Cle 4.2	Chase-NY..............323	Flick-Cle......................372	Davis-Phi 459	Davis-Phi..............815	Flick-Cle...............156	Flick-Cle 40.2
Davis-Phi 3.2	Congalton-Cle.......320	Hartsel-Phi..................363	Flick-Cle 441	Flick-Cle...............813	Davis-Phi 150	Davis-Phi 32.1
Davis-Chi 3.2	Seybold-Phi 316	Davis-Phi 355	Hickman-Was 421	Crawford-Det........747	Hickman-Was 135	Seybold-Phi.........20.0

Runs	Hits	Doubles	Triples	Home Runs	Total Bases	Runs Batted In
Flick-Cle..................98	Lajoie-Cle 214	Lajoie-Cle 48	Flick-Cle..................22	Davis-Phi 12	Stone-StL 291	Davis-Phi 96
Keeler-NY 96	Stone-StL 208	Davis-Phi 42	Stone-StL 20	Hickman-Was 9	Lajoie-Cle 280	Lajoie-Cle 91
Hartsel-Phi 96	Flick-Cle...............194	Flick-Cle 34	Crawford-Det 16	Stone-StL 6	Flick-Cle...............275	Davis-Chi 80
Davis-Phi 94	Chase-NY 193	Murphy-Phi 28	Ferris-Bos 13	Seybold-Phi 5	Davis-Phi 253	Williams-NY 77
Stone-StL 91	Keeler-NY 180	Turner-Cle......................27			Chase-NY 236	Chase-NY..............76

Stolen Bases	Base Stealing Runs	Fielding Runs-Infield	Fielding Runs-Outfield	Wins	Winning Pct.	Complete Games
Flick-Cle..................39		Tannehill-Chi 32.4	Niles-StL.............13.7	Orth-NY 27	Plank-Phi 760	Orth-NY 36
Anderson-Was........39		Lajoie-Cle 21.3	McIntyre-Det........12.3	Chesbro-NY............23	White-Chi 750	Mullin-Det 35
Isbell-Chi 37		Turner-Cle 18.6	Anderson-Was 6.6	Rhoads-Cle 22	Joss-Cle 700	Hess-Cle 33
Altizer-Was 37		Schlafly-Was 16.2	Stahl-Bos 6.5	Owen-Chi................22	Rhoads-Cle 688	Rhoads-Cle 31
Donahue-Chi 36		Williams-NY 13.9	Crawford-Det 5.2	....	Owen-Chi 629	....

Strikeouts	Fewest BB/Game	Games	Saves	Base Runners/9	Adjusted Relief Runs	Relief Ranking
Waddell-Phi 196	Young-Bos 78	Chesbro-NY 49	Hess-Cle 3	White-Chi 8.33		
Falkenberg-Was ..178	Altrock-Chi 1.31	Orth-NY 45	Bender-Phi................3	Joss-Cle 8.49		
Walsh-Chi 171	Joss-Cle 1.37	Waddell-Phi 43		Patterson-Chi 8.87		
Hess-Cle 167	White-Chi 1.56	Hess-Cle........................43		Walsh-Chi 9.05		
Bender-Phi............159	Jacobson-StL 1.57	Owen-Chi 42		Pelty-StL 9.18		

Innings Pitched	Opponents' Avg.	Opponents' OBP	Earned Run Average	Adjusted ERA	Adjusted Starter Runs	Pitcher Wins
Orth-NY 338.2	Pelty-StL...............206	White-Chi.....................249	White-Chi 1.52	White-Chi.............167	Rhoads-Cle 28.5	**White-Chi**............3.9
Hess-Cle............333.2	White-Chi 207	Joss-Cle.......................252	Pelty-StL..............1.59	Pelty-StL 163	Hess-Cle..............28.3	**Joss-Cle**..............3.5
Mullin-Det 330.0	Walsh-Chi.............217	Walsh-Chi 265	Joss-Cle 1.72	Joss-Cle...............152	White-Chi 28.3	**Orth-NY** 3.4
Chesbro-NY 325.0	Joss-Cle 218	Pelty-StL 267	Powell-StL............1.77	Powell-StL 146	Joss-Cle 28.1	**Hess-Cle** 3.3
Rhoads-Cle 315.0	Powell-StL.............223	Powell-StL 275	Rhoads-Cle 1.80	Rhoads-Cle 145	Pelty-StL..............26.9	**Pelty-StL** 2.9

Not Quite Hitless

As August began, six American League clubs boasted records over .500 (all but pathetic Washington and Boston, which had totally collapsed). When the dust cleared, it was the White Sox and the Highlanders jousting in the final weeks. While New York played middling ball down the stretch, the White Sox forged ahead and won by three games. Even with the good pennant race, attendance decreased for first time in the AL's short history.

The fourth-place Philadelphia Athletics debuted two future stars, pitcher Jack Coombs and second baseman Eddie Collins. And despite missing time to illness, sophomore outfielder Ty Cobb of Detroit showed that he would be a force to be reckoned with as he hit .316 in a league that batted just .249.

Although the White Sox were called "hitless wonders" while posting a .230 batting average (worst ever for a pennant winner), that appellation is truly a misnomer. The Chicago offense led the league in walks and actually ranked third in runs—second in scoring on the road. Spacious South Side Park kept their offense to just fifth in home contests, but it certainly helped their already excellent mound staff. Doc White paced the league in ERA, while Ed Walsh led in shutouts. Meanwhile, the second-place Yankees were outscored on the road but blew away their opposition at home.

When the World Series rolled around, it was a Second City delight—the Cubs had won 116 games during the regular season and were heavily favored against the White Sox. Nevertheless, the AL champs won two out of the first three, despite collecting just 9 hits in 27 innings off Cubs pitching.

After the Cubs' Three Finger Brown shut out the Sox on 2 hits to even the Series, the supposed "Hitless Wonders" opened up the baseball world's eyes by teeing off for 8–6 and 8–3 wins against Ed Reulbach and Brown to clinch the Series.

1907 National League

TEAM	W	L	T	PCT	GB	HW	HL	R	OR	PA	H	2B	3B	HR	BB	SO	HB	SH	AVG	OBP	SLG	OPS	AOPS	BR	ABR	PF	SB	CS	BSA	BSR
CHI	107	45	3	.704		**54**	19	574	**390**	5570	1224	**162**	48	13	435		**195**	48	.250	.318	.311	629	98	28	-5	106	235			
PIT	91	63	3	.591	17	47	29	**634**	510	5650	**1261**	133	**78**	19	469		178	46	**.254**	.325	**.324**	**649**	**109**	61	53	101	**264**			
PHI	83	64	2	.565	21.5	45	30	514	476	5320	1113	**162**	65	12	424		130	41	.236	.304	.305	609	99	-9	-1	99	154			
NY	82	71	2	.536	25.5	45	30	574	510	5624	1222	160	48	**23**	**516**		165	**69**	.251	**.331**	.317	648	107	**73**	**54**	103	205			
BRO	65	83	5	.439	40	37	38	446	522	5468	1135	142	63	18	336		197	40	.232	.287	.298	585	98	-64	-25	92	121			
CIN	66	87	3	.431	41.5	43	36	526	519	5567	1226	126	90	15	372		**195**	34	.247	.304	.318	622	98	-1	-22	104	158			
BOS	58	90	4	.392	47	31	42	502	652	5623	1222	142	61	22	413		133	57	.243	.308	.309	617	100	2	4	100	120			
STL	52	101	2	.340	55.5	31	47	419	610	5518	1163	121	52	18	312		156	42	.232	.283	.288	571	88	-91	-76	97	125			
TOT	616					333	271	4189		44340	9566	1148	505	140	3277	4217	377	1349	.243	.308	.309	616					1382			

TEAM	CG	SHO	GR	SV	IP	H	HR	BB	SO	BR/9	ERA	AERA	OAV	OOB	PR	APR	PF	OSB	OCS	FA	E	WPB	DP	FW	PW	BW	BSW	DIF
CHI	114	**32**	45	8	1373.1	**1054**	**11**	402	586	**9.8**	**1.73**	**144**	**.216**	**.281**	**112**	**114**	101	148	*132*	**.967**	**211**	31	110	**3.1**	**13.0**	-.6		15.5
PIT	111	24	51	5	1363.0	1207	12	**368**	497	10.7	2.30	106	.241	.299	25	19	99	**124**	*125*	.959	256	41	75	.2	2.2	6.0		5.6
PHI	110	21	46	4	1299.1	1095	13	422	499	10.9	2.43	99	.233	.304	5	-3	98	136	*139*	.957	256	40	104	-.7	-.3	-.1		10.6
NY	109	22	**63**	**13**	1371.0	1219	24	369	**655**	10.7	2.45	101	.238	.294	2	1	100	135	*121*	.963	232	60	75	1.6	.1	**6.1**		-2.4
BRO	125	20	29	1	1356.1	1218	16	463	479	11.4	2.38	98	.249	.319	12	-9	95	208	*152*	.959	262	41	94	-.7	-1.0	-2.8		-4.5
CIN	118	10	39	2	1351.1	1223	16	444	481	11.5	2.41	107	.251	.322	8	24	105	173	*150*	.963	227	**24**	118	2.1	2.7	-2.5		-12.8
BOS	121	9	38	2	1338.2	1324	28	458	426	12.4	3.33	76	.268	.339	-129	-115	103	238	*163*	.961	249	51	**128**	.1	-13.1	.5		-3.5
STL	**127**	19	29	2	1365.2	1212	20	500	594	11.6	2.70	93	.243	.318	-35	-32	101	220	***167***	.948	340	74	105	-5.8	-3.6	-8.6		-6.5
TOT	935	157	340	37	10818.2					11.1	2.46		.243	.308						.960	2033	362	809					

Batter-Fielder Wins	Batting Average	On-Base Percentage	Slugging Average	On-Base Plus Slugging	Adjusted OPS	Adjusted Batter Runs
Wagner-Pit 6.7	Wagner-Pit 350	Wagner-Pit..................408	Wagner-Pit 513	Wagner-Pit...........921	Wagner-Pit...........186	Wagner-Pit 50.3
Brain-Bos 4.8	Magee-Phi 328	Magee-Phi 396	Magee-Phi 455	Magee-Phi 852	Magee-Phi 169	Magee-Phi.........40.7
Magee-Phi 4.5	Beaumont-Bos 322	Clarke-Pit....................383	Lumley-Bro 425	Beaumont-Bos......790	Beaumont-Bos......148	Beaumont-Bos ..29.3
Mitchell-Cin 3.3	Leach-Pit 303	Devlin-NY....................376	Beaumont-Bos 424	Clarke-Pit.............772	Lumley-Bro 144	Jordan-Bro..........26.3
Beaumont-Bos ..3.0	Seymour-NY.........294	Thomas-Phi 374	Brain-Bos 420	Leach-Pit 756	Jordan-Bro...........141	Clarke-Pit............25.8

Runs	Hits	Doubles	Triples	Home Runs	Total Bases	Runs Batted In
Shannon-NY 104	Beaumont-Bos......187	Wagner-Pit 38	Ganzel-Cin.............16	Brain-Bos...............10	Wagner-Pit...........264	Magee-Phi 85
Leach-Pit 102	Wagner-Pit...........180	Magee-Phi 28	Alperman-Bro 16	Lumley-Bro 9	Beaumont-Bos......246	Wagner-Pit 82
Wagner-Pit.............98	Leach-Pit 166	Steinfeldt-Chi 25	Wagner-Pit.............14	Murray-StL................7	Magee-Phi 229	Abbaticchio-Pit 82
Clarke-Pit................97	Magee-Phi 165	Seymour-NY 25	Beaumont-Bos........14	Wagner-Pit................6	Leach-Pit 221	Seymour-NY..........75
Tenney-Bos 83	Mitchell-Cin 163	Brain-Bos 24	Clarke-Pit................13	Browne-NY 5	Brain-Bos.............214	Steinfeldt-Chi 70

Stolen Bases	Base Stealing Runs	Fielding Runs-Infield	Fielding Runs-Outfield	Wins	Winning Pct.	Complete Games
Wagner-Pit.............61		Evers-Chi 27.1	Mitchell-Cin..........25.1	Mathewson-NY 24	Reulbach-Chi 810	McGlynn-StL 33
Magee-Phi 46		Brain-Bos 22.5	Leach-Pit 8.9	Overall-Chi.............23	Brown-Chi.............769	Ewing-Cin..............32
Evers-Chi...............46		Byrne-StL....................20.6	Clarke-Pit 7.8	Sparks-Phi 22	Overall-Chi 767	Mathewson-NY......31
Leach-Pit 43		Doolan-Phi..................14.8	Magee-Phi 7.8	Willis-Pit..................21	Sparks-Phi 733	Karger-StL 29
Devlin-NY 38		Tinker-Chi 13.4	Beaumont-Bos 4.1		Lundgren-Chi 720	Willis-Pit 27

Strikeouts	Fewest BB/Game	Games	Saves	Base Runners/9	Adjusted Relief Runs	Relief Ranking
Mathewson-NY 178	Phillippe-Pit 1.51	McGinnity-NY 47	McGinnity-NY 4	Mathewson-NY....8.71		
Ewing-Cin 147	Mathewson-NY.....1.51	McGlynn-StL..................45	Overall-Chi...............3	Brown-Chi...........8.73		
Ames-NY 146	Brown-Chi............1.55	Mathewson-NY..............41	Brown-Chi 3	Pfiester-Chi..........9.05		
Overall-Chi............141	McGinnity-NY 1.68	Ewing-Cin 41		Overall-Chi 9.42		
Beebe-StL 141	Sparks-Phi 1.73			Sparks-Phi 9.48		

Innings Pitched	Opponents' Avg.	Opponents' OBP	Earned Run Average	Adjusted ERA	Adjusted Starter Runs	Pitcher Wins
McGlynn-StL......352.1	Lundgren-Chi 185	Mathewson-NY 247	Pfiester-Chi..........1.15	Pfiester-Chi 215	Lundgren-Chi 29.2	**Overall-Chi** 3.9
Ewing-Cin 332.2	Pfiester-Chi...........207	Brown-Chi 262	Lundgren-Chi 1.17	Lundgren-Chi.........212	Brown-Chi.............28.8	**Brown-Chi** 3.7
Mathewson-NY..315.0	Overall-Chi 208	Pfiester-Chi 263	Brown-Chi............1.39	Brown-Chi 179	Overall-Chi 27.9	**Lundgren-Chi** 3.5
Karger-StL 314.0	Camnitz-Pit...........211	Overall-Chi...................268	Leever-Pit 1.66	Ewing-Cin 149	Ewing-Cin............26.1	**Mathewson-NY**..2.7
McGinnity-NY 310.1	Mathewson-NY.....212	Karger-StL 270	Overall-Chi 1.68	Overall-Chi............148	Pfiester-Chi..........20.5	**Ewing-Cin** 2.6

Cubs are World Serious

Prior to the season, the rules committee voted that the strike zone should range from the knee to shoulder. With this on the books, runs continued to drop. The Cubs' 1.73 ERA set an all-time NL record.

Two soon-to-be-prominent New York Giants saw their first action in 1907. Second baseman "Laughing Larry" Doyle would play a dozen seasons for John McGraw, while first baseman Fred Merkle lasted sixteen years in the bigs despite being best remembered for a baserunning gaffe. Future batting star Heinie Zimmerman broke in with Chicago, while first baseman Ed Konetchy, a slick fielder who also collected 2,150 lifetime hits, came up at midseason to start for the Cardinals.

Appearing in their final games during 1907 were first baseman Jake Beckley (who collected 2,934 hits), veteran shortstop Tommy Corcoran, third baseman Lave Cross (who played 21 seasons), and Bobby Lowe (Boston's regular second baseman for eleven years). Boston outfielder Cozy Dolan fell ill at spring training with pneumonia and typhoid fever and died on March 29.

After a great start, the Giants crumbled in May. John McGraw worked quickly to reconstruct his aging club, and New York would be back in 1908. As the Giants rebuilt, the Cubs again ran away and hid from the competition, winning the flag by 17 games over Pittsburgh.

The Cubs steamrolled the Tigers in October in five games (one was a tie). Chicago outscored Detroit 19–6 in the World Series, with Ty Cobb crossing the plate just once. This was the last Series until 1918 when at least one team didn't hit a home run.

Finally, in the year's biggest lie, the Mills Commission—appointed to investigate the beginnings of baseball—concluded with not one iota of reliable evidence that Civil War General Abner Doubleday invented the game in Cooperstown, New York, in 1839. Doubleday, who passed away in 1893, was too dead to be able to deny anything.

1907 American League

TEAM	W	L	T	PCT	GB	HW	HL	R	OR	PA	H	2B	3B	HR	BB	SO	HB	SH	AVG	OBP	SLG	OPS	AOPS	BR	ABR	PF	SB	CS	BSA	BSR
DET	92	58	3	.613		**50**	27	**693**	531	5721	**1383**	179	**75**	11	315		158	44	**.266**	**.313**	**.335**	**648**	**108**	**62**	40	104	196			
PHI	88	57	5	.607	1.5	**50**	20	584	511	5596	1276	**220**	44	**22**	384		175	27	.255	.311	.329	640	106	57	**43**	102	137			
CHI	87	64	6	.576	5.5	48	29	588	**474**	5720	1205	149	33	5	**421**		**181**	48	.238	.302	.283	585	95	-35	-16	97	175			
CLE	85	67	6	.559	8	46	31	531	525	5636	1221	182	68	11	335		177	**56**	.241	.295	.310	605	97	-12	-16	101	193			
NY	70	78	4	.473	21	33	40	605	667	5530	1258	150	67	15	304		129	53	.249	.299	.315	614	93	-1	-42	108	**206**			
STL	69	83	3	.454	24	36	40	541	555	5784	1324	154	63	10	370		151	39	.253	.308	.313	621	103	17	19	100	144			
BOS	59	90	6	.396	32.5	34	41	466	558	5721	1224	154	48	18	305		146	35	.234	.281	.292	573	89	-78	-74	99	125			
WAS	49	102	3	.325	43.5	27	47	506	693	5699	1243	134	57	12	390		137	60	.243	.304	.299	603	105	-10	37	92	223			
TOT	617					324	275	4514		45407	10134	1322	455	104	2824	4479	362	1254	.247	.302	.309	611					1399			

TEAM	CG	SHO	GR	SV	IP	H	HR	BB	SO	BR/9	ERA	AERA	OAV	OOB	PR	APR	PF	OSB	OCS	FA	E	WPB	DP	FW	PW	BW	BSW	DIF
DET	120	15	36	6	1370.2	1281	**8**	380	512	11.2	2.33	**112**	.251	.309	32	**39**	102	160	*137*	.959	260	46	79	1.0	**4.3**	4.4		7.3
PHI	106	**27**	65	6	1354.2	**1106**	13	378	**789**	10.3	2.35	111	**.226**	.290	29	37	102	181	*149*	.958	263	50	67	.4	4.1	**4.7**		6.3
CHI	112	17	53	**9**	1406.1	1279	13	**305**	604	10.3	**2.22**	108	.245	.290	**50**	28	94	**153**	*130*	**.966**	**233**	55	101	**3.4**	3.1	-1.8		6.8
CLE	127	20	36	5	1392.2	1253	**8**	362	513	10.8	2.26	111	.244	.300	43	36	99	174	*115*	.960	264	74	**137**	1.3	4.0	-1.8		5.5
NY	93	10	67	6	1333.2	1327	13	428	511	12.2	3.03	92	.262	.325	-73	-32	110	178	*143*	.947	334	52	79	-4.4	-3.5	-4.6		8.5
STL	**129**	15	28	**9**	1381.1	1254	17	352	463	10.8	2.61	96	.245	.300	-10	-16	99	198	*145*	.959	266	**33**	97	.8	-1.8	2.1		-8.1
BOS	100	17	**70**	7	1414.0	1222	22	337	517	**10.2**	2.45	105	.236	**.288**	14	18	101	160	***155***	.959	274	47	100	.2	2.0	-8.2		-9.5
WAS	106	12	57	5	1351.1	1383	10	344	570	11.8	3.11	78	.268	.320	-86	-111	95	195	*137*	.951	310	76	69	-2.4	-12.3	4.1		-15.9
TOT	893	133	412	53	11004.2					10.9	2.54		.247	.302						.958	2204	433	729					

Batter-Fielder Wins	Batting Average	On-Base Percentage	Slugging Average	On-Base Plus Slugging	Adjusted OPS	Adjusted Batter Runs
Lajoie-Cle 7.0	Cobb-Det 350	Hartsel-Phi..................405	Cobb-Det 468	Cobb-Det 848	Cobb-Det 164	Cobb-Det...........40.4
Cobb-Det 4.9	Crawford-Det 323	Stone-StL....................387	Crawford-Det 460	Crawford-Det........826	Crawford-Det........157	Stone-StL 35.5
Crawford-Det......3.9	Stone-StL 320	Flick-Cle......................386	Flick-Cle 412	Flick-Cle...............798	Flick-Cle...............153	Crawford-Det......35.4
Flick-Cle 3.0	Flick-Cle 302	Cobb-Det 380	Stone-StL 399	Stone-StL 787	Stone-StL 151	Flick-Cle 34.6
Stone-StL 2.6	Nicholls-Phi 302	Crawford-Det 366	Davis-Phi 395	Hartsel-Phi 771	Hartsel-Phi 143	Hartsel-Phi 32.5

Runs	Hits	Doubles	Triples	Home Runs	Total Bases	Runs Batted In
Crawford-Det........102	Cobb-Det..............212	Davis-Phi 35	Flick-Cle..................18	Davis-Phi..................8	Cobb-Det..............283	Cobb-Det 119
D.Jones-Det..........101	Stone-StL.............191	Crawford-Det 34	Crawford-Det..........17	Seybold-Phi..............5	Crawford-Det........268	Seybold-Phi 92
Cobb-Det................97	Crawford-Det........188	Lajoie-Cle 30	Cobb-Det................14	Hoffman-NY..............5	Stone-StL 238	Davis-Phi 87
Hartsel-Phi 93	Ganley-Was..........167	J.Collins-Bos-Phi 29	Unglaub-Bos 13	Cobb-Det...................5	Davis-Phi.............230	Crawford-Det 81
Hahn-Chi 87	Flick-Cle...............166	Seybold-Phi 29	....	....	Flick-Cle...............226	Wallace-StL 70

Stolen Bases	Base Stealing Runs	Fielding Runs-Infield	Fielding Runs-Outfield	Wins	Winning Pct.	Complete Games
Cobb-Det................53		Lajoie-Cle 44.9	D.Jones-Det 12.8	White-Chi................27	Donovan-Det 862	Walsh-Chi.............37
Flick-Cle..................41		Donahue-Chi 20.5	Birmingham-Cle ..12.4	Joss-Cle..................27	Dygert-Phi 724	Mullin-Det.............35
Conroy-NY.............41		Elberfeld-NY 12.8	Cobb-Det 12.0	Killian-Det 25	Joss-Cle 711	Joss-Cle 34
Ganley-Was............40		Isbell-Chi 8.1	Crawford-Det 7.0	Donovan-Det 25	Smith-Chi 697	Young-Bos 33
Altizer-Was 38		Wallace-StL 7.9	Ganley-Was 6.6	....	White-Chi 675	Plank-Phi 33

Strikeouts	Fewest BB/Game	Games	Saves	Base Runners/9	Adjusted Relief Runs	Relief Ranking
Waddell-Phi 232	White-Chi 1.18	Walsh-Chi 56	Dinneen-Bos-StL 4	Young-Bos 9.02		
Walsh-Chi..............206	Altrock-Chi...........1.31	White-Chi 46	Walsh-Chi 4	Joss-Cle 9.04		
Plank-Phi..............183	Young-Bos 1.34	Mullin-Det 46	Hughes-Was 4	Bender-Phi 9.11		
Dygert-Phi............151	Bender-Phi 1.40	Waddell-Phi 44		Winter-Bos 9.19		
Young-Bos.............147	Joss-Cle 1.44			Walsh-Chi............9.29		

Innings Pitched	Opponents' Avg.	Opponents' OBP	Earned Run Average	Adjusted ERA	Adjusted Starter Runs	Pitcher Wins
Walsh-Chi..........422.1	Dygert-Phi 214	Young-Bos 263	Walsh-Chi............1.60	Walsh-Chi 150	Walsh-Chi............32.8	**Walsh-Chi** 4.6
Mullin-Det..........357.1	Winter-Bos 216	Joss-Cle......................264	Killian-Det............1.78	Killian-Det 146	Joss-Cle 26.7	**Killian-Det**..........4.2
Plank-Phi 343.2	Walsh-Chi.............224	Bender-Phi..................265	Joss-Cle 1.83	Joss-Cle................136	Young-Bos 24.9	**Joss-Cle**..............3.0
Young-Bos 343.1	Howell-StL 225	Winter-Bos..................267	Howell-StL 1.93	Howell-StL............130	Killian-Det............24.7	**Howell-StL**..........2.6
Joss-Cle 338.2	Donovan-Det 226	Walsh-Chi 269	Young-Bos 1.99	Young-Bos............129	Plank-Phi 17.1	**Young-Bos**..........2.4

A Peach Takes Root in Motown

Four teams entered September within striking distance of the pennant. While Chicago and Cleveland played .500 ball during the last month and Philadelphia peaked early, Detroit finished the season on a high to take the crown. Rarely has one player made such a difference to an entire league as Ty Cobb did in 1907. In his first season of more than 100 games, Cobb won the first of his 12 batting titles and led in slugging, hits, total bases, RBIs, and steals. His outfield mates, Sam Crawford and Davy Jones, were first and second in runs (Cobb was third). The Tigers leapt from sixth to first, edging the Athletics by 1½ games. Just as importantly, Cobb's speed-based game would usher in a new era of "attack" baseball.

The blow of a bad year can be softened by the gain of a Hall of Famer. Boston playing manager Chick Stahl committed suicide in spring training, but the club gained freshman outfielder Tris Speaker. Washington finished last while summoning 19-year-old pitcher Walter Johnson. While the rookie finished 5–9, his ERA was a sparkling 1.87. The Senators, as well as the Tigers, experienced huge attendance gains, and total spectators for the league increased by 16 percent.

Once again, Topsy Hartsel and Harry Davis provided the Philadelphia offense, and the deep pitching was nearly good enough to overcome the fearsome Tigers attack. In the World Series, however, the Tigers were toothless, as the Cubs completely shut them down in five games, including one tie.

At this time, the strike zone was defined, rather vaguely, as reaching from the knees to the shoulders (no "top" or "bottom" of either to make the definition more precise). Strikeouts fell a bit as homers dropped nearly 25 percent. The AL also ruled in 1907 that anyone appearing as a pinch hitter, pinch runner, or defensive substitute would now receive credit for a game played.

1908 National League

TEAM	W	L	T	PCT	GB	HW	HL	R	OR	PA	H	2B	3B	HR	BB	SO	HB	SH	AVG	OBP	SLG	OPS	AOPS	BR	ABR	PF	SB	CS	BSA	BSR
CHI	99	55	4	.643		47	30	624	461	5813	1267	**196**	56	19	418		**270**	40	.249	.311	.321	632	105	53	29	104	**212**			
PIT	98	56	1	.636	1	42	35	585	468	5753	1263	162	**98**	**25**	420		184	40	.247	.309	.332	641	112	61	61	100	186			
NY	98	56	3	.636	1	**52**	25	**651**	455	5826	**1339**	182	43	20	**494**		250	**76**	**.267**	**.342**	**.333**	**675**	**117**	**144**	**113**	105	181			
PHI	83	71	1	.539	16	43	34	504	**445**	5612	1223	194	68	11	334		213	53	.244	.298	.316	614	100	13	-4	103	200			
CIN	73	81	1	.474	26	40	37	488	543	5511	1108	129	77	14	372		214	46	.227	.288	.294	582	95	-44	-31	97	196			
BOS	63	91	2	.409	36	35	42	537	622	5793	1228	137	43	17	414		194	54	.239	.303	.293	596	99	-12	-4	98	134			
BRO	53	101	0	.344	46	27	50	375	516	5415	1044	110	60	28	323		166	29	.213	.266	.277	543	82	-117	-102	96	113			
STL	49	105	0	.318	50	28	49	372	626	5450	1105	134	57	17	282		164	45	.223	.271	.283	554	87	-99	-79	95	150			
TOT	622					314	302	4136		45173	9577	1244	502	151	3057	4180	383	1655	.239	.299	.306	605					1372			

TEAM	CG	SHO	GR	SV	IP	H	HR	BB	SO	BR/9	ERA	AERA	OAV	OOB	PR	APR	PF	OSB	OCS	FA	E	WPB	DP	FW	PW	BW	BSW	DIF
CHI	108	**29**	60	12	1433.2	**1137**	20	437	**668**	10.1	2.14	109	**.221**	.287	33	30	100	158	*156*	**.969**	**205**	46	76	**3.7**	3.5	3.4		11.4
PIT	100	24	71	9	1402.1	1142	16	406	468	10.3	2.12	108	.223	.287	34	25	97	138	*104*	.964	226	**27**	74	1.9	2.9	7.1		9.1
NY	95	25	76	**18**	1411.0	1210	26	**288**	656	**9.8**	2.14	112	.232	**.277**	32	38	102	135	*125*	.962	250	41	79	.4	4.4	**13.1**		3.0
PHI	116	22	43	6	1393.0	1167	**8**	379	476	10.3	**2.10**	**115**	.234	.294	**38**	**44**	103	**128**	*154*	.963	238	45	75	1.0	**5.1**	-.5		.3
CIN	110	17	50	8	1384.0	1218	19	415	433	10.9	2.37	96	.243	.307	-4	-19	98	154	*137*	.959	255	40	72	-.2	-2.2	-3.6		2.0
BOS	92	14	**77**	1	1404.2	1262	29	423	416	11.2	2.79	86	.245	.310	-70	-66	102	199	*152*	.962	253	34	**90**	.0	-7.7	-.5		-6.0
BRO	**118**	20	43	4	1369.0	1165	17	444	535	11.0	2.47	94	.235	.306	-18	-24	99	203	*162*	.961	247	37	66	.3	-2.8	-11.9		-9.7
STL	97	13	72	4	1368.0	1217	16	430	528	11.1	2.64	89	.232	.296	-44	-51	100	257	***173***	.946	348	57	68	-6.8	-5.9	-9.2		-6.1
TOT	836	164	492	62	11165.2					10.6	2.35		.239	.299						.961	2022	327	600					

Batter-Fielder Wins
- **Wagner-Pit** 6.9
- **Tinker-Chi**............4.5
- **Dahlen-Bos** 4.5
- **Bresnahan-NY** 3.8
- **Ritchey-Bos** 3.1

Batting Average
- Wagner-Pit 354
- Donlin-NY 334
- Doyle-NY 308
- Bransfield-Phi 304
- Evers-Chi 300

On-Base Percentage
- Wagner-Pit...................415
- Evers-Chi.....................402
- Bresnahan-NY 401
- Titus-Phi 365
- Donlin-NY 364

Slugging Average
- Wagner-Pit 542
- Donlin-NY 452
- Magee-Phi 417
- Lobert-Cin 407
- Murray-StL 400

On-Base Plus Slugging
- Wagner-Pit............957
- Donlin-NY 816
- Evers-Chi.............777
- Magee-Phi 776
- Bresnahan-NY......760

Adjusted OPS
- Wagner-Pit............205
- Donlin-NY 153
- Lobert-Cin 145
- Magee-Phi............143
- Evers-Chi..............143

Adjusted Batter Runs
- Wagner-Pit 66.3
- Donlin-NY 32.0
- Lobert-Cin 26.5
- Bresnahan-NY....25.3
- Magee-Phi..........25.3

Runs
- Tenney-NY............101
- Wagner-Pit............100
- Leach-Pit 93
- Evers-Chi................83
- Clarke-Pit................83

Hits
- Wagner-Pit............201
- Donlin-NY 198
- Murray-StL............167
- Lobert-Cin 167
- Bransfield-Phi 160

Doubles
- Wagner-Pit 39
- Magee-Phi 30
- Chance-Chi...................27
- Knabe-Phi......................26
- Donlin-NY 26

Triples
- Wagner-Pit..............19
- Lobert-Cin 18
- Magee-Phi...............16
- Leach-Pit 16

Home Runs
- Jordan-Bro..............12
- Wagner-Pit.............10
- Murray-StL................7
- Tinker-Chi 6
- Donlin-NY 6

Total Bases
- Wagner-Pit............308
- Donlin-NY 268
- Murray-StL............237
- Lobert-Cin 232
- Leach-Pit 222

Runs Batted In
- Wagner-Pit 109
- Donlin-NY............106
- Seymour-NY..........92
- Bransfield-Phi........71
- Tinker-Chi.............68

Stolen Bases
- Wagner-Pit.............53
- Murray-StL..............48
- Lobert-Cin 47
- Magee-Phi 40
- Evers-Chi................36

Base Stealing Runs

Fielding Runs-Infield
- Dahlen-Bos 37.5
- Tinker-Chi 26.4
- Ritchey-Bos 12.9
- Sweeney-Bos.............12.2
- Devlin-NY...................11.9

Fielding Runs-Outfield
- Clarke-Pit 10.2
- Burch-Bro 8.5
- Hummel-Bro 8.1
- Shaw-StL 7.3
- Seymour-NY..........5.3

Wins
- Mathewson-NY 37
- Brown-Chi 29
- Reulbach-Chi..........24

Winning Pct.
- Reulbach-Chi 774
- Mathewson-NY.....771
- Brown-Chi.............763
- Maddox-Pit 742
- Leever-Pit 682

Complete Games
- Mathewson-NY......34
- Wilhelm-Bro 33
- McQuillan-Phi........32
- Wiltse-NY 30
- Rucker-Bro 30

Strikeouts
- Mathewson-NY 259
- Rucker-Bro............199
- Overall-Chi............167
- Raymond-StL.........145
- Reulbach-Chi........133

Fewest BB/Game
- Mathewson-NY.......97
- Brown-Chi...........1.41
- Sparks-Phi 1.74
- Ewing-Cin 1.75
- Campbell-Cin 1.79

Games
- Mathewson-NY 56
- Raymond-StL 48
- McQuillan-Phi 48
- Reulbach-Chi 46

Saves
- McGinnity-NY 5
- Mathewson-NY 5
- Brown-Chi 5
- Overall-Chi................4
- Ewing-Cin 3

Base Runners/9
- Mathewson-NY....7.51
- Brown-Chi.............7.72
- McQuillan-Phi......9.01
- Willis-Pit 9.28
- Ewing-Cin 9.47

Adjusted Relief Runs

Relief Ranking

Innings Pitched
- Mathewson-NY..390.2
- McQuillan-Phi 359.2
- Rucker-Bro 333.1
- Wilhelm-Bro 332.0
- Wiltse-NY 330.0

Opponents' Avg.
- Beebe-StL 193
- Brown-Chi.............195
- Mathewson-NY.....197
- McQuillan-Phi.......207
- Raymond-StL 207

Opponents' OBP
- Mathewson-NY 222
- Brown-Chi 232
- Willis-Pit.......................262
- McQuillan-Phi 263
- Beebe-StL 267

Earned Run Average
- Mathewson-NY....1.43
- Brown-Chi............1.47
- McQuillan-Phi......1.53
- Camnitz-Pit..........1.56
- Coakley-Cin-Chi ..1.78

Adjusted ERA
- Mathewson-NY 168
- Brown-Chi 159
- McQuillan-Phi 158
- Camnitz-Pit 147
- Richie-Phi 132

Adjusted Starter Runs
- Mathewson-NY....40.8
- McQuillan-Phi.......32.7
- Brown-Chi............32.0
- Reulbach-Chi 13.9
- Wilhelm-Bro 13.3

Pitcher Wins
- **Mathewson-NY**..6.5
- **Brown-Chi** 4.4
- **McQuillan-Phi**....3.8
- **Reulbach-Chi** 2.2
- **Wiltse-NY** 2.1

Merkle's Boner Leads to Thrilling Three-Way

By decree, pitchers were no longer allowed to rub dirt on the baseball to deface it. Despite this, scoring dropped to just 3.32 runs per team per game, the lowest since 1901. The league batting average of .239 was also the lowest ever. Rookie Gavvy Cravath, future home run king, hit just one in 94 games, while pitchers Hippo Vaughn and Rube Marquard also debuted. Marquard, who played in New York, is now in the Hall of Fame, but Vaughn was clearly greater. Two old Baltimore Orioles ended their big-league tenure: "Iron Man" Joe McGinnity's arm gave out, while outfielder Joe Kelley was finished at 37.

Despite poor hitting, the first great NL pennant race of the century boosted attendance 33 percent. The Giants were up by 4½ on September 18, but Philadelphia rookie left-hander Harry Coveleski beat New York thrice in the final week, drawing the race tighter. On a fateful September 23 in New York, the Giants scored in the ninth, apparently defeating Chicago, 2-1. While the "winning" run scored, however, Fred Merkle, who had been on first, failed to touch second base after the hit. Cubs infielder John Evers called for the ball; umpire Hank O'Day, who had ruled against the Cubs in a similar play weeks before, called Merkle out as fans poured onto the field. The game was later ruled a tie by NL President Harry Pulliam.

Chicago eliminated Pittsburgh on October 4, finishing the season knotted with the Giants. When the game was replayed on October 8, some 35,000 crazed fans at the Polo Grounds watched the Cubs defeat Christy Mathewson, 4–2. After this exhausting pennant race, Chicago's World Series win was almost anticlimactic. Ty Cobb hit .368, but Chicago took Detroit in five. Certainly, nobody at the time could have dreamed that this would be the mighty Cubs' last world championship of the century.

1908 American League

TEAM	W	L	T	PCT	GB	HW	HL	R	OR	PA	H	2B	3B	HR	BB	SO	HB	SH	AVG	OBP	SLG	OPS	AOPS	BR	ABR	PF	SB	CS	BSA	BSR
DET	90	63	1	.588		44	33	**647**	547	5668	**1347**	**199**	86	19	320		191	42	**.263**	**.312**	**.347**	**659**	**115**	**103**	**77**	104	165			
CLE	90	64	3	.584	0.5	**51**	26	569	**459**	5770	1221	188	58	18	364		**243**	55	.239	.297	.309	606	103	17	15	100	177			
CHI	88	64	4	.579	1.5	**51**	25	537	470	5788	1127	145	41	3	**463**		236	62	.224	.298	.271	569	91	-35	-27	98	**209**			
STL	83	69	3	.546	6.5	46	31	544	483	5726	1261	173	52	20	343		197	35	.245	.296	.310	606	102	14	11	101	126			
BOS	75	79	1	.487	15.5	37	40	564	513	5579	1239	117	**88**	14	289		173	**69**	.245	.295	.312	607	100	7	-8	103	156			
PHI	68	85	4	.444	22	46	30	486	562	5656	1131	183	50	**21**	368		186	37	.223	.281	.292	573	86	-43	-74	107	116			
WAS	67	85	3	.441	22.5	43	32	479	539	5648	1186	132	74	8	368		196	43	.235	.293	.296	589	106	-17	30	92	170			
NY	51	103	1	.331	39.5	30	47	460	713	5533	1190	142	50	13	288		153	45	.236	.283	.291	574	91	-46	-51	101	231			
TOT	622					348	264	4286		45368	9702	1279	499	116	2803	4930	388	1575	.239	.294	.304	598					1350			

TEAM	CG	SHO	GR	SV	IP	H	HR	BB	SO	BR/9	ERA	AERA	OAV	OOB	PR	APR	PF	OSB	OCS	FA	E	WPB	DP	FW	PW	BW	BSW	DIF
DET	**119**	15	38	5	1374.1	1313	12	318	553	11.1	2.40	100	.255	.306	-3	2	101	176	*147*	.953	305	**40**	95	-2.1	.2	**8.8**		6.6
CLE	108	18	61	5	1424.1	1172	16	328	548	9.7	**2.02**	**118**	.229	.280	**59**	**56**	100	**123**	*127*	.962	257	46	95	1.6	**6.4**	1.7		3.3
CHI	107	**23**	62	**10**	1414.0	1165	11	**284**	623	**9.4**	2.22	104	**.225**	**.269**	26	14	97	149	*127*	**.966**	**232**	43	82	**3.2**	1.6	-3.1		10.3
STL	107	15	61	5	1397.0	**1151**	**7**	387	607	10.3	2.15	111	.230	.294	37	36	100	141	*138*	.964	237	45	**97**	2.7	4.1	1.3		-1.1
BOS	102	12	65	7	1380.1	1200	18	364	624	10.5	2.28	108	.238	.295	17	26	103	167	*155*	.955	297	63	71	-1.4	3.0	-.9		-2.6
PHI	102	**23**	74	4	1400.1	1194	10	410	**741**	10.6	2.56	100	.235	.298	-27	-4	107	242	***159***	.957	272	60	68	.6	-.5	-8.4		-.2
WAS	106	15	60	7	1391.2	1236	16	348	649	10.5	2.34	97	.241	.294	7	-13	96	151	*136*	.958	275	63	89	.1	-1.5	3.4		-11.0
NY	90	11	**75**	3	1366.0	1293	26	458	585	12.0	3.16	78	.252	.322	-117	-102	104	201	*140*	.947	337	49	78	-4.1	-11.6	-5.8		-4.4
TOT	841	132	496	46	11148.0					10.5	2.39		.239	.294						.958	2212	409	675					

Batter-Fielder Wins	Batting Average	On-Base Percentage	Slugging Average	On-Base Plus Slugging	Adjusted OPS	Adjusted Batter Runs
Lajoie-Cle 8.0	Cobb-Det 324	Gessler-Bos 394	Cobb-Det 475	Cobb-Det 842	Cobb-Det 166	Cobb-Det 40.0
McIntyre-Det 4.6	Crawford-Det 311	McIntyre-Det 392	Crawford-Det 457	Gessler-Bos.........817	Gessler-Bos.........161	Crawford-Det......34.7
Cobb-Det 4.1	Gessler-Bos 308	Hemphill-NY 374	Gessler-Bos 423	Crawford-Det........812	Crawford-Det........157	McIntyre-Det 33.4
McBride-Was 3.7	Hemphill-NY 297	Hartsel-Phi...................371	Rossman-Det 418	McIntyre-Det 775	McIntyre-Det 146	Gessler-Bos........31.0
Wagner-Bos 3.2	McIntyre-Det.........295	Dougherty-Chi 367	McIntyre-Det.........383	Rossman-Det........748	Rossman-Det........137	Lajoie-Cle 24.3

Runs	Hits	Doubles	Triples	Home Runs	Total Bases	Runs Batted In
McIntyre-Det 105	Cobb-Det 188	Cobb-Det 36	Cobb-Det 20	Crawford-Det 7	Cobb-Det 276	Cobb-Det 108
Crawford-Det........102	Crawford-Det 184	Rossman-Det 33	Stahl-NY-Bos 16	Hinchman-Cle 6	Crawford-Det........270	Crawford-Det 80
Schaefer-Det..........96	McIntyre-Det 168	Crawford-Det 33	Crawford-Det 16	Niles-NY-Bos 5	Rossman-Det........219	Lajoie-Cle 74
Jones-Chi 92	Lajoie-Cle 168	Lajoie-Cle 32	Gessler-Bos............14	Stone-StL 5	McIntyre-Det 218	Ferris-StL 74
Stone-StL 89	Stone-StL 165	Stovall-Cle 29		Davis-Phi 5	Lajoie-Cle 218	Rossman-Det 71

Stolen Bases	Base Stealing Runs	Fielding Runs-Infield	Fielding Runs-Outfield	Wins	Winning Pct.	Complete Games
Dougherty-Chi........47		Lajoie-Cle 46.8	McIntyre-Det........16.4	Walsh-Chi 40	Walsh-Chi 727	Walsh-Chi..............42
Hemphill-NY 42		McBride-Was.............32.6	Murphy-Phi 5.3	Summers-Det 24	Donovan-Det 720	Young-Bos 30
Schaefer-Det 40		Wagner-Bos...............32.4	Hartzell-StL............5.0	Joss-Cle..................24	Joss-Cle 686	Joss-Cle 29
Cobb-Det................39		Tannehill-Chi 16.9	Milan-Was.............4.7	Young-Bos 21	Summers-Det 667	Howell-StL 27
J.Clarke-Cle............37		Wallace-StL 15.2	Stahl-NY-Bos 4.6	Waddell-StL............19	Young-Bos 656	Mullin-Det..............26

Strikeouts	Fewest BB/Game	Games	Saves	Base Runners/9	Adjusted Relief Runs	Relief Ranking
Walsh-Chi 269	Joss-Cle 83	Walsh-Chi 66	Walsh-Chi 6	Joss-Cle 7.31		
Waddell-StL..........232	Burns-Was 99	Vickers-Phi 53	Hughes-Was 4	Steele-Bos 7.70		
Hughes-Was 165	Walsh-Chi 1.09	Chesbro-NY 45	Waddell-StL..............3	Walsh-Chi...........7.91		
Dygert-Phi 164	Young-Bos 1.11	Waddell-StL 43		Young-Bos 8.07		
Johnson-Was........160	Summers-Det 1.64	Hughes-Was 43		Burns-Was 8.62		

Innings Pitched	Opponents' Avg.	Opponents' OBP	Earned Run Average	Adjusted ERA	Adjusted Starter Runs	Pitcher Wins
Walsh-Chi..........464.0	Joss-Cle 197	Joss-Cle.......................218	Joss-Cle 1.16	Joss-Cle................205	Walsh-Chi............42.7	**Walsh-Chi** 6.8
Joss-Cle 325.0	Smith-Chi 203	Walsh-Chi 232	Young-Bos 1.26	Young-Bos 194	Joss-Cle 38.3	**Joss-Cle**..............5.0
Howell-StL 324.1	Walsh-Chi.............203	Young-Bos 240	Walsh-Chi 1.42	Walsh-Chi 163	Young-Bos 36.4	**Young-Bos**..........4.1
Vickers-Phi 317.0	Johnson-Was 211	Smith-Chi.....................256	Summers-Det 1.64	Summers-Det 147	Johnson-Was 17.0	**Rhoads-Cle** 2.5
Summers-Det....301.0	Young-Bos 213	Burns-Was...................257	Johnson-Was 1.65	Johnson-Was........138	Howell-StL 16.5	**Howell-StL**..........2.2

Rained Out of a Flag

Once again, pitchers asserted themselves. The AL's .239 batting average was the league's lowest until 1967, and the league's .598 OPS is the lowest in the history of baseball. Four clubs *slugged* under .300. Boston enlarged the already huge Huntington Avenue Grounds, but run production at the park was barely affected. Their 18-year-old pitching phenom, "Smokey Joe" Wood, made a successful debut.

The aging A's began to rebuild, falling to sixth, but what an eye Connie Mack had for talent! Making their major league debuts for Philly in 1908 were outfielders Joe Jackson and Amos Strunk and infielders Jack Barry and Frank "Home Run" Baker. Three of them would shortly help the club become great again. However, Mack and Jackson never quite got along, and "Shoeless Joe" ended up in Cleveland.

Cleveland, Chicago, and Detroit remained in the pennant chase until the last day. While Detroit led big in midsummer, Cleveland won 16 of 18 to climb ahead in late September. On October 2 the Indians' Addie Joss—whose 1.16 ERA set a league record—tossed a perfect game at Chicago while White Sox hurler Ed Walsh struck out 15 and allowed just 1 run.

The Tigers put on a spurt, though, and won the crown on the last day of the season, October 5. "Wild Bill" Donovan shut out Chicago to clinch the flag by a half-game over the Indians because Detroit was not required to make up a rainout. The ensuing flap led the leagues to establish a new rule mandating that all rainouts and ties critical to a pennant race be replayed.

Once again, Detroit had a fearsome attack, featuring four of the league's five top sluggers and pacing the league in runs by 78. Nevertheless, for the second straight year, the Cubs easily whipped the Tigers in the Fall Classic. This time Detroit won one game and Ty Cobb scored three times.

1909 National League

TEAM	W	L	T	PCT	GB	HW	HL	R	OR	PA	H	2B	3B	HR	BB	SO	HB	SH	AVG	OBP	SLG	OPS	AOPS	BR	ABR	PF	SB	CS	BSA	BSR
PIT	110	42	2	.724		**56**	21	**699**	447	5855	**1332**	**218**	**92**	25	479		211	36	**.260**	.327	**.353**	**680**	**109**	**102**	50	108	185			
CHI	104	49	2	.680	6.5	47	29	635	**390**	5698	1227	203	60	20	420		**248**	31	.245	.308	.322	630	100	9	-4	102	187			
NY	92	61	5	.601	18.5	44	33	624	547	5951	1327	173	68	**26**	**530**		151	**52**	.254	**.329**	.328	657	**109**	71	**61**	102	**240**			
CIN	77	76	4	.503	33.5	39	38	606	599	5816	1273	159	72	22	478		212	38	.250	.319	.323	642	107	34	39	99	280			
PHI	74	79	1	.484	36.5	40	37	517	519	5696	1228	185	53	12	369		239	54	.244	.303	.309	612	95	-25	-29	101	185			
BRO	55	98	2	.359	55.5	34	45	444	627	5579	1157	176	59	16	330		173	20	.229	.279	.296	575	87	-100	-83	96	141			
STL	54	98	2	.355	56	26	48	583	731	5857	1242	148	56	15	568		119	62	.243	.326	.303	629	**109**	26	66	94	163			
BOS	45	108	2	.294	65.5	27	47	435	683	5636	1121	125	43	14	400		189	30	.223	.285	.274	559	76	-120	-139	105	135			
TOT	621					313	298	4543		46088	9907	1387	503	150	3574	4437	323	1542	.244	.310	.314	624					1516			

TEAM	CG	SHO	GR	SV	IP	H	HR	BB	SO	BR/9	ERA	AERA	OAV	OOB	PR	APR	PF	OSB	OCS	FA	E	WPB	DP	FW	PW	BW	BSW	DIF
PIT	93	21	82	11	1401.2	1174	12	**320**	490	9.9	2.07	131	.232	.284	81	95	105	**129**	*143*	**.964**	**228**	**24**	100	**3.5**	10.5	5.5		14.4
CHI	111	**32**	57	11	1399.1	**1094**	6	364	680	**9.6**	**1.75**	**145**	**.215**	**.272**	**131**	**127**	98	148	*146*	.962	244	37	95	2.6	**14.1**	-.4		11.2
NY	105	17	66	**15**	1440.2	1248	28	397	**735**	10.5	2.27	112	.238	.295	51	43	98	167	*153*	.954	307	55	99	-1.1	4.8	6.8		5.1
CIN	91	10	83	8	1407.0	1233	**5**	510	477	11.4	2.52	103	.240	.314	11	9	100	197	*148*	.952	309	56	**120**	-1.4	1.0	4.3		-3.5
PHI	89	17	84	6	1391.0	1190	23	472	612	11.0	2.44	106	.235	.304	23	20	100	184	*153*	.962	241	50	97	2.7	2.2	-3.2		-4.2
BRO	**126**	18	30	3	1384.1	1277	31	528	594	12.1	3.10	83	.256	.333	-79	-82	100	213	***185***	.955	282	34	86	.2	-9.1	-9.2		-3.4
STL	84	5	**92**	4	1379.2	1368	22	483	435	12.4	3.41	74	.263	.331	-126	-142	97	253	*161*	.950	322	61	90	-2.6	-15.7	**7.3**		-11.0
BOS	98	13	69	6	1370.2	1329	23	543	414	12.6	3.20	88	.263	.339	-93	-56	109	225	*169*	.948	342	67	101	-3.7	-6.2	-15.4		-6.1
TOT	797	133	563	64	11174.1					11.2	2.59		.244	.310						.956	2275	384	788					

Batter-Fielder Wins
- **Wagner-Pit** 5.6
- **Gibson-Pit** 3.7
- **Konetchy-StL**......3.6
- **Devlin-NY** 3.5
- **Mitchell-Cin** 3.2

Batting Average
- Wagner-Pit 339
- Mitchell-Cin...........310
- Hoblitzel-Cin 308
- Doyle-NY 302
- Bridwell-NY...........294

On-Base Percentage
- Wagner-Pit...................420
- Bridwell-NY 386
- Clarke-Pit.....................384
- Mitchell-Cin 378
- Evers-Chi 369

Slugging Average
- Wagner-Pit 489
- Mitchell-Cin...........430
- Doyle-NY 419
- Hoblitzel-Cin 418
- McCormick-NY 402

On-Base Plus Slugging
- Wagner-Pit............909
- Mitchell-Cin 808
- Hoblitzel-Cin 782
- Doyle-NY 779
- Konetchy-StL 762

Adjusted OPS
- Wagner-Pit............168
- Mitchell-Cin 152
- Konetchy-StL 145
- Hoblitzel-Cin 144
- Doyle-NY 140

Adjusted Batter Runs
- Wagner-Pit 41.7
- Konetchy-StL......31.0
- Mitchell-Cin 30.5
- Doyle-NY............25.2
- Hoblitzel-Cin 25.1

Runs
- Leach-Pit 126
- Clarke-Pit................97
- Byrne-StL-Pit..........92
- Wagner-Pit..............92

Hits
- Doyle-NY 172
- Grant-Phi 170
- Wagner-Pit.............168
- Konetchy-StL 165
- Burch-Bro 163

Doubles
- Wagner-Pit 39
- Magee-Phi 33
- D.Miller-Pit 31
- Sheckard-Chi 29
- Leach-Pit 29

Triples
- Mitchell-Cin 17
- Magee-Phi...............14
- Konetchy-StL..........14
- D.Miller-Pit 13

Home Runs
- Murray-NY.................7
- Leach-Pit 6
- Doyle-NY...................6
- Becker-Bos 6
- Wagner-Pit.................5

Total Bases
- Wagner-Pit............242
- Doyle-NY 239
- Konetchy-StL 228
- Mitchell-Cin 225
- D.Miller-Pit 222

Runs Batted In
- Wagner-Pit 100
- Murray-NY 91
- D.Miller-Pit 87
- Mitchell-Cin 86
- Konetchy-StL 80

Stolen Bases
- Bescher-Cin............54
- Murray-NY..............48
- Egan-Cin 39
- Magee-Phi 38
- Burch-Bro 38

Base Stealing Runs

Fielding Runs-Infield
- Egan-Cin 23.7
- Doolan-Phi..................23.5
- Tinker-Chi 18.3
- Devlin-NY....................16.9
- Byrne-StL-Pit..............16.5

Fielding Runs-Outfield
- Ellis-StL 12.9
- Clarke-Pit 7.3
- Mitchell-Cin............5.3
- O'Hara-NY 4.2
- Bates-Bos-Phi 3.7

Wins
- M.Brown-Chi 27
- Mathewson-NY 25
- H.Camnitz-Pit 25
- Willis-Pit..................22

Winning Pct.
- Mathewson-NY.....806
- H.Camnitz-Pit.......806
- M.Brown-Chi.........750
- Pfiester-Chi...........739
- Leifield-Pit.............704

Complete Games
- M.Brown-Chi 32
- Bell-Bro 29
- Rucker-Bro 28
- Mathewson-NY......26

Strikeouts
- Overall-Chi............205
- Rucker-Bro............201
- Moore-Phi 173
- M.Brown-Chi 172
- Ames-NY 156

Fewest BB/Game
- Mathewson-NY....1.18
- M.Brown-Chi........1.39
- Wiltse-NY 1.70
- Maddox-Pit 1.73
- McQuillan-Phi......1.96

Games
- M.Brown-Chi.................50
- Mattern-Bos 47
- Gaspar-Cin 44
- Beebe-StL.....................44

Saves
- M.Brown-Chi 7
- Crandall-NY.............6

Base Runners/9
- Mathewson-NY....7.45
- Adams-Pit............7.89
- M.Brown-Chi.........8.04
- H.Camnitz-Pit 8.97
- Curtis-Bos 9.22

Adjusted Relief Runs

Relief Ranking

Innings Pitched
- M.Brown-Chi......342.2
- Mattern-Bos 316.1
- Rucker-Bro 309.1
- Moore-Phi..........299.2
- Willis-Pit 289.2

Opponents' Avg.
- Overall-Chi 198
- Mathewson-NY.....200
- Fromme-Cin 201
- M.Brown-Chi.........202
- Moore-Phi.............210

Opponents' OBP
- Mathewson-NY 228
- M.Brown-Chi 239
- Overall-Chi.................262
- H.Camnitz-Pit 267
- McQuillan-Phi 271

Earned Run Average
- Mathewson-NY....1.14
- M.Brown-Chi........1.31
- Overall-Chi 1.42
- H.Camnitz-Pit 1.62
- Kroh-Chi 1.65

Adjusted ERA
- Mathewson-NY 223
- M.Brown-Chi 193
- Overall-Chi...........178
- H.Camnitz-Pit 167
- Reulbach-Chi........142

Adjusted Starter Runs
- M.Brown-Chi........45.2
- Mathewson-NY....42.2
- Overall-Chi 35.5
- H.Camnitz-Pit......31.3
- Reulbach-Chi 24.4

Pitcher Wins
- **Mathewson-NY**..6.6
- **M.Brown-Chi**......5.3
- **Overall-Chi** 5.2
- **H.Camnitz-Pit**....3.5
- **Fromme-Cin** 3.2

The Great Cobb and Wagner Face Off

Offense increased slightly in the NL, due partly to park changes. On June 30, the Pirates opened Forbes Field, a slightly smaller field than their previous home, Exposition Park. Prior to the season, the Giants significantly reduced the size of center field at the Polo Grounds.

The NL's key rookie was 21-year-old Zack Wheat, who came up late in the season and joined Brooklyn's outfield. He remained with Brooklyn through 1926 before playing a final year with the Athletics while amassing 2,884 hits. John Clarkson, who three times led the NL in victories, died from pneumonia. His 49 wins in 1889, tops in the NL by 21 that year, remains the highest post-1885 total. Another who passed away was Herman Long, Boston's great shortstop of the 1890s, who died at 43 of consumption.

Pittsburgh, Chicago, and New York were again the class of the league. This time the Bucs emerged in May and floated away, finishing 6½ ahead of the Cubs, who themselves won 104 games. It was a return to glory for Honus Wagner, who won his fourth straight batting crown and led the NL in RBIs for the fourth time. Chicago again had the best pitching, but the Pirates sported the top four finishers in runs.

Then there was the league's doormat, the St. Louis Cardinals, who finished 50 or more games out of first for the fourth straight time. A somewhat respectable 43–57 on August 16, the Redbirds lost 15 straight down the stretch. As bad as the Cardinals were, Boston was even worse, ending up 65½ games out.

It was Babe Adams' turn to shine in the fall. The Pittsburgh righty, a fifth starter during the regular season, beat the Tigers three times in a World Series that went seven games. In the match-up of the game's two top stars, Wagner batted .333 with 6 RBIs, while Cobb hit .231 and scored just three times.

1909 American League

TEAM	W	L	T	PCT	GB	HW	HL	R	OR	PA	H	2B	3B	HR	BB	SO	HB	SH	AVG	OBP	SLG	OPS	AOPS	BR	ABR	PF	SB	CS	BSA	BSR
DET	98	54	6	.645		**57**	19	**666**	493	5763	**1360**	**209**	58	19	397		232	39	**.267**	**.325**	.342	**667**	113	**102**	75	104	**280**			
PHI	95	58	0	.621	3.5	49	27	605	**411**	5620	1257	186	**88**	**21**	403		**247**	64	.256	.321	**.343**	664	**115**	92	**80**	102	201			
BOS	88	63	1	.583	9.5	47	28	601	549	5575	1309	151	69	20	348		170	**77**	.263	.321	.333	654	112	73	60	102	215			
CHI	78	74	7	.513	20	42	34	492	464	5759	1109	145	56	4	**441**		243	57	.221	.291	.275	566	89	-72	-51	96	211			
NY	74	77	2	.490	23.5	41	35	589	587	5649	1234	143	61	16	407		198	63	.248	.313	.311	624	103	25	21	101	187			
CLE	71	82	2	.464	27.5	39	37	493	532	5536	1216	173	81	10	283		157	48	.241	.288	.313	601	92	-31	-50	104	173			
STL	61	89	4	.407	36	40	37	441	575	5487	1151	116	45	10	331		141	51	.232	.287	.279	566	91	-82	-48	93	136			
WAS	42	110	4	.276	56	27	48	380	656	5541	1113	149	41	9	321		195	42	.223	.276	.275	551	84	-109	-88	95	136			
TOT	620					342	265	4267		44930	9749	1272	499	109	2931	4918	441	1583	.244	.303	.309	612					1539			

TEAM	CG	SHO	GR	SV	IP	H	HR	BB	SO	BR/9	ERA	AERA	OAV	OOB	PR	APR	PF	OSB	OCS	FA	E	WPB	DP	FW	PW	BW	BSW	DIF
DET	**117**	17	50	12	1420.1	1254	16	359	528	10.6	2.26	111	.238	.293	33	39	102	190	*155*	.959	276	**43**	87	.4	4.4	8.5		8.7
PHI	110	**27**	61	3	1378.0	**1069**	9	386	**728**	**9.9**	**1.93**	**124**	**.217**	**.282**	**82**	**74**	97	**152**	*162*	.961	**245**	45	92	1.8	**8.4**	**9.1**		-.8
BOS	75	11	**95**	**14**	1360.1	1213	18	384	555	10.9	2.59	96	.243	.303	-19	-15	101	167	*153*	.955	292	52	95	-1.3	-1.7	6.8		8.7
CHI	115	26	49	4	1430.1	1182	**8**	**340**	669	**9.9**	2.05	114	.229	.283	67	47	95	210	*158*	**.964**	246	54	101	**2.4**	5.3	-5.8		.0
NY	94	18	64	8	1350.1	1223	21	422	597	11.4	2.65	95	.248	.316	-26	-21	102	207	*156*	.948	330	52	94	-3.6	-2.4	2.4		2.1
CLE	110	15	51	3	1361.0	1212	9	348	568	10.6	2.40	106	.250	.307	11	20	103	180	*164*	.957	278	65	**110**	-.0	2.3	-5.7		-2.0
STL	105	21	55	4	1354.2	1287	16	383	620	11.4	2.88	84	.261	.319	-61	-74	98	203	***169***	.958	267	51	107	.5	-8.4	-5.5		-.6
WAS	99	11	74	2	1374.2	1288	12	424	653	11.6	3.04	80	.248	.312	-87	-98	98	230	*159*	.957	280	72	100	-.0	-11.1	-10.0		-12.8
TOT	825	146	499	50	11029.2					10.8	2.47		.244	.303						.957	2214	434	786					

Batter-Fielder Wins	Batting Average	On-Base Percentage	Slugging Average	On-Base Plus Slugging	Adjusted OPS	Adjusted Batter Runs
Cobb-Det 6.0	Cobb-Det 377	Cobb-Det 431	Cobb-Det 517	Cobb-Det.............947	Cobb-Det.............190	Cobb-Det...........59.2
Collins-Phi 5.9	Collins-Phi 347	Collins-Phi 416	Crawford-Det 452	Collins-Phi 866	Collins-Phi 170	Collins-Phi 48.1
Lajoie-Cle 5.7	Lajoie-Cle 324	Bush-Det 380	Collins-Phi 450	Crawford-Det 817	Stahl-Bos..............153	Crawford-Det.......33.2
Speaker-Bos 4.6	Lord-Bos..............315	Lajoie-Cle 378	Baker-Phi 447	Stahl-Bos.............812	Crawford-Det 151	Speaker-Bos 29.8
Engle-NY 2.3	Crawford-Det 314	Stahl-Bos....................377	Speaker-Bos.........443	Lajoie-Cle 809	Speaker-Bos 151	Stahl-Bos...........27.2

Runs	Hits	Doubles	Triples	Home Runs	Total Bases	Runs Batted In
Cobb-Det.............116	Cobb-Det.............216	Crawford-Det 35	Baker-Phi...............19	Cobb-Det..................9	Cobb-Det.............296	Cobb-Det 107
Bush-Det 114	Collins-Phi 198	Lajoie-Cle 33	Murphy-Phi 14	Speaker-Bos 7	Crawford-Det........266	Crawford-Det 97
Collins-Phi............104	Crawford-Det.........185	Cobb-Det 33	Crawford-Det.........14	Stahl-Bos..................6	Collins-Phi 257	Baker-Phi 85
Lord-Bos 89	Speaker-Bos 168	Collins-Phi 30		Crawford-Det 6	Baker-Phi.............242	Speaker-Bos..........77
Crawford-Det..........83	Lord-Bos 168	Murphy-Phi 28		Murphy-Phi 5	Speaker-Bos 241	Davis-Phi 75

Stolen Bases	Base Stealing Runs	Fielding Runs-Infield	Fielding Runs-Outfield	Wins	Winning Pct.	Complete Games
Cobb-Det................76		Lajoie-Cle 23.3	Speaker-Bos........18.5	Mullin-Det 29	Mullin-Det 784	Smith-Chi 37
Collins-Phi..............63		Parent-Chi 14.4	Engle-NY 14.9	Smith-Chi...............25	Krause-Phi 692	Young-Cle..............30
Bush-Det 53		McBride-Was 13.0	Hartzell-StL...........8.5	Willett-Det 21	Bender-Phi 692	Mullin-Det 29
Lord-Bos 36		Austin-NY....................13.0	Milan-Was.............4.7		Summers-Det 679	Johnson-Was 27
Dougherty-Chi 36		Wallace-StL 11.0	Niles-Bos 2.3		Willett-Det............677	Morgan-Bos-Phi 26

Strikeouts	Fewest BB/Game	Games	Saves	Base Runners/9	Adjusted Relief Runs	Relief Ranking
Smith-Chi.............177	Joss-Cle 1.15	Smith-Chi 51	Arellanes-Bos 8	Walsh-Chi............8.60		
Johnson-Was........164	White-Chi 1.57	Arellanes-Bos 45	Powell-StL 3	Joss-Cle 8.64		
Berger-Cle 162	Powell-StL............1.58	Groom-Was 44		Smith-Chi 8.73		
Bender-Phi............161	Bender-Phi 1.62	Willett-Det.....................41		Bender-Phi 8.86		
Waddell-StL..........141	Summers-Det 1.66			Krause-Phi 9.00		

Innings Pitched	Opponents' Avg.	Opponents' OBP	Earned Run Average	Adjusted ERA	Adjusted Starter Runs	Pitcher Wins
Smith-Chi 365.0	Morgan-Bos-Phi ...202	Walsh-Chi 253	Krause-Phi 1.39	Krause-Phi............172	Walsh-Chi 24.9	**Walsh-Chi** 4.1
Mullin-Det 303.2	Walsh-Chi 203	Bender-Phi..................254	Walsh-Chi 1.41	Walsh-Chi 166	Morgan-Bos-Phi ..24.3	**Smith-Chi** 4.1
Johnson-Was 296.1	Krause-Phi 204	Joss-Cle.......................255	Bender-Phi 1.66	Joss-Cle................149	Krause-Phi 23.3	**Bender-Phi** 2.7
Young-Cle..........294.1	Cicotte-Bos...........207	Smith-Chi.....................257	Joss-Cle 1.71	Killian-Det 147	Smith-Chi 22.9	**Krause-Phi** 2.7
Morgan-Bos-Phi 293.1	Wood-Bos 209	Krause-Phi...................266	Killian-Det 1.71	Bender-Phi............145	Joss-Cle 20.9	**Plank-Phi**............2.6

Bengals Win Battle of Weak Bats

Detroit led the league almost the entire way as Cobb's Tigers captured their third straight AL pennant. Their challengers were the Athletics, led by second baseman Eddie Collins, and the Red Sox, led by center fielder Tris Speaker. Collins was an all-around standout, while Speaker set an AL mark with 35 outfield assists.

Chicago and Cleveland dropped from contention essentially because they couldn't score. Despite fielding just three quality offensive players—Ty Cobb, Donie Bush, and Sam Crawford—Detroit paced the AL in runs by more than 60. Cobb and Bush ranked first and second in runs, Cobb and Crawford first and second in RBIs. Cobb grabbed the Triple Crown and also led in on-base percentage, slugging, total bases, and steals. However, the Tigers magic wore off yet again in the World Series as Detroit fell to the Pirates.

Boston's Harry Hooper spent his rookie year as a part-time outfielder. Starting in 1910, he'd become a regular for sixteen years. Also for the Red Sox, star righty Jack Chesbro was done as a big leaguer at age 35. George Davis, a great shortstop of the nineteenth century, played his last game with the White Sox. Two active players died. Thirty-eight-year-old catcher Doc Powers passed away in April from complications of gangrene, while Jimmy Sebring, an outfielder who played one game for the Senators after five years in the NL, died in December from Bright's disease.

Two AL teams moved into shiny new digs. The Athletics built their revolutionary Shibe Park, which would serve them until they left the city in 1953, while the St. Louis Browns began playing in a new Sportsman's Park. The average AL team scored just 3.44 runs per game, the lowest mark until 1968; three starting pitchers had ERAs below 1.70. The fans apparently found the low-scoring style of play exciting enough, though, as attendance reached a pre-1920 peak.

1910 National League

TEAM	W	L	T	PCT	GB	HW	HL	R	OR	PA	H	2B	3B	HR	BB	SO	HB	SH	AVG	OBP	SLG	OPS	AOPS	BR	ABR	PF	SB	CS	BSA	BSR
CHI	104	50	0	.675		**58**	19	712	**499**	5792	1333	219	**84**	**34**	542	501	**234**	39	.268	.344	**.366**	710	114	84	90	99	173			
NY	91	63	1	.591	13	52	26	**715**	567	5873	**1391**	204	83	31	**562**	**489**	193	**57**	**.275**	**.354**	**.366**	**720**	**116**	**108**	**107**	100	**282**			
PIT	86	67	1	.562	17.5	46	30	655	576	5794	1364	214	83	33	437	524	198	34	.266	.328	.360	688	100	30	-6	106	148			
PHI	78	75	4	.510	25.5	40	36	674	639	5925	1319	**223**	71	22	506	559	205	43	.255	.327	.338	665	97	-1	-21	103	199			
CIN	75	79	2	.487	29	39	37	620	684	5861	1326	150	79	23	529	515	182	29	.259	.332	.333	665	105	-3	26	96	310			
BRO	64	90	2	.416	40	39	39	497	623	5782	1174	166	73	25	434	706	183	40	.229	.294	.305	599	82	-136	-121	97	151			
STL	63	90	0	.412	40.5	35	41	639	718	5798	1217	167	70	15	655	581	153	78	.248	.345	.319	664	103	22	47	96	179			
BOS	53	100	4	.346	50.5	29	48	495	701	5710	1260	173	49	31	359	540	181	47	.246	.301	.317	618	81	-102	-124	105	152			
TOT	621					338	276	5007		46535	10384	1516	592	214	4024	4415	367	1529	.256	.328	.338	666					1594			

TEAM	CG	SHO	GR	SV	IP	H	HR	BB	SO	BR/9	ERA	AERA	OAV	OOB	PR	APR	PF	OSB	OCS	FA	E	WPB	DP	FW	PW	BW	BSW	DIF
CHI	100	**25**	74	13	1378.2	**1171**	18	474	609	**11.0**	**2.51**	**115**	**.235**	**.307**	**79**	**57**	95	**145**	*148*	.963	**230**	46	110	**2.1**	**6.0**	9.5		9.4
NY	96	9	80	10	1391.2	1290	30	397	**717**	11.2	2.68	110	.250	.308	54	45	98	192	*153*	.955	291	52	117	-1.7	4.7	**11.3**		-.3
PIT	73	13	100	12	1376.0	1254	20	**392**	479	11.1	2.83	109	.250	.311	29	37	102	168	*145*	.961	245	**23**	102	1.1	3.9	-.6		5.1
PHI	84	17	**107**	9	1411.1	1297	36	547	657	12.1	3.05	102	.253	.330	-5	9	103	213	*163*	.960	258	49	132	.6	.9	-2.2		2.1
CIN	86	16	88	11	1386.2	1334	27	528	497	12.5	3.08	94	.261	.338	-9	-30	96	153	*145*	.955	291	53	103	-1.6	-3.2	2.7		.0
BRO	**103**	15	65	5	1420.1	1331	**17**	545	555	12.1	3.07	99	.259	.335	-7	-9	100	215	*188*	**.964**	235	54	125	2.0	-.9	-12.7		-1.3
STL	81	4	96	**14**	1337.1	1396	30	541	466	13.3	3.78	79	.275	.350	-112	-122	98	264	*138*	.959	261	61	109	.0	-12.8	4.9		-5.6
BOS	72	12	**107**	9	1390.1	1328	36	599	531	12.8	3.22	103	.265	.349	-30	13	110	244	***192***	.954	305	57	**137**	-2.4	1.4	-13.1		-9.5
TOT	695	111	717	83	11092.1					12.0	3.02		.256	.328						.959	2116	395	935					

Batter-Fielder Wins	Batting Average	On-Base Percentage	Slugging Average	On-Base Plus Slugging	Adjusted OPS	Adjusted Batter Runs
Konetchy-StL 3.9	Magee-Phi .331	Magee-Phi .445	Magee-Phi .507	Magee-Phi .952	Magee-Phi 172	Magee-Phi 52.7
Mowrey-StL 3.6	Campbell-Pit .326	Snodgrass-NY .440	Hofman-Chi .461	Snodgrass-NY .871	Snodgrass-NY 154	Hofman-Chi 33.3
Wagner-Pit 3.5	Hofman-Chi .325	Evers-Chi .413	Schulte-Chi .460	Hofman-Chi .867	Hofman-Chi 154	Snodgrass-NY 33.1
Magee-Phi 3.4	Snodgrass-NY .321	Hofman-Chi .406	Merkle-NY .441	Konetchy-StL .822	Konetchy-StL 145	Konetchy-StL 31.9
Hofman-Chi 2.8	Wagner-Pit .320	Huggins-StL .399	Campbell-Pit .436	Wagner-Pit .822	Schulte-Chi 137	Wagner-Pit 23.7

Runs	Hits	Doubles	Triples	Home Runs	Total Bases	Runs Batted In
Magee-Phi 110	Wagner-Pit 178	Byrne-Pit 43	Mitchell-Cin 18	Schulte-Chi 10	Magee-Phi 263	Magee-Phi 123
Huggins-StL 101	Byrne-Pit 178	Magee-Phi 39	Magee-Phi 17	Beck-Bos 10	Schulte-Chi 257	Mitchell-Cin 88
Byrne-Pit 101	Wheat-Bro 172	Wheat-Bro 36	Konetchy-StL 16	Doyle-NY 8	Byrne-Pit 251	Murray-NY 87
Doyle-NY 97	Magee-Phi 172	Merkle-NY 35	Hofman-Chi 16	Daubert-Bro 8	Wheat-Bro 244	Hofman-Chi 86
Bescher-Cin 95	Hoblitzel-Cin 170	Wagner-Pit 34			Wagner-Pit 240	Wagner-Pit 81

Stolen Bases	Base Stealing Runs	Fielding Runs-Infield	Fielding Runs-Outfield	Wins	Winning Pct.	Complete Games
Bescher-Cin 70		Shean-Bos 43.2	Paskert-Cin 9.6	Mathewson-NY 27	Cole-Chi .833	Rucker-Bro 27
Murray-NY 57		Doolan-Phi 17.8	Sheckard-Chi 8.1	Brown-Chi 25	Crandall-NY .810	Mathewson-NY 27
Paskert-Cin 51		Mowrey-StL 14.3	Collins-Bos 8.1	Moore-Phi 22	Mathewson-NY .750	Brown-Chi 27
Magee-Phi 49		Tinker-Chi 14.3	Murray-NY 5.9	Suggs-Cin 20	Adams-Pit .667	Bell-Bro 25
Devore-NY 43		Knabe-Phi 13.9	Bates-Phi 5.4	Cole-Chi 20	Brown-Chi .641	Barger-Bro 25

Strikeouts	Fewest BB/Game	Games	Saves	Base Runners/9	Adjusted Relief Runs	Relief Ranking
Moore-Phi 185	Suggs-Cin 1.62	Mattern-Bos 51	Gaspar-Cin 7	Phillippe-Pit 9.10		
Mathewson-NY 184	Mathewson-NY 1.70	Gaspar-Cin 48	Brown-Chi 7	McQuillan-Phi 9.57		
Frock-Pit-Bos 171	Crandall-NY 1.86		Crandall-NY 5	Pfiester-Chi 9.78		
Drucke-NY 151	Brown-Chi 1.95		Richie-Bos-Chi 4	Brown-Chi 9.87		
Rucker-Bro 147	Wiltse-NY 1.99		Phillippe-Pit 4	Overall-Chi 10.02		

Innings Pitched	Opponents' Avg.	Opponents' OBP	Earned Run Average	Adjusted ERA	Adjusted Starter Runs	Pitcher Wins
Rucker-Bro 320.1	Cole-Chi .211	Brown-Chi .277	McQuillan-Phi 1.60	Cole-Chi 159	Mathewson-NY 35.4	**Mathewson-NY** 5.3
Mathewson-NY 318.1	Drucke-NY .228	Mathewson-NY .286	Cole-Chi 1.80	Mathewson-NY 156	Cole-Chi 29.3	**Brown-Chi** 4.0
Bell-Bro 310.0	Moore-Phi .228	Crandall-NY .289	Brown-Chi 1.86	Brown-Chi 155	Brown-Chi 28.6	**Cole-Chi** 3.1
Mattern-Bos 305.0	Brown-Chi .232	Adams-Pit .291	Mathewson-NY 1.89	Adams-Pit 138	McQuillan-Phi 22.8	**Moore-Phi** 2.6
Brown-Chi 295.1	Scanlan-Bro .234	Bell-Bro .296	Ames-NY 2.22	Ames-NY 133	Moore-Phi 20.2	**Suggs-Cin** 2.4

End of an Era in Chicago

The rules committee made two codifications that seem oddly obvious: The batting order must be presented before the game and followed, and substitutions can only come when time was out. In addition, the passed ball and wild pitch were first defined.

Christy Mathewson and Three Finger Brown were again the league's top pitchers, maintaining their touch even as team runs per game topped 4.00 for first time in five years. NL batters clubbed 214 homers in 1910, the highest total since 1901. But another runaway by the Cubs dropped attendance 16 percent; attendance would not reach its 1908 level again until 1920.

Jake Daubert debuted as Brooklyn's everyday first baseman, and went on to a fifteen-year career and two batting titles. Catcher Hank Gowdy, who would spend his entire seventeen-year skein with the Giants and Braves, plus another season in France during World War I, played his first game in September 1910. Pirates outfielder Max Carey, who would lead the NL ten times in steals, made The Show at age 20.

Infielder Alan Storke, who split '09 between Pittsburgh and St. Louis, underwent a lung operation in March but died from complications. He was 26. Others playing their last games (but not dying) included Hall of Famer "Wee" Willie Keeler, Pirates hurler Sam Leever, and Vic Willis, who won 249 games in thirteen years.

For the fourth time in five years, the Cubs won more than 100 games, pulling from the pack in May and never looking back. Neither the Pirates, whose pitching staff had aged dangerously, or the rebuilding Giants were serious threats. However, John McGraw had restocked New York with some excellent young players. A loss to the Athletics in the World Series ended the Cubs' era of dominance; they would only win one more flag in the next two decades.

1910 American League

TEAM	W	L	T	PCT	GB	HW	HL	R	OR	PA	H	2B	3B	HR	BB	SO	HB	SH	AVG	OBP	SLG	OPS	AOPS	BR	ABR	PF	SB	CS	BSA	BSR
PHI	102	48	5	.680		**57**	19	674	**442**	5809	**1373**	**191**	**105**	19	409		199	47	**.266**	.326	**.355**	**681**	**120**	**104**	**111**	99	207			
NY	88	63	5	.583	14.5	49	25	626	557	5762	1254	164	75	20	**464**		176	**71**	.248	.320	.322	642	101	45	11	106	**288**			
DET	86	68	1	.558	18	46	31	**679**	584	5746	1317	190	72	28	459		197	51	.261	**.329**	.344	673	110	99	57	107	249			
BOS	81	72	5	.529	22.5	51	28	641	564	5917	1350	175	87	**43**	430		**227**	56	.259	.323	.351	674	114	94	78	102	194			
CLE	71	81	9	.467	32	39	36	548	657	5988	1316	188	64	9	366		190	37	.244	.296	.308	604	94	-39	-46	101	189			
CHI	68	85	3	.444	35.5	41	37	457	479	5661	1058	115	58	7	403		190	44	.211	.275	.261	536	76	-154	-136	96	183			
WAS	66	85	6	.437	36.5	38	35	501	551	5690	1175	145	47	9	449		170	82	.236	.309	.289	598	98	-30	-4	95	192			
STL	47	107	4	.305	57	26	51	451	743	5675	1105	131	60	12	415		147	36	.218	.281	.274	555	84	-120	-90	94	169			
TOT	628					347	262	4577		46248	9948	1299	568	147	3395	5278	424	1496	.243	.308	.313	621					1671			

TEAM	CG	SHO	GR	SV	IP	H	HR	BB	SO	BR/9	ERA	AERA	OAV	OOB	PR	APR	PF	OSB	OCS	FA	E	WPB	DP	FW	PW	BW	BSW	DIF
PHI	**123**	**24**	45	5	1421.2	**1103**	**8**	450	**789**	10.2	**1.79**	**133**	**.221**	.292	**116**	**97**	94	187	*168*	**.965**	**230**	49	**117**	**3.9**	**10.8**	**12.3**		.0
NY	110	14	57	**8**	1399.0	1238	16	**364**	654	10.7	2.61	102	.243	.300	-15	5	106	194	*152*	.956	286	**48**	95	.2	.6	1.2		10.5
DET	108	17	64	5	1380.1	1257	34	460	532	11.6	2.82	93	.248	.319	-47	-26	104	193	*168*	.956	288	**48**	79	-.0	-2.9	6.3		5.6
BOS	100	12	70	6	1430.0	1236	30	414	670	10.7	2.45	104	.235	.297	10	14	101	207	*141*	.954	309	52	80	-1.1	1.6	8.7		-4.6
CLE	92	13	**82**	5	1467.0	1392	10	488	617	11.9	2.88	90	.261	.330	-60	-49	103	259	*190*	.964	248	62	112	3.4	-5.4	-5.1		2.2
CHI	103	23	66	7	1421.0	1130	16	381	785	**9.8**	2.03	118	.222	**.281**	77	59	95	**175**	*158*	.954	314	**48**	100	-1.7	6.6	-15.1		1.8
WAS	119	19	43	3	1373.1	1215	19	375	674	10.8	2.46	101	.244	.304	8	5	99	201	*170*	.959	264	84	99	1.8	.6	-.4		-11.4
STL	101	9	72	3	1391.0	1356	14	532	557	12.6	3.09	80	.265	.341	-89	-97	98	252	***196***	.943	385	**48**	113	-6.3	-10.8	-10.0		-2.9
TOT	856	131	499	42	11283.1					11.0	2.52		.243	.308						.956	2324	439	795					

Batter-Fielder Wins
Lajoie-Cle 8.9
Collins-Phi 7.0
Cobb-Det 6.3
Speaker-Bos 4.8
McBride-Was 4.1

Batting Average
Cobb-Det 383
Lajoie-Cle 384
Speaker-Bos.........340
Collins-Phi 324
Knight-NY.............312

On-Base Percentage
Cobb-Det 456
Lajoie-Cle 445
Speaker-Bos 404
Collins-Phi 382
Milan-Was 379

Slugging Average
Cobb-Det 551
Lajoie-Cle.............514
Speaker-Bos.........468
Murphy-Phi...........436
Oldring-Phi 430

On-Base Plus Slugging
Cobb-Det...........1008
Lajoie-Cle 960
Speaker-Bos 873
Collins-Phi 800
Cree-NY 775

Adjusted OPS
Cobb-Det.............202
Lajoie-Cle 198
Speaker-Bos 169
Collins-Phi 152
Murphy-Phi 143

Adjusted Batter Runs
Lajoie-Cle 69.3
Cobb-Det............61.5
Speaker-Bos 42.5
Collins-Phi 33.9
Murphy-Phi 24.1

Runs
Cobb-Det..............106
Lajoie-Cle 94
Speaker-Bos 92
Bush-Det 90
Milan-Was 89

Hits
Lajoie-Cle 227
Cobb-Det..............194
Collins-Phi.............188
Speaker-Bos 183
Crawford-Det........170

Doubles
Lajoie-Cle 51
Cobb-Det 35
Lewis-Bos.......................29
Murphy-Phi 28
Oldring-Phi 27

Triples
Crawford-Det..........19
Lord-Cle-Phi 18
Murphy-Phi 18
Stahl-Bos................16
Cree-NY 16

Home Runs
Stahl-Bos................10
Lewis-Bos 8
Cobb-Det..................8
Speaker-Bos 7
Crawford-Det............5

Total Bases
Lajoie-Cle 304
Cobb-Det.............279
Speaker-Bos 252
Crawford-Det........249
Murphy-Phi 244

Runs Batted In
Crawford-Det 120
Cobb-Det 91
Collins-Phi 81
Stahl-Bos 77
Lajoie-Cle..............76

Stolen Bases
Collins-Phi 81
Cobb-Det.................65
Zeider-Chi 49
Bush-Det 49
Milan-Was 44

Base Stealing Runs

Fielding Runs-Infield
McBride-Was 32.8
Collins-Phi 29.8
Wallace-StL 22.6
Lajoie-Cle 12.5
Bush-Det 10.4

Fielding Runs-Outfield
Lewis-Bos............11.5
Birmingham-Cle ..10.3
Hooper-Bos 8.8
Speaker-Bos..........8.6
Milan-Was..............7.6

Wins
Coombs-Phi............31
Ford-NY 26
Johnson-Was..........25
Bender-Phi.............23
Mullin-Det 21

Winning Pct.
Bender-Phi 821
Ford-NY 813
Coombs-Phi 775
Donovan-Det 708
Mullin-Det 636

Complete Games
Johnson-Was........38
Coombs-Phi 35
Walsh-Chi.............33
Ford-NY 29
Mullin-Det 27

Strikeouts
Johnson-Was........313
Walsh-Chi 258
Coombs-Phi..........224
Ford-NY 209
Bender-Phi...........155

Fewest BB/Game
Walsh-Chi...........1.49
Young-Cle...........1.49
Collins-Bos 1.51
Bender-Phi 1.69
Johnson-Was 1.85

Games
Walsh-Chi 45
Johnson-Was 45
Coombs-Phi 45
Scott-Chi.......................41

Saves
Walsh-Chi 5
Browning-Det...........3

Base Runners/9
Walsh-Chi............7.47
Ford-NY 8.17
Johnson-Was 8.54
Bender-Phi 8.60
Collins-Bos 9.09

Adjusted Relief Runs

Relief Ranking

Innings Pitched
Johnson-Was 370.0
Walsh-Chi..........369.2
Coombs-Phi 353.0
Ford-NY 299.2
Morgan-Phi........290.2

Opponents' Avg.
Walsh-Chi............187
Ford-NY 188
Coombs-Phi 201
Johnson-Was 205
Hall-Bos 207

Opponents' OBP
Walsh-Chi 226
Ford-NY 245
Bender-Phi....................255
Johnson-Was...............257
Collins-Bos 264

Earned Run Average
Walsh-Chi...............1.27
Coombs-Phi 1.30
Johnson-Was 1.36
Morgan-Phi..........1.55
Bender-Phi 1.58

Adjusted ERA
Walsh-Chi 189
Johnson-Was........183
Coombs-Phi..........182
Ford-NY 161
Collins-Bos 158

Adjusted Starter Runs
Coombs-Phi 46.6
Walsh-Chi...........45.5
Johnson-Was 43.4
Ford-NY 33.9
Bender-Phi 25.2

Pitcher Wins
Walsh-Chi 6.3
Coombs-Phi 5.8
Johnson-Was 5.5
Ford-NY 4.2
Bender-Phi 4.1

Chalmers Promotion Sparks Chicanery and Controversy

The Indians began the season in brand-new League Park, while on July 1, the White Sox moved into Comiskey Park, the "Palace of Baseball." In two years, half of the league had built new concrete-and-steel parks; one more step towards the AL's consolidation of power. Despite this, attendance fell nearly 13 percent.

One of the biggest controversies of the era focused on the batting title, a battle between Cleveland's popular Nap Lajoie and Detroit's *un*popular Ty Cobb. The Chalmers company promised a car to the batting titlist, and on the season's last day, the Browns had their third baseman play deep, allowing Lajoie to bunt for seven hits in a doubleheader and to finish at .384. Even so, Cobb won because of a clerical error that double-counted 2 of his hits, an error not corrected for 70 years. Chalmers awarded each man a car.

Connie Mack's Athletics pulled away from Detroit in early summer and coasted to the title. The Yankees moved from fifth to second with a speed-based attack and good pitching. The Tigers, disheartened by three straight World Series losses, ended third despite Cobb leading the league in runs, slugging, and on-base percentage, edging out Lajoie in those categories without any computation errors or uncontested bunts.

Two standouts played their last games. Outfielder Elmer Flick, a speed demon beset by injuries, was through at 34. Rube Waddell, the overpowering southpaw, could no longer get hitters out consistently, and was released by St. Louis. He would be dead within four years.

Setting an all-time AL record for team ERA at 1.74, Athletics pitchers—Jack Coombs and Chief Bender combined for 54 wins—did not allow a home run at Shibe Park *all season*. But they also had the league's best offense, as well as ERA, in road games. In the World Series, the Mackmen completely destroyed Chicago, mauling the Cubs for 35 runs in five games and allowing just 15.

1911 National League

TEAM	W	L	T	PCT	GB	HW	HL	R	OR	PA	H	2B	3B	HR	BB	SO	HB	SH	AVG	OBP	SLG	OPS	AOPS	BR	ABR	PF	SB	CS	BSA	BSR
NY	99	54	1	.647		**49**	25	756	**542**	5781	**1399**	**225**	103	41	530	**506**	160	**85**	**.279**	**.358**	**.390**	**748**	**113**	**111**	**87**	103	**347**			
CHI	92	62	3	.597	7.5	**49**	32	**757**	607	5959	1335	218	101	54	585	617	**202**	42	.260	.341	.374	715	107	44	43	100	214			
PIT	85	69	1	.552	14.5	48	29	744	557	5907	1345	206	**106**	49	525	583	193	52	.262	.336	.372	708	101	27	1	104	160			
PHI	79	73	1	.520	19.5	42	34	658	669	5751	1307	214	56	**60**	490	588	186	31	.259	.328	.359	687	98	-10	-18	101	153			
STL	75	74	9	.503	22	36	38	671	745	5970	1295	199	86	26	**592**	650	181	65	.252	.337	.340	677	99	-17	2	97	175			
CIN	70	83	6	.458	29	38	42	682	706	6089	1379	180	105	21	578	594	185	35	.261	.337	.346	683	102	-13	13	96	289			
BRO	64	86	4	.427	33.5	31	42	539	659	5680	1198	151	71	28	425	683	157	39	.237	.301	.311	612	80	-157	-135	96	184			
BOS	44	107	5	.291	54	19	54	699	1021	6045	1417	249	54	37	554	577	152	31	.267	.340	.355	695	93	14	-40	108	169			
TOT	623					312	296	5506		47182	10675	1642	682	316	4279	4798	380	1416	.260	.335	.356	691					1691			

TEAM	CG	SHO	GR	SV	IP	H	HR	BB	SO	BR/9	ERA	AERA	OAV	OOB	PR	APR	PF	OSB	OCS	FA	E	WPB	DP	FW	PW	BW	BSW	DIF
NY	**95**	19	80	13	1368.0	1267	33	**369**	**771**	11.0	**2.69**	**125**	.246	**.300**	**106**	**101**	99	146	*117*	.959	256	41	86	.5	**10.1**	**8.7**		3.1
CHI	85	12	97	**16**	1411.0	1270	**26**	525	582	11.7	2.90	114	**.245**	.320	78	63	97	**133**	*152*	.960	260	46	114	.6	6.3	4.3		3.8
PIT	91	13	84	11	1380.1	**1249**	36	375	605	**10.8**	2.84	121	.248	.306	85	87	101	185	*154*	**.963**	232	43	**131**	**2.1**	8.7	.1		-2.9
PHI	90	**20**	78	10	1373.1	1285	43	598	697	12.7	3.30	104	.255	.340	14	19	101	243	*179*	**.963**	**231**	52	113	1.9	1.9	-1.8		1.0
STL	88	6	101	10	1402.1	1296	39	701	561	13.2	3.68	91	.254	.350	-46	-52	99	288	*190*	.960	261	51	106	.6	-5.2	.2		4.9
CIN	77	4	97	12	1425.0	1410	36	476	557	12.3	3.26	101	.265	.332	21	5	97	156	*163*	.955	295	38	108	-1.4	.5	1.3		-6.9
BRO	81	13	91	10	1371.2	1310	27	566	533	12.6	3.39	98	.263	.344	0	-13	98	256	*195*	.962	241	**25**	112	1.4	-1.3	-13.6		2.4
BOS	73	5	**115**	7	1374.0	1570	76	672	486	15.1	5.08	75	.296	.381	-258	-174	113	284	***201***	.947	347	55	110	-5.0	-17.5	-4.0		-5.0
TOT	680	92	743	89	11105.2					12.4	3.39		.260	.335						.958	2123	351	880					

Batter-Fielder Wins
- **Sheckard-Chi**......4.1
- **Wagner-Pit**..........4.1
- **Meyers-NY**..........3.3
- **Sweeney-Bos**......3.1
- **Tinker-Chi**............2.9

Batting Average
- Wagner-Pit 334
- Miller-Bos 333
- Meyers-NY 332
- Clarke-Pit 324
- Fletcher-NY 319

On-Base Percentage
- Sheckard-Chi..............434
- Wagner-Pit...................423
- Bates-Cin.....................415
- Sweeney-Bos...............404
- Doyle-NY 397

Slugging Average
- Schulte-Chi...........534
- Doyle-NY 527
- Wagner-Pit 507
- Clarke-Pit 492
- Magee-Phi 483

On-Base Plus Slugging
- Wagner-Pit............930
- Doyle-NY 924
- Schulte-Chi 918
- Magee-Phi 849
- Wilson-Pit 826

Adjusted OPS
- Schulte-Chi 156
- Wagner-Pit............154
- Doyle-NY..............153
- Magee-Phi............135
- Konetchy-StL........132

Adjusted Batter Runs
- Schulte-Chi 40.4
- Doyle-NY............35.4
- Wagner-Pit 35.2
- Sheckard-Chi 33.5
- Bates-Cin 28.6

Runs
- Sheckard-Chi........121
- Huggins-StL..........106
- Bescher-Cin..........106
- Schulte-Chi 105
- Doyle-NY..............102

Hits
- Miller-Bos..............192
- Hoblitzel-Cin 180
- Daubert-Bro..........176
- Schulte-Chi 173
- Luderus-Phi..........166

Doubles
- Konetchy-StL 38
- Miller-Bos 36
- Wilson-Pit 34
- Herzog-Bos-NY 33
- Sweeney-Bos 33

Triples
- Doyle-NY 25
- Mitchell-Cin 22
- Schulte-Chi 21
- Zimmerman-Chi......17
- Byrne-Pit 17

Home Runs
- Schulte-Chi 21
- Luderus-Phi............16
- Magee-Phi 15
- Doyle-NY 13

Total Bases
- Schulte-Chi 308
- Doyle-NY..............277
- Luderus-Phi..........260
- Hoblitzel-Cin 258
- Wilson-Pit 257

Runs Batted In
- Wilson-Pit............107
- Schulte-Chi..........107
- Luderus-Phi 99
- Magee-Phi 94

Stolen Bases
- Bescher-Cin............81
- Devore-NY..............61
- Snodgrass-NY........51
- Merkle-NY 49

Base Stealing Runs

Fielding Runs-Infield
- Tinker-Chi 21.6
- Doolan-Phi..................17.0
- Merkle-NY 15.5
- Huggins-StL................11.4
- Sweeney-Bos..............11.2

Fielding Runs-Outfield
- Sheckard-Chi 14.8
- Mitchell-Cin..........8.6
- Ingerton-Bos..........8.2
- Leach-Pit 7.8
- Carey-Pit...............7.1

Wins
- Alexander-Phi 28
- Mathewson-NY 26
- Marquard-NY..........24
- Harmon-StL............23

Winning Pct.
- Marquard-NY 774
- Crandall-NY 750
- Cole-Chi 720
- Alexander-Phi.......683
- Mathewson-NY.....667

Complete Games
- Alexander-Phi........31
- Mathewson-NY......29
- Harmon-StL 28
- Leifield-Pit 26
- Adams-Pit..............24

Strikeouts
- Marquard-NY........237
- Alexander-Phi 227
- Rucker-Bro............190
- Moore-Phi 174
- Harmon-StL 144

Fewest BB/Game
- Mathewson-NY....1.11
- Adams-Pit............1.29
- Steele-Pit-Bro 1.71
- Brown-Chi............1.83
- Wiltse-NY 1.87

Games
- Brown-Chi......................53
- Harmon-StL 51
- Rucker-Bro 48
- Alexander-Phi 48

Saves
- Brown-Chi 13
- Crandall-NY.............5

Base Runners/9
- Adams-Pit............9.30
- Ames-NY 10.01
- Mathewson-NY..10.03
- Steele-Pit-Bro 10.33
- Alexander-Phi 10.35

Adjusted Relief Runs

Relief Ranking

Innings Pitched
- Alexander-Phi....367.0
- Harmon-StL 348.0
- Leifield-Pit..........318.0
- Rucker-Bro 315.2
- Moore-Phi 308.1

Opponents' Avg.
- Alexander-Phi.......219
- Marquard-NY 219
- Ames-NY 223
- Rucker-Bro 226
- Keefe-Cin 229

Opponents' OBP
- Adams-Pit 271
- Ames-NY 277
- Mathewson-NY 283
- Wiltse-NY.....................292
- Alexander-Phi 293

Earned Run Average
- Mathewson-NY....1.99
- Richie-Chi............2.31
- Adams-Pit............2.33
- Marquard-NY 2.50
- Alexander-Phi......2.57

Adjusted ERA
- Mathewson-NY 168
- Adams-Pit 147
- Richie-Chi 143
- Marquard-NY........134
- Alexander-Phi 133

Adjusted Starter Runs
- Mathewson-NY....42.4
- Alexander-Phi......37.0
- Adams-Pit............35.4
- Leifield-Pit............29.7
- Rucker-Bro 29.6

Pitcher Wins
- **Mathewson-NY**..5.7
- **Rucker-Bro** 3.9
- **Adams-Pit** 3.9
- **Alexander-Phi**....3.7
- **Leifield-Pit**..........3.4

A Time of Giants

The introduction in both leagues of a new cork-centered baseball led to an increase in scoring. NL runs rose 9.7 percent and homers ballooned to 316, a league record until 1921. However, stolen bases were also up, to 1.36 per game, the highest in NL history. Bob Bescher of the Reds set a league record with 81 steals, while Jimmy Sheckard of the Cubs established a mark with 147 walks, the Senior Circuit's highest until 1947, though bases on balls for hitters were not widely recognized.

New York's Christy Mathewson had another amazing season, while his chief mound rival, Chicago's Mordecai Brown, notched 13 saves, which also set a record. Philadelphia rookie Grover Cleveland Alexander enjoyed one of the more spectacular debuts in history. The righty was 28–13, leading the NL in wins, shutouts, innings, and opponents' average.

On the other side, the last-place Braves became the only NL team until1923 to allow more than 1,000 runs. In context, their staff rates as one of the worst of all time, posting a 5.09 ERA when the league ERA was 3.40, and leading in runs allowed by more than 250. Their hitters finished second in batting average and led in home runs, but it translated into 107 losses. Fans in the Hub showed an appropriate level of support; for the third straight year, attendance dropped more than 20 percent.

On June 28, the Giants moved into a new Polo Grounds, and experienced a huge gain in attendance. Gotham fans were rewarded in September when their club broke away from the Cubs to capture the flag. While much was made of New York's speed-based attack—they broke the league record with 347 swipes—the Giants won with the league's best pitching and hitters who led in batting average, on-base percentage, and slugging percentage. Unfortunately, the Giants didn't hit a lick in the World Series, losing to Philadelphia in five.

1911 American League

TEAM	W	L	T	PCT	GB	HW	HL	R	OR	PA	H	2B	3B	HR	BB	SO	HB	SH	AVG	OBP	SLG	OPS	AOPS	BR	ABR	PF	SB	CS	BSA	BSR
PHI	101	50	1	.669		**54**	20	**861**	**602**	5919	1540	237	93	**35**	424		**231**	65	**.296**	**.357**	**.398**	**755**	**119**	**109**	**124**	98	226			
DET	89	65	0	.578	13.5	51	25	831	777	5995	**1544**	230	**96**	30	471		181	49	.292	.355	.388	743	108	92	53	105	**276**			
CLE	80	73	3	.523	22	46	30	693	712	5885	1501	**238**	81	20	354		160	50	.282	.333	.369	702	101	1	-7	101	209			
CHI	77	74	3	.510	24	40	37	718	624	5850	1401	179	92	20	385		207	48	.269	.325	.350	675	97	-50	-28	97	201			
BOS	78	75	0	.510	24	39	37	680	643	5806	1379	203	66	**35**	**506**		212	**74**	.275	.350	.363	713	106	42	49	99	190			
NY	76	76	1	.500	25.5	36	40	684	723	5793	1374	190	**96**	25	493		184	64	.272	.344	.362	706	97	23	-21	107	269			
WAS	64	90	0	.416	38.5	39	38	624	765	5760	1308	159	54	16	466		149	80	.258	.330	.320	650	89	-75	-63	98	215			
STL	45	107	0	.296	56.5	25	53	567	812	5631	1192	187	63	17	460		141	34	.239	.307	.311	618	81	-143	-121	96	125			
TOT	614					330	280	5658		46639	11239	1623	641	198	3559	5093	464	1465	.273	.338	.358	696					1711			

TEAM	CG	SHO	GR	SV	IP	H	HR	BB	SO	BR/9	ERA	AERA	OAV	OOB	PR	APR	PF	OSB	OCS	FA	E	WPB	DP	FW	PW	BW	BSW	DIF
PHI	97	13	77	**13**	1375.2	1343	**17**	487	739	12.5	3.01	105	.264	.338	50	22	94	184	*171*	**.964**	**225**	**48**	100	**4.9**	2.2	**12.2**		6.3
DET	**108**	8	67	3	1387.2	1514	28	460	538	13.3	3.73	93	.283	.348	-60	-43	104	203	*176*	.951	318	55	78	-.9	-4.2	5.2		12.0
CLE	93	6	74	6	1390.2	1382	**17**	552	675	12.9	3.36	101	.267	.345	-3	7	102	246	***193***	.954	303	88	**108**	.3	.7	-.7		3.2
CHI	85	**17**	**103**	11	1386.1	1349	22	**384**	**752**	**11.5**	2.97	108	**.255**	**.310**	57	39	96	**151**	*150*	.961	252	60	98	3.4	3.8	-2.8		-2.9
BOS	87	10	85	8	1351.2	**1309**	21	473	711	12.2	**2.74**	**119**	.262	.332	**89**	**80**	98	219	*177*	.949	323	60	93	-1.4	**7.9**	4.8		-9.8
NY	90	5	79	3	1360.2	1404	26	406	667	12.3	3.54	101	.270	.329	-30	9	108	219	*170*	.949	328	53	99	-1.7	.9	-2.1		2.9
WAS	106	13	62	3	1353.1	1471	39	410	628	12.8	3.52	93	.277	.334	-27	-38	98	201	*178*	.953	305	96	90	-.0	-3.7	-6.2		-3.0
STL	92	8	80	1	1332.1	1465	28	463	383	13.4	3.86	87	.278	.342	-77	-73	101	291	*186*	.945	358	50	104	-3.8	-7.2	-11.9		-8.1
TOT	758	80	627	48	10938.1					12.6	3.34		.273	.338						.953	2412	510	770					

Batter-Fielder Wins	Batting Average	On-Base Percentage	Slugging Average	On-Base Plus Slugging	Adjusted OPS	Adjusted Batter Runs
Cobb-Det 6.6	Cobb-Det 420	Jackson-Cle 468	Cobb-Det 621	Cobb-Det 1088	Cobb-Det 193	Cobb-Det...........71.7
Jackson-Cle........6.5	Jackson-Cle 408	Cobb-Det 467	Jackson-Cle 590	Jackson-Cle........1058	Jackson-Cle..........192	Jackson-Cle.......71.5
Collins-Phi 4.6	Crawford-Det 378	Collins-Phi 451	Crawford-Det 526	Crawford-Det........964	Collins-Phi 163	Crawford-Det......47.0
Baker-Phi 3.5	Collins-Phi 365	Crawford-Det 438	Cree-NY 513	Collins-Phi 932	Crawford-Det 160	Collins-Phi 45.6
Gardner-Bos 3.3	Cree-NY 348	Speaker-Bos 418	Baker-Phi 508	Cree-NY 928	Speaker-Bos 158	Speaker-Bos 40.5

Runs	Hits	Doubles	Triples	Home Runs	Total Bases	Runs Batted In
Cobb-Det.............147	Cobb-Det.............248	Cobb-Det 47	Cobb-Det................24	Baker-Phi................11	Cobb-Det.............367	Cobb-Det 127
Jackson-Cle..........126	Jackson-Cle..........233	Jackson-Cle 45	Cree-NY 22	Speaker-Bos 8	Jackson-Cle..........337	Crawford-Det 115
Bush-Det 126	Crawford-Det 217	Baker-Phi 42	Jackson-Cle............19	Cobb-Det..................8	Crawford-Det 302	Baker-Phi 115
Milan-Was 109	Baker-Phi..............198	Lord-Phi 37	Lord-Chi..................18		Baker-Phi..............301	Bodie-Chi 97
Crawford-Det 109	Milan-Was 194	LaPorte-StL 37	Wolter-NY 15		Cree-NY 267	Delahanty-Det 94

Stolen Bases	Base Stealing Runs	Fielding Runs-Infield	Fielding Runs-Outfield	Wins	Winning Pct.	Complete Games
Cobb-Det................83		Tannehill-Chi 36.3	Hogan-Phi-StL 12.6	Coombs-Phi...........28	Bender-Phi 773	Johnson-Was 36
Milan-Was 58		McBride-Was 27.4	Cobb-Det 6.7	Walsh-Chi 27	Gregg-Cle.............767	Walsh-Chi..............33
Cree-NY 48		Gardner-Bos 22.7	Milan-Was.............6.6	Johnson-Was..........25	Plank-Phi 742	Ford-NY 26
Callahan-Chi 45		Austin-StL 18.6	Hooper-Bos 5.8		Coombs-Phi 700	Coombs-Phi 26
Lord-Chi..................43		Bush-Det 12.5	Jackson-Cle 5.3		Morgan-Phi...........682	

Strikeouts	Fewest BB/Game	Games	Saves	Base Runners/9	Adjusted Relief Runs	Relief Ranking
Walsh-Chi 255	White-Chi 1.47	Walsh-Chi 56	Walsh-Chi 4	Gregg-Cle............9.86		
Wood-Bos 231	Lake-StL 1.67	Coombs-Phi 47	Plank-Phi 4	Walsh-Chi.............9.91		
Johnson-Was........207	Walsh-Chi 1.76	Wood-Bos......................44	Hall-Bos....................4	Wood-Bos..........10.22		
Coombs-Phi..........185	Warhop-NY..........1.89	Caldwell-NY 41	Wood-Bos 3	Johnson-Was 10.33		
Ford-NY 158	Powell-StL............1.91		Bender-Phi...............3	Ford-NY 10.59		

Innings Pitched	Opponents' Avg.	Opponents' OBP	Earned Run Average	Adjusted ERA	Adjusted Starter Runs	Pitcher Wins
Walsh-Chi..........368.2	Gregg-Cle.............205	Walsh-Chi 280	Gregg-Cle............1.80	Gregg-Cle 189	Johnson-Was 43.1	**Wood-Bos** 5.7
Coombs-Phi 336.2	Wood-Bos.............223	Johnson-Was...............283	Johnson-Was 1.90	Johnson-Was........173	Gregg-Cle............42.8	**Walsh-Chi** 5.5
Johnson-Was 322.1	Krapp-Cle 232	Wood-Bos 284	Wood-Bos............2.02	Wood-Bos 162	Walsh-Chi............42.1	**Johnson-Was** 5.4
Ford-NY 281.1	Ford-NY 237	Gregg-Cle 286	Plank-Phi 2.10	Ford-NY...............158	Wood-Bos............33.7	**Gregg-Cle** 4.6
Wood-Bos..........275.2	Johnson-Was 238	Ford-NY 291	Bender-Phi 2.16	Plank-Phi 150	Ford-NY 30.4	**Plank-Phi**...........3.2

White Elephants on Parade

As the season opened, baseball fans were shocked by the death of Cleveland's mound ace, Addie Joss, from tuberculosis. The two-time league ERA leader died April 14, just two days after his 30th birthday. Cy Young threw his final pitch in the majors in 1911, going 7–9 for two clubs to raise his win total to 511.

The major leagues introduced a new cork-centered baseball, sending the previous rubber-centered ball to the trash bin. As a result, the league batting average rose 30 points. Home runs also increased and runs per game rose to 4.61, the highest total in a decade and the highest until 1920. Who better to benefit from this new ball than Ty Cobb, already the league's best player? The Georgia Peach set new AL marks in 1911 for hits, RBIs, runs, and total bases, and batted .420. Detroit started hot, leading by 9½ games in May, but from July through the end of the season played essentially .500 ball as the Athletics caught fire in August. Connie Mack's White Elephants pulled away and won by 13½ games.

Philadelphia's so-called "$100,000 Infield" of Stuffy McInnis, Eddie Collins, Jack Barry, and Frank Baker, showed good leather and fine stick, and the club's starting pitching was again excellent. The World Series went six games with the Athletics coming out on top for the second straight time. Baker hit two crucial long balls to gain the nickname "Home Run," and Chief Bender, Jack Coombs, and Eddie Plank bested the Giants. It was an exciting Series; the first five games were close, two of them extending into extra innings.

1912 National League

TEAM	W	L	T	PCT	GB	HW	HL	R	OR	PA	H	2B	3B	HR	BB	SO	HB	SH	AVG	OBP	SLG	OPS	AOPS	BR	ABR	PF	SB	CS	BSA	BSR
NY	103	48	3	.682		**49**	25	**823**	571	5802	1451	231	89	**47**	514	**497**	152	**69**	**.286**	**.360**	.395	**755**	**110**	**92**	**69**	103	**319**			
PIT	93	58	1	.616	10	44	31	751	**565**	5879	**1493**	222	**129**	39	420	514	181	26	.284	.340	**.398**	738	**110**	39	50	99	177			
CHI	91	59	2	.607	11.5	46	30	756	668	5830	1398	**245**	91	42	**560**	615	**182**	40	.277	.354	.386	740	109	65	68	100	164			
CIN	75	78	2	.490	29	45	32	656	722	5794	1310	183	89	21	479	492	175	25	.256	.323	.339	662	90	-93	-74	97	248			
PHI	73	79	0	.480	30.5	34	41	670	688	5754	1354	244	68	43	464	615	179	34	.267	.332	.367	699	91	-21	-63	107	159			
STL	63	90	0	.412	41	37	40	659	830	5813	1366	190	77	27	508	620	166	47	.268	.340	.352	692	97	-28	-11	98	193			
BRO	58	95	0	.379	46	33	43	651	744	5830	1377	220	73	32	490	584	159	40	.268	.336	.358	694	100	-27	1	96	179			
BOS	52	101	2	.340	52	31	47	693	871	6031	1465	227	68	35	454	690	168	48	.273	.335	.361	696	94	-27	-39	102	137			
TOT	613					319	289	5659		46733	11214	1762	684	286	3889	4627	329	1362	.272	.340	.369	710					1576			

TEAM	CG	SHO	GR	SV	IP	H	HR	BB	SO	BR/9	ERA	AERA	OAV	OOB	PR	APR	PF	OSB	OCS	FA	E	WPB	DP	FW	PW	BW	BSW	DIF
NY	93	8	76	**16**	1369.2	1352	35	**338**	652	**11.3**	**2.58**	**130**	.259	**.307**	**124**	**120**	99	**141**	*113*	.956	280	49	123	-2.1	**11.8**	**6.8**		11.0
PIT	**94**	**18**	76	7	1385.0	**1268**	**28**	497	**664**	11.8	2.85	114	**.251**	.324	84	63	96	154	*137*	**.972**	**169**	38	125	**6.0**	6.2	4.9		.4
CHI	80	15	104	9	1358.2	1307	33	493	554	12.2	3.42	97	.259	.331	-4	-20	98	153	*150*	.960	249	46	125	-.0	-2.0	6.7		11.3
CIN	86	13	89	10	1377.2	1455	**28**	452	561	12.9	3.42	98	.279	.344	-4	-14	99	202	*153*	.960	249	**35**	102	.4	-1.4	-7.3		6.8
PHI	81	10	99	9	1355.0	1381	43	515	616	12.9	3.25	111	.272	.344	23	50	106	221	*173*	.963	231	61	98	1.3	4.9	-6.2		-3.1
STL	61	6	**134**	12	1353.0	1466	31	560	487	13.7	3.85	89	.286	.361	-68	-63	101	266	***188***	.957	274	41	113	-1.8	-6.2	-1.1		-4.5
BRO	71	10	99	8	1357.0	1399	45	510	553	12.9	3.64	92	.273	.343	-37	-50	98	214	*162*	.959	255	36	96	-.3	-4.9	.0		-13.3
BOS	88	5	94	5	1390.2	1544	43	521	542	13.6	4.17	86	.291	.359	-119	-94	105	225	*176*	.954	297	69	**129**	-3.2	-9.2	-3.8		-8.2
TOT	654	85	771	76	10946.2					12.7	3.40		.272	.340						.960	2004	375	911					

Batter-Fielder Wins	Batting Average	On-Base Percentage	Slugging Average	On-Base Plus Slugging	Adjusted OPS	Adjusted Batter Runs
Wagner-Pit 5.9	Zimmerman-Chi ...372	Evers-Chi 431	Zimmerman-Chi ...571	Zimmerman-Chi....989	Zimmerman-Chi....170	Zimmerman-Chi 51.1
Sweeney-Bos......5.6	Meyers-NY 358	Huggins-StL.................422	Wilson-Pit 513	Wagner-Pit............891	Wagner-Pit............145	Wagner-Pit 34.0
Zimmerman-Chi 5.3	Sweeney-Bos 344	Paskert-Phi 420	Wagner-Pit 496	Evers-Chi..............873	Evers-Chi..............139	Evers-Chi............30.1
Meyers-NY 4.0	Evers-Chi 341	Zimmerman-Chi...........418	Meyers-NY 477	Doyle-NY..............864	Wilson-Pit 134	Sweeney-Bos 29.5
Evers-Chi 3.7	Doyle-NY 330	Sweeney-Bos...............416	Doyle-NY 471	Titus-Phi-Bos........862	Konetchy-StL 134	Meyers-NY 26.4

Runs	Hits	Doubles	Triples	Home Runs	Total Bases	Runs Batted In
Bescher-Cin..........120	Zimmerman-Chi....207	Zimmerman-Chi 41	Wilson-Pit 36	Zimmerman-Chi......14	Zimmerman-Chi....318	Wagner-Pit 102
Carey-Pit 114	Sweeney-Bos 204	Paskert-Phi...................37	Wagner-Pit..............20	Schulte-Chi 12	Wilson-Pit 299	Sweeney-Bos 100
Paskert-Phi 102	Campbell-Bos 185	Wagner-Pit 35	Murray-NY...............20	Wilson-Pit 11	Wagner-Pit............277	Zimmerman-Chi 99
Campbell-Bos 102	Doyle-NY 184	Miller-Pit 33	Daubert-Bro............16	Merkle-NY 11	Sweeney-Bos 264	Wilson-Pit.............95
	Wagner-Pit............181	Doyle-NY 33		Cravath-Phi 11	Doyle-NY 263	Murray-NY 92

Stolen Bases	Base Stealing Runs	Fielding Runs-Infield	Fielding Runs-Outfield	Wins	Winning Pct.	Complete Games
Bescher-Cin............67		Tinker-Chi 26.3	Sheckard-Chi 9.3	Marquard-NY..........26	Hendrix-Pit 727	Cheney-Chi 28
Carey-Pit 45		Sweeney-Bos.............26.0	Magee-StL 5.9	Cheney-Chi 26	Cheney-Chi...........722	Mathewson-NY......27
Snodgrass-NY 43		Herzog-NY..................20.1	Cravath-Phi............5.5	Hendrix-Pit.............24	Tesreau-NY...........708	Suggs-Cin 25
Murray-NY 38		Wagner-Pit..................17.1	Murray-NY 5.3	Mathewson-NY 23	Marquard-NY 703	Hendrix-Pit 25
....		Fletcher-NY 14.5	Miller-Bos-Phi 4.3	Camnitz-Pit 22	Richie-Chi.............667	Alexander-Phi........25

Strikeouts	Fewest BB/Game	Games	Saves	Base Runners/9	Adjusted Relief Runs	Relief Ranking
Alexander-Phi 195	Mathewson-NY.......99	Benton-Cin 50	Sallee-StL 6	Robinson-Pit.........9.57		
Hendrix-Pit............176	Robinson-Pit.........1.54	Sallee-StL 48	Mathewson-NY 5	Mathewson-NY..10.07		
Marquard-NY........175	Suggs-Cin.............1.66	Alexander-Phi 46	Rucker-Bro 4	Rucker-Bro 10.49		
Benton-Cin 162	Ames-NY 1.76	Rucker-Bro 45	Reulbach-Chi............4	Tesreau-NY.......10.85		
Rucker-Bro............151	Adams-Pit............1.85	Seaton-Phi 44		Adams-Pit..........10.94		

Innings Pitched	Opponents' Avg.	Opponents' OBP	Earned Run Average	Adjusted ERA	Adjusted Starter Runs	Pitcher Wins
Alexander-Phi 310.1	Tesreau-NY...........204	Mathewson-NY 281	Tesreau-NY..........1.96	Tesreau-NY 172	Mathewson-NY....43.1	**Mathewson-NY**..5.3
Mathewson-NY..310.0	Cheney-Chi............234	Robinson-Pit 284	Mathewson-NY....2.12	Mathewson-NY 159	Rucker-Bro 37.3	**Rucker-Bro** 5.1
Cheney-Chi........303.1	Robinson-Pit.........237	Rucker-Bro...................298	Rucker-Bro 2.21	Rucker-Bro............151	Tesreau-NY...........33.8	**Hendrix-Pit** 4.0
Suggs-Cin..........303.0	Brown-Bos 239	Tesreau-NY 298	Robinson-Pit........2.26	Rixey-Phi 145	Marquard-NY 30.0	**Marquard-NY** 3.5
Benton-Cin 302.0	O'Toole-Pit 241	Adams-Pit 303	Ames-NY 2.46	Robinson-Pit 144	Alexander-Phi......27.2	**Alexander-Phi**....3.0

The Bats Take Over

Offense continued to increase in 1912 as runs scored reached 4.62 per game, the highest total in a decade. Honus Wagner led the league in RBIs at age 38, while Bob Bescher scored 120 runs and swiped 67 bases for the Reds. But the biggest numbers came from relative obscurities. Owen "Chief" Wilson, a 29-year-old Pittsburgh outfielder, rapped out an amazing 36 triples, the highest total before or since. Previously unheralded Cubs third baseman Heinie Zimmerman stomped the competition in batting average, slugging, hits, and doubles. Zimmerman's was one of the game's great fluke seasons.

There were pitchers of merit. Christy Mathewson, Rube Marquard, and rookie Jeff Tesreau combined to win 66 games for the Giants; Marquard's 19 wins in a row were the most in a season in the twentieth century and tied the all-time mark set by New York ace Tim Keefe in 1888. Two rookies made splashy entries in 1912: Eppa Rixey had 10 victories for Philadelphia, while Wilbur Cooper was a late-season sensation in Pittsburgh.

Two of the game's great personalities debuted, and one died. Casey Stengel started his career with Brooklyn, while Boston brought up 21-year-old shortstop Rabbit Maranville. Former Giants pitcher Bugs Raymond, who had partied his way out of the majors the year before, was beaten to death in September in an altercation during a semi-pro game.

The pennant race held little tension. The Giants won easily, capturing 16 straight at one point. The only early challenger, Cincinnati, dropped to fourth; their new digs, Redland Field, continuing a trend that saw five NL clubs open new parks during the decade. A lack of pennant-race excitement hurt attendance, which fell in six of eight cities and dropped by 15 percent. For the fifth consecutive year, New York, Pittsburgh, and Chicago ranked as the Senior Circuit's top clubs. However, the Giants again failed in the World Series, losing in five to Boston.

1912 American League

TEAM	W	L	T	PCT	GB	HW	HL	R	OR	PA	H	2B	3B	HR	BB	SO	HB	SH	AVG	OBP	SLG	OPS	AOPS	BR	ABR	PF	SB	CS	BSA	BSR
BOS	105	47	2	.691		**57**	20	**799**	**544**	5871	1404	**269**	84	**29**	**565**		190	**45**	.277	**.355**	**.380**	**735**	110	**111**	73	105	185			
WAS	91	61	2	.599	14	45	32	699	581	5729	1298	202	86	20	472		144	38	.256	.324	.341	665	94	-32	-36	101	**273**			
PHI	90	62	1	.592	15	45	31	779	658	5835	**1442**	204	**108**	22	485		**201**	38	**.282**	.349	.377	726	**117**	82	**111**	96	258			
CHI	78	76	4	.506	28	34	43	639	648	5867	1321	174	80	17	423		211	51	.255	.317	.329	646	93	-71	-50	97	213			
CLE	75	78	2	.490	30.5	41	35	677	681	5798	1403	219	77	12	407		208	51	.273	.333	.353	686	98	6	-15	103	194			
DET	69	84	1	.451	36.5	37	39	720	777	5882	1376	189	86	19	530		151	58	.268	.343	.349	692	106	27	51	97	277			
STL	53	101	3	.344	53	27	50	552	764	5710	1262	166	71	19	449		139	42	.248	.315	.320	635	90	-89	-67	96	176			
NY	50	102	1	.329	55	31	44	630	842	5772	1320	168	79	18	463		152	65	.259	.329	.334	663	90	-33	-70	106	247			
TOT	619					317	294	5495		46464	10826	1591	671	156	3794	5157	388	1396	.265	.333	.348	681					1823			

TEAM	CG	SHO	GR	SV	IP	H	HR	BB	SO	BR/9	ERA	AERA	OAV	OOB	PR	APR	PF	OSB	OCS	FA	E	WPB	DP	FW	PW	BW	BSW	DIF
BOS	**108**	**18**	59	6	1362.0	1243	18	**385**	712	**11.0**	2.76	124	.248	**.306**	88	101	103	202	*163*	.957	267	**40**	88	2.4	10.1	7.3		9.2
WAS	98	11	73	7	1376.2	**1219**	24	525	**828**	11.8	**2.69**	**125**	**.242**	.320	**99**	**104**	101	**164**	*178*	.954	297	70	92	.7	**10.4**	-3.6		7.6
PHI	95	11	81	9	1357.0	1273	**12**	518	601	12.3	3.32	93	.258	.336	2	-33	93	171	*172*	**.959**	**263**	55	115	**2.5**	-3.3	**11.1**		3.7
CHI	85	14	**101**	**16**	1413.0	1398	26	426	698	11.8	3.06	105	.264	.322	44	27	96	239	*190*	.956	291	50	102	1.5	2.7	-5.0		1.8
CLE	94	7	80	7	1352.2	1367	15	523	622	12.9	3.30	104	.272	.346	6	20	103	240	*190*	.954	287	65	124	1.4	2.0	-1.5		-3.4
DET	107	7	59	5	1367.1	1438	16	521	512	13.3	3.77	87	.277	.350	-66	-72	98	289	*192*	.950	338	83	91	-1.7	-7.2	5.1		-3.7
STL	85	8	89	5	1369.2	1433	17	442	547	12.7	3.71	90	.277	.341	-56	-55	100	271	***193***	.947	341	54	**127**	-1.6	-5.5	-6.7		-10.3
NY	105	5	60	3	1335.0	1448	28	436	637	13.0	4.13	88	.282	.344	-117	-66	108	248	*186*	.940	382	64	77	-4.4	-6.6	-7.0		-8.0
TOT	777	81	602	58	10933.1					12.3	3.34		.265	.333						.952	2466	481	816					

Batter-Fielder Wins
Speaker-Bos 7.2
Jackson-Cle 7.1
Baker-Phi 6.5
Collins-Phi 6.4
Cobb-Det 5.6

Batting Average
Cobb-Det 409
Jackson-Cle 395
Speaker-Bos 383
Lajoie-Cle 368
Collins-Phi 348

On-Base Percentage
Speaker-Bos 464
Jackson-Cle 458
Cobb-Det 456
Collins-Phi 450
Lajoie-Cle 414

Slugging Average
Cobb-Det 584
Jackson-Cle 579
Speaker-Bos 567
Baker-Phi 541
Crawford-Det 470

On-Base Plus Slugging
Cobb-Det 1040
Jackson-Cle 1036
Speaker-Bos 1031
Baker-Phi 945
Collins-Phi 885

Adjusted OPS
Cobb-Det 203
Jackson-Cle 190
Speaker-Bos 185
Baker-Phi 176
Collins-Phi 159

Adjusted Batter Runs
Cobb-Det 71.5
Speaker-Bos 68.2
Jackson-Cle........66.7
Baker-Phi 54.4
Collins-Phi 49.6

Runs
Collins-Phi 137
Speaker-Bos 136
Jackson-Cle..........121
Cobb-Det 120
Baker-Phi 116

Hits
Jackson-Cle 226
Cobb-Det 226
Speaker-Bos 222
Baker-Phi 200

Doubles
Speaker-Bos 53
Jackson-Cle 44
Baker-Phi 40
Lewis-Bos 36

Triples
Jackson-Cle............26
Cobb-Det 23
Crawford-Det 21
Baker-Phi 21
Gardner-Bos 18

Home Runs
Speaker-Bos 10
Baker-Phi 10
Cobb-Det 7

Total Bases
Jackson-Cle..........331
Speaker-Bos 329
Cobb-Det 323
Baker-Phi 312
Crawford-Det 273

Runs Batted In
Baker-Phi 130
Lewis-Bos 109
Crawford-Det 109
McInnis-Phi 101

Stolen Bases
Milan-Was 88
Collins-Phi 63
Cobb-Det 61
Speaker-Bos 52
Zeider-Chi 48

Base Stealing Runs

Fielding Runs-Infield
McBride-Was 27.8
Bush-Det 27.0
Louden-Det 17.6
Rath-Chi 16.2
Collins-Phi 14.0

Fielding Runs-Outfield
Speaker-Bos........16.4
Jackson-Cle 13.9
Hogan-StL 9.9
Strunk-Phi..............8.2
Milan-Was..............6.8

Wins
Wood-Bos 34
Johnson-Was 33
Walsh-Chi 27
Plank-Phi 26
Groom-Was 24

Winning Pct.
Wood-Bos 872
Plank-Phi 813
Johnson-Was 733
Bedient-Bos 690
Coombs-Phi 677

Complete Games
Wood-Bos..............35
Johnson-Was 34
Walsh-Chi 32
Ford-NY 30

Strikeouts
Johnson-Was........303
Wood-Bos 258
Walsh-Chi 254
Gregg-Cle 184
Groom-Was 179

Fewest BB/Game
Bender-Phi 1.74
Johnson-Was 1.85
Collins-Bos 1.90
Powell-StL............1.99
Warhop-NY 2.06

Games
Walsh-Chi 62
Johnson-Was 50
Wood-Bos 43
Groom-Was 43
Benz-Chi 42

Saves
Walsh-Chi 10
Warhop-NY 3
Mogridge-Chi............3
Lange-Chi 3
Dubuc-Det 3

Base Runners/9
Johnson-Was 8.56
Wood-Bos 9.44
Walsh-Chi 9.78
Bedient-Bos 10.29
Collins-Bos 10.66

Adjusted Relief Runs

Relief Ranking

Innings Pitched
Walsh-Chi..........393.0
Johnson-Was 369.0
Wood-Bos..........344.0
Groom-Was 316.0
Ford-NY 291.2

Opponents' Avg.
Johnson-Was 196
Wood-Bos 216
Walsh-Chi 231
Houck-Phi 234
Dubuc-Det 235

Opponents' OBP
Johnson-Was 248
Wood-Bos 272
Walsh-Chi 279
Bedient-Bos 288
Collins-Bos 297

Earned Run Average
Johnson-Was 1.39
Wood-Bos 1.91
Walsh-Chi 2.15
Plank-Phi 2.22
Collins-Bos 2.53

Adjusted ERA
Johnson-Was........241
Wood-Bos 179
Walsh-Chi 149
Plank-Phi 140
Collins-Bos 135

Adjusted Starter Runs
Johnson-Was 77.1
Wood-Bos............53.1
Walsh-Chi............49.0
Gregg-Cle............27.5
Plank-Phi 24.9

Pitcher Wins
Johnson-Was ..10.6
Wood-Bos 7.6
Walsh-Chi 6.5
Plank-Phi.............3.2
Gregg-Cle 2.8

Glory on the Fens

It was quite a year in Boston. First, the Red Sox opened Fenway Park, a more intimate setting than cavernous Huntington Avenue Grounds. Second, pitcher Smokey Joe Wood finally got the support he needed to harness his dominating fastball. His heroics, and the spectacular play of Tris Speaker, propelled the Red Sox to the pennant. Wood's chief mound rival was Walter Johnson, who won 16 straight for surprising Washington. The two stars met September 5 in Boston, and Wood—also en route to winning 16 in a row—bested Johnson, 1–0.

A hitting slump dropped the Tigers to sixth, and the club fell lower in the public eye after striking in May to protest the suspension of Ty Cobb, who had severely beaten a heckler. With the club AWOL, a makeshift lineup of amateurs and Tigers coaches lost at Philadelphia, 24–2; Detroit ended the walkout the next day under pressure from AL President Ban Johnson. Rookie outfielder Bobby Veach would soon help the club regain its standing.

Earned runs for pitchers were first tabulated this year, but it would be until 1917 before ERA was an official statistic. Offensive players set two new league records: Joe Jackson of Cleveland hit 26 triples, while Washington's Clyde Milan swiped 88 bases. Buck Weaver and Ray Schalk made their debuts in Chicago, while Herb Pennock and Stan Coveleski pitched their first games, both for Philadelphia. Could Connie Mack pick 'em?

The Red Sox-New York Giants October matchup was the best World Series to date, going the full seven with a tie thrown in. Four one-run games kept fans on the edges of their seats. The Series ended with a thrilling duel between Christy Mathewson and Wood, on in relief of Hugh Bedient, went to the 10th before a wild series of plays gave the Red Sox a come-from-behind 3–2 win.

1913 National League

TEAM	W	L	T	PCT	GB	HW	HL	R	OR	PA	H	2B	3B	HR	BB	SO	HB	SH	AVG	OBP	SLG	OPS	AOPS	BR	ABR	PF	SB	CS	BSA	BSR
NY	101	51	4	.664		**54**	23	684	**515**	5837	1427	226	71	31	444	**501**	112	**63**	**.273**	**.338**	.362	700	105	47	42	101	**296**	196	**60**	**-3**
PHI	88	63	8	.583	12.5	43	33	693	636	6001	**1433**	**257**	78	**73**	383	578	**183**	35	.265	.318	**.382**	700	102	31	4	104	156	122	56	-8
CHI	88	65	2	.575	13.5	51	25	**720**	630	5775	1289	195	**96**	59	**554**	634	158	41	.257	.335	.369	**704**	**107**	**53**	**52**	100	181	160	53	-16
PIT	78	71	6	.523	21.5	41	35	673	585	5830	1383	210	86	35	391	545	152	35	.263	.319	.356	675	103	-14	14	96	181	131	58	-6
BOS	69	82	3	.457	31.5	34	40	641	690	5845	1318	191	60	32	488	640	169	43	.256	.326	.335	661	93	-24	-36	102	177	153	54	-15
BRO	65	84	3	.436	34.5	29	47	595	613	5704	1394	193	86	39	361	555	147	31	.270	.321	.363	684	98	1	-16	103	188	150	56	-11
CIN	64	89	3	.418	37.5	32	44	607	717	5781	1339	170	**96**	27	458	579	162	29	.261	.325	.347	672	98	-13	-10	100	226	144	61	-1
STL	51	99	3	.340	49	25	48	528	755	5618	1229	152	72	15	451	573	156	44	.247	.316	.316	632	88	-80	-72	99	171	184	48	-27
TOT	620					309	295	5141		46391	10812	1594	645	311	3530	4605	321	1239	.262	.325	.354	679					1576	1240	56	-87

TEAM	CG	SHO	GR	SV	IP	H	HR	BB	SO	BR/9	ERA	AERA	OAV	OOB	PR	APR	PF	OSB	OCS	FA	E	WPB	DP	FW	PW	BW	BSW	DIF
NY	82	12	94	**17**	1422.0	**1276**	38	**315**	651	**10.2**	**2.42**	**128**	**.243**	**.289**	**122**	**110**	97	**158**	133	.961	254	**34**	107	-.6	**11.4**	4.4	.8	9.0
PHI	77	**20**	**131**	11	1455.1	1407	40	512	**667**	12.1	3.15	105	.261	.330	7	26	104	193	**179**	**.968**	**214**	42	112	**2.2**	2.7	.4	.3	6.9
CHI	89	12	90	15	1373.0	1330	39	478	556	12.1	3.13	101	.260	.328	10	5	99	176	169	.959	260	58	106	-1.1	.5	**5.4**	-.5	7.2
PIT	74	9	109	7	1400.0	1344	**26**	434	590	11.6	2.90	104	.260	.320	46	18	94	222	151	.964	226	42	94	1.1	1.9	1.5	.5	-1.4
BOS	**105**	13	64	3	1373.1	1343	38	419	597	11.8	3.19	103	.263	.324	1	11	103	195	151	.957	273	43	82	-2.0	1.1	-3.7	-.4	-1.4
BRO	71	9	104	7	1373.0	1287	33	439	548	11.6	3.13	105	.255	.321	11	22	103	197	146	.961	243	37	**125**	-.3	2.3	-1.7	.0	-9.8
CIN	71	10	113	10	1380.0	1398	40	456	522	12.4	3.46	94	.273	.338	-40	-35	101	185	146	.961	251	52	104	-.4	-3.6	-1.0	**1.0**	-8.4
STL	74	6	114	11	1351.2	1426	57	477	465	13.0	4.23	76	.280	.348	-156	-150	101	250	165	.965	219	39	113	1.3	-15.6	-7.5	-1.7	-.5
TOT	643	91	819	81	11128.1					11.9	3.20		.262	.325						.962	1940	347	843					

Batter-Fielder Wins
Tinker-Cin............3.8
Evers-Chi 3.4
Zimmerman-Chi 3.3
Cravath-Phi 3.0
Meyers-NY 3.0

Batting Average
Daubert-Bro 350
Cravath-Phi...........341
Viox-Pit 317
Tinker-Cin.............317
Becker-Cin-Phi 316

On-Base Percentage
Huggins-StL.................432
Cravath-Phi 407
Daubert-Bro.................405
Viox-Pit 399
Leach-Chi 391

Slugging Average
Cravath-Phi...........568
Becker-Cin-Phi 502
Zimmerman-Chi ...490
Saier-Chi..............480
Magee-Phi 479

On-Base Plus Slugging
Cravath-Phi 974
Zimmerman-Chi....868
Saier-Chi 850
Magee-Phi 848
Daubert-Bro..........829

Adjusted OPS
Cravath-Phi 169
Zimmerman-Chi....147
Viox-Pit 142
Saier-Chi 141
Magee-Phi............135

Adjusted Batter Runs
Cravath-Phi 46.7
Viox-Pit 30.2
Zimmerman-Chi 26.7
Saier-Chi 26.5
Daubert-Bro 22.9

Runs
Leach-Chi 99
Carey-Pit 99
Lobert-Phi 98
Saier-Chi 94
Magee-Phi..............92

Hits
Cravath-Phi 179
Daubert-Bro..........178
Burns-NY..............173
Lobert-Phi 172
Carey-Pit 172

Doubles
Smith-Bro 40
Burns-NY 37
Magee-Phi 36
Cravath-Phi...................34

Triples
Saier-Chi 21
Miller-Pit..................20
Konetchy-StL..........17
Wilson-Pit 14
Cravath-Phi 14

Home Runs
Cravath-Phi 19
Luderus-Phi............18
Saier-Chi 14
Magee-Phi 11
Wilson-Pit 10

Total Bases
Cravath-Phi 298
Luderus-Phi..........254
Saier-Chi 249
Miller-Pit...............243
Lobert-Phi 243

Runs Batted In
Cravath-Phi 128
Zimmerman-Chi 95
Saier-Chi 92
Miller-Pit 90
Luderus-Phi 86

Stolen Bases
Carey-Pit 61
Myers-Bos 57
Lobert-Phi 41
Burns-NY................40
Cutshaw-Bro 39

Base Stealing Runs
Carey-Pit...............7.5
Myers-Bos 6.2
Marsans-Cin..........4.3
Doyle-NY 3.5
Cutshaw-Bro..........2.6

Fielding Runs-Infield
Evers-Chi...................27.7
Tinker-Cin 20.7
Mowrey-StL 17.5
Maranville-Bos............17.1
Cutshaw-Bro 16.9

Fielding Runs-Outfield
Paskert-Phi..........11.2
Carey-Pit..............10.6
Murray-NY 8.9
Magee-StL 8.7
Wheat-Bro 7.9

Wins
Seaton-Phi.............27
Mathewson-NY 25
Marquard-NY..........23
Tesreau-NY 22
Alexander-Phi 22

Winning Pct.
Humphries-Chi 800
Alexander-Phi.......733
Marquard-NY 697
Mathewson-NY.....694
Seaton-Phi 692

Complete Games
Tyler-Bos 28
Mathewson-NY......25
Cheney-Chi 25
Adams-Pit.............24
Alexander-Phi........23

Strikeouts
Seaton-Phi............168
Tesreau-NY 167
Alexander-Phi 159
Marquard-NY........151
Adams-Pit 144

Fewest BB/Game
Mathewson-NY.......62
Humphries-Chi 1.19
Adams-Pit...........1.41
Marquard-NY 1.53
Suggs-Cin...........1.58

Games
Cheney-Chi...................54
Seaton-Phi 52
Sallee-StL 50
Alexander-Phi 47
Camnitz-Pit-Phi.............45

Saves
Cheney-Chi 11
Crandall-NY.............6
Brown-Cin 6
Sallee-StL 5

Base Runners/9
Mathewson-NY....9.18
Adams-Pit............9.18
Marquard-NY 9.38
Humphries-Chi 9.70
Demaree-NY 9.87

Adjusted Relief Runs
Crandall-NY 2.5

Relief Ranking
Crandall-NY..........2.2

Innings Pitched
Seaton-Phi 322.1
Adams-Pit..........313.2
Alexander-Phi....306.1
Mathewson-NY..306.0
Cheney-Chi........305.0

Opponents' Avg.
Tesreau-NY..........220
Seaton-Phi 226
Allen-Bro..............231
Pierce-Chi.............234
Tyler-Bos 235

Opponents' OBP
Mathewson-NY 266
Adams-Pit 267
Marquard-NY 273
Humphries-Chi............277
Demaree-NY 286

Earned Run Average
Mathewson-NY....2.06
Adams-Pit...........2.15
Tesreau-NY..........2.17
Demaree-NY 2.21
Pierce-Chi...........2.30

Adjusted ERA
Mathewson-NY 151
Tesreau-NY 143
Demaree-NY 141
Adams-Pit 140
Brennan-Phi 139

Adjusted Starter Runs
Mathewson-NY....36.8
Adams-Pit.............33.1
Tesreau-NY..........27.8
Seaton-Phi 24.7
Marquard-NY 23.0

Pitcher Wins
Mathewson-NY..4.6
Adams-Pit...........4.1
Tesreau-NY 3.6
Cheney-Chi 2.6
Marquard-NY 2.4

Change of the Guard

The Phillies paced the loop through June, but the deeper Giants soon took over. Pitching again carried the day for New York, but they had a strong attack and the league's best manager, John McGraw. Despite New York's third straight pennant, and their fifth flag since 1904, it was a year of large-scale change in the Senior Circuit. The Phillies were a legitimate contender, riding the arm of Grover Cleveland Alexander and the bat of Gavvy Cravath, who led in homers with 19 (he learned to push the ball toward Baker Bowl's 272-foot right-field fence). In a decade that saw the Philadelphia's attendance wildly fluctuate each season, 1913 was a good year; fans came out in 80 percent greater numbers to greet the second-place club. On the other side of the state, though, Pittsburgh's attendance declined by 30 percent.

Brooklyn opened their new palace, Ebbets Field, and celebrated by beginning a steady improvement that would bring them the flag in 1916. Meanwhile, the Cubs began five years of misery by dumping several top players without talent ready to replace them. Owner Charlie Murphy caused so much bad PR for the franchise that in 1914 the Federal League was able to get a toehold, using Chicago as its bellwether.

The difference between athletics and baseball was clearly outlined in 1913. Debuting that year was Jim Thorpe, the world's greatest athlete; he could never hit the curve, however, and only exceeded 100 games played once in his six years in the majors. Edd Roush began a career that included three major leagues, two NL batting titles, and 2,376 hits. His only AL hit came with the 1913 White Sox.

Connie Mack's Athletics won the World Series against New York in five relatively easy games. It marked the third time since 1905 that the A's and Giants faced each other; the Mackmen took two of the matchups. It would be seventy-six years before they met again, when both teams resided in California's Bay Area.

1913 American League

TEAM	W	L	T	PCT	GB	HW	HL	R	OR	PA	H	2B	3B	HR	BB	SO	HB	SH	AVG	OBP	SLG	OPS	AOPS	BR	ABR	PF	SB	CS	BSA	BSR
PHI	96	57	0	.627		**50**	26	**794**	592	5817	**1412**	**223**	80	**33**	**534**	547	174	**65**	**.280**	**.356**	**.375**	**731**	**124**	**140**	**157**	98	221			
WAS	90	64	1	.584	6.5	42	35	596	562	5667	1281	156	81	19	440	595	111	42	.252	.317	.326	643	93	-38	-50	102	**287**			
CLE	86	66	3	.566	9.5	45	32	633	536	5712	1349	206	74	16	420	557	**208**	53	.268	.331	.348	679	102	31	13	103	191			
BOS	79	71	1	.527	15.5	41	34	631	610	5649	1334	220	**101**	17	467	**534**	174	39	.268	.336	.364	700	109	67	51	103	189			
CHI	78	74	1	.513	17.5	40	37	488	**498**	5452	1139	157	66	24	398	550	196	36	.236	.299	.311	610	86	-97	-92	99	156			
DET	66	87	0	.431	30	34	42	625	716	5760	1344	180	**101**	24	496	501	154	46	.265	.336	.355	691	111	54	64	99	218			
NY	57	94	2	.377	38	27	47	529	668	5611	1157	155	45	8	**534**	617	140	57	.237	.320	.292	612	85	-73	-75	100	203			
STL	57	96	2	.373	39	31	46	528	642	5667	1193	179	73	18	455	769	138	43	.237	.306	.312	618	90	-81	-66	97	209			
TOT	614					310	299	4824		45335	10209	1476	621	159	3744	4670	381	1295	.256	.325	.336	661					1674			

TEAM	CG	SHO	GR	SV	IP	H	HR	BB	SO	BR/9	ERA	AERA	OAV	OOB	PR	APR	PF	OSB	OCS	FA	E	WPB	DP	FW	PW	BW	BSW	DIF
PHI	69	17	**124**	**22**	1351.1	1200	24	532	630	11.8	3.19	87	.243	.321	-39	-69	94	188	*162*	**.966**	**212**	59	108	**3.3**	-7.3	**16.7**		6.9
WAS	78	**23**	120	20	1396.1	**1177**	35	465	**758**	**11.0**	2.73	108	**.233**	.306	31	34	101	177	*156*	.960	261	57	122	.4	3.6	-5.3		14.3
CLE	93	18	90	5	1386.2	1278	19	502	689	11.8	2.54	119	.251	.324	59	71	104	176	*169*	.962	242	56	124	1.6	7.6	1.4		-.5
BOS	83	12	95	10	1358.1	1323	**6**	442	710	11.9	2.94	100	.262	.325	-2	-3	100	229	*169*	.961	238	52	84	1.4	-.3	5.4		-2.5
CHI	84	17	98	8	1360.1	1190	10	**438**	602	**11.0**	**2.33**	**125**	.239	**.305**	**91**	**89**	100	**166**	*144*	.960	255	51	104	.5	**9.5**	-9.8		1.8
DET	90	4	87	7	1360.0	1359	13	504	468	12.6	3.38	86	.267	.339	-68	-71	100	256	*177*	.954	303	62	105	-2.5	-7.6	6.8		-7.2
NY	75	8	99	7	1344.0	1318	31	455	530	12.2	3.27	91	.262	.330	-51	-41	102	294	***192***	.954	293	56	94	-1.9	-4.4	-8.0		-4.2
STL	**104**	14	60	5	1382.1	1369	21	454	476	12.2	3.06	96	.269	.335	-20	-22	100	191	*184*	.954	301	**45**	**125**	-2.2	-2.3	-7.0		-7.9
TOT	676	113	773	84	10939.1					11.8	2.93		.256	.325						.959	2105	438	866					

Batter-Fielder Wins	Batting Average	On-Base Percentage	Slugging Average	On-Base Plus Slugging	Adjusted OPS	Adjusted Batter Runs
Collins-Phi 7.0	Cobb-Det 390	Cobb-Det 467	Jackson-Cle 551	Jackson-Cle........1011	Cobb-Det 196	Jackson-Cle........63.4
Baker-Phi 6.6	Jackson-Cle 373	Jackson-Cle 460	Cobb-Det 535	Cobb-Det 1002	Jackson-Cle..........190	Speaker-Bos 53.6
Speaker-Bos 6.5	Speaker-Bos.........363	Collins-Phi 441	Speaker-Bos.........533	Speaker-Bos 974	Speaker-Bos 180	Cobb-Det............53.5
Jackson-Cle........5.9	Collins-Phi 345	Speaker-Bos 441	Baker-Phi 493	Baker-Phi.............906	Baker-Phi.............168	Baker-Phi............49.9
Cobb-Det 4.6	Baker-Phi 337	Baker-Phi.....................413	Crawford-Det 489	Collins-Phi 894	Collins-Phi 165	Collins-Phi 49.1

Runs	Hits	Doubles	Triples	Home Runs	Total Bases	Runs Batted In
Collins-Phi 125	Jackson-Cle..........197	Jackson-Cle 39	Crawford-Det 23	Baker-Phi.................12	Crawford-Det........298	Baker-Phi 117
Baker-Phi..............116	Crawford-Det 193	Speaker-Bos..................35	Speaker-Bos 22	Crawford-Det 9	Jackson-Cle..........291	McInnis-Phi 90
Jackson-Cle............109	Baker-Phi..............190	Baker-Phi 34	Jackson-Cle..............17	Bodie-Chi....................8	Baker-Phi..............278	Lewis-Bos..............90
Shotton-StL 105	Speaker-Bos 189	Crawford-Det 32	Williams-StL 16	Jackson-Cle..............7	Speaker-Bos 277	Pratt-StL 87
E.Murphy-Phi........105	Collins-Phi 184		Cobb-Det 16		Collins-Phi 242	Barry-Phi 85

Stolen Bases	Base Stealing Runs	Fielding Runs-Infield	Fielding Runs-Outfield	Wins	Winning Pct.	Complete Games
Milan-Was 75		Weaver-Chi 35.5	Speaker-Bos........18.6	Johnson-Was..........36	Johnson-Was 837	Johnson-Was 29
Moeller-Was............62		Collins-Phi 16.4	Lewis-Bos............11.2	Falkenberg-Cle 23	Bush-Phi...............714	Russell-Chi............26
Collins-Phi 55		Lajoie-Cle 14.5	Johnston-StL 9.8	Russell-Chi 22	Boehling-Was 708	Scott-Chi 25
Cobb-Det.................51		Turner-Cle 13.4	Hooper-Bos 7.7	Bender-Phi.............21	Collins-Bos 704	
Speaker-Bos 46		Baker-Phi.......................9.3	Shotton-StL 7.3		Falkenberg-Cle 697	

Strikeouts	Fewest BB/Game	Games	Saves	Base Runners/9	Adjusted Relief Runs	Relief Ranking
Johnson-Was........243	Johnson-Was 99	Russell-Chi 52	Bender-Phi..............13	Johnson-Was 7.26		
V.Gregg-Cle 166	Collins-Bos 1.35	Scott-Chi.........................48	Hughes-Was 6	Russell-Chi 9.55		
Falkenberg-Cle 166	Mitchell-StL..........1.72	Johnson-Was 48	Bedient-Bos..............5	Scott-Chi............10.00		
Scott-Chi 158	Plank-Phi 2.11	Bender-Phi 48		Cicotte-Chi 10.07		
Groom-Was 156	Weilman-StL 2.15	V.Gregg-Cle 44		Plank-Phi 10.13		

Innings Pitched	Opponents' Avg.	Opponents' OBP	Earned Run Average	Adjusted ERA	Adjusted Starter Runs	Pitcher Wins
Johnson-Was 346.0	Johnson-Was 190	Johnson-Was...............220	Johnson-Was 1.14	Johnson-Was........258	Johnson-Was 69.8	**Johnson-Was** ..10.9
Russell-Chi 316.2	Mitchell-Cle...........202	Russell-Chi 275	Cicotte-Chi 1.58	Cicotte-Chi.............185	Russell-Chi 37.9	**Russell-Chi** 4.7
Scott-Chi............312.1	Engel-Was 218	Cicotte-Chi...................283	Scott-Chi..............1.90	Mitchell-Cle 159	Cicotte-Chi 36.4	**Cicotte-Chi** 4.1
V.Gregg-Cle 285.2	Russell-Chi 220	Scott-Chi 283	Russell-Chi 1.90	Scott-Chi 154	Scott-Chi..............34.5	**Scott-Chi** 3.8
Falkenberg-Cle ..276.0	Caldwell-NY 221	Bender-Phi...................287	Mitchell-Cle..........1.91	Russell-Chi 153	Falkenberg-Cle 27.0	**Falkenberg-Cle**..2.9

Chief Saves the Day

Prior to the season, another big-market AL club shifted its headquarters as New York moved into the Giants' home, the Polo Grounds. The dimensions were smaller than those of Hilltop Park, but the potential gate receipts were much higher.

After a year off, the Athletics won once more, withstanding an August challenge from eventual third-place finishers Cleveland, who had a big year from Joe Jackson. Washington's Walter Johnson won 14 games in a row, helping his Senators finish second again. However, Boston slipped to fourth as Smokey Joe Wood broke his arm.

Chief Bender was 21–10 for the Athletics, and also was credited many years later with 13 saves, which tied the retroactive all-time record. Frank Baker paced the AL in homers and RBIs, and the entire club led the league in hits, doubles, homers, slugging, walks, and, of course, runs. Four Philadelphians scored 100 runs or more; among the other seven clubs, only three players could boast such a feat. It was a year of yet more star debuts for the A's. Pitcher Bob Shawkey, who would go one to glory with the Yankees, was 6–5 for the Mackmen, and catcher Wally Schang played 79 games.

In an entertaining five-game World Series, the A's defeated New York. The Giants' only win came in Game 2, a 10-inning shutout by Christy Mathewson, who drove in the game-deciding run. Three of the Philadelphia wins were by two or fewer runs. Both Mathewson and Eddie Plank were superb, posting identical 0.95 ERAs. Bender won both his games. Joe Bush, winner of Game 3, was the only other A's pitcher used.

Former Cleveland Spiders outfielder Lou "Chief" Sockalexis, who lost his potentially great career to drinking, died at 42 on Christmas Eve. While his life ended sadly, he had a legacy: a few years later, the city's American League club would become known as the "Indians."

1914 National League

TEAM	W	L	T	PCT	GB	HW	HL	R	OR	PA	H	2B	3B	HR	BB	SO	HB	SH	AVG	OBP	SLG	OPS	AOPS	BR	ABR	PF	SB	CS	BSA	BSR
BOS	94	59	5	.614		**51**	25	657	548	5979	1307	213	60	35	**502**	617	**221**	50	.251	.323	.335	658	103	20	24	99	139			
NY	84	70	2	.545	10.5	43	36	**672**	576	5789	1363	**222**	59	30	447	**479**	139	**57**	.265	**.330**	.348	678	**112**	56	**79**	97	**239**			
STL	81	72	4	.529	13	42	34	558	**540**	5720	1249	203	65	33	445	618	187	42	.248	.314	.333	647	100	-7	0	99	204			
CHI	78	76	2	.506	16.5	46	30	605	638	5784	1229	199	74	42	501	577	191	42	.243	.317	.337	654	101	8	10	100	164			
BRO	75	79	0	.487	19.5	45	34	622	618	5751	**1386**	172	**90**	31	376	559	190	33	**.269**	.323	.355	678	106	39	25	102	173			
PHI	74	80	0	.481	20.5	48	30	651	687	5770	1345	211	52	**62**	472	570	161	27	.263	.329	**.361**	**690**	105	**72**	31	107	145			
PIT	69	85	4	.448	25.5	39	36	503	**540**	5753	1197	148	79	18	416	608	156	36	.233	.295	.303	598	88	-106	-84	96	147			
CIN	60	94	3	.390	34.5	34	42	530	651	5635	1178	142	64	16	441	627	149	54	.236	.305	.300	605	83	-81	-96	103	224			
TOT	625					348	267	4798		46181	10254	1510	543	267	3600	4655	341	1394	.251	.317	.334	651					1435			

TEAM	CG	SHO	GR	SV	IP	H	HR	BB	SO	BR/9	ERA	AERA	OAV	OOB	PR	APR	PF	OSB	OCS	FA	E	WPB	DP	FW	PW	BW	BSW	DIF
BOS	**104**	19	69	6	1421.0	1272	38	477	606	11.4	2.74	100	.249	.319	7	1	99	139	*147*	.963	246	54	**143**	1.8	.1	2.6		13.0
NY	88	**20**	89	9	1390.2	1298	47	**367**	563	11.0	2.94	90	.253	**.306**	-25	-49	95	**129**	*121*	.961	254	**36**	119	1.1	-5.3	**8.5**		2.7
STL	84	16	96	12	1424.2	1279	**26**	422	531	11.1	**2.38**	**117**	.250	.313	**64**	**64**	100	176	*139*	.964	239	**36**	109	2.2	**6.9**	.0		-4.6
CHI	70	14	**110**	11	1389.1	**1169**	37	528	**651**	11.2	2.71	103	**.233**	.311	12	9	100	201	*145*	.951	310	89	87	-2.7	1.0	1.1		1.7
BRO	80	11	99	11	1368.1	1282	36	466	605	11.8	2.82	101	.255	.323	-5	7	103	199	*146*	.961	248	42	112	1.2	.8	2.7		-6.7
PHI	85	14	98	7	1379.1	1403	**26**	452	650	12.4	3.06	96	.270	.335	-42	-20	105	241	***170***	.950	324	38	81	-3.9	-2.2	3.3		-.3
PIT	86	10	97	11	1405.0	1272	27	392	488	**10.9**	2.70	98	.249	.308	13	-10	95	170	*133*	**.966**	**223**	39	96	**3.4**	-1.1	-9.1		-1.2
CIN	74	15	106	**15**	1387.1	1259	30	489	607	11.7	2.94	100	.248	.320	-24	-3	105	180	*146*	.952	314	79	113	-2.9	-.3	-10.4		-3.5
TOT	671	119	764	82	11165.2					11.4	2.78		.251	.317						.958	2158	413	860					

Batter-Fielder Wins	Batting Average	On-Base Percentage	Slugging Average	On-Base Plus Slugging	Adjusted OPS	Adjusted Batter Runs
Maranville-Bos ..5.5	Daubert-Bro 329	Stengel-Bro 404	Magee-Phi 509	Cravath-Phi 901	Cravath-Phi 157	Burns-NY............39.3
Herzog-Cin 4.8	Becker-Phi 325	Burns-NY....................403	Cravath-Phi..........499	Magee-Phi 890	Magee-Phi 154	Cravath-Phi 37.5
Magee-Phi 4.2	Dalton-Bro 319	Cravath-Phi................402	Connolly-Bos 494	Wheat-Bro 830	Burns-NY..............149	Magee-Phi..........35.4
Wheat-Bro 3.8	Wheat-Bro 319	Huggins-StL................396	Wheat-Bro 452	Stengel-Bro 829	Stengel-Bro 143	Connolly-Bos......32.5
Smith-Bro-Bos....3.8	Stengel-Bro...........316	Dalton-Bro 396	Becker-Phi 446	Burns-NY..............820	Wheat-Bro 143	Wheat-Bro 27.7

Runs	Hits	Doubles	Triples	Home Runs	Total Bases	Runs Batted In
Burns-NY..............100	Magee-Phi 171	Magee-Phi 39	Carey-Pit 17	Cravath-Phi 19	Magee-Phi............277	Magee-Phi 103
Magee-Phi 96	Wheat-Bro 170	Zimmerman-Chi 36	Zimmerman-Chi......12	Saier-Chi 18	Cravath-Phi 249	Cravath-Phi 100
Daubert-Bro...........89	Burns-NY...............170	Burns-NY 35	Wilson-StL 12	Magee-Phi 15	Wheat-Bro 241	Wheat-Bro 89
Saier-Chi 87	Zimmerman-Chi....167	Connolly-Bos 28	Cutshaw-Bro 12	Luderus-Phi............12	Zimmerman-Chi....239	D.Miller-StL............88
Doyle-NY 87	Becker-Phi 167				Burns-NY..............234	Zimmerman-Chi 87

Stolen Bases	Base Stealing Runs	Fielding Runs-Infield	Fielding Runs-Outfield	Wins	Winning Pct.	Complete Games
Burns-NY................62		Maranville-Bos 49.8	Wheat-Bro 14.5	Alexander-Phi 27	James-Bos 788	Alexander-Phi.........32
Herzog-Cin 46		Herzog-Cin 33.4	Wilson-StL 12.1	Tesreau-NY 26	Doak-StL 760	Rudolph-Bos..........31
Dolan-StL 42		Cutshaw-Bro 27.6	Mann-Bos..............9.5	Rudolph-Bos 26	Tesreau-NY.........722	James-Bos 30
Carey-Pit 38		Smith-Bro-Bos 18.3	Paskert-Phi............9.3	James-Bos...............26	Rudolph-Bos.........722	Mathewson-NY......29
		Sweeney-Chi 15.8	Carey-Pit................6.7	Mathewson-NY 24	Pfeffer-Bro 657	Pfeffer-Bro 27

Strikeouts	Fewest BB/Game	Games	Saves	Base Runners/9	Adjusted Relief Runs	Relief Ranking
Alexander-Phi 214	Mathewson-NY.......66	Cheney-Chi....................50	Sallee-StL 6	Rudolph-Bos........9.45		
Tesreau-NY 189	Adams-Pit..........1.24	Mayer-Phi 48	Ames-Cin.................6	Adams-Pit...........9.51		
Vaughn-Chi 165	Marquard-NY 1.58	Ames-Cin 47	Cheney-Chi 5	Mamaux-Pit 9.57		
Cheney-Chi 157	Rudolph-Bos........1.63		Pfeffer-Bro 4	Mathewson-NY....9.78		
James-Bos............156	Alexander-Phi......1.93		McQuillan-Pit 4	Doak-StL 10.09		

Innings Pitched	Opponents' Avg.	Opponents' OBP	Earned Run Average	Adjusted ERA	Adjusted Starter Runs	Pitcher Wins
Alexander-Phi....355.0	Tesreau-NY...........209	Adams-Pit 276	Doak-StL 1.72	Doak-StL 162	James-Bos 31.0	**James-Bos** 3.6
Rudolph-Bos......336.1	Cheney-Chi...........215	Rudolph-Bos 276	James-Bos 1.90	James-Bos.............145	Pfeffer-Bro 30.4	**Pfeffer-Bro** 3.2
James-Bos 332.1	Doak-StL 216	Mathewson-NY 278	Pfeffer-Bro 1.97	Pfeffer-Bro 145	Doak-StL 27.2	**Alexander-Phi**....3.1
Tesreau-NY........322.1	Vaughn-Chi...........222	Alexander-Phi 290	Vaughn-Chi..........2.05	Vaughn-Chi 135	Sallee-StL............22.4	**Sallee-StL** 3.1
Mayer-Phi 321.0	Douglas-Cin 223	Doak-StL 290	Sallee-StL............2.10	Sallee-StL 133	Alexander-Phi......22.2	**Doak-StL** 2.6

Hub Miracle

In last place on July 18, the Boston Braves suddenly began to win. Taking 34 of their last 44, they not only caught and passed the New York Giants, but they blew away the league and took the flag by an amazing 10½ games. A three-man rotation carried the pitching load, and manager George Stallings made the most of a weak lineup by instituting a platoon system; this strategy was almost unknown at the time.

During the last month of the season, the Braves moved to Fenway Park due to suddenly huge crowds. Braves attendance had risen 72 percent in 1913, and went up another 84 percent in 1914; this led to the construction of massive Braves Field, which opened the following spring. Despite Boston's miracle victory, and the resulting excitement, overall league attendance fell a frightening 40 percent. Total turnstile clicks were under two million for the first time since 1902.

The birth of the Federal League led to player raids on the AL and NL. In the Senior Circuit, the lower talent level meant parity; the Braves' 94 wins were the lowest total for a flag winner in over a decade. But this didn't matter in October, as the heavily favored Philadelphia Athletics did a belly flop. Boston completed its ridiculous, unbelievable season with a four-game World Series sweep. It was the Senior Circuit's first Series win since 1909.

The Cubs' great 1900s infield was in the news in 1914. First baseman Frank Chance retired; second sacker Johnny Evers was the league MVP, hitting .279 with 87 walks for Boston; shortstop Joe Tinker managed the Federal League's Chicago club; and third baseman Harry Steinfeldt, out of the game since 1911, died at 36.

1914 American League

TEAM	W	L	T	PCT	GB	HW	HL	R	OR	PA	H	2B	3B	HR	BB	SO	HB	SH	AVG	OBP	SLG	OPS	AOPS	BR	ABR	PF	SB	CS	BSA	BSR
PHI	99	53	6	.651		**51**	24	**749**	529	5940	**1392**	165	80	**29**	545	**517**	**217**	**52**	**.272**	**.348**	**.352**	**700**	**123**	**113**	**142**	96	**231**	188	55	-15
BOS	91	62	6	.595	8.5	44	31	589	**510**	5816	1278	**226**	**85**	18	490	549	170	39	.250	.320	.338	658	105	28	28	100	177	176	50	-23
WAS	81	73	4	.526	19	40	33	572	519	5801	1245	176	81	18	470	640	177	46	.244	.313	.320	633	93	-19	-40	104	220	163	57	-9
DET	80	73	4	.523	19.5	42	35	615	618	5908	1318	195	84	25	**557**	537	205	44	.258	.336	.344	680	109	78	58	103	211	154	**58**	**-7**
STL	71	82	6	.464	28.5	42	36	523	615	5706	1241	185	75	17	423	863	147	35	.243	.306	.319	625	99	-40	-19	96	233	189	55	-15
NY	70	84	3	.455	30	36	40	537	550	5756	1144	149	52	12	577	711	140	47	.229	.315	.287	602	88	-59	-57	100	251	191	57	-12
CHI	70	84	3	.455	30	43	37	487	560	5698	1205	161	71	19	408	609	204	46	.239	.302	.311	613	92	-62	-55	99	167	152	52	-16
CLE	51	102	4	.333	48.5	32	47	538	709	5800	1262	178	70	10	450	685	154	39	.245	.310	.312	622	90	-40	-60	104	167	157	52	-18
TOT	631					330	283	4610		46425	10085	1435	598	148	3920	5111	348	1414	.248	.319	.323	642					1657	1370	55	-115

TEAM	CG	SHO	GR	SV	IP	H	HR	BB	SO	BR/9	ERA	AERA	OAV	OOB	PR	APR	PF	OSB	OCS	FA	E	WPB	DP	FW	PW	BW	BSW	DIF
PHI	89	24	95	16	1404.0	1264	18	521	720	11.6	2.78	94	.249	.322	-6	-29	95	228	*176*	**.966**	**213**	62	116	**3.5**	-3.2	**15.7**	-.0	7.1
BOS	88	24	92	7	1427.1	1207	18	393	602	**10.3**	**2.36**	**114**	.236	**.295**	**59**	**51**	98	172	*156*	.963	242	**41**	99	1.8	**5.6**	3.1	-1.0	4.9
WAS	75	**25**	120	**19**	1420.2	**1170**	20	520	**784**	11.0	2.54	111	**.233**	.311	31	40	103	196	*166*	.961	254	68	116	1.0	4.4	-4.4	.6	2.4
DET	81	14	117	11	1412.0	1285	17	498	567	11.8	2.86	98	.249	.322	-19	-10	103	230	*171*	.958	286	54	101	-1.1	-1.1	6.4	**.8**	-1.6
STL	81	15	113	9	1410.2	1309	20	540	553	12.1	2.85	95	.251	.327	-17	-23	99	212	*171*	.952	317	71	114	-2.7	-2.5	-2.1	-.0	2.0
NY	**98**	9	83	2	1397.1	1277	30	**390**	563	10.9	2.81	98	.250	.308	-12	-10	101	216	*176*	.963	238	52	93	1.9	-1.1	-6.3	.3	-1.7
CHI	74	17	124	11	1398.2	1207	15	401	660	10.5	2.48	108	.239	.298	40	31	98	**164**	*164*	.955	299	47	90	-1.9	3.4	-6.1	-.2	-2.3
CLE	69	9	**129**	2	1391.2	1365	**10**	666	688	13.4	3.21	90	.267	.357	-74	-53	105	233	***190***	.953	300	76	**119**	-1.9	-5.9	-6.6	-.4	-10.7
TOT	655	137	873	77	11262.1					11.5	2.73		.248	.319						.959	2149	471	848					

Batter-Fielder Wins
Speaker-Bos 7.3
Collins-Phi 6.9
Bush-Det..............5.1
Baker-Phi 5.0
T.Walker-StL 4.2

Batting Average
Cobb-Det 368
Collins-Phi 344
Speaker-Bos.........338
Jackson-Cle 338
Baker-Phi 319

On-Base Percentage
Collins-Phi 452
Speaker-Bos 423
Jackson-Cle.................399
Crawford-Det 388
Baker-Phi.....................380

Slugging Average
Cobb-Det 513
Speaker-Bos.........503
Crawford-Det 483
Jackson-Cle 464
Collins-Phi 452

On-Base Plus Slugging
Speaker-Bos 926
Collins-Phi 904
Crawford-Det.........871
Jackson-Cle..........862
Baker-Phi..............822

Adjusted OPS
Collins-Phi 179
Speaker-Bos 178
Crawford-Det........157
Baker-Phi..............153
Jackson-Cle..........153

Adjusted Batter Runs
Collins-Phi..........57.6
Speaker-Bos 56.7
Cobb-Det............40.7
Crawford-Det......38.0
Baker-Phi............35.3

Runs
Collins-Phi 122
Speaker-Bos 101
Murphy-Phi 101
Bush-Det 97

Hits
Speaker-Bos 193
Crawford-Det........183
Baker-Phi..............182
McInnis-Phi 181
Collins-Phi 181

Doubles
Speaker-Bos..................46
Lewis-Bos......................37
Pratt-StL 34
Collins-Chi 34
Leary-StL 28

Triples
Crawford-Det..........26
Gardner-Bos 19
Speaker-Bos 18
T.Walker-StL............16
Hooper-Bos 15

Home Runs
Baker-Phi..................9
Crawford-Det..............8
T.Walker-StL..............6
Fournier-Chi..............6

Total Bases
Speaker-Bos 287
Crawford-Det........281
Baker-Phi..............252
Pratt-StL 240
Collins-Phi 238

Runs Batted In
Crawford-Det 104
McInnis-Phi 95
Speaker-Bos..........90
Baker-Phi 89
Collins-Phi 85

Stolen Bases
Maisel-NY 74
Collins-Phi 58
Speaker-Bos 42
Shotton-StL 40

Base Stealing Runs
Maisel-NY............10.3
Peckinpaugh-NY....2.4
Collins-Phi 2.3
Moriarty-Det 2.2
Chapman-Cle 2.1

Fielding Runs-Infield
Bush-Det 31.8
Gandil-Was 23.3
Turner-Cle 22.3
Boone-NY 17.7
Moriarty-Det................15.8

Fielding Runs-Outfield
Speaker-Bos........23.0
T.Walker-StL 16.5
Hooper-Bos 9.9
Strunk-Phi..............6.3
Graney-Cle 5.0

Wins
Johnson-Was..........28
Coveleski-Det 22
Collins-Bos 20
Leonard-Bos 19
Dauss-Det 19

Winning Pct.
Bender-Phi 850
Leonard-Bos.........792
Plank-Phi 682
Caldwell-NY 667
Shawkey-Phi.........652

Complete Games
Johnson-Was 33
Coveleski-Det........23
Dauss-Det 22
Caldwell-NY 22

Strikeouts
Johnson-Was........225
Mitchell-Cle 179
Leonard-Bos 176
Shaw-Was 164
Dauss-Det 150

Fewest BB/Game
McHale-NY 1.55
Russell-Chi 1.77
Johnson-Was 1.79
Warhop-NY..........1.83
Ayers-Was 1.83

Games
Johnson-Was 51
Ayers-Was 49
Shaw-Was 48
Benz-Chi.......................48

Saves
Shaw-Was 4
Mitchell-StL 4
Faber-Chi...................4
Bentley-Was 4

Base Runners/9
Leonard-Bos........8.29
Caldwell-NY 8.79
Johnson-Was 9.01
Shore-Bos 9.15
Foster-Bos 9.48

Adjusted Relief Runs

Relief Ranking

Innings Pitched
Johnson-Was 371.2
Coveleski-Det 303.1
Hamilton-StL......302.1
Dauss-Det 302.0
Weilman-StL......299.0

Opponents' Avg.
Leonard-Bos.........180
Caldwell-NY 205
Shaw-Was 216
Johnson-Was 217
Foster-Bos 218

Opponents' OBP
Leonard-Bos 246
Caldwell-NY................260
Johnson-Was..............265
Foster-Bos 274
Benz-Chi 282

Earned Run Average
Leonard-Bos..........96
Foster-Bos 1.70
Johnson-Was 1.72
Caldwell-NY 1.94
Shore-Bos 2.00

Adjusted ERA
Leonard-Bos 279
Johnson-Was........163
Foster-Bos 158
Caldwell-NY..........142
Cicotte-Chi............131

Adjusted Starter Runs
Johnson-Was 45.3
Leonard-Bos........43.3
Caldwell-NY 21.0
Weilman-StL........20.6
Foster-Bos 18.5

Pitcher Wins
Johnson-Was 7.2
Leonard-Bos 4.8
Caldwell-NY 3.0
Coveleski-Det 2.3
Cicotte-Chi 2.1

The End of an A's Era

Moundsmen came to terms with the cork-centered ball by developing techniques to increase movement on their pitches. As a result, in 1914 the AL's batting average dropped sharply for the third straight year to .248, where it would remain until 1918.

Only three players in the league scored 100 runs. Infielder Gus Williams of the Browns fanned 120 times to set new loop record. (His short career ended the next season.) Twenty-two-year-old southpaw Dutch Leonard of the Red Sox was spectacular, finishing 19–5 with an almost inconceivable 0.96 ERA, the best ever. The performance of Leonard, and the purchase from Baltimore of a young pitcher named George Ruth, helped the Red Sox improve to 91–62. Dominating Philadelphia remained out of reach, leading the league from June to the finish. Detroit debuted outfielder Harry Heilmann and improved to fourth, while the slumping Chisox got a good show from rookie hurler Red Faber.

Second baseman Eddie Collins of the Athletics led the AL in runs for the third straight season, cementing his reputation as one of baseball's smartest and most capable men. Once again, the entire A's infield was the class of the game, and seven of the eight regular position players hit at least .272. Seven Philadelphia pitchers had at least 10 wins.

Due to competition from the new Federal League, and a shrinking economy, AL attendance fell by nearly a quarter. Even in pennant-winning Philadelphia, without a Federal League competitor, crowds were down 39 percent. Perhaps the low attendance was a harbinger of doom. The heavily favored Athletics punted the World Series in four straight to the underdog Boston Braves. Conscious of his low box office receipts, and angry for his club's poor October play, the shrewd and thrifty Connie Mack chose to dismantle his dynasty.

1914 Federal League

TEAM	W	L	T	PCT	GB	HW	HL	R	OR	PA	H	2B	3B	HR	BB	SO	HB	SH	AVG	OBP	SLG	OPS	AOPS	BR	ABR	PF	SB	CS	BSA	BSR
IND	88	65	4	.575		**53**	23	**762**	622	5907	**1474**	**230**	**90**	33	470	668	**223**	38	**.285**	**.349**	**.383**	**732**	95	**-37**	-97	111	**273**			
CHI	87	67	3	.565	1.5	41	34	621	**517**	5821	1314	227	50	**52**	**520**	645	162	41	.258	.331	.352	683	**98**	-123	**-90**	94	171			
BAL	84	70	6	.545	4.5	**53**	26	645	628	5831	1374	222	67	32	487	**589**	178	**46**	.268	.337	.357	694	92	-105	-121	103	152			
BUF	80	71	4	.530	7	47	29	620	602	5649	1264	177	74	37	430	761	132	23	.250	.311	.336	647	80	-207	-216	102	228			
BRO	77	77	3	.500	11.5	47	32	662	677	5805	1402	225	85	42	404	665	135	45	.269	.326	.368	694	96	-120	-116	99	220			
KC	67	84	3	.444	20	38	37	644	683	5712	1369	226	77	39	399	621	150	36	.267	.324	.364	688	97	-129	-107	96	171			
PIT	64	86	4	.427	22.5	37	37	605	698	5751	1339	180	**90**	34	410	575	188	39	.262	.321	.352	673	90	-159	-155	99	153			
STL	62	89	3	.411	25	31	44	565	697	5791	1254	193	65	26	503	662	176	34	.247	.319	.326	645	77	-200	-222	105	113			
TOT	624					347	262	5124		46267	10790	1680	598	295	3623	5186	302	1344	.263	.328	.355	682					1481			

TEAM	CG	SHO	GR	SV	IP	H	HR	BB	SO	BR/9	ERA	AERA	OAV	OOB	PR	APR	PF	OSB	OCS	FA	E	WPB	DP	FW	PW	BW	BSW	DIF
IND	**104**	15	67	9	1397.2	1352	**29**	476	664	12.1	3.06	113	.258	.325	23	58	108	197	***159***	.956	289	45	113	-1.2	6.0	-10.1		16.8
CHI	93	**17**	87	8	1420.1	**1204**	43	393	650	**10.3**	**2.44**	**121**	**.233**	**.291**	**121**	**87**	92	**135**	*144*	**.962**	249	**41**	114	1.1	**9.0**	**-9.4**		9.2
BAL	88	15	**93**	13	1392.0	1389	34	**392**	**732**	11.7	3.13	108	.268	.323	12	35	105	175	*144*	.960	263	55	105	.6	3.6	-12.6		15.4
BUF	89	15	91	**16**	1387.0	1249	45	505	662	11.7	3.16	104	.245	.318	7	19	103	154	*149*	**.962**	**242**	55	109	**1.3**	2.0	-22.5		23.7
BRO	91	11	92	9	1385.1	1375	31	559	636	12.9	3.33	96	.264	.341	-20	-22	100	216	*152*	.956	283	49	120	-.9	-2.3	-12.1		15.2
KC	82	10	92	12	1361.0	1387	37	445	600	12.4	3.41	91	.268	.331	-30	-50	96	196	*145*	.957	279	61	**135**	-.9	-5.2	-11.1		8.7
PIT	97	9	71	6	1370.0	1416	38	444	510	12.4	3.56	89	.273	.333	-54	-59	99	182	*151*	.960	253	45	92	.6	-6.1	-16.1		10.7
STL	97	9	73	6	1367.2	1418	38	409	661	12.3	3.59	94	.267	.324	-58	-31	105	226	*155*	.957	273	59	94	-.6	-3.2	-23.1		13.4
TOT	741	101	666	79	11081.0					12.0	3.20		.263	.328						.959	2131	410	882					

Batter-Fielder Wins	Batting Average	On-Base Percentage	Slugging Average	On-Base Plus Slugging	Adjusted OPS	Adjusted Batter Runs
Wilson-Chi 5.4	Kauff-Ind...............370	Kauff-Ind 447	Evans-Bro.............556	Kauff-Ind 981	Evans-Bro 165	Evans-Bro 39.0
Kenworthy-KC 5.1	Evans-Bro.............348	Evans-Bro 416	Kauff-Ind...............534	Evans-Bro 973	Kauff-Ind 150	Kauff-Ind 36.7
Kauff-Ind 3.7	Easterly-KC 335	Lennox-Pit 414	Kenworthy-KC.......525	Lennox-Pit 907	Kenworthy-KC 148	Kenworthy-KC 25.7
Evans-Bro............3.3	Shaw-Bro 324	Meyer-Bal 395	Lennox-Pit 493	Kenworthy-KC 896	Lennox-Pit 148	Lennox-Pit..........24.7
Doolan-Bal 1.7	Campbell-Ind 318	Wilson-Chi 394	Zwilling-Chi...........485	Wilson-Chi 860	Wilson-Chi 142	Wilson-Chi..........21.3

Runs	Hits	Doubles	Triples	Home Runs	Total Bases	Runs Batted In
Kauff-Ind 120	Kauff-Ind 211	Kauff-Ind........................44	Evans-Bro 15	Zwilling-Chi 16	Kauff-Ind 305	LaPorte-Ind 107
McKechnie-Ind......107	Zwilling-Chi 185	Evans-Bro......................41	Esmond-Ind 15	Kenworthy-KC 15	Zwilling-Chi 287	Evans-Bro 96
Duncan-Bal 99	Evans-Bro 179	Kenworthy-KC................40	Kenworthy-KC 14	Hanford-Buf............12	Kenworthy-KC 286	Zwilling-Chi............95
Kenworthy-KC 93	Oakes-Pit..............178	Zwilling-Chi....................38		Evans-Bro 12	Evans-Bro 286	Kauff-Ind................95
Evans-Bro 93	Hanford-Buf..........174				Hanford-Buf..........264	Kenworthy-KC 91

Stolen Bases	Base Stealing Runs	Fielding Runs-Infield	Fielding Runs-Outfield	Wins	Winning Pct.	Complete Games
Kauff-Ind 75		Doolan-Bal.................34.1	Chadbourne-KC 9.2	Hendrix-Chi 29	Ford-Buf 778	Hendrix-Chi 34
McKechnie-Ind........47		McKechnie-Ind............22.5	Kauff-Ind................8.5	Quinn-Bal 26	Hendrix-Chi 744	Falkenberg-Ind 33
Myers-Bro 43		Kenworthy-KC 22.4	Hanford-Buf 6.9	Seaton-Bro 25	Quinn-Bal 650	Moseley-Ind 29
Chadbourne-KC......42		Wisterzil-Bro 16.1	Tobin-StL 5.6	Falkenberg-Ind........25	Seaton-Bro 641	Quinn-Bal 27
		Tinker-Chi 12.3	W.Miller-StL 4.7	Suggs-Bal 24	Suggs-Bal.............632	

Strikeouts	Fewest BB/Game	Games	Saves	Base Runners/9	Adjusted Relief Runs	Relief Ranking
Falkenberg-Ind......236	Ford-Buf 1.49	Hendrix-Chi...................49	Ford-Buf...................6	Hendrix-Chi 8.55		
Moseley-Ind..........205	Suggs-Bal............1.61	Falkenberg-Ind 49	Wilhelm-Bal 5	Ford-Buf 8.66		
Hendrix-Chi 189	Quinn-Bal 1.71	Wilhelm-Bal 47	Packard-KC 5	Johnson-Chi 9.07		
Seaton-Bro 172	Hendrix-Chi 1.91	Suggs-Bal......................46	Hendrix-Chi 5	Falkenberg-Ind ..10.16		
Groom-StL............167	Keupper-StL 2.07	Quinn-Bal 46		Fiske-Chi 10.32		

Innings Pitched	Opponents' Avg.	Opponents' OBP	Earned Run Average	Adjusted ERA	Adjusted Starter Runs	Pitcher Wins
Falkenberg-Ind ..377.1	Hendrix-Chi 203	Hendrix-Chi 251	Johnson-Chi 1.57	Ford-Buf................163	Hendrix-Chi 42.2	**Hendrix-Chi**........5.4
Hendrix-Chi 362.0	Krapp-Buf 210	Ford-Buf........................254	Hendrix-Chi 1.69	Hendrix-Chi 157	Falkenberg-Ind 33.1	**Falkenberg-Ind**..3.2
Quinn-Bal 342.2	Ford-Buf 214	Lange-Chi 282	Ford-Buf 1.82	Falkenberg-Ind......141	Ford-Buf 30.1	**Ford-Buf**.............3.0
Suggs-Bal..........319.1	Lange-Chi.............224	Falkenberg-Ind..............284	Watson-Chi-StL ..2.01	Watson-Chi-StL 137	Watson-Chi-StL ..19.7	**Quinn-Bal** 2.5
Moseley-Ind 316.2	Watson-Chi-StL ...230	Anderson-Buf................297	Falkenberg-Ind 2.22	Lange-Chi 119	Quinn-Bal 15.4	**Suggs-Bal** 1.7

A Federal Case

Chicago coal baron and machinery manufacturer Jim Gilmore, who had never even heard of the Federal League before August 1913, jumped in with both feet and took over the minor league's Chicago franchise late in the season. Gilmore then became league president and immediately escalated plans to become a major league, inducing well-to-do backers to support new franchises.

Robert B. Ward wanted to name his Brooklyn team the Tip-Tops, after his national bakery. Media outrage over such commercialism led to the alternate name Brookfeds. Restaurant chain owner Charles Weeghman took over the Chicago club, convinced by Gilmore it would take no more than $26,000. By the time new Weeghman Park opened in 1914, the franchise's backers had already spent $412,000.

Gilmore was better at landing big money than big players; Browns manager George Stovall was the first major league player to jump to the FL. The Feds also lured black sheep Hal Chase as well as Joe Tinker and Three Finger Brown, both past their prime.

From Terrapin Park in Baltimore, some of the 27,692 Opening Day patrons could see Oriole Park, where only 1,500 watched John McGraw's Giants play the International League Orioles in an exhibition game. Heavy FL-induced losses led Orioles owner Jack Dunn to offer Babe Ruth to Connie Mack; the A's said they couldn't afford Ruth, but new Red Sox owner Joe Lannin could. Dunn, who made $25,000 for selling Ruth and two others to Boston, moved his club to Richmond for 1915.

Good pitchers were rewarded with money, and victories. Ex-Pirates hurler Claude Hendrix won 29 and Jack Quinn, late of the Braves, won 26 in 1914. Chief Johnson, defying a permanent injunction to keep him from jumping from the Reds to the Feds, pitched through 1915 for Stovall's Kansas City Packers. Benny Kauff, whose major league experience consisted of 11 at bats with the Yankees in 1912, was an offensive force and led Indianapolis to the first FL pennant.

1915 Federal League

TEAM	W	L	T	PCT	GB	HW	HL	R	OR	PA	H	2B	3B	HR	BB	SO	HB	SH	AVG	OBP	SLG	OPS	AOPS	BR	ABR	PF	SB	CS	BSA	BSR
CHI	86	66	3	.566		44	32	640	538	5784	1320	185	77	**50**	444	590	177	30	.257	.320	.352	672	101	-113	-82	94	161			
STL	87	67	5	.565		43	34	634	527	5990	1344	199	**81**	23	**576**	**502**	**233**	36	.261	**.340**	.345	685	94	-71	-98	105	195			
PIT	86	67	3	.562	0.5	45	31	592	**524**	5728	1318	180	80	20	448	561	202	38	.262	.326	.341	667	94	-113	-109	99	224			
KC	81	72	0	.529	5.5	**46**	31	547	551	5551	1206	200	66	28	368	503	200	46	.244	.303	.329	632	87	-185	-168	96	144			
NEW	80	72	3	.526	6	40	39	585	562	5771	1283	**210**	80	17	438	550	200	36	.252	.315	.334	649	93	-151	-123	94	184			
BUF	74	78	1	.487	12	37	40	574	634	5620	1261	193	68	40	420	587	116	19	.249	.309	.338	647	85	-161	-170	102	184			
BRO	70	82	1	.461	16	34	40	**647**	673	5707	**1348**	205	75	36	473	654	152	**47**	**.268**	.336	**.360**	**696**	**103**	**-57**	**-53**	99	**249**			
BAL	47	107	0	.305	40	24	51	550	760	5744	1235	196	53	36	470	641	177	37	.244	.313	.325	638	82	-168	-181	103	128			
TOT	619					313	298	4769		45895	10315	1568	580	250	3637	4588	289	1457	.255	.320	.340	661					1469			

TEAM	CG	SHO	GR	SV	IP	H	HR	BB	SO	BR/9	ERA	AERA	OAV	OOB	PR	APR	PF	OSB	OCS	FA	E	WPB	DP	FW	PW	BW	BSW	DIF
CHI	97	21	68	10	1397.2	1232	34	402	576	**10.7**	2.64	106	**.240**	**.299**	61	25	92	164	*129*	.964	233	50	102	.4	2.7	-8.8		15.7
STL	94	**24**	88	9	1426.0	1267	22	396	**698**	**10.7**	2.73	**117**	.243	.300	47	**69**	105	182	*142*	.967	212	47	111	2.0	**7.4**	-10.5		11.1
PIT	88	16	88	12	1382.1	1273	36	441	517	11.4	2.79	108	.253	.317	37	33	99	**152**	*149*	**.971**	**182**	40	98	**3.5**	3.6	-11.7		14.2
KC	95	16	75	11	1359.0	**1210**	29	**390**	526	10.8	2.82	103	.242	.301	32	15	96	192	*150*	.962	246	53	96	-.5	1.6	-18.1		21.5
NEW	**100**	16	76	7	1406.2	1308	**15**	453	581	11.6	**2.60**	109	.253	.319	**67**	40	94	154	*150*	.963	239	39	124	.0	4.3	-13.2		12.9
BUF	79	14	97	11	1360.0	1271	35	553	594	12.3	3.38	92	.254	.331	-53	-40	103	234	***166***	.964	232	48	112	.3	-4.3	-18.3		20.3
BRO	78	10	**99**	**16**	1355.2	1299	27	536	467	12.3	3.37	90	.258	.332	-50	-53	100	211	*148*	.955	290	60	103	-3.1	-5.7	**-5.7**		8.6
BAL	85	5	92	7	1360.1	1455	52	466	570	13.0	3.96	81	.284	.349	-140	-111	105	180	*147*	.957	273	**37**	**140**	-2.0	-11.9	-19.5		3.5
TOT	716	122	683	83	11047.2					11.6	3.03		.255	.320						.963	1907	374	886					

Batter-Fielder Wins
Kauff-Bro 4.7
Rariden-New 4.3
Wilson-Chi 2.6
Cooper-Bro..........2.0
Louden-Buf 1.7

Batting Average
Kauff-Bro 342
Fischer-Chi 329
Magee-Bro 323
Konetchy-Pit 314
Flack-Chi 314

On-Base Percentage
Kauff-Bro 446
W.Miller-StL 400
Borton-StL 395
Evans-Bro-Bal 392
Cooper-Bro 388

Slugging Average
Kauff-Bro 509
Konetchy-Pit 483
Chase-Buf 471
Fischer-Chi 449
Zwilling-Chi...........442

On-Base Plus Slugging
Kauff-Bro 955
Konetchy-Pit 846
Evans-Bro-Bal 818
Zwilling-Chi 808
Mann-Chi..............795

Adjusted OPS
Kauff-Bro 170
Konetchy-Pit 138
Zwilling-Chi 135
Mann-Chi..............131
Flack-Chi 129

Adjusted Batter Runs
Kauff-Bro...........43.0
Wilson-Chi..........21.8
Konetchy-Pit 17.9
Zwilling-Chi 17.3
Evans-Bro-Bal 16.1

Runs
Borton-StL..............97
Berghammer-Pit 96
Evans-Bro-Bal 94
Tobin-StL 92
Kauff-Bro 92

Hits
Tobin-StL 184
Konetchy-Pit 181
Evans-Bro-Bal 171
Kauff-Bro 165
Chase-Buf 165

Doubles
Evans-Bro-Bal 34
Zwilling-Chi 32
Konetchy-Pit 31
Chase-Buf.......................31

Triples
Mann-Chi.................19
Konetchy-Pit 18
Kelly-Pit 17
Gilmore-KC 15

Home Runs
Chase-Buf 17
Zwilling-Chi 13
Kauff-Bro 12
Konetchy-Pit 10
Walsh-Bal-StL 9

Total Bases
Konetchy-Pit 278
Chase-Buf 267
Tobin-StL 254
Kauff-Bro 246
Zwilling-Chi 242

Runs Batted In
Zwilling-Chi............94
Konetchy-Pit...........93
Chase-Buf 89
Kauff-Bro 83
Borton-StL 83

Stolen Bases
Kauff-Bro 55
Mowrey-Pit.............40
Kelly-Pit 38
Flack-Chi 37
Magee-Bro.............34

Base Stealing Runs

Fielding Runs-Infield
Doolan-Bal-Chi 31.0
Johnson-StL...............16.4
Louden-Buf 11.8
Perring-KC 10.9
Halt-Bro 5.9

Fielding Runs-Outfield
Kelly-Pit 13.4
Cooper-Bro...........12.4
Kauff-Bro 11.2
Mann-Chi 5.3
Gilmore-KC............5.1

Wins
McConnell-Chi........25
Allen-Pit 23
Davenport-StL 22
Cullop-KC 22

Winning Pct.
McConnell-Chi 714
Brown-Chi............680
Reulbach-New 677
Cullop-KC 667
Plank-StL 656

Complete Games
Davenport-StL 30
Hendrix-Chi 26
Schulz-Buf 25
Allen-Pit 24

Strikeouts
Davenport-StL......229
Schulz-Buf............160
McConnell-Chi......151
Plank-StL..............147

Fewest BB/Game
Plank-StL 1.81
Bender-Bal 1.87
Hearn-Pit 1.90
Cullop-KC 1.99
Quinn-Bal 2.07

Games
Davenport-StL 55
Bedient-Buf....................53
Crandall-StL 51
Johnson-KC 46

Saves
Bedient-Buf 10
Barger-Pit 6
Wiltse-Bro 5

Base Runners/9
Plank-StL 9.02
Davenport-StL 9.19
Brown-Chi............9.90
Anderson-Buf 10.01
Reulbach-New ..10.17

Adjusted Relief Runs

Relief Ranking

Innings Pitched
Davenport-StL ..392.2
Crandall-StL 312.2
Schulz-Buf 309.2
McConnell-Chi ..303.0
Cullop-KC 302.1

Opponents' Avg.
Davenport-StL 215
Plank-StL 218
Brown-Chi.............220
Main-KC 222
Anderson-Buf 222

Opponents' OBP
Plank-StL.....................262
Davenport-StL 268
Brown-Chi 279
Anderson-Buf..............285
Reulbach-New.............287

Earned Run Average
Moseley-New 1.91
Plank-StL 2.08
Brown-Chi............2.09
McConnell-Chi 2.20
Davenport-StL 2.20

Adjusted ERA
Plank-StL...............138
Moseley-New........134
Davenport-StL 131
Brown-Chi 120
Reulbach-New......115

Adjusted Starter Runs
Davenport-StL 28.3
Plank-StL 22.7
Moseley-New 17.3
Reulbach-New 12.2
Brown-Chi............10.7

Pitcher Wins
Plank-StL............3.0
Crandall-StL 2.2
Brown-Chi 1.8
McConnell-Chi ..1.7
Moseley-New 1.3

The Tightest Race Ever

On the field, the season was thrilling. Eddie Plank and Chief Bender escaped from Connie Mack after pitching the A's to the AL pennant a year earlier. Frank Allen of Pittsburgh pitched the first of four FL no-hitters. The Feds also outhomered the two established leagues in 1914–15, clubbing 545 as the NL hit 492 and the AL just 308. Dutch Zwilling, who would hit one career homer against non-FL pitching, smacked 29 in two years as the new league's home run king. Chicago, St. Louis, and Pittsburgh finished the year 1-2-3 as the Whales took the tightest race in major league history by exactly one percentage point; the Rebels were third by only .004.

Walter Johnson was the Whale that got away, even though Chicago Whales player-manager Joe Tinker signed Johnson to a three-year deal worth $58,500. Despite AL President Ban Johnson's assertion that The Big Train was "damaged goods," Washington owner Clark Griffith knew better. Aided by money from other AL clubs, he lured back his prized pitcher and later signed Johnson to a five-year, $80,000 contract, dimming the FL's long-term chances.

In January 1915 the FL sued the other two leagues for violating the Sherman Antitrust Act. They chose the U.S. District Court of Judge Kenesaw Mountain Landis, a noted trustbuster, as the venue. That proved to be as big a mistake as competing against two established leagues in a time of uncertainty because of the war in Europe. Landis, an ardent Cubs fan, effectively killed the Federal League by sitting on the case.

Absent a legal ruling, the competing leagues negotiated a complicated settlement that resulted in FL owners in St. Louis and Chicago buying the Browns and Cubs, bringing into the NL what would become Wrigley Field. The agreement paid off some—but not all—FL owners. FL players could return, but only eight former Feds later appeared in as many as 500 big league games.

1915 National League

TEAM	W	L	T	PCT	GB	HW	HL	R	OR	PA	H	2B	3B	HR	BB	SO	HB	SH	AVG	OBP	SLG	OPS	AOPS	BR	ABR	PF	SB	CS	BSA	BSR
PHI	90	62	1	.592		49	27	589	**463**	5591	1216	202	39	**58**	460	600	181	34	.247	.316	.340	**656**	104	**35**	29	101	121	113	52	-13
BOS	83	69	5	.546	7	49	27	582	545	5869	1219	**231**	57	17	**549**	620	**194**	**56**	.240	**.321**	.319	640	**105**	22	**50**	96	121	98	55	-8
BRO	80	72	2	.526	10	**51**	26	536	560	5635	1268	165	75	14	313	**496**	175	27	.248	.295	.317	612	89	-61	-70	102	131	126	51	-15
CHI	73	80	3	.477	17.5	42	34	570	620	5730	1246	212	66	53	393	639	182	41	.244	.303	**.342**	645	102	5	4	100	166	124	57	-7
PIT	73	81	2	.474	18	40	37	557	520	5743	1259	197	91	24	419	656	162	49	.246	.309	.334	643	102	7	15	99	**182**	111	**62**	**1**
STL	72	81	4	.471	18.5	42	36	**590**	601	5780	1297	159	**92**	20	457	658	175	42	**.254**	.320	.333	653	104	28	27	100	162	144	53	-15
CIN	71	83	6	.461	20	39	37	516	585	5836	**1323**	194	84	15	360	512	192	53	.253	.308	.331	639	98	-7	-17	102	156	142	52	-15
NY	69	83	3	.454	21	37	38	582	628	5703	1312	195	68	24	315	547	122	48	.251	.300	.329	629	103	-28	5	94	155	137	53	-14
TOT	624					349	262	4522		45887	10140	1555	572	225	3266	4728	350	1383	.248	.309	.331	640					1194	995	55	-86

TEAM	CG	SHO	GR	SV	IP	H	HR	BB	SO	BR/9	ERA	AERA	OAV	OOB	PR	APR	PF	OSB	OCS	FA	E	WPB	DP	FW	PW	BW	BSW	DIF
PHI	**98**	**20**	67	8	1374.1	**1161**	26	342	652	**10.0**	**2.17**	**126**	**.234**	**.288**	**87**	**85**	100	134	*117*	**.966**	216	33	99	.8	**9.4**	3.2	-.3	.8
BOS	95	17	78	**13**	1405.2	1257	23	366	630	10.7	2.57	100	.246	.302	27	1	94	**110**	*124*	**.966**	**213**	34	115	**1.4**	.1	**5.6**	.3	-.4
BRO	87	16	91	8	1389.2	1252	29	473	499	11.6	2.66	104	.245	.318	14	17	101	172	*124*	.963	238	49	96	-.5	1.9	-7.8	-.5	10.9
CHI	71	18	**119**	8	1399.0	1272	28	480	**657**	11.6	3.11	89	.247	.316	-57	-54	101	151	***130***	.958	268	58	94	-2.3	-6.0	.4	.4	4.0
PIT	91	18	91	11	1380.0	1229	**21**	384	544	10.8	2.60	105	.246	.304	23	19	99	164	*126*	**.966**	214	**31**	100	1.2	2.1	1.7	**1.3**	-10.3
STL	79	13	103	9	1400.2	1320	30	402	538	11.3	2.89	96	.256	.314	-22	-17	101	133	*129*	.964	235	34	109	-.0	-1.9	3.0	-.5	-5.1
CIN	80	19	113	12	1432.1	1304	28	497	572	11.6	2.84	101	.250	.321	-15	1	104	163	*125*	**.966**	222	36	**148**	1.1	.1	-1.9	-.5	-4.9
NY	78	15	105	9	1385.0	1350	40	**325**	637	11.2	3.11	82	.260	.308	-57	-92	93	167	*120*	.960	256	56	119	-1.6	-10.2	.6	-.4	4.7
TOT	679	136	767	78	11166.2					11.1	2.75		.248	.309						.964	1862	331	880					

Batter-Fielder Wins	Batting Average	On-Base Percentage	Slugging Average	On-Base Plus Slugging	Adjusted OPS	Adjusted Batter Runs
Cravath-Phi 5.2	Doyle-NY 320	Cravath-Phi 393	Cravath-Phi..........510	Cravath-Phi 902	Cravath-Phi 170	Cravath-Phi 47.3
Luderus-Phi 4.0	Luderus-Phi 315	Luderus-Phi 376	Luderus-Phi 457	Luderus-Phi..........833	Doyle-NY 150	Doyle-NY............33.6
Herzog-Cin 4.0	Griffith-Cin 307	Daubert-Bro................369	Long-StL...............446	Hinchman-Pit........807	Luderus-Phi..........150	Hinchman-Pit.....31.6
Snyder-StL 3.8	Hinchman-Pit 307	Hinchman-Pit..............368	Saier-Chi...............445	Doyle-NY 799	Hinchman-Pit........146	Luderus-Phi........30.7
Fletcher-NY 3.3	Daubert-Bro 301	Doyle-NY 358	Doyle-NY 442	Saier-Chi 795	Saier-Chi 140	Saier-Chi 24.7

Runs	Hits	Doubles	Triples	Home Runs	Total Bases	Runs Batted In
Cravath-Phi 89	Doyle-NY 189	Doyle-NY 40	Long-StL 25	Cravath-Phi 24	Cravath-Phi 266	Cravath-Phi 115
Doyle-NY 86	Griffith-Cin 179	Luderus-Phi 36	H.Wagner-Pit..........17	Williams-Chi 13	Doyle-NY...............261	Magee-Bos............87
Bancroft-Phi............85	Hinchman-Pit........177	Saier-Chi.......................35	Griffith-Cin 16	Schulte-Chi 12	Griffith-Cin 254	Griffith-Cin 85
Burns-NY................83	Groh-Cin 170	Smith-Bos 34	Hinchman-Pit..........14	Saier-Chi 11	Hinchman-Pit.........253	H.Wagner-Pit 78
O'Mara-Bro 77	Burns-NY..............169	Magee-Bos 34	Burns-NY................14	Becker-Phi..............11	H.Wagner-Pit.........239	Hinchman-Pit 77

Stolen Bases	Base Stealing Runs	Fielding Runs-Infield	Fielding Runs-Outfield	Wins	Winning Pct.	Complete Games
Carey-Pit 36	Saier-Chi................3.2	Fletcher-NY 34.8	Carey-Pit.............11.1	Alexander-Phi 31	Alexander-Phi........756	Alexander-Phi........36
Herzog-Cin 35	Bresnahan-Chi 3.1	Herzog-Cin 30.3	Wilson-StL 10.6	Rudolph-Bos 22	Toney-Cin 739	Rudolph-Bos..........30
Saier-Chi 29	Baird-Pit 2.2	Maranville-Bos 20.0	Z.Wheat-Bro..........9.1	Mayer-Phi 21	Mamaux-Pit 724	Pfeffer-Bro 26
Baird-Pit..................29	Herzog-Cin 2.1	Cutshaw-Bro 13.8	Cravath-Phi............8.7	Mamaux-Pit 21	Vaughn-Chi...........625	Harmon-Pit............25
Cutshaw-Bro 28	Carey-Pit................2.0	Groh-Cin 11.6	Magee-Bos............6.3	Vaughn-Chi 20	Coombs-Bro 600	Tesreau-NY 24

Strikeouts	Fewest BB/Game	Games	Saves	Base Runners/9	Adjusted Relief Runs	Relief Ranking
Alexander-Phi 241	Mathewson-NY.......97	Hughes-Bos 50	Hughes-Bos.............9	Alexander-Phi......7.82		
Tesreau-NY 176	Humphries-Chi 1.21	Dale-Cin 49	Benton-Cin-NY 5	Hughes-Bos 8.89		
Hughes-Bos..........171	Adams-Pit............1.25	Alexander-Phi 49	Lavender-Chi 4	Tesreau-NY.........9.26		
Mamaux-Pit 152	Alexander-Phi......1.53	Schneider-Cin...............48	Cooper-Pit 4	Toney-Cin 9.54		
Vaughn-Chi 148	Rudolph-Bos.........1.69	Sallee-StL......................46		Nehf-Bos 9.65		

Innings Pitched	Opponents' Avg.	Opponents' OBP	Earned Run Average	Adjusted ERA	Adjusted Starter Runs	Pitcher Wins
Alexander-Phi....376.1	Alexander-Phi.......191	Alexander-Phi 234	Alexander-Phi......1.22	Alexander-Phi 224	Alexander-Phi......58.3	**Alexander-Phi**.......7.5
Rudolph-Bos......341.1	Toney-Cin 207	Hughes-Bos..................265	Toney-Cin 1.58	Toney-Cin 181	Toney-Cin 32.1	**Toney-Cin** 3.0
Tesreau-NY........306.0	Mamaux-Pit 208	Tesreau-NY 269	Mamaux-Pit 2.04	Mamaux-Pit 134	Pfeffer-Bro 21.6	**Pfeffer-Bro** 2.9
Dale-Cin 296.2	Hughes-Bos 213	Toney-Cin.....................278	Pfeffer-Bro 2.10	Pfeffer-Bro 132	Mamaux-Pit 21.1	**Mayer-Phi** 2.5
Pfeffer-Bro 291.2	Tesreau-NY..........215	Adams-Pit 280	Hughes-Bos 2.12	Hughes-Bos..........122	Hughes-Bos 16.0	**Mamaux-Pit**........2.0

Alexander the Greatest

With Grover Cleveland Alexander dominating on the hill, the Phillies found themselves in first place in mid-July. Withstanding challenges from Boston and Brooklyn down the stretch, Philadelphia won the pennant by 7 games. Playing in a great home run park, the Phillies again paced the league in long balls; Gavvy Cravath slugged an unheard-of 24. Amazingly, pitching half his games in the Baker Bowl, Alexander allowed just *three* taters in 376 innings and posted a 1.22 ERA, the best mark in the majors until 1968.

The level of parity between NL teams was even greater in 1915. Pitchers had made adjustments to the lively ball, and the NL's average continued its drop to .248, the lowest since 1909. Only 21 games separated Philadelphia from last-place New York. The Giants' ignominious tumble to the basement was hell on manager John McGraw and veteran pitcher Christy Mathewson; again Matty was the league's stingiest pitcher with walks, but an 8–14 record marked his last full season. Meanwhile, sixth-place St. Louis saw a flash of better times ahead with the debut of infielder Rogers Hornsby.

Overall league attendance rose 42 percent, with gains of over 100 percent in Brooklyn, Philadelphia, and—surprisingly—seventh-place Cincinnati. Defending world champion Boston finished second, but attendance began a four-year decline just as the club opened cavernous Braves Field (the center-field fence was 550 feet from home plate). Across town, the AL's Red Sox capped off a big year by edging the Phillies in a five-game World Series in which four of the games were settled by one run and the other by two.

Two teammates from the NL's first Chicago club died. Pitcher and sporting goods entrepreneur Al Spalding passed away in San Diego at age 65. Ross Barnes, the National League's inaugural batting champion in 1876, died in Chicago.

1915 American League

TEAM	W	L	T	PCT	GB	HW	HL	R	OR	PA	H	2B	3B	HR	BB	SO	HB	SH	AVG	OBP	SLG	OPS	AOPS	BR	ABR	PF	SB	CS	BSA	BSR
BOS	101	50	4	.669		**55**	20	669	499	5865	1308	202	76	14	527	**476**	265	49	.260	.336	.339	675	110	48	69	97	118	117	50	-15
DET	100	54	2	.649	2.5	51	26	**778**	597	6046	**1372**	**207**	94	23	**681**	527	202	35	**.268**	**.357**	**.358**	**715**	**114**	**135**	**98**	105	**241**	146	62	2
CHI	93	61	1	.604	9.5	54	24	717	509	5838	1269	163	**102**	**25**	583	575	**270**	**71**	.258	.345	.348	693	110	82	62	103	233	183	56	-13
WAS	85	68	2	.556	17	50	29	569	**491**	5719	1225	152	79	12	458	541	187	45	.244	.312	.312	624	90	-55	-65	102	186	106	**64**	**4**
NY	69	83	2	.454	32.5	37	43	584	588	5765	1162	167	50	31	570	669	169	44	.233	.317	.305	622	91	-45	-44	100	198	133	60	-3
STL	63	91	5	.409	39.5	35	38	522	680	5800	1255	166	65	19	472	765	173	43	.246	.315	.315	630	98	-46	-23	96	202	160	56	-12
CLE	57	95	2	.375	44.5	27	50	539	670	5738	1210	169	79	20	490	681	177	37	.240	.312	.317	629	91	-45	-55	102	138	117	54	-11
PHI	43	109	2	.283	58.5	19	53	545	889	5708	1204	183	72	16	436	634	137	54	.237	.304	.311	615	92	-75	-56	97	127	89	59	-3
TOT	621					328	283	4923		46479	10005	1409	617	160	4217	4868	378	1580	.248	.325	.326	651					1443	1051	58	-50

TEAM	CG	SHO	GR	SV	IP	H	HR	BB	SO	BR/9	ERA	AERA	OAV	OOB	PR	APR	PF	OSB	OCS	FA	E	WPB	DP	FW	PW	BW	BSW	DIF
BOS	81	19	99	15	1397.0	1164	18	446	634	10.7	2.39	116	**.231**	.300	84	62	95	157	*125*	.964	226	51	95	2.5	6.6	7.3	-.9	10.1
DET	86	10	109	**19**	1413.1	1259	14	492	550	11.5	2.86	106	.243	.316	11	24	103	179	*121*	.961	258	62	107	.5	2.5	**10.4**	.9	8.7
CHI	91	16	91	9	1401.0	1242	14	**350**	635	**10.4**	2.43	122	.241	**.294**	78	83	101	**101**	*100*	.965	222	**38**	95	2.7	8.8	6.6	-.7	-1.4
WAS	87	**21**	99	13	1393.2	**1161**	**12**	455	**715**	10.7	**2.31**	**129**	.232	.302	**97**	**101**	101	156	*123*	.964	230	50	101	2.2	**10.7**	-6.9	**1.1**	1.4
NY	**101**	12	66	1	1382.2	1272	41	517	559	12.0	3.06	96	.254	.329	-20	-20	100	188	*131*	**.966**	**217**	**38**	118	**2.9**	-2.1	-4.7	.4	-3.5
STL	76	6	131	6	1403.0	1256	21	612	566	12.4	3.04	94	.249	.338	-17	-32	98	196	*141*	.949	336	69	**144**	-4.3	-3.4	-2.4	-.6	-3.2
CLE	62	11	**138**	10	1372.0	1287	18	518	610	12.0	3.13	97	.256	.329	-30	-13	104	170	*135*	.957	280	54	82	-1.2	-1.4	-5.8	-.5	-10.1
PHI	78	6	95	2	1348.1	1358	22	827	588	15.0	4.29	68	.278	.388	-204	-207	100	295	***175***	.947	338	85	118	-5.0	-22.0	-5.9	.4	-.4
TOT	662	101	828	75	11111.0					11.8	2.93		.248	.325						.959	2107	447	860					

Batter-Fielder Wins	Batting Average	On-Base Percentage	Slugging Average	On-Base Plus Slugging	Adjusted OPS	Adjusted Batter Runs
E.Collins-Chi 6.6	Cobb-Det 369	Cobb-Det 486	Fournier-Chi 491	Cobb-Det 973	Cobb-Det 182	Cobb-Det 66.6
Cobb-Det 5.7	E.Collins-Chi.........332	E.Collins-Chi 460	Cobb-Det 487	Fournier-Chi..........920	Fournier-Chi..........170	E.Collins-Chi 49.8
Speaker-Bos 3.6	Fournier-Chi 322	Fournier-Chi................429	Kavanagh-Det.......452	E.Collins-Chi 896	E.Collins-Chi 163	Speaker-Bos 39.2
Fournier-Chi........3.6	Speaker-Bos..........322	Speaker-Bos 416	J.Jackson-Cle-Chi ...445	J.Jackson-Cle-Chi 830	Speaker-Bos 152	Fournier-Chi 38.4
Chapman-Cle......3.4	McInnis-Phi...........314	Shotton-StL 409	Roth-Chi-Cle.........438	Speaker-Bos 827	J.Jackson-Cle-Chi 145	Shotton-StL 32.3

Runs	Hits	Doubles	Triples	Home Runs	Total Bases	Runs Batted In
Cobb-Det..............144	Cobb-Det..............208	Veach-Det.....................40	Crawford-Det..........19	Roth-Chi-Cle 7	Cobb-Det..............274	Veach-Det............112
E.Collins-Chi 118	Crawford-Det 183	Pratt-StL 31	Fournier-Chi...........18	Oldring-Phi 6	Crawford-Det........264	Crawford-Det 112
Vitt-Det..................116	Veach-Det 178	Lewis-Bos 31	Roth-Chi-Cle 17		Veach-Det 247	Cobb-Det 99
Speaker-Bos 108	Speaker-Bos 176	Crawford-Det 31	S.Collins-Chi 17		Pratt-StL 237	S.Collins-Chi..........85
Chapman-Cle 101	Pratt-StL 175	Cobb-Det 31	Chapman-Cle 17		E.Collins-Chi 227	J.Jackson-Cle-Chi 81

Stolen Bases	Base Stealing Runs	Fielding Runs-Infield	Fielding Runs-Outfield	Wins	Winning Pct.	Complete Games
Cobb-Det................96	Cobb-Det 7.8	Boone-NY 20.5	Strunk-Phi............11.1	Johnson-Was..........27	Wood-Bos.............750	Johnson-Was 35
Maisel-NY 51	Maisel-NY..............7.0	Lajoie-Phi...................17.0	Hooper-Bos 8.7	Scott-Chi 24	Shore-Bos 704	Caldwell-NY 31
E.Collins-Chi 46	Moeller-Was 3.5	Pratt-StL 16.0	T.Walker-StL 8.5	Faber-Chi................24	Foster-Bos 704	Dauss-Det 27
Shotton-StL 43	Schang-Phi............2.9	Vitt-Det.......................12.9	Speaker-Bos 7.8	Dauss-Det 24	Ruth-Bos...............692	Scott-Chi 23
C.Milan-Was 40	Chapman-Cle 2.7	E.Collins-Chi 11.3	Shanks-Was 6.6	Coveleski-Det 22	Scott-Chi..............686	Dubuc-Det 22

Strikeouts	Fewest BB/Game	Games	Saves	Base Runners/9	Adjusted Relief Runs	Relief Ranking
Johnson-Was........203	Johnson-Was 1.50	Faber-Chi 50	Mays-Bos..................7	Johnson-Was 8.90		
Faber-Chi..............182	Ayers-Was 1.62	Coveleski-Det 50		Morton-Cle 9.41		
Wyckoff-Phi 157	Benz-Chi..............1.62	Scott-Chi........................48		Wood-Bos.............9.44		
Coveleski-Det 150	Russell-Chi 1.84	Jones-Cle 48		Ayers-Was 9.50		
Mitchell-Cle 149	Cicotte-Chi 1.93			Benz-Chi..............9.63		

Innings Pitched	Opponents' Avg.	Opponents' OBP	Earned Run Average	Adjusted ERA	Adjusted Starter Runs	Pitcher Wins
Johnson-Was 336.2	Leonard-Bos.........208	Johnson-Was...............260	Wood-Bos............1.49	Johnson-Was........191	Johnson-Was 51.1	**Johnson-Was** 7.4
Coveleski-Det 312.2	Ruth-Bos...............212	Morton-Cle...................268	Johnson-Was 1.55	Wood-Bos 186	Scott-Chi..............27.6	**Wood-Bos** 3.9
Dauss-Det 309.2	Johnson-Was 214	Wood-Bos 275	Shore-Bos 1.64	Shore-Bos 169	Shore-Bos 27.2	**Scott-Chi** 2.9
Caldwell-NY 305.0	Morton-Cle 216	Benz-Chi.......................276	Scott-Chi.............2.03	Scott-Chi 146	Morton-Cle 25.0	**Foster-Bos**..........2.9
Faber-Chi 299.2	Wood-Bos.............216	Ayers-Was 276	Fisher-NY 2.11	Morton-Cle 142	Wood-Bos............24.9	**Ruth-Bos** 2.8

What Curse?

All season, the Red Sox and Tigers chased the flag together. For Boston, Smokey Joe Wood paced the league with a 1.49 ERA, while Babe Ruth was 18–6 and also hit .315. Peerless center fielder Tris Speaker served as the offense's one-man wrecking crew. Detroit's Sam Crawford, Bobby Veach, and Ty Cobb—who swiped 96 bases, establishing a big-league record that held until 1962—comprised the league's best outfield, an aggregation that helped make up for a very mediocre Tigers infield.

Chicago finished third, with newly acquired second baseman Eddie Collins enjoying another great season. His former team, the Athletics, declined an unprecedented 56 games from their 1914 performance, landing ignominiously in the AL basement. The club's attendance dropped 58 percent. While Mack divested himself of his talent, third sacker Frank Baker chose to hold out all year. Using a staggering 56 players in 1915, trying futilely to replace his formerly great team, Mack's club became the laughing-stock of baseball and would finish last for the next *seven years*.

Walter Johnson's best efforts (he led the league in wins, strikeouts, and ERA) couldn't bring the Senators in above fourth, but Washington did give future Hall of Famer Sam Rice his first big-league action. Wally Pipp started his first season as New York's regular first baseman, a position he held for a decade until a headache forced him to sit out an afternoon in favor of Lou Gehrig.

The Red Sox held the cards in 1915. Rookie Carl Mays led the league with 7 saves, heading up a superb set of second-line pitchers who gave Boston much more mound depth that Detroit. The Tigers wound up 2½ games back despite winning 100 games. Boston took on the NL's surprise champions, the Phillies, in the World Series. After Philadelphia's opening victory, the Red Sox won four straight one-run contests, three times scoring the deciding run in the ninth inning. Harry Hooper hit .350 with 2 home runs for the Red Sox.

1916 National League

TEAM	W	L	T	PCT	GB	HW	HL	R	OR	PA	H	2B	3B	HR	BB	SO	HB	SH	AVG	OBP	SLG	OPS	AOPS	BR	ABR	PF	SB	CS	BSA	BSR
BRO	94	60	2	.610		**50**	27	585	471	5833	**1366**	195	**80**	28	355	**550**	**203**	41	**.261**	**.313**	**.345**	**658**	105	**46**	30	103	187			
PHI	91	62	1	.595	2.5	**50**	29	581	489	5597	1244	**223**	53	**42**	399	571	179	34	.250	.310	.341	651	102	39	19	104	149			
BOS	89	63	6	.586	4	41	31	542	**453**	5760	1181	166	73	22	**437**	646	202	**46**	.233	.299	.307	606	96	-38	-15	96	141			
NY	86	66	3	.566	7	47	30	**597**	504	5686	1305	188	74	**42**	356	558	134	44	.253	.307	.343	650	**112**	31	**63**	95	**206**			
CHI	67	86	3	.438	26.5	37	41	520	541	5778	1237	194	56	46	399	662	166	34	.239	.298	.325	623	88	-15	-66	111	133			
PIT	65	89	3	.422	29	37	40	484	586	5769	1246	147	91	20	372	618	166	50	.240	.298	.316	614	94	-36	-41	101	173			
STL	60	93	0	.392	33.5	36	40	476	629	5514	1223	155	74	25	335	651	116	33	.243	.295	.318	613	95	-38	-35	99	182			
CIN	60	93	2	.392	33.5	32	44	505	617	5783	1336	187	88	14	362	573	127	40	.254	.307	.331	638	105	11	25	98	157			
TOT	622					330	282	4290		45720	10138	1455	589	239	3015	4829	322	1293	.247	.303	.328	632					1328			

TEAM	CG	SHO	GR	SV	IP	H	HR	BB	SO	BR/9	ERA	AERA	OAV	OOB	PR	APR	PF	OSB	OCS	FA	E	WPB	DP	FW	PW	BW	BSW	DIF
BRO	96	22	92	9	1427.1	**1201**	**24**	372	634	10.2	**2.12**	**126**	**.232**	.289	**78**	**84**	102	162	119	.965	224	53	90	1.2	**9.6**	3.4		2.7
PHI	**97**	**25**	78	9	1382.1	1238	28	**295**	601	10.3	2.36	112	.244	.292	39	43	101	153	117	.963	234	60	119	.4	4.9	2.2		7.0
BOS	**97**	23	82	11	1415.2	1206	**24**	325	**644**	**9.9**	2.19	113	.235	**.285**	66	47	95	**100**	119	**.967**	**212**	**40**	124	**2.1**	5.4	-1.7		7.2
NY	88	22	103	12	1397.1	1267	41	310	638	10.4	2.60	93	.245	.293	2	-30	93	142	98	.966	217	55	108	1.5	-3.4	**7.2**		4.7
CHI	72	17	119	13	1416.2	1265	32	365	616	10.6	2.65	110	.244	.298	-6	35	111	177	134	.957	286	57	104	-2.6	4.0	-7.5		-3.4
PIT	88	11	102	7	1419.2	1277	**24**	443	596	11.1	2.76	97	.247	.311	-24	-14	103	192	142	.959	260	**40**	97	-.9	-1.6	-4.7		-4.8
STL	58	13	**127**	**15**	1355.0	1331	31	445	529	12.1	3.14	84	.265	.330	-80	-76	101	192	137	.957	278	51	124	-2.4	-8.7	-4.0		-1.4
CIN	86	7	98	6	1408.0	1356	35	461	569	11.9	3.10	84	.261	.326	-76	-82	99	210	**159**	.965	228	48	**126**	.9	-9.4	2.9		-10.9
TOT	682	140	801	82	11222.0					10.8	2.61		.247	.303						.963	1939	404	892					

Batter-Fielder Wins	Batting Average	On-Base Percentage	Slugging Average	On-Base Plus Slugging	Adjusted OPS	Adjusted Batter Runs
Groh-Cin 4.8	Chase-Cin .339	Cravath-Phi .379	Z.Wheat-Bro .461	Williams-Chi .831	Chase-Cin 155	Z.Wheat-Bro 32.6
Fletcher-NY 4.7	Daubert-Bro .316	Hinchman-Pit .378	Chase-Cin .459	Z.Wheat-Bro .828	Hornsby-StL 150	Chase-Cin 32.3
Doyle-NY-Chi 3.8	Hinchman-Pit .315	Williams-Chi .372	Williams-Chi .459	Chase-Cin .822	Z.Wheat-Bro 149	Hinchman-Pit 29.9
Hornsby-StL 3.7	Hornsby-StL .313	Daubert-Bro .371	Hornsby-StL .444	Cravath-Phi .819	Cravath-Phi 146	Hornsby-StL 28.2
Z.Wheat-Bro 3.6	Z.Wheat-Bro .312	Groh-Cin .370	Cravath-Phi .440	Hornsby-StL .814	Hinchman-Pit 146	Cravath-Phi 26.8

Runs	Hits	Doubles	Triples	Home Runs	Total Bases	Runs Batted In
Burns-NY 105	Chase-Cin 184	Niehoff-Phi 42	Hinchman-Pit 16	Williams-Chi 12	Z.Wheat-Bro 262	Zimmerman-Chi-NY 83
Carey-Pit 90	Robertson-NY 180	Z.Wheat-Bro 32	Roush-NY-Cin 15	Robertson-NY 12	Robertson-NY 250	Chase-Cin 82
Robertson-NY 88	Z.Wheat-Bro 177	Paskert-Phi 30	Kauff-NY 15	Cravath-Phi 11	Chase-Cin 249	Hinchman-Pit 76
Groh-Cin 85	Hinchman-Pit 175		Hornsby-StL 15	Z.Wheat-Bro 9	Hinchman-Pit 237	Kauff-NY 74
Paskert-Phi 82	Burns-NY 174			Kauff-NY 9	Burns-NY 229	Z.Wheat-Bro 73

Stolen Bases	Base Stealing Runs	Fielding Runs-Infield	Fielding Runs-Outfield	Wins	Winning Pct.	Complete Games
Carey-Pit 63	Carey-Pit 7.2	Betzel-StL 29.4	Carey-Pit 21.9	Alexander-Phi 33	Hughes-Bos .842	Alexander-Phi 38
Kauff-NY 40	Bescher-StL 4.4	Bancroft-Phi 25.3	Snodgrass-Bos 8.9	Pfeffer-Bro 25	Alexander-Phi .733	Pfeffer-Bro 30
Bescher-StL 39	Daubert-Bro 2.2	Maranville-Bos 23.3	Neale-Cin 6.6	Rixey-Phi 22	Pfeffer-Bro .694	Rudolph-Bos 27
Burns-NY 37	Maranville-Bos 1.8	Fletcher-NY 21.6	Z.Wheat-Bro 6.2	Mamaux-Pit 21	Rixey-Phi .688	Mamaux-Pit 26
Herzog-Cin-NY 34	Chase-Cin 1.0	Doyle-NY-Chi 18.0	Stengel-Bro 4.8		Benton-NY .667	Demaree-Phi 25

Strikeouts	Fewest BB/Game	Games	Saves	Base Runners/9	Adjusted Relief Runs	Relief Ranking
Alexander-Phi 167	Rudolph-Bos 1.10	Meadows-StL 51	Ames-StL 8	Schupp-NY 7.76		
Cheney-Bro 166	Alexander-Phi 1.16	Alexander-Phi 48	Packard-Chi 5	Rudolph-Bos 8.86		
Mamaux-Pit 163	Demaree-Phi 1.52	Mamaux-Pit 45	Marquard-Bro 5	Alexander-Phi 8.86		
Toney-Cin 146	Sallee-StL-NY 1.63	Ames-StL 45	Hughes-Bos 5	Prendergast-Chi 8.94		
Vaughn-Chi 144	Marquard-Bro 1.67			Marquard-Bro 9.09		

Innings Pitched	Opponents' Avg.	Opponents' OBP	Earned Run Average	Adjusted ERA	Adjusted Starter Runs	Pitcher Wins
Alexander-Phi 389.0	Cheney-Bro .198	Rudolph-Bos .261	Alexander-Phi 1.55	Alexander-Phi 171	Alexander-Phi 47.0	**Alexander-Phi** 7.2
Pfeffer-Bro 328.2	Cooper-Pit .215	Alexander-Phi .262	Marquard-Bro 1.58	Marquard-Bro 169	Pfeffer-Bro 29.5	**Pfeffer-Bro** 4.1
Rudolph-Bos 312.0	Hughes-Bos .215	Marquard-Bro .267	Rixey-Phi 1.85	Cooper-Pit 144	Schupp-NY 23.7	**Rixey-Phi** 2.5
Mamaux-Pit 310.0	Ragan-Bos .218	Ragan-Bos .270	Cooper-Pit 1.87	Rixey-Phi 143	Marquard-Bro 23.1	**Tyler-Bos** 2.3
Toney-Cin 300.0	McConnell-Chi .223	McConnell-Chi .271	Pfeffer-Bro 1.92	Pfeffer-Bro 140	Rixey-Phi 21.0	**Cooper-Pit** 2.1

Ebbets Field's First Champeens

Offense continued its free fall as runs dropped for the fourth straight year. The average club tallied just 3.45 runs per game, the league's lowest total until 1968. The Federal League's demise meant fewer jobs for more players, and—as a result—lower salaries (and bigger profits) for the owners. The Cubs moved from West Side Grounds to Weeghman Park, and their attendance rose 109 percent.

Cy Williams led the NL in homers for first of four times, while the Pirates gave rookie Burleigh Grimes his first major league action; the right-hander lasted until 1934 and was the last to legally throw a spitball. The end of an era came on September 4, 1916: Three-Finger Brown, bowing out with the Cubs, and Christy Mathewson, now manager of Cincinnati, hooked up for their 25th and final duel. Matty's win gave each pitcher 12 wins against the other. It was the final big league game for both.

Grover Cleveland Alexander was the new breed. His 16 shutouts in '16 remain an all-time record and his 33 wins have not been matched since. "Alex" also paced the NL in strikeouts for the fourth time in five years. His 389 innings were 60 more than anyone else.

Alexander's Phillies opened September in a three-way race with Brooklyn and Boston. While the three clubs remained neck-and-neck into the last week, it was the Robins, so dubbed because of third-year manager Wilbert Robinson, who came out ahead. Philadelphia and Boston knocked each other out of the running. The late-charging Giants, who won a league-record 26 straight, fell just short in fourth.

This was big news for Brooklyn, which had spent most of the century as a league doormat. The Robins did it with balanced pitching and hitting. They had few stars (save Zack Wheat) but no weaknesses, and Jeff Pfeffer was arguably the league's second-best pitcher. In the World Series, however, the NL lost again as the Red Sox knocked out Brooklyn in five games.

1916 American League

TEAM	W	L	T	PCT	GB	HW	HL	R	OR	PA	H	2B	3B	HR	BB	SO	HB	SH	AVG	OBP	SLG	OPS	AOPS	BR	ABR	PF	SB	CS	BSA	BSR
BOS	91	63	2	.591		**49**	28	550	**480**	5758	1246	197	56	14	464	**482**	**238**	38	.248	.317	.318	635	97	-20	-22	100	129			
CHI	89	65	1	.578	2	**49**	28	601	497	5809	1277	194	**100**	17	447	591	221	**60**	.251	.319	.339	658	103	15	9	101	197			
DET	87	67	1	.565	4	**49**	28	**670**	595	5969	**1371**	202	96	17	545	529	202	29	**.264**	**.337**	**.350**	**687**	**109**	**78**	**56**	104	190			
NY	80	74	2	.519	11	46	31	577	561	5905	1277	194	59	**35**	516	632	155	36	.246	.318	.326	644	98	-4	-16	102	179			
STL	79	75	4	.513	12	45	32	588	545	5987	1262	181	50	14	**626**	638	164	42	.245	.331	.307	638	103	5	35	95	**234**			
CLE	77	77	3	.500	14	44	33	630	602	5853	1264	**233**	66	16	522	605	234	33	.250	.324	.331	655	97	21	-12	106	160			
WAS	76	77	6	.497	14.5	**49**	28	536	543	5864	1238	170	60	12	535	597	165	50	.242	.320	.306	626	95	-30	-24	99	185			
PHI	36	117	1	.235	54.5	23	53	447	776	5604	1212	169	65	19	406	631	158	30	.242	.303	.313	616	96	-65	-40	95	151			
TOT	625					354	261	4599		46749	10147	1540	552	144	4061	4705	318	1537	.248	.321	.324	645					1425			

TEAM	CG	SHO	GR	SV	IP	H	HR	BB	SO	BR/9	ERA	AERA	OAV	OOB	PR	APR	PF	OSB	OCS	FA	E	WPB	DP	FW	PW	BW	BSW	DIF
BOS	76	**24**	103	16	1410.2	1221	**10**	463	584	11.0	2.48	112	.239	.307	55	45	98	134	124	**.972**	**183**	40	108	**3.0**	5.0	-2.4		8.4
CHI	73	20	140	15	1412.1	**1189**	14	**405**	644	**10.3**	**2.36**	**117**	**.236**	**.296**	**72**	**63**	98	**113**	118	.968	205	**28**	**134**	1.5	**7.0**	1.0		2.5
DET	81	8	126	13	1410.0	1254	12	578	531	12.1	2.97	96	.248	.333	-23	-18	101	202	113	.968	211	50	110	1.1	-2.0	**6.2**		4.6
NY	84	12	102	**17**	1428.0	1249	37	476	616	11.2	2.77	104	.244	.314	8	17	102	135	160	.967	219	32	119	.7	1.9	-1.8		2.2
STL	74	9	**141**	13	1443.2	1292	15	478	505	11.3	2.58	106	.248	.316	39	27	97	210	114	.963	248	38	120	-.9	3.0	3.9		-3.9
CLE	65	9	140	16	1410.0	1383	16	467	537	12.0	2.90	103	.264	.328	-13	15	106	167	123	.965	232	58	130	.0	1.7	-1.3		-.3
WAS	85	11	107	7	1430.2	1271	14	490	**706**	11.3	2.67	104	.244	.314	25	18	99	178	125	.964	232	76	119	.2	2.0	-2.7		-.0
PHI	**94**	11	80	3	1343.2	1311	26	715	575	13.8	3.92	73	.267	.364	-163	-159	101	286	**184**	.951	314	70	126	-5.5	-17.6	-4.4		-13.0
TOT	632	104	939	100	11289.0					11.6	2.82		.248	.321						.965	1844	392	966					

Batter-Fielder Wins	Batting Average	On-Base Percentage	Slugging Average	On-Base Plus Slugging	Adjusted OPS	Adjusted Batter Runs
Speaker-Cle........5.7	Speaker-Cle 386	Speaker-Cle.................470	Speaker-Cle 502	Speaker-Cle..........972	Speaker-Cle..........181	Speaker-Cle 59.5
Cobb-Det 4.6	Cobb-Det 371	Cobb-Det.....................452	Jackson-Chi 495	Cobb-Det..............944	Cobb-Det..............177	Cobb-Det............54.6
Pratt-StL..............4.0	Jackson-Chi 341	E.Collins-Chi 405	Cobb-Det 493	Jackson-Chi..........888	Jackson-Chi..........165	Jackson-Chi........44.0
Jackson-Chi........3.6	Strunk-Phi.............316	Jackson-Chi.................393	Veach-Det.............433	Strunk-Phi 814	Strunk-Phi 152	Strunk-Phi 35.8
Shotton-StL 3.0	Gardner-Bos 308	Strunk-Phi 393	Baker-NY 428	E.Collins-Chi 802	E.Collins-Chi 139	E.Collins-Chi 29.0

Runs	Hits	Doubles	Triples	Home Runs	Total Bases	Runs Batted In
Cobb-Det..............113	Speaker-Cle..........211	Speaker-Cle 41	Jackson-Chi............21	Pipp-NY 12	Jackson-Chi..........293	Pratt-StL 103
Graney-Cle 106	Jackson-Chi..........202	Graney-Cle 41	E.Collins-Chi 17	Baker-NY 10	Speaker-Cle..........274	Pipp-NY 93
Speaker-Cle..........102	Cobb-Det..............201	Jackson-Chi 40	Witt-Phi 15	Schang-Phi 7	Cobb-Det..............267	Veach-Det..............91
Shotton-StL 97	Sisler-StL..............177	Pratt-StL 35	Veach-Det 15	Felsch-Chi 7	Veach-Det 245	Speaker-Cle 79
Veach-Det 92	Shotton-StL 174	Veach-Det......................33				Jackson-Chi 78

Stolen Bases	Base Stealing Runs	Fielding Runs-Infield	Fielding Runs-Outfield	Wins	Winning Pct.	Complete Games
Cobb-Det................68	Cobb-Det 6.6	Lajoie-Phi....................26.7	Milan-Was............14.1	Johnson-Was..........25	Cicotte-Chi 682	Johnson-Was 36
Marsans-StL 46	Hooper-Bos 2.1	Vitt-Det........................26.3	Shanks-Was 13.5	Shawkey-NY 24	Ruth-Bos...............657	Myers-Phi 31
Shotton-StL 41	Schalk-Chi 2.0	Lavan-StL 25.9	Shotton-StL 8.1	Ruth-Bos 23	Coveleski-Det 656	Bush-Phi................25
E.Collins-Chi 40	Roth-Cle 1.5	Pratt-StL 19.6	Speaker-Cle 5.6	Coveleski-Det 21	Faber-Chi 654	Ruth-Bos 23
Speaker-Cle............35	E.Collins-Chi..........1.5	McBride-Was 13.6	Hooper-Bos 5.2	Dauss-Det 19	Shawkey-NY.........632	Coveleski-Det........22

Strikeouts	Fewest BB/Game	Games	Saves	Base Runners/9	Adjusted Relief Runs	Relief Ranking
Johnson-Was........228	Russell-Chi 1.43	Davenport-StL 59	Shawkey-NY 8	Russell-Chi 8.51		
Myers-Phi 182	Cullop-NY.............1.72	Russell-Chi 56	Russell-NY...............6	Benz-Chi..............9.06		
Ruth-Bos 170	Coveleski-Det 1.75	Shawkey-NY 53	Leonard-Bos 6	Johnson-Was 9.28		
Bush-Phi 157	Shore-Bos 1.95	Gallia-Was 49	Cicotte-Chi...............5	Shawkey-NY........9.47		
Harper-Was 149	Johnson-Was 2.00		Bagby-Cle 5	Coveleski-Det 9.77		

Innings Pitched	Opponents' Avg.	Opponents' OBP	Earned Run Average	Adjusted ERA	Adjusted Starter Runs	Pitcher Wins
Johnson-Was 369.2	Ruth-Bos...............201	Russell-Chi 254	Ruth-Bos..............1.75	Ruth-Bos 158	Ruth-Bos..............35.1	**Ruth-Bos** 5.7
Coveleski-Det 324.1	Shawkey-NY.........209	Johnson-Was..............270	Cicotte-Chi 1.78	Cicotte-Chi............155	Johnson-Was 34.9	**Johnson-Was** 5.2
Ruth-Bos............323.2	Cicotte-Chi 218	Shawkey-NY 273	Johnson-Was 1.90	Johnson-Was........147	Coveleski-Det 26.2	**Shawkey-NY** 3.4
Myers-Phi 315.0	Bush-Phi...............219	Ruth-Bos 280	Coveleski-Det 1.97	Coveleski-Det 145	Shawkey-NY........23.6	**Coveleski-Det**....3.1
Davenport-StL ..290.2	Johnson-Was 220	Coveleski-Det 282	Faber-Chi 2.02	Cullop-NY 141	Cicotte-Chi 18.3	**Mays-Bos**............2.8

Ruth Rises to the Occasion

Could Connie Mack's Athletics get worse? At 36–117, they set an AL record for losses and posted the worst team winning percentage of the twentieth century. Philadelphia dropped 20 in a row at one point. So many teams feasted on Philadelphia's misery that seventh-place Washington finished just one game under .500, and the Senators had even been in first place during May. Jack Nabors of the A's beat defending world champion Boston on May 22 for his first major league win; he lost his next 19 decisions and never won again. Nap Lajoie, 41, had an undignified finish to a great career, batting .246 for the pathetic A's.

On the other side of the pennant race, the Red Sox, White Sox, and Tigers clawed at each other into September. Despite trading Tris Speaker and Smokey Joe Wood to Cleveland in salary disputes, Boston held it together. While their attack was below par, Boston's five starters were extremely productive; Babe Ruth led the AL in ERA and shutouts.

Chicago had the better club on paper, featuring Eddie Collins and Joe Jackson, but lacked pitching depth (although Chisox righty Eddie Cicotte, at 15–7, led the loop in winning percentage and his 1.78 ERA was second). Detroit once again rode Ty Cobb's back into contention, as Sam Crawford began to slow up at age 36. Two future stars enjoyed excellent first full seasons. Stan Coveleski was 16–13 for Cleveland, while first baseman George Sisler won hearts in St. Louis. Both the Indians and Browns saw huge attendance gains as they began rebuilding. League attendance rose 42 percent.

Down the stretch, the Red Sox grabbed the flag with seven straight road victories against the White Sox, Tigers, and Indians. Boston was favored to win the World Series against Brooklyn, but after three one-run decisions—including a complete-game, 14-inning, 2-1 victory from Ruth in Game 2—the Red Sox barely led, two games to one. However, the Red Sox knocked out Rube Marquard and Jeff Pfeffer the next two games to repeat as champions.

1917 National League

TEAM	W	L	T	PCT	GB	HW	HL	R	OR	PA	H	2B	3B	HR	BB	SO	HB	SH	AVG	OBP	SLG	OPS	AOPS	BR	ABR	PF	SB	CS	BSA	BSR
NY	98	56	4	.636		**50**	28	**635**	**457**	5787	1360	170	71	**39**	373	533	151	**52**	.261	**.317**	.343	660	113	**50**	70	97	**162**			
PHI	87	65	2	.572	10	46	29	578	500	5725	1262	**225**	60	38	**435**	533	186	20	.248	.310	.339	649	101	35	12	104	109			
STL	82	70	2	.539	15	38	38	531	567	5626	1271	159	93	26	359	652	160	24	.250	.303	.333	636	104	-1	14	97	159			
CIN	78	76	3	.506	20	39	38	601	611	5728	**1385**	196	**100**	26	312	**477**	131	34	**.264**	.309	**.354**	**663**	**114**	46	**72**	96	153			
CHI	74	80	3	.481	24	35	42	552	567	5775	1229	194	67	17	415	599	**202**	23	.239	.299	.313	612	86	-33	-71	108	127			
BOS	72	81	4	.471	25.5	35	42	536	552	5855	1280	169	75	22	427	587	182	45	.246	.309	.320	629	105	-2	32	94	155			
BRO	70	81	5	.464	26.5	36	38	511	559	5776	1299	159	78	25	334	527	162	29	.247	.296	.322	618	93	-35	-49	103	130			
PIT	51	103	3	.331	47	25	53	464	595	5788	1230	160	61	9	399	580	174	46	.238	.298	.298	596	86	-61	-76	103	150			
TOT	625					304	308	4408		46060	10316	1432	605	202	3054	4488	273	134	8.249	.305	.328	633					1145			

TEAM	CG	SHO	GR	SV	IP	H	HR	BB	SO	BR/9	ERA	AERA	OAV	OOB	PR	APR	PF	OSB	OCS	FA	E	WPB	DP	FW	PW	BW	BSW	DIF
NY	92	18	97	**14**	1426.2	**1221**	29	327	551	**9.9**	**2.27**	112	**.234**	**.283**	**69**	45	94	136	*63*	**.968**	**208**	**31**	122	**1.8**	5.1	7.9		6.2
PHI	102	**22**	65	5	1389.0	1258	25	**325**	616	10.5	2.46	**114**	.246	.295	38	**51**	104	125	*109*	.967	212	36	112	1.2	**5.8**	1.4		2.7
STL	66	16	**140**	10	1392.2	1257	29	421	502	11.1	3.03	89	.248	.311	-51	-55	99	**115**	*124*	.967	221	39	**153**	.6	-6.2	1.6		10.0
CIN	94	12	85	6	1397.1	1358	20	402	488	11.5	2.70	97	.260	.317	1	-15	97	159	*116*	.962	247	40	120	-.7	-1.7	**8.1**		-4.8
CHI	79	16	121	9	1404.0	1303	34	374	**654**	10.9	2.62	110	.253	.307	14	38	107	146	*127*	.959	267	63	121	-1.9	4.3	-8.0		2.6
BOS	**103**	21	81	3	1424.2	1309	19	371	593	10.8	2.77	92	.251	.304	-10	-40	94	126	*116*	.966	224	45	122	.7	-4.5	3.6		-4.3
BRO	99	8	81	9	1421.1	1288	32	405	582	11.0	2.78	100	.247	.307	-12	0	103	144	*106*	.962	245	40	102	-.7	.0	-5.5		.7
PIT	84	17	84	6	1417.2	1318	**14**	432	509	11.3	3.01	94	.253	.314	-48	-28	105	194	***129***	.961	251	43	119	-.9	-3.2	-8.6		-13.3
TOT	719	130	754	62	11273.1					10.9	2.70		.249	.305						.964	1875	337	971					

Batter-Fielder Wins	Batting Average	On-Base Percentage	Slugging Average	On-Base Plus Slugging	Adjusted OPS	Adjusted Batter Runs
Hornsby-StL........7.8	Roush-Cin............341	Groh-Cin 385	Hornsby-StL 484	Hornsby-StL 868	Hornsby-StL 170	Hornsby-StL 42.4
Groh-Cin 5.8	Hornsby-StL 327	Hornsby-StL................385	Cravath-Phi..........473	Cravath-Phi 842	Roush-Cin 162	Groh-Cin 39.7
Fletcher-NY 4.5	Z.Wheat-Bro 312	Burns-NY....................380	Roush-Cin.............454	Roush-Cin 833	Cravath-Phi 151	Burns-NY............36.1
Bancroft-Phi........3.6	Kauff-NY..............308	Roush-Cin 379	Z.Wheat-Bro 423	Groh-Cin 796	Groh-Cin 150	Roush-Cin 35.7
Burns-NY 3.5	Groh-Cin...............304	Kauff-NY 379	Burns-NY 412	Burns-NY..............792	Burns-NY..............148	Cravath-Phi 31.8

Runs	Hits	Doubles	Triples	Home Runs	Total Bases	Runs Batted In
Burns-NY.............103	Groh-Cin 182	Groh-Cin 39	Hornsby-StL 17	Robertson-NY 12	Hornsby-StL 253	Zimmerman-NY ..102
Groh-Cin 91	Burns-NY.............180	Merkle-Bro-Chi 31	Cravath-Phi 16	Cravath-Phi 12	Groh-Cin 246	Chase-Cin 86
Kauff-NY 89	Roush-Cin 178	Smith-Bos 31	Chase-Cin 15	Hornsby-StL 8	Burns-NY..............246	Cravath-Phi 83
Hornsby-StL 86	Zimmerman-NY....174	Cravath-Phi.....................29	Roush-Cin 14		Cravath-Phi 238	Stengel-Bro 73
	Carey-Pit 174	Chase-Cin.......................28	Long-StL 14			Luderus-Phi 72

Stolen Bases	Base Stealing Runs	Fielding Runs-Infield	Fielding Runs-Outfield	Wins	Winning Pct.	Complete Games
Carey-Pit 46		Bancroft-Phi...............28.0	Carey-Pit.............21.3	Alexander-Phi 30	Schupp-NY...........750	Alexander-Phi........34
Burns-NY..................40		Fletcher-NY 27.8	Stengel-Bro...........11.3	Toney-Cin 24	Sallee-NY 720	Toney-Cin 31
Kauff-NY 30		Hornsby-StL...............19.0	Williams-Chi 10.8	Vaughn-Chi 23	Perritt-NY 708	Vaughn-Chi 27
Maranville-Bos........27		Shean-Cin 17.4	King-Pit..................7.6	Schupp-NY 21	Alexander-Phi.......698	Barnes-Bos 26
Baird-Pit-StL 26		Miller-StL 17.2	Griffith-Cin 7.0	Schneider-Cin 20	Nehf-Bos 680	Schupp-NY............25

Strikeouts	Fewest BB/Game	Games	Saves	Base Runners/9	Adjusted Relief Runs	Relief Ranking
Alexander-Phi 200	Alexander-Phi......1.30	Douglas-Chi 51	Sallee-NY 4	Anderson-NY 8.78		
Vaughn-Chi 195	Sallee-NY 1.42	Barnes-Bos....................50		Schupp-NY 9.13		
Douglas-Chi..........151	Nehf-Bos 1.50	Schneider-Cin................46		Alexander-Phi 9.23		
Schupp-NY 147	Barnes-Bos..........1.53	Alexander-Phi 45		Nehf-Bos 9.26		
Schneider-Cin 138	Douglas-Chi 1.53	Doak-StL.......................44		Bender-Phi 9.32		

Innings Pitched	Opponents' Avg.	Opponents' OBP	Earned Run Average	Adjusted ERA	Adjusted Starter Runs	Pitcher Wins
Alexander-Phi 388.0	Schupp-NY...........209	Anderson-NY 255	Alexander-Phi......1.83	Anderson-NY 176	Alexander-Phi.......39.3	**Alexander-Phi**....5.4
Toney-Cin 339.2	Anderson-NY 209	Schupp-NY 265	Anderson-NY 1.44	Alexander-Phi 153	Vaughn-Chi..........25.3	**Vaughn-Chi** 3.4
Schneider-Cin....333.2	Nehf-Bos 231	Alexander-Phi 266	Perritt-NY 1.88	Vaughn-Chi 144	Schupp-NY 21.5	**Schupp-NY** 2.2
Cooper-Pit 297.2	Marquard-Bro 232	Nehf-Bos 268	Schupp-NY...........1.95	Perritt-NY..............135	Anderson-NY 18.1	**Rixey-Phi** 1.8
Vaughn-Chi........295.2	Pfeffer-Bro 234	Barnes-Bos 277	Vaughn-Chi..........2.01	Schupp-NY 130	Toney-Cin 16.7	**Cadore-Bro** 1.7

Trouble Looming

The flag drive was never in doubt after June, as the Giants pulled away from the Phillies to win by 10 games. New York outfielder George Burns was the league's only 100-run man, and John McGraw used six quality starters. In Philadelphia, Grover Cleveland Alexander won 30 games for the third straight season, but his team didn't hit much.

Defending champion Brooklyn left the gate slowly and dropped all the way from first to seventh; their attack was too thin to help a decent pitching rotation. The Pirates dropped into the NL cellar for first time in the twentieth century, finishing 47 games from first place. Honus Wagner, a preseason holdout at 43, played his last season and hit just .265. St. Louis finished third, the franchise's best performance since joining the NL in 1892. Their top performer was infielder Rogers Hornsby. A 20-year-old outfielder named Ross Youngs debuted late in the year for the Giants. Room would be made for him in 1918.

In this, the twilight of the Dead Ball Era, even stolen bases fell to their lowest level yet as pitchers continued to deface, scuff, spit on, and otherwise render the baseball unhitable. No NL club had ever led the league with so few steals as New York's 162.

Following two years of gains, league attendance fell; only rejuvenated St. Louis reported an appreciable gain in tickets sold. For the Senior Circuit, at least, the hoped-for gains of the post-Federal League era had not yet materialized, and the coming conflict in Europe would take another bite out of baseball.

The phonograph record was a recent invention, and the World Series' platter was already skipping. Again the AL defeated the Senior Circuit's representative, with the White Sox putting lumps on the Giants' pitchers in a six-game set.

1917 American League

TEAM	W	L	T	PCT	GB	HW	HL	R	OR	PA	H	2B	3B	HR	BB	SO	HB	SH	AVG	OBP	SLG	OPS	AOPS	BR	ABR	PF	SB	CS	BSA	BSR
CHI	100	54	2	.649		**56**	21	**655**	463	5858	1281	152	**81**	18	522	479	232	**47**	.253	**.329**	.326	655	103	34	22	102	**219**			
BOS	90	62	5	.592	9	45	33	555	**455**	5858	1243	198	64	14	466	**473**	**310**	34	.246	.314	.319	633	100	-9	-3	99	105			
CLE	88	66	2	.571	12	43	34	584	543	5840	1224	**218**	64	13	**549**	596	262	35	.245	.324	.322	646	96	25	-16	107	210			
DET	78	75	1	.510	21.5	34	41	639	577	5814	**1317**	204	77	**25**	483	476	193	45	**.259**	.328	**.344**	**672**	**111**	**62**	**65**	100	163			
WAS	74	79	4	.484	25.5	42	36	544	566	5861	1238	173	70	4	500	574	176	43	.241	.313	.304	617	95	-35	-28	99	166			
NY	71	82	2	.464	28.5	35	40	524	558	5858	1226	172	52	27	496	535	188	38	.239	.310	.308	618	93	-34	-39	101	136			
STL	57	97	1	.370	43	31	46	510	687	5694	1250	183	63	15	405	540	167	31	.246	.305	.315	620	98	-40	-20	96	157			
PHI	55	98	1	.359	44.5	29	47	529	691	5780	1296	177	62	17	435	519	203	33	.254	.316	.323	639	101	-2	6	99	112			
TOT	622					315	298	4540		46563	10075	1477	533	133	3856	4192	306	1731	.248	.318	.320	638					1268			

TEAM	CG	SHO	GR	SV	IP	H	HR	BB	SO	BR/9	ERA	AERA	OAV	OOB	PR	APR	PF	OSB	OCS	FA	E	WPB	DP	FW	PW	BW	BSW	DIF
CHI	78	**22**	112	21	1424.1	1236	**10**	**413**	517	10.6	**2.16**	**123**	.238	.298	**79**	**76**	100	**108**	*110*	.967	204	**22**	117	2.3	**8.5**	2.4		9.8
BOS	**115**	15	51	7	1421.1	**1197**	12	**413**	509	**10.5**	2.20	117	**.231**	**.295**	73	62	97	138	*120*	**.972**	**183**	51	116	**3.9**	6.9	-.3		3.5
CLE	73	20	129	**22**	1412.2	1270	17	438	451	11.1	2.52	112	.247	.310	22	45	106	144	*131*	.964	242	32	136	-.5	5.0	-1.8		8.3
DET	78	20	112	15	1396.1	1209	12	504	516	11.4	2.56	103	.240	.316	16	13	99	178	*112*	.964	234	39	95	-.1	1.4	**7.2**		-7.1
WAS	84	21	98	10	1413.0	1217	12	537	**637**	11.4	2.75	95	.239	.316	-14	-20	99	179	*138*	.961	251	64	127	-1.0	-2.2	-3.1		3.9
NY	87	10	93	6	1411.1	1280	28	427	571	11.1	2.66	101	.252	.314	0	3	101	124	*131*	.965	225	35	129	.6	.3	-4.3		-2.1
STL	66	12	**143**	12	1385.1	1320	19	537	429	12.3	3.20	81	.257	.332	-83	-99	98	188	*130*	.957	281	55	**139**	-3.4	-11.0	-2.2		-3.3
PHI	80	8	95	8	1365.2	1310	23	562	516	12.5	3.27	84	.261	.338	-92	-77	103	209	***151***	.961	251	54	106	-1.4	-8.6	.7		-12.3
TOT	661	128	833	101	11230.				11.4	2.66		.248	.318						.964	1871	352	965						

Batter-Fielder Wins	Batting Average	On-Base Percentage	Slugging Average	On-Base Plus Slugging	Adjusted OPS	Adjusted Batter Runs
Cobb-Det 7.4	Cobb-Det 383	Cobb-Det 444	Cobb-Det 570	Cobb-Det 1014	Cobb-Det 210	Cobb-Det............75.9
Chapman-Cle......5.8	Sisler-StL 353	Speaker-Cle..................432	Speaker-Cle 486	Speaker-Cle..........918	Speaker-Cle.........168	Speaker-Cle 45.4
Sisler-StL 4.3	Speaker-Cle 352	Veach-Det 393	Veach-Det.............457	Veach-Det 850	Sisler-StL 163	Veach-Det 41.2
Speaker-Cle........4.1	Veach-Det.............319	Sisler-StL 390	Sisler-StL 453	Sisler-StL..............843	Veach-Det 160	Sisler-StL............37.9
Veach-Det............4.0	Felsch-Chi 308	E.Collins-Chi 389	Jackson-Chi 429	Jackson-Chi..........805	Jackson-Chi..........142	Jackson-Chi........26.5

Runs	Hits	Doubles	Triples	Home Runs	Total Bases	Runs Batted In
Bush-Det 112	Cobb-Det..............225	Cobb-Det 44	Cobb-Det................24	Pipp-NY 9	Cobb-Det 335	Veach-Det............103
Cobb-Det..............107	Sisler-StL..............190	Speaker-Cle 42	Jackson-Chi............17	Veach-Det 8	Veach-Det 261	Felsch-Chi 102
Chapman-Cle 98	Speaker-Cle..........184	Veach-Det......................31	Judge-Was..............15	Bodie-Phi.....................7	Speaker-Cle..........254	Cobb-Det 102
Jackson-Chi............91	Veach-Det 182	Sisler-StL 30	Chapman-Cle 13		Sisler-StL..............244	Heilmann-Det 86
E.Collins-Chi 91		Roth-Cle 30			Bodie-Phi..............233	Jackson-Chi 75

Stolen Bases	Base Stealing Runs	Fielding Runs-Infield	Fielding Runs-Outfield	Wins	Winning Pct.	Complete Games
Cobb-Det................55		Chapman-Cle 23.6	Felsch-Chi 14.6	Cicotte-Chi.............28	Russell-Chi 750	Ruth-Bos 35
E.Collins-Chi 53		Pratt-StL 17.8	Menosky-Was......10.5	Ruth-Bos 24	Mays-Bos 710	Johnson-Was 30
Chapman-Cle 52		Wambsganss-Cle.......14.8	Shanks-Was 8.4	Johnson-Was..........23	Cicotte-Chi 700	Cicotte-Chi 29
Roth-Cle 51		Lavan-StL 12.8	Bodie-Phi 7.5	Bagby-Cle 23	Williams-Chi 680	Mays-Bos 27
Sisler-StL................37		Baker-NY 9.4	Jackson-Chi 5.5	Mays-Bos................22	Ruth-Bos..............649	

Strikeouts	Fewest BB/Game	Games	Saves	Base Runners/9	Adjusted Relief Runs	Relief Ranking
Johnson-Was........188	Russell-Chi 1.52	Danforth-Chi 50	Danforth-Chi 9	Cicotte-Chi 8.28		
Cicotte-Chi............150	Mogridge-NY 1.79	Cicotte-Chi 49	Bagby-Cle 7	Coveleski-Cle 8.96		
Leonard-Bos 144	Cicotte-Chi 1.82	Bagby-Cle......................49	Boland-Det 6	Johnson-Was 9.11		
Coveleski-Cle 133	Johnson-Was 1.88	Sothoron-StL 48	Coumbe-Cle 5	Benz-Chi.............9.60		
Ruth-Bos 128	Bagby-Cle............2.05			Russell-Chi 9.65		

Innings Pitched	Opponents' Avg.	Opponents' OBP	Earned Run Average	Adjusted ERA	Adjusted Starter Runs	Pitcher Wins
Cicotte-Chi 346.2	Coveleski-Cle 194	Cicotte-Chi...................248	Cicotte-Chi 1.53	Cicotte-Chi...........173	Cicotte-Chi 44.8	**Cicotte-Chi** 5.7
Ruth-Bos............326.1	Cicotte-Chi 203	Coveleski-Cle...............261	Mays-Bos 1.74	Coveleski-Cle 156	Coveleski-Cle 33.3	**Ruth-Bos** 4.9
Johnson-Was 326.0	Ruth-Bos...............211	Johnson-Was...............263	Coveleski-Cle 1.81	Mays-Bos.............148	Bagby-Cle............30.2	**Mays-Bos**............4.0
Bagby-Cle..........320.2	Johnson-Was 211	Russell-Chi 279	Faber-Chi 1.92	Bagby-Cle 142	Mays-Bos 24.7	**Bagby-Cle** 3.9
Coveleski-Cle 298.1	Mays-Bos 221	Mays-Bos.....................282	Russell-Chi 1.95	Faber-Chi..............138	Ruth-Bos..............22.2	**Coveleski-Cle** 3.2

White Sox Play Clean Ball

The waves of World War were causing the good ship baseball to list. America's economy sagged, and as a result, league attendance fell 17 percent. Speculation over an increased war effort led to cries of impending doom for baseball, which could lose much of its talent to conscription and military industry.

Despite a 1.79 ERA, 42-year-old Eddie Plank was 5–6 for seventh-place St. Louis, and his big-league career came to an end. Also finished at 36 was former White Sox ace "Big Ed" Walsh, whose arm was dead after leading the AL four times in a six-year span in innings pitched. No longer would pitchers be asked to shoulder the load that Walsh did in 1912, when he pitched 62 games and 393 innings (although that was actually a step back from his 464-inning, 40-win 1908 season).

Showing excellent all-around effort, Chicago pulled away from second-place Boston in September. The Red Sox were barely.500 down the stretch, while the White Sox came alive when they smelled the flag. Chicago won 100 games with an excellent attack, leading the league in runs scored, and 33-year-old spitballer Eddie Cicotte finally had his first 20-win season—28 to be precise.

Babe Ruth was 24–13 for the Bosox and hit .325, seeing extra duty as a pinch-hitter. The 1917 campaign was his final full season on the mound, as his bat would soon prove too hot to keep on the bench. Boston's attack was substandard; they didn't hit, draw walks, or steal bases.

The White Sox-Giants World Series started as a pitching paradise. Chicago allowed just 3 runs in winning the first pair at home. Back east, New York won the next two by shutouts. But Game 5 at Comiskey saw the Pale Hose outlast New York, 8–5, despite making 6 errors. Chicago then won the next game as the Giants made 3 miscues of their own. White Sox hurler Red Faber went 3–1 in 27 innings.

1918 National League

TEAM	W	L	T	PCT	GB	HW	HL	R	OR	PA	H	2B	3B	HR	BB	SO	HB	SH	AVG	OBP	SLG	OPS	AOPS	BR	ABR	PF	SB	CS	BSA	BSR
CHI	84	45	2	.651		**49**	25	**538**	**393**	4900	1147	164	53	**21**	358	343	**190**	27	.265	.325	.342	667	106	50	37	103	159			
NY	71	53	0	.573	10.5	35	21	480	415	4589	1081	150	53	13	271	365	121	**33**	.260	.310	.330	640	103	2	11	98	130			
CIN	68	60	1	.531	15.5	46	24	530	496	4762	**1185**	**165**	**84**	15	304	303	162	31	**.278**	**.330**	**.366**	**696**	**120**	**86**	**96**	98	128			
PIT	65	60	1	.520	17	42	28	466	412	4667	1016	107	72	15	**371**	**285**	180	25	.248	.315	.321	636	96	-1	-16	103	**200**			
BRO	57	69	0	.452	25.5	33	21	360	463	4578	1052	121	62	10	212	326	118	36	.250	.291	.315	606	90	-57	-55	100	113			
PHI	55	68	2	.447	26	27	29	430	507	4677	1022	158	28	25	346	400	119	20	.244	.305	.313	618	88	-25	-52	107	97			
BOS	53	71	0	.427	28.5	23	29	424	469	4691	1014	107	59	13	350	438	151	28	.244	.307	.307	614	97	-33	-14	96	83			
STL	51	78	2	.395	33	32	40	454	527	4863	1066	147	64	27	329	461	141	24	.244	.301	.325	626	99	-22	-6	97	119			
TOT	508					287	217	3682		37727	8583	1119	475	139	2541	2921	224	1182	.254	.311	.328	638					1029			

TEAM	CG	SHO	GR	SV	IP	H	HR	BB	SO	BR/9	ERA	AERA	OAV	OOB	PR	APR	PF	OSB	OCS	FA	E	WPB	DP	FW	PW	BW	BSW	DIF
CHI	92	**23**	52	8	1197.0	1050	**13**	296	**472**	10.3	**2.18**	**128**	**.239**	.291	**77**	**80**	101	121	*100*	.966	188	31	91	.5	**8.9**	4.1		5.9
NY	74	18	71	**11**	1111.2	**1002**	20	**228**	330	**10.1**	2.64	100	.243	**.287**	15	-1	95	131	*63*	**.971**	**152**	30	78	**2.1**	-.1	1.2		5.8
CIN	84	14	62	6	1142.1	1136	19	381	321	12.1	3.00	89	.268	.332	-30	-44	97	118	*107*	.964	192	30	**127**	.0	-4.9	**10.7**		-1.9
PIT	85	10	52	7	1140.1	1005	**13**	299	367	10.5	2.48	116	.243	.300	36	49	104	**74**	*103*	.966	179	**19**	108	.6	5.5	-1.8		-1.8
BRO	85	17	51	2	1131.1	1024	22	320	395	10.9	2.81	99	.248	.307	-6	-4	101	144	*111*	.963	193	50	74	-.3	-.4	-6.1		.9
PHI	78	10	61	6	1139.2	1086	22	369	312	11.7	3.15	95	.258	.323	-49	-19	109	133	*99*	.961	211	38	91	-1.5	-2.1	-5.8		3.0
BOS	**96**	13	31	0	1117.1	1111	14	277	340	11.4	2.90	93	.266	.316	-17	-28	97	144	*101*	.965	184	21	89	.0	-3.1	-1.6		-4.4
STL	72	3	**79**	5	1193.0	1148	16	352	361	11.6	2.96	91	.261	.321	-27	-34	98	164	***119***	.962	220	21	116	-1.5	-3.8	-.7		-7.5
TOT	666	108	459	45	9172.2					11.1	2.76		.254	.311						.965	1519	240	774					

Batter-Fielder Wins
- **Groh-Cin** 4.1
- **Hornsby-StL** 3.8
- **Fletcher-NY** 3.3
- **Fisher-StL** 3.0
- **R.Smith-Bos** 2.9

Batting Average
- Z.Wheat-Bro 335
- Roush-Cin 333
- Groh-Cin 320
- Hollocher-Chi 316
- Daubert-Bro 308

On-Base Percentage
- Groh-Cin 395
- Hollocher-Chi 379
- R.Smith-Bos 373
- S.Magee-Cin 370
- Z.Wheat-Bro 369

Slugging Average
- Roush-Cin 455
- Daubert-Bro 429
- Hornsby-StL 416
- S.Magee-Cin 415
- Wickland-Bos 398

On-Base Plus Slugging
- Roush-Cin 823
- Groh-Cin 791
- Daubert-Bro 789
- S.Magee-Cin 785
- Hollocher-Chi 775

Adjusted OPS
- Roush-Cin 153
- Groh-Cin 144
- S.Magee-Cin 142
- Daubert-Bro 141
- Wickland-Bos 139

Adjusted Batter Runs
- Groh-Cin 29.5
- Roush-Cin 25.5
- Hollocher-Chi 21.7
- S.Magee-Cin 20.2
- R.Smith-Bos 19.4

Runs
- Groh-Cin 86
- Burns-NY 80
- Flack-Chi 74
- Hollocher-Chi 72

Hits
- Hollocher-Chi 161
- Groh-Cin 158
- Roush-Cin 145
- Youngs-NY 143
- Merkle-Chi 143

Doubles
- Groh-Cin 28
- Mann-Chi 27
- Cravath-Phi 27
- Meusel-Phi 25
- Merkle-Chi 25

Triples
- Daubert-Bro 15
- Wickland-Bos 13
- S.Magee-Cin 13
- L.Magee-Cin 13

Home Runs
- Cravath-Phi 8
- Williams-Phi 6
- Cruise-StL 6

Total Bases
- Hollocher-Chi 202
- Roush-Cin 198
- Groh-Cin 195
- Mann-Chi 188
- Merkle-Chi 187

Runs Batted In
- S.Magee-Cin 76
- Cutshaw-Pit 68
- Luderus-Phi 67
- R.Smith-Bos 65
- Merkle-Chi 65

Stolen Bases
- Carey-Pit 58
- Burns-NY 40
- Hollocher-Chi 26
- Cutshaw-Pit 25
- Baird-StL 25

Base Stealing Runs

Fielding Runs-Infield
- Fletcher-NY 24.8
- Bancroft-Phi 16.3
- Blackburne-Cin 11.1
- Doolan-Bro 9.5
- Hornsby-StL 9.4

Fielding Runs-Outfield
- Carey-Pit 13.0
- Burns-NY 9.2
- Myers-Bro 7.9
- Neale-Cin 6.8
- Roush-Cin 5.0

Wins
- Vaughn-Chi 22
- Hendrix-Chi 20
- Tyler-Chi 19
- Grimes-Bro 19
- Cooper-Pit 19

Winning Pct.
- Hendrix-Chi 741
- Tyler-Chi 704
- Mayer-Phi-Pit 696
- Vaughn-Chi 688
- Grimes-Bro 679

Complete Games
- Nehf-Bos 28
- Vaughn-Chi 27
- Cooper-Pit 26
- Tyler-Chi 22
- Hendrix-Chi 21

Strikeouts
- Vaughn-Chi 148
- Cooper-Pit 117
- Grimes-Bro 113
- Tyler-Chi 102
- Nehf-Bos 96

Fewest BB/Game
- Sallee-NY 82
- Perritt-NY 1.47
- G.Smith-Cin-NY-Bro 1.50
- Toney-Cin-NY 1.54
- Demaree-NY 1.58

Games
- Grimes-Bro 40
- Cooper-Pit 38
- Eller-Cin 37

Saves
- Toney-Cin-NY 3
- Oeschger-Phi 3
- Cooper-Pit 3
- Anderson-NY 3

Base Runners/9
- Sallee-NY 9.14
- Vaughn-Chi 9.27
- Harmon-Pit 9.62
- Grimes-Bro 9.68
- Cooper-Pit 9.68

Adjusted Relief Runs

Relief Ranking

Innings Pitched
- Vaughn-Chi 290.1
- Nehf-Bos 284.1
- Cooper-Pit 273.1
- Grimes-Bro 269.2
- Tyler-Chi 269.1

Opponents' Avg.
- Vaughn-Chi 208
- Grimes-Bro 216
- Cooper-Pit 223
- Tyler-Chi 226
- Jacobs-Pit-Phi 233

Opponents' OBP
- Sallee-NY 259
- Vaughn-Chi 266
- Grimes-Bro 276
- Perritt-NY 278
- Cooper-Pit 279

Earned Run Average
- Vaughn-Chi 1.74
- Tyler-Chi 2.00
- Cooper-Pit 2.11
- Douglas-Chi 2.13
- Grimes-Bro 2.14

Adjusted ERA
- Vaughn-Chi 161
- Tyler-Chi 139
- Cooper-Pit 136
- Douglas-Chi 131
- Grimes-Bro 130

Adjusted Starter Runs
- Vaughn-Chi 34.0
- Tyler-Chi 26.6
- Cooper-Pit 21.6
- Grimes-Bro 15.5
- Hamilton-Pit 11.6

Pitcher Wins
- **Vaughn-Chi** 4.5
- **Tyler-Chi** 3.2
- **Cooper-Pit** 3.0
- **Grimes-Bro** 1.9
- **Hogg-Phi** 1.8

The Abbreviated Race

World War I threatened to shut down the major leagues, and baseball saved face by agreeing to stop play on Labor Day. The loss of many regular players and pitchers to military jobs or combat assignments meant that expectations of who would win were completely thrown off.

The surprising Chicago Cubs, sparked by a big rookie season from infielder Charlie Hollocher, were up by 10½ games when the merry-go-round stopped. A good schedule, crammed with lots of early home games, helped; so did the great season of Jim "Hippo" Vaughn, the league's top pitcher.

The war, and its resultant drain on spectators and disposable income, brought league attendance down another 42 percent. Of course, there were fewer games, which decreased total tickets sold, but average attendance was down everywhere except Pittsburgh. For first time, batters' strikeouts declined to below three per game; they would remain less than three through 1929. Part of the reason strikeouts were down? Grover Cleveland Alexander had entered the service. The war forced some teams to use very old and very young players. Pittsburgh brought back 40-year-old Tommy Leach as a utilityman; 38-year-old Mickey Doolan hit .179 as Brooklyn's second sacker. The last-place Cardinals, hit very hard by the war, used both 19-year-old Charlie Grimm and 44-year-old Bobby Wallace.

In the World Series, played by special government order, the Cubs and Red Sox nearly boycotted over their low shares, but finally took the field. Boston won in six games in the only World Series to end before the second week of September.

First baseman Jack Beckley, owner of 2,934 career hits for four NL clubs, died at age 51, but his death didn't merit quite the attention given Eddie Grant, the first player killed in World War I. The veteran infielder died in October in the Argonne Forest of France.

1918 American League

TEAM	W	L	T	PCT	GB	HW	HL	R	OR	PA	H	2B	3B	HR	BB	SO	HB	SH	AVG	OBP	SLG	OPS	AOPS	BR	ABR	PF	SB	CS	BSA	BSR
BOS	75	51	0	.595		**49**	21	474	**380**	4609	990	159	54	15	407	**324**	**193**	27	.249	.322	.327	649	103	7	15	98	110			
CLE	73	54	2	.575	2.5	38	22	**504**	447	4869	1084	**176**	**67**	9	**491**	386	170	**42**	**.260**	**.344**	**.341**	**685**	102	**70**	23	110	**171**			
WAS	72	56	2	.563	4	41	32	461	412	5017	**1144**	156	49	4	376	361	134	35	.256	.318	.315	633	98	-22	-14	98	137			
NY	60	63	3	.488	13.5	37	29	493	475	4785	1085	160	45	**20**	367	370	171	23	.257	.320	.330	650	99	2	-8	102	92			
STL	58	64	1	.475	15	23	30	426	448	4627	1040	152	40	5	397	340	176	35	.259	.331	.320	651	**105**	13	**28**	97	139			
CHI	57	67	0	.460	17	30	26	457	446	4698	1057	136	55	8	375	358	164	27	.256	.322	.321	643	98	-7	-11	101	119			
DET	55	71	2	.437	20	28	29	476	557	4879	1063	141	56	13	452	380	143	22	.249	.325	.318	643	103	-2	18	96	123			
PHI	52	76	2	.406	24	35	32	412	538	4777	1039	124	44	22	343	485	130	26	.243	.303	.308	611	88	-62	-66	101	83			
TOT	508					281	221	3703		38261	8502	1204	410	96	3208	3004	237	1281	.254	.323	.322	646					974			

TEAM	CG	SHO	GR	SV	IP	H	HR	BB	SO	BR/9	ERA	AERA	OAV	OOB	PR	APR	PF	OSB	OCS	FA	E	WPB	DP	FW	PW	BW	BSW	DIF
BOS	**105**	**26**	28	2	1120.0	**931**	**9**	380	392	10.8	2.31	116	**.231**	.302	58	49	97	112	*92*	**.971**	**152**	38	89	**2.5**	5.5	1.7		2.4
CLE	78	5	67	**13**	1161.0	1126	**9**	343	364	11.5	2.64	114	.262	.319	18	42	108	**93**	*93*	.962	207	**24**	82	-.7	4.7	2.6		2.9
WAS	75	19	74	8	1228.0	1021	10	395	**505**	**10.6**	**2.14**	**127**	**.231**	**.298**	**86**	**81**	98	126	*101*	.960	226	53	95	-1.8	**9.0**	-1.6		2.3
NY	59	8	**88**	**13**	1157.1	1103	25	463	370	12.5	3.00	94	.261	.340	-30	-23	102	106	*92*	.970	161	25	**137**	1.9	-2.6	-.9		.0
STL	67	8	79	8	1111.1	993	11	402	346	11.5	2.75	99	.246	.319	2	-2	99	140	*96*	.963	190	25	86	-.2	-.2	**3.1**		-5.7
CHI	76	9	68	8	1126.0	1092	**9**	**300**	349	11.3	2.73	100	.261	.314	5	-3	99	97	*74*	.967	169	**24**	98	1.2	-.3	-1.2		-4.7
DET	74	8	76	7	1160.2	1130	10	437	374	12.4	3.40	78	.263	.335	-81	-104	96	157	*105*	.960	212	33	77	-1.1	-11.6	2.0		2.7
PHI	80	13	67	9	1156.0	1106	13	486	277	12.7	3.22	91	.266	.348	-58	-37	106	146	***124***	.959	228	27	136	-1.9	-4.1	-7.4		1.4
TOT	614	96	547	68	9220.1					11.7	2.77		.254	.323						.964	1545	249	800					

Batter-Fielder Wins	Batting Average	On-Base Percentage	Slugging Average	On-Base Plus Slugging	Adjusted OPS	Adjusted Batter Runs
T.Cobb-Det 4.3	T.Cobb-Det 382	T.Cobb-Det..................440	Ruth-Bos...............555	T.Cobb-Det............955	T.Cobb-Det...........196	T.Cobb-Det 47.7
Sisler-StL 4.0	Burns-Phi 352	E.Collins-Chi 407	T.Cobb-Det 515	Burns-Phi..............857	Sisler-StL 159	Ruth-Bos 37.5
Burns-Phi 3.8	Sisler-StL 341	Speaker-Cle.................403	Burns-Phi 467	Sisler-StL 841	Burns-Phi..............157	Burns-Phi 31.8
Chapman-Cle......3.0	Speaker-Cle 318	Sisler-StL 400	Sisler-StL 440	Speaker-Cle..........839	Hooper-Bos 142	Sisler-StL............31.5
Baker-NY 2.9	Baker-NY 306	Hooper-Bos 391	Speaker-Cle 435	Hooper-Bos 796	Speaker-Cle..........140	Hooper-Bos 27.3

Runs	Hits	Doubles	Triples	Home Runs	Total Bases	Runs Batted In
Chapman-Cle 84	Burns-Phi.............178	Speaker-Cle 33	T.Cobb-Det..............14	Walker-Phi 11	Burns-Phi..............236	Veach-Det...............78
T.Cobb-Det............83	T.Cobb-Det.............161	Ruth-Bos........................26	Veach-Det 13	Ruth-Bos 11	T.Cobb-Det............217	Burns-Phi 70
Hooper-Bos 81	Sisler-StL 154	Hooper-Bos.....................26	Hooper-Bos 13	Burns-Phi..................6	Baker-NY 206	Wood-Cle 66
Bush-Det 74	Baker-NY 154	Baker-NY 24	Roth-Cle 12	Baker-NY 6	Speaker-Cle..........205	Ruth-Bos 66
Speaker-Cle............73	Speaker-Cle..........150				Sisler-StL 199	T.Cobb-Det 64

Stolen Bases	Base Stealing Runs	Fielding Runs-Infield	Fielding Runs-Outfield	Wins	Winning Pct.	Complete Games
Sisler-StL 45		Peckinpaugh-NY 22.1	S.Collins-Chi........11.8	Johnson-Was..........23	Jones-Bos............762	Perry-Phi 30
Roth-Cle 36		Scott-Bos 20.8	Kopp-Phi................9.8	Coveleski-Cle 22	Johnson-Was 639	Mays-Bos 30
Chapman-Cle 35		Dugan-Phi 16.7	Demmitt-StL 9.2	Mays-Bos.................21	Coveleski-Cle 629	Johnson-Was 29
T.Cobb-Det..............34		Gedeon-StL 15.6	Speaker-Cle 8.4	Perry-Phi 20	Mays-Bos 618	Bush-Bos 26
Speaker-Cle............27		Gardner-Phi 12.8	Leibold-Chi 7.3	Bagby-Cle 17	Shaw-Was 571	Coveleski-Cle 25

Strikeouts	Fewest BB/Game	Games	Saves	Base Runners/9	Adjusted Relief Runs	Relief Ranking
Johnson-Was........162	Cicotte-Chi 1.35	Mogridge-NY 45	Mogridge-NY 7	Johnson-Was 8.81	Houck-StL..............3.2	Houck-StL 2.6
Shaw-Was 129	Mogridge-NY 1.62	Bagby-Cle.......................45	Bagby-Cle 6	Ruth-Bos.............9.52		
Bush-Bos 125	Benz-Chi..............1.64	Perry-Phi........................44	Russell-NY................4	Sothoron-StL 9.56		
Morton-Cle 123	Enzmann-Cle 1.91	Shaw-Was 41	Geary-Phi 4	Matteson-Was 9.71		
Mays-Bos...............114	Johnson-Was 1.93	Ayers-Was 40		Wright-StL...........9.86		

Innings Pitched	Opponents' Avg.	Opponents' OBP	Earned Run Average	Adjusted ERA	Adjusted Starter Runs	Pitcher Wins
Perry-Phi 332.1	Sothoron-StL 205	Johnson-Was...............260	Johnson-Was 1.27	Johnson-Was.........214	Johnson-Was 51.4	**Johnson-Was** 7.6
Johnson-Was 326.0	Johnson-Was 210	Sothoron-StL 274	Coveleski-Cle 1.82	Coveleski-Cle 164	Coveleski-Cle 35.0	**Coveleski-Cle** 3.9
Coveleski-Cle 311.0	Harper-Was 212	Ruth-Bos 277	Sothoron-StL 1.94	Perry-Phi 148	Perry-Phi 32.5	**Mays-Bos**............3.7
Mays-Bos 293.1	Ruth-Bos...............214	Coveleski-Cle...............279	Perry-Phi 1.98	Sothoron-StL 141	Harper-Was 17.3	**Perry-Phi** 3.5
Bush-Bos 272.2	Mays-Bos 221	Mays-Bos.....................284	Bush-Bos 2.11	Mogridge-NY 129	Sothoron-StL 16.9	**Ruth-Bos** 2.9

The Babe Does It All

Baseball's worst nightmare came true in 1918. Baseball had been declared a non-essential industry, forcing many players into military service or war-related jobs. The game shut down before it was forced to by the government. As a result, the Boston Red Sox were able to eke out a pennant when the abbreviated season ended on Labor Day. The defending champion White Sox lost Eddie Collins, Swede Risberg, Happy Felsch, Joe Jackson, Red Faber, and Lefty Williams; Chicago fell to sixth.

Boston had Carl Mays do the majority of heavy mound work, while Babe Ruth was 13–7 on the hill and hit .300 with 11 homers (tied for the league lead) in the outfield. Cleveland nearly scraped out a flag, but aside from Stan Coveleski, the pitching wasn't strong. Walter Johnson again was the league's top hurler, and the Senators were the only team with increased attendance.

This was a deadened form of baseball; homers fell to just .09 per game—only 1907 saw a lower percentage. Never again would a league hit fewer than the AL's 96 home runs. The average AL team tallied just 3.64 runs a game, the lowest production until 1968. The league's watered-down quality also meant parity. Last-place Philadelphia ended up just 24 out, a relative godsend for Connie Mack's sad crew. Eighteen-year-old Waite Hoyt debuted, and Smokey Joe Wood, forced to retire from the mound in 1915 because of a sore arm, resurrected his career as the right fielder for old pal Tris Speaker's Indians.

In a World Series held through special dispensation from the war department, the Red Sox won in six. Ruth and Mays each won twice as no team scored over 3 runs in a game. Boston took the Series despite being outscored (10–9), outhit (.210–.186), and outpitched (the Cubs' ERA was 1.04, Boston's 1.70). This bittersweet victory was one Boston would have to learn to savor. The club's fifth world championship in fifteen years would be their last of the century.

1919 National League

TEAM	W	L	T	PCT	GB	HW	HL	R	OR	PA	H	2B	3B	HR	BB	SO	HB	SH	AVG	OBP	SLG	OPS	AOPS	BR	ABR	PF	SB	CS	BSA	BSR
CIN	96	44	0	.686		**52**	19	577	**401**	5214	1204	135	**83**	20	**405**	368	**199**	33	.263	**.327**	.342	669	110	42	57	97	143			
NY	87	53	0	.621	9	46	23	**605**	470	5157	**1254**	**204**	64	**40**	328	407	128	37	**.269**	.322	**.366**	**688**	**113**	**67**	**73**	99	**157**			
CHI	75	65	0	.536	21	40	31	454	407	5088	1174	166	58	21	298	**359**	167	**42**	.256	.308	.332	640	97	-14	-17	101	150			
PIT	71	68	0	.511	24.5	40	30	472	466	5050	1132	130	82	17	344	381	144	24	.249	.306	.325	631	92	-28	-45	104	196			
BRO	69	71	1	.493	27	36	33	525	513	5283	1272	167	66	25	258	405	153	28	.263	.304	.340	644	97	-15	-25	102	112			
BOS	57	82	1	.410	38.5	29	38	465	563	5299	1201	142	62	24	355	481	156	**42**	.253	.311	.324	635	100	-18	4	96	145			
STL	54	83	1	.394	40.5	34	35	463	552	5053	1175	163	52	18	304	418	143	18	.256	.305	.326	631	101	-28	2	94	148			
PHI	47	90	1	.343	47.5	26	44	510	699	5220	1191	208	50	42	323	469	123	28	.251	.303	.342	645	92	-5	-39	107	114			
TOT	558					303	253	4071		41364	9603	1315	517	207	2615	3288	252	1213	.258	.311	.337	648					1165			

TEAM	CG	SHO	GR	SV	IP	H	HR	BB	SO	BR/9	ERA	AERA	OAV	OOB	PR	APR	PF	OSB	OCS	FA	E	WPB	DP	FW	PW	BW	BSW	DIF
CIN	89	**23**	74	9	1274.0	**1104**	21	298	407	**10.0**	2.23	124	**.239**	**.288**	96	79	95	133	*114*	**.974**	**151**	28	98	**2.7**	8.8	6.3		8.2
NY	72	11	96	**13**	1256.0	1153	34	305	340	10.6	2.70	104	.247	.296	29	14	96	147	*90*	.964	216	27	96	-1.0	1.6	**8.1**		8.4
CHI	80	21	79	5	1265.0	1127	**14**	294	**495**	10.3	**2.21**	**130**	.242	.291	**98**	**94**	99	140	*111*	.969	185	26	87	.7	**10.5**	-1.9		-4.3
PIT	91	17	54	4	1249.0	1113	23	**263**	391	10.2	2.88	104	.244	.290	4	17	104	**108**	*99*	.970	165	**24**	89	1.8	1.9	-5.0		2.8
BRO	**98**	12	50	1	1281.0	1256	21	292	476	11.1	2.73	109	.262	.309	25	32	102	172	*121*	.963	219	39	84	-1.1	3.6	-2.8		-.6
BOS	79	5	74	9	1270.1	1313	29	337	374	11.8	3.17	90	.276	.327	-36	-46	98	147	*133*	.966	204	41	111	-.4	-5.1	.4		-7.5
STL	55	6	**137**	8	1217.1	1146	25	415	414	11.9	3.23	86	.256	.326	-44	-63	96	137	*122*	.963	214	50	**112**	-1.1	-7.0	.2		-6.6
PHI	93	6	57	2	1252.0	1391	40	408	397	13.3	4.14	78	.294	.356	-171	-116	111	181	***135***	.963	218	53	**112**	-1.3	-12.9	-4.3		-2.9
TOT	657	101	621	51	10064.2					11.2	2.91		.258	.311						.967	1572	288	789					

Batter-Fielder Wins	Batting Average	On-Base Percentage	Slugging Average	On-Base Plus Slugging	Adjusted OPS	Adjusted Batter Runs
Hornsby-StL 5.1	Roush-Cin............321	Burns-NY....................396	Myers-Bro............436	Groh-Cin 823	Hornsby-StL 154	Hornsby-StL 34.1
Maranville-Bos ..4.6	Hornsby-StL 318	Groh-Cin 392	Doyle-NY 433	Hornsby-StL 814	Groh-Cin 151	Burns-NY...........32.6
Stock-StL 4.4	Youngs-NY 311	Hornsby-StL................384	Groh-Cin..............431	Roush-Cin 811	Roush-Cin 147	Groh-Cin 29.8
Fletcher-NY 3.4	Groh-Cin...............310	Youngs-NY..................384	Roush-Cin............431	Burns-NY..............801	Burns-NY.............142	Cravath-Phi 29.4
Groh-Cin 3.4	Stock-StL 307	Roush-Cin 380	Hornsby-StL 430	Youngs-NY 799	Youngs-NY 142	Roush-Cin 29.2

Runs	Hits	Doubles	Triples	Home Runs	Total Bases	Runs Batted In
Burns-NY................86	Olson-Bro 164	Youngs-NY 31	Southworth-Pit........14	Cravath-Phi 12	Myers-Bro 223	Myers-Bro.............73
Groh-Cin 79	Hornsby-StL 163	Luderus-Phi 30	Myers-Bro 14	Kauff-NY 10	Hornsby-StL 220	Roush-Cin 71
Daubert-Cin............79	Roush-Cin 162	Burns-NY 30		Williams-Phi.............9	Z.Wheat-Bro 219	Hornsby-StL 71
Rath-Cin 77	Burns-NY..............162	Kauff-NY........................27		Hornsby-StL 8	Roush-Cin 217	Kauff-NY...............67
		Meusel-Phi 26		Doyle-NY 7	Burns-NY.............216	Groh-Cin................63

Stolen Bases	Base Stealing Runs	Fielding Runs-Infield	Fielding Runs-Outfield	Wins	Winning Pct.	Complete Games
Burns-NY................40		Maranville-Bos............26.3	Bigbee-Pit............14.5	J.Barnes-NY 25	Ruether-Cin 760	Cooper-Pit 27
Cutshaw-Pit............36		Fletcher-NY 25.3	Southworth-Pit 5.8	Vaughn-Chi 21	Sallee-Cin.............750	Pfeffer-Bro 26
Bigbee-Pit 31		Stock-StL....................19.4	Roush-Cin.............5.3	Sallee-Cin 21	J.Barnes-NY 735	Vaughn-Chi 25
Smith-StL................30		Rath-Cin 12.9	McHenry-StL 4.4		Eller-Cin 679	Rudolph-Bos..........24
		Luderus-Phi 9.3	Myers-Bro..............3.7		Adams-Pit.............630	

Strikeouts	Fewest BB/Game	Games	Saves	Base Runners/9	Adjusted Relief Runs	Relief Ranking
Vaughn-Chi 141	Adams-Pit...............79	Tuero-StL 45	Tuero-StL..................4	Adams-Pit............8.17		
Eller-Cin................137	Sallee-Cin................79	Meadows-StL-Phi 40		Alexander-Chi.........8.35		
Alexander-Chi 121	J.Barnes-NY 1.07	Vaughn-Chi....................38		J.Barnes-NY 9.13		
Meadows-StL-Phi 116	Cadore-Bro..........1.40	Eller-Cin 38		Fisher-Cin 9.29		
Cooper-Pit 106	Alexander-Chi......1.46	J.Barnes-NY 38		Miller-Pit 9.33		

Innings Pitched	Opponents' Avg.	Opponents' OBP	Earned Run Average	Adjusted ERA	Adjusted Starter Runs	Pitcher Wins
Vaughn-Chi........306.2	Alexander-Chi.......211	Adams-Pit 241	Alexander-Chi......1.72	Alexander-Chi 167	Vaughn-Chi..........36.3	**Alexander-Chi** ..4.6
J.Barnes-NY......295.2	Adams-Pit.............220	Alexander-Chi 245	Vaughn-Chi.........1.79	Vaughn-Chi 161	Alexander-Chi.......33.5	**Vaughn-Chi** 4.3
Cooper-Pit 286.2	Ruether-Cin 223	J.Barnes-NY 260	Ruether-Cin 1.82	Ruether-Cin 152	Adams-Pit............29.7	**Ruether-Cin**........3.1
Rudolph-Bos......273.2	Cooper-Pit 225	Fisher-Cin 271	Toney-NY 1.84	Toney-NY..............152	Ruether-Cin 24.1	**Adams-Pit** 3.0
Nehf-Bos-NY 270.2	Nehf-Bos-NY 225	Miller-Pit......................272	Adams-Pit...........1.98	Adams-Pit 152	Sallee-Cin............20.2	**Sallee-Cin** 2.5

The Reds Were Cheated, Too

With the war's end, attendance shot up 109 percent across the league, rising more than 90 percent in five cities. However, the NL continued to lag behind the AL in attendance, as it had throughout the decade. On the field, teams stole more than one base per game for the last time in NL history. The home run age would soon render the old rules obsolete.

With former Philadelphia skipper Pat Moran at the helm, the Cincinnati Reds used deep pitching and a speed-and-contact offense to coast to the NL flag, leaving John McGraw's Giants behind in August. Classic Dead Ball Era players like Edd Roush, Heinie Groh, and Morrie Rath fueled the attack, while former slugger Sherry Magee ended his career on the Cincinnati bench.

Second-place New York brought up another quality rookie, infielder Frankie Frisch, who soon became a star. McGraw's intellect was certainly in question when he decided to employ veteran game-fixer Hal Chase as his regular first baseman. Not only did the 36-year-old Chase provide below-average offense, he also used his influence to help fix games. For this, he was finally bounced from baseball after the season.

The Phillies, contenders two years before, tumbled into the basement after a series of ill-advised trades. Once a proud franchise, they would be laughingstocks for most of the next four decades.

Oddly enough, the two times in the decade that everyone felt the AL was a World Series cinch, the NL club pulled off an upset. This time, the Reds—who, few people seem to recall, actually had eight more regular-season wins than the White Sox—beat Chicago in eight games in the best-of-nine format. Unfortunately for the Reds, several White Sox weren't playing on the level, so their first world championship would be forever tainted despite their best efforts.

1919 American League

TEAM	W	L	T	PCT	GB	HW	HL	R	OR	PA	H	2B	3B	HR	BB	SO	HB	SH	AVG	OBP	SLG	OPS	AOPS	BR	ABR	PF	SB	CS	BSA	BSR
CHI	88	52	0	.629		**48**	22	**667**	534	5359	**1343**	218	70	25	427	**358**	**223**	34	**.287**	.351	.380	731	111	71	68	100	**150**			
CLE	84	55	0	.604	3.5	44	25	636	537	5322	1268	**254**	72	24	**498**	367	221	38	.278	**.354**	**.381**	**735**	107	**83**	45	106	117			
NY	80	59	2	.576	7.5	46	25	578	**506**	5358	1275	193	49	**45**	386	479	165	32	.267	.326	.356	682	96	-21	-25	101	101			
DET	80	60	0	.571	8	46	24	618	578	5328	1319	222	**84**	23	429	427	209	25	.283	.346	**.381**	727	**113**	61	**76**	98	121			
STL	67	72	1	.482	20.5	40	30	533	567	5299	1234	187	73	31	391	443	201	35	.264	.326	.355	681	95	-24	-37	103	74			
BOS	66	71	1	.482	20.5	35	30	564	552	5254	1188	181	49	33	471	411	190	**45**	.261	.336	.344	680	103	-9	25	94	108			
WAS	56	84	2	.400	32	32	40	533	570	5381	1238	177	63	24	416	511	168	40	.260	.325	.339	664	93	-49	-44	99	142			
PHI	36	104	0	.257	52	21	49	457	742	5230	1156	175	71	35	349	565	121	30	.244	.300	.334	634	82	-113	-118	101	103			
TOT	560					312	245	4586		42531	10021	1607	531	240	3367	3561	279	1498	.268	.333	.359	692					916			

TEAM	CG	SHO	GR	SV	IP	H	HR	BB	SO	BR/9	ERA	AERA	OAV	OOB	PR	APR	PF	OSB	OCS	FA	E	WPB	DP	FW	PW	BW	BSW	DIF
CHI	88	14	73	3	1265.2	1245	24	**342**	468	11.5	3.04	105	.262	.315	26	19	99	92	*84*	.969	176	**15**	116	1.6	2.0	7.1		7.2
CLE	79	10	93	**10**	1245.0	1242	19	362	432	11.8	2.94	**114**	.264	.321	39	51	104	**81**	*75*	.965	201	22	102	-.0	5.3	4.7		4.5
NY	85	14	90	7	1287.0	**1143**	47	433	500	**11.3**	**2.82**	113	**.240**	**.309**	**58**	**54**	99	111	*88*	.968	193	32	108	.7	**5.7**	-2.6		6.8
DET	85	10	74	4	1256.0	1254	35	436	428	12.4	3.30	97	.266	.333	-11	-14	99	128	*76*	.964	205	35	81	-.2	-1.5	**8.0**		3.7
STL	78	14	95	4	1256.0	1255	35	421	415	12.3	3.13	106	.263	.328	13	23	103	121	*94*	.963	215	35	98	-.8	2.4	-3.9		-.2
BOS	**89**	**15**	66	8	1224.1	1251	**16**	421	381	12.5	3.31	91	.275	.341	-12	-44	94	111	*97*	**.975**	**140**	56	**118**	**3.8**	-4.6	2.6		-4.3
WAS	68	13	**97**	**10**	1274.1	1237	20	451	**536**	12.2	3.01	106	.259	.328	30	28	99	120	*104*	.960	227	50	86	-1.4	2.9	-4.6		-10.9
PHI	72	1	89	3	1239.1	1371	44	503	417	13.8	4.26	80	.292	.364	-143	-111	106	144	***118***	.956	257	36	96	-3.5	-11.6	-12.4		-6.5
TOT	644	91	677	49	10047.2					12.2	3.22		.268	.333						.965	1614	281	805					

Batter-Fielder Wins	Batting Average	On-Base Percentage	Slugging Average	On-Base Plus Slugging	Adjusted OPS	Adjusted Batter Runs
Ruth-Bos..............7.3	Cobb-Det 384	Ruth-Bos 456	Ruth-Bos..............657	Ruth-Bos 1114	Ruth-Bos 224	Ruth-Bos 76.3
Peckinpaugh-NY 5.1	Veach-Det............355	Cobb-Det 429	Sisler-StL 530	Cobb-Det 944	Cobb-Det 168	Cobb-Det...........44.7
Veach-Det...........4.5	Sisler-StL 352	Jackson-Chi 422	Veach-Det.............519	Jackson-Chi...........928	Veach-Det 160	Jackson-Chi........41.9
Sisler-StL 4.4	Jackson-Chi 351	Leibold-Chi 404	Cobb-Det 515	Sisler-StL.............921	Jackson-Chi..........159	Veach-Det 40.9
Jackson-Chi........3.3	Flagstead-Det.......331	E.Collins-Chi 400	Jackson-Chi 506	Veach-Det 916	Sisler-StL.............153	Sisler-StL............33.3

Runs	Hits	Doubles	Triples	Home Runs	Total Bases	Runs Batted In
Ruth-Bos 103	Veach-Det 191	Veach-Det.....................45	Veach-Det 17	Ruth-Bos 29	Ruth-Bos 284	Ruth-Bos 114
Sisler-StL 96	Cobb-Det..............191	Speaker-Cle 38	Sisler-StL...............15	T.Walker-Phi...........10	Veach-Det 279	Veach-Det............101
Cobb-Det................92	Jackson-Chi...........181	Cobb-Det 36	Heilmann-Det 15	Sisler-StL...............10	Sisler-StL.............271	Jackson-Chi 96
Weaver-Chi 89	Sisler-StL..............180	O'Neill-Cle 35	Jackson-Chi...........14	Baker-NY 10	Jackson-Chi..........261	Heilmann-Det 93
Peckinpaugh-NY 89	Rice-Was..............179		Cobb-Det................13	Smith-Cle..................9		Lewis-NY 89

Stolen Bases	Base Stealing Runs	Fielding Runs-Infield	Fielding Runs-Outfield	Wins	Winning Pct.	Complete Games
E.Collins-Chi 33		Peckinpaugh-NY 25.5	Felsch-Chi 17.4	Cicotte-Chi.............29	Cicotte-Chi 806	Cicotte-Chi 30
Sisler-StL 28		Pratt-NY.....................24.6	Speaker-Cle 14.8	Coveleski-Cle 24	Dauss-Det 700	Williams-Chi 27
Cobb-Det.................28		Vitt-Bos 17.9	Ruth-Bos...............9.3	Williams-Chi 23	Williams-Chi 676	Johnson-Was 27
Rice-Was 26		Sisler-StL 13.1	Veach-Det.............9.0	Dauss-Det 21	Pennock-Bos 667	Mays-Bos-NY 26
		Wambsganss-Cle 11.1	Leibold-Chi 7.7		Coveleski-Cle 667	Coveleski-Cle 24

Strikeouts	Fewest BB/Game	Games	Saves	Base Runners/9	Adjusted Relief Runs	Relief Ranking
Johnson-Was........147	Cicotte-Chi 1.44	Shaw-Was 45	Russell-NY-Bos 5	Cicotte-Chi 9.01	Phillips-Cle 1.1	Phillips-Cle 9
Shaw-Was 128	Johnson-Was 1.58	Russell-NY-Bos.............44	Shawkey-NY 5	Johnson-Was 9.08		
Williams-Chi 125	Bagby-Cle............1.64	Kinney-Phi 43	Shaw-Was 5	Williams-Chi 10.12		
Shawkey-NY 122	Williams-Chi 1.76	Coveleski-Cle 43	Coveleski-Cle 4	Hoyt-Bos............10.34		
Coveleski-Cle 118	Coveleski-Cle 1.89			Thormahlen-NY 10.49		

Innings Pitched	Opponents' Avg.	Opponents' OBP	Earned Run Average	Adjusted ERA	Adjusted Starter Runs	Pitcher Wins
Shaw-Was 306.2	Johnson-Was 219	Johnson-Was..............259	Johnson-Was 1.49	Johnson-Was........215	Johnson-Was 52.4	**Johnson-Was** 6.7
Cicotte-Chi 306.2	Cicotte-Chi 228	Cicotte-Chi.................261	Cicotte-Chi 1.82	Cicotte-Chi............175	Cicotte-Chi 47.2	**Cicotte-Chi** 5.5
Williams-Chi 297.0	Thormahlen-NY ...228	Williams-Chi................289	Weilman-StL 2.07	Weilman-StL 160	Sothoron-StL 26.7	**Coveleski-Cle** 3.9
Johnson-Was 290.1	Shawkey-NY.........231	Morton-Cle...................293	Mays-Bos-NY 2.10	Sothoron-StL 151	Coveleski-Cle 26.2	**Mays-Bos-NY** 3.1
Coveleski-Cle 286.0	Mays-Bos-NY 233	Quinn-NY.....................295	Sothoron-StL 2.20	Mays-Bos-NY 147	Mays-Bos-NY 25.5	**Sothoron-StL** 2.5

Earthquake

With the war over, and the players back to their teams, baseball could resume as normal. Except nothing about 1919 was normal. First of all, the schedule was set at 140 games, with a nine-game World Series proposed to recoup lost gates. The extra games gave the gamblers infiltrating baseball more incentive to push their agenda, but nobody could see this at the time.

The season's biggest story was the way baseballs flew out of the parks. With Babe Ruth given a chance to play every day for Boston, the game changed entirely as he clouted an amazing 29 homers to set an all-time mark. Other players followed his example; four-baggers increased by 150 percent to 240, setting a new league record that would be broken each of the next three years.

This rise in long balls came with no appreciable rise in strikeouts, but stolen bases—the run-creating method of the scratch-out-a-run Dead Ball Era—fell to a new low. Old-school baseball men pointed out that Ruth's team finished 20½ games out, but part of the reason was because one of the league's best left-handers no longer took his regular turn in the Red Sox rotation. Boston's team ERA increased by a full run; the league ERA was up by half a run.

The peacetime economy and the excitement over Ruth's exploits caused attendance to rise in every AL city, increasing the league's turnstile clicks by 114 percent. Chicago and Detroit saw attendance increases of over 200 percent. While the White Sox had good battles from the Indians and Tigers, Chicago had the most talent in the league and pulled away, withstanding a late Cleveland charge to take the flag by 3½. An aggressive, intelligent bunch, the Sox could hit, run, field, and pitch like nobody's business.

Few knew that this White Sox team, which played so well together, was divided by class, temperament, and greed. Chicago's surprise World Series loss to Cincinnati raised red flags.

1920 National League

TEAM	W	L	T	PCT	GB	HW	HL	R	OR	PA	H	2B	3B	HR	BB	SO	HB	SH	AVG	OBP	SLG	OPS	AOPS	BR	ABR	PF	SB	CS	BSA	BSR
BRO	93	61	1	.604		**49**	29	660	**528**	5966	1493	205	**99**	28	359	391	189	19	.277	.324	.367	691	100	17	-3	103	70	80	47	-13
NY	86	68	1	.558	7	45	35	**682**	543	5891	1427	210	76	**46**	**432**	545	124	26	.269	.327	.363	690	104	25	32	99	131	113	54	-11
CIN	82	71	1	.536	10.5	42	34	639	569	5799	1432	169	76	18	382	**367**	194	**47**	.277	.332	.349	681	102	10	19	99	158	128	55	-10
PIT	79	75	1	.513	14	42	35	530	552	5796	1342	162	90	16	374	405	174	29	.257	.310	.332	642	86	-71	-87	103	**181**	117	**61**	**-1**
STL	75	79	1	.487	18	38	38	675	682	6086	**1589**	**238**	96	32	373	484	192	26	**.289**	**.337**	**.385**	**722**	**117**	**84**	**112**	96	126	114	53	-12
CHI	75	79	0	.487	18	43	34	619	635	5811	1350	223	67	34	428	421	**220**	46	.264	.326	.354	680	98	11	-1	102	115	129	47	-20
BOS	62	90	1	.408	30	36	37	523	670	5802	1358	168	86	23	385	488	166	33	.260	.315	.339	654	97	-47	-22	96	88	98	47	-15
PHI	62	91	0	.405	30.5	32	45	565	714	5742	1385	229	54	64	283	531	159	36	.263	.305	.364	669	93	-28	-54	105	100	83	55	-7
TOT	617					327	287	4893		46893	11376	1604	644	261	3016	3632	262	1418	.270	.322	.357	679					969	862	53	-89

TEAM	CG	SHO	GR	SV	IP	H	HR	BB	SO	BR/9	ERA	AERA	OAV	OOB	PR	APR	PF	OSB	OCS	FA	E	WPB	DP	FW	PW	BW	BSW	DIF
BRO	89	17	93	10	1427.1	1381	**25**	327	**553**	10.9	**2.62**	**122**	.259	.304	**81**	**89**	102	132	99	.966	226	47	118	-.2	**9.5**	-.3	-.2	7.2
NY	86	**18**	103	9	1408.2	1379	44	297	380	**10.8**	2.80	107	.261	.303	51	32	96	**95**	89	.969	210	37	**137**	.8	3.4	3.4	.0	1.4
CIN	90	12	82	9	1391.2	**1327**	26	393	435	11.3	2.90	105	**.256**	.313	36	23	97	108	111	.968	200	32	125	1.3	2.5	2.0	.1	-.4
PIT	92	17	85	10	1415.1	1389	**25**	**280**	444	**10.8**	2.89	111	.261	**.301**	39	49	103	120	99	**.971**	**186**	37	119	**2.2**	5.2	-9.3	**1.1**	2.8
STL	72	9	**135**	**12**	1426.2	1488	30	479	529	12.8	3.43	87	.277	.343	-47	-75	95	141	97	.961	256	39	136	-2.0	-8.0	**12.0**	-.1	-3.9
CHI	**95**	13	93	9	1388.2	1459	37	382	508	12.1	3.27	98	.276	.328	-21	-10	102	115	117	.965	225	**31**	112	-.2	-1.1	-.1	-1.0	.3
BOS	93	14	73	6	1386.1	1464	39	415	368	12.4	3.54	86	.280	.337	-62	-77	97	111	**143**	.964	239	32	125	-1.1	-8.2	-2.4	-.4	-1.9
PHI	77	8	102	11	1380.2	1480	35	444	419	12.8	3.63	94	.284	.345	-76	-32	109	147	107	.964	232	47	135	-.7	-3.4	-5.8	.4	-5.0
TOT	694	108	766	76	11225.1					11.7	3.13		.270	.322						.966	1774	302	1007					

Batter-Fielder Wins	Batting Average	On-Base Percentage	Slugging Average	On-Base Plus Slugging	Adjusted OPS	Adjusted Batter Runs
Hornsby-StL........7.9	Hornsby-StL 370	Hornsby-StL................431	Hornsby-StL 559	Hornsby-StL 990	Hornsby-StL 190	Hornsby-StL 69.0
Bancroft-Phi-NY 5.6	Nicholson-Pit 360	Youngs-NY..................427	Nicholson-Pit 530	Youngs-NY 904	Youngs-NY 161	Youngs-NY 49.2
Youngs-NY 4.1	Youngs-NY 351	Roush-Cin 386	Williams-Phi 497	Williams-Phi.........861	Roush-Cin 142	Roush-Cin 30.7
Roush-Cin............3.1	Roush-Cin.............339	Wheat-Bro 385	Youngs-NY 477	Wheat-Bro 848	Williams-Phi..........139	Wheat-Bro 29.1
Williams-Phi........3.0	Wheat-Bro 328	Groh-Cin 375	Meusel-Phi 473	Roush-Cin 839	Wheat-Bro 138	Williams-Phi 28.4

Runs	Hits	Doubles	Triples	Home Runs	Total Bases	Runs Batted In
Burns-NY..............115	Hornsby-StL 218	Hornsby-StL 44	Myers-Bro 22	Williams-Phi............15	Hornsby-StL 329	Kelly-NY 94
Bancroft-Phi-NY ..102	Youngs-NY 204	Bancroft-Phi-NY 36	Hornsby-StL 20	Meusel-Phi 14	Williams-Phi..........293	Hornsby-StL 94
Daubert-Cin 97	Stock-StL...............204	Williams-Phi 36	Roush-Cin 16	Kelly-NY..................11	Youngs-NY 277	Roush-Cin 90
Hornsby-StL 96	Roush-Cin 196	Myers-Bro 36	Maranville-Bos........15	Robertson-Chi 10	Wheat-Bro 270	Duncan-Cin 83
Youngs-NY 92	Williams-Phi..........192	Burns-NY 35	Bigbee-Pit 15	McHenry-StL 10	Myers-Bro 269	Myers-Bro..............80

Stolen Bases	Base Stealing Runs	Fielding Runs-Infield	Fielding Runs-Outfield	Wins	Winning Pct.	Complete Games
Carey-Pit 52	Carey-Pit................7.9	Bancroft-Phi-NY..........36.8	Neale-Cin 12.0	Alexander-Chi 27	Grimes-Bro 676	Alexander-Chi........33
Roush-Cin 36	Frisch-NY 3.6	Terry-Chi 17.4	Burns-NY 10.9	Cooper-Pit 24	Alexander-Chi.......659	Cooper-Pit 28
Frisch-NY................34	Neale-Cin 2.2	Maranville-Bos............15.3	Roush-Cin............10.2	Grimes-Bro 23	Toney-NY 656	Rixey-Phi 25
Bigbee-Pit 31	Bigbee-Pit..............1.6	Fletcher-NY-Phi 14.4	Williams-Phi 10.2	Toney-NY................21	Pfeffer-Bro 640	Grimes-Bro............25
Neale-Cin 29	Gowdy-Bos............1.0	Deal-Chi.......................11.1	Heathcote-StL 9.8	Nehf-NY..................21	Nehf-NY 636	Vaughn-Chi 24

Strikeouts	Fewest BB/Game	Games	Saves	Base Runners/9	Adjusted Relief Runs	Relief Ranking
Alexander-Chi 173	Adams-Pit...............62	Haines-StL 47	Sherdel-StL 6	Adams-Pit............8.86		
Vaughn-Chi 131	Cooper-Pit 1.43	Douglas-NY 46	McQuillan-Bos 5	Alexander-Chi....10.03		
Grimes-Bro 131	Nehf-NY 1.44	Alexander-Chi 46	Alexander-Chi 5	Luque-Cin..........10.05		
Haines-StL............120	Benton-NY 1.44	Scott-Bos 44	Hubbell-NY-Phi 4	J.Barnes-NY......10.12		
Schupp-StL 119	Marquard-Bro 1.66	Cooper-Pit.....................44	Mamaux-Bro 4	Grimes-Bro........10.14		

Innings Pitched	Opponents' Avg.	Opponents' OBP	Earned Run Average	Adjusted ERA	Adjusted Starter Runs	Pitcher Wins
Alexander-Chi....363.1	Luque-Cin............225	Adams-Pit 259	Alexander-Chi......1.91	Alexander-Chi 168	Alexander-Chi......51.6	**Alexander-Chi** ..6.9
Cooper-Pit 327.0	Grimes-Bro 238	Grimes-Bro 282	Adams-Pit...........2.16	Adams-Pit 149	Grimes-Bro..........30.1	**Grimes-Bro** 4.9
Grimes-Bro 303.2	Adams-Pit............244	Alexander-Chi 285	Grimes-Bro..........2.22	Grimes-Bro 144	Adams-Pit...........27.6	**Smith-Bro** 3.2
Haines-StL 301.2	Ponder-Pit............246	Luque-Cin 286	Cooper-Pit 2.39	Cooper-Pit 134	Cooper-Pit 26.1	**Cooper-Pit**..........3.0
Vaughn-Chi........301.0	Ruether-Cin 247	Ponder-Pit 286	Ruether-Cin 2.47	Vaughn-Chi 126	Ruether-Cin 19.5	**Vaughn-Chi** 2.6

Runs, Hits, and Robins

Runs per game rose 8 percent in 1920, but home runs were not the culprit; the league leader, Cy Williams, hit just 15, and he played in Philadelphia, the league's one home run haven. Stolen bases, meanwhile, dropped to their lowest level yet. The decision by the rules committee to disallow scuffed baseballs was the biggest contributor to increased scoring.

On July 1 the Cardinals moved into Sportsman's Park, owned by the AL Browns. Sportsman's was smaller than Robison Field, a change that helped second sacker Rogers Hornsby compile huge numbers in the coming years. On September 15 third baseman Pie Traynor played the first of his 1,941 major league games—all in Pittsburgh flannels.

The post-war attendance boom continued as league attendance leapt 40 percent. The biggest off-field news of the year, the Black Sox scandal, broke in September after rumors had circulated for a year. While the probe focused on the AL, the Senior Circuit was hit as well. Before the 1921 season started, NL veterans Claude Hendrix, Buck Herzog, and Benny Kauff were banned from baseball due to gambling or racketeering. The scandal also tainted the Reds' 1919 world championship victory.

The lowly Brooklyn Robins—who had managed only three first-division finishes since 1903—found themselves in a surprising September tangle with the mighty Giants and Reds. As the other two clubs treaded water, Brooklyn won 16 of 18 to clinch the pennant. Outfielders Hy Myers (22 triples) and Zack Wheat were the chief offensive weapons, as spitballing Burleigh Grimes paced the league in ERA. The Robins led the NL in ERA though the staff was a patchwork job—manager Wilbert Robinson used six starting pitchers. The 1920 campaign was only temporary balm for Brooklyn fans; the club immediately returned to the NL's nether regions and would not win again until 1941.

1920 American League

TEAM	W	L	T	PCT	GB	HW	HL	R	OR	PA	H	2B	3B	HR	BB	SO	HB	SH	AVG	OBP	SLG	OPS	AOPS	BR	ABR	PF	SB	CS	BSA	BSR
CLE	98	56	0	.636		51	27	**857**	642	6064	1574	**300**	95	35	**576**	379	**256**	36	.303	**.376**	.417	**793**	**113**	**130**	**104**	103	73	93	44	-16
CHI	96	58	0	.623	2	**52**	25	794	665	6032	1574	263	**98**	37	471	355	195	38	.295	.357	.402	759	107	49	49	100	109	96	53	-10
NY	95	59	0	.617	3	49	28	838	**629**	5911	1448	268	71	**115**	539	626	174	22	.280	.350	**.426**	776	107	74	47	104	64	82	44	-15
STL	76	77	1	.497	21.5	40	38	797	766	6032	**1651**	279	83	50	427	**339**	208	**39**	**.308**	.363	.419	782	110	94	70	103	**121**	79	**61**	**-1**
BOS	72	81	1	.471	25.5	41	35	650	698	5997	1397	216	71	22	533	429	219	46	.269	.342	.350	692	93	-71	-41	96	98	111	47	-17
WAS	68	84	1	.447	29	37	38	723	802	5936	1526	233	81	36	433	543	199	53	.291	.351	.386	737	104	5	25	97	160	114	58	-5
DET	61	93	1	.396	37	32	46	652	833	5932	1408	228	72	30	479	391	219	19	.270	.334	.359	693	91	-82	-65	98	76	68	53	-7
PHI	48	106	2	.312	50	25	50	558	834	5823	1324	220	49	44	353	593	169	45	.252	.305	.338	643	74	-192	-197	101	50	67	43	-12
TOT	617					327	287	5869		47727	11902	2007	620	369	3811	3655	298	1639	.284	.347	.387	735					751	710	51	-83

TEAM	CG	SHO	GR	SV	IP	H	HR	BB	SO	BR/9	ERA	AERA	OAV	OOB	PR	APR	PF	OSB	OCS	FA	E	WPB	DP	FW	PW	BW	BSW	DIF
CLE	94	11	100	7	1377.0	1448	**31**	**401**	466	**12.3**	3.41	111	.276	.331	57	58	100	84	70	.971	184	31	124	2.1	5.6	**10.1**	-.5	3.7
CHI	**109**	9	66	10	1386.2	1467	45	405	438	**12.3**	3.59	105	.280	.335	31	24	99	**61**	82	.968	198	27	**142**	1.2	2.3	4.8	.0	10.7
NY	88	**15**	93	11	1368.0	**1414**	48	420	480	**12.3**	**3.32**	**115**	**.270**	**.328**	**72**	**75**	101	87	58	.969	194	31	129	1.4	**7.3**	4.6	-.4	5.2
STL	84	9	102	**14**	1378.2	1481	53	578	444	13.7	4.03	97	.283	.359	-38	-22	103	95	89	.963	233	**23**	119	-1.2	-2.1	6.8	**.9**	-4.8
BOS	92	11	76	6	1395.1	1481	39	461	481	12.7	3.82	95	.279	.339	-5	-31	96	123	83	**.972**	**183**	45	131	**2.2**	-3.0	-4.0	-.6	.9
WAS	81	10	102	10	1367.0	1521	51	520	418	13.7	4.17	89	.288	.357	-58	-71	98	91	99	.963	232	63	95	-1.3	-6.9	2.4	.5	-2.8
DET	74	9	**122**	7	1385.0	1487	46	561	**483**	13.7	4.04	92	.284	.359	-38	-52	98	107	96	.964	230	41	95	-.9	-5.0	-6.3	.3	-4.0
PHI	79	6	104	2	1380.1	1612	56	461	423	13.8	3.93	102	.302	.362	-21	11	106	103	**133**	.959	266	40	125	-3.3	1.1	-19.1	-.2	-7.5
TOT	701	80	765	67	11038.0					13.1	3.79		.284	.347						.966	1720	301	960					

Batter-Fielder Wins
Ruth-NY 9.3
Sisler-StL 7.9
Speaker-Cle 5.4
E.Collins-Chi 5.4
Jackson-Chi 4.5

Batting Average
Sisler-StL 407
Speaker-Cle 388
Jackson-Chi 382
Ruth-NY 376
E.Collins-Chi.........372

On-Base Percentage
Ruth-NY......................532
Speaker-Cle................483
Sisler-StL....................449
Jackson-Chi.................444
E.Collins-Chi 438

Slugging Average
Ruth-NY 847
Sisler-StL 632
Jackson-Chi 589
Speaker-Cle 562
Felsch-Chi 540

On-Base Plus Slugging
Ruth-NY.............1379
Sisler-StL...........1082
Speaker-Cle........1045
Jackson-Chi........1033
E.Collins-Chi 932

Adjusted OPS
Ruth-NY................252
Sisler-StL..............179
Jackson-Chi..........172
Speaker-Cle..........171
E.Collins-Chi 146

Adjusted Batter Runs
Ruth-NY...........110.5
Sisler-StL...........69.4
Speaker-Cle 63.9
Jackson-Chi........59.0
E.Collins-Chi 43.1

Runs
Ruth-NY................158
Speaker-Cle..........137
Sisler-StL.............137
E.Collins-Chi 117

Hits
Sisler-StL.............257
E.Collins-Chi 224
Jackson-Chi..........218
Jacobson-StL........216
Speaker-Cle..........214

Doubles
Speaker-Cle 50
Sisler-StL 49
Jackson-Chi 42

Triples
Jackson-Chi............20
Sisler-StL................18
Hooper-Bos 17

Home Runs
Ruth-NY..................54
Sisler-StL................19
T.Walker-Phi............17
Felsch-Chi 14

Total Bases
Sisler-StL..............399
Ruth-NY................388
Jackson-Chi..........336
Speaker-Cle..........310
Jacobson-StL........305

Runs Batted In
Ruth-NY 137
Sisler-StL 122
Jacobson-StL 122
Jackson-Chi 121
Gardner-Cle 118

Stolen Bases
Rice-Was................63
Sisler-StL...............42
Roth-Was...............24
Menosky-Bos..........23
Tobin-StL 21

Base Stealing Runs
Rice-Was 3.4
Sisler-StL 3.3
E.Collins-Chi..........1.6
Williams-StL 1.2
Burns-Phi-Cle........1.1

Fielding Runs-Infield
Ward-NY 16.5
Dykes-Phi 15.4
Sisler-StL 15.1
Scott-Bos 14.1
Chapman-Cle 13.9

Fielding Runs-Outfield
Rice-Was 17.0
Veach-Det............13.6
Felsch-Chi 12.4
Jacobson-StL 9.6
Speaker-Cle 6.0

Wins
Bagby-Cle 31
Mays-NY 26
Coveleski-Cle 24
Faber-Chi................23
Williams-Chi 22

Winning Pct.
Bagby-Cle............721
Mays-NY...............703
Kerr-Chi 700
Cicotte-Chi 677

Complete Games
Bagby-Cle.............30
Faber-Chi...............28
Cicotte-Chi 28
Mays-NY................26
Coveleski-Cle 26

Strikeouts
Coveleski-Cle 133
Williams-Chi 128
Shawkey-NY 126
Faber-Chi..............108
Shocker-StL..........107

Fewest BB/Game
Quinn-NY 1.71
Coveleski-Cle 1.86
Bagby-Cle...........2.09
Cicotte-Chi 2.20
Perry-Phi 2.22

Games
Bagby-Cle......................48
Ayers-Det 46
Mays-NY........................45
Kerr-Chi 45
Zachary-Was 44

Saves
Shocker-StL..............5
Kerr-Chi 5
Burwell-StL 4

Base Runners/9
Coveleski-Cle 10.09
Mails-Cle 10.23
W.Johnson-Was 10.46
Shocker-StL 10.92
Rommel-Phi 10.99

Adjusted Relief Runs

Relief Ranking

Innings Pitched
Bagby-Cle.........339.2
Faber-Chi 319.0
Coveleski-Cle 315.0
Mays-NY............312.0
Cicotte-Chi 303.1

Opponents' Avg.
Coveleski-Cle 243
Collins-NY 247
Shawkey-NY.........248
Shocker-StL 248
Ehmke-Det 253

Opponents' OBP
Coveleski-Cle..............285
Shocker-StL.................305
Shawkey-NY 308
Quinn-NY.....................308
Rommel-Phi.................309

Earned Run Average
Shawkey-NY........2.45
Coveleski-Cle 2.49
Shocker-StL 2.71
Rommel-Phi 2.85
Bagby-Cle...........2.89

Adjusted ERA
Shawkey-NY 155
Coveleski-Cle 153
Shocker-StL..........144
Rommel-Phi..........141
Bagby-Cle 131

Adjusted Starter Runs
Coveleski-Cle 44.4
Shawkey-NY........41.3
Bagby-Cle............38.9
Shocker-StL 29.6
Mays-NY.............28.0

Pitcher Wins
Coveleski-Cle 5.5
Bagby-Cle 4.7
Shawkey-NY 4.6
Shocker-StL 3.7
Mays-NY 3.5

Scandal, Homers, and Clean Balls

Prior to the season, the major leagues decided that using discolored, lumpy baseballs could be dangerous for the players, offense, and attendance. The previous year's gains in runs per team per game continued, and the 1920 figure of 4.76 was the highest in eighteen years. The AL became the first league to draw five million fans, with the Yankees the first team to crack the million mark.

New rules preventing pitchers from defacing balls only increased the offense and excitement levels at the suddenly fuller parks. (Established spitball pitchers could continue their practice if they registered with the leagues.) St. Louis' George Sisler set an all-time record with 257 hits, and the 54 homers by new Yankee Babe Ruth made him a national hero.

The Indians, White Sox, and Yankees converged in June. Indians shortstop Ray Chapman was killed by an errant pitch thrown by Yankee Carl Mays on August 16, and for a time the Indians slumped. Cleveland, however, pulled shortstop Joe Sewell from the minors, and the Tribe regained its fire, winning seven straight while Chicago kayoed New York. The public outcry following Chapman's death forced umpires to keep clean baseballs in play at all times, which further increased scoring.

On September 27, with Chicago a half-game back, eight White Sox players were indicted for fixing 1919's World Series. Owner Charles Comiskey, who had conspired to squelch the investigation, was forced to suspend the players. The decimated White Sox crumbled while Cleveland clinched. To restore public confidence in baseball, the newly appointed Commissioner Kenesaw Mountain Landis barred the eight Sox, and several other miscreants.

After falling behind two games to one in the best-of-nine World Series, the Indians won four straight from Brooklyn to clinch the title. In those four wins, Brooklyn scored just twice. In Game 5, Cleveland's Elmer Smith hit the first Series grand slam. Four innings later, a line drive at Indians second baseman Bill Wambsganss turned into the second unassisted triple play of the century.

1921 National League

TEAM	W	L	T	PCT	GB	HW	HL	R	OR	PA	H	2B	3B	HR	BB	SO	HB	SH	AVG	OBP	SLG	OPS	AOPS	BR	ABR	PF	SB	CS	BSA	BSR
NY	94	59	0	.614		**53**	26	**840**	637	5946	1575	237	93	75	**469**	390	166	**33**	.298	**.359**	.421	780	112	97	95	100	**137**	114	55	-10
PIT	90	63	1	.588	4	45	31	692	**595**	5946	1533	231	**104**	37	341	**371**	**203**	23	.285	.330	.387	717	93	-40	-57	103	134	93	**59**	**-3**
STL	87	66	1	.569	7	48	29	809	681	5915	**1635**	**260**	88	**83**	382	452	195	29	**.308**	.358	**.437**	**795**	**118**	**116**	**134**	98	94	94	50	-12
BOS	79	74	0	.516	15	42	32	721	697	5982	1561	209	100	61	377	470	198	22	.290	.339	.400	739	107	3	45	95	94	100	48	-14
BRO	77	75	0	.507	16.5	41	37	667	681	5773	1476	209	85	59	325	400	164	21	.280	.325	.386	711	90	-54	-76	104	91	73	55	-6
CIN	70	83	0	.458	24	40	36	618	649	5727	1421	221	94	20	375	308	195	45	.278	.333	.370	703	96	-56	-26	95	117	120	49	-16
CHI	64	89	0	.418	30	32	44	668	773	5907	1553	234	56	37	343	374	208	35	.292	.339	.378	717	95	-29	-30	100	70	97	42	-19
PHI	51	103	0	.331	43.5	29	47	617	919	5760	1512	238	50	88	294	615	112	25	.284	.324	.397	721	89	-36	-84	108	66	80	45	-13
TOT	613					330	282	5632		46956	12266	1839	670	460	2906	3380	233	1441	.289	.338	.397	736					803	771	51	-93

TEAM	CG	SHO	GR	SV	IP	H	HR	BB	SO	BR/9	ERA	AERA	OAV	OOB	PR	APR	PF	OSB	OCS	FA	E	WPB	DP	FW	PW	BW	BSW	DIF
NY	71	9	127	**18**	1372.1	1497	79	**295**	357	11.9	3.55	103	.286	.326	34	17	97	80	94	.971	187	29	**155**	1.3	1.7	9.4	.2	5.0
PIT	**88**	10	91	10	1415.2	**1448**	**37**	322	**500**	**11.5**	**3.17**	**121**	**.271**	**.316**	**96**	**103**	101	**73**	87	.973	172	27	129	2.3	**10.2**	-5.6	**.9**	5.8
STL	70	10	**155**	16	1371.2	1486	61	399	464	12.6	3.62	101	.282	.337	24	5	97	104	94	.965	219	52	130	-.6	.5	**13.2**	-.0	-2.6
BOS	74	**11**	124	12	1385.0	1488	54	420	382	12.6	3.90	94	.280	.337	-18	-40	97	90	**119**	.969	199	**16**	122	.5	-3.9	4.4	-.2	1.7
BRO	82	8	106	12	1363.1	1556	46	361	471	12.9	3.70	105	.293	.342	13	27	103	117	94	.964	232	37	142	-1.5	2.7	-7.5	.6	6.8
CIN	83	7	95	9	1363.0	1500	**37**	305	408	12.0	3.46	103	.287	.328	48	17	95	87	78	.969	193	32	139	.9	1.7	-2.6	-.4	-6.1
CHI	73	7	120	7	1363.0	1605	67	409	441	13.6	4.39	87	.303	.357	-93	-87	101	107	103	**.974**	**166**	24	129	**2.5**	-8.6	-3.0	-.7	-2.8
PHI	82	5	107	8	1348.2	1665	79	371	333	13.8	4.48	94	.308	.356	-105	-35	112	145	102	.955	295	55	127	-5.2	-3.5	-8.3	-.1	-8.9
TOT	623	67	925	92	10982.2					12.6	3.78		.289	.338						.967	1663	272	1073					

Batter-Fielder Wins	Batting Average	On-Base Percentage	Slugging Average	On-Base Plus Slugging	Adjusted OPS	Adjusted Batter Runs
Hornsby-StL........7.7	Hornsby-StL 397	Hornsby-StL................458	Hornsby-StL 639	Hornsby-StL 1097	Hornsby-StL 191	Hornsby-StL 79.2
Bancroft-NY........5.3	Roush-Cin.............352	Youngs-NY..................411	McHenry-StL 531	McHenry-StL 924	McHenry-StL 145	Fournier-StL 37.6
Frisch-NY............4.5	McHenry-StL 350	Fournier-StL................409	Kelly-NY 528	Fournier-StL..........914	Fournier-StL..........144	McHenry-StL 36.8
Johnston-Bro......3.0	Cruise-Bos 346	Grimes-Chi 406	Meusel-Phi-NY 515	Meusel-Phi-NY 895	Kelly-NY................131	Cruise-Bos 29.2
McHenry-StL 2.5	Fournier-StL 343	Carey-Pit 395	Mann-StL 512	Kelly-NY................884	Youngs-NY 129	Roush-Cin 27.2

Runs	Hits	Doubles	Triples	Home Runs	Total Bases	Runs Batted In
Hornsby-StL 131	Hornsby-StL 235	Hornsby-StL 44	Powell-Bos.............18	Kelly-NY..................23	Hornsby-StL 378	Hornsby-StL 126
Frisch-NY..............121	Frisch-NY..............211	Kelly-NY 42	Hornsby-StL 18	Hornsby-StL 21	Kelly-NY................310	Kelly-NY 122
Bancroft-NY..........121	C.Bigbee-Pit 204	Johnston-Bro 41	Grimm-Pit 17	Williams-Phi............18	McHenry-StL 305	Youngs-NY 102
Powell-Bos............114	Johnston-Bro 203	Grimes-Chi 38	Frisch-NY................17	McHenry-StL 17	Meusel-Phi-NY 302	McHenry-StL 102
Burns-NY..............111		McHenry-StL..................37	C.Bigbee-Pit 17	Fournier-StL............16	Frisch-NY..............300	Frisch-NY 100

Stolen Bases	Base Stealing Runs	Fielding Runs-Infield	Fielding Runs-Outfield	Wins	Winning Pct.	Complete Games
Frisch-NY................49	Frisch-NY 6.2	Lavan-StL 20.5	C.Bigbee-Pit 11.8	Grimes-Bro 22	Doak-StL 714	Grimes-Bro............30
Carey-Pit 37	Carey-Pit................3.9	Bancroft-NY 19.1	Williams-Phi 8.7	Cooper-Pit 22	Nehf-NY 667	Cooper-Pit 29
Johnston-Bro 28	Stock-StL 1.4	Deal-Chi......................12.8	Griffith-Bro 7.1	Oeschger-Bos 20	Grimes-Bro 629	Luque-Cin..............25
Bohne-Cin 26	Cutshaw-Pit 1.3	Kelly-NY......................11.7	McHenry-StL 5.2	Nehf-NY..................20	Barnes-NY .625	
Maranville-Pit..........25	Maranville-Pit 1.3	Kilduff-Bro 11.5	Carey-Pit................5.1	Rixey-Cin 19	Toney-NY .621	

Strikeouts	Fewest BB/Game	Games	Saves	Base Runners/9	Adjusted Relief Runs	Relief Ranking
Grimes-Bro 136	Adams-Pit............1.01	Scott-Bos 47	North-StL.................7	Adams-Pit............9.73	North-StL 2.4	North-StL..............2.4
Cooper-Pit 134	Alexander-Chi......1.18	Oeschger-Bos................46	Barnes-NY...............6	J.Morrison-Pit 10.31		
Luque-Cin 102	Barnes-NY 1.53	McQuillan-Bos 45	McQuillan-Bos..........5	Ryan-NY............10.57		
McQuillan-Bos 94	Hubbell-Phi..........1.55	Watson-Bos 44		Donohue-Cin 10.88		
	Doak-StL 1.60	Fillingim-Bos.................44		Glazner-Pit 10.92		

Innings Pitched	Opponents' Avg.	Opponents' OBP	Earned Run Average	Adjusted ERA	Adjusted Starter Runs	Pitcher Wins
Cooper-Pit 327.0	Glazner-Pit 250	Adams-Pit 272	Doak-StL 2.59	Adams-Pit 145	Grimes-Bro..........32.8	**Grimes-Bro** 4.0
Luque-Cin..........304.0	Adams-Pit.............251	Glazner-Pit...................306	Adams-Pit............2.64	Doak-StL 142	Glazner-Pit 26.4	**Adams-Pit** 2.5
Grimes-Bro.........302.1	Pertica-StL 267	Nehf-NY........................311	Glazner-Pit 2.77	Glazner-Pit............138	Rixey-Cin 22.6	**Rixey-Cin**...........2.2
Rixey-Cin 301.0	Watson-Bos 270	Luque-Cin 312	Rixey-Cin 2.78	Grimes-Bro 137	Doak-StL 21.1	**Cooper-Pit**..........2.2
Oeschger-Bos....299.0	Nehf-NY 271	Doak-StL 313	Grimes-Bro..........2.83	Mitchell-Bro 134	Adams-Pit............20.5	**Mitchell-Bro** 1.9

A Powerful Visitation

The home run made a splash in the NL in 1921. Four-baggers nearly doubled, from 261 to 460 as runs per team per game rose 16 percent to 4.59, the highest since 1912. Batters struck out less often, despite the rise of the homer, and stolen bases continued to fade. Prior to 1921, the Braves shortened their left-field fence by 25 feet. Cubs Park, Cincinnati's Redland Field, and St. Louis' Sportsman's Park were also shrunk, though Redland Field remained a home run desert.

The change to power baseball caused casualties. After fifteen years, outfielder Dode Paskert played his last game. Perhaps the quintessential Dead Ball Era player, Paskert's singles, walks, and steals were no longer in vogue. Meanwhile, future Hall of Famer Kiki Cuyler began his eighteen-year career, going 0-for-3 in his only appearance of the season for the Pirates.

Seeking their first flag in twelve years, Pittsburgh topped the league most of the season. The pitching, led by Wilbur Cooper and 39-year-old Babe Adams, was the league's best, and their offense rated well, even in cavernous Forbes Field. Down the stretch, though, John McGraw's Giants came up winners. First baseman Bill Terry paced the NL with 23 homers, but New York did real damage by leading the loop in walks by a margin of nearly 100.

The Giants-Yankees World Series, the last best-of-nine affair, was classic. Each game was close into the late innings, with only two games settled by more than 2 runs. In the end, John McGraw's men were stronger as they gained their first world championship since 1905, in eight games.

1921 American League

TEAM	W	L	T	PCT	GB	HW	HL	R	OR	PA	H	2B	3B	HR	BB	SO	HB	SH	AVG	OBP	SLG	OPS	AOPS	BR	ABR	PF	SB	CS	BSA	BSR
NY	98	55	0	.641		**53**	25	**948**	708	6066	1576	285	87	**134**	588	569	189	40	.300	.375	**.464**	**839**	**116**	**146**	**126**	102	89	64	58	-3
CLE	94	60	0	.610	4.5	51	26	925	712	6275	**1656**	**355**	90	42	**623**	376	**232**	37	**.308**	**.383**	.430	813	111	121	107	102	51	42	55	-3
STL	81	73	0	.526	17.5	43	34	835	845	6096	1655	246	**106**	67	413	407	205	36	.304	.357	.425	782	98	24	-21	106	91	71	56	-5
WAS	80	73	1	.523	18	46	30	704	738	6003	1468	240	96	42	462	472	188	**59**	.277	.342	.383	725	95	-83	-48	95	**112**	66	**63**	**2**
BOS	75	79	0	.487	23.5	41	36	668	**696**	5851	1440	248	69	17	428	**344**	186	31	.277	.335	.361	696	84	-134	-117	97	83	65	56	-4
DET	71	82	1	.464	27	37	40	883	852	6302	1724	268	100	58	582	376	230	29	.316	.385	.433	818	115	121	130	99	95	89	52	-10
CHI	62	92	0	.403	36.5	37	40	683	858	5997	1509	242	82	35	445	474	186	37	.283	.343	.379	722	90	-88	-79	99	94	93	50	-12
PHI	53	100	2	.346	45	28	47	657	894	6067	1497	256	64	82	424	565	135	43	.274	.331	.389	720	88	-103	-106	101	69	56	55	-4
TOT	616					336	278	6303		48657	12525	2140	694	477	3965	3583	312	155	1.292	.357	.408	765					684	546	56	-41

TEAM	CG	SHO	GR	SV	IP	H	HR	BB	SO	BR/9	ERA	AERA	OAV	OOB	PR	APR	PF	OSB	OCS	FA	E	WPB	DP	FW	PW	BW	BSW	DIF
NY	**92**	8	96	15	1364.0	**1461**	51	470	**481**	13.1	**3.82**	**111**	**.277**	**.342**	**70**	**63**	99	82	61	.965	222	36	138	-.3	**5.9**	11.8	.2	3.9
CLE	81	**11**	114	14	1377.0	1534	**43**	**431**	475	**13.0**	3.90	109	.288	.344	58	55	100	96	52	.967	204	32	124	.8	5.1	10.0	.2	.8
STL	77	9	**142**	9	1379.0	1541	71	556	477	13.9	4.61	97	.288	.360	-51	-21	105	79	66	.964	224	**24**	127	-.3	-2.0	-2.0	.0	8.2
WAS	80	10	108	10	1383.2	1568	51	442	452	13.3	3.97	104	.291	.349	47	23	96	**59**	67	.963	235	36	153	-.9	2.2	-4.5	**.7**	6.1
BOS	88	9	82	5	1364.1	1521	53	452	446	13.3	3.98	106	.291	.352	45	38	99	73	71	**.975**	**157**	27	151	**3.5**	3.6	-10.9	.1	1.8
DET	73	4	115	**17**	1386.1	1634	71	495	452	14.2	4.40	97	.297	.361	-18	-20	100	99	75	.963	232	34	107	-.8	-1.9	**12.2**	-.5	-14.6
CHI	84	7	106	9	1365.1	1603	52	549	392	14.4	4.94	86	.303	.372	-99	-109	99	98	79	.969	200	35	**155**	1.0	-10.2	-7.4	-.6	2.2
PHI	75	2	119	7	1400.1	1645	85	548	431	14.3	4.61	97	.300	.367	-52	-24	104	101	**90**	.958	274	48	144	-3.1	-2.2	-9.9	.1	-8.4
TOT	650	60	882	86	11020.0					13.7	4.28		.292	.357						.965	1748	272	1099					

Batter-Fielder Wins	Batting Average	On-Base Percentage	Slugging Average	On-Base Plus Slugging	Adjusted OPS	Adjusted Batter Runs
Ruth-NY 9.4	Heilmann-Det 394	Ruth-NY 512	Ruth-NY 846	Ruth-NY.............1359	Ruth-NY................236	Ruth-NY...........117.7
Cobb-Det 4.8	Cobb-Det 389	Cobb-Det 452	Heilmann-Det 606	Heilmann-Det 1051	Heilmann-Det 167	Heilmann-Det 60.7
Collins-Chi 4.4	Ruth-NY 378	Heilmann-Det..............444	Cobb-Det 596	Cobb-Det...........1048	Cobb-Det 167	Cobb-Det............52.2
Speaker-Cle 3.8	Sisler-StL 371	Speaker-Cle.................439	Williams-StL 561	Williams-StL 990	Speaker-Cle..........146	Speaker-Cle 38.5
Heilmann-Det......3.4	Speaker-Cle 362	Williams-StL.................429	Sisler-StL 560	Speaker-Cle..........977	Williams-StL 142	Williams-StL 36.3

Runs	Hits	Doubles	Triples	Home Runs	Total Bases	Runs Batted In
Ruth-NY................177	Heilmann-Det 237	Speaker-Cle 52	Tobin-StL 18	Ruth-NY..................59	Ruth-NY................457	Ruth-NY 171
Tobin-StL 132	Tobin-StL 236	Ruth-NY 44	Sisler-StL 18	Williams-StL 24	Heilmann-Det 365	Heilmann-Det 139
Peckinpaugh-NY ..128	Sisler-StL..............216	Veach-Det.......................43	Shanks-Was 18	Meusel-NY..............24	Meusel-NY............334	Meusel-NY 135
Sisler-StL...............125	Jacobson-StL.........211	Heilmann-Det 43		T.Walker-Phi............23	Tobin-StL 327	Veach-Det............128
Cobb-Det..............124	Veach-Det 207	Meusel-NY 40		Heilmann-Det 19	Sisler-StL 326	Gardner-Cle 120

Stolen Bases	Base Stealing Runs	Fielding Runs-Infield	Fielding Runs-Outfield	Wins	Winning Pct.	Complete Games
Sisler-StL.................35	Sisler-StL 3.8	Scott-Bos 41.2	Veach-Det............12.9	Shocker-StL 27	Mays-NY 750	Faber-Chi 32
Harris-Was.............29	Harris-Was 3.2	Collins-Chi 30.7	Speaker-Cle 9.2	Mays-NY 27	Shocker-StL 692	Shocker-StL 30
Rice-Was................26	Judge-Was 2.5	Dykes-Phi 21.1	Cobb-Det 6.0	Faber-Chi................25	Bush-Bos 640	Mays-NY................30
Johnson-Chi 22	Meusel-NY 1.6	Johnson-Chi................20.8	Rice-Was 5.9	Jones-Bos 23	Coveleski-Cle 639	Coveleski-Cle 28
Cobb-Det................22	Rice-Was 1.5	Ward-NY 18.8	T.Walker-Phi 5.2	Coveleski-Cle 23	Faber-Chi 625	....

Strikeouts	Fewest BB/Game	Games	Saves	Base Runners/9	Adjusted Relief Runs	Relief Ranking
Johnson-Was........143	Hasty-Phi 2.01	Mays-NY 49	Middleton-Det 7	Faber-Chi 10.53		
Shocker-StL..........132	Mays-NY..............2.03	Shocker-StL 47	Mays-NY 7	Morton-Cle 11.03		
Shawkey-NY 126	Mogridge-Was 2.06	Bayne-StL......................47		Mays-NY..............11.15		
Faber-Chi..............124	Bagby-Cle.............2.07	Rommel-Phi 46		Mogridge-Was ..11.69		
Leonard-Det 120	Zachary-Was 2.12			Shocker-StL 12.04		

Innings Pitched	Opponents' Avg.	Opponents' OBP	Earned Run Average	Adjusted ERA	Adjusted Starter Runs	Pitcher Wins
Mays-NY............336.2	Faber-Chi 242	Faber-Chi.....................297	Faber-Chi 2.48	Faber-Chi.............171	Faber-Chi 64.1	**Faber-Chi**............6.8
Faber-Chi 330.2	Mays-NY...............257	Mays-NY 303	Mogridge-Was 3.00	Mays-NY 139	Mays-NY..............42.6	**Mays-NY** 5.4
Shocker-StL 326.2	Bush-Bos 260	Mogridge-Was 313	Mays-NY...............3.05	Mogridge-Was 137	Mogridge-Was 35.8	**Jones-Bos** 4.3
Coveleski-Cle 315.0	Shawkey-NY.........263	Shocker-StL 319	Hoyt-NY 3.09	Hoyt-NY................137	Hoyt-NY 35.3	**Shocker-StL** 4.2
Kerr-Chi 308.2	Johnson-Was 263	Johnson-Was...............326	Jones-Bos............3.22	Jones-Bos 131	Jones-Bos............34.3	**Hoyt-NY** 3.3

The First of Many

Resurgent New York, riding a one-man power wave, engaged with Cleveland in one of the decade's best races. Neck-and-neck from mid-May onward, the teams counter-punched their way through mid-September. With the two clubs tied on September 23, the Indians started a four-game set at New York. After splitting the first two, the Yankees destroyed Cleveland, 21–7, on September 25, won again the next day, and never looked back. This was the first pennant ever for the Yankees.

Once again, Babe Ruth outhomered most AL clubs. Bob Meusel, Wally Pipp, and Roger Peckinpaugh supported The Bambino ably, as did and a capable mound staff led by pariah Carl Mays. The game had changed almost overnight. Runs rose to 5.12 per team per game, and only Red Faber posted an ERA under 3.00. The overpowering force named Ruth set new major league marks for home runs and RBIs.

Stripped of talent by Judge Landis' lifetime suspensions, the White Sox fell to seventh. Due to the gambling scandal, the public lost confidence in baseball, especially in American League cities. Despite the excitement generated by Babe Ruth, attendance was down 9 percent in 1920; moreover, the perception of the AL as a "dirty league" helped the NL eventually surpass of the Junior Circuit in attendance as AL fans responded to the scandal by voting with their feet. AL attendance in 1930 was substantially less than the NL's, even though the AL had outdrawn the NL by 26 percent in 1920.

The Philadelphia A's expanded Shibe Park's right field by 40 feet in 1921, but that didn't stop the tide of home runs. New York, St. Louis, and Philadelphia were the league's big long-ball parks, but the Yankees led the loop in homers at home *and* on the road. In the crosstown World Series (the final best-of-nine classic), the Giants shut down the mighty Yankees, winning in eight.

1922 National League

TEAM	W	L	T	PCT	GB	HW	HL	R	OR	PA	H	2B	3B	HR	BB	SO	HB	SH	AVG	OBP	SLG	OPS	AOPS	BR	ABR	PF	SB	CS	BSA	BSR
NY	93	61	2	.604		**51**	27	852	**658**	6109	1661	253	90	80	448	421	159	**48**	.305	**.363**	.428	791	109	79	72	101	116	83	58	-4
CIN	86	68	2	.558	7	48	29	766	677	5943	1561	226	99	45	436	381	189	36	.296	.353	.401	754	102	6	21	98	130	136	49	-19
STL	85	69	0	.552	8	42	35	863	819	6061	1634	**280**	88	**107**	447	425	161	28	.301	.357	**.444**	**801**	**118**	**94**	**137**	95	73	63	54	-6
PIT	85	69	1	.552	8	45	33	**865**	736	6151	**1698**	239	**110**	52	423	326	175	32	**.308**	.360	.419	779	106	54	44	101	**145**	59	**71**	**11**
CHI	80	74	2	.519	13	39	37	771	808	6092	1564	248	71	42	**525**	447	**205**	27	.293	.359	.390	749	97	10	-5	102	97	108	47	-16
BRO	76	78	1	.494	17	44	34	743	754	5955	1569	235	76	56	339	**318**	178	25	.290	.335	.392	727	94	-60	-54	99	79	60	57	-4
PHI	57	96	1	.373	35.5	35	41	738	920	6088	1537	268	55	116	450	611	140	39	.282	.341	.415	756	92	1	-67	110	48	60	44	-10
BOS	53	100	1	.346	39.5	32	43	596	822	5750	1355	162	73	32	387	451	174	28	.263	.317	.341	658	78	-184	-158	96	67	65	51	-8
TOT	620					336	279	6194		48149	12579	1911	662	530	3455	3380	263	1381	.292	.348	.404	753					755	634	54	-56

TEAM	CG	SHO	GR	SV	IP	H	HR	BB	SO	BR/9	ERA	AERA	OAV	OOB	PR	APR	PF	OSB	OCS	FA	E	WPB	DP	FW	PW	BW	BSW	DIF
NY	76	7	135	**15**	1396.1	**1454**	71	393	388	12.0	**3.45**	**116**	**.272**	.324	**100**	**85**	98	**70**	58	**.970**	194	40	145	1.1	**8.0**	6.8	.3	-.2
CIN	**88**	8	93	3	1385.2	1481	**49**	**326**	357	**11.9**	3.53	113	.278	**.322**	87	71	97	77	69	.968	205	**18**	147	.4	6.7	2.0	-1.1	1.1
STL	60	8	**172**	12	1362.2	1609	61	447	465	13.9	4.44	87	.299	.358	-52	-93	94	90	83	.961	239	34	122	-2.0	-8.8	**12.9**	.0	5.8
PIT	**88**	**15**	114	7	1387.1	1613	52	358	490	13.0	3.98	102	.296	.343	18	14	99	92	64	**.970**	**187**	31	126	**1.5**	1.3	4.2	**1.7**	-.7
CHI	74	8	138	12	1397.2	1579	77	475	402	13.6	4.34	97	.292	.356	-38	-23	102	79	**104**	.968	204	35	**154**	.5	-2.2	-.5	-.9	6.0
BRO	82	12	115	8	1385.2	1574	74	490	**499**	13.6	4.05	100	.293	.356	8	2	99	128	82	.967	208	42	139	.1	.2	-5.1	.3	3.5
PHI	73	6	118	5	1372.0	1692	89	460	394	14.4	4.64	101	.307	.365	-82	6	114	123	76	.965	225	52	152	-1.1	.6	-6.3	-.3	-12.4
BOS	63	7	146	6	1348.0	1565	57	489	360	13.9	4.37	91	.298	.361	-41	-59	98	96	98	.965	215	34	121	-.4	-5.6	-14.9	-.0	-2.5
TOT	604	71	1031	68	11035.1					13.3	4.10		.292	.348						.967	1677	286	1106					

Batter-Fielder Wins	Batting Average	On-Base Percentage	Slugging Average	On-Base Plus Slugging	Adjusted OPS	Adjusted Batter Runs
Hornsby-StL........8.9	Hornsby-StL 401	Hornsby-StL.................459	Hornsby-StL 722	Hornsby-StL 1181	Hornsby-StL 210	Hornsby-StL 100.4
Bancroft-NY........4.9	Grimes-Chi 354	Grimes-Chi 442	Grimes-Chi 572	Grimes-Chi 1014	Grimes-Chi 157	Grimes-Chi 46.8
O'Farrell-Chi........4.1	Miller-Chi 352	O'Farrell-Chi 439	Lee-Phi 540	Williams-Phi..........905	Daubert-Cin..........130	Daubert-Cin........25.3
Carey-Pit..............3.5	Bigbee-Pit.............350	Carey-Pit 408	Tierney-Pit 515	Miller-Chi 899	Wheat-Bro 129	Wheat-Bro 25.2
Grimes-Chi..........3.2	Tierney-Pit 345	Bigbee-Pit 405	Williams-Phi 514	Walker-Phi 899	Miller-Chi 128	Russell-Pit 23.4

Runs	Hits	Doubles	Triples	Home Runs	Total Bases	Runs Batted In
Hornsby-StL 141	Hornsby-StL 250	Hornsby-StL 46	Daubert-Cin............22	Hornsby-StL 42	Hornsby-StL 450	Hornsby-StL 152
Carey-Pit 140	Bigbee-Pit 215	Grimes-Chi 45	Meusel-NY.............17	Williams-Phi...........26	Meusel-NY............314	Meusel-NY 132
Smith-StL..............117	Bancroft-NY..........209	Duncan-Cin...................44	Maranville-Pit.........15	Lee-Phi 17	Wheat-Bro 302	Wheat-Bro 112
Bancroft-NY..........117	Carey-Pit 207	Bancroft-NY 41	Bigbee-Pit 15	Kelly-NY..................17	Williams-Phi..........300	Kelly-NY 107
Maranville-Pit........115	Daubert-Cin..........205	Hollocher-Chi 37			Daubert-Cin..........300	

Stolen Bases	Base Stealing Runs	Fielding Runs-Infield	Fielding Runs-Outfield	Wins	Winning Pct.	Complete Games
Carey-Pit 51	Carey-Pit.............10.5	Parkinson-Phi 27.9	Bigbee-Pit............13.7	Rixey-Cin 25	Donohue-Cin 667	Cooper-Pit 27
Frisch-NY................31	Traynor-Pit 2.7	Bancroft-NY 22.1	Carey-Pit................9.9	Cooper-Pit 23	Rixey-Cin 658	Ruether-Bro 26
Burns-Cin 30	Kelly-NY 1.6	Pinelli-Cin 21.9	Powell-Bos 6.0	Ruether-Bro.............21	Couch-Cin 640	Rixey-Cin 26
Maranville-Pit..........24	Smith-StL 1.5	Bohne-Cin 12.5	Walker-Phi 4.5	Pfeffer-StL 19	Ruether-Bro .636	
Bigbee-Pit 24	T.Griffith-Bro 1.2	Kelly-NY.......................9.3	Youngs-NY 2.6	Nehf-NY...................19	Cooper-Pit .622	

Strikeouts	Fewest BB/Game	Games	Saves	Base Runners/9	Adjusted Relief Runs	Relief Ranking
Vance-Bro 134	Adams-Pit...............79	North-StL 53	Jonnard-NY 5	McNamara-Bos..10.44	McNamara-Bos....11.8	McNamara-Bos ..10.5
Cooper-Pit 129	Alexander-Chi......1.25	Sherdel-StL...................47	North-StL..................4	Douglas-NY 11.02	Causey-NY 5.2	Causey-NY 4.8
Ring-Phi................116	Rixey-Cin 1.29	Ryan-NY........................46		Adams-Pit...........11.03	Jonnard-NY 3.9	Jonnard-NY 3.0
Morrison-Pit..........104	Donohue-Cin 1.60	Oeschger-Bos................46		Rixey-Cin 11.09	Mamaux-Bro..........2.6	Mamaux-Bro 1.5
Grimes-Bro 99	J.Barnes-NY 1.61	Morrison-Pit 45		Donohue-Cin 11.34	Braxton-Bos 2.4	Braxton-Bos..........1.2

Innings Pitched	Opponents' Avg.	Opponents' OBP	Earned Run Average	Adjusted ERA	Adjusted Starter Runs	Pitcher Wins
Rixey-Cin 313.1	Douglas-NY 257	Douglas-NY 302	Douglas-NY 2.63	Douglas-NY..........152	Cooper-Pit 27.3	**Cooper-Pit**..........3.9
Cooper-Pit 294.2	Luque-Cin.............268	Rixey-Cin 303	Ryan-NY...............3.01	Weinert-Phi 137	Douglas-NY 24.9	**Meadows-Phi** 2.6
Morrison-Pit 286.1	Ryan-NY...............269	Adams-Pit 307	Donohue-Cin 3.12	Ryan-NY 133	Donohue-Cin 21.6	**Nehf-NY**............2.5
Nehf-NY 268.1	Osborne-Chi.........271	J.Barnes-NY 311	Cooper-Pit 3.18	Cooper-Pit 128	Nehf-NY 21.1	**Ruether-Bro** 2.5
Ruether-Bro 267.1	Rixey-Cin 275	Donohue-Cin 312	Nehf-NY 3.29	Donohue-Cin 128	Morrison-Pit 21.0	**Ryan-NY** 2.5

Polo Grounds Potency

Team runs per game rose to 5.00, more than an entire run higher than 1920 and the century's top total to date. The league pounded 530 homers, another all-time high; four-baggers had more than doubled in two years. Meanwhile, the stolen base was at its lowest ebb yet at .61 per game. More runs meant fewer pitchers racking up big totals; just three pitchers won 20, compared to seven in 1920.

John McGraw's Giants, first or second every year since 1917, took their second straight NL flag. Only for a few days did the Giants trail, and they won easily over second-place Cincinnati, which featured 25-game winner Eppa Rixey. Three Giants hurlers graced the top five in ERA, and the club featured seven .300-hitting regulars.

Rogers Hornsby enjoyed arguably his greatest season in 1922, batting .401 and taking the Triple Crown. However, his Cardinals, otherwise weak offensively, tied for third with Pittsburgh. The Pirates topped the league in runs, bucking the trend by leading the loop in average and steals.

Three eventual Hall of Famers debuted. Cubs catcher Gabby Hartnett played the first of his 1,990 career games. Cardinals first baseman Jim Bottomley hit .325 after an August promotion. Finally, shortstop Travis Jackson began his fifteen-year career with a cameo appearance for the Giants. Two significant deaths bridged the old and the new. The great Cap Anson passed away at 70 on April 14. Meanwhile, 27-year-old Cardinals outfielder Austin McHenry, suffering from a brain tumor, died November 27.

The Giants again met—and vanquished—the Yankees at the Polo Grounds, making it 13 straight World Series games played at the same two-team venue. The Giants won in five (including one tie), allowing just 11 runs and batting .309. Nobody sensed that this would be the Giants' last world title for more than a decade.

1922 American League

TEAM	W	L	T	PCT	GB	HW	HL	R	OR	PA	H	2B	3B	HR	BB	SO	HB	SH	AVG	OBP	SLG	OPS	AOPS	BR	ABR	PF	SB	CS	BSA	BSR
NY	94	60	0	.610		50	27	758	**618**	6000	1504	220	75	95	497	532	218	40	.287	.353	.412	765	103	34	17	102	62	59	51	-7
STL	93	61	0	.604	1	**54**	23	**867**	643	6128	**1693**	291	**94**	**98**	473	381	203	36	**.313**	**.372**	**.455**	**827**	**117**	**159**	**128**	104	**136**	76	**64**	**3**
DET	79	75	1	.513	15	43	34	828	791	6170	1641	250	87	54	530	378	**244**	36	.306	**.372**	.415	787	115	94	122	97	78	62	56	-5
CLE	78	76	1	.506	16	44	35	768	817	6095	1544	**320**	73	32	**554**	**331**	203	**45**	.292	.364	.398	762	104	49	43	101	90	58	61	0
CHI	77	77	1	.500	17	43	34	691	691	6023	1463	243	62	45	482	463	231	43	.278	.343	.373	716	92	-52	-49	100	109	84	56	-5
WAS	69	85	0	.448	25	40	39	650	706	5868	1395	229	76	45	458	442	152	57	.268	.334	.367	701	93	-86	-53	95	97	63	61	-1
PHI	65	89	1	.422	29	38	39	705	830	5854	1409	229	63	111	437	591	170	36	.270	.331	.402	733	94	-38	-55	103	60	69	47	-11
BOS	61	93	0	.396	33	31	42	598	769	5859	1392	250	55	45	366	455	161	44	.263	.316	.357	673	82	-151	-146	99	64	67	49	-9
TOT	618					343	273	5865		47997	12041	2032	585	525	3797	3573	337	158	2.285	.348	.398	746					696	538	56	-35

TEAM	CG	SHO	GR	SV	IP	H	HR	BB	SO	BR/9	ERA	AERA	OAV	OOB	PR	APR	PF	OSB	OCS	FA	E	WPB	DP	FW	PW	BW	BSW	DIF
NY	**100**	7	69	14	1393.2	**1402**	73	423	458	**11.9**	3.39	118	**.268**	**.325**	99	92	99	67	72	**.975**	157	37	124	2.0	8.9	1.7	-.3	4.6
STL	79	8	115	**22**	1392.0	1412	71	**419**	**534**	12.1	**3.38**	**122**	**.268**	.327	**101**	**112**	103	**66**	**77**	.968	201	24	158	-.5	**10.9**	**12.4**	**.7**	-7.5
DET	67	7	133	15	1391.0	1554	62	473	461	13.7	4.27	91	.288	.354	-37	-67	96	112	60	.970	191	29	133	.2	-6.5	11.8	-.0	-3.4
CLE	76	**14**	135	7	1383.2	1605	58	464	489	13.7	4.59	87	.296	.356	-85	-93	99	106	48	.968	202	48	147	-.5	-9.0	4.2	.4	5.9
CHI	86	13	99	8	1403.2	1472	57	529	484	13.0	3.94	103	.278	.346	15	15	101	75	76	**.975**	**155**	**19**	143	**2.2**	1.5	-4.8	-.0	1.1
WAS	84	13	97	10	1362.1	1485	49	500	422	13.4	3.81	101	.286	.354	33	6	96	85	74	.969	196	42	**168**	-.2	.6	-5.1	.3	-3.6
PHI	73	4	**147**	6	1362.1	1573	107	469	373	13.7	4.59	92	.297	.357	-85	-52	105	83	75	.966	215	38	118	-1.2	-5.0	-5.3	-.6	.2
BOS	71	10	130	6	1373.1	1508	**48**	503	359	13.5	4.30	95	.287	.354	-41	-31	102	102	56	.965	224	38	145	-1.8	-3.0	-14.2	-.4	3.4
TOT	636	76	925	88	11062.0					13.1	4.03		.285	.348						.969	1541	275	1136					

Batter-Fielder Wins	Batting Average	On-Base Percentage	Slugging Average	On-Base Plus Slugging	Adjusted OPS	Adjusted Batter Runs
Sisler-StL 6.3	Sisler-StL 420	Speaker-Cle 474	Ruth-NY 672	Ruth-NY 1106	Ruth-NY 181	Sisler-StL 60.0
Speaker-Cle 5.1	Cobb-Det 401	Sisler-StL 467	Williams-StL 627	Speaker-Cle 1080	Speaker-Cle 178	Cobb-Det 57.7
Cobb-Det 4.2	Speaker-Cle 378	Cobb-Det 462	Speaker-Cle 606	Sisler-StL 1061	Cobb-Det 172	Speaker-Cle 54.6
Williams-StL 4.1	Heilmann-Det 356	Ruth-NY 434	Heilmann-Det 598	Williams-StL 1040	Heilmann-Det 172	Williams-StL 52.1
Ruth-NY 3.5	Miller-Phi 335	Heilmann-Det 432	Sisler-StL 594	Heilmann-Det 1030	Sisler-StL 169	Ruth-NY 49.2

Runs	Hits	Doubles	Triples	Home Runs	Total Bases	Runs Batted In
Sisler-StL 134	Sisler-StL 246	Speaker-Cle 48	Sisler-StL 18	Williams-StL 39	Williams-StL 367	Williams-StL 155
Blue-Det 131	Cobb-Det 211	Pratt-Bos 44	Jacobson-StL 16	Walker-Phi 37	Sisler-StL 348	Veach-Det 126
Williams-StL 128	Tobin-StL 207	Sisler-StL 42	Cobb-Det 16	Ruth-NY 35	Walker-Phi 310	McManus-StL 109
Tobin-StL 122	Veach-Det 202	Cobb-Det 42	Judge-Was 15	Miller-Phi 21	Cobb-Det 297	Sisler-StL 105
			Mostil-Chi 14	Heilmann-Det 21	Tobin-StL 296	Jacobson-StL 102

Stolen Bases	Base Stealing Runs	Fielding Runs-Infield	Fielding Runs-Outfield	Wins	Winning Pct.	Complete Games
Sisler-StL 51	Sisler-StL 4.6	Harris-Was 31.2	Veach-Det 9.7	Rommel-Phi 27	Bush-NY 788	Faber-Chi 31
Williams-StL 37	Jacobson-StL 2.1	Peckinpaugh-Was 18.3	Menosky-Bos 5.6	Bush-NY 26	Rommel-Phi 675	Shocker-StL 29
Harris-Was 25	Evans-Cle 1.7	Scott-NY 16.6	Miller-Phi 5.2	Shocker-StL 24	Shawkey-NY 625	Uhle-Cle 23
Johnson-Chi 21	Harris-Was 1.7	Sisler-StL 11.7	Hooper-Chi 4.8	Uhle-Cle 22	Pillette-Det 613	Johnson-Was 23
	Veach-Det 1.6	Jones-Det 10.1	Harris-Bos 4.0	Faber-Chi 21	Hoyt-NY 613	

Strikeouts	Fewest BB/Game	Games	Saves	Base Runners/9	Adjusted Relief Runs	Relief Ranking
Shocker-StL 149	Shocker-StL 1.47	Rommel-Phi 51	Jones-NY 8	Faber-Chi 10.82	Murray-NY 1.2	Murray-NY 1.0
Faber-Chi 148	Vangilder-StL 1.76	Uhle-Cle 50	Pruett-StL 7	Shocker-StL 11.02		
Shawkey-NY 130	Mays-NY 1.88	Shocker-StL 48	Wright-StL 5	Rommel-Phi 11.08		
Ehmke-Det 108	Kolp-StL 1.91	Harriss-Phi 47		Vangilder-StL 11.09		
Johnson-Was 105	Hasty-Phi 1.92			Quinn-Bos 11.43		

Innings Pitched	Opponents' Avg.	Opponents' OBP	Earned Run Average	Adjusted ERA	Adjusted Starter Runs	Pitcher Wins
Faber-Chi 352.0	Davis-StL 250	Faber-Chi 299	Faber-Chi 2.81	Faber-Chi 144	Faber-Chi 46.6	**Shocker-StL** 4.9
Shocker-StL 348.0	Bush-NY 252	Shocker-StL 304	Pillette-Det 2.85	Wright-StL 141	Shocker-StL 43.8	**Faber-Chi** 4.6
Shawkey-NY 299.2	Faber-Chi 252	Rommel-Phi 309	Shawkey-NY 2.91	Shocker-StL 139	Shawkey-NY 37.3	**Vangilder-StL** 3.8
Rommel-Phi 294.0	Shawkey-NY 256	Vangilder-StL 310	Wright-StL 2.92	Shawkey-NY 137	Pillette-Det 29.9	**Rommel-Phi** 3.6
Uhle-Cle 287.1	Pillette-Det 258	Quinn-Bos 311	Shocker-StL 2.97	Pillette-Det 136	Rommel-Phi 29.9	**Shawkey-NY** 3.3

Browns Come Close

Apparently deciding that if they couldn't beat 'em, they'd join 'em, the Athletics brought *in* the left-field fences at Shibe Park. As a result, Philadelphia hit the league' most homers in home games. Unfortunately, they also *allowed* the most, and finished seventh. These were hard years to be a Philadelphia baseball fan. The A's and Phillies both finished last in 1919, 1920, and 1921, and were seventh in 1922. Soon, Connie Mack's club would climb back to the top.

AL hitters pounded 525 homers, more than double the total of three years before. But this wasn't sloppy baseball; hitters still made contact (since 1918, no AL pitcher had notched 150 strikeouts). In addition, for the first time, the league's fielding percentage reached .970; it never again fell below .968. And as the 1910s faded into memory, so did two of the decade's standouts. Home Run Baker ended his career with the Yankees, and converted outfielder Smokey Joe Wood hit .297 in his final season for Cleveland.

The Yankees won the flag again. But one misconception about the Yankees teams of the 1920s is that they bludgeoned the opposition. It just isn't so; only twice in the '20s did they romp to the flag. In fact, in 1922, they almost lost—to the Browns. St. Louis was fueled by George Sisler, who set an AL record by hitting in 41 games. He also led the league in hits, runs, triples, while pounding out a .420 average (only surpassed in the AL by Nap Lajoie's .426 in 1901). The Browns scored 100 more runs than New York, had a better ERA, and stole more bases, but the Yankees moved ahead in August and eventually held on by 1 game.

The Yankees struggled without Babe Ruth and Bob Meusel, suspended a month for barnstorming. When the two returned, they carried the club's attack. They did little in October, though. The Yankees lost in five (four losses and one tie) to the pitching-rich Giants, who had served as their landlord at the Polo Grounds for a decade.

1923 National League

TEAM	W	L	T	PCT	GB	HW	HL	R	OR	PA	H	2B	3B	HR	BB	SO	HB	SH	AVG	OBP	SLG	OPS	AOPS	BR	ABR	PF	SB	CS	BSA	BSR
NY	95	58	0	.621		**47**	30	**854**	679	6083	**1610**	248	76	85	**487**	406	113	31	**.295**	**.356**	**.415**	**771**	**110**	**73**	**84**	99	106	70	60	-1
CIN	91	63	0	.591	4.5	46	32	708	**629**	5935	1506	237	95	45	439	367	**185**	33	.285	.344	.392	736	102	-2	13	98	96	105	48	-16
PIT	87	67	0	.565	8.5	**47**	30	786	696	5943	1592	224	**111**	49	407	**362**	103	28	**.295**	.347	.404	751	102	22	6	102	154	75	**67**	**8**
CHI	83	71	0	.539	12.5	46	31	756	704	5896	1516	243	52	**90**	455	485	151	31	.288	.348	.406	754	104	35	34	100	**181**	143	56	-10
STL	79	74	1	.516	16	42	35	746	732	6137	1582	**274**	76	63	438	446	135	**38**	.286	.343	.398	741	103	7	24	98	89	61	59	-2
BRO	76	78	1	.494	19.5	37	40	753	741	6082	1559	214	81	62	425	382	148	33	.285	.340	.387	727	100	-23	-2	97	71	50	59	-2
BOS	54	100	1	.351	41.5	22	55	636	798	5957	1455	213	58	32	429	404	168	31	.273	.331	.353	684	90	-100	-73	96	57	80	42	-15
PHI	50	104	1	.325	45.5	20	55	748	1008	6054	1528	259	39	112	414	556	110	39	.278	.333	.401	734	89	-12	-89	112	70	73	49	-10
TOT	617					307	308	5987		48087	12348	1912	588	538	3494	3408	264	1113	.286	.343	.395	737					824	657	56	-49

TEAM	CG	SHO	GR	SV	IP	H	HR	BB	SO	BR/9	ERA	AERA	OAV	OOB	PR	APR	PF	OSB	OCS	FA	E	WPB	DP	FW	PW	BW	BSW	DIF
NY	62	10	**159**	**18**	1378.0	1440	82	424	453	12.3	3.90	98	.271	.328	15	-14	96	**63**	69	**.972**	**176**	26	141	**2.4**	-1.3	**8.1**	.5	8.9
CIN	88	11	97	9	1391.1	1465	**28**	**359**	450	**12.0**	**3.21**	**120**	.273	**.322**	**121**	**102**	97	98	91	.969	202	31	144	.9	**9.8**	1.3	-1.0	3.0
PIT	92	5	99	9	1376.1	1513	53	402	414	12.7	3.87	103	.284	.337	19	19	100	78	70	.971	179	**25**	157	2.3	1.8	.6	**1.4**	4.0
CHI	80	8	107	11	1366.2	**1419**	86	435	408	12.4	3.82	105	**.269**	.329	27	25	100	80	69	.967	208	**25**	144	.5	2.4	3.3	-.4	.2
STL	77	9	126	7	1398.1	1539	70	456	398	13.1	3.87	101	.284	.344	20	5	98	111	71	.963	232	36	141	-.9	.5	2.3	.4	.2
BRO	**94**	8	92	5	1396.2	1503	55	476	**548**	13.0	3.74	103	.277	.340	39	21	97	131	103	.955	293	49	137	-4.4	2.0	-.2	.4	1.2
BOS	55	**13**	153	7	1392.2	1662	64	394	351	13.5	4.21	94	.302	.352	-34	-41	100	126	**105**	.964	230	32	157	-.7	-3.9	-7.0	-.9	-10.5
PHI	68	3	150	8	1376.1	1801	100	549	384	15.6	5.34	86	.322	.386	-205	-100	115	137	79	.966	217	60	**172**	.0	-9.6	-8.6	-.4	-8.5
TOT	616	67	983	74	11076.1					13.1	3.99		.286	.343						.966	1737	284	1193					

Batter-Fielder Wins	Batting Average	On-Base Percentage	Slugging Average	On-Base Plus Slugging	Adjusted OPS	Adjusted Batter Runs
Fournier-Bro........4.2	Hornsby-StL 384	Hornsby-StL.................459	Hornsby-StL 627	Hornsby-StL 1086	Hornsby-StL 188	Hornsby-StL 55.7
O'Farrell-Chi........3.9	Wheat-Bro 375	Bottomley-StL 425	Fournier-Bro 588	Fournier-Bro 999	Fournier-Bro 165	Fournier-Bro 47.4
Hornsby-StL..........3.8	Bottomley-StL.......371	Youngs-NY..................412	Williams-Phi 576	Bottomley-StL 960	Bottomley-StL 155	Bottomley-StL 42.1
Hargrave-Cin 3.8	Fournier-Bro 351	Fournier-Bro.................411	Barnhart-Pit 563	Williams-Phi..........947	Roush-Cin 149	Roush-Cin 36.9
Traynor-Pit..........3.6	Roush-Cin.............351	O'Farrell-Chi 408	Bottomley-StL.......535	Roush-Cin 938	Frisch-NY..............133	Frisch-NY 30.0

Runs	Hits	Doubles	Triples	Home Runs	Total Bases	Runs Batted In
Youngs-NY 121	Frisch-NY..............223	Roush-Cin......................41	Traynor-Pit 19	Williams-Phi............41	Frisch-NY..............311	Meusel-NY 125
Carey-Pit 120	Statz-Chi 209	Tierney-Pit-Phi 36	Carey-Pit 19	Fournier-Bro 22	Williams-Phi..........308	Williams-Phi 114
Frisch-NY..............116	Traynor-Pit 208	Grantham-Chi 36	Roush-Cin 18	Miller-Chi 20	Fournier-Bro 303	Frisch-NY 111
Johnston-Bro 111	Johnston-Bro 203	Bottomley-StL 34	Southworth-Bos......16	Meusel-NY..............19	Traynor-Pit 301	Kelly-NY 103
Statz-Chi 110	Youngs-NY 200			Hornsby-StL 17	Statz-Chi 288	Fournier-Bro 102

Stolen Bases	Base Stealing Runs	Fielding Runs-Infield	Fielding Runs-Outfield	Wins	Winning Pct.	Complete Games
Carey-Pit 51	Carey-Pit................8.4	Tierney-Pit-Phi...........15.1	Carey-Pit..............12.1	Luque-Cin 27	Luque-Cin.............771	Grimes-Bro............33
Grantham-Chi 43	Smith-StL 3.2	Johnston-Bro 14.4	Statz-Chi...............10.7	Morrison-Pit............25	Ryan-NY...............762	Luque-Cin..............28
Smith-StL................32	Frisch-NY 2.2	Bancroft-NY...............12.4	Bigbee-Pit...............7.7	Alexander-Chi 22	Scott-NY 696	Morrison-Pit 27
Heathcote-Chi 32	Rawlings-Pit 2.0	B.Smith-Bos................11.6	Smith-StL 6.7	Grimes-Bro 21	Morrison-Pit 658	Cooper-Pit 26
	Traynor-Pit 1.6	Maranville-Pit.............10.9	Barnhart-Pit 5.9	Donohue-Cin 21	Alexander-Chi.......647	Alexander-Chi........26

Strikeouts	Fewest BB/Game	Games	Saves	Base Runners/9	Adjusted Relief Runs	Relief Ranking
Vance-Bro 197	Alexander-Chi.........89	Ryan-NY.........................45	Jonnard-NY 5	Alexander-Chi.......9.97	Decatur-Bro 11.1	Decatur-Bro..........6.9
Luque-Cin 151	B.Adams-Pit 1.42	Jonnard-NY....................45	Ryan-NY 4	Luque-Cin.........10.40	Jonnard-NY 3.6	Jonnard-NY 2.8
Grimes-Bro 119	Genewich-Bos 1.82	Oeschger-Bos...............44		Cooney-Bos 10.74		
Morrison-Pit..........114	Rixey-Cin 1.89	J.Barnes-NY-Bos 43		Ryan-NY............11.31		
Ring-Phi................112	Meadows-Phi-Pit 2.15	Genewich-Bos 43		Aldridge-Chi 11.49		

Innings Pitched	Opponents' Avg.	Opponents' OBP	Earned Run Average	Adjusted ERA	Adjusted Starter Runs	Pitcher Wins
Grimes-Bro 327.0	Luque-Cin.............235	Alexander-Chi 277	Luque-Cin............1.93	Luque-Cin 200	Luque-Cin............70.4	**Luque-Cin** 7.6
Luque-Cin..........322.0	Vance-Bro.............250	Luque-Cin 291	Rixey-Cin 2.80	Rixey-Cin 138	Rixey-Cin 36.7	**Rixey-Cin**..............3.3
Rixey-Cin 309.0	Aldridge-Chi 251	Aldridge-Chi..................307	Keen-Chi.............3.00	Keen-Chi 133	Alexander-Chi......28.6	**Alexander-Chi** ...3.1
Alexander-Chi....305.0	Morrison-Pit 253	Ryan-NY 308	Kaufmann-Chi 3.10	Kaufmann-Chi 129	Ring-Phi 25.0	**Kaufmann-Chi** ..2.0
Ring-Phi 304.1	Osborne-Chi.........255	McQuillan-NY 315	Haines-StL 3.11	Alexander-Chi 125	Keen-Chi..............20.2	**Cooper-Pit**..........1.8

Get Out of My Yard

Going wire-to-wire, the New York Giants won their third straight NL crown, beating back occasional challenges from the Reds and Pirates. The Giants again had the league's best offense and pitching in road games, and played well at home as well. They paced the NL in runs by a margin of 68.

As only the Polo Grounds—expanded to 54,000 capacity—made any alterations to its field dimensions, NL pitchers began to gain some control and runs per game decreased by 3 percent. The Cardinals, who fell 5 games in the standings despite the monster season of Rogers Hornsby, suffered a 37 percent attendance drop. Five NL clubs posted double-digit gains, and league turnstile clicks were up.

Cincinnati, on its last legs as a contender, fielded a team comprised mostly of players in their 30s. Pitcher Dolf Luque was the best in the league at 27–8. Two other Reds pitchers won 20 (Eppa Rixey and Pete Donahue), but their second-line pitching was very poor.

Veteran outfielder Burt Shotton, who twice led the AL in walks, played in his last game (for the Cardinals), but he would reemerge some five years later as a manager with the moribund Phillies. Two future Hall of Famers joined the major league fraternity: Bill Terry and Hack Wilson.

New York featured productive performers at nearly every position, with two youngsters—24-year-old second baseman Frankie Frisch and 19-year-old shortstop Travis Jackson—providing special fire. Platoon outfielder Casey Stengel hit .339 and batted .417 with 2 homers in the World Series. The Yankees reveled in their new home, which opened in 1923 because the Giants asked them to vacate the Polo Grounds, and knocked off the Giants on their third try in the World Series.

1923 American League

TEAM	W	L	T	PCT	GB	HW	HL	R	OR	PA	H	2B	3B	HR	BB	SO	HB	SH	AVG	OBP	SLG	OPS	AOPS	BR	ABR	PF	SB	CS	BSA	BSR
NY	98	54	0	.645		**46**	30	823	**622**	6047	1554	231	79	**105**	521	516	145	34	.291	.357	**.422**	779	108	71	57	102	69	74	48	-11
DET	83	71	1	.539	16	45	32	831	741	6173	1579	270	69	41	596	385	**256**	**55**	.300	.377	.401	778	113	94	111	98	87	62	58	-3
CLE	82	71	0	.536	16.5	42	36	**888**	746	6171	**1594**	**301**	75	59	**633**	**384**	199	49	**.301**	**.381**	.420	**801**	**117**	**141**	**143**	100	79	79	50	-10
WAS	75	78	2	.490	23.5	43	34	720	747	6055	1436	224	**93**	26	532	448	232	47	.274	.346	.367	713	98	-49	-12	95	**102**	68	**60**	**-1**
STL	74	78	2	.487	24	40	36	688	720	5975	1489	248	62	82	442	423	209	26	.281	.339	.398	737	94	-17	-55	106	64	54	54	-5
PHI	69	83	1	.454	29	34	41	661	761	5853	1407	229	64	53	445	517	170	42	.271	.333	.370	703	89	-77	-85	101	72	62	54	-6
CHI	69	85	2	.448	30	30	45	692	741	6067	1463	254	57	42	532	458	249	40	.279	.350	.373	723	97	-25	-16	99	191	118	62	1
BOS	61	91	2	.401	37	37	40	584	809	5775	1354	253	54	34	391	480	161	42	.261	.318	.351	669	81	-144	-147	101	79	91	46	-14
TOT	616					317	294	5887		48116	11876	2010	553	442	4092	3611	335	1621	.282	.351	.388	739					743	608	55	-49

TEAM	CG	SHO	GR	SV	IP	H	HR	BB	SO	BR/9	ERA	AERA	OAV	OOB	PR	APR	PF	OSB	OCS	FA	E	WPB	DP	FW	PW	BW	BSW	DIF
NY	**101**	9	68	10	1380.2	**1365**	68	491	**506**	**12.3**	**3.62**	**109**	**.263**	**.330**	**55**	**49**	99	**79**	58	**.977**	**144**	53	131	**3.3**	**4.7**	5.5	-.5	8.9
DET	61	9	**163**	12	1373.2	1502	58	**449**	447	13.1	4.09	94	.283	.345	-16	-35	97	84	**102**	.968	200	30	103	.0	-3.4	10.7	.3	-1.7
CLE	77	**10**	143	11	1376.0	1517	**36**	465	407	13.2	3.91	101	.285	.346	11	4	100	**79**	43	.964	226	28	143	-1.7	.4	**13.8**	-.4	-6.7
WAS	71	8	130	**16**	1374.1	1527	56	563	474	14.0	3.98	95	.291	.364	0	-32	95	91	95	.966	216	31	**182**	-.9	-3.1	-1.2	.5	3.2
STL	83	**10**	126	10	1373.1	1430	59	528	488	13.2	3.93	106	.275	.348	9	35	105	99	79	.971	177	**23**	145	1.4	3.4	-5.3	.1	-1.6
PHI	65	7	131	12	1364.2	1465	68	550	400	13.5	4.08	101	.280	.352	-15	1	103	91	75	.965	221	42	127	-1.4	.0	-8.2	.0	2.5
CHI	74	5	126	11	1397.0	1512	49	534	467	13.4	4.05	98	.283	.353	-10	-13	99	105	66	.971	184	33	138	1.1	-1.3	-1.5	**.7**	-7.0
BOS	77	3	115	11	1372.0	1534	48	520	412	13.9	4.20	98	.294	.366	-33	-15	103	115	89	.963	232	41	126	-2.0	-1.5	-14.2	-.8	3.4
TOT	609	61	1002	93	11011.2					13.3	3.98		.282	.351						.968	1600	281	1095					

Batter-Fielder Wins	Batting Average	On-Base Percentage	Slugging Average	On-Base Plus Slugging	Adjusted OPS	Adjusted Batter Runs
Ruth-NY 10.1	Heilmann-Det 403	Ruth-NY 545	Ruth-NY 764	Ruth-NY.............1309	Ruth-NY................238	Ruth-NY...........119.2
Speaker-Cle 6.5	Ruth-NY 393	Heilmann-Det..............481	Heilmann-Det 632	Heilmann-Det 1113	Heilmann-Det 195	Heilmann-Det 75.5
J.Sewell-Cle 6.2	Speaker-Cle 380	Speaker-Cle.................469	Williams-StL 623	Speaker-Cle........1079	Speaker-Cle..........183	Speaker-Cle 74.1
Heilmann-Det.......6.0	Collins-Chi 360	J.Sewell-Cle.................456	Speaker-Cle 610	Williams-StL 1062	Williams-StL 168	Williams-StL 54.7
Williams-StL........4.7	Williams-StL 357	Collins-Chi 455	Harris-Bos 520	J.Sewell-Cle..........935	J.Sewell-Cle.........147	J.Sewell-Cle........44.9

Runs	Hits	Doubles	Triples	Home Runs	Total Bases	Runs Batted In
Ruth-NY................151	Jamieson-Cle........222	Speaker-Cle 59	Rice-Was 18	Ruth-NY..................41	Ruth-NY................399	Ruth-NY 131
Speaker-Cle..........133	Speaker-Cle..........218	Burns-Bos.....................47	Goslin-Was 18	Williams-StL 29	Speaker-Cle..........350	Speaker-Cle 130
Jamieson-Cle........130	Heilmann-Det 211	Ruth-NY 45	Tobin-StL 15	Heilmann-Det 18	Williams-StL 346	Heilmann-Det......115
Heilmann-Det 121	Ruth-NY...............205	Heilmann-Det 44	Mostil-Chi 15	Speaker-Cle............17	Heilmann-Det 331	J.Sewell-Cle 109
Rice-Was..............117	Tobin-StL 202	J.Sewell-Cle 41		Hauser-Phi.............17	Tobin-StL 303	Pipp-NY 108

Stolen Bases	Base Stealing Runs	Fielding Runs-Infield	Fielding Runs-Outfield	Wins	Winning Pct.	Complete Games
Collins-Chi 48	Mostil-Chi 3.4	Peckinpaugh-Was 21.8	Mostil-Chi 16.0	Uhle-Cle 26	Pennock-NY 760	Uhle-Cle 29
Mostil-Chi 41	Rice-Was 1.6	Harris-Was..................18.6	Flagstead-Det-Bos ..14.4	Jones-NY................21	Jones-NY 724	Ehmke-Bos...........28
Harris-Was.............23	Barrett-Chi 1.6	Lutzke-Cle 16.0	Williams-StL 8.1	Dauss-Det 21	Hoyt-NY 654	Shocker-StL 24
Rice-Was................20	Veach-Det.............1.1	Ward-NY 9.5	Rice-Was 6.7	Shocker-StL............20	Shocker-StL 625	Dauss-Det 22
		Judge-Was....................8.3	Ruth-NY 6.4	Ehmke-Bos 20	Uhle-Cle 619	Bush-NY 22

Strikeouts	Fewest BB/Game	Games	Saves	Base Runners/9	Adjusted Relief Runs	Relief Ranking
Johnson-Was........130	Shocker-StL 1.59	Rommel-Phi 56	Russell-Was.............9	Shocker-StL 11.16		
Shawkey-NY 125	Coveleski-Cle 1.66	Uhle-Cle 54	Quinn-Bos 7	Hoyt-NY 11.20		
Bush-NY 125	Thurston-StL-Chi 1.75	Russell-Was 52	Harriss-Phi...............6	Pennock-NY 11.52		
Ehmke-Bos 121	Quinn-Bos 1.96	Cole-Det 52		Jones-NY 11.63		
	Dauss-Det 2.22	Dauss-Det......................50		Coveleski-Cle 11.64		

Innings Pitched	Opponents' Avg.	Opponents' OBP	Earned Run Average	Adjusted ERA	Adjusted Starter Runs	Pitcher Wins
Uhle-Cle 357.2	Shawkey-NY.........246	Shocker-StL 306	Coveleski-Cle 2.76	Coveleski-Cle 143	Vangilder-StL 27.8	**Uhle-Cle**..............3.4
Ehmke-Bos 316.2	Hoyt-NY 253	Hoyt-NY.......................307	Hoyt-NY 3.02	Vangilder-StL........136	Coveleski-Cle 26.2	**Rommel-Phi** 3.2
Dauss-Det 316.0	Jones-NY 257	Faber-Chi......................311	Russell-Was 3.03	Hoyt-NY................131	Pennock-NY 24.6	**Vangilder-StL** 2.8
Rommel-Phi 297.2	Faber-Chi 259	Jones-NY.....................312	Vangilder-StL 3.06	Thurston-StL-Chi ..127	Shocker-StL 24.1	**Bush-NY** 2.6
Vangilder-StL 282.1	Bush-NY 260	Pennock-NY.................314	Mogridge-Was 3.11	Rommel-Phi..........126	Rommel-Phi 23.7	**Shocker-StL** 2.6

The Year the Yankees Were Born

Kicked out of the Polo Grounds by the Giants the year before, the New York Yankees built their own park, Yankee Stadium, which quickly became a palace of American sport.

The Bronx Bombers put on a show for the million-plus fans that filled the park, running away with the pennant. Babe Ruth had another spectacular season, leading the loop in runs, homers, and RBIs—all while drawing 170 walks to set an AL record that still stands.

While the Yankees didn't score as many runs as the Tigers or Indians, they had much better pitching; New York's deep, if unspectacular, staff was the only one in the league with more strikeouts than walks, and easily led in complete games. New York used rookie Lou Gehrig in a few games, and Earle Combs came up the next year. Both were clearly part of the Yankees' future. The 1923 season also saw the debut of the first great relief pitcher in the game's history, Washington's Firpo Marberry. Ted Lyons of Chicago began a playing career that would last—with three years as a Marine thrown in—until 1946.

The Tigers had a fine outfield. Harry Heilmann batted .403, and rookie Heinie Manush and 36-year-old Ty Cobb kicked in high averages, though Cobb continued to suffer from knee problems. For Cleveland, 35-year-old Tris Speaker set a new big-league record with 53 doubles and Charlie Jamieson notched 222 hits.

The Giants were again the Yankees' World Series opponents, and the NL won Game 1 on Casey Stengel's ninth-inning inside-the-park homer. But the story would end differently. The Yanks rebounded to win three times at their former home park. Trailing 4–1 at the Polo Grounds in Game 6, the Yankees put together a 5-run eighth to win the title. With another pennant, their first Series crown, a ballpark of their own, and the parts of a dynasty firmly coming into place, 1923 was the year the Yankees became the Yankees.

1924 National League

TEAM	W	L	T	PCT	GB	HW	HL	R	OR	PA	H	2B	3B	HR	BB	SO	HB	SH	AVG	OBP	SLG	OPS	AOPS	BR	ABR	PF	SB	CS	BSA	BSR
NY	93	60	1	.608		**51**	26	**857**	641	6067	**1634**	**269**	81	**95**	467	479	127	28	**.300**	**.358**	**.432**	**790**	**120**	**127**	**151**	97	82	53	61	-1
BRO	92	62	0	.597	1.5	46	31	717	679	5951	1534	227	54	72	447	357	143	22	.287	.345	.391	736	105	21	45	97	34	46	43	-9
PIT	90	63	0	.588	3	49	28	724	586	5833	1517	222	**122**	44	366	396	151	28	.287	.336	.400	736	100	7	-4	102	**181**	92	**66**	**8**
CIN	83	70	0	.542	10	43	33	649	**579**	5835	1539	236	111	36	349	**334**	159	26	.290	.337	.397	734	103	5	16	99	103	98	51	-12
CHI	81	72	1	.529	12	46	31	698	699	5796	1419	207	59	66	**469**	521	**163**	**30**	.276	.340	.378	718	96	-9	-15	101	137	149	48	-22
STL	65	89	0	.422	28.5	40	37	740	750	5909	1552	270	87	67	382	418	145	33	.290	.341	.411	752	108	43	57	98	86	86	50	-11
PHI	55	96	1	.364	37	26	49	676	849	5855	1459	256	56	94	382	452	131	36	.275	.328	.397	725	88	-10	-84	112	57	67	46	-11
BOS	53	100	1	.346	40	28	48	520	798	5767	1355	194	52	25	354	451	104	26	.256	.306	.327	633	77	-184	-162	96	74	68	52	-8
TOT	614					329	283	5581		47013	12009	1881	622	499	3216	3408	229	1123	.283	.337	.392	729					754	659	53	-65

TEAM	CG	SHO	GR	SV	IP	H	HR	BB	SO	BR/9	ERA	AERA	OAV	OOB	PR	APR	PF	OSB	OCS	FA	E	WPB	DP	FW	PW	BW	BSW	DIF
NY	71	4	148	**21**	1378.2	1464	77	392	406	12.2	3.62	101	.274	.326	38	7	95	96	74	.971	186	24	160	.4	.7	**15.0**	.7	-.3
BRO	**97**	10	84	5	1376.1	1432	58	403	**638**	12.2	3.64	103	.270	.326	35	17	97	108	95	.968	196	27	121	-.2	1.7	4.5	-.0	9.1
PIT	85	**15**	105	5	1382.0	**1387**	42	323	364	**11.3**	3.27	117	**.267**	.313	92	88	99	**56**	65	.971	183	31	161	.5	8.7	-.4	**1.6**	3.1
CIN	77	14	104	9	1378.0	1408	**30**	**293**	451	**11.3**	**3.12**	**121**	**.267**	**.309**	**115**	**102**	97	95	78	.966	217	**23**	142	-1.4	**10.1**	1.6	-.4	-3.4
CHI	85	4	107	6	1380.2	1459	89	438	416	12.5	3.83	102	.275	.333	6	11	101	76	80	.966	218	30	153	-1.4	1.1	-1.5	-1.4	7.7
STL	79	7	119	6	1364.2	1528	70	486	393	13.5	4.15	91	.290	.354	-43	-58	98	95	75	.969	188	32	162	.3	-5.8	5.7	-.3	-11.9
PHI	59	7	**154**	10	1354.1	1691	84	469	349	14.6	4.87	92	.314	.372	-151	-52	115	109	**97**	.972	175	43	**168**	.8	-5.2	-8.3	-.3	-7.6
BOS	66	10	123	4	1379.1	1607	49	402	364	13.3	4.46	86	.301	.353	-92	-101	99	119	95	**.973**	**168**	39	154	**1.4**	-10.0	-16.1	.0	1.2
TOT	619	71	944	66	10994.0					12.6	3.87		.283	.337						.970	1531	249	1221					

Batter-Fielder Wins	Batting Average	On-Base Percentage	Slugging Average	On-Base Plus Slugging	Adjusted OPS	Adjusted Batter Runs
Hornsby-StL 9.3	Hornsby-StL .424	Hornsby-StL .507	Hornsby-StL .696	Hornsby-StL 1203	Hornsby-StL 223	Hornsby-StL 99.4
Frisch-NY 6.0	Wheat-Bro .375	Youngs-NY .441	Williams-Phi .552	Wheat-Bro 978	Wheat-Bro 165	Wheat-Bro 53.7
Fournier-Bro 4.9	Youngs-NY .356	Fournier-Bro .428	Wheat-Bro .549	Fournier-Bro 965	Fournier-Bro 162	Fournier-Bro 53.7
Wheat-Bro 4.5	Cuyler-Pit .354	Wheat-Bro .428	Cuyler-Pit .539	Youngs-NY 962	Youngs-NY 161	Youngs-NY 49.9
Youngs-NY 3.5	Roush-Cin .348	Williams-Phi .403	Fournier-Bro .536	Williams-Phi 955	Cuyler-Pit 147	Kelly-NY 33.1

Runs	Hits	Doubles	Triples	Home Runs	Total Bases	Runs Batted In
Hornsby-StL 121	Hornsby-StL 227	Hornsby-StL 43	Roush-Cin 21	Fournier-Bro 27	Hornsby-StL 373	Kelly-NY 136
Frisch-NY 121	Wheat-Bro 212	Wheat-Bro 41	Maranville-Pit 20	Hornsby-StL 25	Wheat-Bro 311	Fournier-Bro 116
Carey-Pit 113	Frisch-NY 198	Kelly-NY 37	Wright-Pit 18	Williams-Phi 24	Williams-Phi 308	Wright-Pit 111
Youngs-NY 112	High-Bro 191		Cuyler-Pit 16	Kelly-NY 21	Kelly-NY 303	Bottomley-StL 111
Williams-Phi 101	Fournier-Bro 188		Frisch-NY 15		Fournier-Bro 302	Meusel-NY 102

Stolen Bases	Base Stealing Runs	Fielding Runs-Infield	Fielding Runs-Outfield	Wins	Winning Pct.	Complete Games
Carey-Pit 49	Carey-Pit 6.2	Frisch-NY 27.6	Smith-StL 8.8	Vance-Bro 28	Yde-Pit .842	Vance-Bro 30
Cuyler-Pit 32	Cuyler-Pit 3.2	Pinelli-Cin 24.3	Statz-Chi 8.8	Grimes-Bro 22	Vance-Bro .824	Grimes-Bro 30
Heathcote-Chi 26	Frisch-NY 1.7	Ford-Phi 8.9	Cunningham-Bos 5.3	Mays-Cin 20	Bentley-NY .762	Cooper-Pit 25
Traynor-Pit 24	Hartnett-Chi 1.5	Wright-Pit 8.7	Grigsby-Chi 4.5	Cooper-Pit 20	Mays-Cin .690	Barnes-Bos 21
Smith-StL 24	Freigau-StL 1.1	Groh-NY 7.4	Wheat-Bro 3.5	Kremer-Pit 18	Kremer-Pit .643	Aldridge-Chi 20

Strikeouts	Fewest BB/Game	Games	Saves	Base Runners/9	Adjusted Relief Runs	Relief Ranking
Vance-Bro 262	Benton-Cin 1.33	Morrison-Pit 41	May-Cin 6	Vance-Bro 9.46	Jonnard-NY 10.8	Jonnard-NY 10.0
Grimes-Bro 135	Alexander-Chi 1.33	Kremer-Pit 41	Ryan-NY 5	Ehrhardt-Bro 9.57	May-Cin 9.1	May-Cin 6.2
Luque-Cin 86	Cooper-Pit 1.34	Keen-Chi 40	Jonnard-NY 5	Rixey-Cin 10.12	Stone-Pit 5.3	Stone-Pit 4.4
Morrison-Pit 85	Mays-Cin 1.43	Sheehan-Cin 39		Stone-Pit 10.13		
Kaufmann-Chi 79	Donohue-Cin 1.46			Jonnard-NY 10.64		

Innings Pitched	Opponents' Avg.	Opponents' OBP	Earned Run Average	Adjusted ERA	Adjusted Starter Runs	Pitcher Wins
Grimes-Bro 310.2	Vance-Bro .213	Vance-Bro .269	Vance-Bro 2.16	Vance-Bro 173	Vance-Bro 56.6	**Vance-Bro** 5.9
Vance-Bro 308.1	Yde-Pit .244	Rixey-Cin .285	McQuillan-NY 2.69	Rixey-Cin 137	Rixey-Cin 28.5	**Rixey-Cin** 3.4
Cooper-Pit 268.2	Morrison-Pit .245	Benton-Cin .297	Rixey-Cin 2.76	McQuillan-NY 136	Yde-Pit 22.4	**Mays-Cin** 3.0
Barnes-Bos 267.2	Rixey-Cin .246	Alexander-Chi .299	Benton-Cin 2.77	Benton-Cin 136	Kremer-Pit 21.1	**Cooper-Pit** 2.7
Kremer-Pit 259.1	Doak-StL-Bro .249	Nehf-NY .301	Yde-Pit 2.83	Yde-Pit 136	McQuillan-NY 19.0	**Yde-Pit** 2.2

Big Mac's Last Stand

NL pitchers gained a foothold in 1924 as the league ERA fell to 3.87. Brooklyn's Dazzy Vance won his third straight strikeout title (as well as the win and ERA championships) as his whiffs rose from 197 to 262.

The Giants, gunning for their fourth straight flag, dominated early but blew a 10-game lead over Pittsburgh by sleepwalking through August. Brooklyn rode Vance's golden arm to 15 straight wins—including 11 games in eight days—to establish a three-way tangle.

By late September, the Giants, who led the league in nearly every offensive category, regained their momentum while Brooklyn and Pittsburgh knocked each other around. New York eventually won by 1½ over Brooklyn; Pittsburgh, again using a speed-oriented offense, finished 3 games back.

The race raised attendance in Brooklyn and Pittsburgh, and as a result, NL tickets sold rose for the third straight year. Meanwhile, St. Louis saw a 19 percent decline even as Rogers Hornsby won his fifth batting title in a row—batting .424!—but his club ended sixth.

Two Hall of Famers debuted in 1924. Freddie Lindstrom was a utilityman for John McGraw's Giants, and Cardinals outfielder Chick Hafey got into 24 games down the stretch. Several prominent baseball figures died during the year. Candy Cummings, a 120-pound righty credited with inventing the curve in the 1860s, died at age 76. Pat Moran, 48, who guided the Phillies and the Reds to their first NL pennants, died from Bright's disease in spring training with Cincinnati. Hall of Famer Frank Chance died a year after managing the last-place Red Sox. Two notable active players also breathed their last. Third baseman Tony Boeckel of the Braves became the first player killed in a motor accident. Veteran first baseman Jake Daubert, Cincinnati's team captain who collected 2,326 hits, died October 9 following an appendectomy.

The Giants' loss in the World Series to Washington heralded the end of their dynasty. McGraw managed until 1932, but he never won another pennant.

1924 American League

TEAM	W	L	T	PCT	GB	HW	HL	R	OR	PA	H	2B	3B	HR	BB	SO	HB	SH	AVG	OBP	SLG	OPS	AOPS	BR	ABR	PF	SB	CS	BSA	BSR
WAS	92	62	2	.597		**47**	30	755	**613**	6098	1558	255	**88**	22	513	392	**232**	**49**	.294	.361	.387	748	101	-10	14	97	**116**	85	**58**	**-4**
NY	89	63	1	.586	2	45	32	798	667	5936	1516	248	86	**98**	478	420	189	29	.289	.352	**.426**	**778**	106	25	27	100	69	67	51	-8
DET	86	68	2	.558	6	45	33	**849**	796	6262	**1604**	**315**	76	35	**607**	400	225	41	**.298**	**.373**	.404	777	**108**	**57**	**71**	98	100	77	56	-5
STL	74	78	1	.487	17	41	36	769	807	5923	1543	266	62	67	465	**349**	190	32	.295	.356	.408	764	96	9	-35	106	85	85	50	-11
PHI	71	81	0	.467	20	36	39	685	778	5749	1459	251	59	63	374	484	156	35	.281	.334	.389	723	90	-80	-86	101	77	68	53	-7
CLE	67	86	0	.438	24.5	37	38	755	814	6031	1580	306	59	41	492	371	163	44	.296	.361	.399	760	100	11	1	101	85	57	60	-1
BOS	67	87	3	.435	25	41	36	735	806	6185	1481	302	63	30	603	417	195	47	.277	.356	.374	730	94	-39	-40	100	78	61	56	**-4**
CHI	66	87	1	.431	25.5	37	39	793	858	6125	1512	254	58	41	604	421	**232**	34	.288	.365	.382	747	101	-5	20	97	137	92	60	-2
TOT	617					329	283	6139		48309	12253	2197	551	397	4136	3254	311	1582	.290	.357	.397	754					747	592	56	-43

TEAM	CG	SHO	GR	SV	IP	H	HR	BB	SO	BR/9	ERA	AERA	OAV	OOB	PR	APR	PF	OSB	OCS	FA	E	WPB	DP	FW	PW	BW	BSW	DIF
WAS	74	**13**	128	**25**	1383.0	**1329**	**34**	505	469	**12.2**	**3.34**	**121**	**.259**	**.330**	**136**	**112**	95	**62**	55	.972	171	18	149	1.3	**10.6**	1.3	.1	1.6
NY	76	**13**	112	13	1359.1	1483	59	522	**487**	13.4	3.86	108	.284	.353	56	45	98	88	74	**.974**	**156**	55	131	**2.0**	4.2	2.5	-.2	4.4
DET	60	5	158	20	1394.2	1586	55	**467**	441	13.5	4.19	98	.293	.354	5	-12	97	101	77	.971	187	**17**	142	.4	-1.1	**6.7**	.0	3.0
STL	66	11	**176**	7	1353.1	1511	68	517	386	13.8	4.57	99	.289	.358	-51	-9	107	100	82	.969	184	20	142	.3	-.8	-3.3	-.5	2.4
PHI	68	8	144	10	1345.0	1527	43	597	371	14.4	4.39	98	.292	.368	-24	-15	101	90	63	.971	180	31	**157**	.5	-1.4	-8.1	-.2	4.2
CLE	**87**	7	119	7	1349.0	1603	43	503	315	14.3	4.40	97	.300	.365	-25	-20	101	98	65	.967	205	43	130	-1.0	-1.9	.0	**.4**	-7.1
BOS	73	8	144	16	1391.1	1563	43	523	414	13.9	4.35	100	.290	.359	-19	2	103	100	82	.967	210	46	126	-1.0	.2	-3.8	.1	-5.5
CHI	76	1	118	11	1370.2	1635	52	512	360	14.3	4.74	87	.305	.368	-78	-98	97	108	**94**	.963	229	48	136	-2.4	-9.3	1.9	.3	-1.1
TOT	580	66	1099	109	10946.1					13.7	4.23		.290	.357						.969	1522	278	1113					

Batter-Fielder Wins	Batting Average	On-Base Percentage	Slugging Average	On-Base Plus Slugging	Adjusted OPS	Adjusted Batter Runs
Ruth-NY 8.4	Ruth-NY 378	Ruth-NY 513	Ruth-NY 739	Ruth-NY.............1252	Ruth-NY................221	Ruth-NY...........104.0
J.Sewell-Cle 4.5	Jamieson-Cle 359	Collins-Chi 441	Heilmann-Det 533	Heilmann-Det 961	Heilmann-Det 149	Heilmann-Det 43.5
Heilmann-Det......3.7	Falk-Chi 352	Speaker-Cle.................432	Williams-StL 533	Williams-StL 958	Goslin-Was 145	Goslin-Was 39.2
Rigney-Det 3.5	Collins-Chi 349	Heilmann-Det...............428	Jacobson-StL 528	Speaker-Cle..........943	Speaker-Cle..........141	Collins-Chi..........34.9
Collins-Chi 3.0	Bassler-Det..........346	Sheely-Chi 426	Myatt-Cle 518	Goslin-Was 937	Williams-StL 138	Speaker-Cle 32.2

Runs	Hits	Doubles	Triples	Home Runs	Total Bases	Runs Batted In
Ruth-NY................143	Rice-Was 216	J.Sewell-Cle 45	Pipp-NY 19	Ruth-NY..................46	Ruth-NY................391	Goslin-Was..........129
Cobb-Det..............115	Jamieson-Cle........213	Heilmann-Det 45	Goslin-Was 17	Hauser-Phi..............27	Jacobson-StL........306	Ruth-NY 121
Collins-Chi............108	Cobb-Det..............211	Wambsganss-Bos..........41	Heilmann-Det 16	Jacobson-StL..........19	Heilmann-Det 304	Meusel-NY 120
Hooper-Chi 107	Ruth-NY...............200	Jacobson-StL 41	Rice-Was................14	Williams-StL 18	Goslin-Was 299	Hauser-Phi 115
Heilmann-Det 107	Goslin-Was 199	Meusel-NY 40	Jacobson-StL..........12	Boone-Bos..............13	Hauser-Phi............290	

Stolen Bases	Base Stealing Runs	Fielding Runs-Infield	Fielding Runs-Outfield	Wins	Winning Pct.	Complete Games
Collins-Chi 42	Collins-Chi 3.3	J.Sewell-Cle................21.8	Hooper-Chi 10.4	Johnson-Was..........23	Johnson-Was 767	Thurston-Chi 28
Meusel-NY..............26	Manush-Det 1.3	Lutzke-Cle 16.6	Jacobson-StL 9.9	Pennock-NY 21	Pennock-NY 700	Ehmke-Bos............26
Rice-Was................24	Burns-Cle 1.3	Wambsganss-Bos 13.0	Falk-Chi 7.9	Thurston-Chi 20	Whitehill-Det.........654	Pennock-NY 25
Cobb-Det................23	Heilmann-Det 1.1	Peckinpaugh-Was 11.0	Mostil-Chi 6.6	Shaute-Cle 20	Zachary-Was 625	Shaute-Cle 21
Jamieson-Cle..........21		Scott-NY 10.3	Heilmann-Det 6.5	Ehmke-Bos 19		Rommel-Phi 21

Strikeouts	Fewest BB/Game	Games	Saves	Base Runners/9	Adjusted Relief Runs	Relief Ranking
Johnson-Was........158	Smith-Cle 1.53	Marberry-Was................50	Marberry-Was 15	Johnson-Was 10.37	Speece-Was..........4.0	Speece-Was 2.0
Ehmke-Bos 119	Thurston-Chi.........1.86	Holloway-Det 49	Russell-Was.............8	Collins-Det 11.08		
Shawkey-NY 114	Shocker-StL 1.90	Shaute-Cle 46	Quinn-Bos 7	Zachary-Was 11.28		
Pennock-NY 101	Pennock-NY 2.01	Hoyt-NY 46	Dauss-Det 6	Smith-Cle 11.48		
Shocker-StL............88	Quinn-Bos 2.05	Ehmke-Bos 45	Connally-Chi 6	Pennock-NY 11.54		

Innings Pitched	Opponents' Avg.	Opponents' OBP	Earned Run Average	Adjusted ERA	Adjusted Starter Runs	Pitcher Wins
Ehmke-Bos........315.0	Johnson-Was 224	Johnson-Was..............284	Johnson-Was 2.72	Baumgartner-Phi ..149	Johnson-Was 43.8	**Johnson-Was** 4.9
Thurston-Chi......291.0	Collins-Det 249	Collins-Det..................307	Zachary-Was 2.75	Johnson-Was........148	Pennock-NY.........42.5	**Pennock-NY** 3.8
Pennock-NY 286.1	Marberry-Was.......262	Smith-Cle.....................312	Pennock-NY 2.83	Pennock-NY 147	Ehmke-Bos..........33.3	**Zachary-Was** 3.7
Shaute-Cle 283.0	Wingard-StL 262	Pennock-NY.................314	Baumgartner-Phi 2.88	Zachary-Was........147	Smith-Cle 31.2	**Ehmke-Bos** 3.4
Rommel-Phi 278.0	Davis-StL 263	Zachary-Was 315	Smith-Cle 3.02	Smith-Cle.............142	Zachary-Was 30.2	**Bush-NY** 3.2

First in War, First in Peace, First in Everything

Walter Johnson had pitched for a long time and never won a pennant. But in 1924, the Yankees were far from dominant, and the AL flag was ready for the picking. Washington, New York, and Detroit spent July and August twisted together. By September the Tigers had dropped out, and the Yankees chased the Senators to the end. Washington held on for its first flag thanks to the 36-year-old Johnson, the league's dominant hurler.

Playing in cavernous Griffith Stadium, the Senators lacked homers but hit plenty of triples, and Goose Goslin led the league in RBIs. Righty Firpo Marberry was credited (retroactively) with 15 saves and was the first reliever to lead the AL in appearances.

Homers declined to 397 as only nine players reached double figures. This was the final year in big-league history that either league hit fewer than 400. Fleet Walker, the first African American in the majors, died May 11, his legacy going unnoted for decades. Three Hall of Famers reached the majors in 1924. Al Simmons debuted for Philadelphia; as he became a top slugger, the Athletics returned to contention. Red Ruffing, who would pitch until 1947, bowed for the Red Sox. Charlie Gehringer got into a few games in second base for Detroit.

The Senators and Giants produced a memorable World Series; each of the seven games was close, with four decided by one run. New York appeared to have Game 7 wrapped up until the Senators, down 3–1 in the bottom of the eighth, tied it when a grounder by player-manager Bucky Harris hopped over the head of Giants third baseman Freddie Lindstrom. With the game still knotted in the 12th, the Senators had Muddy Ruel on second, and Johnson, on in relief since the ninth, on first. Rookie Earl McNeely's grounder bounced over Lindstrom's head. Washington had its first, and as it would happen, only world champion.

1925 National League

TEAM	W	L	T	PCT	GB	HW	HL	R	OR	PA	H	2B	3B	HR	BB	SO	HB	SH	AVG	OBP	SLG	OPS	AOPS	BR	ABR	PF	SB	CS	BSA	BSR
PIT	95	58	0	.621		**52**	25	**912**	715	6036	**1651**	**316**	**105**	78	**499**	363	135	**30**	**.307**	**.369**	**.449**	**818**	**108**	**120**	**62**	107	**159**	63	**72**	**13**
NY	86	66	0	.566	8.5	47	29	736	702	5858	1507	239	61	**114**	411	494	95	25	.283	.337	.415	752	101	-28	3	96	79	65	55	-5
CIN	80	73	0	.523	15	44	32	690	**643**	5838	1490	221	90	44	409	**327**	**173**	23	.285	.339	.387	726	93	-71	-54	98	108	107	50	-14
STL	77	76	0	.503	18	48	28	828	764	5936	1592	292	80	109	446	414	134	27	.299	.356	.445	801	**108**	75	56	102	70	51	58	-2
BOS	70	83	0	.458	25	37	39	708	802	5945	1567	260	70	41	405	380	145	**30**	.292	.345	.390	735	102	-48	22	91	77	72	52	-8
PHI	68	85	0	.444	27	38	39	812	930	6035	1598	288	58	100	456	542	133	34	.295	.354	.425	779	96	39	-28	109	48	59	45	-10
BRO	68	85	0	.444	27	40	37	786	866	6045	1617	250	80	64	437	383	114	26	.296	.351	.406	757	102	-8	14	97	37	30	55	-2
CHI	68	86	0	.442	27.5	37	40	723	773	5933	1473	254	70	86	397	470	150	33	.275	.329	.397	726	89	-78	-88	102	94	70	57	-4
TOT	612					343	269	6195		47626	12495	2120	614	636	3460	3373	228	1079	.292	.348	.414	762					672	517	57	-33

TEAM	CG	SHO	GR	SV	IP	H	HR	BB	SO	BR/9	ERA	AERA	OAV	OOB	PR	APR	PF	OSB	OCS	FA	E	WPB	DP	FW	PW	BW	BSW	DIF
PIT	77	2	119	**13**	1354.2	1526	81	387	386	12.9	3.87	115	.287	.339	59	84	105	**54**	51	.964	224	36	**171**	-.9	7.9	**5.8**	**1.6**	4.1
NY	80	6	113	8	1354.0	1532	73	408	446	13.0	3.94	102	.289	.342	49	18	95	91	73	.968	199	**20**	129	.5	1.7	.3	-.0	7.6
CIN	**92**	**11**	103	12	1375.1	**1447**	**35**	**324**	437	**11.8**	**3.38**	**121**	**.272**	**.317**	**135**	**115**	96	107	52	.968	203	32	161	.3	**10.8**	-5.1	-.9	-1.6
STL	82	8	105	7	1335.2	1480	86	470	428	13.4	4.36	99	.283	.347	-14	-7	101	72	57	.966	204	25	156	.3	-.7	5.2	.2	-4.6
BOS	77	5	129	4	1366.2	1567	67	458	351	13.4	4.39	91	.291	.348	-19	-62	94	77	48	.964	221	29	145	-.7	-5.8	2.1	-.4	-1.7
PHI	69	8	**151**	9	1350.2	1753	117	444	371	14.8	5.02	95	.315	.368	-114	-34	112	89	54	.966	211	45	147	-.1	-3.2	-2.6	-.5	-2.0
BRO	82	4	128	4	1350.2	1608	75	477	**518**	14.1	4.77	88	.301	.362	-76	-92	98	122	**107**	.966	210	50	130	-.0	-8.6	1.3	.2	-1.3
CHI	75	5	115	10	1370.0	1575	102	485	435	13.7	4.41	98	.292	.353	-21	-13	101	60	75	**.969**	**198**	21	161	**.7**	-1.2	-8.2	.0	-.3
TOT	634	49	963	67	10857.2					13.4	4.27		.292	.348						.966	1670	258	1200					

Batter-Fielder Wins	Batting Average	On-Base Percentage	Slugging Average	On-Base Plus Slugging	Adjusted OPS	Adjusted Batter Runs
Hornsby-StL........6.8	Hornsby-StL 403	Hornsby-StL.................489	Hornsby-StL 756	Hornsby-StL 1245	Hornsby-StL 208	Hornsby-StL 85.3
Fournier-Bro........4.2	Bottomley-StL 367	Fournier-Bro................446	Cuyler-Pit 598	Cuyler-Pit............1021	Fournier-Bro 162	Fournier-Bro 53.9
Bancroft-Bos 3.9	Wheat-Bro 359	Blades-StL...................423	Wrightstone-Phi ...591	Fournier-Bro 1015	Cuyler-Pit..............148	Cuyler-Pit...........44.1
Traynor-Pit 3.6	Cuyler-Pit 357	Cuyler-Pit.....................423	Bottomley-StL.......578	Bottomley-StL 992	Bottomley-StL 147	Bottomley-StL 43.2
Cuyler-Pit 3.6	Fournier-Bro 350	Carey-Pit 418	Fournier-Bro 569	Blades-StL............958	Wheat-Bro 143	Wheat-Bro 38.8

Runs	Hits	Doubles	Triples	Home Runs	Total Bases	Runs Batted In
Cuyler-Pit.............144	Bottomley-StL 227	Bottomley-StL 44	Cuyler-Pit................26	Hornsby-StL 39	Hornsby-StL 381	Hornsby-StL 143
Hornsby-StL 133	Wheat-Bro 221	Cuyler-Pit 43	Walker-Cin 16	Hartnett-Chi............24	Cuyler-Pit..............369	Fournier-Bro 130
Wheat-Bro............125	Cuyler-Pit..............220	Wheat-Bro 42	Roush-Cin 16	Fournier-Bro 22	Bottomley-StL 358	Bottomley-StL.......128
Traynor-Pit...........114	Hornsby-StL 203	Hornsby-StL 41	Fournier-Bro 16	Meusel-NY..............21	Wheat-Bro 333	Wright-Pit 121
Blades-StL............112	Stock-Bro..............202	Burrus-Bos 41	....	Bottomley-StL 21	Fournier-Bro 310	Barnhart-Pit 114

Stolen Bases	Base Stealing Runs	Fielding Runs-Infield	Fielding Runs-Outfield	Wins	Winning Pct.	Complete Games
Carey-Pit 46	Carey-Pit................6.3	Adams-Chi..................26.5	Felix-Bos................9.5	Vance-Bro 22	Sherdel-StL 714	Donohue-Cin 27
Cuyler-Pit..............41	Cuyler-Pit 4.5	Traynor-Pit 23.3	Blades-StL..............9.3	Rixey-Cin................21	Vance-Bro.............710	Vance-Bro 26
Adams-Chi.............26	Smith-StL 3.7	Critz-Cin......................19.7	Heathcote-Chi 8.3	Donohue-Cin 21	Aldridge-Pit...........682	Rixey-Cin 22
Roush-Cin 22	Moore-Pit 1.7	Kelly-NY......................18.3	Neis-Bos................7.1	Meadows-Pit 19	Kremer-Pit 680	Luque-Cin..............22
Frisch-NY...............21	Grantham-Pit 1.7	Pinelli-Cin 17.0	Welsh-Bos 4.8		Rixey-Cin 656	Ring-Phi 21

Strikeouts	Fewest BB/Game	Games	Saves	Base Runners/9	Adjusted Relief Runs	Relief Ranking
Vance-Bro 221	Alexander-Chi......1.11	Morrison-Pit 44	Morrison-Pit.............4	Fitzsimmons-NY 10.61	Huntzinger-NY 3.9	Huntzinger-NY......3.3
Luque-Cin 140	Donohue-Cin 1.47	Donohue-Cin 42	Bush-Chi 4	Luque-Cin..........10.61		
Ring-Phi..................93	Rixey-Cin 1.47	Bush-Chi.......................42		Donohue-Cin 10.79		
Blake-Chi................93	Cooney-Bos 1.83	Osborne-Bro.................41		Vance-Bro..........10.96		
Aldridge-Pit 88	Sherdel-StL 1.89	Kremer-Pit....................40		Rixey-Cin 11.15		

Innings Pitched	Opponents' Avg.	Opponents' OBP	Earned Run Average	Adjusted ERA	Adjusted Starter Runs	Pitcher Wins
Donohue-Cin 301.0	Luque-Cin.............239	Luque-Cin 291	Luque-Cin...........2.63	Luque-Cin 156	Luque-Cin............48.3	**Luque-Cin** 5.9
Luque-Cin..........291.0	Benton-Bos...........249	Donohue-Cin 299	Rixey-Cin 2.88	Rixey-Cin..............143	Rixey-Cin 43.0	**Donohue-Cin**.....4.6
Rixey-Cin 287.1	Vance-Bro.............250	Vance-Bro 304	Reinhart-StL 3.05	Sherdel-StL 139	Donohue-Cin 38.3	**Rixey-Cin**............4.1
Ring-Phi 270.0	Donohue-Cin 268	Rixey-Cin 307	Donohue-Cin 3.08	Donohue-Cin 133	Sherdel-StL 28.5	**Scott-NY** 3.5
Vance-Bro..........265.1	Scott-NY 269	Cooney-Bos 312	Benton-Bos..........3.09	Benton-Bos 130	Scott-NY 25.5	**Sherdel-StL**........2.8

Fattening Up

NL hitters fattened up on Senior Circuit's hurlers in 1925. Each team averaged 5.06 runs per game, up 11 percent from '24. The biggest reason was the extra 137 home runs that NL batters slugged. The league ERA went up 40 points, and just two qualifying pitchers posted ERAs below 3.00.

The Pittsburgh Pirates shrunk right field at Forbes Field from 372 feet to just 300, which helped the Bucs score 188 more runs than in 1924, accounting for 40 percent of the league's increase. The cozier confines of Forbes Field did not harm Pittsburgh's crack staff at all; five Pirates had 15 or more victories. New York led the NL through June, but Pittsburgh—third-place finishers for the past three years—came on fast and took the lead for good in early July, eventually winning by 8½ games. Kiki Cuyler scored 144 runs and smacked 26 triples and Max Carey stole 46 bases. The Bucs had seven .300 hitters.

The second-place Giants led the league in homers, with Irish Meusel hitting 21 and George Kelly 20, but their lineup featured several offensive dead spots. Perhaps the top 1-2 punch in the league was St. Louis' Rogers Hornsby (league MVP and Triple Crown winner) and Jim Bottomley (the NL leader in hits and doubles), but the rest of the team was thin.

The Washington Senators took three of the first four games of the World Series, but the Bucs weren't done. Pittsburgh won Game 5 at Washington, 6–3, then came from behind to take the final two contests at Forbes Field. Down 7–6 in the eighth inning of Game 7, the Pirates scored three times off 37-year-old Walter Johnson to capture the Series. It would be the Bucs' last World Series appearance until 1960.

1925 American League

TEAM	W	L	T	PCT	GB	HW	HL	R	OR	PA	H	2B	3B	HR	BB	SO	HB	SH	AVG	OBP	SLG	OPS	AOPS	BR	ABR	PF	SB	CS	BSA	BSR
WAS	96	55	1	.636		**53**	22	829	**670**	5994	1577	251	71	56	533	427	208	47	.303	.373	.411	784	106	38	55	98	**135**	92	59	-2
PHI	88	64	1	.579	8.5	51	26	831	713	6071	**1659**	298	79	76	453	432	187	32	**.307**	.364	.434	798	101	53	0	107	67	60	53	-6
STL	82	71	1	.536	15	45	32	900	906	6110	1620	**304**	68	**110**	498	**375**	143	29	.298	.360	**.439**	**799**	103	53	11	105	85	78	52	-9
DET	81	73	2	.526	16.5	43	34	**903**	829	6264	1621	277	**84**	50	640	386	221	32	.302	**.379**	.413	792	**109**	**64**	**78**	99	97	63	**61**	**-1**
CHI	79	75	0	.513	18.5	44	33	811	770	6168	1482	299	59	38	**662**	405	**231**	**51**	.284	.370	.385	755	102	-2	43	95	131	87	60	-2
CLE	70	84	1	.455	27.5	37	39	782	817	6163	1613	285	58	52	520	379	180	27	.297	.361	.399	760	97	-12	-18	101	90	77	54	-7
NY	69	85	2	.448	28.5	42	36	706	774	6021	1471	247	74	**110**	470	482	174	24	.275	.336	.410	746	96	-65	-52	98	69	73	49	-10
BOS	47	105	0	.309	49.5	28	47	639	922	5845	1375	257	64	41	513	422	135	31	.266	.336	.364	700	83	-133	-132	100	42	56	43	-10
TOT	616					343	269	6401		48636	12418	2218	557	533	4289	3308	2731	479	.292	.360	.408	768					716	586	55	-48

TEAM	CG	SHO	GR	SV	IP	H	HR	BB	SO	BR/9	ERA	AERA	OAV	OOB	PR	APR	PF	OSB	OCS	FA	E	WPB	DP	FW	PW	BW	BSW	DIF
WAS	69	10	145	**21**	1358.1	**1434**	49	543	463	**13.3**	**3.70**	114	.278	.351	**105**	82	96	74	64	.972	170	**24**	**166**	1.8	7.6	5.1	.4	5.7
PHI	61	8	**161**	18	1381.2	1468	60	544	**495**	**13.3**	3.87	**120**	**.276**	**.347**	81	**113**	106	93	61	.966	211	41	148	-.6	**10.5**	.0	.0	2.1
STL	67	7	160	10	1379.2	1588	99	675	419	15.0	4.92	95	.298	.380	-80	-37	106	103	**94**	.964	226	44	164	-1.4	-3.4	1.0	-.3	9.6
DET	66	2	142	18	1383.2	1582	70	556	419	14.2	4.61	94	.296	.366	-32	-47	98	103	65	.972	173	34	143	1.9	-4.4	**7.2**	**.5**	-1.2
CHI	71	**12**	129	13	1385.2	1579	69	**489**	374	13.6	4.29	97	.295	.356	17	-23	95	**46**	88	.968	200	26	162	.2	-2.1	4.0	.4	-.4
CLE	**93**	6	103	9	1372.1	1604	**41**	493	345	14.0	4.49	98	.296	.359	-15	-9	101	71	57	.967	210	26	146	-.4	-.8	-1.7	-.0	-4.0
NY	80	8	123	13	1387.2	1560	78	505	492	13.6	4.33	98	.289	.353	10	-11	97	96	89	**.974**	**160**	32	150	**2.7**	-1.0	-4.8	-.4	-4.5
BOS	68	6	128	6	1326.2	1615	67	510	310	14.7	4.97	92	.308	.374	-84	-60	103	130	68	.957	271	28	150	-4.2	-5.6	-12.2	-.4	-6.6
TOT	575	59	1091	108	10975.2					14.0	4.39		.292	.360						.968	1621	255	1229					

Batter-Fielder Wins	Batting Average	On-Base Percentage	Slugging Average	On-Base Plus Slugging	Adjusted OPS	Adjusted Batter Runs
Speaker-Cle 4.3	Heilmann-Det 393	Speaker-Cle 479	Williams-StL 613	Cobb-Det 1066	Cobb-Det 171	Heilmann-Det 55.5
J.Sewell-Cle 3.9	Speaker-Cle 389	Cobb-Det 468	Simmons-Phi 599	Speaker-Cle........1057	Speaker-Cle..........166	Cobb-Det...........47.9
Goslin-Was 3.5	Simmons-Phi 387	Collins-Chi 461	Cobb-Det 598	Heilmann-Det 1026	Heilmann-Det 161	Speaker-Cle 47.7
Cobb-Det 3.5	Cobb-Det 378	Heilmann-Det..............457	Speaker-Cle 578	Simmons-Phi......1018	Wingo-Det 151	Simmons-Phi......42.5
Heilmann-Det......3.4	Wingo-Det 370	Wingo-Det 456	Heilmann-Det 569	Wingo-Det 983	Simmons-Phi........146	Wingo-Det 37.9

Runs	Hits	Doubles	Triples	Home Runs	Total Bases	Runs Batted In
Mostil-Chi 135	Simmons-Phi 253	McManus-StL 44	Goslin-Was 20	Meusel-NY.............33	Simmons-Phi 392	Meusel-NY 138
Simmons-Phi........122	Rice-Was 227	Simmons-Phi 43	Mostil-Chi 16	Williams-StL 25	Meusel-NY............338	Heilmann-Det 134
Combs-NY............117	Heilmann-Det 225	Sheely-Chi 43	Sisler-StL 15	Ruth-NY.................25	Goslin-Was 329	Simmons-Phi 129
Goslin-Was 116	Sisler-StL..............224	Burns-Cle 41		Simmons-Phi..........24	Heilmann-Det 326	Goslin-Was..........113
Rice-Was 111	J.Sewell-Cle..........204			Gehrig-NY 20	Sisler-StL..............311	Sheely-Chi 111

Stolen Bases	Base Stealing Runs	Fielding Runs-Infield	Fielding Runs-Outfield	Wins	Winning Pct.	Complete Games
Mostil-Chi 43	Goslin-Was 3.1	J.Sewell-Cle 15.8	Goslin-Was 14.3	Rommel-Phi............21	Coveleski-Was 800	Smith-Cle 22
Goslin-Was 27	Mostil-Chi 2.5	O'Rourke-Det.............14.7	Flagstead-Bos 14.0	Lyons-Chi 21	Johnson-Was 741	Ehmke-Bos............22
Rice-Was 26	Blue-Det 2.4	Sisler-StL 10.4	Wingo-Det 8.9	Johnson-Was..........20	Ruether-Was.........720	Pennock-NY 21
	Collins-Chi 2.1	Wambsganss-Bos 8.4	Rice-Was 6.8	Coveleski-Was........20	Blankenship-Chi ...680	Lyons-Chi 19
	Haney-Det 2.1	Davis-Chi 6.9	Jamieson-Cle 5.0	Harriss-Phi.............19	Rommel-Phi 677	Wingfield-Bos 18

Strikeouts	Fewest BB/Game	Games	Saves	Base Runners/9	Adjusted Relief Runs	Relief Ranking
Grove-Phi 116	Smith-Cle 1.82	Marberry-Was................55	Marberry-Was 15	Pennock-NY 11.05	Marberry-Was........5.2	Marberry-Was 8.9
Johnson-Was........108	Quinn-Bos-Phi 1.85	Walberg-Phi 53	Doyle-Det.................8	Blankenship-Chi 11.13	Gregg-Was 9	Gregg-Was 5
Harriss-Phi.............95	Shocker-NY 2.14	Vangilder-StL 52	Connally-Chi 8	Coveleski-Was ..11.39		
Ehmke-Bos 95	Faber-Chi 2.23	Rommel-Phi 52	Walberg-Phi.............7	Gray-Phi 11.71		
Jones-NY................92	Pennock-NY 2.31	Pennock-NY 47		Johnson-Was 11.87		

Innings Pitched	Opponents' Avg.	Opponents' OBP	Earned Run Average	Adjusted ERA	Adjusted Starter Runs	Pitcher Wins
Pennock-NY 277.0	Johnson-Was 250	Pennock-NY.................303	Coveleski-Was 2.84	Coveleski-Was......149	Coveleski-Was 40.9	**Johnson-Was** 4.6
Lyons-Chi 262.2	Blankenship-Chi ...253	Blankenship-Chi............308	Pennock-NY 2.96	Pennock-NY 144	Pennock-NY 36.3	**Pennock-NY** 3.3
Rommel-Phi 261.0	Pennock-NY 254	Coveleski-Was 312	Blankenship-Chi ..3.03	Gray-Phi 142	Blankenship-Chi ...31.2	**Harriss-Phi** 3.2
Ehmke-Bos 260.2	Coveleski-Was 255	Johnson-Was 317	Johnson-Was 3.07	Johnson-Was........138	Harriss-Phi 30.6	**Rommel-Phi** 2.9
Wingfield-Bos 254.1	Gray-Phi 260	Gray-Phi.......................319	Dauss-Det 3.16	Blankenship-Chi ..137	Johnson-Was 30.1	**Coveleski-Was** ..2.9

Walter's Disappointment

Has a team ever had a better set of players making their big league debuts than the 1925 A's? Both catcher Mickey Cochrane and pitcher Lefty Grove appeared for the first time on April 14, and first baseman Jimmie Foxx came up two weeks later. With Al Simmons rapping 253 hits in his sophomore season and Ed Rommel leading the league in wins for the second time, Philadelphia vaulted all the way to second.

But once again, it was Washington's year. The Senators broke away from the slumping Athletics in late August and won by 8½ games. A superannuated pitching staff featuring Walter Johnson and Stan Coveleski (aided by Firpo Marberry) was good enough, and outfielder Goose Goslin was spectacular.

The Yankees were no factor; Babe Ruth's wild nightlife shelved him. He collapsed during spring training from an intestinal problem; he missed seven weeks. When he returned, Ruth wasn't the same hitter—he was suspended in September. The undermanned Yanks finished seventh. Lou Gehrig did play his first full season.

The relative pitching calm of 1924 was replaced by a stormy 1925 in which AL batters set a new homer record with 533—even with Ruth out of commission. The league batting and slugging averages were also the highest ever. AL teams scored 5.20 runs per game, the most since 1901.

Former "Clean Sox" outfielders Nemo Leibold and Shano Collins saw their final major league action, as did two other famous gardeners, Harry Hooper and Bobby Veach. In addition, Chief Bender, one of the great hurlers of the early century, pitched his last game.

The Senators went up three games to one on Pittsburgh in the World Series, but couldn't close the deal. With the Series knotted, Johnson started Game 7; he completed the contest, although he shouldn't have. He allowed all 9 runs (5 earned) and 15 hits in a game in which the Senators led 6–4 through the sixth.

1926 National League

TEAM	W	L	T	PCT	GB	HW	HL	R	OR	PA	H	2B	3B	HR	BB	SO	HB	SH	AVG	OBP	SLG	OPS	AOPS	BR	ABR	PF	SB	CS	BSA	BSR
STL	89	65	2	.578		47	30	**817**	678	6104	**1541**	259	82	**90**	**478**	518	212	33	.286	.348	**.415**	**763**	107	**77**	48	104	83			
CIN	87	67	3	.565	2	**53**	23	747	651	6047	**1541**	242	**120**	35	454	**333**	**239**	**34**	**.290**	**.349**	.400	749	**110**	49	**70**	97	51			
PIT	84	69	4	.549	4.5	49	28	769	689	5969	1514	243	106	44	434	350	190	33	.285	.343	.396	739	99	25	-12	105	91			
CHI	82	72	1	.532	7	49	28	682	**602**	5902	1453	**291**	49	66	445	447	199	29	.278	.338	.390	728	100	12	4	101	85			
NY	74	77	0	.490	13.5	43	33	663	668	5667	1435	214	58	73	339	420	139	22	.278	.325	.384	709	97	-39	-31	99	**94**			
BRO	71	82	2	.464	17.5	38	38	623	705	5790	1348	246	62	40	475	464	158	27	.263	.328	.358	686	91	-63	-53	99	76			
BOS	66	86	1	.434	22	43	34	624	719	5870	1444	209	62	16	426	348	199	29	.277	.335	.350	685	99	-67	-5	91	81			
PHI	58	93	1	.384	29.5	33	42	687	900	5851	1479	244	50	75	422	479	153	22	.281	.337	.390	727	96	6	-28	105	47			
TOT	618					355	256	5612		47200	11755	1948	589	439	3473	3359	229	1489	.280	.338	.386	724					608			

TEAM	CG	SHO	GR	SV	IP	H	HR	BB	SO	BR/9	ERA	AERA	OAV	OOB	PR	APR	PF	OSB	OCS	FA	E	WPB	DP	FW	PW	BW	BSW	DIF
STL	**90**	10	118	6	1398.2	1423	76	397	365	11.8	3.67	106	**.269**	.322	24	35	102	60	*64*	.969	198	19	141	.3	3.5	4.7		3.5
CIN	88	**14**	107	8	1408.2	1449	40	**324**	424	**11.5**	3.42	108	.271	**.316**	64	44	97	76	*43*	.972	183	27	160	1.3	4.3	**6.9**		-2.6
PIT	83	12	131	**18**	1379.1	1422	50	455	387	12.5	3.67	107	.272	.334	24	41	103	63	*44*	.965	220	**18**	161	-.9	4.1	-1.2		5.5
CHI	77	13	114	14	1378.1	1407	**39**	486	508	12.6	**3.26**	**118**	.273	.340	**87**	**89**	101	**42**	*68*	**.974**	**162**	37	**174**	**2.4**	**8.8**	.4		-6.6
NY	61	4	135	15	1341.2	**1370**	70	427	419	12.2	3.77	100	**.269**	.328	8	-3	98	84	*54*	.970	186	36	150	.7	-.3	-3.1		1.2
BRO	83	5	108	9	1361.2	1440	50	472	**517**	12.8	3.82	100	.276	.339	1	0	100	97	*63*	.963	229	34	95	-1.5	.0	-5.2		1.3
BOS	60	9	132	9	1365.1	1536	46	455	408	13.4	4.01	88	.294	.354	-28	-76	93	92	***71***	.967	208	42	150	-.5	-7.5	-.5		-1.5
PHI	68	5	**171**	5	1334.1	1699	68	454	331	14.7	5.03	82	.315	.371	-179	-123	108	94	*56*	.964	224	46	153	-1.5	-12.2	-2.8		-1.1
TOT	610	72	1016	84	10968.0					12.7	3.82		.280	.338						.968	1610	259	1184					

Batter-Fielder Wins	Batting Average	On-Base Percentage	Slugging Average	On-Base Plus Slugging	Adjusted OPS	Adjusted Batter Runs
O'Farrell-StL 3.2	Hargrave-Cin 353	Waner-Pit....................413	Williams-Phi 568	Wilson-Chi 944	Wilson-Chi 150	Wilson-Chi..........39.2
Wilson-Chi 2.8	Christensen-Cin ...350	Blades-StL 409	Wilson-Chi 539	Waner-Pit.............941	Waner-Pit..............144	Waner-Pit............34.0
Waner-Pit 2.6	Smith-Pit...............346	Wilson-Chi 406	Waner-Pit 528	L.Bell-StL.............901	Herman-Bro..........136	L.Bell-StL............27.6
Bancroft-Bos 2.6	Williams-Phi 345	Grantham-Pit 400	Hargrave-Cin 525	Grantham-Pit 890	L.Bell-StL..............135	Williams-Phi 26.3
Adams-Chi 2.6	Waner-Pit 336	Bancroft-Bos 399	L.Bell-StL 518	Herman-Bro..........875	Grantham-Pit 131	Herman-Bro........24.3

Runs	Hits	Doubles	Triples	Home Runs	Total Bases	Runs Batted In
Cuyler-Pit.............113	Brown-Bos............201	Bottomley-StL 40	Waner-Pit................22	Wilson-Chi 21	Bottomley-StL 305	Bottomley-StL......120
Waner-Pit..............101	Cuyler-Pit.............197	Roush-Cin.....................37	Walker-Cin 20	Bottomley-StL 19	L.Bell-StL..............301	Wilson-Chi 109
Southworth-NY-StL....99	Adams-Chi............193	Wilson-Chi 36	Traynor-Pit 17	Williams-Phi...........18	Wilson-Chi.............285	L.Bell-StL 100
Sand-Phi 99	L.Bell-StL..............189			L.Bell-StL................17	Waner-Pit..............283	Southworth-NY-StL ..99
				Southworth-NY-StL....16	Cuyler-Pit..............282	Pipp-Cin 99

Stolen Bases	Base Stealing Runs	Fielding Runs-Infield	Fielding Runs-Outfield	Wins	Winning Pct.	Complete Games
Cuyler-Pit...............35		Critz-Cin.....................23.0	Heathcote-Chi 8.5	Rhem-StL 20	Kremer-Pit 769	Mays-Cin 24
Adams-Chi..............27		Friberg-Phi 22.1	Welsh-Bos 8.2	Meadows-Pit 20	Rhem-StL 741	Petty-Bro 23
Frisch-NY................23		Adams-Chi...................20.1	Douthit-StL 7.2	Kremer-Pit 20	Meadows-Pit.........690	Root-Chi 21
Douthit-StL 23		Cooney-Chi 17.8	Cuyler-Pit 6.7	Donohue-Cin 20	Mays-Cin 613	Rhem-StL 20
Youngs-NY 21		Thevenow-StL 16.2	Leach-Phi 6.0	Mays-Cin 19	Donohue-Cin 588	Carlson-Phi 20

Strikeouts	Fewest BB/Game	Games	Saves	Base Runners/9	Adjusted Relief Runs	Relief Ranking
Vance-Bro 140	Donohue-Cin 1.23	Scott-NY 50	Davies-NY 6	Alexander-Chi-StL 10.06	Hallahan-StL..........1.7	Hallahan-StL 1.3
Root-Chi 127	Alexander-Chi-StL ..1.39	Willoughby-Phi 47	Scott-NY 5	H.Bell-StL 10.69		
May-Cin 103	Carlson-Phi..........1.58	Donohue-Cin 47	Kremer-Pit 5	Petty-Bro............10.71		
Benton-Bos 103	Mays-Cin 1.70	Ulrich-Phi 45	Ehrhardt-Bro 4	Kremer-Pit 10.74		
Petty-Bro 101	Lucas-Cin 1.75	May-Cin 45		Bush-Pit 10.90		

Innings Pitched	Opponents' Avg.	Opponents' OBP	Earned Run Average	Adjusted ERA	Adjusted Starter Runs	Pitcher Wins
Donohue-Cin 285.2	Petty-Bro..............240	Alexander-Chi-StL 281	Kremer-Pit 2.61	Kremer-Pit 151	Kremer-Pit 34.4	**Kremer-Pit** 3.9
Mays-Cin 281.0	Alexander-Chi-StL ...250	Petty-Bro 296	Root-Chi 2.82	Root-Chi 136	Root-Chi 30.1	**Root-Chi** 3.1
Petty-Bro...........275.2	Rhem-StL 250	Kremer-Pit 296	Petty-Bro.............2.84	Petty-Bro 134	Petty-Bro..............25.2	**Mays-Cin** 2.9
Root-Chi 271.1	Greenfield-NY.......251	Donohue-Cin 298	Bush-Chi..............2.86	Bush-Chi 134	Carlson-Phi..........24.9	**Carlson-Phi**........2.6
Carlson-Phi........267.1	Kremer-Pit 252	Rhem-StL 305	Barnes-NY 2.87	Barnes-NY............131	Mays-Cin 20.9	**Petty-Bro** 2.4

Cardinals Nest at the Top

It had been a long upward crawl for the St. Louis Cardinals. Since joining the NL in 1892, the franchise had never won and rarely even contended. With slugging Rogers Hornsby taking the managerial reins, however, 1926 was different. St. Louis' powerful offense, led by Hornsby and Bottomley, bludgeoned its opponents into submission. Unheralded Les Bell (.325, 17 homers, 100 RBIs) turned in one of the best hitting performances by a third baseman to that time. Lowly Boston spiced things up by beating up on St. Louis in early September. The Braves in turn knocked Cincinnati, Chicago, and Pittsburgh out of the race.

Attendance again hit an all-time high. Since 1904, AL attendance had topped the NL's every season. But in 1926 the Senior Circuit outdrew its rival and would remain better attended for seven more seasons. Since five NL teams actually lost attendance in '26, the gains came from just three clubs: the Cardinals (60 percent increase), the Reds (69 percent), and the Cubs (70 percent).

Giants outfielder Ross Youngs came down with Bright's disease at midseason. He died in November 1927. However, 17-year-old Mel Ott moved in, hitting .383 in 35 games for the Giants. Two stellar Pittsburgh, hurlers, Babe Adams and Wilbur Cooper, ended their careers with 416 combined victories. But the Bucs welcomed outfielder Paul Waner, who had a tremendous start to his Hall of Fame career. He led the NL in on-base percentage and went 6-for-6 against St. Louis on August 26.

The Cardinals-Yankees World Series was a thriller. Down three games to two in New York, St. Louis blew out the Bombers in Game 6 and held on for a thrilling Game 7 victory. Summoned in relief, Grover Cleveland Alexander quelled two New York rallies in the final contest after winning Games 2 and 6. Babe Ruth hit 4 homers, but he was thrown out stealing second to end the Series!

1926 American League

TEAM	W	L	T	PCT	GB	HW	HL	R	OR	PA	H	2B	3B	HR	BB	SO	HB	SH	AVG	OBP	SLG	OPS	AOPS	BR	ABR	PF	SB	CS	BSA	BSR
NY	91	63	1	.591		**50**	25	**847**	713	6104	1508	262	75	**121**	**642**	580	218	23	.289	**.369**	**.437**	**806**	**119**	**124**	**138**	98	79	62	56	-4
CLE	88	66	0	.571	3	49	31	738	612	6005	1529	**333**	49	27	455	**332**	222	35	.289	.349	.386	735	97	-13	-19	101	88	42	**68**	**5**
PHI	83	67	0	.553	6	44	27	677	**570**	5833	1359	259	65	61	523	452	**239**	25	.269	.341	.383	724	90	-39	-75	106	56	45	55	-3
WAS	81	69	2	.540	8	42	30	802	761	6011	1525	244	**97**	43	555	369	195	**38**	**.292**	.364	.401	765	109	46	66	98	117	91	56	-6
CHI	81	72	2	.529	9.5	47	31	730	665	6039	1508	314	60	32	556	381	229	34	.289	.361	.390	751	106	29	58	96	**123**	78	61	0
DET	79	75	3	.513	12	39	41	793	830	6184	**1547**	281	90	36	599	423	236	34	.291	.367	.398	765	105	53	43	101	88	71	55	-5
STL	62	92	1	.403	29	40	39	682	845	5936	1449	253	78	72	437	472	205	35	.276	.335	.394	729	92	-42	-73	105	64	66	49	-9
BOS	46	107	1	.301	44.5	25	51	562	835	5848	1325	249	54	32	465	454	165	33	.256	.321	.343	664	82	-158	-140	97	52	48	52	-5
TOT	616					336	275	5831		47960	11750	2195	568	424	4232	3463	257	1709	.281	.351	.392	743					667	503	57	-29

TEAM	CG	SHO	GR	SV	IP	H	HR	BB	SO	BR/9	ERA	AERA	OAV	OOB	PR	APR	PF	OSB	OCS	FA	E	WPB	DP	FW	PW	BW	BSW	DIF
NY	63	4	147	20	1372.1	1442	56	478	486	12.8	3.86	100	.274	.337	24	-1	96	95	67	.966	210	36	117	-1.1	-.0	**13.4**	-.0	1.9
CLE	**96**	**11**	81	4	1374.0	1412	49	**450**	381	12.5	3.40	119	.271	.334	94	100	101	**49**	41	.972	173	28	153	1.1	9.7	-1.8	**.8**	1.3
PHI	62	10	156	16	1346.0	**1362**	**38**	451	**571**	**12.3**	**3.00**	**139**	**.268**	**.331**	**153**	**168**	104	78	64	.972	171	35	131	.9	**16.3**	-7.3	.0	-1.9
WAS	65	5	143	**26**	1348.1	1489	45	566	418	14.0	4.34	89	.287	.361	-48	-74	96	80	59	.969	184	**21**	129	.2	-7.2	6.4	-.2	6.8
CHI	85	**11**	100	12	1380.0	1426	47	506	458	12.7	3.74	103	.271	.336	43	17	96	59	55	**.973**	**165**	**21**	122	**1.6**	1.6	5.6	.4	-4.7
DET	57	10	**164**	18	1394.2	1570	58	555	469	14.0	4.41	92	.292	.363	-61	-53	101	100	70	.969	193	24	151	.0	-5.1	4.2	-.1	3.0
STL	64	5	139	9	1368.0	1549	86	654	337	14.7	4.66	92	.297	.379	-98	-55	107	67	**86**	.963	235	38	**167**	-2.6	-5.3	-7.1	-.5	.5
BOS	53	6	163	5	1362.0	1520	45	546	336	13.9	4.72	86	.294	.365	-107	-99	101	139	59	.970	193	34	143	-.2	-9.6	-13.6	-.1	-7.1
TOT	545	62	1093	110	10945.1					13.3	4.02		.281	.351						.969	1524	237	1113					

Batter-Fielder Wins	Batting Average	On-Base Percentage	Slugging Average	On-Base Plus Slugging	Adjusted OPS	Adjusted Batter Runs
Ruth-NY 8.5	Manush-Det 378	Ruth-NY 516	Ruth-NY 737	Ruth-NY.............1253	Ruth-NY................228	Ruth-NY...........102.8
Mostil-Chi 7.8	Ruth-NY 372	Heilmann-Det...............445	Simmons-Phi 564	Manush-Det..........985	Goslin-Was 155	Gehrig-NY 47.5
Goslin-Was 4.4	Fothergill-Det 367	Bishop-Phi 431	Manush-Det 564	Heilmann-Det 979	Gehrig-NY 154	Goslin-Was 45.0
Rigney-Bos..........4.3	Heilmann-Det 367	Goslin-Was 425	Gehrig-NY 549	Gehrig-NY 969	Manush-Det..........153	Heilmann-Det 41.8
J.Sewell-Cle 3.4	Burns-Cle 358	Manush-Det.................421	Goslin-Was 542	Goslin-Was 967	Heilmann-Det 153	Manush-Det........37.3

Runs	Hits	Doubles	Triples	Home Runs	Total Bases	Runs Batted In
Ruth-NY................139	Rice-Was 216	Burns-Cle 64	Gehrig-NY 20	Ruth-NY.................47	Ruth-NY...............365	Ruth-NY 146
Gehrig-NY 135	Burns-Cle 216	Simmons-Phi 53	Gehringer-Det 17	Simmons-Phi 19	Simmons-Phi........329	Lazzeri-NY 114
Mostil-Chi 120	Goslin-Was 201	Speaker-Cle 52	Mostil-Chi 15	Lazzeri-NY..............18	Gehrig-NY 314	Burns-Cle 114
Combs-NY............113	Simmons-Phi........199	Jacobson-StL-Bos 51	Goslin-Was 15	Williams-StL 17	Goslin-Was 308	Gehrig-NY 112
Goslin-Was 105	Mostil-Chi 197	Gehrig-NY.....................47		Goslin-Was 17	Burns-Cle 298	Simmons-Phi 109

Stolen Bases	Base Stealing Runs	Fielding Runs-Infield	Fielding Runs-Outfield	Wins	Winning Pct.	Complete Games
Mostil-Chi 35	Mostil-Chi 2.8	Rigney-Bos 21.1	Mostil-Chi 49.6	Uhle-Cle 27	Uhle-Cle 711	Uhle-Cle 32
Rice-Was................24	Hunnefield-Chi 2.1	Dykes-Phi 16.3	Goslin-Was..........11.6	Pennock-NY 23	Pennock-NY 676	Lyons-Chi 24
Hunnefield-Chi........24	McNeely-Was 1.9	Kamm-Chi 16.1	Falk-Chi 8.3	Shocker-NY 19	Shocker-NY 633	Johnson-Was 22
McNeely-Was 18	Simmons-Phi 1.4	Regan-Bos.................15.7	Rice-Was 7.8	Lyons-Chi 18	Faber-Chi 625	Grove-Phi 20
J.Sewell-Cle............17	J.Sewell-Cle 1.3	McManus-StL 11.9	Summa-Cle 5.7		Hoyt-NY 571	Pennock-NY 19

Strikeouts	Fewest BB/Game	Games	Saves	Base Runners/9	Adjusted Relief Runs	Relief Ranking
Grove-Phi 194	Pennock-NY 1.45	Marberry-Was...............64	Marberry-Was 22	Russell-Bos 10.93	Pate-Phi 19.6	Marberry-Was 21.2
Uhle-Cle 159	Smith-Cle 1.48	Pate-Phi 47	Dauss-Det 9	Pennock-NY 11.52	Marberry-Was......13.3	Pate-Phi..............16.4
Thomas-Chi..........127	Quinn-Phi 1.98	Grove-Phi 45	Pate-Phi...................6	Rommel-Phi 11.55	Braxton-NY............7.6	Braxton-NY 6.6
Johnson-Was........125	Rommel-Phi 2.22	Thomas-Chi 44	Grove-Phi 6	Johnson-Was 11.64	Russell-Bos 7.6	Russell-Bos 3.8
Whitehill-Det 109	Wingfield-Bos 2.36		Jones-NY..................5	Grove-Phi 11.65		

Innings Pitched	Opponents' Avg.	Opponents' OBP	Earned Run Average	Adjusted ERA	Adjusted Starter Runs	Pitcher Wins
Uhle-Cle 318.1	Thomas-Chi 244	Pennock-NY................313	Grove-Phi 2.51	Grove-Phi 166	Uhle-Cle 44.6	**Uhle-Cle**............5.4
Lyons-Chi 283.2	Grove-Phi 244	Rommel-Phi................314	Uhle-Cle 2.83	Uhle-Cle 143	Grove-Phi 43.7	**Grove-Phi** 3.7
Pennock-NY 266.1	Lyons-Chi 252	Hoyt-NY 316	Lyons-Chi 3.01	Rommel-Phi..........135	Lyons-Chi 28.8	**Lyons-Chi** 3.3
Johnson-Was 260.2	Uhle-Cle 253	Johnson-Was..............317	Rommel-Phi 3.08	Buckeye-Cle 131	Rommel-Phi 27.1	**Walberg-Phi** 2.3
Shocker-NY 258.1	Levsen-Cle 261	Shocker-NY 318	Buckeye-Cle 3.10	Lyons-Chi 128	Walberg-Phi 19.3	**Rommel-Phi** 2.2

The Yankees Are Back

Due to the calamitous (at least for pitchers) rise in offense, the rules committee decided that any flyball over an outfield fence less than 250 feet from home was a ground-rule double. Three clubs also tried to curb production; St. Louis, a home run haven in '25, pushed out the fences by 10 feet. Boston enlarged Fenway Park's right field by 45 feet, and the White Sox grew center field by 30. Philadelphia, however, hoping to spur on their young power, shrunk Shibe Park to all fields. The Senators also chopped Griffith Stadium's left field by 66 feet. But the upshot to all these moves was a decline in scoring by nearly half a run and a loss of more than 100 homers.

Into this environment moved the Yankees, bolstered by the hitting of a healthy Babe Ruth, rookie infielder Tony Lazzeri, and 23-year-old Lou Gehrig, making his first appearance among the league leaders—although he actually hit more triples than homers. Miller Huggins' lineup destroyed the competition, but they just held off second-place Cleveland, whose first baseman George Burns rapped out a major league record 64 doubles.

The Indians and third-place Athletics played in inhospitable home run parks, and couldn't compete with New York's fire-power, and their pitching wasn't good enough to overcome this. Washington fell to fourth as Walter Johnson finally went over the hill.

Shortstop Everett Scott retired with the record for most consecutive games played (1,307), and Hall of Fame hurler Eddie Plank died at age 50 of a stroke. Joe Cronin, later a standout with the Senators, debuted for the Pittsburgh Pirates—who soon gave up on him.

In addition to the Yankees' tough World Series loss to the Cardinals, 1926 was an ignominious year for the Junior Circuit in another way: the NL moved ahead in attendance for the first time since 1903. The Senior Circuit remained ahead until 1934.

1927 National League

TEAM	W	L	T	PCT	GB	HW	HL	R	OR	PA	H	2B	3B	HR	BB	SO	HB	SH	AVG	OBP	SLG	OPS	AOPS	BR	ABR	PF	SB	CS	BSA	BSR
PIT	94	60	2	.610		48	31	**817**	659	6077	**1648**	258	78	54	437	355	214	29	**.305**	**.361**	.412	773	106	100	46	107	65			
STL	92	61	0	.601	1.5	**55**	25	754	665	5888	1450	264	**79**	84	**484**	511	171	26	.278	.343	.408	751	104	50	27	103	**110**			
NY	92	62	1	.597	2	49	25	**817**	720	6045	1594	251	62	**109**	461	462	180	**32**	.297	.356	**.427**	**783**	**116**	**115**	**117**	100	73			
CHI	85	68	0	.556	8.5	50	28	750	661	6018	1505	**266**	63	74	481	492	207	27	.284	.346	.400	746	106	47	45	100	65			
CIN	75	78	0	.490	18.5	45	35	643	**653**	5827	1439	222	77	29	402	**332**	**219**	21	.278	.332	.367	699	96	-49	-28	97	62			
BRO	65	88	1	.425	28.5	34	39	541	619	5752	1314	195	74	39	368	494	166	25	.253	.306	.342	648	79	-157	-159	100	106			
BOS	60	94	1	.390	34	32	41	651	771	5941	1498	216	61	37	346	363	197	28	.279	.326	.363	689	98	-76	-23	92	100			
PHI	51	103	1	.331	43	34	43	678	903	5956	1487	216	46	57	434	482	177	28	.280	.337	.370	707	94	-30	-39	101	68			
TOT	617					347	267	5651		47504	11935	1888	540	483	3413	3491	216	1531	.282	.339	.386	725					649			

TEAM	CG	SHO	GR	SV	IP	H	HR	BB	SO	BR/9	ERA	AERA	OAV	OOB	PR	APR	PF	OSB	OCS	FA	E	WPB	DP	FW	PW	BW	BSW	DIF
PIT	**90**	10	107	10	1385.0	1400	58	418	435	12.0	3.66	112	.267	.324	39	65	105	63	*36*	.969	187	32	130	.6	6.4	4.5		5.4
STL	89	**14**	110	11	1367.1	1416	72	363	394	**11.8**	3.57	110	.271	**.320**	52	56	101	85	*64*	.966	213	**21**	**170**	-1.0	5.5	2.7		8.3
NY	65	7	147	**16**	1381.2	1520	77	453	442	13.0	3.97	97	.283	.341	-8	-18	98	70	*54*	.969	195	34	160	.1	-1.8	**11.5**		5.1
CHI	75	11	114	5	1385.0	1439	50	514	465	12.9	3.65	106	.273	.342	40	32	99	**52**	*58*	.971	181	31	152	.8	3.2	4.4		.1
CIN	87	12	93	12	1368.0	1472	**36**	**316**	407	11.9	3.54	107	.281	.325	57	38	97	100	*31*	**.973**	**165**	34	160	**1.6**	3.8	-2.8		-4.1
BRO	74	7	131	10	1375.1	**1382**	63	418	**574**	11.9	**3.36**	**118**	**.265**	.323	**85**	**89**	101	99	*68*	.963	229	25	117	-1.8	**8.8**	-15.7		-2.8
BOS	52	3	**156**	11	1390.0	1602	43	468	402	13.6	4.22	88	.296	.356	-48	-83	95	81	***71***	.963	231	40	130	-1.8	-8.2	-2.3		-4.7
PHI	81	5	112	6	1355.1	1710	84	462	377	14.7	5.36	77	.317	.374	-218	-177	106	99	*42*	.972	169	35	152	1.5	-17.5	-3.8		-6.2
TOT	613	69	970	81	11007.2					12.7	3.91		.282	.339						.969	1570	252	1171					

Batter-Fielder Wins	Batting Average	On-Base Percentage	Slugging Average	On-Base Plus Slugging	Adjusted OPS	Adjusted Batter Runs
Frisch-StL............7.2	P.Waner-Pit 380	Hornsby-NY 448	Hafey-StL 590	Hornsby-NY........1035	Hornsby-NY..........175	Hornsby-NY........64.1
Hornsby-NY 6.8	Hornsby-NY 361	P.Waner-Pit 437	Hornsby-NY 586	P.Waner-Pit 986	Wilson-Chi 159	P.Waner-Pit 47.1
Jackson-NY 5.4	L.Waner-Pit..........355	Harper-NY 435	Wilson-Chi 579	Wilson-Chi 980	P.Waner-Pit 152	Wilson-Chi..........46.1
P.Waner-Pit..........3.9	Stephenson-Chi ...344	Stephenson-Chi..........415	P.Waner-Pit 549	Harper-NY 930	Harper-NY 149	Harper-NY 38.1
Dressen-Cin 3.3	Traynor-Pit 342	Harris-Pit 402	Terry-NY 529	Terry-NY 907	Stephenson-Chi....141	Stephenson-Chi 37.3

Runs	Hits	Doubles	Triples	Home Runs	Total Bases	Runs Batted In
L.Waner-Pit 133	P.Waner-Pit 237	Stephenson-Chi 46	P.Waner-Pit 18	Wilson-Chi 30	P.Waner-Pit 342	P.Waner-Pit..........131
Hornsby-NY..........133	L.Waner-Pit 223	P.Waner-Pit 42	Bottomley-StL 15	Williams-Phi............30	Hornsby-NY..........333	Wilson-Chi 129
Wilson-Chi 119	Frisch-StL 208	Lindstrom-NY 36	Thompson-Phi 14	Hornsby-NY............26	Wilson-Chi 319	Hornsby-NY 125
P.Waner-Pit 114	Hornsby-NY..........205	Dressen-Cin 36	Terry-NY 13	Terry-NY 20	Terry-NY 307	Bottomley-StL......124
Frisch-StL 112	Stephenson-Chi....199	Brown-Bos 35	Wilson-Chi 12	Bottomley-StL 19	Bottomley-StL 292	Terry-NY.............121

Stolen Bases	Base Stealing Runs	Fielding Runs-Infield	Fielding Runs-Outfield	Wins	Winning Pct.	Complete Games
Frisch-StL 48		Frisch-StL 49.3	Leach-Phi 16.3	Root-Chi 26	Benton-Bos-NY ...708	Vance-Bro 25
Carey-Bro 32		Jackson-NY...............26.3	Statz-Bro 9.9	Haines-StL.............24	Haines-StL 706	Meadows-Pit 25
Hendrick-Bro 29		Friberg-Phi.................20.3	Welsh-Bos 8.1	Hill-Pit 22	Kremer-Pit 704	Haines-StL 25
Adams-Chi.............26		Traynor-Pit 14.3	P.Waner-Pit 6.7	Alexander-StL 21	Grimes-NY 704	Hill-Pit...................22
Richbourg-Bos........24		Cooney-Chi-Phi 13.2	Bressler-Cin 5.2		Alexander-StL.......677	Alexander-StL........22

Strikeouts	Fewest BB/Game	Games	Saves	Base Runners/9	Adjusted Relief Runs	Relief Ranking
Vance-Bro 184	Alexander-StL......1.28	Scott-Phi.........................48	Sherdel-StL 6	Miljus-Pit.............9.40	Clark-Bro 13.2	Clark-Bro...........15.3
Root-Chi 145	Lucas-Cin 1.46	Root-Chi 48	Nehf-Cin-Chi 5	Alexander-StL....10.07	Ehrhardt-Bro..........4.0	Ehrhardt-Bro 3.9
May-Cin 121	Donohue-Cin 1.51	Ehrhardt-Bro 46	Mogridge-Bos 5	Lucas-Cin 10.14	Cvengros-Pit..........3.6	Cvengros-Pit 2.0
Grimes-NY............102	Carlson-Phi-Chi ..1.63	Henry-NY 45	Henry-NY..................4	Kremer-Pit 10.27	Morrison-Pit 4	Morrison-Pit............4
Petty-Bro 101	Henry-NY 1.70	May-Cin 44		Vance-Bro..........10.44		

Innings Pitched	Opponents' Avg.	Opponents' OBP	Earned Run Average	Adjusted ERA	Adjusted Starter Runs	Pitcher Wins
Root-Chi 309.0	Vance-Bro............239	Alexander-StL 286	Kremer-Pit 2.47	Kremer-Pit 166	Alexander-StL......41.3	**Alexander-StL** ..5.0
Haines-StL 300.2	Kremer-Pit 244	Lucas-Cin 287	Alexander-StL......2.52	Alexander-StL 157	Haines-StL 39.4	**Kremer-Pit** 4.2
Meadows-Pit......299.1	Haines-StL 245	Kremer-Pit 289	Vance-Bro...........2.70	Vance-Bro 147	Kremer-Pit 39.0	**Haines-StL** 4.1
Hill-Pit 277.2	Hill-Pit...................249	Vance-Bro 291	Haines-StL 2.72	Haines-StL............145	Vance-Bro............38.1	**Vance-Bro** 3.9
Vance-Bro..........273.1	Bush-Chi..............250	Petty-Bro 293	Petty-Bro.............2.98	Petty-Bro 133	Petty-Bro.............29.4	**Lucas-Cin** 3.1

Raising the Skull and Crossbones

Once again, the Pittsburgh Pirates showed their facility in developing young players by debuting two more future stars: outfielder Lloyd Waner and shortstop Dick Bartell. Waner, and older brother Paul, would star in Pittsburgh for many years, but Bartell, sent to Philly in a poor 1930 trade, did most of his damage for other clubs. The great seasons of the Waners, and a big year from obscure pitcher Carmen Hill, propelled Pittsburgh to its second flag in three seasons.

The Cardinals finished 1_ games out after dealing productive but cranky Rogers Hornsby to the Giants for another second sacker, Frankie Frisch. While Frisch played well offensively and defensively for St. Louis, Mound City fans lambasted the deal. New York was third, 2 games back, with mediocre starting pitching and a power-based offense.

Several Senior Circuit veterans played their final seasons. First baseman Jacques Fournier was gone after 1,503 games, while 38-year-old Heinie Groh was released by the Pirates. Rifle-armed outfielder Irish Meusel's career careened to a premature end in Brooklyn, while future Hall of Famer Zach Wheat bowed out with a .324 season as a part-timer in Philadelphia. In addition, August "Garry" Herrmann, president of the Reds since 1902 and a kingpin of the National League, bowed out due to poor health that would lead to his death in 1931.

The Chicago Cubs, reconsidering an earlier promise to keep Wrigley Field single decked, decided to double-deck their park, and as a result became the first NL team to break the million mark in attendance. Their 1,159,168 turnstile clicks helped the entire league once again set a new high. The last-place Phillies, meanwhile, had to play at the Athletics' home, Shibe Park, for a few games after a section of Baker Bowl bleachers collapsed on May 14. Forbes Field took in a club-record 869,720, plus another 83,000 for the World Series, but on the field the Pirates were no match for the Yankees.

1927 American League

TEAM	W	L	T	PCT	GB	HW	HL	R	OR	PA	H	2B	3B	HR	BB	SO	HB	SH	AVG	OBP	SLG	OPS	AOPS	BR	ABR	PF	SB	CS	BSA	BSR
NY	110	44	1	.714		**57**	19	**975**	**599**	6207	**1644**	**291**	**103**	**158**	**635**	605	203	22	**.307**	**.383**	**.489**	**872**	**135**	**236**	**268**	97	90	64	58	-3
PHI	91	63	1	.591	19	50	27	841	726	6094	1606	281	70	56	551	**326**	**217**	30	.303	.372	.414	786	103	80	35	106	101	63	62	0
WAS	85	69	3	.552	25	51	28	782	730	6117	1549	268	87	29	498	359	199	**31**	.287	.351	.386	737	97	-27	-18	99	**133**	52	**72**	**11**
DET	82	71	3	.536	27.5	44	32	845	805	6112	1533	282	100	51	587	420	202	24	.289	.363	.409	772	105	46	35	101	139	73	66	5
CHI	70	83	0	.458	39.5	38	37	662	708	5910	1433	285	61	36	493	389	234	26	.278	.344	.378	722	94	-53	-35	98	89	75	54	-7
CLE	66	87	0	.431	43.5	35	42	668	766	5843	1471	321	52	26	381	366	212	48	.283	.337	.379	716	90	-68	-73	101	65	72	47	-11
STL	59	94	2	.386	50.5	38	38	724	904	5897	1440	262	59	55	443	420	191	43	.276	.338	.380	718	88	-69	-91	103	90	66	58	-3
BOS	51	103	0	.331	59	29	49	597	856	5867	1348	271	78	28	430	456	191	39	.259	.320	.357	677	82	-152	-139	98	81	46	64	2
TOT	619					342	272	6094		48047	12024	2261	610	439	4018	3341	263	1649	.285	.351	.399	751					788	511	61	-5

TEAM	CG	SHO	GR	SV	IP	H	HR	BB	SO	BR/9	ERA	AERA	OAV	OOB	PR	APR	PF	OSB	OCS	FA	E	WPB	DP	FW	PW	BW	BSW	DIF
NY	82	**11**	109	20	1389.2	**1403**	42	**409**	431	**11.9**	**3.20**	**120**	**.267**	**.323**	**145**	**107**	93	94	44	.969	195	22	123	.7	**10.2**	**25.5**	-.2	-3.1
PHI	65	8	160	**24**	1384.0	1467	65	442	**553**	12.6	3.97	107	.278	.338	26	44	103	**84**	47	.970	190	27	124	1.0	4.2	3.3	.0	5.4
WAS	62	10	**163**	23	1402.0	1434	53	491	497	12.6	3.97	102	.269	.335	26	14	98	86	55	.969	195	**18**	125	.8	1.3	-1.7	**1.1**	6.4
DET	75	5	131	17	1387.2	1542	52	577	421	14.0	4.14	102	.290	.364	0	9	102	100	62	.968	206	33	**173**	.1	.9	3.3	.5	.7
CHI	**85**	10	95	8	1367.0	1467	55	440	365	12.7	3.91	103	.283	.342	34	20	98	86	68	**.971**	**178**	20	131	**1.6**	1.9	-3.3	-.6	-6.0
CLE	72	5	132	8	1353.1	1542	**37**	508	366	13.9	4.27	98	.295	.361	-20	-11	102	86	91	.968	201	39	146	.2	-1.0	-6.9	-1.0	-1.7
STL	80	4	121	8	1353.1	1592	79	604	385	14.7	4.95	88	.304	.378	-122	-87	105	94	**92**	.960	248	48	166	-2.5	-8.3	-8.6	-.2	2.1
BOS	63	6	134	7	1366.1	1603	56	558	381	14.5	4.72	89	.305	.376	-88	-76	102	158	52	.964	228	34	167	-1.4	-7.2	-13.2	.3	-4.5
TOT	584	59	1045	115	11003.1					13.4	4.14		.285	.351						.967	1641	241	1155					

Batter-Fielder Wins
Ruth-NY 8.8
Gehrig-NY...........8.4
Heilmann-Det......4.1
Lazzeri-NY 3.5
Simmons-Phi 3.3

Batting Average
Heilmann-Det 398
Simmons-Phi 392
Gehrig-NY 373
Fothergill-Det 359
Cobb-Phi 357

On-Base Percentage
Ruth-NY.......................486
Heilmann-Det..............475
Gehrig-NY 474
Bishop-Phi 442
Cobb-Phi 440

Slugging Average
Ruth-NY 772
Gehrig-NY 765
Simmons-Phi 645
Heilmann-Det 616
Williams-StL 525

On-Base Plus Slugging
Ruth-NY.............1258
Gehrig-NY 1240
Heilmann-Det 1091
Fothergill-Det........929
Williams-StL 928

Adjusted OPS
Ruth-NY................229
Gehrig-NY 224
Heilmann-Det 179
Combs-NY............143
Fothergill-Det........138

Adjusted Batter Runs
Gehrig-NY 108.8
Ruth-NY...........108.0
Heilmann-Det 62.6
Combs-NY..........40.3
Simmons-Phi......39.3

Runs
Ruth-NY................158
Gehrig-NY 149
Combs-NY.............137
Gehringer-Det 110
Heilmann-Det 106

Hits
Combs-NY............231
Gehrig-NY 218
Sisler-StL..............201
Heilmann-Det 201
Goslin-Was 194

Doubles
Gehrig-NY......................52
Burns-Cle 51
Heilmann-Det 50
J.Sewell-Cle 48
Meusel-NY 47

Triples
Combs-NY.............23
Manush-Det...........18
Gehrig-NY 18
Goslin-Was 15
Rice-Was 14

Home Runs
Ruth-NY..................60
Gehrig-NY 47
Lazzeri-NY.............18
Williams-StL 17
Simmons-Phi..........15

Total Bases
Gehrig-NY 447
Ruth-NY...............417
Combs-NY...........331
Heilmann-Det 311
Goslin-Was 300

Runs Batted In
Gehrig-NY 175
Ruth-NY 164
Heilmann-Det 120
Goslin-Was..........120
Fothergill-Det 114

Stolen Bases
Sisler-StL................27
Meusel-NY.............24
Neun-Det................22
Lazzeri-NY.............22
Cobb-Phi 22

Base Stealing Runs
Sisler-StL 3.5
Harris-Was 2.9
Goslin-Was...........2.5
Neun-Det 2.4
Rice-Was 2.1

Fielding Runs-Infield
Gehringer-Det 17.1
Bluege-Was 14.8
Sisler-StL 12.1
Koenig-NY 12.1
O'Rourke-StL..............11.2

Fielding Runs-Outfield
Falk-Chi 18.1
Rice-StL 10.9
Metzler-Chi 7.2
Barrett-Chi 6.9
Williams-StL 5.8

Wins
Lyons-Chi 22
Hoyt-NY..................22
Grove-Phi 20

Winning Pct.
Hoyt-NY 759
Shocker-NY 750
Moore-NY 731
Pennock-NY 704
Lisenbee-Was.......667

Complete Games
Lyons-Chi 30
Thomas-Chi 24
Hoyt-NY 23
Gaston-StL 21

Strikeouts
Grove-Phi 174
Walberg-Phi..........136
Thomas-Chi..........107
Lisenbee-Was 105
Braxton-Was 96

Fewest BB/Game
Quinn-Phi 1.65
Shocker-NY 1.85
Hoyt-NY 1.90
Braxton-Was........1.91
Lyons-Chi 1.96

Games
Braxton-Was..................58
Marberry-Was................56
Grove-Phi 51
Moore-NY 50
Walberg-Phi 46

Saves
Moore-NY 13
Braxton-Was 13
Marberry-Was 9
Grove-Phi 9

Base Runners/9
Moore-NY..........10.35
Braxton-Was.......10.37
Lyons-Chi 10.47
Hoyt-NY 10.53
Thomas-Chi 10.71

Adjusted Relief Runs
Braxton-Was........18.7
Burke-Was 2.9
G.Smith-Det 2.7

Relief Ranking
Braxton-Was 24.1
G.Smith-Det...........1.7
Burke-Was............1.4

Innings Pitched
Thomas-Chi 307.2
Lyons-Chi 307.2
Hudlin-Cle..........264.2
Grove-Phi 262.1
Hoyt-NY 256.1

Opponents' Avg.
Moore-NY 234
Thomas-Chi 244
Hadley-Was 244
Lisenbee-Was.......245
Braxton-Was.........246

Opponents' OBP
Moore-NY 289
Braxton-Was 289
Lyons-Chi.....................292
Hoyt-NY 294
Thomas-Chi 303

Earned Run Average
Moore-NY...........2.28
Hoyt-NY 2.63
Shocker-NY 2.84
Lyons-Chi 2.84
Hadley-Was 2.85

Adjusted ERA
Moore-NY 169
Hoyt-NY................146
Lyons-Chi 143
Hadley-Was..........142
Braxton-Was 137

Adjusted Starter Runs
Thomas-Chi 42.0
Moore-NY 38.8
Lyons-Chi 38.2
Hoyt-NY 37.6
Hadley-Was 28.2

Pitcher Wins
Lyons-Chi 4.7
Moore-NY 4.5
Hoyt-NY 3.8
Thomas-Chi 3.8
Grove-Phi 3.0

Murder by Bat

Some felt that Babe Ruth's better days were behind him. But in 1927, he exploded again, tagging 60 home runs to set a mark that lasted until 1961. Lou Gehrig chipped in 175 RBIs, which still tops the AL list. Earle Combs led the league in hits and triples. The remainder of the offense assisted in the bludgeoning, and Murderer's Row outscored its closest rivals by 134. In addition, the Yankees pitching staff was the stingiest in the league by a margin of 109 runs. This dominating team was one of the best in baseball history.

Needless to say, the rest of the AL provided no challenge to the Yankees, whose 110 wins set a league record. Ruth and Gehrig, together, smacked 107 homers; Washington, Cleveland, Chicago, and Boston *combined* for only 119. The Red Sox, Ruth's former employer, finished 59 games behind, last for the third straight season.

As the Yankees eradicated the rest of the league, some of the great players of the pre-Ruth era called it quits. Walter Johnson pitched his last game at 39; first baseman Stuffy McInnis and shortstop Roger Peckinpaugh hung 'em up; and hurler Bob Shawkey, a consistent winner for New York even before the Babe's arrival, pitched his last game. On the horizon were the second-place Athletics, who continued to improve as Lefty Grove, Al Simmons, Mickey Cochrane, and Jimmie Foxx developed. But they were two years away.

The Pirates were a fine club, winning a tight NL race with solid hitting from the Waner brothers. But Pittsburgh was no match for the Yankees in the World Series, losing in four. While two games were decided by one run, the Bucs scored just 10 times in the Series; the Yankees tallied 23. Ruth batted .400 and hit the lone 2 homers of the Series.

1928 National League

TEAM	W	L	T	PCT	GB	HW	HL	R	OR	PA	H	2B	3B	HR	BB	SO	HB	SH	AVG	OBP	SLG	OPS	AOPS	BR	ABR	PF	SB	CS	BSA	BSR
STL	95	59	0	.617		42	35	807	636	6144	1505	**292**	70	113	**568**	438	187	**32**	.281	.353	.425	778	108	77	63	102	82			
NY	93	61	1	.604	2	51	26	807	653	6103	1600	276	59	**118**	444	376	173	27	.293	.349	**.430**	779	**110**	69	**66**	100	62			
CHI	91	63	0	.591	4	**52**	25	714	**615**	6009	1460	251	64	92	508	517	210	31	.278	.345	.402	747	103	12	22	99	**83**			
PIT	85	67	0	.559	9	47	30	**837**	704	6037	**1659**	246	**100**	52	435	352	202	29	**.309**	**.364**	.421	**785**	108	**86**	55	104	64			
CIN	78	74	1	.513	16	44	33	648	686	5808	1449	229	67	32	386	**330**	**212**	26	.280	.333	.368	701	91	-80	-70	98	**83**			
BRO	77	76	2	.503	17.5	41	35	665	640	5992	1393	229	70	66	557	510	160	**32**	.266	.340	.374	714	94	-47	-37	99	81			
BOS	50	103	0	.327	44.5	25	51	631	878	5893	1439	241	41	52	447	377	191	27	.275	.335	.367	702	95	-70	-35	95	60			
PHI	43	109	0	.283	51	26	49	660	957	5917	1396	257	47	85	503	510	159	21	.267	.333	.382	715	90	-48	-70	103	53			
TOT	614					328	284	5769		47903	11901	2021	518	610	3848	3410	225	1494	.281	.344	.397	741					568			

TEAM	CG	SHO	GR	SV	IP	H	HR	BB	SO	BR/9	ERA	AERA	OAV	OOB	PR	APR	PF	OSB	OCS	FA	E	WPB	DP	FW	PW	BW	BSW	DIF
STL	**83**	4	119	**21**	1415.1	1470	86	**399**	422	**12.1**	3.38	118	.270	**.323**	97	98	100	55	*53*	.974	160	25	134	1.3	9.6	6.2		.9
NY	79	7	126	16	1394.0	1454	77	405	399	**12.1**	3.67	107	.273	.327	50	38	98	53	*35*	.972	178	29	175	.3	3.7	**6.4**		5.5
CHI	75	12	122	14	1380.2	1383	**56**	508	531	12.5	3.40	113	.267	.336	91	72	96	**38**	***70***	**.975**	**156**	26	176	**1.6**	7.0	2.1		3.3
PIT	82	8	112	11	1354.0	1422	66	446	385	12.6	3.95	103	.274	.335	7	16	102	88	*55*	.967	201	33	123	-1.3	1.6	5.4		3.3
CIN	68	11	120	11	1371.2	1516	58	410	355	12.7	3.94	100	.289	.342	8	2	99	67	*61*	.974	162	21	**194**	1.1	.2	-6.8		7.5
BRO	75	**16**	141	15	1396.0	**1378**	59	468	**551**	**12.1**	**3.25**	**122**	**.261**	.324	**115**	**113**	100	93	*58*	.965	217	**18**	113	-2.0	**11.0**	-3.6		-4.9
BOS	54	1	168	6	1360.0	1596	100	524	343	14.2	4.83	81	.298	.363	-127	-142	98	79	*54*	.969	193	36	141	-.7	-13.9	-3.4		-8.5
PHI	42	4	**189**	11	1346.2	1664	108	675	402	15.9	5.61	76	.315	.397	-242	-188	107	95	***70***	.971	181	29	171	-.0	-18.4	-6.8		-7.7
TOT	558	63	1097	105	11018.1					13.0	3.99		.281	.344						.971	1448	217	1227					

Batter-Fielder Wins	Batting Average	On-Base Percentage	Slugging Average	On-Base Plus Slugging	Adjusted OPS	Adjusted Batter Runs
Hornsby-Bos 6.1	Hornsby-Bos.........387	Hornsby-Bos 498	Hornsby-Bos.........632	Hornsby-Bos 1130	Hornsby-Bos 204	Hornsby-Bos 83.4
Lindstrom-NY 4.9	P.Waner-Pit 370	P.Waner-Pit 446	Bottomley-StL.......628	Bottomley-StL 1030	Bottomley-StL 163	Bottomley-StL 50.6
Hartnett-Chi........4.7	Lindstrom-NY 358	Grantham-Pit 408	Hafey-StL 604	Wilson-Chi 992	Wilson-Chi 159	P.Waner-Pit 49.4
Jackson-NY 4.2	Sisler-Bos 340	Stephenson-Chi..........407	Wilson-Chi 588	P.Waner-Pit 992	Hafey-StL..............152	Wilson-Chi..........44.6
P.Waner-Pit..........3.9	Herman-Bro 340	Wilson-Chi 404	P.Waner-Pit 547	Hafey-StL..............990	P.Waner-Pit 152	Bissonette-Bro....38.2

Runs	Hits	Doubles	Triples	Home Runs	Total Bases	Runs Batted In
P.Waner-Pit 142	Lindstrom-NY 231	P.Waner-Pit 50	Bottomley-StL 20	Wilson-Chi..............31	Bottomley-StL 362	Bottomley-StL......136
Bottomley-StL 123	P.Waner-Pit 223	Hafey-StL.......................46	P.Waner-Pit 19	Bottomley-StL 31	Lindstrom-NY 330	Traynor-Pit 124
L.Waner-Pit 121	L.Waner-Pit 221	Hornsby-Bos.................42	L.Waner-Pit 14	Hafey-StL................27	P.Waner-Pit 329	Wilson-Chi 120
Douthit-StL 111	Richbourg-Bos......206	Bottomley-StL 42	Bressler-Bro............13	Bissonette-Bro........25	Bissonette-Bro......319	Hafey-StL 111
Frisch-StL 107	Traynor-Pit 192	Lindstrom-NY 39	Bissonette-Bro........13	Hornsby-Bos 21	Hafey-StL..............314	Lindstrom-NY 107

Stolen Bases	Base Stealing Runs	Fielding Runs-Infield	Fielding Runs-Outfield	Wins	Winning Pct.	Complete Games
Cuyler-Chi 37		Maguire-Chi 49.1	Douthit-StL 13.3	Grimes-Pit 25	Benton-NY 735	Grimes-Pit 28
Frisch-StL 29		Jackson-NY 28.0	Leach-Phi 5.6	Benton-NY..............25	Haines-StL 714	Benton-NY 28
Walker-Cin 19		Lindstrom-NY.............14.6	P.Waner-Pit 5.4	Vance-Bro 22	Bush-Chi...............714	Vance-Bro 24
Thompson-Phi 19		Ford-Cin......................14.5	Sothern-Phi 5.3	Sherdel-StL 21	Fitzsimmons-NY ...690	Sherdel-StL 20
		Kelly-Cin 7.9	Richbourg-Bos 3.8		Vance-Bro.............688	Haines-StL 20

Strikeouts	Fewest BB/Game	Games	Saves	Base Runners/9	Adjusted Relief Runs	Relief Ranking
Vance-Bro 200	Alexander-StL......1.37	Grimes-Pit.....................48	Sherdel-StL 5	Vance-Bro...........9.79		
Malone-Chi 155	Sherdel-StL 2.03	Kolp-Cin 44	Haid-StL 5	Hubbell-NY..........10.23		
Root-Chi 122	Benton-NY 2.06	Rixey-Cin 43	Carlson-Chi 4	Benton-NY 10.73		
Grimes-Pit 97	Rixey-Cin 2.07		Benton-NY................4	Grimes-Pit 10.81		
Benton-NY..............90	Grimes-Pit 2.10			Lucas-Cin 11.08		

Innings Pitched	Opponents' Avg.	Opponents' OBP	Earned Run Average	Adjusted ERA	Adjusted Starter Runs	Pitcher Wins
Grimes-Pit 330.2	Vance-Bro............221	Vance-Bro 277	Vance-Bro............2.09	Vance-Bro 191	Vance-Bro...........60.5	**Vance-Bro** 7.2
Benton-NY 310.1	McWeeny-Bro.......235	Grimes-Pit 297	Blake-Chi 2.47	Blake-Chi 156	Benton-NY 42.6	**Grimes-Pit**..........4.9
Rixey-Cin 291.1	Malone-Chi...........236	Benton-NY...................300	Nehf-Chi 2.65	Clark-Bro 148	Blake-Chi 37.4	**Benton-NY**..........4.1
Vance-Bro..........280.1	Blake-Chi 240	Sherdel-StL 303	Clark-Bro 2.68	Nehf-Chi 145	Grimes-Pit 32.0	**Blake-Chi**............4.0
Fitzsimmons-NY ..261.1	Root-Chi 242	Lucas-Cin 304	Benton-NY 2.73	Benton-NY............144	Sherdel-StL 30.9	**Sherdel-StL**........3.9

Holding off the Giants

St. Louis, featuring an aging pitching staff and a veteran lineup, didn't lead the league in batting average, home runs, or ERA, but drew more walks than any other team and allowed fewer walks as well. First sacker Jim Bottomley was the club's best hitter, and 41-year-old Grover Cleveland Alexander finished 16–9. Moving ahead for good in early June, the Cardinals won the flag despite the dogged efforts of the Giants, who went 25–8 in September. John McGraw had found he could not get along with irascible Rogers Hornsby and dealt the him to seventh-place Boston in the off-season. As a result, New York's offense suffered. Hornsby, meanwhile, won his seventh (and last) batting title in near-obscurity for the pathetic Bees.

The Cubs continued to rise into contention, finishing just four games out as Hack Wilson hit 31 homers to tie Bottomley for the lead. The hard-drinking Wilson also fanned 94 times, a modern NL record. On the mound, Brooklyn's Dazzy Vance led the NL in strikeouts for the seventh (and last) time, but another outstanding pitcher debuted on July 26 when lefty Carl Hubbell pitched his first game for the Giants. Four days later, the Phillies gave slugging outfielder Chuck Klein his first major league action.

Six teams in the NL finished over .500, while Philadelphia and Boston—who desperately named Hornsby player-manager in midseason—ended a combined 95 games back. Large ticket sale drops in Boston, Philadelphia, and Pittsburgh, who dropped to fourth, led attendance to dip 8 percent.

Hitting was on the rise again as runs increased by 2.6 percent. Although league average fell a point, home runs skyrocketed by more than 25 percent and strikeouts decreased. Another indication of increased hitting? NL pitchers tossed just 558 complete games, by far the lowest total to date.

1928 American League

TEAM	W	L	T	PCT	GB	HW	HL	R	OR	PA	H	2B	3B	HR	BB	SO	HB	SH	AVG	OBP	SLG	OPS	AOPS	BR	ABR	PF	SB	CS	BSA	BSR
NY	101	53	0	.656		**52**	25	**894**	685	6070	**1578**	269	**79**	**133**	**562**	544	146	25	**.296**	**.365**	**.450**	**815**	**124**	**147**	**177**	97	51	52	50	-7
PHI	98	55	0	.641	2.5	**52**	25	829	**615**	5990	1540	**323**	75	89	533	**442**	200	**31**	.295	.363	.436	799	112	120	97	103	59	55	52	-6
STL	82	72	0	.532	19	44	33	772	742	6007	1431	276	76	63	548	479	**214**	28	.274	.346	.393	739	97	3	-19	103	**78**	43	**64**	**2**
WAS	75	79	1	.487	26	37	43	718	705	6009	1510	277	93	40	481	390	180	28	.284	.346	.393	739	101	0	5	99	108	63	63	**2**
CHI	72	82	1	.468	29	37	40	656	725	5907	1405	231	77	24	469	488	200	**31**	.270	.334	.358	692	88	-92	-83	99	144	88	62	1
DET	68	86	0	.442	33	36	41	744	804	5949	1476	265	97	62	469	438	163	25	.279	.340	.401	741	99	-5	-16	102	113	79	59	-3
CLE	62	92	1	.403	39	29	48	674	830	5984	1535	299	61	34	377	426	191	30	.285	.335	.382	717	93	-49	-56	101	50	52	49	-7
BOS	57	96	1	.373	43.5	26	47	589	770	5754	1356	260	62	38	395	512	206	21	.264	.319	.361	680	86	-119	-108	98	97	68	59	-2
TOT	617					313	302	5876		47670	11831	2200	620	483	3834	3719	219	150	0.281	.344	.397	741					700	500	58	-21

TEAM	CG	SHO	GR	SV	IP	H	HR	BB	SO	BR/9	ERA	AERA	OAV	OOB	PR	APR	PF	OSB	OCS	FA	E	WPB	DP	FW	PW	BW	BSW	DIF
NY	82	13	112	**21**	1375.1	1466	59	452	487	12.7	3.74	101	.276	.335	46	3	93	102	64	.968	194	28	136	-.0	.3	**17.1**	-.4	7.1
PHI	81	**15**	103	16	1367.2	**1349**	66	**424**	**607**	**11.8**	**3.36**	**119**	**.259**	**.318**	**103**	**98**	99	83	45	.970	181	29	124	.6	**9.5**	9.4	-.3	2.3
STL	80	6	128	15	1374.1	1487	93	454	456	12.8	4.17	101	.282	.340	-20	3	104	98	51	.969	189	19	146	.2	.3	-1.8	**.4**	5.9
WAS	77	**15**	118	10	1384.0	1420	**40**	466	462	12.5	3.88	103	.272	.335	25	19	99	72	62	**.972**	**178**	30	146	**1.0**	1.8	.5	**.4**	-5.7
CHI	**88**	6	93	11	1378.0	1518	66	501	418	13.4	3.98	102	.287	.352	8	8	100	**59**	60	.970	186	27	149	.5	.8	-8.0	**.4**	1.4
DET	65	5	130	16	1372.0	1481	58	567	451	13.7	4.32	95	.281	.355	-42	-33	102	86	71	.965	218	31	140	-1.5	-3.2	-1.5	-.0	-2.8
CLE	71	4	122	15	1378.0	1615	52	511	416	14.2	4.47	93	.303	.369	-66	-51	103	90	72	.965	221	41	**187**	-1.6	-4.9	-5.4	-.4	-2.7
BOS	70	5	**131**	9	1352.0	1492	49	452	407	13.2	4.39	93	.288	.349	-53	-44	102	110	**77**	.971	**178**	**18**	139	.9	-4.3	-10.4	.0	-5.8
TOT	614	69	937	113	10981.1					13.0	4.04		.281	.344						.969	1545	223	1167					

Batter-Fielder Wins	Batting Average	On-Base Percentage	Slugging Average	On-Base Plus Slugging	Adjusted OPS	Adjusted Batter Runs
Ruth-NY 7.1	Goslin-Was 379	Gehrig-NY 467	Ruth-NY 709	Ruth-NY.............1172	Ruth-NY................211	Ruth-NY.............92.1
Gehrig-NY............5.9	Manush-StL 378	Ruth-NY.......................463	Gehrig-NY 648	Gehrig-NY 1115	Gehrig-NY 196	Gehrig-NY 83.3
J.Sewell-Cle 5.3	Gehrig-NY 374	Goslin-Was 442	Goslin-Was...........614	Goslin-Was 1056	Goslin-Was 176	Goslin-Was 50.7
Goslin-Was 4.9	Simmons-Phi 351	Bishop-Phi 438	Manush-StL 575	Manush-StL 989	Manush-StL 153	Manush-StL........46.3
Manush-StL 3.3	Lazzeri-NY 332	Manush-StL 414	Simmons-Phi 558	Simmons-Phi........954	Simmons-Phi........144	Foxx-Phi 28.9

Runs	Hits	Doubles	Triples	Home Runs	Total Bases	Runs Batted In
Ruth-NY................163	Manush-StL 241	Manush-StL 47	Combs-NY.............21	Ruth-NY..................54	Ruth-NY...............380	Ruth-NY 142
Gehrig-NY 139	Gehrig-NY 210	Gehrig-NY......................47	Manush-StL 20	Gehrig-NY 27	Manush-StL 367	Gehrig-NY 142
Combs-NY............118	Rice-Was 202	Meusel-NY 45	Gehringer-Det 16	Goslin-Was 17	Gehrig-NY 364	Meusel-NY 113
Blue-StL................116	Combs-NY............194	Schulte-StL 44		Hauser-Phi..............16	Combs-NY............290	Manush-StL 108
Gehringer-Det 108	Gehringer-Det 193	Lind-Cle 42		Simmons-Phi 15	Heilmann-Det 283	

Stolen Bases	Base Stealing Runs	Fielding Runs-Infield	Fielding Runs-Outfield	Wins	Winning Pct.	Complete Games
Myer-Bos 30	Rice-Was 2.5	Gerber-StL-Bos 25.7	Jamieson-Cle 15.9	Pipgras-NY 24	Crowder-StL 808	Ruffing-Bos 25
Mostil-Chi 23	Goslin-Was 2.5	J.Sewell-Cle...............25.5	Mostil-Chi 11.9	Grove-Phi 24	Hoyt-NY 767	Thomas-Chi 24
Rice-Det 20	Reynolds-Chi 2.3	Regan-Bos...................15.1	Schulte-StL............9.9	Hoyt-NY..................23	Grove-Phi 750	Grove-Phi 24
Cissell-Chi 18	Judge-Was 2.1	Tavener-Det 12.1	Goslin-Was 7.6	Crowder-StL 21	Pennock-NY 739	Pipgras-NY............22
Bluege-Was 18		Bluege-Was 10.1	Taitt-Bos 6.0	Gray-StL 20	Quinn-Phi 720	

Strikeouts	Fewest BB/Game	Games	Saves	Base Runners/9	Adjusted Relief Runs	Relief Ranking
Grove-Phi 183	Rommel-Phi 1.35	Marberry-Was...............48	Hoyt-NY....................8	Braxton-Was........9.32		
Pipgras-NY 139	Quinn-Phi 1.45	Morris-Bos 47	Hudlin-Cle 7	Grove-Phi 10.08		
Thomas-Chi 129	Pennock-NY 1.71	Pipgras-NY 46	Lyons-Chi 6	Rommel-Phi 10.62		
Ruffing-Bos 118	Braxton-Was........1.81	Rommel-Phi 43	Braxton-Was 6	Pennock-NY 10.88		
Earnshaw-Phi 117	Russell-Bos 1.83			Heimach-NY 10.99		

Innings Pitched	Opponents' Avg.	Opponents' OBP	Earned Run Average	Adjusted ERA	Adjusted Starter Runs	Pitcher Wins
Pipgras-NY........300.2	Braxton-Was.........222	Braxton-Was 267	Braxton-Was........2.51	Braxton-Was 159	Grove-Phi 40.7	**Grove-Phi** 4.7
Ruffing-Bos........289.1	Grove-Phi 229	Grove-Phi.....................277	Pennock-NY 2.56	Grove-Phi 155	Braxton-Was........34.0	**Thomas-Chi** 3.5
Thomas-Chi 283.0	Earnshaw-Phi.......240	Rommel-Phi.................295	Grove-Phi 2.58	Pennock-NY 147	Thomas-Chi 30.7	**Jones-Was**..........3.3
Hoyt-NY 273.0	Johnson-NY 250	Pennock-NY.................302	Jones-Was 2.84	Jones-Was............141	Pennock-NY 30.6	**Braxton-Was**......3.2
Gray-StL 262.2	Jones-Was 252	Thomas-Chi 310	Quinn-Phi 2.90	Quinn-Phi 138	Jones-Was 27.1	**Pennock-NY** 3.1

Murderer's Row Survives A's, Kills Cards

Once again the Yankees enjoyed a great attack, leading the league both individually and collectively in nearly every offensive category. Lou Gehrig was now Babe Ruth's equal at bat, and the supporting cast continued to shine. Rookie catcher Bill Dickey made his first appearance and would soon join the fearsome lineup. While the Yankees' pitching was not nearly as strong as in the previous season, they were deep enough to withstand the loss (and, later that year, death from heart disease) of veteran righty Urban Shocker.

It wasn't easy, however. The Athletics were a worthy opponent, and after a late-season hot streak actually took a half-game lead over New York on September 8. The next day, more than 85,000 fans crammed into Yankee Stadium to see the two teams meet in a doubleheader; it was the most important regular-season matchup that baseball had seen in years, and the largest crowd to that point ever to watch a major league game. New York swept the twin bill, and despite a late flurry by Philadelphia, clinched the flag on September 28.

The Athletics, a fascinating mix of young and old, had seven Hall of Famers on the club. Lefty Grove had become the league's best pitcher, and he was well supported by 28-year-old rookie George Earnshaw, who held opponents to a .240 average. Earnshaw and Grove were 1-2 in the league in strikeouts per game, while teammates Eddie Rommel and Jack Quinn were the two stingiest in walks.

Offensively, the entire A's lineup contributed, and the bench sported a group of all-time greats. Three of them retired after the season: pitcher "Bullet Joe" Bush and two of the game's greatest center fielders, Ty Cobb and Tris Speaker. Forty-year-old Eddie Collins would hang around with Philadelphia until 1930.

But it was still the Yankees' show. Showing no signs of weakness, New York blew by the St. Louis Cardinals in four straight World Series games. Babe Ruth, who batted .625, and Gehrig, who hit .545, homered in the same game three times.

1929 National League

TEAM	W	L	T	PCT	GB	HW	HL	R	OR	PA	H	2B	3B	HR	BB	SO	HB	SH	AVG	OBP	SLG	OPS	AOPS	BR	ABR	PF	SB	CS	BSA	BSR
CHI	98	54	4	.645		**52**	25	**982**	758	6252	1655	**310**	46	**139**	**589**	567	163	29	**.303**	**.373**	**.452**	**825**	**111**	**98**	**96**	100	**103**			
PIT	88	65	1	.575	10.5	45	31	904	780	6198	**1663**	285	**116**	60	503	**335**	**176**	29	**.303**	.364	.430	794	101	25	5	102	94			
NY	84	67	1	.556	13.5	39	37	897	**709**	6060	1594	251	47	136	482	405	154	**36**	.296	.358	.436	794	103	18	21	100	85			
STL	78	74	2	.513	20	43	32	831	806	6030	1569	**310**	84	100	490	455	154	22	.293	.354	.438	792	101	13	5	101	72			
PHI	71	82	1	.464	27.5	39	37	897	1032	6216	1693	305	51	153	573	470	135	24	.309	.377	.467	844	108	130	70	107	59			
BRO	70	83	0	.458	28.5	42	35	755	888	5954	1535	282	69	99	504	454	155	22	.291	.355	.427	782	102	-1	16	98	80			
CIN	66	88	1	.429	33	38	39	686	760	5882	1478	258	79	34	412	347	175	26	.281	.336	.379	715	87	-137	-104	95	134			
BOS	56	98	0	.364	43	34	43	657	876	5923	1481	252	77	33	408	432	197	27	.280	.335	.375	710	85	-146	-118	96	65			
TOT	616					332	279	6609		48515	12668	2253	569	754	3961	3465	215	1309	.294	.357	.426	783					692			

TEAM	CG	SHO	GR	SV	IP	H	HR	BB	SO	BR/9	ERA	AERA	OAV	OOB	PR	APR	PF	OSB	OCS	FA	E	WPB	DP	FW	PW	BW	BSW	DIF
CHI	79	**14**	139	21	1398.2	1542	77	537	548	13.5	4.16	111	**.284**	.350	86	71	98	67	*72*	**.975**	**154**	36	**169**	**1.4**	6.5	**8.7**		5.4
PIT	79	5	134	13	1379.0	**1530**	96	439	409	13.0	4.36	109	**.284**	.340	54	61	101	87	*67*	.970	181	31	136	-.2	5.5	.5		5.7
NY	68	9	131	13	1372.0	1536	102	**387**	431	**12.7**	**3.97**	**115**	.287	**.337**	**113**	**96**	97	**63**	*26*	**.975**	158	24	163	.9	**8.7**	1.9		-3.1
STL	**83**	6	115	8	1359.2	1604	101	474	453	13.9	4.66	100	.297	.357	8	-1	99	76	*63*	.971	174	26	149	.2	-.0	.5		1.5
PHI	45	5	**204**	**24**	1348.0	1743	122	616	369	16.0	6.13	85	.319	.391	-212	-129	110	96	*64*	.969	191	30	153	-.8	-11.7	6.4		.7
BRO	59	8	173	16	1358.0	1553	92	549	**549**	14.2	4.92	94	.290	.360	-32	-49	98	146	*65*	.968	192	45	113	-.9	-4.5	1.5		-2.6
CIN	75	5	121	8	1369.1	1558	**61**	413	347	13.1	4.41	103	.292	.345	46	23	97	73	***74***	.974	162	**19**	148	.9	2.1	-9.5		-4.5
BOS	78	4	108	12	1352.2	1604	103	530	366	14.4	5.12	91	.302	.367	-62	-69	99	84	*66*	.967	204	32	146	-1.5	-6.3	-10.7		-2.5
TOT	566	56	1125	115	10937.1					13.8	4.71		.294	.357						.971	1416	243	1177					

Batter-Fielder Wins
- **Hornsby-Chi**........6.8
- **Ott-NY**..................5.0
- **O'Doul-Phi**..........4.5
- **Whitney-Phi**........3.7
- **Wilson-Chi**..........3.6

Batting Average
- O'Doul-Phi 398
- Herman-Bro 381
- Hornsby-Chi 380
- Terry-NY 372
- Stephenson-Chi ...362

On-Base Percentage
- O'Doul-Phi 465
- Hornsby-Chi.................459
- Ott-NY 449
- Stephenson-Chi...........445
- Cuyler-Chi 438

Slugging Average
- Hornsby-Chi 679
- Klein-Phi 657
- Ott-NY 635
- Hafey-StL 632
- O'Doul-Phi 622

On-Base Plus Slugging
- Hornsby-Chi 1139
- O'Doul-Phi..........1087
- Ott-NY 1084
- Klein-Phi 1065
- Herman-Bro........1047

Adjusted OPS
- Hornsby-Chi 178
- Ott-NY 166
- Herman-Bro..........160
- O'Doul-Phi 157
- Wilson-Chi 155

Adjusted Batter Runs
- Hornsby-Chi 75.7
- Ott-NY 61.1
- O'Doul-Phi..........59.1
- Herman-Bro.......53.1
- Wilson-Chi..........49.4

Runs
- Hornsby-Chi 156
- O'Doul-Phi............152
- Ott-NY 138
- Wilson-Chi............135
- L.Waner-Pit 134

Hits
- O'Doul-Phi............254
- L.Waner-Pit 234
- Hornsby-Chi 229
- Terry-NY 226
- Klein-Phi 219

Doubles
- Frederick-Bro 52
- Hornsby-Chi 47
- Hafey-StL 47
- Klein-Phi 45
- Kelly-Cin 45

Triples
- L.Waner-Pit 20
- P.Waner-Pit 15
- Walker-Cin 15
- Whitney-Phi 14

Home Runs
- Klein-Phi 43
- Ott-NY 42
- Wilson-Chi 39
- Hornsby-Chi 39
- O'Doul-Phi 32

Total Bases
- Hornsby-Chi 409
- Klein-Phi 405
- O'Doul-Phi............397
- Wilson-Chi............355
- Herman-Bro..........348

Runs Batted In
- Wilson-Chi 159
- Ott-NY 151
- Hornsby-Chi........149
- Klein-Phi..............145
- Bottomley-StL......137

Stolen Bases
- Cuyler-Chi 43
- Swanson-Cin 33
- Frisch-StL 24
- Herman-Bro............21
- Allen-Cin 21

Base Stealing Runs

Fielding Runs-Infield
- Whitney-Phi 23.4
- Maranville-Bos 21.4
- Jackson-NY 15.2
- English-Chi 14.0
- Thompson-Phi 11.1

Fielding Runs-Outfield
- Ott-NY 7.8
- L.Waner-Pit...........7.2
- Orsatti-StL 6.9
- Allen-Cin 4.6
- Richbourg-Bos 4.5

Wins
- Malone-Chi 22
- Root-Chi 19
- Lucas-Cin 19

Winning Pct.
- Root-Chi 760
- Bush-Chi...............720
- Grimes-Pit 708
- Malone-Chi 688
- Kremer-Pit 643

Complete Games
- Lucas-Cin 28

Strikeouts
- Malone-Chi 166
- Clark-Bro 140
- Vance-Bro 126
- Root-Chi 124
- Hubbell-NY 106

Fewest BB/Game
- Vance-Bro...........1.83
- Lucas-Cin 1.93
- Petty-Pit 2.05
- Hubbell-NY..........2.25
- Clark-Bro 2.29

Games
- Bush-Chi........................50
- Willoughby-Phi 49
- Sweetland-Phi.................43
- Root-Chi 43
- Collins-Phi 43

Saves
- Morrison-Bro 8
- Bush-Chi 8
- Koupal-Bro-Phi 6

Base Runners/9
- Lucas-Cin 10.87
- Scott-NY............11.39
- Hubbell-NY.........11.62
- Kremer-Pit 11.65
- Petty-Pit 11.67

Adjusted Relief Runs
- Hill-Pit-StL 5

Relief Ranking
- Hill-Pit-StL 3

Innings Pitched
- Clark-Bro 279.0
- Root-Chi 272.0
- Bush-Chi............270.2
- Lucas-Cin 270.0
- Hubbell-NY........268.0

Opponents' Avg.
- Lucas-Cin 257
- Johnson-StL 265
- Hubbell-NY 265
- Bush-Chi...............265
- Grimes-Pit 269

Opponents' OBP
- Lucas-Cin 297
- Hubbell-NY 313
- Clark-Bro 316
- Vance-Bro 316
- Petty-Pit 317

Earned Run Average
- Walker-NY 3.09
- Grimes-Pit 3.13
- Root-Chi 3.47
- Malone-Chi..........3.57
- Lucas-Cin 3.60

Adjusted ERA
- Grimes-Pit 152
- Walker-NY............148
- Root-Chi 133
- Johnson-StL 129
- Malone-Chi 129

Adjusted Starter Runs
- Root-Chi 36.5
- Grimes-Pit 36.1
- Malone-Chi 33.4
- Lucas-Cin 31.3
- Walker-NY 30.5

Pitcher Wins
- **Lucas-Cin** 4.3
- **Grimes-Pit**..........4.0
- **Malone-Chi**..........3.5
- **Root-Chi** 2.7
- **Clark-Bro**............2.7

Blowup

The big story was hitting, as teams scored an astounding 5.36 runs per game while league batters clubbed 754 home runs and hit .294—all historical highs. The Phillies' pitchers posted a ghastly 6.13 ERA, allowing more than 1,000 runs (the first time a team ever did this), but still finished fifth by clubbing 153 homers. Braves Field was shrunk 30 feet in center and 67 in right, but hitting increased just as much elsewhere. Raising the left-field wall at Baker Bowl to 12 feet didn't cut decrease extra-base hits.

The outmanned Reds tried the running game, swiping 134 bases, but still finished seventh. This year was the death knell for the steal; no NL club would steal even 100 sacks until 1941, and it would be 1962 before a team would best Cincinnati's total.

As the defending champion Cardinals slumped, and were forced to retool, the Cubs sailed into the breach, running away with the NL flag after overtaking the Pirates in July. In winning their first title since 1918, Chicago became the fourth team to take a chance on Rogers Hornsby in four years, and the star second sacker enjoyed his last great season.

Pitcher Bobo Newsom began his twenty-year, nine-team major league odyssey with the Robins/Dodgers. Pitching their last seasons were Carl Mays, 7–2 at 38 for the Giants, and Art Nehf, 8–5 for the Cubs at 37. It was also sayonara for Dead Ball Era standout Max Carey, 39, who led the NL in steals ten times.

Catcher Peck Lerian, following his second season as Phillies catcher, died October 22 after being hit by a car. George Stallings, superstitious skipper of the 1914 "Miracle Braves," died in Georgia. "Iron Man" Joe McGinnity, who had consecutive 30-wins seasons for the 1903–04 Giants, breathed his last in Brooklyn. Plenty of current pitchers wished they could do the same.

1929 American League

TEAM	W	L	T	PCT	GB	HW	HL	R	OR	PA	H	2B	3B	HR	BB	SO	HB	SH	AVG	OBP	SLG	OPS	AOPS	BR	ABR	PF	SB	CS	BSA	BSR
PHI	104	46	1	.693		**57**	16	**901**	**615**	5988	1539	288	76	122	543	440	**213**	**28**	**.296**	**.365**	**.451**	**816**	111	**115**	84	104	63	39	**62**	0
NY	88	66	0	.571	18	49	28	899	775	6103	**1587**	262	74	**142**	554	518	145	25	.295	.364	.450	814	**123**	111	**174**	93	52	50	51	-6
CLE	81	71	0	.533	24	44	32	717	736	5868	1525	**294**	**79**	62	453	**363**	202	26	.294	.354	.417	771	100	27	0	104	**75**	87	46	-14
STL	79	73	2	.520	26	41	36	733	713	5976	1426	277	64	46	**589**	431	191	22	.276	.352	.381	733	91	-31	-58	104	70	47	60	-1
WAS	71	81	1	.467	34	37	40	730	776	5995	1445	244	66	48	556	400	185	17	.276	.347	.375	722	90	-56	-61	101	89	63	59	-2
DET	70	84	1	.455	36	38	39	926	928	6253	1671	339	97	110	521	496	122	18	.299	.360	.453	813	114	112	108	100	95	75	56	-5
CHI	59	93	0	.388	46	35	41	627	792	5849	1406	240	74	37	425	436	154	22	.268	.325	.363	688	83	-138	-131	99	109	65	63	1
BOS	58	96	1	.377	48	32	45	605	803	5778	1377	285	69	28	413	494	177	**28**	.267	.325	.365	690	85	-131	-116	98	86	82	51	-10
TOT	613					333	277	6138		47810	11976	2229	599	595	4054	3578	186	1389	.284	.349	.407	757					639	508	56	-37

TEAM	CG	SHO	GR	SV	IP	H	HR	BB	SO	BR/9	ERA	AERA	OAV	OOB	PR	APR	PF	OSB	OCS	FA	E	WPB	DP	FW	PW	BW	BSW	DIF
PHI	70	9	126	**24**	1357.0	**1371**	73	487	**573**	**12.4**	**3.44**	**123**	**.264**	**.329**	**121**	**119**	100	89	44	**.975**	**146**	38	117	**2.6**	**11.2**	7.9	.4	6.8
NY	64	12	**144**	18	1366.2	1475	83	485	484	13.1	4.19	92	.278	.341	7	-57	91	78	54	.971	178	27	153	.8	-5.4	**16.4**	-.1	-.7
CLE	80	8	102	10	1352.0	1570	56	488	389	13.9	4.05	109	.295	.357	28	54	105	88	66	.968	198	24	**162**	-.6	5.1	.0	-.9	1.4
STL	83	**15**	117	10	1371.0	1469	100	**462**	415	12.8	4.08	108	.279	.340	25	49	104	**59**	61	**.975**	156	**22**	148	2.2	4.6	-5.5	.3	1.3
WAS	62	3	138	17	1354.2	1429	**48**	496	494	12.9	4.34	98	.276	.342	-15	-16	100	66	74	.968	195	38	156	-.3	-1.5	-5.8	.3	2.3
DET	82	5	139	9	1390.1	1641	73	646	467	15.0	4.96	86	.301	.377	-111	-104	101	110	71	.961	242	44	149	-3.0	-9.8	10.2	-.0	-4.3
CHI	78	5	100	7	1357.2	1481	84	505	328	13.4	4.41	97	.284	.351	-26	-22	101	75	61	.970	188	33	153	.0	-2.1	-12.4	**.5**	-3.2
BOS	**84**	9	105	5	1366.2	1537	78	496	416	13.6	4.43	96	.291	.355	-28	-25	101	74	**77**	.965	218	44	159	-1.6	-2.4	-10.9	-.5	-3.6
TOT	603	66	971	100	10916.0					13.4	4.24		.284	.349						.969	1521	270	1197					

Batter-Fielder Wins
Ruth-NY 5.4
Lazzeri-NY 5.2
Simmons-Phi 5.1
Gehrig-NY...........4.5
Foxx-Phi 4.3

Batting Average
Fonseca-Cle 369
Simmons-Phi 365
Manush-StL 355
Lazzeri-NY 354
Foxx-Phi 354

On-Base Percentage
Foxx-Phi.......................463
Gehrig-NY 431
Ruth-NY........................430
Lazzeri-NY 429
Fonseca-Cle 427

Slugging Average
Ruth-NY 697
Simmons-Phi 642
Foxx-Phi 625
Gehrig-NY 584
Alexander-Det.......580

On-Base Plus Slugging
Ruth-NY.............1128
Foxx-Phi...............1088
Simmons-Phi......1040
Gehrig-NY 1015
Lazzeri-NY............991

Adjusted OPS
Ruth-NY................199
Foxx-Phi...............171
Gehrig-NY 170
Lazzeri-NY............164
Simmons-Phi........158

Adjusted Batter Runs
Ruth-NY...............72.3
Gehrig-NY 63.0
Foxx-Phi 58.9
Lazzeri-NY..........53.7
Simmons-Phi......46.1

Runs
Gehringer-Det 131
Johnson-Det 128
Gehrig-NY 127
Foxx-Phi................123
Ruth-NY................121

Hits
Gehringer-Det 215
Alexander-Det 215
Simmons-Phi 212
Fonseca-Cle 209
Manush-StL 204

Doubles
Manush-StL 45
Johnson-Det 45
Gehringer-Det.................45
Fonseca-Cle 44

Triples
Gehringer-Det 19
Scarritt-Bos 17
B.Miller-Phi 16

Home Runs
Ruth-NY.................46
Gehrig-NY 35
Simmons-Phi 34
Foxx-Phi..................33
Alexander-Det 25

Total Bases
Simmons-Phi........373
Alexander-Det 363
Ruth-NY................348
Gehringer-Det 337

Runs Batted In
Simmons-Phi 157
Ruth-NY 154
Alexander-Det 137
Gehrig-NY 126
Heilmann-Det 120

Stolen Bases
Gehringer-Det 27
Cissell-Chi 25
Rothrock-Bos..........24
B.Miller-Phi 24
Johnson-Det 20

Base Stealing Runs
Gehringer-Det........2.4
B.Miller-Phi 1.8
Myer-Was 1.7
Goslin-Was 1.4
Reynolds-Chi 1.0

Fielding Runs-Infield
Melillo-StL 20.4
Durocher-NY 20.2
Kerr-Chi 17.1
J.Sewell-Cle...............14.4
McManus-Det 6.9

Fielding Runs-Outfield
Simmons-Phi 19.6
West-Was 13.2
B.Barrett-Chi-Bos......6.9
Johnson-Det..........6.3
Schulte-StL............6.2

Wins
Earnshaw-Phi 24
Ferrell-Cle 21
Grove-Phi 20
Marberry-Was 19

Winning Pct.
Grove-Phi 769
Earnshaw-Phi.......750
Ferrell-Cle............677
Walberg-Phi 621
Marberry-Was.......613

Complete Games
Thomas-Chi 24
Uhle-Det 23
Gray-StL 23
Hudlin-Cle 22
Lyons-Chi 21

Strikeouts
Grove-Phi 170
Earnshaw-Phi 149
Pipgras-NY 125
Marberry-Was 121

Fewest BB/Game
Russell-Bos 1.58
Pennock-NY 1.60
Thomas-Chi 2.08
Uhle-Det 2.10
Quinn-Phi 2.18

Games
Marberry-Was...............49
Earnshaw-Phi 44
Gray-StL 43
Ferrell-Cle 43

Saves
Marberry-Was 11
Moore-NY 8
Shores-Phi...............7
Ferrell-Cle 5

Base Runners/9
Marberry-Was....11.07
Stewart-StL.......11.43
Thomas-Chi 11.44
Heimach-NY......11.56
Grove-Phi 11.83

Adjusted Relief Runs

Relief Ranking

Innings Pitched
Gray-StL 305.0
Hudlin-Cle..........280.1
Grove-Phi 275.1
Walberg-Phi 267.2
Crowder-StL 266.2

Opponents' Avg.
Earnshaw-Phi.......241
Wells-NY..............248
Marberry-Was.......252
Walberg-Phi 254
Grove-Phi 262

Opponents' OBP
Marberry-Was 308
Thomas-Chi 310
Grove-Phi.....................316
Hudlin-Cle 318
Walberg-Phi.................320

Earned Run Average
Grove-Phi 2.81
Marberry-Was.......3.06
Thomas-Chi 3.19
Earnshaw-Phi......3.29
Hudlin-Cle............3.34

Adjusted ERA
Grove-Phi 150
Marberry-Was 139
Thomas-Chi..........134
Hudlin-Cle 133
Earnshaw-Phi 129

Adjusted Starter Runs
Grove-Phi 42.6
Hudlin-Cle............34.2
Marberry-Was......33.3
Earnshaw-Phi......26.9
Gray-StL 23.9

Pitcher Wins
Marberry-Was....4.0
Grove-Phi 3.6
Hudlin-Cle 3.5
Ferrell-Cle 3.3
Thomas-Chi 2.7

Mack Is Back

Babe Ruth led the league in homers again; Lou Gehrig hit .300 with 126 RBIs. But it was the Yankees' turn to be blown away. The Athletics pulled away in June and the race was never in doubt. Philadelphia had five players score 100 runs or more, and they scored just 2 runs more than New York for the season. The pitching was the difference. Lefty Grove, George Earnshaw, and Rube Walberg were Philadelphia's leading starters, and Connie Mack used relief pitchers efficiently.

Meanwhile, the Yankees dealt with the sudden death, due to blood poisoning, of manager Miller Huggins in late September. His passing effectively ended the first phase of the club's dynasty. The Indians improved 20 games and leapt to third, largely due to batting titlist Lew Fonseca and the heroics of rookie outfielder Earl Averill. Fifth-place Detroit had the loop's best offense and worst pitching, with only some of this attributable to their home field.

The game was changing—again. AL hitters set a new record with 595 homers, but 1929 was also the last year that batter strikeouts were fewer than three per game. From now on, there would be more whiffs as well as long balls.

The Athletics were distinct underdogs to the Cubs in the World Series. But Mack's surprising Game 1 starter—35-year-old Howard Ehmke, who appeared just 11 times all year—shut down Chicago, 3–1. The A's also won the next day. The Cubs captured Game 3 at Philadelphia, and led 8–0 in the seventh the next afternoon. But the Athletics exploded for a 10-run rally, ignited when Hack Wilson lost a flyball in the sun that scored three runs. The comeback, never equaled in Series history, turned the tide. Philadelphia rallied in the ninth inning of Game 5; Mule Haas' two-run shot tied things up. Al Simmons and Bing Miller doubled to give the Athletics their first title since 1913.

1930 National League

TEAM	W	L	T	PCT	GB	HW	HL	R	OR	PA	H	2B	3B	HR	BB	SO	HB	SH	AVG	OBP	SLG	OPS	AOPS	BR	ABR	PF	SB	CS	BSA	BSR
STL	92	62	0	.597		**53**	24	**1004**	784	6204	1732	**373**	89	104	479	496	185	28	.314	.372	.471	843	105	77	46	103	72			
CHI	90	64	2	.584	2	51	26	998	870	6354	1722	305	72	**171**	**588**	635	148	**37**	.309	**.378**	**.481**	**859**	**111**	**113**	**106**	101	70			
NY	87	67	0	.565	5	46	31	959	814	6161	**1769**	264	83	143	422	**382**	165	21	**.319**	.369	.473	842	110	63	83	98	59			
BRO	86	68	0	.558	6	49	28	871	**738**	6088	1654	303	73	122	481	541	147	27	.304	.364	.454	818	103	22	33	99	53			
PIT	80	74	0	.519	12	42	35	891	928	6058	1622	285	**119**	86	494	449	**196**	22	.303	.365	.449	814	101	12	9	100	**76**			
BOS	70	84	0	.455	22	39	38	693	835	5870	1503	246	78	66	332	397	154	28	.281	.326	.393	719	81	-192	-169	97	69			
CIN	59	95	0	.383	33	37	40	665	857	5880	1475	265	67	74	445	489	174	16	.281	.339	.400	739	87	-137	-100	95	48			
PHI	52	102	2	.338	40	35	42	944	1199	6288	1783	345	44	126	450	459	148	23	.315	.367	.458	825	97	42	-21	107	34			
TOT	618					352	264	7025		48903	13260	2386	625	892	3691	3848	202	1317	.303	.360	.448	808					481			

TEAM	CG	SHO	GR	SV	IP	H	HR	BB	SO	BR/9	ERA	AERA	OAV	OOB	PR	APR	PF	OSB	OCS	FA	E	WPB	DP	FW	PW	BW	BSW	DIF
STL	63	5	150	**21**	1380.2	1594	87	476	**639**	13.7	4.39	114	.293	.353	89	94	101	52	***57***	.970	183	53	**176**	.2	8.3	4.1		2.5
CHI	67	6	174	12	1403.2	1642	111	528	601	14.1	4.80	102	.294	.357	26	14	98	**47**	*49*	.973	170	41	167	1.0	1.2	**9.4**		1.4
NY	64	6	157	19	1363.1	1546	117	439	522	13.3	4.61	103	.290	.348	54	19	95	59	*44*	**.974**	164	**26**	144	1.3	1.7	7.3		-.3
BRO	74	**13**	138	15	1372.0	**1480**	115	**394**	526	**12.4**	**4.03**	**122**	**.278**	**.330**	**144**	**136**	99	59	*46*	.972	174	32	167	.7	**12.0**	2.9		-6.6
PIT	**80**	7	107	13	1361.1	1730	128	438	393	14.5	5.24	95	.313	.367	-41	-40	100	61	*55*	.965	216	33	164	-1.8	-3.5	.8		7.5
BOS	71	6	124	11	1361.0	1624	117	475	424	14.0	4.91	100	.302	.360	9	3	99	51	*33*	.971	178	**26**	167	.4	.3	-14.9		7.2
CIN	61	6	149	11	1335.0	1650	**75**	**394**	361	13.9	5.08	95	.310	.361	-15	-38	97	65	*46*	.973	**161**	42	164	**1.4**	-3.4	-8.8		-7.2
PHI	54	3	**201**	7	1372.2	1993	142	543	384	16.8	6.71	81	.346	.405	-266	-172	110	87	*42*	.962	239	34	169	-3.0	-15.2	-1.9		-5.0
TOT	534	52	1200	109	10949.2					14.1	4.97		.303	.360						.970	1485	287	1318					

Batter-Fielder Wins	Batting Average	On-Base Percentage	Slugging Average	On-Base Plus Slugging	Adjusted OPS	Adjusted Batter Runs
Klein-Phi.............5.7	Terry-NY...............401	Ott-NY.........................458	Wilson-Chi 723	Wilson-Chi..........1177	Wilson-Chi...........177	Wilson-Chi.........75.7
Terry-NY.............5.6	Herman-Bro 393	Herman-Bro................455	Klein-Phi 687	Herman-Bro........1132	Herman-Bro..........171	Herman-Bro.........72.1
Lindstrom-NY 4.7	Klein-Phi 386	Wilson-Chi 454	Herman-Bro 678	Klein-Phi 1123	Terry-NY 159	Terry-NY 61.3
Wilson-Chi 4.7	O'Doul-Phi 383	O'Doul-Phi 453	Hafey-StL 652	Terry-NY 1071	Klein-Phi 155	Klein-Phi 57.7
Hartnett-Chi........4.1	Lindstrom-NY 379	Terry-NY 452	Hartnett-Chi 630	Hafey-StL...........1059	Ott-NY 152	Ott-NY 50.2

Runs	Hits	Doubles	Triples	Home Runs	Total Bases	Runs Batted In
Klein-Phi 158	Terry-NY 254	Klein-Phi 59	Comorosky-Pit........23	Wilson-Chi 56	Klein-Phi 445	Wilson-Chi 191
Cuyler-Chi 155	Klein-Phi 250	Cuyler-Chi.....................50	P.Waner-Pit 18	Klein-Phi 40	Wilson-Chi............423	Klein-Phi..............170
English-Chi 152	Herman-Bro..........241	Herman-Bro 48	English-Chi 17	Berger-Bos 38	Herman-Bro..........416	Cuyler-Chi 134
Wilson-Chi 146	Lindstrom-NY 231	Comorosky-Pit 47	Cuyler-Chi 17	Hartnett-Chi............37	Terry-NY 392	Herman-Bro 130
Herman-Bro...........143	Cuyler-Chi 228	Frisch-StL 46	Terry-NY 15	Herman-Bro............35	Cuyler-Chi 351	Terry-NY.............129

Stolen Bases	Base Stealing Runs	Fielding Runs-Infield	Fielding Runs-Outfield	Wins	Winning Pct.	Complete Games
Cuyler-Chi 37		Frisch-StL 22.3	Klein-Phi 21.2	Malone-Chi 20	Fitzsimmons-NY ...731	Malone-Chi...........22
P.Waner-Pit 18		Whitney-Phi 20.8	Heilmann-Cin 11.3	Kremer-Pit 20	Malone-Chi 690	Brame-Pit 22
Herman-Bro............18		Terry-NY 13.9	Welsh-Bos 7.0	Fitzsimmons-NY 19	Brame-Pit 680	French-Pit.............21
		Durocher-Cin 11.3	Sothern-Phi-Pit......6.6		Kremer-Pit 625	Vance-Bro 20
		Gilbert-Bro 9.3	Bressler-Bro 6.1		Hallahan-StL.........625	Seibold-Bos 20

Strikeouts	Fewest BB/Game	Games	Saves	Base Runners/9	Adjusted Relief Runs	Relief Ranking
Hallahan-StL 177	Clark-Bro 1.71	Elliott-Phi 48	Bell-StL 8	Vance-Bro..........10.47	Bell-StL................11.2	Lindsey-StL 8.4
Vance-Bro 173	Kolp-Cin 1.82	Collins-Phi 47	Heving-NY 6	Thurston-Bro 10.78	Lindsey-StL............7.5	Bell-StL 7.9
Malone-Chi 142	Johnson-StL 1.82	Bush-Chi.........................46	Clark-Bro 6	Clark-Bro 11.11		
Root-Chi 124	Lucas-Cin 1.88	Pruett-NY 45		Kolp-Cin 11.44		
Hubbell-NY 117	Vance-Bro............1.91	Malone-Chi 45		Fitzsimmons-NY ..11.63		

Innings Pitched	Opponents' Avg.	Opponents' OBP	Earned Run Average	Adjusted ERA	Adjusted Starter Runs	Pitcher Wins
Kremer-Pit 276.0	Vance-Bro.............246	Vance-Bro 289	Vance-Bro...........2.61	Vance-Bro 188	Vance-Bro............64.1	**Vance-Bro** 6.4
French-Pit..........274.2	Hallahan-StL.........260	Clark-Bro 306	Hubbell-NY 3.87	Elliott-Bro..............124	Malone-Chi..........26.1	**Malone-Chi** 2.6
Malone-Chi........271.2	Fitzsimmons-NY ...266	Fitzsimmons-NY 314	Walker-NY 3.93	Malone-Chi 124	Hubbell-NY 24.8	**Seibold-Bos** 2.0
Vance-Bro..........258.2	Walker-NY 268	Kolp-Cin.......................314	Malone-Chi..........3.94	Grimes-Bos-StL....123	Elliott-Bro 23.4	**Clark-Bro**............2.0
Seibold-Bos 251.0	Malone-Chi...........271	Hubbell-NY 327	Elliott-Bro 3.95	Hubbell-NY 122	Seibold-Bos 20.3	**Root-Chi** 1.9

Truly Offensive

If 1929 was a bad dream for pitchers, 1930 was hell. The league changed the ball, winding it tighter and reducing the size of the stitches, which impaired the pitcher's grip. The resulting league average rose to .303, the OPS .808, and runs per team per game to 5.68. None of these numbers have ever been topped.

For the Phillies, Chuck Klein scored 158 runs and hit .386 with 40 homers, and Lefty O'Doul scored 122 runs. The team hit .315 but finished last—with a 6.71 team ERA. Philadepia's *average* game was a 7–6 loss. Even Grover Cleveland Alexander—back where he started—was finished after a short trial at age 43; his 9.14 ERA was almost equal to his ERAs added together with the Phils from 1913–17.

The true star of 1930 was Brooklyn's Dazzy Vance, whose 2.61 ERA led the league by more than a run; the league average was 4.98. Chicago's Hack Wilson was a slugging machine. His 56 homers survived as an NL record until 1998, and his RBI mark still stands—later research, in fact, resulted in his total *improving* to 191 almost seven decades after the fact.

St. Louis bounced back to top the league in runs, thanks to Jim Bottomley, Chick Hafey, Frankie Frisch, and an excellent bench. The Cardinals went 21–4 in September, passing the Cubs and the surprising Robins. Giants first baseman Bill Terry became the last NLer to hit over .400, but McGraw's men finished 5 games back.

Hall of Fame shortstop Dave Bancroft hung 'em up, as did Cy Williams, who hit 251 career homers. Cubs pitcher Hal Carlson died suddenly May 30 of a stomach hemorrhage, while rookie Lon Warneke of Chicago began his 192-win career. Dizzy Dean debuted with a 3-hitter for St. Louis on September 28.

Most believed that attendance would drop because of 1929's financial crash, but a 50 percent gain in Brooklyn helped overall attendance jump 10.6 percent. This unexpected leap was whistling in the dark—the bad times were about to begin.

1930 American League

TEAM	W	L	T	PCT	GB	HW	HL	R	OR	PA	H	2B	3B	HR	BB	SO	HB	SH	AVG	OBP	SLG	OPS	AOPS	BR	ABR	PF	SB	CS	BSA	BSR
PHI	102	52	0	.662		**58**	18	951	751	6158	1573	319	74	125	599	531	**182**	32	.294	.369	.452	821	108	106	66	104	48	33	59	**-1**
WAS	94	60	0	.610	8	56	21	892	**689**	6116	1620	300	98	57	537	**438**	171	**38**	.302	.369	.426	795	106	59	55	100	**101**	67	**60**	**-1**
NY	86	68	0	.558	16	47	29	**1062**	898	6272	**1683**	298	**110**	**152**	**644**	569	161	19	**.309**	**.384**	**.488**	**872**	**131**	**208**	**259**	96	91	60	**60**	**-1**
CLE	81	73	0	.526	21	44	33	890	915	6130	1654	**358**	59	72	490	461	175	26	.304	.364	.431	795	102	60	27	104	51	47	52	-5
DET	75	79	0	.487	27	45	33	783	833	5927	1504	298	90	82	461	508	144	25	.284	.344	.421	765	96	-19	-34	102	98	70	58	-3
STL	64	90	0	.416	38	38	40	751	886	5941	1415	289	67	75	497	550	151	15	.268	.333	.391	724	85	-96	-120	103	93	71	57	-4
CHI	62	92	0	.403	40	34	44	729	884	5995	1496	256	90	63	389	479	155	32	.276	.328	.391	719	89	-117	-92	97	74	40	65	2
BOS	52	102	0	.338	50	30	46	612	814	5807	1393	257	68	47	358	552	144	19	.264	.313	.365	678	79	-197	-172	96	42	35	55	-3
TOT	616					352	264	6670		48346	12338	2375	656	673	3975	4088	206	1283	.288	.351	.421	772					598	423	59	-16

TEAM	CG	SHO	GR	SV	IP	H	HR	BB	SO	BR/9	ERA	AERA	OAV	OOB	PR	APR	PF	OSB	OCS	FA	E	WPB	DP	FW	PW	BW	BSW	DIF
PHI	72	**8**	136	**21**	1371.0	1457	84	488	**672**	12.9	4.28	109	.274	.337	56	58	101	79	44	**.975**	**145**	36	121	**3.0**	5.2	6.0	.0	10.7
WAS	**78**	6	111	14	1369.0	**1367**	**52**	504	524	**12.5**	**3.96**	**116**	**.264**	**.332**	**104**	**97**	99	57	53	.974	157	19	150	2.3	**8.8**	5.0	.0	.9
NY	65	7	**150**	15	1367.2	1566	93	524	572	13.9	4.88	88	.287	.352	-36	-98	93	82	48	.965	207	50	132	-.7	-8.9	**23.4**	.0	-4.9
CLE	68	5	139	14	1360.0	1663	85	528	442	14.6	4.88	99	.305	.368	-36	-9	104	92	51	.962	237	31	156	-2.5	-.8	2.4	-.3	5.2
DET	68	4	137	17	1351.2	1507	86	570	574	14.0	4.70	102	.286	.359	-8	13	103	105	47	.967	192	44	156	.2	1.2	-3.1	-.0	-.2
STL	68	5	122	10	1371.2	1639	124	449	470	13.9	5.07	96	.300	.356	-65	-29	105	59	**64**	.970	188	**14**	152	.4	-2.6	-10.9	-.2	.3
CHI	63	2	146	10	1361.0	1629	74	**407**	471	13.6	4.71	98	.300	.352	-10	-15	99	78	61	.962	235	31	136	-2.4	-1.4	-8.3	**.4**	-3.3
BOS	**78**	4	92	5	1360.1	1515	75	488	356	13.4	4.68	98	.286	.348	-6	-12	99	**50**	55	.968	196	30	**161**	-.0	-1.1	-15.6	-.0	-8.2
TOT	560	41	1033	106	10912.1					13.6	4.65		.288	.351						.968	1557	255	1164					

Batter-Fielder Wins
- **Gehrig-NY** 7.7
- **Ruth-NY** 7.6
- **Cronin-Was** 6.9
- **Simmons-Phi** 4.5
- **Cochrane-Phi** 3.8

Batting Average
- Simmons-Phi 381
- Gehrig-NY 379
- Ruth-NY 359
- Reynolds-Chi 359
- Cochrane-Phi 357

On-Base Percentage
- Ruth-NY 493
- Gehrig-NY 473
- Foxx-Phi 429
- Bishop-Phi 426
- Combs-NY 424

Slugging Average
- Ruth-NY 732
- Gehrig-NY 721
- Simmons-Phi 708
- Foxx-Phi 637

On-Base Plus Slugging
- Ruth-NY 1225
- Gehrig-NY 1194
- Simmons-Phi 1130
- Foxx-Phi 1066
- Morgan-Cle 1014

Adjusted OPS
- Ruth-NY 216
- Gehrig-NY 207
- Simmons-Phi 173
- Foxx-Phi 159
- Morgan-Cle 148

Adjusted Batter Runs
- Ruth-NY 100.0
- Gehrig-NY 98.5
- Simmons-Phi 58.1
- Foxx-Phi 51.3
- Morgan-Cle 42.3

Runs
- Simmons-Phi 152
- Ruth-NY 150
- Gehringer-Det 144
- Gehrig-NY 143
- Combs-NY 129

Hits
- Hodapp-Cle 225
- Gehrig-NY 220
- Simmons-Phi 211
- Rice-Was 207
- Morgan-Cle 204

Doubles
- Hodapp-Cle 51
- Manush-StL-Was 49
- Morgan-Cle 47
- Gehringer-Det 47

Triples
- Combs-NY 22
- Reynolds-Chi 18
- Gehrig-NY 17
- Simmons-Phi 16

Home Runs
- Ruth-NY 49
- Gehrig-NY 41
- Goslin-Was-StL 37
- Foxx-Phi 37
- Simmons-Phi 36

Total Bases
- Gehrig-NY 419
- Simmons-Phi 392
- Ruth-NY 379
- Foxx-Phi 358

Runs Batted In
- Gehrig-NY 174
- Simmons-Phi 165
- Foxx-Phi 156
- Ruth-NY 153
- Goslin-Was-StL 138

Stolen Bases
- McManus-Det 23
- Gehringer-Det 19
- Goslin-Was-StL 17
- Johnson-Det 17
- Cronin-Was 17

Base Stealing Runs
- Lary-NY 2.4
- McManus-Det 2.3
- Reynolds-Chi 2.1
- Simmons-Phi 1.3
- Dickey-NY 1.2

Fielding Runs-Infield
- Cronin-Was 26.5
- Melillo-StL 24.7
- Goldman-Cle 15.3
- Kamm-Chi 12.5
- Hodapp-Cle 10.3

Fielding Runs-Outfield
- Haas-Phi 7.4
- Oliver-Bos 6.0
- Johnson-Det 4.9
- Goslin-Was-StL 4.5
- Harris-Chi-Was 4.1

Wins
- Grove-Phi 28
- Ferrell-Cle 25
- Lyons-Chi 22
- Earnshaw-Phi 22
- Stewart-StL 20

Winning Pct.
- Grove-Phi 848
- Marberry-Was 750
- Jones-Was 682
- Ferrell-Cle 658
- Ruffing-Bos-NY 652

Complete Games
- Lyons-Chi 29
- Crowder-StL-Was 25
- Ferrell-Cle 25
- Stewart-StL 23
- Grove-Phi 22

Strikeouts
- Grove-Phi 209
- Earnshaw-Phi 193
- Hadley-Was 162
- Ferrell-Cle 143
- Ruffing-Bos-NY 131

Fewest BB/Game
- Pennock-NY 1.15
- Lyons-Chi 1.72
- Grove-Phi 1.86
- Russell-Bos 2.08
- Brown-Cle 2.15

Games
- Grove-Phi 50
- Earnshaw-Phi 49
- Pipgras-NY 44
- Johnson-NY 44
- Ferrell-Cle 43

Saves
- Grove-Phi 9
- Braxton-Was-Chi 6
- Quinn-Phi 6
- Sullivan-Det 5
- McKain-Chi 5

Base Runners/9
- Grove-Phi 10.45
- Burke-Was 11.38
- Stewart-StL 11.69
- Rommel-Phi 11.74
- Lyons-Chi 11.79

Adjusted Relief Runs
- Quinn-Phi 2.4

Relief Ranking
- Quinn-Phi 4.2

Innings Pitched
- Lyons-Chi 297.2
- Ferrell-Cle 296.2
- Earnshaw-Phi 296.0
- Grove-Phi 291.0
- Crowder-StL-Was 279.2

Opponents' Avg.
- Grove-Phi 247
- Hadley-Was 247
- Crowder-StL-Was 259
- Collins-StL 259
- Gaston-Bos 259

Opponents' OBP
- Grove-Phi 288
- Stewart-StL 315
- Lyons-Chi 319
- Marberry-Was 321
- Crowder-StL-Was 321

Earned Run Average
- Grove-Phi 2.54
- Ferrell-Cle 3.31
- Stewart-StL 3.45
- Uhle-Det 3.65
- Hadley-Was 3.73

Adjusted ERA
- Grove-Phi 184
- Ferrell-Cle 146
- Stewart-StL 141
- Uhle-Det 131
- Sorrell-Det 124

Adjusted Starter Runs
- Grove-Phi 65.8
- Ferrell-Cle 45.9
- Stewart-StL 40.8
- Uhle-Det 31.3
- Crowder-StL-Was 29.6

Pitcher Wins
- **Grove-Phi** 6.9
- **Ferrell-Cle** 5.9
- **Stewart-StL** 4.4
- **Lyons-Chi** 3.7
- **Uhle-Det** 3.4

Hitters Explode, but Pitching Carries the A's

Manager Walter Johnson's Senators, fifth in 1929, improved by 22 games and kept the race close until mid-July. Despite playing in a huge park, the Senators had good hitters like young shortstop Joe Cronin. But once again, the Athletics won by plenty.

Philadelphia enlarged Shibe Park in left and right field before the season, which helps explain how Lefty Grove's ERA declined from 2.81 to 2.54. But those changes don't explain how he dominated a league where offense increased by 8 percent. The incredible Grove was supported ably by George Earnshaw. Jimmie Foxx and Al Simmons provided the power, but the entire lineup added value.

The AL's 673 long balls set a new mark, while runs per team per game increased to 5.41, also an all-time record. Washington's 3.97 ERA was the highest to that point to lead the league. Foxx topped batters with 66 strikeouts, the lowest league-leading total for which figures are available. Despite becoming the first team in the twentieth century to top 1,000 runs, the Yankees floundered due to substandard pitching. Rookie Lefty Gomez and new acquisition Red Ruffing soon helped sort things out.

It was a tough time, though, at the box office. The Yankees were the last AL club to draw one million fans until 1935. The depression cut attendance nearly everywhere; despite the quality of the club, crowds fell each year from 1930–32 in Philadelphia. Hoping that fans would embrace hitting, speed and defense went out the window. This was the age of Smead Jolley, Zeke Bonura, and Buzz Arlett—sluggers whose modest hitting gifts are overstated by the offensive inflation of the era.

Grove and Earnshaw each won twice in the six-game World Series, allowing St. Louis just 7 runs in 5 starts between them. Only in Game 3 did anyone besides Grove or Earnshaw throw a pitch for the Athletics.

1931 National League

TEAM	W	L	T	PCT	GB	HW	HL	R	OR	PA	H	2B	3B	HR	BB	SO	HB	SH	AVG	OBP	SLG	OPS	AOPS	BR	ABR	PF	SB	CS	BSA	BSR
STL	101	53	0	.656		**54**	24	815	614	5989	1554	**353**	74	60	432	475	90	**32**	.286	.342	.411	753	105	66	37	104	**114**			
NY	87	65	1	.572	13	50	27	768	**599**	5840	1554	251	64	**101**	383	**395**	59	26	**.289**	.340	.416	756	112	59	78	98	83			
CHI	84	70	2	.545	17	50	27	**828**	710	6178	**1578**	340	66	84	**577**	641	**125**	25	**.289**	**.360**	**.422**	**782**	**115**	**138**	**124**	102	49			
BRO	79	73	1	.520	21	46	29	681	673	5814	1464	240	**77**	71	409	512	69	27	.276	.331	.390	721	101	-7	-2	99	45			
PIT	75	79	1	.487	26	44	33	636	691	5999	1425	243	70	41	493	454	130	16	.266	.330	.360	690	93	-56	-49	99	59			
PHI	66	88	1	.429	35	40	36	684	828	5935	1502	299	52	81	437	492	100	23	.279	.336	.400	736	96	29	-24	108	42			
BOS	64	90	2	.416	37	36	41	533	680	5809	1367	221	59	34	368	430	123	22	.258	.309	.341	650	84	-142	-122	96	46			
CIN	58	96	0	.377	43	38	39	592	742	5861	1439	241	70	21	403	463	93	22	.269	.323	.352	675	94	-88	-50	94	24			
TOT	618					358	256	5537		47425	11883	2188	532	493	3502	3862	193	789	.277	.334	.387	721					462			

TEAM	CG	SHO	GR	SV	IP	H	HR	BB	SO	BR/9	ERA	AERA	OAV	OOB	PR	APR	PF	OSB	OCS	FA	E	WPB	DP	FW	PW	BW	BSW	DIF
STL	80	**17**	111	**20**	1384.2	1470	65	449	**626**	12.6	3.45	**114**	.273	.332	63	**72**	102	51	*67*	**.974**	160	41	169	**1.0**	**7.2**	3.7		12.2
NY	**90**	**17**	105	12	1360.2	**1341**	71	422	570	**11.8**	**3.30**	112	**.255**	**.313**	**85**	61	96	**37**	*40*	**.974**	**159**	28	126	**1.0**	6.1	7.8		-3.8
CHI	80	8	144	8	1385.2	1448	54	524	541	13.0	3.97	97	.268	.337	-17	-19	100	49	*52*	.973	169	38	141	.6	-1.9	**12.3**		-4.0
BRO	64	9	142	18	1356.0	1520	56	**351**	546	12.5	3.84	99	.283	.329	3	-5	99	57	*46*	.969	187	27	154	-.7	-.5	-.2		4.4
PIT	89	9	97	5	1390.0	1489	55	442	345	12.6	3.66	105	.274	.331	32	28	100	59	*38*	.968	194	30	167	-.9	2.8	-4.9		1.0
PHI	60	6	**163**	16	1360.1	1603	75	511	499	14.2	4.58	93	.293	.358	-108	-46	110	79	*53*	.966	210	38	149	-1.9	-4.6	-2.4		-2.2
BOS	78	12	122	9	1380.1	1465	66	406	419	12.3	3.90	97	.272	.325	-5	-18	98	57	*42*	.973	170	29	141	.5	-1.8	-12.1		.4
CIN	70	7	133	6	1345.0	1545	**51**	399	317	13.1	4.22	89	.294	.346	-53	-75	97	73	*40*	.973	165	**23**	**194**	.7	-7.5	-5.0		-7.3
TOT	611	85	1017	94	10962.2					12.8	3.86		.277	.334						.971	1414	254	1241					

Batter-Fielder Wins	Batting Average	On-Base Percentage	Slugging Average	On-Base Plus Slugging	Adjusted OPS	Adjusted Batter Runs
Terry-NY 3.7	Hafey-StL 349	Hafey-StL....................404	Klein-Phi 584	Klein-Phi 982	Ott-NY 153	Terry-NY 42.0
Berger-Bos.........3.6	Terry-NY...............349	Cuyler-Chi 404	Hornsby-Chi 574	Hafey-StL.............973	Hafey-StL..............153	Klein-Phi 40.0
Cuccinello-Cin....3.5	Bottomley-StL.......348	P.Waner-Pit 404	Hafey-StL 569	Ott-NY 937	Terry-NY 150	Ott-NY 38.1
Ott-NY 3.4	Klein-Phi 337	Grantham-Pit 400	Ott-NY 545	Terry-NY 926	Klein-Phi 149	Berger-Bos 36.7
P.Waner-Pit..........3.1	O'Doul-Bro 336	Klein-Phi 398	Arlett-Phi..............538	Berger-Bos 892	Berger-Bos 143	Hornsby-Chi 34.2

Runs	Hits	Doubles	Triples	Home Runs	Total Bases	Runs Batted In
Terry-NY 121	L.Waner-Pit 214	Adams-StL 46	Terry-NY 20	Klein-Phi 31	Klein-Phi 347	Klein-Phi.............121
Klein-Phi 121	Terry-NY 213	Berger-Bos 44	Herman-Bro...........16	Ott-NY 29	Terry-NY 323	Ott-NY 115
English-Chi 117	English-Chi 202	Terry-NY 43	Traynor-Pit 15	Berger-Bos 19	Herman-Bro...........320	Terry-NY..............112
Cuyler-Chi 110	Cuyler-Chi 202	Herman-Bro 43	Bissonette-Bro........14	Herman-Bro............18	Berger-Bos 316	Traynor-Pit 103
Ott-NY 104	Klein-Phi 200	Bartell-Phi.....................43		Arlett-Phi 18	Cuyler-Chi 290	Herman-Bro 97

Stolen Bases	Base Stealing Runs	Fielding Runs-Infield	Fielding Runs-Outfield	Wins	Winning Pct.	Complete Games
Frisch-StL 28		Hurst-Phi 11.4	P.Waner-Pit 13.8	Meine-Pit 19	Derringer-StL 692	Lucas-Cin 24
Herman-Bro............17		Frisch-StL 10.9	Crabtree-Cin.........10.3	Hallahan-StL 19	Hallahan-StL.........679	Brandt-Bos 23
Martin-StL 16		Terry-NY 10.3	L.Waner-Pit...........10.1	J.Elliott-Phi.............19	Bush-Chi...............667	Meine-Pit 22
Adams-StL..............16		Maguire-Bos 10.1	Berger-Bos 4.1		Grimes-StL 654	Hubbell-NY............21
Watkins-StL 15		Jackson-NY 9.7	Ott-NY 2.5			French-Pit.............20

Strikeouts	Fewest BB/Game	Games	Saves	Base Runners/9	Adjusted Relief Runs	Relief Ranking
Hallahan-StL 159	Johnson-StL 1.40	J.Elliott-Phi 52	Quinn-Bro 15	Hubbell-NY........10.23	Lindsey-StL............7.2	Quinn-Bro 10.3
Hubbell-NY 155	Lucas-Cin 1.47	Johnson-Cin 42	Lindsey-StL 7	Walker-NY 10.49	Quinn-Bro 5.8	Lindsey-StL 10.1
Vance-Bro 150	Cantwell-Bos 1.96	Collins-Phi 42	J.Elliott-Phi..............5	Johnson-StL 10.50	May-Chi 1.8	May-Chi................2.1
Derringer-StL........134	Clark-Bro 2.01		Hallahan-StL 4	Fitzsimmons-NY 10.79		
Root-Chi 131	Zachary-Bos........2.08		Collins-Phi 4	Mooney-NY........11.05		

Innings Pitched	Opponents' Avg.	Opponents' OBP	Earned Run Average	Adjusted ERA	Adjusted Starter Runs	Pitcher Wins
Meine-Pit 284.0	Hubbell-NY 227	Hubbell-NY 282	Walker-NY 2.26	Walker-NY 164	Walker-NY 37.3	**Hubbell-NY** 3.4
French-Pit..........275.2	Walker-NY 231	Walker-NY 283	Hubbell-NY 2.65	Hubbell-NY 139	Hubbell-NY 29.9	**Brandt-Bos** 3.4
Johnson-Cin 262.1	Brandt-Bos 244	Johnson-StL.................286	Brandt-Bos 2.92	Benge-Phi 134	Benge-Phi...........25.7	**Fitzsimmons-NY**2.9
Fitzsimmons-NY ..253.2	Fitzsimmons-NY ...251	Fitzsimmons-NY 296	Meine-Pit 2.98	Johnson-StL 131	Meine-Pit 25.0	**Walker-NY** 2.9
Root-Chi 251.0	Root-Chi 252	Cantwell-Bos 301	Johnson-StL 3.00	Brandt-Bos............130	Brandt-Bos 23.8	**Benge-Phi** 2.9

Wild Horses

Several Senior Circuit clubs altered their ballparks in 1931, but this alone could not have been responsible for the spectacular decrease in offense. NL teams plated just 4.48 runs a game, the smallest output in more than a decade, with homers dropping a stunning 45 percent. The league also adopted a rule abolishing home runs on fair balls bouncing into the stands; they'd be doubles instead, as was already the law in the AL.

Into this new environment stepped the Cardinals, who led wire to wire. A tough, gritty team with homespun, rural players who liked to raise a ruckus on and off the diamond, St. Louis hit only 60 homers—fourth in the loop—but led in steals and finished second in runs. Hard-nosed competitors like Frankie Frisch, Pepper Martin, Ripper Collins, and Burleigh Grimes defined the club, and rookie Paul Derringer was 18–8 to give the team a strong second starter behind Wild Bill Hallahan.

The second-place Giants ended 13 out. The lack of a pennant race, and the fifth through eight place clubs each finishing between 26 and 43 games behind, factored in a frightening attendance drop of 15.6 percent, the biggest fall since 1918.

Along with Derringer, several key players debuted in 1931. Boston third baseman Bucky Walters eventually washed out as a hitter, then became the dominant NL right-hander of the early 1940s. Ernie Lombardi, who would later catch Walters (as well as Derringer) in Cincinnati, hit .297 for Brooklyn. Dixie Walker, later a favorite in Brooklyn, collected the first of his 2,064 hits. Wilbert Robinson finally stepped down in Brooklyn, allowing the team to change names, from Robins back to Dodgers, as well as managers; with a 1,399–1,398 career record, "Uncle Robbie" quit while he was ahead, barely.

St. Louis took home the NL's first World Series title since the Cards' win in 1926. Martin ran wild in the Series, hitting .500 and scoring 5 runs. This seven-game loss was it for Mack's club; after 1932, the Athletics never again contended in Philadelphia.

1931 American League

TEAM	W	L	T	PCT	GB	HW	HL	R	OR	PA	H	2B	3B	HR	BB	SO	HB	SH	AVG	OBP	SLG	OPS	AOPS	BR	ABR	PF	SB	CS	BSA	BSR
PHI	107	45	1	.704		**60**	15	858	**626**	6019	1544	**311**	64	118	528	543	79	**35**	.287	.355	.435	790	107	96	45	106	25	23	52	-3
NY	94	59	2	.614	13.5	51	25	**1067**	760	6471	**1667**	277	78	**155**	**748**	554	87	28	**.297**	**.383**	**.457**	**840**	**135**	**222**	**285**	94	**138**	68	**67**	**7**
WAS	92	62	2	.597	16	55	22	843	690	6183	1588	308	**93**	49	481	**459**	**96**	30	.285	.345	.400	745	100	6	2	101	72	64	53	-7
CLE	78	76	1	.506	30	45	31	885	833	6112	1612	321	69	71	555	433	91	21	.296	.363	.419	782	105	95	48	106	63	60	51	-7
STL	63	91	0	.409	45	39	38	721	870	5935	1455	287	62	76	488	580	61	12	.271	.333	.390	723	92	-41	-66	104	73	80	48	-12
BOS	62	90	1	.408	45	39	40	625	800	5864	1409	289	34	37	405	565	68	12	.262	.315	.349	664	85	-155	-119	95	42	43	49	-6
DET	61	93	0	.396	47	36	41	651	836	5993	1456	292	69	43	480	468	63	20	.268	.330	.371	701	87	-80	-103	103	117	75	61	-1
CHI	56	97	3	.366	51.5	31	45	704	939	6099	1423	238	69	27	483	445	105	30	.260	.323	.343	666	86	-151	-111	94	94	39	71	**7**
TOT	618					356	257	6354		48676	12154	2323	538	576	4168	4047	188	650	.278	.344	.396	740					624	452	58	-21

TEAM	CG	SHO	GR	SV	IP	H	HR	BB	SO	BR/9	ERA	AERA	OAV	OOB	PR	APR	PF	OSB	OCS	FA	E	WPB	DP	FW	PW	BW	BSW	DIF
PHI	**97**	**12**	82	16	1365.1	**1342**	73	457	574	**11.9**	**3.47**	**130**	**.256**	**.316**	**138**	**152**	103	66	51	**.976**	**141**	30	151	3.2	**14.2**	4.2	-.0	9.5
NY	78	4	132	17	1410.1	1461	67	543	**686**	12.9	4.20	94	.263	.332	28	-41	91	71	54	.972	169	24	131	1.7	-3.8	**26.5**	**.9**	-7.8
WAS	60	7	145	**24**	1394.1	1434	73	498	582	12.6	3.76	114	.264	.327	95	83	98	**65**	45	**.976**	142	28	148	**3.3**	7.7	.2	-.4	4.2
CLE	76	6	124	9	1354.2	1577	64	561	470	14.4	4.63	100	.286	.355	-38	-2	106	76	64	.963	232	30	143	-2.0	-.2	4.5	-.4	-.8
STL	65	4	129	10	1362.0	1623	84	**448**	436	13.8	4.76	97	.293	.348	-57	-17	106	69	51	.963	232	**20**	**160**	-2.1	-1.6	-6.1	-.9	-3.3
BOS	61	5	161	10	1366.2	1559	**54**	473	365	13.5	4.60	94	.285	.344	-33	-45	98	70	56	.970	188	28	127	.4	-4.2	-11.1	-.3	1.2
DET	86	5	92	6	1384.1	1549	79	597	511	14.1	4.59	100	.282	.355	-32	-1	105	95	**72**	.964	220	33	139	-1.4	-.0	-9.6	.2	-5.1
CHI	54	6	**170**	10	1390.1	1613	82	588	421	14.5	5.04	85	.287	.358	-101	-125	97	112	59	.961	245	29	131	-2.7	-11.6	-10.3	**.9**	3.3
TOT	577	49	1035	102	11028.0					13.5	4.38		.278	.344						.968	1569	222	1130					

Batter-Fielder Wins	Batting Average	On-Base Percentage	Slugging Average	On-Base Plus Slugging	Adjusted OPS	Adjusted Batter Runs
Ruth-NY 8.1	Simmons-Phi .390	Ruth-NY .495	Ruth-NY .700	Ruth-NY 1195	Ruth-NY 223	Ruth-NY 104.4
Gehrig-NY 6.0	Ruth-NY .373	Morgan-Cle .451	Gehrig-NY .662	Gehrig-NY 1108	Gehrig-NY 199	Gehrig-NY 91.0
Simmons-Phi 4.6	Morgan-Cle .351	Gehrig-NY .446	Simmons-Phi .641	Simmons-Phi 1085	Simmons-Phi 172	Simmons-Phi 52.4
Cochrane-Phi 4.5	Cochrane-Phi .349	Simmons-Phi .444	Averill-Cle .576	Averill-Cle 979	Webb-Bos 151	Webb-Bos 47.0
Cronin-Was 4.5	Gehrig-NY .341	Blue-Chi .430	Foxx-Phi .567	Cochrane-Phi 976	Goslin-StL 147	Goslin-StL 41.3

Runs	Hits	Doubles	Triples	Home Runs	Total Bases	Runs Batted In
Gehrig-NY 163	Gehrig-NY 211	Webb-Bos 67	Johnson-Det 19	Ruth-NY 46	Gehrig-NY 410	Gehrig-NY 184
Ruth-NY 149	Averill-Cle 209	Alexander-Det 47	Gehrig-NY 15	Gehrig-NY 46	Ruth-NY 374	Ruth-NY 163
Averill-Cle 140	Simmons-Phi 200	Kress-StL 46	Blue-Chi 15	Averill-Cle 32	Averill-Cle 361	Averill-Cle 143
Combs-NY 120	Ruth-NY 199	Cronin-Was 44	Vosmik-Cle 14	Foxx-Phi 30	Simmons-Phi 329	Simmons-Phi 128
Chapman-NY 120	Webb-Bos 196		Reynolds-Chi 14	Goslin-StL 24	Goslin-StL 328	Cronin-Was 126

Stolen Bases	Base Stealing Runs	Fielding Runs-Infield	Fielding Runs-Outfield	Wins	Winning Pct.	Complete Games
Chapman-NY 61	Chapman-NY 5.4	Melillo-StL 35.3	West-Was 13.6	Grove-Phi 31	Grove-Phi .886	Grove-Phi 27
Johnson-Det 33	Cissell-Chi 1.9	Burns-StL 18.8	Johnson-Det 11.4	Ferrell-Cle 22	Marberry-Was .800	Ferrell-Cle 27
Burns-StL 19	H.Walker-Det 1.9	Rhyne-Bos 18.0	Oliver-Bos 5.8	Gomez-NY 21	Mahaffey-Phi .789	Earnshaw-Phi 23
Lazzeri-NY 18	Blue-Chi 1.8	Hodapp-Cle 15.2	Simmons-Phi 5.5	Earnshaw-Phi 21	Earnshaw-Phi .750	Whitehill-Det 22
Cissell-Chi 18	Reynolds-Chi 1.6	McManus-Det-Bos 13.1	Chapman-NY 5.3	Walberg-Phi 20	Gomez-NY .700	Stewart-StL 20

Strikeouts	Fewest BB/Game	Games	Saves	Base Runners/9	Adjusted Relief Runs	Relief Ranking
Grove-Phi 175	Pennock-NY 1.43	Hadley-Was 55	Moore-Bos 10	Grove-Phi 9.73	Kimsey-StL 7	Kimsey-StL 8
Earnshaw-Phi 152	Gray-StL 1.88	Moore-Bos 53	Hadley-Was 8	Earnshaw-Phi 10.64		
Gomez-NY 150	Grove-Phi 1.93	Caraway-Chi 51	Marberry-Was 7	Gomez-NY 10.93		
Ruffing-NY 132	Brown-Cle 2.12	Frasier-Chi 46	Kimsey-StL 7	Coffman-StL 11.27		
Hadley-Was 124	Blaeholder-StL 2.23	Fischer-Was 46	Earnshaw-Phi 6	Uhle-Det 11.33		

Innings Pitched	Opponents' Avg.	Opponents' OBP	Earned Run Average	Adjusted ERA	Adjusted Starter Runs	Pitcher Wins
Walberg-Phi 291.0	Hadley-Was .218	Grove-Phi .271	Grove-Phi 2.06	Grove-Phi 218	Grove-Phi 73.9	**Grove-Phi** 8.2
Grove-Phi 288.2	Gomez-NY .226	Earnshaw-Phi .288	Gomez-NY 2.67	Gomez-NY 149	Gomez-NY 36.5	**Ferrell-Cle** 5.0
Earnshaw-Phi 281.2	Grove-Phi .229	Gomez-NY .295	Hadley-Was 3.06	Hadley-Was 140	Walberg-Phi 28.2	**Gomez-NY** 3.6
Ferrell-Cle 276.1	Johnson-NY .234	Coffman-StL .298	Brown-Was 3.20	Brown-Was 134	Earnshaw-Phi 27.8	**Earnshaw-Phi** 3.1
Whitehill-Det 271.1	Earnshaw-Phi .236	Uhle-Det .304	Marberry-Was 3.45	Uhle-Det 131	Brown-Was 27.2	**Brown-Was** 3.0

A Sticky End

There was little drama in the American League race, as Connie Mack's Athletics wiped up the competition. New York, with Joe McCarthy over to manage from the Cubs, finished 13_ games out despite a late charge. Led by Babe Ruth and Lou Gehrig again, the Yankees outscored their opponents at home and on the road. But New York's pitching wasn't nearly up to the Athletics' standards, and Mack's club had its own three-pronged attack of Jimmie Foxx, Al Simmons, and Mickey Cochrane. Philly also had 20-game winners Rube Walberg and George Earnshaw—and Lefty Grove, who set a major league mark for winning percentage and dominated other mound categories as well.

Homers fell 14 percent and overall scoring dropped 5 percent. Part of this change was due to park adjustments. The Tigers enlarged Navin Field's left field by 28 feet, and runs and homers fell dramatically. The Senators removed left-field seats at Griffith Stadium, relocating the wall to 407 feet, and scoring dropped slightly. On the other hand, Boston brought in Fenway's right-field fence by 33 feet, and runs in their home games increased slightly, though homers did not. (They moved the fence back in 1933.)

Reflecting the downfall of the running game, the 0.5 stolen bases per game was the *highest* rate of the decade. Boston's unheralded Earl Webb set an all-time mark with 67 doubles. And in a frightening development, AL attendance fell 17 percent in 1931, and the league had its lowest total since 1919.

White Sox owner Charles Comiskey died in October after his team pulled up last. The Old Roman had to be pleased to outlive AL founder and adversary Ban Johnson by eight months. In addition, October was the effective end of the Athletics dynasty, which began crumbling in a surprising seven-game World Series loss to St. Louis.

1932 National League

TEAM	W	L	T	PCT	GB	HW	HL	R	OR	PA	H	2B	3B	HR	BB	SO	HB	SH	AVG	OBP	SLG	OPS	AOPS	BR	ABR	PF	SB	CS	BSA	BSR
CHI	90	64	0	.584		**53**	24	720	**633**	6006	1519	296	60	69	398	514	118	28	.278	.330	.392	722	101	1	8	99	48			
PIT	86	68	0	.558	4	45	31	701	711	5906	1543	274	**90**	48	358	**385**	96	**31**	.285	.333	.395	728	103	7	20	98	71			
BRO	81	73	0	.526	9	44	34	752	747	5944	1538	296	59	110	388	574	99	24	.283	.334	.420	754	**110**	56	**72**	98	61			
PHI	78	76	0	.506	12	45	32	**844**	796	6108	**1608**	**330**	67	**122**	**446**	547	**125**	27	**.292**	**.348**	**.442**	**790**	105	**136**	44	112	71			
BOS	77	77	1	.500	13	44	33	649	655	5977	1460	262	53	63	347	496	105	19	.265	.311	.366	677	90	-96	-72	96	36			
STL	72	82	2	.468	18	42	35	684	717	5972	1467	307	51	76	420	514	69	25	.269	.324	.385	709	93	-24	-43	103	**92**			
NY	72	82	0	.468	18	37	40	755	706	5950	1527	263	54	116	348	391	49	23	.276	.322	.406	728	103	-1	14	98	31			
CIN	60	94	1	.390	30	33	44	575	715	5999	1429	265	68	47	436	436	100	20	.263	.320	.362	682	92	-78	-56	97	35			
TOT	618					343	273	5680		47862	12091	2293	502	651	3141	3857	197	761	.276	.328	.396	724					445			

TEAM	CG	SHO	GR	SV	IP	H	HR	BB	SO	BR/9	ERA	AERA	OAV	OOB	PR	APR	PF	OSB	OCS	FA	E	WPB	DP	FW	PW	BW	BSW	DIF
CHI	79	9	132	7	1401.0	**1444**	68	409	527	12.1	**3.44**	**109**	**.264**	.319	**68**	**51**	97	**29**	*47*	.973	173	43	146	.4	**5.0**	.8		6.8
PIT	71	12	126	12	1377.0	1472	86	338	377	11.9	3.75	102	.270	.314	20	11	98	63	*30*	.969	185	33	124	-.4	1.1	2.0		6.3
BRO	61	7	153	16	1379.2	1538	72	403	497	12.8	4.27	89	.282	.334	-60	-69	98	57	*52*	.971	183	31	**169**	-.3	-6.8	**7.1**		4.0
PHI	59	4	**160**	**17**	1384.0	1589	107	450	459	13.5	4.47	99	.287	.344	-91	-8	114	60	*33*	.968	194	23	133	-.9	-.8	4.4		-1.6
BOS	72	8	124	8	1414.0	1483	**61**	420	440	12.3	3.53	107	.272	.328	55	37	97	43	*45*	**.976**	**152**	**22**	145	**1.7**	3.7	-7.1		1.7
STL	70	**13**	139	9	1396.0	1533	76	455	**681**	13.0	3.97	99	.282	.340	-14	-5	101	68	***63***	.971	175	43	155	.4	-.5	-4.3		-.6
NY	57	3	156	16	1375.1	1533	112	387	506	12.7	3.83	97	.280	.330	8	-19	96	60	*37*	.969	191	33	143	-.7	-1.9	1.4		-3.8
CIN	**83**	6	112	6	1394.2	1505	69	**276**	359	**11.6**	3.79	102	.274	**.311**	14	10	99	65	*43*	.971	178	35	129	.1	1.0	-5.5		-12.6
TOT	552	62	1102	91	11121.2					12.5	3.88		.276	.328						.971	1431	263	1144					

Batter-Fielder Wins
- **Ott-NY** 5.2
- **Klein-Phi** 4.9
- **Terry-NY** 4.8
- **Herman-Cin** 4.5
- **O'Doul-Bro** 4.0

Batting Average
- O'Doul-Bro 368
- Terry-NY 350
- Klein-Phi 348
- P.Waner-Pit 341
- Hurst-Phi 339

On-Base Percentage
- Ott-NY 424
- O'Doul-Bro 423
- Hurst-Phi 412
- Klein-Phi 404
- P.Waner-Pit 397

Slugging Average
- Klein-Phi 646
- Ott-NY 601
- Terry-NY 580
- O'Doul-Bro 555
- Hurst-Phi 547

On-Base Plus Slugging
- Klein-Phi 1050
- Ott-NY 1025
- O'Doul-Bro 978
- Terry-NY 962
- Hurst-Phi 959

Adjusted OPS
- Ott-NY 175
- O'Doul-Bro 164
- Klein-Phi 158
- Terry-NY 158
- Herman-Cin 152

Adjusted Batter Runs
- Ott-NY 64.0
- O'Doul-Bro 54.3
- Klein-Phi 52.8
- Terry-NY 49.3
- Herman-Cin 41.9

Runs
- Klein-Phi 152
- Terry-NY 124
- O'Doul-Bro 120
- Ott-NY 119
- Bartell-Phi 118

Hits
- Klein-Phi 226
- Terry-NY 225
- O'Doul-Bro 219
- P.Waner-Pit 215
- Herman-Chi 206

Doubles
- P.Waner-Pit 62
- Klein-Phi 50
- Stephenson-Chi 49
- Bartell-Phi 48

Triples
- Herman-Cin 19
- Suhr-Pit 16
- Klein-Phi 15

Home Runs
- Ott-NY 38
- Klein-Phi 38
- Terry-NY 28
- Hurst-Phi 24
- Wilson-Bro 23

Total Bases
- Klein-Phi 420
- Terry-NY 373
- Ott-NY 340
- O'Doul-Bro 330
- P.Waner-Pit 321

Runs Batted In
- Hurst-Phi 143
- Klein-Phi 137
- Whitney-Phi 124
- Wilson-Bro 123
- Ott-NY 123

Stolen Bases
- Klein-Phi 20
- Piet-Pit 19
- Watkins-StL 18
- Frisch-StL 18
- K.Davis-Phi 16

Base Stealing Runs

Fielding Runs-Infield
- Jurges-Chi 30.0
- Cuccinello-Bro 20.8
- Frisch-StL 15.8
- Stripp-Bro 15.6
- Terry-NY 15.1

Fielding Runs-Outfield
- Herman-Cin 13.2
- Lee-Phi 9.2
- L.Waner-Pit 9.0
- K.Davis-Phi 8.1
- Klein-Phi 6.7

Wins
- Warneke-Chi 22
- Clark-Bro 20
- Bush-Chi 19

Winning Pct.
- Warneke-Chi 786
- Bush-Chi 633
- Rhem-StL-Phi 625
- Clark-Bro 625
- Hubbell-NY 621

Complete Games
- Lucas-Cin 28
- Warneke-Chi 25
- Hubbell-NY 22

Strikeouts
- Dean-StL 191
- Hubbell-NY 137
- Malone-Chi 120
- Carleton-StL 113
- Brown-Bos 110

Fewest BB/Game
- Swift-Pit 1.09
- Lucas-Cin 1.17
- Hubbell-NY 1.27
- Benton-Cin 1.35
- Betts-Bos 1.42

Games
- French-Pit 47
- Dean-StL 46
- Carleton-StL 44
- Collins-Phi 43

Saves
- Quinn-Bro 8
- Benge-Phi 6
- Luque-NY 5
- Cantwell-Bos 5

Base Runners/9
- Hubbell-NY 9.63
- Swift-Pit 9.78
- Lucas-Cin 9.92
- Warneke-Chi 10.17
- Rixey-Cin 10.32

Adjusted Relief Runs
- Quinn-Bro 5.3
- Frankhouse-Bos 2

Relief Ranking
- Quinn-Bro 6.6
- Frankhouse-Bos 2

Innings Pitched
- Dean-StL 286.0
- Hubbell-NY 284.0
- Warneke-Chi 277.0
- French-Pit 274.1
- Clark-Bro 273.0

Opponents' Avg.
- Swetonic-Pit 221
- Warneke-Chi 237
- Hubbell-NY 238
- Brown-Bos 238
- Malone-Chi 244

Opponents' OBP
- Hubbell-NY 268
- Swift-Pit 272
- Lucas-Cin 274
- Warneke-Chi 283
- Swetonic-Pit 286

Earned Run Average
- Warneke-Chi 2.37
- Hubbell-NY 2.50
- Betts-Bos 2.80
- Swetonic-Pit 2.82
- Lucas-Cin 2.94

Adjusted ERA
- Warneke-Chi 159
- Hubbell-NY 148
- Swetonic-Pit 135
- Betts-Bos 134
- Lucas-Cin 131

Adjusted Starter Runs
- Warneke-Chi 45.2
- Hubbell-NY 39.6
- Lucas-Cin 26.4
- Betts-Bos 23.3
- Swetonic-Pit 20.8

Pitcher Wins
- **Hubbell-NY** 4.7
- **Lucas-Cin** 4.4
- **Warneke-Chi** 4.3
- **Cantwell-Bos** 2.6
- **Dean-StL** 2.5

Managerial Ch-Ch-Ch-Ch-Changes

The Chicago Cubs led in the early going, but by August were in second and scuffling with brusque manager Rogers Hornsby. Charlie Grimm assumed the reins on August 7, and the Cubs reeled off a 14-game winning streak, rolling to the NL title. While the Cubs lacked a world-class offense, rookie Lon Warneke was arguably the league's top pitcher. Stan Hack began his long career as a part-time third baseman.

Home runs rose 30 percent, but overall scoring did not change significantly from 1931. Brooklyn's Ebbets Field was shrunk significantly in left and center fields, which increased runs, while the Pirates heightened Forbes Field's right-field wall, which had little effect.

The Pirates led the league for six weeks, but fell off the pace and finished second. Twenty-year-old rookie Arky Vaughan would become the team's best shortstop since Honus Wagner, while Paul Waner took advantage of spacious Forbes Field to hit 62 doubles. Led by slugger Chuck Klein, the Phillies led the NL in scoring, finishing .500 for first time since 1917. Cardinals rookie Joe Medwick batted .349 in a late-season trial.

New York saw the end of an era as manager John McGraw, in ill health and feuding with his players, quit with the Giants in last. Despite a sixth-place finish in 1932, the team improved quickly under Bill Terry.

Parity ruled the day; the Cubs' 90 wins were the fewest for an NL flag winner since 1915, and the distance from first to seventh in the standings was just 18 games. The lack of overwhelming skill from the NL champs showed in the World Series as the Yankees swept Chicago. Although the pennant race was interesting, NL attendance dropped another 16 percent as the true level of the economic depression sank in.

1932 American League

TEAM	W	L	T	PCT	GB	HW	HL	R	OR	PA	H	2B	3B	HR	BB	SO	HB	SH	AVG	OBP	SLG	OPS	AOPS	BR	ABR	PF	SB	CS	BSA	BSR
NY	107	47	2	.695		**62**	15	**1002**	724	6346	1564	279	82	160	**766**	527	76	27	.286	**.376**	.454	**830**	**128**	**176**	**232**	95	**77**	66	54	-6
PHI	94	60	0	.610	13	51	26	981	752	6299	**1606**	303	52	**172**	647	630	94	21	**.290**	.366	**.457**	823	115	153	119	104	38	23	**62**	0
WAS	93	61	0	.604	14	51	26	840	**716**	6141	1565	303	**100**	61	505	**442**	95	26	.284	.347	.408	755	102	6	17	99	70	47	60	-1
CLE	87	65	1	.572	19	43	33	845	747	6121	1544	**310**	74	78	566	454	**110**	**33**	.285	.357	.413	770	99	46	-6	107	52	54	49	-7
DET	76	75	2	.503	29.5	42	34	799	787	5993	1479	291	80	80	486	523	85	13	.273	.335	.401	736	92	-37	-66	104	103	49	68	6
STL	63	91	0	.409	44	33	42	736	898	6065	1502	274	69	67	507	528	90	19	.276	.339	.388	727	89	-47	-88	106	69	62	53	-7
CHI	49	102	1	.325	56.5	28	49	667	897	5903	1426	274	56	36	459	386	89	19	.267	.327	.360	687	90	-124	-78	94	89	58	61	-1
BOS	43	111	0	.279	64	27	50	566	915	5856	1331	253	57	53	469	539	80	12	.251	.314	.351	665	80	-175	-158	97	46	46	50	-6
TOT	615					337	275	6436		48724	12017	2287	570	707	4405	4029	170	719	.277	.346	.404	750					544	405	57	-22

TEAM	CG	SHO	GR	SV	IP	H	HR	BB	SO	BR/9	ERA	AERA	OAV	OOB	PR	APR	PF	OSB	OCS	FA	E	WPB	DP	FW	PW	BW	BSW	DIF
NY	**96**	**11**	93	15	1408.0	1425	93	561	**780**	**12.8**	**3.98**	102	**.260**	.331	**78**	17	91	65	38	.969	188	37	124	.2	1.6	**21.5**	-.3	7.1
PHI	95	10	92	10	1386.0	1477	112	511	595	13.0	4.45	102	.271	.336	4	11	101	68	49	**.979**	**124**	36	142	**3.8**	1.0	11.0	.3	.9
WAS	66	10	139	**22**	1383.1	1463	73	526	437	13.0	4.16	104	.271	.337	49	25	96	**44**	48	**.979**	125	**23**	157	**3.8**	2.3	1.6	.2	8.2
CLE	94	6	92	8	1377.1	1506	**70**	**446**	439	**12.8**	4.12	**115**	.273	**.329**	55	**90**	106	57	41	.969	191	24	129	-.2	**8.3**	-.6	-.4	3.8
DET	67	9	120	17	1362.2	**1421**	89	592	521	13.5	4.30	109	.269	.346	27	58	105	67	51	.969	187	31	154	.0	5.4	-6.1	**.8**	.4
STL	63	8	150	11	1376.2	1592	103	574	496	14.3	5.01	97	.290	.359	-81	-22	108	61	53	.969	188	29	156	.0	-2.0	-8.1	-.4	-3.5
CHI	50	2	166	12	1348.2	1551	88	580	379	14.4	4.82	90	.287	.359	-52	-77	97	76	**67**	.958	264	37	**170**	-4.6	-7.1	-7.2	.2	-7.7
BOS	42	3	**188**	7	1362.0	1574	79	612	365	14.6	5.02	90	.289	.364	-81	-79	100	106	58	.963	233	33	165	-2.6	-7.3	-14.6	-.3	-9.2
TOT	573	59	1040	102	11004.2					13.6	4.48		.277	.346						.969	1500	250	1197					

Batter-Fielder Wins	Batting Average	On-Base Percentage	Slugging Average	On-Base Plus Slugging	Adjusted OPS	Adjusted Batter Runs
Foxx-Phi 6.7	Alexander-Det-Bos ...367	Ruth-NY 489	Foxx-Phi 749	Foxx-Phi 1218	Ruth-NY 206	Foxx-Phi 91.5
Ruth-NY 6.5	Foxx-Phi 364	Foxx-Phi 469	Ruth-NY 661	Ruth-NY 1150	Foxx-Phi 203	Ruth-NY 80.5
Gehrig-NY 5.1	Gehrig-NY 349	Gehrig-NY 451	Gehrig-NY 621	Gehrig-NY 1072	Gehrig-NY 184	Gehrig-NY 79.4
Cochrane-Phi 4.2	Manush-Was 342	Bishop-Phi 412	Averill-Cle 569	Averill-Cle 961	Lazzeri-NY 140	Alexander-Det-Bos 34.5
Lazzeri-NY 3.9	Ruth-NY 341	Cochrane-Phi 412	Simmons-Phi 548	Cochrane-Phi 921	Averill-Cle 137	Averill-Cle 33.0

Runs	Hits	Doubles	Triples	Home Runs	Total Bases	Runs Batted In
Foxx-Phi 151	Simmons-Phi 216	McNair-Phi 47	Cronin-Was 18	Foxx-Phi 58	Foxx-Phi 438	Foxx-Phi 169
Simmons-Phi 144	Manush-Was 214	Gehringer-Det 44	Myer-Was 16	Ruth-NY 41	Gehrig-NY 370	Simmons-Phi 151
Combs-NY 143	Foxx-Phi 213	Cronin-Was 43	Lazzeri-NY 16	Simmons-Phi 35	Simmons-Phi 367	Gehrig-NY 151
Gehrig-NY 138	Gehrig-NY 208		Chapman-NY 15	Gehrig-NY 34	Averill-Cle 359	Ruth-NY 137
Manush-Was 121	Averill-Cle 198			Averill-Cle 32	Manush-Was 325	Averill-Cle 124

Stolen Bases	Base Stealing Runs	Fielding Runs-Infield	Fielding Runs-Outfield	Wins	Winning Pct.	Complete Games
Chapman-NY 38	Walker-Det 4.5	Warstler-Bos 22.8	Vosmik-Cle 18.9	Crowder-Was 26	Allen-NY 810	Grove-Phi 27
Walker-Det 30	Johnson-Det-Bos ..2.3	Appling-Chi 14.8	West-Was 14.7	Grove-Phi 25	Gomez-NY 774	Ferrell-Cle 26
Johnson-Det-Bos 20	Chapman-NY 2.1	Rogell-Det 11.3	Funk-Chi 5.5	Gomez-NY 24	Ruffing-NY 720	Ruffing-NY 22
Cissell-Chi-Cle 18	Blue-Chi 1.6	Melillo-StL 11.3	Goslin-StL 4.8	Ferrell-Cle 23	Grove-Phi 714	
	Schuble-Det 1.3	Kamm-Cle 9.3	Chapman-NY 4.1	Weaver-Was 22	Weaver-Was 688	

Strikeouts	Fewest BB/Game	Games	Saves	Base Runners/9	Adjusted Relief Runs	Relief Ranking
Ruffing-NY 190	Brown-Cle 1.71	Marberry-Was 54	Marberry-Was 13	Grove-Phi 10.77	Kimsey-StL-Chi 7.7	Kimsey-StL-Chi 7.2
Grove-Phi 188	Crowder-Was 2.12	Gray-StL 52	Moore-Bos-NY 8	Crowder-Was 10.90	Faber-Chi 4.5	Faber-Chi 5.6
Gomez-NY 176	Gray-StL 2.31	Crowder-Was 50	Hogsett-Det 7	Allen-NY 11.39	Krausse-Phi 0	Krausse-Phi 0
Hadley-Chi-StL 145	Harder-Cle 2.40		Grove-Phi 7	Ruffing-NY 11.71		
Pipgras-NY 111	Grove-Phi 2.44		Faber-Chi 6	Sorrell-Det 12.06		

Innings Pitched	Opponents' Avg.	Opponents' OBP	Earned Run Average	Adjusted ERA	Adjusted Starter Runs	Pitcher Wins
Crowder-Was 327.0	Ruffing-NY 226	Grove-Phi 292	Grove-Phi 2.84	Grove-Phi 159	Grove-Phi 54.0	**Grove-Phi** 5.9
Grove-Phi 291.2	Allen-NY 228	Crowder-Was 295	Ruffing-NY 3.09	Bridges-Det 140	Crowder-Was 36.9	**Ferrell-Cle** 4.0
Ferrell-Cle 287.2	Bridges-Det 233	Allen-NY 306	Lyons-Chi 3.28	Hogsett-Det 133	Ferrell-Cle 31.8	**Ruffing-NY** 4.0
Walberg-Phi 272.0	Grove-Phi 241	Ruffing-NY 311	Crowder-Was 3.33	Lyons-Chi 132	Ruffing-NY 31.8	**Crowder-Was** 3.8
Gomez-NY 265.1	Crowder-Was 252	Brown-Cle 314	Bridges-Det 3.36	Ruffing-NY 132	Lyons-Chi 27.9	**Lyons-Chi** 3.1

The Babe's Last Hurrah

While the AL's slugging torch passed from Babe Ruth to the younger Jimmie Foxx and Lou Gehrig, the Yankees were on the way up. Bill Dickey, Ben Chapman, and rookie shortstop Frankie Crosetti provided vital shots of youth, and New York no longer depended on one or two sluggers to carry the club.

The Athletics were strong hitters, but their pitching (besides Lefty Grove) was no longer the best in the league. As a result, the Yankees—with terrific mound work from Red Ruffing and Johnny Allen, as well as 24 wins from "Goofy" Gomez—won comfortably, giving skipper Joe McCarthy his first AL title.

A record 707 homers flew from AL parks in 1932, and for the first time since 1922, a non-Yankee (Foxx) captured the individual crown. The Red Sox scored the league's fewest runs, allowed the most, and absorbed 111 losses to finish last for the seventh time in eight years. Several canny trades soon lifted the club into the first division.

Attendance dropped another 19 percent, and the AL suffered its worst full season totals since 1915. Chicago's plight during the 1930s was especially strange. Attendance for the mostly moribund team ping-ponged each year: down 42 percent, up 71, down 41, up 98, down 6, up 33, down 42, and so on until 1939–40, when they had two straight years of growth. The Indians, finishing fourth for the third of four straight years, opened new Lakefront Stadium on July 31. The cavernous park, the first built with public money, was a failure from the start—it had been commissioned in the hopes of drawing the Olympics. Oddly shaped League Park housed the Tribe's weekday games until 1946.

Ruth's last, and greatest, October show resulted in New York's third World Series sweep since 1927. The 37-year-old star, ripped mercilessly by Cubs bench jockeys, hit .333 with 2 homers while Lou Gehrig batted .529 with 3 bombs. Ruth's "called shot" at Wrigley Field in Game 3 has passed into baseball lore.

1933 National League

TEAM	W	L	T	PCT	GB	HW	HL	R	OR	PA	H	2B	3B	HR	BB	SO	HB	SH	AVG	OBP	SLG	OPS	AOPS	BR	ABR	PF	SB	CS	BSA	BSR
NY	91	61	4	.599		48	27	636	**515**	5939	1437	204	41	**82**	377	477	86	15	.263	.312	.361	673	100	-16	-6	98	31			
PIT	87	67	0	.565	5	50	27	667	619	5962	**1548**	249	**84**	39	366	**334**	**147**	20	**.285**	**.333**	**.383**	**716**	**111**	**70**	**71**	100	34			
CHI	86	68	0	.558	6	**56**	23	646	536	5785	1422	**256**	51	72	**392**	475	108	30	.271	.325	.380	705	107	50	52	100	52			
BOS	83	71	2	.539	9	45	31	552	531	5728	1320	217	56	54	326	428	134	25	.252	.299	.345	644	98	-73	-26	92	25			
STL	82	71	1	.536	9.5	47	30	**687**	609	5911	1486	**256**	61	57	391	528	101	**32**	.276	.329	.378	707	103	55	22	105	**99**			
BRO	65	88	4	.425	26.5	36	41	617	695	5872	1413	224	51	62	397	453	90	18	.263	.316	.359	675	103	-8	19	96	82			
PHI	60	92	0	.395	31	32	40	607	760	5796	1439	240	41	60	381	479	125	29	.274	.326	.369	695	93	34	-39	113	55			
CIN	58	94	1	.382	33	37	42	496	643	5653	1267	208	37	34	349	354	115	33	.246	.298	.320	618	83	-111	-104	99	30			
TOT	618					351	261	4908		46646	11332	1854	422	460	2979	3528	202	906	.266	.317	.362	679					408			

TEAM	CG	SHO	GR	SV	IP	H	HR	BB	SO	BR/9	ERA	AERA	OAV	OOB	PR	APR	PF	OSB	OCS	FA	E	WPB	DP	FW	PW	BW	BSW	DIF
NY	75	**23**	126	15	1408.2	**1280**	61	400	555	**10.9**	**2.71**	**118**	**.242**	**.299**	**98**	**81**	96	53	*45*	.973	178	42	156	-.5	**8.6**	-.6		7.5
PIT	70	16	144	12	1373.1	1417	54	313	401	11.5	3.27	101	.264	.308	10	7	99	69	*36*	.972	166	24	133	.2	.7	**7.5**		1.6
CHI	**95**	16	97	9	1362.0	1316	51	413	488	11.6	2.93	112	.254	.312	62	53	98	35	*43*	.973	168	37	**163**	.0	5.6	5.5		-2.2
BOS	85	15	102	**16**	1403.0	1391	54	355	383	11.3	2.96	103	.261	.309	58	15	92	**29**	*37*	**.978**	**138**	**20**	148	**2.1**	1.6	-2.8		5.0
STL	73	11	128	**16**	1382.2	1391	55	452	**635**	12.1	3.37	103	.261	.321	-5	15	104	51	*42*	.973	162	37	119	.4	1.6	2.3		1.2
BRO	71	9	133	10	1386.1	1502	51	374	415	12.4	3.73	86	.275	.326	-60	-82	96	49	***52***	.971	177	38	120	-.3	-8.7	2.0		-4.5
PHI	52	10	**170**	13	1336.2	1563	87	410	341	13.6	4.34	88	.293	.348	-150	-69	114	66	*45*	.970	183	41	156	-1.1	-7.3	-4.1		-3.5
CIN	74	13	113	8	1352.0	1470	**47**	**257**	310	11.6	3.42	99	.279	.314	-13	-5	102	56	*39*	.971	177	37	139	-.6	-.5	-11.0		-5.8
TOT	595	113	1013	99	11004.2					11.9	3.34		.266	.317						.973	1349	276	1134					

Batter-Fielder Wins	Batting Average	On-Base Percentage	Slugging Average	On-Base Plus Slugging	Adjusted OPS	Adjusted Batter Runs
Klein-Phi 5.6	Klein-Phi .368	Klein-Phi .422	Klein-Phi .602	Klein-Phi 1025	Berger-Bos 177	Klein-Phi 54.9
Berger-Bos 4.7	Davis-Phi .349	Davis-Phi .395	Berger-Bos .566	Berger-Bos .932	Klein-Phi 168	Berger-Bos 50.4
Vaughan-Pit 3.8	Stephenson-Chi .329	Vaughan-Pit .388	B.Herman-Chi .502	Davis-Phi .867	Vaughan-Pit 146	Vaughan-Pit 35.3
B.Herman-Chi 3.7	Piet-Pit .323	Martin-StL .387	Medwick-StL .497	Vaughan-Pit .866	B.Herman-Chi 142	Ott-NY 31.7
Critz-NY 3.1	Terry-NY .322	Terry-NY .375	Vaughan-Pit .478	B.Herman-Chi .855	Ott-NY 139	P.Waner-Pit 29.3

Runs	Hits	Doubles	Triples	Home Runs	Total Bases	Runs Batted In
Martin-StL 122	Klein-Phi 223	Klein-Phi 44	Vaughan-Pit 19	Klein-Phi 28	Klein-Phi 365	Klein-Phi 120
P.Waner-Pit 101	Fullis-Phi 200	Medwick-StL 40	P.Waner-Pit 16	Berger-Bos 27	Berger-Bos 299	Berger-Bos 106
Klein-Phi 101	P.Waner-Pit 191	Lindstrom-Pit 39	Martin-StL 12	Ott-NY 23	Medwick-StL 296	Ott-NY 103
Ott-NY 98	Traynor-Pit 190	P.Waner-Pit 38	B.Herman-Chi 12	Medwick-StL 18	P.Waner-Pit 282	Medwick-StL 98
Medwick-StL 92	Martin-StL 189	Berger-Bos 37			Vaughan-Pit 274	Vaughan-Pit 97

Stolen Bases	Base Stealing Runs	Fielding Runs-Infield	Fielding Runs-Outfield	Wins	Winning Pct.	Complete Games
Martin-StL 26		Critz-NY 45.0	Klein-Phi 8.1	Hubbell-NY 23	Cantwell-Bos .667	Warneke-Chi 26
Fullis-Phi 18		B.Herman-Chi 29.0	Medwick-StL 7.3	Dean-StL 20	Hubbell-NY .657	Dean-StL 26
Frisch-StL 18		Jurges-Chi 22.8	Lindstrom-Pit 6.3	Cantwell-Bos 20	Meine-Pit .652	Brandt-Bos 23
Klein-Phi 15		Ryan-NY 16.5	Hafey-Cin 6.2	Bush-Chi 20	Bush-Chi .625	Hubbell-NY 22
Orsatti-StL 14		Bartell-Phi 8.8	Rice-Cin 4.1	Schumacher-NY 19	Schumacher-NY .613	

Strikeouts	Fewest BB/Game	Games	Saves	Base Runners/9	Adjusted Relief Runs	Relief Ranking
Dean-StL 199	Lucas-Cin .74	Dean-StL 48	Collins-Phi 6	Hubbell-NY 8.92	Bell-NY 13.3	Bell-NY 13.9
Hubbell-NY 156	Hubbell-NY 1.37	French-Pit 47	Hubbell-NY 5	Schumacher-NY 9.88	Luque-NY 5.7	Luque-NY 7.1
Carleton-StL 147	Swift-Pit 1.48	Liska-Phi 45	Harris-Pit 5	Betts-Bos 10.41		
Warneke-Chi 133	Hansen-Phi 1.60	Hubbell-NY 45	Bell-NY 5	Bell-NY 10.42		
Parmelee-NY 132	French-Pit 1.70	Carleton-StL 44		Swift-Pit 10.47		

Innings Pitched	Opponents' Avg.	Opponents' OBP	Earned Run Average	Adjusted ERA	Adjusted Starter Runs	Pitcher Wins
Hubbell-NY 308.2	Schumacher-NY .214	Hubbell-NY .260	Hubbell-NY 1.66	Hubbell-NY 193	Hubbell-NY 55.3	**Hubbell-NY** 7.3
Dean-StL 293.0	Hubbell-NY .227	Schumacher-NY .280	Warneke-Chi 2.00	Warneke-Chi 163	Warneke-Chi 38.9	**Warneke-Chi** 5.8
French-Pit 291.1	Parmelee-NY .232	Swift-Pit .285	Schumacher-NY 2.16	Schumacher-NY 149	Schumacher-NY 33.3	**Schumacher-NY** 4.4
Brandt-Bos 287.2	Mungo-Bro .236	Betts-Bos .290	Brandt-Bos 2.60	Root-Chi 126	Brandt-Bos 21.1	**Brandt-Bos** 3.5
Warneke-Chi 287.1	Warneke-Chi .244	Cantwell-Bos .291	Root-Chi 2.60	French-Pit 122	French-Pit 20.7	**Bush-Chi** 2.0

Pitching Royalty and a Guy Named Mel

Three members of the Giants made the job easier for player-manager Bill Terry. Slugger Mel Ott led the league in walks and finished top five in runs, homers, and RBIs, while "King Carl" Hubbell and "Prince Hal" Schumacher were the pitching top twosome in the league. New York surged ahead in mid-June and never looked back, improving from seventh to win the flag.

Pittsburgh, Chicago, Boston (which set a new NL mark with a .978 fielding percentage), and St. Louis bunched together fighting for second. The Pirates were the eventual runners-up, finishing 5 games back.

Despite Chuck Klein winning the Triple Crown, the Phillies ended seventh. Philadelphia sold Klein to the Cubs for $125,000 after the season; they finished seventh again in 1934 and lost one more game than the previous year. Last-place Cincinnati was the final stop for two great pitchers. Eppa Rixey went 6–3 at age 42, while 23-year-vet Jack Quinn pitched his last game at the age of 50.

Due to the depression, major league teams cut their rosters to 23, and even Commissioner Landis took a pay cut. The average yearly salary for a major league player was $6,000. NL attendance fell another 18 percent in 1933, bringing league totals to their lowest since 1919. During the 1930s, the Cubs and Giants were the loop's only consistent draws. Both Chicago and New York had good ballparks, large populations, charismatic players, and were competitive most of the decade. In 1933 Cubs President William L. Veeck proposed a midseason slate of interleague games and a split season to spark more interest; he died a few months later.

Defeating the Washington Senators in five games, the Giants captured their first World Series since 1922. Hubbell pitched 20 innings without allowing an earned run, capturing Games 1 and 4. Ott's homer in the 10th -inning was the deciding blow in the final contest.

1933 American League

TEAM	W	L	T	PCT	GB	HW	HL	R	OR	PA	H	2B	3B	HR	BB	SO	HB	SH	AVG	OBP	SLG	OPS	AOPS	BR	ABR	PF	SB	CS	BSA	BSR
WAS	99	53	1	.651		46	30	850	**665**	6212	**1586**	281	**86**	60	539	**395**	**128**	**21**	**.287**	.353	.402	755	107	46	55	99	65	50	57	**-3**
NY	91	59	2	.607	7	**51**	23	**927**	768	6069	1495	241	75	**144**	**700**	506	78	17	.283	**.369**	**.440**	**809**	**129**	**156**	**215**	94	**76**	59	56	-4
PHI	79	72	1	.523	19.5	46	29	875	853	6051	1519	**297**	57	139	625	618	80	16	.285	.362	**.440**	802	118	140	131	101	34	34	50	-4
CLE	75	76	0	.497	23.5	45	32	654	669	5806	1366	218	77	50	448	426	101	17	.261	.321	.360	681	82	-109	-136	105	36	40	47	-6
DET	75	79	1	.487	25	43	35	722	733	6091	1479	283	78	57	475	523	93	**21**	.269	.329	.380	709	92	-55	-68	102	68	50	**58**	**-3**
CHI	67	83	1	.447	31	35	41	683	814	5991	1448	231	53	43	538	416	108	27	.272	.342	.360	702	96	-51	-20	96	43	46	48	-7
BOS	63	86	0	.423	34.5	32	40	700	758	5857	1407	294	56	50	525	464	116	15	.271	.339	.377	716	97	-25	-18	99	58	37	61	0
STL	55	96	2	.364	43.5	30	46	669	820	5907	1337	244	64	64	520	556	87	15	.253	.322	.360	682	81	-104	-142	106	72	60	55	-5
TOT	608					328	276	6080		47984	11637	2089	546	607	4370	3904	149	791	.273	.342	.390	732					452	376	55	-32

TEAM	CG	SHO	GR	SV	IP	H	HR	BB	SO	BR/9	ERA	AERA	OAV	OOB	PR	APR	PF	OSB	OCS	FA	E	WPB	DP	FW	PW	BW	BSW	DIF
WAS	68	5	150	**26**	1389.2	1415	64	**452**	447	**12.2**	3.82	109	**.263**	**.322**	71	57	98	**31**	30	**.979**	**131**	22	149	**2.6**	5.4	5.2	.0	9.7
NY	70	8	123	22	1354.2	1426	66	612	**711**	13.6	4.36	89	.267	.344	-13	-80	91	35	39	.972	165	45	122	.4	-7.6	**20.4**	.0	2.8
PHI	69	6	142	14	1343.2	1523	77	644	423	14.6	4.81	89	.283	.361	-79	-78	100	67	38	.966	203	42	121	-1.9	-7.4	12.4	.0	.4
CLE	**74**	**12**	124	7	1350.0	**1382**	**60**	465	437	12.4	**3.71**	**120**	.264	.325	**86**	**107**	104	43	**65**	.974	156	**18**	127	.9	**10.1**	-12.9	-.2	1.5
DET	69	6	129	17	1398.0	1415	84	561	575	12.9	3.95	109	**.263**	.335	52	56	101	93	55	.971	178	21	**167**	-.2	5.3	-6.4	.0	-.8
CHI	53	8	**167**	13	1371.1	1505	85	519	423	13.5	4.45	95	.277	.343	-26	-33	99	70	37	.970	186	41	143	-1.0	-3.1	-1.9	-.3	-1.7
BOS	60	4	146	14	1327.2	1396	75	591	467	13.6	4.35	101	.271	.348	-10	4	102	68	60	.966	204	22	133	-2.2	.4	-1.7	**.4**	-8.3
STL	55	7	147	10	1360.2	1574	96	531	426	14.0	4.82	97	.289	.354	-82	-23	109	45	52	.976	149	30	162	1.5	-2.2	-13.4	-.0	-6.3
TOT	518	56	1128	123	10895.2					13.3	4.28		.273	.342						.972	1372	241	1124					

Batter-Fielder Wins	Batting Average	On-Base Percentage	Slugging Average	On-Base Plus Slugging	Adjusted OPS	Adjusted Batter Runs
Foxx-Phi 6.9	Foxx-Phi .356	Cochrane-Phi .459	Foxx-Phi .703	Foxx-Phi 1153	Foxx-Phi 199	Foxx-Phi 82.4
Ruth-NY 4.7	Manush-Was .336	Foxx-Phi .449	Gehrig-NY .605	Gehrig-NY 1030	Gehrig-NY 181	Gehrig-NY 70.1
Gehrig-NY 4.7	Gehrig-NY .334	Bishop-Phi .446	Ruth-NY .582	Ruth-NY 1023	Ruth-NY 180	Ruth-NY 58.8
Cochrane-Phi 4.1	Simmons-Chi .331	Ruth-NY .442	Cochrane-Phi .515	Cochrane-Phi 974	Cochrane-Phi 156	Cochrane-Phi 42.6
Cronin-Was 3.9	Gehringer-Det .325	Gehrig-NY .424	Johnson-Phi .505	Johnson-Phi 892	Dickey-NY 138	Johnson-Phi 27.7

Runs	Hits	Doubles	Triples	Home Runs	Total Bases	Runs Batted In
Gehrig-NY 138	Manush-Was 221	Cronin-Was 45	Manush-Was 17	Foxx-Phi 48	Foxx-Phi 403	Foxx-Phi 163
Foxx-Phi 125	Gehringer-Det 204	Johnson-Phi 44	Combs-NY 16	Ruth-NY 34	Gehrig-NY 359	Gehrig-NY 139
Manush-Was 115	Foxx-Phi 204	Burns-StL 43	Averill-Cle 16	Gehrig-NY 32	Manush-Was 302	Simmons-Chi 119
Chapman-NY 112	Simmons-Chi 200	Rogell-Det 42	Myer-Was 15	Johnson-Phi 21	Gehringer-Det 294	Cronin-Was 118
Cramer-Phi 109	Gehrig-NY 198	Gehringer-Det 42	Reynolds-StL 14	Lazzeri-NY 18	Simmons-Chi 291	Kuhel-Was 107

Stolen Bases	Base Stealing Runs	Fielding Runs-Infield	Fielding Runs-Outfield	Wins	Winning Pct.	Complete Games
Chapman-NY 27	Walker-Det 2.6	Melillo-StL 22.3	Chapman-NY 14.1	Grove-Phi 24	Grove-Phi .750	Grove-Phi 21
Walker-Det 26	Werber-NY-Bos 1.5	Rogell-Det 18.9	Simmons-Chi 9.4	Crowder-Was 24	Whitehill-Was .733	Whitehill-Was 19
Swanson-Chi 19	Kuhel-Was 9	Scharein-StL 16.1	Schulte-Was 7.6	Whitehill-Was 22	Stewart-Was .714	Hadley-StL 19
Kuhel-Was 17	Stumpf-Bos 9	Appling-Chi 8.5	West-StL 5.2		Allen-NY .682	Ruffing-NY 18
	Lazzeri-NY 9	Foxx-Phi 6.8	Goslin-Was 4.6			

Strikeouts	Fewest BB/Game	Games	Saves	Base Runners/9	Adjusted Relief Runs	Relief Ranking
Gomez-NY 163	Brown-Cle 1.65	Crowder-Was 52	Russell-Was 13	Heving-Chi 10.83	Russell-Was 19.6	Russell-Was 30.3
Hadley-StL 149	Marberry-Det 2.30	Russell-Was 50	Hogsett-Det 9	Russell-Was 11.03	Heving-Chi 17.4	Heving-Chi 17.9
Ruffing-NY 122	Stewart-Was 2.34	Welch-Bos 47	Moore-NY 8	Pearson-Cle 11.04	Gray-StL 7.3	Gray-StL 7.1
Bridges-Det 120	Harder-Cle 2.38	Kline-Bos 46	Heving-Chi 6	Marberry-Det 11.10	Faber-Chi 7.2	Faber-Chi 6.2
Allen-NY 119	Blaeholder-StL 2.43		Grove-Phi 6	Stewart-Was 11.24	Burke-Was 5.5	Burke-Was 5.4

Innings Pitched	Opponents' Avg.	Opponents' OBP	Earned Run Average	Adjusted ERA	Adjusted Starter Runs	Pitcher Wins
Hadley-StL 316.2	Bridges-Det .226	Marberry-Det .302	Pearson-Cle 2.33	Harder-Cle 151	Harder-Cle 35.1	**Harder-Cle** 4.4
Crowder-Was 299.1	Gomez-NY .240	Stewart-Was .304	Harder-Cle 2.95	Bridges-Det 140	Grove-Phi 34.5	**Bridges-Det** 3.2
Grove-Phi 275.1	Allen-NY .242	Harder-Cle .309	Bridges-Det 3.09	Grove-Phi 134	Pearson-Cle 29.5	**Pearson-Cle** 3.1
Whitehill-Was 270.0	Weiland-Bos .244	Brown-Cle .310	Gomez-NY 3.18	Marberry-Det 131	Marberry-Det 29.5	**Grove-Phi** 3.1
Blaeholder-StL 255.2	Hildebrand-Cle .245	Grove-Phi .316	Grove-Phi 3.20	Brown-Cle 130	Bridges-Det 28.8	**Russell-Was** 3.1

Last Gasp for the Senators and A's

Following up on a strong finish in 1932, the Washington Senators moved ahead of the Yankees in June, withstood a challenge in late July, and then pulled away at the end. Player-manager Joe Cronin, just 26, keyed a line-drive power offense, three 30-something starters combined for 59 wins, and Jack Russell carried on the relief tradition of Firpo Marberry (departed to Detroit), winning 12 and being credited retroactively with 13 saves.

Prior to the season, Connie Mack looked at the finances and decided to tear apart his A's. After trading Al Simmons, Jimmy Dykes, and Mule Haas, the Athletics only finished third because of Jimmie Foxx (the Triple Crown winner), Lefty Grove, and Mickey Cochrane. After another attendance dip in '33, Mack finished the destruction by dealing Grove to Boston and Cochrane to Detroit. It was the finish of the Athletics as a competitive team in Philadelphia.

The Tigers spent 1933 in fifth place, breaking in two rookie pitchers who would soon be very important: Schoolboy Rowe and Elden Auker. Though the White Sox were a sixth-place crew, they remained in the news. Comiskey Park was the site of the first midsummer All-Star game. The AL won the game before a packed house, 4–2; Ruth christened the event with the first All-Star homer.

Red Faber, 44, the last active player from the 1919 White Sox and still a mainstay of the club, pitched in his last game. The same year, "Black Sox" manager Kid Gleason died, his heart still broken from the betrayal carried out by "his boys."

Although Lou Gehrig was outstanding, and Babe Ruth had his final big year, it was the Senators' grand finale. For 1920s holdovers Ossie Bluege, Sam Rice, and Goose Goslin (brought back for one year by owner Clark Griffith), it was their third flag in a decade—and the franchise's last in the capital. Washington's five-game World Series loss to the Giants was the end, rather than the beginning, of the excitement in D.C.

1934 National League

TEAM	W	L	T	PCT	GB	HW	HL	R	OR	PA	H	2B	3B	HR	BB	SO	HB	SH	AVG	OBP	SLG	OPS	AOPS	BR	ABR	PF	SB	CS	BSA	BSR
STL	95	58	1	.621		48	29	**799**	656	5988	**1582**	**294**	75	104	392	535	76	18	**.288**	.337	**.425**	**762**	102	**63**	15	107	**69**			
NY	93	60	0	.608	2	**49**	26	760	**583**	5934	1485	240	41	**126**	406	526	**108**	24	.275	.329	.405	734	**105**	7	**25**	98	19			
CHI	86	65	1	.570	8	47	30	705	639	5841	1494	263	44	101	375	630	93	26	.279	.330	.402	732	103	5	20	98	59			
BOS	78	73	1	.517	16	40	35	683	714	5854	1460	233	44	83	375	440	81	**28**	.272	.323	.378	701	101	-54	-1	93	30			
PIT	74	76	1	.493	19.5	45	32	735	713	5878	1541	281	**77**	52	**440**	**398**	59	18	.287	**.344**	.398	742	102	34	17	102	44			
BRO	71	81	1	.467	23.5	43	33	748	795	6074	1526	284	52	79	548	555	77	22	.281	.350	.396	746	112	55	97	95	55			
PHI	56	93	0	.376	37	35	36	675	794	5724	1480	286	35	56	398	534	79	29	.284	.338	.384	722	87	0	-81	113	52			
CIN	52	99	1	.344	42	30	47	590	801	5785	1428	227	65	55	313	532	78	33	.266	.311	.364	675	88	-111	-97	98	34			
TOT	608					337	268	5695		47078	11996	2108	433	656	3247	4150	198	651	.279	.333	.394	727					362			

TEAM	CG	SHO	GR	SV	IP	H	HR	BB	SO	BR/9	ERA	AERA	OAV	OOB	PR	APR	PF	OSB	OCS	FA	E	WPB	DP	FW	PW	BW	BSW	DIF
STL	**78**	**15**	146	16	1386.2	1463	77	411	**689**	12.4	3.69	115	.268	.323	58	79	104	41	*32*	.972	166	31	**141**	.3	7.7	1.5		9.0
NY	68	13	129	**30**	1370.0	**1384**	75	**351**	499	**11.5**	**3.19**	**121**	**.260**	**.308**	**132**	**107**	95	45	*37*	.972	179	46	**141**	-.5	**10.4**	2.4		4.2
CHI	73	11	129	9	1361.1	1432	80	417	633	12.3	3.76	103	.269	.325	46	19	95	37	***48***	**.977**	**137**	45	135	**1.9**	1.9	1.9		4.8
BOS	62	12	138	20	1359.2	1512	78	405	462	12.8	4.11	93	.279	.331	-7	-47	94	43	*38*	.972	169	**19**	120	.0	-4.6	-.0		7.2
PIT	63	8	159	8	1329.2	1523	78	354	487	12.9	4.20	98	.284	.332	-20	-13	101	66	*-4*	.975	145	22	118	1.4	-1.3	1.7		-2.8
BRO	66	6	166	12	1354.1	1540	81	475	520	13.6	4.48	87	.285	.346	-63	-91	96	47	*36*	.970	180	53	**141**	-.6	-8.9	**9.4**		-5.0
PHI	52	8	175	15	1297.0	1501	126	437	416	13.6	4.76	99	.288	.347	-101	-3	116	**36**	*32*	.966	197	28	140	-1.8	-.3	-7.9		-8.5
CIN	51	3	**182**	19	1347.2	1645	**61**	389	438	13.8	4.37	93	.299	.348	-46	-43	101	47	*37*	.970	181	35	136	-.7	-4.2	-9.4		-9.2
TOT	513	76	1224	129	10806.1					12.9	4.06		.279	.333						.972	1354	279	1072					

Batter-Fielder Wins	Batting Average	On-Base Percentage	Slugging Average	On-Base Plus Slugging	Adjusted OPS	Adjusted Batter Runs
Vaughan-Pit 5.5	P.Waner-Pit 362	Vaughan-Pit 431	Collins-StL 615	Collins-StL 1008	Ott-NY 170	Ott-NY 59.1
P.Waner-Pit.........4.3	Terry-NY 354	P.Waner-Pit 429	Ott-NY 591	Ott-NY 1006	Collins-StL 155	P.Waner-Pit 47.3
Collins-StL 3.7	Cuyler-Chi............338	Ott-NY 415	DeLancey-StL.......565	P.Waner-Pit 968	P.Waner-Pit 154	Collins-StL.........45.7
Ott-NY 3.6	Vaughan-Pit 333	Terry-NY 414	Berger-Bos 546	Vaughan-Pit..........942	Koenecke-Bro 152	Vaughan-Pit........43.1
Hartnett-Chi 3.5	Collins-StL 333	Koenecke-Bro 411	P.Waner-Pit 539	Koenecke-Bro 919	Berger-Bos 148	Berger-Bos 38.4

Runs	Hits	Doubles	Triples	Home Runs	Total Bases	Runs Batted In
P.Waner-Pit 122	P.Waner-Pit 217	Cuyler-Chi......................42	Medwick-StL 18	Ott-NY 35	Collins-StL 369	Ott-NY 135
Ott-NY 119	Terry-NY 213	Allen-Phi 42	P.Waner-Pit 16	Collins-StL 35	Ott-NY 344	Collins-StL 128
Collins-StL 116	Collins-StL 200	Vaughan-Pit 41	Suhr-Pit 13	Berger-Bos 34	Berger-Bos 336	Berger-Bos 121
Vaughan-Pit...........115	Medwick-StL 198	Medwick-StL 40	Collins-StL 12	Hartnett-Chi..............22	Medwick-StL 328	Medwick-StL........106
Medwick-StL 110		Collins-StL 40		Klein-Chi 20	P.Waner-Pit 323	Suhr-Pit 103

Stolen Bases	Base Stealing Runs	Fielding Runs-Infield	Fielding Runs-Outfield	Wins	Winning Pct.	Complete Games
Martin-StL 23		Critz-NY 27.3	K.Davis-StL-Phi ..13.7	D.Dean-StL 30	D.Dean-StL...........811	Hubbell-NY............25
Cuyler-Chi 15		Bartell-Phi 18.4	Allen-Phi 10.6	Schumacher-NY 23	Hoyt-Pit..................714	D.Dean-StL............24
Bartell-Phi 13		Ryan-NY 10.3	Boyle-Bro 8.6	Warneke-Chi 22	Schumacher-NY ...697	Warneke-Chi 23
Taylor-Bro 12		Jackson-NY 9.6	J.Moore-Cin-Phi 7.8	Hubbell-NY 21	Warneke-Chi.........688	Mungo-Bro 22
		Frey-Bro.........................9.5	Thompson-Bos 7.7		Frankhouse-Bos ...654	Brandt-Bos 20

Strikeouts	Fewest BB/Game	Games	Saves	Base Runners/9	Adjusted Relief Runs	Relief Ranking
D.Dean-StL 195	Hubbell-NY..........1.06	C.Davis-Phi...................51	Hubbell-NY 8	Hubbell-NY..........9.35	Haines-StL 6.3	Haines-StL 5.2
Mungo-Bro............184	Freitas-Cin 1.47	Hansen-Phi...................50	Luque-NY 7	S.Johnson-Cin-Phi 10.00	Bell-NY 1.9	Bell-NY 2.6
P.Dean-StL.............150	Frey-Cin 1.54	D.Dean-StL 50	D.Dean-StL 7	Warneke-Chi......10.53		
Warneke-Chi 143	Leonard-Bro 1.62	Hubbell-NY 49	Bell-NY 6	D.Dean-StL 10.66		
Derringer-Cin........122	Fitzsimmons-NY ..1.74	French-Pit 49		Hoyt-Pit..............10.81		

Innings Pitched	Opponents' Avg.	Opponents' OBP	Earned Run Average	Adjusted ERA	Adjusted Starter Runs	Pitcher Wins
Mungo-Bro 315.1	Parmelee-NY 238	Hubbell-NY 263	Hubbell-NY 2.30	Hubbell-NY 168	Hubbell-NY..........55.5	**D.Dean-StL** 6.1
Hubbell-NY 313.0	Hubbell-NY...........239	Warneke-Chi 287	D.Dean-StL 2.66	C.Davis-Phi 160	D.Dean-StL...........50.6	**Hubbell-NY** 5.9
D.Dean-StL 311.2	D.Dean-StL...........241	D.Dean-StL 289	Hoyt-Pit................2.93	D.Dean-StL 159	C.Davis-Phi..........42.8	**C.Davis-Phi** 5.7
Schumacher-NY ..297.0	Warneke-Chi.........244	P.Dean-StL 292	C.Davis-Phi...........2.95	Hoyt-Pit 141	Hoyt-Pit................23.3	**Schumacher-NY**3.3
Warneke-Chi......291.1	P.Dean-StL 248	Hoyt-Pit 296	Fitzsimmons-NY ..3.04	Walker-StL 135	Warneke-Chi........22.9	**Fitzsimmons-NY**3.2

Dizzy, My Head Is Spinning

Dizzy Dean served notice of his greatness in 1934, becoming the last pitcher to win 30 games until 1968. With Dizzy and rookie brother Paul "Daffy" leading the mound staff, and an attack boasting Joe Medwick and Ripper Collins, St. Louis mounted a thrilling late-season comeback.

The Giants—sparked by Mel Ott and Carl Hubbell, who won 21 and saved 8—took the lead in June, but St. Louis won 33 of its last 45 while New York played .500 ball down the stretch. Dizzy clinched the pennant by shutting out Cincinnati on September 30.

It was a disappointing season for the Giants, who led by seven on September 5, but a great triumph for the "Gashouse Gang" Cardinals and their all-out style of play.

Third-place Chicago debuted Augie Galan, Bill Lee, and Phil Cavaretta, all of whom would contribute in 1935. The Reds finished last for the fourth straight year, but new owner Powel Crosley served notice that he would pay for quality players. Two great New York managers died in 1933. John McGraw succumbed two years after leaving the Giants, while Little Napoleon's one-time pal and longtime adversary Wilbert Robinson passed on three years after departing Brooklyn.

Perhaps the top pitcher of 1934 was Philadelphia rookie Curt Davis, who led the league in appearances and went 19–17 with a seventh-place team playing in the tiny Baker Bowl. Scoring increased by 18 percent, making performances like Davis' less common; only four pitchers had sub-3.00 ERAs.

The World Series was wild and woolly, with a few routs and a few nail biters. In the seventh game, St. Louis blew out Elden Auker en route to an 11–0 shellacking of the Tigers. Pepper Martin, Collins, and Medwick each had 11 hits in the Series, while the Deans—as promised by Dizzy—earned all the wins. The Cardinals' victory was the Senior Circuit's final world title of the decade.

1934 American League

TEAM	W	L	T	PCT	GB	HW	HL	R	OR	PA	H	2B	3B	HR	BB	SO	HB	SH	AVG	OBP	SLG	OPS	AOPS	BR	ABR	PF	SB	CS	BSA	BSR
DET	101	53	0	.656		**54**	26	**958**	708	6239	**1644**	**349**	53	74	639	528	**101**	**24**	**.300**	**.376**	**.424**	**800**	113	**119**	117	100	**125**	55	69	8
NY	94	60	0	.610	7	53	24	842	**669**	6177	1494	226	61	**135**	**700**	597	89	20	.278	.364	.419	783	**117**	69	**133**	93	71	46	61	0
CLE	85	69	0	.552	16	47	31	814	763	6028	1550	340	46	100	526	**433**	87	19	.287	.353	.423	776	105	48	36	102	52	32	62	0
BOS	76	76	1	.500	24	42	35	820	775	6045	1465	287	**70**	51	610	535	85	11	.274	.350	.383	733	90	-27	-77	107	116	47	**71**	**9**
PHI	68	82	3	.453	31	34	40	764	838	5920	1491	236	50	144	491	584	99	13	.280	.343	.425	768	108	16	46	96	57	35	62	0
STL	67	85	2	.441	33	36	39	674	800	5922	1417	252	59	62	514	631	**101**	19	.268	.335	.373	708	82	-87	-140	108	43	31	58	-1
WAS	66	86	3	.434	34	34	40	729	806	6170	1512	278	**70**	51	570	447	131	21	.278	.348	.382	730	99	-36	-6	96	47	42	53	-4
CHI	53	99	1	.349	47	29	46	704	946	5994	1395	237	40	71	565	524	111	17	.263	.336	.363	699	84	-99	-119	103	36	27	57	-2
TOT	615					329	281	6305		48495	11968	2205	449	688	4615	4279	144	804	.279	.351	.399	750					547	315	63	10

TEAM	CG	SHO	GR	SV	IP	H	HR	BB	SO	BR/9	ERA	AERA	OAV	OOB	PR	APR	PF	OSB	OCS	FA	E	WPB	DP	FW	PW	BW	BSW	DIF
DET	74	**13**	128	14	1370.2	1467	86	**488**	640	12.9	4.06	108	.273	.335	67	52	98	**43**	44	**.974**	159	25	150	1.2	4.8	10.9	.6	6.5
NY	**83**	**13**	111	10	1382.2	**1349**	71	542	**656**	**12.4**	**3.76**	108	**.254**	**.324**	**114**	53	90	68	32	.973	**157**	**22**	151	**1.3**	4.9	**12.4**	-.1	-1.4
CLE	72	8	143	19	1367.0	1476	**70**	582	554	13.7	4.28	106	.275	.349	33	40	101	64	30	.972	172	49	164	.4	3.7	3.3	-.1	.6
BOS	68	9	138	9	1361.0	1527	**70**	543	538	13.8	4.32	**111**	.283	.351	27	**68**	107	61	30	.969	188	36	141	-.5	**6.3**	-7.2	**.7**	.6
PHI	68	8	144	8	1337.0	1429	84	693	480	14.4	5.01	87	.275	.363	-77	-97	97	80	41	.967	196	45	166	-1.0	-9.0	4.3	-.1	-1.2
STL	50	6	**172**	**20**	1350.0	1499	94	632	499	14.3	4.49	**111**	.283	.361	1	**68**	111	68	**48**	.969	187	37	160	-.4	**6.3**	-13.0	-.2	-1.7
WAS	61	4	163	12	1381.1	1622	74	503	412	13.9	4.68	92	.295	.355	-28	-57	96	49	42	**.974**	162	36	**167**	1.0	-5.3	-.6	-.5	-4.7
CHI	72	5	118	8	1355.0	1599	139	628	506	14.9	5.41	88	.292	.367	-137	-96	105	114	**48**	.966	207	60	126	-1.6	-8.9	-11.1	-.3	-1.1
TOT	548	66	1117	100	10904.2					13.8	4.50		.279	.351						.970	1428	310	1225					

Batter-Fielder Wins	Batting Average	On-Base Percentage	Slugging Average	On-Base Plus Slugging	Adjusted OPS	Adjusted Batter Runs
Gehrig-NY 7.9	Gehrig-NY 363	Gehrig-NY 465	Gehrig-NY 706	Gehrig-NY 1172	Gehrig-NY 213	Gehrig-NY 100.4
Foxx-Phi 6.1	Gehringer-Det.......356	Gehringer-Det 450	Foxx-Phi 653	Foxx-Phi.............1102	Foxx-Phi................188	Foxx-Phi 73.4
Gehringer-Det 6.0	Manush-Was 349	Foxx-Phi.......................449	Greenberg-Det 600	Greenberg-Det ..1005	Greenberg-Det 156	Gehringer-Det 49.6
Averill-Cle............4.1	Simmons-Chi 344	Cochrane-Det 428	Trosky-Cle 598	Trosky-Cle 987	Trosky-Cle 149	Greenberg-Det ..48.7
Werber-Bos 3.9	Vosmik-Cle 341	Myer-Was.....................419	Averill-Cle 569	Averill-Cle 982	Averill-Cle 149	Averill-Cle 45.5

Runs	Hits	Doubles	Triples	Home Runs	Total Bases	Runs Batted In
Gehringer-Det 134	Gehringer-Det 214	Greenberg-Det 63	Chapman-NY..........13	Gehrig-NY 49	Gehrig-NY 409	Gehrig-NY 165
Werber-Bos 129	Gehrig-NY 210	Gehringer-Det................50	Manush-Was 11	Foxx-Phi..................44	Trosky-Cle 374	Trosky-Cle 142
Gehrig-NY 128	Trosky-Cle 206	Averill-Cle 48		Trosky-Cle 35	Greenberg-Det 356	Greenberg-Det....139
Averill-Cle 128	Cramer-Phi 202	Trosky-Cle......................45		Johnson-Phi...........34	Foxx-Phi................352	Foxx-Phi 130
Foxx-Phi................120	Greenberg-Det 201	Hale-Cle.........................44		Averill-Cle 31	Averill-Cle 340	Gehringer-Det......127

Stolen Bases	Base Stealing Runs	Fielding Runs-Infield	Fielding Runs-Outfield	Wins	Winning Pct.	Complete Games
Werber-Bos 40	White-Det 4.1	Hale-Cle......................25.9	Johnson-Phi 8.6	Gomez-NY..............26	Gomez-NY 839	Gomez-NY 25
White-Det 28	Werber-Bos............3.5	Werber-Bos 17.1	Byrd-NY 6.1	Rowe-Det................24	Rowe-Det 750	Bridges-Det 23
Chapman-NY..........26	Lazzeri-NY 2.1	Melillo-StL 16.6	Stone-Was 4.7	Bridges-Det 22	Marberry-Det 750	Lyons-Chi 21
Fox-Det 25	Fox-Det...................2.0	Warstler-Phi 15.8	West-StL................4.6	Harder-Cle..............20	Auker-Det 682	Rowe-Det 20
Walker-Det.............20	Rogell-Det..............1.8	Cronin-Was 13.4	Chapman-NY 4.1	Ruffing-NY..............19	Bridges-Det..........667	

Strikeouts	Fewest BB/Game	Games	Saves	Base Runners/9	Adjusted Relief Runs	Relief Ranking
Gomez-NY............158	W.Ferrell-Bos 2.44	Russell-Was 54	Russell-Was.............7	Gomez-NY 10.19	Pennock-Bos 8.9	Pennock-Bos 4.5
Bridges-Det 151	Auker-Det 2.46	Newsom-StL 47	L.Brown-Cle.............6	Rowe-Det 11.54	McColl-Was 5.0	Bean-Cle 4.5
Ruffing-NY............149	Blaeholder-StL 2.61	Rowe-Det 45	Newsom-StL 5	Bridges-Det........11.65	Bean-Cle 4.2	McColl-Was 2.9
Rowe-Det..............149	Rowe-Det 2.74	Knott-StL.......................45		Murphy-NY 11.66	Wells-StL 1.2	Wells-StL 9
Pearson-Cle..........140	Weaver-Was 2.77			Harder-Cle 11.77	Russell-Was 9	Russell-Was 8

Innings Pitched	Opponents' Avg.	Opponents' OBP	Earned Run Average	Adjusted ERA	Adjusted Starter Runs	Pitcher Wins
Gomez-NY 281.2	Gomez-NY 215	Gomez-NY...................282	Gomez-NY 2.33	Harder-Cle............174	Gomez-NY 59.3	**Harder-Cle**..........5.7
Bridges-Det........275.0	Ruffing-NY 236	Ruffing-NY 310	Harder-Cle 2.61	Gomez-NY............174	Harder-Cle 50.1	**Gomez-NY** 5.5
Rowe-Det 266.0	Bridges-Det...........241	Rowe-Det.....................312	Murphy-NY 3.13	Ostermueller-Bos 138	Rowe-Det 31.5	**Rowe-Det**............4.5
Newsom-StL......262.1	Burke-Was 245	Bridges-Det 312	Burke-Was 3.21	Burke-Was............134	Bridges-Det..........27.7	**Newsom-StL** 2.9
Ruffing-NY 256.1	Benton-Phi 249	Harder-Cle 316	Auker-Det 3.42	W.Ferrell-Bos 132	Ostermueller-Bos 26.5	**W.Ferrell-Bos** 2.8

Tigers Have AL by the Tail

For the first six weeks of the season, the Detroit Tigers, pennant-less since 1909, looked like nothing special. Then they began to win and shot up in the AL standings. By July, only the Yankees were a threat, and Detroit's 23–6 August put away the New Yorkers.

While the acquisitions of player-manager Mickey Cochrane and left fielder Goose Goslin helped push the Tigers over the hump, second baseman Charlie Gehringer and first baseman Hank Greenberg did most of the damage. Tommy Bridges won 16 straight games, and the pitching was deep if not spectacular. Second-place New York relied, uncharacteristically, on pitching rather than offense to contend. Lefty Gomez was now the league's top hurler and, aside from Triple Crown winner Lou Gehrig, the Yanks lacked big thumpers.

As the A's and Senators fell back into the second division, the Red Sox—last place finishers for most of the previous decade—bounded into fourth as new owner Tom Yawkey spent money on players like Billy Werber and Wes Ferrell. The pennant fever surrounding the Tigers and the increased interest in the Red Sox brought huge attendance gains as the overall league gate rose 29 percent.

Three ballparks were made smaller for the 1934 season. The Red Sox, who also replaced the wooden grandstands with concrete and steel, brought in the right-field fences at Fenway by 24 feet (after the fence had been pushed back a year earlier); the White Sox shrunk left and right field at Comiskey by 20 feet; and Detroit decreased left field at Briggs by 28 feet as AL ERA increased from 4.29 to 4.50.

The boisterous Cardinals bested the Tigers in a seven-game World Series, with the denouement an 11–0 debacle in Detroit. Angry fans threw so much debris at St. Louis left fielder Joe "Ducky" Medwick that he was removed from the game by Commissioner Landis for his own safety. The hometown crowd was mostly frustrated with their club, though, which couldn't win either of the final two games at home.

1935 National League

TEAM	W	L	T	PCT	GB	HW	HL	R	OR	PA	H	2B	3B	HR	BB	SO	HB	SH	AVG	OBP	SLG	OPS	AOPS	BR	ABR	PF	SB	CS	BSA	BSR
CHI	100	54	0	.649		**56**	21	**847**	**597**	6133	1581	**303**	62	88	**464**	471	**150**	**33**	**.288**	**.347**	.414	**761**	**110**	**86**	**81**	101	66			
STL	96	58	0	.623	4	53	24	829	625	5977	1548	286	59	86	404	521	97	19	.284	.335	.405	740	101	35	6	104	**71**			
NY	91	62	3	.595	8.5	50	27	770	675	6163	**1608**	248	56	**123**	392	479	116	32	.286	.336	**.416**	752	**110**	53	68	98	32			
PIT	86	67	0	.562	13.5	46	31	743	647	5973	1543	255	**90**	66	457	**437**	77	24	.285	.343	.402	745	103	48	24	103	30			
BRO	70	83	1	.458	29.5	38	38	711	767	5937	1496	235	62	59	430	520	70	27	.277	.333	.376	709	99	-23	-7	98	60			
CIN	68	85	1	.444	31.5	41	35	646	772	5798	1403	244	68	73	392	547	80	30	.265	.319	.378	697	96	-53	-32	97	72			
PHI	64	89	3	.418	35.5	35	43	685	871	5944	1466	249	32	92	392	661	84	26	.269	.322	.378	700	85	-47	-109	110	52			
BOS	38	115	0	.248	61.5	25	50	575	852	5761	1396	233	33	75	353	436	80	19	.263	.311	.362	673	93	-99	-47	92	20			
TOT	617					344	269	5806		47686	12041	2053	462	662	3284	4072	210	754	.277	.331	.391	722					403			

TEAM	CG	SHO	GR	SV	IP	H	HR	BB	SO	BR/9	ERA	AERA	OAV	OOB	PR	APR	PF	OSB	OCS	FA	E	WPB	DP	FW	PW	BW	BSW	DIF
CHI	**81**	12	118	14	1394.1	**1417**	85	400	589	11.9	**3.26**	**121**	.263	.317	**118**	**106**	98	45	*54*	.970	186	45	**163**	.3	**10.3**	**7.9**		4.5
STL	73	10	139	18	1384.2	1445	68	377	**602**	12.0	3.52	116	.267	.318	76	87	102	43	*12*	**.972**	**164**	34	133	**1.6**	8.5	.6		8.4
NY	76	10	134	11	1403.2	1433	106	411	524	12.0	3.78	102	**.262**	.318	37	12	96	46	*40*	**.972**	174	46	129	1.1	1.2	6.6		5.6
PIT	76	**15**	118	11	1365.2	1428	**63**	**312**	549	**11.6**	3.42	120	.265	**.307**	91	101	102	64	*41*	.968	190	34	94	.0	9.8	2.3		-2.7
BRO	62	11	145	**20**	1358.0	1519	88	436	480	13.1	4.22	94	.281	.337	-31	-37	99	**42**	*44*	.969	188	49	146	.2	-3.6	-.7		-2.4
CIN	59	9	161	12	1356.0	1490	65	438	500	13.0	4.30	93	.278	.336	-43	-50	99	52	*50*	.966	204	40	139	-.7	-4.9	-3.1		.2
PHI	53	8	**202**	15	1374.2	1652	106	505	475	14.4	4.76	95	.295	.358	-113	-31	113	50	*34*	.963	228	28	145	-2.0	-3.0	-10.6		3.1
BOS	54	6	136	5	1330.0	1645	81	404	355	14.0	4.93	77	.303	.354	-135	-180	94	61	*33*	.967	197	**21**	101	-.4	-17.5	-4.6		-16.0
TOT	534	81	1153	106	10967.0					12.7	4.02		.277	.331						.968	1531	297	1050					

Batter-Fielder Wins
- **Vaughan-Pit** 6.6
- **Herman-Chi** 5.2
- **Hartnett-Chi**........4.7
- **Berger-Bos**..........4.4
- **Ott-NY** 4.2

Batting Average
- Vaughan-Pit 385
- Medwick-StL.........353
- Hartnett-Chi 344
- Lombardi-Cin 343
- Herman-Chi 341

On-Base Percentage
- Vaughan-Pit 491
- Ott-NY 407
- Hack-Chi 406
- Galan-Chi 399
- P.Waner-Pit 392

Slugging Average
- Vaughan-Pit 607
- Medwick-StL.........576
- Ott-NY 555
- Berger-Bos 548
- Hartnett-Chi 545

On-Base Plus Slugging
- Vaughan-Pit........1098
- Medwick-StL 962
- Ott-NY 962
- R.Collins-StL 915
- Berger-Bos 903

Adjusted OPS
- Vaughan-Pit..........187
- Ott-NY 159
- Berger-Bos 151
- Medwick-StL 149
- Leiber-NY 143

Adjusted Batter Runs
- Vaughan-Pit........69.2
- Ott-NY 51.1
- Medwick-StL 41.6
- Berger-Bos 40.3
- Leiber-NY 37.4

Runs
- Galan-Chi 133
- Medwick-StL 132
- Martin-StL 121
- Ott-NY 113
- Herman-Chi..........113

Hits
- Herman-Chi..........227
- Medwick-StL 224

Doubles
- Herman-Chi 57
- Medwick-StL.................46
- Allen-Phi 46
- Martin-StL.....................41
- Galan-Chi 41

Triples
- Goodman-Cin 18
- L.Waner-Pit 14
- Medwick-StL 13

Home Runs
- Berger-Bos 34
- Ott-NY 31
- Camilli-Phi 25
- Medwick-StL 23
- R.Collins-StL 23

Total Bases
- Medwick-StL 365
- Ott-NY 329
- Berger-Bos 323
- Herman-Chi..........317
- Leiber-NY 314

Runs Batted In
- Berger-Bos 130
- Medwick-StL.........126
- R.Collins-StL 122
- Ott-NY 114
- Leiber-NY 107

Stolen Bases
- Galan-Chi 22
- Martin-StL...............20
- Bordagaray-Bro 18
- Hack-Chi 14
- Goodman-Cin 14

Base Stealing Runs

Fielding Runs-Infield
- Jurges-Chi 24.9
- Herman-Chi 16.0
- Cuccinello-Bro 8.1
- Riggs-Cin......................8.1
- Stripp-Bro 7.1

Fielding Runs-Outfield
- Allen-Phi 12.7
- Berger-Bos 9.2
- T.Moore-StL 6.8
- Lee-Bos 6.1
- Goodman-Cin 5.1

Wins
- D.Dean-StL 28
- Hubbell-NY 23
- Derringer-Cin..........22
- Warneke-Chi 20
- Lee-Chi 20

Winning Pct.
- Lee-Chi.................769
- Castleman-NY 714
- D.Dean-StL..........700
- Schumacher-NY ...679
- Hubbell-NY...........657

Complete Games
- D.Dean-StL...........29
- Hubbell-NY...........24
- Blanton-Pit 23
- Warneke-Chi 20
- Derringer-Cin 20

Strikeouts
- D.Dean-StL 190
- Hubbell-NY 150
- Mungo-Bro............143
- P.Dean-StL............143
- Blanton-Pit............142

Fewest BB/Game
- Clark-Bro 1.22
- Hubbell-NY..........1.46
- Hoyt-Pit................1.48
- Derringer-Cin 1.59
- Johnson-Phi 1.60

Games
- Jorgens-Phi....................53
- D.Dean-StL 50
- Bivin-Phi 47
- Smith-Bos 46
- P.Dean-StL 46

Saves
- Leonard-Bro 8
- Johnson-Phi.............6
- Hoyt-Pit 6

Base Runners/9
- Blanton-Pit 9.80
- Swift-Pit 10.21
- Clark-Bro 10.61
- Warneke-Chi......10.66
- Schumacher-NY 10.66

Adjusted Relief Runs

Relief Ranking

Innings Pitched
- D.Dean-StL........325.1
- Hubbell-NY........302.2
- Derringer-Cin 276.2
- P.Dean-StL 269.2

Opponents' Avg.
- Blanton-Pit 229
- Schumacher-NY ...238
- Hollingsworth-Cin ...243
- Swift-Pit 247
- P.Dean-StL 249

Opponents' OBP
- Blanton-Pit 272
- Swift-Pit 282
- Clark-Bro 289
- Schumacher-NY 292
- P.Dean-StL 292

Earned Run Average
- Blanton-Pit 2.58
- Swift-Pit 2.70
- Schumacher-NY ..2.89
- French-Chi 2.96
- Lee-Chi...............2.96

Adjusted ERA
- Blanton-Pit............159
- Swift-Pit 152
- D.Dean-StL 135
- Schumacher-NY ..133
- French-Chi............133

Adjusted Starter Runs
- Blanton-Pit 41.3
- D.Dean-StL..........37.8
- Swift-Pit 31.2
- French-Chi 27.9
- Schumacher-NY ..27.5

Pitcher Wins
- **D.Dean-StL** 4.5
- **Blanton-Pit** 4.4
- **Swift-Pit**..............3.3
- **Warneke-Chi** 3.3
- **Schumacher-NY**3.2

And there Was Light

Once again, the Giants started fast but flattened; by August, the dangerous Cardinals took over the league lead. But the Cubs had a surprise in store. In third place on Labor Day, Chicago captured 21 straight and won the pennant by besting Dizzy and Paul Dean in St. Louis September 25–26. Lon Warneke and Bill Lee won 20 apiece for Chicago, which led the league in both runs and ERA.

Other than Joe Medwick and Ripper Collins, St. Louis lacked offense, despite playing in a hitter's park. Chicago had a great defensive infield and topped the loop in walks and doubles. Third-place New York had Carl Hubbell and Mel Ott, but lacked depth. On the other side of the world, the Boston Braves were the NL's worst team ever, declining 40 games from their previous year's performance. Even a cameo by Babe Ruth couldn't save a team that posted just one good position player, outfielder Wally Berger.

The majors' first night game took place at Cincinnati on May 24. The Reds played 8 night games in 1935, and the excitement helped to raise team attendance 117 percent. Other clubs with poor gates noted Cincinnati's success and planned accordingly. League attendance rose 14 percent and would continue to increase throughout the decade.

Dodgers outfielder Len Koenecke, fifth in the NL in on-base percentage in 1934, had a mediocre season. On September 17 he became violent on a plane after being sent to the minors. When he assaulted a pilot, he was beaten to death with a fire extinguisher. Three longtime stars played their final games. Complications from a broken leg shut down shortstop Rabbit Maranville, while pitchers Dolf Luque and Dazzy Vance made their last appearances.

The Cubs outhomered the Tigers in the World Series, 5–1, but the 25 walks issued by Chicago made the difference in a tight six-game affair. Although Warneke won twice, the Cubs were left standing on the field—as they had been in 1929—to watch a foe celebrate a bottom-of-the-ninth clincher.

1935 American League

TEAM	W	L	T	PCT	GB	HW	HL	R	OR	PA	H	2B	3B	HR	BB	SO	HB	SH	AVG	OBP	SLG	OPS	AOPS	BR	ABR	PF	SB	CS	BSA	BSR
DET	93	58	1	.616		**53**	25	**919**	665	6179	**1573**	301	**83**	**106**	**627**	456	110	19	**.290**	**.366**	**.435**	**801**	**116**	**97**	**129**	97	70	45	61	0
NY	89	60	0	.597	3	41	33	818	**632**	5917	1462	255	70	104	604	469	71	**28**	.280	.358	.416	774	111	42	89	94	68	46	60	-1
CLE	82	71	3	.536	12	48	29	776	739	6099	**1573**	**324**	77	93	460	567	88	17	.284	.341	.421	762	100	3	-11	102	63	54	54	-5
BOS	78	75	1	.510	16	41	37	718	732	6055	1458	281	63	69	609	470	**137**	21	.276	.353	.392	745	92	-9	-57	107	**91**	59	61	-1
CHI	74	78	1	.487	19.5	42	34	738	750	6025	1460	262	42	74	580	**405**	112	19	.275	.348	.382	730	92	-40	-58	103	46	28	**62**	0
WAS	67	86	1	.438	27	37	39	823	903	6299	1591	255	95	32	596	406	74	37	.285	.357	.381	738	99	-22	5	97	54	37	59	-1
STL	65	87	3	.428	28.5	31	44	718	930	6088	1446	291	51	73	593	561	116	14	.270	.344	.384	728	90	-47	-79	105	45	25	64	1
PHI	58	91	0	.389	34	30	42	710	869	5847	1470	243	44	112	475	602	86	17	.279	.341	.406	747	99	-25	-19	99	43	35	55	-3
TOT	611					323	283	6220		48509	12033	2212	525	663	4544	3936	172	794	.280	.351	.402	753					480	329	59	-10

TEAM	CG	SHO	GR	SV	IP	H	HR	BB	SO	BR/9	ERA	AERA	OAV	OOB	PR	APR	PF	OSB	OCS	FA	E	WPB	DP	FW	PW	BW	BSW	DIF
DET	**87**	**16**	95	11	1364.0	1440	78	522	584	13.1	3.82	109	.271	.339	96	57	94	**44**	41	**.978**	**128**	26	154	**2.3**	5.3	**12.1**	.1	-2.3
NY	76	12	120	13	1331.0	**1276**	91	516	**594**	**12.2**	**3.60**	112	**.251**	**.321**	**126**	72	91	**44**	35	.974	151	30	114	.8	6.7	8.3	.0	-1.4
CLE	67	12	138	**21**	1396.0	1527	68	**457**	498	12.9	4.15	108	.278	.335	47	54	101	54	37	.972	177	**24**	147	-.3	5.1	-1.0	-.4	2.1
BOS	82	6	138	11	1376.0	1520	**67**	520	470	13.5	4.05	**117**	.280	.346	62	**100**	107	49	**55**	.969	194	33	136	-1.4	**9.4**	-5.3	.0	-1.2
CHI	80	8	102	8	1360.2	1443	105	574	436	13.5	4.38	106	.272	.346	12	35	104	71	43	.976	146	44	133	1.3	3.3	-5.4	.1	-1.3
WAS	67	5	143	12	1378.2	1672	89	613	456	15.1	5.25	82	.302	.374	-122	-146	97	80	34	.972	171	44	**186**	-.0	-13.7	.5	.0	3.7
STL	42	4	**219**	15	1380.1	1667	92	641	435	15.2	5.26	91	.297	.371	-124	-67	108	54	35	.970	187	38	138	-.9	-6.3	-7.4	**.2**	3.4
PHI	58	7	148	10	1326.1	1486	73	704	469	15.0	5.12	89	.285	.372	-97	-83	102	84	49	.968	190	46	150	-1.4	-7.8	-1.8	-.2	-5.3
TOT	559	70	1103	101	10913.0					13.8	4.46		.280	.351						.972	1344	285	1158					

Batter-Fielder Wins	Batting Average	On-Base Percentage	Slugging Average	On-Base Plus Slugging	Adjusted OPS	Adjusted Batter Runs
Foxx-Phi 5.9	Myer-Was .349	Gehrig-NY .466	Foxx-Phi .636	Foxx-Phi 1096	Foxx-Phi 182	Gehrig-NY 71.7
Myer-Was 5.3	Vosmik-Cle .348	Foxx-Phi .461	Greenberg-Det .628	Gehrig-NY 1049	Gehrig-NY 180	Foxx-Phi 70.0
Gehrig-NY 5.3	Foxx-Phi .346	Cochrane-Det .452	Gehrig-NY .583	Greenberg-Det 1039	Greenberg-Det 171	Greenberg-Det 63.7
Appling-Chi 5.1	Cramer-Phi .332	Myer-Was .440	Vosmik-Cle .537	Vosmik-Cle 946	Vosmik-Cle 140	Myer-Was 41.8
Greenberg-Det 5.0	Gehringer-Det .330	Appling-Chi .437	Fox-Det .513	Gehringer-Det 911	Myer-Was 139	Gehringer-Det 36.8

Runs	Hits	Doubles	Triples	Home Runs	Total Bases	Runs Batted In
Gehrig-NY 125	Vosmik-Cle 216	Vosmik-Cle 47	Vosmik-Cle 20	Greenberg-Det 36	Greenberg-Det 389	Greenberg-Det 170
Gehringer-Det 123	Myer-Was 215	Greenberg-Det 46	Stone-Was 18	Foxx-Phi 36	Foxx-Phi 340	Gehrig-NY 119
Greenberg-Det 121	Cramer-Phi 214	Solters-Bos-StL 45	Greenberg-Det 16	Gehrig-NY 30	Vosmik-Cle 333	Foxx-Phi 115
Foxx-Phi 118	Greenberg-Det 203	Fox-Det 38	Cronin-Bos 14	Johnson-Phi 28	Solters-Bos-StL 314	Trosky-Cle 113
Chapman-NY 118		Chapman-NY 38	Averill-Cle 13	Trosky-Cle 26	Gehrig-NY 312	Solters-Bos-StL 112

Stolen Bases	Base Stealing Runs	Fielding Runs-Infield	Fielding Runs-Outfield	Wins	Winning Pct.	Complete Games
Werber-Bos 29	Lary-Was-StL 4.8	Appling-Chi 24.9	Solters-Bos-StL 13.5	W.Ferrell-Bos 25	Auker-Det .720	W.Ferrell-Bos 31
Lary-Was-StL 28	Werber-Bos 3.9	Travis-Was 19.2	Chapman-NY 13.4	Harder-Cle 22	Broaca-NY .682	Grove-Bos 23
Almada-Bos 20	Hughes-Cle 1.8	Melillo-StL-Bos 17.0	West-StL 11.4	Bridges-Det 21	Bridges-Det .677	Bridges-Det 23
White-Det 19	Solters-Bos-StL 1.7	Werber-Bos 13.6	Selkirk-NY 5.0	Grove-Bos 20	Harder-Cle .667	Rowe-Det 21
Chapman-NY 17		Berger-Cle 12.1	Johnson-Phi 4.1	Rowe-Det 19	Lyons-Chi .652	

Strikeouts	Fewest BB/Game	Games	Saves	Base Runners/9	Adjusted Relief Runs	Relief Ranking
Bridges-Det 163	Harder-Cle 1.66	VanAtta-NY-StL 58	Knott-StL 7	Grove-Bos 11.11	L.Brown-Cle 13.7	L.Brown-Cle 16.2
Rowe-Det 140	Grove-Bos 2.14	Walkup-StL 55		Rowe-Det 11.17	Hogsett-Det 6.6	Hogsett-Det 8.2
Gomez-NY 138	Rowe-Det 2.22	Andrews-StL 50		Ruffing-NY 11.27	DeShong-NY 6.5	DeShong-NY 4.9
Grove-Bos 121	Andrews-StL 2.24	Thomas-StL 49		Allen-NY 11.37	Wilson-Bos 3.7	Wilson-Bos 3.8
Allen-NY 113	Hudlin-Cle 2.37	Knott-StL 48		Gomez-NY 11.38		

Innings Pitched	Opponents' Avg.	Opponents' OBP	Earned Run Average	Adjusted ERA	Adjusted Starter Runs	Pitcher Wins
W.Ferrell-Bos 322.1	Allen-NY .238	Rowe-Det .301	Grove-Bos 2.70	Grove-Bos 176	Grove-Bos 55.0	**W.Ferrell-Bos** 6.8
Harder-Cle 287.1	Ruffing-NY .239	Grove-Bos .302	Lyons-Chi 3.02	Lyons-Chi 153	W.Ferrell-Bos 41.2	**Grove-Bos** 5.5
Whitehill-Was 279.1	Gomez-NY .242	Ruffing-NY .303	Ruffing-NY 3.12	Harder-Cle 137	Harder-Cle 38.6	**Ruffing-NY** 4.2
Rowe-Det 275.2	Whitehead-Chi .250	Allen-NY .307	Gomez-NY 3.18	Andrews-StL 135	Lyons-Chi 29.9	**Harder-Cle** 4.1
Bridges-Det 274.1	Broaca-NY .254	Harder-Cle .307	Harder-Cle 3.29	W.Ferrell-Bos 135	Andrews-StL 28.3	**Rowe-Det** 3.2

Tigers Finally Destroy Prey

After a quick start by the White Sox, the AL race became a five-team mess in June. The Yankees tried to pull away, but a hot July propelled the Detroit Tigers into the lead. Detroit kept winning, and despite a late slump held off New York to win its second straight pennant. The Yankees had an excellent strikeout-oriented pitching staff, but couldn't score runs like the Tigers, who had offense from seven lineup spots and boasted four quality starting pitchers. The Tigers' success led to a financial windfall as they became the first AL club to draw one million fans since 1930.

Meanwhile, in St. Louis, the Browns drew just 80,000 fans. This horrible total is partially due to club's playing 19 home doubleheaders. Three times during the 1930s, however, the Brownies pulled in fewer than 100,000 fans for the season. The last team before the Browns to draw less than six figures was the 1917 Senators; when St. Louis drew 93,000 a year later, it marked the last time anyone has gone below six figures. Connie Mack's Athletics, all their talent now distributed through the league, predictably drew 62 percent fewer fans than had come to witness the A's last pennant four years earlier. They would finish either last or seventh every year until 1943.

It was the end of an era as three glory-days Yankees retired. Babe Ruth played his last game not in the Bronx, but for the Boston Braves; center fielder Earle Combs' career was ended by a broken collarbone; and pitcher Sad Sam Jones was done at 43.

The six-game World Series featured three games decided by one-run, with Detroit winning two in its final turn. Game 6, played to 48,420 screaming fans in Detroit, climaxed with Goose Goslin's ninth-inning single scoring Mickey Cochrane for the Series-winning run. It was the Tigers' first world championship in their thirty-five-year history. Tommy Bridges won twice for Detroit, while unheralded outfielder Pete Fox batted .385.

1936 National League

TEAM	W	L	T	PCT	GB	HW	HL	R	OR	PA	H	2B	3B	HR	BB	SO	HB	SH	AVG	OBP	SLG	OPS	AOPS	BR	ABR	PF	SB	CS	BSA	BSR
NY	92	62	0	.597		**52**	26	742	621	6038	1529	237	48	**97**	431	**452**	123	**35**	.281	.337	.395	732	104	18	26	99	31			
STL	87	67	1	.565	5	43	33	795	794	6065	1554	**332**	60	88	442	577	71	15	.281	.336	**.410**	**746**	**106**	44	**47**	100	**69**			
CHI	87	67	0	.565	5	50	27	755	**603**	6069	1545	275	36	76	491	462	**137**	32	**.286**	**.349**	.392	741	104	48	31	102	68			
PIT	84	70	2	.545	8	46	30	**804**	718	6211	**1596**	283	**80**	60	**517**	502	82	26	**.286**	**.349**	.397	**746**	105	**57**	39	102	37			
CIN	74	80	0	.481	18	42	34	722	760	5904	1476	224	73	82	410	584	67	34	.274	.329	.388	717	**106**	-18	29	94	68			
BOS	71	83	3	.461	21	35	43	631	715	6041	1450	207	45	67	433	582	99	31	.265	.322	.356	678	94	-90	-46	94	23			
BRO	67	87	2	.435	25	37	40	662	752	6068	1518	263	43	33	390	458	79	25	.272	.323	.353	676	87	-93	-99	101	55			
PHI	54	100	0	.351	38	30	48	726	874	6040	1538	250	46	103	451	586	103	21	.281	.339	.401	740	95	32	-37	110	50			
TOT	620					335	281	5837		48436	12206	2071	431	606	3565	4203	219	761	.278	.335	.386	722					401			

TEAM	CG	SHO	GR	SV	IP	H	HR	BB	SO	BR/9	ERA	AERA	OAV	OOB	PR	APR	PF	OSB	OCS	FA	E	WPB	DP	FW	PW	BW	BSW	DIF
NY	60	12	148	22	1385.2	1458	75	401	500	12.2	**3.46**	**113**	.273	.327	**86**	**69**	97	40	*48*	.974	168	34	164	1.1	**6.7**	2.5		4.6
STL	65	5	166	**24**	1398.0	1610	89	434	559	13.4	4.47	88	.289	.344	-71	-85	98	41	*39*	.974	156	50	134	1.9	-8.3	**4.6**		11.9
CHI	**77**	**18**	139	10	1382.1	**1413**	77	434	597	12.2	3.54	**113**	**.265**	.324	74	**69**	99	39	*46*	**.976**	**146**	34	156	**2.4**	**6.7**	3.0		-2.1
PIT	67	5	137	12	1395.1	1475	74	**379**	559	**12.1**	3.89	104	.269	**.319**	20	25	101	68	*44*	.967	199	31	113	-.5	2.4	3.8		1.3
CIN	50	6	161	23	1367.1	1576	**51**	418	459	13.3	4.22	91	.287	.341	-31	-64	95	48	*46*	.969	191	46	150	-.2	-6.2	2.8		.6
BOS	61	7	134	13	1413.1	1566	69	451	421	13.0	3.94	97	.281	.337	12	-18	95	**38**	*43*	.971	189	**26**	**175**	.1	-1.8	-4.5		.1
BRO	59	7	**169**	18	1403.0	1466	84	528	**651**	13.0	3.98	104	.266	.333	5	21	103	76	*47*	.966	208	43	107	-1.0	2.0	-9.7		-1.4
PHI	51	7	**169**	14	1365.1	1630	87	515	454	14.4	4.64	98	.292	.356	-95	-15	113	51	*33*	.959	252	33	144	-3.7	-1.5	-3.6		-14.3
TOT	490	67	1223	136	11110.1					12.9	4.02		.278	.335						.969	1509	297	1143					

Batter-Fielder Wins
Bartell-NY............5.7
Medwick-StL 5.2
Herman-Chi 5.2
Ott-NY 4.8
P.Waner-Pit.........4.7

Batting Average
P.Waner-Pit 373
Phelps-Bro 367
Medwick-StL.........351
Demaree-Chi 350
Vaughan-Pit 335

On-Base Percentage
Vaughan-Pit.................453
Ott-NY 448
P.Waner-Pit 446
Camilli-Phi 441
Suhr-Pit 410

Slugging Average
Ott-NY 588
Camilli-Phi 577
Mize-StL 577
Medwick-StL.........577
P.Waner-Pit 520

On-Base Plus Slugging
Ott-NY 1036
Camilli-Phi 1018
P.Waner-Pit 965
Medwick-StL 964
Vaughan-Pit..........927

Adjusted OPS
Ott-NY 179
Medwick-StL 157
Camilli-Phi 156
P.Waner-Pit 156
Vaughan-Pit..........146

Adjusted Batter Runs
Ott-NY 65.1
P.Waner-Pit 50.7
Medwick-StL 49.1
Camilli-Phi..........46.7
Vaughan-Pit........45.7

Runs
Vaughan-Pit..........122
P.Martin-StL 121
Ott-NY 120
Medwick-StL 115
Suhr-Pit 111

Hits
Medwick-StL 223
P.Waner-Pit 218
Demaree-Chi........212
Herman-Chi..........211
Moore-NY 205

Doubles
Medwick-StL.................64
Herman-Chi 57
P.Waner-Pit 53
Moore-StL.....................39
Moore-Bos 38

Triples
Goodman-Cin 14
Medwick-StL 13
Camilli-Phi 13

Home Runs
Ott-NY 33
Camilli-Phi 28
Klein-Chi-Phi 25
Berger-Bos 25
Mize-StL 19

Total Bases
Medwick-StL 367
Ott-NY 314
Klein-Chi-Phi 308
Camilli-Phi 306
P.Waner-Pit 304

Runs Batted In
Medwick-StL........138
Ott-NY 135
Suhr-Pit 118
Klein-Chi-Phi 104

Stolen Bases
P.Martin-StL 23
S.Martin-StL 17
Hack-Chi 17
Chiozza-Phi 17

Base Stealing Runs

Fielding Runs-Infield
Bartell-NY 42.6
Whitehead-NY 32.1
Kampouris-Cin............22.4
Cuccinello-Bos............17.6
Herman-Chi 17.0

Fielding Runs-Outfield
Medwick-StL........14.0
Moore-Bos 13.1
Moore-StL............13.0
Cooney-Bro 8.5
Moore-NY 8.3

Wins
Hubbell-NY 26
D.Dean-StL 24
Derringer-Cin..........19

Winning Pct.
Hubbell-NY...........813
Lucas-Pit 789
French-Chi 667
D.Dean-StL 649
Lee-Chi.................621

Complete Games
D.Dean-StL............28
Hubbell-NY............25
Mungo-Bro 22
MacFayden-Bos 21
Lee-Chi..................20

Strikeouts
Mungo-Bro............238
D.Dean-StL 195
Blanton-Pit............127
Hubbell-NY 123
Derringer-Cin........121

Fewest BB/Game
Lucas-Pit 1.33
Derringer-Cin 1.34
D.Dean-StL 1.51
Hubbell-NY 1.69
Gabler-NY............1.89

Games
Derringer-Cin 51
D.Dean-StL 51
Passeau-Phi 49
Brown-Pit 47

Saves
D.Dean-StL 11
Brennan-Cin 9
Smith-Bos 8
Johnson-Phi.............7
Coffman-NY..............7

Base Runners/9
Hubbell-NY..........9.68
D.Dean-StL.........10.46
Lucas-Pit 10.61
Hoyt-Pit.............10.65
Blanton-Pit 11.19

Adjusted Relief Runs
Johnson-Phi 4.6
Bryant-Chi 3.6
Root-Chi 3

Relief Ranking
Johnson-Phi 5.1
Bryant-Chi 1.8
Root-Chi 3

Innings Pitched
D.Dean-StL........315.0
Mungo-Bro 311.2
Hubbell-NY........304.0
Derringer-Cin 282.1
MacFayden-Bos 266.2

Opponents' Avg.
Mungo-Bro 234
Hubbell-NY...........236
Lee-Chi.................246
D.Dean-StL...........253
Blanton-Pit 257

Opponents' OBP
Hubbell-NY 276
D.Dean-StL 285
Lucas-Pit 287
Blanton-Pit...................301
Mungo-Bro...................305

Earned Run Average
Hubbell-NY..........2.31
MacFayden-Bos ..2.87
Gabler-NY............3.12
D.Dean-StL..........3.17
Lucas-Pit 3.18

Adjusted ERA
Hubbell-NY 169
MacFayden-Bos....134
Passeau-Phi 130
Lucas-Pit 128
Gabler-NY 125

Adjusted Starter Runs
Hubbell-NY 59.6
MacFayden-Bos ..30.4
Mungo-Bro 27.6
D.Dean-StL 26.9
Lee-Chi................19.3

Pitcher Wins
Hubbell-NY 6.2
D.Dean-StL 3.0
MacFayden-Bos 2.8
Mungo-Bro 2.7
Passeau-Phi 2.4

King Carl Reigns

After two years of late-season collapses, it was the Giants' turn to make a big run down the stretch. Tied for fourth place with a .500 record in mid-July, the Giants went on a 34–5 tear, moving from 10_ down to 3 up by the end of August. New York held on for dear life in September to claim the pennant.

The Giants rode to the flag on the left arm of King Carl Hubbell, who won his last 15 decisions, paced the league in ERA by more than half a run, and garnered league MVP honors. Seven Giants pitchers made 10 or more starts as manager Bill Terry searched for rotation depth. Shortstop Dick Bartell had a big year in the field and at bat, while Mel Ott led the league in homers for third of his six times. Three Giants of classic vintage—Travis Jackson, Freddie Lindstrom, and Terry—played in their last big league games.

While the second-place Cubs had excellent and very deep starting pitching, their attack was poor. Charlie Grimm ended his 20-year playing career as a player, but Jolly Cholly, the 1935 pennant still under his belt, remained as manager in his first of three stints at the helm of the Cubbies. Joe Medwick of the third-place Cardinals led the league in hits, RBIs, and doubles (64, a league record). St. Louis also benefited from the efforts of rookie first baseman Johnny Mize, who hit .329 with 19 homers.

While the Pirates had two great offensive players in Paul Waner, who won his third batting title, and shortstop Arky Vaughan, who paced the NL in on-base percentage for the third straight season. Mediocre pitching doomed the Bucs to fourth.

In the World Series, the thin Giants staff was battered around by the Yankees, who won in six games. Only Hubbell, 1–1 with a 2.25 ERA, escaped relatively unscathed.

1936 American League

TEAM	W	L	T	PCT	GB	HW	HL	R	OR	PA	H	2B	3B	HR	BB	SO	HB	SH	AVG	OBP	SLG	OPS	AOPS	BR	ABR	PF	SB	CS	BSA	BSR
NY	102	51	2	.667		**56**	21	**1065**	**731**	6391	1676	315	83	**182**	**700**	594	67	33	.300	**.381**	**.483**	**864**	**124**	**164**	**203**	97	77	40	66	3
DET	83	71	0	.539	19.5	44	33	921	871	6226	1638	326	55	94	640	462	88	**34**	.300	.377	.431	808	106	61	58	100	73	49	60	-1
CHI	81	70	2	.536	20	43	32	920	873	6283	1597	282	56	60	684	417	**107**	26	.292	.374	.397	771	94	-8	-39	104	66	29	69	4
WAS	82	71	0	.536	20	42	35	889	799	6094	1601	293	**84**	62	576	**398**	61	24	.295	.365	.414	779	105	-9	42	94	**104**	42	**71**	**8**
CLE	80	74	3	.519	22.5	49	30	921	862	6253	**1715**	**357**	82	123	514	470	77	16	**.304**	.364	.461	825	109	71	63	101	66	53	55	-4
BOS	74	80	1	.481	28.5	47	29	775	764	6098	1485	288	62	86	584	465	108	23	.276	.349	.400	749	86	-73	-116	106	55	44	56	-3
STL	57	95	3	.375	44.5	31	43	804	1064	6107	1502	299	66	79	625	627	72	19	.279	.356	.403	759	91	-51	-73	103	62	20	76	7
PHI	53	100	1	.346	49	31	46	714	1045	5990	1443	240	60	72	524	590	74	19	.269	.336	.376	712	84	-156	-142	98	59	43	58	-2
TOT	618					343	269	7009		49442	12657	2400	548	758	4847	4023	194	654	.289	.363	.421	784					562	320	64	12

TEAM	CG	SHO	GR	SV	IP	H	HR	BB	SO	BR/9	ERA	AERA	OAV	OOB	PR	APR	PF	OSB	OCS	FA	E	WPB	DP	FW	PW	BW	BSW	DIF
NY	77	6	119	**21**	1400.1	**1474**	84	663	**624**	13.8	**4.17**	112	**.271**	.351	**135**	81	92	**47**	43	.973	163	41	148	.8	7.2	**17.9**	.1	-.5
DET	76	**13**	127	13	1360.0	1568	100	562	526	14.2	5.00	99	.289	.358	6	-7	98	58	30	**.975**	**153**	49	159	**1.3**	-.6	5.1	-.2	.4
CHI	**80**	5	104	8	1365.0	1603	104	578	414	14.5	5.06	103	.293	.363	-4	20	103	58	46	.973	168	43	**174**	.4	1.8	-3.4	.2	6.6
WAS	78	8	112	14	1345.2	1484	**73**	588	462	14.0	4.58	104	.279	.353	68	31	95	73	**47**	.970	182	47	163	-.4	2.7	3.7	**.6**	-1.1
CLE	74	6	155	12	1389.1	1604	**73**	607	619	14.5	4.83	104	.289	.362	32	32	100	75	46	.971	178	59	154	.0	2.8	5.6	-.5	-5.0
BOS	78	11	143	9	1372.1	1501	78	**552**	584	**13.6**	4.39	**121**	.277	**.346**	99	**134**	106	81	44	.972	165	**37**	139	.7	**11.8**	-10.2	-.4	-4.9
STL	54	3	**193**	13	1348.1	1776	115	609	399	16.2	6.24	86	.314	.385	-180	-122	107	69	25	.969	188	53	143	-.6	-10.8	-6.4	.5	-1.6
PHI	68	3	130	12	1352.1	1645	131	696	405	15.7	6.08	84	.300	.381	-156	-144	101	101	39	.965	209	91	152	-1.9	-12.7	-12.5	-.3	3.9
TOT	585	55	1083	102	10933.1					14.6	5.04		.289	.363						.971	1406	420	1232					

Batter-Fielder Wins
- **Gehrig-NY**............6.6
- **Gehringer-Det** 6.1
- **Appling-Chi** 5.4
- **Dickey-NY** 4.2
- **Averill-Cle**............3.8

Batting Average
- Appling-Chi...........388
- Averill-Cle 378
- Dickey-NY.............362
- Gehringer-Det.......354
- Gehrig-NY 354

On-Base Percentage
- Gehrig-NY 478
- Appling-Chi 474
- Foxx-Bos 440
- Averill-Cle....................438
- Gehringer-Det 431

Slugging Average
- Gehrig-NY 696
- Trosky-Cle 644
- Foxx-Bos...............631
- Averill-Cle 627
- Dickey-NY.............617

On-Base Plus Slugging
- Gehrig-NY 1174
- Foxx-Bos 1071
- Averill-Cle 1065
- Trosky-Cle 1026
- Gehringer-Det 987

Adjusted OPS
- Gehrig-NY 193
- Averill-Cle 159
- Foxx-Bos 153
- Trosky-Cle 148
- Stone-Was............145

Adjusted Batter Runs
- Gehrig-NY 90.9
- Averill-Cle 55.2
- Foxx-Bos 49.2
- Gehringer-Det 44.4
- Trosky-Cle 40.9

Runs
- Gehrig-NY 167
- Clift-StL 145
- Gehringer-Det 144
- Crosetti-NY 137
- Averill-Cle 136

Hits
- Averill-Cle 232
- Gehringer-Det 227
- Trosky-Cle 216
- Bell-StL 212
- Radcliff-Chi 207

Doubles
- Gehringer-Det................60
- Walker-Det 55
- Chapman-NY-Was 50
- Hale-Cle 50

Triples
- Rolfe-NY 15
- DiMaggio-NY..........15
- Averill-Cle 15
- B.Johnson-Phi 14

Home Runs
- Gehrig-NY 49
- Trosky-Cle 42
- Foxx-Bos 41
- DiMaggio-NY..........29
- Averill-Cle 28

Total Bases
- Trosky-Cle 405
- Gehrig-NY 403
- Averill-Cle 385
- Foxx-Bos 369
- DiMaggio-NY........367

Runs Batted In
- Trosky-Cle 162
- Gehrig-NY 152
- Foxx-Bos 143
- Bonura-Chi..........138
- Solters-StL 134

Stolen Bases
- Lary-StL..................37
- Powell-Was-NY 26
- Werber-Bos 23
- Chapman-NY-Was..20
- Hughes-Cle 20

Base Stealing Runs
- Lary-StL 5.0
- Hill-Was 2.4
- Powell-Was-NY......1.9
- Stone-Was 1.8
- Sewell-Chi 1.7

Fielding Runs-Infield
- Hale-Cle.......................16.7
- Gehringer-Det 15.6
- Appling-Chi 14.8
- Hayes-Chi 13.4
- Bonura-Chi..................11.0

Fielding Runs-Outfield
- Solters-StL 12.5
- Cramer-Bos 11.4
- DiMaggio-NY 8.1
- West-StL................6.4
- Stone-Was 5.8

Wins
- Bridges-Det 23
- Kennedy-Chi 21
- Ruffing-NY..............20
- W.Ferrell-Bos 20
- Allen-Cle 20

Winning Pct.
- Pearson-NY 731
- Kennedy-Chi.........700
- Bridges-Det..........676
- Allen-Cle..............667
- Rowe-Det 655

Complete Games
- W.Ferrell-Bos 28
- Bridges-Det 26
- Ruffing-NY 25
- Newsom-Was........24
- Grove-Bos 22

Strikeouts
- Bridges-Det 175
- Allen-Cle 165
- Newsom-Was 156
- Grove-Bos 130
- Pearson-NY..........118

Fewest BB/Game
- Lyons-Chi 2.23
- Grove-Bos 2.31
- Rowe-Det 2.35
- Andrews-StL........2.35
- Marcum-Bos 2.69

Games
- VanAtta-StL 52
- Knott-StL.......................47

Saves
- Malone-NY 9
- Knott-StL 6
- Murphy-NY 5
- Brown-Chi 5
- Hildebrand-Cle..........4

Base Runners/9
- Grove-Bos 10.87
- Walberg-Bos......12.11
- Rowe-Det 12.18
- Ruffing-NY 12.19
- Allen-Cle...........12.30

Adjusted Relief Runs
- Brown-Chi..............2.9
- Gumpert-Phi.............5

Relief Ranking
- Brown-Chi 2.9
- Gumpert-Phi 2

Innings Pitched
- W.Ferrell-Bos 301.0
- Bridges-Det........294.2
- Newsom-Was 285.2
- Kennedy-Chi......274.1
- Ruffing-NY 271.0

Opponents' Avg.
- Pearson-NY 233
- Grove-Bos 246
- Gomez-NY 254
- Appleton-Was.........254
- Bridges-Det...........255

Opponents' OBP
- Grove-Bos 297
- Rowe-Det.....................321
- Ruffing-NY...................323
- Appleton-Was 324
- Bridges-Det 326

Earned Run Average
- Grove-Bos 2.81
- Allen-Cle..............3.44
- Appleton-Was......3.53
- Bridges-Det..........3.60
- Pearson-NY 3.71

Adjusted ERA
- Grove-Bos 189
- Allen-Cle 146
- Bridges-Det 137
- Appleton-Was 135
- Kelley-Phi 132

Adjusted Starter Runs
- Grove-Bos 67.0
- Allen-Cle.............42.8
- Bridges-Det..........42.8
- W.Ferrell-Bos 35.7
- Kelley-Phi 33.6

Pitcher Wins
- **Grove-Bos** 6.6
- **W.Ferrell-Bos** 4.4
- **Allen-Cle** 4.3
- **Bridges-Det**........4.2
- **Ruffing-NY** 3.9

The Dominators

The defending world champion Tigers stumbled out of the gate when first baseman Hank Greenberg broke his wrist in April and was lost for the year. The loss a few weeks later of catcher Mickey Cochrane to an emotional breakdown shot the club's chances.

That was enough to clear the way for the Yankees, who led the league in runs by 140 and fewest runs allowed by 33. Seven New Yorkers reached double figures in homers, while six hurlers won in double figures. After a brief challenge from Boston, which had imported stars like Jimmie Foxx and Joe Cronin, New York widened the gap and eventually won by 19_ games. The Red Sox were sixth.

League hitters continued their feast, setting new records for home runs and scoring. The 5.67 runs tallied by the average AL team has never been equaled, much less surpassed. For the first time, no club had an ERA under 4.00, and Lefty Grove—working in the unfriendly atmosphere of Fenway Park—was the only pitcher to record an ERA under 3.44. St. Louis and Philadelphia each posted ERAs over 6.00.

Fans saw the future of baseball as two of the greats in history, Joe DiMaggio and Bob Feller, debuted in 1936. DiMaggio, already famous for his exploits in the Pacific Coast League, hit .323 with 88 extra-base hits, tying for the lead in triples with Yankees teammate Red Rolfe. Feller, just 17, fanned 76 men in just 62 innings with Cleveland. Baseball began to officially celebrate its history in 1936, electing five players to the newly created Hall of Fame in Cooperstown, New York. Three of the five were AL stalwarts: Ty Cobb, Babe Ruth, and Walter Johnson.

The World Series went six games, with the Yankees defeating the Giants. Five of the games were close, but in the late innings, the Bronx Bombers and their unstoppable attack were able to salt things away.

1937 National League

TEAM	W	L	T	PCT	GB	HW	HL	R	OR	PA	H	2B	3B	HR	BB	SO	HB	SH	AVG	OBP	SLG	OPS	AOPS	BR	ABR	PF	SB	CS	BSA	BSR
NY	95	57	0	.625		**50**	25	732	602	5862	1484	251	41	**111**	412	492	90	**31**	.278	.334	.403	737	105	41	32	101	45			
CHI	93	61	0	.604	3	46	32	**811**	682	6028	1537	253	74	96	**538**	496	**119**	22	**.287**	**.355**	**.416**	**771**	**111**	**118**	**85**	104	71			
PIT	86	68	0	.558	10	46	32	704	647	5996	**1550**	223	**86**	47	463	**480**	89	11	.285	.343	.384	727	104	27	27	100	32			
STL	81	73	3	.526	15	45	33	789	733	5966	1543	**264**	67	94	385	569	89	16	.282	.331	.406	737	104	35	21	102	**78**			
BOS	79	73	0	.520	16	43	33	579	**556**	5740	1265	200	41	63	485	707	113	18	.247	.314	.339	653	91	-110	-54	91	45			
BRO	62	91	2	.405	33.5	36	39	616	772	5893	1401	258	53	37	469	583	109	20	.265	.327	.354	681	90	-55	-65	102	69			
PHI	61	92	2	.399	34.5	29	45	724	869	5993	1482	258	37	103	478	640	75	16	.273	.334	.391	725	95	24	-31	108	66			
CIN	56	98	1	.364	40	28	51	612	706	5763	1329	215	59	73	437	586	72	24	.254	.315	.360	675	94	-80	-49	95	53			
TOT	617					323	290	5567		47241	11591	1922	458	624	3667	4553	158	756	.272	.332	.382	714					459			

TEAM	CG	SHO	GR	SV	IP	H	HR	BB	SO	BR/9	ERA	AERA	OAV	OOB	PR	APR	PF	OSB	OCS	FA	E	WPB	DP	FW	PW	BW	BSW	DIF
NY	67	11	142	17	1361.0	**1341**	86	404	**653**	11.7	3.43	**113**	**.258**	.314	73	**70**	99	36	***55***	.974	159	35	143	.9	**6.9**	3.2		8.0
CHI	73	11	148	13	1381.1	1434	91	502	596	12.8	3.97	100	.267	.332	-10	0	102	47	*50*	**.975**	**151**	44	141	**1.5**	.0	**8.4**		6.1
PIT	67	12	149	17	1366.1	1398	71	428	643	12.2	3.56	108	.264	.321	53	46	99	99	*47*	.970	181	29	135	-.2	4.6	2.7		1.9
STL	81	10	141	4	1392.0	1546	95	448	571	13.0	3.98	100	.281	.337	-10	-1	102	62	*51*	.973	164	43	127	1.0	-.0	2.1		1.1
BOS	**85**	**16**	103	10	1359.1	1344	60	**372**	387	**11.4**	**3.22**	111	.259	**.310**	**105**	60	92	**30**	*52*	**.975**	157	**14**	128	1.0	6.0	-5.4		1.4
BRO	63	5	160	8	1362.2	1470	68	476	592	13.0	4.13	98	.274	.336	-33	-14	103	65	*51*	.964	217	42	127	-2.2	-1.4	-6.4		-4.5
PHI	59	6	**178**	15	1373.2	1629	115	501	529	14.2	5.05	86	.297	.359	-174	-103	111	42	*41*	.970	184	27	**157**	-.3	-10.2	-3.1		-1.9
CIN	64	10	162	**18**	1358.1	1428	**38**	533	581	13.1	3.94	95	.270	.339	-4	-33	95	78	*48*	.966	208	47	139	-1.6	-3.3	-4.9		-11.2
TOT	559	81	1183	102	10954.2					12.7	3.91		.272	.332						.971	1421	281	1097					

Batter-Fielder Wins
Bartell-NY............6.1
Medwick-StL 6.0
Herman-Chi 4.9
Camilli-Phi 3.8
Ott-NY 3.5

Batting Average
Medwick-StL 374
Mize-StL 364
Hartnett-Chi 354
P.Waner-Pit 354
Whitney-Phi 341

On-Base Percentage
Camilli-Phi 446
Mize-StL.......................427
Medwick-StL 414
P.Waner-Pit 413
Ott-NY 408

Slugging Average
Medwick-StL.........641
Mize-StL 595
Camilli-Phi 587
Hartnett-Chi 548
Ott-NY 523

On-Base Plus Slugging
Medwick-StL 1056
Camilli-Phi 1034
Mize-StL 1021
Ott-NY 931
Herman-Chi..........875

Adjusted OPS
Medwick-StL 179
Mize-StL 171
Camilli-Phi 165
Ott-NY 149
P.Waner-Pit 132

Adjusted Batter Runs
Medwick-StL 67.6
Mize-StL 56.2
Camilli-Phi...........46.7
Ott-NY 41.4
P.Waner-Pit 30.1

Runs
Medwick-StL 111
Herman-Chi..........106
Hack-Chi 106
Galan-Chi 104
Demaree-Chi........104

Hits
Medwick-StL 237
P.Waner-Pit 219
Mize-StL 204
Demaree-Chi........199
Herman-Chi..........189

Doubles
Medwick-StL..................56
Mize-StL 40
Bartell-NY.......................38
Phelps-Bro 37
Moore-NY 37

Triples
Vaughan-Pit............17
Suhr-Pit 14
Handley-Pit 12
Goodman-Cin 12
Herman-Chi............11

Home Runs
Ott-NY 31
Medwick-StL 31
Camilli-Phi 27
Mize-StL 25
Galan-Chi 18

Total Bases
Medwick-StL 406
Mize-StL 333
Demaree-Chi.........298
Ott-NY 285
Camilli-Phi 279

Runs Batted In
Medwick-StL........154
Demaree-Chi 115
Mize-StL 113
Suhr-Pit 97
Ott-NY 95

Stolen Bases
Galan-Chi 23
Hack-Chi 16

Base Stealing Runs

Fielding Runs-Infield
Bartell-NY 35.5
Whitehead-NY 28.4
Riggs-Cin....................18.1
Herman-Chi................15.4
Young-Pit 13.0

Fielding Runs-Outfield
Moore-Bos 11.2
T.Moore-StL 7.7
DiMaggio-Bos.........7.5
Arnovich-Phi..........6.8
Galan-Chi 5.4

Wins
Hubbell-NY 22
Turner-Bos..............20
Melton-NY 20
Fette-Bos 20
Warneke-StL 18

Winning Pct.
Hubbell-NY 733
Melton-NY 690
Fette-Bos 667
Carleton-Chi 667
Turner-Bos 645

Complete Games
Turner-Bos 24
Fette-Bos 23
Weiland-StL 21

Strikeouts
Hubbell-NY 159
Grissom-Cin 149
Blanton-Pit............143
Melton-NY 142

Fewest BB/Game
D.Dean-StL 1.51
Root-Chi 1.61
Hoyt-Pit-Bro 1.66
Turner-Bos 1.82
Castleman-NY 1.85

Games
Mulcahy-Phi 56
Jorgens-Phi....................52

Saves
Melton-NY 7
Brown-Pit..................7
Grissom-Cin 6
Root-Chi 5
Hollingsworth-Cin........5

Base Runners/9
Turner-Bos 9.82
Melton-NY 10.05
Castleman-NY ..10.16
Root-Chi 10.53
Tobin-Pit 10.66

Adjusted Relief Runs
Coffman-NY 5.6

Relief Ranking
Coffman-NY 7.4

Innings Pitched
Passeau-Phi......292.1
Lee-Chi..............272.1
Weiland-StL 264.1
Hubbell-NY........261.2
Fette-Bos 259.0

Opponents' Avg.
Mungo-Bro 229
Grissom-Cin 232
Melton-NY 233
Turner-Bos 235
Carleton-Chi.........236

Opponents' OBP
Turner-Bos 274
Melton-NY 280
Castleman-NY 287
Root-Chi.......................290
D.Dean-StL 291

Earned Run Average
Turner-Bos 2.38
Melton-NY 2.61
D.Dean-StL 2.69
Bauers-Pit............2.88
Fette-Bos 2.88

Adjusted ERA
Turner-Bos...........150
Melton-NY 149
D.Dean-StL 148
Mungo-Bro............139
Bauers-Pit 134

Adjusted Starter Runs
Turner-Bos 36.2
Melton-NY 32.5
D.Dean-StL..........25.4
Fette-Bos 22.9
Bauers-Pit............21.5

Pitcher Wins
Turner-Bos 4.8
Melton-NY 3.4
D.Dean-StL 2.8
Fette-Bos............2.8
Mungo-Bro 2.8

Cardinals Sing Bye-Bye as Giants Tread

As the rest of the league floundered, the Cubs and Giants emerged in July. Chicago was up by 6_ as late as August 13, but the Cubs fell apart for the second straight year as the Giants shot to the top. New York won 37 of its final 51. Carl Hubbell was spectacular again, and unheralded Cliff Melton—who won 20 and saved 7—was even better, giving the Giants a devastating 1-2 lefty combo. Mel Ott led the league in homers and walks, while Chicago lacked anyone up to the level of New York's stars.

The already popular All-Star Game claimed its first serious casualty. Earl Averill's liner broke Dizzy Dean's big toe, causing the popular Cardinals hurler to alter his delivery, which in turn ruined his arm. With Dean's effectiveness curtailed, the Cardinals fell to fourth despite Joe Medwick's Triple Crown. Dean's injury marked the end of the first great St. Louis era. Five classic Cardinals ended their careers in 1937: Jim Bottomley, Frankie Frisch, Chick Hafey, Jesse Haines, and Rogers Hornsby. In addition, Pittsburgh's Pie Traynor, considered the league's finest third baseman until the 1960s, retired.

The Boston Braves, who had improved 41 games in two years, ended fifth as two 30-year old rookies, Lou Fette and Jim Turner, won 20 each (Turner also led the league in ERA). The Reds finished in the cellar for the last time until 1982. Strikeouts per game rose to 3.69, the highest level between 1916 and 1948. Oddly enough, league leader Hubbell whiffed just 159—the 1936 leader, Van Mungo, struck out 238—and Boston rookie Vince DiMaggio was the sole player to fan more than 100 times.

Once again, however, the Giants did nothing with the Yankees in the World Series, falling in five games, only one of which was close. The Giants did not hit a home run until the final game of the Series when Ott hit a two-run homer.

1937 American League

TEAM	W	L	T	PCT	GB	HW	HL	R	OR	PA	H	2B	3B	HR	BB	SO	HB	SH	AVG	OBP	SLG	OPS	AOPS	BR	ABR	PF	SB	CS	BSA	BSR
NY	102	52	3	.662		**57**	20	**979**	**671**	6291	1554	282	73	**174**	**709**	607	61	**34**	.283	.369	**.456**	**825**	**113**	**113**	**107**	101	60	36	63	1
DET	89	65	1	.578	13	49	28	935	841	6264	**1611**	**309**	62	150	656	711	70	22	**.292**	**.370**	.452	822	111	109	89	102	**89**	45	66	**4**
CHI	86	68	0	.558	16	47	30	780	730	5956	1478	280	**76**	67	549	**447**	**111**	19	.280	.350	.400	750	95	-39	-38	100	70	34	**67**	**4**
CLE	83	71	2	.539	19	50	28	817	768	6040	1499	304	**76**	103	570	551	96	21	.280	.352	.423	775	100	5	0	101	78	51	60	-1
BOS	80	72	2	.526	21	44	29	821	775	6084	1506	269	64	100	601	557	103	26	.281	.357	.411	768	96	-1	-31	104	79	61	56	-4
WAS	73	80	5	.477	28.5	43	35	757	841	6259	1559	245	84	47	591	503	67	23	.279	.351	.379	730	94	-79	-44	96	61	35	64	1
PHI	54	97	3	.358	46.5	27	50	699	854	5886	1398	278	60	94	583	557	70	5	.267	.341	.397	738	93	-64	-52	98	95	48	66	**4**
STL	46	108	2	.299	56	25	51	715	1023	6123	1573	327	44	71	514	510	85	14	.285	.348	.399	747	93	-45	-50	101	30	27	53	-3
TOT	622					342	271	6503		48903	12178	2294	539	806	4773	4443	164	663	.281	.355	.415	770					562	337	63	6

TEAM	CG	SHO	GR	SV	IP	H	HR	BB	SO	BR/9	ERA	AERA	OAV	OOB	PR	APR	PF	OSB	OCS	FA	E	WPB	DP	FW	PW	BW	BSW	DIF
NY	**82**	**15**	100	**21**	1396.0	**1417**	92	**506**	652	**12.5**	**3.65**	**122**	**.261**	**.325**	**151**	**128**	96	**52**	39	.972	170	**23**	134	.2	**11.7**	**9.8**	.0	3.2
DET	70	6	132	11	1378.0	1521	102	635	485	14.2	4.87	96	.279	.357	-38	-30	101	75	35	**.976**	**147**	43	149	**1.4**	-2.8	8.2	**.3**	4.9
CHI	70	**15**	108	**21**	1351.1	1435	115	532	533	13.2	4.17	110	.273	.341	68	65	100	59	43	.971	174	34	173	-.2	6.0	-3.5	**.3**	6.5
CLE	64	4	**160**	15	1364.2	1529	**61**	566	630	14.0	4.39	105	.285	.356	35	33	100	81	**54**	.974	159	26	153	.8	3.0	.0	-.2	2.4
BOS	74	6	132	14	1366.0	1518	92	597	**682**	14.0	4.48	106	.279	.352	21	39	103	62	32	.970	177	31	139	-.4	3.6	-2.8	-.4	4.1
WAS	75	5	122	14	1398.2	1498	96	671	524	14.1	4.58	97	.275	.357	7	-24	96	74	51	.972	170	36	**181**	.3	-2.2	-4.0	.0	2.5
PHI	65	6	143	9	1335.0	1490	105	613	469	14.3	4.85	97	.281	.358	-35	-20	102	75	38	.967	198	55	150	-1.7	-1.8	-4.8	**.3**	-13.5
STL	55	2	157	8	1363.0	1768	143	653	468	16.2	6.00	80	.315	.390	-209	-170	105	84	45	.972	173	42	166	-.0	-15.6	-4.6	-.3	-10.4
TOT	555	59	1054	113	10952.2					14.1	4.62		.281	.355						.972	1368	290	1245					

Batter-Fielder Wins	Batting Average	On-Base Percentage	Slugging Average	On-Base Plus Slugging	Adjusted OPS	Adjusted Batter Runs
Clift-StL.......7.4	Gehringer-Det.......371	Gehrig-NY.......473	DiMaggio-NY.......673	Gehrig-NY.......1116	Gehrig-NY.......177	Gehrig-NY.......74.1
DiMaggio-NY.......5.7	Gehrig-NY.......351	Gehringer-Det.......458	Greenberg-Det.......668	Greenberg-Det..1105	Greenberg-Det.......171	Greenberg-Det..65.3
Dickey-NY.......5.6	DiMaggio-NY.......346	Greenberg-Det.......436	York-Det.......651	DiMaggio-NY.......1085	DiMaggio-NY.......168	DiMaggio-NY.......60.1
Greenberg-Det.......5.1	Bonura-Chi.......345	Johnson-Phi.......425	Gehrig-NY.......643	Dickey-NY.......987	Johnson-Phi.......147	Gehringer-Det...43.0
Gehrig-NY.......4.8	Travis-Was.......344	Dickey-NY.......417	Bonura-Chi.......573	Bonura-Chi.......984	Bonura-Chi.......146	Johnson-Phi.......38.2

Runs	Hits	Doubles	Triples	Home Runs	Total Bases	Runs Batted In
DiMaggio-NY.......151	Bell-StL.......218	Bell-StL.......51	Walker-Chi.......16	DiMaggio-NY.......46	DiMaggio-NY.......418	Greenberg-Det.......183
Rolfe-NY.......143	DiMaggio-NY.......215	Greenberg-Det.......49	Kreevich-Chi.......16	Greenberg-Det.......40	Greenberg-Det.......397	DiMaggio-NY.......167
Gehrig-NY.......138	Walker-Det.......213	Moses-Phi.......48	Stone-Was.......15	Gehrig-NY.......37	Gehrig-NY.......366	Gehrig-NY.......159
Greenberg-Det.......137	Lewis-Was.......210	Vosmik-StL.......47	DiMaggio-NY.......15	Foxx-Bos.......36	Moses-Phi.......357	Dickey-NY.......133
Gehringer-Det.......133	Gehringer-Det.......209	Lary-Cle.......46	Greenberg-Det.......14	York-Det.......35	Trosky-Cle.......329	Trosky-Cle.......128

Stolen Bases	Base Stealing Runs	Fielding Runs-Infield	Fielding Runs-Outfield	Wins	Winning Pct.	Complete Games
Chapman-Was-Bos.......35	Chapman-Was-Bos..3.5	Clift-StL.......41.3	Johnson-Phi.......9.6	Gomez-NY.......21	Allen-Cle.......938	W.Ferrell-Bos-Was.......26
Werber-Phi.......35	Werber-Phi.......3.2	Hayes-Chi.......23.4	West-StL.......9.2	Ruffing-NY.......20	Stratton-Chi.......750	Gomez-NY.......25
Walker-Det.......23	Walker-Det.......2.6	Hale-Cle.......22.4	Almada-Bos-Was..7.5	Lawson-Det.......18	Ruffing-NY.......741	Ruffing-NY.......22
	Hill-Was-Phi.......2.6	Appling-Chi.......16.7	Stone-Was.......7.2	Grove-Bos.......17	Lawson-Det.......720	Grove-Bos.......21
	Kreevich-Chi.......1.9	Foxx-Bos.......11.4	Vosmik-StL.......7.0	Auker-Det.......17	Gomez-NY.......656	DeShong-Was.......20

Strikeouts	Fewest BB/Game	Games	Saves	Base Runners/9	Adjusted Relief Runs	Relief Ranking
Gomez-NY.......194	Stratton-Chi.......2.02	Brown-Chi.......53	Brown-Chi.......18	Stratton-Chi.......9.89	Brown-Chi.......12.0	Brown-Chi.......20.0
Newsom-Was-Bos 166	Hudlin-Cle.......2.20	Wilson-Bos.......51	Murphy-NY.......10	Gomez-NY.......10.57	Fink-Phi.......5.7	Murphy-NY.......6.6
Grove-Bos.......153	Marcum-Bos.......2.30	Newsom-Was-Bos.......41	Wilson-Bos.......7	Ruffing-NY.......10.92	Cohen-Was.......5.1	Cohen-Was.......5.8
Feller-Cle.......150	Ruffing-NY.......2.39	Kelley-Phi.......41	Malone-NY.......6	Chandler-NY.......10.93	Murphy-NY.......4.1	Fink-Phi.......2.8
Bridges-Det.......138	Lyons-Chi.......2.39	Heving-Cle.......40		Allen-Cle.......11.55	Wyatt-Cle.......2.9	Wyatt-Cle.......1.8

Innings Pitched	Opponents' Avg.	Opponents' OBP	Earned Run Average	Adjusted ERA	Adjusted Starter Runs	Pitcher Wins
W.Ferrell-Bos-Was 281.0	Gomez-NY.......223	Stratton-Chi.......280	Gomez-NY.......2.33	Stratton-Chi.......191	Gomez-NY.......66.9	**Gomez-NY**.......6.8
Gomez-NY.......278.1	Stratton-Chi.......234	Gomez-NY.......287	Stratton-Chi.......2.40	Gomez-NY.......191	Grove-Bos.......48.5	**Stratton-Chi**.......4.3
Newsom-Was-Bos 275.1	Smith-Phi.......242	Ruffing-NY.......296	Allen-Cle.......2.55	Allen-Cle.......181	Ruffing-NY.......43.2	**Ruffing-NY**.......4.0
DeShong-Was..264.1	Allen-Cle.......244	Lee-Chi.......312	Ruffing-NY.......2.98	Grove-Bos.......157	Allen-Cle.......40.3	**Grove-Bos**.......3.9
Grove-Bos.......262.0	Ruffing-NY.......247	Allen-Cle.......313	Grove-Bos.......3.02	Ruffing-NY.......149	Stratton-Chi.......38.8	**Allen-Cle**.......2.7

Goofy, Joe D., and Another Title

New York broke from the pack in June and coasted to another easy pennant. Despite excellent defense and the bats of Charlie Gehringer and Hank Greenberg, Detroit didn't have the firepower to contend with the Yankees. New York had the three top run scorers, three of the top four RBI men, and the league's best pitchers in Lefty Gomez and Red Ruffing. The multi-dimensional Joe DiMaggio had become the league's gem, and Lou Gehrig enjoyed his last great season. The Yankees also added two rookies, pitcher Spud Chandler and outfielder Tommy Henrich.

Attendance rose in every AL city but Boston; ironically, the Red Sox had their best year since 1918. Finishing 80–72, they added their first real homegrown star, second baseman Bobby Doerr. Detroit once again drew a million fans, and the league's overall turnstile clicks were the most in over a decade.

While overall runs fell by 500, AL hitters established another new record for homers. Hitters were both walking and striking out more than ever as the uppercut swing became better established. Cleveland's Johnny Allen set an all-time single-season record for winning percentage at .938, while the last-place Browns had a staff ERA over 6.00 for the second straight year. They'd once again reach that low in 1939.

The White Sox enlarged Comiskey Park, which significantly cut scoring, but Detroit shrunk its left field, which increased run production. Yankee Stadium's formerly cavernous center field was cut from 26 feet to a still huge 461 feet, and scoring there *increased* slightly.

The Yankees again wiped the floor with the Giants in the World Series. After three easy wins by the Yankees, the Giants staved off elimination in Game 4 behind Carl Hubbell, 7–2. Goofy Gomez shut down the Giants in Game 5 and also drove in the winning run.

1938 National League

TEAM	W	L	T	PCT	GB	HW	HL	R	OR	PA	H	2B	3B	HR	BB	SO	HB	SH	AVG	OBP	SLG	OPS	AOPS	BR	ABR	PF	SB	CS	BSA	BSR
CHI	89	63	2	.586		44	33	713	**597**	5972	1435	242	70	65	522	476	88	29	.269	.338	.377	715	100	26	7	103	49			
PIT	86	64	2	.573	2	44	33	707	630	6007	1511	265	66	65	485	**409**	81	19	**.279**	**.340**	.388	728	106	49	44	101	47			
NY	83	67	2	.553	5	43	30	705	637	5841	1424	210	36	**125**	465	528	88	**33**	.271	.334	.396	730	106	45	39	101	31			
CIN	82	68	1	.547	6	43	34	723	634	5878	1495	251	57	110	366	518	**89**	32	.277	.327	.406	733	**110**	42	**62**	97	19			
BOS	77	75	1	.507	12	**45**	30	561	618	5775	1311	199	39	54	424	548	78	23	.250	.309	.333	642	91	-121	-61	90	49			
STL	71	80	5	.470	17.5	36	41	**725**	722	6039	**1542**	**288**	74	91	412	492	83	16	**.279**	.331	**.407**	**738**	103	**56**	16	106	55			
BRO	69	80	2	.463	18.5	31	41	704	710	5853	1322	225	**79**	61	**611**	615	80	20	.257	.338	.367	705	98	14	-1	102	**66**			
PHI	45	105	1	.300	43	26	48	550	840	5713	1318	233	29	40	423	507	86	12	.254	.312	.333	645	85	-111	-95	97	38			
TOT	610					312	290	5388		47078	11358	1913	450	611	3708	4093	184	673	.267	.329	.376	705					354			

TEAM	CG	SHO	GR	SV	IP	H	HR	BB	SO	BR/9	ERA	AERA	OAV	OOB	PR	APR	PF	OSB	OCS	FA	E	WPB	DP	FW	PW	BW	BSW	DIF
CHI	67	**16**	148	**18**	1396.2	1414	71	454	**583**	12.1	**3.37**	**113**	.262	.322	**64**	**66**	101	40	*30*	**.978**	**135**	42	151	**2.3**	**6.6**	.7		3.4
PIT	57	8	144	15	1379.2	1406	71	432	557	12.2	3.46	109	.266	.324	49	50	100	44	***45***	.974	163	24	**168**	.5	5.0	4.4		1.1
NY	59	8	142	**18**	1349.0	1370	87	**389**	497	**11.9**	3.62	104	.261	**.314**	24	20	99	37	*24*	.973	168	**20**	147	.2	2.0	3.9		1.9
CIN	72	11	130	16	1362.0	**1329**	75	463	542	**11.9**	3.62	101	**.254**	.316	25	3	96	37	*33*	.971	172	39	133	-.1	.3	**6.2**		.6
BOS	**83**	15	109	12	1380.0	1375	**66**	465	413	12.2	3.40	101	.258	.322	58	3	91	**27**	*42*	.972	173	23	136	-.0	.3	-6.1		6.9
STL	58	10	**179**	16	1384.2	1482	77	474	534	12.8	3.84	103	.272	.333	-9	16	104	48	*43*	.967	199	36	145	-1.4	1.6	1.6		-6.3
BRO	56	12	155	14	1332.0	1464	88	446	469	13.1	4.07	96	.278	.338	-42	-25	103	47	*31*	.973	157	52	148	.8	-2.5	-.1		-3.6
PHI	68	3	140	6	1329.1	1516	76	582	492	14.4	4.93	79	.285	.358	-169	-151	103	74	*35*	.966	201	40	135	-1.8	-15.2	-9.6		-3.4
TOT	520	83	1147	115	10913.1					12.6	3.78		.267	.329						.972	1368	276	1163					

Batter-Fielder Wins	Batting Average	On-Base Percentage	Slugging Average	On-Base Plus Slugging	Adjusted OPS	Adjusted Batter Runs
Ott-NY 6.4	Lombardi-Cin 342	Ott-NY 442	Mize-StL 614	Mize-StL 1036	Ott-NY 178	Ott-NY 62.3
Vaughan-Pit 6.4	Mize-StL 337	Vaughan-Pit 433	Ott-NY 583	Ott-NY 1024	Mize-StL 172	Mize-StL 53.0
Lombardi-Cin 4.1	McCormick-Cin 327	Mize-StL 422	Medwick-StL 536	Lombardi-Cin 915	Lombardi-Cin 154	Vaughan-Pit 37.6
Hack-Chi 4.0	Medwick-StL 322	Hack-Chi 411	Goodman-Cin 533	Medwick-StL 905	Goodman-Cin 149	Goodman-Cin 36.5
Mize-StL 3.9	Vaughan-Pit 322	Suhr-Pit 394	Lombardi-Cin 524	Goodman-Cin 901	Vaughan-Pit 140	Lombardi-Cin 35.3

Runs	Hits	Doubles	Triples	Home Runs	Total Bases	Runs Batted In
Ott-NY 116	McCormick-Cin 209	Medwick-StL 47	Mize-StL 16	Ott-NY 36	Mize-StL 326	Medwick-StL 122
Hack-Chi 109	Hack-Chi 195	McCormick-Cin 40	Gutteridge-StL 15	Goodman-Cin 30	Medwick-StL 316	Ott-NY 116
Camilli-Bro 106	L.Waner-Pit 194	Young-Pit 36	Suhr-Pit 14	Mize-StL 27	Ott-NY 307	Rizzo-Pit 111
Goodman-Cin 103	Medwick-StL 190	Martin-Phi 36	Riggs-Cin 13	Camilli-Bro 24	Goodman-Cin 303	McCormick-Cin 106
Medwick-StL 100	Mize-StL 179		Koy-Bro 13	Rizzo-Pit 23	Rizzo-Pit 285	Mize-StL 102

Stolen Bases	Base Stealing Runs	Fielding Runs-Infield	Fielding Runs-Outfield	Wins	Winning Pct.	Complete Games
Hack-Chi 16		Bartell-NY 25.9	Arnovich-Phi 17.4	Lee-Chi 22	Lee-Chi 710	Derringer-Cin 26
Lavagetto-Bro 15		Young-Pit 25.1	DiMaggio-Bos 10.5	Derringer-Cin 21	Bryant-Chi 633	Turner-Bos 22
Koy-Bro 15		Herman-Chi 21.5	Rosen-Bro 9.1	Bryant-Chi 19	Brown-Pit 625	Walters-Phi-Cin 20
Vaughan-Pit 14		Vaughan-Pit 16.7	Medwick-StL 8.0	Weiland-StL 16	VanderMeer-Cin 600	MacFayden-Bos 19
Gutteridge-StL 14		Kampouris-Cin-NY 13.2	Craft-Cin 7.1		Derringer-Cin 600	Lee-Chi 19

Strikeouts	Fewest BB/Game	Games	Saves	Base Runners/9	Adjusted Relief Runs	Relief Ranking
Bryant-Chi 135	Davis-StL 1.40	Coffman-NY 51	Coffman-NY 12	Dean-Chi 8.68	Brown-NY 17.6	Brown-NY 16.3
Derringer-Cin 132	Derringer-Cin 1.44	Brown-Pit 51	Root-Chi 8	Brown-NY 9.40	Russell-Chi 5.6	Coffman-NY 4.5
VanderMeer-Cin 125	Hubbell-NY 1.66	McGee-StL 47	Hamlin-Bro 6	Hubbell-NY 10.36	Coffman-NY 3.7	Russell-Chi 3.8
Lee-Chi 121	Root-Chi 1.68	Mulcahy-Phi 46	Errickson-Bos 6	Johnson-Phi 10.63	Shoun-StL 7	Shoun-StL 7
	Turner-Bos 1.81			Derringer-Cin 10.67		

Innings Pitched	Opponents' Avg.	Opponents' OBP	Earned Run Average	Adjusted ERA	Adjusted Starter Runs	Pitcher Wins
Derringer-Cin 307.0	VanderMeer-Cin 213	Hubbell-NY 285	Lee-Chi 2.66	Lee-Chi 144	Lee-Chi 38.6	**Lee-Chi** 4.1
Lee-Chi 291.0	Bauers-Pit 233	Derringer-Cin 291	Root-Chi 2.86	Root-Chi 134	Derringer-Cin 27.8	**Derringer-Cin** 2.9
Bryant-Chi 270.1	Bryant-Chi 235	Root-Chi 294	Derringer-Cin 2.93	Fitzsimmons-Bro 129	Bryant-Chi 22.1	**Bryant-Chi** 2.6
Turner-Bos 268.0	MacFayden-Bos 247	Lohrman-NY 294	MacFayden-Bos 2.95	Klinger-Pit 127	Fitzsimmons-Bro 18.0	**Bauers-Pit** 2.1
Mulcahy-Phi 267.1	Schumacher-NY 248	Schumacher-NY 299	Klinger-Pit 2.99	Derringer-Cin 124	Bauers-Pit 17.8	**Fitzsimmons-Bro** 1.8

Cubs Glow One Last Time

For all intents and purposes, 1938 looked like Pittsburgh's year. A 24–7 record in July allowed them to overtake the sliding Giants, and the Pirates led for all of August and most of September. Then the elements took over. A mid-September hurricane stopped play for four days and gave tired Chicago time to recover; the team the reeled off seven straight wins to catch the stumbling Pirates, who had led by seven on Labor Day.

Chicago knocked Pittsburgh out with a three-game sweep September 27–29 at Wrigley Field. Player-manager Gabby Hartnett's dramatic "homer in the gloamin'," hit just before the umpires were set to call the game by darkness, provided the key hit in the second game. Pittsburgh had great relief pitching from Mace Brown, and a solid line-drive offense, but didn't have Chicago's rotation: Bill Lee of the Cubs led the NL in wins and ERA, while 19-game winner Clay Bryant had a superior season in an otherwise nondescript career.

Cincinnati leapt to fourth, raising attendance by 72 percent. Overpowering Johnny Vander Meer threw no-hitters in consecutive starts, while catcher Ernie Lombardi was MVP. Rebuilding St. Louis debuted future stars Mort Cooper and Enos Slaughter.

Stolen bases fell to just .29 per contest, the lowest total to that point in history. Vince DiMaggio again paced the league with 138 strikeouts, setting a record that lasted until 1956. Several teams altered their ballparks in 1938. The Cubs redesigned Wrigley Field, adding the bleachers still in use, while the Giants chopped 50 feet from center field with a temporary fence. The Phillies moved into Shibe Park, the Athletics' headquarters, on July 4; Shibe was much larger than the tiny Baker Bowl.

The Cubs had no more luck in the World Series than other NL teams of the period, losing to the Yankees in four. While 1938 was the Cubs' eleventh straight year among the NL's top three, it was also the *end* of the franchise as a consistent winner; Chicago did not contend again until 1945.

1938 American League

TEAM	W	L	T	PCT	GB	HW	HL	R	OR	PA	H	2B	3B	HR	BB	SO	HB	SH	AVG	OBP	SLG	OPS	AOPS	BR	ABR	PF	SB	CS	BSA	BSR
NY	99	53	5	.651		**55**	22	**966**	**710**	6259	1480	283	63	**174**	**749**	616	61	**39**	.274	.366	**.446**	**812**	**111**	81	**86**	100	**91**	28	**76**	**10**
BOS	88	61	1	.591	9.5	52	23	902	751	6004	1566	298	56	98	650	463	**112**	13	**.299**	**.378**	.434	**812**	105	**91**	51	105	55	51	52	-6
CLE	86	66	1	.566	13	46	30	847	782	6000	1506	**300**	**89**	113	550	605	78	16	.281	.350	.434	784	104	8	25	98	83	36	70	6
DET	84	70	1	.545	16	48	31	862	795	6060	1434	219	52	137	693	581	75	22	.272	.359	.411	770	94	-2	-46	106	76	41	65	2
WAS	75	76	1	.497	23.5	44	33	814	873	6158	**1602**	278	72	85	573	**379**	93	18	.293	.362	.416	778	108	11	74	93	65	37	64	1
CHI	65	83	1	.439	32	33	39	709	752	5805	1439	239	55	67	514	489	78	14	.277	.343	.383	726	86	-94	-110	102	56	39	59	-1
STL	55	97	4	.362	44	31	43	755	962	6049	1498	273	36	92	590	528	106	20	.281	.355	.397	752	95	-36	-34	100	51	40	56	-3
PHI	53	99	2	.349	46	28	47	726	956	5934	1410	243	62	98	605	590	78	22	.270	.348	.396	744	95	-58	-38	97	65	53	55	-4
TOT	613					337	268	6581		48269	11935	2133	485	864	4924	4251	164	681	.281	.358	.415	773					542	325	63	5

TEAM	CG	SHO	GR	SV	IP	H	HR	BB	SO	BR/9	ERA	AERA	OAV	OOB	PR	APR	PF	OSB	OCS	FA	E	WPB	DP	FW	PW	BW	BSW	DIF
NY	**91**	**11**	91	13	1382.0	1436	**85**	566	567	**13.1**	**3.91**	**116**	**.268**	**.339**	**134**	**101**	95	52	37	.973	169	39	177	.5	**9.1**	**7.8**	**.8**	4.8
BOS	67	10	147	15	1316.1	1472	102	**528**	484	13.8	4.46	111	.281	.349	48	67	103	63	35	.968	190	**27**	172	-1.1	6.1	4.6	-.6	4.6
CLE	68	5	145	**17**	1353.0	**1416**	100	681	**717**	14.1	4.60	101	**.268**	.355	29	7	97	82	**49**	.974	151	39	145	1.2	.6	2.3	.5	5.4
DET	75	3	134	11	1348.1	1532	110	608	435	14.4	4.79	104	.287	.361	1	31	104	**48**	35	**.976**	147	37	172	1.6	2.8	-4.2	.1	6.6
WAS	59	6	**156**	11	1360.1	1472	92	655	515	14.3	4.94	91	.276	.358	-22	-68	94	64	39	.970	180	60	**179**	-.5	-6.1	6.7	.0	-.6
CHI	83	5	84	9	1316.1	1449	101	550	432	13.8	4.36	112	.279	.350	62	76	102	57	42	.967	196	33	155	-1.6	6.9	-9.9	-.2	-4.2
STL	71	3	134	7	1344.2	1584	132	737	632	15.7	5.80	86	.295	.382	-151	-120	104	89	**49**	.975	**145**	37	163	**1.8**	-10.8	-3.1	-.3	-8.5
PHI	56	4	143	12	1324.0	1573	142	599	473	14.9	5.48	88	.292	.365	-101	-94	101	87	39	.965	206	43	119	-1.8	-8.5	-3.4	-.4	-8.9
TOT	570	47	1034	95	10745.0					14.3	4.79		.281	.358						.971	1384	315	1282					

Batter-Fielder Wins	Batting Average	On-Base Percentage	Slugging Average	On-Base Plus Slugging	Adjusted OPS	Adjusted Batter Runs
Foxx-Bos.............5.8	Foxx-Bos..............349	Foxx-Bos 462	Foxx-Bos..............704	Foxx-Bos 1166	Foxx-Bos 180	Foxx-Bos 71.9
Clift-StL...............5.3	Heath-Cle 343	Myer-Was...................454	Greenberg-Det 683	Greenberg-Det ..1122	Greenberg-Det 167	Greenberg-Det ..58.3
Greenberg-Det....4.5	Chapman-Bos 340	Greenberg-Det............438	Heath-Cle 602	York-Det...............995	Heath-Cle 146	Clift-StL 38.9
Cronin-Bos..........4.4	Myer-Was 336	Averill-Cle....................429	DiMaggio-NY 581	Heath-Cle 985	Dickey-NY 144	Johnson-Phi 36.0
Dickey-NY 4.1	Travis-Was 335	Cronin-Bos..................428	York-Det 579	Dickey-NY 981	Clift-StL 143	Myer-Was 34.1

Runs	Hits	Doubles	Triples	Home Runs	Total Bases	Runs Batted In
Greenberg-Det 144	Vosmik-Bos 201	Cronin-Bos 51	Heath-Cle 18	Greenberg-Det 58	Foxx-Bos 398	Foxx-Bos 175
Foxx-Bos 139	Cramer-Bos 198	McQuinn-StL.................42	Averill-Cle 15	Foxx-Bos 50	Greenberg-Det 380	Greenberg-Det 146
Gehringer-Det 133	Almada-Was-StL ..197	Trosky-Cle......................40	DiMaggio-NY..........13	Clift-StL 34	DiMaggio-NY........348	DiMaggio-NY 140
Rolfe-NY 132	Foxx-Bos 197	Chapman-Bos...............40		York-Det..................33	Johnson-Phi..........311	York-Det 127
DiMaggio-NY........129	Rolfe-NY 196	Vosmik-Bos...................37		DiMaggio-NY 32	Heath-Cle 302	Clift-StL 118

Stolen Bases	Base Stealing Runs	Fielding Runs-Infield	Fielding Runs-Outfield	Wins	Winning Pct.	Complete Games
Crosetti-NY 27	Lary-Cle 3.0	Gordon-NY 20.5	Johnson-Phi 9.6	Ruffing-NY..............21	Ruffing-NY 750	Newsom-StL..........31
Lary-Cle..................23	Gehringer-Det........2.7	Crosetti-NY 18.4	Cramer-Bos 5.5	Newsom-StL 20	Pearson-NY 696	Ruffing-NY 22
Werber-Phi.............19	Rolfe-NY 2.5	Clift-StL 15.2	Chapman-Bos 5.4	Gomez-NY..............18	Harder-Cle 630	Gomez-NY 20
Lewis-Was 17	Crosetti-NY............1.7	Rogell-Det 9.8	Moses-Phi 4.3	Harder-Cle 17	Stratton-Chi 625	Feller-Cle 20
Fox-Det 16	Moses-Phi 1.5	Doerr-Bos 9.0	Vosmik-Bos............3.5	Feller-Cle 17	Feller-Cle 607	Caster-Phi 20

Strikeouts	Fewest BB/Game	Games	Saves	Base Runners/9	Adjusted Relief Runs	Relief Ranking
Feller-Cle 240	Leonard-Was 2.14	Humphries-Cle 45	Murphy-NY 11	Leonard-Was 11.32	Murphy-NY 4.9	Murphy-NY 6.1
Newsom-StL 226	Harder-Cle 2.33	Newsom-StL..................44	McKain-Bos..............6	Eisenstat-Det 11.56	McKain-Bos 3.5	McKain-Bos..........3.3
L.Mills-StL 134	Lyons-Chi 2.40	E.Smith-Phi...................43	Humphries-Cle 6	Harris-Bos 11.76		
Gomez-NY............129	Chandler-NY........2.46	Bagby-Bos 43	Potter-Phi.................5	Ruffing-NY 11.94		
Ruffing-NY............127	Thomas-Phi 2.63	Appleton-Was 43	Appleton-Was 5	Stratton-Chi 12.03		

Innings Pitched	Opponents' Avg.	Opponents' OBP	Earned Run Average	Adjusted ERA	Adjusted Starter Runs	Pitcher Wins
Newsom-StL......329.2	Feller-Cle 220	Leonard-Was 305	Grove-Bos 3.08	Grove-Bos 160	Ruffing-NY 37.1	**Ruffing-NY** 4.5
Caster-Phi.........281.1	Allen-Cle...............246	Stratton-Chi 315	Ruffing-NY 3.31	Lee-Chi 140	Lee-Chi.................33.0	**Lee-Chi** 3.4
Feller-Cle 277.2	Hadley-NY 254	Ruffing-NY...................317	Gomez-NY 3.35	Rigney-Chi............138	Grove-Bos 32.5	**Gomez-NY**..........3.2
Ruffing-NY 247.1	Stratton-Chi 255	Harder-Cle 319	Leonard-Was 3.43	Ruffing-NY............137	Gomez-NY 31.0	**Grove-Bos** 3.0
Lee-Chi..............245.1	Rigney-Chi 256	Grove-Bos 319	Lee-Chi................3.49	Gomez-NY............135	Rigney-Chi 25.9	**Leonard-Was** 2.8

Crushing the Competition

While it was again a Yankees year, fans in Boston and Cleveland had plenty to cheer about. Both teams hung in with New York through late July, but couldn't compete with the Yankees' 48–13 record from July 1 through August 30. With the great all-around play of Joe DiMaggio, catcher Bill Dickey contributing another fine year at bat, and rookie Joe Gordon at second base, the Yankees were able to withstand the sudden decline of Lou Gehrig. Joe McCarthy began using Johnny Murphy in tough relief situations, which made the aging starting staff look even better.

Boston got great seasons from Jimmie Foxx and Joe Cronin, but a punchless outfield and thin pitching doomed the club. Cleveland's Bob Feller, a 19-year-old fireballer with a great fastball and a large ego, led the league in both walks and strikeouts. The Indians also gave 20-year-old infielder Lou Boudreau his first taste of the big leagues. St. Louis had one spectacular pitcher—30-year-old Bobo Newsom, who was 20–16 for the 55–97 Browns and led the league in starts and complete games. Two former star outfielders, Goose Goslin and Mule Haas, saw their careers grind to a halt with the clubs of their youth, Washington and Philadelphia, respectively.

While hitters set yet another new home run record, stolen bases continued to plummet; just two players swiped more than 20 sacks. However, the Yankees cornered the market in this field, as well, leading the loop in stolen bases as well as runs, home runs, and bases on balls.

When the New York met up with the Cubs in the World Series, nobody gave Chicago a chance. They were right. The Bombers' sweep was still impressive—the Yankees outscored the Cubs, 22–9, and put together late-inning rallies to break open close contests in Games 2 and 4.

1939 National League

TEAM	W	L	T	PCT	GB	HW	HL	R	OR	PA	H	2B	3B	HR	BB	SO	HB	SH	AVG	OBP	SLG	OPS	AOPS	BR	ABR	PF	SB	CS	BSA	BSR
CIN	97	57	2	.630		**55**	25	767	**595**	6106	1493	269	60	98	500	538	**193**	**35**	.278	.343	.405	748	106	52	48	101	46			
STL	92	61	2	.601	4.5	51	27	**779**	633	6116	**1601**	**332**	**62**	98	475	566	167	27	**.294**	**.354**	**.432**	**786**	**110**	**127**	**79**	106	44			
BRO	84	69	4	.549	12.5	51	27	708	645	6047	1420	265	57	78	**564**	639	107	26	.265	.338	.380	718	96	2	-22	104	59			
CHI	84	70	2	.545	13	44	34	724	678	5990	1407	263	**62**	91	523	553	140	34	.266	.336	.391	727	99	11	-1	102	**61**			
NY	77	74	0	.510	18.5	41	33	703	685	5767	1395	211	38	**116**	498	**499**	108	32	.272	.340	.396	736	103	27	22	101	26			
PIT	68	85	0	.444	28.5	35	42	666	721	5923	1453	261	60	63	477	420	156	21	.276	.338	.384	722	102	4	15	98	44			
BOS	63	88	1	.417	32.5	37	35	572	659	5795	1395	199	39	56	366	494	122	21	.264	.314	.348	662	91	-122	-80	93	41			
PHI	45	106	1	.298	50.5	29	44	553	856	5707	1341	232	40	49	421	486	144	9	.261	.318	.351	669	89	-100	-83	97	47			
TOT	616					343	267	5472		47451	11505	2032	418	649	3824	4195	205	1137	.272	.335	.386	721					368			

TEAM	CG	SHO	GR	SV	IP	H	HR	BB	SO	BR/9	ERA	AERA	OAV	OOB	PR	APR	PF	OSB	OCS	FA	E	WPB	DP	FW	PW	BW	BSW	DIF
CIN	**86**	13	143	9	1403.2	**1340**	81	499	**637**	12.0	**3.27**	**117**	**.255**	.322	**101**	**89**	98	42	*43*	.974	162	45	170	.6	**8.9**	4.8		5.7
STL	45	**18**	**210**	**32**	1384.2	1377	76	498	603	12.3	3.59	115	.260	.326	50	76	105	39	*31*	.971	177	43	140	-.2	7.6	**7.9**		.2
BRO	69	9	138	13	1410.1	1431	93	**399**	528	**11.9**	3.64	110	.263	**.317**	43	58	103	42	*39*	.972	176	30	157	-.0	5.8	-2.2		3.9
CHI	72	8	136	13	1392.1	1504	74	430	584	12.6	3.80	104	.276	.331	18	20	101	34	***44***	.970	186	33	126	-.6	2.0	-.1		5.7
NY	55	6	163	20	1319.0	1412	86	477	505	13.1	4.07	96	.275	.340	-22	-20	100	57	*36*	**.975**	**153**	40	151	**.8**	-2.0	2.2		.5
PIT	53	10	157	15	1354.0	1537	70	423	464	13.2	4.15	92	.287	.342	-36	-51	98	41	*35*	.972	168	**26**	153	.1	-5.1	1.5		-5.0
BOS	68	11	144	15	1358.1	1400	**63**	513	430	12.8	3.71	100	.271	.339	31	-3	94	**32**	*41*	.971	181	30	**178**	-.6	-.3	-8.0		-3.6
PHI	67	3	133	12	1326.2	1502	106	579	447	14.4	5.17	77	.289	.365	-185	-167	102	81	*38*	.970	171	47	136	-.0	-16.7	-8.3		-5.4
TOT	515	78	1224	129	10949.0					12.8	3.92		.272	.335						.972	1374	294	1211					

Batter-Fielder Wins	Batting Average	On-Base Percentage	Slugging Average	On-Base Plus Slugging	Adjusted OPS	Adjusted Batter Runs
Mize-StL 4.3	Mize-StL 349	Ott-NY 449	Mize-StL 626	Mize-StL 1070	Mize-StL 174	Mize-StL 61.8
Frey-Cin 4.0	McCormick-Cin 332	Mize-StL 444	Ott-NY 581	Ott-NY 1030	Ott-NY 173	Ott-NY 46.8
Vaughan-Pit 4.0	Medwick-StL 332	Camilli-Bro 409	Leiber-Chi 556	Camilli-Bro 933	Camilli-Bro 144	Camilli-Bro 38.5
Ott-NY 3.4	P.Waner-Pit 328	Goodman-Cin 401	Camilli-Bro 524	Goodman-Cin 916	Goodman-Cin 144	Goodman-Cin 29.9
Camilli-Bro 3.2	Arnovich-Phi 324	Arnovich-Phi 397	Goodman-Cin 515	Medwick-StL 886	West-Bos 139	Leiber-Chi 29.8

Runs	Hits	Doubles	Triples	Home Runs	Total Bases	Runs Batted In
Werber-Cin 115	McCormick-Cin 209	Slaughter-StL 52	Herman-Chi 18	Mize-StL 28	Mize-StL 353	McCormick-Cin 128
Hack-Chi 112	Medwick-StL 201	Medwick-StL 48	Goodman-Cin 16	Ott-NY 27	McCormick-Cin 312	Medwick-StL 117
Herman-Chi 111	Mize-StL 197	Mize-StL 44	Mize-StL 14	Camilli-Bro 26	Medwick-StL 307	Mize-StL 108
Camilli-Bro 105	Slaughter-StL 193	McCormick-Cin 41	Camilli-Bro 12	Leiber-Chi 24	Camilli-Bro 296	Camilli-Bro 104
	Brown-StL 192			Lombardi-Cin 20	Slaughter-StL 291	Leiber-Chi 88

Stolen Bases	Base Stealing Runs	Fielding Runs-Infield	Fielding Runs-Outfield	Wins	Winning Pct.	Complete Games
Handley-Pit 17		Jurges-NY 19.5	Arnovich-Phi 14.3	Walters-Cin 27	Derringer-Cin 781	Walters-Cin 31
Hack-Chi 17		Frey-Cin 14.1	Slaughter-StL 13.2	Derringer-Cin 25	Walters-Cin 711	Derringer-Cin 28
Werber-Cin 15		Vaughan-Pit 11.3	Moore-StL 7.6	Davis-StL 22	French-Chi 652	Lee-Chi 20
Lavagetto-Bro 14		Hassett-Bos 10.6	Goodman-Cin 6.6	Hamlin-Bro 20	Gumbert-NY 621	Hamlin-Bro 19
Hassett-Bos 13		May-Phi 9.9	Medwick-StL 4.8	Lee-Chi 19	Hamlin-Bro 606	Posedel-Bos 18

Strikeouts	Fewest BB/Game	Games	Saves	Base Runners/9	Adjusted Relief Runs	Relief Ranking
Passeau-Phi-Chi ..137	Derringer-Cin 1.05	Shoun-StL 53	Shoun-StL 9	Hubbell-NY 10.29	Shoun-StL 3.2	J.Russell-Chi 2.2
Walters-Cin 137	Hubbell-NY 1.40	Sewell-Pit 52	Bowman-StL 9	Walters-Cin 10.30	J.Russell-Chi 2.1	Shoun-StL 1.7
Cooper-StL 130	Davis-StL 1.74	Bowman-StL 51	Davis-StL 7	Hamlin-Bro 10.31		
Derringer-Cin 128	Hamlin-Bro 1.80	Davis-StL 49	Brown-NY 7	Johnson-Phi 10.38		
Lee-Chi 105	Root-Chi 1.83	Brown-Pit 47	Brown-Pit 7	Wyatt-Bro 10.65		

Innings Pitched	Opponents' Avg.	Opponents' OBP	Earned Run Average	Adjusted ERA	Adjusted Starter Runs	Pitcher Wins
Walters-Cin 319.0	Walters-Cin 220	Hubbell-NY 280	Walters-Cin 2.29	Walters-Cin 168	Walters-Cin 54.4	**Walters-Cin** 8.2
Derringer-Cin 301.0	Bowman-StL 232	Hamlin-Bro 285	Bowman-StL 2.60	Bowman-StL 158	Derringer-Cin 30.5	**Derringer-Cin** 2.9
Lee-Chi 282.1	Hamlin-Bro 248	Walters-Cin 291	Hubbell-NY 2.75	Hubbell-NY 143	Bowman-StL 27.9	**Davis-StL** 2.8
Passeau-Phi-Chi 274.1	Hubbell-NY 249	Derringer-Cin 295	Casey-Bro 2.93	Casey-Bro 137	Casey-Bro 25.0	**Bowman-StL** 2.7
Hamlin-Bro 269.2	Moore-Cin 254	Bowman-StL 302	Derringer-Cin 2.93	Derringer-Cin 131	Thompson-Cin 21.9	**Casey-Bro** 2.7

Queen City Renaissance

Just 3_ games separated the eight teams in mid-May. From this point, however, the Cincinnati Reds asserted their dominance under second-year manager Bill McKechnie by winning 12 straight to leap to the top of the league. The Reds continued to lead the league, but slowed down, playing just .500 ball in August while the St. Louis Cardinals caught fire, taking 19 of 21 games. Responding to the challenge, Cincinnati recovered in September and clinched the pennant.

For the Reds, who captured their first flag since 1919, Bucky Walters (the league's MVP) and Paul Derringer combined for 52 victories; their progress made up for Johnny Vander Meer's slump. Bill Werber, purchased from the Athletics, proved an outstanding leadoff man, while first baseman Frank McCormick developed into a star. Cincinnati also enjoyed good defense. The pitching was efficient, and whenever runners got on, infielders Lonny Frey, Billy Myers, and Werber erased them; the Reds' 170 double plays were the third-highest total ever for an NL pennant winner.

Second-place St. Louis, playing in small Sportsman's Park, again had good offensive numbers. Their real strength, however, was the pitching of Curt Davis, Lon Warneke, and Mort Cooper. Slugger Johnny Mize didn't hurt; he won the first of his four home run crowns and his lone batting title in 1939.

Leo Durocher was hired to get the Brooklyn Dodgers out of the doldrums; this he did, moving the club from seventh to third and goosing the gate by 44 percent. Ebbets Field was also the site, on August 26, of the first-ever baseball telecast. The Dodgers had a decent enough offense, but a patchwork pitching staff provided the strength.

The Hall of Fame was dedicated in Cooperstown, New York. The opening lineup of inductees (alive and dead) elected since 1936 included National Leaguers Honus Wagner, Christy Mathewson, Grover Cleveland Alexander, Cy Young, John McGraw, Wee Willie Keeler, Buck Ewing, Al Spalding, Charley Radbourn, and Cap Anson. The World Series downstate was ho hum. The Yankees swept the Reds, who scored but 8 runs and only led for four innings of the entire series.

1939 American League

TEAM	W	L	T	PCT	GB	HW	HL	R	OR	PA	H	2B	3B	HR	BB	SO	HB	SH	AVG	OBP	SLG	OPS	AOPS	BR	ABR	PF	SB	CS	BSA	BSR
NY	106	45	1	.702		**52**	25	**967**	**556**	6129	1521	259	55	**166**	**701**	543	92	**36**	.287	**.374**	**.451**	**825**	**119**	**137**	**152**	98	72	37	66	3
BOS	89	62	1	.589	17	42	32	890	795	6054	**1543**	287	57	124	591	505	140	15	**.291**	.363	.436	799	106	81	49	104	42	44	49	-6
CLE	87	67	0	.565	20.5	44	33	797	700	6007	1490	**291**	**79**	85	557	574	120	14	.280	.350	.413	763	105	4	33	97	72	46	61	0
CHI	85	69	1	.552	22.5	50	27	755	737	6033	1451	220	56	64	579	**502**	**154**	21	.275	.349	.374	723	89	-64	-83	103	**113**	61	65	4
DET	81	73	1	.526	26.5	42	35	849	762	6108	1487	277	67	124	620	592	146	16	.279	.356	.426	782	99	45	-14	108	88	38	**70**	**6**
WAS	65	87	1	.428	41.5	37	39	702	797	6026	1483	249	**79**	44	547	460	134	11	.278	.346	.379	725	98	-65	-7	93	94	47	67	4
PHI	55	97	1	.362	51.5	28	48	711	1022	5965	1438	282	55	98	503	532	138	15	.271	.336	.400	736	96	-55	-39	98	60	34	64	1
STL	43	111	2	.279	64.5	18	59	733	1035	6133	1453	242	50	91	559	606	132	20	.268	.339	.381	720	88	-81	-96	102	48	38	56	-3
TOT	615					313	298	6404		48455	11866	2107	498	796	4657	4314	148	1056	.279	.352	.407	759					589	345	63	9

TEAM	CG	SHO	GR	SV	IP	H	HR	BB	SO	BR/9	ERA	AERA	OAV	OOB	PR	APR	PF	OSB	OCS	FA	E	WPB	DP	FW	PW	BW	BSW	DIF
NY	**87**	**15**	93	**26**	1348.2	**1208**	85	567	565	**11.9**	**3.31**	**132**	**.241**	**.319**	**196**	**166**	94	49	32	**.978**	**126**	**29**	159	**2.9**	**15.3**	**14.0**	.2	-1.9
BOS	52	4	**187**	20	1350.2	1533	77	543	539	14.0	4.56	104	.287	.355	9	25	102	85	43	.970	180	31	147	.0	2.3	4.5	-.7	7.2
CLE	69	10	142	13	1364.2	1394	**75**	602	614	13.3	4.08	108	.267	.344	81	51	95	67	43	.970	180	37	148	.2	4.7	3.0	-.1	2.1
CHI	62	5	125	21	1377.0	1470	99	**454**	535	12.7	4.31	110	.275	.333	48	63	102	73	41	.972	167	35	140	1.0	5.8	-7.6	.3	8.6
DET	64	8	150	16	1367.1	1430	104	574	**633**	13.3	4.29	114	.268	.341	50	86	106	65	53	.967	198	47	147	-.6	7.9	-1.3	**.5**	-2.4
WAS	72	4	122	10	1354.2	1420	**75**	602	521	13.6	4.60	94	.271	.348	2	-41	94	**47**	34	.966	205	70	**167**	-1.1	-3.8	-.6	.3	-5.7
PHI	50	6	155	12	1342.2	1687	148	579	397	15.3	5.79	81	.307	.375	-175	-159	102	103	43	.964	210	49	131	-1.4	-14.7	-3.6	.0	-1.4
STL	56	3	181	3	1371.1	1724	133	739	516	16.4	6.01	81	.310	.393	-212	-166	105	100	**56**	.968	199	49	144	-.6	-15.3	-8.8	-.4	-8.8
TOT	512	55	1155	121	10877.0					13.8	4.62		.279	.352						.969	1465	347	1183					

Batter-Fielder Wins	Batting Average	On-Base Percentage	Slugging Average	On-Base Plus Slugging	Adjusted OPS	Adjusted Batter Runs
DiMaggio-NY 5.5	DiMaggio-NY 381	Foxx-Bos 464	Foxx-Bos..............694	Foxx-Bos 1158	DiMaggio-NY 185	Foxx-Bos 62.0
Foxx-Bos.............5.2	Foxx-Bos..............360	Selkirk-NY 452	DiMaggio-NY 671	DiMaggio-NY......1119	Foxx-Bos 185	DiMaggio-NY......59.0
Johnson-Phi........4.8	Johnson-Phi 338	DiMaggio-NY 448	Greenberg-Det 622	Williams-Bos 1045	Williams-Bos 158	Williams-Bos 52.7
Dickey-NY 4.5	Trosky-Cle 335	Keller-NY 447	Williams-Bos.........609	Greenberg-Det ..1042	Trosky-Cle 157	Johnson-Phi 49.4
Williams-Bos 4.1	Rolfe-NY...............329	Johnson-Phi................440	Trosky-Cle 589	Trosky-Cle 994	Johnson-Phi...........156	Greenberg-Det ...40.1

Runs	Hits	Doubles	Triples	Home Runs	Total Bases	Runs Batted In
Rolfe-NY 139	Rolfe-NY 213	Rolfe-NY 46	Lewis-Was 16	Foxx-Bos 35	Williams-Bos 344	Williams-Bos 145
Williams-Bos 131	McQuinn-StL 195	Williams-Bos 44	McCosky-Det.........14	Greenberg-Det 33	Foxx-Bos 324	DiMaggio-NY 126
Foxx-Bos 130	Keltner-Cle............191	Greenberg-Det 42	McQuinn-StL 13	Williams-Bos 31	Rolfe-NY 321	Johnson-Phi 114
McCosky-Det........120	McCosky-Det.........190	McQuinn-StL..................37	Campbell-Cle..........13	DiMaggio-NY...........30	McQuinn-StL 318	Greenberg-Det 112
Johnson-Phi..........115	Williams-Bos 185	Keltner-Cle 35		Gordon-NY 28	Greenberg-Det 311	

Stolen Bases	Base Stealing Runs	Fielding Runs-Infield	Fielding Runs-Outfield	Wins	Winning Pct.	Complete Games
Case-Was 51	Case-Was..............5.3	Doerr-Bos 26.5	Johnson-Phi 9.7	Feller-Cle 24	Grove-Bos 789	Newsom-StL-Det ..24
Kreevich-Chi 23	McCosky-Det 3.0	Clift-StL 12.9	Kreevich-Chi..........9.5	Ruffing-NY..............21	Ruffing-NY 750	Feller-Cle 24
Fox-Det 23	Kuhel-Chi 2.2	Trosky-Cle 11.5	Fox-Det..................8.4	Newsom-StL-Det....20	Feller-Cle 727	Ruffing-NY 22
McCosky-Det..........20	Welaj-Was 2.2	Lewis-Was 10.9	Walker-Chi 7.6	Leonard-Was 20	Leonard-Was 714	Leonard-Was 21
	Chapman-Cle 1.9	Crosetti-NY 9.8	DiMaggio-NY 4.5	Bridges-Det 17	Bridges-Det...........708	Grove-Bos 17

Strikeouts	Fewest BB/Game	Games	Saves	Base Runners/9	Adjusted Relief Runs	Relief Ranking
Feller-Cle 246	Lyons-Chi 1.36	Brown-Chi......................61	Murphy-NY 19	Lyons-Chi 9.85	Brown-Chi............10.5	Brown-Chi 20.4
Newsom-StL-Det..192	Leonard-Was 1.97	Dean-Phi........................54	Brown-Chi 18	Russo-NY 9.93	Heving-Bos............6.1	Heving-Bos 8.1
Bridges-Det 129	Beckmann-Phi 2.38	Dickman-Bos 48	Heving-Bos 7	Hildebrand-NY ..10.23	Dickman-Bos 1.5	Dickman-Bos........1.5
Rigney-Chi.............119	Lee-Chi................2.68	Heving-Bos 46	Dean-Phi 7	Ruffing-NY 11.11		
Chase-Was 118	Grove-Bos 2.73		Appleton-Was 6	Leonard-Was 11.26		

Innings Pitched	Opponents' Avg.	Opponents' OBP	Earned Run Average	Adjusted ERA	Adjusted Starter Runs	Pitcher Wins
Feller-Cle 296.2	Feller-Cle 210	Lyons-Chi.....................276	Grove-Bos 2.54	Grove-Bos 186	Feller-Cle 54.2	**Feller-Cle**............6.0
Newsom-StL-Det291.2	Gomez-NY 235	Ruffing-NY 301	Lyons-Chi 2.76	Lyons-Chi 171	Grove-Bos 45.2	**Ruffing-NY** 4.8
Leonard-Was 269.1	Hadley-NY 237	Feller-Cle 303	Feller-Cle 2.85	Feller-Cle.............154	Newsom-StL-Det 42.2	**Grove-Bos** 3.7
Lee-Chi..............235.0	Ruffing-NY 240	Bridges-Det 304	Ruffing-NY 2.93	Ruffing-NY............149	Ruffing-NY 37.8	**Lyons-Chi** 3.7
Ruffing-NY 233.1	Bridges-Det...........243	Leonard-Was 305	Hadley-NY 2.98	Hadley-NY 146	Lyons-Chi 31.7	**Newsom-StL-Det**3.5

Williams Can't Unseat Yankees

An unparalleled rookie class graced the American League in 1939. Say hello to Ted Williams, Charlie Keller, Dizzy Trout, Mickey Vernon, Early Wynn, and Hal Newhouser, all of whom affected baseball in the 1940s and beyond. Let's focus on Williams, a lithe 20-year-old from San Diego. He was second in the league in doubles and walks, fifth in hits, and third in homers. The Red Sox ended up second, their best finish in two decades, on his hitting, that of Jimmie Foxx, and the ninth and final ERA crown won by ageless Lefty Grove.

But New York again rolled over the competition, leaving the Red Sox 17 games behind. It is a tribute to the Yankees that they kept winning even when Lou Gehrig was forced to retire due to a condition eventually defined as Amyotrophic Lateral Sclerosis. The disease would kill him in 1941, shortly before he would have turned 38. (Three other greats also left the active ranks in '39: Jimmy Dykes, Tony Lazzeri, and Heinie Manush.)

How did the Yanks do it? Balance, again, was the secret. All eight regulars hit at least 10 homers, and the Yankees led the league in runs, ERA, and saves. Keller, Joe DiMaggio, and George Selkirk comprised a top outfield, while manager Joe McCarthy gave seven pitchers at least 10 starts—and each won at least 10 games.

Another four-game World Series sweep, this one over Cincinnati, established the Yankees as perhaps the AL's greatest team to date. Bill Dickey, DiMaggio, and Keller did the damage as New York outscored the Reds 20–8. It was New York's eighth world championship since 1923, and even more dominating, it was their fifth sweep.

But even perfection becomes boring; attendance at Yankee Stadium dropped 11 percent. The Athletics, hoping to increase their gate, hosted the league's first night game on May 16. And while scoring dropped, the league's 512 complete games still ranked as the lowest total ever.

1940 National League

TEAM	W	L	T	PCT	GB	HW	HL	R	OR	PA	H	2B	3B	HR	BB	SO	HB	SH	AVG	OBP	SLG	OPS	AOPS	BR	ABR	PF	SB	CS	BSA	BSR
CIN	100	53	2	.654		**55**	21	707	**528**	5986	1427	264	38	89	453	503	**125**	**36**	.266	.327	.379	706	100	9	2	101	72			
BRO	88	65	3	.575	12	41	37	697	621	6089	1421	256	**70**	93	522	570	77	20	.260	.327	.383	710	96	15	-26	106	56			
STL	84	69	3	.549	16	41	36	747	699	6087	**1514**	266	61	**119**	479	610	88	21	.275	.336	**.411**	**747**	106	84	42	106	**97**			
PIT	78	76	2	.506	22.5	40	34	**809**	783	6115	1511	**276**	68	76	**553**	**494**	63	33	**.276**	**.346**	.394	740	**112**	**87**	**93**	99	69			
CHI	75	79	0	.487	25.5	40	37	681	636	5970	1441	272	48	86	482	566	70	29	.267	.331	.384	715	106	28	42	98	63			
NY	72	80	0	.474	27.5	33	43	663	659	5900	1423	201	46	91	453	478	86	37	.267	.329	.374	703	99	1	-4	101	45			
BOS	65	87	0	.428	34.5	35	40	623	745	5810	1366	219	50	59	402	581	62	17	.256	.311	.349	660	93	-86	-53	95	48			
PHI	50	103	0	.327	50	24	55	494	750	5673	1225	180	35	75	435	527	87	14	.238	.300	.331	631	83	-137	-116	96	25			
TOT	617					309	303	5421		47630	11328	1934	416	688	3779	4329	207	658	.264	.326	.376	702					475			

TEAM	CG	SHO	GR	SV	IP	H	HR	BB	SO	BR/9	ERA	AERA	OAV	OOB	PR	APR	PF	OSB	OCS	FA	E	WPB	DP	FW	PW	BW	BSW	DIF
CIN	**91**	10	106	11	1407.2	**1263**	73	445	557	**11.0**	**3.05**	**124**	**.240**	**.302**	**125**	**117**	98	51	*29*	**.981**	**117**	22	158	**2.9**	**11.8**	.2		8.6
BRO	65	**17**	169	14	1433.0	1366	101	**393**	**639**	11.2	3.50	114	.248	**.302**	56	76	104	52	*35*	.970	183	22	110	-.3	7.7	-2.6		6.8
STL	71	10	168	14	1396.0	1457	83	488	550	12.7	3.83	104	.266	.329	3	23	104	63	*51*	.971	174	45	134	.1	2.3	4.2		.8
PIT	49	8	**215**	**24**	1388.2	1569	**72**	492	491	13.6	4.36	87	.283	.345	-79	-86	99	80	*55*	.966	217	32	161	-2.0	-8.7	**9.4**		2.3
CHI	69	12	151	14	1392.0	1418	74	430	564	12.1	3.54	106	.262	.319	47	33	97	58	*48*	.968	199	**21**	143	-1.2	3.3	4.2		-8.4
NY	57	11	166	18	1360.1	1383	110	473	606	12.4	3.79	102	.262	.325	9	14	101	**44**	*49*	.977	139	36	132	1.6	1.4	-.4		-6.6
BOS	76	9	148	12	1359.0	1444	83	573	435	13.6	4.36	85	.274	.349	-77	-100	97	58	***61***	.970	184	31	**169**	-.6	-10.1	-5.4		5.1
PHI	66	5	133	8	1357.0	1429	92	475	485	12.8	4.40	89	.270	.333	-83	-74	101	69	*43*	.970	181	48	136	-.4	-7.5	-11.7		-6.9
TOT	544	82	1256	115	11093.2					12.4	3.85		.264	.326						.972	1394	257	1143					

Batter-Fielder Wins	Batting Average	On-Base Percentage	Slugging Average	On-Base Plus Slugging	Adjusted OPS	Adjusted Batter Runs
Vaughan-Pit 5.1	Garms-Pit 355	Fletcher-Pit 418	Mize-StL 636	Mize-StL 1039	Mize-StL 173	Mize-StL 56.9
Hack-Chi.............4.5	Davis-Pit 326	Ott-NY 407	Nicholson-Chi 534	Camilli-Bro...........926	Nicholson-Chi 148	Fletcher-Pit 33.9
Mize-StL 3.6	Lombardi-Cin 319	Mize-StL......................404	Camilli-Bro 529	Nicholson-Chi 899	Camilli-Bro............144	Camilli-Bro.........33.2
Miller-Bos 3.4	Cooney-Bos 318	Camilli-Bro...................397	DiMaggio-Cin-Pit .519	Slaughter-StL........874	Gleeson-Chi 139	Ott-NY 32.2
Danning-NY 3.1	Hack-Chi...............317	Hack-Chi 395	Slaughter-StL 504	Ott-NY 864	Fletcher-Pit 137	Nicholson-Chi 30.9

Runs	Hits	Doubles	Triples	Home Runs	Total Bases	Runs Batted In
Vaughan-Pit..........113	F.McCormick-Cin ..191	F.McCormick-Cin...........44	Vaughan-Pit............15	Mize-StL 43	Mize-StL 368	Mize-StL 137
Mize-StL 111	Hack-Chi 191	Vaughan-Pit 40	Ross-Bos 14	Nicholson-Chi 25	F.McCormick-Cin ..298	F.McCormick-Cin 127
Werber-Cin 105	Mize-StL 182	Gleeson-Chi 39	Slaughter-StL..........13	Rizzo-Pit-Cin-Phi 24	Medwick-StL-Bro ..280	VanRobays-Pit 116
Frey-Cin................102	Vaughan-Pit..........178	Hack-Chi........................38	Mize-StL 13	Camilli-Bro..............23	Camilli-Bro............271	Fletcher-Pit..........104
Hack-Chi 101	Medwick-StL-Bro ..175	Walker-Bro 37	Camilli-Bro..............13		Vaughan-Pit..........269	Young-NY 101

Stolen Bases	Base Stealing Runs	Fielding Runs-Infield	Fielding Runs-Outfield	Wins	Winning Pct.	Complete Games
Frey-Cin.................22		Herman-Chi 20.3	Moore-StL............13.0	Walters-Cin 22	Fitzsimmons-Bro .889	Walters-Cin............29
Hack-Chi 21		Witek-NY 16.2	Moore-Bro-Bos 5.4	Passeau-Chi 20	Sewell-Pit 762	Derringer-Cin 26
Moore-StL 18		May-Phi 15.8	Ross-Bos 5.4	Derringer-Cin..........20	Walters-Cin...........688	Mulcahy-Phi 21
Werber-Cin 16		Frey-Cin 15.0	West-Bos 4.8		Thompson-Cin 640	Passeau-Chi..........20
Reese-Bro 15		Miller-Bos....................14.8	Slaughter-StL 4.5		Derringer-Cin 625	Higbe-Phi 20

Strikeouts	Fewest BB/Game	Games	Saves	Base Runners/9	Adjusted Relief Runs	Relief Ranking
Higbe-Phi..............137	Derringer-Cin 1.46	Shoun-StL......................54	Brown-NY 7	Fitzsimmons-Bro 9.78	Beggs-Cin............15.4	Beggs-Cin 30.3
Wyatt-Bro..............124	Turner-Cin...........1.54	Brown-Pit 48	Brown-Pit..................7	Derringer-Cin 9.95	Russell-StL 6.8	Russell-StL 8.2
Passeau-Chi 124	Hamlin-Bro 1.68	Passeau-Chi 46	Beggs-Cin 7	Walters-Cin..........9.97	Raffensberger-Chi 3.1	Raffensberger-Chi....4.0
Schumacher-NY ..123	Davis-StL-Bro 1.79	Casey-Bro......................44	Shoun-StL 5	Pressnell-Bro 10.14	Hutchings-Cin........2.8	Pressnell-Bro........3.6
....	Warneke-StL........1.82	Raffensberger-Chi 43	Passeau-Chi 5	Passeau-Chi......10.33	Brown-NY 2.5	Brown-NY 3.1

Innings Pitched	Opponents' Avg.	Opponents' OBP	Earned Run Average	Adjusted ERA	Adjusted Starter Runs	Pitcher Wins
Walters-Cin........305.0	Walters-Cin..........220	Derringer-Cin 276	Walters-Cin..........2.48	Walters-Cin 153	Walters-Cin..........44.1	**Passeau-Chi** 5.1
Derringer-Cin 296.2	Higbe-Phi 232	Passeau-Chi 278	Passeau-Chi........2.50	Passeau-Chi 150	Passeau-Chi........37.1	**Walters-Cin** 4.7
Higbe-Phi 283.0	Thompson-Cin 233	Walters-Cin 283	Sewell-Pit 2.80	Sewell-Pit.............136	Derringer-Cin 25.0	**Beggs-Cin** 3.2
Passeau-Chi......280.2	Passeau-Chi.........237	Tamulis-Bro 288	Fitzsimmons-Bro 2.81	Turner-Cin 131	Sewell-Pit 20.5	**Olsen-Chi**............2.5
Mulcahy-Phi 280.0	Casey-Bro............237	Hamlin-Bro..................292	Turner-Cin...........2.89	Hamlin-Bro 131	Fitzsimmons-Bro 18.7	**Sewell-Pit** 2.5

Reds Take It All

The dominant NL teams of the 1940s were St. Louis and Brooklyn. Listing the top debut players for the teams in 1940 tells why: The Cardinals brought up shortstop Marty Marion and pitchers Harry Brecheen and Walker Cooper, while the Dodgers summoned shortstop Pee Wee Reese and outfielder Pete Reiser.

While AL attendance rose, the NL's fell nearly 7 percent. To increase ticket sales, the Giants, Cardinals, and Pirates added lights to their parks, while the Braves changed their park's dimensions, moving in the foul lines and the center-field fences.

The Reds and Dodgers were the early leaders in the '40 race. In mid-July, once the surprising Giants fell from the race, Brooklyn began to slump. The Reds, meanwhile, took 19 of 21 to surge ahead. Brooklyn continued to stumble, and Cincinnati kept winning. The pitching-and-defense Reds set a new NL record with a .981 fielding percentage. Bucky Walters led the NL in wins, ERA, and innings, and was ably supported by Paul Derringer. Frank McCormick sparked a mediocre attack by topping the loop in hits and doubles.

There was one casualty. On August 2, following a tough loss, backup catcher Willard Hershberger took his life. By World Series time, everyday receiver Ernie Lombardi was too banged-up to play. Therefore, with Hershberger out of the picture, 40-year-old coach Jimmie Wilson was forced into action for six of the seven games. He hit .353.

The Tigers won their three games by an aggregate of 22–6, and led 1–0, 2–1, and 3–2 in games, but the Reds won the last two contests at home, clinching their first world championship since 1919. Derringer and Walters won all four games for Cincinnati. Detroit's Bobo Newsom won Game 5 three days after his father died, then fell 2–1 in a tension-filled finale.

1940 American League

TEAM	W	L	T	PCT	GB	HW	HL	R	OR	PA	H	2B	3B	HR	BB	SO	HB	SH	AVG	OBP	SLG	OPS	AOPS	BR	ABR	PF	SB	CS	BSA	BSR
DET	90	64	1	.584		50	29	**888**	717	6183	1549	**312**	65	134	**664**	**556**	77	24	**.286**	**.366**	.442	**808**	105	**130**	50	110	**66**	39	**63**	**1**
CLE	89	65	1	.578	1	51	30	710	**637**	5957	1422	287	61	101	519	597	61	16	.265	.332	.398	730	98	-43	-22	97	53	36	60	-1
NY	88	66	1	.571	2	**52**	24	817	671	6046	1371	243	66	**155**	648	606	76	**36**	.259	.344	.418	762	107	25	58	96	59	36	62	0
CHI	82	72	1	.532	8	41	36	735	672	6002	1499	238	63	73	496	569	**110**	10	.278	.340	.387	727	93	-45	-54	101	52	60	46	-10
BOS	82	72	0	.532	8	45	34	872	825	6174	**1566**	301	**80**	145	590	597	91	12	**.286**	.356	**.449**	805	**110**	110	**76**	104	55	49	53	-5
STL	67	87	2	.435	23	37	39	757	882	6051	1423	278	58	118	556	642	63	16	.263	.333	.401	734	94	-35	-50	102	51	40	56	-3
WAS	64	90	0	.416	26	36	41	665	811	5912	1453	266	67	52	468	504	61	18	.271	.331	.374	705	95	-87	-41	94	94	40	70	7
PHI	54	100	0	.351	36	29	42	703	932	5948	1391	242	53	105	556	656	69	19	.262	.334	.387	721	95	-55	-40	98	48	33	59	-1
TOT	619					341	275	6147		48273	11674	2167	513	883	4497	4727	151	608	.271	.342	.407	750					478	333	59	-11

TEAM	CG	SHO	GR	SV	IP	H	HR	BB	SO	BR/9	ERA	AERA	OAV	OOB	PR	APR	PF	OSB	OCS	FA	E	WPB	DP	FW	PW	BW	BSW	DIF
DET	59	10	171	**23**	1375.1	1425	102	570	**752**	13.2	4.01	**119**	.266	.338	57	**105**	109	54	**56**	.968	194	33	116	-.7	**9.9**	4.7	.2	-1.2
CLE	72	**13**	151	22	1375.0	**1328**	**86**	512	686	12.2	**3.63**	116	.254	.324	**115**	93	96	**42**	47	**.975**	**149**	33	164	**1.7**	8.8	-2.1	.0	3.5
NY	76	10	125	14	1373.0	1389	119	511	559	12.6	3.89	104	.261	.328	76	24	92	43	43	**.975**	152	**28**	158	1.6	2.3	5.5	.1	1.6
CHI	**83**	10	91	18	1386.2	1335	111	**480**	574	**11.9**	3.74	118	**.250**	**.313**	99	**105**	101	55	32	.969	185	46	125	-.2	**9.9**	-5.1	-.8	1.2
BOS	51	4	178	16	1379.2	1568	124	625	613	14.5	4.89	92	.284	.359	-77	-58	103	64	32	.972	173	48	156	.4	-5.5	**7.2**	-.3	3.2
STL	64	4	**180**	9	1373.1	1592	113	646	439	14.8	5.12	89	.290	.367	-113	-79	105	63	33	.974	158	60	**179**	1.3	-7.5	-4.7	-.1	1.0
WAS	74	6	122	7	1350.0	1494	93	618	618	14.2	4.59	91	.281	.359	-31	-67	95	65	54	.968	194	70	166	-.7	-6.3	-3.9	**.8**	-2.9
PHI	72	4	117	12	1345.0	1543	135	534	488	14.0	5.22	85	.283	.348	-125	-114	101	92	36	.960	238	55	131	-3.1	-10.8	-3.8	.0	-5.4
TOT	551	61	1135	121	10958.0					13.4	4.38		.271	.342						.970	1443	373	1195					

Batter-Fielder Wins	Batting Average	On-Base Percentage	Slugging Average	On-Base Plus Slugging	Adjusted OPS	Adjusted Batter Runs
DiMaggio-NY 4.5	DiMaggio-NY 352	Williams-Bos 442	Greenberg-Det 670	Greenberg-Det ..1103	DiMaggio-NY........176	Greenberg-Det ..57.4
Greenberg-Det....4.5	Appling-Chi...........348	Greenberg-Det............433	DiMaggio-NY 626	DiMaggio-NY......1051	Greenberg-Det 166	DiMaggio-NY......56.3
Williams-Bos 4.0	Williams-Bos.........344	Gehringer-Det 428	Williams-Bos.........594	Williams-Bos 1036	Williams-Bos 159	Williams-Bos 53.1
Gordon-NY 3.8	Radcliff-StL...........342	DiMaggio-NY 425	York-Det 583	York-Det................993	Foxx-Bos 148	Foxx-Bos 39.2
Boudreau-Cle......3.5	Greenberg-Det 340	Appling-Chi 420	Foxx-Bos..............581	Foxx-Bos 993	Keller-NY 142	York-Det 37.3

Runs	Hits	Doubles	Triples	Home Runs	Total Bases	Runs Batted In
Williams-Bos 134	Radcliff-StL 200	Greenberg-Det 50	McCosky-Det..........19	Greenberg-Det 41	Greenberg-Det 384	Greenberg-Det 150
Greenberg-Det 129	McCosky-Det........200	York-Det 46	Keller-NY 15	Foxx-Bos 36	York-Det................343	York-Det 134
McCosky-Det........123	Cramer-Bos 200	Boudreau-Cle 46	Finney-Bos 15	York-Det.................33	Williams-Bos 333	DiMaggio-NY 133
Gordon-NY 112	Appling-Chi 197	Williams-Bos.................43	Williams-Bos 14	Johnson-Phi............31	DiMaggio-NY........318	Foxx-Bos 119
Kuhel-Chi.............111	Wright-Chi 196	Moses-Phi.....................41	Appling-Chi 13	DiMaggio-NY 31	Gordon-NY 315	Williams-Bos 113

Stolen Bases	Base Stealing Runs	Fielding Runs-Infield	Fielding Runs-Outfield	Wins	Winning Pct.	Complete Games
Case-Was 35	Case-Was.............4.2	Heffner-StL 15.7	Kreevich-Chi..........6.9	Feller-Cle 27	Rowe-Det 842	Feller-Cle 31
Walker-Was 21	Walker-Was 3.2	Gordon-NY 13.8	Solters-Chi 6.2	Newsom-Det 21	Newsom-Det.........808	Lee-Chi..................24
Gordon-NY 18	Gehringer-Det........2.2	Bloodworth-Was 13.7	Johnson-Phi 5.6	Milnar-Cle 18	Feller-Cle 711	Leonard-Was 23
Lewis-Was.............15	Bartell-Det 1.9	Doerr-Bos 13.4	DiMaggio-Bos........5.6	Hudson-Was 17	Smith-Cle 682	
Kreevich-Chi 15	Rosar-NY 1.2	Bartell-Det 13.4	Moses-Phi 4.7		Milnar-Cle 643	

Strikeouts	Fewest BB/Game	Games	Saves	Base Runners/9	Adjusted Relief Runs	Relief Ranking
Feller-Cle 261	Lyons-Chi 1.79	Feller-Cle 43	Benton-Det 17	Bonham-NY 8.70	Eisenstat-Cle 10.6	Brown-Chi 10.3
Newsom-Det 164	Lee-Chi................2.21	Benton-Det 42	Brown-Chi 10	Feller-Cle 10.34	Brown-Chi.............6.0	Eisenstat-Cle........8.0
Rigney-Chi............141	Rowe-Det 2.29	Wilson-Bos 41	Murphy-NY 9	Murphy-NY 10.37	Trotter-StL..............4.4	Murphy-NY 7.5
Bridges-Det 133	Leonard-Was 2.43	Heusser-Phi 41		Rigney-Chi 10.65	Murphy-NY 3.7	Benton-Det 6.7
Chase-Was 129	Russo-NY 2.61	Dobson-Cle...................40		Lyons-Chi 10.87	Benton-Det 3.3	Trotter-StL 5.5

Innings Pitched	Opponents' Avg.	Opponents' OBP	Earned Run Average	Adjusted ERA	Adjusted Starter Runs	Pitcher Wins
Feller-Cle 320.1	Feller-Cle 210	Feller-Cle 285	Feller-Cle 2.61	Newsom-Det 168	Feller-Cle 61.5	**Feller-Cle**............6.8
Leonard-Was 289.0	Smith-Chi 228	Lyons-Chi......................287	Newsom-Det........2.83	Feller-Cle 161	Newsom-Det........47.0	**Rigney-Chi** 4.1
Rigney-Chi 280.2	Bridges-Det...........229	Rigney-Chi 292	Rigney-Chi 3.11	Rigney-Chi............142	Rigney-Chi 38.9	**Newsom-Det**......3.9
Newsom-Det......264.0	Rigney-Chi 230	Lee-Chi 300	Smith-Chi 3.21	Bridges-Det 141	Bridges-Det..........27.1	**Rowe-Det**............3.1
Auker-StL 263.2	Newsom-Det.........238	Russo-NY 303	Chase-Was..........3.23	Smith-Chi..............138	Rowe-Det 25.6	**Bonham-NY**........2.8

Tigers Fill Their Tank

The AL race of 1940 was made possible by a poor start from the usually dominant Yankees. Detroit and Cleveland made hay while New York struggled, and the Indians led into September. The Tribe—a league laughingstock due to a much-publicized player rebellion against autocratic manager Ossie Vitt—dropped five straight (three to the Tigers) while the Yankees won 19 of 23 to create a three-way tie on September 9. New York dropped out, but the Tigers and Indians clustered until Detroit took three of four from Cleveland in late September. In the clincher, unknown Floyd Giebell shut out Bob Feller and the Indians for his third (and last) major league victory.

Hank Greenberg led the AL in doubles, homers, and RBIs for overpowering Detroit, while 21-year-old Feller took the pitching Triple Crown. New York had deep pitching and power, but several regulars slumped. Fourth-place Boston made rookie Dom, the youngest DiMaggio, their center fielder.

Each AL team had an attendance bump, sending league sales to their highest total to date. The Tigers, the only AL team to top the million mark in the 1930s, became the only AL team to do so in the new decade until 1945, when they did it again. While homers rose to 883, a new league high that would last until 1950, runs per team fell to 4.97 per game—the top rate in what would be a pitching-friendly decade.

White Sox second baseman Jackie Hayes began to lose his sight, and was forced to retire midseason at age 33. Another veteran infielder, Billy Rogell, 35, finished his fourteen-season career but would live another 63 years.

The World Series was one of the best in years. The teams traded wins until the Reds pulled out Game 7. Detroit's Bobo Newsom, whose father died midway through the Series, was 2–1 with a 1.38 ERA.

1941 National League

TEAM	W	L	T	PCT	GB	HW	HL	R	OR	PA	H	2B	3B	HR	BB	SO	HB	SH	AVG	OBP	SLG	OPS	AOPS	BR	ABR	PF	SB	CS	BSA	BSR
BRO	100	54	3	.649		52	25	**800**	581	6218	**1494**	**286**	**69**	**101**	**600**	535	106	27	**.272**	**.347**	**.405**	**752**	**113**	**132**	**98**	104	36			
STL	97	56	2	.634	2.5	**53**	24	734	589	6151	1482	254	56	70	540	543	**126**	**28**	**.272**	.340	.377	717	102	63	17	107	47			
CIN	88	66	0	.571	12	45	34	616	**564**	5819	1288	213	33	64	477	**428**	102	22	.247	.313	.337	650	89	-74	-76	100	**68**			
PIT	81	73	2	.526	19	45	32	690	643	5954	1417	233	65	56	547	516	95	15	.268	.338	.368	706	105	38	41	100	59			
NY	74	79	3	.484	25.5	38	39	667	706	6018	1401	248	35	95	504	518	96	23	.260	.326	.371	697	101	16	3	102	36			
CHI	70	84	1	.455	30	38	39	666	670	5902	1323	239	25	99	559	670	99	14	.253	.327	.365	692	105	11	36	96	39			
BOS	62	92	2	.403	38	32	44	592	720	5968	1357	231	38	48	471	608	70	13	.251	.312	.334	646	92	-84	-59	96	61			
PHI	43	111	1	.279	57	23	52	501	793	5796	1277	188	38	64	451	596	90	22	.244	.307	.331	638	89	-101	-80	96	65			
TOT	622					326	289	5266		47826	11039	1892	359	597	4149	4414	164	784	.258	.326	.361	688					411			

TEAM	CG	SHO	GR	SV	IP	H	HR	BB	SO	BR/9	ERA	AERA	OAV	OOB	PR	APR	PF	OSB	OCS	FA	E	WPB	DP	FW	PW	BW	BSW	DIF
BRO	66	17	157	**22**	1421.0	**1236**	81	495	603	**11.1**	**3.14**	117	**.233**	**.300**	**78**	82	101	**34**	*40*	.974	162	**29**	125	.9	8.4	**10.1**		3.6
STL	64	15	171	20	1416.1	1289	85	502	**659**	11.5	3.19	**118**	.242	.310	70	**87**	104	42	*48*	.973	172	32	146	.2	**8.9**	1.7		9.6
CIN	**89**	**19**	112	10	1386.2	1300	61	510	627	11.9	3.17	114	.250	.319	72	67	99	64	*46*	**.975**	**152**	39	147	**1.3**	6.9	-7.8		10.7
PIT	71	8	150	12	1374.1	1392	66	492	410	12.4	3.48	104	.260	.323	23	19	99	47	*42*	.968	196	33	130	-1.1	2.0	4.2		-1.0
NY	55	12	175	18	1391.2	1455	90	539	566	13.0	3.94	94	.269	.337	-48	-38	102	46	*41*	.974	160	37	144	.9	-3.9	.3		.2
CHI	74	8	145	9	1364.2	1431	**60**	**449**	548	12.5	3.72	94	.267	.327	-13	-34	97	59	*39*	.970	180	30	139	-.3	-3.5	3.7		-6.9
BOS	62	10	176	9	1385.2	1440	75	554	446	13.2	3.95	90	.269	.341	-49	-59	98	53	*47*	.969	191	36	**174**	-.9	-6.1	-6.1		-2.0
PHI	35	4	**201**	9	1372.1	1499	79	606	552	14.0	4.50	82	.279	.355	-132	-119	102	66	***52***	.969	187	46	147	-.7	-12.2	-8.2		-12.9
TOT	516	93	1287	109	11112.2					12.4	3.63		.258	.326						.972	1400	282	1152					

Batter-Fielder Wins	Batting Average	On-Base Percentage	Slugging Average	On-Base Plus Slugging	Adjusted OPS	Adjusted Batter Runs
Reiser-Bro 4.5	Reiser-Bro 343	Fletcher-Pit 421	Reiser-Bro 558	Reiser-Bro 964	Reiser-Bro 163	Camilli-Bro.........46.5
Fletcher-Pit 3.6	Cooney-Bos 319	Hack-Chi 417	Camilli-Bro 556	Camilli-Bro...........962	Camilli-Bro...........162	Reiser-Bro 43.7
Camilli-Bro 3.3	Medwick-Bro........318	Camilli-Bro 407	Mize-StL 535	Mize-StL 941	Mize-StL 153	Fletcher-Pit 39.8
Hack-Chi.............3.1	Hack-Chi..............317	Reiser-Bro 406	Medwick-Bro.........517	Ott-NY 898	Ott-NY 149	Hack-Chi 39.5
Ott-NY 3.0	Mize-StL 317	Mize-StL......................406	Slaughter-StL 496	Slaughter-StL........886	Fletcher-Pit 148	Ott-NY 38.2

Runs	Hits	Doubles	Triples	Home Runs	Total Bases	Runs Batted In
Reiser-Bro 117	Hack-Chi 186	Reiser-Bro.....................39	Reiser-Bro 17	Camilli-Bro.............34	Reiser-Bro 299	Camilli-Bro 120
Hack-Chi 111	Reiser-Bro 184	Mize-StL 39	Fletcher-Pit 13	Ott-NY 27	Camilli-Bro............294	Young-NY 104
Medwick-Bro 100	Litwhiler-Phi..........180	Rucker-NY.....................38	Hopp-StL 11	Nicholson-Chi 26	Medwick-Bro 278	Mize-StL 100
Rucker-NY 95	Rucker-NY 179	Dallessandro-Chi 36	Medwick-Bro 10	Young-NY 25	Litwhiler-Phi..........275	DiMaggio-Pit........100
Fletcher-Pit 95	Medwick-Bro 171		Elliott-Pit 10	Dahlgren-Bos-Chi ..23	Young-NY 265	Nicholson-Chi........98

Stolen Bases	Base Stealing Runs	Fielding Runs-Infield	Fielding Runs-Outfield	Wins	Winning Pct.	Complete Games
Murtaugh-Phi..........18		May-Phi 23.9	Litwhiler-Phi 13.3	Wyatt-Bro...............22	E.Riddle-Cin 826	Walters-Cin...........27
Benjamin-Phi 17		Stringer-Chi 23.8	Walker-Bro 9.9	Higbe-Bro 22	Higbe-Bro 710	Wyatt-Bro 23
Handley-Pit 16		Miller-Bos....................13.3	VanRobays-Pit 6.1	Walters-Cin 19	White-StL 708	Tobin-Bos 20
Frey-Cin 16		Werber-Cin..................10.1	West-Bos 5.4	E.Riddle-Cin 19	Wyatt-Bro 688	Passeau-Chi..........20
Hopp-StL 15		Fletcher-Pit 9.9	Moore-Bos 5.2		Warneke-StL.........654	

Strikeouts	Fewest BB/Game	Games	Saves	Base Runners/9	Adjusted Relief Runs	Relief Ranking
VanderMeer-Cin ..202	Passeau-Chi........2.03	Higbe-Bro 48	Brown-NY 8	Wyatt-Bro 9.58	Pressnell-Chi 4.5	Pressnell-Chi........4.8
Wyatt-Bro..............176	Derringer-Cin 2.13	Pearson-Phi 46	Crouch-Phi-StL 7	Davis-Bro 9.91	Brown-NY 2.9	Brown-NY 3.7
Walters-Cin 129	Lohrman-NY 2.26	Casey-Bro.....................45	Casey-Bro 7	E.Riddle-Cin 10.14	Crouch-Phi-StL..........7	Crouch-Phi-StL 6
Higbe-Bro 121	Tobin-Bos 2.27	Hutchings-Cin-Bos...........44	Pearson-Phi.............6	White-StL 10.50		
M.Cooper-StL 118	Lee-Chi................2.31	Johnson-Bos.................43		Pollet-StL 10.67		

Innings Pitched	Opponents' Avg.	Opponents' OBP	Earned Run Average	Adjusted ERA	Adjusted Starter Runs	Pitcher Wins
Walters-Cin........302.0	Wyatt-Bro 212	Wyatt-Bro....................270	E.Riddle-Cin 2.24	E.Riddle-Cin 160	Wyatt-Bro 41.6	**Wyatt-Bro** 5.3
Higbe-Bro 298.0	VanderMeer-Cin ...214	E.Riddle-Cin 282	Wyatt-Bro 2.34	White-StL.............157	E.Riddle-Cin 30.5	**E.Riddle-Cin** 3.5
Wyatt-Bro 288.1	White-StL 217	White-StL.....................287	White-StL 2.40	Wyatt-Bro.............157	White-StL 28.1	**Walters-Cin** 3.3
Sewell-Pit 249.0	Higbe-Bro 220	Sewell-Pit....................299	VanderMeer-Cin ..2.82	VanderMeer-Cin ..127	Walters-Cin..........26.7	**White-StL** 3.0
Warneke-StL.......246.0	E.Riddle-Cin 224	Tobin-Bos....................300	Walters-Cin..........2.83	Walters-Cin 127	VanderMeer-Cin ..19.2	**VanderMeer-Cin** 2.1

Brooklyn Celebrates

The first thrilling Cardinals-Dodgers confrontation of the decade took place in 1941. From Opening Day, the two clubs clung to one another, soaring high above the rest of the league; defending champ Cincinnati never quite got it together, finishing third only with a late surge.

Joe Medwick's midseason trade from St. Louis to Brooklyn sparked controversy, and Ducky went on to finish third in the league in runs. As August rolled into September, the Redbirds and Bums stood in a flat-footed tie. A September 4 doubleheader loss at Chicago, however, started the Cardinals on a downswing from which they could not recover. Leo Durocher's Dodgers kept the pressure on down the stretch and on September 25 clinched Brooklyn's first flag since 1920.

Dodger hurlers Kirby Higbe and Whitlow Wyatt tied for the league lead in victories, and Pete Reiser played like the game's next big star. Meanwhile, the Dodgers became the first NL team since 1931 to draw a million fans, and, thanks to a series of bean-ball scares, they also were the first to don batting helmets.

St. Louis, weak offensively except for first sacker Johnny Mize, hung in the race on the wings of their deep pitching staff. Despite the pennant loss, a late-season .426 showing from 20-year-old rookie Stan Musial showed that the Cardinals had much to anticipate.

Catcher Gabby Hartnett ended his career for fifth-place New York. The floundering Braves, showing indecision typical of a loser, again fiddled with their field dimensions—as they would continue to do throughout the decade.

The World Series was painful for Dodgers fans. Just one strike away from a Series-tying win in Game 4, a wild pitch by Hugh Casey set off a Yankees rally that won that game and carried into the next. New York's 3–1 win the next day clinched the Series.

1941 American League

TEAM	W	L	T	PCT	GB	HW	HL	R	OR	PA	H	2B	3B	HR	BB	SO	HB	SH	AVG	OBP	SLG	OPS	AOPS	BR	ABR	PF	SB	CS	BSA	BSR
NY	101	53	2	.656		**51**	26	830	**631**	6137	1464	243	**60**	**151**	616	565	49	**28**	.269	.346	.419	765	111	64	75	99	51	33	61	0
BOS	84	70	1	.545	17	47	30	**865**	750	6177	**1517**	**304**	55	124	**683**	567	**115**	20	**.283**	**.366**	**.430**	**796**	**115**	**142**	**121**	102	67	51	57	-3
CHI	77	77	2	.500	24	38	39	638	649	6012	1376	245	47	47	510	**476**	74	24	.255	.322	.343	665	84	-130	-122	99	**91**	53	**63**	**1**
DET	75	79	1	.487	26	43	34	686	743	6077	1412	247	55	81	602	584	82	23	.263	.340	.375	715	87	-27	-92	110	43	28	61	0
CLE	75	79	1	.487	26	42	35	677	668	5914	1350	249	84	103	512	605	101	18	.256	.323	.393	716	101	-43	-8	95	63	47	57	-3
WAS	70	84	2	.455	31	40	37	728	798	6067	1502	257	80	52	470	488	62	14	.272	.331	.376	707	99	-58	-25	95	79	36	69	5
STL	70	84	3	.455	31	40	37	765	823	6285	1440	281	58	91	775	552	89	13	.266	.360	.390	750	103	61	35	103	50	39	56	-3
PHI	64	90	0	.416	37	36	41	713	840	5994	1431	240	69	85	574	588	76	8	.268	.340	.387	727	102	-9	9	98	27	36	43	-7
TOT	622					337	279	5902		48663	11492	2066	508	734	4742	4425	148	648	.266	.341	.389	730					471	323	59	-9

TEAM	CG	SHO	GR	SV	IP	H	HR	BB	SO	BR/9	ERA	AERA	OAV	OOB	PR	APR	PF	OSB	OCS	FA	E	WPB	DP	FW	PW	BW	BSW	DIF
NY	75	13	119	**26**	1396.1	**1309**	81	598	589	12.4	3.53	112	**.248**	.325	96	66	95	**44**	36	.973	165	35	**196**	.5	6.4	7.3	.1	9.7
BOS	70	8	137	11	1372.0	1453	88	611	574	13.7	4.19	100	.270	.347	-6	-3	101	54	34	.972	172	42	139	.0	-.3	**11.7**	-.2	-4.3
CHI	**106**	**14**	63	4	1416.0	1362	89	**521**	564	**12.1**	**3.52**	**116**	.252	**.320**	**99**	**92**	99	54	46	.971	180	50	145	-.3	**8.9**	-11.8	.2	3.0
DET	52	8	157	16	1381.2	1399	80	645	**697**	13.4	4.18	109	.260	.341	-4	52	110	69	46	.969	186	39	129	-.7	5.0	-8.9	.1	2.5
CLE	68	10	133	19	1377.0	1366	71	660	617	13.4	3.90	101	.259	.344	39	7	95	50	37	**.976**	**142**	**34**	158	**1.7**	.7	-.8	-.2	-3.4
WAS	69	8	140	7	1389.1	1524	**69**	603	544	13.9	4.35	93	.279	.353	-32	-49	98	59	**48**	.969	187	68	169	-.7	-4.7	-2.4	**.6**	.3
STL	65	7	**158**	10	1389.0	1563	120	549	454	13.8	4.72	91	.283	.350	-88	-62	104	64	38	.975	151	41	156	1.3	-6.0	3.4	-.2	-5.5
PHI	64	3	125	18	1365.1	1516	136	557	386	13.8	4.83	87	.279	.348	-104	-97	101	77	38	.967	200	69	150	-1.6	-9.4	.9	-.6	-2.3
TOT	569	71	1032	111	11086.2					13.3	4.15		.266	.341						.972	1383	378	1242					

Batter-Fielder Wins	Batting Average	On-Base Percentage	Slugging Average	On-Base Plus Slugging	Adjusted OPS	Adjusted Batter Runs
Williams-Bos 8.5	Williams-Bos.........406	Williams-Bos 553	Williams-Bos.........735	Williams-Bos 1287	Williams-Bos 232	Williams-Bos 101.7
DiMaggio-NY 6.6	Travis-Was 359	Cullenbine-StL 452	DiMaggio-NY 643	DiMaggio-NY......1083	DiMaggio-NY........186	DiMaggio-NY......67.7
Travis-Was 5.1	DiMaggio-NY 357	DiMaggio-NY 440	Heath-Cle 586	Keller-NY 996	Heath-Cle 165	Heath-Cle 50.4
Keller-NY 4.0	Heath-Cle 340	Keller-NY 416	Keller-NY 580	Heath-Cle 982	Keller-NY 163	Keller-NY 48.0
S.Chapman-Phi ..3.7	Siebert-Phi 334	Foxx-Bos 412	S.Chapman-Phi ...543	Travis-Was............930	Travis-Was............152	Travis-Was.........43.6

Runs	Hits	Doubles	Triples	Home Runs	Total Bases	Runs Batted In
Williams-Bos 135	Travis-Was............218	Boudreau-Cle 45	Heath-Cle 20	Williams-Bos 37	DiMaggio-NY........348	DiMaggio-NY 125
DiMaggio-NY........122	Heath-Cle 199	DiMaggio-NY 43	Travis-Was..............19	Keller-NY 33	Heath-Cle 343	Heath-Cle..............123
DiMaggio-Bos 117	DiMaggio-NY........193	Judnich-StL....................40	Keltner-Cle..............13	Henrich-NY 31	Williams-Bos 335	Keller-NY 122
Clift-StL 108	Appling-Chi 186	Travis-Was 39		DiMaggio-NY..........30	Travis-Was............316	Williams-Bos 120
	Williams-Bos 185	Kuhel-Chi 39		York-Det..................27	S.Chapman-Phi 300	York-Det 111

Stolen Bases	Base Stealing Runs	Fielding Runs-Infield	Fielding Runs-Outfield	Wins	Winning Pct.	Complete Games
Case-Was 33	Case-Was..............4.1	Bloodworth-Was 27.2	Case-Was............11.7	Feller-Cle 25	Gomez-NY 750	Lee-Chi..................30
Kuhel-Chi................20	Kuhel-Chi 2.7	Keltner-Cle..................20.3	S.Chapman-Phi ..11.7	Lee-Chi.....................22	Ruffing-NY 714	Feller-Cle 28
Heath-Cle 18	Kreevich-Chi..........2.0	Rizzuto-NY 19.0	Lewis-Was 11.4	D.Newsome-Bos 19	Benton-Det 714	Smith-Chi 21
Tabor-Bos 17	Rizzuto-NY 1.3	Boudreau-Cle 13.4	B.Johnson-Phi 8.7	Leonard-Was..........18	Lee-Chi.................667	Lyons-Chi 19
Kreevich-Chi 17	Fox-Bos 1.3	Gordon-NY 8.6	Moses-Phi 7.8		Feller-Cle 658	Leonard-Was 19

Strikeouts	Fewest BB/Game	Games	Saves	Base Runners/9	Adjusted Relief Runs	Relief Ranking
Feller-Cle 260	Lyons-Chi 1.78	Feller-Cle 44	Murphy-NY 15	Humphries-Chi ..10.55	Murphy-NY 17.5	Murphy-NY 30.1
Newsom-Det 175	Leonard-Was 1.90	Newsom-Det.................43	Ferrick-Phi 7	Lee-Chi..............10.61	Heving-Cle 13.2	Heving-Cle.........13.9
Lee-Chi 130	Muncrief-StL 2.23	Brown-Cle......................41	Benton-Det 7	Bonham-NY 10.66	Carrasquel-Was 6.6	Brown-Cle 5.2
Rigney-Chi............119	Ruffing-NY 2.62	Ryba-Bos 40	Ryba-Bos..................6	Ruffing-NY 11.25	Brown-Cle.............6.0	Carrasquel-Was ..5.2
	Lee-Chi................2.76	Benton-Det 38		Benton-Det 11.30	Thomas-Det 3	Thomas-Det 1

Innings Pitched	Opponents' Avg.	Opponents' OBP	Earned Run Average	Adjusted ERA	Adjusted Starter Runs	Pitcher Wins
Feller-Cle 343.0	Benton-Det...........221	Lee-Chi 293	Lee-Chi................2.37	Lee-Chi 173	Lee-Chi................56.1	**Lee-Chi** 6.5
Lee-Chi..............300.1	Feller-Cle 226	Benton-Det 302	Benton-Det 2.97	Benton-Det 153	Feller-Cle 34.3	**Feller-Cle**............3.6
Smith-Chi 263.1	Lee-Chi.................232	Ruffing-NY...................306	Wagner-Bos 3.07	Wagner-Bos..........136	Smith-Chi 28.1	**Smith-Chi** 3.4
Leonard-Was 256.0	Donald-NY 237	Chandler-NY 307	Russo-NY............3.09	Smith-Chi..............129	Benton-Det..........24.1	**Murphy-NY** 2.9
Newsom-Det......250.1	Chandler-NY.........239	Lyons-Chi.....................308	Feller-Cle 3.15	Harris-Bos 128	Wagner-Bos 22.3	**Benton-Det** 2.6

Joltin' Joe and Teddy Ballgame

The final year of normal baseball before America entered World War II was the stuff of legend, as immortals like Joe DiMaggio and Ted Williams grabbed the headlines and Mickey Owen grabbed the goat's horns. The Yankees returned to the top after a season in third place. Emerging from a five-team scramble in July, New York left everyone in the dust as they took league honors by 17 games.

The old Yankees were gone; in their place were a passel of new stars, including DiMaggio, Phil Rizzuto, Charlie Keller, Joe Gordon, and Tommy Henrich. DiMaggio hit .357 and enthralled the nation with his 56-game hitting streak. Keller batted .298 with 33 homers and 122 RBIs, and Johnny "Grandma" Murphy—one of the first true relief aces—saved 15 games.

Lacking a staff anchor, Joe McCarthy used seven starting pitchers at least 14 times, getting excellent performance from most of them. Both 32-year-old Lefty Gomez and Red Ruffing, 37, won 15. Finishing in second place were the Red Sox, who couldn't turn Williams' season (.406 average, 37 homers, 145 walks, and 135 runs—all of which led the AL) into a pennant because of mediocre pitching.

A few players left for the military during the season, most notably three-time home run champ Hank Greenberg. Fans were also busy in other matters. It was the first of three consecutive seasons of decreasing league attendance; NL attendance actually increased by 8 percent in 1941 before falling the next two years.

The Yankees won the World Series from the Dodgers in five games, four of which were decided by only one run. The one that wasn't (Game 4) featured a ninth-inning, four-run rally that began when Dodgers catcher Owen dropped a third strike that would have ended the game in favor of Brooklyn and tied the Series.

1942 National League

TEAM	W	L	T	PCT	GB	HW	HL	R	OR	PA	H	2B	3B	HR	BB	SO	HB	SH	AVG	OBP	SLG	OPS	AOPS	BR	ABR	PF	SB	CS	BSA	BSR
STL	106	48	2	.688		**60**	17	**755**	**480**	6124	**1454**	**282**	**69**	60	551	507	**130**	22	**.268**	**.338**	**.379**	**717**	109	**112**	61	108	71			
BRO	104	50	1	.675	2	57	22	742	512	5990	1398	263	34	62	**572**	**484**	119	14	.265	**.338**	.362	700	**110**	85	**74**	102	**81**			
NY	85	67	2	.559	20	47	31	675	600	5879	1323	162	35	**109**	558	511	77	**34**	.254	.330	.361	691	108	58	55	101	39			
CIN	76	76	2	.500	29	38	39	527	545	5860	1216	198	39	66	483	549	94	23	.231	.299	.321	620	88	-83	-82	100	42			
PIT	66	81	4	.449	36.5	41	34	585	631	5754	1250	173	49	54	537	536	87	26	.245	.320	.330	650	95	-17	-31	103	41			
CHI	68	86	1	.442	38	36	41	591	665	5984	1360	224	41	75	509	607	104	19	.254	.321	.353	674	108	24	49	96	63			
BOS	59	89	2	.399	44	33	36	515	645	5661	1216	210	19	68	474	507	90	20	.240	.307	.329	636	94	-47	-36	98	49			
PHI	42	109	0	.278	62.5	23	51	394	706	5567	1174	168	37	44	392	488	99	16	.232	.289	.306	595	84	-130	-107	95	37			
TOT	613					335	271	4784		46819	10391	1680	323	538	4076	4189	174	800	.249	.318	.343	661					423			

TEAM	CG	SHO	GR	SV	IP	H	HR	BB	SO	BR/9	ERA	AERA	OAV	OOB	PR	APR	PF	OSB	OCS	FA	E	WPB	DP	FW	PW	BW	BSW	DIF
STL	70	**18**	149	15	1410.1	**1192**	49	473	**651**	**10.7**	**2.55**	**134**	**.228**	**.294**	**120**	**133**	103	**33**	*56*	.972	169	43	137	-.1	**14.3**	6.5		8.3
BRO	67	16	165	**24**	1398.2	1205	73	493	612	11.1	2.84	115	.231	.302	73	65	98	35	*39*	**.977**	**138**	**19**	150	**1.7**	7.0	**7.9**		10.4
NY	70	12	153	13	1370.0	1299	94	493	497	11.9	3.31	101	.250	.316	0	7	101	43	*34*	**.977**	**138**	29	128	1.6	.8	5.9		.7
CIN	**80**	12	115	8	1411.2	1213	**47**	526	616	11.2	2.82	117	.230	.302	78	74	99	57	*45*	.971	177	28	**158**	-.7	7.9	-8.8		1.6
PIT	64	13	156	11	1351.1	1376	62	**435**	426	12.1	3.58	94	.262	.320	-41	-30	102	61	*42*	.969	184	29	128	-1.3	-3.2	-3.3		.4
CHI	71	10	150	14	1400.2	1447	70	525	507	12.8	3.60	89	.267	.334	-44	-65	97	48	*48*	.973	170	37	136	-.2	-7.0	5.3		-7.1
BOS	68	9	162	8	1334.0	1326	82	518	414	12.6	3.76	89	.260	.331	-66	-62	101	67	*41*	.976	142	40	138	1.1	-6.7	-3.9		-5.6
PHI	51	2	**184**	6	1341.0	1328	61	605	472	13.1	4.12	80	.260	.342	-120	-122	100	79	*45*	.968	194	36	147	-1.9	-13.1	-11.5		-7.0
TOT	541	92	1234	99	11017.2					11.9	3.31		.249	.318						.973	1312	261	1122					

Batter-Fielder Wins	Batting Average	On-Base Percentage	Slugging Average	On-Base Plus Slugging	Adjusted OPS	Adjusted Batter Runs
Nicholson-Chi 4.1	Lombardi-Bos 330	Fletcher-Pit 417	Mize-NY 521	Ott-NY 912	Ott-NY 165	Ott-NY 50.1
Ott-NY 3.9	Slaughter-StL 318	Ott-NY 415	Ott-NY 497	Slaughter-StL........906	Mize-NY................161	Slaughter-StL 41.8
Slaughter-StL 3.5	Musial-StL 315	Slaughter-StL..............412	Slaughter-StL 494	Mize-NY................901	Nicholson-Chi 156	Nicholson-Chi 41.8
Reese-Bro...........3.3	Reiser-Bro 310	Hack-Chi 402	Musial-StL 490	Musial-StL 888	Slaughter-StL........153	Mize-NY..............40.5
Musial-StL 3.2	Mize-NY 305	Musial-StL 397	Lombardi-Bos.......482	Nicholson-Chi 859	Musial-StL 148	Hack-Chi 35.6

Runs	Hits	Doubles	Triples	Home Runs	Total Bases	Runs Batted In
Ott-NY 118	Slaughter-StL........188	Marion-StL 38	Slaughter-StL..........17	Ott-NY 30	Slaughter-StL........292	Mize-NY 110
Slaughter-StL........100	Nicholson-Chi 173	Medwick-Bro.................37	Nicholson-Chi 11	Mize-NY..................26	Mize-NY................282	Camilli-Bro 109
Mize-NY..................97	Medwick-Bro 166	Hack-Chi.......................36	Musial-StL 10	Camilli-Bro..............26	Nicholson-Chi 280	Slaughter-StL 98
Hack-Chi 91	Hack-Chi 166	Herman-Bro 34	Litwhiler-Phi.............9	Nicholson-Chi 21	Ott-NY 273	Medwick-Bro 96
	Elliott-Pit 166	Reiser-Bro.....................33		West-Bos 16	Camilli-Bro............247	Ott-NY 93

Stolen Bases	Base Stealing Runs	Fielding Runs-Infield	Fielding Runs-Outfield	Wins	Winning Pct.	Complete Games
Reiser-Bro 20		May-Phi 19.1	DiMaggio-Pit........12.0	M.Cooper-StL 22	French-Bro 789	Tobin-Bos 28
Reese-Bro 15		Reese-Bro 18.2	Musial-StL 7.4	Beazley-StL 21	Beazley-StL 778	Passeau-Chi..........24
Fernandez-Bos 15		Fletcher-Pit 11.1	Nicholson-Chi 6.9	Wyatt-Bro................19	M.Cooper-StL 759	M.Cooper-StL 22
Merullo-Chi 14		Glossop-Phi................10.4	Barrett-Pit 5.5	Passeau-Chi 19	Wyatt-Bro 731	Walters-Cin............21
Hopp-StL 14		Bragan-Phi...................8.9	Holmes-Bos 5.2	VanderMeer-Cin 18	Davis-Bro 714	VanderMeer-Cin 21

Strikeouts	Fewest BB/Game	Games	Saves	Base Runners/9	Adjusted Relief Runs	Relief Ranking
VanderMeer-Cin ..186	Warneke-StL-Chi 1.79	Adams-NY 61	Casey-Bro 13	M.Cooper-StL 9.04	Adams-NY 14.0	Adams-NY..........19.7
M.Cooper-StL 152	Lohrman-StL-NY 1.85	Casey-Bro.....................50	Adams-NY 11	Shoun-StL-Cin 9.69	Casey-Bro...........13.0	Beggs-Cin 14.0
Higbe-Bro 115	Hubbell-NY..........1.94	Podgajny-Phi.................43	Beggs-Cin 8	Melton-NY 9.84	Beggs-Cin............10.6	Casey-Bro 12.8
Walters-Cin 109	Derringer-Cin 2.11	Beazley-StL 43	Sain-Bos 6	Beggs-Cin............10.05	Shoun-StL-Cin 8.6	Shoun-StL-Cin.......4.3
Melton-Phi 107	M.Cooper-StL 2.20		Gumbert-StL 5	Lohrman-StL-NY10.07	Webber-Bro 2.9	Webber-Bro 2.7

Innings Pitched	Opponents' Avg.	Opponents' OBP	Earned Run Average	Adjusted ERA	Adjusted Starter Runs	Pitcher Wins
Tobin-Bos 287.2	M.Cooper-StL 204	M.Cooper-StL 258	M.Cooper-StL 1.78	M.Cooper-StL 193	M.Cooper-StL 46.6	**M.Cooper-StL** 4.7
M.Cooper-StL 278.2	VanderMeer-Cin 208	Lohrman-StL-NY 281	Beazley-StL 2.13	Beazley-StL 161	Beazley-StL 27.6	**Beazley-StL**........3.5
Passeau-Chi 278.1	Higbe-Bro 223	Wyatt-Bro.......................286	Davis-Bro 2.36	Davis-Bro..............138	VanderMeer-Cin ..24.6	**French-Bro** 3.3
Starr-Cin 276.2	Wyatt-Bro 225	Warneke-StL-Chi 286	VanderMeer-Cin ..2.43	Lohrman-StL-NY ..136	Starr-Cin 24.5	**VanderMeer-Cin** 3.1
Javery-Bos 261.0	Starr-Cin 226	Davis-Bro.......................287	Lohrman-StL-NY 2.48	VanderMeer-Cin ..135	French-Bro 22.0	**Walters-Cin** 2.5

Where Did *You* Come From?

It looked like a cinch. On August 15 Brooklyn, starring 23-year-olds Pee Wee Reese and Pete Reiser, held a 9_ game lead over second-place St. Louis, which had played well all season but recently stumbled. But from that point, the Bums never knew what hit them. The Cardinals went 43–8 down the stretch, overtaking Brooklyn in mid-September. In winning 12 of their final 13, they held off the late-charging Dodgers. St. Louis pulled it off despite a starting infield with just 9 homers and only two pitchers with more than 13 wins. But they still led the league in runs and ERA.

For the third consecutive season, scoring dropped, this time to 3.90 runs per game. For the only time between 1918 and 1963, the league average sank below .250. As a result, the performances of Cardinals outfielders Enos Slaughter and Stan Musial look especially good. MVP Mort Cooper led the league in wins, shutouts, and ERA, and rookie Johnny Beazley won 21.

Relief pitching gained some definition in 1942 as Giants right-hander Ace Adams set a record with 61 bullpen appearances (he broke it the next year). While some teams continued to shuttle their best starters in and out of late-inning jobs, many clubs were already using a particular reliever in clutch situations.

Seeing their first action were two Braves pitchers who blossomed after the war: Warren Spahn and Johnny Sain. But 21-year-old Al Montgomery, Boston's backup catcher in 1941, was killed April 26 in a car wreck.

The World Series was highly anticipated; both the Cardinals and Yankees cleared 100 wins. But the classic went just five games; after losing the first contest, St. Louis took the next four to stun the New Yorkers. All five games were entertaining and close. Beazley twice fired complete-game victories, including the clincher.

1942 American League

TEAM	W	L	T	PCT	GB	HW	HL	R	OR	PA	H	2B	3B	HR	BB	SO	HB	SH	AVG	OBP	SLG	OPS	AOPS	BR	ABR	PF	SB	CS	BSA	BSR
NY	103	51	0	.669		**58**	19	**801**	**507**	6009	1429	223	57	**108**	591	556	84	**29**	.269	.346	.394	740	**118**	105	**122**	98	**69**	33	**68**	**4**
BOS	93	59	0	.612	9	53	24	761	594	5984	**1451**	**244**	55	103	591	**508**	**123**	22	**.276**	**.352**	**.403**	**755**	116	**135**	109	103	68	61	53	-6
STL	82	69	0	.543	19.5	40	37	730	637	5947	1354	239	**62**	98	**609**	607	96	13	.259	.338	.385	723	109	70	59	102	37	38	49	-5
CLE	75	79	2	.487	28	39	39	590	659	5931	1344	223	58	50	500	544	90	24	.253	.320	.345	665	100	-45	-7	94	**69**	74	48	-11
DET	73	81	2	.474	30	43	34	589	587	5928	1313	217	37	76	509	476	73	19	.246	.314	.344	658	85	-58	-103	108	39	40	49	-5
CHI	66	82	0	.446	34	35	35	538	609	5552	1215	214	36	25	497	427	90	16	.246	.316	.318	634	87	-87	-75	98	114	70	62	1
WAS	62	89	0	.411	39.5	35	42	653	817	5949	1364	224	49	40	581	536	54	19	.258	.333	.341	674	98	-14	-7	99	98	29	77	11
PHI	55	99	0	.357	48	25	51	549	801	5822	1315	213	46	33	440	490	74	23	.249	.309	.325	634	86	-104	-101	99	44	45	49	-6
TOT	611					328	281	5211		47122	10785	1797	400	533	4318	4144	165	684	.257	.329	.357	686					538	390	58	-18

TEAM	CG	SHO	GR	SV	IP	H	HR	BB	SO	BR/9	ERA	AERA	OAV	OOB	PR	APR	PF	OSB	OCS	FA	E	WPB	DP	FW	PW	BW	BSW	DIF
NY	**88**	**18**	89	**17**	1375.0	**1259**	71	**431**	558	**11.2**	**2.91**	118	**.244**	**.304**	**115**	87	94	**37**	50	**.976**	**142**	**21**	**190**	**2.0**	8.9	**12.5**	.6	1.9
BOS	84	11	108	**17**	1358.2	1260	65	553	500	12.1	3.44	108	.247	.322	32	42	102	62	48	.974	157	34	156	1.0	4.3	11.2	-.4	.9
STL	68	12	140	13	1363.0	1387	63	505	488	12.7	3.59	103	.262	.330	10	17	101	86	43	.972	167	51	143	.4	1.7	6.0	-.3	-1.4
CLE	61	12	**162**	11	1402.2	1353	61	560	448	12.4	3.59	96	.254	.327	10	-24	94	63	36	.974	163	24	175	1.0	-2.5	-.7	-.9	1.1
DET	65	12	126	14	1399.1	1321	60	598	**671**	12.5	3.13	**126**	.248	.326	82	**118**	108	71	56	.969	194	42	142	-.8	**12.1**	-10.6	-.3	-4.5
CHI	86	8	75	8	1314.1	1304	74	473	432	12.3	3.58	100	.258	.325	11	3	98	58	31	.970	173	43	144	-.1	.3	-7.7	.3	-.9
WAS	68	12	125	11	1346.2	1496	**50**	558	496	13.8	4.58	80	.279	.349	-139	-139	100	65	**66**	.962	222	41	133	-2.7	-14.2	-.7	**1.4**	2.7
PHI	67	5	114	9	1374.2	1404	89	639	546	13.5	4.45	85	.263	.344	-120	-99	103	96	60	.969	188	58	124	-.6	-10.1	-10.3	-.4	-.6
TOT	587	90	939	100	10934.1					12.6	3.66		.257	.329						.971	1406	314	1207					

Batter-Fielder Wins	Batting Average	On-Base Percentage	Slugging Average	On-Base Plus Slugging	Adjusted OPS	Adjusted Batter Runs
Williams-Bos 8.5	Williams-Bos.........356	Williams-Bos 499	Williams-Bos.........648	Williams-Bos 1147	Williams-Bos 214	Williams-Bos 89.9
Gordon-NY 5.8	Pesky-Bos 331	Keller-NY 417	Keller-NY 513	Keller-NY 930	Keller-NY 164	Keller-NY 50.4
Rizzuto-NY 4.6	Spence-Was 323	Judnich-StL 413	Judnich-StL..........499	Judnich-StL 912	Gordon-NY 156	Gordon-NY 41.9
Pesky-Bos 4.5	Gordon-NY 322	Fleming-Cle 412	DiMaggio-NY 498	Gordon-NY 900	Judnich-StL 153	Fleming-Cle 40.1
Keller-NY 4.2	Case-Was.............320	Gordon-NY 409	Laabs-StL 498	Laabs-StL 878	DiMaggio-NY........148	DiMaggio-NY......36.6

Runs	Hits	Doubles	Triples	Home Runs	Total Bases	Runs Batted In
Williams-Bos 141	Pesky-Bos 205	Kolloway-Chi..................40	Spence-Was 15	Williams-Bos 36	Williams-Bos 338	Williams-Bos 137
DiMaggio-NY........123	Spence-Was 203	Clift-StL...........................39	Heath-Cle 13	Laabs-StL 27	DiMaggio-NY.........304	DiMaggio-NY 114
DiMaggio-Bos 110	Williams-Bos 186	Heath-Cle 37	DiMaggio-NY..........13	Keller-NY 26	Keller-NY 279	Keller-NY 108
Clift-StL 108	DiMaggio-NY 186	DiMaggio-Bos 36	McQuillen-StL 12	York-Det..................21	Spence-Was 272	Gordon-NY 103
Keller-NY 106	Keltner-Cle............179			DiMaggio-NY..........21	DiMaggio-Bos 272	Doerr-Bos 102

Stolen Bases	Base Stealing Runs	Fielding Runs-Infield	Fielding Runs-Outfield	Wins	Winning Pct.	Complete Games
Case-Was 44	Case-Was.............7.6	Rizzuto-NY 30.0	DiMaggio-Bos......13.1	Hughson-Bos..........22	Bonham-NY 808	Hughson-Bos 22
Vernon-Was...........25	Vernon-Was 3.4	Pesky-Bos 19.6	Moses-Chi 6.1	Bonham-NY............21	Borowy-NY 789	Bonham-NY 22
Rizzuto-NY 22	Rizzuto-NY 2.7	York-Det....................15.3	Johnson-Phi 5.4	Marchildon-Phi 17	Hughson-Bos 786	Lyons-Chi 20
Kuhel-Chi................22	Keller-NY 2.4	Doerr-Bos 12.0	Chartak-NY-Was-StL 5.4	Bagby-Cle 17	Chandler-NY.........762	Hudson-Was..........19
	Appling-Chi............2.0	Keltner-Cle.................11.3	Cullenbine-SL-W-NY 4.7	Chandler-NY 16	Bagby-Cle.............654	

Strikeouts	Fewest BB/Game	Games	Saves	Base Runners/9	Adjusted Relief Runs	Relief Ranking
Newsom-Was 113	Bonham-NY 96	Haynes-Chi...................40	Murphy-NY 11	Bonham-NY 8.92	Ferrick-Cle 14.5	Haynes-Chi 13.3
Hughson-Bos........113	Lyons-Chi 1.30	Caster-StL.....................39	Haynes-Chi 6	Lyons-Chi 9.73	Haynes-Chi..........10.5	Caster-StL 9.5
Marchildon-Phi 110	Ruffing-NY 1.91		Brown-Bos 6	Ferrick-Cle 9.74	Caster-StL 7.5	Ferrick-Cle............9.2
Benton-Det 110	Breuer-NY............2.03		Newhouser-Det 5	Butland-Bos 9.78	Brown-Bos 1.7	Brown-Bos............3.3
Niggeling-StL........107	Bagby-Cle............2.13		Caster-StL 5	Ruffing-NY 10.55		

Innings Pitched	Opponents' Avg.	Opponents' OBP	Earned Run Average	Adjusted ERA	Adjusted Starter Runs	Pitcher Wins
Hughson-Bos 281.0	Newhouser-Det.....207	Bonham-NY 259	Lyons-Chi 2.10	Lyons-Chi 172	Hughson-Bos 35.0	**Lyons-Chi** 3.8
Bagby-Cle.........270.2	Niggeling-StL 226	Lyons-Chi...................275	Bonham-NY 2.27	Newhouser-Det 161	Bonham-NY 31.3	**Hughson-Bos** 3.7
Auker-StL 249.0	Dobson-Bos 231	Ruffing-NY..................292	Chandler-NY........2.38	Bonham-NY..........152	Lyons-Chi 29.2	**Bonham-NY**........3.0
Marchildon-Phi ..244.0	Trucks-Det 231	Breuer-NY 295	Newhouser-Det....2.45	Chandler-NY 145	White-Det 24.9	**Chandler-NY**......3.0
Hudson-Was......239.1	Borowy-NY 233	Hughson-Bos...............296	Borowy-NY 2.52	Trucks-Det 144	Benton-Det 24.9	**Newhouser-Det** 2.9

You're in the Army Now

At no point after mid-May was the pennant race close, as the Yankees buzzed their way to an even better record than in 1941. Joe McCarthy wielded deep pitching, with seven men starting 13 or more games, and a peerless outfield of Tommy Henrich, Joe DiMaggio, and Charlie Keller to lead in runs by 40 and ERA by 22 points.

The Red Sox, again a strong second, added another piece by promoting rookie shortstop Johnny Pesky, who hit .331. Ted Williams had another spectacular year, taking the Triple Crown, but the Bosox were weak at key positions, and their pitching wasn't up to standard. While the race featured little drama, the third-place team caused a buzz. The St. Louis Browns, 43–111 in 1939 and sixth the next two years, improved by 12_ games with a strong second half. Rookie shortstop Vern Stephens was a keeper. What the Browns showed most, though, was how World War II was affecting baseball.

When the war hit home in December 1941, the country needed healthy bodies. Therefore, many great players got the call; between 1943–45 Cleveland lost Bob Feller, Boston sacrificed Williams, Pesky, and Dom DiMaggio, and the Yankees lost Joe DiMaggio and Henrich. Detroit's Hank Greenberg, who joined the military before the U.S. was even in the war, played less than 100 games between 1941–45. Teammate Charlie Gehringer's career ended when he was called into service. Browns pitcher Elden Auker retired to devote time to a war job. Washington infielder Cecil Travis never recovered from his service. Johnny Sturm, the Yankees' first baseman in 1941, spent the next four years in the military and never returned to the majors. Two men who appeared briefly in the major leagues, Elmer Gedeon (Senators) and Harry O'Neill (Athletics), were killed in action.

Previously "good" teams were no longer a lock. Until the war was over, it was every club for itself. The Yankees' surprise five-game loss in the World Series to St. Louis showed that teams with good farm systems were in the best shape.

1943 National League

TEAM	W	L	T	PCT	GB	HW	HL	R	OR	PA	H	2B	3B	HR	BB	SO	HB	SH	AVG	OBP	SLG	OPS	AOPS	BR	ABR	PF	SB	CS	BSA	BSR
STL	105	49	3	.682		**58**	21	679	**475**	6057	**1515**	259	72	**70**	428	438	**172**	19	**.279**	.333	**.391**	**724**	**110**	**92**	62	104	40			
CIN	87	67	1	.565	18	48	29	608	543	5910	1362	229	47	43	445	476	119	17	.256	.315	.340	655	96	-36	-28	99	49			
BRO	81	72	0	.529	23.5	46	31	**716**	675	6009	1444	**263**	35	39	**580**	**422**	99	**21**	.272	**.346**	.357	703	**110**	76	**75**	100	58			
PIT	80	74	3	.519	25	47	30	669	605	6030	1401	240	**73**	42	573	566	86	18	.262	.335	.357	692	103	46	24	103	**64**			
CHI	74	79	1	.484	30.5	36	38	632	599	5970	1380	207	56	52	574	522	96	**21**	.261	.336	.351	687	107	38	48	99	53			
BOS	68	85	0	.444	36.5	38	39	465	612	5780	1213	202	36	39	469	609	98	17	.233	.299	.309	608	82	-122	-115	99	56			
PHI	64	90	3	.416	41	33	43	571	676	5918	1321	186	36	66	499	556	101	**21**	.249	.316	.335	651	98	-39	-15	96	29			
NY	55	98	3	.359	49.5	34	43	558	713	5900	1309	153	33	81	480	470	107	23	.247	.313	.335	648	92	-52	-56	101	35			
TOT	621					340	274	4898		47574	10945	1739	388	432	4048	4059	157	878	.258	.324	.347	672					384			

TEAM	CG	SHO	GR	SV	IP	H	HR	BB	SO	BR/9	ERA	AERA	OAV	OOB	PR	APR	PF	OSB	OCS	FA	E	WPB	DP	FW	PW	BW	BSW	DIF
STL	**94**	**21**	104	15	1427.0	**1246**	**33**	477	**639**	**11.0**	**2.57**	**131**	**.237**	**.303**	**129**	**127**	99	**30**	*34*	.976	151	33	183	.9	**13.6**	6.6		6.9
CIN	78	18	119	17	1404.0	1299	38	579	498	12.1	3.13	106	.251	.328	39	28	98	41	***50***	**.980**	**125**	21	**193**	**2.2**	3.0	-3.0		7.8
BRO	50	13	182	**22**	1369.2	1326	59	637	588	13.1	3.88	86	.254	.338	-76	-80	99	46	*39*	.972	168	35	137	-.3	-8.5	**8.0**		5.4
PIT	74	11	157	12	1404.0	1424	44	422	396	11.9	3.08	113	.264	.319	47	58	103	33	*44*	.973	170	24	159	-.2	6.2	2.6		-5.5
CHI	67	13	160	14	1386.0	1379	53	**394**	513	11.6	3.31	101	.258	.311	11	4	99	37	*19*	.973	168	34	138	-.3	.4	5.1		-7.8
BOS	87	13	99	4	1397.2	1361	66	441	409	11.8	3.25	105	.255	.314	20	25	101	81	*40*	.972	176	**18**	139	-.8	2.7	-12.3		1.9
PHI	66	10	140	14	1392.2	1436	59	451	431	12.3	3.79	89	.267	.326	-62	-64	100	55	*38*	.969	189	39	143	-1.3	-6.8	-1.6		-3.3
NY	35	6	**208**	19	1394.2	1474	80	626	588	13.7	4.08	84	.272	.350	-108	-97	102	61	*35*	.973	166	43	140	-.0	-10.4	-6.0		-5.1
TOT	551	105	1169	117	11175.2					12.2	3.38		.258	.324						.974	1313	247	1232					

Batter-Fielder Wins	Batting Average	On-Base Percentage	Slugging Average	On-Base Plus Slugging	Adjusted OPS	Adjusted Batter Runs
Musial-StL 5.7	Musial-StL 357	Musial-StL 425	Musial-StL 562	Musial-StL 988	Musial-StL 176	Musial-StL 60.7
Nicholson-Chi 4.5	Herman-Bro 330	Galan-Bro 412	Nicholson-Chi 531	Nicholson-Chi 917	Nicholson-Chi 166	Nicholson-Chi 50.1
Mueller-Cin..........3.8	W.Cooper-StL 318	Herman-Bro 398	W.Cooper-StL 463	Elliott-Pit 820	Tipton-Cin 138	Galan-Bro 29.9
Galan-Bro 3.6	Elliott-Pit 315	Fletcher-Pit 395	Elliott-Pit 444	Tipton-Cin 819	Galan-Bro 136	Herman-Bro..........29.6
Witek-NY 3.2	Witek-NY 314	Tipton-Cin 395	Triplett-StL-Phi 439	Galan-Bro 818	Herman-Bro..........135	Tipton-Cin 28.1

Runs	Hits	Doubles	Triples	Home Runs	Total Bases	Runs Batted In
Vaughan-Bro 112	Musial-StL 220	Musial-StL.....................48	Musial-StL 20	Nicholson-Chi 29	Musial-StL 347	Nicholson-Chi......128
Musial-StL 108	Witek-NY 195	Herman-Bro 41	Klein-StL 14	Ott-NY 18	Nicholson-Chi 323	Elliott-Pit 101
Nicholson-Chi 95	Herman-Bro............193	DiMaggio-Pit.................41	Lowrey-Chi 12	Northey-Phi 16	Elliott-Pit 258	Herman-Bro 100
Cavarretta-Chi 93	Nicholson-Chi 188	Vaughan-Bro.................39	Elliott-Pit 12	Triplett-StL-Phi........15	Klein-StL 257	DiMaggio-Pit..........88
Stanky-Chi.............92	Vaughan-Bro 186	Holmes-Bos 33		DiMaggio-Pit 15		

Stolen Bases	Base Stealing Runs	Fielding Runs-Infield	Fielding Runs-Outfield	Wins	Winning Pct.	Complete Games
Vaughan-Bro 20		Miller-Cin 23.8	DiMaggio-Pit........11.9	Sewell-Pit................21	M.Cooper-StL 724	Sewell-Pit 25
Lowrey-Chi 13		Wietelmann-Bos 18.2	Litwhiler-Phi-StL 6.9	Riddle-Cin 21	Sewell-Pit 700	Tobin-Bos 24
Workman-Bos 12		Marion-StL 16.2	Galan-Bro 6.4	M.Cooper-StL 21	Lanier-StL.............682	M.Cooper-StL 24
Russell-Pit 12		Witek-NY 15.3	Lowrey-Chi 5.7	Bithorn-Chi 18	Riddle-Cin.............656	Andrews-Bos 23
Gustine-Pit..............12		Frey-Cin 12.9	Musial-StL 4.5	Javery-Bos.............17	Bithorn-Chi 600	

Strikeouts	Fewest BB/Game	Games	Saves	Base Runners/9	Adjusted Relief Runs	Relief Ranking
VanderMeer-Cin ..174	Rowe-Phi 1.31	Adams-NY 70	Webber-Bro 10	Pollet-StL 8.90	Beggs-Cin............10.6	Adams-NY 12.2
M.Cooper-StL 141	Wyse-Chi 1.96	Webber-Bro...................54	Adams-NY 9	Wyatt-Bro 9.07	Adams-NY 9.4	Beggs-Cin 12.0
Javery-Bos............134	Derringer-Chi 2.02	Head-Bro 47	Shoun-Cin 7	Brecheen-StL 9.31	Prim-Chi 3.6	Prim-Chi 3.9
Lanier-StL 123	Davis-Bro 2.14	Shoun-Cin......................45	Head-Bro 6	Gumbert-StL........9.95	Brandt-Pit 2.2	Brandt-Pit 1.7
Higbe-Bro 108	Wyatt-Bro 2.14	Mungo-NY 45	Beggs-Cin 6	Warneke-Chi......10.19		

Innings Pitched	Opponents' Avg.	Opponents' OBP	Earned Run Average	Adjusted ERA	Adjusted Starter Runs	Pitcher Wins
Javery-Bos 303.0	Wyatt-Bro 207	Wyatt-Bro.....................255	Pollet-StL 1.75	Lanier-StL 177	M.Cooper-StL 32.9	**Sewell-Pit** 3.9
VanderMeer-Cin 289.0	VanderMeer-Cin ...224	Rowe-Phi 279	Lanier-StL 1.90	M.Cooper-StL 146	Lanier-StL............30.8	**M.Cooper-StL** 3.3
Andrews-Bos 283.2	M.Cooper-StL 226	M.Cooper-StL 286	M.Cooper-StL 2.30	Sewell-Pit.............137	Sewell-Pit 26.9	**Rowe-Phi** 3.3
M.Cooper-StL 274.0	Krist-StL 233	Andrews-Bos 291	Wyatt-Bro 2.49	Wyatt-Bro.............135	Andrews-Bos 25.6	**Andrews-Bos** 3.2
Sewell-Pit 265.1	Barrett-Chi-Phi 237	Bithorn-Chi...................294	Sewell-Pit 2.54	Butcher-Pit............134	Bithorn-Chi 23.2	**Tobin-Bos** 3.1

Life During Wartime

World War II was taking a bite out of baseball's economy. Attendance fell 13 percent further after dropping 9 percent in 1942. And it took a bite out of the ball, too—with cork and rubber unavailable to Spalding, the 1943 baseballs were made from a cork substitute called balata. The ball was deader than vaudeville, and public outcry soon forced the manufacture of a livelier spheroid.

Talent was draining from baseball as well. The Dodgers, losing Hugh Casey, Larry French, Pee Wee Reese, and Pete Reiser to military service, dropped to a distant third. The Reds sacrificed Ewell Blackwell to the war for three years; the Cubs lost Eddie Waitkus for four. Johnny Sain and Warren Spahn departed Boston from 1943–45, and the Giants lived without Johnny Mize for the same span.

St. Louis' excellent farm system produced Harry Brecheen, Lou Klein, and Al Brazle to supplement a club that lost Johnny Beazley, Frank Crespi, Terry Moore, and Enos Slaughter for three seasons. Buoyed by big years from Stan Musial and Mort Cooper, the Cardinals ran away with the pennant. Only a late flurry by second-place Cincinnati cut St. Louis' winning margin under 20; this was the league's least competitive race in nearly forty years.

Breaking his own record for relief appearances, Ace Adams of the Giants became the first pitcher to appear in 70 games since 1883. The Phillies changed their name to the Blue Jays, but didn't get any better. In Brooklyn, 19-year-old first baseman Gil Hodges got his first major league at bats, while across town at the Polo Grounds, Carl Hubbell retired at 40 with arm problems. The Giants finished last.

Despite their great regular season, the Cardinals—perhaps challenged for competition—lost to the Yankees in a five-game World Series. The Cards, who batted just .224, actually outhit New York—only not when it counted. They scored 2 runs or less in all four losses.

1943 American League

TEAM	W	L	T	PCT	GB	HW	HL	R	OR	PA	H	2B	3B	HR	BB	SO	HB	SH	AVG	OBP	SLG	OPS	AOPS	BR	ABR	PF	SB	CS	BSA	BSR
NY	98	56	1	.636		**54**	23	**669**	**542**	6024	1350	218	**59**	**100**	**624**	562	93	25	.256	**.337**	**.376**	**713**	**114**	**98**	**93**	101	46	60	43	-11
WAS	84	69	0	.549	13.5	44	32	666	595	5965	1328	245	50	47	605	579	88	**39**	.254	.336	.347	683	110	49	74	96	142	55	**72**	**12**
CLE	82	71	0	.536	15.5	44	33	600	577	5968	1344	**246**	45	55	567	**521**	121	11	.255	.329	.350	679	112	35	76	94	47	58	45	-10
CHI	82	72	1	.532	16	40	36	573	594	5909	1297	193	46	33	561	581	72	22	.247	.322	.320	642	94	-34	-33	100	**173**	87	67	8
DET	78	76	1	.506	20	45	32	632	560	5983	**1401**	200	47	77	483	553	**123**	13	**.261**	.324	.359	683	98	29	-16	108	40	43	48	-6
STL	72	80	1	.474	25	44	33	596	604	5865	1269	229	36	78	569	646	106	15	.245	.322	.349	671	100	16	3	102	37	43	46	-7
BOS	68	84	3	.447	29	39	36	563	607	6010	1314	223	42	57	486	591	113	19	.244	.308	.332	640	92	-49	-58	102	86	61	59	-2
PHI	49	105	1	.318	49	27	51	497	717	5798	1219	174	44	26	430	465	95	29	.232	.294	.297	591	78	-143	-141	100	55	42	57	-3
TOT	617					337	276	4796		47522	10522	1728	369	473	4325	4498	173	811	.249	.322	.341	663					626	449	58	-19

TEAM	CG	SHO	GR	SV	IP	H	HR	BB	SO	BR/9	ERA	AERA	OAV	OOB	PR	APR	PF	OSB	OCS	FA	E	WPB	DP	FW	PW	BW	BSW	DIF
NY	**83**	14	98	13	1415.1	1229	60	489	653	**11.0**	**2.93**	110	**.234**	**.301**	**58**	47	98	**48**	50	.974	160	31	166	.2	5.1	**10.1**	-.9	6.5
WAS	61	16	134	**21**	1388.0	1293	**48**	540	495	12.0	3.18	101	.246	.318	17	3	97	59	51	.971	179	49	145	-1.0	.3	8.0	**1.6**	-1.4
CLE	64	14	**158**	20	1406.1	1234	52	606	585	11.9	3.15	99	.239	.322	23	-7	94	57	61	.975	157	**13**	**183**	.3	-.8	8.2	-.8	-1.4
CHI	70	12	109	19	1400.1	1352	54	501	476	12.1	3.20	104	.255	.324	15	21	101	66	43	.973	166	35	167	-.0	2.3	-3.6	1.1	5.3
DET	67	**18**	130	20	1411.2	**1226**	51	549	**706**	11.4	3.00	**117**	**.234**	.308	46	**76**	107	84	**80**	.971	177	32	130	-.7	**8.2**	-1.7	-.4	-4.4
STL	64	10	130	14	1385.0	1397	74	**488**	572	12.4	3.41	97	.263	.327	-18	-13	101	124	54	.975	**152**	32	127	**.6**	-1.4	.3	-.5	-3.0
BOS	62	13	140	16	1426.1	1369	61	615	513	12.6	3.45	96	.257	.335	-25	-22	101	80	55	**.976**	153	45	179	**.6**	-2.4	-6.3	.0	-.0
PHI	73	5	107	13	1394.0	1421	73	536	503	12.9	4.05	84	.265	.336	-117	-98	103	108	55	.973	162	43	148	.1	-10.6	-15.3	-.0	-2.2
TOT	544	102	1006	136	11227.0					12.0	3.30		.249	.322						.973	1306	280	1245					

Batter-Fielder Wins
Boudreau-Cle......6.8
Appling-Chi 6.3
Gordon-NY 5.6
York-Det 4.6
Keller-NY 4.0

Batting Average
Appling-Chi...........328
Wakefield-Det.......316
Hodgin-Chi 314
Cramer-Det...........300
Case-Was.............294

On-Base Percentage
Appling-Chi 419
Cullenbine-Cle 407
Keller-NY 396
Boudreau-Cle 388
Curtright-Chi 382

Slugging Average
York-Det 527
Keller-NY 525
Stephens-StL 482
Heath-Cle 481
Wakefield-Det 434

On-Base Plus Slugging
Keller-NY 922
York-Det...............893
Heath-Cle 850
Stephens-StL........839
Appling-Chi 825

Adjusted OPS
Keller-NY 167
Heath-Cle 157
York-Det...............148
Cullenbine-Cle......146
Appling-Chi 142

Adjusted Batter Runs
Keller-NY 45.1
Appling-Chi 36.7
Cullenbine-Cle....34.4
York-Det 33.3
Heath-Cle 30.4

Runs
Case-Was 102
Keller-NY 97
Wakefield-Det 91
York-Det..................90
Vernon-Was............89

Hits
Wakefield-Det 200
Appling-Chi 192
Cramer-Det 182
Case-Was 180

Doubles
Wakefield-Det 38
Case-Was 36
Gutteridge-StL 35
Etten-NY 35

Triples
Moses-Chi 12
Lindell-NY 12
York-Det..................11
Keller-NY 11
Spence-Was 10

Home Runs
York-Det..................34
Keller-NY 31
Stephens-StL..........22
Heath-Cle 18

Total Bases
York-Det................301
Wakefield-Det 275
Keller-NY 269
Doerr-Bos 249
Stephens-StL........247

Runs Batted In
York-Det 118
Etten-NY..............107
Johnson-NY 94
Stephens-StL 91
Spence-Was..........88

Stolen Bases
Case-Was 61
Moses-Chi...............56
Tucker-Chi 29
Appling-Chi 27
Vernon-Was............24

Base Stealing Runs
Case-Was.............8.5
Moses-Chi 7.4
Appling-Chi............3.1
Culberson-Bos 3.1
Vernon-Was 2.5

Fielding Runs-Infield
Boudreau-Cle 25.1
Gordon-NY 24.7
York-Det......................18.6
Clift-StL-Was 15.4
Bloodworth-Det 15.4

Fielding Runs-Outfield
Tucker-Chi 9.2
Byrnes-StL 6.9
Moses-Chi 6.6
Johnson-Was 6.5
Laabs-StL 4.6

Wins
Trout-Det 20
Chandler-NY 20
Wynn-Was 18
Smith-Cle................17
Bagby-Cle 17

Winning Pct.
Chandler-NY.........833
Smith-Cle.............708
Bonham-NY 652
Trout-Det..............625
Grove-Chi 625

Complete Games
Hughson-Bos 20
Chandler-NY..........20
Wensloff-NY 18
Trout-Det 18
Grove-Chi 18

Strikeouts
Reynolds-Cle........151
Newhouser-Det 144
Chandler-NY 134
Bridges-Det 124
Trucks-Det............118

Fewest BB/Game
Leonard-Was 1.88
Chandler-NY.......1.92
Bonham-NY 2.07
Muncrief-StL 2.11
Trucks-Det 2.31

Games
Brown-Bos 49
Trout-Det......................44
Wolff-Phi 41
Ryba-Bos 40
Carrasquel-Was 39

Saves
Maltzberger-Chi......14
Heving-Cle...............9
Brown-Bos 9
Murphy-NY 8
Caster-StL 8

Base Runners/9
Chandler-NY........9.07
Murphy-NY 9.79
Trucks-Det 9.90
Bonham-NY 9.97
Wensloff-NY 10.07

Adjusted Relief Runs
Brown-Bos 11.6
Maltzberger-Chi ...10.8
Caster-StL 9.6
Murphy-NY 5.6
Heving-Cle 4.3

Relief Ranking
Caster-StL...........18.0
Brown-Bos..........15.9
Maltzberger-Chi..14.3
Murphy-NY 11.2
Naymick-Cle 5.0

Innings Pitched
Bagby-Cle..........273.0
Hughson-Bos 266.0
Wynn-Was 256.2
Chandler-NY......253.0
Trout-Det...........246.2

Opponents' Avg.
Reynolds-Cle 202
Niggeling-StL-Was ...204
Haefner-Was.........208
Chandler-NY.........215
Wensloff-NY 219

Opponents' OBP
Chandler-NY 261
Trucks-Det 276
Wensloff-NY................282
Bonham-NY 282
Niggeling-StL-Was 282

Earned Run Average
Chandler-NY........1.64
Bonham-NY 2.27
Haefner-Was........2.29
Bridges-Det.........2.39
Trout-Det.............2.48

Adjusted ERA
Chandler-NY 197
Bridges-Det 147
Trout-Det 142
Bonham-NY..........141
Haefner-Was 140

Adjusted Starter Runs
Chandler-NY.......42.1
Bonham-NY 26.0
Trout-Det.............25.8
Bridges-Det.........23.9
Hughson-Bos 19.6

Pitcher Wins
Chandler-NY......5.3
Trout-Det............4.1
Bridges-Det........2.6
Bonham-NY.........2.5
Caster-StL..........2.0

Fathers Playing Catch with Sons

On September 6, 16-year-old Carl Scheib debuted as a pitcher for the Philadelphia A's. He became the youngest player in AL history, and joined others, like 20-year-olds Gene Woodling and George Kell, 18-year-old Vern Benson, and 17-year-old Cass Michaels in 1943's force-feeding derby.

In addition, several graybeards profited from the lack of available bodies. Forty-year-old Mike Ryba pitched 40 times for the Red Sox, who also used 41-year-old Al Simmons in the outfield. Joe Kuhel, Chicago's 37-year-old first baseman, batted .213 in 153 games. Johnny Niggeling, at 39, made 26 starts.

The Yankees won the pennant once more—but with Nick Etten at first base, outfielders Bud Matheny and Johnny Lindell replacing Joe DiMaggio and Tommy Henrich, and, again, a deep veteran pitching staff. Boston dropped into seventh and the Browns to sixth, leaving the Senators, Indians, and White Sox as the Yankees' closest pursuers.

For the third straight year, attendance declined, and average scoring fell for the fifth straight season to 3.89 runs per team—the fewest until 1966. As a result, speed became a factor. The Senators and White Sox both stole more bases than any AL club since 1923. Washington outfielder George Case's 61 steals were the highest individual total in more than a decade. The Yankees were the exception, with a major league-high 100 home runs.

Spud Chandler was a very good pitcher—but his 20–4 record and 1.64 ERA for the Yankees are reflective of the talent he was facing during the war years. Only three AL players hit 20 home runs in 1943. Yankees pitching was the World Series secret . St. Louis scored just 9 runs as New York won easily in five games. Chandler notched 2 complete-game victories, allowing just 1 earned run. Bill Dickey played in his last of eight Fall Classics and collected 4 RBIs.

1944 National League

TEAM	W	L	T	PCT	GB	HW	HL	R	OR	PA	H	2B	3B	HR	BB	SO	HB	SH	AVG	OBP	SLG	OPS	AOPS	BR	ABR	PF	SB	CS	BSA	BSR
STL	105	49	3	.682		**54**	22	**772**	**490**	6170	**1507**	**274**	59	**100**	544	473	**124**	**27**	**.275**	**.344**	**.402**	**746**	**114**	**113**	**99**	102	37			
PIT	90	63	5	.588	14.5	49	28	744	662	6099	1441	248	**80**	70	**573**	616	80	18	.265	.338	.379	717	104	58	29	104	**87**			
CIN	89	65	1	.578	16	45	33	573	537	5821	1340	229	31	51	423	**391**	100	**27**	.254	.313	.338	651	92	-74	-52	96	51			
CHI	75	79	3	.487	30	35	42	702	669	6108	1425	236	46	71	520	521	105	21	.261	.328	.360	688	101	-1	3	99	53			
NY	67	87	1	.435	38	39	36	682	773	5953	1398	191	47	93	512	480	115	20	.263	.331	.370	701	103	20	22	100	39			
BOS	65	89	1	.422	40	38	40	593	674	5868	1299	250	39	79	456	509	112	18	.246	.308	.353	661	88	-60	-83	104	37			
BRO	63	91	1	.409	42	37	39	690	832	6011	1450	255	51	56	486	451	118	14	.269	.331	.366	697	104	17	29	98	45			
PHI	61	92	1	.399	43.5	29	49	539	658	5911	1331	199	42	55	470	500	109	31	.251	.316	.336	652	92	-73	-53	97	32			
TOT	623					326	289	5295		47941	11191	1882	395	575	3984	3941	176	863	.261	.326	.363	689					381			

TEAM	CG	SHO	GR	SV	IP	H	HR	BB	SO	BR/9	ERA	AERA	OAV	OOB	PR	APR	PF	OSB	OCS	FA	E	WPB	DP	FW	PW	BW	BSW	DIF
STL	89	**26**	113	12	1427.0	**1228**	55	468	**637**	**10.8**	**2.67**	**132**	**.233**	**.298**	**148**	**138**	98	35	*30*	**.982**	**112**	22	**162**	**3.7**	**14.2**	**10.2**		-.0
PIT	77	10	140	19	1414.1	1466	65	435	452	12.2	3.44	108	.265	.321	27	43	103	43	*35*	.970	191	23	122	-1.1	4.4	3.0		7.2
CIN	**93**	17	96	12	1398.1	1292	60	**390**	369	10.9	2.97	117	.246	.300	99	83	97	**31**	*19*	.978	137	**14**	153	2.0	8.5	-5.3		6.8
CHI	70	11	156	13	1400.2	1484	75	458	545	12.5	3.59	98	.274	.331	4	-9	98	49	***44***	.970	186	35	151	-.8	-.9	.3		-.5
NY	47	4	**200**	**21**	1363.2	1413	116	587	499	13.4	4.29	85	.265	.342	-103	-93	102	45	*35*	.971	179	49	128	-.5	-9.5	2.3		-2.2
BOS	70	13	132	12	1388.1	1430	80	527	454	12.8	3.67	104	.267	.335	-9	21	106	76	*41*	.971	182	23	160	-.7	2.2	-8.5		-4.9
BRO	50	4	187	13	1367.2	1471	75	660	487	14.3	4.68	76	.274	.357	-162	-175	98	54	*35*	.966	197	48	112	-1.7	-18.0	3.0		2.6
PHI	66	11	155	6	1395.1	1407	**49**	459	496	12.2	3.64	99	.261	.321	-4	-4	100	48	*33*	.972	177	41	138	-.5	-.4	-5.4		-9.2
TOT	562	96	1179	108	11155.1					12.4	3.61		.261	.326						.972	1361	255	1126					

Batter-Fielder Wins	Batting Average	On-Base Percentage	Slugging Average	On-Base Plus Slugging	Adjusted OPS	Adjusted Batter Runs
Musial-StL 5.5	Walker-Bro 357	Musial-StL 440	Musial-StL 549	Musial-StL 990	Musial-StL 174	Musial-StL 60.7
Walker-Bro 4.9	Musial-StL 347	Walker-Bro..................434	Nicholson-Chi 545	Ott-NY 967	Walker-Bro............173	Walker-Bro..........54.8
Galan-Bro 4.5	Medwick-NY 337	Galan-Bro 426	Ott-NY 544	Walker-Bro............963	Ott-NY 171	Galan-Bro 50.8
McCormick-Cin ..3.8	Hopp-StL 336	Ott-NY 423	Walker-Bro 529	Nicholson-Chi 935	Nicholson-Chi 162	Nicholson-Chi 49.5
Nicholson-Chi 3.8	Cavarretta-Chi 321	Hopp-StL 404	Weintraub-NY.......524	Galan-Bro 922	Galan-Bro 162	Ott-NY 41.7

Runs	Hits	Doubles	Triples	Home Runs	Total Bases	Runs Batted In
Nicholson-Chi 116	Musial-StL 197	Musial-StL......................51	Barrett-Pit 19	Nicholson-Chi 33	Nicholson-Chi 317	Nicholson-Chi......122
Musial-StL 112	Cavarretta-Chi......197	Galan-Bro 43	Elliott-Pit 16	Ott-NY 26	Musial-StL 312	Elliott-Pit..............108
Russell-Pit 109	Holmes-Bos..........195	Holmes-Bos 42	Cavarretta-Chi........15	Northey-Phi 22	Holmes-Bos..........288	Northey-Phi 104
Hopp-StL 106	Walker-Bro............191		Russell-Pit 14	McCormick-Cin 20	Walker-Bro............283	Sanders-StL 102
Cavarretta-Chi......106	Russell-Pit 181		Musial-StL 14	Kurowski-StL 20	Northey-Phi 283	McCormick-Cin....102

Stolen Bases	Base Stealing Runs	Fielding Runs-Infield	Fielding Runs-Outfield	Wins	Winning Pct.	Complete Games
Barrett-Pit 28		Kerr-NY 19.3	Pafko-Chi 10.2	Walters-Cin 23	Wilks-StL 810	Tobin-Bos 28
Lupien-Phi 18		Williams-Cin...............15.6	Russell-Pit 9.1	M.Cooper-StL 22	Brecheen-StL 762	Walters-Cin.............27
Hughes-Chi 16		Hughes-Chi 13.4	Medwick-NY 7.1	Voiselle-NY 21	M.Cooper-StL 759	Voiselle-NY............25
Hopp-StL 15		Luby-NY......................12.5	Olmo-Bro 5.2	Sewell-Pit................21	Walters-Cin...........742	Sewell-Pit 24
Kerr-NY 14		McCormick-Cin 12.3	Musial-StL 3.3	Tobin-Bos................18	Sewell-Pit 636	M.Cooper-StL........22

Strikeouts	Fewest BB/Game	Games	Saves	Base Runners/9	Adjusted Relief Runs	Relief Ranking
Voiselle-NY 161	Raffensberger-Phi ..1.57	Adams-NY 65	Adams-NY..............13	Wilks-StL 9.66	Karl-Phi................10.5	Karl-Phi 5.8
Lanier-StL 141	Strincevich-Pit......1.75	Webber-Bro...................48	Schmidt-StL.............5	Heusser-Cin 9.72	Donnelly-StL..........9.9	Donnelly-StL 4.9
Javery-Bos............137	Davis-Bro 1.81	Rescigno-Pit 48	Rescigno-Pit 5	Karl-Phi................9.91		
Raffensberger-Phi 136	Shoun-Cin 1.87	Voiselle-NY 43	Davis-Bro.................4	Munger-StL........10.04		
	Derringer-Chi 1.95	Tobin-Bos 43	Cuccurullo-Pit 4	DeLaCruz-Cin....10.16		

Innings Pitched	Opponents' Avg.	Opponents' OBP	Earned Run Average	Adjusted ERA	Adjusted Starter Runs	Pitcher Wins
Voiselle-NY........312.2	Walters-Cin...........219	Wilks-StL 275	Heusser-Cin 2.38	Heusser-Cin..........146	Walters-Cin..........34.0	**Walters-Cin** 4.7
Tobin-Bos 299.1	Wilks-StL 227	Heusser-Cin.................275	Walters-Cin..........2.40	Walters-Cin 145	M.Cooper-StL 33.1	**Tobin-Bos** 3.8
Sewell-Pit 286.0	Heusser-Cin 231	Walters-Cin 281	M.Cooper-StL 2.46	M.Cooper-StL 143	Munger-StL...........29.1	**M.Cooper-StL** 3.7
Walters-Cin........285.0	Voiselle-NY...........232	DeLaCruz-Cin 284	Wilks-StL 2.64	Wilks-StL 133	Wilks-StL 25.0	**Munger-StL** 3.4
Raffensberger-Phi 258.2	Lanier-StL.............234	Raffensberger-Phi...........285	Lanier-StL............2.65	Lanier-StL 133	Heusser-Cin 24.6	**Heusser-Cin** 3.1

Baby Face

The use of young players, by now a cliché of wartime baseball, reached a crest on June 10 when 15-year-old Joe Nuxhall pitched for the Cincinnati Reds. He remains the youngest big leaguer in history. Sixteen-year-old Tommy Brown played shortstop for the Dodgers, with 17-year-old Eddie Miksis filling in at both short and third. Eighteen-year-olds Cal McLish and Ralph Branca pitched for Brooklyn, who fell to seventh, crushed by wartime losses. The Phillies showcased infielders Putsy Caballero, 16, and Granny Hamner, 17, as well as hurler Rogers McKee, also 17. New York had two 19-year-old pitchers, and the Braves used two 17-year-olds.

Tellingly, the Cardinals, who became the first NL team to win 100 games three straight seasons, had no teenagers on their team. St. Louis was in control by May and coasted to another pennant. Outfielder Stan Musial and Johnny Hopp fattened up on wartime pitching, but the MVP went to their teammate, slick-fielding shortstop Marty Marion. Pittsburgh finished a surprising second; a patchwork pitching staff and a line-drive attack helped them finish just above Cincinnati, for whom hurler Bucky Walters had another dominating season.

In the game's only all-St. Louis World Series, the Cardinals snuffed out their crosstown rivals' attack, and the Browns committed 10 errors. The Cardinals came back from a two-games-to-one deficit to take the next three, allowing the Browns but 2 runs in the process. Four of the six games were decided by 1 or 2 runs, and excellent pitching—allowing the Browns just a .183 average—carried the day.

Judge Kenesaw Mountain Landis died on November 25 at age 78. The autocratic Commissioner served baseball for nearly a quarter-century, but with declining power; he could not stop the subjugation of the minors to the majors. But never again would the game be commanded by a strong, independent voice.

1944 American League

TEAM	W	L	T	PCT	GB	HW	HL	R	OR	PA	H	2B	3B	HR	BB	SO	HB	SH	AVG	OBP	SLG	OPS	AOPS	BR	ABR	PF	SB	CS	BSA	BSR
STL	89	65	0	.578		**54**	23	684	587	5928	1328	223	45	72	531	604	107	21	.252	.323	.352	675	94	-3	-37	106	44	33	57	-2
DET	88	66	2	.571	1	43	34	658	**581**	6011	1405	220	44	60	**532**	500	111	**24**	.263	.332	.354	686	97	22	-12	106	61	55	53	-6
NY	83	71	0	.539	6	47	31	674	617	5978	1410	216	**74**	**96**	523	627	102	22	.264	.333	**.387**	**720**	108	74	51	103	**91**	31	**75**	**9**
BOS	77	77	2	.500	12	47	30	**739**	676	6052	1456	**277**	56	69	522	505	110	20	**.270**	**.336**	.380	716	**112**	**77**	**86**	99	60	40	60	-1
PHI	72	82	1	.468	17	39	37	525	594	5873	1364	169	47	36	422	490	**122**	17	.257	.314	.327	641	90	-78	-70	99	42	32	57	-2
CLE	72	82	1	.468	17	39	38	643	677	6119	**1458**	270	50	70	512	593	107	19	.266	.331	.372	703	111	50	78	96	48	42	53	-4
CHI	71	83	0	.461	18	41	36	543	662	5819	1307	210	55	23	439	**448**	67	21	.247	.307	.320	627	86	-99	-92	99	66	47	58	-2
WAS	64	90	0	.416	25	40	37	592	664	5926	1386	186	42	33	470	477	108	29	.261	.324	.330	654	97	-43	-15	96	127	59	68	7
TOT	619					350	266	5058		47706	11114	1771	413	459	3951	4244	173	834	.260	.325	.353	678					539	339	61	0

TEAM	CG	SHO	GR	SV	IP	H	HR	BB	SO	BR/9	ERA	AERA	OAV	OOB	PR	APR	PF	OSB	OCS	FA	E	WPB	DP	FW	PW	BW	BSW	DIF
STL	71	16	127	17	1397.1	1392	58	469	**581**	12.1	3.17	114	.259	.320	41	63	105	76	31	.972	171	**30**	142	.5	6.6	-3.9	-.2	9.0
DET	**87**	**20**	119	8	1400.0	1373	**39**	452	568	11.9	**3.09**	**116**	.257	.318	**54**	**72**	104	**37**	**60**	.970	190	32	184	-.5	**7.6**	-1.3	-.6	5.8
NY	78	9	111	13	1390.1	1351	82	532	529	12.3	3.39	103	.257	.326	7	15	102	57	40	**.974**	**156**	38	170	**1.3**	1.6	5.4	**.9**	-3.2
BOS	58	7	150	17	1394.1	1404	66	592	524	13.0	3.82	89	.263	.339	-60	-66	99	69	38	.972	171	40	154	.6	-6.9	**9.0**	-.1	-2.6
PHI	72	10	107	14	1397.1	**1345**	58	**390**	534	**11.4**	3.26	107	**.252**	**.307**	27	35	102	98	50	.971	176	42	127	.2	3.7	-7.4	-.2	-1.3
CLE	48	7	**200**	**18**	1419.1	1428	40	621	524	13.2	3.65	90	.265	.344	-35	-58	96	78	45	**.974**	165	40	**192**	.9	-6.1	8.2	-.4	-7.6
CHI	64	5	112	17	1390.2	1411	68	420	481	12.0	3.58	96	.264	.320	-23	-23	100	56	40	.970	183	44	154	-.2	-2.4	-9.7	-.2	6.5
WAS	83	13	110	11	1381.0	1410	48	475	503	12.4	3.49	93	.264	.327	-10	-38	95	68	35	.964	218	62	156	-2.3	-4.0	-1.6	.7	-5.9
TOT	561	87	1036	115	11170.1					12.3	3.43		.260	.325						.971	1430	328	1279					

Batter-Fielder Wins
Boudreau-Cle......7.5
Stirnweiss-NY 6.8
Spence-Was........5.4
B.Johnson-Bos ..5.3
Doerr-Bos............5.1

Batting Average
Boudreau-Cle 327
Doerr-Bos 325
B.Johnson-Bos 324
Stirnweiss-NY.......319
Spence-Was 316

On-Base Percentage
B.Johnson-Bos............431
Boudreau-Cle 406
Doerr-Bos 399
Etten-NY 399
Byrnes-StL..................396

Slugging Average
Doerr-Bos 528
B.Johnson-Bos 528
Lindell-NY.............500
Spence-Was.........486

On-Base Plus Slugging
B.Johnson-Bos 959
Doerr-Bos 927
Spence-Was 877
Etten-NY 865
Lindell-NY 851

Adjusted OPS
B.Johnson-Bos 175
Doerr-Bos 166
Spence-Was 157
Boudreau-Cle 146
Etten-NY 142

Adjusted Batter Runs
B.Johnson-Bos ..56.6
Spence-Was 44.0
Doerr-Bos 39.9
Boudreau-Cle 39.4
Etten-NY 34.8

Runs
Stirnweiss-NY 125
B.Johnson-Bos 106
Cullenbine-Cle........98
Doerr-Bos 95
Metkovich-Bos........94

Hits
Stirnweiss-NY 205
Boudreau-Cle 191
Spence-Was 187
Lindell-NY 178
Rocco-Cle 174

Doubles
Boudreau-Cle 45
Keltner-Cle....................41
B.Johnson-Bos 40
Fox-Bos..........................37
Stirnweiss-NY 35

Triples
Stirnweiss-NY 16
Lindell-NY 16
Gutteridge-StL 11
Doerr-Bos 10

Home Runs
Etten-NY 22
Stephens-StL..........20
York-Det..................18
Spence-Was 18
Lindell-NY 18

Total Bases
Lindell-NY 297
Stirnweiss-NY 296
Spence-Was 288
B.Johnson-Bos 277

Runs Batted In
Stephens-StL 109
B.Johnson-Bos 106
Lindell-NY............103
Spence-Was........100
York-Det 98

Stolen Bases
Stirnweiss-NY 55
Case-Was 49
Myatt-Was 26
Moses-Chi 21
Gutteridge-StL 20

Base Stealing Runs
Stirnweiss-NY........8.3
Case-Was..............4.5
Myatt-Was 2.2
Moses-Chi 2.2
Gutteridge-StL 1.6

Fielding Runs-Infield
Mayo-Det 33.5
Boudreau-Cle 20.2
Stirnweiss-NY 18.0
Rocco-Cle 16.6
Hoover-Det..................14.8

Fielding Runs-Outfield
Spence-Was........15.4
Tucker-Chi 10.8
B.Johnson-Bos 5.2
Garrison-Bos-Phi ..4.9
Lindell-NY 4.0

Wins
Newhouser-Det 29
Trout-Det 27
Potter-StL................19
Hughson-Bos..........18

Winning Pct.
Hughson-Bos 783
Newhouser-Det.....763
Potter-StL 731
Trout-Det..............659
Borowy-NY 586

Complete Games
Trout-Det 33
Newhouser-Det 25

Strikeouts
Newhouser-Det 187
Trout-Det 144
Newsom-Phi 142
Kramer-StL 124
Niggeling-Was 121

Fewest BB/Game
Harris-Phi 1.34
Leonard-Was 1.45
Bonham-NY 1.73
Gorsica-Det 1.78
Hamlin-Phi 1.80

Games
Heving-Cle 63
Berry-Phi 53
Trout-Det........................49
Newhouser-Det..............47
Klieman-Cle 47

Saves
Maltzberger-Chi......12
Caster-StL 12
Berry-Phi 12
Heving-Cle..............10
Barrett-Bos 8

Base Runners/9
Berry-Phi 8.33
Hughson-Bos 9.52
Maltzberger-Chi ..9.95
Trout-Det...........10.24
Leonard-Was 10.28

Adjusted Relief Runs
Berry-Phi 17.2
Heving-Cle 13.5
Maltzberger-Chi 6.8
Caster-StL 5.6

Relief Ranking
Berry-Phi 29.2
Heving-Cle..........13.7
Maltzberger-Chi..12.1
Caster-StL 9.3

Innings Pitched
Trout-Det............352.1
Newhouser-Det..312.1
Newsom-Phi 265.0
Kramer-StL 257.0
Borowy-NY 252.2

Opponents' Avg.
Gromek-Cle 219
Niggeling-Was 221
Hughson-Bos 225
Newhouser-Det.....230
Borowy-NY 236

Opponents' OBP
Hughson-Bos...............267
Leonard-Was 284
Trout-Det 284
Gromek-Cle 290
Newhouser-Det 293

Earned Run Average
Trout-Det..............2.12
Newhouser-Det....2.22
Hughson-Bos 2.26
Niggeling-Was 2.32
Kramer-StL 2.49

Adjusted ERA
Trout-Det 168
Newhouser-Det 161
Hughson-Bos........151
Kramer-StL 145
Niggeling-Was 141

Adjusted Starter Runs
Trout-Det.............53.1
Newhouser-Det.....44.7
Hughson-Bos 26.6
Kramer-StL 26.6
Niggeling-Was 23.0

Pitcher Wins
Trout-Det............8.2
Newhouser-Det 6.1
Kramer-StL.........3.4
Berry-Phi............3.2
Hughson-Bos 3.1

Brownout

In a year that stretched baseball's ability to take itself seriously, a squad of especially unlikely heroes won the flag. The perpetually bad St. Louis Browns took advantage of a war-decimated league and climbed atop a four-team tangle by mid-August. Shortstop Vern Stephens was the club's only real threat at bat, but a veteran pitching staff, quality infield defense, and other teams' shortcomings kept the Brownies in the hunt.

At that point, the Red Sox dropped out. The Yankees got hot, but cooled off again, leaving the race to the Browns and Tigers. Detroit was fueled by Hal Newhouser and Dizzy Trout's pitching and outfielder Dick Wakefield's activation from the military rolls.

Both teams were on fire the last two weeks, but the Brownies came out on top, taking four straight from New York while the Tigers fell to Washington on the season's last day. This would be St. Louis' only AL crown, and the fact that it was accomplished by a collection of military-deferred 4-Fs, alcoholics, and graybeards is almost irrelevant.

The first big league player to die in World War II was 27-year-old Elmer Gedeon. A captain in the Army Air Corps, Gedeon's plane was shot down over France on April 20. He had played the outfield for the 1939 Senators.

During the 1940s, few teams altered their ballparks; due to the war, most construction was out. But this year, Detroit reconfigured its grounds, giving Tiger Stadium the dimensions it retained until closing in 1999. Total tickets sold skyrocketed 30 percent for the AL in 1944, and for the first time since 1925, the Browns didn't finish last in attendance. They came in fifth.

As if adhering to the demands of the war on travel, Sportsman's Park was the site for all six World Series games. The first all-St. Louis World Series was a much closer affair than anyone expected. The Browns actually went up two games to one before the deeper Cardinals took the next three.

1945 National League

TEAM	W	L	T	PCT	GB	HW	HL	R	OR	PA	H	2B	3B	HR	BB	SO	HB	SH	AVG	OBP	SLG	OPS	AOPS	BR	ABR	PF	SB	CS	BSA	BSR
CHI	98	56	1	.636		**49**	26	735	**532**	6034	1465	229	52	57	554	462	**150**	32	**.277**	**.349**	.372	721	**109**	54	70	98	69			
STL	95	59	1	.617	3	48	29	756	582	6166	**1498**	256	44	64	515	488	138	26	.273	.338	.371	709	102	27	10	102	55			
BRO	87	67	1	.565	11	48	30	**795**	724	6183	1468	257	**71**	57	**629**	**434**	111	25	.271	**.349**	.376	**725**	**109**	**69**	**75**	99	77			
PIT	82	72	1	.532	16	45	34	753	686	6038	1425	**259**	56	72	590	480	88	17	.267	.342	.377	719	102	48	20	104	**81**			
NY	78	74	2	.513	19	47	30	668	701	5991	1439	175	35	**114**	501	457	100	**40**	.269	.336	**.379**	715	103	30	19	102	38			
BOS	67	85	2	.441	30	36	38	721	728	6078	1453	229	25	101	520	510	91	26	.267	.334	.374	708	102	21	17	101	82			
CIN	61	93	0	.396	37	36	41	536	694	5796	1317	221	26	56	392	532	95	26	.249	.304	.333	637	85	-124	-112	98	71			
PHI	46	108	0	.299	52	22	55	548	865	5738	1278	197	27	56	449	501	71	15	.246	.307	.326	633	84	-125	-110	97	54			
TOT	618					331	283	5512		48024	11343	1823	336	577	4150	3864	207	844	.265	.333	.364	696					527			

TEAM	CG	SHO	GR	SV	IP	H	HR	BB	SO	BR/9	ERA	AERA	OAV	OOB	PR	APR	PF	OSB	OCS	FA	E	WPB	DP	FW	PW	BW	BSW	DIF
CHI	**86**	15	135	14	1366.1	**1301**	**57**	**385**	541	**11.3**	**2.98**	**123**	**.249**	**.304**	**125**	**106**	96	**43**	*33*	**.980**	**121**	**24**	124	**3.4**	**10.6**	7.0		.0
STL	77	**18**	156	9	1408.2	1351	70	497	510	12.0	3.24	116	.253	.320	88	80	99	70	*53*	.977	137	**24**	150	2.4	8.0	1.0		6.6
BRO	61	7	163	18	1392.1	1357	74	586	**557**	12.8	3.70	101	.253	.331	15	7	99	60	*36*	.962	230	41	144	-3.2	.7	**7.5**		5.0
PIT	73	8	142	16	1387.1	1477	61	455	518	12.7	3.76	105	.272	.331	6	26	104	77	*42*	.971	178	**24**	141	-.0	2.6	2.0		.5
NY	53	13	179	21	1374.2	1401	85	528	529	12.8	4.06	96	.263	.332	-40	-22	103	**43**	*42*	.973	166	33	112	.6	-2.2	1.9		1.7
BOS	57	7	166	13	1391.2	1474	99	557	404	13.3	4.04	95	.272	.342	-37	-32	101	64	***54***	.969	193	25	**160**	-1.1	-3.2	1.7		-6.4
CIN	77	11	132	6	1365.2	1438	70	534	372	13.2	4.00	94	.271	.340	-31	-37	99	76	*36*	.976	146	31	138	1.8	-3.7	-11.2		-2.9
PHI	31	4	**212**	**26**	1352.2	1544	61	608	432	14.5	4.64	83	.285	.360	-126	-122	101	94	*45*	.962	234	50	150	-3.5	-12.2	-11.0		-4.2
TOT	515	83	1285	123	11039.1					12.8	3.80		.265	.333						.971	1405	252	1119					

Batter-Fielder Wins	Batting Average	On-Base Percentage	Slugging Average	On-Base Plus Slugging	Adjusted OPS	Adjusted Batter Runs
Hack-Chi.............5.3	Cavarretta-Chi 355	Cavarretta-Chi 449	Holmes-Bos 577	Holmes-Bos..........997	Holmes-Bos..........175	Holmes-Bos........63.9
Holmes-Bos 5.1	Holmes-Bos 352	Galan-Bro 423	Kurowski-StL 511	Cavarretta-Chi......949	Cavarretta-Chi......167	Cavarretta-Chi....50.2
Cavarretta-Chi....4.1	Rosen-Bro 325	Hack-Chi 420	Cavarretta-Chi 500	Ott-NY 910	Ott-NY 150	Galan-Bro 39.6
Stanky-Bro..........3.7	Hack-Chi...............323	Holmes-Bos 420	Ott-NY 499	Kurowski-StL 894	Kurowski-StL 144	Ott-NY................33.2
Lombardi-NY 2.8	Kurowski-StL 323	Stanky-Bro..................417	Olmo-Bro 462	Galan-Bro 864	Galan-Bro 142	Hack-Chi 32.7

Runs	Hits	Doubles	Triples	Home Runs	Total Bases	Runs Batted In
Stanky-Bro............128	Holmes-Bos.........224	Holmes-Bos 47	Olmo-Bro 13	Holmes-Bos............28	Holmes-Bos..........367	Walker-Bro 124
Rosen-Bro 126	Rosen-Bro 197	Walker-Bro 42	Pafko-Chi 12	Workman-Bos 25	Adams-Phi-StL 279	Holmes-Bos 117
Holmes-Bos..........125	Hack-Chi 193	Galan-Bro 36	Rucker-NY 11	Adams-Phi-StL 22	Rosen-Bro 279	Pafko-Chi 110
Galan-Bro 114	Clay-Cin...............184	Elliott-Pit 36	Rosen-Bro 11	Ott-NY 21	Walker-Bro...........266	Olmo-Bro 110
Hack-Chi 110		Cavarretta-Chi 34	Cavarretta-Chi........10	Kurowski-StL 21	Kurowski-StL 261	Adams-Phi-StL 109

Stolen Bases	Base Stealing Runs	Fielding Runs-Infield	Fielding Runs-Outfield	Wins	Winning Pct.	Complete Games
Schoendienst-StL ..26		Kerr-NY 30.2	Gillenwater-Bos ..17.0	Barrett-Bos-StL 23	Brecheen-StL 789	Barrett-Bos-StL 24
Barrett-Pit 25		Coscarart-Pit 21.2	Walker-Bro 9.6	Wyse-Chi................22	Burkhart-StL 692	Wyse-Chi 23
Clay-Cin.................19		Hack-Chi 19.6	DiMaggio-Phi 9.0	Gregg-Bro 18	Wyse-Chi 688	Passeau-Chi..........19
		Johnson-Chi................15.4	Russell-Pit 5.0	Burkhart-StL 18	Barrett-Bos-StL.....657	Strincevich-Pit 18
		Mesner-Cin 15.0	Schoendienst-StL ..4.7	Passeau-Chi 17	Passeau-Chi.........654	Heusser-Cin 18

Strikeouts	Fewest BB/Game	Games	Saves	Base Runners/9	Adjusted Relief Runs	Relief Ranking
Roe-Pit..................148	Prim-Chi 1.25	Karl-Phi.........................67	Karl-Phi 15	Prim-Chi 9.04	Karl-Phi................14.5	Karl-Phi 14.3
Gregg-Bro 139	Barrett-Bos-StL....1.71	Adams-NY 65	Adams-NY 15	Beck-Cin-Pit 10.00	Buker-Bro 4.2	Adams-NY 6.0
Voiselle-NY 115	Roe-Pit 1.76	Hutchings-Bos 57	Rescigno-Pit 9	Maglie-NY..........10.25	Adams-NY 3.2	Buker-Bro 4.5
Mungo-NY 101	Wyse-Chi 1.78	Barrett-Bos-StL.............45		Roe-Pit 10.53		
Hutchings-Bos........99	Strincevich-Pit......1.93	Fox-Cin 45		Passeau-Chi......10.55		

Innings Pitched	Opponents' Avg.	Opponents' OBP	Earned Run Average	Adjusted ERA	Adjusted Starter Runs	Pitcher Wins
Barrett-Bos-StL..284.2	Prim-Chi 228	Prim-Chi.......................256	Borowy-Chi..........2.13	Prim-Chi 152	Passeau-Chi........32.6	**Passeau-Chi** 3.9
Wyse-Chi 278.1	Gregg-Bro.............232	Passeau-Chi 289	Prim-Chi 2.40	Brecheen-StL 149	Wyse-Chi 32.3	**Wyse-Chi** 3.3
Gregg-Bro..........254.1	Brecheen-StL 238	Barrett-Bos-StL 295	Passeau-Chi 2.46	Passeau-Chi 149	Roe-Pit 31.7	**Roe-Pit**...............3.2
Roe-Pit 235.0	Mungo-NY 238	Wyse-Chi 296	Brecheen-StL 2.52	Walters-Cin 140	Barrett-Bos-StL....24.6	**Prim-Chi** 2.9
Voiselle-NY........232.1	Passeau-Chi.........238	Roe-Pit.........................296	Walters-Cin..........2.68	Roe-Pit.................137	Brecheen-StL 22.9	**Walters-Cin** 2.6

Chicago's Last Stand

With the war drawing to a merciful close, NL attendance rose 32 percent to its highest total since 1930. Many veterans, such as Paul Derringer, Leo Durocher, Lloyd Waner, and Lon Warneke, played their last innings in 1945, as did Dick Sipek, a deaf outfielder employed by the Reds.

The surprise team of the season was Chicago, which improved by 23 games. In early July the Cubs were stalled in fourth place, but Chicago then won 16 of 17 to pass the Dodgers for the league lead. Holding off a late St. Louis challenge, the Cubs won their last NL pennant of the century. Phil Cavaretta won the batting title and was named league MVP. Stan Hack, Andy Pafko and Bill Nicholson provided punch, but the team's real strength was pitching. Graybeards Ray Prim, Claude Passeau, and Paul Derringer combined for 46 wins, Hank Wyse was 22-10, and Hank Borowy—who came over from New York in an odd midseason waiver deal—went 11–2 with Chicago while leading the NL in ERA. Chicago's favorite patsies were the seventh-place Reds, who dropped 21 of 22 to the Cubs. Chicago was also very good at doubling up opponents, winning 20 doubleheaders.

While the Cardinals remained strong, they too were hit hard by the war; outfielders Danny Litwhiler and Stan Musial were finally inducted after several deferrals. Rookie Red Schoendienst filled in ably, pacing the NL in steals, but the missing big bats, and several pitching injuries, proved too much. Ace Adams of the Giants was again the league's top reliever. Boston's Tommy Holmes, whose 37-game hitting streak was the NL's longest since 1897, led the league in doubles, hits, and homers. The Phillies finished last for the eighth time in ten years, but their stock would soon rise.

A sloppy but entertaining World Series saw the Tigers walk away with the victory. Borowy, 2–2 in the Series, got the decision in each of the last three games; he won Game 6 for the Cubs in relief but was hit hard in Games 5 and 7.

1945 American League

TEAM	W	L	T	PCT	GB	HW	HL	R	OR	PA	H	2B	3B	HR	BB	SO	HB	SH	AVG	OBP	SLG	OPS	AOPS	BR	ABR	PF	SB	CS	BSA	BSR
DET	88	65	2	.575		**50**	26	633	565	5885	1345	**227**	47	77	517	533	102	9	.256	.324	.361	685	98	21	-16	106	60	54	53	-6
WAS	87	67	2	.565	1.5	46	31	622	562	6008	1375	197	**63**	27	545	489	114	23	.258	.330	.334	664	107	-9	47	92	**110**	65	**63**	**1**
STL	81	70	3	.536	6	47	27	597	**548**	5866	1302	215	37	63	500	555	**124**	15	.249	.316	.341	657	91	-29	-56	105	25	31	45	-5
NY	81	71	0	.533	6.5	48	28	**676**	606	5925	1343	189	61	**93**	**618**	567	95	**36**	.259	**.343**	**.373**	**716**	108	**90**	**59**	105	64	43	60	-1
CLE	73	72	2	.503	11	44	33	557	**548**	5536	1249	216	48	65	505	578	119	14	.255	.326	.359	685	**109**	24	50	96	19	31	38	-7
CHI	71	78	1	.477	15	44	29	596	633	5661	1330	204	55	22	470	**467**	100	14	**.262**	.326	.337	663	101	-14	2	97	78	54	59	-2
BOS	71	83	3	.461	17.5	42	35	599	674	6018	**1393**	225	44	50	541	534	87	23	.260	.330	.346	676	100	14	0	102	72	50	59	-2
PHI	52	98	3	.347	34.5	39	35	494	638	5861	1297	201	37	33	449	463	96	20	.245	.306	.316	622	86	-98	-96	100	25	45	36	-10
TOT	612					360	244	4774		46760	10634	1674	392	430	4145	4186	154	837	.255	.325	.346	671					453	373	55	-31

TEAM	CG	SHO	GR	SV	IP	H	HR	BB	SO	BR/9	ERA	AERA	OAV	OOB	PR	APR	PF	OSB	OCS	FA	E	WPB	DP	FW	PW	BW	BSW	DIF
DET	78	**19**	131	**16**	1393.2	1305	48	538	**588**	12.1	2.99	**118**	.250	.322	58	**78**	105	49	52	.975	158	40	173	.4	**8.4**	-1.7	-.2	4.7
WAS	82	**19**	110	11	1412.1	1307	42	**440**	550	**11.2**	**2.92**	106	**.242**	**.301**	**69**	30	92	45	33	.970	183	58	124	-1.0	3.2	5.0	**.5**	2.2
STL	**91**	10	110	8	1382.2	1307	59	506	570	11.8	3.14	112	.249	.316	34	55	105	60	36	.976	143	**23**	123	1.2	5.9	-6.0	-.1	4.6
NY	78	9	102	14	1355.0	1277	66	485	474	11.8	3.45	100	.250	.316	-13	1	103	74	53	.971	175	35	170	-.7	.1	**6.3**	.3	-1.0
CLE	76	14	116	12	1302.1	**1269**	**39**	501	497	12.4	3.31	98	.257	.328	8	-9	97	68	45	**.977**	**126**	41	149	**1.7**	-1.0	5.4	-.3	-5.3
CHI	84	13	86	13	1330.2	1400	63	448	486	12.7	3.69	90	.270	.332	-49	-56	99	**35**	50	.970	180	26	139	-1.1	-6.0	.2	.2	3.2
BOS	71	15	**135**	13	1390.2	1389	58	656	490	13.4	3.80	90	.264	.348	-67	-60	101	52	**56**	.973	169	48	**198**	-.1	-6.4	.0	.2	.3
PHI	65	11	120	8	1381.0	1380	55	571	531	12.9	3.62	95	.262	.337	-40	-29	102	70	48	.973	168	27	160	-.3	-3.1	-10.3	-.7	-8.7
TOT	625	110	910	95	10948.1					12.3	3.36		.255	.325						.973	1302	298	1236					

Batter-Fielder Wins	Batting Average	On-Base Percentage	Slugging Average	On-Base Plus Slugging	Adjusted OPS	Adjusted Batter Runs
Stirnweiss-NY 7.2	Stirnweiss-NY.......309	Lake-Bos 412	Stirnweiss-NY.......476	Stirnweiss-NY 862	Stirnweiss-NY 143	Stirnweiss-NY 33.9
Lake-Bos 6.5	Cuccinello-Chi 308	Cullenbine-Cle-Det 402	Stephens-StL 473	Cullenbine-Cle-Det ..846	Estalella-Phi 142	Heath-Cle 33.0
Mayo-Det 3.5	Dickshot-Chi 302	Estalella-Phi.................399	Cullenbine-Cle-Det ...444	Estalella-Phi 834	Kuhel-Was 137	Cullenbine-Cle-Det 30.9
Cullenbine-Cle-Det ..3.1	Estalella-Phi 299	Grimes-NY...................395	Etten-NY...............437	Stephens-StL........825	Cullenbine-Cle-Det ..137	Lake-Bos 28.6
Boudreau-Cle......2.7	Myatt-Was 296	Etten-NY 387	Estalella-Phi 435	Etten-NY 824	Lake-Bos 136	Kuhel-Was..........27.5

Runs	Hits	Doubles	Triples	Home Runs	Total Bases	Runs Batted In
Stirnweiss-NY 107	Stirnweiss-NY 195	Moses-Chi 35	Stirnweiss-NY 22	Stephens-StL..........24	Stirnweiss-NY 301	Etten-NY.............111
Stephens-StL..........90	Moses-Chi 168	Stirnweiss-NY 32	Moses-Chi 15	Cullenbine-Cle-Det 18	Stephens-StL........270	Cullenbine-Cle-Det....93
Cullenbine-Cle-Det 83	Stephens-StL........165	Binks-Was.....................32	Kuhel-Was 13	York-Det..................18	Etten-NY 247	Stephens-StL 89
	Hall-Phi 161	McQuinn-StL.................31	Dickshot-Chi 10	Etten-NY 18	York-Det................246	York-Det 87
	Etten-NY 161		Peck-Phi 9	Heath-Cle 15	Moses-Chi 239	Binks-Was 81

Stolen Bases	Base Stealing Runs	Fielding Runs-Infield	Fielding Runs-Outfield	Wins	Winning Pct.	Complete Games
Stirnweiss-NY 33	Dickshot-Chi 2.9	Stirnweiss-NY 25.2	Cullenbine-Cle-Det 9.1	Newhouser-Det 25	Newhouser-Det.....735	Newhouser-Det 29
Myatt-Was 30	Myatt-Was 2.8	Lake-Bos 23.7	Case-Was................8.6	Ferriss-Bos 21	Leonard-Was 708	Ferriss-Bos 26
Case-Was 30	Metkovich-Bos 2.1	Kell-Phi 21.8	Mackiewicz-Cle 7.3	Wolff-Was 20	Gromek-Cle 679	Wolff-Was.............21
Metkovich-Bos 19	Stirnweiss-NY........1.3	Mayo-Det 20.3	Byrnes-StL 6.5	Gromek-Cle............19	Ferriss-Bos 677	Potter-StL 21
Dickshot-Chi 18	Crosetti-NY............1.2	Hall-Phi 20.1	Moses-Chi 6.2		Wolff-Was............667	Gromek-Cle 21

Strikeouts	Fewest BB/Game	Games	Saves	Base Runners/9	Adjusted Relief Runs	Relief Ranking
Newhouser-Det 212	Bonham-NY 1.10	Berry-Phi 52	Turner-NY 10	Wolff-Was............9.14	Berry-Phi 15.0	Berry-Phi............16.8
Potter-StL.............129	Leonard-Was 1.46	Reynolds-Cle 44	Berry-Phi 5	Potter-StL 9.90	Holcombe-NY 7.4	Holcombe-NY 7.2
Newsom-Phi 127	Wolff-Was 1.91	Pieretti-Was 44		Newhouser-Det..10.02	Barrett-Bos 6.9	Barrett-Bos 5.6
Reynolds-Cle 112	Overmire-Det 2.33	Trout-Det......................41		Leonard-Was 10.21	Zoldak-StL 1	Zoldak-StL...............0
	Gromek-Cle 2.37	Newhouser-Det..............40		Bonham-NY 10.41		

Innings Pitched	Opponents' Avg.	Opponents' OBP	Earned Run Average	Adjusted ERA	Adjusted Starter Runs	Pitcher Wins
Newhouser-Det..313.1	Newhouser-Det.....211	Wolff-Was 258	Newhouser-Det....1.81	Newhouser-Det 194	Newhouser-Det....58.4	**Newhouser-Det** 7.6
Ferriss-Bos 264.2	Wolff-Was 215	Potter-StL....................279	Benton-Det 2.02	Benton-Det 174	Wolff-Was 31.3	**Potter-StL** 3.6
Newsom-Phi 257.1	Potter-StL 226	Leonard-Was 279	Wolff-Was 2.12	Wolff-Was 146	Potter-StL 30.4	**Wolff-Was** 3.3
Potter-StL 255.1	Niggeling-Was 240	Newhouser-Det 281	Leonard-Was 2.13	Leonard-Was 146	Benton-Det 24.4	**Ferriss-Bos** 3.0
Gromek-Cle 251.0	Benton-Det 241	Bonham-NY.................288	Lee-Chi................2.44	Potter-StL.............143	Leonard-Was 21.2	**Gromek-Cle**........2.6

End of the Tin Era

During the last and possibly most ridiculous baseball season of the war years, the AL debuted a one-armed player (outfielder Pete Gray of St. Louis) and a one-legged player (pitcher Bert Shepard of Washington). And both their usually mediocre clubs were, again, in the pennant race. For the fifth straight season, home runs dropped. Only one player, Vern Stephens of the Browns, even hit 20, while the entire White Sox squad hit just 22—Chicago had slugged 25 in 1919.

The fourth-place Yankees again topped the AL in runs, with second baseman George "Snuffy" Stirnweiss beating up on substandard pitching. St. Louis had excellent hurling, but an even poorer attack than in 1944, and finished third. Second-place Washington boasted a speed-based offense and Roger Wolff, one of the most obscure 20-game winners of modern times.

Detroit's Hal Newhouser won his second straight MVP, this time with a 25–9 season that helped carry the Tigers over the top with the lowest winning percentage ever for an AL champ. Hank Greenberg, who returned at midseason from the military, hit a grand slam against St. Louis on September 30 to clinch the flag.

The World Series, an entertaining, sloppy, uneven affair, featured the Tigers and the equally-not-great Cubs. (Asked for his pre-Series prediction, Chicago sportswriter Warren Brown opined, "I don't think either team can win it.") The clubs went to the brink, although the quality of play was far from solid. Game 6, a sloppy, 8–7, error-filled 12-inning affair won by Chicago on the brink of elimination, sapped their pitching; the Tigers won the final contest 9–3, behind Newhouser.

Harry O'Neill of the 1939 Athletics perished at Iwo Jima on March 6. He was the second and final big leaguer to die in World War II, but more than 50 American professional ballplayers were killed in the conflict.

1946 National League

TEAM	W	L	T	PCT	GB	HW	HL	R	OR	PA	H	2B	3B	HR	BB	SO	HB	SH	AVG	OBP	SLG	OPS	AOPS	BR	ABR	PF	SB	CS	BSA	BSR
STL	98	58	0	.628		49	29	**712**	**545**	6020	**1426**	**265**	56	**81**	530	537	97	21	**.265**	.334	**.381**	**715**	105	56	28	104	58			
BRO	96	60	1	.615	2	**56**	22	701	570	6134	1376	233	**66**	55	**691**	575	**141**	17	.260	**.348**	.361	709	**106**	**63**	**56**	101	**100**			
CHI	82	71	2	.536	14.5	44	33	626	581	6024	1344	223	50	56	586	599	116	**24**	.254	.331	.346	677	100	-8	5	98	43			
BOS	81	72	1	.529	15.5	45	31	630	592	5940	1377	238	48	44	558	**468**	135	22	.264	.337	.353	690	101	18	11	101	60			
PHI	69	85	1	.448	28	41	36	560	705	5772	1351	209	40	80	417	590	103	19	.258	.315	.359	674	100	-32	-15	97	41			
CIN	67	87	2	.435	30	35	42	523	570	5934	1262	206	33	65	493	604	122	28	.239	.307	.327	634	88	-102	-82	96	82			
PIT	63	91	1	.409	34	37	40	552	668	5907	1300	202	52	60	592	555	101	15	.250	.328	.344	672	95	-19	-33	103	48			
NY	61	93	0	.396	36	38	39	612	685	5836	1326	176	37	121	532	546	86	27	.255	.328	.374	702	104	25	21	101	46			
TOT	621					345	272	4916		47567	10762	1752	382	562	4399	4474	173	901	.256	.329	.355	684					478			

TEAM	CG	SHO	GR	SV	IP	H	HR	BB	SO	BR/9	ERA	AERA	OAV	OOB	PR	APR	PF	OSB	OCS	FA	E	WPB	DP	FW	PW	BW	BSW	DIF
STL	**75**	**18**	180	15	1397.0	1326	63	493	607	11.9	**3.01**	**115**	.254	.322	**63**	**69**	101	41	*36*	**.980**	**124**	29	167	**2.1**	**7.3**	3.0		7.6
BRO	52	14	**223**	**28**	1418.0	**1280**	58	671	**647**	12.5	3.05	111	**.243**	.331	58	53	99	**37**	***60***	.972	174	44	154	-.9	5.6	**5.9**		7.3
CHI	59	15	187	11	1393.0	1370	58	527	619	12.4	3.24	102	.256	.325	26	15	97	56	*37*	.976	146	28	119	.7	1.6	.5		2.7
BOS	74	10	167	12	1371.0	1291	76	478	566	11.7	3.35	102	.249	**.314**	10	13	101	74	*39*	.972	169	32	129	-.8	1.4	1.2		2.7
PHI	55	11	185	23	1369.0	1442	73	542	490	13.3	3.99	86	.273	.344	-88	-85	101	66	*49*	.975	148	44	144	.6	-9.0	-1.6		2.1
CIN	69	17	146	11	1413.1	1334	70	**467**	506	**11.6**	3.08	109	.252	**.314**	53	43	98	47	*58*	.975	155	**17**	**192**	.2	4.6	-8.7		-6.1
PIT	61	10	181	6	1370.0	1406	**50**	561	458	13.1	3.72	95	.269	.342	-46	-28	103	88	*48*	.970	184	28	127	-1.6	-3.0	-3.5		-5.9
NY	47	8	216	13	1353.1	1313	114	660	581	13.2	3.92	88	.256	.343	-76	-71	101	69	*43*	.973	159	38	121	-.2	-7.5	2.2		-10.5
TOT	492	103	1485	119	11084.2					12.5	3.41		.256	.329						.974	1259	260	1153					

Batter-Fielder Wins	Batting Average	On-Base Percentage	Slugging Average	On-Base Plus Slugging	Adjusted OPS	Adjusted Batter Runs
Musial-StL 5.8	Musial-StL 365	Stanky-Bro 436	Musial-StL 587	Musial-StL 1021	Musial-StL 180	Musial-StL 66.0
Mize-NY 4.8	Hopp-Bos 333	Musial-StL 434	Ennis-Phi 485	Kurowski-StL 853	Ennis-Phi 144	Mize-NY.............43.8
Cavarretta-Chi....3.0	Walker-Bro 319	Cavarretta-Chi 401	Slaughter-StL 465	Ennis-Phi 849	Cavarretta-Chi 140	Cavarretta-Chi....30.4
Stanky-Bro..........2.9	Ennis-Phi 313	Herman-Bro-Bos 395	Kurowski-StL 462	Walker-Bro............839	Walker-Bro............136	Walker-Bro..........28.2
Ennis-Phi 2.9	Holmes-Bos 310	Walker-Bro 391	Walker-Bro 448	Slaughter-StL........838	Kurowski-StL 136	Ennis-Phi............28.2

Runs	Hits	Doubles	Triples	Home Runs	Total Bases	Runs Batted In
Musial-StL 124	Musial-StL 228	Musial-StL......................50	Musial-StL 20	Kiner-Pit.................23	Musial-StL 366	Slaughter-StL 130
Slaughter-StL........100	Walker-Bro............184	Holmes-Bos 35	Reese-Bro 10	Mize-NY..................22	Slaughter-StL........283	Walker-Bro 116
Stanky-Bro.............98	Slaughter-StL........183	Kurowski-StL..................32	Cavarretta-Chi 10	Slaughter-StL..........18	Ennis-Phi 262	Musial-StL 103
Schoendienst-StL ..94	Holmes-Bos..........176	Herman-Bro-Bos............31	Walker-Bro................9	Ennis-Phi 17	Walker-Bro............258	Kurowski-StL 89
Cavarretta-Chi 89	Schoendienst-StL 170				Holmes-Bos..........241	Kiner-Pit 81

Stolen Bases	Base Stealing Runs	Fielding Runs-Infield	Fielding Runs-Outfield	Wins	Winning Pct.	Complete Games
Reiser-Bro 34		Marion-StL.................18.1	Ennis-Phi 10.1	Pollet-StL 21	Dickson-StL 714	Sain-Bos................24
Haas-Cin 22		Handley-Pit 12.0	Furillo-Bro...............8.7	Sain-Bos 20	Higbe-Bro 680	Pollet-StL 22
Hopp-Bos 21		Gustine-Pit....................7.8	Gilbert-Chi-Phi 6.0	Higbe-Bro 17	Pollet-StL 677	Koslo-NY 17
Adams-Cin..............16		Kerr-NY 7.6	Holmes-Bos 5.4	Dickson-StL............15	Sain-Bos...............588	Ostermueller-Pit 16
Walker-Bro..............14		McCormick-Phi 4.8	Wyrostek-Phi 4.7	Brecheen-StL 15	Brecheen-StL 500	Cooper-Bos 15

Strikeouts	Fewest BB/Game	Games	Saves	Base Runners/9	Adjusted Relief Runs	Relief Ranking
Schmitz-Chi..........135	Cooper-Bos 1.76	Trinkle-NY......................48	Raffensberger-Phi 6	Rowe-Phi 9.20	Casey-Bro............13.5	Casey-Bro 21.1
Higbe-Bro 134	Raffensberger-Phi ..1.79	Dickson-StL 47	Pollet-StL 5	Cooper-Bos 9.95	Thompson-NY 11.6	Thompson-NY....18.4
Sain-Bos 129	Beggs-Cin............1.85	Behrman-Bro 47	Karl-Phi 5	Beggs-Cin..........10.18	Malloy-Cin..............3.5	Malloy-Cin 3.3
Koslo-NY 121	Heusser-Cin 2.09	Casey-Bro.......................46	Herring-Bro 5	Spahn-Bos 10.31	Budnick-NY 1.1	Wilks-StL 7
Brecheen-StL 117	Strincevich-Pit......2.25		Casey-Bro 5	Sain-Bos............10.66	Wilks-StL 9	Budnick-NY 6

Innings Pitched	Opponents' Avg.	Opponents' OBP	Earned Run Average	Adjusted ERA	Adjusted Starter Runs	Pitcher Wins
Pollet-StL 266.0	Schmitz-Chi 221	Cooper-Bos 276	Pollet-StL 2.10	Pollet-StL..............165	Pollet-StL 34.7	**Sain-Bos** 5.4
Koslo-NY 265.1	Kennedy-NY 224	Beggs-Cin 287	Sain-Bos.............2.21	Sain-Bos 155	Sain-Bos..............33.9	**Pollet-StL**..............4.3
Sain-Bos...........265.0	Blackwell-Cin 226	Sain-Bos 294	Beggs-Cin............2.32	Beggs-Cin 144	Brecheen-StL 25.2	**Brecheen-StL** 3.1
Brecheen-StL 231.1	Higbe-Bro 229	Dickson-StL 295	Blackwell-Cin 2.45	Brecheen-StL 139	Blackwell-Cin 19.9	**Beggs-Cin** 2.6
Schmitz-Chi 224.1	Sain-Bos..............230	Pollet-StL 300	Brecheen-StL 2.49	Blackwell-Cin........136	Beggs-Cin............19.8	**Ostermueller-Pit**2.5

Contract Jumping, Integration, and More!

The Dodgers and Cardinals, rejuvenated by players returning from the service, hung together at the top of the NL for the entire 1946 season, working in lockstep from July to the end. The teams matched win for win and ended the year in a tie—the first in major league history. Both teams blew chances to win outright in the final regular-season weekend. In a best-of-three playoff, the Cardinals got fine pitching from Howie Pollet, Murry Dickson, and Harry Brecheen to win the series in two.

Once again attendance reached an all-time NL record, increasing 69 percent. Five teams drew a million, an unprecedented total; the Dodgers set an all-time league record. Even with many veterans returning, several impressive youngsters debuted, including Carl Furillo, Ralph Kiner, Alvin Dark, and Bobby Thomson.

One of the year's odder stories involved the Mexican League, headed by entrepreneur Jorge Pasquel. Determined to make his league a serious player, he and his cohorts spent many thousands to lure away key players from the Cardinals, Dodgers, and Giants. New Commissioner Happy Chandler banned all jumpers from returning for five years, although this edict was softened when the Mexican League began to have problems paying its contracts.

The World Series was one of the best in history, with the Cardinals and Red Sox trading victories in the first six contests. In Game 7 Boston tied the score with 2 runs in the visiting eighth, but the Cardinals won in the bottom of the frame when Harry Walker's single scored the hustling Enos Slaughter from first. Brecheen had 3 wins, allowing just 1 earned run in 20 innings.

For all the exciting baseball played during the season, the most significant event of the year occurred out of the country. In Montreal, Dodgers farmhand Jackie Robinson became the first African American in professional ball in more than sixty years.

1946 American League

TEAM	W	L	T	PCT	GB	HW	HL	R	OR	PA	H	2B	3B	HR	BB	SO	HB	SH	AVG	OBP	SLG	OPS	AOPS	BR	ABR	PF	SB	CS	BSA	BSR
BOS	104	50	2	.675		**61**	16	**792**	594	6126	**1441**	**268**	**50**	109	**687**	661	**106**	15	**.271**	**.356**	**.402**	**758**	**113**	**142**	**100**	106	45	36	56	-3
DET	92	62	1	.597	12	48	30	704	567	6057	1373	212	41	108	622	**616**	104	13	.258	.337	.374	711	100	43	4	106	**65**	41	**61**	0
NY	87	67	0	.565	17	47	30	684	**547**	5879	1275	208	**50**	**136**	627	706	80	**33**	.248	.334	.387	721	107	56	47	101	48	35	58	-2
WAS	76	78	1	.494	28	38	38	608	706	5958	1388	260	63	60	511	641	86	24	.260	.327	.366	693	106	2	42	94	51	50	50	-6
CHI	74	80	1	.481	30	40	38	562	595	5911	1364	206	44	37	501	600	78	20	.257	.323	.333	656	94	-66	-44	96	78	64	55	-5
CLE	68	86	2	.442	36	36	41	537	638	5857	1285	233	56	79	506	697	96	13	.245	.313	.356	669	99	-50	-10	94	57	49	54	-5
STL	66	88	2	.429	38	35	41	621	710	5921	1350	220	46	84	465	713	67	16	.251	.313	.356	669	89	-55	-82	105	23	35	40	-7
PHI	49	105	1	.318	55	31	46	529	680	5796	1317	220	51	40	482	594	105	9	.253	.318	.338	656	91	-70	-67	99	39	30	57	-2
TOT	621					336	280	5037		47505	10793	1827	401	653	4401	5228	143	722	.256	.328	.364	692					406	340	54	-30

TEAM	CG	SHO	GR	SV	IP	H	HR	BB	SO	BR/9	ERA	AERA	OAV	OOB	PR	APR	PF	OSB	OCS	FA	E	WPB	DP	FW	PW	BW	BSW	DIF
BOS	79	15	151	**20**	1396.2	1359	89	501	667	12.1	3.38	108	.254	.319	19	42	105	**39**	28	**.977**	**139**	24	163	**1.5**	4.4	**10.5**	.0	10.6
DET	**94**	**18**	101	15	1402.0	1277	97	**497**	**896**	**11.5**	3.22	**114**	**.241**	**.307**	45	**65**	104	47	37	.974	155	35	138	.5	**6.8**	.4	**.4**	6.9
NY	68	17	152	17	1361.0	**1232**	**66**	552	653	11.9	3.13	110	.243	.319	56	49	99	42	49	.975	150	23	**174**	.7	5.1	4.9	.2	-.9
WAS	71	8	157	10	1396.1	1459	81	547	537	13.1	3.74	89	.269	.339	-36	-64	96	55	46	.966	211	64	162	-2.8	-6.7	4.4	-.2	4.4
CHI	62	9	142	16	1392.1	1348	80	508	550	12.1	**3.10**	110	.255	.323	**63**	50	97	55	43	.972	175	49	170	-.7	5.2	-4.6	-.1	-2.8
CLE	63	16	170	13	1388.2	1282	84	649	789	12.6	3.62	91	.245	.331	-17	-51	94	42	42	.975	147	36	147	1.0	-5.3	-1.0	-.1	-3.5
STL	63	13	**193**	12	1382.1	1465	73	573	574	13.3	3.95	94	.272	.343	-69	-32	107	84	41	.974	159	46	157	.3	-3.4	-8.6	-.3	1.0
PHI	61	10	145	5	1342.2	1371	83	577	562	13.2	3.90	91	.264	.340	-59	-52	101	42	**54**	.971	167	**20**	141	-.2	-5.4	-7.0	.2	-15.5
TOT	561	106	1211	108	11062.0					12.5	3.50		.256	.328						.973	1303	297	1252					

Batter-Fielder Wins
Williams-Bos 8.1
Doerr-Bos 4.8
Pesky-Bos 4.6
Vernon-Was 4.3
Greenberg-Det.....3.9

Batting Average
Vernon-Was 353
Williams-Bos.........342
Pesky-Bos 335
Kell-Phi-Det 322
DiMaggio-Bos.......316

On-Base Percentage
Williams-Bos 497
Keller-NY 405
Vernon-Was 403
Pesky-Bos 401
DiMaggio-Bos 393

Slugging Average
Williams-Bos.........667
Greenberg-Det 604
Keller-NY 533
DiMaggio-NY 511
Edwards-Cle 509

On-Base Plus Slugging
Williams-Bos 1164
Greenberg-Det 977
Keller-NY 938
Vernon-Was..........910
DiMaggio-NY 878

Adjusted OPS
Williams-Bos 211
Vernon-Was..........163
Greenberg-Det 160
Keller-NY 158
Edwards-Cle 151

Adjusted Batter Runs
Williams-Bos 88.3
Vernon-Was........48.9
Keller-NY 45.6
Greenberg-Det ..40.6
Cullenbine-Det ..38.9

Runs
Williams-Bos 142
Pesky-Bos 115
Lake-Det 105
Keller-NY 98
Doerr-Bos 95

Hits
Pesky-Bos 208
Vernon-Was..........207
Appling-Chi 180
Williams-Bos 176
Lewis-Was 170

Doubles
Vernon-Was 51
Spence-Was 50
Pesky-Bos......................43
Williams-Bos..................37
Doerr-Bos 34

Triples
Edwards-Cle 16
Lewis-Was 13
Kell-Phi-Det 10
Spence-Was 10
Keller-NY 10

Home Runs
Greenberg-Det 44
Williams-Bos 38
Keller-NY 30
Seerey-Cle..............26
DiMaggio-NY..........25

Total Bases
Williams-Bos 343
Greenberg-Det 316
Vernon-Was..........298
Spence-Was 287
Keller-NY 287

Runs Batted In
Greenberg-Det 127
Williams-Bos 123
York-Bos 119
Doerr-Bos............116
Keller-NY 101

Stolen Bases
Case-Cle 28
Stirnweiss-NY 18
Lake-Det 15

Base Stealing Runs
Case-Cle 2.3
Stirnweiss-NY.........1.9
Dillinger-StL 1.4
Evers-Det 1.2
Wright-Chi..............1.1

Fielding Runs-Infield
Doerr-Bos 27.3
Gordon-NY 18.1
Boudreau-Cle 17.2
Rizzuto-NY 16.7
Pesky-Bos 12.3

Fielding Runs-Outfield
Zarilla-StL 9.6
Chapman-Phi 8.1
Judnich-StL............5.3
Lewis-Was 2.4
Williams-Bos..........2.4

Wins
Newhouser-Det 26
Feller-Cle 26
Ferriss-Bos 25
Hughson-Bos..........20
Chandler-NY 20

Winning Pct.
Ferriss-Bos 806
Newhouser-Det.....743
Chandler-NY.........714
Harris-Bos 654
Hughson-Bos 645

Complete Games
Feller-Cle 36
Newhouser-Det 29
Ferriss-Bos 26
Trout-Det 23
Hughson-Bos 21

Strikeouts
Feller-Cle 348
Newhouser-Det 275
Hughson-Bos........172
Trucks-Det............161
Trout-Det 151

Fewest BB/Game
Hughson-Bos 1.65
Lopat-Chi 1.87
Leonard-Was 2.00
Flores-Phi 2.21
Ferriss-Bos 2.33

Games
Feller-Cle 48
Savage-Phi 40
Ferriss-Bos 40
Hughson-Bos 39
Caldwell-Chi 39

Saves
Klinger-Bos 9
Caldwell-Chi 8
Murphy-NY 7
Ferrick-Cle-StL 6

Base Runners/9
Ruffing-NY 8.85
Caldwell-Chi 8.93
Newhouser-Det....9.66
Gumpert-NY 9.84
Hughson-Bos 9.87

Adjusted Relief Runs
Caldwell-Chi 12.9
Klinger-Bos 8.3
Kinder-StL..............4.7
Lemon-Cle 4.3

Relief Ranking
Caldwell-Chi 24.4
Klinger-Bos 9.5
Lemon-Cle............3.8
Kinder-StL 3.0

Innings Pitched
Feller-Cle 371.1
Newhouser-Det..292.2
Hughson-Bos 278.0
Trout-Det...........276.1
Ferriss-Bos 274.0

Opponents' Avg.
Newhouser-Det.....201
Feller-Cle 208
Chandler-NY.........218
Embree-Cle 227
Bevens-NY 232

Opponents' OBP
Newhouser-Det 269
Hughson-Bos..............274
Chandler-NY 288
Lopat-Chi 288
Feller-Cle 291

Earned Run Average
Newhouser-Det....1.94
Chandler-NY........2.10
Feller-Cle 2.18
Bevens-NY 2.23
Flores-Phi 2.32

Adjusted ERA
Newhouser-Det ...189
Chandler-NY 164
Trout-Det 156
Bevens-NY 154
Flores-Phi 153

Adjusted Starter Runs
Newhouser-Det....51.1
Feller-Cle 50.1
Chandler-NY........38.5
Trout-Det.............37.0
Bevens-NY 33.6

Pitcher Wins
Newhouser-Det 6.4
Feller-Cle............5.4
Trout-Det...........4.7
Chandler-NY......4.5
Bevens-NY 3.2

Goodbye and Hello

Boston improved by 33 games, leaping from seventh to first. The core of the club—Ted Williams, Bobby Doerr, Johnny Pesky, Tex Hughson, Mickey Harris, and Dom DiMaggio—came home and made up for lost time. Despite two offensive dead spots, the Red Sox led the AL in runs by nearly 100, leaving second-place Detroit in the dust. Former contenders Washington, St. Louis, and Chicago all finished below .500.

With the boys back home, attendance shot up 72 percent to establish a new league record. This was the first time that the *average* AL team drew more than a million fans. In 1946 five clubs topped a million, and even St. Louis had its second-best attendance ever. The Yankees became the first club ever to draw two million customers. (New York's 1946 attendance was higher than the totals for the previous three seasons combined.)

Home runs increased by more than half, and continued to rise until 1950. Not coincidentally, strikeouts also reached a new high. Hal Newhouser, dispelling criticism that he was just a wartime star, set an AL mark with 8.46 whiffs per game. Two top catchers debuted in 1946, Sherm Lollar with the Indians and Yogi Berra, arguably the best in league history, with the Yankees. With Berra on the way, Bill Dickey retired. Ted Lyons, Chicago's 46-year-old "Sunday pitcher," retired following three years in the army—he went 1–4 but still had a 2.32 ERA.

Former Yankees star Tony Lazzeri died after falling down a flight of stairs, while Walter Johnson succumbed from a brain tumor. Manager Joe McCarthy departed the Yankees in midseason amid clashes with owner Larry MacPhail. And in another shocking departure, the Tigers waived Hank Greenberg, who wanted a $20,000 raise. Pittsburgh convinced Greenberg to play in 1947 by making him the game's first $100,000 player.

The World Series was a classic, with the St. Louis Cardinals winning in seven games. The final contest was a nail-biter all the way as the lead changed hands three times.

1947 National League

TEAM	W	L	T	PCT	GB	HW	HL	R	OR	PA	H	2B	3B	HR	BB	SO	HB	SH	AVG	OBP	SLG	OPS	AOPS	BR	ABR	PF	SB	CS	BSA	BSR
BRO	94	60	1	.610		**52**	25	774	667	6125	1428	241	50	83	**732**	561	115	**29**	.272	**.364**	.384	748	102	67	38	104	**88**			
STL	89	65	2	.578	5	46	31	780	634	6131	**1462**	235	**65**	115	612	511	68	**29**	.270	.347	.401	748	101	41	9	104	28			
BOS	86	68	0	.558	8	50	27	701	**626**	5954	1444	**265**	42	85	558	**500**	**129**	14	**.275**	.346	.390	736	105	22	40	98	58			
NY	81	73	1	.526	13	45	31	**830**	761	5924	1446	220	48	**221**	494	568	64	23	.271	.335	**.454**	**789**	**114**	**93**	**88**	101	29			
CIN	73	81	0	.474	21	42	35	681	755	5954	1372	242	43	95	539	530	95	21	.259	.330	.375	705	95	-47	-42	99	46			
CHI	69	85	1	.448	25	36	43	569	722	5859	1373	231	48	71	471	578	64	19	.259	.321	.361	682	91	-95	-70	96	22			
PIT	62	92	2	.403	32	32	45	745	817	6008	1385	216	44	156	607	687	70	24	.261	.340	.406	746	102	31	11	103	30			
PHI	62	92	1	.403	32	38	38	589	687	5828	1354	210	52	60	464	594	82	26	.258	.321	.352	673	88	-112	-90	96	60			
TOT	620					341	275	5669		47783	11264	1860	392	886	4477	4529	185	687	.265	.338	.390	729					361			

TEAM	CG	SHO	GR	SV	IP	H	HR	BB	SO	BR/9	ERA	AERA	OAV	OOB	PR	APR	PF	OSB	OCS	FA	E	WPB	DP	FW	PW	BW	BSW	DIF
BRO	47	**14**	**223**	**34**	1375.0	**1299**	104	626	592	12.8	3.82	108	**.251**	.336	37	48	102	42	38	.978	129	47	**169**	.9	4.7	3.7		7.6
STL	65	12	187	20	1397.2	1417	106	495	**642**	12.4	**3.53**	**117**	.266	.330	**83**	**92**	102	39	27	**.979**	**128**	33	**169**	**1.1**	**9.0**	.9		1.0
BOS	**74**	**14**	167	13	1362.2	1342	**93**	**453**	494	**11.9**	3.62	108	.255	**.316**	67	43	96	52	37	.974	153	**22**	124	-.6	4.2	3.9		1.4
NY	58	6	212	14	1363.2	1428	122	590	553	13.4	4.44	92	.267	.342	-58	-56	100	**29**	27	.974	155	40	136	-.7	-5.5	**8.7**		1.5
CIN	54	13	190	13	1365.1	1442	102	589	633	13.5	4.41	93	.274	.349	-53	-46	101	45	**41**	.977	138	**22**	134	.3	-4.5	-4.1		4.3
CHI	46	8	216	15	1367.0	1449	106	618	571	13.7	4.04	98	.274	.353	4	-13	97	43	34	.975	150	40	159	-.4	-1.3	-6.9		.5
PIT	44	9	211	13	1374.0	1488	155	592	530	13.9	4.68	90	.278	.354	-95	-68	104	52	39	.975	149	47	131	-.2	-6.7	1.1		-9.2
PHI	70	8	161	14	1362.0	1399	98	513	514	12.8	3.96	101	.276	.346	15	8	99	59	38	.974	152	52	140	-.5	.8	-8.9		-6.5
TOT	458	84	1567	136	10967.1					13.1	4.06		.265	.338						.976	1154	303	1162					

Batter-Fielder Wins	Batting Average	On-Base Percentage	Slugging Average	On-Base Plus Slugging	Adjusted OPS	Adjusted Batter Runs
Kiner-Pit 5.3	Walker-StL-Phi .363	Galan-Cin .449	Kiner-Pit .639	Kiner-Pit 1055	Kiner-Pit 172	Kiner-Pit 58.3
Mize-NY 5.0	B.Elliott-Bos .317	Walker-StL-Phi .436	Mize-NY .614	Mize-NY 998	Mize-NY 160	Mize-NY 48.0
B.Elliott-Bos 3.8	Cavarretta-Chi .314	Kurowski-StL .420	W.Cooper-NY .586	Kurowski-StL 964	Walker-StL-Phi 150	B.Elliott-Bos 40.9
Walker-StL-Phi 3.8	Kiner-Pit .313	Kiner-Pit .417	Kurowski-StL .544	B.Elliott-Bos 927	B.Elliott-Bos 148	Walker-StL-Phi 38.9
Marshall-NY 3.0	Musial-StL .312	Walker-Bro .415	Marshall-NY .528	W.Cooper-NY 926	Kurowski-StL 148	Kurowski-StL 37.9

Runs	Hits	Doubles	Triples	Home Runs	Total Bases	Runs Batted In
Mize-NY 137	Holmes-Bos 191	Miller-Cin 38	Walker-StL-Phi 16	Mize-NY 51	Kiner-Pit 361	Mize-NY 138
Robinson-Bro 125	Walker-StL-Phi 186	B.Elliott-Bos 35	Slaughter-StL 13	Kiner-Pit 51	Mize-NY 360	Kiner-Pit 127
Kiner-Pit 118	Musial-StL 183	Ryan-Bos 33	Musial-StL 13	Marshall-NY 36	Marshall-NY 310	W.Cooper-NY 122
Musial-StL 113	Gustine-Pit 183	Holmes-Bos 33	Schoendienst-StL 9	W.Cooper-NY 35	W.Cooper-NY 302	B.Elliott-Bos 113
Kurowski-StL 108	Baumholtz-Cin 182	Baumholtz-Cin 32	Baumholtz-Cin 9	Thomson-NY 29	Musial-StL 296	Marshall-NY 107

Stolen Bases	Base Stealing Runs	Fielding Runs-Infield	Fielding Runs-Outfield	Wins	Winning Pct.	Complete Games
Robinson-Bro 29		Verban-Phi 17.5	Marshall-NY 9.4	Blackwell-Cin 22	Jansen-NY .808	Blackwell-Cin 23
Reiser-Bro 14		Gustine-Pit 16.4	Kiner-Pit 8.4	Spahn-Bos 21	Munger-StL .762	Spahn-Bos 22
Walker-StL-Phi 13		Marion-StL 15.6	Holmes-Bos 5.5	Sain-Bos 21	Blackwell-Cin .733	Sain-Bos 22
Hopp-Bos 13		Kerr-NY 11.9	Ennis-Phi 4.2	Jansen-NY 21	Hatten-Bro .680	Jansen-NY 20
Torgeson-Bos 11		Lowrey-Chi 10.2	Walker-StL-Phi 4.2	Branca-Bro 21	Spahn-Bos .677	Leonard-Phi 19

Strikeouts	Fewest BB/Game	Games	Saves	Base Runners/9	Adjusted Relief Runs	Relief Ranking
Blackwell-Cin 193	Jansen-NY 2.07	Trinkle-NY 62	Casey-Bro 18	Poat-NY 9.90	Lanfranconi-Bos 7.4	Lanfranconi-Bos 8.6
Branca-Bro 148	Rowe-Phi 2.07	Higbe-Bro-Pit 50	Trinkle-NY 10	Spahn-Bos 10.25	Kush-Chi 7.0	Kush-Chi 8.5
Sain-Bos 132	Leonard-Phi 2.18	Behrman-Bro-Pt-Bro 50	Gumbert-Cin 10	Blackwell-Cin 10.75	Gumbert-Cin 3.1	Gumbert-Cin 6.1
Spahn-Bos 123	Barrett-Bos 2.26	Kush-Chi 47	Behrman-Bro-Pt-Bro 8	Leonard-Phi 10.84	Casey-Bro 2.4	Casey-Bro 4.9
Munger-StL 123	Brazle-StL 2.57	Dickson-StL 47		Jansen-NY 10.85	Trinkle-NY 2.1	Trinkle-NY 2.9

Innings Pitched	Opponents' Avg.	Opponents' OBP	Earned Run Average	Adjusted ERA	Adjusted Starter Runs	Pitcher Wins
Spahn-Bos 289.2	Taylor-Bro .225	Spahn-Bos .283	Spahn-Bos 2.33	Spahn-Bos 167	Spahn-Bos 51.9	**Spahn-Bos** 5.3
Branca-Bro 280.0	Spahn-Bos .226	Barrett-Bos .292	Blackwell-Cin 2.47	Blackwell-Cin 166	Blackwell-Cin 46.2	**Blackwell-Cin** 4.5
Blackwell-Cin 273.0	Blackwell-Cin .234	Blackwell-Cin .304	Branca-Bro 2.67	Branca-Bro 155	Branca-Bro 42.6	**Branca-Bro** 4.2
Sain-Bos 266.0	Branca-Bro .240	Leonard-Phi .306	Leonard-Phi 2.68	Leonard-Phi 149	Leonard-Phi 32.6	**Leonard-Phi** 3.9
Jansen-NY 248.0	Lombardi-Bro .241	Jansen-NY .306	Brazle-StL 2.84	Brazle-StL 146	Jansen-NY 23.5	**Brazle-StL** 3.0

Hello to the Modern Era

Money, race, and television—they were the biggest issues of 1947, perhaps baseball's first true modern season. The Pirates, flush with money from new investor Bing Crosby, opened their wallets to lure Hank Greenberg east with an unprecedented $100,000 deal. The club shortened the left field fences to aid him (and Ralph Kiner), but Pittsburgh tied for last anyway.

On the other side of the pennant race were the Dodgers, who overtook the surprising Braves in midsummer and held off the Cardinals. Blessed with excellent pitching from 21-year old Ralph Branca and reliever Hugh Casey, Brooklyn had a lineup full of on-base machines and a 28-year-old rookie first baseman named Jackie Robinson.

Robinson, the majors' first twentieth-century African American, withstood heckling and threats to lead the Dodgers' efforts. His performance was spectacular enough to make him the first official Rookie of the Year. Several other future stars debuted, including Duke Snider, Ted Kluzewski, and Curt Simmons.

Former favorites Billy Herman, Ernie Lombardi, and Mel Ott ended their careers, and two stars from the first part of the century, Johnny Evers and Hal Chase, passed away. (Evers' double-play partner Joe Tinker died the next year.)

From 1947–49, six NL teams drew more than a million fans every year—everyone but Cincinnati and Philadelphia. Scoring rose 15 percent in 1947, with homers up 58 percent. Johnny Mize and Kiner became the first NLers with 50 homers since 1930. Cincinnati's Ewell "The Whip" Blackwell won 16 straight and nearly threw back-to-back no-hitters.

In the first televised World Series, and one of the most entertaining ever, the Yankees defeated the Dodgers in seven. Six of the games were nail-biters, and for the first time, any American with access to a TV could look in. And for that, and many other, reasons, the game was never the same.

1947 American League

TEAM	W	L	T	PCT	GB	HW	HL	R	OR	PA	H	2B	3B	HR	BB	SO	HB	SH	AVG	OBP	SLG	OPS	AOPS	BR	ABR	PF	SB	CS	BSA	BSR
NY	97	57	1	.630		**55**	22	**794**	**568**	6031	**1439**	230	**72**	**115**	610	581	86	**27**	**.271**	.349	**.407**	**756**	**117**	**110**	**118**	99	27	23	**54**	**-2**
DET	85	69	4	.552	12	46	31	714	642	6148	1363	**234**	42	103	**762**	565	97	13	.258	**.353**	.377	730	106	82	61	103	**52**	60	46	-10
BOS	83	71	3	.539	14	49	30	720	669	6099	1412	206	54	103	666	590	95	16	.265	.349	.382	731	102	72	21	107	41	35	**54**	-3
CLE	80	74	3	.519	17	38	39	687	588	5976	1392	**234**	51	112	502	609	93	14	.259	.324	.385	709	106	8	26	97	29	25	**54**	**-2**
PHI	78	76	2	.506	19	39	38	633	614	5971	1311	218	52	61	605	**563**	**144**	24	.252	.333	.349	682	94	-23	-35	102	37	33	53	-3
CHI	70	84	1	.455	27	32	43	553	661	5837	1350	211	41	53	492	527	56	15	.256	.321	.342	663	93	-71	-49	96	91	57	61	0
WAS	64	90	0	.416	33	36	41	496	675	5717	1234	186	48	42	525	534	72	8	.241	.313	.321	634	84	-121	-107	97	53	51	51	-6
STL	59	95	0	.383	38	29	48	564	744	5819	1238	189	52	90	583	664	76	15	.241	.320	.350	670	90	-57	-68	102	69	49	58	**-2**
TOT	623					324	292	5161		47598	10739	1708	412	679	4745	4633	132	719	.256	.333	.364	698					399	333	55	-29

TEAM	CG	SHO	GR	SV	IP	H	HR	BB	SO	BR/9	ERA	AERA	OAV	OOB	PR	APR	PF	OSB	OCS	FA	E	WPB	DP	FW	PW	BW	BSW	DIF
NY	73	14	140	21	1374.1	**1221**	95	628	**691**	**12.2**	**3.39**	104	**.238**	**.323**	**48**	23	95	61	32	.981	109	27	151	1.5	2.4	**12.2**	.2	3.7
DET	**77**	**15**	137	18	1398.2	1382	79	**531**	648	12.4	3.57	106	.258	.326	21	30	102	41	36	.975	155	35	142	-1.0	3.1	6.3	-.7	.2
BOS	64	13	**184**	19	1391.1	1383	84	575	586	12.8	3.81	102	.261	.335	-16	11	105	57	29	.977	137	47	172	-.0	1.1	2.2	.0	2.6
CLE	55	13	182	**29**	1402.1	1244	94	628	590	**12.2**	3.44	101	.240	.325	41	7	94	**31**	48	**.983**	**104**	36	178	**1.9**	.7	2.7	.2	-2.5
PHI	70	12	125	15	1391.1	1291	85	597	493	12.3	3.51	**109**	.247	.326	30	**45**	103	37	**55**	.976	143	**19**	161	-.4	**4.7**	-3.6	.0	.3
CHI	47	11	**184**	27	1391.0	1384	76	603	522	13.0	3.64	100	.261	.339	11	3	99	58	40	.975	155	48	**180**	-1.2	.3	-5.1	**.4**	-1.5
WAS	67	**15**	143	12	1362.0	1408	**63**	579	551	13.2	3.97	94	.267	.342	-40	-37	101	51	48	.976	143	23	151	-.5	-3.8	-11.1	-.2	2.7
STL	50	7	141	13	1365.0	1426	103	604	552	13.4	4.33	90	.272	.348	-94	-65	105	63	45	.977	134	28	169	.0	-6.7	-7.0	.2	-4.4
TOT	503	100	1236	154	11076.0					12.7	3.71		.256	.333						.977	1080	263	1304					

Batter-Fielder Wins
Williams-Bos 7.2
Boudreau-Cle......5.3
Cullenbine-Det ..3.6
Doerr-Bos............3.3
Stephens-StL......3.1

Batting Average
Williams-Bos.........343
McCosky-Phi 328
Pesky-Bos 324
Wright-Chi............324
Kell-Det.................320

On-Base Percentage
Williams-Bos 499
Fain-Phi 414
Cullenbine-Det............401
McCosky-Phi 395
McQuinn-NY 395

Slugging Average
Williams-Bos.........634
DiMaggio-NY 522
Gordon-Cle...........496
Henrich-NY...........485
Heath-StL.............485

On-Base Plus Slugging
Williams-Bos 1133
DiMaggio-NY........913
Henrich-NY 857
Heath-StL 850
Gordon-Cle 842

Adjusted OPS
Williams-Bos 199
DiMaggio-NY 154
Henrich-NY 139
Gordon-Cle 136
Heath-StL 133

Adjusted Batter Runs
Williams-Bos 82.7
DiMaggio-NY......38.0
Henrich-NY 27.9
McQuinn-NY 25.0
Fain-Phi..............24.4

Runs
Williams-Bos 125
Henrich-NY............109
Pesky-Bos 106
Stirnweiss-NY 102
DiMaggio-NY..........97

Hits
Pesky-Bos 207
Kell-Det 188
Williams-Bos 181
McCosky-Phi 179

Doubles
Boudreau-Cle 45
Williams-Bos..................40
Henrich-NY.....................35
DiMaggio-NY 31

Triples
Henrich-NY 13
Vernon-Was............12
Philley-Chi 11

Home Runs
Williams-Bos 32
Gordon-Cle 29
Heath-StL 27
Cullenbine-Det........24
York-Bos-Chi 21

Total Bases
Williams-Bos 335
Gordon-Cle 279
DiMaggio-NY........279
Henrich-NY 267
Pesky-Bos 250

Runs Batted In
Williams-Bos 114
Henrich-NY............98
DiMaggio-NY 97
Jones-Chi-Bos 96

Stolen Bases
Dillinger-StL............34
Philley-Chi 21
Vernon-Was............12
Pesky-Bos 12

Base Stealing Runs
Dillinger-StL 2.9
Valo-Phi 1.4
Binks-Phi 1.1
Kolloway-Chi..........1.0
Tucker-Chi 8

Fielding Runs-Infield
Doerr-Bos 25.2
Boudreau-Cle 18.8
Rizzuto-NY 17.7
Cullenbine-Det...........17.5
Kell-Det 16.2

Fielding Runs-Outfield
DiMaggio-Bos......15.0
Chapman-Phi 8.2
Spence-Was..........6.2
Lindell-NY..............5.6
Henrich-NY............4.6

Wins
Feller-Cle 20
Reynolds-NY 19
Marchildon-Phi 19
Hutchinson-Det 18
Dobson-Bos.............18

Winning Pct.
Reynolds-NY 704
Dobson-Bos 692
Marchildon-Phi 679
Feller-Cle 645
Hutchinson-Det.....643

Complete Games
Newhouser-Det 24
Wynn-Was 22
Lopat-Chi 22
Marchildon-Phi 21
Feller-Cle 20

Strikeouts
Feller-Cle..............196
Newhouser-Det 176
Masterson-Was 135
Reynolds-NY 129
Marchildon-Phi 128

Fewest BB/Game
Galehouse-StL-Bos 2.48
Hutchinson-Det....2.50
Lopat-Chi 2.60
Muncrief-StL 2.60
Dobson-Bos 2.87

Games
Klieman-Cle 58
Page-NY 56
Johnson-Bos..................45
Savage-Phi 44
Christopher-Phi..............44

Saves
Page-NY 17
Klieman-Cle............17
Christopher-Phi 12
Ferrick-Was 9

Base Runners/9
Chandler-NY........9.91
Feller-Cle 10.87
Dobson-Bos 10.90
Raschi-NY 11.01
Shea-NY............11.08

Adjusted Relief Runs
Page-NY 18.1
Christopher-Phi......7.7
Murphy-Bos 7.3
Klieman-Cle 5.9
Ferrick-Was 3.6

Relief Ranking
Page-NY 30.3
Christopher-Phi ..15.4
Klieman-Cle..........7.6
Ferrick-Was 5.6
Murphy-Bos..........3.6

Innings Pitched
Feller-Cle 299.0
Newhouser-Det..285.0
Marchildon-Phi ..276.2
Masterson-Was 253.0
Lopat-Chi 252.2

Opponents' Avg.
Shea-NY..............200
Feller-Cle 215
Marchildon-Phi 224
Reynolds-NY 227
Embree-Cle 233

Opponents' OBP
Dobson-Bos................299
Feller-Cle 300
Shea-NY 303
Hutchinson-Det 304
Lopat-Chi.....................307

Earned Run Average
Haynes-Chi..........2.42
Chandler-NY........2.46
Feller-Cle 2.68
Fowler-Phi...........2.81
Lopat-Chi 2.81

Adjusted ERA
Haynes-Chi 151
Fowler-Phi 136
Dobson-Bos..........132
Newhouser-Det 131
Feller-Cle 130

Adjusted Starter Runs
Feller-Cle 28.7
Newhouser-Det....28.0
Lopat-Chi 26.0
Fowler-Phi...........26.0
Dobson-Bos 23.1

Pitcher Wins
Newhouser-Det 3.7
Hutchinson-Det 3.7
Page-NY..............3.3
Feller-Cle............3.2
Lopat-Chi............2.9

It's...the Yankees

In April the Indians brought the power alleys at Municipal Stadium in by 70 feet, then a few weeks later shortened center field by 58. While this significantly increased home run production, the team made a much more important alteration July 5, when owner Bill Veeck made Larry Doby the league's first African American player. Cleveland also broke in rookie pitcher Bob Lemon, while infielder Nellie Fox began his career in Philadelphia. Red Ruffing, 43, retired with 273 wins, while catcher Al Lopez hung it up at 39.

The pennant race held few thrills. In late June New York emerged from a crowded field and pulled away. Under new manager Bucky Harris the Yankees led the league in runs and in fewest allowed. While few players had statistically impressive seasons, there were no weak spots. Joe Page, 29, became the league's dominant reliever. The second-place Tigers felt the loss of Hank Greenberg. Boston, with several offensive black holes, fell to third despite Ted Williams' Triple Crown. The Philadelphia A's improved by 29 games and had their first winning record since 1933.

The advance in glove technology, improvements in groundskeeping, and better defensive skill helped AL fielders, for the first time ever, complete more double plays than they made errors. Stolen bases, which had increased during World War II, dropped to the lowest level in league history—only to drop again in 1948.

Three of the seven games in an exciting Dodgers-Yankees World Series were one-run affairs. New York took the first two, then Brooklyn captured the following pair at Ebbets Field, including a thrilling Game 4 in which Yankees pitcher Bill Bevens lost his no-hitter, and the game, on Cookie Lavagetto's ninth-inning two-run pinch-double. After the well-matched clubs split the next two, the final contest took place at Yankee Stadium. Brooklyn's weary pitching staff couldn't hold off the Yankees, and Page saved the 5–2 win with five scoreless relief innings.

1948 National League

TEAM	W	L	T	PCT	GB	HW	HL	R	OR	PA	H	2B	3B	HR	BB	SO	HB	SH	AVG	OBP	SLG	OPS	AOPS	BR	ABR	PF	SB	CS	BSA	BSR
BOS	91	62	1	.595		45	31	739	**584**	6125	**1458**	**272**	49	95	**671**	536	**140**	17	**.275**	**.359**	.399	**758**	**114**	**101**	**115**	98	43			
STL	85	69	1	.552	6.5	44	33	742	646	5994	1396	238	**58**	105	594	**521**	76	**22**	.263	.340	.389	729	98	31	-8	106	24			
BRO	84	70	1	.545	7.5	36	41	744	669	6047	1393	256	54	91	601	684	100	18	.261	.338	.381	719	98	15	-8	103	**114**			
PIT	83	71	2	.539	8.5	**47**	31	706	701	5943	1388	191	54	108	580	578	56	21	.263	.338	.380	718	99	7	-7	102	68			
NY	78	76	1	.506	13.5	37	40	**780**	703	5960	1352	210	49	**164**	599	648	65	19	.256	.334	**.408**	742	106	45	41	101	51			
PHI	66	88	1	.429	25.5	32	44	591	728	5830	1367	227	39	91	440	598	82	21	.259	.318	.368	686	94	-65	-54	98	68			
CIN	64	89	0	.418	27	32	45	588	751	5700	1266	221	37	104	478	586	79	16	.247	.313	.365	678	92	-77	-57	97	42			
CHI	64	90	1	.416	27.5	35	42	597	705	5894	1402	225	44	87	443	578	70	29	.262	.322	.369	691	97	-55	-29	96	39			
TOT	619					308	307	5487		47493	11022	1840	384	845	4406	4729	163	668	.261	.333	.383	716					449			

TEAM	CG	SHO	GR	SV	IP	H	HR	BB	SO	BR/9	ERA	AERA	OAV	OOB	PR	APR	PF	OSB	OCS	FA	E	WPB	DP	FW	PW	BW	BSW	DIF
BOS	**70**	10	167	17	1389.1	1354	93	**430**	579	**11.6**	**3.37**	**114**	**.249**	**.306**	**89**	**73**	97	63	*35*	.976	143	**19**	132	.7	**7.3**	**11.5**		-5.0
STL	60	13	205	18	1368.0	1392	103	476	625	12.4	3.91	105	.262	.324	7	27	103	**20**	*33*	**.980**	**119**	30	138	**2.1**	2.7	-.8		4.0
BRO	52	9	211	**22**	1392.2	**1328**	119	633	**670**	12.9	3.75	106	.253	.337	31	36	101	37	*43*	.973	161	49	151	-.2	3.6	-.8		4.4
PIT	65	5	166	19	1371.2	1373	120	564	543	12.9	4.15	98	.261	.335	-29	-12	103	53	***49***	.977	137	56	150	1.2	-1.2	-.7		6.7
NY	54	**15**	**230**	21	1373.0	1425	122	556	527	13.2	3.93	100	.269	.342	4	0	100	49	*25*	.974	156	30	134	.1	.0	4.1		-3.2
PHI	61	6	162	15	1362.1	1385	95	556	550	13.0	4.08	97	.262	.335	-18	-20	100	86	*46*	.964	210	45	126	-2.8	-2.0	-5.4		-.8
CIN	40	8	211	20	1343.1	1410	104	572	599	13.4	4.47	87	.270	.344	-77	-86	99	80	*26*	.973	158	30	135	-.1	-8.6	-5.7		1.9
CHI	51	7	220	10	1355.1	1355	**89**	619	636	13.2	4.00	97	.261	.342	-7	-15	99	61	*41*	.972	172	38	**152**	-.7	-1.5	-2.9		-7.9
TOT	453	73	1572	142	10955.2					12.8	3.95		.261	.333						.974	1256	297	1118					

Batter-Fielder Wins	Batting Average	On-Base Percentage	Slugging Average	On-Base Plus Slugging	Adjusted OPS	Adjusted Batter Runs
Musial-StL 7.2	Musial-StL .376	Musial-StL .450	Musial-StL .702	Musial-StL 1152	Musial-StL 196	Musial-StL 82.1
Pafko-Chi 4.2	Ashburn-Phi .333	B.Elliott-Bos .423	Mize-NY .564	Mize-NY 959	Mize-NY 156	Mize-NY 44.8
Mize-NY 4.2	Holmes-Bos .325	Ashburn-Phi .410	Gordon-NY .537	Gordon-NY 927	Gordon-NY 148	B.Elliott-Bos 41.3
Gordon-NY 3.0	Dark-Bos .322	Slaughter-StL .409	Kiner-Pit .533	Kiner-Pit 924	Kiner-Pit 145	Kiner-Pit 36.8
B.Elliott-Bos 2.9	Slaughter-StL .321	Mize-NY .395	Ennis-Phi .525	B.Elliott-Bos 897	B.Elliott-Bos 145	Gordon-NY 35.1

Runs	Hits	Doubles	Triples	Home Runs	Total Bases	Runs Batted In
Musial-StL 135	Musial-StL 230	Musial-StL 46	Musial-StL 18	Mize-NY 40	Musial-StL 429	Musial-StL 131
Lockman-NY 117	Holmes-Bos 190	Ennis-Phi 40	Hopp-Pit 12	Kiner-Pit 40	Mize-NY 316	Mize-NY 125
Mize-NY 110	Rojek-Pit 186	Dark-Bos 39	Slaughter-StL 11	Musial-StL 39	Ennis-Phi 309	Kiner-Pit 123
Robinson-Bro 108	Slaughter-StL 176	Robinson-Bro 38	Waitkus-Chi 10	Sauer-Cin 35	Kiner-Pit 296	Gordon-NY 107
Kiner-Pit 104	Dark-Bos 175	Holmes-Bos 35	Lockman-NY 10		Pafko-Chi 283	Pafko-Chi 101

Stolen Bases	Base Stealing Runs	Fielding Runs-Infield	Fielding Runs-Outfield	Wins	Winning Pct.	Complete Games
Ashburn-Phi 32		Gustine-Pit 12.6	Ashburn-Phi 9.1	Sain-Bos 24	Brecheen-StL .741	Sain-Bos 28
Reese-Bro 25		Smalley-Chi 10.7	Furillo-Bro 7.2	Brecheen-StL 20	Jones-NY .667	Brecheen-StL 21
Rojek-Pit 24		Pafko-Chi 10.3	Hermanski-Bro 5.8	Schmitz-Chi 18	Sain-Bos .615	Schmitz-Chi 18
Robinson-Bro 22		Marion-StL 10.3	Sauer-Cin 4.4	Jansen-NY 18	Jansen-NY .600	Spahn-Bos 16
Torgeson-Bos 19		Waitkus-Chi 8.0	Jeffcoat-Chi 3.4	VanderMeer-Cin 17	Schmitz-Chi .581	Leonard-Phi 16

Strikeouts	Fewest BB/Game	Games	Saves	Base Runners/9	Adjusted Relief Runs	Relief Ranking
Brecheen-StL 149	Roe-Bro 1.67	Gumbert-Cin 61	Gumbert-Cin 17	Potter-Bos 9.00	Wilks-StL 21.3	Wilks-StL 22.3
Barney-Bro 138	Jansen-NY 1.75	Wilks-StL 57	Wilks-StL 13	Brecheen-StL 9.41	Hansen-NY 10.2	Minner-Bro 9.6
Sain-Bos 137	Raffensberger-Cin 1.85	Higbe-Pit 56	Higbe-Pit 10	Roe-Bro 9.68	Minner-Bro 9.2	Trinkle-NY 8.9
Jansen-NY 126	Brecheen-StL 1.89	Jones-NY 55	Trinkle-NY 7	Wilks-StL 10.47	Dobernic-Chi 8.1	Dobernic-Chi 7.9
Branca-Bro 122	Leonard-Phi 2.15	Dobernic-Chi 54	Behrman-Bro 7	Schmitz-Chi 10.60	Higbe-Pit 7.9	Higbe-Pit 7.9

Innings Pitched	Opponents' Avg.	Opponents' OBP	Earned Run Average	Adjusted ERA	Adjusted Starter Runs	Pitcher Wins
Sain-Bos 314.2	Schmitz-Chi .215	Brecheen-StL .265	Brecheen-StL 2.24	Brecheen-StL 183	Brecheen-StL 46.9	**Sain-Bos** 5.3
Jansen-NY 277.0	Barney-Bro .217	Roe-Bro .271	Leonard-Phi 2.51	Leonard-Phi 157	Sain-Bos 43.0	**Brecheen-StL** 5.3
Spahn-Bos 257.0	Brecheen-StL .222	Schmitz-Chi .295	Sain-Bos 2.60	Roe-Bro 152	Leonard-Phi 31.4	**Schmitz-Chi** 3.8
Dickson-StL 252.1	Branca-Bro .232	Sain-Bos .296	Roe-Bro 2.63	Schmitz-Chi 148	Schmitz-Chi 30.5	**Leonard-Phi** 3.7
Barney-Bro 246.2	Roe-Bro .233	Raffensberger-Cin .296	Schmitz-Chi 2.64	Sain-Bos 147	Roe-Bro 26.5	**Roe-Bro** 2.6

Triumph of the Brave

Brooklyn general manager Branch Rickey was glad that things worked out with Jackie Robinson. For 1948 he imported catcher Roy Campanella from the Negro Leagues. But despite bringing in their left and center field fences, Dodgers hitters slumped, and the team fell to third. Manager Leo Durocher quit at midseason and took the helm of the hated Giants.

Stan Musial won his third batting title in six years, and led the NL in hits, runs, doubles, triples, and RBIs, while Harry Brecheen was arguably the league's top pitcher. However, teammate Murry Dickson gave up 39 homers, a new major league record, and the rest of the staff didn't give Brecheen much support; the Cardinals finished second.

The NL's class club was in Boston, which hadn't had a Senior Circuit champ since 1914. MVP Bob Elliott and a supporting cast including Alvin Dark, Tommy Holmes, and Jeff Heath, provided the hitting. Even with Johnny Sain and Warren Spahn combining to complete 44 games, the pitching was thin; the staff completed just 70, the lowest league-leading total to date.

And the Braves were no sure thing; on September 1, they were tied with Dodgers for the lead, with the Cardinals and surprising Pirates close behind. But a 14-of-15 streak, nine of them won by Spahn or Sain, put Boston ahead to stay.

Former stars Arky Vaughan and Joe Medwick retired, while Philadelphia's Richie Ashburn and Brooklyn's Carl Erskine made impressive major league debuts. And the Chicago Cubs fell into the cellar for first time since 1925, beginning a 20-year period of intense frustration.

Despite good pitching, the Braves couldn't do much in the World Series; five of the games were close, but aside from an 11–5 Game 5 blowout, Boston had no offense. Within just a few years, the Braves fell out of contention and attendance sagged, forcing a move to Milwaukee.

1948 American League

TEAM	W	L	T	PCT	GB	HW	HL	R	OR	PA	H	2B	3B	HR	BB	SO	HB	SH	AVG	OBP	SLG	OPS	AOPS	BR	ABR	PF	SB	CS	BSA	BSR
CLE	97	58	1	.626		48	30	840	**568**	6201	**1534**	242	54	**155**	646	575	85	24	**.282**	.360	.431	**791**	**119**	113	**136**	97	**54**	44	55	-4
BOS	96	59	0	.619	1	**55**	23	**907**	720	6284	1471	**277**	40	121	**823**	552	66	**32**	.274	**.374**	.409	783	109	**124**	82	105	38	17	**69**	**2**
NY	94	60	0	.610	2.5	50	27	857	633	6048	1480	251	**75**	139	623	**478**	78	23	.278	.356	**.432**	788	116	99	107	99	24	24	50	-3
PHI	84	70	0	.545	12.5	36	41	729	735	6049	1345	231	47	68	726	523	120	22	.260	.353	.362	715	96	-18	-19	100	40	32	56	-2
DET	78	76	0	.506	18.5	39	38	700	726	6063	1396	219	58	78	671	504	**130**	27	.267	.353	.375	728	96	-1	-20	103	22	32	41	-6
STL	59	94	2	.386	37	34	42	671	849	6013	1438	251	62	63	578	572	113	19	.271	.345	.378	723	96	-21	-39	103	63	44	59	-2
WAS	56	97	1	.366	40	29	48	578	796	5783	1245	203	**75**	31	568	572	84	20	.244	.322	.331	653	81	-156	-140	97	76	48	61	0
CHI	51	101	2	.336	44.5	27	48	559	814	5872	1303	172	39	55	595	528	73	12	.251	.329	.331	660	84	-138	-118	97	46	47	49	-6
TOT	618					318	297	5841		48313	11212	1846	450	710	5230	4304	179	749	.266	.349	.382	731					363	288	56	-21

TEAM	CG	SHO	GR	SV	IP	H	HR	BB	SO	BR/9	ERA	AERA	OAV	OOB	PR	APR	PF	OSB	OCS	FA	E	WPB	DP	FW	PW	BW	BSW	DIF
CLE	66	**26**	196	**30**	1409.1	**1246**	82	625	593	**12.1**	**3.22**	**126**	**.239**	**.323**	**167**	**138**	95	**31**	31	**.982**	114	**24**	183	**1.4**	**13.4**	**13.2**	-.1	-8.3
BOS	70	11	141	13	1379.1	1445	83	592	513	13.4	4.26	103	.270	.345	4	20	102	40	28	.981	116	31	174	1.2	1.9	7.9	**.4**	7.0
NY	62	16	162	24	1365.2	1289	94	641	654	12.9	3.75	109	.250	.336	82	53	95	49	40	.979	120	40	161	.9	5.1	10.4	-.0	.6
PHI	**74**	7	137	18	1368.2	1456	86	638	486	13.9	4.43	97	.275	.355	-21	-20	100	39	34	.981	**113**	42	180	1.3	-1.9	-1.8	.0	9.4
DET	60	5	187	22	1377.0	1367	92	**589**	**678**	12.9	4.15	105	.259	.335	21	33	102	49	28	.974	155	44	143	-.9	3.2	-1.9	-.3	1.0
STL	35	4	**243**	20	1373.1	1513	103	737	531	14.9	5.01	91	.281	.371	-109	-65	106	67	30	.972	168	54	**190**	-1.6	-6.3	-3.8	.0	-5.9
WAS	42	4	201	22	1357.1	1439	**81**	734	446	14.6	4.65	93	.273	.364	-55	-46	101	35	**59**	.974	154	31	144	-.9	-4.5	-13.6	.3	-1.8
CHI	35	2	210	23	1345.2	1454	89	673	403	14.4	4.89	87	.280	.365	-90	-95	99	53	38	.974	160	47	176	-1.2	-9.2	-11.4	-.3	-2.8
TOT	444	75	1477	172	10976.1					13.6	4.29		.266	.349						.977	1100	313	1351					

Batter-Fielder Wins	Batting Average	On-Base Percentage	Slugging Average	On-Base Plus Slugging	Adjusted OPS	Adjusted Batter Runs
Boudreau-Cle......7.1	Williams-Bos.........369	Williams-Bos 497	Williams-Bos.........615	Williams-Bos 1112	Williams-Bos 185	Williams-Bos 71.5
Williams-Bos 5.9	Boudreau-Cle 355	Boudreau-Cle 453	DiMaggio-NY 598	DiMaggio-NY........994	Boudreau-Cle 166	Boudreau-Cle 57.8
DiMaggio-NY 4.5	Mitchell-Cle...........336	Appling-Chi 423	Henrich-NY...........554	Boudreau-Cle 987	DiMaggio-NY........164	DiMaggio-NY......49.7
Priddy-StL 4.5	Zarilla-StL.............329	Goodman-Bos 414	Boudreau-Cle 534	Henrich-NY 945	Henrich-NY 151	Henrich-NY 40.8
Doerr-Bos............3.7	McCosky-Phi 326	Fain-Phi 412	Keltner-Cle 522	Keltner-Cle............917	Keltner-Cle............146	Keltner-Cle 36.5

Runs	Hits	Doubles	Triples	Home Runs	Total Bases	Runs Batted In
Henrich-NY 138	Dillinger-StL 207	Williams-Bos.................44	Henrich-NY 14	DiMaggio-NY 39	DiMaggio-NY........355	DiMaggio-NY 155
DiMaggio-Bos 127	Mitchell-Cle 204	Henrich-NY 42	Stewart-NY-Was 13	Gordon-Cle 32	Henrich-NY 326	Stephens-Bos......137
Williams-Bos 124	Boudreau-Cle 199	Majeski-Phi 41	Yost-Was 11	Keltner-Cle.............31	Williams-Bos 313	Williams-Bos 127
Pesky-Bos 124	DiMaggio-NY 190	Priddy-StL......................40	Mullin-Det 11	Stephens-Bos 29	Stephens-Bos 299	Gordon-Cle..........124
Boudreau-Cle 116	Williams-Bos 188	DiMaggio-Bos...............40	DiMaggio-NY..........11	Doerr-Bos 27	Boudreau-Cle 299	Majeski-Phi..........120

Stolen Bases	Base Stealing Runs	Fielding Runs-Infield	Fielding Runs-Outfield	Wins	Winning Pct.	Complete Games
Dillinger-StL............28	Dillinger-StL 2.3	Priddy-StL 22.5	Coan-Was............11.9	Newhouser-Det 21	Kramer-Bos 783	Lemon-Cle 20
Coan-Was 23	Coan-Was..............1.9	Pellagrini-StL 17.9	Philley-Chi 9.6	Lemon-Cle.............20	Bearden-Cle 741	Newhouser-Det 19
Vernon-Was............15	Robertson-Was 1.8	Michaels-Chi 16.3	DiMaggio-Bos........8.7	Bearden-Cle 20	Raschi-NY 704	Raschi-NY 18
Mitchell-Cle 13	Tucker-Cle 1.7	Baker-Chi.....................15.8	Hodgin-Chi 2.5	Raschi-NY 19	Reynolds-NY 696	Feller-Cle 18
	DiMaggio-Bos........1.5	Appling-Chi 13.4	Henrich-NY............1.8	Feller-Cle 19		

Strikeouts	Fewest BB/Game	Games	Saves	Base Runners/9	Adjusted Relief Runs	Relief Ranking
Feller-Cle 164	Hutchinson-Det....1.95	Page-NY 55	Christopher-Cle 17	Paige-Cle 10.40	Klieman-Cle 13.6	Christopher-Cle ..11.6
Lemon-Cle.............147	Zoldak-StL-Cle 2.42	Widmar-StL...................49	Page-NY 16	Hutchinson-Det..11.08	Christopher-Cle 8.2	Klieman-Cle............9.2
Newhouser-Det 143	Lopat-NY 2.62	Biscan-StL 47	Houtteman-Det 10	Lemon-Cle 11.12	Thompson-Was 4.1	Thompson-Was 4.7
Brissie-Phi 127	Kramer-Bos 2.81	Thompson-Was 46	Ferrick-Was 10	Gumpert-NY-Chi 11.18	Widmar-StL............2.3	Ferrick-Was 2.6
Raschi-NY 124	Houtteman-Det....2.85		Judson-Chi 8	Gromek-Cle 11.49	Ferrick-Was 2.2	Widmar-StL 2.1

Innings Pitched	Opponents' Avg.	Opponents' OBP	Earned Run Average	Adjusted ERA	Adjusted Starter Runs	Pitcher Wins
Lemon-Cle 293.2	Shea-NY...............208	Hutchinson-Det 297	Bearden-Cle 2.43	Bearden-Cle 167	Bearden-Cle 42.9	**Lemon-Cle**..........6.6
Feller-Cle 280.1	Lemon-Cle 216	Lemon-Cle....................302	Scarborough-Was2.82	Scarborough-Was 154	Lemon-Cle 42.5	**Bearden-Cle** 5.5
Newhouser-Det..272.1	Bearden-Cle 229	Scarborough-Was 307	Lemon-Cle 2.82	Newhouser-Det 145	Newhouser-Det....38.3	**Newhouser-Det** 4.5
Dobson-Bos 245.1	Scarborough-Was.233	Newhouser-Det 309	Newhouser-Det....3.01	Lemon-Cle............144	Scarborough-Was28.8	**Scarborough-Was**3.4
Reynolds-NY 236.1	Trucks-Det 240	Raschi-NY 310	Parnell-Bos..........3.14	Parnell-Bos 140	Parnell-Bos..........26.4	**Parnell-Bos** 2.2

A Real Tribe

Bill Veeck was baseball's master showman, but he brought the crowds back to Cleveland not with stunts, but by building an integrated club that would contend for the next decade.

In early August the Indians, Red Sox, Yankees, and the surprising Athletics sat atop the AL in a virtual knot. While Philadelphia dropped out in early September, the other three teams kept winning, landing in a three-way tie September 23.

Cleveland attempted to pull away, but Boston knocked out New York October 2 and moved into a tie with the Indians, losers of two of three to Detroit, on the season's final day. In the league's first-ever playoff, the Indians invaded Fenway Park and whipped the Red Sox, 8–3, with rookie Gene Bearden winning his 20th.

The Indians, who had the league's best pitching and a strong offense, debuted two great pitchers: Negro Leagues legend Satchel Paige and Mike Garcia, the "Big Bear." Cleveland shortstop Lou Boudreau, nearing the end of his great playing career, was league MVP. Cleveland also set a new record by drawing 2,620,627 fans. Boston's excellent attack couldn't quite negate a mediocre pitching staff, while the Yankees didn't hit enough and had a poor season from Joe Page. Both clubs set new attendance marks for their parks as league attendance rose another 17 percent to the highest total yet.

Babe Ruth's death from cancer on August 16 set America into mourning. The Bambino was still a beloved hero and his body was visited by more than 100,000 at Yankee Stadium.

The World Series pitted faux Native Americans from Cleveland and Boston. Despite Bob Feller's two losses, the Indians won with fine pitching from Bob Lemon and Bearden. While the Braves took Game 5, 11–5, they scored but six times in the other five contests. Larry Doby, at .318, was the hottest Cleveland hitter.

1949 National League

TEAM	W	L	T	PCT	GB	HW	HL	R	OR	PA	H	2B	3B	HR	BB	SO	HB	SH	AVG	OBP	SLG	OPS	AOPS	BR	ABR	PF	SB	CS	BSA	BSR
BRO	97	57	2	.630		48	29	**879**	651	6173	1477	236	47	**152**	638	570	**102**	**33**	.274	**.354**	**.419**	**773**	**110**	**106**	**73**	104	**117**			
STL	96	58	3	.623	1	**51**	26	766	**616**	6151	**1513**	**281**	54	102	569	**482**	94	25	**.277**	.348	.404	752	103	64	29	105	17			
PHI	81	73	0	.526	16	40	37	662	668	5935	1349	232	**55**	122	528	670	74	26	.254	.325	.388	713	100	-28	-9	97	27			
BOS	75	79	3	.487	22	43	34	706	719	6139	1376	246	33	103	**684**	656	96	23	.258	.345	.374	719	105	10	51	95	28			
NY	73	81	2	.474	24	43	34	736	693	6009	1383	203	52	147	613	523	64	24	.261	.340	.401	741	105	35	36	100	43			
PIT	71	83	0	.461	26	36	41	681	760	5870	1350	191	41	126	548	554	86	22	.259	.332	.384	716	96	-16	-33	103	48			
CIN	62	92	2	.403	35	35	42	627	770	5994	1423	264	35	86	429	559	76	20	.260	.316	.368	684	88	-84	-91	101	31			
CHI	61	93	0	.396	36	33	44	593	773	5723	1336	212	53	97	396	573	87	26	.256	.312	.373	685	91	-88	-72	97	53			
TOT	622					329	287	5650		47994	11207	1865	370	935	4405	4587	199	679	.262	.334	.389	723					364			

TEAM	CG	SHO	GR	SV	IP	H	HR	BB	SO	BR/9	ERA	AERA	OAV	OOB	PR	APR	PF	OSB	OCS	FA	E	WPB	DP	FW	PW	BW	BSW	DIF
BRO	62	**15**	193	17	1408.2	**1306**	132	582	**743**	12.2	3.80	108	**.246**	.324	37	46	102	**25**	*31*	**.980**	**122**	31	162	**1.5**	4.6	**7.2**		6.7
STL	64	13	188	**19**	1407.2	1356	**87**	507	606	**12.1**	**3.44**	**121**	.252	**.319**	**94**	**110**	103	40	*25*	.976	146	**29**	149	.3	**10.9**	2.9		5.0
PHI	58	12	190	15	1391.2	1389	104	**502**	495	12.4	3.89	101	.268	.335	23	9	98	56	*39*	.974	156	35	141	-.5	.9	-.9		4.5
BOS	**68**	12	159	11	1400.0	1466	110	520	589	12.9	3.99	95	.268	.334	8	-35	94	49	*32*	.976	148	30	144	.1	-3.5	5.1		-3.7
NY	**68**	10	186	9	1374.1	1328	132	544	516	12.4	3.82	104	.249	.321	33	25	99	50	*26*	.973	161	43	134	-.6	2.5	3.6		-9.4
PIT	53	9	179	15	1356.0	1452	142	535	556	13.4	4.57	92	.274	.344	-79	-53	104	35	*38*	.978	132	34	**173**	.9	-5.3	-3.3		1.7
CIN	55	10	**210**	6	1401.2	1423	124	640	538	13.4	4.34	96	.264	.345	-47	-24	104	41	*39*	.977	138	48	150	.6	-2.4	-9.0		-4.2
CHI	44	8	200	17	1357.2	1487	104	575	544	13.8	4.50	90	.279	.351	-70	-71	100	68	***43***	.970	186	56	160	-2.1	-7.0	-7.1		.3
TOT	472	89	1505	109	11097.2					12.8	4.04		.262	.334						.975	1189	306	1213					

Batter-Fielder Wins	Batting Average	On-Base Percentage	Slugging Average	On-Base Plus Slugging	Adjusted OPS	Adjusted Batter Runs
Kiner-Pit 5.1	Robinson-Bro .342	Musial-StL .438	Kiner-Pit .658	Kiner-Pit 1089	Kiner-Pit 183	Kiner-Pit 67.0
Musial-StL 5.1	Musial-StL .338	Robinson-Bro .432	Musial-StL .624	Musial-StL 1062	Musial-StL 174	Musial-StL 66.9
Robinson-Bro 5.0	Slaughter-StL .336	Kiner-Pit .432	Robinson-Bro .528	Robinson-Bro 960	Robinson-Bro 150	Robinson-Bro 45.7
B.Elliott-Bos 4.0	Furillo-Bro .322	Slaughter-StL .418	Ennis-Phi .525	Slaughter-StL 929	Gordon-NY 142	Slaughter-StL 35.5
Campanella-Bro 3.1	Kiner-Pit .310	Stanky-Bos .417	Thomson-NY .518	Gordon-NY 909	Slaughter-StL 141	Gordon-NY 33.1

Runs	Hits	Doubles	Triples	Home Runs	Total Bases	Runs Batted In
Reese-Bro 132	Musial-StL 207	Musial-StL 41	Slaughter-StL 13	Kiner-Pit 54	Musial-StL 382	Kiner-Pit 127
Musial-StL 128	Robinson-Bro 203	Ennis-Phi 39	Musial-StL 13	Musial-StL 36	Kiner-Pit 361	Robinson-Bro 124
Robinson-Bro 122	Thomson-NY 198	Robinson-Bro 38	Robinson-Bro 12	Sauer-Cin-Chi 31	Thomson-NY 332	Musial-StL 123
Kiner-Pit 116	Slaughter-StL 191	Hatton-Cin 38	Ennis-Phi 11	Thomson-NY 27	Ennis-Phi 320	Hodges-Bro 115
Schoendienst-StL 102	Schoendienst-StL 190		Ashburn-Phi 11	Gordon-NY 26	Robinson-Bro 313	Ennis-Phi 110

Stolen Bases	Base Stealing Runs	Fielding Runs-Infield	Fielding Runs-Outfield	Wins	Winning Pct.	Complete Games
Robinson-Bro 37		Schoendienst-StL 27.5	Ashburn-Phi 10.4	Spahn-Bos 21	Roe-Bro .714	Spahn-Bos 25
Reese-Bro 26		Smalley-Chi 17.6	Thomson-NY 7.6	Pollet-StL 20	Pollet-StL .690	Raffensberger-Cin 20
		Marion-StL 12.4	Holmes-Bos 6.2	Raffensberger-Cin 18	Newcombe-Bro .680	Newcombe-Bro 19
		Reich-Chi 12.2	Diering-StL 6.2		Meyer-Phi .680	Pollet-StL 17
		B.Elliott-Bos 11.4	Sauer-Cin-Chi 4.5		Munger-StL .652	Jansen-NY 17

Strikeouts	Fewest BB/Game	Games	Saves	Base Runners/9	Adjusted Relief Runs	Relief Ranking
Spahn-Bos 151	Koslo-NY 1.83	Wilks-StL 59	Wilks-StL 9	Koslo-NY 10.02	Konstanty-Phi 8.1	Konstanty-Phi 11.8
Newcombe-Bro 149	Roe-Bro 1.86	Konstanty-Phi 53	Potter-Bos 7	Staley-StL 10.40	Erautt-Cin 7.8	Erautt-Cin 9.5
Jansen-NY 113	Werle-Pit 2.08	Palica-Bro 49	Konstanty-Phi 7	Roe-Bro 10.45	Wilks-StL 7.3	Palica-Bro 8.5
Roe-Bro 109	Jansen-NY 2.15	Banta-Bro 48	Staley-StL 6	Bonham-Pit 10.52	Hogue-Bos 5.1	Wilks-StL 8.5
Branca-Bro 109	Leonard-Chi 2.15	Muncrief-Pit-Chi 47	Palica-Bro 6	Wilks-StL 10.88	Palica-Bro 5.0	Hogue-Bos 3.0

Innings Pitched	Opponents' Avg.	Opponents' OBP	Earned Run Average	Adjusted ERA	Adjusted Starter Runs	Pitcher Wins
Spahn-Bos 302.1	Staley-StL .238	Koslo-NY .278	Koslo-NY 2.50	Koslo-NY 159	Pollet-StL 35.2	**Pollet-StL** 4.2
Raffensberger-Cin 284.0	Koslo-NY .239	Staley-StL .286	Staley-StL 2.73	Staley-StL 152	Koslo-NY 34.5	**Koslo-NY** 4.1
Jansen-NY 259.2	Kennedy-NY .242	Roe-Bro .293	Pollet-StL 2.77	Pollet-StL 150	Roe-Bro 31.9	**Newcombe-Bro** 2.9
Heintzelman-Phi 250.0	Newcombe-Bro .243	Spahn-Bos .299	Roe-Bro 2.79	Roe-Bro 147	Newcombe-Bro 27.3	**Staley-StL** 2.9
Newcombe-Bro 244.1	Spahn-Bos .245	Newcombe-Bro .301	Heintzelman-Phi 3.02	Brazle-StL 131	Heintzelman-Phi 24.9	**Roe-Bro** 2.6

Jackie's Back

Some had labeled Jackie Robinson a one-year wonder after he slumped in 1948. But he had not yet begun to fight; his comeback season netted MVP honors and sparked the Dodgers in their thrilling pennant drive against the Cardinals.

Both contenders played in extreme hitters' parks. Brooklyn won with an overwhelming offense and mediocre hurling, while St. Louis had a spectacularly good staff and several weak hitters. The Cardinals were in the driver's seat, up 1_ games with one week left, but four straight losses doomed them to second place as the Dodgers capitalized. Once again, outfielders Stan Musial and Enos Slaughter had to carry the Cardinals attack. In a sign of what was to come, the Phillies improved by 15 games and leapt into to third place.

For the third straight season, the Dodgers debuted an impressive African American player as pitcher Don Newcombe won Rookie of the Year. Del Crandall and former Negro Leaguer Monte Irvin also made their first appearances in the majors, while it was the last year of service for Mort Cooper and Dixie Walker.

Ralph Kiner's 54 homers were the most in the majors since 1930, and NL home runs rose to 935, a new mark. For the first time, six clubs hit over 100 homers each. There was tragedy off the field. Pirates hurler Tiny Bonham died September 15 after an emergency appendectomy, and Phillies first baseman Eddie Waitkus was shot by a crazed admirer in a Chicago hotel room—he recovered to play six more years in the majors. In the face of a lawsuit that threatened baseball's reserve clause, Happy Chandler rescinded the ban on players who jumped to the Mexican League in 1946.

For the third time in the decade, the Yankees beat the Dodgers in the World Series, this time in five games. All were tight contests but the last, when the Brooklyn pitching collapsed.

1949 American League

TEAM	W	L	T	PCT	GB	HW	HL	R	OR	PA	H	2B	3B	HR	BB	SO	HB	SH	AVG	OBP	SLG	OPS	AOPS	BR	ABR	PF	SB	CS	BSA	BSR
NY	97	57	1	.630		54	23	829	637	6043	1396	215	**60**	115	731	539	84	**32**	.269	.362	.400	762	108	59	59	100	**58**	30	**66**	**2**
BOS	96	58	1	.623	1	**61**	16	**896**	667	6250	**1500**	**272**	36	**131**	**835**	510	78	17	**.282**	**.381**	**.420**	**801**	**111**	**154**	**93**	107	43	25	63	1
CLE	89	65	0	.578	8	49	28	675	**574**	5958	1358	194	58	112	601	534	113	23	.260	.339	.384	723	99	-35	-21	98	44	40	52	-4
DET	87	67	1	.565	10	50	27	751	655	6140	1405	215	51	88	751	502	107	23	.267	.361	.378	739	102	21	19	100	39	52	43	-10
PHI	81	73	0	.526	16	52	25	726	725	6048	1331	214	49	82	783	**493**	**117**	25	.260	.361	.369	730	104	8	34	97	36	25	59	-1
CHI	63	91	0	.409	34	32	45	648	737	6003	1340	207	66	43	702	596	84	13	.257	.347	.347	694	93	-68	-46	97	62	55	53	-6
STL	53	101	1	.344	44	36	41	667	913	5847	1301	213	30	117	631	700	83	21	.254	.339	.377	716	92	-41	-68	104	38	39	49	-5
WAS	50	104	0	.325	47	26	51	584	868	5912	1330	207	41	81	593	495	63	22	.254	.333	.356	689	90	-96	-82	98	46	33	58	-1
TOT	618					360	256	5776		48201	10961	1737	391	769	5627	4369	176	729	.263	.353	.379	732					366	299	55	-24

TEAM	CG	SHO	GR	SV	IP	H	HR	BB	SO	BR/9	ERA	AERA	OAV	OOB	PR	APR	PF	OSB	OCS	FA	E	WPB	DP	FW	PW	BW	BSW	DIF
NY	59	12	159	**36**	1371.1	**1231**	98	812	**671**	13.6	3.69	110	**.242**	.351	77	56	96	54	**42**	.977	138	40	195	.0	5.4	5.7	**.5**	8.3
BOS	84	16	120	16	1377.0	1375	82	661	598	13.5	3.97	110	.262	.347	34	57	104	35	28	.980	120	31	207	1.1	5.5	**9.1**	.4	2.9
CLE	65	10	168	19	1383.2	1275	82	**611**	594	**12.4**	**3.36**	**119**	.247	**.329**	**129**	**103**	95	**32**	37	**.983**	**103**	**27**	192	**2.1**	**10.0**	-2.0	-.0	2.1
DET	70	**19**	152	12	1393.2	1338	102	628	631	12.8	3.77	110	.254	.335	66	61	99	45	37	.978	131	40	174	.4	5.9	1.8	-.7	2.5
PHI	**85**	9	107	11	1365.0	1359	105	758	490	14.1	4.23	97	.263	.360	-5	-19	98	46	40	.976	140	43	**217**	-.1	-1.8	3.3	.2	2.5
CHI	57	10	174	17	1363.1	1362	108	693	502	13.7	4.30	97	.264	.353	-15	-19	99	51	38	.977	141	34	180	-.2	-1.8	-4.5	-.3	-7.2
STL	43	3	**231**	16	1341.1	1583	113	685	432	15.4	5.21	87	.294	.377	-151	-94	108	47	38	.971	166	41	154	-1.6	-9.1	-6.6	-.2	-6.4
WAS	44	9	206	9	1345.2	1438	**79**	779	451	15.0	5.10	84	.276	.373	-134	-124	101	56	39	.973	161	47	168	-1.4	-12.1	-8.0	.2	-5.7
TOT	507	88	1317	136	10941.0					13.8	4.20		.263	.353						.977	1100	303	1487					

Batter-Fielder Wins	Batting Average	On-Base Percentage	Slugging Average	On-Base Plus Slugging	Adjusted OPS	Adjusted Batter Runs
Williams-Bos 6.4	Kell-Det................343	Williams-Bos 490	Williams-Bos.........650	Williams-Bos 1141	Williams-Bos 187	Williams-Bos 79.9
Doerr-Bos 5.1	Williams-Bos.........343	Appling-Chi 439	Stephens-Bos.......539	Henrich-NY 942	Henrich-NY 148	Joost-Phi 37.8
Joost-Phi 5.1	Dillinger-StL 324	Joost-Phi 429	Henrich-NY...........526	Stephens-Bos 930	Joost-Phi 138	DiMaggio-NY......32.1
Michaels-Chi 4.5	Mitchell-Cle...........317	Kell-Det 424	Doerr-Bos.............497	Kell-Det 892	Kell-Det 136	Henrich-NY 30.6
Stephens-Bos 3.9	Doerr-Bos 309	Michaels-Chi 417	Berra-NY 480	Doerr-Bos 890	Stephens-Bos 135	Stephens-Bos 29.6

Runs	Hits	Doubles	Triples	Home Runs	Total Bases	Runs Batted In
Williams-Bos 150	Mitchell-Cle 203	Williams-Bos.................39	Mitchell-Cle 23	Williams-Bos 43	Williams-Bos 368	Williams-Bos 159
Joost-Phi 128	Williams-Bos 194	Kell-Det.........................38	Dillinger-StL 13	Stephens-Bos 39	Stephens-Bos 329	Stephens-Bos......159
DiMaggio-Bos 126	DiMaggio-Bos 186	DiMaggio-Bos 34	Valo-Phi 12		Wertz-Det 283	Wertz-Det............133
Stephens-Bos 113	Wertz-Det 185	Zarilla-StL-Bos 33			Mitchell-Cle 274	Doerr-Bos.............109
Pesky-Bos 111	Pesky-Bos 185	Stephens-Bos 31			Doerr-Bos 269	Chapman-Phi 108

Stolen Bases	Base Stealing Runs	Fielding Runs-Infield	Fielding Runs-Outfield	Wins	Winning Pct.	Complete Games
Dillinger-StL 20	Rizzuto-NY 1.9	Doerr-Bos 27.1	Valo-Phi 9.5	Parnell-Bos 25	Kinder-Bos 793	Parnell-Bos............27
Rizzuto-NY 18	Philley-Chi 1.5	Pesky-Bos 18.9	Evers-Det 8.0	Kinder-Bos..............23	Parnell-Bos...........781	Newhouser-Det 22
Valo-Phi..................14	Tebbetts-Bos.........1.4	Vernon-Cle.................16.1	Kokos-StL 7.4	Lemon-Cle..............22	Reynolds-NY 739	Lemon-Cle 22
Philley-Chi 13	Fain-Phi 1.4	Michaels-Chi 15.0	Mapes-NY 6.4	Raschi-NY 21	Lemon-Cle 688	Raschi-NY 21
	Mapes-NY 1.3	Baker-Chi....................11.0	DiMaggio-Bos........5.8	Kellner-Phi 20		

Strikeouts	Fewest BB/Game	Games	Saves	Base Runners/9	Adjusted Relief Runs	Relief Ranking
Trucks-Det 153	Hutchinson-Det....2.48	Page-NY 60	Page-NY 27	Hutchinson-Det..10.49	Page-NY..............22.7	Page-NY 41.9
Newhouser-Det 144	Houtteman-Det....2.61	Welteroth-Was 52	Benton-Cle 10	Trucks-Det 11.03	Paige-Cle 10.3	Paige-Cle............13.7
Lemon-Cle.............138	Lopat-NY 2.88	Ferrick-StL 50	Ferrick-StL................6	Garcia-Cle 11.07	Ferrick-StL 7.7	Ferrick-StL............7.6
Kinder-Bos............138	Garcia-Cle 3.07	Kennedy-StL 48	Paige-Cle..................5	Benton-Cle 11.14	Papish-Cle 6.0	Papish-Cle............3.0
Byrne-NY..............129	Wynn-Cle 3.12	Surkont-Chi...................44		Paige-Cle 11.28	Starr-StL 2.2	Starr-StL 1.9

Innings Pitched	Opponents' Avg.	Opponents' OBP	Earned Run Average	Adjusted ERA	Adjusted Starter Runs	Pitcher Wins
Parnell-Bos........295.1	Byrne-NY 183	Hutchinson-Det 290	Garcia-Cle 2.36	Garcia-Cle 169	Parnell-Bos..........49.2	**Lemon-Cle**..........5.6
Newhouser-Det..292.0	Lemon-Cle 211	Trucks-Det 301	Parnell-Bos.........2.77	Parnell-Bos 157	Trucks-Det 42.1	**Parnell-Bos** 5.2
Lemon-Cle 279.2	Trucks-Det 211	Garcia-Cle 308	Trucks-Det 2.81	Trucks-Det 148	Lemon-Cle 33.8	**Page-NY**..............4.0
Trucks-Det 275.0	Gray-Det..............227	Lemon-Cle 309	Hutchinson-Det....2.96	Hutchinson-Det 141	Garcia-Cle 33.6	**Garcia-Cle**..........3.7
Raschi-NY 274.2	Pierce-Chi.............228	Gumpert-Chi 318	Lemon-Cle 2.99	Lemon-Cle............133	Benton-Cle 30.9	**Trucks-Det** 3.5

The First of Casey

While Cleveland stumbled early, Boston and New York put on a show. The oft-injured Yankees, with skipper Casey Stengel taking the helm, held a steady lead from July into late August, when the consistently improving Red Sox cut sagging New York's lead from 8 games to 1_ in a month.

New York hung on through September, then lost three straight at Boston with a week left. In the season's final series at New York, the Yankees, one game behind, won two pressure-packed games from the Red Sox to steal the crown from Boston skipper Joe McCarthy, who had enjoyed his share of New York glory.

Boston led the league in runs, thanks to Ted Williams, and got fine pitching from Mel Parnell and Ellis Kinder. Despite using a patchwork lineup, New York's offense was just fine; Joe DiMaggio was great when healthy and Yogi Berra developed into a terrific two-way player. Yankees pitching was deep and Joe Page's 27 saves set a new mark.

The White Sox brought in Comiskey Park's fences by 20 feet, and then returned them in early May. They finished sixth anyway. Third-place Cleveland debuted two more black players: Cuban outfielder Minnie Minoso and first baseman Luke Easter.

Baseball was now ruled by the slugging strategy of waiting for a good pitch and uppercutting it. In 1949, seven AL pitching staffs walked more hitters than they struck out. Behemoths Walt Dropo, Gus Zernial, and Roy Sievers debuted in '49, and similar lead-footed boppers ruled the game for much of the coming decade.

A strong Dodgers club was favored in the World Series, but Yankees pitching carried the day in a five-game victory. Joe Page again worked his magic in the late innings, and Allie Reynolds tossed 12.1 scoreless innings. This improbable season thus kicked off the next phase of Bronx Bombers' greatness.

1950 National League

TEAM	W	L	T	PCT	GB	HW	HL	R	OR	PA	H	2B	3B	HR	BB	SO	HB	SH	AVG	OBP	SLG	OPS	AOPS	BR	ABR	PF	SB	CS	BSA	BSR
PHI	91	63	3	.591		47	30	722	**624**	6051	1440	225	**55**	125	535	**569**	66	24	.265	.334	.396	730	100	-16	-4	98	33			
BRO	89	65	1	.578	2	**48**	30	**847**	724	6086	**1461**	247	46	**194**	607	632	**88**	27	**.272**	**.349**	**.444**	**793**	**113**	**109**	**92**	102	**77**			
NY	86	68	0	.558	5	44	32	735	643	5981	1352	204	50	133	**627**	629	75	**41**	.258	.342	.392	734	100	3	-1	101	42			
BOS	83	71	2	.539	8	46	31	785	736	6079	1411	246	36	148	615	616	74	27	.263	.342	.405	747	110	26	78	94	71			
STL	78	75	0	.510	12.5	47	29	693	670	5917	1353	**255**	50	102	606	604	73	23	.259	.339	.386	725	93	-12	-44	105	23			
CIN	66	87	0	.431	24.5	38	38	654	734	5845	1366	257	27	99	504	497	72	16	.260	.327	.376	703	91	-64	-66	100	37			
CHI	64	89	1	.418	26.5	35	42	643	772	5794	1298	224	47	161	479	767	54	31	.248	.315	.401	716	95	-56	-48	99	46			
PIT	57	96	1	.373	33.5	33	44	681	857	5976	1404	227	59	138	564	693	54	31	.264	.338	.406	744	99	11	-12	103	43			
TOT	618					338	276	5760		47729	11085	1885	370	1100	4537	5007	220	556	.261	.336	.401	737					372			

TEAM	CG	SHO	GR	SV	IP	H	HR	BB	SO	BR/9	ERA	AERA	OAV	OOB	PR	APR	PF	OSB	OCS	FA	E	WPB	DP	FW	PW	BW	BSW	DIF
PHI	57	13	167	**27**	1406.0	1324	122	**530**	620	**12.0**	**3.50**	**116**	.250	**.320**	**101**	**88**	98	47	*29*	.975	151	34	155	.1	**8.6**	-.4		5.7
BRO	62	10	195	21	1389.2	1397	163	591	**772**	13.0	4.28	96	.263	.339	-22	-29	99	33	*38*	**.979**	**127**	35	**183**	**1.4**	-2.8	**9.0**		4.5
NY	70	**19**	179	15	1375.0	**1268**	140	536	596	**12.0**	3.71	110	**.246**	**.320**	66	59	99	**31**	*38*	.977	137	37	181	.8	5.8	-.0		2.6
BOS	**88**	7	135	10	1385.1	1411	129	554	615	13.0	4.14	93	.263	.336	0	-48	93	53	***44***	.970	182	35	146	-1.7	-4.7	7.6		4.7
STL	57	10	185	14	1356.0	1398	**119**	535	603	13.0	3.97	108	.268	.339	26	47	104	37	*30*	.978	130	**31**	172	1.1	4.6	-4.3		.1
CIN	67	7	157	13	1357.2	1363	145	582	686	13.2	4.32	98	.259	.338	-26	-13	102	64	*31*	.976	140	49	132	.5	-1.3	-6.5		-3.3
CHI	55	9	199	19	1371.1	1452	130	593	559	13.6	4.28	98	.271	.347	-21	-11	101	70	*42*	.968	201	43	169	-2.8	-1.1	-4.7		-3.9
PIT	42	6	**213**	16	1368.2	1472	152	616	556	13.9	4.96	88	.275	.353	-124	-83	106	37	*38*	.977	136	39	165	.8	-8.1	-1.2		-11.0
TOT	498	81	1430	135	11009.2					13.0	4.14		.261	.336						.975	1204	303	1303					

Batter-Fielder Wins	Batting Average	On-Base Percentage	Slugging Average	On-Base Plus Slugging	Adjusted OPS	Adjusted Batter Runs
Robinson-Bro......5.0	Musial-StL 346	Stanky-NY 460	Musial-StL 596	Musial-StL 1034	Musial-StL 161	Musial-StL 52.7
Stanky-NY 4.6	Robinson-Bro 328	Musial-StL 437	Pafko-Chi 591	Kiner-Pit................998	Gordon-Bos 160	Kiner-Pit.............45.4
Musial-StL 3.8	Snider-Bro 321	Robinson-Bro..............423	Kiner-Pit 590	Pafko-Chi..............989	Pafko-Chi..............158	Gordon-Bos 43.8
Gordon-Bos 3.6	Ennis-Phi 311	Glaviano-StL 421	Gordon-Bos 557	Gordon-Bos 960	Kiner-Pit................154	Pafko-Chi............43.1
Seminick-Phi 3.6	Kluszewski-Cin 307	Torgeson-Bos...............412	Snider-Bro 553	Snider-Bro 932	Elliott-Bos 143	Torgeson-Bos 40.7

Runs	Hits	Doubles	Triples	Home Runs	Total Bases	Runs Batted In
Torgeson-Bos 120	Snider-Bro 199	Schoendienst-StL 43	Ashburn-Phi............14	Kiner-Pit..................47	Snider-Bro 343	Ennis-Phi 126
Stanky-NY 115	Musial-StL 192	Musial-StL......................41	Bell-Pit 11	Pafko-Chi 36	Musial-StL 331	Kiner-Pit 118
Kiner-Pit................112	Furillo-Bro 189	Robinson-Bro 39	Snider-Bro 10	Sauer-Chi 32	Ennis-Phi 328	Hodges-Bro 113
Snider-Bro 109	Ennis-Phi 185	Kluszewski-Cin 37	Smalley-Chi 9	Hodges-Bro 32	Kiner-Pit.................323	Kluszewski-Cin 111
Musial-StL 105	Waitkus-Phi 182	Dark-NY 36	Schoendienst-StL 9		Pafko-Chi..............304	Musial-StL 109

Stolen Bases	Base Stealing Runs	Fielding Runs-Infield	Fielding Runs-Outfield	Wins	Winning Pct.	Complete Games
Jethroe-Bos 35		Smalley-Chi 19.6	Bell-Pit 4.5	Spahn-Bos..............21	Maglie-NY.............818	Bickford-Bos..........27
Reese-Bro 17		Cox-Bro 12.1	Lockman-NY..........4.1	Sain-Bos 20	Konstanty-Phi 696	Spahn-Bos 25
Snider-Bro 16		Schoendienst-StL 11.8	Marshall-Bos 3.6	Roberts-Phi 20	Simmons-Phi 680	Sain-Bos................25
Torgeson-Bos 15		Robinson-Bro.............10.9	Gordon-Bos 3.5		Roberts-Phi 645	Roberts-Phi 21
Ashburn-Phi............14		Thompson-NY 8.2	Adcock-Cin 3.5			Jansen-NY 21

Strikeouts	Fewest BB/Game	Games	Saves	Base Runners/9	Adjusted Relief Runs	Relief Ranking
Spahn-Bos............191	Raffensberger-Cin ..1.51	Konstanty-Phi 74	Konstanty-Phi 22	Hearn-StL-NY......8.60	Konstanty-Phi 24.1	Konstanty-Phi 40.6
Blackwell-Cin........188	Jansen-NY 1.80	Dickson-Pit 51	Werle-Pit 8	Konstanty-Phi 9.36	Smith-Cin 4.0	Smith-Cin 3.9
Jansen-NY............161	Sain-Bos..............2.26	Werle-Pit.........................48	Hogue-Bos 7	Jansen-NY 9.62	Kramer-NY 2.2	Kramer-NY 2.1
Simmons-Phi 146	Roberts-Phi 2.28	Maglie-NY.......................47	Branca-Bro 7	Roberts-Phi 10.68	Leonard-Chi 1.7	Leonard-Chi 1.5
Roberts-Phi 146	Roe-Bro 2.37	Brazle-StL.......................46		Church-Phi 10.71		

Innings Pitched	Opponents' Avg.	Opponents' OBP	Earned Run Average	Adjusted ERA	Adjusted Starter Runs	Pitcher Wins
Bickford-Bos......311.2	Blackwell-Cin 210	Jansen-NY...................271	Hearn-StL-NY......2.49	Maglie-NY 151	Roberts-Phi 37.7	**Konstanty-Phi**....3.8
Roberts-Phi 304.1	Simmons-Phi 223	Roberts-Phi 297	Maglie-NY............2.71	Blackwell-Cin........143	Jansen-NY 32.8	**Blackwell-Cin** 3.6
Spahn-Bos 293.0	Maglie-NY.............226	Brecheen-StL...............298	Blackwell-Cin 2.97	Lanier-StL 137	Blackwell-Cin 32.5	**Jansen-NY**..........3.6
Sain-Bos............278.1	Spahn-Bos 227	Spahn-Bos....................299	Jansen-NY 3.01	Jansen-NY............136	Maglie-NY............31.8	**Roberts-Phi**........3.2
Jansen-NY 275.0	Jansen-NY 232	Blackwell-Cin 301	Roberts-Phi 3.02	Roberts-Phi 134	Roe-Bro 24.5	**Maglie-NY** 3.1

Whizzing Into a Title

Prior to the season, the strike zone was shrunk to a range from the armpits to the top of knees. While league scoring rose 2.6 percent, which was predictable, strikeouts also increased by 10 percent—to an all-time NL high of 4.05 per game—which was not. Homers skyrocketed another 18 percent to 1,100, marking the first time either league had cracked four digits. Seven NL clubs cleared 100 long balls; the Reds hit 99.

Boston's farm system was producing players; Joe Adcock and Sam Jethroe made their debuts, and in 1951, Johnny Logan made his first appearance. Grover Cleveland Alexander, perhaps the NL's greatest right-hander ever, died destitute in a Nebraska rooming house at age 63. Meanwhile, two fine pitchers of the 1940s, Kirby Higbe and Bucky Walters, were finished.

The Phillies, nicknamed the "Whiz Kids" because of youngsters Robin Roberts, Curt Simmons, Granny Hamner, Willie Jones, and Richie Ashburn, emerged from the pack in July. However, a veteran—33-year-old reliever Jim Konstanty—was league MVP, appearing in relief a record 74 times and saving 22, an NL mark.

Philly was well in front until the fence-busting Dodgers, led by Duke Snider and Gil Hodges, made their move. Nine games down on September 18, the Dodgers won 13 of 15 while the Phils slumped. The lead was just one game with only one left to play—a showdown at Ebbets Field. But the Whiz Kids came through, defeating Brooklyn 4–1 on a Dick Sisler homer in the 10th. The heroics were through for the Phillies, however. The Yankees took them out in four straight in a competitive, but short, World Series.

For baseball, the postwar boom was over; for the third straight season, NL attendance dropped sharply. Owners in the minors and majors began worrying about television and the exodus to the suburbs.

1950 American League

TEAM	W	L	T	PCT	GB	HW	HL	R	OR	PA	H	2B	3B	HR	BB	SO	HB	SH	AVG	OBP	SLG	OPS	AOPS	BR	ABR	PF	SB	CS	BSA	BSR
NY	98	56	1	.636		53	24	914	691	6164	1511	234	**70**	159	687	**463**	85	31	.282	.367	.441	808	**116**	92	**118**	97	**41**	28	59	-1
DET	95	59	3	.617	3	50	30	837	713	6232	1518	285	50	114	**722**	480	**110**	19	.282	.369	.417	786	104	65	38	103	23	40	37	-9
BOS	94	60	0	.610	4	**55**	22	**1027**	804	6322	**1665**	**287**	61	161	719	582	62	25	**.302**	**.385**	**.464**	**849**	112	**189**	101	110	32	17	**65**	**1**
CLE	92	62	1	.597	6	49	28	806	**654**	6080	1417	222	46	**164**	693	624	86	**38**	.269	.358	.422	780	109	40	68	97	40	34	54	-3
WAS	67	87	1	.435	31	35	42	690	813	6028	1365	190	53	76	671	606	74	32	.260	.347	.360	707	91	-96	-62	95	42	25	63	0
CHI	60	94	2	.390	38	35	42	625	749	5945	1368	172	47	93	551	566	106	28	.260	.333	.364	697	86	-131	-113	97	19	22	46	-4
STL	58	96	0	.377	40	27	47	684	916	5970	1269	235	43	106	690	744	97	20	.246	.337	.370	707	84	-101	-125	104	39	40	49	-5
PHI	52	102	0	.338	46	29	48	670	913	5993	1361	204	53	100	685	493	73	23	.261	.349	.378	727	94	-58	-44	98	42	25	63	0
TOT	620					333	283	6253		48734	11474	1829	423	973	5418	4558	216	693	.271	.356	.402	759					278	231	55	-20

TEAM	CG	SHO	GR	SV	IP	H	HR	BB	SO	BR/9	ERA	AERA	OAV	OOB	PR	APR	PF	OSB	OCS	FA	E	WPB	DP	FW	PW	BW	BSW	DIF
NY	66	**12**	141	**31**	1372.2	1322	118	708	**712**	13.5	4.15	103	.255	.348	65	23	94	26	29	.980	119	**27**	188	1.3	2.2	**11.0**	.1	6.4
DET	**72**	9	153	20	1407.1	1444	141	**553**	576	13.0	4.12	114	.267	.339	71	86	102	26	26	**.981**	120	33	194	1.3	8.1	3.6	-.6	5.7
BOS	66	6	183	28	1362.1	1413	121	748	630	14.4	4.88	100	.270	.364	-46	2	107	31	22	**.981**	**111**	38	181	**1.7**	.2	9.5	**.3**	5.4
CLE	69	11	184	16	1378.2	**1289**	120	647	674	**12.8**	**3.75**	**115**	**.248**	**.333**	**126**	**94**	95	**24**	36	.978	129	29	160	.7	**8.8**	6.4	-.0	-.8
WAS	59	7	156	18	1364.2	1479	**99**	648	486	14.2	4.66	96	.278	.359	-12	-25	98	49	29	.972	167	37	181	-1.4	-2.3	-5.8	.2	-.7
CHI	62	7	182	9	1365.2	1370	107	734	566	14.0	4.41	102	.263	.356	26	12	98	49	32	.977	140	36	181	.2	1.1	-10.6	-.1	-7.6
STL	56	7	**188**	14	1365.1	1629	129	651	448	15.2	5.20	95	.295	.372	-94	-35	108	36	**38**	.967	196	37	155	-3.1	-3.3	-11.7	-.2	-.7
PHI	50	3	153	18	1346.1	1528	138	729	466	15.3	5.49	83	.287	.376	-136	-141	99	37	19	.974	155	49	**208**	-.8	-13.2	-4.1	.2	-7.1
TOT	500	62	1340	154	10963.0					14.0	4.58		.271	.356						.976	1137	286	1448					

Batter-Fielder Wins	Batting Average	On-Base Percentage	Slugging Average	On-Base Plus Slugging	Adjusted OPS	Adjusted Batter Runs
Rizzuto-NY 4.0	Goodman-Bos .354	Doby-Cle .442	DiMaggio-NY .585	Doby-Cle .986	Doby-Cle 156	Doby-Cle 46.9
Rosen-Cle 4.0	Kell-Det .340	Yost-Was .440	Dropo-Bos .583	DiMaggio-NY .979	DiMaggio-NY 152	DiMaggio-NY 39.5
Berra-NY 3.8	DiMaggio-Bos .328	Pesky-Bos .437	Evers-Det .551	Dropo-Bos .961	Rosen-Cle 146	Rosen-Cle 39.2
Doby-Cle 3.2	Doby-Cle .326	Fain-Phi .430	Doby-Cle .545	Evers-Det .959	Evers-Det 139	Williams-Bos 34.1
Priddy-Det 3.0	Zarilla-Bos .325	Goodman-Bos .427	Rosen-Cle .543	Rosen-Cle .948	Berra-NY 136	Yost-Was 31.7

Runs	Hits	Doubles	Triples	Home Runs	Total Bases	Runs Batted In
DiMaggio-Bos 131	Kell-Det 218	Kell-Det 56	Evers-Det 11	Rosen-Cle 37	Dropo-Bos 326	Stephens-Bos 144
Stephens-Bos 125	Rizzuto-NY 200	Wertz-Det 37	Doerr-Bos 11	Dropo-Bos 34	Stephens-Bos 321	Dropo-Bos 144
Rizzuto-NY 125	DiMaggio-Bos 193	Rizzuto-NY 36	DiMaggio-Bos 11	DiMaggio-NY 32	Berra-NY 318	Berra-NY 124
Berra-NY 116	Berra-NY 192	Evers-Det 35		Stephens-Bos 30	Kell-Det 310	Wertz-Det 123
	Stephens-Bos 185	Stephens-Bos 34		Zernial-Chi 29	DiMaggio-NY 307	DiMaggio-NY 122

Stolen Bases	Base Stealing Runs	Fielding Runs-Infield	Fielding Runs-Outfield	Wins	Winning Pct.	Complete Games
DiMaggio-Bos 15	DiMaggio-Bos 1.9	Priddy-Det 27.9	Woodling-NY 12.4	B.Lemon-Cle 23	Raschi-NY .724	B.Lemon-Cle 22
Valo-Phi 12	Vernon-Cle-Was 1.4	Pesky-Bos 16.4	Noren-Was 9.2	Raschi-NY 21	Wynn-Cle .692	Garver-StL 22
Rizzuto-NY 12	Collins-NY 1.1	Carrasquel-Chi 10.7	Sievers-StL 7.3	Houtteman-Det 19	Lopat-NY .692	Parnell-Bos 21
Coan-Was 10	Avila-Cle 1.1	Fain-Phi 10.7	Chapman-Phi 5.2		Hutchinson-Det .680	Houtteman-Det 21
Lipon-Det 9	Jensen-NY .9	Doerr-Bos 9.4	Philley-Chi 4.6		B.Lemon-Cle .676	

Strikeouts	Fewest BB/Game	Games	Saves	Base Runners/9	Adjusted Relief Runs	Relief Ranking
B.Lemon-Cle 170	Hutchinson-Det 1.86	Harris-Was 53	Harris-Was 15	Gromek-Cle 10.56	Judson-Chi 7.8	Ferrick-StL-NY 10.6
Reynolds-NY 160	Lopat-NY 2.48	Kinder-Bos 48	Page-NY 13	Ford-NY 11.33	Aloma-Chi 5.7	Aloma-Chi 5.8
Raschi-NY 155	Overmire-StL 2.52	Ferrick-StL-NY 46	Ferrick-StL-NY 11	Ferrick-StL-NY 11.38	Ferrick-StL-NY 5.3	Flores-Cle 5.0
Wynn-Cle 143	Trout-Det 3.12	Judson-Chi 46	Kinder-Bos 9	Wynn-Cle 11.41	Flores-Cle 4.2	Benton-Cle 4.0
Feller-Cle 119	Houtteman-Det 3.24	Brissie-Phi 46	Brissie-Phi 8	Ostrowski-StL-NY 11.50	Benton-Cle 4.0	Judson-Chi 3.9

Innings Pitched	Opponents' Avg.	Opponents' OBP	Earned Run Average	Adjusted ERA	Adjusted Starter Runs	Pitcher Wins
B.Lemon-Cle 288.0	Wynn-Cle .212	Wynn-Cle .305	Wynn-Cle 3.20	Garver-StL 146	Garver-StL 39.1	**Garver-StL** 4.9
Houtteman-Det 274.2	Pierce-Chi .228	Lopat-NY .317	Garver-StL 3.39	Parnell-Bos 136	Houtteman-Det 37.5	**Wynn-Cle** 3.7
Garver-StL 260.0	Reynolds-NY .242	Houtteman-Det .322	Feller-Cle 3.43	Wynn-Cle 135	Parnell-Bos 30.1	**Houtteman-Det** 3.7
Raschi-NY 256.2	Raschi-NY .243	Feller-Cle .325	Lopat-NY 3.47	Houtteman-Det 132	Wynn-Cle 27.6	**B.Lemon-Cle** 3.4
Parnell-Bos 249.0	Cain-Chi .244	Raschi-NY .327	Houtteman-Det 3.54	Feller-Cle 126	Feller-Cle 27.2	**Parnell-Bos** 3.1

Casey, Part II

A four-way race rolled into September with the clubs holding the exact positions in which they finished: New York, Detroit, Boston, and Cleveland. First, the seventh-place Browns knocked out the Indians, who then damaged the Red Sox and Tigers as the Yankees turned on the juice in the last week. While Yogi Berra and Joe DiMaggio enjoyed spectacular seasons for New York, shortstop Phil Rizzuto's surprise performance garnered him the MVP trophy.

Detroit used control pitching and on-base ability to finish just 3 games back. Cleveland led the league in ERA and homers, but Joe Gordon and Jim Hegan hit .235 and .219 in a league that batted .271.

The third-place Red Sox trampled their opponents at home, but were barely .500 on the road. Their offense scored a staggering 1,027 runs overall, by far highest in the AL, but ranked just fourth in scoring away from home. Mostly because Boston scored a ridiculous 8.16 runs per game at Fenway, league runs per contest jumped to 5.04, the most between 1939 and 1994. Homers also increased 27 percent to 973, another new record.

Whitey Ford successfully debuted for the Yankees while Tommy Henrich retired. Veteran middle infielders Gordon and Luke Appling also called it quits, and Philadelphia manager Connie Mack stepped down at age 87; he had managed the Athletics for half a century.

Many AL teams were slow to sign blacks, and for several years the Junior Circuit developed few impressive youngsters. The top rookie of 1950 was 27-year-old first baseman Walt Dropo.

The Yankees got a tougher bargain than they counted on in the World Series against the Phillies, but swept anyway. The first three games were one-run affairs, and in Game 4 Ford led, 5–0, in the ninth until Philly scored twice. Allie Reynolds, the Game 2 winner, came in to save the day. New York held Philadelphia to just 5 runs overall.

1951 National League

TEAM	W	L	T	PCT	GB	HW	HL	R	OR	PA	H	2B	3B	HR	BB	SO	HB	SH	AVG	OBP	SLG	OPS	AOPS	BR	ABR	PF	SB	CS	BSA	BSR
NY	98	59	0	.624		**50**	28	781	**641**	6153	1396	201	53	179	**671**	624	82	40	.260	.347	.418	765	111	92	86	101	55	34	62	0
BRO	97	60	1	.618	1	49	29	**855**	672	6214	**1511**	**249**	37	**184**	603	649	75	**44**	**.275**	**.352**	**.434**	**786**	**116**	**134**	**117**	102	**89**	70	56	-5
STL	81	73	1	.526	15.5	44	34	683	671	6003	1404	230	**57**	95	569	**492**	**86**	31	.264	.339	.382	721	99	8	4	101	30	30	50	-4
BOS	76	78	1	.494	20.5	42	35	723	662	5968	1385	234	37	130	565	617	79	31	.262	.336	.394	730	111	22	76	93	80	34	**70**	**6**
PHI	73	81	0	.474	23.5	38	39	648	644	5961	1384	199	47	108	505	525	103	21	.260	.326	.375	701	96	-41	-31	99	63	28	69	4
CIN	68	86	1	.442	28.5	35	42	559	667	5775	1309	215	33	88	415	577	64	11	.248	.304	.351	655	81	-137	-145	102	44	40	52	-4
PIT	64	90	1	.416	32.5	32	45	689	845	5973	1372	218	56	137	557	615	76	22	.258	.331	.397	728	99	11	-9	103	29	27	52	-3
CHI	62	92	1	.403	34.5	32	45	614	750	5862	1327	200	47	103	477	647	56	22	.250	.315	.364	679	86	-89	-99	102	63	30	68	3
TOT	622					322	297	5552		47909	11088	1746	367	1024	4362	4746	222	621	.260	.331	.390	721					453	293	61	-3

TEAM	CG	SHO	GR	SV	IP	H	HR	BB	SO	BR/9	ERA	AERA	OAV	OOB	PR	APR	PF	OSB	OCS	FA	E	WPB	DP	FW	PW	BW	BSW	DIF
NY	64	9	189	18	1412.2	**1334**	148	**482**	625	**11.7**	**3.48**	**113**	**.248**	**.313**	**75**	**69**	99	41	40	.972	171	35	175	-1.0	**6.9**	8.6	.0	5.0
BRO	64	10	179	13	1423.1	1360	150	549	**693**	12.2	3.88	101	.253	.326	13	8	99	**21**	36	.979	129	39	**192**	**1.3**	.8	**11.7**	-.5	5.2
STL	58	9	183	**23**	1387.2	1391	119	568	546	12.8	3.95	100	.264	.338	1	2	100	49	30	**.980**	**125**	**26**	187	**1.3**	.2	.4	-.4	2.4
BOS	**73**	16	164	12	1389.0	1378	**96**	595	604	13.0	3.75	98	.259	.337	33	-12	93	67	**47**	.976	145	44	157	.3	-1.2	7.6	**.6**	-8.3
PHI	57	**19**	179	15	1384.2	1373	110	497	570	12.3	3.81	101	.258	.324	23	6	97	50	30	.977	138	46	146	.6	.6	-3.1	.4	-2.5
CIN	55	14	204	**23**	1390.2	1357	119	490	584	12.2	3.70	110	.255	.323	40	56	103	75	29	.977	140	48	141	.5	5.6	-14.5	-.4	-.2
PIT	40	9	**226**	22	1380.1	1479	157	609	580	13.8	4.79	88	.274	.350	-128	-82	107	58	36	.972	170	36	178	-1.1	-8.2	-.9	-.3	-2.5
CHI	48	10	185	10	1385.2	1416	125	572	544	13.1	4.34	94	.265	.340	-58	-36	103	92	45	.971	181	60	161	-1.7	-3.6	-9.9	.3	-.1
TOT	459	96	1509	136	11154.0					12.6	3.96		.260	.331						.975	1199	334	1337					

Batter-Fielder Wins	Batting Average	On-Base Percentage	Slugging Average	On-Base Plus Slugging	Adjusted OPS	Adjusted Batter Runs
Robinson-Bro......7.3	Musial-StL 355	Kiner-Pit.......................452	Kiner-Pit 627	Kiner-Pit.............1079	Musial-StL 182	Musial-StL 70.1
Musial-StL 6.1	Ashburn-Phi 344	Musial-StL 449	Musial-StL 614	Musial-StL 1063	Kiner-Pit................182	Kiner-Pit.............68.7
Campanella-Bro 5.9	Robinson-Bro 338	Robinson-Bro..............429	Campanella-Bro ...590	Campanella-Bro ..983	Campanella-Bro ..158	Robinson-Bro 44.7
Kiner-Pit 5.0	Campanella-Bro ...325	Irvin-NY 415	Thomson-NY 562	Robinson-Bro........957	Robinson-Bro.........153	Campanella-Bro 40.8
Ashburn-Phi 4,2	Irvin-NY 312	Stanky-NY 401	Hodges-Bro 527	Thomson-NY 947	Thomson-NY 150	Irvin-NY 39.9

Runs	Hits	Doubles	Triples	Home Runs	Total Bases	Runs Batted In
Musial-StL 124	Ashburn-Phi..........221	Dark-NY 41	Musial-StL 12	Kiner-Pit..................42	Musial-StL 355	Irvin-NY 121
Kiner-Pit................124	Musial-StL 205	Kluszewski-Cin 35	Bell-Pit 12	Hodges-Bro 40	Kiner-Pit................333	Kiner-Pit 109
Hodges-Bro 118	Furillo-Bro 197	Robinson-Bro 33	Irvin-NY 11	Campanella-Bro 33	Hodges-Bro 307	Gordon-Bos 109
Dark-NY................114	Dark-NY................196	Campanella-Bro 33	Jethroe-Bos 10	Thomson-NY 32	Campanella-Bro ..298	Musial-StL 108
Robinson-Bro........106	Robinson-Bro........185		Baumholtz-Chi 10	Musial-StL 32		Campanella-Bro ..108

Stolen Bases	Base Stealing Runs	Fielding Runs-Infield	Fielding Runs-Outfield	Wins	Winning Pct.	Complete Games
Jethroe-Bos 35	Jethroe-Bos 5.9	Robinson-Bro.............19.1	Ashburn-Phi 21.4	Maglie-NY 23	Roe-Bro 880	Spahn-Bos 26
Ashburn-Phi............29	Ashburn-Phi 4.3	Schoendienst-StL 16.8	Furillo-Bro............12.4	Jansen-NY..............23	Maglie-NY.............793	Roberts-Phi 22
Robinson-Bro...........25	Robinson-Bro 2.7	Hemus-StL..................12.1	Sauer-Chi 8.4	Spahn-Bos..............22	Newcombe-Bro.....690	Maglie-NY 22
Torgeson-Bos 20	Jackson-Chi 2.0	Johnson-StL.................9.6	Merriman-Cin 6.0	Roe-Bro 22	Jansen-NY 676	Roe-Bro 19
Reese-Bro 20	Irvin-NY 1.9	Strickland-Pit 8.6	Musial-StL 5.2	Roberts-Phi 21	Hearn-NY 654	Dickson-Pit............19

Strikeouts	Fewest BB/Game	Games	Saves	Base Runners/9	Adjusted Relief Runs	Relief Ranking
Spahn-Bos............164	Raffensberger-Cin ..1.38	Wilks-StL-Pit 65	Wilks-StL-Pit 13	Labine-Bro 9.92	Wilks-StL-Pit........13.8	Leonard-Chi 21.0
Newcombe-Bro 164	Jansen-NY 1.81	Werle-Pit 59	Smith-Cin................11	Raffensberger-Cin ..9.99	Brazle-StL.............13.8	Wilks-StL-Pit 13.9
Maglie-NY 146	Roberts-Phi 1.83	Konstanty-Phi 58	Konstanty-Phi 9	Roberts-Phi 10.03	Perkowski-Cin......11.9	Brazle-StL 10.2
Jansen-NY............145	Roe-Bro 2.24	Spencer-NY 57	Brazle-StL 7	Jansen-NY 10.11	Leonard-Chi 11.4	Smith-Cin 10.0
Rush-Chi 129	Sain-Bos..............2.53	Brazle-StL......................56		Maglie-NY..........10.45	Kennedy-NY 10.6	Perkowski-Cin 9.7

Innings Pitched	Opponents' Avg.	Opponents' OBP	Earned Run Average	Adjusted ERA	Adjusted Starter Runs	Pitcher Wins
Roberts-Phi 315.0	Maglie-NY.............230	Roberts-Phi 278	Nichols-Bos 2.88	Maglie-NY 134	Maglie-NY............34.7	**Roberts-Phi**........3.8
Spahn-Bos 310.2	Newcombe-Bro.......230	Jansen-NY...................279	Maglie-NY............2.93	Roe-Bro 129	Jansen-NY 31.1	**Spahn-Bos** 3.6
Maglie-NY..........298.0	Blackwell-Cin 233	Raffensberger-Cin 279	Spahn-Bos 2.98	Jansen-NY.............129	Roberts-Phi 30.2	**Jansen-NY**..........3.2
Dickson-Pit........288.2	Queen-Pit 233	Maglie-NY 289	Roberts-Phi 3.03	Nichols-Bos 127	Spahn-Bos 29.0	**Maglie-NY** 3.0
Jansen-NY 278.2	Branca-Bro 237	Newcombe-Bro 297	Jansen-NY 3.04	Roberts-Phi 127	Roe-Bro 27.6	**Blackwell-Cin**....2.5

Thomson's Blast Caps the Greatest Rally

The 1951 race looked like a cakewalk for Brooklyn; on August 12 the Dodgers led the slumping Giants by 13_ as Roy Campanella, Don Newcombe, Gil Hodges, Jackie Robinson, and Duke Snider were enjoying great seasons. At that point, however, the Giants, sparked by eventual Rookie of the Year Willie Mays and RBI champ Monte Irvin, won 16 straight to cut the lead to 5 games by Labor Day. Giants pitchers Larry Jansen and Sal Maglie were nearly unbeatable down the stretch.

On closing day, with both teams tied, New York won and Brooklyn managed a dramatic 14-inning victory at Philadelphia to force a best-of-three playoff. The teams split the first two, but the Dodgers jumped out in the third game and led, 4–1, in the last of the ninth. The Giants, though, rallied off Newcombe; with two on, two out, and the Giants up by two, Ralph Branca came in to face Bobby Thomson, who unloaded a three-run blast into the left field seats.

This, the first baseball game televised coast-to-coast, acquired a mythical quality over the years. Even in defeat, the Dodgers were honored; Campanella was voted MVP. What 1950s chauvinists don't admit is that fan interest sagged even during this great race; NL attendance dropped 13 percent. Boston's attendance fell by nearly half as rumors had the club moving to Milwaukee.

Commissioner Happy Chandler was forced out after trying to keep owners from signing high school players; Ford Frick, NL president, took the job and promised to keep out of the way. Warren Giles was voted the NL's new prexy.

Even though the charging Giants won two of the first three, the Yankees won the World Series in six. Bronx bats hammered Jansen and Maglie mercilessly. Irvin and Alvin Dark both batted over .400, but no other Giants regular even surpassed .240

1951 American League

TEAM	W	L	T	PCT	GB	HW	HL	R	OR	PA	H	2B	3B	HR	BB	SO	HB	SH	AVG	OBP	SLG	OPS	AOPS	BR	ABR	PF	SB	CS	BSA	BSR
NY	98	56	0	.636		**56**	22	798	621	5927	1395	208	48	**140**	605	547	91	37	.269	.349	**.408**	**757**	**113**	61	**90**	96	78	39	**67**	**4**
CLE	93	61	1	.604	5	53	24	696	**594**	5946	1346	208	35	**140**	606	632	63	27	.256	.336	.389	725	106	-1	41	94	52	35	60	-1
BOS	87	67	0	.565	11	50	25	**804**	725	6211	1428	**233**	32	127	**756**	594	59	18	.266	**.358**	.392	750	98	**67**	-4	110	20	21	49	-3
CHI	81	73	1	.526	17	39	38	714	644	6128	**1453**	229	**64**	86	596	**524**	**103**	**51**	**.270**	.349	.385	734	105	22	38	98	**99**	70	59	-3
DET	73	81	0	.474	25	36	41	685	741	6008	1413	231	35	104	568	525	86	18	.265	.338	.380	718	99	-15	-18	100	37	34	52	-4
PHI	70	84	0	.455	28	38	41	736	745	6049	1381	262	43	102	677	565	61	34	.262	.349	.386	735	101	33	18	102	47	36	57	-2
WAS	62	92	0	.403	36	32	44	672	764	5979	1399	242	45	54	560	515	64	26	.263	.336	.355	691	93	-60	-48	98	45	38	54	-3
STL	52	102	0	.338	46	24	53	611	882	5848	1288	223	47	86	521	693	92	16	.247	.317	.357	674	84	-105	-122	103	35	38	48	-6
TOT	617					328	288	5716		48096	11103	1836	349	839	4889	4595	227	619	.262	.342	.381	723					413	311	57	-18

TEAM	CG	SHO	GR	SV	IP	H	HR	BB	SO	BR/9	ERA	AERA	OAV	OOB	PR	APR	PF	OSB	OCS	FA	E	WPB	DP	FW	PW	BW	BSW	DIF
NY	66	**24**	158	22	1367.0	1290	92	562	**664**	12.4	3.56	107	.250	.328	85	44	93	41	47	.975	144	28	190	.3	4.3	**8.9**	**.6**	6.9
CLE	**76**	10	135	19	1391.1	**1287**	**85**	577	642	**12.2**	**3.38**	112	**.245**	**.323**	**114**	68	92	54	36	**.978**	**134**	29	151	**.9**	6.7	4.0	.1	4.2
BOS	46	7	**210**	**24**	1399.0	1413	99	599	658	13.2	4.14	108	.264	.342	-2	46	108	47	27	.977	141	37	184	.5	4.5	-.4	-.0	5.5
CHI	74	11	150	14	1418.1	1353	109	**549**	572	**12.2**	3.50	**115**	.252	**.323**	97	**86**	98	57	25	.975	151	25	176	.0	**8.5**	3.7	-.0	-8.1
DET	51	8	195	17	1384.0	1385	103	602	597	13.2	4.29	97	.262	.342	-26	-18	101	71	43	.973	163	53	166	-.7	-1.8	-1.8	-.2	.4
PHI	52	7	157	22	1358.0	1421	109	569	437	13.4	4.47	96	.272	.347	-52	-27	104	**34**	46	**.978**	136	42	**204**	.8	-2.7	1.8	.0	-6.9
WAS	58	6	160	13	1366.1	1429	110	630	475	13.7	4.49	91	.269	.348	-55	-59	99	52	36	.973	160	**23**	148	-.5	-5.8	-4.7	-.0	-3.9
STL	56	5	180	9	1370.1	1525	132	801	550	15.5	5.18	85	.282	.379	-160	-112	107	58	**51**	.971	172	41	179	-1.2	-11.0	-12.0	-.4	-.4
TOT	479	78	1345	140	11054.1					13.2	4.12		.262	.342						.975	1201	278	1398					

Batter-Fielder Wins	Batting Average	On-Base Percentage	Slugging Average	On-Base Plus Slugging	Adjusted OPS	Adjusted Batter Runs
Fain-Phi 4.3	Fain-Phi .344	Williams-Bos .464	Williams-Bos .556	Williams-Bos 1019	Doby-Cle 163	Williams-Bos 52.1
Joost-Phi 4.3	Minoso-Cle-Chi .326	Fain-Phi .451	Doby-Cle .512	Doby-Cle 941	Williams-Bos 159	Doby-Cle 44.7
Williams-Bos 4.1	Kell-Det .319	Doby-Cle .428	Zernial-Chi-Phi .511	Minoso-Cle-Chi 922	Minoso-Cle-Chi 152	Minoso-Cle-Chi 41.5
Doby-Cle 3.8	Williams-Bos .318	Yost-Was .423	Wertz-Det .511	Fain-Phi 921	Fain-Phi 146	Yost-Was 34.5
Berra-NY 3.5	Fox-Chi .313	Minoso-Cle-Chi .422	Minoso-Cle-Chi .500	Wertz-Det 894	Wertz-Det 140	Fain-Phi 33.4

Runs	Hits	Doubles	Triples	Home Runs	Total Bases	Runs Batted In
DiMaggio-Bos 113	Kell-Det 191	Yost-Was 36	Minoso-Cle-Chi 14	Zernial-Chi-Phi 33	Williams-Bos 295	Zernial-Chi-Phi 129
Minoso-Cle-Chi 112	Fox-Chi 189	Mele-Was 36	Coleman-StL-Chi 12	Williams-Bos 30	Zernial-Chi-Phi 292	Williams-Bos 126
Yost-Was 109	DiMaggio-Bos 189	Kell-Det 36	Fox-Chi 12	Robinson-Chi 29	Robinson-Chi 279	Robinson-Chi 117
Williams-Bos 109	Minoso-Cle-Chi 173		Young-StL 9		Berra-NY 269	Easter-Cle 103
Joost-Phi 107	Williams-Bos 169				DiMaggio-Bos 267	Rosen-Cle 102

Stolen Bases	Base Stealing Runs	Fielding Runs-Infield	Fielding Runs-Outfield	Wins	Winning Pct.	Complete Games
Minoso-Cle-Chi 31	Minoso-Cle-Chi 3.3	Fain-Phi 16.2	Coan-Was 18.4	Feller-Cle 22	Feller-Cle .733	Garver-StL 24
Busby-Chi 26	Rizzuto-NY 2.9	Stephens-Bos 11.8	Noren-Was 12.3	Raschi-NY 21	Lopat-NY .700	Wynn-Cle 21
Rizzuto-NY 18	Busby-Chi 1.9	Carrasquel-Chi 11.6	Zernial-Chi-Phi 8.5	Lopat-NY 21	Reynolds-NY .680	Lopat-NY 20
	Carrasquel-Chi 1.7	Priddy-Det 11.3	Delsing-StL 7.7		Raschi-NY .677	Pierce-Chi 18
	McDougald-NY 1.3	Rizzuto-NY 11.2	Busby-Chi 6.7		Shantz-Phi .643	

Strikeouts	Fewest BB/Game	Games	Saves	Base Runners/9	Adjusted Relief Runs	Relief Ranking
Raschi-NY 164	Hutchinson-Det 1.29	Kinder-Bos 63	Kinder-Bos 14	Aloma-Chi 10.13	Kinder-Bos 24.3	Kinder-Bos 28.4
Wynn-Cle 133	Lopat-NY 2.72	Brissie-Phi-Cle 56	Scheib-Phi 10	Zoldak-Phi 10.62	Aloma-Chi 18.5	Aloma-Chi 16.2
Lemon-Cle 132	Pierce-Chi 2.73	Garcia-Cle 47	Brissie-Phi-Cle 9	Lopat-NY 10.85	Masterson-Bos 7.2	Brissie-Phi-Cle 4.2
Gray-Det 131	Hooper-Phi 2.90	Scheib-Phi 46	Reynolds-NY 7	Kinder-Bos 10.91	Brissie-Phi-Cle 5.2	Masterson-Bos 3.8
McDermott-Bos 127	Garcia-Cle 2.91		Garcia-Cle 6	Rogovin-Det-Chi 10.97	Ostrowski-NY 3.1	Ostrowski-NY 3.3

Innings Pitched	Opponents' Avg.	Opponents' OBP	Earned Run Average	Adjusted ERA	Adjusted Starter Runs	Pitcher Wins
Wynn-Cle 274.1	Reynolds-NY .213	Lopat-NY .298	Rogovin-Det-Chi 2.78	Rogovin-Det-Chi 146	Rogovin-Det-Chi 29.7	**Parnell-Bos** 3.3
Lemon-Cle 263.1	Wynn-Cle .225	Rogovin-Det-Chi .301	Lopat-NY 2.91	Parnell-Bos 137	Pierce-Chi 28.0	**Lopat-NY** 3.3
Raschi-NY 258.1	McDermott-Bos .226	Wynn-Cle .301	Wynn-Cle 3.02	McDermott-Bos 133	Wynn-Cle 26.7	**Pierce-Chi** 3.1
Garcia-Cle 254.0	Rogovin-Det-Chi .235	Hutchinson-Det .302	Pierce-Chi 3.03	Pierce-Chi 133	Lopat-NY 26.2	**Wynn-Cle** 3.1
Feller-Cle 249.2	Lopat-NY .239	Reynolds-NY .304	Reynolds-NY 3.05	Lopat-NY 131	Parnell-Bos 23.7	**Garver-StL** 2.9

Goodbye and Hello

Perennial doormat Chicago jumped out in front and led the league during June. Outfielder Minnie Minoso helped manager Paul Richards turn the White Sox around. Chicago faded while the Yankees, Red Sox, and Indians took over. Cleveland and New York stayed neck-and-neck, with Boston close behind. On September 15–16, with the Indians up one game, New York took two from the Tribe at Yankee Stadium, starting Cleveland on a fatal slide.

Despite losing Whitey Ford to military service, New York pitchers led in shutouts and strikeouts, and catcher Yogi Berra was MVP. Casey Stengel continued his successful platoon system, supplementing what appeared to be an unprepossessing lineup. Bob Feller, Mike Garcia, and Early Wynn each won 20 for Cleveland, but three offensive dead spots negated Larry Doby and Al Rosen's hitting. Despite their big bats—Vern Stephens, Ted Williams, and Bobby Doerr (whose career was ended by knee problems)—the Red Sox didn't hit enough.

Bill Veeck, now owner of the St. Louis Browns, had to get creative to draw fans to his poor team. On August 19 he sent three-foot , seven-inch Eddie Gaedel to the plate as a pinch hitter. Five days later fans voted on in-game decisions with placards. The Browns drew 16 percent more fans than in 1950, but the club finished last both on the field and in attendance.

The Yankees took six games to win a defensive-oriented World Series from the Giants. The heroes were Eddie Lopat, who allowed 1 run in 18 innings, and four relievers who tossed 7.2 scoreless innings. Bob Kuzava saved decisive Game 6 for Vic Raschi.

After hitting .261 in the Series, 36-year-old Joe DiMaggio retired; injuries rendered him unable to play to his own standards. The Yankees had already broken in his successor, Mickey Mantle.

Hy Turkin and S.C. Thompson's *Official Encyclopedia of Baseball*, the first modern baseball reference, was published. In December "Shoeless" Joe Jackson, 62, became the first of the Black Sox to die.

1952 National League

TEAM	W	L	T	PCT	GB	HW	HL	R	OR	PA	H	2B	3B	HR	BB	SO	HB	SH	AVG	OBP	SLG	OPS	AOPS	BR	ABR	PF	SB	CS	BSA	BSR
BRO	96	57	2	.627		45	33	**775**	603	6068	1380	199	32	**153**	**663**	699	104	35	.262	**.348**	**.399**	**747**	**113**	**111**	**103**	101	**90**	49	**65**	**3**
NY	92	62	0	.597	4.5	**50**	27	722	639	5891	1337	186	**56**	151	536	672	88	38	.256	.329	**.399**	728	107	54	49	101	30	31	49	-4
STL	88	66	0	.571	8.5	48	29	677	630	5845	1386	**247**	54	97	537	**479**	65	**43**	**.267**	.340	.391	731	110	71	70	100	33	32	51	-4
PHI	87	67	0	.565	9.5	47	29	657	**552**	5875	1353	237	45	93	540	534	**107**	23	.260	.332	.376	708	104	28	35	99	60	41	59	-1
CHI	77	77	1	.500	19.5	42	35	628	631	5836	**1408**	223	45	107	422	712	63	21	.264	.321	.383	704	101	4	-4	101	50	40	56	-3
CIN	69	85	0	.448	27.5	38	39	615	659	5785	1303	212	45	104	480	709	53	18	.249	.314	.366	680	95	-37	-35	100	32	42	43	-8
BOS	64	89	2	.418	32	31	45	569	651	5828	1214	187	31	110	483	711	92	32	.233	.301	.343	644	88	-104	-85	97	58	34	63	1
PIT	42	112	1	.273	54.5	23	54	515	793	5775	1201	181	30	92	486	724	70	26	.231	.300	.331	631	79	-127	-140	103	43	41	51	-5
TOT	618					324	291	5158		46903	10582	1672	338	907	4147	5240	236	642	.253	.323	.374	697					396	310	56	-21

TEAM	CG	SHO	GR	SV	IP	H	HR	BB	SO	BR/9	ERA	AERA	OAV	OOB	PR	APR	PF	OSB	OCS	FA	E	WPB	DP	FW	PW	BW	BSW	DIF
BRO	45	11	196	24	1399.1	1295	121	544	**773**	12.0	3.53	103	.247	.321	31	17	98	29	38	**.982**	**106**	37	169	**2.0**	1.8	**10.6**	**.6**	4.5
NY	49	12	**226**	**31**	1371.0	1282	121	538	655	12.2	3.59	103	.248	.323	22	17	99	**28**	40	.974	158	37	**175**	-.8	1.8	5.1	-.1	9.1
STL	49	12	208	27	1361.1	1274	119	501	712	11.9	3.66	101	.247	.317	11	8	100	36	36	.977	141	31	159	.1	.8	7.2	-.1	3.0
PHI	**80**	**17**	142	16	1386.2	1306	**96**	**373**	609	**11.0**	**3.07**	**119**	.249	**.301**	**102**	**92**	98	50	34	.975	150	**17**	145	-.4	**9.5**	3.6	.2	-2.9
CHI	59	15	168	15	1386.1	**1265**	101	534	661	11.9	3.58	107	**.240**	.314	23	40	103	83	30	.976	146	65	123	-.1	4.1	-.4	-.0	-3.6
CIN	56	11	173	12	1363.1	1377	111	517	579	12.8	4.01	94	.267	.338	-43	-36	101	56	41	**.982**	107	24	145	1.9	-3.7	-3.6	-.6	-2.0
BOS	63	11	175	13	1396.0	1388	106	525	687	12.5	3.78	96	.259	.329	-7	-27	97	51	42	.975	154	45	143	-.5	-2.8	-8.8	.4	-.8
PIT	43	5	204	8	1363.2	1395	132	615	564	13.4	4.65	86	.265	.345	-139	-92	107	63	**49**	.970	182	34	167	-2.0	-9.5	-14.5	-.2	-8.8
TOT	444	94	1492	146	11027.2					12.2	3.73		.253	.323						.976	1144	290	1226					

Batter-Fielder Wins	Batting Average	On-Base Percentage	Slugging Average	On-Base Plus Slugging	Adjusted OPS	Adjusted Batter Runs
Robinson-Bro......5.7	Musial-StL 336	Robinson-Bro..............440	Musial-StL 538	Musial-StL 970	Musial-StL 167	Musial-StL 57.7
Schoendienst-StL 5.4	Baumholtz-Chi 325	Musial-StL 432	Sauer-Chi 531	Robinson-Bro........904	Robinson-Bro........149	Robinson-Bro 41.9
Musial-StL 4.2	Kluszewski-Cin 320	Hemus-StL...................392	Kluszewski-Cin 509	Kluszewski-Cin 892	Kluszewski-Cin 146	Hodges-Bro 32.9
Hemus-StL 3.9	Robinson-Bro 308	Hodges-Bro 386	Kiner-Pit 500	Sauer-Chi 892	Gordon-Bos 144	Gordon-Bos 32.6
Sauer-Chi 3.1	Snider-Bro 303	Slaughter-StL..............386	Hodges-Bro 500	Hodges-Bro..........886	Sauer-Chi 143	Sauer-Chi 32.6

Runs	Hits	Doubles	Triples	Home Runs	Total Bases	Runs Batted In
Musial-StL 105	Musial-StL 194	Musial-StL......................42	Thomson-NY 14	Sauer-Chi 37	Musial-StL 311	Sauer-Chi 121
Hemus-StL 105	Schoendienst-StL 188	Schoendienst-StL 40	Slaughter-StL..........12	Kiner-Pit..................37	Sauer-Chi 301	Thomson-NY 108
Robinson-Bro........104	Adams-Cin............180	McMillan-Cin..................32	Kluszewski-Cin 11	Hodges-Bro 32	Thomson-NY 293	Ennis-Phi 107
Lockman-NY 99	Dark-NY................177	Sauer-Chi 31	Ennis-Phi................10	Mathews-Bos..........25	Ennis-Phi 281	Hodges-Bro 102
Reese-Bro 94	Lockman-NY 176	Ashburn-Phi 31		Gordon-Bos 25	Snider-Bro 264	Slaughter-StL 101

Stolen Bases	Base Stealing Runs	Fielding Runs-Infield	Fielding Runs-Outfield	Wins	Winning Pct.	Complete Games
Reese-Bro 30	Reese-Bro 4.8	Schoendienst-StL 35.6	Sauer-Chi 10.3	Roberts-Phi 28	Wilhelm-NY 833	Roberts-Phi 30
Jethroe-Bos 28	Jethroe-Bos 3.0	Logan-Bos 12.5	Jeffcoat-Chi 10.0	Maglie-NY 18	Roberts-Phi 800	Dickson-Pit............21
Robinson-Bro..........24	Robinson-Bro 2.8	McMillan-Cin 10.3	Ashburn-Phi 7.9	Staley-StL 17	Black-Bro 789	Spahn-Bos 19
Ashburn-Phi............16	Davis-Pit 1.3	Adams-Cin....................7.0	Adcock-Cin 6.8	Rush-Chi 17	Maglie-NY.............692	Raffensberger-Cin 18
	Ryan-Phi.................1.1	Hemus-StL....................5.0	Wyrostek-Cin-Phi ..6.8	Raffensberger-Cin......17	Hacker-Chi 625	Rush-Chi 17

Strikeouts	Fewest BB/Game	Games	Saves	Base Runners/9	Adjusted Relief Runs	Relief Ranking
Spahn-Bos............183	Roberts-Phi 1.23	Wilhelm-NY....................71	Brazle-StL 16	Hacker-Chi 8.56	Black-Bro 22.9	Black-Bro............33.0
Rush-Chi 157	Hacker-Chi 1.51	Black-Bro 56	Black-Bro................15	Black-Bro 9.11	Wilhelm-NY 18.5	Wilhelm-NY 21.7
Roberts-Phi 148	Raffensberger-Cin ..1.64	Yuhas-StL 54	Wilhelm-NY 11	Miller-StL 9.31	Leonard-Chi 12.3	Brazle-StL 20.7
Mizell-StL..............146	Staley-StL 1.95	Smith-Cin 53	Leonard-Chi............11	Roberts-Phi 9.33	Brazle-StL............12.0	Yuhas-StL 15.0
Simmons-Phi 141	Drews-Phi............2.05	Main-Pit 48		Ramsdell-Chi 9.40	Yuhas-StL 10.7	Leonard-Chi 11.2

Innings Pitched	Opponents' Avg.	Opponents' OBP	Earned Run Average	Adjusted ERA	Adjusted Starter Runs	Pitcher Wins
Roberts-Phi 330.0	Hacker-Chi 212	Hacker-Chi...................247	Wilhelm-NY 2.43	Wilhelm-NY 152	Roberts-Phi 42.8	**Roberts-Phi**........4.6
Spahn-Bos 290.0	Rush-Chi...............216	Roberts-Phi 263	Hacker-Chi 2.58	Hacker-Chi............149	Hacker-Chi 27.3	**Rush-Chi** 4.0
Dickson-Pit 277.2	Wilhelm-NY 220	Rush-Chi 282	Roberts-Phi 2.59	Rush-Chi 143	Raffensberger-Cin ..25.6	**Black-Bro** 3.3
Rush-Chi............250.1	Erskine-Bro...........220	Erskine-Bro 289	Loes-Bro..............2.69	Roberts-Phi...........141	Rush-Chi..............25.5	**Hacker-Chi** 3.1
Raffensberger-Cin 247.0	Loes-Bro...............224	Spahn-Bos...................291	Rush-Chi..............2.70	Loes-Bro 135	Drews-Phi............25.0	**Drews-Phi** 2.9

Dodgers Blue Again

The Dodgers were again the class of the league early on, but this time didn't crumble down the stretch. Only for a short time in mid-September, when the Dodgers slumped and the Giants turned on the heat, was the race close.

League batting average was just .253, the lowest between 1942 and 1963, and runs per game fell to 4.17, the fewest of the decade. NL home runs dipped below 1,000 for the first time since 1950, and for the last time to date. Strikeouts rose once more. Despite this, complete games dropped to a new low, and two 28-year-old freshman relievers were the league's sensations. Despite leading the NL in appearances, ERA, and winning percentage, the Giants' Hoyt Wilhelm lost Rookie of the Year balloting to Brooklyn's Joe Black.

Philadelphia's Robin Roberts won 28, the most by a Senior Circuit hurler since 1935, while Stan Musial took his third straight batting title for the third-place Cardinals. Pittsburgh did a full swan dive into the basement, posting the league's worst record since 1935 despite Ralph Kiner's seventh straight home run crown.

League attendance fell another 12.5 percent. Boston's gate dropped another 42 percent as the club announced its move to Milwaukee—the first major league franchise relocation since 1903. The Braves added to their growing arsenal with the debut of third baseman Eddie Mathews, who tied for fourth in the league in homers.

Recently retired Arky Vaughan, one of the greatest shortstops in baseball history, drowned in a fishing accident. And outfielder Pete Reiser, robbed of a potentially great career by catastrophic injuries, played his last game.

In the fourth all-New York World Series in five years, the Dodgers led the Yankees three games to two and had the final two games in Ebbets Field, but they couldn't close the deal despite Duke Snider's .345 average, 4 homers, and 8 RBIs. Brooklyn fans were starting to wonder if next year would ever come.

1952 American League

TEAM	W	L	T	PCT	GB	HW	HL	R	OR	PA	H	2B	3B	HR	BB	SO	HB	SH	AVG	OBP	SLG	OPS	AOPS	BR	ABR	PF	SB	CS	BSA	BSR
NY	95	59	0	.617		49	28	727	**557**	5990	**1411**	221	**56**	129	566	652	94	36	**.267**	.341	.403	744	121	89	136	94	52	42	55	-3
CLE	93	61	1	.604	2	49	28	**763**	606	6060	1399	211	49	**148**	626	749	84	20	.262	.342	**.404**	**746**	**122**	**95**	**147**	94	46	39	54	-4
CHI	81	73	2	.526	14	44	33	610	568	6036	1337	199	38	80	541	**521**	**121**	**58**	.252	.327	.348	675	93	-36	-41	101	**61**	38	**62**	0
PHI	79	75	1	.513	16	45	32	664	723	5975	1305	212	35	89	**683**	561	102	27	.253	**.343**	.359	702	96	29	-11	106	52	43	55	-4
WAS	78	76	3	.506	17	42	35	598	608	6046	1282	225	44	50	580	607	79	30	.239	.317	.326	643	88	-98	-78	97	48	37	56	-2
BOS	76	78	0	.494	19	**50**	27	668	658	5885	1338	**233**	34	113	542	739	66	31	.255	.328	.377	705	96	16	-31	108	59	47	56	-3
STL	64	90	1	.416	31	42	35	604	733	6001	1340	225	46	82	540	720	86	22	.250	.322	.356	678	92	-39	-56	103	30	34	47	-5
DET	50	104	2	.325	45	32	45	557	738	5914	1278	190	37	103	553	605	80	23	.243	.318	.352	670	92	-54	-59	101	27	38	42	-7
TOT	621					353	263	5191		47907	10690	1716	339	794	4631	5154	247	712	.253	.330	.365	695					375	318	54	-29

TEAM	CG	SHO	GR	SV	IP	H	HR	BB	SO	BR/9	ERA	AERA	OAV	OOB	PR	APR	PF	OSB	OCS	FA	E	WPB	DP	FW	PW	BW	BSW	DIF
NY	72	**21**	143	27	1381.0	**1240**	94	581	666	12.1	**3.14**	106	.243	.324	**82**	31	90	49	40	.979	127	**21**	**199**	.8	3.2	14.1	.0	-.2
CLE	**80**	19	143	18	1407.0	1278	94	556	671	11.9	3.32	101	.241	**.316**	55	4	91	50	40	.975	155	34	141	-.8	.4	**15.3**	-.0	1.2
CHI	53	15	**190**	**28**	1416.2	1251	86	578	**774**	**11.7**	3.25	**112**	**.238**	**.316**	66	**63**	99	63	34	**.980**	**123**	37	158	**1.1**	**6.5**	-4.3	**.4**	.2
PHI	73	11	137	15	1384.1	1402	113	**526**	562	12.8	4.15	95	.263	.333	-74	-28	108	37	**48**	.977	140	32	148	.0	-2.9	-1.1	-.0	6.0
WAS	75	10	137	15	1429.2	1405	**78**	577	574	12.7	3.37	105	.258	.332	48	30	97	42	31	.978	132	34	152	.6	3.1	-8.1	.2	5.2
BOS	53	7	176	24	1372.1	1332	107	623	624	13.1	3.80	104	.256	.340	-20	19	107	**35**	37	.976	145	37	181	-.3	2.0	-3.2	.0	.5
STL	48	6	181	18	1399.0	1388	111	598	581	13.0	4.12	95	.260	.339	-69	-30	107	51	47	.974	155	38	176	-.8	-3.1	-5.8	-.1	-3.1
DET	51	10	182	14	1388.1	1394	111	591	702	13.0	4.25	90	.262	.338	-89	-66	104	48	41	.975	152	50	145	-.6	-6.8	-6.1	-.4	-13.1
TOT	505	99	1289	159	11178.1					12.5	3.67		.253	.330						.977	1129	283	1300					

Batter-Fielder Wins	Batting Average	On-Base Percentage	Slugging Average	On-Base Plus Slugging	Adjusted OPS	Adjusted Batter Runs
Fain-Phi..............4.5	Fain-Phi 327	Fain-Phi 438	Doby-Cle..............541	Mantle-NY 924	Doby-Cle 166	Mantle-NY 48.4
Doby-Cle.............4.4	Mitchell-Cle..........323	Valo-Phi 432	Mantle-NY 530	Doby-Cle 924	Mantle-NY 166	Rosen-Cle 47.1
Mantle-NY...........3.9	Mantle-NY 311	Mantle-NY 394	Rosen-Cle............524	Rosen-Cle 911	Rosen-Cle 162	Doby-Cle 45.8
Berra-NY.............3.5	Kell-Det-Bos 311	Joost-Phi 388	Easter-Cle............513	Wertz-Det-StL 887	Easter-Cle 144	Fain-Phi 32.5
Goodman-Bos 3.4	Woodling-NY 309	Rosen-Cle 387	Wertz-Det-StL.......506	Fain-Phi 867	Wertz-Det-StL 143	Woodling-NY 28.7

Runs	Hits	Doubles	Triples	Home Runs	Total Bases	Runs Batted In
Doby-Cle 104	Fox-Chi 192	Fain-Phi 43	Avila-Cle 11	Doby-Cle 32	Rosen-Cle 297	Rosen-Cle 105
Avila-Cle 102	Avila-Cle 179	Mantle-NY.....................37	Simpson-Cle 10	Easter-Cle 31	Mantle-NY 291	Robinson-Chi 104
Rosen-Cle 101	Robinson-Chi.........176	Vernon-Was 33	Rizzuto-NY 10	Berra-NY 30	Dropo-Bos-Det 282	Doby-Cle 104
Berra-NY 97	Fain-Phi 176	Robinson-Chi 33	Fox-Chi 10	Dropo-Bos-Det 29	Doby-Cle 281	Zernial-Phi 100
Minoso-Chi 96				Zernial-Phi..............29	Robinson-Chi........277	Berra-NY 98

Stolen Bases	Base Stealing Runs	Fielding Runs-Infield	Fielding Runs-Outfield	Wins	Winning Pct.	Complete Games
Minoso-Chi 22	Jensen-NY-Was 1.9	Goodman-Bos 23.0	Philley-Phi.............6.9	Shantz-Phi..............24	Shantz-Phi 774	Lemon-Cle 28
Rivera-StL-Chi 21	Rizzuto-NY 1.6	Rizzuto-NY 21.4	Busby-Chi-Was......6.7	Wynn-Cle................23	Raschi-NY 727	Shantz-Phi 27
Jensen-NY-Was......18	Rivera-StL-Chi 1.5	Martin-NY 18.3	Woodling-NY 5.9	Lemon-Cle..............22	Reynolds-NY 714	Reynolds-NY 24
Rizzuto-NY 17	Throneberry-Bos ..1.1	Fain-Phi 17.9	Rivera-StL-Chi 4.6	Garcia-Cle 22	Lemon-Cle 667	Wynn-Cle 19
Throneberry-Bos 16	Goodman-Bos 1.1	McDougald-NY 16.2	Jensen-NY-Was 2.3	Reynolds-NY 20	Garcia-Cle 667	Garcia-Cle 19

Strikeouts	Fewest BB/Game	Games	Saves	Base Runners/9	Adjusted Relief Runs	Relief Ranking
Reynolds-NY 160	Shantz-Phi 2.03	Kennedy-Chi.................47	Dorish-Chi 11	Shantz-Phi 9.56	Dorish-Chi 11.9	Dorish-Chi 17.3
Wynn-Cle..............153	Pillette-StL 2.41	Paige-StL......................46	Paige-StL................10	Dobson-Chi 10.05	Kennedy-Chi..........5.5	Kennedy-Chi 3.7
Shantz-Phi............152	Marrero-Was........2.59	Garcia-Cle 46	Sain-NY 7	Lemon-Cle 10.09	Littlefield-Det-SL 3.6	Consuegra-Was ..3.1
Pierce-Chi 144	Houtteman-Det 2.65	Hooper-Phi 43		Gromek-Cle 10.20	Consuegra-Was 3.5	Littlefield-Det-SL 2.9
Garcia-Cle 143	Garcia-Cle 2.68			Pierce-Chi..........10.43	Newsom-Was-Phi..1.7	Newsom-Was-Phi 2.3

Innings Pitched	Opponents' Avg.	Opponents' OBP	Earned Run Average	Adjusted ERA	Adjusted Starter Runs	Pitcher Wins
Lemon-Cle 309.2	Lemon-Cle 208	Shantz-Phi 272	Reynolds-NY 2.06	Reynolds-NY 161	Shantz-Phi 42.7	**Shantz-Phi**..........5.1
Garcia-Cle 292.1	Raschi-NY 216	Lemon-Cle 279	Garcia-Cle 2.37	Shantz-Phi............160	Reynolds-NY 35.3	**Lemon-Cle**..........4.4
Wynn-Cle 285.2	Reynolds-NY 218	Dobson-Chi 280	Shantz-Phi 2.48	Dobson-Chi 145	Garcia-Cle 33.3	**Reynolds-NY**......4.1
Shantz-Phi 279.2	Dobson-Chi 222	Pierce-Chi 289	Lemon-Cle 2.50	Pierce-Chi 142	Pierce-Chi............33.0	**Garcia-Cle**..........3.7
Pierce-Chi..........255.1	Shantz-Phi 225	Reynolds-NY 300	Dobson-Chi 2.51	Garcia-Cle 141	Lemon-Cle 30.2	**Pierce-Chi** 3.5

By the Skin of Their Teeth

The Indians spent August and September shadowing the Yankees, and both clubs were 19–5 in the final month, with the Yankees only clinching in the final weekend. However, the Tribe's mediocre play in August had already doomed them. Once again, the Indians had a trio of 20-game winners, but Bob Feller began to show signs of wear. The Yankees had the better pitching despite the military-related absence of Whitey Ford and Tom Morgan; Allie Reynolds led the AL in ERA and strikeouts. Twenty-year-old Mickey Mantle became the club's offensive lynchpin.

Cleveland again had power to spare, with Larry Doby and Luke Easter finishing 1-2 in homers. The third-place White Sox didn't hit, but had speed and a fine bullpen. Ferris Fain won his second straight batting title, and his Athletics ended a surprising fourth.

For the third straight year, the Yankees lost an outfielder as Charlie Keller retired due to back problems. Boston player-manager Lou Boudreau also hung up his glove. Runs fell for the second year in a row, decreasing to just 4.18 per game, and the top five ERA qualifiers all had better averages than 1951's ERA champ.

Bob Neighbors, who had played for the 1939 Browns, went missing in action in Korea on August 8. Neighbors was the only major league player lost to the Korean War.

In a seesaw World Series dominated by home runs, the Dodgers had a three-games-to-two lead, but the Yankees worked their magic again, taking the final two games at Ebbets Field. Vic Raschi started and won Game 6 with relief help from Reynolds, and both came in to relieve the next day. Bob Kuzava saved the deciding game for the second straight season. The Yankees hit 10 homers in the Series: Johnny Mize slugged 3, Yogi Berra and Mantle added 2 apiece. Once again, Stengel's boys had scraped by.

1953 National League

TEAM	W	L	T	PCT	GB	HW	HL	R	OR	PA	H	2B	3B	HR	BB	SO	HB	SH	AVG	OBP	SLG	OPS	AOPS	BR	ABR	PF	SB	CS	BSA	BSR
BRO	105	49	1	.682		**60**	17	**955**	689	6138	**1529**	274	59	**208**	**655**	686	75	35	**.285**	**.366**	**.474**	**840**	**121**	**194**	**173**	102	**90**	47	66	**3**
MIL	92	62	3	.597	13	45	31	738	**589**	5895	1422	227	52	156	439	637	**80**	27	.266	.325	.415	740	104	-24	23	94	46	27	63	1
STL	83	71	3	.539	22	48	30	768	713	6065	1474	**281**	56	140	574	617	55	**39**	.273	.347	.424	771	107	58	59	100	18	22	45	-4
PHI	83	71	2	.539	22	48	29	716	666	5916	1400	228	**62**	115	530	**597**	67	29	.265	.335	.396	731	97	-25	-21	99	42	21	**67**	2
NY	70	84	1	.455	35	38	39	768	747	5956	1452	195	45	176	499	608	67	28	.271	.336	.422	758	101	18	5	102	31	21	60	-1
CIN	68	86	1	.442	37	38	39	714	788	5912	1396	190	34	166	485	701	68	16	.261	.325	.403	728	94	-45	-50	101	25	20	56	-1
CHI	65	89	1	.422	40	43	34	633	835	5873	1372	204	57	137	514	746	73	14	.260	.328	.399	727	93	-43	-58	102	49	21	70	**3**
PIT	50	104	0	.325	55	26	51	622	887	5902	1297	178	49	99	524	715	89	36	.247	.319	.356	675	82	-133	-129	99	41	39	51	-5
TOT	622					346	270	5914		47657	11342	1777	414	1197	4220	5307	224	574	.266	.335	.411	747					342	218	61	-1

TEAM	CG	SHO	GR	SV	IP	H	HR	BB	SO	BR/9	ERA	AERA	OAV	OOB	PR	APR	PF	OSB	OCS	FA	E	WPB	DP	FW	PW	BW	BSW	DIF
BRO	51	11	212	29	1380.2	1337	169	509	**817**	12.1	4.10	104	.253	.320	29	25	99	**22**	25	**.980**	**118**	28	161	**1.7**	2.4	**16.7**	**.3**	7.0
MIL	72	**14**	159	15	1387.0	**1282**	**107**	539	738	**12.0**	**3.30**	**119**	**.245**	**.318**	**153**	**105**	92	48	33	.976	143	31	169	.4	**10.1**	2.2	.1	2.2
STL	51	11	234	**36**	1386.2	1406	139	533	732	12.9	4.23	101	.262	.333	9	5	99	53	29	.977	138	40	161	.7	.5	5.7	-.4	-.4
PHI	**76**	13	165	15	1369.2	1410	138	**410**	637	12.1	3.80	111	.265	.320	74	63	98	40	16	.975	147	33	161	.0	6.1	-2.0	.2	1.7
NY	46	10	217	20	1365.2	1403	146	610	647	13.4	4.25	101	.264	.343	5	6	100	33	30	.975	151	51	151	-.2	.6	.5	-.0	-7.8
CIN	47	7	202	15	1365.0	1484	179	488	506	13.2	4.64	94	.279	.343	-53	-42	102	35	18	.978	129	**24**	**176**	1.1	-4.0	-4.8	-.0	-1.1
CHI	38	3	**238**	22	1359.0	1491	151	554	623	13.8	4.79	93	.276	.347	-76	-49	104	47	**34**	.967	193	35	141	-2.5	-4.7	-5.6	**.3**	.5
PIT	49	4	211	10	1358.0	1529	168	577	607	14.1	5.22	86	.285	.356	-141	-108	104	64	33	.973	163	76	139	-.9	-10.4	-12.4	-.5	-2.8
TOT	430	73	1638	162	10971.2					12.9	4.29		.266	.335						.975	1182	318	1259					

Batter-Fielder Wins
Schoendienst-StL 6.5
Mathews-Mil........6.1
Campanella-Bro 5.0
Musial-StL 4.4
Snider-Bro 3.9

Batting Average
Furillo-Bro............344
Schoendienst-StL .342
Musial-StL 337
Snider-Bro 336
Mueller-NY 333

On-Base Percentage
Musial-StL 437
Robinson-Bro...............425
Snider-Bro 419
Irvin-NY 406
Mathews-Mil 406

Slugging Average
Snider-Bro 627
Mathews-Mil 627
Campanella-Bro ...611
Musial-StL 609
Furillo-Bro.............580

On-Base Plus Slugging
Snider-Bro 1046
Musial-StL 1046
Mathews-Mil 1033
Campanella-Bro 1006
Furillo-Bro 973

Adjusted OPS
Mathews-Mil 175
Musial-StL 169
Snider-Bro 165
Campanella-Bro ..154
Furillo-Bro 146

Adjusted Batter Runs
Musial-StL 65.6
Mathews-Mil 65.3
Snider-Bro 57.8
Campanella-Bro 41.2
Kluszewski-Cin ..34.7

Runs
Snider-Bro 132
Musial-StL 127
Dark-NY.................126
Gilliam-Bro............125

Hits
Ashburn-Phi..........205
Musial-StL 200
Snider-Bro 198
Dark-NY.................194
Schoendienst-StL 193

Doubles
Musial-StL......................53
Dark-NY 41
Snider-Bro......................38
Furillo-Bro 38
Bell-Cin 37

Triples
Gilliam-Bro.............17
Bruton-Mil 14
Hemus-StL 11
Fondy-Chi 11

Home Runs
Mathews-Mil 47
Snider-Bro 42
Campanella-Bro 41
Kluszewski-Cin 40
Kiner-Pit-Chi 35

Total Bases
Snider-Bro 370
Mathews-Mil 363
Musial-StL 361
Kluszewski-Cin 325
Bell-Cin 320

Runs Batted In
Campanella-Bro ..142
Mathews-Mil........135
Snider-Bro 126
Ennis-Phi 125
Hodges-Bro 122

Stolen Bases
Bruton-Mil 26
Reese-Bro 22
Gilliam-Bro..............21
Robinson-Bro..........17
Snider-Bro 16

Base Stealing Runs
Reese-Bro 2.7
Robinson-Bro 2.3
Bruton-Mil.............1.9
Miksis-Chi..............1.5
Torgeson-Phi 1.2

Fielding Runs-Infield
Schoendienst-StL 28.6
Logan-Mil....................20.8
Bridges-Cin 13.8
McMillan-Cin 10.0
Bilko-StL 9.2

Fielding Runs-Outfield
Ashburn-Phi 17.7
Thomas-Pit 6.4
Marshall-Cin 4.9
Jeffcoat-Chi 4.7
Bell-Cin..................4.6

Wins
Spahn-Mil 23
Roberts-Phi 23
Haddix-StL..............20
Erskine-Bro 20
Staley-StL 18

Winning Pct.
Erskine-Bro...........769
Spahn-Mil 767
Meyer-Bro.............750
Burdette-Mil 750
Haddix-StL 690

Complete Games
Roberts-Phi 33
Spahn-Mil.............24
Simmons-Phi 19
Haddix-StL 19
Erskine-Bro 16

Strikeouts
Roberts-Phi 198
Erskine-Bro 187
Mizell-StL..............173
Haddix-StL............163
Spahn-Mil 148

Fewest BB/Game
Roberts-Phi 1.58
Raffensberger-Cin ..1.71
Minner-Chi 1.79
Staley-StL 2.11
Hacker-Chi 2.19

Games
Wilhelm-NY....................68
Brazle-StL......................60
Hetki-Pit 54
Smith-Cin 50

Saves
Brazle-StL 18
Wilhelm-NY 15
Hughes-Bro 9
Leonard-Chi..............8
Burdette-Mil..............8

Base Runners/9
Spahn-Mil 9.55
Labine-Bro 9.95
Roberts-Phi 10.05
Milliken-Bro........10.40
Haddix-StL 10.42

Adjusted Relief Runs
Wilhelm-NY 18.3
Labine-Bro 17.5
White-StL 11.5
Johnson-Mil 9.4
Hughes-Bro 9.0

Relief Ranking
Labine-Bro..........26.8
Wilhelm-NY 21.3
White-StL 15.6
Hughes-Bro 8.8
Johnson-Mil..........7.3

Innings Pitched
Roberts-Phi 346.2
Spahn-Mil 265.2
Haddix-StL 253.0
Erskine-Bro........246.2
Simmons-Phi 238.0

Opponents' Avg.
Spahn-Mil 217
Gomez-NY 218
Mizell-StL 227
Erskine-Bro...........230
Haddix-StL 232

Opponents' OBP
Spahn-Mil 270
Roberts-Phi 276
Haddix-StL...................287
Hacker-Chi...................299
Simmons-Phi 302

Earned Run Average
Spahn-Mil 2.10
Roberts-Phi 2.75
Haddix-StL 3.06
Antonelli-Mil 3.18
Simmons-Phi 3.21

Adjusted ERA
Spahn-Mil 187
Roberts-Phi 153
Haddix-StL............139
Simmons-Phi........131
Gomez-NY............126

Adjusted Starter Runs
Roberts-Phi 58.5
Spahn-Mil 57.3
Haddix-StL 32.6
Simmons-Phi 25.0
Gomez-NY 20.3

Pitcher Wins
Spahn-Mil 7.0
Roberts-Phi........6.4
Haddix-StL.........4.5
Labine-Bro 2.5
Simmons-Phi 2.3

Brooklyn Blast

The Dodgers became the NL's first repeat champions since 1944, winning a race that wasn't close after mid-July. With MVP winner Roy Campanella and yet another African American Rookie of the Year in Jim Gilliam, Brooklyn easily outclassed the surprising Braves. The Dodgers were the league's last 100-game winner until 1962. Brooklyn again led the world in runs, in both home and road games, while Milwaukee sported the league's best pitching. The Dodgers dominated at Ebbets Field with a .779 winning percentage. No NL team had compiled a better home record since 1902.

Boston's move to Milwaukee, and the team's sudden rise to contention, juiced up NL attendance; the Braves drew league record crowds, causing tickets sales to increase 17 percent although attendance fell in five other cities. Turnout in Milwaukee, when compared to Boston in '52, was up an absurd 549 percent.

The Braves added two more impressive rookies to the mix, outfielder Bill Bruton and pitcher Bob Buhl, while the Cubs debuted Ernie Banks and last-place Pittsburgh introduced Elroy Face. The Cardinals began a dry spell, due to poor pitching, as several of their great 1940s stars—Harry Brecheen, Marty Marion, and Johnny Mize—played their last games, all for other clubs. The Pirates lost youngsters Vern Law and Dick Groat to military service, while the Giants did without Willie Mays and the Dodgers lost Don Newcombe, as the Korean conflict took its toll.

Runs per game rose to 4.75, the highest of the 1950s, as league batters yet again set an all-time record for home runs. The league ERA leapt more than a half a run, with only Warren Spahn and Robin Roberts finishing under the 3.00 mark, and bullpen use continued to increase.

The World Series was a high-scoring affair, with New York and Brooklyn combining for 17 homers in six games. Predictably, the Yankees came out on top.

1953 American League

TEAM	W	L	T	PCT	GB	HW	HL	R	OR	PA	H	2B	3B	HR	BB	SO	HB	SH	AVG	OBP	SLG	OPS	AOPS	BR	ABR	PF	SB	CS	BSA	BSR
NY	99	52	0	.656		50	27	**801**	**547**	5961	1420	226	52	139	**656**	644	77	34	**.273**	**.359**	**.417**	**776**	**120**	**115**	**144**	97	34	44	44	-8
CLE	92	62	1	.597	8.5	**53**	24	770	627	6019	**1426**	201	29	**160**	609	683	90	35	.270	.349	.410	759	114	77	98	97	33	29	53	-3
CHI	89	65	2	.578	11.5	41	36	716	592	5987	1345	226	**53**	74	601	**530**	**120**	**54**	.258	.341	.364	705	93	-17	-37	103	**73**	55	57	-3
BOS	84	69	0	.549	16	38	38	656	632	5879	1385	**255**	37	101	496	601	99	38	.264	.332	.384	716	94	-9	-43	105	33	45	42	-8
WAS	76	76	0	.500	23.5	39	36	687	614	5858	1354	230	**53**	69	596	604	82	31	.263	.343	.368	711	100	-5	12	98	65	36	**64**	**2**
DET	60	94	4	.390	40.5	30	47	695	923	6152	1479	259	44	108	506	603	63	30	.266	.331	.387	718	100	-10	-1	99	30	35	46	-6
PHI	59	95	3	.383	41.5	27	50	632	799	6028	1398	205	38	116	498	602	51	24	.256	.321	.372	693	89	-64	-87	104	41	24	63	1
STL	54	100	0	.351	46.5	23	54	555	778	5877	1310	214	25	112	507	644	89	17	.249	.317	.363	680	87	-85	-96	102	17	34	33	-8
TOT	618					301	312	5512		47761	11117	1816	331	879	4469	4911	263	671	.262	.337	.383	720					326	302	52	-34

TEAM	CG	SHO	GR	SV	IP	H	HR	BB	SO	BR/9	ERA	AERA	OAV	OOB	PR	APR	PF	OSB	OCS	FA	E	WPB	DP	FW	PW	BW	BSW	DIF
NY	50	**18**	176	**39**	1358.1	**1286**	94	500	604	**12.1**	**3.20**	115	.251	**.321**	**120**	80	92	33	31	.979	126	**25**	182	.3	8.0	**14.4**	-.4	1.1
CLE	**81**	11	135	15	1373.0	1311	**92**	519	586	12.2	3.64	103	.253	.325	53	17	94	46	30	.979	127	37	**197**	.4	1.7	9.8	.1	2.9
CHI	57	17	184	33	1403.2	1299	113	583	**714**	12.2	3.41	**118**	**.246**	.324	91	**95**	101	41	35	**.980**	125	41	144	.6	**9.5**	-3.7	.1	5.5
BOS	41	15	214	37	1373.0	1333	**92**	584	642	12.7	3.58	**118**	.254	.331	63	91	105	39	32	.975	148	36	173	-.9	9.1	-4.3	-.4	3.9
WAS	76	16	132	10	1344.2	1313	112	**478**	515	12.2	3.66	106	.258	.324	50	36	98	35	32	.979	**120**	28	173	**.7**	3.6	1.2	**.6**	-6.1
DET	50	2	218	16	1415.0	1633	154	585	645	14.4	5.25	77	.291	.363	-198	-183	102	55	47	.978	135	63	149	.1	-18.3	-.1	-.2	1.5
PHI	51	7	165	11	1409.0	1475	121	594	566	13.6	4.67	92	.271	.349	-106	-56	107	**28**	**53**	.977	137	66	161	-.0	-5.6	-8.7	.5	-4.2
STL	28	10	**250**	24	1383.2	1467	101	626	639	13.8	4.48	94	.273	.351	-74	-40	105	49	42	.974	152	41	165	-1.0	-4.0	-9.6	-.4	-8.0
TOT	434	96	1474	185	11060.1					12.9	3.99		.262	.337						.978	1070	337	1344					

Batter-Fielder Wins	Batting Average	On-Base Percentage	Slugging Average	On-Base Plus Slugging	Adjusted OPS	Adjusted Batter Runs
Rosen-Cle 7.4	Vernon-Was .337	Woodling-NY .429	Rosen-Cle .613	Rosen-Cle 1034	Rosen-Cle 181	Rosen-Cle 68.0
Berra-NY 3.8	Rosen-Cle .336	Rosen-Cle .422	Zernial-Phi .559	Vernon-Was 921	Vernon-Was 151	Vernon-Was 43.5
Boone-Cle-Det 3.6	Goodman-Bos .313	Minoso-Chi .410	Berra-NY .523	Zernial-Phi 914	Woodling-NY 147	Boone-Cle-Det 31.9
Strickland-Cle 3.3	Minoso-Chi .313	Fain-Chi .405	Boone-Cle-Det .519	Boone-Cle-Det 909	Boone-Cle-Det 146	Woodling-NY 31.7
Vernon-Was 3.0	Busby-Was .312	Yost-Was .403	Vernon-Was .518	Woodling-NY 898	Mantle-NY 145	Mantle-NY 31.4

Runs	Hits	Doubles	Triples	Home Runs	Total Bases	Runs Batted In
Rosen-Cle 115	Kuenn-Det 209	Vernon-Was 43	Rivera-Chi 16	Rosen-Cle 43	Rosen-Cle 367	Rosen-Cle 145
Yost-Was 107	Vernon-Was 205	Kell-Bos 41	Vernon-Was 11	Zernial-Phi 42	Vernon-Was 315	Vernon-Was 115
Mantle-NY 105	Rosen-Cle 201	White-Bos 34	Piersall-Bos 9	Doby-Cle 29	Zernial-Phi 311	Boone-Cle-Det 114
Minoso-Chi 104	Philley-Phi 188	Kuenn-Det 33	Philley-Phi 9	Berra-NY 27	Philley-Phi 263	Zernial-Phi 108
Vernon-Was 101	Busby-Was 183	Goodman-Bos 33		Boone-Cle-Det 26	Berra-NY 263	Berra-NY 108

Stolen Bases	Base Stealing Runs	Fielding Runs-Infield	Fielding Runs-Outfield	Wins	Winning Pct.	Complete Games
Minoso-Chi 25	Michaels-Phi 1.5	Strickland-Cle 21.0	Busby-Was 12.9	Porterfield-Was 22	Lopat-NY .800	Porterfield-Was 24
Rivera-Chi 22	Coan-Was 1.5	Hunter-StL 13.9	Groth-StL 12.2	Parnell-Bos 21	Ford-NY .750	B.Lemon-Cle 23
Jensen-Was 18	Jensen-Was 1.2	Dropo-Det 12.5	Piersall-Bos 10.9	B.Lemon-Cle 21	Parnell-Bos .724	Garcia-Cle 21
Philley-Phi 13	Philley-Phi 1.1	Avila-Cle 12.5	Zernial-Phi 5.3	Trucks-StL-Chi 20	Porterfield-Was .688	Pierce-Chi 19
Busby-Was 13	Zernial-Phi .9	Rosen-Cle 9.4	Lund-Det 5.1			Trucks-StL-Chi 17

Strikeouts	Fewest BB/Game	Games	Saves	Base Runners/9	Adjusted Relief Runs	Relief Ranking
Pierce-Chi 186	Lopat-NY 1.61	Kinder-Bos 69	Kinder-Bos 27	Raschi-NY 10.24	Kinder-Bos 24.7	Kinder-Bos 47.3
Trucks-StL-Chi 149	Sain-NY 2.14	Stuart-StL 60	Dorish-Chi 18	Lopat-NY 10.35	Dorish-Chi 11.0	Dorish-Chi 14.0
Wynn-Cle 138	A.Kellner-Phi 2.28	Martin-Phi 58	Reynolds-NY 13	Kinder-Bos 10.43	Paige-StL 8.7	Paige-StL 9.9
Parnell-Bos 136	Porterfield-Was 2.58	Paige-StL 57	Paige-StL 11	Keegan-Chi 10.49	Kuzava-NY 5.9	Kuzava-NY 6.9
Garcia-Cle 134	Hoeft-Det 2.64	Dorish-Chi 55	Sain-NY 9	Pierce-Chi 10.65	Bearden-Chi 4.4	Bearden-Chi 4.1

Innings Pitched	Opponents' Avg.	Opponents' OBP	Earned Run Average	Adjusted ERA	Adjusted Starter Runs	Pitcher Wins
B.Lemon-Cle 286.2	Pierce-Chi .218	Raschi-NY .283	Lopat-NY 2.42	Lopat-NY 152	Pierce-Chi 37.8	**Kinder-Bos** 5.2
Garcia-Cle 271.2	McDermott-Bos .224	Lopat-NY .288	Pierce-Chi 2.72	Pierce-Chi 148	Trucks-StL-Chi 31.8	**McDermott-Bos** 4.1
Pierce-Chi 271.1	Raschi-NY .224	Pierce-Chi .292	Trucks-StL-Chi 2.93	McDermott-Bos 140	Parnell-Bos 27.8	**Trucks-StL-Chi** 3.6
Trucks-StL-Chi 264.1	Masterson-Was .232	Masterson-Was .304	Sain-NY 3.00	Trucks-StL-Chi 139	Lopat-NY 25.5	**Pierce-Chi** 3.5
Porterfield-Was 255.0	Trucks-StL-Chi .238	Garcia-Cle .307	Ford-NY 3.00	Parnell-Bos 137	McDermott-Bos 25.2	**Porterfield-Was** 3.3

Ho-Hum

The pennant race wasn't close in 1953, with the Yankees easily shaking off the Indians and White Sox to capture their 20th AL crown in 33 seasons. More than in previous years, the Yankees had a stable lineup, although per usual, manager Casey Stengel had six pitchers make at least 15 starts—one of whom was also his relief ace, Allie Reynolds. New York led the AL in runs and ERA by healthy margins.

Cleveland third baseman Al Rosen nearly won the Triple Crown, leading in the power categories and losing the batting championship to Washington's Mickey Vernon by less than a point. Rosen's MVP trophy didn't make up for another second-place finish, however.

Boston's Ellis Kinder racked up 27 saves (figured retroactively), tying Joe Page's record, helping his team finish fourth even with Ted Williams spending most of the season in the marines—Teddy Ballgame even survived his plane being shot down in Korea. Eighteen-year-old outfielder Al Kaline of sixth-place Detroit made his debut, and to honor the Athletics' retired owner-manager, Shibe Park was renamed Connie Mack Stadium. The A's, however, tumbled to seventh and attendance fell by half. Overall, league attendance dropped for the fifth straight year as New York's victory routine proved tiresome. Football was already making huge inroads into the American postwar consciousness.

The St. Louis Browns' final season didn't pass without more weirdness. Alva "Bobo" Holloman pitched a no-hitter in his first major league start, May 6, but was subsequently shelled back to the minors. The AL forced Bill Veeck to sell the club, and the Browns moved to Baltimore.

The World Series went six games, with Stengel calling on five different starters. In an even more power-dominated Series than in 1952, the Yankees used big innings to win Games 1 and 5, then captured the deciding contest in the last of the ninth on Billy Martin's record-setting 12th hit. For the Yankees, it was their fifth straight world title.

1954 National League

TEAM	W	L	T	PCT	GB	HW	HL	R	OR	PA	H	2B	3B	HR	BB	SO	HB	SH	AVG	OBP	SLG	OPS	AOPS	BR	ABR	PF	SB	CS	BSA	BSR
NY	97	57	0	.630		**53**	23	732	**550**	5936	1386	194	42	**186**	522	**561**	84	33	.264	.332	.424	756	101	15	11	101	30	23	57	-1
BRO	92	62	0	.597	5	45	32	**778**	740	6058	**1418**	**246**	56	**186**	**634**	625	79	**35**	**.270**	**.349**	**.444**	**793**	**109**	**103**	**78**	103	46	39	54	-4
MIL	89	65	0	.578	8	43	34	670	556	5921	1395	217	41	139	471	619	**110**	**35**	.265	.327	.401	728	102	-34	12	94	**54**	31	**64**	**1**
PHI	75	79	0	.487	22	39	39	659	614	5937	1384	243	**58**	102	604	620	84	10	.267	.341	.395	736	98	0	1	100	30	27	53	-3
CIN	74	80	0	.481	23	41	36	729	763	5972	1369	221	46	147	557	645	101	29	.262	.333	.406	739	95	-8	-27	103	47	30	61	0
STL	72	82	0	.468	25	33	44	799	790	6127	1518	285	**58**	119	582	586	44	30	.281	.350	.421	771	106	69	63	101	63	46	58	-2
CHI	64	90	0	.416	33	40	37	700	766	5965	1412	229	45	159	478	693	56	32	.263	.325	.412	737	96	-22	-29	101	46	31	60	-1
PIT	53	101	0	.344	44	31	46	557	845	5836	1260	181	57	76	566	737	99	25	.248	.323	.350	673	82	-122	-113	99	21	13	62	0
TOT	616					325	291	5624		47752	11142	1816	403	1114	4414	5086	229	657	.265	.335	.407	742					337	240	58	-10

TEAM	CG	SHO	GR	SV	IP	H	HR	BB	SO	BR/9	ERA	AERA	OAV	OOB	PR	APR	PF	OSB	OCS	FA	E	WPB	DP	FW	PW	BW	BSW	DIF
NY	45	**19**	235	33	1390.0	**1258**	113	613	692	12.3	**3.09**	**130**	**.243**	.326	**151**	**147**	99	29	31	.975	154	38	172	-.5	**14.6**	1.1	.0	4.9
BRO	39	8	231	**36**	1393.2	1399	164	533	**762**	12.6	4.31	95	.261	.328	-36	-34	100	28	29	.978	129	32	138	.8	-3.4	**7.7**	-.3	10.1
MIL	63	13	193	21	1394.2	1296	**106**	553	698	12.1	3.19	117	.250	.323	137	91	92	42	32	**.981**	**116**	33	171	**1.5**	9.0	1.2	**.2**	.0
PHI	**78**	14	139	12	1365.1	1329	133	**450**	570	**11.8**	3.59	112	.256	**.315**	73	68	99	37	21	.975	145	**29**	133	-.0	6.7	.0	-.2	-8.6
CIN	34	8	235	27	1367.1	1491	169	547	537	13.6	4.50	93	.282	.351	-65	-45	103	**24**	31	.977	137	33	**194**	.4	-4.5	-2.7	.1	3.6
STL	40	11	**262**	18	1390.1	1484	170	535	680	13.4	4.50	91	.275	.343	-66	-59	101	27	24	.976	146	43	178	-.0	-5.8	6.2	-.0	-5.2
CHI	41	6	210	19	1374.1	1375	131	619	622	13.2	4.51	93	.264	.340	-66	-45	103	71	31	.974	154	49	164	-.5	-4.5	-2.9	.0	-5.2
PIT	37	4	195	15	1346.0	1510	128	564	525	14.0	4.92	85	.287	.354	-127	-106	103	79	**41**	.971	173	46	136	-1.6	-10.5	-11.2	.1	-.9
TOT	377	83	1700	181	11021.2					12.9	4.07		.265	.335						.976	1154	303	1286					

Batter-Fielder Wins	Batting Average	On-Base Percentage	Slugging Average	On-Base Plus Slugging	Adjusted OPS	Adjusted Batter Runs
Mays-NY 6.2	Mays-NY .345	Ashburn-Phi .441	Mays-NY .667	Mays-NY 1078	Mathews-Mil 177	Snider-Bro 61.5
Mathews-Mil 5.4	Mueller-NY .342	Musial-StL .428	Snider-Bro .647	Snider-Bro 1071	Mays-NY 176	Mays-NY 61.4
Musial-StL 4.7	Snider-Bro .341	Snider-Bro .423	Kluszewski-Cin .642	Kluszewski-Cin 1049	Snider-Bro 170	Musial-StL 61.4
Schoendienst-StL 4.5	Musial-StL .330	Mathews-Mil .423	Musial-StL .607	Musial-StL 1036	Musial-StL 166	Mathews-Mil 58.3
Snider-Bro 4.3	Kluszewski-Cin .326	Mays-NY .411	Mathews-Mil .603	Mathews-Mil 1026	Kluszewski-Cin 165	Kluszewski-Cin 54.3

Runs	Hits	Doubles	Triples	Home Runs	Total Bases	Runs Batted In
Snider-Bro 120	Mueller-NY 212	Musial-StL 41	Mays-NY 13	Kluszewski-Cin 49	Snider-Bro 378	Kluszewski-Cin 141
Musial-StL 120	Snider-Bro 199	Snider-Bro 39	Hamner-Phi 11	Hodges-Bro 42	Mays-NY 377	Snider-Bro 130
Mays-NY 119	Musial-StL 195	Repulski-StL 39	Snider-Bro 10	Sauer-Chi 41	Kluszewski-Cin 368	Hodges-Bro 130
Ashburn-Phi 111	Mays-NY 195	Hamner-Phi 39		Mays-NY 41	Musial-StL 359	Musial-StL 126
Gilliam-Bro 107	Moon-StL 193				Hodges-Bro 335	Ennis-Phi 119

Stolen Bases	Base Stealing Runs	Fielding Runs-Infield	Fielding Runs-Outfield	Wins	Winning Pct.	Complete Games
Bruton-Mil 34	Bruton-Mil 2.9	Schoendienst-StL 27.7	Ashburn-Phi 13.2	Roberts-Phi 23	Antonelli-NY .750	Roberts-Phi 29
Temple-Cin 21	Fondy-Chi 2.7	Grammas-StL 22.2	Mays-NY 9.5	Spahn-Mil 21	Lawrence-StL .714	Spahn-Mil 23
Fondy-Chi 20	Temple-Cin 2.2	Logan-Mil 12.6	Thomas-Pit 7.2	Antonelli-NY 21	Gomez-NY .654	Simmons-Phi 21
Moon-StL 18	Torgeson-Phi 1.2	Fondy-Chi 8.4	Furillo-Bro 4.0	Haddix-StL 18	Spahn-Mil .636	Antonelli-NY 18
Ashburn-Phi 11	Mathews-Mil 1.1	Hodges-Bro 6.8	Gordon-Pit 3.1	Erskine-Bro 18	Roberts-Phi .605	

Strikeouts	Fewest BB/Game	Games	Saves	Base Runners/9	Adjusted Relief Runs	Relief Ranking
Roberts-Phi 185	Roberts-Phi 1.50	Hughes-Bro 60	Hughes-Bro 24	Roberts-Phi 9.36	Wilhelm-NY 23.2	Grissom-NY 36.8
Haddix-StL 184	Minner-Chi 2.06	Hetki-Pit 58	Smith-Cin 20	Johnson-Mil 10.15	Grissom-NY 23.0	Wilhelm-NY 33.3
Erskine-Bro 166	Hacker-Chi 2.10	Brazle-StL 58	Grissom-NY 19	Smith-Cin 10.22	Jolly-Mil 16.5	Jolly-Mil 26.0
Antonelli-NY 152	Burdette-Mil 2.34	Wilhelm-NY 57	Jolly-Mil 10	Poholsky-StL 10.61	Smith-Cin 12.4	Smith-Cin 24.8
Spahn-Mil 136	Meyer-Bro 2.45	Grissom-NY 56	Hetki-Pit 9	Antonelli-NY 10.72	Johnson-Mil 11.5	Hughes-Bro 14.2

Innings Pitched	Opponents' Avg.	Opponents' OBP	Earned Run Average	Adjusted ERA	Adjusted Starter Runs	Pitcher Wins
Roberts-Phi 336.2	Antonelli-NY .219	Roberts-Phi .266	Antonelli-NY 2.30	Antonelli-NY 176	Antonelli-NY 49.5	**Antonelli-NY** 5.3
Spahn-Mil 283.1	Roberts-Phi .231	Antonelli-NY .292	Burdette-Mil 2.76	Simmons-Phi 144	Roberts-Phi 44.5	**Roberts-Phi** 4.3
Erskine-Bro 260.1	Simmons-Phi .239	Hacker-Chi .299	Simmons-Phi 2.81	Gomez-NY 140	Simmons-Phi 29.5	**Grissom-NY** 3.7
Haddix-StL 259.2	Littlefield-Pit .239	Spahn-Mil .300	Gomez-NY 2.88	Roberts-Phi 136	Gomez-NY 27.2	**Wilhelm-NY** 3.2
Antonelli-NY 258.2	Wehmeier-Cin-Phi .239	Burdette-Mil .300	Conley-Mil 2.96	Burdette-Mil 135	Burdette-Mil 25.6	**Spahn-Mil** 3.2

New York Life

Prior to the season, the Braves traded young hurler Johnny Antonelli to the Giants for outfielder Bobby Thomson. While Thomson broke his leg in spring training and played just 43 games, Antonelli broke out for New York, winning 21 and pacing the NL in ERA. With Willie Mays back from the army and winning MVP honors with his first great season, the Giants didn't miss Thomson. Pulling away from Brooklyn with superb pitching and the league's best home run offense, the Giants won their last pennant in New York. Thomson's injury did help Milwaukee, however. When the veteran went down, manager Charlie Grimm filled the gap with rookie Hank Aaron.

Attendance rose another 8 percent as the third-place Braves were the first NL team ever to draw two million. The game became a little less homespun in 1954, as players were no longer allowed to leave their gloves on the field. In addition, the use of relief pitching continued to gain steam as complete games fell sharply to an all-time low of 377.

After trading slugger Ralph Kiner, the Pirates removed the temporary fencing in left field, restoring Forbes Field to its larger dimensions. It didn't help the team, which again finished last, but Pittsburgh was beginning to rebuild.

In the World Series, the Giants blew away favored Cleveland in a four-game sweep. Three huge pinch hits by New York's Dusty Rhodes—one a three-run homer that won Game 1—provided the offensive difference. Willie Mays' catch of Vic Wertz' tremendous drive to center field in the opening game remains one of the great plays ever made in the postseason. The Giants effectively shut down the Indians' offense, allowing just 9 runs—and 4 of those runs came after New York had built a 7–0 lead in Game 4. The surprise win triggered a short period of NL dominance, as the Senior Circuit won five world titles in seven seasons.

1954 American League

TEAM	W	L	T	PCT	GB	HW	HL	R	OR	PA	H	2B	3B	HR	BB	SO	HB	SH	AVG	OBP	SLG	OPS	AOPS	BR	ABR	PF	SB	CS	BSA	BSR
CLE	111	43	2	.721		**59**	18	746	**504**	6048	1368	188	39	**156**	637	668	**107**	23	.262	.341	.403	744	108	77	65	102	30	33	48	-5
NY	103	51	1	.669	8	54	23	**805**	563	6027	**1400**	**215**	**59**	133	**650**	632	84	20	**.268**	**.348**	**.408**	**756**	**118**	**103**	**131**	97	34	41	45	-7
CHI	94	60	1	.610	17	45	32	711	521	5972	1382	203	47	94	604	**536**	96	**51**	.267	.347	.379	726	103	53	30	103	**98**	58	**63**	**1**
BOS	69	85	2	.448	42	38	39	700	728	6207	1436	244	41	123	654	660	78	23	.266	.345	.395	740	98	78	3	111	51	30	**63**	**1**
DET	68	86	1	.442	43	35	42	584	664	5865	1351	**215**	41	90	492	603	80	19	.258	.322	.367	689	97	-37	-25	98	48	44	52	-5
WAS	66	88	1	.429	45	37	41	632	680	6005	1292	188	69	81	610	719	77	27	.246	.325	.355	680	97	-47	-12	95	37	21	64	**1**
BAL	54	100	0	.351	57	32	45	483	668	5838	1309	195	49	52	468	634	99	21	.251	.313	.338	651	91	-107	-64	93	30	31	49	-4
PHI	51	103	2	.331	60	29	47	542	875	5823	1228	191	41	94	504	677	54	28	.236	.305	.342	647	83	-119	-121	100	30	29	51	-4
TOT	621					329	287	5203		47785	10766	1639	386	823	4619	5129	212	675	.257	.331	.373	704					358	287	56	-22

TEAM	CG	SHO	GR	SV	IP	H	HR	BB	SO	BR/9	ERA	AERA	OAV	OOB	PR	APR	PF	OSB	OCS	FA	E	WPB	DP	FW	PW	BW	BSW	DIF
CLE	**77**	12	160	36	1419.1	**1220**	89	**486**	678	**10.9**	**2.78**	**132**	**.232**	**.297**	**148**	**142**	99	43	35	.979	128	**19**	148	.7	**14.7**	6.7	-.2	12.1
NY	51	16	182	**37**	1379.1	1284	86	552	655	12.2	3.26	105	.251	.325	71	29	92	34	33	.979	126	27	**198**	.8	3.0	**13.5**	-.4	9.1
CHI	60	**23**	176	33	1383.0	1255	94	517	701	11.6	3.05	122	.244	.312	103	105	100	**32**	35	**.982**	**108**	27	149	**1.8**	10.8	3.1	**.4**	.9
BOS	41	10	**224**	22	1412.1	1434	118	612	**707**	13.3	4.01	102	.265	.341	-46	14	110	57	36	.972	176	37	163	-2.0	1.4	.3	**.4**	-8.2
DET	58	13	179	13	1383.0	1375	138	506	603	12.5	3.81	97	.261	.328	-13	-18	99	34	40	.978	129	**19**	131	.6	-1.9	-2.6	-.2	-4.9
WAS	69	10	158	7	1383.1	1396	79	573	562	13.0	3.84	93	.265	.338	-18	-46	96	51	29	.977	137	33	172	.2	-4.8	-1.2	**.4**	-5.6
BAL	58	6	156	8	1373.1	1279	**78**	688	668	13.0	3.88	92	.250	.338	-24	-47	96	56	**46**	.975	147	32	152	-.4	-4.9	-6.6	-.1	-11.0
PHI	49	3	182	13	1371.1	1523	141	685	555	14.7	5.18	75	.285	.366	-222	-185	105	51	33	.972	169	52	163	-1.6	-19.1	-12.5	-.1	7.3
TOT	463	93	1417	169	11105.0					12.6	3.72		.257	.331						.977	1120	246	1276					

Batter-Fielder Wins
Williams-Bos 5.1
Avila-Cle 4.8
Berra-NY...............4.4
Minoso-Chi..........4.1
Mantle-NY...........3.8

Batting Average
Avila-Cle 341
Minoso-Chi 320
Noren-NY 319
Fox-Chi 319
Berra-NY 307

On-Base Percentage
Williams-Bos 513
Minoso-Chi 411
Mantle-NY 408
Yost-Was 405
Rosen-Cle 404

Slugging Average
Minoso-Chi 535
Mantle-NY 525
Rosen-Cle.............506
Vernon-Was 492
Berra-NY 488

On-Base Plus Slugging
Williams-Bos 1148
Minoso-Chi 946
Mantle-NY 933
Rosen-Cle 910
Avila-Cle 880

Adjusted OPS
Williams-Bos 193
Mantle-NY 160
Minoso-Chi 154
Rosen-Cle 148
Noren-NY 140

Adjusted Batter Runs
Williams-Bos 60.7
Mantle-NY 46.9
Minoso-Chi 43.5
Rosen-Cle 33.6
Avila-Cle 30.5

Runs
Mantle-NY 129
Minoso-Chi 119
Avila-Cle 112
Fox-Chi 111
Carrasquel-Chi 106

Hits
Kuenn-Det 201
Fox-Chi 201
Avila-Cle 189
Busby-Was 187
Minoso-Chi 182

Doubles
Vernon-Was 33
Smith-Cle 29
Minoso-Chi 29

Triples
Minoso-Chi 18
Runnels-Was..........15
Vernon-Was...........14
Mantle-NY 12
Tuttle-Det 11

Home Runs
Doby-Cle 32
Williams-Bos 29
Mantle-NY 27
Jensen-Bos 25

Total Bases
Minoso-Chi 304
Vernon-Was..........294
Mantle-NY 285
Berra-NY 285
Doby-Cle 279

Runs Batted In
Doby-Cle 126
Berra-NY 125
Jensen-Bos 117
Minoso-Chi..........116

Stolen Bases
Jensen-Bos 22
Rivera-Chi 18
Minoso-Chi 18
Jacobs-Phi..............17
Busby-Was 17

Base Stealing Runs
Busby-Was 3.0
Jacobs-Phi 2.7
Jensen-Bos............2.4
Cavarretta-Chi 9
Michaels-Chi.............8

Fielding Runs-Infield
Coleman-NY 14.6
Carrasquel-Chi 13.2
Carey-NY...................12.5
McDougald-NY 10.2
Terwilliger-Was...........10.0

Fielding Runs-Outfield
Diering-Bal 9.8
Power-Phi 8.0
Kaline-Det..............7.3
Sievers-Was 7.2
Renna-Phi..............6.1

Wins
Wynn-Cle................23
Lemon-Cle..............23
Grim-NY 20
Trucks-Chi 19
Garcia-Cle 19

Winning Pct.
Consuegra-Chi 842
Grim-NY 769
Lemon-Cle 767
Garcia-Cle 704
Houtteman-Cle 682

Complete Games
Porterfield-Was......21
Lemon-Cle 21
Wynn-Cle 20
Gromek-Det 17

Strikeouts
Turley-Bal 185
Wynn-Cle.............155
Trucks-Chi 152
Pierce-Chi 148
Harshman-Chi 134

Fewest BB/Game
Lopat-NY 1.75
Gromek-Det 2.03
Garver-Det 2.27
Garcia-Cle 2.47
Zuverink-Det........2.75

Games
Dixon-Was-Phi 54
Martin-Phi-Chi 48
Pascual-Was.................48
Kinder-Bos 48

Saves
Sain-NY..................22
Kinder-Bos.............15
Narleski-Cle............13

Base Runners/9
Mossi-Cle 9.29
Sain-NY 9.47
Dorish-Chi 9.74
Garcia-Cle 10.19
Wynn-Cle 10.24

Adjusted Relief Runs
Mossi-Cle 18.6
Narleski-Cle 14.6
Dorish-Chi 12.9
Miller-Det 8.1
Kinder-Bos 6.4

Relief Ranking
Mossi-Cle 15.8
Narleski-Cle.........13.7
Dorish-Chi 12.3
Kinder-Bos..........10.6
Sain-NY................8.5

Innings Pitched
Wynn-Cle 270.2
Trucks-Chi 264.2
Garcia-Cle 258.2
Lemon-Cle 258.1
Gromek-Det 252.2

Opponents' Avg.
Turley-Bal 203
Wynn-Cle 225
Ford-NY 227
Trucks-Chi 228
Garcia-Cle 229

Opponents' OBP
Garcia-Cle 282
Wynn-Cle....................283
Garver-Det...................286
Gromek-Det 294
Trucks-Chi 296

Earned Run Average
Garcia-Cle 2.64
Lemon-Cle 2.72
Wynn-Cle 2.73
Gromek-Det 2.74
Trucks-Chi 2.79

Adjusted ERA
Garcia-Cle 139
Lemon-Cle............135
Wynn-Cle..............135
Gromek-Det..........135
Trucks-Chi 134

Adjusted Starter Runs
Garcia-Cle 31.0
Trucks-Chi 29.6
Wynn-Cle 29.4
Gromek-Det 28.0
Lemon-Cle 25.4

Pitcher Wins
Gromek-Det 3.7
Lemon-Cle..........3.7
Wynn-Cle............3.6
Trucks-Chi 3.3
Garcia-Cle..........3.0

Tribal Gathering

The Indians, bridesmaids three straight times, stormed the altar in 1954. By July Cleveland, New York, and Chicago were the only three contenders. The Tribe would not be denied, pulling away in August and leaving two very good clubs in the dust. Cleveland allowed fewer runs than any full-season AL team since 1917. Featuring five top-flight right-handed starters, a lefty-righty relief duo, and a veteran southpaw middleman, the Indians had one of the greatest staffs ever. And the offense wasn't shoddy, featuring Al Rosen, Larry Doby, and batting champ Bobby Avila.

And Cleveland handily beat Casey Stengel's best team. The Yankees won 103 games and were the only major league team to score 800 runs, but they still lost by 8 games. Despite the Indians' victory, Yogi Berra won his second MVP award, and Mickey Mantle consolidated his position as the league's top center fielder.

The poor got poorer in 1954: there had not been a 60-game spread from first to last since 1939. Even in New York, winning was tired, as Yankees attendance declined each of the last six years. The league champion Indians' attendance was just half of the club's 1948 total.

White Sox third baseman Cass Michaels' career was ended by a beanball that fractured his skull, while Johnny Pesky played out the string in Washington. Thirty-nine-year-old Allie Reynolds retired after another excellent season in New York. The sixth-place Senators called on two rookies who make considerable impact in the coming years: pitcher Camilo Pascual and infielder Harmon Killebrew. In their first season in Baltimore, the Orioles finished seventh. Following the season, the Mack family sold the last-place A's to Arnold Johnson, who moved the club to Kansas City.

While Cleveland set league records for victories and winning percentage, they crumbled in the World Series. The New York Giants ripped apart Tribe pitching and snuffed out their powerful offense, winning in four straight. It was the most shocking sweep since the 1914 "Miracle" Braves

1955 National League

TEAM	W	L	T	PCT	GB	HW	HL	R	OR	PA	H	2B	3B	HR	BB	SO	HB	SH	AVG	OBP	SLG	OPS	AOPS	BR	ABR	PF	SB	CS	BSA	BSR
BRO	98	55	1	.641		**56**	21	**857**	**650**	6037	1406	**230**	44	**201**	**674**	718	75	**41**	**.271**	**.356**	**.448**	**804**	**115**	**147**	**124**	103	**79**	56	59	-2
MIL	85	69	0	.552	13.5	46	31	743	668	5920	1377	219	**55**	182	504	735	72	28	.261	.326	.427	753	109	26	64	95	42	27	61	0
NY	80	74	0	.519	18.5	44	35	702	673	5940	1377	173	34	169	497	**581**	69	36	.260	.325	.402	727	97	-17	-18	100	38	22	**63**	**1**
PHI	77	77	0	.500	21.5	46	31	675	666	5864	1300	214	50	132	652	673	53	24	.255	.340	.395	735	102	16	29	98	44	32	58	-2
CIN	75	79	0	.487	23.5	46	31	761	684	5978	**1424**	216	28	181	556	657	**76**	33	.270	.341	.425	766	102	65	23	106	51	36	59	-1
CHI	72	81	1	.471	26	43	33	626	713	5766	1287	187	**55**	164	428	806	69	22	.247	.305	.398	703	90	-79	-77	100	37	35	51	-4
STL	68	86	0	.442	30.5	41	36	654	757	5855	1375	228	36	143	458	597	56	31	.261	.321	.400	721	95	-30	-29	100	64	59	52	-7
PIT	60	94	0	.390	38.5	36	39	560	767	5790	1262	210	60	91	471	652	93	21	.244	.308	.361	669	83	-129	-121	99	22	22	50	-3
TOT	616					358	257	5578		47150	10808	1677	362	1263	4240	5419	236	563	.259	.328	.407	735					377	289	57	-18

TEAM	CG	SHO	GR	SV	IP	H	HR	BB	SO	BR/9	ERA	AERA	OAV	OOB	PR	APR	PF	OSB	OCS	FA	E	WPB	DP	FW	PW	BW	BSW	DIF
BRO	46	11	209	**37**	1378.0	1296	168	483	**773**	**11.7**	**3.68**	**110**	**.248**	**.313**	**54**	**58**	101	**36**	24	.978	133	40	156	.5	**5.8**	**12.3**	.0	2.9
MIL	**61**	5	203	12	1383.0	1339	**138**	591	654	12.7	3.85	98	.256	.331	29	-15	93	38	45	.975	152	40	155	-.6	-1.5	6.4	.2	3.5
NY	52	6	246	14	1386.2	1347	155	560	721	12.7	3.77	107	.257	.332	41	39	100	42	37	.976	142	42	165	.0	3.9	-1.8	**.3**	.6
PHI	58	11	193	21	1356.2	**1291**	161	477	657	11.9	3.93	101	.251	.315	17	6	98	43	29	**.981**	**110**	46	117	**1.8**	.6	2.9	.0	-5.3
CIN	38	**12**	245	22	1363.0	1373	161	**443**	576	12.1	3.95	107	.264	.322	13	41	105	37	28	.977	139	**38**	169	.2	4.1	2.3	.1	-8.6
CHI	47	10	209	23	1378.1	1306	153	601	686	12.6	4.17	98	.251	.330	-21	-13	101	73	42	.975	147	52	147	-.3	-1.3	-7.6	-.2	4.9
STL	42	10	**274**	15	1376.2	1376	185	549	730	12.9	4.56	89	.262	.334	-80	-76	101	42	35	.975	146	45	152	-.2	-7.5	-2.9	-.5	2.1
PIT	41	5	199	16	1362.0	1480	142	536	622	13.5	4.39	94	.281	.347	-54	-41	102	66	**49**	.972	166	49	**175**	-1.4	-4.1	-12.0	-.0	.5
TOT	385	70	1778	160	10984.1					12.5	4.04		.259	.328						.976	1135	352	1236					

Batter-Fielder Wins	Batting Average	On-Base Percentage	Slugging Average	On-Base Plus Slugging	Adjusted OPS	Adjusted Batter Runs
Mays-NY 6.8	Ashburn-Phi .338	Ashburn-Phi .449	Mays-NY .659	Mays-NY 1059	Mays-NY 176	Mays-NY 61.6
Banks-Chi 5.1	Mays-NY .319	Snider-Bro .418	Snider-Bro .628	Snider-Bro 1046	Mathews-Mil 175	Mathews-Mil 57.8
Mathews-Mil 4.9	Musial-StL .319	Mathews-Mil .413	Mathews-Mil .601	Mathews-Mil 1014	Snider-Bro 169	Snider-Bro 57.0
Snider-Bro 4.5	Campanella-Bro .318	Musial-StL .408	Banks-Chi .596	Campanella-Bro 978	Musial-StL 156	Musial-StL 47.7
Musial-StL 4.5	Aaron-Mil .314	Mays-NY .400	Kluszewski-Cin .585	Musial-StL 974	Campanella-Bro 153	Ashburn-Phi 40.5

Runs	Hits	Doubles	Triples	Home Runs	Total Bases	Runs Batted In
Snider-Bro 126	Kluszewski-Cin 192	Logan-Mil 37	Mays-NY 13	Mays-NY 51	Mays-NY 382	Snider-Bro 136
Mays-NY 123	Aaron-Mil 189	Aaron-Mil 37	Long-Pit 13	Kluszewski-Cin 47	Kluszewski-Cin 358	Mays-NY 127
Post-Cin 116	Bell-Cin 188	Snider-Bro 34	Bruton-Mil 12	Banks-Chi 44	Banks-Chi 355	Ennis-Phi 120
Kluszewski-Cin 116	Post-Cin 186	Post-Cin 33	Clemente-Pit 11	Snider-Bro 42	Post-Cin 345	Banks-Chi 117
Gilliam-Bro 110		Ashburn-Phi 32		Mathews-Mil 41	Snider-Bro 338	Kluszewski-Cin 113

Stolen Bases	Base Stealing Runs	Fielding Runs-Infield	Fielding Runs-Outfield	Wins	Winning Pct.	Complete Games
Bruton-Mil 25	Mays-NY 3.9	McMillan-Cin 17.9	Mays-NY 11.7	Roberts-Phi 23	Newcombe-Bro .800	Roberts-Phi 26
Mays-NY 24	Temple-Cin 2.8	Groat-Pit 16.7	Clemente-Pit 10.8	Newcombe-Bro 20	Roberts-Phi .622	Newcombe-Bro 17
Boyer-StL 22	Bruton-Mil 1.7	O'Connell-Mil 14.3	Bruton-Mil 8.7	Spahn-Mil 17	Nuxhall-Cin .586	Spahn-Mil 16
Temple-Cin 19	Robinson-Bro 1.6	Robinson-Bro 11.0	King-Chi 6.5	Nuxhall-Cin 17	Spahn-Mil .548	
Gilliam-Bro 15	Blaylock-Phi 1.0	Musial-StL 8.3	Greengrass-Cin-Phi 5.8			

Strikeouts	Fewest BB/Game	Games	Saves	Base Runners/9	Adjusted Relief Runs	Relief Ranking
Jones-Chi 198	Newcombe-Bro 1.46	Labine-Bro 60	Meyer-Phi 16	Rogovin-Phi 9.49	Freeman-Cin 17.7	Freeman-Cin 23.9
Roberts-Phi 160	Roberts-Phi 1.56	Wilhelm-NY 59	Roebuck-Bro 12	Newcombe-Bro 10.05	Miller-Phi 16.3	Miller-Phi 20.0
Haddix-StL 150	Hacker-Chi 1.82	LaPalme-StL 56	Labine-Bro 11	Crone-Mil 10.20	Labine-Bro 12.6	Labine-Bro 16.3
Newcombe-Bro 143	Friend-Pit 2.34	Grissom-NY 55	Freeman-Cin 11	Bessent-Bro 10.23	Bessent-Bro 10.8	Bessent-Bro 14.9
Antonelli-NY 143	Spahn-Mil 2.38	Freeman-Cin 52	Grissom-NY 8	Roberts-Phi 10.24	LaPalme-StL 10.7	Jeffcoat-Chi 11.8

Innings Pitched	Opponents' Avg.	Opponents' OBP	Earned Run Average	Adjusted ERA	Adjusted Starter Runs	Pitcher Wins
Roberts-Phi 305.0	Jones-Chi .206	Newcombe-Bro .279	Friend-Pit 2.83	Friend-Pit 145	Friend-Pit 24.9	**Newcombe-Bro** 4.0
Nuxhall-Cin 257.0	Buhl-Mil .227	Roberts-Phi .279	Newcombe-Bro 3.20	Newcombe-Bro 127	Nuxhall-Cin 23.1	**Roberts-Phi** 3.4
Spahn-Mil 245.2	Rush-Chi .234	Hacker-Chi .282	Buhl-Mil 3.21	Nuxhall-Cin 122	Schmidt-StL 20.0	**Nuxhall-Cin** 2.8
Jones-Chi 241.2	Antonelli-NY .234	Friend-Pit .291	Spahn-Mil 3.26	Roberts-Phi 121	Newcombe-Bro 19.2	**Friend-Pit** 2.7
Antonelli-NY 235.1	Dickson-Phi .238	Rush-Chi .293	Roberts-Phi 3.28	Antonelli-NY 121	Roberts-Phi 18.4	**Freeman-Cin** 2.5

Is It Next Year Already?

There was no pennant race in 1955 as the Dodgers, 22–2 on May 10, cruised to an easy title over Milwaukee and New York. For the victorious Dodgers, Roy Campanella won his third MVP trophy, while 19-year-old lefty Sandy Koufax made his major league debut for his hometown team. Brooklyn's pitching was superb, especially considering the bandbox that was Ebbets Field.

The league saw another all-time high in homers in 1955; this was the only season until 1999 in which teams hit more than one per game. The uppercut era was in full "swing"—strikeouts rose and did so until 1960. Philadelphia's Robin Roberts illustrated the era: for the fourth straight year he led the NL in wins and also allowed a major league record 41 homers.

The Cardinals finished seventh but showcased promising youngsters Ken Boyer and Lindy McDaniel. Phil Cavaretta and Ralph Kiner ended their storied careers. Attendance fell for the seventh straight year in Pittsburgh, but the Pirates added rookie outfielder Roberto Clemente. And as a new icon came to Steeltown, a past one left: the beloved Honus Wagner died at age 81.

The 1955 World Series offered a surprise ending for people who had become accustomed to the Yankees-Dodgers plots of 1941, '47, '49, '52, and '53. It started familiarly with the Yankees winning the first two games at home, just as they had done when the teams last met. Brooklyn, though, came back to take the next three at home, blowing apart New York pitching. For Game 6 Dodgers manager Walter Alston used his sixth starting pitcher of the series, but Karl Spooner didn't finish the first as the Yankees won, 5–1.

The Dodgers, who had twice lost seventh games to the Yanks in the past, sent Johnny Podres against Whitey Ford in the finale. Gil Hodges drove in runs in the fourth and sixth, and Sandy Amoros' great running catch snuffed out a sixth-inning Yankees rally. Podres went all the way for the 2–0 win that finally brought "next year" to Flatbush.

1955 American League

TEAM	W	L	T	PCT	GB	HW	HL	R	OR	PA	H	2B	3B	HR	BB	SO	HB	SH	AVG	OBP	SLG	OPS	AOPS	BR	ABR	PF	SB	CS	BSA	BSR
NY	96	58	0	.623		**52**	25	762	569	5944	1342	179	**55**	**175**	609	658	79	46	.260	.340	**.418**	**758**	**112**	70	**82**	98	55	25	69	3
CLE	93	61	0	.604	3	49	28	698	601	6050	1325	195	31	148	**723**	715	87	35	.257	.349	.394	743	102	63	36	104	28	24	54	-2
CHI	91	63	1	.591	5	49	28	725	**557**	5999	1401	204	36	116	567	595	**111**	**58**	**.268**	.344	.388	732	100	32	12	103	**69**	45	61	-1
BOS	84	70	0	.545	12	47	31	755	652	6131	1392	**241**	39	137	707	733	69	29	.264	**.351**	.402	753	100	**83**	18	109	43	17	**72**	**4**
DET	79	75	0	.513	17	46	31	**775**	658	6073	**1407**	211	38	130	641	**583**	71	21	.266	.345	.394	739	107	48	66	98	41	22	65	1
KC	63	91	1	.409	33	33	43	638	911	5916	1395	189	46	121	463	725	58	26	.261	.322	.382	704	94	-44	-51	101	22	36	38	-8
BAL	57	97	2	.370	39	30	47	540	754	5933	1263	177	39	54	560	742	70	19	.240	.314	.320	634	83	-162	-123	93	34	46	43	-9
WAS	53	101	0	.344	43	28	49	598	789	5833	1277	178	54	80	538	654	79	36	.248	.322	.351	673	92	-89	-56	95	25	32	44	-6
TOT	618					334	282	5491		47879	10802	1574	338	961	4808	5405	270	624	.258	.336	.381	717					317	247	56	-17

TEAM	CG	SHO	GR	SV	IP	H	HR	BB	SO	BR/9	ERA	AERA	OAV	OOB	PR	APR	PF	OSB	OCS	FA	E	WPB	DP	FW	PW	BW	BSW	DIF
NY	52	19	190	33	1372.1	**1163**	108	688	731	12.3	**3.23**	116	**.232**	.326	**111**	82	95	**27**	25	.978	128	31	**180**	.5	8.2	**8.2**	.5	1.6
CLE	45	15	215	**36**	1386.1	1285	111	558	**877**	12.1	3.39	**118**	.245	.319	88	**92**	101	36	28	**.981**	**108**	48	152	**1.7**	**9.2**	3.6	.0	1.5
CHI	55	**20**	202	23	1378.0	1301	111	**497**	720	**11.9**	3.37	117	.251	**.317**	90	89	100	30	23	**.981**	111	**25**	147	1.5	8.9	1.2	.1	2.2
BOS	44	9	187	34	1384.1	1333	128	582	674	12.7	3.72	115	.253	.329	37	81	108	47	34	.977	136	34	140	.0	8.1	1.8	**.6**	-3.5
DET	**66**	16	185	12	1380.1	1381	126	517	629	12.6	3.79	101	.261	.328	26	8	97	40	36	.976	139	38	159	-.2	.8	6.6	.3	-5.6
KC	29	9	**255**	23	1382.0	1486	175	707	572	14.6	5.35	78	.278	.363	-214	-172	105	36	23	.976	146	50	174	-.5	-17.2	-5.1	-.6	9.5
BAL	35	10	235	22	1388.2	1403	103	625	595	13.4	4.21	91	.266	.344	-39	-64	96	53	38	.972	167	64	159	-1.7	-6.4	-12.3	-.7	1.1
WAS	37	10	229	16	1354.2	1450	**99**	634	607	14.2	4.62	83	.279	.359	-100	-124	97	48	**40**	.974	154	45	170	-1.0	-12.4	-5.6	-.4	-4.5
TOT	363	108	1698	199	11026.2					13.0	3.96		.258	.336						.977	1089	335	1281					

Batter-Fielder Wins	Batting Average	On-Base Percentage	Slugging Average	On-Base Plus Slugging	Adjusted OPS	Adjusted Batter Runs
Mantle-NY............5.5	Kaline-Det............340	Mantle-NY 431	Mantle-NY 611	Mantle-NY 1042	Mantle-NY 181	Mantle-NY 62.2
Kaline-Det 4.9	Power-KC 319	Kaline-Det 421	Kaline-Det............546	Kaline-Det 967	Kaline-Det 163	Kaline-Det 53.6
Fox-Chi 4.4	Kell-Chi 312	Smith-Cle.....................407	Zernial-KC 508	Smith-Cle.............880	Sievers-Was 136	Williams-Bos 52.2
Williams-Bos 4.3	Fox-Chi 311	Yost-Was 407	Doby-Cle...............505	Doby-Cle 874	Vernon-Was..........133	Smith-Cle 31.6
McDougald-NY ..3.7	Kuenn-Det 306	Goodman-Bos 394	Power-KC 505	Power-KC..............859	Smith-Cle..............132	Vernon-Was........25.7

Runs	Hits	Doubles	Triples	Home Runs	Total Bases	Runs Batted In
Smith-Cle..............123	Kaline-Det 200	Kuenn-Det......................38	Mantle-NY 11	Mantle-NY 37	Kaline-Det 321	Jensen-Bos 116
Mantle-NY 121	Fox-Chi 198	Power-KC 34	Carey-NY...............11	Zernial-KC 30	Mantle-NY 316	Boone-Det 116
Kaline-Det 121	Power-KC..............190	Goodman-Bos 31	Power-KC................10	Williams-Bos 28	Power-KC..............301	Berra-NY 108
Tuttle-Det.............102	Kuenn-Det 190	White-Bos 30			Smith-Cle..............287	Sievers-Was 106
Kuenn-Det 101	Smith-Cle..............186	Finigan-KC 30			Jensen-Bos 275	Kaline-Det 102

Stolen Bases	Base Stealing Runs	Fielding Runs-Infield	Fielding Runs-Outfield	Wins	Winning Pct.	Complete Games
Rivera-Chi 25	Torgeson-Det 2.0	Fox-Chi 31.1	Rivera-Chi............11.4	F.Sullivan-Bos 18	Byrne-NY 762	Ford-NY 18
Minoso-Chi 19	Busby-Was-Chi......1.6	McDougald-NY 22.3	Minoso-Chi 5.6	Lemon-Cle..............18	Ford-NY 720	Hoeft-Det 17
Jensen-Bos 16	Mantle-NY 1.4	Miranda-Bal 20.3	Zernial-KC 5.1	Ford-NY..................18	Hoeft-Det 696	
Busby-Was-Chi 12	Minoso-Chi 1.4	Power-KC....................14.2	Bauer-NY 5.1	Wynn-Cle................17	Lemon-Cle 643	
Smith-Cle................11	Klaus-Bos 1.3	Carey-NY....................10.2	Tuttle-Det 4.8	Turley-NY................17	Donovan-Chi.........625	

Strikeouts	Fewest BB/Game	Games	Saves	Base Runners/9	Adjusted Relief Runs	Relief Ranking
Score-Cle 245	Gromek-Det 1.84	Narleski-Cle 60	Narleski-Cle............19	Kinder-Bos 9.85	Consuegra-Chi 17.5	Kinder-Bos..........21.0
Turley-NY..............210	Donovan-Chi........2.31	Mossi-Cle 57	Kinder-Bos..............18	Consuegra-Chi 9.97	Kiely-Bos 14.1	Hurd-Bos 17.1
Pierce-Chi 157	Garcia-Cle 2.39	Gorman-KC....................57	Gorman-KC 18	Pierce-Chi..........10.02	Mossi-Cle 12.9	Consuegra-Chi ..15.9
Ford-NY 137	Garver-Det 2.61	Dorish-Chi-Bal 48	Konstanty-NY 11	Ford-NY 10.71	Kinder-Bos 10.7	Konstanty-NY 13.7
Hoeft-Det.............133	Porterfield-Was....2.73	Moore-Bal 46	Morgan-NY 10	Hoeft-Det 10.96	Dorish-Chi-Bal 10.1	Mossi-Cle 13.2

Innings Pitched	Opponents' Avg.	Opponents' OBP	Earned Run Average	Adjusted ERA	Adjusted Starter Runs	Pitcher Wins
F.Sullivan-Bos 260.0	Turley-NY 193	Pierce-Chi 277	Pierce-Chi............1.97	Pierce-Chi 201	Pierce-Chi............44.7	**Pierce-Chi** 5.3
Ford-NY 253.2	Score-Cle 194	Ford-NY 296	Ford-NY 2.63	F.Sullivan-Bos 148	Ford-NY 34.4	**Ford-NY** 3.4
Turley-NY 246.2	Ford-NY 208	Hoeft-Det 296	Wynn-Cle 2.82	Ford-NY 143	F.Sullivan-Bos 33.9	**F.Sullivan-Bos**....3.4
Wilson-Bal 235.1	Pierce-Chi.............213	Wilson-Bal 297	Score-Cle 2.85	Wynn-Cle..............142	Wynn-Cle 28.4	**Wynn-Cle**...........3.3
Lary-Det 235.0	Harshman-Chi 224	Wynn-Cle.....................304	F.Sullivan-Bos 2.91	Score-Cle 140	Score-Cle 27.6	**Hoeft-Det**............2.7

Pinstripe Changes

Cleveland, the Yankees, the White Sox, and the Red Sox were bunched together by late August. The standings changed almost hourly from August 25 to September 5. Boston and Chicago dropped out after Labor Day, but the Indians got hot and the Yankees hung tough. With the race in hand, Cleveland promptly lost five straight, including three to fifth-place Detroit while the New York swept Boston, starting a nine-game winning streak. The Yankees clinched on September 23.

The Yankees again had spectacular pitching, with seven men making 10 or more starts. Mickey Mantle was the league's top hitter. Injuries and age began to erode Cleveland's lineup and pitching staff, and the club didn't recover. As Yogi Berra won his third MVP, his eventual successor, Elston Howard, was the Yankees' first African American player. Other rookies on the scene included Jim Bunning, Rocky Colavito, and 18-year-old Brooks Robinson. The most impressive freshman, Cleveland's fireballing Herb Score, set a record, fanning 9.70 hitters per game.

Boston first baseman Harry Agganis passed away on June 27 of a heart problem, sending the Hub into mourning. The great Cy Young, who threw the first pitch in the modern World Series as well as seemingly every other pitch from 1890–1911, died at 88. Three outstanding pitchers appeared in their final games: Hal Newhouser, Vic Raschi, and Johnny Sain.

Al Kaline of the Tigers became the youngest batting champion in history, while the sixth-place Athletics, in their first season in Kansas City, ranked second in attendance. Complete games fell by 100 to an all-time low, while saves rose to a new high; for the first time, the complete games leader, Whitey Ford, had fewer than 20.

Ford won Game 6 of the World Series with a nine-inning performance, but for the first time since 1942, the Yankees lost a Series. The Brooklyn Dodgers won their first title with a 2–0 Game 7 victory at Yankee Stadium.

1956 National League

TEAM	W	L	T	PCT	GB	HW	HL	R	OR	PA	H	2B	3B	HR	BB	SO	HB	SH	AVG	OBP	SLG	OPS	AOPS	BR	ABR	PF	SB	CS	BSA	BSR
BRO	93	61	0	.604		**52**	25	720	601	5884	1315	212	36	179	**649**	738	86	17	.258	**.342**	.419	761	102	86	32	108	**65**	37	64	1
MIL	92	62	1	.597	1	47	29	709	**569**	5897	1350	212	**54**	177	486	714	**142**	20	.259	.323	.423	746	**112**	38	**83**	94	29	20	59	-1
CIN	91	63	1	.591	2	51	26	**775**	658	6003	1406	201	32	**221**	528	760	90	**51**	.266	.336	**.441**	**777**	107	**105**	58	106	45	22	**67**	**2**
STL	76	78	2	.494	17	43	34	678	698	5986	**1443**	**234**	49	124	503	**622**	41	33	**.268**	.333	.399	732	102	26	26	100	41	35	54	-3
PHI	71	83	0	.461	22	40	37	668	738	5910	1313	207	49	121	585	673	52	27	.252	.329	.381	710	99	-11	2	98	45	23	66	**2**
NY	67	87	0	.435	26	37	40	540	650	5709	1268	192	45	145	402	659	59	21	.244	.299	.382	681	89	-88	-84	99	67	34	66	3
PIT	66	88	3	.429	27	35	43	588	653	5757	1340	199	57	110	383	752	95	18	.257	.307	.380	687	92	-74	-61	98	24	33	42	-6
CHI	60	94	3	.390	33	39	38	597	708	5852	1281	202	50	142	446	776	87	13	.244	.302	.382	684	91	-82	-71	98	55	38	59	-1
TOT	621					344	272	5275		46998	10716	1659	372	1219	3982	5694	200	652	.256	.321	.401	722					371	242	61	-3

TEAM	CG	SHO	GR	SV	IP	H	HR	BB	SO	BR/9	ERA	AERA	OAV	OOB	PR	APR	PF	OSB	OCS	FA	E	WPB	DP	FW	PW	BW	BSW	DIF
BRO	46	**12**	201	**30**	1368.2	**1251**	171	441	**772**	**11.3**	3.57	**111**	**.244**	**.305**	31	57	105	**32**	27	**.981**	**111**	51	149	**1.4**	5.8	3.3	.1	5.3
MIL	**64**	**12**	177	27	1393.1	1295	**133**	467	639	11.5	**3.11**	**111**	.247	.309	**102**	**59**	92	33	30	.979	130	29	159	.3	**6.0**	**8.5**	-.0	.2
CIN	47	4	231	29	1389.0	1406	141	458	653	12.3	3.85	103	.265	.325	-12	19	106	50	31	**.981**	113	26	147	1.3	1.9	5.9	.2	4.5
STL	41	**12**	234	**30**	1388.2	1339	155	546	709	12.3	3.97	95	.257	.327	-30	-28	100	52	26	.978	134	53	**172**	.1	-2.9	2.7	-.3	-.7
PHI	57	4	212	15	1377.1	1407	172	**437**	750	12.2	4.20	89	.266	.323	-66	-74	99	63	23	.975	144	**23**	140	-.6	-7.6	.2	.2	1.7
NY	31	9	263	28	1378.0	1287	144	551	765	12.2	3.78	100	.250	.324	-1	1	100	35	30	.976	144	48	143	-.6	.1	-8.6	**.3**	-1.3
PIT	37	8	**266**	24	1376.1	1406	142	469	662	12.4	3.74	101	.267	.327	5	5	100	47	35	.973	162	54	140	-1.5	.5	-6.2	-.6	-3.2
CHI	37	6	220	17	1392.0	1325	161	613	744	12.7	3.96	95	.252	.332	-29	-29	100	59	**40**	.976	144	41	141	-.4	-3.0	-7.3	-.0	-6.3
TOT	360	67	1804	200	11063.1					12.1	3.77		.256	.321						.977	1082	325	1191					

Batter-Fielder Wins	Batting Average	On-Base Percentage	Slugging Average	On-Base Plus Slugging	Adjusted OPS	Adjusted Batter Runs
Aaron-Mil 4.1	Aaron-Mil 328	Snider-Bro 399	Snider-Bro 598	Snider-Bro 997	Adcock-Mil............154	Snider-Bro 43.3
Mays-NY 4.1	Virdon-StL-Pit 319	Gilliam-Bro..................399	Adcock-Mil 597	Robinson-Cin........936	Aaron-Mil 154	Aaron-Mil............43.1
McMillan-Cin 3.7	Clemente-Pit.........311	Moon-StL 390	Aaron-Mil 558	Adcock-Mil............934	Snider-Bro 152	Mathews-Mil 37.4
Musial-StL 3.6	Musial-StL 310	Musial-StL 386	Robinson-Cin 558	Mays-NY 926	Mays-NY 146	Musial-StL 37.3
Snider-Bro 3.2	Boyer-StL 306	Ashburn-Phi................384	Mays-NY...............557	Aaron-Mil..............923	Mathews-Mil 146	Mays-NY 37.0

Runs	Hits	Doubles	Triples	Home Runs	Total Bases	Runs Batted In
Robinson-Cin........122	Aaron-Mil..............200	Aaron-Mil 34	Bruton-Mil 15	Snider-Bro 43	Aaron-Mil..............340	Musial-StL 109
Snider-Bro 112	Ashburn-Phi..........190	Snider-Bro......................33	Aaron-Mil 14	Robinson-Cin..........38	Snider-Bro 324	Adcock-Mil 103
Aaron-Mil..............106	Virdon-StL-Pit 185	Musial-StL......................33	Walls-Pit 11	Adcock-Mil.............38	Mays-NY 322	Kluszewski-Cin....102
Mathews-Mil 103	Musial-StL 184	Lopata-Phi 33	Moon-StL.................11	Mathews-Mil 37	Robinson-Cin........319	Snider-Bro 101
Gilliam-Bro............102	Boyer-StL..............182	Bell-Cin 31	Virdon-StL-Pit 10		Musial-StL 310	Boyer-StL 98

Stolen Bases	Base Stealing Runs	Fielding Runs-Infield	Fielding Runs-Outfield	Wins	Winning Pct.	Complete Games
Mays-NY 40	Mays-NY................5.3	McMillan-Cin 28.5	Ennis-Phi 22.8	Newcombe-Bro 27	Newcombe-Bro.....794	Roberts-Phi 22
Gilliam-Bro.............21	Ashburn-Phi 1.9	Robinson-Bro..............19.0	Ashburn-Phi 18.7	Spahn-Mil 20	Buhl-Mil 692	Spahn-Mil 20
White-NY................15	Temple-Cin 1.7	Blasingame-StL 16.5	King-Chi 10.0	Antonelli-NY 20	Lawrence-Cin 655	Friend-Pit 19
Temple-Cin 14	Gilliam-Bro 1.5	Baker-Chi....................13.4	Irvin-Chi 7.6		Burdette-Mil 655	Newcombe-Bro......18
Reese-Bro 13	Reese-Bro 1.5	Gilliam-Bro..................11.3	Moryn-Chi.............6.4		Spahn-Mil 645	Burdette-Mil 16

Strikeouts	Fewest BB/Game	Games	Saves	Base Runners/9	Adjusted Relief Runs	Relief Ranking
Jones-Chi 176	Roberts-Phi 1.21	Face-Pit 68	Labine-Bro.............19	Newcombe-Bro....9.00	Grissom-NY 20.2	Freeman-Cin 14.2
Haddix-StL-Phi 170	Newcombe-Bro....1.54	Wilhelm-NY...................64	Freeman-Cin 18	Spahn-Mil 9.73	Acker-Cin 14.8	Bessent-Bro 13.5
Friend-Pit.............166	Spahn-Mil 1.66	Freeman-Cin.................64	Lown-Chi 13	Acker-Cin 9.79	Bessent-Bro 12.9	Labine-Bro..........12.0
Roberts-Phi 157	Fowler-Cin 1.77	Labine-Bro 62	Jackson-StL.............9	Grissom-NY 9.82	Labine-Bro 7.4	Acker-Cin............11.5
Mizell-StL.............153	Burdette-Mil 1.83	Lown-Chi 61	Bessent-Bro.............9	Maglie-Bro 9.94	Freeman-Cin..........7.3	Grissom-NY........10.1

Innings Pitched	Opponents' Avg.	Opponents' OBP	Earned Run Average	Adjusted ERA	Adjusted Starter Runs	Pitcher Wins
Friend-Pit 314.1	Newcombe-Bro.....221	Newcombe-Bro 257	Burdette-Mil 2.70	Maglie-Bro...........138	Spahn-Mil 28.1	**Newcombe-Bro** 4.1
Roberts-Phi 297.1	Jones-Chi 221	Spahn-Mil 275	Spahn-Mil 2.78	Antonelli-NY 132	Antonelli-NY 26.1	**Spahn-Mil** 3.7
Spahn-Mil 281.1	Mizell-StL 222	Rush-Chi 280	Antonelli-NY 2.86	Newcombe-Bro 130	Newcombe-Bro....25.7	**Antonelli-NY** 3.5
Newcombe-Bro..268.0	Maglie-Bro 222	Maglie-Bro..................281	Maglie-Bro 2.87	Burdette-Mil.........128	Maglie-Bro 23.1	**Burdette-Mil** 2.6
Kline-Pit 264.0	Craig-Bro 231	Burdette-Mil 281	Newcombe-Bro....3.06	Spahn-Mil 124	Burdette-Mil 23.0	**Dickson-Phi-StL** 1.9

The Last of Flatbush

The Braves streaked to a big lead by Labor Day, but lost five straight to give hope to Brooklyn and Cincinnati (sparked by Rookie of the Year Frank Robinson). While Cincy dropped five straight, and couldn't recover, Brooklyn and Milwaukee juggled the lead until the last weekend. Brooklyn swept three from Pittsburgh at Ebbets Field while the Braves dropped two of three at St. Louis. Don Newcombe of the Dodgers was voted Most Valuable Player as well as winner of the first Cy Young Award, which was only given to one pitcher in the major leagues until 1967.

The Braves had blossoming star Hank Aaron as well as the league's best pitching. The Dodgers countered with Clem Labine, the NL's best reliever, and 19-year-old rookie Don Drysdale, who pitched well. Cincinnati's 3.85 ERA was middle of the pack, but the lineup's 221 homers tied the all-time record.

Nineteen-year-old Bill Mazeroski took over at second base for the Pirates, who improved to seventh after four straight years in the basement. The Phillies moved in their center field fence, and Robin Roberts promptly served up 46 homers, setting a mark that lasted three decades.

After winning the first two World Series games, Brooklyn looked to rack up another championship. But it was not to be. Don Larsen's Game 5 perfecto, and a 9–0 Game 7 embarrassment at Ebbets, gave the Yankees yet another title.

The golden era for both New York teams was over. Ralph Branca and Monte Irvin played their final games, and when Walter O'Malley traded Jackie Robinson to the Giants following the Series, Robinson chose to retire. Brooklyn had the league's second-highest attendance in both 1955 and 1956, but the Giants' gate was dropping. The success of the Braves in Milwaukee, and problems getting new facilities built in New York, led O'Malley and Horace Stoneham to consider relocating.

En route to winter ball, Cardinals outfielder Charlie Peete—expected to contend for a starting job in 1957—was killed in an airplane crash.

1956 American League

TEAM	W	L	T	PCT	GB	HW	HL	R	OR	PA	H	2B	3B	HR	BB	SO	HB	SH	AVG	OBP	SLG	OPS	AOPS	BR	ABR	PF	SB	CS	BSA	BSR
NY	97	57	0	.630		**49**	28	**857**	631	6075	1433	193	**55**	**190**	615	755	82	30	.270	.347	**.434**	**781**	**115**	78	**105**	97	51	37	58	-2
CLE	88	66	1	.571	9	46	31	712	**581**	5988	1256	199	23	153	681	764	81	40	.244	.335	.381	716	92	-34	-49	102	40	32	56	-2
CHI	85	69	0	.552	12	46	31	776	634	6122	1412	218	43	128	619	660	**86**	**75**	.267	.349	.397	746	101	31	20	101	**70**	33	**68**	**4**
BOS	84	70	1	.545	13	43	34	780	751	6215	1473	**261**	45	139	**727**	687	68	25	.275	**.362**	.419	**781**	100	**106**	14	112	28	19	60	0
DET	82	72	1	.532	15	37	40	789	699	6144	**1494**	209	50	150	644	**618**	58	28	**.279**	.356	.420	776	110	84	82	100	43	26	62	0
BAL	69	85	0	.448	28	41	36	571	705	5790	1242	198	34	91	563	725	84	22	.244	.320	.350	670	89	-125	-78	92	39	42	48	-6
WAS	59	95	1	.383	38	32	45	652	924	6043	1302	198	62	112	690	877	75	41	.250	.341	.377	718	95	-28	-27	100	37	34	52	-4
KC	52	102	0	.338	45	22	55	619	831	5860	1325	204	41	112	480	727	67	20	.252	.315	.370	685	86	-111	-113	100	40	30	57	-2
TOT	618					316	300	5756		48237	10937	1680	353	1075	5019	5813	281	601	.260	.341	.394	735					348	253	58	-12

TEAM	CG	SHO	GR	SV	IP	H	HR	BB	SO	BR/9	ERA	AERA	OAV	OOB	PR	APR	PF	OSB	OCS	FA	E	WPB	DP	FW	PW	BW	BSW	DIF
NY	50	10	181	**35**	1382.0	1285	114	652	732	12.9	3.63	107	.249	.335	82	40	93	34	32	.977	136	**31**	**214**	.6	3.9	**10.3**	-.0	5.3
CLE	**67**	**17**	182	24	1384.0	**1233**	116	564	**845**	**11.9**	**3.32**	**127**	**.238**	**.314**	**129**	**134**	101	51	23	.978	129	41	130	1.0	**13.1**	-4.8	-.0	1.7
CHI	65	11	196	13	1389.0	1351	118	**524**	722	12.3	3.73	110	.255	.324	67	59	99	**28**	21	**.979**	**122**	42	160	**1.3**	5.8	2.0	**.5**	-1.6
BOS	50	8	178	20	1398.0	1354	130	668	712	13.3	4.17	111	.254	.340	-1	64	111	39	29	.972	169	41	168	-1.2	6.3	1.4	.1	.4
DET	62	10	187	15	1379.0	1389	140	655	788	13.6	4.06	101	.264	.348	15	9	99	32	35	.976	140	40	151	.4	.9	8.0	.1	-4.5
BAL	38	10	231	24	1360.2	1362	**99**	547	715	12.8	4.20	93	.263	.334	-6	-45	94	58	33	.977	137	40	142	.5	-4.4	-7.6	-.4	4.0
WAS	36	1	244	18	1368.2	1539	171	730	663	15.1	5.33	81	.287	.373	-179	-147	104	55	**40**	.972	171	50	173	-1.3	-14.4	-2.6	-.2	.6
KC	30	3	**251**	18	1370.1	1424	187	679	636	14.1	4.86	89	.271	.357	-107	-78	104	51	**40**	.973	166	57	187	-1.1	-7.6	-11.1	-.0	-5.2
TOT	398	70	1650	167	11031.2					13.2	4.16		.260	.341						.975	1170	342	1325					

Batter-Fielder Wins	Batting Average	On-Base Percentage	Slugging Average	On-Base Plus Slugging	Adjusted OPS	Adjusted Batter Runs
Mantle-NY............8.1	Mantle-NY 353	Williams-Bos 479	Mantle-NY 705	Mantle-NY 1169	Mantle-NY 213	Mantle-NY 90.0
Berra-NY..............4.3	Williams-Bos.........345	Mantle-NY 464	Williams-Bos.........605	Williams-Bos 1084	Williams-Bos 164	Williams-Bos 43.6
Kaline-Det 3.9	Kuenn-Det 332	Nieman-Chi-Bal 436	Maxwell-Det 534	Minoso-Chi 950	Nieman-Chi-Bal 156	Minoso-Chi 42.5
McDougald-NY ..3.5	Maxwell-Det 326	Minoso-Chi 425	Berra-NY 534	Maxwell-Det..........948	Maxwell-Det..........150	Nieman-Chi-Bal ..40.0
Maxwell-Det........3.4	Nieman-Chi-Bal ...320	Maxwell-Det 414	Kaline-Det............530	Nieman-Chi-Bal 931	Minoso-Chi 149	Maxwell-Det........37.5

Runs	Hits	Doubles	Triples	Home Runs	Total Bases	Runs Batted In
Mantle-NY 132	Kuenn-Det 196	Piersall-Bos 40	Simpson-KC...........11	Mantle-NY 52	Mantle-NY 376	Mantle-NY 130
Fox-Chi 109	Kaline-Det 194	Kuenn-Det.....................32	Minoso-Chi 11	Wertz-Cle 32	Kaline-Det 327	Kaline-Det 128
Minoso-Chi 106	Fox-Chi 192	Kaline-Det.....................32	Lemon-Was 11	Berra-NY 30	Jensen-Bos 287	Wertz-Cle 106
	Mantle-NY 188		Jensen-Bos 11	Sievers-Was 29	Minoso-Chi 286	Simpson-KC 105
	Jensen-Bos 182			Maxwell-Det............28		Berra-NY 105

Stolen Bases	Base Stealing Runs	Fielding Runs-Infield	Fielding Runs-Outfield	Wins	Winning Pct.	Complete Games
Aparicio-Chi...........21	Aparicio-Chi 3.2	McDougald-NY 8.8	Kaline-Det............12.2	Lary-Det..................21	Ford-NY 760	Pierce-Chi 21
Rivera-Chi 20	Avila-Cle 2.3	DeMaestri-KC 8.8	Piersall-Bos 7.3		Wynn-Cle 690	Lemon-Cle 21
Avila-Cle 17	Mantle-NY 1.9	Yost-Was 8.3	Maxwell-Det 6.4		Score-Cle 690	Lary-Det 20
Minoso-Chi 12	Jensen-Bos............1.4	Power-KC......................7.8	Lemon-Was 4.2		Pierce-Chi............690	
	Pilarcik-KC 1.3	Buddin-Bos 6.9	Stephens-Bos........3.5		Brewer-Bos...........679	

Strikeouts	Fewest BB/Game	Games	Saves	Base Runners/9	Adjusted Relief Runs	Relief Ranking
Score-Cle 263	Stobbs-Was 2.03	Zuverink-Bal 62	Zuverink-Bal 16	Score-Cle 10.58	Narleski-Cle 17.7	Narleski-Cle........16.1
Pierce-Chi 192	Donovan-Chi........2.26	Crimian-KC 54	Mossi-Cle 11	Donovan-Chi........10.62	Grim-NY 9.3	Delock-Bos 11.1
Foytack-Det 184	Kucks-NY 2.89	Gorman-KC....................52	Morgan-NY 11	Wynn-Cle 10.66	Byerly-Was 7.7	Mossi-Cle 9.4
Hoeft-Det 172	Wynn-Cle 2.95	Mossi-Cle 48	Shantz-KC 9	Brown-Bal..........10.68	Delock-Bos............7.1	Byerly-Was 9.4
Lary-Det................165	Sturdivant-NY 2.96	Delock-Bos 48	Delock-Bos 9	Sturdivant-NY 10.80	Mossi-Cle 6.7	Grim-NY 9.3

Innings Pitched	Opponents' Avg.	Opponents' OBP	Earned Run Average	Adjusted ERA	Adjusted Starter Runs	Pitcher Wins
Lary-Det 294.0	Score-Cle 186	Donovan-Chi..............290	Ford-NY 2.47	Score-Cle 166	Wynn-Cle 46.3	**Wynn-Cle**............5.1
Wynn-Cle 277.2	Larsen-NY 204	Score-Cle.....................290	Score-Cle 2.53	Ford-NY 156	Score-Cle 44.9	**Score-Cle** 4.9
Pierce-Chi..........276.1	Brewer-Bos...........220	Wynn-Cle.....................291	Wynn-Cle 2.72	Wynn-Cle.............154	Ford-NY 37.7	**Lemon-Cle**...........4.6
Foytack-Det 256.0	Harshman-Chi 221	Sturdivant-NY 291	Lemon-Cle 3.03	Lemon-Cle............139	Lary-Det 31.7	**Ford-NY** 4.6
Lemon-Cle 255.1	Sturdivant-NY.......224	Ford-NY 301	Harshman-Chi 3.10	Sullivan-Bos..........135	Lemon-Cle 30.7	**Brewer-Bos**........3.9

His Favorite Year

Mickey Mantle had perhaps his greatest season, winning the Triple Crown and MVP honors, as the Yankees won another flag. Yogi Berra, Moose Skowron, and Gil McDougald contributed significantly on offense, and Whitey Ford captured the ERA title. These are the Yankees that people remember, with Mantle doing it all, Elston Howard and Joe Collins platooning, hard-nosed Hank Bauer in right field, Billy Martin at second, and otherwise undistinguished pitchers like Johnny Kucks, Don Larsen, and Tom Sturdivant enjoying their greatest moments.

The second-place Indians again had a trio of 20-game winners, but their offense had declined sharply. The race was never close. Third-place Chicago added shortstop Luis Aparicio, whose speed and defense garnered him Rookie of the Year honors.

For the first time, AL homers rose over 1,000; every team had a slow-footed slugger or two. Jim Lemon of the Senators whiffed 138 times to set a new record, while his teammate, Eddie Yost, collected 151 walks.

Orioles catcher Tom Gastall died September 20 in a private plane crash. Beloved A's owner-manager Connie Mack passed away at age 93; Mack's longtime lieutenant, Al Simmons, died three months later of a heart attack. Injured Al Rosen and aging Bob Feller retired from the Indians, and down the pennant stretch, the Yankees released Phil Rizzuto. The Scooter would start a forty-season run in the broadcast booth the following spring.

It didn't look like a great World Series for the Yankees, however, as they lost the first two at Ebbets Field. However, after New York tied things up with Ford and Sturdivant tossing complete-game victories, Don Larsen threw a perfect game at Brooklyn in Game 5, fanning Dale Mitchell for the last out. Clem Labine blanked the Yankees in Game 6, but Kucks breezed to a 9–0 win to give the Bronx its sixth championship in eight years. And after 13 "Subway Series" between New York's three teams since 1921—the Yankees winning 10 times—this would be the last of its kind until 2000.

1957 National League

TEAM	W	L	T	PCT	GB	HW	HL	R	OR	PA	H	2B	3B	HR	BB	SO	HB	SH	AVG	OBP	SLG	OPS	AOPS	BR	ABR	PF	SB	CS	BSA	BSR
MIL	95	59	1	.617		**45**	32	**772**	613	6050	1469	221	**62**	**199**	461	729	64	30	.269	.327	**.442**	769	**120**	81	**140**	93	35	16	**69**	2
STL	87	67	0	.565	8	42	35	737	666	6082	**1497**	235	43	132	493	**672**	45	18	**.274**	.333	.405	738	102	37	23	102	58	44	57	-3
BRO	84	70	0	.545	11	43	34	690	**591**	5944	1325	188	38	147	**550**	848	78	33	.253	.325	.387	712	89	-11	-69	110	**60**	34	64	1
CIN	80	74	0	.519	15	**45**	32	747	781	6104	1452	**251**	33	187	546	752	**84**	37	.269	**.338**	.432	**770**	105	**102**	50	107	51	36	59	-1
PHI	77	77	2	.500	18	38	39	623	656	5921	1311	213	44	117	534	758	52	**45**	.250	.322	.375	697	96	-38	-18	97	57	26	**69**	**3**
NY	69	85	0	.448	26	37	40	643	701	5892	1349	171	54	157	447	669	32	25	.252	.311	.393	704	94	-46	-44	100	64	38	63	1
PIT	62	92	1	.403	33	36	41	586	696	5942	1447	231	60	92	374	733	97	23	.268	.315	.384	699	96	-48	-29	97	46	35	57	-2
CHI	62	92	2	.403	33	31	46	628	722	5947	1312	223	31	147	461	989	58	26	.244	.305	.380	685	90	-77	-67	98	28	25	53	-3
TOT	619					317	299	5426		47882	11162	1733	365	1178	3866	6150	237	510	.260	.322	.400	722					399	254	61	-1

TEAM	CG	SHO	GR	SV	IP	H	HR	BB	SO	BR/9	ERA	AERA	OAV	OOB	PR	APR	PF	OSB	OCS	FA	E	WPB	DP	FW	PW	BW	BSW	DIF
MIL	**60**	9	183	24	1411.0	1347	**124**	570	693	12.3	3.47	101	.253	.325	64	5	90	57	37	.981	120	**31**	173	1.0	.5	**14.2**	.2	2.0
STL	46	11	229	**29**	1413.1	1385	140	506	778	12.2	3.78	105	.257	.322	16	29	102	45	29	.979	131	62	168	.4	2.9	2.3	-.3	4.6
BRO	44	**18**	204	**29**	1399.0	**1285**	144	456	**891**	**11.4**	**3.35**	**124**	**.244**	**.305**	**82**	**118**	107	**37**	31	.979	127	38	136	.6	**12.0**	-7.0	.1	1.3
CIN	40	5	**279**	**29**	1395.2	1486	179	429	707	12.7	4.62	89	.275	.331	-116	-75	106	44	26	**.982**	**107**	36	139	**1.7**	-7.6	5.1	-.0	4.0
PHI	54	9	209	23	1401.2	1363	139	**412**	858	11.5	3.79	100	.254	.307	13	1	98	71	24	.976	136	37	117	.2	.1	-1.8	**.3**	1.2
NY	35	9	270	20	1398.2	1436	150	471	701	12.5	4.01	98	.267	.327	-20	-12	101	**37**	30	.974	161	40	**180**	-1.3	-1.2	-4.5	.1	-1.1
PIT	47	9	264	15	1395.0	1463	158	421	663	12.3	3.88	98	.270	.323	0	-14	98	45	27	.972	170	40	143	-1.7	-1.4	-2.9	-.2	-8.7
CHI	30	5	263	26	1403.1	1397	144	601	859	13.0	4.13	94	.261	.336	-39	-41	100	63	**50**	.975	149	53	140	-.5	-4.2	-6.8	-.3	-3.2
TOT	356	75	1901	195	11217.2					12.2	3.88		.260	.322						.977	1101	337	1196					

Batter-Fielder Wins	Batting Average	On-Base Percentage	Slugging Average	On-Base Plus Slugging	Adjusted OPS	Adjusted Batter Runs
Mays-NY 5.6	Musial-StL .351	Musial-StL .422	Mays-NY .626	Musial-StL 1034	Mays-NY 174	Mays-NY 60.6
Musial-StL 4.6	Mays-NY .333	Mays-NY .407	Musial-StL .612	Mays-NY 1033	Musial-StL 172	Aaron-Mil 58.1
Aaron-Mil 4.3	Robinson-Cin .322	Bouchee-Phi .394	Aaron-Mil .600	Aaron-Mil 978	Aaron-Mil 170	Musial-StL 53.7
Mathews-Mil 4.3	Aaron-Mil .322	Ashburn-Phi .390	Snider-Bro .587	Snider-Bro 955	Mathews-Mil 157	Mathews-Mil 47.9
Banks-Chi 3.9	Groat-Pit .315	Temple-Cin .387	Banks-Chi .579	Banks-Chi 939	Banks-Chi 150	Banks-Chi 41.4

Runs	Hits	Doubles	Triples	Home Runs	Total Bases	Runs Batted In
Aaron-Mil 118	Schoendienst-NY-Mil 200	Hoak-Cin 39	Mays-NY 20	Aaron-Mil 44	Aaron-Mil 369	Aaron-Mil 132
Banks-Chi 113	Aaron-Mil 198	Musial-StL 38	Virdon-Pit 11	Banks-Chi 43	Mays-NY 366	Ennis-StL 105
Mays-NY 112	Robinson-Cin 197	Bouchee-Phi 35	Mathews-Mil 9	Snider-Bro 40	Banks-Chi 344	Musial-StL 102
Mathews-Mil 109	Mays-NY 195	Banks-Chi 34	Bruton-Mil 9	Mays-NY 35	Robinson-Cin 323	Banks-Chi 102
Blasingame-StL 108	Ashburn-Phi 186	Moryn-Chi 33		Mathews-Mil 32	Mathews-Mil 309	Hodges-Bro 98

Stolen Bases	Base Stealing Runs	Fielding Runs-Infield	Fielding Runs-Outfield	Wins	Winning Pct.	Complete Games
Mays-NY 38	Temple-Cin 2.4	Logan-Mil 21.6	Ashburn-Phi 25.0	Spahn-Mil 21	Buhl-Mil .720	Spahn-Mil 18
Gilliam-Bro 26	Gilliam-Bro 2.2	Blasingame-StL 19.8	Robinson-Cin 11.5	Sanford-Phi 19	Sanford-Phi .704	Friend-Pit 17
Blasingame-StL 21	Fernandez-Phi 2.2	O'Connell-Mil-NY 11.6	Post-Cin 9.3	Buhl-Mil 18	Spahn-Mil .656	Gomez-NY 16
Temple-Cin 19	Mays-NY 1.7	Spencer-NY 10.9	Thomas-Pit 8.0	Drysdale-Bro 17	Drysdale-Bro .654	Sanford-Phi 15
Fernandez-Phi 18	Robinson-Cin 1.5	Schoendienst-NY-Mil 8.7	Moryn-Chi 7.3	Burdette-Mil 17	Burdette-Mil .654	

Strikeouts	Fewest BB/Game	Games	Saves	Base Runners/9	Adjusted Relief Runs	Relief Ranking
Sanford-Phi 188	Newcombe-Bro 1.49	Lown-Chi 67	Labine-Bro 17	Podres-Bro 9.78	Roebuck-Bro 12.8	Farrell-Phi 17.8
Drott-Chi 170	Roberts-Phi 1.55	Face-Pit 59	Grissom-NY 14	Roberts-Phi 10.45	Farrell-Phi 11.4	Roebuck-Bro 14.4
Drabowsky-Chi 170	Law-Pit 1.67	Labine-Bro 58	Lown-Chi 12	Newcombe-Bro 10.56	Miller-Phi 8.6	Miller-Phi 10.9
Jones-StL 154	Purkey-Pit 1.90	Worthington-NY 55	Wilhelm-StL 11	Spahn-Mil 10.66	Grissom-NY 8.0	Grissom-NY 10.0
Drysdale-Bro 148	Jeffcoat-Cin 2.00	Grissom-NY 55		V.McDaniel-StL 10.70	Brosnan-Chi 7.0	Labine-Bro 8.3

Innings Pitched	Opponents' Avg.	Opponents' OBP	Earned Run Average	Adjusted ERA	Adjusted Starter Runs	Pitcher Wins
Friend-Pit 277.0	Sanford-Phi .221	Podres-Bro .273	Podres-Bro 2.66	Podres-Bro 156	Drysdale-Bro 33.3	**Drysdale-Bro** 4.1
Spahn-Mil 271.0	Podres-Bro .230	Roberts-Phi .283	Drysdale-Bro 2.69	Drysdale-Bro 155	Podres-Bro 31.2	**Podres-Bro** 3.4
Burdette-Mil 256.2	Drott-Chi .234	Newcombe-Bro .288	Spahn-Mil 2.69	Law-Pit 132	Spahn-Mil 25.6	**Spahn-Mil** 3.1
Lawrence-Cin 250.1	Drysdale-Bro .236	Law-Pit .290	Buhl-Mil 2.74	Spahn-Mil 130	Buhl-Mil 18.9	**Newcombe-Bro** 2.1
Roberts-Phi 249.2	Spahn-Mil .237	Spahn-Mil .291	Law-Pit 2.87	Buhl-Mil 128	Sanford-Phi 17.5	**Farrell-Phi** 1.9

On, Wisconsin!

All-Star ballot stuffing led Commissioner Ford Frick to override the election of eight Cincinnati players in the All-Star Game. He inserted Hank Aaron, Willie Mays, and Stan Musial into the lineup—the NL only had 4 hits and lost in Baltimore. Players, coaches, and managers were subsequently awarded the voting. Fans lost the franchise until 1970. Cincy All-Star shortstop Roy McMillan was a recipient of the inaugural Gold Glove, an award for fielders; Gil Hodges and Mays were the other NL choices. After just one player was honored at each position, the leagues awarded individual sets of winners in 1958.

The pennant chase was a quagmire, involving the Braves, Dodgers, Cardinals, Redlegs (it was the Communist-scared '50s), and Phillies. However, a 17–2 August spurt lifted the Braves up to stay. When the Cardinals threatened in September, Milwaukee won eight in a row to wrap things up. Unheralded rookie Bob "Hurricane" Hazle hit .403 in 41 games down the stretch, but a mid-season deal to acquire second baseman Red Schoendienst really put the Braves over the top. Despite playing in a pitcher's park, Milwaukee led the NL in runs.

For just the second time since 1946, an NL team outside New York played in the World Series, and Milwaukee was fit for battle. Down two games to one, the Braves came back from a 5–4 deficit in the bottom of the 10th to win, 7–5, on a home run by Eddie Mathews. Milwaukee then took Game 5 behind Lew Burdette, 1-0. The Yanks won at home in Game 6, but Burdette, who had a 0.67 ERA in 27 innings, won for the third time to clinch. Aaron hit .393 with 3 homers.

Both the Dodgers and Giants departed for the West Coast following the 1957 season. Willie Mays said goodbye to New York by hitting 20 triples, a feat unmatched in the NL until 1996. Dodgers catcher Roy Campanella would never play in Los Angeles, however; in January 1958, he was paralyzed in a car accident.

1957 American League

TEAM	W	L	T	PCT	GB	HW	HL	R	OR	PA	H	2B	3B	HR	BB	SO	HB	SH	AVG	OBP	SLG	OPS	AOPS	BR	ABR	PF	SB	CS	BSA	BSR
NY	98	56	0	.636		**48**	29	**723**	**534**	5993	**1412**	200	**54**	145	562	709	93	24	**.268**	.339	**.409**	**748**	**112**	75	**87**	98	49	38	56	-3
CHI	90	64	1	.584	8	45	32	707	566	6083	1369	208	41	106	**633**	745	75	**68**	.260	**.345**	.375	720	102	42	38	101	**109**	51	**68**	**6**
BOS	82	72	0	.532	16	44	33	721	668	5995	1380	**231**	32	**153**	624	739	41	25	.262	.341	.405	746	104	**80**	40	106	29	21	58	-1
DET	78	76	0	.506	20	45	32	614	614	6005	1376	224	37	116	504	**643**	96	27	.257	.323	.378	701	95	-18	-34	103	36	47	43	-9
BAL	76	76	2	.500	21	42	33	597	588	5966	1326	191	39	87	504	699	**110**	34	.252	.318	.353	671	95	-68	-29	94	57	35	62	0
CLE	76	77	0	.497	21.5	40	37	682	722	5919	1304	199	26	140	591	786	78	26	.252	.329	.382	711	101	11	18	99	40	47	46	-8
KC	59	94	1	.386	38.5	37	40	563	710	5656	1262	195	40	166	364	760	62	24	.244	.295	.394	689	91	-64	-73	102	35	27	56	-2
WAS	55	99	0	.357	43	28	49	603	808	5895	1274	215	38	111	527	733	50	46	.244	.316	.363	679	92	-55	-48	99	13	38	25	-10
TOT	616					329	285	5210		47512	10703	1663	307	1024	4309	5814	274	605	.255	.326	.382	708					368	304	55	-25

TEAM	CG	SHO	GR	SV	IP	H	HR	BB	SO	BR/9	ERA	AERA	OAV	OOB	PR	APR	PF	OSB	OCS	FA	E	WPB	DP	FW	PW	BW	BSW	DIF
NY	41	13	179	**42**	1395.1	**1198**	110	580	**810**	11.7	**3.00**	**120**	**.234**	.315	**122**	**96**	95	40	**51**	.980	123	39	**183**	.2	**9.9**	**9.0**	.0	1.8
CHI	**59**	**16**	200	27	1401.2	1305	124	**470**	665	11.6	3.35	112	.248	.311	69	62	99	38	31	**.982**	**107**	42	169	**1.1**	6.4	3.9	**.9**	.6
BOS	55	9	171	23	1376.2	1391	116	498	692	12.6	3.88	103	.264	.329	-14	16	105	34	31	.976	149	34	179	-1.2	1.7	4.1	.2	.2
DET	52	9	209	21	1417.2	1330	147	505	756	11.9	3.56	108	.250	.318	37	46	102	**33**	31	.980	121	**31**	151	.3	4.8	-3.5	-.6	.0
BAL	44	13	195	25	1408.0	1272	**95**	493	767	**11.5**	3.46	104	.243	**.310**	51	21	95	41	49	.981	112	43	159	.8	2.2	-3.0	.3	-.3
CLE	46	7	204	23	1380.2	1381	130	618	807	13.3	4.06	92	.261	.340	-42	-54	98	61	34	.974	153	60	154	-1.4	-5.6	1.9	-.5	5.1
KC	26	6	**250**	19	1369.2	1344	153	565	626	12.7	4.19	94	.260	.333	-61	-34	104	53	28	.979	125	67	162	.1	-3.5	-7.5	.1	-6.7
WAS	31	5	234	16	1377.0	1482	149	580	691	13.7	4.85	80	.278	.349	-162	-142	103	68	49	.979	128	44	159	-.0	-14.7	-5.0	-.7	-1.6
TOT	354	78	1642	196	11126.2					12.4	3.79		.255	.326						.979	1018	360	1316					

Batter-Fielder Wins	Batting Average	On-Base Percentage	Slugging Average	On-Base Plus Slugging	Adjusted OPS	Adjusted Batter Runs
Mantle-NY............8.2	Williams-Bos.........388	Williams-Bos 526	Williams-Bos.........731	Williams-Bos 1257	Williams-Bos 227	Mantle-NY 94.0
Williams-Bos 7.1	Mantle-NY 365	Mantle-NY 512	Mantle-NY 665	Mantle-NY 1177	Mantle-NY 223	Williams-Bos 84.3
Fox-Chi 6.1	Woodling-Cle 321	Woodling-Cle 408	Sievers-Was 579	Sievers-Was 967	Sievers-Was 163	Sievers-Was 49.1
McDougald-NY ..4.4	Boyd-Bal 318	Minoso-Chi 408	Woodling-Cle 521	Woodling-Cle 929	Woodling-Cle 155	Woodling-Cle......35.0
Sievers-Was 3.9	Fox-Chi 317	Fox-Chi 403	Wertz-Cle 485	Minoso-Chi 862	Minoso-Chi 136	Minoso-Chi 33.9

Runs	Hits	Doubles	Triples	Home Runs	Total Bases	Runs Batted In
Mantle-NY 121	Fox-Chi 196	Minoso-Chi 36	Simpson-KC-NY 9	Sievers-Was 42	Sievers-Was 331	Sievers-Was 114
Fox-Chi 110	Malzone-Bos 185	Gardner-Bal 36	McDougald-NY 9	Williams-Bos 38	Mantle-NY 315	Wertz-Cle 105
Piersall-Bos 103	Minoso-Chi 176	Malzone-Bos..................31	Bauer-NY..................9	Mantle-NY 34	Williams-Bos 307	Minoso-Chi............103
Sievers-Was 99	Mantle-NY 173	Kuenn-Det......................30	Fox-Chi 8	Wertz-Cle 28	Kaline-Det 276	Malzone-Bos 103
	Kuenn-Det 173		Boyd-Bal 8	Zernial-KC 27	Malzone-Bos 271	Jensen-Bos 103

Stolen Bases	Base Stealing Runs	Fielding Runs-Infield	Fielding Runs-Outfield	Wins	Winning Pct.	Complete Games
Aparicio-Chi............28	Aparicio-Chi 3.4	Fox-Chi 25.0	Maxwell-Det 9.7	Pierce-Chi 20	Sturdivant-NY.......727	Pierce-Chi 16
Rivera-Chi 18	Rivera-Chi..............3.3	Bridges-Was 22.6	Colavito-Cle 7.9	Bunning-Det 20	Donovan-Chi.........727	Donovan-Chi 16
Minoso-Chi 18	Mantle-NY 2.5	Malzone-Bos 21.0	Woodling-Cle 6.9	Sturdivant-NY 16	Bunning-Det 714	Brewer-Bos............15
Mantle-NY 16	Landis-Chi 1.7	Klaus-Bos 18.6	Maris-Cle 6.7	Donovan-Chi 16	Wilson-Chi 652	
	Martin-NY-KC 1.3	McDougald-NY 16.9	Kaline-Det..............5.1	Brewer-Bos 16	Pierce-Chi.............625	

Strikeouts	Fewest BB/Game	Games	Saves	Base Runners/9	Adjusted Relief Runs	Relief Ranking
Wynn-Cle..............184	F.Sullivan-Bos 1.80	Zuverink-Bal 56	Grim-NY 19	O'Dell-Bal 9.68	Staley-Chi............19.4	Zuverink-Bal 19.1
Bunning-Det 182	Donovan-Chi........1.84	Hyde-Was 52	Narleski-Cle............16	F.Sullivan-Bos 9.76	Zuverink-Bal 13.1	Grim-NY 18.2
Johnson-Bal..........177	Shantz-NY 2.08	Clevenger-Was 52	Delock-Bos 11	Bunning-Det 10.00	Trucks-KC 10.8	Trucks-KC 14.9
Pierce-Chi 171	Loes-Bal 2.14	Delock-Bos 49	Zuverink-Bal 9	Brown-Bal..........10.26	Grim-NY 9.1	Staley-Chi 12.9
Turley-NY..............152	Bunning-Det 2.42	Trucks-KC 48	Clevenger-Was 8	Donovan-Chi......10.44	Lehman-Bal 7.3	Lehman-Bal........12.1

Innings Pitched	Opponents' Avg.	Opponents' OBP	Earned Run Average	Adjusted ERA	Adjusted Starter Runs	Pitcher Wins
Bunning-Det 267.1	Turley-NY 194	F.Sullivan-Bos 273	Shantz-NY 2.45	Shantz-NY 147	F.Sullivan-Bos 34.5	**F.Sullivan-Bos**....3.5
Wynn-Cle 263.0	Bunning-Det 218	Bunning-Det.................277	Sturdivant-NY 2.54	F.Sullivan-Bos 146	Bunning-Det 32.5	**Bunning-Det** 3.4
Pierce-Chi..........257.0	Foytack-Det 226	Pierce-Chi 287	Bunning-Det 2.69	Bunning-Det 143	Sturdivant-NY 24.9	**Shantz-NY** 2.7
Johnson-Bal 242.0	F.Sullivan-Bos 230	Johnson-Bal.................287	Turley-NY 2.71	Sturdivant-NY 141	Donovan-Chi........22.9	**Sturdivant-NY**....2.6
F.Sullivan-Bos 240.2	Sturdivant-NY 232	Donovan-Chi 291	F.Sullivan-Bos 2.73	Donovan-Chi 135	Shantz-NY 21.3	**Donovan-Chi** 2.4

The Battle of Mickey and Teddy

The Yankees were again the class of the league. New York had 21-year-old Bobby Richardson at second and 20-year-old utility infielder Tony Kubek meshing with 41-year-old outfielder Enos Slaughter, the usual veterans like Yogi Berra and Hank Bauer, and a staff of reasonably talented arms. Mickey Mantle again was voted Most Valuable Player, hitting .365 with 146 walks, and three New York hurlers finished among the league's top five in ERA.

Al Lopez left Cleveland, where he had managed for six years, to take over the White Sox, who finished second after leading the league through June. Chicago became the first club since 1945 to steal more than 100 bases, more than doubling the number of steals of the runner-up (Orioles). Chicago's middle infield duo of Luis Aparicio (the league steals leader) and Nellie Fox (AL-high 196 hits) were turning heads. Meanwhile, the last-place Senators stole just 13 bases in 154 games, the fewest ever.

Ted Williams, 39, became the oldest player ever to win a batting crown; his .388 mark was the highest average in the game since his own .406 in '41. Just to make things a little sweeter, he kicked in 119 walks and 38 homers, but lost to Mantle in a much-disputed MVP vote. Boston finished a surprise third despite a mediocre—at best—pitching corps.

The Indians sank to sixth as their pitching fell apart, but the Tribe did install 22-year-old rookie Roger Maris in the outfield. The tragedy of the season involved Cleveland's Herb Score, who took a Gil McDougald line drive to his right eye on May 7. After a layoff, he returned, hurt his arm, and was never again effective.

A disappointing World Series loss to Milwaukee again showed that the Yankees were, indeed, human. Oddly, they outscored and outhit the Braves in the Series and had a better ERA, but the Braves came up in the clinches.

1958 National League

TEAM	W	L	T	PCT	GB	HW	HL	R	OR	PA	H	2B	3B	HR	BB	SO	HB	SH	AVG	OBP	SLG	OPS	AOPS	BR	ABR	PF	SB	CS	BSA	BSR
MIL	92	62	0	.597		48	29	675	**541**	5859	1388	221	21	167	478	646	**79**	36	**.266**	.329	.412	741	**110**	15	**79**	92	26	8	**76**	3
PIT	84	70	0	.545	8	**49**	28	662	607	5779	1386	229	**68**	134	396	753	68	28	.264	.317	.410	727	100	-24	-6	97	30	15	67	1
SF	80	74	0	.519	12	44	33	**727**	698	5996	1399	**250**	42	170	531	817	68	34	.263	.331	.422	753	106	**40**	57	98	64	29	69	**4**
CIN	76	78	0	.494	16	40	37	695	621	5980	1359	242	40	123	572	765	76	21	.258	.331	.389	720	91	-16	-50	105	61	38	62	0
STL	72	82	0	.468	20	39	38	619	704	5891	1371	216	39	111	533	**637**	44	20	.261	.329	.380	709	90	-37	-61	104	44	43	51	-5
CHI	72	82	0	.468	20	35	42	709	725	5902	1402	207	49	**182**	487	853	42	**45**	.265	.330	**.426**	**756**	107	38	50	98	39	23	63	1
LA	71	83	0	.461	21	39	38	668	761	5804	1297	166	50	172	495	850	68	25	.251	.317	.402	719	92	-37	-56	103	**73**	47	61	0
PHI	69	85	0	.448	23	35	42	664	762	6081	**1424**	238	56	124	**573**	871	70	38	**.266**	**.339**	.400	739	102	22	32	99	51	33	61	0
TOT	616					329	287	5419		47292	11026	1769	365	1183	4065	6192	247	515	.262	.328	.405	733					388	236	62	3

TEAM	CG	SHO	GR	SV	IP	H	HR	BB	SO	BR/9	ERA	AERA	OAV	OOB	PR	APR	PF	OSB	OCS	FA	E	WPB	DP	FW	PW	BW	BSW	DIF
MIL	**72**	**16**	149	17	1376.0	**1261**	125	426	773	**11.2**	**3.21**	110	**.244**	**.303**	**113**	53	89	41	34	.980	120	27	152	.8	5.3	**8.0**	.3	.6
PIT	43	10	222	**41**	1367.0	1344	**123**	470	679	12.1	3.56	109	.261	.323	59	47	98	45	36	.978	133	45	173	.1	4.7	-.6	.0	2.7
SF	38	7	255	25	1389.1	1400	166	512	775	12.6	3.98	96	.263	.330	-4	-26	97	41	**37**	.975	152	41	156	-.9	-2.6	5.7	**.4**	.4
CIN	50	7	219	20	1385.1	1422	148	**419**	705	12.1	3.73	**111**	.267	.322	34	**61**	105	37	28	**.983**	**100**	**25**	148	**1.9**	**6.2**	-5.0	-.0	-4.0
STL	45	6	240	25	1381.2	1398	158	567	822	13.1	4.12	100	.264	.338	-25	2	105	74	23	.974	153	48	163	-.9	.2	-6.2	-.5	2.4
CHI	27	5	**293**	24	1361.0	1322	142	619	805	13.1	4.22	93	.254	.336	-40	-46	99	61	25	.975	150	48	161	-.8	-4.6	5.0	.0	-4.7
LA	30	7	284	31	1368.1	1399	173	606	**855**	13.4	4.47	92	.267	.344	-79	-55	104	**33**	31	.975	146	76	**198**	-.6	-5.5	-5.6	-.0	5.8
PHI	51	6	221	15	1397.0	1480	148	446	778	12.5	4.32	92	.272	.326	-58	-56	100	56	22	.978	129	58	136	.3	-5.6	3.2	-.0	-5.9
TOT	356	64	1883	198	11025.2					12.5	3.95		.262	.328						.977	1083	368	1287					

Batter-Fielder Wins	Batting Average	On-Base Percentage	Slugging Average	On-Base Plus Slugging	Adjusted OPS	Adjusted Batter Runs
Mays-SF 6.3	Ashburn-Phi .350	Ashburn-Phi .440	Banks-Chi .614	Mays-SF 1002	Mays-SF 167	Mays-SF 59.2
Banks-Chi 5.9	Mays-SF .347	Musial-StL .423	Mays-SF .583	Banks-Chi .980	Banks-Chi 157	Aaron-Mil 48.4
Ashburn-Phi 4.5	Musial-StL .337	Mays-SF .419	Aaron-Mil .546	Musial-StL .950	Aaron-Mil 157	Banks-Chi 47.0
Boyer-StL 4.0	Aaron-Mil .326	Temple-Cin .405	Thomas-Pit .528	Aaron-Mil .931	Musial-StL 145	Ashburn-Phi 38.5
Aaron-Mil 3.6	Skinner-Pit .321	Skinner-Pit .387	Musial-StL .528	H.Anderson-Phi .897	H.Anderson-Phi 137	Musial-StL 34.7

Runs	Hits	Doubles	Triples	Home Runs	Total Bases	Runs Batted In
Mays-SF 121	Ashburn-Phi 215	Cepeda-SF 38	Ashburn-Phi 13	Banks-Chi 47	Banks-Chi 379	Banks-Chi 129
Banks-Chi 119	Mays-SF 208	Groat-Pit 36	Virdon-Pit 11	Thomas-Pit 35	Mays-SF 350	Thomas-Pit 109
Aaron-Mil 109	Aaron-Mil 196	Musial-StL 35	Mays-SF 11	Robinson-Cin 31	Aaron-Mil 328	H.Anderson-Phi 97
Boyer-StL 101	Banks-Chi 193	H.Anderson-Phi 34	Banks-Chi 11	Mathews-Mil 31	Cepeda-SF 309	Mays-SF 96
Ashburn-Phi 98	Cepeda-SF 188	Aaron-Mil 34		Aaron-Mil 30	Thomas-Pit 297	Cepeda-SF 96

Stolen Bases	Base Stealing Runs	Fielding Runs-Infield	Fielding Runs-Outfield	Wins	Winning Pct.	Complete Games
Mays-SF 31	Mays-SF 4.7	Zimmer-LA 24.1	Clemente-Pit 19.1	Spahn-Mil 22	Spahn-Mil .667	Spahn-Mil 23
Ashburn-Phi 30	Blasingame-StL 2.7	Boyer-StL 24.1	Flood-StL 13.1	Friend-Pit 22	Burdette-Mil .667	Roberts-Phi 21
T.Taylor-Chi 21	T.Taylor-Chi 2.5	Mazeroski-Pit 17.7	Ashburn-Phi 11.5	Burdette-Mil 20	Friend-Pit .611	Burdette-Mil 19
Blasingame-StL 20	Ashburn-Phi 2.4	Logan-Mil 14.5	Mays-SF 7.0	Roberts-Phi 17	Purkey-Cin .607	Purkey-Cin 17
Gilliam-LA 18	Zimmer-LA 2.4	Neal-LA 13.3	Skinner-Pit 6.7	Purkey-Cin 17	Antonelli-SF .552	Friend-Pit 16

Strikeouts	Fewest BB/Game	Games	Saves	Base Runners/9	Adjusted Relief Runs	Relief Ranking
Jones-StL 225	Burdette-Mil 1.63	Elston-Chi 69	Face-Pit 20	Henry-Chi 8.96	Elston-Chi 11.4	Elston-Chi 20.6
Spahn-Mil 150	Roberts-Phi 1.70	Klippstein-Cin-LA 57	Labine-LA 14	Jay-Mil 9.68	Henry-Chi 10.6	Henry-Chi 12.3
Podres-LA 143	Law-Pit 1.73	Face-Pit 57	Farrell-Phi 11	Porterfield-Pit 10.06	Face-Pit 9.4	Face-Pit 12.1
Antonelli-SF 143	Purkey-Cin 1.76	Hobbie-Chi 55		Spahn-Mil 10.40	Schmidt-Cin 7.2	Farrell-Phi 11.0
Friend-Pit 135	Newcombe-LA-Cin 1.93			Miller-SF 10.43	Porterfield-Pit 7.1	Porterfield-Pit 8.2

Innings Pitched	Opponents' Avg.	Opponents' OBP	Earned Run Average	Adjusted ERA	Adjusted Starter Runs	Pitcher Wins
Spahn-Mil 290.0	Koufax-LA .220	Miller-SF .286	Miller-SF 2.47	Miller-SF 154	Jones-StL 30.7	**Spahn-Mil** 4.1
Burdette-Mil 275.1	Jones-StL .223	Spahn-Mil .287	Jones-StL 2.88	Jones-StL 143	Witt-Pit 26.8	**Burdette-Mil** 2.9
Friend-Pit 274.0	Miller-SF .233	Roberts-Phi .292	Burdette-Mil 2.91	Roberts-Phi 122	Miller-SF 26.7	**Roberts-Phi** 2.6
Roberts-Phi 269.2	Spahn-Mil .237	Burdette-Mil .300	Spahn-Mil 3.07	Brosnan-Chi-StL 121	Roberts-Phi 20.8	**Witt-Pit** 2.5
	Antonelli-SF .239	Purkey-Cin .304	Roberts-Phi 3.24	Burdette-Mil 121	Burdette-Mil 19.0	**Jones-StL** 2.5

Last of the Braves

Milwaukee spent the first half of the season underachieving, but turned on the burners in August and strolled to another relatively easy NL crown. Both Warren Spahn and Lew Burdette won 20 for the Braves, but most of the lineup slumped. The Giants and Dodgers, in their new California surroundings, had fallen into rebuilding mode. East Coast stalwarts Pee Wee Reese and Sal Maglie retired. San Francisco finished a surprising third despite playing youngsters, including Orlando Cepeda (a unanimous Rookie of the Year) and Felipe Alou.

Pittsburgh leapt from seventh to second, improving 22 games under manager Danny Murtaugh. While the team, featuring a cadre of players in their mid-20s, still had a few holes to fill, the Pirates had served notice that their days as a joke were through.

St. Louis' Sam Jones won his third strikeout crown, while Ernie Banks of the fifth-place Cubs took MVP honors. The Phillies, sparked by batting titlist Richie Ashburn, became the first last-place team to lead the NL in batting average; they also paced in hits, walks, and on-base percentage. Philadelphia pitchers, on the other hand, allowed the most runs and the highest opponent batting average in the league.

Unfortunately, the bloom was coming off the rose in Milwaukee, as attendance began to fall even as the Braves won their second straight league title. In fact, fans dropped the team like a hot potato; attendance fell by 11 percent or more every year until 1963. Once again, however, franchise shifting pumped league coffers as the Dodgers' and Giants' moves to the West Coast—and the surprising rise of the Pirates—lifted NL attendance 15 percent.

In retrospect, the World Series was the beginning of the end for the Braves in Milwaukee; up three games to one, and with the final two contests at County Stadium, the Braves lost three straight to the Yankees. This time, Burdette was racked. It was the franchise's last World Series appearance until 1991.

1958 American League

TEAM	W	L	T	PCT	GB	HW	HL	R	OR	PA	H	2B	3B	HR	BB	SO	HB	SH	AVG	OBP	SLG	OPS	AOPS	BR	ABR	PF	SB	CS	BSA	BSR
NY	92	62	1	.597		44	33	**759**	577	5971	**1418**	212	39	**164**	537	822	72	26	**.268**	.336	**.416**	**752**	**116**	**89**	**117**	96	48	32	60	-1
CHI	82	72	1	.532	10	47	30	634	615	5935	1348	191	42	101	518	**669**	72	**49**	.257	.327	.367	694	99	-14	-1	98	**101**	33	**75**	**11**
BOS	79	75	1	.513	13	**49**	28	697	691	5972	1335	**229**	30	155	**638**	820	60	27	.256	**.338**	.400	738	102	75	28	107	29	22	57	-1
CLE	77	76	0	.503	14.5	42	34	694	635	5840	1340	210	31	161	494	819	69	40	.258	.325	.403	728	108	39	56	98	50	49	51	-6
DET	77	77	0	.500	15	43	34	659	606	5805	1384	**229**	41	109	463	678	**75**	22	.266	.326	.389	715	95	21	-24	107	48	32	60	-1
BAL	74	79	1	.484	17.5	46	31	521	**575**	5720	1233	195	19	108	483	731	62	28	.241	.308	.350	658	91	-85	-55	95	33	35	49	-5
KC	73	81	2	.474	19	43	34	642	713	5845	1297	196	**50**	138	452	747	64	25	.247	.307	.381	688	92	-43	-54	102	22	36	38	-8
WAS	61	93	2	.396	31	33	44	553	747	5763	1240	161	38	121	477	751	57	35	.240	.307	.357	664	90	-82	-71	98	22	41	35	-10
TOT	619					347	268	5159		46851	10595	1623	290	1057	4062	6037	252	531	.254	.322	.383	705					353	280	56	-20

TEAM	CG	SHO	GR	SV	IP	H	HR	BB	SO	BR/9	ERA	AERA	OAV	OOB	PR	APR	PF	OSB	OCS	FA	E	WPB	DP	FW	PW	BW	BSW	DIF
NY	53	**21**	184	**33**	1379.0	**1201**	116	557	796	11.8	**3.22**	110	**.235**	.313	**85**	51	94	43	**45**	.978	128	**33**	**182**	-.1	5.3	**12.1**	.2	-2.4
CHI	55	15	204	25	1389.2	1296	152	515	751	11.8	3.61	101	.250	.317	25	5	97	37	34	.981	114	39	160	.7	.5	-.1	**1.4**	2.5
BOS	44	5	201	28	1380.0	1396	121	521	695	12.7	3.92	102	.264	.332	-23	13	106	36	38	.976	145	37	172	-1.1	1.3	2.9	.2	-1.3
CLE	51	2	221	20	1373.1	1283	123	604	766	12.5	3.73	98	.249	.328	6	-13	97	50	33	.974	152	68	171	-1.5	-1.3	5.8	-.4	-2.0
DET	**59**	8	220	19	1357.1	1294	133	437	**797**	11.8	3.59	**112**	.252	.314	26	**62**	107	40	32	**.982**	**106**	43	140	**1.1**	**6.4**	-2.5	.2	-5.2
BAL	55	15	183	28	1369.2	1277	**106**	**403**	749	**11.3**	3.40	106	.249	**.306**	57	32	95	**28**	25	.980	114	46	159	.6	3.3	-5.7	-.3	-.5
KC	42	9	**237**	25	1398.1	1405	150	467	721	12.2	4.15	94	.262	.323	-59	-36	104	39	34	.979	125	66	166	.1	-3.7	-5.6	-.6	5.8
WAS	28	6	222	28	1376.2	1443	156	558	762	13.3	4.53	84	.272	.341	-116	-108	101	80	39	.980	118	58	163	.5	-11.2	-7.3	-.8	2.8
TOT	387	81	1672	206	11024.0					12.2	3.77		.254	.322						.979	1002	390	1313					

Batter-Fielder Wins	Batting Average	On-Base Percentage	Slugging Average	On-Base Plus Slugging	Adjusted OPS	Adjusted Batter Runs
Mantle-NY 6.0	Williams-Bos .328	Williams-Bos .458	Colavito-Cle .620	Williams-Bos 1042	Mantle-NY 189	Mantle-NY 71.2
Colavito-Cle 5.1	Runnels-Bos .322	Mantle-NY .443	Cerv-KC .592	Mantle-NY 1035	Colavito-Cle 183	Colavito-Cle 57.1
Cerv-KC 4.6	Kuenn-Det .319	Runnels-Bos .416	Mantle-NY .592	Colavito-Cle 1024	Williams-Bos 174	Williams-Bos 48.3
Runnels-Bos 3.7	Kaline-Det .313	Colavito-Cle .405	Williams-Bos .584	Cerv-KC 963	Cerv-KC 158	Cerv-KC 38.7
Kaline-Det 3.7	Power-KC-Cle .312	Jensen-Bos .396	Sievers-Was .544	Jensen-Bos 931	Sievers-Was 148	Jensen-Bos 37.1

Runs	Hits	Doubles	Triples	Home Runs	Total Bases	Runs Batted In
Mantle-NY 127	Fox-Chi 187	Kuenn-Det 39	Power-KC-Cle 10	Mantle-NY 42	Mantle-NY 307	Jensen-Bos 122
Runnels-Bos 103	Malzone-Bos 185	Power-KC-Cle 37	Tuttle-KC 9	Colavito-Cle 41	Cerv-KC 305	Colavito-Cle 113
Power-KC-Cle 98	Power-KC-Cle 184	Kaline-Det 34	Lemon-Was 9	Sievers-Was 39	Colavito-Cle 303	Sievers-Was 108
Minoso-Cle 94	Runnels-Bos 183	Runnels-Bos 32	Aparicio-Chi 9	Cerv-KC 38	Sievers-Was 299	Cerv-KC 104
Cerv-KC 93	Kuenn-Det 179	Jensen-Bos 31	Harris-Det 8	Jensen-Bos 35	Jensen-Bos 293	Mantle-NY 97

Stolen Bases	Base Stealing Runs	Fielding Runs-Infield	Fielding Runs-Outfield	Wins	Winning Pct.	Complete Games
Aparicio-Chi 29	Aparicio-Chi 4.3	Kubek-NY 20.4	Kaline-Det 19.8	Turley-NY 21	Turley-NY .750	Turley-NY 19
Rivera-Chi 21	Rivera-Chi 3.6	Malzone-Bos 16.6	Cerv-KC 14.8	Pierce-Chi 17	McLish-Cle .667	Pierce-Chi 19
Landis-Chi 19	Mantle-NY 2.9	Buddin-Bos 14.0	Minoso-Cle 5.8	McLish-Cle 16	Pierce-Chi .607	Lary-Det 19
Mantle-NY 18	Wilson-Det 2.2	Aparicio-Chi 11.5	Kuenn-Det 3.5	Lary-Det 16	Portocarrero-Bal .577	Harshman-Bal 17
Minoso-Cle 14		F.Bolling-Det 11.1	Williams-Bal 2.9		Foytack-Det .536	

Strikeouts	Fewest BB/Game	Games	Saves	Base Runners/9	Adjusted Relief Runs	Relief Ranking
Wynn-Chi 179	Donovan-Chi 1.92	Clevenger-Was 55	Duren-NY 20	Wilhelm-Cle-Bal 9.76	Hyde-Was 21.3	Hyde-Was 32.6
Bunning-Det 177	O'Dell-Bal 2.07	Tomanek-Cle-KC 54	Hyde-Was 18	Ford-NY 9.81	Duren-NY 13.5	Duren-NY 24.1
Turley-NY 168	Sullivan-Bos 2.21	Hyde-Was 53	Kiely-Bos 12	Pierce-Chi 9.96	Kiely-Bos 8.5	Kiely-Bos 9.5
Harshman-Bal 161	Lary-Det 2.35	Wall-Bos 52	Wall-Bos 10	Portocarrero-Bal 10.25	Wall-Bos 5.4	Wall-Bos 8.3
Pascual-Was 146	Pierce-Chi 2.42			Hyde-Was 10.40	Daley-KC 4.4	Morgan-Det 4.5

Innings Pitched	Opponents' Avg.	Opponents' OBP	Earned Run Average	Adjusted ERA	Adjusted Starter Runs	Pitcher Wins
Lary-Det 260.1	Turley-NY .206	Ford-NY .276	Ford-NY 2.01	Ford-NY 176	Ford-NY 37.4	**Ford-NY** 3.9
Ramos-Was 259.1	Bell-Cle .213	Pierce-Chi .279	Pierce-Chi 2.68	Lary-Det 139	Lary-Det 31.8	**Lary-Det** 3.5
Donovan-Chi 248.0	Ford-NY .217	O'Dell-Bal .284	Harshman-Bal 2.89	Pierce-Chi 136	Pierce-Chi 25.8	**Hyde-Was** 3.4
Turley-NY 245.1	Pierce-Chi .227	Portocarrero-Bal .284	Lary-Det 2.90	Harshman-Bal 124	Turley-NY 22.1	**Harshman-Bal** 3.3
Pierce-Chi 245.0	Grant-Cle .228	Harshman-Bal .292	O'Dell-Bal 2.97	McLish-Cle 122	Wilhelm-Cle-Bal 18.1	**Pierce-Chi** 3.0

Yankees Take Rematch

The New York Yankees were again AL champs, this time with no challenges. As the Yankees started ferociously, the rest of the league was so bad that the Kansas City Athletics held second for nearly a month. New York drew well—with no National League competition for the first time—but few other teams boasted strong gates.

Those who went to games didn't see an overabundance of offense. Teams scored an average of just 4.17 times per game, the lowest total in a decade. Mickey Mantle led the AL in walks and runs and finished fourth in steals (the top three thieves were Chicagoans—only the White Sox used stolen bases as a weapon). Ted Williams hit .328 and won his final batting title at age 40.

Yankees righty Bob Turley won 21 games despite leading the AL with 128 walks, but Whitey Ford, just 14–7, was New York's top twirler, towering over the league with a 2.01 ERA. The second-place White Sox, just 82–72, rate as one of the worst-ever pre-expansion runners-up. The Yankees' poor late-season performance—they were barely .500 the last two months, and Hoyt Wilhelm no-hit them on September 20—foreshadowed New York's 1959 collapse.

Hall of Famer Tris Speaker and star outfielder Harry Heilmann died in 1958. Meanwhile, Norm Cash and Johnny Callison debuted with the White Sox. They soon departed for other teams, one reason why Chicago didn't win in the 1960s.

Down three games to one in the World Series, the Yankees appeared headed for a second straight Series loss to the Braves. But Turley shut out Milwaukee, 7–0 in Game 5; then, back in Wisconsin, the Yankees—using Turley in relief twice—took the final two contests. The inability to win just one more Series game was, in essence, the end of the Milwaukee Braves.

1959 National League

TEAM	W	L	T	PCT	GB	HW	HL	R	OR	PA	H	2B	3B	HR	BB	SO	HB	SH	AVG	OBP	SLG	OPS	AOPS	BR	ABR	PF	SB	CS	BSA	BSR
LA	88	68	0	.564		46	32	705	670	6033	1360	196	46	148	**591**	891	**100**	28	.257	.334	.396	730	94	16	-32	107	**84**	51	62	1
MIL	86	70	1	.551	2	**49**	29	724	623	6010	1426	216	36	**177**	488	765	64	27	.265	.326	.417	743	**114**	31	**97**	92	41	14	**75**	4
SF	83	71	0	.539	4	42	35	705	**613**	5890	1377	239	35	167	473	875	73	25	.261	.322	.414	736	104	17	33	98	81	34	70	**6**
PIT	78	76	1	.506	9	47	30	651	680	5952	1414	230	42	112	442	**715**	77	24	.263	.320	.384	704	95	-41	-35	99	32	26	55	-2
CIN	74	80	0	.481	13	43	34	**764**	738	5922	**1448**	**258**	34	161	499	763	53	32	**.274**	**.337**	**.427**	**764**	107	**80**	59	103	65	28	70	5
CHI	74	80	1	.481	13	38	39	673	688	5939	1321	209	44	163	498	911	62	**43**	.249	.317	.398	715	97	-24	-17	99	32	19	63	0
STL	71	83	0	.461	16	42	35	641	725	5907	1432	244	**49**	118	485	747	60	19	.269	.331	.400	731	95	14	-28	106	65	53	55	-4
PHI	64	90	1	.416	23	37	40	599	725	5735	1237	196	38	113	498	858	59	34	.242	.312	.362	674	85	-94	-103	102	39	46	46	-8
TOT	620					344	274	5462		47388	11015	1788	324	1159	3974	6525	232	548	.260	.325	.400	725					439	271	62	2

TEAM	CG	SHO	GR	SV	IP	H	HR	BB	SO	BR/9	ERA	AERA	OAV	OOB	PR	APR	PF	OSB	OCS	FA	E	WPB	DP	FW	PW	BW	BSW	DIF
LA	43	14	241	**26**	1411.2	1317	157	614	**1077**	12.6	3.79	**111**	.247	.329	24	**64**	107	**24**	32	**.981**	**114**	59	154	**1.5**	**6.4**	-3.2	.0	5.3
MIL	**69**	**18**	167	18	1400.2	1406	**128**	429	775	11.9	3.51	101	.260	.315	68	6	90	36	30	.979	127	**30**	138	.8	.6	**9.8**	.4	-3.5
SF	52	12	205	23	1376.1	**1279**	139	500	873	**11.8**	**3.47**	110	**.246**	**.314**	**74**	54	97	50	35	.974	152	36	118	-.8	5.4	3.3	**.6**	-2.6
PIT	48	7	225	17	1393.1	1432	134	**418**	730	12.1	3.90	99	.267	.320	7	-5	98	56	32	.975	154	53	**165**	-.8	-.5	-3.5	-.2	6.1
CIN	44	7	232	**26**	1357.1	1460	162	456	690	12.9	4.31	94	.275	.335	-55	-38	103	40	**39**	.978	126	35	157	.7	-3.8	5.9	.5	-6.3
CHI	30	11	**250**	25	1391.0	1337	152	519	765	12.2	4.01	98	.254	.321	-10	-10	100	107	28	.977	140	46	142	-.0	-1.0	-1.7	-.0	-.2
STL	36	8	231	21	1363.0	1427	137	564	846	13.3	4.34	98	.271	.341	-59	-14	107	53	38	.975	146	61	158	-.4	-1.4	-2.8	-.4	-.9
PHI	54	8	190	15	1354.0	1357	150	474	769	12.4	4.27	96	.261	.324	-49	-24	104	73	38	.973	154	53	132	-.8	-2.4	-10.4	-.8	1.4
TOT	376	85	1741	171	11047.1					12.4	3.95		.260	.325						.977	1113	373	1164					

Batter-Fielder Wins	Batting Average	On-Base Percentage	Slugging Average	On-Base Plus Slugging	Adjusted OPS	Adjusted Batter Runs
Aaron-Mil 6.8	Aaron-Mil .355	Cunningham-StL .453	Aaron-Mil .636	Aaron-Mil 1037	Aaron-Mil 188	Aaron-Mil 77.3
Banks-Chi 6.2	Cunningham-StL .345	Aaron-Mil .401	Banks-Chi .596	Mathews-Mil 983	Mathews-Mil 172	Mathews-Mil 59.6
Mathews-Mil 6.0	Cepeda-SF .317	Moon-LA .394	Mathews-Mil .593	Robinson-Cin 975	Mays-SF 157	Mays-SF 46.9
Mays-SF 4.1	Pinson-Cin .316	Robinson-Cin .391	Robinson-Cin .583	Banks-Chi 970	Banks-Chi 156	Banks-Chi 45.9
Boyer-StL 3.5	Mays-SF .313	Mathews-Mil .390	Mays-SF .583	Mays-SF 964	Robinson-Cin 152	Robinson-Cin 41.8

Runs	Hits	Doubles	Triples	Home Runs	Total Bases	Runs Batted In
Pinson-Cin 131	Aaron-Mil 223	Pinson-Cin 47	Neal-LA 11	Mathews-Mil 46	Aaron-Mil 400	Banks-Chi 143
Mays-SF 125	Pinson-Cin 205	Aaron-Mil 46	Moon-LA 11	Banks-Chi 45	Mathews-Mil 352	Robinson-Cin 125
Mathews-Mil 118	Cepeda-SF 192	Mays-SF 43	White-StL 9	Aaron-Mil 39	Banks-Chi 351	Aaron-Mil 123
Aaron-Mil 116	Temple-Cin 186	Cimoli-StL 40	Pinson-Cin 9	Robinson-Cin 36	Mays-SF 335	Bell-Cin 115
Robinson-Cin 106	Mathews-Mil 182		Dark-Chi 9	Mays-SF 34	Pinson-Cin 330	Mathews-Mil 114

Stolen Bases	Base Stealing Runs	Fielding Runs-Infield	Fielding Runs-Outfield	Wins	Winning Pct.	Complete Games
Mays-SF 27	Mays-SF 4.5	Blasingame-StL 19.9	Virdon-Pit 13.9	Spahn-Mil 21	Face-Pit .947	Spahn-Mil 21
T.Taylor-Chi 23	Pinson-Cin 2.5	Neal-LA 18.4	H.Anderson-Phi 10.0	S.Jones-SF 21	Law-Pit .667	Law-Pit 20
Gilliam-LA 23	Temple-Cin 2.0	Boyer-StL 12.7	Pinson-Cin 8.8	Burdette-Mil 21	Antonelli-SF .655	Burdette-Mil 20
Cepeda-SF 23	T.Taylor-Chi 1.9	Kasko-Cin 10.2	Post-Phi 6.7	Antonelli-SF 19	Buhl-Mil .625	Roberts-Phi 19
Pinson-Cin 21	Cepeda-SF 1.9	Adcock-Mil 9.8	Bell-Cin 3.7			

Strikeouts	Fewest BB/Game	Games	Saves	Base Runners/9	Adjusted Relief Runs	Relief Ranking
Drysdale-LA 242	Newcombe-Cin 1.09	Henry-Chi 65	McMahon-Mil 15	Henry-Chi 9.25	Henry-Chi 20.0	Face-Pit 27.0
S.Jones-SF 209	Burdette-Mil 1.18	Elston-Chi 65	McDaniel-StL 15	Haddix-Pit 9.63	Miller-SF 16.5	Henry-Chi 26.8
Koufax-LA 173	Roberts-Phi 1.22	McDaniel-StL 62	Elston-Chi 13	Craig-LA 9.90	Face-Pit 13.5	Miller-SF 15.1
Antonelli-SF 165	Purkey-Cin 1.78	McMahon-Mil 60	Henry-Chi 12	Newcombe-Cin 10.05	McMahon-Mil 9.9	Elston-Chi 13.3
McCormick-SF 151	Law-Pit 1.79	Miller-SF 59		Conley-Phi 10.15	Elston-Chi 6.8	McMahon-Mil 12.9

Innings Pitched	Opponents' Avg.	Opponents' OBP	Earned Run Average	Adjusted ERA	Adjusted Starter Runs	Pitcher Wins
Spahn-Mil 292.0	S.Jones-SF .228	Haddix-Pit .271	S.Jones-SF 2.83	Conley-Phi 137	Law-Pit 30.5	**S.Jones-SF** 3.6
Burdette-Mil 289.2	Haddix-Pit .228	Newcombe-Cin .279	Miller-SF 2.84	S.Jones-SF 135	S.Jones-SF 30.3	**Newcombe-Cin** 3.6
Antonelli-SF 282.0	Antonelli-SF .233	Conley-Phi .280	Buhl-Mil 2.86	Miller-SF 134	Craig-LA 30.3	**Spahn-Mil** 3.4
S.Jones-SF 270.2	Drysdale-LA .233	Law-Pit .281	Spahn-Mil 2.96	Law-Pit 130	Antonelli-SF 25.5	**Law-Pit** 3.1
Drysdale-LA 270.2	Conley-Phi .235	Antonelli-SF .285	Law-Pit 2.98	Jackson-StL 128	Jackson-StL 25.1	**Drysdale-LA** 2.9

The Sun-Kissed Dodgers

San Francisco, enjoying great years from Willie Mays and Orlando Cepeda, looked to have the race wrapped up in mid-August, but Los Angeles and underachieving Milwaukee caught fire around Labor Day. In mid-September the Dodgers came into San Francisco and swept three, and the Giants dropped like a stone. Milwaukee stayed hot, the Dodgers kept winning, and the season ended in a deadlock.

The resulting playoff was just as close. Underdog Los Angeles won two one-run games, the second in 12 innings, to take the pennant, effectively ending Milwaukee's run of success.

Don Drysdale, winning his first strikeout title, led Los Angeles' patchwork mound staff, and 26-year-old midseason call-up Maury Wills anchored an unspectacular infield. Milwaukee's Warren Spahn led the NL in wins for the sixth time, but Red Schoendienst's illness, and manager Fred Haney's use of weak-hitting first baseman Frank Torre, hamstrung a great attack.

An amazing rookie class sewed the seeds of success for many 1960s clubs. St. Louis debuted Bob Gibson and Tim McCarver, while the Phillies welcomed Chris Short. The Cubs brought up Billy Williams, while the Dodgers summoned Wills and Tommy Davis. San Francisco's Willie McCovey, the most impressive of all, won Rookie of the Year honors.

The Los Angeles Coliseum's ridiculous 252-foot left field fence led baseball to enact a rule that new ballparks must reach 325 feet at all fences and 400 to center. Still, the Dodgers were only fifth in home runs. Chicago's Ernie Banks won MVP honors again. Pittsburgh's Roy Face set an all-time winning percentage mark, while Cincinnati's Vada Pinson blossomed into a star.

Larry Sherry pitched just 14 times in relief (with 9 starts) during the regular season, but he was a bullpen wizard in the World Series. Sherry had 2 wins and 2 saves as Los Angeles wiped out the favored White Sox in six games. Second baseman Charlie Neal hit .370 with 2 homers and Gil Hodges batted .391.

1959 American League

TEAM	W	L	T	PCT	GB	HW	HL	R	OR	PA	H	2B	3B	HR	BB	SO	HB	SH	AVG	OBP	SLG	OPS	AOPS	BR	ABR	PF	SB	CS	BSA	BSR
CHI	94	60	2	.610		**47**	30	669	**588**	6054	1325	220	**46**	97	580	**634**	84	**49**	.250	.327	.364	691	96	-19	-10	99	**113**	53	68	**6**
CLE	89	65	0	.578	5	43	34	**745**	646	5860	1390	216	25	**167**	433	721	60	39	**.263**	.321	**.408**	729	**109**	31	**59**	96	33	36	48	-5
NY	79	75	1	.513	15	40	37	687	647	5980	**1397**	224	40	153	457	828	76	30	.260	.319	.402	721	107	16	41	97	45	22	67	2
DET	76	78	0	.494	18	41	36	713	732	5948	1346	196	30	160	580	737	73	44	.258	**.335**	.400	**735**	102	**58**	20	105	34	17	67	2
BOS	75	79	0	.487	19	43	34	726	696	5985	1335	**248**	28	125	**626**	810	65	23	.256	**.335**	.385	720	98	41	9	105	68	25	**73**	**6**
BAL	74	80	1	.481	20	38	39	551	621	5883	1240	182	23	109	536	690	**88**	20	.238	.310	.345	655	87	-98	-85	98	36	24	60	0
KC	66	88	0	.429	28	37	40	681	760	5885	1383	231	43	117	481	780	69	33	**.263**	.326	.390	716	100	16	4	102	34	24	59	-1
WAS	63	91	0	.409	31	34	43	619	701	5734	1205	173	32	163	517	881	64	26	.237	.308	.379	687	93	-45	-42	100	51	34	60	-1
TOT	618					323	293	5391		47329	10621	1690	267	1091	4210	6081	264	579	.253	.323	.384	707					414	235	64	9

TEAM	CG	SHO	GR	SV	IP	H	HR	BB	SO	BR/9	ERA	AERA	OAV	OOB	PR	APR	PF	OSB	OCS	FA	E	WPB	DP	FW	PW	BW	BSW	DIF
CHI	44	13	**242**	**36**	1425.1	1297	129	525	761	11.7	**3.29**	**114**	.242	**.311**	**91**	**76**	97	56	28	**.979**	130	**31**	141	.6	**7.7**	-1.0	**.5**	9.2
CLE	**58**	7	190	23	1383.2	**1230**	148	635	799	12.3	3.75	98	**.239**	.323	18	-10	95	60	30	.978	127	51	138	.7	-1.0	**6.0**	-.6	7.0
NY	38	**15**	222	28	1399.0	1281	120	594	**836**	12.2	3.60	101	.244	.322	40	7	94	42	32	.978	131	41	160	.5	.7	4.2	.0	-3.5
DET	53	9	197	24	1360.0	1327	177	**432**	829	11.9	4.20	97	.254	.315	-52	-20	105	45	32	.978	**124**	38	131	**.9**	-2.0	2.0	.0	-2.0
BOS	38	9	222	25	1364.0	1386	135	589	724	13.2	4.17	97	.266	.341	-47	-16	105	**37**	28	.978	131	51	**167**	.5	-1.6	.9	**.5**	-2.3
BAL	45	**15**	180	30	1400.1	1290	**111**	476	735	**11.5**	3.56	106	.246	**.311**	47	35	98	40	**43**	.976	146	85	163	-.4	3.5	-8.6	-.1	2.5
KC	44	8	241	21	1360.2	1452	148	492	703	13.2	4.35	92	.274	.338	-74	-51	104	49	20	.973	160	56	156	-1.2	-5.2	.4	-.2	-4.8
WAS	46	10	214	21	1360.0	1358	123	467	694	12.3	4.01	98	.259	.321	-23	-14	101	85	22	.973	162	56	140	-1.4	-1.4	-4.3	-.2	-6.7
TOT	366	86	1708	208	11053.0					12.3	3.86		.253	.323						.977	1111	409	1196					

Batter-Fielder Wins	Batting Average	On-Base Percentage	Slugging Average	On-Base Plus Slugging	Adjusted OPS	Adjusted Batter Runs
Mantle-NY 3.6	Kuenn-Det .353	Yost-Det .435	Kaline-Det .530	Kaline-Det .940	Mantle-NY 152	Mantle-NY 40.7
Runnels-Bos 3.6	Kaline-Det .327	Runnels-Bos .415	Killebrew-Was .516	Mantle-NY .904	Kaline-Det 149	Francona-Cle 40.3
Kaline-Det 3.3	Runnels-Bos .314	Kaline-Det .410	Mantle-NY .514	Kuenn-Det .903	Kuenn-Det 140	Kaline-Det 36.5
Francona-Cle 3.2	Fox-Chi .306	Kuenn-Det .402	Colavito-Cle .512	Yost-Det .871	Woodling-Bal 139	Yost-Det 33.8
Jensen-Bos 3.1	Minoso-Cle .302	Woodling-Bal .402	Lemon-Was .510	Killebrew-Was .870	Killebrew-Was 137	Kuenn-Det 31.8

Runs	Hits	Doubles	Triples	Home Runs	Total Bases	Runs Batted In
Yost-Det 115	Kuenn-Det 198	Kuenn-Det 42	Allison-Was 9	Killebrew-Was 42	Colavito-Cle 301	Jensen-Bos 112
Mantle-NY 104	Fox-Chi 191	Malzone-Bos 34	McDougald-NY 8	Colavito-Cle 42	Killebrew-Was 282	Colavito-Cle 111
Power-Cle 102	Runnels-Bos 176	Fox-Chi 34		Lemon-Was 33	Kuenn-Det 281	Killebrew-Was 105
Jensen-Bos 101	Power-Cle 172	Williams-KC 33		Maxwell-Det 31	Mantle-NY 278	Lemon-Was 100
Kuenn-Det 99	Minoso-Cle 172	Runnels-Bos 33		Mantle-NY 31	Allison-Was 275	Maxwell-Det 95

Stolen Bases	Base Stealing Runs	Fielding Runs-Infield	Fielding Runs-Outfield	Wins	Winning Pct.	Complete Games
Aparicio-Chi 56	Aparicio-Chi 7.8	Gardner-Bal 22.6	Tuttle-KC 9.2	Wynn-Chi 22	Shaw-Chi .750	Pascual-Was 17
Mantle-NY 21	Mantle-NY 3.6	Power-Cle 9.9	Minoso-Cle 9.2	McLish-Cle 19	McLish-Cle .704	Pappas-Bal 15
Landis-Chi 20	Jensen-Bos 2.7	Malzone-Bos 9.7	Jensen-Bos 8.4	Shaw-Chi 18	Wynn-Chi .688	Mossi-Det 15
Jensen-Bos 20	Malzone-Bos 1.3	McDougald-NY 9.0	Landis-Chi 6.7		Mossi-Det .654	Wynn-Chi 14
Allison-Was 13	Yost-Det 1.3	Runnels-Bos 6.3	Colavito-Cle 4.5			Bunning-Det 14

Strikeouts	Fewest BB/Game	Games	Saves	Base Runners/9	Adjusted Relief Runs	Relief Ranking
Bunning-Det 201	Brown-Bal 1.76	Staley-Chi 67	Lown-Chi 15	Shantz-NY 9.22	Staley-Chi 17.2	Duren-NY 23.7
Pascual-Was 185	Lary-Det 1.86	Lown-Chi 60	Staley-Chi 14	Ditmar-NY 9.62	Duren-NY 16.2	Staley-Chi 22.0
Wynn-Chi 179	Garver-KC 1.88	Clevenger-Was 50	Loes-Bal 14	Pascual-Was 10.33	Shantz-NY 12.2	Lown-Chi 14.3
Score-Cle 147	Mossi-Det 1.93	Shaw-Chi 47	Duren-NY 14	Mossi-Det 10.34	Lown-Chi 10.1	Shantz-NY 12.5
Wilhelm-Bal 139	Ramos-Was 2.00		Fornieles-Bos 11	O'Dell-Bal 10.43	Fornieles-Bos 9.3	Fornieles-Bos 11.0

Innings Pitched	Opponents' Avg.	Opponents' OBP	Earned Run Average	Adjusted ERA	Adjusted Starter Runs	Pitcher Wins
Wynn-Chi 255.2	Score-Cle .210	Ditmar-NY .268	Wilhelm-Bal 2.19	Wilhelm-Bal 173	Wilhelm-Bal 39.8	**Pascual-Was** 4.7
Bunning-Det 249.2	Ditmar-NY .211	Pascual-Was .282	Pascual-Was 2.64	Pascual-Was 148	Pascual-Was 33.8	**Wilhelm-Bal** 3.7
Foytack-Det 240.1	Wynn-Chi .216	O'Dell-Bal .284	Shaw-Chi 2.69	Shaw-Chi 140	Shaw-Chi 30.7	**Shaw-Chi** 2.9
Pascual-Was 238.2	O'Dell-Bal .220	Mossi-Det .284	Ditmar-NY 2.90	Walker-Bal 130	Mossi-Det 19.5	**Daley-KC** 2.9
McLish-Cle 235.1	Wilhelm-Bal .224	Brown-Bal .289	Walker-Bal 2.92	O'Dell-Bal 129	O'Dell-Bal 18.7	**Perry-Cle** 2.7

Going to a Go-Go

All eight teams were bunched together until late June, when the White Sox and Indians forged ahead. Up by 1_ games on August 26, Chicago invaded Cleveland and took four straight, effectively ending the race. The "Go-Go" White Sox were called hitless, but outside cavernous Comiskey Park, Chicago had the league's third-best offense. Sherm Lollar's power, Luis Aparicio's defense and speed, and MVP Nellie Fox and Jim Landis' on-base ability supported a short pitching staff. Early Wynn won 22.

Despite Rocky Colavito's 42 homers, the Indians fell again. Cleveland hero Nap Lajoie died at 84, and former Indian Larry Doby ended his career as a part-timer in Chicago.

A slow start put the Yankees in seventh, and Casey Stengel's club never really came together. The pitching was mediocre; what worked with Tom Sturdivant and Bob Turley didn't with Duke Maas and Eli Grba. Mickey Mantle's slump and the aging of Hank Bauer and Yogi Berra contributed to New York distant third-place finish. Perhaps as a result of New York's sputtering, AL attendance was its highest since 1949. Crowds increased in seven cities, doubling in Cleveland and nearly doing so in Chicago (now owned by Bill Veeck).

Even as steals rose to their highest level since the war, home runs increased as well; strikeouts rose for the sixth straight year to 4.92, a new high. Two pitchers who won 498 games between them—Jim Perry and Jim Kaat—debuted. The Red Sox became the last club to integrate, two years after Detroit had done so. The AL remained far behind the NL in employment of African Americans and dark-skinned Latinos, but would soon shorten the gap.

While the White Sox won Game 1 of the World Series, 11–0, they were outscored by the Dodgers the rest of the way, 21–12. Both teams batted .261, but Los Angeles won in six games. Chicago hasn't reached the Series since.

1960 National League

TEAM	W	L	T	PCT	GB	HW	HL	R	OR	PA	H	2B	3B	HR	BB
PIT	95	59	1	.617		**52**	25	**734**	**593**	6029	**1493**	**236**	56	120	486
MIL	88	66	0	.571	7	51	26	724	658	5868	1393	198	48	**170**	463
STL	86	68	1	.558	9	51	26	639	616	5806	1317	213	48	138	501
LA	82	72	0	.532	13	42	35	662	**593**	5935	1333	216	38	126	**529**
SF	79	75	2	.513	16	45	32	671	631	5923	1357	220	**62**	130	467
CIN	67	87	0	.435	28	37	40	640	692	5940	1324	230	40	140	512
CHI	60	94	2	.390	35	33	44	634	776	5960	1293	213	48	119	531
PHI	59	95	0	.383	36	31	46	546	691	5748	1235	196	44	99	448
TOT	619					342	274	5250		47209	10745	1722	384	1042	3937

TEAM	SO	HB	SH	AVG	OBP	SLG	OPS	AOPS	BR	ABR	PF	SB	CS	BSA	BSR
PIT	**747**	69	20	**.276**	**.335**	.407	**742**	108	**73**	69	101	34	24	59	-1
MIL	793	59	23	.265	.323	**.417**	740	**117**	58	**116**	93	69	37	65	2
STL	792	52	31	.254	.321	.393	714	93	14	-38	109	48	35	58	-2
LA	837	**102**	27	.255	.324	.383	707	93	7	-33	106	**95**	53	64	2
SF	846	60	**33**	.255	.317	.393	710	106	-1	41	94	86	45	**66**	**3**
CIN	858	60	34	.250	.318	.388	706	97	0	-11	102	73	37	**66**	**3**
CHI	897	64	19	.243	.313	.369	682	93	-48	-41	99	51	34	60	-1
PHI	1054	66	**33**	.239	.302	.351	653	84	-103	-104	100	45	48	48	-7
TOT	6824	220	532	.255	.319	.388	707					501	313	62	1

TEAM	CG	SHO	GR	SV	IP	H	HR	BB	SO	BR/9	ERA	AERA	OAV	OOB	PR
PIT	47	11	205	33	1399.2	1363	**105**	**386**	811	**11.3**	3.49	107	.257	**.307**	42
MIL	**55**	13	182	28	1387.1	1327	130	518	807	12.2	3.76	91	.251	.320	0
STL	37	11	217	30	1371.0	1316	127	511	906	12.1	3.64	112	.253	.319	18
LA	46	13	204	20	1398.0	**1218**	154	564	**1122**	11.7	**3.40**	**117**	**.234**	.311	**56**
SF	**55**	**16**	214	26	1396.0	1288	107	512	897	11.8	3.44	101	.245	.313	50
CIN	33	8	253	**35**	1390.1	1417	134	442	740	12.3	4.00	96	.267	.326	-37
CHI	36	6	**260**	25	1402.2	1393	152	565	805	12.8	4.35	87	.260	.333	-92
PHI	45	6	199	16	1375.1	1423	133	439	736	12.3	4.01	97	.270	.325	-38
TOT	354	84	1734	213	11120.1					12.1	3.76		.255	.319	

TEAM	APR	PF	OSB	OCS	FA	E	WPB	DP	FW	PW	BW	BSW	DIF
PIT	41	100	44	32	**.979**	128	**35**	**163**	.7	4.2	7.1	-.1	6.1
MIL	-57	91	**38**	33	.976	141	57	137	-.0	-5.9	**11.9**	.2	4.8
STL	64	109	50	37	.976	141	48	152	.0	6.6	-3.9	-.2	6.5
LA	**84**	106	42	34	**.979**	**125**	63	142	**.9**	**8.6**	-3.4	.2	-1.3
SF	6	93	77	20	.972	166	55	117	-1.3	.6	4.2	**.3**	-1.8
CIN	-27	102	56	43	**.979**	**125**	43	155	**.9**	-2.8	-1.1	**.3**	-7.2
CHI	-89	100	91	**59**	.977	143	54	133	-.0	-9.2	-4.2	-.1	-3.5
PHI	-19	103	103	55	.974	155	53	129	-.8	-2.0	-10.7	-.7	-3.8
TOT					.977	1124	408	1128					

Batter-Fielder Wins	Batting Average	On-Base Percentage	Slugging Average	On-Base Plus Slugging	Adjusted OPS	Adjusted Batter Runs
Banks-Chi 6.0	Groat-Pit .325	Ashburn-Chi .415	Robinson-Cin .595	Robinson-Cin 1002	Mathews-Mil 170	Mathews-Mil 56.6
Mays-SF 5.0	Larker-LA .323	Robinson-Cin .407	Aaron-Mil .566	Mathews-Mil 948	Robinson-Cin 169	Mays-SF 51.1
Aaron-Mil 4.5	Mays-SF .319	Mathews-Mil .397	Boyer-StL .562	Mays-SF 936	Mays-SF 164	Robinson-Cin 47.7
Boyer-StL 4.5	Clemente-Pit .314	Moon-LA .383	Mays-SF .555	Boyer-StL 932	Aaron-Mil 161	Aaron-Mil 45.8
Robinson-Cin 4.4	Boyer-StL .304	Mays-SF .381	Banks-Chi .554	Aaron-Mil 919	Banks-Chi 145	Banks-Chi 36.3

Runs	Hits	Doubles	Triples	Home Runs	Total Bases	Runs Batted In
Bruton-Mil 112	Mays-SF 190	Pinson-Cin 37	Bruton-Mil 13	Banks-Chi 41	Aaron-Mil 334	Aaron-Mil 126
Mathews-Mil 108	Pinson-Cin 187	Cepeda-SF 36	Pinson-Cin 12	Aaron-Mil 40	Banks-Chi 331	Mathews-Mil 124
Pinson-Cin 107	Groat-Pit 186	Skinner-Pit 33	Mays-SF 12	Mathews-Mil 39	Mays-SF 330	Banks-Chi 117
Mays-SF 107	Bruton-Mil 180	Robinson-Cin 33	Aaron-Mil 11	Boyer-StL 32	Boyer-StL 310	Mays-SF 103
Aaron-Mil 102	Clemente-Pit 179	Banks-Chi 32		Robinson-Cin 31	Pinson-Cin 308	Boyer-StL 97

Stolen Bases	Base Stealing Runs	Fielding Runs-Infield	Fielding Runs-Outfield	Wins	Winning Pct.	Complete Games
Wills-LA 50	Wills-LA 6.8	Mazeroski-Pit 26.9	Walters-Phi 11.7	Spahn-Mil 21	Broglio-StL .700	Spahn-Mil 18
Pinson-Cin 32	Pinson-Cin 2.8	Wills-LA 19.9	Cepeda-SF 4.6	Broglio-StL 21	Law-Pit .690	Law-Pit 18
T.Taylor-Chi-Phi 26	Javier-StL 2.8	Boyer-StL 16.1	Robinson-Cin 4.3	Law-Pit 20	Spahn-Mil .677	Burdette-Mil 18
Mays-SF 25	Blasingame-SF 2.4	Groat-Pit 13.1	Virdon-Pit 4.2	Burdette-Mil 19	Buhl-Mil .640	Hobbie-Chi 16
Bruton-Mil 22	Ashburn-Chi 2.1	Grammas-StL 12.8	Mays-SF 4.1		Purkey-Cin .607	Friend-Pit 16

Strikeouts	Fewest BB/Game	Games	Saves	Base Runners/9	Adjusted Relief Runs	Relief Ranking
Drysdale-LA 246	Burdette-Mil 1.14	Face-Pit 68	McDaniel-StL 26	McDaniel-StL 8.51	McDaniel-StL 24.7	McDaniel-StL 42.9
Koufax-LA 197	Roberts-Phi 1.29	McDaniel-StL 65	Face-Pit 24	Brosnan-Cin 9.18	Brosnan-Cin 15.0	Face-Pit 21.6
S.Jones-SF 190	Law-Pit 1.33	Elston-Chi 60	Henry-Cin 17	Face-Pit 9.58	Roebuck-LA 14.0	Farrell-Phi 20.8
Broglio-StL 188	Friend-Pit 1.47	Farrell-Phi 59	Brosnan-Cin 12	Marichal-SF 9.63	Farrell-Phi 12.7	Brosnan-Cin 16.3
Friend-Pit 183	Haddix-Pit 1.98	Roebuck-LA 58		Drysdale-LA 9.90	Face-Pit 11.5	Roebuck-LA 14.0

Innings Pitched	Opponents' Avg.	Opponents' OBP	Earned Run Average	Adjusted ERA	Adjusted Starter Runs	Pitcher Wins
Jackson-StL 282.0	Koufax-LA .207	Drysdale-LA .274	McCormick-SF 2.70	Broglio-StL 149	Drysdale-LA 32.9	**McDaniel-StL** 4.7
Friend-Pit 275.2	Williams-LA .210	Friend-Pit .280	Broglio-StL 2.74	Drysdale-LA 140	Broglio-StL 31.5	**Broglio-StL** 4.4
Burdette-Mil 275.2	Broglio-StL .213	Williams-LA .280	Drysdale-LA 2.84	Simmons-Phi-StL 134	McCormick-SF 24.9	**Drysdale-LA** 4.0
Law-Pit 271.2	Drysdale-LA .215	Law-Pit .286	Williams-LA 3.00	Williams-LA 133	Friend-Pit 24.6	**McCormick-SF** 3.0
Drysdale-LA 269.0	Buhl-Mil .229	Burdette-Mil .287	Friend-Pit 3.00	Podres-LA 129	Podres-LA 21.1	**Face-Pit** 2.6

The Wait Is Over

Pittsburgh took an early lead in the NL race, trying to win for the first time in 35 seasons. Milwaukee caught Pittsburgh in July, but then dropped 11 of 15. Victory was sweet for Pirates fans, not far removed from the horror of the early 1950s. Pittsburgh had it all: four quality starters, a bullpen ace, a solid everyday lineup, and a strong bench. Vernon Law won the Cy Young, while scrappy shortstop Dick Groat took MVP honors with equally fiery teammate Don Hoak second.

Milwaukee wasted Henry Aaron, Eddie Mathews, and Warren Spahn's great years; lousy middle-infield production doomed the Braves to second. The third-place Cardinals got nothing from their entire outfield, including 39-year-old Stan Musial. Fifth-place San Francisco moved into windy Candlestick Park, where Juan Marichal debuted July 19 with a one-hitter. Ron Santo joined the Cubs, but the Dodgers' Frank Howard was Rookie of the Year.

Gotham's NL glory days were quickly turning to memory; Alvin Dark, Carl Furillo, and Don Newcombe played their last games. Meanwhile, Dodgers hurler Sandy Koufax set a mark for strikeouts per game, then broke it in 1962. Bespectacled Reds reliever Jim Brosnan penned *The Long Season*, a diary of the 1959 campaign. Some dubbed Brosnan a "traitor" for discussing the goings-on of a major league clubhouse.

The Pirates certainly didn't *look* like a league champion in the three World Series games they lost to the Yankees: 16–3, 10–0, and 12–0. Pittsburgh captured three close ones, however. After taking a 4–0 lead in Game 7, the Pirates fell behind. Down 7–4 in the eighth, Hal Smith's homer put Pittsburgh ahead, 9–7. But the Yankees tied things in the ninth. The baseball season ended suddenly when Bill Mazeroski led off the home ninth with a home run. The last time the Pirates had won the World Series, in 1925, they counted two world championships to the Yankees' one; by the time Mazeroski touched home plate in the bedlam of Forbes Field, the tally was 19–3 in favor of New York—but the Bucs enjoyed their day.

1960 American League

TEAM	W	L	T	PCT	GB	HW	HL	R	OR	PA	H	2B	3B	HR	BB	SO	HB	SH	AVG	OBP	SLG	OPS	AOPS	BR	ABR	PF	SB	CS	BSA	BSR
NY	97	57	1	.630		**55**	22	**746**	627	5981	1377	215	40	**193**	537	818	81	28	.260	.329	**.426**	**755**	**115**	**62**	**106**	94	37	23	62	0
BAL	89	65	0	.578	8	44	33	682	**606**	5911	1307	206	33	123	**596**	801	72	36	.253	.332	.377	709	99	-7	2	99	37	24	61	0
CHI	87	67	0	.565	10	51	26	741	617	5966	1402	**242**	38	112	567	648	95	**54**	**.270**	**.345**	.396	741	107	60	67	99	**122**	48	**72**	**10**
CLE	76	78	0	.494	21	39	38	667	693	5921	**1415**	218	20	127	444	**573**	**97**	32	.267	.325	.388	713	101	-12	9	97	58	25	70	4
WAS	73	81	0	.474	24	32	45	672	696	6004	1283	205	**43**	147	584	883	86	48	.244	.324	.384	708	98	-19	-12	99	52	43	55	-4
DET	71	83	0	.461	26	40	37	633	644	5990	1243	188	34	150	636	728	85	33	.239	.324	.375	699	93	-32	-49	103	66	32	67	3
BOS	65	89	0	.422	32	36	41	658	775	5931	1359	234	32	124	570	798	70	25	.261	.333	.389	722	98	18	-5	104	34	28	55	-2
KC	58	96	1	.377	39	34	43	615	756	5858	1303	212	34	110	513	744	75	12	.249	.316	.366	682	89	-70	-74	101	16	11	59	0
TOT	617					331	285	5414		47562	10689	1720	274	1086	4447	5993	268	661	.255	.328	.388	716					422	234	64	11

TEAM	CG	SHO	GR	SV	IP	H	HR	BB	SO	BR/9	ERA	AERA	OAV	OOB	PR	APR	PF	OSB	OCS	FA	E	WPB	DP	FW	PW	BW	BSW	DIF
NY	38	**16**	**263**	**42**	1398.0	1225	123	609	712	12.0	**3.52**	102	**.238**	.320	**55**	11	93	43	30	.979	129	52	162	.2	1.1	**10.7**	-.1	8.1
BAL	**48**	11	177	22	1375.2	**1222**	**117**	552	785	**11.8**	**3.52**	108	.241	.317	54	45	98	54	23	**.982**	**108**	58	172	**1.4**	4.6	.2	-.1	6.0
CHI	42	11	254	26	1381.0	1338	127	533	695	12.3	3.60	105	.258	.326	41	28	98	41	31	**.982**	109	**28**	**175**	**1.4**	2.8	6.8	**.9**	-1.8
CLE	32	10	219	30	1382.1	1308	161	636	771	12.8	3.95	95	.252	.334	-12	-34	97	59	32	.978	128	51	165	.2	-3.4	.9	.3	1.1
WAS	34	10	258	35	1405.1	1392	130	538	775	12.6	3.77	103	.260	.329	16	18	100	**40**	**40**	.973	165	54	159	-2.1	1.8	-1.2	-.5	-1.9
DET	40	7	209	25	1405.2	1336	141	**474**	**824**	11.9	3.64	**109**	.251	**.316**	37	**49**	102	53	32	.977	138	50	138	-.5	**5.0**	-5.0	.2	-5.7
BOS	34	6	252	23	1361.0	1440	127	580	767	13.6	4.62	87	.273	.346	-113	-84	104	49	25	.976	141	67	156	-.6	-8.5	-.5	-.3	-2.0
KC	44	4	227	14	1374.0	1428	160	525	664	13.1	4.38	91	.271	.339	-77	-59	103	83	21	.979	127	54	149	.3	-6.0	-7.5	-.1	-5.7
TOT	312	75	1859	217	11083.0					12.5	3.87		.255	.328						.978	1045	414	1276					

Batter-Fielder Wins	Batting Average	On-Base Percentage	Slugging Average	On-Base Plus Slugging	Adjusted OPS	Adjusted Batter Runs
Mantle-NY............3.8	Runnels-Bos 320	Yost-Det 414	Maris-NY 581	Mantle-NY 957	Mantle-NY 166	Mantle-NY 51.4
Maris-NY..............3.6	Smith-Chi 315	Woodling-Bal 401	Mantle-NY 558	Maris-NY 952	Maris-NY 164	Maris-NY 42.4
Williams-Bos 3.6	Minoso-Chi 311	Runnels-Bos 401	Killebrew-Was.......534	Sievers-Chi 930	Sievers-Chi 152	Williams-Bos 41.7
Aparicio-Chi........3.4	Skowron-NY 309	Mantle-NY 399	Sievers-Chi...........534	Killebrew-Was 909	Killebrew-Was 145	Sievers-Chi 34.1
Skowron-NY........3.1	Kuenn-Cle.............308	Sievers-Chi 396	Skowron-NY 528	Skowron-NY 881	Skowron-NY 144	Skowron-NY 30.5

Runs	Hits	Doubles	Triples	Home Runs	Total Bases	Runs Batted In
Mantle-NY 119	Minoso-Chi 184	Francona-Cle 36	Fox-Chi 10	Mantle-NY 40	Mantle-NY 294	Maris-NY 112
Maris-NY 98	Robinson-Bal........175	Skowron-NY 34	Robinson-Bal............9	Maris-NY 39	Maris-NY 290	Minoso-Chi..........105
Minoso-Chi 89	Fox-Chi 175	Minoso-Chi 32		Lemon-Was 38	Skowron-NY 284	Wertz-Bos 103
Landis-Chi 89	Smith-Chi..............169	Freese-Chi 32		Colavito-Det............35	Minoso-Chi 284	Lemon-Was 100
Sievers-Chi 87	Runnels-Bos 169			Killebrew-Was 31	Lemon-Was 268	Gentile-Bal 98

Stolen Bases	Base Stealing Runs	Fielding Runs-Infield	Fielding Runs-Outfield	Wins	Winning Pct.	Complete Games
Aparicio-Chi............51	Aparicio-Chi 8.4	Aparicio-Chi 28.9	Tuttle-KC 7.1	Perry-Cle 18	Perry-Cle 643	Lary-Det 15
Landis-Chi 23	Landis-Chi 3.0	Boyer-NY 20.6	Piersall-Cle 5.9	Estrada-Bal 18	Ditmar-NY.............625	Ramos-Was 14
Green-Was 21	Kaline-Det..............2.8	Power-Cle 20.0	Allison-Was.............5.0	B.Daley-KC 16	Estrada-Bal...........621	Herbert-KC 14
Kaline-Det 19	Piersall-Cle 2.2	Fox-Chi 17.0	Cerv-KC-NY 4.9		Pappas-Bal...........577	Wynn-Chi 13
Piersall-Cle 18	Mantle-NY 2.0	Robinson-Bal 15.4	Landis-Chi 3.7			B.Daley-KC............13

Strikeouts	Fewest BB/Game	Games	Saves	Base Runners/9	Adjusted Relief Runs	Relief Ranking
Bunning-Det 201	Brown-Bal............1.25	Fornieles-Bos 70	Klippstein-Cle 14	Staley-Chi............9.52	Staley-Chi............15.4	Staley-Chi 28.2
Ramos-Was..........160	Mossi-Det 1.82	Staley-Chi......................64	Fornieles-Bos 14	Brown-Bal............10.08	Fornieles-Bos 15.2	Fornieles-Bos 23.1
Wynn-Chi..............158	Hall-KC 1.88	Clevenger-Was 53	Moore-Chi-Was 13	Wilhelm-Bal 10.10	Sisler-Det 13.7	Sisler-Det............20.9
Lary-Det................149	Lary-Det 2.03	Moore-Chi-Was..............51	B.Shantz-NY 11	Aguirre-Det........10.27	Aguirre-Det..........12.7	Aguirre-Det 12.7
Estrada-Bal 144	Pierce-Chi............2.11	Kutyna-KC.......................51	....	Stafford-NY........10.35	Stobbs-Was 6.7	B.Shantz-NY 10.1

Innings Pitched	Opponents' Avg.	Opponents' OBP	Earned Run Average	Adjusted ERA	Adjusted Starter Runs	Pitcher Wins
Lary-Det 274.1	Estrada-Bal...........218	Brown-Bal 283	Baumann-Chi 2.67	Bunning-Det 142	Bunning-Det 30.6	**Staley-Chi** 3.2
Ramos-Was 274.0	Turley-NY 222	Bunning-Det..................292	Bunning-Det 2.79	Baumann-Chi 141	Baumann-Chi 20.8	**Fornieles-Bos** 2.6
Perry-Cle 261.1	Barber-Bal 226	Mossi-Det 293	Brown-Bal............3.06	Brown-Bal 125	Herbert-KC 18.4	**Bunning-Det** 2.5
Herbert-KC 252.2	Ford-NY 235	Ford-NY 297	Ditmar-NY............3.06	Herbert-KC 121	Kralick-Was 16.8	**Herbert-KC** 2.3
Bunning-Det 252.0	Bunning-Det 236	Hall-KC.........................299	Ford-NY 3.08	Barber-Bal 118	Brown-Bal............13.4	**Sisler-Det** 2.2

Casey's Last Flag

The Yankees, eerily resembling the 1959 model, sleepwalked through much of the season, but eventually woke up; they overtook surprising Baltimore in September and brought it home by winning their final 15 contests. Right fielder Roger Maris won the MVP award for the Yankees, who set a league record with 193 homers. New York was the only AL club to draw more than one million fans each year of the decade. Once again, Casey Stengel manipulated a staff of largely undistinguished pitchers into a cohesive unit, and the starting lineup was successfully rebuilt.

Baltimore's "Baby Birds" staff, including four starting pitchers aged 21 or 22, propelled the Orioles from seventh place to second. Third-place Chicago reacquired Minnie Minoso, but had a poorly constructed offense and thin starting pitching. Washington, with young talent beginning to jell, rose from last to fifth, and announced plans to move to the Twin Cities for 1961. The AL scheduled a new expansion club for the capital, with another slated for Los Angeles; the move from eight to ten teams proved a seismic shift.

Owner Arnold Johnson of last-place Kansas City had, for years, been feeding talent to the Yankees—including Roger Maris—for very little in return. Johnson's death in 1960 ended that. Charlie Finley bought the club in 1961.

Boston's Ted Williams homered in his last at bat at Fenway to close out a spectacular career. The Yankees also lost Gil McDougald to the rocking chair, while two-time batting titlist Mickey Vernon hung 'em up to manage the new Senators.

Following the Yankees' disappointing World Series loss to the Pirates, New York management pulled what would later be called a "Steinbrenner" and sacked Stengel, the most successful manager in history. It was arguable that the game had passed The Old Professor by, but still…

1961 National League

TEAM	W	L	T	PCT	GB	HW	HL	R	OR	PA	H	2B	3B	HR	BB	SO	HB	SH	AVG	OBP	SLG	OPS	AOPS	BR	ABR	PF	SB	CS	BSA	BSR
CIN	93	61	0	.604		47	30	710	**653**	5796	1414	**247**	35	158	423	761	50	29	.270	.325	.421	746	102	20	11	101	70	33	**68**	**4**
LA	89	65	0	.578	4	45	32	735	697	5940	1358	193	40	157	**596**	796	**96**	23	.262	**.338**	.405	743	95	30	-29	109	**86**	45	66	3
SF	85	69	1	.552	8	45	32	**773**	655	5887	1379	219	32	183	506	764	70	30	.264	.329	**.423**	**752**	108	**36**	64	96	79	54	59	-2
MIL	83	71	1	.539	10	45	32	712	656	5958	1365	199	34	**188**	534	880	62	**34**	.258	.328	.415	743	**109**	19	**66**	94	70	43	62	0
STL	80	74	1	.519	13	**48**	29	703	668	5944	1436	236	51	103	494	745	70	33	.271	.334	.393	727	89	-3	-66	110	46	28	62	0
PIT	75	79	0	.487	18	38	39	694	675	5867	**1448**	232	**57**	128	428	**721**	64	27	**.273**	.328	.410	738	101	7	5	100	26	30	46	-5
CHI	64	90	2	.416	29	40	37	689	800	6000	1364	238	51	176	539	1027	52	32	.255	.325	.418	743	101	17	8	101	35	25	58	-1
PHI	47	107	1	.305	46	22	55	584	796	5870	1265	185	50	103	475	928	108	46	.243	.310	.357	667	83	-126	-118	99	56	30	65	2
TOT	619					330	286	5600		47262	11029	1749	350	1196	3995	6622	254	572	.262	.327	.405	732					468	288	62	2

TEAM	CG	SHO	GR	SV	IP	H	HR	BB	SO	BR/9	ERA	AERA	OAV	OOB	PR	APR	PF	OSB	OCS	FA	E	WPB	DP	FW	PW	BW	BSW	DIF
CIN	46	**12**	210	**40**	1370.0	**1300**	147	500	829	12.0	3.78	107	.250	.318	38	42	101	68	34	.977	134	63	124	.7	4.2	1.1	**.4**	9.7
LA	40	10	239	35	1378.1	1346	167	544	**1105**	12.7	4.04	107	.256	.329	-2	43	108	53	32	.975	144	80	162	.1	4.3	-2.9	.3	10.2
SF	39	9	235	30	1388.0	1306	152	502	924	**11.9**	3.77	101	**.249**	**.316**	40	6	95	63	30	.977	133	43	126	.8	.6	6.4	-.2	.5
MIL	**57**	8	194	16	1391.1	1357	153	493	652	12.1	3.89	96	.258	.322	21	-26	93	**42**	33	**.982**	**111**	**41**	152	**2.0**	-2.6	**6.5**	-.0	.0
STL	49	10	184	24	1368.2	1334	136	570	823	12.7	**3.74**	**118**	.256	.330	**44**	**92**	109	68	41	.972	166	61	165	-1.1	**9.1**	-6.5	-.0	1.5
PIT	34	9	236	29	1362.0	1442	**121**	**400**	759	12.3	3.92	102	.274	.326	17	10	99	44	25	.975	150	58	**187**	-.2	1.0	.5	-.5	-2.7
CHI	34	6	248	25	1385.0	1492	165	465	755	12.9	4.48	93	.277	.336	-70	-45	104	61	34	.970	183	85	175	-2.0	-4.5	.8	-.1	-7.2
PHI	29	9	**257**	13	1383.1	1452	155	521	775	13.1	4.61	88	.273	.340	-88	-81	101	69	**59**	.976	146	80	179	.0	-8.0	-11.7	.2	-10.5
TOT	328	73	1803	212	11026.2					12.5	4.03		.262	.327						.976	1167	511	1270					

Batter-Fielder Wins
Robinson-Cin......4.9
Mays-SF 4.7
Aaron-Mil 4.6
Mathews-Mil........4.2
Boyer-StL 4.0

Batting Average
Clemente-Pit.........351
Pinson-Cin 343
Boyer-StL 329
Moon-LA...............328
Aaron-Mil 327

On-Base Percentage
Moon-LA 434
Robinson-Cin..............404
Mathews-Mil 402
Boyer-StL....................397
Mays-SF 393

Slugging Average
Robinson-Cin 611
Cepeda-SF 609
Aaron-Mil 594
Mays-SF 584
Stuart-Pit 581

On-Base Plus Slugging
Robinson-Cin......1015
Mays-SF 977
Aaron-Mil 974
Cepeda-SF 970
Clemente-Pit 949

Adjusted OPS
Aaron-Mil 165
Robinson-Cin........164
Mays-SF 162
Cepeda-SF 158
Mathews-Mil 156

Adjusted Batter Runs
Aaron-Mil 54.9
Robinson-Cin......51.9
Mays-SF 51.8
Mathews-Mil 48.9
Cepeda-SF 45.4

Runs
Mays-SF 129
Robinson-Cin........117
Aaron-Mil 115
Boyer-StL.............109

Hits
Pinson-Cin............208
Clemente-Pit 201
Aaron-Mil 197
Boyer-StL.............194
Cepeda-SF 182

Doubles
Aaron-Mil 39
Pinson-Cin 34
Santo-Chi 32
Robinson-Cin 32
Mays-SF 32

Triples
Altman-Chi.............12
White-StL...............11
Callison-Phi 11
Boyer-StL...............11

Home Runs
Cepeda-SF 46
Mays-SF 40
Robinson-Cin.........37
Stuart-Pit 35
Adcock-Mil.............35

Total Bases
Aaron-Mil 358
Cepeda-SF 356
Mays-SF 334
Robinson-Cin........333
Clemente-Pit 320

Runs Batted In
Cepeda-SF..........142
Robinson-Cin 124
Mays-SF.............123
Aaron-Mil 120
Stuart-Pit 117

Stolen Bases
Wills-LA 35
Pinson-Cin.............23
Robinson-Cin..........22
Aaron-Mil 21
Mays-SF 18

Base Stealing Runs
Robinson-Cin 3.8
Wills-LA 2.5
Maye-Mil 1.9
Pinson-Cin 1.6
Gonzalez-Phi 1.5

Fielding Runs-Infield
Mazeroski-Pit.............35.7
Boyer-StL..................13.6
Banks-Chi 13.2
Amaro-Phi 13.1
Groat-Pit 10.8

Fielding Runs-Outfield
Clemente-Pit........10.0
Pinson-Cin 8.7
Robinson-Cin 4.6
Musial-StL 3.9
Flood-StL 3.8

Wins
Spahn-Mil 21
Jay-Cin 21
O'Toole-Cin 19

Winning Pct.
Podres-LA............783
O'Toole-Cin...........679
Jay-Cin 677
Burdette-Mil 621
Spahn-Mil 618

Complete Games
Spahn-Mil 21
Koufax-LA.............15
Jay-Cin 14
Burdette-Mil 14

Strikeouts
Koufax-LA 269
Williams-LA 205
Drysdale-LA.........182
O'Toole-Cin 178
Gibson-StL 166

Fewest BB/Game
Burdette-Mil 1.09
Friend-Pit 1.72
Purkey-Cin 1.86
Spahn-Mil 2.19
Ellsworth-Chi 2.31

Games
Baldschun-Phi 65
Miller-SF 63
Face-Pit 62
Elston-Chi 58
Anderson-Chi 57

Saves
Miller-SF 17
Face-Pit 17
Henry-Cin 16
Brosnan-Cin 16
L.Sherry-LA 15

Base Runners/9
Miller-SF 9.81
Face-Pit 10.27
K.Johnson-Cin ..10.30
Sturdivant-Pit 10.40
Spahn-Mil 10.42

Adjusted Relief Runs
Miller-SF 16.3
Perranoski-LA......15.7
Henry-Cin 9.6
McMahon-Mil 8.3
Brosnan-Cin 7.6

Relief Ranking
Miller-SF 28.0
Perranoski-LA 20.9
Brosnan-Cin 15.1
Schultz-Chi 13.8
Henry-Cin 11.3

Innings Pitched
Burdette-Mil 272.1
Spahn-Mil 262.2
Cardwell-Chi......259.1
Koufax-LA.........255.2
O'Toole-Cin........252.2

Opponents' Avg.
Koufax-LA............222
Jay-Cin 236
Sadecki-StL 238
Gibson-StL 239
O'Toole-Cin..........240

Opponents' OBP
Spahn-Mil 291
Koufax-LA 295
Burdette-Mil 295
Purkey-Cin 296
Jackson-StL 301

Earned Run Average
Spahn-Mil 3.02
O'Toole-Cin..........3.10
Simmons-StL 3.13
McCormick-SF 3.20
Gibson-StL 3.24

Adjusted ERA
Simmons-StL........141
Gibson-StL 136
O'Toole-Cin 131
Spahn-Mil 124
Koufax-LA 123

Adjusted Starter Runs
O'Toole-Cin..........25.8
Gibson-StL 24.3
Spahn-Mil 22.8
Simmons-StL 21.0
Koufax-LA............19.9

Pitcher Wins
Spahn-Mil 4.1
Miller-SF 3.1
Gibson-StL 2.9
O'Toole-Cin 2.6
Simmons-StL 2.5

Cincinnati Surprise

Cincinnati took the flag in one of the oddest seasons ever. The Reds were 17 games over .500 at home despite being outscored at Crosley Field. Cincinnati had the league's best pitching—as well as a more efficient offense—on the road. The club had Vada Pinson, the major league leader in hits, and MVP Frank Robinson, plus a few other decent regulars. Jerry Lynch enjoyed one of the all-time great seasons for a bench player, and five pitchers—three starters and two relievers—carried the load.

Second-place Los Angeles, mixing the unproven and the elderly, never capitalized despite the Reds' early-season sputtering. For the third straight year, however, Dodgers hurlers paced the NL in strikeouts.

The aging Pirates fell to eighth, although Roberto Clemente won his first of four batting titles. Chicago debuted Lou Brock and Kenny Hubbs on September 10. Neither would be around when the Cubs finally turned it around years later. Meanwhile, the Phillies lost 23 straight, falling far into the basement with the NL's worst record in a decade.

As runs per game rose to 4.52, the highest of the 1960s, complete games dropped to a new low; only Warren Spahn finished more than 15. Despite excellent seasons by Spahn and Hank Aaron, Milwaukee's classic era was over. Fans deserted the Braves; attendance plunged 26 percent, then 30 more in 1962. Attendance fell in every NL city except Cincinnati, so the league decided to pre-empt a proposed rival, the Continental League, by expanding to New York and Houston for 1962.

The Yankees blew apart the Reds, taking the World Series in five games. "Embarrassing, wasn't it?" wrote Cincy reliever Jim Brosnan the next year in a *Sports Illustrated* article. Just a few months after throwing out the first pitch at Game 3, former Reds outfielder Dummy Hoy died at age 99.

1961 American League

TEAM	W	L	T	PCT	GB	HW	HL	R	OR	PA	H	2B	3B	HR	BB	SO	HB	SH	AVG	OBP	SLG	OPS	AOPS	BR	ABR	PF	SB	CS	BSA	BSR
NY	109	53	1	.673		**65**	16	827	612	6239	1461	194	40	**240**	543	785	57	35	.263	.330	**.442**	**772**	**118**	79	**124**	95	28	18	61	0
DET	101	61	1	.623	8	50	31	**841**	671	6378	**1481**	215	**53**	180	**673**	867	64	38	**.266**	**.347**	.421	768	108	**96**	73	103	98	36	**73**	**9**
BAL	95	67	1	.586	14	48	33	691	**588**	6211	1393	**227**	36	149	581	902	**78**	23	.254	.326	.390	716	101	-16	10	97	39	30	57	-2
CHI	86	76	1	.531	23	53	28	765	726	6285	1475	216	46	138	550	**612**	71	**57**	.265	.335	.395	730	103	16	28	98	**100**	40	71	8
CLE	78	83	0	.484	30.5	40	41	737	752	6252	1493	257	39	150	492	720	73	28	**.266**	.326	.406	732	104	9	30	97	34	11	76	4
BOS	76	86	1	.469	33	50	31	729	792	6307	1401	251	37	112	647	847	81	29	.254	.334	.374	708	94	-19	-36	102	56	36	61	0
MIN	70	90	1	.438	38	36	44	707	778	6156	1353	215	40	167	597	840	67	33	.250	.326	.397	723	94	-5	-43	106	47	43	52	-5
LA	70	91	1	.435	38.5	46	36	744	784	6252	1331	218	22	189	681	1068	80	30	.245	.331	.398	729	91	15	-61	111	37	28	57	-2
WAS	61	100	0	.379	47.5	33	46	618	776	6062	1307	217	44	119	558	917	73	21	.244	.315	.367	682	89	-84	-74	99	81	47	63	1
KC	61	100	1	.379	47.5	33	47	683	863	6164	1342	216	47	90	580	772	89	25	.247	.320	.354	674	84	-91	-102	102	58	22	**73**	5
TOT	811					454	353	7342		62306	14037	2226	404	1534	5902	8330	319	733	.256	.329	.395	724					578	311	65	18

TEAM	CG	SHO	GR	SV	IP	H	HR	BB	SO	BR/9	ERA	AERA	OAV	OOB	PR	APR	PF	OSB	OCS	FA	E	WPB	DP	FW	PW	BW	BSW	DIF
NY	47	14	201	**39**	1451.0	1288	137	542	866	**11.5**	3.46	107	.239	.311	91	45	92	**43**	31	**.980**	**124**	46	**180**	**1.6**	4.5	**12.3**	-.2	9.8
DET	**62**	12	220	30	1459.1	1404	170	**469**	836	11.7	3.55	116	.252	.311	78	88	102	45	**39**	.976	146	42	147	.3	8.7	7.2	**.7**	3.0
BAL	54	**21**	168	33	1471.1	**1226**	**109**	617	926	**11.5**	**3.22**	**120**	**.227**	**.308**	**132**	**108**	96	52	31	**.980**	128	75	173	1.4	**10.7**	1.0	-.4	1.3
CHI	39	3	260	33	1448.2	1491	158	498	814	12.4	4.06	97	.268	.326	-5	-23	97	48	32	**.980**	128	**35**	138	1.4	-2.3	2.8	.6	2.5
CLE	35	12	228	23	1443.1	1426	178	599	801	12.8	4.15	95	.258	.331	-20	-34	98	53	38	.977	139	58	142	.6	-3.4	3.0	.2	-2.9
BOS	35	6	231	30	1442.2	1472	167	679	831	13.5	4.29	97	.266	.345	-43	-19	104	68	24	.977	144	55	170	.4	-1.9	-3.6	-.2	.2
MIN	49	14	217	23	1432.1	1415	163	570	914	12.8	4.28	99	.256	.329	-41	-6	105	56	24	.972	174	58	150	-1.4	-.6	-4.3	-.7	-3.0
LA	25	5	**311**	34	1438.0	1391	180	713	**973**	13.4	4.31	105	.254	.341	-46	28	112	78	32	.969	192	77	154	-2.4	2.8	-6.0	-.4	-4.4
WAS	39	8	220	21	1425.0	1405	131	586	666	12.8	4.23	95	.260	.333	-33	-34	100	83	34	.975	156	78	171	-.4	-3.4	-7.3	-.0	-8.3
KC	32	5	268	23	1415.0	1519	141	629	703	14.0	4.74	88	.275	.351	-113	-85	104	52	26	.972	175	75	160	-1.4	-8.4	-10.1	.3	.2
TOT	417	100	2324	289	14426.2					12.6	4.02		.256	.329						.976	1506	599	1585					

Batter-Fielder Wins	Batting Average	On-Base Percentage	Slugging Average	On-Base Plus Slugging	Adjusted OPS	Adjusted Batter Runs
Cash-Det.............7.6	Cash-Det 361	Cash-Det 487	Mantle-NY 687	Cash-Det 1148	Mantle-NY 210	Mantle-NY 85.6
Mantle-NY...........7.4	Kaline-Det............324	Mantle-NY 448	Cash-Det 662	Mantle-NY 1135	Cash-Det 198	Cash-Det 83.0
Gentile-Bal..........5.6	Piersall-Cle 322	Gentile-Bal.................423	Gentile-Bal 646	Gentile-Bal..........1069	Gentile-Bal............189	Gentile-Bal 65.4
Colavito-Det........4.7	Mantle-NY 317	Pearson-LA 420	Maris-NY 620	Killebrew-Min......1012	Maris-NY 170	Maris-NY 56.8
Howard-NY..........4.3	Gentile-Bal 302	Killebrew-Min 405	Killebrew-Min 606	Maris-NY 993	Killebrew-Min........159	Colavito-Det........49.4

Runs	Hits	Doubles	Triples	Home Runs	Total Bases	Runs Batted In
Maris-NY 132	Cash-Det 193	Kaline-Det.....................41	Wood-Det 14	Maris-NY 61	Maris-NY 366	Maris-NY 142
Mantle-NY 132	B.Robinson-Bal 192	B.Robinson-Bal.............38	Lumpe-KC 9	Mantle-NY 54	Cash-Det 354	Gentile-Bal 141
Colavito-Det..........129	Kaline-Det 190	Kubek-NY 38	Keough-Was 9	Killebrew-Min.........46	Mantle-NY 353	Colavito-Det 140
Cash-Det 119	Francona-Cle........178	Siebern-KC 36		Gentile-Bal.............46	Colavito-Det..........338	Cash-Det 132
Kaline-Det 116	Richardson-NY 173	Power-Cle 34		Colavito-Det............45	Killebrew-Min........328	Mantle-NY 128

Stolen Bases	Base Stealing Runs	Fielding Runs-Infield	Fielding Runs-Outfield	Wins	Winning Pct.	Complete Games
Aparicio-Chi............53	Aparicio-Chi 7.1	Boyer-NY 27.6	Kaline-Det............10.6	Ford-NY 25	Ford-NY 862	Lary-Det 22
Howser-KC 37	Howser-KC 5.0	Lumpe-KC 19.1	Colavito-Det 8.3	Lary-Det..................23	Terry-NY 842	Pascual-Min 15
Wood-Det 30	Wood-Det 3.5	Power-Cle 13.8	Landis-Chi 7.7	Barber-Bal 18	Arroyo-NY.............750	Barber-Bal 14
Hinton-Was 22	Hinton-Was............3.1	Kubek-NY 13.7	Jensen-Bos............6.7	Bunning-Det 17	Lary-Det 719	
Bruton-Det..............22	Bruton-Det 2.7	Schilling-Bos 11.8	Bruton-Det 6.5	Terry-NY 16		

Strikeouts	Fewest BB/Game	Games	Saves	Base Runners/9	Adjusted Relief Runs	Relief Ranking
Pascual-Min..........221	Mossi-Det 1.76	Arroyo-NY.....................65	Arroyo-NY 29	Donovan-Was......9.39	Arroyo-NY...........20.7	Arroyo-NY 41.5
Ford-NY 209	Brown-Bal 1.78	Morgan-LA 59	Wilhelm-Bal 18	Morgan-LA 9.43	Morgan-LA 18.1	Wilhelm-Bal 30.3
Bunning-Det 194	Donovan-Was......1.87	Lown-Chi 59	Fornieles-Bos 15	Hall-Bal 9.71	Wilhelm-Bal 18.0	Fox-Det 25.4
Pizarro-Chi 188	Terry-NY 2.01	Kunkel-KC.....................58	Moore-Min 14	Terry-NY 9.80	Fox-Det 16.2	Morgan-LA..........22.3
McBride-LA 180	McClain-Was 2.04	Fornieles-Bos 57	Fox-Det 12	Fowler-LA 9.81	Hillman-Bos 12.4	Funk-Cle 16.2

Innings Pitched	Opponents' Avg.	Opponents' OBP	Earned Run Average	Adjusted ERA	Adjusted Starter Runs	Pitcher Wins
Ford-NY 283.0	Estrada-Bal..........207	Donovan-Was 267	Donovan-Was.........2.40	Donovan-Was 167	Hoeft-Bal 28.2	**Arroyo-NY** 4.4
Lary-Det 275.1	Pappas-Bal...........208	Terry-NY 275	Stafford-NY.........2.68	Stafford-NY 139	Mossi-Det 27.9	**Lary-Det**..............3.3
Bunning-Det 268.0	Pascual-Min 217	Bunning-Det.................284	Mossi-Det 2.96	Mossi-Det 139	Donovan-Was......26.9	**Donovan-Was** 3.3
Ramos-Min 264.1	Barber-Bal 218	Brown-Bal 284	Pappas-Bal..........3.04	Archer-KC 131	Bunning-Det 25.7	**Wilhelm-Bal** 3.0
Pascual-Min 252.1	Donovan-Was.......224	Lary-Det.......................290	Pizarro-Chi 3.05	Schwall-Bos..........129	Lary-Det 25.3	**Stafford-NY**.......2.8

As the Records Fall

Expansion to ten teams and 162 games meant more games, more traveling, and many new faces. Debuts included Carl Yastrzemski, who replaced Ted Williams in Boston; new Yankees Al Downing and Tom Tresh; Angels Dean Chance and Jim Fregosi; Cleveland's Sam McDowell; Detroit's Bill Freehan; and Baltimore's Boog Powell. By the mid-1960s, all had made significant contributions.

Playing more games, hitters clubbed 41 percent more homers—but home runs per contest also rose 8 percent, due largely to Los Angeles' tiny Wrigley Field, home to more than 3 homers *per game*. Expansion raised total attendance, but most teams' admissions declined; Chicago, Boston, Cleveland, and Baltimore experienced frightening decreases. One team that didn't draw, in 1961 or later, was the "new" Washington Senators, arguably the least successful franchise in league history.

Roger Maris and Mickey Mantle spent the summer chasing Babe Ruth's single-season homer record. Mantle dropped out due to injury, but Maris took it to the wire, clubbing No. 61 on closing day. Maris won his second straight MVP, but he lost a lot of hair in the grueling chase. The Yankees' 240 homers set an all-time record.

Detroit's rookie infielder Jake Wood broke the strikeout record; whiffs rose to 5.14 per game, a new high, and would keep rising. Yankee Luis Arroyo's 29 (unofficial) saves also established a new mark. The changes in baseball reflected strongly against the death of Dead Ball Era denizen Ty Cobb.

Detroit, flush with offense from Norm Cash, Al Kaline, and newly acquired Rocky Colavito, hung neck-and-neck with New York until early September. The Yankees simply out-clubbed them.

Under new manager Ralph Houk, the Bronx Bombers won a fairly easy five-game World Series from Cincinnati, blowing apart the Reds in the final two contests, 7–0, and 13–5. Whitey Ford broke Babe Ruth's mark for consecutive scoreless innings in Series play.

1962 National League

TEAM	W	L	T	PCT	GB	HW	HL	R	OR	PA	H	2B	3B	HR	BB	SO	HB	SH	AVG	OBP	SLG	OPS	AOPS	BR	ABR	PF	SB	CS	BSA	BSR
SF	103	62	0	.624		**61**	21	**878**	690	6277	**1552**	235	32	**204**	523	**822**	76	42	**.278**	**.341**	**.441**	**782**	**118**	**126**	**141**	98	73	50	59	-1
LA	102	63	0	.618	1	54	29	842	697	6362	1510	192	**65**	140	572	886	**83**	32	.268	.337	.400	737	111	39	90	94	**198**	43	**82**	**29**
CIN	98	64	0	.605	3.5	58	23	802	685	6273	1523	**252**	40	167	498	903	57	41	.270	.332	.417	749	104	57	32	103	66	39	63	1
PIT	93	68	0	.578	8	51	30	706	**626**	6035	1468	240	**65**	108	432	836	54	17	.268	.321	.394	715	98	-16	-17	100	50	39	56	-3
MIL	86	76	0	.531	15.5	49	32	730	665	6155	1376	204	38	181	**581**	975	47	34	.252	.326	.403	729	105	17	37	97	57	27	68	3
STL	84	78	1	.519	17.5	44	37	774	664	6307	1528	221	31	137	515	846	69	45	.271	.335	.394	729	93	23	-44	110	86	41	68	5
PHI	81	80	0	.503	20	46	34	705	759	6131	1410	199	39	142	531	923	**83**	**53**	.260	.330	.390	720	103	5	27	97	79	42	65	3
HOU	64	96	2	.400	36.5	32	48	592	717	6198	1370	170	47	105	493	806	75	38	.246	.310	.351	661	91	-120	-71	93	42	30	58	-1
CHI	59	103	0	.364	42.5	32	49	632	827	6173	1398	196	56	126	504	1044	54	39	.253	.317	.377	694	89	-55	-78	104	78	50	61	0
NY	40	120	1	.250	60.5	22	58	617	948	6242	1318	166	40	139	616	991	58	32	.240	.318	.361	679	88	-76	-86	102	59	48	55	-4
TOT	812					449	361	7278		62153	14453	2075	453	1449	5265	9032	373	656	.261	.327	.393	720					788	409	66	30

TEAM	CG	SHO	GR	SV	IP	H	HR	BB	SO	BR/9	ERA	AERA	OAV	OOB	PR	APR	PF	OSB	OCS	FA	E	WPB	DP	FW	PW	BW	BSW	DIF
SF	**62**	10	216	39	1461.2	1399	148	503	886	11.9	3.79	100	.251	**.314**	24	0	96	65	26	.977	142	**47**	153	1.0	.0	**14.1**	-.4	5.9
LA	44	8	249	**46**	1488.2	**1386**	115	588	**1104**	12.1	3.62	100	**.245**	.317	54	3	92	59	34	.970	193	71	144	-2.1	.3	9.0	**2.6**	9.7
CIN	51	13	222	35	1460.2	1397	149	567	964	12.4	3.75	107	.254	.327	31	43	102	75	36	.977	145	67	144	.6	4.3	3.2	-.2	9.1
PIT	40	13	263	41	1432.1	1433	118	466	897	12.1	**3.37**	117	.262	.320	**90**	89	100	86	31	.976	152	66	**177**	.2	8.9	-1.7	-.6	5.8
MIL	59	10	206	24	1434.2	1443	151	**407**	802	**11.8**	3.68	103	.262	.315	42	20	96	**49**	44	**.980**	**124**	50	154	**1.9**	2.0	3.7	.0	-2.6
STL	53	**17**	208	25	1463.1	1394	149	517	914	11.9	3.55	**120**	.252	.318	64	**108**	108	73	40	.979	132	76	170	1.5	**10.8**	-4.4	.2	-5.0
PHI	43	7	247	24	1426.2	1469	155	574	863	13.2	4.28	90	.268	.341	-53	-66	98	67	47	.977	138	89	167	1.0	-6.6	2.7	.0	3.4
HOU	34	9	264	19	1453.2	1446	**113**	471	1047	12.1	3.83	98	.259	.319	19	-15	95	119	43	.973	173	99	149	-1.0	-1.5	-7.1	-.4	-6.0
CHI	29	4	**309**	26	1438.1	1509	159	601	783	13.5	4.54	91	.272	.346	-95	-59	105	101	**58**	.977	146	99	171	.6	-5.9	-7.8	-.3	-8.6
NY	43	4	254	10	1430.0	1577	192	571	772	13.8	5.04	83	.281	.349	-175	-129	106	94	50	.967	210	97	167	-3.3	-12.9	-8.6	-.7	-14.5
TOT	458	95	2438	289	14490.0					12.5	3.94		.261	.327						.975	1555	761	1596					

Batter-Fielder Wins
Mays-SF 6.2
Robinson-Cin 5.6
H.Aaron-Mil 4.8
Mazeroski-Pit......4.7
T.Davis-LA 3.7

Batting Average
T.Davis-LA 346
Robinson-Cin 342
Musial-StL 330
White-StL 324
H.Aaron-Mil 323

On-Base Percentage
Robinson-Cin 421
Musial-StL 416
Skinner-Pit 395
Altman-Chi 393
H.Aaron-Mil 390

Slugging Average
Robinson-Cin 624
H.Aaron-Mil 618
Mays-SF 615
Howard-LA 560
T.Davis-LA 535

On-Base Plus Slugging
Robinson-Cin......1045
H.Aaron-Mil 1008
Mays-SF 999
Musial-StL 924
T.Davis-LA 910

Adjusted OPS
Robinson-Cin........172
H.Aaron-Mil 171
Mays-SF 167
T.Davis-LA 151
Howard-LA............149

Adjusted Batter Runs
Robinson-Cin......64.8
H.Aaron-Mil 58.3
Mays-SF 57.7
T.Davis-LA 44.4
Mathews-Mil 31.6

Runs
Robinson-Cin........134
Wills-LA 130
Mays-SF 130
H.Aaron-Mil 127
T.Davis-LA 120

Hits
T.Davis-LA 230
Wills-LA 208
Robinson-Cin........208
White-StL..............199
Groat-Pit 199

Doubles
Robinson-Cin 51
Mays-SF 36
Groat-Pit 34

Triples
Wills-LA 10
Virdon-Pit.................10
W.Davis-LA 10
Callison-Phi 10

Home Runs
Mays-SF 49
H.Aaron-Mil 45
Robinson-Cin..........39
Banks-Chi 37
Cepeda-SF 35

Total Bases
Mays-SF 382
Robinson-Cin........380
H.Aaron-Mil 366
T.Davis-LA 356
Cepeda-SF 324

Runs Batted In
T.Davis-LA 153
Mays-SF..............141
Robinson-Cin 136
H.Aaron-Mil 128
Howard-LA 119

Stolen Bases
Wills-LA 104
W.Davis-LA 32
Pinson-Cin..............26
Javier-StL 26
Taylor-Phi................20

Base Stealing Runs
Wills-LA 18.3
W.Davis-LA............4.6
Mays-SF 3.3
Pinson-Cin 2.9
Javier-StL 2.6

Fielding Runs-Infield
Mazeroski-Pit..............40.2
Groat-Pit 16.1
Santo-Chi...................16.1
Lillis-Hou 10.0
Wine-Phi 7.8

Fielding Runs-Outfield
Callison-Phi 18.8
Mays-SF 7.3
Clemente-Pit..........7.1
Flood-StL 5.2
W.Davis-LA............5.1

Wins
Drysdale-LA............25
Sanford-SF 24
Purkey-Cin..............23
Jay-Cin 21

Winning Pct.
Purkey-Cin 821
Sanford-SF 774
Drysdale-LA 735
Pierce-SF 727
Shaw-Mil..............625

Complete Games
Spahn-Mil 22
O'Dell-SF 20
Mahaffey-Phi 20
Drysdale-LA 19

Strikeouts
Drysdale-LA..........232
Koufax-LA 216
Gibson-StL 208
Farrell-Hou............203
O'Dell-SF 195

Fewest BB/Game
Shaw-Mil.............1.76
Friend-Pit 1.82
Spahn-Mil 1.84
Pierce-SF 1.94
Purkey-Cin 2.00

Games
Perranoski-LA................70
Baldschun-Phi 67
Roebuck-LA 64
Face-Pit 63
Olivo-Pit 62

Saves
Face-Pit 28
Perranoski-LA 20
Miller-SF 19
McDaniel-StL..........14

Base Runners/9
Face-Pit 9.20
Umbricht-Hou 9.40
Koufax-LA............9.42
Shantz-Hou-StL ..9.88
Farrell-Hou 10.06

Adjusted Relief Runs
Face-Pit 20.4
McMahon-Mil-Hou19.5
Shantz-Hou-StL ..15.1
Umbricht-Hou 12.8
Baldschun-Phi 11.8

Relief Ranking
Face-Pit...............40.9
McMahon-Mil-Hou28.6
Baldschun-Phi 21.1
Shantz-Hou-StL..19.1
Elston-Chi 19.1

Innings Pitched
Drysdale-LA 314.1
Purkey-Cin 288.1
O'Dell-SF 280.2
Mahaffey-Phi 274.0
Jay-Cin 273.0

Opponents' Avg.
Koufax-LA............197
Gibson-StL 204
Bennett-Phi..........224
Drysdale-LA 230
Farrell-Hou 233

Opponents' OBP
Koufax-LA 261
Farrell-Hou..................279
Drysdale-LA.................282
Pierce-SF.....................283
Spahn-Mil 284

Earned Run Average
Koufax-LA...............2.54
Shaw-Mil...............2.80
Purkey-Cin 2.81
Drysdale-LA 2.83
Gibson-StL 2.85

Adjusted ERA
Gibson-StL 150
Purkey-Cin...........143
Koufax-LA 143
Broglio-StL...........142
Shaw-Mil 136

Adjusted Starter Runs
Purkey-Cin 34.7
Gibson-StL 34.5
Broglio-StL 31.1
Friend-Pit 27.4
Drysdale-LA 27.1

Pitcher Wins
Gibson-StL 4.7
Face-Pit 4.1
Spahn-Mil 3.5
Drysdale-LA 3.3
Purkey-Cin 3.0

Shades of '51

The new ten-team National League had great teams, mediocre teams, and the Mets, perhaps the worst ever. Between first and last lay 60_ games, the largest gap in 27 years.

The Giants, Reds, and Dodgers battled at the top. Cincinnati hung close, but down the stretch the New York transplants provided the thrills.

Los Angeles, playing in new Chavez Ravine, saw attendance increase by 56 percent; solid pitching and expansive surroundings translated into the club's first 100-win season since 1953. Despite Maury Wills' record 104 steals and MVP award, Tommy Davis was the Dodgers' key. Don Drysdale took the Cy Young, while Sandy Koufax led in ERA. The two were 1-2 in strikeouts although Koufax missed two months with circulatory problems.

The Giants scored more runs than any team since 1953. Willie Mays, second in MVP voting, and Orlando Cepeda each drove in and scored more than 100. Meanwhile, 20-homer man Willie McCovey sat on the bench.

The Phillies improved nearly 30 games, and Pittsburgh debuted Willie Stargell and Bob Veale. Chicago's Ken Hubbs was Rookie of the Year—teammate Billy Williams had won the award the previous year. Richie Ashburn, the first batter in Mets history, retired rather than risk another 120-loss season.

While home runs rose to a record high, they decreased per game due to large new parks. Sparked by Wills, the stolen base made a comeback. Steals per game reached their highest level since the 1920s. League attendance rose annually through 1966; the Dodgers drew two million each year. In yet another honor, Jackie Robinson became the first African American Hall of Famer.

LA led by 4 games in mid-September. At that point, the Dodgers began losing, and despite playing .500 ball over the last two weeks, the Giants forced a tie. With their three-game playoff tied one game each, the Dodgers took a 4–2 lead to the top of the ninth in the third game. The Giants capitalized on walks and bobbles to win the game, and the pennant, 6–4. The World Series went to the Yankees in seven tight games.

1962 American League

TEAM	W	L	T	PCT	GB	HW	HL	R	OR	PA	H	2B	3B	HR	BB	SO	HB	SH	AVG	OBP	SLG	OPS	AOPS	BR	ABR	PF	SB	CS	BSA	BSR
NY	96	66	0	.593		**50**	30	**817**	680	6393	**1509**	240	29	199	584	842	79	32	**.267**	.337	**.426**	**763**	**115**	**89**	**116**	97	42	29	59	-1
MIN	91	71	1	.562	5	45	36	798	713	6362	1445	215	39	185	649	823	71	31	.260	**.338**	.412	750	104	68	39	104	33	20	62	0
LA	86	76	0	.531	10	40	41	718	706	6255	1377	232	35	137	602	917	**82**	29	.250	.325	.380	705	99	-22	1	97	46	27	63	1
DET	85	76	0	.528	10.5	49	33	758	692	6234	1352	191	36	**209**	**651**	894	56	33	.248	.330	.411	741	101	41	15	104	69	21	77	8
CHI	85	77	0	.525	11	43	38	707	**658**	6297	1415	250	56	92	620	**674**	**82**	41	.257	.334	.372	706	96	-11	-7	100	**76**	40	66	3
CLE	80	82	0	.494	16	43	38	682	745	6137	1341	202	22	180	502	939	52	**54**	.245	.312	.388	700	97	-48	-27	97	35	16	69	2
BAL	77	85	0	.475	19	44	38	652	680	6158	1363	225	34	156	516	931	75	32	.248	.314	.387	701	100	-43	2	94	45	32	58	-1
BOS	76	84	0	.475	19	39	40	707	756	6177	1429	**257**	53	146	525	923	59	27	.258	.324	.403	727	98	10	-12	103	39	33	54	-3
KC	72	90	0	.444	24	39	42	745	837	6302	1467	220	**58**	116	556	803	78	42	.263	.332	.386	718	95	2	-31	105	**76**	21	**78**	**9**
WAS	60	101	1	.373	35.5	27	53	599	716	6072	1370	206	38	132	466	789	71	15	.250	.308	.373	681	90	-85	-80	99	99	53	65	3
TOT	809					419	389	7183		62387	14068	2238	400	1552	5671	8535	336	705	.255	.325	.394	719					560	292	66	21

TEAM	CG	SHO	GR	SV	IP	H	HR	BB	SO	BR/9	ERA	AERA	OAV	OOB	PR	APR	PF	OSB	OCS	FA	E	WPB	DP	FW	PW	BW	BSW	DIF
NY	33	10	248	42	1470.1	1375	146	499	838	**11.6**	3.70	101	**.247**	**.310**	44	8	94	**34**	26	.979	131	**34**	151	.4	.8	**11.7**	-.3	2.5
MIN	**53**	11	241	27	1463.1	1400	166	**493**	**948**	11.9	3.89	105	.253	.317	13	30	103	41	31	.980	129	68	**173**	.5	3.0	3.9	-.2	2.8
LA	23	**15**	**345**	**47**	1466.0	1412	**118**	616	858	12.8	3.70	104	.253	.330	**45**	27	97	52	35	.973	175	55	153	-2.2	2.7	.1	-.1	4.5
DET	46	8	245	35	1443.2	1452	169	503	873	12.4	3.81	**107**	.259	.321	26	**41**	103	47	26	.974	156	45	114	-1.1	**4.1**	1.5	.6	-.6
CHI	50	13	265	28	1451.2	1380	123	537	821	12.0	3.73	105	.251	.317	38	29	98	72	24	**.982**	**110**	46	153	**1.6**	2.9	-.7	.0	.1
CLE	45	12	242	31	1441.0	1410	174	594	780	12.7	4.14	94	.258	.331	-27	-44	98	54	**37**	.978	139	43	168	-.1	-4.4	-2.7	-.0	6.2
BAL	32	8	253	33	1462.1	**1373**	147	549	898	12.0	**3.69**	100	.249	.318	**45**	1	93	80	**37**	.980	122	78	152	.9	.1	.2	-.3	-4.9
BOS	34	12	222	40	1437.2	1416	159	632	923	13.1	4.22	98	.258	.337	-40	-14	104	70	19	.979	131	60	152	.3	-1.4	-1.2	-.5	-1.1
KC	32	4	274	33	1434.0	1450	199	655	825	13.5	4.79	88	.263	.343	-131	-85	106	65	25	.979	132	88	131	.3	-8.5	-3.1	**.7**	1.7
WAS	38	11	266	13	1445.0	1400	151	593	771	12.5	4.04	100	.256	.328	-12	-1	102	45	32	.978	139	46	160	-.1	-.1	-8.0	.0	-12.3
TOT	386	104	2601	329	14515.0					12.4	3.97		.255	.325						.978	1364	563	1507					

Batter-Fielder Wins	Batting Average	On-Base Percentage	Slugging Average	On-Base Plus Slugging	Adjusted OPS	Adjusted Batter Runs
Mantle-NY............5.0	Runnels-Bos.........326	Mantle-NY..................486	Mantle-NY...........605	Mantle-NY..........1091	Mantle-NY............198	Mantle-NY..........62.9
Bressoud-Bos....3.9	Mantle-NY...........321	Siebern-KC.................412	Killebrew-Min.......545	Killebrew-Min........912	Siebern-KC..........138	Siebern-KC.........36.5
Boyer-NY............3.4	Robinson-Chi........312	Cunningham-Chi.........410	Colavito-Det.........514	Siebern-KC..........907	Killebrew-Min.......137	Killebrew-Min......30.1
Colavito-Det........3.1	Hinton-Was...........310	Runnels-Bos...............408	Cash-Det.............513	Cash-Det..............894	Cash-Det..............134	Colavito-Det........28.7
B.Robinson-Bal..3.0	Siebern-KC...........308	Robinson-Chi..............384	Allison-Min...........511	Colavito-Det..........885	Colavito-Det..........132	Robinson-Chi......28.7

Runs	Hits	Doubles	Triples	Home Runs	Total Bases	Runs Batted In
Pearson-LA..........115	Richardson-NY....209	Robinson-Chi................45	Cimoli-KC................15	Killebrew-Min..........48	Colavito-Det..........309	Killebrew-Min......126
Siebern-KC..........114	Lumpe-KC............193	Yastrzemski-Bos...........43	Robinson-Chi..........10	Cash-Det................39	B.Robinson-Bal....308	Siebern-KC..........117
Allison-Min...........102	B.Robinson-Bal....192	Bressoud-Bos...............40	Lumpe-KC...............10	Wagner-LA..............37	Wagner-LA............306	Colavito-Det........112
Yastrzemski-Bos....99	Yastrzemski-Bos..191	Richardson-NY.............38	Clinton-Bos............10	Colavito-Det............37	Yastrzemski-Bos..303	Robinson-Chi......109
Richardson-NY......99	Robinson-Chi........187				Killebrew-Min........301	Wagner-LA..........107

Stolen Bases	Base Stealing Runs	Fielding Runs-Infield	Fielding Runs-Outfield	Wins	Winning Pct.	Complete Games
Aparicio-Chi...........31	Wood-Det.............4.2	Boyer-NY...................33.0	Colavito-Det........11.8	Terry-NY................23	Herbert-Chi...........690	Pascual-Min..........18
Hinton-Was............28	Howser-KC............3.5	Versalles-Min.............29.9	DelGreco-KC........9.8	Pascual-Min............20	Ford-NY...............680	Kaat-Min...............16
Wood-Det..............24	Charles-KC............3.0	Bressoud-Bos............24.5	Yastrzemski-Bos....8.3	Herbert-Chi.............20	Donovan-Cle.........667	Donovan-Cle........16
Charles-KC............20	Hinton-Was...........2.7	Cottier-Was...............19.9	Bruton-Det...........6.6	Donovan-Cle...........20	Aguirre-Det...........667	Terry-NY................14
	Aparicio-Chi..........2.6	Kindall-Cle.................18.9	Kirkland-Cle..........6.3	Bunning-Det..........19	Terry-NY..............657	

Strikeouts	Fewest BB/Game	Games	Saves	Base Runners/9	Adjusted Relief Runs	Relief Ranking
Pascual-Min..........206	Donovan-Cle........1.69	Radatz-Bos..................62	Radatz-Bos............24	Hall-Bal................9.20	Radatz-Bos..........26.4	Radatz-Bos........39.8
Bunning-Det........184	Terry-NY.............1.72	Wyatt-KC......................59	Bridges-NY............18	Terry-NY................9.55	Hall-Bal...............21.4	Wilhelm-Bal.......34.1
Terry-NY.............176	Mossi-Det............1.80		Fox-Det.................16	Aguirre-Det..........9.67	Wilhelm-Bal.........17.0	Hall-Bal..............22.0
Pizarro-Chi..........173	Roberts-Bal........1.93		Wilhelm-Bal...........15	Wilhelm-Bal........9.77	Fox-Det................14.6	Fox-Det..............18.0
Kaat-Min.............173	Pascual-Min........2.06		Bell-Cle.................12	Pena-KC.............9.94	Fowler-LA...........10.7	Fowler-LA..........10.2

Innings Pitched	Opponents' Avg.	Opponents' OBP	Earned Run Average	Adjusted ERA	Adjusted Starter Runs	Pitcher Wins
Terry-NY............298.2	Aguirre-Det...........205	Aguirre-Det.................267	Aguirre-Det..........2.21	Aguirre-Det..........184	Aguirre-Det..........40.6	**Radatz-Bos**........3.9
Kaat-Min............269.0	Cheney-Was..........213	Terry-NY.....................268	Roberts-Bal..........2.78	Roberts-Bal..........133	Ford-NY...............27.3	**Kaat-Min**............3.8
Bunning-Det......258.0	Belinsky-LA...........216	Pascual-Min.................285	Ford-NY..............2.90	Chance-LA...........130	Kaat-Min..............27.3	**Pascual-Min**......3.7
Pascual-Min......257.2	Terry-NY...............231	Roberts-Bal.................288	Chance-LA..........2.96	Kaat-Min..............130	Pascual-Min.........24.4	**Wilhelm-Bal**......3.5
Ford-NY............257.2	Wilson-Bos...........231	Fisher-Chi...................291	Fisher-Chi...........3.10	Ford-NY...............129	Roberts-Bal.........22.9	**Aguirre-Det**........3.4

Carrying the Mantle

The Indians led the AL at the start of July, but Cleveland soon dropped into the second division as the Yankees took over. Minnesota and Los Angeles hung around until September, although neither got close enough to scare New York. Mickey Mantle took home his third MVP trophy, even though he missed nearly 40 games with knee problems. The team's balanced attack led the AL in scoring. But New Yorkers again seemed blasé about success; with National League baseball back in the city, the Yankees' attendance dropped every year from 1962 through 1966.

The Twins finished second as Harmon Killebrew captured his first home run title (and set a new strikeout mark). All eight Minnesota regulars hit homers in double figures, and Camilo Pascual paced the AL in strikeouts, shutouts, and complete games. Outfielder Tony Oliva went 4-for-9 in his first big league action.

The surprising Angels ended up third. Moving from tiny Wrigley Field to huge Chavez Ravine, the Angels saw attendance increase 90 percent to break the million mark. Rookie pitcher Bo Belinsky took Tinseltown by storm, throwing a no-hitter and dating starlet Mamie Van Doren, though the nightlife led to a quick loss of effectiveness for the pitcher.

Boston's Pete Runnells won his second batting crown, but the Red Sox, beginning a fallow period, ended to eighth. The Orioles dropped to seventh as their young pitchers began to crumble under heavy workloads.

All seven games in the Yankees-Giants World Series were close. The big stars—Mantle, Maris, Mays, and McCovey—were non-factors. Unlikely heroes like Chuck Hiller, Bill Stafford, and Clete Boyer dominated the entertaining Series. With the Yankees up three games to two, California rain delayed the proceedings by three days. The Giants won Game 6, but Raph Terry shut out the Giants on 4 hits to win the decider, 1–0. The Series ended when second baseman Bobby Richardson caught McCovey's hard liner with the tying and winning runs in scoring position.

1963 National League

TEAM	W	L	T	PCT	GB	HW	HL	R	OR	PA	H	2B	3B	HR	BB	SO	HB	SH	AVG	OBP	SLG	OPS	AOPS	BR	ABR	PF	SB	CS	BSA	BSR
LA	99	63	1	.611		**53**	28	640	**550**	6045	1361	178	34	110	453	**867**	85	26	.251	.309	.357	666	106	-3	42	93	**124**	70	64	**3**
STL	93	69	0	.574	6	**53**	28	**747**	628	6283	**1540**	**231**	**66**	128	458	915	85	25	**.271**	**.326**	.403	729	107	**119**	55	109	77	42	**65**	2
SF	88	74	0	.543	11	50	31	725	641	6176	1442	206	35	**197**	441	889	72	45	.258	.316	**.414**	**730**	**118**	112	**120**	99	55	49	53	-5
PHI	87	75	0	.537	12	45	36	642	578	6092	1390	228	54	126	403	955	**87**	44	.252	.306	.381	687	105	28	36	99	56	39	59	-1
CIN	86	76	0	.531	13	46	35	648	594	6040	1333	225	44	122	474	960	62	**47**	.246	.310	.371	681	100	28	9	103	92	58	61	0
MIL	84	78	1	.519	15	45	36	677	603	6211	1345	204	39	139	**525**	954	82	43	.244	.312	.370	682	104	32	39	99	75	52	59	-2
CHI	82	80	0	.506	17	43	38	570	578	5987	1286	205	44	127	439	1049	64	36	.238	.297	.363	660	91	-21	-51	105	68	60	53	-6
PIT	74	88	0	.457	25	42	39	567	595	6110	1385	181	49	108	454	940	63	29	.250	.309	.359	668	98	-4	-8	101	57	41	58	-2
HOU	66	96	0	.407	33	44	37	464	640	5983	1184	170	39	62	456	938	86	30	.220	.283	.301	584	80	-161	-131	94	39	30	57	-2
NY	51	111	0	.315	48	34	47	501	774	5921	1168	156	35	96	457	1078	46	**47**	.219	.285	.315	600	78	-131	-138	102	41	52	44	-9
TOT	811					455	355	6181		60848	13434	1984	439	1215	4560	9545	372	732	.245	.306	.364	669					684	493	58	-22

TEAM	CG	SHO	GR	SV	IP	H	HR	BB	SO	BR/9	ERA	AERA	OAV	OOB	PR	APR	PF	OSB	OCS	FA	E	WPB	DP	FW	PW	BW	BSW	DIF
LA	51	**24**	209	29	1469.2	1329	111	402	**1095**	**10.8**	**2.85**	106	.239	**.293**	**71**	30	92	**48**	31	.975	159	60	129	-.0	3.3	4.6	**.6**	9.6
STL	49	17	243	32	1463.0	1329	124	463	978	11.3	3.32	107	.241	.303	-5	34	108	84	44	.976	147	69	136	.6	3.7	6.0	.5	1.3
SF	46	9	247	30	1469.0	1380	126	464	954	11.5	3.35	96	.246	.306	-9	-24	97	69	39	.975	156	**53**	113	.1	-2.6	**13.0**	-.3	-3.2
PHI	45	12	242	31	1457.1	**1262**	113	553	1052	11.4	3.09	105	**.235**	.309	32	24	98	79	61	.978	142	62	147	.9	2.6	3.9	.1	-1.6
CIN	55	22	182	**36**	1439.2	1307	117	425	1048	11.1	3.29	102	.242	.300	-1	8	102	69	46	.978	135	81	127	1.3	.9	1.0	.2	1.6
MIL	**56**	18	262	25	1471.2	1327	149	489	924	11.3	3.27	99	.241	.304	4	-8	98	62	45	**.980**	**129**	69	161	**1.8**	-.9	4.2	.0	-2.1
CHI	45	15	217	28	1457.0	1357	119	400	851	11.0	3.08	**114**	.249	.301	34	**66**	107	**48**	**65**	.976	155	62	172	.2	**7.2**	-5.5	-.4	-.4
PIT	34	16	**292**	33	1448.0	1350	99	457	900	11.5	3.10	107	.249	.311	31	33	100	82	53	.972	182	57	**195**	-1.4	3.6	-.9	.0	-8.3
HOU	36	16	232	20	1450.1	1341	**95**	**378**	937	10.9	3.44	92	.245	.295	-24	-48	96	82	49	.974	162	65	100	-.3	-5.2	-14.2	.0	4.7
NY	42	5	233	12	1427.2	1452	162	529	806	12.8	4.12	85	.263	.330	-132	-95	106	61	60	.967	210	81	151	-3.1	-10.3	-15.0	-.7	-.9
TOT	459	154	2359	276	14553.1					11.4	3.29		.245	.306						.975	1577	659	1431					

Batter-Fielder Wins	Batting Average	On-Base Percentage	Slugging Average	On-Base Plus Slugging	Adjusted OPS	Adjusted Batter Runs
Mays-SF 6.1	T.Davis-LA 326	Mathews-Mil 399	H.Aaron-Mil 586	H.Aaron-Mil 977	H.Aaron-Mil 180	H.Aaron-Mil 65.6
H.Aaron-Mil 5.6	Clemente-Pit.........320	H.Aaron-Mil 391	Mays-SF 582	Mays-SF 962	Mays-SF 176	Mays-SF 58.1
Mazeroski-Pit......5.3	Groat-StL 319	Mays-SF 380	McCovey-SF.........566	Cepeda-SF 929	Cepeda-SF 166	Cepeda-SF 47.5
Mathews-Mil........5.1	H.Aaron-Mil 319	Robinson-Cin..............379	Cepeda-SF...........563	McCovey-SF 915	McCovey-SF 161	McCovey-SF 42.3
Callison-Phi 4.1	Cepeda-SF...........316	Groat-StL.....................377	Pinson-Cin 514	Pinson-Cin............861	Mathews-Mil 147	Mathews-Mil 40.6

Runs	Hits	Doubles	Triples	Home Runs	Total Bases	Runs Batted In
H.Aaron-Mil 121	Pinson-Cin............204	Groat-StL 43	Pinson-Cin.............14	McCovey-SF 44	H.Aaron-Mil 370	H.Aaron-Mil 130
Mays-SF 115	Groat-StL.............201	Pinson-Cin 37	Gonzalez-Phi.........12	H.Aaron-Mil 44	Mays-SF 347	Boyer-StL............111
Flood-StL..............112	H.Aaron-Mil 201	Williams-Chi 36	Groat-StL................11	Mays-SF 38	Pinson-Cin............335	White-StL............109
White-StL..............106	White-StL.............200	Gonzalez-Phi 36	Callison-Phi 11	Cepeda-SF 34	Cepeda-SF 326	Pinson-Cin 106
McCovey-SF 103	Flood-StL..............200	Callison-Phi 36	Brock-Chi................11	Howard-LA..............28	White-StL..............323	Mays-SF..............103

Stolen Bases	Base Stealing Runs	Fielding Runs-Infield	Fielding Runs-Outfield	Wins	Winning Pct.	Complete Games
Wills-LA 40	H.Aaron-Mil 5.1	Mazeroski-Pit.............51.4	Callison-Phi 18.2	Marichal-SF............25	Perranoski-LA.......842	Spahn-Mil..............22
H.Aaron-Mil 31	Pinson-Cin..............3.1	Hubbs-Chi 21.2	W.Davis-LA..........10.7	Koufax-LA 25	Koufax-LA.............833	Koufax-LA..............20
Pinson-Cin..............27	Gilliam-LA..............2.4	Harkness-NY 16.6	Brock-Chi 9.5	Spahn-Mil 23	Spahn-Mil 767	Ellsworth-Chi 19
Robinson-Cin..........26	Maye-Mil................2.4	Schofield-Pit 16.3	Flood-StL 7.3	Maloney-Cin 23	Maloney-Cin 767	Marichal-SF 18
W.Davis-LA 25	Harper-Cin..............2.3	Santo-Chi...................13.9	Robinson-Cin 6.2	Ellsworth-Chi..........22	Marichal-SF 758	Drysdale-LA 17

Strikeouts	Fewest BB/Game	Games	Saves	Base Runners/9	Adjusted Relief Runs	Relief Ranking
Koufax-LA 306	Friend-Pit 1.47	Perranoski-LA...............69	McDaniel-Chi..........22	Koufax-LA............7.96	Perranoski-LA......20.2	Perranoski-LA 34.2
Maloney-Cin 265	Farrell-Hou 1.56	Baldschun-Phi 65	Perranoski-LA 21	Shantz-StL 8.39	Veale-Pit 17.6	Woodeshick-Hou 27.6
Drysdale-LA..........251	Nuxhall-Cin...........1.62	Bearnarth-NY 58	Face-Pit..................16	Umbricht-Hou 8.76	Klippstein-Phi 16.4	Baldschun-Phi 18.3
Marichal-SF 248	Drysdale-LA 1.63	Sisk-Pit 57	Baldschun-Phi 16	Farrell-Hou 8.81	Woodeshick-Hou 15.5	Klippstein-Phi 17.1
Gibson-StL 204	Koufax-LA............1.68	McDaniel-Chi 57	Henry-Cin 14	Marichal-SF 9.02	Taylor-StL 11.7	Veale-Pit 15.8

Innings Pitched	Opponents' Avg.	Opponents' OBP	Earned Run Average	Adjusted ERA	Adjusted Starter Runs	Pitcher Wins
Marichal-SF 321.1	Koufax-LA.............189	Koufax-LA 230	Koufax-LA............1.88	Ellsworth-Chi 167	Koufax-LA...........46.9	**Ellsworth-Chi** 5.0
Drysdale-LA 315.1	Maloney-Cin 202	Farrell-Hou...................255	Ellsworth-Chi 2.11	Koufax-LA 161	Ellsworth-Chi 44.0	**Koufax-LA** 4.1
Koufax-LA..........311.0	Culp-Phi 206	Marichal-SF 255	Friend-Pit 2.34	Simmons-StL........143	Marichal-SF 28.6	**Perranoski-LA** ..3.9
Ellsworth-Chi 290.2	Ellsworth-Chi 210	Ellsworth-Chi 262	Marichal-SF 2.41	Friend-Pit..............141	Friend-Pit 27.0	**Woodeshick-Hou**3.2
Sanford-SF........284.1	Broglio-StL 216	Friend-Pit......................267	Simmons-StL 2.48	Jackson-Chi..........137	Jackson-Chi 22.7	**Jackson-Chi** 3.1

Roger, Dodgers!

For the first several months, the Giants, Reds, Cardinals, and Dodgers jousted. Eventually, Los Angeles won 17 of 20 and made some space. But in late August, the Cardinals started their own streak, winning 19 of 20. This set up a crucial three-game set at St. Louis, which the Dodgers swept to end the race. St. Louis fans then had to deal with another disappointment as Stan Musial retired.

A healthy Sandy Koufax took the Cy Young and MVP, capitalizing on the newly enlarged strike zone and the comfortable dimensions of Chavez Ravine. The Dodgers, sixth in runs, were the NL's second-best offense on the road—better even than St. Louis, which led the league in scoring due to small Busch Stadium. While sore-legged Maury Wills' steals dropped to 40, Tommy Davis' batting title and Frank Howard's homers carried the day for the Dodgers.

The league batting average of .245 was the worst in fifty-four years, and the new hitting conditions sorted the haves from the have-nots. The last-place Mets' .219 average was the lowest of any team since 1908.

On September 10 Felipe, Matty, and Jesus Alou all played in the Giants' outfield. On September 27 Houston fielded an all-rookie lineup including Joe Morgan, Jimmy Wynn, and Jerry Grote. They sat another frosh, Rusty Staub, already the Colts' regular first baseman.

Milwaukee's Henry Aaron won his second of four home run titles. Cincinnati's scrappy second baseman Pete Rose was Rookie of the Year, and Gil Hodges retired to go into managing. Prior to the season, Rogers Hornsby, one of the game's greatest hitters, died.

Fittingly, the World Series was all pitching. Holding New York to a .171 average, the Dodgers pinned the Yankees with their first-ever four-game sweep. (The 1922 Giants also kept the Yankees from the win column, but that Series featured a tie). Koufax fanned 15 in Game 1 and captured the decisive fourth game as well.

1963 American League

TEAM	W	L	T	PCT	GB	HW	HL	R	OR	PA	H	2B	3B	HR	BB	SO	HB	SH	AVG	OBP	SLG	OPS	AOPS	BR	ABR	PF	SB	CS	BSA	BSR
NY	104	57	0	.646		**58**	22	714	547	6067	1387	197	35	188	434	**808**	66	31	.252	.309	.403	712	105	25	31	99	42	26	62	0
CHI	94	68	0	.580	10.5	49	33	683	**544**	6242	1379	208	**40**	114	571	896	79	40	.250	.323	.365	688	101	5	17	98	64	28	70	4
MIN	91	70	0	.565	13	48	33	**767**	602	6233	**1408**	**223**	35	**225**	547	912	84	**41**	**.255**	.325	**.430**	**755**	**115**	**118**	**103**	102	32	14	70	2
BAL	86	76	0	.531	18.5	48	33	644	621	6055	1359	207	32	146	469	940	73	28	.249	.310	.380	690	103	-7	18	96	**97**	34	**74**	**9**
DET	79	83	0	.488	25.5	47	34	700	703	6242	1388	195	36	148	**592**	908	64	38	.252	**.327**	.382	709	102	44	21	103	73	32	70	5
CLE	79	83	0	.488	25.5	41	40	635	702	6136	1314	214	29	169	469	1102	**88**	40	.239	.301	.381	682	97	-26	-20	99	59	36	62	0
BOS	76	85	0	.472	28	44	36	666	704	6145	1403	247	34	171	475	954	44	26	.252	.312	.400	712	102	33	12	103	27	16	63	0
KC	73	89	0	.451	31.5	36	45	615	704	6172	1356	225	38	95	529	829	77	25	.247	.313	.353	666	88	-40	-73	106	47	26	64	1
LA	70	91	0	.435	34	39	42	597	660	6127	1378	208	38	95	448	916	84	43	.250	.309	.354	663	97	-54	-16	94	43	30	59	-1
WAS	56	106	0	.346	48.5	31	49	578	812	6069	1237	190	35	138	497	963	57	30	.227	.293	.351	644	86	-98	-96	100	68	28	71	5
TOT	808					441	367	6599		61488	13609	2114	352	1489	5031	9228	342	716	.247	.312	.380	692					552	270	67	27

TEAM	CG	SHO	GR	SV	IP	H	HR	BB	SO	BR/9	ERA	AERA	OAV	OOB	PR	APR	PF	OSB	OCS	FA	E	WPB	DP	FW	PW	BW	BSW	DIF
NY	**59**	19	180	31	1449.0	**1239**	115	476	965	**10.8**	3.07	114	**.232**	**.295**	89	73	97	**36**	18	.982	110	**42**	162	1.4	7.7	3.3	-.3	11.5
CHI	49	**21**	211	39	1469.0	1311	**100**	**440**	932	10.9	**2.97**	**118**	.239	.297	**107**	**90**	97	51	32	.979	131	60	163	.3	**9.5**	1.8	.1	1.4
MIN	58	13	234	30	1446.1	1322	162	459	941	11.2	3.28	111	.242	.302	56	58	100	43	23	.976	144	70	140	-.5	6.1	**10.8**	-.0	-5.8
BAL	35	8	248	**43**	1452.0	1353	137	507	913	11.7	3.45	101	.248	.314	29	4	96	47	24	**.984**	**99**	**42**	157	**2.1**	.4	1.9	**.7**	-.0
DET	42	7	240	28	1456.1	1407	195	477	930	11.9	3.90	96	.253	.315	-44	-25	103	38	25	.982	113	63	124	1.3	-2.6	2.2	.2	-3.1
CLE	40	14	257	25	1469.0	1390	176	478	**1018**	11.6	3.79	95	.249	.309	-27	-28	100	51	34	.977	143	50	129	-.4	-2.9	-2.1	-.3	3.7
BOS	29	7	241	32	1449.2	1367	152	539	1009	12.0	3.97	95	.248	.316	-55	-29	104	62	17	.978	135	62	119	-.0	-3.0	1.3	-.3	-2.4
KC	35	11	247	29	1458.0	1417	156	540	887	12.4	3.92	100	.256	.324	-47	-3	108	96	26	.980	127	54	131	.5	-.3	-7.7	-.2	-.3
LA	30	13	**315**	31	1455.1	1317	120	578	889	12.0	3.52	97	.242	.318	17	-17	94	56	**41**	.974	163	66	155	-1.6	-1.8	-1.7	-.4	-5.0
WAS	29	8	276	25	1447.0	1486	176	537	744	12.8	4.42	84	.266	.331	-126	-111	102	73	28	.971	182	66	**165**	-2.6	-11.7	-10.1	.2	-.9
TOT	406	121	2449	313	14551.2					11.7	3.63		.247	.312						.978	1347	575	1445					

Batter-Fielder Wins	Batting Average	On-Base Percentage	Slugging Average	On-Base Plus Slugging	Adjusted OPS	Adjusted Batter Runs
Yastrzemski-Bos 4.2	Yastrzemski-Bos ...321	Yastrzemski-Bos 418	Killebrew-Min 555	Allison-Min............911	Allison-Min............150	Yastrzemski-Bos....40.7
Battey-Min 4.0	Kaline-Det.............312	Pearson-LA 402	Allison-Min 533	Killebrew-Min........904	Killebrew-Min........147	Allison-Min..........37.7
Hansen-Chi 3.9	Rollins-Min 307	Cash-Det 386	Howard-NY 528	Yastrzemski-Bos ..894	Yastrzemski-Bos ..145	Killebrew-Min......32.2
Allison-Min 3.8	Pearson-LA............304	Allison-Min 378	Stuart-Bos 521	Kaline-Det 889	Kaline-Det 142	Kaline-Det 31.4
Howard-NY..........3.4	Ward-Chi 295	Kaline-Det 375	Hall-Min 521	Howard-NY 869	Howard-NY 141	Pearson-LA 31.2

Runs	Hits	Doubles	Triples	Home Runs	Total Bases	Runs Batted In
Allison-Min..............99	Yastrzemski-Bos ..183	Yastrzemski-Bos 40	Versalles-Min..........13	Killebrew-Min..........45	Stuart-Bos 319	Stuart-Bos 118
Pearson-LA 92	Ward-Chi 177	Ward-Chi.........................34	Hinton-Was 12	Stuart-Bos 42	Ward-Chi 289	Kaline-Det 101
Yastrzemski-Bos 91	Pearson-LA 176	Torres-LA 32	Fregosi-LA 12	Allison-Min...............35	Killebrew-Min........286	Killebrew-Min 96
Tresh-NY 91	Kaline-Det 172	Causey-KC 32	Cimoli-KC................11	Hall-Min 33	Kaline-Det 283	Colavito-Det 91
Colavito-Det............91	Fregosi-LA 170	Alvis-Cle 32		Howard-NY 28	Allison-Min............281	Allison-Min 91

Stolen Bases	Base Stealing Runs	Fielding Runs-Infield	Fielding Runs-Outfield	Wins	Winning Pct.	Complete Games
Aparicio-Bal 40	Aparicio-Bal 6.7	Hansen-Chi 27.5	Hall-Min 10.3	Ford-NY 24	Ford-NY 774	Terry-NY 18
Hinton-Was 25	Tartabull-KC 3.2	Boyer-NY 21.9	Yastrzemski-Bos....8.7	Pascual-Min.............21	Bouton-NY 750	Pascual-Min 18
Wood-Det 18	Weis-Chi 3.0	Causey-KC..................14.9	Allison-Min 8.3	Bouton-NY...............21	Radatz-Bos...........714	Stigman-Min 15
Snyder-Bal..............18	Richardson-NY 3.0	Richardson-NY 12.9	Geiger-Bos 7.5	Monbouquette-Bos 20	Peters-Chi.............704	Herbert-Chi 14
Pearson-LA 17	Hinton-Was............2.3	Moran-LA.....................12.2	Hinton-Was............6.8	Barber-Bal 20	Pascual-Min 700	Aguirre-Det............14

Strikeouts	Fewest BB/Game	Games	Saves	Base Runners/9	Adjusted Relief Runs	Relief Ranking
Pascual-Min..........202	Donovan-Cle........1.22	S.Miller-Bal 71	S.Miller-Bal 27	Dailey-Min............8.20	Radatz-Bos..........26.0	Radatz-Bos 48.1
Bunning-Det 196	Terry-NY..............1.31	Radatz-Bos....................66	Radatz-Bos 25	Hall-Bal 8.95	Dailey-Min............20.5	Dailey-Min 24.2
Stigman-Min 193	Herbert-Chi...........1.40	Dailey-Min......................66	Wyatt-KC 21	Fowler-LA 8.97	S.Miller-Bal 13.8	S.Miller-Bal 21.8
Peters-Chi 189	Monbouquette-Bos1.42	Lamabe-Bos 65	Wilhelm-Chi 21	Wilhelm-Chi 9.24	Wilhelm-Chi 12.6	Wilhelm-Chi........15.2
Ford-NY 189	Roberts-Bal 1.43	Wyatt-KC.........................63	Dailey-Min 21	Cheney-Was........9.24	Fowler-LA 11.4	Fowler-LA 12.1

Innings Pitched	Opponents' Avg.	Opponents' OBP	Earned Run Average	Adjusted ERA	Adjusted Starter Runs	Pitcher Wins
Ford-NY 269.1	Downing-NY 184	Terry-NY 271	Peters-Chi............2.33	Peters-Chi 150	Peters-Chi............33.6	**Radatz-Bos** 5.0
Terry-NY............268.0	Morehead-Bos 211	Ramos-Cle...................272	Pizarro-Chi 2.39	Pascual-Min...........148	Pascual-Min 33.2	**Peters-Chi** 4.8
Monbouquette-Bos266.2	Bouton-NY 212	Roberts-Bal 272	Pascual-Min 2.46	Pizarro-Chi 147	Bouton-NY 27.5	**Pascual-Min** 4.7
Barber-Bal 258.2	Drabowsky-KC 214	Downing-NY 277	Bouton-NY 2.53	Bouton-NY............139	Pizarro-Chi 25.2	**Pizarro-Chi** 3.0
Roberts-Bal 251.1	Peters-Chi.............216	Peters-Chi 277	Downing-NY 2.56	Stange-Min 139	Ford-NY 22.3	**Dailey-Min** 2.9

Brother, Can You Spare a Bat?

Baseball authorities decided that the game had become too dependent on home runs. Therefore, to balance the game in favor of the pitcher, the strike zone was enlarged before the season and would now range from the top of the shoulders to the top of the knees. The result was an offensive disaster. Scoring fell to its lowest since 1946, and would continue to decline through 1968.

The odd thing? Home runs didn't decrease much. Strikeouts, however, shot up; the Indians set an all-time high for whiffs, and for the third straight year, a wild swinger broke the individual record. Chicago slugger Dave Nicholson's 175 strikeouts shattered the mark by 33.

Despite Nicholson's whiffs, the White Sox finished second on big seasons from rookies Gary Peters and Pete Ward. Minnesota, with a fearsome attack that topped the AL in homers both at home and on the road, led in scoring, but had very poor second-line pitching.

Early Wynn won his 300th career game, and then was immediately released by Cleveland, who also gave lefty Tommy John his first exposure to the majors. And in a year in which Harmon Killebrew won his third home run crown, Frank "Home Run" Baker, who had captured four such titles, died at 77.

Once again, the Yankees won, and easily. Excellent pitching and Elston Howard's MVP performance sprung the club from a tangle in June. They never looked back despite losing Mickey Mantle to injury. For the first time since 1951, the Yankees had two 20-game winners—Whitey Ford and Jim Bouton. But neither pitcher won in the World Series; in fact, no Yankee won. The Yankees, with six World Series sweeps to their credit, were themselves swept by the Dodgers. New York scored just 4 runs. Mantle batted just .133; Hank Bauer hit .077.

1964 National League

TEAM	W	L	T	PCT	GB	HW	HL	R	OR	PA	H	2B	3B	HR	BB	SO	HB	SH	AVG	OBP	SLG	OPS	AOPS	BR	ABR	PF	SB	CS	BSA	BSR
STL	93	69	0	.574		**48**	33	715	652	6196	**1531**	240	53	109	427	925	94	18	**.272**	.324	.392	716	99	62	4	109	73	51	59	-2
PHI	92	70	0	.568	1	46	35	693	632	6116	1415	241	51	130	440	924	97	**40**	.258	.315	.391	706	106	42	51	99	30	35	46	-6
CIN	92	70	1	.568	1	47	34	660	**566**	6153	1383	220	38	130	457	974	65	33	.249	.308	.372	680	95	-10	-32	104	90	36	**71**	7
SF	90	72	0	.556	3	44	37	656	587	6194	1360	185	38	**165**	**505**	900	78	33	.246	.310	.382	692	99	15	1	102	64	35	65	2
MIL	88	74	0	.543	5	45	36	**803**	744	6206	1522	**274**	32	159	486	**825**	54	38	**.272**	**.333**	**.418**	**751**	**117**	**138**	**133**	101	53	41	56	-3
PIT	80	82	0	.494	13	42	39	663	636	6119	1469	225	**54**	121	408	970	87	24	.264	.315	.389	704	105	34	35	100	39	33	54	-3
LA	80	82	2	.494	13	41	40	614	572	6120	1375	180	39	79	438	893	**120**	19	.250	.305	.340	645	95	-73	-28	93	**141**	60	70	**10**
CHI	76	86	0	.469	17	40	41	649	724	6157	1391	239	50	145	499	1041	55	25	.251	.314	.390	704	101	39	12	104	70	49	59	-2
HOU	66	96	0	.407	27	41	40	495	628	5859	1214	162	41	70	381	872	87	49	.229	.285	.315	600	80	-163	-135	94	40	48	45	-8
NY	53	109	1	.327	40	33	48	569	776	6045	1372	195	31	103	353	932	52	48	.246	.296	.348	644	90	-87	-73	98	36	31	54	-3
TOT	812					427	383	6517		61165	14032	2161	427	1211	4394	9256	327	789	.254	.311	.374	685					636	419	60	-7

TEAM	CG	SHO	GR	SV	IP	H	HR	BB	SO	BR/9	ERA	AERA	OAV	OOB	PR	APR	PF	OSB	OCS	FA	E	WPB	DP	FW	PW	BW	BSW	DIF
STL	47	10	232	38	1445.1	1405	133	410	877	11.5	3.43	111	.255	.308	17	56	108	57	27	.973	172	49	147	-.7	5.9	.4	-.1	6.5
PHI	37	17	273	**41**	1461.0	1402	129	440	1009	11.7	3.36	103	.252	.312	28	17	98	58	45	.975	157	72	150	.0	1.8	5.4	-.6	4.3
CIN	54	14	203	35	1467.0	1306	112	436	**1122**	10.9	3.07	**118**	.238	.296	75	**86**	102	70	43	**.979**	**130**	69	137	**1.6**	**9.1**	-3.4	.8	2.9
SF	48	17	251	30	1476.1	1348	118	480	1023	11.4	3.19	112	.241	.304	57	61	101	70	36	.975	159	**45**	136	-.0	6.4	.1	.3	2.2
MIL	45	14	268	39	1434.2	1411	160	452	906	11.8	4.12	86	.257	.314	-92	-95	100	49	33	.977	143	87	139	.8	-10.0	**14.0**	-.2	2.4
PIT	42	14	**274**	29	1443.2	1429	92	476	951	12.1	3.52	100	.260	.320	2	-2	99	67	36	.972	177	74	**179**	-1.0	-.2	3.7	-.2	-3.2
LA	47	**19**	213	27	1483.2	**1289**	**88**	458	1062	**10.8**	**2.95**	110	**.232**	**.292**	**96**	51	92	**39**	44	.973	170	65	126	-.5	5.4	-3.0	**1.1**	-4.0
CHI	**58**	11	255	19	1445.0	1510	144	423	737	12.1	4.08	91	.270	.321	-87	-56	105	52	51	.975	162	65	147	-.2	-5.9	1.3	-.1	-.0
HOU	30	9	248	31	1428.0	1421	105	**353**	852	11.4	3.41	100	.260	.306	20	1	97	95	38	.976	149	62	124	.5	.1	-14.3	-.8	-.6
NY	40	10	266	15	1438.2	1511	130	466	717	12.7	4.25	84	.272	.332	-115	-107	101	79	**66**	.974	167	85	154	-.4	-11.3	-7.7	-.2	-8.4
TOT	448	135	2483	304	14523.1					11.6	3.54		.254	.311						.975	1586	673	1439					

Batter-Fielder Wins
Santo-Chi 7.1
Allen-Phi 5.9
Mays-SF 5.8
Menke-Mil 4.8
Aaron-Mil 4.5

Batting Average
Clemente-Pit.........339
Carty-Mil...............330
Aaron-Mil 328
Torre-Mil 321
Allen-Phi...............318

On-Base Percentage
Santo-Chi....................398
Robinson-Cin..............396
Aaron-Mil 393
Clemente-Pit 388
Carty-Mil 388

Slugging Average
Mays-SF 607
Santo-Chi 564
Allen-Phi 557
Carty-Mil..............554
Robinson-Cin 548

On-Base Plus Slugging
Mays-SF 990
Santo-Chi 962
Robinson-Cin........943
Carty-Mil 942
Allen-Phi 939

Adjusted OPS
Mays-SF 171
Allen-Phi 163
Santo-Chi 162
Carty-Mil 162
Robinson-Cin........158

Adjusted Batter Runs
Mays-SF 54.2
Allen-Phi 52.9
Santo-Chi 50.9
Robinson-Cin......47.1
Aaron-Mil...........41.3

Runs
Allen-Phi 125
Mays-SF 121
Brock-Chi-StL 111
Robinson-Cin........103
Aaron-Mil 103

Hits
Flood-StL.............211
Clemente-Pit 211
Williams-Chi 201
Allen-Phi 201
Brock-Chi-StL 200

Doubles
Maye-Mil.......................44
Clemente-Pit..................40
Williams-Chi 39
Robinson-Cin 38
Allen-Phi 38

Triples
Santo-Chi 13
Allen-Phi 13
Brock-Chi-StL 11
Pinson-Cin.............11

Home Runs
Mays-SF 47
Williams-Chi 33
Hart-SF 31
Cepeda-SF 31
Callison-Phi 31

Total Bases
Allen-Phi 352
Mays-SF 351
Williams-Chi 343
Santo-Chi 334
Callison-Phi..........322

Runs Batted In
Boyer-StL 119
Santo-Chi 114
Mays-SF..............111
Torre-Mil 109
Callison-Phi 104

Stolen Bases
Wills-LA 53
Brock-Chi-StL 43
W.Davis-LA 42
Harper-Cin..............24
Robinson-Cin.........23

Base Stealing Runs
Wills-LA 5.7
W.Davis-LA............4.7
Harper-Cin 4.2
Aaron-Mil 3.4
Robinson-Cin 3.3

Fielding Runs-Infield
Mazeroski-Pit.............34.5
Santo-Chi...................19.4
Rodgers-Chi...............15.3
Kasko-Hou.................14.8
Banks-Chi 10.2

Fielding Runs-Outfield
Callison-Phi 13.7
W.Davis-LA.........12.8
Altman-NY 9.4
Aaron-Mil 9.2
T.Davis-LA 6.2

Wins
Jackson-Chi...........24
Marichal-SF 21
Sadecki-StL 20

Winning Pct.
Koufax-LA............792
Marichal-SF 724
O'Toole-Cin...........708
Bunning-Phi 704
Jackson-Chi 686

Complete Games
Marichal-SF 22
Drysdale-LA 21
Jackson-Chi 19
Gibson-StL 17
Ellsworth-Chi 16

Strikeouts
Veale-Pit 250
Gibson-StL 245
Drysdale-LA..........237
Koufax-LA 223
Bunning-Phi..........219

Fewest BB/Game
Bunning-Phi 1.46
Bruce-Hou 1.47
Law-Pit 1.50
Marichal-SF 1.74
Jackson-Chi 1.75

Games
B.Miller-LA 74
Perranoski-LA................72
Baldschun-Phi 71
Taylor-StL 63
McDaniel-Chi 63

Saves
Woodeshick-Hou 23
McBean-Pit 22
Baldschun-Phi 21
McDaniel-Chi..........15

Base Runners/9
Koufax-LA...........8.35
Drysdale-LA 8.96
Short-Phi 9.34
Ellis-Cin 9.56
McCool-Cin............9.67

Adjusted Relief Runs
McBean-Pit...........15.4
Ellis-Cin 14.5
McCool-Cin...........11.7
Roebuck-Phi..........11.4
B.Miller-LA 9.5

Relief Ranking
McBean-Pit 25.5
Ellis-Cin 17.6
McCool-Cin 15.0
Roebuck-Phi 14.7
B.Miller-LA..........10.1

Innings Pitched
Drysdale-LA 321.1
Jackson-Chi 297.2
Gibson-StL 287.1
Bunning-Phi 284.1
Veale-Pit 279.2

Opponents' Avg.
Koufax-LA............191
Drysdale-LA 207
Veale-Pit 217
Short-Phi 217
Bolin-SF 220

Opponents' OBP
Koufax-LA 240
Drysdale-LA.................255
Short-Phi 266
Jackson-Chi.................272
Marichal-SF 272

Earned Run Average
Koufax-LA...........1.74
Drysdale-LA 2.18
Short-Phi 2.20
Marichal-SF 2.48
Bunning-Phi 2.63

Adjusted ERA
Koufax-LA 187
Short-Phi 157
Drysdale-LA..........148
Marichal-SF 144
O'Toole-Cin 136

Adjusted Starter Runs
Drysdale-LA 41.4
Koufax-LA...........41.4
Short-Phi 31.4
Marichal-SF 29.6
Gibson-StL 26.6

Pitcher Wins
Drysdale-LA 5.0
Koufax-LA 4.3
Short-Phi 3.6
Marichal-SF........3.1
McBean-Pit 2.9

A Philly Disappointment

The 1964 season has gone into legend as one of the NL's great races, but all the excitement came in the last two weeks. Boasting top rookie Richie Allen, outfielder Johnny Callison, and pitchers Jim Bunning and Chris Short, Philadelphia broke away from San Francisco in midsummer and led by 6_ on September 20. But with World Series tickets printed, Philadelphia dropped 10 straight, including three to hard-charging Cincinnati, winners of nine straight, and three to St. Louis, which had risen from the depths in August.

With the Giants awakening from their doldrums on the strength of Willie Mays, Juan Marichal, and rookie Japanese reliever Masanori Murakami, a four-way tie loomed in the last weekend. The Mets, of all teams, beat the Cardinals in the first two games of the season-ending series before St. Louis held on to take the finale. The Reds—aware that manager Fred Hutchinson was dying of cancer—lost to the Phillies. Philadelphia and Cincinnati both finished 1 game out.

Lou Brock, acquired midseason from the Cubs, ignited the Redbirds' attack. Ken Boyer was MVP, and Ray Sadecki and Bob Gibson combined for 39 wins. Veteran reliever Barney Schultz, like Pedro Ramos in the AL, was vital down the stretch. The Phillies seized up at the finish line as manager Gene Mauch relied almost solely on Bunning and Short.

Several longtime NL stars began their careers in 1964, including Phil Niekro, Tony Perez, and Larry Dierker. Duke Snider retired. Prior to the season, Cubs infielder Ken Hubbs was killed in a plane crash, and Colts reliever Jim Umbricht died of cancer

The World Series went seven games. Both the Cardinals and Yankees blew leads, had exciting late-inning rallies, hit crucial home runs, and boasted great pitching performances. However, St. Louis' two wins at New York helped withstand Jim Bouton's two victories for the Yankees. Tim McCarver hit .478 and slugged a 10th inning homer to win Game 5. Gibson went all the way in Game 7 for a 7–5 win.

1964 American League

TEAM	W	L	T	PCT	GB	HW	HL	R	OR	PA	H	2B	3B	HR	BB	SO	HB	SH	AVG	OBP	SLG	OPS	AOPS	BR	ABR	PF	SB	CS	BSA	BSR
NY	99	63	2	.611		50	31	730	577	6358	**1442**	208	35	162	520	976	68	31	**.253**	.317	.387	704	100	12	1	102	54	18	**75**	**6**
CHI	98	64	0	.605	1	**52**	29	642	**501**	6246	1356	184	40	106	**562**	**902**	**96**	**52**	.247	.320	.353	673	97	-33	-15	97	75	39	66	3
BAL	97	65	1	.599	2	49	32	679	567	6143	1357	**229**	20	162	537	1019	69	27	.248	.316	.387	703	101	17	20	100	78	38	67	4
DET	85	77	1	.525	14	46	35	699	678	6183	1394	199	**57**	157	517	912	71	40	**.253**	.319	.395	714	102	33	23	102	60	27	69	4
LA	82	80	0	.506	17	45	36	544	551	5975	1297	186	27	102	472	920	78	26	.242	.304	.344	648	95	-91	-31	90	49	39	56	-3
MIN	79	83	1	.488	20	40	41	**737**	678	6318	1413	227	46	**221**	553	1019	74	44	.252	**.322**	**.427**	**749**	**113**	**99**	**94**	101	46	22	68	2
CLE	79	83	2	.488	20	41	40	689	693	6257	1386	208	22	164	500	1063	63	49	.247	.312	.380	692	99	-8	-3	99	**79**	51	61	0
BOS	72	90	0	.444	27	45	36	688	793	6106	1425	253	29	186	504	917	35	28	.258	**.322**	.416	738	106	79	45	105	18	16	53	-2
WAS	62	100	0	.383	37	31	50	578	733	6037	1246	199	28	125	514	1124	66	28	.231	.299	.348	647	86	-95	-92	100	47	30	61	0
KC	57	105	1	.352	42	26	55	621	836	6192	1321	216	29	166	548	1104	53	42	.239	.311	.379	690	95	-13	-32	103	34	20	63	0
TOT	814					425	385	6607		61815	13637	2109	333	1551	5227	9956	367	673	.247	.315	.382	696					540	300	64	14

TEAM	CG	SHO	GR	SV	IP	H	HR	BB	SO	BR/9	ERA	AERA	OAV	OOB	PR	APR	PF	OSB	OCS	FA	E	WPB	DP	FW	PW	BW	BSW	DIF
NY	46	18	215	**45**	1506.2	1312	129	504	989	11.0	3.15	115	.234	.299	79	78	100	33	25	.983	109	55	158	1.1	8.2	.1	**.5**	8.1
CHI	44	20	219	**45**	1467.2	**1216**	124	**401**	955	**10.1**	**2.72**	**127**	**.226**	**.282**	**147**	**125**	95	31	27	.981	122	84	164	.2	**13.1**	-1.6	.2	5.0
BAL	44	17	238	41	1458.2	1292	129	456	939	11.0	3.16	113	.239	.300	76	68	99	62	26	**.985**	**95**	51	159	**1.9**	7.2	2.1	.3	4.6
DET	35	11	248	35	1453.0	1343	164	536	993	12.0	3.84	95	.244	.316	-35	-29	101	**25**	31	.982	111	59	137	1.0	-3.0	2.4	.3	3.4
LA	30	**28**	285	41	1450.2	1273	**100**	530	965	11.5	2.91	113	.236	.309	115	67	91	52	**37**	.978	138	**50**	**168**	-.7	7.0	-3.3	-.5	-1.6
MIN	**47**	4	277	29	1477.2	1361	181	545	1099	11.8	3.58	100	.243	.312	8	1	99	51	35	.977	145	91	131	-1.1	.1	**9.9**	.0	-11.0
CLE	37	16	277	37	1487.2	1443	154	565	**1162**	12.3	3.75	96	.255	.324	-21	-25	99	61	31	.981	118	83	149	.6	-2.6	-.3	-.1	.5
BOS	21	9	252	38	1422.0	1464	178	571	1094	13.1	4.50	86	.266	.336	-138	-95	106	75	26	.977	138	61	123	-.7	-10.0	4.7	-.4	-2.7
WAS	27	5	291	26	1435.1	1417	172	505	794	12.2	3.98	93	.259	.322	-57	-44	102	54	36	.979	127	63	145	-.0	-4.6	-9.7	-.1	-4.5
KC	18	6	**344**	27	1455.2	1516	220	614	966	13.5	4.71	81	.269	.344	-175	-136	105	96	26	.975	158	73	152	-1.9	-14.3	-3.4	-.1	-4.3
TOT	349	134	2646	364	14615.0					11.8	3.63		.247	.315						.980	1261	670	1486					

Batter-Fielder Wins	Batting Average	On-Base Percentage	Slugging Average	On-Base Plus Slugging	Adjusted OPS	Adjusted Batter Runs
Fregosi-LA 5.6	Oliva-Min .323	Mantle-NY .423	Powell-Bal .606	Mantle-NY 1015	Mantle-NY 177	Mantle-NY 52.9
Powell-Bal 4.7	B.Robinson-Bal .317	Allison-Min .404	Mantle-NY .591	Powell-Bal 1005	Powell-Bal 176	Allison-Min 45.7
Hansen-Chi 4.4	Howard-NY .313	Powell-Bal .399	Oliva-Min .557	Allison-Min 957	Allison-Min 163	Powell-Bal 45.5
Allison-Min 4.4	Mantle-NY .303	Robinson-Chi .388	Allison-Min .553	Killebrew-Min 924	Killebrew-Min 153	Oliva-Min 42.6
Howard-NY 3.8	Robinson-Chi .301	Kaline-Det .383	Killebrew-Min .548	Oliva-Min 916	Oliva-Min 150	Killebrew-Min 42.6

Runs	Hits	Doubles	Triples	Home Runs	Total Bases	Runs Batted In
Oliva-Min 109	Oliva-Min 217	Oliva-Min 43	Versalles-Min 10	Killebrew-Min 49	Oliva-Min 374	B.Robinson-Bal 118
Howser-Cle 101	B.Robinson-Bal 194	Bressoud-Bos 41	Rollins-Min 10	Powell-Bal 39	B.Robinson-Bal 319	Stuart-Bos 114
Killebrew-Min 95	Richardson-NY 181	B.Robinson-Bal 35	Yastrzemski-Bos 9	Mantle-NY 35	Killebrew-Min 316	Mantle-NY 111
Wagner-Cle 94	Howard-NY 172	Versalles-Min 33	Oliva-Min 9	Colavito-KC 34	Colavito-KC 298	Killebrew-Min 111
Versalles-Min 94	Versalles-Min 171		Fregosi-LA 9	Stuart-Bos 33	Stuart-Bos 296	Colavito-KC 102

Stolen Bases	Base Stealing Runs	Fielding Runs-Infield	Fielding Runs-Outfield	Wins	Winning Pct.	Complete Games
Aparicio-Bal 57	Aparicio-Bal 6.6	Knoop-LA 33.3	Yastrzemski-Bos 16.5	Peters-Chi 20	Bunker-Bal .792	Chance-LA 15
Weis-Chi 22	Tresh-NY 2.9	Hansen-Chi 14.2	Hall-Min 9.3	Chance-LA 20	Ford-NY .739	Pascual-Min 14
Davalillo-Cle 21	Weis-Chi 2.4	Green-KC 13.1	Lock-Was 8.7	Wickersham-Det 19	Peters-Chi .714	Pappas-Bal 13
Howser-Cle 20	Wagner-Cle 2.4	Boyer-NY 12.3	King-Was 7.9	Pizarro-Chi 19	Pappas-Bal .696	Osteen-Was 13
Hinton-Was 17	Howser-Cle 2.0	Fregosi-LA 9.6	Brandt-Bal 6.6	Bunker-Bal 19	Chance-LA .690	Kaat-Min 13

Strikeouts	Fewest BB/Game	Games	Saves	Base Runners/9	Adjusted Relief Runs	Relief Ranking
Downing-NY 217	Monbouquette-Bos 1.54	Wyatt-KC 81	Radatz-Bos 29	Hall-Bal 7.60	B.Lee-LA 27.9	Radatz-Bos 46.7
Pascual-Min 213	Pappas-Bal 1.72	Radatz-Bos 79	Wilhelm-Chi 27	Horlen-Chi 8.59	Radatz-Bos 25.9	Wilhelm-Chi 39.6
Chance-LA 207	Newman-LA 1.85	Wilhelm-Chi 73	Miller-Bal 23	Wilhelm-Chi 8.63	Wilhelm-Chi 21.4	B.Lee-LA 27.9
Peters-Chi 205	Bouton-NY 1.99	McMahon-Cle 70	Wyatt-KC 20	Fisher-Chi 8.71	Stock-Bal-KC 19.4	Worthington-Min 27.5
Lolich-Det 192	Pizarro-Chi 2.07	Miller-Bal 66	B.Lee-LA 19	Chance-LA 9.12	Hall-Bal 17.5	Hall-Bal 20.7

Innings Pitched	Opponents' Avg.	Opponents' OBP	Earned Run Average	Adjusted ERA	Adjusted Starter Runs	Pitcher Wins
Chance-LA 278.1	Horlen-Chi .190	Horlen-Chi .248	Chance-LA 1.65	Chance-LA 199	Chance-LA 57.7	**Chance-LA** 5.6
Peters-Chi 273.2	Chance-LA .195	Chance-LA .260	Horlen-Chi 1.88	Horlen-Chi 184	Ford-NY 38.8	**Radatz-Bos** 4.9
Bouton-NY 271.1	Bunker-Bal .207	Pizarro-Chi .267	Ford-NY 2.13	Ford-NY 170	Horlen-Chi 36.7	**Wilhelm-Chi** 4.2
Pascual-Min 267.1	Peters-Chi .219	Bunker-Bal .267	Peters-Chi 2.50	Peters-Chi 138	Peters-Chi 29.0	**Horlen-Chi** 4.0
Osteen-Was 257.0	Pizarro-Chi .219	Bouton-NY .272	Pizarro-Chi 2.56	Pizarro-Chi 135	Pizarro-Chi 24.3	**Peters-Chi** 3.9

Ragged End of the String

The Yankees struggled most of the way under new skipper Yogi Berra. Dissension racked the ranks in New York as the Orioles and White Sox ran the roost. On August 28 the Yankees were in third, 4_ games out. But a great September, which included 11 straight wins, propelled New York to the top. Baltimore and Chicago suffered key losses to second-division teams down the stretch.

Mickey Mantle and Roger Maris were great again for New York, and despite just three regular starters, the pitching was good enough. Veteran reliever Pedro Ramos was sterling in September.

The White Sox nearly pulled it out with a strong rotation and spectacular 40-year-old reliever Hoyt Wilhelm. Orioles third baseman Brooks Robinson dazzled with bat and glove to garner MVP honors. Baltimore also had Boog Powell, Luis Aparicio, and moundsmen Robin Roberts and Harvey Haddix.

The Twins fell to sixth, but Rookie of the Year Tony Oliva hit 32 homers, led the AL in runs, hits, and doubles, and won the batting title. Another rookie, 19-year-old Tony Conigliaro, hit 24 homers in only 111 games. Luis Tiant, Bert Campaneris, Mickey Lolich, Denny McLain, and Mel Stottlemyre also made impressive debuts.

Los Angeles' Dean Chance, pitching in spacious Chavez Ravine, won the Cy Young, leading the league in several key categories. In the bullpen, John Wyatt established a new major league best with 81 appearances for last-place Kansas City, and Boston's hard-throwing Dick Radatz had 29 saves. Six clubs had relief aces, the most to that point, and save totals were rising.

Once again, the Yankees looked human in the World Series, losing a seven-game tilt to the Cardinals. Nobody knew it at the time, but New York's long dynasty was over. Berra was canned after the Series—replaced by St. Louis manager Johnny Keane—Mantle's injuries had taken their toll, and several young players' careers quickly fell apart.

1965 National League

TEAM	W	L	T	PCT	GB	HW	HL	R	OR	PA	H	2B	3B	HR	BB	SO	HB	SH	AVG	OBP	SLG	OPS	AOPS	BR	ABR	PF	SB	CS	BSA	BSR
LA	97	65	0	.599		50	31	608	**521**	6107	1329	193	32	78	492	891	**103**	**52**	.245	.312	.335	647	95	-61	-19	93	**172**	77	**69**	**11**
SF	95	67	1	.586	2	**51**	30	682	593	6119	1384	169	43	159	476	**844**	80	31	.252	.313	.385	698	100	21	3	103	47	27	64	1
PIT	90	72	1	.556	7	49	32	675	580	6249	1506	217	57	111	419	1008	67	35	.265	.317	.382	699	102	25	22	101	51	38	57	-2
CIN	89	73	0	.549	8	49	32	**825**	704	6355	**1544**	**268**	**61**	183	**538**	1003	73	50	**.273**	**.339**	**.439**	**778**	**118**	**192**	**136**	107	82	40	67	4
MIL	86	76	0	.531	11	44	37	708	633	6077	1419	243	28	**196**	408	976	58	37	.256	.310	.416	726	109	69	65	101	64	37	63	1
PHI	85	76	1	.528	11.5	45	35	654	667	6172	1380	205	53	144	494	1091	75	36	.250	.313	.384	697	105	23	35	98	46	32	59	-1
STL	80	81	1	.497	16.5	42	39	707	674	6204	1415	234	46	109	477	882	72	35	.254	.314	.371	685	91	4	-53	109	100	52	66	4
CHI	72	90	2	.444	25	40	41	635	723	6205	1316	202	33	134	532	948	48	43	.238	.307	.358	665	92	-33	-48	102	65	47	58	-2
HOU	65	97	0	.401	32	36	45	569	711	6122	1299	188	42	97	502	877	57	46	.237	.305	.340	645	95	-74	-31	93	90	37	71	7
NY	50	112	2	.309	47	29	52	495	752	5976	1202	203	27	107	392	1129	76	39	.221	.277	.327	604	79	-166	-148	96	28	42	40	-9
TOT	813					435	374	6558		61586	13794	2122	422	1318	4730	9649	404	709	.249	.311	.374	685					745	429	63	14

TEAM	CG	SHO	GR	SV	IP	H	HR	BB	SO	BR/9	ERA	AERA	OAV	OOB	PR	APR	PF	OSB	OCS	FA	E	WPB	DP	FW	PW	BW	BSW	DIF
LA	**58**	**23**	202	34	1476.0	**1223**	127	425	1079	**10.3**	**2.81**	116	**.224**	**.283**	**119**	80	92	**53**	33	.979	134	**60**	135	.8	8.5	-2.0	**1.0**	7.7
SF	42	17	262	**42**	1465.1	1325	137	408	1060	10.9	3.20	112	.238	.293	55	64	102	65	30	.976	148	75	124	.0	6.8	.3	-.0	6.9
PIT	49	17	246	27	1479.0	1324	**89**	469	882	11.2	3.01	**117**	.241	.304	87	**83**	99	54	33	.977	152	65	**189**	-.1	**8.8**	2.3	-.4	-1.6
CIN	43	9	244	34	1457.1	1355	136	587	**1113**	12.3	3.88	96	.247	.322	-56	-21	106	91	46	**.981**	**117**	98	142	**1.8**	-2.2	**14.4**	.3	-6.2
MIL	43	4	266	38	1447.2	1336	123	541	966	11.8	3.52	100	.246	.316	3	1	100	84	**58**	.978	140	96	145	.5	.1	6.9	-.0	-2.4
PHI	50	18	246	21	1468.2	1426	116	466	1071	12.0	3.53	98	.256	.318	2	-12	98	74	54	.975	157	63	153	-.5	-1.3	3.7	-.3	2.8
STL	40	11	261	35	1461.1	1414	166	467	916	11.8	3.77	102	.255	.315	-37	11	109	80	35	.979	130	70	152	1.1	1.2	-5.6	.3	2.6
CHI	33	9	292	35	1472.0	1470	154	481	855	12.1	3.78	98	.260	.320	-39	-15	104	82	49	.974	171	65	166	-1.2	-1.6	-5.1	-.4	-.8
HOU	29	7	256	26	1461.0	1459	123	**388**	931	11.6	3.84	87	.260	.310	-49	-84	95	70	42	.974	166	78	130	-1.0	-8.9	-3.3	.6	-3.5
NY	29	11	**301**	14	1454.2	1462	147	498	776	12.4	4.06	87	.262	.326	-84	-86	100	92	49	.974	171	72	153	-1.2	-9.1	-15.6	-1.1	-4.0
TOT	416	126	2576	306	14643.0					11.6	3.54		.249	.311						.977	1486	742	1489					

Batter-Fielder Wins	Batting Average	On-Base Percentage	Slugging Average	On-Base Plus Slugging	Adjusted OPS	Adjusted Batter Runs
Mays-SF 6.6	Clemente-Pit .329	Mays-SF .398	Mays-SF .645	Mays-SF 1043	Mays-SF 184	Mays-SF 61.8
Santo-Chi 6.2	H.Aaron-Mil .318	Robinson-Cin .386	H.Aaron-Mil .560	H.Aaron-Mil 938	H.Aaron-Mil 161	Williams-Chi 47.5
Wynn-Hou 5.2	Mays-SF .317	Rose-Cin .382	Williams-Chi .552	Williams-Chi 929	Williams-Chi 155	H.Aaron-Mil 47.1
H.Aaron-Mil 4.8	Williams-Chi .315	McCovey-SF .381	Robinson-Cin .540	Robinson-Cin 925	McCovey-SF 152	Robinson-Cin 39.6
Allen-Phi 4.0	Rose-Cin .312	H.Aaron-Mil .379	McCovey-SF .539	McCovey-SF 920	Robinson-Cin 148	McCovey-SF 39.5

Runs	Hits	Doubles	Triples	Home Runs	Total Bases	Runs Batted In
Harper-Cin 126	Rose-Cin 209	H.Aaron-Mil 40	Callison-Phi 16	Mays-SF 52	Mays-SF 360	Johnson-Cin 130
Mays-SF 118	Pinson-Cin 204	Williams-Chi 39	Clendenon-Pit 14	McCovey-SF 39	Williams-Chi 356	Robinson-Cin 113
Rose-Cin 117	Williams-Chi 203	Rose-Cin 35	Clemente-Pit 14	Williams-Chi 34	Pinson-Cin 324	Mays-SF 112
Williams-Chi 115	Clemente-Pit 194	Brock-StL 35	Allen-Phi 14	Santo-Chi 33	H.Aaron-Mil 319	Williams-Chi 108
	Flood-StL 191	Pinson-Cin 34	Morgan-Hou 12	Robinson-Cin 33	Johnson-Cin 317	Stargell-Pit 107

Stolen Bases	Base Stealing Runs	Fielding Runs-Infield	Fielding Runs-Outfield	Wins	Winning Pct.	Complete Games
Wills-LA 94	Wills-LA 9.8	Mazeroski-Pit 26.7	Callison-Phi 15.1	Koufax-LA 26	Koufax-LA .765	Koufax-LA 27
Brock-StL 63	Wynn-Hou 8.1	Alley-Pit 25.0	Wynn-Hou 10.1	Cloninger-Mil 24	Maloney-Cin .690	Marichal-SF 24
Wynn-Hou 43	Harper-Cin 5.6	Santo-Chi 22.0	Shannon-StL 7.0	Drysdale-LA 23	Ellis-Cin .688	Gibson-StL 20
Harper-Cin 35	Brock-StL 4.4	Wine-Phi 17.1	Mays-SF 6.4	Marichal-SF 22	Cloninger-Mil .686	Drysdale-LA 20
W.Davis-LA 25	H.Aaron-Mil 3.9	Wills-LA 15.1	H.Aaron-Mil 5.8	Ellis-Cin 22	Bunning-Phi .679	Cloninger-Mil 16

Strikeouts	Fewest BB/Game	Games	Saves	Base Runners/9	Adjusted Relief Runs	Relief Ranking
Koufax-LA 382	Marichal-SF 1.40	Abernathy-Chi 84	Abernathy-Chi 31	Koufax-LA 7.83	Linzy-SF 17.5	Linzy-SF 33.3
Veale-Pit 276	Law-Pit 1.45	Woodeshick-Hou-StL 78	McCool-Cin 21	Marichal-SF 8.35	McBean-Pit 16.0	O'Dell-Mil 24.0
Gibson-StL 270	Bruce-Hou 1.49	McDaniel-Chi 71	Linzy-SF 21	Roberts-Hou 8.41	Abernathy-Chi 14.8	Woodeshick-Hou-StL 21.8
Bunning-Phi 268	Farrell-Hou 1.51	Baldschun-Phi 65		Law-Pit 9.11	O'Dell-Mil 14.5	McBean-Pit 20.9
Maloney-Cin 244	Johnson-Hou-Mil 1.87			O'Dell-Mil 9.62	McDaniel-Chi 14.3	Perranoski-LA 19.0

Innings Pitched	Opponents' Avg.	Opponents' OBP	Earned Run Average	Adjusted ERA	Adjusted Starter Runs	Pitcher Wins
Koufax-LA 335.2	Koufax-LA .179	Koufax-LA .227	Koufax-LA 2.04	Marichal-SF 169	Marichal-SF 48.0	**Marichal-SF** 6.0
Drysdale-LA 308.1	Marichal-SF .205	Marichal-SF .239	Marichal-SF 2.13	Law-Pit 163	Koufax-LA 47.6	**Koufax-LA** 5.5
Gibson-StL 299.0	Maloney-Cin .206	Law-Pit .261	Law-Pit 2.15	Koufax-LA 160	Maloney-Cin 33.9	**Maloney-Cin** 4.6
Short-Phi 297.1	Bolin-SF .214	Drysdale-LA .279	Maloney-Cin 2.54	Maloney-Cin 148	Law-Pit 30.9	**Law-Pit** 4.3
Marichal-SF 295.1	Gibson-StL .222	Bunning-Phi .279	Bunning-Phi 2.60	Shaw-SF 136	Bunning-Phi 30.8	**Drysdale-LA** 4.2

Batting Around

The pennant race got ugly on August 22, when Giants pitcher Juan Marichal smashed Dodgers catcher John Roseboro in the head with a bat. The incident resulted in a fine and suspension for Marichal, and cemented tensions between the clubs.

San Francisco appeared to have the race in control, reeling off 14 straight wins in mid-September as Los Angeles foundered, but the Dodgers came back with 13 victories in a row, tying things up on September 26. While the Giants struggled over the last weekend, the Dodgers took the crown by winning three of four from Milwaukee, allowing only 3 runs in the series.

Cy Young winner Sandy Koufax outdid himself, fanning a record 382; he also pitched his fourth no-hitter—a perfect game—on September 9. When Tommy Davis broke an ankle, Rookie of the Year Jim Lefebvre and veteran outfielder Lou Johnson picked up the slack. Mays powered the Giants, winning his second MVP; he was the league's first 50-homer man since 1947. When Orlando Cepeda went down with knee troubles, Willie McCovey stepped in and hit 39 homers.

Chicago's Ted Abernanthy pitched 85 times and notched 31 saves to set records. Cincinnati's hard-throwing Jim Maloney threw two extra-inning no-hitters, one of which he won. Warren Spahn, 44, retired with totals—notably 363 wins and 382 complete games—that would have been extraordinary even in the Dead Ball Era.

The Mets opened Shea Stadium in 1964, and this season Houston moved into the Astrodome. The first domed ballpark drew two million fans—and spawned millions of complaints about AstroTurf. Disappointed Phillies fans, meanwhile, began staying away; the club's attendance fell each year through 1969. The fifth-place Braves announced they would move to Atlanta for 1966.

A seven-game World Series against Minnesota should have been called The Sandy Koufax Show. After losing Game 2—he did not pitch in the opener in observance of Yom Kippur—Koufax shut out the Twins in Games 5 and 7. The final contest, a dominating 3-hitter pitched on just two days' rest, gave the Dodgers their third title in seven years.

1965 American League

TEAM	W	L	T	PCT	GB	HW	HL	R	OR	PA	H	2B	3B	HR	BB	SO	HB	SH	AVG	OBP	SLG	OPS	AOPS	BR	ABR	PF	SB	CS	BSA	BSR
MIN	102	60	0	.630		51	30	**774**	600	6213	**1396**	**257**	**42**	150	**554**	969	77	35	**.254**	**.324**	**.399**	**723**	**107**	**87**	**56**	104	92	33	**74**	**9**
CHI	95	67	0	.586	7	48	33	647	**555**	6217	1354	200	38	125	533	916	89	**43**	.246	.315	.364	679	105	1	43	94	50	33	60	-1
BAL	94	68	0	.580	8	46	33	641	578	6138	1299	227	38	125	529	907	**95**	28	.238	.307	.363	670	94	-20	-32	102	67	31	68	4
DET	89	73	0	.549	13	47	34	680	602	6064	1278	190	27	**162**	**554**	952	69	37	.238	.312	.374	686	100	11	4	101	57	41	58	-2
CLE	87	75	0	.537	15	**52**	30	663	613	6138	1367	198	21	156	506	**857**	90	33	.250	.315	.379	694	102	26	21	101	**109**	46	70	8
NY	77	85	0	.475	25	40	43	611	604	6081	1286	196	31	149	489	951	72	19	.235	.299	.364	663	95	-44	-40	99	35	20	64	1
CAL	75	87	0	.463	27	46	34	527	569	5956	1279	200	36	92	443	973	93	22	.239	.297	.341	638	89	-83	-70	98	107	57	65	4
WAS	70	92	0	.432	32	36	45	591	721	6078	1227	179	33	136	570	1125	63	34	.228	.304	.350	654	93	-48	-39	99	30	19	61	0
BOS	62	100	0	.383	40	34	47	669	791	6220	1378	244	40	165	607	964	57	30	.251	.327	.400	727	**107**	99	57	106	47	24	66	2
KC	59	103	0	.364	43	33	48	585	755	6058	1294	186	59	110	521	1020	74	35	.240	.309	.358	667	97	-28	-19	99	110	51	68	6
TOT	810					433	377	6388		61163	13158	2077	365	1370	5306	9634	316	779	.242	.311	.369	680					704	355	66	31

TEAM	CG	SHO	GR	SV	IP	H	HR	BB	SO	BR/9	ERA	AERA	OAV	OOB	PR	APR	PF	OSB	OCS	FA	E	WPB	DP	FW	PW	BW	BSW	DIF
MIN	32	12	299	45	1457.1	1278	166	503	934	11.2	3.14	113	.235	.301	52	66	103	53	34	.973	172	60	158	-2.3	7.0	6.0	**.6**	9.6
CHI	21	14	267	**53**	1481.2	1261	122	**460**	946	**10.6**	2.99	107	**.231**	**.292**	76	35	92	80	38	.980	127	108	156	.6	3.7	4.6	-.4	5.6
BAL	32	**15**	228	41	1477.2	1268	120	510	939	11.0	**2.98**	**116**	.233	.300	**78**	**79**	100	71	41	.980	126	**48**	152	.6	**8.4**	-3.4	.0	7.3
DET	**45**	14	240	31	1455.0	1283	137	509	1069	11.4	3.35	104	.237	.306	17	20	101	**51**	33	**.981**	116	71	126	1.3	2.1	.4	-.5	4.7
CLE	41	13	282	41	1458.1	**1254**	129	500	**1156**	11.0	3.30	106	.232	.298	26	30	101	**51**	40	**.981**	**114**	74	127	**1.4**	3.2	2.2	.5	-1.3
NY	41	11	252	31	1459.2	1337	126	511	1001	11.6	3.28	104	.245	.311	29	20	98	69	34	.978	137	59	**166**	-.0	2.1	-4.3	-.2	-1.6
CAL	39	14	236	33	1441.2	1259	**91**	563	847	11.5	3.17	107	.237	.312	46	37	98	57	29	**.981**	123	72	149	.8	3.9	-7.5	.0	-3.4
WAS	21	8	327	40	1435.2	1376	160	633	867	12.8	3.93	88	.254	.334	-75	-72	101	74	**43**	.977	143	70	148	-.4	-7.7	-4.2	-.3	1.6
BOS	33	9	268	25	1439.1	1443	158	543	993	12.6	4.24	88	.260	.327	-125	-76	108	101	36	.974	162	58	129	-1.6	-8.1	**6.1**	-.1	-15.2
KC	18	7	**378**	32	1433.0	1399	161	574	882	12.6	4.24	82	.256	.329	-124	-118	101	97	27	.977	139	87	142	-.2	-12.6	-2.0	.3	-7.5
TOT	323	117	2777	372	14539.1					11.6	3.46		.242	.311						.978	1359	707	1453					

Batter-Fielder Wins	Batting Average	On-Base Percentage	Slugging Average	On-Base Plus Slugging	Adjusted OPS	Adjusted Batter Runs
Buford-Chi 4.1	Oliva-Min 321	Yastrzemski-Bos 395	Yastrzemski-Bos...536	Yastrzemski-Bos ..932	Yastrzemski-Bos ..154	Yastrzemski-Bos....38.1
Yastrzemski-Bos 3.5	Yastrzemski-Bos...312	Colavito-Cle 383	Conigliaro-Bos 512	Cash-Det 883	Cash-Det 147	Colavito-Cle........34.7
Fregosi-Cal..........3.4	Davalillo-Cle 301	Blefary-Bal..................381	Cash-Det 512	Oliva-Min 870	Wagner-Cle 143	Oliva-Min 32.2
Versalles-Min......3.2	Robinson-Bal 297	Oliva-Min 378	Wagner-Cle 495	Wagner-Cle 864	Oliva-Min 141	Cash-Det 31.2
Knoop-Cal 3.0	Wagner-Cle 294	Mantilla-Bos.................374	Oliva-Min 491	Colavito-Cle..........851	Colavito-Cle..........140	Wagner-Cle 29.1

Runs	Hits	Doubles	Triples	Home Runs	Total Bases	Runs Batted In
Versalles-Min........126	Oliva-Min 185	Yastrzemski-Bos 45	Versalles-Min..........12	Conigliaro-Bos........32	Versalles-Min........308	Colavito-Cle 108
Oliva-Min 107	Versalles-Min........182	Versalles-Min 45	Campaneris-KC 12	Cash-Det 30	Tresh-NY 287	Horton-Det 104
Tresh-NY 94	Colavito-Cle..........170	Oliva-Min.........................40	Aparicio-Bal 10	Horton-Det..............29	Oliva-Min 283	Oliva-Min 98
Buford-Chi 93	Tresh-NY 168	Tresh-NY..........................29	W.Smith-Cal.............9	Wagner-Cle 28	Colavito-Cle...........277	Mantilla-Bos 92
Colavito-Cle............92	Fregosi-Cal 167	Richardson-NY 28			Conigliaro-Bos......267	Whitfield-Cle..........90

Stolen Bases	Base Stealing Runs	Fielding Runs-Infield	Fielding Runs-Outfield	Wins	Winning Pct.	Complete Games
Campaneris-KC 51	Campaneris-KC 4.6	Boyer-NY 24.7	Conigliaro-Bos 8.9	Grant-Min................21	Grant-Min 750	Stottlemyre-NY......18
Cardenal-Cal 37	Versalles-Min 4.2	Knoop-Cal 18.0	Allison-Min 8.4	Stottlemyre-NY 20	McLain-Det 727	McDowell-Cle 14
Versalles-Min..........27	Davalillo-Cle 3.3	Hansen-Chi 13.3	Hershberger-KC 6.3	Kaat-Min 18	Stottlemyre-NY 690	Grant-Min 14
Davalillo-Cle 26	Aparicio-Bal 3.3	Buford-Chi 9.5	Davalillo-Cle 4.2	McDowell-Cle 17	Fisher-Chi.............682	McLain-Det............13
Aparicio-Bal 26	Cardenal-Cal 2.9	Adair-Bal 9.1	Berry-Chi 3.2		Siebert-Cle 667	

Strikeouts	Fewest BB/Game	Games	Saves	Base Runners/9	Adjusted Relief Runs	Relief Ranking
McDowell-Cle 325	Terry-Cle.............1.25	Fisher-Chi......................82	Kline-Was 29	Wilhelm-Chi 7.63	Wilhelm-Chi 23.3	S.Miller-Bal 44.3
Lolich-Det 226	Monbouquette-Bos1.57	Kline-Was 74	S.Miller-Bal 24	Fisher-Chi...........8.87	S.Miller-Bal 22.4	B.Lee-Cal 29.3
McLain-Det 192	Horlen-Chi 1.60	B.Lee-Cal 69	Fisher-Chi 24	S.Miller-Bal 9.05	B.Lee-Cal 20.3	Wilhelm-Chi..........26.7
Siebert-Cle 191	Ford-NY 1.84	Dickson-KC......................68	B.Lee-Cal...............23	Siebert-Cle 9.06	Fisher-Chi............15.2	Worthington-Min 22.7
Downing-NY 179	Grant-Min 2.03	S.Miller-Bal 67	Radatz-Bos 22	Hall-Bal.................9.13	Hamilton-NY 12.5	Fisher-Chi 22.5

Innings Pitched	Opponents' Avg.	Opponents' OBP	Earned Run Average	Adjusted ERA	Adjusted Starter Runs	Pitcher Wins
Stottlemyre-NY..291.0	McDowell-Cle 185	Siebert-Cle 259	McDowell-Cle 2.18	McDowell-Cle 160	McDowell-Cle 37.5	**S.Miller-Bal** 4.9
McDowell-Cle 273.0	Fisher-Chi.............205	Fisher-Chi 259	Fisher-Chi............2.40	Siebert-Cle 143	Stottlemyre-NY 24.3	**McDowell-Cle** 3.8
Grant-Min 270.1	Siebert-Cle 206	Terry-Cle 268	Siebert-Cle 2.43	Perry-Min..............135	Siebert-Cle 22.0	**B.Lee-Cal**............3.2
Kaat-Min 264.1	Brunet-Cal 209	McLain-Det 273	Brunet-Cal 2.56	Richert-Was..........134	McLain-Det..........20.1	**Stottlemyre-NY** 2.8
Newman-Cal......260.2	Richert-Was 210	Horlen-Chi 279	Richert-Was 2.60	Pappas-Bal 133	Richert-Was 19.0	**Wilhelm-Chi** 2.7

New Favorites

As scoring decreased, teams brought back "small-ball" strategy. Stolen bases increased 30 percent. Tellingly, however, the powerful Twins won the AL by 7 games, pulling away from Chicago and Baltimore in September. Minnesota had surprise MVP Zoilo Versalles, and four teammates connected for at least 20 home runs. In addition, the Twins posted the league's third-best ERA despite allowing the most homers in the majors.

The Yankees stumbled out of the gate and couldn't recover, finishing sixth—their worst placing since 1925—even as Mel Stottlemyre and Whitey Ford racked up 36 wins. Certainly the Yankees were unlucky. Tony Kubek was forced to retire due to a back problem, and injuries shelved Mickey Mantle, Roger Maris, and Elston Howard. But the team's reticence (some called it racism) to develop blacks and Latins had caught up.

Chicago's Eddie Fisher broke the mark for appearances with 82. Cleveland lefty "Sudden Sam" McDowell fanned 10.71 men per nine innings, a record that stood until 1984. Baltimore's Mark Belanger, Davey Johnson, and Jim Palmer made their major league debuts, as did Catfish Hunter of Kansas City and Roy White and Bobby Murcer of New York.

In the first amateur draft—designed to filter unsigned players through a system that would check ever-escalating bonuses—the Athletics made outfielder Rick Monday the initial pick. For an execrable last-place club, the A's made plenty of news. Satchel Paige, activated at age 58 to qualify for a pension, pitched 3 scoreless innings. Kansas City's 1965 attendance was the lowest of any franchise during the decade, and blowhard owner Charley Finley endlessly threatened to move the team.

A thrilling World Series went to the Dodgers, who shut out the Twins three times. Sandy Koufax allowed just 3 hits in winning the clincher at Metropolitan Stadium, the only game won by the visiting team.

1966 National League

TEAM	W	L	T	PCT	GB	HW	HL	R	OR	PA	H	2B	3B	HR	BB	SO	HB	SH	AVG	OBP	SLG	OPS	AOPS	BR	ABR	PF	SB	CS	BSA	BSR
LA	95	67	0	.586		**53**	28	606	**490**	6066	1399	201	27	108	430	**830**	84	**49**	.256	.314	.362	676	102	-36	17	92	94	64	59	-2
SF	93	68	0	.578	1.5	47	34	675	626	6083	1373	195	31	181	414	860	70	32	.248	.303	.392	695	95	-16	-34	103	29	30	49	-4
PIT	92	70	0	.568	3	46	35	759	641	6229	**1586**	**238**	**66**	158	405	1011	73	35	**.279**	**.329**	**.428**	**757**	**116**	**116**	**115**	100	64	60	52	-7
PHI	87	75	0	.537	8	48	33	696	640	6256	1448	224	49	117	510	969	78	29	.258	.322	.378	700	101	13	12	100	56	42	57	-2
ATL	85	77	1	.525	10	43	38	**782**	683	6286	1476	220	32	**207**	**512**	913	72	40	.263	.326	.424	750	112	108	96	102	59	47	56	-3
STL	83	79	0	.512	12	43	38	571	577	5963	1377	196	61	108	345	977	59	35	.251	.298	.368	666	90	-70	-73	101	**144**	61	**70**	**10**
CIN	76	84	0	.475	18	46	33	692	702	6043	1434	232	33	149	394	877	69	20	.260	.309	.395	704	93	8	-45	109	70	50	58	-2
HOU	72	90	1	.444	23	45	36	612	695	6170	1405	203	35	112	491	885	**97**	34	.255	.318	.365	683	103	-18	29	93	90	47	66	3
NY	66	95	0	.410	28.5	32	49	587	761	5951	1286	187	35	98	446	992	63	42	.239	.301	.342	643	87	-100	-87	98	55	46	54	-4
CHI	59	103	0	.364	36	32	49	644	809	6213	1418	203	43	140	457	998	80	47	.254	.313	.380	693	97	-6	-14	101	76	47	62	0
TOT	809					435	373	6624		61260	14202	2099	412	1378	4404	9312	363	745	.256	.313	.384	697					737	494	60	-11

TEAM	CG	SHO	GR	SV	IP	H	HR	BB	SO	BR/9	ERA	AERA	OAV	OOB	PR	APR	PF	OSB	OCS	FA	E	WPB	DP	FW	PW	BW	BSW	DIF
LA	**52**	**20**	214	35	1458.0	**1287**	**84**	**356**	**1084**	**10.3**	**2.62**	**126**	**.237**	**.286**	**159**	**119**	91	**54**	42	.979	133	**53**	128	.9	**12.5**	1.8	-.0	-1.0
SF	**52**	14	250	27	1476.2	1370	140	359	973	10.7	3.24	113	.244	.292	61	69	102	84	43	.974	168	67	131	-1.2	7.2	-3.6	-.3	10.3
PIT	35	12	285	**43**	1463.1	1445	125	463	898	12.0	3.52	101	.261	.321	13	8	99	71	35	.978	141	58	**215**	.4	.8	**12.1**	-.6	-1.7
PHI	**52**	15	245	23	1459.2	1439	137	412	928	11.8	3.57	101	.258	.315	6	4	100	69	51	**.982**	**113**	60	147	**2.0**	.4	1.3	-.0	2.4
ATL	37	10	**290**	36	1469.1	1430	129	485	884	11.9	3.68	99	.257	.317	-12	-7	101	69	**64**	.976	154	110	139	-.3	-.7	10.1	-.2	-4.9
STL	47	19	261	32	1459.2	1345	130	448	892	11.3	3.11	115	.246	.306	80	77	100	55	49	.977	145	**53**	166	.2	8.1	-7.7	**1.2**	.2
CIN	28	10	270	35	1436.0	1408	153	490	1043	12.2	4.08	96	.258	.322	-76	-26	108	102	57	.980	122	65	133	1.4	-2.7	-4.7	-.0	2.2
HOU	34	13	261	26	1443.2	1468	130	391	929	11.8	3.76	91	.262	.313	-24	-57	95	70	44	.972	174	85	126	-1.4	-6.0	3.0	.4	-5.1
NY	37	9	288	22	1427.0	1497	166	521	773	12.9	4.17	87	.272	.337	-89	-84	101	85	51	.975	159	92	171	-.6	-8.8	-9.1	-.3	4.4
CHI	28	6	285	24	1458.0	1513	184	479	908	12.5	4.33	85	.268	.326	-118	-104	102	78	58	.974	166	58	132	-1.0	-10.9	-1.5	.1	-8.8
TOT	402	128	2649	303	14551.1					11.7	3.61		.256	.313						.977	1475	701	1488					

Batter-Fielder Wins	Batting Average	On-Base Percentage	Slugging Average	On-Base Plus Slugging	Adjusted OPS	Adjusted Batter Runs
Santo-Chi 7.3	Alou-Pit .342	Santo-Chi .412	Allen-Phi .632	Allen-Phi 1027	Allen-Phi 181	Allen-Phi 57.2
Allen-Phi 5.2	Alou-Atl .327	Morgan-Hou .410	McCovey-SF .586	McCovey-SF 977	Stargell-Pit 164	Santo-Chi 50.5
Mazeroski-Pit 4.7	Carty-Atl .326	Allen-Phi .396	Stargell-Pit .581	Stargell-Pit 962	McCovey-SF 163	McCovey-SF 44.9
Torre-Atl 4.6	Allen-Phi .317	McCovey-SF .391	Torre-Atl .560	Santo-Chi 950	Santo-Chi 161	Stargell-Pit 42.4
Aaron-Atl 3.8	Clemente-Pit .317	Carty-Atl .391	Mays-SF .556	Torre-Atl 943	Torre-Atl 157	Torre-Atl 41.8

Runs	Hits	Doubles	Triples	Home Runs	Total Bases	Runs Batted In
Alou-Atl 122	Alou-Atl 218	Callison-Phi 40	McCarver-StL 13	Aaron-Atl 44	Alou-Atl 355	Aaron-Atl 127
Aaron-Atl 117	Rose-Cin 205	Rose-Cin 38	Brock-StL 12	Allen-Phi 40	Clemente-Pit 342	Clemente-Pit 119
Allen-Phi 112	Clemente-Pit 202	Pinson-Cin 35	Clemente-Pit 11	Mays-SF 37	Allen-Phi 331	Allen-Phi 110
Clemente-Pit 105	Beckert-Chi 188	Alou-Atl 32		Torre-Atl 36	Aaron-Atl 325	White-Phi 103
Williams-Chi 100				McCovey-SF 36	Mays-SF 307	Mays-SF 103

Stolen Bases	Base Stealing Runs	Fielding Runs-Infield	Fielding Runs-Outfield	Wins	Winning Pct.	Complete Games
Brock-StL 74	Brock-StL 10.0	Mazeroski-Pit 40.3	Clemente-Pit 10.1	Koufax-LA 27	Marichal-SF .806	Koufax-LA 27
Jackson-Hou 49	Jackson-Hou 5.9	Santo-Chi 21.8	Aaron-Atl 8.6	Marichal-SF 25	Koufax-LA .750	Marichal-SF 25
Wills-LA 38	Aaron-Atl 3.6	Maxvill-StL 17.0	Staub-Hou 5.7	Perry-SF 21	Perry-SF .724	Gibson-StL 20
Phillips-Phi-Chi 32	Harper-Cin 2.9	Lanier-SF 16.1	Shannon-StL 5.7	Gibson-StL 21	Short-Phi .667	Short-Phi 19
Harper-Cin 29	Phillips-Phi-Chi 1.8	Groat-Phi 15.4	Phillips-Phi-Chi 5.0	Short-Phi 20	Maloney-Cin .667	Bunning-Phi 16

Strikeouts	Fewest BB/Game	Games	Saves	Base Runners/9	Adjusted Relief Runs	Relief Ranking
Koufax-LA 317	Marichal-SF 1.05	Carroll-Atl 73	Regan-LA 21	Marichal-SF 7.88	Regan-LA 23.9	Regan-LA 37.3
Bunning-Phi 252	Law-Pit 1.22	Mikkelsen-Pit 71	McCool-Cin 18	Regan-LA 8.41	Carroll-Atl 19.4	McCool-Cin 26.4
Veale-Pit 229	Perry-SF 1.41	Knowles-Phi 69	Face-Pit 18	Jarvis-Atl 8.52	Hoerner-StL 16.9	Carroll-Atl 21.5
Gibson-StL 225	Drysdale-LA 1.48	Regan-LA 65	Raymond-Hou 16	Koufax-LA 8.86	McCool-Cin 15.1	Hoerner-StL 18.5
Marichal-SF 222	Bunning-Phi 1.58	McDaniel-SF 64	Linzy-SF 16	Gibson-StL 9.41	Woodeshick-StL 13.2	Linzy-SF 14.4

Innings Pitched	Opponents' Avg.	Opponents' OBP	Earned Run Average	Adjusted ERA	Adjusted Starter Runs	Pitcher Wins
Koufax-LA 323.0	Marichal-SF .202	Marichal-SF .230	Koufax-LA 1.73	Koufax-LA 191	Koufax-LA 60.4	**Koufax-LA** 6.1
Bunning-Phi 314.0	Koufax-LA .205	Koufax-LA .252	Cuellar-Hou 2.22	Marichal-SF 165	Marichal-SF 49.1	**Marichal-SF** 5.8
Marichal-SF 307.1	Gibson-StL .207	Gibson-StL .265	Marichal-SF 2.23	Cuellar-Hou 154	Bunning-Phi 42.4	**Gibson-StL** 4.4
Gibson-StL 280.1	Bolin-SF .211	Bunning-Phi .268	Bunning-Phi 2.41	Bunning-Phi 149	Gibson-StL 34.6	**Bunning-Phi** 4.4
Drysdale-LA 273.2	Maloney-Cin .214	Cuellar-Hou .273	Gibson-StL 2.44	Gibson-StL 147	Maloney-Cin 25.5	**Regan-LA** 4.1

The Last Roundup

Prior to the season, Don Drysdale and Sandy Koufax staged a joint holdout. The Dodgers eventually paid each more than $100,000. Koufax won his third Cy Young and finished just behind Roberto Clemente in MVP voting. As Drysdale struggled, rookie Don Sutton provided a solid fourth starter.

Since winning the 1960 World Series, Pittsburgh had rebuilt with blacks and Latinos, becoming the game's colorblind franchise. The '66 Pirates took the league lead in August, with Los Angeles and San Francisco close behind. Matty Alou, Willie Stargell, and Clemente provided the firepower for the Bucs.

The Dodgers reeled off seven straight wins in mid-September to grab first place. Though the Giants, keyed by 20-game winners Juan Marichal and Gaylord Perry, surged in the final week, the Dodgers again took the flag on closing day. The Giants swept three from Pittsburgh to finish second. Any of the three teams could have won going into the last weekend.

Nolan Ryan made his major league debut with the Mets in 1966; he would later eclipse Koufax for most strikeouts in a season and Walter Johnson for most strikeouts ever. Veterans Robin Roberts, Frank Thomas, Del Crandall, and Joe Adcock ended their careers in '66. Rebuilding St. Louis opened up new Busch Stadium. The Cubs fell to last, but acquired Fergie Jenkins, Bill Hands, and Randy Hundley.

The league posted its highest average attendance until 1977. Eight NL teams surpassed one million. Interest in baseball history was galvanized by *The Glory of Their Times*, an essential book of interviews with players from the early twentieth century.

Los Angeles fell apart in the World Series, fielding poorly and scoring nothing in the final three games to suffer an unceremonious sweep at the hands of the Orioles. Following the season, Koufax retired due to chronic damage in his pitching elbow. Jim Gilliam also called it quits and Maury Wills and Tommy Davis were traded, bringing the golden era of Dodgers baseball—which began twenty years earlier in Brooklyn—to a climactic end.

1966 American League

TEAM	W	L	T	PCT	GB	HW	HL	R	OR	PA	H	2B	3B	HR	BB	SO	HB	SH	AVG	OBP	SLG	OPS	AOPS	BR	ABR	PF	SB	CS	BSA	BSR
BAL	97	63	0	.606		48	31	**755**	601	6199	**1426**	**243**	35	175	514	926	82	39	**.258**	**.324**	**.409**	**733**	**118**	**118**	**130**	98	55	43	56	-3
MIN	89	73	0	.549	9	**49**	32	663	581	6035	1341	219	33	144	513	**844**	49	39	.249	.316	.382	698	100	52	11	106	67	42	61	0
DET	88	74	0	.543	10	42	39	719	698	6195	1383	224	45	**179**	**551**	987	67	33	.251	.321	.406	727	111	105	88	102	41	34	55	-3
CHI	83	79	1	.512	15	45	36	574	**517**	6021	1235	193	40	87	476	872	**109**	**44**	.231	.297	.331	628	92	-84	-45	93	**153**	78	66	6
CLE	81	81	0	.500	17	41	40	574	586	6040	1300	156	25	155	450	914	56	27	.237	.297	.360	657	94	-41	-41	100	53	41	56	-3
CAL	80	82	0	.494	18	42	39	604	643	6038	1244	179	54	122	525	1062	69	38	.232	.303	.354	657	98	-31	-14	97	80	54	60	-1
KC	74	86	0	.463	23	42	39	564	648	5873	1259	212	**56**	70	421	982	71	26	.236	.294	.337	631	90	-85	-68	97	132	50	**73**	**12**
WAS	71	88	0	.447	25.5	42	36	557	659	5905	1245	185	40	126	450	1069	84	20	.234	.295	.355	650	93	-52	-46	99	53	37	59	-1
BOS	72	90	0	.444	26	40	41	655	731	6175	1318	228	44	145	542	1020	65	32	.240	.310	.376	686	93	26	-36	110	35	24	59	-1
NY	70	89	1	.440	26.5	35	46	611	612	5936	1254	182	36	162	485	817	58	21	.235	.299	.374	673	103	-7	16	96	49	29	63	1
TOT	806					426	379	6276		60417	13005	2021	408	1365	4927	9493	319	710	.240	.306	.369	674					718	432	62	7

TEAM	CG	SHO	GR	SV	IP	H	HR	BB	SO	BR/9	ERA	AERA	OAV	OOB	PR	APR	PF	OSB	OCS	FA	E	WPB	DP	FW	PW	BW	BSW	DIF
BAL	23	13	253	**51**	1466.1	1267	127	514	1070	11.1	3.32	100	.233	.301	19	2	97	82	**49**	**.981**	**115**	76	142	**1.3**	.2	**14.0**	-.4	1.9
MIN	**52**	11	202	28	1438.2	1246	139	**392**	1015	10.4	3.13	115	.232	.286	48	71	105	72	42	.977	139	57	118	.0	7.6	1.2	-.0	-.8
DET	36	11	271	38	1454.1	1356	185	520	1026	11.9	3.85	90	.247	.315	-67	-59	101	57	33	.980	120	63	142	1.1	-6.3	9.5	-.4	3.2
CHI	38	**22**	239	34	1475.1	**1229**	**101**	403	896	**10.2**	**2.68**	**118**	**.226**	**.282**	**123**	**86**	92	81	41	.976	159	92	149	-1.1	**9.2**	-4.8	.6	-1.9
CLE	49	15	226	28	1467.1	1260	129	489	**1111**	10.9	3.23	107	.232	.297	34	35	100	**49**	44	.978	138	67	132	.0	3.8	-4.4	-.4	1.0
CAL	31	12	296	40	1457.1	1364	136	511	836	11.8	3.56	94	.251	.317	-21	-34	98	72	46	.979	136	65	**186**	.2	-3.7	-1.5	-.2	4.1
KC	19	11	306	47	1435.0	1281	106	630	854	12.2	3.56	96	.241	.323	-19	-25	99	82	43	.977	139	72	154	-.0	-2.7	-7.3	**1.2**	2.9
WAS	25	6	295	35	1419.0	1282	154	448	866	11.1	3.70	93	.242	.302	-42	-38	101	56	47	.977	142	57	139	-.3	-4.1	-4.9	-.2	1.0
BOS	32	10	**311**	31	1463.2	1402	164	577	977	12.4	3.92	97	.253	.325	-78	-16	111	114	**49**	.975	155	66	153	-.9	-1.7	-3.9	-.2	-2.3
NY	29	7	227	32	1415.2	1318	124	443	842	11.3	3.41	97	.248	.306	3	-15	97	53	38	.977	142	**45**	142	-.3	-1.6	1.7	.0	-9.4
TOT	334	118	2626	364	14492.2					11.3	3.44		.240	.306						.978	1385	660	1457					

Batter-Fielder Wins	Batting Average	On-Base Percentage	Slugging Average	On-Base Plus Slugging	Adjusted OPS	Adjusted Batter Runs
F.Robinson-Bal ..6.5	F.Robinson-Bal 316	F.Robinson-Bal............410	F.Robinson-Bal 637	F.Robinson-Bal ..1047	F.Robinson-Bal 200	F.Robinson-Bal ..78.0
Fregosi-Cal..........4.0	Oliva-Min 307	Kaline-Det 392	Killebrew-Min 538	Killebrew-Min........929	Kaline-Det 161	Killebrew-Min......44.2
Kaline-Det 3.9	Kaline-Det.............288	Killebrew-Min 391	Kaline-Det.............534	Kaline-Det 927	Powell-Bal 159	Kaline-Det 41.6
Tresh-NY.............3.7	Powell-Bal.............287	McAuliffe-Det..............373	Powell-Bal.............532	Powell-Bal 903	Killebrew-Min........155	Powell-Bal 38.5
McAuliffe-Det......3.2	Killebrew-Min 281	Powell-Bal 372	McAuliffe-Det 509	McAuliffe-Det........882	McAuliffe-Det........148	Mantle-NY 32.0

Runs	Hits	Doubles	Triples	Home Runs	Total Bases	Runs Batted In
F.Robinson-Bal 122	Oliva-Min 191	Yastrzemski-Bos 39	Knoop-Cal 11	F.Robinson-Bal 49	F.Robinson-Bal 367	F.Robinson-Bal 122
Oliva-Min 99	F.Robinson-Bal 182	B.Robinson-Bal..............35	Campaneris-KC 10	Killebrew-Min..........39	Oliva-Min 312	Killebrew-Min 110
Cash-Det 98	Aparicio-Bal..........182	F.Robinson-Bal 34	Brinkman-Was..........9	Powell-Bal 34	Killebrew-Min.........306	Powell-Bal..............109
Agee-Chi 98	Agee-Chi 172	Oliva-Min.......................32		Cash-Det 32	Cash-Det 288	B.Robinson-Bal....100
	Cash-Det 168	Fregosi-Cal 32		Pepitone-NY 31	Agee-Chi 281	Horton-Det 100

Stolen Bases	Base Stealing Runs	Fielding Runs-Infield	Fielding Runs-Outfield	Wins	Winning Pct.	Complete Games
Campaneris-KC 52	Campaneris-KC 7.9	Weis-Chi 21.8	Yastrzemski-Bos 9.4	Kaat-Min 25	Siebert-Cle 667	Kaat-Min................19
Buford-Chi 51	Buford-Chi 3.5	Knoop-Cal 20.6	Hershberger-KC 8.3	McLain-Det 20	Kaat-Min 658	McLain-Det...........14
Agee-Chi 44	Agee-Chi...............3.4	Boyer-NY 16.7	Northrup-Det 8.1	Wilson-Bos-Det 18	Wilson-Bos-Det ...621	Wilson-Bos-Det 13
Aparicio-Bal............25	Tartabull-KC-Bos ..2.8	Tresh-NY 15.2	Lock-Was 7.7	Siebert-Cle 16	Palmer-Bal 600	Bell-Cle..................12
Cardenal-Cal 24	Salmon-Cle............1.9	Fregosi-Cal 15.1	Oliva-Min 7.2	Palmer-Bal..............15	McLain-Det...........588	

Strikeouts	Fewest BB/Game	Games	Saves	Base Runners/9	Adjusted Relief Runs	Relief Ranking
McDowell-Cle 225	Kaat-Min 1.62	Fisher-Chi-Bal................67	Aker-KC 32	Wilhelm-Chi 7.52	Aker-KC 18.6	Aker-KC 28.2
Kaat-Min 205	Peterson-NY 1.67	Cox-Was 66	Kline-Was 23	Drabowsky-Bal 8.63	Wilhelm-Chi 13.2	S.Miller-Bal 20.1
Wilson-Bos-Det 200	Grant-Min 1.77	Aker-KC 66	Sherry-Det...............20	S.Miller-Bal 8.90	Worthington-Min ..12.2	McMahon-Cle-Bos17.5
Richert-Was..........195	Peters-Chi............1.98	Worthington-Min 65	Fisher-Chi-Bal 19	Aker-KC 8.92	S.Miller-Bal 12.1	Worthington-Min 15.1
Bell-Cle 194	Hargan-Cle 2.11	Kline-Was 63	S.Miller-Bal 18	Peters-Chi............8.97	Lines-Was............11.1	Locker-Chi..........13.8

Innings Pitched	Opponents' Avg.	Opponents' OBP	Earned Run Average	Adjusted ERA	Adjusted Starter Runs	Pitcher Wins
Kaat-Min............304.2	McDowell-Cle 188	Peters-Chi 260	Peters-Chi............1.98	Peters-Chi 160	Peters-Chi............28.9	**Peters-Chi** 4.0
McLain-Det........264.1	Boswell-Min 197	Richert-Was.................270	Horlen-Chi 2.43	Perry-Min...............142	Kaat-Min..............24.9	**Kaat-Min** 3.6
Wilson-Bos-Det 264.0	Peters-Chi............212	Kaat-Min 270	Hargan-Cle 2.48	Hargan-Cle 138	Perry-Min 20.4	**Wilson-Bos-Det** 3.6
Chance-Cal 259.2	McLain-Det...........214	Ortega-Was 274	Perry-Min 2.54	Kaat-Min 131	Horlen-Chi 20.2	**Aker-KC** 3.2
Bell-Cle..............254.1	Richert-Was 215	Siebert-Cle 276	John-Chi 2.62	Horlen-Chi 130	Hargan-Cle..........19.9	**Perry-Min**............2.4

Rare Birds

Cleveland reeled off 10 wins to open the season, and led the league through May, but a poor attack proved their undoing. The Orioles, meanwhile, used a 21–6 run to zoom ahead and never looked back. MVP Frank Robinson, acquired the past winter from the Reds, collected the Triple Crown, and the Orioles got good performances from a young rotation; former "Baby Bird" Steve Barber was the old hand at 27. This was a team built for the long term; four position regulars were 24 or younger.

Minnesota, Detroit, and Chicago scrambled for the crumbs. The Twins came up second, with Oliva and Killebrew the big hitters. Detroit moved up with starters Denny McLain and Mickey Lolich, but saw managers Chuck Dressen and Bob Swift die during the same year; impressively, the Tigers still finished third with 88 wins. Fourth-place Chicago, playing in the league's worst run environment, had pitching but predictably feeble hitting.

Seventh-place Kansas City premiered Sal Bando and Rick Monday; Jack Aker saved 32 games to set a new mark. The ninth-place Red Sox decided to promote minor league skipper Dick Williams; they had already made George Scott and Joe Foy regulars with Mike Andrews and Reggie Smith en route. The Angels moved to a new park in Anaheim.

The American League was wide open; the Yankees had collapsed into the cellar. New York lost Bobby Richardson to retirement, with Roger Maris, Mickey Mantle, Whitey Ford, and Jim Bouton pulling up lame.

Emmett Ashford was the game's first black umpire, giving the AL a much-overdue chance to show some vision. By this time, Robinson, Oliva, Willie Horton, and Rookie of the Year Tommie Agee were among the game's biggest stars, and the AL's best teams had gotten the message on integration.

The Birds swept the Dodgers to collect their first-ever world title. Los Angeles didn't score after the third inning of Game 1. Frank Robinson smacked 2 homers, including a blast in the clincher that provided the margin of victory in Dave McNally's 1–0 shutout.

1967 National League

TEAM	W	L	T	PCT	GB	HW	HL	R	OR	PA	H	2B	3B	HR	BB	SO	HB	SH	AVG	OBP	SLG	OPS	AOPS	BR	ABR	PF	SB	CS	BSA	BSR
STL	101	60	0	.627		49	32	695	557	6152	1462	225	40	115	443	919	54	**45**	.263	.320	.379	699	**108**	53	**62**	99	**102**	54	65	**4**
SF	91	71	0	.562	10.5	**51**	31	652	**551**	6205	1354	201	39	140	520	978	92	42	.245	.313	.372	685	104	24	33	99	22	30	42	-6
CHI	87	74	1	.540	14	49	34	**702**	624	6148	1373	211	49	128	509	**912**	**93**	34	.251	.316	.378	694	100	45	16	105	63	50	56	-4
CIN	87	75	0	.537	14.5	49	32	604	563	6012	1366	**251**	54	109	372	969	56	31	.248	.297	.372	669	88	-20	-80	111	92	63	59	-2
PHI	82	80	0	.506	19.5	45	35	612	581	6096	1306	221	47	103	**545**	1033	90	27	.242	.313	.357	670	98	1	-5	101	79	62	56	-4
PIT	81	81	1	.500	20.5	49	32	679	693	6255	**1585**	193	**62**	91	387	914	63	36	**.277**	**.324**	**.380**	**704**	**108**	**58**	55	101	79	37	**68**	**4**
ATL	77	85	0	.475	24.5	48	33	631	640	6088	1307	191	29	**158**	512	947	57	33	.240	.307	.372	679	102	10	19	99	55	45	55	-4
LA	73	89	0	.451	28.5	42	39	519	595	6110	1285	203	38	82	485	881	91	43	.236	.301	.332	633	96	-74	-25	92	56	47	54	-4
HOU	69	93	0	.426	32.5	46	35	626	742	6177	1372	259	46	93	537	934	65	26	.249	.317	.364	681	106	24	47	97	88	38	70	6
NY	61	101	0	.377	40.5	36	42	498	672	5928	1288	178	23	83	362	981	68	37	.238	.288	.325	613	83	-121	-113	98	58	44	57	-3
TOT	810					464	345	6218		61171	13698	2133	427	1102	4672	9468	354	729	.249	.310	.363	673					694	470	60	-12

TEAM	CG	SHO	GR	SV	IP	H	HR	BB	SO	BR/9	ERA	AERA	OAV	OOB	PR	APR	PF	OSB	OCS	FA	E	WPB	DP	FW	PW	BW	BSW	DIF
STL	44	17	272	**45**	1465.0	1313	97	431	956	10.9	3.05	108	.239	.297	54	40	97	**45**	48	.978	140	48	127	.0	4.3	**6.7**	.6	8.9
SF	**64**	17	215	25	1474.1	**1283**	113	453	990	**10.8**	**2.92**	113	**.234**	**.294**	**75**	62	97	75	47	.979	134	66	149	.4	6.7	3.6	-.5	-.2
CHI	47	7	244	28	1457.0	1352	142	463	888	11.4	3.48	102	.246	.306	-17	9	105	57	38	**.981**	**121**	**39**	143	**1.1**	1.0	1.7	-.3	3.0
CIN	34	**18**	235	39	1468.0	1328	101	498	**1065**	11.5	3.05	**123**	.241	.306	54	**103**	111	81	44	.980	**121**	71	124	**1.1**	**11.2**	-8.7	-.0	2.5
PHI	46	17	214	23	1453.2	1372	**86**	403	967	11.2	3.10	110	.250	.304	44	49	101	63	41	.978	137	53	174	.2	5.3	-.5	-.3	-3.7
PIT	35	5	283	35	1458.1	1439	108	561	820	12.5	3.74	90	.261	.330	-59	-61	100	60	44	.978	141	55	**186**	.0	-6.6	6.0	.6	.0
ATL	35	5	276	32	1454.0	1377	118	449	862	11.6	3.47	96	.251	.310	-16	-25	98	86	54	.978	138	101	148	.2	-2.7	2.1	-.3	-3.2
LA	41	17	229	24	1473.0	1421	93	**393**	967	11.3	3.21	96	.254	.306	27	-20	92	58	48	.975	160	52	144	-1.1	-2.2	-2.7	-.3	-1.7
HOU	35	8	**294**	21	1445.2	1444	120	485	1060	12.3	4.03	82	.260	.322	-105	-117	98	82	48	.974	159	92	120	-1.0	-12.7	5.1	**.8**	-4.2
NY	36	10	277	19	1433.2	1369	124	536	893	12.1	3.73	91	.253	.321	-56	-54	100	87	**58**	.975	157	76	147	-.9	-5.8	-12.2	-.2	-.8
TOT	417	121	2539	291	14582.2					11.6	3.38		.249	.310						.978	1408	653	1462					

Batter-Fielder Wins
- **Santo-Chi** 7.6
- **Aaron-Atl** 5.2
- **Clemente-Pit** 5.0
- **Cepeda-StL** 4.6
- **Allen-Phi** 4.5

Batting Average
- Clemente-Pit.........357
- Gonzalez-Phi 339
- Alou-Pit.................338
- Flood-StL 335
- Staub-Hou 333

On-Base Percentage
- Allen-Phi 404
- Clemente-Pit 400
- Cepeda-StL 399
- Staub-Hou 398
- Gonzalez-Phi 396

Slugging Average
- Aaron-Atl 573
- Allen-Phi 566
- Clemente-Pit.........554
- McCovey-SF 535
- Cepeda-StL 524

On-Base Plus Slugging
- Allen-Phi 970
- Clemente-Pit 954
- Aaron-Atl 943
- Cepeda-StL 923
- McCovey-SF 913

Adjusted OPS
- Allen-Phi 173
- Clemente-Pit 170
- Aaron-Atl 169
- Cepeda-StL 166
- McCovey-SF 162

Adjusted Batter Runs
- Aaron-Atl 53.1
- Clemente-Pit 51.5
- Cepeda-StL 50.7
- Allen-Phi 46.3
- Santo-Chi 43.6

Runs
- Brock-StL..............113
- Aaron-Atl 113
- Santo-Chi 107
- Clemente-Pit 103
- Wynn-Hou 102

Hits
- Clemente-Pit 209
- Brock-StL..............206
- Pinson-Cin............187
- Wills-Pit 186
- Alou-Pit 186

Doubles
- Staub-Hou 44
- Cepeda-StL 37
- Aaron-Atl.......................37

Triples
- Pinson-Cin.............13
- Williams-Chi 12
- Brock-StL...............12
- Morgan-Hou............11

Home Runs
- Aaron-Atl 39
- Wynn-Hou 37
- Santo-Chi 31
- McCovey-SF 31
- Hart-SF 29

Total Bases
- Aaron-Atl 344
- Brock-StL..............325
- Clemente-Pit 324
- Williams-Chi 305
- Santo-Chi 300

Runs Batted In
- Cepeda-StL 111
- Clemente-Pit 110
- Aaron-Atl 109
- Wynn-Hou 107
- Perez-Cin 102

Stolen Bases
- Brock-StL................52
- Wills-Pit 29
- Morgan-Hou.............29
- Pinson-Cin..............26
- Phillips-Chi 24

Base Stealing Runs
- Brock-StL 5.1
- Morgan-Hou 4.6
- Pinson-Cin 2.9
- Wills-Pit 2.9
- Allen-Phi 2.7

Fielding Runs-Infield
- Santo-Chi....................30.7
- Wine-Phi 23.3
- Lanier-SF 21.4
- Mazeroski-Pit..............18.8
- Fuentes-SF 18.0

Fielding Runs-Outfield
- Phillips-Chi 7.6
- Gonzalez-Phi 5.0
- Aaron-Atl 4.9
- Callison-Phi 4.7
- Flood-StL 3.9

Wins
- McCormick-SF........22
- Jenkins-Chi 20
- Osteen-LA 17
- Bunning-Phi............17

Winning Pct.
- Hughes-StL 727
- McCormick-SF 688
- Veale-Pit...............667
- Jenkins-Chi...........606
- Jarvis-Atl..............600

Complete Games
- Jenkins-Chi............20
- Seaver-NY 18
- Perry-SF...............18
- Marichal-SF 18

Strikeouts
- Bunning-Phi..........253
- Jenkins-Chi 236
- Perry-SF 230
- Nolan-Cin 206
- Cuellar-Hou 203

Fewest BB/Game
- Pappas-Cin..........1.57
- Osteen-LA 1.62
- Johnson-Atl..........1.63
- Niekro-Chi 1.70
- L.Jackson-Phi......1.86

Games
- Perranoski-LA................70
- Abernathy-Cin................70
- Willis-StL.......................65
- Face-Pit 61

Saves
- Abernathy-Cin 28
- Linzy-SF 17
- Face-Pit 17
- Perranoski-LA 16
- Hoerner-StL............15

Base Runners/9
- Hughes-StL 8.78
- Abernathy-Cin 9.23
- Linzy-SF 9.50
- Farrell-Hou-Phi ...9.64
- Lamabe-NY-StL ..9.64

Adjusted Relief Runs
- Abernathy-Cin 25.6
- Linzy-SF 18.3
- McBean-Pit..........12.6
- Nottebart-Cin 12.2
- Farrell-Hou-Phi.....11.2

Relief Ranking
- Abernathy-Cin....34.7
- Linzy-SF 31.5
- Hall-Phi 19.8
- Farrell-Hou-Phi ..18.4
- Face-Pit..............15.3

Innings Pitched
- Bunning-Phi 302.1
- Perry-SF............293.0
- Jenkins-Chi........289.1
- Osteen-LA 288.1
- Drysdale-LA 282.0

Opponents' Avg.
- Hughes-StL 203
- Wilson-Hou...........209
- Perry-SF 214
- Queen-Cin 215
- Bunning-Phi 217

Opponents' OBP
- Hughes-StL 251
- Bunning-Phi.................271
- Queen-Cin 271
- Perry-SF 273
- Niekro-Atl....................275

Earned Run Average
- Niekro-Atl 1.87
- Bunning-Phi 2.29
- Short-Phi 2.39
- Nolan-Cin 2.58
- Perry-SF..............2.61

Adjusted ERA
- Niekro-Atl..............178
- Bunning-Phi............149
- Nolan-Cin 145
- Short-Phi 142
- Queen-Cin 136

Adjusted Starter Runs
- Bunning-Phi 35.2
- Niekro-Atl 27.3
- Nolan-Cin 26.8
- Short-Phi 25.1
- Perry-SF 22.6

Pitcher Wins
- **Bunning-Phi** 3.9
- **Abernathy-Cin** ..3.8
- **Linzy-SF**............3.5
- **Niekro-Atl** 3.0
- **Jenkins-Chi**........2.8

Gibson the Head Bird

St. Louis improved 18 games to win another flag despite losing ace Bob Gibson for much of the season to a broken leg. First sacker Orlando "El Toro" Cepeda, liberated from the Giants the previous year, was the league's unanimous MVP both for his hitting and his infectious charm. Tim McCarver, perhaps the game's top all-around receiver, finished second. The Cardinals were fast, strong defensively, deep in pitching, and blessed with racial harmony; they also benefited from an excellent outfield of Lou Brock, Curt Flood, and Roger Maris.

Cincinnati led the league through May and much of June, but injuries destroyed their chances. The Giants only began to hit late in the season. San Francisco was the NL's hottest club in the last month and finished second.

As pitcher Ferguson Jenkins enjoyed his first of six straight 20-win seasons, the Cubs—sparked by veterans Billy Williams and Ron Santo—improved 28_ games and leapt from last to third. Despite pitching in a good hitting park, Atlanta's Phil Niekro won the ERA crown.

The last-place Mets showed impressive arms, debuting Rookie of the Year Tom Seaver as well as 1968's runner-up, Jerry Koosman. Nolan Ryan, Tug McGraw, and Dick Selma quickly followed.

The 1967 season was first time that the leagues had separate Cy Young awards. The award had resided in southern California since 1962, thanks to Don Drysdale, Sandy Koufax, and Dean Chance; in 1967 it moved north up the freeway. San Francisco lefty Mike McCormick, the runaway winner, may be the least remembered Cy Young recipient ever. This was the last go-round for several key veterans of earlier seasons, including Lew Burdette, Dick Groat, Vern Law, and Curt Simmons.

The World Series was Bob Gibson's stage. Tossing complete-game victories in Games 1, 4, and 7, he allowed only 2 runs in 27 innings. Brock hit .414 and scored 8 runs. The dogged Red Sox came back to win Games 5 and 6, but Gibson himself homered in the 7–2 deciding game.

1967 American League

TEAM	W	L	T	PCT	GB	HW	HL	R	OR	PA	H	2B	3B	HR	BB	SO	HB	SH	AVG	OBP	SLG	OPS	AOPS	BR	ABR	PF	SB	CS	BSA	BSR
BOS	92	70	0	.568		49	32	**722**	614	6149	**1394**	**216**	39	**158**	522	1020	85	31	**.255**	.321	**.395**	**716**	109	**120**	66	108	68	59	54	-6
MIN	91	71	2	.562	1	52	29	671	590	6116	1309	**216**	**48**	131	512	976	66	46	.240	.309	.369	678	98	45	-4	108	55	37	60	-1
DET	91	71	1	.562	1	52	29	683	587	6200	1315	192	36	152	**626**	994	78	**51**	.243	**.325**	.376	701	**111**	103	**84**	103	37	21	**64**	**1**
CHI	89	73	0	.549	3	49	33	531	**491**	6000	1209	181	34	89	480	**849**	67	38	.225	.291	.320	611	90	-82	-62	96	**124**	82	60	-1
CAL	84	77	0	.522	7.5	**53**	30	567	587	5902	1265	170	37	114	453	1021	**88**	31	.238	.301	.349	650	102	-15	7	96	40	36	53	-4
WAS	76	85	0	.472	15.5	40	40	550	637	6044	1211	168	25	115	472	1037	63	37	.223	.288	.326	614	91	-83	-62	96	53	37	59	-1
BAL	76	85	0	.472	15.5	35	42	654	592	6164	1312	215	44	138	531	1002	82	41	.240	.310	.372	682	109	56	61	99	54	37	59	-1
CLE	75	87	0	.463	17	36	45	559	613	6037	1282	213	35	131	413	984	85	50	.235	.293	.359	652	97	-15	-20	101	53	65	45	-11
NY	72	90	1	.444	20	43	38	522	621	6118	1225	166	17	100	532	1043	78	30	.225	.296	.317	613	90	-75	-55	96	63	37	63	**1**
KC	62	99	0	.385	29.5	37	44	533	660	5938	1244	212	50	69	452	1019	59	42	.233	.296	.330	626	94	-55	-37	97	132	59	69	8
TOT	810					446	362	5992		60668	12766	1949	365	1197	4993	9945	397	751	.236	.303	.351	654					679	470	59	-15

TEAM	CG	SHO	GR	SV	IP	H	HR	BB	SO	BR/9	ERA	AERA	OAV	OOB	PR	APR	PF	OSB	OCS	FA	E	WPB	DP	FW	PW	BW	BSW	DIF
BOS	41	9	254	44	1459.1	1307	142	477	1010	11.3	3.36	104	.239	.304	-21	19	108	63	38	.977	142	64	142	-.6	2.1	7.3	-.5	2.7
MIN	**58**	18	219	24	1461.0	1336	115	**396**	1089	10.9	3.14	110	.243	.296	15	49	107	70	48	.978	132	63	123	.1	5.4	-.4	.0	4.8
DET	46	17	254	40	1443.2	1230	151	472	1038	10.8	3.32	98	.230	.295	-14	-9	101	79	38	.978	132	63	126	.0	-1.0	**9.3**	.3	1.4
CHI	36	**24**	292	39	1490.1	**1197**	**87**	465	927	**10.4**	**2.45**	**127**	**.219**	**.287**	**129**	**112**	96	70	53	.979	138	84	149	-.3	**12.4**	-6.8	.0	2.8
CAL	19	14	301	**46**	1430.1	1246	118	525	892	11.4	3.19	98	.237	.308	6	-8	97	**49**	**63**	**.982**	**111**	74	135	**1.3**	-.9	.8	-.3	2.6
WAS	24	14	**330**	39	1473.1	1334	113	495	878	11.4	3.38	93	.242	.307	-25	-37	98	57	46	.978	144	60	**167**	-.8	-4.1	-6.8	.0	7.1
BAL	29	17	248	36	1457.1	1218	116	566	1034	11.2	3.32	95	.228	.304	-15	-28	98	79	48	.980	124	76	144	.5	-3.1	6.7	.0	-8.7
CLE	49	14	236	27	1477.2	1258	120	559	**1189**	11.3	3.25	101	.231	.305	-3	3	101	65	47	.981	116	93	138	1.0	.3	-2.2	-1.0	-4.1
NY	37	16	251	27	1480.2	1375	110	480	898	11.5	3.24	97	.249	.310	-2	-19	97	71	54	.976	154	**40**	144	-1.3	-2.1	-6.1	.3	.2
KC	26	10	265	34	1428.0	1265	125	558	990	11.7	3.68	87	.238	.313	-71	-80	99	76	36	.978	132	61	120	-.0	-8.8	-4.1	**1.0**	-6.6
TOT	365	153	2650	356	14601.2					11.2	3.23		.236	.303						.979	1325	678	1388					

Batter-Fielder Wins	Batting Average	On-Base Percentage	Slugging Average	On-Base Plus Slugging	Adjusted OPS	Adjusted Batter Runs
Yastrzemski-Bos 6.9	Yastrzemski-Bos ...326	Yastrzemski-Bos 418	Yastrzemski-Bos ...622	Yastrzemski-Bos 1040	Yastrzemski-Bos ..189	Yastrzemski-Bos....67.2
B.Robinson-Bal ..5.3	F.Robinson-Bal 311	Kaline-Det 411	F.Robinson-Bal 576	F.Robinson-Bal 979	F.Robinson-Bal 189	F.Robinson-Bal ..55.1
Kaline-Det 5.1	Kaline-Det............308	Killebrew-Min 408	Killebrew-Min 558	Killebrew-Min........965	Kaline-Det 176	Killebrew-Min......54.5
F.Robinson-Bal ..4.3	Scott-Bos 303	F.Robinson-Bal............403	Kaline-Det.............541	Kaline-Det 952	Killebrew-Min.......170	Kaline-Det 47.4
Killebrew-Min 4.2	Blair-Bal 293	Mantle-NY 391	Howard-Was.........511	Mincher-Cal 854	Mincher-Cal 156	Mincher-Cal........35.6

Runs	Hits	Doubles	Triples	Home Runs	Total Bases	Runs Batted In
Yastrzemski-Bos ..112	Yastrzemski-Bos ..189	Oliva-Min.......................34	Blair-Bal 12	Yastrzemski-Bos 44	Yastrzemski-Bos ..360	Yastrzemski-Bos..121
Killebrew-Min........105	Tovar-Min 173	Tovar-Min 32	Buford-Chi 9	Killebrew-Min..........44	Killebrew-Min........305	Killebrew-Min 113
Tovar-Min................98	Scott-Bos...............171	Yastrzemski-Bos 31		Howard-Was 36	F.Robinson-Bal 276	F.Robinson-Bal 94
Kaline-Det 94	Fregosi-Cal 171	D.Johnson-Bal 30		F.Robinson-Bal 30	B.Robinson-Bal 265	Howard-Was..........89
McAuliffe-Det..........92	B.Robinson-Bal 164	Campaneris-KC 29			Howard-Was 265	Oliva-Min 83

Stolen Bases	Base Stealing Runs	Fielding Runs-Infield	Fielding Runs-Outfield	Wins	Winning Pct.	Complete Games
Campaneris-KC 55	Campaneris-KC 6.5	B.Robinson-Bal 32.1	Blair-Bal 9.1	Wilson-Det..............22	Horlen-Chi 731	Chance-Min 18
Buford-Chi 34	Clarke-NY 3.2	Clarke-NY 16.3	Monday-KC............8.5	Lonborg-Bos 22	Lonborg-Bos.........710	Lonborg-Bos..........15
Agee-Chi 28	Valentine-Was 2.7	Cullen-Was 14.6	Oliva-Min 7.8	Chance-Min.............20	Wilson-Det 667	Hargan-Cle 15
McCraw-Chi............24	Agee-Chi...............2.7	Oyler-Det 13.4	Hershberger-KC 7.6	Horlen-Chi 19	Sparma-Det 640	....
Clarke-NY 21	Aparicio-Bal 2.2	McCraw-Chi................11.0	Kaline-Det..............7.2	McLain-Det 17	Peters-Chi.............593	....

Strikeouts	Fewest BB/Game	Games	Saves	Base Runners/9	Adjusted Relief Runs	Relief Ranking
Lonborg-Bos 246	Merritt-Min 1.19	Locker-Chi 77	Rojas-Cal................27	Horlen-Chi 8.72	Wilhelm-Chi 16.1	Wilhelm-Chi........22.4
McDowell-Cle 236	Kaat-Min..............1.44	Rojas-Cal 72	Wyatt-Bos 20	Drabowsky-Bal 8.78	Drabowsky-Bal 15.7	Drabowsky-Bal ..21.9
Chance-Min..........220	Stange-Bos..........1.59	Kelso-Cal 69	Locker-Chi 20	Hiller-Det..............9.14	Locker-Chi 15.0	Locker-Chi 17.9
Tiant-Cle 219	Horlen-Chi 2.02	Womack-NY 65	Womack-NY 18	Merritt-Min 9.21	McMahon-Bos-Chi14.2	Wyatt-Bos 17.3
Peters-Chi 215	Peterson-NY 2.13	McMahon-Bos-Chi 63	Worthington-Min 16	Watt-Bal 9.29	Watt-Bal 11.8	Gladding-Det......15.2

Innings Pitched	Opponents' Avg.	Opponents' OBP	Earned Run Average	Adjusted ERA	Adjusted Starter Runs	Pitcher Wins
Chance-Min 283.2	Peters-Chi............199	Horlen-Chi 253	Horlen-Chi 2.06	Horlen-Chi 151	Horlen-Chi 33.5	**Horlen-Chi**..........3.8
Lonborg-Bos......273.1	Boswell-Min 202	Merritt-Min 260	Peters-Chi...........2.28	Siebert-Cle 137	Peters-Chi............24.1	**Peters-Chi**..........3.6
Wilson-Det 264.0	Siebert-Cle 202	Siebert-Cle 266	Siebert-Cle 2.38	Merritt-Min 137	Merritt-Min 22.8	**Drabowsky-Bal**..2.8
Kaat-Min 263.1	Horlen-Chi 203	John-Chi 275	John-Chi 2.47	Peters-Chi 136	Chance-Min 17.8	**Wilhelm-Chi** 2.4
Peters-Chi..........260.0	Downing-NY 217	Peters-Chi 276	Merritt-Min 2.53	Chance-Min..........127	Siebert-Cle 16.9	**Siebert-Cle** 2.2

Boston's Summer of Love

In possibly the greatest and nuttiest pennant race of all time, four clubs converged in late July and bunched closer as the year went on. Chicago had excellent pitching and terrible hitting, even outside of cavernous Comiskey Park, but lacked a fourth starter. Boston featured a passel of young talent, led by Cy Young winner Jim Lonborg and slugger Carl Yastrzemski. Minnesota had Harmon Killebrew and Rookie of the Year Rod Carew, while Detroit's lineup sported four players with 20 or more homers. The Orioles slid to sixth as their young pitchers came up lame.

From early August until late September, the closely packed teams changed positions nearly hourly. The ongoing dramas and great performances added to the character of the race.

Chicago, in a position to win, dropped five straight to Kansas City and Washington in the last week to fall from contention. Minnesota came into the last two days of the season leading Boston and Detroit by 1 game. As the Tigers split two home doubleheaders with California, the Red Sox won their last two games at Fenway—over Minnesota. MVP Yastrzemski's hitting carried the day; rarely had one player so impacted a close pennant race. Yaz is the last player to date to collect a Triple Crown. Fittingly, AL attendance rose to an all-time high.

As the dissension-ridden A's sank to last, Charlie Finley finally swung a deal to move the franchise to Oakland, which gave the Angels a West Coast partner. Finley gave rookies Joe Rudi and Reggie Jackson a taste of major league baseball—Kansas City style; they hit .186 and .178 in their respective debuts.

The Red Sox magic faded in the World Series, as the Cardinals won in seven. It was the Junior Circuit's fifth Series defeat of the decade. Bob Gibson threw 3 complete-game wins for St. Louis, while Lonborg tossed a one-hitter in Game 2.

1968 National League

TEAM	W	L	T	PCT	GB	HW	HL	R	OR	PA	H	2B	3B	HR	BB	SO	HB	SH	AVG	OBP	SLG	OPS	AOPS	BR	ABR	PF	SB	CS	BSA	BSR
STL	97	65	0	.599		**47**	34	583	**472**	6080	1383	227	**48**	73	378	897	67	32	.249	.298	.346	644	101	2	9	99	110	45	**71**	**8**
SF	88	74	1	.543	9	42	39	599	529	6132	1301	162	33	108	**508**	904	92	**47**	.239	.307	.341	648	102	20	21	100	50	37	57	-2
CHI	84	78	1	.519	13	**47**	34	612	611	6020	1319	203	43	**130**	415	854	74	36	.242	.298	.366	664	99	36	-1	107	41	30	58	-1
CIN	83	79	1	.512	14	40	41	**690**	673	6286	**1573**	**281**	36	106	379	938	64	37	**.273**	**.320**	**.389**	**709**	**113**	**134**	**91**	106	59	55	52	-6
ATL	81	81	1	.500	16	41	40	514	549	6118	1399	179	31	80	414	**782**	86	36	.252	.307	.339	646	101	8	6	100	83	44	65	3
PIT	80	82	1	.494	17	40	41	583	532	6163	1404	180	44	80	422	953	**96**	33	.252	.306	.343	649	104	16	25	99	**130**	59	69	**8**
PHI	76	86	0	.469	21	38	43	543	615	5966	1253	178	30	100	462	1003	64	22	.233	.294	.333	627	95	-24	-24	100	58	51	53	-5
LA	76	86	0	.469	21	41	40	470	509	5935	1234	202	36	67	439	980	79	18	.230	.289	.319	608	96	-61	-21	92	57	43	57	-3
NY	73	89	1	.451	24	32	49	473	499	6027	1252	178	30	81	379	1203	75	43	.228	.281	.315	596	85	-93	-95	101	72	45	62	0
HOU	72	90	0	.444	25	42	39	510	588	5994	1233	205	28	66	479	988	97	48	.231	.298	.317	615	94	-38	-28	98	44	51	46	-8
TOT	813					410	400	5577		60721	13351	1995	359	891	4275	9502	352	794	.243	.300	.341	641					704	460	60	-6

TEAM	CG	SHO	GR	SV	IP	H	HR	BB	SO	BR/9	ERA	AERA	OAV	OOB	PR	APR	PF	OSB	OCS	FA	E	WPB	DP	FW	PW	BW	BSW	DIF
STL	63	**30**	196	32	1479.1	1282	82	375	971	10.3	**2.49**	**116**	.234	.285	**82**	**69**	97	**50**	36	.978	140	**40**	135	-.0	**7.9**	1.0	**1.0**	6.1
SF	**77**	20	167	16	1469.0	1302	86	**344**	942	**10.2**	2.71	109	.236	**.282**	45	39	99	93	47	.975	162	79	125	-1.3	4.5	2.4	-.2	1.6
CHI	46	12	221	32	1453.2	1399	138	392	894	11.3	3.41	93	.254	.304	-69	-38	106	**50**	49	**.981**	**119**	50	149	**1.2**	-4.4	-.1	-.0	6.3
CIN	24	16	**321**	**38**	1490.1	1399	114	573	963	12.2	3.56	89	.250	.321	-96	-63	106	62	49	.978	144	79	144	-.2	-7.2	**10.4**	-.6	-.3
ATL	44	16	199	29	1474.2	1326	87	362	871	10.5	2.92	103	.241	.290	11	12	100	88	34	.980	125	68	139	.9	1.4	.7	.4	-3.3
PIT	42	19	244	30	1487.0	1322	73	485	897	11.2	2.74	107	.240	.304	40	31	98	61	50	.979	139	62	162	.0	3.6	2.9	**1.0**	-8.5
PHI	42	12	227	27	1448.1	1416	91	421	935	11.7	3.36	89	.257	.313	-61	-57	101	56	56	.980	127	49	**163**	.7	-6.5	-2.8	-.5	4.1
LA	38	23	218	31	1448.2	1293	**65**	414	994	10.8	2.69	103	.241	.297	48	13	93	65	**62**	.977	144	60	144	-.3	1.5	-2.4	-.3	-3.5
NY	45	25	212	32	1483.1	**1250**	87	430	1014	10.5	2.72	111	**.230**	.290	43	48	101	71	49	.979	133	70	142	.4	5.5	-10.9	.0	-3.1
HOU	50	12	243	23	1446.2	1362	68	479	**1021**	11.7	3.26	91	.249	.311	-44	-49	99	108	28	.975	156	89	129	-1.0	-5.6	-3.2	-.8	1.7
TOT	471	185	2248	290	14681.0					11.0	2.99		.243	.300						.978	1389	646	1432					

Batter-Fielder Wins	Batting Average	On-Base Percentage	Slugging Average	On-Base Plus Slugging	Adjusted OPS	Adjusted Batter Runs
McCovey-SF 5.0	Rose-Cin .335	Rose-Cin .391	McCovey-SF .545	McCovey-SF .923	McCovey-SF 176	McCovey-SF 49.4
H.Aaron-Atl 4.7	Alou-Pit .332	McCovey-SF .378	Allen-Phi .520	Allen-Phi .872	Allen-Phi 160	Wynn-Hou 41.5
Wynn-Hou 4.6	Alou-Atl .317	Wynn-Hou .376	Williams-Chi .500	Rose-Cin .861	Mays-SF 158	H.Aaron-Atl 39.8
Santo-Chi 4.4	A.Johnson-Cin .312	Staub-Hou .373	H.Aaron-Atl .498	Mays-SF .860	Wynn-Hou 158	Rose-Cin 39.5
Mays-SF 4.0	Flood-StL .301	Mays-SF .372	Mays-SF .488	H.Aaron-Atl .852	H.Aaron-Atl 154	Allen-Phi 38.0

Runs	Hits	Doubles	Triples	Home Runs	Total Bases	Runs Batted In
Beckert-Chi 98	Rose-Cin 210	Brock-StL 46	Brock-StL 14	McCovey-SF 36	Williams-Chi 321	McCovey-SF 105
Rose-Cin 94	Alou-Atl 210	Rose-Cin 42	Clemente-Pit 12	Allen-Phi 33	H.Aaron-Atl 302	Williams-Chi 98
Perez-Cin 93	Beckert-Chi 189	Bench-Cin 40	Davis-LA 10	Banks-Chi 32	Rose-Cin 294	Santo-Chi 98
Brock-StL 92	A.Johnson-Cin 188	Staub-Hou 37	Allen-Phi 9	Williams-Chi 30	Alou-Atl 290	Perez-Cin 92
Williams-Chi 91	Flood-StL 186	Alou-Atl 37	Williams-Chi 8	H.Aaron-Atl 29	McCovey-SF 285	Allen-Phi 90

Stolen Bases	Base Stealing Runs	Fielding Runs-Infield	Fielding Runs-Outfield	Wins	Winning Pct.	Complete Games
Brock-StL 62	Brock-StL 9.4	Kessinger-Chi 23.6	H.Aaron-Atl 9.4	Marichal-SF 26	Blass-Pit .750	Marichal-SF 30
Wills-Pit 52	Davis-LA 4.4	Alley-Pit 20.7	Flood-StL 9.1	Gibson-StL 22	Marichal-SF .743	Gibson-StL 28
Davis-LA 36	H.Aaron-Atl 4.4	Mazeroski-Pit 20.2	Wynn-Hou 8.9	Jenkins-Chi 20	Gibson-StL .710	Jenkins-Chi 20
H.Aaron-Atl 28	Wills-Pit 4.1	Santo-Chi 19.8	Clemente-Pit 6.6		Briles-StL .633	Perry-SF 19
Jones-NY 23	Taylor-Phi 3.1	Rojas-Phi 15.0	Rose-Cin 4.2			Koosman-NY 17

Strikeouts	Fewest BB/Game	Games	Saves	Base Runners/9	Adjusted Relief Runs	Relief Ranking
Gibson-StL 268	Hands-Chi 1.25	Abernathy-Cin 78	Regan-LA-Chi 25	Gibson-StL 7.89	Kline-Pit 15.4	Kline-Pit 23.0
Jenkins-Chi 260	Marichal-SF 1.27	Regan-LA-Chi 73	Carroll-Atl-Cin 17	Jarvis-Atl 8.93	Regan-LA-Chi 12.0	Regan-LA-Chi 18.6
Singer-LA 227	Seaver-NY 1.56	Carroll-Atl-Cin 68	Hoerner-StL 17	Bolin-SF 9.07	Abernathy-Cin 9.4	Linzy-SF 14.3
Marichal-SF 218	Pappas-Cin-Atl 1.57	Taylor-NY 58	Brewer-LA 14	Seaver-NY 9.08	Linzy-SF 7.5	Abernathy-Cin 12.7
Sadecki-SF 206	Niekro-Atl 1.58	Linzy-SF 57		Hands-Chi 9.15	Koonce-NY 7.3	Koonce-NY 8.7

Innings Pitched	Opponents' Avg.	Opponents' OBP	Earned Run Average	Adjusted ERA	Adjusted Starter Runs	Pitcher Wins
Marichal-SF 326.0	Gibson-StL .184	Gibson-StL .233	Gibson-StL 1.12	Gibson-StL 258	Gibson-StL 59.6	**Gibson-StL** 7.6
Jenkins-Chi 308.0	Bolin-SF .200	Jarvis-Atl .252	Bolin-SF 1.99	Bolin-SF 148	Seaver-NY 26.1	**Seaver-NY** 3.0
Gibson-StL 304.2	Veale-Pit .211	Bolin-SF .258	Veale-Pit 2.05	Koosman-NY 145	Koosman-NY 25.3	**Koosman-NY** 2.8
Perry-SF 291.0	Jarvis-Atl .214	Seaver-NY .261	Koosman-NY 2.08	Veale-Pit 142	Veale-Pit 23.7	**Marichal-SF** 2.5
Seaver-NY 277.2	Moose-Pit .218	Hands-Chi .262	Blass-Pit 2.12	Blass-Pit 138	Bolin-SF 20.2	**Jenkins-Chi** 2.5

No Hitting, Please

They called '68 the "Year of the Pitcher." And for good reason. Batting average fell to an all-time low, and slugging percentage was the lowest since 1919. Runs per game were just 3.43, the fewest in sixty years. It was really the Year of Bob Gibson. His 1.12 ERA is the best since 1914, and hasn't been matched. Only two pitchers have ever topped his 13 shutouts. Gibson was a unanimous Cy Young pick and won a close MVP vote.

Juan Marichal won 26 and threw 30 complete games, the most since 1952. Don Drysdale didn't allow an earned run for a record 58.2 consecutive innings. The Cubs didn't score in 48 innings; Fergie Jenkins lost 1–0 five times. Willie McCovey's 105 RBIs were the fewest for a league leader since 1920.

With the Cardinals dominating, the race was never close. The Giants were again bridesmaids, and the Cubs scraped into third. Cincinnati catcher Johnny Bench was Rookie of the Year, and New York improved 12 games due to an excellent young mound staff under new manager Gil Hodges. The difference from first to last was just 25 games, the fewest in a decade.

St. Louis magic ran out in the World Series as the Tigers, down three games to one, won it all. St. Louis scored just twice in the final two games at Busch Stadium. Cardinals owner Augie Busch, incensed, began disassembling his club.

The NL announced that new franchises in San Diego and Montreal would join the league in 1969. Not all went smoothly; veteran pitcher Larry Jackson retired after being selected by Montreal in the expansion draft. Bowie Kuhn was the new commissioner, combining a willingness to do the owners' bidding with the baseball knowledge lacking in predecessor William "Spike" Eckert. Kuhn inherited a troubled game. Attendance had dropped again in 1968, and the newly galvanized Players Association was making noises.

1968 American League

TEAM	W	L	T	PCT	GB	HW	HL	R	OR	PA	H	2B	3B	HR	BB	SO	HB	SH	AVG	OBP	SLG	OPS	AOPS	BR	ABR	PF	SB	CS	BSA	BSR
DET	103	59	2	.636		**56**	25	**671**	**492**	6179	1292	190	39	**185**	521	964	73	**61**	.235	.307	**.385**	**692**	**113**	**102**	**82**	103	26	32	45	-5
BAL	91	71	0	.562	12	47	33	579	497	6022	1187	**215**	28	133	570	1019	**80**	48	.225	.304	.352	656	105	45	44	100	78	32	**71**	6
CLE	86	75	1	.534	16.5	43	37	516	504	5988	1266	210	36	75	427	**858**	69	39	.234	.293	.327	620	95	-34	-26	99	115	61	65	4
BOS	86	76	0	.531	17	46	35	614	611	6036	1253	207	17	125	**582**	974	77	33	.236	**.313**	.352	665	101	67	28	107	76	62	55	-5
NY	83	79	2	.512	20	39	42	536	531	5992	1137	154	34	109	566	958	56	30	.214	.292	.318	610	94	-48	-32	97	90	50	64	2
OAK	82	80	1	.506	21	44	38	569	544	6026	**1300**	192	40	94	472	1022	78	35	**.240**	.304	.343	647	108	19	48	95	**147**	61	**71**	**11**
MIN	79	83	0	.488	24	41	40	562	546	5974	1274	207	**41**	105	445	966	69	49	.237	.299	.350	649	98	20	-7	105	98	54	64	3
CAL	67	95	0	.414	36	32	49	498	615	5942	1209	170	33	83	447	1080	75	52	.227	.291	.318	609	94	-53	-34	96	62	50	55	-4
CHI	67	95	0	.414	36	36	45	463	527	5965	1233	169	33	71	397	840	90	40	.228	.284	.311	595	86	-85	-90	101	90	50	64	2
WAS	65	96	0	.404	37.5	34	47	524	665	5971	1208	160	37	124	454	960	46	39	.224	.287	.336	623	98	-35	-18	97	29	19	60	0
TOT	812					418	391	5532		60095	12359	1874	338	1104	4881	9641	426	713	.230	.297	.339	637					811	471	63	14

TEAM	CG	SHO	GR	SV	IP	H	HR	BB	SO	BR/9	ERA	AERA	OAV	OOB	PR	APR	PF	OSB	OCS	FA	E	WPB	DP	FW	PW	BW	BSW	DIF
DET	**59**	19	238	29	1489.2	1180	129	486	1115	**10.3**	2.71	**111**	.217	**.284**	44	49	101	80	40	**.983**	**105**	50	133	**2.0**	5.6	**9.4**	-.7	5.7
BAL	53	16	234	31	1451.0	1111	101	502	1044	**10.3**	**2.66**	110	.212	.285	51	43	98	80	**59**	.981	120	77	131	1.0	4.9	5.0	.5	-1.5
CLE	48	**23**	222	32	1464.1	**1087**	98	540	**1157**	**10.3**	**2.66**	**111**	**.206**	.285	**53**	**50**	99	61	44	.979	127	64	130	.6	**5.7**	-3.0	.3	1.8
BOS	55	17	225	31	1447.0	1303	115	523	972	11.7	3.33	95	.241	.312	-57	-27	106	104	42	.979	128	92	147	.6	-3.1	3.2	-.7	5.1
NY	45	14	204	27	1467.1	1308	99	424	831	10.8	2.79	104	.240	.297	31	19	97	**57**	48	.979	139	**34**	142	.0	2.2	-3.7	.0	3.4
OAK	45	18	252	29	1455.2	1220	124	505	997	10.9	2.94	96	.227	.295	6	-21	95	92	38	.977	145	75	136	-.4	-2.4	5.5	**1.1**	-2.8
MIN	46	14	229	29	1433.1	1224	**92**	**414**	996	10.5	2.89	107	.229	.288	13	30	104	78	36	.973	170	61	117	-2.0	3.4	-.8	.2	-2.9
CAL	29	11	320	31	1437.0	1234	131	519	869	11.2	3.43	85	.233	.303	-72	-85	98	84	56	.977	140	86	**156**	-.2	-9.7	-3.9	-.6	.4
CHI	20	11	**322**	**40**	1468.0	1290	97	451	834	11.1	2.75	110	.236	.301	38	45	102	88	55	.977	151	56	152	-.8	5.2	-10.3	.0	-8.1
WAS	26	11	296	28	1439.2	1402	118	517	826	12.3	3.64	80	.258	.325	-106	-119	98	86	54	.976	148	82	144	-.7	-13.6	-2.1	-.2	1.1
TOT	426	154	2542	307	14553.0					10.9	2.98		.230	.297						.978	1373	677	1388					

Batter-Fielder Wins	Batting Average	On-Base Percentage	Slugging Average	On-Base Plus Slugging	Adjusted OPS	Adjusted Batter Runs
Yastrzemski-Bos 6.2	Yastrzemski-Bos ...301	Yastrzemski-Bos 426	F.Howard-Was 552	Yastrzemski-Bos ..922	F.Howard-Was 172	Yastrzemski-Bos 52.5
Freehan-Det 5.2	Cater-Oak.............290	F.Robinson-Bal.............390	Horton-Det 543	Horton-Det............895	Yastrzemski-Bos ..168	F.Howard-Was 49.2
F.Howard-Was 4.5	Oliva-Min 289	Mantle-NY 385	Harrelson-Bos 518	F.Howard-Was 890	Horton-Det............165	Horton-Det 38.8
Campaneris-Oak 4.3	Horton-Det 285	Monday-Oak 371	Yastrzemski-Bos ...495	Harrelson-Bos 874	Harrelson-Bos 153	Harrelson-Bos 34.4
B.Robinson-Bal ..3.3	Uhlaender-Min 283	Andrews-Bos 368	Oliva-Min 477	F.Robinson-Bal 834	F.Robinson-Bal 153	F.Robinson-Bal ..31.7

Runs	Hits	Doubles	Triples	Home Runs	Total Bases	Runs Batted In
McAuliffe-Det..........95	Campaneris-Oak ..177	Smith-Bos 37	Fregosi-Cal 13	F.Howard-Was 44	F.Howard-Was 330	Harrelson-Bos 109
Yastrzemski-Bos 90	Tovar-Min..............167	B.Robinson-Bal..............36	McCraw-Chi............12	Horton-Det..............36	Horton-Det............278	F.Howard-Was 106
White-NY 89	F.Howard-Was 164	Yastrzemski-Bos 32	Stroud-Was 10	Harrelson-Bos 35	Harrelson-Bos 277	Northrup-Det 90
Tovar-Min................89	Aparicio-Chi 164	Tovar-Min 31	McAuliffe-Det..........10	Jackson-Oak 29	Yastrzemski-Bos ..267	Powell-Bal..............85
Stanley-Det 88	Yastrzemski-Bos ..162		Campaneris-Oak 9		Northrup-Det 259	Horton-Det 85

Stolen Bases	Base Stealing Runs	Fielding Runs-Infield	Fielding Runs-Outfield	Wins	Winning Pct.	Complete Games
Campaneris-Oak 62	Campaneris-Oak ..5.9	Clarke-NY 29.0	Yastrzemski-Bos ..11.2	McLain-Det 31	McLain-Det...........838	McLain-Det............28
Cardenal-Cle 40	Tovar-Min 3.2	Aparicio-Chi................20.1	Unser-Was 10.0	McNally-Bal 22	Culp-Bos...............727	Tiant-Cle................19
Tovar-Min................35	Foy-Bos 2.9	Belanger-Bal 19.3	Davalillo-Cle-Cal 6.6	Tiant-Cle 21	Tiant-Cle...............700	Stottlemyre-NY 19
Buford-Bal 27	McCraw-Chi 2.7	Knoop-Cal 19.1	Cardenal-Cle 6.6	Stottlemyre-NY 21	Ellsworth-Bos 696	McNally-Bal 18
Foy-Bos 26	Nelson-Cle 2.6	B.Robinson-Bal 18.6	Jackson-Oak..........6.3	Hardin-Bal 18	McNally-Bal 688	Hardin-Bal 16

Strikeouts	Fewest BB/Game	Games	Saves	Base Runners/9	Adjusted Relief Runs	Relief Ranking
McDowell-Cle 283	Peterson-NY 1.23	Wood-Chi 88	Worthington-Min 18	McNally-Bal 7.91	Wood-Chi 20.1	Wood-Chi 32.9
McLain-Det 280	McLain-Det.........1.69	Wilhelm-Chi 72	Wood-Chi...............16	Tiant-Cle...............7.98	Wilhelm-Chi 13.8	Romo-Cle 16.1
Tiant-Cle 264	Ellsworth-Bos 1.70	Locker-Chi 70	Higgins-Was 13	McLain-Det..........8.30	Romo-Cle 13.6	Wilhelm-Chi........14.6
Chance-Min 234	Kaat-Min 1.73	Perranoski-Min 66		Romo-Cle 8.32	McMahon-Chi-Det10.7	Drabowsky-Bal 8.9
McNally-Bal 202	McNally-Bal 1.81			Messersmith-Cal 8.85	Locker-Chi 7.3	McMahon-Chi-Det 8.5

Innings Pitched	Opponents' Avg.	Opponents' OBP	Earned Run Average	Adjusted ERA	Adjusted Starter Runs	Pitcher Wins
McLain-Det........336.0	Tiant-Cle...............168	McNally-Bal 232	Tiant-Cle..............1.60	Tiant-Cle 185	Tiant-Cle..............39.5	**Tiant-Cle** 4.4
Chance-Min 292.0	McNally-Bal 182	Tiant-Cle 233	McDowell-Cle 1.81	McDowell-Cle 164	McLain-Det...........36.2	**McLain-Det** 4.4
Stottlemyre-NY ..278.2	McDowell-Cle 189	McLain-Det 243	McNally-Bal 1.95	McLain-Det 154	McNally-Bal 30.9	**McNally-Bal** 4.3
McNally-Bal 273.0	Siebert-Cle 198	Chance-Min 260	McLain-Det 1.96	John-Chi 153	McDowell-Cle 28.2	**Wood-Chi**............3.8
McDowell-Cle 269.0	McLain-Det...........200	Nash-Oak 269	John-Chi 1.98	McNally-Bal 150	Bahnsen-NY.........25.5	**McDowell-Cle** 3.3

Burning Bright

The pennant-winning Tigers helped unite a riot-torn city, becoming the only AL team in the decade to draw more than two million fans. Denny McLain won 31 games, capturing the Cy Young and MVP trophies, and Detroit had the league's top attack—but that wasn't saying much.

The league batting average of .230 is the lowest ever recorded, and the 3.41 runs scored per game per team remains the fewest in AL history. As clubs tried to create runs by any means possible, stolen bases rose again by 19 percent. Cleveland's Luis Tiant allowed just 5.30 hits a game, a new record.

Chicago's Wilbur Wood pitched 88 games, another record, as his White Sox fell 22 games into eighth place. Gigantic Frank Howard won the home run title, but the Senators still finished last. Oakland improved 19_ games with a very young (and cheap) club. Catfish Hunter pitched the AL's first perfect game in the regular season since 1922.

For the World Series, Detroit manager Mayo Smith wanted shortstop Ray Oyler and his weak bat out of the lineup, so he shifted outfielder Mickey Stanley to short. The move allowed the Tigers to get Al Kaline into the lineup; the veteran hit .379 with 2 homers.

The Tigers trailed three games to one before capturing Game 5, behind Mickey Lolich; McLain won Game 6 in St. Louis, 13–1. Jim Northrup's three-run triple broke open a scoreless tie in the deciding contest, and Lolich won his third game of the Series, defeating Bob Gibson, 4–1.

Prior to the 1969 season, Mickey Mantle announced his retirement. Elston Howard and Roger Maris, already with other clubs, also hung up the spikes. The AL and NL announced expansion to 12 clubs each for 1969, with each loop split into six-team divisions, with playoffs used to determine the league champion. And baseball felt obliged to correct the obvious pitching domination prior to the next season.

1969 National League

TEAM	W	L	T	PCT	GB	HW	HL	R	OR	PA	H	2B	3B	HR	BB	SO	HB	SH	AVG	OBP	SLG	OPS	AOPS	BR	ABR	PF	SB	CS	BSA	BSR
EAST																														
NY	100	62	0	.617		**52**	30	632	541	6102	1311	184	41	109	527	1089	82	33	.242	.311	.351	662	90	-53	-65	102	66	43	61	-1
CHI	92	70	1	.568	8	49	32	720	611	6243	1400	215	40	142	559	928	72	36	.253	.323	.384	707	93	38	-42	113	30	32	48	-5
PIT	88	74	0	.543	12	47	34	725	652	6235	1557	220	**52**	119	454	944	73	46	**.277**	.334	.398	732	**114**	83	**99**	98	74	34	**69**	**4**
STL	87	75	0	.537	13	42	38	595	**540**	6152	1403	**228**	44	90	503	876	57	23	.253	.316	.359	675	96	-25	-27	100	87	49	64	2
PHI	63	99	0	.389	37	30	51	645	745	6080	1304	227	35	137	549	1130	61	26	.241	.312	.372	684	101	-10	8	97	73	49	60	-1
MON	52	110	0	.321	48	24	57	582	791	6073	1300	202	33	125	529	962	57	38	.240	.310	.359	669	94	-40	-42	100	52	52	50	-7
WEST																														
ATL	93	69	0	.574		50	31	691	631	6098	1411	195	22	141	485	**665**	87	32	.258	.321	.380	701	103	20	18	100	59	48	55	-4
SF	90	72	0	.556	3	**52**	29	713	636	6375	1325	187	28	136	**711**	1054	82	**66**	.242	.334	.361	695	104	35	48	98	71	32	**69**	**4**
CIN	89	73	1	.549	4	50	31	**798**	768	6301	**1558**	224	42	**171**	474	1042	**100**	46	**.277**	**.335**	**.422**	**757**	113	**133**	94	105	79	56	59	-2
LA	85	77	0	.525	8	50	31	645	561	6166	1405	185	**52**	97	484	823	96	21	.254	.315	.359	674	102	-35	13	93	80	51	61	0
HOU	81	81	0	.500	12	**52**	29	676	668	6196	1284	208	40	104	699	972	68	41	.240	.330	.352	682	100	10	24	98	**101**	58	64	2
SD	52	110	0	.321	41	28	53	468	746	5891	1203	180	42	99	423	1143	56	35	.225	.285	.329	614	81	-158	-138	96	45	44	51	-5
TOT	973					526	446	7890		73912	16461	2455	471	1470	6397	11628	443	891	.250	.319	.369	688					817	548	60	-12

TEAM	CG	SHO	GR	SV	IP	H	HR	BB	SO	BR/9	ERA	AERA	OAV	OOB	PR	APR	PF	OSB	OCS	FA	E	WPB	DP	FW	PW	BW	BSW	DIF
EAST																												
NY	51	**28**	203	35	1468.1	**1217**	119	517	1012	**10.8**	2.99	**122**	**.227**	**.296**	99	**107**	102	55	48	.980	122	63	146	1.4	**11.2**	-6.8	.0	13.2
CHI	58	22	245	27	1454.1	1366	118	475	1017	11.6	3.34	120	.248	.310	41	98	112	59	54	.979	136	**50**	149	.6	10.3	-4.4	-.4	4.9
PIT	39	9	267	33	1445.2	1348	**96**	553	1124	12.1	3.61	97	.248	.320	-3	-21	97	62	50	.975	155	**50**	169	-.5	-2.2	**10.4**	**.5**	-1.2
STL	63	12	183	26	1460.1	1289	99	511	1004	11.3	**2.94**	121	.237	.305	**106**	103	99	77	40	.978	138	60	144	.5	10.8	-2.8	.3	-2.8
PHI	47	14	236	21	1434.0	1494	134	570	921	13.2	4.14	86	.270	.340	-88	-97	99	68	47	.978	137	76	157	.5	-10.2	.8	.0	-9.2
MON	26	8	299	21	1426.0	1429	145	702	973	13.8	4.33	85	.263	.350	-117	-101	102	92	49	.971	184	87	**179**	-2.1	-10.6	-4.4	-.6	-11.2
WEST																												
ATL	38	7	221	42	1445.0	1334	144	438	893	11.2	3.53	102	.245	.302	11	13	100	78	27	**.981**	**115**	71	114	**1.8**	1.4	1.9	-.3	7.3
SF	**71**	15	174	17	1473.2	1381	120	461	906	11.5	3.26	108	.248	.307	55	41	97	64	43	.974	169	73	155	-1.3	4.3	5.0	**.5**	.4
CIN	23	11	307	**44**	1465.0	1478	149	611	818	13.2	4.11	92	.262	.338	-84	-54	105	**42**	43	.974	167	93	158	-1.1	-5.7	9.9	-.1	5.0
LA	47	20	190	31	1457.0	1324	122	**420**	975	11.0	3.08	108	.242	.299	83	42	93	80	43	.980	126	68	130	1.2	4.4	1.4	.1	-3.0
HOU	52	11	256	34	1435.2	1347	111	547	**1221**	12.1	3.60	98	.247	.318	-1	-10	99	66	**55**	.975	153	88	136	-.4	-1.0	2.5	.3	-1.4
SD	16	9	**322**	25	1422.1	1454	113	592	764	13.2	4.24	83	.267	.341	-102	-113	98	74	49	.975	156	86	140	-.5	-11.9	-14.5	-.4	-1.7
TOT	531	166	2903	356	17387.1					12.1	3.59		.250	.319						.977	1758	865	1777					

Batter-Fielder Wins	Batting Average	On-Base Percentage	Slugging Average	On-Base Plus Slugging	Adjusted OPS	Adjusted Batter Runs
McCovey-SF 6.6	Rose-Cin .348	McCovey-SF .453	McCovey-SF .656	McCovey-SF 1108	McCovey-SF 212	McCovey-SF 81.0
Wynn-Hou 5.9	Clemente-Pit .345	Wynn-Hou .436	H.Aaron-Atl .607	H.Aaron-Atl 1003	H.Aaron-Atl 177	H.Aaron-Atl 57.3
H.Aaron-Atl 5.2	Jones-NY .340	Rose-Cin .428	Allen-Phi .573	Clemente-Pit 955	Clemente-Pit 170	Wynn-Hou 55.5
Staub-Mon 4.9	Alou-Pit .331	Staub-Mon .426	Stargell-Pit .556	Staub-Mon 952	Wynn-Hou 168	Staub-Mon 53.8
Clemente-Pit 4.8	McCovey-SF .320	Jones-NY .422	Clemente-Pit .544	Allen-Phi 949	Allen-Phi 168	Rose-Cin 50.4

Runs	Hits	Doubles	Triples	Home Runs	Total Bases	Runs Batted In
Rose-Cin 120	Alou-Pit 231	Alou-Pit 41	Clemente-Pit 12	McCovey-SF 45	H.Aaron-Atl 332	McCovey-SF 126
Bonds-SF 120	Rose-Cin 218	Kessinger-Chi 38	Rose-Cin 11	H.Aaron-Atl 44	Perez-Cin 331	Santo-Chi 123
Wynn-Hou 113	Brock-StL 195	Williams-Chi 33	Williams-Chi 10	May-Cin 38	McCovey-SF 322	Perez-Cin 122
Kessinger-Chi 109	Tolan-Cin 194	Rose-Cin 33	Tolan-Cin 10	Perez-Cin 37	Rose-Cin 321	May-Cin 110
Alou-Pit 105	Williams-Chi 188	Brock-StL 33	Brock-StL 10	Wynn-Hou 33	May-Cin 321	Banks-Chi 106

Stolen Bases	Base Stealing Runs	Fielding Runs-Infield	Fielding Runs-Outfield	Wins	Winning Pct.	Complete Games
Brock-StL 53	Bonds-SF 8.5	Kessinger-Chi 24.8	Callison-Phi 11.9	Seaver-NY 25	Seaver-NY .781	Gibson-StL 28
Morgan-Hou 49	Brock-StL 6.8	Lanier-SF 23.6	Gaspar-NY 7.8	Niekro-Atl 23	Marichal-SF .656	Marichal-SF 27
Bonds-SF 45	Morgan-Hou 5.9	Wine-Mon 19.6	Flood-StL 7.0	Marichal-SF 21	Merritt-Cin .654	Perry-SF 26
Wills-Mon-LA 40	Wynn-Hou 2.6	Money-Phi 17.6	Hisle-Phi 6.9	Jenkins-Chi 21	Koosman-NY .654	Jenkins-Chi 23
Tolan-Cin 26	Alou-Pit 2.0	Maxvill-StL 14.3	Lum-Atl 6.7		Reed-Atl .643	Niekro-Atl 21

Strikeouts	Fewest BB/Game	Games	Saves	Base Runners/9	Adjusted Relief Runs	Relief Ranking
Jenkins-Chi 273	Marichal-SF 1.62	Granger-Cin 90	Gladding-Hou 29	Marichal-SF 9.13	McGraw-NY 14.1	McGraw-NY 19.0
Gibson-StL 269	Niekro-Atl 1.80	McGinn-Mon 74	Upshaw-Atl 27	Dierker-Hou 9.23	Granger-Cin 9.6	Taylor-NY 17.1
Singer-LA 247	Jenkins-Chi 2.05	Regan-Chi 71	Granger-Cin 27	Singer-LA 9.35	Upshaw-Atl 9.0	Brewer-LA 13.5
Wilson-Hou 235	Niekro-Chi-SD 2.07	Carroll-Cin 71	Brewer-LA 20	Niekro-Atl 9.40	Taylor-NY 8.9	Granger-Cin 12.9
Perry-SF 233	Osteen-LA 2.07	Reberger-SD 67	Regan-Chi 17	Seaver-NY 9.58	DiLauro-NY 8.7	Upshaw-Atl 12.9

Innings Pitched	Opponents' Avg.	Opponents' OBP	Earned Run Average	Adjusted ERA	Adjusted Starter Runs	Pitcher Wins
Perry-SF 325.1	Seaver-NY .207	Dierker-Hou .261	Marichal-SF 2.10	Marichal-SF 167	Gibson-StL 50.0	**Gibson-StL** 6.3
Osteen-LA 321.0	Maloney-Cin .208	Marichal-SF .261	Carlton-StL 2.17	Seaver-NY 166	Marichal-SF 45.1	**Seaver-NY** 5.3
Singer-LA 315.2	Singer-LA .210	Singer-LA .261	Gibson-StL 2.18	Carlton-StL 165	Seaver-NY 43.2	**Marichal-SF** 5.0
Gibson-StL 314.0	Dierker-Hou .214	Niekro-Atl .264	Seaver-NY 2.21	Gibson-StL 164	Hands-Chi 42.7	**Carlton-StL** 5.0
Jenkins-Chi 311.1	Carlton-StL .216	Seaver-NY .272	Koosman-NY 2.28	Hands-Chi 162	Dierker-Hou 39.7	**Niekro-Atl** 4.5

Magical Mystery Mets

The wackiest decade in American history reached an appropriate end as the New York Mets, of all teams, rallied in September to win the NL East, the NL playoffs, and the World Series. The Mets made a run at the Cubs in July, but sagged as Chicago—with four fine starters and strong hitters in Ron Santo and Billy Williams—built a 9_ game lead in late August. But the Cubs lost 10 of 11 down the stretch as the Mets rallied furiously. With Tom Seaver winning nine times in the last five weeks, the pitching-rich Mets won going away.

Five teams in the NL West, meanwhile, stood poised to win. In fact, on September 10, first-place San Francisco and fifth-place Houston were separated by just 2 games. By September 22, though, only the Giants and Braves remained, but San Francisco lost four to the brutal Padres as Atlanta won 10 straight to clinch. This was the Giants' fifth consecutive second-place finish.

Seaver was a near-unanimous Cy Young and finished a close second in MVP voting behind the Giants' Willie McCovey. Bobby Bonds fanned a new record 187 times, and Jimmy Wynn walked 148 times, also setting an NL mark. Pitcher Wayne Granger made history with his 90 appearances. For the first time, saves were an official statistic.

A sore arm forced Don Drysdale to retire, and Ken Boyer was released. It was also goodbye to former top relievers Roy Face, Dick Radatz, and John Wyatt. Gene Mauch reappeared in a new country with a new team: the Montreal Expos. Almost eight years of experience in Philly prepared him for the 110 losses.

The first National League Championship Series packed surprising power as New York swept the Braves. The World Series was another shock; after Baltimore took Game 1, the Mets roared back to win the next four. Great catches by Tommie Agee and Ron Swoboda, clutch homers from Donn Clendenon and Al Weis, and excellent pitching buried the Orioles.

1969 American League

TEAM	W	L	T	PCT	GB	HW	HL	R	OR	PA	H	2B	3B	HR	BB	SO	HB	SH	AVG	OBP	SLG	OPS	AOPS	BR	ABR	PF	SB	CS	BSA	BSR
EAST																														
BAL	109	53	0	.673		**60**	21	779	**517**	6328	1465	234	29	175	634	**806**	**74**	43	.265	**.343**	.414	**757**	**117**	**139**	**132**	101	82	45	65	2
DET	90	72	0	.556	19	46	35	701	601	6155	1316	188	29	182	578	922	63	30	.242	.316	.387	703	99	17	-11	104	35	28	56	-2
BOS	87	75	0	.537	22	46	35	743	736	6294	1381	234	37	**197**	**658**	923	67	32	.251	.333	**.415**	748	109	113	73	105	41	47	47	-7
WAS	86	76	0	.531	23	47	34	694	644	6196	1365	171	**40**	148	630	900	51	32	.251	.330	.378	708	110	36	74	95	52	40	57	-3
NY	80	81	1	.497	28.5	48	32	562	587	5990	1247	210	44	94	565	840	63	14	.235	.308	.344	652	91	-74	-52	96	119	74	62	0
CLE	62	99	0	.385	46.5	33	48	573	717	6014	1272	173	24	119	535	906	47	24	.237	.307	.345	652	85	-79	-97	103	85	37	70	6
WEST																														
MIN	97	65	0	.599		57	24	**790**	618	6424	**1520**	**246**	32	163	599	906	65	43	**.268**	.340	.408	748	114	121	104	102	**115**	70	62	1
OAK	88	74	0	.543	9	49	32	740	678	6403	1400	210	28	148	617	953	**74**	**63**	.249	.329	.376	705	109	33	65	96	100	39	**72**	**8**
CAL	71	91	1	.438	26	43	38	528	652	5980	1221	151	29	88	516	929	75	32	.230	.300	.319	619	83	-142	-116	95	54	39	58	-2
KC	69	93	1	.426	28	36	45	586	688	6122	1311	179	32	98	522	901	57	43	.240	.309	.338	647	86	-87	-90	101	129	70	65	4
CHI	68	94	0	.420	29	41	40	625	723	6158	1346	210	27	112	552	844	70	49	.247	.320	.357	677	92	-24	-54	105	54	22	71	4
SEA	64	98	1	.395	33	34	47	639	799	6205	1276	179	27	125	626	1015	72	34	.234	.316	.346	662	93	-54	-43	98	167	59	74	16
TOT	973					540	431	7960		74269	16120	2385	378	1649	7032	10845	439	778	.246	.321	.369	690					1033	570	64	28

TEAM	CG	SHO	GR	SV	IP	H	HR	BB	SO	BR/9	ERA	AERA	OAV	OOB	PR	APR	PF	OSB	OCS	FA	E	WPB	DP	FW	PW	BW	BSW	DIF
EAST																												
BAL	50	**20**	235	36	1473.2	**1194**	**117**	**498**	897	**10.5**	**2.83**	**126**	**.223**	**.290**	**130**	**123**	98	**48**	51	**.984**	**101**	**48**	145	**2.2**	**12.9**	**13.8**	-.0	-.9
DET	**55**	**20**	251	28	1455.1	1250	128	586	**1032**	11.6	3.31	113	.232	.310	50	65	103	109	44	.979	130	60	130	.5	6.8	-1.2	-.5	3.3
BOS	30	7	298	41	1466.2	1423	155	685	935	13.2	3.92	97	.256	.341	-49	-18	105	84	51	.975	157	82	**178**	-1.0	-1.9	7.7	-1.0	2.2
WAS	28	10	311	41	1447.1	1310	135	656	835	12.4	3.49	99	.244	.328	22	-4	96	84	**58**	.978	140	70	159	-.0	-.4	7.8	-.6	-1.7
NY	53	13	199	20	1440.2	1258	118	522	801	11.2	3.23	108	.236	.304	63	41	96	76	43	.979	131	65	158	.5	4.3	-5.5	-.2	.4
CLE	35	7	294	22	1437.0	1330	134	681	1000	12.9	3.94	96	.248	.335	-51	-26	104	87	53	.976	145	71	153	-.4	-2.7	-10.2	.4	-5.6
WEST																												
MIN	41	8	302	**43**	1497.2	1388	119	524	906	11.7	3.24	113	.246	.313	64	68	101	70	35	.977	150	66	177	-.6	7.1	10.9	-.1	-1.3
OAK	42	14	276	36	1480.2	1356	163	586	887	12.0	3.71	93	.245	.320	-15	-48	95	84	48	.979	136	81	162	.2	-5.0	6.8	.6	4.4
CAL	25	9	285	39	1438.1	1294	126	517	885	11.7	3.54	98	.242	.313	13	-9	96	89	56	.978	136	94	164	.2	-.9	-12.2	-.5	3.3
KC	42	10	249	25	1464.2	1357	136	560	894	11.9	3.72	99	.246	.316	-15	-5	102	75	43	.975	157	69	114	-1.0	-.5	-9.4	.2	-1.3
CHI	29	10	265	25	1437.2	1470	146	564	810	12.9	4.21	92	.267	.337	-93	-52	107	109	47	.981	122	95	163	1.0	-5.5	-5.7	.2	-3.1
SEA	21	6	**357**	33	1463.2	1490	172	653	963	13.5	4.35	84	.264	.343	-118	-116	100	117	46	.974	167	82	149	-1.5	-12.2	-4.5	**1.4**	-.2
TOT	451	134	3322	389	17503.1					12.1	3.62		.246	.321						.978	1672	883	1852					

Batter-Fielder Wins
- **Petrocelli-Bos** 7.5
- **Jackson-Oak** 6.4
- **Aparicio-Chi**........5.4
- **Cardenas-Min** 5.0
- **Killebrew-Min** 4.7

Batting Average
- Carew-Min 332
- Smith-Bos.............309
- Oliva-Min 309
- F.Robinson-Bal 308
- Powell-Bal.............304

On-Base Percentage
- Killebrew-Min 427
- F.Robinson-Bal.............415
- Jackson-Oak 410
- Petrocelli-Bos...............403
- Howard-Was 402

Slugging Average
- Jackson-Oak.........608
- Petrocelli-Bos 589
- Killebrew-Min 584
- Howard-Was.........574
- Powell-Bal.............559

On-Base Plus Slugging
- Jackson-Oak 1018
- Killebrew-Min......1011
- Petrocelli-Bos 992
- Howard-Was 976
- F.Robinson-Bal 955

Adjusted OPS
- Jackson-Oak 190
- Howard-Was 180
- Killebrew-Min........177
- Petrocelli-Bos 167
- F.Robinson-Bal 164

Adjusted Batter Runs
- Jackson-Oak 70.5
- Howard-Was 64.7
- Killebrew-Min......64.4
- Petrocelli-Bos 50.2
- F.Robinson-Bal ..49.5

Runs
- Jackson-Oak 123
- F.Robinson-Bal 111
- Howard-Was 111
- Killebrew-Min........106
- Bando-Oak 106

Hits
- Oliva-Min 197
- Clarke-NY 183
- Blair-Bal................178
- Howard-Was 175
- Horton-Cle............174

Doubles
- Oliva-Min.........................39
- Jackson-Oak...................36
- Johnson-Bal 34
- Petrocelli-Bos 32
- Blair-Bal 32

Triples
- Unser-Was................8
- Smith-Bos 7
- Clarke-NY 7

Home Runs
- Killebrew-Min..........49
- Howard-Was 48
- Jackson-Oak 47
- Yastrzemski-Bos 40
- Petrocelli-Bos 40

Total Bases
- Howard-Was 340
- Jackson-Oak 334
- Killebrew-Min........324
- Oliva-Min 316
- Petrocelli-Bos 315

Runs Batted In
- Killebrew-Min 140
- Powell-Bal............121
- Jackson-Oak 118
- Bando-Oak 113

Stolen Bases
- Harper-Sea 73
- Campaneris-Oak 62
- Tovar-Min................45
- Kelly-KC..................40
- Foy-KC....................37

Base Stealing Runs
- Campaneris-Oak 10.8
- Harper-Sea............9.8
- Cardenal-Cle 5.8
- Tovar-Min 5.7
- Kelly-KC 4.3

Fielding Runs-Infield
- Knoop-Cal-Chi 32.5
- Aparicio-Chi................32.5
- Cardenas-Min 23.2
- McMullen-Was 21.4
- Brinkman-Was 19.7

Fielding Runs-Outfield
- Blair-Bal 11.7
- Piniella-KC 10.1
- Tovar-Min 9.4
- Kirkpatrick-KC........7.9
- Kelly-KC 7.4

Wins
- McLain-Det 24
- Cuellar-Bal.............23

Winning Pct.
- Palmer-Bal 800
- Perry-Min 769
- McNally-Bal 741
- McLain-Det 727
- Odom-Oak 714

Complete Games
- Stottlemyre-NY......24
- McLain-Det.............23
- McDowell-Cle 18
- Cuellar-Bal 18
- Peterson-NY..........16

Strikeouts
- McDowell-Cle 279
- Lolich-Det 271
- Messersmith-Cal ..211
- Boswell-Min 190
- ....

Fewest BB/Game
- Peterson-NY........1.42
- Bosman-Was 1.82
- McLain-Det..........1.86
- Perry-Min 2.27
- Cuellar-Bal 2.45

Games
- Wood-Chi 76
- Perranoski-Min 75
- Lyle-Bos 71
- Locker-Chi-Sea..............68
- Segui-Sea.......................66

Saves
- Perranoski-Min 31
- K.Tatum-Cal...........22
- Lyle-Bos..................17
- Watt-Bal..................16
- Higgins-Was 16

Base Runners/9
- Hall-Bal................8.09
- Wilhelm-Cal 9.05
- Peterson-NY........9.07
- Cuellar-Bal 9.07
- Drabowsky-KC 9.18

Adjusted Relief Runs
- K.Tatum-Cal 22.2
- Perranoski-Min 20.4
- Lyle-Bos 13.9
- Watt-Bal 13.8
- Hall-Bal................13.0

Relief Ranking
- Perranoski-Min ..40.9
- K.Tatum-Cal 33.5
- Watt-Bal.............19.2
- Drabowsky-KC....19.1
- Lyle-Bos 18.6

Innings Pitched
- McLain-Det........325.0
- Stottlemyre-NY ..303.0
- Cuellar-Bal 290.2
- McDowell-Cle 285.0
- Lolich-Det 280.2

Opponents' Avg.
- Messersmith-Cal .190
- Palmer-Bal 200
- Cuellar-Bal 204
- Lolich-Det 210
- McDowell-Cle 213

Opponents' OBP
- Cuellar-Bal..................260
- Bosman-Was 260
- Peterson-NY 261
- Palmer-Bal 272
- Messersmith-Cal 274

Earned Run Average
- Bosman-Was 2.19
- Palmer-Bal 2.34
- Cuellar-Bal 2.38
- Messersmith-Cal 2.52
- Peterson-NY........2.55

Adjusted ERA
- Bosman-Was........158
- Palmer-Bal...........153
- Cuellar-Bal...........150
- Messersmith-Cal ..138
- Peterson-NY 137

Adjusted Starter Runs
- McLain-Det..........36.4
- Cuellar-Bal 35.2
- Messersmith-Cal 27.8
- Palmer-Bal 27.2
- Perry-Min 27.0

Pitcher Wins
- **Perranoski-Min** .4.4
- **K.Tatum-Cal** 4.1
- **Cuellar-Bal** 3.7
- **Stottlemyre-NY** 3.7
- **Peterson-NY** 3.3

A Whole New Game

In less than a decade, the league had expanded by a third, added divisions, and instituted a set of postseason playoffs. It was a shock to the system. Responding to pressure from fans, hitters, and the media, the leagues shrunk the strike zone, which now ranged from the armpits to the top of the knees. AL scoring per game increased 20 percent.

Reggie Jackson of Oakland was on a record home run pace, but settled for "just" 47, third best in the AL. For the first time, five men hit 40 or more homers. Sam McDowell of Cleveland took his fourth strikeout crown, and Lou Piniella was Rookie of the Year for expansion Kansas City, which finished ahead of Chicago and fellow expansion team Seattle in the West.

Three future catching mainstays debuted: Thurman Munson, Carlton Fisk, and Rick Dempsey. Meanwhile, pitcher Paul Edmondson of Chicago perished in an accident traveling to 1970 spring training.

Minnesota's Rod Carew won the first of his seven batting titles, and under the tutelage of rookie manager Billy Martin, Carew stole home seven times. Tony Oliva led the AL in hits, Harmon Killebrew was MVP, and the Twins won the West. They were no match, however, for the Orioles, who took the inaugural American League Championship Series in three straight. Neither division race was close.

Feisty Earl Weaver, in his first full season as manager in Baltimore, knew how to structure a lineup. His club led the East in runs and its pitching was the league's best. Mike Cuellar (co-Cy Young winner with Denny McLain) and Dave McNally each earned 20 wins. However, the Orioles were a surprise World Series loser as the Cinderella New York Mets won in five. The Orioles tallied just 9 runs.

With two new clubs added, AL attendance again reached an all-time high. But most clubs' attendance fell, with seven clubs drawing fewer than a million, as football—busily merging the AFL and NFL—made further inroads on the American psyche.

1970 National League

TEAM	W	L	T	PCT	GB	HW	HL	R	OR	PA	H	2B	3B	HR	BB	SO	HB	SH	AVG	OBP	SLG	OPS	AOPS	BR	ABR	PF	SB	CS	BSA	BSR
EAST																														
PIT	89	73	0	.549		50	32	729	664	6231	**1522**	235	**70**	130	444	871	53	44	**.270**	.325	.406	731	104	8	24	98	66	34	66	3
CHI	84	78	0	.519	5	46	34	806	679	6229	1424	228	44	179	607	844	75	20	.259	.333	.415	748	95	50	-34	112	39	16	71	3
NY	83	79	0	.512	6	44	38	695	**630**	6275	1358	211	42	120	684	1062	74	26	.249	.333	.370	703	95	-21	-22	100	118	54	69	7
STL	76	86	0	.469	13	34	47	744	747	6376	1497	218	51	113	569	961	52	26	.263	.331	.379	710	95	-22	-37	102	117	47	71	9
PHI	73	88	0	.453	15.5	40	40	594	730	6099	1299	224	58	101	519	1066	62	25	.238	.305	.356	661	85	-127	-110	97	72	64	53	-7
MON	73	89	0	.451	16	39	41	687	807	6251	1284	211	35	136	659	972	**107**	39	.237	.323	.365	688	91	-61	-60	100	65	45	59	-1
WEST																														
CIN	102	60	0	.630		**57**	24	775	681	6222	1498	253	45	**191**	547	984	58	29	**.270**	.336	**.436**	**772**	**113**	95	93	100	115	52	69	7
LA	87	74	0	.540	14.5	39	42	749	684	6293	1515	233	67	87	541	841	72	24	**.270**	.334	.382	716	103	-6	28	96	**138**	57	71	10
SF	86	76	0	.531	16	48	33	**831**	826	6469	1460	**257**	35	165	**729**	1005	66	**56**	.262	**.351**	.409	760	111	**98**	**108**	99	83	27	**75**	9
HOU	79	83	0	.488	23	44	37	744	763	6305	1446	250	47	129	598	911	63	27	.259	.332	.391	723	104	6	39	96	114	41	74	**11**
ATL	76	86	0	.469	26	42	39	736	772	6202	1495	215	24	160	522	**736**	54	38	**.270**	.334	.404	738	98	32	-10	106	58	34	63	1
SD	63	99	0	.389	39	31	50	681	788	6145	1353	208	36	172	500	1164	83	39	.246	.312	.391	703	98	-51	-23	96	60	45	57	-3
TOT	971					514	457	8771		75097	17151	2743	554	1683	6919	11417	393	819	.258	.329	.392	721					1045	516	67	49

TEAM	CG	SHO	GR	SV	IP	H	HR	BB	SO	BR/9	ERA	AERA	OAV	OOB	PR	APR	PF	OSB	OCS	FA	E	WPB	DP	FW	PW	BW	BSW	DIF
EAST																												
PIT	36	13	288	43	1453.2	1386	106	625	990	12.7	3.70	106	.255	.334	56	34	96	64	56	.979	137	55	**195**	.3	3.4	2.4	-.1	2.0
CHI	**59**	9	205	25	1435.0	1402	143	**475**	1000	11.9	3.76	**120**	.256	.316	46	**106**	111	71	48	.978	137	59	146	.3	**10.6**	-3.4	-.1	-4.4
NY	47	10	228	32	1459.2	**1260**	135	575	**1064**	**11.5**	**3.45**	117	**.233**	**.307**	**97**	94	99	64	42	.979	124	54	136	1.0	9.4	-2.2	.3	-6.5
STL	51	11	278	20	1475.2	1483	**102**	632	960	13.0	4.06	101	.263	.337	-2	9	102	86	45	.977	150	86	159	-.4	.9	-3.7	.5	-2.3
PHI	24	8	277	36	1461.0	1483	132	538	1047	12.7	4.17	96	.265	.330	-20	-30	99	122	47	**.981**	**114**	71	134	**1.5**	-3.0	-11.0	-1.1	6.0
MON	29	10	285	32	1438.2	1434	162	716	914	13.8	4.50	91	.261	.349	-73	-62	102	78	45	.977	141	61	193	.0	-6.2	-6.0	-.5	4.6
WEST																												
CIN	32	15	252	**60**	1444.2	1370	118	592	843	12.4	3.69	109	.251	.325	57	56	100	**46**	38	.976	151	53	173	-.5	5.6	9.3	.3	6.3
LA	37	**17**	227	42	1458.2	1394	164	496	880	11.9	3.82	100	.250	.314	37	2	95	106	28	.978	135	66	135	.4	.2	2.8	.6	2.6
SF	50	7	253	30	1457.2	1514	156	604	931	13.3	4.50	88	.267	.339	-74	-87	98	114	31	.973	170	106	153	-1.5	-8.7	**10.8**	.5	4.0
HOU	36	6	**302**	35	1456.0	1491	131	577	942	13.0	4.23	92	.265	.336	-30	-61	96	78	**58**	.978	140	103	144	.1	-6.1	3.9	**.7**	-.6
ATL	45	9	204	24	1430.2	1451	185	478	960	12.3	4.33	99	.261	.320	-45	-6	106	123	32	.977	141	74	118	.0	-.6	-1.0	-.3	-3.2
SD	24	9	279	32	1440.1	1483	149	611	886	13.3	4.36	91	.267	.341	-50	-62	98	93	46	.975	158	**42**	159	-.9	-6.2	-2.3	-.7	-8.0
TOT	470	124	3078	411	17411.2					12.6	4.05		.258	.329						.977	1698	830	1845					

Batter-Fielder Wins
McCovey-SF 6.5
Bench-Cin............6.0
Perez-Cin 4.6
Carty-Atl 4.0
Morgan-Hou 3.9

Batting Average
Carty-Atl 366
Torre-StL...............325
Sanguillen-Pit 325
Williams-Chi 322
Parker-LA 319

On-Base Percentage
Carty-Atl 454
McCovey-SF 444
Dietz-SF.......................426
Hickman-Chi 419
Perez-Cin.....................401

Slugging Average
McCovey-SF 612
Perez-Cin 589
Bench-Cin.............587
Williams-Chi 586
Carty-Atl 584

On-Base Plus Slugging
McCovey-SF 1056
Carty-Atl 1037
Hickman-Chi 1001
Perez-Cin.............990
Williams-Chi 977

Adjusted OPS
McCovey-SF 183
Carty-Atl 167
Perez-Cin..............162
Dietz-SF 154
Hickman-Chi 148

Adjusted Batter Runs
McCovey-SF 66.8
Perez-Cin 52.4
Carty-Atl 48.7
Dietz-SF 44.7
Carbo-Cin 41.6

Runs
Williams-Chi 137
Bonds-SF 134
Rose-Cin 120
Brock-StL.............114
Tolan-Cin 112

Hits
Williams-Chi 205
Rose-Cin 205
Torre-StL.............203
Brock-StL.............202
Alou-Pit 201

Doubles
Parker-LA 47
McCovey-SF 39
Rose-Cin.......................37
Dietz-SF 36
Bonds-SF 36

Triples
Davis-LA 16
Kessinger-Chi 14
Clemente-Pit 10
Bonds-SF 10

Home Runs
Bench-Cin 45
Williams-Chi 42
Perez-Cin...............40
McCovey-SF 39

Total Bases
Williams-Chi 373
Bench-Cin 355
Perez-Cin..............346
Bonds-SF 334
Gaston-SD............317

Runs Batted In
Bench-Cin 148
Williams-Chi........129
Perez-Cin 129
McCovey-SF.......126
H.Aaron-Atl..........118

Stolen Bases
Tolan-Cin 57
Brock-StL...............51
Bonds-SF 48
Morgan-Hou............42
Davis-LA 38

Base Stealing Runs
Bonds-SF 7.1
Brock-StL 6.0
Tolan-Cin 5.5
Morgan-Hou 4.7
Harrelson-NY 3.7

Fielding Runs-Infield
Alley-Pit 31.4
Maxvill-StL 27.6
Rader-Hou 25.3
Mazeroski-Pit..............20.1
Wine-Mon 18.7

Fielding Runs-Outfield
Briggs-Phi.............6.8
Staub-Mon 6.3
Bonds-SF 5.8
Jones-NY 5.8
Davis-LA...............5.7

Wins
Perry-SF 23
Gibson-StL 23
Jenkins-Chi 22
Merritt-Cin 20

Winning Pct.
Gibson-StL 767
Nolan-Cin 720
Walker-Pit 714
Perry-SF 639
Merritt-Cin............625

Complete Games
Jenkins-Chi...........24
Perry-SF...............23
Gibson-StL 23
Seaver-NY 19
Dierker-Hou 17

Strikeouts
Seaver-NY 283
Jenkins-Chi 274
Gibson-StL 274
Perry-SF 214
Holtzman-Chi........202

Fewest BB/Game
Jenkins-Chi.........1.73
Marichal-SF 1.78
Osteen-LA 1.81
McAndrew-NY 1.86
Merritt-Cin...........2.04

Games
Herbel-SD-NY...............76
Selma-Phi 73
Linzy-SF-StL.................67
Granger-Cin 67
Giusti-Pit 66

Saves
Granger-Cin...........35
Giusti-Pit 26
Brewer-LA 24
Raymond-Mon........23
Selma-Phi 22

Base Runners/9
Jenkins-Chi.........9.55
Singer-LA 9.56
Seaver-NY 9.82
Brewer-LA..........10.01
McAndrew-NY ..10.06

Adjusted Relief Runs
Selma-Phi............20.0
Carroll-Cin 15.3
Gullett-Cin 14.4
C.Taylor-StL 14.3
McMahon-SF 12.3

Relief Ranking
Selma-Phi 29.7
Granger-Cin........22.3
Carroll-Cin..........22.1
McMahon-SF......21.7
Giusti-Pit 16.6

Innings Pitched
Perry-SF...........328.2
Jenkins-Chi.........313.0
Gibson-StL 294.0
Seaver-NY 290.2
Holtzman-Chi 287.2

Opponents' Avg.
Simpson-Cin........198
Seaver-NY 214
Walker-Pit 219
Jenkins-Chi...........224
Gentry-NY 224

Opponents' OBP
Jenkins-Chi 264
Seaver-NY...................272
McAndrew-NY 279
Perry-SF 289
Gibson-StL...................293

Earned Run Average
Seaver-NY 2.82
Simpson-Cin.........3.02
Walker-Pit 3.04
Gibson-StL 3.12
Koosman-NY 3.14

Adjusted ERA
Seaver-NY............143
Simpson-Cin 134
Pappas-Atl-Chi 134
Holtzman-Chi.......133
Jenkins-Chi 133

Adjusted Starter Runs
Seaver-NY 39.0
Jenkins-Chi...........37.1
Gibson-StL 33.7
Holtzman-Chi 31.4
Perry-SF..............26.5

Pitcher Wins
Gibson-StL 4.5
Seaver-NY..........4.4
Jenkins-Chi........3.9
Selma-Phi 3.1
Holtzman-Chi 3.0

A Change Is Gonna Come

Veteran outfielder Curt Flood sat out the season, refusing a trade from St. Louis to Philadelphia. Instead he filed suit to challenge baseball's reserve clause, which bound him to the team that first signed him. Flood lost, but he laid the groundwork for free agency.

Two rust-belt clubs built new "cereal bowl" artificial turf parks in midseason: the Reds opened Riverfront Stadium and the Pirates debuting Three Rivers Stadium. In April 1970 only one NL team used turf; by 1979 half did. Great crowds in New York and the new parks helped spike NL attendance. Scoring rose nearly a half-run per game, with homers an all-time high until 1987. But it wasn't just slugging; speed was also back, with steals per game the highest since 1929.

The top NL shortstops of the decade debuted on consecutive days: Dave Concepcion and Larry Bowa. Twenty-year-old Houston outfielder Cesar Cedeno was an immediate sensation. MacMillan published *The Baseball Encyclopedia*, setting the standard for sports reference.

In a closely bunched NL East, the Pirates pulled away from the Cubs and Mets in September. Last-place Montreal improved 21 games and finished just 16 out. Willie Stargell and Roberto Clemente's bats, and deep pitching, won for Pittsburgh.

Cincinnati, finally showing its tremendous talent, led from opening day and was never challenged. Johnny Bench was the MVP for his awesome power and fine defense, and Tony Perez and Lee May also dented the fences. Wayne Granger's 35 saves established a new mark. The Reds won the NLCS in three nail-biters, allowing just 3 runs to the vaunted Pirates.

During the playoffs, umpires in both leagues briefly went on strike—the first-ever arbiter walkout. A few days later, the Reds hosted the first World Series game on plastic, but the Baltimore Orioles won the Fall Classic in five games, including three one-run affairs.

1970 American League

TEAM	W	L	T	PCT	GB	HW	HL	R	OR	PA	H	2B	3B	HR	BB	SO	HB	SH	AVG	OBP	SLG	OPS	AOPS	BR	ABR	PF	SB	CS	BSA	BSR
EAST																														
BAL	108	54	0	.667		**59**	22	**792**	**574**	6416	1424	213	25	179	**717**	952	64	**44**	.257	**.344**	.401	745	**111**	105	**96**	101	84	39	68	5
NY	93	69	1	.574	15	53	28	680	612	6211	1381	208	**41**	111	588	**808**	60	25	.251	.324	.365	689	101	-18	18	95	105	61	63	2
BOS	87	75	0	.537	21	52	29	786	722	6250	**1450**	**252**	28	**203**	594	855	34	40	**.262**	.335	**.428**	**763**	108	**123**	70	107	50	48	51	-6
DET	79	83	0	.488	29	42	39	666	731	6199	1282	207	38	148	656	825	83	34	.238	.322	.374	696	97	-3	-8	101	29	30	49	-4
CLE	76	86	0	.469	32	43	38	649	675	6124	1358	197	23	183	503	909	76	37	.249	.314	.394	708	96	1	-30	105	25	36	41	-7
WAS	70	92	0	.432	38	40	41	626	689	6223	1302	184	28	138	635	989	44	46	.238	.321	.358	679	98	-36	-4	95	72	42	63	1
WEST																														
MIN	98	64	0	.605		51	30	744	605	6143	1438	230	**41**	153	501	905	**79**	42	**.262**	.327	.403	730	106	50	40	101	57	52	52	-6
OAK	89	73	0	.549	9	49	32	678	593	6105	1338	208	24	171	584	977	73	36	.249	.325	.392	717	108	30	56	96	**131**	68	66	5
CAL	86	76	0	.531	12	43	38	631	630	6114	1391	197	40	114	447	922	69	29	.251	.309	.363	672	94	-68	-46	97	69	27	**72**	**6**
MIL	65	97	1	.401	33	38	42	613	751	6170	1305	202	24	126	592	985	115	36	.242	.319	.358	677	92	-41	-45	101	91	73	55	-6
KC	65	97	0	.401	33	35	44	611	705	6128	1341	202	**41**	97	514	958	63	21	.244	.309	.348	657	87	-91	-90	100	97	53	65	3
CHI	56	106	0	.346	42	31	53	633	822	6132	1394	192	20	123	477	872	51	42	.253	.315	.362	677	90	-52	-75	104	53	33	62	0
TOT	973					536	436	8109		74215	16404	2492	373	1746	6808	10957	432	811	.250	.322	.379	701					863	562	61	-7

TEAM	CG	SHO	GR	SV	IP	H	HR	BB	SO	BR/9	ERA	AERA	OAV	OOB	PR	APR	PF	OSB	OCS	FA	E	WPB	DP	FW	PW	BW	BSW	DIF
EAST																												
BAL	**60**	12	228	31	1478.2	1317	139	469	941	**11.0**	**3.15**	**116**	.240	**.300**	**93**	**84**	98	55	43	.981	117	56	148	**1.1**	**8.7**	**10.0**	.6	6.7
NY	36	6	239	49	1471.2	1386	**130**	**451**	777	11.4	3.24	108	.249	.306	77	47	95	**40**	41	.980	130	**44**	146	.4	4.9	1.9	.3	4.6
BOS	38	8	284	44	1446.1	1391	156	594	1003	12.6	3.87	102	.251	.327	-25	13	107	73	34	.974	156	83	131	-1.2	1.3	7.3	-.6	-.9
DET	33	9	288	39	1447.1	1443	153	623	1045	13.1	4.09	91	.260	.336	-61	-59	100	68	54	.978	133	71	142	.2	-6.1	-.8	-.4	5.1
CLE	34	8	312	35	1451.1	1333	163	689	**1076**	12.8	3.91	101	.247	.335	-31	8	107	57	54	.979	133	76	168	.2	.8	-3.1	-.7	-2.2
WAS	20	11	**316**	40	1457.2	1375	139	611	823	12.4	3.80	94	.252	.328	-13	-41	96	56	49	**.982**	**116**	63	173	**1.1**	-4.3	-.4	.2	-7.6
WEST																												
MIN	26	12	269	**58**	1448.1	1329	**130**	486	940	11.5	3.23	115	.244	.308	78	79	100	55	49	.980	123	49	130	.7	8.2	4.1	-.6	4.5
OAK	33	**15**	309	40	1442.2	**1253**	134	542	858	11.4	3.30	107	**.234**	.307	66	40	95	70	39	.977	141	68	152	-.3	4.1	5.8	.6	-2.2
CAL	21	10	314	49	1462.1	1280	154	559	922	11.6	3.48	104	.237	.312	37	22	97	77	41	.980	127	79	169	.5	2.3	-4.8	**.7**	6.3
MIL	31	2	283	27	1446.2	1397	146	587	895	12.6	4.21	90	.255	.330	-79	-66	102	106	51	.978	136	55	142	.0	-6.8	-4.7	-.6	-4.0
KC	30	11	268	25	1463.2	1346	138	641	915	12.4	3.78	99	.247	.328	-11	-7	101	100	**62**	.976	152	72	162	-.9	-.7	-9.3	.4	-5.4
CHI	20	6	280	30	1430.1	1554	164	556	762	13.6	4.54	86	.280	.347	-132	-98	105	106	45	.975	165	90	**187**	-1.7	-10.2	-7.8	.0	-5.4
TOT	382	110	3390	467	17447.0					12.2	3.71		.250	.322						.978	1629	806	1850					

Batter-Fielder Wins	Batting Average	On-Base Percentage	Slugging Average	On-Base Plus Slugging	Adjusted OPS	Adjusted Batter Runs
Harper-Mil 5.5	Johnson-Cal 329	Yastrzemski-Bos 452	Yastrzemski-Bos ...592	Yastrzemski-Bos 1044	Yastrzemski-Bos ..174	Yastrzemski-Bos 64.2
Yastrzemski-Bos 5.5	Yastrzemski-Bos ...329	Howard-Was 416	Powell-Bal............549	Howard-Was 962	Howard-Was 173	Howard-Was 61.9
Aparicio-Chi........5.3	Oliva-Min 325	Powell-Bal 412	Killebrew-Min 546	Powell-Bal 962	Powell-Bal 163	Powell-Bal 49.7
Fregosi-Cal.........4.7	Aparicio-Chi 313	Killebrew-Min 411	Howard-Was.........546	Killebrew-Min........957	Killebrew-Min........161	Killebrew-Min......49.3
Howard-Was........4.4	F.Robinson-Bal 306	Bando-Oak 407	Harper-Mil.............522	F.Robinson-Bal 918	F.Robinson-Bal 151	White-NY 39.4

Runs	Hits	Doubles	Triples	Home Runs	Total Bases	Runs Batted In
Yastrzemski-Bos ..125	Oliva-Min 204	Tovar-Min 36	Tovar-Min................13	Howard-Was 44	Yastrzemski-Bos ..335	Howard-Was........126
Tovar-Min..............120	Johnson-Cal 202	Otis-KC 36	Stanley-Det 11	Killebrew-Min..........41	Oliva-Min 323	T.Conigliaro-Bos ..116
White-NY...............109	Tovar-Min...............195	Oliva-Min..........................36	Otis-KC 9	Yastrzemski-Bos 40	Harper-Mil 315	Powell-Bal.............114
Smith-Bos 109	Yastrzemski-Bos ..186	Harper-Mil.......................35		T.Conigliaro-Bos 36	Howard-Was 309	Killebrew-Min 113
Harper-Mil 104	White-NY..............180	Cardenas-Min 34		Powell-Bal 35	Powell-Bal 289	Oliva-Min 107

Stolen Bases	Base Stealing Runs	Fielding Runs-Infield	Fielding Runs-Outfield	Wins	Winning Pct.	Complete Games
Campaneris-Oak 42	Otis-KC 6.6	Brinkman-Was 31.4	Oliva-Min 13.3	Perry-Min................24	Cuellar-Bal 750	Cuellar-Bal 21
Harper-Mil 38	Campaneris-Oak ..5.7	Knoop-Chi 27.3	Blair-Bal 12.1	McNally-Bal 24	McNally-Bal 727	McDowell-Cle 19
Alomar-Cal..............35	Stroud-Was............3.6	Nettles-Cle.................26.0	Alou-Oak 7.8	Cuellar-Bal..............24	Perry-Min 667	Palmer-Bal 17
Kelly-KC..................34	Alomar-Cal 3.5	Aparicio-Chi 25.3	Tovar-Min 7.5	Wright-Cal 22	Palmer-Bal 667	McNally-Bal 16
Otis-KC 33	Johnson-Cal 3.0	Leon-Cle 16.8	Smith-Bos..............6.8		Siebert-Bos 652	Culp-Bos 15

Strikeouts	Fewest BB/Game	Games	Saves	Base Runners/9	Adjusted Relief Runs	Relief Ranking
McDowell-Cle 304	Peterson-NY........1.38	Wood-Chi 77	Perranoski-Min 34	Hall-Bal..................8.36	Grant-Oak............25.7	McDaniel-NY 31.7
Lolich-Det 230	Perry-Min 1.84	Grant-Oak......................72	McDaniel-NY 29	McDaniel-NY 8.95	Hall-Min 22.5	Knowles-Was 30.0
Johnson-KC..........206	Cox-Was...............2.06	Knowles-Was 71	Timmermann-Det ..27	Sanders-Mil 9.06	Sanders-Mil 20.9	Perranoski-Min ...26.1
Palmer-Bal............199	Cuellar-Bal 2.09	Williams-Min 68	Knowles-Was..........27	Hall-Min 9.39	Williams-Min........19.8	Grant-Oak 24.3
Culp-Bos 197	Horlen-Chi 2.14	....	Grant-Oak 24	Williams-Min..........9.69	McDaniel-NY 19.6	Hall-Min..............23.2

Innings Pitched	Opponents' Avg.	Opponents' OBP	Earned Run Average	Adjusted ERA	Adjusted Starter Runs	Pitcher Wins
Palmer-Bal 305.0	Messersmith-Cal .205	Peterson-NY 279	Segui-Oak 2.56	Segui-Oak 139	Palmer-Bal 34.2	**McDaniel-NY**......3.4
McDowell-Cle 305.0	McDowell-Cle 213	Cuellar-Bal 284	Palmer-Bal 2.71	McDowell-Cle 136	McDowell-Cle 32.3	**Knowles-Was** 3.1
Cuellar-Bal 297.2	Segui-Oak 222	Perry-Min.....................286	Wright-Cal............2.83	Palmer-Bal............134	Culp-Bos...............21.7	**Perry-Min**............3.1
McNally-Bal 296.0	Culp-Bos...............224	Blyleven-Min 288	Peterson-NY 2.90	Culp-Bos 130	Wright-Cal............20.8	**Palmer-Bal** 3.1
Perry-Min 278.2	Johnson-KC 228	Messersmith-Cal 289	McDowell-Cle 2.92	Wright-Cal 128	Perry-Min 20.2	**Wright-Cal**..........2.9

This One's for the Birds

As spring training adjourned, the expansion Seattle Pilots—the subject of pitcher Jim Bouton's controversial book *Ball Four*—were sold to car salesman Bud Selig, moved to Milwaukee, and rechristened the Brewers.

Once again, Baltimore was the class of the league, pacing the East from May on. The Yankees had a brief flurry in June, but the Orioles pulled away as the Senators and Tigers declined 16 and 17 games apiece. Baltimore boasted no league leaders in the hitting categories, but with MVP Boog Powell and Frank Robinson, they topped the loop in scoring. The Birds had a deep rotation and a solid bullpen that garnered few saves; the starters completed 60 games, the AL's most in a decade. The rich got richer as the Orioles also welcomed rookies Bobby Grich and Don Baylor. The league's top freshman, however, was Yankees catcher Thurman Munson.

Sparked by the arms of Cy Young winner Jim Perry and 19-year-old Bert Blyleven, Minnesota won its second straight West title. California made a brief run in July but fell back, and the Athletics came on too late. Chicago fell into the basement for the first time since 1948.

Baltimore swept the Twins in the ALCS, then stomped the Reds in a five-game World Series. Brooks Robinson grabbed the headlines with several great defensive plays, but the key was that the Orioles battered Cincinnati pitching and came back from deficits of three or more runs in three of their victories.

Neither division champ escaped tragedy, however. The Twins lost two outfielders, veteran Bob Allison to retirement and rookie Herm Hill to a drowning in Venezuela during winter ball. Former Orioles catcher Dick Brown, forced from the game in 1966 with a brain tumor, also died.

1971 National League

TEAM	W	L	T	PCT	GB	HW	HL	R	OR	PA	H	2B	3B	HR	BB	SO	HB	SH	AVG	OBP	SLG	OPS	AOPS	BR	ABR	PF	SB	CS	BSA	BSR
EAST																														
PIT	97	65	0	.599		**52**	28	**788**	599	6283	**1555**	223	**61**	**154**	469	919	62	29	.274	.330	**.416**	**746**	**118**	**120**	**124**	100	65	31	68	3
STL	90	72	1	.556	7	45	36	739	699	6300	1542	225	54	95	543	757	63	25	**.275**	**.338**	.385	723	107	92	64	104	**124**	53	70	9
NY	83	79	0	.512	14	44	37	588	**550**	6178	1365	203	29	98	547	958	91	28	.249	.319	.351	670	97	-20	-11	99	89	43	67	5
CHI	83	79	0	.512	14	44	37	637	648	6131	1401	202	34	128	527	772	**92**	34	.258	.325	.378	703	92	42	-43	115	44	32	58	-2
MON	71	90	1	.441	25.5	36	44	622	729	6098	1312	197	29	88	543	800	102	78	.246	.322	.343	665	95	-18	-20	100	51	43	54	-4
PHI	67	95	0	.414	30	34	47	558	688	6171	1289	209	35	123	499	1031	55	34	.233	.298	.350	648	89	-75	-74	100	63	39	62	0
WEST																														
SF	90	72	0	.556		51	30	706	644	6258	1348	224	36	140	**654**	1042	69	**37**	.247	.329	.378	707	108	61	72	98	101	36	**74**	**10**
LA	89	73	0	.549	1	42	39	663	587	6155	1469	213	38	95	489	755	72	21	.266	.325	.370	695	110	28	70	94	76	40	66	3
ATL	82	80	0	.506	8	43	39	643	699	6172	1434	192	30	153	434	**747**	91	28	.257	.312	.385	697	97	16	-23	106	57	46	55	-4
HOU	79	83	0	.488	11	39	42	585	567	6105	1319	**230**	52	71	478	888	65	29	.240	.302	.340	642	90	-81	-66	97	101	51	66	4
CIN	79	83	0	.488	11	46	35	586	581	5973	1306	203	28	138	438	907	69	27	.241	.300	.366	666	96	-46	-34	98	59	33	64	1
SD	61	100	0	.379	28.5	33	48	486	610	5935	1250	184	31	96	438	966	87	25	.233	.293	.332	625	89	-120	-84	93	70	45	61	0
TOT	972					509	462	7601		73759	16590	2505	457	1379	6059	10542	395	918	.252	.316	.366	683					900	492	65	26

TEAM	CG	SHO	GR	SV	IP	H	HR	BB	SO	BR/9	ERA	AERA	OAV	OOB	PR	APR	PF	OSB	OCS	FA	E	WPB	DP	FW	PW	BW	BSW	DIF
EAST																												
PIT	43	15	229	**48**	1461.0	1426	108	470	813	11.9	3.31	102	.257	.316	26	12	98	**42**	45	.979	133	54	164	.0	1.3	**13.3**	.0	1.2
STL	56	14	**274**	22	1467.0	1482	104	576	911	12.9	3.85	93	.263	.333	-63	-39	104	54	36	.978	142	80	155	-.4	-4.2	6.9	.7	6.0
NY	42	13	211	22	1466.1	**1227**	100	529	**1157**	**11.0**	**2.99**	**114**	**.227**	**.299**	**78**	**69**	98	78	28	.981	114	54	135	1.2	**7.4**	-1.2	.3	-5.7
CHI	**75**	17	202	13	1444.0	1458	132	411	900	11.8	3.61	109	.262	.314	-23	46	114	81	52	.980	126	56	150	.5	4.9	-4.6	-.4	1.6
MON	49	8	215	25	1434.1	1418	133	658	829	13.2	4.12	86	.260	.341	-104	-92	102	87	43	.976	150	74	164	-.9	-9.9	-2.1	-.7	4.1
PHI	31	10	253	25	1470.2	1396	132	525	838	12.0	3.71	95	.254	.320	-41	-30	102	110	**60**	.981	122	80	158	.7	-3.2	-7.9	-.2	-3.3
WEST																												
SF	45	14	252	30	1454.2	1324	128	471	831	11.3	3.32	102	.242	.303	24	13	98	74	23	.972	179	65	153	-2.6	1.4	7.7	**.8**	1.6
LA	48	**18**	187	33	1449.2	1363	110	**399**	853	11.1	3.23	100	.250	.301	37	-1	93	77	42	.979	131	56	159	.2	-.1	7.5	.0	.3
ATL	40	11	224	31	1474.2	1529	152	485	823	12.5	3.75	99	.269	.328	-46	-5	107	84	33	.977	146	89	**180**	-.7	-.5	-2.5	-.7	5.3
HOU	43	10	245	25	1471.1	1318	**75**	475	914	11.3	3.13	107	.241	.307	55	39	97	68	44	.983	106	82	152	1.6	4.2	-7.1	.2	-.9
CIN	27	11	255	38	1444.0	1298	112	501	750	11.4	3.35	100	.243	.310	18	0	97	50	32	**.984**	**103**	**44**	174	**1.8**	.0	-3.6	-.1	-.0
SD	47	10	237	17	1438.0	1351	93	559	923	12.1	3.22	102	.249	.321	39	12	95	95	54	.974	161	70	144	-1.6	1.3	-9.0	-.2	-10.0
TOT	546	151	2784	329	17475.2					11.9	3.47		.252	.316						.979	1613	804	1888					

Batter-Fielder Wins	Batting Average	On-Base Percentage	Slugging Average	On-Base Plus Slugging	Adjusted OPS	Adjusted Batter Runs
Stargell-Pit 5.1	Torre-StL..............363	Mays-SF 425	H.Aaron-Atl 669	H.Aaron-Atl 1079	H.Aaron-Atl 190	Stargell-Pit..........60.8
H.Aaron-Atl 4.3	Garr-Atl................343	Torre-StL 421	Stargell-Pit 628	Stargell-Pit..........1026	Stargell-Pit............188	H.Aaron-Atl 58.7
Torre-StL 3.8	Beckert-Chi..........342	H.Aaron-Atl 410	Torre-StL..............555	Torre-StL 976	Torre-StL 169	Torre-StL 58.2
Mays-SF 3.7	Clemente-Pit..........341	Hunt-Mon....................402	May-Cin 532	Mays-SF 907	Mays-SF 160	Allen-LA................42.7
Staub-Mon 3.6	H.Aaron-Atl 327	Stargell-Pit..................398	Bonds-SF 512	Williams-Chi 888	Allen-LA................154	Mays-SF 41.0

Runs	Hits	Doubles	Triples	Home Runs	Total Bases	Runs Batted In
Brock-StL..............126	Torre-StL 230	Cedeno-Hou 40	Morgan-Hou............11	Stargell-Pit 48	Torre-StL 352	Torre-StL 137
Bonds-SF 110	Garr-Atl 219	Brock-StL 37	Metzger-Hou 11	H.Aaron-Atl 47	H.Aaron-Atl 331	Stargell-Pit 125
Stargell-Pit............104	Brock-StL..............200	Torre-StL.......................34	Davis-LA 10	May-Cin 39	Stargell-Pit............321	H.Aaron-Atl.........118
Garr-Atl 101	Davis-LA 198	Staub-Mon 34	Gaston-SD...............9	Johnson-Phi...........34	Bonds-SF 317	Bonds-SF 102
Torre-StL 97		Davis-LA 33			Williams-Chi 300	Montanez-Phi 99

Stolen Bases	Base Stealing Runs	Fielding Runs-Infield	Fielding Runs-Outfield	Wins	Winning Pct.	Complete Games
Brock-StL................64	Brock-StL 7.4	Helms-Cin 26.1	Lum-Atl 8.7	Jenkins-Chi 24	Gullett-Cin 727	Jenkins-Chi............30
Morgan-Hou............40	Morgan-Hou 6.0	Sizemore-StL..............17.6	Garr-Atl...................8.5	Seaver-NY 20	Downing-LA 690	Seaver-NY 21
Garr-Atl 30	Agee-NY 4.1	Harrelson-NY..............14.7	Alou-Hou 7.7	Downing-LA............20	Carlton-StL 690	Stoneman-Mon.......20
	Mays-SF 4.0	Robertson-Pit.............13.7	Stahl-SD 7.6	Carlton-StL 20	Ellis-Pit 679	Gibson-StL 20
	Harrelson-NY 3.7	Kessinger-Chi 11.3	Clemente-Pit..........7.3	Ellis-Pit 19	Seaver-NY 667	

Strikeouts	Fewest BB/Game	Games	Saves	Base Runners/9	Adjusted Relief Runs	Relief Ranking
Seaver-NY 289	Jenkins-Chi..........1.02	Granger-Cin 70	Giusti-Pit 30	Seaver-NY 8.64	McGraw-NY 22.2	McGraw-NY........30.6
Jenkins-Chi 263	Marichal-SF 1.81	J.Johnson-SF 67	Marshall-Mon..........23	Brewer-LA...........8.74	Miller-Chi-SD-Pit 17.7	Brewer-LA 25.8
Stoneman-Mon 251	Stone-Atl..............1.82	Marshall-Mon 66	Brewer-LA 22	Wilson-Hou..........9.44	Brewer-LA.............14.1	Miller-Chi-SD-Pit ..25.0
Kirby-SD 231	Hands-Chi 1.86	McMahon-SF 61	J.Johnson-SF..........18	McGraw-NY 9.49	Ray-Hou 13.3	Frisella-NY..........19.3
Sutton-LA 194	Sutton-LA 1.87	Carroll-Cin 61	Upshaw-Atl 17	Jenkins-Chi..........9.58	Frisella-NY 12.1	Ray-Hou 18.0

Innings Pitched	Opponents' Avg.	Opponents' OBP	Earned Run Average	Adjusted ERA	Adjusted Starter Runs	Pitcher Wins
Jenkins-Chi........325.0	Wilson-Hou...........202	Seaver-NY 252	Seaver-NY 1.76	Seaver-NY 194	Seaver-NY 54.4	**Seaver-NY**..........6.7
Stoneman-Mon..294.2	Seaver-NY 206	Wilson-Hou 266	Roberts-SD..........2.10	Roberts-SD 157	Jenkins-Chi...........36.4	**Jenkins-Chi**..........5.6
Seaver-NY 286.1	Kirby-SD 216	Jenkins-Chi 269	Wilson-Hou..........2.45	Jenkins-Chi 142	Roberts-SD...........35.7	**Roberts-SD** 4.6
Perry-SF............280.0	Cumberland-SF ...223	Marichal-SF 273	Forsch-Hou..........2.53	Wilson-Hou 137	Wilson-Hou..........28.5	**McGraw-NY**........3.6
Marichal-SF 279.0	Gentry-NY 224	Nolan-Cin......................275	Sutton-LA 2.54	Forsch-Hou 133	Sutton-LA 21.6	**Brewer-LA** 3.0

Pittsburgh's Glory

San Francisco looked like a shoo-in for NL West honors, leading by 8_ in early September, but a late slide and a furious Los Angeles rally closed the gap. But the Dodgers could get no closer as the Giants held a 1-game lead over the final five days. Willie Mays and Willie McCovey were declining and injured, respectively, but Bobby Bonds, Ken Henderson, and Dick Dietz provided the hitting; Juan Marichal headed a very thin rotation.

An 11-game July winning streak put the Bucs over the top in the East. Seven Pittsburgh pitchers made at least 13 starts, and Willie Stargell was the league's dominant power hitter. On the other side of the state, and the standings, the Phillies opened Veterans Stadium, another bowl-shaped artificial turf stadium; their attendance more than doubled. The league reached a new all-time attendance high, with everyone but San Diego clearing a million.

MVP Joe Torre of the Cardinals hit .363, the NL's highest since 1948. Atlanta's Earl Williams was Rookie of the Year. Fergie Jenkins captured the Cy Young, but the Cubs lacked the offense to win. Ernie Banks and Jim Bunning retired, neither ever appearing in a World Series.

The Pirates disposed of the Giants in four games—the first League Championship Series in six tries that did not end in a sweep. Bucs first baseman Bob Robertson hit 4 homers in the NLCS, including 3 long balls at Candlestick in Game 2. Pittsburgh lost the first two World Series games at Baltimore as the Orioles tallied 16 runs. The Pirates, however, won the next three with pitching and big rallies (Game 4 was the first World Series game played at night).

The Orioles came back from a 2–0 deficit to win a 10-inning thriller in Game 6. Roberto Clemente, who hit .414 in the Series and played astounding defense, clubbed a homer the next day in the deciding 2–1 victory. Steve Blass, who allowed just 7 hits—and 4 walks—in 18 innings, racked up his second complete-game victory of the Series.

1971 American League

TEAM	W	L	T	PCT	GB	HW	HL	R	OR	PA	H	2B	3B	HR	BB	SO	HB	SH	AVG	OBP	SLG	OPS	AOPS	BR	ABR	PF	SB	CS	BSA	BSR
EAST																														
BAL	101	57	0	.639		53	24	**742**	**530**	6143	1382	207	25	158	**672**	844	**85**	46	**.261**	**.347**	.398	**745**	**119**	**137**	**144**	99	66	38	63	1
DET	91	71	0	.562	12	**54**	27	701	645	6196	**1399**	214	38	**179**	540	854	62	**55**	.254	.325	**.405**	730	109	88	61	104	35	43	45	-7
BOS	85	77	0	.525	18	47	33	691	667	6107	1360	**246**	28	161	552	871	75	32	.252	.322	.397	719	103	72	26	107	51	34	60	-1
NY	82	80	0	.506	21	44	37	648	641	6164	1377	195	**43**	97	581	**717**	77	37	.254	.328	.360	688	109	22	64	94	75	55	58	-3
WAS	63	96	0	.396	38.5	35	46	537	660	5986	1219	189	30	86	575	956	58	28	.230	.307	.326	633	91	-86	-54	94	68	45	60	-1
CLE	60	102	0	.370	43	29	52	543	747	6061	1303	200	20	109	467	868	67	31	.238	.300	.342	642	81	-85	-130	109	57	37	61	0
WEST																														
OAK	101	60	0	.627		46	35	691	564	6191	1383	195	25	160	542	1018	80	37	.252	.321	.384	705	108	41	55	98	80	53	60	-1
KC	85	76	0	.528	16	44	37	603	566	5914	1323	225	40	80	490	819	45	25	.250	.313	.353	666	96	-28	-23	99	**130**	46	**74**	**13**
CHI	79	83	0	.488	22.5	39	42	617	597	6114	1346	185	30	138	562	870	81	51	.250	.325	.373	698	101	33	13	103	83	65	56	-4
CAL	76	86	0	.469	25.5	35	46	511	576	6079	1271	213	18	96	441	827	83	29	.231	.290	.329	619	87	-132	-94	93	72	34	68	4
MIN	74	86	0	.463	26.5	37	42	654	670	6072	1406	197	31	116	512	846	64	25	.260	.323	.372	695	100	27	7	103	66	44	60	-1
MIL	69	92	0	.429	32	34	48	534	609	5904	1188	160	23	104	543	924	107	30	.229	.304	.329	633	86	-90	-84	99	82	53	61	-1
TOT	966					497	469	7472		72931	15957	2426	351	1484	6477	10414	426	884	.247	.317	.364	681					865	547	61	-1

TEAM	CG	SHO	GR	SV	IP	H	HR	BB	SO	BR/9	ERA	AERA	OAV	OOB	PR	APR	PF	OSB	OCS	FA	E	WPB	DP	FW	PW	BW	BSW	DIF
EAST																												
BAL	**71**	15	177	22	1415.1	1257	125	**416**	793	**10.8**	**2.99**	112	.239	**.295**	**74**	59	97	56	51	.981	112	53	148	.7	6.3	**15.5**	.1	-.6
DET	53	11	265	32	1468.1	1355	126	609	**1000**	12.3	3.63	99	.247	.325	-28	-7	104	81	41	**.983**	**106**	52	156	**1.2**	-.8	6.6	-.7	3.7
BOS	44	11	247	35	1443.0	1424	136	535	871	12.5	3.80	97	.259	.327	-55	-17	107	78	31	.981	116	55	149	.6	-1.8	2.8	-.0	2.5
NY	67	15	189	12	1452.0	1382	126	423	707	11.3	3.43	94	.252	.306	4	-35	93	**38**	40	.981	125	58	159	.1	-3.8	6.9	-.3	-1.9
WAS	30	10	315	26	1418.2	1376	132	554	762	12.5	3.70	89	.258	.331	-37	-65	96	84	45	.977	141	66	170	-1.0	-7.0	-5.8	-.0	-2.6
CLE	21	7	**325**	32	1440.0	1352	154	770	937	13.6	4.28	89	.252	.348	-130	-65	111	73	52	.981	116	84	159	.6	-7.0	-14.0	.0	-.7
WEST																												
OAK	57	18	227	36	1469.1	**1229**	131	501	999	**10.8**	3.05	109	**.228**	.296	67	48	96	72	33	.981	117	54	157	.5	5.2	5.9	-.0	9.0
KC	34	15	264	**44**	1420.1	1301	**84**	496	775	11.6	3.25	106	.247	.314	33	29	99	68	43	.979	132	52	**178**	-.4	3.1	-2.5	**1.4**	2.8
CHI	46	19	259	32	1450.1	1348	100	468	976	11.4	3.12	**115**	.247	.307	55	**73**	104	102	48	.975	160	75	128	-1.9	**7.9**	1.4	-.4	-8.9
CAL	39	11	243	32	1481.0	1246	101	607	904	11.5	3.10	104	.230	.310	60	24	94	85	49	.980	131	85	159	-.2	2.6	-10.1	.4	2.3
MIN	43	9	252	25	1416.2	1384	139	529	895	12.4	3.81	93	.257	.326	-55	-40	103	73	44	.980	118	54	134	.4	-4.3	.8	-.0	-2.8
MIL	32	**23**	238	32	1416.1	1303	130	569	795	12.1	3.38	103	.247	.321	13	14	100	55	**70**	.977	138	**41**	152	-.7	1.5	-9.0	-.0	-3.2
TOT	537	164	3001	360	17291.1					11.9	3.46		.247	.317						.980	1512	729	1849					

Batter-Fielder Wins	Batting Average	On-Base Percentage	Slugging Average	On-Base Plus Slugging	Adjusted OPS	Adjusted Batter Runs
Nettles-Cle 5.9	Oliva-Min .337	Murcer-NY .427	Oliva-Min .546	Murcer-NY .969	Murcer-NY 185	Murcer-NY 62.4
Melton-Chi 4.8	Murcer-NY .331	Rettenmund-Bal .422	Murcer-NY .543	Oliva-Min .915	White-NY 155	White-NY 40.8
Murcer-NY 4.7	Rettenmund-Bal .318	Kaline-Det .416	Cash-Det .531	Cash-Det .903	F.Robinson-Bal 154	Rettenmund-Bal 36.8
Patek-KC 4.3	Tovar-Min .311	Buford-Bal .413	F.Robinson-Bal .510	F.Robinson-Bal .894	Buford-Bal 153	Buford-Bal 36.3
White-NY 3.9	Carew-Min .307	White-NY .388	Jackson-Oak .508	Buford-Bal .890	Oliva-Min 152	F.Robinson-Bal 34.4

Runs	Hits	Doubles	Triples	Home Runs	Total Bases	Runs Batted In
Buford-Bal 99	Tovar-Min 204	Smith-Bos 33	Patek-KC 11	Melton-Chi 33	Smith-Bos 302	Killebrew-Min 119
Tovar-Min 94	Alomar-Cal 179	Schaal-KC 31	Carew-Min 10	Jackson-Oak 32	Jackson-Oak 288	F.Robinson-Bal 99
Murcer-NY 94	Carew-Min 177	Rodriguez-Det 30	Blair-Bal 8	Cash-Det 32	Murcer-NY 287	Smith-Bos 96
Carew-Min 88	Smith-Bos 175	Oliva-Min 30		Smith-Bos 30	Melton-Chi 267	Murcer-NY 94
Jackson-Oak 87	Murcer-NY 175				Oliva-Min 266	Bando-Oak 94

Stolen Bases	Base Stealing Runs	Fielding Runs-Infield	Fielding Runs-Outfield	Wins	Winning Pct.	Complete Games
Otis-KC 52	Otis-KC 8.6	Nettles-Cle 46.1	Tovar-Min 14.1	Lolich-Det 25	McNally-Bal .808	Lolich-Det 29
Patek-KC 49	Patek-KC 5.9	Michael-NY 24.6	Yastrzemski-Bos 10.7	Blue-Oak 24	Dobson-Oak .750	Blue-Oak 24
Alomar-Cal 39	Alomar-Cal 5.1	Melton-Chi 23.7	Unser-Was 9.6	Wood-Chi 22	Blue-Oak .750	Wood-Chi 22
Campaneris-Oak 34	Campaneris-Oak 5.0	Alomar-Cal 22.8	Stanley-Det 9.3	McNally-Bal 21	Dobson-Bal .714	Cuellar-Bal 21
	Harper-Mil 4.4	Patek-KC 21.6	Otis-KC 8.2	Hunter-Oak 21		Palmer-Bal 20

Strikeouts	Fewest BB/Game	Games	Saves	Base Runners/9	Adjusted Relief Runs	Relief Ranking
Lolich-Det 308	Peterson-NY 1.38	Sanders-Mil 83	Sanders-Mil 31	Blue-Oak 8.68	Sanders-Mil 22.8	Sanders-Mil 40.3
Blue-Oak 301	Kline-NY 1.50	Scherman-Det 69	Abernathy-KC 23	Fingers-Oak 9.19	Burgmeier-KC 14.9	Burgmeier-KC 29.9
Coleman-Det 236	Kaat-Min 1.62	Burgmeier-KC 67	Scherman-Det 20	Wood-Chi 9.19	Mingori-Cle 13.6	Scherman-Det 18.0
Blyleven-Min 224	Wood-Chi 1.67	Abernathy-KC 63	Fingers-Oak 17	Grzenda-Was 9.21	Grzenda-Was 10.5	Abernathy-KC 11.9
Wood-Chi 210	Drago-KC 1.72		Burgmeier-KC 17	Sanders-Mil 9.84	Queen-Cal 10.3	Allen-Cal 11.3

Innings Pitched	Opponents' Avg.	Opponents' OBP	Earned Run Average	Adjusted ERA	Adjusted Starter Runs	Pitcher Wins
Lolich-Det 376.0	Blue-Oak .189	Blue-Oak .251	Blue-Oak 1.82	Wood-Chi 188	Wood-Chi 55.8	**Wood-Chi** 5.8
Wood-Chi 334.0	McDowell-Cle .207	Wood-Chi .263	Wood-Chi 1.91	Blue-Oak 184	Blue-Oak 53.9	**Blue-Oak** 5.3
Blue-Oak 312.0	May-Cal .213	Kline-NY .275	Palmer-Bal 2.68	Siebert-Bos 127	Lolich-Det 27.1	**Sanders-Mil** 4.4
Cuellar-Bal 292.1	Messersmith-Cal .218	Dobson-Bal .278	Hedlund-KC 2.71	Hedlund-KC 127	Blyleven-Min 23.3	**Burgmeier-KC** 3.7
Coleman-Det 286.0	Palmer-Bal .221	Hunter-Oak .281	Blyleven-Min 2.81	Blyleven-Min 126	Palmer-Bal 22.0	**Siebert-Bos** 3.2

The Beltway Bandit

After missing the 1970 season as his case against baseball's reserve clause went to Federal Court, Curt Flood joined Washington but retired after 13 games. Those Senators were a sad bunch. As manager Ted Williams fumed, owner Bob Short hauled in problems and rejects like Denny McLain, Don Wert, Jerry Janeski, and Joe Foy; things worked out as well as could be expected. The Senators lost 96 games, but Cleveland kept them out the basement.

Boston made an early run at the AL East title, but the Orioles again improved as the weather got hotter, clearing 100 wins for the third consecutive season. Earl Weaver's club again paced in runs and fewest allowed, with four 20-game winners in his rotation and Don Buford and Merv Rettenmund ranking among the league's top four in on-base percentage.

With Aurelio Rodriguez, Ed Brinkman, and Joe Coleman heisted from Washington, the Tigers improved under Billy Martin. Yankees center fielder Bobby Murcer enjoyed a breakout season.

Oakland won the franchise's first crown since 1931 on the left arm of MVP and Cy Young winner Vida Blue, who led the AL in ERA and shutouts. Only Reggie Jackson starred on offense, but everyone in Dick Williams' lineup made a solid contribution. Defending champion Minnesota collapsed to fifth, declining 23 games amidst poor pitching; Tony Oliva won the batting title but tore up his knee. Kansas City finished second but never contended.

Baltimore swept the A's in a three-game playoff, then lost a painful seven-game World Series to the Pirates.

Following the season, the carpetbagging Short—refusing to pay his rent bills and citing poor attendance—moved the Senators to Dallas for 1972 and renamed them the Texas Rangers. As Short left the nation's capital without a major league team for the first time since 1900, it was fitting, then, that two great Senators of years past, Goose Goslin and Heinie Manush, died.

1972 National League

TEAM	W	L	T	PCT	GB	HW	HL	R	OR	PA	H	2B	3B	HR	BB	SO	HB	SH	AVG	OBP	SLG	OPS	AOPS	BR	ABR	PF	SB	CS	BSA	BSR
EAST																														
PIT	96	59	0	.619		**49**	29	691	**512**	6021	**1505**	**251**	**47**	110	404	871	52	25	**.274**	.324	**.397**	**721**	113	75	90	98	49	30	62	0
CHI	85	70	1	.548	11	46	31	685	567	5950	1346	206	40	133	565	815	67	28	.257	**.330**	.387	717	99	76	10	111	69	47	59	-1
NY	83	73	0	.532	13.5	41	37	528	578	5883	1154	175	31	105	589	990	86	34	.225	.307	.332	639	90	-67	-53	97	41	41	50	-5
STL	75	81	0	.481	21.5	40	37	568	600	5884	1383	214	42	70	437	793	58	27	.260	.317	.355	672	98	-14	-6	99	104	48	68	6
MON	70	86	0	.449	26.5	35	43	513	609	5817	1205	156	22	91	474	828	108	49	.234	.303	.325	628	84	-94	-102	102	68	66	51	-8
PHI	59	97	0	.378	37.5	28	51	503	635	5862	1240	200	36	98	487	930	69	22	.236	.302	.344	646	88	-66	-79	103	42	50	46	-8
WEST																														
CIN	95	59	0	.617		42	34	707	557	6003	1317	214	44	124	**606**	914	65	**37**	.251	**.330**	.380	710	**115**	70	**112**	94	**140**	63	**69**	**9**
HOU	84	69	0	.549	10.5	41	36	**708**	636	5936	1359	233	38	**134**	524	907	62	32	.258	.326	.393	719	113	**78**	93	98	111	56	66	5
LA	85	70	0	.548	10.5	41	34	584	527	5903	1349	178	39	98	480	**786**	**89**	24	.256	.319	.360	679	101	-1	14	98	82	39	68	4
ATL	70	84	1	.455	25	36	41	628	730	5938	1363	186	17	144	532	770	55	35	.258	.328	.382	710	99	62	5	109	47	35	57	-2
SF	69	86	0	.445	26.5	34	43	662	649	5858	1281	211	36	150	480	964	64	30	.244	.309	.384	693	102	18	9	101	123	45	73	11
SD	58	95	0	.379	36.5	26	54	488	665	5750	1181	168	38	102	407	976	90	15	.227	.283	.332	615	86	-135	-100	93	78	46	63	1
TOT	930					459	470	7265		70805	15683	2392	430	1359	5985	10544	358	865	.248	.315	.365	680					954	566	63	12

TEAM	CG	SHO	GR	SV	IP	H	HR	BB	SO	BR/9	ERA	AERA	OAV	OOB	PR	APR	PF	OSB	OCS	FA	E	WPB	DP	FW	PW	BW	BSW	DIF
EAST																												
PIT	39	15	205	48	1414.1	1282	90	433	838	11.1	2.81	118	.243	.302	102	84	96	54	41	.978	136	**40**	**171**	-.0	9.0	9.7	-.1	-.0
CHI	54	19	197	32	1398.2	1329	112	**421**	824	11.5	3.22	118	.251	.309	37	83	110	95	46	.979	132	44	148	.2	8.9	1.1	-.2	-2.5
NY	32	12	207	41	1414.2	1263	118	486	**1059**	11.3	3.26	103	.240	.306	30	16	97	60	61	.980	116	60	122	1.1	1.7	-5.7	-.6	8.5
STL	**64**	13	216	13	1399.2	1290	87	531	912	11.8	3.42	99	.247	.317	5	-3	99	91	55	.977	141	71	146	-.3	-.3	-.6	.5	-2.3
MON	39	11	217	23	1401.1	1281	103	579	888	12.1	3.59	99	.245	.321	-21	-6	103	73	**67**	.978	134	58	141	.0	-.6	-11.0	-1.0	4.5
PHI	43	13	263	15	1400.0	1318	117	536	927	12.1	3.66	98	.251	.321	-33	-11	104	87	45	.981	116	66	142	1.1	-1.2	-8.5	-1.0	-9.4
WEST																												
CIN	25	15	239	**60**	1412.2	1313	129	435	806	11.3	3.21	100	.247	.305	38	0	93	**31**	40	**.982**	**110**	47	143	**1.3**	.0	**12.0**	.9	3.8
HOU	38	14	245	31	1385.1	1340	114	498	971	12.2	3.77	89	.256	.323	-48	-64	97	99	37	.980	116	75	151	.9	-6.9	10.0	.4	3.0
LA	50	**23**	176	29	1403.0	**1196**	**83**	429	856	**10.6**	**2.78**	**120**	**.230**	**.291**	**104**	**89**	97	79	37	.974	162	55	145	-1.5	**9.6**	1.5	.3	-2.4
ATL	40	4	220	27	1377.0	1412	155	512	732	12.7	4.27	89	.266	.331	-126	-67	110	96	37	.974	156	105	130	-1.1	-7.2	.5	-.3	1.1
SF	44	8	219	23	1386.1	1309	130	507	771	12.0	3.69	94	.250	.318	-37	-32	101	87	53	.974	156	63	121	-1.1	-3.4	1.0	**1.1**	-6.0
SD	39	17	**270**	19	1403.2	1350	121	618	960	12.9	3.78	87	.255	.334	-50	-80	95	98	46	.976	144	75	146	-.6	-8.6	-10.8	.0	1.4
TOT	507	164	2674	361	16796.2					11.8	3.45		.248	.315						.978	1619	759	1706					

Batter-Fielder Wins	Batting Average	On-Base Percentage	Slugging Average	On-Base Plus Slugging	Adjusted OPS	Adjusted Batter Runs
Bench-Cin............6.6	Williams-Chi 333	Morgan-Cin 417	Williams-Chi 606	Williams-Chi 1005	Bench-Cin 171	Bench-Cin 52.1
Morgan-Cin..........5.9	Garr-Atl.................325	Williams-Chi................398	Stargell-Pit 558	Stargell-Pit............930	Stargell-Pit............166	Williams-Chi 49.8
Cedeno-Hou........5.2	Baker-Atl...............321	Santo-Chi....................391	Bench-Cin.............541	Cedeno-Hou 921	Williams-Chi 166	Cedeno-Hou 46.4
Santo-Chi 3.9	Cedeno-Hou 320	Aaron-Atl 390	Cedeno-Hou 537	Bench-Cin 920	Cedeno-Hou 163	Morgan-Cin 45.3
Williams-Chi........3.8	Watson-Hou 312	Wynn-Hou 389	Aaron-Atl 514	Aaron-Atl 904	Hebner-Pit 155	Stargell-Pit..........42.8

Runs	Hits	Doubles	Triples	Home Runs	Total Bases	Runs Batted In
Morgan-Cin 122	Rose-Cin 198	Montanez-Phi 39	Bowa-Phi 13	Bench-Cin 40	Williams-Chi 348	Bench-Cin 125
Bonds-SF 118	Brock-StL.............193	Cedeno-Hou 39	Rose-Cin 11	Colbert-SD 38	Cedeno-Hou 300	Williams-Chi 122
Wynn-Hou 117	Williams-Chi 191	Simmons-StL 36	Sanguillen-Pit 8	Williams-Chi 37	Bench-Cin 291	Stargell-Pit 112
Rose-Cin 107	Simmons-StL........180	Williams-Chi 34	Cedeno-Hou 8	Aaron-Atl 34	May-Hou 290	Colbert-SD 111
Cedeno-Hou 103	Garr-Atl 180		Brock-StL..................8	Stargell-Pit.............33	Colbert-SD 286	May-Hou................98

Stolen Bases	Base Stealing Runs	Fielding Runs-Infield	Fielding Runs-Outfield	Wins	Winning Pct.	Complete Games
Brock-StL................63	Bonds-SF 7.6	Helms-Hou..................28.8	Baker-Atl..............12.3	Carlton-Phi 27	Nolan-Cin 750	Carlton-Phi 30
Morgan-Cin 58	Brock-StL 7.6	Foli-Mon 18.4	Rose-Cin.................9.9	Seaver-NY 21	Carlton-Phi 730	Jenkins-Chi............23
Cedeno-Hou 55	Morgan-Cin............6.8	Rader-Hou 17.6	Henderson-SF 8.5	Osteen-LA 20	Pappas-Chi............708	Gibson-StL 23
Bonds-SF 44	Cedeno-Hou 4.8	Kessinger-Chi 16.7	Montanez-Phi 8.1	Jenkins-Chi 20	Blass-Pit 704	Wise-StL.................20
Tolan-Cin 42	Hernandez-SD 4.2	Santo-Chi....................14.6	Carbo-Cin-StL 6.8	....	Ellis-Pit 682	Sutton-LA 18

Strikeouts	Fewest BB/Game	Games	Saves	Base Runners/9	Adjusted Relief Runs	Relief Ranking
Carlton-Phi 310	Pappas-Chi..........1.34	Marshall-Mon 65	Carroll-Cin 37	Brewer-LA............7.81	Marshall-Mon 21.7	Marshall-Mon 43.5
Seaver-NY............249	Nolan-Cin 1.53	Carroll-Cin 65	McGraw-NY............27	Sutton-LA 8.35	McGraw-NY 18.6	Brewer-LA 35.1
Gibson-StL 208	Niekro-Atl 1.69	Borbon-Cin 62	Giusti-Pit 22	Carlton-Phi 8.97	Brewer-LA.............17.6	McGraw-NY.........32.7
Sutton-LA 207	Ellis-Pit 1.82	Ross-SD 60	Marshall-Mon..........18	Willoughby-SF 9.03	R.Hernandez-Pit..13.8	Giusti-Pit 24.4
Jenkins-Chi 184	Moose-Pit 1.87			Nolan-Cin 9.10	Giusti-Pit..............12.3	Carroll-Cin..........19.5

Innings Pitched	Opponents' Avg.	Opponents' OBP	Earned Run Average	Adjusted ERA	Adjusted Starter Runs	Pitcher Wins
Carlton-Phi 346.1	Sutton-LA 189	Sutton-LA.....................240	Carlton-Phi 1.97	Carlton-Phi 182	Carlton-Phi 60.2	**Carlton-Phi** 7.3
Jenkins-Chi........289.1	Carlton-Phi 206	Carlton-Phi..................257	Nolan-Cin 1.99	Nolan-Cin 161	Sutton-LA 38.8	**Marshall-Mon** 4.9
Niekro-Atl 282.1	Gibson-StL 224	Nolan-Cin....................259	Sutton-LA 2.08	Sutton-LA 160	Gibson-StL 30.8	**Gibson-StL** 4.4
Gibson-StL 278.0	Seaver-NY 224	Niekro-Atl....................274	Matlack-NY..........2.32	Matlack-NY 145	Matlack-NY..........25.2	**Osteen-LA** 4.2
Sutton-LA 272.2	Bryant-SF 224	McAndrew-NY 276	Gibson-StL 2.46	Gibson-StL 138	Blass-Pit 24.1	**Brewer-LA**..........4.0

Best Pitcher on the Worst Team

Prior to the season, the penny-pinching Cardinals sent Steve Carlton to the Phillies for Rick Wise. In addition to completing St. Louis' post-1968 destruction, the deal also helped Philadelphia build a powerhouse. Carlton was 27–10 for a horrible Phillies club in 1972, earning Cy Young honors and finishing fifth in MVP voting. Future Phils debuting around Lefty included Bob Boone and Mike Schmidt; Greg Luzinski hit 18 homers in his first year as a regular.

There was doubt, however, that the season would begin. For the first time, players went on strike, wiping out the first 12 days of the season. Mets manager Gil Hodges died of a heart attack during spring training; Yogi Berra took charge of the club. Chicago's Billy Williams finished second in MVP voting in both 1970 and 1972, but the Cubs couldn't catch the Pirates either year. The '72 Bucs boasted deep pitching and seven regulars who hit at least .280.

The Reds pulled away from surprising Houston in July and coasted to a division crown. Johnny Bench again was MVP, with Clay Carroll saving an all-time record 37. Pete Rose and new acquisition Joe Morgan set the table like perhaps no other combination in history.

Pittsburgh and Cincinnati traded wins through the first four NLCS contests. In Game 5, with Cincinnati down 3–2 in the last of the ninth, Bench led off with a game-tying homer; two outs and two singles later, Bob Moose's wild pitch gave the game—and pennant—to the Reds. Cincinnati was denied again in the World Series, however, as Oakland won a tight Series in seven.

Following the season, Bill Mazeroski, Hoyt Wilhelm, and Maury Wills retired. Pie Traynor, Jackie Robinson, and Gabby Hartnett passed away. The most shocking death of the year, however, was that of Roberto Clemente, lost in a December 31 air crash en route to earthquake-torn Nicaragua. Clemente had collected his 3,000th and final hit on September 30.

1972 American League

TEAM	W	L	T	PCT	GB	HW	HL	R	OR	PA	H	2B	3B	HR	BB	SO	HB	SH	AVG	OBP	SLG	OPS	AOPS	BR	ABR	PF	SB	CS	BSA	BSR
EAST																														
DET	86	70	0	.551		44	34	558	514	5721	1206	179	32	122	483	793	74	31	.237	.305	.356	661	100	17	0	103	17	21	45	-4
BOS	85	70	0	.548	0.5	52	26	**640**	620	5871	1289	**229**	**34**	124	522	858	56	37	.248	.318	**.376**	**694**	107	**86**	53	106	66	30	**69**	**4**
BAL	80	74	0	.519	5	38	39	519	**430**	5676	1153	193	29	100	507	935	65	36	.229	.302	.339	641	95	-11	-24	103	78	41	66	3
NY	79	76	0	.510	6.5	46	31	557	527	5793	1288	201	24	103	491	**689**	74	29	.249	.316	.357	673	111	47	68	97	71	42	63	1
CLE	72	84	0	.462	14	43	34	472	519	5769	1220	187	18	91	420	762	83	26	.234	.293	.330	623	88	-55	-70	103	49	53	48	-8
MIL	65	91	0	.417	21	37	42	493	595	5733	1204	167	22	88	472	868	78	29	.235	.302	.328	630	96	-37	-27	98	64	57	53	-6
WEST																														
OAK	93	62	0	.600		48	29	604	457	5846	1248	195	29	**134**	463	886	**100**	**47**	.240	.306	.366	672	**112**	37	69	95	87	48	64	2
CHI	87	67	0	.565	5.5	**55**	23	566	538	5721	1208	170	28	108	511	991	68	34	.238	.310	.346	656	100	14	3	102	**100**	52	66	**4**
MIN	77	77	0	.500	15.5	42	32	537	535	5848	1277	182	31	93	478	905	73	35	.244	.310	.344	654	96	8	-18	105	53	41	56	-3
KC	76	78	0	.494	16.5	44	33	580	545	5845	**1317**	220	26	78	**534**	711	72	34	**.255**	**.327**	.353	680	110	68	**71**	100	85	44	66	3
CAL	75	80	0	.484	18	44	36	454	533	5639	1249	171	26	78	358	850	66	25	.242	.293	.330	623	97	-59	-31	94	57	37	61	0
TEX	54	100	0	.351	38.5	31	46	461	628	5680	1092	166	17	56	503	926	84	30	.217	.290	.290	580	83	-115	-96	96	126	73	63	2
TOT	929					524	405	6441		69142	14751	2260	316	1175	5742	10174	393	893	.239	.306	.343	649					853	539	61	-1

TEAM	CG	SHO	GR	SV	IP	H	HR	BB	SO	BR/9	ERA	AERA	OAV	OOB	PR	APR	PF	OSB	OCS	FA	E	WPB	DP	FW	PW	BW	BSW	DIF
EAST																												
DET	46	11	248	33	1388.1	1212	101	465	952	11.2	2.96	106	.236	.304	15	28	103	87	46	**.984**	**96**	55	137	**1.9**	3.2	.0	-.4	3.3
BOS	48	20	216	25	1382.2	1309	101	512	918	12.1	3.47	93	.251	.321	-63	-37	105	66	40	.978	130	42	141	-.0	-4.2	6.0	**.5**	5.3
BAL	**62**	20	167	21	1371.2	1116	**85**	**395**	788	**10.0**	**2.53**	**121**	.224	**.282**	**81**	**82**	100	44	44	.983	100	41	150	1.6	**9.3**	-2.7	.4	-5.6
NY	35	19	188	39	1373.1	1306	87	419	625	11.5	3.05	97	.252	.310	2	-16	96	**42**	34	.978	134	57	**179**	-.3	-1.8	7.7	.1	-4.2
CLE	47	13	255	25	1410.0	1232	123	534	846	11.5	2.92	110	.237	.311	23	45	105	66	43	.981	116	59	157	.8	5.1	-8.0	-.9	-3.0
MIL	37	14	216	32	1391.2	1289	116	486	740	11.7	3.45	88	.247	.312	-61	-66	99	65	43	.977	139	51	145	-.5	-7.5	-3.1	-.7	-1.2
WEST																												
OAK	42	**23**	236	**43**	1417.2	1170	96	418	862	10.2	2.58	110	.226	.284	76	45	93	72	38	.979	130	42	146	-.0	5.1	7.8	.2	2.4
CHI	36	14	248	42	1385.1	1269	94	431	936	11.2	3.12	100	.245	.305	-9	1	102	75	**60**	.977	135	70	136	-.4	.1	.3	**.5**	9.5
MIN	37	17	203	34	1399.1	1188	105	444	838	10.7	2.84	113	.230	.294	35	55	105	69	48	.974	159	**33**	133	-1.8	6.3	-2.0	-.3	-2.1
KC	44	16	242	28	1381.1	1293	**85**	405	801	11.3	3.24	94	.251	.307	-27	-32	99	86	42	.981	116	54	164	.7	-3.6	**8.1**	.4	-6.5
CAL	57	18	192	16	1377.2	**1109**	90	620	**1000**	11.5	3.06	95	**.222**	.310	0	-25	95	102	44	.981	114	70	135	.8	-2.8	-3.5	.0	3.0
TEX	11	8	**324**	34	1374.2	1258	92	613	868	12.6	3.53	85	.246	.329	-71	-81	98	77	56	.972	166	58	147	-2.2	-9.2	-10.9	.2	-.9
TOT	502	193	2735	372	16653.2					11.3	3.06		.239	.306						.979	1535	632	1770					

Batter-Fielder Wins	Batting Average	On-Base Percentage	Slugging Average	On-Base Plus Slugging	Adjusted OPS	Adjusted Batter Runs
D.Allen-Chi 5.8	Carew-Min .318	D.Allen-Chi .420	D.Allen-Chi .603	D.Allen-Chi 1023	D.Allen-Chi 199	D.Allen-Chi 65.2
Fisk-Bos 5.1	Piniella-KC .312	May-Chi .405	Fisk-Bos .538	Fisk-Bos 909	Murcer-NY 171	Murcer-NY 49.2
Murcer-NY 4.5	D.Allen-Chi .308	Mayberry-KC .394	Murcer-NY .537	Mayberry-KC 900	Mayberry-KC 168	Mayberry-KC 44.5
Patek-KC 4.2	May-Chi .308	White-NY .384	Mayberry-KC .507	Murcer-NY 898	Epstein-Oak 166	Epstein-Oak 38.6
Mayberry-KC 3.5	Rudi-Oak .305	Scheinblum-KC .383	Epstein-Oak .490	Epstein-Oak 866	Fisk-Bos 159	May-Chi 36.1

Runs	Hits	Doubles	Triples	Home Runs	Total Bases	Runs Batted In
Murcer-NY 102	Rudi-Oak 181	Piniella-KC 33	Rudi-Oak 9	D.Allen-Chi 37	Murcer-NY 314	D.Allen-Chi 113
Rudi-Oak 94	Piniella-KC 179	Rudi-Oak 32	Fisk-Bos 9	Murcer-NY 33	D.Allen-Chi 305	Mayberry-KC 100
Harper-Bos 92	Murcer-NY 171	Murcer-NY 30	Blair-Bal 8	Killebrew-Min 26	Rudi-Oak 288	Murcer-NY 96
D.Allen-Chi 90	Carew-Min 170	White-NY 29	Murcer-NY 7	Epstein-Oak 26	Mayberry-KC 255	Scott-Mil 88
Tovar-Min 86	May-Chi 161	Harper-Bos 29	Kelly-Chi 7		Piniella-KC 253	Powell-Bal 81

Stolen Bases	Base Stealing Runs	Fielding Runs-Infield	Fielding Runs-Outfield	Wins	Winning Pct.	Complete Games
Campaneris-Oak 52	Campaneris-Oak 6.5	Patek-KC 37.7	Berry-Cal 8.0	Wood-Chi 24	Hunter-Oak .750	Perry-Cle 29
Nelson-Tex 51	Nelson-Tex 5.3	Michael-NY 24.0	Ford-Tex 7.4	Perry-Cle 24	Tiant-Bos .714	Lolich-Det 23
Patek-KC 33	Patek-KC 4.8	Rodriguez-Det 20.2	Blair-Bal 5.3	Lolich-Det 22	Odom-Oak .714	Wood-Chi 20
Kelly-Chi 32	Baylor-Bal 4.6	Clarke-NY 15.3	May-Mil 5.2		Palmer-Bal .677	Ryan-Cal 20
Otis-KC 28	Kelly-Chi 3.9	Killebrew-Min 10.9	G.Brown-Det 5.2		Kline-NY .640	Palmer-Bal 18

Strikeouts	Fewest BB/Game	Games	Saves	Base Runners/9	Adjusted Relief Runs	Relief Ranking
Ryan-Cal 329	Peterson-NY 1.58	Lindblad-Tex 66	Lyle-NY 35	Nelson-KC 7.89	Lyle-NY 13.3	Lyle-NY 25.4
Lolich-Det 250	Nelson-KC 1.61	Fingers-Oak 65	Forster-Chi 29	Hunter-Oak 8.32	Knowles-Oak 11.3	Forster-Chi 13.7
Perry-Cle 234	Kline-NY 1.68	Granger-Min 63	Fingers-Oak 21	Kaat-Min 9.05	Bell-Mil 10.7	Knowles-Oak 13.5
Blyleven-Min 228	Holtzman-Oak 1.76		Granger-Min 19	Perry-Cle 9.11	Harrison-Bal 9.4	Abernathy-KC 9.5
Coleman-Det 222	Wood-Chi 1.77		Sanders-Mil 17	Alexander-Bal 9.23	Forster-Chi 8.3	Fingers-Oak 9.1

Innings Pitched	Opponents' Avg.	Opponents' OBP	Earned Run Average	Adjusted ERA	Adjusted Starter Runs	Pitcher Wins
Wood-Chi 376.2	Ryan-Cal .171	Nelson-KC .234	Tiant-Bos 1.91	Tiant-Bos 169	Perry-Cle 48.5	**Perry-Cle** 6.7
Perry-Cle 342.2	Hunter-Oak .189	Hunter-Oak .241	Perry-Cle 1.92	Perry-Cle 168	Palmer-Bal 29.5	**Palmer-Bal** 4.1
Lolich-Det 327.1	Nelson-KC .196	Perry-Cle .261	Hunter-Oak 2.04	Palmer-Bal 149	Hunter-Oak 29.3	**Hunter-Oak** 3.1
Hunter-Oak 295.1	Tiant-Bos .202	Palmer-Bal .268	Palmer-Bal 2.07	Nelson-KC 146	Wood-Chi 25.1	**Lyle-NY** 3.0
Blyleven-Min 287.1	Perry-Cle .205	Tiant-Bos .275	Nelson-KC 2.08	Hunter-Oak 140	Tiant-Bos 24.4	**Tiant-Bos** 2.9

First Strike

Players went on strike in spring training, canceling the first 13 days of action. Once the strike ended, the AL East saw its first close race. New York, Baltimore, Boston, and Detroit bunched together in August, with the division lead switching seemingly every hour through Labor Day. The Yankees and Orioles faded while the Red Sox and Tigers split four in mid-September at Fenway and met three times to close the schedule at Detroit. The Tigers took the first two to win by a mere half-game.

The West again went to Oakland, although the resurgent White Sox—with knuckleballer Wilbur Wood, who made 49 starts, and MVP Dick Allen—made a run in August. Nolan Ryan, in his first year as an Angel, set a new record for fewest hits allowed per game; he also recorded his first of six 300-strikeout seasons. Minnesota's Rod Carew won his first of six batting titles in the decade. Moving from Washington to Texas, the Rangers had an attendance bump…of just 6,000.

With labor strife taking games off the schedule as well as a continued scoring reduction—only Bobby Murcer cleared 100 runs—attendance dipped for the third straight year. The Yankees failed to draw one million for the first time since 1945. Boston, second to Detroit in attendance and the standings, boasted Rookie of the Year Carlton Fisk plus Sparky Lyle, whose 35 saves set a league record.

In a thrilling ALCS, each team came back once in the bottom of the 10th to win. Oakland prevailed, winning the first two on the coast, then losing two and taking the deciding game in Detroit as Blue Moon Odom and Vida Blue held off the Tigers, 2–1. However, Reggie Jackson injured his knee and missed the World Series.

Six of the seven games in the see-saw Reds-A's Series were one-run affairs. Each team had dramatic come-from-behind wins and good pitching; the unlikely hero was Oakland's Gene Tenace, who hit 4 homers, including long balls in his first 2 at bats. Catfish Hunter won Game 7 in relief, holding off the Reds, 3–2.

1973 National League

TEAM	W	L	T	PCT	GB	HW	HL	R	OR	PA	H	2B	3B	HR	BB	SO	HB	SH	AVG	OBP	SLG	OPS	AOPS	BR	ABR	PF	SB	CS	BSA	BSR
EAST																														
NY	82	79	0	.509		43	38	608	588	6164	1345	198	24	85	540	805	108	23	.246	.315	.338	653	88	-82	-72	98	27	22	55	-2
STL	81	81	0	.500	1.5	43	38	643	603	6177	1418	240	35	75	531	796	89	29	.259	.325	.357	682	95	-23	-21	100	100	46	68	6
PIT	80	82	0	.494	2.5	41	40	704	693	6167	1465	**257**	44	154	432	842	60	27	.261	.315	.405	720	108	29	48	97	23	30	43	-5
MON	79	83	0	.488	3.5	43	38	668	702	6251	1345	190	23	125	**695**	**777**	**115**	**44**	.251	**.340**	.364	704	98	32	7	104	77	68	53	-7
CHI	77	84	0	.478	5	41	39	614	655	6070	1322	201	21	117	575	855	75	20	.247	.320	.357	677	88	-35	-78	107	65	58	53	-6
PHI	71	91	0	.438	11.5	38	43	642	717	6156	1381	218	29	134	476	979	56	33	.249	.310	.371	681	92	-41	-57	103	51	47	52	-5
WEST																														
CIN	99	63	0	.611		**50**	31	741	621	6304	1398	232	34	137	639	947	78	31	.254	.332	.383	715	**110**	46	**86**	95	**148**	55	**73**	**13**
LA	95	66	1	.590	3.5	**50**	31	675	**565**	6267	1473	219	29	110	497	795	81	28	.263	.323	.371	694	103	-6	25	96	109	50	69	6
SF	88	74	0	.543	11	47	34	739	702	6274	1452	212	**52**	161	590	913	75	35	.262	.335	.407	742	108	87	57	104	112	52	68	6
HOU	82	80	0	.506	17	41	40	681	672	6153	1391	216	35	134	469	962	83	33	.251	.312	.376	688	96	-30	-28	100	92	48	66	3
ATL	76	85	1	.472	22.5	40	40	**799**	774	6384	**1497**	219	34	**206**	608	870	65	34	**.266**	.339	**.427**	**766**	**110**	**136**	78	108	84	40	68	4
SD	60	102	0	.370	39	31	50	548	770	5985	1330	198	26	112	401	966	73	21	.244	.296	.351	647	92	-114	-67	92	88	36	71	7
TOT	971					508	462	8062		74352	16817	2600	386	1550	6453	10507	358	958	.254	.322	.376	698					976	552	64	22

TEAM	CG	SHO	GR	SV	IP	H	HR	BB	SO	BR/9	ERA	AERA	OAV	OOB	PR	APR	PF	OSB	OCS	FA	E	WPB	DP	FW	PW	BW	BSW	DIF
EAST																												
NY	47	15	194	40	1465.0	1345	127	490	**1027**	11.4	3.26	111	.245	.307	65	58	99	67	43	.980	126	**46**	140	1.1	6.0	-7.5	-.4	2.3
STL	42	14	264	36	1460.2	1366	**105**	486	867	11.6	3.25	112	.248	.310	66	63	100	74	53	.975	159	72	149	-.7	6.6	-2.2	.4	-4.1
PIT	26	11	284	**44**	1450.2	1426	110	564	839	12.6	3.73	94	.258	.329	-12	-36	96	84	39	.976	151	51	156	-.3	-3.7	5.0	-.7	-1.3
MON	26	6	272	38	1451.2	1356	128	681	866	12.8	3.71	103	.250	.334	-9	16	104	76	50	.974	163	83	156	-.9	1.7	.7	-.9	-2.5
CHI	27	13	249	40	1437.2	1471	128	**438**	885	12.1	3.66	108	.267	.322	1	43	108	78	53	.975	157	54	155	-.7	4.5	-8.1	-.8	1.6
PHI	**49**	11	257	22	1447.1	1435	131	632	919	13.1	3.99	95	.263	.341	-53	-30	104	65	**60**	.979	134	80	**179**	.7	-3.1	-5.9	-.7	-.9
WEST																												
CIN	39	**17**	267	43	1473.0	1389	135	518	801	11.8	3.40	100	.252	.318	42	0	93	**43**	33	**.982**	**115**	49	162	**1.8**	.0	**9.0**	**1.2**	6.1
LA	45	15	212	38	1491.0	**1270**	129	461	961	**10.6**	**3.00**	**115**	**.231**	**.292**	**109**	**77**	94	74	36	.981	125	71	166	1.2	**8.0**	2.6	.4	2.2
SF	33	8	252	**44**	1452.1	1442	145	485	787	12.1	3.79	101	.257	.318	-21	4	104	103	34	.974	163	73	138	-.9	.4	5.9	.4	1.2
HOU	45	14	268	26	1460.2	1389	111	575	907	12.3	3.75	97	.252	.323	-14	-19	99	102	43	.981	116	67	140	1.7	-2.0	-2.9	.1	4.0
ATL	34	9	**287**	35	1462.0	1467	144	575	803	12.7	4.25	93	.263	.332	-95	-48	107	119	**60**	.974	166	75	142	-1.1	-5.0	8.1	.2	-6.7
SD	34	10	269	23	1430.0	1461	157	548	845	12.8	4.16	83	.267	.334	-79	-116	95	84	44	.973	170	67	152	-1.3	-12.1	-7.0	.5	-1.1
TOT	447	143	3075	429	17482.0					12.2	3.66		.254	.322						.977	1745	788	1835					

Batter-Fielder Wins	Batting Average	On-Base Percentage	Slugging Average	On-Base Plus Slugging	Adjusted OPS	Adjusted Batter Runs
Morgan-Cin 7.5	Rose-Cin .338	Singleton-Mon .425	Stargell-Pit .646	Stargell-Pit 1038	Stargell-Pit 189	Stargell-Pit 63.3
Evans-Atl 6.3	Cedeno-Hou .320	Fairly-Mon .422	Evans-Atl .556	Evans-Atl .959	Perez-Cin 162	Morgan-Cin 50.2
Stargell-Pit 5.8	Maddox-SF .319	Morgan-Cin .406	Johnson-Atl .546	Perez-Cin .919	Morgan-Cin 157	Perez-Cin 48.7
Cedeno-Hou 4.6	Perez-Cin .314	Watson-Hou .403	Cedeno-Hou .537	Johnson-Atl .916	Evans-Atl 153	Evans-Atl 46.4
Ferguson-LA 4.0	Watson-Hou .312	Evans-Atl .403	Bonds-SF .530	Cedeno-Hou .913	Cedeno-Hou 151	Singleton-Mon 42.4

Runs	Hits	Doubles	Triples	Home Runs	Total Bases	Runs Batted In
Bonds-SF 131	Rose-Cin 230	Stargell-Pit 43	Metzger-Hou 14	Stargell-Pit 44	Bonds-SF 341	Stargell-Pit 119
Morgan-Cin 116	Garr-Atl 200	Oliver-Pit 38	Matthews-SF 10	Johnson-Atl 43	Stargell-Pit 337	May-Hou 105
Rose-Cin 115	Brock-StL 193	Staub-NY 36	Maddox-SF 10	Evans-Atl 41	Evans-Atl 331	Evans-Atl 104
Evans-Atl 114	Simmons-StL 192	Simmons-StL 36	Davis-LA 9	Aaron-Atl 40	Johnson-Atl 305	Bench-Cin 104
Brock-StL 110	Oliver-Pit 191	Rose-Cin 36		Bonds-SF 39	Oliver-Pit 303	Singleton-Mon 103

Stolen Bases	Base Stealing Runs	Fielding Runs-Infield	Fielding Runs-Outfield	Wins	Winning Pct.	Complete Games
Brock-StL 70	Morgan-Cin 9.5	Kessinger-Chi 26.7	Unser-Phi 14.3	Bryant-SF 24	John-LA .696	Seaver-NY 18
Morgan-Cin 67	Brock-StL 8.4	Foli-Mon 18.3	Rose-Cin 7.6	Seaver-NY 19	Gullett-Cin .692	Carlton-Phi 18
Cedeno-Hou 56	Cedeno-Hou 7.1	Schmidt-Phi 18.1	Williams-Chi 6.3	Billingham-Cin 19	Bryant-SF .667	Billingham-Cin 16
Bonds-SF 43	Baker-Atl 4.2	Evans-Atl 17.2	Bonds-SF 5.9	Sutton-LA 18	Seaver-NY .655	
Lopes-LA 36	Garr-Atl 3.8	Stennett-Pit 16.5	Cedeno-Hou 5.5	Gullett-Cin 18	Billingham-Cin .655	

Strikeouts	Fewest BB/Game	Games	Saves	Base Runners/9	Adjusted Relief Runs	Relief Ranking
Seaver-NY 251	Marichal-SF 1.61	Marshall-Mon 92	Marshall-Mon 31	Seaver-NY 8.91	Marshall-Mon 22.1	Marshall-Mon 35.6
Carlton-Phi 223	Jenkins-Chi 1.89	Borbon-Cin 80	McGraw-NY 25	Sutton-LA 9.02	Borbon-Cin 17.7	Borbon-Cin 23.9
Matlack-NY 205	Barr-SF 1.91	Sosa-SF 71	Giusti-Pit 20	Rogers-Mon 9.60	Moffitt-SF 15.4	Locker-Chi 21.9
Sutton-LA 200	Sutton-LA 1.97	Giusti-Pit 67	Brewer-LA 20	R.Hernandez-Pit 10.04	Locker-Chi 12.9	Giusti-Pit 17.9
	Seaver-NY 1.99	Segui-StL 65		Messersmith-LA 10.06	Giusti-Pit 12.7	Moffitt-SF 15.4

Innings Pitched	Opponents' Avg.	Opponents' OBP	Earned Run Average	Adjusted ERA	Adjusted Starter Runs	Pitcher Wins
Carlton-Phi 293.1	Seaver-NY .206	Seaver-NY .252	Seaver-NY 2.08	Seaver-NY 174	Seaver-NY 50.4	**Seaver-NY** 5.5
Billingham-Cin 293.1	Sutton-LA .209	Sutton-LA .257	Sutton-LA 2.42	Twitchell-Phi 152	Rogers-Mon 32.1	**Marshall-Mon** 4.1
Seaver-NY 290.0	Wilson-Hou .213	Messersmith-LA .278	Twitchell-Phi 2.50	Marshall-Mon 144	Sutton-LA 31.3	**Rogers-Mon** 3.8
Reuss-Hou 279.1	Messersmith-LA .214	Gibson-StL .281	Marshall-Mon 2.66	Sutton-LA 142	Twitchell-Phi 30.5	**Renko-Mon** 3.5
Jenkins-Chi 271.0	Renko-Mon .218	Briles-Pit .287	Messersmith-LA 2.70	Renko-Mon 136	Renko-Mon 25.8	**Sutton-LA** 3.2

Power of Belief

The Dodgers cruised along atop the NL West through August, but they picked the wrong time to slump. Cincinnati, barely over .500 through June, had two separate seven-game September win streaks as Los Angeles' pitching rusted down the stretch. The Reds scraped out the division title with just four good hitters; MVP Pete Rose and Joe Morgan again did the heavy lifting.

Dave Winfield joined the Padres without visiting the minors, while Dave Parker debuted in Pittsburgh and Ken Griffey with Cincinnati. The Expos' Mike Marshall was the league's most discussed pitcher, setting a new record with 92 appearances, winning 14, and saving 31. But the biggest number of the year was 713—Henry Aaron's end-of-season career home run total.

The NL East had a nutty race. As no team seemed to be able to clear .500, everyone but Philadelphia had a chance to win in the last week. The Cubs blew a big lead in July; the Cardinals surged ahead in August but fell back. New York sputtered until late August when they won 19 of 26, moving from last to first in 27 days. On September 23 just 2_ separated the front-running Mets from the fifth-place Cubs.

Despite challenges from St. Louis and Pittsburgh, the Mets clinched the day after the season's scheduled ending—thanks to a rainout—as Tom Seaver won in Chicago. New York finished with the lowest winning percentage ever for a champion (.509). Seaver took his second Cy Young in a close vote, while Rusty Staub headed a mediocre offense.

The underdog Mets (slogan: "Ya Gotta Believe!") then took out the favored Reds in a five-game NLCS. Cincinnati won 2–1 twice, but New York won three blowouts, two behind Seaver—shortstop Bud Harrelson did lose a one-sided brawl with Rose. In the World Series, New York fell in seven, with Willie Mays, now a Mets reserve, playing for the last time in the major leagues.

1973 American League

TEAM	W	L	T	PCT	GB	HW	HL	R	OR	PA	H	2B	3B	HR	BB	SO	HB	SH	AVG	OBP	SLG	OPS	AOPS	BR	ABR	PF	SB	CS	BSA	BSR
EAST																														
BAL	97	65	0	.599		**50**	31	754	**561**	6335	1474	229	**48**	119	**648**	752	58	**43**	.266	**.345**	.389	734	107	**63**	**69**	99	**146**	64	70	**10**
BOS	89	73	0	.549	8	48	33	738	647	6223	1472	235	30	147	581	799	54	31	.267	.338	**.401**	**739**	101	60	18	106	114	45	**72**	9
DET	85	77	0	.525	12	47	34	642	674	6135	1400	213	32	**157**	509	722	48	39	.254	.320	.390	710	93	-10	-52	107	28	30	48	-4
NY	80	82	0	.494	17	**50**	31	641	610	6064	1435	212	17	131	489	**680**	27	22	.261	.322	.378	700	101	-25	-1	97	47	43	52	-5
MIL	74	88	0	.457	23	40	41	708	731	6227	1399	229	40	145	563	977	61	42	.253	.325	.388	713	102	2	18	98	110	66	63	1
CLE	71	91	0	.438	26	34	47	680	826	6178	1429	205	29	158	471	793	40	32	.256	.315	.387	702	95	-30	-41	102	60	68	47	-11
WEST																														
OAK	94	68	0	.580		**50**	31	**758**	615	6257	1431	216	28	147	595	919	**67**	35	.260	.333	.389	722	**109**	29	**69**	95	128	57	69	8
KC	88	74	0	.543	6	48	33	755	752	6274	1440	239	40	114	644	696	49	26	.261	.339	.381	720	95	34	-19	108	105	69	60	-1
MIN	81	81	0	.500	13	37	44	738	692	6331	**1521**	**240**	44	120	598	954	34	34	**.270**	.342	.393	735	102	58	29	104	87	46	65	3
CAL	79	83	0	.488	15	43	38	629	657	6153	1395	183	29	93	509	816	60	34	.253	.318	.348	666	94	-87	-37	92	59	47	56	-3
CHI	77	85	0	.475	17	40	41	652	705	6135	1400	228	38	111	537	952	49	32	.256	.324	.372	696	93	-28	-50	103	83	73	53	-7
TEX	57	105	0	.352	37	35	46	619	844	6113	1397	195	29	110	503	791	45	27	.255	.318	.361	679	95	-65	-38	96	91	53	63	1
TOT	972					522	450	8314		74425	17193	2624	404	1552	6647	9851	397	592	.259	.328	.381	710					1058	661	62	1

TEAM	CG	SHO	GR	SV	IP	H	HR	BB	SO	BR/9	ERA	AERA	OAV	OOB	PR	APR	PF	OSB	OCS	FA	E	WPB	DP	FW	PW	BW	BSW	DIF
EAST																												
BAL	67	14	140	26	1461.2	**1297**	124	475	715	**11.0**	**3.07**	**122**	**.240**	**.302**	**122**	**111**	98	70	54	.981	119	43	184	1.3	**11.4**	**7.1**	**1.0**	-4.7
BOS	67	10	144	33	1440.1	1417	158	499	808	12.2	3.65	110	.259	.323	27	56	105	72	45	.979	127	**30**	162	.8	5.7	1.8	.9	-1.3
DET	39	11	211	**46**	1447.2	1468	154	493	911	12.4	3.90	105	.265	.326	-13	28	107	107	71	**.982**	**112**	58	144	**1.7**	2.9	-5.3	-.4	5.2
NY	47	16	143	39	1427.2	1379	109	**457**	708	11.7	3.34	110	.254	.313	75	53	96	61	52	.976	156	54	172	-.8	5.4	-.1	-.5	-5.0
MIL	50	11	217	28	1454.0	1476	119	623	671	13.2	3.98	94	.265	.340	-27	-36	99	81	**73**	.977	145	66	167	-.2	-3.7	1.8	.0	-5.1
CLE	55	9	206	21	1464.2	1532	172	602	883	13.4	4.58	85	.271	.343	-125	-105	103	109	47	.978	139	114	174	.2	-10.7	-4.2	-1.1	5.9
WEST																												
OAK	46	16	203	41	1457.1	1311	143	494	797	11.3	3.29	108	.241	.305	86	45	93	**54**	60	.978	137	61	170	.3	4.6	**7.1**	.8	.3
KC	40	7	213	41	1449.1	1521	114	617	790	13.5	4.19	98	.273	.346	-60	-12	108	86	49	.974	167	51	**192**	-1.4	-1.2	-1.9	-.1	11.7
MIN	48	**18**	190	34	1451.2	1443	115	519	879	12.4	3.77	105	.259	.324	7	29	104	93	54	.978	139	80	147	.2	3.0	3.0	.3	-6.4
CAL	**72**	13	164	19	1456.1	1351	**104**	614	**1010**	12.4	3.53	100	.246	.324	46	3	93	105	40	.975	156	72	153	-.8	.3	-3.8	-.3	2.6
CHI	48	15	176	35	1456.0	1484	110	574	848	13.0	3.86	102	.266	.336	-8	15	104	110	57	.977	144	71	165	-.1	1.5	-5.1	-.7	.4
TEX	35	10	**241**	27	1430.0	1514	130	680	831	14.1	4.64	80	.273	.353	-131	-150	98	109	58	.974	161	70	164	-1.1	-15.3	-3.9	.0	-3.8
TOT	614	150	2248	390	17396.2					12.5	3.82		.259	.328						.977	1702	770	1994					

Batter-Fielder Wins	Batting Average	On-Base Percentage	Slugging Average	On-Base Plus Slugging	Adjusted OPS	Adjusted Batter Runs
Carew-Min 5.8	Carew-Min 350	Mayberry-KC 417	Jackson-Oak.........531	Jackson-Oak 914	Jackson-Oak 165	Jackson-Oak 47.9
Grich-Bal 5.5	Scott-Mil 306	Carew-Min 411	Bando-Oak 498	Mayberry-KC 895	Robinson-Cal........153	Bando-Oak 42.9
Munson-NY..........5.0	Davis-Bal 306	Yastrzemski-Bos 407	Robinson-Cal 489	Carew-Min 881	Bando-Oak 153	Robinson-Cal......40.2
Jackson-Oak 4.2	Murcer-NY 304	Tenace-Oak 387	Scott-Mil 488	Bando-Oak 873	Scott-Mil 144	Carew-Min..........35.0
Patek-KC.............4.1	May-Mil..................303	Jackson-Oak 383	Munson-NY 487	Yastrzemski-Bos ..870	Carew-Min............143	Scott-Mil 34.5

Runs	Hits	Doubles	Triples	Home Runs	Total Bases	Runs Batted In
Jackson-Oak 99	Carew-Min............203	Garcia-Mil 32	Carew-Min.............11	Jackson-Oak 32	Scott-Mil 295	Jackson-Oak 117
Scott-Mil 98	May-Mil 189	Bando-Oak 32	Bumbry-Bal 11	Robinson-Cal..........30	May-Mil 295	Scott-Mil 107
North-Oak 98	Murcer-NY 187	Scott-Mil 30	Orta-Chi.................10	Burroughs-Tex........30	Bando-Oak 295	Mayberry-KC 100
Carew-Min..............98	Scott-Mil 185	Chambliss-Cle 30	Coggins-Bal.............9	Bando-Oak 29	Murcer-NY............286	Bando-Oak............98
Bando-Oak 97	Johnson-Tex 179	Carew-Min 30	Coluccio-Mil.............8		Jackson-Oak 286	Robinson-Cal 97

Stolen Bases	Base Stealing Runs	Fielding Runs-Infield	Fielding Runs-Outfield	Wins	Winning Pct.	Complete Games
Harper-Bos 54	Harper-Bos 7.0	Patek-KC 39.8	North-Oak...........15.4	Wood-Chi................24	Hunter-Oak...........808	Perry-Cle 29
North-Oak 53	North-Oak.............4.7	Nettles-NY 32.7	Burroughs-Tex 9.7	Coleman-Det 23	Palmer-Bal 710	Ryan-Cal 26
Nelson-Tex.............43	Campaneris-Oak ..4.0	Bell-Cle 27.2	Coluccio-Mil 8.4	Palmer-Bal.............22	Blue-Oak 690	Blyleven-Min..........25
Carew-Min..............41	Baylor-Bal..............3.9	Grich-Bal 26.8	Blair-Bal 5.6		Splittorff-KC 645	Tiant-Bos 23
Patek-KC 36	Nelson-Tex 3.9	Clarke-NY 16.2	Stanley-Det...........4.9		Colborn-Mil..........625	Colborn-Mil............22

Strikeouts	Fewest BB/Game	Games	Saves	Base Runners/9	Adjusted Relief Runs	Relief Ranking
Ryan-Cal 383	Kaat-Min-Chi 1.73	Hiller-Det.......................65	Hiller-Det 38	Jackson-Bal 8.74	Hiller-Det.............34.8	Hiller-Det 61.1
Blyleven-Min 258	Blyleven-Min 1.86	Fingers-Oak 62	Lyle-NY 27	Lyle-NY...............9.18	Reynolds-Bal 22.5	Acosta-Chi..........31.9
Singer-Cal 241	Holtzman-Oak 2.00	Bird-KC 54	Fingers-Oak...........22	Hiller-Det.............9.19	Fingers-Oak 20.2	Fingers-Oak 29.4
Perry-Cle 238	Wood-Chi 2.28	Knowles-Oak 52	Bird-KC 20	Beene-NY...........9.40	Jackson-Bal 17.2	Reynolds-Bal......26.0
Lolich-Det 214	Lolich-Det 2.30		Acosta-Chi.............18	Reynolds-Bal 9.65	Acosta-Chi 16.8	Jackson-Bal........19.8

Innings Pitched	Opponents' Avg.	Opponents' OBP	Earned Run Average	Adjusted ERA	Adjusted Starter Runs	Pitcher Wins
Wood-Chi 359.1	Bibby-Tex 192	Tiant-Bos 278	Palmer-Bal 2.40	Blyleven-Min 157	Blyleven-Min........48.0	**Hiller-Det**...........6.7
Perry-Cle 344.0	Ryan-Cal...............203	Hunter-Oak 282	Blyleven-Min 2.52	Palmer-Bal...........156	Palmer-Bal 46.2	**Blyleven-Min**......5.3
Ryan-Cal...........326.0	Palmer-Bal...........211	Blyleven-Min 284	Lee-Bos 2.75	Lee-Bos 146	Lee-Bos 36.7	**Palmer-Bal** 4.7
Blyleven-Min 325.0	Tiant-Bos 219	Holtzman-Oak 286	Ryan-Cal..............2.87	Medich-NY...........124	Ryan-Cal..............29.1	**Lee-Bos** 3.6
Singer-Cal..........315.2	Blue-Oak 224	Palmer-Bal 288	Medich-NY 2.95	Ryan-Cal 124	Holtzman-Oak 22.8	**Acosta-Chi** 3.3

All A's Again

With the AL adopting the designated hitter, scoring increased 23 percent, the biggest rise since 1911. Perhaps not coincidentally, attendance leapt to a new all-time high. Oakland took the AL West lead in July. When the Royals made a run in August, the A's responded, winning 13 of 14. Reggie Jackson won his only MVP, and four teammates scored 89 or more runs while three starters won 20.

Kansas City's new stadium sported artificial turf and a much smaller outfield, which helped center fielder Amos Otis develop. In addition, the Royals debuted George Brett and Frank White. California's Nolan Ryan, an overpowering pitcher in a great pitcher's park, threw his first no-hitter and set an all-time mark with 383 strikeouts.

With an offense that appeared unprepossessing but was quite effective, Baltimore won 14 straight in August to break open a tough AL East race with Boston and Detroit. Jim Palmer was the Cy Young winner, as again Earl Weaver let his starters finish their business. Detroit's John Hiller saved 38, setting a record that lasted until 1983, but the aging Tigers were slowing up. Boston and Luis Aparicio parted ways in a postseason salary dispute, ending the 39-year-old's career.

Four of the five ALCS games were close, but Catfish Hunter came through with a Game 5 shutout (his second win of the series) to send Oakland to the World Series. Despite being outhit, outscored, and outpitched by the Mets, Oakland won the Series in seven. Two games went extra innings and there was much human drama. New York's Rusty Staub played right field with a dead arm, Oakland owner Charlie Finley forced Mike Andrews off the roster after 2 errors, and Willie Mays ended his career. Darold Knowles, the only pitcher to appear in seven games, and Rollie Fingers pitched 20 innings of relief between them, allowing the Mets 1 run.

1974 National League

TEAM	W	L	T	PCT	GB	HW	HL	R	OR	PA	H	2B	3B	HR	BB	SO	HB	SH	AVG	OBP	SLG	OPS	AOPS	BR	ABR	PF	SB	CS	BSA	BSR
EAST																														
PIT	88	74	0	.543		**52**	29	751	657	6361	**1560**	238	46	114	514	828	54	38	**.274**	.335	.391	726	113	65	94	96	55	31	64	1
STL	86	75	0	.534	1.5	44	37	677	643	6318	1492	216	46	83	531	752	68	**44**	.265	.331	.365	696	101	7	13	99	**172**	62	74	**16**
PHI	80	82	0	.494	8	46	35	676	701	6117	1434	233	**50**	95	469	822	84	26	.261	.320	.373	693	95	-9	-35	104	115	58	66	5
MON	79	82	0	.491	8.5	42	38	662	657	6190	1355	201	29	86	652	812	106	33	.254	.335	.350	685	92	3	-32	106	124	49	72	10
NY	71	91	0	.438	17	36	45	572	646	6226	1286	183	22	96	597	**735**	87	29	.235	.311	.329	640	85	-100	-90	98	43	23	65	1
CHI	66	96	0	.407	22	32	49	669	826	6344	1397	221	42	110	621	857	80	29	.251	.327	.365	692	95	0	-27	104	78	73	52	-8
WEST																														
LA	102	60	0	.630		**52**	29	**798**	**561**	6332	1511	231	34	**139**	597	820	86	28	.272	.342	**.401**	**743**	**119**	**105**	**139**	96	149	75	67	7
CIN	98	64	1	.605	4	50	31	776	631	6372	1437	**271**	35	135	**693**	940	68	30	.260	**.343**	.394	737	114	101	113	99	146	49	**75**	15
ATL	88	74	1	.543	14	46	35	661	563	6279	1375	202	37	120	571	772	**109**	24	.249	.319	.363	682	92	-25	-52	104	72	44	62	0
HOU	81	81	0	.500	21	46	35	653	632	6120	1441	222	41	110	471	864	83	29	.263	.322	.378	700	106	4	34	96	108	65	62	1
SF	72	90	0	.444	30	37	44	634	723	6159	1380	228	38	93	548	869	75	30	.252	.322	.358	680	92	-28	-57	105	107	51	68	6
SD	60	102	0	.370	42	36	45	541	830	6117	1239	196	27	99	564	900	83	20	.229	.302	.330	632	86	-124	-100	96	85	45	65	3
TOT	972					519	452	8070		74935	16907	2642	447	1280	6828	9971	360	983	.255	.326	.367	693					1254	625	67	57

TEAM	CG	SHO	GR	SV	IP	H	HR	BB	SO	BR/9	ERA	AERA	OAV	OOB	PR	APR	PF	OSB	OCS	FA	E	WPB	DP	FW	PW	BW	BSW	DIF
EAST																												
PIT	**51**	9	229	17	1466.0	1428	93	543	721	12.3	3.49	99	.256	.323	21	-7	95	85	54	.975	162	58	154	-.5	-.7	9.8	-.4	-1.2
STL	37	13	293	20	1473.1	1399	97	616	794	12.5	3.48	103	.254	.329	22	15	99	119	57	.977	147	57	**192**	.4	1.6	1.4	**1.2**	1.1
PHI	46	4	283	19	1447.1	1394	111	682	892	13.1	3.91	97	.257	.341	-47	-21	104	122	52	.976	148	75	168	.4	-2.2	-3.6	.0	4.5
MON	35	8	223	**27**	1429.0	1340	99	544	822	12.0	3.60	107	.249	.319	3	36	106	89	64	.976	153	74	157	.0	3.7	-3.3	.5	-2.5
NY	46	15	212	14	1470.1	1433	99	504	908	12.0	3.42	104	.257	.320	33	24	99	113	48	.975	158	52	150	-.2	2.5	-9.4	-.4	-2.5
CHI	23	6	347	26	1466.1	1593	122	576	895	13.6	4.28	89	.277	.344	-108	-72	105	126	54	.969	199	81	141	-2.6	-7.5	-2.8	-1.3	-.7
WEST																												
LA	33	19	209	23	1465.1	**1272**	112	**464**	**943**	**10.8**	**2.97**	114	**.233**	**.294**	**105**	74	94	76	47	.975	157	55	122	-.2	7.7	**14.5**	.2	-1.2
CIN	34	11	256	**27**	1466.1	1364	126	536	875	11.8	3.41	102	.247	.314	33	13	96	**56**	41	.979	134	59	151	1.2	1.4	11.8	1.1	1.6
ATL	46	**21**	215	22	1474.1	1343	97	488	772	11.3	3.05	**124**	.244	.307	93	**114**	104	107	50	.979	132	64	161	1.3	**11.9**	-5.4	-.5	-.3
HOU	36	18	272	18	1450.2	1396	**84**	601	738	12.6	3.46	100	.255	.331	25	0	96	123	56	**.982**	**113**	65	161	**2.4**	.0	3.5	-.4	-5.5
SF	27	11	292	25	1439.0	1409	116	559	756	12.5	3.78	101	.257	.325	-26	3	105	107	36	.972	175	**51**	153	-1.2	.3	-5.9	.1	-2.3
SD	25	7	**352**	19	1445.2	1536	124	715	855	14.3	4.58	78	.275	.359	-155	-168	98	131	**65**	.973	170	71	126	-.9	-17.5	-10.4	-.2	8.0
TOT	439	142	3183	257	17493.2					12.4	3.62		.255	.326						.976	1848	762	1836					

Batter-Fielder Wins	Batting Average	On-Base Percentage	Slugging Average	On-Base Plus Slugging	Adjusted OPS	Adjusted Batter Runs
Schmidt-Phi 7.4	Garr-Atl 353	Morgan-Cin 427	Schmidt-Phi 546	Stargell-Pit 944	Stargell-Pit 169	Stargell-Pit 50.6
Morgan-Cin 7.0	Oliver-Pit 321	Stargell-Pit 407	Stargell-Pit 537	Schmidt-Phi 941	Morgan-Cin 160	Morgan-Cin 49.1
Bench-Cin 5.7	Gross-Hou 314	Bailey-Mon 396	Smith-StL 528	Morgan-Cin 921	Smith-StL 158	Schmidt-Phi 44.5
Evans-Atl 4.7	Buckner-LA 314	Schmidt-Phi 395	Bench-Cin 507	Smith-StL 917	Schmidt-Phi 156	Wynn-LA 41.6
Cash-Phi 4.4	Madlock-Chi 313	Gross-Hou 393	Garr-Atl 503	Garr-Atl 886	Wynn-LA 154	Smith-StL 39.8

Runs	Hits	Doubles	Triples	Home Runs	Total Bases	Runs Batted In
Rose-Cin 110	Garr-Atl 214	Rose-Cin 45	Garr-Atl 17	Schmidt-Phi 36	Bench-Cin 315	Bench-Cin 129
Schmidt-Phi 108	Cash-Phi 206	Oliver-Pit 38	Oliver-Pit 12	Bench-Cin 33	Schmidt-Phi 310	Schmidt-Phi 116
Bench-Cin 108	Garvey-LA 200	Bench-Cin 38	Cash-Phi 11	Wynn-LA 32	Garr-Atl 305	Garvey-LA 111
Morgan-Cin 107	Oliver-Pit 198	Stargell-Pit 37	Metzger-Hou 10	Perez-Cin 28	Garvey-LA 301	Wynn-LA 108
Brock-StL 105	Stennett-Pit 196		Bowa-Phi 10	Cedeno-Hou 26	Oliver-Pit 293	Simmons-StL 103

Stolen Bases	Base Stealing Runs	Fielding Runs-Infield	Fielding Runs-Outfield	Wins	Winning Pct.	Complete Games
Brock-StL 118	Brock-StL 14.4	Foli-Mon 34.8	Geronimo-Cin 10.5	P.Niekro-Atl 20	Messersmith-LA ...769	P.Niekro-Atl 18
Lopes-LA 59	Morgan-Cin 8.6	Cash-Phi 30.7	Anderson-Phi 9.8	Messersmith-LA 20	Sutton-LA 679	Carlton-Phi 17
Morgan-Cin 58	Lintz-Mon 8.6	Schmidt-Phi 28.3	Rose-Cin 9.3	Sutton-LA 19	Capra-Atl 667	Lonborg-Phi 16
Cedeno-Hou 57	Concepcion-Cin 6.9	Evans-Atl 26.6	Zisk-Pit 6.9	Billingham-Cin 19	Torrez-Mon 652	Rooker-Pit 15
Lintz-Mon 50	Lopes-LA 6.7	Stennett-Pit 20.9	Cedeno-Hou 6.4		Billingham-Cin 633	

Strikeouts	Fewest BB/Game	Games	Saves	Base Runners/9	Adjusted Relief Runs	Relief Ranking
Carlton-Phi 240	Barr-SF 1.76	Marshall-LA 106	Marshall-LA 21	Murray-Mon 8.91	Marshall-LA 23.9	Marshall-LA 33.3
Messersmith-LA ..221	Reed-Atl 1.98	Hardy-SD 76	Moffitt-SF 15	House-Atl 9.12	Taylor-Mon 20.1	C.Carroll-Cin 26.1
Seaver-NY 201	Ellis-Pit 2.09	Borbon-Cin 73	Borbon-Cin 14	Leon-Atl 9.96	House-Atl 19.8	House-Atl 18.6
P.Niekro-Atl 195	Lonborg-Phi 2.23	Forsch-Hou 70	Giusti-Pit 12	Messersmith-LA ..9.97	Murray-Mon 19.4	Taylor-Mon..........18.1
Matlack-NY 195	Marshall-LA 2.42	Sosa-SF 68		P.Niekro-Atl 10.21	C.Carroll-Cin.........15.8	Leon-Atl 14.6

Innings Pitched	Opponents' Avg.	Opponents' OBP	Earned Run Average	Adjusted ERA	Adjusted Starter Runs	Pitcher Wins
P.Niekro-Atl 302.1	Capra-Atl 208	Messersmith-LA...........277	Capra-Atl 2.28	Capra-Atl 166	P.Niekro-Atl 44.8	**P.Niekro-Atl** 5.0
Messersmith-LA 292.1	Messersmith-LA ...212	Matlack-NY 283	P.Niekro-Atl 2.38	P.Niekro-Atl 159	Matlack-NY...........35.0	**Messersmith-LA** 3.8
Carlton-Phi 291.0	Gullett-Cin 222	P.Niekro-Atl 284	Matlack-NY...........2.41	Matlack-NY 148	Capra-Atl 32.6	**Marshall-LA**.........3.6
Lonborg-Phi 283.0	P.Niekro-Atl 225	Reed-Atl 285	Marshall-LA 2.42	Marshall-LA 141	Messersmith-LA ..30.4	**Capra-Atl** 3.5
Sutton-LA 276.0	Matlack-NY...........226	Capra-Atl 286	Messersmith-LA ..2.59	Barr-SF 139	Barr-SF 29.5	**Rooker-Pit** 3.3

Records, Records, Records

Henry Aaron, boosted by a mid-career move to hitter-friendly Fulton County Stadium, had slowly closed in on Babe Ruth's all-time home run record. Despite the media pressure, the hate mail, and the nagging injuries, the 40-year-old Aaron tied the record on Opening Day in Cincinnati and then broke it in Atlanta against Los Angeles on April 8.

The Braves finished third with surprising pitching, but Atlanta never contended. Cincinnati was excellent, but the Dodgers were even better. Los Angeles, led from start to finish. The Dodgers shored up a mediocre bullpen by acquiring Mike Marshall from Montreal, and the muttonchopped screwballer set a big-league mark with 106 appearances and became the first reliever to win the Cy Young. The Dodgers also got big production from center fielder Jimmy Wynn and first baseman Steve Garvey, an All-Star write-in starter and eventual MVP.

With Willies Mays and McCovey departed, the Giants sank to fifth. Their attendance, just 50 percent of their 1971 total, was the league's lowest figure of the decade. Both Felipe and Matty Alou ended their major league careers. Catastrophic control problems forced Pirates hurler Steve Blass from the game, while Orlando Cepeda and Ron Santo's careers ground to disappointing halts in the AL. Former Cardinals pitching great—and beloved TV announcer—Dizzy Dean passed away, and Kent Tekulve, Keith Hernandez, and Gary Carter made their major league bows.

Lou Brock of St. Louis used his 35-year-old legs to steal 118 bases, shattering Ty Cobb's record, and his club almost took the NL East crown. But the Cardinals didn't hit enough, and Willie Stargell's Pirates, sometimes known as the Pittsburgh Lumber Company, led the league in batting average and took a see-saw race.

A four-game NLCS went easily to the Dodgers; Pirates reliever Dave Giusti allowed 13 hits in 3.1 innings of "relief." The World Series, however, was no celebration as the Oakland A's beat Los Angeles in five. Four of the games were decided by 3–2 scores.

1974 American League

TEAM	W	L	T	PCT	GB	HW	HL	R	OR	PA	H	2B	3B	HR	BB	SO	HB	SH	AVG	OBP	SLG	OPS	AOPS	BR	ABR	PF	SB	CS	BSA	BSR
EAST																														
BAL	91	71	0	.562		46	35	659	612	6230	1418	226	27	116	509	770	72	**58**	.256	.322	.370	692	102	-1	20	97	145	58	**71**	**12**
NY	89	73	0	.549	2	47	34	671	623	6181	1451	220	30	101	515	**690**	49	21	.263	.324	.368	692	101	1	13	98	53	35	60	-1
BOS	84	78	0	.519	7	46	35	**696**	661	6214	1449	**236**	31	109	**569**	811	64	33	.264	.333	.377	710	97	42	-5	107	104	58	64	3
CLE	77	85	0	.475	14	40	41	662	694	6019	1395	201	19	131	432	756	56	26	.255	.311	.370	681	96	-38	-32	99	79	68	54	-6
MIL	76	86	0	.469	15	40	41	647	660	6090	1335	228	**49**	120	500	909	56	27	.244	.309	.369	678	95	-42	-38	99	106	75	59	-3
DET	72	90	0	.444	19	36	45	620	768	6106	1375	200	35	131	436	784	41	24	.247	.303	.366	669	89	-68	-88	104	67	38	64	1
WEST																														
OAK	90	72	0	.556		**49**	32	689	**551**	6048	1315	205	37	132	568	876	60	38	.247	.321	.373	694	106	2	48	94	**164**	93	64	4
TEX	84	76	1	.525	5	42	38	690	698	6123	1482	198	39	99	508	710	**81**	38	**.272**	**.336**	.377	713	**108**	41	**59**	98	113	80	59	-3
MIN	82	80	1	.506	8	48	33	673	669	6302	**1530**	190	37	111	520	791	64	46	**.272**	**.336**	.378	714	102	42	20	103	74	45	62	1
CHI	80	80	3	.500	9	46	34	684	721	6235	1492	225	23	**135**	519	858	70	26	.268	.330	**.389**	**719**	104	**50**	33	102	64	53	55	-4
KC	77	85	0	.475	13	40	41	667	662	6263	1448	232	42	89	550	768	56	32	.259	.327	.364	691	94	-1	-37	106	146	76	66	6
CAL	68	94	1	.420	22	36	45	618	657	6085	1372	203	31	95	509	801	82	45	.254	.321	.356	677	101	-30	8	94	119	79	60	-1
TOT	973					516	454	7976		73896	17062	2564	400	1369	6135	9524	414	751	.258	.323	.371	694					1234	758	62	6

TEAM	CG	SHO	GR	SV	IP	H	HR	BB	SO	BR/9	ERA	AERA	OAV	OOB	PR	APR	PF	OSB	OCS	FA	E	WPB	DP	FW	PW	BW	BSW	DIF
EAST																												
BAL	57	**16**	185	25	1474.0	1393	101	480	701	11.6	3.27	105	.253	.314	56	31	95	91	58	**.980**	128	50	174	1.0	3.2	2.1	**1.2**	2.5
NY	53	13	182	24	1455.1	1402	104	528	829	12.1	3.31	106	.256	.323	50	36	97	**80**	55	.977	142	54	158	.2	3.8	1.4	-.2	2.8
BOS	**71**	12	139	18	1455.1	1462	126	463	751	12.1	3.72	103	.262	.320	-16	19	106	108	60	.977	145	51	156	.0	2.0	-.5	.3	1.2
CLE	45	9	214	27	1445.2	1419	138	479	650	12.0	3.80	95	.260	.320	-30	-31	100	92	48	.977	146	**30**	157	-.0	-3.2	-3.3	-.7	3.3
MIL	43	11	189	24	1457.2	1476	126	493	621	12.3	3.76	96	.266	.326	-23	-23	100	103	56	**.980**	**127**	62	168	**1.1**	-2.4	-4.0	-.4	.7
DET	54	7	154	15	1455.2	1443	148	621	869	13.0	4.16	91	.262	.338	-88	-55	105	134	79	.975	158	75	155	-.7	-5.8	-9.2	.0	6.6
WEST																												
OAK	49	12	**216**	28	1439.2	**1322**	**90**	**430**	755	**11.1**	**2.95**	**112**	**.246**	**.302**	**107**	**64**	92	83	59	.977	141	37	154	.3	**6.7**	5.0	.4	-3.3
TEX	62	**16**	189	12	1433.2	1423	126	449	871	12.0	3.82	93	.260	.318	-33	-42	99	99	60	.974	163	59	164	-1.1	-4.4	**6.2**	-.4	3.6
MIN	43	11	189	**29**	1455.1	1436	115	513	934	12.3	3.64	102	.260	.325	-4	13	103	119	**86**	.976	151	43	164	-.3	1.4	2.1	.0	-2.2
CHI	55	11	201	**29**	1465.2	1470	103	548	826	12.7	3.94	95	.263	.332	-52	-33	103	111	69	.977	147	60	**188**	-.0	-3.5	3.5	-.5	.5
KC	54	13	209	17	1471.2	1477	91	482	731	12.2	3.51	109	.263	.322	17	47	106	115	55	.976	152	71	166	-.4	4.9	-3.9	.6	-5.2
CAL	64	13	190	12	1439.0	1339	101	649	**986**	12.7	3.52	98	.248	.332	15	-14	95	98	72	.976	147	73	150	-.0	-1.5	.8	-.2	-12.2
TOT	650	144	2257	260	17448.2					12.2	3.62		.258	.323						.977	1747	665	1954					

Batter-Fielder Wins	Batting Average	On-Base Percentage	Slugging Average	On-Base Plus Slugging	Adjusted OPS	Adjusted Batter Runs
Carew-Min 6.9	Carew-Min 364	Carew-Min 433	D.Allen-Chi 563	D.Allen-Chi............938	Jackson-Oak 171	Burroughs-Tex....50.2
Grich-Bal 6.1	Orta-Chi 316	Yastrzemski-Bos 414	Jackson-Oak.........514	Jackson-Oak 905	Burroughs-Tex......164	Jackson-Oak 49.9
Jackson-Oak 5.4	McRae-KC 310	Burroughs-Tex 397	Burroughs-Tex 504	Burroughs-Tex......901	D.Allen-Chi............164	Carew-Min..........42.0
Harrah-Tex 3.3	Piniella-NY 305	Maddox-NY 395	Rudi-Oak 484	Carew-Min 879	Carew-Min 149	D.Allen-Chi 37.8
Burroughs-Tex....3.0	Maddox-NY...........303	Jackson-Oak 391	Freehan-Det 479	Yastrzemski-Bos ..859	Robinson-Cal-Cle 143	Grich-Bal 32.8

Runs	Hits	Doubles	Triples	Home Runs	Total Bases	Runs Batted In
Yastrzemski-Bos 93	Carew-Min 218	Rudi-Oak.......................39	Rivers-Cal 11	D.Allen-Chi..............32	Rudi-Oak 287	Burroughs-Tex 118
Grich-Bal 92	Davis-Bal..............181	Scott-Mil 36	Otis-KC 9	Jackson-Oak 29	K.Henderson-Chi..281	Bando-Oak 103
Jackson-Oak 90	Money-Mil 178	McRae-KC 36		Tenace-Oak 26	Burroughs-Tex......279	Rudi-Oak 99
Otis-KC 87	K.Henderson-Chi..176	K.Henderson-Chi 35		Darwin-Min 25	Carew-Min 267	K.Henderson-Chi ..95
Carew-Min 86	Rudi-Oak 174	Burroughs-Tex 33		Burroughs-Tex.........25		Darwin-Min 94

Stolen Bases	Base Stealing Runs	Fielding Runs-Infield	Fielding Runs-Outfield	Wins	Winning Pct.	Complete Games
North-Oak 54	Jackson-Oak..........3.8	Nettles-NY 20.3	Evans-Bos 11.6	Jenkins-Tex 25	Cuellar-Bal 688	Jenkins-Tex............29
Carew-Min...............38	Coggins-Bal 3.6	Doyle-Cal......................17.8	North-Oak.............11.4	Hunter-Oak 25	Jenkins-Tex...........676	G.Perry-Cle 28
Lowenstein-Cle 36	Pinson-KC..............2.9	Grich-Bal 15.6	Maddox-NY..........10.0		Hunter-Oak...........676	Lolich-Det 27
Campaneris-Oak 34	Blair-Bal 2.8	Rodriguez-Det 15.0	Piniella-NY 9.3		Tiant-Bos 629	Ryan-Cal 26
Patek-KC 33	North-Oak..............2.8	Bell-Cle 14.5	Miller-Bos 9.0			Tiant-Bos 25

Strikeouts	Fewest BB/Game	Games	Saves	Base Runners/9	Adjusted Relief Runs	Relief Ranking
Ryan-Cal 367	Jenkins-Tex..........1.23	Fingers-Oak 76	Forster-Chi.............24	Hunter-Oak.........8.99	Murphy-Mil 24.1	Murphy-Mil 44.0
Blyleven-Min 249	Hunter-Oak...........1.30	Murphy-Mil 70	Murphy-Mil.............20	Jenkins-Tex.........9.29	Lyle-NY.................21.9	Hiller-Det 36.3
Jenkins-Tex 225	Holtzman-Oak 1.80	Foucault-Tex 69	Campbell-Min 19	G.Perry-Cle..........9.35	Hiller-Det..............18.2	Lyle-NY 27.2
G.Perry-Cle 216	Kaat-Chi 2.04	Lyle-NY 66	Buskey-NY-Cle 18	Jackson-Bal 9.59	Foucault-Tex 17.2	Campbell-Min 23.1
Lolich-Det 202	Wright-Mil 2.09	Campbell-Min 63	Fingers-Oak............18	Garland-Bal 9.59	Campbell-Min 15.7	Foucault-Tex 21.4

Innings Pitched	Opponents' Avg.	Opponents' OBP	Earned Run Average	Adjusted ERA	Adjusted Starter Runs	Pitcher Wins
Ryan-Cal............332.2	Ryan-Cal...............190	Hunter-Oak 258	Hunter-Oak.........2.49	G.Perry-Cle 144	G.Perry-Cle..........41.4	**Murphy-Mil** 4.9
Jenkins-Tex........328.1	G.Perry-Cle...........204	Jenkins-Tex 262	G.Perry-Cle..........2.51	Blyleven-Min 140	Hunter-Oak...........34.8	**G.Perry-Cle** 4.5
G.Perry-Cle.........322.1	DalCanton-KC.......211	G.Perry-Cle 270	Hassler-Cal..........2.61	Fitzmorris-KC........137	Tiant-Bos 32.5	**Hiller-Det**............3.8
Wood-Chi 320.1	Hassler-Cal...........225	Blyleven-Min 290	Blyleven-Min 2.66	Hunter-Oak 134	Blyleven-Min 30.6	**Hunter-Oak**........3.8
Hunter-Oak........318.1	Hunter-Oak...........229	Tiant-Bos 291	Fitzmorris-KC 2.79	Hassler-Cal 132	Jenkins-Tex..........27.9	**Blyleven-Min**......3.7

Sprinting to a Dynasty

Following the 1973 World Series, A's manager Dick Williams quit, unable to stomach capricious owner Charlie Finley. Under Alvin Dark, who'd worked for Finley back in the 1960s, the A's won their fourth consecutive AL West title. Catfish Hunter led an extraordinary staff and earned Cy Young honors. Four Oakland batters hit 20 or more homers. Oakland also brought Finley's long-standing speed obsession to fruition, using former Olympic sprinter Herb Washington 92 times as a pinch runner—he never batted or took the field.

Under new skipper Billy Martin, the Rangers leapt from last to second as Fergie Jenkins won 25 games and Jeff Burroughs was MVP. Nolan Ryan fanned 357 hitters for the last-place Angels, but he walked 202.

The Red Sox, leading by 8 games near the end of August, crumbled. Cozy Fenway Park disguised a mediocre offense, and Luis Tiant's heroics weren't enough. Meanwhile, Baltimore caught fire the last two weeks, rising from fourth at the beginning of September to win; the Birds captured 16 of their final 18. Mike Cuellar and Dave McNally were a combined 10–0 with a sub-2.00 ERA in September.

New York finished second on strong pitching, although shoulder troubles ended Mel Stottlemyre's career. Due to stadium renovations, the Yankees played at Shea Stadium in 1974–75; the Yankees drew more people than they had in a decade. Milwaukee gave a job to 18-year-old rookie shortstop Robin Yount, who stayed in the lineup until 1993. Detroit's great era ended as Norm Cash and Al Kaline, who garnered his 3,000th hit, retired.

Oakland wrapped up the ALCS in four, then edged Los Angeles in a competitive five-game World Series. Four of the A's-Dodgers contests were decided by one run. It was Oakland's third straight Series crown, a feat unmatched since the 1951–53 Yankees. Over the winter, though, Finley "forgot" a payment on Hunter's contract, and the pitcher was ruled a free agent.

1975 National League

TEAM	W	L	T	PCT	GB	HW	HL	R	OR	PA	H	2B	3B	HR	BB	SO	HB	SH	AVG	OBP	SLG	OPS	AOPS	BR	ABR	PF	SB	CS	BSA	BSR
EAST																														
PIT	92	69	0	.571		52	28	712	565	6111	1444	255	**47**	**138**	468	832	76	**38**	.263	.323	**.402**	725	108	43	49	99	49	28	64	1
PHI	86	76	0	.531	6.5	51	30	735	694	6363	1506	**283**	42	125	610	960	88	31	.269	.342	**.402**	744	109	102	72	104	126	57	69	8
NY	82	80	0	.506	10.5	42	39	646	625	6237	1430	217	34	101	501	805	75	37	.256	.319	.361	680	100	-38	-8	95	32	26	55	-2
STL	82	80	1	.506	10.5	45	36	662	689	6207	**1527**	239	46	81	444	**649**	92	29	**.273**	.327	.375	702	98	5	-18	104	116	49	70	8
MON	75	87	0	.463	17.5	39	42	601	690	6272	1346	216	31	98	579	954	110	27	.244	.317	.348	665	87	-64	-89	104	108	58	65	3
CHI	75	87	0	.463	17.5	42	39	712	827	6323	1419	229	41	95	650	802	107	30	.259	.338	.368	706	98	34	4	104	67	55	55	-5
WEST																														
CIN	108	54	0	.667		**64**	17	**840**	586	6418	1515	278	37	124	**691**	916	66	35	.271	**.353**	.401	**754**	**114**	**134**	**119**	102	**168**	36	**82**	**24**
LA	88	74	0	.543	20	49	32	648	**534**	6246	1355	217	31	118	611	825	104	31	.248	.325	.365	690	102	-9	21	96	138	52	73	12
SF	80	81	0	.497	27.5	46	35	659	671	6186	1412	235	45	84	604	775	62	22	.259	.333	.365	698	96	11	-16	104	99	47	68	5
SD	71	91	0	.438	37	38	43	552	683	6151	1324	215	22	78	506	754	**133**	37	.244	.310	.335	645	91	-101	-64	94	85	50	63	1
ATL	67	94	0	.416	40.5	37	43	583	739	6092	1323	179	28	107	543	759	72	18	.244	.313	.346	659	86	-78	-98	104	55	38	59	-1
HOU	64	97	1	.398	43.5	37	44	664	711	6211	1401	218	54	84	523	762	97	32	.254	.320	.359	679	101	-39	10	93	133	62	68	8
TOT	971					542	428	8014		74817	17002	2781	458	1233	6730	9793	367	1082	.257	.327	.369	696					1176	558	68	63

TEAM	CG	SHO	GR	SV	IP	H	HR	BB	SO	BR/9	ERA	AERA	OAV	OOB	PR	APR	PF	OSB	OCS	FA	E	WPB	DP	FW	PW	BW	BSW	DIF
EAST																												
PIT	43	14	226	31	1437.1	1302	**79**	551	768	11.7	3.01	**118**	.243	.313	98	**87**	98	81	35	.976	151	56	147	.2	**9.1**	5.1	-.4	-2.5
PHI	33	11	283	30	1455.0	1353	111	546	897	11.9	3.82	98	.249	.317	-33	-15	103	69	52	.976	152	60	156	.2	-1.6	7.5	.3	-1.4
NY	40	14	229	31	1466.0	1344	99	580	**989**	12.0	3.39	102	.246	.319	38	11	95	116	63	.976	151	56	144	.3	1.1	-.8	-.8	1.2
STL	33	13	272	36	1454.2	1452	98	571	824	12.7	3.57	105	.260	.328	8	29	104	110	39	.973	171	86	140	-.8	3.0	-1.9	.3	.4
MON	30	12	271	25	1480.0	1448	102	665	831	13.1	3.72	103	.259	.339	-17	16	106	78	46	.973	180	85	**179**	-1.3	1.7	-9.3	-.2	3.2
CHI	27	8	**298**	33	1444.1	1587	130	551	850	13.6	4.49	86	.281	.347	-140	-99	106	93	54	.972	179	**50**	152	-1.3	-10.3	.4	-1.1	6.3
WEST																												
CIN	22	8	277	**50**	1459.0	1422	112	487	663	12.0	3.37	107	.257	.319	41	37	99	**61**	29	**.984**	**102**	52	173	**3.0**	3.9	**12.4**	**2.0**	5.8
LA	**51**	**18**	169	21	1469.2	**1215**	104	**448**	894	**10.4**	**2.92**	116	**.225**	**.285**	**114**	83	94	68	33	.979	127	51	106	1.6	8.7	2.2	.7	-6.2
SF	37	9	259	24	1432.2	1406	92	612	856	12.9	3.74	102	.259	.336	-19	9	105	114	47	.976	146	64	164	.5	.9	-1.7	-.0	-.2
SD	40	12	290	20	1463.1	1494	99	521	713	12.5	3.48	100	.266	.329	23	-2	96	118	51	.971	188	51	163	-1.8	-.2	-6.7	-.4	-.9
ATL	32	4	267	24	1430.0	1543	101	519	669	13.3	3.91	96	.278	.341	-47	-22	104	147	44	.972	175	90	147	-1.1	-2.3	-10.2	-.7	.8
HOU	39	6	265	25	1458.1	1436	106	679	839	13.3	4.04	83	.262	.343	-67	-117	93	125	**65**	.979	137	113	166	1.1	-12.2	1.0	.3	-6.7
TOT	427	129	3106	350	17450.1					12.4	3.62		.257	.327						.976	1859	814	1837					

Batter-Fielder Wins	Batting Average	On-Base Percentage	Slugging Average	On-Base Plus Slugging	Adjusted OPS	Adjusted Batter Runs
Morgan-Cin..........8.0	Madlock-Chi 354	Morgan-Cin 466	Parker-Pit 541	Morgan-Cin 974	Morgan-Cin 168	Morgan-Cin 56.9
Bench-Cin............5.4	Simmons-StL 332	Rose-Cin 406	Luzinski-Phi 540	Luzinski-Phi..........934	Luzinski-Phi..........152	Luzinski-Phi........44.2
Schmidt-Phi 5.3	Sanguillen-Pit 328	Wynn-LA 403	Schmidt-Phi 523	Parker-Pit..............898	Watson-Hou..........152	Thornton-Chi 33.1
Evans-Atl 4.3	Morgan-Cin...........327	Madlock-Chi................402	Bench-Cin.............519	Stargell-Pit............891	Parker-Pit..............148	Simmons-StL......32.9
Simmons-StL......3.6	Watson-Hou 324	Cardenal-Chi 397	Foster-Cin.............518	Schmidt-Phi..........890	Stargell-Pit............147	Rose-Cin 32.9

Runs	Hits	Doubles	Triples	Home Runs	Total Bases	Runs Batted In
Rose-Cin 112	Cash-Phi 213	Rose-Cin........................47	Garr-Atl 11	Schmidt-Phi............38	Luzinski-Phi 322	Luzinski-Phi 120
Cash-Phi 111	Rose-Cin 210	Cash-Phi........................40	Parker-Pit................10	Kingman-NY 36	Garvey-LA 314	Bench-Cin 110
Lopes-LA 108	Garvey-LA 210	Oliver-Pit 39	Kessinger-Chi 10	Luzinski-Phi............34	Parker-Pit.............302	Perez-Cin 109
Morgan-Cin 107	Simmons-StL........193	Bench-Cin......................39	Joshua-SF 10	Bench-Cin 28	Schmidt-Phi 294	Staub-NY 105
Thomas-SF 99	Millan-NY..............191	Garvey-LA......................38	Gross-Hou 10		Rose-Cin 286	

Stolen Bases	Base Stealing Runs	Fielding Runs-Infield	Fielding Runs-Outfield	Wins	Winning Pct.	Complete Games
Lopes-LA 77	Lopes-LA 12.7	Evans-Atl 31.3	Maddox-SF-Phi....14.5	Seaver-NY 22	Gullett-Cin 789	Messersmith-LA 19
Morgan-Cin 67	Morgan-Cin..........11.2	Stennett-Pit 25.7	Geronimo-Cin........11.4	Jones-SD.................20	Seaver-NY 710	Jones-SD 18
Brock-StL................56	Brock-StL 6.7	Schmidt-Phi 18.7	Foster-Cin 9.6	Messersmith-LA 19	Hooton-Chi-LA 667	Seaver-NY 15
Cedeno-Hou 50	Concepcion-Cin 5.2	Trillo-Chi......................18.0	Cardenal-Chi 9.3	Hooton-Chi-LA........18	Murray-Mon 652	Reuss-Pit 15
Cardenal-Chi 34	Cedeno-Hou..........5.1	Cash-Phi 17.6	Unser-NY 8.6	Reuss-Pit................18		

Strikeouts	Fewest BB/Game	Games	Saves	Base Runners/9	Adjusted Relief Runs	Relief Ranking
Seaver-NY 243	Nolan-Cin 1.24	Garber-Phi 71	Hrabosky-StL..........22	Jones-SD 9.41	Hrabosky-StL 19.7	Hrabosky-StL......39.1
Montefusco-SF 215	Jones-SD 1.77	McEnaney-Cin 70	Eastwick-Cin 22	Sutton-LA 9.45	Apodaca-NY........18.5	Apodaca-NY 20.1
Messersmith-LA ..213	Reed-Atl-StL 1.91	Tomlin-SD 67	Giusti-Pit 17	Messersmith-LA ..9.65	Hilgendorf-Phi.......14.0	Eastwick-Cin 14.9
Carlton-Phi 192	Rau-LA 2.13	Borbon-Cin 67	McEnaney-Cin........15	Hrabosky-StL 9.80	Eastwick-Cin........11.0	Garman-StL........14.2
Richard-Hou 176	Barr-SF 2.14	Garman-StL 66	Knowles-Chi 15	Hooton-Chi-LA 9.89	C.Carroll-Cin........10.7	McGraw-Phi........13.8

Innings Pitched	Opponents' Avg.	Opponents' OBP	Earned Run Average	Adjusted ERA	Adjusted Starter Runs	Pitcher Wins
Messersmith-LA 321.2	Messersmith-LA ...213	Sutton-LA......................263	Jones-SD 2.24	Jones-SD.............155	Messersmith-LA ..42.4	**Seaver-NY**..........4.5
Jones-SD 285.0	Sutton-LA 213	Jones-SD......................269	Messersmith-LA ..2.29	Messersmith-LA ..149	Jones-SD 37.1	**Messersmith-LA**4.5
Seaver-NY 280.1	Seaver-NY 214	Hooton-Chi-LA.............274	Seaver-NY 2.38	Seaver-NY............146	Seaver-NY 36.8	**Jones-SD**..........4.5
Morton-Atl..........277.2	Warthen-Mon 217	Messersmith-LA...........275	Reuss-Pit 2.54	Reuss-Pit.............140	Reuss-Pit 29.7	**Hrabosky-StL** 4.2
Niekro-Atl 275.2	Hooton-Chi-LA 219	Nolan-Cin.....................275	Forsch-StL 2.86	Montefusco-SF 132	Montefusco-SF 25.3	**Reuss-Pit**...........4.1

Free and Clear

The Reds cruised in a lopsided pennant "race." Joe Morgan was an easy MVP, enjoying one of the greatest seasons ever for a second baseman. Everyone in Cincinnati's lineup contributed offensively and defensively, and the deep pitching featured left-right relief combo Will McEnaney and Rawly Eastwick.

The NL East was again tightly packed, with just 17_ games separating first from last. Pittsburgh used six strong starting pitchers, including rookie John Candelaria, to withstand Philadelphia's challenge to win its fourth crown in five years. The Pirates favored power and boasted little speed. Philadelphia stole 126 bases, but could hit the long ball, too; third baseman Mike Schmidt won the second of his eight NL home run crowns.

The Cardinals lost 1930s star Joe Medwick, who passed away, and Bob Gibson, who hung up the spikes. Claude Osteen and Vada Pinson also retired. Astros pitcher Don Wilson died in his car of carbon monoxide poisoning.

Pirates second baseman Rennie Stennett had one of the great afternoons of all time, going 7-for-7 in a 22–0 massacre at Wrigley Field to tie Wilbert Robinson's 1892 mark. Giants mainstay Juan Marichal retired, while the club welcomed Jack Clark and Rookie of the Year John Montefusco.

The Pirates were no match for the Reds, who took the NLCS in three games. But the 1975 World Series was different; packed with drama, controversy, great plays, and unexpected heroes, five of the seven games were one-run affairs. The Reds won Games 2, 3, and 7 with dramatic rallies in their last at bats; the Red Sox won two games with big innings and took a nail-biting, 12-inning, Game 6 on Carlton Fisk's barely-fair homer. The next night Morgan's ninth-inning single plated Pete Rose with the Series-winning run.

The biggest change of the year came December 23, when federal arbitrator Peter Seitz ruled baseball's reserve clause invalid, opening the door for free agency, distribution of talent, and increased salaries. Litigant Andy Messersmith (and the newly retired Dave McNally) first benefited from the ruling, but the doors soon blew out and nearly every club entered the market.

1975 American League

TEAM	W	L	T	PCT	GB	HW	HL	R	OR	PA	H	2B	3B	HR	BB	SO	HB	SH	AVG	OBP	SLG	OPS	AOPS	BR	ABR	PF	SB	CS	BSA	BSR
EAST																														
BOS	95	65	0	.594		47	34	**796**	709	6175	**1500**	**284**	44	134	565	741	75	34	**.275**	**.344**	**.417**	**761**	105	**112**	49	109	66	58	53	-6
BAL	90	69	0	.566	4.5	44	33	682	**553**	6211	1382	224	33	124	580	834	73	38	.252	.326	.373	699	104	-13	34	94	104	55	65	4
NY	83	77	0	.519	12	43	35	681	588	6038	1430	230	39	110	486	710	54	30	.264	.325	.382	707	101	-3	9	98	102	59	63	2
CLE	79	80	0	.497	15.5	41	39	688	703	6057	1409	201	25	**153**	525	**667**	64	24	.261	.327	.392	719	102	16	17	100	106	89	54	-8
MIL	68	94	0	.420	28	36	45	675	792	6081	1343	242	34	146	553	922	73	28	.250	.320	.389	709	100	-1	-4	101	65	64	50	-8
DET	57	102	0	.358	37.5	31	49	570	786	5852	1338	171	39	125	383	872	37	28	.249	.301	.366	667	84	-101	-124	104	63	57	53	-6
WEST																														
OAK	98	64	0	.605		**54**	27	758	606	6184	1376	220	33	151	609	846	74	**51**	.254	.333	.391	724	**106**	35	**52**	98	183	82	**69**	**12**
KC	91	71	0	.562	7	51	30	710	649	6230	1431	263	**58**	118	591	675	68	29	.261	.333	.394	727	102	42	23	103	155	75	67	8
TEX	79	83	0	.488	19	39	41	714	733	6342	1431	208	17	134	**613**	863	64	25	.256	.330	.371	701	99	-9	-3	99	102	62	62	1
MIN	76	83	0	.478	20.5	39	43	724	736	6225	1497	215	28	121	563	746	62	40	.271	.341	.386	727	104	47	37	101	81	48	63	1
CHI	75	86	0	.466	22.5	42	39	655	703	6243	1400	209	38	94	611	800	50	40	.255	.331	.358	689	94	-24	-33	101	101	54	65	3
CAL	72	89	0	.447	25.5	35	46	628	723	6141	1324	195	41	55	593	811	**97**	27	.246	.322	.328	650	90	-100	-56	93	**220**	108	67	11
TOT	963					502	461	8281		73779	16861	2662	429	1465	6672	9487	394	791	.258	.328	.379	707					1348	811	62	13

TEAM	CG	SHO	GR	SV	IP	H	HR	BB	SO	BR/9	ERA	AERA	OAV	OOB	PR	APR	PF	OSB	OCS	FA	E	WPB	DP	FW	PW	BW	BSW	DIF
EAST																												
BOS	62	11	167	31	1436.2	1463	145	**490**	720	12.4	3.98	102	.265	.325	-33	13	108	111	60	.977	139	**37**	142	.9	1.3	5.0	-.7	8.5
BAL	**70**	**19**	149	21	1451.0	1285	110	500	717	**11.1**	**3.17**	111	.242	**.306**	**98**	59	93	93	62	**.983**	**107**	47	**175**	**2.6**	6.0	3.5	.3	-1.9
NY	**70**	11	147	20	1424.0	1325	104	502	809	11.7	3.29	**112**	.249	.314	78	**64**	97	**80**	71	.978	135	48	148	1.1	**6.5**	.9	.0	-5.6
CLE	37	6	218	33	1435.1	1395	136	599	800	12.7	3.84	98	.258	.333	-10	-10	100	121	74	.978	134	66	156	1.1	-1.0	1.7	-.9	-1.4
MIL	36	10	223	34	1431.2	1496	133	624	643	13.7	4.34	88	.271	.348	-89	-79	101	118	73	.971	180	85	162	-1.4	-8.1	-.4	-.9	-2.2
DET	52	10	155	17	1396.0	1496	137	533	787	13.3	4.27	94	.275	.340	-77	-38	106	123	68	.972	173	59	141	-1.1	-3.9	-12.7	-.7	-4.1
WEST																												
OAK	36	10	**245**	**44**	1448.0	**1267**	**102**	523	784	11.4	3.27	111	**.236**	**.306**	82	60	96	110	50	.977	143	60	140	.7	6.1	**5.3**	**1.1**	3.7
KC	52	11	204	25	1456.2	1422	108	498	815	12.0	3.47	111	.258	.320	50	61	102	119	64	.976	155	53	151	.0	6.2	2.3	.7	.6
TEX	60	16	224	17	1465.2	1456	123	518	792	12.4	3.86	97	.261	.327	-14	-18	99	96	71	.971	191	60	173	-2.0	-1.8	-.3	.0	2.1
MIN	57	7	163	22	1423.0	1381	137	617	846	12.9	4.05	94	.257	.335	-43	-35	101	119	79	.973	170	58	147	-.9	-3.6	3.8	.0	-2.7
CHI	34	7	209	39	1452.1	1489	107	655	799	13.5	3.93	99	.268	.347	-24	-9	103	109	**80**	.978	140	38	155	.9	-.9	-3.4	.2	-2.3
CAL	59	**19**	192	16	1453.1	1386	123	613	**975**	12.6	3.89	91	.253	.330	-18	-59	94	150	65	.971	184	74	164	-1.6	-6.0	-5.7	1.0	3.9
TOT	625	137	2296	319	17273.2					12.5	3.78		.258	.328						.975	1851	685	1854					

Batter-Fielder Wins	Batting Average	On-Base Percentage	Slugging Average	On-Base Plus Slugging	Adjusted OPS	Adjusted Batter Runs
Harrah-Tex 6.8	Carew-Min 359	Carew-Min 421	Lynn-Bos 566	Lynn-Bos 967	Mayberry-KC 167	Mayberry-KC 55.2
Carew-Min 6.7	Lynn-Bos 331	Mayberry-KC 416	Mayberry-KC 547	Mayberry-KC 963	Carew-Min............159	Singleton-Bal......51.9
Grich-Bal 6.5	Munson-NY 318	Singleton-Bal 415	Powell-Cle............524	Carew-Min 919	Lynn-Bos 158	Carew-Min..........43.5
Munson-NY..........4.5	Rice-Bos...............309	Harrah-Tex....................403	Scott-Mil 515	Powell-Cle 901	Singleton-Bal 156	Lynn-Bos 42.0
Mayberry-KC 4.5	C.Washington-Oak.308	Lynn-Bos 401	Bonds-NY 512	Bonds-NY 888	Powell-Cle 154	Bonds-NY 38.3

Runs	Hits	Doubles	Triples	Home Runs	Total Bases	Runs Batted In
Lynn-Bos 103	Brett-KC................195	Lynn-Bos.........................47	Rivers-Cal 13	Scott-Mil 36	Scott-Mil 318	Scott-Mil 109
Mayberry-KC 95	Carew-Min 192	Jackson-Oak...................39	Brett-KC..................13	Jackson-Oak 36	Mayberry-KC 303	Mayberry-KC 106
Bonds-NY 93	Munson-NY 190	McRae-KC 38	Orta-Chi..................10	Mayberry-KC 34	Jackson-Oak 303	Lynn-Bos 105
Rice-Bos 92	C.Washington-Oak182	Mayberry-KC..................38	Cowens-KC 8	Bonds-NY 32	Lynn-Bos 299	Jackson-Oak 104
		Chambliss-NY................38			Brett-KC................289	

Stolen Bases	Base Stealing Runs	Fielding Runs-Infield	Fielding Runs-Outfield	Wins	Winning Pct.	Complete Games
Rivers-Cal 70	Rivers-Cal............10.5	Belanger-Bal 29.5	Evans-Bos 18.7	Palmer-Bal..............23	Torrez-Bal.............690	Hunter-NY 30
C.Washington-Oak 40	Otis-KC 4.7	Rodriguez-Det 26.5	North-Oak.............11.4	Hunter-NY...............23	Leonard-KC 682	G.Perry-Cle-Tex 25
Otis-KC 39	Patek-KC 4.6	Grich-Bal 26.3	Sharp-Chi-Mil 11.1	Blue-Oak 22	Palmer-Bal 676	Palmer-Bal 25
Carew-Min 35	Carew-Min 4.6	Dent-Chi 18.2	Manning-Cle 10.2	Torrez-Bal 20	Blue-Oak 667	Jenkins-Tex.............22
Remy-Cal.................34	Alomar-NY 4.1	Harrah-Tex...................16.5	White-NY 8.1	Kaat-Chi 20	Lee-Bos 654	Blyleven-Min..........20

Strikeouts	Fewest BB/Game	Games	Saves	Base Runners/9	Adjusted Relief Runs	Relief Ranking
Tanana-Cal 269	Jenkins-Tex..........1.87	Fingers-Oak 75	Gossage-Chi 26	Hunter-NY............9.22	Gossage-Chi 31.4	Gossage-Chi 46.9
G.Perry-Cle-Tex....233	G.Perry-Cle-Tex ..2.06	Lindblad-Oak 68	Fingers-Oak............24	Palmer-Bal............9.33	Todd-Oak.............17.0	Fingers-Oak 18.5
Blyleven-Min 233	Grimsley-Bal 2.15	Gossage-Chi....................62	Murphy-Mil..............20	Fingers-Oak 9.52	Hiller-Det..............13.8	LaRoche-Cle 17.9
Palmer-Bal............193	Palmer-Bal 2.23	LaRoche-Cle...................61	LaRoche-Cle 17	Blyleven-Min......10.02	LaRoche-Cle 13.3	Todd-Oak............17.6
Blue-Oak 189	Hunter-NY............2.28	Foucault-Tex 59	Drago-Bos 15	Tanana-Cal........10.18	Lindblad-Oak 12.2	Hiller-Det 14.9

Innings Pitched	Opponents' Avg.	Opponents' OBP	Earned Run Average	Adjusted ERA	Adjusted Starter Runs	Pitcher Wins
Hunter-NY..........328.0	Hunter-NY.............208	Hunter-NY 261	Palmer-Bal 2.09	Palmer-Bal...........168	Palmer-Bal 52.3	**Palmer-Bal** 5.6
Palmer-Bal 323.0	Ryan-Cal................213	Palmer-Bal....................266	Hunter-NY............2.58	Eckersley-Cle 146	Hunter-NY............41.3	**Gossage-Chi** 5.1
G.Perry-Cle-Tex 305.2	Eckersley-Cle 215	Blyleven-Min 281	Eckersley-Cle 2.60	Hunter-NY 143	Tanana-Cal..........31.4	**Hunter-NY** 4.3
Kaat-Chi 303.2	Palmer-Bal 216	G.Perry-Cle-Tex...........284	Tanana-Cal..........2.62	Tanana-Cal 136	Blyleven-Min........25.7	**Tanana-Cal** 3.1
Wood-Chi 291.1	Blyleven-Min.........219	Tanana-Cal 286	Figueroa-Cal........2.91	Blyleven-Min 128	Eckersley-Cle 25.0	**Busby-KC** 2.9

The Red and the Black

Boston had no trouble after June, pulling away while the Brewers and Yankees sagged, and the Orioles didn't get going until it was too late. Red Sox center fielder Fred Lynn was an immediate sensation, winning Rookie of the Year as well as MVP honors. Fellow freshman Jim Rice was nearly as good.

It was a fine season all around for rookies. Dennis Eckersley, Jerry Remy, and Lyman Bostock all played well, and Butch Hobson and Willie Randolph also made their first appearances. It was the end, however, for Harmon Killebrew, who hit .199 in Kansas City.

New York owner George Steinbrenner came out with a huge contract for free agent Catfish Hunter, but his 23 wins couldn't carry a mediocre staff. Cleveland made Frank Robinson the game's first African American manager; Robby also served as a part-time DH and homered in his first at bat Opening Day.

Kansas City's John Mayberry, Hal McRae, and George Brett blossomed, but the Royals, couldn't deter the A's from their fifth straight division title. A 13-of-14 stretch in June put Oakland well ahead. Despite playing in a pitcher's park, the offense was superb, boasting power, speed, and on-base ability. Alvin Dark used seven starters 10 or more times, and Vida Blue won 20 games for the third time. Nolan Ryan went down with elbow problems, allowing his Angels teammate, 21-year-old Frank Tanana, to lead the AL in strikeouts.

Boston easily crushed the A's to win the league pennant, but the World Series was another Hub disappointment. Indelible moments—Luis Tiant's twisting, Bernie Carbo's swinging, Dwight Evans' leaping, Carlton Fisk's gesturing—made the seven-game loss to Cincinnati even tougher to swallow.

Lefty Grove and Casey Stengel died, and the Oakland dynasty also came to an end. A's owner Charlie Finley—not unlike franchise predecessor Connie Mack—would be forced to trade or sell his stars. Many of Finley's "mustache gang" eventually walked away as free agents, happily moving to greener, calmer, but less storied pastures.

1976 National League

TEAM	W	L	T	PCT	GB	HW	HL	R	OR	PA	H	2B	3B	HR	BB	SO	HB	SH	AVG	OBP	SLG	OPS	AOPS	BR	ABR	PF	SB	CS	BSA	BSR
EAST																														
PHI	101	61	0	.623		**53**	28	770	557	6236	1505	259	45	110	542	793	59	**40**	.272	.338	.395	733	111	110	88	103	127	70	64	3
PIT	92	70	0	.568	9	47	34	708	630	6177	1499	249	56	110	433	807	61	29	.267	.321	.391	712	107	49	43	101	130	45	74	13
NY	86	76	0	.531	15	45	37	615	**538**	6129	1334	198	34	102	561	797	**92**	28	.246	.319	.352	671	102	-20	18	94	66	58	53	-6
CHI	75	87	0	.463	26	42	39	611	728	6155	1386	216	24	105	490	834	75	30	.251	.313	.356	669	88	-27	-78	109	74	74	50	-10
STL	72	90	0	.444	29	37	44	629	671	6181	1432	243	57	63	512	860	86	22	.260	.323	.359	682	99	1	-5	101	123	55	69	8
MON	55	107	0	.340	46	27	53	531	734	5992	1275	224	32	94	433	841	75	16	.235	.291	.340	631	81	-110	-131	104	86	44	66	4
WEST																														
CIN	102	60	0	.630		49	32	**857**	633	6538	**1599**	**271**	**63**	**141**	**681**	902	67	28	**.280**	**.357**	**.424**	**781**	**125**	**219**	**198**	102	**210**	57	**79**	**26**
LA	92	70	0	.568	10	49	32	608	543	6125	1371	200	34	91	486	744	91	29	.251	.313	.349	662	96	-41	-29	98	144	55	72	12
HOU	80	82	0	.494	22	46	36	625	657	6111	1401	195	50	66	530	**719**	57	21	.256	.322	.347	669	105	-22	39	91	150	57	72	13
SF	74	88	0	.457	28	40	41	595	686	6123	1340	211	37	85	518	778	80	25	.246	.312	.345	657	89	-49	-66	103	88	55	62	0
SD	73	89	0	.451	29	42	38	570	662	6047	1327	216	37	64	488	716	125	23	.247	.310	.337	647	97	-66	-16	92	92	46	67	4
ATL	70	92	0	.432	32	34	47	620	700	6107	1309	170	30	82	589	811	107	19	.245	.320	.334	654	87	-45	-80	106	74	61	55	-5
TOT	972					511	461	7739		73921	16778	2652	499	1113	6263	9602	310	975	.255	.320	.361	681					1364	677	67	63

TEAM	CG	SHO	GR	SV	IP	H	HR	BB	SO	BR/9	ERA	AERA	OAV	OOB	PR	APR	PF	OSB	OCS	FA	E	WPB	DP	FW	PW	BW	BSW	DIF
EAST																												
PHI	34	9	247	44	1459.0	1377	98	**397**	918	11.1	3.08	**115**	.250	.301	69	**75**	101	103	38	.981	115	44	148	1.7	**8.0**	9.3	-.2	1.2
PIT	45	12	237	35	1466.1	1402	95	460	762	11.5	3.36	104	.253	.310	22	20	100	94	66	.975	163	**39**	142	-1.0	2.1	4.6	.8	4.5
NY	**53**	**18**	183	25	1449.0	**1248**	97	419	**1025**	**10.5**	**2.94**	112	**.233**	**.290**	**91**	61	94	103	58	.979	131	51	116	.8	6.5	1.9	-1.2	-3.0
CHI	27	12	**329**	33	1471.1	1511	123	490	850	12.4	3.93	98	.268	.327	-71	-11	110	112	59	.978	140	49	145	.3	-1.2	-8.3	-1.6	4.8
STL	35	15	298	26	1453.2	1416	91	581	731	12.5	3.60	98	.258	.329	-16	-11	101	**87**	**72**	.973	174	77	163	-1.7	-1.2	-.5	.3	-5.9
MON	26	10	309	21	1440.0	1442	89	659	783	13.4	3.99	93	.266	.347	-79	-41	106	113	69	.976	155	74	**179**	-.6	-4.4	-13.9	-.1	-7.0
WEST																												
CIN	33	12	274	**45**	1471.0	1436	100	491	790	11.9	3.51	100	.258	.318	-1	0	100	94	51	**.984**	**102**	49	157	**2.5**	.0	**21.0**	**2.2**	-4.7
LA	47	17	182	28	1470.2	1330	97	479	747	11.2	3.02	112	.243	.305	79	62	97	114	55	.980	128	46	154	1.0	6.6	-3.1	.7	5.8
HOU	42	17	235	29	1444.1	1349	82	662	780	12.7	3.56	90	.250	.332	-9	-64	91	166	59	.978	140	89	155	.3	-6.8	4.1	.8	.5
SF	27	**18**	304	31	1461.2	1464	**68**	518	746	12.3	3.53	103	.263	.325	-4	16	104	136	46	.971	186	62	153	-2.4	1.7	-7.0	-.6	1.2
SD	47	11	258	18	1432.1	1368	87	543	652	12.1	3.65	90	.253	.321	-24	-65	93	104	53	.978	141	57	148	.2	-6.9	-1.7	-.1	.5
ATL	33	13	264	27	1438.0	1435	86	564	818	12.8	3.86	98	.261	.332	-58	-11	108	138	51	.973	167	98	151	-1.3	-1.2	-8.5	-1.1	1.0
TOT	449	164	3120	362	17457.1					12.0	3.50		.255	.320						.977	1742	735	1811					

Batter-Fielder Wins	Batting Average	On-Base Percentage	Slugging Average	On-Base Plus Slugging	Adjusted OPS	Adjusted Batter Runs
Morgan-Cin 6.7	Madlock-Chi .339	Morgan-Cin .444	Morgan-Cin .576	Morgan-Cin 1020	Morgan-Cin 186	Morgan-Cin 60.5
Schmidt-Phi 6.0	Griffey-Cin .336	Madlock-Chi .412	Foster-Cin .530	Madlock-Chi .912	Watson-Hou 151	Schmidt-Phi 40.7
Concepcion-Cin 4.2	Maddox-Phi .330	Rose-Cin .404	Schmidt-Phi .524	Schmidt-Phi .900	Schmidt-Phi 150	Watson-Hou 39.9
Cey-LA 4.0	Rose-Cin .323	Griffey-Cin .401	Monday-Chi .507	Foster-Cin .894	Foster-Cin 149	Rose-Cin 38.4
Maddox-Phi 3.8	Morgan-Cin .320	Cey-LA .386	Kingman-NY .506	Rose-Cin .854	Madlock-Chi 146	Foster-Cin 34.0

Runs	Hits	Doubles	Triples	Home Runs	Total Bases	Runs Batted In
Rose-Cin 130	Rose-Cin 215	Rose-Cin 42	Cash-Phi 12	Schmidt-Phi 38	Schmidt-Phi 306	Foster-Cin 121
Morgan-Cin 113	Montanez-SF-Atl 206	Johnstone-Phi 38	Geronimo-Cin 11	Kingman-NY 37	Rose-Cin 299	Morgan-Cin 111
Schmidt-Phi 112	Garvey-LA 200	Maddox-Phi 37	Parker-Pit 10	Monday-Chi 32	Foster-Cin 298	Schmidt-Phi 107
Griffey-Cin 111	Buckner-LA 193	Garvey-LA 37	W.Davis-SD 10	Foster-Cin 29	Garvey-LA 284	Watson-Hou 102
Monday-Chi 107				Morgan-Cin 27		Luzinski-Phi 95

Stolen Bases	Base Stealing Runs	Fielding Runs-Infield	Fielding Runs-Outfield	Wins	Winning Pct.	Complete Games
Lopes-LA 63	Lopes-LA 10.4	Royster-Atl 25.0	Maddox-Phi 14.1	Jones-SD 22	Carlton-Phi .741	Jones-SD 25
Morgan-Cin 60	Morgan-Cin 10.1	Stennett-Pit 23.8	Johnstone-Phi 8.9	Sutton-LA 21	Candelaria-Pit .696	Koosman-NY 17
Taveras-Pit 58	Taveras-Pit 8.9	Schmidt-Phi 18.1	Winfield-SD 7.6	Koosman-NY 21	Sutton-LA .677	Matlack-NY 16
Cedeno-Hou 58	Cedeno-Hou 7.5	Foli-Mon 16.9	Cruz-Hou 7.1	Richard-Hou 20	Koosman-NY .677	Sutton-LA 15
Brock-StL 56	Brock-StL 5.7	Concepcion-Cin 16.8	Wynn-Atl 7.1	Carlton-Phi 20	Rooker-Pit .652	Richard-Hou 14

Strikeouts	Fewest BB/Game	Games	Saves	Base Runners/9	Adjusted Relief Runs	Relief Ranking
Seaver-NY 235	Nolan-Cin 1.02	Murray-Mon 81	Eastwick-Cin 26	Reed-Phi 8.58	Hough-LA 17.2	Eastwick-Cin 29.9
Richard-Hou 214	Kaat-Phi 1.27	Metzger-SD 77	Lockwood-NY 19	Lockwood-NY 9.35	Eastwick-Cin 15.9	Hough-LA 26.7
Koosman-NY 200	Jones-SD 1.43	Hough-LA 77	Forsch-Hou 19	Jones-SD 9.36	Reed-Phi 15.2	Reed-Phi 19.8
Carlton-Phi 195	Matlack-NY 1.96	Eastwick-Cin 71	Hough-LA 18	Sutter-Chi 9.61	Moffitt-SF 13.1	Lavelle-SF 18.8
Niekro-Atl 173	Lonborg-Phi 2.03	Borbon-Cin 69	Metzger-SD 16	Candelaria-Pit 9.61	Forsch-Hou 12.8	Moffitt-SF 17.7

Innings Pitched	Opponents' Avg.	Opponents' OBP	Earned Run Average	Adjusted ERA	Adjusted Starter Runs	Pitcher Wins
Jones-SD 315.1	Richard-Hou .212	Jones-SD .265	Denny-StL 2.52	Denny-StL 140	Seaver-NY 25.3	**Hough-LA** 3.1
Richard-Hou 291.0	Seaver-NY .213	Candelaria-Pit .271	Rau-LA 2.57	Rau-LA 132	Montefusco-SF 23.8	**Eastwick-Cin** 2.9
Seaver-NY 271.0	Candelaria-Pit .216	Seaver-NY .272	Seaver-NY 2.59	Zachry-Cin 128	Rau-LA 22.5	**Rau-LA** 2.8
Niekro-Atl 270.2	Messersmith-Atl .219	Nolan-Cin .275	Koosman-NY 2.69	Montefusco-SF 128	Denny-StL 21.4	**Koosman-NY** 2.8
Sutton-LA 267.2	Falcone-StL .222	Koosman-NY .278	Zachry-Cin 2.74	Seaver-NY 127	Jones-SD 20.2	**Denny-StL** 2.4

Red Moon Rising

There were no pennant races in the NL's centennial season; the Phillies and Reds ran away with their respective divisions. This was the Phillies' first title of any kind in more than a quarter-century, and they did it convincingly. An extraordinary bullpen supported a lefty-loaded rotation, while Mike Schmidt won his third straight homer crown and a .300-hitting outfield (Jay Johnstone, Garry Maddox, and Greg Luzinski) chipped in. Philadelphia was also defensively strong where it counted.

Cincinnati easily outclassed the Dodgers again in the West as Joe Morgan was a repeat MVP. Pete Rose enjoyed another terrific season, and George Foster began to blossom into a fine power hitter. Walter Alston retired from second-place Los Angeles in September following twenty-three seasons as the franchise's manager.

At midseason of otherwise bad campaigns, the Cubs and Cardinals brought up rookies Bruce Sutter and Garry Templeton. Stolen bases continue to rise as homers fell to their lowest level since 1968. The Cardinals hit just 63 homers, fewest for an NL club since 1963. It was especially tough to homer in Busch Stadium, the Astrodome, or San Diego Stadium.

San Diego's finesse lefty Randy Jones won Cy Young honors, and Houston's hard-throwing starter J.R. Richard blossomed at age 26. Former Cub Billy Williams ended his career in Oakland as the A's dynasty ground to a halt.

The postseason was all Reds. Cincy swept the NLCS in three, and then blew out the Yankees in four to win back-to-back World Series crowns. Foster hit 2 homers in the playoffs, while Johnny Bench homered twice in Game 4 to clinch the World Series sweep.

The Pirates were hit hard after the season. Hurler Bob Moose was killed in an auto crash on October 9, while manager Danny Murtaugh, who had just retired after fifteen seasons, died less than two months later.

1976 American League

TEAM	W	L	T	PCT	GB	HW	HL	R	OR	PA	H	2B	3B	HR	BB	SO	HB	SH	AVG	OBP	SLG	OPS	AOPS	BR	ABR	PF	SB	CS	BSA	BSR
EAST																														
NY	97	62	0	.610		45	35	730	**575**	6156	1496	231	36	120	470	**616**	50	35	.269	.328	.389	717	**110**	65	**72**	99	163	65	71	13
BAL	88	74	0	.543	10.5	42	39	619	598	6091	1326	213	28	119	519	883	57	23	.243	.310	.358	668	101	-33	7	94	150	61	71	12
BOS	83	79	0	.512	15.5	46	35	716	660	6154	1448	257	53	**134**	500	832	55	29	.263	.324	**.402**	**726**	100	**81**	2	112	95	70	58	-4
CLE	81	78	0	.509	16	44	35	615	615	6029	1423	189	38	85	479	631	67	11	.263	.321	.359	680	100	-4	3	99	75	69	52	-8
DET	74	87	0	.460	24	36	44	609	709	6018	1401	207	38	101	450	730	46	31	.257	.315	.365	680	95	-9	-32	104	107	59	64	3
MIL	66	95	0	.410	32	36	45	570	655	6056	1326	170	38	88	511	909	78	23	.246	.311	.340	651	93	-60	-49	98	62	61	50	-8
WEST																														
KC	90	72	0	.556		49	32	713	611	6197	1490	**259**	**57**	65	484	650	71	31	.269	.327	.371	698	103	39	34	101	218	106	67	11
OAK	87	74	0	.540	2.5	**51**	30	686	598	6106	1319	208	33	113	**592**	818	58	**45**	.246	.323	.361	684	104	15	43	96	**341**	123	**73**	**32**
MIN	85	77	0	.525	5	44	37	**743**	704	6307	**1526**	222	51	81	550	714	**93**	41	**.274**	**.341**	.375	716	108	79	64	102	146	75	66	6
TEX	76	86	0	.469	14	39	42	616	652	6269	1390	213	26	80	568	809	72	29	.250	.321	.341	662	92	-31	-44	102	87	45	66	3
CAL	76	86	0	.469	14	38	43	550	631	6101	1265	210	23	63	534	812	92	42	.235	.306	.318	624	89	-104	-68	94	126	80	61	0
CHI	64	97	0	.398	25.5	35	45	586	745	6171	1410	209	46	73	471	739	79	34	.255	.314	.349	663	93	-38	-42	101	120	53	69	8
TOT	967					505	462	7753		73655	16820	2588	467	1122	6128	9143	374	818	.256	.320	.361	681					1690	867	66	68

TEAM	CG	SHO	GR	SV	IP	H	HR	BB	SO	BR/9	ERA	AERA	OAV	OOB	PR	APR	PF	OSB	OCS	FA	E	WPB	DP	FW	PW	BW	BSW	DIF
EAST																												
NY	62	15	156	37	1455.0	**1300**	97	448	674	**10.9**	**3.19**	107	**.241**	**.298**	**53**	37	97	**110**	67	.980	126	55	141	.9	3.9	**7.6**	.8	4.3
BAL	59	16	171	23	1468.2	1396	**80**	489	678	11.7	3.32	99	.255	.315	33	-8	93	127	65	**.982**	**118**	44	157	**1.5**	-.8	.7	.7	5.0
BOS	49	13	195	27	1458.0	1495	109	**409**	673	12.0	3.52	**111**	.267	.318	-1	**56**	111	115	60	.978	141	41	148	.2	**5.9**	.2	-1.0	-3.3
CLE	30	**17**	237	**46**	1432.0	1361	**80**	533	928	12.1	3.47	101	.255	.324	8	3	99	163	72	.980	121	51	159	1.2	.3	.3	-1.5	1.2
DET	55	12	164	20	1431.1	1426	101	550	738	12.6	3.87	96	.263	.331	-56	-24	105	140	71	.974	168	52	161	-1.4	-2.5	-3.4	-.3	1.2
MIL	45	10	202	27	1435.1	1406	99	567	677	12.6	3.64	96	.260	.331	-20	-24	99	144	69	.975	152	70	160	-.5	-2.5	-5.2	-1.5	-4.8
WEST																												
KC	41	12	**248**	35	1472.1	1356	83	493	735	11.5	3.21	109	.247	.309	51	48	100	146	66	.978	139	**38**	147	.3	5.1	3.6	.6	-.6
OAK	39	15	233	29	1459.1	1412	96	415	711	11.5	3.26	103	.255	.308	42	16	95	126	63	.977	144	51	130	-.0	1.7	4.6	**2.8**	-2.5
MIN	29	11	221	23	1459.0	1421	89	610	762	12.8	3.69	97	.259	.335	-29	-19	102	157	81	.973	172	72	**182**	-1.6	-2.0	6.8	.0	.8
TEX	63	15	196	15	1472.0	1464	106	461	773	12.0	3.45	104	.262	.320	10	21	102	120	82	.976	156	57	142	-.7	2.2	-4.7	-.3	-1.6
CAL	**64**	15	177	17	1477.1	1323	95	553	**992**	11.7	3.36	99	**.241**	.313	26	-6	95	191	**88**	.977	150	42	139	-.3	-.6	-7.2	-.6	3.8
CHI	54	10	166	22	1448.0	1460	87	600	802	13.0	4.25	84	.266	.338	-118	-109	101	151	82	.979	130	45	155	.7	-11.6	-4.5	.2	-1.5
TOT	590	161	2366	321	17468.1					12.0	3.52		.256	.320						.977	1717	618	1821					

Batter-Fielder Wins	Batting Average	On-Base Percentage	Slugging Average	On-Base Plus Slugging	Adjusted OPS	Adjusted Batter Runs
Grich-Bal 4.9	Brett-KC 333	McRae-KC 407	R.Jackson-Bal 502	McRae-KC 868	R.Jackson-Bal 158	McRae-KC..........39.6
Nettles-NY 4.3	McRae-KC 332	Hargrove-Tex 397	Rice-Bos..............482	Carew-Min 858	McRae-KC............154	Carew-Min..........38.0
Brett-KC 4.1	Carew-Min 331	Carew-Min 395	Nettles-NY 475	R.Jackson-Bal 853	Tenace-Oak..........150	R.Jackson-Bal 35.5
Belanger-Bal 3.8	Bostock-Min 323	Staub-Det 386	Lynn-Bos 467	Brett-KC................839	Carew-Min 149	Brett-KC..............35.4
McRae-KC 3.7	LeFlore-Det...........316	Carty-Cle 379	Carew-Min 463	Lynn-Bos 835	Brett-KC................145	Carty-Cle............32.4

Runs	Hits	Doubles	Triples	Home Runs	Total Bases	Runs Batted In
White-NY.............104	Brett-KC................215	Otis-KC..........................40	Brett-KC..................14	Nettles-NY.............32	Brett-KC................298	L.May-Bal............109
Carew-Min.............97	Carew-Min............200	McRae-KC 34	Garner-Oak 12	R.Jackson-Bal 27	Chambliss-NY 283	Munson-NY 105
Rivers-NY 95	Chambliss-NY 188	Evans-Bos 34	Carew-Min 12	Bando-Oak 27	Rice-Bos 280	Yastrzemski-Bos..102
Brett-KC..................94	Munson-NY 186	Carty-Cle 34	Poquette-KC 10		Carew-Min 280	
	Rivers-NY 184	Brett-KC 34	Bostock-Min.............9		Nettles-NY 277	

Stolen Bases	Base Stealing Runs	Fielding Runs-Infield	Fielding Runs-Outfield	Wins	Winning Pct.	Complete Games
North-Oak 75	Campaneris-Oak ..7.7	Remy-Cal...................19.2	Beniquez-Tex 12.9	Palmer-Bal.............22	Campbell-Min 773	Fidrych-Det...........24
LeFlore-Det 58	Baylor-Oak 7.2	White-KC...................18.2	Hisle-Min 10.9	Tiant-Bos 21	Garland-Bal 741	Tanana-Cal............23
Campaneris-Oak 54	Rivers-NY 7.0	Nettles-NY 16.9	Lemon-Chi 7.5	Garland-Bal 20	Ellis-NY.................680	Palmer-Bal 23
Baylor-Oak.............52	North-Oak..............6.3	Kuiper-Cle 16.8	Evans-Bos 7.2		Fidrych-Det...........679	
Patek-KC 51	Patek-KC 6.0	Belanger-Bal 16.3	Lezcano-Mil 5.8			

Strikeouts	Fewest BB/Game	Games	Saves	Base Runners/9	Adjusted Relief Runs	Relief Ranking
Ryan-Cal 327	Bird-KC 1.41	Campbell-Min 78	Lyle-NY 23	Tanana-Cal..........9.18	Littell-KC.............17.4	Hiller-Det.............29.3
Tanana-Cal 261	Jenkins-Bos 1.85	Fingers-Oak 70	LaRoche-Cle 21	Gura-KC 9.77	Hiller-Det.............16.9	Fingers-Oak 28.6
Blyleven-Min-Tex ..219	Perry-Tex 1.87	Lindblad-Oak 65	Fingers-Oak............20	G.Jackson-Bal-NY9.81	Fingers-Oak 14.8	Littell-KC 24.1
Eckersley-Cle 200	Blue-Oak 1.90	Lyle-NY 64	Campbell-Min 20	Fidrych-Det..........9.81	LaRoche-Cle 14.3	Lyle-NY 21.5
Hunter-NY 173	Fidrych-Det..........1.91	LaRoche-Cle...................61	Littell-KC 16	Burgmeier-Min 9.83	Burgmeier-Min 14.2	Kern-Cle 20.9

Innings Pitched	Opponents' Avg.	Opponents' OBP	Earned Run Average	Adjusted ERA	Adjusted Starter Runs	Pitcher Wins
Palmer-Bal 315.0	Ryan-Cal...............195	Tanana-Cal 261	Fidrych-Det..........2.34	Fidrych-Det 159	Fidrych-Det..........35.8	**Fidrych-Det**........4.4
Hunter-NY..........298.2	Tanana-Cal...........203	Fidrych-Det 277	Blue-Oak 2.35	Blue-Oak 143	Blue-Oak 34.2	**Blue-Oak** 3.4
Blue-Oak 298.1	Eckersley-Cle 214	Palmer-Bal...................278	Tanana-Cal..........2.43	Tanana-Cal 137	Tanana-Cal..........30.9	**Tanana-Cal** 3.3
Blyleven-Min-Tex297.2	Palmer-Bal 224	Blue-Oak 279	Torrez-Oak 2.50	Torrez-Oak............134	Palmer-Bal 26.9	**Fingers-Oak** 3.2
Slaton-Mil 292.2	Brett-NY-Chi 233	Bird-KC 279	Palmer-Bal 2.51	Palmer-Bal............130	Tiant-Bos 24.8	**Hiller-Det**............3.2

New York State of Mind

Prior to the season, Oakland owner Charlie Finley traded Reggie Jackson and Ken Holtzman to Baltimore. During the year, he tried to sell Vida Blue, Rollie Fingers, and Joe Rudi, but Bowie Kuhn blocked the sales—thus forcing the stubborn Finley, unwilling to pay high salaries, to watch his players test free agency.

Free agency came at a time when the AL set a new attendance record, which invalidated the poormouth cries of many successful owners. Detroit's fortunes were temporarily improved by Mark "The Bird" Fidrych, whose baffling deliveries made him Rookie of the Year and one of the league's best attractions. Tigers attendance increased 38 percent and tickets for his starts were hard to find. But as the economics changed, more stars of the 1960s retired, including Hank Aaron, Bill Freehan, Tony Oliva, and Frank Robinson.

In renovated Yankee Stadium, East champ New York led the league in attendance for the first time since 1964, and did so the remainder of the decade. Thurman Munson was MVP and in-season acquisitions Holtzman, Grant Jackson, and Doyle Alexander bolstered the staff.

The three-time bridesmaid Royals won the West. George Brett won his first batting title, and Whitey Herzog's Royals used a line-drive and speed-based attack. But the real runners were the A's, who swiped an all-time record 341 bases, with eight players in double figures. Bill North, Bert Campaneris, and Don Baylor all topped 50. For all that, the team didn't score much and had just three solid pitchers.

Come-from-behind victories and seesawing leads defined the ALCS. In Game 5 at Yankee Stadium, John Mayberry's two-run homer put Kansas City in front, but New York rallied for a 6–3 lead. Brett's dramatic three-run homer tied the score in the eighth. Yankees first baseman Chris Chambliss ended the series with a homer in the last of the ninth. The momentum didn't carry, as the Yankees lost in four to the overpowering Reds, but the swagger was back.

Texas infielder Danny Thompson died of leukemia after the season.

1977 National League

TEAM	W	L	T	PCT	GB	HW	HL	R	OR	PA	H	2B	3B	HR	BB	SO	HB	SH	AVG	OBP	SLG	OPS	AOPS	BR	ABR	PF	SB	CS	BSA	BSR
EAST																														
PHI	101	61	0	.623		**60**	21	**847**	668	6290	1548	266	56	186	573	806	59	38	**.279**	**.346**	**.448**	**794**	**113**	**145**	**109**	104	135	68	67	6
PIT	96	66	0	.593	5	58	23	734	665	6262	**1550**	**278**	57	133	474	878	49	34	.274	.331	.413	744	101	36	16	103	**260**	120	68	15
STL	83	79	0	.512	18	52	31	737	688	6136	1490	252	56	96	489	823	66	25	.270	.330	.388	718	100	-14	-1	98	134	112	54	-10
CHI	81	81	0	.500	20	46	35	692	739	6286	1489	271	37	111	534	**796**	69	27	.266	.330	.387	717	88	-10	-81	111	64	45	59	-2
MON	75	87	0	.463	26	38	43	665	736	6282	1474	294	50	138	478	877	69	21	.260	.318	.402	720	101	-20	1	97	88	50	64	2
NY	64	98	0	.395	37	35	44	587	663	6069	1319	227	30	88	529	887	63	30	.244	.313	.346	659	86	-126	-98	95	98	81	55	-7
WEST																														
LA	98	64	0	.605		51	30	769	**582**	6327	1484	223	28	**191**	588	896	**83**	23	.266	.336	.418	754	108	58	62	100	114	62	65	3
CIN	88	74	0	.543	10	48	33	802	725	6261	1513	269	42	181	**600**	911	62	25	.274	.345	.436	781	112	118	103	102	170	64	**73**	15
HOU	81	81	0	.500	17	46	35	680	650	6200	1405	263	**60**	114	515	839	76	**40**	.254	.320	.385	705	103	-42	23	91	187	72	72	**16**
SF	75	87	0	.463	23	38	43	673	711	6215	1392	227	41	134	568	842	78	21	.253	.323	.383	706	94	-37	-34	100	90	59	60	-1
SD	69	93	0	.426	29	35	46	692	834	6353	1397	245	49	120	602	1057	90	29	.249	.324	.375	699	104	-49	30	90	133	57	70	9
ATL	61	101	0	.377	37	40	41	678	895	6205	1404	218	20	139	537	876	**83**	17	.254	.320	.376	696	82	-60	-129	112	82	53	61	-1
TOT	972					547	425	8556		74886	17465	3033	526	1631	6487	10488	330	847	.262	.328	.396	724					1555	843	65	47

TEAM	CG	SHO	GR	SV	IP	H	HR	BB	SO	BR/9	ERA	AERA	OAV	OOB	PR	APR	PF	OSB	OCS	FA	E	WPB	DP	FW	PW	BW	BSW	DIF
EAST																												
PHI	31	7	246	**47**	1455.2	1451	134	482	856	12.1	3.71	108	.263	.323	32	46	102	119	62	.981	120	48	168	1.3	4.7	**11.0**	.2	2.8
PIT	25	**15**	278	39	1481.2	1406	149	485	890	11.6	3.61	110	.252	.311	50	61	102	102	63	.977	145	57	137	-.0	6.2	1.6	1.1	6.2
STL	26	10	305	31	1446.0	1420	139	532	768	12.3	3.81	101	.260	.326	16	6	98	117	62	.978	139	53	**174**	.3	.6	-.1	-1.4	2.6
CHI	16	10	319	44	1468.0	1500	128	489	**942**	12.3	4.01	109	.266	.325	-16	55	112	134	85	.977	153	63	147	-.5	5.6	-8.2	-.6	3.7
MON	31	11	307	33	1481.0	1426	135	579	856	12.3	4.01	95	.255	.325	-17	-34	97	135	63	.980	129	62	128	.8	-3.4	.1	-.2	-3.3
NY	27	12	248	28	1433.2	**1378**	118	490	911	11.9	3.77	99	.254	.317	22	-6	96	127	70	.978	134	**36**	132	.5	-.6	-9.9	-1.1	-5.9
WEST																												
LA	34	13	238	39	1475.1	1393	119	**438**	930	**11.3**	**3.22**	**119**	**.251**	**.308**	**113**	**101**	98	108	59	.981	124	48	160	1.1	**10.2**	6.3	-.0	-.5
CIN	33	12	261	32	1437.1	1469	156	544	868	12.8	4.21	93	.267	.334	-49	-45	101	**87**	54	**.984**	**95**	61	154	**2.7**	-4.6	10.4	1.1	-2.7
HOU	**37**	11	234	28	1465.2	1384	**110**	545	871	12.0	3.54	101	**.251**	.319	61	5	91	143	80	.978	142	70	136	.0	.5	2.3	**1.2**	-4.1
SF	27	10	312	33	1459.0	1501	114	529	854	12.7	3.75	104	.267	.331	26	26	100	158	75	.972	179	43	136	-2.0	2.6	-3.4	-.5	-2.7
SD	6	5	**382**	44	1466.1	1556	160	673	827	13.8	4.43	80	.276	.353	-85	-161	91	120	**87**	.971	189	67	142	-2.5	-16.3	3.0	.5	3.3
ATL	28	5	327	31	1445.1	1581	169	701	915	14.5	4.85	92	.279	.360	-151	-57	114	205	83	.972	175	98	127	-1.7	-5.8	-13.1	-.5	1.1
TOT	321	121	3457	429	17515.0					12.5	3.91		.262	.328						.977	1724	706	1741					

Batter-Fielder Wins	Batting Average	On-Base Percentage	Slugging Average	On-Base Plus Slugging	Adjusted OPS	Adjusted Batter Runs
Schmidt-Phi 6.5	Parker-Pit 338	Smith-LA 427	Foster-Cin 631	Foster-Cin 1013	Smith-LA 168	Foster-Cin 54.2
Foster-Cin 5.9	Templeton-StL 322	Morgan-Cin 417	Luzinski-Phi 594	Smith-LA 1003	Foster-Cin 165	Smith-LA 52.4
Parker-Pit 5.1	Foster-Cin 320	Tenace-SD 415	Smith-LA 576	Luzinski-Phi 988	Luzinski-Phi 155	Luzinski-Phi 44.7
Morgan-Cin 4.6	Griffey-Cin 318	Simmons-StL 408	Schmidt-Phi 574	Schmidt-Phi 967	Schmidt-Phi 151	Schmidt-Phi 41.3
Hendrick-SD 4.2	Simmons-StL 318	Parker-Pit 397	Bench-Cin 540	Parker-Pit 927	Hendrick-SD 148	Parker-Pit 39.8

Runs	Hits	Doubles	Triples	Home Runs	Total Bases	Runs Batted In
Foster-Cin 124	Parker-Pit 215	Parker-Pit 44	Templeton-StL 18	Foster-Cin 52	Foster-Cin 388	Foster-Cin 149
Griffey-Cin 117	Rose-Cin 204	Cash-Mon 42	Schmidt-Phi 11	Burroughs-Atl 41	Parker-Pit 338	Luzinski-Phi 130
Schmidt-Phi 114	Templeton-StL 200	Hernandez-StL 41	Richards-SD 11	Luzinski-Phi 39	Luzinski-Phi 329	Garvey-LA 115
Morgan-Cin 113	Foster-Cin 197	Cromartie-Mon 41	Almon-SD 11	Schmidt-Phi 38	Garvey-LA 322	Burroughs-Atl 114
Parker-Pit..............107	Garvey-LA 192			Garvey-LA 33	Schmidt-Phi 312	

Stolen Bases	Base Stealing Runs	Fielding Runs-Infield	Fielding Runs-Outfield	Wins	Winning Pct.	Complete Games
Taveras-Pit.............70	Taveras-Pit 9.1	DeJesus-Chi 45.5	Parker-Pit 23.2	Carlton-Phi 23	Candelaria-Pit.......800	Niekro-Atl 20
Cedeno-Hou 61	Cedeno-Hou 8.5	Trillo-Chi.....................30.1	Winfield-SD 11.6	Seaver-NY-Cin........21	Seaver-NY-Cin 778	Seaver-NY-Cin 19
Richards-SD 56	Richards-SD 8.1	Schmidt-Phi 26.6	Foster-Cin.............10.9		Christenson-Phi ...760	Rogers-Mon 17
Moreno-Pit..............53	Morgan-Cin............7.3	Tyson-StL 23.9	Hendrick-SD 7.9		John-LA 741	Carlton-Phi 17
Morgan-Cin 49	Lopes-LA 6.1	Russell-LA 16.7	Thomas-SF............7.7		Forsch-StL 741	Richard-Hou 13

Strikeouts	Fewest BB/Game	Games	Saves	Base Runners/9	Adjusted Relief Runs	Relief Ranking
Niekro-Atl..............262	Candelaria-Pit......1.95	Fingers-SD 78	Fingers-SD 35	Sosa-LA 7.77	Gossage-Pit 34.2	Gossage-Pit 60.0
Richard-Hou 214	John-LA 2.04	Tomlin-SD 76	Sutter-Chi 31	Sutter-Chi 7.80	Sutter-Chi 31.3	Sutter-Chi 44.6
Rogers-Mon..........206	Rau-LA 2.08	Spillner-SD 76	Gossage-Pit...........26	Gossage-Pit 8.73	Lavelle-SF 23.0	Lavelle-SF 32.4
Carlton-Phi 198	Barr-SF 2.15	Metzger-SD-StL 75	Hough-LA 22	Seaver-NY-Cin 9.13	Garber-Phi 18.6	Garber-Phi..........29.6
Seaver-NY-Cin......196	Lemongello-Hou ..2.18			Garber-Phi 9.32	Reed-Phi.............17.5	Reed-Phi 19.5

Innings Pitched	Opponents' Avg.	Opponents' OBP	Earned Run Average	Adjusted ERA	Adjusted Starter Runs	Pitcher Wins
Niekro-Atl 330.1	Seaver-NY-Cin 209	Seaver-NY-Cin 258	Candelaria-Pit......2.34	Candelaria-Pit 170	Candelaria-Pit......42.8	**Gossage-Pit** 6.4
Rogers-Mon 301.2	Richard-Hou 218	Candelaria-Pit 274	Seaver-NY-Cin 2.58	R.Reuschel-Chi 158	R.Reuschel-Chi ..41.7	**Carlton-Phi** 5.5
Carlton-Phi 283.0	Carlton-Phi 223	Hooton-LA 279	Hooton-LA 2.62	Carlton-Phi 152	Seaver-NY-Cin ...39.8	**R.Reuschel-Chi** 5.3
Richard-Hou 267.0	Hooton-LA 225	Carlton-Phi...................286	Carlton-Phi 2.64	Seaver-NY-Cin......150	Carlton-Phi 39.0	**Candelaria-Pit** ..4.9
Seaver-NY-Cin ..261.1	Koosman-NY 232	Sutton-LA.....................289	John-LA 2.78	Hooton-LA 146	Hooton-LA 29.6	**Sutter-Chi** 4.7

Runs, Runs, Runs

Scoring leapt to its highest since 1970, and although the Astros and Cardinals both pushed their outfield fences out, homers rose 27 percent. More homers were hit in every NL park except Wrigley Field. Stolen bases also rose again, reaching their highest per-game total since 1919.

Larry Dierker, Al Downing, Doug Rader, Ray Sadecki, Joe Torre, and Jimmy Wynn hung 'em up. All had been reduced to part-time status. And with great teams came terrible ones: the last-place Mets, managed by Torre, and Braves, managed for one night by maverick owner Ted Turner, both finished 37 games out of first.

The Expos moved from cozy Jarry Park to Olympic Stadium, a smaller field but with far more seats; attendance more than doubled for Montreal, which showed signs of life under Dick Williams. Outfielder Andre Dawson was Rookie of the Year.

Lou Brock shattered Ty Cobb's career steals mark, but the champ speed demons were the second-place Pirates, whose 260 swipes were the highest NL total since 1913. Despite the thievery, the Bucs scored 113 runs fewer than the division champion Phillies, who boasted seven players with double-figure home runs; Mike Schmidt (who became the first $500,000-a-year player) and Greg Luzinski combined for 77. Steve Carlton won his second Cy Young. Chicago led until August, but crumbled when Bruce Sutter went down with a shoulder injury and Philadelphia won 19 of 20.

While MVP George Foster of Cincinnati was spectacular, the Dodgers were better. Under rookie manager Tommy Lasorda, Los Angeles led by 11_ on May 15, and the Reds never got much closer. Steve Garvey, Ron Cey, Reggie Smith, and Dusty Baker each hit 30 homers, and the superb infield of Garvey, Davey Lopes, Bill Russell, and Cey could not be matched.

While the Dodgers convincingly beat the Phillies in a four-game NLCS, the World Series went to the Yankees in six despite Smith's 3 homers. A different Reggie hit 3 homers in Game 6.

1977 American League

TEAM	W	L	T	PCT	GB	HW	HL	R	OR	PA	H	2B	3B	HR	BB	SO	HB	SH	AVG	OBP	SLG	OPS	AOPS	BR	ABR	PF	SB	CS	BSA	BSR
EAST																														
NY	100	62	0	.617		**55**	26	831	**651**	6260	1576	267	47	184	533	681	46	28	.281	.344	.444	788	**114**	106	**115**	99	93	57	62	1
BAL	97	64	0	.602	2.5	54	27	719	653	6173	1433	231	25	148	560	945	48	24	.261	.329	.393	722	102	-22	25	94	90	51	64	2
BOS	97	64	0	.602	2.5	51	29	859	712	6184	1551	258	56	**213**	528	905	45	42	.281	.345	**.465**	**810**	106	**145**	53	112	66	47	58	-2
DET	74	88	0	.457	26	39	42	714	751	6177	1480	228	45	166	452	764	45	20	.264	.318	.410	728	92	-28	-63	105	60	46	57	-3
CLE	71	90	0	.441	28.5	37	44	676	739	6204	1476	221	46	100	531	688	94	34	.269	.334	.380	714	97	-32	-9	97	87	87	50	-11
MIL	67	95	0	.414	33	37	44	639	765	6087	1425	255	46	125	443	862	60	22	.258	.314	.389	703	90	-74	-73	100	85	67	56	-5
TOR	54	107	0	.335	45.5	25	55	605	822	6055	1367	230	41	100	499	819	81	23	.252	.316	.365	681	84	-107	-115	101	65	55	54	-5
WEST																														
KC	102	60	0	.630		**55**	26	822	**651**	6268	1549	**299**	**77**	146	522	687	49	**45**	.277	.340	.436	776	109	84	77	101	**170**	87	**66**	**7**
TEX	94	68	0	.580	8	44	37	767	657	6342	1497	265	39	135	**596**	904	**116**	39	.270	.342	.405	747	102	38	30	101	154	85	64	4
CHI	90	72	0	.556	12	48	33	844	771	6322	1568	254	52	192	559	**666**	33	34	.278	.344	.444	788	113	108	110	100	42	44	49	-6
MIN	84	77	0	.522	17.5	48	32	**867**	776	6382	**1588**	273	60	123	563	754	81	43	**.282**	**.348**	.417	765	109	73	86	99	105	65	62	0
CAL	74	88	0	.457	28	39	42	675	695	6113	1380	233	40	131	542	880	74	36	.255	.324	.386	710	97	-47	-19	96	159	89	64	4
SEA	64	98	0	.395	38	29	52	624	855	6044	1398	218	33	133	426	769	81	35	.256	.312	.381	693	89	-94	-88	99	110	67	62	1
OAK	63	98	0	.391	38.5	35	46	605	749	6020	1284	176	37	117	516	910	64	36	.240	.308	.352	660	80	-149	-140	99	176	89	**66**	8
TOT	1131					596	535	10247		86631	20572	3408	644	2013	7270	11234	461	917	.266	.330	.405	735					1462	936	61	-6

TEAM	CG	SHO	GR	SV	IP	H	HR	BB	SO	BR/9	ERA	AERA	OAV	OOB	PR	APR	PF	OSB	OCS	FA	E	WPB	DP	FW	PW	BW	BSW	DIF
EAST																												
NY	52	16	154	34	1449.1	1395	139	486	758	11.8	3.61	109	.254	**.315**	73	55	97	89	60	.979	132	52	151	.6	5.5	**11.4**	.1	1.4
BAL	**65**	11	169	23	1451.0	1414	124	494	737	12.0	3.74	101	.260	.322	51	9	93	77	72	**.983**	**106**	37	**189**	**2.0**	.9	2.5	.2	10.9
BOS	40	13	209	40	1428.0	1555	158	**378**	758	12.3	4.11	109	.278	.325	-8	54	111	**69**	54	.978	133	**19**	162	.5	5.4	5.3	-.2	5.5
DET	44	3	198	23	1457.0	1526	162	470	784	12.5	4.13	104	.271	.327	-11	24	106	90	69	.978	142	43	153	.0	2.4	-6.3	-.3	-2.9
CLE	45	8	230	30	1452.1	1441	136	550	876	12.5	4.10	96	.261	.329	-6	-26	97	158	64	.979	130	55	145	.7	-2.6	-.9	-1.1	-5.6
MIL	38	6	215	25	1431.0	1461	136	566	719	13.0	4.32	94	.268	.337	-42	-40	100	105	59	.978	139	61	165	.2	-4.0	-7.3	-.5	-2.5
TOR	40	3	187	20	1428.1	1538	152	623	771	13.7	4.57	92	.278	.350	-81	-57	103	85	75	.974	164	69	133	-1.2	-5.7	-11.4	-.5	-7.7
WEST																												
KC	41	15	219	**42**	1460.2	**1377**	**110**	499	850	11.8	**3.52**	**115**	**.251**	**.315**	**88**	**84**	99	84	51	.978	137	69	145	.3	**8.3**	7.6	.7	3.9
TEX	49	**17**	200	31	1472.1	1412	134	471	864	**11.7**	3.56	114	.255	**.315**	81	**84**	101	**69**	60	.982	117	49	156	1.5	**8.3**	3.0	.4	-.2
CHI	34	3	221	40	1444.2	1557	136	516	842	13.2	4.25	96	.277	.339	-31	-27	101	130	77	.974	159	50	125	-.9	-2.7	10.9	-.6	2.2
MIN	35	4	242	25	1442.0	1546	151	507	737	13.0	4.36	91	.278	.340	-48	-61	98	107	67	.978	143	58	184	-.0	-6.1	8.5	.0	1.0
CAL	53	13	185	26	1437.2	1383	136	572	**965**	12.5	3.72	105	.256	.330	54	32	96	129	78	.976	147	61	137	-.2	3.2	-1.9	.4	-8.5
SEA	18	1	**280**	31	1433.0	1508	194	578	785	13.5	4.83	85	.272	.344	-123	-113	101	146	60	.976	147	64	162	-.2	-11.2	-8.7	.1	3.1
OAK	32	4	249	26	1436.2	1459	145	560	788	12.8	4.04	100	.265	.333	3	-3	99	123	**91**	.970	190	67	136	-2.7	-.3	-13.9	**.8**	-1.4
TOT	586	117	2958	416	20224.0					12.6	4.06		.266	.330						.977	1986	754	2143					

Batter-Fielder Wins
Carew-Min 6.6
Singleton-Bal 4.7
Brett-KC 4.6
Fisk-Bos 4.6
Page-Oak 4.5

Batting Average
Carew-Min .... .388
Bostock-Min .... .336
Singleton-Bal .... .328
Rivers-NY .... .326
LeFlore-Det .... .325

On-Base Percentage
Carew-Min .... .449
Singleton-Bal .... .438
Hargrove-Tex .... .420
Page-Oak .... .405
Fisk-Bos .... .402

Slugging Average
Rice-Bos .... .593
Carew-Min .... .570
Jackson-NY .... .550
Hisle-Min .... .533
Brett-KC .... .532

On-Base Plus Slugging
Carew-Min 1019
Rice-Bos 969
Singleton-Bal 945
Page-Oak 926
Jackson-NY 925

Adjusted OPS
Carew-Min 179
Singleton-Bal 168
Page-Oak 153
Jackson-NY 151
Thornton-Cle 149

Adjusted Batter Runs
Carew-Min 70.0
Singleton-Bal 58.6
Page-Oak 40.0
Jackson-NY 38.7
Hargrove-Tex 38.3

Runs
Carew-Min 128
Fisk-Bos 106
Brett-KC 105

Hits
Carew-Min 239
LeFlore-Det 212
Rice-Bos 206
Bostock-Min 199
Burleson-Bos 194

Doubles
McRae-KC 54
Jackson-NY 39
Lemon-Chi 38
Carew-Min 38

Triples
Carew-Min 16
Rice-Bos 15
Cowens-KC 14
Brett-KC 13
Bostock-Min 12

Home Runs
Rice-Bos 39
Nettles-NY 37
Bonds-Cal 37
Scott-Bos 33
Jackson-NY 32

Total Bases
Rice-Bos 382
Carew-Min 351
McRae-KC 330
Cowens-KC 318
LeFlore-Det 310

Runs Batted In
Hisle-Min 119
Bonds-Cal 115
Rice-Bos 114
Hobson-Bos 112
Cowens-KC 112

Stolen Bases
Patek-KC 53
Page-Oak 42
Remy-Cal 41
Bonds-Cal 41
LeFlore-Det 39

Base Stealing Runs
Page-Oak 7.5
Patek-KC 7.1
Harrah-Tex 4.2
White-KC 3.3
Remy-Cal 3.1

Fielding Runs-Infield
Campaneris-Tex 26.1
Burleson-Bos 20.1
Smalley-Min 19.7
Belanger-Bal 18.9
Brett-KC 18.0

Fielding Runs-Outfield
Lemon-Chi 23.1
Yastrzemski-Bos 9.7
R.Jones-Sea 9.4
Armas-Oak 8.8
Lezcano-Mil 8.6

Wins
Palmer-Bal 20
Leonard-KC 20
Goltz-Min 20
Ryan-Cal 19

Winning Pct.
Splittorff-KC .... .727
T.Johnson-Min ..... .696
Guidry-NY .... .696
Rozema-Det .... .682

Complete Games
Ryan-Cal 22
Palmer-Bal 22
Leonard-KC 21
Garland-Cle 21
Tanana-Cal 20

Strikeouts
Ryan-Cal 341
Leonard-KC 244
Tanana-Cal 205
Palmer-Bal 193
Eckersley-Cle 191

Fewest BB/Game
Rozema-Det 1.40
Jenkins-Bos 1.68
Hartzell-Cal 1.81
Eckersley-Cle 1.96
Cleveland-Bos 2.03

Games
Lyle-NY 72
T.Johnson-Min 71
Campbell-Bos 69
McClure-Mil 68
LaGrow-Chi 66

Saves
Campbell-Bos 31
Lyle-NY 26
LaGrow-Chi 25
Kern-Cle 18
LaRoche-Cle-Cal 17

Base Runners/9
Foucault-Det 9.81
Blyleven-Tex 9.86
Eckersley-Cle 10.01
Guidry-NY 10.21
Tanana-Cal 10.22

Adjusted Relief Runs
Lyle-NY 26.1
Campbell-Bos 22.5
LaGrow-Chi 17.1
Romo-Sea 16.2
Torrealba-Oak 16.0

Relief Ranking
Campbell-Bos 42.9
Lyle-NY 42.0
Romo-Sea 28.0
LaGrow-Chi 25.4
T.Johnson-Min 23.1

Innings Pitched
Palmer-Bal 319.0
Goltz-Min 303.0
Ryan-Cal 299.0
Leonard-KC 292.2
Garland-Cle 282.2

Opponents' Avg.
Ryan-Cal .... .193
Blyleven-Tex .... .214
Guidry-NY .... .224
Tanana-Cal .... .227
Leonard-KC .... .227

Opponents' OBP
Eckersley-Cle .... .276
Blyleven-Tex .... .278
Leonard-KC .... .283
Guidry-NY .... .283
Tanana-Cal .... .284

Earned Run Average
Tanana-Cal 2.54
Blyleven-Tex 2.72
Ryan-Cal 2.77
Guidry-NY 2.82
Palmer-Bal 2.91

Adjusted ERA
Tanana-Cal 155
Blyleven-Tex 150
Ryan-Cal 142
Guidry-NY 140
Rozema-Det 139

Adjusted Starter Runs
Tanana-Cal 41.7
Ryan-Cal 38.3
Palmer-Bal 36.7
Blyleven-Tex 35.1
Leonard-KC 30.7

Pitcher Wins
Campbell-Bos 4.5
Lyle-NY 4.3
Ryan-Cal 4.3
Tanana-Cal 4.1
Blyleven-Tex 3.7

Room for Two More

The AL expanded to 14 teams, adding Seattle and Toronto. Runs per team per game rose 13 percent to its highest rate since 1961—not so coincidentally, another expansion year. League attendance was up five million, and two AL teams—the Yankees and Red Sox—drew two million fans in the same year for the first time since 1949.

With free agents Reggie Jackson and Don Gullett, plus holdovers Graig Nettles, Thurman Munson, and Sparky Lyle (the first AL reliever to win a Cy Young), the Yankees leapt from third place in August to win the division. As Boog Powell and Brooks Robinson retired, Baltimore finished second. First baseman Eddie Murray was the league's top rookie, but the Birds' lineup was mediocre. Third-place Boston had an ordinary offense away from Fenway Park. Meanwhile, the awful Tigers debuted Alan Trammell, Lou Whitaker, Lance Parrish, and Jack Morris.

Bill Veeck's ramshackle White Sox led the West for much of the year, but slumped just as the other contenders turned hot. Texas won 14 straight, but Kansas City captured 17 in a row to take the division. The Royals had six players with double-digit homers, excellent defense, and a very deep bullpen. Rod Carew's .388 was the highest batting average since 1941. Nolan Ryan fanned 341 but walked 204, the most since Bob Feller in 1938. With their key players gone, Oakland finished last, below the expansion Mariners, and their attendance was the league's lowest since 1970.

The Yanks and Royals traded booming hits, and wins, in the first four ALCS games. The Royals led the decisive fifth contest at Kansas City, 3–1, after seven. A Yankees run in the eighth tightened the game, and in the ninth, New York scored three times off three pitchers (handing Sparky Lyle his second victory) to move to the World Series.

New York then took it to the Dodgers, winning in six games. Jackson hit 3 home runs in the deciding game, but just as important to the Yankees were pitchers Lyle, Mike Torrez, and Ron Guidry.

1978 National League

TEAM	W	L	T	PCT	GB	HW	HL	R	OR	PA	H	2B	3B	HR	BB	SO	HB	SH	AVG	OBP	SLG	OPS	AOPS	BR	ABR	PF	SB	CS	BSA	BSR
EAST																														
PHI	90	72	0	.556		54	28	708	586	6152	1404	248	32	133	552	866	61	**42**	.258	.328	.388	716	105	51	45	101	152	58	72	13
PIT	88	73	0	.547	1.5	**55**	26	684	637	6038	1390	239	**54**	115	480	874	64	**42**	.257	.320	.385	705	99	20	-8	105	**213**	90	70	15
CHI	79	83	0	.488	11	44	38	664	724	6258	**1461**	224	48	72	562	746	84	21	**.264**	.331	.361	692	89	10	-62	112	110	58	65	4
MON	76	86	0	.469	14	41	39	633	611	6063	1404	269	31	121	396	881	62	35	.254	.306	.379	685	98	-27	-20	99	80	42	66	3
STL	69	93	0	.426	21	37	44	600	657	5965	1351	263	44	79	420	**713**	55	22	.249	.303	.358	661	91	-67	-58	99	97	42	70	7
NY	66	96	0	.407	24	33	47	607	690	6132	1332	227	47	86	549	829	71	24	.245	.314	.352	666	95	-48	-26	96	100	77	56	-5
WEST																														
LA	95	67	0	.586		54	27	**727**	**573**	6225	1435	251	27	**149**	610	818	111	20	**.264**	**.338**	**.402**	**740**	**113**	**102**	**105**	100	137	52	72	12
CIN	92	69	0	.571	2.5	49	31	710	688	6192	1378	**270**	32	136	**636**	899	84	26	.256	.334	.393	727	109	80	80	100	137	58	70	10
SF	89	73	0	.549	6	50	31	613	594	6102	1331	240	41	117	554	814	**127**	17	.248	.318	.374	692	103	-1	25	96	87	54	62	0
SD	84	78	0	.519	11	50	31	591	598	6081	1349	208	42	75	536	848	114	32	.252	.321	.348	669	101	-38	13	92	152	70	68	9
HOU	74	88	0	.457	21	50	31	605	634	6034	1408	231	45	70	434	743	76	22	.258	.313	.355	668	101	-52	-5	93	178	59	**75**	**19**
ATL	69	93	0	.426	26	39	42	600	750	6066	1313	191	39	123	550	874	61	27	.244	.315	.363	678	85	-30	-92	111	90	65	58	-3
TOT	971					556	415	7742		73308	16556	2861	482	1276	6279	9905	330	970	.254	.320	.372	692					1533	725	68	84

TEAM	CG	SHO	GR	SV	IP	H	HR	BB	SO	BR/9	ERA	AERA	OAV	OOB	PR	APR	PF	OSB	OCS	FA	E	WPB	DP	FW	PW	BW	BSW	DIF
EAST																												
PHI	38	9	234	29	1436.1	1343	118	**393**	813	**11.0**	3.33	107	.251	**.303**	39	37	100	**91**	56	**.983**	**104**	**35**	156	**2.0**	3.9	4.8	.6	-2.3
PIT	30	13	272	44	1444.2	1366	103	499	880	11.8	3.41	108	.249	.313	26	44	104	138	47	.973	167	53	133	-1.4	4.7	-.8	.9	4.3
CHI	24	7	**327**	38	1455.1	1475	125	539	768	12.7	4.05	99	.265	.331	-77	-4	113	118	62	.978	144	62	154	-.2	-.4	-6.6	-.3	5.5
MON	42	13	267	32	1446.0	1332	117	572	740	12.0	3.42	103	.249	.323	24	16	99	108	61	.979	134	43	150	.4	1.7	-2.1	-.4	-4.5
STL	32	13	258	22	1437.2	**1300**	94	600	859	12.1	3.58	98	**.245**	.323	-1	-11	98	162	**78**	.978	136	72	155	.3	-1.2	-6.1	.0	-5.0
NY	21	7	270	26	1455.1	1447	114	531	775	12.4	3.87	90	.265	.330	-48	-64	98	111	69	.979	132	49	160	.5	-6.8	-2.8	-1.3	-4.7
WEST																												
LA	46	16	198	38	1440.1	1362	107	440	800	11.4	**3.12**	**112**	.250	.307	**73**	**63**	98	105	56	.978	140	45	138	.0	**6.7**	**11.1**	.5	-4.4
CIN	16	10	299	46	1448.1	1437	122	567	908	12.6	3.81	93	.261	.329	-38	-43	99	106	60	.978	134	53	120	.3	-4.5	8.5	.3	6.9
SF	42	**17**	239	29	1455.0	1377	84	453	840	11.5	3.30	104	.252	.309	44	24	96	159	54	.977	146	38	118	-.3	2.5	2.6	-.7	3.8
SD	21	10	265	**55**	1433.2	1385	**74**	483	744	11.8	3.28	101	.257	.317	47	8	93	102	65	.975	160	44	**171**	-1.0	.8	1.4	.2	1.6
HOU	**48**	**17**	218	23	1440.1	1328	86	578	**930**	12.1	3.63	91	.247	.320	-9	-56	93	167	59	.978	133	69	109	.4	-5.9	-.5	**1.3**	-2.3
ATL	29	12	293	32	1440.1	1404	132	624	848	12.9	4.08	99	.257	.335	-81	-5	113	166	57	.975	153	99	126	-.6	-.5	-9.7	-1.1	-.0
TOT	389	144	3140	414	17333.1					12.0	3.57		.254	.320						.978	1683	662	1690					

Batter-Fielder Wins	Batting Average	On-Base Percentage	Slugging Average	On-Base Plus Slugging	Adjusted OPS	Adjusted Batter Runs
Parker-Pit 4.5	Parker-Pit .334	Burroughs-Atl .432	Parker-Pit .585	Parker-Pit .979	Smith-LA 164	Parker-Pit 47.8
Lopes-LA 4.3	Garvey-LA .316	Parker-Pit .394	Smith-LA .559	Burroughs-Atl .961	Parker-Pit 163	Luzinski-Phi 41.6
Templeton-StL 4.3	Cruz-Hou .315	Tenace-SD .392	Foster-Cin .546	Smith-LA .942	Clark-SF 155	Clark-SF 41.2
Clark-SF 4.2	Madlock-SF .309	Luzinski-Phi .388	Clark-SF .537	Luzinski-Phi .914	Winfield-SD 153	Burroughs-Atl 40.2
Simmons-StL 4.1	Winfield-SD .308	Smith-LA .382	Burroughs-Atl .529	Foster-Cin .906	Luzinski-Phi 152	Winfield-SD 39.3

Runs	Hits	Doubles	Triples	Home Runs	Total Bases	Runs Batted In
DeJesus-Chi 104	Garvey-LA 202	Rose-Cin 51	Templeton-StL 13	Foster-Cin 40	Parker-Pit 340	Foster-Cin 120
Rose-Cin 103	Rose-Cin 198	Clark-SF 46	Richards-SD 12	Luzinski-Phi 35	Foster-Cin 330	Parker-Pit 117
Parker-Pit 102	Cabell-Hou 195	Simmons-StL 40	Parker-Pit 12	Parker-Pit 30	Garvey-LA 319	Garvey-LA 113
Foster-Cin 97	Parker-Pit 194	Parrish-Mon 39		Smith-LA 29	Clark-SF 318	Luzinski-Phi 101
Moreno-Pit 95	Bowa-Phi 192	Perez-Mon 38			Winfield-SD 293	Clark-SF 98

Stolen Bases	Base Stealing Runs	Fielding Runs-Infield	Fielding Runs-Outfield	Wins	Winning Pct.	Complete Games
Moreno-Pit 71	Lopes-LA 8.5	Templeton-StL 32.6	Cromartie-Mon 17.6	Perry-SD 21	Perry-SD .778	Niekro-Atl 22
Taveras-Pit 46	Moreno-Pit 7.9	Smith-SD 29.7	Valentine-Mon 10.6	Grimsley-Mon 20	Hooton-LA .655	Grimsley-Mon 19
Lopes-LA 45	McBride-Phi 5.1	Trillo-Chi 29.4	S.Henderson-NY 7.9	Niekro-Atl 19	Grimsley-Mon .645	Richard-Hou 16
DeJesus-Chi 41	Cruz-Hou 5.0	Russell-LA 21.4	Clark-SF 7.7	Hooton-LA 19	Blue-SF .643	Knepper-SF 16
Smith-SD 40	DeJesus-Chi 4.8	DeJesus-Chi 15.3	Youngblood-NY 6.9		John-LA .630	

Strikeouts	Fewest BB/Game	Games	Saves	Base Runners/9	Adjusted Relief Runs	Relief Ranking
Richard-Hou 303	Christenson-Phi 1.86	Tekulve-Pit 91	Fingers-SD 37	Garber-Phi-Atl 8.69	Garber-Phi-Atl 20.2	Bair-Cin 32.4
Niekro-Atl 248	Barr-SF 1.93	Littell-StL 72	Tekulve-Pit 31	Reed-Phi 9.52	Tekulve-Pit 18.6	Tekulve-Pit 27.6
Seaver-Cin 226	R.Reuschel-Chi 2.00	Moore-Chi 71	Bair-Cin 28	Fingers-SD 9.56	Bair-Cin 18.5	Garber-Phi-Atl 26.2
Blyleven-Pit 182	Halicki-SF 2.04	Moffitt-SF 70	Sutter-Chi 27	Welch-LA 9.62	Reed-Phi 15.2	Fingers-SD 22.1
Montefusco-SF 177	Sutton-LA 2.04	Bair-Cin 70	Garber-Phi-Atl 25	Swan-NY 9.72	D'Acquisto-SD 13.9	Forster-LA 20.3

Innings Pitched	Opponents' Avg.	Opponents' OBP	Earned Run Average	Adjusted ERA	Adjusted Starter Runs	Pitcher Wins
Niekro-Atl 334.1	Richard-Hou .196	Halicki-SF .270	Swan-NY 2.43	Swan-NY 144	Niekro-Atl 35.9	**Niekro-Atl** 4.6
Richard-Hou 275.1	Swan-NY .219	Swan-NY .275	Rogers-Mon 2.47	Rogers-Mon 143	Rogers-Mon 27.4	**Bair-Cin** 3.4
Grimsley-Mon 263.0	Halicki-SF .221	Hooton-LA .275	Vuckovich-StL 2.54	Niekro-Atl 141	Swan-NY 24.9	**Hooton-LA** 3.1
Perry-SD 260.2	Hooton-LA .226	Christenson-Phi .282	Knepper-SF 2.63	Vuckovich-StL 139	Hooton-LA 24.8	**Tekulve-Pit** 3.0
Knepper-SF 260.0	Seaver-Cin .227	D.Robinson-Pit .283	Hooton-LA 2.71	Knepper-SF 131	Knepper-SF 24.4	**Carlton-Phi** 3.0

Coming into Los Angeles

The Dodgers, who lost coach Jim Gilliam to cancer, became the first team in history to draw more than three million fans. While the AL surpassed the NL in overall attendance, thanks to the addition of two extra teams in 1977, the average Senior Circuit team drew approximately 200,000 more than their counterparts in the other league in '78.

The NL East compressed to a 24-game first-to-last gap, with the Phillies barely holding off the Pirates, who rose from fourth place with a torrid August stretch. Pittsburgh's Dave Parker was MVP, but the Bucs lacked the starting pitching or power to win. Amazingly, the Cubs had just one player—Dave Kingman—to hit more than 9 homers, ranking 11th in the league in long balls despite playing 81 games in the cozy confines of Wrigley Field.

Deep pitching and big power won the Dodgers another crown. Los Angeles didn't take the division lead until late August, but the Reds had just one top starter (Tom Seaver) and suffered poor performances from key regulars. Pete Rose did make the news, however, collecting his 3,000th hit and fashioning a 44-game hitting streak.

Last-place Atlanta showcased Rookie of the Year Bob Horner and catcher Dale Murphy, playing his first full season. Phil Niekro, at 39, was 19–18 for a team that won just 69 games. Another 39-year-old, San Diego's Gaylord Perry, became the first pitcher to win a Cy Young in each league, and teammate Rollie Fingers paced the NL in saves for the second straight season. The surprising Padres also broke in rookie Ozzie Smith at shortstop.

The NLCS was another breeze for the Dodgers, who hit Phillies starters very hard; only the fourth and final NLCS game was close. Once again, though, Los Angeles couldn't solve the Yankees in the World Series. After winning the first two, the Dodgers were outscored 28–8 as they dropped the last four.

1978 American League

TEAM	W	L	T	PCT	GB	HW	HL	R	OR	PA	H	2B	3B	HR	BB	SO	HB	SH	AVG	OBP	SLG	OPS	AOPS	BR	ABR	PF	SB	CS	BSA	BSR
EAST																														
NY	100	63	0	.613		55	26	735	**582**	6219	1489	228	38	125	505	695	37	42	.267	.329	.388	717	103	13	30	98	98	42	70	7
BOS	99	64	0	.607	1	**59**	23	796	657	6316	1493	270	46	172	582	835	65	24	.267	.336	.424	760	101	98	21	111	74	51	59.	-2
MIL	93	69	0	.574	6.5	54	27	**804**	650	6227	**1530**	265	38	**173**	520	805	**89**	32	**.276**	**.339**	**.432**	**771**	**115**	**116**	**114**	100	95	53	64	2
BAL	90	71	0	.559	9	51	30	659	633	6079	1397	248	19	154	552	864	41	22	.258	.326	.396	722	109	21	67	94	75	61	55	-5
DET	86	76	0	.531	13.5	47	34	714	653	6299	1520	218	34	129	563	695	57	31	.271	**.339**	.392	731	102	44	23	103	90	38	70	7
CLE	69	90	0	.434	29	42	36	639	694	6011	1400	223	45	106	488	698	92	26	.261	.323	.379	702	98	-21	-13	99	64	63	50	-8
TOR	59	102	0	.366	40	37	44	590	775	6015	1358	217	39	98	448	645	77	23	.250	.308	.359	667	85	-97	-108	102	28	52	35	-12
WEST																														
KC	92	70	0	.568		56	25	743	634	6129	1469	**305**	**59**	98	498	**644**	55	30	.268	.329	.399	728	101	37	19	103	**216**	84	**72**	**18**
TEX	87	75	0	.537	5	52	30	692	632	6141	1353	216	36	132	**624**	779	83	32	.253	.332	.381	713	100	12	11	100	196	91	68	11
CAL	87	75	0	.537	5	50	31	691	666	6206	1417	226	28	108	539	682	72	**67**	.259	.330	.370	700	100	-13	14	96	86	69	55	-5
MIN	73	89	0	.451	19	38	43	666	678	6323	1472	259	47	82	604	684	109	33	.267	**.339**	.375	714	99	23	10	102	99	56	64	2
CHI	71	90	0	.441	20.5	38	42	634	731	5955	1423	221	41	106	409	625	63	33	.264	.317	.379	696	94	-38	-44	101	83	68	55	-6
OAK	69	93	0	.426	23	38	42	532	690	5914	1304	200	31	100	433	800	108	25	.245	.303	.351	654	88	-121	-92	95	144	117	55	-9
SEA	56	104	0	.350	35	32	49	614	834	6023	1327	229	37	97	522	702	68	22	.248	.314	.359	673	90	-74	-70	99	123	47	**72**	11
TOT	1131					649	482	9509		85857	19952	3325	538	1680	7287	10153	442	1016	.261	.326	.385	711					1471	892	62	11

TEAM	CG	SHO	GR	SV	IP	H	HR	BB	SO	BR/9	ERA	AERA	OAV	OOB	PR	APR	PF	OSB	OCS	FA	E	WPB	DP	FW	PW	BW	BSW	DIF
EAST																												
NY	39	16	188	**36**	1460.2	**1321**	111	478	817	**11.3**	**3.18**	114	**.243**	**.306**	**95**	74	96	83	61	**.982**	113	54	134	1.5	7.6	3.1	.6	5.6
BOS	57	15	178	26	1472.2	1530	137	464	706	12.4	3.54	**116**	.270	.327	37	**86**	109	114	55	.977	146	**24**	171	-.3	**8.9**	2.2	-.3	7.1
MIL	62	**19**	173	24	1436.0	1442	109	**398**	577	11.8	3.65	103	.262	.313	17	17	100	**80**	46	.977	150	38	144	-.6	1.8	**11.7**	.1	-1.0
BAL	**65**	16	161	33	1429.0	1340	107	509	754	11.7	3.56	98	.251	.316	32	-12	93	81	68	**.982**	**110**	51	166	**1.6**	-1.2	6.9	-.6	2.8
DET	60	12	157	21	1455.2	1441	135	503	684	12.2	3.64	106	.263	.325	20	35	103	85	59	.981	118	58	**177**	1.2	3.6	2.4	.6	-2.8
CLE	36	6	214	28	1407.1	1397	**100**	568	739	12.7	3.97	94	.261	.332	-33	-37	99	129	59	.980	123	71	142	.8	-3.8	-1.3	-.9	-5.2
TOR	35	5	213	23	1429.1	1529	149	614	758	13.6	4.54	86	.279	.351	-123	-94	104	101	66	.979	131	63	163	.4	-9.7	-11.1	-1.3	.2
WEST																												
KC	53	14	208	33	1439.0	1350	108	478	657	11.6	3.44	111	.251	.313	52	60	102	90	52	.976	150	48	153	-.6	6.2	2.0	**1.8**	1.7
TEX	54	12	170	25	1456.1	1431	108	421	776	11.6	3.36	112	.259	.312	66	63	100	84	75	.976	153	47	140	-.8	6.5	1.1	1.0	-1.9
CAL	44	13	193	33	1455.2	1382	125	599	**892**	12.4	3.65	99	.253	.327	19	-7	96	154	**80**	.978	136	41	136	.2	-.7	1.4	-.6	5.7
MIN	48	9	176	26	1459.2	1468	102	520	703	12.5	3.69	103	.266	.330	11	20	102	91	76	.977	146	58	171	-.4	2.1	1.0	.1	-10.8
CHI	38	9	200	33	1409.1	1380	128	586	710	12.8	4.21	90	.259	.334	-71	-64	101	129	60	.977	139	51	130	-.0	-6.6	-4.5	-.7	2.4
OAK	26	11	**271**	29	1433.1	1401	106	582	750	12.6	3.62	100	.259	.330	22	3	97	110	**80**	.971	179	47	145	-2.3	.3	-9.5	-1.0	.5
SEA	28	4	249	20	1419.1	1540	155	567	630	13.6	4.67	81	.280	.348	-144	-135	101	140	55	.978	141	37	174	-.2	-13.9	-7.2	1.0	-3.7
TOT	645	161	2751	390	20163.1					12.4	3.76		.261	.326						.978	1935	688	2146					

Batter-Fielder Wins	Batting Average	On-Base Percentage	Slugging Average	On-Base Plus Slugging	Adjusted OPS	Adjusted Batter Runs
Smalley-Min 5.2	Carew-Min 333	Carew-Min 411	Rice-Bos 600	Rice-Bos 970	Singleton-Bal 154	Rice-Bos 44.2
DeCinces-Bal......4.3	Oliver-Tex 324	Singleton-Bal 409	Hisle-Mil 533	Hisle-Mil.................906	Rice-Bos 153	Singleton-Bal......41.9
Rice-Bos 4.1	Rice-Bos...............315	Hargrove-Tex 388	DeCinces-Bal 526	Otis-KC 905	Hisle-Mil................153	Thornton-Cle 37.7
Yount-Mil.............4.1	Piniella-NY 314	Randolph-NY 381	Otis-KC 525	Thornton-Cle 893	Thornton-Cle 152	Hisle-Mil 36.8
Otis-KC 3.9	Oglivie-Mil.............303	Lynn-Bos 380	Thornton-Cle 516	Roberts-Sea 879	DeCinces-Bal 152	Murray-Bal..........34.8

Runs	Hits	Doubles	Triples	Home Runs	Total Bases	Runs Batted In
LeFlore-Det 126	Rice-Bos 213	Brett-KC 45	Rice-Bos 15	Rice-Bos 46	Rice-Bos 406	Rice-Bos..............139
Rice-Bos 121	LeFlore-Det 198	McRae-KC 39	Ford-Min 10	Hisle-Mil.................34	Murray-Bal............293	Staub-Det 121
Baylor-Cal 103	Carew-Min............188	Fisk-Bos 39	Carew-Min 10	Baylor-Cal 34	Staub-Det 279	Hisle-Mil 115
Thornton-Cle 97	Munson-NY 183	DeCinces-Bal 37	Yount-Mil 9	Thornton-Cle 33	Baylor-Cal 279	Thornton-Cle 105
Hisle-Mil..................96	Staub-Det 175	Ford-Min 36	Garr-Chi.....................9	Thomas-Mil 32	Thompson-Det......278	

Stolen Bases	Base Stealing Runs	Fielding Runs-Infield	Fielding Runs-Outfield	Wins	Winning Pct.	Complete Games
LeFlore-Det 68	Cruz-Sea 9.5	Belanger-Bal 30.3	Bosetti-Tor 14.4	Guidry-NY 25	Guidry-NY.............893	Caldwell-Mil 23
Cruz-Sea 59	LeFlore-Det............9.4	Bell-Cle 26.5	Bailor-Tor 9.7	Caldwell-Mil 22	Stanley-Bos 882	Leonard-KC 20
Wills-Tex 52	Wills-Tex 6.5	Wills-Tex 21.7	R.Miller-Cal............8.0	Palmer-Bal..............21	Gura-KC 800	Palmer-Bal 19
Dilone-Oak 50	Wilson-KC...............5.9	Yount-Mil 20.6	Wilson-KC..............7.1	Leonard-KC 21	Eckersley-Bos.......714	Matlack-Tex 18
Wilson-KC 46	Randolph-NY 5.5	Whitaker-Det 20.0	Roberts-Sea 6.1		Caldwell-Mil 710	

Strikeouts	Fewest BB/Game	Games	Saves	Base Runners/9	Adjusted Relief Runs	Relief Ranking
Ryan-Cal 260	Jenkins-Tex..........1.48	Lacey-Oak 74	Gossage-NY 27	Guidry-NY............8.55	Gossage-NY........21.9	Gossage-NY 40.7
Guidry-NY 248	Sorensen-Mil 1.60	Heaverlo-Oak 69	LaRoche-Cal 25	Hiller-Det.............9.65	Stanley-Bos 20.6	Marshall-Min 29.5
Leonard-KC 183	Caldwell-Mil 1.66	Sosa-Oak 68	Stanhouse-Bal........24	Caldwell-Mil 9.79	Hiller-Det..............15.1	Stanley-Bos........25.5
Flanagan-Bal........167	Matlack-Tex 1.70	Gossage-NY 63	Marshall-Min 21	Jenkins-Tex.........9.83	Marshall-Min.......14.7	Hiller-Det 24.7
Eckersley-Bos 162	Rozema-Det 1.76		Hrabosky-KC 20	Gossage-NY.........9.92	Sosa-Oak 13.2	Hrabosky-KC.......18.9

Innings Pitched	Opponents' Avg.	Opponents' OBP	Earned Run Average	Adjusted ERA	Adjusted Starter Runs	Pitcher Wins
Palmer-Bal 296.0	Guidry-NY............193	Guidry-NY 249	Guidry-NY...........1.74	Guidry-NY 209	Guidry-NY............59.2	**Guidry-NY** 6.4
Leonard-KC 294.2	Ryan-Cal...............220	Caldwell-Mil 273	Matlack-Tex 2.27	Matlack-Tex 166	Caldwell-Mil 44.2	**Caldwell-Mil** 4.8
Caldwell-Mil 293.1	Palmer-Bal 227	Jenkins-Tex 278	Caldwell-Mil 2.36	Caldwell-Mil 160	Matlack-Tex 38.2	**Gossage-NY** 4.3
Flanagan-Bal 281.1	Gura-KC 229	Matlack-Tex 283	Palmer-Bal 2.46	Goltz-Min..............154	Palmer-Bal 35.4	**Matlack-Tex** 4.0
Sorensen-Mil 280.2	Tiant-Bos 234	Gura-KC.......................283	Goltz-Min 2.49	Palmer-Bal............143	Eckersley-Bos......32.0	**Palmer-Bal** 3.9

The Boston Massacre

Hoping to wipe out the past once and for all, Boston surged to a 14_-game lead by July 19. But when Bob Lemon replaced Billy Martin as New York's manager on July 24, the Yankees began winning. In just 12 days, they cut Boston's lead to 6_, where it remained until early September. With a four-game sweep of the Red Sox at Fenway (dubbed "The Boston Massacre"; no game was close), New York eventually plowed to a 3_-game advantage over the demoralized Sox.

Boston turned it on during the last week, though, winning their final eight to force a tie on the season's last day. In a classic one-game playoff, the Yankees overcame a 2–0 seventh-inning deficit on homers by Bucky Dent and Reggie Jackson to win, 5–4.

Ron Guidry—a remarkable 25–3 with a 1.74 ERA—won the Cy Young for the mostly veteran Yankees. Jim Rice took MVP honors for Boston. Lou Whitaker of Detroit was Rookie of the Year over impressive Milwaukee freshman Paul Molitor. Lost in all the Yankees-Red Sox hysteria was a 93-win season by the Brewers.

The slumping Royals and overachieving Angels were close heading into September, but Kansas City was great in the last month while California went 7–11 in a critical stretch. The Angels were devastated on September 24 when outfielder Lyman Bostock was murdered near Chicago. California finished tied with Texas for second. Jim Fregosi, the last original active Angel, retired as a player on June 1 to take California's managing job, and guided the club to a 62–54 mark.

The ALCS was tight; the last two games were one-run affairs, with the Yankees beating the Royals in four. The second straight Yankees-Dodgers World Series featured another New York comeback. After Los Angeles took the first two at home, New York took the next four. The clincher was a blowout of Don Sutton at Dodger Stadium. Dent and fill-in second baseman Brian Doyle both batted over .400; Reggie Jackson tormented the Dodgers with 2 more homers and drove in 8 runs.

1979 National League

TEAM	W	L	T	PCT	GB	HW	HL	R	OR	PA	H	2B	3B	HR	BB	SO	HB	SH	AVG	OBP	SLG	OPS	AOPS	BR	ABR	PF	SB	CS	BSA	BSR
EAST																														
PIT	98	64	1	.605		48	33	**775**	643	6330	1541	264	52	148	483	855	98	32	.272	.330	**.416**	**746**	104	**68**	34	105	180	66	**73**	**17**
MON	95	65	0	.594	2	**56**	25	701	**581**	6029	1445	273	42	143	432	890	67	27	.264	.319	.408	727	105	24	30	99	121	56	68	7
STL	86	76	1	.531	12	42	39	731	693	6347	**1594**	**279**	**63**	100	460	838	63	27	**.278**	.331	.401	732	104	46	40	101	116	69	63	1
PHI	84	78	1	.519	14	43	38	683	718	6219	1453	250	53	119	602	764	60	**37**	.266	**.340**	.396	736	104	65	42	103	128	76	63	2
CHI	80	82	0	.494	18	45	36	706	707	6182	1494	250	43	135	478	762	77	35	.269	.329	.403	732	96	40	-23	110	73	52	58	-2
NY	63	99	1	.389	35	28	53	593	706	6230	1399	255	41	74	498	817	66	35	.250	.313	.350	663	90	-90	-67	96	135	79	63	2
WEST																														
CIN	90	71	0	.559		48	32	731	644	6218	1445	266	31	132	**614**	902	62	19	.264	.338	.396	734	105	60	56	101	99	47	68	5
HOU	89	73	0	.549	1.5	52	29	583	582	6029	1382	224	52	49	461	**745**	**109**	22	.256	.315	.344	659	91	-96	-61	94	**190**	95	67	9
LA	79	83	0	.488	11.5	46	35	739	717	6188	1443	220	24	**183**	556	834	83	23	.263	.331	.412	743	**110**	63	**74**	99	106	46	70	7
SF	71	91	0	.438	19.5	38	43	672	751	6131	1328	192	36	125	580	925	89	20	.246	.319	.365	684	99	-47	-1	93	140	73	66	5
SD	68	93	0	.422	22	39	42	603	681	6168	1316	193	53	93	534	770	113	32	.242	.311	.348	659	91	-101	-64	94	100	58	63	2
ATL	66	94	0	.413	23.5	34	45	669	763	6035	1389	220	28	126	490	818	62	23	.256	.318	.377	695	88	-31	-75	107	98	50	66	4
TOT	971					519	450	8186		74106	17229	2886	518	1427	6188	9920	332	949	.261	.325	.385	709					1486	767	66	58

TEAM	CG	SHO	GR	SV	IP	H	HR	BB	SO	BR/9	ERA	AERA	OAV	OOB	PR	APR	PF	OSB	OCS	FA	E	WPB	DP	FW	PW	BW	BSW	DIF
EAST																												
PIT	24	7	326	**52**	1493.1	1424	125	504	904	11.8	3.41	114	.254	.316	53	74	104	108	52	.979	134	62	163	.4	7.6	3.5	**1.3**	4.2
MON	33	18	260	39	1447.1	1379	116	**450**	813	11.5	**3.14**	**117**	.253	.310	**95**	**86**	98	103	77	.979	131	**32**	123	.4	**8.9**	3.1	.2	2.4
STL	38	10	275	25	1486.2	1449	127	501	788	11.9	3.72	101	.258	.318	1	6	101	134	52	.980	132	61	166	.5	.6	4.1	-.4	.1
PHI	33	14	261	29	1441.1	1455	135	477	787	12.2	4.16	92	.266	.325	-69	-52	103	**95**	68	**.983**	**106**	41	148	**2.1**	-5.4	4.3	-.3	2.3
CHI	20	11	287	44	1446.2	1500	127	521	**933**	12.8	3.88	106	.270	.335	-24	34	110	123	67	.975	159	48	163	-1.1	3.5	-2.4	-.7	-.3
NY	16	10	**328**	36	1482.2	1486	120	607	819	12.9	3.84	95	.266	.338	-18	-35	98	136	**82**	.978	140	60	**168**	.0	-3.6	-6.9	-.3	-7.2
WEST																												
CIN	27	10	281	40	1440.1	1415	103	485	773	12.0	3.58	104	.260	.319	24	24	100	110	55	.980	124	39	152	.9	2.5	5.8	.0	.3
HOU	**55**	**19**	237	31	1447.2	**1278**	**90**	504	854	**11.2**	3.20	110	**.237**	**.304**	86	54	94	127	50	.978	138	73	146	.1	5.6	-6.3	.4	8.2
LA	30	6	240	34	1444.0	1425	101	555	811	12.5	3.83	95	.260	.329	-15	-32	97	118	63	.981	118	65	123	1.3	-3.3	**7.6**	.2	-7.9
SF	25	6	302	34	1436.0	1484	143	577	880	13.1	4.16	84	.269	.338	-69	-114	94	144	76	.974	163	67	138	-1.4	-11.8	-.1	.0	3.2
SD	29	7	279	25	1453.0	1438	108	513	779	12.2	3.69	96	.263	.326	6	-28	95	107	76	.978	141	35	154	-.1	-2.9	-6.6	-.3	-2.6
ATL	32	3	283	34	1407.2	1496	132	494	779	13.0	4.18	97	.272	.335	-70	-19	109	181	48	.970	183	70	139	-2.7	-2.0	-7.7	-.0	-1.5
TOT	362	121	3359	423	17426.2					12.3	3.73		.261	.325						.978	1669	653	1783					

Batter-Fielder Wins	Batting Average	On-Base Percentage	Slugging Average	On-Base Plus Slugging	Adjusted OPS	Adjusted Batter Runs
Schmidt-Phi 5.8	Hernandez-StL .344	Rose-Phi .418	Kingman-Chi .613	Kingman-Chi .956	Winfield-SD 167	Winfield-SD 55.6
Hernandez-StL 5.4	Rose-Phi .331	Hernandez-StL .417	Schmidt-Phi .564	Winfield-SD .953	Foster-Cin 155	Hernandez-StL 47.8
Winfield-SD 5.2	Knight-Cin .318	Tenace-SD .403	Foster-Cin .561	Schmidt-Phi .950	Schmidt-Phi 153	Schmidt-Phi 42.5
Templeton-StL 5.0	Garvey-LA .315	Mazzilli-NY .395	Winfield-SD .558	Foster-Cin .948	Hernandez-StL 152	Parker-Pit 35.4
Concepcion-Cin 4.5	Horner-Atl .314	Winfield-SD .395	Horner-Atl .552	Hernandez-StL .930	Parrish-Mon 146	Foster-Cin 33.5

Runs	Hits	Doubles	Triples	Home Runs	Total Bases	Runs Batted In
Hernandez-StL 116	Templeton-StL 211	Hernandez-StL 48	Templeton-StL 19	Kingman-Chi 48	Winfield-SD 333	Winfield-SD 118
Moreno-Pit 110	Hernandez-StL 210	Cromartie-Mon 46	Moreno-Pit 12	Schmidt-Phi 45	Parker-Pit 327	Kingman-Chi 115
Schmidt-Phi 109	Rose-Phi 208	Parker-Pit 45	McBride-Phi 12	Winfield-SD 34	Kingman-Chi 326	Schmidt-Phi 114
Parker-Pit 109	Garvey-LA 204	Reitz-StL 41	Dawson-Mon 12	Horner-Atl 33	Garvey-LA 322	Garvey-LA 110
Lopes-LA 109	Moreno-Pit 196	Rose-Phi 40		Stargell-Pit 32	Matthews-Atl 317	Hernandez-StL 105

Stolen Bases	Base Stealing Runs	Fielding Runs-Infield	Fielding Runs-Outfield	Wins	Winning Pct.	Complete Games
Moreno-Pit 77	Moreno-Pit 9.6	Royster-Atl 29.3	Maddox-Phi 17.2	Niekro-Atl 21	Seaver-Cin .727	Niekro-Atl 23
North-SF 58	Lopes-LA 8.3	Templeton-StL 24.2	McBride-Phi 13.1	Niekro-Hou 21	Niekro-Hou .656	Richard-Hou 19
Taveras-Pit-NY 44	Royster-Atl 4.9	Concepcion-Cin 20.1	Youngblood-NY 10.3	Richard-Hou 18	Martinez-StL .652	Rogers-Mon 13
Lopes-LA 44	Scott-Mon 4.4	Smith-SD 19.5	Cromartie-Mon 9.8	Reuschel-Chi 18	Sutcliffe-LA .630	Carlton-Phi 13
Scott-Mon 39	North-SF 4.4	Trillo-Phi 18.3	Geronimo-Cin 6.3	Carlton-Phi 18	Carlton-Phi .621	Hooton-LA 12

Strikeouts	Fewest BB/Game	Games	Saves	Base Runners/9	Adjusted Relief Runs	Relief Ranking
Richard-Hou 313	Forsch-Hou 1.77	Tekulve-Pit 94	Sutter-Chi 37	Sutter-Chi 8.79	Sutter-Chi 19.1	Sambito-Hou 37.5
Carlton-Phi 213	Candelaria-Pit 1.78	Romo-Pit 84	Tekulve-Pit 31	Fulgham-StL 9.37	Sambito-Hou 19.0	Sutter-Chi 34.8
Niekro-Atl 208	Hume-Cin 1.82	Jackson-Pit 72	Garber-Atl 25	Forsch-Hou 9.62	Sosa-Mon 18.9	Sosa-Mon 33.6
Blyleven-Pit 172	Lee-Mon 1.86	Lavelle-SF 70	Sambito-Hou 22	Richard-Hou 9.88	Hume-Cin 18.6	Tekulve-Pit 27.8
McGlothen-Chi 147	Swan-NY 2.04	Garber-Atl 68	Lavelle-SF 20	Minton-SF 9.94	Tekulve-Pit 16.5	Littell-StL 25.5

Innings Pitched	Opponents' Avg.	Opponents' OBP	Earned Run Average	Adjusted ERA	Adjusted Starter Runs	Pitcher Wins
Niekro-Atl 342.0	Richard-Hou .209	Forsch-Hou .273	Richard-Hou 2.71	Hume-Cin 135	Richard-Hou 28.8	**Sambito-Hou** 4.4
Richard-Hou 292.1	Carlton-Phi .219	Richard-Hou .276	Hume-Cin 2.76	Richard-Hou 130	Fulgham-StL 19.6	**Sutter-Chi** 3.8
Niekro-Hou 263.2	Schatzeder-Mon .225	Sutton-LA .288	Schatzeder-Mon 2.83	Schatzeder-Mon 130	Niekro-Atl 19.5	**Sosa-Mon** 3.5
Jones-SD 263.0	Niekro-Hou .228	Seaver-Cin .289	Hooton-LA 2.97	Hooton-LA 123	Rogers-Mon 18.2	**Tekulve-Pit** 3.0
Swan-NY 251.1	Andujar-Hou .233	Candelaria-Pit .290	Niekro-Hou 3.00	Rogers-Mon 122	Schatzeder-Mon 16.1	**Richard-Hou** 2.9

Family Affair

After ten years, Montreal began to grow up. Under Dick Williams, the young Expos featured catcher Gary Carter and one of baseball's best outfields: Warren Cromartie, Andrew Dawson, and Ellis Valentine. The Pirates—adopting Sister Sledge's dance anthem "We Are Family"—led the division most of the season. In a crazy two-week stretch, the Bucs defeated the Expos five of six and took the NL East by two games.

Aging Cincinnati squeezed out one last title, with George Foster and Tom Seaver the stars. Relievers Doug Bair and Tom Hume did yeoman work as the Reds surged ahead of the Astros in September. Houston contended on little ball, their 49 homers were the NL's fewest since 1946. Outfielders Jeffrey Leonard, Jose Cruz, and Terry Puhl provided line drives, steals, and on-base ability. Poor second-line pitching was Houston's downfall.

There were just two 20-game winners—ironically, brothers Phil (at 40!) and Joe Niekro. Dominating Cubs reliever Bruce Sutter won Cy Young honors. Houston's J.R. Richard led in ERA and strikeouts.

Cardinals left fielder Lou Brock sprinted into the sunset, ending his career shortly after collecting his 3,000th hit. The NL's superior leadoff man of the 1980s, Montreal's Tim Raines, debuted. Another rookie was skinny 22-year-old Mets reliever Jesse Orosco.

The Pirates eliminated the Reds in three straight, but the Orioles appeared to have the World Series in hand, winning three of the first four. However, Pittsburgh pitchers suddenly became stingy, permitting Baltimore but twice over the final three games. The Pirates got the key hits, including Willie Stargell's Series winner, a two-run homer in Game 7 at Baltimore. Kent Tekulve, who pitched 94 times during the season, racked up 3 saves for the "Fam-i-lee."

Stargell was elected league co-MVP with Cardinals first baseman and batting champion Keith Hernandez. Voting "Pops" as the league's best player in '79 was a sentimental selection; few would argue, though, about his choice as NLCS and World Series MVP. He batted .455 against Cincinnati and hit .400 with all 3 Pirates home runs against Baltimore.

1979 American League

TEAM	W	L	T	PCT	GB	HW	HL	R	OR	PA	H	2B	3B	HR	BB	SO	HB	SH	AVG	OBP	SLG	OPS	AOPS	BR	ABR	PF	SB	CS	BSA	BSR
EAST																														
BAL	102	57	0	.642		**55**	24	757	**582**	6106	1401	258	24	181	608	847	42	31	.261	.336	.419	755	106	28	58	96	99	49	67	5
MIL	95	66	0	.590	8	52	29	807	722	6227	1552	291	41	185	549	745	72	20	.280	.345	.448	793	112	98	98	100	100	53	65	3
BOS	91	69	0	.569	11.5	51	29	841	711	6184	1567	**310**	34	**194**	512	708	42	33	**.283**	.344	**.456**	**800**	108	**112**	67	106	60	43	58	-2
NY	89	71	0	.556	13.5	51	30	734	672	6061	1443	226	40	150	509	**590**	50	18	.266	.328	.406	734	99	-23	-7	98	65	46	59	-2
DET	85	76	0	.528	18	46	34	770	738	6080	1446	221	35	164	575	814	56	22	.269	.339	.415	754	99	23	-1	103	176	86	67	9
CLE	81	80	0	.503	22	47	34	760	805	6205	1388	206	29	138	**657**	786	70	**42**	.258	.340	.384	724	95	-20	-23	100	143	90	61	0
TOR	53	109	0	.327	50.5	32	49	613	862	6010	1362	253	34	95	448	663	65	36	.251	.311	.363	674	80	-143	-149	101	75	56	57	-3
WEST																														
CAL	88	74	0	.543		49	32	**866**	768	6311	1563	242	43	164	589	843	79	37	.282	**.351**	.429	780	**113**	84	**114**	97	100	53	65	3
KC	85	77	0	.525	3	46	35	851	816	6349	**1596**	286	**79**	116	528	675	57	35	.282	.343	.422	765	103	51	36	102	**207**	76	**73**	**19**
TEX	83	79	0	.512	5	44	37	750	698	6193	1549	252	26	140	461	607	78	33	.278	.334	.409	743	100	-1	8	99	79	51	61	0
MIN	82	80	0	.506	6	39	42	764	725	6296	1544	256	46	112	526	693	**142**	31	.278	.341	.402	743	96	7	-21	104	66	45	59	-1
CHI	73	87	0	.456	14	33	46	730	748	6056	1505	290	33	127	454	668	58	36	.275	.333	.410	743	99	-2	-2	100	97	62	61	0
SEA	67	95	0	.414	21	36	45	711	820	6202	1490	250	52	132	515	725	61	28	.269	.331	.404	735	95	-19	-31	102	126	52	71	10
OAK	54	108	0	.333	34	31	50	573	860	5971	1276	188	32	108	482	751	75	20	.239	.302	.346	648	78	-195	-165	95	104	69	60	-1
TOT	1128					612	516	10527		86251	20682	3529	548	2006	7413	10115	422	947	.270	.334	.408	743					1497	831	64	38

TEAM	CG	SHO	GR	SV	IP	H	HR	BB	SO	BR/9	ERA	AERA	OAV	OOB	PR	APR	PF	OSB	OCS	FA	E	WPB	DP	FW	PW	BW	BSW	DIF
EAST																												
BAL	52	**12**	167	30	1434.1	**1279**	133	467	786	**11.0**	**3.26**	**123**	**.241**	**.301**	**152**	**125**	95	88	58	.980	125	46	161	.8	**12.2**	5.7	.2	3.7
MIL	**61**	**12**	204	23	1439.2	1563	162	**381**	580	12.3	4.03	103	.279	.324	29	22	99	97	60	.980	127	58	153	.7	2.1	9.6	.0	2.0
BOS	47	11	198	29	1431.1	1487	133	463	731	12.5	4.03	110	.270	.328	29	58	105	116	41	.977	142	51	166	-.2	5.7	6.5	-.5	-.6
NY	43	10	217	37	1432.1	1446	123	455	731	12.0	3.83	106	.268	.323	61	39	97	83	55	**.981**	122	60	183	1.0	3.8	-.7	-.5	5.4
DET	25	5	221	37	1423.1	1429	167	547	802	12.8	4.27	101	.265	.335	-9	8	103	97	65	**.981**	**120**	75	184	**1.1**	.8	-.0	.6	2.1
CLE	28	7	241	32	1431.2	1502	138	570	781	13.2	4.57	93	.272	.339	-56	-50	101	146	47	.978	134	60	149	.3	-4.9	-2.2	-.3	7.5
TOR	44	7	195	11	1417.0	1537	165	594	613	13.8	4.82	90	.281	.353	-95	-73	103	85	56	.975	159	72	187	-1.0	-7.1	-14.5	-.6	-4.8
WEST																												
CAL	46	9	209	33	1436.0	1463	131	573	**820**	13.0	4.34	94	.267	.336	-19	-44	97	138	51	.978	135	65	172	.3	-4.3	**11.1**	.0	-.2
KC	42	7	239	27	1448.1	1477	165	536	640	12.7	4.45	96	.267	.331	-38	-30	101	**75**	59	.977	146	55	160	-.3	-2.9	3.5	**1.6**	2.1
TEX	26	10	217	**42**	1437.0	1371	135	532	773	12.1	3.86	107	.253	.321	56	46	98	90	58	.979	130	45	151	.6	4.5	.8	-.3	-3.6
MIN	31	6	214	33	1444.1	1590	128	452	721	12.8	4.13	106	.285	.338	14	38	104	77	71	.979	134	**44**	**203**	.4	3.7	-2.0	-.4	-.7
CHI	28	9	236	37	1409.0	1365	**114**	618	675	12.9	4.10	104	.256	.334	18	23	101	135	66	.972	173	67	142	-1.9	2.2	-.2	-.3	-6.9
SEA	37	7	217	26	1438.0	1567	165	571	736	13.6	4.58	95	.281	.348	-57	-33	103	152	58	.978	141	50	170	.0	-3.2	-3.0	.7	-8.5
OAK	41	4	**243**	20	1429.1	1606	147	654	726	14.5	4.75	85	.288	.363	-84	-117	96	117	**86**	.972	174	87	137	-1.9	-11.4	-16.1	-.4	2.7
TOT	551	116	3018	417	20051.2					12.8	4.22		.270	.334						.978	1962	835	2318					

Batter-Fielder Wins	Batting Average	On-Base Percentage	Slugging Average	On-Base Plus Slugging	Adjusted OPS	Adjusted Batter Runs
Smalley-Min 5.6	Lynn-Bos 333	Lynn-Bos 423	Lynn-Bos 637	Lynn-Bos 1059	Lynn-Bos 173	Lynn-Bos 57.1
Lynn-Bos.............5.3	Brett-KC 329	Porter-KC 421	Rice-Bos 596	Lezcano-Mil 987	Lezcano-Mil 165	Singleton-Bal 50.9
Porter-KC 5.1	Downing-Cal 326	Downing-Cal 418	Lezcano-Mil 573	Rice-Bos 977	Singleton-Bal 158	Lezcano-Mil 45.9
Brett-KC 4.9	Rice-Bos 325	Lezcano-Mil 414	Brett-KC 563	Kemp-Det 941	Rice-Bos 152	Rice-Bos 44.0
Grich-Cal 3.9	Oliver-Tex 323	Singleton-Bal 405	Jackson-NY 544	Brett-KC 939	Jackson-NY 151	Baylor-Cal 41.8

Runs	Hits	Doubles	Triples	Home Runs	Total Bases	Runs Batted In
Baylor-Cal 120	Brett-KC 212	Lemon-Chi 44	Brett-KC 20	Thomas-Mil 45	Rice-Bos 369	Baylor-Cal...........139
Brett-KC 119	Rice-Bos 201	Cooper-Mil 44	Molitor-Mil 16	Rice-Bos 39	Brett-KC 363	Rice-Bos...............130
Rice-Bos 117	Bell-Tex 200	Lynn-Bos.....................42	Wilson-KC 13	Lynn-Bos 39	Lynn-Bos 338	Thomas-Mil 123
Lynn-Bos 116	Molitor-Mil 188	Brett-KC 42	Randolph-NY 13	Baylor-Cal 36	Baylor-Cal 333	Lynn-Bos 122
Lansford-Cal 114	Lansford-Cal 188	Bell-Tex 42		Singleton-Bal 35	Singleton-Bal 304	Porter-KC 112

Stolen Bases	Base Stealing Runs	Fielding Runs-Infield	Fielding Runs-Outfield	Wins	Winning Pct.	Complete Games
Wilson-KC 83	Wilson-KC...........14.1	Smalley-Min 32.6	Wilson-KC............13.1	Flanagan-Bal 23	Caldwell-Mil 727	D.Martinez-Bal 18
LeFlore-Det 78	LeFlore-Det...........12.3	Dent-NY 31.8	Rivera-Min 9.4	John-NY 21	Flanagan-Bal 719	Ryan-Cal 17
Cruz-Sea 49	Cruz-Sea 7.6	Burleson-Bos 30.2	Bosetti-Tor 9.2	Koosman-Min 20	Morris-Det.............708	John-NY 17
Bumbry-Bal 37	Otis-KC 4.8	Bell-Tex 28.4	R.Miller-Cal............8.0	Guidry-NY 18	John-NY 700	Eckersley-Bos 17
Wills-Tex 35	Bumbry-Bal...........3.9	Cruz-Sea 19.9	Bonds-Cle..............7.0		Guidry-NY.............692	

Strikeouts	Fewest BB/Game	Games	Saves	Base Runners/9	Adjusted Relief Runs	Relief Ranking
Ryan-Cal 223	McGregor-Bal 1.19	Marshall-Min 90	Marshall-Min 32	McGregor-Bal 9.79	Kern-Tex 38.8	Kern-Tex 61.7
Guidry-NY 201	Caldwell-Mil 1.49	Monge-Cle 76	Kern-Tex 29	Darwin-Tex 9.81	Monge-Cle 27.6	Marshall-Min 52.1
Flanagan-Bal 190	Sorensen-Mil 1.61	Kern-Tex 71	Stanhouse-Bal........21	Lyle-Tex 10.04	Lopez-Det 26.6	Monge-Cle..........50.8
Jenkins-Tex 164	Stanley-Bos 1.83	Lyle-Tex..........................67	Lopez-Det 21	Kern-Tex 10.26	Marshall-Min........26.0	Lopez-Det 38.2
Koosman-Min 157	John-NY 2.12	Heaverlo-Oak 62	Monge-Cle.............19	Guidry-NY..........10.43	Stoddard-Bal 15.8	Drago-Bos 25.9

Innings Pitched	Opponents' Avg.	Opponents' OBP	Earned Run Average	Adjusted ERA	Adjusted Starter Runs	Pitcher Wins
D.Martinez-Bal ..292.1	Ryan-Cal..............212	McGregor-Bal 273	Guidry-NY...........2.78	Eckersley-Bos 148	Eckersley-Bos......38.5	**Kern-Tex** 6.3
John-NY 276.1	Kravec-Chi 233	Guidry-NY 292	John-NY 2.96	Guidry-NY 147	Guidry-NY............34.1	**Marshall-Min**......5.4
Flanagan-Bal 265.2	Guidry-NY............236	Flanagan-Bal 296	Eckersley-Bos......2.99	John-NY................138	John-NY 31.3	**Monge-Cle**..........5.1
Koosman-Min 263.2	Baumgarten-Chi ...243	Eckersley-Bos 297	Flanagan-Bal 3.08	Morris-Det 132	Koosman-Min 28.5	**Eckersley-Bos** ..4.0
Jenkins-Tex........259.0	Morris-Det............244	Leonard-KC 297	Morris-Det...........3.28	Flanagan-Bal 131	Flanagan-Bal 26.6	**Lopez-Det** 3.8

Gimme an "O"

As scoring reached its highest level since 1950, four teams—Boston, New York, Kansas City, and California—attracted two million fans. Last-place Oakland, on the other hand, drew just over 300,000 fans. No team had drawn that few fans since, well, the A's—in 1954, their last year in Philadelphia. There was only one reason to watch these A's: rookie outfielder Rickey Henderson.

Although six clubs in the AL East finished over .500, the Orioles had no serious challenge after July. Underrated Ken Singleton had a superb season at bat and was ably supported by a mix of youngsters and veterans. Lefty Mike Flanagan took Cy Young honors; he came up big when Jim Palmer went down with elbow problems. The Brewers, led by home run champ Gorman Thomas, won 95 games, but finished 8 games back.

Toronto, miserable in its first two seasons, was even worse in year three. The Blue Jays ended 50_ out, the deepest last-place finish since 1954; rookie Dave Stieb was an impressive 8–8. Ron Guidry led the AL in ERA for the second straight time, but the Yankees' season ended when Thurman Munson was killed in an airplane crash on August 2. Catfish Hunter retired after the season.

California won a poor AL West; their record would have placed them fifth in the East. The Angels, fortified by trades that brought Rod Carew and Dan Ford, led the league in runs: MVP Don Baylor, Carney Lansford, and Ford each scored more than 100 times. California pitching was very thin, but it was good enough. The pitching-poor Royals couldn't turn it on early enough, the Rangers didn't hit, and the Twins just didn't have the horses, although reliever Mike Marshall pitched an AL-record 90 times.

Baltimore defeated the Angels in four games, three of them close, to win the ALCS. The Orioles lost the World Series in seven despite being up three games to one; just like 1971, the O's dropped Game 7 to the Pirates at home. It was Earl Weaver's last trip to the Fall Classic.

1980 National League

TEAM	W	L	T	PCT	GB	HW	HL	R	OR	PA	H	2B	3B	HR	BB	SO	HB	SH	AVG	OBP	SLG	OPS	AOPS	BR	ABR	PF	SB	CS	BSA	BSR
EAST																														
PHI	91	71	0	.562		49	32	728	639	6265	1517	272	54	117	472	**708**	77	**33**	.270	.327	**.400**	727	102	62	24	106	140	62	69	9
MON	90	72	0	.556	1	51	29	694	629	6164	1407	250	61	114	547	865	76	20	.257	.324	.388	712	104	36	35	100	237	82	74	23
PIT	83	79	0	.512	8	47	34	666	646	6125	1469	249	38	116	452	760	75	25	.266	.322	.388	710	101	27	17	102	209	102	67	10
STL	74	88	0	.457	17	41	40	**738**	710	6202	**1541**	**300**	49	101	451	781	73	21	**.275**	**.328**	**.400**	**728**	105	**66**	44	103	117	54	68	7
NY	67	95	0	.414	24	38	44	611	702	6130	1407	218	41	61	501	840	73	25	.257	.319	.345	664	94	-53	-36	97	158	99	61	0
CHI	64	98	0	.395	27	37	44	614	728	6217	1411	251	35	107	471	912	69	18	.251	.309	.365	674	87	-47	-89	107	93	64	59	-2
WEST																														
HOU	93	70	0	.571		**55**	26	637	**589**	6253	1455	231	**67**	75	540	755	89	13	.261	.326	.367	693	**107**	0	**57**	92	194	74	72	17
LA	92	71	0	.564	1	**55**	27	663	591	6221	1462	209	24	**148**	492	846	96	24	.263	.323	.388	711	106	29	42	98	123	72	63	2
CIN	89	73	1	.549	3.5	44	37	707	670	6208	1445	256	45	113	537	852	78	23	.262	.327	.386	713	104	41	41	100	156	43	**78**	19
ATL	81	80	0	.503	11	50	30	630	660	5958	1352	226	22	144	434	899	69	20	.250	.307	.380	687	94	-27	-46	103	73	52	58	-2
SF	75	86	0	.466	17	44	37	573	634	6045	1310	199	44	80	509	840	**100**	14	.244	.308	.342	650	89	-84	-71	98	100	58	63	2
SD	73	89	1	.451	19.5	45	36	591	654	6254	1410	195	43	67	**563**	791	92	21	.255	.324	.342	666	98	-50	-12	94	**239**	73	77	**27**
TOT	973					556	416	7852		74042	17186	2856	523	1243	5969	9849	257	967	.259	.320	.374	695					1839	835	69	112

TEAM	CG	SHO	GR	SV	IP	H	HR	BB	SO	BR/9	ERA	AERA	OAV	OOB	PR	APR	PF	OSB	OCS	FA	E	WPB	DP	FW	PW	BW	BSW	DIF
EAST																												
PHI	25	8	277	40	1480.0	1419	87	530	889	12.0	3.43	**110**	.255	.319	28	**56**	105	166	79	.979	136	59	136	.2	**5.9**	2.5	-.0	1.3
MON	33	15	280	36	1456.2	1447	100	460	823	11.9	3.48	102	.261	.317	20	14	99	**116**	71	.977	144	44	126	-.2	1.5	3.7	1.4	2.6
PIT	25	8	271	**43**	1458.1	1422	110	**451**	832	11.7	3.58	102	.259	.316	4	10	101	125	64	.978	137	**34**	154	.2	1.1	1.8	.0	-1.1
STL	**34**	9	297	27	1447.0	1454	90	495	664	12.3	3.93	94	.265	.326	-53	-38	103	169	68	.981	122	51	**174**	1.0	-4.0	4.6	-.2	-8.4
NY	17	9	324	33	1451.1	1473	140	510	886	12.4	3.85	92	.267	.328	-40	-49	99	132	80	.975	154	40	132	-.7	-5.2	-3.8	-1.0	-3.3
CHI	13	6	**344**	35	1479.0	1525	109	589	923	13.0	3.89	101	.272	.340	-47	4	109	154	**105**	.974	174	51	149	-1.7	.4	-9.4	-1.2	-5.1
WEST																												
HOU	31	18	246	41	1482.2	1367	**69**	466	**929**	**11.3**	**3.10**	106	**.246**	**.305**	**82**	34	91	157	47	.978	140	62	145	.0	3.6	**6.0**	.8	1.0
LA	24	**19**	266	42	1472.2	**1358**	105	480	835	**11.3**	3.25	108	.247	.306	58	42	97	168	51	.981	123	44	149	1.0	4.4	4.4	-.8	1.4
CIN	30	12	262	37	1459.1	1404	113	506	833	11.9	3.85	93	.255	.317	-40	-44	99	187	57	**.983**	**106**	47	144	**1.9**	-4.6	4.3	1.0	5.4
ATL	29	9	289	37	1428.0	1397	131	454	696	11.8	3.77	99	.258	.316	-27	-4	104	144	64	.975	162	50	156	-1.2	-.4	-4.9	-1.2	8.1
SF	27	10	288	35	1448.1	1446	92	492	811	12.2	3.46	102	.261	.323	24	13	98	156	74	.975	159	38	124	-1.0	1.4	-7.5	-.8	2.4
SD	19	9	296	39	1466.1	1474	97	536	728	12.4	3.65	94	.267	.331	-8	-38	95	165	75	.980	132	45	157	.5	-4.0	-1.3	**1.9**	-5.1
TOT	307	132	3440	445	17529.2					12.0	3.60		.259	.320						.978	1689	565	1746					

Batter-Fielder Wins	Batting Average	On-Base Percentage	Slugging Average	On-Base Plus Slugging	Adjusted OPS	Adjusted Batter Runs
Schmidt-Phi 6.9	Buckner-Chi 324	Hernandez-StL 408	Schmidt-Phi 624	Schmidt-Phi 1004	Schmidt-Phi 169	Schmidt-Phi 50.5
Templeton-StL....5.4	Hernandez-StL 321	Cedeno-Hou 389	Clark-SF 517	Hernandez-StL 902	Clark-SF 155	Hernandez-StL ..41.3
Carter-Mon..........5.2	Templeton-StL 319	Clark-SF 382	Murphy-Atl 510	Clark-SF 900	Cedeno-Hou 150	Easler-Pit...........36.9
Smith-SD 4.1	McBride-Phi 309	Schmidt-Phi 380	Simmons-StL 505	Simmons-StL........880	Hernandez-StL 147	Cedeno-Hou 35.0
Dawson-Mon 4.0	Cedeno-Hou 309	Driessen-Cin 377	Baker-LA...............503	Murphy-Atl 858	Simmons-StL.........140	Clark-SF 33.6

Runs	Hits	Doubles	Triples	Home Runs	Total Bases	Runs Batted In
Hernandez-StL 111	Garvey-LA 200	Rose-Phi.......................42	Scott-Mon 13	Schmidt-Phi 48	Schmidt-Phi 342	Schmidt-Phi 121
Schmidt-Phi 104	Richards-SD 193	Dawson-Mon 41	Moreno-Pit.............13	Horner-Atl 35	Garvey-LA 307	Hendrick-StL 109
Murphy-Atl 98	Hernandez-StL 191	Buckner-Chi 41	LeFlore-Mon 11	Murphy-Atl 33	Hernandez-StL 294	Garvey-LA 106
Dawson-Mon 96	Buckner-Chi..........187	Knight-Cin.....................39	Herndon-SF............11	Carter-Mon 29	Baker-LA 291	Carter-Mon..........101
		Hernandez-StL 39		Baker-LA 29	Murphy-Atl 290	Hernandez-StL......99

Stolen Bases	Base Stealing Runs	Fielding Runs-Infield	Fielding Runs-Outfield	Wins	Winning Pct.	Complete Games
LeFlore-Mon 97	LeFlore-Mon 14.7	Smith-SD 38.5	Youngblood-NY ..19.4	Carlton-Phi 24	Bibby-Pit 760	Rogers-Mon 14
Moreno-Pit.............96	Collins-Cin 10.0	Templeton-StL 35.5	Moreno-Pit 11.3	Niekro-Hou 20	Reuss-LA 750	Carlton-Phi 13
Collins-Cin 79	Mumphrey-SD 9.7	Trillo-Phi.....................24.3	Puhl-Hou 9.5	Bibby-Pit 19	Carlton-Phi 727	Niekro-Atl 11
Scott-Mon 63	Moreno-Pit 9.6	Hubbard-Atl 21.2	Lacy-Pit 7.7	Reuss-LA 18	Ruthven-Phi 630	Niekro-Hou 11
Richards-SD 61	Scott-Mon 9.3	Schmidt-Phi 18.5	Dawson-Mon 7.3	Ruthven-Phi............17	Niekro-Hou 625	

Strikeouts	Fewest BB/Game	Games	Saves	Base Runners/9	Adjusted Relief Runs	Relief Ranking
Carlton-Phi 286	Forsch-StL 1.38	Tidrow-Chi 84	Sutter-Chi 28	Richard-Hou 8.31	McGraw-Phi 23.1	McGraw-Phi........30.1
Ryan-Hou 200	Reuss-LA 1.57	Tekulve-Pit 78	Hume-Cin 25	McGraw-Phi 8.48	Caudill-Chi 22.0	Camp-Atl 25.9
Soto-Cin 182	Forsch-Hou..........1.66	Hume-Cin 78	Fingers-SD 23	Sambito-Hou 8.87	Camp-Atl 21.0	Hume-Cin 23.6
Niekro-Atl.............176	Candelaria-Pit.......1.93	Camp-Atl.........................77	Camp-Atl 22	Sutton-LA 8.99	Smith-Hou 17.7	Sutter-Chi 22.0
Blyleven-Pit 168	Sutton-LA 1.99	Romo-Pit.........................74	Allen-NY 22	Reuss-LA 9.14	Holland-SF 15.5	Smith-Hou 22.0

Innings Pitched	Opponents' Avg.	Opponents' OBP	Earned Run Average	Adjusted ERA	Adjusted Starter Runs	Pitcher Wins
Carlton-Phi 304.0	Soto-Cin 187	Sutton-LA....................257	Sutton-LA 2.20	Carlton-Phi 162	Carlton-Phi 47.5	**Carlton-Phi** 5.2
Rogers-Mon 281.0	Sutton-LA 211	Reuss-LA......................260	Carlton-Phi 2.34	Sutton-LA 159	Sutton-LA 32.3	**McGraw-Phi** 3.3
Niekro-Atl 275.0	Carlton-Phi 218	Pastore-Cin 275	Reuss-LA 2.51	Reuss-LA..............140	Reuss-LA 24.6	**Camp-Atl** 3.0
Reuschel-Chi 257.0	Seaver-Cin 225	Carlton-Phi...................276	Blue-SF 2.97	Rogers-Mon..........120	Rogers-Mon 20.0	**Hume-Cin** 2.7
Niekro-Hou 256.0	Reuss-LA 227	Soto-Cin........................276	Rogers-Mon 2.98	Blue-SF 119	Richard-Hou 17.7	**Reuss-LA** 2.6

Finally, Philly

Defending world champion Pittsburgh, leading the East in late August, suddenly dropped 13 of 15 to fall from contention. The Phillies and Expos took the mantle, and the season went down to the last three games of the year—in Montreal. Philly captured the first two to clinch. Mike Schmidt, whose homer won the division-clinching game, was MVP, while Steve Carlton won his third Cy Young. Montreal's Gary Carter finished second in MVP voting.

Houston gave free agent Nolan Ryan the first $1 million annual salary. As it turned out, they really needed Ryan; fireballer J.R. Richard suffered a career-ending stroke on July 30. The Astros and Dodgers traded the West lead from June onward, spending six straight days tied in mid-September. Los Angeles lost five straight late in the month, but then swept a season-ending home series (with three one-run games) against Houston to force a playoff, also at Dodger Stadium. The Astros won, 7–1, behind Joe Niekro, for their first title.

The Dodgers, who led the NL league in attendance each year until 1986, had the Rookie of the Year in Steve Howe. Giants mainstay Willie McCovey retired. Game-winning RBI became an official statistic and would remain so through 1988.

Houston and Philadelphia hooked up in a wild five-game NLCS, with the last four contests decided in extra innings. After the Phillies' Game 1 win, the Astros won the next two. Philadelphia staved off elimination in Game 4 with three in the eighth and two in the 10th. In Game 5 Houston scored three in the seventh to go up, 5–2, but Philadelphia plated five in the eighth, and the Astros scored twice to tie it. The Phillies won in the 10th when Garry Maddox doubled home Del Unser.

The Phillies finally won their first World Series ever with a six-game triumph over Kansas City. Every game was close, with late-inning magic on both sides, but Carlton's two wins and great relief from Tug McGraw cinched it for the Phils.

1980 American League

TEAM	W	L	T	PCT	GB	HW	HL	R	OR	PA	H	2B	3B	HR	BB	SO	HB	SH	AVG	OBP	SLG	OPS	AOPS	BR	ABR	PF	SB	CS	BSA	BSR
EAST																														
NY	103	59	0	.636		**53**	28	820	662	6329	1484	239	34	189	643	739	51	28	.267	.343	.425	768	111	81	95	98	86	36	70	6
BAL	100	62	0	.617	3	50	31	805	**640**	6281	1523	258	29	156	587	766	42	21	.273	.342	.413	755	107	55	63	99	111	38	74	11
MIL	86	76	0	.531	17	40	42	811	682	6242	1555	**298**	36	**203**	455	745	58	25	.275	.329	**.448**	**777**	**115**	80	**107**	97	131	56	70	9
BOS	83	77	0	.519	19	36	45	757	767	6200	1588	297	36	162	475	720	40	32	.283	.340	.436	776	106	**89**	49	105	79	48	62	1
DET	84	78	1	.519	19	43	38	**830**	757	6444	1543	232	53	143	**645**	844	63	33	.273	.348	.409	757	105	66	48	102	75	68	52	-7
CLE	79	81	0	.494	23	44	35	738	807	6258	1517	221	40	89	617	**625**	60	37	.277	**.350**	.381	731	100	27	24	100	118	58	67	6
TOR	67	95	0	.414	36	35	46	624	762	6149	1398	249	53	126	448	813	63	33	.251	.309	.383	692	84	-95	-122	105	67	72	48	-10
WEST																														
KC	97	65	0	.599		49	32	809	694	6357	**1633**	266	**59**	115	508	709	34	**38**	**.286**	.345	.413	758	106	62	56	101	**185**	43	**81**	**26**
OAK	83	79	0	.512	14	46	35	686	642	6160	1424	212	35	137	506	824	**99**	19	.259	.322	.385	707	100	-54	-4	93	175	82	68	10
MIN	77	84	0	.478	19.5	44	36	670	724	6130	1468	252	46	99	436	703	92	21	.265	.319	.381	700	85	-67	-111	107	62	46	57	-2
TEX	76	85	2	.472	20.5	39	41	756	752	6319	1616	263	27	124	480	589	70	23	.284	.339	.405	744	106	31	55	97	91	49	65	3
CHI	70	90	2	.438	26	37	42	587	722	6000	1408	255	38	91	399	670	67	39	.259	.311	.370	681	86	-105	-102	100	68	54	56	-4
CAL	65	95	0	.406	31	30	51	698	797	6134	1442	236	32	106	539	889	71	32	.265	.332	.378	710	96	-32	-14	98	91	63	59	-2
SEA	59	103	1	.364	38	36	45	610	793	6141	1359	211	35	104	483	727	106	19	.248	.308	.356	664	80	-139	-144	101	116	62	65	4
TOT	1132					582	547	10201		87144	20958	3489	553	1844	7221	10363	400	916	.269	.331	.399	731					1455	775	65	49

TEAM	CG	SHO	GR	SV	IP	H	HR	BB	SO	BR/9	ERA	AERA	OAV	OOB	PR	APR	PF	OSB	OCS	FA	E	WPB	DP	FW	PW	BW	BSW	DIF
EAST																												
NY	29	**15**	210	**50**	1464.1	1433	**102**	463	845	11.8	3.58	109	.259	.316	73	56	97	**64**	**69**	.978	138	61	160	.0	5.6	9.5	.3	6.7
BAL	42	10	190	41	1460.0	1438	134	507	789	12.1	3.64	109	.261	.323	63	51	98	93	67	**.985**	**95**	54	178	**2.4**	5.1	6.3	.7	4.4
MIL	48	14	231	30	1450.0	1530	137	**420**	575	12.3	3.71	104	.273	.323	53	27	96	81	46	.977	147	39	189	-.5	2.7	**10.7**	.6	-8.4
BOS	30	8	238	43	1441.1	1557	129	481	696	12.9	4.38	96	.279	.337	-55	-25	105	107	45	.977	149	**34**	**206**	-.7	-2.5	4.9	-.2	1.6
DET	40	9	210	30	1467.1	1505	152	558	741	12.8	4.25	97	.267	.334	-35	-22	102	102	45	.979	133	78	165	.3	-2.2	4.8	-1.0	1.1
CLE	35	8	225	32	1428.0	1519	137	552	843	13.3	4.68	87	.275	.341	-103	-96	101	124	56	.983	105	69	143	1.8	-9.6	2.4	.3	4.2
TOR	39	9	**286**	23	1466.0	1523	135	635	705	13.4	4.19	103	.274	.348	-26	16	107	115	53	.979	133	49	**206**	.3	1.6	-12.2	-1.3	-2.4
WEST																												
KC	37	10	201	42	1459.1	1496	129	465	614	12.2	3.83	106	.267	.323	33	36	100	109	56	.978	141	50	150	-.2	3.6	5.6	**2.2**	4.7
OAK	**94**	9	146	13	1471.2	**1347**	142	521	769	**11.6**	**3.46**	109	**.244**	**.310**	**94**	54	93	87	66	.979	130	60	115	.5	5.4	-.4	.6	-4.1
MIN	35	9	213	30	1451.0	1502	120	468	744	12.4	3.93	**111**	.272	.328	16	**63**	108	76	59	.977	148	40	192	-.6	**6.3**	-11.1	-.5	2.5
TEX	35	6	256	25	1451.2	1561	119	519	**890**	13.1	4.02	97	.277	.339	2	-22	97	112	60	.977	147	79	169	-.5	-2.2	5.5	-.0	-7.3
CHI	32	12	236	42	1435.1	1434	108	563	724	12.8	3.92	103	.263	.333	18	17	100	124	58	.973	171	61	162	-1.9	1.7	-10.2	-.7	1.1
CAL	22	6	268	30	1428.1	1548	141	529	725	13.3	4.52	87	.278	.342	-77	-96	97	147	41	.978	134	42	144	.1	-9.6	-1.4	-.5	-3.6
SEA	31	7	236	26	1457.1	1565	159	540	703	13.2	4.38	94	.278	.341	-56	-39	102	114	54	.977	149	44	189	-.6	-3.9	-14.4	.0	-3.2
TOT	549	132	3146	457	20331.2					12.7	4.03		.269	.331						.978	1920	760	2368					

Batter-Fielder Wins	Batting Average	On-Base Percentage	Slugging Average	On-Base Plus Slugging	Adjusted OPS	Adjusted Batter Runs
G.Brett-KC 6.6	G.Brett-KC 390	G.Brett-KC 454	G.Brett-KC 664	G.Brett-KC 1118	G.Brett-KC 202	G.Brett-KC 64.9
Henderson-Oak ..5.7	Cooper-Mil 352	Randolph-NY 427	Jackson-NY 597	Jackson-NY 995	Jackson-NY 172	Jackson-NY 51.8
Bell-Tex 5.2	Dilone-Cle.............341	Henderson-Oak 420	Oglivie-Mil.............563	Cooper-Mil............926	Cooper-Mil............157	Cooper-Mil.........47.3
Randolph-NY 5.0	Rivers-Tex.............333	Hargrove-Cle 415	Cooper-Mil 539	Oglivie-Mil 925	Oglivie-Mil 156	Oglivie-Mil 43.3
Oglivie-Mil 4.8	Carew-Cal 331	Thompson-Det-Cal 398	Yount-Mil...............519	Singleton-Bal 882	Singleton-Bal 143	Henderson-Oak..38.2

Runs	Hits	Doubles	Triples	Home Runs	Total Bases	Runs Batted In
Wilson-KC 133	Wilson-KC 230	Yount-Mil 49	Wilson-KC 15	Oglivie-Mil 41	Cooper-Mil............335	Cooper-Mil 122
Yount-Mil 121	Cooper-Mil............219	Oliver-Tex 43	Griffin-Tor................15	Jackson-NY 41	Oglivie-Mil 333	Oglivie-Mil............118
Bumbry-Bal 118	Rivers-Tex 210	Morrison-Chi 40	Washington-KC 11	Thomas-Mil 38	Murray-Bal............322	G.Brett-KC 118
Henderson-Oak 111	Oliver-Tex.............209	McRae-KC 39	Landreaux-Min 11	Armas-Oak 35	Yount-Mil 317	Oliver-Tex 117
Trammell-Det 107	Bumbry-Bal 205	Evans-Bos 37	Yount-Mil 10	Murray-Bal..............32	Oliver-Tex..............315	Murray-Bal 116

Stolen Bases	Base Stealing Runs	Fielding Runs-Infield	Fielding Runs-Outfield	Wins	Winning Pct.	Complete Games
Henderson-Oak....100	Wilson-KC............13.9	Burleson-Bos 31.2	Wilson-KC............13.9	Stone-Bal................25	Stone-Bal 781	Langford-Oak 28
Wilson-KC 79	Henderson-Oak ..12.9	Bell-Tex 26.6	Henderson-Oak ..13.9	Norris-Oak 22	May-NY..................750	Norris-Oak 24
Dilone-Cle 61	Cruz-Sea 7.4	Smalley-Min 26.2	Harlow-Cal 13.2	John-NY 22	McGregor-Bal 714	Keough-Oak 20
Cruz-Sea 45	Dilone-Cle..............7.1	DeCinces-Bal..............26.1	Oglivie-Mil............12.9	McGregor-Bal 20	Norris-Oak 710	John-NY 16
Bumbry-Bal 44	Bumbry-Bal............5.8	Castino-Min 21.4	Bailor-Tor 12.9	Leonard-KC 20	John-NY 710	Gura-KC 16

Strikeouts	Fewest BB/Game	Games	Saves	Base Runners/9	Adjusted Relief Runs	Relief Ranking
Barker-Cle 187	Matlack-Tex 1.84	Quisenberry-KC 75	Quisenberry-KC.......33	May-NY................9.39	Corbett-Min..........34.8	Corbett-Min 45.2
Norris-Oak............180	Splittorff-KC 1.90	Corbett-Min....................73	Gossage-NY 33	Corbett-Min...........9.57	Burgmeier-Bos 20.8	Burgmeier-Bos ...28.2
Guidry-NY 166	John-NY 1.90	Monge-Cle 67	Farmer-Chi 30	Norris-Oak 9.62	Gossage-NY..........18.5	Quisenberry-KC 28.0
Leonard-KC 155	Tanana-Cal 1.99	Lopez-Det 67	Stoddard-Bal 26	Burgmeier-Bos 9.91	Garvin-Tor............17.6	Gossage-NY 27.1
Bannister-Sea 155	Langford-Oak 1.99		Burgmeier-Bos........24	Lacey-Oak 10.17	Darwin-Tex 16.1	Darwin-Tex 25.0

Innings Pitched	Opponents' Avg.	Opponents' OBP	Earned Run Average	Adjusted ERA	Adjusted Starter Runs	Pitcher Wins
Langford-Oak 290.0	Norris-Oak 209	May-NY 268	May-NY................2.46	May-NY 159	Norris-Oak 43.0	**Corbett-Min**........4.8
Norris-Oak 284.1	May-NY.................224	Norris-Oak 270	Norris-Oak 2.53	Norris-Oak............149	Burns-Chi 33.3	**Norris-Oak**..........4.7
Gura-KC 283.1	Clancy-Tor 233	Eckersley-Bos 289	Burns-Chi 2.84	Burns-Chi 142	Gura-KC 33.1	**Burns-Chi** 3.7
Leonard-KC 280.1	Keough-Oak 236	Burns-Chi.....................293	Keough-Oak 2.92	Gura-KC................137	May-NY................28.7	**May-NY** 3.2
John-NY 265.1	Underwood-NY.....237	Langford-Oak...............294	Gura-KC 2.95	Erickson-Min 135	Keough-Oak 24.2	**Gura-KC**..............3.2

.390

Kansas City's George Brett *looked* like a .400 hitter, with quick wrists, strong power, and in a good ballpark for his stroke. And despite various injuries, he was over .400 in early September, though a late slump brought him to .390—still the highest mark in the majors over a full season since 1941. An easy MVP, Brett helped the Royals destroy the West Division.

Prior to the season, Charlie Finley sold the A's. The new owners hired Billy Martin to pump up the team and the gate. With Rickey Henderson stealing 100 bases, the A's improved 29 games to second, and their attendance skyrocketed. Part of Martin's "win now" regimen involved his best pitchers doing all the work; his staff completed 94 games, most of any AL team since 1946. Most of the team's top pitchers soon came up lame.

The White Sox brought up rookie Harold Baines, and used 57-year-old Minnie Minoso for 2 at bats. While Reggie Jackson got the acclaim for the Yankees' division title, Willie Randolph, Tommy John, and Rich Gossage were also key performers. New York lost a member of its family as Elston Howard succumbed to cancer.

The Orioles were the league's first second-place 100-game winner since 1961. Steve Stone won 14 in a row and captured the Cy Young. The next year, he was finished by arm problems. Three big-name Tigers retired: Mark Fidrych with shoulder trouble and John Hiller and Willie Horton due to age.

Kansas City avenged their three ALCS defeats at New York's hands by sweeping the Yankees in three. The Royals supplemented their booming bats with excellent starting pitching and help from submarining reliever Dan Quisenberry. The World Series, however, went Philadelphia's way as they defeated Kansas City in six.

1981 National League

TEAM	W	L	T	PCT	GB	HW	HL	R	OR	PA	H	2B	3B	HR	BB	SO	HB	SH	AVG	OBP	SLG	OPS	AOPS	BR	ABR	PF	SB	CS	BSA	BSR
EAST	*Split Season: First-half Winner PHI (34-21); Second-half Winner MON (30-23)*																													
STL	59	43	1	.578		32	21	464	417	4013	936	158	**45**	50	379	495	46	16	.265	.336	.377	713	105	43	31	103	88	45	66	4
MON	60	48	0	.556	2	**38**	18	443	394	4068	883	146	28	81	368	498	63	16	.246	.316	.370	686	99	2	-3	101	**138**	40	**78**	**16**
PHI	59	48	0	.551	2.5	36	19	**491**	472	4141	**1002**	165	25	69	372	**432**	44	**23**	**.273**	**.341**	**.389**	**730**	**108**	**68**	47	104	103	46	69	7
PIT	46	56	1	.451	13	22	28	407	425	3959	920	176	30	55	278	494	54	15	.257	.311	.369	680	95	-9	-21	103	122	52	70	9
NY	41	62	2	.398	18.5	24	27	348	432	3885	868	136	35	57	304	603	41	13	.248	.308	.356	664	96	-28	-22	98	103	42	71	8
CHI	38	65	3	.369	21.5	27	30	370	483	3984	838	138	29	57	342	611	53	13	.236	.303	.340	643	84	-53	-68	104	72	41	64	1
WEST	*Split Season: First-half Winner LA (36-21); Second-half Winner HOU (33-20)*																													
CIN	66	42	0	.611		32	22	464	440	4123	972	**190**	24	64	375	553	53	18	.267	.335	.385	720	**108**	57	**49**	102	58	37	61	0
LA	63	47	0	.573	4	33	23	450	356	4188	984	133	20	**82**	331	550	62	17	.262	.323	.374	697	107	15	32	96	73	46	61	0
HOU	61	49	0	.555	6	31	20	394	**331**	4155	948	160	35	45	340	488	**79**	8	.257	.318	.356	674	102	-13	9	95	81	43	65	3
SF	56	55	0	.505	11.5	29	24	427	414	4258	941	161	26	63	**386**	543	65	14	.250	.320	.357	677	100	-7	1	98	89	50	64	2
ATL	50	56	1	.472	15	22	27	395	416	4055	886	148	22	64	321	540	56	18	.243	.306	.349	655	89	-42	-51	103	98	39	72	8
SD	41	69	0	.373	26	20	35	382	455	4184	963	170	35	32	311	525	72	14	.256	.313	.346	659	99	-34	-3	93	83	62	57	-3
TOT	644					346	294	5035		49013	11141	1881	354	719	4107	6332	185	688	.255	.319	.364	683					1108	543	67	54

TEAM	CG	SHO	GR	SV	IP	H	HR	BB	SO	BR/9	ERA	AERA	OAV	OOB	PR	APR	PF	OSB	OCS	FA	E	WPB	DP	FW	PW	BW	BSW	DIF
EAST																												
STL	11	5	219	**33**	943.0	902	52	290	388	11.5	3.63	98	.255	.312	-14	-7	102	94	40	**.981**	82	**27**	108	.6	-.8	3.3	-.0	4.8
MON	20	12	183	23	975.0	902	58	**268**	520	11.0	3.30	106	.247	.300	21	21	100	**65**	48	.980	81	33	88	.9	2.3	-.3	**1.2**	1.9
PHI	19	5	184	23	960.1	967	72	347	580	12.4	4.05	90	.267	.329	-60	-43	104	124	41	.980	86	34	90	.6	-4.6	5.1	.3	4.2
PIT	11	5	201	29	942.0	953	60	346	492	12.6	3.56	101	.266	.331	-8	3	103	**65**	34	.979	86	39	106	.4	.3	-2.3	.5	-4.0
NY	7	3	234	24	926.1	906	74	336	490	12.2	3.55	98	.259	.323	-6	-7	100	68	39	.968	130	31	89	-1.6	-.8	-2.4	.4	-6.1
CHI	6	2	**263**	20	956.2	983	59	388	532	13.1	4.01	92	.270	.340	-55	-31	106	109	55	.974	113	48	103	-.8	-3.3	-7.3	-.4	-1.7
WEST																												
CIN	25	14	182	20	965.2	863	67	393	593	11.8	3.73	95	.241	.315	-26	-18	102	107	35	**.981**	**80**	30	99	**1.0**	-1.9	**5.3**	-.5	8.2
LA	**26**	**19**	187	24	997.0	904	54	302	603	11.0	3.01	110	.245	.302	54	36	95	80	45	.980	87	32	101	.7	3.9	3.4	-.5	.5
HOU	23	**19**	164	25	990.0	**842**	**40**	300	**610**	**10.5**	**2.66**	**124**	**.231**	**.289**	**91**	**74**	94	86	52	.980	87	44	81	.7	**8.0**	1.0	-.2	-3.5
SF	8	9	211	**33**	1009.1	970	57	393	561	12.4	3.28	105	.256	.327	23	17	98	117	43	.977	102	43	102	.0	1.8	.1	-.3	-1.2
ATL	11	4	215	24	968.0	936	62	330	471	11.9	3.45	104	.257	.318	4	14	103	98	**58**	.976	102	35	93	-.2	1.5	-5.5	.4	.8
SD	9	6	239	23	1002.0	1013	64	414	492	13.0	3.72	88	.268	.341	-25	-55	93	95	53	.977	102	35	**117**	-.0	-5.9	-.3	-.8	-6.9
TOT	176	103	2482	301	11635.1					11.9	3.49		.255	.319						.978	1138	431	1177					

Batter-Fielder Wins	Batting Average	On-Base Percentage	Slugging Average	On-Base Plus Slugging	Adjusted OPS	Adjusted Batter Runs
Schmidt-Phi 7.2	Madlock-Pit...........341	Schmidt-Phi 435	Schmidt-Phi 644	Schmidt-Phi........1080	Schmidt-Phi..........195	Schmidt-Phi........47.3
Dawson-Mon 4.6	Rose-Phi...............325	Madlock-Pit 412	Dawson-Mon 553	Dawson-Mon 918	Dawson-Mon 157	Dawson-Mon 28.4
Concepcion-Cin 3.1	Baker-LA...............320	Hernandez-StL 401	Foster-Cin.............519	Madlock-Pit 907	Madlock-Pit 153	Foster-Cin 27.2
Foster-Cin...........2.7	Schmidt-Phi 316	Matthews-Phi..............398	Madlock-Pit...........495	Foster-Cin 892	Foster-Cin 150	Hernandez-StL ...24.1
Trillo-Phi.............2.7	Buckner-Chi 311	Rose-Phi 391	Hendrick-StL.........485	Hernandez-StL 864	Cey-LA..................145	Madlock-Pit 21.5

Runs	Hits	Doubles	Triples	Home Runs	Total Bases	Runs Batted In
Schmidt-Phi............78	Rose-Phi 140	Buckner-Chi 35	Richards-SD 12	Schmidt-Phi............31	Schmidt-Phi..........228	Schmidt-Phi 91
Rose-Phi 73	Buckner-Chi..........131	Jones-SD 34	Reynolds-Hou 12	Dawson-Mon...........24	Dawson-Mon 218	Foster-Cin...............90
Dawson-Mon 71	Concepcion-Cin....129	Concepcion-Cin 28	Herr-StL....................9	Kingman-NY 22	Foster-Cin 215	Buckner-Chi 75
Hendrick-StL 67	Baker-LA 128	Hernandez-StL 27		Foster-Cin 22	Buckner-Chi..........202	Carter-Mon............68
	Griffey-Cin 123	Chambliss-Atl 25		Hendrick-StL 18	Hendrick-StL 191	

Stolen Bases	Base Stealing Runs	Fielding Runs-Infield	Fielding Runs-Outfield	Wins	Winning Pct.	Complete Games
Raines-Mon 71	Raines-Mon 11.8	Schmidt-Phi 22.8	Dawson-Mon 12.0	Seaver-Cin..............14	Seaver-Cin 875	Valenzuela-LA 11
Moreno-Pit.............39	Dawson-Mon 4.3	Smith-SD 22.2	Maddox-Phi 7.6	Valenzuela-LA 13	Carlton-Phi 765	Soto-Cin 10
Scott-Mon 30	Lacy-Pit 4.2	Trillo-Phi.....................18.1	Easler-Pit 6.4	Carlton-Phi 13	Ryan-Hou 688	Carlton-Phi 10
	Scott-Mon 4.2	Flynn-NY 14.0	Lacy-Pit 5.2		Valenzuela-LA 650	Reuss-LA 8
	Lopes-LA 3.7	Templeton-StL 10.6	Gross-Phi 5.0		Hooton-LA 647	Rogers-Mon 7

Strikeouts	Fewest BB/Game	Games	Saves	Base Runners/9	Adjusted Relief Runs	Relief Ranking
Valenzuela-LA 180	Perry-Atl 1.43	Lucas-SD 57	Sutter-StL 25	Reardon-NY-Mon 9.09	Camp-Atl 14.8	Camp-Atl 27.3
Carlton-Phi 179	Reuss-LA 1.59	Minton-SF 55	Minton-SF 21	Sutton-Hou 9.19	Reardon-NY-Mon 11.6	Lucas-SD 19.3
Soto-Cin 151	Sutton-Hou 1.64	Tidrow-Chi 51	Allen-NY 18	Valenzuela-LA 9.45	Lucas-SD 11.5	Sambito-Hou 16.9
Ryan-Hou 140	Sorensen-StL 1.67	Hume-Cin 51	Camp-Atl 17	Sambito-Hou 9.47	Holland-SF 11.3	Sutter-StL 13.7
Gullickson-Mon 115	Solomon-Pit 1.91	Sambito-Hou.................49		D.Smith-Hou 9.48	Falcone-NY............9.9	Holland-SF 13.6

Innings Pitched	Opponents' Avg.	Opponents' OBP	Earned Run Average	Adjusted ERA	Adjusted Starter Runs	Pitcher Wins
Valenzuela-LA ..192.1	Ryan-Hou 188	Sutton-Hou 265	Ryan-Hou 1.69	Ryan-Hou 195	Ryan-Hou 27.0	**Ryan-Hou** 3.4
Carlton-Phi 190.0	Valenzuela-LA 205	Valenzuela-LA 270	Knepper-Hou 2.18	Knepper-Hou 151	Carlton-Phi 23.2	**Camp-Atl** 2.9
Soto-Cin 175.0	Seaver-Cin 205	Knepper-Hou 278	Hooton-LA 2.28	Carlton-Phi 150	Knepper-Hou 21.4	**Valenzuela-LA** ..2.6
Seaver-Cin 166.1	Berenyi-Cin...........211	Sanderson-Mon...........278	Reuss-LA 2.30	Hooton-LA 146	Valenzuela-LA 19.7	**Seaver-Cin** 2.2
Niekro-Hou 166.0	Blue-SF 217	Ryan-Hou.....................280	Carlton-Phi 2.42	Reuss-LA..............144	Seaver-Cin 18.7	**Hooton-LA**..........2.1

One Strike Away

Pushed by the owners on the free-agent compensation issue, the players went on strike in June and the game didn't resume until August. As a result, the owners instituted a "split season" with the winners in each half declared division co-champs, with a playoff to decide who played in the Championship Series. Unfortunately, the worst came to pass: Cincinnati and St. Louis posted the best overall division records but didn't "win" either half. The flawed system did, however, provide Montreal with its only post-season appearance to date.

Portly rookie southpaw Fernando Valenzuela of the Dodgers went a long way toward erasing the game's black eye. "Fernandomania" struck parks all over the league, giving fans a new idol—and the Dodgers a great pitcher who won Cy Young and Rookie of the Year honors. Philadelphia's 40-year-old Pete Rose shattered Stan Musial's NL hit record, but this time Charlie Hustle broke a record as a first baseman with little power rather than as a second baseman, third baseman, left fielder, or right fielder.

Los Angeles, first-half winners by a smidgen, scraped by Houston, sparked by Nolan Ryan and Don Sutton, in a five-game West playoff. The Expos, with Andre Dawson and rookie Tim Raines providing the stickwork, defeated Philadelphia in the East. Mike Schmidt won another MVP; Carlton was great during the season, but 0–2 in the playoff.

The Montreal-Los Angeles NLCS went the full five. In the deciding contest, Ray Burris—a shutout winner in Game 2—went eight innings for Montreal against Valenzuela. With the game tied in the ninth, 1–1, Expos manager Jim Fanning brought in starter Steve Rogers on two days' rest, even though he had a rested bullpen. Rogers promptly allowed Rick Monday's pinch-homer that won the series.

The Yankees took the first two World Series games in New York, but the Dodgers roared back with three consecutive one-run victories. In Game 6 they walloped Tommy John and five relievers, 9–2, earning the Dodgers their first title since 1965.

1981 American League

TEAM	W	L	T	PCT	GB	HW	HL	R	OR	PA	H	2B	3B	HR	BB	SO	HB	SH	AVG	OBP	SLG	OPS	AOPS	BR	ABR	PF	SB	CS	BSA	BSR
EAST	*Split Season: First-half Winner NY (34-22); Second-half Winner MIL (31-22)*																													
MIL	62	47	0	.569		28	21	493	459	4152	961	173	20	96	300	461	35	29	.257	.313	.391	704	108	9	34	95	39	36	52	-4
BAL	59	46	0	.562	1	33	22	429	437	3985	883	165	11	88	**404**	454	26	15	.251	.329	.379	708	103	25	26	100	41	34	55	-3
NY	59	48	0	.551	2	32	19	421	**343**	3994	889	148	22	100	391	434	40	7	.252	.325	.391	716	106	30	37	99	47	30	61	0
DET	60	49	0	.550	2	32	23	427	404	4109	922	148	**29**	65	**404**	500	50	18	.256	.331	.368	699	97	15	-1	104	61	37	62	0
BOS	59	49	0	.546	2.5	30	23	**519**	481	4281	**1052**	168	17	90	378	520	37	13	**.275**	**.340**	**.399**	**739**	106	**67**	37	106	32	31	51	-4
CLE	52	51	0	.505	7	25	29	431	442	3952	922	150	21	39	343	**379**	46	13	.263	.327	.351	678	96	-11	-5	99	**119**	37	**76**	**13**
TOR	37	69	0	.349	23.5	17	36	329	466	3887	797	137	23	61	284	556	44	20	.226	.286	.330	616	72	-106	-125	106	66	57	54	-5
WEST	*Split Season: First-half Winner OAK (37-23); Second-half Winner KC (30-23)*																													
OAK	64	45	0	.587		**35**	21	458	403	4113	910	119	26	**104**	342	647	46	16	.247	.312	.379	691	103	-11	11	95	98	47	68	5
TEX	57	48	0	.543	5	32	24	452	389	3972	968	**178**	15	49	295	396	36	21	.270	.326	.369	695	106	7	31	95	46	41	53	-4
CHI	54	52	0	.509	8.5	25	24	476	423	4064	982	135	27	76	322	518	48	**43**	.272	.335	.387	722	**110**	40	**50**	98	86	44	66	4
KC	50	53	0	.485	11	19	28	397	405	3941	952	169	**29**	61	301	419	28	17	.267	.325	.383	708	104	17	21	99	100	53	65	3
CAL	51	59	0	.464	13.5	26	28	476	453	4191	944	134	16	97	393	571	**51**	29	.256	.330	.380	710	104	26	26	100	44	33	57	-2
SEA	44	65	1	.404	20	20	37	426	521	4201	950	148	13	89	329	553	41	27	.251	.314	.368	682	92	-19	-36	104	100	50	67	5
MIN	41	68	1	.376	23	24	36	378	486	4025	884	147	36	47	275	497	36	11	.240	.293	.338	631	76	-90	-112	107	34	27	56	-2
TOT	750					378	371	6112		56867	13016	2119	305	1062	4761	6905	279	564	.256	.321	.373	693					913	557	62	6

TEAM	CG	SHO	GR	SV	IP	H	HR	BB	SO	BR/9	ERA	AERA	OAV	OOB	PR	APR	PF	OSB	OCS	FA	E	WPB	DP	FW	PW	BW	BSW	DIF
EAST																												
MIL	11	4	**199**	**35**	986.0	994	72	352	448	12.4	3.91	88	.266	.328	-27	-57	94	70	40	.982	79	40	**135**	.3	-6.0	3.6	-.5	10.0
BAL	25	10	133	23	940.0	923	83	347	489	12.3	3.70	98	.260	.326	-4	-7	99	50	41	.983	68	40	114	.8	-.7	2.7	-.4	4.1
NY	16	**13**	161	30	948.0	**827**	**64**	287	**606**	**10.7**	**2.90**	**123**	**.235**	**.293**	**80**	**73**	98	70	35	.982	72	30	100	.7	**7.7**	3.9	-.0	-6.7
DET	33	**13**	146	22	969.1	840	83	373	476	11.5	3.53	107	.236	.310	14	25	103	58	40	**.984**	**67**	32	109	**1.0**	2.6	-.1	-.0	2.0
BOS	19	4	157	24	987.1	983	90	354	536	12.4	3.81	102	.262	.328	-17	6	106	93	35	.979	91	27	108	-.4	.6	3.9	-.5	1.4
CLE	33	10	111	13	931.0	989	67	311	569	12.7	3.88	94	.274	.330	-23	-26	99	**48**	46	.978	87	38	91	-.4	-2.7	-.5	**1.3**	2.8
TOR	20	4	189	18	953.1	908	72	377	451	12.5	3.81	103	.252	.326	-17	12	108	55	36	.975	105	45	102	-1.3	1.3	-13.1	-.6	-2.3
WEST																												
OAK	**60**	11	112	10	993.0	883	80	370	505	11.6	3.30	105	.240	.311	40	21	95	50	45	.980	81	32	74	.2	2.2	1.2	.5	5.4
TEX	23	**13**	142	18	940.1	851	67	322	488	11.4	3.40	102	.243	.308	27	8	95	50	38	**.984**	69	28	102	.7	.8	3.3	-.5	.1
CHI	20	8	173	23	940.2	891	73	336	529	12.0	3.47	103	.252	.319	19	11	98	74	37	.979	87	26	113	-.3	1.2	**5.2**	.4	-5.5
KC	24	8	127	24	922.1	909	75	**273**	404	11.7	3.56	101	.260	.313	10	5	99	72	26	.982	72	**20**	94	.5	.5	2.2	.3	-5.0
CAL	27	8	155	19	971.1	958	81	323	426	12.1	3.70	99	.261	.321	-4	-5	100	73	49	.977	101	24	120	-.9	-.5	2.7	-.3	-5.1
SEA	10	5	**199**	23	997.1	1039	76	360	478	12.8	4.23	91	.271	.334	-64	-40	105	85	35	.979	91	49	122	-.3	-4.2	-3.8	.5	-2.7
MIN	13	6	165	22	979.2	1021	79	376	500	13.0	3.98	99	.272	.338	-35	-3	108	65	**53**	.978	96	22	103	-.6	-.3	-11.8	-.3	-.6
TOT	334	117	2169	304	13459.2					12.1	3.66		.256	.321						.980	1166	453	1487					

Batter-Fielder Wins	Batting Average	On-Base Percentage	Slugging Average	On-Base Plus Slugging	Adjusted OPS	Adjusted Batter Runs
Grich-Cal 5.2	Lansford-Bos 336	Hargrove-Cle 424	Grich-Cal 543	Evans-Bos 937	Grich-Cal 164	Evans-Bos 35.4
Bell-Tex 5.2	Paciorek-Sea 326	Evans-Bos 415	Murray-Bal 534	Grich-Cal 921	Evans-Bos 160	Henderson-Oak ..31.3
Yount-Mil 4.7	Cooper-Mil 320	Henderson-Oak 408	Evans-Bos 522	Murray-Bal 895	Murray-Bal 156	Cooper-Mil 28.8
Henderson-Oak ..4.7	Henderson-Oak ...319	Kemp-Det 389	Paciorek-Sea 509	Paciorek-Sea 888	Lemon-Chi 155	Grich-Cal 28.5
Burleson-Cal 4.6	Hargrove-Cle 317	Lansford-Bos 389	Cooper-Mil 495	Lemon-Chi 874	Cooper-Mil 154	Murray-Bal 26.6

Runs	Hits	Doubles	Triples	Home Runs	Total Bases	Runs Batted In
Henderson-Oak 89	Henderson-Oak 135	Cooper-Mil 35	Castino-Min 9	Murray-Bal 22	Evans-Bos 215	Murray-Bal 78
Evans-Bos 84	Lansford-Bos 134	Oliver-Tex 29	Wilson-KC 7	Grich-Cal 22	Armas-Oak 211	Armas-Oak 76
Cooper-Mil 70	Wilson-KC 133	Paciorek-Sea 28	Henderson-Oak 7	Evans-Bos 22	Paciorek-Sea 206	Oglivie-Mil 72
Harrah-Cle 64	Cooper-Mil 133	Dauer-Bal 27	G.Brett-KC 7	Armas-Oak 22	Cooper-Mil 206	Evans-Bos 71
Rivers-Tex 62	Paciorek-Sea 132	G.Brett-KC 27	Baines-Chi 7		Murray-Bal 202	Winfield-NY 68

Stolen Bases	Base Stealing Runs	Fielding Runs-Infield	Fielding Runs-Outfield	Wins	Winning Pct.	Complete Games
Henderson-Oak 56	Cruz-Sea 6.7	Bell-Tex 34.3	Wilson-KC 17.6	Vuckovich-Mil 14	Vuckovich-Mil 778	Langford-Oak 18
Cruz-Sea 43	Wilson-KC 4.7	Yount-Mil 30.0	Henderson-Oak ..14.8	Morris-Det 14	D.Martinez-Bal 737	McCatty-Oak 16
LeFlore-Chi 36	Henderson-Oak 4.6	Burleson-Cal 27.4	Manning-Cle 7.8	McCatty-Oak 14	McGregor-Bal 722	Morris-Det 15
Wilson-KC 34	Manning-Cle 4.4	Grich-Cal 18.3	Evans-Bos 6.1	D.Martinez-Bal 14	Guidry-NY 688	Norris-Oak 12
Dilone-Cle 29	LeFlore-Chi 4.1	Castino-Min 17.3	Roenicke-Bal 4.6			Gura-KC 12

Strikeouts	Fewest BB/Game	Games	Saves	Base Runners/9	Adjusted Relief Runs	Relief Ranking
Barker-Cle 127	Honeycutt-Tex 1.20	Corbett-Min 54	Fingers-Mil 28	Fingers-Mil 7.96	Fingers-Mil 22.5	Fingers-Mil 41.2
Burns-Chi 108	Forsch-Cal 1.59	Fingers-Mil 47	Gossage-NY 20	Davis-NY 8.88	Gossage-NY 14.2	Gossage-NY 27.2
Leonard-KC 107	Gura-KC 1.83	Rawley-Sea 46	Quisenberry-KC 18	Guidry-NY 9.00	Corbett-Min 12.1	Saucier-Det 17.8
Blyleven-Cle 107	Leonard-KC 1.83	Easterly-Mil 44	Corbett-Min 17	Gura-KC 9.30	Quisenberry-KC ..12.0	Quisenberry-KC 16.3
Guidry-NY 104	Guidry-NY 1.84		Saucier-Det 13	Righetti-NY 9.66	Saucier-Det 10.5	Aase-Cal 15.5

Innings Pitched	Opponents' Avg.	Opponents' OBP	Earned Run Average	Adjusted ERA	Adjusted Starter Runs	Pitcher Wins
Leonard-KC 201.2	McCatty-Oak 211	Guidry-NY 256	McCatty-Oak 2.33	Stewart-Bal 156	McCatty-Oak 26.6	**Fingers-Mil** 4.6
Morris-Det 198.0	Guidry-NY 214	Gura-KC 265	Stewart-Bal 2.32	McCatty-Oak 150	Righetti-NY 19.2	**Gossage-NY** 3.0
Langford-Oak 195.1	Darwin-Tex 218	Honeycutt-Tex 272	Lamp-Chi 2.41	Lamp-Chi 149	Burns-Chi 17.2	**McCatty-Oak** 3.0
McCatty-Oak 185.2	Morris-Det 218	McCatty-Oak 277	John-NY 2.63	John-NY 136	Morris-Det 16.5	**Righetti-NY** 2.2
Stieb-Tor 183.2	Lamp-Chi 222	Forsch-Cal 286	Burns-Chi 2.64	Burns-Chi 136	Stieb-Tor 16.4	**Saucier-Det** 1.9

Shattered Season

On June 12 players called the first in-season strike in baseball history. Owners provoked the action by trying to force free-agent compensation onto the bargaining table through the courts. Once the owners' strike insurance ran out, they compromised, and the season resumed August 10. To revive interest in the destroyed season, the owners instituted a "split" format—the standings before the strike would stand, with the leading clubs declared first-half winners. The rest of the schedule would produce its own "winners."

The folly of the "split season" was palpable—why expect a team to push if it had *already clinched* a playoff berth? All four divisions had "split" championships. The extra round of playoffs—a format later adopted for the Division Series—helped the owners and NBC turn the strike into extra profits. Attendance was down almost everywhere, of course. Oakland's attendance had been so bad that their gate went up 55 percent *despite* the strike.

The league's biggest surprise was Toronto, which played at a .276 pre-strike clip. In the second half, playing sophomore Lloyd Moseby and rookies George Bell and Jesse Barfield, the Jays went 21–27; they would no longer be patsies.

Oakland, the West's first-half winner, had homer and steal leaders in Tony Armas and Rickey Henderson. They swept the Royals in the three-game West playoff.

The Brewers and Yankees won the East, with Milwaukee's Rollie Fingers winning Cy Young and MVP honors. New York, however, won the East playoff, in five hotly-contested games. The Yankees defeated Oakland in four for the AL title before falling to the Dodgers in the World Series.

Postseason excitement aside, this was a disaster of historic proportions for baseball. With football and college sports taking over media and public consciousness, the last thing the major leagues needed was a crippling strike when it should have been the only game in town. Forgiveness came hard, and some people never returned to baseball.

1982 National League

TEAM	W	L	T	PCT	GB	HW	HL	R	OR	PA	H	2B	3B	HR	BB	SO	HB	SH	AVG	OBP	SLG	OPS	AOPS	BR	ABR	PF	SB	CS	BSA	BSR
EAST																														
STL	92	70	0	.568		46	35	685	**609**	6196	1439	239	**52**	67	569	805	87	30	.264	**.334**	.364	698	100	25	18	101	**200**	91	69	12
PHI	89	73	0	.549	3	**51**	30	664	654	6107	1417	245	25	112	506	831	85	24	.260	.323	.376	699	99	16	2	102	128	76	63	2
MON	86	76	0	.531	6	40	41	697	616	6221	1454	270	38	133	503	816	85	**35**	.262	.325	.396	721	105	55	42	102	156	56	**74**	**15**
PIT	84	78	0	.519	8	42	39	724	696	6234	**1535**	**272**	40	134	447	862	78	28	**.273**	.327	**.408**	**735**	108	**81**	59	103	161	75	68	9
CHI	73	89	0	.451	19	38	43	676	709	6141	1436	239	46	102	460	869	76	25	.260	.317	.375	692	96	-5	-22	103	132	70	65	5
NY	65	97	0	.401	27	33	48	609	723	6108	1361	227	26	97	456	1005	64	25	.247	.305	.350	655	90	-76	-72	99	137	58	70	10
WEST																														
ATL	89	73	0	.549		42	39	**739**	702	6229	1411	215	22	**146**	554	869	96	29	.256	.325	.383	708	100	34	6	104	151	77	66	6
LA	88	74	0	.543	1	43	38	691	612	6361	1487	222	32	138	528	**804**	**106**	30	.264	.327	.388	715	**109**	47	**66**	98	151	56	73	14
SF	87	75	0	.537	2	45	36	673	687	6227	1393	213	30	133	**607**	915	59	17	.253	.327	.376	703	102	28	29	100	130	56	70	9
SD	81	81	0	.500	8	43	38	675	658	6159	1435	217	**52**	81	429	877	86	22	.257	.311	.359	670	98	-53	-19	95	165	77	68	9
HOU	77	85	0	.475	12	43	38	569	620	6008	1342	236	48	74	435	830	68	19	.247	.302	.349	651	94	-87	-41	92	140	61	70	9
CIN	61	101	0	.377	28	33	48	545	661	6099	1375	228	34	82	470	817	88	21	.251	.310	.350	660	88	-64	-76	102	131	69	66	5
TOT	972					499	473	7947		74090	17085	2823	445	1299	5964	10300	305	978	.258	.319	.373	692					1782	822	68	104

TEAM	CG	SHO	GR	SV	IP	H	HR	BB	SO	BR/9	ERA	AERA	OAV	OOB	PR	APR	PF	OSB	OCS	FA	E	WPB	DP	FW	PW	BW	BSW	DIF
EAST																												
STL	25	10	318	47	1465.1	1420	94	502	689	11.9	3.37	107	.258	.320	37	40	101	149	64	**.981**	124	60	169	.9	4.2	1.9	.3	3.6
PHI	**38**	13	287	33	1456.1	1395	86	472	**1002**	11.7	3.61	102	.255	.314	-1	9	102	154	64	**.981**	**121**	60	138	**1.1**	.9	.2	-.7	6.4
MON	34	10	250	43	1460.2	1371	110	**448**	936	11.3	3.31	**110**	.250	.306	46	**52**	101	121	75	.980	122	55	117	**1.1**	**5.5**	4.4	**.7**	-6.6
PIT	19	7	280	39	1466.2	1434	118	521	933	12.2	3.81	97	.257	.321	-34	-17	103	**108**	72	.977	145	71	133	-.3	-1.8	6.2	.0	-1.2
CHI	9	7	**354**	43	1447.1	1510	125	452	764	12.4	3.92	95	.272	.327	-51	-28	104	156	76	.979	132	45	110	.5	-2.9	-2.3	-.4	-2.8
NY	15	5	278	37	1447.1	1508	119	582	759	13.1	3.88	94	.273	.341	-45	-40	101	153	86	.972	175	**38**	134	-2.0	-4.2	-7.6	.1	-2.4
WEST																												
ATL	15	11	314	**51**	1463.0	1484	126	502	813	12.4	3.82	98	.267	.328	-36	-14	104	167	67	.979	137	50	**186**	.2	-1.5	.6	-.3	8.9
LA	37	**16**	295	28	1488.1	1356	**81**	468	932	**11.2**	**3.26**	106	**.244**	**.303**	**56**	36	96	127	69	.979	139	51	131	.0	3.8	**6.9**	.6	-4.4
SF	18	4	323	45	1465.1	1507	109	466	810	12.3	3.64	99	.270	.326	-6	-7	100	185	**96**	.973	173	40	125	-1.9	-.7	3.0	.0	5.5
SD	20	11	277	41	1476.0	1348	139	502	765	11.4	3.52	97	**.244**	.307	13	-17	95	136	43	.976	152	39	142	-.7	-1.8	-2.0	.0	4.4
HOU	37	**16**	244	31	1446.2	**1338**	87	479	899	11.5	3.42	97	.247	.310	30	-17	92	177	57	.978	136	93	154	.3	-1.8	-4.3	.0	1.8
CIN	22	7	293	31	1460.1	1414	105	570	998	12.4	3.66	101	.258	.328	-10	6	103	149	53	.980	128	62	158	.7	.6	-8.0	-.4	-13.0
TOT	289	117	3513	469	17543.1					12.0	3.60		.258	.319						.978	1684	664	1697					

Batter-Fielder Wins	Batting Average	On-Base Percentage	Slugging Average	On-Base Plus Slugging	Adjusted OPS	Adjusted Batter Runs
Carter-Mon 6.9	Oliver-Mon .331	Schmidt-Phi .403	Schmidt-Phi .547	Schmidt-Phi 949	Schmidt-Phi 161	Schmidt-Phi 46.2
Schmidt-Phi 6.5	Madlock-Pit .319	Morgan-SF .400	Guerrero-LA .536	Guerrero-LA 914	Guerrero-LA 157	Guerrero-LA 43.6
O.Smith-StL 4.8	Durham-Chi .312	Hernandez-StL .397	Durham-Chi .521	Durham-Chi 909	Oliver-Mon 149	Oliver-Mon 42.1
Guerrero-LA 4.3	L.Smith-StL .307	Oliver-Mon .392	Oliver-Mon .514	Oliver-Mon 906	Lezcano-SD 149	Thompson-Pit 39.2
Thon-Hou 4.3	Buckner-Chi .306	Thompson-Pit .391	Thompson-Pit .511	Thompson-Pit 902	Durham-Chi 148	Carter-Mon 36.2

Runs	Hits	Doubles	Triples	Home Runs	Total Bases	Runs Batted In
L.Smith-StL 120	Oliver-Mon 204	Oliver-Mon 43	Thon-Hou 10	Kingman-NY 37	Oliver-Mon 317	Oliver-Mon 109
Murphy-Atl 113	Buckner-Chi 201	Kennedy-SD 42	Wilson-NY 9	Murphy-Atl 36	Guerrero-LA 308	Murphy-Atl 109
Schmidt-Phi 108	Dawson-Mon 183	Dawson-Mon 37	Puhl-Hou 9	Schmidt-Phi 35	Murphy-Atl 303	Buckner-Chi 105
Dawson-Mon 107	L.Smith-StL 182	Knight-Hou 36	Moreno-Pit 9	Horner-Atl 32	Dawson-Mon 303	Hendrick-StL 104
Sandberg-Chi 103	Ray-Pit 182			Guerrero-LA 32	Buckner-Chi 290	Clark-SF 103

Stolen Bases	Base Stealing Runs	Fielding Runs-Infield	Fielding Runs-Outfield	Wins	Winning Pct.	Complete Games
Raines-Mon 78	Raines-Mon 11.6	O.Smith-StL 35.5	Lezcano-SD 9.4	Carlton-Phi 23	Niekro-Atl .810	Carlton-Phi 19
L.Smith-StL 68	Wilson-NY 7.2	Concepcion-Cin 18.8	Dawson-Mon 8.2	Valenzuela-LA 19	Rogers-Mon .704	Valenzuela-LA 18
Moreno-Pit 60	L.Smith-StL 5.9	Hubbard-Atl 18.5	Dernier-Phi 7.9	Rogers-Mon 19	Carlton-Phi .676	Niekro-Hou 16
Wilson-NY 58	Thon-Hou 5.3	Schmidt-Phi 18.5	Householder-Cin 7.9	Reuss-LA 18	Lollar-SD .640	Rogers-Mon 14
S.Sax-LA 49	Wiggins-SD 5.2	Thon-Hou 18.4	Wilson-NY 7.7		Forsch-StL .625	Soto-Cin 13

Strikeouts	Fewest BB/Game	Games	Saves	Base Runners/9	Adjusted Relief Runs	Relief Ranking
Carlton-Phi 286	Bird-Chi 1.41	Tekulve-Pit 85	Sutter-StL 36	DeLeon-SD 8.29	Minton-SF 24.2	Minton-SF 35.7
Soto-Cin 274	Hammaker-SF 1.44	Minton-SF 78	Minton-SF 30	Howe-LA 9.42	Bedrosian-Atl 20.7	Garber-Atl 28.9
Ryan-Hou 245	Andujar-StL 1.69	Scurry-Pit 76	Garber-Atl 30	Soto-Cin 9.68	Scurry-Pit 20.5	DeLeon-SD 26.1
Valenzuela-LA 199	Reuss-LA 1.77	Reardon-Mon 75	Reardon-Mon 26	Niekro-Hou 9.77	Reardon-Mon 19.2	Reardon-Mon 26.0
Rogers-Mon 179	Candelaria-Pit 1.91	Hernandez-Chi 75	Tekulve-Pit 20	Andujar-StL 9.96	DeLeon-SD 17.3	Bedrosian-Atl 22.0

Innings Pitched	Opponents' Avg.	Opponents' OBP	Earned Run Average	Adjusted ERA	Adjusted Starter Runs	Pitcher Wins
Carlton-Phi 295.2	Ryan-Hou .213	Soto-Cin .271	Rogers-Mon 2.40	Rogers-Mon 152	Rogers-Mon 38.0	**Minton-SF** 3.9
Valenzuela-LA 285.0	Soto-Cin .215	Sutton-Hou .277	Niekro-Hou 2.47	Andujar-StL 147	Andujar-StL 32.1	**Rogers-Mon** 3.7
Rogers-Mon 277.0	Lea-Mon .222	Reuss-LA .277	Andujar-StL 2.47	Niekro-Hou 135	Niekro-Hou 30.1	**Garber-Atl** 3.2
Niekro-Hou 270.0	Lollar-SD .224	Niekro-Hou .278	Soto-Cin 2.79	Soto-Cin 133	Soto-Cin 25.8	**Andujar-StL** 2.9
Andujar-StL 265.2	Niekro-Hou .229	Andujar-StL .281	Valenzuela-LA 2.87	Candelaria-Pit 126	Valenzuela-LA 18.7	**DeLeon-SD** 2.9

My Beer's Better Than Yours

The NL West was nothing if not streaky. Atlanta, featuring Bob Horner and MVP Dale Murphy, won its first 13 games of the season under new manager Joe Torre. The Braves then fell apart in late July, losing 19 of 21 to sag below the streaking Dodgers. Meanwhile, San Francisco, featuring veterans Reggie Smith (in his last season), Joe Morgan, and Jack Clark plus rookie Chili Davis, won 10 straight in August, and then 18 of 21 in September.

With the title in sight, Los Angeles lost eight straight; on September 26, one game separated the Braves, Giants, and Dodgers. Atlanta won five of their final seven to capture the division as Los Angeles and San Francisco knocked each other out.

Steve Sax was the fourth successive Dodger to be Rookie of the Year. A superior crew of freshmen became regulars in '82, including Davis, Ryne Sandberg, Willie McGee, and Tony Gwynn. Willie Stargell ended his career as a pinch hitter for Pittsburgh, a team ready for collapse amid shady characters and an aging lineup. The Mets, hoping for a quick fix, traded for George Foster and then made him the first $2 million player. He didn't help.

Whitey Herzog's Cardinals battled the Phillies starting in July, and then pulled away in September. Lonnie Smith sparked the offense, and Bruce Sutter led the NL in saves for the fourth consecutive time. Steve Carlton won his fourth Cy Young for the Phillies, but Mike Schmidt aside, Philadelphia's lineup couldn't deliver.

St. Louis easily swept Atlanta in the NLCS. The Cardinals then played a rollicking, entertaining seven-game World Series against Milwaukee. The final contest between beer towns was a seesaw affair; St. Louis came back in the late innings to win. This was the NL's fourth straight Series victory.

NL owners worked to bounce Bowie Kuhn from the commissioner's chair, feeling that he was too weak in negotiations and had no long-term vision. The game had no full-time commissioner until 1984.

1982 American League

TEAM	W	L	T	PCT	GB	HW	HL	R	OR	PA	H	2B	3B	HR	BB	SO	HB	SH	AVG	OBP	SLG	OPS	AOPS	BR	ABR	PF	SB	CS	BSA	BSR
EAST																														
MIL	95	67	1	.586		48	34	**891**	717	6337	1599	277	41	**216**	484	714	56	18	.279	.335	**.455**	**790**	**122**	109	**165**	94	84	52	62	0
BAL	94	68	1	.580	1	53	28	774	687	6325	1478	259	27	179	634	796	57	25	.266	.341	.419	760	107	71	74	100	49	38	56	-3
BOS	89	73	0	.549	6	49	32	753	713	6262	1536	271	31	136	547	736	53	28	.274	.340	.407	747	98	42	0	106	42	39	52	-4
DET	83	79	0	.512	12	47	34	729	685	6166	1489	237	40	177	470	807	41	26	.266	.324	.418	742	102	13	10	100	93	66	58	-3
NY	79	83	0	.488	16	42	39	709	716	6244	1417	225	37	161	590	719	55	24	.256	.328	.398	726	100	-5	7	98	69	45	61	-1
TOR	78	84	0	.481	17	44	37	651	701	6067	1447	262	45	106	415	749	48	28	.262	.314	.383	697	82	-72	-126	109	118	81	59	-2
CLE	78	84	0	.481	17	41	40	683	748	6359	1458	225	32	109	**651**	**625**	74	**35**	.262	.341	.373	714	96	-11	-7	100	**151**	68	69	9
WEST																														
CAL	93	69	0	.574		52	29	814	**670**	6350	1518	268	26	186	613	760	**114**	**35**	.274	**.347**	.433	780	113	**113**	113	100	55	53	51	-6
KC	90	72	0	.556	3	**56**	25	784	717	6177	**1603**	**295**	**58**	132	442	758	32	25	**.285**	.337	.428	765	108	68	67	100	133	48	**73**	**12**
CHI	87	75	0	.537	6	49	31	786	710	6242	1523	266	52	136	533	866	54	30	.273	.337	.413	750	105	44	44	100	136	58	70	10
SEA	76	86	0	.469	17	42	39	651	712	6181	1431	259	33	130	456	806	42	22	.254	.311	.381	692	87	-85	-102	103	131	82	62	0
OAK	68	94	0	.420	25	36	45	691	819	6154	1286	211	27	149	582	948	50	20	.236	.309	.367	676	89	-107	-79	96	232	87	**73**	21
TEX	64	98	0	.395	29	38	43	590	749	6020	1354	204	26	115	447	750	64	32	.249	.308	.359	667	86	-131	-101	95	63	45	58	-2
MIN	60	102	0	.370	33	37	44	657	819	6115	1427	234	44	148	474	887	22	24	.257	.316	.396	712	92	-46	-64	103	38	33	54	-3
TOT	1135					634	500	10163		86999	20566	3493	519	2080	7338	10921	372	762	.264	.328	.402	730					1394	795	64	28

TEAM	CG	SHO	GR	SV	IP	H	HR	BB	SO	BR/9	ERA	AERA	OAV	OOB	PR	APR	PF	OSB	OCS	FA	E	WPB	DP	FW	PW	BW	BSW	DIF
EAST																												
MIL	34	6	213	**47**	1467.1	1514	152	511	717	12.5	3.98	95	.270	.330	15	-35	93	121	62	.980	125	56	**185**	.1	-3.5	**16.5**	-.2	1.1
BAL	38	8	231	34	1462.1	1436	147	488	719	**12.0**	3.99	101	.257	**.317**	14	7	99	98	51	**.984**	**101**	42	140	**1.4**	.7	7.4	-.5	4.0
BOS	23	11	214	33	1453.0	1557	155	478	816	12.8	4.03	107	.276	.334	7	42	106	101	55	.981	121	**40**	172	.3	4.2	.0	-.6	4.1
DET	**45**	5	228	27	1451.0	**1371**	172	554	740	12.1	**3.80**	107	**.251**	.321	**44**	42	100	84	63	.981	117	68	165	.5	4.2	1.0	-.5	-3.2
NY	24	8	251	39	1459.0	1471	113	491	939	12.2	3.99	100	.264	.323	13	-1	98	98	44	.979	128	56	158	-.0	-.1	.7	-.3	-2.2
TOR	41	**13**	220	25	1443.2	1428	147	493	776	12.1	3.95	**113**	.257	.319	20	**77**	110	78	46	.978	136	45	146	-.5	**7.7**	-12.6	-.4	2.8
CLE	31	9	221	30	1468.1	1433	122	589	882	12.5	4.11	99	.257	.327	-5	-5	100	125	60	.980	123	62	129	.2	-.5	-.7	.7	-2.7
WEST																												
CAL	40	10	248	27	1464.0	1436	124	482	728	**12.0**	3.82	106	.259	.321	42	38	100	**66**	**77**	.983	108	**40**	171	1.0	3.8	11.3	-.8	-3.3
KC	16	12	228	45	1431.0	1443	163	471	650	12.2	4.08	100	.262	.320	-1	0	100	85	53	.979	127	49	140	-.0	.0	6.7	1.0	1.3
CHI	30	10	258	41	1439.0	1502	**99**	**460**	753	12.4	3.87	104	.270	.326	33	27	99	102	60	.976	154	41	173	-1.5	2.7	4.4	.8	-.4
SEA	23	11	**303**	39	1476.1	1431	173	547	**1002**	12.2	3.88	109	.256	.324	32	57	104	118	51	.978	139	57	158	-.7	5.7	-10.2	-.2	.4
OAK	42	6	239	22	1456.0	1506	177	648	697	13.5	4.54	86	.268	.343	-76	-107	96	97	58	.974	160	66	140	-1.8	-10.7	-7.9	**1.9**	5.5
TEX	32	5	214	24	1431.0	1554	128	483	690	13.1	4.28	90	.280	.339	-33	-69	95	93	59	.981	121	53	169	.3	-6.9	-10.1	-.4	.1
MIN	26	7	244	30	1433.0	1484	208	643	812	13.4	4.72	90	.269	.344	-103	-74	104	128	57	.982	108	51	162	1.0	-7.4	-6.4	-.5	-7.7
TOT	445	121	3312	463	20335.0					12.5	4.07		.264	.328						.980	1768	726	2208					

Batter-Fielder Wins	Batting Average	On-Base Percentage	Slugging Average	On-Base Plus Slugging	Adjusted OPS	Adjusted Batter Runs
Yount-Mil.............7.3	Wilson-KC.............332	Evans-Bos 402	Yount-Mil..............578	Yount-Mil 957	Yount-Mil 170	Yount-Mil 59.9
DeCinces-Cal......5.9	Yount-Mil..............331	Harrah-Cle...................398	Winfield-NY 560	Murray-Bal...........940	Murray-Bal...........157	Murray-Bal.........44.0
Bell-Tex...............5.7	Carew-Cal 319	Henderson-Oak 398	Murray-Bal 549	Evans-Bos 936	DeCinces-Cal 149	Evans-Bos.........42.7
Grich-Cal..............4.3	Murray-Bal 316	Carew-Cal 396	DeCinces-Cal 548	DeCinces-Cal 916	R.Jackson-Cal......147	Harrah-Cle..........39.6
Bernazard-Chi....4.2	Cooper-Mil 313	Murray-Bal...................391	McRae-KC 542	McRae-KC 910	McRae-KC 146	DeCinces-Cal 39.5

Runs	Hits	Doubles	Triples	Home Runs	Total Bases	Runs Batted In
Molitor-Mil 136	Yount-Mil 210	Yount-Mil.........................46	Wilson-KC 15	Thomas-Mil 39	Yount-Mil 367	McRae-KC 133
Yount-Mil 129	Cooper-Mil............205	McRae-KC 46	Herndon-Det 13	R.Jackson-Cal........39	Cooper-Mil............345	Cooper-Mil 121
Evans-Bos..............122	Molitor-Mil 201	White-KC.........................45	Yount-Mil 12	Winfield-NY 37	McRae-KC.............332	Thornton-Cle 116
Henderson-Oak....119	Wilson-KC 194	DeCinces-Cal 42	Mumphrey-NY........10	Oglivie-Mil 34	Evans-Bos 325	Yount-Mil 114
Downing-Cal 109	McRae-KC 189	Cowens-Sea 39			DeCinces-Cal 315	Thomas-Mil 112

Stolen Bases	Base Stealing Runs	Fielding Runs-Infield	Fielding Runs-Outfield	Wins	Winning Pct.	Complete Games
Henderson-Oak....130	Henderson-Oak ..13.9	Bell-Tex 37.7	Brunansky-Min 11.3	Hoyt-Chi..................19	Vuckovich-Mil 750	Stieb-Tor................19
Garcia-Tor 54	Molitor-Mil..............5.9	Bernazard-Chi 31.1	Wilson-KC.............11.0	Zahn-Cal 18	Palmer-Bal 750	Morris-Det 17
J.Cruz-Sea.............46	J.Cruz-Sea 5.6	DeCinces-Cal 22.8	Mitchell-Min 10.6	Vuckovich-Mil..........18	Zahn-Cal...............692	Langford-Oak 15
Molitor-Mil 41	Dilone-Cle...............5.5	Almon-Chi 19.7	Ward-Min 10.6	Gura-KC...................18	Petry-Det 625	Hoyt-Chi 14
Wilson-KC 37	Garcia-Tor..............4.9	Grich-Cal 16.6	Murphy-Oak 9.9	....	Gura-KC 600	

Strikeouts	Fewest BB/Game	Games	Saves	Base Runners/9	Adjusted Relief Runs	Relief Ranking
Bannister-Sea 209	John-NY-Cal 1.58	VandeBerg-Sea 78	Quisenberry-KC......35	Gossage-NY........8.81	Quisenberry-KC ..23.1	Caudill-Sea 41.2
Barker-Cle 187	Eckersley-Bos......1.73	T.Martinez-Bal..............76	Gossage-NY 30	Quisenberry-KC ..9.09	Stanley-Bos 23.0	Spillner-Cle 40.9
Righetti-NY 163	Hoyt-Chi 1.80	Quisenberry-KC 72	Fingers-Mil..............29	Stoddard-Sea 9.22	Spillner-Cle 22.4	Quisenberry-KC 37.4
Guidry-NY 162	Haas-Mil 1.82	Caudill-Sea 70	Caudill-Sea 26	Fingers-Mil 9.49	Burgmeier-Bos 21.1	Gossage-NY 31.3
Tudor-Bos 146	Langford-Oak 1.86	Spillner-Cle 65	Davis-Min................22	Caudill-Sea..........9.50	Caudill-Sea..........20.6	Clear-Bos 28.4

Innings Pitched	Opponents' Avg.	Opponents' OBP	Earned Run Average	Adjusted ERA	Adjusted Starter Runs	Pitcher Wins
Stieb-Tor 288.1	Sutcliffe-Cle 226	Palmer-Bal 286	Sutcliffe-Cle 2.96	Stanley-Bos 139	Stieb-Tor 35.8	**Caudill-Sea** 4.2
Clancy-Tor 266.2	Righetti-NY...........229	Eckersley-Bos 296	Stanley-Bos 3.10	Stieb-Tor 138	Sutcliffe-Cle 26.2	**Quisenberry-KC** 4.2
Morris-Det..........266.1	Ujdur-Det 230	Stieb-Tor 298	Palmer-Bal 3.13	Sutcliffe-Cle...........138	Petry-Det 23.3	**Spillner-Cle**..........4.1
Caldwell-Mil 258.0	Palmer-Bal 231	Barker-Cle 299	Petry-Det 3.22	Palmer-Bal............129	Palmer-Bal 22.6	**Stieb-Tor** 3.9
D.Martinez-Bal ..252.0	Barker-Cle 232	Hoyt-Chi.......................301	Stieb-Tor 3.25	Beattie-Sea 127	Clancy-Tor 20.8	**Gossage-NY** 3.2

Harvey's Wallbangers

With Rotisserie® baseball gaining popularity, and *The Bill James Baseball Abstract* first printed by a major publisher, interest in the analytical side of the game began to grow. But there was no accounting for streaks.

In early September, the white-hot Royals seemed poised to win, but they cooled while the Angels caught fire. California, featuring a veteran lineup acquired through trades and free agency, led the league in attendance, almost doubling their 1981 total, and setting a new league mark. Newest Angel Reggie Jackson led the league in homers, and set the career record for strikeouts, which he still holds. Manager Gene Mauch seemed to keep together his shaky pitching staff with duct tape and bailing wire.

Oakland began to crumble, falling to fifth despite Rickey Henderson's record 130 steals. In their last season at Metropolitan Stadium, the Twins were terrible, but rookies Gary Gaetti, Tom Brunansky, and Kent Hrbek developed camaraderie amidst the rebuilding. In Boston, Wade Boggs debuted at .349; Don Mattingly got in his first swings for the Yankees.

MVP Robin Yount headed the Brewers' bruising offense, and the pitching was barely good enough. Milwaukee got hot in June shortly after Harvey Kuenn was named manager; the Brewers took over the East in mid-July. Baltimore, riding Eddie Murray and top rookie Cal Ripken, took three from the Brewers on the last weekend to tie the race. On the season's last day, Milwaukee stretch pickup Don Sutton defeated Jim Palmer.

California took the first two ALCS contests with complete games from Tommy John and Bruce Kison. Their pitching collapsed in Milwaukee as the Brewers won the next two games with big innings. In the deciding tilt, California took a 3–1 lead, but Cecil Cooper's seventh-inning, bases-loaded single gave Milwaukee a 4–3 win. The Brewers went to their first—and to date, only—World Series and played valiantly, but they lost to the Cardinals in seven.

1983 National League

TEAM	W	L	T	PCT	GB	HW	HL	R	OR	PA	H	2B	3B	HR	BB	SO	HB	SH	AVG	OBP	SLG	OPS	AOPS	BR	ABR	PF	SB	CS	BSA	BSR
EAST																														
PHI	90	72	1	.556		**50**	31	696	635	6218	1352	209	45	125	**640**	906	80	26	.249	.329	.373	702	102	17	25	99	143	75	66	5
PIT	84	78	0	.519	6	41	40	659	648	6169	1460	238	29	121	497	873	84	19	.264	.325	.383	708	100	18	1	103	124	77	62	0
MON	82	80	1	.506	8	46	35	677	646	6293	1482	**297**	41	102	509	**733**	78	**38**	.264	.326	.386	712	104	34	38	99	138	44	**76**	15
STL	79	83	0	.488	11	44	37	679	710	6238	**1496**	262	**63**	83	543	879	72	24	.270	.335	.384	719	**105**	48	**48**	100	**207**	89	70	14
CHI	71	91	0	.438	19	43	38	701	719	6132	1436	272	42	140	470	868	71	29	.261	.319	**.401**	720	100	37	5	105	84	40	68	4
NY	68	94	0	.420	22	41	41	575	680	6009	1314	172	26	112	436	1031	66	31	.241	.300	.344	644	85	-118	-113	99	141	64	69	9
WEST																														
LA	91	71	1	.562		48	32	654	**609**	6129	1358	197	34	**146**	541	925	86	22	.250	.318	.379	697	100	-7	-3	99	166	76	69	10
ATL	88	74	0	.543	3	46	34	**746**	640	6195	1489	218	45	130	582	847	78	17	**.272**	**.341**	.400	**741**	104	**91**	39	107	146	88	62	1
HOU	85	77	0	.525	6	46	36	643	646	6173	1412	239	60	97	517	869	81	19	.257	.320	.375	695	104	-8	36	94	164	95	63	3
SD	81	81	1	.500	10	47	34	653	653	6163	1384	207	34	93	482	822	**89**	20	.250	.311	.351	662	92	-77	-56	97	179	67	73	**16**
SF	79	83	0	.488	12	43	38	687	697	6126	1324	206	30	142	619	990	64	28	.247	.325	.375	700	103	12	34	97	140	78	64	4
CIN	74	88	0	.457	17	36	45	623	710	6057	1274	236	35	107	588	1006	72	19	.239	.314	.356	670	89	-47	-68	104	154	77	67	7
TOT	974					531	441	7993		73902	16781	2753	484	1398	6424	10749	292	921	.255	.322	.376	698					1786	870	67	88

TEAM	CG	SHO	GR	SV	IP	H	HR	BB	SO	BR/9	ERA	AERA	OAV	OOB	PR	APR	PF	OSB	OCS	FA	E	WPB	DP	FW	PW	BW	BSW	DIF
EAST																												
PHI	20	10	300	41	1461.2	1429	111	**464**	**1092**	11.8	3.34	107	.256	.314	47	38	98	167	79	.976	152	57	117	-.7	4.0	2.6	-.2	3.4
PIT	25	14	290	41	1462.1	1378	109	563	1061	12.1	3.55	104	.252	.321	12	24	102	126	64	**.982**	115	61	165	1.4	2.5	.1	-.8	-.3
MON	**38**	**15**	252	34	1471.0	1406	120	479	899	11.7	3.58	100	.254	.315	8	1	99	115	86	.981	116	46	130	1.4	.1	4.0	.8	-5.3
STL	22	10	327	27	1460.2	1479	115	525	709	12.5	3.79	96	.266	.330	-26	-28	100	**110**	64	.976	152	74	173	-.8	-2.9	**5.0**	.7	-4.0
CHI	9	10	**369**	42	1428.2	1496	117	498	807	12.7	4.08	93	.274	.335	-71	-43	105	152	66	**.982**	115	67	164	1.4	-4.5	.5	-.4	-7.1
NY	18	7	274	33	1451.0	1384	97	615	717	12.5	3.68	99	.256	.331	-8	-8	100	194	73	.976	151	58	171	-.7	-.8	-11.8	.2	.2
WEST																												
LA	27	12	278	40	1464.0	1336	97	495	1000	**11.4**	**3.10**	**116**	.244	**.307**	**85**	**80**	99	114	**88**	.974	168	58	132	-1.7	**8.4**	-.3	.3	3.4
ATL	18	4	305	**48**	1440.2	1412	132	540	895	12.3	3.67	106	.260	.327	-7	30	107	172	68	.978	137	**40**	**176**	.1	3.1	4.1	-.7	.3
HOU	22	14	261	**48**	1466.1	**1276**	**94**	570	904	11.5	3.45	99	**.236**	.309	29	-8	94	182	54	.977	147	84	165	-.5	-.8	3.8	-.5	2.0
SD	23	5	294	44	1467.2	1389	144	528	850	11.9	3.62	96	.253	.320	1	-23	96	152	74	.979	129	42	135	.6	-2.4	-5.9	**.9**	6.7
SF	20	9	276	47	1445.2	1431	127	520	881	12.3	3.70	96	.259	.323	-11	-27	97	167	73	.973	171	64	109	-1.9	-2.8	3.6	-.4	-.5
CIN	34	5	271	29	1441.1	1365	135	627	934	12.6	3.98	95	.253	.330	-57	-27	105	135	81	.981	**114**	43	121	**1.5**	-2.8	-7.1	-.0	1.5
TOT	276	115	3497	474	17461.0					12.1	3.63		.255	.322						.978	1667	694	1758					

Batter-Fielder Wins	Batting Average	On-Base Percentage	Slugging Average	On-Base Plus Slugging	Adjusted OPS	Adjusted Batter Runs
Schmidt-Phi 6.5	Madlock-Pit..........323	Schmidt-Phi 399	Murphy-Atl 540	Murphy-Atl 933	Schmidt-Phi 156	Schmidt-Phi........45.6
Thon-Hou 6.3	L.Smith-StL..........321	Hernandez-StL-NY 396	Dawson-Mon 539	Schmidt-Phi 923	Evans-SF.............151	Guerrero-LA 38.9
Raines-Mon 4.6	Cruz-Hou 318	Murphy-Atl 393	Guerrero-LA 531	Guerrero-LA 904	Guerrero-LA 150	Murphy-Atl..........38.5
Carter-Mon.........4.4	Hendrick-StL.........318	Raines-Mon 393	Schmidt-Phi 524	Evans-SF.............894	Murphy-Atl 146	Evans-SF 37.4
Guerrero-LA........4.3	Knight-Hou 304	Madlock-Pit 386	Evans-SF 516	Dawson-Mon 877	Cruz-Hou 143	Cruz-Hou.............35.0

Runs	Hits	Doubles	Triples	Home Runs	Total Bases	Runs Batted In
Raines-Mon 133	Dawson-Mon 189	Ray-Pit 38	Butler-Atl 13	Schmidt-Phi............40	Dawson-Mon 341	Murphy-Atl 121
Murphy-Atl 131	Cruz-Hou..............189	Oliver-Mon 38	Moreno-Hou 11	Murphy-Atl 36	Murphy-Atl 318	Dawson-Mon 113
Schmidt-Phi..........104	Ramirez-Atl 185	Buckner-Chi 38	Green-StL 10	Guerrero-LA 32	Guerrero-LA 310	Schmidt-Phi 109
Dawson-Mon 104	Oliver-Mon 184	Carter-Mon 37	Dawson-Mon 10	Dawson-Mon 32	Thon-Hou 283	Guerrero-LA 103
	Raines-Mon 183			Evans-SF................30	Schmidt-Phi 280	Kennedy-SD 98

Stolen Bases	Base Stealing Runs	Fielding Runs-Infield	Fielding Runs-Outfield	Wins	Winning Pct.	Complete Games
Raines-Mon 90	Raines-Mon 14.9	Sandberg-Chi 44.3	Milner-Cin 12.8	Denny-Phi 19	Denny-Phi.............760	Soto-Cin 18
Wiggins-SD 66	Wiggins-SD 10.0	Bowa-Chi 25.6	Cromartie-Mon 11.4	Soto-Cin 17	Perez-Atl 652	Rogers-Mon 13
S.Sax-LA 56	Wilson-NY 6.3	Hubbard-Atl 24.9	Raines-Mon 9.4	Rogers-Mon............17	McWilliams-Pit 652	Gullickson-Mon 10
Wilson-NY 54	McGee-StL 5.8	Buckner-Chi.................21.8	Wiggins-SD 7.4	Gullickson-Mon 17	Candelaria-Pit.......652	
L.Smith-StL 43	Dernier-Phi 5.3	Schmidt-Phi 21.7	Butler-Atl...............5.7	Lea-Mon 16	McMurtry-Atl.........625	

Strikeouts	Fewest BB/Game	Games	Saves	Base Runners/9	Adjusted Relief Runs	Relief Ranking
Carlton-Phi 275	Hammaker-SF 1.67	Campbell-Chi 82	Smith-Chi...............29	Niedenfuer-LA 8.08	Orosco-NY 23.7	Orosco-NY 45.5
Soto-Cin 242	Ruthven-Phi-Chi ..1.87	Tekulve-Pit 76	Holland-Phi 25	Dawley-Hou 8.36	Smith-Chi 22.8	Smith-Chi 39.5
McWilliams-Pit......199	Denny-Phi............1.97	Hernandez-Chi-Phi 74	Minton-SF 22	Howe-LA..............8.91	Tekulve-Pit 19.4	Howe-LA 30.6
Valenzuela-LA 189	Reuss-LA 2.01	Scherrer-Cin 73	Sutter-StL 21	Holland-Phi...........9.13	Niedenfuer-LA 18.9	Tekulve-Pit..........27.7
Ryan-Hou 183	Candelaria-Pit.......2.05	Minton-SF 73	Reardon-Mon..........21	DiPino-Hou 9.21	Howe-LA...............15.9	Niedenfuer-LA 23.8

Innings Pitched	Opponents' Avg.	Opponents' OBP	Earned Run Average	Adjusted ERA	Adjusted Starter Runs	Pitcher Wins
Carlton-Phi 283.2	Ryan-Hou 195	Hammaker-SF 266	Hammaker-SF 2.25	Hammaker-SF 158	Denny-Phi............32.0	**Orosco-NY**..........5.2
Soto-Cin 273.2	Soto-Cin 208	Soto-Cin.......................278	Denny-Phi............2.37	Denny-Phi 151	Soto-Cin 30.1	**Smith-Chi** 4.2
Rogers-Mon 273.0	Welch-LA 222	Pena-LA........................283	Welch-LA 2.65	Soto-Cin 141	Hammaker-SF 22.4	**Howe-LA** 3.4
Niekro-Hou 263.2	Hammaker-SF 228	Welch-LA......................291	Soto-Cin 2.70	Welch-LA..............136	Welch-LA 21.5	**Denny-Phi** 3.4
Valenzuela-LA ..257.0	Pena-LA 229	Denny-Phi 293	Pena-LA 2.75	Pena-LA................131	McMurtry-Atl........17.8	**Soto-Cin**.............2.9

One More for Cincinnati East

With the departure of Joe Morgan, Tony Perez, Pete Rose, and others, the Reds had declined. In 1982 they had crashed into the basement. Following the 1983 season, Johnny Bench, shifted uncomfortably to third base, retired at 35. The Big Red Machine was dead.

But it lived, one last time, in Philadelphia. With a hot Septembers under new manager Paul Owens, the Phillies squeezed out one last division title as Cincinnati East. Morgan, Rose, and Perez all played key roles for the Phillies. Von Hayes was the only young regular, and the pitching depended heavily on graybeards and reliever Al Holland.

For the first time (excluding 1981) since 1931, the NL had no 20-game winner. As a result, Phillies right-hander John Denny was voted the Cy Young winner. His career was effectively destroyed by elbow problems the next season. Thirty-nine-year-old Fergie Jenkins had the second-best ERA among Cubs starters, but chose to retire. Mets right field prospect Darryl Strawberry lived up to the hype, winning Rookie of the Year honors.

The Dodgers edged Atlanta in the West, getting hot in August just as the Braves cooled. Dale Murphy won his second straight MVP for the Braves, but the late-season acquisition of Len Barker backfired in Atlanta; the club was demoralized when news leaked that Brett Butler was the player to be named going to Cleveland.

Pedro Guerrero was the main cog in Los Angeles' offense. Fernando Valenzuela was not as sharp as he was in his first two seasons, although he remained among the leaders in strikeouts and innings; Bob Welch and Alejandro Pena provided solid rotation support. In the playoffs, though, the Dodgers didn't get much hitting or pitching—Valenzuela won their lone game against Philadelphia. Los Angeles dropped the last two games by 7–2 tallies. Steve Carlton was excellent in two starts, and he also pitched well in the World Series. Unfortunately for the Phillies, the offense was out to lunch, and they lost to the Orioles in five games.

1983 American League

TEAM	W	L	T	PCT	GB	HW	HL	R	OR	PA	H	2B	3B	HR	BB	SO	HB	SH	AVG	OBP	SLG	OPS	AOPS	BR	ABR	PF	SB	CS	BSA	BSR
EAST																														
BAL	98	64	0	.605		50	31	799	652	6272	1492	283	27	**168**	**601**	800	46	23	.269	**.340**	.421	761	110	74	90	98	61	33	65	2
DET	92	70	0	.568	6	48	33	789	679	6246	1530	283	53	156	508	831	48	39	.274	.335	.427	762	111	68	89	97	93	53	64	2
NY	91	71	0	.562	7	51	30	770	703	6279	1535	269	40	153	533	686	37	37	.273	.337	.416	753	110	53	83	96	84	42	67	4
TOR	89	73	0	.549	9	48	33	795	726	6213	1546	268	**58**	167	510	810	36	32	**.277**	.338	**.436**	**774**	105	**88**	41	106	131	72	65	4
MIL	87	75	0	.537	11	52	29	764	708	6240	**1556**	281	57	132	475	**665**	**61**	27	**.277**	.333	.418	751	**114**	43	**107**	92	101	49	67	5
BOS	78	84	0	.481	20	38	43	724	775	6251	1512	**287**	32	142	536	758	49	28	.270	.335	.409	744	97	37	-15	107	30	26	54	-2
CLE	70	92	0	.432	28	36	45	704	785	6222	1451	249	31	86	605	691	48	29	.265	.338	.369	707	91	-21	-47	104	109	71	61	-1
WEST																														
CHI	99	63	0	.611		**55**	26	**800**	650	6163	1439	270	42	157	527	888	53	**43**	.262	.329	.413	742	99	27	0	104	165	50	77	19
KC	79	83	1	.488	20	45	36	696	767	6083	1515	273	54	109	397	722	32	23	.271	.320	.397	717	96	-34	-35	100	182	47	**79**	**24**
TEX	77	85	1	.475	22	44	37	639	**609**	6161	1429	242	33	106	442	767	38	29	.255	.310	.366	676	87	-111	-99	98	119	60	66	5
OAK	74	88	0	.457	25	42	39	708	782	6188	1447	237	28	121	524	872	55	31	.262	.326	.381	707	100	-35	8	94	**235**	98	71	17
CAL	70	92	0	.432	29	35	46	722	779	6294	1467	241	22	154	509	835	68	31	.260	.322	.393	715	97	-30	-24	99	41	39	51	-5
MIN	70	92	0	.432	29	37	44	709	822	6171	1463	280	41	141	467	802	29	29	.261	.319	.401	720	94	-23	-47	104	44	29	60	0
SEA	60	102	0	.370	39	30	51	558	740	5905	1280	247	31	111	460	840	40	24	.240	.301	.360	661	78	-137	-157	104	144	80	64	4
TOT	1135					611	523	10177		86688	20662	3710	549	1903	7094	10967	425	640	.266	.328	.401	728					1539	749	67	.76

TEAM	CG	SHO	GR	SV	IP	H	HR	BB	SO	BR/9	ERA	AERA	OAV	OOB	PR	APR	PF	OSB	OCS	FA	E	WPB	DP	FW	PW	BW	BSW	DIF
EAST																												
BAL	36	**15**	225	38	1452.1	1451	130	452	774	11.9	3.63	109	.261	.316	70	54	97	98	47	.981	121	41	159	.5	5.4	9.0	-.3	2.4
DET	42	9	205	28	1451.0	**1318**	170	522	875	11.6	3.80	103	**.242**	.309	42	17	96	**80**	**63**	.980	125	71	142	.3	1.7	8.9	-.3	.4
NY	**47**	12	202	32	1456.2	1449	116	455	892	11.9	3.86	101	.260	.315	33	6	96	110	52	.978	139	42	157	-.5	.6	8.3	-.1	1.7
TOR	43	8	257	32	1445.1	1434	145	517	835	12.4	4.12	104	.259	.325	-10	27	106	83	47	.981	115	**32**	148	.9	2.7	4.1	-.1	.5
MIL	35	10	211	43	1454.0	1513	133	491	689	12.6	4.02	93	.270	.329	6	-50	92	157	47	**.982**	**113**	37	162	**1.0**	-5.0	**10.7**	-.0	-.6
BOS	29	7	201	42	1446.1	1572	158	493	767	13.0	4.34	100	.279	.337	-44	2	107	155	53	.979	130	36	168	.0	.2	-1.5	-.7	-1.0
CLE	34	8	226	25	1441.2	1531	120	529	794	13.1	4.43	96	.275	.339	-60	-30	104	101	56	.980	122	70	174	.5	-3.0	-4.7	-.6	-3.2
WEST																												
CHI	35	12	243	48	1445.1	1355	128	**447**	877	**11.4**	3.67	114	.248	**.307**	63	81	103	99	45	.981	120	50	158	.6	8.1	.0	1.4	8.0
KC	19	8	229	**49**	1437.2	1535	133	471	593	12.7	4.25	96	.274	.330	-30	-28	100	109	53	.974	165	44	178	-1.9	-2.8	-3.5	**1.9**	4.3
TEX	43	11	190	32	1466.2	1392	**97**	471	826	11.7	**3.31**	**121**	.252	.313	**122**	**114**	99	101	**63**	**.982**	**113**	50	151	**1.0**	**11.4**	-9.9	-.0	-6.5
OAK	22	12	**287**	33	1454.1	1462	135	626	719	13.1	4.34	89	.263	.337	-46	-84	95	95	50	.974	157	57	157	-1.5	-8.4	.8	1.2	.9
CAL	39	7	237	23	1474.0	1636	130	496	668	13.2	4.31	93	.284	.341	-41	-49	99	83	61	.977	154	57	**190**	-1.3	-4.9	-2.4	-1.0	-1.4
MIN	20	5	268	39	1437.1	1559	163	580	748	13.6	4.66	91	.280	.348	-96	-64	105	136	57	.980	121	52	170	.5	-6.4	-4.7	-.5	.0
SEA	25	9	282	39	1418.1	1455	145	544	**910**	12.9	4.12	103	.268	.337	-9	21	105	132	55	.978	136	64	159	-.3	2.1	-15.7	-.1	-7.0
TOT	469	133	3263	503	20281.0					12.5	4.06		.266	.328						.979	1831	703	2273					

Batter-Fielder Wins	Batting Average	On-Base Percentage	Slugging Average	On-Base Plus Slugging	Adjusted OPS	Adjusted Batter Runs
Ripken-Bal 7.1	Boggs-Bos 361	Boggs-Bos 444	Brett-KC 563	Brett-KC 947	Murray-Bal...........158	Murray-Bal.........48.4
Yount-Mil.............5.7	Carew-Cal 339	Henderson-Oak 414	Rice-Bos..............550	Boggs-Bos...........931	Brett-KC 157	Yount-Mil 45.3
Henderson-Oak..5.2	Whitaker-Det.........320	Carew-Cal 409	Murray-Bal 538	Murray-Bal...........930	Yount-Mil 155	Boggs-Bos.........43.7
Grich-Cal 5.0	Trammell-Det 319	Singleton-Bal 393	Fisk-Chi 518	Rice-Bos 911	Boggs-Bos............147	Ripken-Bal.........40.8
Boggs-Bos 4.4	Ripken-Bal 318	Murray-Bal..................393	Ripken-Bal 517	Ripken-Bal...........888	Ripken-Bal............145	Brett-KC.............37.7

Runs	Hits	Doubles	Triples	Home Runs	Total Bases	Runs Batted In
Ripken-Bal............121	Ripken-Bal............211	Ripken-Bal 47	Yount-Mil 10	Rice-Bos 39	Rice-Bos 344	Rice-Bos.................126
Murray-Bal............115	Boggs-Bos............210	Boggs-Bos 44	Herndon-Det 9	Armas-Bos.............36	Ripken-Bal............343	Cooper-Mil 126
Cooper-Mil............106	Whitaker-Det 206	Yount-Mil.......................42	Griffin-Tor.....................9	Kittle-Chi 35	Cooper-Mil............336	Winfield-NY 116
Henderson-Oak....105	Cooper-Mil............203	Parrish-Det 42	Gibson-Det 9	Murray-Bal.............33	Murray-Bal............313	Parrish-Det..........114
Moseby-Tor 104	Rice-Bos 191				Winfield-NY 307	Murray-Bal 111

Stolen Bases	Base Stealing Runs	Fielding Runs-Infield	Fielding Runs-Outfield	Wins	Winning Pct.	Complete Games
Henderson-Oak....108	Henderson-Oak ..17.1	T.Cruz-Sea-Bal 24.2	Ward-Min 18.5	Hoyt-Chi.................24	Dotson-Chi 759	Guidry-NY 21
R.Law-Chi 77	R.Law-Chi...........12.7	Fletcher-Chi 22.9	Brunansky-Min 13.4	Dotson-Chi 22	McGregor-Bal.......720	Morris-Det 20
Wilson-KC 59	Wilson-KC............10.2	White-KC 22.2	Davis-Oak...........10.8	Guidry-NY 21	Hoyt-Chi 706	Stieb-Tor................14
J.Cruz-Sea-Chi 57	J.Cruz-Sea-Chi......8.3	J.Cruz-Sea-Chi 18.5	Collins-Tor.............9.9	Morris-Det 20	Guidry-NY.............700	Rawley-NY 13
Sample-Tex 44	Sample-Tex............6.9	Grich-Cal 17.8	Rice-Bos.................9.7	Petry-Det 19	Boddicker-Bal 667	McGregor-Bal........12

Strikeouts	Fewest BB/Game	Games	Saves	Base Runners/9	Adjusted Relief Runs	Relief Ranking
Morris-Det 232	Hoyt-Chi 1.07	Quisenberry-KC 69	Quisenberry-KC......45	Quisenberry-KC ..8.35	Quisenberry-KC ..32.5	Quisenberry-KC 38.2
Bannister-Chi........193	McGregor-Bal......1.56	VandeBerg-Sea 68	Stanley-Bos 33	Hoyt-Chi 9.25	Stanley-Bos 20.8	Stanley-Bos........32.8
Stieb-Tor 187	John-Cal 1.88	Davis-Min 66	Davis-Min...............30	Warren-Oak 9.59	T.Martinez-Bal......19.0	Gossage-NY 30.9
Righetti-NY 169	Honeycutt-Tex......1.91	T.Martinez-Bal...............65	Caudill-Sea 26	Boddicker-Bal 9.70	Barojas-Chi...........17.3	T.Martinez-Bal 27.7
Sutcliffe-Cle 160	Eckersley-Bos.......1.99	Stanley-Bos 64	Ladd-Mil.................25	T.Martinez-Bal.......9.84	Lopez-Det.............16.5	Lopez-Det 27.2

Innings Pitched	Opponents' Avg.	Opponents' OBP	Earned Run Average	Adjusted ERA	Adjusted Starter Runs	Pitcher Wins
Morris-Det..........293.2	Boddicker-Bal 216	Hoyt-Chi.......................260	Honeycutt-Tex......2.42	Honeycutt-Tex 166	Stieb-Tor 36.3	**Quisenberry-KC** 4.0
Stieb-Tor 278.0	Stieb-Tor 219	Boddicker-Bal 273	Boddicker-Bal 2.77	Boddicker-Bal 143	Honeycutt-Tex......28.7	**Honeycutt-Tex** ..3.7
Petry-Det 266.1	Conroy-Oak 232	Morris-Det 287	Stieb-Tor 3.04	Stieb-Tor 142	Dotson-Chi 26.4	**Stieb-Tor** 3.6
Hoyt-Chi 260.2	Bannister-Chi 233	Guidry-NY 288	Hough-Tex 3.18	Young-Sea...........131	Hough-Tex 25.8	**Stanley-Bos** 3.3
McGregor-Bal 260.0	Morris-Det............233	Stieb-Tor 291	McGregor-Bal......3.18	Dotson-Chi 130	McGregor-Bal......23.7	**Dotson-Chi** 3.2

Ripken the Best Bird

This was the year of the great shortstop parade. Greg Gagne, Tony Fernandez, Spike Owen, and Dick Schofield all made their major league debuts. For the first time, five AL clubs drew more than two million fans—and two other clubs barely missed the mark.

Five teams clustered atop the AL East in August. While the Blue Jays and Brewers slid from contention, the Orioles turned it on and had no competition in September. Joe Altobelli struck it rich in his first season as Orioles manager. Cal Ripken, setting a new standard for shortstops, was a deserving MVP, and Eddie Murray could have been. When Jim Palmer came up lame, 21-year-old Storm Davis stepped into the rotation.

The White Sox routed the West; their 20-game winning margin was the largest in league history. But it was a war of attrition; Texas and California had shots at the top in June, but tanked as Chicago began winning. The White Sox, who reached the postseason for the first time since 1959, were the only division club to clear .500. Dan Quisenberry saved 45 games for the second-place Royals, establishing a new record and voiding the preconception that relief aces were sideburned, fire-tossing behemoths.

In his final season, Boston's Carl Yastrzemski set the all-time games played record—he still holds the AL mark. Gaylord Perry retired after winning his 300th game; Jim Kaat called it quits at 44; and Bert Campaneris and Bobby Murcer closed it out with the Yankees.

Baltimore beat Chicago in the ALCS, holding the White Sox to 4 runs and taking the deciding Game 4 in 10 innings on a Tito Landrum homer. The Orioles took that momentum into the World Series. After losing the opener, 2–1, Baltimore roared back to take three close games before blowing out the Phillies, 5–0, to clinch its first title since 1971. Scott McGregor and Mike Boddicker combined to allow just 2 runs in 26 innings for the Orioles.

1984 National League

TEAM	W	L	T	PCT	GB	HW	HL	R	OR	PA	H	2B	3B	HR	BB	SO	HB	SH	AVG	OBP	SLG	OPS	AOPS	BR	ABR	PF	SB	CS	BSA	BSR
EAST																														
CHI	96	65	0	.596		**51**	29	**762**	658	6143	1415	240	47	136	**567**	967	59	**29**	.260	.331	.397	728	101	80	18	109	154	66	70	11
NY	90	72	0	.556	6.5	48	33	652	676	6066	1400	235	25	107	500	1001	59	20	.257	.320	.369	689	101	2	12	99	149	54	73	14
STL	84	78	0	.519	12.5	44	37	652	645	6086	1369	225	44	75	516	924	68	23	.252	.317	.351	668	97	-36	-20	97	**220**	71	76	**24**
PHI	81	81	0	.500	15.5	39	42	720	690	6283	**1494**	**248**	51	**147**	555	1084	39	**29**	**.266**	**.333**	**.407**	**740**	**112**	**103**	**91**	102	186	60	76	20
MON	78	83	0	.484	18	39	42	593	585	6042	1367	242	36	96	470	**782**	74	25	.251	.312	.362	674	99	-32	-3	96	131	38	**78**	16
PIT	75	87	0	.463	21.5	41	40	615	**567**	6119	1412	237	33	98	438	841	81	19	.255	.310	.363	673	95	-38	-38	100	96	62	61	-1
WEST																														
SD	92	70	0	.568		48	33	686	634	6119	1425	207	42	109	472	810	64	24	.259	.317	.371	688	99	-4	-3	100	152	68	69	10
HOU	80	82	0	.494	12	43	38	693	630	6201	1465	222	**67**	79	494	837	87	17	.264	.323	.371	694	109	11	63	93	105	61	63	2
ATL	80	82	0	.494	12	38	43	632	655	6106	1338	234	27	111	555	896	64	20	.247	.317	.361	678	90	-16	-59	107	140	85	62	1
LA	79	83	0	.488	13	40	41	580	600	6041	1316	213	23	102	488	829	**92**	14	.244	.306	.348	654	90	-69	-63	99	109	69	61	0
CIN	70	92	0	.432	22	39	42	627	747	6200	1342	238	30	106	566	978	71	12	.244	.313	.356	669	90	-33	-60	105	160	63	72	13
SF	66	96	0	.407	26	35	46	682	807	6290	1499	229	26	112	528	980	51	17	.265	.328	.375	703	108	31	55	97	126	76	62	1
TOT	971					505	466	7894		73696	16842	2770	451	1278	6149	10929	249	809	.255	.319	.369	688					1728	773	69	110

TEAM	CG	SHO	GR	SV	IP	H	HR	BB	SO	BR/9	ERA	AERA	OAV	OOB	PR	APR	PF	OSB	OCS	FA	E	WPB	DP	FW	PW	BW	BSW	DIF
EAST																												
CHI	19	8	271	50	1434.0	1458	99	**442**	879	12.1	3.75	104	.267	.321	-26	23	109	134	69	.981	121	50	137	1.1	2.4	1.9	.2	9.9
NY	12	15	278	50	1442.2	1371	104	573	1028	12.3	3.60	98	.252	.324	-2	-11	99	150	64	.979	129	55	154	.7	-1.2	1.3	.5	7.7
STL	19	12	313	**51**	1449.0	1427	94	494	808	12.1	3.58	97	.262	.324	1	-19	97	125	65	**.982**	**118**	64	**184**	**1.3**	-2.0	-2.1	**1.6**	4.2
PHI	11	6	287	35	1458.1	1416	101	448	904	11.6	3.62	100	.253	**.308**	-5	2	101	145	50	.975	161	51	112	-1.2	.2	**9.6**	1.1	-9.7
MON	19	10	272	48	1431.0	1333	114	474	861	11.5	3.31	103	.249	.310	45	19	95	138	67	.978	132	48	147	.4	2.0	-.3	.7	-5.3
PIT	27	13	246	34	1470.0	1344	102	502	995	**11.4**	**3.11**	**116**	.246	**.308**	**78**	**80**	100	**115**	71	.980	128	49	142	.7	**8.4**	-4.0	-1.1	-10.1
WEST																												
SD	13	**17**	285	44	1460.1	**1327**	122	563	812	11.8	3.48	102	**.244**	.315	17	14	99	125	46	.978	138	56	144	.1	1.5	-.3	.0	9.6
HOU	24	13	312	29	1449.1	1350	91	502	950	11.6	3.32	100	.248	.311	44	1	93	188	68	.979	133	83	160	.4	.1	6.6	-.7	-7.4
ATL	17	7	278	49	1447.0	1401	122	525	859	12.1	3.57	108	.257	.322	3	42	107	155	63	.978	139	**44**	153	.0	4.4	-6.2	-.9	1.6
LA	**39**	16	259	27	1460.2	1381	**76**	499	**1033**	11.7	3.17	111	.250	.313	68	60	98	132	**74**	.975	163	52	146	-1.3	6.3	-6.6	-1.0	.6
CIN	25	6	327	25	1461.1	1445	128	578	946	12.6	4.16	91	.259	.328	-92	-58	105	149	70	.977	139	51	116	.0	-6.1	-6.3	.4	.9
SF	9	7	**359**	38	1461.0	1589	125	549	854	13.4	4.39	80	.278	.342	-131	-147	98	172	66	.973	173	76	134	-1.9	-15.4	5.8	-.9	-2.5
TOT	234	130	3487	480	17424.2					12.0	3.59		.255	.319						.978	1674	679	1729					

Batter-Fielder Wins	Batting Average	On-Base Percentage	Slugging Average	On-Base Plus Slugging	Adjusted OPS	Adjusted Batter Runs
Sandberg-Chi 6.5	Gwynn-SD .351	Matthews-Chi .410	Murphy-Atl .547	Schmidt-Phi .919	Schmidt-Phi 155	Schmidt-Phi 40.4
O.Smith-StL 5.1	Lacy-Pit .321	Gwynn-SD .410	Schmidt-Phi .536	Murphy-Atl .919	C.Davis-SF 149	Hernandez-NY 38.9
Raines-Mon 4.9	C.Davis-SF .315	Hernandez-NY .409	Sandberg-Chi .520	Sandberg-Chi .887	Cruz-Hou 148	Cruz-Hou 38.7
Schmidt-Phi 4.7	Sandberg-Chi .314	Raines-Mon .393	C.Davis-SF .507	C.Davis-SF .875	Murphy-Atl 145	Raines-Mon 36.7
Hernandez-NY 4.7	Ray-Pit .312	Schmidt-Phi .383	Durham-Chi .505	Durham-Chi .874	Hernandez-NY 145	Murphy-Atl 36.4

Runs	Hits	Doubles	Triples	Home Runs	Total Bases	Runs Batted In
Sandberg-Chi 114	Gwynn-SD 213	Ray-Pit 38	Sandberg-Chi 19	Schmidt-Phi 36	Murphy-Atl 332	Schmidt-Phi 106
Wiggins-SD 106	Sandberg-Chi 200	Raines-Mon 38	Samuel-Phi 19	Murphy-Atl 36	Sandberg-Chi 331	Carter-Mon 106
Raines-Mon 106	Raines-Mon 192	Sandberg-Chi 36	Cruz-Hou 13	Carter-Mon 27	Samuel-Phi 310	Murphy-Atl 100
Samuel-Phi 105	Samuel-Phi 191	Samuel-Phi 36		Strawberry-NY 26	Carter-Mon 290	Strawberry-NY 97
Matthews-Chi 101	Cruz-Hou 187			Cey-Chi 25	Schmidt-Phi 283	Cey-Chi 97

Stolen Bases	Base Stealing Runs	Fielding Runs-Infield	Fielding Runs-Outfield	Wins	Winning Pct.	Complete Games
Raines-Mon 75	Raines-Mon 13.0	O.Smith-StL 31.5	Milner-Cin 13.8	Andujar-StL 20	Sutcliffe-Chi .941	Soto-Cin 13
Samuel-Phi 72	Samuel-Phi 10.6	Reynolds-Hou 24.1	Lacy-Pit 13.7	Soto-Cin 18	Soto-Cin .720	Valenzuela-LA 12
Wiggins-SD 70	Wiggins-SD 8.1	Sax-LA 22.9	Martinez-SD 11.0	Gooden-NY 17	Gooden-NY .654	Andujar-StL 12
L.Smith-StL 50	Wilson-NY 7.0	Wallach-Mon 22.4	McReynolds-SD 9.9	Sutcliffe-Chi 16	Show-SD .625	Knepper-Hou 11
	Redus-Cin 6.7	Sandberg-Chi 22.3	Wilson-NY 9.5	Niekro-Hou 16		Mahler-Atl 9

Strikeouts	Fewest BB/Game	Games	Saves	Base Runners/9	Adjusted Relief Runs	Relief Ranking
Gooden-NY 276	Gullickson-Mon 1.47	Power-Cin 78	Sutter-StL 45	Denny-Phi 9.04	Sutter-StL 26.1	Sutter-StL 40.4
Valenzuela-LA 240	Candelaria-Pit 1.65	Lavelle-SF 77	Smith-Chi 33	Smith-Hou 9.43	Dawley-Hou 16.7	Bedrosian-Atl 25.5
Ryan-Hou 197	Whitson-SD 2.00	Minton-SF 74	Orosco-NY 31	Lefferts-SD 9.62	Lefferts-SD 16.6	Dawley-Hou 24.6
Soto-Cin 185	Pena-LA 2.08	Tekulve-Pit 72	Holland-Phi 29	Orosco-NY 9.72	Bedrosian-Atl 13.8	Orosco-NY 18.7
Carlton-Phi 163	Knepper-Hou 2.12	Sutter-StL 71	Gossage-SD 25	Gooden-NY 9.74	Sisk-NY 11.4	Power-Cin 17.1

Innings Pitched	Opponents' Avg.	Opponents' OBP	Earned Run Average	Adjusted ERA	Adjusted Starter Runs	Pitcher Wins
Andujar-StL 261.1	Gooden-NY .202	Gooden-NY .269	Pena-LA 2.48	Pena-LA 142	Gooden-NY 23.6	**Sutter-StL** 4.3
Valenzuela-LA 261.0	Soto-Cin .209	Hershiser-LA .278	Gooden-NY 2.60	Gooden-NY 136	Rhoden-Pit 23.1	**Rhoden-Pit** 3.4
Niekro-Hou 248.1	Ryan-Hou .211	Andujar-StL .284	Hershiser-LA 2.66	Hershiser-LA 133	Pena-LA 22.4	**Gooden-NY** 2.9
Rhoden-Pit 238.1	DeLeon-Pit .214	Soto-Cin .284	Rhoden-Pit 2.72	Rhoden-Pit 133	Hershiser-LA 18.9	**Dawley-Hou** 2.8
Soto-Cin 237.1	Hershiser-LA .225	Ryan-Hou .286	Candelaria-Pit 2.72	Candelaria-Pit 133	Denny-Phi 18.6	**Bedrosian-Atl** 2.6

Padres Castigate Cubs

In the thirty-nine years since the Cubs had won, television, rock music, computers, and black voting rights had come along. It was about time for Chicago, and they pulled away from the surprising Mets in August. MVP second baseman Ryne Sandberg starred in all facets and was ably supported by a veteran Cubs lineup. Midseason trades brought in Dennis Eckersley, still a dependable starter, and Rick Sutcliffe, who went 16–1 for the Cubs and took home the Cy Young.

Mets hurler Dwight Gooden, just 19, was Rookie of the Year and finished second in Cy Young balloting. First baseman Keith Hernandez was outstanding, and rookie manager Davey Johnson eagerly inserted talented youngsters into New York's lineup and rotation.

Cubs attendance rose 42 percent, while Mets crowds increased 66 percent. League attendance, however, decreased in eight cities and fell 3.6 percent. Peter Ueberroth was tabbed as the new commissioner to bring financial sensibility to the game, and he *did* help baseball garner more television money. Terry Pendleton debuted for St. Louis, while the Reds welcomed Jose Rijo and Eric Davis. It was the end, though, for Joe Morgan and Tug McGraw.

San Diego, strong defensively and deep in decent pitchers, won the West by July. Tony Gwynn nailed down his first batting crown. Manager Dick Williams moved outfielder Alan Wiggins to second base, creating an instant leadoff man.

Chicago easily won the first two NLCS games at Wrigley Field, winning by a combined score of 17–2. Back in San Diego, the Padres walloped the Cubs in Game 3, and then won a seesaw Game 4 on Steve Garvey's ninth-inning homer. Chicago led the deciding game, 3–2, until Cubs errors and big hits gave San Diego a four-run seventh and their first pennant. It almost didn't matter that the Padres lost to the Tigers in the World Series. San Diego fans had no expectations of glory.

1984 American League

TEAM	W	L	T	PCT	GB	HW	HL	R	OR	PA	H	2B	3B	HR	BB	SO	HB	SH	AVG	OBP	SLG	OPS	AOPS	BR	ABR	PF	SB	CS	BSA	BSR
EAST																														
DET	104	58	0	.642		**53**	29	**829**	**643**	6373	1529	254	46	**187**	602	941	48	34	.271	**.342**	.432	774	**114**	105	**111**	99	106	68	61	0
TOR	89	73	1	.549	15	49	32	750	696	6283	1555	**275**	**68**	143	460	816	35	**52**	.273	.331	.421	752	102	51	24	104	**193**	67	**74**	**19**
NY	87	75	0	.537	17	51	30	758	679	6356	1560	**275**	32	130	534	**673**	64	38	.276	.339	.404	743	109	50	82	96	62	38	62	0
BOS	86	76	0	.531	18	41	40	810	764	6250	**1598**	259	45	181	500	842	36	20	**.283**	.341	**.441**	**782**	110	**113**	76	105	38	25	60	0
BAL	85	77	0	.525	19	44	37	681	667	6186	1374	234	23	160	**620**	884	45	22	.252	.328	.391	719	100	-2	14	98	51	36	59	-1
CLE	75	87	1	.463	29	41	39	761	766	6374	1498	222	39	123	600	815	37	27	.265	.335	.384	719	96	4	-8	102	126	77	62	1
MIL	67	94	0	.416	36.5	38	43	641	734	6057	1446	232	36	96	432	**673**	42	26	.262	.317	.370	687	93	-77	-51	96	52	57	48	-9
WEST																														
KC	84	78	0	.519		44	37	673	686	6063	1487	269	52	117	400	832	41	24	.268	.317	.399	716	96	-25	-30	101	106	64	62	1
CAL	81	81	0	.500	3	37	44	696	697	6166	1363	211	30	150	556	928	**65**	29	.249	.319	.381	700	94	-47	-42	99	80	51	61	0
MIN	81	81	0	.500	3	47	34	673	675	6107	1473	259	33	114	437	735	26	24	.265	.318	.385	703	89	-45	-74	105	39	30	57	-2
OAK	77	85	0	.475	7	44	37	738	796	6161	1415	257	29	158	568	871	37	22	.259	.327	.404	731	108	21	74	93	145	64	69	10
SEA	74	88	0	.457	10	42	39	682	774	6211	1429	244	34	129	519	871	66	42	.258	.324	.384	708	96	-31	-22	99	116	62	65	4
CHI	74	88	0	.457	10	43	38	679	736	6156	1360	225	38	172	523	883	37	39	.247	.314	.395	709	91	-38	-67	105	109	49	69	7
TEX	69	92	0	.429	14.5	34	46	656	714	6099	1452	227	29	120	420	807	47	20	.261	.313	.377	690	87	-78	-97	103	81	50	62	0
TOT	1134					608	525	10027		86842	20539	3443	534	1980	7171	11571	419	626	.264	.326	.398	724					1304	738	64	29

TEAM	CG	SHO	GR	SV	IP	H	HR	BB	SO	BR/9	ERA	AERA	OAV	OOB	PR	APR	PF	OSB	OCS	FA	E	WPB	DP	FW	PW	BW	BSW	DIF
EAST																												
DET	19	8	268	**51**	1464.0	**1358**	130	489	914	**11.5**	**3.49**	**112**	**.246**	**.308**	**81**	**71**	98	**68**	52	.979	127	63	162	.3	**7.1**	**11.2**	-.2	4.6
TOR	34	10	257	33	1464.0	1433	140	528	875	12.3	3.86	106	.257	.323	21	37	103	75	40	.980	123	51	166	.6	3.7	2.4	**1.7**	-.4
NY	15	12	287	43	1465.1	1485	**120**	518	**992**	12.4	3.78	100	.264	.325	35	2	95	88	60	.977	142	41	**177**	-.5	.2	8.2	-.2	-1.7
BOS	40	12	201	32	1442.0	1524	141	517	927	12.9	4.18	100	.270	.332	-29	-2	104	111	**67**	.977	143	47	128	-.6	-.2	7.6	-.2	-1.6
BAL	**48**	**13**	208	32	1439.1	1393	137	512	714	12.1	3.71	104	.256	.320	44	26	97	99	48	**.981**	123	67	166	.5	2.6	1.4	-.3	-.2
CLE	21	7	**308**	35	1467.2	1523	141	545	803	12.8	4.26	96	.269	.332	-43	-27	102	100	47	.977	146	60	163	-.7	-2.7	-.8	-.1	-1.7
MIL	13	7	283	41	1433.0	1532	137	480	785	12.8	4.06	95	.274	.331	-10	-35	96	96	59	.978	136	53	156	-.3	-3.5	-5.1	-1.1	-3.5
WEST																												
KC	18	9	214	50	1444.0	1426	136	**433**	724	11.8	3.92	103	.258	.312	11	17	101	94	51	.979	131	**34**	157	.0	1.7	-3.0	-.1	4.3
CAL	36	12	203	26	1458.0	1526	143	474	754	12.5	3.96	100	.271	.328	6	2	99	71	49	.980	128	48	170	.2	.2	-4.2	-.2	4.0
MIN	32	9	249	38	1437.2	1429	159	463	713	12.1	3.85	109	.260	.319	23	54	105	92	58	.980	**120**	42	134	**.7**	5.4	-7.4	-.4	1.7
OAK	15	6	282	44	1430.0	1554	155	592	695	13.7	4.48	84	.278	.348	-78	-125	94	94	**67**	.975	146	56	159	-.8	-12.6	7.4	.8	1.1
SEA	26	4	292	35	1442.0	1497	138	619	972	13.5	4.31	93	.270	.345	-50	-51	100	88	58	.979	128	64	143	.2	-5.1	-2.2	.2	-.1
CHI	43	9	238	32	1454.1	1416	155	483	840	12.0	4.13	101	.256	.317	-23	4	104	100	41	**.981**	122	43	160	.6	.4	-6.7	.5	-1.7
TEX	38	6	190	21	1438.2	1443	148	518	863	12.5	3.91	106	.260	.325	13	36	104	128	41	.977	138	95	138	-.4	3.6	-9.8	-.2	-4.8
TOT	398	124	3480	513	20280.0					12.5	3.99		.264	.326						.979	1853	764	2179					

Batter-Fielder Wins	Batting Average	On-Base Percentage	Slugging Average	On-Base Plus Slugging	Adjusted OPS	Adjusted Batter Runs
Ripken-Bal 9.4	Mattingly-NY.........343	Murray-Bal..................410	Baines-Chi 541	Evans-Bos.............920	Mattingly-NY 159	Murray-Bal..........51.0
Mattingly-NY 5.4	Winfield-NY 340	Boggs-Bos..................407	Mattingly-NY.........537	Murray-Bal............918	Murray-Bal............157	Mattingly-NY 47.5
Yount-Mil.............5.3	Boggs-Bos 325	Henderson-Oak 399	Evans-Bos 532	Mattingly-NY 918	Winfield-NY 156	Winfield-NY 43.8
Murray-Bal 5.2	Bell-Tex.................315	Winfield-NY 393	Armas-Bos 531	Winfield-NY 908	Henderson-Oak....147	Evans-Bos..........42.0
Henderson-Oak..4.7	Trammell-Det 314	Davis-Sea....................391	Hrbek-Min.............522	Hrbek-Min 906	Davis-Sea.............147	Davis-Sea...........40.8

Runs	Hits	Doubles	Triples	Home Runs	Total Bases	Runs Batted In
Evans-Bos............121	Mattingly-NY 207	Mattingly-NY.................44	Moseby-Tor 15	Armas-Bos..............43	Armas-Bos............339	Armas-Bos 123
Henderson-Oak....113	Boggs-Bos............203	Parrish-Tex 42	Collins-Tor 15	Kingman-Oak 35	Evans-Bos 335	Rice-Bos..............122
Boggs-Bos............109	Ripken-Bal............195	Bell-Tor 39	Gibson-Det 10	Thornton-Cle 33	Ripken-Bal............327	Kingman-Oak 118
Butler-Cle............108	Winfield-NY 193	Ripken-Bal 37	Baines-Chi..............10	Parrish-Det 33	Mattingly-NY 324	Davis-Sea............116
Armas-Bos............107		Evans-Bos 37		Murphy-Oak............33	Easler-Bos 310	

Stolen Bases	Base Stealing Runs	Fielding Runs-Infield	Fielding Runs-Outfield	Wins	Winning Pct.	Complete Games
Henderson-Oak......66	Wilson-KC..............8.6	Ripken-Bal 39.3	Vukovich-Cle........18.8	Boddicker-Bal 20	Alexander-Tor 739	Hough-Tex 17
Collins-Tor 60	Collins-Tor..............8.3	White-KC 29.0	Puckett-Min..........17.8	Morris-Det 19	Blyleven-Cle 731	Boddicker-Bal........16
Butler-Cle...............52	Henderson-Oak 8.2	Bell-Tex 23.8	Murphy-Oak 11.0	Blyleven-Cle 19	Petry-Det 692	Dotson-Chi 14
Pettis-Cal 48	Garcia-Tor..............5.9	Cruz-Chi 23.6	Hatcher-Min............9.9	Viola-Min 18	Wilcox-Det 680	Blyleven-Cle 12
Wilson-KC 47	Moseby-Tor............5.4	Boggs-Bos..................22.3	D.Henderson-Sea ..8.4	Petry-Det.................18		Beattie-Sea 12

Strikeouts	Fewest BB/Game	Games	Saves	Base Runners/9	Adjusted Relief Runs	Relief Ranking
Langston-Sea 204	Hoyt-Chi 1.64	Hernandez-Det.............80	Quisenberry-KC......44	Hernandez-Det....8.72	Hernandez-Det....33.6	Hernandez-Det ..41.1
Stieb-Tor 198	Smithson-Min 1.93	Quisenberry-KC 72	Caudill-Oak 36	Quisenberry-KC ..9.26	Quisenberry-KC ..20.9	Camacho-Cle 30.1
Witt-Cal 196	Guidry-NY............2.02	Lopez-Det......................71	Hernandez-Det 32	Waddell-Cle 9.84	Corbett-Cal..........17.5	Quisenberry-KC 27.2
Blyleven-Cle 170	Alexander-Tor.......2.03	Camacho-Cle 69	Righetti-NY 31	Saberhagen-KC 10.05	Camacho-Cle 17.5	Righetti-NY 26.3
Hough-Tex 164	Haas-Mil 2.04	Caudill-Oak...................68	Davis-Min...............29	Caudill-Oak........10.09	Righetti-NY 15.7	Caudill-Oak 26.1

Innings Pitched	Opponents' Avg.	Opponents' OBP	Earned Run Average	Adjusted ERA	Adjusted Starter Runs	Pitcher Wins
Stieb-Tor............267.0	Stieb-Tor...............221	Black-KC 283	Boddicker-Bal 2.79	Stieb-Tor 145	Stieb-Tor 39.3	**Hernandez-Det**..4.2
Hough-Tex 266.0	Blyleven-Cle 224	Alexander-Tor 284	Stieb-Tor 2.83	Blyleven-Cle 143	Blyleven-Cle 32.7	**Boddicker-Bal** ..3.8
Alexander-Tor 261.2	Boddicker-Bal 228	Blyleven-Cle.................285	Blyleven-Cle 2.87	Boddicker-Bal 139	Boddicker-Bal......30.7	**Stieb-Tor** 3.4
Boddicker-Bal 261.1	Langston-Sea 230	Mason-Tex 285	Niekro-NY.............3.09	Alexander-Tor 131	Alexander-Tor.......28.2	**Blyleven-Cle** 3.3
Viola-Min............257.2	Berenguer-Det 232	Seaver-Chi...................288	Zahn-Cal...............3.12	Viola-Min 131	Viola-Min..............27.0	**Camacho-Cle** 3.1

Runaway Tigers

Riding a 35–5 start, the Detroit Tigers dominated the league. Drawing league-leading crowds to the corner of Michigan and Trumbull, the Tigers led the league in scoring and ERA. Under Sparky Anderson, Detroit won 104 games with a great middle infield of Lou Whitaker and Alan Trammell, star left fielder Kirk Gibson, and slugging catcher Lance Parrish. Three strong starters were supplemented by reliever Willie Hernandez, who won the Cy Young and MVP trophies. Lefty Hernandez and righty Aurelio Lopez appeared in a combined 151 games.

On-base percentage became an official statistic, and the AL's first declared leader was Eddie Murray of the Orioles. While stolen bases dipped to their lowest level since 1973, strikeouts were their highest since the inception of the DH. Seattle rookie Mark Langston paced the league in whiffs and walks. Toronto rose to second in the East, using speed and power while debuting south-paw Jimmy Key as a co-closer. Shoulder miseries forced Jim Palmer to retire from the Orioles, but AL hitters found an equally annoying successor in Boston's 21-year-old rookie Roger Clemens.

The Angels contended with four 20-homer hitters, but again lacked a solid bullpen. The Twins, showing improvement in their third year in the Metrodome, welcomed rookie center fielder Kirby Puckett. Chicago crumbled to fifth. Kansas City was the West's only team over .500. The Royals, riding a hot September, made their sixth postseason appearance since 1976 despite 1) losing Willie Wilson to a drug suspension 2) George Brett playing just 104 games due to injury, 3) using rookie starters Bret Saberhagen, Mark Gubicza, and Danny Jackson, and 4) allowing more runs than they scored. Dan Quisenberry was again a late-inning savior.

Detroit swept the Royals easily in the ALCS. In the World Series Jack Morris twice went the distance in victories, and Trammell and Gibson were the hitting stars. The five-game win against the Padres sparked celebrations and rioting all over the Motor City.

1985 National League

TEAM	W	L	T	PCT	GB	HW	HL	R	OR	PA	H	2B	3B	HR	BB	SO	HB	SH	AVG	OBP	SLG	OPS	AOPS	BR	ABR	PF	SB	CS	BSA	BSR
EAST																														
STL	101	61	0	.623		**54**	27	**747**	572	6182	1446	245	**59**	87	**586**	853	70	18	**.264**	**.335**	.379	**714**	**107**	**52**	58	99	**314**	96	77	**35**
NY	98	64	0	.605	3	51	30	695	**568**	6248	1425	239	35	134	546	872	89	20	.257	.323	.385	708	**107**	32	50	98	117	53	69	7
MON	84	77	0	.522	16.5	44	37	633	636	6053	1342	242	49	118	492	880	61	26	.247	.310	.375	685	103	-20	19	94	169	77	69	10
CHI	77	84	1	.478	23.5	41	39	686	729	6177	1397	239	28	**150**	562	937	66	18	.254	.324	**.390**	**714**	95	42	-28	111	182	49	**79**	23
PHI	75	87	0	.463	26	41	40	667	673	6122	1343	238	47	141	527	1095	49	25	.245	.312	.383	695	97	-1	-18	103	122	51	71	9
PIT	57	104	0	.354	43.5	35	45	568	708	6099	1340	251	28	80	514	842	91	14	.247	.311	.347	658	91	-63	-57	99	110	60	65	3
WEST																														
LA	95	67	0	.586		48	33	682	579	6222	1434	226	28	129	539	846	**104**	**31**	.261	.328	.382	710	**107**	38	**60**	97	136	58	70	10
CIN	89	72	1	.553	5.5	47	34	677	666	6143	1385	249	34	114	576	856	72	23	.255	.327	.376	703	98	28	-5	105	159	70	69	10
SD	83	79	0	.512	12	44	37	650	622	6150	1405	241	28	109	513	**809**	75	23	.255	.320	.368	688	99	-8	2	99	60	39	61	0
HOU	83	79	0	.512	12	44	37	706	691	6192	**1457**	**261**	42	121	477	873	66	23	.261	.319	.388	707	106	25	46	97	96	56	63	2
ATL	66	96	0	.407	29	32	49	632	781	6207	1359	213	28	126	553	849	65	22	.246	.315	.363	678	90	-29	-65	106	72	52	58	-2
SF	62	100	0	.383	33	38	43	556	674	6063	1263	217	31	115	488	962	93	37	.233	.299	.348	647	90	-95	-66	95	99	55	64	3
TOT	971					519	451	7899		73858	16596	2861	437	1424	6373	10674	280	901	.252	.319	.374	692					1636	716	70	109

TEAM	CG	SHO	GR	SV	IP	H	HR	BB	SO	BR/9	ERA	AERA	OAV	OOB	PR	APR	PF	OSB	OCS	FA	E	WPB	DP	FW	PW	BW	BSW	DIF
EAST																												
STL	**37**	20	296	44	1464.0	1343	**98**	453	798	11.2	3.10	114	.246	.305	79	71	98	104	37	**.983**	**108**	48	166	**1.7**	7.5	6.1	**2.7**	2.0
NY	32	19	243	37	1488.0	1306	111	515	**1039**	11.1	3.11	111	.237	.302	80	59	96	122	65	.982	115	50	138	1.3	6.2	5.3	-.2	4.5
MON	13	13	323	**53**	1457.0	1346	99	509	870	11.6	3.55	96	.247	.312	7	-27	94	189	45	.981	121	62	152	.8	-2.8	2.0	.0	3.4
CHI	20	8	313	42	1442.1	1492	156	519	820	12.7	4.16	96	.271	.333	-91	-24	111	137	**82**	.979	134	48	150	.1	-2.5	-2.9	1.5	.4
PHI	24	9	315	30	1447.0	1424	115	596	899	12.7	3.68	100	.259	.331	-15	0	103	164	55	.978	139	49	142	-.2	.0	-1.9	-.0	-3.9
PIT	15	6	297	29	1445.1	1406	107	584	962	12.6	3.97	90	.255	.329	-61	-64	100	105	72	.979	133	54	127	.1	-6.7	-6.0	-.6	-10.3
WEST																												
LA	**37**	**21**	250	36	1465.0	**1280**	102	462	979	**10.8**	**2.96**	**117**	**.234**	**.295**	**102**	**86**	97	**99**	67	.974	166	49	131	-1.8	**9.0**	**6.3**	.0	.4
CIN	24	11	287	45	1451.1	1347	131	535	910	11.8	3.71	102	.248	.315	-19	12	105	133	57	.980	122	52	142	.8	1.3	-.5	.0	6.8
SD	26	19	283	44	1451.1	1399	127	**443**	727	11.6	3.40	104	.257	.313	30	21	98	138	65	.980	124	**29**	158	.7	2.2	.2	-1.0	-.2
HOU	17	9	282	42	1458.0	1393	119	543	909	12.1	3.66	95	.254	.321	-11	-34	96	144	59	.976	152	105	159	-1.0	-3.6	4.8	-.7	2.5
ATL	9	9	**351**	29	1457.1	1512	134	642	776	13.5	4.19	92	.271	.347	-98	-53	107	158	59	.976	159	43	**197**	-1.4	-5.6	-6.8	-1.2	-.0
SF	13	5	321	24	1448.0	1348	125	572	985	12.1	3.61	95	.247	.319	-3	-29	96	143	53	.976	148	77	134	-.7	-3.1	-6.9	-.6	-7.6
TOT	267	149	3561	455	17474.2					12.0	3.59		.252	.319						.979	1621	666	1796					

Batter-Fielder Wins	Batting Average	On-Base Percentage	Slugging Average	On-Base Plus Slugging	Adjusted OPS	Adjusted Batter Runs
Guerrero-LA 5.9	McGee-StL 353	Guerrero-LA................422	Guerrero-LA 577	Guerrero-LA 999	Guerrero-LA 183	Guerrero-LA 57.4
Hubbard-Atl 5.6	Guerrero-LA 320	Scioscia-LA 407	Parker-Cin.............551	Murphy-Atl 927	Raines-Mon 155	Raines-Mon........44.5
Raines-Mon 5.4	Raines-Mon 320	Raines-Mon 405	Murphy-Atl 539	Parker-Cin 916	Clark-StL 151	Murphy-Atl..........41.7
Sandberg-Chi......5.3	Gwynn-SD 317	Rose-Cin 395	Schmidt-Phi 532	Schmidt-Phi..........907	McGee-StL 148	Parker-Cin 37.9
Carter-NY 4.6	Parker-Cin.............312	Clark-StL 393	Marshall-LA 515	Clark-StL 895	Murphy-Atl 148	Schmidt-Phi........36.7

Runs	Hits	Doubles	Triples	Home Runs	Total Bases	Runs Batted In
Murphy-Atl 118	McGee-StL 216	Parker-Cin......................42	McGee-StL 18	Murphy-Atl 37	Parker-Cin 350	Parker-Cin 125
Raines-Mon 115	Parker-Cin 198	Wilson-Phi 39	Samuel-Phi 13	Parker-Cin 34	Murphy-Atl 332	Murphy-Atl 111
McGee-StL 114	Gwynn-SD 197	Herr-StL 38	Raines-Mon 13	Schmidt-Phi............33	McGee-StL 308	Herr-StL 110
Sandberg-Chi 113	Sandberg-Chi 186	Wallach-Mon..................36	Garner-Hou 10	Guerrero-LA 33	Sandberg-Chi 307	Moreland-Chi 106
Coleman-StL 107	Murphy-Atl 185		Coleman-StL 10	Carter-NY 32	Schmidt-Phi..........292	Wilson-Phi 102

Stolen Bases	Base Stealing Runs	Fielding Runs-Infield	Fielding Runs-Outfield	Wins	Winning Pct.	Complete Games
Coleman-StL 110	Coleman-StL 15.4	Hubbard-Atl 59.9	Wilson-Phi 15.8	Gooden-NY 24	Hershiser-LA.........864	Gooden-NY 16
Raines-Mon 70	Raines-Mon 12.3	Wallach-Mon 35.8	Milner-Cin 14.3	Tudor-StL 21	Gooden-NY 857	Valenzuela-LA 14
McGee-StL 56	Lopes-Chi 8.9	Pendleton-StL 25.9	Gwynn-SD 10.6	Andujar-StL 21	Smith-Mon 783	Tudor-StL 14
Sandberg-Chi 54	Sandberg-Chi 8.0	O.Smith-StL 18.1	McReynolds-SD 8.8	Browning-Cin..........20	Darling-NY 727	Cox-StL 10
Samuel-Phi 53	McGee-StL 6.7	Reynolds-Hou 15.5	Hayes-Phi 7.8	Hershiser-LA 19	Tudor-StL 724	Andujar-StL 10

Strikeouts	Fewest BB/Game	Games	Saves	Base Runners/9	Adjusted Relief Runs	Relief Ranking
Gooden-NY 268	Hoyt-SD 86	Burke-Mon 78	Reardon-Mon..........41	Tudor-StL 8.61	Franco-Cin 16.7	Franco-Cin...........26.7
Soto-Cin 214	Eckersley-Chi 1.01	M.Davis-SF 77	Smith-Chi...............33	Gooden-NY 8.75	Burke-Mon 15.9	Gossage-SD 21.7
Ryan-Hou 209	Lynch-NY 1.27	Garrelts-SF 74	Smith-Hou 27	Eckersley-Chi 8.88	Gossage-SD.........14.0	Carman-Phi 21.2
Valenzuela-LA 208	Tudor-StL 1.60	Carman-Phi 71	Power-Cin 27	Gossage-SD.........9.34	Carman-Phi 14.0	Niedenfuer-LA 20.4
Fernandez-NY 180	Smith-Mon 1.66	Minton-SF 68	Gossage-SD 26	Niedenfuer-LA 9.39	Lahti-StL 13.5	Lahti-StL 19.6

Innings Pitched	Opponents' Avg.	Opponents' OBP	Earned Run Average	Adjusted ERA	Adjusted Starter Runs	Pitcher Wins
Gooden-NY 276.2	Fernandez-NY 181	Tudor-StL 249	Gooden-NY 1.53	Gooden-NY 226	Gooden-NY 62.2	**Gooden-NY** 7.5
Tudor-StL 275.0	Gooden-NY 201	Eckersley-Chi...............254	Tudor-StL 1.93	Tudor-StL 183	Tudor-StL 49.4	**Tudor-StL** 5.6
Valenzuela-LA ..272.1	Hershiser-LA.........206	Gooden-NY 254	Hershiser-LA........2.03	Hershiser-LA 172	Hershiser-LA........36.5	**Hershiser-LA** 3.8
Andujar-StL........269.2	Tudor-StL 209	Hershiser-LA 267	Reuschel-Pit 2.27	Reuschel-Pit 158	Valenzuela-LA 30.5	**Reuschel-Pit** 3.6
Mahler-Atl 266.2	Soto-Cin 211	Smith-Mon 268	Welch-LA 2.31	Welch-LA 151	Reuschel-Pit 26.7	**Valenzuela-LA** ..3.5

Cardinal Numbers

After sliding in 1983–84, did the Cardinals have anything left? Yes. The NL East was a two-horse race after early August, and the Redbirds outran the Mets. The pundits said it was all about speed, but Cardinals baseball was multi-faceted. While Rookie of the Year Vince Coleman swiped 110 bases, and the team combined for 314 (most in the NL since 1912), MVP Willie McGee's .353 average, Jack Clark's power, and Tommy Herr and Ozzie Smith's on-base skills proved just as important. John Tudor and Joaquin Andujar each won 20 games with a good bullpen in reserve.

Again the Mets were bridesmaids, and New York waved goodbye to 23-year vet Rusty Staub, but attendance rose another 50 percent. Dwight Gooden, 24–4 with a 1.53 ERA, was a unanimous Cy Young. Chicago's pitching crumbled, and the club released Larry Bowa in favor of rookie Shawon Dunston. Montreal began building a roof over Olympic Stadium in September.

Los Angeles, with an excellent offense despite a big ballpark, had few problems after July as the Padres fell apart. Four excellent Dodgers starters benefited from Pedro Guerrero's bat. Cincinnati improved to second on Dave Parker's comeback season. The club's most emotional moment came September 11, when Pete Rose became "hit king," collecting safety No. 4,192 against the Padres.

The Dodgers won the first two NLCS games at home on fine pitching; however, the Cardinals bats evened the series. Smith won Game 5 with a ninth-inning blast off Tom Niedenfuer (the Wizard's first career home run batting left-handed). In Game 6 Los Angeles lost a 4–1 lead, moved ahead in the eighth, but lost in the ninth. Clark's three-run homer (also off Niedenfuer) gave St. Louis a 7–5 win and the pennant. The Cardinals blew a three-to-one lead in games to the Royals and lost the World Series, but the franchise had reasserted itself.

1985 American League

TEAM	W	L	T	PCT	GB	HW	HL	R	OR	PA	H	2B	3B	HR	BB	SO	HB	SH	AVG	OBP	SLG	OPS	AOPS	BR	ABR	PF	SB	CS	BSA	BSR
EAST																														
TOR	99	62	0	.615		54	26	759	**588**	6106	1482	281	**53**	158	503	807	21	30	.269	.331	.425	756	102	44	25	103	144	77	65	5
NY	97	64	0	.602	2	**58**	22	**839**	660	6236	1458	272	31	176	620	**771**	48	**50**	.267	.344	.425	769	**112**	86	**106**	98	**155**	53	**75**	**16**
DET	84	77	0	.522	15	44	37	729	688	6221	1413	254	45	202	526	926	40	27	.253	.318	.424	742	102	7	12	99	75	41	65	2
BAL	83	78	0	.516	16	45	36	818	764	6211	1451	234	22	**214**	604	908	31	19	.263	.336	**.430**	766	111	65	87	97	69	43	62	0
BOS	81	81	1	.500	18.5	43	37	800	720	6419	**1615**	**292**	31	162	562	816	50	30	**.282**	**.347**	.429	**776**	107	**100**	66	104	66	27	71	5
MIL	71	90	0	.441	28	40	40	690	802	6158	1467	250	44	101	462	746	54	19	.263	.319	.379	698	90	-71	-68	100	69	34	67	3
CLE	60	102	0	.370	39.5	38	43	729	861	6120	1465	254	31	116	492	817	38	15	.265	.324	.385	709	94	-44	-38	99	132	72	65	4
WEST																														
KC	91	71	0	.562		50	32	687	639	6094	1384	261	49	154	473	840	44	36	.252	.313	.401	714	94	-49	-51	100	128	48	73	11
CAL	90	72	0	.556	1	49	30	732	703	6263	1364	215	31	153	**648**	902	**99**	39	.251	.333	.386	719	96	-17	-13	100	106	51	68	5
CHI	85	77	1	.525	6	45	36	736	720	6088	1386	247	37	146	471	843	59	43	.253	.315	.392	707	89	-56	-81	104	108	56	66	4
MIN	77	85	0	.475	14	49	35	705	782	6128	1453	282	41	141	502	779	39	31	.264	.326	.407	733	94	0	-39	106	68	44	61	0
OAK	77	85	0	.475	14	43	36	757	787	6215	1475	230	34	155	508	861	63	16	.264	.325	.401	726	105	-17	41	93	117	58	67	5
SEA	74	88	0	.457	17	42	41	719	818	6185	1410	277	38	171	564	942	28	31	.255	.326	.412	738	99	9	5	101	94	35	73	8
TEX	62	99	0	.385	28.5	37	43	617	785	6003	1359	213	41	129	530	819	34	33	.253	.322	.381	703	91	-57	-65	101	130	76	63	2
TOT	1132					637	494	10317		86447	20182	3562	528	2178	7465	11777	419	648	.261	.327	.406	733					1461	715	67	71

TEAM	CG	SHO	GR	SV	IP	H	HR	BB	SO	BR/9	ERA	AERA	OAV	OOB	PR	APR	PF	OSB	OCS	FA	E	WPB	DP	FW	PW	BW	BSW	DIF
EAST																												
TOR	18	9	316	47	1448.0	**1312**	147	484	823	**11.3**	**3.31**	**127**	.243	**.306**	**135**	**143**	102	83	44	.980	125	39	164	.2	**14.1**	2.5	.0	1.7
NY	25	9	271	**49**	1440.1	1373	157	518	907	11.9	3.69	109	.251	.316	74	52	97	107	46	.979	126	52	172	.2	5.1	**10.5**	**1.1**	-.4
DET	31	**11**	250	40	1456.0	1313	141	556	943	11.7	3.78	108	**.240**	.311	59	48	98	93	53	.977	143	72	152	-.8	4.7	1.2	-.3	-1.3
BAL	32	6	238	33	1427.1	1480	160	568	793	13.1	4.38	92	.270	.338	-36	-56	97	130	37	.979	129	**36**	168	-.0	-5.5	8.6	-.5	-.0
BOS	35	8	202	29	1461.1	1487	130	540	913	12.7	4.06	106	.265	.331	14	35	103	94	**62**	.977	145	48	161	-.8	3.5	6.5	.0	-9.2
MIL	34	5	248	37	1437.0	1510	175	499	777	12.8	4.39	95	.271	.331	-39	-36	100	109	56	.977	142	63	153	-.7	-3.6	-6.7	-.2	1.7
CLE	24	7	306	28	1421.0	1556	170	547	702	13.6	4.91	84	.281	.346	-121	-124	100	134	53	.977	141	59	161	-.6	-12.3	-3.8	-.1	-4.2
WEST																												
KC	27	**11**	216	41	1461.0	1433	**103**	463	846	11.9	3.49	119	.257	.315	107	109	100	92	50	.980	127	52	160	.1	10.8	-5.0	.6	3.5
CAL	22	8	250	41	1457.1	1453	171	514	767	12.3	3.91	105	.263	.326	38	33	99	**79**	56	**.982**	112	53	**202**	1.0	3.3	-1.3	.0	6.0
CHI	20	8	305	39	1451.2	1411	161	569	**1023**	12.5	4.07	106	.256	.327	13	39	104	112	55	**.982**	**111**	65	152	**1.1**	3.9	-8.0	-.1	7.2
MIN	**41**	7	237	34	1426.1	1468	164	**462**	767	12.4	4.48	98	.268	.326	-53	-11	106	100	54	.980	120	64	139	.5	-1.1	-3.9	-.5	.9
OAK	10	6	299	41	1453.0	1451	172	607	785	12.9	4.41	87	.259	.331	-43	-96	93	104	51	.977	140	67	137	-.6	-9.5	4.1	.0	2.0
SEA	23	8	**335**	30	1432.0	1456	154	637	868	13.4	4.68	90	.265	.343	-84	-72	102	105	57	.980	122	83	156	.4	-7.1	.5	.3	-1.1
TEX	18	5	264	33	1411.2	1479	173	501	863	12.9	4.56	93	.269	.331	-65	-51	102	119	41	.980	120	66	145	.5	-5.0	-6.4	-.3	-7.2
TOT	360	108	3737	522	20184.0					12.5	4.15		.261	.327						.979	1803	819	2222					

Batter-Fielder Wins	Batting Average	On-Base Percentage	Slugging Average	On-Base Plus Slugging	Adjusted OPS	Adjusted Batter Runs
Henderson-NY....7.0	Boggs-Bos 368	Boggs-Bos..................450	Brett-KC 585	Brett-KC.............1022	Brett-KC...............178	Brett-KC.............65.1
Brett-KC 6.7	Brett-KC 335	Brett-KC.....................436	Mattingly-NY.........567	Mattingly-NY 939	Henderson-NY......159	Mattingly-NY 52.3
Boggs-Bos 5.6	Mattingly-NY.........324	Harrah-Tex..................432	Barfield-Tor...........536	Henderson-NY......934	Mattingly-NY 159	Boggs-Bos..........51.0
Ripken-Bal 4.6	Henderson-NY......314	Henderson-NY.............419	Murray-Bal 523	Boggs-Bos...........928	Murray-Bal............150	Henderson-NY ..49.7
Murray-Bal 4.5	Butler-Cle 311	Murray-Bal..................383	Evans-Det.............519	Murray-Bal...........906	Boggs-Bos............149	Murray-Bal.........43.3

Runs	Hits	Doubles	Triples	Home Runs	Total Bases	Runs Batted In
Henderson-NY......146	Boggs-Bos............240	Mattingly-NY.................48	Wilson-KC 21	Evans-Det 40	Mattingly-NY 370	Mattingly-NY.......145
Ripken-Bal............116	Mattingly-NY 211	Buckner-Bos.................46	Butler-Cle...............14	Fisk-Chi 37	Brett-KC 322	Murray-Bal 124
Murray-Bal............111	Buckner-Bos 201	Boggs-Bos 42	Puckett-Min 13	Balboni-KC.............36	Bradley-Sea..........319	Winfield-NY 114
Evans-Bos 110	Puckett-Min 199	Cooper-Mil 39	Fernandez-Tor 10	Mattingly-NY 35	Boggs-Bos............312	Baines-Chi 113
Brett-KC.................108	Baines-Chi............198			G.Thomas-Sea 32	Murray-Bal............305	Brett-KC 112

Stolen Bases	Base Stealing Runs	Fielding Runs-Infield	Fielding Runs-Outfield	Wins	Winning Pct.	Complete Games
Henderson-NY........80	Henderson-NY 14.1	Buckner-Bos 25.4	Barfield-Tor 15.1	Guidry-NY 22	Guidry-NY..............786	Blyleven-Cle-Min ..24
Pettis-Cal................56	Pettis-Cal 9.2	Owen-Sea 24.6	Butler-Cle 13.9	Saberhagen-KC......20	Saberhagen-KC ...769	Moore-Sea 14
Butler-Cle................47	Smith-KC 6.3	White-KC 22.5	Jones-Cal 11.1	Viola-Min 18	Leibrandt-KC.........654	Hough-Tex 14
Wilson-KC 43	Perconte-Sea 6.1	Gaetti-Min 17.5	Henderson-NY 10.0	Burns-Chi 18	Higuera-Mil 652	Morris-Det 13
Smith-KC..................40	Wilson-KC.............5.6	Barrett-Bos 16.3	Puckett-Min.............9.8			Boyd-Bos 13

Strikeouts	Fewest BB/Game	Games	Saves	Base Runners/9	Adjusted Relief Runs	Relief Ranking
Blyleven-Cle-Min ..206	Haas-Mil 1.39	Quisenberry-KC 84	Quisenberry-KC......37	Ontiveros-Oak 7.96	James-Chi 24.7	Moore-Cal 47.0
Bannister-Chi........198	Saberhagen-KC ..1.45	VandeBerg-Sea 76	James-Chi 32	Hernandez-Det.....8.18	Quisenberry-KC ..24.4	James-Chi 44.2
Morris-Det 191	Guidry-NY............1.46	Righetti-NY 74	Moore-Cal 31	James-Chi 9.41	Moore-Cal............23.7	Quisenberry-KC 42.6
Hurst-Bos 189	Butcher-Min 1.86	Hernandez-Det..............74	Hernandez-Det 31	Saberhagen-KC ..9.56	Cliburn-Cal 22.7	Hernandez-Det ..31.2
Witt-Cal 180	Key-Tor 2.12	Nunez-Sea 70		Fisher-NY 9.70	Harris-Tex............21.3	Righetti-NY 31.1

Innings Pitched	Opponents' Avg.	Opponents' OBP	Earned Run Average	Adjusted ERA	Adjusted Starter Runs	Pitcher Wins
Blyleven-Cle-Min293.2	Stieb-Tor 213	Saberhagen-KC 271	Stieb-Tor 2.48	Stieb-Tor 170	Stieb-Tor 46.5	**Moore-Cal** 4.8
Boyd-Bos 272.1	Hough-Tex 215	Guidry-NY 277	Leibrandt-KC........2.69	Leibrandt-KC 155	Saberhagen-KC ..36.2	**Stieb-Tor** 4.8
Stieb-Tor 265.0	Petry-Det 217	Key-Tor 282	Saberhagen-KC ..2.87	Saberhagen-KC....145	Leibrandt-KC........36.2	**James-Chi** 4.5
Alexander-Tor 260.2	Morris-Det.............225	Hough-Tex 283	Key-Tor 3.00	Key-Tor 140	Blyleven-Cle-Min 31.7	**Quisenberry-KC** 4.4
Guidry-NY..........259.0	Higuera-Mil 235	Petry-Det 285	Blyleven-Cle-Min 3.16	Seaver-Chi............136	Key-Tor 28.7	**Leibrandt-KC** 4.0

Cards Get Royal Flush

California, with Rod Carew collecting his 3,000th hit in his final season, led the West in early September, but Kansas City took 12 of 13 to forge ahead, then three of four from the Angels in the final week to clinch. The Royals essentially won with a six-man staff: five starters (including 21-year-old Cy Young winner Bret Saberhagen) and Dan Quisenberry. George Brett had another great year, while Steve Balboni provided unexpected power.

Toronto used three big streaks to motor ahead of the Yankees, clinching on the penultimate day with a home win over New York. (The following day, Yankees hurler Phil Niekro won his 300th game.) Yankee Don Mattingly was MVP, but the Blue Jays' outfield of Jesse Barfield, Lloyd Moseby, and George Bell defeated all comers. Despite cold weather and a bad ballpark, Toronto boasted the league's second-best attendance.

Tom Seaver won his 300th game in New York—at Yankee Stadium as a member of the White Sox. A rotator cuff tear ended Rollie Fingers' career, while declining production finished Al Oliver's. Smokey Joe Wood passed on at 95 and cancer-stricken Roger Maris died at just 51.

In the first year of a best-of-seven League Championship Series, the Jays and Royals went the limit. Big rallies gave Toronto three wins in the first four games, which would have ended the series a year earlier. The opportunistic Royals took full advantage, winning Games 5 and 6 with good pitching. Kansas City blew out the home Jays with a four-run sixth in the decisive game. Brett hit .348 with 3 homers.

In the "I-85" World Series Kansas City again fell behind three games to one as St. Louis won three close contests. Unfazed, Danny Jackson won 6–1 in Game 5 to send the Series back to Kansas City. Trailing 1–0 in the ninth of Game 6, the Royals rallied—with the help of a controversial call—and Dane Iorg's two-run single sent the Series to a seventh game. Kansas City, with momentum, big bats, and Saberhagen, captured its first championship, 11–0.

1986 National League

TEAM	W	L	T	PCT	GB	HW	HL	R	OR	PA	H	2B	3B	HR	BB	SO	HB	SH	AVG	OBP	SLG	OPS	AOPS	BR	ABR	PF	SB	CS	BSA	BSR
EAST																														
NY	108	54	0	.667		**55**	26	**783**	578	6348	**1462**	261	31	148	**631**	968	75	31	**.263**	**.339**	**.401**	**740**	**113**	**87**	**110**	97	118	48	71	9
PHI	86	75	0	.534	21.5	49	31	739	713	6229	1386	266	**39**	**154**	589	1154	66	**40**	.253	.327	.400	727	102	52	27	104	153	59	72	13
STL	79	82	0	.491	28.5	42	39	601	611	6120	1270	216	48	58	568	905	108	20	.236	.309	.327	636	82	-123	-118	99	262	78	**77**	30
MON	78	83	0	.484	29.5	36	44	637	688	6173	1401	255	50	110	537	1016	53	33	.254	.322	.379	701	100	-2	4	99	193	95	67	9
CHI	70	90	0	.438	37	42	38	680	781	6127	1409	258	27	155	508	966	54	15	.256	.318	.398	716	96	21	-29	108	132	62	68	7
PIT	64	98	0	.395	44	31	50	663	700	6157	1366	273	33	111	569	929	68	20	.250	.321	.374	695	96	-10	-25	102	152	84	64	4
WEST																														
HOU	96	66	0	.593		52	29	654	**569**	6095	1388	244	32	125	536	**916**	53	24	.255	.322	.381	703	103	2	21	97	163	75	68	10
CIN	86	76	0	.531	10	43	38	732	717	6246	1404	237	35	144	586	920	65	18	.254	.325	.387	712	98	20	-9	104	**177**	53	**77**	**20**
SF	83	79	0	.512	13	46	35	698	618	6209	1394	**269**	29	114	536	1087	**101**	37	.253	.322	.375	697	103	-7	28	95	148	93	61	0
SD	74	88	0	.457	22	43	38	656	723	6118	1442	239	25	136	484	917	66	18	.261	.321	.388	709	103	8	23	98	96	68	59	-3
LA	73	89	0	.451	23	46	35	638	679	6101	1373	232	14	130	478	966	81	32	.251	.313	.370	683	101	-43	4	93	155	67	70	11
ATL	72	89	0	.447	23.5	41	40	615	719	6067	1348	241	24	138	538	904	79	24	.250	.319	.381	700	94	-5	-40	106	93	76	55	-6
TOT	969					526	443	8096		73990	16643	2991	387	1523	6560	11648	312	869	.253	.322	.380	702					1842	858	68	105

TEAM	CG	SHO	GR	SV	IP	H	HR	BB	SO	BR/9	ERA	AERA	OAV	OOB	PR	APR	PF	OSB	OCS	FA	E	WPB	DP	FW	PW	BW	BSW	DIF
EAST																												
NY	27	11	252	46	1484.0	1304	**103**	509	1083	11.2	**3.11**	**114**	.236	.302	**100**	73	95	159	55	.978	138	48	145	.1	7.6	**11.4**	.0	7.9
PHI	22	11	321	39	1451.2	1473	130	553	874	12.7	3.85	100	.265	.331	-22	0	104	216	70	.978	137	68	157	.1	.0	2.8	.4	2.1
STL	17	4	287	46	1466.1	1364	135	**485**	761	11.5	3.37	108	.250	.311	56	45	98	**91**	60	**.981**	**123**	**47**	178	**.9**	4.7	-12.3	**2.2**	3.0
MON	15	9	326	50	1466.1	1350	119	566	1051	12.0	3.78	98	.246	.318	-11	-15	99	200	54	.979	133	70	132	.3	-1.6	.4	.0	-1.7
CHI	11	6	346	42	1445.0	1546	143	557	962	13.2	4.49	90	.279	.344	-124	-67	109	132	**102**	.980	124	72	147	.8	-7.0	-3.0	-.2	-.6
PIT	17	9	**356**	30	1450.2	1397	138	570	924	12.4	3.90	98	.255	.327	-30	-11	103	137	80	.978	143	68	134	-.2	-1.1	-2.6	-.5	-12.6
WEST																												
HOU	18	**19**	299	**51**	1456.1	**1203**	116	523	**1160**	**10.8**	3.15	**114**	**.225**	**.295**	92	**76**	97	176	62	.979	130	59	108	.6	**7.9**	2.2	.1	4.2
CIN	14	8	313	45	1468.0	1465	136	524	924	12.3	3.91	99	.264	.326	-32	-7	104	135	69	.978	140	52	160	.0	-.7	-.9	1.2	5.5
SF	18	10	346	35	1460.1	1264	121	591	992	11.6	3.33	106	.236	.313	62	32	95	137	88	.977	143	70	149	-.2	3.3	2.9	-.9	-3.2
SD	13	7	350	32	1443.1	1406	150	607	934	12.7	3.99	92	.258	.333	-44	-55	98	159	65	.978	137	52	135	.2	-5.7	2.4	-1.2	-2.6
LA	**35**	14	280	25	1454.1	1428	115	499	1051	12.1	3.76	92	.256	.319	-7	-55	93	123	73	.971	181	62	118	-2.2	-5.7	.4	.2	-.7
ATL	17	5	309	39	1424.2	1443	117	576	932	12.9	3.97	100	.266	.338	-41	0	107	177	80	.978	141	55	**181**	-.1	.0	-4.2	-1.5	-2.7
TOT	224	113	3785	480	17471.0					12.1	3.72		.253	.322						.978	1670	723	1744					

Batter-Fielder Wins	Batting Average	On-Base Percentage	Slugging Average	On-Base Plus Slugging	Adjusted OPS	Adjusted Batter Runs
Sax-LA 4.9	Raines-Mon 334	Raines-Mon 413	Schmidt-Phi 547	Schmidt-Phi..........937	Schmidt-Phi..........152	Schmidt-Phi........41.2
Raines-Mon 4.8	Sax-LA 332	Hernandez-NY............413	Strawberry-NY 507	Raines-Mon 889	Raines-Mon 146	Raines-Mon........39.7
Hernandez-NY....4.7	Gwynn-SD 329	Sax-LA..........................390	McReynolds-SD ...504	Strawberry-NY......865	Strawberry-NY......142	Hernandez-NY ..37.0
Gwynn-SD 4.2	Bass-Hou 311	Schmidt-Phi 390	Davis-Hou.............493	McReynolds-SD....862	Hernandez-NY......141	Sax-LA 34.9
Hubbard-Atl 3.7	Hernandez-NY 310	Gwynn-SD...................381	Bass-Hou 486	Hayes-Phi 859	McReynolds-SD....140	Gwynn-SD..........30.6

Runs	Hits	Doubles	Triples	Home Runs	Total Bases	Runs Batted In
Hayes-Phi 107	Gwynn-SD............211	Hayes-Phi 46	Webster-Mon 13	Schmidt-Phi............37	Parker-Cin 304	Schmidt-Phi 119
Gwynn-SD............107	Sax-LA...................210	Sax-LA 43	Samuel-Phi 12	Parker-Cin 31	Schmidt-Phi...........302	Parker-Cin 116
Schmidt-Phi............97	Raines-Mon..........194	Dunston-Chi 37	Raines-Mon 10	Davis-Hou 31	Gwynn-SD 300	Carter-NY............105
Davis-Cin................97	Hayes-Phi 186	Bream-Pit 37	Coleman-StL 8	Murphy-Atl 29	Murphy-Atl 293	Davis-Hou............101
	Bass-Hou..............184	Samuel-Phi 36			Hayes-Phi 293	Hayes-Phi..............98

Stolen Bases	Base Stealing Runs	Fielding Runs-Infield	Fielding Runs-Outfield	Wins	Winning Pct.	Complete Games
Coleman-StL 107	Coleman-StL 18.6	Hubbard-Atl 39.6	Wilson-Phi 14.8	Valenzuela-LA 21	Ojeda-NY 783	Valenzuela-LA 20
Davis-Cin................80	Davis-Cin 13.8	Ramirez-Atl 22.9	Gwynn-SD 14.3	Krukow-SF.............20	Gooden-NY 739	Rhoden-Pit 12
Raines-Mon 70	Raines-Mon 12.3	Bream-Pit.....................21.4	Wilson-NY 9.0	Scott-Hou 18	Fernandez-NY 727	Gooden-NY 12
Duncan-LA 48	Duncan-LA 6.0	Dunston-Chi.................21.2	VanSlyke-StL 5.5	Ojeda-NY................18	Darling-NY 714	Krukow-SF 10
	Bonds-Pit 5.5	Pendleton-StL 19.0	Dykstra-NY.............4.0		Krukow-SF 690	

Strikeouts	Fewest BB/Game	Games	Saves	Base Runners/9	Adjusted Relief Runs	Relief Ranking
Scott-Hou 306	Eckersley-Chi 1.93	Lefferts-SD 83	Worrell-StL.............36	Scott-Hou 8.37	Worrell-StL 17.3	Worrell-StL 34.6
Valenzuela-LA 242	Sanderson-Chi 1.96	McDowell-NY 75	Reardon-Mon..........35	Horton-StL 9.33	Horton-StL 17.2	Orosco-NY 23.5
Youmans-Mon 202	Krukow-SF 2.02	Worrell-StL 74	Smith-Hou 33	Krukow-SF 9.66	McGaffigan-Mon..15.8	Tekulve-Phi 21.7
Gooden-NY 200	Welch-LA 2.10	Franco-Cin 74	Smith-Chi................31	Ojeda-NY 9.90	Tekulve-Phi...........15.8	Garber-Atl 21.5
Fernandez-NY 200	Ojeda-NY 2.15	Tekulve-Phi 73		Gooden-NY 10.12	McCullers-SD 14.2	McCullers-SD 19.7

Innings Pitched	Opponents' Avg.	Opponents' OBP	Earned Run Average	Adjusted ERA	Adjusted Starter Runs	Pitcher Wins
Scott-Hou 275.1	Scott-Hou 186	Scott-Hou.....................242	Scott-Hou 2.22	Scott-Hou 162	Scott-Hou 45.1	**Scott-Hou** 4.5
Valenzuela-LA ..269.1	Ryan-Hou 188	Krukow-SF 269	Ojeda-NY 2.57	Ojeda-NY..............138	Rhoden-Pit 30.5	**Rhoden-Pit** 4.3
Knepper-Hou 258.0	Youmans-Mon 188	Ojeda-NY......................278	Darling-NY 2.81	Rhoden-Pit 135	Ojeda-NY 23.8	**Worrell-StL** 3.6
Rhoden-Pit 253.2	Gooden-NY 215	Gooden-NY 278	Rhoden-Pit 2.84	Darling-NY............126	Darling-NY 20.0	**Orosco-NY**..........2.5
Gooden-NY 250.0	Fernandez-NY 216	Ryan-Hou......................283	Gooden-NY 2.84	Cox-StL 126	Gooden-NY 19.0	**Garber-Atl** 2.3

Fast Forward to October

Mike Schmidt won his third MVP, eighth homer crown, and 10th Gold Glove. The Giants debuted rookies Will Clark and Robby Thompson on the same day, while Pittsburgh welcomed Barry Bonds. Other future stars taking bows included Rookie of the Year Todd Worrell, Reds shortstop Barry Larkin, and Chicago's Greg Maddux and Rafael Palmeiro. Veterans Pete Rose, Tony Perez, and Cesar Cedeno all retired. But the whole season seemed like window dressing for the titanic clashes of October.

New York, which captured the East by 21_ games, the league's biggest margin since 1902, faced Houston in the NLCS. The Astros also won the West going away, as Cy Young winner Mike Scott no-hit the Giants to clinch the division title.

Despite Scott's two victories, the Mets took the NLCS, winning three times in their last at bat. Houston blew a 4–0 lead and lost Game 3 on Lenny Dykstra's two-run homer in the home ninth. The Mets won Game 5 in the 12th; 2–1. In Game 6—perhaps the best playoff game ever—Houston led 3–0 in the ninth when New York tied the score. Both teams tallied in the 14th. The Mets scored three in the top of the 16th; Houston rebounded with two. Finally, Jesse Orosco fanned Kevin Bass with two on, sending the Mets to the World Series.

After Boston won the first two World Series games in New York, the Mets snagged a pair at Fenway Park. Boston won a tight Game 5, and led 2–0, 3–2, and 5–3 (with two out in the 10th) in quest of the Series-clinching victory, but the Mets kept coming back, and won miraculously to force Game 7. The Red Sox leapt in front 3–0, but the Mets battered five Red Sox pitchers over the last three innings to win the clincher, 8–5.

1986 American League

TEAM	W	L	T	PCT	GB	HW	HL	R	OR	PA	H	2B	3B	HR	BB	SO	HB	SH	AVG	OBP	SLG	OPS	AOPS	BR	ABR	PF	SB	CS	BSA	BSR
EAST																														
BOS	95	66	0	.590		**51**	30	794	696	6255	1488	**320**	21	144	595	**707**	44	**66**	.271	.346	.415	761	106	67	65	100	41	34	55	-3
NY	90	72	0	.556	5.5	41	39	797	738	6325	1512	275	23	188	645	911	36	28	.271	**.347**	**.430**	**777**	**111**	**93**	**103**	99	139	48	**74**	**14**
DET	87	75	0	.537	8.5	49	32	798	714	6269	1447	234	30	**198**	613	885	52	43	.263	.338	.424	762	106	53	56	100	138	58	70	10
TOR	86	76	1	.531	9.5	42	39	809	733	6318	1540	285	35	181	496	848	24	33	.269	.329	.427	756	102	30	11	102	110	59	65	4
CLE	84	78	1	.519	11.5	45	35	**831**	841	6287	**1620**	270	**45**	157	456	944	56	24	**.284**	.337	**.430**	767	109	55	70	98	**141**	54	72	12
MIL	77	84	0	.478	18	41	39	667	734	6124	1393	255	38	127	530	986	53	27	.255	.321	.385	706	88	-60	-80	103	100	50	67	5
BAL	73	89	0	.451	22.5	37	42	708	760	6202	1425	223	13	169	563	862	33	31	.258	.327	.395	722	96	-28	-17	99	64	34	65	2
WEST																														
CAL	92	70	0	.568		50	32	786	684	6296	1387	236	36	167	**671**	860	**91**	40	.255	.338	.404	742	102	23	32	99	109	42	72	9
TEX	87	75	0	.537	5	**51**	30	771	743	6148	1479	248	43	184	511	1088	31	35	.267	.331	.428	759	103	35	17	102	103	85	55	-7
KC	76	86	0	.469	16	45	36	654	**673**	6128	1403	264	**45**	137	474	919	24	36	.252	.313	.390	703	88	-79	-91	102	97	46	68	5
OAK	76	86	0	.469	16	47	36	731	760	6127	1370	213	25	163	553	983	56	32	.252	.322	.390	712	101	-50	6	93	139	61	70	9
CHI	72	90	0	.444	20	41	40	644	699	6030	1335	197	34	121	487	940	50	34	.247	.310	.363	673	80	-130	-148	103	115	54	68	6
MIN	71	91	0	.438	21	43	38	741	839	6151	1446	257	39	196	501	977	44	37	.261	.325	.428	753	100	20	1	103	81	61	57	-4
SEA	67	95	0	.414	25	41	41	718	835	6185	1392	243	41	158	572	1148	52	34	.253	.326	.399	725	95	-29	-34	101	93	76	55	-6
TOT	1134					624	509	10449		86845	20237	3520	468	2290	7667	13058	500	646	.262	.330	.408	737					1470	762	66	57

TEAM	CG	SHO	GR	SV	IP	H	HR	BB	SO	BR/9	ERA	AERA	OAV	OOB	PR	APR	PF	OSB	OCS	FA	E	WPB	DP	FW	PW	BW	BSW	DIF
EAST																												
BOS	36	6	254	41	1429.2	1469	167	**474**	1033	12.4	3.93	106	.266	.325	38	36	100	79	62	.979	129	71	146	-.2	3.5	6.4	-.7	5.4
NY	13	8	289	**58**	1443.1	1461	175	492	878	12.3	4.11	99	.263	.323	11	-4	98	95	45	.979	127	57	153	.0	-.4	**10.1**	**1.0**	-1.7
DET	33	12	239	38	1443.2	1374	183	571	880	12.3	4.02	102	.251	.323	25	16	99	87	49	.982	108	62	163	1.1	1.6	5.5	.6	-2.8
TOR	16	12	290	44	1476.0	1467	164	487	1002	12.2	4.08	103	.261	.322	16	22	101	95	46	**.984**	**100**	**47**	150	**1.7**	2.2	1.1	.0	.1
CLE	31	7	290	34	1447.2	1548	167	605	744	13.7	4.58	91	.273	.346	-64	-70	99	113	41	.975	157	83	148	-1.7	-6.9	6.9	.8	3.9
MIL	29	12	237	32	1431.2	1478	158	494	952	12.6	4.01	108	.267	.328	26	48	104	95	**75**	.976	146	72	146	-1.2	4.7	-7.9	.0	.7
BAL	17	6	262	39	1436.2	1451	177	535	954	12.6	4.30	96	.263	.328	-20	-27	99	123	56	.978	135	59	163	-.5	-2.7	-1.7	-.2	-3.0
WEST																												
CAL	29	12	246	40	1456.0	1356	153	478	955	**11.5**	3.84	107	.248	**.309**	54	44	98	**61**	56	.983	107	56	156	1.2	4.3	3.1	.5	1.8
TEX	15	8	**328**	41	1450.1	1356	145	736	**1059**	13.2	4.11	105	.249	.340	11	30	103	165	51	.980	122	119	160	.3	2.9	1.7	-1.1	2.2
KC	24	**13**	230	31	1440.2	1413	**121**	479	888	12.1	**3.82**	**111**	.258	.319	**56**	**67**	102	85	66	.980	123	59	153	.2	**6.6**	-8.9	.0	-3.0
OAK	22	8	286	37	1433.0	**1334**	166	667	937	12.8	4.31	90	**.247**	.330	-21	-76	93	139	53	.978	135	78	120	-.5	-7.5	.6	.5	1.9
CHI	18	8	297	38	1442.1	1361	143	561	895	12.2	3.93	110	.251	.323	39	59	103	116	56	.981	117	69	142	.6	5.8	-14.6	.2	-1.0
MIN	**39**	6	240	24	1432.2	1579	200	503	937	13.4	4.77	90	.281	.342	-94	-72	103	111	44	.980	118	70	168	.5	-7.1	.0	-.8	-2.8
SEA	33	5	281	27	1439.2	1590	171	585	944	13.9	4.65	91	.283	.353	-76	-64	102	106	62	.975	156	63	**191**	-1.7	-6.3	-3.3	-1.0	-1.7
TOT	355	123	3769	524	20203.1					12.7	4.18		.262	.330						.979	1780	965	2159					

Batter-Fielder Wins	Batting Average	On-Base Percentage	Slugging Average	On-Base Plus Slugging	Adjusted OPS	Adjusted Batter Runs
Boggs-Bos 5.4	Boggs-Bos 357	Boggs-Bos 453	Mattingly-NY 573	Mattingly-NY 967	Mattingly-NY 163	Mattingly-NY 59.1
Ripken-Bal 4.7	Mattingly-NY 352	P.Bradley-Sea..............405	Barfield-Tor 559	Boggs-Bos............939	Boggs-Bos............156	Boggs-Bos..........53.9
Mattingly-NY 4.6	Puckett-Min..........328	Brett-KC 401	Puckett-Min...........537	Barfield-Tor 927	Barfield-Tor 145	Barfield-Tor 37.3
Trammell-Det......4.6	Tabler-Cle 326	Murray-Bal 396	Bell-Tor 532	Puckett-Min 903	Puckett-Min 138	Puckett-Min 34.1
Barfield-Tor 4.3	Rice-Bos 324	Mattingly-NY 394	Gaetti-Min 518	Brett-KC................881	Rice-Bos 137	Rice-Bos 33.4

Runs	Hits	Doubles	Triples	Home Runs	Total Bases	Runs Batted In
Henderson-NY......130	Mattingly-NY 238	Mattingly-NY 53	Butler-Cle................14	Barfield-Tor 40	Mattingly-NY 388	Carter-Cle............121
Puckett-Min 119	Puckett-Min 223	Boggs-Bos 47	Sierra-Tex 10	Kingman-Oak 35	Puckett-Min 365	Canseco-Oak 117
Mattingly-NY 117	Fernandez-Tor 213	Rice-Bos 39	Fernandez-Tor 9	Gaetti-Min 34	Carter-Cle 341	Mattingly-NY........113
Carter-Cle 108	Boggs-Bos............207	Buckner-Bos 39	Carter-Cle 9	Deer-Mil..................33	Bell-Tor 341	Rice-Bos...............110
		Barrett-Bos 39		Canseco-Oak 33	Barfield-Tor 329	

Stolen Bases	Base Stealing Runs	Fielding Runs-Infield	Fielding Runs-Outfield	Wins	Winning Pct.	Complete Games
Henderson-NY........87	Henderson-NY 12.8	Owen-Sea-Bos 35.8	Barfield-Tor 16.0	Clemens-Bos..........24	Clemens-Bos 857	Candiotti-Cle 17
Pettis-Cal 50	Pettis-Cal 6.4	Reynolds-Sea 30.2	Pettis-Cal 10.5	Morris-Det 21	Rasmussen-NY ...750	Blyleven-Min..........16
Cangelosi-Chi 50	Gibson-Det 5.4	Buckner-Bos 19.5	Rice-Bos 8.4	Higuera-Mil 20	Morris-Det............724	Morris-Det 15
Wilson-KC 34	Cangelosi-Chi........5.1	Guillen-Chi.................18.3	Henderson-Sea-Bos ..7.8	Witt-Cal 18	Higuera-Mil...........645	Higuera-Mil............15
Gibson-Det 34	Wilson-KC..............4.7	Gaetti-Min 17.0	Baines-Chi 7.5	Rasmussen-NY 18	Witt-Cal.................643	Witt-Cal 14

Strikeouts	Fewest BB/Game	Games	Saves	Base Runners/9	Adjusted Relief Runs	Relief Ranking
Langston-Sea 245	Guidry-NY.............1.78	Williams-Tex 80	Righetti-NY 46	Clemens-Bos 8.86	Eichhorn-Tor........43.7	Eichhorn-Tor 55.5
Clemens-Bos........238	Boyd-Bos 1.89	Righetti-NY 74	Aase-Bal 34	Eichhorn-Tor........9.00	Righetti-NY..........20.7	Righetti-NY 41.3
Morris-Det 223	Blyleven-Min 1.92	Harris-Tex 73	Henke-Tor 27	Henke-Tor............9.46	Harris-Tex 17.5	Harris-Tex 31.5
Blyleven-Min 215	Wegman-Mil 1.95	Eichhorn-Tor 69	Hernandez-Det 24	Candelaria-Cal 9.52	Clear-Mil..............15.9	Plesac-Mil 26.7
Witt-Cal 208	Sutton-Cal 2.13		Moore-Cal 21	Haas-Oak..............9.71	Mohorcic-Tex 15.2	Clear-Mil 26.1

Innings Pitched	Opponents' Avg.	Opponents' OBP	Earned Run Average	Adjusted ERA	Adjusted Starter Runs	Pitcher Wins
Blyleven-Min......271.2	Clemens-Bos 195	Clemens-Bos 252	Clemens-Bos 2.48	Clemens-Bos.........168	Clemens-Bos 48.4	**Eichhorn-Tor**......5.8
Witt-Cal.............269.0	Rasmussen-NY ...217	Witt-Cal 275	Higuera-Mil 2.79	Higuera-Mil 155	Higuera-Mil 42.9	**Higuera-Mil** 5.1
Morris-Det..........267.0	Witt-Cal................221	Morris-Det 287	Witt-Cal................2.84	Witt-Cal 145	Witt-Cal...............38.0	**Clemens-Bos** 5.1
Moore-Sea 266.0	Hough-Tex 221	Sutton-Cal 287	Hurst-Bos 2.99	Hurst-Bos 139	Morris-Det............27.0	**Righetti-NY** 4.1
Clemens-Bos 254.0	Correa-Tex 223	Rasmussen-NY 289	D.Jackson-KC 3.20	D.Jackson-KC 133	Hurst-Bos 23.6	**Witt-Cal** 3.8

Sorrow in Beantown

Despite Dave Righetti's record 46 saves and amazing seasons from Don Mattingly and Rickey Henderson, it wasn't the Yankees' year. The AL East went to Boston. Roger Clemens, who primed Hub hysteria in April with the major leagues' first 20-K nine-inning game, was both MVP and Cy Young. Wade Boggs led the league in both batting and on-base percentage for the third time; four Red Sox drove in 90 or more runs. Boston wrapped it up with an 11-game win streak starting August 30.

Kansas City collapsed in the West, and the Angels easily stepped into the breach. Rookie first baseman Wally Joyner was a surprise, leavening an old team with a young bat. Four California regulars were 35 or older, and the bench and bullpen were stocked with graybeards as well. Rookies also sparked second-place Texas; Ruben Sierra impressed with power and speed, while Pete Incaviglia slugged 30 homers but fanned an AL-record 185 times. The Rookie of the Year, however, was Jose Canseco of third-place Oakland. Others making their first major league appearances included Mark McGwire, Jamie Moyer, Kevin Brown, Fred McGriff, and Chuck Finley. Minnesota's Bert Blyleven allowed 50 home runs, a new record, but ended 17–14; his team finished 20 games under .500.

The playoffs again went seven games. Each team blew out the other, and then the Angels took the next two in Anaheim with dramatic late-inning rallies. California couldn't pull the trigger. Boston, trailing 5–2 in the ninth in Game 5, took the lead on Dave Henderson's home run; the Angels tied it, but the Red Sox won in the 11th. Back at Fenway, the Red Sox twice blasted the Angels to reach the World Series. The Fall Classic, however, was painful for Boston fans. Just one strike away from winning, the Red Sox found a way to lose Game 6 to the Mets; another lead slipped away in Game 7.

Two Tigers first basemen, Hank Greenberg and Norm Cash, passed on. Following the season, Bobby Grich and Tom Seaver retired.

1987 National League

TEAM	W	L	T	PCT	GB	HW	HL	R	OR	PA	H	2B	3B	HR	BB	SO	HB	SH	AVG	OBP	SLG	OPS	AOPS	BR	ABR	PF	SB	CS	BSA	BSR
EAST																														
STL	95	67	0	.586		**49**	32	798	693	6297	1449	252	49	94	**644**	933	**84**	18	.263	**.340**	.378	718	95	-9	-23	102	**248**	72	78	**29**
NY	92	70	0	.568	3	**49**	32	**823**	698	6333	**1499**	287	34	192	592	1012	70	31	**.268**	.339	**.434**	**773**	**116**	**84**	**130**	95	159	49	76	18
MON	91	71	0	.562	4	48	33	741	720	6162	1467	**310**	39	120	501	918	57	35	.265	.328	.401	729	96	-4	-25	103	166	74	69	11
PIT	80	82	0	.494	15	47	34	723	744	6222	1464	282	45	131	535	**914**	71	29	.264	.330	.403	733	99	4	0	101	140	58	71	11
PHI	80	82	0	.494	15	43	38	702	749	6190	1390	248	**51**	169	587	1109	63	25	.254	.327	.410	737	98	7	-16	103	111	49	69	7
CHI	76	85	0	.472	18.5	40	40	720	801	6197	1475	244	33	**209**	504	1064	59	21	.264	.326	.432	758	102	38	9	104	109	48	69	7
WEST																														
SF	90	72	0	.556		46	35	783	**669**	6248	1458	274	32	205	511	1094	55	**39**	.260	.324	.430	754	110	33	72	95	126	97	57	-6
CIN	84	78	0	.519	6	42	39	783	752	6196	1478	262	29	192	514	928	57	31	.266	.330	.427	757	102	42	9	104	169	46	**79**	21
HOU	76	86	0	.469	14	47	34	648	678	6143	1386	238	28	122	526	936	58	24	.253	.318	.373	691	93	-79	-54	96	162	46	78	20
LA	73	89	0	.451	17	40	41	635	675	6114	1389	236	23	125	445	923	82	31	.252	.309	.371	680	87	-111	-95	97	128	59	68	8
ATL	69	92	0	.429	20.5	42	39	747	829	6227	1401	284	24	152	641	834	86	38	.258	.339	.403	742	97	33	-3	105	135	68	67	6
SD	65	97	0	.401	25	37	44	668	763	6177	1419	209	48	113	577	992	81	27	.260	.332	.378	710	98	-37	-11	96	198	91	69	12
TOT	971					530	441	8771		74506	17275	3126	435	1824	6577	11657	349	823	.261	.328	.404	732					1851	757	71	142

TEAM	CG	SHO	GR	SV	IP	H	HR	BB	SO	BR/9	ERA	AERA	OAV	OOB	PR	APR	PF	OSB	OCS	FA	E	WPB	DP	FW	PW	BW	BSW	DIF
EAST																												
STL	10	7	362	48	1466.0	1484	**129**	533	873	12.5	3.91	106	.265	.331	28	39	102	**100**	49	**.982**	**116**	62	172	**.9**	3.9	-2.3	**1.7**	9.8
NY	16	7	308	**51**	1454.0	1407	135	510	1032	12.1	3.84	98	.254	.319	38	-12	93	161	57	.978	137	51	137	-.3	-1.2	**12.9**	.6	-1.0
MON	16	8	335	50	1450.1	1428	145	**446**	1012	**11.8**	3.92	**107**	.257	**.312**	26	**45**	103	202	46	.976	147	55	122	-.9	**4.5**	-2.5	-.0	9.0
PIT	25	**13**	313	39	1445.0	1377	164	562	914	12.2	4.20	98	.253	.323	-19	-14	101	134	84	.980	123	70	147	.5	-1.4	.0	-.0	.0
PHI	13	7	389	48	1448.1	1453	167	587	877	12.9	4.18	101	.263	.335	-16	9	104	184	63	.980	121	52	137	.6	.9	-1.6	-.5	-.4
CHI	11	5	327	48	1434.2	1524	159	628	1024	13.7	4.55	94	.275	.349	-76	-42	105	169	69	.979	130	71	154	.0	-4.2	.9	-.5	-.8
WEST																												
SF	19	10	348	38	1471.0	1407	146	547	1038	12.1	**3.68**	105	.255	.323	**66**	29	94	132	**87**	.980	129	74	**183**	.1	2.9	7.2	-1.8	.6
CIN	7	6	**392**	44	1452.1	1486	170	485	919	12.4	4.24	100	.267	.326	-27	0	104	139	75	.979	130	**46**	137	.0	.0	.9	.9	1.1
HOU	13	**13**	316	33	1441.1	**1363**	141	525	**1137**	12.0	3.84	102	**.250**	.317	38	13	96	199	54	.981	**116**	50	113	**.9**	1.3	-5.4	.8	-2.6
LA	**29**	8	281	32	1455.0	1415	130	565	1097	12.4	3.72	**107**	.255	.325	59	41	97	120	65	.975	155	62	144	-1.3	4.1	-9.5	-.4	-.9
ATL	16	4	324	32	1427.2	1529	163	587	837	13.6	4.63	94	.276	.347	-87	-42	107	185	57	**.982**	**116**	53	170	.8	-4.2	-.3	-.6	-7.3
SD	14	10	335	33	1433.1	1402	175	602	897	12.8	4.27	93	.256	.332	-30	-52	97	126	51	.976	147	77	135	-.9	-5.2	-1.1	.0	-8.9
TOT	189	98	4030	496	17379.0					12.5	4.08		.261	.328						.979	1567	723	1751					

Batter-Fielder Wins	Batting Average	On-Base Percentage	Slugging Average	On-Base Plus Slugging	Adjusted OPS	Adjusted Batter Runs
Davis-Cin 5.8	Gwynn-SD 370	Clark-StL 459	Clark-StL 597	Clark-StL 1055	Clark-StL 174	Gwynn-SD..........55.1
Gwynn-SD 5.8	Guerrero-LA 338	Gwynn-SD 447	Davis-Cin 593	Murphy-Atl 997	Strawberry-NY......165	Clark-StL 54.1
Raines-Mon 5.0	Raines-Mon 330	Raines-Mon 429	Strawberry-NY 583	Davis-Cin 991	Gwynn-SD 160	Strawberry-NY ..52.7
Murphy-Atl 4.5	Kruk-SD 313	Murphy-Atl 417	Clark-SF 580	Strawberry-NY......981	Guerrero-LA 156	Murphy-Atl 48.4
Strawberry-NY ..4.4	James-Atl 312	Guerrero-LA................416	Murphy-Atl 580	Gwynn-SD 958	Clark-SF 155	Guerrero-LA 46.4

Runs	Hits	Doubles	Triples	Home Runs	Total Bases	Runs Batted In
Raines-Mon 123	Gwynn-SD 218	Wallach-Mon.................42	Samuel-Phi 15	Dawson-Chi............49	Dawson-Chi..........353	Dawson-Chi 137
Coleman-StL 121	Guerrero-LA 184	Smith-StL 40	Gwynn-SD 13	Murphy-Atl 44	Samuel-Phi 329	Wallach-Mon 123
Davis-Cin 120	Smith-StL.............182	Galarraga-Mon 40	VanSlyke-Pit 11	Strawberry-NY........39	Murphy-Atl 328	Schmidt-Phi 113
Gwynn-SD 119	Coleman-StL 180		McGee-StL 11	Davis-Cin 37	Strawberry-NY......310	Clark-StL 106
Murphy-Atl 115			Coleman-StL 10	Johnson-NY............36	Clark-SF 307	

Stolen Bases	Base Stealing Runs	Fielding Runs-Infield	Fielding Runs-Outfield	Wins	Winning Pct.	Complete Games
Coleman-StL 109	Coleman-StL 16.3	Hubbard-Atl 28.3	Bonds-Pit 16.4	Sutcliffe-Chi............18	Gooden-NY 682	Reuschel-Pit-SF 12
Gwynn-SD 56	Raines-Mon 9.3	Hernandez-NY............16.3	Davis-Cin 15.5	Rawley-Phi 17	Sutcliffe-Chi 643	Valenzuela-LA 12
Hatcher-Hou 53	Davis-Cin 8.9	Templeton-SD 13.4	Wilson-Phi 9.9	Scott-Hou 16	Welch-LA 625	Hershiser-LA 10
Raines-Mon 50	Hatcher-Hou..........8.5	Santana-NY 12.6	Raines-Mon 6.9	Hershiser-LA 16	Rawley-Phi 607	Z.Smith-Atl 9
Davis-Cin 50	Gwynn-SD 8.1	Smith-StL....................11.8	Hatcher-Hou..........5.1		Z.Smith-Atl 600	Scott-Hou 8

Strikeouts	Fewest BB/Game	Games	Saves	Base Runners/9	Adjusted Relief Runs	Relief Ranking
Ryan-Hou 270	Reuschel-Pit-SF ..1.67	Tekulve-Phi 90	Bedrosian-Phi 40	Burke-Mon 8.01	Burke-Mon 27.8	Worrell-StL 31.2
Scott-Hou 233	Heaton-Mon 1.72	Murphy-Cin 87	Smith-Chi...............36	Perez-Mon 8.83	McGaffigan-Mon ..22.9	Franco-Cin..........29.6
Welch-LA 196	Gullickson-Cin 2.13	Williams-Cin 85	Worrell-StL.............33	Smith-Hou 9.15	Williams-Cin 18.8	Burke-Mon..........29.0
Valenzuela-LA 190	Forsch-StL 2.26	J.Robinson-SF-Pit 81	Franco-Cin 32	Perry-StL-Cin 9.78	Worrell-StL 16.1	J.Robinson-SF-Pit ..22.6
Hershiser-LA 190	Drabek-Pit 2.35	McCullers-SD 78	McDowell-NY..........25	Reuschel-Pit-SF 10.19	J.Robinson-SF-Pit ..15.7	Smith-Hou 22.3

Innings Pitched	Opponents' Avg.	Opponents' OBP	Earned Run Average	Adjusted ERA	Adjusted Starter Runs	Pitcher Wins
Hershiser-LA......264.2	Ryan-Hou 199	Scott-Hou......................281	Ryan-Hou 2.76	Ryan-Hou 142	Ryan-Hou 26.8	**Hershiser-LA** 3.5
Welch-LA 251.2	Scott-Hou 217	Reuschel-Pit-SF..........282	Dunne-Pit 3.03	Dunne-Pit 136	Hershiser-LA........25.8	**Worrell-StL** 3.1
Valenzuela-LA ..251.0	Welch-LA 221	Ryan-Hou.......................284	Hershiser-LA........3.06	Reuschel-Pit-SF ..131	Welch-LA 24.9	**Franco-Cin** 2.9
Scott-Hou 247.2	Darling-NY 233	Welch-LA 289	Reuschel-Pit-SF ..3.09	Hershiser-LA 130	Reuschel-Pit-SF ..23.1	**Burke-Mon** 2.9
Z.Smith-Atl 242.0	Dunne-Pit 240	Drabek-Pit 294	Gooden-NY 3.21	Welch-LA..............123	Scott-Hou 21.6	**Ryan-Hou** 2.4

Hum-Birds

Prior to the season, some very attractive free agents found surprisingly little interest. "Unwanted" Andre Dawson gave the Cubs a blank contract, then for a relatively small salary hit 49 homers and captured MVP honors. He couldn't carry Chicago out of last place, however. St. Louis jumped to an early lead, and then held off the Mets to win Whitey Herzog's last title.

Vince Coleman cleared 100 steals for the third time, Jack Clark led the NL in slugging and on-base percentage, and Ozzie Smith finished second in MVP voting. No St. Louis pitcher won more than 11, but eight won at least eight. The Cardinals—along with the Mets—became the first besides Los Angeles to draw three million; league attendance increased 10 percent.

Mets sluggers Darryl Strawberry and Howard Johnson did their best, but Dwight Gooden was suspended for drug possession and several hurlers suffered injuries. Philadelphia's Steve Bedrosian won an extraordinarily close Cy Young vote over Ricks Sutcliffe and Reuschel.

Last in 1985, Roger Craig's "Hum Baby" Giants acquired Reuschel, Kevin Mitchell, Dave Dravecky, and Don Robinson in midseason deals and won the West Division. Will Clark led the attack. The remarkable Eric Davis couldn't quite carry Cincinnati to the division crown; the Reds lacked pitching. Padres receiver Benito Santiago took Rookie of the Year. Houston's Nolan Ryan was 8–16 but fanned a record 11.48 hitters per game.

The .261 league average was the decade's highest, as was the scoring rate. Homers also increased 19 percent. Former Dodgers infielders Ron Cey, Steve Garvey, and Davey Lopes all retired, as did 48-year-old Phil Niekro.

San Francisco went up three games to two in the NLCS on timely hitting and veteran pitching, but John Tudor and Danny Cox shut out the Giants in Games 6 and 7 at Busch Stadium. St. Louis couldn't win the World Series, however, falling in seven to Minnesota.

1987 American League

TEAM	W	L	T	PCT	GB	HW	HL	R	OR	PA	H	2B	3B	HR	BB	SO	HB	SH	AVG	OBP	SLG	OPS	AOPS	BR	ABR	PF	SB	CS	BSA	BSR
EAST																														
DET	98	64	0	.605		54	27	**896**	735	6443	1535	274	32	**225**	**653**	913	39	46	.272	.349	**.451**	**800**	**115**	**94**	**136**	96	106	50	68	6
TOR	96	66	0	.593	2	52	29	845	**655**	6293	1514	277	38	215	555	970	30	38	.269	.336	.446	782	103	43	27	102	126	50	72	10
MIL	91	71	0	.562	7	48	33	862	817	6368	1552	272	46	163	598	1040	63	32	.276	.346	.428	774	101	41	19	103	**176**	74	70	**13**
NY	89	73	0	.549	9	51	30	788	758	6219	1445	239	16	196	604	949	38	28	.262	.336	.418	754	99	-5	5	99	105	43	71	8
BOS	78	84	0	.481	20	50	30	842	825	6359	**1554**	273	26	174	606	**825**	52	**57**	**.278**	**.352**	.430	782	103	64	42	103	77	45	63	1
BAL	67	95	0	.414	31	31	51	729	880	6185	1437	219	20	211	524	939	31	22	.258	.322	.418	740	97	-50	-30	97	69	45	61	-1
CLE	61	101	0	.377	37	35	46	742	957	6212	1476	267	30	187	489	977	44	31	.263	.324	.422	746	95	-36	-40	101	140	54	72	12
WEST																														
MIN	85	77	0	.525		**56**	25	786	806	6088	1422	258	35	196	523	898	47	38	.261	.328	.430	758	96	-8	-34	104	113	65	63	2
KC	83	79	0	.512	2	46	35	715	691	6128	1443	239	40	168	523	1034	34	30	.262	.328	.412	740	92	-42	-59	102	125	43	**74**	12
OAK	81	81	0	.500	4	42	39	806	789	6238	1432	263	33	199	593	1056	50	36	.260	.333	.428	761	107	5	63	93	140	63	69	9
SEA	78	84	0	.481	7	40	41	760	801	6139	1499	282	**48**	161	500	863	38	43	.272	.335	.428	763	95	9	-29	105	174	73	70	**13**
CHI	77	85	0	.475	8	38	43	748	746	6164	1427	**283**	36	173	487	971	54	33	.258	.319	.415	734	91	-57	-73	102	138	52	73	12
TEX	75	87	0	.463	10	43	38	823	849	6248	1478	264	35	194	567	1081	42	24	.266	.333	.430	763	100	9	8	100	120	71	63	2
CAL	75	87	0	.463	10	38	43	770	803	6301	1406	257	26	172	590	926	**70**	35	.252	.326	.401	727	94	-64	-37	97	125	44	**74**	12
TOT	1134					624	510	11112		87385	20620	3667	461	2634	7812	13442	493	632	.265	.333	.425	759					1734	772	69	111

TEAM	CG	SHO	GR	SV	IP	H	HR	BB	SO	BR/9	ERA	AERA	OAV	OOB	PR	APR	PF	OSB	OCS	FA	E	WPB	DP	FW	PW	BW	BSW	DIF
EAST																												
DET	33	10	247	31	1456.0	1430	180	563	976	12.5	4.02	105	.256	.325	70	33	95	118	43	.980	122	85	147	.1	3.1	**13.0**	-.2	1.0
TOR	18	8	**336**	43	1454.0	**1323**	158	567	1064	**11.8**	**3.74**	**120**	**.244**	**.316**	**115**	**120**	101	123	59	.982	111	69	148	.8	**11.4**	2.6	.2	.0
MIL	28	6	282	45	1464.0	1548	169	529	1039	12.9	4.62	99	.271	.333	-27	-8	103	119	58	.976	145	58	155	-1.3	-.8	1.8	**.5**	9.8
NY	19	10	278	**47**	1446.1	1475	179	542	900	12.8	4.36	101	.266	.332	16	5	98	114	63	.983	102	83	155	1.3	.5	.5	.0	5.7
BOS	**47**	**13**	236	16	1436.0	1584	190	517	1034	13.4	4.77	95	.282	.344	-50	-37	102	109	60	.982	110	67	158	.8	-3.5	4.0	-.7	-3.7
BAL	17	6	294	30	1439.2	1555	226	547	870	13.3	5.01	88	.276	.341	-88	-99	99	145	57	.982	111	57	**174**	.8	-9.4	-2.9	-.9	-1.6
CLE	24	8	308	25	1422.2	1566	219	606	849	14.1	5.28	86	.278	.351	-131	-118	102	111	51	.975	153	90	128	-1.8	-11.2	-3.8	.4	-3.5
WEST																												
MIN	16	4	289	39	1427.1	1465	210	564	990	13.1	4.63	100	.266	.337	-27	-2	104	168	46	**.984**	**98**	83	147	**1.6**	-.2	-3.2	-.6	6.4
KC	44	11	225	26	1424.0	1424	**128**	548	923	12.7	3.86	118	.261	.330	95	108	102	124	**66**	.979	131	71	151	-.5	10.3	-5.6	.4	-2.6
OAK	18	6	328	40	1445.2	1442	176	531	1042	12.5	4.32	96	.258	.324	22	-34	93	117	54	.977	142	70	122	-1.1	-3.2	6.0	.1	-1.7
SEA	39	10	251	33	1430.2	1503	199	**497**	919	12.8	4.49	105	.272	.332	-5	35	106	111	50	.980	122	51	150	.1	3.3	-2.8	**.5**	-4.2
CHI	29	12	270	37	1447.2	1436	189	537	792	12.5	4.30	107	.259	.327	26	45	103	98	51	.981	116	**46**	**174**	.5	4.3	-7.0	.4	-2.2
TEX	20	3	329	27	1444.1	1388	199	760	**1103**	13.7	4.63	97	.253	.347	-28	-25	100	205	56	.976	151	134	148	-1.7	-2.4	.8	-.6	-2.1
CAL	20	7	244	36	1457.1	1481	212	504	941	12.5	4.38	98	.264	.327	13	-13	97	**72**	58	.981	117	65	162	.4	-1.2	-3.5	.4	-2.0
TOT	372	114	3917	475	20195.2					12.9	4.46		.265	.333						.980	1731	1029	2119					

Batter-Fielder Wins	Batting Average	On-Base Percentage	Slugging Average	On-Base Plus Slugging	Adjusted OPS	Adjusted Batter Runs
Boggs-Bos 6.5	Boggs-Bos .363	Boggs-Bos .461	McGwire-Oak .618	Boggs-Bos 1049	Boggs-Bos 173	Boggs-Bos 64.8
Trammell-Det 6.1	Molitor-Mil .353	Molitor-Mil .438	Bell-Tor .605	Molitor-Mil 1003	McGwire-Oak 168	McGwire-Oak 53.9
Fernandez-Tor 4.1	Trammell-Det .343	Evans-Bos .417	Boggs-Bos .588	McGwire-Oak 987	Molitor-Mil 159	Trammell-Det 50.4
Molitor-Mil 4.0	Puckett-Min .332	Randolph-NY .411	Evans-Bos .569	Evans-Bos 986	Trammell-Det 157	Evans-Bos 48.2
McGwire-Oak 3.5	Mattingly-NY .327	Trammell-Det .402	Molitor-Mil .566	Bell-Tor 957	Evans-Bos 155	Molitor-Mil 43.7

Runs	Hits	Doubles	Triples	Home Runs	Total Bases	Runs Batted In
Molitor-Mil 114	Seitzer-KC 207	Molitor-Mil 41	Wilson-KC 15	McGwire-Oak 49	Bell-Tor 369	Bell-Tor 134
Bell-Tor 111	Puckett-Min 207	Boggs-Bos 40	Polonia-Oak 10	Bell-Tor 47	McGwire-Oak 344	Evans-Bos 123
Whitaker-Det 110	Trammell-Det 205		P.Bradley-Sea 10		Puckett-Min 333	McGwire-Oak 118
Downing-Cal 110	Boggs-Bos 200		Yount-Mil 9		Trammell-Det 329	Joyner-Cal 117
	Yount-Mil 198				Boggs-Bos 324	Mattingly-NY 115

Stolen Bases	Base Stealing Runs	Fielding Runs-Infield	Fielding Runs-Outfield	Wins	Winning Pct.	Complete Games
Reynolds-Sea 60	Wilson-KC 9.1	Barrett-Bos 32.6	White-Cal 17.6	Stewart-Oak 20	Clemens-Bos .690	Clemens-Bos 18
Wilson-KC 59	Redus-Chi 7.6	Reynolds-Sea 24.0	Kingery-Sea 13.6	Clemens-Bos 20	Key-Tor .680	Saberhagen-KC 15
Redus-Chi 52	Molitor-Mil 6.4	White-KC 22.1	Barfield-Tor 13.4	Langston-Sea 19	Saberhagen-KC .643	Hurst-Bos 15
Molitor-Mil 45	Henderson-NY 6.2	Salazar-KC 20.3	Braggs-Mil 10.2		Higuera-Mil .643	Langston-Sea 14
Henderson-NY 41	Reynolds-Sea 6.2	Gagne-Min 19.3	Felder-Mil 8.2			Higuera-Mil 14

Strikeouts	Fewest BB/Game	Games	Saves	Base Runners/9	Adjusted Relief Runs	Relief Ranking
Langston-Sea 262	Long-Chi 1.49	Eichhorn-Tor 89	Henke-Tor 34	Henke-Tor 8.33	Henke-Tor 21.4	Henke-Tor 29.0
Clemens-Bos 256	Saberhagen-KC 1.86	Williams-Tex 85	Righetti-NY 31	Alexander-Det 9.07	Eichhorn-Tor 19.6	Thigpen-Chi 28.1
Higuera-Mil 240	Sutton-Cal 1.93	Mohorcic-Tex 74	Reardon-Min 31	Eckersley-Oak 9.26	Mohorcic-Tex 18.1	Plesac-Mil 27.6
Hough-Tex 223	Bannister-Chi 1.93	Henke-Tor 72	Plesac-Mil 23	Key-Tor 9.59	Thigpen-Chi 17.6	Mohorcic-Tex 27.6
Morris-Det 208	Young-Oak 1.95	Musselman-Tor 68	Buice-Cal 17	Wilkinson-Sea 9.67	Eckersley-Oak 16.6	Eichhorn-Tor 23.4

Innings Pitched	Opponents' Avg.	Opponents' OBP	Earned Run Average	Adjusted ERA	Adjusted Starter Runs	Pitcher Wins
Hough-Tex 285.1	Key-Tor .221	Key-Tor .272	Key-Tor 2.76	Key-Tor 163	Clemens-Bos 48.9	**Clemens-Bos** 4.5
Clemens-Bos 281.2	Hough-Tex .223	Bannister-Chi .285	Viola-Min 2.90	Viola-Min 160	Key-Tor 47.4	**Viola-Min** 4.5
Langston-Sea 272.0	Morris-Det .228	Morris-Det .293	Clemens-Bos 2.97	Clemens-Bos 153	Viola-Min 45.6	**Key-Tor** 4.3
Blyleven-Min 267.0	Stewart-Oak .229	Young-Oak .293	Saberhagen-KC 3.36	Saberhagen-KC 136	Saberhagen-KC 37.8	**Saberhagen-KC** 3.8
Morris-Det 266.0	DeLeon-Chi .230	Viola-Min .293	Morris-Det 3.38	Leibrandt-KC 134	Leibrandt-KC 29.8	**Leibrandt-KC** 3.3

Twinkies in a Box

Milwaukee won 13 straight to start the season, but the Brewers fell off the pace despite Paul Molitor's 39-game hitting streak. Boston didn't win despite Roger Clemens' second consecutive Cy Young. The real race was at the border.

The Tigers and Blue Jays hung close into September. Toronto's George Bell was MVP, while Doyle Alexander went 9–0 for Detroit when acquired from Atlanta in August (for farmhand John Smoltz). Detroit was old; only one regular and one starter were under 29. Toronto, meanwhile, struggled to find starting pitching. From September 24–26, the Jays swept the Tigers to build a lead of 3_; from that point, Toronto lost four straight while Detroit perked up. In a thrilling Jays-Tigers set on the final weekend at Detroit, the Tigers won to move into a tie on Friday, moved ahead with a comeback victory Saturday, and clinched on Frank Tanana's 1–0 shutout on Sunday.

Hitters bashed a record 2,634 homers; Rookie of the Year Mark McGwire led the league with 49. Strikeouts also rose to their highest levels since 1968; Nolan Ryan established a big league mark for whiffs per game. Reggie Jackson retired from Oakland. Hal McRae hung it up for Kansas City, which also lost manager Dick Howser to cancer.

The A's and Royals struck around in the race until the end, but the title went to Minnesota, 29–52 on the road but great in the Metrodome. Minnesota was carried by four position players—Kirby Puckett, Tom Brunansky, Kent Hrbek, and Gary Gaetti—and starting pitchers Bert Blyleven and Frank Viola. Others helped in limited roles, and the Twins ground out a title.

Then Minnesota surprised Detroit in five for the league title as Brunansky hit .412 with 9 RBIs. Few expected the "Twinkies" to beat the Cardinals in the World Series, but—true to form—the Twins lost all three on the road but won their four in the dome. Viola, Blyleven, and reliever Jeff Reardon were magnificent.

1988 National League

TEAM	W	L	T	PCT	GB	HW	HL	R	OR	PA	H	2B	3B	HR	BB	SO	HB	SH	AVG	OBP	SLG	OPS	AOPS	BR	ABR	PF	SB	CS	BSA	BSR
EAST																														
NY	100	60	0	.625		**56**	24	**703**	**532**	6105	1387	251	24	**152**	544	842	65	32	.256	**.325**	**.396**	**721**	**119**	**99**	**136**	95	140	51	73	13
PIT	85	75	0	.531	15	43	38	651	616	6090	1327	240	45	110	**553**	947	66	32	.247	.317	.369	686	104	34	43	99	119	60	66	5
MON	81	81	1	.500	20	43	38	628	592	6169	1400	260	**48**	107	454	1053	66	32	.251	.309	.373	682	98	12	-16	105	189	89	68	10
CHI	77	85	1	.475	24	39	42	660	694	6202	**1481**	**262**	46	113	403	910	57	21	**.261**	.310	.383	693	100	30	1	105	120	46	72	10
STL	76	86	0	.469	25	41	40	578	633	6177	1373	207	33	71	484	**827**	105	22	.249	.309	.337	646	91	-49	-55	101	**234**	64	**79**	**29**
PHI	65	96	1	.404	35.5	38	42	597	734	6054	1294	246	31	106	489	981	67	47	.239	.306	.355	661	94	-21	-33	102	112	49	70	7
WEST																														
LA	94	67	1	.584		45	36	628	544	6045	1346	217	25	99	437	947	95	32	.248	.305	.352	657	98	-33	-14	97	131	46	74	13
CIN	87	74	0	.540	7	45	35	641	596	6062	1334	246	25	122	479	922	69	37	.246	.309	.368	677	96	7	-17	104	207	56	**79**	26
SD	83	78	0	.516	11	47	34	594	583	6032	1325	205	35	94	494	892	**106**	21	.247	.310	.351	661	98	-21	-10	98	123	50	71	10
SF	83	79	0	.512	11.5	45	36	670	626	6175	1353	227	44	113	550	1023	91	33	.248	.318	.368	686	108	32	62	96	121	78	61	-1
HOU	82	80	0	.506	12.5	44	37	617	631	6127	1338	239	31	96	474	840	77	**38**	.244	.306	.351	657	99	-32	-8	96	198	71	74	19
ATL	54	106	0	.338	39.5	28	51	555	741	6013	1319	228	28	96	432	848	74	21	.242	.298	.348	646	87	-57	-84	105	95	69	58	-3
TOT	969					514	453	7522		73251	16277	2828	415	1279	5793	11032	368	938	.248	.310	.363	673					1789	729	71	138

TEAM	CG	SHO	GR	SV	IP	H	HR	BB	SO	BR/9	ERA	AERA	OAV	OOB	PR	APR	PF	OSB	OCS	FA	E	WPB	DP	FW	PW	BW	BSW	DIF
EAST																												
NY	31	22	241	46	1439.0	**1253**	**78**	**404**	**1100**	**10.6**	**2.91**	111	**.235**	**.291**	**86**	53	93	204	52	**.981**	**115**	56	127	**.9**	5.7	**14.7**	.2	-1.4
PIT	12	11	313	46	1440.2	1349	108	469	790	11.6	3.47	98	.250	.311	-3	-11	99	142	58	.980	125	74	128	.3	-1.2	4.6	-.7	1.9
MON	18	12	307	43	1482.2	1310	122	476	923	11.1	3.08	**117**	.238	.301	60	**81**	104	194	58	.978	142	53	145	-.5	**8.7**	-1.7	-.2	-6.3
CHI	30	10	290	29	1464.1	1494	115	490	897	12.4	3.84	94	.265	.325	-64	-37	105	139	**77**	.980	125	71	128	.5	-4.0	.1	-.2	-.4
STL	17	14	333	42	1470.2	1387	91	486	881	11.6	3.47	100	.252	.312	-4	1	101	118	62	**.981**	121	69	131	.6	.1	-5.9	**1.9**	-1.7
PHI	16	6	336	36	1433.0	1447	118	628	859	13.3	4.14	86	.265	.341	-110	-89	103	185	66	.976	145	70	139	-.7	-9.6	-3.6	-.5	-1.1
WEST																												
LA	**32**	**24**	295	**49**	1463.1	1291	84	473	1029	11.0	2.96	112	.237	.299	78	61	97	126	74	.977	142	50	126	-.5	6.6	-1.5	.2	8.8
CIN	24	13	**343**	43	1455.0	1271	121	504	934	11.1	3.35	107	.237	.303	16	37	104	129	72	.980	125	46	131	.4	4.0	-1.8	1.6	2.4
SD	30	9	238	39	1449.0	1332	112	439	885	11.1	3.28	104	.247	.304	27	19	99	**74**	56	**.981**	120	52	**147**	.6	2.0	-1.1	-.2	1.0
SF	25	13	290	42	1462.1	1323	99	422	875	10.9	3.39	96	.242	.298	10	-21	95	119	44	.980	129	63	145	.2	-2.3	6.7	-1.4	-1.3
HOU	21	15	284	40	1474.2	1339	123	478	1049	11.3	3.41	97	.242	.304	7	-15	96	211	47	.978	138	**39**	124	-.3	-1.6	-.9	.8	3.0
ATL	14	4	318	25	1446.0	1481	108	524	810	12.7	4.09	90	.268	.334	-103	-63	107	148	62	.976	151	57	138	-1.1	-6.8	-9.1	-1.6	-7.4
TOT	270	153	3588	480	17480.2					11.6	3.45		.248	.310						.979	1578	700	1609					

Batter-Fielder Wins	Batting Average	On-Base Percentage	Slugging Average	On-Base Plus Slugging	Adjusted OPS	Adjusted Batter Runs
Strawberry-NY ..5.1	Gwynn-SD 313	Daniels-Cin 397	Strawberry-NY 545	Strawberry-NY......911	Strawberry-NY......168	Clark-SF 50.8
Smith-StL 4.6	Palmeiro-Chi..........307	Butler-SF 393	Galarraga-Mon 540	Clark-SF 894	Clark-SF 163	Strawberry-NY ..48.6
Gibson-LA 4.4	Dawson-Chi 303	Clark-SF 386	Clark-SF 508	Galarraga-Mon 893	Gibson-LA 151	Gibson-LA 38.1
Larkin-Cin............4.2	Galarraga-Mon 302	Gibson-LA 377	VanSlyke-Pit 506	Gibson-LA 860	Bonds-Pit..............147	Galarraga-Mon ..35.2
VanSlyke-Pit 4.1	Perry-Atl 300	Gwynn-SD 373	Dawson-Chi 504	Daniels-Cin 860	Galarraga-Mon 147	Bonilla-Pit 34.5

Runs	Hits	Doubles	Triples	Home Runs	Total Bases	Runs Batted In
Butler-SF 109	Galarraga-Mon 184	Galarraga-Mon 42	VanSlyke-Pit 15	Strawberry-NY........39	Galarraga-Mon 329	Clark-SF 109
Gibson-LA 106	Dawson-Chi..........179	Palmeiro-Chi..................41	Coleman-StL 10	Davis-Hou 30	Dawson-Chi..........298	Strawberry-NY 101
Clark-SF 102	Palmeiro-Chi 178	Sabo-Cin.........................40	Young-Hou................9	Galarraga-Mon 29	VanSlyke-Pit 297	VanSlyke-Pit........100
VanSlyke-Pit 101	Sax-LA...................175	Bream-Pit 37	Samuel-Phi 9	Clark-SF 29	Strawberry-NY......296	Bonilla-Pit............100
Strawberry-NY......101	Larkin-Cin 174		Butler-SF 9	McReynolds-NY......27	Clark-SF 292	

Stolen Bases	Base Stealing Runs	Fielding Runs-Infield	Fielding Runs-Outfield	Wins	Winning Pct.	Complete Games
Coleman-StL 81	Smith-StL 9.4	Smith-StL.....................21.0	Murphy-Atl 10.6	Jackson-Cin............23	Cone-NY...............870	Jackson-Cin 15
Young-Hou..............65	Coleman-StL 8.4	Wallach-Mon 19.3	Martinez-SD 7.2	Hershiser-LA 23	Browning-Cin 783	Hershiser-LA 15
Smith-StL................57	McGee-StL 6.9	Bream-Pit....................19.0	Thompson-Phi 6.9	Cone-NY 20	Jackson-Cin 742	Show-SD 13
Sabo-Cin 46	Davis-Cin 6.7	R.Alomar-SD 15.5	James-Phi...............5.8	Reuschel-SF 19	Hershiser-LA.........742	Sutcliffe-Chi 12
Nixon-Mon 46	Larkin-Cin 6.3	Pendleton-StL 13.8	McReynolds-NY 5.5		Maddux-Chi 692	Gooden-NY 10

Strikeouts	Fewest BB/Game	Games	Saves	Base Runners/9	Adjusted Relief Runs	Relief Ranking
Ryan-Hou 228	B.Smith-Mon........1.45	Murphy-Cin...................76	Franco-Cin.............39	Myers-NY 8.47	Franco-Cin 17.9	Franco-Cin..........35.9
Cone-NY 213	Mahler-Atl 1.52	Robinson-Pit..................75	Gott-Pit 34	Perez-Mon 8.81	Davis-SD 15.5	Davis-SD 29.4
DeLeon-StL 208	Reuschel-SF........1.54	Agosto-Hou....................75	Worrell-StL.............32	Franco-Cin 9.10	Holton-LA 15.5	Myers-NY 24.2
Scott-Hou 190	Ojeda-NY 1.56	Tekulve-Phi....................70	Davis-SD 28	J.Howell-LA..........9.14	Harris-Phi 12.7	Pena-LA 18.5
Fernandez-NY 189	Tudor-StL-LA 1.87	Franco-Cin 70	Bedrosian-Phi 28	Scott-Hou 9.18	Pena-LA 12.6	Parrett-Mon 17.3

Innings Pitched	Opponents' Avg.	Opponents' OBP	Earned Run Average	Adjusted ERA	Adjusted Starter Runs	Pitcher Wins
Hershiser-LA......267.0	Fernandez-NY 191	Perez-Mon 252	Magrane-StL........2.18	Magrane-StL 160	Hershiser-LA........34.3	**Hershiser-LA** 4.5
Jackson-Cin 260.2	Perez-Mon 196	Scott-Hou.....................260	Cone-NY.............2.22	Rijo-Cin 150	Cone-NY..............26.9	**Franco-Cin** 4.0
Browning-Cin 250.2	Scott-Hou 204	Ojeda-NY.....................261	Hershiser-LA........2.26	Tudor-StL-LA 148	Jackson-Cin 24.5	**Davis-SD** 3.6
Mahler-Atl 249.0	Rijo-Cin.................209	Hershiser-LA 269	Tudor-StL-LA 2.32	Hershiser-LA 148	Tudor-StL-LA 23.7	**Jackson-Cin** 3.1
Maddux-Chi 249.0	Cone-NY...............213	Fernandez-NY 271	Rijo-Cin................2.39	Perez-Mon 148	Perez-Mon 23.3	**Cone-NY** 2.8

"I Don't Believe What I Just Saw"

Despite an undermanned offense and several pitching injuries, Los Angeles clung to the West Division lead. Free agent signing Kirk Gibson was MVP, while Orel Hershiser's record 59 scoreless innings won him a unanimous Cy Young. John Tudor's late-season acquisition buffed up the rotation.

The Mets, meanwhile, easily wrapped up the East. Darryl Strawberry enjoyed another spectacular season, as did Kevin McReynolds. Five Mets starters won in double figures. Manager Davey Johnson effectively platooned Mookie Wilson and Lenny Dykstra and found a position for late-season sensation Gregg Jefferies.

New York led in attendance, while second-place Pittsburgh's gate increased 61 percent. Wrigley Field saw its first night game on August 9; lights were difficult for many fans to accept. Cincinnati's Chris Sabo was Rookie of the Year, but several players not as impressive as freshmen had longer careers: Mark Grace, Roberto Alomar, Tom Glavine, Craig Biggio, and John Smoltz.

Owners were found guilty of collusion against 1987 free agents. This greased the path for Peter Ueberroth's resignation. Several "new-look" free agents were also granted their freedom and the owners paid hundreds of millions in damages.

Scoring dropped 14 percent to 3.88 runs per game, the lowest since 1968, and homers fell 30 percent. Both Los Angeles and New York played in great pitchers' parks. Injuries ended Bruce Sutter's career, while Steve Carlton, Dave Concepcion, Ted Simmons, and Don Sutton retired. Giants 1930s ace Carl Hubbell passed away at 85.

Nobody expected the Dodgers to win the NLCS, but Tommy Lasorda's boys hung in, winning a 12-inning Game 4 to knot the series. In Game 7 Hershiser threw yet another complete-game shutout—he had eight during the season and added a final one in the World Series. Los Angeles then shocked prohibitive favorite Oakland in the World Series. An injured Gibson limped off the bench and ripped Dennis Eckersley for a magical game-winning homer in the opener, sparking the five-game upset. Most games were close, and Los Angeles pitchers held the A's to just 11 runs.

1988 American League

TEAM	W	L	T	PCT	GB	HW	HL	R	OR	PA	H	2B	3B	HR	BB	SO	HB	SH	AVG	OBP	SLG	OPS	AOPS	BR	ABR	PF	SB	CS	BSA	BSR
EAST																														
BOS	89	73	0	.549		53	28	**813**	689	6334	**1569**	**310**	39	124	**623**	**728**	66	45	**.283**	**.357**	.420	**777**	**112**	**146**	**111**	104	65	36	64	2
DET	88	74	0	.543	1	50	31	703	658	6153	1358	213	28	143	588	841	66	29	.250	.324	.378	702	100	-21	6	96	87	42	67	4
TOR	87	75	0	.537	2	45	36	763	680	6193	1491	271	**47**	**158**	521	935	34	31	.268	.332	.419	751	109	69	66	100	107	36	75	11
MIL	87	75	0	.537	2	47	34	682	**616**	6064	1409	258	26	113	439	911	59	37	.257	.314	.375	689	91	-57	-62	101	**159**	55	74	16
NY	85	76	0	.528	3.5	46	34	772	748	6297	1469	272	12	148	588	935	36	30	.263	.333	.395	728	104	37	43	99	146	39	**79**	**18**
CLE	78	84	0	.481	11	44	37	666	731	6045	1435	235	28	134	416	866	36	37	.261	.314	.387	701	93	-38	-55	103	97	50	66	4
BAL	54	107	0	.335	34.5	34	46	550	789	5979	1275	199	20	137	504	869	40	32	.238	.305	.359	664	87	-105	-88	97	69	44	61	0
WEST																														
OAK	104	58	0	.642		**54**	27	800	620	6356	1474	251	22	156	580	926	54	**65**	.263	.336	.399	735	109	51	79	97	129	54	70	9
MIN	91	71	0	.562	13	47	34	759	672	6180	1508	294	31	151	528	832	37	55	.274	.340	**.421**	761	109	97	74	103	107	63	63	1
KC	84	77	0	.522	19.5	44	36	704	648	6085	1419	275	40	121	486	944	46	33	.259	.321	.391	712	97	-9	-15	101	137	54	72	11
CAL	75	87	0	.463	29	35	46	714	771	6215	1458	258	31	124	469	819	63	49	.261	.321	.385	706	100	-19	0	97	86	52	62	1
CHI	71	90	0	.441	32.5	40	41	631	757	6039	1327	224	35	132	446	908	**67**	34	.244	.303	.370	673	87	-96	-94	100	98	46	68	5
TEX	70	91	0	.435	33.5	38	43	637	735	6157	1378	227	39	112	542	1022	48	35	.252	.320	.368	688	90	-50	-65	102	130	57	70	9
SEA	68	93	0	.422	35.5	37	44	664	744	6017	1397	271	27	148	461	787	40	38	.257	.317	.398	715	95	-6	-35	104	95	61	61	0
TOT	1131					614	517	9858		86114	19967	3558	425	1901	7191	12323	550	692	.259	.324	.391	715					1512	689	69	91

TEAM	CG	SHO	GR	SV	IP	H	HR	BB	SO	BR/9	ERA	AERA	OAV	OOB	PR	APR	PF	OSB	OCS	FA	E	WPB	DP	FW	PW	BW	BSW	DIF
EAST																												
BOS	26	14	250	37	1426.1	1415	143	493	**1085**	12.3	3.97	104	.259	.322	-1	22	104	107	48	.984	93	59	123	1.6	2.2	**11.2**	-.5	-6.6
DET	34	8	220	36	1445.2	1361	150	497	890	11.8	3.71	103	.248	.312	41	17	96	**80**	43	.982	109	65	129	.6	1.7	.6	-.3	4.3
TOR	16	**17**	294	47	1449.0	1404	143	528	904	12.4	3.80	104	.256	.326	27	22	99	120	55	.982	110	60	170	.6	2.2	6.7	.5	-3.9
MIL	30	8	252	51	1449.1	1355	125	**437**	832	**11.2**	3.45	**115**	.248	**.303**	84	**85**	100	95	45	.981	120	46	146	-.0	**8.6**	-6.3	1.0	2.7
NY	16	5	**304**	43	1456.0	1512	157	487	861	12.7	4.26	92	.267	.328	-48	-52	99	85	29	.978	134	**41**	161	-.9	-5.3	4.4	**1.2**	5.1
CLE	35	10	230	46	1434.0	1501	120	442	812	12.4	4.16	99	.270	.326	-31	-8	104	99	53	.980	124	46	131	-.3	-.8	-5.6	-.3	3.9
BAL	20	7	287	26	1416.0	1506	153	523	709	13.2	4.54	86	.274	.340	-90	-102	98	136	56	.980	119	60	172	.0	-10.3	-8.9	-.7	-6.6
WEST																												
OAK	22	9	290	**64**	1489.1	1376	116	553	983	11.8	**3.44**	110	.247	.316	**87**	59	95	93	56	.983	105	75	151	.9	6.0	8.0	.2	7.9
MIN	18	9	265	52	1431.2	1457	146	453	897	12.3	3.93	104	.266	.325	6	22	103	112	41	**.986**	**84**	56	155	**2.1**	2.2	7.5	-.6	-1.2
KC	29	12	253	32	1428.1	1415	**102**	465	886	12.1	3.65	109	.258	.318	49	52	101	117	42	.980	124	67	147	-.3	5.3	-1.5	.5	-.4
CAL	26	9	262	33	1455.2	1503	135	568	817	13.1	4.32	89	.270	.338	-57	-76	97	98	**64**	.979	135	81	175	-.9	-7.7	.0	-.6	3.1
CHI	11	9	293	43	1439.0	1467	138	533	754	12.7	4.12	96	.266	.331	-25	-24	100	108	53	.976	154	71	**177**	-2.1	-2.4	-9.5	-.2	4.7
TEX	**41**	11	251	31	1438.2	**1310**	129	654	912	12.6	4.05	101	**.244**	.329	-13	5	103	145	52	.979	131	108	145	-.7	.5	-6.6	.2	-4.0
SEA	28	11	292	28	1428.0	1385	144	558	981	12.5	4.15	100	.256	.327	-30	1	105	117	52	.980	123	66	168	-.2	.1	-3.5	-.7	-8.2
TOT	352	139	3743	569	20187.0					12.4	3.97		.259	.324						.981	1665	901	2150					

Batter-Fielder Wins	Batting Average	On-Base Percentage	Slugging Average	On-Base Plus Slugging	Adjusted OPS	Adjusted Batter Runs
Boggs-Bos 6.4	Boggs-Bos 366	Boggs-Bos 476	Canseco-Oak 569	Boggs-Bos...........965	Canseco-Oak 172	Boggs-Bos..........62.6
Canseco-Oak 6.0	Puckett-Min..........356	Greenwell-Bos 416	McGriff-Tor 552	Canseco-Oak 959	Boggs-Bos 165	Canseco-Oak 60.4
Puckett-Min 4.9	Greenwell-Bos 325	Davis-Sea 412	Gaetti-Min 551	Greenwell-Bos......946	Winfield-NY 159	Greenwell-Bos....49.5
Greenwell-Bos....4.8	Winfield-NY 322	Winfield-NY 398	Puckett-Min...........545	McGriff-Tor............928	Greenwell-Bos......158	Winfield-NY 45.8
C.Ripken-Bal 4.2	Molitor-Mil 312	Henderson-NY.............394	Greenwell-Bos 531	Winfield-NY 927	McGriff-Tor............156	Puckett-Min 42.3

Runs	Hits	Doubles	Triples	Home Runs	Total Bases	Runs Batted In
Boggs-Bos............128	Puckett-Min 234	Boggs-Bos 45	Yount-Mil 11	Canseco-Oak 42	Puckett-Min 358	Canseco-Oak 124
Canseco-Oak 120	Boggs-Bos............214	Ray-Cal.........................42	Wilson-KC 11	McGriff-Tor.............34	Canseco-Oak 347	Puckett-Min 121
Henderson-NY......118	Greenwell-Bos......192	Puckett-Min...................42	Reynolds-Sea 11	McGwire-Oak 32	Greenwell-Bos......313	Greenwell-Bos 119
Molitor-Mil 115	Yount-Mil 190	Brett-KC 42	Greenwell-Bos..........8	Murray-Bal.............28	Brett-KC 300	Evans-Bos 111
Puckett-Min 109	Molitor-Mil 190	Fernandez-Tor 41		Gaetti-Min 28	Carter-Cle 297	Winfield-NY 107

Stolen Bases	Base Stealing Runs	Fielding Runs-Infield	Fielding Runs-Outfield	Wins	Winning Pct.	Complete Games
Henderson-NY........93	Henderson-NY 15.9	Guillen-Chi..................40.8	Barfield-Tor 13.1	Viola-Min 24	Viola-Min..............774	Stewart-Oak..........14
Pettis-Det...............44	Pettis-Det 6.2	Gruber-Tor 26.4	Gladden-Min........12.1	Stewart-Oak 21	Hurst-Bos 750	Clemens-Bos 14
Molitor-Mil 41	Molitor-Mil..............5.5	Schofield-Cal 21.7	Snyder-Cle 9.6	Gubicza-KC 20	Gubicza-KC 714	Witt-Tex 13
Canseco-Oak 40	Wilson-KC..............5.3	White-KC 20.9	Puckett-Min............9.3		Davis-Oak............696	Witt-Cal 12
	Redus-Chi.............5.0	Randolph-NY 13.9	White-Cal 8.5		Stieb-Tor..............667	Swindell-Cle 12

Strikeouts	Fewest BB/Game	Games	Saves	Base Runners/9	Adjusted Relief Runs	Relief Ranking
Clemens-Bos........291	Anderson-Min......1.65	Crim-Mil 70	Eckersley-Oak 45	Eckersley-Oak 7.93	Henneman-Det....19.6	Henneman-Det ..37.5
Langston-Sea 235	Swindell-Cle 1.67	Thigpen-Chi 68	Reardon-Min 42	Higuera-Mil..........9.22	Mirabella-Mil........15.6	Harvey-Cal 25.7
Viola-Min 193	Alexander-Det......1.81	Williams-Tex 67	Jones-Cle 37	McMurtry-Tex 9.30	Jones-Cle 15.2	Jones-Cle 23.6
Stewart-Oak 192	Bosio-Mil..............1.88	Henneman-Det 65	Thigpen-Chi...........34	Jones-Cle 9.40	Jackson-Sea........14.3	Eckersley-Oak....23.1
Higuera-Mil 192	Viola-Min..............1.90		Plesac-Mil 30	Harvey-Cal 9.47	Harvey-Cal 14.1	Reardon-Min 22.9

Innings Pitched	Opponents' Avg.	Opponents' OBP	Earned Run Average	Adjusted ERA	Adjusted Starter Runs	Pitcher Wins
Stewart-Oak 275.2	Robinson-Det 197	Higuera-Mil 263	Anderson-Min 2.45	Anderson-Min 167	Viola-Min.............39.9	**Viola-Min** 4.7
Gubicza-KC 269.2	Higuera-Mil 207	Clemens-Bos 270	Higuera-Mil 2.45	Higuera-Mil 162	Higuera-Mil...........39.9	**Higuera-Mil** 4.4
Clemens-Bos 264.0	Stieb-Tor 210	Robinson-Det...............282	Viola-Min..............2.64	Viola-Min 154	Gubicza-KC 37.0	**Gubicza-KC**.........3.9
Langston-Sea 261.1	Witt-Tex.................216	Viola-Min 286	Gubicza-KC 2.70	Gubicza-KC 148	Clemens-Bos 34.1	**Henneman-Det**..3.9
Saberhagen-KC 260.2	Clemens-Bos 220	Swindell-Cle.................286	Clemens-Bos 2.93	Clemens-Bos........141	Anderson-Min 30.8	**Anderson-Min**....3.8

Oakland Surprise

Some years, it's better just to stay home. The Baltimore Orioles lost their first 21 games of the season and finished a deep last. As scoring dropped 11 percent to its lowest full-season total since 1978, several big names from that time retired: Don Baylor, Chris Chambliss, Ron Guidry, Graig Nettles, and Joe Niekro.

The balance of power in the AL switched from East to West in the late 1980s; the league's best teams were now Oakland and Minnesota. The A's had a veteran staff led by 21-game winner Dave Stewart, who survived a record 16 balks called by umpires trying to enforce a short-lived edict from the commissioner's office. "Bash Brothers" Mark McGwire and MVP Jose Canseco (the first player with 40 homers and 40 steals in the same year), plowed up enough runs for 104 wins, the franchise's highest total since Connie Mack's Philadelphia juggernaut of 1931. The Twins actually won six more games than their world championship team of '87, but Oakland kept them at arm's length. Cy Young winner Frank Viola couldn't make up for lineup gaps and a lack of quality pitching.

Early in the schedule, the Yankees and Tigers paced the East. Slumping Boston fired manager John McNamara, and got hot under new skipper Joe Morgan. With Wade Boggs claiming his fifth batting title in six years, and Dwight Evans, Ellis Burks, and Mike Greenwell fashioning the league's top outfield, Boston won even though the team didn't have a dependable *third* starter until Mike Boddicker's arrival in July. Detroit, Milwaukee, Toronto, and New York all finished within 5 games. A second-place finish was the end of the road for the Tigers, the oldest team in the league and about to collapse.

Oakland took care of business in the ALCS, sweeping Boston in four with excellent pitching and Canseco's 3 homers. The World Series against the Dodgers, however, was anything but businesslike. After Kirk Gibson's pinch-homer sunk the A's in Game 1, Oakland fell in five.

1989 National League

TEAM	W	L	T	PCT	GB	HW	HL	R	OR	PA	H	2B	3B	HR	BB	SO	HB	SH	AVG	OBP	SLG	OPS	AOPS	BR	ABR	PF	SB	CS	BSA	BSR
EAST																														
CHI	93	69	0	.574		48	33	**702**	623	6141	**1438**	235	45	124	472	921	80	26	**.261**	.319	.387	**706**	100	**52**	4	107	136	57	70	10
NY	87	75	0	.537	6	51	30	683	595	6130	1351	**280**	21	**147**	504	934	56	33	.246	.311	.385	696	109	33	67	95	158	53	**75**	**16**
STL	86	76	2	.531	7	46	35	632	608	6141	1418	263	47	73	507	**848**	78	21	.258	**.321**	.363	684	98	17	-3	103	155	54	74	15
MON	81	81	0	.500	12	44	37	632	630	6206	1353	267	30	100	**572**	958	71	35	.247	.319	.361	680	99	16	7	101	**160**	70	70	11
PIT	74	88	2	.457	19	39	42	637	680	6260	1334	263	**53**	95	563	914	83	24	.241	.311	.359	670	101	-12	11	97	155	69	69	10
PHI	67	95	1	.414	26	38	42	629	735	6126	1324	215	36	123	558	926	57	22	.243	.314	.364	678	99	0	0	100	106	50	68	6
WEST																														
SF	92	70	0	.568		**53**	28	699	600	6138	1365	241	52	141	508	1071	82	**40**	.250	.316	**.390**	**706**	**110**	49	**69**	97	87	54	62	0
SD	89	73	0	.549	3	46	35	642	626	6119	1360	215	32	120	552	1013	**95**	9	.251	.319	.369	688	102	21	20	100	136	67	67	6
HOU	86	76	0	.531	6	47	35	647	669	6200	1316	239	28	97	530	860	83	27	.239	.306	.345	651	95	-50	-28	97	144	62	70	10
LA	77	83	0	.481	14	44	37	554	**536**	6123	1313	241	17	89	507	885	83	27	.240	.306	.339	645	92	-60	-50	98	81	54	60	-1
CIN	75	87	0	.463	17	38	43	632	691	6158	1362	243	28	128	493	1028	66	30	.247	.309	.370	679	96	1	-20	103	128	71	64	3
ATL	63	97	1	.394	28	33	46	584	680	6079	1281	201	22	128	485	996	65	24	.234	.298	.350	648	89	-67	-81	103	83	54	61	-1
TOT	973					527	443	7673		73821	16215	2903	411	1365	6251	11354	318	899	.246	.312	.365	678					1529	715	68	86

TEAM	CG	SHO	GR	SV	IP	H	HR	BB	SO	BR/9	ERA	AERA	OAV	OOB	PR	APR	PF	OSB	OCS	FA	E	WPB	DP	FW	PW	BW	BSW	DIF
EAST																												
CHI	18	10	338	**55**	1460.1	1369	106	532	918	11.9	3.43	110	.250	.316	11	50	108	87	56	.980	124	56	130	.6	5.3	.4	.3	5.3
NY	24	12	274	38	1454.1	**1260**	115	532	**1108**	11.3	3.29	99	**.231**	**.301**	33	-5	93	158	57	.976	144	61	110	-.6	-.5	7.2	**.9**	-1.0
STL	18	18	**358**	43	1461.0	1330	**84**	482	844	11.3	3.36	108	.243	.306	21	41	104	133	55	**.982**	**112**	52	134	**1.4**	4.4	-.3	.8	-1.3
MON	20	13	287	35	1468.1	1344	120	519	1059	11.6	3.48	102	.245	.312	3	9	101	166	70	.979	136	51	126	-.1	1.0	.7	.4	-2.0
PIT	20	9	325	40	1487.2	1394	121	539	827	11.9	3.64	92	.248	.314	-24	-49	96	190	56	.975	160	74	130	-1.4	-5.2	1.2	.3	-1.9
PHI	10	10	348	33	1433.1	1408	127	613	899	12.9	4.04	88	.259	.335	-87	-79	101	113	66	.979	133	97	136	.1	-8.4	.0	-.1	-5.5
WEST																												
SF	12	16	318	47	1457.0	1320	120	471	802	11.2	3.30	102	.243	.304	31	11	97	96	56	**.982**	114	48	135	1.2	1.2	**7.4**	-.8	2.1
SD	21	11	245	52	1457.1	1359	133	481	933	11.5	3.38	103	.249	.310	19	19	100	**68**	44	.976	154	56	147	-1.1	2.0	2.1	-.1	5.1
HOU	19	12	346	38	1479.1	1379	105	551	965	11.9	3.64	93	.247	.315	-25	-44	97	170	40	.977	142	64	121	-.4	-4.7	-3.0	.3	12.8
LA	**25**	**19**	285	36	1463.1	1278	95	504	1052	**11.1**	**2.95**	**116**	.237	.304	**89**	**78**	98	99	72	.981	118	63	**153**	.8	**8.3**	-5.3	-.9	-6.0
CIN	16	9	339	37	1464.1	1404	125	559	981	12.3	3.73	96	.253	.323	-38	-21	103	141	65	.980	121	**47**	108	.8	-2.2	-2.1	-.4	-1.9
ATL	15	8	340	33	1447.2	1370	114	**468**	966	11.5	3.70	99	.250	.309	-33	-8	104	108	**78**	.976	152	62	124	-1.1	-.9	-8.7	-.9	-5.5
TOT	218	147	3803	487	17534.0					11.7	3.49		.246	.312						.978	1610	731	1554					

Batter-Fielder Wins	Batting Average	On-Base Percentage	Slugging Average	On-Base Plus Slugging	Adjusted OPS	Adjusted Batter Runs
Mitchell-SF 6.2	Gwynn-SD 336	L.Smith-Atl 415	Mitchell-SF 635	Mitchell-SF 1023	Mitchell-SF 194	Mitchell-SF 67.2
Clark-SF 5.1	Clark-SF 333	J.Clark-SD 410	Johnson-NY 559	Clark-SF 953	Clark-SF 177	Clark-SF 60.3
L.Smith-Atl 4.8	L.Smith-Atl 315	Clark-SF 407	Clark-SF 546	L.Smith-Atl............948	Johnson-NY..........171	Johnson-NY........53.1
Oquendo-StL 4.3	Grace-Chi 314	Grace-Chi 405	Davis-Cin 541	Johnson-NY..........928	L.Smith-Atl............166	L.Smith-Atl..........45.9
Bonilla-Pit............4.2	Guerrero-StL 311	Raines-Mon 395	L.Smith-Atl 533	Davis-Cin..............908	Davis-Cin..............154	J.Clark-SD 37.4

Runs	Hits	Doubles	Triples	Home Runs	Total Bases	Runs Batted In
Sandberg-Chi 104	Gwynn-SD 203	Wallach-Mon.................42	Thompson-SF 11	Mitchell-SF 47	Mitchell-SF 345	Mitchell-SF 125
Johnson-NY..........104	Clark-SF 196	Guerrero-StL.................42	Bonilla-Pit 10	Johnson-NY............36	Clark-SF 321	Guerrero-StL 117
Clark-SF 104	R.Alomar-SD 184	Johnson-NY 41	VanSlyke-Pit 9	Davis-Hou 34	Johnson-NY..........319	Clark-SF 111
Mitchell-SF 100	Guerrero-StL 177	Clark-SF 38	Coleman-StL 9	Davis-Cin 34	Bonilla-Pit 302	Johnson-NY 101
Butler-SF 100	Sandberg-Chi 176	Bonilla-Pit 37	Clark-SF 9	Sandberg-Chi 30	Sandberg-Chi 301	Davis-Cin 101

Stolen Bases	Base Stealing Runs	Fielding Runs-Infield	Fielding Runs-Outfield	Wins	Winning Pct.	Complete Games
Coleman-StL 65	Coleman-StL 10.8	Pendleton-StL 34.9	Young-Hou 14.2	Scott-Hou 20	Bielecki-Chi 720	Hurst-SD 10
Samuel-Phi-NY 42	Johnson-NY 6.2	Oquendo-StL 24.9	Bonds-Pit 12.2	Maddux-Chi 19	D.Martinez-Mon ...696	Belcher-LA 10
R.Alomar-SD 42	Raines-Mon 5.9	Thon-Phi 19.6	McReynolds-NY 7.6	Magrane-StL 18	Reuschel-SF.........680	Scott-Hou 9
Raines-Mon 41	Samuel-Phi-NY......5.0	Uribe-SF 17.3	Strawberry-NY 4.9	Bielecki-Chi 18	Scott-Hou 667	Magrane-StL 9
Johnson-NY............41	Nixon-Mon 3.9	Foley-Mon 15.5	Dykstra-NY-Phi 4.3	Reuschel-SF 17	Magrane-StL..........667	Browning-Cin 9

Strikeouts	Fewest BB/Game	Games	Saves	Base Runners/9	Adjusted Relief Runs	Relief Ranking
DeLeon-StL 201	Robinson-SF........1.69	Williams-Chi 76	Davis-SD 44	Andersen-Hou 8.93	Lancaster-Chi 18.2	Davis-SD 26.6
Belcher-LA............200	Lilliquist-Atl 1.85	Dibble-Cin 74	Williams-Chi 36	Garrelts-SF...........9.08	Andersen-Hou 17.6	Howell-LA 26.0
Fernandez-NY 198	D.Martinez-Mon ..1.90	Parrett-Phi 72	Franco-Cin.............32	Howell-LA 9.26	Dibble-Cin............17.5	Dibble-Cin 24.5
Cone-NY 190	Whitson-SD 1.90	Dayley-StL 71	Howell-LA 28	Lancaster-Chi 9.29	Davis-SD 17.4	Burke-Mon..........19.3
Hurst-SD 179	Glavine-Atl 1.94	Agosto-Hou 71	Burke-Mon..............28	Darwin-Hou 9.37	Howell-LA 17.0	Darwin-Hou 18.4

Innings Pitched	Opponents' Avg.	Opponents' OBP	Earned Run Average	Adjusted ERA	Adjusted Starter Runs	Pitcher Wins
Hershiser-LA......256.2	DeLeon-StL 197	Garrelts-SF 258	Garrelts-SF 2.28	Garrelts-SF 148	Hershiser-LA........31.8	**Hershiser-LA** 4.4
Browning-Cin 249.2	Fernandez-NY 198	Scott-Hou.....................267	Hershiser-LA.........2.31	Hershiser-LA 148	Garrelts-SF..........23.0	**Maddux-Chi**.........2.9
Hurst-SD............244.2	Smoltz-Atl 212	DeLeon-StL 268	Langston-Mon 2.39	Langston-Mon 148	Hurst-SD..............21.9	**Howell-LA** 2.8
DeLeon-StL 244.2	Garrelts-SF...........212	Fernandez-NY 271	Whitson-SD 2.66	Whitson-SD 132	Whitson-SD 21.1	**Davis-SD** 2.7
Drabek-Pit 244.1	Scott-Hou 212	Smiley-Pit.....................273	Hurst-SD...............2.69	Hurst-SD 130	Langston-Mon 20.0	**Dibble-Cin** 2.5

I Wouldn't Bet You

Just before Opening Day, NL President Bart Giamatti was appointed commissioner, and Bill White became the first African American league president. Giamatti immediately was presented with serious allegations against Pete Rose, accused of gambling on baseball games in which he was involved. Despite being Cincinnati's manager since 1984, Rose's shady dealings made him appear guilty to many.

In late August Rose—with no other option—signed an agreement banning him for life from the game, even though he denied gambling on baseball. Nine days later, Giamatti died of a heart attack, and Fay Vincent became the new commissioner.

Horror also visited the playing field. Giants pitcher Dave Dravecky suffered a broken arm while pitching, ending his career. He eventually lost the arm. Darrell Evans, Mike Schmidt, and Kent Tekulve also called it quits. Late in the season, Montreal debuted Larry Walker and Marquis Grissom, but the Expos goofed by trading Randy Johnson for Mark Langston, who soon departed via free agency.

San Francisco won again, with a veteran pitching staff and Kevin Mitchell's MVP season; Will Clark finished second in the voting. Despite Tony Gwynn's fourth batting title and reliever Mark Davis' Cy Young, the Padres fell just short.

Chicago, in another potentially earth-shaking event, captured the East despite a string of injuries. Outfielders Jerome Walton was Rookie of the Year, but Ryne Sandberg and Greg Maddux did most of the heavy lifting.

The Giants beat Chicago in a five-game NLCS. First basemen Clark and Mark Grace put on hitting shows, but San Francisco won three straight squeakers at home to wrap things up. The Bay Area was struck by an earthquake in the middle of a four-game A's World Series sweep of the Giants. Baseball's core had been shaken, and it would get worse.

1989 American League

TEAM	W	L	T	PCT	GB	HW	HL	R	OR	PA	H	2B	3B	HR	BB	SO	HB	SH	AVG	OBP	SLG	OPS	AOPS	BR	ABR	PF	SB	CS	BSA	BSR
EAST																														
TOR	89	73	0	.549		46	35	731	651	6216	1449	265	40	142	521	923	30	31	.260	.323	.398	721	104	19	33	98	144	58	71	11
BAL	87	75	0	.537	2	47	34	708	686	6173	1369	238	33	129	593	957	63	30	.252	.326	.379	705	101	-5	17	97	118	55	68	7
BOS	83	79	0	.512	6	46	35	**774**	735	6455	**1571**	**326**	30	108	**643**	755	52	36	**.277**	**.351**	**.403**	**754**	**105**	**114**	**65**	106	56	35	62	0
MIL	81	81	0	.500	8	45	36	707	679	6083	1415	235	32	126	455	791	51	**50**	.259	.318	.382	700	97	-23	-16	99	**165**	62	73	15
NY	74	87	0	.460	14.5	41	40	698	792	6094	1470	229	23	130	502	831	58	27	.269	.331	.391	722	104	25	34	99	137	60	70	9
CLE	73	89	0	.451	16	41	40	604	654	6110	1340	221	26	127	499	934	72	35	.245	.310	.365	675	89	-74	-84	102	74	51	59	-2
DET	59	103	0	.364	30	38	43	617	816	6132	1315	198	24	116	585	899	35	37	.242	.318	.351	669	90	-75	-60	98	103	50	67	5
WEST																														
OAK	99	63	0	.611		54	27	712	**576**	6110	1414	220	25	127	562	855	36	34	.261	.331	.381	712	104	12	38	96	157	55	74	15
KC	92	70	0	.568	7	**55**	26	690	635	6150	1428	227	41	101	554	897	42	29	.261	.329	.373	702	97	-10	-7	100	154	51	**75**	**16**
CAL	91	71	0	.562	8	52	29	669	578	6102	1422	208	37	**145**	429	1011	54	28	.256	.311	.386	697	97	-43	-31	98	89	40	69	6
TEX	83	79	0	.512	16	45	36	695	714	6098	1433	260	**46**	122	503	989	63	34	.263	.326	.394	720	100	18	7	102	101	49	67	5
MIN	80	82	0	.494	19	45	36	740	738	6207	1542	278	35	117	478	**743**	51	39	.276	.334	.402	736	99	55	8	107	111	53	68	6
SEA	73	89	0	.451	26	40	41	694	728	6133	1417	237	29	134	489	838	35	45	.257	.320	.384	704	95	-16	-37	103	81	55	60	-1
CHI	69	92	0	.429	29.5	35	45	693	750	6132	1493	262	36	94	464	873	**85**	28	.271	.328	.383	711	102	4	21	98	97	52	65	3
TOT	1133					630	503	9732		86195	20078	3404	457	1718	7277	12296	483	727	.261	.326	.384	709					1587	726	69	95

TEAM	CG	SHO	GR	SV	IP	H	HR	BB	SO	BR/9	ERA	AERA	OAV	OOB	PR	APR	PF	OSB	OCS	FA	E	WPB	DP	FW	PW	BW	BSW	DIF
EAST																												
TOR	12	12	277	38	1467.0	1408	99	478	849	11.8	3.58	105	.255	.317	49	31	97	115	54	.980	127	74	164	-.1	3.2	3.4	.4	1.2
BAL	16	7	312	44	1448.1	1518	134	486	676	12.6	4.00	95	.272	.331	-19	-34	98	114	51	**.986**	**87**	**46**	163	**2.3**	-3.5	1.7	.0	5.4
BOS	14	9	297	42	1460.1	1448	131	548	1054	12.5	4.01	102	.261	.328	-20	15	106	161	58	.980	127	51	162	-.1	1.5	**6.6**	-.7	-5.3
MIL	16	8	291	45	1432.1	1463	129	457	812	12.2	3.80	101	.265	.321	14	7	99	113	46	.975	155	**46**	164	-1.8	.7	-1.6	.8	1.9
NY	15	9	278	44	1414.2	1550	150	521	787	13.4	4.50	86	.281	.344	-98	-100	100	81	51	.980	122	49	**183**	.1	-10.2	3.5	.2	-.2
CLE	23	13	287	38	1453.0	1423	107	**452**	844	11.8	3.65	109	.257	.313	38	49	102	126	50	.981	118	60	126	.4	5.0	-8.6	-.9	-4.0
DET	24	4	252	26	1427.1	1514	150	652	831	13.9	4.53	84	.274	.352	-103	-116	98	126	**65**	.979	130	60	153	-.3	-11.8	-6.1	-.2	-3.6
WEST																												
OAK	17	**20**	317	**57**	1448.1	1287	103	510	930	**11.3**	**3.09**	**119**	**.238**	**.305**	**128**	**101**	95	89	48	.979	129	84	159	-.2	**10.3**	3.9	.8	3.2
KC	27	13	264	38	1451.2	1415	**86**	455	978	11.7	3.55	109	.257	.314	54	49	99	**79**	56	.982	114	68	139	.7	5.0	-.7	**.9**	5.1
CAL	**32**	**20**	252	38	1454.1	1384	113	465	897	11.6	3.28	116	.253	.312	97	88	98	111	42	.985	96	65	173	1.7	9.0	-3.2	-.0	2.5
TEX	26	7	321	44	1434.1	**1279**	119	654	**1112**	12.4	3.91	101	.239	.324	-4	9	102	140	51	.978	136	107	137	-.6	.9	.7	-.2	1.2
MIN	19	8	297	38	1429.1	1495	139	500	851	12.8	4.28	97	.269	.332	-63	-21	107	115	49	.982	107	54	141	1.1	-2.1	.8	-.0	-.7
SEA	15	10	**330**	44	1438.0	1422	114	560	897	12.7	4.00	101	.259	.330	-19	4	104	115	52	.977	143	57	168	-1.1	.4	-3.8	-.8	-2.8
CHI	9	5	321	46	1422.0	1472	144	539	778	12.9	4.23	90	.269	.335	-54	-68	98	102	53	.975	151	71	176	-1.6	-6.9	2.1	-.4	-4.7
TOT	265	145	4096	582	20181.0					12.4	3.88		.261	.326						.980	1742		892	2208				

Batter-Fielder Wins	Batting Average	On-Base Percentage	Slugging Average	On-Base Plus Slugging	Adjusted OPS	Adjusted Batter Runs
R.Henderson-NY-Oak 4.6	Puckett-Min 339	Boggs-Bos 430	Sierra-Tex 543	McGriff-Tor 924	McGriff-Tor 162	McGriff-Tor 50.8
Boggs-Bos 4.3	Lansford-Oak 336	Davis-Sea 424	McGriff-Tor 525	Davis-Sea 920	Davis-Sea 155	Yount-Mil 43.1
Molitor-Mil 4.2	Boggs-Bos 330	R.Henderson-NY-Oak.......411	Yount-Mil 511	Yount-Mil 896	Yount-Mil 152	Davis-Sea 42.6
McGriff-Tor..........4.1	Yount-Mil 318	McGriff-Tor 399	Esasky-Bos 500	Sierra-Tex 889	Sierra-Tex 146	Boggs-Bos 41.6
Yount-Mil..............4.0	Franco-Tex 316	Lansford-Oak 398	Davis-Sea 496	Boggs-Bos 879	Baines-Chi-Tex 144	Sierra-Tex 35.2

Runs	Hits	Doubles	Triples	Home Runs	Total Bases	Runs Batted In
R.Henderson-NY-Oak 113	Puckett-Min 215	Boggs-Bos 51	Sierra-Tex 14	McGriff-Tor 36	Sierra-Tex 344	Sierra-Tex 119
Boggs-Bos 113	Sax-NY 205	Puckett-Min 45	White-Cal 13	Carter-Cle 35	Yount-Mil 314	Mattingly-NY 113
Yount-Mil 101	Boggs-Bos 205	Reed-Bos 42	Bradley-Bal 10	McGwire-Oak 33	Carter-Cle 303	Esasky-Bos 108
Sierra-Tex 101	Yount-Mil 195	Bell-Tor 41		Jackson-KC 32	Mattingly-NY 301	Jackson-KC 105
McGriff-Tor..............98		Yount-Mil 38		Esasky-Bos 30	Puckett-Min 295	Carter-Cle............105

Stolen Bases	Base Stealing Runs	Fielding Runs-Infield	Fielding Runs-Outfield	Wins	Winning Pct.	Complete Games
R.Henderson-NY-Oak 77	R.Henderson-NY-Oak 12.0	Reynolds-Sea 24.6	Snyder-Cle 12.9	Saberhagen-KC......23	Saberhagen-KC ...793	Saberhagen-KC 12
Espy-Tex 45	Pettis-Det 4.2	Howell-Cal 24.1	Puckett-Min............10.7	Stewart-Oak 21	Blyleven-Cal 773	Morris-Det 10
White-Cal................44	White-Cal 4.1	Buechele-Tex 18.8	Barfield-Tor-NY 9.9	Moore-Oak 19	Davis-Oak.............731	Finley-Cal 9
Sax-NY 43	Felder-Mil 4.0	Espinoza-NY 18.5	Polonia-Oak-NY 8.8	Davis-Oak 19	Stewart-Oak 700	
Pettis-Det................43	Franco-Tex 3.6	Gantner-Mil 17.8	Orsulak-Bal............6.0	Ballard-Bal 18	Ballard-Bal 692	

Strikeouts	Fewest BB/Game	Games	Saves	Base Runners/9	Adjusted Relief Runs	Relief Ranking
Ryan-Tex 301	Key-Tor 1.13	Crim-Mil 76	Russell-Tex 38	Saberhagen-KC ..8.71	Montgomery-KC ..25.5	Montgomery-KC 33.6
Clemens-Bos.........230	Saberhagen-KC ..1.48	Murphy-Bos 74	Thigpen-Chi.............34	Burns-Oak 8.88	Olson-Bal 20.4	Henke-Tor 29.3
Saberhagen-KC....193	Blyleven-Cal 1.64	Rogers-Tex 73	Schooler-Sea..........33	Russell-Tex 8.92	Henke-Tor 19.5	Russell-Tex 29.2
Gubicza-KC 173	Bosio-Mil..............1.84	Russell-Tex 71	Plesac-Mil 33	Montgomery-KC ..9.10	Lamp-Bos 19.4	Jones-Cle 27.1
Bosio-Mil 173	Witt-Cal................1.96	Guetterman-NY 70	Eckersley-Oak 33	Plesac-Mil............9.39	Minton-Cal 17.5	Olson-Bal 26.5

Innings Pitched	Opponents' Avg.	Opponents' OBP	Earned Run Average	Adjusted ERA	Adjusted Starter Runs	Pitcher Wins
Saberhagen-KC 262.1	Ryan-Tex 187	Saberhagen-KC 251	Saberhagen-KC ..2.16	Saberhagen-KC....178	Saberhagen-KC ..48.0	**Saberhagen-KC** 5.3
Stewart-Oak 257.2	Gordon-KC 210	Ryan-Tex 275	Finley-Cal 2.57	Finley-Cal 149	Blyleven-Cal 31.6	**Moore-Oak** 3.7
Gubicza-KC 255.0	Saberhagen-KC ...217	Moore-Oak 286	Moore-Oak 2.61	Moore-Oak 142	Moore-Oak 29.8	**Montgomery-KC** 3.5
Clemens-Bos 253.1	Stieb-Tor 219	Blyleven-Cal................287	Blyleven-Cal 2.73	Blyleven-Cal 140	Finley-Cal 27.5	**Finley-Cal** 3.2
Milacki-Bal 243.0	Moore-Oak 219	Bosio-Mil 289	McCaskill-Cal 2.93	Clemens-Bos.........131	Clemens-Bos 25.6	**Russell-Tex** 3.1

Get Outta My Nest, It's Starting to Rumble

Baltimore, last-place finishers the year before, led the East for most of the summer on Jeff Ballard's 18–8 surprise season and a balanced lineup. Toronto, after a 12–24 start, hired Cito Gaston as manager. While the Orioles came to earth, the Blue Jays stayed hot and pulled into a first-place tie on August 31. Through the final month, both teams played well, and Toronto won the title by taking two thrilling contests from Baltimore at SkyDome on the season's last weekend.

In their new domed stadium, Toronto—featuring sluggers Fred McGriff and George Bell—topped three million fans, an AL first. Robin Yount won his second MVP for Milwaukee. Tommy John retired at 46, and Jim Rice quit with elbow problems. Former Angels hurler Donnie Moore was a suicide, and on Christmas, Billy Martin perished in a car crash.

Despite another Cy Young for Kansas City's Bret Saberhagen, Tony LaRussa's A's easily won the West. Dave Stewart enjoyed his third straight 20-win season, and Dennis Eckersley was dominating in relief. A thrill for third-place California was the rookie season of lefty Jim Abbott, born without a right hand. Seattle debuted two rookies, Omar Vizquel and Ken Griffey Jr., on Opening Day. Texas gave cups of coffee to kid outfielders Juan Gonzalez and Sammy Sosa.

Rickey Henderson, back in the A's fold after a midseason deal, went to town in the ALCS: Henderson reached base 15 times, stole 8 bases, scored 8 runs, and even hit 2 homers. While Oakland beat Toronto in five, the final two were nail-biters.

The A's-Giants World Series was longer and more earth-shaking than anyone would have guessed. Prior to Game 3, with Oakland up two games to none, a deadly earthquake hit the Bay Area. After a ten-day hiatus, the series resumed. The Athletics twice more wiped the floor with the Giants to sweep the Series, outscoring the NL champs, 32–14.

1990 National League

TEAM	W	L	T	PCT	GB	HW	HL	R	OR	PA	H	2B	3B	HR	BB	SO	HB	SH	AVG	OBP	SLG	OPS	AOPS	BR	ABR	PF	SB	CS	BSA	BSR
EAST																														
PIT	95	67	0	.586		49	32	733	619	6156	1395	**288**	42	138	**582**	914	**96**	24	.259	**.330**	.405	**735**	**112**	**68**	**98**	96	137	52	72	12
NY	91	71	0	.562	4	**52**	29	**775**	613	6182	1410	278	21	**172**	536	**851**	54	32	.256	.323	**.408**	731	106	52	54	100	110	33	**77**	13
MON	85	77	0	.525	10	47	34	662	598	6189	1363	227	**43**	114	576	1024	87	26	.250	.322	.370	692	100	-19	7	96	**235**	99	70	**17**
PHI	77	85	0	.475	18	41	40	646	729	6245	1410	237	27	103	**582**	915	59	30	.255	.327	.363	690	96	-18	-16	100	108	35	76	12
CHI	77	85	0	.475	18	39	42	690	774	6148	**1474**	240	36	136	406	869	61	30	.263	.314	.392	706	92	-10	-56	107	151	50	75	16
STL	70	92	0	.432	25	34	47	599	698	6127	1398	255	41	73	517	844	77	21	.256	.320	.358	678	92	-46	-49	100	221	74	75	23
WEST																														
CIN	91	71	0	.562		46	35	693	**597**	6163	1466	284	40	125	466	913	88	**42**	**.265**	.325	.399	724	101	37	8	104	166	66	72	13
LA	86	76	0	.531	5	47	34	728	685	6179	1436	222	27	129	538	952	71	31	.262	.328	.382	710	104	17	37	97	141	65	68	8
SF	85	77	0	.525	6	49	32	719	710	6215	1459	221	35	152	488	973	76	33	.262	.323	.396	719	107	22	48	96	109	56	66	4
SD	75	87	0	.463	16	37	44	673	673	6218	1429	243	35	123	509	902	79	28	.257	.320	.380	700	97	-9	-14	101	138	59	70	10
HOU	75	87	0	.463	16	49	32	573	656	6075	1301	209	32	94	548	997	79	28	.242	.313	.345	658	90	-85	-67	97	179	83	68	10
ATL	65	97	0	.401	26	37	44	682	821	6084	1376	263	26	162	473	1010	49	27	.250	.311	.396	707	94	-8	-44	106	92	55	63	1
TOT	972					527	445	8173		73981	16917	2967	405	1521	6221	11164	352	876	.256	.321	.383	704					1787	727	71	139

TEAM	CG	SHO	GR	SV	IP	H	HR	BB	SO	BR/9	ERA	AERA	OAV	OOB	PR	APR	PF	OSB	OCS	FA	E	WPB	DP	FW	PW	BW	BSW	DIF
EAST																												
PIT	18	8	364	43	1447.0	1367	135	**413**	848	**11.3**	3.40	106	.251	.305	63	37	95	135	68	.979	134	51	125	-.4	3.8	**10.1**	.0	.5
NY	18	**14**	268	41	1440.0	1339	119	444	**1217**	**11.3**	3.42	109	.246	**.304**	59	51	99	201	71	.978	132	71	107	-.3	5.3	5.6	.1	-.6
MON	18	11	341	**50**	1473.1	1349	127	510	991	11.6	**3.37**	108	**.245**	.311	**70**	48	96	194	45	.982	110	**48**	134	.9	4.9	.7	.6	-3.2
PHI	18	7	**374**	35	1449.0	1381	124	651	840	12.8	4.07	94	.253	.333	-45	-39	101	104	56	.981	117	77	**150**	.5	-4.0	-1.6	.0	1.1
CHI	13	7	346	42	1442.2	1510	121	572	877	13.2	4.34	94	.271	.340	-87	-39	108	**98**	56	.980	124	86	136	.1	-4.0	-5.8	.5	5.2
STL	8	13	364	39	1443.1	1432	**98**	475	833	12.1	3.87	98	.261	.320	-13	-9	101	144	**76**	.979	130	56	114	-.2	-.9	-5.1	**1.2**	-6.0
WEST																												
CIN	14	12	316	**50**	1456.1	**1338**	124	543	1029	11.8	3.39	**116**	.246	.316	64	**86**	104	135	60	**.983**	**102**	67	126	**1.4**	**8.9**	.8	.1	-1.3
LA	**29**	12	339	29	1442.0	1364	137	478	1021	11.7	3.72	98	.249	.310	11	-10	97	134	59	.979	130	73	123	-.2	-1.0	3.8	-.4	2.8
SF	14	6	335	45	1446.1	1477	131	553	788	12.8	4.08	89	.267	.333	-46	-72	96	147	53	**.983**	107	**48**	148	1.1	-7.4	4.9	-.8	6.1
SD	21	12	288	35	1461.2	1437	147	507	928	12.1	3.68	104	.258	.320	19	23	101	132	60	.977	141	**48**	141	-.8	2.4	-1.4	-.2	-5.9
HOU	12	6	348	37	1450.0	1396	130	496	854	12.0	3.61	103	.255	.318	30	17	98	182	61	.978	131	54	124	-.3	1.8	-6.9	-.2	-.4
ATL	17	8	346	30	1429.2	1527	128	579	938	13.4	4.58	88	.275	.343	-125	-81	106	181	62	.974	158	76	133	-1.8	-8.4	-4.5	-1.1	-.2
TOT	200	116	4029	476	17381.1					12.2	3.79		.256	.321						.980	1516	755	1561					

Batter-Fielder Wins	Batting Average	On-Base Percentage	Slugging Average	On-Base Plus Slugging	Adjusted OPS	Adjusted Batter Runs
Bonds-Pit 6.5	McGee-StL 335	Dykstra-Phi 418	Bonds-Pit 565	Bonds-Pit.............970	Bonds-Pit.............172	Bonds-Pit...........54.3
Dykstra-Phi 4.8	Murray-LA............330	Magadan-NY 417	Sandberg-Chi 559	Murray-LA 934	Murray-LA 160	Murray-LA 48.6
Sandberg-Chi......4.2	Magadan-NY 328	Murray-LA 414	Mitchell-SF 544	Daniels-LA...........920	Daniels-LA...........156	J.Clark-SD 37.1
Larkin-Cin...........4.1	Dykstra-Phi..........325	Bonds-Pit....................406	Gant-Atl 539	Sandberg-Chi 913	Mitchell-SF 151	Dykstra-Phi 36.1
Murray-LA 4.0	Dawson-Chi 310	Butler-SF 397	Justice-Atl............535	Justice-Atl 908	Magadan-NY 143	Daniels-LA...........35.8

Runs	Hits	Doubles	Triples	Home Runs	Total Bases	Runs Batted In
Sandberg-Chi 116	Dykstra-Phi 192	Jefferies-NY 40	Duncan-Cin 11	Sandberg-Chi 40	Sandberg-Chi 344	Williams-SF 122
Bonilla-Pit 112	Butler-SF 192	Bonilla-Pit 39	Gwynn-SD 10	Strawberry-NY........37	Bonilla-Pit 324	Bonilla-Pit 120
Butler-SF 108	Sandberg-Chi 188	Sabo-Cin.......................38	L.Smith-Atl...............9	Mitchell-SF 35	Gant-Atl 310	Carter-SD 115
Gant-Atl 107	Wallach-Mon 185	Wallach-Mon..................37	Coleman-StL 9	Williams-SF 33	Williams-SF 301	Bonds-Pit 114
Dykstra-Phi 106	Larkin-Cin 185	Johnson-NY 37	Butler-SF 9	Bonds-Pit................33	Wallach-Mon 295	Strawberry-NY 108

Stolen Bases	Base Stealing Runs	Fielding Runs-Infield	Fielding Runs-Outfield	Wins	Winning Pct.	Complete Games
Coleman-StL 77	Coleman-StL 11.0	Grace-Chi 25.3	Wilson-Hou..........10.0	Drabek-Pit 22	Drabek-Pit 786	Martinez-LA 12
Yelding-Hou 64	Bonds-Pit 6.9	Treadway-Atl 23.9	Bonds-Pit 7.8	Viola-NY 20	Martinez-LA 769	Hurst-SD 9
Bonds-Pit................52	Nixon-Mon 6.4	Larkin-Cin 21.0	Hatcher-Cin 7.4	Martinez-LA...........20	Gooden-NY 731	Drabek-Pit 9
Butler-SF 51	Roberts-SD...........5.9	Thompson-SF 20.1	Dykstra-Phi............6.8	Gooden-NY 19	Viola-NY 625	Maddux-Chi 8
Nixon-Mon 50	Dykstra-Phi............5.5	Lind-Pit 19.8	Walker-Mon 6.4		Browning-Cin 625	

Strikeouts	Fewest BB/Game	Games	Saves	Base Runners/9	Adjusted Relief Runs	Relief Ranking
Cone-NY 233	Darwin-Hou 1.72	Agosto-Hou...................82	Franco-NY 33	Tomlin-Pit 8.69	Dibble-Cin............22.5	Myers-Cin 27.7
Martinez-LA..........223	Whitson-SD 1.85	Assenmacher-Chi 74	Myers-Cin 31	Dibble-Cin............8.91	Brantley-SF..........20.1	Dibble-Cin 27.4
Gooden-NY 223	Leibrandt-Atl 1.94	Harris-SD 73	L.Smith-StL 27	Tudor-StL 9.35	Harris-SD 19.2	Harris-SD 26.3
Viola-NY 182	D.Martinez-Mon ..1.95	McDowell-Phi 72	Smith-Hou 23	Darwin-Hou 9.46	Charlton-Cin 19.1	Brantley-SF 24.8
Fernandez-NY 181	Browning-Cin 2.06	Akerfelds-Phi 71	Lefferts-SD 23	Drabek-Pit 9.69	Myers-Cin 16.3	Charlton-Cin 23.8

Innings Pitched	Opponents' Avg.	Opponents' OBP	Earned Run Average	Adjusted ERA	Adjusted Starter Runs	Pitcher Wins
Viola-NY 249.2	Fernandez-NY 200	Darwin-Hou 266	Darwin-Hou 2.21	Darwin-Hou 168	Whitson-SD 31.6	**Viola-NY** 3.7
Maddux-Chi 237.0	Rijo-Cin................212	Drabek-Pit 274	Smith-Mon-Pit......2.55	Whitson-SD 147	Viola-NY 30.3	**Drabek-Pit**..........3.6
Martinez-LA 234.1	Martinez-LA 220	D.Martinez-Mon 274	Whitson-SD 2.60	Rijo-Cin 147	Darwin-Hou 29.1	**Whitson-SD**..........3.3
Gooden-NY 232.2	Drabek-Pit 225	Fernandez-NY 277	Viola-NY 2.67	Smith-Mon-Pit 143	Rijo-Cin................26.0	**Myers-Cin** 3.0
	Darwin-Hou 225	Martinez-LA.................278	Rijo-Cin................2.70	Viola-NY 140	Drabek-Pit 24.3	**Rijo-Cin** 2.9

Hunt for a Reds October

The season began a week late as players scrambled to get in condition after the owners ended their lockout of spring training camps. By adding doubleheaders and extending the season three days, all teams played a full 162-game schedule. The NL announced in June that it would expand to fourteen teams, the same number as the AL, for 1993. The finalist cities were Buffalo, Denver, Miami, Orlando, Tampa-St. Petersburg, and Washington, D.C.

The decline and fall of Pete Rose continued, as the former superstar pled guilty to filing false income tax returns and was sentenced to five months in federal prison. Moises Alou, Felipe's son, debuted in June, while Luis Gonzalez made his first appearance in September. Keith Hernandez hung up the spikes after seventeen seasons. Bo Diaz, former catcher for the Phillies and Reds, died one year after retiring when he was crushed by a satellite dish he was installing.

Cincinnati led the West wire-to-wire, sparked by the Nasty Boys bullpen trio of Randy Myers, Rob Dibble and Norm Charlton. Pittsburgh, behind Barry Bonds' MVP performance (his first of a record six), won 10 of 11 games late in the season to hold off the Mets in the East. Doug Drabek, enjoying a career year with 22 wins and the Cy Young Award, led a pedestrian Pirates staff.

While the Reds dropped the first game of the NLCS to Pittsburgh, they rallied to take four of the next five. Cincinnati then brought back memories of the Big Red Machine by sweeping heavily favored Oakland in the World Series. Series MVP Jose Rijo dominated Oakland hitters, winning Games 1 and 4, while Billy Hatcher set offensive records by getting hits in seven consecutive at bats and bating .750 (9-for-12).

1990 American League

TEAM	W	L	T	PCT	GB	HW	HL	R	OR	PA	H	2B	3B	HR	BB	SO	HB	SH	AVG	OBP	SLG	OPS	AOPS	BR	ABR	PF	SB	CS	BSA	BSR
EAST																														
BOS	88	74	0	.543		**51**	30	699	664	6234	**1502**	298	31	106	598	795	48	28	**.272**	**.344**	.395	739	101	61	27	105	53	52	50	-7
TOR	86	76	0	.531	2	44	37	**767**	661	6223	1479	263	**50**	167	526	970	18	28	.265	.328	**.419**	**747**	105	54	41	102	111	52	68	6
DET	79	83	0	.488	9	39	42	750	754	6224	1418	241	32	**172**	634	952	36	34	.259	.337	.409	746	**107**	**63**	58	101	82	57	59	-2
CLE	77	85	0	.475	11	41	40	732	737	6087	1465	266	41	110	458	836	54	29	.267	.324	.391	715	99	-7	-4	100	107	52	67	5
BAL	76	85	0	.472	11.5	40	40	669	698	6223	1328	234	22	132	**660**	962	72	40	.245	.330	.370	700	98	-20	3	97	94	52	64	2
MIL	74	88	0	.457	14	39	42	732	760	6185	1408	247	36	128	519	821	59	33	.256	.320	.384	704	97	-26	-21	99	**164**	72	69	11
NY	67	95	0	.414	21	37	44	603	749	6036	1322	208	19	147	427	1027	37	**53**	.241	.300	.366	666	85	-114	-116	100	119	45	**73**	10
WEST																														
OAK	103	59	0	.636		**51**	30	733	**570**	6238	1379	209	22	164	651	992	60	46	.254	.336	.391	727	**107**	31	**62**	96	141	54	72	**12**
CHI	94	68	0	.580	9	49	31	682	633	6038	1393	251	44	106	478	903	**75**	36	.258	.320	.379	699	97	-37	-22	98	140	90	61	-1
TEX	83	79	0	.512	20	47	35	676	696	6176	1416	257	27	110	575	1054	54	34	.259	.331	.376	707	97	-10	-11	100	115	48	71	9
CAL	80	82	0	.494	23	42	39	690	706	6267	1448	237	27	147	566	1000	58	28	.260	.329	.391	720	103	9	24	98	69	43	62	0
SEA	77	85	0	.475	26	38	43	640	680	6205	1419	251	26	107	596	**749**	41	40	.259	.333	.373	706	96	-5	-13	101	105	51	67	5
KC	75	86	0	.466	27.5	45	36	707	709	6098	1465	**316**	44	100	498	879	31	27	.267	.328	.395	723	103	16	27	98	107	62	63	2
MIN	74	88	0	.457	29	41	40	666	729	6086	1458	281	39	100	445	**749**	40	**53**	.265	.324	.385	709	91	-17	-58	107	96	53	64	3
TOT	1133					604	529	9746		86320	19900	3559	460	1796	7631	12689	509	683	.259	.327	.388	715					1503	783	66	57

TEAM	CG	SHO	GR	SV	IP	H	HR	BB	SO	BR/9	ERA	AERA	OAV	OOB	PR	APR	PF	OSB	OCS	FA	E	WPB	DP	FW	PW	BW	BSW	DIF
EAST																												
BOS	15	13	323	44	1442.0	1439	**92**	519	997	12.5	3.72	110	.261	.327	30	54	104	127	58	.980	123	70	154	-.2	5.5	2.7	-1.1	.0
TOR	6	9	317	48	1454.0	1434	143	**445**	892	11.9	3.84	103	.260	.317	11	16	101	95	67	**.986**	**86**	57	144	**2.0**	1.6	4.2	.2	-3.0
DET	15	12	300	45	1430.1	1401	154	661	856	13.3	4.39	90	.259	.341	-76	-67	101	136	59	.979	131	91	178	-.7	-6.8	5.9	-.6	.2
CLE	12	10	301	47	1427.1	1491	163	518	860	12.9	4.26	92	.270	.334	-57	-55	100	97	53	.981	117	64	146	.2	-5.6	-.4	.0	1.7
BAL	10	5	357	43	1435.1	1445	161	537	776	12.5	4.04	94	.264	.328	-21	-40	97	103	44	.985	93	**39**	151	1.6	-4.1	.3	-.2	-2.1
MIL	23	13	340	42	1445.0	1558	121	469	771	12.9	4.08	95	.275	.331	-28	-34	99	111	45	.976	149	58	152	-1.8	-3.5	-2.1	.7	-.3
NY	15	6	342	41	1444.2	1430	144	618	909	12.9	4.21	94	.261	.336	-49	-38	102	106	**83**	.980	126	110	164	-.4	-3.9	-11.8	.6	1.5
WEST																												
OAK	18	**16**	303	64	1456.0	**1287**	123	494	831	**11.2**	**3.18**	**117**	**.238**	**.302**	**118**	**91**	95	**73**	44	**.986**	87	64	152	**2.0**	**9.3**	**6.3**	**.8**	3.7
CHI	17	10	**367**	**68**	1449.1	1313	106	548	914	11.8	3.61	106	.244	.316	48	35	98	89	60	.980	124	48	169	-.3	3.6	-2.2	-.5	12.5
TEX	**25**	9	302	36	1444.2	1343	113	623	997	12.5	3.83	102	.248	.327	12	14	100	131	52	.979	133	96	161	-.8	1.4	-1.1	.5	2.0
CAL	21	13	269	42	1454.0	1482	106	544	944	12.8	3.79	101	.267	.334	18	4	98	91	69	.978	142	65	**186**	-1.4	.4	2.4	-.4	-2.1
SEA	21	7	312	41	1443.1	1319	120	606	**1064**	12.3	3.69	107	.243	.321	34	42	101	120	56	.979	130	87	152	-.6	4.3	-1.3	.0	-6.4
KC	18	8	312	33	1420.2	1449	116	560	1006	13.0	3.93	97	.264	.334	-5	-17	98	115	28	.980	122	72	161	-.2	-1.7	2.7	-.2	-6.1
MIN	13	13	310	43	1435.2	1509	134	489	872	12.7	4.12	101	.273	.332	-35	4	106	109	65	.983	101	66	161	1.1	.4	-5.9	-.1	-2.5
TOT	229	144	4455	637	20182.1					12.5	3.91		.259	.327						.981	1664	987	2231					

Batter-Fielder Wins	Batting Average	On-Base Percentage	Slugging Average	On-Base Plus Slugging	Adjusted OPS	Adjusted Batter Runs
R.Henderson-Oak 7.8	Brett-KC 329	R.Henderson-Oak 439	Fielder-Det 592	R.Henderson-Oak 1016	R.Henderson-Oak 190	R.Henderson-Oak 64.9
Fielder-Det 4.5	R.Henderson-Oak .325	McGriff-Tor.................400	R.Henderson-Oak .577	Fielder-Det...........969	Fielder-Det...........167	Fielder-Det.........51.2
McGriff-Tor.........4.4	Palmeiro-Tex.........319	E.Martinez-Sea 397	J.Canseco-Oak.....543	McGriff-Tor...........930	J.Canseco-Oak 160	McGriff-Tor 44.1
Fisk-Chi...............4.1	Trammell-Det 304	Brett-KC 387	McGriff-Tor 530	J.Canseco-Oak 914	McGriff-Tor...........156	Brett-KC.............40.1
Parrish-Cal 3.8	Boggs-Bos 302	Davis-Sea 387	Brett-KC 515	Brett-KC...............902	Brett-KC 154	J.Canseco-Oak ..38.5

Runs	Hits	Doubles	Triples	Home Runs	Total Bases	Runs Batted In
R.Henderson-Oak 119	Palmeiro-Tex 191	J.Reed-Bos 45	Fernandez-Tor 17	Fielder-Det.............51	Fielder-Det...........339	Fielder-Det 132
Fielder-Det...........104	Boggs-Bos...........187	Brett-KC 45	Sosa-Chi 10	McGwire-Oak 39	Gruber-Tor 303	Gruber-Tor 118
Reynolds-Sea 100	Kelly-NY...............183	Calderon-Chi 44	Polonia-NY-Cal 9	J.Canseco-Oak 37	McGriff-Tor...........295	McGwire-Oak 108
Yount-Mil 98	Greenwell-Bos......181	Boggs-Bos 44	Liriano-Tor-Min..........9	McGriff-Tor.............35	Griffey-Sea 287	J.Canseco-Oak....101
Phillips-Det 97		Harper-Min 42	Johnson-Chi 9	Gruber-Tor 31	Burks-Bos 286	Sierra-Tex 96

Stolen Bases	Base Stealing Runs	Fielding Runs-Infield	Fielding Runs-Outfield	Wins	Winning Pct.	Complete Games
R.Henderson-Oak ..65	R.Henderson-Oak 10.8	Espinoza-NY 22.9	Orsulak-Bal...........8.9	Welch-Oak.............27	Welch-Oak 818	Stewart-Oak 11
Sax-NY 43	Sax-NY 6.3	Reynolds-Sea 20.1	Deer-Mil 8.5	Stewart-Oak 22	Clemens-Bos 778	Morris-Det 11
Kelly-NY.................42	Cole-Cle 5.7	Whitaker-Det 17.7	Gladden-Min..........8.5	Clemens-Bos..........21	Stieb-Tor...............750	
Cole-Cle 40	Wilson-Tor.............3.7	Phillips-Det 15.4	Webster-Cle 8.0		Boddicker-Bos 680	
Pettis-Tex 38	Cotto-Sea 3.6	Quintana-Bos.............13.2	Mack-Min 8.0			

Strikeouts	Fewest BB/Game	Games	Saves	Base Runners/9	Adjusted Relief Runs	Relief Ranking
Ryan-Tex 232	Anderson-Min......1.86	Thigpen-Chi 77	Thigpen-Chi............57	Eckersley-Oak 5.52	Farr-KC 26.7	Eckersley-Oak 44.6
Witt-Tex 221	Swindell-Cle 1.97	Ward-Tor 73	Eckersley-Oak 48	Nelson-Oak 9.04	Eckersley-Oak 25.0	Thigpen-Chi........40.0
Hanson-Sea 211	Clemens-Bos 2.13	Montgomery-KC 73	Jones-Cle 43	McDonald-Bal......9.33	Thigpen-Chi 20.0	Farr-KC 38.2
Clemens-Bos.........209	Knudson-Mil 2.14	Rogers-Tex 69	Olson-Bal...............37	Henke-Tor.............9.40	Nelson-Oak 19.0	Olson-Bal 24.9
Langston-Cal........195	Wells-Tor..............2.14	Henneman-Det 69	Righetti-NY 36	Thigpen-Chi 9.44	Swift-Sea 19.0	Jones-Cle 24.2

Innings Pitched	Opponents' Avg.	Opponents' OBP	Earned Run Average	Adjusted ERA	Adjusted Starter Runs	Pitcher Wins
Stewart-Oak 267.0	Ryan-Tex 188	Ryan-Tex 267	Clemens-Bos 1.93	Clemens-Bos........212	Clemens-Bos 50.5	**Clemens-Bos** 6.2
Morris-Det..........249.2	Johnson-Sea 216	Clemens-Bos 278	Finley-Cal 2.40	Finley-Cal 159	Stewart-Oak 36.4	**Eckersley-Oak** ..4.7
Welch-Oak 238.0	Clemens-Bos 228	Wells-Tor 283	Stewart-Oak 2.56	Stewart-Oak 145	Finley-Cal 36.1	**Stewart-Oak** 4.3
Hanson-Sea 236.0	Stieb-Tor 230	Hanson-Sea.................287	Appier-KC 2.76	Appier-KC 139	Stieb-Tor 23.2	**Thigpen-Chi** 4.2
Finley-Cal 236.0	Stewart-Oak 231	Black-Cle-Tor 290	Stieb-Tor 2.93	Stieb-Tor 135	Hanson-Sea 22.6	**Farr-KC** 4.1

Another Round of Labor

Owners, angry about salaries, locked out the players in spring training. However, Commissioner Fay Vincent, fearing that a work stoppage would affect the newly signed television contract, ended the lockout. This further inflamed hard-line owners and ensured that Vincent's tenure would be short.

Toronto led the East by 1 game in late September, but lost six of its last eight and fell to Boston. Roger Clemens was again outstanding for the Red Sox, leading the league in ERA while pitching in Fenway Park. The Jays had a more impressive club than Boston but suffered from a lack of lefty relief and inconsistent starting pitching (David Wells shuttled between both roles and won 11 games). Behemoth first baseman Cecil Fielder of Detroit, signed after playing in Japan, hit 51 homers.

Oakland's Rickey Henderson shattered Ty Cobb's career AL steals record. Teammate Bob Welch won the Cy Young with 27 victories, the AL's most since 1968, although Clemens probably deserved the award. With Mark McGwire and Jose Canseco combining for 76 homers, the A's had little trouble in the West. Texas' 43-year-old Nolan Ryan won his 300th game and pitched his sixth no-hitter. The second-place White Sox, in their final season at venerable Comiskey Park, won 90 games for the first time since 1983. Chicago was led by Bobby Thigpen's record 57-save season plus rookie slugger Frank Thomas.

The AL West's top clubs of the 1980s, California and Kansas City, lost two players each to retirement: Bob Boone, Fred Lynn, Dan Quisenberry, and Frank White all sat down. The A's swept Boston in the ALCS, allowing just 4 runs, but they were in turn broomed out by the Reds in the World Series.

1991 National League

TEAM	W	L	T	PCT	GB	HW	HL	R	OR	PA	H	2B	3B	HR	BB	SO	HB	SH	AVG	OBP	SLG	OPS	AOPS	BR	ABR	PF	SB	CS	BSA	BSR
EAST																														
PIT	98	64	0	.605		52	32	**768**	632	6269	**1433**	**259**	50	126	**620**	901	**99**	35	**.263**	**.338**	.398	**736**	**115**	**107**	**120**	98	124	46	73	**11**
STL	84	78	0	.519	14	52	32	651	648	6020	1366	239	**53**	68	532	857	58	21	.255	.322	.357	679	96	-13	-17	101	**202**	110	65	6
PHI	78	84	0	.481	20	47	36	629	680	6133	1332	248	33	111	490	1026	52	21	.241	.303	.358	661	92	-60	-53	99	92	30	**75**	10
CHI	77	83	0	.481	20	46	37	695	734	6130	1395	232	26	159	442	879	75	36	.253	.309	.390	699	96	9	-21	105	123	64	66	5
NY	77	84	0	.478	20.5	40	42	640	646	6076	1305	250	24	117	578	**789**	60	27	.244	.317	.365	682	98	-6	-1	99	153	70	69	9
MON	71	90	0	.441	26.5	33	35	579	655	6035	1329	236	42	95	484	1056	64	28	.246	.308	.357	665	93	-48	-39	99	221	100	69	14
WEST																														
ATL	94	68	0	.580		48	33	749	644	6182	1407	255	30	141	563	906	86	32	.258	.328	.393	721	102	68	27	106	165	76	68	10
LA	93	69	0	.574	1	**54**	27	665	**565**	6159	1366	191	29	108	583	957	94	28	.253	.326	.359	685	100	0	16	98	126	68	65	4
SD	84	78	0	.519	10	42	39	636	646	6057	1321	204	36	121	501	1069	78	32	.244	.310	.362	672	91	-38	-56	103	101	64	61	0
SF	75	87	0	.463	19	43	38	649	697	6097	1345	215	48	141	471	973	90	**40**	.246	.309	.381	690	102	-12	10	97	95	57	63	1
CIN	74	88	0	.457	20	39	42	689	691	6134	1419	250	27	**164**	488	1006	72	32	.258	.320	**.403**	723	104	58	32	104	124	56	69	8
HOU	65	97	0	.401	29	37	44	605	717	6147	1345	240	43	79	502	1027	63	35	.244	.309	.347	656	96	-65	-28	94	125	68	65	4
TOT	970					533	437	7955		73439	16363	2819	441	1430	6254	11446	367	891	.250	.317	.373	689					1651	809	67	80

TEAM	CG	SHO	GR	SV	IP	H	HR	BB	SO	BR/9	ERA	AERA	OAV	OOB	PR	APR	PF	OSB	OCS	FA	E	WPB	DP	FW	PW	BW	BSW	DIF
EAST																												
PIT	**18**	11	353	**51**	1456.2	1411	117	**401**	919	11.4	3.44	104	.256	.308	39	21	97	142	73	.981	120	49	134	.4	2.2	**12.5**	.5	1.5
STL	9	5	**369**	**51**	1435.1	1367	114	454	822	11.7	3.69	101	.255	.315	0	5	101	121	81	**.982**	**107**	**41**	133	**1.1**	.5	-1.8	-.0	3.2
PHI	16	11	321	35	1463.0	1346	111	670	988	12.7	3.86	95	.246	.329	-29	-32	100	151	47	.981	119	90	111	.4	-3.3	-5.5	.3	5.1
CHI	12	4	360	40	1456.2	1415	117	542	927	12.3	4.03	96	.257	.324	-57	-23	105	139	64	**.982**	113	67	120	.7	-2.4	-2.2	-.2	1.1
NY	12	11	314	39	1437.1	1403	108	410	1028	11.5	3.56	102	.257	.309	20	14	99	134	75	.977	143	71	112	-1.0	1.5	-.1	.2	-4.1
MON	12	**14**	367	39	1440.1	**1304**	111	584	909	12.0	3.64	99	.244	.320	7	-4	98	149	81	.979	133	73	128	-.4	-.4	-4.1	**.8**	-5.3
WEST																												
ATL	**18**	7	345	48	1452.2	**1304**	118	481	969	**11.2**	3.49	111	**.240**	**.303**	32	61	106	149	59	.978	138	80	122	-.7	6.4	2.8	.3	4.1
LA	15	**14**	367	40	1458.0	1312	**96**	500	1028	11.4	**3.06**	**117**	.241	.306	**101**	**88**	98	145	60	.980	123	56	126	.2	**9.2**	1.7	-.3	1.2
SD	14	11	334	47	1452.2	1385	139	457	921	11.5	3.57	106	.252	.308	18	35	103	**109**	65	**.982**	113	58	130	.8	3.7	-5.9	-.7	5.1
SF	10	10	334	45	1442.0	1397	143	544	905	12.3	4.03	89	.257	.326	-56	-74	97	129	**83**	**.982**	109	53	**151**	1.0	-7.7	1.0	-.6	.3
CIN	7	11	354	43	1440.0	1372	127	560	997	12.3	3.83	99	.253	.323	-24	-4	103	140	60	.979	125	80	131	.0	-.4	3.3	.1	-10.1
HOU	7	13	365	36	1453.0	1347	129	651	**1033**	12.6	4.00	88	.247	.328	-51	-84	95	143	61	.974	161	62	129	-2.0	-8.8	-2.9	-.3	-2.0
TOT	150	122	4183	514	17387.2					11.9	3.68		.250	.317						.980	1504	780	1527					

Batter-Fielder Wins	Batting Average	On-Base Percentage	Slugging Average	On-Base Plus Slugging	Adjusted OPS	Adjusted Batter Runs
Larkin-Cin............6.2	Pendleton-Atl 319	Bonds-Pit 410	Clark-SF 536	Bonds-Pit.............924	Bonds-Pit..............163	Bonds-Pit............48.9
Bonds-Pit 5.7	Morris-Cin............318	Butler-LA 401	Johnson-NY 535	Clark-SF 895	Clark-SF 154	Bonilla-Pit 43.3
Pendleton-Atl......5.1	Gwynn-SD 317	McGriff-SD...................396	Pendleton-Atl 517	McGriff-SD............890	Bonilla-Pit 151	Clark-SF 38.5
Bonilla-Pit............4.4	McGee-SF 312	Bonilla-Pit 391	Bonds-Pit 514	Larkin-Cin 884	Johnson-NY..........147	McGriff-SD 36.2
Thompson-SF 3.6	Jose-StL 305	Bagwell-Hou 387	Larkin-Cin.............506	Bonilla-Pit 883	McGriff-SD............146	Johnson-NY........34.5

Runs	Hits	Doubles	Triples	Home Runs	Total Bases	Runs Batted In
Butler-LA 112	Pendleton-Atl 187	Bonilla-Pit 44	Lankford-StL 15	Johnson-NY............38	Pendleton-Atl 303	Johnson-NY 117
Johnson-NY..........108	Butler-LA 182	Jose-StL 40	Gwynn-SD 11	Williams-SF 34	Clark-SF 303	Clark-SF 116
Sandberg-Chi 104	Sabo-Cin 175	Zeile-StL 36	Finley-Hou 10	Gant-Atl 32	Johnson-NY..........302	Bonds-Pit 116
Bonilla-Pit 102	Bonilla-Pit 174	O'Neill-Cin 36	Grissom-Mon...........9	McGriff-SD.............31	Williams-SF 294	McGriff-SD 106
Gant-Atl 101	Jose-StL 173		Gonzalez-Hou 9	Dawson-Chi............31	Sabo-Cin 294	Gant-Atl 105

Stolen Bases	Base Stealing Runs	Fielding Runs-Infield	Fielding Runs-Outfield	Wins	Winning Pct.	Complete Games
Grissom-Mon..........76	Grissom-Mon 10.8	Lind-Pit 25.8	Thompson-StL 9.4	Smiley-Pit 20	Smiley-Pit 714	D.Martinez-Mon 9
Nixon-Atl 72	Nixon-Atl................8.5	Larkin-Cin 22.9	Gonzalez-Hou 8.9	Glavine-Atl 20	Rijo-Cin..................714	Glavine-Atl 9
DeShields-Mon 56	Bonds-Pit 4.9	Griffin-LA 20.8	O'Neill-Cin 8.8	Avery-Atl 18	Avery-Atl 692	Mulholland-Phi 8
Lankford-StL 44	O.Smith-StL 4.6	Pendleton-Atl 19.6	Grissom-Mon 8.2	Martinez-LA............17	Hurst-SD................652	Maddux-Chi 7
Bonds-Pit................43	DeShields-Mon.......4.3	Grace-Chi 16.8	Walker-Mon 7.6		Glavine-Atl 645	

Strikeouts	Fewest BB/Game	Games	Saves	Base Runners/9	Adjusted Relief Runs	Relief Ranking
Cone-NY 241	Smith-Pit..............1.14	Jones-Mon 77	L.Smith-StL 47	Berenguer-Atl 9.23	McElroy-Chi 17.1	Williams-Phi 27.0
Maddux-Chi 198	Tewksbury-StL 1.79	Assenmacher-Chi 75	Dibble-Cin 31	Innis-NY 9.46	Maddux-SD 14.3	L.Smith-StL 23.9
Glavine-Atl 192	Mulholland-Phi 1.90	Stanton-Atl 74	Williams-Phi.............30	Maddux-SD 9.67	Williams-Phi 13.5	Pena-NY-Atl.........16.0
Rijo-Cin.................172	Smiley-Pit 1.91	Burke-Mon-NY 72	Franco-NY 30	Stanton-Atl 9.69	Brantley-SF...........12.8	McElroy-Chi..........13.0
Harnisch-Hou 172	B.Smith-StL 2.04	Agosto-StL 72	Righetti-SF 24	Harris-SD 9.74	Pena-NY-Atl 12.4	Maddux-SD 13.0

Innings Pitched	Opponents' Avg.	Opponents' OBP	Earned Run Average	Adjusted ERA	Adjusted Starter Runs	Pitcher Wins
Maddux-Chi 263.0	Harnisch-Hou 212	Rijo-Cin 272	D.Martinez-Mon ..2.39	Glavine-Atl 152	Glavine-Atl 33.4	**Glavine-Atl** 4.9
Glavine-Atl 246.2	Rijo-Cin.................219	Glavine-Atl 277	Rijo-Cin..................2.51	Rijo-Cin 152	D.Martinez-Mon ..29.2	**D.Martinez-Mon** 3.6
Morgan-LA 236.1	Glavine-Atl 222	Morgan-LA...................278	Glavine-Atl 2.55	D.Martinez-Mon 151	Rijo-Cin................26.4	**Williams-Phi** 2.8
Drabek-Pit 234.2	Hill-StL 224	D.Martinez-Mon 282	Belcher-LA 2.62	DeLeon-StL 137	Benes-SD 22.0	**Rijo-Cin** 2.8
Cone-NY............232.2	DeJesus-Phi 224	Benes-SD 285	Harnisch-Hou 2.70	Belcher-LA............137	Morgan-LA 21.1	**L.Smith-StL**..........2.5

Pete Rose Just Won't Go Away

On New Year's Day Pete Rose was released from federal prison after serving five months for income tax evasion. The Hall of Fame caused much controversy less than two weeks later by announcing a change in eligibility rules. No player on the permanently ineligible list, as Rose had been for eighteen months, could now be listed on the annual ballot. In more pleasant news, especially for fans in Denver and Miami, the NL announced that those cities would receive expansion franchises for the 1993 season.

Baseball lost one of its most colorful characters when Leo Durocher passed away the day before the postseason began. Durocher, who won more than 2,000 games as a big league skipper, titled his autobiography, *Nice Guys Finish Last*. Meanwhile, Houston rookie Jeff Bagwell began his journey to 400–plus home runs. Mark Wohlers also made his debut later in the year. It was the last season for Dave Parker, Rick Reuschel, and Ken Griffey Sr., the first major leaguer to play alongside his son.

The Pirates, with Barry Bonds, Andy Van Slyke, and Bobby Bonilla spearheading the league's best offense, had no trouble repeating as NL champs, finishing 14 games ahead of St. Louis. Atlanta, which finished last in the West in 1990, battled Los Angeles all season and didn't eliminate the Dodgers until the next to last game. The Braves had great seasons from outfielder Ron Gant, MVP Terry Pendleton, and a devastating young pitching trio of Tom Glavine, Steve Avery, and John Smoltz.

Those hurlers, especially Avery, made the difference in a thrilling NLCS, hurling 3 shutouts, including back-to-back blankings in Games 6 and 7 in Pittsburgh. The Braves lost a heartbreaking World Series to Minnesota, dropping the final two games in extra innings.

1991 American League

TEAM	W	L	T	PCT	GB	HW	HL	R	OR	PA	H	2B	3B	HR	BB	SO	HB	SH	AVG	OBP	SLG	OPS	AOPS	BR	ABR	PF	SB	CS	BSA	BSR
EAST																														
TOR	91	71	0	.562		46	35	684	**622**	6167	1412	295	45	133	499	1043	56	**58**	.257	.322	.400	722	95	-6	-31	104	148	53	74	**14**
DET	84	78	0	.519	7	49	32	817	794	6359	1372	259	26	**209**	**699**	1185	38	31	.247	.333	.416	749	105	52	41	101	109	47	70	8
BOS	84	78	0	.519	7	43	38	731	712	6256	1486	**305**	25	126	593	820	50	32	.269	.340	.401	741	99	47	11	105	59	39	60	-1
MIL	83	79	0	.512	8	43	37	799	744	6308	1523	247	**53**	116	556	802	52	23	.271	.336	.396	732	105	21	40	98	106	68	61	0
NY	71	91	0	.438	20	39	42	674	777	6140	1418	249	19	147	473	861	37	39	.256	.316	.387	703	93	-49	-50	100	109	36	**75**	11
BAL	67	95	0	.414	24	33	48	686	796	6257	1421	256	29	170	528	974	47	33	.254	.319	.401	720	102	-18	12	96	50	33	60	-1
CLE	57	105	0	.352	34	30	52	576	759	6070	1390	236	26	79	449	888	62	43	.254	.313	.350	663	83	-122	-125	101	84	58	59	-2
WEST																														
MIN	95	67	0	.586		**51**	30	776	652	6215	**1557**	270	42	140	526	**747**	44	40	**.280**	**.344**	.420	764	105	82	47	105	107	68	61	0
CHI	87	75	0	.537	8	46	35	758	681	6358	1464	226	39	139	610	896	**76**	37	.262	.336	.391	727	102	10	28	98	134	74	64	4
TEX	85	77	0	.525	10	46	35	**829**	814	6441	1539	288	31	177	596	1039	59	42	.270	.341	**.424**	**765**	**112**	**87**	**102**	98	102	50	67	5
OAK	84	78	0	.519	11	47	34	760	776	6192	1342	246	19	159	642	981	41	50	.248	.331	.389	720	104	0	44	94	**151**	64	70	11
SEA	83	79	0	.512	12	45	36	702	674	6236	1400	268	29	126	588	811	55	37	.255	.328	.383	711	96	-19	-20	100	97	44	69	6
KC	82	80	0	.506	13	40	41	727	722	6242	1475	290	41	117	523	969	53	35	.264	.328	.394	722	99	-4	-7	100	119	68	64	2
CAL	81	81	0	.500	14	40	41	653	649	6050	1396	245	29	115	448	928	63	38	.255	.314	.374	688	89	-81	-80	100	94	56	63	1
TOT	1134					598	536	10172		87291	20195	3680	453	1953	7730	12944	538	733	.260	.329	.395	724					1469	758	66	58

TEAM	CG	SHO	GR	SV	IP	H	HR	BB	SO	BR/9	ERA	AERA	OAV	OOB	PR	APR	PF	OSB	OCS	FA	E	WPB	DP	FW	PW	BW	BSW	DIF
EAST																												
TOR	10	**16**	347	**60**	1462.2	**1301**	121	523	971	**11.5**	**3.50**	**120**	**.238**	**.307**	**96**	**111**	103	118	53	.980	127	76	115	-.6	**11.1**	-3.1	**1.0**	1.6
DET	18	8	326	38	1450.1	1570	148	593	739	13.6	4.51	92	.280	.348	-66	-56	101	88	56	.983	104	62	171	.7	-5.6	4.1	.4	3.4
BOS	15	13	328	45	1439.2	1405	147	530	999	12.3	4.01	107	.257	.323	13	43	105	97	53	.981	116	**53**	165	.0	4.3	1.1	-.5	-1.9
MIL	23	11	341	41	1463.2	1498	147	527	859	12.7	4.14	96	.266	.332	-8	-29	97	115	47	.981	118	69	176	-.0	-2.9	4.0	-.4	1.4
NY	3	11	377	37	1444.0	1510	152	506	936	12.8	4.42	94	.271	.334	-52	-44	101	134	51	.979	133	66	181	-.9	-4.4	-5.0	.7	-.3
BAL	8	8	372	42	1457.2	1534	147	504	868	12.8	4.59	86	.273	.333	-80	-107	97	111	51	**.985**	**91**	57	172	**1.4**	-10.7	1.2	-.5	-5.4
CLE	22	8	289	33	1441.1	1551	110	**441**	862	12.7	4.23	98	.276	.329	-22	-13	101	102	47	.976	149	67	150	-1.8	-1.3	-12.5	-.6	-7.8
WEST																												
MIN	21	12	291	53	1449.1	1402	139	488	876	11.9	3.69	115	.255	.317	64	88	104	118	43	**.985**	95	69	161	1.2	8.8	4.7	-.4	-.3
CHI	**28**	8	338	40	1478.0	1302	154	601	923	11.8	3.79	105	.239	.315	50	31	97	96	67	.982	116	64	151	.0	3.1	2.8	-.0	.0
TEX	9	10	386	41	1479.0	1486	151	662	**1022**	13.3	4.47	90	.262	.341	-61	-73	98	107	58	.979	134	92	138	-1.0	-7.3	**10.2**	.0	2.0
OAK	14	10	**397**	49	1444.1	1425	155	655	892	13.3	4.57	84	.260	.342	-77	-127	94	116	60	.982	107	68	150	.5	-12.7	4.4	.7	10.1
SEA	10	13	383	48	1464.1	1387	136	628	1003	12.7	3.79	109	.253	.332	50	54	101	**84**	44	.983	110	106	**187**	.3	5.4	-2.0	.2	-1.9
KC	17	12	295	41	1466.0	1473	**105**	529	1004	12.6	3.92	105	.261	.327	28	32	101	94	56	.980	125	58	141	-.5	3.2	-.7	-.2	-.8
CAL	18	10	310	50	1441.2	1351	141	543	990	12.1	3.69	111	.250	.321	65	66	100	89	**72**	.984	102	72	156	.8	6.6	-8.0	-.3	.9
TOT	216	150	4780	618	20382.0					12.6	4.09		.260	.329						.981	1627	979	2214					

Batter-Fielder Wins	Batting Average	On-Base Percentage	Slugging Average	On-Base Plus Slugging	Adjusted OPS	Adjusted Batter Runs
C.Ripken-Bal 8.6	Franco-Tex 341	Thomas-Chi 453	Tartabull-KC 593	Thomas-Chi.......1006	Thomas-Chi..........181	Thomas-Chi........71.8
Thomas-Chi 5.9	Boggs-Bos 332	Randolph-Mil 424	C.Ripken-Bal.........566	Tartabull-KC.........990	Tartabull-KC..........170	C.Ripken-Bal 55.2
Griffey-Sea..........4.6	Randolph-Mil 327	Boggs-Bos 421	Canseco-Oak 556	C.Ripken-Bal 940	C.Ripken-Bal 164	Palmeiro-Tex 49.7
Phillips-Det.........4.2	Griffey-Sea 327	Franco-Tex 408	Thomas-Chi 553	Griffey-Sea 926	Canseco-Oak 159	Tartabull-KC 47.3
Boggs-Bos 3.8	Molitor-Mil............325	E.Martinez-Sea 405	Palmeiro-Tex.........532	Palmeiro-Tex 922	Palmeiro-Tex 156	Canseco-Oak 46.1

Runs	Hits	Doubles	Triples	Home Runs	Total Bases	Runs Batted In
Molitor-Mil 133	Molitor-Mil 216	Palmeiro-Tex..................49	Molitor-Mil 13	Fielder-Det.............44	C.Ripken-Bal 368	Fielder-Det 133
Palmeiro-Tex 115	C.Ripken-Bal.........210	C.Ripken-Bal..................46	Johnson-Chi 13	Canseco-Oak 44	Palmeiro-Tex 336	Canseco-Oak 122
Canseco-Oak 115	Sierra-Tex 203	Sierra-Tex 44	Alomar-Tor..............11	C.Ripken-Bal 34	Sierra-Tex 332	Sierra-Tex............116
White-Tor..............110	Palmeiro-Tex 203		White-Tor.................10	Carter-Tor 33	Molitor-Mil 325	C.Ripken-Bal 114
Sierra-Tex 110	Franco-Tex............201		Devereaux-Bal........10	Thomas-Chi............32	Carter-Tor 321	Thomas-Chi 109

Stolen Bases	Base Stealing Runs	Fielding Runs-Infield	Fielding Runs-Outfield	Wins	Winning Pct.	Complete Games
R.Henderson-Oak ..58	Alomar-Tor 7.8	Sojo-Cal......................26.6	Orsulak-Bal..........17.2	Gullickson-Det 20	Erickson-Min.........714	McDowell-Chi 15
Alomar-Tor..............53	R.Henderson-Oak 6.5	Vizquel-Sea 26.1	Whiten-Tor-Cle 10.4	Erickson-Min 20	Langston-Cal 704	Clemens-Bos 13
Raines-Chi..............51	Raines-Chi 6.0	Espinoza-NY 21.0	Bichette-Mil...........8.9	Langston-Cal 19	Gullickson-Det 690	Navarro-Mil............10
Polonia-Cal 48	Cuyler-Det 5.5	C.Ripken-Bal 19.5	Buhner-Sea 7.2		Wegman-Mil 682	Morris-Min 10
Cuyler-Det 41	Franco-Tex 4.8	Phillips-Det 18.1	R.Henderson-Oak 6.5		Moore-Oak 680	Terrell-Det................8

Strikeouts	Fewest BB/Game	Games	Saves	Base Runners/9	Adjusted Relief Runs	Relief Ranking
Clemens-Bos........241	Swindell-Cle 1.17	D.Ward-Tor 81	Harvey-Cal.............46	Gray-Bos 7.30	Frohwirth-Bal 21.9	Harvey-Cal 32.7
Johnson-Sea 228	Sanderson-NY 1.25	Olson-Bal 72	Eckersley-Oak 43	Harvey-Cal 7.89	Swift-Sea 21.2	Aguilera-Min 28.1
Ryan-Tex 203	Tapani-Min 1.48	Jackson-Sea 72	Aguilera-Min 42	Eckersley-Oak 8.29	Harvey-Cal 19.8	Farr-NY 27.2
McDowell-Chi 191	Gullickson-Det 1.75	Swift-Sea 71	Reardon-Bos 40	Eichhorn-Cal.........8.60	Eichhorn-Cal.........18.7	D.Ward-Tor 24.3
Langston-Cal........183	Wegman-Mil 1.86		Montgomery-KC 33	Frohwirth-Bal 8.78	Flanagan-Bal 18.3	Radinsky-Chi......22.8

Innings Pitched	Opponents' Avg.	Opponents' OBP	Earned Run Average	Adjusted ERA	Adjusted Starter Runs	Pitcher Wins
Clemens-Bos 271.1	Ryan-Tex 172	Ryan-Tex 263	Clemens-Bos 2.62	Clemens-Bos........164	Clemens-Bos 46.1	**Clemens-Bos** 4.7
McDowell-Chi 253.2	Johnson-Sea 213	Clemens-Bos 270	Candiotti-Cle-Tor 2.65	Candiotti-Cle-Tor.......158	Candiotti-Cle-Tor 38.7	**Candiotti-Cle-Tor** 4.0
Morris-Min 246.2	Langston-Cal 215	Tapani-Min 277	Wegman-Mil 2.84	Tapani-Min...........143	Tapani-Min 35.6	**J.Abbott-Cal** 4.0
Langston-Cal 246.1	Clemens-Bos 221	Sanderson-NY 279	J.Abbott-Cal 2.89	J.Abbott-Cal.........142	J.Abbott-Cal 33.2	**Tapani-Min** 3.4
Tapani-Min 244.0	Candiotti-Cle-Tor 228	Saberhagen-KC 280	Ryan-Tex 2.91	Wegman-Mil 140	Langston-Cal 30.9	**Harvey-Cal** 3.3

Morris Dance

The year began sadly as Hall of Fame shortstop Luke Appling passed away two days after New Year's Day at age 83, then three days later, 32-year-old Alan Wiggins died of AIDS complications. Also passing was Hall of Fame outfielder James "Cool Papa" Bell, a Negro Leagues superstar. The terrible run of bad luck off the field continued in July when respected umpire Steve Palermo, was partially paralyzed when shot in the back during a restaurant robbery.

Baltimore hurler Jim Palmer, already elected to the Hall of Fame, attempted a brief and unsuccessful comeback during spring training. Chicago's "New" Comiskey Park opened to trumpet fanfare, though the stadium would be horribly outdated within a few years as more fashionable "retro" ballparks opened.

May 1 was a historic night. In Texas Nolan Ryan extended his own record by throwing a seventh no-hitter, and in Oakland Rickey Henderson copped Lou Brock's all-time stolen base record. As Dwight Evans was concluding his memorable twenty-year career, future postseason heroes Mike Mussina, Ivan Rodriguez, and Bernie Williams were making their first appearances.

Minnesota, last-place finishers the year before, and Toronto had easy times winning their respective division titles. The Twins, buffed up by free agent Jack Morris and rookie Chuck Knoblauch, had three strong starters and a solid all-around club, while the Blue Jays sported a spectacular three-man bullpen in Tom Henke, Duane Ward, and Mike Timlin.

Behind Kirby Puckett's bat and Jack Morris' arm, Minnesota cruised past the Blue Jays in five games in the ALCS, then beat Atlanta in one of the game's most memorable World Series. Both the Twins and Braves had heroes galore, but Morris' 10-inning, complete-game shutout in Game 7 took the cake.

1992 National League

TEAM	W	L	T	PCT	GB	HW	HL	R	OR	PA	H	2B	3B	HR	BB	SO	HB	SH	AVG	OBP	SLG	OPS	AOPS	BR	ABR	PF	SB	CS	BSA	BSR
EAST																														
PIT	96	66	0	.593		**53**	28	**693**	595	6266	1409	272	**54**	106	569	872	89	25	.255	.324	.381	705	106	50	**58**	99	110	53	67	6
MON	87	75	0	.537	9	43	38	648	581	6120	1381	263	37	102	463	976	82	43	.252	.313	.370	683	100	-3	3	99	196	63	**76**	**21**
STL	83	79	0	.512	13	45	36	631	604	6230	**1464**	262	44	94	495	996	68	32	**.262**	.323	.375	698	**107**	30	51	97	**208**	118	64	4
CHI	78	84	0	.481	18	43	38	593	624	6156	1420	221	41	104	417	**816**	78	31	.254	.307	.364	671	93	-35	-50	103	77	51	60	-1
NY	72	90	0	.444	24	41	40	599	653	6059	1254	259	17	93	**572**	956	74	28	.235	.310	.342	652	91	-50	-42	99	129	52	71	10
PHI	70	92	0	.432	26	41	40	686	717	6171	1392	255	36	118	509	1059	64	52	.253	.320	.377	697	103	28	30	100	127	31	80	17
WEST																														
ATL	98	64	0	.605		51	30	682	**569**	6142	1391	223	48	**138**	493	924	93	26	.254	.316	**.388**	704	99	32	-6	106	126	60	68	7
CIN	90	72	0	.556	8	**53**	28	660	609	6162	1418	**281**	44	99	563	888	66	21	.260	**.328**	.382	**710**	104	**61**	43	103	125	65	66	5
SD	82	80	0	.506	16	45	36	617	636	6074	1396	255	30	135	453	864	78	26	.255	.313	.386	699	101	23	12	102	69	52	57	-3
HOU	81	81	0	.500	17	47	34	608	668	6162	1350	255	38	96	506	1025	88	**48**	.246	.313	.359	672	101	-19	10	96	139	54	72	12
SF	72	90	0	.444	26	42	39	574	647	6070	1330	220	36	105	435	1067	**101**	39	.244	.302	.355	657	96	-60	-27	94	112	64	64	2
LA	63	99	0	.389	35	37	44	548	636	6037	1333	201	34	72	503	899	102	24	.248	.313	.339	652	92	-57	-48	98	142	78	65	4
TOT	972					541	431	7539		73649	16538	2967	459	1262	5978	11342	395	983	.252	.315	.368	684					1560	741	68	84

TEAM	CG	SHO	GR	SV	IP	H	HR	BB	SO	BR/9	ERA	AERA	OAV	OOB	PR	APR	PF	OSB	OCS	FA	E	WPB	DP	FW	PW	BW	BSW	DIF
EAST																												
PIT	20	20	354	43	1479.2	1410	101	455	844	11.5	3.35	103	.254	.312	25	15	98	124	**73**	.984	101	63	144	.9	1.6	**6.2**	-.1	6.4
MON	11	14	349	49	1468.0	**1296**	92	525	1014	11.5	3.25	107	**.238**	.309	41	35	99	199	68	.980	124	57	113	-.4	3.8	.3	**1.5**	.8
STL	10	9	**424**	47	1480.0	1405	118	**400**	842	**11.2**	3.38	100	.252	**.303**	20	1	97	124	39	**.985**	**94**	49	146	**1.3**	.1	5.5	-.3	-4.6
CHI	16	11	372	37	1469.0	1337	107	575	901	12.0	3.39	106	.246	.320	18	33	103	116	72	.982	114	82	142	.2	3.6	-5.4	-.9	-.5
NY	17	13	333	34	1446.2	1404	98	482	1025	12.0	3.66	95	.256	.318	-25	-30	99	148	67	.981	116	44	134	.0	-3.2	-4.5	.3	-1.6
PHI	**27**	7	323	34	1428.0	1387	113	549	851	12.4	4.11	85	.257	.325	-96	-99	100	111	53	.978	131	56	128	-.8	-10.7	3.2	1.1	-3.8
WEST																												
ATL	26	**24**	338	41	1460.0	1321	89	489	948	11.3	**3.14**	**116**	.242	.305	**58**	**80**	104	149	66	.982	109	71	121	.4	**8.6**	-.6	.0	8.6
CIN	9	11	357	**55**	1449.2	1362	109	470	**1060**	11.5	3.46	104	.251	.312	6	21	103	104	54	.984	96	62	128	1.2	2.3	4.6	-.2	1.2
SD	9	11	363	46	1461.1	1444	111	439	971	11.7	3.56	100	.261	.315	-9	3	102	141	69	.982	115	**27**	127	.0	.3	1.3	-1.1	.4
HOU	5	12	422	45	1459.1	1386	114	539	978	12.1	3.72	90	.252	.320	-35	-61	96	129	54	.981	114	58	125	.2	-6.6	1.1	.5	4.8
SF	9	12	386	30	1461.0	1385	128	502	927	11.8	3.61	91	.253	.318	-17	-53	94	**74**	64	.982	113	50	**174**	.2	-5.7	-2.9	-.5	-.0
LA	18	13	353	29	1438.0	1401	**82**	553	981	12.4	3.41	101	.257	.326	15	5	98	141	62	.972	174	84	136	-3.2	.5	-5.2	-.3	-9.8
TOT	177	157	4374	490	17500.2					11.8	3.50		.252	.315						.981	1401	703	1618					

Batter-Fielder Wins	Batting Average	On-Base Percentage	Slugging Average	On-Base Plus Slugging	Adjusted OPS	Adjusted Batter Runs
Bonds-Pit 8.0	Sheffield-SD 330	Bonds-Pit 456	Bonds-Pit 624	Bonds-Pit............1080	Bonds-Pit..............207	Bonds-Pit............76.1
Sheffield-SD........6.0	VanSlyke-Pit 324	Kruk-Phi.......................423	Sheffield-SD 580	Sheffield-SD 965	Sheffield-SD 168	Sheffield-SD 49.1
Sandberg-Chi......5.6	Kruk-Phi 323	Butler-LA 413	McGriff-SD 556	McGriff-SD............950	McGriff-SD............164	McGriff-SD 47.5
Larkin-Cin............5.5	Roberts-Cin 323	McGriff-SD...................394	Daulton-Phi............524	Daulton-Phi 908	Daulton-Phi 157	VanSlyke-Pit 42.3
Daulton-Phi 4.9	Gwynn-SD 317	Roberts-Cin 393	Sandberg-Chi 510	VanSlyke-Pit 886	Clark-SF 153	Kruk-Phi 40.3

Runs	Hits	Doubles	Triples	Home Runs	Total Bases	Runs Batted In
Bonds-Pit.............109	VanSlyke-Pit 199	VanSlyke-Pit 45	Sanders-Atl 14	McGriff-SD.............35	Sheffield-SD 323	Daulton-Phi 109
Hollins-Phi 104	Pendleton-Atl........199	Lankford-StL 40	Finley-Hou 13	Bonds-Pit................34	Sandberg-Chi 312	Pendleton-Atl 105
VanSlyke-Pit 103	Sandberg-Chi 186	Duncan-Phi....................40	VanSlyke-Pit 12	Sheffield-SD 33	VanSlyke-Pit 310	McGriff-SD 104
Sandberg-Chi 100	Grace-Chi 185	Clark-SF 40	Butler-LA 11	Hollins-Phi 27	Pendleton-Atl........303	Bonds-Pit 103
Grissom-Mon..........99	Sheffield-SD 184		Alicea-StL 11	Daulton-Phi 27		Sheffield-SD........100

Stolen Bases	Base Stealing Runs	Fielding Runs-Infield	Fielding Runs-Outfield	Wins	Winning Pct.	Complete Games
Grissom-Mon..........78	Grissom-Mon 12.6	Thompson-SF 25.5	Jackson-SD 14.4	Maddux-Chi............20	Tewksbury-StL 762	Mulholland-Phi 12
DeShields-Mon 46	Finley-Hou 6.5	Wallach-Mon 18.7	Gonzalez-Hou 13.5	Glavine-Atl..............20	Glavine-Atl 714	Schilling-Phi 10
Roberts-Cin 44	O.Smith-StL 6.3	Sharperson-LA 18.2	Sanders-Cin 10.7		Leibrandt-Atl.........682	Drabek-Pit 10
Finley-Hou..............44	Bonds-Pit 5.8	Harris-LA 15.8	Javier-LA-Phi 10.1		Morgan-Chi...........667	Smoltz-Atl..................9
O.Smith-StL 43	DeShields-Mon......4.9	O.Smith-StL 15.8	Nixon-Atl 9.5		Maddux-Chi 645	Maddux-Chi 9

Strikeouts	Fewest BB/Game	Games	Saves	Base Runners/9	Adjusted Relief Runs	Relief Ranking
Smoltz-Atl 215	Tewksbury-StL 77	Boever-Hou....................81	L.Smith-StL 43	Beck-SF 7.73	Rojas-Mon 23.3	D.Jones-Hou 35.7
Cone-NY 214	Cormier-StL 1.60	D.Jones-Hou 80	Myers-SD................38	Schilling-Phi 8.95	D.Jones-Hou........17.8	Rojas-Mon 20.8
Maddux-Chi 199	Swindell-Cin 1.73	Perez-StL 77	Wetteland-Mon 37	Tewksbury-StL 9.27	Beck-SF 16.7	Perez-StL 18.0
Fernandez-NY 193	Mulholland-Phi 1.81	Hernandez-Hou 77	D.Jones-Hou 36	D.Jones-Hou.........9.51	Perez-StL 15.5	Beck-SF 15.3
Drabek-Pit 177	Tomlin-Pit 1.81	Innis-NY 76	M.Williams-Phi........29	Rojas-Mon 9.57	Hernandez-Hou ..15.1	Hernandez-Hou..13.9

Innings Pitched	Opponents' Avg.	Opponents' OBP	Earned Run Average	Adjusted ERA	Adjusted Starter Runs	Pitcher Wins
Maddux-Chi 268.0	Schilling-Phi 201	Schilling-Phi.................253	Swift-SF 2.08	Maddux-Chi..........165	Maddux-Chi 43.5	**Maddux-Chi**........6.0
Drabek-Pit 256.2	Maddux-Chi 210	Tewksbury-StL.............265	Tewksbury-StL 2.16	Swift-SF 159	Tewksbury-StL 31.9	**D.Jones-Hou**......3.8
Smoltz-Atl.........246.2	Fernandez-NY 210	Martinez-Mon 271	Maddux-Chi 2.18	Tewksbury-StL.......157	Schilling-Phi 27.9	**Glavine-Atl** 3.0
Morgan-Chi........240.0	Martinez-Mon 211	Maddux-Chi 272	Schilling-Phi 2.35	Schilling-Phi..........149	Morgan-Chi...........25.9	**Schilling-Phi** 3.0
Avery-Atl 233.2	Cone-NY...............223	Fernandez-NY 273	Martinez-Mon 2.47	Morgan-Chi 141	Swift-SF 24.4	**Rijo-Cin** 3.0

Pirates Leave Their Heart with Francisco

Commissioner Fay Vincent announced his plan to realign the divisions, which would have put Atlanta and Cincinnati in the East and St. Louis and Chicago in the West, making the layout geographical. The Reds and Cubs vehemently opposed the move, which was later blocked by a U.S. District Court judge. That debacle, combined with an inability to break the union, sealed the commish's fate as owners voted 18–9 to fire Vincent, who finally resigned in September. One of Vincent's most outspoken critics was Milwaukee owner Bud Selig, who effectively became commissioner as chair of the owners' Executive Council. Owners also prevented the Giants from moving to Tampa-St. Petersburg.

The Reds were in turmoil again, with skipper Lou Piniella and reliever Rob Dibble fighting in the clubhouse, and owner Marge Schott accused of making anti-Semitic remarks. Pedro Martinez and Mike Piazza, debuted for the Dodgers in September, while Gary Carter, Jack Clark and Pedro Guerrero called it a career. Hall of Fame second baseman Billy Herman passed away. Philadelphia's Mickey Morandini turned the league's first unassisted triple play since 1927.

Barry Bonds won his second MVP award and led the Pirates and an unheralded mound staff to a third consecutive East title. Atlanta, with strong starters and a mix-and-match bullpen, took its second straight West crown. The Braves again eliminated Pittsburgh in a thrilling seven-game NLCS. The Braves were down 2–0 in the last of the ninth of Game 7. But the Pirates fell apart on the hill and in the field, and Sid Bream slid in with the winning run with two outs on pinch hitter Francisco Cabrera's two-run single. After this emotional peak, however, Atlanta lost the World Series again, this time to Toronto in six games.

1992 American League

TEAM	W	L	T	PCT	GB	HW	HL	R	OR	PA	H	2B	3B	HR	BB	SO	HB	SH	AVG	OBP	SLG	OPS	AOPS	BR	ABR	PF	SB	CS	BSA	BSR
EAST																														
TOR	96	66	0	.593		**53**	28	780	682	6224	1458	265	40	163	561	933	26	47	.263	.333	**.414**	**747**	103	63	30	105	129	39	**77**	15
MIL	92	70	0	.568	4	**53**	28	740	**604**	6181	1477	272	35	82	511	779	61	33	.268	.330	.375	705	99	-11	4	98	**256**	115	69	**16**
BAL	89	73	0	.549	7	43	38	705	656	6292	1423	243	36	148	647	827	50	51	.259	.340	.398	738	103	56	37	103	89	48	65	3
NY	76	86	0	.469	20	41	40	733	746	6252	1462	281	18	163	536	903	26	42	.261	.328	.406	734	105	35	41	99	78	37	68	4
CLE	76	86	0	.469	20	41	40	674	746	6199	1495	227	24	127	448	885	42	45	.266	.323	.383	706	99	-27	-15	98	144	67	68	8
DET	75	87	0	.463	21	38	42	**791**	794	6310	1411	256	16	**182**	675	1055	43	24	.256	.337	.407	744	106	**65**	61	101	66	45	59	-1
BOS	73	89	0	.451	23	44	37	599	669	6186	1343	259	21	84	591	865	60	31	.246	.321	.347	668	82	-83	-121	107	44	48	48	-7
WEST																														
OAK	96	66	0	.593		51	30	745	672	6274	1389	219	24	142	**707**	831	**72**	49	.258	**.346**	.386	732	**111**	55	**98**	95	143	59	71	11
MIN	90	72	0	.556	6	48	33	747	653	6267	**1544**	275	27	104	527	834	46	**53**	**.277**	.341	.391	732	102	47	24	103	123	74	62	1
CHI	86	76	0	.531	10	50	32	738	690	6267	1434	269	36	110	622	784	47	31	.261	.336	.383	719	102	21	31	99	160	57	74	15
TEX	77	85	0	.475	19	36	45	682	753	6238	1387	266	23	159	550	1036	56	50	.250	.321	.393	714	103	-5	21	96	81	44	65	2
KC	72	90	0	.444	24	44	37	610	667	6082	1411	**284**	**42**	75	439	**741**	45	51	.256	.315	.364	679	88	-74	-90	103	131	71	65	4
CAL	72	90	0	.444	24	41	40	579	671	5916	1306	202	20	88	416	882	56	40	.243	.301	.338	639	79	-158	-161	101	160	101	61	0
SEA	64	98	0	.395	32	38	43	679	799	6179	1466	278	24	149	474	841	52	38	.263	.323	.402	725	101	13	9	101	100	55	65	3
TOT	1134					621	513	9802		86867	20006	3596	386	1776	7704	12196	585	682	.259	.328	.385	713					1704	860	66	74

TEAM	CG	SHO	GR	SV	IP	H	HR	BB	SO	BR/9	ERA	AERA	OAV	OOB	PR	APR	PF	OSB	OCS	FA	E	WPB	DP	FW	PW	BW	BSW	DIF
EAST																												
TOR	18	14	284	49	1440.2	1346	124	541	954	12.1	3.91	104	.248	.318	5	26	104	144	63	.985	93	81	109	1.4	2.6	3.1	1.0	6.9
MIL	19	14	338	39	1457.0	**1344**	127	**435**	793	**11.3**	**3.43**	112	**.246**	**.305**	**82**	67	97	96	53	**.986**	**89**	**42**	146	**1.6**	6.8	.4	**1.1**	1.1
BAL	20	**16**	290	48	1464.0	1419	124	518	846	12.1	3.79	106	.256	.322	25	38	102	131	44	.985	93	60	168	1.4	3.9	3.8	-.2	-.8
NY	20	9	308	44	1452.2	1453	129	612	851	13.0	4.21	93	.263	.338	-43	-47	99	164	62	.982	114	68	165	.2	-4.8	4.2	-.1	-4.5
CLE	13	7	379	46	1470.0	1507	159	566	890	12.9	4.11	95	.268	.336	-28	-34	99	109	64	.978	141	62	**176**	-1.3	-3.5	-1.5	.3	1.0
DET	10	4	355	36	1435.2	1534	155	564	693	13.3	4.60	86	.277	.343	-105	-102	100	102	62	.981	116	65	164	.1	-10.4	6.2	-.6	-1.3
BOS	22	13	328	39	1448.2	1403	107	535	943	12.3	3.58	**117**	.255	.323	57	**94**	107	114	51	.978	139	58	170	-1.2	**9.6**	-12.3	-1.3	-2.9
WEST																												
OAK	8	9	**400**	**58**	1447.0	1396	129	601	843	12.7	3.73	100	.256	.331	34	3	95	118	76	.979	125	75	158	-.4	.3	**10.0**	.6	4.5
MIN	16	13	323	50	1453.0	1391	121	479	923	11.8	3.70	109	.254	.316	38	55	103	152	60	.985	95	66	155	1.3	5.6	2.4	-.4	.0
CHI	21	5	292	52	1461.2	1400	123	550	810	12.3	3.82	101	.252	.323	19	6	98	120	57	.979	129	48	134	-.6	.6	3.2	1.0	.8
TEX	19	3	359	42	1460.1	1471	113	598	**1034**	13.0	4.09	93	.264	.337	-24	-49	96	**87**	**84**	.975	154	91	153	-2.0	-5.0	2.1	-.3	1.2
KC	9	12	340	44	1447.1	1426	**106**	512	834	12.3	3.81	106	.259	.323	21	38	103	107	52	.980	122	56	164	-.2	3.9	-9.2	-.1	-3.4
CAL	**26**	13	297	42	1446.0	1449	130	532	888	12.6	3.84	104	.264	.331	16	23	101	120	70	.979	134	47	172	-.9	2.3	-16.4	-.5	6.5
SEA	21	9	372	30	1445.0	1467	129	661	894	13.6	4.55	87	.266	.348	-97	-92	101	140	62	.982	112	70	170	.3	-9.4	.9	-.2	-8.7
TOT	242	141	4665	619	20329.0					12.5	3.94		.259	.328						.981	1656	889	2204					

Batter-Fielder Wins	Batting Average	On-Base Percentage	Slugging Average	On-Base Plus Slugging	Adjusted OPS	Adjusted Batter Runs
Ventura-Chi 5.1	E.Martinez-Sea ...343	Thomas-Chi 439	McGwire-Oak 585	Thomas-Chi..........975	McGwire-Oak 180	Thomas-Chi........67.3
E.Martinez-Sea ..4.9	Puckett-Min...........329	Tartabull-NY................409	E.Martinez-Sea ...544	McGwire-Oak 970	Thomas-Chi..........176	McGwire-Oak 51.7
R.Henderson-Oak4.6	Thomas-Chi 323	Alomar-Tor 405	Thomas-Chi 536	E.Martinez-Sea 948	E.Martinez-Sea 164	E.Martinez-Sea ..46.2
Thomas-Chi 4.5	Molitor-Mil.............320	E.Martinez-Sea 404	Griffey-Sea 535	Tartabull-NY 898	Tartabull-NY 152	R.Henderson-Oak37.0
Baerga-Cle 3.8	Mack-Min..............315	Mack-Min.....................394	Gonzalez-Tex 529	Griffey-Sea 896	Griffey-Sea 148	Molitor-Mil 36.5

Runs	Hits	Doubles	Triples	Home Runs	Total Bases	Runs Batted In
Phillips-Det 114	Puckett-Min 210	Thomas-Chi 46	Johnson-Chi 12	Gonzalez-Tex..........43	Puckett-Min 313	Fielder-Det 124
Thomas-Chi..........108	Baerga-Cle 205	E.Martinez-Sea.............46	Devereaux-Bal.......11	McGwire-Oak 42	Carter-Tor 310	Carter-Tor............119
Alomar-Tor............105	Molitor-Mil 195	Yount-Mil.........................40	Anderson-Bal..........10	Fielder-Det.............35	Gonzalez-Tex.........309	Thomas-Chi 115
Puckett-Min 104	Mack-Min...............189	Mattingly-NY..................40	Raines-Chi...............9	Carter-Tor 34	Thomas-Chi...........307	Belle-Cle..............112
Knoblauch-Min 104	Thomas-Chi..........185	Griffey-Sea 39		Belle-Cle 34	Devereaux-Bal......303	Bell-Chi..................112

Stolen Bases	Base Stealing Runs	Fielding Runs-Infield	Fielding Runs-Outfield	Wins	Winning Pct.	Complete Games
Lofton-Cle 66	Lofton-Cle............10.3	Reed-Bos....................30.4	Raines-Chi 9.6	Morris-Tor 21	Mussina-Bal 783	McDowell-Chi 13
Listach-Mil 54	Raines-Chi 7.8	Ventura-Chi 26.1	Wilson-Oak............8.1	Brown-Tex 21	Morris-Tor.............778	Clemens-Bos 11
Anderson-Bal..........53	Alomar-Tor 7.6	Gagne-Min.....................19.3	White-Tor 7.3	McDowell-Chi 20	Guzman-Tor 762	Brown-Tex 11
Polonia-Cal 51	White-Tor 6.7	Gaetti-Cal 13.7	Lofton-Cle...............7.0	Mussina-Bal............18	Bosio-Mil..............727	Perez-NY 10
Alomar-Tor..............49	R.Henderson-Oak 6.7	Joyner-KC 12.8	Anderson-Bal 5.4	Clemens-Bos 18	McDowell-Chi 667	Nagy-Cle 10

Strikeouts	Fewest BB/Game	Games	Saves	Base Runners/9	Adjusted Relief Runs	Relief Ranking
Johnson-Sea 241	Bosio-Mil.............1.71	Rogers-Tex 81	Eckersley-Oak 51	Eckersley-Oak 8.32	D.Ward-Tor 21.9	Eckersley-Oak 35.5
Perez-NY 218	Mussina-Bal 1.79	D.Ward-Tor 79	Aguilera-Min 41	Lilliquist-Cle 8.61	Eckersley-Oak 18.2	Olin-Cle 29.5
Clemens-Bos........208	Wegman-Mil 1.89	Olin-Cle..........................72	Montgomery-KC 39	Hernandez-Chi 8.75	Harris-Bos 17.7	J.Russell-Tex-Oak ..28.0
Guzman-Tex 179	Tapani-Min 1.96	Lilliquist-Cle 71	Olson-Bal...............36	Eldred-Mil 9.06	Hernandez-Chi 17.6	Hernandez-Chi ..27.2
McDowell-Chi 178	Gullickson-Det 2.03	Harris-Bos......................70	Henke-Tor 34	Willis-Min 9.53	Frohwirth-Bal 17.1	D.Ward-Tor 25.6

Innings Pitched	Opponents' Avg.	Opponents' OBP	Earned Run Average	Adjusted ERA	Adjusted Starter Runs	Pitcher Wins
Brown-Tex..........265.2	Johnson-Sea 206	Mussina-Bal.................278	Clemens-Bos 2.41	Clemens-Bos........175	Clemens-Bos 44.7	**Clemens-Bos** 5.3
Wegman-Mil 261.2	Guzman-Tor 207	Clemens-Bos...............278	Appier-KC 2.46	Appier-KC 165	Mussina-Bal 40.2	**Appier-KC** 4.1
McDowell-Chi 260.2	Appier-KC 217	Appier-KC 281	Mussina-Bal 2.54	Mussina-Bal..........159	Appier-KC 37.4	**Eckersley-Oak** ..3.7
Nagy-Cle 252.0	Clemens-Bos 224	Smiley-Min...................286	Guzman-Tor 2.64	Guzman-Tor..........155	Guzman-Tor 28.9	**Mussina-Bal** 3.7
Perez-NY 247.2	Smiley-Min 231	Guzman-Tor.................286	Abbott-Cal 2.77	Abbott-Cal 144	Nagy-Cle 27.3	**Eldred-Mil** 3.2

A Special on Canadian Club

Oriole Park at Camden Yards opened in April, making several other parks instantly obsolete. It started a craze for ballparks designed with idiosyncrasies, asymmetrical dimensions, and memorable features, like the Baltimore & Ohio Warehouse beyond right field. Camden Yards drew three million people for every non-strike season through 2001.

In August Bret Boone debuted with Seattle. Following grandfather Ray and dad Bob, Bret became the first third-generation player in big league history. Rookie Jeff Kent was part of the year's biggest trading deadline deal, going from Toronto to the Mets for David Cone. It was the final season for Bert Blyleven, Brian Downing, and Willie Randolph. Jean Yawkey, Red Sox owner since 1976, died without an heir, leaving the club out of family control for the first time since 1933.

Milwaukee's Robin Yount and Kansas City's George Brett each surpassed 3,000 career hits. Texas' Juan Gonzalez hammered 43 long balls to become, at 22, the youngest home run champ ever. Oakland reliever Dennis Eckersley won both the MVP and Cy Young awards.

Bolstered by Mark McGwire's 42 homers, Oakland, which traded Jose Canseco to Texas at midseason, again won the West. The A's were denied a fourth straight World Series appearance by Toronto, winners in the East by just 4 games over surprising Milwaukee.

The Blue Jays were sparked by a great season from second sacker Roberto Alomar and won four of the last five ALCS contests, slugging 10 home runs and hitting Eckersley hard. Toronto capped its magic season by beating the Braves in six games in the World Series. Pat Borders' timely hitting and some excellent bullpen work helped the Jays win a low-scoring series, bringing the World Series trophy north of the border for the first time.

1993 National League

TEAM	W	L	T	PCT	GB	HW	HL	R	OR	PA	H	2B	3B	HR	BB	SO	HB	SH	AVG	OBP	SLG	OPS	AOPS	BR	ABR	PF	SB	CS	BSA	BSR
EAST																														
PHI	97	65	0	.599		52	29	**877**	740	6527	**1555**	**297**	**51**	156	**665**	1049	84	42	.274	**.351**	.426	**777**	**115**	**121**	**134**	99	91	32	74	9
MON	94	68	1	.580	3	**55**	26	732	682	6233	1410	270	36	122	542	**860**	100	48	.257	.326	.386	712	92	-23	-52	104	**228**	56	**80**	**31**
STL	87	75	0	.537	10	49	32	758	744	6279	1508	262	34	118	588	882	59	27	.272	.341	.395	736	104	35	52	98	153	72	68	8
CHI	84	78	1	.519	13	43	38	738	739	6216	1521	259	32	161	446	923	67	34	.270	.325	.414	739	104	17	30	98	100	43	70	7
PIT	75	87	0	.463	22	40	41	707	806	6268	1482	267	50	110	536	972	76	**55**	.267	.335	.393	728	100	11	13	100	92	55	63	1
FLA	64	98	0	.395	33	35	46	581	724	6125	1356	197	31	94	498	1054	58	51	.248	.314	.346	660	78	-128	-159	106	117	56	68	6
NY	59	103	0	.364	38	28	53	672	744	6056	1350	228	37	158	448	879	89	24	.248	.305	.390	695	91	-76	-68	99	79	50	61	0
WEST																														
ATL	104	58	0	.642		51	30	767	**559**	6234	1444	239	29	**169**	560	946	73	36	.262	.331	.408	739	102	27	20	101	125	48	72	11
SF	103	59	0	.636	1	50	31	808	636	6271	1534	269	33	168	516	930	102	46	**.276**	.340	**.427**	767	114	83	109	97	120	65	65	4
HOU	85	77	0	.525	19	44	37	716	630	6130	1459	288	37	138	497	911	82	40	.267	.330	.409	739	107	26	55	96	103	60	63	2
LA	81	81	0	.500	23	41	40	675	662	6261	1458	234	28	130	492	937	**107**	27	.261	.321	.383	704	99	-47	-4	94	126	61	67	6
CIN	73	89	0	.451	31	41	40	722	785	6163	1457	261	28	137	485	1025	63	32	.264	.324	.396	720	97	-12	-13	100	142	59	71	11
COL	67	95	0	.414	37	39	42	758	967	6073	1507	278	59	142	388	944	70	46	.273	.323	.422	745	89	26	-78	116	146	90	62	1
SD	61	101	0	.377	43	34	47	679	772	6135	1386	239	28	153	443	1046	80	59	.252	.312	.389	701	90	-60	-71	102	92	41	69	6
TOT	1135					602	532	10190		86971	20427	3588	513	1956	7104	13358	567	1110	.264	.327	.399	726					1714	788	69	101

TEAM	CG	SHO	GR	SV	IP	H	HR	BB	SO	BR/9	ERA	AERA	OAV	OOB	PR	APR	PF	OSB	OCS	FA	E	WPB	DP	FW	PW	BW	BSW	DIF
EAST																												
PHI	**24**	11	350	46	1472.2	1419	129	573	**1117**	12.4	3.95	100	.251	.322	14	1	98	101	49	.977	141	86	123	-.4	.0	**13.4**	.2	2.8
MON	8	7	385	**61**	1456.2	1369	119	521	934	12.0	3.55	118	.249	.317	80	98	103	172	51	.975	159	60	144	-1.4	9.8	-5.2	**2.4**	7.4
STL	5	7	423	54	1453.0	1553	152	**383**	775	12.3	4.09	97	.276	.324	-8	-21	98	112	54	.975	159	54	157	-1.4	-2.1	5.2	.0	4.3
CHI	8	5	422	56	1449.2	1514	153	470	905	12.6	4.18	95	.273	.332	-22	-31	99	84	**69**	.982	115	57	162	1.1	-3.1	3.0	-.0	2.0
PIT	12	5	384	34	1445.2	1557	153	485	832	13.0	4.77	85	.280	.339	-117	-116	100	148	51	.983	105	74	161	1.7	-11.6	1.3	-.6	3.2
FLA	4	5	409	48	1440.1	1437	135	598	945	12.9	4.13	105	.261	.334	-14	28	107	118	51	.980	125	114	130	.5	2.8	-15.9	-.1	-4.3
NY	16	8	297	22	1438.0	1483	139	434	867	12.3	4.05	99	.269	.324	-2	-6	99	143	56	.975	156	**36**	143	-1.3	-.6	-6.8	-.7	-12.6
WEST																												
ATL	18	**16**	353	46	1455.0	**1297**	**101**	480	1036	**11.1**	**3.14**	**128**	**.240**	**.303**	**146**	**143**	99	121	53	.983	108	59	146	1.5	**14.3**	2.0	.4	4.9
SF	4	9	414	50	1456.2	1385	168	442	982	11.6	3.61	108	.253	.313	69	49	97	**81**	66	**.984**	**101**	48	**169**	**1.9**	4.9	10.9	-.3	4.7
HOU	18	14	324	42	1441.1	1363	117	476	1056	11.7	3.49	111	.251	.313	88	63	96	110	42	.979	126	67	141	.5	6.3	5.5	-.5	-7.7
LA	17	9	346	36	1472.2	1406	103	567	1043	12.3	3.50	109	.254	.324	88	54	94	129	66	.979	133	62	141	.0	5.4	-.4	-.1	-4.9
CIN	11	8	375	37	1434.0	1510	158	508	996	12.9	4.51	89	.272	.336	-74	-77	100	134	56	.980	121	59	133	.8	-7.7	-1.3	.4	-.1
COL	9	0	**453**	35	1431.1	1664	181	609	913	14.6	5.41	88	.294	.362	-218	-86	118	119	56	.973	167	93	149	-1.9	-8.6	-7.8	-.6	4.9
SD	8	6	397	32	1437.2	1470	148	558	957	12.9	4.23	98	.266	.334	-30	-15	102	142	68	.974	160	77	129	-1.5	-1.5	-7.1	-.1	-9.8
TOT	162	110	5332	599	20284.2					12.5	4.04		.264	.327						.978	1876	946	2028					

Batter-Fielder Wins
Bonds-SF 8.0
Dykstra-Phi 5.6
Bell-Pit 5.4
Wilkins-Chi..........5.4
Piazza-LA 5.3

Batting Average
Galarraga-Col.......370
Gwynn-SD 358
Jefferies-StL 342
Bonds-SF 336
Grace-Chi 325

On-Base Percentage
Bonds-SF.......................458
Kruk-Phi..........................430
Dykstra-Phi 420
Merced-Pit 414
Jefferies-StL 408

Slugging Average
Bonds-SF 677
Galarraga-Col.......602
Williams-SF 561
Piazza-LA.............561
McGriff-SD-Atl 549

On-Base Plus Slugging
Bonds-SF 1136
Galarraga-Col 1005
Piazza-LA 932
McGriff-SD-Atl 924
Kruk-Phi................905

Adjusted OPS
Bonds-SF 207
Piazza-LA 155
Bagwell-Hou 146
Kruk-Phi................145
Dykstra-Phi 144

Adjusted Batter Runs
Bonds-SF 89.7
Dykstra-Phi 47.7
Kruk-Phi 41.6
Piazza-LA 40.8
Bagwell-Hou 36.7

Runs
Dykstra-Phi 143
Bonds-SF 129
Gant-Atl 113
McGriff-SD-Atl 111
Blauser-Atl............110

Hits
Dykstra-Phi 194
Grace-Chi 193
Grissom-Mon........188
Bell-Pit.................187
Jefferies-StL 186

Doubles
Hayes-Col.......................45
Dykstra-Phi....................44
Bichette-Col 43
Gwynn-SD 41
Biggio-Hou 41

Triples
Finley-Hou 13
Butler-LA 10
Morandini-Phi 9
Bell-Pit 9

Home Runs
Bonds-SF 46
Justice-Atl 40
Williams-SF 38
McGriff-SD-Atl 37
Gant-Atl 36

Total Bases
Bonds-SF 365
Williams-SF 325
Gant-Atl 309
Piazza-LA 307
Dykstra-Phi 307

Runs Batted In
Bonds-SF 123
Justice-Atl............120
Gant-Atl 117
Piazza-LA............112
Williams-SF 110

Stolen Bases
Carr-Fla 58
Grissom-Mon..........53
Nixon-Atl 47
Lewis-SF 46
Jefferies-StL 46

Base Stealing Runs
Grissom-Mon 8.2
Jefferies-StL 7.0
DeShields-Mon......6.0
Nixon-Atl 5.8
Davis-LA................5.5

Fielding Runs-Infield
O.Smith-StL 23.4
Bell-Pit 21.5
Lemke-Atl.....................18.4
Thompson-SF 16.8
Vizcaino-Chi................15.2

Fielding Runs-Outfield
Gonzalez-Hou 14.9
Plantier-SD 9.9
Bichette-Col 9.1
Merced-Pit 8.8
Carr-Fla 7.1

Wins
Glavine-Atl..............22
Burkett-SF 22
Swift-SF..................21
Maddux-Atl 20

Winning Pct.
Portugal-Hou 818
Greene-Phi..........800
Glavine-Atl 786
Burkett-SF 759
Avery-Atl 750

Complete Games
Maddux-Atl..............8

Strikeouts
Rijo-Cin 227
Smoltz-Atl 208
Maddux-Atl 197
Schilling-Phi..........186
Harnisch-Hou 185

Fewest BB/Game
Tewksbury-StL 84
Arocha-StL 1.48
Burkett-SF 1.55
Avery-Atl 1.73
Maddux-Atl 1.75

Games
Jackson-SF...................81
West-Phi 76
Beck-SF 76
McMichael-Atl 74

Saves
Myers-Chi 53
Beck-SF.................48
Harvey-Fla 45

Base Runners/9
Harvey-Fla 7.57
Beck-SF 8.28
S.Fernandez-NY ..9.10
Wetteland-Mon 9.28
McMichael-Atl......9.52

Adjusted Relief Runs
Fassero-Mon 28.5
Wetteland-Mon 25.1
McMichael-Atl......20.6
Harvey-Fla 18.9
Beck-SF 16.3

Relief Ranking
Wetteland-Mon ..50.3
Harvey-Fla..........35.9
Fassero-Mon 29.4
Gott-LA 26.7
Beck-SF 24.2

Innings Pitched
Maddux-Atl 267.0
Rijo-Cin..............257.1
Smoltz-Atl 243.2
Glavine-Atl 239.1
Drabek-Hou 237.2

Opponents' Avg.
Harnisch-Hou 214
Swift-SF 226
Rijo-Cin.................230
Smoltz-Atl 230
Maddux-Atl 232

Opponents' OBP
Maddux-Atl 273
Swift-SF 277
Rijo-Cin 278
Mulholland-Phi.............282
Harnisch-Hou...............289

Earned Run Average
Maddux-Atl 2.36
Rijo-Cin................2.48
Portugal-Hou 2.77
Swift-SF 2.82
Avery-Atl 2.94

Adjusted ERA
Maddux-Atl 170
Rijo-Cin 162
Portugal-Hou 140
Swift-SF 139
Avery-Atl 137

Adjusted Starter Runs
Maddux-Atl 46.0
Rijo-Cin................45.1
Swift-SF 27.7
Avery-Atl 26.7
Portugal-Hou 25.4

Pitcher Wins
Maddux-Atl 5.3
Wetteland-Mon..5.1
Rijo-Cin 4.8
Swift-SF...............4.0
Harvey-Fla..........3.7

A Race for the Ages

The NL expanded for the first time since 1969, adding the Colorado Rockies and Florida Marlins. More than 80,000 watched Colorado's opener in Denver's Mile High Stadium as the Rockies went on to draw more than 4.4 million fans, shattering the individual club record. The Marlins also surpassed three million, propelling MLB to a new all-time record. Aided substantially by Denver's thin air, NL offense increased tremendously. Runs per game jumped 16 percent, and home runs per game were up 33 percent. Conspiracy theorists blamed their favorite chimera, a "juiced ball."

Cincinnati's problems continued as owner Marge Schott was suspended from daily activities for a year because of racist comments, and new Reds skipper Tony Perez was fired after only 44 games. Houston hired Bob Watson as baseball's first black general manager. Mets hurler Anthony Young lost 16 straight decisions and a record 27 straight over two years. Dodgers stars Roy Campanella and Don Drysdale died, as did Johnny Mize. Dale Murphy retired in Colorado; Trevor Hoffman debuted in Florida.

In the last year before the Wild Card, the NL West experienced one of the greatest races ever. The Braves and Giants battled all season, both winning more than 100 games, and the clubs were tied going into the final day. The Braves beat the Rockies, meaning that the Giants knew as their game with the Dodgers began they had to beat their bitter rivals to force a one-game playoff. But Los Angeles overpowered San Francisco, 12–1, spoiling what had been a magical season for the Bay Area. Philadelphia edged out Montreal in the East, then upset the mighty Braves in six games in the NLCS. However, the fightin' Phils' mojo evaporated ten days later, north of the border, in the World Series against Toronto.

1993 American League

TEAM	W	L	T	PCT	GB	HW	HL	R	OR	PA	H	2B	3B	HR	BB	SO	HB	SH	AVG	OBP	SLG	OPS	AOPS	BR	ABR	PF	SB	CS	BSA	BSR
EAST																														
TOR	95	67	0	.586		48	33	847	742	6319	1556	317	42	159	588	861	46	52	**.279**	.350	**.436**	786	109	88	84	101	**170**	49	**78**	**20**
NY	88	74	0	.543	7	**50**	31	821	761	6359	**1568**	294	24	178	629	910	22	43	**.279**	.353	.435	788	**114**	96	126	97	39	35	53	-4
BAL	85	77	0	.525	10	48	33	786	745	6309	1470	287	24	157	655	930	49	41	.267	.346	.413	759	99	39	7	104	73	54	57	-3
DET	85	77	0	.525	10	44	37	**899**	837	6505	1546	282	38	178	**765**	1122	33	35	.275	**.362**	.434	**796**	**114**	**124**	**130**	99	104	63	62	1
BOS	80	82	0	.494	15	43	38	686	698	6195	1451	**319**	29	114	508	871	**80**	**62**	.264	.330	.395	725	89	-39	-81	106	73	38	66	3
CLE	76	86	0	.469	19	46	35	790	813	6267	1547	264	31	141	488	843	39	49	.275	.335	.409	744	99	-7	-4	100	159	55	74	16
MIL	69	93	0	.426	26	38	43	733	792	6222	1426	240	25	125	555	932	57	40	.258	.328	.378	706	90	-80	-70	99	138	93	60	-2
WEST																														
CHI	94	68	0	.580		45	36	776	**664**	6253	1454	228	**44**	162	604	**834**	72	33	.265	.338	.411	749	102	7	24	98	106	57	65	3
TEX	86	76	0	.531	8	**50**	31	835	751	6166	1472	284	39	**181**	483	984	69	48	.267	.329	.431	760	106	15	46	96	113	67	63	1
KC	84	78	0	.519	10	43	38	675	694	6101	1455	294	35	125	428	936	48	52	.263	.320	.397	717	86	-69	-107	106	100	75	57	-4
SEA	82	80	0	.506	12	46	35	734	731	6288	1429	272	24	161	624	901	63	56	.260	.339	.406	745	98	4	-7	101	91	68	57	-4
CAL	71	91	0	.438	23	44	37	684	770	6089	1399	259	24	114	564	930	50	38	.260	.331	.380	711	88	-63	-85	103	169	100	63	2
MIN	71	91	0	.438	23	36	45	693	830	6209	1480	261	27	121	493	850	27	51	.264	.327	.385	712	91	-72	-74	100	83	59	58	-2
OAK	68	94	0	.420	26	38	43	715	846	6293	1408	260	21	158	622	1048	46	33	.254	.330	.394	724	100	-43	3	94	131	59	69	8
TOT	1134					619	515	10674		87575	20661	3861	427	2074	8006	12952	633	701	.267	.337	.408	745					1549	872	64	36

TEAM	CG	SHO	GR	SV	IP	H	HR	BB	SO	BR/9	ERA	AERA	OAV	OOB	PR	APR	PF	OSB	OCS	FA	E	WPB	DP	FW	PW	BW	BSW	DIF
EAST																												
TOR	11	11	344	**50**	1441.1	1441	134	620	1023	13.1	4.21	103	.261	.336	18	17	100	136	64	.982	107	89	144	.5	1.7	8.2	**1.7**	2.0
NY	11	**13**	332	38	1438.1	1467	170	552	899	12.8	4.35	95	.266	.333	-5	-33	96	115	47	.983	105	**40**	166	.6	-3.2	12.3	-.6	-2.0
BAL	21	10	329	42	1442.2	1427	153	579	900	12.8	4.31	104	.261	.333	2	25	104	96	64	.984	100	47	171	.9	2.4	.7	-.5	.6
DET	11	7	375	36	1436.2	1547	188	542	828	13.4	4.65	92	.276	.342	-52	-58	99	102	57	.979	132	76	148	-1.0	-5.6	**12.7**	-.2	-1.9
BOS	9	11	389	44	1452.1	**1379**	127	552	997	**12.3**	3.77	**122**	**.252**	**.322**	88	**127**	107	92	44	.980	122	53	155	-.4	**12.4**	-7.9	.0	-5.1
CLE	7	8	410	45	1445.2	1591	182	591	888	13.8	4.58	95	.281	.351	-41	-40	100	113	68	.976	148	50	**174**	-1.9	-3.9	-.4	1.3	-.0
MIL	**26**	6	353	29	1447.0	1511	153	522	810	13.0	4.45	95	.271	.336	-21	-34	98	115	51	.979	131	57	148	-.9	-3.3	-6.8	-.4	-.5
WEST																												
CHI	16	11	322	48	1454.0	1398	125	566	974	12.4	**3.70**	113	.255	.328	**100**	80	97	**82**	**82**	.982	112	66	153	.2	7.8	2.3	.0	2.7
TEX	20	6	359	45	1438.1	1476	144	562	957	13.0	4.28	97	.267	.337	6	-22	96	95	67	.979	132	70	145	-1.0	-2.1	4.5	-.2	3.8
KC	16	6	303	48	1445.1	**1379**	**105**	571	985	12.4	4.04	113	.254	.327	45	82	106	119	71	.984	97	91	150	1.0	8.0	-10.4	-.6	5.0
SEA	22	10	353	41	1453.2	1421	135	605	**1083**	13.0	4.20	105	.259	.337	20	32	102	105	68	**.985**	**90**	70	173	**1.5**	3.1	-.7	-.6	-2.2
CAL	**26**	6	320	41	1430.1	1482	153	550	843	13.1	4.34	104	.270	.339	-3	25	104	122	52	.980	120	65	161	-.3	2.4	-8.3	-.0	-3.8
MIN	5	3	356	44	1444.1	1591	148	**514**	901	13.4	4.71	92	.283	.344	-63	-57	101	137	66	.984	100	64	160	.9	-5.5	-7.2	-.4	2.3
OAK	8	2	**424**	42	1452.1	1551	157	680	864	14.1	4.90	83	.276	.356	-94	-142	94	120	71	.982	111	54	161	.2	-13.8	.3	.5	-.2
TOT	209	110	4969	593	20222.1					13.0	4.32		.267	.337						.981	1607	892	2209					

Batter-Fielder Wins	Batting Average	On-Base Percentage	Slugging Average	On-Base Plus Slugging	Adjusted OPS	Adjusted Batter Runs
Olerud-Tor 5.8	Olerud-Tor .363	Olerud-Tor .473	Gonzalez-Tex .632	Olerud-Tor 1072	Olerud-Tor 186	Olerud-Tor 77.1
Hoiles-Bal 5.3	Molitor-Tor .332	Phillips-Det .443	Griffey-Sea .617	Thomas-Chi 1033	Thomas-Chi 180	Thomas-Chi 67.7
Griffey-Sea 5.1	Alomar-Tor .326	Henderson-Oak-Tor .432	Thomas-Chi .607	Griffey-Sea 1025	Gonzalez-Tex 170	Griffey-Sea 59.7
Palmeiro-Tex 4.9	Lofton-Cle .325	Thomas-Chi .426	Olerud-Tor .599	Hoiles-Bal 1001	Griffey-Sea 170	Gonzalez-Tex 49.7
Henderson-Oak-Tor 4.6	Baerga-Cle .321	Hoiles-Bal .416	Hoiles-Bal .585	Gonzalez-Tex 1000	Hoiles-Bal 160	Palmeiro-Tex 44.2

Runs	Hits	Doubles	Triples	Home Runs	Total Bases	Runs Batted In
Palmeiro-Tex 124	Molitor-Tor 211	Olerud-Tor 54	Johnson-Chi 14	Gonzalez-Tex 46	Griffey-Sea 359	Belle-Cle 129
Molitor-Tor 121	Olerud-Tor 200	White-Tor 42	Cora-Chi 13	Griffey-Sea 45	Gonzalez-Tex 339	Thomas-Chi 128
White-Tor 116	Baerga-Cle 200	Valentin-Bos 40	Hulse-Tex 10	Thomas-Chi 41	Thomas-Chi 333	Carter-Tor 121
Lofton-Cle 116	Alomar-Tor 192	Palmeiro-Tex 40	McRae-KC 9	Belle-Cle 38	Palmeiro-Tex 331	Gonzalez-Tex 118
Henderson-Oak-Tor 114	Lofton-Cle 185	Puckett-Min 39	Fernandez-Tor 9	Palmeiro-Tex 37	Olerud-Tor 330	Fielder-Det 117

Stolen Bases	Base Stealing Runs	Fielding Runs-Infield	Fielding Runs-Outfield	Wins	Winning Pct.	Complete Games
Lofton-Cle 70	Lofton-Cle 10.5	Gallego-NY 26.2	Kirby-Cle 14.1	McDowell-Chi 22	Key-NY .750	Finley-Cal 13
Polonia-Cal 55	Henderson-Oak-Tor 8.9	Boggs-NY 21.3	Hamilton-Mil 10.7	Johnson-Sea 19	Johnson-Sea .704	Brown-Tex 12
Alomar-Tor 55	Alomar-Tor 6.8	Vizquel-Sea 19.7	Belle-Cle 10.6	Hentgen-Tor 19	Appier-KC .692	McDowell-Chi 10
Henderson-Oak-Tor 53	White-Tor 6.1	Joyner-KC 19.2	McLemore-Bal 9.0		McDowell-Chi .688	Johnson-Sea 10
Curtis-Cal 48	Johnson-Chi 5.3	Whitaker-Det 18.3	Mack-Min 8.9		Hentgen-Tor .679	Eldred-Mil 8

Strikeouts	Fewest BB/Game	Games	Saves	Base Runners/9	Adjusted Relief Runs	Relief Ranking
Johnson-Sea 308	Key-NY 1.64	Harris-Bos 80	D.Ward-Tor 45	Montgomery-KC 9.27	Montgomery-KC 22.0	Montgomery-KC 44.0
Langston-Cal 196	Darwin-Bos 1.92	Radinsky-Chi 73	Montgomery-KC 45	Aguilera-Min 9.33	D.Ward-Tor 18.3	D.Ward-Tor 31.2
Guzman-Tor 194	Wells-Det 2.02	D.Ward-Tor 71	Henke-Tex 40	D.Ward-Tor 9.42	Hernandez-Chi 17.7	Hernandez-Chi 28.9
Cone-KC 191	Tapani-Min 2.27	Nelson-Sea 71	Hernandez-Chi 38	Darwin-Bos 9.73	Lilliquist-Cle 13.8	Henke-Tex 22.9
Finley-Cal 187	Doherty-Det 2.34	Fossas-Bos 71	Eckersley-Oak 36	Hernandez-Chi 9.84	Mills-Bal 13.4	Lilliquist-Cle 19.2

Innings Pitched	Opponents' Avg.	Opponents' OBP	Earned Run Average	Adjusted ERA	Adjusted Starter Runs	Pitcher Wins
Eldred-Mil 258.0	Johnson-Sea .203	Darwin-Bos .272	Appier-KC 2.56	Appier-KC 179	Appier-KC 50.2	**Appier-KC** 5.1
McDowell-Chi 256.2	Appier-KC .212	Appier-KC .279	Alvarez-Chi 2.95	Viola-Bos 148	Langston-Cal 36.7	**Montgomery-KC** 4.5
Langston-Cal 256.1	Cone-KC .223	Key-NY .279	Key-NY 3.00	Finley-Cal 143	Johnson-Sea 33.6	**Langston-Cal** 3.7
Johnson-Sea 255.1	McDonald-Bal .228	Johnson-Sea .290	Fernandez-Chi 3.13	Alvarez-Chi 142	Darwin-Bos 33.3	**Finley-Cal** 3.5
Cone-KC 254.0	Bosio-Sea .229	Langston-Cal .295	Viola-Bos 3.14	Darwin-Bos 142	Cone-KC 33.0	**Darwin-Bos** 3.5

Walk-Off to the North

Tragedy struck in spring training as Cleveland pitchers Tim Crews and Steve Olin were killed in a boating accident. Indians hurler Bob Ojeda also was badly hurt in the crash. Cliff Young, another Cleveland pitcher, died in a truck accident in November. Also passing were second baseman Charlie Gehringer and catcher Bill Dickey, both Hall of Famers, and Royals owner Ewing Kauffman. It was the last season for George Brett, Robin Yount, Carlton Fisk and Nolan Ryan, all future Hall of Famers.

On the bright side, Bo Jackson made a remarkable comeback from hip replacement surgery, hitting 16 homers for the White Sox. Minnesota's Dave Winfield collected his 3,000th hit. Toronto first baseman John Olerud carried a .400 batting average into August; Olerud, Paul Molitor, and Roberto Alomar finished 1-2-3 in the batting race, a first for teammates. Outfielders Shawn Green (Blue Jays) and Jim Edmonds (Angels) began their careers.

Toronto in the East and Chicago in the West were runaway division winners. The visiting team won the first four games of the ALCS before Toronto finally won at home in Game 5. The Jays then won their second straight AL pennant by scoring 3 runs in the top of the ninth inning of Game 6. Alomar and Molitor were the hitting stars in an offensively-charged World Series against the Phillies, but it was Joe Carter's dramatic walk-off home run against "Wild Thing" Mitch Williams in the bottom of the ninth inning in Game 6 that gave the Jays their second consecutive world championship.

Ominously, Congress considered legislation that would take away baseball's exemption from antitrust laws as dark storm clouds gathered on the labor front. The silver lining was that the exciting 1993 season was played to completion in front of a record number of fans.

1994 National League

TEAM	W	L	T	PCT	GB	HW	HL	R	OR	PA	H	2B	3B	HR	BB	SO	HB	SH	AVG	OBP	SLG	OPS	AOPS	BR	ABR	PF	SB	CS	BSA	BSR
EAST																														
MON	74	40	0	.649		32	20	585	454	4514	1111	246	30	108	379	669	53	40	.278	.343	.435	778	106	51	46	101	**137**	36	**79**	**18**
ATL	68	46	0	.596	6	31	24	542	**448**	4349	1031	198	18	**137**	377	**668**	60	22	.267	.333	.434	767	102	26	15	102	48	31	61	0
NY	55	58	0	.487	18.5	23	30	506	526	4347	966	164	21	117	336	807	59	52	.250	.316	.394	710	90	-59	-54	99	25	26	49	-4
PHI	54	61	0	.470	20.5	34	26	521	497	4436	1028	208	28	80	396	711	51	31	.262	.332	.390	722	91	-30	-41	102	67	24	74	6
FLA	51	64	0	.443	23.5	25	34	468	576	4387	1043	180	24	94	349	746	42	40	.266	.330	.396	726	91	-31	-44	103	65	26	71	5
CENTRAL																														
CIN	66	48	1	.579		**37**	22	**609**	490	4511	**1142**	211	**36**	124	388	738	53	29	**.286**	**.350**	**.449**	**799**	114	**79**	86	99	119	51	70	8
HOU	66	49	0	.574	0.5	**37**	22	602	503	4500	1099	**252**	25	120	**394**	718	**73**	**43**	.278	.347	.445	792	**117**	71	**104**	95	124	44	74	12
STL	53	61	1	.465	13	23	33	535	621	4450	1026	213	27	108	434	686	44	33	.263	.339	.414	753	103	16	27	98	76	46	62	1
PIT	53	61	0	.465	13	32	29	466	580	4299	1001	198	23	80	349	725	36	22	.259	.322	.384	706	88	-57	-62	101	53	25	68	3
CHI	49	64	0	.434	16.5	20	39	500	549	4386	1015	189	26	109	364	750	54	27	.259	.325	.404	729	95	-30	-22	99	69	53	57	-3
WEST																														
LA	58	56	0	.509		33	22	532	509	4371	1055	160	29	115	366	687	51	19	.270	.333	.414	747	106	-2	35	93	74	37	67	3
SF	55	60	0	.478	3.5	29	31	504	500	4364	963	159	32	123	364	719	65	39	.249	.318	.402	720	97	-47	-23	95	114	40	74	11
COL	53	64	0	.453	6.5	25	32	573	638	4493	1098	206	39	125	378	761	50	23	.274	.337	.439	776	91	39	-42	116	91	53	63	1
SD	47	70	0	.402	12.5	26	31	479	531	4518	1117	200	19	92	319	762	67	31	.275	.330	.401	731	98	-25	-9	97	79	37	68	4
TOT	803					407	395	7422		61925	14695	2784	377	1532	5193	10147	451	758	.267	.333	.415	747					1141	529	68	66

TEAM	CG	SHO	GR	SV	IP	H	HR	BB	SO	BR/9	ERA	AERA	OAV	OOB	PR	APR	PF	OSB	OCS	FA	E	WPB	DP	FW	PW	BW	BSW	DIF
EAST																												
MON	4	**8**	259	**46**	1036.2	970	100	**288**	805	**11.3**	**3.56**	**119**	.247	**.302**	**75**	**76**	100	99	32	.979	94	**35**	90	-.5	**7.5**	4.5	**1.3**	4.2
ATL	**16**	**8**	244	26	1026.1	**929**	**76**	378	**865**	11.7	3.57	**119**	**.242**	.311	73	**76**	101	90	32	.982	81	46	85	.3	**7.5**	1.5	-.5	2.2
NY	7	3	238	35	1023.0	1069	117	332	640	12.5	4.13	101	.271	.328	9	4	99	68	34	.980	89	36	112	-.2	.4	-5.3	-.9	4.5
PHI	7	6	243	30	1024.1	1028	98	377	699	12.6	3.85	111	.261	.328	41	49	102	87	30	.978	94	56	96	-.4	4.8	-4.0	.1	-4.0
FLA	5	7	300	30	1015.0	1069	120	428	649	13.6	4.50	97	.274	.349	-32	-14	104	**59**	**52**	.978	95	75	111	-.5	-1.4	-4.3	.0	-.4
CENTRAL																												
CIN	6	6	261	27	1038.1	1037	117	339	799	12.2	3.78	109	.262	.322	50	41	98	78	39	.983	73	58	91	.8	4.0	8.5	.3	-4.6
HOU	9	6	268	29	1029.2	1043	102	367	739	12.6	3.97	100	.265	.331	28	-2	94	85	36	.983	76	51	110	.6	-.2	**10.2**	.7	-2.9
STL	7	7	**330**	29	1018.0	1154	134	355	632	13.7	5.14	81	.289	.351	-105	-113	99	70	40	.982	80	46	119	.4	-11.1	2.7	-.4	4.4
PIT	8	2	285	24	1005.2	1094	117	370	650	13.5	4.64	93	.281	.347	-47	-35	103	78	31	.980	91	**35**	**131**	-.3	-3.4	-6.1	-.2	6.0
CHI	5	5	286	27	1023.2	1054	120	392	717	12.9	4.47	93	.268	.335	-29	-36	99	75	46	.982	81	51	110	.2	-3.5	-2.2	-.8	-1.3
WEST																												
LA	14	5	239	20	1014.0	1041	90	354	732	12.7	4.17	94	.267	.331	4	-30	93	90	33	.980	88	54	104	-.1	-3.0	3.4	-.2	.8
SF	2	4	288	33	1025.1	1014	122	372	655	12.5	3.99	100	.262	.330	26	2	95	76	35	**.985**	**68**	38	113	**1.1**	.2	-2.3	.6	-2.1
COL	4	5	329	28	1031.0	1185	120	448	703	14.7	5.15	96	.292	.366	-108	-18	118	87	44	.981	84	55	117	.2	-1.8	-4.1	-.4	.5
SD	8	6	273	27	1045.2	1008	99	393	862	12.3	4.08	101	.252	.321	15	3	98	99	45	.975	111	59	82	-1.3	.3	-.9	-.0	-9.5
TOT	102	78	3843	411	14356.2					12.8	4.21		.267	.333						.980	1205	695	1471					

Batter-Fielder Wins	Batting Average	On-Base Percentage	Slugging Average	On-Base Plus Slugging	Adjusted OPS	Adjusted Batter Runs
Bagwell-Hou 7.7	Gwynn-SD 394	Gwynn-SD 454	Bagwell-Hou 750	Bagwell-Hou 1201	Bagwell-Hou 220	Bagwell-Hou 73.1
Bonds-SF 4.9	Bagwell-Hou 368	Bagwell-Hou 451	Mitchell-Cin...........681	Mitchell-Cin 1110	Mitchell-Cin 188	Bonds-SF 50.9
Gwynn-SD 3.9	Alou-Mon 339	Mitchell-Cin 429	Bonds-SF 647	Bonds-SF 1073	Bonds-SF 184	Gwynn-SD.........46.8
Mitchell-Cin 3.8	Morris-Cin............335	Justice-Atl 427	McGriff-Atl 623	Gwynn-SD 1022	Gwynn-SD 171	Mitchell-Cin 42.2
Biggio-Hou 3.7	Mitchell-Cin...........326	Bonds-SF.....................426	Williams-SF 607	McGriff-Atl 1012	McGriff-Atl 156	McGriff-Atl 34.3

Runs	Hits	Doubles	Triples	Home Runs	Total Bases	Runs Batted In
Bagwell-Hou 104	Gwynn-SD 165	Walker-Mon...................44	Lewis-SF 9	Williams-SF 43	Bagwell-Hou 300	Bagwell-Hou........116
Grissom-Mon.........96	Bichette-Col 147	Biggio-Hou 44	Butler-LA 9	Bagwell-Hou 39	Williams-SF 270	Williams-SF 96
Lankford-StL 89	Bagwell-Hou 147	Gwynn-SD 35	R.Sanders-Cin.........8	Bonds-SF 37	Bichette-Col 265	Bichette-Col 95
Bonds-SF 89	Morris-Cin 146	Bell-Pit 35	Mondesi-LA 8	McGriff-Atl 34	McGriff-Atl 264	McGriff-Atl 94
Biggio-Hou..............88	Conine-Fla 144	Bichette-Col 33	Kingery-Col 8	Galarraga-Col 31	Bonds-SF 253	Piazza-LA...............92

Stolen Bases	Base Stealing Runs	Fielding Runs-Infield	Fielding Runs-Outfield	Wins	Winning Pct.	Complete Games
Biggio-Hou.............39	Biggio-Hou.............7.2	Sanchez-Chi 20.4	Whiten-StL 11.2	Maddux-Atl 16	Saberhagen-NY ...778	Maddux-Atl 10
D.Sanders-Atl-Cin 38	Grissom-Mon 5.8	Garcia-Pit...................18.0	Grissom-Mon 9.0	Hill-Mon 16	Hill-Mon 762	Drabek-Hou 6
Grissom-Mon..........36	Larkin-Cin 5.0	Bell-Pit 17.7	R.Sanders-Cin 6.4	Saberhagen-NY......14	Maddux-Atl 727	Candiotti-LA 5
Carr-Fla 32	Carr-Fla 4.2	Bagwell-Hou 15.4	Carr-Fla 6.1	Jackson-Phi............14	Jackson-Phi 700	
Lewis-SF 30	Clayton-SF 4.0	Karros-LA 13.3	Gonzalez-Hou 5.7	Glavine-Atl 13	Martinez-Mon 688	

Strikeouts	Fewest BB/Game	Games	Saves	Base Runners/9	Adjusted Relief Runs	Relief Ranking
Benes-SD 189	Saberhagen-NY 66	Reed-Col.......................61	Franco-NY 30	Maddux-Atl 8.33	Jones-Phi 12.9	Brantley-Cin........24.8
Rijo-Cin 171	Tewksbury-StL 1.27	Rojas-Mon 58	Beck-SF.................28	Saberhagen-NY ..9.44	McElroy-Cin 12.6	Jones-Phi 24.1
Maddux-Atl 156	Maddux-Atl 1.38	Bautista-Chi 58	Jones-Phi................27	Drabek-Hou 9.78	Brantley-Cin 12.4	Carrasco-Cin......22.5
Saberhagen-NY....143	Reynolds-Hou......1.52	Munoz-Col 57	Wetteland-Mon 25	Jones-Hou 9.78	Jackson-SF..........12.3	Hoffman-SD 20.5
Martinez-Mon 142	Swindell-Hou 1.58	Burba-SF 57	....	Wetteland-Mon 9.90	Carrasco-Cin 11.6	Wetteland-Mon ..19.9

Innings Pitched	Opponents' Avg.	Opponents' OBP	Earned Run Average	Adjusted ERA	Adjusted Starter Runs	Pitcher Wins
Maddux-Atl 202.0	Maddux-Atl 207	Maddux-Atl 243	Maddux-Atl 1.56	Maddux-Atl 272	Maddux-Atl 57.5	**Maddux-Atl** 6.8
Jackson-Phi 179.1	Martinez-Mon 220	Saberhagen-NY...........271	Saberhagen-NY ..2.74	Saberhagen-NY....153	Saberhagen-NY ..29.6	**Saberhagen-NY** 3.1
Saberhagen-NY 177.1	Drabek-Hou 220	Drabek-Hou 275	Drabek-Hou 2.84	Fassero-Mon 142	Freeman-Col........22.7	**Drabek-Hou**........2.7
Rijo-Cin.............172.1	Avery-Atl 227	Ashby-SD.....................285	Fassero-Mon 2.99	Drabek-Hou 139	Henry-Mon 22.3	**Brantley-Cin** 2.5
Benes-SD 172.1	Fassero-Mon 229	Fassero-Mon 285	Reynolds-Hou......3.05	Rijo-Cin 134	Drabek-Hou 21.6	**Jones-Phi** 2.5

Summertime Strikeout

The 1994 season was like a wonderful outdoor party held under a black sky. Major league per-game attendance was even higher than 1993's record rate, San Diego's Tony Gwynn flirted with .400, San Francisco third baseman Matt Williams was on pace to possibly break Roger Maris' single-season home run record, Greg Maddux of Atlanta was enjoying his best season to that point, and Jeff Bagwell, hitting in the pitcher-dominant Astrodome, had 116 RBIs in 110 games. A broken hand ended Bagwell's season early; everyone else waited helplessly for the storm. It hit on August 12.

The strike ended Montreal's dream season, as les Expos owned the best record in baseball and had a 6-game lead in the East over the Braves, who held a slight advantage over the Astros in the new Wild Card standings. The star-crossed Expos seemed a lock to make the postseason for the first time since 1981. Felipe Alou's club, with All-Stars Moises Alou, Wil Cordero, Marquis Grissom, Darrin Fletcher, and 16-game winner Ken Hill, plus dominant seasons from Larry Walker and John Wetteland, would never look the same again.

Central leader Cincinnati and West frontrunner Los Angeles led tight races as of the strike, though Major League Baseball declined to officially name any division winners. The decision by owners to cancel the remainder of the season meant the first year with no World Series since 1904. In December owners declared an impasse in negotiations and implemented new rules, including a salary cap. Players appealed to the National Labor Relations Board, which also heard unfair labor practice claims by owners against players.

1994 American League

TEAM	W	L	T	PCT	GB	HW	HL	R	OR	PA	H	2B	3B	HR	BB	SO	HB	SH	AVG	OBP	SLG	OPS	AOPS	BR	ABR	PF	SB	CS	BSA	BSR
EAST																														
NY	70	43	0	.619		33	24	670	534	4611	1155	238	16	139	**530**	660	27	31	**.290**	**.374**	.462	**836**	**119**	**102**	**130**	96	55	40	58	-2
BAL	63	49	0	.563	6.5	28	27	589	**497**	4384	1047	185	20	139	438	655	16	39	.272	.349	.438	787	96	12	-16	105	69	13	**84**	11
TOR	55	60	0	.478	16	33	26	566	579	4461	1064	210	30	115	387	691	30	38	.269	.336	.424	760	94	-31	-33	100	79	26	75	8
BOS	54	61	0	.470	17	31	33	552	621	4446	1038	222	19	120	404	723	38	31	.263	.334	.421	755	89	-38	-63	105	81	38	68	5
DET	53	62	0	.461	18	34	24	652	671	4574	1048	216	25	161	520	897	17	34	.265	.352	.454	806	106	44	41	100	46	33	58	-1
CENTRAL																														
CHI	67	46	0	.593		34	19	633	498	4556	1133	175	**39**	121	497	**568**	**51**	20	.287	.366	.444	810	110	56	69	98	77	27	74	7
CLE	66	47	0	.584	1	**35**	16	**679**	562	4493	**1165**	**240**	20	**167**	382	629	33	18	**.290**	.351	**.484**	835	112	75	74	100	131	48	73	**12**
KC	64	51	0	.557	4	**35**	24	574	532	4390	1051	211	38	100	376	698	32	33	.269	.335	.419	754	89	-40	-61	104	**140**	62	69	9
MIN	53	60	0	.469	14	32	27	594	688	4408	1092	239	23	103	359	635	22	**41**	.276	.340	.427	767	96	-19	-19	100	94	30	76	10
MIL	53	62	0	.461	15	24	32	547	586	4494	1045	238	21	99	417	680	28	33	.263	.335	.408	743	86	-52	-76	105	59	37	61	0
WEST																														
TEX	52	62	0	.456		31	32	613	697	4531	1114	198	27	124	437	730	41	36	.280	.353	.436	789	102	19	21	100	82	35	70	6
OAK	51	63	0	.447	1	24	32	549	589	4395	1009	178	13	113	417	686	24	18	.260	.330	.399	729	95	-70	-22	92	91	39	70	6
SEA	49	63	0	.438	2	22	22	569	616	4361	1045	211	18	153	372	652	48	26	.269	.335	.451	786	98	-2	-13	102	48	21	70	3
CAL	47	68	0	.409	5.5	23	40	543	660	4443	1042	178	16	120	402	715	42	27	.264	.334	.409	743	89	-56	-63	101	65	54	55	-5
TOT	797					419	378	8330		62547	15048	2939	325	1774	5938	9619	425	449	.273	.345	.434	779					1117	503	69	70

TEAM	CG	SHO	GR	SV	IP	H	HR	BB	SO	BR/9	ERA	AERA	OAV	OOB	PR	APR	PF	OSB	OCS	FA	E	WPB	DP	FW	PW	BW	BSW	DIF
EAST																												
NY	8	2	241	31	1019.2	1045	120	398	656	12.9	4.34	105	.267	.335	52	27	95	55	29	.982	80	56	122	.1	2.5	**12.0**	-.6	-.5
BAL	13	4	234	37	997.2	1005	131	**351**	666	12.5	4.31	116	.263	.327	54	74	104	61	28	**.986**	**57**	**23**	103	**1.5**	6.8	-1.5	**.6**	-.4
TOR	13	4	221	26	1025.0	1053	127	482	**832**	13.8	4.70	103	.266	.348	12	14	100	101	43	.981	81	68	105	.2	1.3	-3.0	.3	-1.2
BOS	6	3	**308**	30	1029.1	1104	120	450	729	13.9	4.93	102	.276	.351	-15	11	105	98	38	.981	81	62	124	.2	1.0	-5.8	.0	1.1
DET	15	1	246	20	1018.0	1139	148	449	560	14.3	5.38	90	.282	.356	-66	-61	101	94	36	.981	82	67	90	.1	-5.6	3.8	-.6	-2.2
CENTRAL																												
CHI	13	**9**	239	20	1011.1	**964**	115	377	754	**12.1**	**3.96**	**118**	**.250**	**.317**	**94**	81	97	81	30	.981	79	31	91	.2	7.5	6.4	.2	-3.8
CLE	**17**	5	222	21	1018.2	1097	**94**	404	666	13.6	4.36	108	.275	.346	49	41	98	75	33	.980	90	65	119	-.4	3.8	6.8	**.6**	-1.3
KC	5	6	247	**38**	1031.2	1018	95	392	717	12.6	4.23	**118**	.260	.328	65	**85**	104	91	30	.982	80	65	102	.2	**7.9**	-5.6	.4	3.7
MIN	6	4	272	29	1005.0	1197	153	388	602	14.5	5.68	86	.299	.361	-98	-89	101	85	**53**	.982	75	48	99	.4	-8.2	-1.8	.5	5.6
MIL	11	3	252	23	1036.0	1071	127	421	577	13.2	4.62	109	.269	.340	20	45	105	117	28	.981	85	41	**130**	-.0	4.2	-7.0	-.5	-1.1
WEST																												
TEX	10	4	301	26	1023.0	1176	157	394	683	14.1	5.45	88	.288	.351	-75	-72	100	**47**	33	.976	106	59	106	-1.4	-6.7	1.9	.0	1.0
OAK	12	**9**	**308**	23	1003.1	979	128	510	732	13.7	4.80	92	.257	.347	0	-45	92	60	45	.979	88	47	105	-.3	-4.2	-2.0	.0	.4
SEA	13	7	252	21	984.0	1051	109	486	763	14.3	4.99	98	.274	.357	-21	-12	102	69	39	.977	95	49	102	-.8	-1.1	-1.2	-.2	-3.7
CAL	11	4	257	21	1027.0	1149	150	436	682	14.3	5.42	90	.287	.360	-70	-59	102	83	38	.983	76	59	110	.5	-5.5	-5.8	-.9	1.2
TOT	153	65	3600	366	14229.2					13.5	4.80		.273	.345						.981	1155	740	1508					

Batter-Fielder Wins	Batting Average	On-Base Percentage	Slugging Average	On-Base Plus Slugging	Adjusted OPS	Adjusted Batter Runs
Thomas-Chi 5.2	O'Neill-NY............359	Thomas-Chi 487	Thomas-Chi 729	Thomas-Chi.......1217	Thomas-Chi.........214	Thomas-Chi........76.6
Belle-Cle..............4.5	Belle-Cle..............357	O'Neill-NY 460	Belle-Cle..............714	Belle-Cle 1152	Belle-Cle 191	Belle-Cle 57.5
Griffey-Sea.........4.2	Thomas-Chi 353	Belle-Cle 438	Griffey-Sea 674	Griffey-Sea 1076	O'Neill-NY 179	O'Neill-NY 48.2
O'Neill-NY...........4.0	Lofton-Cle............349	Boggs-NY 433	O'Neill-NY............603	O'Neill-NY 1064	Griffey-Sea 168	Griffey-Sea 43.0
Lofton-Cle 3.8	Boggs-NY.............342	Clark-Tex 431	Hamelin-KC 599	Hamelin-KC 987	Davis-Cal..............147	Lofton-Cle 30.8

Runs	Hits	Doubles	Triples	Home Runs	Total Bases	Runs Batted In
Thomas-Chi..........106	Lofton-Cle 160	Knoblauch-Min 45	L.Johnson-Chi 14	Griffey-Sea 40	Belle-Cle 294	Puckett-Min 112
Lofton-Cle............105	Molitor-Tor 155	Belle-Cle.......................35	Coleman-KC 12	Thomas-Chi...........38	Griffey-Sea 292	Carter-Tor...........103
Griffey-Sea 94	Belle-Cle 147	Thomas-Chi 34	Lofton-Cle 9	Belle-Cle 36	Thomas-Chi..........291	Thomas-Chi 101
Phillips-Det 91	Thomas-Chi..........141	Fryman-Det...................34	Diaz-Mil 7	Canseco-Tex 31	Lofton-Cle 246	Belle-Cle.............101
Belle-Cle 90				Fielder-Det.............28	Palmeiro-Bal 240	Franco-Chi 98

Stolen Bases	Base Stealing Runs	Fielding Runs-Infield	Fielding Runs-Outfield	Wins	Winning Pct.	Complete Games
Lofton-Cle 60	Lofton-Cle.............9.0	Valentin-Mil 21.3	Edmonds-Cal 8.3	Key-NY 17	Bere-Chi 857	Johnson-Sea 9
Coleman-KC 50	Coleman-KC...........8.2	Espinoza-Cle 15.8	Curtis-Cal 7.3	Mussina-Bal...........16	Key-NY 810	Martinez-Cle...........7
Nixon-Bos 42	Anderson-Bal 6.5	Gallego-NY 15.7	L.Johnson-Chi 7.3	Cone-KC 16	Clark-Cle 786	Finley-Cal 7
Knoblauch-Min 35	Nixon-Bos.............5.7	Fielder-Det.................15.5	Ward-Mil 6.1	McDonald-Bal 14	Mussina-Bal 762	
Anderson-Bal..........31	Knoblauch-Min 5.6	Gagne-KC 13.4	Puckett-Min............5.9		Cone-KC...............762	

Strikeouts	Fewest BB/Game	Games	Saves	Base Runners/9	Adjusted Relief Runs	Relief Ranking
Johnson-Sea 204	Gubicza-KC 1.80	Wickman-NY.................53	L.Smith-Bal 33	Ontiveros-Oak 9.75	Eichhorn-Bal........21.0	Eichhorn-Bal 29.9
Clemens-Bos.........168	Gullickson-Det 1.95	Mesa-Cle 51	Montgomery-KC 27	Cone-KC...........10.01	Castillo-Tor 16.7	Plunk-Cle............20.2
Finley-Cal 148	Wegman-Mil 2.02	Guthrie-Min..................50	Aguilera-Min 23	Clemens-Bos 10.49	Plunk-Cle 16.5	Ryan-Bos............19.6
Hentgen-Tor..........147	Ontiveros-Oak 2.03	Brewer-KC 50	Eckersley-Oak 19	Mussina-Bal 10.51	Ryan-Bos 13.3	Fetters-Mil 19.5
Appier-KC 145	McDowell-Chi 2.09	Willis-Min 49	Ayala-Sea 18	Wickman-NY 10.54	Howe-NY 13.3	Risley-Sea..........18.8

Innings Pitched	Opponents' Avg.	Opponents' OBP	Earned Run Average	Adjusted ERA	Adjusted Starter Runs	Pitcher Wins
Finley-Cal 183.1	Clemens-Bos 203	Ontiveros-Oak 271	Ontiveros-Oak 2.65	Clemens-Bos........177	Cone-KC..............38.5	**Cone-KC** 4.3
McDowell-Chi 181.0	Cone-KC..............209	Cone-KC 277	Clemens-Bos 2.85	Cone-KC 171	Clemens-Bos 38.4	**Mussina-Bal** 4.0
Eldred-Mil 179.0	Johnson-Sea 216	Clemens-Bos 288	Cone-KC..............2.94	Ontiveros-Oak 167	Mussina-Bal 36.4	**Johnson-Sea**......3.5
Martinez-Cle......176.2	Ontiveros-Oak 217	Mussina-Bal.................291	Mussina-Bal 3.06	Mussina-Bal..........164	Johnson-Sea 33.5	**Clemens-Bos** 3.2
Mussina-Bal 176.1	Bere-Chi 229	Martinez-Cle 298	Johnson-Sea 3.19	Johnson-Sea 153	Bones-Mil 27.2	**Eichhorn-Bal**......2.9

Crossing the Rubicon

The high-velocity rhetoric started flying early in the year as owners tried to link revenue sharing to a salary cap in labor negotiations. Players steadfastly refused a cap, however. Milwaukee owner Bud Selig, now interim commissioner, was given total control over negotiations. Talks were fruitless, and the players went on strike on August 12. The season, including the postseason, was officially pronounced kaput on September 14.

Before the catastrophe, two new ballparks opened: Jacobs Field in Cleveland and the Ballpark in Arlington in Texas. Also new was baseball's revamped postseason format, which included three divisions in each league for the first time and a Wild Card post-season berth for the second place team with the best record.

Cleveland slugger Albert Belle was caught using a corked bat. Basketball superstar Michael Jordan, in what proved to be a temporary retirement from basketball, signed a minor league contract with White Sox. The glory of the NBA spent the summer struggling at Double-A, hitting only .202 and slugging .266 in his lone season in baseball. Goose Gossage, Kent Hrbek, Bo Jackson, and Jack Morris retired. Eighteen-year-old shortstop Alex Rodriguez debuted for Seattle.

Seattle's Ken Griffey Jr. led the league with 40 home runs, and was close to a pace needed to break Roger Maris' revered record. Chicago's Frank Thomas (38) and Belle (36) were right behind Griffey. For all the immense damage it wrought, the strike saved baseball the embarrassment of a division champion 10 games under .500: the Rangers, who led the four-team West. Baseball's decision not to officially declare division champions robbed deserving AL leaders Chicago (Central) and New York (East) of titles. Cleveland, which had not reached the postseason since 1954, was the leading Wild Card team.

1995 National League

TEAM	W	L	T	PCT	GB	HW	HL	R	OR	PA	H	2B	3B	HR	BB	SO	HB	SH	AVG	OBP	SLG	OPS	AOPS	BR	ABR	PF	SB	CS	BSA	BSR
EAST																														
ATL	90	54	0	.625		**44**	28	645	**540**	5464	1202	210	27	168	520	933	56	40	.250	.326	.409	735	95	-11	-31	103	73	43	63	1
NY	69	75	0	.479	21	40	32	657	618	5581	1323	218	34	125	446	994	**92**	42	.267	.330	.400	730	100	-17	5	97	58	39	60	-1
PHI	69	75	0	.479	21	35	37	615	658	5611	1296	263	30	94	497	884	77	46	.262	.332	.384	716	93	-31	-35	101	72	25	74	7
FLA	67	76	0	.469	22.5	37	34	673	673	5569	1278	214	29	144	517	916	69	49	.262	.335	.406	741	100	8	6	100	131	53	71	10
MON	66	78	0	.458	24	31	41	621	638	5451	1268	265	24	118	400	901	58	56	.259	.320	.394	714	90	-48	-68	104	120	49	71	9
CENTRAL																														
CIN	85	59	0	.590		**44**	28	747	623	5574	1326	**277**	35	161	519	946	62	40	.270	.342	.440	782	111	80	84	100	**190**	68	74	**18**
HOU	76	68	0	.528	9	36	36	747	674	5857	1403	260	22	109	**566**	992	78	**69**	.275	**.353**	.399	752	**112**	47	**103**	93	176	60	**75**	**18**
CHI	73	71	0	.507	12	34	38	693	671	5543	1315	267	39	158	440	953	71	34	.265	.327	.430	757	106	23	36	98	105	37	74	10
STL	62	81	0	.434	22.5	39	33	563	658	5349	1182	238	24	107	436	920	48	46	.247	.314	.374	688	86	-90	-88	100	79	46	63	1
PIT	58	86	0	.403	27	31	41	629	736	5501	1281	245	27	125	456	972	51	24	.259	.323	.396	719	92	-39	-50	102	84	55	60	-1
WEST																														
LA	78	66	0	.542		39	33	634	609	5543	1303	191	31	140	468	1023	68	30	.264	.329	.400	729	106	-23	40	91	127	45	74	12
COL	77	67	0	.535	1	**44**	28	**785**	783	5647	**1406**	259	**43**	**200**	484	943	82	56	**.282**	.350	**.471**	**821**	93	**142**	-41	129	125	59	68	7
SD	70	74	0	.486	8	40	32	668	672	5526	1345	231	20	116	447	**872**	56	35	.272	.334	.397	731	102	-12	12	97	124	46	73	11
SF	67	77	0	.465	11	37	35	652	776	5603	1256	229	33	152	472	1060	79	57	.253	.323	.404	727	99	-29	-8	97	138	46	**75**	14
TOT	1007					531	476	9329		77819	18184	3367	418	1917	6668	13309	624	947	.263	.331	.408	739					1602	671	70	118

TEAM	CG	SHO	GR	SV	IP	H	HR	BB	SO	BR/9	ERA	AERA	OAV	OOB	PR	APR	PF	OSB	OCS	FA	E	WPB	DP	FW	PW	BW	BSW	DIF
EAST																												
ATL	**18**	11	339	34	1291.2	**1184**	**107**	436	**1087**	**11.5**	**3.44**	**124**	.244	**.309**	**106**	**116**	102	132	37	.982	100	46	113	.6	**11.4**	-3.0	-.7	9.7
NY	9	9	298	36	1291.0	1296	133	**401**	901	12.1	3.88	104	.262	.319	44	25	97	127	40	.979	115	53	125	-.3	2.5	.5	-.9	-4.8
PHI	8	8	341	41	1290.1	1241	134	538	980	12.8	4.21	100	.254	.333	-4	3	101	137	38	.982	97	76	139	.8	.3	-3.4	-.1	-.5
FLA	12	7	400	29	1286.0	1299	139	562	994	13.3	4.27	99	.264	.343	-13	-8	101	**82**	53	.979	115	**44**	143	-.3	-.8	.6	.2	-4.2
MON	7	9	396	42	1283.2	1286	128	416	950	12.3	4.11	104	.262	.325	10	26	103	145	56	.980	109	51	119	.1	2.6	-6.7	.0	-2.0
CENTRAL																												
CIN	8	10	330	38	1289.1	1270	131	424	903	12.0	4.03	102	.260	.320	21	12	99	92	30	**.986**	**79**	69	140	**1.9**	1.2	8.3	**.9**	.7
HOU	6	8	394	32	1320.1	1357	118	460	1056	12.7	4.06	95	.266	.331	17	-31	93	120	49	.979	121	67	120	-.6	-3.0	**10.1**	**.9**	-3.4
CHI	6	**12**	414	**45**	1301.0	1313	162	518	926	12.9	4.13	99	.262	.333	7	-4	98	123	56	.979	115	57	115	-.3	-.4	3.5	.2	-2.0
STL	4	6	377	38	1265.2	1290	135	445	842	12.6	4.09	102	.268	.333	13	14	100	132	**64**	.980	113	60	**156**	-.2	1.4	-8.7	-.7	-1.3
PIT	11	7	391	29	1275.1	1407	130	477	871	13.7	4.70	92	.283	.350	-74	-55	103	125	61	.978	122	77	138	-.7	-5.4	-4.9	-.9	-2.1
WEST																												
LA	16	11	355	37	1295.0	1188	125	462	1060	11.7	3.66	104	**.243**	.311	76	22	91	108	45	.976	130	68	120	-1.2	2.2	3.9	.4	.7
COL	1	1	**456**	43	1288.1	1443	160	512	891	13.9	4.97	108	.286	.355	-113	47	129	100	43	.981	107	72	146	.2	4.6	-4.0	-.1	4.3
SD	6	10	337	35	1284.2	1242	142	512	1047	12.6	4.13	97	.255	.331	7	-15	96	91	54	.980	108	68	130	.2	-1.5	1.2	.3	-2.1
SF	12	5	381	34	1293.2	1368	173	505	801	13.4	4.86	84	.275	.345	-98	-115	98	88	45	.980	108	50	142	.2	-11.3	-.8	.6	6.4
TOT	124	114	5209	513	18056.0					12.7	4.18		.263	.331						.980	1539	858	1846					

Batter-Fielder Wins	Batting Average	On-Base Percentage	Slugging Average	On-Base Plus Slugging	Adjusted OPS	Adjusted Batter Runs
Bonds-SF 5.7	Gwynn-SD 368	Bonds-SF......................431	Bichette-Col 620	Bonds-SF 1009	Piazza-LA 177	Bonds-SF 57.1
Piazza-LA 5.0	Piazza-LA.............346	Biggio-Hou...................406	Walker-Col 607	Piazza-LA 1006	Bonds-SF 169	Piazza-LA 46.2
Caminiti-SD 4.6	Bichette-Col 340	Gwynn-SD 404	Piazza-LA.............606	Walker-Col............988	R.Sanders-Cin......155	Biggio-Hou 40.8
Biggio-Hou 4.5	Bell-Hou 334	Weiss-Col 403	R.Sanders-Cin 579	Bichette-Col..........984	Karros-LA 149	R.Sanders-Cin....40.4
R.Sanders-Cin 4.1	Grace-Chi 326	Piazza-LA 400	Bonds-SF 577	R.Sanders-Cin......975	Gant-Cin 146	Karros-LA 37.9

Runs	Hits	Doubles	Triples	Home Runs	Total Bases	Runs Batted In
Biggio-Hou............123	Gwynn-SD 197	Grace-Chi 51	Butler-NY-LA 9	Bichette-Col............40	Bichette-Col..........359	Bichette-Col 128
Bonds-SF 109	Bichette-Col..........197	McRae-Chi 38	Young-Col 9	Walker-Col...............36	Walker-Col............300	Sosa-Chi 119
Finley-SD..............104	Grace-Chi 180	Bichette-Col 38	D.Sanders-Cin-SF 8	Sosa-Chi 36	Castilla-Col 297	Galarraga-Col......106
Bichette-Col..........102		R.Sanders-Cin 36	Gonzalez-Hou-Chi....8	Bonds-SF 33	Karros-LA 295	Karros-LA.............105
Larkin-Cin 98			Finley-SD..................8		Bonds-SF 292	Conine-Fla 105

Stolen Bases	Base Stealing Runs	Fielding Runs-Infield	Fielding Runs-Outfield	Wins	Winning Pct.	Complete Games
Veras-Fla 56	Larkin-Cin 9.5	Bagwell-Hou 17.7	Mondesi-LA 8.9	Maddux-Atl 19	Maddux-Atl 905	Maddux-Atl 10
Larkin-Cin 51	Sosa-Chi.................5.0	Reed-SD 17.7	Sosa-Chi.................8.3	Schourek-Cin...........18	Schourek-Cin 720	Leiter-SF..................7
DeShields-LA 39	Veras-Fla 5.0	Vizcaino-NY................15.4	Gonzalez-Hou-Chi 7.0	Martinez-LA.............17	Martinez-LA 708	Valdes-LA..................6
R.Sanders-Cin........36	Mondesi-LA 4.5	Lansing-Mon 15.1	Carr-Fla 6.4	Glavine-Atl 16	Glavine-Atl 696	Neagle-Pit 5
Finley-SD................36	Lansing-Mon..........4.5	Weiss-Col 13.9	D.Lewis-SF-Cin......5.1			

Strikeouts	Fewest BB/Game	Games	Saves	Base Runners/9	Adjusted Relief Runs	Relief Ranking
Nomo-LA 236	Maddux-Atl 99	Leskanic-Col..................76	Myers-Chi 38	Maddux-Atl 7.47	Reed-Col 22.8	Wohlers-Atl 31.1
Smoltz-Atl 193	Reynolds-Hou.......1.76	Veres-Hou......................72	Henke-StL 36	Reed-Col 8.89	Veres-Hou............20.1	Worrell-LA 23.0
Maddux-Atl 181	Neagle-Pit............1.93	Reed-Col.........................71	Beck-SF..................33	Brantley-Cin 9.47	Leskanic-Col........17.8	Henke-StL 22.5
Reynolds-Hou 175	Saberhagen-NY-Col 1.94	Perez-Fla 69	Worrell-LA 32	Schilling-Phi 9.70	Bottalico-Phi 17.6	Reed-Col 18.6
Martinez-Mon 174	Smiley-Cin 1.99		Slocumb-Phi 32	Nomo-LA 9.74	Wohlers-Atl..........15.5	Leskanic-Col 17.9

Innings Pitched	Opponents' Avg.	Opponents' OBP	Earned Run Average	Adjusted ERA	Adjusted Starter Runs	Pitcher Wins
Neagle-Pit..........209.2	Nomo-LA 182	Maddux-Atl 224	Maddux-Atl 1.63	Maddux-Atl 262	Maddux-Atl 61.4	**Maddux-Atl** 6.4
Maddux-Atl 209.2	Maddux-Atl 197	Nomo-LA 269	Nomo-LA 2.54	Nomo-LA 149	Nomo-LA 29.1	**Glavine-Atl** 3.2
Martinez-LA 206.1	Martinez-Mon 227	Valdes-LA 277	Ashby-SD 2.94	Glavine-Atl............139	Glavine-Atl 24.9	**Wohlers-Atl** 3.1
Hamilton-SD 204.1	Valdes-LA.............228	Schourek-Cin...............281	Valdes-LA............3.05	Ashby-SD 137	Smoltz-Atl 22.2	**Schourek-Cin** 2.6
Navarro-Chi 200.1	Schourek-Cin 228	Reynolds-Hou 300	Glavine-Atl 3.08	Smoltz-Atl 134	Ashby-SD 20.8	**Worrell-LA** 2.3

Brave New World

Players' union head Donald Fehr claimed all 835 players without signed contracts were free agents because baseball imposed new work rules, including a salary cap. Owners, of course, said no. Baseball officials must have figured that with no players, they needed no umpires, and with players still on strike, locked out its arbiters. Replacements—umpires, that is—were used for a week once the players came to terms.

Suspended for sixty days for violating MLB's drug policy, Darryl Strawberry was released by the Giants, then pleaded guilty to tax evasion. The Dodgers had to forfeit a game to St. Louis in August after Los Angeles fans flung giveaway baseballs onto the field following a controversial call. Hideo Nomo, 13–6 and leading the league in strikeouts for those Dodgers, became the first Japanese player in thirty-one years to debut in the big leagues.

Former Reds outfielders Vada Pinson and Gus Bell died, but Cincinnati, sparked by MVP Barry Larkin, won the Central and swept Los Angeles in the Division Series. Colorado, in only its third season, had four 30-homer men at new Coors Field and claimed the Wild Card despite a league-worst 4.97 ERA. Atlanta, with 19–2 Greg Maddux, had the best record in the league and lost only once in reaching the World Series, besting the Rockies in the Division Series and sweeping the Reds in the NLCS.

Atlanta pitchers dominated the World Series, holding Cleveland's potent offense to a collective .179 average. Tom Glavine and Mark Wohlers combined on a 1–0, 1-hit shutout in Game 6, with Dave Justice's home run providing the difference. The win gave the Braves their first Series crown since 1957 and made them the first franchise to win world championships in three different cities.

1995 American League

TEAM	W	L	T	PCT	GB	HW	HL	R	OR	PA	H	2B	3B	HR	BB	SO	HB	SH	AVG	OBP	SLG	OPS	AOPS	BR	ABR	PF	SB	CS	BSA	BSR
EAST																														
BOS	86	58	0	.597		42	30	791	698	5716	1399	**286**	31	175	560	923	45	**65**	.280	.357	.455	812	106	79	53	103	99	44	69	6
NY	79	65	1	.549	7	46	26	749	688	5699	1365	280	34	122	**625**	851	20	39	.276	.357	.420	777	102	31	40	99	50	30	63	1
BAL	71	73	0	.493	15	36	36	704	640	5531	1267	229	27	173	574	803	40	39	.262	.342	.428	770	98	-4	-15	102	92	45	67	4
DET	60	84	0	.417	26	35	37	654	844	5535	1204	228	29	159	551	987	35	41	.247	.327	.404	731	90	-80	-76	99	73	36	67	3
TOR	56	88	0	.389	30	29	43	642	777	5650	1309	275	27	140	492	906	33	44	.260	.328	.409	737	91	-70	-65	99	75	16	82	**11**
CENTRAL																														
CLE	100	44	0	.694		**54**	18	**840**	**607**	5684	**1461**	279	23	**207**	542	**766**	31	35	**.291**	**.361**	**.479**	**840**	**114**	**125**	**113**	101	**132**	53	71	10
KC	70	74	0	.486	30	35	37	629	691	5526	1275	240	35	119	475	849	**66**	43	.260	.328	.396	724	86	-91	-99	101	120	53	69	8
CHI	68	76	1	.472	32	38	34	755	758	5770	1417	252	37	146	576	767	46	32	.280	.354	.431	785	108	32	70	95	110	39	**74**	**11**
MIL	65	79	0	.451	35	33	39	740	747	5631	1329	249	**42**	128	502	800	41	46	.266	.336	.409	745	88	-52	-88	106	105	40	72	9
MIN	56	88	0	.389	44	29	43	703	889	5588	1398	270	34	120	471	916	18	58	.279	.346	.419	765	98	-11	-12	100	105	57	65	3
WEST																														
SEA	79	66	0	.545		46	27	796	708	5670	1377	276	20	182	549	871	52	39	.276	.350	.448	798	105	47	40	101	110	41	73	10
CAL	78	67	0	.538	1	39	33	801	697	5690	1390	252	25	186	564	889	33	36	.277	.352	.448	800	107	52	60	99	58	39	60	-1
TEX	74	70	0	.514	4.5	41	31	691	720	5566	1304	247	24	138	526	877	49	33	.265	.338	.410	748	91	-43	-58	102	90	47	66	3
OAK	67	77	0	.465	11.5	38	34	730	761	5616	1296	228	18	169	565	911	32	45	.264	.341	.420	761	103	-15	27	95	112	46	71	9
TOT	1010					541	468	10225		78872	18791	3591	406	2164	7572	12116	595	541	.270	.344	.427	771					1331	586	69	88

TEAM	CG	SHO	GR	SV	IP	H	HR	BB	SO	BR/9	ERA	AERA	OAV	OOB	PR	APR	PF	OSB	OCS	FA	E	WPB	DP	FW	PW	BW	BSW	DIF
EAST																												
BOS	7	9	370	39	1292.2	1338	**127**	476	888	12.9	4.39	111	.268	.334	46	66	103	80	41	.978	120	86	151	-1.2	6.2	5.0	-.0	4.1
NY	18	5	302	35	1284.2	1286	159	535	908	13.0	4.56	101	.261	.334	22	8	98	117	40	**.986**	74	70	121	**1.4**	.8	3.8	-.5	1.6
BAL	**19**	**10**	336	29	1267.0	**1165**	149	523	930	12.3	4.31	110	**.245**	.322	56	61	101	98	43	**.986**	**72**	**38**	141	**1.4**	5.7	-1.4	-.2	-6.5
DET	5	3	366	38	1275.0	1509	170	536	729	14.8	5.49	87	.296	.365	-110	-103	101	102	38	.981	106	70	143	-.4	-9.7	-7.1	-.3	5.5
TOR	16	8	265	22	1292.2	1336	145	654	894	14.2	4.88	96	.267	.356	-24	-25	100	98	50	.982	97	104	131	.0	-2.3	-6.1	**.4**	-8.1
CENTRAL																												
CLE	10	**10**	335	**50**	1301.0	1261	135	**445**	926	**12.1**	**3.83**	**122**	.255	**.320**	**127**	**125**	100	117	38	.982	101	59	142	-.2	**11.7**	**10.6**	**.4**	5.5
KC	11	**10**	308	37	1288.0	1323	142	503	763	13.0	4.49	107	.268	.338	32	42	102	78	29	.984	90	56	168	.4	3.9	-9.3	.2	2.7
CHI	12	4	**373**	36	1284.2	1374	164	617	892	14.2	4.85	92	.275	.356	-20	-61	95	106	**59**	.980	108	57	131	-.5	-5.7	6.6	**.4**	-4.8
MIL	7	4	321	31	1286.0	1391	146	603	699	14.3	4.82	103	.280	.360	-16	22	106	110	36	.981	105	79	**186**	-.4	2.1	-8.3	.3	-.7
MIN	7	2	336	27	1272.2	1450	210	533	790	14.3	5.76	83	.287	.356	-149	-139	101	102	25	.981	100	63	141	-.1	-13.0	-1.1	-.3	-1.4
WEST																												
SEA	9	8	324	39	1289.1	1343	149	591	**1068**	13.8	4.50	105	.268	.347	31	34	101	88	46	.980	104	63	108	-.3	3.2	3.8	**.4**	-.5
CAL	8	9	368	42	1284.1	1310	163	486	901	12.9	4.52	104	.265	.333	28	25	100	88	46	.982	95	55	120	.2	2.3	5.6	-.7	-2.0
TEX	14	4	310	34	1285.0	1385	152	514	838	13.6	4.66	104	.278	.346	8	23	102	**55**	44	.982	98	70	156	.0	2.2	-5.4	-.3	5.6
OAK	8	4	358	34	1273.0	1320	153	556	890	13.6	4.93	91	.269	.347	-31	-70	95	92	51	.981	102	60	151	-.2	-6.6	2.5	.3	-1.0
TOT	151	90	4672	493	17976.0					13.5	4.71		.270	.344						.982	1372	930	1990					

Batter-Fielder Wins
E.Martinez-Sea ..5.7
Belle-Cle 5.1
Salmon-Cal 5.0
Valentin-Bos 4.6
F.Thomas-Chi......4.5

Batting Average
E.Martinez-Sea ...356
Knoblauch-Min 333
Salmon-Cal...........330
Boggs-NY............324
Murray-Cle 323

On-Base Percentage
E.Martinez-Sea 479
F.Thomas-Chi..............454
Thome-Cle....................438
Salmon-Cal 429
Davis-Cal 429

Slugging Average
Belle-Cle...............690
E.Martinez-Sea ...628
F.Thomas-Chi 606
Salmon-Cal..........594
Palmeiro-Bal.........583

On-Base Plus Slugging
E.Martinez-Sea ..1107
Belle-Cle 1091
F.Thomas-Chi 1061
Salmon-Cal 1024
Thome-Cle............996

Adjusted OPS
E.Martinez-Sea 184
F.Thomas-Chi 184
Belle-Cle 175
Salmon-Cal 165
Thome-Cle............155

Adjusted Batter Runs
E.Martinez-Sea ..73.7
F.Thomas-Chi 71.2
Belle-Cle 61.0
Salmon-Cal 55.4
McGwire-Oak 52.1

Runs
E.Martinez-Sea 121
Belle-Cle 121
Edmonds-Cal........120
Phillips-Cal 119
Salmon-Cal 111

Hits
Johnson-Chi 186
E.Martinez-Sea 182
Knoblauch-Min 179
Salmon-Cal 177
Baerga-Cle 175

Doubles
E.Martinez-Sea.............52
Belle-Cle.......................52
Puckett-Min...................39
Valentin-Bos 37
T.Martinez-Sea 35

Triples
Lofton-Cle 13
Johnson-Chi 12
Anderson-Bal..........10
B.Williams-NY 9
Knoblauch-Min 8

Home Runs
Belle-Cle 50
F.Thomas-Chi 40
Buhner-Sea 40

Total Bases
Belle-Cle 377
Palmeiro-Bal 323
E.Martinez-Sea 321
Salmon-Cal 319
Vaughn-Bos..........316

Runs Batted In
Vaughn-Bos 126
Belle-Cle.............126
Buhner-Sea 121
E.Martinez-Sea ..113

Stolen Bases
Lofton-Cle 54
Nixon-Tex.................50
Goodwin-KC 50
Knoblauch-Min 46
Coleman-KC-Sea....42

Base Stealing Runs
Johnson-Chi 6.7
Lofton-Cle..............6.6
Javier-Oak 6.2
Alomar-Tor 5.6
Goodwin-KC 4.7

Fielding Runs-Infield
Fryman-Det 27.3
Gil-Tex 18.3
Alicea-Bos 14.9
Gagne-KC 12.4
Vina-Mil 12.2

Fielding Runs-Outfield
Cordova-Min........13.8
Edmonds-Cal 11.7
Javier-Oak 8.6
G.Williams-NY 7.8
Becker-Min 7.4

Wins
Mussina-Bal...........19
Cone-Tor-NY 18
Johnson-Sea 18
Rogers-Tex 17

Winning Pct.
Johnson-Sea 900
Hanson-Bos 750
Nagy-Cle 727
Hershiser-Cle 727
Rogers-Tex...........708

Complete Games
McDowell-NY 8
Erickson-Min-Bal 7
Mussina-Bal 7

Strikeouts
Johnson-Sea 294
Stottlemyre-Oak....205
Finley-Cal 195
Cone-Tor-NY 191
Appier-KC 185

Fewest BB/Game
Mussina-Bal 2.03
Martinez-Cle 2.21
Radke-Min 2.34
K.Brown-Bal 2.51
Gubicza-KC 2.62

Games
Orosco-Bal 65
McDowell-Tex 64
Wickman-NY..................63
Belinda-Bos 63
Ayala-Sea 63

Saves
Mesa-Cle 46
Smith-Cal...............37
Aguilera-Min-Bos 32
Hernandez-Chi 32

Base Runners/9
Percival-Cal 7.78
Wetteland-NY 7.92
Mesa-Cle 9.28
Johnson-Sea 9.66
Mussina-Bal 9.66

Adjusted Relief Runs
Mesa-Cle 25.4
Nelson-Sea.........22.3
Percival-Cal 21.9
Tavarez-Cle 16.5
Plunk-Cle 15.3

Relief Ranking
Mesa-Cle............44.4
Aguilera-Min-Bos27.6
Nelson-Sea 26.5
Tavarez-Cle 21.0
Wetteland-NY 20.5

Innings Pitched
Cone-Tor-NY......229.1
Mussina-Bal 221.2
McDowell-NY 217.2
Johnson-Sea 214.1
Gubicza-KC 213.1

Opponents' Avg.
Johnson-Sea 201
Appier-KC 221
Mussina-Bal 226
Wakefield-Bos.......227
Cone-Tor-NY.........228

Opponents' OBP
Johnson-Sea 266
Mussina-Bal.................270
Wakefield-Bos 300
K.Brown-Bal................302
Martinez-Cle 302

Earned Run Average
Johnson-Sea 2.48
Wakefield-Bos.......2.95
Martinez-Cle........3.08
Mussina-Bal 3.29
Rogers-Tex 3.38

Adjusted ERA
Johnson-Sea 191
Wakefield-Bos 165
Martinez-Cle 153
Mussina-Bal..........145
Rogers-Tex 143

Adjusted Starter Runs
Johnson-Sea 53.5
Wakefield-Bos......38.1
Mussina-Bal 35.6
Martinez-Cle........33.4
Rogers-Tex..........31.7

Pitcher Wins
Johnson-Sea......4.6
Mesa-Cle 4.3
Wakefield-Bos ..4.2
Mussina-Bal 4.0
Rogers-Tex 3.3

Ripken Pulls Baseball from Its Deathbed

Owners announced plans to use replacement players if a labor deal wasn't reached by Opening Day. Baltimore owner Peter Angelos refused to sign replacements players, thus the O's played no exhibition contests. His stated motive: preserving Cal Ripken's consecutive games streak. Angelos' stand led to his being virtually ostracized by other owners.

A March 31 injunction against MLB by U.S. District Court judge Sonia Sotomayor ended the strike. Fans were understandably bitter and jaded all summer, but the harsh feeling seemed to relent for one magical night at Camden Yards. On September 6, on national television, Ripken broke Lou Gehrig's record by playing in his 2,131st consecutive game.

Yankees great Mickey Mantle died in August, two months after receiving a liver transplant, while colorful umpire Ron Luciano committed suicide. Two Yankees greats retired—Dave Winfield and Don Mattingly—as Derek Jeter and Jason Giambi debuted. Eddie Murray collected his 3,000th hit.

Sparked by Albert Belle, the first player to hit 50 homers and 50 doubles in a season, Cleveland won the Central by an amazing 30 games and swept Boston to reach the ALCS. Seattle climaxed a furious comeback by winning a one-game playoff against California to reach the postseason for the first time. The Mariners then outlasted the Wild Card Yankees in the other inaugural AL Division Series. Game 5 ended with starters Randy Johnson and Jack McDowell pitching in relief. Edgar Martinez drove home the tying and winning runs in the home 11th, sending the Kingdome into a frenzy. Despite Jay Buhner's 3 homers for Seattle, Cleveland's outstanding starting pitching prevailed in a six-game ALCS. The Tribe, however, ran out of steam in the World Series, losing to Atlanta in six.

1996 National League

TEAM	W	L	T	PCT	GB	HW	HL	R	OR	PA	H	2B	3B	HR	BB	SO	HB	SH	AVG	OBP	SLG	OPS	AOPS	BR	ABR	PF	SB	CS	BSA	BSR
EAST																														
ATL	96	66	0	.593		**56**	25	773	**648**	6290	1514	264	28	197	530	1032	69	27	.270	.333	.432	765	100	48	6	106	83	43	66	3
MON	88	74	0	.543	8	50	31	741	668	6170	1441	297	27	148	492	1077	79	58	.262	.327	.406	733	96	-12	-29	102	108	34	**76**	12
FLA	80	82	0	.494	16	52	29	688	703	6192	1413	240	30	150	553	1122	41	55	.257	.329	.393	722	98	-30	-5	97	99	46	68	6
NY	71	91	0	.438	25	42	39	746	779	6220	1515	267	47	147	445	1069	75	33	.270	.324	.412	736	103	-14	22	95	97	48	67	5
PHI	67	95	0	.414	29	35	46	650	790	6171	1405	249	39	132	536	1092	54	45	.256	.325	.387	712	92	-54	-61	101	117	41	74	11
CENTRAL																														
STL	88	74	0	.543		48	33	759	706	6177	1468	281	31	142	495	1089	**88**	44	.267	.330	.407	737	100	-4	4	99	149	58	72	12
HOU	82	80	0	.506	6	48	33	753	792	6269	1445	297	29	129	554	1057	68	**84**	.262	.336	.397	733	**106**	2	**67**	92	180	63	74	18
CIN	81	81	0	.500	7	46	35	778	773	6213	1398	259	36	191	**604**	1134	71	34	.256	.331	.422	753	103	29	26	100	171	63	73	16
CHI	76	86	0	.469	12	43	38	772	771	6229	1388	267	19	175	523	1090	66	61	.251	.320	.401	721	92	-39	-56	103	108	50	68	6
PIT	73	89	0	.451	15	36	44	776	833	6336	1509	**319**	33	138	510	**989**	72	40	.266	.329	.407	736	96	-4	-23	103	126	49	72	11
WEST																														
SD	91	71	0	.562		45	36	771	682	6417	1499	285	24	147	601	1014	59	50	.265	.338	.402	740	**106**	15	65	94	109	55	66	5
LA	90	72	0	.556	1	47	34	703	652	6185	1396	215	33	150	516	1190	74	22	.252	.316	.384	700	97	-85	-28	92	124	40	**76**	13
COL	83	79	0	.512	8	55	26	**961**	964	6332	**1607**	297	**37**	**221**	527	1108	81	82	**.287**	**.355**	**.472**	**827**	99	**181**	0	124	**201**	66	75	**21**
SF	68	94	0	.420	23	38	44	752	862	6316	1400	245	21	153	615	1189	77	48	.253	.331	.388	719	99	-32	-2	96	113	53	68	6
TOT	1134					641	493	10623		87517	20398	3782	434	2220	7501	15252	683	974	.262	.330	.408	738					1785	709	72	145

TEAM	CG	SHO	GR	SV	IP	H	HR	BB	SO	BR/9	ERA	AERA	OAV	OOB	PR	APR	PF	OSB	OCS	FA	E	WPB	DP	FW	PW	BW	BSW	DIF
EAST																												
ATL	**14**	9	408	46	1469.0	1372	120	**451**	**1245**	**11.3**	3.52	**125**	**.247**	**.304**	113	**137**	104	116	44	.980	130	60	143	-.1	**13.4**	.6	-.7	1.9
MON	11	7	433	43	1441.1	**1353**	152	482	1206	11.8	3.78	114	**.247**	.312	70	84	102	156	48	.980	126	56	121	.0	8.2	-2.8	.2	1.4
FLA	8	**13**	417	41	1443.0	1386	**113**	598	1050	12.7	3.95	103	.256	.334	42	19	97	**84**	57	.982	111	61	**187**	1.0	1.9	-.5	-.4	-3.0
NY	10	10	335	41	1440.0	1517	159	532	999	13.1	4.22	95	.272	.337	-1	-36	95	125	33	.974	159	70	163	-1.9	-3.5	2.1	-.5	-6.2
PHI	12	6	387	42	1423.1	1463	160	510	1044	12.7	4.48	96	.267	.331	-42	-26	102	88	44	.981	116	81	145	.7	-2.5	-6.0	.0	-6.3
CENTRAL																												
STL	13	11	413	43	1452.1	1380	173	539	1050	12.1	3.97	105	.251	.319	39	34	99	104	54	.980	125	**51**	139	.2	3.3	.4	.2	3.0
HOU	13	4	371	35	1447.0	1541	154	539	1163	13.4	4.37	89	.274	.342	-24	-88	92	115	55	.978	138	79	130	-.6	-8.6	**6.5**	.8	2.9
CIN	6	8	425	**52**	1443.0	1447	167	591	1089	13.0	4.32	98	.263	.336	-16	-14	100	146	50	.980	121	73	145	.4	-1.4	2.5	.6	-2.1
CHI	10	10	439	34	1456.1	1447	184	546	1027	12.7	4.36	99	.260	.330	-23	-5	103	129	50	**.983**	**104**	61	147	**1.4**	-.5	-5.5	-.4	-.0
PIT	5	7	422	37	1453.1	1602	183	479	1044	13.2	4.61	95	.281	.339	-63	-39	103	185	57	.980	128	72	144	-.0	-3.8	-2.2	.0	-2.0
WEST																												
SD	5	11	411	47	1489.0	1395	138	506	1194	11.8	3.72	107	.248	.313	81	43	94	136	54	.981	118	73	136	.6	4.2	6.4	-.5	-.6
LA	6	9	383	50	1466.1	1378	125	534	1212	12.0	**3.46**	111	.249	.317	**123**	70	92	171	39	.980	125	54	143	.2	6.8	-2.7	.3	4.5
COL	5	4	**447**	34	1422.2	1597	198	624	932	14.5	5.59	93	.285	.361	-218	-48	124	122	55	.976	149	85	167	-1.3	-4.7	.0	**1.0**	7.0
SF	9	8	425	35	1442.1	1520	194	570	997	13.5	4.71	87	.273	.345	-80	-103	97	108	**69**	.978	136	71	165	-.5	-10.1	-.2	-.4	-1.8
TOT	127	117	5716	580	20289.0					12.7	4.21		.262	.330						.979	1786	947	2075					

Batter-Fielder Wins	Batting Average	On-Base Percentage	Slugging Average	On-Base Plus Slugging	Adjusted OPS	Adjusted Batter Runs
Bonds-SF 7.8	Gwynn-SD .353	Sheffield-Fla .465	Burks-Col .639	Sheffield-Fla 1090	Sheffield-Fla 192	Sheffield-Fla 80.4
Caminiti-SD 7.7	Burks-Col .344	Bonds-SF .461	Sheffield-Fla .624	Bonds-SF 1076	Bonds-SF 189	Bagwell-Hou 79.6
Bagwell-Hou 7.1	Piazza-LA .336	Bagwell-Hou .451	Caminiti-SD .621	Burks-Col 1047	Bagwell-Hou 182	Bonds-SF 77.6
Larkin-Cin 6.2	Johnson-NY .333	Piazza-LA .422	Bonds-SF .615	Caminiti-SD 1028	Caminiti-SD 179	Caminiti-SD 64.0
Gilkey-NY 5.8	Grace-Chi .331	Henderson-SD .410	Galarraga-Col .601	Bagwell-Hou 1021	Piazza-LA 171	Piazza-LA 57.7

Runs	Hits	Doubles	Triples	Home Runs	Total Bases	Runs Batted In
Burks-Col 142	Johnson-NY 227	Bagwell-Hou 48	Johnson-NY 21	Galarraga-Col 47	Burks-Col 392	Galarraga-Col 150
Finley-SD 126	Burks-Col 211	Finley-SD 45	Howard-Cin 10	Sheffield-Fla 42	Galarraga-Col 376	Bichette-Col 141
Bonds-SF 122	Grissom-Atl 207	Burks-Col 45	Grissom-Atl 10	Bonds-SF 42	Finley-SD 348	Caminiti-SD 130
Galarraga-Col 119	Grudzielanek-Mon 201	Gilkey-NY 44	Finley-SD 9	Hundley-NY 41	Castilla-Col 345	Bonds-SF 129
Sheffield-Fla 118	Bichette-Col 198	Rodriguez-Mon 42			Caminiti-SD 339	Burks-Col 128

Stolen Bases	Base Stealing Runs	Fielding Runs-Infield	Fielding Runs-Outfield	Wins	Winning Pct.	Complete Games
Young-Col 53	Johnson-NY 6.8	Castilla-Col 33.8	Gilkey-NY 17.5	Smoltz-Atl 24	Smoltz-Atl .750	Schilling-Phi 8
Johnson-NY 50	DeShields-LA 6.7	Young-Col 27.4	Jordan-StL 10.8	A.Benes-StL 18	Martinez-LA .714	Smoltz-Atl 6
DeShields-LA 48	Bonds-SF 6.3	Andrews-Mon 16.2	Merced-Pit 10.0	Ritz-Col 17	Valdes-LA .682	
Bonds-SF 40	Bell-Hou 5.3	Caminiti-SD 14.8	Santangelo-Mon 7.3	Brown-Fla 17	A.Benes-StL .643	
Martin-Pit 38	Lankford-StL 5.3	Gagne-LA 13.8	Mondesi-LA 6.9		Neagle-Pit-Atl .640	

Strikeouts	Fewest BB/Game	Games	Saves	Base Runners/9	Adjusted Relief Runs	Relief Ranking
Smoltz-Atl 276	Maddux-Atl 1.03	Clontz-Atl 81	Worrell-LA 44	Hoffman-SD 8.49	Nen-Fla 19.8	Hoffman-SD 37.1
Nomo-LA 234	Brown-Fla 1.27	Patterson-Chi 79	Brantley-Cin 44	Smoltz-Atl 9.08	Shaw-Cin 19.4	Nen-Fla 27.6
Martinez-Mon 222	Darwin-Pit-Hou 1.48	Shaw-Cin 78	Hoffman-SD 42	Brown-Fla 9.12	Hoffman-SD 18.6	J.Franco-NY 25.4
Fassero-Mon 222	Reynolds-Hou 1.66	Dewey-SF 78	Wohlers-Atl 39	Maddux-Atl 9.40	Ryan-Phi 16.0	Shaw-Cin 24.7
Kile-Hou 219	Tewksbury-SD 1.87	Wohlers-Atl 77	Rojas-Mon 36	Rojas-Mon 9.56	Adams-Chi 15.3	Brantley-Cin 21.2

Innings Pitched	Opponents' Avg.	Opponents' OBP	Earned Run Average	Adjusted ERA	Adjusted Starter Runs	Pitcher Wins
Smoltz-Atl 253.2	Leiter-Fla .202	Smoltz-Atl .260	Brown-Fla 1.89	Brown-Fla 215	Brown-Fla 55.9	**Brown-Fla** 6.9
Maddux-Atl 245.0	Smoltz-Atl .216	Brown-Fla .262	Maddux-Atl 2.72	Maddux-Atl 162	Maddux-Atl 43.3	**Smoltz-Atl** 5.2
Reynolds-Hou 239.0	Nomo-LA .218	Maddux-Atl .264	Leiter-Fla 2.93	Smoltz-Atl 150	Smoltz-Atl 39.6	**Maddux-Atl** 4.8
Navarro-Chi 236.2	Brown-Fla .220	Schilling-Phi .278	Smoltz-Atl 2.94	Glavine-Atl 148	Glavine-Atl 34.3	**Glavine-Atl** 4.3
Glavine-Atl 235.1	Schilling-Phi .223	Reynolds-Hou .288	Glavine-Atl 2.98	Trachsel-Chi 143	Leiter-Fla 30.2	**Hoffman-SD** 3.6

Schott Herself in the Foot

Cincinnati owner Marge Schott was removed from day-to-day operations of the Reds for a second time after telling a reporter that Adolf Hitler was good at first, but then "went too far." Schott also looked petty after the tragic death of umpire John McSherry on Opening Day. McSherry, working the plate for Cincy's game against Montreal, collapsed behind home plate and died from a massive heart attack only minutes into the contest. Schott protested the cancellation of the game, saying, "I feel cheated."

In August the Mets and Padres played a regular-season series in Monterey, Mexico. They were the first big league games played outside the U.S. or Canada. It was the final season for Ozzie Smith, Andre Dawson, and longtime Dodgers skipper Tommy Lasorda. Scott Rolen, Vladimir Guerrero, and Andruw Jones debuted. San Diego third baseman Ken Caminiti, who later admitted he took steroids regularly during the 1996 season, was the overwhelming choice for MVP.

Both Division Series ended quickly. The Braves easily swept the Dodgers, who won the Wild Card despite losing their final three regular-season games to the division-winning Padres. San Diego lost three straight to St. Louis to set up a classic NLCS. Atlanta won the first game, but allowed 5 runs in the seventh inning the next night and squandered leads in Games 3 and 4 to fall behind three games to one. However, Atlanta's bats and arms came alive at the same time as the Braves outscored St. Louis, 32–1, in the final three games. The Braves were denied a second straight World Series title, falling in six games to the Yankees.

1996 American League

TEAM	W	L	T	PCT	GB	HW	HL	R	OR	PA	H	2B	3B	HR	BB	SO	HB	SH	AVG	OBP	SLG	OPS	AOPS	BR	ABR	PF	SB	CS	BSA	BSR
EAST																														
NY	92	70	0	.568		49	31	871	787	6414	1621	293	28	162	632	909	41	41	.288	.360	.436	796	100	17	18	100	96	46	68	5
BAL	88	74	1	.543	4	43	38	949	903	6493	1557	299	29	**257**	645	915	31	61	.274	.350	.472	822	106	50	57	99	76	40	66	3
BOS	85	77	0	.525	7	47	34	928	921	6545	1631	308	31	209	642	1020	33	67	.283	.359	.457	816	102	48	31	102	91	44	67	5
TOR	74	88	0	.457	18	35	46	766	809	6295	1451	302	35	177	529	1105	38	**92**	.259	.331	.420	751	88	-103	-99	100	116	38	75	12
DET	53	109	0	.327	39	27	54	783	1103	6202	1413	257	21	204	546	1268	48	29	.256	.323	.420	743	86	-126	-124	100	87	50	64	2
CENTRAL																														
CLE	99	62	0	.615		**51**	29	952	**769**	6486	**1665**	335	23	218	671	**844**	34	43	**.293**	**.369**	.475	844	**112**	114	120	99	160	50	**76**	**18**
CHI	85	77	0	.525	14.5	44	37	898	794	6497	1586	284	33	195	**701**	927	56	34	.281	.360	.447	807	107	35	82	95	105	41	72	9
MIL	80	82	0	.494	19.5	38	43	894	899	6434	1578	304	40	178	624	986	45	53	.279	.353	.441	794	95	0	-31	104	101	48	68	5
MIN	78	84	0	.481	21.5	39	43	877	900	6397	1633	332	**47**	118	576	958	20	65	.288	.357	.425	782	96	-14	-27	102	143	53	73	13
KC	75	86	0	.466	24	37	43	746	786	6229	1477	286	38	123	529	943	**66**	43	.267	.332	.398	730	83	-136	-134	100	**195**	85	70	13
WEST																														
TEX	90	72	1	.556		50	31	928	799	6494	1622	323	32	221	660	1041	32	31	.284	.358	.469	827	102	69	23	105	83	26	**76**	9
SEA	85	76	0	.528	4.5	43	38	**993**	895	6517	1625	**343**	19	245	670	1052	46	75	.287	.366	**.484**	**850**	**112**	**123**	**124**	100	90	39	70	6
OAK	78	84	0	.481	12	40	41	861	900	6402	1492	283	21	243	640	1114	35	58	.265	.344	.452	796	101	-9	9	98	58	35	62	1
CAL	70	91	0	.435	19.5	43	38	762	943	6320	1571	256	24	192	527	974	45	29	.276	.339	.431	770	93	-67	-69	100	53	39	58	-2
TOT	1133					586	546	12208		89725	21922	4205	421	2742	8592	14056	721	570	.277	.350	.445	795					1454	634	70	98

TEAM	CG	SHO	GR	SV	IP	H	HR	BB	SO	BR/9	ERA	AERA	OAV	OOB	PR	APR	PF	OSB	OCS	FA	E	WPB	DP	FW	PW	BW	BSW	DIF
EAST																												
NY	6	**9**	411	**52**	1440.0	**1469**	**143**	610	1139	13.3	4.65	106	**.265**	.341	55	46	99	120	42	.985	91	72	146	1.2	4.2	1.6	-.2	4.1
BAL	13	1	378	44	1468.2	1604	209	597	1047	13.7	5.14	96	.280	.349	-25	-37	99	135	37	.984	97	52	173	.9	-3.4	5.2	-.4	4.6
BOS	17	5	409	37	1458.0	1606	185	722	**1165**	14.7	4.98	102	.279	.360	1	14	102	147	36	.978	135	74	152	-1.2	1.3	2.8	-.2	1.3
TOR	**19**	7	303	35	1445.2	1476	187	610	1033	13.2	4.57	109	.266	.340	68	69	100	74	41	.982	110	77	187	.2	6.3	-9.0	.5	-4.9
DET	10	4	**426**	22	1432.2	1699	241	784	957	16.1	6.38	79	.296	.384	-221	-209	101	117	54	.978	137	89	157	-1.4	-19.0	-11.3	-.5	4.2
CENTRAL																												
CLE	13	**9**	382	46	1452.1	1530	173	484	1033	**12.7**	**4.34**	**113**	.271	**.331**	**105**	**90**	98	104	52	.980	124	60	156	-.7	**8.2**	10.9	**1.0**	-1.0
CHI	7	4	391	43	1461.0	1529	174	616	1039	13.4	4.52	105	.270	.343	77	39	95	105	55	.982	109	67	145	.2	3.6	7.5	.2	-7.4
MIL	6	4	384	42	1447.1	1570	213	635	846	14.1	5.14	101	.278	.354	-23	8	104	96	40	.978	134	65	180	-1.2	.7	-2.8	-.2	2.5
MIN	13	5	387	31	1439.2	1561	233	581	959	13.6	5.28	97	.277	.346	-46	-26	102	84	42	.984	94	60	142	1.1	-2.4	-2.5	.5	.2
KC	17	8	322	35	1450.0	1563	176	**460**	926	12.9	4.55	110	.277	.335	71	73	100	69	42	.982	111	67	184	.0	6.7	-12.2	.5	-.6
WEST																												
TEX	**19**	6	347	43	1449.1	1569	168	582	976	13.6	4.65	**113**	.278	.347	55	**90**	105	**62**	**56**	**.986**	**87**	48	150	**1.5**	**8.2**	2.1	.2	-3.0
SEA	4	4	403	34	1431.2	1562	216	605	1000	14.0	5.21	95	.279	.353	-35	-43	99	78	42	.982	110	**45**	155	.1	-3.9	**11.3**	-.0	-2.9
OAK	7	5	418	34	1456.1	1638	205	644	884	14.4	5.20	95	.287	.362	-33	-45	99	117	41	.984	103	71	**195**	.6	-4.1	.8	-.5	.3
CAL	12	8	383	38	1439.0	1546	219	662	1052	14.3	5.30	94	.275	.357	-49	-47	100	146	54	.979	128	92	156	-.9	-4.3	-6.3	-.8	1.8
TOT	163	79	5344	536	20271.2					13.9	4.99		.277	.350						.982	1570	939	2278					

Batter-Fielder Wins	Batting Average	On-Base Percentage	Slugging Average	On-Base Plus Slugging	Adjusted OPS	Adjusted Batter Runs
Alomar-Bal..........6.1	Rodriguez-Sea 358	McGwire-Oak..............467	McGwire-Oak 730	McGwire-Oak 1198	McGwire-Oak 201	F.Thomas-Chi 72.5
Rodriguez-Sea....5.7	F.Thomas-Chi 349	E.Martinez-Sea 464	Gonzalez-Tex 643	F.Thomas-Chi 1085	F.Thomas-Chi 181	McGwire-Oak 72.0
Thome-Cle 5.4	Molitor-Min 341	F.Thomas-Chi..............459	Anderson-Bal 637	Thome-Cle..........1062	Thome-Cle...........166	E.Martinez-Sea ..60.7
McGwire-Oak......5.0	Knoblauch-Min 341	Thome-Cle..................450	Rodriguez-Sea 631	E.Martinez-Sea ..1059	E.Martinez-Sea 166	Thome-Cle 57.9
F.Thomas-Chi......4.9	Greer-Tex 332	Knoblauch-Min............448	Griffey-Sea 628	Rodriguez-Sea....1045	Rodriguez-Sea......160	Rodriguez-Sea ..56.6

Runs	Hits	Doubles	Triples	Home Runs	Total Bases	Runs Batted In
Rodriguez-Sea......141	Molitor-Min............225	Rodriguez-Sea 54	Knoblauch-Min 14	McGwire-Oak 52	Rodriguez-Sea......379	Belle-Cle..............148
Knoblauch-Min 140	Rodriguez-Sea......215	E.Martinez-Sea.............52	Vina-Mil 10	Anderson-Bal..........50	Belle-Cle 375	Gonzalez-Tex 144
Lofton-Cle 132	Lofton-Cle 210	Rodriguez-Tex................47		Griffey-Sea 49	Vaughn-Bos...........370	Vaughn-Bos 143
Alomar-Bal............132	Vaughn-Bos..........207	Cordova-Min 46		Belle-Cle 48	Anderson-Bal........369	Palmeiro-Bal........142
Griffey-Sea 125	Knoblauch-Min 197	Cirillo-Mil.......................46		Gonzalez-Tex..........47	Gonzalez-Tex........348	Griffey-Sea 140

Stolen Bases	Base Stealing Runs	Fielding Runs-Infield	Fielding Runs-Outfield	Wins	Winning Pct.	Complete Games
Lofton-Cle 75	Lofton-Cle............10.6	Gonzalez-Tor 28.4	Becker-Min 17.2	Pettitte-NY 21	Nagy-Cle 773	Hentgen-Tor 10
Goodwin-KC 66	Nixon-Tor 7.3	McLemore-Tex............23.7	Phillips-Chi 9.4	Hentgen-Tor...............20	Pettitte-NY 724	Pavlik-Tex 7
Nixon-Tor 54	Goodwin-KC 6.8	Fryman-Det 22.6	Green-Tor 7.8	Mussina-Bal............19	Hentgen-Tor 667	Hill-Tex 7
Knoblauch-Min 45	Durham-Chi 5.2	Alomar-Bal...................22.0	Mieske-Mil 7.0	Nagy-Cle 17	Pavlik-Tex 652	
Vizquel-Cle 35	Knoblauch-Min 5.0	Vina-Mil 18.2	Bragg-Sea-Bos......6.1		Mussina-Bal 633	

Strikeouts	Fewest BB/Game	Games	Saves	Base Runners/9	Adjusted Relief Runs	Relief Ranking
Clemens-Bos........257	Haney-KC 2.01	Myers-Det 83	Wetteland-NY 43	Percival-Cal 8.64	M.Rivera-NY........35.2	Hernandez-Chi ..54.6
Finley-Cal 215	Wells-Bal 2.05	Guardado-Min..................83	Mesa-Cle 39	M.Rivera-NY..........9.11	Hernandez-Chi 27.3	M.Rivera-NY 35.5
Appier-KC 207	Radke-Min 2.21	Stanton-Bos-Tex............81	Hernandez-Chi 38	Guzman-Tor 10.45	Plunk-Cle 22.6	Slocumb-Bos......34.1
Mussina-Bal..........204	Nagy-Cle 2.47	Slocumb-Bos 75	Percival-Cal 36	Wetteland-NY 10.60	Percival-Cal 22.6	Wetteland-NY 28.4
Fernandez-Chi......200	Fernandez-Chi 2.51		Fetters-Mil 32	Cone-NY............10.75	James-Cal 20.9	Percival-Cal........26.4

Innings Pitched	Opponents' Avg.	Opponents' OBP	Earned Run Average	Adjusted ERA	Adjusted Starter Runs	Pitcher Wins
Hentgen-Tor 265.2	Guzman-Tor 228	Guzman-Tor.................289	Guzman-Tor 2.93	Guzman-Tor..........171	Hentgen-Tor 52.6	**Hentgen-Tor** 5.2
Fernandez-Chi ..258.0	Clemens-Bos 237	Radke-Min 302	Hentgen-Tor 3.22	Hentgen-Tor..........156	Guzman-Tor 43.0	**Hernandez-Chi** ..5.1
Hill-Tex 250.2	Hentgen-Tor 241	Nagy-Cle 306	Nagy-Cle 3.41	Hill-Tex..................145	Hill-Tex 41.9	**Hill-Tex**.................3.8
Mussina-Bal 243.1	Appier-KC 245	Fernandez-Chi.............307	Fernandez-Chi 3.45	Nagy-Cle 144	Clemens-Bos 40.7	**Guzman-Tor** 3.8
Clemens-Bos 242.2	Fernandez-Chi 253	Hentgen-Tor.................308	Appier-KC 3.62	Clemens-Bos........140	Nagy-Cle 39.0	**Appier-KC** 3.5

The Yankee Ride Again

Home runs were hit at a record pace; the 2,742 long balls at the rate of 1.21 per team per game remain AL marks. Oakland's Mark McGwire and Baltimore's Brady Anderson, who never before or after surpassed 24 homers, each surpassed 50. It was the first season since 1961 that two players had reached that plateau.

Baltimore's Roberto Alomar spat in the face of umpire John Hirschbeck during a heated argument in the final series of the year. Although Alomar was suspended, umps were incensed that Alomar was allowed to play in the postseason. Mel Allen, the longtime radio voice of the Yankees, and narrator of *This Week in Baseball*, died, as did former A's owner Charlie Finley. Nomar Garciaparra made his debut.

Both Division Series were decided in four games. Despite owning the league's best record, Cleveland was thwarted by Orioles second baseman Roberto Alomar, who tied Game 4 in the ninth and won it with a homer in the 12th. Texas, playing in the post-season for the first time, won Game 1 of the other Division Series and got 5 home runs from Juan Gonzalez, but the Yankees took three close games. New York then cruised past Baltimore in five games in the ALCS.

The Yankees appeared dead after scoring only once against Atlanta in two World Series losses at Yankee Stadium. New York won Game 3, but fell behind 6–0 to the Braves in Game 4, and many conceded Atlanta its second straight world championship. The Yankees, however, mounted a fierce comeback, tying the game on a Jim Leyritz homer and winning in 10 innings. Momentum shifted, and the Yankees captured their first Series title since 1978.

1997 National League

TEAM	W	L	T	PCT	GB	HW	HL	R	OR	PA	H	2B	3B	HR	BB	SO	HB	SH	AVG	OBP	SLG	OPS	AOPS	BR	ABR	PF	SB	CS	BSA	BSR
EAST																														
ATL	101	61	0	.623		50	31	791	**581**	6312	1490	268	37	174	597	1160	83	52	.270	.343	.426	769	104	56	40	102	108	58	65	3
FLA	92	70	0	.568	9	**52**	29	740	669	6299	1410	272	28	136	**686**	**1074**	71	61	.259	.346	.395	741	104	14	51	95	115	58	66	5
NY	88	74	0	.543	13	50	31	777	709	6248	1448	274	28	153	550	1029	58	57	.262	.332	.405	737	102	-11	17	96	97	74	57	-5
MON	78	84	0	.481	23	45	36	691	740	6131	1423	**339**	34	172	420	1084	72	73	.258	.316	.425	741	98	-22	-18	100	75	46	62	0
PHI	68	94	0	.420	33	38	43	668	840	6126	1390	290	35	116	519	1032	74	40	.255	.322	.385	707	90	-72	-70	100	92	56	62	1
CENTRAL																														
HOU	84	78	0	.519		46	35	777	660	6362	1427	314	40	133	633	1085	74	**100**	.259	.344	.403	747	105	25	57	96	171	74	70	12
PIT	79	83	0	.488	5	43	38	725	760	6200	1440	291	**52**	129	481	1161	77	92	.262	.329	.404	733	95	-25	-36	102	160	50	**76**	**18**
CIN	76	86	0	.469	8	40	41	651	764	6152	1386	269	27	142	518	1113	75	45	.253	.321	.389	710	89	-73	-80	101	**190**	67	74	**18**
STL	73	89	0	.451	11	41	40	689	708	6211	1409	269	39	144	543	1191	58	42	.255	.324	.396	720	94	-52	-44	99	164	60	73	15
CHI	68	94	0	.420	16	42	39	687	759	6095	1444	269	39	127	451	1003	83	34	.263	.321	.396	717	90	-64	-79	102	116	60	66	5
WEST																														
SF	90	72	0	.556		48	33	784	793	6296	1415	266	37	172	642	1120	64	46	.258	.337	.414	751	104	22	45	97	121	49	71	9
LA	88	74	0	.543	2	47	34	742	645	6216	1488	242	33	174	498	1079	**105**	33	.268	.330	.418	748	108	-1	62	92	131	64	67	6
COL	83	79	0	.512	7	47	34	**923**	908	6336	**1611**	269	40	**239**	562	1060	73	63	**.288**	**.357**	**.478**	**835**	100	**180**	6	123	137	65	68	7
SD	76	86	0	.469	14	39	42	795	891	6369	1519	275	16	152	604	1129	63	35	.271	.342	.407	749	**109**	22	**85**	93	140	60	70	10
TOT	1134					628	506	10440		87353	20300	3907	485	2163	7704	15320	773	1030	.263	.333	.410	744					1817	841	68	105

TEAM	CG	SHO	GR	SV	IP	H	HR	BB	SO	BR/9	ERA	AERA	OAV	OOB	PR	APR	PF	OSB	OCS	FA	E	WPB	DP	FW	PW	BW	BSW	DIF
EAST																												
ATL	21	**17**	374	37	1465.2	**1319**	**111**	**450**	1196	**11.1**	**3.18**	**132**	**.241**	**.301**	**166**	**166**	100	124	54	.982	114	49	136	.3	**16.3**	3.9	-.4	-.2
FLA	12	10	404	39	1446.2	1353	131	639	1188	12.8	3.83	105	.250	.334	60	34	96	95	70	.981	116	48	167	.2	3.3	5.0	-.2	2.7
NY	7	8	376	**49**	1459.1	1452	160	504	982	12.4	3.95	102	.262	.326	41	14	96	106	44	.981	120	57	165	-.0	1.4	1.7	-1.2	5.2
MON	**27**	14	390	37	1447.0	1365	149	557	1138	12.3	4.14	101	.250	.325	10	9	100	192	42	.979	132	65	150	-.7	.9	-1.8	-.7	-.7
PHI	13	7	409	35	1420.1	1441	171	616	1209	13.4	4.85	88	.265	.342	-102	-95	101	107	57	.982	108	89	134	.7	-9.4	-6.9	-.6	3.2
CENTRAL																												
HOU	16	12	354	37	1459.0	1379	134	511	1138	12.0	3.66	109	.251	.319	87	56	95	**92**	57	.979	131	52	169	-.7	5.5	5.6	.4	-7.9
PIT	6	8	451	41	1436.0	1503	143	560	1080	13.3	4.28	100	.271	.342	-13	1	102	109	66	.979	131	72	149	-.7	.0	-3.5	**1.0**	1.1
CIN	5	8	423	**49**	1449.0	1408	173	558	1159	12.7	4.41	97	.255	.330	-34	-23	102	139	48	.982	**106**	77	129	**.8**	-2.3	-7.9	**1.0**	3.3
STL	5	3	399	39	1455.2	1422	124	536	1130	12.5	3.88	107	.259	.328	52	44	99	134	66	.980	123	66	156	-.2	4.3	-4.3	.7	-8.5
CHI	6	4	441	37	1429.0	1451	185	590	1072	13.1	4.44	97	.266	.339	-38	-22	102	146	59	.981	112	51	117	.5	-2.2	-7.8	-.2	-3.3
WEST																												
SF	5	9	**481**	45	1446.0	1494	160	578	1044	13.1	4.39	93	.270	.340	-31	-52	97	108	73	.980	125	57	157	-.3	-5.1	4.4	.1	9.8
LA	6	6	412	45	1459.1	1325	163	546	**1232**	11.8	3.62	106	**.241**	.313	94	41	92	118	58	.981	116	**47**	104	.2	4.0	6.1	-.2	-3.2
COL	9	5	426	38	1432.2	1697	196	566	870	14.6	5.25	98	.300	.367	-167	-11	123	130	54	**.983**	111	55	**202**	.5	-1.1	.6	-.0	2.0
SD	5	2	426	43	1450.0	1581	172	596	1059	13.9	4.98	78	.280	.352	-125	-192	92	171	**75**	.979	132	66	132	-.7	-18.9	**8.4**	.2	6.0
TOT	143	113	5766	571	20255.2					12.8	4.20		.263	.333						.981	1677	851	2067					

Batter-Fielder Wins	Batting Average	On-Base Percentage	Slugging Average	On-Base Plus Slugging	Adjusted OPS	Adjusted Batter Runs
Biggio-Hou 8.3	Gwynn-SD 372	Walker-Col 452	Walker-Col 720	Walker-Col..........1172	Piazza-LA 191	Piazza-LA 75.0
Piazza-LA 7.8	Walker-Col 366	Bonds-SF.....................446	Piazza-LA.............638	Piazza-LA 1070	Bonds-SF 173	Bagwell-Hou 66.1
Bonds-SF 6.3	Piazza-LA 362	Piazza-LA 431	Bagwell-Hou 592	Bonds-SF 1031	Bagwell-Hou 171	Bonds-SF 66.0
Bagwell-Hou 6.0	Lofton-Atl 333	Bagwell-Hou 425	Galarraga-Col.......585	Bagwell-Hou 1017	Walker-Col............164	Walker-Col..........56.1
Caminiti-SD 5.2	Joyner-SD.............327	Sheffield-Fla 424	Lankford-StL.........585	Lankford-StL 996	Gwynn-SD 162	Gwynn-SD..........53.9

Runs	Hits	Doubles	Triples	Home Runs	Total Bases	Runs Batted In
Biggio-Hou............146	Gwynn-SD 220	Grudzielanek-Mon 54	DeShields-StL 14	Walker-Col..............49	Walker-Col 409	Galarraga-Col......140
Walker-Col............143	Walker-Col 208	Gwynn-SD 49	Perez-Col................10	Bagwell-Hou 43	Piazza-LA 355	Bagwell-Hou........135
Bonds-SF 123	Piazza-LA 201	Walker-Col 46	Womack-Pit 9	Galarraga-Col 41	Galarraga-Col 351	Walker-Col 130
Galarraga-Col 120		Lansing-Mon..................45	Randa-Pit..................9		Castilla-Col 335	Piazza-LA............124
Bagwell-Hou 109		Mondesi-LA 42	Guerrero-LA 9		Bagwell-Hou 335	Kent-SF 121

Stolen Bases	Base Stealing Runs	Fielding Runs-Infield	Fielding Runs-Outfield	Wins	Winning Pct.	Complete Games
Womack-Pit 60	Womack-Pit 10.8	Young-Col 25.5	A.Jones-Atl 17.3	Neagle-Atl 20	Maddux-Atl 826	Martinez-Mon........13
D.Sanders-Cin 56	D.Sanders-Cin 7.8	Biggio-Hou..................25.4	Glanville-Chi 9.2	Maddux-Atl 19	Neagle-Atl.............800	Perez-Mon 8
DeShields-StL 55	DeShields-StL 7.2	Weiss-Col 19.0	Mondesi-LA 8.6	Kile-Hou.................19	Estes-SF...............792	Smoltz-Atl................7
Biggio-Hou.............47	Biggio-Hou 6.8	Randa-Pit....................18.6	Sosa-Chi................7.4	Estes-SF 19	Kile-Hou 731	Schilling-Phi 7
Young-Col-LA 45	Bonds-SF 5.3	Rolen-Phi....................18.5	Finley-SD 5.8		Martinez-Mon 680	Hampton-Hou..........7

Strikeouts	Fewest BB/Game	Games	Saves	Base Runners/9	Adjusted Relief Runs	Relief Ranking
Schilling-Phi..........319	Maddux-Atl 77	Tavarez-SF 89	Shaw-Cin 42	Martinez-Mon 8.73	Shaw-Cin 20.0	Shaw-Cin............27.4
Martinez-Mon 305	Reed-NY..............1.34	Belinda-Cin 84	Hoffman-SD...........37	Maddux-Atl 8.74	Frascatore-StL 15.0	Hoffman-SD 24.7
Smoltz-Atl 241	Neagle-Atl............1.89	Shaw-Cin 78	Beck-SF..................37	Shaw-Cin 8.75	Osuna-LA 13.2	J.Franco-NY 21.4
Nomo-LA 233	Schilling-Phi 2.05	Rojas-Chi-NY 77	J.Franco-NY............36	Hoffman-SD 9.18	Martin-Hou 13.2	McMichael-NY....18.6
	Perez-Mon 2.09		Eckersley-StL 36	Schilling-Phi 9.59	Hoffman-SD 12.8	Wagner-Hou 18.1

Innings Pitched	Opponents' Avg.	Opponents' OBP	Earned Run Average	Adjusted ERA	Adjusted Starter Runs	Pitcher Wins
Smoltz-Atl..........256.0	Martinez-Mon 184	Martinez-Mon 249	Martinez-Mon 1.90	Martinez-Mon 221	Martinez-Mon 58.0	**Martinez-Mon** 5.9
Kile-Hou..............255.2	Park-LA................213	Maddux-Atl 256	Maddux-Atl 2.20	Maddux-Atl 191	Maddux-Atl 54.4	**Maddux-Atl** 5.3
Schilling-Phi 254.1	Estes-SF..............223	Schilling-Phi................271	Kile-Hou 2.57	Kile-Hou................156	Kile-Hou 39.9	**Kile-Hou** 4.0
Martinez-Mon 241.1	Schilling-Phi 224	Reed-NY 272	Valdes-LA 2.65	Brown-Fla 150	Brown-Fla 37.0	**Smoltz-Atl** 3.9
Glavine-Atl 240.0	Kile-Hou 225	Neagle-Atl 277	Brown-Fla 2.69	Valdes-LA 145	Glavine-Atl 34.3	**Brown-Fla** 3.8

Wild Things

Acting Commissioner Bud Selig failed to pass his radical realignment plan. Several clubs were adamantly against the idea, which would have created divisions based solely on geographic location. On April 15, the 50th anniversary of Jackie Robinson's momentous debut, baseball permanently retired Robinson's uniform number 42 during a Dodgers-Mets game at Shea Stadium. Bud Selig's surprise announcement upstaged President Bill Clinton, who spoke during a break in the fifth inning.

The Braves opened Turner Field, the rebuilt former outdoor track stadium used in the 1996 Olympics. Outfielders Brett Butler and Eric Davis returned to action after cancer treatments, while pitcher Pete Harnisch recovered from clinical depression. Butler, Ryne Sandberg, and Fernando Valenzuela retired. Former Phillies star Richie Ashburn and Curt Flood, whose holdout ultimately led to players gaining free agent rights, died.

Atlanta had the best record in baseball and was expecting another trip to the Fall Classic following a dominating NLDS sweep of Houston. But the Marlins, who swept San Francisco in the other Division Series, pounded Greg Maddux for 5 runs early in NLCS opener and the Braves never really recovered. Livian Hernandez won once in relief and fanned 15 as a starter—aided by a liberal strike zone—as Florida, in just its fifth season of existence, headed to the World Series.

Six lackluster Series games were shine outshone by Game 7. Cleveland led by a run heading into the ninth, but Craig Counsell's sacrifice fly tied the game. Edgar Renteria singled with the bases loaded in the bottom of the 11th to make the Marlins the first Wild Card world champion. Victory celebrations would be short and sweet, however, as the Marlins quickly dismantled their expensive team simply to cut payroll.

1997 American League

TEAM	W	L	T	PCT	GB	HW	HL	R	OR	PA	H	2B	3B	HR	BB	SO	HB	SH	AVG	OBP	SLG	OPS	AOPS	BR	ABR	PF	SB	CS	BSA	BSR
EAST																														
BAL	98	64	0	.605		46	35	812	**681**	6340	1498	264	22	196	586	952	46	**65**	.268	.341	.429	770	103	5	30	97	63	26	71	5
NY	96	66	0	.593	2	**47**	33	891	688	6527	1636	325	23	161	**676**	954	34	37	.287	**.362**	.436	798	108	85	93	99	99	58	63	1
DET	79	83	0	.488	19	42	39	784	790	6189	1415	268	32	176	578	1164	34	49	.258	.332	.415	747	95	-48	-41	99	**161**	72	69	10
BOS	78	84	0	.481	20	39	42	851	857	6430	**1684**	**373**	32	185	514	1044	21	59	**.291**	.352	.463	815	109	100	83	102	68	48	59	-2
TOR	76	86	0	.469	22	42	39	654	694	6109	1333	275	**41**	147	487	1138	38	59	.244	.310	.389	699	81	-154	-157	101	134	50	**73**	**12**
CENTRAL																														
CLE	86	75	0	.534		44	37	868	815	6304	1589	301	22	220	617	955	45	37	.286	.358	.467	825	109	120	89	104	118	59	67	5
CHI	80	81	0	.497	6	45	36	779	833	6200	1498	260	28	158	569	**901**	47	33	.273	.341	.417	758	101	-17	16	96	106	52	67	5
MIL	78	83	0	.484	8	**47**	33	681	742	6096	1415	294	27	135	494	967	**48**	58	.260	.325	.398	723	87	-93	-98	101	103	55	65	3
MIN	68	94	0	.420	18.5	35	46	772	861	6265	1522	305	40	132	495	1121	20	60	.270	.333	.409	742	92	-57	-66	101	151	52	74	15
KC	67	94	0	.416	19	33	47	747	820	6295	1478	256	35	158	561	1061	51	42	.264	.333	.407	740	90	-62	-79	102	130	66	66	6
WEST																														
SEA	90	72	0	.556		45	36	**925**	833	6384	1574	312	21	**264**	626	1110	46	49	.280	.355	**.485**	**840**	**118**	**143**	**153**	99	89	40	69	6
ANA	84	78	0	.519	6	46	36	829	794	6387	1531	279	25	161	617	953	40	45	.272	.346	.416	762	98	-4	-2	100	126	72	64	3
TEX	77	85	0	.475	13	39	42	807	823	6265	1547	311	27	187	500	1116	28	34	.274	.334	.438	772	95	-4	-44	105	72	37	66	3
OAK	65	97	0	.401	25	35	46	764	946	6369	1451	274	23	197	642	1181	49	49	.260	.339	.423	762	100	-14	0	98	71	36	66	3
TOT	1132					585	547	11164		88160	21171	4097	398	2477	7962	14617	676	547	.271	.340	.428	768					1491	723	67	75

TEAM	CG	SHO	GR	SV	IP	H	HR	BB	SO	BR/9	ERA	AERA	OAV	OOB	PR	APR	PF	OSB	OCS	FA	E	WPB	DP	FW	PW	BW	BSW	DIF
EAST																												
BAL	8	10	400	**59**	1461.0	**1404**	164	563	1139	**12.3**	3.91	112	**.253**	**.323**	106	82	96	149	50	.984	97	**50**	148	.8	7.8	2.9	-.0	5.5
NY	11	10	368	51	1467.2	1463	**144**	532	1165	12.5	**3.84**	116	.260	.327	**118**	102	97	111	47	.983	104	81	156	.5	9.7	8.8	-.4	-3.6
DET	13	8	417	42	1445.2	1476	178	552	982	12.9	4.56	101	.266	.334	1	4	100	130	48	**.985**	92	62	146	**1.1**	.4	-3.9	.4	-.0
BOS	7	4	417	40	1451.2	1569	149	611	987	13.9	4.85	96	.277	.351	-46	-34	102	171	53	.978	135	87	**179**	-1.3	-3.2	7.9	-.7	-5.7
TOR	**19**	**16**	336	34	1442.2	1453	167	497	1150	12.4	3.92	**117**	.263	.326	104	**107**	101	77	64	.984	94	65	150	1.0	**10.2**	-14.9	.6	-1.9
CENTRAL																												
CLE	4	3	428	39	1425.2	1528	181	575	1036	13.6	4.73	99	.276	.347	-26	-6	103	126	54	.983	106	67	159	.3	-.6	8.5	-.0	-2.7
CHI	6	7	389	52	1422.1	1505	175	575	961	13.4	4.73	93	.271	.340	-27	-58	96	119	52	.978	127	87	131	-.9	-5.5	1.5	-.0	4.4
MIL	6	8	367	44	1427.1	1419	177	542	1016	12.7	4.22	109	.261	.333	55	62	101	106	52	.980	121	57	171	-.5	5.9	-9.3	-.2	1.7
MIN	10	4	390	30	1434.0	1596	187	**495**	908	13.3	5.00	93	.283	.342	-69	-54	102	85	46	.983	101	80	170	.6	-5.1	-6.3	**.9**	-3.1
KC	11	5	393	29	1443.0	1530	186	531	961	13.2	4.70	100	.274	.340	-21	2	103	72	42	**.985**	**91**	76	168	**1.1**	.2	-7.5	.0	-7.4
WEST																												
SEA	9	8	392	38	1447.2	1500	192	598	**1207**	13.5	4.78	94	.267	.342	-35	-47	99	99	**66**	.979	126	60	143	-.8	-4.5	**14.6**	.0	-.4
ANA	9	5	400	39	1454.2	1506	202	605	1050	13.4	4.52	101	.269	.343	8	8	100	101	63	.980	123	76	140	-.6	.8	-.2	-.2	3.3
TEX	8	9	382	33	1429.2	1598	169	541	925	13.7	4.69	102	.283	.347	-20	15	105	**60**	56	.980	121	61	155	-.5	1.4	-4.2	-.2	-.5
OAK	2	1	**480**	38	1445.1	1734	197	642	953	15.2	5.48	83	.301	.372	-147	-155	99	131	48	.980	122	56	170	-.6	-14.7	.0	-.2	-.5
TOT	123	98	5559	568	20198.1					13.3	4.56		.271	.340						.982	1560	965	2186					

Batter-Fielder Wins	Batting Average	On-Base Percentage	Slugging Average	On-Base Plus Slugging	Adjusted OPS	Adjusted Batter Runs
Griffey-Sea 6.0	F.Thomas-Chi .347	F.Thomas-Chi .456	Griffey-Sea .646	F.Thomas-Chi 1067	F.Thomas-Chi 184	F.Thomas-Chi 73.1
F.Thomas-Chi 5.1	E.Martinez-Sea .330	E.Martinez-Sea .456	F.Thomas-Chi .611	Griffey-Sea 1028	Griffey-Sea 165	E.Martinez-Sea 60.7
E.Martinez-Sea 4.6	Justice-Cle .329	Thome-Cle .423	Justice-Cle .596	Justice-Cle 1013	E.Martinez-Sea 164	Griffey-Sea 57.4
Valentin-Bos 4.0	Williams-NY .328	Vaughn-Bos .420	Gonzalez-Tex .589	E.Martinez-Sea 1009	Justice-Cle 156	Thome-Cle 44.7
Rodriguez-Tex 4.0	Ramirez-Cle .328	Justice-Cle .418	Thome-Cle .579	Thome-Cle 1001	Thome-Cle 154	Justice-Cle 43.5

Runs	Hits	Doubles	Triples	Home Runs	Total Bases	Runs Batted In
Griffey-Sea 125	Garciaparra-Bos 209	Valentin-Bos 47	Garciaparra-Bos 11	Griffey-Sea 56	Griffey-Sea 393	Griffey-Sea 147
Garciaparra-Bos 122	Greer-Tex 193	Cirillo-Mil 46	Knoblauch-Min 10	Martinez-NY 44	Garciaparra-Bos 365	Martinez-NY 141
Knoblauch-Min 117	Jeter-NY 190	Belle-Chi 45	Damon-KC 8	Gonzalez-Tex 42	Martinez-NY 343	Gonzalez-Tex 131
Jeter-NY 116	Anderson-Ana 189	Garciaparra-Bos 44	Burnitz-Mil 8	Thome-Cle 40	F.Thomas-Chi 324	Salmon-Ana 129
	Rodriguez-Tex 187			Buhner-Sea 40	Greer-Tex 319	F.Thomas-Chi 125

Stolen Bases	Base Stealing Runs	Fielding Runs-Infield	Fielding Runs-Outfield	Wins	Winning Pct.	Complete Games
Hunter-Det 74	Knoblauch-Min 10.1	Cirillo-Mil 24.0	Cameron-Chi 13.0	Clemens-Tor 21	Johnson-Sea .833	Hentgen-Tor 9
Knoblauch-Min 62	Hunter-Det 10.0	King-KC 21.2	Salmon-Ana 10.1	Radke-Min 20	Moyer-Sea .773	Clemens-Tor 9
Goodwin-KC-Tex 50	Nixon-Tor 6.8	Brosius-Oak 18.8	Anderson-Ana 9.9	Johnson-Sea 20	Clemens-Tor .750	Wells-NY 5
Nixon-Tor 47	Goodwin-KC-Tex 5.4	Gil-Tex 18.0	Higginson-Det 8.6	Pettitte-NY 18	Pettitte-NY .720	Tewksbury-Min 5
Vizquel-Cle 43	Vizquel-Cle 5.3	Valentin-Bos 17.7	Edmonds-Ana 7.4	Moyer-Sea 17	Erickson-Bal .696	Johnson-Sea 5

Strikeouts	Fewest BB/Game	Games	Saves	Base Runners/9	Adjusted Relief Runs	Relief Ranking
Clemens-Tor 292	Burkett-Tex 1.43	Myers-Det 88	Myers-Bal 45	Jones-Mil 8.29	Quantrill-Tor 24.0	Jones-Mil 45.9
Johnson-Sea 291	Tewksbury-Min 1.65	Groom-Oak 78	Rivera-NY 43	Wetteland-Tex 8.86	Jones-Mil 23.0	Rivera-NY 41.5
Cone-NY 222	Radke-Min 1.80	Quantrill-Tor 77	Jones-Mil 36	Clemens-Tor 9.68	Rivera-NY 20.8	Myers-Bal 38.6
Mussina-Bal 218	Wells-NY 1.86	Nelson-NY 77	Wetteland-Tex 31	Johnson-Sea 9.89	Wickman-Mil 19.9	Wetteland-Tex 37.1
Appier-KC 196	Moyer-Sea 2.05	Slocumb-Bos-Sea 76	Jones-Det 31	Rhodes-Bal 9.91	Myers-Bal 19.3	Quantrill-Tor 34.3

Innings Pitched	Opponents' Avg.	Opponents' OBP	Earned Run Average	Adjusted ERA	Adjusted Starter Runs	Pitcher Wins
Hentgen-Tor 264.0	Johnson-Sea .194	Clemens-Tor .273	Clemens-Tor 2.05	Clemens-Tor 225	Clemens-Tor 74.9	**Clemens-Tor** 7.9
Clemens-Tor 264.0	Clemens-Tor .213	Johnson-Sea .277	Johnson-Sea 2.28	Johnson-Sea 197	Johnson-Sea 52.6	**Johnson-Sea** 5.6
Pettitte-NY 240.1	Cone-NY .218	Mussina-Bal .282	Cone-NY 2.82	Cone-NY 158	Pettitte-NY 42.3	**Jones-Mil** 4.5
Radke-Min 239.2	Gordon-Bos .226	Thompson-Det .289	Pettitte-NY 2.88	Pettitte-NY 154	Thompson-Det 38.2	**Pettitte-NY** 4.1
Appier-KC 235.2	Thompson-Det .233	Radke-Min .293	Thompson-Det 3.02	Thompson-Det 152	Cone-NY 36.4	**Rivera-NY** 4.1

Interleague Affair

Interleague play began during the regular season for the first time in history. Pushed for by acting commissioner Bud Selig, it was decried by purists and led to some dramatic differences in schedule for competing teams. From the start, interest and attendance was high for some matchups and less for others. New York and Chicago enthusiasts have sold out every Mets-Yankees and Cubs-White Sox game to date.

Before the season Cleveland outfielder Albert Belle jumped to a division rival and became the first eight-figure player. He signed as a free agent with the White Sox for $11 million per year (plus an escape clause if he did not remain among the top three MLB players in salary). A midseason trade sent Oakland slugger Mark McGwire to St. Louis. McGwire hit a combined 58 home runs, making him the second player to slug at least 50 in consecutive seasons after Babe Ruth in 1927–28; ironically, McGwire did not lead either league in homers. Bartolo Colon, Magglio Ordonez, and Miguel Tejada all debuted.

Cleveland, Central champs for the third straight season, had a fierce battle with the Wild Card Yankees in the ALDS. Facing elimination in Game 4, Cleveland rallied for a run in the eighth and another in the ninth to survive. The Indians nearly blew an early four-run lead in Game 5, but held on to advance. Baltimore shut down Seattle's potent offense to win the other ALDS in four games. Though the O's blanked Cleveland in the ALCS opener, Cleveland scored the winning run in the eighth inning or later four times to take the series in six. The Indians came within two outs of winning their first World Series title since 1948, but dropped a heartbreaker to Florida in Game 7.

1998 National League

TEAM	W	L	T	PCT	GB	HW	HL	R	OR	PA	H	2B	3B	HR	BB	SO	HB	SH	AVG	OBP	SLG	OPS	AOPS	BR	ABR	PF	SB	CS	BSA	BSR
EAST																														
ATL	106	56	0	.654		**56**	25	826	**581**	6215	1489	297	26	215	548	1062	76	61	.272	.342	**.453**	**795**	113	104	104	100	98	43	70	7
NY	88	74	0	.543	18	47	34	706	645	6255	1425	289	24	136	572	1049	88	37	.259	.330	.394	724	97	-29	-17	98	62	46	57	-2
PHI	75	87	0	.463	31	40	41	713	808	6300	1482	286	36	126	508	1080	65	45	.264	.326	.395	721	93	-38	-48	101	97	45	68	6
MON	65	97	0	.401	41	39	42	644	783	6041	1348	280	32	147	439	1058	87	60	.249	.310	.394	704	90	-86	-76	98	91	46	66	4
FLA	54	108	0	.333	52	31	50	667	923	6227	1381	277	36	114	525	1120	70	45	.248	.317	.373	690	91	-107	-73	95	115	57	67	5
CENTRAL																														
HOU	102	60	0	.630		55	26	**874**	620	6441	**1578**	**326**	28	166	621	1122	58	**72**	**.280**	**.356**	.436	792	**116**	**121**	**147**	97	**155**	51	75	**16**
CHI	90	73	0	.552	12.5	51	31	831	792	6393	1494	250	**34**	212	601	1223	67	39	.264	.337	.433	770	103	56	29	103	65	44	60	-1
STL	83	79	1	.512	19	48	34	810	782	6413	1444	292	30	**223**	676	1179	68	42	.258	.341	.441	782	111	84	93	99	133	41	**76**	15
CIN	77	85	0	.475	25	39	42	750	760	6268	1441	298	28	138	608	1107	78	37	.262	.337	.402	739	98	7	-1	101	95	42	69	6
MIL	74	88	0	.457	28	38	43	707	812	6232	1439	266	17	152	532	1039	61	66	.260	.330	.396	726	96	-28	-29	100	81	59	58	-3
PIT	69	93	1	.426	33	40	40	650	718	6111	1395	271	35	107	393	1060	78	91	.254	.311	.374	685	83	-116	-123	101	159	51	**76**	17
WEST																														
SD	98	64	0	.605		54	27	749	635	6243	1390	292	30	167	604	1072	56	48	.253	.330	.409	739	107	-2	60	92	79	37	68	4
SF	89	74	0	.546	9.5	49	32	845	739	6484	1540	292	26	161	**678**	**1040**	81	44	.274	.353	.421	774	**116**	87	141	94	102	51	67	5
LA	83	79	0	.512	15	48	33	669	678	6076	1374	209	27	159	447	1056	**91**	36	.252	.310	.387	697	93	-102	-62	94	137	53	72	12
COL	77	85	0	.475	21	42	39	826	855	6277	1640	333	36	183	469	949	98	37	.291	.347	.461	808	95	132	-24	122	67	47	59	-2
ARI	65	97	0	.401	33	34	47	665	812	6116	1353	235	46	159	489	1239	45	64	.246	.314	.393	707	90	-83	-81	100	73	38	66	3
TOT	1298					711	586	11932		100092	23213	4493	491	2565	8710	17455	824	1167	.262	.331	.410	741					1609	751	68	91

TEAM	CG	SHO	GR	SV	IP	H	HR	BB	SO	BR/9	ERA	AERA	OAV	OOB	PR	APR	PF	OSB	OCS	FA	E	WPB	DP	FW	PW	BW	BSW	DIF
EAST																												
ATL	**24**	**23**	354	45	1438.2	**1291**	**117**	467	**1232**	**11.2**	**3.25**	**128**	**.240**	**.303**	**156**	**147**	98	85	40	**.985**	**91**	64	139	**1.3**	**14.5**	10.3	.1	-1.2
NY	9	16	399	46	1458.0	1381	152	532	1129	12.2	3.76	110	.253	.325	76	62	98	117	**64**	.984	101	51	151	.8	6.1	-1.7	-.8	2.5
PHI	21	10	385	32	1463.0	1476	188	544	1176	12.8	4.64	93	.262	.331	-66	-49	102	87	33	.982	110	88	131	.3	-4.8	-4.7	.0	3.2
MON	4	5	443	39	1427.0	1448	156	533	1017	12.9	4.38	96	.264	.332	-24	-29	99	132	**64**	.975	155	68	127	-2.1	-2.9	-7.5	-.2	-3.3
FLA	11	3	420	24	1449.2	1617	182	715	1016	14.8	5.18	78	.287	.370	-153	-189	96	109	54	.979	129	80	177	-.7	-18.7	-7.2	-.0	-.4
CENTRAL																												
HOU	12	11	340	44	1471.1	1435	147	**465**	1187	11.9	3.50	116	.256	.315	119	94	96	**75**	42	.983	108	59	144	.4	9.3	**14.5**	1.0	-4.2
CHI	7	7	**449**	56	1477.1	1528	180	575	1207	13.1	4.47	99	.266	.336	-39	-11	104	120	43	.984	101	55	107	.8	-1.1	2.9	-.7	6.6
STL	6	10	428	44	1469.2	1513	151	558	972	13.0	4.31	97	.268	.337	-12	-19	99	92	44	.978	142	**48**	160	-1.4	-1.9	9.2	.9	-4.8
CIN	6	8	366	42	1441.1	1400	170	573	1098	12.6	4.44	96	.256	.330	-34	-26	101	117	46	.980	122	70	142	-.3	-2.6	-.0	.0	-1.0
MIL	2	2	416	39	1451.0	1538	188	550	1063	13.3	4.63	92	.275	.344	-64	-59	101	125	34	.982	110	62	192	.3	-5.8	-2.9	-.9	2.2
PIT	7	10	395	41	1449.0	1433	147	530	1112	12.4	3.91	110	.259	.324	52	61	102	95	39	.977	140	59	161	-1.3	6.0	-12.1	**1.1**	-5.7
WEST																												
SD	14	11	369	**59**	1454.2	1384	139	501	1217	12.0	3.63	108	.252	.318	97	48	92	94	40	.983	104	80	155	.6	4.7	5.9	-.2	5.9
SF	6	6	433	44	1477.0	1457	171	562	1089	12.6	4.18	95	.259	.330	8	-38	94	97	39	.984	101	71	157	.8	-3.7	13.9	-.0	-3.4
LA	16	10	342	47	1447.1	1332	135	587	1178	12.3	3.81	104	.246	.324	68	26	94	93	57	.978	134	54	154	-1.0	2.6	-6.1	.6	5.9
COL	9	5	406	36	1432.2	1583	174	562	951	13.9	4.99	104	.285	.355	-121	23	122	108	52	.984	102	56	**193**	.7	2.3	-2.4	-.8	-3.9
ARI	7	6	368	37	1432.1	1463	188	489	908	12.5	4.63	91	.266	.328	-64	-68	100	93	63	.984	100	58	125	.8	-6.7	-8.0	-.3	-1.9
TOT	161	143	6313	675	23240.0					12.7	4.23		.262	.331						.981	1850	1023	2415					

Batter-Fielder Wins	Batting Average	On-Base Percentage	Slugging Average	On-Base Plus Slugging	Adjusted OPS	Adjusted Batter Runs
McGwire-StL 7.1	Walker-Col 363	McGwire-StL 470	McGwire-StL.........752	McGwire-StL 1222	McGwire-StL 218	McGwire-StL 97.0
Bonds-SF 6.8	Olerud-NY 354	Olerud-NY 447	Sosa-Chi..............647	Walker-Col 1075	Bonds-SF 184	Bonds-SF 75.4
Piazza-LA-Fla-NY5.9	Bichette-Col 331	Walker-Col 445	Walker-Col 630	Bonds-SF 1047	Olerud-NY 165	Olerud-NY 58.5
Biggio-Hou 5.6	Piazza-LA-Fla-NY.328	Bonds-SF.......................438	Bonds-SF 609	Sosa-Chi 1024	Bagwell-Hou 161	Bagwell-Hou 53.5
Rolen-Phi 5.1	Kendall-Pit 327	Sheffield-Fla-LA...........428	Vaughn-SD 597	Olerud-NY 998	Sheffield-Fla-LA.....160	Alou-Hou 51.7

Runs	Hits	Doubles	Triples	Home Runs	Total Bases	Runs Batted In
Sosa-Chi 134	Bichette-Col..........219	Biggio-Hou 51	Dellucci-Ari 12	McGwire-StL 70	Sosa-Chi 416	Sosa-Chi 158
McGwire-StL 130	Biggio-Hou............210	Young-Cin 48	B.Larkin-Cin............10	Sosa-Chi 66	McGwire-StL 383	McGwire-StL 147
Bagwell-Hou 124	Castilla-Col 206	Bichette-Col 48	W.Guerrero-LA-Mon 9	Vaughn-SD 50	Castilla-Col 380	Castilla-Col..........144
C.Jones-Atl 123	V.Guerrero-Mon 202	Walker-Col 46	Perez-Col..................9	Castilla-Col 46	V.Guerrero-Mon 367	Kent-SF 128
Biggio-Hou............123				Galarraga-Atl 44	Vaughn-SD 342	Burnitz-Mil 125

Stolen Bases	Base Stealing Runs	Fielding Runs-Infield	Fielding Runs-Outfield	Wins	Winning Pct.	Complete Games
Womack-Pit 58	Womack-Pit 10.0	Perez-Col....................29.4	A.Jones-Atl 20.0	Glavine-Atl 20	Smoltz-Atl 850	Schilling-Phi 15
Biggio-Hou..............50	Biggio-Hou 8.2	Vina-Mil 28.4	Kotsay-Fla............18.5	Tapani-Chi 19	Glavine-Atl 769	Maddux-Atl 9
Young-LA.................42	Young-LA 4.7	Cirillo-Mil 21.7	Rodriguez-Chi........9.4	Reynolds-Hou 19	Leiter-NY 739	Hernandez-Fla 9
Renteria-Fla............41	B.Larkin-Cin 4.7	Veras-SD 20.3	Dunwoody-Fla 7.4	Maddux-Atl 18	Brown-SD 720	C.Perez-Mon-LA......7
Bonds-SF 28	A.Jones-Atl 4.5	Andrews-Mon 18.2	Sosa-Chi................7.4	Brown-SD 18	Reynolds-Hou.........704	Brown-SD.................7

Strikeouts	Fewest BB/Game	Games	Saves	Base Runners/9	Adjusted Relief Runs	Relief Ranking
Schilling-Phi..........300	Anderson-Ari 1.04	Beck-Chi 81	Hoffman-SD............53	Hoffman-SD 7.77	Nen-SF 23.3	Nen-SF 46.6
Brown-SD 257	Reed-NY..............1.23	Nen-SF 78	Beck-Chi 51	Nen-SF 8.63	Urbina-Mon..........22.7	Urbina-Mon 45.4
Wood-Chi..............233	Lima-Hou 1.23	McElroy-Col 78	Shaw-Cin-LA 48	Maddux-Atl 9.07	Hoffman-SD 21.9	Hoffman-SD 43.6
Reynolds-Hou 209	Maddux-Atl 1.61	Kline-Mon 78	Nen-SF 40	Urbina-Mon..........9.09	Shaw-Cin-LA 19.3	Shaw-Cin-LA......38.7
Maddux-Atl 204	Brown-SD.............1.72	Telford-Mon.....................77	J.Franco-NY............38	R.Johnson-Hou.....9.18	Acevedo-StL 18.5	Acevedo-StL 23.5

Innings Pitched	Opponents' Avg.	Opponents' OBP	Earned Run Average	Adjusted ERA	Adjusted Starter Runs	Pitcher Wins
Schilling-Phi 268.2	Wood-Chi 196	Maddux-Atl 260	Maddux-Atl 2.22	Maddux-Atl 187	Maddux-Atl 52.4	**Maddux-Atl** 6.4
Brown-SD 257.0	Leiter-NY 216	Brown-SD 279	Brown-SD 2.38	Glavine-Atl 168	Brown-SD 45.7	**Glavine-Atl** 5.6
Maddux-Atl 251.0	Maddux-Atl 220	Schilling-Phi..................282	Leiter-NY 2.47	Leiter-NY 167	Glavine-Atl 45.4	**Brown-SD** 4.8
C.Perez-Mon-LA241.0	Harnisch-Cin.........228	Smoltz-Atl 285	Glavine-Atl 2.47	Brown-SD 164	Leiter-NY 37.1	**Nen-SF**................4.7
Hernandez-Fla ..234.1	Smoltz-Atl 231	Lima-Hou 285	Daal-Ari 2.88	Daal-Ari 147	Schilling-Phi 33.0	**Urbina-Mon** 4.5

The Year They'll All Remember

Sluggers Mark McGwire and Sammy Sosa put on a season-long show. McGwire broke Roger Maris' record first, smashing his 62nd homer on September 8 against the Cubs. Sosa briefly took the league lead on the third-to-last day of the season when he smacked his 66th homer. Not to be outdone, McGwire tied Sosa that night and clubbed four more in the final two games to finish with 70. Some felt the record was tainted after it was learned McGwire was taking androstenedione. While "andro" was a legal, over-the-counter supplement, it was banned by the NFL and NCAA and many believed McGwire had an unfair edge.

The addition of two teams, the Diamondbacks and (surprise!) the Brewers, brought a record 2,565 homers to the sixteen-team NL, but scoring per game remained essentially unchanged. Chicago rookie Kerry Wood fanned 20 Astros in only his fifth start, tying the single-game record. Rupert Murdoch, head of the FOX media empire, bought the Dodgers from Peter O'Malley, whose family had controlled the franchise since 1950. Chicago lost two legendary broadcasters: Harry Caray died in February, while Jack Brickhouse passed in August.

Sosa's power helped the Cubs win the Wild Card after a one-game playoff with the Giants, who overtook the Mets in a furious final week. The Division Series saw Atlanta sweep Chicago, while San Diego, allowing 1 run in each of its victories, beat Houston in four. The Padres won the first three games of the NLCS and closed it out with a 5–0 shutout over the Braves in Game 6, only to be swept by the powerful Yankees in the Series.

1998 American League

TEAM	W	L	T	PCT	GB	HW	HL	R	OR	PA	H	2B	3B	HR	BB	SO	HB	SH	AVG	OBP	SLG	OPS	AOPS	BR	ABR	PF	SB	CS	BSA	BSR
EAST																														
NY	114	48	0	.704		**62**	19	**965**	**656**	6444	1625	290	31	207	**653**	**1025**	32	57	.288	**.364**	.460	**824**	**117**	**125**	**163**	96	153	63	**71**	**12**
BOS	92	70	0	.568	22	51	30	876	729	6299	1568	**338**	**35**	205	541	1049	35	70	.280	.348	**.463**	811	107	79	61	102	72	39	65	2
TOR	88	74	1	.543	26	51	30	816	768	6323	1482	316	19	**221**	564	1132	**43**	**87**	.266	.340	.448	788	103	31	28	100	**184**	81	69	**12**
BAL	79	83	0	.488	35	42	39	817	785	6304	1520	303	11	214	593	903	44	58	.273	.347	.447	794	107	48	61	99	86	48	64	2
TB	63	99	0	.389	51	33	48	620	751	6156	1450	267	43	111	473	1107	53	37	.261	.321	.385	706	81	-141	-153	102	120	73	62	1
CENTRAL																														
CLE	89	73	0	.549		46	35	850	779	6376	1530	334	30	198	630	1061	30	41	.272	.347	.448	795	102	55	27	103	143	60	70	10
CHI	80	82	1	.494	9	44	37	861	931	6280	1516	291	38	198	551	916	38	47	.271	.339	.444	783	105	17	41	97	127	46	73	**12**
KC	72	89	0	.447	16.5	29	51	714	899	6191	1459	274	40	134	475	984	45	60	.263	.324	.399	723	85	-101	-119	103	135	50	73	**12**
MIN	70	92	0	.432	19	35	46	734	818	6262	1499	285	32	115	506	915	18	45	.266	.328	.389	717	85	-111	-121	102	112	54	67	6
DET	65	97	0	.401	24	32	49	722	863	6242	1494	306	29	165	455	1070	16	62	.264	.323	.415	738	89	-80	-84	101	122	62	66	5
WEST																														
TEX	88	74	0	.543		48	33	940	871	6401	**1637**	314	32	201	595	1045	41	39	**.289**	.357	.462	819	107	104	67	104	82	47	64	2
ANA	85	77	0	.525	3	42	39	787	783	6278	1530	314	27	147	510	1028	49	48	.272	.335	.415	750	93	-43	-48	101	93	45	67	5
SEA	76	85	0	.472	11.5	42	39	859	855	6327	1553	321	28	234	558	1081	36	57	.276	.345	.468	813	109	78	78	100	115	39	75	**12**
OAK	74	88	0	.457	14	39	42	804	866	6282	1413	295	13	149	633	1122	58	55	.257	.338	.397	735	93	-62	-44	98	131	47	74	**12**
TOT	1134					596	537	11365		88165	21276	4248	408	2499	7737	14438	763	538	.271	.340	.432	771					1675	754	69	105

TEAM	CG	SHO	GR	SV	IP	H	HR	BB	SO	BR/9	ERA	AERA	OAV	OOB	PR	APR	PF	OSB	OCS	FA	E	WPB	DP	FW	PW	BW	BSW	DIF
EAST																												
NY	**22**	**16**	334	48	1456.2	**1357**	**156**	466	1080	**11.7**	**3.82**	**114**	**.247**	**.312**	**133**	**95**	94	102	51	.984	98	49	146	.9	**9.0**	**15.4**	**.4**	7.4
BOS	5	8	432	**53**	1436.0	1406	168	504	1025	12.3	4.18	113	.255	.321	75	83	101	132	58	.983	105	97	128	.5	7.8	5.7	-.5	-2.5
TOR	10	11	384	47	1465.0	1443	169	587	1154	12.7	4.28	109	.256	.329	60	62	100	149	47	.979	125	**43**	131	-.6	5.8	2.6	**.4**	-1.3
BAL	16	10	402	37	1431.1	1505	169	535	1065	13.1	4.74	96	.272	.338	-15	-31	98	182	53	**.987**	**81**	63	144	**1.8**	-2.9	5.7	-.5	-6.1
TB	7	7	410	28	1443.0	1425	171	643	1008	13.4	4.35	110	.261	.345	47	68	103	97	61	.985	94	62	**178**	1.1	6.4	-14.4	-.6	-10.5
CENTRAL																												
CLE	9	4	423	47	1460.0	1552	171	563	1037	13.5	4.44	107	.274	.344	33	51	103	110	47	.982	110	**43**	146	.2	4.8	2.5	.2	.2
CHI	8	4	405	42	1438.2	1569	211	580	911	13.8	5.22	87	.278	.348	-92	-111	98	122	59	.977	140	67	161	-1.4	-10.5	3.9	**.4**	6.6
KC	6	5	388	46	1436.1	1590	196	568	999	13.9	5.15	94	.281	.350	-80	-51	104	80	43	.980	125	83	172	-.7	-4.8	-11.2	**.4**	7.8
MIN	7	8	432	42	1447.2	1622	180	**457**	952	13.2	4.75	100	.284	.338	-16	2	103	101	45	.982	108	66	135	.3	.2	-11.4	-.1	.0
DET	9	4	**446**	32	1446.1	1551	185	595	947	13.6	4.93	96	.277	.348	-45	-34	101	120	**69**	.982	115	74	164	-.0	-3.2	-7.9	-.2	-4.6
WEST																												
TEX	10	8	402	46	1431.1	1624	164	519	994	13.8	4.99	97	.285	.346	-55	-26	104	**64**	55	.980	121	72	140	-.4	-2.5	6.3	-.5	4.0
ANA	3	5	415	52	1444.0	1481	164	630	1091	13.5	4.49	104	.267	.344	26	32	101	156	65	.983	106	98	146	.4	3.0	-4.5	-.2	5.3
SEA	17	7	368	31	1424.1	1530	196	528	**1156**	13.4	4.93	94	.273	.340	-45	-49	100	127	49	.979	125	72	139	-.7	-4.6	7.4	**.4**	-7.0
OAK	12	4	408	39	1434.0	1555	179	529	922	13.4	4.81	95	.276	.342	-25	-39	98	103	48	.977	141	81	155	-1.5	-3.7	-4.1	**.4**	1.9
TOT	141	101	5649	590	20194.2					13.2	4.65		.271	.340						.981	1594	970	2085					

Batter-Fielder Wins	Batting Average	On-Base Percentage	Slugging Average	On-Base Plus Slugging	Adjusted OPS	Adjusted Batter Runs
Belle-Chi.............5.9	Williams-NY 339	Martinez-Sea 429	Belle-Chi...............655	Belle-Chi 1055	Belle-Chi 175	Belle-Chi 68.7
Griffey-Sea..........5.1	Vaughn-Bos 337	Williams-NY 422	Gonzalez-Tex 630	Thome-Cle............997	Williams-NY 163	Martinez-Sea......52.9
Rodriguez-Sea....4.6	Belle-Chi..............328	Thome-Cle...................413	Griffey-Sea 611	Williams-NY 997	Martinez-Sea.........157	Williams-NY........48.9
Martinez-Sea 4.1	Davis-Bal 327	Salmon-Ana.................410	M.Ramirez-Cle 599	Gonzalez-Tex........997	Thome-Cle............151	Vaughn-Bos........46.1
Williams-NY 3.9	Jeter-NY 324	Offerman-KC 403	Delgado-Tor 592	Vaughn-Bos..........993	Davis-Bal..............151	Griffey-Sea 43.4

Runs	Hits	Doubles	Triples	Home Runs	Total Bases	Runs Batted In
Jeter-NY 127	Rodriguez-Sea......213	Gonzalez-Tex 50	Offerman-KC 13	Griffey-Sea 56	Belle-Chi 399	Gonzalez-Tex 157
Durham-Chi 126	Vaughn-Bos..........205	Belle-Chi.........................48	Damon-KC..............10	Belle-Chi 49	Griffey-Sea 387	Belle-Chi..............152
Rodriguez-Sea.......123	Jeter-NY 203	Martinez-Sea 46	Winn-TB 9	Canseco-Tor 46	Rodriguez-Sea......384	Griffey-Sea 146
Griffey-Sea 120	Belle-Chi 200	Valentin-Bos 44		M.Ramirez-Cle........45	Gonzalez-Tex.........382	M.Ramirez-Cle 145
Knoblauch-NY 117	Garciaparra-Bos ..195	Delgado-Tor 43		Gonzalez-Tex..........45	Vaughn-Bos..........360	Rodriguez-Sea 124

Stolen Bases	Base Stealing Runs	Fielding Runs-Infield	Fielding Runs-Outfield	Wins	Winning Pct.	Complete Games
Henderson-Oak......66	Henderson-Oak ..10.0	Easley-Det................25.7	Lawton-Min..........14.3	Helling-Tex..............20	Wells-NY.................818	Erickson-Bal..........11
Lofton-Cle 54	Lofton-Cle.............8.4	Alomar-Bal................21.0	Griffey-Sea 7.6	Cone-NY 20	Clemens-Tor 769	Wells-NY 8
Stewart-Tor 51	Offerman-KC 5.7	Bordick-Bal 20.9	Anderson-Ana 5.3	Clemens-Tor 20	Helling-Tex 741	Rogers-Oak 7
Rodriguez-Sea........46	Nixon-Min 5.7	Valentin-Bos 18.2	Ordonez-Chi..........4.6	Sele-Tex...................19	Cone-NY.................741	Fassero-Sea............7
Offerman-KC 45	Rodriguez-Sea 5.6	Segui-Sea 17.6	McCracken-TB 4.6	Martinez-Bos 19	Martinez-Bos 731	

Strikeouts	Fewest BB/Game	Games	Saves	Base Runners/9	Adjusted Relief Runs	Relief Ranking
Clemens-Tor 271	Wells-NY.............1.22	Runyan-Det...................88	Gordon-Bos 46	Jackson-Cle 8.44	Jackson-Cle 22.8	Gordon-Bos.........36.7
Martinez-Bos.........251	Saberhagen-Bos 1.49	Quantrill-Tor 82	Wetteland-Tex 42	Wetteland-Tex.......8.85	Gordon-Bos 18.3	Wetteland-Tex 31.3
Johnson-Sea 213	Moyer-Sea 1.61	Swindell-Min-Bos 81	Percival-Ana 42	Gordon-Bos 9.08	Rivera-NY 18.3	Jackson-Cle........31.0
Finley-Ana 212	Mussina-Bal 1.79	Guardado-Min................79	Jackson-Cle............40	Wells-NY...............9.45	Quantrill-Tor 18.1	Rivera-NY 26.7
Cone-NY 209	Radke-Min 1.81	Plesac-Tor.....................78	Aguilera-Min 38	Brocail-Det............9.48	Wetteland-Tex......17.8	Lopez-TB.............20.3

Innings Pitched	Opponents' Avg.	Opponents' OBP	Earned Run Average	Adjusted ERA	Adjusted Starter Runs	Pitcher Wins
Erickson-Bal......251.1	Clemens-Tor 197	Wells-NY 265	Clemens-Tor 2.65	Clemens-Tor 176	Clemens-Tor 51.6	**Clemens-Tor** 5.2
Rogers-Oak 238.2	Martinez-Bos 217	Clemens-Tor 277	Martinez-Bos 2.89	Martinez-Bos 163	Martinez-Bos 46.8	**Martinez-Bos** 4.6
Clemens-Tor......234.2	Irabu-NY 233	Martinez-Bos 278	Rogers-Oak 3.17	Rogers-Oak 144	Rogers-Oak 37.4	**Rogers-Oak**........3.7
Moyer-Sea 234.1	Cone-NY................237	Mussina-Bal................282	Finley-Ana 3.39	Finley-Ana 139	Finley-Ana 29.6	**Gordon-Bos**........3.5
Belcher-KC 234.0	Wells-NY...............239	Moyer-Sea 295	Wells-NY..............3.49	Arrojo-TB 135	Moyer-Sea 29.5	**Arrojo-TB**............3.3

Selig Not Acting Anymore

Expansion took place for the second time in five years with the addition of Tampa Bay and Arizona. Milwaukee agreed to move to the National League so the Devil Rays and Diamondbacks could be placed in different leagues, marking the first time an AL team had joined the NL. Brewers owner Bud Selig, acting commissioner since 1992, finally was given the title full time.

Chicago's Albert Belle smacked 97 extra-base hits—49 homers and 48 doubles—the second highest total in history behind his 1995 record of 102. Baltimore's Cal Ripken voluntarily ended his consecutive games played streak at 2,632 when he took himself out of the starting lineup just before Baltimore's final home game of the season. Paul Molitor and Dennis Eckersley retired; Dan Quisenberry and Mark Belanger died a week apart.

The Yankees won 114 games, an AL record, and breezed through the postseason. Texas led the league in hitting and placed second in runs, but scored just once in a three-game Division Series sweep by the Yankees. Cleveland rallied for three straight wins over Boston to win the other ALDS in four. The Tribe won two of the first three against the Yankees, but New York blanked Cleveland, 4–0, in Game 4, and then won the next two games to take the ALCS in six. New York cruised through San Diego in the World Series. Although the Padres took three-run leads into the seventh in Games 1 and 3, the Yankees won both times. The Series ended with a 3–0 shutout of the Padres in Game 4.

1999 National League

TEAM	W	L	T	PCT	GB	HW	HL	R	OR	PA	H	2B	3B	HR	BB	SO	HB	SH	AVG	OBP	SLG	OPS	AOPS	BR	ABR	PF	SB	CS	BSA	BSR
EAST																														
ATL	103	59	0	.636		**56**	25	840	**661**	6351	1481	309	23	197	608	**962**	74	53	.266	.341	.436	777	100	11	12	100	148	66	69	9
NY	97	66	0	.595	6.5	49	32	853	711	6454	1553	297	14	181	717	994	63	48	**.279**	**.363**	.434	797	110	**75**	105	97	150	61	71	12
PHI	77	85	0	.475	26	41	40	841	846	6386	1539	302	44	161	631	1081	70	46	.275	.351	.431	782	99	27	4	103	125	35	**78**	15
MON	68	94	0	.420	35	35	46	718	853	6149	1473	320	47	163	438	939	71	53	.265	.323	.427	750	96	-63	-42	97	70	51	58	-2
FLA	64	98	0	.395	39	35	45	691	852	6216	1465	266	44	128	479	1145	44	59	.263	.325	.395	720	91	-114	-72	94	92	46	67	4
CENTRAL																														
HOU	97	65	0	.599		50	32	823	675	6402	1463	293	23	168	**728**	1138	79	52	.267	.355	.420	775	103	28	42	98	**166**	75	69	10
CIN	96	67	0	.589	1.5	45	37	865	711	6377	1536	**312**	37	209	569	1125	70	45	.272	.341	.451	792	101	34	12	103	164	54	75	**17**
PIT	78	83	0	.484	18.5	45	36	775	782	6233	1417	282	40	171	573	1197	**87**	**60**	.259	.334	.419	753	94	-43	-40	100	112	44	72	9
STL	75	86	0	.466	21.5	38	42	809	838	6353	1461	274	27	194	613	1202	75	51	.262	.338	.426	764	97	-18	-21	100	134	48	74	13
MIL	74	87	0	.460	22.5	32	48	815	886	6433	1524	299	30	165	658	1065	**87**	55	.273	.353	.426	779	103	27	38	99	81	33	71	6
CHI	67	95	0	.414	30	34	47	747	920	6201	1411	255	35	189	571	1170	65	39	.257	.329	.420	749	95	-55	-42	98	60	44	58	-2
WEST																														
ARI	100	62	0	.617		52	29	**908**	676	6415	**1566**	289	**46**	**216**	588	1045	61	48	.277	.347	**.459**	**806**	107	64	60	101	137	39	**78**	16
SF	86	76	0	.531	14	49	32	872	831	6448	1507	307	18	188	696	1028	**87**	**60**	.271	.356	.434	790	**112**	52	**121**	93	109	56	66	4
LA	77	85	0	.475	23	37	44	793	787	6338	1480	253	23	187	594	1030	74	52	.266	.339	.420	759	102	-25	24	94	167	68	71	13
SD	74	88	0	.457	26	46	35	710	781	6136	1360	256	22	153	631	1169	36	35	.252	.332	.393	725	96	-90	-30	92	174	67	72	15
COL	72	90	0	.444	28	39	42	906	1028	6368	1644	305	39	223	508	863	54	43	.288	.348	.472	820	87	87	-104	127	70	43	62	0
TOT	1295					683	612	12966		101260	23880	4619	512	2893	9602	17153	799	1097	.268	.342	.429	771					1959	830	70	140

TEAM	CG	SHO	GR	SV	IP	H	HR	BB	SO	BR/9	ERA	AERA	OAV	OOB	PR	APR	PF	OSB	OCS	FA	E	WPB	DP	FW	PW	BW	BSW	DIF
EAST																												
ATL	9	9	394	45	1471.0	1398	142	507	1197	**11.8**	**3.63**	**124**	.251	**.314**	**152**	**143**	99	108	45	.982	111	**44**	127	.6	**13.5**	1.1	.0	6.8
NY	5	7	439	49	1456.2	1372	167	617	1172	12.6	4.27	103	.252	.331	47	18	96	134	44	**.989**	**68**	48	147	**3.3**	1.7	9.9	.3	.3
PHI	11	6	441	32	1438.1	1494	212	627	1030	13.6	4.92	96	.269	.347	-58	-32	103	94	35	.983	100	80	144	1.3	-3.0	.4	.6	-3.2
MON	6	4	432	44	1434.1	1505	152	572	1043	13.4	4.69	96	.270	.342	-21	-34	98	157	47	.974	160	62	125	-2.4	-3.2	-4.0	-1.0	-2.4
FLA	6	5	453	33	1435.2	1560	171	655	943	14.2	4.90	89	.281	.359	-54	-90	96	94	67	.979	127	56	150	-.4	-8.5	-6.8	-.5	-.8
CENTRAL																												
HOU	12	8	339	48	1458.2	1485	**128**	**478**	**1204**	12.4	3.83	115	.267	.326	119	98	97	94	43	.983	106	63	175	.9	9.3	4.0	.1	1.8
CIN	6	**11**	381	**55**	1462.0	**1309**	190	636	1081	12.3	3.98	117	**.241**	.324	94	107	102	124	34	.983	105	76	139	1.0	10.1	1.1	**.8**	1.5
PIT	8	3	425	34	1433.1	1444	160	633	1083	13.4	4.33	106	.263	.343	37	38	100	99	50	.976	147	63	179	-1.7	3.6	-3.8	.0	-.7
STL	5	3	**454**	38	1445.1	1519	161	667	1025	14.0	4.74	96	.273	.355	-29	-27	100	**80**	**69**	.978	132	68	163	-.8	-2.6	-2.0	.4	-.6
MIL	2	5	453	40	1442.2	1618	213	616	987	14.3	5.07	89	.284	.356	-82	-87	99	177	44	.979	127	77	146	-.4	-8.2	3.6	-.3	-1.2
CHI	11	6	441	32	1430.2	1619	221	529	980	13.7	5.27	86	.286	.346	-112	-121	99	100	43	.977	139	73	135	-1.1	-11.4	-4.0	-1.0	3.6
WEST																												
ARI	**16**	9	382	42	1467.1	1387	176	543	1198	12.1	3.77	121	.249	.320	128	130	100	138	66	.983	104	56	132	1.0	12.3	5.7	.7	-.6
SF	6	3	450	42	1456.1	1486	194	655	1076	13.5	4.71	89	.265	.345	-24	-89	92	129	53	.983	105	70	155	.9	-8.4	**11.4**	-.5	1.5
LA	8	6	399	37	1453.0	1438	192	594	1077	13.0	4.45	96	.258	.334	18	-28	94	156	56	.978	137	66	137	-1.0	-2.6	2.3	.4	-3.0
SD	5	6	403	43	1420.1	1454	193	529	1078	12.8	4.47	94	.266	.332	15	-47	92	114	45	.979	129	88	151	-.5	-4.4	-2.8	.6	.2
COL	12	2	420	33	1429.0	1700	237	737	1032	15.7	6.01	97	.301	.384	-231	-26	127	163	63	.981	118	79	**189**	.1	-2.5	-9.8	-.8	4.0
TOT	128	93	6706	647	23134.2					13.3	4.56		.268	.342						.980	1915	1069	2394					

Batter-Fielder Wins	Batting Average	On-Base Percentage	Slugging Average	On-Base Plus Slugging	Adjusted OPS	Adjusted Batter Runs
Bagwell-Hou 5.3	Walker-Col 379	Walker-Col 458	Walker-Col 710	Walker-Col 1168	McGwire-StL 177	Bagwell-Hou 66.7
Ventura-NY..........4.5	Gonzalez-Ari.........336	Bagwell-Hou 454	McGwire-StL.........697	McGwire-StL 1120	C.Jones-Atl 168	C.Jones-Atl 65.6
Biggio-Hou..........4.3	Abreu-Phi 335	Abreu-Phi.....................446	Sosa-Chi...............635	C.Jones-Atl 1074	Bagwell-Hou 165	McGwire-StL 64.3
Sosa-Chi 4.2	Casey-Cin.............332	C.Jones-Atl 441	C.Jones-Atl 633	Bagwell-Hou 1045	Giles-Pit................159	Giles-Pit..............49.5
McGwire-StL 4.2	Cirillo-Mil...............326	Olerud-NY 427	Giles-Pit 614	Giles-Pit..............1032	Walker-Col 151	Abreu-Phi 44.6

Runs	Hits	Doubles	Triples	Home Runs	Total Bases	Runs Batted In
Bagwell-Hou 143	Gonzalez-Ari 206	Biggio-Hou 56	Perez-Col................11	McGwire-StL 65	Sosa-Chi 397	McGwire-StL 147
Bell-Ari..................132	Glanville-Phi 204	Vidro-Mon 45	Abreu-Phi 11	Sosa-Chi 63	V.Guerrero-Mon 366	Williams-Ari 142
Biggio-Hou............123	Cirillo-Mil 198	Gonzalez-Ari...................45	Womack-Ari............10	Vaughn-Cin 45	McGwire-StL 363	Sosa-Chi 141
Alfonzo-NY 123	Casey-Cin 197	Grace-Chi 44	Finley-Ari 10	C.Jones-Atl 45	C.Jones-Atl 359	Bichette-Col 133
		Jenkins-Mil 43			Helton-Col 339	V.Guerrero-Mon ..131

Stolen Bases	Base Stealing Runs	Fielding Runs-Infield	Fielding Runs-Outfield	Wins	Winning Pct.	Complete Games
Womack-Ari............72	Womack-Ari 11.3	Benjamin-Pit 34.8	A.Jones-Atl 17.3	Hampton-Hou 22	Hampton-Hou 846	Johnson-Ari 12
Cedeno-NY 66	Cedeno-NY.............8.6	Perez-Col....................26.7	Kotsay-Fla............12.4	Lima-Hou.................21	Millwood-Atl 720	Schilling-Phi 8
Young-LA................51	Glanville-Phi 6.8	Ventura-NY 18.5	Jenkins-Mil 10.6	Maddux-Atl 19	Bottenfield-StL 720	Astacio-Col..............7
Castillo-Fla.............50	Reese-Cin..............5.9	Biggio-Hou..................17.7	Sosa-Chi.................9.3		Schilling-Phi 714	Brown-LA 5
	Renteria-StL 5.3	Reese-Cin 16.9	Hidalgo-Hou 8.5		Maddux-Atl 679	

Strikeouts	Fewest BB/Game	Games	Saves	Base Runners/9	Adjusted Relief Runs	Relief Ranking
Johnson-Ari 364	Reynolds-Hou......1.44	Kline-Mon 82	Urbina-Mon 41	Wagner-Hou 7.11	Wagner-Hou 24.5	Williamson-Cin ..44.3
Brown-LA.............221	Maddux-Atl 1.52	Wendell-NY.....................80	Hoffman-SD............40	Hoffman-SD 8.42	Benitez-NY 22.6	Wagner-Hou 38.0
Astacio-Col 210	Lima-Hou 1.61	Telford-Mon....................79	Wagner-Hou 39	Millwood-Atl 9.12	Williamson-Cin 22.2	Graves-Cin 31.4
Millwood-Atl 205	Woodard-Mil 1.75	Sullivan-Cin....................79	Rocker-Atl 38	Benitez-NY 9.35	Sullivan-Cin 20.8	Rocker-Atl 31.1
Reynolds-Hou 197	Smoltz-Atl 1.93	Benitez-NY 77		Williamson-Cin 9.45	Remlinger-Atl 20.3	Benitez-NY 29.9

Innings Pitched	Opponents' Avg.	Opponents' OBP	Earned Run Average	Adjusted ERA	Adjusted Starter Runs	Pitcher Wins
Johnson-Ari 271.2	Millwood-Atl 202	Millwood-Atl 258	Johnson-Ari 2.48	Johnson-Ari 184	Johnson-Ari 61.4	**Hampton-Hou** 5.3
Brown-LA 252.1	Johnson-Ari 208	Johnson-Ari 266	Millwood-Atl 2.68	Millwood-Atl 168	Millwood-Atl 44.6	**Johnson-Ari** 5.1
Lima-Hou 246.1	Brown-LA 222	Brown-LA.......................273	Hampton-Hou 2.90	Hampton-Hou 152	Hampton-Hou 40.5	**Millwood-Atl** 4.4
Hampton-Hou 239.0	Daal-Ari 236	Schilling-Phi..................287	Brown-LA 3.00	Brown-LA..............143	Brown-LA 35.2	**Williamson-Cin** ..4.2
Glavine-Atl 234.0	Schilling-Phi 237	Smoltz-Atl 288	Smoltz-Atl 3.19	Smoltz-Atl 141	Smoltz-Atl 29.0	**Wagner-Hou** 3.7

An All-Century Re-Pete

Under pressure from its corporate sponsor, Commissioner Bud Selig agreed to let Pete Rose participate in on-field ceremonies during the World Series for baseball's All-Century Team. Rose, in the 10th year of lifetime ban for "conduct relating to gambling," was overwhelmingly voted to the team by fans. Marge Schott, Cincinnati's twice-suspended owner, was forced to sell controlling interest to Carl Lindner, one of the team's limited partners.

Mark McGwire hit 65 homers and Sammy Sosa slammed 63 as they became the first players in history to belt 60 or more in two different seasons. Three workers were killed at the Miller Park construction site in Milwaukee when a crane collapsed. The accident ultimately delayed opening of the new park by a year. Dodgers star Pee Wee Reese died.

Arizona won 100 games and became the first team to make the postseason in its second year. Yet the Diamondbacks were surprised in four games by the Mets, who reached the NLDS by winning a one-game playoff with the Reds for the Wild Card. The Braves advanced to the NLCS for the fifth straight year with a four-game Division Series win against Houston. Atlanta defeated New York in six games, but the Braves had to work for it. After dropping the first three games, the Mets rallied for two wins; 15-inning, rain-drenched Game 5 ended on Robin Ventura's grand slam that changed to an RBI-single when one of the celebrating runners passed Ventura during his trot. The Braves won Game 6, and the series, in 11 innings, but Atlanta was swept by the Yankees in the World Series.

1999 American League

TEAM	W	L	T	PCT	GB	HW	HL	R	OR	PA	H	2B	3B	HR	BB	SO	HB	SH	AVG	OBP	SLG	OPS	AOPS	BR	ABR	PF	SB	CS	BSA	BSR
EAST																														
NY	98	64	0	.605		48	33	900	731	6416	1568	302	36	193	718	978	22	55	.282	.366	.453	819	**109**	84	**95**	99	104	57	65	3
BOS	94	68	0	.580	4	49	32	836	**718**	6321	1551	334	**42**	176	597	928	34	55	.278	.350	.448	798	99	27	1	103	67	39	63	1
TOR	84	78	0	.519	14	40	41	883	862	6369	1580	**337**	14	212	578	1077	28	**76**	.280	.352	.457	809	103	50	37	102	119	48	71	9
BAL	78	84	0	.481	20	41	40	851	815	6409	1572	299	21	203	615	890	41	61	.279	.353	.447	800	107	34	68	96	107	46	70	7
TB	69	93	0	.426	29	33	48	772	913	6272	1531	272	29	145	544	1042	30	64	.274	.343	.411	754	91	-65	-73	101	73	49	60	-1
CENTRAL																														
CLE	97	65	0	.599		47	34	**1009**	860	6553	1629	309	32	209	743	1099	**54**	55	.289	**.373**	.467	**840**	108	**135**	91	105	**147**	50	**75**	**15**
CHI	75	86	1	.466	21.5	38	42	777	870	6262	1563	298	37	162	499	**810**	40	34	.277	.337	.429	766	94	-52	-54	100	110	50	69	7
DET	69	92	0	.429	27.5	38	43	747	882	6095	1433	289	34	212	458	1049	35	82	.261	.326	.443	769	94	-60	-64	101	108	70	61	-1
KC	64	97	0	.398	32.5	33	47	856	921	6325	1584	294	52	151	535	932	46	64	.282	.348	.433	781	96	-12	-30	102	127	39	77	14
MIN	63	97	1	.394	33	31	50	686	845	6124	1450	285	30	105	500	978	24	49	.264	.328	.384	712	78	-151	-173	104	118	60	66	5
WEST																														
TEX	95	67	0	.586		51	30	945	859	6388	**1653**	304	29	230	611	937	35	29	**.293**	.361	**.479**	**840**	107	112	71	105	111	54	67	6
OAK	87	75	0	.537	8	**52**	29	893	846	6440	1430	287	20	235	**770**	1129	39	71	.259	.355	.446	801	108	39	78	96	70	37	65	2
SEA	79	83	0	.488	16	43	38	859	905	6310	1499	263	21	**244**	610	1095	38	42	.269	.343	.455	798	105	13	34	98	130	45	74	13
ANA	70	92	0	.432	25	37	44	711	826	6131	1404	248	22	158	511	1022	41	43	.256	.322	.395	717	82	-154	-150	99	71	45	61	0
TOT	1132					581	551	11725		88415	21447	4121	419	2635	8289	13966	780	507	.275	.347	.439	786					1462	689	68	80

TEAM	CG	SHO	GR	SV	IP	H	HR	BB	SO	BR/9	ERA	AERA	OAV	OOB	PR	APR	PF	OSB	OCS	FA	E	WPB	DP	FW	PW	BW	BSW	DIF
EAST																												
NY	6	10	359	**50**	1439.2	1402	**158**	581	1111	12.8	4.13	114	.255	.330	116	97	97	131	48	.982	111	67	132	.2	9.0	**8.8**	-.3	-.7
BOS	6	**12**	412	**50**	1436.2	**1396**	160	**469**	**1131**	**12.0**	**4.00**	**124**	**.253**	**.315**	**137**	**151**	102	159	58	.979	127	59	132	-.6	**14.0**	.0	-.4	.0
TOR	14	9	377	39	1439.0	1582	191	575	1009	13.8	4.92	100	.280	.349	-11	0	101	124	53	.983	106	68	165	.4	.0	3.4	.3	-1.2
BAL	**17**	11	393	33	1435.0	1468	198	647	982	13.6	4.77	98	.269	.348	14	-14	96	93	50	**.986**	**89**	60	191	**1.3**	-1.3	6.3	.1	-9.4
TB	6	5	453	45	1433.0	1606	172	695	1055	14.9	5.06	98	.286	.370	-32	-15	102	101	**69**	.978	135	64	**198**	-1.1	-1.4	-6.8	-.6	-2.2
CENTRAL																												
CLE	3	6	**466**	46	1450.1	1503	197	634	1120	13.6	4.89	103	.268	.346	-5	22	104	118	46	.983	106	62	154	.4	2.0	8.4	**.9**	4.2
CHI	6	3	409	39	1438.1	1608	210	596	968	14.2	4.92	99	.282	.353	-10	-8	100	102	46	.977	136	74	149	-1.1	-.7	-5.0	.1	1.2
DET	4	6	421	33	1421.0	1528	209	583	976	13.8	5.17	95	.276	.349	-50	-37	102	81	44	.982	106	55	156	.4	-3.4	-5.9	-.6	-1.9
KC	11	3	416	29	1420.2	1607	202	643	831	14.7	5.35	94	.288	.365	-78	-53	103	111	49	.980	125	70	188	-.6	-4.9	-2.8	.8	-9.0
MIN	13	8	417	34	1423.1	1591	208	487	927	13.3	5.00	102	.283	.341	-23	12	105	73	37	.985	92	69	150	1.1	1.1	-16.0	-.0	-3.2
WEST																												
TEX	6	9	439	47	1436.1	1626	186	509	979	13.6	5.07	100	.286	.346	-34	0	104	**47**	52	.981	119	**52**	169	-.2	.0	6.6	.0	7.6
OAK	6	5	406	48	1438.1	1537	160	569	967	13.5	4.69	99	.274	.344	26	-9	96	110	51	.980	122	75	166	-.4	-.8	7.2	-.3	.4
SEA	7	6	346	40	1433.2	1613	191	684	980	14.9	5.24	90	.287	.368	-60	-84	97	107	50	.981	113	71	182	.0	-7.8	3.1	.7	1.9
ANA	4	7	400	37	1431.1	1472	177	624	877	13.5	4.79	101	.269	.346	10	8	100	103	62	.983	106	85	156	.4	.7	-13.9	-.5	2.2
TOT	109	100	5714	570	20076.2					13.7	4.86		.275	.347						.981	1593	931	2288					

Batter-Fielder Wins	Batting Average	On-Base Percentage	Slugging Average	On-Base Plus Slugging	Adjusted OPS	Adjusted Batter Runs
R.Alomar-Cle 5.2	Garciaparra-Bos ...357	Martinez-Sea 447	M.Ramirez-Cle 663	M.Ramirez-Cle....1105	M.Ramirez-Cle......171	M.Ramirez-Cle ..59.9
Garciaparra-Bos 4.7	Jeter-NY 349	M.Ramirez-Cle............442	Palmeiro-Tex.........630	Palmeiro-Tex 1050	Martinez-Sea........158	Jeter-NY 55.1
M.Ramirez-Cle....4.5	Williams-NY 342	Jeter-NY......................438	Garciaparra-Bos...603	Garciaparra-Bos 1022	Palmeiro-Tex 157	Giambi-Oak........52.3
Rodriguez-Tex 4.3	Martinez-Sea 337	Williams-NY 435	Gonzalez-Tex 601	Martinez-Sea......1001	Giambi-Oak 154	Palmeiro-Tex 51.3
Williams-NY 4.2	M.Ramirez-Cle 333	Fernandez-Tor 427	Green-Tor 588	Jeter-NY 989	Jeter-NY 153	Martinez-Sea......50.7

Runs	Hits	Doubles	Triples	Home Runs	Total Bases	Runs Batted In
R.Alomar-Cle........138	Jeter-NY 219	Green-Tor 45	Offerman-Bos 11	Griffey-Sea 48	Green-Tor 361	M.Ramirez-Cle 165
Jeter-NY 134	Surhoff-Bal 207	Sweeney-KC 44	Jeter-NY 9	Palmeiro-Tex 47	Palmeiro-Tex 356	Palmeiro-Tex........148
Green-Tor 134	Williams-NY.........202	Dye-KC 44	Febles-KC 9	M.Ramirez-Cle.......44	Griffey-Sea 349	Griffey-Sea 134
M.Ramirez-Cle......131	Velarde-Ana-Oak..200	Garciaparra-Bos 42	Damon-KC 9	Delgado-Tor 44	M.Ramirez-Cle......346	Delgado-Tor 134
Griffey-Sea 123	Rodriguez-Tex 199				Jeter-NY 346	Gonzalez-Tex 128

Stolen Bases	Base Stealing Runs	Fielding Runs-Infield	Fielding Runs-Outfield	Wins	Winning Pct.	Complete Games
Hunter-Det-Sea 44	Hunter-Det-Sea 6.9	Bordick-Bal 35.1	Dye-KC 14.3	P.Martinez-Bos........23	P.Martinez-Bos 852	D.Wells-Tor 7
Vizquel-Cle 42	Vizquel-Cle 6.1	Sanchez-KC...............29.4	Singleton-Chi 11.9	Sele-Tex.................18	Colon-Cle 783	Ponson-Bal.............6
Goodwin-Tex 39	R.Alomar-Cle 6.0	Cairo-TB 27.4	Erstad-Ana 11.9	Mussina-Bal............18	Mussina-Bal 720	Erickson-Bal 6
Stewart-Tor 37	Damon-KC 5.8	Valentin-Bos 12.4	Hunter-Det-Sea 9.9	Colon-Cle 18	Garcia-Sea 680	
R.Alomar-Cle..........37	Anderson-Bal 5.5	Bush-Tor 10.1	Ordonez-Chi..........7.4		Sele-Tex 667	

Strikeouts	Fewest BB/Game	Games	Saves	Base Runners/9	Adjusted Relief Runs	Relief Ranking
P.Martinez-Bos......313	Heredia-Oak........1.53	Wells-Min 76	Rivera-NY 45	Zimmerman-Tex ..7.70	Foulke-Chi 31.4	Rivera-NY 46.3
Finley-Ana 200	P.Martinez-Bos 1.56	Groom-Oak...................76	Wetteland-Tex 43	Foulke-Chi 8.20	Lowe-Bos 28.3	Zimmerman-Tex 33.1
Sele-Tex................186	Radke-Min 1.81	Trombley-Min 75	Hernandez-TB........43	Rivera-NY 8.35	Zimmerman-Tex ..25.6	Lowe-Bos 27.9
Cone-NY 177	Moyer-Sea 1.89	Lowe-Bos 74	Jackson-Cle...........39	P.Martinez-Bos 8.69	Rivera-NY 23.1	Hernandez-TB....26.1
Burba-Cle 174	Mussina-Bal 2.30	Lloyd-Tor.......................74	Mesa-Sea 33	Lowe-Bos 9.30	Brocail-Det 22.5	Karsay-Cle..........23.9

Innings Pitched	Opponents' Avg.	Opponents' OBP	Earned Run Average	Adjusted ERA	Adjusted Starter Runs	Pitcher Wins
D.Wells-Tor 231.2	P.Martinez-Bos 205	P.Martinez-Bos............248	P.Martinez-Bos 2.07	P.Martinez-Bos......241	P.Martinez-Bos 67.2	**P.Martinez-Bos**..8.0
Erickson-Bal 230.1	Cone-NY...............229	Milton-Min 299	Cone-NY.............3.44	Cone-NY 138	Radke-Min 31.2	**Rivera-NY** 4.5
Moyer-Sea 228.0	Hernandez-NY 233	Hernandez-NY............311	Mussina-Bal 3.50	Radke-Min 136	Cone-NY.............27.4	**Radke-Min**..........3.3
Burba-Cle 220.0	Colon-Cle 242	Moyer-Sea 311	Radke-Min 3.75	Mussina-Bal..........134	Saberhagen-Bos 26.6	**Saberhagen-Bos**3.2
Helling-Tex 219.1	Milton-Min............243	Mussina-Bal.................312	Rosado-KC 3.85	Rosado-KC 130	Mussina-Bal 26.5	**Mussina-Bal** 3.2

The Umps Definitely Blew That Call

The Orioles traveled to Cuba for a spring exhibition game against the Cuban national team, the first game involving American pros there in forty years. The Mariners gleefully moved into Safeco Field in mid-July, while teary-eyed fans in Detroit said farewell to beloved Tiger Stadium. Yankees legend Joe DiMaggio died in March, while an awe-struck Ted Williams was lauded at the All-Star Game at Fenway Park.

In what was perhaps the game's worst negotiating tactic ever, most of baseball's umpires resigned en masse in July, attempting to get around a no-strike clause in their contract. Many resignations were accepted and twenty-two umps wound up losing their jobs.

Pedro Martinez averaged a record 13.2 strikeouts per game. Tampa Bay's 35-year-old reliever Jim Morris became the oldest rookie in nearly forty years.

The Yankees were postseason juggernauts again. For the second straight year, they permitted Texas 1 run in a three-game Division Series sweep. After losing the first two games in the other ALDS, the Red Sox pummeled Cleveland pitchers in the final three games, including the greatest scoring display in postseason history: a 23–7 rout in Game 4. Aside from a lopsided Boston win in Game 3, it was all New York in the ALCS. In the other games the Yanks outscored the Red Sox, 22–8, in the first meeting between the long-time rivals in the postseason. The Yankees crushed Atlanta for their 25th world championship, and eighth by sweep. The Braves held eighth-inning leads in Games 1 and 3, but New York rallied to win both times.

2000 National League

TEAM	W	L	T	PCT	GB	HW	HL	R	OR	PA	H	2B	3B	HR	BB	SO	HB	SH	AVG	OBP	SLG	OPS	AOPS	BR	ABR	PF	SB	CS	BSA	BSR
EAST																														
ATL	95	67	0	.586		51	30	810	**714**	6275	1490	274	26	179	595	1010	**87**	59	.271	.346	.429	775	100	7	8	100	148	56	73	13
NY	94	68	0	.580	1	**55**	26	807	738	6327	1445	281	20	198	675	1037	70	45	.263	.346	.430	776	105	13	52	96	66	46	59	-2
FLA	79	82	0	.491	15.5	43	38	731	797	6202	1441	274	29	160	540	1184	42	60	.262	.331	.409	740	96	-70	-33	95	**168**	55	**75**	**18**
MON	67	95	0	.414	28	37	44	738	902	6152	1475	310	35	178	476	1048	78	29	.266	.326	.432	758	93	-49	-66	102	58	48	55	-4
PHI	65	97	0	.401	30	34	47	708	830	6273	1386	304	40	144	611	1117	70	44	.251	.329	.400	729	88	-92	-95	100	102	30	77	12
CENTRAL																														
STL	95	67	0	.586		50	31	887	771	6369	1481	259	25	235	675	1253	79	**84**	.270	.356	.455	811	109	84	83	100	87	51	63	1
CIN	85	77	1	.525	10	43	38	825	765	6372	1545	302	36	200	559	995	56	64	.274	.343	.447	790	101	32	17	102	100	38	72	9
MIL	73	89	1	.451	22	42	39	740	826	6354	1366	297	25	177	620	1245	61	61	.246	.325	.403	728	90	-95	-78	98	72	44	62	0
HOU	72	90	0	.444	23	39	42	938	944	6444	1547	289	36	**249**	673	1129	57	83	.278	.361	**.477**	**838**	109	**137**	90	105	114	52	69	7
PIT	69	93	0	.426	26	37	44	793	888	6369	1506	**320**	31	168	564	1032	59	66	.267	.339	.424	763	98	-24	-14	99	86	40	68	5
CHI	65	97	0	.401	30	38	43	764	904	6397	1426	272	23	183	632	1120	89	54	.256	.335	.411	746	94	-56	-36	97	93	37	72	8
WEST																														
SF	97	65	0	.599		**55**	26	925	747	6418	1535	304	44	226	**709**	1032	73	51	.278	**.362**	.472	834	**124**	133	**213**	92	79	39	67	4
LA	86	76	0	.531	11	44	37	798	729	6312	1408	265	28	211	668	1083	66	51	.257	.341	.431	772	106	-4	50	94	95	42	69	6
ARI	85	77	0	.525	12	47	34	792	754	6240	1466	282	44	179	535	975	61	59	.265	.333	.429	762	94	-29	-49	103	97	44	69	6
COL	82	80	0	.506	15	48	33	**968**	897	6453	**1664**	**320**	**53**	161	601	**907**	75	42	**.294**	**.362**	.455	817	89	102	-83	125	131	61	68	7
SD	76	86	0	.469	21	41	40	752	815	6290	1413	279	37	157	602	1177	39	46	.254	.330	.402	732	96	-87	-31	93	131	53	71	10
TOT	1296					704	592	12976		101247	23594	4632	532	3005	9735	17344	898	1062	.266	.342	.432	773					1627	736	69	100

TEAM	CG	SHO	GR	SV	IP	H	HR	BB	SO	BR/9	ERA	AERA	OAV	OOB	PR	APR	PF	OSB	OCS	FA	E	WPB	DP	FW	PW	BW	BSW	DIF
EAST																												
ATL	13	9	376	**53**	1440.1	1428	165	**484**	1093	**12.2**	**4.05**	**113**	.258	**.319**	**93**	**86**	99	99	33	.979	129	**32**	138	-.6	**8.1**	.8	.6	5.1
NY	8	10	411	49	1450.0	1398	164	574	1164	12.6	4.16	106	**.252**	.327	76	41	95	133	46	.980	118	42	121	-.0	3.9	4.9	-.8	5.0
FLA	5	4	429	48	1429.2	1477	169	650	1051	13.7	4.59	97	.269	.348	6	-26	96	104	55	.980	125	61	144	-.5	-2.5	-3.1	**1.1**	3.4
MON	4	7	452	39	1424.2	1575	181	579	1011	14.0	5.13	93	.282	.353	-79	-52	104	123	38	.978	132	74	151	-.8	-4.9	-6.2	-1.0	-1.1
PHI	8	6	414	34	1438.2	1458	201	640	1123	13.4	4.77	98	.265	.343	-23	-18	101	77	44	.983	100	58	136	1.0	-1.7	-9.0	.5	-6.8
CENTRAL																												
STL	10	7	386	37	1433.2	1403	196	606	1100	13.0	4.38	105	.259	.338	39	36	100	**70**	**66**	.981	111	57	148	.4	3.4	7.8	-.5	2.9
CIN	8	7	387	42	1456.1	1446	190	659	1015	13.3	4.33	109	.261	.341	49	59	102	81	33	.982	111	108	156	.4	5.6	1.6	.3	-3.8
MIL	2	7	433	29	1466.1	1501	174	728	967	14.1	4.63	98	.269	.357	-1	-14	98	86	58	.981	118	72	**187**	.0	-1.3	-7.4	-.6	1.3
HOU	8	2	410	30	1437.2	1596	234	598	1064	14.1	5.42	90	.281	.352	-125	-85	105	111	32	.978	133	61	149	-.9	-8.0	8.5	.0	-8.7
PIT	5	7	466	27	1449.0	1554	163	711	1070	14.4	4.94	93	.277	.361	-50	-56	99	101	42	.979	132	79	169	-.8	-5.3	-1.3	-.1	-4.5
CHI	10	5	421	39	1454.2	1505	231	658	1143	13.8	5.25	86	.268	.348	-101	-119	98	94	54	.983	100	51	139	1.0	-11.2	-3.4	.2	-2.5
WEST																												
SF	9	**15**	384	47	1444.1	1452	**151**	623	1076	13.2	4.21	100	.266	.342	68	4	91	97	48	**.985**	**93**	58	173	**1.3**	.4	**20.1**	-.2	-5.6
LA	9	11	371	36	1445.0	**1379**	176	600	1154	12.8	4.10	105	**.252**	.332	84	38	94	106	52	.978	135	75	151	-1.0	3.6	4.7	-.0	-2.3
ARI	**16**	8	390	38	1443.2	1441	190	500	**1220**	12.4	4.35	108	.262	.326	45	55	102	102	56	.982	107	34	138	.6	5.2	-4.6	-.0	2.9
COL	7	2	**479**	33	1430.0	1568	221	588	1001	14.0	5.26	110	.281	.354	-99	68	125	102	35	**.985**	94	55	176	**1.3**	6.4	-7.8	.0	1.1
SD	5	5	443	46	1459.1	1443	191	649	1071	13.3	4.52	95	.258	.340	18	-36	93	106	50	.977	141	79	155	-1.3	-3.4	-2.9	.4	2.3
TOT	127	112	6652	627	23103.1					13.4	4.63		.266	.342						.981	1879	996	2431					

Batter-Fielder Wins	Batting Average	On-Base Percentage	Slugging Average	On-Base Plus Slugging	Adjusted OPS	Adjusted Batter Runs
Bonds-SF 7.0	Helton-Col 372	Helton-Col 463	Helton-Col 698	Helton-Col 1162	Bonds-SF 195	Bonds-SF 75.1
Kent-SF 6.6	Alou-Hou 355	Bonds-SF.....................440	Bonds-SF 688	Bonds-SF 1127	Sheffield-LA..........180	Sheffield-LA.........65.8
Alfonzo-NY 5.5	V.Guerrero-Mon ...345	Sheffield-LA.................438	V.Guerrero-Mon ...664	Sheffield-LA.........1081	Kent-SF 168	Kent-SF 64.9
Helton-Col 5.1	Hammonds-Col ...335	Giles-Pit.......................432	Sheffield-LA 643	V.Guerrero-Mon ..1074	Sosa-Chi 162	Sosa-Chi 58.7
Hidalgo-Hou........5.0	Castillo-Fla 334	Alfonzo-NY...................425	Hidalgo-Hou 636	Sosa-Chi 1040	V.Guerrero-Mon 162	Giles-Pit..............55.5

Runs	Hits	Doubles	Triples	Home Runs	Total Bases	Runs Batted In
Bagwell-Hou 152	Helton-Col 216	Helton-Col.........................59	Womack-Ari 14	Sosa-Chi 50	Helton-Col 405	Helton-Col 147
Helton-Col 138	Vidro-Mon 200	Cirillo-Col 53	Perez-Col.................11	Bonds-SF 49	Sosa-Chi 383	Sosa-Chi 138
Edmonds-StL........129	A.Jones-Atl 199	Vidro-Mon 51	V.Guerrero-Mon 11	Bagwell-Hou 47	V.Guerrero-Mon 379	Bagwell-Hou........132
Bonds-SF 129	V.Guerrero-Mon 197	Gonzalez-Ari.....................47	Abreu-Phi 10	Hidalgo-Hou 44	Bagwell-Hou 363	Kent-SF 125
A.Jones-Atl 122	Kent-SF 196	Green-LA 44		V.Guerrero-Mon 44		

Stolen Bases	Base Stealing Runs	Fielding Runs-Infield	Fielding Runs-Outfield	Wins	Winning Pct.	Complete Games
Castillo-Fla..............62	E.Young-Chi 9.4	Perez-Col....................36.5	Hidalgo-Hou 14.3	Glavine-Atl..............21	Johnson-Ari 731	Schilling-Phi-Ari 8
Goodwin-Col-LA 55	Goodwin-Col-LA 8.6	Meares-Pit 21.7	Kotsay-Fla............11.2	Kile-StL 20	Estes-SF...............714	Johnson-Ari 8
E.Young-Chi 54	Womack-Ari 6.1	Morris-Pit 19.3	Abreu-Phi 10.6	Maddux-Atl 19	Elarton-Hou 708	Maddux-Atl 6
Womack-Ari............45	Castillo-Fla 5.9	Helton-Col 18.7	Jenkins-Mil 7.1	Johnson-Ari 19	Glavine-Atl 700	Lieber-Chi.................6
Furcal-Atl 40	Reese-Cin..............5.3	Beltre-LA 16.9	Jordan-Atl 6.2	Park-LA 18	Kile-StL.................690	

Strikeouts	Fewest BB/Game	Games	Saves	Base Runners/9	Adjusted Relief Runs	Relief Ranking
Johnson-Ari 347	Maddux-Atl 1.52	Kline-Mon 83	Alfonseca-Fla..........45	Nen-SF 7.91	White-Cin-Col 25.8	Nen-SF 41.1
Park-LA 217	Anderson-Ari 1.65	Sullivan-Cin.....................79	Hoffman-SD............43	White-Cin-Col 8.79	Nen-SF 20.5	Graves-Cin 40.6
Brown-LA..............216	Reed-NY..............1.66	Myers-Col 78	Nen-SF 41	Hoffman-SD 8.96	Graves-Cin 20.3	White-Cin-Col 38.8
Dempster-Fla........209	Brown-LA 1.84	Wendell-NY......................77	Benitez-NY 41	Benitez-NY 9.12	Leskanic-Mil 18.0	Benitez-NY 31.3
Leiter-NY 200	Schilling-Phi-Ari 1.93		Graves-Cin..............30	Brown-LA 9.27	Williamson-Cin 17.2	Leskanic-Mil 30.2

Innings Pitched	Opponents' Avg.	Opponents' OBP	Earned Run Average	Adjusted ERA	Adjusted Starter Runs	Pitcher Wins
Lieber-Chi..........251.0	Brown-LA 213	Brown-LA.....................261	Brown-LA 2.58	Johnson-Ari 178	Johnson-Ari 51.5	**Maddux-Atl** 5.2
Maddux-Atl 249.1	Park-LA................214	Maddux-Atl 276	Johnson-Ari 2.64	D'Amico-Mil 171	Brown-LA.............46.5	**Johnson-Ari** 4.8
Johnson-Ari 248.2	Ankiel-StL 219	Johnson-Ari 288	D'Amico-Mil 2.66	Brown-LA.............168	Maddux-Atl 44.7	**Graves-Cin** 4.2
Glavine-Atl 241.0	Johnson-Ari 224	Schilling-Phi-Ari 294	Maddux-Atl 3.00	Maddux-Atl 153	D'Amico-Mil 33.7	**Nen-SF**................4.0
Hernandez-SF ..240.0	Leiter-NY 228	Glavine-Atl 296	Hampton-NY........3.14	Hampton-NY 140	Glavine-Atl 31.8	**Park-LA** 3.8

Rocking the Boat

Atlanta reliever John Rocker, who saved 38 games the previous season, was suspended for two weeks after making incendiary and racist comments in an interview with *Sports Illustrated.* Rocker instantly became the most hated player in baseball, and was booed vociferously in every road ballpark—especially in his least favorite city, New York.

The Reds pulled off the last "Deal of the Century," acquiring hometown legend Ken Griffey Jr., and sending Seattle four relatively unknown players. Griffey signed a long-term deal with Cincinnati at a below-market rate, and later became the youngest player to hit 400 homers. The Cubs and Mets opened the year in Tokyo, the first regular-season games played outside North America. Chicago's Sammy Sosa hit 50 homers for the third straight year and Todd Helton of the Rockies hit the most doubles since 1936. Will Clark, Dwight Gooden, and Orel Hershiser retired.

Atlanta's vaunted pitching fell apart in the Division Series against the Cardinals, giving up 24 runs in the St. Louis sweep. The Cards won Game 1 despite starter Rick Ankiel's postseason-record 5 wild pitches in the third inning. The Wild Card Mets scraped by San Francisco in four games, clinching the NLDS with a complete-game, 1-hit shutout by unheralded Bobby Jones. Ankiel's control problems played a part in the Cardinals' five-game NLCS loss. He walked 3, threw 2 wild pitches, and allowed 2 runs in the first inning of Game 2, ultimately a 6–5 New York victory. Mets fans were ecstatic over their first pennant since 1986, but the club was dismissed in five games by the hated Yankees in the World Series.

2000 American League

TEAM	W	L	T	PCT	GB	HW	HL	R	OR	PA	H	2B	3B	HR	BB	SO	HB	SH	AVG	OBP	SLG	OPS	AOPS	BR	ABR	PF	SB	CS	BSA	BSR
EAST																														
NY	87	74	0	.540		44	36	871	814	6310	1541	294	25	205	631	1007	16	57	.277	.354	.450	804	103	28	34	99	99	48	67	5
BOS	85	77	0	.525	2.5	42	39	792	**745**	6371	1503	316	32	167	611	1019	40	42	.267	.341	.423	764	89	-59	-83	103	43	30	59	-1
TOR	83	79	0	.512	4.5	45	36	861	908	6326	1562	328	21	**244**	526	1026	29	**60**	.275	.341	.469	810	100	21	-7	103	89	34	72	8
BAL	74	88	0	.457	13.5	44	37	794	913	6237	1508	310	22	184	558	900	27	49	.272	.341	.435	776	100	-37	3	95	**126**	65	66	5
TB	69	92	0	.429	18	36	44	733	842	6206	1414	253	22	162	558	1022	52	51	.257	.329	.399	728	85	-138	-132	99	90	46	66	4
CENTRAL																														
CHI	95	67	0	.586		46	35	**978**	839	6406	1615	325	33	216	591	960	55	53	.286	.356	.470	826	105	70	55	102	119	42	74	11
CLE	90	72	0	.556	5	**48**	33	950	816	6512	1639	310	30	221	685	1057	41	51	**.288**	**.367**	.470	**837**	**108**	**105**	**85**	102	113	34	77	13
DET	79	83	0	.488	16	43	38	823	827	6340	1553	307	41	177	562	982	42	43	.275	.343	.438	781	99	-29	-7	97	83	38	69	5
KC	77	85	0	.475	18	42	39	879	930	6394	**1644**	281	27	150	511	**840**	56	48	**.288**	.348	.425	773	92	-36	-64	104	121	35	**78**	**14**
MIN	69	93	0	.426	26	36	45	748	880	6281	1516	325	**49**	116	556	1021	24	35	.270	.337	.407	744	85	-99	-128	104	90	45	67	4
WEST																														
OAK	91	70	0	.565		47	34	947	813	6432	1501	281	23	239	750	1159	26	52	.270	.360	.458	818	**108**	59	80	98	40	15	73	4
SEA	91	71	0	.562	0.5	47	34	907	780	6444	1481	300	26	198	**775**	1073	**63**	48	.269	.361	.442	803	105	41	69	97	122	56	69	7
ANA	82	80	0	.506	9.5	46	35	864	869	6373	1574	309	34	236	608	1024	47	47	.280	.352	**.472**	824	104	60	36	103	93	52	64	2
TEX	71	91	0	.438	20.5	42	39	848	974	6363	1601	**330**	35	173	580	922	48	39	.283	.352	.446	798	100	13	0	102	69	47	59	-1
TOT	1132					608	524	11995		88995	21652	4269	420	2688	8502	14012	675	566	.276	.349	.443	792					1297	587	69	80

TEAM	CG	SHO	GR	SV	IP	H	HR	BB	SO	BR/9	ERA	AERA	OAV	OOB	PR	APR	PF	OSB	OCS	FA	E	WPB	DP	FW	PW	BW	BSW	DIF
EAST																												
NY	9	6	382	40	1424.1	1458	177	577	1040	13.2	4.76	102	.263	.336	24	12	98	91	37	.981	109	62	132	.2	1.1	3.1	-.0	2.2
BOS	7	**12**	425	**46**	1452.2	**1433**	173	498	1121	**12.3**	**4.23**	**119**	**.257**	**.322**	**110**	**127**	103	159	47	.982	109	59	120	.2	**11.6**	-7.6	-.6	.4
TOR	**15**	4	388	37	1437.1	1615	195	560	978	14.0	5.14	99	.285	.354	-37	-10	103	99	38	.984	100	**48**	176	.7	-.9	-.6	.2	2.6
BAL	14	6	396	33	1433.1	1547	202	665	1017	14.1	5.37	88	.275	.352	-73	-108	96	104	31	.981	116	57	151	-.2	-9.9	.3	-.0	2.9
TB	10	8	401	38	1431.1	1553	198	533	955	13.5	4.86	102	.277	.345	8	12	101	114	46	.981	118	71	169	-.4	1.1	-12.1	-.2	.0
CENTRAL																												
CHI	5	7	**466**	43	1450.1	1509	195	614	1037	13.5	4.66	107	.270	.346	41	52	102	79	**58**	.978	133	56	**190**	-1.2	4.8	5.0	.5	4.9
CLE	6	5	462	34	1442.1	1511	173	666	**1213**	13.8	4.84	103	.270	.350	12	21	101	109	42	**.988**	**72**	60	147	**2.4**	1.9	**7.8**	.7	-3.8
DET	6	6	429	44	1443.1	1583	177	**496**	978	13.3	4.71	102	.280	.340	33	18	98	**55**	42	.983	105	58	171	.5	1.6	-.6	-.0	-3.4
KC	10	6	329	29	1439.1	1585	239	693	927	14.5	5.48	93	.282	.362	-90	-55	104	118	38	.983	102	84	185	.6	-5.0	-5.9	**.8**	5.5
MIN	6	4	412	35	1432.2	1634	212	516	1042	13.7	5.14	100	.287	.347	-37	1	105	64	33	.983	102	81	155	.6	.0	-11.7	-.2	-.8
WEST																												
OAK	7	11	381	43	1435,1	1535	**158**	615	963	13.8	4.58	104	.274	.348	53	27	97	92	39	.978	134	54	164	-1.3	2.5	7.3	-.2	2.1
SEA	4	10	383	44	1441.2	1442	167	634	998	13.2	4.49	105	.262	.339	67	35	96	82	38	.984	99	51	176	.8	3.2	6.3	.1	-.5
ANA	5	3	441	**46**	1448.0	1534	228	662	846	13.9	5.00	101	.273	.351	-15	10	103	101	56	.978	134	53	182	-1.2	.9	3.3	-.3	-1.6
TEX	3	4	415	39	1429.0	1683	202	661	918	15.2	5.52	91	.294	.369	-96	-81	102	65	37	.978	135	**48**	162	-1.3	-7.4	.0	-.6	-.7
TOT	107	92	5710	551	20141.0					13.7	4.91		.276	.349						.982	1568	842	2280					

Batter-Fielder Wins	Batting Average	On-Base Percentage	Slugging Average	On-Base Plus Slugging	Adjusted OPS	Adjusted Batter Runs
A.Rodriguez-Sea 6.8	Garciaparra-Bos ...372	J.Giambi-Oak..............476	M.Ramirez-Cle 697	M.Ramirez-Cle....1154	J.Giambi-Oak........187	J.Giambi-Oak 78.1
J.Giambi-Oak......5.2	Erstad-Ana 355	Delgado-Tor 470	Delgado-Tor 664	Delgado-Tor........1134	M.Ramirez-Cle......184	Delgado-Tor........76.8
Glaus-Ana............5.0	M.Ramirez-Cle 351	M.Ramirez-Cle............457	J.Giambi-Oak 647	J.Giambi-Oak......1123	Delgado-Tor..........178	Thomas-Chi........61.5
Garciaparra-Bos 5.0	Delgado-Tor 344	Thomas-Chi 436	Thomas-Chi 625	Thomas-Chi........1061	Thomas-Chi..........163	M.Ramirez-Cle ..60.1
Delgado-Tor 4.6	Jeter-NY 339	Garciaparra-Bos 434	A.Rodriguez-Sea .606	Garciaparra-Bos 1033	A.Rodriguez-Sea ..163	A.Rodriguez-Sea 56.8

Runs	Hits	Doubles	Triples	Home Runs	Total Bases	Runs Batted In
Damon-KC...........136	Erstad-Ana 240	Delgado-Tor 57	Guzman-Min 20	Glaus-Ana 47	Delgado-Tor..........378	Martinez-Sea 145
A.Rodriguez-Sea ..134	Damon-KC............214	Garciaparra-Bos 51	Kennedy-Ana..........11	Thomas-Chi...........43	Erstad-Ana 366	Sweeney-KC........144
Erstad-Ana 121	Sweeney-KC 206	D.Cruz-Det 46	Damon-KC..............10	J.Giambi-Oak.........43	Thomas-Chi..........364	Thomas-Chi 143
Durham-Chi 121	Jeter-NY 201	Olerud-Sea 45	Durham-Chi 9		Glaus-Ana 340	J.Giambi-Oak 137
Glaus-Ana 120	Garciaparra-Bos ..197				Dye-KC 337	Delgado-Tor 137

Stolen Bases	Base Stealing Runs	Fielding Runs-Infield	Fielding Runs-Outfield	Wins	Winning Pct.	Complete Games
Damon-KC.............46	R.Alomar-Cle 7.2	Velarde-Oak................22.0	Martinez-TB-Tx-Tor 11.5	D.Wells-Tor 20	Hudson-Oak 769	D.Wells-Tor 9
R.Alomar-Cle..........39	Damon-KC 7.0	Sanchez-KC...............19.1	Higginson-Det........9.7	Hudson-Oak 20	P.Martinez-Bos 750	P.Martinez-Bos 7
DeShields-Bal 37	DeShields-Bal........4.6	Valentin-Chi 17.9	Erstad-Ana 8.6	Pettitte-NY 19	Burba-Cle 727	Ponson-Bal..............6
Henderson-Sea 31	Lofton-Cle.............4.2	Olerud-Sea 14.5	Jones-Min 7.1	P.Martinez-Bos........18	D.Wells-Tor 714	Mussina-Bal 6
	Cairo-TB 3.7	R.Alomar-Cle 14.3	Salmon-Ana 5.8	Sele-Sea 17	Pettitte-NY 679	

Strikeouts	Fewest BB/Game	Games	Saves	Base Runners/9	Adjusted Relief Runs	Relief Ranking
P.Martinez-Bos......284	D.Wells-Tor 1.21	Wunsch-Chi 83	Lowe-Bos...............42	P.Martinez-Bos 7.22	Lowe-Bos 25.2	Lowe-Bos 41.5
Colon-Cle 212	P.Martinez-Bos 1.33	Venafro-Tex...................77	Jones-Det 42	Foulke-Chi 9.20	Foulke-Chi 20.1	Koch-Tor 39.1
Mussina-Bal..........210	Mussina-Bal 1.74	Wells-Min 76	Sasaki-Sea 37	Rivera-NY 9.87	Tam-Oak.............19.9	Rivera-NY 33.9
Finley-Cle 189	Milton-Min............1.98	Trombley-Bal.................75	Rivera-NY 36	Wells-Min 10.32	Koch-Tor 19.6	Mecir-TB-Oak 27.1
Clemens-NY 188	Moehler-Det 2.02	Lowe-Bos 74		Rhodes-Sea 10.38	Mecir-TB-Oak 18.2	Nelson-NY..........26.6

Innings Pitched	Opponents' Avg.	Opponents' OBP	Earned Run Average	Adjusted ERA	Adjusted Starter Runs	Pitcher Wins
Mussina-Bal 237.2	P.Martinez-Bos 167	P.Martinez-Bos............213	P.Martinez-Bos 1.74	P.Martinez-Bos......290	P.Martinez-Bos 78.5	**P.Martinez-Bos**..8.4
D.Wells-Tor 229.2	Hudson-Oak 227	Mussina-Bal................291	Clemens-NY........3.70	Sirotka-Chi............132	Mussina-Bal 26.7	**Lowe-Bos** 3.9
Rogers-Tex 227.1	Colon-Cle 233	Hernandez-NY.............298	Mussina-Bal 3.79	Clemens-NY 131	D.Wells-Tor 24.1	**Koch-Tor** 3.7
Radke-Min 226.2	Clemens-NY 236	Milton-Min 303	Sirotka-Chi 3.79	Colon-Cle 128	Clemens-NY 23.9	**Rivera-NY** 3.3
Ponson-Bal........222.0	Abbott-Sea 243	Hudson-Oak 306	Colon-Cle 3.88	Mussina-Bal..........125	F.Castillo-Tor 23.3	**Mecir-TB-Oak** 2.5

Three Times for Yankees

Umpires formed a new union to replace the one broken a year earlier in their botched mass resignation. One of its first duties was to agree to merge the league staffs, so arbiters could work games in both leagues. New parks opened in Detroit, San Francisco, Houston and Pittsburgh, lifting average attendance to near pre-strike levels. Slugger Albert Belle had to retire because of a degenerative hip condition. Pitching sensations Mark Mulder and Barry Zito debuted with Oakland; Hall of Famer Bob Lemon died.

The Yankees had the worst record of any team in the postseason, but their veteran-laden squad held off upstart Oakland in the Division Series. While the A's defeated Roger Clemens twice, they did not win at home after the opener. Following an overnight trip to Oakland for Game 5, the Yankees scored 6 runs in the top of the first and then held on. Seattle, which didn't clinch the Wild Card until the season's final day, swept the White Sox in the other ALDS. The Yankees dispatched the Mariners in six games, including the first complete-game ALCS shutout in fifteen years—a 15-strikeout, 1-hit masterpiece by Clemens.

New York's first Subway Series since 1956 was big on talk, low on ratings, and just five games start to finish—although three games were decided in the eighth inning or later. The Mets broke the Yankees' 14-game World Series winning streak but little else as the Yanks claimed baseball's first "three-peat" since the 1972–74 A's. After the season Alex Rodriguez signed a 10-year, $252 million contract with Texas, the richest deal in American pro sports history.

2001 National League

TEAM	W	L	T	PCT	GB	HW	HL	R	OR	PA	H	2B	3B	HR	BB	SO	HB	SH	AVG	OBP	SLG	OPS	AOPS	BR	ABR	PF	SB	CS	BSA	BSR
EAST																														
ATL	88	74	0	.543		40	41	729	**643**	6152	1432	263	24	174	493	1039	64	45	.260	.324	.412	736	92	-45	-58	102	85	46	65	3
PHI	86	76	0	.531	2	47	34	746	719	6219	1431	295	29	164	551	1125	67	43	.260	.329	.414	743	99	-22	-1	97	**153**	47	**77**	**17**
NY	82	80	0	.506	6	44	37	642	713	6156	1361	273	18	147	545	1062	52	65	.249	.323	.387	710	93	-89	-52	95	66	48	58	-2
FLA	76	86	0	.469	12	46	34	742	744	6184	1461	**325**	30	166	470	1145	60	67	.264	.326	.423	749	101	-17	11	96	89	40	69	6
MON	68	94	0	.420	20	34	47	670	812	6026	1361	320	28	131	478	1071	64	60	.253	.319	.396	715	88	-81	-92	102	101	51	66	4
CENTRAL																														
HOU	93	69	0	.574		44	37	847	769	6325	1500	313	29	208	581	1119	71	**89**	.271	.347	.451	798	105	95	53	105	64	49	57	-3
STL	93	69	0	.574		**54**	28	814	684	6177	1469	274	32	199	529	1089	83	65	.270	.339	.441	780	106	47	56	99	91	35	72	8
CHI	88	74	0	.543	5	48	33	777	701	6219	1409	268	32	194	577	1077	**117**	66	.261	.336	.430	766	108	23	67	95	67	36	65	2
MIL	68	94	0	.420	25	36	45	740	806	6148	1378	273	30	209	488	1399	65	72	.251	.319	.426	745	99	-36	-17	97	66	36	65	2
CIN	66	96	0	.407	27	27	54	735	850	6222	1464	304	22	176	468	1172	66	65	.262	.324	.419	743	92	-31	-60	104	103	54	66	4
PIT	62	100	0	.383	31	38	43	657	858	6027	1333	256	25	161	467	1106	60	67	.247	.313	.393	706	84	-107	-118	102	93	73	56	-5
WEST																														
ARI	92	70	0	.568		48	33	818	677	6346	1494	284	35	208	587	1052	71	57	.267	.341	.442	783	100	55	9	106	71	38	65	2
SF	90	72	0	.556	2	49	32	799	748	6408	1493	304	40	**235**	625	1090	67	50	.266	.342	.460	802	**120**	95	**166**	93	57	42	58	-2
LA	86	76	0	.531	6	44	37	758	744	6169	1399	264	27	206	519	1062	57	56	.255	.323	.425	748	105	-25	35	92	89	42	68	5
SD	79	83	0	.488	13	35	46	789	812	6278	1379	273	26	161	**678**	**1273**	29	41	.252	.336	.399	735	104	-28	44	91	129	44	75	13
COL	73	89	0	.451	19	41	40	**923**	906	6393	**1663**	324	**61**	213	511	1027	81	61	**.292**	**.354**	**.483**	**837**	98	**166**	-6	122	132	54	71	10
TOT	1296					675	621	12186		99449	23027	4613	488	2952	8567	17908	969	1074	.261	.331	.425	756					1456	735	66	63

TEAM	CG	SHO	GR	SV	IP	H	HR	BB	SO	BR/9	ERA	AERA	OAV	OOB	PR	APR	PF	OSB	OCS	FA	E	WPB	DP	FW	PW	BW	BSW	DIF
EAST																												
ATL	5	13	411	41	1447.1	1363	153	499	1133	11.8	**3.59**	**123**	.250	.314	**123**	**129**	101	102	50	.983	103	50	133	.4	**12.6**	-5.6	-.0	-.2
PHI	8	7	473	47	1445.1	1417	170	527	1086	12.5	4.15	102	.259	.329	33	15	98	57	32	.985	91	49	145	1.1	1.5	-.0	**1.3**	1.3
NY	6	**14**	397	**48**	1445.2	1418	186	**438**	1191	11.8	4.07	101	.257	.314	46	10	95	131	40	.983	101	64	132	.5	1.0	-5.1	-.6	5.1
FLA	5	11	430	32	1438.0	1397	151	617	1119	13.0	4.32	97	.257	.338	5	-19	97	75	51	.983	103	50	**174**	.4	-1.8	1.1	.2	-4.8
MON	5	11	**491**	28	1431.1	1509	190	525	1103	13.2	4.68	95	.272	.339	-52	-35	102	128	33	.982	108	67	139	.1	-3.4	-9.0	.0	-.8
CENTRAL																												
HOU	7	6	405	**48**	1454.2	1453	221	486	1228	12.4	4.37	104	.261	.325	-3	30	105	66	49	.982	110	**46**	138	.0	2.9	5.2	-.7	4.6
STL	8	11	484	38	1435.1	1389	196	526	1083	12.5	3.93	108	.256	.328	68	54	98	**51**	37	.982	110	52	156	.0	5.3	5.4	.4	.9
CHI	8	6	452	41	1437.0	1357	164	550	**1344**	12.3	4.03	103	.249	.321	53	19	95	106	46	.982	109	61	113	.0	1.8	6.5	-.2	-1.3
MIL	3	8	489	28	1436.1	1452	197	667	1057	13.7	4.64	93	.265	.350	-45	-56	99	93	47	.983	103	69	156	.4	-5.4	-1.7	-.2	-6.1
CIN	2	2	461	35	1442.2	1572	198	515	943	13.3	4.77	95	.279	.341	-67	-34	105	75	**62**	.978	138	74	136	-1.5	-3.3	-5.8	.0	-4.3
PIT	8	9	410	36	1416.1	1493	167	549	908	13.5	5.05	89	.272	.344	-108	-85	103	97	37	.978	133	58	168	-1.3	-8.3	-11.5	-.9	2.9
WEST																												
ARI	**12**	13	421	34	1459.2	**1352**	195	461	1297	**11.5**	3.87	118	**.247**	**.311**	79	109	105	107	55	**.986**	**84**	57	148	**1.5**	10.6	.9	-.2	-1.8
SF	3	8	439	47	1463.1	1437	**145**	579	1080	12.6	4.18	95	.258	.329	28	-36	91	86	45	.981	118	58	170	-.4	-3.5	**16.2**	-.6	-2.7
LA	3	5	408	46	1450.2	1387	184	524	1212	12.3	4.25	94	.252	.323	17	-42	92	82	51	.981	116	53	138	-.3	-4.1	3.4	.1	5.9
SD	5	6	422	46	1440.2	1519	219	476	1088	12.8	4.52	88	.269	.330	-27	-91	92	94	52	.976	145	61	127	-1.9	-8.9	4.3	.9	3.6
COL	8	8	476	26	1430.0	1522	239	598	1058	13.7	5.29	101	.275	.350	-149	5	122	100	36	.984	96	52	167	.8	.5	-.6	.6	-9.3
TOT	96	138	7069	621	23074.1					12.7	4.36		.261	.331						.982	1768	921	2340					

Batter-Fielder Wins	Batting Average	On-Base Percentage	Slugging Average	On-Base Plus Slugging	Adjusted OPS	Adjusted Batter Runs
Bonds-SF 12.0	L.Walker-Col .350	Bonds-SF .515	Bonds-SF .863	Bonds-SF 1379	Bonds-SF 267	Bonds-SF 136.0
Sosa-Chi 8.9	Helton-Col .336	L.Walker-Col .449	Sosa-Chi .737	Sosa-Chi 1174	Sosa-Chi 208	Sosa-Chi 97.5
Gonzalez-Ari 5.9	Alou-Hou .331	Sosa-Chi .437	Gonzalez-Ari .688	Gonzalez-Ari 1117	Gonzalez-Ari 172	Gonzalez-Ari 68.4
Nevin-SD 5.4	Berkman-Hou .331	Helton-Col .432	Helton-Col .685	Helton-Col 1116	Sheffield-LA 168	Berkman-Hou 56.5
Pujols-StL 5.4	C.Jones-Atl .330	Berkman-Hou .430	L.Walker-Col .662	L.Walker-Col 1111	Nevin-SD 162	Sheffield-LA 56.1

Runs	Hits	Doubles	Triples	Home Runs	Total Bases	Runs Batted In
Sosa-Chi 146	Aurilia-SF 206	Berkman-Hou 55	Rollins-Phi 12	Bonds-SF 73	Sosa-Chi 425	Sosa-Chi 160
Helton-Col 132	Pierre-Col 202	Helton-Col 54	Uribe-Col 11	Sosa-Chi 64	Gonzalez-Ari 419	Helton-Col 146
Bonds-SF 129	Gonzalez-Ari 198	Kent-SF 49	Pierre-Col 11	Gonzalez-Ari 57	Bonds-SF 411	Gonzalez-Ari 142
Gonzalez-Ari 128	Helton-Col 197	Abreu-Phi 48	Castillo-Fla 10	Helton-Col 49	Helton-Col 402	Bonds-SF 137
Bagwell-Hou 126	Pujols-StL 194	Pujols-StL 47		Green-LA 49	Green-LA 370	

Stolen Bases	Base Stealing Runs	Fielding Runs-Infield	Fielding Runs-Outfield	Wins	Winning Pct.	Complete Games
Rollins-Phi 46	Rollins-Phi 7.3	Cabrera-Mon 29.0	Shinjo-NY 12.7	Schilling-Ari 22	Schilling-Ari .786	Schilling-Ari 6
Pierre-Col 46	Pierre-Col 4.2	Polanco-StL 24.3	A.Jones-Atl 11.1	Morris-StL 22	Johnson-Ari .778	Vazquez-Mon 5
Guerrero-Mon 37	Reese-Cin 4.1	Cirillo-Col 17.9	Jordan-Atl 10.2	Johnson-Ari 21	Lieber-Chi .769	Lieber-Chi 5
Abreu-Phi 36	Glanville-Phi 4.1	Nunez-Pit 17.3	Glanville-Phi 6.3	Lieber-Chi 20	Morris-StL .733	
Castillo-Fla 33	Womack-Ari 3.7	Lugo-Hou 15.6	Sosa-Chi 5.9		Glavine-Atl .696	

Strikeouts	Fewest BB/Game	Games	Saves	Base Runners/9	Adjusted Relief Runs	Relief Ranking
Johnson-Ari 372	Maddux-Atl 1.04	Kline-StL 89	Nen-SF 45	Rodriguez-SF 9.07	Rodriguez-SF 22.8	Wagner-Hou 25.9
Schilling-Ari 293	Schilling-Ari 1.37	Lloyd-Mon 84	Shaw-LA 43	Reed-NY 9.16	Kline-StL 21.2	Rodriguez-SF 25.5
Park-LA 218	Lieber-Chi 1.59	King-Mil 82	Hoffman-SD 43	Nen-SF 9.39	Dotel-Hou 20.7	Kim-Ari 24.9
Wood-Chi 217	Jones-SD 1.75	Fassero-Chi 82	Benitez-NY 43	Schilling-Ari 9.71	Weathers-Mil-Chi 18.6	Mesa-Phi 22.9
Vazquez-Mon 208	Vazquez-Mon 1.77		Mesa-Phi 42	Johnson-Ari 9.73	Kim-Ari 18.1	Dotel-Hou 22.1

Innings Pitched	Opponents' Avg.	Opponents' OBP	Earned Run Average	Adjusted ERA	Adjusted Starter Runs	Pitcher Wins
Schilling-Ari 256.2	Wood-Chi .202	Schilling-Ari .273	Johnson-Ari 2.49	Johnson-Ari 184	Johnson-Ari 55.4	**Johnson-Ari** 5.3
Johnson-Ari 249.2	Johnson-Ari .203	Johnson-Ari .274	Schilling-Ari 2.98	Schilling-Ari 154	Schilling-Ari 45.9	**Maddux-Atl** 4.4
Park-LA 234.0	Park-LA .216	Vazquez-Mon .274	Burkett-Atl 3.04	Burkett-Atl 145	Maddux-Atl 35.6	**Schilling-Ari** 4.3
Maddux-Atl 233.0	Burkett-Atl .230	Maddux-Atl .278	Maddux-Atl 3.05	Maddux-Atl 145	Burkett-Atl 32.8	**Kile-StL** 3.6
Lieber-Chi 232.1	Burnett-Fla .231	Lieber-Chi .290	Kile-StL 3.09	Kile-StL 138	Kile-StL 31.2	**Vazquez-Mon** 3.4

Bonds Is Best

New ballparks opened in Pittsburgh and Milwaukee. Compared to recent openings, attendance was good the first season, but the numbers for both also-rans dropped by one-quarter the following season—a new stadium was no longer a cure-all. Umpire Al Clark was fired following allegations he broke MLB rules: exchanging first-class plane tickets for economy class (and pocketing the difference) and soliciting players' autographs to sell as memorabilia.

Barry Bonds had one of the most impressive seasons ever, breaking Mark McGwire's record with 73 home runs, and setting single-season marks for walks (177) and slugging percentage (.863). Sammy Sosa became the first player with 60 or more homers in three seasons. McGwire retired after the season, fifth on the all-time home run list; Tony Gwynn also hung up the spikes. Hall of Famers Eddie Mathews and Willie Stargell died.

Arizona won the West for the second time in four years, behind the pitching duo of Randy Johnson and Curt Schilling. Johnson fanned 20 Reds in May, equaling the nine-inning record, but he was removed when the game went into extra innings. Schilling, who won 22 during the season, tossed a complete-game in Game 5 of the Division Series as the Diamondbacks beat St. Louis in the bottom of the ninth. Atlanta swept Houston in the other Division Series. Johnson won both his starts in the D-backs' five-game NLCS victory over the Braves. Arizona and the Yankees played a seven-game World Series thriller, with Johnson winning three times, including Game 7 in relief. It took a ninth-inning rally, capped by a broken-bat hit by Luis Gonzalez, to give Arizona the title.

2001 American League

TEAM	W	L	T	PCT	GB	HW	HL	R	OR	PA	H	2B	3B	HR	BB	SO	HB	SH	AVG	OBP	SLG	OPS	AOPS	BR	ABR	PF	SB	CS	BSA	BSR
EAST																														
NY	95	65	1	.594		51	28	804	713	6233	1488	289	20	203	519	1035	30	64	.267	.334	.435	769	100	12	1	101	161	53	75	17
BOS	82	79	0	.509	13.5	41	40	772	745	6264	1493	316	29	198	520	1131	28	70	.266	.334	.439	773	101	21	13	101	46	35	57	-2
TOR	80	82	0	.494	16	40	42	767	753	6284	1489	287	36	195	470	1094	34	74	.263	.325	.430	755	95	-25	-44	103	156	55	74	15
BAL	63	98	1	.391	32.5	30	50	687	829	6150	1359	262	24	136	514	**989**	38	77	.248	.319	.380	699	89	-123	-87	95	133	53	72	11
TB	62	100	0	.383	34	37	44	672	887	6104	1426	311	21	121	456	1116	45	54	.258	.320	.388	708	87	-111	-102	99	115	52	69	7
CENTRAL																														
CLE	91	71	0	.562		44	36	897	821	6357	1559	294	37	212	577	1076	49	69	.278	.350	.458	808	110	100	88	101	79	41	66	3
MIN	85	77	0	.525	6	47	34	771	766	6182	1514	328	**38**	164	495	1083	25	64	.272	.337	.433	770	99	17	-2	103	146	67	69	9
CHI	83	79	0	.512	8	46	35	798	795	6150	1463	300	29	214	520	998	**63**	52	.268	.334	.451	785	101	42	14	104	123	59	68	6
DET	66	96	0	.407	25	37	44	724	876	6144	1439	291	60	139	466	972	41	51	.260	.320	.409	729	95	-72	-40	96	133	61	69	8
KC	65	97	0	.401	26	35	46	729	858	6176	1503	277	37	152	406	898	36	44	.266	.318	.409	727	83	-82	-137	109	100	42	70	7
WEST																														
SEA	116	46	0	.716		**57**	24	**927**	**627**	6474	**1637**	310	**38**	169	614	**989**	48	62	**.288**	**.360**	.445	805	**118**	**112**	**168**	94	**174**	42	**81**	**24**
OAK	102	60	0	.630	14	53	28	884	645	6385	1469	**334**	22	199	**640**	1021	25	**88**	.264	.345	.439	784	105	61	58	100	68	29	70	5
ANA	75	87	0	.463	41	39	42	691	730	6221	1447	275	26	158	494	1001	46	77	.261	.327	.405	732	90	-59	-77	103	116	52	69	7
TEX	73	89	0	.451	43	41	41	890	968	6388	1566	326	23	**246**	548	1093	25	75	.275	.344	**.471**	**815**	108	109	77	104	97	32	75	10
TOT	1133					598	534	11013		87512	20852	4200	440	2506	7239	14496	921	533	.267	.334	.428	762					1647	673	71	127

TEAM	CG	SHO	GR	SV	IP	H	HR	BB	SO	BR/9	ERA	AERA	OAV	OOB	PR	APR	PF	OSB	OCS	FA	E	WPB	DP	FW	PW	BW	BSW	DIF
EAST																												
NY	7	9	362	**57**	1451.1	1429	158	465	**1266**	12.1	4.02	112	.257	.318	72	75	100	146	45	.982	109	75	132	.3	7.2	.0	.8	6.7
BOS	3	9	424	48	1448.0	1412	**146**	544	1259	12.7	4.15	108	.254	.329	53	54	100	223	51	.981	113	77	129	.0	5.2	1.2	-1.1	-3.9
TOR	7	10	471	41	1462.2	1553	165	490	1041	13.0	4.28	107	.275	.339	31	49	103	112	47	.985	97	**43**	184	1.0	4.7	-4.2	.6	-3.1
BAL	10	6	392	31	1432.1	1504	194	528	938	13.2	4.67	92	.269	.337	-32	-65	96	157	51	.979	125	52	137	-.6	-6.2	-8.3	.2	-2.5
TB	1	6	370	30	1423.2	1513	207	569	1030	13.6	4.94	91	.273	.345	-73	-71	100	113	44	.977	139	83	144	-1.4	-6.8	-9.8	-.2	-.8
CENTRAL																												
CLE	3	4	**483**	42	1446.2	1512	148	573	1218	13.3	4.64	97	.270	.341	-27	-20	101	128	60	.982	107	70	137	.4	-1.9	8.4	-.6	3.6
MIN	12	8	402	45	1441.1	1494	192	445	965	12.5	4.51	102	.268	.325	-6	13	103	**73**	43	.982	108	62	118	.4	1.2	-.2	.0	2.6
CHI	8	9	406	51	1433.1	1465	181	500	921	12.9	4.55	101	.266	.334	-13	9	103	107	40	.981	118	70	149	-.2	.9	1.3	-.3	.3
DET	**16**	2	391	34	1429.1	1624	180	553	859	14.2	5.01	87	.288	.357	-85	-109	97	104	50	.979	131	70	164	-1.0	-10.4	-3.8	-.1	.4
KC	5	1	396	30	1440.0	1537	209	576	911	13.6	4.87	101	.276	.348	-63	5	110	105	45	.981	117	83	**204**	-.2	.5	-13.1	-.2	-3.0
WEST																												
SEA	8	**14**	391	56	1465.0	**1293**	160	465	1051	**11.2**	**3.54**	117	**.236**	**.301**	**152**	107	93	**73**	29	**.986**	**83**	46	137	**1.8**	10.3	**16.1**	**1.4**	5.4
OAK	13	9	416	44	1463.1	1384	153	**440**	1117	11.5	3.59	**123**	.249	.308	144	**137**	99	124	55	.980	125	46	151	-.6	**13.1**	5.6	-.4	3.3
ANA	6	1	384	43	1437.2	1452	168	525	947	12.8	4.20	109	.263	.331	44	56	102	109	59	.983	103	62	142	.7	5.4	-7.4	-.2	-4.4
TEX	4	3	410	37	1438.1	1670	222	596	951	14.6	5.71	82	.293	.362	-198	-161	104	79	**66**	.981	114	72	167	.0	-15.4	7.4	.0	-.0
TOT	103	91	5698	589	20213.0					12.9	4.47		.267	.334						.981	1589	911	2095					

Batter-Fielder Wins	Batting Average	On-Base Percentage	Slugging Average	On-Base Plus Slugging	Adjusted OPS	Adjusted Batter Runs
A.Rodriguez-Tex 6.9	Suzuki-Sea 350	J.Giambi-Oak...............477	J.Giambi-Oak 660	J.Giambi-Oak......1137	J.Giambi-Oak........197	J.Giambi-Oak 84.6
J.Giambi-Oak......6.3	J.Giambi-Oak 342	Martinez-Sea 423	Thome-Cle 624	Thome-Cle...........1040	Thome-Cle...........167	A.Rodriguez-Tex 55.3
Alomar-Cle 5.9	Alomar-Cle 336	Thome-Cle...................416	A.Rodriguez-Tex ...622	A.Rodriguez-Tex 1021	Martinez-Sea........163	Thome-Cle 55.3
Martinez-Sea 4.0	Boone-Sea 331	Alomar-Cle...................415	Ramirez-Bos.........609	Ramirez-Bos 1014	Ramirez-Bos 161	Martinez-Sea......50.4
Boone-Sea 3.8	Catalanotto-Tex ...330	Delgado-Tor 408	Gonzalez-Cle 590	Martinez-Sea........966	A.Rodriguez-Tex ..159	Boone-Sea 49.2

Runs	Hits	Doubles	Triples	Home Runs	Total Bases	Runs Batted In
A.Rodriguez-Tex ..133	Suzuki-Sea 242	J.Giambi-Oak 47	Guzman-Min 14	A.Rodriguez-Tex 52	A.Rodriguez-Tex ..393	Boone-Sea 141
Suzuki-Sea 127	Boone-Sea 206	Sweeney-KC 46	Beltran-KC 12	Thome-Cle.............49	Boone-Sea 360	Gonzalez-Cle 140
Boone-Sea 118	Stewart-Tor 202	Stewart-Tor 44	Alomar-Cle...............12	Palmeiro-Tex 47	J.Giambi-Oak.........343	A.Rodriguez-Tex..135
Alomar-Cle............113	A.Rodriguez-Tex ..201	Chavez-Oak 43	Cedeno-Det 11	Ramirez-Bos 41	Palmeiro-Tex 338	Ramirez-Bos........125
Jeter-NY 110	Anderson-Ana 194	Durham-Chi 42	Durham-Chi 10	Glaus-Ana 41	Thome-Cle............328	Thome-Cle 124

Stolen Bases	Base Stealing Runs	Fielding Runs-Infield	Fielding Runs-Outfield	Wins	Winning Pct.	Complete Games
Suzuki-Sea 56	Suzuki-Sea 7.4	Gonzalez-Tor 33.3	Hunter-Min 18.6	Mulder-Oak 21	Clemens-NY 870	Sparks-Det 8
Cedeno-Det............55	Cedeno-Det 6.8	Menechino-Oak 17.6	Singleton-Chi 7.3	Moyer-Sea 20	Abbott-Sea 810	Radke-Min 6
Soriano-NY 43	Beltran-KC 6.5	Halter-Det 14.4	Suzuki-Sea 7.0	Clemens-NY 20	Sabathia-Cle.........773	Mulder-Oak.............6
McLemore-Sea 39	McLemore-Sea......6.1	Easley-Det 12.7	Higginson-Det........6.7	Hudson-Oak 18	Moyer-Sea 769	Weaver-Det.............5
Knoblauch-NY 38	Cameron-Sea 5.7	Chavez-Oak..................12.3	Salmon-Ana 6.2	Garcia-Sea 18		

Strikeouts	Fewest BB/Game	Games	Saves	Base Runners/9	Adjusted Relief Runs	Relief Ranking
Nomo-Bos 220	Radke-Min 1.04	Quantrill-Tor 80	M.Rivera-NY 50	Rhodes-Sea 7.81	Foulke-Chi 20.8	Foulke-Chi 41.7
Mussina-NY..........214	Mussina-NY 1.65	Stanton-NY....................76	Sasaki-Sea 45	M.Rivera-NY.........8.26	Rhodes-Sea 19.9	M.Rivera-NY 37.6
Clemens-NY 213	Pettitte-NY 1.84	Grimsley-KC 73	Foulke-Chi 42	Sasaki-Sea 8.51	M.Rivera-NY 18.8	Levine-Ana 33.2
Zito-Oak................205	Moyer-Sea 1.89	Foulke-Chi......................72	Percival-Ana 39	Zimmerman-Tex ..8.58	Zimmerman-Tex ..17.8	Zimmerman-Tex 30.1
Colon-Cle 201	Loaiza-Tor............1.89		Koch-Tor 36	Pineiro-Sea..........8.84	Stanton-NY..........17.2	Stanton-NY 25.0

Innings Pitched	Opponents' Avg.	Opponents' OBP	Earned Run Average	Adjusted ERA	Adjusted Starter Runs	Pitcher Wins
Garcia-Sea 238.2	Garcia-Sea 225	Mussina-NY 274	Garcia-Sea 3.05	Mays-Min 146	Mays-Min 36.4	**Mays-Min**............4.2
Hudson-Oak 235.0	Sabathia-Cle.........228	Buehrle-Chi 279	Mussina-NY 3.15	Mussina-NY...........143	Mussina-NY 34.4	**Foulke-Chi**..........4.1
Mays-Min 233.2	Zito-Oak 230	Garcia-Sea 283	Mays-Min 3.16	Buehrle-Chi 140	Garcia-Sea 31.5	**Mussina-NY**........3.9
Sparks-Det 232.0	Buehrle-Chi 230	Moyer-Sea 285	Buehrle-Chi 3.29	Garcia-Sea 136	Buehrle-Chi 31.5	**M.Rivera-NY** 3.8
	Nomo-Bos 231	Mays-Min 289	Hudson-Oak 3.37	Hudson-Oak 131	Martinez-Bos 27.8	**Buehrle-Chi**........3.3

Tragedy Affects All

Baseball, like the rest of the world, was affected by the September 11 terrorist attacks in New York, Washington, D.C., and Pennsylvania. Games were postponed for six days while the nation evaluated its new travel procedures. No contests were lost, however, as the season was extended by a week. That meant a first-ever November finish for the World Series.

Texas and Toronto began the season in Puerto Rico, the third consecutive season opener outside the U.S. or Canada. Cal Ripken, Harold Baines, and Paul O'Neill retired; Lou Boudreau died.

Seattle's Ichiro Suzuki, a former Japanese superstar, finished the year with 242 hits, the highest total since 1930. The right fielder, known simply as Ichiro on two continents, helped the Mariners to a league-record 116 wins. Oakland, a distant second, won 102 games to take the Wild Card.

The Yankees, East champs again, looked in trouble against the A's in the Division Series. Oakland won the first two games, but New York came back, thanks to one of the most replayed defensive gems in postseason history. With the Yankees leading Game 3, 1–0, shortstop Derek Jeter ranged across the diamond to corral a throw from right field, and threw off balance to catcher Jorge Posada to nail Jeremy Giambi. Like New York, Seattle survived a five-game ALDS. Jamie Moyer and three relievers held Cleveland to 4 hits and 1 run in the deciding game. New York became the first club to win an LCS four straight times—spoiling a guarantee by Mariners manager Lou Piniella—but the Yankees were finally beaten in the World Series by Arizona.

2002 National League

TEAM	W	L	T	PCT	GB	HW	HL	R	OR	PA	H	2B	3B	HR	BB	SO	HB	SH	AVG	OBP	SLG	OPS	AOPS	BR	ABR	PF	SB	CS	BSA	BSR
EAST																														
ATL	101	59	1	.631		52	28	708	**565**	6223	1428	280	25	164	558	1028	67	54	.260	.331	.409	740	98	0	-5	101	76	39	66	3
MON	83	79	0	.512	19	49	32	735	718	6250	1432	300	36	162	575	1104	**108**	46	.261	.334	.418	752	94	23	-34	108	118	64	65	4
PHI	80	81	0	.497	21.5	40	40	710	724	6322	1428	**325**	**41**	165	640	1095	67	53	.259	.339	.422	761	110	46	85	95	104	43	71	8
FLA	79	83	0	.488	23	46	35	699	763	6260	1433	280	32	146	595	1130	59	61	.261	.337	.403	740	103	5	36	96	**177**	73	71	**13**
NY	75	86	0	.466	26.5	38	43	690	703	6150	1409	238	22	160	486	1044	75	63	.256	.322	.395	717	97	-56	-28	96	87	42	67	4
CENTRAL																														
STL	97	65	0	.599		52	29	787	648	6246	**1475**	285	26	175	542	**927**	83	**67**	**.268**	.338	.425	763	108	45	66	97	86	42	67	4
HOU	84	78	0	.519	13	47	34	749	695	6252	1441	291	32	167	589	1120	64	59	.262	.338	.417	755	99	31	-2	105	71	27	72	6
CIN	78	84	0	.481	19	38	43	709	774	6254	1386	297	21	169	583	1188	95	66	.253	.330	.408	738	96	-3	-21	103	116	52	69	7
PIT	72	89	0	.447	24.5	38	42	641	730	6049	1300	263	20	142	537	1109	68	73	.244	.319	.381	700	88	-80	-84	101	86	49	64	2
CHI	67	95	0	.414	30	36	45	706	759	6242	1351	259	29	200	585	1269	78	44	.246	.321	.413	734	99	-24	-9	98	63	21	75	7
MIL	56	106	0	.346	41	31	50	627	821	6083	1369	269	29	139	500	1125	79	55	.253	.320	.390	710	92	-65	-55	99	94	50	65	3
WEST																														
ARI	98	64	0	.605		**55**	26	**819**	674	6316	1471	283	**41**	165	**643**	1016	62	50	.267	**.346**	.423	769	98	67	2	109	92	46	67	4
SF	95	66	1	.590	2.5	50	31	783	616	6298	1465	300	35	**198**	616	961	68	65	.267	.344	**.442**	**786**	**116**	**95**	**136**	95	74	21	**78**	9
LA	92	70	0	.568	6	46	35	713	643	6146	1464	286	29	155	428	940	67	53	.264	.320	.409	729	103	-36	13	93	96	37	72	8
COL	73	89	0	.451	25	47	34	778	898	6164	1508	283	**41**	152	497	1043	49	56	.274	.337	.423	760	90	35	-66	116	103	53	66	4
SD	66	96	0	.407	32	41	40	662	815	6178	1393	243	29	136	547	1062	45	30	.253	.321	.381	702	98	-81	-17	91	71	44	62	0
TOT	1294					706	587	11516		99433	22753	4482	488	2595	8921	17161	895	1134	.259	.331	.410	741					1514	703	68	87

TEAM	CG	SHO	GR	SV	IP	H	HR	BB	SO	BR/9	ERA	AERA	OAV	OOB	PR	APR	PF	OSB	OCS	FA	E	WPB	DP	FW	PW	BW	BSW	DIF
EAST																												
ATL	3	**15**	469	**57**	1467.1	**1302**	123	554	1058	11.6	**3.13**	**130**	**.240**	.313	**158**	**156**	100	96	55	.982	114	52	170	-.3	**15.6**	-.5	-.2	6.4
MON	9	3	437	39	1453.0	1475	165	508	1088	12.6	3.97	112	.265	.329	22	73	109	85	44	.978	139	63	160	-1.7	7.3	-3.4	-.1	-.0
PHI	5	9	450	47	1449.2	1381	153	570	1075	12.5	4.17	94	.252	.328	-10	-46	95	74	34	**.986**	88	80	156	1.2	-4.6	8.5	.3	-5.8
FLA	11	12	461	36	1456.1	1449	151	631	1104	13.2	4.36	90	.262	.341	-42	-72	96	93	**61**	.983	106	61	163	.2	-7.2	3.6	**.8**	.7
NY	9	10	451	36	1442.2	1408	163	543	1107	12.5	3.89	102	.256	.327	34	11	96	151	53	.976	144	**33**	138	-2.0	1.1	-2.8	-.1	-1.7
CENTRAL																												
STL	4	9	472	42	1446.1	1355	141	547	1009	12.2	3.70	107	.251	.323	65	42	96	86	34	.983	103	49	168	.4	4.2	6.6	-.1	5.0
HOU	2	11	480	43	1445.0	1423	151	546	1219	12.6	4.00	107	.260	.330	17	41	104	104	36	**.986**	**83**	43	149	**1.5**	4.1	-.2	.0	-2.4
CIN	2	8	462	42	1453.2	1502	173	550	980	13.1	4.27	99	.269	.338	-27	-5	103	**67**	42	.981	120	80	169	-.6	-.5	-2.1	.2	.0
PIT	2	7	458	47	1412.2	1447	163	572	920	13.2	4.23	99	.268	.342	-20	-9	102	94	44	.982	115	46	**177**	-.4	-.9	-8.4	-.3	1.5
CHI	11	9	390	23	1441.1	1373	167	606	**1333**	12.7	4.29	94	.253	.331	-30	-45	98	112	54	.981	114	59	144	-.3	-4.5	-.9	.2	-8.5
MIL	7	4	446	32	1432.1	1468	199	666	1026	13.8	4.73	87	.268	.352	-99	-102	100	109	49	.983	103	76	154	.4	-10.2	-5.5	-.2	-9.4
WEST																												
ARI	**14**	10	422	40	1446.2	1361	170	**421**	1303	**11.4**	3.92	113	.247	**.305**	30	76	108	77	43	.985	89	61	116	1.1	7.6	.2	-.1	8.2
SF	10	13	417	43	1437.1	1349	**116**	523	992	11.9	3.54	109	.251	.319	90	56	94	87	36	.985	90	43	166	1.1	5.6	**13.6**	.4	-6.2
LA	4	**15**	423	56	1457.2	1311	165	555	1132	11.8	3.69	103	.241	.315	67	21	93	110	53	.985	90	45	134	1.1	2.1	1.3	.3	6.3
COL	1	8	**506**	43	1426.2	1554	225	582	920	13.9	5.20	92	.277	.349	-174	-59	116	87	23	.982	112	54	158	-.2	-5.9	-6.6	-.1	4.8
SD	5	10	459	40	1436.1	1522	177	582	1108	13.6	4.62	82	.274	.346	-82	-149	92	76	40	.979	128	65	162	-1.1	-14.9	-1.7	-.5	3.2
TOT	99	153	7203	666	23105.0					12.7	4.11		.259	.331						.982	1738	910	2484					

Batter-Fielder Wins	Batting Average	On-Base Percentage	Slugging Average	On-Base Plus Slugging	Adjusted OPS	Adjusted Batter Runs
Bonds-SF 11.7	Bonds-SF 370	Bonds-SF....................582	Bonds-SF 799	Bonds-SF 1381	Bonds-SF 272	Bonds-SF 128.9
Giles-Pit 5.7	Walker-Col 338	Giles-Pit 450	Giles-Pit 622	Giles-Pit..............1072	Giles-Pit................179	Giles-Pit.............65.4
Edmonds-StL......5.2	V.Guerrero-Mon ...336	C.Jones-Atl 435	Walker-Col 602	Walker-Col..........1023	Sosa-Chi 161	Sosa-Chi 50.6
Kent-SF................5.0	Helton-Col 329	Helton-Col 429	Sosa-Chi..............594	V.Guerrero-Mon ..1010	Edmonds-StL........161	C.Jones-Atl 49.1
Rolen-Phi-StL......4.5	C.Jones-Atl 327	Walker-Col 421	V.Guerrero-Mon ...593	Helton-Col 1006	Green-LA..............156	Abreu-Phi 49.0

Runs	Hits	Doubles	Triples	Home Runs	Total Bases	Runs Batted In
Sosa-Chi 122	V.Guerrero-Mon 206	Abreu-Phi 50	Rollins-Phi 10	Sosa-Chi 49	V.Guerrero-Mon 364	Berkman-Hou 128
Pujols-StL 118	Kent-SF 195	Lowell-Fla 44	Rolen-Phi-StL 8	Bonds-SF 46	Kent-SF 352	Pujols-StL 127
Bonds-SF 117	Vidro-Mon 190	Vidro-Mon 43	Wilkerson-Mon..........8	Green-LA................42	Berkman-Hou 334	Burrell-Phi 116
Green-LA..............110	Pujols-StL 185	Cabrera-Mon 43	McCracken-Ari..........8	Berkman-Hou 42	Pujols-StL 331	Green-LA 114
Helton-Col 107	Castillo-Fla............185		Furcal-Atl..................8	V.Guerrero-Mon 39	Sosa-Chi 330	V.Guerrero-Mon ..111

Stolen Bases	Base Stealing Runs	Fielding Runs-Infield	Fielding Runs-Outfield	Wins	Winning Pct.	Complete Games
Castillo-Fla..............48	Roberts-LA 6.4	Reese-Pit....................27.8	Shinjo-SF 12.1	Johnson-Ari 24	Johnson-Ari 828	Johnson-Ari 8
Pierre-Col 47	Pierre-Col 6.1	Uribe-Col 26.5	Sanders-SF 8.7	Schilling-Ari 23	Miller-Hou 789	Burnett-Fla 7
Roberts-LA 45	Castillo-Fla 5.3	Cabrera-Mon 21.2	Owens-Fla 8.6	Oswalt-Hou 19	Schilling-Ari 767	Schilling-Ari 5
V.Guerrero-Mon......40	Fox-Fla 4.4	Rolen-Phi-StL 20.2	Perez-NY 6.8	Millwood-Atl 18	Nomo-LA 727	Hernandez-SF 5
Sanchez-Mil.............37	Boone-Cin 4.2	J.Wilson-Pit 19.9	Sanchez-Mil 5.8	Glavine-Atl 18	Maddux-Atl 727	

Strikeouts	Fewest BB/Game	Games	Saves	Base Runners/9	Adjusted Relief Runs	Relief Ranking
Johnson-Ari 334	Schilling-Ari 1.15	Quantrill-LA....................86	Smoltz-Atl 55	Gagne-LA............7.98	Dotel-Hou 25.5	Kim-Ari 40.4
Schilling-Ari 316	Perez-LA..............1.54	Dotel-Hou 83	Gagne-LA 52	Dotel-Hou 8.23	Hammond-Atl 23.9	Gagne-LA 31.3
Wood-Chi..............217	Vazquez-Mon 1.91	Worrell-SF.......................80	M.Williams-Pit 46	Timlin-StL-Phi......8.75	Kim-Ari 20.9	Nen-SF 29.8
Clement-Chi 215	Maddux-Atl 2.03	Jones-Col 79	Mesa-Phi 45	Schilling-Ari 8.81	Gagne-LA............18.9	Dotel-Hou 26.3
Oswalt-Hou 208	Ohka-Mon..............2.10		Nen-SF 43	Isringhausen-StL 8.95	Eischen-Mon 16.3	Hammond-Atl 25.5

Innings Pitched	Opponents' Avg.	Opponents' OBP	Earned Run Average	Adjusted ERA	Adjusted Starter Runs	Pitcher Wins
Johnson-Ari 260.0	Johnson-Ari 208	Schilling-Ari 251	Johnson-Ari 2.32	Johnson-Ari 191	Johnson-Ari 54.0	**Johnson-Ari** 5.6
Schilling-Ari 259.1	Burnett-Fla 209	Perez-LA 262	Maddux-Atl 2.62	Maddux-Atl 156	Schilling-Ari 34.2	**Kim-Ari** 4.2
Oswalt-Hou........233.0	Clement-Chi 215	Johnson-Ari 273	Glavine-Atl 2.96	Oswalt-Hou 142	Maddux-Atl 31.6	**Maddux-Atl** 3.7
Vazquez-Mon 230.1	Schmidt-SF..........218	Wolf-Phi 285	Perez-LA.............3.00	Ohka-Mon 141	Oswalt-Hou...........30.7	**Schilling-Ari** 3.5
Glavine-Atl 224.2	Moss-Atl 221	Millwood-Atl 292	Oswalt-Hou.........3.01	Dessens-Cin 140	Glavine-Atl 27.0	**Oswalt-Hou** 3.5

Monty Hall Would Have Been Proud

In a transaction worthy of *Let's Make a Deal*, Florida owner John Henry bought the Red Sox and sold the Marlins to Montreal owner Jeffrey Loria. What was behind door number three? The Expos. The other 29 clubs took ownership of Montreal, rather than sell to an owner who would oppose contraction. Several Latin players were found to be older than previously thought. The discrepancies were discovered during increased background checks following the 2001 terrorist attacks.

The Rockies began treating baseballs in a Coors Field "humidor" in an attempt to decrease scoring. It seemed to work and helped league scoring drop to its lowest level since 1992, the last season BC: Before Colorado. Even so, Barry Bonds became only the fourth player to hit 600 home runs. Tragedy claimed the life of two active players: San Diego outfielder Mike Darr was killed in a car wreck during spring training, and St. Louis pitcher Darryl Kile died of heart problems in midseason. Hall of Famer Enos Slaughter and legendary Cardinals broadcaster Jack Buck also passed.

St. Louis overpowered Randy Johnson in Game 1 of the NLDS and wound up sweeping their series with Arizona. Three Bonds homers helped San Francisco beat Atlanta in a five-game Division Series. Bonds homered only once in the NLCS, as he was walked 10 times, but the Giants beat St. Louis in five with clutch hitting by the rest of the lineup. San Francisco was a win away from a World Series title, but the Giants dropped two heartbreakers and lost to Anaheim in seven.

2002 American League

TEAM	W	L	T	PCT	GB	HW	HL	R	OR	PA	H	2B	3B	HR	BB	SO	HB	SH	AVG	OBP	SLG	OPS	AOPS	BR	ABR	PF	SB	CS	BSA	BSR
EAST																														
NY	103	58	0	.640		52	28	**897**	697	6377	1540	314	12	**223**	**640**	1171	23	72	.275	**.354**	**.455**	**809**	**114**	**124**	**130**	99	100	38	72	9
BOS	93	69	0	.574	10.5	42	39	859	665	6332	1560	**348**	33	177	545	944	22	72	.277	.345	.444	789	106	78	62	102	80	28	74	8
TOR	78	84	0	.481	25.5	42	39	813	828	6230	1457	305	**38**	187	522	1142	17	53	.261	.327	.430	757	96	-1	-28	104	71	18	**80**	9
BAL	67	95	0	.414	36.5	34	47	667	773	6096	1353	311	27	165	452	993	40	64	.246	.309	.403	712	93	-98	-62	95	110	48	70	7
TB	55	106	0	.342	48	30	51	673	918	6198	1418	297	35	133	456	1115	44	58	.253	.314	.390	704	88	-112	-100	98	102	45	69	7
CENTRAL																														
MIN	94	67	0	.584		**54**	27	768	712	6196	1518	**348**	36	167	472	1089	34	56	.272	.332	.437	769	101	26	18	101	79	62	56	-4
CHI	81	81	0	.500	13.5	47	34	856	798	6207	1475	289	29	217	555	952	48	49	.268	.338	.449	787	105	62	50	102	75	31	71	6
CLE	74	88	0	.457	20.5	39	42	739	837	6099	1349	255	26	192	542	1000	39	56	.249	.321	.412	733	95	-51	-38	98	52	37	58	-2
KC	62	100	0	.383	32.5	37	44	737	891	6206	1415	285	42	140	524	921	44	52	.256	.323	.398	721	81	-68	-142	112	140	65	68	8
DET	55	106	0	.342	39	33	47	575	864	5920	1340	265	37	124	363	1035	30	64	.248	.300	.379	679	84	-163	-127	94	65	44	60	-1
WEST																														
OAK	103	59	0	.636		**54**	27	800	654	6291	1450	279	28	205	609	1008	20	68	.261	.339	.432	771	103	35	34	100	46	20	70	3
ANA	99	63	0	.611	4	**54**	27	851	**644**	6327	**1603**	333	32	152	462	**805**	**49**	**74**	**.282**	.341	.433	774	104	44	45	100	117	51	70	8
SEA	93	69	0	.574	10	48	33	814	699	6362	1531	285	31	152	629	1003	41	51	.275	.350	.419	769	108	49	81	96	**137**	58	70	**10**
TEX	72	90	0	.444	31	42	39	843	882	6332	1510	304	27	230	554	1055	48	62	.269	.338	**.455**	793	104	76	34	105	62	34	65	2
TOT	1132					608	524	10892		87173	20519	4218	433	2464	7325	14233	851	499	.264	.331	.424	755					1236	579	68	69

TEAM	CG	SHO	GR	SV	IP	H	HR	BB	SO	BR/9	ERA	AERA	OAV	OOB	PR	APR	PF	OSB	OCS	FA	E	WPB	DP	FW	PW	BW	BSW	DIF
EAST																												
NY	9	11	334	53	1452.0	1441	144	**403**	1135	11.7	3.87	113	.256	.309	94	81	98	92	39	.979	127	69	117	-1.2	7.8	**12.5**	.4	3.0
BOS	5	17	338	51	1446.0	**1339**	146	430	**1157**	**11.5**	3.75	**120**	**.246**	**.308**	113	118	101	118	50	.983	104	51	140	.2	11.4	6.0	.3	-5.8
TOR	6	6	461	41	1438.1	1504	177	590	991	13.5	4.80	96	.269	.344	-55	-29	103	107	41	.982	107	75	159	.0	-2.8	-2.7	.4	2.1
BAL	8	3	407	31	1450.2	1491	208	549	967	13.0	4.46	96	.266	.336	0	-32	96	103	44	.985	91	76	**173**	.9	-3.1	-6.0	.2	-6.1
TB	**12**	3	306	25	1440.1	1567	215	620	925	14.3	5.29	84	.279	.357	-133	-133	100	92	53	.979	126	75	168	-1.2	-12.8	-9.6	.2	-2.1
CENTRAL																												
MIN	8	9	435	47	1444.2	1454	184	439	1026	12.1	4.12	109	.261	.318	54	58	101	**57**	27	**.987**	**74**	67	124	**1.9**	5.6	1.7	-.9	5.2
CHI	7	7	423	35	1423.0	1422	190	528	945	12.7	4.53	100	.260	.330	-11	-3	101	99	38	.984	97	63	157	.6	-.3	4.8	.1	-5.2
CLE	9	4	421	34	1424.2	1508	142	603	1058	13.7	4.91	89	.274	.348	-71	-83	99	126	**59**	.981	113	67	161	-.4	-8.0	-3.7	-.7	5.7
KC	**12**	6	421	30	1441.0	1587	212	572	909	13.8	5.21	96	.281	.349	-120	-28	113	90	36	.979	130	76	153	-1.4	-2.7	-13.7	.3	-1.6
DET	11	7	372	33	1414.0	1593	163	463	794	13.5	4.92	87	.285	.343	-73	-101	97	72	34	.977	142	82	148	-2.1	-9.7	-12.2	-.6	-.9
WEST																												
OAK	9	**19**	408	48	1452.0	1391	**135**	474	1021	11.9	**3.68**	119	.252	.315	**126**	117	99	68	46	.984	102	**49**	144	.3	11.3	3.3	-.2	7.4
ANA	7	14	400	**54**	1452.1	1345	169	509	999	11.8	3.69	**120**	.247	.314	124	**120**	99	78	51	.986	87	59	151	1.2	**11.5**	4.3	.3	.7
SEA	8	12	343	43	1445.1	1422	178	441	1063	11.9	4.07	104	.257	.315	62	25	95	66	35	.985	88	**49**	134	1.1	2.4	7.8	**.5**	.2
TEX	4	4	**487**	33	1439.2	1528	194	669	1030	14.2	5.15	92	.272	.355	-111	-65	106	74	28	.984	99	95	152	.5	-6.3	3.3	-.3	-6.2
TOT	115	122	5556	558	20164.0					12.8	4.46		.264	.331						.982	1487	953	2081					

Batter-Fielder Wins	Batting Average	On-Base Percentage	Slugging Average	On-Base Plus Slugging	Adjusted OPS	Adjusted Batter Runs
A.Rodriguez-Tex 7.1	Ramirez-Bos.........349	Ramirez-Bos 450	Thome-Cle 677	Thome-Cle..........1122	Thome-Cle............197	Thome-Cle 73.6
Thome-Cle 5.5	Sweeney-KC.........340	Thome-Cle..................445	Ramirez-Bos.........647	Ramirez-Bos 1097	Ramirez-Bos 183	Giambi-NY..........65.5
Garciaparra-Bos 5.4	B.Williams-NY.......333	Giambi-NY..................435	A.Rodriguez-Tex ...623	Giambi-NY..........1034	Giambi-NY............173	Ramirez-Bos 56.4
Ramirez-Bos 4.5	Suzuki-Sea..........321	Sweeney-KC 417	Giambi-NY 598	A.Rodriguez-Tex 1015	A.Rodriguez-Tex ..156	A.Rodriguez-Tex 51.0
Giambi-NY 4.3	Ordonez-Chi.........320	B.Williams-NY 415	Ordonez-Chi 597	Sweeney-KC 979	Ordonez-Chi 153	Ordonez-Chi 44.8

Runs	Hits	Doubles	Triples	Home Runs	Total Bases	Runs Batted In
Soriano-NY 128	Soriano-NY 209	Garciaparra-Bos 56	Damon-Bos 11	A.Rodriguez-Tex 57	A.Rodriguez-Tex ..389	A.Rodriguez-Tex..142
A.Rodriguez-Tex ..125	Suzuki-Sea 208	Anderson-Ana...............56	Winn-TB 9	Thome-Cle............52	Soriano-NY 381	Ordonez-Chi.........135
Jeter-NY 124	B.Williams-NY 204	Soriano-NY...................51	Young-Tex 8	Palmeiro-Tex 43	Ordonez-Chi 352	Tejada-Oak..........131
Giambi-NY...........120	Tejada-Oak 204	Ordonez-Chi 47	Suzuki-Sea 8	Giambi-NY.............41	Anderson-Ana 344	Anderson-Ana 123
Damon-Bos 118	Garciaparra-Bos ..197	Beltran-KC 44	Beltran-KC 7	Soriano-NY 39	Tejada-Oak 336	Giambi-NY 122

Stolen Bases	Base Stealing Runs	Fielding Runs-Infield	Fielding Runs-Outfield	Wins	Winning Pct.	Complete Games
Soriano-NY 41	Jeter-NY 6.0	Bordick-Bal 26.2	Erstad-Ana 19.4	Zito-Oak.................23	Martinez-Bos 833	Byrd-KC 7
Beltran-KC 35	Beltran-KC 5.3	Garciaparra-Bos 18.8	Jones-Min 13.3	Lowe-Bos.................21	Zito-Oak 821	Kennedy-TB 5
Jeter-NY 32	Damon-Bos 4.7	Sweeney-KC 14.4	Fick-Det 9.3	Martinez-Bos 20	Washburn-Ana 750	Buehrle-Chi 5
	Soriano-NY...........4.5	Young-Tex 13.9	Mora-Bal.................8.6			
	Cameron-Sea 4.0	Vizquel-Cle 12.7	Suzuki-Sea 6.7			

Strikeouts	Fewest BB/Game	Games	Saves	Base Runners/9	Adjusted Relief Runs	Relief Ranking
Martinez-Bos........239	Reed-Min 1.24	Koch-Oak 84	Guardado-Min 45	Rhodes-Sea 7.49	Romero-Min 23.9	Percival-Ana 32.7
Clemens-NY 192	Byrd-KC 1.50	Romero-Min 81	Koch-Oak................44	Groom-Bal 8.42	Hawkins-Min.........19.8	Julio-Bal.............30.5
Zito-Oak...............182	Milton-Min............1.58	Stanton-NY...................79	Urbina-Bos 40	Hawkins-Min........8.74	Groom-Bal 19.7	Rhodes-Sea 30.1
Mussina-NY..........182	Martinez-Bos 1.81	Karsay-NY 78	Percival-Ana 40	Martinez-Bos 8.98	Percival-Ana 16.3	Romero-Min........29.8
Garcia-Sea 181	Lidle-Oak 1.83	Escobar-Tor 76	Escobar-Tor 38	Lowe-Bos 9.26	Rhodes-Sea 16.2	Koch-Oak 23.4

Innings Pitched	Opponents' Avg.	Opponents' OBP	Earned Run Average	Adjusted ERA	Adjusted Starter Runs	Pitcher Wins
Halladay-Tor 239.1	Martinez-Bos 198	Martinez-Bos 254	Martinez-Bos 2.26	Martinez-Bos 199	Lowe-Bos 48.5	**Lowe-Bos** 6.3
Buehrle-Chi 239.0	Wakefield-Bos.......204	Lowe-Bos....................266	Lowe-Bos 2.58	Lowe-Bos..............174	Martinez-Bos 46.2	**Martinez-Bos** 5.3
Hudson-Oak 238.1	Lowe-Bos 211	Wakefield-Bos 276	Zito-Oak 2.75	Wakefield-Bos 160	Zito-Oak 41.8	**Zito-Oak**.............4.8
Moyer-Sea 230.2	Zito-Oak 218	Moyer-Sea 278	Wakefield-Bos......2.81	Zito-Oak................160	Halladay-Tor 39.3	**Halladay-Tor**......4.0
Zito-Oak 229.1	Moyer-Sea 230	Reed-Min 288	Halladay-Tor 2.93	Halladay-Tor 157	Hudson-Oak 38.0	**Hudson-Oak** 3.6

(Labor) Peace of Mind

Commissioner Bud Selig found it hard to do much right. First, his plan to contract two teams failed because of Minnesota state court rulings. Then, in what he hoped would be a glorious homecoming in Milwaukee, he had to declare the All-Star Game a tie when both leagues ran out of pitchers after the 11th inning. The thing that worried the most people, though, actually worked out: a deadline deal averted a strike by the players.

Texas superstar Alex Rodriguez became the first shortstop with back-to-back 50 home runs seasons. Ted Williams, called by many—including himself—the greatest hitter ever, died.

The Twins, who would have been contracted if Selig had his way, won the Central. Many expected a quick exit, but the Twins survived a five-game ALDS against Oakland, which rode a league-record 20-game winning streak to the West title. The A's had the tying run on base with two outs in the ninth, but Twins closer "Everyday" Eddie Guardado finally shut the door. Wild Card Anaheim pounded the Yankees in the other ALDS, batting .376 and scoring 31 runs in four games. The Angels' hitting continued in a five-game win over the Twins in the ALCS.

The Angels capped a magical season with a seven-game triumph over San Francisco in the World Series. Facing elimination, Anaheim rallied from a 5–0 deficit in Game 6, and then won the next night behind rookie starter John Lackey. Francisco Rodriguez, aka K-Rod, didn't make his big league debut until September 18, but he had 5 wins during Anaheim's unlikely October run and led an outstanding bullpen.

2003 National League

TEAM	W	L	T	PCT	GB	HW	HL	R	OR	PA	H	2B	3B	HR	BB	SO	HB	SH	AVG	OBP	SLG	OPS	AOPS	BR	ABR	PF	SB	CS	BSA	BSR
EAST																														
ATL	101	61	0	.623		55	26	**907**	740	6378	**1608**	321	31	**235**	545	**933**	65	49	**.284**	.349	**.475**	**824**	118	**152**	153	100	68	22	**76**	7
FLA	91	71	0	.562	10	53	28	751	692	6185	1459	292	44	157	515	978	82	57	.266	.333	.421	754	106	7	41	96	**150**	74	67	7
PHI	86	76	0	.531	15	49	32	791	697	6333	1448	325	27	166	**651**	1155	46	55	.261	.343	.419	762	110	39	93	94	72	29	71	6
MON	83	79	0	.512	18	52	29	711	716	6116	1404	294	25	144	522	990	72	45	.258	.326	.401	727	86	-43	-102	109	100	39	72	**8**
NY	66	95	0	.410	34.5	34	46	642	754	6007	1317	262	24	124	489	1035	78	54	.247	.314	.374	688	87	-120	-98	97	70	31	69	5
CENTRAL																														
CHI	88	74	0	.543		44	37	724	683	6187	1431	302	24	172	492	1158	80	50	.259	.323	.416	739	98	-25	-12	98	73	31	70	5
HOU	87	75	0	.537	1	48	33	805	677	6320	1466	308	30	191	557	1021	61	**81**	.263	.336	.431	767	100	38	5	104	66	30	69	4
STL	85	77	0	.525	3	48	33	876	796	6466	1580	**342**	32	196	580	952	**87**	73	.279	**.350**	.454	804	**119**	122	**160**	96	82	32	72	7
PIT	75	87	0	.463	13	39	42	753	801	6314	1492	275	45	163	529	1049	79	87	.267	.338	.420	758	100	20	6	102	86	37	70	6
CIN	69	93	0	.426	19	35	46	694	886	6210	1349	239	21	182	524	1326	66	79	.245	.318	.395	713	92	-81	-68	98	80	34	70	6
MIL	68	94	0	.420	20	31	50	714	873	6268	1423	266	24	196	547	1221	62	71	.256	.329	.419	748	101	-6	11	98	99	39	72	**8**
WEST																														
SF	100	61	0	.621		**57**	24	755	638	6204	1440	281	29	180	593	980	76	40	.264	.338	.425	763	106	32	55	97	53	37	59	-1
LA	85	77	0	.525	15.5	46	35	574	**556**	6036	1328	260	25	124	407	985	71	72	.243	.303	.368	671	84	-167	-133	94	80	36	69	5
ARI	84	78	0	.519	16.5	45	36	717	685	6261	1467	303	**47**	152	531	1006	63	45	.263	.330	.417	747	90	-7	-73	110	76	38	67	3
COL	74	88	0	.457	26.5	49	32	853	892	6282	1472	330	31	198	619	1134	55	52	.267	.344	.445	789	97	87	-15	114	63	37	63	1
SD	64	98	0	.395	36.5	35	46	678	831	6245	1442	257	32	128	565	1073	50	57	.261	.333	.388	721	102	-48	23	91	76	39	66	3
TOT	1295					720	575	11945		99812	23126	4657	491	2708	8666	16996	967	1093	.262	.332	.417	749					1294	585	69	80

TEAM	CG	SHO	GR	SV	IP	H	HR	BB	SO	BR/9	ERA	AERA	OAV	OOB	PR	APR	PF	OSB	OCS	FA	E	WPB	DP	FW	PW	BW	BSW	DIF
EAST																												
ATL	4	7	489	51	1456.1	1425	147	555	992	12.5	4.10	103	.257	.327	29	20	99	91	34	.981	121	60	**166**	-.8	2.0	15.0	.2	3.6
FLA	7	11	395	36	1445.1	1415	128	530	1132	12.4	4.04	101	.258	.325	39	10	96	70	25	**.987**	78	62	162	**1.6**	1.0	4.0	.2	3.2
PHI	9	13	437	33	1443.2	1386	142	536	1060	12.5	4.04	99	.253	.327	38	-8	93	112	24	.984	97	69	146	.5	-.8	9.1	.0	-4.0
MON	**15**	10	437	42	1437.2	1467	181	**463**	1028	12.5	4.01	117	.264	.327	43	98	109	**40**	38	.983	102	82	152	.3	9.6	-10.0	**.3**	1.8
NY	3	10	412	38	1413.1	1497	168	576	907	13.5	4.48	93	.273	.345	-32	-53	97	98	52	.980	118	50	158	-.7	-5.2	-9.6	.0	1.0
CENTRAL																												
CHI	13	14	420	36	1456.1	1304	143	617	**1404**	12.3	3.83	110	.241	.324	73	63	98	70	42	.983	106	75	157	.0	6.2	-1.2	.0	1.9
HOU	1	5	**502**	50	1450.0	1350	161	565	1139	12.3	3.86	115	.248	.326	67	89	104	86	48	.985	95	**44**	149	.6	8.8	.5	-.0	-3.8
STL	9	10	460	41	1463.2	1544	210	508	969	13.0	4.60	88	.271	.336	-52	-92	95	55	24	**.987**	**77**	60	138	**1.6**	-9.0	**15.7**	.2	-4.5
PIT	7	10	457	44	1444.1	1527	178	502	926	13.0	4.64	94	.272	.336	-57	-40	102	69	26	.980	123	60	159	-.9	-3.9	.6	.0	-1.8
CIN	4	5	475	38	1446.1	1578	209	590	932	13.8	5.09	84	.278	.349	-130	-133	100	77	28	.977	141	55	152	-1.9	-13.1	-6.7	.0	9.6
MIL	5	3	460	44	1452.0	1590	219	575	1034	13.8	5.02	85	.279	.348	-120	-126	99	100	37	.981	114	71	142	-.4	-12.4	1.1	**.3**	-1.6
WEST																												
SF	7	10	461	43	1437.1	1349	136	546	1006	12.1	3.73	110	.250	.321	88	63	96	67	29	**.987**	80	76	163	1.4	6.2	5.4	-.6	7.0
LA	3	**17**	438	**58**	1457.2	**1254**	**127**	526	1289	**11.2**	**3.16**	**127**	**.234**	**.306**	**182**	**148**	94	117	**75**	.981	119	58	164	-.7	**14.6**	-13.1	.0	3.2
ARI	7	11	452	42	1455.0	1379	150	526	1291	12.2	3.84	121	.250	.322	71	122	109	84	38	.983	107	67	132	-.0	12.0	-7.2	-.2	-1.6
COL	3	4	500	34	1420.0	1629	200	552	866	14.4	5.20	94	.290	.359	-146	-41	115	73	42	.981	116	59	165	-.5	-4.0	-1.5	-.4	-.6
SD	2	10	473	31	1431.1	1458	208	611	1091	13.4	4.87	81	.264	.341	-94	-161	92	95	25	.983	102	79	141	.3	-15.8	2.3	-.2	-3.5
TOT	99	150	7268	661	23110.1					12.8	4.28		.262	.332						.983	1696	1027	2446					

Batter-Fielder Wins	Batting Average	On-Base Percentage	Slugging Average	On-Base Plus Slugging	Adjusted OPS	Adjusted Batter Runs
Bonds-SF 8.8	Pujols-StL .359	Bonds-SF .529	Bonds-SF .749	Bonds-SF 1278	Bonds-SF 235	Bonds-SF 93.7
Pujols-StL 7.5	Helton-Col .358	Helton-Col .458	Pujols-StL .667	Pujols-StL 1106	Pujols-StL 192	Pujols-StL 83.1
Helton-Col 5.8	Bonds-SF .341	Pujols-StL .439	Helton-Col .630	Helton-Col 1088	Sheffield-Atl 164	Sheffield-Atl 57.2
Giles-Atl 5.7	Renteria-StL .330	Giles-Pit-SD .427	Edmonds-StL .617	Sheffield-Atl 1023	Edmonds-StL 163	Helton-Col 57.0
Lopez-Atl 5.4	Sheffield-Atl .330	Walker-Col .422	Sheffield-Atl .604	Edmonds-StL 1002	Helton-Col 159	Thome-Phi 49.5

Runs	Hits	Doubles	Triples	Home Runs	Total Bases	Runs Batted In
Pujols-StL 137	Pujols-StL 212	Pujols-StL 51	Furcal-Atl 10	Thome-Phi 47	Pujols-StL 394	Wilson-Col 141
Helton-Col 135	Helton-Col 209	Rolen-StL 49	Finley-Ari 10	Sexson-Mil 45	Helton-Col 367	Sheffield-Atl 132
Furcal-Atl 130	Pierre-Fla 204	Helton-Col 49	Lofton-Pit-Chi 8	Bonds-SF 45	Sheffield-Atl 348	Thome-Phi 131
Sheffield-Atl 126	Renteria-StL 194	Green-LA 49	Podsednik-Mil 8	Pujols-StL 43	Sexson-Mil 332	Sexson-Mil 124
	Furcal-Atl 194	Giles-Atl 49		Lopez-Atl 43	Thome-Phi 331	Pujols-StL 124

Stolen Bases	Base Stealing Runs	Fielding Runs-Infield	Fielding Runs-Outfield	Wins	Winning Pct.	Complete Games
Pierre-Fla 65	Pierre-Fla 7.3	Cora-LA 30.8	Cruz-SF 14.7	Ortiz-Atl 21	Schmidt-SF .773	Hernandez-Mon 8
Podsednik-Mil 43	Podsednik-Mil 6.0	Gonzalez-Chi 25.6	Hidalgo-Hou 14.3	Williams-StL 18	Prior-Chi .750	Schmidt-SF 5
Roberts-LA 40	Renteria-StL 5.0	Perez-SF 22.2	Kotsay-SD 13.7	Prior-Chi 18	Ortiz-Atl .750	Morris-StL 5
Renteria-StL 34	Furcal-Atl 4.8	Helton-Col 19.8	Edmonds-StL 12.8	Schmidt-SF 17	Williams-StL .667	Millwood-Phi 5
Lofton-Pit-Chi 30	Cabrera-Mon 4.6	Giles-Atl 18.3	Encarnacion-Fla 5.7			

Strikeouts	Fewest BB/Game	Games	Saves	Base Runners/9	Adjusted Relief Runs	Relief Ranking
Wood-Chi 266	Maddux-Atl 1.36	Quantrill-LA 89	Gagne-LA 55	Gagne-LA 6.56	Gagne-LA 27.5	Gagne-LA 47.6
Prior-Chi 245	Schilling-Ari 1.71	Villarreal-Ari 86	Smoltz-Atl 45	Smoltz-Atl 7.83	Mota-LA 26.5	Wagner-Hou 35.5
Vazquez-Mon 241	Sheets-Mil 1.75	Martin-LA 80	Wagner-Hou 44	Wagner-Hou 8.16	Wagner-Hou 24.8	Smoltz-Atl 34.3
Schmidt-SF 208	Schmidt-SF 1.99	King-Atl 80	Worrell-SF 38	Cormier-Phi 8.50	Cormier-Phi 22.7	Villarreal-Ari 26.8
Schilling-Ari 194	Ohka-Mon 2.04		Biddle-Mon 34	Schmidt-SF 8.80	Smoltz-Atl 22.5	Mantei-Ari 23.6

Innings Pitched	Opponents' Avg.	Opponents' OBP	Earned Run Average	Adjusted ERA	Adjusted Starter Runs	Pitcher Wins
Hernandez-Mon 233.1	Schmidt-SF .200	Schmidt-SF .250	Schmidt-SF 2.34	Schmidt-SF 176	Schmidt-SF 43.5	**Prior-Chi** 4.9
Vazquez-Mon 230.2	Wood-Chi .203	Schilling-Ari .270	Brown-LA 2.39	Prior-Chi 174	Prior-Chi 40.8	**Gagne-LA** 4.9
Millwood-Phi 222.0	Webb-Ari .212	Vazquez-Mon .278	Prior-Chi 2.43	Brown-LA 168	Brown-LA 37.8	**Brown-LA** 4.1
Williams-StL 220.2	Ortiz-Atl .223	Prior-Chi .283	Webb-Ari 2.84	Webb-Ari 165	Hernandez-Mon 35.5	**Schmidt-SF** 3.9
Sheets-Mil 220.2	Nomo-LA .223	Brown-LA .290	Schilling-Ari 2.95	Schilling-Ari 159	Vazquez-Mon 33.9	**Hernandez-Mon** 3.7

Reeling in the Prize Fish

The Hall of Fame canceled an anniversary retrospective on *Bull Durham*, one of the most popular baseball movies ever, because lead actors Susan Sarandon and Tim Robbins, both political activists, were critical of the U.S.-led war in Iraq. Sammy Sosa clubbed his 500th career homer during the season's first week, though his hitting prowess came under scrutiny in June when he was caught using a corked bat.

Cincinnati opened Great American Ball Park, which instantly became one of the homer-happiest parks, while the Expos played 22 "home" games in San Juan, Puerto Rico. Bobby Bonds, Barry's father, and Hall of Famer Warren Spahn died.

Florida was 16–22 when skipper Jeff Torborg was fired and replaced with 72-year-old Jack McKeon. That move, and the help of rookie midseason call-ups Dontrelle Willis and Miguel Cabrera, made Florida the best team after the All-Star break. Ivan Rodriguez drove in 6 runs and withstood a series-ending collision to lead the Marlins over the Giants in a four-game NLDS. Chicago eliminated Atlanta in a five-game Division Series.

The Cubs were just five outs away from their first World Series appearance since 1945 when disaster struck in Game 6 of the NLCS. A fan prevented left fielder Moises Alou from reaching into the stands for a foul ball, which, compounded by an error, opened the door for 8 runs. Chicago led 5–3 early in Game 7, but Florida came back again. The Marlins bested the Yankees in six games in the World Series, with Brad Penny winning twice and brash Josh Beckett tossing a complete-game shutout in the clincher.

2003 American League

TEAM	W	L	T	PCT	GB	HW	HL	R	OR	PA	H	2B	3B	HR	BB	SO	HB	SH	AVG	OBP	SLG	OPS	AOPS	BR	ABR	PF	SB	CS	BSA	BSR
EAST																														
NY	101	61	1	.623		50	32	877	716	6430	1518	304	14	230	**684**	1042	25	81	.271	.356	.453	809	114	116	131	98	98	33	75	10
BOS	95	67	0	.586	6	53	28	**961**	809	6530	**1667**	**371**	40	**238**	620	943	24	53	**.289**	**.360**	**.491**	**851**	**119**	**199**	**175**	102	88	35	72	7
TOR	86	76	0	.531	15	41	40	894	826	6364	1580	357	33	190	546	1081	11	**90**	.279	.349	.455	804	108	98	82	102	37	25	60	-1
BAL	71	91	1	.438	30	40	40	743	820	6241	1516	277	24	152	431	902	51	54	.268	.323	.405	728	95	-73	-45	96	89	36	71	7
TB	63	99	0	.389	38	36	45	715	852	6212	1501	298	38	137	420	1030	32	56	.265	.320	.404	724	92	-82	-70	98	142	42	**77**	17
CENTRAL																														
MIN	90	72	0	.556		48	33	801	758	6324	1567	318	**45**	155	512	1027	42	63	.277	.341	.431	772	101	29	22	101	94	44	68	5
CHI	86	76	0	.531	4	51	30	791	715	6148	1445	303	19	220	519	916	43	58	.263	.331	.446	777	102	26	18	101	77	29	73	7
KC	83	79	0	.512	7	40	40	836	867	6239	1526	288	39	162	476	926	**63**	75	.274	.336	.427	763	88	7	-87	113	120	42	74	**12**
CLE	68	94	0	.420	22	38	43	699	778	6187	1413	296	26	158	466	1062	46	62	.254	.316	.401	717	91	-96	-73	97	86	61	59	-2
DET	43	119	0	.265	47	23	58	591	928	6070	1312	201	39	153	443	1099	65	47	.240	.300	.375	675	83	-188	-141	92	98	63	61	0
WEST																														
OAK	96	66	0	.593		**57**	24	768	643	6187	1398	317	24	176	556	898	22	59	.254	.327	.417	744	94	-33	-40	101	48	14	**77**	6
SEA	93	69	0	.574	3	50	31	795	**637**	6281	1509	290	33	139	586	989	35	53	.271	.344	.410	754	101	1	27	97	108	37	74	11
ANA	77	85	0	.475	19	45	37	736	743	6119	1473	276	33	150	476	**838**	50	56	.268	.330	.413	743	99	-35	-6	96	**129**	61	68	7
TEX	71	91	0	.438	25	43	38	826	969	6293	1506	274	36	239	488	1052	24	75	.266	.330	.454	784	96	32	-35	109	65	25	72	6
TOT	1135					615	519	11033		87625	20931	4170	443	2499	7223	13805	882	533	.267	.333	.428	761					1279	547	70	90

TEAM	CG	SHO	GR	SV	IP	H	HR	BB	SO	BR/9	ERA	AERA	OAV	OOB	PR	APR	PF	OSB	OCS	FA	E	WPB	DP	FW	PW	BW	BSW	DIF
EAST																												
NY	8	12	367	**49**	1462.0	1512	145	**375**	1119	11.9	4.02	109	.265	.314	82	60	97	92	37	.981	114	**46**	126	-.4	5.7	12.5	.3	1.8
BOS	5	6	437	36	1464.2	1503	153	488	**1141**	12.7	4.48	102	.263	.327	7	13	101	101	35	.982	113	64	130	-.4	1.2	**16.8**	.0	-3.6
TOR	14	6	443	36	1435.0	1560	184	485	984	13.2	4.69	98	.276	.337	-27	-16	102	126	32	.981	117	66	161	-.7	-1.5	7.9	-.7	.0
BAL	9	3	425	41	1449.2	1579	198	526	981	13.6	4.76	92	.278	.346	-38	-62	97	121	37	.983	105	54	164	.0	-5.9	-4.3	.0	.1
TB	7	7	372	30	1436.2	1454	196	639	877	13.7	4.93	92	.264	.347	-65	-65	100	65	41	.983	103	74	158	.1	-6.2	-6.7	**1.0**	-6.2
CENTRAL																												
MIN	7	8	399	45	1462.0	1526	187	402	997	12.2	4.41	103	.268	.319	19	22	100	70	27	.985	87	72	114	1.0	2.1	2.1	-.1	3.9
CHI	12	4	361	36	1431.0	1364	162	518	1056	12.2	4.17	109	.253	.321	56	59	100	**58**	29	.984	93	52	154	.7	5.6	1.7	.0	-3.1
KC	7	10	407	36	1438.2	1569	190	566	865	13.8	5.05	102	.279	.348	-85	16	114	95	42	.982	108	68	143	-.1	1.5	-8.3	.5	8.4
CLE	5	7	428	34	1459.1	1477	179	501	943	12.6	4.21	105	.264	.329	52	35	98	84	43	.980	126	60	178	-1.2	3.4	-7.0	-.8	-7.4
DET	3	5	451	27	1438.2	1616	195	557	764	13.9	5.30	81	.286	.352	-124	-166	95	128	**54**	.978	138	63	**194**	-1.8	-15.9	-13.5	-.6	-6.2
WEST																												
OAK	**16**	14	364	48	1441.2	**1336**	**140**	499	1018	11.8	**3.63**	**124**	**.246**	.314	**143**	**142**	100	91	43	.983	107	50	145	-.0	**13.6**	-3.8	-.0	5.4
SEA	8	**15**	366	38	1441.0	1340	173	466	1001	**11.6**	3.76	115	.247	**.311**	122	95	96	62	32	**.989**	**65**	47	159	**2.3**	9.1	2.6	.4	-2.4
ANA	5	9	375	39	1431.1	1444	190	486	980	12.6	4.28	101	.261	.327	40	6	95	80	48	.982	105	64	138	.0	.6	-.6	.0	-4.1
TEX	4	3	**494**	43	1433.1	1625	208	603	1009	14.4	5.67	88	.288	.360	-182	-103	110	96	45	.985	94	62	168	.6	-9.9	-3.4	-.0	2.6
TOT	110	109	5689	538	20225.0					12.9	4.52		.267	.333						.983	1475	842	2132					

Batter-Fielder Wins	Batting Average	On-Base Percentage	Slugging Average	On-Base Plus Slugging	Adjusted OPS	Adjusted Batter Runs
Rodriguez-Tex 6.5	Mueller-Bos 326	Ramirez-Bos 427	Rodriguez-Tex 600	Delgado-Tor........1019	Delgado-Tor..........163	Delgado-Tor........58.6
Posada-NY 5.1	Ramirez-Bos.........325	Delgado-Tor.................426	Delgado-Tor 593	Ramirez-Bos 1014	Ramirez-Bos 161	Ramirez-Bos 55.0
Ramirez-Bos 4.3	Jeter-NY 324	Giambi-NY 412	Ortiz-Bos 592	Rodriguez-Tex 995	Nixon-Bos 150	Giambi-NY..........45.4
Delgado-Tor 4.2	Wells-Tor...............317	Martinez-Sea 406	Ramirez-Bos.........587	Nixon-Bos 975	Giambi-NY............149	Rodriguez-Tex 41.5
Chavez-Oak 4.2	Ordonez-Chi 317	Posada-NY 405	Nixon-Bos 578	Ortiz-Bos 961	D.Young-Det 148	Thomas-Chi........40.2

Runs	Hits	Doubles	Triples	Home Runs	Total Bases	Runs Batted In
Rodriguez-Tex 124	Wells-Tor 215	Wells-Tor.......................49	Guzman-Min 14	Rodriguez-Tex 47	Wells-Tor 373	Delgado-Tor 145
Garciaparra-Bos ..120	Suzuki-Sea 212	Anderson-Ana...............49	Garciaparra-Bos 13	Thomas-Chi............42	Rodriguez-Tex 364	Rodriguez-Tex 118
Wells-Tor 118	Young-Tex 204	Huff-TB 47	Beltran-KC 10	Delgado-Tor............42	Soriano-NY 358	Wells-Tor..............117
Ramirez-Bos 117	Anderson-Ana 201	Ordonez-Chi 46		Giambi-NY..............41	Huff-TB 353	Boone-Sea 117
Delgado-Tor..........117						Anderson-Ana 116

Stolen Bases	Base Stealing Runs	Fielding Runs-Infield	Fielding Runs-Outfield	Wins	Winning Pct.	Complete Games
Crawford-TB 55	Crawford-TB 8.6	Hudson-Tor 44.6	Cameron-Sea......16.2	Halladay-Tor 22	Halladay-Tor 759	Mulder-Oak..............9
Sanchez-Det 44	Beltran-KC 7.6	Ellis-Oak 30.0	Anderson-Ana 13.3	Pettitte-NY 21	Moyer-Sea 750	Halladay-Tor 9
Beltran-KC 41	Soriano-NY.............4.9	Chavez-Oak.................23.1	Crawford-TB 10.6	Moyer-Sea 21	Pettitte-NY 724	Colon-Chi 9
Soriano-NY 35	Suzuki-Sea 4.7	B.Phillips-Cle 15.7	Baldelli-TB 10.3	Loaiza-Chi 21	Lowe-Bos 708	
Suzuki-Sea 34	Damon-Bos 4.5	Valentin-Chi 13.7	Suzuki-Sea 9.2		Loaiza-Chi 700	

Strikeouts	Fewest BB/Game	Games	Saves	Base Runners/9	Adjusted Relief Runs	Relief Ranking
Loaiza-Chi 207	Wells-NY...................85	Miller-Tor........................79	Foulke-Oak 43	Foulke-Oak 8.72	Marte-Chi 25.7	Foulke-Oak 47.4
Martinez-Bos........206	Halladay-Tor 1.08	Walker-Det 78	Guardado-Min 41	Guardado-Min 8.82	Hasegawa-Sea 24.5	M.Rivera-NY 42.5
Halladay-Tor 204	Radke-Min 1.19	Ryan-Bal..........................76	M.Rivera-NY 40	Riske-Cle 9.04	Foulke-Oak 24.1	Hawkins-Min 31.1
Mussina-NY..........195	Mussina-NY 1.68	Grimsley-KC 76	Julio-Bal...................36	F.Rodriguez-Ana ..9.10	Donnelly-Ana 23.7	Hasegawa-Sea ..28.2
Clemens-NY 190	Mulder-Oak..........1.93	Hawkins-Min 74	Percival-Ana 33	Mateo-Sea 9.14	M.Rivera-NY 21.8	Cordero-Tex........26.8

Innings Pitched	Opponents' Avg.	Opponents' OBP	Earned Run Average	Adjusted ERA	Adjusted Starter Runs	Pitcher Wins
Halladay-Tor 266.0	Martinez-Bos 215	Martinez-Bos 272	Martinez-Bos 2.22	Martinez-Bos........206	Martinez-Bos 47.8	**Loaiza-Chi**..........5.4
Colon-Chi 242.0	Zito-Oak 219	Mussina-NY.................275	Hudson-Oak 2.70	Hudson-Oak 167	Hudson-Oak 46.6	**Foulke-Oak** 4.7
Hudson-Oak 240.0	Hudson-Oak 223	Halladay-Tor................275	Loaiza-Chi 2.90	Loaiza-Chi 157	Loaiza-Chi 42.9	**Hudson-Oak** 4.4
Zito-Oak 231.2	Loaiza-Chi 233	Hudson-Oak 280	Mulder-Oak..........3.13	Mulder-Oak 144	Halladay-Tor 37.1	**Martinez-Bos** 4.3
Buehrle-Chi 230.1	Zambrano-TB 237	Loaiza-Chi 286	Halladay-Tor 3.25	Halladay-Tor 142	Mulder-Oak..........31.5	**M.Rivera-NY** 4.3

When Push Came to Shove

Boston surprised traditionalists by adding 278 seats atop the Green Monster. They quickly became the hottest ticket in baseball. Baltimore pitcher Steve Bechler died in spring training after collapsing during a workout. An over-the-counter diet supplement containing ephedra was linked to his death. Larry Doby, the AL's first black player, also died.

The season-opening series in Tokyo between Seattle and Oakland was canceled because of security concerns related to the U.S.-led war in Iraq. Yankees hurler Roger Clemens won his 300th game and recorded his 4,000th strikeout on the same night against the Cardinals. Toronto's Roy Halladay won 15 straight decisions, a victory shy of the league record for one season. Rafael Palmeiro smacked career homer number 500 for Texas, which led the league in long balls hit as well as allowed.

The small-market Twins won the Central for the second straight year, but they were dispatched in four games in the ALDS by the Yankees. The Red Sox rallied to win Games 3, 4, and 5 to beat Oakland in the other Division Series. The ALCS was marred by a bench-clearing brawl in Game 3; New York bench coach Don Zimmer charged Pedro Martinez, Boston's starting pitcher, who casually moved aside and pushed Zimmer to the ground. Two Yankees later were involved in a bullpen brawl between innings with a partisan groundskeeper. Aaron Boone's leadoff homer in the bottom of the 11th of Game 7 sent the Yankees to the World Series again. New York was shocked in the Fall Classic for the second time in three years as the Marlins won in six games.

MIDSUMMER CLASSICS: THE ALL-STAR GAMES

The All-Star Game was born in 1933 as a one-time event to bring sports fans to Chicago's Century of Progress Exposition. Arch Ward, the sports editor of the Chicago Tribune, thought up the idea of "the game of the century" and convinced the two major leagues as well as sportswriters across the country to make it happen. The event's success persuaded everyone in baseball to make the game an annual affair, and there has been at least one All-Star Game almost every year since then. The lone exception was 1945, when the game was cancelled due to wartime travel restrictions. There were two games each season from 1960–1962.

The debate over who should elect or select the All-Star teams, over how to vote, and over who to vote for has become an annual tradition. Over the years, the power of the ballot has switched back and forth between fans, managers, and players. Meanwhile, fans and the media have continually debated about whether the most popular players or the best players should be voted onto the teams, and whether voting should be based on a player's recent performance or his whole career.

Wall-to-wall national and regional television coverage of baseball in recent decades made the All-Star Game less of a special event, as dramatically declining Nielsen ratings have shown. The advent of interleague play in 1997 has also clearly diminished interest in what was once "must-see" TV.

Nevertheless, Major League Baseball's annual Midsummer Classic is still by far the most popular all-star game in American sports. The event has been expanded into a weeklong festival of activity, including a very popular home run-hitting contest and a "Futures Game" that showcases top minor league talent.

Key to All-Star Game table. The All-Star Game table is straightforward enough. Innings are shown in the third column only if the game was shorter or longer than 9 innings. MVP winners and the teams they represented are shown in the last column. MVPs from the losing team are in italics. Our Ex Post Facto MVP choices are shown prior to the inception of the official award in 1962. Tie games are underlined; no MVP selections were made for those games.

Year (No.)	Host/League	Result (Innings)	MVP, Team [Ex Post Facto MVP]
1933	Chicago/AL	AL 4, NL 2	[Lefty Gomez, NY]
1934	New York/NL	AL 9, NL 7	[*Carl Hubbell, NY*]
1935	Cleveland/AL	AL 4, NL 1	[Jimmie Foxx, Phi]
1936	Boston/NL	NL 4, AL 3	[Dizzy Dean, StL]
1937	Washington/AL	AL 8, NL 3	[Lou Gehrig, NY]
1938	Cincinnati/NL	NL 4, AL 1	[Johnny Vander Meer, Cin]
1939	New York/AL	AL 3, NL 1	[Bob Feller, Cle]
1940	St. Louis/NL	NL 4, AL 0	[Billy Herman, Chi]
1941	Detroit/AL	AL 7, NL 5	[Ted Williams, Bos]
1942	New York/NL	AL 3, NL 1	[Spud Chandler, NY]
1943	Philadelphia/AL	AL 5, NL 3	[Bobby Doerr, Bos]
1944	Pittsburgh/NL	NL 7, AL 1	[Rip Sewell, Pit]
1946	Boston/AL	AL 12, NL 0	[Ted Williams, Bos]
1947	Chicago/NL	AL 2, NL 1	[Hal Newhouser, Det]
1948	St. Louis/AL	AL 5, NL 2	[Vic Raschi, NY]
1949	Brooklyn/NL	AL 11, NL 7	[Joe DiMaggio, NY]
1950	Chicago/AL	NL 4, AL 3 (14)	[Red Schoendienst, StL]
1951	Detroit/AL	NL 8, AL 3	[Richie Ashburn, Phi]
1952	Philadelphia/NL	NL 3, AL 2 (5)	[Hank Sauer, Chi]
1953	Cincinnati/NL	NL 5, AL 1	[Enos Slaughter, StL]
1954	Cleveland/AL	AL 11, NL 9	[Al Rosen, Cle]
1955	Milwaukee/NL	NL 6, AL 5 (12)	[Stan Musial, StL]
1956	Washington/AL	NL 7, AL 3	[Willie Mays, NY]
1957	St. Louis/NL	AL 6, NL 5	[Jim Bunning, Det]
1958	Baltimore/AL	AL 4, NL 3	[Billy O'Dell, Bal]
1959 (1)	Pittsburgh/NL	NL 5, AL 4	[Hank Aaron, Mil]
1959 (2)	Los Angeles/NL	AL 5, NL 3	[Yogi Berra, NY]
1960 (1)	Kansas City/AL	NL 5, AL 3	[Ernie Banks, Chi]
1960 (2)	New York/AL	NL 6, AL 0	[Willie Mays, SF]
1961 (1)	San Francisco/NL	NL 5, AL 4 (10)	[Roberto Clemente, Pit]
1961 (2)	Boston/AL	AL 1, NL 1	[None]
1962 (1)	Washington/AL	NL 3, AL 1	Maury Wills, LA
1962 (2)	Chicago/NL	AL 9, NL 4	Leon Wagner, LA
1963	Cleveland/AL	NL 5, AL 3	Willie Mays, SF
1964	New York/NL	NL 7, AL 4	Johnny Callison, Phi
1965	Minnesota/AL	NL 6, AL 5	Juan Marichal, SF
1966	St. Louis/NL	NL 2, AL 1 (10)	*Brooks Robinson, Bal*
1967	California/AL	NL 2, AL 1 (15)	Tony Perez, Cin
1968	Houston/NL	NL 1, AL 0	Willie Mays, SF
1969	Washington/AL	NL 9, AL 3	Willie McCovey, SF
1970	Cincinnati/NL	NL 5, AL 4 (12)	*Carl Yastrzemski, Bos*
1971	Detroit/AL	AL 6, NL 4	Frank Robinson, Bal
1972	Atlanta/NL	NL 4, AL 3 (10)	Joe Morgan, Cin
1973	Kansas City/AL	NL 7, AL 1	Bobby Bonds, SF
1974	Pittsburgh/NL	NL 7, AL 2	Steve Garvey, LA
1975	Milwaukee/AL	NL 6, AL 3	Bill Madlock, Chi & Jon Matlack, NY
1976	Philadelphia/NL	NL 7, AL 1	George Foster, Cin
1977	New York/AL	NL 7, AL 5	Don Sutton, LA
1978	San Diego/NL	NL 7, AL 3	Steve Garvey, LA
1979	Seattle/AL	NL 7, AL 6	Dave Parker, Pit
1980	Los Angeles/NL	NL 4, AL 2	Ken Griffey, Sr., Cin
1981	Cleveland/AL	NL 5, AL 4	Gary Carter, Mon
1982	Montreal/NL	NL 4, AL 1	Dave Concepcion, Cin
1983	Chicago/AL	AL 13, NL 3	Fred Lynn, Cal
1984	San Francisco/NL	NL 3, AL 1	Gary Carter, Mon
1985	Minnesota/AL	NL 6, AL 1	La Marr Hoyt, SD
1986	Houston/NL	AL 3, NL 2	Roger Clemens, Bos
1987	Oakland/AL	NL 2, AL 0 (13)	Tim Raines, Mon
1988	Cincinnati/NL	AL 2, NL 1	Terry Steinbach, Oak
1989	California/AL	AL 5, NL 3	Bo Jackson, KC
1990	Chicago/NL	AL 2, NL 0	Julio Franco, Tex
1991	Toronto/AL	AL 4, NL 2	Cal Ripken, Bal
1992	San Diego/NL	AL 13, NL 6	Ken Griffey, Jr., Sea
1993	Baltimore/AL	AL 9, NL 3	Kirby Puckett, Min
1994	Pittsburgh/NL	NL 8, AL 7 (10)	Fred McGriff, Atl
1995	Texas/AL	NL 3, AL 2	Jeff Conine, Fla
1996	Philadelphia/NL	NL 6, AL 0	Mike Piazza, LA
1997	Cleveland/AL	AL 3, NL 1	Sandy Alomar, Jr., Cle
1998	Colorado/NL	AL 13, NL 8	Roberto Alomar, Bal
1999	Boston/AL	AL 4, NL 1	Pedro Martinez, Bos
2000	Atlanta/NL	AL 6, NL 3	Derek Jeter, NY
2001	Seattle/AL	AL 4, NL 1	Cal Ripken, Bal
2002	Milwaukee/NL	AL 7, NL 7 (11)	[None]
2003	Chicago/AL	AL 7, NL 6	Garret Anderson, Ana

OCTOBER CLASSICS: POSTSEASON SERIES AND PLAYOFFS

In 2003 Major League Baseball celebrated the 100th anniversary of the World Series, citing the 1903 World Series between the Boston Red Sox and the Pittsburgh Pirates as the first of its kind. As a modern World Series, the 1903 affair was the first of its kind, but it was definitely not the first World Series.

Postseason play is almost as old as baseball itself. In the 1870s, National Association teams would play exhibition games against local teams after the regular season was over. The first series between two league champions occurred in 1882, when National League champion Chicago faced American Association champion St. Louis in two exhibition games. Starting in 1884, the regular-season winners of these two competing leagues officially met to determine the championship of professional baseball.

These nineteenth century championship series, often referred to today as "World Series" since they pitted two league winners against each other, were played in a variety of formats. The 1884 Series was a simple best-of-five arrangement; the 1885 and 1886 Series changed to the best out of seven games. The 1887 Series was stretched to an epic best-of-15 affair, with the NL's Detroit Wolverines and the AA's St. Louis Browns playing in ten different cities! Even after the Wolverines clinched the Series with their eighth win in the eleventh game, the two teams still played out the final four games. The 1888 battle between the NL Giants and the AA Browns was downsized to a 10-game series played in four cities. The last year for this nineteenth century World Series was 1890, as the collapse of the American Association in 1891 left the National League as the only major league.

Without another league, the NL tried several different approaches to postseason play. In 1892 the season was deliberately divided into two halves for the only time in big-league history, with the winner of the first half facing the second-half winner in the NL championship series. From 1894–1897 the first place team in the NL faced the second place team in a postseason trophy series started by wealthy sportsman William Temple. While the "Temple Cup" format did attract paying fans to the ballpark, it never generated that much excitement. (No surprise there, as the first-place team had already shown itself superior during the regular season.) After the demise of the Temple Cup, Pittsburgh's *Chronicle-Telegraph* newspaper sponsored a five-game match-up in 1900 between the second-place Pirates and the first-place Brooklyn Superbas.

In 1901 the American League emerged as an alternative major league. By outbidding the senior National League to most of the game's best players, and by putting a more refined game on the field, the AL quickly surpassed the NL in popularity. By 1903 the established league agreed to a ceasefire with its upstart rival. This agreement allowed the NL champion Pittsburgh Pirates to challenge the AL champion Boston Americans.

This first modern World Series was an enormous success in virtually every way, with Boston winning the series, five games to three. American baseball fans fully expected—but did not get—another World Series the next year. The 1903 arrangement was the result of an agreement between the two clubs involved: it was not officially sanctioned by either league. New York was the runaway NL winner in 1904, but Giants manager John McGraw, who disliked the AL and despised Ban Johnson, had no intention of playing an AL team in the postseason if he didn't have to.

Giants owner John Brush, who had problems of his own with the AL and Ban Johnson, backed McGraw's stand in 1904, then changed his mind over the off-season and proposed an annual, officially sanctioned World Series starting in 1905. The National Commission, which had been formed to oversee the two leagues as a result of the 1903 ceasefire agreement, adopted most of Brush's suggestions, and so the World Series became a permanent fixture of the National Pastime.

The World Series has run relatively smoothly ever since. There have been only two major crises involving the Fall Classic. The first was the infamous Black Sox scandal, where members of the Chicago White Sox were involved in a game-fixing plot during the 1919 World Series. The credibility of professional baseball and the World Series was severely damaged by this imbroglio; only the harsh actions of new commissioner Judge Landis and the emergence of Babe Ruth as an international superstar kept the major leagues from falling from grace. In 1994 the titanic labor dispute between owners and players resulted in another strike. During the strike, Commissioner Bud Selig canceled the 1994 World Series, marking the first time in eighty-nine years that the Series had not been played.

For more than sixty years after the World Series was granted the imprimatur of the major leagues, baseball's postseason stayed the course with little significant change. However, in the 1960s baseball had to face increasing competition from other sports, its own declining popularity, and the demands of expansion. The AL and NL separately expanded to ten teams in the early 1960s without changing the postseason. As both leagues planned to go to twelve teams in 1969, MLB felt that the leagues could no longer maintain their traditional structures and keep most of the fans interested in the pennant races. Therefore, each league was split into Eastern and Western Divisions (though geography didn't always determine which division teams were placed in), and the League Championship Series was created to determine who would make it to the World Series. Initially, the LCS were devised as best-of-five matchups; in 1985 they were expanded to a best-of-seven format.

The other anomalous postseason in the twentieth century resulted from the 1981 strike and its ad hoc split season. First-half winners of each division faced second-half winners in best-of-five series in order to qualify for the LCS that year.

After the 1993 NL expansion, each league had fourteen teams, with further expansion expected soon. Therefore, baseball owners decided to add another postseason round, ushering in the era of Division Series. In 1994 MLB adopted a three-division structure out of which the division winners and one "wild card" team from each league would make it into the postseason. This meant that a World Series champion would now have to win three short series—a best-of-five Division series, a best-of-seven League Championship Series, and the best-of-seven World Series. Since a wild card team has won the World Series in three out of the first nine years this system has been in place, it is clear that winning a regular-season title is no longer necessary.

While many traditionalists have been disappointed by the way the expanded postseason has reduced the importance of the regular season, MLB and many others feel that the Wild Card has boosted interest in many cities late in the season. The remarkably tight 2003 NL wild card race—in which seven teams were competing into the final month of the reason—has also added fuel to the movement to expand the postseason even further by adding more wild card berths.

While there is little question that interest in places like South Florida in 2003 is fueled by having a Wild Card race, the long-term damage to the pennant races and to the postseason is substantial, even though less clear. Division Series attendance has been mediocre at best in many places as fans wait to see if their team will survive the lightning round and play for the pennant. Even worse, the magnitude of baseball's showcase event, the World Series, has dimmed dramatically since the 1980s.

Key to Postseason and Playoff Tables. The first World Series Most Valuable Player Award was created in 1949 by the New York chapter of the Baseball Writers Association of America in honor of Babe Ruth, who had died the previous year. In 1955 the

editors of *SPORT* Magazine started choosing their own World Series MVP. That MVP Award often came with a Corvette, courtesy of General Motors' Chevrolet division.

Eventually, the winners of the *Sport* award came to be determined by baseball writers and executives present at the World Series. Now MLB's official World Series MVP Award greatly overshadows the Babe Ruth Award, whose winner is generally not selected until several weeks after the Series ends. *SPORT's* involvement with the World Series MVP Award ended with the magazine's demise in 2000. Prior to 1955 we have selected Ex Post Facto MVPs: the players who we think would have won the World Series MVP Award if it had existed. Selections in italics designate MVPs from losing teams.

MVPs for the League Championship Series have been awarded by the NL since 1977 and the AL since 1980. No MVP Award has been established for the more recent Division Series. We have made Ex Post Facto MVP picks for all Division Series and for the ALCS and NLCS prior to the league awards.

The following tables show the results of all postseason series in baseball history. From 1969–2003, the division for each team is indicated by a letter code (E–Eastern Division; C–Central Division; W–Western Division), while a bullet (#) indicates a Wild Card team. First-half winners in 1892 and 1981 are indicated by (1H); second-half winners by (2H). For the 1894–1900 "Cup" series, (1) indicates the team finished first-during the regular season; (2) indicates the team finished second.

Also shown are the results of the four NL playoff series and the six-single game playoffs. Prior to the advent of divisional play in 1969, NL first-place ties were broken by playing a three-game series, while the AL used a single-game playoff format. Since 1969 all ties for postseason qualification have been broken by one-game playoffs. MLB considers any playoff game or series to determine who advances to the postseason to be part of the regular season.

National League Playoff Series

Year	Games Won (Scores)
1946	St. Louis 2, Brooklyn 0 (4-2, 8-4)
1951	New York 2, Brooklyn 1 (3-1, 0-10, 5-4)
1959	Los Angeles 2, Milwaukee 0 (3-2, 6-5)
1962	San Francisco 2, Los Angeles 1 (8-0, 7-8, 6-4)

Single-Game Playoffs

Year	Title	Score
1948	AL	Cleveland 8, Boston 3
1978	AL East	New York 5, Boston 4
1980	NL West	Houston 7, Los Angeles 1
1995	AL West	Seattle 9, California 1
1998	NL Wild Card	Chicago 5, San Francisco 3
1999	NL Wild Card	New York 5, Cincinnati 0

Division Series

Year	American League (Division) Games Won	Ex Post Facto MVP	National League (Division) Games Won	Ex Post Facto MVP
1981	New York (E/1H) 3, Milwaukee (E/2H) 2	[Goose Gossage]	Montreal (E/2H) 3, Philadelphia (E/1H) 2	[Steve Rogers]
	Oakland (W/1H) 3, Kansas City (W/2H) 0	[Dwayne Murphy]	Los Angeles (W/1H) 3, Houston (W/2H) 2	[Jerry Reuss]
1995	Cleveland (C) 3, Boston (E) 0	[Eddie Murray]	Atlanta (E) 3, Colorado (W#) 1	[Marquis Grissom]
	Seattle (W) 3, New York (E#) 2	[Edgar Martinez]	Cincinnati (C) 3, Los Angeles (W) 0	[Hal Morris]
1996	Baltimore (E#) 3, Cleveland (C) 1	[Brady Anderson]	Atlanta (E) 3, Los Angeles (W#) 0	[Mark Wohlers]
	New York (E) 3, Texas (W) 1	[*Juan Gonzalez*]	St. Louis (C) 3, San Diego (W) 0	[Brian Jordan]
1997	Cleveland (C) 3, New York (E#) 2	[Mike Mussina]	Florida (E#) 3, San Francisco (W) 0	[Gary Sheffield]
	Baltimore (E) 3, Seattle (W) 1	[Omar Vizquel]	Atlanta (E) 3, Houston (C) 0	[Chipper Jones]
1998	New York (E) 3, Texas (W) 0	[Scott Brosius]	Atlanta (E) 3, Chicago (C#) 0	[Javy Lopez]
	Cleveland (C) 3, Boston (E#) 1	[Manny Ramirez]	San Diego (W) 3, Houston (C) 1	[Kevin Brown]
1999	New York (E) 3, Texas (W) 0	[Bernie Williams]	New York (E#) 3, Arizona (W) 1	[Edgardo Alfonzo]
	Boston (E#) 3, Cleveland (C) 2	[Pedro Martinez]	Atlanta (W) 3, Houston (C) 1	[Brian Jordan]
2000	New York (E) 3, Oakland (W) 2	[Mariano Rivera]	St. Louis (C) 3, Atlanta (E) 0	[Jim Edmonds]
	Seattle (W#) 3, Chicago (C) 0	[Edgar Martinez]	New York (E#) 3, San Francisco (W) 1	[Bobby Jones]
2001	Seattle (W) 3, Cleveland (C) 2	[Edgar Martinez]	Atlanta (E) 3, Houston (C) 0	[Chipper Jones]
	New York (E) 3, Oakland (W#) 2	[Derek Jeter]	Arizona (W) 3, St. Louis (C#) 2	[Curt Schilling]
2002	Minnesota (C) 3, Oakland (W) 2	[A.J. Pierzynski]	St. Louis (C) 3, Arizona (W) 0	[Fernando Vina]
	Anaheim (W#) 3, New York (E) 1	[Scott Spiezio]	San Francisco (W#)3, Atlanta (E) 2	[Barry Bonds]
2003	Boston (E#) 3, Oakland (W) 2	[Todd Walker]	Chicago (C) 3, Atlanta (E) 2	[Kerry Wood]
	New York (E) 3, Minnesota (C) 1	[Derek Jeter]	Florida (E#) 3, San Francisco (W) 2	[Ivan Rodriguez]

E: East Division; C: Central Division; W: West Division; #: Wildcard; 1H: First-half winner; 2H: Second-half winner.

National League Championship Series

Year	Games Won	Ex Post Facto MVP
1892	Boston (1H) 5, Cleveland (2H) 0, 1 Tie	[Hugh Duffy]
1894	New York (2) 4, Baltimore (1) 0 (Temple Cup)	[Amos Rusie]
1895	Cleveland (2) 4, Baltimore (1) 1 (Temple Cup)	[Cy Young]
1896	Baltimore (1) 4, Cleveland (2) 0 (Temple Cup)	[Willie Keeler]
1897	Baltimore (2) 4, Boston (1) 1 (Temple Cup)	[Jack Doyle]
1900	Brooklyn (1) 3, Pittsburgh (2) 1 (Chronicle-Telegraph Cup)	[Joe McGinnity]

(1) Finished first-in regular season; (2) Finished second in regular season; 1H: First-half winner; 2H: Second-half winner.

American League & National League Championship Series

Year	ALCS (Division) Games Won	MVP [Ex Post Facto]	NLCS (Division) Games Won	MVP [Ex Post Facto]
1969	Baltimore (E) 3, Minnesota (W) 0	[Dave McNally]	New York (E) 3, Atlanta (W) 0	[Ken Boswell]
1970	Baltimore (E) 3, Minnesota (W) 0	[Boog Powell]	Cincinnati (W) 3, Pittsburgh (E) 0	[Bobby Tolan]
1971	Baltimore (E) 3, Oakland (W) 0	[Boog Powell]	Pittsburgh (E) 3, San Francisco (W) 1	[Bob Robertson]
1972	Oakland (W) 3, Detroit (E) 2	[Blue Moon Odom]	Cincinnati (W) 3, Pittsburgh (E) 2	[Johnny Bench]
1973	Oakland (W) 3, Baltimore (E) 2	[Catfish Hunter]	New York (E) 3, Cincinnati (W) 2	[Rusty Staub]
1974	Oakland (W) 3, Baltimore (E) 1	[Sal Bando]	Los Angeles (W) 3, Pittsburgh (E) 1	[Don Sutton]
1975	Boston (E) 3, Oakland (W) 0	[Carl Yastrzemski]	Cincinnati (W) 3, Pittsburgh (E) 0	[Tony Perez]
1976	New York (E) 3, Kansas City (W) 2	[Chris Chambliss]	Cincinnati (W) 3, Philadelphia (E) 0	[Pete Rose]
1977	New York (E) 3, Kansas City (W) 2	[Sparky Lyle]	Los Angeles (W) 3, Philadelphia (E) 1	Dusty Baker
1978	New York (E) 3, Kansas City (W) 1	[Reggie Jackson]	Los Angeles (W) 3, Philadelphia (E) 1	Steve Garvey
1979	Baltimore (E) 3, California (W) 1	[Eddie Murray]	Pittsburgh (E) 3, Cincinnati (W) 0	Willie Stargell
1980	Kansas City (W) 3, New York (E) 0	Frank White	Philadelphia (E) 3, Houston (W) 2	Manny Trillo
1981	New York (E) 3, Oakland (W) 0	Graig Nettles	Los Angeles (W) 3, Montreal (E) 2	Burt Hooton
1982	Milwaukee (E) 3, California (W) 2	*Fred Lynn*	St. Louis (E) 3, Atlanta (W) 0	Darrell Porter
1983	Baltimore (E) 3, Chicago (W) 1	Mike Boddicker	Philadelphia (E) 3, Los Angeles (W) 1	Gary Matthews
1984	Detroit (E) 3, Kansas City (W) 0	Kirk Gibson	San Diego (W) 3, Chicago (E) 2	Steve Garvey
1985	Kansas City (W) 4, Toronto (E) 3	George Brett	St. Louis (E) 4, Los Angeles (W) 2	Ozzie Smith
1986	Boston (E) 4, California (W) 3	Marty Barrett	New York (E) 4, Houston (W) 2	*Mike Scott*
1987	Minnesota (W) 4, Detroit (E) 1	Gary Gaetti	St. Louis (E) 4, San Francisco (W) 3	*Jeffrey Leonard*
1988	Oakland (W) 4, Boston (E) 0	Dennis Eckersley	Los Angeles (W) 4, New York (E) 3	Orel Hershiser
1989	Oakland (W) 4, Toronto (E) 1	Rickey Henderson	San Francisco (W) 4, Chicago (E) 1	Will Clark
1990	Oakland (W) 4, Boston (E) 0	Dave Stewart	Cincinnati (W) 4, Pittsburgh (E) 2	Rob Dibble & Randy Myers
1991	Minnesota (W) 4, Toronto (E) 1	Kirby Puckett	Atlanta (W) 4, Pittsburgh (E) 3	Steve Avery
1992	Toronto (E) 4, Oakland (W) 2	Roberto Alomar	Atlanta (W) 4, Pittsburgh (E) 3	John Smoltz
1993	Toronto (E) 4, Chicago (W) 2	Dave Stewart	Philadelphia (E) 4, Atlanta (W) 2	Curt Schilling
1995	Cleveland (C) 4, Seattle (W) 2	Orel Hershiser	Atlanta (E) 4, Cincinnati (C) 0	Mike Devereaux
1996	New York (E) 4, Baltimore (E#) 1	Bernie Williams	Atlanta (E) 4, St. Louis (C) 3	Javier Lopez
1997	Cleveland (C) 4, Baltimore (E) 2	Marquis Grissom	Florida (E#) 4, Atlanta (E) 2	Livan Hernandez
1998	New York (E) 4, Cleveland (C) 2	David Wells	San Diego (W) 4, Atlanta (E) 2	Sterling Hitchcock
1999	New York (E) 4, Boston (E#) 1	Orlando Hernandez	Atlanta (E) 4, New York (E#) 2	Eddie Perez
2000	New York (E) 4, Seattle (W) 2	David Justice	New York (E#) 4, St. Louis (C) 1	Mike Hampton
2001	New York (E) 4, Seattle (W) 1	Alfonso Soriano	Arizona (W) 4, Atlanta (E) 1	Craig Counsell
2002	Anaheim (W#) 4, Minnesota (C) 1	Adam Kennedy	San Francisco (W#) 4, St. Louis (C) 1	Benito Santiago
2003	New York (E) 4, Boston (E#) 3	Mariano Rivera	Florida (E#) 4, Chicago (C) 3	Ivan Rodriguez

E: East Division; C: Central Division; W: West Division; #: Wildcard.

World Series

Year	Team (League) Games Won	Sport Magazine Award [Ex Post Facto MVP]	Babe Ruth Award
1884	Providence (NL) 3, New York (AA) 0	[Charles Radbourn]	
1885	St. Louis (AA) 3, Chicago (NL) 3, 1 tie	[Cap Anson]	
1886	St. Louis (AA) 4, Chicago (NL) 2	[Bob Caruthers]	
1887	Detroit (NL) 10, St. Louis (AA) 5	[Lady Baldwin]	
1888	New York (NL) 6, St. Louis (AA) 4	[Tim Keefe]	
1889	New York (NL) 6, Brooklyn (AA) 3	[Monte Ward]	
1890	Brooklyn (NL) 3, Louisville (AA) 3, 1 tie	[Red Ehret]	
1903	Boston (AL) 5, Pittsburgh (NL) 3	[Bill Dineen]	
1905	New York (NL) 4, Philadelphia (AL) 1	[Christy Mathewson]	
1906	Chicago (AL) 4, Chicago (NL) 2	[George Davis]	
1907	Chicago (NL) 4, Detroit (AL) 0, 1 tie	[Harry Steinfeldt]	
1908	Chicago (NL) 4, Detroit (AL) 1	[Orval Overall]	
1909	Pittsburgh (NL) 4, Detroit (AL) 3	[Babe Adams]	
1910	Philadelphia (AL) 4, Chicago (NL) 1	[Jack Coombs]	
1911	Philadelphia (AL) 4, New York (NL) 2	[Frank Baker]	
1912	Boston (AL) 4, New York (NL) 3, 1 tie	[Joe Wood]	
1913	Philadelphia (AL) 4, New York (NL) 1	[Frank Baker]	
1914	Boston (NL) 4, Philadelphia (AL) 0	[Hank Gowdy]	
1915	Boston (AL) 4, Philadelphia (NL) 1	[Harry Hooper]	
1916	Boston (AL) 4, Brooklyn (NL) 1	[Ernie Shore]	
1917	Chicago (AL) 4, New York (NL) 2	[Red Faber]	
1918	Boston (AL) 4, Chicago (NL) 2	[Carl Mays]	
1919	Cincinnati (NL) 5, Chicago (AL) 3	[Hod Eller]	
1920	Cleveland (AL) 5, Brooklyn (NL) 2	[Stan Coveleski]	
1921	New York (NL) 5, New York (AL) 3	[Waite Hoyt]	

Year	Team (League) Games Won	Sport Magazine Award [Ex Post Facto MVP]	Babe Ruth Award
1922	New York (NL) 4, New York (AL) 0, 1 tie	[Irish Meusel]	
1923	New York (AL) 4, New York (NL) 2	[Babe Ruth]	
1924	Washington (AL) 4, New York (NL) 3	[Goose Goslin]	
1925	Pittsburgh (NL) 4, Washington (AL) 3	[Max Carey]	
1926	St. Louis (NL) 4, New York (AL) 3	[Grover Alexander]	
1927	New York (AL) 4, Pittsburgh (NL) 0	[Babe Ruth]	
1928	New York (AL) 4, St. Louis (NL) 0	[Lou Gehrig]	
1929	Philadelphia (AL) 4, Chicago (NL) 1	[Jimmie Foxx]	
1930	Philadelphia (AL) 4, St. Louis (NL) 2	[George Earnshaw]	
1931	St. Louis (NL) 4, Philadelphia (AL) 3	[Pepper Martin]	
1932	New York (AL) 4, Chicago (NL) 0	[Lou Gehrig]	
1933	New York (NL) 4, Washington (AL) 1	[Carl Hubbell]	
1934	St. Louis (NL) 4, Detroit (AL) 3	[Dizzy Dean]	
1935	Detroit (AL) 4, Chicago (NL) 2	[Tommy Bridges]	
1936	New York (AL) 4, New York (NL) 2	[Jake Powell]	
1937	New York (AL) 4, New York (NL) 1	[Lefty Grove]	
1938	New York (AL) 4, Chicago (NL) 0	[Joe Gordon]	
1939	New York (AL) 4, Cincinnati (NL) 0	[Charlie Keller]	
1940	Cincinnati (NL) 4, Detroit (AL) 3	[Jimmy Ripple]	
1941	New York (AL) 4, Brooklyn (NL) 1	[Charlie Keller]	
1942	St. Louis (NL) 4, New York (AL) 1	[Johnny Beazley]	
1943	New York (AL) 4, St. Louis (NL) 1	[Spud Chandler]	
1944	St. Louis (NL) 4, St. Louis (AL) 2	[Mort Cooper]	
1945	Detroit (AL) 4, Chicago (NL) 3	[Hank Greenberg]	
1946	St. Louis (NL) 4, Boston (AL) 3	[Harry Brecheen]	
1947	New York (AL) 4, Brooklyn (NL) 3	[Johnny Lindell]	
1948	Cleveland (AL) 4, Boston (NL) 2	[Bob Lemon]	
1949	New York (AL) 4, Brooklyn (NL) 1	[Allie Reynolds]	Joe Page
1950	New York (AL) 4, Philadelphia (NL) 0	[Jerry Coleman]	Jerry Coleman
1951	New York (AL) 4, New York (NL) 2	[Ed Lopat]	Phil Rizzuto
1952	New York (AL) 4, Brooklyn (NL) 3	[Mickey Mantle]	Johnny Mize
1953	New York (AL) 4, Brooklyn (NL) 2	[Billy Martin]	Billy Martin
1954	New York (NL) 4, Cleveland (AL) 0	[Dusty Rhodes]	Dusty Rhodes
1955	Brooklyn (NL) 4, New York (AL) 3	Johnny Podres	Johnny Podres
1956	New York (AL) 4, Brooklyn (NL) 3	Don Larsen	Don Larsen
1957	Milwaukee (NL) 4, New York (AL) 3	Lew Burdette	Lew Burdette
1958	New York (AL) 4, Milwaukee (NL) 3	Bob Turley	Elston Howard
1959	Los Angeles (NL) 4, Chicago (AL) 2	Larry Sherry	Larry Sherry
1960	Pittsburgh (NL) 4, New York (AL) 3	*Bobby Richardson*	Bill Mazeroski
1961	New York (AL) 4, Cincinnati (NL) 1	Whitey Ford	Whitey Ford
1962	New York (AL) 4, San Francisco (NL) 3	Ralph Terry	Ralph Terry
1963	Los Angeles (NL) 4, New York (AL) 0	Sandy Koufax	Sandy Koufax
1964	St. Louis (NL) 4, New York (AL) 3	Bob Gibson	Bob Gibson
1965	Los Angeles (NL) 4, Minnesota (AL) 3	Sandy Koufax	Sandy Koufax
1966	Baltimore (AL) 4, Los Angeles (NL) 0	Frank Robinson	Frank Robinson
1967	St. Louis (NL) 4, Boston (AL) 3	Bob Gibson	Lou Brock
1968	Detroit (AL) 4, St. Louis (NL) 3	Mickey Lolich	Mickey Lolich
1969	New York (NL) 4, Baltimore (AL) 1	Donn Clendenon	Al Weis
1970	Baltimore (AL) 4, Cincinnati (NL) 1	Brooks Robinson	Brooks Robinson
1971	Pittsburgh (NL) 4, Baltimore (AL) 3	Roberto Clemente	Roberto Clemente
1972	Oakland (AL) 4, Cincinnati (NL)3	Gene Tenace	Gene Tenace
1973	Oakland (AL) 4, New York (NL) 3	Reggie Jackson	Bert Campaneris
1974	Oakland (AL) 4, Los Angeles (NL) 1	Rollie Fingers	Dick Green
1975	Cincinnati (NL) 4, Boston (AL) 3	Pete Rose	*Luis Tiant*
1976	Cincinnati (NL) 4, New York (AL) 0	Johnny Bench	Johnny Bench
1977	New York (AL) 4, Los Angeles (NL) 2	Reggie Jackson	Reggie Jackson
1978	New York (AL) 4, Los Angeles (NL) 2	Bucky Dent	Bucky Dent
1979	Pittsburgh (NL) 4, Baltimore (AL) 3	Willie Stargell	Willie Stargell
1980	Philadelphia (NL) 4, Kansas City (AL) 2	Mike Schmidt	Tug McGraw
1981	Los Angeles (NL) 4, New York (AL) 2	Ron Cey & Pedro Guerrero & Steve Yeager	Ron Cey
1982	St. Louis (NL) 4, Milwaukee (AL) 3	Darrell Porter	Bruce Sutter
1983	Baltimore (AL) 4, Philadelphia (NL) 1	Rick Dempsey	Rick Dempsey
1984	Detroit (AL) 4, San Diego (NL) 1	Alan Trammell	Jack Morris
1985	Kansas City (AL) 4, St. Louis (NL) 3	Bret Saberhagen	Bret Saberhagen
1986	New York (NL) 4, Boston (AL) 3	Ray Knight	Ray Knight
1987	Minnesota (AL) 4, St. Louis (NL) 3	Frank Viola	Frank Viola
1988	Los Angeles (NL) 4, Oakland (AL) 1	Orel Hershiser	Orel Hershiser
1989	Oakland (AL) 4, San Francisco (NL) 0	Dave Stewart	Dave Stewart
1990	Cincinnati (NL) 4, Oakland (AL) 0	Jose Rijo	Billy Hatcher
1991	Minnesota (AL) 4, Atlanta (NL) 3	Jack Morris	Jack Morris
1992	Toronto (AL) 4, Atlanta (NL) 2	Pat Borders	Dave Winfield
1993	Toronto (AL) 4, Philadelphia (NL) 2	Paul Molitor	Paul Molitor
1995	Atlanta (NL) 4, Cleveland (AL) 2	Tom Glavine	Tom Glavine
1996	New York (AL) 4, Atlanta (NL) 2	John Wetteland	Cecil Fielder
1997	Florida (NL) 4, Cleveland (AL) 3	Livan Hernandez	Moises Alou
1998	New York (AL) 4, San Diego (NL) 0	Scott Brosius	Scott Brosius
1999	New York (AL) 4, Atlanta (NL) 0	Mariano Rivera	Mariano Rivera
2000	New York (AL) 4, New York (NL) 1	Derek Jeter	Derek Jeter
2001	Arizona (NL) 4, New York (AL) 3	Randy Johnson	Randy Johnson & Curt Schilling
2002	Anaheim (AL) 4, San Francisco (NL) 3	Troy Glaus	David Eckstein
2003	Florida (NL) 4, New York (AL) 2	Josh Beckett	Josh Beckett

THE GLORY OF THEIR TIMES: THE ALL-TIME LEADERS

The history of baseball is so appealing partly because it is possible to compare achievements from eras that are many years apart. While baseball has certainly evolved over time, it has not undergone radical changes that would make the sport unrecognizable. A fan from 1903 transported to a 2003 major league game would not have a problem understanding what was happening on the field (though he might not be carrying a week's wages to pay for a hot dog).

The unchanging nature of the game is why the leaders section is often the first place a reader turns upon opening a book such as this. Most baseball statistics have maintained enough of their meaning over time so as to make comparisons between players of different eras possible, either directly or indirectly (by comparing to the league average). Only a few statistical categories have changed continually in one direction over baseball history. Those few include innings pitched, which has generally declined on a seasonal basis along with parallel statistics such as complete games; fielding average, which has risen due to improvements in gloves, better groundskeeping, and more lenient official scoring; and strikeouts, which have risen due to changes in the style of play. Most other statistics rise and fall with variances in the balance between offense and defense but haven't fundamentally changed over the years.

Some of the lists in this section are divided by time period in order to more clearly highlight the standout performers of each era. Eight significant eras in baseball history have been defined for this purpose—each is distinguished by major rules changes, by large changes in the number of leagues or teams, or by other important factors.

- The first era covers 1876–91, a period that started with the formation of the National League and ended with the collapse of the American Association;
- The next period, 1892–1900, marks the short period during which the National League stood unchallenged by any rival major league;
- The third era, 1901–20, covers the Dead Ball Era, World War I, the banning of the spitball, and the Black Sox scandal. It concludes as offensive levels start to jump (which came later in the NL than in the AL);
- The next period, 1921–42, takes the major leagues through the period in which offense dominated until World War II started to seriously deplete the majors;
- The fifth era, 1943–60, starts with the peak war years and continues through baseball's integration and the migration of the major leagues to the West Coast;
- The next period, 1961–72, is highlighted by the expansion of both leagues as well the change to division play, the expansion of the strike zone (and its subsequent reversion), and the resulting collapse of offense;
- The seventh era, 1973–1987, starts with the implementation of the designated hitter rule and includes the heyday of the multipurpose stadiums. This era is highlighted by the return of offense—as well as significantly higher attendance—to the game;
- The current era, which covers 1988 to the present, is marked by the explosion of home runs, the wave of retro ballparks, and a new period of expansion.

Players are only eligible to be listed in only one era each, even if their careers spanned several eras. They are placed in the era during which they played the most games or pitched the most innings. However, their lifetime totals or averages are used to rank them in the era they played the most.

A quick perusal of these leader lists will reveal the names of all of the National Pastime's immortals along with the all-time greats and numerous perennial all-stars. They recount the exploits of more than a few lucky players who happened to catch lightning in a bottle once or twice. The greatest players live on in the memories of most baseball fans; the lucky ones sometimes live on only in the pages of the record books. Regardless of the type of player, the vast majority of ballplayers who show up on these lists were truly the glory of their times.

The Glory of Their Times is one of the greatest baseball books ever published. In its pages, Lawrence Ritter captured the sweet essence of men in the twilight of their lives—men whose glory may have faded but whose memories have not. By recording the names of these all-time leaders, we hope to honor them as well as the game they played so well.

A few notes about some of the leader lists:

On-Base Percentage is calculated by the current official definition for every season since 1954. However, since a distinct sacrifice fly category was not kept before 1954, they are not included in the calculations for seasons before 1954, except for the years during which sacrifice flies were not counted as sacrifice hits. (1908–30 and 1939 were the other years when sac flies were awarded; in other years pre–1954, a sacrifice fly was counted as an at bat.)

Plate Appearances count every time a batter completes an at bat, including hits, outs, walks, sacrifices, hit-by-pitches, etc.

Strikeout Percentage divides strikeouts by at bats to indicate what percentage of the time a batter strikes out.

At Bats per Strikeout indicates how infrequently a batter strikes out.

Relative Batting Average is a player's batting average compared to the league's batting average where the latter is 1.0.

Home Run Percentage divides home runs by at bats to show the percentage of times a batter hits a home run.

Runs/150 Games and **RBI/150 Games** show a player's typical production in a full season. While today the regular season lasts 162 games, for most of baseball history the regular season was 154 games or less.

Total Chances consist of assists plus putouts plus errors.

Relief Wins and **Relief Losses** include only decisions for pitchers who did not start the game.

Blown Saves and **Save Percentage** are available for 1969 to the present only.

The minimums for Single-Season leaders include:

- Starting Pitchers (for rate statistics): 1 inning pitched per scheduled game;
- Relief Pitchers (for rate statistics): 0.5 inning pitched per scheduled game;
- Pitcher Winning Percentage: 15 wins;
- Save Percentage: 20 saves;
- Batters (for rate statistics): 3.1 plate appearances per scheduled game;
- Pinch-Hit Batting Average: 30 at bats;
- Pitcher Batting Average: 20 hits;
- Stolen Base Percentage: 20 stolen bases;

- Fielding Statistics: 0.66 games played per scheduled game (exception: for outfielders with a 1.000 Fielding Average, a minimum of 250 total chances, and for pitchers with a 1.000 Fielding Average, a minimum of 50 total chances);
- Catcher Fielding Statistics: 0.5 games played per scheduled game.

The minimums for Career leaders include:

- Starting Pitchers (for rate statistics): 1,500 innings pitched;
- Relief Pitchers (for rate statistics): 750 innings pitched;
- Save Percentage: 50 Saves;
- Batters (for rate statistics): 1,000 games;
- Pinch-Hit Batting Average: 150 at bats;
- Pitcher Batting Average: 80 hits;
- Stolen Base Percentage: 100 stolen bases.

Games

1	Pete Rose	3562
2	Carl Yastrzemski	3308
3	Hank Aaron	3298
4	**Rickey Henderson**	**3081**
5	Ty Cobb	3035
6	Eddie Murray	3026
	Stan Musial	3026
8	Cal Ripken	3001
9	Willie Mays	2992
10	Dave Winfield	2973
11	Rusty Staub	2951
12	Brooks Robinson	2896
13	Robin Yount	2856
14	Al Kaline	2834
15	Harold Baines	2830
16	Eddie Collins	2826
17	Reggie Jackson	2820
18	Frank Robinson	2808
19	Honus Wagner	2794
20	Tris Speaker	2789
21	Tony Perez	2777
22	Mel Ott	2730
23	George Brett	2707
24	Graig Nettles	2700
25	Darrell Evans	2687
26	Paul Molitor	2683
27	Rabbit Maranville	2670
28	Joe Morgan	2649
29	Andre Dawson	2627
30	Lou Brock	2616
31	Dwight Evans	2606
32	Luis Aparicio	2599
33	Willie McCovey	2588
34	Ozzie Smith	2573
35	**Barry Bonds**	**2569**
36	**Rafael Palmeiro**	**2567**
37	Paul Waner	2549
38	Ernie Banks	2528
39	Bill Buckner	2517
	Sam Crawford	2517
41	Gary Gaetti	2507
42	Babe Ruth	2503
43	Tim Raines	2502
44	Carlton Fisk	2499
45	Dave Concepcion	2488
	Billy Williams	2488
47	Nap Lajoie	2480
48	Max Carey	2476
49	Rod Carew	2469
	Vada Pinson	2469
51	Dave Parker	2466
52	Ted Simmons	2456
53	Bill Dahlen	2444
54	Ron Fairly	2442
55	Wade Boggs	2440
	Tony Gwynn	2440
57	Chili Davis	2436
58	Harmon Killebrew	2435
59	Roberto Clemente	2433
	Fred McGriff	**2433**
61	Willie Davis	2429
62	Luke Appling	2422
63	Zack Wheat	2410
64	Mickey Vernon	2409
65	Buddy Bell	2405
66	Sam Rice	2404
	Mike Schmidt	2404
68	Mickey Mantle	2401
69	Eddie Mathews	2391
70	Lou Whitaker	2390
71	Jake Beckley	2389
72	Bobby Wallace	2383
73	Enos Slaughter	2380
74	George Davis	2372
75	Al Oliver	2368
76	Nellie Fox	2367
77	Willie Stargell	2360
78	Jose Cruz	2353
79	Brian Downing	2344
80	Steve Garvey	2332
81	Bert Campaneris	2328
82	Frank White	2324
83	**Roberto Alomar**	**2323**
	Charlie Gehringer	2323
85	Jimmie Foxx	2317
86	Frankie Frisch	2311
87	Harry Hooper	2309
88	Gary Carter	2296
89	Alan Trammell	2293
90	Don Baylor	2292
	Ted Williams	2292
92	Goose Goslin	2287
93	Jimmy Dykes	2282
94	Lave Cross	2278
95	Cap Anson	2277
96	Bob Boone	2264
97	Chris Speier	2260
98	Rogers Hornsby	2259
99	**Craig Biggio**	**2253**
100	**Andres Galarraga**	**2250**

Plate Appearances

1	Pete Rose	15861
2	Carl Yastrzemski	13991
3	Hank Aaron	13940
4	**Rickey Henderson**	**13346**
5	Ty Cobb	13068
6	Cal Ripken	12883
7	Eddie Murray	12817
8	Stan Musial	12712
9	Willie Mays	12493
10	Dave Winfield	12358
11	Robin Yount	12249
12	Paul Molitor	12160
13	Eddie Collins	12037
14	Tris Speaker	11988
15	Brooks Robinson	11782
16	Honus Wagner	11748
17	Frank Robinson	11743
18	George Brett	11624
19	Al Kaline	11597
20	Reggie Jackson	11416
21	Mel Ott	11337
22	Joe Morgan	11329
23	Rabbit Maranville	11256
24	Lou Brock	11235
25	Luis Aparicio	11230
26	Rusty Staub	11229
27	Harold Baines	11092
28	**Rafael Palmeiro**	**10973**
29	**Barry Bonds**	**10967**
30	Tony Perez	10861
31	Ozzie Smith	10778
32	Max Carey	10770
33	Andre Dawson	10769
34	Paul Waner	10762
35	Wade Boggs	10740
36	Darrell Evans	10737
37	Babe Ruth	10617
38	Sam Crawford	10594
39	Dwight Evans	10569
40	Rod Carew	10550
41	Billy Williams	10519
42	Jake Beckley	10504
43	Nap Lajoie	10460
44	Bill Dahlen	10405
45	Vada Pinson	10403
46	Ernie Banks	10395
47	Tim Raines	10359
48	Nellie Fox	10349
49	Sam Rice	10246
50	Harry Hooper	10244
51	Luke Appling	10243
52	Charlie Gehringer	10237
53	Tony Gwynn	10232
54	Graig Nettles	10226
55	Roberto Clemente	10212
56	**Roberto Alomar**	**10210**
57	Dave Parker	10184
58	George Davis	10178
59	Cap Anson	10123
60	Eddie Mathews	10101
61	Frankie Frisch	10100
62	**Fred McGriff**	**10093**
63	Mike Schmidt	10062
64	Bill Buckner	10033
65	Buddy Bell	10009
66	Chili Davis	9996
	Zack Wheat	9996
68	**Craig Biggio**	**9990**
69	Lou Whitaker	9967
70	Doc Cramer	9933
71	Mickey Mantle	9909
72	Carlton Fisk	9853
73	Fred Clarke	9838
74	Mickey Vernon	9834
75	Harmon Killebrew	9831
76	Willie Davis	9822
	Goose Goslin	9822
78	Gary Gaetti	9817
79	Ted Williams	9791
80	Al Oliver	9778
81	Lave Cross	9742
82	Richie Ashburn	9736
83	Willie McCovey	9686
84	Ted Simmons	9685
85	Jimmie Foxx	9670
86	Lou Gehrig	9660
87	Dave Concepcion	9640
88	Bert Campaneris	9625
89	Jesse Burkett	9620
90	Bobby Wallace	9612
91	Willie Keeler	9610
92	Brett Butler	9545
93	Al Simmons	9515
94	Rogers Hornsby	9475
95	Pee Wee Reese	9470
96	Steve Garvey	9466
97	Willie Randolph	9462
98	Bid McPhee	9430
99	Don Baylor	9401
100	Ron Santo	9396

At Bats

1	Pete Rose	14053
2	Hank Aaron	12364
3	Carl Yastrzemski	11988
4	Cal Ripken	11551
5	Ty Cobb	11434
6	Eddie Murray	11336
7	Robin Yount	11008
8	Dave Winfield	11003
9	Stan Musial	10972
10	**Rickey Henderson**	**10961**
11	Willie Mays	10881
12	Paul Molitor	10835
13	Brooks Robinson	10654
14	Honus Wagner	10439
15	George Brett	10349
16	Lou Brock	10332
17	Luis Aparicio	10230
18	Tris Speaker	10195
19	Al Kaline	10116
20	Rabbit Maranville	10078
21	Frank Robinson	10006
22	Eddie Collins	9949
23	Andre Dawson	9927
24	Harold Baines	9908
25	Reggie Jackson	9864
26	Tony Perez	9778
27	Rusty Staub	9720
28	Vada Pinson	9645
29	Nap Lajoie	9589
30	Sam Crawford	9570
31	**Rafael Palmeiro**	**9553**
32	Jake Beckley	9538
33	Paul Waner	9459
34	Mel Ott	9456
35	Roberto Clemente	9454
36	Ernie Banks	9421
37	Bill Buckner	9397
38	Ozzie Smith	9396
39	Max Carey	9363
40	Dave Parker	9358
41	Billy Williams	9350
42	Rod Carew	9315
43	Tony Gwynn	9288
44	Joe Morgan	9277
45	Sam Rice	9269
46	Nellie Fox	9232
47	Wade Boggs	9180
48	Willie Davis	9174
49	Doc Cramer	9140
50	Frankie Frisch	9112
51	Zack Wheat	9106
52	Cap Anson	9104
53	Lave Cross	9085
54	Al Oliver	9049
55	George Davis	9045
56	Bill Dahlen	9036
57	Dwight Evans	8996
58	Buddy Bell	8995
59	Graig Nettles	8986
60	Darrell Evans	8973
61	Gary Gaetti	8951
62	**Roberto Alomar**	**8902**
63	Tim Raines	8872
64	Charlie Gehringer	8860
65	Luke Appling	8856
66	Steve Garvey	8835
67	Tommy Corcoran	8812
68	Harry Hooper	8785
69	Al Simmons	8759
70	Carlton Fisk	8756
71	Mickey Vernon	8731
72	**Barry Bonds**	**8725**
73	Dave Concepcion	8723
74	**Fred McGriff**	**8685**
75	Bert Campaneris	8684
76	Ted Simmons	8680
77	Chili Davis	8673
78	Goose Goslin	8656
79	Bobby Wallace	8618
80	Willie Keeler	8591
81	**Craig Biggio**	**8588**
82	Fred Clarke	8584
83	Lou Whitaker	8570
84	Eddie Mathews	8537
85	Red Schoendienst	8479
86	Jesse Burkett	8426
87	Joe Carter	8422
88	Larry Bowa	8418
89	Babe Ruth	8399
90	Ryne Sandberg	8385
91	Richie Ashburn	8365
92	Mike Schmidt	8352
93	Bid McPhee	8304
94	Alan Trammell	8288
95	George Sisler	8267
96	Jim Rice	8225
97	Don Baylor	8198
98	Willie McCovey	8197
99	Brett Butler	8180
100	Rogers Hornsby	8173

Runs

1	**Rickey Henderson**	**2295**
2	Ty Cobb	2246
3	Hank Aaron	2174
	Babe Ruth	2174
5	Pete Rose	2165
6	Willie Mays	2062
7	Stan Musial	1949
8	**Barry Bonds**	**1941**
9	Lou Gehrig	1888
10	Tris Speaker	1882
11	Mel Ott	1859
12	Frank Robinson	1829
13	Eddie Collins	1821
14	Carl Yastrzemski	1816
15	Ted Williams	1798
16	Paul Molitor	1782
17	Charlie Gehringer	1774
18	Jimmie Foxx	1751
19	Honus Wagner	1739
20	Cap Anson	1722
21	Jesse Burkett	1720
22	Willie Keeler	1719
23	Billy Hamilton	1697
24	Bid McPhee	1684
25	Mickey Mantle	1677
26	Dave Winfield	1669
27	Joe Morgan	1650
28	Cal Ripken	1647
29	Jimmy Ryan	1643
30	George Van Haltren	1642
31	Robin Yount	1632
32	Eddie Murray	1627
	Paul Waner	1627
34	Fred Clarke	1622
	Al Kaline	1622
36	Roger Connor	1620
37	Lou Brock	1610
38	Jake Beckley	1602
39	Ed Delahanty	1600
40	Bill Dahlen	1590
41	George Brett	1583
42	Rogers Hornsby	1579
43	Tim Raines	1571
44	Hugh Duffy	1554
45	Reggie Jackson	1551
46	**Rafael Palmeiro**	**1548**
47	Max Carey	1545
	George Davis	1545
49	Frankie Frisch	1532
50	Dan Brouthers	1523
	Tom Brown	1523
52	Sam Rice	1514
53	Wade Boggs	1513
54	Eddie Mathews	1509
55	Al Simmons	1507
56	Mike Schmidt	1506
57	Nap Lajoie	1504
58	**Craig Biggio**	**1503**
59	Harry Stovey	1492
60	**Roberto Alomar**	**1490**
61	Goose Goslin	1483
62	Arlie Latham	1481
63	Dwight Evans	1470
64	Herman Long	1456
65	Jim O'Rourke	1446
66	Harry Hooper	1429
	Dummy Hoy	1429
68	Rod Carew	1424
69	Joe Kelley	1421
70	Roberto Clemente	1416
71	John Ward	1410
	Billy Williams	1410
73	Mike Griffin	1406
74	**Jeff Bagwell**	**1402**
75	Sam Crawford	1391
76	Joe DiMaggio	1390
77	Lou Whitaker	1386
78	Tony Gwynn	1383
79	Andre Dawson	1373
80	Vada Pinson	1366
81	Brett Butler	1359
82	Doc Cramer	1357
	King Kelly	1357
84	Tommy Leach	1355
85	Darrell Evans	1344
86	**Fred McGriff**	**1342**
87	Lave Cross	1338
	Pee Wee Reese	1338
89	Luis Aparicio	1335
90	George Gore	1327
91	Richie Ashburn	1322
92	Patsy Donovan	1321
93	Luke Appling	1319
94	Ryne Sandberg	1318
95	Mike Tiernan	1316
96	**Sammy Sosa**	**1314**
97	Ernie Banks	1305
	Kiki Cuyler	1305
99	Tony Phillips	1300
100	Harold Baines	1299

Runs by era

1988-2003

1	**Rickey Henderson**	**2295**
2	**Barry Bonds**	**1941**
3	Paul Molitor	1782
4	Cal Ripken	1647
5	Tim Raines	1571
6	**Rafael Palmeiro**	**1548**
7	Wade Boggs	1513
8	**Craig Biggio**	**1503**
9	**Roberto Alomar**	**1490**
10	**Jeff Bagwell**	**1402**

1973-1987

1	Pete Rose	2165
2	Dave Winfield	1669
3	Joe Morgan	1650
4	Robin Yount	1632
5	Eddie Murray	1627
6	George Brett	1583
7	Reggie Jackson	1551
8	Mike Schmidt	1506
9	Dwight Evans	1470
10	Rod Carew	1424

1961-1972

1	Hank Aaron	2174
2	Willie Mays	2062
3	Frank Robinson	1829
4	Carl Yastrzemski	1816
5	Al Kaline	1622
6	Lou Brock	1610
7	Roberto Clemente	1416
8	Billy Williams	1410
9	Vada Pinson	1366
10	Luis Aparicio	1335

1943-1960

1	Stan Musial	1949
2	Ted Williams	1798
3	Mickey Mantle	1677
4	Eddie Mathews	1509
5	Pee Wee Reese	1338
6	Richie Ashburn	1322
7	Nellie Fox	1279
8	Duke Snider	1259
9	Enos Slaughter	1247
10	Red Schoendienst	1223

1921-1942

1	Babe Ruth	2174
2	Lou Gehrig	1888
3	Mel Ott	1859
4	Charlie Gehringer	1774
5	Jimmie Foxx	1751
6	Paul Waner	1627
7	Rogers Hornsby	1579
8	Frankie Frisch	1532
9	Sam Rice	1514
10	Al Simmons	1507

1901-1920

1	Ty Cobb	2246
2	Tris Speaker	1882
3	Eddie Collins	1821
4	Honus Wagner	1739
5	Willie Keeler	1719
6	Fred Clarke	1622
7	Bill Dahlen	1590
8	Max Carey	1545
9	Nap Lajoie	1504
10	Harry Hooper	1429

1893-1900

1	Jesse Burkett	1720
2	Billy Hamilton	1697
3	Jimmy Ryan	1643
4	George Van Haltren	1642
5	Jake Beckley	1602
6	Ed Delahanty	1600
7	Hugh Duffy	1554
8	George Davis	1545
9	Tom Brown	1523
10	Herman Long	1456

1876-1892

1	Cap Anson	1722
2	Bid McPhee	1684
3	Roger Connor	1620
4	Dan Brouthers	1523
5	Harry Stovey	1492
6	Arlie Latham	1481
7	Jim O'Rourke	1446
8	John Ward	1410
9	King Kelly	1357
10	George Gore	1327

Runs/150 Games by era

1988-2003

1	**Alex Rodriguez**	**118.7**
2	**Derek Jeter**	**114.6**
3	**Kenny Lofton**	**113.5**
4	**Barry Bonds**	**113.3**
5	**Rickey Henderson**	**111.7**
6	**Jeff Bagwell**	**107.6**
7	Chuck Knoblauch	104.0
8	**Manny Ramirez**	**104.0**
9	**Bernie Williams**	**103.5**
10	**Chipper Jones**	**103.1**

1973-1987

1	Bobby Bonds	102.1
2	Ron LeFlore	99.8
3	Mike Schmidt	94.0
4	Joe Morgan	93.4
5	Pete Rose	91.2
6	Kirk Gibson	90.4
7	Jim Rice	89.7
8	George Brett	87.7
9	Lou Whitaker	87.0
10	Rod Carew	86.5

1961-1972

1	Willie Mays	103.4
2	Hank Aaron	98.9
3	Frank Robinson	97.7
4	Dick Allen	94.3
5	Lou Brock	92.3
6	Roberto Clemente	87.3
7	Jimmy Wynn	86.3
8	Al Kaline	85.9
9	Billy Williams	85.0
10	Roger Maris	84.7

1943-1960

1	Ted Williams	117.7
2	Dom DiMaggio	112.2
3	Mickey Mantle	104.8
4	Jackie Robinson	102.8
5	Johnny Pesky	102.4
6	Ralph Kiner	98.9
7	Eddie Stanky	96.6
8	Stan Musial	96.6
9	Eddie Mathews	94.7
10	Larry Doby	93.9

1921-1942

1	Lou Gehrig	130.9
2	Babe Ruth	130.3
3	Earle Combs	122.3
4	Red Rolfe	120.3
5	Joe DiMaggio	120.1
6	Charlie Gehringer	114.6
7	Jimmie Foxx	113.4
8	Hank Greenberg	113.1
9	Earl Averill	110.0
10	Max Bishop	108.3

1901-1920

1	Willie Keeler	121.5
2	Ty Cobb	111.0
3	Fred Clarke	108.3
4	Roy Thomas	103.2
5	Tris Speaker	101.2
6	Fielder Jones	99.0
7	Chick Stahl	98.7
8	Donie Bush	98.7
9	Joe Jackson	98.3
10	Ginger Beaumont	97.9

1893-1900

1	Billy Hamilton	159.7
2	John McGraw	139.8
3	Mike Griffin	139.4
4	Hugh Duffy	134.1
5	Mike Tiernan	133.6
6	Ed Delahanty	130.6
7	Tom Brown	127.8
8	Tommy McCarthy	125.6
9	Cupid Childs	125.0
10	Jesse Burkett	124.8

1876-1892

1	George Gore	151.9
2	Harry Stovey	150.6
3	King Kelly	139.9
4	Dan Brouthers	136.6
5	Arlie Latham	136.4
6	Sam Thompson	134.3
7	Buck Ewing	128.8
8	Hardy Richardson	126.2
9	Tip O'Neill	125.3
10	Denny Lyons	124.6

Hits

1	Pete Rose	4256
2	Ty Cobb	4189
3	Hank Aaron	3771
4	Stan Musial	3630
5	Tris Speaker	3514
6	Honus Wagner	3420
7	Carl Yastrzemski	3419
8	Paul Molitor	3319
9	Eddie Collins	3315
10	Willie Mays	3283
11	Eddie Murray	3255
12	Nap Lajoie	3242
13	Cal Ripken	3184
14	George Brett	3154
15	Paul Waner	3152
16	Robin Yount	3142
17	Tony Gwynn	3141
18	Dave Winfield	3110
19	**Rickey Henderson**	**3055**
20	Rod Carew	3053
21	Lou Brock	3023
22	Cap Anson	3012
23	Wade Boggs	3010
24	Al Kaline	3007
25	Roberto Clemente	3000
26	Sam Rice	2987
27	Sam Crawford	2961
28	Frank Robinson	2943
29	Jake Beckley	2934
30	Willie Keeler	2932
31	Rogers Hornsby	2930
32	Al Simmons	2927
33	Zack Wheat	2884
34	Frankie Frisch	2880
35	Mel Ott	2876
36	Babe Ruth	2873
37	Harold Baines	2866
38	Jesse Burkett	2850
39	Brooks Robinson	2848
40	Charlie Gehringer	2839
41	George Sisler	2812
42	**Rafael Palmeiro**	**2780**
43	Andre Dawson	2774
44	Vada Pinson	2757
45	Luke Appling	2749
46	Al Oliver	2743
47	Goose Goslin	2735
48	Tony Perez	2732
49	Lou Gehrig	2721
50	Rusty Staub	2716
51	Bill Buckner	2715
52	Dave Parker	2712
53	Billy Williams	2711
54	Doc Cramer	2705
55	**Roberto Alomar**	**2679**
56	Fred Clarke	2678
57	Luis Aparicio	2677
58	Max Carey	2665
	George Davis	2665
60	Nellie Fox	2663
61	Harry Heilmann	2660
62	Ted Williams	2654
63	Lave Cross	2651
64	Jimmie Foxx	2646
65	Rabbit Maranville	2605
	Tim Raines	2605
67	Steve Garvey	2599
68	Ed Delahanty	2597
69	**Barry Bonds**	**2595**
70	Reggie Jackson	2584
71	Ernie Banks	2583
72	Richie Ashburn	2574
73	Willie Davis	2561
74	George Van Haltren	2544
75	Heinie Manush	2524
76	Joe Morgan	2517
77	Buddy Bell	2514
78	Jimmy Ryan	2513
79	Mickey Vernon	2495
80	**Fred McGriff**	**2477**
81	Ted Simmons	2472
82	Joe Medwick	2471
83	Roger Connor	2467
84	Harry Hooper	2466
85	**Craig Biggio**	**2461**
	Bill Dahlen	2461
87	Ozzie Smith	2460
88	Lloyd Waner	2459
89	Jim Rice	2452
90	Red Schoendienst	2449
91	Dwight Evans	2446
92	**Mark Grace**	**2445**
93	Pie Traynor	2416
94	Mickey Mantle	2415
95	Stuffy McInnis	2405
96	Ryne Sandberg	2386
97	Enos Slaughter	2383
98	Chili Davis	2380
99	Edd Roush	2376
100	Brett Butler	2375

Doubles

1	Tris Speaker	792
2	Pete Rose	746
3	Stan Musial	725
4	Ty Cobb	724
5	George Brett	665
6	Nap Lajoie	657
7	Carl Yastrzemski	646
8	Honus Wagner	643
9	Hank Aaron	624
10	Paul Molitor	605
	Paul Waner	605
12	Cal Ripken	603
13	Robin Yount	583
14	Wade Boggs	578
15	Charlie Gehringer	574
16	Eddie Murray	560
17	Tony Gwynn	543
	Rafael Palmeiro	**543**
19	Harry Heilmann	542
20	Rogers Hornsby	541
21	Joe Medwick	540
	Dave Winfield	540
23	Al Simmons	539
24	**Barry Bonds**	**536**
25	Lou Gehrig	534
26	Cap Anson	529
	Al Oliver	529
28	Frank Robinson	528
29	Dave Parker	526
30	Ted Williams	525
31	Willie Mays	523
32	Ed Delahanty	522
33	**Craig Biggio**	**517**
34	Joe Cronin	515
35	**Mark Grace**	**511**
36	**Rickey Henderson**	**510**
37	Babe Ruth	506
38	Tony Perez	505
39	Andre Dawson	503
40	Goose Goslin	500
41	Rusty Staub	499
42	**Roberto Alomar**	**498**
	Bill Buckner	498
	Al Kaline	498
	Sam Rice	498
46	Heinie Manush	491
	Edgar Martinez	**491**
48	Mickey Vernon	490
49	Harold Baines	488
	Mel Ott	488
51	Lou Brock	486
	Billy Herman	486
53	Vada Pinson	485
54	Hal McRae	484
55	Dwight Evans	483
	Ted Simmons	483
57	Brooks Robinson	482
58	Zack Wheat	476
59	Jake Beckley	473
	John Olerud	**473**
61	Frankie Frisch	466
62	Jim Bottomley	465
63	Reggie Jackson	463
64	Dan Brouthers	460
65	Sam Crawford	458
	Jimmie Foxx	458
67	**Jeff Bagwell**	**455**
68	George Davis	453
	Jimmy Dykes	453
70	Paul O'Neill	451
	Jimmy Ryan	451
72	Joe Morgan	449
73	Rod Carew	445
74	George Burns	444
	Andres Galarraga	**444**
76	Gary Gaetti	443
77	Dick Bartell	442
	Don Mattingly	442
79	Roger Connor	441
80	Luke Appling	440
	Will Clark	440
	Roberto Clemente	440
	Steve Garvey	440
84	Eddie Collins	438
	Fred McGriff	**438**
86	Cesar Cedeno	436
	Joe Sewell	436
88	Wally Moses	435
	Larry Walker	**435**
90	Billy Williams	434
91	Joe Judge	433
92	Joe Carter	432
	Tim Wallach	432
94	**Luis Gonzalez**	**430**
	Tim Raines	430
96	**Frank Thomas**	**428**
97	Red Schoendienst	427
98	Keith Hernandez	426
	Barry Larkin	**426**
100	3 players tied	425

Doubles by era

1988-2003

1	Paul Molitor	605
2	Cal Ripken	603
3	Wade Boggs	578
4	Tony Gwynn	543
	Rafael Palmeiro	**543**
6	**Barry Bonds**	**536**
7	**Craig Biggio**	**517**
8	**Mark Grace**	**511**
9	**Rickey Henderson**	**510**
10	**Roberto Alomar**	**498**

1973-1987

1	Pete Rose	746
2	George Brett	665
3	Robin Yount	583
4	Eddie Murray	560
5	Dave Winfield	540
6	Al Oliver	529
7	Dave Parker	526
8	Tony Perez	505
9	Andre Dawson	503
10	Rusty Staub	499

1961-1972

1	Carl Yastrzemski	646
2	Hank Aaron	624
3	Frank Robinson	528
4	Willie Mays	523
5	Al Kaline	498
6	Lou Brock	486
7	Vada Pinson	485
8	Brooks Robinson	482
9	Roberto Clemente	440
10	Billy Williams	434

1943-1960

1	Stan Musial	725
2	Ted Williams	525
3	Mickey Vernon	490
4	Red Schoendienst	427
5	Enos Slaughter	413
6	Lou Boudreau	385
	George Kell	385
8	Bob Elliott	382
9	Bobby Doerr	381
10	Dixie Walker	376

1921-1942

1	Paul Waner	605
2	Charlie Gehringer	574
3	Harry Heilmann	542
4	Rogers Hornsby	541
5	Joe Medwick	540
6	Al Simmons	539
7	Lou Gehrig	534
8	Joe Cronin	515
9	Babe Ruth	506
10	Goose Goslin	500

1901-1920

1	Tris Speaker	792
2	Ty Cobb	724
3	Nap Lajoie	657
4	Honus Wagner	643
5	Zack Wheat	476
6	Sam Crawford	458
7	Eddie Collins	438
8	Sherry Magee	425
9	Max Carey	419
10	Bill Dahlen	413

1893-1900

1	Ed Delahanty	522
2	Jake Beckley	473
3	George Davis	453
4	Jimmy Ryan	451
5	Lave Cross	412
6	Joe Kelley	358
7	Herman Long	342
8	Hugh Duffy	325
9	Jesse Burkett	320
10	Jack Doyle	316

1876-1892

1	Cap Anson	529
2	Dan Brouthers	460
3	Roger Connor	441
4	Jim O'Rourke	414
5	Paul Hines	368
6	King Kelly	359
7	Harry Stovey	347
8	Sam Thompson	343
9	Jack Glasscock	313
10	Bid McPhee	303
	Hardy Richardson	303

Triples

1	Sam Crawford	309
2	Ty Cobb	295
3	Honus Wagner	252
4	Jake Beckley	244
5	Roger Connor	233
6	Tris Speaker	222
7	Fred Clarke	220
8	Dan Brouthers	205
9	Joe Kelley	194
10	Paul Waner	191
11	Bid McPhee	189
12	Eddie Collins	187
13	Ed Delahanty	186
14	Sam Rice	184
15	Jesse Burkett	182
	Ed Konetchy	182
	Edd Roush	182
18	Buck Ewing	178
19	Rabbit Maranville	177
	Stan Musial	177
21	Harry Stovey	174
22	Goose Goslin	173
23	Tommy Leach	172
	Zack Wheat	172
25	Rogers Hornsby	169
26	Joe Jackson	168
27	Roberto Clemente	166
	Sherry Magee	166
29	Jake Daubert	165
30	Elmer Flick	164
	George Sisler	164
	Pie Traynor	164
33	Bill Dahlen	163
	George Davis	163
	Lou Gehrig	163
	Nap Lajoie	163
37	Mike Tiernan	162
38	Sam Thompson	161
	George Van Haltren	161
40	Harry Hooper	160
	Heinie Manush	160
42	Max Carey	159
	Joe Judge	159
44	Ed McKean	158
45	Kiki Cuyler	157
	Jimmy Ryan	157
47	Tommy Corcoran	155
48	Earle Combs	154
49	Jim Bottomley	151
	Harry Heilmann	151
51	Kip Selbach	149
	Al Simmons	149
53	Wally Pipp	148
	Enos Slaughter	148
55	Bobby Veach	147
	Willie Wilson	147
57	Charlie Gehringer	146
58	Harry Davis	145
	Willie Keeler	145
60	Bobby Wallace	143
61	Lou Brock	141
62	Willie Mays	140
63	John Reilly	139
64	Tom Brown	138
	Willie Davis	138
	Frankie Frisch	138
	Jimmy Williams	138
68	George Brett	137
69	Lave Cross	136
	Babe Ruth	136
	Jimmy Sheckard	136
	Elmer Smith	136
73	Pete Rose	135
74	Shano Collins	133
75	Jim O'Rourke	132
	George Wood	132
77	Brett Butler	131
	Joe DiMaggio	131
	Buck Freeman	131
80	Buddy Myer	130
81	Tommy Burns	129
	Larry Gardner	129
83	Earl Averill	128
	Arky Vaughan	128
85	Vada Pinson	127
86	Hardy Richardson	126
	Robin Yount	126
88	Jimmie Foxx	125
89	John Anderson	124
	Cap Anson	124
	Hal Chase	124
	Frank Schulte	124
93	Larry Doyle	123
	Duke Farrell	123
95	Dummy Hoy	121
96	Fred Pfeffer	120
	Mickey Vernon	120
98	Hugh Duffy	119
99	3 players tied	118

Triples by era

1988-2003
1 Brett Butler ... 131
2 Lance Johnson ... 117
3 Paul Molitor ... 114
4 Tim Raines ... 113
5 Steve Finley ... 108
6 Juan Samuel ... 102
7 Willie McGee ... 94
8 Tony Fernandez ... 92
9 Andy Van Slyke ... 91
10 Vince Coleman ... 89

1973-1987
1 Willie Wilson ... 147
2 George Brett ... 137
3 Pete Rose ... 135
4 Robin Yount ... 126
5 Rod Carew ... 112
6 Garry Templeton ... 106
7 Larry Bowa ... 99
8 Andre Dawson ... 98
9 Joe Morgan ... 96
10 Jose Cruz ... 94

1961-1972
1 Roberto Clemente ... 166
2 Lou Brock ... 141
3 Willie Mays ... 140
4 Willie Davis ... 138
5 Vada Pinson ... 127
6 Hank Aaron ... 98
7 Luis Aparicio ... 92
8 Ernie Banks ... 90
9 Johnny Callison ... 89
10 Billy Williams ... 88

1943-1960
1 Stan Musial ... 177
2 Enos Slaughter ... 148
3 Mickey Vernon ... 120
4 Nellie Fox ... 112
5 Richie Ashburn ... 109
6 Bill Bruton ... 102
Jeff Heath ... 102
8 Phil Cavarretta ... 99
9 Dixie Walker ... 96
10 Bob Elliott ... 94

1921-1942
1 Paul Waner ... 191
2 Sam Rice ... 184
3 Edd Roush ... 182
4 Rabbit Maranville ... 177
5 Goose Goslin ... 173
6 Rogers Hornsby ... 169
7 George Sisler ... 164
Pie Traynor ... 164
9 Lou Gehrig ... 163
10 Heinie Manush ... 160

1901-1920
1 Sam Crawford ... 309
2 Ty Cobb ... 295
3 Honus Wagner ... 252
4 Tris Speaker ... 222
5 Fred Clarke ... 220
6 Eddie Collins ... 187
7 Ed Konetchy ... 182
8 Tommy Leach ... 172
Zack Wheat ... 172
10 Joe Jackson ... 168

1893-1900
1 Jake Beckley ... 244
2 Joe Kelley ... 194
3 Ed Delahanty ... 186
4 Jesse Burkett ... 182
5 George Davis ... 163
6 Mike Tiernan ... 162
7 George Van Haltren ... 161
8 Ed McKean ... 158
9 Jimmy Ryan ... 157
10 Tommy Corcoran ... 155

1876-1892
1 Roger Connor ... 233
2 Dan Brouthers ... 205
3 Bid McPhee ... 189
4 Buck Ewing ... 178
5 Harry Stovey ... 174
6 Sam Thompson ... 161
7 John Reilly ... 139
8 Jim O'Rourke ... 132
George Wood ... 132
10 Tommy Burns ... 129

Home Runs
1 Hank Aaron ... 755
2 Babe Ruth ... 714
3 Willie Mays ... 660
4 Barry Bonds ... 658
5 Frank Robinson ... 586
6 Mark McGwire ... 583
7 Harmon Killebrew ... 573
8 Reggie Jackson ... 563
9 Mike Schmidt ... 548
10 Sammy Sosa ... 539
11 Mickey Mantle ... 536
12 Jimmie Foxx ... 534
13 Rafael Palmeiro ... 528
14 Willie McCovey ... 521
Ted Williams ... 521
16 Ernie Banks ... 512
Eddie Mathews ... 512
18 Mel Ott ... 511
19 Eddie Murray ... 504
20 Lou Gehrig ... 493
21 Fred McGriff ... 491
22 Ken Griffey ... 481
23 Stan Musial ... 475
Willie Stargell ... 475
25 Dave Winfield ... 465
26 Jose Canseco ... 462
27 Carl Yastrzemski ... 452
28 Dave Kingman ... 442
29 Andre Dawson ... 438
30 Cal Ripken ... 431
31 Juan Gonzalez ... 429
32 Billy Williams ... 426
33 Jeff Bagwell ... 419
34 Frank Thomas ... 418
35 Darrell Evans ... 414
36 Duke Snider ... 407
37 Al Kaline ... 399
38 Andres Galarraga ... 398
Dale Murphy ... 398
40 Joe Carter ... 396
41 Graig Nettles ... 390
42 Johnny Bench ... 389
43 Dwight Evans ... 385
44 Harold Baines ... 384
45 Frank Howard ... 382
Jim Rice ... 382
47 Albert Belle ... 381
Jim Thome ... 381
49 Orlando Cepeda ... 379
Tony Perez ... 379
Gary Sheffield ... 379
52 Matt Williams ... 378
53 Norm Cash ... 377
54 Carlton Fisk ... 376
55 Rocky Colavito ... 374
56 Gil Hodges ... 370
57 Ralph Kiner ... 369
58 Joe DiMaggio ... 361
59 Gary Gaetti ... 360
60 Johnny Mize ... 359
61 Yogi Berra ... 358
Mike Piazza ... 358
63 Greg Vaughn ... 355
64 Lee May ... 354
65 Dick Allen ... 351
Ellis Burks ... 351
Larry Walker ... 351
68 Chili Davis ... 350
69 George Foster ... 348
70 Manny Ramirez ... 347
71 Alex Rodriguez ... 345
72 Ron Santo ... 342
73 Jack Clark ... 340
74 Dave Parker ... 339
Boog Powell ... 339
76 Don Baylor ... 338
77 Joe Adcock ... 336
78 Darryl Strawberry ... 335
79 Bobby Bonds ... 332
80 Hank Greenberg ... 331
81 Mo Vaughn ... 328
82 Willie Horton ... 325
83 Gary Carter ... 324
Lance Parrish ... 324
85 Ron Gant ... 321
86 Cecil Fielder ... 319
87 Roy Sievers ... 318
88 George Brett ... 317
89 Ron Cey ... 316
90 Reggie Smith ... 314
91 Jay Buhner ... 310
92 Greg Luzinski ... 307
Al Simmons ... 307
94 Fred Lynn ... 306
95 David Justice ... 305
96 Carlos Delgado ... 304
97 Rogers Hornsby ... 301
98 Chuck Klein ... 300
99 Tino Martinez ... 299
100 2 players tied ... 297

Home Runs by era

1988-2003
1 Barry Bonds ... 658
2 Mark McGwire ... 583
3 Sammy Sosa ... 539
4 Rafael Palmeiro ... 528
5 Fred McGriff ... 491
6 Ken Griffey ... 481
7 Jose Canseco ... 462
8 Cal Ripken ... 431
9 Juan Gonzalez ... 429
10 Jeff Bagwell ... 419

1973-1987
1 Reggie Jackson ... 563
2 Mike Schmidt ... 548
3 Eddie Murray ... 504
4 Dave Winfield ... 465
5 Dave Kingman ... 442
6 Andre Dawson ... 438
7 Darrell Evans ... 414
8 Dale Murphy ... 398
9 Graig Nettles ... 390
10 Johnny Bench ... 389

1961-1972
1 Hank Aaron ... 755
2 Willie Mays ... 660
3 Frank Robinson ... 586
4 Harmon Killebrew ... 573
5 Willie McCovey ... 521
6 Ernie Banks ... 512
7 Willie Stargell ... 475
8 Carl Yastrzemski ... 452
9 Billy Williams ... 426
10 Al Kaline ... 399

1943-1960
1 Mickey Mantle ... 536
2 Ted Williams ... 521
3 Eddie Mathews ... 512
4 Stan Musial ... 475
5 Duke Snider ... 407
6 Gil Hodges ... 370
7 Ralph Kiner ... 369
8 Yogi Berra ... 358
9 Joe Adcock ... 336
10 Roy Sievers ... 318

1921-1942
1 Babe Ruth ... 714
2 Jimmie Foxx ... 534
3 Mel Ott ... 511
4 Lou Gehrig ... 493
5 Joe DiMaggio ... 361
6 Johnny Mize ... 359
7 Hank Greenberg ... 331
8 Al Simmons ... 307
9 Rogers Hornsby ... 301
10 Chuck Klein ... 300

1901-1920
1 Zack Wheat ... 132
2 Gavy Cravath ... 119
3 Tilly Walker ... 118
4 Ty Cobb ... 117
Tris Speaker ... 117
6 Honus Wagner ... 101
7 Sam Crawford ... 97
8 Frank Baker ... 96
9 Frank Schulte ... 92
10 Bill Dahlen ... 84
Fred Luderus ... 84

1893-1900
1 Jimmy Ryan ... 118
2 Hugh Duffy ... 106
Mike Tiernan ... 106
4 Ed Delahanty ... 101
5 Herman Long ... 91
6 Jake Beckley ... 87
7 Jack Clements ... 77
8 Jesse Burkett ... 75
9 George Davis ... 73
10 Bobby Lowe ... 71

1876-1892
1 Roger Connor ... 138
2 Sam Thompson ... 126
3 Harry Stovey ... 122
4 Dan Brouthers ... 106
5 Cap Anson ... 97
6 Fred Pfeffer ... 94
7 Jerry Denny ... 74
8 Buck Ewing ... 71
9 Hardy Richardson ... 70
10 King Kelly ... 69
John Reilly ... 69

Home Run Pct.
1 Mark McGwire ... 9.42
2 Babe Ruth ... 8.50
3 Barry Bonds ... 7.54
4 Jim Thome ... 7.30
5 Sammy Sosa ... 7.15
6 Ralph Kiner ... 7.09
7 Harmon Killebrew ... 7.03
8 Manny Ramirez ... 6.93
9 Alex Rodriguez ... 6.92
10 Ken Griffey ... 6.79
11 Ted Williams ... 6.76
12 Mike Piazza ... 6.69
13 Carlos Delgado ... 6.68
14 Juan Gonzalez ... 6.67
15 Dave Kingman ... 6.62
16 Mickey Mantle ... 6.62
17 Jimmie Foxx ... 6.57
18 Mike Schmidt ... 6.56
19 Jose Canseco ... 6.55
20 Albert Belle ... 6.51
21 Hank Greenberg ... 6.37
22 Willie McCovey ... 6.36
23 Frank Thomas ... 6.32
24 Vladimir Guerrero ... 6.22
25 Cecil Fielder ... 6.19
26 Jay Buhner ... 6.18
27 Darryl Strawberry ... 6.18
28 Lou Gehrig ... 6.16
29 Hank Aaron ... 6.11
30 Willie Mays ... 6.07
31 Hank Sauer ... 6.01
32 Eddie Mathews ... 6.00
33 Willie Stargell ... 5.99
34 Jason Giambi ... 5.99
35 Brian Giles ... 5.94
36 Mo Vaughn ... 5.93
37 Rob Deer ... 5.93
38 Frank Howard ... 5.89
39 Jeff Bagwell ... 5.88
40 Frank Robinson ... 5.86
41 Greg Vaughn ... 5.82
42 Bob Horner ... 5.77
43 Roy Campanella ... 5.76
44 Matt Stairs ... 5.75
45 Rocky Colavito ... 5.75
46 Gus Zernial ... 5.74
47 Gorman Thomas ... 5.73
48 Reggie Jackson ... 5.71
49 Dick Stuart ... 5.70
50 Duke Snider ... 5.68
51 Jim Edmonds ... 5.66
52 Kevin Mitchell ... 5.66
53 Fred McGriff ... 5.65
54 Gary Sheffield ... 5.63
55 Norm Cash ... 5.62
56 Dean Palmer ... 5.61
57 Jeromy Burnitz ... 5.60
58 Johnny Mize ... 5.57
59 Ryan Klesko ... 5.57
60 Dick Allen ... 5.54
61 Larry Walker ... 5.54
62 Rafael Palmeiro ... 5.53
63 Chipper Jones ... 5.44
64 Ernie Banks ... 5.43
65 David Justice ... 5.42
66 Mel Ott ... 5.40
67 Matt Williams ... 5.40
68 Roger Maris ... 5.39
69 Andruw Jones ... 5.37
70 Todd Hundley ... 5.36
71 Javy Lopez ... 5.35
72 Eric Davis ... 5.30
73 Joe DiMaggio ... 5.29
74 Gil Hodges ... 5.26
75 Wally Post ... 5.24
76 Danny Tartabull ... 5.23
77 Mickey Tettleton ... 5.21
78 Tim Salmon ... 5.20
79 Al Rosen ... 5.15
80 Shawn Green ... 5.13
81 Hack Wilson ... 5.13
82 Glenn Davis ... 5.11
83 Bob Allison ... 5.09
84 Joe Adcock ... 5.09
85 Johnny Bench ... 5.08
86 Boog Powell ... 5.07
87 Jesse Barfield ... 5.06
88 Nate Colbert ... 5.06
89 Glenallen Hill ... 5.01
90 Dale Murphy ... 5.00
91 Charlie Keller ... 4.99
92 Roy Sievers ... 4.98
93 Ron Gant ... 4.98
94 Cliff Johnson ... 4.97
95 Don Mincher ... 4.97
96 Jack Clark ... 4.97
97 George Foster ... 4.96
98 Tony Batista ... 4.94
99 Scott Rolen ... 4.94
100 Andres Galarraga ... 4.92

Home Run Pct. by era

1988-2003
1 Mark McGwire ... 9.42
2 Barry Bonds ... 7.54
3 Jim Thome ... 7.30
4 Sammy Sosa ... 7.15
5 Manny Ramirez ... 6.93
6 Alex Rodriguez ... 6.92
7 Ken Griffey ... 6.79
8 Mike Piazza ... 6.69
9 Carlos Delgado ... 6.68
10 Juan Gonzalez ... 6.67

1973-1987
1 Dave Kingman ... 6.62
2 Mike Schmidt ... 6.56
3 Bob Horner ... 5.77
4 Gorman Thomas ... 5.73
5 Reggie Jackson ... 5.71
6 Johnny Bench ... 5.08
7 Jesse Barfield ... 5.06
8 Dale Murphy ... 5.00
9 Cliff Johnson ... 4.97
10 Jack Clark ... 4.97

1961-1972
1 Harmon Killebrew ... 7.03
2 Willie McCovey ... 6.36
3 Hank Aaron ... 6.11
4 Willie Mays ... 6.07
5 Willie Stargell ... 5.99
6 Frank Howard ... 5.89
7 Frank Robinson ... 5.86
8 Rocky Colavito ... 5.75
9 Dick Stuart ... 5.70
10 Norm Cash ... 5.62

1943-1960
1 Ralph Kiner ... 7.09
2 Ted Williams ... 6.76
3 Mickey Mantle ... 6.62
4 Hank Sauer ... 6.01
5 Eddie Mathews ... 6.00
6 Roy Campanella ... 5.76
7 Gus Zernial ... 5.74
8 Duke Snider ... 5.68
9 Gil Hodges ... 5.26
10 Wally Post ... 5.24

1921-1942
1 Babe Ruth ... 8.50
2 Jimmie Foxx ... 6.57
3 Hank Greenberg ... 6.37
4 Lou Gehrig ... 6.16
5 Johnny Mize ... 5.57
6 Mel Ott ... 5.40
7 Joe DiMaggio ... 5.29
8 Hack Wilson ... 5.13
9 Rudy York ... 4.70
10 Wally Berger ... 4.69

1901-1920
1 Gavy Cravath ... 3.01
2 Tilly Walker ... 2.33
3 Elmer Smith ... 2.19
4 Buck Freeman ... 1.95
5 Fred Luderus ... 1.73
6 Frank Baker ... 1.60
7 Charlie Hickman ... 1.48
8 Zack Wheat ... 1.45
9 Frank Schulte ... 1.41
10 Casey Stengel ... 1.40

1893-1900
1 Jack Clements ... 1.79
2 Mike Tiernan ... 1.79
3 Hugh Duffy ... 1.50
4 Jimmy Ryan ... 1.44
5 Ed Delahanty ... 1.34
6 Herman Long ... 1.19
7 Billy Nash ... 1.02
8 Bobby Lowe ... 1.00
9 Ed McKean ... 0.97
10 Joe Kelley ... 0.93

1876-1892
1 Sam Thompson ... 2.10
2 Harry Stovey ... 1.99
3 Roger Connor ... 1.77
4 Dan Brouthers ... 1.58
5 Jerry Denny ... 1.50
6 John Reilly ... 1.47
7 Denny Lyons ... 1.44
8 Charlie Bennett ... 1.44
9 Fred Pfeffer ... 1.43
10 Ed Williamson ... 1.41

Extra Base Hits

1	Hank Aaron	1477
2	Stan Musial	1377
3	Babe Ruth	1356
4	Willie Mays	1323
5	**Barry Bonds**	**1268**
6	Lou Gehrig	1190
7	Frank Robinson	1186
8	Carl Yastrzemski	1157
9	Ty Cobb	1136
10	Tris Speaker	1131
11	George Brett	1119
12	Jimmie Foxx	1117
	Ted Williams	1117
14	**Rafael Palmeiro**	**1109**
15	Eddie Murray	1099
16	Dave Winfield	1093
17	Cal Ripken	1078
18	Reggie Jackson	1075
19	Mel Ott	1071
20	Pete Rose	1041
21	Andre Dawson	1039
22	Mike Schmidt	1015
23	Rogers Hornsby	1011
24	Ernie Banks	1009
25	Honus Wagner	996
26	Al Simmons	995
27	Al Kaline	972
28	Tony Perez	963
29	Robin Yount	960
30	**Fred McGriff**	**953**
	Paul Molitor	953
	Willie Stargell	953
33	Mickey Mantle	952
34	Billy Williams	948
35	Dwight Evans	941
36	Dave Parker	940
37	Eddie Mathews	938
38	Harold Baines	921
	Goose Goslin	921
40	Willie McCovey	920
41	Paul Waner	909
42	**Jeff Bagwell**	**904**
	Charlie Gehringer	904
44	Nap Lajoie	902
45	**Sammy Sosa**	**901**
46	**Ken Griffey**	**899**
47	Harmon Killebrew	887
48	Joe Carter	881
	Joe DiMaggio	881
50	Harry Heilmann	876
51	**Andres Galarraga**	**874**
52	**Rickey Henderson**	**873**
53	Vada Pinson	868
54	Sam Crawford	864
55	Joe Medwick	858
56	**Frank Thomas**	**857**
57	Duke Snider	850
58	Roberto Clemente	846
59	Carlton Fisk	844
60	**Larry Walker**	**843**
61	Gary Gaetti	842
62	Mark McGwire	841
63	Rusty Staub	838
64	**Juan Gonzalez**	**837**
65	Jim Bottomley	835
66	Jim Rice	834
67	Al Oliver	825
68	Orlando Cepeda	823
69	Brooks Robinson	818
70	**Ellis Burks**	**816**
	Jose Canseco	816
72	Joe Morgan	813
73	Roger Connor	812
74	Ed Delahanty	809
	Johnny Mize	809
76	Jake Beckley	804
	Chili Davis	804
78	Joe Cronin	803
	Edgar Martinez	**803**
80	Johnny Bench	794
81	Albert Belle	791
82	Dale Murphy	787
83	**Roberto Alomar**	**782**
	Mickey Vernon	782
85	Hank Greenberg	781
86	Zack Wheat	780
87	Darrell Evans	779
	Bob Johnson	779
89	**Craig Biggio**	**778**
	Ted Simmons	778
91	Lou Brock	776
92	Ron Santo	774
93	Chuck Klein	772
94	Dan Brouthers	771
	Will Clark	771
96	Earl Averill	767
97	**Luis Gonzalez**	**763**
	Tony Gwynn	763
99	Heinie Manush	761
	Ryne Sandberg	761

Total Bases

1	Hank Aaron	6856
2	Stan Musial	6134
3	Willie Mays	6066
4	Ty Cobb	5854
5	Babe Ruth	5793
6	Pete Rose	5752
7	Carl Yastrzemski	5539
8	Eddie Murray	5397
9	Frank Robinson	5373
10	**Barry Bonds**	**5253**
11	Dave Winfield	5221
12	Cal Ripken	5168
13	Tris Speaker	5101
14	Lou Gehrig	5060
15	George Brett	5044
16	Mel Ott	5041
17	**Rafael Palmeiro**	**4983**
18	Jimmie Foxx	4956
19	Ted Williams	4884
20	Honus Wagner	4870
21	Paul Molitor	4854
22	Al Kaline	4852
23	Reggie Jackson	4834
24	Andre Dawson	4787
25	Robin Yount	4730
26	Rogers Hornsby	4712
27	Ernie Banks	4706
28	Al Simmons	4685
29	Harold Baines	4604
30	Billy Williams	4599
31	**Rickey Henderson**	**4588**
32	Tony Perez	4532
33	Mickey Mantle	4511
34	Roberto Clemente	4492
35	Paul Waner	4478
36	Nap Lajoie	4471
37	**Fred McGriff**	**4436**
38	Dave Parker	4405
39	Mike Schmidt	4404
40	Eddie Mathews	4349
41	Sam Crawford	4328
42	Goose Goslin	4325
43	Brooks Robinson	4270
44	Eddie Collins	4268
45	Vada Pinson	4264
46	Tony Gwynn	4259
47	Charlie Gehringer	4257
48	Lou Brock	4238
49	Dwight Evans	4230
50	Willie McCovey	4219
51	Willie Stargell	4190
52	Rusty Staub	4185
53	Jake Beckley	4156
54	Harmon Killebrew	4143
55	Jim Rice	4129
56	**Sammy Sosa**	**4121**
57	Zack Wheat	4100
58	Al Oliver	4083
59	Cap Anson	4080
60	Wade Boggs	4064
61	Harry Heilmann	4053
62	**Andres Galarraga**	**4032**
63	Carlton Fisk	3999
64	Rod Carew	3998
65	**Ken Griffey**	**3977**
66	Joe Morgan	3962
67	Orlando Cepeda	3959
68	Sam Rice	3955
69	**Roberto Alomar**	**3951**
70	Joe DiMaggio	3948
71	Steve Garvey	3941
72	Frankie Frisch	3937
73	Chili Davis	3914
74	Joe Carter	3910
75	**Jeff Bagwell**	**3909**
76	Gary Gaetti	3881
77	George Sisler	3871
78	Darrell Evans	3866
79	Duke Snider	3865
80	Joe Medwick	3852
81	Bill Buckner	3833
82	Ed Delahanty	3794
83	Ted Simmons	3793
84	Roger Connor	3788
85	Ryne Sandberg	3787
86	Graig Nettles	3779
	Ron Santo	3779
88	Willie Davis	3778
89	Tim Raines	3771
90	Jesse Burkett	3759
91	**Frank Thomas**	**3752**
92	Mickey Vernon	3741
93	Jim Bottomley	3737
94	Dale Murphy	3733
95	**Craig Biggio**	**3710**
96	**Ellis Burks**	**3682**
97	Fred Clarke	3680
98	Heinie Manush	3665
99	George Davis	3663
100	Buddy Bell	3654

Runs Batted In

1	Hank Aaron	2297
2	Babe Ruth	2213
3	Lou Gehrig	1995
4	Stan Musial	1951
5	Ty Cobb	1938
6	Jimmie Foxx	1922
7	Eddie Murray	1917
8	Willie Mays	1903
9	Cap Anson	1880
10	Mel Ott	1860
11	Carl Yastrzemski	1844
12	Ted Williams	1839
13	Dave Winfield	1833
14	Al Simmons	1827
15	Frank Robinson	1812
16	**Barry Bonds**	**1742**
17	Honus Wagner	1733
18	Reggie Jackson	1702
19	Cal Ripken	1695
20	**Rafael Palmeiro**	**1687**
21	Tony Perez	1652
22	Ernie Banks	1636
23	Harold Baines	1628
24	Goose Goslin	1609
25	Nap Lajoie	1599
26	George Brett	1595
	Mike Schmidt	1595
28	Andre Dawson	1591
29	Rogers Hornsby	1584
	Harmon Killebrew	1584
31	Al Kaline	1583
32	Jake Beckley	1578
33	Willie McCovey	1555
34	**Fred McGriff**	**1543**
35	Willie Stargell	1540
36	Harry Heilmann	1539
37	Joe DiMaggio	1537
38	Tris Speaker	1529
39	Sam Crawford	1525
40	Mickey Mantle	1509
41	Dave Parker	1493
42	Billy Williams	1475
43	Ed Delahanty	1466
	Rusty Staub	1466
45	Eddie Mathews	1453
46	Jim Rice	1451
47	**Sammy Sosa**	**1450**
48	Joe Carter	1445
49	George Davis	1440
50	Yogi Berra	1430
51	Charlie Gehringer	1427
52	Joe Cronin	1424
53	**Andres Galarraga**	**1423**
54	Jim Bottomley	1422
55	**Jeff Bagwell**	**1421**
56	Mark McGwire	1414
57	Jose Canseco	1407
58	Robin Yount	1406
59	**Frank Thomas**	**1390**
60	Ted Simmons	1389
61	**Juan Gonzalez**	**1387**
62	Dwight Evans	1384
	Ken Griffey	**1384**
64	Joe Medwick	1383
65	Lave Cross	1378
66	Johnny Bench	1376
67	Chili Davis	1372
68	Orlando Cepeda	1365
69	Brooks Robinson	1357
70	Darrell Evans	1354
71	Gary Gaetti	1341
72	Johnny Mize	1337
73	Duke Snider	1333
74	Ron Santo	1331
75	Carlton Fisk	1330
76	Al Oliver	1326
77	Roger Connor	1323
78	Graig Nettles	1314
	Pete Rose	1314
80	Mickey Vernon	1311
81	Paul Waner	1309
82	Steve Garvey	1308
83	Paul Molitor	1307
84	Roberto Clemente	1305
	Sam Thompson	1305
86	Enos Slaughter	1304
87	Hugh Duffy	1302
88	Eddie Collins	1300
89	Dan Brouthers	1296
90	Del Ennis	1284
91	Bob Johnson	1283
92	Don Baylor	1276
	Hank Greenberg	1276
94	Gil Hodges	1274
95	Pie Traynor	1273
96	Paul O'Neill	1269
97	Dale Murphy	1266
98	Zack Wheat	1248
99	Bobby Doerr	1247
100	2 players tied	1244

Runs Batted In by era

1988-2003

1	**Barry Bonds**	**1742**
2	Cal Ripken	1695
3	**Rafael Palmeiro**	**1687**
4	Harold Baines	1628
5	**Fred McGriff**	**1543**
6	**Sammy Sosa**	**1450**
7	Joe Carter	1445
8	**Andres Galarraga**	**1423**
9	**Jeff Bagwell**	**1421**
10	Mark McGwire	1414

1973-1987

1	Eddie Murray	1917
2	Dave Winfield	1833
3	Reggie Jackson	1702
4	Tony Perez	1652
5	George Brett	1595
	Mike Schmidt	1595
7	Andre Dawson	1591
8	Dave Parker	1493
9	Rusty Staub	1466
10	Jim Rice	1451

1961-1972

1	Hank Aaron	2297
2	Willie Mays	1903
3	Carl Yastrzemski	1844
4	Frank Robinson	1812
5	Ernie Banks	1636
6	Harmon Killebrew	1584
7	Al Kaline	1583
8	Willie McCovey	1555
9	Willie Stargell	1540
10	Billy Williams	1475

1943-1960

1	Stan Musial	1951
2	Ted Williams	1839
3	Mickey Mantle	1509
4	Eddie Mathews	1453
5	Yogi Berra	1430
6	Duke Snider	1333
7	Mickey Vernon	1311
8	Enos Slaughter	1304
9	Del Ennis	1284
10	Gil Hodges	1274

1921-1942

1	Babe Ruth	2213
2	Lou Gehrig	1995
3	Jimmie Foxx	1922
4	Mel Ott	1860
5	Al Simmons	1827
6	Goose Goslin	1609
7	Rogers Hornsby	1584
8	Harry Heilmann	1539
9	Joe DiMaggio	1537
10	Charlie Gehringer	1427

1901-1920

1	Ty Cobb	1938
2	Honus Wagner	1733
3	Nap Lajoie	1599
4	Tris Speaker	1529
5	Sam Crawford	1525
6	Eddie Collins	1300
7	Zack Wheat	1248
8	Bill Dahlen	1234
9	Sherry Magee	1176
10	Bobby Veach	1166

1893-1900

1	Jake Beckley	1578
2	Ed Delahanty	1466
3	George Davis	1440
4	Lave Cross	1378
5	Hugh Duffy	1302
6	Joe Kelley	1194
7	Tommy Corcoran	1135
8	Ed McKean	1124
9	Jimmy Ryan	1093
10	Herman Long	1055

1876-1892

1	Cap Anson	1880
2	Roger Connor	1323
3	Sam Thompson	1305
4	Dan Brouthers	1296
5	Bid McPhee	1072
6	Fred Pfeffer	1021
7	Jim O'Rourke	1010
8	King Kelly	950
9	Harry Stovey	908
10	Charlie Comiskey	883
	Buck Ewing	883

RBI/150 Games by era

1988-2003

1	**Juan Gonzalez**	**125.7**
2	**Manny Ramirez**	**123.6**
3	Albert Belle	120.8
4	**Alex Rodriguez**	**116.5**
5	**Mike Piazza**	**113.7**
6	Mark McGwire	113.2
7	**Frank Thomas**	**112.6**
8	Jose Canseco	111.8
9	**Carlos Delgado**	**111.1**
10	**Jeff Bagwell**	**109.0**

1973-1987

1	Jim Rice	104.2
2	Bob Horner	100.7
3	Mike Schmidt	99.5
4	Johnny Bench	95.6
5	Eddie Murray	95.0
6	George Foster	94.0
7	Dave Kingman	93.5
8	Kent Hrbek	93.2
9	Greg Luzinski	92.9
10	Dave Winfield	92.5

1961-1972

1	Hank Aaron	104.5
2	Dick Stuart	100.2
3	Willie Stargell	97.9
4	Harmon Killebrew	97.6
5	Ernie Banks	97.1
6	Frank Robinson	96.8
7	Orlando Cepeda	96.4
8	Dick Allen	96.0
9	Willie Mays	95.4
10	Rocky Colavito	94.4

1943-1960

1	Ted Williams	120.4
2	Roy Campanella	105.7
3	Ralph Kiner	103.4
4	Al Rosen	103.0
5	Vern Stephens	102.4
6	Del Ennis	101.2
7	Yogi Berra	101.2
8	Bobby Doerr	100.3
9	Charlie Keller	97.4
10	Jackie Jensen	96.9

1921-1942

1	Lou Gehrig	138.3
2	Hank Greenberg	137.3
3	Joe DiMaggio	132.8
4	Babe Ruth	132.6
5	Jimmie Foxx	124.4
6	Al Simmons	123.7
7	Hack Wilson	118.3
8	Bob Meusel	113.8
9	Hal Trosky	112.7
10	Rudy York	107.8

1901-1920

1	Nap Lajoie	96.7
2	Bobby Veach	96.0
3	Ty Cobb	95.8
4	Buck Freeman	95.0
5	Frank Baker	94.0
6	Honus Wagner	93.0
7	Sam Mertes	90.9
8	Sam Crawford	90.9
9	John Anderson	89.7
10	Gavy Cravath	88.4

1893-1900

1	Ed Delahanty	119.7
2	Hugh Duffy	112.4
3	Ed McKean	101.9
4	Jake Beckley	99.1
5	Hughie Jennings	98.1
6	Joe Kelley	96.7
7	Billy Nash	94.7
8	Patsy Tebeau	94.5
9	Steve Brodie	93.9
10	Jack Doyle	92.8

1876-1892

1	Sam Thompson	138.8
2	Cap Anson	123.8
3	Dan Brouthers	116.2
4	Tip O'Neill	107.9
5	Henry Larkin	105.9
6	Tommy Burns	105.3
7	Denny Lyons	101.0
8	Buck Ewing	100.7
9	Roger Connor	99.3
10	Dave Foutz	99.0

Walks

1	**Rickey Henderson**	**2190**
2	**Barry Bonds**	**2070**
3	Babe Ruth	2062
4	Ted Williams	2021
5	Joe Morgan	1865
6	Carl Yastrzemski	1845
7	Mickey Mantle	1733
8	Mel Ott	1708
9	Eddie Yost	1614
10	Darrell Evans	1605
11	Stan Musial	1599
12	Pete Rose	1566
13	Harmon Killebrew	1559
14	Lou Gehrig	1508
15	Mike Schmidt	1507
16	Eddie Collins	1499
17	Willie Mays	1464
18	Jimmie Foxx	1452
19	Eddie Mathews	1444
20	Frank Robinson	1420
21	Wade Boggs	1412
22	Hank Aaron	1402
23	Dwight Evans	1391
24	**Frank Thomas**	**1386**
25	Tris Speaker	1381
26	Reggie Jackson	1375
27	Willie McCovey	1345
28	Eddie Murray	1333
29	Tim Raines	1330
30	Tony Phillips	1319
31	Mark McGwire	1317
32	Luke Appling	1302
33	**Fred McGriff**	**1296**
34	**Jeff Bagwell**	**1287**
35	Al Kaline	1277
36	Ken Singleton	1263
37	Jack Clark	1262
38	Rusty Staub	1255
39	Ty Cobb	1249
40	Willie Randolph	1243
41	**Edgar Martinez**	**1225**
42	**Rafael Palmeiro**	**1224**
	Jimmy Wynn	1224
44	Dave Winfield	1216
45	Pee Wee Reese	1210
46	Richie Ashburn	1198
	John Olerud	**1198**
48	Brian Downing	1197
	Lou Whitaker	1197
50	Chili Davis	1194
51	Billy Hamilton	1189
52	Charlie Gehringer	1186
53	Donie Bush	1158
54	Max Bishop	1156
55	Toby Harrah	1153
56	Harry Hooper	1136
57	Jimmy Sheckard	1135
58	Brett Butler	1129
	Cal Ripken	1129
60	**Gary Sheffield**	**1110**
61	Ron Santo	1108
	Jim Thome	**1108**
63	George Brett	1096
64	Paul Molitor	1094
65	Lu Blue	1092
	Stan Hack	1092
67	Paul Waner	1091
68	Graig Nettles	1088
69	Bobby Grich	1087
70	**Mark Grace**	**1075**
	Bob Johnson	1075
72	Ozzie Smith	1072
73	Harlond Clift	1070
	Keith Hernandez	1070
75	Bill Dahlen	1064
76	Harold Baines	1062
77	Joe Cronin	1059
78	**Robin Ventura**	**1053**
79	Ron Fairly	1052
80	Billy Williams	1045
81	Norm Cash	1043
	Eddie Joost	1043
83	Roy Thomas	1042
84	Max Carey	1040
85	Rogers Hornsby	1038
86	Jim Gilliam	1036
87	Sal Bando	1031
88	Jesse Burkett	1029
89	**Craig Biggio**	**1020**
90	**Roberto Alomar**	**1018**
	Rod Carew	1018
	Enos Slaughter	1018
93	Ron Cey	1012
94	Ralph Kiner	1011
95	Dummy Hoy	1006
96	Miller Huggins	1003
97	Roger Connor	1002
98	Boog Powell	1001
99	Eddie Stanky	996
100	Cupid Childs	991

Walk Percentage (BB/PA)

1	Ted Williams	20.64
2	Max Bishop	20.00
3	Babe Ruth	19.42
4	**Barry Bonds**	**18.87**
5	Ferris Fain	18.43
6	Eddie Stanky	18.33
7	Roy Cullenbine	17.82
8	Gene Tenace	17.81
9	Eddie Yost	17.59
10	Mickey Mantle	17.49
11	**Jim Thome**	**17.26**
12	Mark McGwire	17.19
13	Charlie Keller	17.03
14	**Frank Thomas**	**16.97**
15	John McGraw	16.92
16	Mickey Tettleton	16.52
17	Joe Morgan	16.46
18	**Rickey Henderson**	**16.41**
19	**Brian Giles**	**16.23**
20	Earl Torgeson	16.23
21	Bernie Carbo	16.20
22	Ralph Kiner	16.16
23	Harmon Killebrew	15.86
24	Roy Thomas	15.85
25	Billy Hamilton	15.63
26	Lou Gehrig	15.61
27	Harlond Clift	15.52
28	Joe Ferguson	15.51
29	Elmer Valo	15.47
30	Eddie Joost	15.38
31	Jack Clark	15.34
32	Jimmy Wynn	15.28
33	Lu Blue	15.15
34	**Jason Giambi**	**15.09**
35	**Edgar Martinez**	**15.08**
36	Mel Ott	15.07
37	Jimmie Foxx	15.02
38	Mike Schmidt	14.98
39	Darrell Evans	14.95
40	**Bobby Abreu**	**14.94**
41	**Jeff Bagwell**	**14.91**
42	Dolph Camilli	14.91
43	Ken Singleton	14.76
44	Joe Cunningham	14.75
45	Miller Huggins	14.75
46	John Cangelosi	14.72
47	Cupid Childs	14.65
48	Elbie Fletcher	14.61
49	Darren Daulton	14.51
50	Tony Phillips	14.48
51	Merv Rettenmund	14.48
52	Dave Magadan	14.47
53	Topsy Hartsel	14.45
54	Mike Hargrove	14.42
55	Jason Thompson	14.35
56	Wayne Garrett	14.34
57	**John Olerud**	**14.31**
58	Eddie Mathews	14.30
59	Dwayne Murphy	14.25
60	John Kruk	14.10
61	**Tim Salmon**	**14.07**
62	**Chipper Jones**	**14.06**
63	Augie Galan	13.98
64	Hank Greenberg	13.98
65	Gene Woodling	13.93
66	Andy Thornton	13.92
67	Willie McCovey	13.89
68	**Carlos Delgado**	**13.87**
69	Larry Doby	13.82
70	**Gary Sheffield**	**13.81**
71	Mickey Cochrane	13.81
72	Darrell Porter	13.77
73	Johnny Briggs	13.71
74	David Justice	13.68
75	Alvin Davis	13.67
76	John Mayberry	13.67
77	Paul Radford	13.57
78	Billy North	13.57
79	Steve Braun	13.48
80	Norm Siebern	13.44
81	**Dave Hansen**	**13.43**
82	Bob Allison	13.43
83	Al Rosen	13.42
84	**Manny Ramirez**	**13.40**
85	Jay Buhner	13.36
86	Bob Johnson	13.36
87	Lee Mazzilli	13.29
88	Roger Bresnahan	13.29
89	Donie Bush	13.26
90	Bobby Grich	13.22
91	Wally Schang	13.22
92	Mike Jorgensen	13.19
93	Carl Yastrzemski	13.19
94	Norm Cash	13.19
95	Rick Ferrell	13.16
96	Tommy Henrich	13.16
97	Dwight Evans	13.16
98	Toby Harrah	13.15
99	Grady Hatton	13.15
100	Wade Boggs	13.15

Strikeouts

1	Reggie Jackson	2597
2	**Andres Galarraga**	**2000**
3	**Sammy Sosa**	**1977**
4	Jose Canseco	1942
5	Willie Stargell	1936
6	Mike Schmidt	1883
7	Tony Perez	1867
8	**Fred McGriff**	**1863**
9	Dave Kingman	1816
10	Bobby Bonds	1757
11	Dale Murphy	1748
12	Lou Brock	1730
13	Mickey Mantle	1710
14	Harmon Killebrew	1699
15	Chili Davis	1698
16	Dwight Evans	1697
17	**Rickey Henderson**	**1694**
18	Dave Winfield	1686
19	Gary Gaetti	1602
20	Mark McGwire	1596
21	Lee May	1570
22	**Jim Thome**	**1559**
23	Dick Allen	1556
24	Willie McCovey	1550
25	Dave Parker	1537
26	Frank Robinson	1532
27	Lance Parrish	1527
28	Willie Mays	1526
	Devon White	1526
30	Eddie Murray	1516
31	Rick Monday	1513
	Greg Vaughn	**1513**
33	Andre Dawson	1509
34	Tony Phillips	1499
35	Ray Lankford	1495
	Greg Luzinski	1495
37	Eddie Mathews	1487
38	Frank Howard	1460
39	**Jay Bell**	**1443**
40	Juan Samuel	1442
41	Harold Baines	1441
	Jack Clark	1441
43	**Mo Vaughn**	**1429**
44	Jimmy Wynn	1427
45	Jim Rice	1423
46	George Foster	1419
47	George Scott	1418
48	**Ron Gant**	**1411**
49	Darrell Evans	1410
50	Rob Deer	1409
51	**Jeff Bagwell**	**1406**
	Jay Buhner	1406
53	Eric Davis	1398
54	Carl Yastrzemski	1393
55	**Barry Bonds**	**1387**
	Joe Carter	1387
57	Carlton Fisk	1386
58	Hank Aaron	1383
59	**Craig Biggio**	**1373**
60	Travis Fryman	1369
61	**Matt Williams**	**1363**
62	Danny Tartabull	1362
63	Larry Parrish	1359
64	Darryl Strawberry	1352
65	Robin Yount	1350
66	Ron Santo	1343
67	Gorman Thomas	1339
68	**Ellis Burks**	**1332**
	Dean Palmer	**1332**
70	Babe Ruth	1330
71	**Reggie Sanders**	**1320**
72	Deron Johnson	1318
73	Cecil Fielder	1316
74	Willie Horton	1313
75	Jimmie Foxx	1311
76	Mickey Tettleton	1307
	Tim Wallach	1307
78	Cal Ripken	1305
79	Kirk Gibson	1285
80	Johnny Bench	1278
	Bobby Grich	1278
82	Pete Incaviglia	1277
83	**Tim Salmon**	**1275**
84	Claudell Washington	1266
85	Ryne Sandberg	1260
86	**Ken Griffey**	**1256**
87	**Juan Gonzalez**	**1254**
88	Ken Singleton	1246
89	Paul Molitor	1244
	Rafael Palmeiro	**1244**
91	Willie McGee	1238
92	Duke Snider	1237
93	Ernie Banks	1236
94	Ron Cey	1235
	Benito Santiago	**1235**
96	Jesse Barfield	1234
97	Roberto Clemente	1230
	Jose Hernandez	**1230**
99	Boog Powell	1226
100	Graig Nettles	1209

At Bats per Strikeout

1	Joe Sewell	62.6
2	Lloyd Waner	44.9
3	Nellie Fox	42.7
4	Tommy Holmes	40.9
5	Andy High	33.8
6	Sam Rice	33.7
7	Frankie Frisch	33.5
8	Dale Mitchell	33.5
9	Johnny Cooney	31.5
10	Frank McCormick	30.3
11	Don Mueller	29.9
12	Billy Southworth	29.5
13	Rip Radcliff	28.9
14	Edd Roush	28.3
15	Pie Traynor	27.2
16	Doc Cramer	26.5
17	Carson Bigbee	26.0
18	Hank Severeid	25.5
19	George Sisler	25.3
20	Paul Waner	25.2
21	Sparky Adams	24.9
22	Lou Finney	24.9
23	Deacon White	24.8
24	Jack Rowe	24.8
25	Irish Meusel	24.6
26	Ezra Sutton	24.6
27	Red Schoendienst	24.5
28	Vic Power	24.5
29	Arky Vaughan	24.0
30	Felix Millan	23.9
31	Mickey Cochrane	23.8
32	Charlie Gehringer	23.8
33	John Ward	23.5
34	George Kell	23.4
35	George Cutshaw	23.2
36	Jack Tobin	23.1
37	Taffy Wright	23.1
38	Hughie Critz	23.1
39	Mark Koenig	22.5
40	Ernie Lombardi	22.3
41	Heinie Manush	22.2
42	Bobby Richardson	22.2
43	Jo-Jo Moore	22.0
44	Earl Sheely	21.8
45	Bill Dickey	21.8
46	Johnny Pesky	21.8
47	Rick Ferrell	21.8
48	Glenn Beckert	21.4
49	Tony Gwynn	21.4
50	Dick Siebert	21.2

Strikeout Percentage

1	Rob Deer	36.31
2	**Jose Hernandez**	**30.59**
3	Pete Incaviglia	30.17
4	**Jim Thome**	**29.88**
5	Gorman Thomas	28.63
6	Jay Buhner	28.05
7	Mickey Tettleton	27.82
8	Jose Canseco	27.52
9	**Mike Cameron**	**27.49**
10	Dave Kingman	27.20
11	Danny Tartabull	27.18
12	**Dean Palmer**	**27.17**
13	Cory Snyder	27.13
14	Ray Lankford	26.95
15	Gary Pettis	26.40
16	Nate Colbert	26.36
17	Reggie Jackson	26.33
18	Eric Davis	26.27
19	**Todd Hundley**	**26.21**
20	**Sammy Sosa**	**26.21**
21	Jesse Barfield	25.93
22	**Reggie Sanders**	**25.87**
23	**Mo Vaughn**	**25.83**
24	Mark McGwire	25.80
25	**Charles Johnson**	**25.68**
26	Cecil Fielder	25.52
27	**Jeromy Burnitz**	**25.14**
28	**John Vander Wal**	**25.11**
29	Lee Stevens	24.97
30	Darryl Strawberry	24.95
31	Bobby Bonds	24.95
32	**Greg Vaughn**	**24.79**
33	**Carlos Delgado**	**24.77**
34	Paul Sorrento	24.74
35	**Andres Galarraga**	**24.73**
36	Rick Monday	24.66
37	Dick Allen	24.57
38	Donn Clendenon	24.53
39	Mack Jones	24.46
40	**Jim Edmonds**	**24.43**
41	Willie Stargell	24.42
42	Dick Stuart	23.94
43	**Michael Tucker**	**23.92**
44	Juan Samuel	23.71
45	**Alex Gonzalez**	**23.61**
46	Woodie Held	23.49
47	Tommie Agee	23.47
48	Tony Armas	23.26
49	**Jose Valentin**	**23.18**
50	**Tim Salmon**	**23.03**

Batting Average

1	Ty Cobb	.366
2	Rogers Hornsby	.358
3	Joe Jackson	.356
4	Ed Delahanty	.346
5	Tris Speaker	.345
6	Billy Hamilton	.344
7	Ted Williams	.344
8	Dan Brouthers	.342
9	Babe Ruth	.342
10	Harry Heilmann	.342
11	Pete Browning	.341
12	Willie Keeler	.341
13	Bill Terry	.341
14	George Sisler	.340
15	Lou Gehrig	.340
16	Jesse Burkett	.338
17	Tony Gwynn	.338
18	Nap Lajoie	.338
19	Riggs Stephenson	.336
20	Al Simmons	.334
21	John McGraw	.334
22	Paul Waner	.333
23	Eddie Collins	.333
24	Mike Donlin	.333
25	Sam Thompson	.331
26	Cap Anson	.331
27	Stan Musial	.331
28	Heinie Manush	.330
29	Wade Boggs	.328
30	Rod Carew	.328
31	Honus Wagner	.328
32	Tip O'Neill	.326
33	Hugh Duffy	.326
34	Bob Fothergill	.325
35	Jimmie Foxx	.325
36	Earle Combs	.325
37	Joe DiMaggio	.325
38	Babe Herman	.324
39	Joe Medwick	.324
40	**Vladimir Guerrero**	**.323**
41	Edd Roush	.323
42	Sam Rice	.322
43	Ross Youngs	.322
44	Kiki Cuyler	.321
45	Charlie Gehringer	.320
46	Chuck Klein	.320
47	Pie Traynor	.320
48	Mickey Cochrane	.320
49	**Mike Piazza**	**.319**
50	Ken Williams	.319
51	Kirby Puckett	.318
52	Earl Averill	.318
53	Arky Vaughan	.318
54	**Derek Jeter**	**.317**
55	Roberto Clemente	.317
56	Chick Hafey	.317
57	Joe Kelley	.317
58	**Manny Ramirez**	**.317**
59	Zack Wheat	.317
60	Roger Connor	.316
61	Lloyd Waner	.316
62	George Van Haltren	.316
63	Frankie Frisch	.316
64	Goose Goslin	.315
65	**Edgar Martinez**	**.315**
66	**Larry Walker**	**.314**
67	Bibb Falk	.314
68	Cecil Travis	.314
69	Hank Greenberg	.313
70	Jack Fournier	.313
71	Elmer Flick	.313
72	Bill Dickey	.313
73	Dale Mitchell	.312
74	Johnny Mize	.312
75	Joe Sewell	.312
76	Fred Clarke	.312
77	Barney McCosky	.312
78	Hughie Jennings	.312
79	Freddie Lindstrom	.311
80	Bing Miller	.311
81	Jackie Robinson	.311
82	Baby Doll Jacobson	.311
83	Taffy Wright	.311
84	Rip Radcliff	.311
85	Ginger Beaumont	.311
86	Mike Tiernan	.311
87	Luke Appling	.310
88	Irish Meusel	.310
89	Elmer Smith	.310
90	Denny Lyons	.310
91	Bobby Veach	.310
92	Jim O'Rourke	.310
93	**Frank Thomas**	**.310**
94	Jim Bottomley	.310
95	John Stone	.310
96	Sam Crawford	.309
97	Bob Meusel	.309
98	Jack Tobin	.309
99	**Chipper Jones**	**.309**
100	Spud Davis	.308

Batting Average by era

1988-2003

1	Tony Gwynn	.338
2	Wade Boggs	.328
3	**Vladimir Guerrero**	**.323**
4	**Mike Piazza**	**.319**
5	Kirby Puckett	.318
6	**Derek Jeter**	**.317**
7	**Manny Ramirez**	**.317**
8	**Edgar Martinez**	**.315**
9	**Larry Walker**	**.314**
10	**Frank Thomas**	**.310**

1973-1987

1	Rod Carew	.328
2	Ralph Garr	.306
3	George Brett	.305
4	Bill Madlock	.305
5	Al Oliver	.303
6	Pete Rose	.303
7	Pedro Guerrero	.300
8	Bake McBride	.299
9	Cecil Cooper	.298
10	Jim Rice	.298

1961-1972

1	Roberto Clemente	.317
2	Matty Alou	.307
3	Hank Aaron	.305
4	Tony Oliva	.304
5	Manny Mota	.304
6	Willie Mays	.302
7	Rico Carty	.299
8	Joe Torre	.297
9	Al Kaline	.297
10	Orlando Cepeda	.297

1943-1960

1	Ted Williams	.344
2	Stan Musial	.331
3	Dale Mitchell	.312
4	Barney McCosky	.312
5	Jackie Robinson	.311
6	Richie Ashburn	.308
7	Johnny Pesky	.307
8	George Kell	.306
9	Dixie Walker	.306
10	Harvey Kuenn	.303

1921-1942

1	Rogers Hornsby	.358
2	Babe Ruth	.342
3	Harry Heilmann	.342
4	Bill Terry	.341
5	George Sisler	.340
6	Lou Gehrig	.340
7	Riggs Stephenson	.336
8	Al Simmons	.334
9	Paul Waner	.333
10	Heinie Manush	.330

1901-1920

1	Ty Cobb	.366
2	Joe Jackson	.356
3	Tris Speaker	.345
4	Willie Keeler	.341
5	Nap Lajoie	.338
6	Eddie Collins	.333
7	Mike Donlin	.333
8	Honus Wagner	.328
9	Zack Wheat	.317
10	Elmer Flick	.313

1893-1900

1	Ed Delahanty	.346
2	Billy Hamilton	.344
3	Jesse Burkett	.338
4	John McGraw	.334
5	Hugh Duffy	.326
6	Joe Kelley	.317
7	George Van Haltren	.316
8	Hughie Jennings	.312
9	Mike Tiernan	.311
10	Elmer Smith	.310

1876-1892

1	Dan Brouthers	.342
2	Pete Browning	.341
3	Sam Thompson	.331
4	Cap Anson	.331
5	Tip O'Neill	.326
6	Roger Connor	.316
7	Denny Lyons	.310
8	Jim O'Rourke	.310
9	King Kelly	.308
10	Deacon White	.303

On-Base Percentage

1	Ted Williams	.482
2	Babe Ruth	.474
3	John McGraw	.466
4	Billy Hamilton	.455
5	Lou Gehrig	.447
6	Rogers Hornsby	.434
7	**Barry Bonds**	**.433**
	Ty Cobb	.433
9	Jimmie Foxx	.428
	Tris Speaker	.428
	Frank Thomas	**.428**
12	Eddie Collins	.424
	Ferris Fain	.424
14	Max Bishop	.423
	Dan Brouthers	.423
	Joe Jackson	.423
	Edgar Martinez	**.423**
18	Mickey Mantle	.421
19	Mickey Cochrane	.419
20	**Brian Giles**	**.417**
	Stan Musial	.417
22	Cupid Childs	.416
23	Wade Boggs	.415
	Jesse Burkett	.415
	Jason Giambi	**.415**
26	Mel Ott	.414
27	**Manny Ramirez**	**.413**
	Roy Thomas	.413
29	Hank Greenberg	.412
30	**Jeff Bagwell**	**.411**
	Ed Delahanty	.411
	Jim Thome	**.411**
33	Harry Heilmann	.410
	Charlie Keller	.410
	Eddie Stanky	.410
36	**Bobby Abreu**	**.409**
	Jackie Robinson	.409
38	Roy Cullenbine	.408
39	Denny Lyons	.407
	Riggs Stephenson	.407
41	Arky Vaughan	.406
42	Charlie Gehringer	.404
	Chipper Jones	**.404**
	Paul Waner	.404
45	Pete Browning	.403
	Joe Cunningham	.403
47	Lu Blue	.402
	Joe Kelley	.402
	John Olerud	**.402**
50	**Rickey Henderson**	**.401**
	Gary Sheffield	**.401**
52	**Larry Walker**	**.400**
53	Luke Appling	.399
	Ross Youngs	.399
55	Joe DiMaggio	.398
	Ralph Kiner	.398
	Elmer Smith	.398
	Elmer Valo	.398
59	Earle Combs	.397
	Roger Connor	.397
	John Kruk	.397
	Johnny Mize	.397
63	Cap Anson	.396
	Richie Ashburn	.396
	Mike Hargrove	.396
66	Earl Averill	.395
	Carlos Delgado	**.395**
	Hack Wilson	.395
69	Frank Chance	.394
	Stan Hack	.394
	Mark McGwire	.394
	Johnny Pesky	.394
	Eddie Yost	.394
74	Rod Carew	.393
	Bob Johnson	.393
	Wally Schang	.393
	Bill Terry	.393
	Ken Williams	.393
79	Jack Fournier	.392
	George Grantham	.392
	Joe Morgan	.392
	Tip O'Neill	.392
	Mike Tiernan	.392
84	Hughie Jennings	.391
	Joe Sewell	.391
	Honus Wagner	.391
87	Harlond Clift	.390
	Joe Cronin	.390
	Augie Galan	.390
	Vladimir Guerrero	**.390**
	Dave Magadan	.390
	Bernie Williams	**.390**
93	Elmer Flick	.389
	Derek Jeter	**.389**
	Minnie Minoso	.389
	Buddy Myer	.389
	Frank Robinson	.389
	Tim Salmon	**.389**
99	7 players tied	.388

Slugging Average

1	Babe Ruth	.690
2	Ted Williams	.634
3	Lou Gehrig	.632
4	Jimmie Foxx	.609
5	Hank Greenberg	.605
6	**Barry Bonds**	**.602**
7	**Manny Ramirez**	**.598**
8	Mark McGwire	.588
9	**Vladimir Guerrero**	**.588**
10	**Alex Rodriguez**	**.581**
11	Joe DiMaggio	.579
12	Rogers Hornsby	.577
13	**Mike Piazza**	**.572**
14	**Jim Thome**	**.568**
15	**Frank Thomas**	**.568**
16	**Larry Walker**	**.567**
17	Albert Belle	.564
18	**Juan Gonzalez**	**.563**
19	**Brian Giles**	**.563**
20	Johnny Mize	.562
21	**Ken Griffey**	**.562**
22	Stan Musial	.559
23	**Carlos Delgado**	**.558**
24	Willie Mays	.557
25	Mickey Mantle	.557
26	Hank Aaron	.555
27	**Jason Giambi**	**.549**
28	**Jeff Bagwell**	**.549**
29	Ralph Kiner	.548
30	**Sammy Sosa**	**.546**
31	Hack Wilson	.545
32	Chuck Klein	.543
33	**Chipper Jones**	**.541**
34	Duke Snider	.540
35	Frank Robinson	.537
36	Al Simmons	.535
37	Dick Allen	.534
38	Earl Averill	.534
39	Mel Ott	.533
40	**Jim Edmonds**	**.533**
41	Babe Herman	.532
42	Ken Williams	.530
43	Willie Stargell	.529
44	Mike Schmidt	.527
45	**Gary Sheffield**	**.527**
46	Chick Hafey	.526
47	**Edgar Martinez**	**.525**
48	**Mo Vaughn**	**.523**
49	**Rafael Palmeiro**	**.522**
50	Hal Trosky	.522
51	Wally Berger	.522
52	**Ryan Klesko**	**.521**
53	Harry Heilmann	.520
54	Kevin Mitchell	.520
55	Dan Brouthers	.519
56	Charlie Keller	.518
57	Joe Jackson	.517
58	Willie McCovey	.515
59	Jose Canseco	.515
60	**Shawn Green**	**.513**
61	**Bobby Abreu**	**.513**
62	Ty Cobb	.512
63	**Ellis Burks**	**.511**
64	**Fred McGriff**	**.511**
65	**Scott Rolen**	**.510**
66	Eddie Mathews	.509
67	Jeff Heath	.509
68	Harmon Killebrew	.509
69	**Moises Alou**	**.508**
70	**Tim Salmon**	**.506**
71	Bob Johnson	.506
72	Bill Terry	.506
73	Darryl Strawberry	.505
74	Sam Thompson	.505
75	Ed Delahanty	.505
76	Joe Medwick	.505
77	**Jeff Kent**	**.503**
78	Jim Rice	.502
79	**Javy Lopez**	**.502**
80	Tris Speaker	.500
81	David Justice	.500
82	Jim Bottomley	.500
83	**Matt Stairs**	**.500**
84	Goose Goslin	.500
85	Roy Campanella	.500
86	Ernie Banks	.500
87	Orlando Cepeda	.499
88	Bob Horner	.499
89	Dante Bichette	.499
90	**Andres Galarraga**	**.499**
91	Frank Howard	.499
92	Ted Kluszewski	.498
93	Bob Meusel	.497
94	Will Clark	.497
95	Hank Sauer	.496
96	**Cliff Floyd**	**.496**
97	Danny Tartabull	.496
98	Al Rosen	.495
99	**Andruw Jones**	**.494**
100	Jay Buhner	.494

On-Base plus Slugging

1	Babe Ruth	1164
2	Ted Williams	1116
3	Lou Gehrig	1079
4	Jimmie Foxx	1037
5	**Barry Bonds**	**1035**
6	Hank Greenberg	1017
7	Rogers Hornsby	1011
	Manny Ramirez	**1011**
9	**Frank Thomas**	**996**
10	Mark McGwire	982
11	**Brian Giles**	**980**
12	**Jim Thome**	**979**
13	**Vladimir Guerrero**	**978**
	Mickey Mantle	978
15	Joe DiMaggio	977
16	Stan Musial	976
17	**Larry Walker**	**967**
18	**Jason Giambi**	**964**
19	**Alex Rodriguez**	**963**
20	**Jeff Bagwell**	**960**
	Mike Piazza	**960**
22	Johnny Mize	959
23	**Carlos Delgado**	**953**
24	**Edgar Martinez**	**948**
25	Mel Ott	947
26	Ralph Kiner	946
27	Ty Cobb	945
	Chipper Jones	**945**
29	Dan Brouthers	942
30	**Ken Griffey**	**941**
	Willie Mays	941
32	Joe Jackson	940
	Hack Wilson	940
34	Albert Belle	933
35	Harry Heilmann	930
36	Hank Aaron	929
	Earl Averill	929
38	Charlie Keller	928
	Gary Sheffield	**928**
	Tris Speaker	928
41	Frank Robinson	926
42	Ken Williams	923
43	**Bobby Abreu**	**922**
44	Chuck Klein	922
45	Duke Snider	920
46	Ed Delahanty	916
47	Al Simmons	915
48	Babe Herman	915
49	**Jim Edmonds**	**913**
50	Dick Allen	912
51	**Juan Gonzalez**	**907**
52	Mike Schmidt	907
53	**Mo Vaughn**	**906**
54	Bob Johnson	899
	Bill Terry	899
56	Chick Hafey	898
57	Mickey Cochrane	897
58	**Rafael Palmeiro**	**895**
	Tim Salmon	**895**
	Sammy Sosa	**895**
61	Hal Trosky	893
62	**Ryan Klesko**	**891**
63	Willie McCovey	889
	Willie Stargell	889
	Sam Thompson	889
66	**Fred McGriff**	**889**
67	Billy Hamilton	887
68	Goose Goslin	887
69	Harmon Killebrew	885
	Eddie Mathews	885
71	Charlie Gehringer	884
	Scott Rolen	**884**
73	Roger Connor	883
	Jackie Robinson	883
75	**Bernie Williams**	**882**
76	Wally Berger	881
	Will Clark	881
78	Dolph Camilli	880
	Kevin Mitchell	880
	Riggs Stephenson	880
81	Jeff Heath	879
	Al Rosen	879
83	David Justice	878
84	Paul Waner	877
85	Larry Doby	876
86	John McGraw	876
87	**Moises Alou**	**875**
	Ellis Burks	**875**
	Jack Fournier	875
90	Tommy Henrich	873
	John Olerud	**873**
92	Pete Browning	870
	Shawn Green	**870**
94	Jim Bottomley	869
95	Jose Canseco	868
	Bill Dickey	868
97	Joe Medwick	867
98	Rusty Greer	865
99	Danny Tartabull	864
100	3 players tied	862

Adjusted OPS

1	Babe Ruth	209
2	Ted Williams	186
3	Lou Gehrig	182
4	**Barry Bonds**	**181**
5	Rogers Hornsby	176
6	Mickey Mantle	173
7	Dan Brouthers	169
	Joe Jackson	169
9	Ty Cobb	167
10	Mark McGwire	165
11	Pete Browning	164
	Frank Thomas	**164**
13	Jimmie Foxx	161
14	Hank Greenberg	157
	Willie Mays	157
	Johnny Mize	157
	Stan Musial	157
18	Hank Aaron	156
	Dick Allen	156
	Joe DiMaggio	156
	Mike Piazza	**156**
	Manny Ramirez	**156**
	Tris Speaker	156
24	Mel Ott	155
25	**Jeff Bagwell**	**154**
	Roger Connor	154
	Frank Robinson	154
28	Ed Delahanty	152
	Jason Giambi	**152**
	Charlie Keller	152
31	**Edgar Martinez**	**151**
	Jim Thome	**151**
33	**Brian Giles**	**150**
	Nap Lajoie	150
	Honus Wagner	150
36	Gavy Cravath	149
	Elmer Flick	149
38	Harry Heilmann	148
	Ralph Kiner	148
	Willie McCovey	148
	Gary Sheffield	**148**
42	Mike Schmidt	147
	Willie Stargell	147
44	**Vladimir Guerrero**	**146**
	Sam Thompson	146
46	**Ken Griffey**	**145**
	Eddie Mathews	145
	Hack Wilson	145
49	Albert Belle	144
	Alex Rodriguez	**144**
51	Sam Crawford	143
	Jack Fournier	143
	Frank Howard	143
	Kevin Mitchell	143
55	Eddie Collins	142
	Carlos Delgado	**142**
	Mike Donlin	142
	Chipper Jones	**142**
	Harmon Killebrew	142
	Henry Larkin	142
61	Babe Herman	141
	Harry Stovey	141
63	**Bobby Abreu**	**140**
	Wally Berger	140
	Jesse Burkett	140
	Jeff Heath	140
	Reggie Jackson	140
	Tip O'Neill	140
69	Cap Anson	139
	Billy Hamilton	139
	Bob Johnson	139
	Darryl Strawberry	139
73	Norm Cash	138
	Jack Clark	138
	Will Clark	138
	Pedro Guerrero	138
	Denny Lyons	138
	Al Rosen	138
	Duke Snider	138
	Mike Tiernan	138
81	Larry Doby	137
	Sherry Magee	137
	Gene Tenace	137
	Bill Terry	137
85	Frank Baker	136
	King Kelly	136
	Reggie Smith	136
	Arky Vaughan	136
	Ken Williams	136
90	George Brett	135
	Tommy Burns	135
	Frank Chance	135
	Jim Edmonds	**135**
	Chuck Klein	135
	John McGraw	135
	Larry Walker	**135**
97	8 players tied	134

Adjusted Batting Wins

1	Babe Ruth	135.2
2	**Barry Bonds**	**111.1**
3	Ty Cobb	103.4
4	Ted Williams	103.0
5	Hank Aaron	95.2
6	Lou Gehrig	93.7
7	Stan Musial	92.5
8	Mickey Mantle	89.4
9	Rogers Hornsby	87.6
10	Willie Mays	87.3
11	Tris Speaker	82.9
12	Frank Robinson	78.9
13	Mel Ott	78.2
14	Jimmie Foxx	70.0
15	Honus Wagner	66.0
16	**Frank Thomas**	**65.2**
17	Eddie Collins	64.4
18	**Jeff Bagwell**	**60.3**
19	Eddie Mathews	58.3
20	Mark McGwire	58.3
21	Nap Lajoie	57.9
22	Mike Schmidt	57.7
23	Willie McCovey	57.5
24	Reggie Jackson	54.3
25	**Edgar Martinez**	**54.2**
26	**Rickey Henderson**	**54.0**
27	Dan Brouthers	53.4
28	Harry Heilmann	52.7
29	Carl Yastrzemski	52.3
30	Joe Morgan	52.1
31	Willie Stargell	52.1
32	Harmon Killebrew	51.3
33	Joe DiMaggio	50.2
34	George Brett	50.1
35	**Gary Sheffield**	**50.0**
36	Dick Allen	49.9
37	Al Kaline	49.6
38	Johnny Mize	49.5
39	Sam Crawford	48.7
40	Ed Delahanty	48.5
41	Roger Connor	48.3
42	Eddie Murray	47.0
43	Paul Waner	46.6
44	**Rafael Palmeiro**	**46.0**
45	Tony Gwynn	45.5
46	Wade Boggs	45.1
47	Joe Jackson	45.0
48	Dave Winfield	44.9
49	**Ken Griffey**	**43.7**
50	**Fred McGriff**	**43.4**
51	Jesse Burkett	43.1
52	Rod Carew	42.8
53	**Mike Piazza**	**41.4**
54	Hank Greenberg	40.8
55	**Jim Thome**	**40.7**
56	**Manny Ramirez**	**40.4**
57	Jack Clark	40.3
58	Will Clark	40.2
59	Pete Rose	40.2
60	Billy Williams	39.6
61	Duke Snider	39.6
62	Cap Anson	39.6
63	Frank Howard	38.3
64	Ken Singleton	38.1
65	Norm Cash	37.8
66	Bob Johnson	37.7
67	**John Olerud**	**37.2**
68	Reggie Smith	37.0
69	Billy Hamilton	37.0
70	Roberto Clemente	37.0
71	Rusty Staub	36.8
72	Ralph Kiner	36.5
73	Orlando Cepeda	35.9
74	Elmer Flick	35.9
75	Arky Vaughan	35.8
76	Sherry Magee	35.7
77	**Jason Giambi**	**35.7**
78	Fred Clarke	35.6
79	Albert Belle	35.4
80	Dwight Evans	35.1
81	Zack Wheat	34.8
82	Keith Hernandez	34.6
83	Paul Molitor	34.3
84	Pete Browning	34.0
85	Tim Raines	33.8
86	Boog Powell	33.7
87	Al Simmons	33.6
88	**Chipper Jones**	**33.5**
89	**Sammy Sosa**	**33.3**
90	**Larry Walker**	**33.1**
91	Bill Terry	32.6
92	Goose Goslin	32.4
93	Charlie Gehringer	32.0
94	Joe Medwick	32.0
95	Jimmy Wynn	31.7
96	Babe Herman	31.7
97	Joe Torre	31.6
98	Jack Fournier	31.2
99	Minnie Minoso	30.7
100	Rocky Colavito	30.6

Adjusted Batting Wins

101	Jose Canseco	30.6
102	Hack Wilson	30.4
103	Joe Kelley	30.3
104	**Bernie Williams**	**30.1**
105	**Alex Rodriguez**	**30.1**
106	Sam Thompson	29.9
107	Chuck Klein	29.9
108	Darryl Strawberry	29.8
109	Charlie Keller	29.3
110	Pedro Guerrero	29.2
111	Ron Santo	29.0
112	Bobby Bonds	29.0
113	Brian Downing	28.9
114	**Carlos Delgado**	**28.8**
115	Tony Perez	28.7
116	Larry Doby	28.7
117	Gene Tenace	28.7
118	Harold Baines	28.2
119	Johnny Bench	28.2
120	Greg Luzinski	28.1
121	Darrell Evans	28.0
122	Bobby Grich	28.0
123	Fred Lynn	27.9
124	Jim Rice	27.8
125	Earl Averill	27.7
126	Jake Beckley	27.6
127	**Brian Giles**	**27.5**
128	Mike Tiernan	27.2
129	Willie Keeler	27.1
130	Dolph Camilli	26.9
131	Ernie Banks	26.9
132	Gavy Cravath	26.8
133	Don Mattingly	26.8
134	Wally Berger	26.6
135	Harry Stovey	26.5
136	Enos Slaughter	26.5
137	Frank Baker	26.4
138	**Tim Salmon**	**26.3**
139	Jim O'Rourke	26.3
140	Bob Watson	26.2
141	Bob Elliott	26.2
142	**Juan Gonzalez**	**26.2**
143	**Craig Biggio**	**25.9**
144	Jeff Heath	25.9
145	Chili Davis	25.9
146	**Mark Grace**	**25.6**
147	Bobby Bonilla	25.6
148	Tony Oliva	25.5
149	Rico Carty	25.4
150	Roy Thomas	25.4
151	Jimmy Sheckard	25.2
152	Bill Nicholson	25.1
153	Stan Hack	25.1
154	Kiki Cuyler	25.1
155	Jose Cruz	25.0
156	Jackie Robinson	24.9
157	Al Oliver	24.9
158	**Mo Vaughn**	**24.7**
159	**Ellis Burks**	**24.7**
160	George Davis	24.6
161	Dave Parker	24.5
162	George Sisler	24.3
163	Yogi Berra	24.3
164	Jim Bottomley	24.2
165	**Vladimir Guerrero**	**24.2**
166	Cesar Cedeno	24.2
167	Kevin Mitchell	24.0
168	Bill Dickey	24.0
169	Edd Roush	23.8
170	Kent Hrbek	23.7
171	Danny Tartabull	23.7
172	Ken Williams	23.6
173	Ron Cey	23.5
174	George Foster	23.5
175	Gabby Hartnett	23.5
176	**Luis Gonzalez**	**23.4**
177	Bobby Veach	23.4
178	Bobby Murcer	23.4
179	David Justice	23.4
180	**Jim Edmonds**	**23.3**
181	Mickey Cochrane	23.2
182	John McGraw	23.1
183	Paul O'Neill	23.0
184	Roy White	22.9
185	**Bobby Abreu**	**22.9**
186	Lou Whitaker	22.8
187	Robin Yount	22.6
188	King Kelly	22.5
189	Sid Gordon	22.4
190	Paul Hines	22.4
191	Rick Monday	22.4
192	Hal McRae	22.4
193	Ted Simmons	22.4
194	Augie Galan	22.4
195	Earle Combs	22.4
196	**Jeff Kent**	**22.4**
197	Larry Doyle	22.4
198	**Roberto Alomar**	**22.4**
199	Joe Cronin	22.3
200	Frank Chance	22.2

Pinch Hits

1	**Lenny Harris**	**181**
2	Manny Mota	150
3	Smoky Burgess	145
4	Greg Gross	143
5	**Dave Hansen**	**129**
6	**John Vander Wal**	**125**
7	Jose Morales	123
8	Jerry Lynch	116
9	Red Lucas	114
10	Steve Braun	113
11	Terry Crowley	108
	Denny Walling	108
13	Gates Brown	107
14	Mike Lum	103
15	Jim Dwyer	102
16	Rusty Staub	100
17	**Mark Sweeney**	**97**
18	Dave Clark	96
19	Larry Biittner	95
	Vic Davalillo	95
	Gerald Perry	95
22	Jerry Hairston	94
23	Dave Philley	93
	Joel Youngblood	93
25	Jay Johnstone	92
	Dave Magadan	92

Pinch Hit Average

(150 at-bats minimum)

1	**Greg Colbrunn**	**.322**
2	Alex Arias	.320
3	Tommy Davis	.320
4	Frenchy Bordagaray	.312
5	Harold Baines	.311
6	Frankie Baumholtz	.307
7	Sid Bream	.306
8	Mark Carreon	.306
9	Red Schoendienst	.303
10	Bob Fothergill	.300
11	Dave Philley	.299
12	**Matt Stairs**	**.298**
13	Manny Mota	.297
14	Ted Easterly	.296
15	Harvey Hendrick	.295
16	Larry Herndon	.294
17	Rance Mulliniks	.292
18	Terry Puhl	.289
19	Chip Hale	.289
20	**Orlando Palmeiro**	**.288**
21	Manny Sanguillen	.288
22	Glenallen Hill	.287
23	Smoky Burgess	.286
24	Rick Miller	.286
25	Johnny Mize	.283

Pinch Hit Home Runs

1	Cliff Johnson	20
2	Jerry Lynch	18
	John Vander Wal	**17**
4	Gates Brown	16
	Smoky Burgess	16
	Willie McCovey	16
7	George Crowe	14
	Dave Hansen	**14**
9	Glenallen Hill	13
10	Joe Adcock	12
	Bob Cerv	12
	Jose Morales	12
	Graig Nettles	12
14	Jeff Burroughs	11
	Jay Johnstone	11
	Candy Maldonado	11
	Orlando Merced	**11**
	Fred Whitfield	11
	Cy Williams	11
19	Mark Carreon	10
	Dave Clark	10
	Jim Dwyer	10
	Mike Lum	10
	Ken McMullen	10
	Don Mincher	10
	Wally Post	10
	Champ Summers	10
	Jerry Turner	10
	Gus Zernial	10

Stolen Bases

1	**Rickey Henderson**	**1406**
2	Lou Brock	938
3	Billy Hamilton	914
4	Ty Cobb	897
5	Tim Raines	808
6	Vince Coleman	752
7	Arlie Latham	742
8	Eddie Collins	741
9	Max Carey	738
10	Honus Wagner	723
11	Joe Morgan	689
12	Willie Wilson	668
13	Tom Brown	657
14	Bert Campaneris	649
15	Otis Nixon	620
16	George Davis	619
17	Dummy Hoy	596
18	Maury Wills	586
19	George Van Haltren	583
20	Ozzie Smith	580
21	Hugh Duffy	574
22	Bid McPhee	568
23	Brett Butler	558
24	Davey Lopes	557
25	Cesar Cedeno	550
26	Bill Dahlen	548
27	John Ward	540
28	**Kenny Lofton**	**538**
29	Herman Long	537
30	Patsy Donovan	518
	Jack Doyle	518
32	Fred Clarke	509
	Harry Stovey	509
34	Luis Aparicio	506
35	Paul Molitor	504
36	**Barry Bonds**	**500**
37	Willie Keeler	495
	Clyde Milan	495
39	Omar Moreno	487
40	**Roberto Alomar**	**474**
41	Mike Griffin	473
42	Tommy McCarthy	468
43	Jimmy Sheckard	465
44	Delino DeShields	463
45	Bobby Bonds	461
46	Ed Delahanty	455
	Ron LeFlore	455
48	Curt Welch	453
49	Steve Sax	444
50	Joe Kelley	443
51	Sherry Magee	441
52	John McGraw	436
	Tris Speaker	436
	Eric Young	**436**
55	Bob Bescher	428
	Mike Tiernan	428
57	**Marquis Grissom**	**425**
58	Frankie Frisch	419
	Jimmy Ryan	419
60	Charlie Comiskey	416
61	Tommy Harper	408
62	Chuck Knoblauch	407
63	Donie Bush	406
64	Frank Chance	403
65	Bill Lange	400
66	Willie Davis	398
67	Sam Mertes	396
	Juan Samuel	396
69	Dave Collins	395
	Billy North	395
71	**Craig Biggio**	**389**
	Jesse Burkett	389
73	Tommy Corcoran	387
74	Tom Daly	385
	Freddie Patek	385
76	George Burns	383
	Hugh Nicol	383
	Fred Pfeffer	383
	Walt Wilmot	383
80	Nap Lajoie	380
81	**Barry Larkin**	**377**
82	Harry Hooper	375
	George Sisler	375
84	Jack Glasscock	372
85	Lonnie Smith	370
86	Tommy Dowd	368
	King Kelly	368
88	Sam Crawford	367
89	**Tom Goodwin**	**364**
90	Hal Chase	363
91	Tommy Leach	361
92	Hughie Jennings	359
	Fielder Jones	359
94	Buck Ewing	354
	Gary Pettis	354
96	Rod Carew	353
97	Willie McGee	352
	Tommy Tucker	352
99	Sam Rice	351
100	2 players tied	349

Stolen Base Average

1	**Carlos Beltran**	**88.2**
2	**Pokey Reese**	**85.2**
3	Tim Raines	84.7
4	Eric Davis	84.1
5	Henry Cotto	83.3
6	Willie Wilson	83.3
7	**Tony Womack**	**83.1**
8	**Barry Larkin**	**83.0**
9	Davey Lopes	83.0
10	Stan Javier	82.8
11	**Doug Glanville**	**81.6**
12	Julio Cruz	81.5
13	**Brian Hunter**	**81.0**
14	Joe Morgan	81.0
15	Vince Coleman	80.9
16	**Roberto Alomar**	**80.9**
17	**Rickey Henderson**	**80.8**
18	Andy Van Slyke	80.6
19	Mickey Mantle	80.1
20	Lenny Dykstra	79.8
21	Ozzie Smith	79.7
22	Enzo Hernandez	79.6
23	Gary Redus	79.5
24	**Alex Rodriguez**	**79.4**
25	Paul Molitor	79.4
26	**Kenny Lofton**	**79.1**
27	R. J. Reynolds	79.0
28	**Marquis Grissom**	**78.8**
29	Luis Aparicio	78.8
30	**Derek Jeter**	**78.8**
31	**Johnny Damon**	**78.7**
32	Amos Otis	78.6
33	**Mike Cameron**	**78.5**
34	Kirk Gibson	78.5
35	**Barry Bonds**	**78.1**
36	Alan Wiggins	78.1
37	Devon White	77.9
38	Tommy Harper	77.9
39	Rudy Law	77.8
40	Joe Carter	77.8
	Mike Felder	77.8
42	Chuck Knoblauch	77.7
43	**Roger Cedeno**	**77.6**
44	Bob Dernier	77.6
45	**Damian Jackson**	**77.5**
46	Miguel Dilone	77.4
47	Gary Pettis	77.3
48	**Alfonso Soriano**	**77.1**
49	**Craig Biggio**	**77.0**
50	Mookie Wilson	76.9

Base Stealing Wins

1	**Rickey Henderson**	**18.7**
2	Tim Raines	12.7
3	Vince Coleman	10.6
4	Lou Brock	10.4
5	Willie Wilson	10.0
6	Joe Morgan	9.8
7	Davey Lopes	8.5
8	Ozzie Smith	7.9
9	Bert Campaneris	7.7
10	Otis Nixon	7.1
11	Luis Aparicio	6.7
12	**Kenny Lofton**	**6.5**
13	Paul Molitor	6.3
14	**Roberto Alomar**	**6.3**
15	Cesar Cedeno	6.1
16	**Barry Bonds**	**6.0**
17	Maury Wills	5.9
18	**Barry Larkin**	**5.6**
19	Eric Davis	5.4
20	**Marquis Grissom**	**5.3**
21	Tommy Harper	5.2
22	Ron LeFlore	5.1
23	Delino DeShields	5.0
24	Julio Cruz	4.9
25	Chuck Knoblauch	4.6
26	Omar Moreno	4.5
27	**Tony Womack**	**4.5**
28	**Craig Biggio**	**4.5**
29	Willie Davis	4.4
30	Amos Otis	4.4
31	Bobby Bonds	4.3
32	Gary Redus	4.3
33	**Eric Young**	**4.2**
34	Gary Pettis	4.2
35	Devon White	4.1
36	Freddie Patek	4.1
37	Ryne Sandberg	3.9
38	Dave Collins	3.9
39	Mookie Wilson	3.9
40	Willie Mays	3.9
41	George Case	3.9
42	Lenny Dykstra	3.8
43	Juan Samuel	3.8
44	**Tom Goodwin**	**3.7**
45	Steve Sax	3.7
46	Willie McGee	3.6
47	Stan Javier	3.6
48	Larry Bowa	3.5
49	Kirk Gibson	3.5
50	**Brian Hunter**	**3.5**

Pitcher Batting Average by era

1988-2003

1	**Mike Hampton**	**.247**
2	**Livan Hernandez**	**.234**
3	**Russ Ortiz**	**.223**
4	Orel Hershiser	.201
5	Mark Portugal	.198
6	Dwight Gooden	.196
7	Jose Rijo	.191
8	**Tom Glavine**	**.185**
9	Sid Fernandez	.182
10	**Greg Maddux**	**.178**

1973-1987

1	Ken Brett	.262
2	Rick Rhoden	.238
3	Don Robinson	.231
4	Steve Renko	.215
5	Bob Forsch	.213
6	Jim Rooker	.201
7	Steve Carlton	.201
8	Fernando Valenzuela	.200
9	Dave Roberts	.194
10	Mike Krukow	.193

1961-1972

1	Catfish Hunter	.226
2	Gary Peters	.222
3	Bob Gibson	.206
4	Camilo Pascual	.205
5	Juan Pizarro	.202
6	Jim Maloney	.201
7	Jim Perry	.199
8	Rick Wise	.195
9	Earl Wilson	.195
10	Tony Cloninger	.192

1943-1960

1	Fred Hutchinson	.276
2	Don Newcombe	.266
3	Mickey McDermott	.250
	Carl Scheib	.250
5	Tommy Byrne	.246
6	Johnny Sain	.245
7	Willard Nixon	.242
8	Don Larsen	.240
9	Bob Lemon	.233
10	Murry Dickson	.231

1921-1942

1	George Uhle	.286
2	Wes Ferrell	.284
3	Jack Scott	.276
4	Sloppy Thurston	.270
5	Red Ruffing	.269
6	Carl Mays	.268
7	Johnny Marcum	.265
8	Dutch Ruether	.264
9	Joe Shaute	.260
10	Schoolboy Rowe	.257

1901-1920

1	Babe Ruth	.299
2	Doc Crandall	.279
3	Al Orth	.277
4	George Mullin	.262
5	Jesse Tannehill	.256
6	Joe Wood	.241
7	Claude Hendrix	.241
8	Ray Caldwell	.241
9	Frank Kitson	.240
10	Wilbur Cooper	.239

1893-1900

1	Cy Seymour	.280
2	Win Mercer	.261
3	Brickyard Kennedy	.261
4	Nixey Callahan	.260
5	Jack Taylor	.252
6	Al Maul	.246
7	Jack Dunn	.244
8	Jouett Meekin	.243
9	Frank Killen	.241
10	Pink Hawley	.241

1876-1892

1	Guy Hecker	.297
2	Jack Stivetts	.295
3	Jim Devlin	.293
4	Charlie Ferguson	.288
5	Charlie Sweeney	.284
6	Bob Caruthers	.276
7	Ben Sanders	.275
8	Scott Stratton	.275
9	Ad Gumbert	.274
10	Dave Foutz	.262

Pitcher Batting Runs

1	Red Ruffing	143
2	Bob Caruthers	111
3	Wes Ferrell	100
4	Walter Johnson	99
5	Red Lucas	98
6	George Uhle	92
7	Guy Hecker	90
	Bob Lemon	90
9	Jim Whitney	89
10	Warren Spahn	88
11	George Mullin	87
12	Don Newcombe	79
13	Babe Ruth	78
14	Schoolboy Rowe	76
15	Early Wynn	72
16	Bob Gibson	65
	Jack Stivetts	65
18	Carl Mays	64
19	Al Orth	63
20	Don Drysdale	60
21	Christy Mathewson	59
22	Gary Peters	57
	Bucky Walters	57
	Earl Wilson	57
25	Doc Crandall	54
	Jesse Tannehill	54
	Jim Tobin	54
28	Ad Gumbert	53
29	Burleigh Grimes	52
30	Claude Hendrix	50
	Tony Mullane	50
32	Joe Bush	49
	Steve Carlton	49
	Charlie Ferguson	49
35	Bob Forsch	48
	Mike Hampton	**48**
	Scott Stratton	48
38	Don Larsen	46
39	Dave Foutz	45
	Vern Law	45
	Rick Rhoden	45
	Dutch Ruether	45
	Adonis Terry	45
44	Frank Killen	44
	Jack Scott	44
46	Tommy Byrne	41
	Jim Kaat	41
	Don Robinson	41
49	Johnny Sain	40
50	Wilbur Cooper	39
	Fred Hutchinson	39
52	Claude Osteen	38
	Charley Radbourn	38
	Sloppy Thurston	38
55	Dolf Luque	37
	Doc White	37
57	Jack Coombs	36
	Mickey McDermott	36
59	Clark Griffith	35
	Harvey Haddix	35
	Win Mercer	35
	Frank Smith	35
63	Art Nehf	34
	Robin Roberts	34
	Jack Taylor	34
	Rick Wise	34
67	Chief Bender	33
	Erv Brame	33
	Ken Brett	33
	Orel Hershiser	33
	Catfish Hunter	33
	Ben Sanders	33
73	Hooks Dauss	32
	Ted Lyons	32
	Al Maul	32
	Fernando Valenzuela	32
77	Ray Caldwell	31
	Russ Ortiz	**31**
	Dizzy Trout	31
	John Ward	31
	Joe Wood	31
82	Ed Brandt	30
	Lew Burdette	30
	Dwight Gooden	30
	Lefty Tyler	30
86	Jack Harshman	29
	Ed Lopat	29
	Jouett Meekin	29
	Camilo Pascual	29
	Juan Pizarro	29
91	Jack Bentley	28
	Livan Hernandez	**28**
	Joe Nuxhall	28
	Tom Seaver	28
	Urban Shocker	28
96	7 players tied	27

Games

First Base

1	Eddie Murray	2413
2	Jake Beckley	2380
3	Mickey Vernon	2237
4	**Fred McGriff**	**2233**
5	**Mark Grace**	**2162**
6	Lou Gehrig	2137
7	Charlie Grimm	2131
8	**Andres Galarraga**	**2105**
9	Joe Judge	2084
10	Ed Konetchy	2073

Second Base

1	Eddie Collins	2650
2	Joe Morgan	2527
3	Lou Whitaker	2308
4	Nellie Fox	2295
5	**Roberto Alomar**	**2279**
6	Charlie Gehringer	2206
7	Willie Randolph	2152
8	Frank White	2150
9	Bid McPhee	2129
10	Bill Mazeroski	2094

Shortstop

1	Luis Aparicio	2581
2	Ozzie Smith	2511
3	Cal Ripken	2302
4	Larry Bowa	2222
5	Luke Appling	2218
6	Dave Concepcion	2178
7	Rabbit Maranville	2153
8	Alan Trammell	2139
9	Bill Dahlen	2133
10	Bert Campaneris	2097

Third Base

1	Brooks Robinson	2870
2	Graig Nettles	2412
3	Gary Gaetti	2282
4	Wade Boggs	2215
5	Mike Schmidt	2212
6	Buddy Bell	2183
7	Eddie Mathews	2181
8	Ron Santo	2130
9	Tim Wallach	2054
10	Eddie Yost	2008

Outfield

1	Ty Cobb	2934
2	Willie Mays	2842
3	**Rickey Henderson**	**2826**
4	Hank Aaron	2760
5	Tris Speaker	2698
6	Lou Brock	2507
7	**Barry Bonds**	**2502**
8	Al Kaline	2488
9	Dave Winfield	2469
10	Max Carey	2421
11	Vada Pinson	2403
12	Roberto Clemente	2370
13	Zack Wheat	2337
14	Tony Gwynn	2326
15	Willie Davis	2323
	Andre Dawson	2323
17	Mel Ott	2313
18	Sam Crawford	2299
19	Paul Waner	2288
20	Harry Hooper	2284

Catcher

1	Carlton Fisk	2226
2	Bob Boone	2225
3	Gary Carter	2056
4	Tony Pena	1950
5	Jim Sundberg	1927
6	Al Lopez	1918
7	**Benito Santiago**	**1862**
8	Lance Parrish	1818
9	Rick Ferrell	1806
10	Gabby Hartnett	1793

Pitcher

1	**Jesse Orosco**	**1252**
2	Dennis Eckersley	1071
3	Hoyt Wilhelm	1070
4	**Dan Plesac**	**1064**
5	Kent Tekulve	1050
6	**John Franco**	**1036**
7	Lee Smith	1022
8	Rich Gossage	1002
9	Lindy McDaniel	987
10	Mike Jackson	960

Fielding Average

First Base

1	Steve Garvey	.996
2	Don Mattingly	.996
3	Wes Parker	.996
4	**J. T. Snow**	**.995**
5	**David Segui**	**.995**
6	**Tino Martinez**	**.995**
7	**John Olerud**	**.995**
8	Dan Driessen	.995
9	Jim Spencer	.995
10	Frank McCormick	.995

Second Base

1	Ryne Sandberg	.989
2	Tom Herr	.989
3	Mickey Morandini	.989
4	Jose Lind	.988
5	Jody Reed	.988
6	**Bret Boone**	**.987**
7	Jim Gantner	.985
8	Craig Biggio	.984
9	Frank White	.984
10	Bobby Grich	.984

Shortstop

1	**Omar Vizquel**	**.983**
2	**Mike Bordick**	**.982**
3	Larry Bowa	.980
4	Tony Fernandez	.980
5	Cal Ripken	.979
6	Ozzie Smith	.978
7	**Alex Rodriguez**	**.977**
8	Spike Owen	.977
9	Alan Trammell	.977
10	Mark Belanger	.977

Third Base

1	Brooks Robinson	.971
2	Ken Reitz	.970
3	George Kell	.969
4	Steve Buechele	.968
5	Don Money	.968
6	Don Wert	.968
7	Willie Kamm	.967
8	Heinie Groh	.967
9	**Jeff Cirillo**	**.966**
10	Carney Lansford	.966

Outfield

1	Darryl Hamilton	.995
2	Darren Lewis	.994
3	Terry Puhl	.993
4	Brett Butler	.993
5	Pete Rose	.991
6	Amos Otis	.991
7	Joe Rudi	.991
8	**Tom Goodwin**	**.991**
9	Mickey Stanley	.991
10	Robin Yount	.990
11	Jim Piersall	.990
12	**Johnny Damon**	**.990**
13	Brian McRae	.990
14	**Bernie Williams**	**.990**
15	Jim Landis	.989
16	Ken Berry	.989
17	Otis Nixon	.989
18	**Garret Anderson**	**.989**
19	Brady Anderson	.989
20	Tommy Holmes	.989
21	Kirby Puckett	.989

Catcher

1	**Dan Wilson**	**.995**
2	**Charles Johnson**	**.994**
3	Darrin Fletcher	.993
4	Bill Freehan	.993
5	**Brad Ausmus**	**.993**
6	**Brent Mayne**	**.993**
7	Elston Howard	.993
8	Jim Sundberg	.993
9	Sherm Lollar	.992
10	**Javy Lopez**	**.992**

Pitcher

1	Don Mossi	.990
2	**Brad Radke**	**.990**
3	Gary Nolan	.990
4	Rick Rhoden	.989
5	**Kirk Rueter**	**.989**
6	Lon Warneke	.988
7	Jim Wilson	.988
8	Woodie Fryman	.988
9	**Mike Mussina**	**.986**
10	Larry Gura	.986

Total Chances/Game (Infield)

First Base

1	Tom Jones	11.38
2	George Stovall	11.30
3	George Kelly	11.09
4	Wally Pipp	11.05
5	Ed Konetchy	11.04
6	Candy LaChance	11.04
7	George Burns	10.92
8	Bill Terry	10.91
9	Cap Anson	10.85
10	Walter Holke	10.83
11	Bill Phillips	10.83
12	Fred Tenney	10.83
13	Hal Chase	10.82
14	Charlie Comiskey	10.82
15	Dan Brouthers	10.74
16	Roger Connor	10.74
17	Jake Beckley	10.73
18	Lu Blue	10.73
19	Stuffy McInnis	10.71
20	Fred Luderus	10.69
21	Fred Merkle	10.68
22	John Reilly	10.68
23	Kitty Bransfield	10.67
24	Dan McGann	10.65
25	Jack Doyle	10.63

Second Base

1	Fred Pfeffer	6.95
2	Bid McPhee	6.70
3	Cub Stricker	6.59
4	Lou Bierbauer	6.49
5	Cupid Childs	6.32
6	Ski Melillo	6.16
7	Hughie Critz	6.07
8	Frankie Frisch	6.05
9	Bobby Lowe	6.01
10	Bucky Harris	6.00
11	Nap Lajoie	6.00
12	Billy Herman	5.97
13	Jerry Priddy	5.93
14	Bobby Doerr	5.86
15	Kid Gleason	5.83
16	Hobe Ferris	5.82
17	Buddy Myer	5.79
18	Tony Cuccinello	5.78
19	Charlie Gehringer	5.78
20	Joe Quinn	5.78
21	Tom Daly	5.77
22	Bill Wambsganss	5.77
23	George Cutshaw	5.75
24	Bill Hallman	5.70
25	Bill Mazeroski	5.67

Shortstop

1	Herman Long	6.38
2	Dave Bancroft	6.33
3	Bill Dahlen	6.26
4	George Davis	6.22
5	Rabbit Maranville	6.10
6	Bobby Wallace	6.10
7	Tommy Corcoran	6.09
8	Monte Cross	6.06
9	Bones Ely	6.06
10	Honus Wagner	5.99
11	Germany Smith	5.98
12	Travis Jackson	5.96
13	Dick Bartell	5.92
14	Joe Tinker	5.88
15	Art Fletcher	5.87
16	Donie Bush	5.81
17	Mickey Doolan	5.81
18	Doc Lavan	5.81
19	Ivy Olson	5.81
20	Freddy Parent	5.77
21	George McBride	5.75
22	Jack Glasscock	5.71
23	Glenn Wright	5.69
24	Joe Sewell	5.64
25	Luke Appling	5.53

Third Base

1	Jerry Denny	4.21
2	Billy Shindle	4.15
3	Billy Nash	4.07
4	Arlie Latham	4.04
5	Denny Lyons	3.98
6	Jimmy Collins	3.89
7	Hick Carpenter	3.81
8	Jimmy Austin	3.74
9	Lave Cross	3.73
10	Frank Baker	3.64
11	Bill Bradley	3.63
12	Harry Steinfeldt	3.57
13	George Pinkney	3.56
14	Doc Casey	3.48
15	Art Devlin	3.48
16	Bobby Byrne	3.44
17	Harlond Clift	3.44
18	Red Smith	3.42
19	Billy Werber	3.42
20	Eddie Foster	3.41
21	Willie Kamm	3.40
22	Clete Boyer	3.38
23	Larry Gardner	3.32
24	Mike Mowrey	3.31
25	Pie Traynor	3.30

Assists (Infield)

First Base

1	Eddie Murray	1865
2	Keith Hernandez	1682
3	**Mark Grace**	**1665**
4	**Jeff Bagwell**	**1592**
5	George Sisler	1529
6	Wally Joyner	1470
7	Mickey Vernon	1448
8	**Fred McGriff**	**1444**
9	**Rafael Palmeiro**	**1434**
10	**Andres Galarraga**	**1375**
11	Fred Tenney	1363
12	Bill Buckner	1351
	Chris Chambliss	1351
14	**Eric Karros**	**1342**
15	Norm Cash	1317
16	Jake Beckley	1316
17	Joe Judge	1301
	John Olerud	**1301**
19	Will Clark	1294
20	Ed Konetchy	1292
21	Gil Hodges	1281
22	Stuffy McInnis	1238
23	Jimmie Foxx	1222
	Willie McCovey	1222
25	Charlie Grimm	1214

Second Base

1	Eddie Collins	7630
2	Charlie Gehringer	7068
3	Joe Morgan	6967
4	Bid McPhee	6919
5	Bill Mazeroski	6685
6	Lou Whitaker	6653
7	**Roberto Alomar**	**6439**
8	Nellie Fox	6373
9	Ryne Sandberg	6363
10	Willie Randolph	6336
11	Nap Lajoie	6262
12	Frank White	6250
13	Frankie Frisch	6026
14	Bobby Doerr	5710
15	Billy Herman	5681
16	Bobby Grich	5381
17	Red Schoendienst	5243
18	Rogers Hornsby	5166
19	Hughie Critz	5138
20	Johnny Evers	5124
21	Fred Pfeffer	5108
22	Del Pratt	5075
23	Steve Sax	4805
24	Kid Gleason	4776
25	Joe Gordon	4706

Shortstop

1	Ozzie Smith	8375
2	Luis Aparicio	8016
3	Bill Dahlen	7505
4	Rabbit Maranville	7354
5	Luke Appling	7218
6	Tommy Corcoran	7110
7	Cal Ripken	6977
8	Larry Bowa	6857
9	Dave Concepcion	6594
10	Dave Bancroft	6561
11	Roger Peckinpaugh	6337
12	Bobby Wallace	6303
13	Don Kessinger	6212
14	Roy McMillan	6191
15	Alan Trammell	6172
16	Germany Smith	6166
17	Bert Campaneris	6160
18	Herman Long	6137
19	Donie Bush	6119
20	Garry Templeton	6041
	Honus Wagner	6041
22	Pee Wee Reese	5891
23	Joe Tinker	5856
24	Joe Cronin	5814
25	Dick Groat	5811

Third Base

1	Brooks Robinson	6205
2	Graig Nettles	5279
3	Mike Schmidt	5045
4	Buddy Bell	4925
5	Ron Santo	4581
6	Gary Gaetti	4531
7	Eddie Mathews	4322
8	Wade Boggs	4246
9	Aurelio Rodriguez	4150
10	Ron Cey	4018
11	Tim Wallach	3992
12	Terry Pendleton	3891
13	Sal Bando	3720
14	Lave Cross	3715
15	Jimmy Collins	3702
16	George Brett	3674
17	Eddie Yost	3659
18	Ken Boyer	3652
19	Arlie Latham	3546
20	**Robin Ventura**	**3541**
21	Pie Traynor	3521
22	Stan Hack	3494
23	Larry Gardner	3408
24	**Matt Williams**	**3376**
25	Willie Kamm	3345

Assists/Game (Infield)

First Base

1	Bill Buckner	0.87
2	Ferris Fain	0.84
3	Keith Hernandez	0.84
4	**Jeff Bagwell**	**0.83**
5	Vic Power	0.83
6	**Eric Karros**	**0.81**
7	**Mark Grace**	**0.78**
8	Eddie Murray	0.78
9	Pete O'Brien	0.78
10	George Sisler	0.78
11	Wally Joyner	0.77
12	Rudy York	0.77
13	Fred Tenney	0.76
14	Mike Hargrove	0.75
15	**Rafael Palmeiro**	**0.75**
16	Dick Stuart	0.75
17	Willie Upshaw	0.74
18	Elbie Fletcher	0.71
19	George McQuinn	0.71
20	**John Olerud**	**0.71**
21	Bill Terry	0.71
22	Frank McCormick	0.70
23	George Stovall	0.70
24	Chris Chambliss	0.69
25	Will Clark	0.69
26	Donn Clendenon	0.69
27	**David Segui**	**0.69**
28	Eddie Waitkus	0.69

Second Base

1	Hughie Critz	3.54
2	Frankie Frisch	3.42
3	Ski Melillo	3.38
4	Lou Bierbauer	3.35
5	Glenn Hubbard	3.34
6	Fred Pfeffer	3.33
7	Rogers Hornsby	3.31
8	Bid McPhee	3.25
9	Tony Cuccinello	3.23
10	Cupid Childs	3.22
11	Charlie Gehringer	3.21
12	Bill Mazeroski	3.20
13	Ryne Sandberg	3.19
14	Bobby Lowe	3.17
15	Max Bishop	3.14
16	Billy Herman	3.14
17	Hobe Ferris	3.10
18	Joe Gordon	3.10
19	Manny Trillo	3.10
20	Bobby Doerr	3.09
21	Nap Lajoie	3.08
22	Bucky Harris	3.07
23	Miller Huggins	3.07
24	Julio Cruz	3.06
25	Tony Lazzeri	3.06

Shortstop

1	Germany Smith	3.70
2	Art Fletcher	3.55
3	Bill Dahlen	3.52
4	Dave Bancroft	3.51
5	Bones Ely	3.50
6	Travis Jackson	3.50
7	George Davis	3.49
8	Jack Glasscock	3.46
9	Bobby Wallace	3.46
10	Tommy Corcoran	3.43
11	Herman Long	3.42
12	Rabbit Maranville	3.42
13	Freddy Parent	3.36
14	Joe Tinker	3.36
15	Ozzie Smith	3.34
16	Dick Bartell	3.33
17	Glenn Wright	3.31
18	Donie Bush	3.28
19	Luke Appling	3.26
20	Mickey Doolan	3.26
21	Rick Burleson	3.25
22	George McBride	3.25
23	Robin Yount	3.25
24	Joe Sewell	3.24
25	Billy Jurges	3.23
26	Doc Lavan	3.23
27	Eddie Miller	3.23

Third Base

1	Mike Schmidt	2.29
2	Billy Shindle	2.27
3	Buddy Bell	2.26
4	Arlie Latham	2.26
5	Clete Boyer	2.24
6	Jimmy Collins	2.20
7	Graig Nettles	2.19
8	George Brett	2.18
9	Terry Pendleton	2.18
10	Darrell Evans	2.17
11	Brooks Robinson	2.17
12	Lave Cross	2.16
13	Ron Santo	2.16
14	Doug Rader	2.15
15	Billy Nash	2.14
16	Bill Bradley	2.12
17	Billy Werber	2.12
18	Harlond Clift	2.11
19	Jerry Denny	2.11
20	Frank Malzone	2.11
21	Aurelio Rodriguez	2.10
22	Doug DeCinces	2.09
23	Art Devlin	2.09
24	Ken McMullen	2.08
25	Jimmy Austin	2.07

Double Plays

First Base

1	Mickey Vernon	2044
2	Eddie Murray	2033
3	**Fred McGriff**	**1770**
4	Joe Kuhel	1769
5	Charlie Grimm	1733
6	Chris Chambliss	1687
7	Keith Hernandez	1654
8	**Andres Galarraga**	**1646**
9	Gil Hodges	1614
10	Wally Joyner	1611

Second Base

1	Bill Mazeroski	1706
2	Nellie Fox	1619
3	Willie Randolph	1547
4	Lou Whitaker	1527
5	Bobby Doerr	1507
6	Joe Morgan	1505
7	Charlie Gehringer	1444
8	**Roberto Alomar**	**1383**
9	Frank White	1382
10	Red Schoendienst	1368

Shortstop

1	Ozzie Smith	1590
2	Cal Ripken	1565
3	Luis Aparicio	1553
4	Luke Appling	1424
5	**Omar Vizquel**	**1308**
6	Alan Trammell	1307
7	Roy McMillan	1304
8	Dave Concepcion	1290
9	Larry Bowa	1265
10	Pee Wee Reese	1246

Third Base

1	Brooks Robinson	618
2	Graig Nettles	470
3	Gary Gaetti	460
4	Mike Schmidt	450
5	Buddy Bell	430
6	Wade Boggs	423
7	Aurelio Rodriguez	408
8	Ron Santo	395
9	Eddie Mathews	369
10	Ken Boyer	355

Outfield

1	Tris Speaker	139
2	Ty Cobb	107
3	Max Carey	86
4	Tom Brown	85
5	Harry Hooper	81
6	Jimmy Sheckard	80
7	Mike Griffin	75
8	Dummy Hoy	72
9	Jimmy Ryan	71
10	Fielder Jones	70
11	Patsy Donovan	69
12	Sam Rice	67
13	George Van Haltren	64
14	Jesse Burkett	62
15	Sam Thompson	61
16	Willie Keeler	60
	Willie Mays	60
	Tommy McCarthy	60
	Mel Ott	60
20	Sam Crawford	59

Catcher

1	Ray Schalk	226
2	Steve O'Neill	193
3	Yogi Berra	175
4	Gabby Hartnett	163
5	Tony Pena	156
6	Bob Boone	154
7	Jimmie Wilson	153
8	Gary Carter	149
	Wally Schang	149
10	Carlton Fisk	147

Pitcher

1	Phil Niekro	83
2	Warren Spahn	82
3	Freddie Fitzsimmons	79
4	Bob Lemon	78
5	Bucky Walters	76
6	Burleigh Grimes	74
7	Walter Johnson	72
8	**Greg Maddux**	**71**
9	Tommy John	69
10	Jim Kaat	65

Putouts (Outfield)

Outfield

1	Willie Mays	7095
2	Tris Speaker	6788
3	**Rickey Henderson**	**6468**
4	Max Carey	6363
5	Ty Cobb	6361
6	Richie Ashburn	6089
7	Hank Aaron	5539
8	Willie Davis	5449
9	Doc Cramer	5412
10	Brett Butler	5296
11	Andre Dawson	5158
12	Vada Pinson	5097
13	Willie Wilson	5060
14	**Barry Bonds**	**5055**
15	Al Kaline	5035
16	Zack Wheat	4996
17	Chet Lemon	4993
18	Al Simmons	4988
19	Dave Winfield	4975
20	Amos Otis	4936
21	Paul Waner	4872
22	Lloyd Waner	4860
23	Fred Clarke	4795
24	Goose Goslin	4792
25	Sam Rice	4774
26	Devon White	4739
27	**Steve Finley**	**4706**
28	Roberto Clemente	4696
29	Fred Lynn	4556
30	Edd Roush	4537
31	Joe DiMaggio	4516
32	Tony Gwynn	4512
33	Mel Ott	4511
34	**Marquis Grissom**	**4470**
35	Garry Maddox	4449
36	Babe Ruth	4444
37	Mickey Mantle	4438
38	**Ken Griffey**	**4396**
39	Lou Brock	4394
40	Kirby Puckett	4392
41	Jose Cruz	4391
42	Dwight Evans	4371
43	Paul Blair	4343
44	Sam West	4300
45	Willie McGee	4260
46	Jimmy Sheckard	4203
47	Tim Raines	4201
48	Cy Williams	4180
49	Ted Williams	4158
50	Cesar Cedeno	4131
	Sammy Sosa	**4131**
52	**Bernie Williams**	**4116**
53	Duke Snider	4099
54	Clyde Milan	4095
55	Reggie Jackson	4062
56	Dale Murphy	4053
57	Kiki Cuyler	4034
58	Curt Flood	4021
59	Bob Johnson	4003
60	Wally Moses	4000
61	Joe Medwick	3994
62	Harry Hooper	3981
63	Frank Robinson	3978
64	Earl Averill	3968
65	Dummy Hoy	3964
	Kenny Lofton	**3964**
67	Jesse Burkett	3961
68	Carl Yastrzemski	3941
69	Enos Slaughter	3925
70	George Burns	3918
71	Jimmy Wynn	3912
72	Bill Bruton	3905
73	Dom DiMaggio	3859
74	Jim Piersall	3851
75	Heinie Manush	3841
76	Rick Manning	3831
77	George Foster	3809
78	Sherry Magee	3800
79	Dave Parker	3791
80	Bill Virdon	3777
81	Lloyd Moseby	3765
82	Bobby Veach	3754
83	George Hendrick	3751
84	Dode Paskert	3734
85	Stan Musial	3730
86	Paul O'Neill	3724
87	Brady Anderson	3713
88	Jimmy Ryan	3701
89	Reggie Smith	3676
90	Joe Carter	3669
91	Dusty Baker	3663
92	Gee Walker	3661
93	Bobby Bonds	3659
94	Tom Brown	3629
95	Sam Crawford	3626
96	Del Ennis	3621
97	Larry Doby	3616
98	Fielder Jones	3580
99	Sam Chapman	3579
	Dwayne Murphy	3579

Putouts/Game (Outfield)

Outfield

1	Taylor Douthit	3.01
2	Richie Ashburn	2.90
3	Dom DiMaggio	2.82
4	Dwayne Murphy	2.82
5	Mike Kreevich	2.81
6	Sam Chapman	2.74
7	Sam West	2.74
8	Fred Schulte	2.70
9	Lloyd Waner	2.68
10	**Mike Cameron**	**2.67**
11	Billy North	2.65
12	Garry Maddox	2.64
13	Max Carey	2.63
14	Joe DiMaggio	2.63
15	Vince DiMaggio	2.63
16	**Andruw Jones**	**2.63**
17	Terry Moore	2.63
18	Robin Yount	2.63
19	Gary Pettis	2.62
20	Chet Lemon	2.60
21	Kirby Puckett	2.59
22	Omar Moreno	2.58
23	Wally Berger	2.57
24	Jim Busby	2.57
25	Amos Otis	2.57
26	Lenny Dykstra	2.55
27	Rick Manning	2.55
28	Ruppert Jones	2.54
29	Devon White	2.54
30	**Bernie Williams**	**2.54**
31	Doc Cramer	2.53
32	Baby Doll Jacobson	2.53
33	Lance Johnson	2.53
34	Larry Doby	2.52
35	Mickey Rivers	2.52
36	Tris Speaker	2.52
37	Bill Bruton	2.51
38	**Jim Edmonds**	**2.51**
39	Gorman Thomas	2.51
40	Earl Averill	2.50
41	Fred Lynn	2.50
42	Willie Mays	2.50
43	Willie Wilson	2.50
44	Earle Combs	2.49
45	Lloyd Moseby	2.47
46	Brett Butler	2.46
47	Hy Myers	2.46
48	Edd Roush	2.46
49	Ethan Allen	2.45
50	**Kenny Lofton**	**2.45**
51	Bill Virdon	2.45
52	Mule Haas	2.44
53	**Ken Griffey**	**2.43**
54	Ron LeFlore	2.43
55	Jimmy McAleer	2.43
56	Mookie Wilson	2.43
57	Cesar Cedeno	2.41
58	Dave Henderson	2.41
59	Barney McCosky	2.41
60	Al Bumbry	2.40
61	Ira Flagstead	2.40
62	Mike Griffin	2.40
63	Jim Piersall	2.39
64	Tony Armas	2.37
65	George Case	2.37
66	Curt Flood	2.37
67	Tommy Leach	2.37
68	Bobby Thomson	2.37
69	**Johnny Damon**	**2.36**
70	Brian McRae	2.36
71	Willie Davis	2.35
72	**Marquis Grissom**	**2.35**
73	Ben Chapman	2.33
74	Hoot Evers	2.33
75	Al Simmons	2.33
76	Paul Blair	2.32
77	Mike Devereaux	2.32
78	Jim Landis	2.32
79	Tommy Holmes	2.30
80	Roy Thomas	2.30
81	Cy Williams	2.30
82	**Rickey Henderson**	**2.29**
83	Dode Paskert	2.29
84	Carl Reynolds	2.29
85	**Steve Finley**	**2.28**
86	Ray Lankford	2.28
87	Al Oliver	2.28
88	Ken Williams	2.28
89	**Garret Anderson**	**2.27**
90	Cliff Heathcote	2.27
91	Bob Johnson	2.27
92	Bill Tuttle	2.27
93	Gee Walker	2.27
94	Roberto Kelly	2.26
95	Carson Bigbee	2.24
96	Kiki Cuyler	2.24
97	Rick Miller	2.24
98	Wally Moses	2.24
99	Hack Wilson	2.24
100	5 players tied	2.23

Fielding Runs (by position)

First Base

Rank	Player	Runs
1	Keith Hernandez	133
2	Fred Tenney	130
3	Vic Power	124
4	Bill Buckner	114
5	**Jeff Bagwell**	**95**
6	George Sisler	93
7	**Todd Helton**	**80**
8	Darrell Evans	75
9	Sid Bream	73
	Rafael Palmeiro	**73**

Second Base

Rank	Player	Runs
1	Bill Mazeroski	353
2	Nap Lajoie	341
3	Bid McPhee	283
4	Fred Pfeffer	240
5	Glenn Hubbard	213
6	Bobby Doerr	175
7	Manny Trillo	170
8	Bobby Knoop	158
9	Ski Melillo	149
10	Bobby Grich	139

Shortstop

Rank	Player	Runs
1	Ozzie Smith	279
2	Bill Dahlen	273
3	Jack Glasscock	256
4	George Davis	182
5	Joe Tinker	181
6	Dave Bancroft	177
7	George McBride	171
8	Art Fletcher	170
9	Tim Foli	159
10	Dick Bartell	154
	Rey Sanchez	**154**

Third Base

Rank	Player	Runs
1	Mike Schmidt	236
2	Buddy Bell	227
3	Clete Boyer	185
4	Ron Santo	168
5	Terry Pendleton	160
6	Lave Cross	136
7	Tim Wallach	134
8	Darrell Evans	132
9	Aurelio Rodriguez	129
10	Jimmy Collins	123
	Graig Nettles	123

Outfield

Rank	Player	Runs
1	Tris Speaker	154
2	Max Carey	127
3	Richie Ashburn	120
4	Jesse Barfield	101
	Roberto Clemente	101
6	Jimmy Sheckard	100
7	Jim Fogarty	97
8	Johnny Callison	86
9	**Rickey Henderson**	**84**
10	Bob Johnson	83
11	Ed Delahanty	82
12	Sam West	80
13	Johnny Mostil	79
14	**Andruw Jones**	**77**
15	Curt Welch	74
16	Orator Shafer	70
17	Harry Hooper	69
	Carl Yastrzemski	69
19	Kip Selbach	68
20	Al Kaline	67
	Mark Kotsay	**67**

Catcher

Rank	Player	Runs
1	Tony Pena	180
2	**Ivan Rodriguez**	**165**
3	Chief Zimmer	164
4	Gary Carter	145
5	Pop Snyder	144
6	Lou Criger	137
7	Johnny Bench	125
8	Lance Parrish	123
9	Ray Schalk	122
10	Jim Sundberg	119

Pitcher

Rank	Player	Runs
1	**Greg Maddux**	**93**
2	Ed Walsh	80
3	Carl Mays	72
4	Christy Mathewson	65
5	Tommy John	62
6	Freddie Fitzsimmons	60
7	Bob Lemon	58
8	Burleigh Grimes	57
9	**Kenny Rogers**	**53**
10	Harry Gumbert	50

Fielding Wins

Rank	Player	Wins
1	Bill Mazeroski	36.4
2	Nap Lajoie	34.2
3	Bill Dahlen	29.2
4	Ozzie Smith	29.1
5	Bid McPhee	24.5
6	Mike Schmidt	24.4
7	Buddy Bell	23.4
8	Glenn Hubbard	22.1
9	George Davis	21.9
10	Jack Glasscock	21.8
11	Fred Pfeffer	21.4
12	Darrell Evans	21.2
13	Clete Boyer	20.8
14	Bobby Wallace	20.2
15	Joe Tinker	19.0
16	Tony Pena	18.2
17	George McBride	18.2
18	Dave Bancroft	18.1
19	Art Fletcher	18.0
20	Ron Santo	17.6
21	Manny Trillo	17.5
22	Bobby Doerr	17.4
23	Tim Foli	17.4
24	Mickey Doolan	17.2
25	**Rey Sanchez**	**17.1**
26	Bobby Knoop	16.9
27	Dick Bartell	16.8
28	Terry Pendleton	16.3
29	Lee Tannehill	16.1
30	**Neifi Perez**	**15.8**
31	**Ivan Rodriguez**	**15.6**
32	Tris Speaker	15.5
33	Gene Alley	14.9
34	Frank White	14.9
35	Gary Carter	14.6
36	Lave Cross	14.5
37	Ski Melillo	14.2
38	Chief Zimmer	14.2
39	Aurelio Rodriguez	14.1
40	Keith Hernandez	13.8
41	Tim Wallach	13.7
42	Lou Criger	13.5
43	Lou Boudreau	13.4
44	Red Schoendienst	13.4
45	Willie Randolph	13.3
46	Fred Tenney	13.3
47	Frankie Frisch	13.1
48	Joe Gerhardt	13.0
49	Max Carey	12.9
50	Pop Snyder	12.9
51	Vic Power	12.9
52	Billy Jurges	12.8
53	Rabbit Maranville	12.8
54	Graig Nettles	12.8
55	Rick Burleson	12.8
56	Bobby Grich	12.8
57	Hughie Jennings	12.8
58	Bobby Wine	12.7
59	Danny Richardson	12.4
60	Ray Schalk	12.3
61	Fred Dunlap	12.3
62	Jim Sundberg	12.2
63	Harold Reynolds	12.1
64	Hughie Critz	12.1
65	Mark Belanger	12.0
66	Jim Hegan	11.9
67	Richie Ashburn	11.9
68	Lance Parrish	11.8
69	Phil Rizzuto	11.7
70	Jimmy Collins	11.7
71	Germany Smith	11.7
72	**Omar Vizquel**	**11.6**
73	Bill Holbert	11.6
74	Bill Buckner	11.5
75	Gary Gaetti	11.2
76	Everett Scott	11.1
77	Lou Bierbauer	11.0
78	John Ward	10.8
79	Mike Scioscia	10.5
80	Julio Cruz	10.4
81	Roberto Clemente	10.3
82	Gabby Hartnett	10.3
83	Hobe Ferris	10.2
84	Ryne Sandberg	10.2
85	Mike Benjamin	10.0
86	Jesse Barfield	10.0
87	Brooks Robinson	10.0
88	Jody Reed	9.9
89	Roger Peckinpaugh	9.8
90	Don Kessinger	9.8
91	Ron Hansen	9.8
92	Carlton Fisk	9.7
93	Del Pratt	9.6
94	Rennie Stennett	9.6
95	Johnny Logan	9.5
96	Burgess Whitehead	9.4
97	Jerry Denny	9.4
98	**Jeff Bagwell**	**9.3**
99	George Sisler	9.1
100	Buddy Kerr	9.0

Fielding Wins

Rank	Player	Wins
101	Hardy Richardson	9.0
102	Buck Ewing	9.0
103	Charlie Bennett	9.0
104	Miller Huggins	8.9
105	Joe Sewell	8.9
106	Jimmy Sheckard	8.8
107	Johnny Callison	8.8
108	Eddie Miller	8.7
109	Travis Jackson	8.7
110	Frank Malzone	8.6
111	Bill Killefer	8.6
112	Art Devlin	8.6
113	Buck Herzog	8.6
114	Gil McDougald	8.6
115	**Matt Williams**	**8.6**
116	Honus Wagner	8.5
117	Dave Cash	8.5
118	Ted Sizemore	8.5
119	Davy Force	8.4
120	**Robin Ventura**	**8.4**
121	Thurman Munson	8.4
122	Johnny Bench	8.3
123	Steve Yeager	8.3
124	Billy Shindle	8.2
125	**Rickey Henderson**	**8.2**
126	Wade Boggs	8.1
127	Cupid Childs	8.1
128	Dal Maxvill	8.1
129	Carl Yastrzemski	8.0
130	Johnny Edwards	8.0
131	Hal Lanier	8.0
132	**Brad Ausmus**	**8.0**
133	Pinky May	8.0
134	Rick Dempsey	7.9
135	Bill Bergen	7.9
136	Rollie Hemsley	7.8
137	Charlie O'Brien	7.8
138	Scott Fletcher	7.8
139	John Valentin	7.8
140	**Javy Lopez**	**7.7**
141	Tommy Corcoran	7.7
142	Jerry Grote	7.6
143	John Farrell	7.6
144	**Todd Helton**	**7.5**
145	Bob Johnson	7.5
146	Rocky Bridges	7.5
147	**Damian Miller**	**7.5**
148	Babe Pinelli	7.5
149	**Andruw Jones**	**7.5**
150	Billy Rogell	7.4
151	Sid Bream	7.4
152	Doug Rader	7.4
153	**Orlando Cabrera**	**7.4**
154	Yogi Berra	7.4
155	Luis Aparicio	7.4
156	Johnny Mostil	7.3
157	Sam West	7.3
158	**Scott Rolen**	**7.3**
159	Willie Kamm	7.3
160	Ernie Whitt	7.2
161	Billy Clingman	7.2
162	Jim Fogarty	7.2
163	Roy McMillan	7.2
164	Wid Conroy	7.2
165	Harlond Clift	7.1
166	Tommy Leach	7.1
167	Jerry Priddy	7.0
168	Nellie Fox	7.0
169	Bill Sweeney	7.0
170	Harry Hooper	6.9
171	Al Lopez	6.9
172	**Rafael Palmeiro**	**6.9**
173	Al Kaline	6.9
174	Bill Terry	6.9
175	Muddy Ruel	6.9
176	Dick Groat	6.8
177	**Mike Bordick**	**6.8**
178	Bob Boone	6.8
179	Freddie Maguire	6.7
180	Alvaro Espinoza	6.7
181	Marty Marion	6.7
182	Jerry Royster	6.6
183	Eddie Murray	6.5
184	Pinky Whitney	6.5
185	**Eric Karros**	**6.5**
186	Luke Appling	6.5
187	Ken Boyer	6.5
188	Dave Shean	6.5
189	**Pokey Reese**	**6.4**
190	Charlie Ganzel	6.4
191	**Mark Kotsay**	**6.4**
192	Ed Konetchy	6.4
193	Garry Templeton	6.4
194	Horace Clarke	6.4
195	Curt Welch	6.4
196	**Jose Valentin**	**6.3**
197	Del Crandall	6.3
198	Bob Allen	6.3
199	Kip Selbach	6.3
200	Norm Cash	6.3

Batter-Fielder Wins by era

1988-2003

Rank	Player	Wins
1	**Barry Bonds**	**112.6**
2	**Rickey Henderson**	**72.0**
3	**Jeff Bagwell**	**53.6**
4	Wade Boggs	51.1
5	**Frank Thomas**	**46.0**
6	**Edgar Martinez**	**44.5**
7	**Ken Griffey**	**44.1**
	Cal Ripken	44.1
9	**Barry Larkin**	**42.9**
10	**Alex Rodriguez**	**42.5**
11	**Mike Piazza**	**42.0**
12	Tony Gwynn	38.8
13	Tim Raines	38.7
14	**Gary Sheffield**	**38.2**
15	**Roberto Alomar**	**37.8**
16	Paul Molitor	37.0
17	Ryne Sandberg	36.7
18	Mark McGwire	35.7
19	**Ivan Rodriguez**	**34.7**
20	**Rafael Palmeiro**	**34.4**
21	**Craig Biggio**	**33.8**
22	**Jim Thome**	**31.7**
23	**Manny Ramirez**	**30.5**
24	**Larry Walker**	**30.1**
25	Albert Belle	29.8

1973-1987

Rank	Player	Wins
1	Mike Schmidt	78.6
2	Joe Morgan	67.4
3	Bobby Grich	51.6
4	Ozzie Smith	45.7
5	George Brett	43.4
6	Johnny Bench	42.5
7	Darrell Evans	41.2
	Robin Yount	41.2
9	Rod Carew	40.3
10	Reggie Jackson	39.5
11	Gary Carter	39.2
12	Carlton Fisk	38.8
13	Willie Randolph	37.1
14	Lou Whitaker	35.6
15	Eddie Murray	35.4
16	Keith Hernandez	34.8
17	Reggie Smith	31.9
18	Alan Trammell	31.7
19	Dave Winfield	30.5
20	Jack Clark	29.6
21	Buddy Bell	28.7
22	Bobby Bonds	27.2
23	Gene Tenace	26.3
24	Thurman Munson	25.4
25	Dwight Evans	24.8

1961-1972

Rank	Player	Wins
1	Willie Mays	84.6
2	Hank Aaron	81.3
3	Frank Robinson	64.3
4	Ron Santo	45.3
5	Al Kaline	43.1
6	Carl Yastrzemski	42.3
7	Dick Allen	39.2
8	Willie McCovey	39.0
9	Roberto Clemente	34.0
	Bill Mazeroski	34.0
11	Harmon Killebrew	32.6
12	Willie Stargell	30.8
13	Norm Cash	30.5
14	Jimmy Wynn	30.0
15	Ernie Banks	27.2
16	Jim Fregosi	25.5
17	Billy Williams	23.8
18	Rocky Colavito	22.7
19	Frank Howard	22.6
20	Joe Torre	22.3
21	Tony Oliva	20.3
22	Ken Boyer	19.7
23	Orlando Cepeda	19.1
24	Gene Alley	18.8
25	Boog Powell	18.7

1943-1960

Rank	Player	Wins
1	Ted Williams	87.0
2	Stan Musial	76.0
3	Mickey Mantle	72.9
4	Eddie Mathews	52.1
5	Lou Boudreau	43.6
6	Bobby Doerr	40.3
7	Yogi Berra	38.6
8	Jackie Robinson	34.3
9	Joe Gordon	28.8
10	Ralph Kiner	24.2
11	Roy Campanella	24.1
12	Duke Snider	23.0
13	Richie Ashburn	22.6
14	Gil McDougald	22.2
15	Charlie Keller	22.1
16	Bob Elliott	21.4
17	Minnie Minoso	21.0
18	Vern Stephens	20.7
19	Eddie Stanky	20.1
20	Roy Cullenbine	18.8
	Ferris Fain	18.8
22	Phil Rizzuto	18.7
23	Larry Doby	18.1
24	Jeff Heath	17.2
	Bill Nicholson	17.2

Batter-Fielder Wins by era

1921-1942

Rank	Player	Wins
1	Babe Ruth	112.0
2	Rogers Hornsby	86.0
3	Lou Gehrig	70.9
4	Mel Ott	60.7
5	Jimmie Foxx	58.3
6	Joe DiMaggio	45.8
7	Charlie Gehringer	45.1
8	Gabby Hartnett	44.3
9	Arky Vaughan	43.3
10	Luke Appling	42.4
11	Joe Cronin	39.6
12	Bill Dickey	38.5
13	Johnny Mize	37.7
14	Frankie Frisch	37.3
15	Dave Bancroft	36.2
16	Bob Johnson	35.7
17	Joe Sewell	35.2
18	Mickey Cochrane	34.7
19	Paul Waner	33.8
20	Harry Heilmann	33.2
21	Hank Greenberg	32.6
22	Billy Herman	31.6
23	Stan Hack	29.4
24	Dick Bartell	28.2
25	Bill Terry	26.7

1901-1920

Rank	Player	Wins
1	Nap Lajoie	95.1
2	Ty Cobb	85.5
3	Tris Speaker	82.1
	Honus Wagner	82.1
5	Eddie Collins	72.5
6	Bill Dahlen	48.5
7	Joe Jackson	38.3
8	Bobby Wallace	35.4
9	Frank Baker	33.7
10	Heinie Groh	30.4
11	Elmer Flick	29.7
12	Sam Crawford	29.3
13	Fred Clarke	27.7
14	Art Fletcher	27.2
15	Sherry Magee	26.2
16	Zack Wheat	24.1
17	Jimmy Collins	23.0
	Fred Tenney	23.0
19	Roy Thomas	22.7
20	Frank Chance	22.6
21	Roger Bresnahan	22.5
	Del Pratt	22.5
23	Miller Huggins	22.3
24	Ed Konetchy	21.2
25	Jimmy Sheckard	20.7

1893-1900

Rank	Player	Wins
1	George Davis	50.7
2	Ed Delahanty	42.6
3	Jesse Burkett	31.1
4	Cupid Childs	30.5
5	Billy Hamilton	27.3
6	Hughie Jennings	26.8
7	Jake Beckley	23.0
8	Chief Zimmer	20.7
9	Joe Kelley	20.0
10	John McGraw	19.5
11	Bill Joyce	19.3
12	Mike Griffin	18.0
13	Lave Cross	16.4
14	Mike Tiernan	14.4
15	Kip Selbach	13.5
16	Jack Clements	12.9
17	Jimmy Ryan	12.6
18	Billy Nash	11.3
19	Ed McFarland	10.3
20	Heinie Peitz	10.1
	George Van Haltren	10.1
22	Jack Crooks	9.9
23	Duke Farrell	9.8
24	Bill Lange	7.8
25	Mike Grady	7.7

1876-1892

Rank	Player	Wins
1	Roger Connor	43.4
2	Dan Brouthers	43.2
3	Bid McPhee	38.3
4	Jack Glasscock	36.6
5	Cap Anson	35.4
6	Sam Thompson	29.5
7	Buck Ewing	29.1
8	King Kelly	28.9
9	Fred Dunlap	28.1
10	Pete Browning	27.9
11	Hardy Richardson	26.6
12	Charlie Bennett	23.9
13	Harry Stovey	21.5
14	Fred Pfeffer	20.6
15	Denny Lyons	19.6
16	Charley Jones	19.4
17	Jim O'Rourke	16.0
18	Henry Larkin	15.3
19	Paul Hines	14.5
20	Dave Orr	13.8
21	Jocko Milligan	13.6
22	George Gore	13.5
23	Fred Carroll	12.6
24	Orator Shafer	12.1
25	Deacon White	11.3

Batter-Fielder Wins

1	**Barry Bonds**	**112.6**
2	Babe Ruth	112.0
3	Nap Lajoie	95.1
4	Ted Williams	87.0
5	Rogers Hornsby	86.0
6	Ty Cobb	85.5
7	Willie Mays	84.6
8	Tris Speaker	82.1
	Honus Wagner	82.1
10	Hank Aaron	81.3
11	Mike Schmidt	78.6
12	Stan Musial	76.0
13	Mickey Mantle	72.9
14	Eddie Collins	72.5
15	**Rickey Henderson**	**72.0**
16	Lou Gehrig	70.9
17	Joe Morgan	67.4
18	Frank Robinson	64.3
19	Mel Ott	60.7
20	Jimmie Foxx	58.3
21	**Jeff Bagwell**	**53.6**
22	Eddie Mathews	52.1
23	Bobby Grich	51.6
24	Wade Boggs	51.1
25	George Davis	50.7
26	Bill Dahlen	48.5
27	**Frank Thomas**	**46.0**
28	Joe DiMaggio	45.8
29	Ozzie Smith	45.7
30	Ron Santo	45.3
31	Charlie Gehringer	45.1
32	**Edgar Martinez**	**44.5**
33	Gabby Hartnett	44.3
34	**Ken Griffey**	**44.1**
	Cal Ripken	44.1
36	Lou Boudreau	43.6
37	George Brett	43.4
	Roger Connor	43.4
39	Arky Vaughan	43.3
40	Dan Brouthers	43.2
41	Al Kaline	43.1
42	**Barry Larkin**	**42.9**
43	Ed Delahanty	42.6
44	Johnny Bench	42.5
	Alex Rodriguez	**42.5**
46	Luke Appling	42.4
47	Carl Yastrzemski	42.3
48	**Mike Piazza**	**42.0**
49	Darrell Evans	41.2
	Robin Yount	41.2
51	Rod Carew	40.3
	Bobby Doerr	40.3
53	Joe Cronin	39.6
54	Reggie Jackson	39.5
55	Dick Allen	39.2
	Gary Carter	39.2
57	Willie McCovey	39.0
58	Carlton Fisk	38.8
	Tony Gwynn	38.8
60	Tim Raines	38.7
61	Yogi Berra	38.6
62	Bill Dickey	38.5
63	Joe Jackson	38.3
	Bid McPhee	38.3
65	**Gary Sheffield**	**38.2**
66	**Roberto Alomar**	**37.8**
67	Johnny Mize	37.7
68	Frankie Frisch	37.3
69	Willie Randolph	37.1
70	Paul Molitor	37.0
71	Ryne Sandberg	36.7
72	Jack Glasscock	36.6
73	Dave Bancroft	36.2
74	Bob Johnson	35.7
	Mark McGwire	35.7
76	Lou Whitaker	35.6
77	Cap Anson	35.4
	Eddie Murray	35.4
	Bobby Wallace	35.4
80	Joe Sewell	35.2
81	Keith Hernandez	34.8
82	Mickey Cochrane	34.7
	Ivan Rodriguez	**34.7**
84	**Rafael Palmeiro**	**34.4**
85	Jackie Robinson	34.3
86	Roberto Clemente	34.0
	Bill Mazeroski	34.0
88	**Craig Biggio**	**33.8**
	Paul Waner	33.8
90	Frank Baker	33.7
91	Harry Heilmann	33.2
92	Hank Greenberg	32.6
	Harmon Killebrew	32.6
94	Reggie Smith	31.9
95	**Jim Thome**	**31.7**
	Alan Trammell	31.7
97	Billy Herman	31.6
98	Jesse Burkett	31.1
99	Willie Stargell	30.8
100	Norm Cash	30.5

Batter-Fielder Wins

	Cupid Childs	30.5
	Manny Ramirez	**30.5**
	Dave Winfield	30.5
104	Heinie Groh	30.4
105	**Larry Walker**	**30.1**
106	Jimmy Wynn	30.0
107	Albert Belle	29.8
108	Elmer Flick	29.7
109	Jack Clark	29.6
110	Sam Thompson	29.5
111	Stan Hack	29.4
112	Sam Crawford	29.3
113	Buck Ewing	29.1
114	King Kelly	28.9
115	Joe Gordon	28.8
116	Buddy Bell	28.7
	Sammy Sosa	**28.7**
118	**Jeff Kent**	**28.5**
119	**Jim Edmonds**	**28.4**
120	Dick Bartell	28.2
121	Fred Dunlap	28.1
122	Pete Browning	27.9
123	Fred Clarke	27.7
124	Billy Hamilton	27.3
125	Ernie Banks	27.2
	Bobby Bonds	27.2
	Art Fletcher	27.2
128	Hughie Jennings	26.8
	Bernie Williams	**26.8**
130	Bill Terry	26.7
131	Hardy Richardson	26.6
132	Harlond Clift	26.3
	Gene Tenace	26.3
134	Sherry Magee	26.2
135	**Scott Rolen**	**26.1**
136	**Robin Ventura**	**25.8**
137	Joe Medwick	25.6
138	Jim Fregosi	25.5
139	**Nomar Garciaparra**	**25.4**
	Thurman Munson	25.4
141	Will Clark	24.8
	Dwight Evans	24.8
	Brian Giles	**24.8**
	George Sisler	24.8
145	Jack Fournier	24.4
146	**John Olerud**	**24.3**
147	Ralph Kiner	24.2
148	Roy Campanella	24.1
	Zack Wheat	24.1
150	Charlie Bennett	23.9
	Pete Rose	23.9
152	Billy Williams	23.8
153	Kirby Puckett	23.7
154	Goose Goslin	23.1
	Darryl Strawberry	23.1
156	Jake Beckley	23.0
	Jose Canseco	23.0
	Jimmy Collins	23.0
	Lenny Dykstra	23.0
	Duke Snider	23.0
	Rusty Staub	23.0
	Fred Tenney	23.0
163	**Fred McGriff**	**22.9**
164	Rocky Colavito	22.7
	Roy Thomas	22.7
166	Richie Ashburn	22.6
	Frank Chance	22.6
	Frank Howard	22.6
169	Roger Bresnahan	22.5
	Del Pratt	22.5
	Al Simmons	22.5
172	Cesar Cedeno	22.3
	Miller Huggins	22.3
	Tim Salmon	**22.3**
	Joe Torre	22.3
176	Gil McDougald	22.2
	Lance Parrish	22.2
178	Charlie Keller	22.1
179	Travis Jackson	22.0
180	Ted Simmons	21.7
181	Ken Caminiti	21.6
	Graig Nettles	21.6
183	**Jason Giambi**	**21.5**
	Harry Stovey	21.5
185	Bob Elliott	21.4
	Tony Fernandez	21.4
187	Ron Cey	21.3
188	Jose Cruz	21.2
	Ed Konetchy	21.2
190	**Vladimir Guerrero**	**21.1**
	Chuck Klein	21.1
192	Wally Berger	21.0
	Minnie Minoso	21.0
194	**Chipper Jones**	**20.9**
	Darrell Porter	20.9
196	Jimmy Sheckard	20.7
	Vern Stephens	20.7
	Chief Zimmer	20.7
199	Ernie Lombardi	20.6
	Kevin Mitchell	20.6

Batter-Fielder Wins

	Fred Pfeffer	20.6
202	Wally Schang	20.4
	Ken Singleton	20.4
204	Eric Davis	20.3
	Brian Downing	20.3
	Tony Oliva	20.3
207	Glenn Hubbard	20.2
208	**Javy Lopez**	**20.1**
	Eddie Stanky	20.1
210	Art Devlin	20.0
	Luis Gonzalez	**20.0**
	Joe Kelley	20.0
213	Ken Boyer	19.7
	Todd Helton	**19.7**
	Fred Lynn	19.7
	Matt Williams	**19.7**
217	Denny Lyons	19.6
218	John McGraw	19.5
	Joe Tinker	19.5
220	Toby Harrah	19.4
	Charley Jones	19.4
222	Bill Joyce	19.3
	Chet Lemon	19.3
	Tony Phillips	19.3
225	Orlando Cepeda	19.1
226	**Bobby Abreu**	**19.0**
227	Gene Alley	18.8
	Roy Cullenbine	18.8
	Ferris Fain	18.8
	Ray Lankford	18.8
231	Boog Powell	18.7
	Phil Rizzuto	18.7
233	**Juan Gonzalez**	**18.6**
	Jim Rice	18.6
235	George Foster	18.5
236	Gavy Cravath	18.4
	Pie Traynor	18.4
238	Mike Scioscia	18.3
239	Hack Wilson	18.2
240	Rico Carty	18.1
	Andre Dawson	18.1
	Larry Doby	18.1
243	Max Carey	18.0
	Bill Freehan	18.0
	Mike Griffin	18.0
	Pedro Guerrero	18.0
247	Dave Concepcion	17.9
	Bobby Veach	17.9
249	Tony Lazzeri	17.8
250	John Valentin	17.6
251	Babe Herman	17.5
	Ken Williams	17.5
253	Earl Averill	17.3
	Ellis Burks	**17.3**
255	Jeff Heath	17.2
	Chief Meyers	17.2
	Bill Nicholson	17.2
	Roy Smalley	17.2
259	Rick Burleson	17.0
260	Andy Van Slyke	16.9
261	**Kenny Lofton**	**16.7**
262	Ray Chapman	16.6
263	Johnny Logan	16.5
264	Bobby Bonilla	16.4
	Lave Cross	16.4
266	Bobby Knoop	16.3
	Pee Wee Reese	16.3
268	**Jay Bell**	**16.2**
	Al Rosen	16.2
270	Brett Butler	16.1
	Mike Hargrove	16.1
	Ray Schalk	16.1
273	Paul O'Neill	16.0
	Jim O'Rourke	16.0
	Jorge Posada	**16.0**
276	Johnny Evers	15.9
	Don Mattingly	15.9
278	Dwayne Murphy	15.8
	Red Schoendienst	15.8
280	**Andruw Jones**	**15.7**
	Willie Kamm	15.7
282	David Justice	15.5
	Johnny Pesky	15.5
284	Ron Hansen	15.4
	Rico Petrocelli	15.4
	Jimmy Williams	15.4
287	Augie Galan	15.3
	Henry Larkin	15.3
	Roy White	15.3
290	**Julio Franco**	**15.2**
	Jason Kendall	**15.2**
292	**Carlos Delgado**	**15.0**
	Tommy Henrich	15.0
	Willie Keeler	15.0
	Dave Parker	15.0
296	Doug DeCinces	14.9
297	Chili Davis	14.8
	Sid Gordon	14.8
299	Hal McRae	14.7
300	Ben Chapman	14.5

Batter-Fielder Wins

	Paul Hines	14.5
	Enos Slaughter	14.5
303	Nellie Fox	14.4
	Johnny Kling	14.4
	Mike Tiernan	14.4
306	Bert Campaneris	14.3
	Buddy Myer	14.3
	Roger Peckinpaugh	14.3
	Brooks Robinson	14.3
310	Jesse Barfield	14.1
	Davey Johnson	14.1
312	Kid Elberfeld	14.0
313	**Shawn Green**	**13.8**
	Gil Hodges	13.8
	Dave Orr	13.8
316	John Titus	13.7
317	Lonny Frey	13.6
	Jocko Milligan	13.6
319	Kiki Cuyler	13.5
	George Gore	13.5
	Chick Hafey	13.5
	Kip Selbach	13.5
	Red Smith	13.5
324	Dolph Camilli	13.4
325	Harold Baines	13.3
	Rudy York	13.3
327	Hank Gowdy	13.2
	Robby Thompson	13.2
329	Riggs Stephenson	13.1
330	Danny Tartabull	13.0
331	Bob Allison	12.9
	Jack Clements	12.9
	Tom Haller	12.9
	Stan Spence	12.9
335	Greg Luzinski	12.8
	Tony Pena	12.8
337	Earl Battey	12.7
	Don Buford	12.7
	Mark Grace	**12.7**
	Ken Keltner	12.7
341	Fred Carroll	12.6
	Sherm Lollar	12.6
	Lefty O'Doul	12.6
	Jimmy Ryan	12.6
	Roy Sievers	12.6
346	Davey Lopes	12.5
	Lonnie Smith	12.5
348	Luis Aparicio	12.4
	Dan McGann	12.4
	George Stone	12.4
351	**Miguel Tejada**	**12.3**
	Andy Thornton	12.3
	Jose Valentin	**12.3**
	Omar Vizquel	**12.3**
	Bob Watson	12.3
356	Joe Harris	12.2
	Tommy Holmes	12.2
358	**Moises Alou**	**12.1**
	Kirk Gibson	12.1
	John Kruk	12.1
	Orator Shafer	12.1
	Tim Wallach	12.1
363	Jim Gentile	12.0
	Harry Hooper	12.0
	Kent Hrbek	12.0
	Tommy Leach	12.0
	Amos Otis	12.0
368	Lou Criger	11.9
	Gene Woodling	11.9
370	Darren Daulton	11.8
	Oscar Gamble	11.8
372	Tony Cuccinello	11.7
	Joe Ferguson	11.7
	Johnny Mostil	11.7
	Jerry Priddy	11.7
	Jim Sundberg	11.7
	Dixie Walker	11.7
378	Heinie Zimmerman	11.6
379	Earle Combs	11.5
	Kal Daniels	11.5
	Rick Ferrell	11.5
382	Walker Cooper	11.4
383	Chris Hoiles	11.3
	Billy Nash	11.3
	Reggie Sanders	**11.3**
	Deacon White	11.3
387	Don Baylor	11.2
	Lance Berkman	**11.2**
	Ron Hunt	11.2
	Ernie Whitt	11.2
	Ross Youngs	11.2
392	Tommy Burns	11.0
	Dave Cash	11.0
	Mike Donlin	11.0
	Johnny Romano	11.0
	Ed Swartwood	11.0
397	Max Bishop	10.9
	Bill Bradley	10.9
	Eric Chavez	**10.9**
	Jake Daubert	10.9

Batter-Fielder Wins

	Harry Davis	10.9
	Benny Kauff	10.9
	Dick McAuliffe	10.9
	Richie Zisk	10.9
405	Sixto Lezcano	10.8
	Vic Wertz	10.8
407	Smoky Burgess	10.7
	Charlie Hickman	10.7
	Kevin McReynolds	10.7
	Tip O'Neill	10.7
411	Larry Doyle	10.6
	Buck Herzog	10.6
	Maggio Ordonez	**10.6**
	Ed Williamson	10.6
415	Dick Groat	10.5
	Dale Murphy	10.5
	Bob Nieman	10.5
	Snuffy Stirnweiss	10.5
419	Jody Reed	10.4
420	**Cliff Floyd**	**10.3**
	Rabbit Maranville	10.3
	Ed McFarland	10.3
	Tony Perez	10.3
	Johnny Ray	10.3
	Andy Seminick	10.3
	Bump Wills	10.3
	Jimmy Wolf	10.3
428	Wally Joyner	10.2
	Pinky May	10.2
	Bob O'Farrell	10.2
	Cecil Travis	10.2
432	Johnny Callison	10.1
	Dom DiMaggio	10.1
	Heinie Peitz	10.1
	George Van Haltren	10.1
	Quilvio Veras	10.1
437	**Steve Finley**	**10.0**
	Chris Speier	10.0
439	Jack Crooks	9.9
	Solly Hemus	9.9
	Elston Howard	9.9
	Freddie Lindstrom	9.9
	Cy Seymour	9.9
	Maury Wills	9.9
445	**Jeff Cirillo**	**9.8**
	Duke Farrell	9.8
	Ryan Klesko	**9.8**
	Don Money	9.8
449	Larry Hisle	9.7
	Marty McManus	9.7
	Danny Murphy	9.7
	Doug Rader	9.7
	Edd Roush	9.7
	Mickey Tettleton	9.7
	Billy Werber	9.7
456	Sal Bando	9.6
	Clete Boyer	9.6
	Bernie Carbo	9.6
	Roger Maris	9.6
460	Ken Griffey	9.5
	Bill Sweeney	9.5
	Garry Templeton	9.5
463	Donie Bush	9.4
	Topsy Hartsel	9.4
	Charlie Hollocher	9.4
	Cy Williams	9.4
467	Von Hayes	9.3
	Billy Jurges	9.3
	Socks Seybold	9.3
470	Alvin Davis	9.2
	Jackie Jensen	9.2
	Tim McCarver	9.2
	Kevin Seitzer	9.2
	Frank White	9.2
475	**Mike Cameron**	**9.1**
	Richard Hidalgo	**9.1**
	Wes Westrum	9.1
478	Del Crandall	9.0
	Jerry Denny	9.0
	Freddie Patek	9.0
	Art Wilson	9.0
482	Jay Buhner	8.9
	Larry Gardner	8.9
484	**Edgardo Alfonzo**	**8.8**
	Cecil Cooper	8.8
	Bubbles Hargrave	8.8
	Fred Luderus	8.8
	Bobby Murcer	8.8
	Al Oliver	8.8
490	Mark Belanger	8.7
491	Monte Irvin	8.6
	Whitey Kurowski	8.6
	Steve O'Neill	8.6
	Earl Smith	8.6
	Pinky Whitney	8.6
496	Elbie Fletcher	8.5
	George Kell	8.5
	Chuck Knoblauch	8.5
	Manny Trillo	8.5
500	3 players tied	8.4

Wins

1	Cy Young	511
2	Walter Johnson	417
3	Grover Alexander	373
	Christy Mathewson	373
5	Warren Spahn	363
6	Jim Galvin	361
	Kid Nichols	361
8	Tim Keefe	342
9	Steve Carlton	329
10	John Clarkson	328
11	Eddie Plank	326
12	Nolan Ryan	324
	Don Sutton	324
14	Phil Niekro	318
15	Gaylord Perry	314
16	Tom Seaver	311
17	**Roger Clemens**	**310**
18	Charley Radbourn	309
19	Mickey Welch	307
20	Lefty Grove	300
	Early Wynn	300
22	**Greg Maddux**	**289**
23	Tommy John	288
24	Bert Blyleven	287
25	Robin Roberts	286
26	Fergie Jenkins	284
	Tony Mullane	284
28	Jim Kaat	283
29	Red Ruffing	273
30	Burleigh Grimes	270
31	Jim Palmer	268
32	Bob Feller	266
	Eppa Rixey	266
34	Jim McCormick	265
35	Gus Weyhing	264
36	Ted Lyons	260
37	Red Faber	254
	Jack Morris	254
39	Carl Hubbell	253
40	Bob Gibson	251
	Tom Glavine	**251**
42	Vic Willis	249
43	Jack Quinn	247
44	Joe McGinnity	246
	Amos Rusie	246
46	Dennis Martinez	245
	Jack Powell	245
48	Juan Marichal	243
49	Herb Pennock	241
50	Frank Tanana	240
51	Mordecai Brown	239
52	Clark Griffith	237
	Waite Hoyt	237
54	Whitey Ford	236
55	Charlie Buffinton	233
56	**Randy Johnson**	**230**
57	Sam Jones	229
	Luis Tiant	229
	Will White	229
60	George Mullin	228
61	Jim Bunning	224
	Catfish Hunter	224
63	Hooks Dauss	223
	Paul Derringer	223
	Mel Harder	223
66	Jerry Koosman	222
67	Joe Niekro	221
68	Jerry Reuss	220
69	Bob Caruthers	218
	Earl Whitehill	218
71	Freddie Fitzsimmons	217
	Mickey Lolich	217
73	Wilbur Cooper	216
	Charlie Hough	216
75	Stan Coveleski	215
	Jim Perry	215
77	Rick Reuschel	214
78	Chief Bender	212
79	Bobo Newsom	211
	Billy Pierce	211
	Bob Welch	211
82	Jesse Haines	210
83	Vida Blue	209
	Eddie Cicotte	209
	Don Drysdale	209
	Milt Pappas	209
87	Carl Mays	208
88	Bob Lemon	207
	Hal Newhouser	207
90	Orel Hershiser	204
	Al Orth	204
92	Lew Burdette	203
	Silver King	203
	Jack Stivetts	203
95	Rube Marquard	201
	Charlie Root	201
97	Chuck Finley	200
	George Uhle	200
	David Wells	**200**
100	**Mike Mussina**	**199**

Losses

1	Cy Young	316
2	Jim Galvin	308
3	Nolan Ryan	292
4	Walter Johnson	279
5	Phil Niekro	274
6	Gaylord Perry	265
7	Don Sutton	256
8	Jack Powell	254
9	Eppa Rixey	251
10	Bert Blyleven	250
11	Robin Roberts	245
	Warren Spahn	245
13	Steve Carlton	244
	Early Wynn	244
15	Jim Kaat	237
16	Frank Tanana	236
17	Gus Weyhing	232
18	Tommy John	231
19	Bob Friend	230
	Ted Lyons	230
21	Fergie Jenkins	226
22	Tim Keefe	225
	Red Ruffing	225
24	Bobo Newsom	222
25	Tony Mullane	220
26	Jack Quinn	218
27	Sam Jones	217
28	Charlie Hough	216
29	Jim McCormick	214
30	Red Faber	213
31	Paul Derringer	212
	Chick Fraser	212
	Burleigh Grimes	212
34	Mickey Welch	210
35	Jerry Koosman	209
36	Grover Alexander	208
	Kid Nichols	208
38	Tom Seaver	205
	Vic Willis	205
40	Joe Niekro	204
	Jim Whitney	204
42	George Mullin	196
	Adonis Terry	196
44	Claude Osteen	195
45	Eddie Plank	194
	Charley Radbourn	194
47	Dennis Martinez	193
48	Mickey Lolich	191
	Rick Reuschel	191
	Jerry Reuss	191
	Tom Zachary	191
52	Al Orth	189
53	Christy Mathewson	188
54	Mel Harder	186
	Mike Morgan	186
	Jack Morris	186
57	Earl Whitehill	185
58	Jim Bunning	184
	Joe Bush	184
60	Larry Jackson	183
	Curt Simmons	183
62	Danny Darwin	182
	Hooks Dauss	182
	Waite Hoyt	182
65	Murry Dickson	181
	Dutch Leonard	181
	Rick Wise	181
68	Lee Meadows	180
69	Pink Hawley	179
	Dolf Luque	179
71	John Clarkson	178
	Wilbur Cooper	178
73	Bill Dinneen	177
	Rube Marquard	177
75	Mike Moore	176
76	Red Donahue	175
77	Doyle Alexander	174
	Bob Gibson	174
	Tom Hughes	174
	Jim Perry	174
	Amos Rusie	174
82	Chuck Finley	173
83	Luis Tiant	172
84	Dennis Eckersley	171
	Larry French	171
86	Ted Breitenstein	170
	Camilo Pascual	170
88	Billy Pierce	169
89	Red Ames	167
	Jim Clancy	167
	Bert Cunningham	167
	Red Ehret	167
93	Don Drysdale	166
	Howard Ehmke	166
	Catfish Hunter	166
	George Uhle	166
	Will White	166
98	Mark Baldwin	165
	Bump Hadley	165
	Si Johnson	165

Winning Percentage

1	**Pedro Martinez**	**.712**
2	Dave Foutz	.690
3	Whitey Ford	.690
4	Bob Caruthers	.688
5	Lefty Grove	.680
6	**Randy Johnson**	**.669**
7	Vic Raschi	.667
8	Larry Corcoran	.665
9	Christy Mathewson	.665
10	Sam Leever	.660
11	**Roger Clemens**	**.660**
12	Sal Maglie	.657
13	**Andy Pettitte**	**.656**
14	Sandy Koufax	.655
15	Johnny Allen	.654
16	Ron Guidry	.651
17	Lefty Gomez	.649
18	John Clarkson	.648
19	Mordecai Brown	.648
20	**Mike Mussina**	**.644**
21	Dizzy Dean	.644
22	Grover Alexander	.642
23	**Greg Maddux**	**.639**
24	Jim Palmer	.638
25	Kid Nichols	.634
26	Deacon Phillippe	.634
27	Joe McGinnity	.634
28	Dwight Gooden	.634
29	Ed Reulbach	.632
30	Juan Marichal	.631
31	Mort Cooper	.631
32	Allie Reynolds	.630
33	Jesse Tannehill	.627
34	Ray Kremer	.627
35	Firpo Marberry	.627
36	Eddie Plank	.627
37	Tommy Bond	.627
38	Chief Bender	.625
39	Don Newcombe	.623
40	Nig Cuppy	.623
41	Carl Mays	.623
42	Addie Joss	.623
43	Fred Goldsmith	.622
44	Doc Crandall	.622
45	Carl Hubbell	.622
46	Bob Feller	.621
47	Mel Parnell	.621
48	**Kirk Rueter**	**.620**
49	John Tudor	.619
50	Clark Griffith	.619
51	Bob Lemon	.618
52	Cy Young	.618
53	**Tom Glavine**	**.615**
54	Urban Shocker	.615
55	Jeff Tesreau	.615
56	Jim Maloney	.615
57	Charley Radbourn	.614
58	John Ward	.614
59	Jimmy Key	.614
60	Lon Warneke	.613
61	Gary Nolan	.611
62	Schoolboy Rowe	.610
63	Carl Erskine	.610
64	**David Wells**	**.610**
65	Ed Walsh	.607
66	Charlie Ferguson	.607
67	Dave McNally	.607
68	Hooks Wiltse	.607
69	**David Cone**	**.606**
70	Jack Stivetts	.606
71	Ramon Martinez	.605
72	Art Nehf	.605
73	Charlie Buffinton	.605
74	Orval Overall	.603
75	Tim Keefe	.603
76	Tom Seaver	.603
77	Stan Coveleski	.602
78	Preacher Roe	.602
79	Wes Ferrell	.601
80	J.R. Richard	.601
81	**Kevin Brown**	**.601**
82	Jack Chesbro	.600
83	Walter Johnson	.599
84	Herb Pennock	.598
85	Freddie Fitzsimmons	.598
86	Ed Lopat	.597
87	Warren Spahn	.597
88	Rip Sewell	.596
89	Mike Garcia	.594
90	Mickey Welch	.594
91	Jack McDowell	.593
92	Pat Malone	.593
93	Alvin Crowder	.592
94	John Candelaria	.592
95	Harry Brecheen	.591
96	Bob Welch	.591
97	Bob Gibson	.591
98	Dutch Ruether	.591
99	Denny McLain	.590
100	Eddie Rommel	.590

Games

1	**Jesse Orosco**	**1252**
2	Dennis Eckersley	1071
3	Hoyt Wilhelm	1070
4	**Dan Plesac**	**1064**
5	Kent Tekulve	1050
6	**John Franco**	**1036**
7	Lee Smith	1022
8	Rich Gossage	1002
9	Lindy McDaniel	987
10	Mike Jackson	960
11	Rollie Fingers	944
12	Gene Garber	931
13	Cy Young	906
14	Sparky Lyle	899
15	Jim Kaat	898
16	**Mike Stanton**	**885**
17	Paul Assenmacher	884
18	Jeff Reardon	880
19	Don McMahon	874
20	Phil Niekro	864
21	Charlie Hough	858
22	Roy Face	848
23	Doug Jones	846
24	Tug McGraw	824
25	Nolan Ryan	807
26	Walter Johnson	802
27	Rick Honeycutt	797
28	Gaylord Perry	777
29	Don Sutton	774
30	**Mark Guthrie**	**765**
	Darold Knowles	765
32	**Roberto Hernandez**	**762**
	Jose Mesa	**762**
34	Tommy John	760
35	Jack Quinn	756
36	Ron Reed	751
37	Warren Spahn	750
38	Tom Burgmeier	745
	Gary Lavelle	745
40	Willie Hernandez	744
41	Steve Carlton	741
42	**Steve Reed**	**738**
43	Ron Perranoski	737
44	Ron Kline	736
	Mike Timlin	**736**
46	Rick Aguilera	732
	Steve Bedrosian	732
48	Clay Carroll	731
49	Randy Myers	728
50	Mike Marshall	723
	Roger McDowell	723
52	Dave Righetti	718
53	Danny Darwin	716
54	**Jeff Nelson**	**714**
	Eric Plunk	714
56	Johnny Klippstein	711
57	Greg Minton	710
58	**Paul Quantrill**	**705**
59	Stu Miller	704
60	Greg Harris	703
61	Joe Niekro	702
62	Bill Campbell	700
	Jeff Montgomery	700
64	Larry Andersen	699
65	Bob McClure	698
66	Jim Galvin	697
67	Grover Alexander	696
	Craig Lefferts	696
69	Bob Miller	694
70	Bert Blyleven	692
	Grant Jackson	692
	Dennis Martinez	692
	Eppa Rixey	692
74	Early Wynn	691
75	Eddie Fisher	690
76	Ted Abernathy	681
77	**Buddy Groom**	**679**
78	**Rod Beck**	**678**
79	Robin Roberts	676
80	Waite Hoyt	674
	Dan Quisenberry	674
82	Red Faber	669
83	Dave Giusti	668
84	**Todd Jones**	**666**
85	Dennis Cook	665
86	Fergie Jenkins	664
	Greg Swindell	664
88	Bruce Sutter	661
89	Tom Seaver	656
90	Paul Lindblad	655
91	Chuck McElroy	654
92	Wilbur Wood	651
93	Sam Jones	647
	Dave LaRoche	647
95	Robb Nen	643
96	Tom Henke	642
97	**Trevor Hoffman**	**641**
98	Dutch Leonard	640
	Gerry Staley	640
100	3 players tied	639

Games Started

1	Cy Young	815
2	Nolan Ryan	773
3	Don Sutton	756
4	Phil Niekro	716
5	Steve Carlton	709
6	Tommy John	700
7	Gaylord Perry	690
8	Bert Blyleven	685
9	Jim Galvin	681
10	Walter Johnson	666
11	Warren Spahn	665
12	Tom Seaver	647
13	Jim Kaat	625
14	Frank Tanana	616
15	Early Wynn	612
16	Robin Roberts	609
17	**Roger Clemens**	**606**
18	Grover Alexander	600
19	Fergie Jenkins	594
	Tim Keefe	594
21	**Greg Maddux**	**571**
22	Dennis Martinez	562
	Kid Nichols	562
24	Eppa Rixey	554
25	Christy Mathewson	552
26	Mickey Welch	549
27	Jerry Reuss	547
28	Red Ruffing	538
29	**Tom Glavine**	**537**
30	Eddie Plank	529
	Rick Reuschel	529
32	Jerry Koosman	527
	Jack Morris	527
34	Jim Palmer	521
35	Jim Bunning	519
36	John Clarkson	518
37	Jack Powell	516
38	Gus Weyhing	505
39	Tony Mullane	504
40	Charley Radbourn	502
41	Joe Niekro	500
42	Bob Friend	497
	Burleigh Grimes	497
44	Mickey Lolich	496
45	Claude Osteen	488
46	Sam Jones	487
47	Jim McCormick	485
48	Bob Feller	484
	Ted Lyons	484
	Luis Tiant	484
51	Red Faber	483
	Bobo Newsom	483
53	Bob Gibson	482
54	Catfish Hunter	476
55	Vida Blue	473
	Earl Whitehill	473
57	Vic Willis	471
58	Chuck Finley	467
59	Orel Hershiser	466
60	Don Drysdale	465
	Milt Pappas	465
62	Doyle Alexander	464
63	Curt Simmons	462
	Bob Welch	462
65	Mike Torrez	458
66	Lefty Grove	457
	Juan Marichal	457
68	Rick Wise	455
69	Jim Perry	447
70	Paul Derringer	445
71	**Randy Johnson**	**444**
72	Jack Quinn	443
73	**Kevin Brown**	**441**
74	Charlie Hough	440
	Mike Moore	440
76	Whitey Ford	438
77	Mel Harder	433
	Carl Hubbell	433
79	Billy Pierce	432
80	Larry Jackson	429
81	Mark Langston	428
	George Mullin	428
83	Amos Rusie	427
84	Freddie Fitzsimmons	425
	Waite Hoyt	425
86	Fernando Valenzuela	424
87	**John Burkett**	**423**
88	Bob Forsch	422
89	**Jamie Moyer**	**420**
	Frank Viola	420
91	**David Cone**	**419**
	Herb Pennock	419
93	Bob Knepper	413
94	Dave Stieb	412
95	Mike Morgan	411
96	Tom Candiotti	410
	Dwight Gooden	410
	Ken Holtzman	410
99	Tom Zachary	408
100	2 players tied	407

Games Started by era

1988-2003

1	**Roger Clemens**	**606**
2	**Greg Maddux**	**571**
3	**Tom Glavine**	**537**
4	Chuck Finley	467
5	Orel Hershiser	466
6	**Randy Johnson**	**444**
7	**Kevin Brown**	**441**
8	Mike Moore	440
9	Mark Langston	428
10	**John Burkett**	**423**

1973-1987

1	Nolan Ryan	773
2	Don Sutton	756
3	Phil Niekro	716
4	Steve Carlton	709
5	Tommy John	700
6	Gaylord Perry	690
7	Bert Blyleven	685
8	Tom Seaver	647
9	Frank Tanana	616
10	Fergie Jenkins	594

1961-1972

1	Jim Kaat	625
2	Jim Bunning	519
3	Mickey Lolich	496
4	Claude Osteen	488
5	Bob Gibson	482
6	Catfish Hunter	476
7	Don Drysdale	465
	Milt Pappas	465
9	Juan Marichal	457
10	Jim Perry	447

1943-1960

1	Warren Spahn	665
2	Early Wynn	612
3	Robin Roberts	609
4	Bob Friend	497
5	Bob Feller	484
6	Curt Simmons	462
7	Whitey Ford	438
8	Billy Pierce	432
9	Dutch Leonard	375
10	Hal Newhouser	374

1921-1942

1	Eppa Rixey	554
2	Red Ruffing	538
3	Burleigh Grimes	497
4	Sam Jones	487
5	Ted Lyons	484
6	Red Faber	483
	Bobo Newsom	483
8	Earl Whitehill	473
9	Lefty Grove	457
10	Paul Derringer	445

1901-1920

1	Cy Young	815
2	Walter Johnson	666
3	Grover Alexander	600
4	Christy Mathewson	552
5	Eddie Plank	529
6	Jack Powell	516
7	Vic Willis	471
8	George Mullin	428
9	Rube Marquard	407
10	Wilbur Cooper	406

1893-1900

1	Kid Nichols	562
2	Amos Rusie	427
3	Clark Griffith	372
4	Brickyard Kennedy	354
5	Pink Hawley	344
6	Ted Breitenstein	342
7	Frank Dwyer	318
8	Bert Cunningham	311
9	Red Ehret	309
10	Jouett Meekin	308

1876-1892

1	Jim Galvin	681
2	Tim Keefe	594
3	Mickey Welch	549
4	John Clarkson	518
5	Gus Weyhing	505
6	Tony Mullane	504
7	Charley Radbourn	502
8	Jim McCormick	485
9	Adonis Terry	406
10	Will White	401

Complete Games

1	Cy Young	749
2	Jim Galvin	639
3	Tim Keefe	554
4	Kid Nichols	532
5	Walter Johnson	531
6	Mickey Welch	525
7	Charley Radbourn	488
8	John Clarkson	485
9	Tony Mullane	468
10	Jim McCormick	466
11	Gus Weyhing	449
12	Grover Alexander	437
13	Christy Mathewson	435
14	Jack Powell	422
15	Eddie Plank	410
16	Will White	394
17	Amos Rusie	393
18	Vic Willis	388
19	Warren Spahn	382
20	Jim Whitney	377
21	Adonis Terry	367
22	Ted Lyons	356
23	George Mullin	353
24	Charlie Buffinton	351
25	Chick Fraser	342
26	Clark Griffith	337
27	Red Ruffing	335
28	Silver King	328
29	Al Orth	324
30	Bill Hutchison	321
31	Burleigh Grimes	314
	Joe McGinnity	314
33	Red Donahue	312
	Guy Hecker	312
35	Bill Dinneen	306
36	Robin Roberts	305
37	Gaylord Perry	303
38	Ted Breitenstein	301
39	Bob Caruthers	298
	Lefty Grove	298
41	Pink Hawley	297
	Ed Morris	297
43	Mark Baldwin	295
44	Tommy Bond	294
	Brickyard Kennedy	294
46	Eppa Rixey	290
	Early Wynn	290
48	Bill Donovan	289
	Bobby Mathews	289
50	Bert Cunningham	287
51	Wilbur Cooper	279
	Bob Feller	279
	Sadie McMahon	279
	Jack Taylor	279
55	Jack Stivetts	278
56	Charlie Getzien	277
57	Red Faber	273
58	Mordecai Brown	271
	Frank Dwyer	271
60	Jouett Meekin	270
61	Fergie Jenkins	267
62	Elton Chamberlain	264
	Matt Kilroy	264
	Jesse Tannehill	264
65	Doc White	262
66	Rube Waddell	261
67	Jack Chesbro	260
	Red Ehret	260
	Carl Hubbell	260
70	Larry Corcoran	256
71	Chief Bender	255
	Bob Gibson	255
73	Steve Carlton	254
74	Frank Killen	253
	Win Mercer	253
76	Paul Derringer	251
77	Sam Jones	250
	Ed Walsh	250
79	Eddie Cicotte	249
	Stump Wiedman	249
81	Herb Pennock	247
82	Bobo Newsom	246
83	George Bradley	245
	Hooks Dauss	245
	Phil Niekro	245
	John Ward	245
87	Harry Howell	244
	Juan Marichal	244
89	Jack Quinn	243
90	Bert Blyleven	242
	Deacon Phillippe	242
	Bucky Walters	242
93	Sam Leever	241
94	Kid Gleason	240
95	Addie Joss	234
96	George Uhle	232
97	Carl Mays	231
	Tom Seaver	231
	Harry Staley	231
100	Earl Moore	230

Complete Games by era

1988-2003

1	**Roger Clemens**	**117**
2	**Greg Maddux**	**103**
3	**Randy Johnson**	**88**
4	Mark Langston	81
5	Mike Moore	79
	Curt Schilling	**79**
7	Bret Saberhagen	76
8	Frank Viola	74
9	**Kevin Brown**	**72**
10	Tom Candiotti	68
	Dwight Gooden	68
	Orel Hershiser	68

1973-1987

1	Gaylord Perry	303
2	Fergie Jenkins	267
3	Steve Carlton	254
4	Phil Niekro	245
5	Bert Blyleven	242
6	Tom Seaver	231
7	Nolan Ryan	222
8	Jim Palmer	211
9	Luis Tiant	187
10	Don Sutton	178

1961-1972

1	Bob Gibson	255
2	Juan Marichal	244
3	Mickey Lolich	195
4	Catfish Hunter	181
5	Jim Kaat	180
6	Mike Cuellar	172
7	Don Drysdale	167
8	Mel Stottlemyre	152
9	Jim Bunning	151
10	Larry Jackson	149

1943-1960

1	Warren Spahn	382
2	Robin Roberts	305
3	Early Wynn	290
4	Bob Feller	279
5	Hal Newhouser	212
6	Billy Pierce	193
7	Dutch Leonard	192
8	Bob Lemon	188
9	Ed Lopat	164
10	Bob Friend	163
	Curt Simmons	163

1921-1942

1	Ted Lyons	356
2	Red Ruffing	335
3	Burleigh Grimes	314
4	Lefty Grove	298
5	Eppa Rixey	290
6	Red Faber	273
7	Carl Hubbell	260
8	Paul Derringer	251
9	Sam Jones	250
10	Herb Pennock	247

1901-1920

1	Cy Young	749
2	Walter Johnson	531
3	Grover Alexander	437
4	Christy Mathewson	435
5	Jack Powell	422
6	Eddie Plank	410
7	Vic Willis	388
8	George Mullin	353
9	Chick Fraser	342
10	Al Orth	324

1893-1900

1	Kid Nichols	532
2	Amos Rusie	393
3	Clark Griffith	337
4	Ted Breitenstein	301
5	Pink Hawley	297
6	Brickyard Kennedy	294
7	Bert Cunningham	287
8	Frank Dwyer	271
9	Jouett Meekin	270
10	Red Ehret	260

1876-1892

1	Jim Galvin	639
2	Tim Keefe	554
3	Mickey Welch	525
4	Charley Radbourn	488
5	John Clarkson	485
6	Tony Mullane	468
7	Jim McCormick	466
8	Gus Weyhing	449
9	Will White	394
10	Jim Whitney	377

Shutouts

1	Grover Alexander	90
2	Christy Mathewson	79
3	Cy Young	76
4	Eddie Plank	69
5	Warren Spahn	63
6	Nolan Ryan	61
	Tom Seaver	61
8	Bert Blyleven	60
9	Don Sutton	58
10	Jim Galvin	57
	Ed Walsh	57
12	Bob Gibson	56
13	Mordecai Brown	55
	Steve Carlton	55
15	Jim Palmer	53
	Gaylord Perry	53
17	Juan Marichal	52
18	Rube Waddell	50
	Vic Willis	50
20	Don Drysdale	49
	Fergie Jenkins	49
	Luis Tiant	49
	Early Wynn	49
24	Kid Nichols	48
25	**Roger Clemens**	**46**
	Tommy John	46
	Jack Powell	46
28	Whitey Ford	45
	Addie Joss	45
	Phil Niekro	45
	Robin Roberts	45
	Red Ruffing	45
	Doc White	45
34	Babe Adams	44
	Bob Feller	44
36	Milt Pappas	43
37	Catfish Hunter	42
	Bucky Walters	42
39	Mickey Lolich	41
	Hippo Vaughn	41
	Mickey Welch	41
42	Chief Bender	40
	Jim Bunning	40
	Larry French	40
	Sandy Koufax	40
	Claude Osteen	40
	Ed Reulbach	40
	Mel Stottlemyre	40
49	Tim Keefe	39
	Sam Leever	39
	Jerry Reuss	39
52	Stan Coveleski	38
	Billy Pierce	38
	Nap Rucker	38
55	Vida Blue	37
	John Clarkson	37
	Larry Jackson	37
	Eppa Rixey	37
	Steve Rogers	37
60	Mike Cuellar	36
	Bob Friend	36
	Carl Hubbell	36
	Sam Jones	36
	Camilo Pascual	36
	Allie Reynolds	36
	Curt Simmons	36
	Will White	36
68	Tommy Bond	35
	Joe Bush	35
	Jack Chesbro	35
	Eddie Cicotte	35
	Jack Coombs	35
	Wilbur Cooper	35
	Bill Donovan	35
	Burleigh Grimes	35
	Lefty Grove	35
	Randy Johnson	**35**
	George Mullin	35
	Herb Pennock	35
	Charley Radbourn	35
81	Bill Doak	34
	Greg Maddux	**34**
	Earl Moore	34
	Frank Tanana	34
	Jesse Tannehill	34
86	Tommy Bridges	33
	Lew Burdette	33
	Dean Chance	33
	Mort Cooper	33
	Jerry Koosman	33
	Dutch Leonard	33
	Jim McCormick	33
	Dave McNally	33
	Hal Newhouser	33
	Bob Shawkey	33
	Virgil Trucks	33
97	Paul Derringer	32
	Lefty Leifield	32
	Joe McGinnity	32
	Jim Perry	32

Saves

1	Lee Smith	478
2	**John Franco**	**424**
3	Dennis Eckersley	390
4	Jeff Reardon	367
5	**Trevor Hoffman**	**352**
6	Randy Myers	347
7	Rollie Fingers	341
8	John Wetteland	330
9	**Roberto Hernandez**	**320**
10	Rick Aguilera	318
11	Robb Nen	314
12	Tom Henke	311
13	Rich Gossage	310
14	Jeff Montgomery	304
15	Doug Jones	303
16	Bruce Sutter	300
17	**Rod Beck**	**286**
18	**Troy Percival**	**283**
	Mariano Rivera	**283**
20	Todd Worrell	256
21	Dave Righetti	252
22	**Jose Mesa**	**249**
23	Dan Quisenberry	244
24	Sparky Lyle	238
25	Hoyt Wilhelm	227
26	**Billy Wagner**	**225**
27	Gene Garber	218
28	Gregg Olson	217
29	Dave Smith	216
30	**Ugueth Urbina**	**206**
31	Jeff Shaw	203
32	Bobby Thigpen	201
33	**Armando Benitez**	**197**
34	Roy Face	193
	Mike Henneman	193
36	Mitch Williams	192
37	Mike Marshall	188
38	Jeff Russell	186
39	Steve Bedrosian	184
	Todd Jones	**184**
	Kent Tekulve	184
42	Tug McGraw	180
43	Ron Perranoski	179
44	Bryan Harvey	177
45	Jeff Brantley	172
	Lindy McDaniel	172
47	Roger McDowell	159
48	**Dan Plesac**	**158**
49	Bob Wickman	156
50	Jay Howell	155
	Billy Koch	**155**
52	Stu Miller	154
53	Don McMahon	153
54	Greg Minton	150
55	Ted Abernathy	148
56	Willie Hernandez	147
57	Dave Giusti	145
58	**Jesse Orosco**	**144**
	Mike Williams	**144**
60	Clay Carroll	143
	Keith Foulke	**143**
	Darold Knowles	143
63	Mike Jackson	142
64	Gary Lavelle	136
65	Jim Brewer	132
	Steve Farr	132
	Bob Stanley	132
68	**Danny Graves**	**131**
69	Ron Davis	130
	Jason Isringhausen	**130**
71	**Kazuhiro Sasaki**	**129**
72	Terry Forster	127
73	Bill Campbell	126
	Dave LaRoche	126
	Mel Rojas	126
76	John Hiller	125
77	Jack Aker	123
78	Dick Radatz	122
79	**Antonio Alfonseca**	**121**
	Duane Ward	121
81	Mark Wohlers	119
82	**Eddie Guardado**	**116**
	Mike Timlin	**116**
84	Tippy Martinez	115
85	**Ricky Bottalico**	**114**
86	Frank Linzy	111
87	**Tom Gordon**	**110**
	John Smoltz	**110**
	Al Worthington	110
90	Fred Gladding	109
91	Wayne Granger	108
	Ron Kline	108
93	**Eric Gagne**	**107**
	Johnny Murphy	107
95	Bill Caudill	106
96	Ron Reed	103
	John Wyatt	103
98	4 players tied	102

Saves by era

1988-2003

1	**John Franco**	**424**
2	**Trevor Hoffman**	**352**
3	Randy Myers	347
4	John Wetteland	330
5	**Roberto Hernandez**	**320**
6	Rick Aguilera	318
7	Robb Nen	314
8	Tom Henke	311
9	Jeff Montgomery	304
10	Doug Jones	303

1973-1987

1	Lee Smith	478
2	Dennis Eckersley	390
3	Jeff Reardon	367
4	Rollie Fingers	341
5	Rich Gossage	310
6	Bruce Sutter	300
7	Dave Righetti	252
8	Dan Quisenberry	244
9	Sparky Lyle	238
10	Gene Garber	218

1961-1972

1	Ron Perranoski	179
2	Lindy McDaniel	172
3	Don McMahon	153
4	Ted Abernathy	148
5	Dave Giusti	145
6	Clay Carroll	143
	Darold Knowles	143
8	Jim Brewer	132
9	Jack Aker	123
10	Dick Radatz	122

1943-1960

1	Hoyt Wilhelm	227
2	Roy Face	193
3	Stu Miller	154
4	Al Worthington	110
5	Ron Kline	108
6	Ellis Kinder	102
7	Clem Labine	96
8	Bill Henry	90
9	Joe Page	76
10	Jim Konstanty	74

1921-1942

1	Johnny Murphy	107
2	Firpo Marberry	101
3	Al Benton	66
4	Clint Brown	64
5	Joe Heving	63
6	Jack Quinn	57
7	Hugh Casey	55
	Lefty Grove	55
9	Waite Hoyt	52
10	Wilcy Moore	49

1901-1920

1	Mordecai Brown	49
2	Allan Russell	42
3	Hooks Dauss	39
4	Red Ames	36
	Slim Sallee	36
6	Ed Walsh	35
7	Chief Bender	34
	Walter Johnson	34
9	Hooks Wiltse	33
10	Grover Alexander	32

1893-1900

1	Kid Nichols	17
2	Win Mercer	10
3	Brickyard Kennedy	9
	Jack Taylor	9
5	Fred Anderson	8
	Clark Griffith	8
7	Frank Dwyer	6
	George Hemming	6
9	Nick Cullop	5
	Nig Cuppy	5
	Duke Esper	5
	Amos Rusie	5

1876-1892

1	Tony Mullane	15
2	Kid Gleason	6
	Silver King	6
	Adonis Terry	6
5	Mark Baldwin	5
	John Clarkson	5
	Jack Stivetts	5
8	Charlie Ferguson	4
	Frank Foreman	4
	Dave Foutz	4
	Bill Hutchison	4
	Sadie McMahon	4
	Hank O'Day	4
	Billy Taylor	4
	Mickey Welch	4
	Gus Weyhing	4

Save percentage

1	**Eric Gagne**	**96.40**
2	**John Smoltz**	**92.44**
3	**Trevor Hoffman**	**88.89**
4	**Mariano Rivera**	**86.54**
5	**Troy Percival**	**86.28**
6	**Keith Foulke**	**85.63**
7	**Billy Wagner**	**85.55**
8	**Kazuhiro Sasaki**	**85.43**
9	Robb Nen	85.33
10	**Jose Mesa**	**85.27**
11	Randy Myers	85.26
12	**Mike Williams**	**85.21**
13	**Billy Koch**	**85.16**
14	Tom Henke	84.97
15	**Armando Benitez**	**84.91**
16	**Ugueth Urbina**	**84.77**
17	**Matt Mantei**	**84.76**
18	Bryan Harvey	84.69
19	Dennis Eckersley	84.60
20	**Jason Isringhausen**	**84.42**
21	John Wetteland	83.97
22	**Rod Beck**	**83.87**
23	**Jose Jimenez**	**82.93**
24	Mark Wohlers	82.07
25	**Danny Graves**	**81.88**
26	**Eddie Guardado**	**81.69**
27	**John Franco**	**81.07**
28	Dave Smith	80.60
29	**Kelvim Escobar**	**80.56**
30	Jeff Russell	80.52
31	Rick Aguilera	80.51
32	Jeff Montgomery	80.42
33	Mike Henneman	80.42
34	**Jorge Julio**	**80.26**
	Dan Quisenberry	80.26
36	**Roberto Hernandez**	**80.00**
	John Rocker	**80.00**
	Billy Taylor	80.00
39	Jeff Shaw	79.92
40	Doug Jones	79.74
41	Mike Schooler	79.67
42	**Byung-Hyun Kim**	**79.63**
43	Alejandro Pena	79.57
44	Gregg Olson	79.49
45	Bobby Thigpen	79.45
46	**Todd Jones**	**78.97**
47	Jeff Brantley	78.90
48	**Derek Lowe**	**78.70**
49	**Tom Gordon**	**78.57**
50	Bill Caudill	78.52

Blown Saves

1	**John Franco**	**99**
2	Gene Garber	82
3	Kent Tekulve	81
4	**Roberto Hernandez**	**80**
	Gary Lavelle	80
6	Rick Aguilera	77
	Doug Jones	77
8	**Jesse Orosco**	**76**
9	Jeff Montgomery	74
	Dan Plesac	**74**
	Dave Righetti	74
12	Bill Campbell	72
13	Dennis Eckersley	71
	Todd Worrell	71
15	John Wetteland	63
16	**Mike Timlin**	**61**
17	Randy Myers	60
	Dan Quisenberry	60
19	Paul Assenmacher	59
	Mike Jackson	59
21	Steve Bedrosian	57
22	Gregg Olson	56
	Mitch Williams	56
24	**Rod Beck**	**55**
	Tom Henke	55
	Roger McDowell	55
	Bob Stanley	55
28	Greg Minton	54
	Robb Nen	54
30	Dave Smith	52
	Bobby Thigpen	52
	Bob Wickman	52
33	Jeff Shaw	51
34	Jay Howell	49
	Todd Jones	**49**
36	Mike Henneman	47
37	Jeff Brantley	46
	Greg Harris	46
39	Tim Burke	45
	Jeff Nelson	**45**
	Troy Percival	**45**
	Jeff Russell	45
43	**Trevor Hoffman**	**44**
	Mariano Rivera	**44**
45	Ron Davis	43
	Willie Hernandez	43
	Jose Mesa	**43**
	Elias Sosa	43
	Mike Stanton	**43**
50	2 players tied	42

Innings Pitched

1	Cy Young	7356.0
2	Jim Galvin	5941.1
3	Walter Johnson	5914.1
4	Phil Niekro	5404.1
5	Nolan Ryan	5386.0
6	Gaylord Perry	5350.1
7	Don Sutton	5282.1
8	Warren Spahn	5243.3
9	Steve Carlton	5217.1
10	Grover Alexander	5190.0
11	Kid Nichols	5067.1
12	Tim Keefe	5049.3
13	Bert Blyleven	4970.0
14	Mickey Welch	4802.0
15	Christy Mathewson	4788.3
16	Tom Seaver	4782.3
17	Tommy John	4710.1
18	Robin Roberts	4688.3
19	Early Wynn	4564.0
20	John Clarkson	4536.1
21	Tony Mullane	4531.1
22	Jim Kaat	4530.1
23	Charley Radbourn	4527.1
24	Fergie Jenkins	4500.3
25	Eddie Plank	4495.3
26	Eppa Rixey	4494.3
27	Jack Powell	4389.0
28	Red Ruffing	4344.0
29	Gus Weyhing	4337.0
30	**Roger Clemens**	**4278.3**
31	Jim McCormick	4275.3
32	Frank Tanana	4188.1
33	Burleigh Grimes	4179.3
34	Ted Lyons	4161.0
35	Red Faber	4086.3
36	Dennis Martinez	3999.3
37	Vic Willis	3996.0
38	**Greg Maddux**	**3968.3**
39	Jim Palmer	3948.0
40	Lefty Grove	3940.3
41	Jack Quinn	3920.1
42	Bob Gibson	3884.1
43	Sam Jones	3883.0
44	Jerry Koosman	3839.1
45	Bob Feller	3827.0
46	Jack Morris	3824.0
47	Charlie Hough	3801.1
48	Amos Rusie	3778.3
49	Waite Hoyt	3762.1
50	Jim Bunning	3760.1
51	Bobo Newsom	3759.1
52	George Mullin	3686.3
53	Jerry Reuss	3669.3
54	Paul Derringer	3645.0
55	Mickey Lolich	3638.1
56	Bob Friend	3611.0
57	Carl Hubbell	3590.1
58	Joe Niekro	3584.0
59	Herb Pennock	3571.3
60	Earl Whitehill	3564.3
61	Rick Reuschel	3548.1
62	Will White	3542.3
63	**Tom Glavine**	**3528.0**
64	Adonis Terry	3514.1
65	Juan Marichal	3507.1
66	Jim Whitney	3496.1
67	Luis Tiant	3486.1
68	Wilbur Cooper	3480.0
69	Claude Osteen	3460.1
70	Catfish Hunter	3449.1
71	Joe McGinnity	3441.1
72	Don Drysdale	3432.0
73	Mel Harder	3426.1
74	Charlie Buffinton	3404.0
75	Hooks Dauss	3390.3
76	Clark Griffith	3385.3
77	Doyle Alexander	3367.3
78	Chick Fraser	3364.0
79	Al Orth	3354.3
80	Curt Simmons	3348.1
81	Vida Blue	3343.1
82	Rube Marquard	3306.3
	Billy Pierce	3306.3
84	Dennis Eckersley	3285.3
	Jim Perry	3285.3
86	Larry Jackson	3262.3
87	Eddie Cicotte	3226.0
88	Freddie Fitzsimmons	3223.3
89	Dolf Luque	3220.1
90	Dutch Leonard	3218.1
91	Jesse Haines	3208.3
92	Red Ames	3198.0
93	Chuck Finley	3197.1
	Charlie Root	3197.1
95	Milt Pappas	3186.0
96	Silver King	3180.3
97	Mordecai Brown	3172.1
98	Whitey Ford	3170.1
99	Lee Meadows	3160.3
100	Larry French	3152.0

Innings Pitched by era

1988-2003

1	**Roger Clemens**	**4278.3**
2	**Greg Maddux**	**3968.3**
3	**Tom Glavine**	**3528.0**
4	Chuck Finley	3197.1
5	Orel Hershiser	3130.1
6	**Randy Johnson**	**3122.1**
7	**Kevin Brown**	**3051.0**
8	Danny Darwin	3016.3
9	Mark Langston	2962.3
10	**David Cone**	**2898.3**

1973-1987

1	Phil Niekro	5404.1
2	Nolan Ryan	5386.0
3	Gaylord Perry	5350.1
4	Don Sutton	5282.1
5	Steve Carlton	5217.1
6	Bert Blyleven	4970.0
7	Tom Seaver	4782.3
8	Tommy John	4710.1
9	Fergie Jenkins	4500.3
10	Frank Tanana	4188.1

1961-1972

1	Jim Kaat	4530.1
2	Bob Gibson	3884.1
3	Jim Bunning	3760.1
4	Mickey Lolich	3638.1
5	Juan Marichal	3507.1
6	Claude Osteen	3460.1
7	Catfish Hunter	3449.1
8	Don Drysdale	3432.0
9	Jim Perry	3285.3
10	Larry Jackson	3262.3

1943-1960

1	Warren Spahn	5243.3
2	Robin Roberts	4688.3
3	Early Wynn	4564.0
4	Bob Feller	3827.0
5	Bob Friend	3611.0
6	Curt Simmons	3348.1
7	Billy Pierce	3306.3
8	Dutch Leonard	3218.1
9	Whitey Ford	3170.1
10	Lew Burdette	3067.1

1921-1942

1	Eppa Rixey	4494.3
2	Red Ruffing	4344.0
3	Burleigh Grimes	4179.3
4	Ted Lyons	4161.0
5	Red Faber	4086.3
6	Lefty Grove	3940.3
7	Jack Quinn	3920.1
8	Sam Jones	3883.0
9	Waite Hoyt	3762.1
10	Bobo Newsom	3759.1

1901-1920

1	Cy Young	7356.0
2	Walter Johnson	5914.1
3	Grover Alexander	5190.0
4	Christy Mathewson	4788.3
5	Eddie Plank	4495.3
6	Jack Powell	4389.0
7	Vic Willis	3996.0
8	George Mullin	3686.3
9	Wilbur Cooper	3480.0
10	Joe McGinnity	3441.1

1893-1900

1	Kid Nichols	5067.1
2	Amos Rusie	3778.3
3	Clark Griffith	3385.3
4	Brickyard Kennedy	3030.0
5	Pink Hawley	3012.3
6	Ted Breitenstein	2973.1
7	Frank Dwyer	2819.0
8	Red Ehret	2754.1
9	Bert Cunningham	2734.3
10	Jouett Meekin	2605.1

1876-1892

1	Jim Galvin	5941.1
2	Tim Keefe	5049.3
3	Mickey Welch	4802.0
4	John Clarkson	4536.1
5	Tony Mullane	4531.1
6	Charley Radbourn	4527.1
7	Gus Weyhing	4337.0
8	Jim McCormick	4275.3
9	Will White	3542.3
10	Adonis Terry	3514.1

Fewest Hits/Game

1	Nolan Ryan	6.56
2	**Pedro Martinez**	**6.72**
3	Sandy Koufax	6.79
4	Sid Fernandez	6.85
5	J.R. Richard	6.88
6	Andy Messersmith	6.94
7	Hoyt Wilhelm	7.01
8	**Randy Johnson**	**7.02**
9	Sam McDowell	7.03
10	Ed Walsh	7.12
11	Bob Turley	7.18
12	Orval Overall	7.22
13	Jeff Tesreau	7.24
14	Ed Reulbach	7.24
15	Mario Soto	7.26
16	Addie Joss	7.30
17	Jose DeLeon	7.38
18	Jim Maloney	7.39
19	Rich Gossage	7.45
20	Tom Seaver	7.47
21	Rube Waddell	7.48
22	Walter Johnson	7.48
23	Bob Gibson	7.60
24	Don Wilson	7.61
25	Jim Palmer	7.63
26	Larry Cheney	7.68
27	Mordecai Brown	7.68
28	Sam Jones	7.68
29	**Hideo Nomo**	**7.68**
30	Johnny Vander Meer	7.69
31	Bob Feller	7.69
32	Catfish Hunter	7.72
33	Al Downing	7.72
34	Jim Scott	7.73
35	**Roger Clemens**	**7.73**
36	**John Smoltz**	**7.74**
37	Charlie Hough	7.77
38	**David Cone**	**7.77**
39	Stan Williams	7.79
40	Bobby Bolin	7.79
41	Rollie Fingers	7.80
42	Dean Chance	7.81
43	Frank Smith	7.82
44	Tug McGraw	7.83
45	Barney Pelty	7.84
46	Whitey Ford	7.85
47	Denny McLain	7.85
48	Bob Veale	7.87
49	George McQuillan	7.89
50	Chief Bender	7.89
51	Jack Coombs	7.89
52	Moe Drabowsky	7.90
53	Tim Keefe	7.91
54	Vida Blue	7.91
55	Nap Rucker	7.91
56	Allie Reynolds	7.92
57	Eddie Plank	7.92
58	Christy Mathewson	7.93
59	Luis Tiant	7.94
60	Rudy May	7.94
61	Ray Culp	7.95
62	**Curt Schilling**	**7.96**
63	Bill Donovan	7.99
64	Howie Camnitz	7.99
65	Juan Pizarro	7.99
66	Don Sutton	7.99
67	Dave Stieb	7.99
68	Gary Bell	8.01
69	Earl Moore	8.02
70	Sonny Siebert	8.03
71	Ramon Martinez	8.03
72	Lefty Tyler	8.03
73	Hal Newhouser	8.04
74	Claude Hendrix	8.06
75	Steve Carlton	8.06
76	Hooks Wiltse	8.06
77	**Al Leiter**	**8.07**
78	Amos Rusie	8.07
79	Willie Mitchell	8.07
80	Larry Corcoran	8.08
81	Bill Singer	8.08
82	Bob Lemon	8.08
83	Eddie Cicotte	8.08
84	Mike Scott	8.08
85	Stu Miller	8.09
86	Gary Nolan	8.09
87	Don Drysdale	8.09
88	Juan Marichal	8.09
89	Doc White	8.10
90	Virgil Trucks	8.11
91	Hippo Vaughn	8.11
92	Blue Moon Odom	8.12
93	Kirby Higbe	8.13
94	Jim Shaw	8.13
95	Mike Cuellar	8.13
96	Billy Pierce	8.13
97	Mort Cooper	8.15
98	Red Ames	8.15
99	Vic Willis	8.16
100	Harry Brecheen	8.17

Fewest Hits/Game by era

1988-2003

1	**Pedro Martinez**	**6.72**
2	Sid Fernandez	6.85
3	**Randy Johnson**	**7.02**
4	Jose DeLeon	7.38
5	**Hideo Nomo**	**7.68**
6	**Roger Clemens**	**7.73**
7	**John Smoltz**	**7.74**
8	**David Cone**	**7.77**
9	**Curt Schilling**	**7.96**
10	Ramon Martinez	8.03

1973-1987

1	Nolan Ryan	6.56
2	J.R. Richard	6.88
3	Andy Messersmith	6.94
4	Mario Soto	7.26
5	Rich Gossage	7.45
6	Tom Seaver	7.47
7	Jim Palmer	7.63
8	Charlie Hough	7.77
9	Rollie Fingers	7.80
10	Tug McGraw	7.83

1961-1972

1	Sandy Koufax	6.79
2	Sam McDowell	7.03
3	Jim Maloney	7.39
4	Bob Gibson	7.60
5	Don Wilson	7.61
6	Catfish Hunter	7.72
7	Al Downing	7.72
8	Stan Williams	7.79
9	Bobby Bolin	7.79
10	Dean Chance	7.81

1943-1960

1	Hoyt Wilhelm	7.01
2	Bob Turley	7.18
3	Sam Jones	7.68
4	Johnny Vander Meer	7.69
5	Bob Feller	7.69
6	Whitey Ford	7.85
7	Allie Reynolds	7.92
8	Hal Newhouser	8.04
9	Bob Lemon	8.08
10	Stu Miller	8.09

1921-1942

1	Kirby Higbe	8.13
2	Mort Cooper	8.15
3	Lefty Gomez	8.23
4	Van Mungo	8.34
5	Tommy Bridges	8.52
6	Dazzy Vance	8.52
7	Johnny Allen	8.53
8	Whit Wyatt	8.61
9	Bucky Walters	8.67
10	Carl Hubbell	8.68

1901-1920

1	Ed Walsh	7.12
2	Orval Overall	7.22
3	Jeff Tesreau	7.24
4	Ed Reulbach	7.24
5	Addie Joss	7.30
6	Rube Waddell	7.48
7	Walter Johnson	7.48
8	Larry Cheney	7.68
9	Mordecai Brown	7.68
10	Jim Scott	7.73

1893-1900

1	Amos Rusie	8.07
2	Kid Nichols	8.75
3	Ed Stein	9.18
4	Billy Rhines	9.33
5	Ted Breitenstein	9.39
6	Brickyard Kennedy	9.75
7	Clark Griffith	9.76
8	Frank Killen	9.78
9	Jouett Meekin	9.80
10	Nixey Callahan	9.81

1876-1892

1	Tim Keefe	7.91
2	Larry Corcoran	8.08
3	Ed Morris	8.29
4	Dave Foutz	8.30
5	Toad Ramsey	8.32
6	Charlie Ferguson	8.33
7	Tony Mullane	8.33
8	John Ward	8.47
9	Bob Caruthers	8.52
10	John Clarkson	8.52

Fewest HR Allowed/Game by era

1988-2003

1	**Greg Maddux**	**0.53**
2	**Kevin Brown**	**0.56**
3	Zane Smith	0.57
4	Danny Jackson	0.58
5	Mark Gubicza	0.63
6	**Pedro Martinez**	**0.65**
7	Bill Swift	0.65
8	Dwight Gooden	0.67
9	**Roger Clemens**	**0.68**
10	Orel Hershiser	0.68

1973-1987

1	J.R. Richard	0.41
2	Steve Rogers	0.48
3	Mike LaCoss	0.51
4	Nolan Ryan	0.54
5	Steve Trout	0.54
6	Rick Reuschel	0.56
7	John Denny	0.57
8	Tommy John	0.58
9	Rich Gossage	0.59
10	Dock Ellis	0.59

1961-1972

1	Bob Veale	0.43
2	Dean Chance	0.51
3	Bill Singer	0.55
4	Steve Barber	0.56
5	Mel Stottlemyre	0.58
6	Bob Miller	0.59
7	Sam McDowell	0.59
8	Bob Gibson	0.60
9	Don Wilson	0.61
10	Blue Moon Odom	0.61

1943-1960

1	Max Lanier	0.36
2	Dizzy Trout	0.37
3	Hal Newhouser	0.41
4	Bill Wight	0.43
5	Johnny Vander Meer	0.43
6	Dutch Leonard	0.44
7	Allie Reynolds	0.48
8	Johnny Schmitz	0.48
9	Rip Sewell	0.49
10	Mike Garcia	0.50

1921-1942

1	Eppa Rixey	0.18
2	Stan Coveleski	0.19
3	Jakie May	0.20
4	Dutch Ruether	0.23
5	Jack Quinn	0.23
6	Lee Meadows	0.24
7	Red Faber	0.24
8	Sherry Smith	0.25
9	Al Hollingsworth	0.28
10	Pete Donohue	0.29

1901-1920

1	Ed Killian	0.05
2	Ed Walsh	0.07
3	Addie Joss	0.07
4	Willie Mitchell	0.08
5	Eddie Plank	0.08
6	Eddie Cicotte	0.09
7	Cy Falkenberg	0.09
8	Bill Donovan	0.09
9	Orval Overall	0.09
10	Harry Howell	0.09

1893-1900

1	Billy Rhines	0.12
2	Amos Rusie	0.18
3	Pink Hawley	0.18
4	Nixey Callahan	0.19
5	Frank Killen	0.20
6	Clark Griffith	0.20
7	Bert Cunningham	0.20
8	Red Ehret	0.21
9	Jouett Meekin	0.23
10	Win Mercer	0.23

1876-1892

1	Terry Larkin	0.07
2	John Ward	0.09
3	Tommy Bond	0.10
4	Jumbo McGinnis	0.12
5	Hardie Henderson	0.13
6	Tim Keefe	0.13
7	Ed Morris	0.14
8	Lee Richmond	0.15
9	Guy Hecker	0.15
10	George Bradley	0.16

Walks

1	Nolan Ryan	2795
2	Steve Carlton	1833
3	Phil Niekro	1809
4	Early Wynn	1775
5	Bob Feller	1764
6	Bobo Newsom	1732
7	Amos Rusie	1707
8	Charlie Hough	1665
9	Gus Weyhing	1570
10	Red Ruffing	1541
11	Bump Hadley	1442
12	Warren Spahn	1434
13	Earl Whitehill	1431
14	Tony Mullane	1408
15	Sam Jones	1396
16	Jack Morris	1390
	Tom Seaver	1390
18	**Roger Clemens**	**1379**
	Gaylord Perry	1379
20	Bobby Witt	1375
21	Mike Torrez	1371
22	Walter Johnson	1363
23	Don Sutton	1343
24	Chick Fraser	1338
25	Bob Gibson	1336
26	Chuck Finley	1332
27	Bert Blyleven	1322
28	Sam McDowell	1312
29	Jim Palmer	1311
30	Mark Baldwin	1307
31	Adonis Terry	1298
32	Mickey Welch	1297
33	Burleigh Grimes	1295
34	Mark Langston	1289
35	Kid Nichols	1272
36	Joe Bush	1263
37	Joe Niekro	1262
38	Allie Reynolds	1261
39	Tommy John	1259
40	**Randy Johnson**	**1258**
41	Frank Tanana	1255
42	Bob Lemon	1251
43	Hal Newhouser	1249
44	George Mullin	1238
45	Tim Keefe	1233
46	Cy Young	1217
47	Red Faber	1213
48	Vic Willis	1212
49	Ted Breitenstein	1207
50	**Tom Glavine**	**1206**
51	Brickyard Kennedy	1203
52	Jerry Koosman	1198
53	Tommy Bridges	1192
54	John Clarkson	1191
55	Lefty Grove	1187
56	Vida Blue	1185
57	Billy Pierce	1178
58	Dennis Martinez	1165
59	Mike Moore	1156
60	Jack Stivetts	1155
61	Fernando Valenzuela	1151
62	**David Cone**	**1137**
63	Bill Hutchison	1132
	Johnny Vander Meer	1132
65	Jerry Reuss	1127
66	Ted Lyons	1121
	Bucky Walters	1121
68	Mel Harder	1118
69	Earl Moore	1108
70	Bob Buhl	1105
71	Luis Tiant	1104
72	Mickey Lolich	1099
73	Lefty Gomez	1095
74	Virgil Trucks	1088
75	Whitey Ford	1086
76	Jim Kaat	1083
77	Eppa Rixey	1082
78	Rick Sutcliffe	1081
79	Eddie Plank	1072
80	Camilo Pascual	1069
81	Bob Turley	1068
82	Hooks Dauss	1067
83	Elton Chamberlain	1065
84	Bert Cunningham	1064
85	Curt Simmons	1063
86	Bill Donovan	1059
87	Murry Dickson	1058
88	Jouett Meekin	1056
89	Vern Kennedy	1049
90	Dizzy Trout	1046
91	Howard Ehmke	1042
92	Wes Ferrell	1040
93	Tommy Byrne	1037
94	Red Ames	1034
	Dave Stewart	1034
	Dave Stieb	1034
	Bob Welch	1034
98	Rube Walberg	1031
99	Jack Powell	1021
100	Bob Shawkey	1018

Strikeouts

1	Nolan Ryan	5714
2	Steve Carlton	4136
3	**Roger Clemens**	**4099**
4	**Randy Johnson**	**3871**
5	Bert Blyleven	3701
6	Tom Seaver	3640
7	Don Sutton	3574
8	Gaylord Perry	3534
9	Walter Johnson	3509
10	Phil Niekro	3342
11	Fergie Jenkins	3192
12	Bob Gibson	3117
13	Jim Bunning	2855
14	Mickey Lolich	2832
15	Cy Young	2803
16	Frank Tanana	2773
17	**Greg Maddux**	**2765**
18	**David Cone**	**2668**
19	Chuck Finley	2610
20	Warren Spahn	2583
21	Bob Feller	2581
22	Tim Keefe	2564
23	Jerry Koosman	2556
24	**Curt Schilling**	**2542**
25	Christy Mathewson	2507
26	Don Drysdale	2486
27	Jack Morris	2478
28	Mark Langston	2464
29	Jim Kaat	2461
30	Sam McDowell	2453
31	**Pedro Martinez**	**2426**
32	Luis Tiant	2416
33	Dennis Eckersley	2401
34	Sandy Koufax	2396
35	Charlie Hough	2362
36	Robin Roberts	2357
37	Early Wynn	2334
38	Rube Waddell	2316
39	**John Smoltz**	**2313**
40	Juan Marichal	2303
41	Dwight Gooden	2293
42	Lefty Grove	2266
43	**Kevin Brown**	**2264**
44	Eddie Plank	2246
45	Tommy John	2245
46	Jim Palmer	2212
47	Grover Alexander	2198
48	Vida Blue	2175
49	Camilo Pascual	2167
50	Dennis Martinez	2149
51	**Tom Glavine**	**2136**
52	**Mike Mussina**	**2126**
53	Bobo Newsom	2082
54	Fernando Valenzuela	2074
55	Dazzy Vance	2045
56	Rick Reuschel	2015
57	Orel Hershiser	2014
58	Catfish Hunter	2012
59	Andy Benes	2000
60	Billy Pierce	1999
61	**Kevin Appier**	**1992**
62	Red Ruffing	1987
63	John Clarkson	1978
64	Bob Welch	1969
65	Whitey Ford	1956
66	Bobby Witt	1955
67	Amos Rusie	1950
68	Danny Darwin	1942
69	Jerry Reuss	1907
70	Kid Nichols	1881
71	**David Wells**	**1873**
72	Mickey Welch	1850
73	Frank Viola	1844
74	Charley Radbourn	1830
75	Tony Mullane	1803
76	**Hideo Nomo**	**1802**
77	Jim Galvin	1799
78	Hal Newhouser	1796
79	Ron Guidry	1778
80	**John Burkett**	**1766**
81	**Al Leiter**	**1760**
	Rudy May	1760
83	Joe Niekro	1747
84	Sid Fernandez	1743
85	Dave Stewart	1741
86	Ed Walsh	1736
87	Tom Candiotti	1735
88	Bob Friend	1734
89	Joe Coleman	1728
	Milt Pappas	1728
91	Kevin Gross	1727
92	Floyd Bannister	1723
93	Bret Saberhagen	1715
94	Chief Bender	1711
95	Larry Jackson	1709
96	Jim McCormick	1704
97	Bob Veale	1703
98	Red Ames	1702
99	Charlie Buffinton	1700
100	Curt Simmons	1697

Strikeouts/Game

1	**Randy Johnson**	**11.16**
2	**Pedro Martinez**	**10.50**
3	Nolan Ryan	9.55
4	Sandy Koufax	9.28
5	**Hideo Nomo**	**9.07**
6	Sam McDowell	8.86
7	**Curt Schilling**	**8.85**
8	**Roger Clemens**	**8.62**
9	Sid Fernandez	8.40
10	J.R. Richard	8.37
11	**David Cone**	**8.28**
12	**Tom Gordon**	**8.15**
13	Bob Veale	7.96
14	**John Smoltz**	**7.95**
15	Jim Maloney	7.81
16	Jose Rijo	7.69
17	**Al Leiter**	**7.63**
18	Jose DeLeon	7.56
19	Mario Soto	7.54
20	Sam Jones	7.54
21	**Jeff Fassero**	**7.51**
22	Mark Langston	7.48
23	Rich Gossage	7.47
24	Dwight Gooden	7.37
25	Chuck Finley	7.35
26	Bob Gibson	7.22
27	Andy Benes	7.18
28	**Mike Mussina**	**7.17**
29	Bobby Witt	7.14
30	Steve Carlton	7.13
31	**Dave Burba**	**7.13**
32	**Shane Reynolds**	**7.05**
33	Rube Waddell	7.04
34	**Pedro Astacio**	**7.02**
35	Mickey Lolich	7.01
36	Darryl Kile	6.93
37	**Kevin Appier**	**6.92**
38	Rollie Fingers	6.87
39	Tom Seaver	6.85
40	Jim Bunning	6.83
41	**Wilson Alvarez**	**6.80**
42	Erik Hanson	6.80
43	Ramon Martinez	6.77
44	**Denny Neagle**	**6.74**
45	Juan Pizarro	6.73
46	Bobby Bolin	6.71
47	Bert Blyleven	6.70
48	Ron Guidry	6.69
49	Ray Culp	6.69
50	Jon Lieber	6.68
51	**Kevin Brown**	**6.68**
52	Stan Williams	6.66
53	Camilo Pascual	6.65
54	Bob Turley	6.65
55	Don Wilson	6.60
56	Tug McGraw	6.59
57	Dennis Eckersley	6.58
58	Denny Lemaster	6.57
59	Andy Messersmith	6.56
60	Don Drysdale	6.52
61	Todd Stottlemyre	6.52
62	Al Downing	6.50
63	Floyd Bannister	6.49
64	Toad Ramsey	6.49
65	Diego Segui	6.46
66	Dean Chance	6.43
67	Hoyt Wilhelm	6.43
68	Mark Gardner	6.41
69	Alex Fernandez	6.40
70	**Andy Pettitte**	**6.40**
71	Mike Scott	6.39
72	Fergie Jenkins	6.38
73	Moe Drabowsky	6.37
74	Fernando Valenzuela	6.37
75	Earl Wilson	6.37
76	Harvey Haddix	6.34
77	**Tim Wakefield**	**6.34**
78	Sonny Siebert	6.32
79	Chris Short	6.31
80	Bruce Hurst	6.29
81	Pete Harnisch	6.28
82	**Woody Williams**	**6.28**
83	Bill Singer	6.27
84	**Greg Maddux**	**6.27**
85	**Aaron Sele**	**6.27**
86	Kevin Gross	6.25
87	Jack McDowell	6.25
88	Luis Tiant	6.24
89	Greg Swindell	6.21
90	Turk Farrell	6.21
91	Frank Castillo	6.21
92	Dazzy Vance	6.20
93	Stu Miller	6.18
94	Clay Kirby	6.17
95	**Steve Trachsel**	**6.16**
96	Gary Bell	6.15
97	Gary Peters	6.14
98	Denny McLain	6.12
99	Don Sutton	6.09
100	Mike Krukow	6.07

Earned Run Average

1	Ed Walsh	1.82
2	Addie Joss	1.89
3	Mordecai Brown	2.06
4	John Ward	2.10
5	Christy Mathewson	2.13
6	Rube Waddell	2.16
7	Walter Johnson	2.17
8	Orval Overall	2.23
9	Tommy Bond	2.25
10	Ed Reulbach	2.28
	Will White	2.28
12	Jim Scott	2.30
13	Eddie Plank	2.35
14	Larry Corcoran	2.36
15	Eddie Cicotte	2.38
	Ed Killian	2.38
	George McQuillan	2.38
18	Doc White	2.39
19	Nap Rucker	2.42
20	Terry Larkin	2.43
	Jim McCormick	2.43
	Jeff Tesreau	2.43
23	Chief Bender	2.46
24	Sam Leever	2.47
	Lefty Leifield	2.47
	Hooks Wiltse	2.47
27	Bob Ewing	2.49
	Hippo Vaughn	2.49
29	George Bradley	2.50
30	Hoyt Wilhelm	2.52
31	Noodles Hahn	2.55
32	Grover Alexander	2.56
	Slim Sallee	2.56
34	**Pedro Martinez**	**2.58**
35	Deacon Phillippe	2.59
	Frank Smith	2.59
37	Ed Siever	2.60
38	Bob Rhoads	2.61
39	Red Ames	2.63
	Tim Keefe	2.63
	Barney Pelty	2.63
	Vic Willis	2.63
	Cy Young	2.63
44	Claude Hendrix	2.65
	Jack Taylor	2.65
46	Joe McGinnity	2.66
	Dick Rudolph	2.66
48	Nick Altrock	2.67
	Charlie Ferguson	2.67
	Carl Weilman	2.67
51	Jack Chesbro	2.68
	Cy Falkenberg	2.68
	Charley Radbourn	2.68
54	Bill Donovan	2.69
	Fred Toney	2.69
56	Larry Cheney	2.70
57	Mickey Welch	2.71
58	Fred Goldsmith	2.73
59	Harry Howell	2.74
60	Howie Camnitz	2.75
	Whitey Ford	2.75
	Dummy Taylor	2.75
63	Babe Adams	2.76
	Sandy Koufax	2.76
	Dutch Leonard	2.76
66	Jeff Pfeffer	2.77
67	Jack Coombs	2.78
	Earl Moore	2.78
69	Phil Douglas	2.80
	Jesse Tannehill	2.80
71	John Clarkson	2.81
72	Ray Fisher	2.82
	Ed Morris	2.82
	George Mullin	2.82
	Tully Sparks	2.82
76	Bob Caruthers	2.83
77	Dave Foutz	2.84
78	Andy Messersmith	2.86
	Jim Palmer	2.86
	Tom Seaver	2.86
81	Jim Galvin	2.87
	George Winter	2.87
83	Willie Mitchell	2.88
84	Wilbur Cooper	2.89
	Stan Coveleski	2.89
	Greg Maddux	**2.89**
	Juan Marichal	2.89
88	Rollie Fingers	2.90
89	Bob Gibson	2.91
90	Harry Brecheen	2.92
	Dean Chance	2.92
	Doc Crandall	2.92
	Carl Mays	2.92
94	Dave Davenport	2.93
	Guy Hecker	2.93
96	Don Drysdale	2.95
	Jumbo McGinnis	2.95
	Lefty Tyler	2.95
99	Charlie Buffinton	2.96
	Kid Nichols	2.96

Adjusted Earned Run Average

1	**Pedro Martinez**	**174**
2	Lefty Grove	148
3	Walter Johnson	147
4	Hoyt Wilhelm	146
5	Ed Walsh	145
6	**Randy Johnson**	**143**
	Greg Maddux	**143**
8	Addie Joss	142
9	**Roger Clemens**	**140**
10	Kid Nichols	139
11	Cy Young	138
12	Mordecai Brown	137
13	Christy Mathewson	136
14	Grover Alexander	135
	Rube Waddell	135
16	John Clarkson	134
17	Harry Brecheen	133
	Whitey Ford	133
	Noodles Hahn	133
20	**Kevin Brown**	**131**
	Sandy Koufax	131
22	Dizzy Dean	130
	Carl Hubbell	130
	Hal Newhouser	130
	Amos Rusie	130
26	**Mike Mussina**	**129**
	Curt Schilling	**129**
28	Stan Coveleski	128
29	Nig Cuppy	127
	Bob Gibson	127
	Sal Maglie	127
	Tom Seaver	127
33	Tommy Bridges	126
	Rich Gossage	126
	Bret Saberhagen	126
36	Lefty Gomez	125
	Tim Keefe	125
	Max Lanier	125
	Jim Palmer	125
	Mel Parnell	125
	Dazzy Vance	125
42	Dave Foutz	124
	Urban Shocker	124
	John Smoltz	**124**
	Dizzy Trout	124
	John Tudor	124
47	Bob Caruthers	123
	Eddie Cicotte	123
	Mort Cooper	123
	Larry Corcoran	123
	Sam Leever	123
	Orval Overall	123
53	**Kevin Appier**	**122**
	Bob Feller	122
	Charlie Ferguson	122
	Jimmy Key	122
	Silver King	122
	Juan Marichal	122
	Eddie Plank	122
	Ed Reulbach	122
	Eddie Rommel	122
	Dave Stieb	122
63	Don Drysdale	121
	Tom Glavine	**121**
	Clark Griffith	121
	Andy Messersmith	121
	Jack Stivetts	121
68	Tiny Bonham	120
	David Cone	**120**
	Joe McGinnity	120
	Deacon Phillippe	120
	Charley Radbourn	120
	Jose Rijo	120
	Jim Scott	120
	Hippo Vaughn	120
	Will White	120
77	Dean Chance	119
	Red Faber	119
	Rollie Fingers	119
	Ron Guidry	119
	Thornton Lee	119
	Bob Lemon	119
	Dutch Leonard	119
	Carl Mays	119
	Billy Pierce	119
	Nap Rucker	119
	Bobby Shantz	119
	Lon Warneke	119
89	Babe Adams	118
	Bert Blyleven	118
	Ted Lyons	118
	Sadie McMahon	118
	Tony Mullane	118
	Warren Spahn	118
	Bob Stanley	118
	John Ward	118
	Vic Willis	118
98	8 players tied	117

Adjusted ERA by era

1988-2003		
1	**Pedro Martinez**	**174**
2	**Randy Johnson**	**143**
	Greg Maddux	**143**
4	**Roger Clemens**	**140**
5	**Kevin Brown**	**131**
6	**Mike Mussina**	**129**
	Curt Schilling	**129**
8	Bret Saberhagen	126
9	**John Smoltz**	**124**
10	**Kevin Appier**	**122**
	Jimmy Key	122
1973-1987		
1	Tom Seaver	127
2	Rich Gossage	126
3	Jim Palmer	125
4	John Tudor	124
5	Dave Stieb	122
6	Andy Messersmith	121
7	Rollie Fingers	119
	Ron Guidry	119
9	Bert Blyleven	118
	Bob Stanley	118
1961-1972		
1	Sandy Koufax	131
2	Bob Gibson	127
3	Juan Marichal	122
4	Don Drysdale	121
5	Dean Chance	119
6	Gary Nolan	116
7	Jim Maloney	115
8	Jim Bunning	114
	Bill Hands	114
10	Larry Jackson	113
	Bob Veale	113
	Wilbur Wood	113
1943-1960		
1	Hoyt Wilhelm	146
2	Harry Brecheen	133
	Whitey Ford	133
4	Hal Newhouser	130
5	Sal Maglie	127
6	Max Lanier	125
	Mel Parnell	125
8	Dizzy Trout	124
9	Bob Feller	122
10	Tiny Bonham	120
1921-1942		
1	Lefty Grove	148
2	Dizzy Dean	130
	Carl Hubbell	130
4	Stan Coveleski	128
5	Tommy Bridges	126
6	Lefty Gomez	125
	Dazzy Vance	125
8	Urban Shocker	124
9	Mort Cooper	123
10	Eddie Rommel	122
1901-1920		
1	Walter Johnson	147
2	Ed Walsh	145
3	Addie Joss	142
4	Cy Young	138
5	Mordecai Brown	137
6	Christy Mathewson	136
7	Grover Alexander	135
	Rube Waddell	135
9	Noodles Hahn	133
10	Eddie Cicotte	123
	Sam Leever	123
	Orval Overall	123
1893-1900		
1	Kid Nichols	139
2	Amos Rusie	130
3	Nig Cuppy	127
4	Clark Griffith	121
5	Frank Dwyer	115
6	Billy Rhines	114
7	Ted Breitenstein	109
	Nixey Callahan	109
	Frank Killen	109
10	Pink Hawley	107
	Win Mercer	107
1876-1892		
1	John Clarkson	134
2	Tim Keefe	125
3	Dave Foutz	124
4	Bob Caruthers	123
	Larry Corcoran	123
6	Charlie Ferguson	122
	Silver King	122
8	Jack Stivetts	121
9	Charley Radbourn	120
	Will White	120

Opponent Batting Average

1	Nolan Ryan	.204
2	Sandy Koufax	.205
3	**Pedro Martinez**	**.206**
4	Sid Fernandez	.209
5	Andy Messersmith	.212
	J.R. Richard	.212
7	**Randy Johnson**	**.215**
	Sam McDowell	.215
9	Hoyt Wilhelm	.216
10	Ed Walsh	.218
11	Mario Soto	.220
	Bob Turley	.220
13	Addie Joss	.223
	Orval Overall	.223
	Jeff Tesreau	.223
16	Jose DeLeon	.224
	Jim Maloney	.224
	Ed Reulbach	.224
19	Larry Corcoran	.226
	Tim Keefe	.226
	Tom Seaver	.226
22	Walter Johnson	.227
23	Bob Gibson	.228
	Rich Gossage	.228
	Rube Waddell	.228
	Don Wilson	.228
27	Sam Jones	.230
	Jim Palmer	.230
29	Bobby Bolin	.231
	Roger Clemens	**.231**
	Bob Feller	.231
	Catfish Hunter	.231
	Hideo Nomo	**.231**
34	**David Cone**	**.232**
	Al Downing	.232
	John Smoltz	**.232**
	Johnny Vander Meer	.232
	Stan Williams	.232
39	Mordecai Brown	.233
	Charlie Ferguson	.233
	Charlie Hough	.233
42	Dean Chance	.234
	Larry Cheney	.234
	Denny McLain	.234
	Toad Ramsey	.234
	Amos Rusie	.234
	John Ward	.234
48	Ray Culp	.235
	Rollie Fingers	.235
	Whitey Ford	.235
	Dave Foutz	.235
	Ed Morris	.235
	Tony Mullane	.235
54	Moe Drabowsky	.236
	Christy Mathewson	.236
	Curt Schilling	**.236**
	Don Sutton	.236
	Luis Tiant	.236
	Bob Veale	.236
60	Vida Blue	.237
	Juan Marichal	.237
	Tug McGraw	.237
	Juan Pizarro	.237
	Frank Smith	.237
65	Rudy May	.238
	Allie Reynolds	.238
	Jim Scott	.238
	Sonny Siebert	.238
69	Gary Bell	.239
	Chief Bender	.239
	Bill Donovan	.239
	Don Drysdale	.239
	Ramon Martinez	.239
	Hal Newhouser	.239
	Gary Nolan	.239
	Barney Pelty	.239
	Eddie Plank	.239
	Dupee Shaw	.239
	Dave Stieb	.239
	Will White	.239
81	Steve Carlton	.240
	Bob Caruthers	.240
	John Clarkson	.240
	Mort Cooper	.240
	Billy Pierce	.240
	Mike Scott	.240
	Bill Singer	.240
	Virgil Trucks	.240
89	Jack Coombs	.241
	Kirby Higbe	.241
	Al Leiter	**.241**
	Bob Lemon	.241
	George McQuillan	.241
	Earl Moore	.241
	Charley Radbourn	.241
	Hooks Wiltse	.241
97	10 players tied	.242

Opponent On-Base Pct.

1	John Ward	.254
2	Addie Joss	.260
3	George Bradley	.262
4	Terry Larkin	.263
5	Larry Corcoran	.264
	Ed Walsh	.264
7	Tommy Bond	.267
8	**Pedro Martinez**	**.268**
	Will White	.268
10	Charlie Ferguson	.270
11	Christy Mathewson	.273
	Ed Morris	.273
13	Jim McCormick	.274
14	Fred Goldsmith	.275
	Tim Keefe	.275
	Sandy Koufax	.275
	Jim Whitney	.275
18	Juan Marichal	.277
19	Mordecai Brown	.278
	Charley Radbourn	.278
21	Walter Johnson	.279
	Dupee Shaw	.279
23	Guy Hecker	.281
	Jumbo McGinnis	.281
25	**Curt Schilling**	**.282**
26	Deacon Phillippe	.283
	Tom Seaver	.283
28	Babe Adams	.284
	Jim Galvin	.284
30	Bob Caruthers	.285
	Catfish Hunter	.285
	Bobby Mathews	.285
	Gary Nolan	.285
34	Sid Fernandez	.286
	Dave Foutz	.286
	Don Sutton	.286
37	Fergie Jenkins	.287
	Greg Maddux	**.287**
	Andy Messersmith	.287
	Cy Young	.287
41	Grover Alexander	.288
	Rube Waddell	.288
	Hoyt Wilhelm	.288
44	Tiny Bonham	.289
	Henry Boyle	.289
	Noodles Hahn	.289
	Jack Lynch	.289
	Bret Saberhagen	.289
49	Dennis Eckersley	.290
	Denny McLain	.290
	Mike Mussina	**.290**
	Hooks Wiltse	.290
53	Nick Altrock	.291
	John Clarkson	.291
	Carl Hubbell	.291
56	Chief Bender	.292
	Charlie Buffinton	.292
	Rollie Fingers	.292
	Ron Guidry	.292
	Robin Roberts	.292
	John Smoltz	**.292**
	Mickey Welch	.292
	Doc White	.292
64	Don Drysdale	.293
	Sam Leever	.293
	Eddie Plank	.293
67	George McQuillan	.294
	Jim Palmer	.294
	Mario Soto	.294
	Ralph Terry	.294
71	John Candelaria	.295
	Toad Ramsey	.295
	Jeff Tesreau	.295
74	**Roger Clemens**	**.296**
	Gaylord Perry	.296
	Warren Spahn	.296
77	Jim Bunning	.297
	Jack Chesbro	.297
	Eddie Cicotte	.297
	Mike Cuellar	.297
	Eddie Fisher	.297
	Bob Gibson	.297
	Don Mossi	.297
	Mike Scott	.297
	Frank Smith	.297
	Jack Taylor	.297
	Luis Tiant	.297
	George Winter	.297
89	Harry Brecheen	.298
	Dizzy Dean	.298
	Tony Mullane	.298
	Don Newcombe	.298
	Orval Overall	.298
	Fritz Peterson	.298
	Lee Richmond	.298
	Dick Rudolph	.298
97	5 players tied	.299

Adjusted Pitching Wins

1	Cy Young	77.8
2	Walter Johnson	70.8
3	**Roger Clemens**	**61.1**
4	Lefty Grove	60.8
5	Kid Nichols	55.1
6	Grover Alexander	55.0
7	**Greg Maddux**	**54.6**
8	Tom Seaver	46.8
9	**Randy Johnson**	**44.9**
10	**Pedro Martinez**	**44.7**
11	Christy Mathewson	41.3
12	John Clarkson	39.6
13	Warren Spahn	38.2
14	Carl Hubbell	38.2
15	Bob Gibson	36.8
16	Jim Palmer	35.5
17	Whitey Ford	34.6
18	Bert Blyleven	34.2
19	Amos Rusie	33.9
20	Tim Keefe	33.1
21	**Kevin Brown**	**32.7**
22	Bob Feller	32.3
23	Gaylord Perry	32.3
24	**Mike Mussina**	**30.5**
25	Ed Walsh	30.0
26	Hal Newhouser	29.7
27	Eddie Plank	29.1
28	Hoyt Wilhelm	28.8
29	**Tom Glavine**	**28.8**
30	Dazzy Vance	28.5
31	**Curt Schilling**	**28.5**
32	Charley Radbourn	27.8
33	Mordecai Brown	27.7
34	Steve Carlton	27.3
35	Ted Lyons	27.3
36	Phil Niekro	27.2
37	Robin Roberts	27.2
38	Stan Coveleski	27.0
39	Tommy Bridges	26.8
40	Fergie Jenkins	26.5
41	Bret Saberhagen	26.4
42	Sandy Koufax	25.9
43	Juan Marichal	25.8
44	Don Drysdale	25.2
45	Billy Pierce	24.6
46	Red Faber	24.6
47	**John Smoltz**	**24.5**
48	Nolan Ryan	24.5
49	Rube Waddell	24.4
50	Eppa Rixey	23.7
51	Dave Stieb	23.7
52	Tony Mullane	23.5
53	Lefty Gomez	23.4
54	Clark Griffith	23.3
55	Urban Shocker	23.1
56	**David Cone**	**23.0**
57	Addie Joss	22.9
58	**Kevin Appier**	**22.8**
59	Silver King	22.3
60	Dennis Eckersley	21.9
61	Jimmy Key	21.6
62	Harry Brecheen	21.5
63	Eddie Cicotte	21.5
64	Vic Willis	21.4
65	Dizzy Trout	21.3
66	Jim Bunning	21.0
67	Dolf Luque	20.8
68	Joe McGinnity	20.7
69	Dutch Leonard	20.6
70	Eddie Rommel	20.5
71	Dizzy Dean	19.9
72	Bob Lemon	19.7
73	Carl Mays	19.6
74	Don Sutton	19.4
75	Bob Caruthers	19.4
76	Luis Tiant	19.4
77	Jim McCormick	19.4
78	Chuck Finley	19.3
79	Red Ruffing	19.2
80	Mickey Welch	19.1
81	Nig Cuppy	19.1
82	Lon Warneke	19.0
83	Ron Guidry	19.0
84	Rick Reuschel	18.7
85	Noodles Hahn	18.1
86	Jack Stivetts	18.1
87	Babe Adams	17.9
88	Sam Leever	17.7
89	Virgil Trucks	17.6
90	Wes Ferrell	17.5
91	Waite Hoyt	17.5
92	Bucky Walters	17.2
93	Tommy John	17.1
94	Ed Reulbach	17.0
95	Will White	16.9
96	Sal Maglie	16.9
97	Wilbur Cooper	16.8
98	Steve Rogers	16.7
99	Mel Harder	16.6
100	Rich Gossage	16.3

Relief Wins

1	Hoyt Wilhelm	124
2	Lindy McDaniel	119
3	Rich Gossage	115
4	Rollie Fingers	107
5	Sparky Lyle	99
6	Roy Face	96
7	Gene Garber	94
	Kent Tekulve	94
9	Mike Marshall	92
10	Don McMahon	90
11	Tug McGraw	89
12	Clay Carroll	88
	John Franco	**88**
14	**Jesse Orosco**	**87**
15	Bob Stanley	85
16	Bill Campbell	80
	Gary Lavelle	80
18	Tom Burgmeier	79
	Stu Miller	79
	Ron Perranoski	79
21	Johnny Murphy	73
	Jeff Reardon	73
23	John Hiller	72
24	Mark Clear	71
	Dick Hall	71
	Lee Smith	71
27	Willie Hernandez	70
	Roger McDowell	70
29	Pedro Borbon	69
30	Bruce Sutter	68
31	Doug Jones	66
32	Steve Bedrosian	65
33	Al Hrabosky	64
34	Darold Knowles	63
	Clem Labine	63
	Dave LaRoche	63
	Eric Plunk	63
38	Jim Brewer	62
	Turk Farrell	62
	Eddie Fisher	62
	Grant Jackson	62
	Paul Lindblad	62
	Frank Linzy	62
	Dan Plesac	**62**
45	Paul Assenmacher	61
46	Joe Heving	60
47	Mike Jackson	59
	Johnny Klippstein	59
	Elias Sosa	59
50	2 players tied	58

Relief Losses

1	Gene Garber	108
2	Hoyt Wilhelm	103
3	Rollie Fingers	101
4	Mike Marshall	98
5	Kent Tekulve	90
6	Lindy McDaniel	88
7	Lee Smith	87
8	Rich Gossage	85
9	Roy Face	82
10	**John Franco**	**79**
11	Doug Jones	78
	Jesse Orosco	**78**
13	Jeff Reardon	77
14	Sparky Lyle	76
15	Gary Lavelle	75
16	Ron Perranoski	74
17	Darold Knowles	71
	Bruce Sutter	71
19	Roger McDowell	69
	Tug McGraw	69
21	Stu Miller	67
	Dan Plesac	**67**
23	Clay Carroll	66
	Don McMahon	66
25	Bill Campbell	65
26	Mike Jackson	63
27	Greg Minton	62
28	Steve Bedrosian	61
	Bob Stanley	61
30	John Hiller	58
31	Frank Linzy	57
	Randy Myers	57
33	Mitch Williams	56
34	Willie Hernandez	55
35	**Roberto Hernandez**	**54**
	Craig Lefferts	54
37	Tom Burgmeier	53
	Ron Davis	53
	Greg Harris	53
	Dave Smith	53
	Mike Timlin	**53**
42	Rick Aguilera	52
	Jim Kern	52
	Randy Moffitt	52
	Dave Righetti	52
	Todd Worrell	52
47	6 players tied	51

Relief Games

1	**Jesse Orosco**	**1248**
2	**Dan Plesac**	**1050**
	Kent Tekulve	1050
4	**John Franco**	**1036**
5	Hoyt Wilhelm	1018
6	Lee Smith	1016
7	Rich Gossage	965
8	Mike Jackson	953
9	Gene Garber	922
10	Lindy McDaniel	913
11	Rollie Fingers	907
12	Sparky Lyle	899
13	**Mike Stanton**	**884**
14	Paul Assenmacher	883
15	Jeff Reardon	880
16	Don McMahon	872
17	Doug Jones	842
18	Roy Face	821
19	Tug McGraw	785
20	**Roberto Hernandez**	**759**
21	Darold Knowles	757
22	Tom Burgmeier	742
	Gary Lavelle	742
24	**Steve Reed**	**738**
25	Ron Perranoski	736
26	Willie Hernandez	733
27	**Mike Timlin**	**732**
28	**Mark Guthrie**	**722**
29	Roger McDowell	721
30	Randy Myers	716
31	**Jeff Nelson**	**714**
32	Dennis Eckersley	710
33	Clay Carroll	703
	Greg Minton	703
35	Mike Marshall	699
	Jeff Montgomery	699
37	Larry Andersen	698
38	Bill Campbell	691
39	Steve Bedrosian	686
40	**Rod Beck**	**678**
41	Dan Quisenberry	674
42	Eric Plunk	673
43	**Jose Mesa**	**667**
44	**Todd Jones**	**665**
45	**Buddy Groom**	**664**
46	Bruce Sutter	661
47	Craig Lefferts	651
48	Ted Abernathy	647
	Chuck McElroy	647
50	Rick Aguilera	643

Relief Innings Pitched

1	Hoyt Wilhelm	1871.0
2	Lindy McDaniel	1694.0
3	Rich Gossage	1556.2
4	Rollie Fingers	1500.1
5	Gene Garber	1452.2
6	Kent Tekulve	1436.2
7	Sparky Lyle	1390.1
8	Tug McGraw	1301.1
9	Don McMahon	1297.0
10	**Jesse Orosco**	**1277.0**
11	Mike Marshall	1259.1
12	Lee Smith	1252.1
13	Tom Burgmeier	1248.2
14	Roy Face	1212.1
15	Clay Carroll	1204.2
16	Eddie Fisher	1186.0
17	**John Franco**	**1184.2**
18	Bill Campbell	1177.1
19	Ron Perranoski	1170.2
20	Bob Stanley	1157.0
21	Jeff Reardon	1132.1
22	Mike Jackson	1108.0
23	Doug Jones	1097.1
24	Stu Miller	1094.2
25	Greg Minton	1087.1
26	Gary Lavelle	1077.2
27	Darold Knowles	1052.1
28	Paul Lindblad	1043.1
	Dan Quisenberry	1043.1
30	Bruce Sutter	1042.0
31	Johnny Klippstein	1040.2
32	Roger McDowell	1039.2
33	Pedro Borbon	1016.1
34	**Dan Plesac**	**1003.0**
35	Willie Hernandez	994.1
36	Bob Miller	992.2
37	Larry Andersen	990.2
38	Dave LaRoche	976.0
39	Ted Abernathy	970.0
40	John Hiller	962.2
41	Steve Bedrosian	931.0
42	Greg Harris	923.0
43	Eric Plunk	919.0
44	Elias Sosa	905.0
45	Dale Murray	901.1
46	Doug Bair	889.1
47	Terry Forster	888.0
48	Craig Lefferts	881.2
49	Bob Locker	879.0
50	Dennis Lamp	876.0

Adjusted Relievers' Runs

1	Hoyt Wilhelm	252
2	Rich Gossage	183
3	**Mariano Rivera**	**164**
4	**John Franco**	**156**
5	Dan Quisenberry	147
6	Kent Tekulve	139
7	Lee Smith	136
8	John Wetteland	134
9	Tom Henke	131
10	Rollie Fingers	129
11	**Paul Quantrill**	**127**
12	Mark Eichhorn	125
13	Mike Jackson	124
14	**Roberto Hernandez**	**122**
15	Sparky Lyle	121
16	**Jesse Orosco**	**120**
17	Doug Jones	118
18	Bob Stanley	115
19	Tug McGraw	113
20	John Hiller	110
	Jeff Montgomery	110
	Bruce Sutter	110
23	Dennis Eckersley	109
24	**Trevor Hoffman**	**107**
25	**Keith Foulke**	**105**
	Lindy McDaniel	105
27	Mike Marshall	103
28	**Troy Percival**	**102**
29	**Steve Reed**	**100**
30	**Billy Wagner**	**99**
31	Clay Carroll	98
32	Gary Lavelle	97
	Jeff Nelson	**97**
34	Robb Nen	96
35	Rick Aguilera	93
	Ellis Kinder	93
37	**Armando Benitez**	**90**
	Gene Garber	90
39	Bob Wickman	89
40	Greg Harris	88
	Ron Perranoski	88
42	**Shigetoshi Hasegawa**	**87**
	Mike Timlin	**87**
44	Don McMahon	86
	Eric Plunk	86
46	Tom Burgmeier	85
	Stu Miller	85
48	Willie Hernandez	84
	Jeff Reardon	84
50	2 players tied	80

Relief Ranking

1	Hoyt Wilhelm	366
2	Rich Gossage	314
3	**Mariano Rivera**	**282**
4	**John Franco**	**277**
5	John Wetteland	248
6	**Roberto Hernandez**	**228**
7	Lee Smith	219
8	Dan Quisenberry	218
9	Rollie Fingers	215
10	Tom Henke	212
11	**Trevor Hoffman**	**202**
12	Robb Nen	199
	Kent Tekulve	199
14	Doug Jones	190
15	Sparky Lyle	187
16	Dennis Eckersley	186
17	Mike Marshall	185
18	John Hiller	179
19	**Jesse Orosco**	**178**
20	Rick Aguilera	175
21	Jeff Montgomery	173
22	Bruce Sutter	172
23	Tug McGraw	162
24	Bob Stanley	156
	Billy Wagner	**156**
26	**Troy Percival**	**155**
	Ron Perranoski	155
28	Ellis Kinder	154
29	Mike Jackson	147
	Gary Lavelle	147
31	**Paul Quantrill**	**143**
32	Lindy McDaniel	142
33	Stu Miller	141
34	Mark Eichhorn	137
	Roy Face	137
	Keith Foulke	**137**
37	**Dan Plesac**	**133**
38	Gene Garber	132
	Gregg Olson	132
40	**Armando Benitez**	**130**
	Mike Henneman	130
	Randy Myers	130
	Jeff Reardon	130
44	Clay Carroll	127
	Bob Wickman	127
46	Dave Righetti	125
47	Jeff Shaw	122
48	Bryan Harvey	119
	Jeff Russell	119
	Mike Timlin	**119**

Pitcher Wins by era

1988-2003

1	**Greg Maddux**	**62.2**
2	**Roger Clemens**	**61.7**
3	**Pedro Martinez**	**44.7**
4	**Randy Johnson**	**42.4**
5	**Tom Glavine**	**35.4**
6	**Kevin Brown**	**34.3**
7	**Mike Mussina**	**32.6**
8	**John Smoltz**	**29.4**
9	Bret Saberhagen	27.8
10	**Mariano Rivera**	**26.9**

1973-1987

1	Tom Seaver	49.1
2	Jim Palmer	34.3
3	Steve Carlton	33.2
4	Gaylord Perry	32.8
5	Bert Blyleven	31.1
6	Fergie Jenkins	30.3
7	Dennis Eckersley	29.8
8	Rich Gossage	29.5
9	Phil Niekro	29.2
10	Dave Stieb	25.1

1961-1972

1	Bob Gibson	44.9
2	Don Drysdale	32.4
3	Juan Marichal	27.5
4	Sandy Koufax	22.3
5	Jim Bunning	16.4
6	Jim Kaat	16.1
	Mel Stottlemyre	16.1
8	Larry Jackson	16.0
9	Ron Perranoski	14.9
10	Wilbur Wood	14.8

1943-1960

1	Warren Spahn	51.4
2	Whitey Ford	37.2
	Hal Newhouser	37.2
4	Hoyt Wilhelm	37.1
5	Bob Lemon	34.2
6	Bob Feller	31.6
7	Robin Roberts	30.3
8	Dizzy Trout	29.7
9	Billy Pierce	25.6
10	Harry Brecheen	24.9

1921-1942

1	Lefty Grove	59.1
2	Carl Hubbell	40.2
3	Ted Lyons	33.5
4	Red Ruffing	31.4
5	Wes Ferrell	31.1
6	Dazzy Vance	29.2
7	Tommy Bridges	27.3
8	Urban Shocker	27.0
9	Bucky Walters	26.7
10	Dolf Luque	26.2

1901-1920

1	Walter Johnson	89.9
2	Cy Young	77.0
3	Grover Alexander	62.9
4	Christy Mathewson	56.3
5	Ed Walsh	37.7
6	Mordecai Brown	32.7
7	Carl Mays	31.7
8	Eddie Plank	30.3
9	Eddie Cicotte	24.3
10	Addie Joss	23.0

1893-1900

1	Kid Nichols	56.2
2	Amos Rusie	36.7
3	Clark Griffith	28.3
4	Nig Cuppy	20.4
5	Frank Dwyer	13.6
6	Ted Breitenstein	10.9
	Frank Killen	10.9
8	Nixey Callahan	9.3
9	Pink Hawley	8.3
10	Win Mercer	8.0

1876-1892

1	John Clarkson	42.5
2	Tim Keefe	35.6
3	Charley Radbourn	31.5
4	Tony Mullane	30.2
5	Bob Caruthers	30.0
6	Jack Stivetts	25.1
7	Silver King	23.0
8	Guy Hecker	22.5
9	Jim McCormick	21.1
10	Charlie Buffinton	19.6

Pitcher Wins

1 Walter Johnson 89.9
2 Cy Young..........................77.0
3 Grover Alexander 62.9
4 Greg Maddux 62.2
5 Roger Clemens 61.7
6 Lefty Grove.......................59.1
7 Christy Mathewson 56.3
8 Kid Nichols 56.2
9 Warren Spahn...................51.4
10 Tom Seaver......................49.1
11 Bob Gibson 44.9
12 Pedro Martinez 44.7
13 John Clarkson 42.5
14 Randy Johnson 42.4
15 Carl Hubbell 40.2
16 Ed Walsh..........................37.7
17 Whitey Ford......................37.2
Hal Newhouser 37.2
19 Hoyt Wilhelm....................37.1
20 Amos Rusie......................36.7
21 Tim Keefe.........................35.6
22 Tom Glavine 35.4
23 Kevin Brown................34.3
Jim Palmer 34.3
25 Bob Lemon.......................34.2
26 Ted Lyons.........................33.5
27 Steve Carlton 33.2
28 Gaylord Perry...................32.8
29 Mordecai Brown...............32.7
30 Mike Mussina 32.6
31 Don Drysdale 32.4
32 Carl Mays.........................31.7
33 Bob Feller.........................31.6
34 Charley Radbourn.............31.5
35 Red Ruffing......................31.4
36 Bert Blyleven....................31.1
Wes Ferrell.......................31.1
38 Fergie Jenkins..................30.3
Eddie Plank.......................30.3
Robin Roberts...................30.3
41 Tony Mullane....................30.2
42 Bob Caruthers..................30.0
43 Dennis Eckersley 29.8
44 Dizzy Trout 29.7
45 Rich Gossage 29.5
46 John Smoltz 29.4
47 Phil Niekro.........................29.2
Dazzy Vance 29.2
49 Clark Griffith.....................28.3
50 Bret Saberhagen..............27.8
51 Juan Marichal....................27.5
52 Tommy Bridges 27.3
53 Urban Shocker 27.0
54 Mariano Rivera...........26.9
55 Bucky Walters 26.7
56 Dolf Luque 26.2
57 Stan Coveleski 26.0
58 Curt Schilling.............25.8
59 Billy Pierce 25.6
60 Dave Stieb.........................25.1
Jack Stivetts 25.1
62 Harry Brecheen 24.9
63 Eddie Cicotte....................24.3
64 Eppa Rixey........................24.2
65 Red Faber.........................23.3
66 David Cone..................23.1
67 Addie Joss 23.0
Silver King.........................23.0
Eddie Rommel 23.0
70 Jimmy Key........................22.8
71 Rollie Fingers....................22.7
72 Lon Warneke.....................22.6
73 Guy Hecker.......................22.5
Rick Reuschel 22.5
75 Lee Smith..........................22.4
76 Dizzy Dean........................22.3
Sandy Koufax.....................22.3
78 Dutch Leonard 22.2
Rube Waddell......................22.2
80 Red Lucas..........................21.5
Nolan Ryan 21.5
Luis Tiant 21.5
83 Joe Wood 21.4
84 Roberto Hernandez 21.1
Jim McCormick 21.1
86 John Hiller.........................20.7
John Wetteland 20.7
88 Nig Cuppy 20.4
89 Kevin Appier 20.2
Jesse Tannehill 20.2
91 Lefty Gomez......................20.1
Tommy John.......................20.1
93 Vic Willis............................20.0
94 Ron Guidry..........................19.9
95 Wilbur Cooper 19.7
96 Charlie Buffinton 19.6
97 Early Wynn.........................19.5
98 Jack Quinn 19.4
99 Chuck Finley 19.3
Doug Jones 19.3

Pitcher Wins

101 Mike Marshall....................19.2
102 Spud Chandler 19.1
103 Freddie Fitzsimmons........19.0
104 Orel Hershiser..................18.9
Joe McGinnity 18.9
Robb Nen...........................18.9
Mickey Welch 18.9
108 Schoolboy Rowe 18.8
Doc White 18.8
110 Bobby Shantz 18.7
111 Ed Lopat 18.6
Don Newcombe 18.6
113 Burleigh Grimes 18.3
Jesse Orosco 18.3
115 Curt Davis 18.2
116 Babe Adams 17.7
Dwight Gooden 17.7
118 Andy Messersmith 17.5
119 Ed Reulbach 17.3
120 Dave Foutz 17.2
Jeff Montgomery...............17.2
122 Noodles Hahn 17.0
Mel Harder 17.0
Babe Ruth 17.0
125 Rick Aguilera.....................16.8
Larry French 16.8
Don Sutton 16.8
Virgil Trucks 16.8
129 Bob Shawkey 16.7
130 Jim Bunning 16.4
131 Hippo Vaughn 16.3
132 John Candelaria 16.2
Murry Dickson.....................16.2
134 Jim Kaat 16.1
Sam Leever.........................16.1
Mel Stottlemyre 16.1
John Tudor 16.1
138 Larry Jackson 16.0
139 George Uhle......................15.9
140 Thornton Lee 15.8
141 Mike Garcia........................15.7
Waite Hoyt..........................15.7
Max Lanier 15.7
Jack Taylor 15.7
145 Deacon Phillippe 15.6
146 Mel Parnell.........................15.5
Nap Rucker 15.5
148 Johnny Antonelli................15.4
Frank Viola 15.4
150 Stu Miller............................15.3
151 Ned Garver 15.2
Hal Schumacher 15.2
153 Chief Bender......................14.9
Ellis Kinder 14.9
Claude Passeau..................14.9
Ron Perranoski 14.9
157 Steve Rogers 14.8
Bob Stanley.........................14.8
Wilbur Wood.......................14.8
160 Derek Lowe 14.7
161 Jerry Koosman...................14.6
Randy Myers 14.6
163 Tim Hudson................14.5
164 Mort Cooper 14.3
Charlie Ferguson................14.3
Claude Hendrix 14.3
167 Mark Eichhorn....................14.1
Tug McGraw.........................14.1
169 Mike Jackson 13.9
170 Sal Maglie 13.8
Dave Righetti.......................13.8
172 Fred Hutchinson.................13.7
Firpo Marberry....................13.7
Jose Rijo 13.7
175 Frank Dwyer.......................13.6
Jim Maloney........................13.6
177 Bartolo Colon..............13.5
Charlie Root 13.5
David Wells 13.5
180 Gary Lavelle 13.4
Claude Osteen 13.4
Andy Pettitte 13.4
183 Roy Face 13.2
Gene Garber.........................13.2
185 Sadie McMahon 13.0
John Ward 13.0
187 Milt Pappas 12.9
188 Vida Blue..............................12.8
Keith Foulke...............12.8
Will White 12.8
191 Al Leiter......................12.7
192 Lindy McDaniel 12.6
Orval Overall 12.6
Gary Peters..........................12.6
195 Larry Corcoran 12.5
Willie Hernandez..................12.5
Harry Howell 12.5
198 Frank Lary 12.4
Barry Zito 12.4
200 Howie Pollet 12.3

Pitcher Wins

201 Steve Farr 12.2
Jeff Pfeffer 12.2
Jake Weimer 12.2
204 Van Mungo.........................12.1
Dan Plesac 12.1
206 Frank Tanana 12.0
Jim Whitney 12.0
208 Clay Carroll 11.9
Alex Fernandez 11.9
George Mullin.......................11.9
211 Charlie Hough 11.7
Frank Linzy...........................11.7
213 Mike Hampton.............11.6
Mike Timlin 11.6
215 Tom Burgmeier.....................11.5
216 Tom Gordon 11.4
Harvey Haddix 11.4
Jon Matlack...........................11.4
Jim Tobin..............................11.4
220 Bill Hutchison 11.3
221 Jim Devlin 11.2
Mark Langston 11.2
Johnny Sain 11.2
224 Jim Perry...............................11.1
Curt Simmons 11.1
226 Jack Chesbro 11.0
Jamie Moyer..................11.0
Ugueth Urbina 11.0
Hooks Wiltse 11.0
230 Ted Breitenstein 10.9
Frank Killen 10.9
Don McMahon.........................10.9
233 Tiny Bonham..........................10.8
Dave Smith..............................10.8
235 Ray Kremer............................10.7
236 Jim Brewer 10.6
Brad Radke 10.6
Tom Zachary 10.6
239 Teddy Higuera........................10.5
Matt Morris...................10.5
Johnny Murphy.........................10.5
Paul Quantrill 10.5
243 Tex Hughson 10.4
244 Al Brazle..................................10.3
Dennis Martinez.........................10.3
Greg Minton 10.3
Bob Wickman.............................10.3
248 Ewell Blackwell 10.2
Dutch Ruether............................10.2
Slim Sallee 10.2
Jeff Shaw....................................10.2
252 Jay Howell..................................10.1
Lefty Leifield 10.1
254 Bob Ewing..................................10.0
Jim Kern 10.0
256 Camilo Pascual 9.9
Monte Pearson..............................9.9
258 Jim Galvin 9.8
Jack McDowell 9.8
Ed Morris 9.8
Kenny Rogers 9.8
262 Elton Chamberlain 9.7
Al Orth..9.7
Fritz Ostermueller 9.7
Sherry Smith 9.7
266 Joe Dobson.....................................9.6
267 Wilson Alvarez 9.5
Jim Bagby 9.5
Dean Chance 9.5
Russ Ford...9.5
Terry Forster 9.5
Dutch Leonard 9.5
Sam McDowell 9.5
Bob Rush 9.5
275 Mike Boddicker....................................9.4
Sid Fernandez.......................................9.4
Mark Gubicza..9.4
Catfish Hunter 9.4
Byung-Hyun Kim..........9.4
Ben Sanders 9.4
281 Johnny Allen...9.3
Nixey Callahan 9.3
Watty Clark 9.3
Art Nehf...9.3
Fernando Valenzuela 9.3
286 Shigetoshi Hasegawa...9.2
Larry Jansen 9.2
Dave McNally 9.2
Gary Nolan...9.2
290 Bill Campbell 9.1
Dick Hall...9.1
Johnny Rigney 9.1
Jim Scott 9.1
Bob Welch...9.1
295 Preacher Roe...9.0
296 Paul Assenmacher...8.9
Allie Reynolds 8.9
298 Paul Derringer..8.8
Jeff Tesreau 8.8
300 8 players tied 8.7

Player Overall Wins by era

1988-2003

1 Barry Bonds.............112.6
2 Rickey Henderson 72.0
3 Greg Maddux 62.2
4 Roger Clemens 61.7
5 Jeff Bagwell................53.6
6 Wade Boggs 51.1
7 Frank Thomas............46.0
8 Pedro Martinez 44.7
9 Edgar Martinez 44.5
10 Ken Griffey 44.1
Cal Ripken 44.1
12 Barry Larkin 42.9
13 Alex Rodriguez 42.5
14 Randy Johnson............42.4
15 Mike Piazza 42.0
16 Tony Gwynn 38.8
17 Tim Raines.........................38.7
18 Gary Sheffield............38.2
19 Roberto Alomar 37.8
20 Paul Molitor 37.0
21 Ryne Sandberg....................36.7
22 Mark McGwire......................35.7
23 Tom Glavine 35.4
24 Ivan Rodriguez...........34.7
25 Rafael Palmeiro 34.4

1973-1987

1 Mike Schmidt 78.6
2 Joe Morgan 67.4
3 Bobby Grich 51.6
4 Tom Seaver..........................49.1
5 Ozzie Smith..........................45.7
6 George Brett 43.4
7 Johnny Bench 42.5
8 Darrell Evans 41.2
Robin Yount...........................41.2
10 Rod Carew 40.3
11 Reggie Jackson 39.5
12 Gary Carter...........................39.2
13 Carlton Fisk...........................38.8
14 Willie Randolph 37.1
15 Lou Whitaker..........................35.6
16 Eddie Murray..........................35.4
17 Keith Hernandez 34.8
18 Jim Palmer 34.3
19 Steve Carlton 33.2
20 Gaylord Perry..........................32.8
21 Reggie Smith 31.9
22 Alan Trammell 31.7
23 Bert Blyleven...........................31.1
24 Dave Winfield 30.5
25 Fergie Jenkins.........................30.3

1961-1972

1 Willie Mays.........................84.6
2 Hank Aaron 81.3
3 Frank Robinson.....................64.3
4 Ron Santo 45.3
5 Bob Gibson 44.9
6 Al Kaline 43.1
7 Carl Yastrzemski 42.3
8 Dick Allen 39.2
9 Willie McCovey.......................39.0
10 Roberto Clemente.................34.0
Bill Mazeroski 34.0
12 Harmon Killebrew 32.6
13 Don Drysdale 32.4
14 Willie Stargell 30.8
15 Norm Cash.............................30.5
16 Jimmy Wynn 30.0
17 Juan Marichal.........................27.5
18 Ernie Banks 27.2
19 Jim Fregosi............................25.5
20 Billy Williams 23.8
21 Rocky Colavito.......................22.7
22 Frank Howard........................22.6
23 Sandy Koufax.........................22.3
Joe Torre 22.3
25 Tony Oliva 20.3

1943-1960

1 Ted Williams.........................87.0
2 Stan Musial 76.0
3 Mickey Mantle 72.9
4 Eddie Mathews 52.1
5 Warren Spahn 51.4
6 Lou Boudreau 43.6
7 Bobby Doerr............................40.3
8 Yogi Berra 38.6
9 Whitey Ford 37.2
Hal Newhouser 37.2
11 Hoyt Wilhelm...........................37.1
12 Jackie Robinson......................34.3
13 Bob Lemon..............................34.0
14 Bob Feller................................31.6
15 Robin Roberts.........................30.3
16 Dizzy Trout 29.7
17 Joe Gordon 28.8
18 Billy Pierce 25.6
19 Harry Brecheen 24.9
20 Ralph Kiner 24.2
21 Roy Campanella 24.1
22 Duke Snider 23.0
23 Richie Ashburn 22.6
24 Dutch Leonard 22.2
Gil McDougald 22.2

Player Overall Wins by era

1921-1942

1 Babe Ruth 129.0
2 Rogers Hornsby 86.0
3 Lou Gehrig 70.9
4 Mel Ott 60.7
5 Lefty Grove..........................59.1
6 Jimmie Foxx 58.7
7 Joe DiMaggio 45.8
8 Charlie Gehringer.................45.1
9 Gabby Hartnett 44.3
10 Arky Vaughan.......................43.3
11 Luke Appling 42.4
12 Carl Hubbell 40.2
13 Joe Cronin............................39.6
14 Bill Dickey.............................38.5
15 Johnny Mize 37.7
16 Frankie Frisch.......................37.3
17 Dave Bancroft 36.2
18 Bob Johnson 35.7
19 Joe Sewell.............................35.2
20 Mickey Cochrane 34.7
21 Paul Waner 33.8
22 Ted Lyons 33.5
23 Harry Heilmann......................33.2
24 Hank Greenberg 32.6
25 Billy Herman 31.6

1901-1920

1 Nap Lajoie..........................95.1
2 Walter Johnson 89.9
3 Ty Cobb..............................85.5
4 Tris Speaker 82.1
Honus Wagner 82.1
6 Cy Young.............................77.0
7 Eddie Collins 72.5
8 Grover Alexander 62.9
9 Christy Mathewson 56.3
10 Bill Dahlen...........................48.5
11 Bobby Wallace 38.4
12 Joe Jackson 38.3
13 Ed Walsh..............................37.7
14 Frank Baker..........................33.7
15 Mordecai Brown 32.7
16 Carl Mays.............................31.7
17 Heinie Groh..........................30.4
18 Eddie Plank..........................30.3
19 Elmer Flick 29.7
20 Sam Crawford 29.3
21 Fred Clarke 27.7
22 Art Fletcher 27.2
23 Sherry Magee 26.2
24 Eddie Cicotte........................24.3
25 Zack Wheat...........................24.1

1893-1900

1 Kid Nichols.........................56.2
2 George Davis 50.7
3 Ed Delahanty 42.6
4 Amos Rusie.........................36.7
5 Cupid Childs........................30.5
6 Jesse Burkett 29.1
7 Clark Griffith.........................28.3
8 Billy Hamilton 27.3
9 Hughie Jennings 26.8
10 Jake Beckley 23.0
11 Chief Zimmer........................20.7
12 Nig Cuppy 20.4
13 Joe Kelley.............................20.0
14 John McGraw........................19.5
15 Bill Joyce 19.3
16 Mike Griffin............................18.0
17 Lave Cross 16.4
18 Elmer Smith 14.2
19 Frank Dwyer..........................13.6
20 Kip Selbach...........................13.5
21 Mike Tiernan 13.3
22 Jimmy Ryan 13.0
23 Jack Clements 12.9
24 George Van Haltren 11.7
25 Billy Nash 11.3

1876-1892

1 Roger Connor 43.4
2 John Clarkson.....................42.5
Dan Brouthers.....................42.5
4 Bid McPhee.........................38.3
5 Jack Glasscock 36.6
6 Tim Keefe.............................35.6
7 Cap Anson 35.4
8 Bob Caruthers.......................33.5
Bob Caruthers........................33.5
10 Charley Radbourn..................31.5
11 Tony Mullane 30.0
12 Sam Thompson......................29.5
13 Buck Ewing 29.3
14 King Kelly 28.4
15 Fred Dunlap 28.1
16 Pete Browning........................27.9
17 Hardy Richardson 26.5
18 Charlie Bennett 23.9
19 Jack Stivetts 23.6
20 Silver King 23.0
21 Guy Hecker 21.9
22 Harry Stovey 21.5
23 Jim McCormick 21.1
24 Fred Pfeffer 20.8
25 John Ward 20.7

Player	Overall Wins alpha
Hank Aaron	81.3
Bobby Abreu	**19.0**
Babe Adams	17.7
Rick Aguilera	16.8
Grover Alexander	62.9
Dick Allen	39.2
Gene Alley	18.8
Roberto Alomar	**37.8**
Cap Anson	35.4
Johnny Antonelli	15.4
Kevin Appier	**20.2**
Luke Appling	42.4
Richie Ashburn	22.6
Earl Averill	17.3
Jeff Bagwell	**53.6**
Frank Baker	33.7
Dave Bancroft	36.2
Ernie Banks	27.2
Jesse Barfield	14.1
Dick Bartell	28.2
Jake Beckley	23.0
Buddy Bell	28.7
Jay Bell	**16.2**
Albert Belle	29.8
Johnny Bench	42.5
Chief Bender	14.9
Charlie Bennett	23.9
Wally Berger	21.0
Yogi Berra	38.6
Craig Biggio	**33.8**
Bert Blyleven	31.1
Wade Boggs	51.1
Barry Bonds	**112.6**
Bobby Bonds	27.2
Bobby Bonilla	16.4
Lou Boudreau	43.6
Ken Boyer	19.7
Harry Brecheen	24.9
Roger Bresnahan	22.8
George Brett	43.4
Tommy Bridges	27.3
Dan Brouthers	42.5
Kevin Brown	**34.3**
Mordecai Brown	32.7
Pete Browning	27.9
Charlie Buffinton	16.2
Jim Bunning	16.4
Jesse Burkett	29.1
Ellis Burks	**17.3**
Rick Burleson	17.0
Brett Butler	16.1
Ken Caminiti	21.6
Roy Campanella	24.1
Bert Campaneris	14.3
John Candelaria	16.2
Jose Canseco	23.0
Rod Carew	40.3
Max Carey	18.0
Steve Carlton	33.2
Gary Carter	39.2
Rico Carty	18.1
Bob Caruthers	33.5
Norm Cash	30.5
Cesar Cedeno	22.3
Orlando Cepeda	19.1
Ron Cey	21.3
Frank Chance	22.6
Spud Chandler	19.1
Ray Chapman	16.6
Ben Chapman	14.4
Cupid Childs	30.5
Eddie Cicotte	24.3
Jack Clark	29.6
Will Clark	24.8
Fred Clarke	27.7
John Clarkson	42.5
Roger Clemens	**61.7**
Roberto Clemente	34.0
Harlond Clift	26.3
Ty Cobb	85.5
Mickey Cochrane	34.7
Rocky Colavito	22.7
Eddie Collins	72.5
Jimmy Collins	23.0
Dave Concepcion	17.9
David Cone	**23.1**
Roger Connor	43.4
Wilbur Cooper	19.7
Mort Cooper	14.3
Stan Coveleski	26.0
Gavy Cravath	18.4
Sam Crawford	29.3
Joe Cronin	39.6
Lave Cross	16.4
Jose Cruz	21.2
Roy Cullenbine	18.8
Nig Cuppy	20.4
Bill Dahlen	48.5
Curt Davis	18.2
Chili Davis	14.8
Eric Davis	20.3
George Davis	50.7
Andre Dawson	18.1
Dizzy Dean	22.3
Doug DeCinces	14.9
Ed Delahanty	42.6
Carlos Delgado	**15.0**
Art Devlin	20.0
Bill Dickey	38.5
Murry Dickson	16.2
Joe DiMaggio	45.8
Larry Doby	18.1
Bobby Doerr	40.3
Brian Downing	20.3
Don Drysdale	32.4
Fred Dunlap	28.1
Frank Dwyer	13.6
Lenny Dykstra	23.0
Dennis Eckersley	29.8
Jim Edmonds	**28.4**
Mark Eichhorn	14.1
Kid Elberfeld	14.0
Bob Elliott	21.4
Darrell Evans	41.2
Dwight Evans	24.8
Johnny Evers	15.9
Buck Ewing	29.3
Red Faber	23.3
Ferris Fain	18.8
Bob Feller	31.6
Charlie Ferguson	14.3
Tony Fernandez	21.4
Wes Ferrell	31.2
Rollie Fingers	22.7
Chuck Finley	19.3
Carlton Fisk	38.8
Freddie Fitzsimmons	19.0
Art Fletcher	27.2
Elmer Flick	29.7
Whitey Ford	37.2
George Foster	18.5
Jack Fournier	24.4
Nellie Fox	14.4
Jimmie Foxx	58.7
Julio Franco	**15.2**
Bill Freehan	18.0
Jim Fregosi	25.5
Larry French	16.8
Lonny Frey	13.6
Frankie Frisch	37.3
Augie Galan	15.3
Mike Garcia	15.7
Nomar Garciaparra	**25.4**
Ned Garver	15.2
Lou Gehrig	70.9
Charlie Gehringer	45.1
Jason Giambi	**21.5**
Bob Gibson	44.9
Brian Giles	**24.8**
Jack Glasscock	36.6
Tom Glavine	**35.4**
Lefty Gomez	20.1
Juan Gonzalez	**18.6**
Luis Gonzalez	**20.0**
Dwight Gooden	17.7
Joe Gordon	28.8
Sid Gordon	14.8
Goose Goslin	23.1
Rich Gossage	29.5
Shawn Green	**13.8**
Hank Greenberg	32.6
Bobby Grich	51.6
Ken Griffey	**44.1**
Mike Griffin	18.0
Clark Griffith	28.3
Burleigh Grimes	18.3
Heinie Groh	30.4
Lefty Grove	59.1
Pedro Guerrero	18.0
Vladimir Guerrero	**21.1**
Ron Guidry	19.9
Tony Gwynn	38.8
Stan Hack	29.4
Noodles Hahn	17.0
Billy Hamilton	27.3
Ron Hansen	15.4
Mel Harder	17.0
Mike Hargrove	16.1
Toby Harrah	19.4
Gabby Hartnett	44.3
Jeff Heath	17.2
Guy Hecker	21.9
Harry Heilmann	33.2
Todd Helton	**19.7**
Rickey Henderson	**72.0**
Claude Hendrix	14.3
Tommy Henrich	15.0
Babe Herman	17.5
Billy Herman	31.6
Roberto Hernandez	**21.1**
Keith Hernandez	34.8
Orel Hershiser	18.9
John Hiller	20.7
Paul Hines	14.5
Gil Hodges	13.8
Rogers Hornsby	86.0
Frank Howard	22.6
Waite Hoyt	15.7
Glenn Hubbard	20.2
Carl Hubbell	40.2
Tim Hudson	**14.5**
Miller Huggins	22.3
Fred Hutchinson	13.7
Larry Jackson	16.0
Mike Jackson	13.9
Joe Jackson	38.3
Reggie Jackson	39.5
Travis Jackson	22.0
Fergie Jenkins	30.3
Hughie Jennings	26.8
Tommy John	20.1
Randy Johnson	**42.4**
Walter Johnson	89.9
Davey Johnson	14.1
Bob Johnson	35.7
Doug Jones	19.3
Andruw Jones	**15.7**
Charley Jones	19.4
Chipper Jones	**20.9**
Addie Joss	23.0
Bill Joyce	19.3
David Justice	15.5
Jim Kaat	16.1
Al Kaline	43.1
Willie Kamm	15.7
Tim Keefe	35.6
Willie Keeler	15.0
Charlie Keller	22.1
Joe Kelley	20.0
King Kelly	28.4
Jason Kendall	**15.2**
Jeff Kent	**28.5**
Jimmy Key	22.8
Harmon Killebrew	32.6
Ellis Kinder	14.9
Ralph Kiner	24.2
Silver King	23.0
Chuck Klein	21.1
Johnny Kling	14.4
Bobby Knoop	16.3
Ed Konetchy	21.2
Jerry Koosman	14.6
Sandy Koufax	22.3
Nap Lajoie	95.1
Max Lanier	15.7
Ray Lankford	18.8
Barry Larkin	**42.9**
Henry Larkin	15.3
Tony Lazzeri	17.8
Thornton Lee	15.8
Sam Leever	16.1
Bob Lemon	34.0
Chet Lemon	19.3
Dutch Leonard	22.2
Kenny Lofton	**16.7**
Johnny Logan	16.5
Ernie Lombardi	20.6
Ed Lopat	18.6
Javy Lopez	**20.1**
Derek Lowe	**14.7**
Red Lucas	20.8
Dolf Luque	26.2
Fred Lynn	19.7
Ted Lyons	33.5
Denny Lyons	19.6
Greg Maddux	**62.2**
Sherry Magee	26.2
Sal Maglie	13.8
Jim Maloney	13.6
Mickey Mantle	72.9
Firpo Marberry	13.7
Juan Marichal	27.5
Mike Marshall	19.2
Pedro Martinez	**44.7**
Edgar Martinez	**44.5**
Eddie Mathews	52.1
Christy Mathewson	56.3
Don Mattingly	15.9
Carl Mays	31.7
Willie Mays	84.6
Bill Mazeroski	34.0
Jim McCormick	21.1
Willie McCovey	39.0
Gil McDougald	22.2
Joe McGinnity	18.9
Tug McGraw	14.1
John McGraw	19.5
Fred McGriff	**22.9**
Mark McGwire	35.7
Bid McPhee	38.3
Hal McRae	14.7
Joe Medwick	25.6
Andy Messersmith	17.5
Chief Meyers	17.2
Stu Miller	15.3
Jocko Milligan	13.6
Minnie Minoso	21.0
Kevin Mitchell	20.6
Johnny Mize	37.7
Paul Molitor	37.0
Jeff Montgomery	17.2
Joe Morgan	67.4
Tony Mullane	30.0
Thurman Munson	25.4
Dwayne Murphy	15.8
Eddie Murray	35.4
Stan Musial	76.0
Mike Mussina	**32.6**
Buddy Myer	14.3
Randy Myers	14.6
Robb Nen	18.9
Graig Nettles	21.6
Don Newcombe	18.6
Hal Newhouser	37.2
Kid Nichols	56.2
Bill Nicholson	17.2
Phil Niekro	29.2
John Olerud	**24.3**
Tony Oliva	20.3
Paul O'Neill	16.0
Jesse Orosco	**18.3**
Jim O'Rourke	16.0
Dave Orr	13.6
Mel Ott	60.7
Rafael Palmeiro	**34.4**
Jim Palmer	34.3
Dave Parker	15.0
Mel Parnell	15.5
Lance Parrish	22.2
Claude Passeau	14.9
Roger Peckinpaugh	14.3
Ron Perranoski	14.9
Gaylord Perry	32.8
Johnny Pesky	15.5
Rico Petrocelli	15.4
Fred Pfeffer	20.8
Deacon Phillippe	15.6
Tony Phillips	19.3
Mike Piazza	**42.0**
Billy Pierce	25.6
Eddie Plank	30.3
Darrell Porter	20.9
Jorge Posada	**16.0**
Boog Powell	18.7
Del Pratt	22.5
Kirby Puckett	23.7
Jack Quinn	19.4
Charley Radbourn	31.5
Tim Raines	38.7
Manny Ramirez	**30.5**
Willie Randolph	37.1
Pee Wee Reese	16.3
Ed Reulbach	17.3
Rick Reuschel	22.5
Jim Rice	18.6
Hardy Richardson	26.5
Dave Righetti	13.8
Jose Rijo	13.7
Cal Ripken	44.1
Mariano Rivera	**26.9**
Eppa Rixey	24.2
Phil Rizzuto	18.7
Robin Roberts	30.3
Brooks Robinson	14.3
Frank Robinson	64.3
Jackie Robinson	34.3
Alex Rodriguez	**42.5**
Ivan Rodriguez	**34.7**
Steve Rogers	14.8
Scott Rolen	**26.1**
Eddie Rommel	23.0
Pete Rose	23.9
Al Rosen	16.2
Schoolboy Rowe	18.8
Nap Rucker	15.5
Red Ruffing	31.2
Amos Rusie	36.7
Babe Ruth	129.0
Nolan Ryan	21.5
Bret Saberhagen	27.8
Tim Salmon	**22.3**
Ryne Sandberg	36.7
Ron Santo	45.3
Ray Schalk	16.1
Wally Schang	20.4
Curt Schilling	**25.8**
Mike Schmidt	78.6
Red Schoendienst	15.8
Hal Schumacher	15.2
Mike Scioscia	18.3
Tom Seaver	49.1
Joe Sewell	35.2
Cy Seymour	14.9
Bobby Shantz	18.7
Bob Shawkey	16.7
Jimmy Sheckard	20.7
Gary Sheffield	**38.2**
Urban Shocker	27.0
Al Simmons	22.5
Ted Simmons	21.7
Ken Singleton	20.4
George Sisler	26.5
Enos Slaughter	14.5
Roy Smalley	17.2
Lee Smith	22.4
Reggie Smith	31.9
Ozzie Smith	45.7
John Smoltz	**29.4**
Duke Snider	23.0
Sammy Sosa	**28.7**
Warren Spahn	51.4
Tris Speaker	82.1
Eddie Stanky	20.1
Bob Stanley	14.8
Willie Stargell	30.8
Rusty Staub	23.0
Vern Stephens	20.7
Dave Stieb	25.1
Jack Stivetts	23.6
Mel Stottlemyre	16.1
Harry Stovey	21.5
Darryl Strawberry	23.1
Don Sutton	16.8
Jesse Tannehill	20.0
Jack Taylor	15.7
Gene Tenace	26.3
Fred Tenney	23.0
Bill Terry	26.7
Frank Thomas	**46.0**
Roy Thomas	22.7
Jim Thome	**31.7**
Sam Thompson	29.5
Luis Tiant	21.5
Joe Tinker	19.5
John Titus	13.7
Joe Torre	22.3
Alan Trammell	31.7
Pie Traynor	18.4
Dizzy Trout	29.7
Virgil Trucks	16.8
John Tudor	16.1
George Uhle	15.9
John Valentin	17.6
Dazzy Vance	29.2
Andy Van Slyke	16.9
Arky Vaughan	43.3
Hippo Vaughn	16.3
Bobby Veach	17.9
Robin Ventura	**25.8**
Frank Viola	15.4
Rube Waddell	22.2
Honus Wagner	82.1
Larry Walker	**30.1**
Bobby Wallace	38.4
Ed Walsh	37.7
Bucky Walters	24.8
Paul Waner	33.8
John Ward	20.7
Lon Warneke	22.6
Mickey Welch	18.9
John Wetteland	20.7
Zack Wheat	24.1
Lou Whitaker	35.6
Doc White	19.3
Roy White	15.3
Hoyt Wilhelm	37.1
Bernie Williams	**26.8**
Billy Williams	23.8
Jimmy Williams	15.4
Ken Williams	17.5
Matt Williams	**19.7**
Ted Williams	87.0
Vic Willis	20.0
Hack Wilson	18.2
Dave Winfield	30.5
Joe Wood	22.1
Wilbur Wood	14.8
Early Wynn	19.5
Jimmy Wynn	30.0
Carl Yastrzemski	42.3
Cy Young	77.0
Robin Yount	41.2
Chief Zimmer	20.7

	Player	Overall Wins
1	Babe Ruth	129.0
2	**Barry Bonds**	**112.6**
3	Nap Lajoie	95.1
4	Walter Johnson	89.9
5	Ted Williams	87.0
6	Rogers Hornsby	86.0
7	Ty Cobb	85.5
8	Willie Mays	84.6
9	Tris Speaker	82.1
	Honus Wagner	82.1
11	Hank Aaron	81.3
12	Mike Schmidt	78.6
13	Cy Young	77.0
14	Stan Musial	76.0
15	Mickey Mantle	72.9
16	Eddie Collins	72.5
17	**Rickey Henderson**	**72.0**
18	Lou Gehrig	70.9
19	Joe Morgan	67.4
20	Frank Robinson	64.3
21	Grover Alexander	62.9
22	**Greg Maddux**	**62.2**
23	**Roger Clemens**	**61.7**
24	Mel Ott	60.7
25	Lefty Grove	59.1
26	Jimmie Foxx	58.7
27	Christy Mathewson	56.3
28	Kid Nichols	56.2
29	**Jeff Bagwell**	**53.6**
30	Eddie Mathews	52.1
31	Bobby Grich	51.6
32	Warren Spahn	51.4
33	Wade Boggs	51.1
34	George Davis	50.7
35	Tom Seaver	49.1
36	Bill Dahlen	48.5
37	**Frank Thomas**	**46.0**
38	Joe DiMaggio	45.8
39	Ozzie Smith	45.7
40	Ron Santo	45.3
41	Charlie Gehringer	45.1
42	Bob Gibson	44.9
43	**Pedro Martinez**	**44.7**
44	**Edgar Martinez**	**44.5**
45	Gabby Hartnett	44.3
46	**Ken Griffey**	**44.1**
	Cal Ripken	44.1
48	Lou Boudreau	43.6
49	George Brett	43.4
	Roger Connor	43.4
51	Arky Vaughan	43.3
52	Al Kaline	43.1
53	**Barry Larkin**	**42.9**
54	Ed Delahanty	42.6
55	John Clarkson	42.5
	Johnny Bench	42.5
	Dan Brouthers	42.5
	Alex Rodriguez	**42.5**
59	**Randy Johnson**	**42.4**
	Luke Appling	42.4
61	Carl Yastrzemski	42.3
62	**Mike Piazza**	**42.0**
63	Darrell Evans	41.2
	Robin Yount	41.2
65	Rod Carew	40.3
	Bobby Doerr	40.3
67	Carl Hubbell	40.2
68	Joe Cronin	39.6
69	Reggie Jackson	39.5
70	Dick Allen	39.2
	Gary Carter	39.2
72	Willie McCovey	39.0
73	Carlton Fisk	38.8
	Tony Gwynn	38.8
75	Tim Raines	38.7
76	Yogi Berra	38.6
77	Bill Dickey	38.5
78	Bobby Wallace	38.4
79	Joe Jackson	38.3
	Bid McPhee	38.3
81	**Gary Sheffield**	**38.2**
82	**Roberto Alomar**	**37.8**
83	Ed Walsh	37.7
	Johnny Mize	37.7
85	Frankie Frisch	37.3
86	Whitey Ford	37.2
	Hal Newhouser	37.2
88	Hoyt Wilhelm	37.1
	Willie Randolph	37.1
90	Paul Molitor	37.0
91	Amos Rusie	36.7
	Ryne Sandberg	36.7
93	Jack Glasscock	36.6
94	Dave Bancroft	36.2
95	Bob Johnson	35.7
	Mark McGwire	35.7
97	Tim Keefe	35.6
	Lou Whitaker	35.6
99	**Tom Glavine**	**35.4**
	Cap Anson	35.4

	Player	Overall Wins
	Eddie Murray	35.4
102	Joe Sewell	35.2
103	Keith Hernandez	34.8
104	Mickey Cochrane	34.7
	Ivan Rodriguez	**34.7**
106	**Rafael Palmeiro**	**34.4**
107	**Kevin Brown**	**34.3**
	Jim Palmer	34.3
	Jackie Robinson	34.3
110	Bob Lemon	34.0
	Roberto Clemente	34.0
	Bill Mazeroski	34.0
113	**Craig Biggio**	**33.8**
	Paul Waner	33.8
115	Frank Baker	33.7
116	Bob Caruthers	33.5
	Ted Lyons	33.5
118	Steve Carlton	33.2
	Harry Heilmann	33.2
120	Gaylord Perry	32.8
121	Mordecai Brown	32.7
122	**Mike Mussina**	**32.6**
	Hank Greenberg	32.6
	Harmon Killebrew	32.6
125	Don Drysdale	32.4
126	Reggie Smith	31.9
127	Carl Mays	31.7
	Jim Thome	**31.7**
	Alan Trammell	31.7
130	Bob Feller	31.6
	Billy Herman	31.6
132	Charley Radbourn	31.5
133	Wes Ferrell	31.2
	Red Ruffing	31.2
135	Bert Blyleven	31.1
136	Willie Stargell	30.8
137	Norm Cash	30.5
	Cupid Childs	30.5
	Manny Ramirez	**30.5**
	Dave Winfield	30.5
141	Heinie Groh	30.4
142	Fergie Jenkins	30.3
	Eddie Plank	30.3
	Robin Roberts	30.3
145	**Larry Walker**	**30.1**
146	Tony Mullane	30.0
	Jimmy Wynn	30.0
148	Dennis Eckersley	29.8
	Albert Belle	29.8
150	Dizzy Trout	29.7
	Elmer Flick	29.7
152	Jack Clark	29.6
153	Rich Gossage	29.5
	Sam Thompson	29.5
155	**John Smoltz**	**29.4**
	Stan Hack	29.4
157	Sam Crawford	29.3
	Buck Ewing	29.3
159	Phil Niekro	29.2
	Dazzy Vance	29.2
161	Jesse Burkett	29.1
162	Joe Gordon	28.8
163	Buddy Bell	28.7
	Sammy Sosa	**28.7**
165	**Jeff Kent**	**28.5**
166	**Jim Edmonds**	**28.4**
	King Kelly	28.4
168	Clark Griffith	28.3
169	Dick Bartell	28.2
170	Fred Dunlap	28.1
171	Pete Browning	27.9
172	Bret Saberhagen	27.8
173	Fred Clarke	27.7
174	Juan Marichal	27.5
175	Tommy Bridges	27.3
	Billy Hamilton	27.3
177	Ernie Banks	27.2
	Bobby Bonds	27.2
	Art Fletcher	27.2
180	Urban Shocker	27.0
181	**Mariano Rivera**	**26.9**
182	Hughie Jennings	26.8
	Bernie Williams	**26.8**
184	Bill Terry	26.7
185	Hardy Richardson	26.5
	George Sisler	26.5
187	Harlond Clift	26.3
	Gene Tenace	26.3
189	Dolf Luque	26.2
	Sherry Magee	26.2
191	**Scott Rolen**	**26.1**
192	Stan Coveleski	26.0
193	**Curt Schilling**	**25.8**
	Robin Ventura	**25.8**
195	Billy Pierce	25.6
	Joe Medwick	25.6
197	Jim Fregosi	25.5
198	**Nomar Garciaparra**	**25.4**
	Thurman Munson	25.4
200	Dave Stieb	25.1

	Player	Overall Wins
201	Harry Brecheen	24.9
202	Bucky Walters	24.8
	Will Clark	24.8
	Dwight Evans	24.8
	Brian Giles	**24.8**
206	Jack Fournier	24.4
207	Eddie Cicotte	24.3
	John Olerud	**24.3**
209	Eppa Rixey	24.2
	Ralph Kiner	24.2
211	Roy Campanella	24.1
	Zack Wheat	24.1
213	Charlie Bennett	23.9
	Pete Rose	23.9
215	Billy Williams	23.8
216	Kirby Puckett	23.7
217	Jack Stivetts	23.6
218	Red Faber	23.3
219	**David Cone**	**23.1**
	Goose Goslin	23.1
	Darryl Strawberry	23.1
222	Addie Joss	23.0
	Silver King	23.0
	Eddie Rommel	23.0
	Jake Beckley	23.0
	Jose Canseco	23.0
	Jimmy Collins	23.0
	Lenny Dykstra	23.0
	Duke Snider	23.0
	Rusty Staub	23.0
	Fred Tenney	23.0
232	**Fred McGriff**	**22.9**
233	Jimmy Key	22.8
	Roger Bresnahan	22.8
235	Rollie Fingers	22.7
	Rocky Colavito	22.7
	Roy Thomas	22.7
238	Lon Warneke	22.6
	Richie Ashburn	22.6
	Frank Chance	22.6
	Frank Howard	22.6
242	Rick Reuschel	22.5
	Del Pratt	22.5
	Al Simmons	22.5
245	Lee Smith	22.4
246	Dizzy Dean	22.3
	Sandy Koufax	22.3
	Cesar Cedeno	22.3
	Miller Huggins	22.3
	Tim Salmon	**22.3**
	Joe Torre	22.3
252	Dutch Leonard	22.2
	Rube Waddell	22.2
	Gil McDougald	22.2
	Lance Parrish	22.2
256	Joe Wood	22.1
	Charlie Keller	22.1
258	Travis Jackson	22.0
259	Guy Hecker	21.9
260	Ted Simmons	21.7
261	Ken Caminiti	21.6
	Graig Nettles	21.6
263	Nolan Ryan	21.5
	Luis Tiant	21.5
	Jason Giambi	**21.5**
	Harry Stovey	21.5
267	Bob Elliott	21.4
	Tony Fernandez	21.4
269	Ron Cey	21.3
270	Jose Cruz	21.2
	Ed Konetchy	21.2
272	**Roberto Hernandez**	**21.1**
	Jim McCormick	21.1
	Vladimir Guerrero	**21.1**
	Chuck Klein	21.1
276	Wally Berger	21.0
	Minnie Minoso	21.0
278	**Chipper Jones**	**20.9**
	Darrell Porter	20.9
280	Red Lucas	20.8
	Fred Pfeffer	20.8
282	John Hiller	20.7
	John Ward	20.7
	John Wetteland	20.7
	Jimmy Sheckard	20.7
	Vern Stephens	20.7
	Chief Zimmer	20.7
288	Ernie Lombardi	20.6
	Kevin Mitchell	20.6
290	Nig Cuppy	20.4
	Wally Schang	20.4
	Ken Singleton	20.4
293	Eric Davis	20.3
	Brian Downing	20.3
	Tony Oliva	20.3
296	**Kevin Appier**	**20.2**
	Glenn Hubbard	20.2
298	Lefty Gomez	20.1
	Tommy John	20.1
	Javy Lopez	**20.1**

	Player	Overall Wins
	Eddie Stanky	20.1
302	Jesse Tannehill	20.0
	Vic Willis	20.0
	Art Devlin	20.0
	Luis Gonzalez	**20.0**
	Joe Kelley	20.0
307	Ron Guidry	19.9
308	Wilbur Cooper	19.7
	Ken Boyer	19.7
	Todd Helton	**19.7**
	Fred Lynn	19.7
	Matt Williams	**19.7**
313	Denny Lyons	19.6
314	Early Wynn	19.5
	John McGraw	19.5
	Joe Tinker	19.5
317	Jack Quinn	19.4
	Toby Harrah	19.4
	Charley Jones	19.4
320	Chuck Finley	19.3
	Doug Jones	19.3
	Doc White	19.3
	Bill Joyce	19.3
	Chet Lemon	19.3
	Tony Phillips	19.3
326	Mike Marshall	19.2
327	Spud Chandler	19.1
	Orlando Cepeda	19.1
329	Freddie Fitzsimmons	19.0
	Bobby Abreu	**19.0**
331	Orel Hershiser	18.9
	Joe McGinnity	18.9
	Robb Nen	18.9
	Mickey Welch	18.9
335	Schoolboy Rowe	18.8
	Gene Alley	18.8
	Roy Cullenbine	18.8
	Ferris Fain	18.8
	Ray Lankford	18.8
340	Bobby Shantz	18.7
	Boog Powell	18.7
	Phil Rizzuto	18.7
343	Ed Lopat	18.6
	Don Newcombe	18.6
	Juan Gonzalez	**18.6**
	Jim Rice	18.6
347	George Foster	18.5
348	Gavy Cravath	18.4
	Pie Traynor	18.4
350	Burleigh Grimes	18.3
	Jesse Orosco	**18.3**
	Mike Scioscia	18.3
353	Curt Davis	18.2
	Hack Wilson	18.2
355	Rico Carty	18.1
	Andre Dawson	18.1
	Larry Doby	18.1
358	Max Carey	18.0
	Bill Freehan	18.0
	Mike Griffin	18.0
	Pedro Guerrero	18.0
362	Dave Concepcion	17.9
	Bobby Veach	17.9
364	Tony Lazzeri	17.8
365	Babe Adams	17.7
	Dwight Gooden	17.7
367	John Valentin	17.6
368	Andy Messersmith	17.5
	Babe Herman	17.5
	Ken Williams	17.5
371	Ed Reulbach	17.3
	Earl Averill	17.3
	Ellis Burks	**17.3**
374	Jeff Montgomery	17.2
	Jeff Heath	17.2
	Chief Meyers	17.2
	Bill Nicholson	17.2
	Roy Smalley	17.2
379	Noodles Hahn	17.0
	Mel Harder	17.0
	Rick Burleson	17.0
382	Andy Van Slyke	16.9
383	Rick Aguilera	16.8
	Larry French	16.8
	Don Sutton	16.8
	Virgil Trucks	16.8
387	Bob Shawkey	16.7
	Kenny Lofton	**16.7**
389	Ray Chapman	16.6
390	Johnny Logan	16.5
391	Jim Bunning	16.4
	Bobby Bonilla	16.4
	Lave Cross	16.4
394	Hippo Vaughn	16.3
	Bobby Knoop	16.3
	Pee Wee Reese	16.3
397	Charlie Buffinton	16.2
	John Candelaria	16.2
	Murry Dickson	16.2
	Jay Bell	**16.2**

	Player	Overall Wins
	Al Rosen	16.2
402	Jim Kaat	16.1
	Sam Leever	16.1
	Mel Stottlemyre	16.1
	John Tudor	16.1
	Brett Butler	16.1
	Mike Hargrove	16.1
	Ray Schalk	16.1
409	Larry Jackson	16.0
	Paul O'Neill	16.0
	Jim O'Rourke	16.0
	Jorge Posada	**16.0**
413	George Uhle	15.9
	Johnny Evers	15.9
	Don Mattingly	15.9
416	Thornton Lee	15.8
	Dwayne Murphy	15.8
	Red Schoendienst	15.8
419	Mike Garcia	15.7
	Waite Hoyt	15.7
	Max Lanier	15.7
	Jack Taylor	15.7
	Andruw Jones	**15.7**
	Willie Kamm	15.7
425	Deacon Phillippe	15.6
426	Mel Parnell	15.5
	Nap Rucker	15.5
	David Justice	15.5
	Johnny Pesky	15.5
430	Johnny Antonelli	15.4
	Frank Viola	15.4
	Ron Hansen	15.4
	Rico Petrocelli	15.4
	Jimmy Williams	15.4
435	Stu Miller	15.3
	Augie Galan	15.3
	Henry Larkin	15.3
	Roy White	15.3
439	Ned Garver	15.2
	Hal Schumacher	15.2
	Julio Franco	**15.2**
	Jason Kendall	**15.2**
443	**Carlos Delgado**	**15.0**
	Tommy Henrich	15.0
	Willie Keeler	15.0
	Dave Parker	15.0
447	Chief Bender	14.9
	Ellis Kinder	14.9
	Claude Passeau	14.9
	Ron Perranoski	14.9
	Doug DeCinces	14.9
	Cy Seymour	14.9
453	Steve Rogers	14.8
	Bob Stanley	14.8
	Wilbur Wood	14.8
	Chili Davis	14.8
	Sid Gordon	14.8
458	**Derek Lowe**	**14.7**
	Hal McRae	14.7
460	Jerry Koosman	14.6
	Randy Myers	14.6
462	**Tim Hudson**	**14.5**
	Paul Hines	14.5
	Enos Slaughter	14.5
465	Ben Chapman	14.4
	Nellie Fox	14.4
	Johnny Kling	14.4
468	Mort Cooper	14.3
	Charlie Ferguson	14.3
	Claude Hendrix	14.3
	Bert Campaneris	14.3
	Buddy Myer	14.3
	Roger Peckinpaugh	14.3
	Brooks Robinson	14.3
475	Mark Eichhorn	14.1
	Tug McGraw	14.1
	Jesse Barfield	14.1
	Davey Johnson	14.1
479	Kid Elberfeld	14.0
480	Mike Jackson	13.9
481	Sal Maglie	13.8
	Dave Righetti	13.8
	Shawn Green	**13.8**
	Gil Hodges	13.8
485	Fred Hutchinson	13.7
	Firpo Marberry	13.7
	Jose Rijo	13.7
	John Titus	13.7
489	Frank Dwyer	13.6
	Jim Maloney	13.6
	Lonny Frey	13.6
	Jocko Milligan	13.6
	Dave Orr	13.6
494	8 players tied	13.5

Plate Appearances

1 Lenny Dykstra, 1993........773
2 Pete Rose, 1974..............770
3 Dave Cash, 1975..............766
4 Pete Rose, 1975..............764
5 Maury Wills, 1962............759
Pete Rose, 1976...............759
7 Wade Boggs, 1985...........758
8 Frankie Crosetti, 1938.......757
Pete Rose, 1965...............757
Omar Moreno, 1979............757
11 Dom DiMaggio, 1948........756
12 Woody English, 1930........755
13 Bobby Richardson, 1962...754
14 Taylor Douthit, 1928..........752
Pete Rose, 1973...............752
Mo Vaughn, 1996.........752
17 Paul Molitor, 1982.............751
18 Paul Molitor, 1991.............749
Brady Anderson, 1992.........749
Craig Biggio, 1999.......749
21 Taylor Douthit, 1930..........748
Augie Galan, 1935............748
Derek Jeter, 1997.......748
Alex Rodriguez, 1998..748
25 Rabbit Maranville, 1922.........747
Darin Erstad, 2000.......747
27 Matty Alou, 1969..............746
Jim Rice, 1978.................746
Juan Pierre, 2003........746
30 Dave Bancroft, 1922.........745
Lyn Lary, 1936..................745
Tommy Harper, 1965...........745
Bobby Bonds, 1970............745
Dave Cash, 1974...............745
Omar Moreno, 1980............745
Willie Wilson, 1980............745
37 Jo-Jo Moore, 1935...........744
Dwight Evans, 1985...........744
Kirby Puckett, 1985............744
Craig Biggio, 1997.......744
41 Frankie Crosetti, 1939.......743
Pee Wee Reese, 1949.......743
Felix Millan, 1975..............743
44 Charlie Jamieson, 1923....742
Don Mattingly, 1986..........742
Wade Boggs, 1989............742
47 Kiki Cuyler, 1930.............741
Lyn Lary, 1937..................741
Ron LeFlore, 1978............741
Johnny Damon, 2000..741
Alfonso Soriano, 2002.......741
52 Frankie Crosetti, 1936.......740
Red Rolfe, 1937...............740
54 Curt Flood, 1964.............739
Sandy Alomar, 1971.........739
Derek Jeter, 1999........739
57 Lou Gehrig, 1931.............738
Chuck Schilling, 1961.......738
Bobby Bonds, 1973...........738
Al Bumbry, 1980...............738
Dwight Evans, 1984..........738
Brian Hunter, 1997......738
Craig Biggio, 1998.......738
Ichiro Suzuki, 2001......738
65 Don Kessinger, 1969.........737
Juan Samuel, 1984............737
Harold Reynolds, 1990.....737
68 Brooks Robinson, 1961.....736
Kenny Lofton, 1996.....736
70 Billy Herman, 1935...........735
Phil Rizzuto, 1950.............735
Dick Howser, 1964............735
Sandy Alomar, 1970..........735
Pete Rose, 1980...............735
Doug Glanville, 1998...735
Vernon Wells, 2003......735
77 Eddie Yost, 1952..............734
Sal Bando, 1969...............734
Rusty Staub, 1978.............734
Nomar Garciaparra, 1997....734
Rafael Furcal, 2003.....734
Alfonso Soriano, 2003.........734
83 Buddy Lewis, 1937...........733
Darrell Evans, 1973...........733
Tony Phillips, 1992............733
86 Max Carey, 1922..............732
Eddie Lake, 1947..............732
Horace Clarke, 1970.........732
Brett Butler, 1990.............732
Rafael Palmeiro, 1996.........732
Neifi Perez, 1999.........732
Alex Rodriguez, 2001..732
93 12 players tied.................731

At Bats

1 Willie Wilson, 1980...........705
2 Juan Samuel, 1984...........701
3 Dave Cash, 1975..............699
4 Matty Alou, 1969..............698
5 Woody Jensen, 1936........696
Alfonso Soriano, 2002.........696
7 Maury Wills, 1962.............695
Omar Moreno, 1979...........695
9 Bobby Richardson, 1962...692
Ichiro Suzuki, 2001......692
11 Kirby Puckett, 1985...........691
12 Neifi Perez, 1999.........690
13 Lou Brock, 1967...............689
Sandy Alomar, 1971..........689
15 Dave Cash, 1974..............687
Tony Fernandez, 1986........687
17 Horace Clarke, 1970.........686
Alex Rodriguez, 1998..686
19 Nomar Garciaparra, 1997.....684
20 Lance Johnson, 1996........682
Alfonso Soriano, 2003.........682
22 Lloyd Waner, 1931............681
Jo-Jo Moore, 1935............681
24 Pete Rose, 1973...............680
Frank Taveras, 1979..........680
Kirby Puckett, 1986............680
27 Harvey Kuenn, 1953.........679
Curt Flood, 1964...............679
Bobby Richardson, 1964...679
Ichiro Suzuki, 2003......679
31 Dick Groat, 1962...............678
Doug Glanville, 1998....678
Vernon Wells, 2003......678
34 Matty Alou, 1970..............677
Jim Rice, 1978..................677
Don Mattingly, 1986..........677
37 Felix Millan, 1975.............676
Omar Moreno, 1980...........676
Darin Erstad, 2000.......676
40 Rennie Stennett, 1974......673
Bill Buckner, 1985.............673
B.J. Surhoff, 1999........673
43 Rabbit Maranville, 1922.....672
Tony Oliva, 1964...............672
Sandy Alomar, 1970...........672
Garry Templeton, 1979......672
Garret Anderson, 2001.........672
48 Jack Tobin, 1921...............671
Marquis Grissom, 1996.......671
50 Al Simmons, 1932.............670
Pete Rose, 1965...............670
Buddy Bell, 1979...............670
53 Vada Pinson, 1965...........669
Larry Bowa, 1974..............669
55 Buddy Lewis, 1937...........668
Brooks Robinson, 1961.....668
Ralph Garr, 1973..............668
Juan Pierre, 2003........668
59 Carl Furillo, 1951.............667
60 Billy Herman, 1935...........666
Zoilo Versalles, 1965.........666
Felipe Alou, 1966.............666
Dave Cash, 1976..............666
Ron LeFlore, 1978............666
Paul Molitor, 1982.............666
Mike Young, 2003........666
67 Tommy Davis, 1962...........665
Pete Rose, 1976...............665
Paul Molitor, 1991.............665
70 Taylor Douthit, 1930..........664
Bobby Richardson, 1965...664
Don Kessinger, 1969........664
Lou Brock, 1970...............664
Rafael Furcal, 2003.....664
75 Jake Wood, 1961.............663
Bill Virdon, 1962...............663
Bobby Bonds, 1970...........663
Rick Burleson, 1977..........663
Cal Ripken, 1983..............663
Juan Samuel, 1985...........663
Joe Carter, 1986..............663
Carlos Beltran, 1999...663
83 Lloyd Waner, 1929...........662
Hughie Critz, 1930............662
Richie Ashburn, 1949........662
Granny Hamner, 1949.......662
Bobby Richardson, 1961...662
Curt Flood, 1963...............662
Felipe Alou, 1968.............662
Pete Rose, 1975...............662
Kenny Lofton, 1996.....662
Dante Bichette, 1998........662
Miguel Tejada, 2002....662
94 Doc Cramer, 1933............661
Doc Cramer, 1940.............661
Ken Hubbs, 1962..............661
Cecil Cooper, 1983...........661
Ruben Sierra, 1991......661
99 5 players tied..................660

Runs

1 Billy Hamilton, 1894..........198
2 Tom Brown, 1891.............177
Babe Ruth, 1921...............177
4 Tip O'Neill, 1887..............167
Lou Gehrig, 1936..............167
6 Billy Hamilton, 1895..........166
7 Willie Keeler, 1894...........165
Joe Kelley, 1894...............165
9 Arlie Latham, 1887...........163
Babe Ruth, 1928...............163
Lou Gehrig, 1931..............163
12 Willie Keeler, 1895...........162
13 Hugh Duffy, 1890.............161
14 Fred Dunlap, 1884...........160
Hugh Duffy, 1894..............160
Jesse Burkett, 1896..........160
17 Hughie Jennings, 1895.....159
18 Bobby Lowe, 1894............158
Babe Ruth, 1920...............158
Babe Ruth, 1927...............158
Chuck Klein, 1930.............158
22 John McGraw, 1894..........156
Rogers Hornsby, 1929.......156
24 King Kelly, 1886...............155
Kiki Cuyler, 1930..............155
26 Dan Brouthers, 1887.........153
Jesse Burkett, 1895..........153
Billy Hamilton, 1896...........153
Willie Keeler, 1896............153
30 Arlie Latham, 1886...........152
Mike Griffin, 1889..............152
Harry Stovey, 1889............152
Billy Hamilton, 1897...........152
Lefty O'Doul, 1929............152
Woody English, 1930.........152
Al Simmons, 1930.............152
Chuck Klein, 1932.............152
Jeff Bagwell, 2000......152
39 Babe Ruth, 1923..............151
Jimmie Foxx, 1932............151
Joe DiMaggio, 1937..........151
42 George Gore, 1886...........150
Bill Dahlen, 1894...............150
Jake Stenzel, 1894............150
Babe Ruth, 1930...............150
Ted Williams, 1949............150
47 Herman Long, 1893..........149
Ed Delahanty, 1895...........149
Lou Gehrig, 1927..............149
Babe Ruth, 1931...............149
51 Hub Collins, 1890.............148
Ed Delahanty, 1894...........148
Joe Kelley, 1895...............148
Joe Kelley, 1896...............148
55 Mike Tiernan, 1889...........147
Hugh Duffy, 1893..............147
Patsy Donovan, 1894.........147
Ty Cobb, 1911..................147
59 Darby O'Brien, 1889.........146
Tom Brown, 1890..............146
Hack Wilson, 1930.............146
Rickey Henderson, 1985......146
Craig Biggio, 1997.......146
Sammy Sosa, 2001......146
65 Jesse Burkett, 1893..........145
Cupid Childs, 1893............145
Ed Delahanty, 1893...........145
Willie Keeler, 1897............145
Nap Lajoie, 1901...............145
Harlond Clift, 1936.............145
71 Hugh Duffy, 1889..............144
Billy Hamilton, 1889...........144
Ty Cobb, 1915..................144
Kiki Cuyler, 1925..............144
Charlie Gehringer, 1930......144
Al Simmons, 1932.............144
Charlie Gehringer, 1936......144
Hank Greenberg, 1938.....144
79 Cupid Childs, 1894............143
John McGraw, 1898...........143
Babe Ruth, 1924...............143
Babe Herman, 1930...........143
Lou Gehrig, 1930..............143
Earle Combs, 1932...........143
Red Rolfe, 1937...............143
Lenny Dykstra, 1993.........143
Larry Walker, 1997......143
Jeff Bagwell, 1999......143
89 Mike Griffin, 1887.............142
Harry Stovey, 1890............142
Jesse Burkett, 1901..........142
Paul Waner, 1928.............142
Ted Williams, 1946............142
Ellis Burks, 1996..........142
95 Billy Hamilton, 1891.........141
Rogers Hornsby, 1922.......141
Ted Williams, 1942............141
Alex Rodriguez, 1996..141
99 9 players tied...................140

Runs by era

1988-2003

1 Jeff Bagwell, 2000......152
2 Craig Biggio, 1997.......146
Sammy Sosa, 2001......146
4 Lenny Dykstra, 1993.........143
Larry Walker, 1997......143
Jeff Bagwell, 1999......143
7 Ellis Burks, 1996..........142
8 Alex Rodriguez, 1996..141
9 Chuck Knoblauch, 1996....140
10 Roberto Alomar, 1999........138
Todd Helton, 2000.......138

1973-1987

1 Rickey Henderson, 1985......146
2 Paul Molitor, 1982.............136
3 Willie Wilson, 1980...........133
Tim Raines, 1983..............133
5 Bobby Bonds, 1973...........131
Dale Murphy, 1983............131
7 Pete Rose, 1976...............130
Rickey Henderson, 1986......130
9 Robin Yount, 1982.............129
10 Rod Carew, 1977..............128

1961-1972

1 Billy Williams, 1970...........137
2 Frank Robinson, 1962.........134
Bobby Bonds, 1970............134
4 Mickey Mantle, 1961.........132
Roger Maris, 1961.............132
6 Willie Mays, 1962..............130
Maury Wills, 1962..............130
8 Willie Mays, 1961..............129
Rocky Colavito, 1961.........129
10 Hank Aaron, 1962.............127

1943-1960

1 Ted Williams, 1949............150
2 Ted Williams, 1946............142
3 Tommy Henrich, 1948.......138
4 Johnny Mize, 1947............137
5 Stan Musial, 1948.............135
6 Pee Wee Reese, 1949.......132
Duke Snider, 1953.............132
Mickey Mantle, 1956..........132
9 Dom DiMaggio, 1950.........131
Vada Pinson, 1959.............131

1921-1942

1 Babe Ruth, 1921...............177
2 Lou Gehrig, 1936..............167
3 Babe Ruth, 1928...............163
Lou Gehrig, 1931..............163
5 Babe Ruth, 1927...............158
Chuck Klein, 1930.............158
7 Rogers Hornsby, 1929.......156
8 Kiki Cuyler, 1930..............155
9 Lefty O'Doul, 1929............152
Woody English, 1930.........152
Al Simmons, 1930.............152
Chuck Klein, 1932.............152

1901-1920

1 Babe Ruth, 1920...............158
2 Ty Cobb, 1911..................147
3 Nap Lajoie, 1901...............145
4 Ty Cobb, 1915..................144
5 Jesse Burkett, 1901..........142
6 Ginger Beaumont, 1903....137
Eddie Collins, 1912...........137
Tris Speaker, 1920............137
George Sisler, 1920..........137
10 Tris Speaker, 1912...........136

1893-1900

1 Billy Hamilton, 1894..........198
2 Billy Hamilton, 1895..........166
3 Willie Keeler, 1894...........165
Joe Kelley, 1894...............165
5 Willie Keeler, 1895...........162
6 Hugh Duffy, 1894..............160
Jesse Burkett, 1896..........160
8 Hughie Jennings, 1895.....159
9 Bobby Lowe, 1894............158
10 John McGraw, 1894..........156

1876-1892

1 Tom Brown, 1891.............177
2 Tip O'Neill, 1887..............167
3 Arlie Latham, 1887...........163
4 Hugh Duffy, 1890..............161
5 Fred Dunlap, 1884............160
6 King Kelly, 1886...............155
7 Dan Brouthers, 1887.........153
8 Arlie Latham, 1886...........152
Mike Griffin, 1889..............152
Harry Stovey, 1889............152

Hits

1 George Sisler, 1920..........257
2 Lefty O'Doul, 1929...........254
Bill Terry, 1930.................254
4 Al Simmons, 1925............253
5 Rogers Hornsby, 1922.......250
Chuck Klein, 1930.............250
7 Ty Cobb, 1911..................248
8 George Sisler, 1922..........246
9 Ichiro Suzuki, 2001......242
10 Heinie Manush, 1928........241
Babe Herman, 1930...........241
12 Jesse Burkett, 1896.........240
Wade Boggs, 1985............240
Darin Erstad, 2000.......240
15 Willie Keeler, 1897...........239
Rod Carew, 1977..............239
17 Ed Delahanty, 1899..........238
Don Mattingly, 1986..........238
19 Hugh Duffy, 1894.............237
Harry Heilmann, 1921.......237
Paul Waner, 1927.............237
Joe Medwick, 1937...........237
23 Jack Tobin, 1921.............236
24 Rogers Hornsby, 1921......235
25 Lloyd Waner, 1929...........234
Kirby Puckett, 1988...........234
27 Joe Jackson, 1911...........233
28 Nap Lajoie, 1901..............232
Earl Averill, 1936..............232
30 Earle Combs, 1927...........231
Freddie Lindstrom, 1928.......231
Freddie Lindstrom, 1930.......231
Matty Alou, 1969...............231
34 Stan Musial, 1948............230
Tommy Davis, 1962...........230
Joe Torre, 1971................230
Pete Rose, 1973...............230
Willie Wilson, 1980...........230
39 Rogers Hornsby, 1929......229
40 Kiki Cuyler, 1930.............228
Stan Musial, 1946............228
42 Nap Lajoie, 1910..............227
Rogers Hornsby, 1924.......227
Jim Bottomley, 1925.........227
Sam Rice, 1925................227
Billy Herman, 1935...........227
Charlie Gehringer, 1936.......227
Lance Johnson, 1996........227
49 Jesse Burkett, 1901.........226
Joe Jackson, 1912...........226
Ty Cobb, 1912..................226
Bill Terry, 1929.................226
Chuck Klein, 1932.............226
54 Tip O'Neill, 1887...............225
Billy Hamilton, 1894...........225
Jesse Burkett, 1895..........225
Ty Cobb, 1917..................225
Harry Heilmann, 1925.......225
Johnny Hodapp, 1930.......225
Bill Terry, 1932.................225
Paul Molitor, 1996.............225
62 Eddie Collins, 1920..........224
George Sisler, 1925..........224
Joe Medwick, 1935...........224
Tommy Holmes, 1945........224
66 Frankie Frisch, 1923.........223
Lloyd Waner, 1927...........223
Paul Waner, 1928.............223
Chuck Klein, 1933.............223
Joe Medwick, 1936...........223
Hank Aaron, 1959.............223
Kirby Puckett, 1986...........223
73 Sam Thompson, 1893......222
Tris Speaker, 1912...........222
Charlie Jamieson, 1923....222
76 Jesse Burkett, 1899.........221
Zack Wheat, 1925.............221
Lloyd Waner, 1928...........221
Heinie Manush, 1933........221
Richie Ashburn, 1951.......221
81 Pete Browning, 1887.........220
Jimmy Williams, 1899.......220
Kiki Cuyler, 1925..............220
Lou Gehrig, 1930..............220
Stan Musial, 1943.............220
Tony Gwynn, 1997............220
87 Ed Delahanty, 1893...........219
Willie Keeler, 1894............219
Cy Seymour, 1905............219
Chuck Klein, 1929.............219
Lefty O'Doul, 1932............219
Paul Waner, 1937.............219
Ralph Garr, 1971..............219
Cecil Cooper, 1980...........219
Dante Bichette, 1998........219
Derek Jeter, 1999........219
97 12 players tied.................218

Doubles

1 Earl Webb, 1931 67
2 George Burns, 1926 64
Joe Medwick, 1936 64
4 Hank Greenberg, 1934 63
5 Paul Waner, 1932 62
6 Charlie Gehringer, 1936 60
7 Tris Speaker, 1923 59
Chuck Klein, 1930 59
Todd Helton, 2000 59
10 Billy Herman, 1935 57
Billy Herman, 1936 57
Carlos Delgado, 2000 57
13 Joe Medwick, 1937 56
George Kell, 1950 56
Craig Biggio, 1999 56
Garret Anderson, 2002 56
Nomar Garciaparra, 2002 56
18 Ed Delahanty, 1899 55
Gee Walker, 1936 55
Lance Berkman, 2001 55
21 Hal McRae, 1977 54
John Olerud, 1993 54
Alex Rodriguez, 1996 54
Mark Grudzielanek, 1997 54
Todd Helton, 2001 54
26 Tris Speaker, 1912 53
Al Simmons, 1926 53
Paul Waner, 1936 53
Stan Musial, 1953 53
Don Mattingly, 1986 53
Jeff Cirillo, 2000 53
32 Tip O'Neill, 1887 52
Tris Speaker, 1921 52
Tris Speaker, 1926 52
Lou Gehrig, 1927 52
Johnny Frederick, 1929 52
Enos Slaughter, 1939 52
Albert Belle, 1995 52
Edgar Martinez, 1995 52
Edgar Martinez, 1996 52
41 Hugh Duffy, 1894 51
Nap Lajoie, 1910 51
Baby Doll Jacobson, 1926 51
George Burns, 1927 51
Johnny Hodapp, 1930 51
Beau Bell, 1937 51
Joe Cronin, 1938 51
Stan Musial, 1944 51
Mickey Vernon, 1946 51
Frank Robinson, 1962 51
Pete Rose, 1978 51
Wade Boggs, 1989 51
Mark Grace, 1995 51
Craig Biggio, 1998 51
Jose Vidro, 2000 51
Nomar Garciaparra, 2000 51
Alfonso Soriano, 2002 51
Albert Pujols, 2003 51
59 Tris Speaker, 1920 50
Harry Heilmann, 1927 50
Paul Waner, 1928 50
Kiki Cuyler, 1930 50
Chuck Klein, 1932 50
Charlie Gehringer, 1934 50
Odell Hale, 1936 50
Ben Chapman, 1936 50
Hank Greenberg, 1940 50
Stan Musial, 1946 50
Stan Spence, 1946 50
Juan Gonzalez, 1998 50
Bobby Abreu, 2002 50
72 Ed Williamson, 1883 49
Ed Delahanty, 1895 49
Nap Lajoie, 1904 49
George Sisler, 1920 49
Heinie Manush, 1930 49
Riggs Stephenson, 1932 49
Hank Greenberg, 1937 49
Robin Yount, 1980 49
Rafael Palmeiro, 1991 49
Tony Gwynn, 1997 49
Jeff Kent, 2001 49
Marcus Giles, 2003 49
Shawn Green, 2003 49
Todd Helton, 2003 49
Scott Rolen, 2003 49
Garret Anderson, 2003 49
Vernon Wells, 2003 49
89 18 players tied 48

Doubles by era

1988-2003

1 Todd Helton, 2000 59
2 Carlos Delgado, 2000 57
3 Craig Biggio, 1999 56
Garret Anderson, 2002 56
Nomar Garciaparra, 2002 56
6 Lance Berkman, 2001 55
7 John Olerud, 1993 54
Alex Rodriguez, 1996 54
Mark Grudzielanek, 1997 54
Todd Helton, 2001 54

1973-1987

1 Hal McRae, 1977 54
2 Don Mattingly, 1986 53
3 Pete Rose, 1978 51
4 Robin Yount, 1980 49
5 Keith Hernandez, 1979 48
Don Mattingly, 1985 48
7 Pete Rose, 1975 47
Fred Lynn, 1975 47
Cal Ripken, 1983 47
Wade Boggs, 1986 47

1961-1972

1 Frank Robinson, 1962 51
2 Wes Parker, 1970 47
3 Lou Brock, 1968 46
4 Floyd Robinson, 1962 45
Zoilo Versalles, 1965 45
Carl Yastrzemski, 1965 45
7 Lee Maye, 1964 44
Rusty Staub, 1967 44
9 Carl Yastrzemski, 1962 43
Dick Groat, 1963 43
Tony Oliva, 1964 43

1943-1960

1 George Kell, 1950 56
2 Stan Musial, 1953 53
3 Stan Musial, 1944 51
Mickey Vernon, 1946 51
5 Stan Musial, 1946 50
Stan Spence, 1946 50
7 Stan Musial, 1943 48
8 Tommy Holmes, 1945 47
Vada Pinson, 1959 47
10 Stan Musial, 1948 46
Hank Aaron, 1959 46

1921-1942

1 Earl Webb, 1931 67
2 George Burns, 1926 64
Joe Medwick, 1936 64
4 Hank Greenberg, 1934 63
5 Paul Waner, 1932 62
6 Charlie Gehringer, 1936 60
7 Tris Speaker, 1923 59
Chuck Klein, 1930 59
9 Billy Herman, 1935 57
Billy Herman, 1936 57

1901-1920

1 Tris Speaker, 1912 53
2 Nap Lajoie, 1910 51
3 Tris Speaker, 1920 50
4 Nap Lajoie, 1904 49
George Sisler, 1920 49
6 Nap Lajoie, 1901 48
Nap Lajoie, 1906 48
8 Harry Davis, 1905 47
Ty Cobb, 1911 47
10 John Anderson, 1901 46
Tris Speaker, 1914 46

1893-1900

1 Ed Delahanty, 1899 55
2 Hugh Duffy, 1894 51
3 Ed Delahanty, 1895 49
4 Joe Kelley, 1894 48
5 Walt Wilmot, 1894 45
Sam Thompson, 1895 45
Honus Wagner, 1899 45
Honus Wagner, 1900 45
9 Ed Delahanty, 1896 44
10 Jake Stenzel, 1897 43
Nap Lajoie, 1898 43

1876-1892

1 Tip O'Neill, 1887 52
2 Ed Williamson, 1883 49
3 Denny Lyons, 1887 43
4 Dan Brouthers, 1883 41
King Kelly, 1889 41
Sam Thompson, 1890 41
7 Orator Shafer, 1884 40
Dan Brouthers, 1886 40
Jack Glasscock, 1889 40
Pete Browning, 1890 40

Triples

1 Chief Wilson, 1912 36
2 Dave Orr, 1886 31
Heinie Reitz, 1894 31
4 Perry Werden, 1893 29
5 Sam Thompson, 1894 28
Harry Davis, 1897 28
7 George Davis, 1893 27
Jimmy Williams, 1899 27
9 John Reilly, 1890 26
George Treadway, 1894 26
Joe Jackson, 1912 26
Sam Crawford, 1914 26
Kiki Cuyler, 1925 26
14 Roger Connor, 1894 25
Buck Freeman, 1899 25
Sam Crawford, 1903 25
Larry Doyle, 1911 25
Tom Long, 1915 25
19 Ed McKean, 1893 24
Ty Cobb, 1911 24
Ty Cobb, 1917 24
22 Harry Stovey, 1884 23
Sam Thompson, 1887 23
Elmer Smith, 1893 23
Dan Brouthers, 1894 23
Nap Lajoie, 1897 23
Ty Cobb, 1912 23
Sam Crawford, 1913 23
Earle Combs, 1927 23
Adam Comorosky, 1930 23
Dale Mitchell, 1949 23
32 Roger Connor, 1887 22
Bid McPhee, 1890 22
Jake Beckley, 1890 22
Joe Visner, 1890 22
Willie Keeler, 1894 22
Kip Selbach, 1895 22
John Anderson, 1898 22
Honus Wagner, 1900 22
Tommy Leach, 1902 22
Sam Crawford, 1902 22
Bill Bradley, 1903 22
Elmer Flick, 1906 22
Mike Mitchell, 1911 22
Birdie Cree, 1911 22
Tris Speaker, 1913 22
Hy Myers, 1920 22
Jake Daubert, 1922 22
Paul Waner, 1926 22
Earle Combs, 1930 22
Snuffy Stirnweiss, 1945 22
52 Dave Orr, 1885 21
Mike Tiernan, 1890 21
Billy Shindle, 1890 21
Tom Brown, 1891 21
Ed Delahanty, 1892 21
Sam Thompson, 1895 21
Mike Tiernan, 1895 21
Tom McCreery, 1896 21
George Van Haltren, 1896 21
Bobby Wallace, 1897 21
Jimmy Williams, 1901 21
Bill Keister, 1901 21
Jimmy Williams, 1902 21
Cy Seymour, 1905 21
Frank Schulte, 1911 21
Frank Baker, 1912 21
Sam Crawford, 1912 21
Vic Saier, 1913 21
Joe Jackson, 1916 21
Edd Roush, 1924 21
Earle Combs, 1928 21
Willie Wilson, 1985 21
Lance Johnson, 1996 21
75 37 players tied 20

Triples by era

1988-2003

1 Lance Johnson, 1996 21
2 Cristian Guzman, 2000 20
3 Tony Fernandez, 1990 17
4 Andy Van Slyke, 1988 15
Ray Lankford, 1991 15
6 Ruben Sierra, 1989 14
Deion Sanders, 1992 14
Lance Johnson, 1993 14
Lance Johnson, 1994 14
Chuck Knoblauch, 1996 14
Delino DeShields, 1997 14
Tony Womack, 2000 14
Cristian Guzman, 2001 14
Cristian Guzman, 2003 14

1973-1987

1 Willie Wilson, 1985 21
2 George Brett, 1979 20
3 Garry Templeton, 1979 19
Juan Samuel, 1984 19
Ryne Sandberg, 1984 19
6 Garry Templeton, 1977 18
Willie McGee, 1985 18
8 Ralph Garr, 1974 17
9 Rod Carew, 1977 16
Paul Molitor, 1979 16

1961-1972

1 Johnny Callison, 1965 16
Willie Davis, 1970 16
3 Gino Cimoli, 1962 15
4 Jake Wood, 1961 14
Vada Pinson, 1963 14
Dick Allen, 1965 14
Roberto Clemente, 1965 14
Donn Clendenon, 1965 14
Lou Brock, 1968 14
Don Kessinger, 1970 14

1943-1960

1 Dale Mitchell, 1949 23
2 Snuffy Stirnweiss, 1945 22
3 Stan Musial, 1943 20
Stan Musial, 1946 20
Willie Mays, 1957 20
6 Johnny Barrett, 1944 19
7 Stan Musial, 1948 18
Minnie Minoso, 1954 18
9 Jim Gilliam, 1953 17
10 Bob Elliott, 1944 16
Snuffy Stirnweiss, 1944 16
Johnny Lindell, 1944 16
Hank Edwards, 1946 16
Harry Walker, 1947 16
Jim Rivera, 1953 16

1921-1942

1 Kiki Cuyler, 1925 26
2 Earle Combs, 1927 23
Adam Comorosky, 1930 23
4 Jake Daubert, 1922 22
Paul Waner, 1926 22
Earle Combs, 1930 22
7 Edd Roush, 1924 21
Earle Combs, 1928 21
9 Rabbit Maranville, 1924 20
Goose Goslin, 1925 20
Curt Walker, 1926 20
Lou Gehrig, 1926 20
Jim Bottomley, 1928 20
Heinie Manush, 1928 20
Lloyd Waner, 1929 20
Bill Terry, 1931 20
Joe Vosmik, 1935 20
Jeff Heath, 1941 20

1901-1920

1 Chief Wilson, 1912 36
2 Joe Jackson, 1912 26
Sam Crawford, 1914 26
4 Sam Crawford, 1903 25
Larry Doyle, 1911 25
Tom Long, 1915 25
7 Ty Cobb, 1911 24
Ty Cobb, 1917 24
9 Ty Cobb, 1912 23
Sam Crawford, 1913 23

1893-1900

1 Heinie Reitz, 1894 31
2 Perry Werden, 1893 29
3 Sam Thompson, 1894 28
Harry Davis, 1897 28
5 George Davis, 1893 27
Jimmy Williams, 1899 27
7 George Treadway, 1894 26
8 Roger Connor, 1894 25
Buck Freeman, 1899 25
10 Ed McKean, 1893 24

1876-1892

1 Dave Orr, 1886 31
2 John Reilly, 1890 26
3 Harry Stovey, 1884 23
Sam Thompson, 1887 23
5 Roger Connor, 1887 22
Bid McPhee, 1890 22
Jake Beckley, 1890 22
Joe Visner, 1890 22
9 Dave Orr, 1885 21
Mike Tiernan, 1890 21
Billy Shindle, 1890 21
Tom Brown, 1891 21
Ed Delahanty, 1892 21

Home Runs

1 Barry Bonds, 2001 73
2 Mark McGwire, 1998 70
3 Sammy Sosa, 1998 66
4 Mark McGwire, 1999 65
5 Sammy Sosa, 2001 64
6 Sammy Sosa, 1999 63
7 Roger Maris, 1961 61
8 Babe Ruth, 1927 60
9 Babe Ruth, 1921 59
10 Mark McGwire, 1997 58
Jimmie Foxx, 1932 58
Hank Greenberg, 1938 58
13 Luis Gonzalez, 2001 57
Alex Rodriguez, 2002 57
15 Hack Wilson, 1930 56
Ken Griffey, 1997 56
Ken Griffey, 1998 56
18 Babe Ruth, 1920 54
Babe Ruth, 1928 54
Ralph Kiner, 1949 54
Mickey Mantle, 1961 54
22 Mickey Mantle, 1956 52
Willie Mays, 1965 52
George Foster, 1977 52
Mark McGwire, 1996 52
Alex Rodriguez, 2001 52
Jim Thome, 2002 52
28 Ralph Kiner, 1947 51
Johnny Mize, 1947 51
Willie Mays, 1955 51
Cecil Fielder, 1990 51
32 Jimmie Foxx, 1938 50
Albert Belle, 1995 50
Brady Anderson, 1996 50
Greg Vaughn, 1998 50
Sammy Sosa, 2000 50
37 Babe Ruth, 1930 49
Lou Gehrig, 1934 49
Lou Gehrig, 1936 49
Ted Kluszewski, 1954 49
Willie Mays, 1962 49
Harmon Killebrew, 1964 49
Frank Robinson, 1966 49
Harmon Killebrew, 1969 49
Andre Dawson, 1987 49
Mark McGwire, 1987 49
Ken Griffey, 1996 49
Larry Walker, 1997 49
Albert Belle, 1998 49
Barry Bonds, 2000 49
Shawn Green, 2001 49
Todd Helton, 2001 49
Jim Thome, 2001 49
Sammy Sosa, 2002 49
55 Jimmie Foxx, 1933 48
Harmon Killebrew, 1962 48
Frank Howard, 1969 48
Willie Stargell, 1971 48
Dave Kingman, 1979 48
Mike Schmidt, 1980 48
Albert Belle, 1996 48
Ken Griffey, 1999 48
63 Babe Ruth, 1926 47
Lou Gehrig, 1927 47
Ralph Kiner, 1950 47
Eddie Mathews, 1953 47
Ted Kluszewski, 1955 47
Ernie Banks, 1958 47
Willie Mays, 1964 47
Reggie Jackson, 1969 47
Hank Aaron, 1971 47
George Bell, 1987 47
Kevin Mitchell, 1989 47
Andres Galarraga, 1996 47
Juan Gonzalez, 1996 47
Rafael Palmeiro, 1999 47
Jeff Bagwell, 2000 47
Troy Glaus, 2000 47
Rafael Palmeiro, 2001 47
Jim Thome, 2003 47
Alex Rodriguez, 2003 47
82 Babe Ruth, 1924 46
Babe Ruth, 1929 46
Babe Ruth, 1931 46
Lou Gehrig, 1931 46
Joe DiMaggio, 1937 46
Eddie Mathews, 1959 46
Orlando Cepeda, 1961 46
Jim Gentile, 1961 46
Harmon Killebrew, 1961 46
Jim Rice, 1978 46
Barry Bonds, 1993 46
Juan Gonzalez, 1993 46
Vinny Castilla, 1998 46
Jose Canseco, 1998 46
Barry Bonds, 2002 46
97 16 players tied 45

Home Runs by era

1988-2003

1 Barry Bonds, 2001........73
2 Mark McGwire, 1998..........70
3 Sammy Sosa, 1998........66
4 Mark McGwire, 1999...........65
5 Sammy Sosa, 2001........64
6 Sammy Sosa, 1999........63
7 Mark McGwire, 1997............58
8 Luis Gonzalez, 2001......57
Alex Rodriguez, 2002....57
10 Ken Griffey, 1997...........56
Ken Griffey, 1998...........56

1973-1987

1 George Foster, 1977 52
2 Andre Dawson, 1987 49
Mark McGwire, 1987...........49
4 Dave Kingman, 1979 48
Mike Schmidt, 1980 48
6 George Bell, 1987...............47
7 Jim Rice, 1978 46
8 Mike Schmidt, 1979 45
Gorman Thomas, 1979.........45
10 Willie Stargell, 1973 44
Dale Murphy, 1987 44

1961-1972

1 Roger Maris, 1961 61
2 Mickey Mantle, 1961 54
3 Willie Mays, 1965.................52
4 Willie Mays, 1962................49
Harmon Killebrew, 1964......49
Frank Robinson, 1966.........49
Harmon Killebrew, 1969......49
8 Harmon Killebrew, 1962......48
Frank Howard, 1969............48
Willie Stargell, 1971 48

1943-1960

1 Ralph Kiner, 1949................54
2 Mickey Mantle, 1956 52
3 Ralph Kiner, 1947................51
Johnny Mize, 1947 51
Willie Mays, 1955................51
6 Ted Kluszewski, 1954 49
7 Ralph Kiner, 1950................47
Eddie Mathews, 1953 47
Ted Kluszewski, 1955 47
Ernie Banks, 1958 47

1921-1942

1 Babe Ruth, 1927.................60
2 Babe Ruth, 1921.................59
3 Jimmie Foxx, 1932..............58
Hank Greenberg, 1938 58
5 Hack Wilson, 1930...............56
6 Babe Ruth, 1928.................54
7 Jimmie Foxx, 1938..............50
8 Babe Ruth, 1930.................49
Lou Gehrig, 1934 49
Lou Gehrig, 1936 49

1901-1920

1 Babe Ruth, 1920.................54
2 Babe Ruth, 1919.................29
3 Gavy Cravath, 1915............24
4 Frank Schulte, 1911 21
5 Gavy Cravath, 1913............19
Gavy Cravath, 1914............19
George Sisler, 1920 19
8 Fred Luderus, 1913.............18
Vic Saier, 1914....................18
10 Hal Chase, 1915.................17
Tilly Walker, 1920................17

1893-1900

1 Buck Freeman, 1899...........25
2 Ed Delahanty, 1893.............19
3 Hugh Duffy, 1894 18
Sam Thompson, 1895 18
5 Jack Clements, 1893 17
Bill Joyce, 1894 17
Bobby Lowe, 1894 17
Bill Joyce, 1895....................17
9 Bill Dahlen, 1894.................15
Jimmy Collins, 1898............15

1876-1892

1 Ed Williamson, 1884...........27
2 Fred Pfeffer, 1884 25
3 Abner Dalrymple, 1884.......22
4 Cap Anson, 1884................21
5 Sam Thompson, 1889 20
6 Billy O'Brien, 1887 19
Bug Holliday, 1889..............19
Harry Stovey, 1889..............19
9 Jerry Denny, 1889...............18
10 Roger Connor, 1887............17
Jimmy Ryan, 1889 17

Home Run Pct.

1 Barry Bonds, 2001....15.34
2 Mark McGwire, 1998......13.75
3 Mark McGwire, 1999......12.48
4 Mark McGwire, 1996......12.29
5 Babe Ruth, 1920............11.79
6 Barry Bonds, 2003....11.54
7 Barry Bonds, 2002....11.41
8 Babe Ruth, 1927............11.11
9 Sammy Sosa, 2001...11.09
10 Babe Ruth, 1921............10.93
11 Jim Thome, 2002......10.83
12 Mark McGwire, 1997.......10.74
13 Mickey Mantle, 1961 ......10.51
14 Hank Greenberg, 1938 ..10.43
15 Roger Maris, 1961 ....10.34
16 Sammy Sosa, 1998...10.26
17 Barry Bonds, 2000....10.21
18 Sammy Sosa, 1999...10.08
19 Babe Ruth, 1928............10.07
20 Jimmie Foxx, 1932...........9.91
21 Ralph Kiner, 1949.............9.84
22 Mickey Mantle, 1956........9.76
23 Jeff Bagwell, 1994 .....9.75
24 Kevin Mitchell, 1994.........9.68
25 Matt Williams, 1994....9.66
26 Hack Wilson, 1930...........9.57
27 Frank Thomas, 1994...9.52
28 Babe Ruth, 1926..............9.49
Hank Aaron, 1971............9.49
30 Jim Gentile, 1961 ....9.47
31 Barry Bonds, 1994......9.46
32 Babe Ruth, 1930..............9.46
33 Willie Stargell, 1971 ....9.39
34 Luis Gonzalez, 2001 ...9.36
35 Willie Mays, 1965.............9.32
36 Jim Thome, 2001 ....9.32
37 Ken Griffey, 1994........9.24
38 Babe Ruth, 1929..............9.22
39 Ken Griffey, 1997........9.21
40 Boog Powell, 1964...........9.20
41 Willie McCovey, 1969.......9.16
42 Albert Belle, 1995 ....9.16
43 Alex Rodriguez, 2002 ....9.13
44 Ted Williams, 1957...........9.05
45 Ralph Kiner, 1947.............9.03
46 Dave Kingman, 1979 ....9.02
47 Mark McGwire, 1992........8.99
48 Ken Griffey, 1996........8.99
49 Babe Ruth, 1932..............8.97
50 Cecil Fielder, 1990 ....8.90
51 Jimmie Foxx, 1938...........8.85
52 Ken Griffey, 1998........8.85
53 Harmon Killebrew, 1969...8.83
54 Sammy Sosa, 2002.....8.81
55 Mark McGwire, 1987........8.80
56 Willie Mays, 1955.............8.79
57 Mike Schmidt, 1980 ....8.76
58 Mike Schmidt, 1981 ....8.76
59 Harmon Killebrew, 1963...8.74
Albert Belle, 1994 ....8.74
61 Greg Vaughn, 1998.....8.73
62 Jim Edmonds, 2003....8.72
63 Johnny Mize, 1947 ....8.70
64 Babe Ruth, 1924..............8.70
Harmon Killebrew, 1962...8.70
66 Juan Gonzalez, 1996..8.69
67 Manny Ramirez, 2000 ....8.66
68 Kevin Mitchell, 1989.........8.66
69 Brady Anderson, 1996.....8.64
70 Larry Walker, 1997 .....8.63
71 Babe Ruth, 1922..............8.62
72 Babe Ruth, 1931..............8.61
73 Ralph Kiner, 1950.............8.59
74 Gary Sheffield, 2000 ..8.58
75 Juan Gonzalez, 1993..8.58
76 Reggie Jackson, 1969 ......8.56
77 Ted Kluszewski, 1954 ......8.55
78 Barry Bonds, 1993......8.53
79 Jay Buhner, 1995 ....8.51
80 Frank Robinson, 1966.......8.51
81 Harmon Killebrew, 1961...8.50
82 Harmon Killebrew, 1964...8.49
83 Lou Gehrig, 1934 ....8.46
Lou Gehrig, 1936 ....8.46
85 George Foster, 1977 ....8.46
86 Larry Walker, 1999 .....8.45
87 Jason Giambi, 2000....8.43
88 Willie Stargell, 1973 ....8.43
Manny Ramirez, 1999 ....8.43
90 Hank Greenberg, 1946 .....8.41
91 Eddie Mathews, 1954 ....8.40
92 Gary Sheffield, 1994 ..8.39
93 Rocky Colavito, 1958 ....8.38
94 Jimmie Foxx, 1933............8.38
95 Joe Adcock, 1956 ....8.37
96 Alex Rodriguez, 1999 ....8.37
97 Jack Clark, 1987 ....8.35
98 Troy Glaus, 2000.........8.35
99 Todd Helton, 2001 ......8.35
100 Rafael Palmeiro, 1999........8.32

Home Run Pct. by era

1988-2003

1 Barry Bonds, 2001....15.34
2 Mark McGwire, 1998......13.75
3 Mark McGwire, 1999......12.48
4 Mark McGwire, 1996......12.29
5 Barry Bonds, 2003....11.54
6 Barry Bonds, 2002....11.41
7 Sammy Sosa, 2001...11.09
8 Jim Thome, 2002......10.83
9 Mark McGwire, 1997......10.74
10 Sammy Sosa, 1998...10.26

1973-1987

1 Dave Kingman, 1979 ....9.02
2 Mark McGwire, 1987........8.80
3 Mike Schmidt, 1980 ....8.76
4 Mike Schmidt, 1981 ....8.76
5 George Foster, 1977 ....8.46
6 Willie Stargell, 1973 ....8.43
7 Jack Clark, 1987 ....8.35
8 Mike Schmidt, 1979 ....8.32
9 Gorman Thomas, 1979....8.08
10 Reggie Jackson, 1980 .....7.98

1961-1972

1 Mickey Mantle, 1961 ......10.51
2 Roger Maris, 1961 ....10.34
3 Hank Aaron, 1971 ....9.49
4 Jim Gentile, 1961 ....9.47
5 Willie Stargell, 1971 ....9.39
6 Willie Mays, 1965.............9.32
7 Boog Powell, 1964...........9.20
8 Willie McCovey, 1969.......9.16
9 Harmon Killebrew, 1969...8.83
10 Harmon Killebrew, 1963...8.74

1943-1960

1 Ralph Kiner, 1949.............9.84
2 Mickey Mantle, 1956........9.76
3 Ted Williams, 1957...........9.05
4 Ralph Kiner, 1947.............9.03
5 Willie Mays, 1955.............8.79
6 Johnny Mize, 1947 ....8.70
7 Ralph Kiner, 1950.............8.59
8 Ted Kluszewski, 1954 ......8.55
9 Hank Greenberg, 1946 ....8.41
10 Eddie Mathews, 1954 ......8.40

1921-1942

1 Babe Ruth, 1927............11.11
2 Babe Ruth, 1921............10.93
3 Hank Greenberg, 1938 ..10.43
4 Babe Ruth, 1928............10.07
5 Jimmie Foxx, 1932...........9.91
6 Hack Wilson, 1930...........9.57
7 Babe Ruth, 1926..............9.49
8 Babe Ruth, 1930..............9.46
9 Babe Ruth, 1929..............9.22
10 Babe Ruth, 1932..............8.97

1901-1920

1 Babe Ruth, 1920............11.79
2 Babe Ruth, 1919..............6.71
3 Gavy Cravath, 1915.........4.60
4 Gavy Cravath, 1914.........3.81
5 Frank Schulte, 1911.........3.64
6 Gavy Cravath, 1913.........3.62
7 Sherry Magee, 1911 ....3.37
8 Vic Saier, 1914.................3.35
9 Sam Crawford, 1901 ....3.11
10 Socks Seybold, 1902 ....3.07

1893-1900

1 Bill Joyce, 1894 ....4.79
2 Jack Clements, 1893 ....4.52
3 Buck Freeman, 1899.........4.25
4 Jim Canavan, 1894 ....3.57
5 Bill Joyce, 1895................3.55
6 Sam Thompson, 1895 .....3.35
7 Hugh Duffy, 1894 ....3.34
8 Ed Delahanty, 1893...........3.19
9 Bill Dahlen, 1894...............2.96
10 Sam Thompson, 1894 .....2.88

1876-1892

1 Ed Williamson, 1884 ....6.47
2 Fred Pfeffer, 1884 ....5.35
3 Cap Anson, 1884 ....4.42
4 Abner Dalrymple, 1884 ....4.22
5 Billy O'Brien, 1887 ....4.19
6 Sam Thompson, 1889 ......3.75
7 Roger Connor, 1887..........3.61
8 Dan Brouthers, 1884........3.52
9 Harry Stovey, 1889...........3.42
10 Bug Holliday, 1889 ....3.37

Extra Base Hits

1 Babe Ruth, 1921...............119
2 Lou Gehrig, 1927 117
3 Chuck Klein, 1930............107
Barry Bonds, 2001.......107
5 Todd Helton, 2001 105
6 Chuck Klein, 1932.............103
Hank Greenberg, 1937 103
Stan Musial, 1948 103
Albert Belle, 1995 103
Todd Helton, 2000 103
Sammy Sosa, 2001......103
12 Rogers Hornsby, 1922 102
13 Lou Gehrig, 1930 100
Jimmie Foxx, 1932............100
Luis Gonzalez, 2001 100
16 Babe Ruth, 1920.................99
Babe Ruth, 1923.................99
Hank Greenberg, 1940 99
Larry Walker, 1997 99
Albert Belle, 1998 99
Carlos Delgado, 2000 99
22 Hank Greenberg, 1935 98
23 Babe Ruth, 1927.................97
Hack Wilson, 1930..............97
Joe Medwick, 1937 97
Juan Gonzalez, 1998 97
27 Hank Greenberg, 1934 96
Hal Trosky, 1936.................96
Joe DiMaggio, 1937 96
30 Lou Gehrig, 1934 95
Joe Medwick, 1936 95
Albert Pujols, 2003........95
33 Rogers Hornsby, 1929 94
Chuck Klein, 1929...............94
Babe Herman, 1930............94
Jimmie Foxx, 1933..............94
Lance Berkman, 2001 ...94
38 Jim Bottomley, 1928...........93
Al Simmons, 1930...............93
Lou Gehrig, 1936 93
Ellis Burks, 1996...........93
Ken Griffey, 1997..........93
43 Babe Ruth, 1924.................92
Lou Gehrig, 1931 92
Jimmie Foxx, 1938..............92
Stan Musial, 1953...............92
Hank Aaron, 1959...............92
Frank Robinson, 1962.........92
Brady Anderson, 1996 92
Ken Griffey, 1998..........92
Alfonso Soriano, 2002 92
52 Babe Ruth, 1928.................91
Alex Rodriguez, 1996....91
Mark McGwire, 1998............91
55 Rogers Hornsby, 1925 90
Stan Musial, 1949...............90
Willie Mays, 1962...............90
Willie Stargell, 1973 90
59 Hal Trosky, 1934.................89
Duke Snider, 1954..............89
Andres Galarraga, 1996............89
Albert Belle, 1996 89
Sammy Sosa, 1999........89
Richard Hidalgo, 2000..........89
Sammy Sosa, 2000........89
66 Joe DiMaggio, 1936 88
Barry Bonds, 1993.........88
Barry Bonds, 1998.........88
Albert Pujols, 2001........88
Garret Anderson, 2002...........88
71 Tris Speaker, 1923 87
Kiki Cuyler, 1925 87
Lou Gehrig, 1928 87
Ripper Collins, 1934............87
Charlie Gehringer, 1936 87
Johnny Mize, 1940..............87
Willie Mays, 1954................87
Robin Yount, 1982...............87
Kevin Mitchell, 1989............87
Chipper Jones, 1999 87
Mark McGwire, 1999...........87
Shawn Green, 1999.......87
Frank Thomas, 2000.......87
Jason Giambi, 2001.......87
Alex Rodriguez, 2001 87
Todd Helton, 2003 87
Vernon Wells, 2003........87
88 17 players tied 86

Total Bases

1 Babe Ruth, 1921...............457
2 Rogers Hornsby, 1922 450
3 Lou Gehrig, 1927 447
4 Chuck Klein, 1930.............445
5 Jimmie Foxx, 1932............438
6 Stan Musial, 1948 429
7 Sammy Sosa, 2001......425
8 Hack Wilson, 1930.............423
9 Chuck Klein, 1932.............420
10 Lou Gehrig, 1930 419
Luis Gonzalez, 2001 419
12 Joe DiMaggio, 1937 418
13 Babe Ruth, 1927...............417
14 Babe Herman, 1930..........416
Sammy Sosa, 1998......416
16 Barry Bonds, 2001.......411
17 Lou Gehrig, 1931 410
18 Rogers Hornsby, 1929 409
Lou Gehrig, 1934 409
Larry Walker, 1997 409
21 Joe Medwick, 1937 406
Jim Rice, 1978 406
23 Chuck Klein, 1929.............405
Hal Trosky, 1936...............405
Todd Helton, 2000 405
26 Jimmie Foxx, 1933............403
Lou Gehrig, 1936 403
28 Todd Helton, 2001 402
29 Hank Aaron, 1959.............400
30 George Sisler, 1920 399
Babe Ruth, 1923...............399
Albert Belle, 1998 399
33 Jimmie Foxx, 1938............398
34 Lefty O'Doul, 1929 397
Hank Greenberg, 1937 397
Sammy Sosa, 1999......397
37 Albert Pujols, 2003......394
38 Ken Griffey, 1997.........393
Alex Rodriguez, 2001 ..393
40 Al Simmons, 1925.............392
Bill Terry, 1930 392
Al Simmons, 1930.............392
Ellis Burks, 1996..........392
44 Babe Ruth, 1924...............391
45 Hank Greenberg, 1935 389
Alex Rodriguez, 2002 ..389
47 Babe Ruth, 1920...............388
George Foster, 1977 388
Don Mattingly, 1986 388
50 Ken Griffey, 1998.........387
51 Earl Averill, 1936 385
52 Hank Greenberg, 1940 384
Alex Rodriguez, 1998 ..384
54 Mark McGwire, 1998.........383
Sammy Sosa, 2000......383
56 Stan Musial, 1949 382
Willie Mays, 1955..............382
Willie Mays, 1962..............382
Jim Rice, 1977 382
Juan Gonzalez, 1998...382
61 Rogers Hornsby, 1925 381
Alfonso Soriano, 2002 381
63 Babe Ruth, 1928...............380
Hank Greenberg, 1938 380
Frank Robinson, 1962.......380
Vinny Castilla, 1998 380
67 Babe Ruth, 1930...............379
Ernie Banks, 1958 379
Alex Rodriguez, 1996 ..379
Vladimir Guerrero, 2000.......379
71 Rogers Hornsby, 1921 378
Duke Snider, 1954.............378
Carlos Delgado, 2000..378
74 Willie Mays, 1954..............377
Albert Belle, 1995 377
76 Mickey Mantle, 1956 376
Andres Galarraga, 1996.......376
78 Albert Belle, 1996 375
79 Hugh Duffy, 1894 374
Babe Ruth, 1931...............374
Hal Trosky, 1934...............374
Tony Oliva, 1964 374
83 Rogers Hornsby, 1924 373
Al Simmons, 1929.............373
Bill Terry, 1932 373
Billy Williams, 1970...........373
Vernon Wells, 2003......373
88 Lou Gehrig, 1932 370
Duke Snider, 1953.............370
Hank Aaron, 1963..............370
Don Mattingly, 1985 370
Mo Vaughn, 1996.........370
Shawn Green, 2001.......370
94 Kiki Cuyler, 1925 369
Ripper Collins, 1934..........369
Jimmie Foxx, 1936............369
Hank Aaron, 1957..............369
Jim Rice, 1979 369
George Bell, 1987 369
Brady Anderson, 1996 369

Runs Batted In

1 Hack Wilson, 1930...........191
2 Lou Gehrig, 1931.............184
3 Hank Greenberg, 1937.....183
4 Lou Gehrig, 1927.............175
Jimmie Foxx, 1938............175
6 Lou Gehrig, 1930.............174
7 Babe Ruth, 1921..............171
8 Chuck Klein, 1930............170
Hank Greenberg, 1935.......170
10 Jimmie Foxx, 1932...........169
11 Joe DiMaggio, 1937..........167
12 Sam Thompson, 1887......166
13 Sam Thompson, 1895......165
Al Simmons, 1930.............165
Lou Gehrig, 1934..............165
Manny Ramirez, 1999..165
17 Babe Ruth, 1927...............164
18 Babe Ruth, 1931...............163
Jimmie Foxx, 1933............163
20 Hal Trosky, 1936..............162
21 Sammy Sosa, 2001......160
22 Hack Wilson, 1929............159
Lou Gehrig, 1937...............159
Ted Williams, 1949............159
Vern Stephens, 1949.........159
26 Sammy Sosa, 1998......158
27 Al Simmons, 1929.............157
Juan Gonzalez, 1998...157
29 Jimmie Foxx, 1930............156
30 Ken Williams, 1922...........155
Joe DiMaggio, 1948..........155
32 Babe Ruth, 1929...............154
Joe Medwick, 1937............154
34 Babe Ruth, 1930...............153
Tommy Davis, 1962...........153
36 Rogers Hornsby, 1922......152
Lou Gehrig, 1936...............152
Albert Belle, 1998..............152
39 Mel Ott, 1929....................151
Lou Gehrig, 1932...............151
Al Simmons, 1932.............151
42 Hank Greenberg, 1940.....150
Andres Galarraga, 1996.......150
44 Rogers Hornsby, 1929......149
George Foster, 1977..........149
46 Johnny Bench, 1970.........148
Albert Belle, 1996..............148
Rafael Palmeiro, 1999.........148
49 Cap Anson, 1886..............147
Sam Thompson, 1894......147
Ken Griffey, 1997.........147
Mark McGwire, 1998..........147
Mark McGwire, 1999..........147
Todd Helton, 2000.......147
55 Hardy Richardson, 1890...146
Ed Delahanty, 1893...........146
Babe Ruth, 1926...............146
Hank Greenberg, 1938.....146
Ken Griffey, 1998.........146
Todd Helton, 2001.......146
61 Hugh Duffy, 1894.............145
Chuck Klein, 1929............145
Ted Williams, 1939............145
Al Rosen, 1953.................145
Don Mattingly, 1985..........145
Manny Ramirez, 1998..145
Edgar Martinez, 2000..145
Carlos Delgado, 2003..145
69 Walt Dropo, 1950.............144
Vern Stephens, 1950........144
Juan Gonzalez, 1996...144
Vinny Castilla, 1998....144
Mike Sweeney, 2000....144
74 Rogers Hornsby, 1925......143
Earl Averill, 1931..............143
Don Hurst, 1932................143
Jimmie Foxx, 1936............143
Ernie Banks, 1959............143
Mo Vaughn, 1996.........143
Frank Thomas, 2000....143
81 Lou Gehrig, 1928.............142
Babe Ruth, 1928...............142
Hal Trosky, 1934...............142
Roy Campanella, 1953.......142
Orlando Cepeda, 1961.....142
Roger Maris, 1961............142
Rafael Palmeiro, 1996.........142
Matt Williams, 1999.....142
Luis Gonzalez, 2001....142
Alex Rodriguez, 2002..142
91 Ted Kluszewski, 1954.......141
Jim Gentile, 1961..............141
Willie Mays, 1962..............141
Dante Bichette, 1996.......141
Tino Martinez, 1997....141
Sammy Sosa, 1999......141
Bret Boone, 2001.........141
Preston Wilson, 2003..141
99 6 players tied....................140

Runs Batted In by era

1988-2003

1 Manny Ramirez, 1999..165
2 Sammy Sosa, 2001......160
3 Sammy Sosa, 1998......158
4 Juan Gonzalez, 1998...157
5 Albert Belle, 1998............152
6 Andres Galarraga, 1996.......150
7 Albert Belle, 1996............148
Rafael Palmeiro, 1999.........148
9 Ken Griffey, 1997.........147
Mark McGwire, 1998.........147
Mark McGwire, 1999.........147
Todd Helton, 2000.......147

1973-1987

1 George Foster, 1977.........149
2 Don Mattingly, 1985..........145
3 Jim Rice, 1978..................139
Don Baylor, 1979..............139
5 Andre Dawson, 1987........137
6 George Bell, 1987.............134
7 Hal McRae, 1982..............133
8 Greg Luzinski, 1977..........130
Jim Rice, 1979..................130
10 Johnny Bench, 1974.........129

1961-1972

1 Tommy Davis, 1962..........153
2 Johnny Bench, 1970.........148
3 Orlando Cepeda, 1961.....142
Roger Maris, 1961............142
5 Jim Gentile, 1961.............141
Willie Mays, 1962.............141
7 Rocky Colavito, 1961........140
Harmon Killebrew, 1969....140
9 Joe Torre, 1971.................137
10 Frank Robinson, 1962.......136

1943-1960

1 Ted Williams, 1949...........159
Vern Stephens, 1949.......159
3 Joe DiMaggio, 1948..........155
4 Al Rosen, 1953.................145
5 Walt Dropo, 1950.............144
Vern Stephens, 1950........144
7 Ernie Banks, 1959............143
8 Roy Campanella, 1953......142
9 Ted Kluszewski, 1954........141
10 Johnny Mize, 1947...........138

1921-1942

1 Hack Wilson, 1930............191
2 Lou Gehrig, 1931..............184
3 Hank Greenberg, 1937......183
4 Lou Gehrig, 1927..............175
Jimmie Foxx, 1938............175
6 Lou Gehrig, 1930..............174
7 Babe Ruth, 1921...............171
8 Chuck Klein, 1930.............170
Hank Greenberg, 1935.....170
10 Jimmie Foxx, 1932...........169

1901-1920

1 Babe Ruth, 1920...............137
2 Frank Baker, 1912.............130
3 Gavy Cravath, 1913..........128
4 Ty Cobb, 1911....................127
5 Honus Wagner, 1901........126
6 Nap Lajoie, 1901..............125
7 Sherry Magee, 1910.........123
8 George Sisler, 1920..........122
Baby Doll Jacobson, 1920.....122
10 Buck Freeman, 1902.........121
Cy Seymour, 1905.............121
Joe Jackson, 1920............121

1893-1900

1 Sam Thompson, 1895......165
2 Sam Thompson, 1894......147
3 Ed Delahanty, 1893..........146
4 Hugh Duffy, 1894..............145
5 Ed Delahanty, 1899..........137
6 George Davis, 1897..........135
7 Steve Brodie, 1895...........134
Joe Kelley, 1895...............134
9 Ed McKean, 1893..............133
Ed Delahanty, 1894..........133

1876-1892

1 Sam Thompson, 1887......166
2 Cap Anson, 1886..............147
3 Hardy Richardson, 1890...146
4 Roger Connor, 1889..........130
5 Tommy Burns, 1890..........128
6 Dave Orr, 1890..................124
Dan Brouthers, 1892.........124
8 Tip O'Neill, 1887...............123
9 Jake Beckley, 1890...........120
Cap Anson, 1891...............120

Walks

1 Barry Bonds, 2002.......198
2 Barry Bonds, 2001.......177
3 Babe Ruth, 1923...............170
4 Ted Williams, 1947...........162
Ted Williams, 1949...........162
Mark McGwire, 1998.........162
7 Ted Williams, 1946...........156
8 Eddie Yost, 1956..............151
Barry Bonds, 1996.......151
10 Babe Ruth, 1920..............150
11 Eddie Joost, 1949............149
Jeff Bagwell, 1999......149
13 Eddie Stanky, 1945..........148
Jimmy Wynn, 1969...........148
Barry Bonds, 2003.......148
16 Jimmy Sheckard, 1911.....147
Ted Williams, 1941...........147
18 Mickey Mantle, 1957.........146
19 Babe Ruth, 1921...............145
Ted Williams, 1942...........145
Harmon Killebrew, 1969....145
Barry Bonds, 1997.......145
23 Babe Ruth, 1926...............144
Eddie Stanky, 1950..........144
Ted Williams, 1951...........144
26 Babe Ruth, 1924...............142
Gary Sheffield, 1996...142
28 Eddie Yost, 1950..............141
29 Frank Thomas, 1991....138
30 Babe Ruth, 1927...............137
Babe Ruth, 1928...............137
Eddie Stanky, 1946..........137
Roy Cullenbine, 1947........137
Ralph Kiner, 1951..............137
Willie McCovey, 1970........137
Jason Giambi, 2000.....137
37 Jack Crooks, 1892...........136
Babe Ruth, 1930...............136
Ferris Fain, 1949..............136
Ted Williams, 1954...........136
Jack Clark, 1987...............136
Frank Thomas, 1995....136
43 Eddie Yost, 1959..............135
Jeff Bagwell, 1996......135
Brian Giles, 2002.........135
46 Ferris Fain, 1950..............133
Mark McGwire, 1999.........133
48 Lou Gehrig, 1935..............132
Frank Howard, 1970..........132
Joe Morgan, 1975.............132
Jack Clark, 1989...............132
Tony Phillips, 1993...........132
53 Bob Elliott, 1948...............131
Eddie Yost, 1954..............131
Harmon Killebrew, 1967....131
56 Babe Ruth, 1932...............130
Lou Gehrig, 1936...............130
Barry Bonds, 1998.......130
59 Eddie Yost, 1952..............129
Mickey Mantle, 1958.........129
Lenny Dykstra, 1993.........129
Jason Giambi, 2001.....129
Jason Giambi, 2003.....129
64 Billy Hamilton, 1894.........128
Max Bishop, 1929.............128
Max Bishop, 1930.............128
Babe Ruth, 1931...............128
Harmon Killebrew, 1970....128
Carl Yastrzemski, 1970.....128
Mike Schmidt, 1983...........128
Adam Dunn, 2002........128
72 Lu Blue, 1931....................127
Lou Gehrig, 1937...............127
Eddie Stanky, 1951...........127
Jimmy Wynn, 1976............127
Barry Bonds, 1992.......127
Jeff Bagwell, 1997.......127
Jim Thome, 1999.........127
79 Lu Blue, 1929....................126
Ted Williams, 1948...........126
Eddie Yost, 1951..............126
Mickey Mantle, 1961.........126
Darrell Evans, 1974..........126
Rickey Henderson, 1989......126
Barry Bonds, 1993.......126
Chipper Jones, 1999...126
87 Richie Ashburn, 1954.......125
Eddie Yost, 1960..............125
Gene Tenace, 1977...........125
Wade Boggs, 1988............125
Rickey Henderson, 1996......125
Tony Phillips, 1996............125
John Olerud, 1999.......125
94 John McGraw, 1899..........124
Norm Cash, 1961..............124
Eddie Mathews, 1963.......124
Darrell Evans, 1973..........124
98 6 players tied...................123

Walk Percentage (BB/PA)

1 Barry Bonds, 2002....32.35
2 Barry Bonds, 2003....26.91
3 Barry Bonds, 2001....26.66
4 Ted Williams, 1954.........25.86
5 Jack Clark, 1987.............24.37
6 Babe Ruth, 1920.............24.35
7 Babe Ruth, 1923.............24.32
8 Mickey Mantle, 1962......24.30
9 Ted Williams, 1941.........24.26
10 Mark McGwire, 1998......23.79
11 Mickey Mantle, 1957......23.43
12 Ted Williams, 1947.........23.38
13 Jack Crooks, 1892..........23.33
14 Ted Williams, 1946.........23.21
15 John McGraw, 1899........23.01
16 Jimmy Wynn, 1969..........22.66
17 Roy Cullenbine, 1947.....22.57
18 Barry Bonds, 1996....22.37
19 Jack Clark, 1989............22.26
20 Ted Williams, 1949.........22.19
21 Babe Ruth, 1926............22.09
22 Eddie Yost, 1956............22.08
23 Babe Ruth, 1932............22.07
24 Max Bishop, 1926...........21.93
25 Eddie Joost, 1949..........21.85
26 Mickey Tettleton, 1994...21.85
27 Ted Williams, 1957.........21.79
28 Max Bishop, 1930...........21.77
29 Jimmy Wynn, 1976..........21.75
30 Toby Harrah, 1985..........21.69
31 Ted Williams, 1942.........21.61
32 Gene Tenace, 1977.........21.51
33 Willie McCovey, 1970.....21.47
34 Max Bishop, 1927...........21.47
35 Eddie Stanky, 1946........21.34
36 Ted Williams, 1951.........21.33
37 Mark McGwire, 1996.......21.17
38 Frank Thomas, 1994.21.08
39 Max Bishop, 1932...........21.07
40 Frank Thomas, 1995.21.02
41 Barry Bonds, 1997....21.01
42 Max Bishop, 1933...........20.99
43 Gary Sheffield, 1996 20.97
44 Brian Giles, 2002......20.96
45 Jack Crooks, 1893..........20.93
46 Babe Ruth, 1921............20.92
47 Jimmy Sheckard, 1911..20.88
48 Willie Mays, 1971...........20.86
49 Babe Ruth, 1924............20.85
50 Eddie Stanky, 1950........20.84
51 Jimmy Wynn, 1975.........20.79
52 Gary Sheffield, 1997 20.79
53 Max Bishop, 1929...........20.78
54 Rickey Henderson, 1996...20.76
55 Barry Bonds, 1992....20.75
56 Joe Morgan, 1975...........20.66
57 Jason Giambi, 2000..20.63
58 Yank Robinson, 1889.....20.49
59 Harmon Killebrew, 1969.20.45
60 Ralph Kiner, 1951...........20.45
61 Jeff Bagwell, 1999...20.44
62 Elmer Valo, 1952...........20.40
63 Hank Greenberg, 1947..20.39
64 Eddie Stanky, 1945........20.39
65 Ted Williams, 1956.........20.28
66 Ferris Fain, 1949............20.24
67 Ferris Fain, 1950............20.21
68 Jim Thome, 1999......20.19
69 Mark McGwire, 1999.......20.12
70 Babe Ruth, 1930............20.12
71 Babe Ruth, 1928............20.03
72 Eddie Yost, 1959............20.00
73 Jim Thome, 2002......19.90
74 Yank Robinson, 1888.....19.90
75 Babe Ruth, 1927............19.83
76 Babe Ruth, 1933............19.83
77 Ted Williams, 1948.........19.75
78 Mickey Mantle, 1958......19.72
79 Frank Thomas, 1991.19.71
80 Bill Joyce, 1890.............19.71
81 Mel Ott, 1943..................19.71
82 Cupid Childs, 1893.........19.70
83 Mel Ott, 1939..................19.69
84 Rickey Henderson, 1993...19.67
85 Eddie Yost, 1960............19.65
86 Lou Gehrig, 1935............19.64
87 Gene Tenace, 1978........19.61
88 Danny Tartabull, 1992....19.58
89 Mickey Tettleton, 1995...19.56
90 Mickey Cochrane, 1933.19.56
91 Luke Appling, 1949........19.55
92 John McGraw, 1897.......19.53
93 Mickey Mantle, 1961......19.50
94 Eddie Stanky, 1951........19.45
95 Johnny Evers, 1910.......19.42
96 Willie McCovey, 1969....19.42
97 Bob Elliott, 1948.............19.41
98 Edgar Martinez, 1996......19.40
99 Eddie Yost, 1955............19.39
100 Mickey Mantle, 1968......19.38

Strikeouts

1 Bobby Bonds, 1970...........189
2 Jose Hernandez, 2002........188
3 Bobby Bonds, 1969...........187
Preston Wilson, 2000..187
5 Rob Deer, 1987.................186
6 Pete Incaviglia, 1986.........185
Jose Hernandez, 2001 185
Jim Thome, 2001.........185
9 Cecil Fielder, 1990............182
Jim Thome, 2003.........182
11 Mo Vaughn, 2000.........181
12 Mike Schmidt, 1975...........180
13 Rob Deer, 1986.................179
14 Richie Sexson, 2001....178
15 Jose Hernandez, 2003........177
16 Mike Cameron, 2002...176
17 Dave Nicholson, 1963........175
Gorman Thomas, 1979.....175
Jose Canseco, 1986.........175
Rob Deer, 1991.................175
Jay Buhner, 1997..............175
22 Sammy Sosa, 1997......174
23 Jim Presley, 1986.............172
Bo Jackson, 1989.............172
25 Reggie Jackson, 1968......171
Sammy Sosa, 1998......171
Sammy Sosa, 1999......171
Jim Thome, 1999.........171
Jim Thome, 2000.........171
30 Gorman Thomas, 1980.....170
Adam Dunn, 2002.........170
32 Andres Galarraga, 1990.......169
Rob Deer, 1993.................169
34 Juan Samuel, 1984...........168
Pete Incaviglia, 1987.........168
Sammy Sosa, 2000......168
37 Jim Edmonds, 2000.....167
38 Gary Alexander, 1978.......166
Steve Balboni, 1985..........166
Cory Snyder, 1987............166
41 Derrek Lee, 2002.........164
42 Donn Clendenon, 1968.....163
Troy Glaus, 2000..........163
44 Butch Hobson, 1977.........162
Juan Samuel, 1987...........162
Ron Gant, 1997............162
Pat Burrell, 2001..........162
48 Dick Allen, 1968................161
Reggie Jackson, 1971......161
Brad Wilkerson, 2002...161
51 Mickey Tettleton, 1990......160
Henry Rodriguez, 1996.....160
53 Mark McGwire, 1997..........159
Richie Sexson, 2000.....159
Jay Buhner, 1996..............159
Jose Canseco, 1998.........159
Ben Grieve, 2001.........159
58 Bo Jackson, 1987.............158
Andres Galarraga, 1989.......158
Rob Deer, 1989.................158
Jose Canseco, 1990.........158
Melvin Nieves, 1996..........158
Jeromy Burnitz, 1998..158
Troy Glaus, 2001..........158
65 Danny Tartabull, 1986.......157
Jose Canseco, 1987.........157
Jim Presley, 1987.............157
Andres Galarraga, 1996.......157
Melvin Nieves, 1997..........157
Lee Stevens, 2001............157
Alfonso Soriano, 2002.........157
72 Tommie Agee, 1970..........156
Dave Kingman, 1982.........156
Reggie Jackson, 1982......156
Tony Armas, 1984.............156
Danny Tartabull, 1993.......156
Preston Wilson, 1999..156
78 Frank Howard, 1967..........155
Jeff Burroughs, 1975........155
Mark McGwire, 1998..........155
Mike Cameron, 2001...155
Brad Wilkerson, 2003..155
83 Willie Stargell, 1971..........154
Larry Parrish, 1987............154
Dean Palmer, 1992.......154
Dean Palmer, 1993.......154
Mo Vaughn, 1996.........154
Mo Vaughn, 1997.........154
89 Dave Kingman, 1975..........153
Andres Galarraga, 1988.......153
Rob Deer, 1988.................153
Pete Incaviglia, 1988.........153
Dean Palmer, 1999.......153
Sammy Sosa, 2001......153
Pat Burrell, 2002..........153
96 George Scott, 1966...........152
Larry Hisle, 1969...............152
Jose Canseco, 1991.........152
99 10 players tied..................151

Strikeout Percentage

1988-2003

Rank	Player	Pct
1	Rob Deer, 1991	39.06
2	Rob Deer, 1993	36.27
3	Mickey Tettleton, 1990	36.04
4	**Jose Hernandez, 2002**	**35.81**
5	**Benji Gil, 1995**	**35.42**
6	**Jim Thome, 2001**	**35.17**
7	**Jim Thome, 1999**	**34.62**
8	**Jose Hernandez, 2001**	**34.13**
9	**Jose Hernandez, 2003**	**34.10**
10	Rob Deer, 1989	33.91

1973-1987

Rank	Player	Pct
1	Rob Deer, 1987	39.24
2	Rob Deer, 1986	38.41
3	Pete Incaviglia, 1986	34.26
4	Gary Alexander, 1978	33.33
5	Jack Clark, 1987	33.17
6	Pete Incaviglia, 1987	33.01
7	Mike Schmidt, 1975	32.03
8	Gorman Thomas, 1979	31.42
9	Danny Tartabull, 1986	30.72
10	Dave Kingman, 1975	30.48

1961-1972

Rank	Player	Pct
1	Dave Nicholson, 1963	38.98
2	Dick Allen, 1969	32.88
3	Reggie Jackson, 1970	31.69
4	Larry Hisle, 1969	31.54
5	Reggie Jackson, 1968	30.92
6	Dick Allen, 1968	30.90
7	Willie Stargell, 1971	30.14
8	Bobby Bonds, 1969	30.06
9	Frank Howard, 1967	29.87
10	Rick Monday, 1968	29.67

1943-1960

Rank	Player	Pct
1	Pancho Herrera, 1960	26.56
2	Jim Lemon, 1956	25.65
3	Dick Stuart, 1960	24.43
4	Frank Howard, 1960	24.11
5	Harmon Killebrew, 1960	23.98
6	Jim Lemon, 1958	23.95
7	Mickey Mantle, 1960	23.72
8	Larry Doby, 1953	23.59
9	Pat Seerey, 1945	23.43
10	Mickey Mantle, 1959	23.29

1921-1942

Rank	Player	Pct
1	Vince DiMaggio, 1938	24.81
2	Vince DiMaggio, 1937	22.52
3	Chet Ross, 1940	22.32
4	Dolph Camilli, 1941	21.74
5	Joe Orengo, 1940	21.69
6	Jimmie Foxx, 1941	21.15
7	Boze Berger, 1935	21.04
8	Jimmie Foxx, 1936	20.34
9	Dolph Camilli, 1938	19.84
10	Babe Ruth, 1922	19.70

1901-1920

Rank	Player	Pct
1	Gus Williams, 1914	24.05
2	Grover Gilmore, 1914	20.38
3	Gavy Cravath, 1916	19.87
4	Ed McDonald, 1912	19.83
5	Art Wilson, 1914	18.18
6	Gavy Cravath, 1912	17.66
7	Cozy Dolan, 1914	17.58
8	Max Carey, 1911	17.56
9	Danny Moeller, 1913	17.49
10	Babe Ruth, 1920	17.47

1893-1900

Rank	Player	Pct
1	Billy Lush, 1896	13.92
2	Tom Daly, 1893	13.83
3	Tom Brown, 1894	13.68
4	Tom McCreery, 1896	13.15
5	Tom Brown, 1895	12.27
6	Billy Clingman, 1896	12.06
7	Tom Brown, 1893	11.91
8	Bill Joyce, 1895	11.69
9	Tom Daly, 1895	11.30
10	Tom Brown, 1896	11.26

1876-1892

Rank	Player	Pct
1	Frank Meinke, 1884	26.10
2	Jim Galvin, 1883	24.53
3	Sam Wise, 1884	24.41
4	Jim Galvin, 1879	21.13
5	Charlie Bastian, 1885	21.08
6	Will White, 1878	20.81
7	Silver Flint, 1883	20.78
8	John Morrill, 1884	19.86
9	John Morrill, 1885	19.80
10	Charlie Bastian, 1886	19.57

Batting Average

Rank	Player	Avg
1	Hugh Duffy, 1894	.440
2	Tip O'Neill, 1887	.435
3	Ross Barnes, 1876	.429
4	Nap Lajoie, 1901	.426
5	Willie Keeler, 1897	.424
6	Rogers Hornsby, 1924	.424
7	George Sisler, 1922	.420
8	Ty Cobb, 1911	.420
9	Sam Thompson, 1894	.415
10	Fred Dunlap, 1884	.412
11	Ed Delahanty, 1899	.410
12	Jesse Burkett, 1896	.410
13	Ty Cobb, 1912	.409
14	Joe Jackson, 1911	.408
15	George Sisler, 1920	.407
16	Ted Williams, 1941	.406
17	Jesse Burkett, 1895	.405
18	Ed Delahanty, 1895	.404
19	Ed Delahanty, 1894	.404
20	Billy Hamilton, 1894	.403
21	Rogers Hornsby, 1925	.403
22	Harry Heilmann, 1923	.403
23	Pete Browning, 1887	.402
24	Rogers Hornsby, 1922	.401
25	Bill Terry, 1930	.401
26	Hughie Jennings, 1896	.401
27	Ty Cobb, 1922	.401
28	Cap Anson, 1881	.399
29	Lefty O'Doul, 1929	.398
30	Harry Heilmann, 1927	.398
31	Rogers Hornsby, 1921	.397
32	Ed Delahanty, 1896	.397
33	Jesse Burkett, 1899	.396
34	Joe Jackson, 1912	.395
35	Tony Gwynn, 1994	.394
36	Harry Heilmann, 1921	.394
37	Babe Ruth, 1923	.393
38	Harry Heilmann, 1925	.393
39	Babe Herman, 1930	.393
40	Joe Kelley, 1894	.393
41	Sam Thompson, 1895	.392
42	John McGraw, 1899	.391
43	Ty Cobb, 1913	.390
44	Al Simmons, 1931	.390
45	George Brett, 1980	.390
46	Fred Clarke, 1897	.390
47	Tris Speaker, 1925	.389
48	Bill Lange, 1895	.389
49	Billy Hamilton, 1895	.389
50	Ty Cobb, 1921	.389
51	Ted Williams, 1957	.388
52	King Kelly, 1886	.388
53	Rod Carew, 1977	.388
54	Luke Appling, 1936	.388
55	Tris Speaker, 1920	.388
56	Lave Cross, 1894	.387
57	Deacon White, 1877	.387
58	Al Simmons, 1925	.387
59	Rogers Hornsby, 1928	.387
60	Tris Speaker, 1916	.386
61	Willie Keeler, 1896	.386
62	Chuck Klein, 1930	.386
63	Hughie Jennings, 1895	.386
64	Willie Keeler, 1898	.385
65	Arky Vaughan, 1935	.385
66	Rogers Hornsby, 1923	.384
67	Ty Cobb, 1919	.384
68	Nap Lajoie, 1910	.384
69	Ty Cobb, 1910	.383
70	Jesse Burkett, 1897	.383
71	Tris Speaker, 1912	.383
72	Ty Cobb, 1917	.383
73	Lefty O'Doul, 1930	.383
74	Joe Jackson, 1920	.382
75	Ty Cobb, 1918	.382
76	Honus Wagner, 1900	.381
77	Babe Herman, 1929	.381
78	Joe DiMaggio, 1939	.381
79	Al Simmons, 1930	.381
80	Paul Waner, 1927	.380
81	Rogers Hornsby, 1929	.380
82	Billy Hamilton, 1893	.380
83	Tris Speaker, 1923	.380
84	Goose Goslin, 1928	.379
85	Freddie Lindstrom, 1930	.379
86	**Larry Walker, 1999**	**.379**
87	Willie Keeler, 1899	.379
88	Lou Gehrig, 1930	.379
89	John Cassidy, 1877	.378
90	Pete Browning, 1882	.378
91	Ty Cobb, 1925	.378
92	Babe Ruth, 1924	.378
93	Sam Crawford, 1911	.378
94	Tris Speaker, 1922	.378
95	Earl Averill, 1936	.378
96	Babe Ruth, 1921	.378
97	Heinie Manush, 1928	.378
98	Heinie Manush, 1926	.378
99	Ed Delahanty, 1897	.377
100	Willie Keeler, 1895	.377

Batting Average by era

1988-2003

Rank	Player	Avg
1	Tony Gwynn, 1994	.394
2	**Larry Walker, 1999**	**.379**
3	**Todd Helton, 2000**	**.372**
4	**Nomar Garciaparra, 2000**	**.372**
5	Tony Gwynn, 1997	.372
6	**Andres Galarraga, 1993**	**.370**
7	**Barry Bonds, 2002**	**.370**
8	Tony Gwynn, 1995	.368
9	**Jeff Bagwell, 1994**	**.368**
10	Wade Boggs, 1988	.366

1973-1987

Rank	Player	Avg
1	George Brett, 1980	.390
2	Rod Carew, 1977	.388
3	Tony Gwynn, 1987	.370
4	Wade Boggs, 1985	.368
5	Rod Carew, 1974	.364
6	Wade Boggs, 1987	.363
7	Wade Boggs, 1983	.361
8	Rod Carew, 1975	.359
9	Wade Boggs, 1986	.357
10	Bill Madlock, 1975	.354

1961-1972

Rank	Player	Avg
1	Rico Carty, 1970	.366
2	Joe Torre, 1971	.363
3	Norm Cash, 1961	.361
4	Roberto Clemente, 1967	.357
5	Roberto Clemente, 1961	.351
6	Pete Rose, 1969	.348
7	Tommy Davis, 1962	.346
8	Roberto Clemente, 1969	.345
9	Ralph Garr, 1971	.343
10	Vada Pinson, 1961	.343

1943-1960

Rank	Player	Avg
1	Ted Williams, 1957	.388
2	Stan Musial, 1948	.376
3	Ted Williams, 1948	.369
4	Stan Musial, 1946	.365
5	Mickey Mantle, 1957	.365
6	Harry Walker, 1947	.363
7	Dixie Walker, 1944	.357
8	Stan Musial, 1943	.357
9	Phil Cavarretta, 1945	.355
10	Lou Boudreau, 1948	.355

1921-1942

Rank	Player	Avg
1	Rogers Hornsby, 1924	.424
2	George Sisler, 1922	.420
3	Ted Williams, 1941	.406
4	Rogers Hornsby, 1925	.403
5	Harry Heilmann, 1923	.403
6	Rogers Hornsby, 1922	.401
7	Bill Terry, 1930	.401
8	Ty Cobb, 1922	.401
9	Lefty O'Doul, 1929	.398
10	Harry Heilmann, 1927	.398

1901-1920

Rank	Player	Avg
1	Nap Lajoie, 1901	.426
2	Ty Cobb, 1911	.420
3	Ty Cobb, 1912	.409
4	Joe Jackson, 1911	.408
5	George Sisler, 1920	.407
6	Joe Jackson, 1912	.395
7	Ty Cobb, 1913	.390
8	Tris Speaker, 1920	.388
9	Tris Speaker, 1916	.386
10	Ty Cobb, 1919	.384

1893-1900

Rank	Player	Avg
1	Hugh Duffy, 1894	.440
2	Willie Keeler, 1897	.424
3	Sam Thompson, 1894	.415
4	Ed Delahanty, 1899	.410
5	Jesse Burkett, 1896	.410
6	Jesse Burkett, 1895	.405
7	Ed Delahanty, 1895	.404
8	Ed Delahanty, 1894	.404
9	Billy Hamilton, 1894	.403
10	Hughie Jennings, 1896	.401

1876-1892

Rank	Player	Avg
1	Tip O'Neill, 1887	.435
2	Ross Barnes, 1876	.429
3	Fred Dunlap, 1884	.412
4	Pete Browning, 1887	.402
5	Cap Anson, 1881	.399
6	King Kelly, 1886	.388
7	Deacon White, 1877	.387
8	John Cassidy, 1877	.378
9	Pete Browning, 1882	.378
10	Dan Brouthers, 1883	.374

Relative Batting Average

Rank	Player	Rel. Avg
1	Ross Barnes, 1876	1.608
2	Tip O'Neill, 1887	1.564
3	Nap Lajoie, 1910	1.537
4	Ty Cobb, 1910	1.534
5	Pete Browning, 1882	1.526
6	Cap Anson, 1881	1.512
7	King Kelly, 1886	1.508
8	Roger Connor, 1885	1.506
9	Tris Speaker, 1916	1.506
10	Ty Cobb, 1917	1.501
11	Ty Cobb, 1912	1.501
12	Nap Lajoie, 1901	1.501
13	Nap Lajoie, 1904	1.499
14	Ty Cobb, 1911	1.493
15	Ty Cobb, 1909	1.492
16	Ted Williams, 1957	1.476
17	Ty Cobb, 1913	1.475
18	Ted Williams, 1941	1.472
19	Ty Cobb, 1918	1.469
20	George Gore, 1880	1.462
21	Rogers Hornsby, 1924	1.461
22	Rod Carew, 1977	1.458
23	**Barry Bonds, 2002**	**1.457**
24	Dan Brouthers, 1885	1.455
25	Joe Jackson, 1911	1.452
26	Joe Jackson, 1912	1.451
27	Dan Brouthers, 1882	1.449
28	Dave Orr, 1884	1.448
29	George Brett, 1980	1.448
30	Ty Cobb, 1915	1.448
31	Pete Browning, 1887	1.446
32	Ty Cobb, 1916	1.445
33	Cap Anson, 1886	1.442
34	Pete Browning, 1885	1.439
35	Dan Brouthers, 1886	1.439
36	Tony Gwynn, 1994	1.436
37	Honus Wagner, 1908	1.434
38	George Sisler, 1922	1.433
39	Cap Anson, 1882	1.428
40	Cy Seymour, 1905	1.425
41	Willie Keeler, 1897	1.423
42	Ed Delahanty, 1899	1.414
43	Wade Boggs, 1988	1.413
44	King Kelly, 1884	1.411
45	Joe Jackson, 1913	1.411
46	Rod Carew, 1974	1.408
47	Wade Boggs, 1985	1.407
48	Tris Speaker, 1912	1.406
49	Deacon White, 1877	1.405
50	Dan Brouthers, 1883	1.402
51	Jimmy Wolf, 1890	1.401
52	George Stone, 1906	1.400
53	Stan Musial, 1948	1.400
54	Cap Anson, 1888	1.399
55	George Sisler, 1920	1.398
56	Joe Torre, 1971	1.397
57	Hugh Duffy, 1894	1.393
58	Stan Musial, 1946	1.393
59	Ed Swartwood, 1883	1.392
60	Ty Cobb, 1919	1.392
61	Rod Carew, 1975	1.391
62	Tommy Tucker, 1889	1.391
63	Nap Lajoie, 1906	1.390
64	John Reilly, 1884	1.389
65	Harry Heilmann, 1923	1.389
66	Mickey Mantle, 1957	1.388
67	Willie Keeler, 1898	1.387
68	Honus Wagner, 1907	1.387
69	Roberto Clemente, 1967	1.385
70	George Sisler, 1917	1.383
71	Jim O'Rourke, 1884	1.383
72	Pete Browning, 1886	1.382
73	Tris Speaker, 1917	1.380
74	Ezra Sutton, 1884	1.380
75	Ty Cobb, 1907	1.379
76	Hick Carpenter, 1882	1.379
77	Roger Connor, 1886	1.378
78	Jesse Burkett, 1896	1.378
79	Paul Hines, 1879	1.377
80	Tony Gwynn, 1987	1.375
81	**Larry Walker, 1999**	**1.375**
82	Pete Browning, 1884	1.374
83	Tris Speaker, 1913	1.374
84	Tony Gwynn, 1997	1.374
85	Kirby Puckett, 1988	1.374
86	John Cassidy, 1877	1.373
87	Eddie Collins, 1909	1.373
88	Honus Wagner, 1905	1.372
89	Dave Orr, 1886	1.372
90	Rico Carty, 1970	1.372
91	George Hall, 1876	1.372
92	Tip O'Neill, 1888	1.370
93	Wade Boggs, 1987	1.370
94	Ty Cobb, 1922	1.370
95	Dan Brouthers, 1889	1.370
96	Cap Anson, 1880	1.368
97	Norm Cash, 1961	1.368
98	Jesse Burkett, 1899	1.367
99	**Andres Galarraga, 1993**	**1.366**
100	Jesse Burkett, 1901	1.365

On-Base Percentage

Rank	Player	OBP
1	**Barry Bonds, 2002**	**.582**
2	Ted Williams, 1941	.553
3	John McGraw, 1899	.547
4	Babe Ruth, 1923	.545
5	Babe Ruth, 1920	.532
6	**Barry Bonds, 2003**	**.529**
7	Ted Williams, 1957	.526
8	Billy Hamilton, 1894	.522
9	Babe Ruth, 1926	.516
10	**Barry Bonds, 2001**	**.515**
11	Ted Williams, 1954	.513
12	Babe Ruth, 1924	.513
13	Babe Ruth, 1921	.512
14	Mickey Mantle, 1957	.512
15	Rogers Hornsby, 1924	.507
16	John McGraw, 1900	.505
17	Joe Kelley, 1894	.502
18	Hugh Duffy, 1894	.502
19	Ed Delahanty, 1895	.500
20	Ted Williams, 1942	.499
21	Ted Williams, 1947	.499
22	Rogers Hornsby, 1928	.498
23	Ted Williams, 1946	.497
24	Ted Williams, 1948	.497
25	Bill Joyce, 1894	.496
26	Babe Ruth, 1931	.495
27	Babe Ruth, 1930	.493
28	Arky Vaughan, 1935	.491
29	Ted Williams, 1949	.490
30	Billy Hamilton, 1895	.490
31	Billy Hamilton, 1893	.490
32	Tip O'Neill, 1887	.490
33	Rogers Hornsby, 1925	.489
	Babe Ruth, 1932	.489
35	**Frank Thomas, 1994**	**.487**
36	Norm Cash, 1961	.487
37	Ty Cobb, 1915	.486
38	Mickey Mantle, 1962	.486
39	Babe Ruth, 1927	.486
40	Tris Speaker, 1920	.483
41	King Kelly, 1886	.483
42	Jesse Burkett, 1895	.482
43	Harry Heilmann, 1923	.481
44	Billy Hamilton, 1898	.480
45	Tris Speaker, 1925	.479
	Ted Williams, 1956	.479
47	**Edgar Martinez, 1995**	**.479**
48	Billy Hamilton, 1896	.478
49	Lou Gehrig, 1936	.478
50	**Jason Giambi, 2001**	**.477**
51	**Jason Giambi, 2000**	**.476**
52	Wade Boggs, 1988	.476
53	Cupid Childs, 1894	.475
54	John McGraw, 1898	.475
55	Ed Delahanty, 1894	.475
56	Harry Heilmann, 1927	.475
57	Tris Speaker, 1922	.474
58	Lou Gehrig, 1927	.474
59	Luke Appling, 1936	.474
60	Lou Gehrig, 1930	.473
61	Lou Gehrig, 1937	.473
62	**John Olerud, 1993**	**.473**
63	Hughie Jennings, 1896	.472
64	Ed Delahanty, 1896	.472
65	John McGraw, 1897	.471
66	Dan Brouthers, 1891	.471
67	Tris Speaker, 1916	.470
68	Bill Joyce, 1896	.470
69	Mark McGwire, 1998	.470
70	**Carlos Delgado, 2000**	**.470**
71	Joe Kelley, 1896	.469
72	Tris Speaker, 1923	.469
73	Jimmie Foxx, 1932	.469
74	Jesse Burkett, 1897	.468
75	Ty Cobb, 1925	.468
76	Joe Jackson, 1911	.468
77	Lou Gehrig, 1928	.467
78	Ty Cobb, 1913	.467
79	Mark McGwire, 1996	.467
80	George Sisler, 1922	.467
81	Cupid Childs, 1896	.467
82	Ty Cobb, 1911	.467
83	Joe Morgan, 1975	.466
84	Dan Brouthers, 1890	.466
85	Lou Gehrig, 1935	.466
86	**Gary Sheffield, 1996**	**.465**
87	Lou Gehrig, 1934	.465
88	Lefty O'Doul, 1929	.465
89	Mike Griffin, 1894	.465
90	Sam Thompson, 1894	.465
91	Jimmie Foxx, 1939	.464
92	Tris Speaker, 1912	.464
93	Ed Delahanty, 1899	.464
94	Pete Browning, 1887	.464
95	Mickey Mantle, 1956	.464
96	**Edgar Martinez, 1996**	**.464**
97	Ted Williams, 1951	.464
98	Willie Keeler, 1897	.464
99	**Todd Helton, 2000**	**.463**
100	Bob Caruthers, 1887	.463

Slugging Average

1 Barry Bonds, 2001 .863
2 Babe Ruth, 1920 .847
3 Babe Ruth, 1921 .846
4 Barry Bonds, 2002 .799
5 Babe Ruth, 1927 .772
6 Lou Gehrig, 1927 .765
7 Babe Ruth, 1923 .764
8 Rogers Hornsby, 1925 .756
9 Mark McGwire, 1998 .752
10 Jeff Bagwell, 1994 .750
11 Jimmie Foxx, 1932 .749
Barry Bonds, 2003 .749
13 Babe Ruth, 1924 .739
14 Babe Ruth, 1926 .737
15 Sammy Sosa, 2001 .737
16 Ted Williams, 1941 .735
17 Babe Ruth, 1930 .732
18 Ted Williams, 1957 .731
19 Mark McGwire, 1996 .730
20 Frank Thomas, 1994 .729
21 Hack Wilson, 1930 .723
22 Rogers Hornsby, 1922 .722
23 Lou Gehrig, 1930 .721
24 Larry Walker, 1997 .720
25 Albert Belle, 1994 .714
26 Larry Walker, 1999 .710
27 Babe Ruth, 1928 .709
28 Al Simmons, 1930 .708
29 Lou Gehrig, 1934 .706
30 Mickey Mantle, 1956 .705
31 Jimmie Foxx, 1938 .704
32 Jimmie Foxx, 1933 .703
33 Stan Musial, 1948 .702
34 Babe Ruth, 1931 .700
35 Todd Helton, 2000 .698
36 Babe Ruth, 1929 .697
37 Manny Ramirez, 2000 .697
38 Mark McGwire, 1999 .697
39 Sam Thompson, 1894 .696
40 Lou Gehrig, 1936 .696
41 Rogers Hornsby, 1924 .696
42 Hugh Duffy, 1894 .694
43 Jimmie Foxx, 1939 .694
44 Tip O'Neill, 1887 .691
45 Albert Belle, 1995 .690
46 Luis Gonzalez, 2001 .688
47 Barry Bonds, 2000 .688
48 Mickey Mantle, 1961 .687
49 Chuck Klein, 1930 .687
50 Todd Helton, 2001 .685
51 Hank Greenberg, 1938 .683
52 Kevin Mitchell, 1994 .681
53 Rogers Hornsby, 1929 .679
54 Babe Herman, 1930 .678
55 Barry Bonds, 1993 .677
56 Jim Thome, 2002 .677
57 Ken Griffey, 1994 .674
58 Joe DiMaggio, 1937 .673
59 Babe Ruth, 1922 .672
60 Joe DiMaggio, 1939 .671
61 Hank Greenberg, 1940 .670
62 Hank Aaron, 1971 .669
63 Hank Greenberg, 1937 .668
64 Ted Williams, 1946 .667
65 Willie Mays, 1954 .667
66 Albert Pujols, 2003 .667
67 Mickey Mantle, 1957 .665
68 Carlos Delgado, 2000 .664
69 Vladimir Guerrero, 2000 .664
70 George Brett, 1980 .664
71 Manny Ramirez, 1999 .663
72 Lou Gehrig, 1931 .662
73 Larry Walker, 2001 .662
74 Norm Cash, 1961 .662
75 Babe Ruth, 1932 .661
76 Jason Giambi, 2001 .660
77 Willie Mays, 1955 .659
78 Ralph Kiner, 1949 .658
79 Chuck Klein, 1929 .657
80 Babe Ruth, 1919 .657
81 Willie McCovey, 1969 .656
82 Albert Belle, 1998 .655
83 Sam Thompson, 1895 .654
84 Jimmie Foxx, 1934 .653
85 Chick Hafey, 1930 .652
86 Ted Williams, 1949 .650
87 Bill Joyce, 1894 .648
88 Lou Gehrig, 1928 .648
89 Ted Williams, 1942 .648
90 Duke Snider, 1954 .647
91 Barry Bonds, 1994 .647
Jason Giambi, 2000 .647
93 Sammy Sosa, 1998 .647
94 Manny Ramirez, 2002 .647
95 Ken Griffey, 1997 .646
96 Mark McGwire, 1997 .646
97 Chuck Klein, 1932 .646
98 Jim Gentile, 1961 .646
99 Willie Stargell, 1973 .646
100 Willie Mays, 1965 .645

On-Base plus Slugging

1 Barry Bonds, 2002 1381
2 Babe Ruth, 1920 1379
3 Barry Bonds, 2001 1379
4 Babe Ruth, 1921 1359
5 Babe Ruth, 1923 1309
6 Ted Williams, 1941 1287
7 Barry Bonds, 2003 1278
8 Babe Ruth, 1927 1258
9 Ted Williams, 1957 1257
10 Babe Ruth, 1926 1253
11 Babe Ruth, 1924 1252
12 Rogers Hornsby, 1925 1245
13 Lou Gehrig, 1927 1240
14 Babe Ruth, 1930 1225
15 Mark McGwire, 1998 1222
16 Jimmie Foxx, 1932 1218
17 Frank Thomas, 1994 1217
18 Rogers Hornsby, 1924 1203
19 Jeff Bagwell, 1994 1201
20 Mark McGwire, 1996 1198
21 Hugh Duffy, 1894 1196
22 Babe Ruth, 1931 1195
23 Lou Gehrig, 1930 1194
24 Rogers Hornsby, 1922 1181
25 Tip O'Neill, 1887 1180
26 Hack Wilson, 1930 1177
27 Mickey Mantle, 1957 1177
28 Sammy Sosa, 2001 1174
29 Lou Gehrig, 1936 1174
30 Babe Ruth, 1928 1172
31 Larry Walker, 1997 1172
32 Lou Gehrig, 1934 1172
33 Mickey Mantle, 1956 1169
34 Larry Walker, 1999 1168
35 Jimmie Foxx, 1938 1166
36 Ted Williams, 1946 1164
37 Todd Helton, 2000 1162
38 Sam Thompson, 1894 1161
39 Jimmie Foxx, 1939 1158
40 Manny Ramirez, 2000 1154
41 Jimmie Foxx, 1933 1153
42 Stan Musial, 1948 1152
43 Albert Belle, 1994 1152
44 Babe Ruth, 1932 1150
45 Norm Cash, 1961 1148
46 Ted Williams, 1954 1148
47 Ted Williams, 1942 1147
48 Bill Joyce, 1894 1143
49 Ted Williams, 1949 1141
50 Rogers Hornsby, 1929 1139
51 Jason Giambi, 2001 1137
52 Barry Bonds, 1993 1136
53 Mickey Mantle, 1961 1135
54 Carlos Delgado, 2000 1134
55 Ted Williams, 1947 1133
56 Babe Herman, 1930 1132
57 Al Simmons, 1930 1130
58 Rogers Hornsby, 1928 1130
59 Babe Ruth, 1929 1128
60 Barry Bonds, 2000 1127
61 Chuck Klein, 1930 1123
62 Jason Giambi, 2000 1123
63 Jim Thome, 2002 1122
64 Hank Greenberg, 1938 1122
65 Mark McGwire, 1999 1120
66 Joe DiMaggio, 1939 1119
67 George Brett, 1980 1118
68 Ed Delahanty, 1895 1117
69 Luis Gonzalez, 2001 1117
70 Todd Helton, 2001 1116
71 Lou Gehrig, 1937 1116
72 Lou Gehrig, 1928 1115
73 Babe Ruth, 1919 1114
74 Harry Heilmann, 1923 1113
75 Ted Williams, 1948 1112
76 Larry Walker, 2001 1111
77 Kevin Mitchell, 1994 1110
78 Willie McCovey, 1969 1108
79 Lou Gehrig, 1931 1108
80 Edgar Martinez, 1995 1107
81 Nap Lajoie, 1901 1106
82 Babe Ruth, 1922 1106
83 Albert Pujols, 2003 1106
84 Manny Ramirez, 1999 1105
85 Hank Greenberg, 1937 1105
86 Joe Kelley, 1894 1104
87 Hank Greenberg, 1940 1103
88 Ed Delahanty, 1896 1103
89 Jimmie Foxx, 1934 1102
90 Arky Vaughan, 1935 1098
91 Rogers Hornsby, 1921 1097
92 Manny Ramirez, 2002 1097
93 Jimmie Foxx, 1935 1096
94 Albert Belle, 1995 1091
95 Mickey Mantle, 1962 1091
96 Harry Heilmann, 1927 1091
97 Gary Sheffield, 1996 1090
98 Ralph Kiner, 1949 1089
99 Jimmie Foxx, 1929 1088
100 Ty Cobb, 1911 1088

Adjusted OPS

1 Barry Bonds, 2002 278
2 Barry Bonds, 2001 267
3 Babe Ruth, 1920 252
4 Babe Ruth, 1923 238
5 Babe Ruth, 1921 236
6 Barry Bonds, 2003 235
7 Ted Williams, 1941 232
8 Babe Ruth, 1927 229
9 Pete Browning, 1882 229
10 Babe Ruth, 1926 228
11 Ted Williams, 1957 227
12 Lou Gehrig, 1927 224
13 Babe Ruth, 1919 224
14 Babe Ruth, 1931 223
15 Mickey Mantle, 1957 223
16 Rogers Hornsby, 1924 223
17 Ross Barnes, 1876 222
18 Babe Ruth, 1924 221
19 Jeff Bagwell, 1994 220
20 Mark McGwire, 1998 218
21 Babe Ruth, 1930 216
22 Frank Thomas, 1994 214
23 Ted Williams, 1942 214
24 Lou Gehrig, 1934 213
25 Mickey Mantle, 1956 213
26 Willie McCovey, 1969 212
27 Ted Williams, 1946 211
28 Babe Ruth, 1928 211
29 Mickey Mantle, 1961 210
30 Rogers Hornsby, 1922 210
31 Ty Cobb, 1917 210
32 Sammy Sosa, 2001 208
33 George Hall, 1876 208
34 Rogers Hornsby, 1925 208
35 Lou Gehrig, 1930 207
36 Barry Bonds, 1993 207
37 Barry Bonds, 1992 207
38 Babe Ruth, 1932 206
39 Tip O'Neill, 1887 205
40 Honus Wagner, 1908 205
41 Rogers Hornsby, 1928 204
42 Nap Lajoie, 1904 204
43 Ty Cobb, 1912 203
44 Jimmie Foxx, 1932 203
45 Roger Connor, 1885 203
46 Dan Brouthers, 1886 203
47 George Brett, 1980 203
48 Ty Cobb, 1910 202
49 Mark McGwire, 1996 201
50 Frank Robinson, 1966 200
51 Jimmie Foxx, 1933 199
52 Ted Williams, 1947 199
53 Lou Gehrig, 1931 199
54 Dan Brouthers, 1885 199
55 Babe Ruth, 1929 199
56 Dick Allen, 1972 199
57 Norm Cash, 1961 198
58 Mickey Mantle, 1962 198
59 Dan Brouthers, 1882 198
60 Nap Lajoie, 1910 198
61 Jim Thome, 2002 197
62 Jason Giambi, 2001 197
63 Ed Swartwood, 1882 197
64 Lou Gehrig, 1928 197
65 Stan Musial, 1948 196
66 Ty Cobb, 1918 196
67 Ty Cobb, 1913 196
68 Nap Lajoie, 1901 196
69 Orator Shafer, 1878 196
70 Mike Schmidt, 1981 195
71 George Stone, 1906 195
72 Harry Heilmann, 1923 195
73 Dave Orr, 1884 195
74 Barry Bonds, 2000 195
75 Kevin Mitchell, 1989 194
76 Dave Orr, 1886 193
77 Lou Gehrig, 1936 193
78 Ed Delahanty, 1899 193
79 Ty Cobb, 1911 193
80 Ted Williams, 1954 193
81 Joe Jackson, 1911 192
82 Albert Pujols, 2003 192
83 Gary Sheffield, 1996 192
84 Ed Delahanty, 1896 192
85 Mike Piazza, 1997 191
86 Rogers Hornsby, 1921 191
87 Albert Belle, 1994 191
88 Ty Cobb, 1909 190
89 Joe Jackson, 1913 190
90 Rickey Henderson, 1990 190
91 Pete Browning, 1885 190
92 Hank Aaron, 1971 190
93 Reggie Jackson, 1969 190
94 Deacon White, 1877 190
95 Joe Jackson, 1912 190
96 Rogers Hornsby, 1920 190
97 Dave Orr, 1885 189
98 Jim Gentile, 1961 189
99 Cupid Childs, 1890 189
100 Carl Yastrzemski, 1967 189

Adjusted Batting Wins

1 Barry Bonds, 2001 12.7
2 Barry Bonds, 2002 12.3
3 Babe Ruth, 1923 11.1
4 Babe Ruth, 1921 10.6
5 Babe Ruth, 1920 10.2
6 Lou Gehrig, 1927 10.0
7 Babe Ruth, 1927 9.9
8 Babe Ruth, 1926 9.6
9 Ted Williams, 1941 9.5
10 Babe Ruth, 1924 9.5
11 Rogers Hornsby, 1924 9.5
12 Babe Ruth, 1931 9.4
13 Mickey Mantle, 1957 9.4
14 Mark McGwire, 1998 9.3
15 Sammy Sosa, 2001 9.2
16 Rogers Hornsby, 1922 9.1
17 Lou Gehrig, 1934 9.0
18 Barry Bonds, 2003 8.9
19 Ted Williams, 1942 8.9
20 Ted Williams, 1946 8.9
21 Babe Ruth, 1930 8.8
22 Barry Bonds, 1993 8.7
23 Lou Gehrig, 1930 8.7
24 Babe Ruth, 1928 8.6
25 Mickey Mantle, 1956 8.5
26 Ted Williams, 1957 8.4
27 Ted Williams, 1947 8.3
28 Mickey Mantle, 1961 8.3
29 Lou Gehrig, 1931 8.2
30 Willie McCovey, 1969 8.2
31 Jimmie Foxx, 1932 8.2
32 Ty Cobb, 1917 8.2
33 Frank Robinson, 1966 8.1
34 Norm Cash, 1961 8.0
35 Stan Musial, 1948 8.0
36 Albert Pujols, 2003 8.0
37 Jason Giambi, 2001 7.9
38 Barry Bonds, 1992 7.9
39 Rogers Hornsby, 1928 7.9
40 Lou Gehrig, 1936 7.8
41 Lou Gehrig, 1928 7.8
42 Rogers Hornsby, 1925 7.7
43 Babe Ruth, 1919 7.7
44 Jeff Bagwell, 1996 7.6
45 Gary Sheffield, 1996 7.6
46 Rogers Hornsby, 1921 7.6
47 Ted Williams, 1949 7.6
48 Jimmie Foxx, 1933 7.6
49 Hank Aaron, 1959 7.5
50 Nap Lajoie, 1910 7.4
51 Barry Bonds, 1996 7.4
52 Honus Wagner, 1908 7.4
53 John Olerud, 1993 7.3
54 Babe Ruth, 1932 7.3
55 Reggie Jackson, 1969 7.2
56 Barry Bonds, 1998 7.2
57 Mike Piazza, 1997 7.2
58 Carl Yastrzemski, 1967 7.2
59 Rogers Hornsby, 1920 7.2
60 Dick Allen, 1972 7.2
61 Harry Heilmann, 1923 7.2
62 Mickey Mantle, 1958 7.1
63 Lou Gehrig, 1932 7.1
64 Frank Thomas, 1991 7.0
65 Ty Cobb, 1912 7.0
66 Jason Giambi, 2000 7.0
67 Hank Aaron, 1963 7.0
68 Tris Speaker, 1923 7.0
69 Kevin Mitchell, 1989 7.0
70 Jim Thome, 2002 7.0
71 Nap Lajoie, 1904 6.9
72 Jeff Bagwell, 1994 6.9
73 Ty Cobb, 1915 6.9
74 Carlos Delgado, 2000 6.9
75 Barry Bonds, 2000 6.9
76 Frank Thomas, 1994 6.9
77 Ty Cobb, 1911 6.9
78 Stan Musial, 1951 6.8
79 Stan Musial, 1946 6.8
80 Joe Jackson, 1911 6.8
81 Rod Carew, 1977 6.8
82 Frank Thomas, 1997 6.8
83 Edgar Martinez, 1995 6.8
84 Rogers Hornsby, 1929 6.8
85 Ralph Kiner, 1951 6.7
86 George Stone, 1906 6.7
87 Ed Delahanty, 1899 6.7
88 Ted Williams, 1948 6.7
89 Frank Thomas, 1992 6.7
90 Frank Howard, 1969 6.7
91 Al Rosen, 1953 6.6
92 Lou Gehrig, 1937 6.6
93 Tris Speaker, 1912 6.6
94 Jimmie Foxx, 1934 6.6
95 Babe Ruth, 1929 6.6
96 Lou Gehrig, 1935 6.6
97 Joe Medwick, 1937 6.6
98 Ty Cobb, 1910 6.6
99 Hack Wilson, 1930 6.6
100 Harmon Killebrew, 1969 6.6

Pinch Hits

1 John Vander Wal, 1995 28
2 Lenny Harris, 1999 26
3 Jose Morales, 1976 25
4 Dave Philley, 1961 24
Vic Davalillo, 1970 24
Rusty Staub, 1983 24
Gerald Perry, 1993 24
8 Greg Norton, 2003 23
9 Sam Leslie, 1932 22
Peanuts Lowrey, 1953 22
Red Schoendienst, 1962 22
Wallace Johnson, 1988 22
Mark Sweeney, 1997 22
Lenny Harris, 2002 22
15 Doc Miller, 1913 21
Smoky Burgess, 1966 21
Merv Rettenmund, 1977 21
18 Ed Coleman, 1936 20
Frenchy Bordagaray, 1938 20
Joe Frazier, 1954 20
Smoky Burgess, 1965 20
Ken Boswell, 1976 20
Jerry Turner, 1978 20
Thad Bosley, 1985 20
Chris Chambliss, 1986 20
Dave Clark, 1997 20

Pinch Hit Average

(30 at-bats minimum)

1 Ed Kranepool, 1974 .486
2 Smead Jolley, 1931 .467
3 Frenchy Bordagaray, 1938 .465
4 Rick Miller, 1983 .457
5 Bill Spiers, 1997 .455
6 Jose Pagan, 1969 .452
7 Elmer Valo, 1955 .452
Mark Johnson, 1996 .452
9 Gates Brown, 1968 .450
10 Ted Easterly, 1912 .433
Milt Thompson, 1985 .433
Randy Bush, 1986 .433
13 Joe Cronin, 1943 .429
Don Dillard, 1961 .429
15 Candy Maldonado, 1986 .425
16 Richie Ashburn, 1962 .419
Dick Williams, 1962 .419
18 Merritt Ranew, 1963 .415
Carl Taylor, 1969 .415
20 Kurt Bevacqua, 1983 .412
21 Jerry Turner, 1978 .408
22 Bob Bowman, 1958 .406
Chico Walker, 1991 .406
Sid Bream, 1994 .406
25 Frankie Baumholtz, 1955 .405

Pinch Hit Home Runs

1 Dave Hansen, 2000 7
Craig Wilson, 2001 7
3 Johnny Frederick, 1932 6
4 Joe Cronin, 1943 5
Butch Nieman, 1945 5
Gene Freese, 1959 5
Jerry Lynch, 1961 5
Cliff Johnson, 1974 5
Lee Lacy, 1978 5
Jerry Turner, 1978 5
Billy Ashley, 1996 5
David Dellucci, 2001 5
Erubiel Durazo, 2001 5
14 Ernie Lombardi, 1946 4
Del Wilber, 1953 4
Bill Taylor, 1955 4
Bob Thurman, 1957 4
Rip Repulski, 1958 4
George Crowe, 1959 4
George Crowe, 1960 4
Johnny Blanchard, 1961 4
Carl Sawatski, 1961 4
Jerry Lynch, 1963 4
Don Mincher, 1964 4
Hal Breeden, 1973 4
Mike Ivie, 1978 4
Del Unser, 1979 4
Jeff Burroughs, 1982 4
Danny Heep, 1983 4
Candy Maldonado, 1986 4
Mark Carreon, 1989 4
Tommy Gregg, 1990 4
Ernest Riles, 1990 4
Howard Johnson, 1994 4
John Vander Wal, 1995 4
Jack Howell, 1996 4
Mark Johnson, 1996 4
Bob Hamelin, 1998 4
Angelo Echevarria, 1999 4
Bubba Trammell, 2000 4
Orlando Merced, 2001 4
Greg Norton, 2003 4

Stolen Bases

1 Hugh Nicol, 1887 138
2 Rickey Henderson, 1982 130
3 Arlie Latham, 1887............129
4 Lou Brock, 1974................118
5 Charlie Comiskey, 1887 117
6 John Ward, 1887...............111
Billy Hamilton, 1889 111
Billy Hamilton, 1891 111
9 Vince Coleman, 1985........110
10 Arlie Latham, 1888............109
Vince Coleman, 1987........109
12 Rickey Henderson, 1983 108
13 Vince Coleman, 1986........107
14 Tom Brown, 1891..............106
15 Maury Wills, 1962 104
16 Pete Browning, 1887.........103
Hugh Nicol, 1888 103
18 Jim Fogarty, 1887..............102
Billy Hamilton, 1890 102
20 Billy Hamilton, 1894 100
Rickey Henderson, 1980 100
22 Jim Fogarty, 1889................99
23 Harry Stovey, 1890..............97
Billy Hamilton, 1895 97
Ron LeFlore, 1980 97
26 Ty Cobb, 1915......................96
Omar Moreno, 1980..............96
28 Bid McPhee, 1887................95
Curt Welch, 1888 95
30 Mike Griffin, 1887................94
Maury Wills, 1965 94
32 Tommy McCarthy, 1888 93
Rickey Henderson, 1988 93
34 Darby O'Brien, 1889 91
35 Tim Raines, 1983..................90
36 Curt Welch, 1887 89
Herman Long, 1889 89
38 Tom Poorman, 1887.............88
Blondie Purcell, 1887...........88
John Ward, 1892..................88
Clyde Milan, 1912 88
42 Harry Stovey, 1888..............87
Arlie Latham, 1891...............87
Joe Kelley, 1896 87
Rickey Henderson, 1986 87
46 Cub Stricker, 1887...............86
47 Tommy Tucker, 1887 85
Hub Collins, 1890.................85
Hugh Duffy, 1891 85
50 King Kelly, 1887 84
Chippy McGarr, 1887 84
Billy Sunday, 1890................84
Bill Lange, 1896 84
54 Tommy McCarthy, 1890 83
Billy Hamilton, 1896 83
Ty Cobb, 1911.......................83
Willie Wilson, 1979 83
58 Dummy Hoy, 1888................82
John Reilly, 1888 82
60 Eddie Collins, 1910..............81
Bob Bescher, 1911...............81
Vince Coleman, 1988...........81
63 Emmett Seery, 1888 80
Hugh Nicol, 1889 80
Rickey Henderson, 1985 80
Eric Davis, 1986....................80
67 Tom Brown, 1890..................79
Dave Collins, 1980................79
Willie Wilson, 1980 79
70 Hugh Duffy, 1890..................78
Tom Brown, 1892..................78
John McGraw, 1894 78
Ron LeFlore, 1979 78
Tim Raines, 1982..................78
Marquis Grissom, 1992 78
76 Ted Scheffler, 1890 77
Jimmy Sheckard, 1899 77
Davey Lopes, 1975 77
Omar Moreno, 1979..............77
Rudy Law, 1983 77
Rickey Henderson, 1989 77
Vince Coleman, 1990...........77
83 Ed McKean, 1887 76
Walt Wilmot, 1890.................76
Walt Wilmot, 1894.................76
Dusty Miller, 1896.................76
Ty Cobb, 1909.......................76
Marquis Grissom, 1991 76
89 Yank Robinson, 1887...........75
George Van Haltren, 1891..........75
Clyde Milan, 1913 75
Benny Kauff, 1914 75
Billy North, 1976 75
Tim Raines, 1984..................75
Kenny Lofton, 1996 75
96 Frank Fennelly, 1887 74
Harry Stovey, 1887...............74
Fritz Maisel, 1914..................74
Lou Brock, 1966....................74
Brian Hunter, 1997 74

Stolen Base Average

1 Kevin McReynolds, 1988 ....100.0
Paul Molitor, 1994 ....100.0
3 Brady Anderson, 1994 .....96.9
Carlos Beltran, 2001 ..96.9
5 Max Carey, 1922 ....96.2
6 Ken Griffey, 1980 ....95.8
7 Stan Javier, 1988 ....95.2
8 Doug Glanville, 1999 ..94.4
9 Amos Otis, 1970 ....94.3
10 Jack Perconte, 1985 ....93.9
11 Miguel Dilone, 1984 ....93.1
Bob Dernier, 1986 ....93.1
13 Kirk Gibson, 1990 ....92.9
Barry Larkin, 1994 .....92.9
15 Rafael Furcal, 2003 ....92.6
16 Don Baylor, 1972..............92.3
Oddibe McDowell, 1987...92.3
Orlando Cabrera, 2003.........92.3
19 Davey Lopes, 1985 ....92.2
20 Eric Davis, 1988...............92.1
21 Delino DeShields, 2001 ...92.0
Henry Cotto, 1992.............92.0
Mike Cameron, 1997 ..92.0
24 Bobby Bonds, 1969..........91.8
Davey Lopes, 1978 ....91.8
26 Davey Lopes, 1979 ....91.7
Marquis Grissom, 1990 ......91.7
28 Jimmy Wynn, 1965 ....91.5
29 Larry Bowa, 1977 ....91.4
Derek Jeter, 2002 ....91.4
31 Ryne Sandberg, 1987 ......91.3
Alan Trammell, 1987 ....91.3
Rich Amaral, 1995 ....91.3
34 Jerry Mumphrey, 1980 .....91.2
35 Tom Herr, 1985 ....91.2
36 Carlos Beltran, 2003 ..91.1
37 Barry Larkin, 1995 .....91.1
38 Jack Smith, 1925 ....90.9
Davey Lopes, 1981 ....90.9
Tim Raines, 1987..............90.9
Bip Roberts, 1995 ....90.9
Roberto Alomar, 1995 ....90.9
Chris Singleton, 2002 ....90.9
44 Craig Biggio, 1994......90.7
Roberto Alomar, 2000 ....90.7
46 Derek Bell, 1996 ....90.6
Pokey Reese, 2000 .....90.6
48 Willie Wilson, 1984 ....90.4
49 Bake McBride, 1978..........90.3
50 Devon White, 1992............90.2

Base Stealing Wins

1 Vince Coleman, 1986.........2.0
2 Maury Wills, 1962 ....1.8
3 Rickey Henderson, 1983 ....1.7
4 Vince Coleman, 1985...........1.6
5 Vince Coleman, 1987...........1.6
6 Rickey Henderson, 1988 ....1.6
7 Ron LeFlore, 1980 ....1.6
8 Tim Raines, 1983.................1.5
9 Lou Brock, 1974...................1.5
10 Eric Davis, 1986...................1.4
11 Willie Wilson, 1980 ....1.4
12 Rickey Henderson, 1982 ....1.4
13 Willie Wilson, 1979 ....1.4
14 Rickey Henderson, 1985 ....1.4
15 Marquis Grissom, 1992 ....1.4
16 Tim Raines, 1984.................1.3
17 Davey Lopes, 1975 ....1.3
18 Rudy Law, 1983 ....1.3
19 Rickey Henderson, 1980 ....1.3
20 Tim Raines, 1985.................1.3
21 Rickey Henderson, 1986 ....1.3
22 Tim Raines, 1986.................1.3
23 Tim Raines, 1981.................1.3
24 Tim Raines, 1982.................1.2
25 Rickey Henderson, 1989 ....1.2
26 Ron LeFlore, 1979 ....1.2
27 Vince Coleman, 1989...........1.2
28 Bert Campaneris, 1969........1.1
29 Joe Morgan, 1975 ....1.1
30 Fritz Maisel, 1914.................1.1
31 Vince Coleman, 1990...........1.1
32 Marquis Grissom, 1991 ....1.1
33 Juan Samuel, 1984 ....1.1
34 Davey Lopes, 1976 ....1.1
35 Tony Womack, 1999 .....1.1
36 Lou Brock, 1968...................1.1
37 Mickey Rivers, 1975 ....1.1
38 Rickey Henderson, 1990 ....1.1
39 Tony Womack, 1997 .....1.1
40 Dave Collins, 1980...............1.1
41 Kenny Lofton, 1992......1.0
42 Lou Brock, 1966...................1.0
43 Alan Wiggins, 1983..............1.0
44 Maury Wills, 1965 ....1.0
45 Joe Morgan, 1976 ....1.0
46 Tommy Harper, 1969...........1.0
47 Willie Wilson, 1983 ....1.0
48 Jerry Mumphrey, 1980 ....1.0
49 Omar Moreno, 1980.............1.0
50 Kenny Lofton, 1993 ......1.0

Pitcher Batting Average by era

1988-2003

1 Orel Hershiser, 1993 356
2 Mike Hampton, 2002 ...344
3 Mike Hampton, 1999 ...311
4 Fernando Valenzuela, 1990 304
5 Livan Hernandez, 2001.....296
6 Mike Hampton, 2001 ...291
7 Tom Glavine, 1996.......289
8 Mike Hampton, 2000 ...274
Darren Oliver, 1999 274
10 Jose Rijo, 1993 268

1973-1987

1 Rick Rhoden, 1984 333
2 Ken Brett, 1974 310
3 Bob Forsch, 1975..............308
Rick Rhoden, 1976 308
5 Jim Rooker, 1974 305
6 Rick Mahler, 1984 296
7 Bob Forsch, 1980..............295
8 Tom Griffin, 1974 294
9 Steve Carlton, 1978 291
10 Don Robinson, 1982 282

1961-1972

1 Catfish Hunter, 1971 350
2 Curt Simmons, 1961 303
3 Bob Gibson, 1970 303
4 Don Drysdale, 1965 300
5 Claude Osteen, 1972 273
6 Gary Peters, 1971 271
7 Rick Wise, 1969 270
8 Camilo Pascual, 1962 268
9 Blue Moon Odom, 1969 266
Sonny Siebert, 1971 266

1943-1960

1 Don Newcombe, 1955 359
2 Gene Bearden, 1952 354
3 Johnny Sain, 1947 346
4 Warren Spahn, 1958..........333
5 Fritz Ostermueller, 1946 328
6 Fred Hutchinson, 1950......326
7 Oscar Judd, 1946..............316
8 Fred Hutchinson, 1946.......315
9 Rip Sewell, 1945 313
Tom Sturdivant, 1956 313

1921-1942

1 Walter Johnson, 1925 433
2 Jack Bentley, 1923 427
3 Curt Davis, 1939 381
4 Red Ruffing, 1930 374
5 George Uhle, 1923.............361
6 Erv Brame, 1930 353
7 Dutch Ruether, 1921 351
8 Wes Ferrell, 1935..............347
9 Wilbur Cooper, 1924 346
Dolf Luque, 1926 346

1901-1920

1 Snake Wiltse, 1901 373
2 Doc Crandall, 1910 342
3 Bill Phillips, 1902...............342
4 Nixey Callahan, 1901 331
5 Babe Ruth, 1917................325
6 Frank Foreman, 1901 325
George Mullin, 1902...........325
8 Al Orth, 1907 324
9 Claude Hendrix, 1912 322
10 Cy Young, 1903.................321

1893-1900

1 Ad Gumbert, 1895 361
2 Ted Breitenstein, 1899 352
3 Kid Gleason, 1894 349
4 Adonis Terry, 1894 347
5 Jack Stivetts, 1896............347
6 Tom Parrott, 1895 343
7 Jack Taylor, 1894 338
8 Jesse Tannehill, 1900 336
9 Al Orth, 1897 329
10 Jack Stivetts, 1894 328

1876-1892

1 Billy Taylor, 1884 366
2 Guy Hecker, 1886 341
3 Charlie Ferguson, 1887 337
4 Bob Caruthers, 1886..........334
5 Scott Stratton, 1890 323
6 Jim Whitney, 1882.............323
7 Charlie Sweeney, 1884 316
8 Jim Devlin, 1876 315
9 Ed Crane, 1890 315
Curry Foley, 1879..............315

Pitcher Batting Runs

1 Guy Hecker, 1884 ....27.5
2 Bob Caruthers, 1886........23.4
3 Jim Whitney, 1882............22.2
4 Don Drysdale, 1965 ....21.6
5 Wes Ferrell, 1935 ....20.2
6 Don Newcombe, 1955 .....19.6
7 Guy Hecker, 1886 ....18.4
8 Jim Whitney, 1883............17.7
9 Schoolboy Rowe, 1943 ....17.4
10 Warren Spahn, 1958........17.4
11 Charlie Ferguson, 1885 ...17.1
12 Wes Ferrell, 1931 ....16.9
13 Babe Ruth, 1917...............16.5
14 Scott Stratton, 1890 ....16.4
15 George Uhle, 1923............16.4
16 Red Ruffing, 1930 ....16.4
17 Walter Johnson, 1925 ......16.2
18 Tony Mullane, 1884...........16.2
19 Bob Lemon, 1950 ....16.1
20 Bob Caruthers, 1889.........15.7
21 Bob Caruthers, 1887.........15.7
22 Red Lucas, 1930...............15.4
23 Bob Lemon, 1949 ....15.0
24 Jack Bentley, 1923 ....15.0
25 Babe Ruth, 1915...............15.0
26 John Ward, 1879...............15.0
27 Claude Hendrix, 1912........14.8
28 Don Newcombe, 1959 .....14.7
29 Red Ruffing, 1936 ....14.3
30 Jim Tobin, 1942.................14.3
31 Red Lucas, 1932...............14.2
32 Frank Killen, 1893 ....14.2
33 Robin Roberts, 1955.........13.9
34 Jack Stivetts, 1892 ....13.8
35 Pink Hawley, 1895.............13.7
36 Scott Stratton, 1888 ....13.4
37 Pete Conway, 1888 ....13.4
38 Charlie Ferguson, 1887 ...13.3
39 Red Ruffing, 1932 ....13.2
40 Jack Coombs, 1911 ....13.1
41 Clark Griffith, 1901 ....13.1
42 Jack Stivetts, 1890 ....13.1
43 Joe Bush, 1924 ....13.1
44 Babe Ruth, 1916...............13.0
45 Adonis Terry, 1890 ....13.0
46 Schoolboy Rowe, 1935 ....12.9
47 Bob Lemon, 1948 ....12.9
48 Red Ruffing, 1935 ....12.9
49 Elam Vangilder, 1922 ....12.9
50 Dave Foutz, 1887 ....12.9
51 Terry Larkin, 1878.............12.8
52 Red Lucas, 1933...............12.7
53 Bucky Walters, 1939 ....12.7
54 Red Ruffing, 1928 ....12.4
55 Catfish Hunter, 1971 ....12.3
56 Ad Gumbert, 1891 ....12.2
57 Johnny Sain, 1947 ....12.0
58 Joe Bowman, 1939 ....12.0
59 Bob Gibson, 1970 ....11.9
60 Jouett Meekin, 1896..........11.8
61 Doc Crandall, 1915 ....11.8
62 Babe Ruth, 1918...............11.8
63 Jim Whitney, 1887............11.7
64 Cy Young, 1903................11.7
65 George Mullin, 1904.........11.7
66 Curt Davis, 1939 ....11.6
67 Red Lucas, 1931...............11.6
68 Jim Whitney, 1881............11.5
69 Charley Radbourn, 1883..11.5
70 Tim Keefe, 1884................11.4
71 Billy Taylor, 1884 ....11.4
72 Wes Ferrell, 1936 ....11.3
73 Red Lucas, 1929...............11.3
74 Erv Brame, 1929 ....11.3
75 Dizzy Trout, 1944 ....11.3
76 Adonis Terry, 1889 ....11.2
77 Schoolboy Rowe, 1934 ....11.2
78 Frank Foreman, 1891.......11.2
79 Dutch Ruether, 1921 ....11.2
80 Jack Stivetts, 1896............11.1
81 Charlie Ferguson, 1886 ...11.1
82 Ad Gumbert, 1895 ....11.1
83 Guy Hecker, 1883 ....11.0
84 Blue Moon Odom, 1969...10.9
85 Red Ruffing, 1941 ....10.9
86 Bob Caruthers, 1891.........10.9
87 Jack Scott, 1921 ....10.9
88 Charlie Buffinton, 1884 ....10.8
89 Ben Sanders, 1892 ....10.8
90 Guy Hecker, 1887 ....10.8
91 Scott Stratton, 1892 ....10.8
92 Carl Mays, 1921 ....10.7
93 Erv Brame, 1930 ....10.7
94 Ken Brett, 1974 ....10.7
95 Dave Ferriss, 1945 ....10.6
96 Mike Hampton, 1999 ..10.6
97 Tony Mullane, 1882...........10.5
98 Claude Hendrix, 1915 ....10.5
99 Al Maul, 1893 ....10.5
100 George Van Haltren, 1888.....10.4

Fielding Average

First Base

1 Steve Garvey, 1984.........1.000
2 Stuffy McInnis, 1921 999
3 Frank McCormick, 1946....999
4 David Segui, 1998 999
5 J. T. Snow, 1998................999
6 Steve Garvey, 1981...........999
7 Jim Spencer, 1973 999
8 Wes Parker, 1968..............999

Second Base

1 Bret Boone, 1997.........997
2 Bobby Grich, 1985 997
3 Jose Oquendo, 1990..........996
4 Ryne Sandberg, 1991 995
5 Jody Reed, 1994...............995
6 Rob Wilfong, 1980 995
7 Bobby Grich, 1973 995
8 Frank White, 1988..............994
9 Mark Lemke, 1994..............994
10 Jose Oquendo, 1989..........994

Shortstop

1 Mike Bordick, 2002 998
2 Cal Ripken, 1990 996
3 Omar Vizquel, 2000.....995
4 Rey Sanchez, 2000......994
5 Rey Ordonez, 1999 994
6 Omar Vizquel, 1998.....993
7 Tony Fernandez, 1989 992
8 Rey Sanchez, 2001......991
9 Larry Bowa, 1979 991
10 Ed Brinkman, 1972 990

Third Base

1 Tony Fernandez, 1994 991
2 Don Money, 1974...............989
3 Hank Majeski, 1947 988
4 Aurelio Rodriguez, 1978..........987
5 Willie Kamm, 1933.............984
6 Steve Buechele, 1991........983
7 Gary Gaetti, 1998...............983
8 George Kell, 1946 983
9 Heinie Groh, 1924 983
10 Carney Lansford, 1979 983

Outfield (250 chances accepted)

1 Danny Litwhiler, 1942.....1.000
Tony Gonzalez, 1962 .....1.000
Rocky Colavito, 1965 .....1.000
Curt Flood, 1966............1.000
Mickey Stanley, 1968 .....1.000
Mickey Stanley, 1970 .....1.000
Roy White, 1971 ....1.000
Ken Berry, 1972 ....1.000
Carl Yastrzemski, 1977 ..1.000
Terry Puhl, 1979 ....1.000
Brian Downing, 1982.......1.000
Brian Downing, 1984.......1.000
Brett Butler, 1991 ....1.000
Darryl Hamilton, 1992.....1.000
Brett Butler, 1993 ....1.000
Darren Lewis, 1993.........1.000
Lance Johnson, 1994.......1.000
Stan Javier, 1995 ....1.000
Darryl Hamilton, 1996......1.000
Paul O'Neill, 1996 ....1.000
Darryl Hamilton, 1999......1.000
B.J. Surhoff, 1999.....1.000
Eric Owens, 2000 .....1.000
Bernie Williams, 2000.....1.000
Luis Gonzalez, 2001.......1.000
Dave Roberts, 2002 ....1.000
Juan Encarnacion, 2003......1.000

Catcher

1 Spud Davis, 1939...........1.000
Buddy Rosar, 1946.........1.000
Lou Berberet, 1957 ....1.000
Pete Daley, 1957 ....1.000
Yogi Berra, 1958 ....1.000
Rick Cerone, 1988 ....1.000
Charles Johnson, 1997 .....1.000
Chris Hoiles, 1997...........1.000
Mike Matheny, 2003 .1.000

Pitcher (90 chances accepted)

1 Kid Nichols, 1896...........1.000
Frank Owen, 1904...........1.000
Mordecai Brown, 1908...1.000
Grover Alexander, 1913 .1.000
Walter Johnson, 1913 ....1.000
Eppa Rixey, 1917 ....1.000
Walter Johnson, 1917 ....1.000
Grover Alexander, 1919 .1.000
Jesse Barnes, 1921 ....1.000
Hal Schumacher, 1935...1.000
Larry Jackson, 1964 ....1.000
Randy Jones, 1976 ....1.000
Greg Maddux, 1990..1.000

Total Chances/Game (Infield)

First Base

1	Joe Gerhardt, 1876	13.28
2	Jiggs Donahue, 1907	12.73
3	Oscar Walker, 1879	12.60
4	Joe Start, 1878	12.54
5	Tim Murnane, 1878	12.52
6	Joe Start, 1879	12.49
7	Jake Goodman, 1878	12.45
8	Herman Dehlman, 1876	12.36
9	Phil Todt, 1926	12.36
10	Joe Start, 1877	12.35
11	George Burns, 1914	12.32
12	George Stovall, 1908	12.20
13	Stuffy McInnis, 1918	12.19
14	Juice Latham, 1877	12.19
15	Bill Phillips, 1888	12.12
16	Joe Start, 1880	12.11
17	Tom Jones, 1905	12.09
18	George Kelly, 1920	12.08
19	Gene Paulette, 1918	12.08
20	George Stovall, 1907	12.08
21	Hal Chase, 1919	12.07
22	Cap Anson, 1885	12.04
23	Bill Everitt, 1899	12.01
24	Charlie Comiskey, 1883	11.96
25	Jiggs Donahue, 1905	11.95

Second Base

1	Thorny Hawkes, 1879	8.44
2	Chick Fulmer, 1879	8.34
3	Jack Burdock, 1878	8.30
4	Ed Somerville, 1876	8.28
5	Joe Gerhardt, 1877	8.12
6	Fred Pfeffer, 1884	8.08
7	Jack Burdock, 1879	7.88
8	Joe Quest, 1878	7.81
9	Pop Smith, 1885	7.74
10	Joe Quest, 1879	7.73
11	Jack Farrell, 1879	7.67
12	Pop Smith, 1883	7.66
13	Joe Gerhardt, 1883	7.65
14	Hardy Richardson, 1883	7.62
15	Jack Burdock, 1880	7.59
16	Bid McPhee, 1886	7.56
17	Bid McPhee, 1884	7.54
18	Fred Pfeffer, 1883	7.53
19	Cub Stricker, 1882	7.53
20	Jack Burdock, 1877	7.53
21	Joe Gerhardt, 1884	7.51
22	Fred Dunlap, 1882	7.48
23	George Wright, 1877	7.47
24	Hardy Richardson, 1882	7.45
25	Bob Ferguson, 1880	7.40

Shortstop

1	Herman Long, 1889	7.27
2	Hughie Jennings, 1895	7.16
3	Dave Bancroft, 1918	7.14
4	Phil Tomney, 1889	7.12
5	George Davis, 1899	7.10
6	Hughie Jennings, 1896	7.07
7	Hughie Jennings, 1897	7.03
8	Bobby Wallace, 1901	6.97
9	Monte Cross, 1897	6.97
10	Bill Dahlen, 1895	6.93
11	Gene DeMontreville, 1897	6.91
12	Rabbit Maranville, 1919	6.89
13	Bill Dahlen, 1893	6.82
	George Davis, 1898	6.82
15	Herman Long, 1893	6.81
16	Bob Allen, 1890	6.81
17	Hughie Jennings, 1894	6.79
18	George Davis, 1900	6.77
19	Kid Elberfeld, 1901	6.77
20	Honus Wagner, 1903	6.76
21	Herman Long, 1896	6.74
22	Bill Dahlen, 1898	6.73
23	Monte Cross, 1898	6.73
24	Bill Dahlen, 1900	6.71
25	Rabbit Maranville, 1914	6.71
	Dave Bancroft, 1922	6.71

Third Base

1	Al Nichols, 1876	5.81
2	Bob Ferguson, 1877	5.61
3	Jumbo Davis, 1888	5.13
4	Billy Alvord, 1891	5.03
5	Cap Anson, 1876	5.03
6	George Bradley, 1880	4.93
7	Billy Shindle, 1892	4.93
8	Jack Gleason, 1882	4.90
9	Bill Bradley, 1900	4.87
10	Will Foley, 1877	4.79
11	Levi Meyerle, 1876	4.78
12	Joe Battin, 1876	4.76
13	Harry Schafer, 1876	4.73
14	Jerry Denny, 1882	4.73
15	Patsy Tebeau, 1890	4.69
16	Joe Battin, 1883	4.68
17	Arlie Latham, 1884	4.67
18	Frank Hankinson, 1878	4.65
19	Ed Williamson, 1883	4.64
20	Billy Shindle, 1889	4.61
21	Arlie Latham, 1891	4.61
22	Billy Shindle, 1891	4.59
23	Hick Carpenter, 1880	4.58
24	Charlie Reilly, 1890	4.58
25	Jerry Denny, 1881	4.55

Assists (Infield)

First Base

1	Bill Buckner, 1985	184
2	**Mark Grace, 1990**	**180**
3	**Mark Grace, 1991**	**167**
4	Sid Bream, 1986	166
5	Bill Buckner, 1983	161
6	Bill Buckner, 1982	159
7	Bill Buckner, 1986	157
8	**Todd Helton, 2003**	**156**
9	Mickey Vernon, 1949	155
10	Fred Tenney, 1905	152
	Eddie Murray, 1985	152
12	Ferris Fain, 1952	150
13	Rudy York, 1943	149
	Keith Hernandez, 1986	149
	Keith Hernandez, 1987	149
	Todd Helton, 2000	**149**
17	Keith Hernandez, 1983	147
	Eric Karros, 1993	**147**
	Rafael Palmeiro, 1993	**147**
	Jeff King, 1997	147
21	Rudy York, 1942	146
	Keith Hernandez, 1979	146
	Pete O'Brien, 1987	146
	Todd Helton, 1998	**146**
25	Vic Power, 1960	145
	Eddie Murray, 1987	145
	Wally Joyner, 1993	145

Second Base

1	Frankie Frisch, 1927	641
2	Hughie Critz, 1926	588
3	Rogers Hornsby, 1927	582
4	Ski Melillo, 1930	572
5	Ryne Sandberg, 1983	571
6	Rabbit Maranville, 1924	568
7	Frank Parkinson, 1922	562
8	Tony Cuccinello, 1936	559
9	Johnny Hodapp, 1930	557
10	Lou Bierbauer, 1892	555
11	Pep Young, 1938	554
12	Burgess Whitehead, 1936	552
13	Sparky Adams, 1925	551
14	Ryne Sandberg, 1984	550
15	Rogers Hornsby, 1929	547
16	Hod Ford, 1924	543
	Ski Melillo, 1931	543
	Bill Mazeroski, 1964	543
19	Hughie Critz, 1925	542
	Charlie Gehringer, 1933	542
	Woody Williams, 1944	542
	Jerry Priddy, 1950	542
23	Hughie Critz, 1933	541
24	Glenn Hubbard, 1985	539
	Ryne Sandberg, 1992	539

Shortstop

1	Ozzie Smith, 1980	621
2	Glenn Wright, 1924	601
3	Dave Bancroft, 1920	598
4	Tommy Thevenow, 1926	597
5	Ivan DeJesus, 1977	595
6	Cal Ripken, 1984	583
7	Whitey Wietelmann, 1943	581
8	Dave Bancroft, 1922	579
9	Rabbit Maranville, 1914	574
10	Don Kessinger, 1968	573
11	Roy Smalley, 1979	572
12	Terry Turner, 1906	570
	Joe Tinker, 1908	570
	Leo Cardenas, 1969	570
	Ozzie Guillen, 1988	570
16	Heinie Wagner, 1908	569
	Ed Brinkman, 1970	569
18	George McBride, 1908	568
19	Donie Bush, 1909	567
20	Art Fletcher, 1917	565
21	Luis Aparicio, 1969	563
22	Germany Smith, 1892	561
	Tommy Corcoran, 1898	561
24	Larry Bowa, 1971	560
	Bill Russell, 1973	560

Third Base

1	Graig Nettles, 1971	412
2	Graig Nettles, 1973	410
	Brooks Robinson, 1974	410
4	Harlond Clift, 1937	405
	Brooks Robinson, 1967	405
6	Mike Schmidt, 1974	404
7	Doug DeCinces, 1982	399
8	Clete Boyer, 1962	396
	Mike Schmidt, 1977	396
	Buddy Bell, 1982	396
11	Ron Santo, 1967	393
12	Terry Pendleton, 1989	392
13	Ron Santo, 1966	391
14	Aurelio Rodriguez, 1974	389
	Vinny Castilla, 1996	**389**
16	Ossie Vitt, 1916	386
17	Graig Nettles, 1976	383
	Buddy Bell, 1983	383
	Tim Wallach, 1985	383
20	Billy Shindle, 1892	382
21	Darrell Evans, 1975	381
22	Graig Nettles, 1975	379
23	Frank Malzone, 1958	378
	Ron Santo, 1968	378
25	Aurelio Rodriguez, 1970	377
	Graig Nettles, 1974	377
	Mike Schmidt, 1976	377

Assists/Game (Infield)

First Base

1	**Mark Grace, 1990**	**1.18**
2	Bill Buckner, 1986	1.14
3	Bill Buckner, 1985	1.14
4	**Jeff Bagwell, 1995**	**1.13**
5	Bill Buckner, 1983	1.12
6	**Jeff Bagwell, 1994**	**1.10**
7	Sid Bream, 1986	1.08
8	**Eric Karros, 1994**	**1.08**
9	Cecil Fielder, 1994	1.06
10	Ferris Fain, 1951	1.05
11	**Mark Grace, 1991**	**1.04**
12	Ferris Fain, 1952	1.04
13	Wally Joyner, 1993	1.04
14	Fred Tenney, 1905	1.03
15	Keith Hernandez, 1983	1.02
16	Bob Robertson, 1971	1.02
17	Sid Bream, 1988	1.01
18	Mickey Vernon, 1949	1.01
19	Darrell Evans, 1985	1.01
20	Roy Cullenbine, 1947	1.01
21	Vic Power, 1961	1.01
22	Keith Hernandez, 1986	1.00
	Todd Helton, 1998	**1.00**
24	Bill Buckner, 1982	0.99
25	Eddie Murray, 1985	0.99

Second Base

1	Joe Gerhardt, 1877	4.28
2	Frankie Frisch, 1927	4.19
3	Thorny Hawkes, 1879	4.13
4	Hughie Critz, 1933	4.07
5	Frank Parkinson, 1922	4.04
6	Joe Quest, 1879	3.99
7	Chick Fulmer, 1879	3.96
8	Ed Somerville, 1876	3.92
9	Ski Melillo, 1930	3.86
10	Glenn Hubbard, 1985	3.85
11	Frankie Frisch, 1930	3.85
12	Jack Farrell, 1883	3.84
13	Sparky Adams, 1925	3.83
14	Freddie Maguire, 1928	3.80
15	Hughie Critz, 1926	3.79
16	Fred Pfeffer, 1884	3.77
17	Hughie Critz, 1925	3.76
18	Danny Richardson, 1891	3.76
19	John Kerr, 1929	3.76
20	Frankie Frisch, 1924	3.76
21	Rogers Hornsby, 1927	3.75
22	Hod Ford, 1924	3.74
23	Hardy Richardson, 1883	3.74
24	Rabbit Maranville, 1924	3.74
25	Charley Bassett, 1887	3.73

Shortstop

1	Germany Smith, 1885	4.21
2	Arthur Irwin, 1880	4.13
3	Art Fletcher, 1919	4.10
4	Bill Dahlen, 1895	4.09
5	Phil Tomney, 1889	4.05
6	Bobby Wallace, 1901	4.04
7	Jack Glasscock, 1887	4.04
8	Germany Smith, 1892	4.04
9	Henry Easterday, 1888	3.99
10	Dave Bancroft, 1920	3.99
11	Rogers Hornsby, 1918	3.98
12	Robin Yount, 1981	3.98
13	Germany Smith, 1894	3.98
14	Bob Ferguson, 1878	3.96
15	Shorty Fuller, 1895	3.96
16	George Davis, 1900	3.95
17	Ozzie Smith, 1980	3.93
18	Glenn Wright, 1924	3.93
19	Garry Templeton, 1980	3.92
20	Monte Cross, 1897	3.91
21	Art Fletcher, 1918	3.90
22	Hughie Jennings, 1894	3.90
23	Sadie Houck, 1885	3.89
24	Bill Dahlen, 1900	3.89
25	Davy Force, 1876	3.89

Third Base

1	Jumbo Davis, 1888	2.96
2	Buddy Bell, 1981	2.93
3	George Bradley, 1880	2.89
4	Bill Hague, 1878	2.85
5	Billy Shindle, 1892	2.85
6	Bob Ferguson, 1877	2.77
7	Ed Williamson, 1879	2.76
8	Arlie Latham, 1884	2.75
9	Bill Bradley, 1900	2.75
10	Arlie Latham, 1891	2.74
11	Buddy Bell, 1982	2.73
12	Brooks Robinson, 1974	2.68
13	Aaron Ward, 1920	2.66
14	Mike Schmidt, 1977	2.66
15	Joe Battin, 1883	2.63
16	Harlond Clift, 1937	2.61
17	Arlie Latham, 1883	2.61
18	Graig Nettles, 1973	2.61
19	Doug DeCinces, 1982	2.61
20	Graig Nettles, 1971	2.61
21	Billy Nash, 1892	2.60
22	Ed Williamson, 1883	2.60
23	Charlie Reilly, 1890	2.58
24	Ron Santo, 1966	2.57
25	Brooks Robinson, 1967	2.56

Double Plays

First Base

1	Ferris Fain, 1949	194
2	Ferris Fain, 1950	192
3	Donn Clendenon, 1966	182
4	**Andres Galarraga, 1997**	**176**
5	Ron Jackson, 1979	175
6	Gil Hodges, 1951	171
7	Mickey Vernon, 1949	168
8	Ted Kluszewski, 1954	166
	Carlos Delgado, 2001	**166**
10	Rudy York, 1944	163

Second Base

1	Bill Mazeroski, 1966	161
2	Jerry Priddy, 1950	150
3	Bill Mazeroski, 1961	144
4	Nellie Fox, 1957	141
	Dave Cash, 1974	141
6	Buddy Myer, 1935	138
	Bill Mazeroski, 1962	138
	Carlos Baerga, 1992	**138**
9	Jerry Coleman, 1950	137
	Jackie Robinson, 1951	137
	Red Schoendienst, 1954	137

Shortstop

1	Rick Burleson, 1980	147
2	Roy Smalley, 1979	144
3	Bobby Wine, 1970	137
4	Lou Boudreau, 1944	134
5	Spike Owen, 1986	133
6	**Mike Bordick, 1999**	**132**
7	Rafael Ramirez, 1982	130
8	Roy McMillan, 1954	129
9	Hod Ford, 1928	128
	Vern Stephens, 1949	128
	Gene Alley, 1966	128

Third Base

1	Graig Nettles, 1971	54
2	Harlond Clift, 1937	50
3	Johnny Pesky, 1949	48
	Paul Molitor, 1982	48
5	Sammy Hale, 1927	46
	Clete Boyer, 1965	46
	Gary Gaetti, 1983	46
8	Eddie Yost, 1950	45
	Frank Malzone, 1961	45
	Darrell Evans, 1974	45
	Jeff Cirillo, 1998	**45**

Outfield

1	Happy Felsch, 1919	15
2	Jimmy Sheckard, 1899	14
3	Tom Brown, 1893	13
4	Tom Brown, 1886	12
	Tommy McCarthy, 1888	12
	Jimmy Bannon, 1894	12
	Mike Griffin, 1895	12
	Danny Green, 1899	12
	Cy Seymour, 1905	12
	Ginger Beaumont, 1907	12
	Ty Cobb, 1907	12
	Tris Speaker, 1909	12
	Jimmy Sheckard, 1911	12
	Tris Speaker, 1914	12
	Mel Ott, 1929	12
16	Sam Thompson, 1886	11
	Tommy McCarthy, 1889	11
	Billy Sunday, 1890	11
	Sam Thompson, 1896	11
	Bill Lange, 1899	11
	Fielder Jones, 1902	11
	Jimmy Sebring, 1903	11
	Phil Geier, 1904	11
	Ben Koehler, 1905	11
	Burt Shotton, 1913	11
	Chief Wilson, 1914	11

Catcher

1	Steve O'Neill, 1916	36
2	Frankie Hayes, 1945	29
3	Ray Schalk, 1916	25
	Yogi Berra, 1951	25
5	Jack Lapp, 1915	23
	Muddy Ruel, 1924	23
	Tom Haller, 1968	23
8	Steve O'Neill, 1914	22
	Bob O'Farrell, 1922	22
10	Gabby Hartnett, 1927	21
	Wes Westrum, 1950	21

Pitcher

1	Bob Lemon, 1953	15
2	Eddie Rommel, 1924	12
	Curt Davis, 1934	12
	Randy Jones, 1976	12
5	Scott Perry, 1919	11
	Tom Rogers, 1919	11
	Art Nehf, 1920	11
	Burleigh Grimes, 1925	11
	Gene Bearden, 1948	11
	Kirk Rueter, 2001	**11**

Putouts

First Base

1	Jiggs Donahue, 1907	1846
2	George Kelly, 1920	1759
3	Phil Todt, 1926	1755
4	Wally Pipp, 1926	1710
5	Jiggs Donahue, 1906	1697
6	Candy LaChance, 1904	1691
7	Tom Jones, 1907	1687
8	Ernie Banks, 1965	1682
9	Wally Pipp, 1922	1667
10	Lou Gehrig, 1927	1662

Second Base

1	Bid McPhee, 1886	529
2	Bobby Grich, 1974	484
3	Bucky Harris, 1922	483
4	Nellie Fox, 1956	478
5	Lou Bierbauer, 1889	472
6	Billy Herman, 1933	466
7	Bill Wambsganss, 1924	463
8	Cub Stricker, 1887	461
9	Buddy Myer, 1935	460
10	Bill Sweeney, 1912	459

Shortstop

1	Hughie Jennings, 1895	425
	Donie Bush, 1914	425
3	Joe Cassidy, 1905	408
4	Rabbit Maranville, 1914	407
5	Dave Bancroft, 1922	405
	Eddie Miller, 1940	405
7	Monte Cross, 1898	404
8	Dave Bancroft, 1921	396
9	Mickey Doolan, 1906	395
10	Buck Weaver, 1913	392

Third Base

1	Denny Lyons, 1887	255
2	Jimmy Williams, 1899	251
	Jimmy Collins, 1900	251
4	Jimmy Collins, 1898	243
	Willie Kamm, 1928	243
6	Willie Kamm, 1927	236
7	Frank Baker, 1913	233
8	Bill Coughlin, 1901	232
9	Ernie Courtney, 1905	229
10	Jimmy Austin, 1911	228

Outfield

1	Taylor Douthit, 1928	547
2	Richie Ashburn, 1951	538
3	Richie Ashburn, 1949	514
4	Chet Lemon, 1977	512
5	Dwayne Murphy, 1980	507
6	Dom DiMaggio, 1948	503
	Richie Ashburn, 1956	503
8	Richie Ashburn, 1957	502
9	Richie Ashburn, 1953	496
10	Richie Ashburn, 1958	495
11	Andruw Jones, 1999	492
12	Jim Busby, 1954	491
13	Omar Moreno, 1979	490
14	Baby Doll Jacobson, 1924	488
	Bobby Thomson, 1949	488
	Al Bumbry, 1980	488
17	**Mike Cameron, 2003**	**485**
18	Lloyd Waner, 1931	484
19	Richie Ashburn, 1954	483
20	Jim Busby, 1953	482
	Willie Wilson, 1980	482

Catcher

1	Johnny Edwards, 1969	1135
2	**Mike Piazza, 1996**	**1055**
3	**Dan Wilson, 1997**	**1051**
4	**Mike Piazza, 1997**	**1045**
5	**Jason Kendall, 1998**	**1015**
6	**Paul LoDuca, 2003**	**1014**
7	Johnny Edwards, 1963	1008
8	**Jorge Posada, 2001**	**996**
9	**Javy Lopez, 1996**	**993**
10	**Jason Kendall, 2000**	**990**

Pitcher

1	Dave Foutz, 1886	57
2	Tony Mullane, 1882	54
3	George Bradley, 1876	50
	Guy Hecker, 1884	50
5	Mike Boddicker, 1984	49
6	Larry Corcoran, 1884	47
7	Ted Breitenstein, 1895	46
8	Al Spalding, 1876	45
9	Jim Devlin, 1876	44
	Dave Foutz, 1887	44
	Bill Hutchison, 1890	44

Putouts per Game

First Base

1 Joe Gerhardt, 1876........12.30
2 Joe Start, 1879.............11.98
3 Joe Start, 1878.............11.79
4 Jiggs Donahue, 1907.....11.76
5 Joe Start, 1877.............11.73
6 Herman Dehlman, 1876.11.72
7 Joe Start, 1880.............11.63
8 Jake Goodman, 1878......11.55
9 George Burns, 1914......11.53
10 Oscar Walker, 1879........11.50

Second Base

1 Jack Burdock, 1878.........4.08
2 Jack Burdock, 1880.........3.81
3 Bid McPhee, 1886...........3.78
4 Bid McPhee, 1884...........3.71
5 Joe Quest, 1878..............3.68
6 Cub Stricker, 1887...........3.66
7 Lou Bierbauer, 1889.........3.63
8 Jack Burdock, 1879..........3.61
9 Chick Fulmer, 1879..........3.59
10 Bob Ferguson, 1880........3.59

Shortstop

1 Hughie Jennings, 1895....3.24
2 Dave Bancroft, 1918........2.97
3 George Davis, 1899.........2.91
4 Hughie Jennings, 1896....2.90
5 Hughie Jennings, 1897....2.89
6 George Davis, 1898.........2.88
7 Rabbit Maranville, 1919........2.76
8 Honus Wagner, 1913........2.75
9 Kid Elberfeld, 1901...........2.74
10 Buck Weaver, 1914..........2.74

Third Base

1 Al Nichols, 1876..............2.16
2 Cap Anson, 1876.............2.05
3 Hick Carpenter, 1880.......2.03
4 Bob Ferguson, 1877.........1.95
5 Denny Lyons, 1887..........1.86
6 Patsy Tebeau, 1890.........1.85
7 Cap Anson, 1877.............1.85
8 Joe Battin, 1876...............1.83
9 Jerry Denny, 1883............1.82
10 Frank Hankinson, 1881....1.80

Outfield

1 Taylor Douthit, 1928.........3.55
2 Fred Treacey, 1876...........3.54
3 Richie Ashburn, 1951........3.49
4 Thurman Tucker, 1944.....3.45
5 Chet Lemon, 1977...........3.44
6 Kirby Puckett, 1984..........3.42
7 Richie Ashburn, 1949......3.34
8 Irv Noren, 1951.................3.33
9 Sam West, 1935...............3.33
10 Mike Cameron, 2003..3.30
11 Jim Busby, 1952..............3.28
12 Richie Ashburn, 1956......3.27
13 Richie Ashburn, 1958......3.26
14 Lloyd Waner, 1932...........3.25
15 Dom DiMaggio, 1948.......3.25
16 Carden Gillenwater, 1945......3.22
17 Richie Ashburn, 1957......3.22
18 Jim Busby, 1953...............3.21
19 Baby Doll Jacobson, 1924.....3.21
20 Dwayne Murphy, 1980.....3.21

Catcher

1 Damian Miller, 2003....8.25
2 Paul LoDuca, 2003.....8.24
3 Sam Trott, 1884...............8.18
4 Damian Miller, 2001....7.98
5 Bill Holbert, 1883.............7.75
6 Javy Lopez, 1998........7.64
7 Jorge Posada, 2001....7.60
8 Duffy Dyer, 1972..............7.58
9 Dan Wilson, 1995.........7.52
10 Mike Piazza, 1997.......7.52

Pitcher

1 Kevin Brown, 1995.....1.54
2 Mike Boddicker, 1984.......1.44
3 Oil Can Boyd, 1985..........1.20
4 Kevin Brown, 1999.....1.17
5 Nick Altrock, 1904............1.13
6 Greg Maddux, 1990....1.11
7 Dave Foutz, 1887..............1.10
8 Dwight Gooden, 1986......1.09
Kevin Brown, 1997.....1.09
10 Dan Petry, 1984..............1.09

Fielding Runs

First Base

1 Bill Buckner, 1985...............25
2 Mark Grace, 1990..........25
3 Chick Gandil, 1914.............23
4 Fred Tenney, 1905..............22
5 Bill Buckner, 1983...............22
6 Sid Bream, 1986.................21
7 Jeff King, 1997...................21
8 Vic Power, 1960..................20
9 Jiggs Donahue, 1907..........20
10 Jake Beckley, 1892............20

Second Base

1 Glenn Hubbard, 1985.........60
2 Bill Mazeroski, 1963............51
3 Frankie Frisch, 1927...........49
4 Freddie Maguire, 1928........49
5 Nap Lajoie, 1908.................45
6 Hughie Critz, 1933..............45
7 Orlando Hudson, 2003..45
8 Ryne Sandberg, 1983.........44
9 Danny Richardson, 1891....43
10 Fred Pfeffer, 1884..............43

Shortstop

1 Rabbit Maranville, 1914..........50
2 George Davis, 1899............46
3 Ivan DeJesus, 1977............45
4 Dick Bartell, 1936...............43
5 Everett Scott, 1921.............41
6 Ozzie Guillen, 1988.............41
7 Germany Smith, 1885.........40
8 Freddie Patek, 1973............40
9 Cal Ripken, 1984.................39
10 Jack Glasscock, 1887.........39

Third Base

1 Graig Nettles, 1971.............46
2 Harlond Clift, 1937..............41
3 Billy Shindle, 1892..............40
4 Buddy Bell, 1982..................38
5 Billy Shindle, 1888...............38
6 Arlie Latham, 1884..............37
7 Tommy Leach, 1904.............36
8 Tim Wallach, 1985...............36
9 Lave Cross, 1899.................36
10 Terry Pendleton, 1989.........35

Outfield

1 Johnny Mostil, 1926............50
2 Jim Fogarty, 1887................30
3 Jesse Burkett, 1896.............29
4 Tom Brown, 1893..................26
5 Tommy McCarthy, 1888.......26
6 Jimmy Sheckard, 1903.........25
7 Mike Mitchell, 1907...............25
8 Richie Ashburn, 1957...........25
9 Ed Delahanty, 1893..............24
10 Dave Parker, 1977..............23
11 Chet Lemon, 1977...............23
12 Tris Speaker, 1914.............23
13 Del Ennis, 1956...................23
14 Dick Johnston, 1887...........23
15 Hardy Richardson, 1881......22
16 Max Carey, 1916.................22
17 Richie Ashburn, 1951..........21
18 Max Carey, 1917.................21
19 Chuck Klein, 1930...............21
20 Dummy Hoy, 1892..............21

Catcher

1 Bill Holbert, 1883.................34
2 Jim Sundberg, 1977............32
3 John Warner, 1897..............32
4 Paul LoDuca, 2003..........31
5 Damian Miller, 2001.......29
6 Tom Daly, 1887....................28
7 Duke Farrell, 1894...............27
8 John Kerins, 1886................27
9 Morgan Murphy, 1891..........27
10 Chief Zimmer, 1894............27

Pitcher

1 Ed Walsh, 1907....................21
2 Harry Howell, 1905...............17
3 Ed Walsh, 1911....................14
4 Ed Walsh, 1908....................13
5 Will White, 1882...................12
6 John Clarkson, 1889............11
7 Tony Mullane, 1882..............10
8 Sadie McMahon, 1890.........10
9 Carl Mays, 1926...................10
10 Ed Walsh, 1910..................10

Fielding Wins

1 Glenn Hubbard, 1985........6.3
2 Bill Mazeroski, 1963...........5.6
3 Rabbit Maranville, 1914..........5.4
4 Nap Lajoie, 1908.................5.3
5 Graig Nettles, 1971............4.9
6 Nap Lajoie, 1907.................4.9
7 Freddie Maguire, 1928.......4.8
8 Frankie Frisch, 1927..........4.8
9 Hughie Critz, 1933.............4.8
10 Johnny Mostil, 1926...........4.7
11 Ryne Sandberg, 1983.........4.7
12 Ivan DeJesus, 1977............4.6
13 Dave Shean, 1910..............4.6
14 Bill Dahlen, 1908................4.3
15 Freddie Patek, 1972...........4.3
16 Orlando Hudson, 2003.........4.3
17 Bill Mazeroski, 1966...........4.2
18 Danny Richardson, 1892...4.2
19 Ozzie Guillen, 1988............4.2
20 George Davis, 1899............4.2
21 Dick Bartell, 1936...............4.1
22 Glenn Hubbard, 1986.........4.1
23 Ozzie Smith, 1980...............4.1
24 Freddie Patek, 1973...........4.1
25 Bill Mazeroski, 1962...........4.0
26 Danny Richardson, 1891....4.0
27 Nap Lajoie, 1903.................4.0
28 Dave Bancroft, 1920...........3.9
29 Cal Ripken, 1984................3.9
30 Everett Scott, 1921............3.9
31 Art Fletcher, 1915...............3.9
32 Joe Cassidy, 1905..............3.9
33 Fred Pfeffer, 1884..............3.8
34 Miller Huggins, 1905..........3.8
35 Rey Sanchez, 2001.......3.8
36 Buck Weaver, 1913............3.8
37 Tommy Leach, 1904............3.8
38 Harlond Clift, 1937..............3.8
39 Tim Wallach, 1985..............3.7
40 Garry Templeton, 1980......3.7
41 Ozzie Smith, 1982..............3.7
42 Buddy Bell, 1982.................3.7
43 Terry Pendleton, 1989........3.7
44 George McBride, 1908........3.7
45 Heinie Wagner, 1908..........3.7
46 Fred Pfeffer, 1888..............3.7
47 Red Schoendienst, 1952....3.7
48 Tim Foli, 1974.....................3.7
49 Bill Mazeroski, 1964...........3.7
50 George McBride, 1910.......3.6
51 Germany Smith, 1885.........3.6
52 Lee Tannehill, 1906............3.6
53 Buck Herzog, 1914.............3.6
54 Lee Tannehill, 1911.............3.6
55 Mickey Doolan, 1914..........3.6
56 Bill Mazeroski, 1961...........3.6
57 Buddy Bell, 1981.................3.6
58 Spike Owen, 1986..............3.6
59 Eddie Mayo, 1944...............3.5
60 Billy Shindle, 1888..............3.5
61 Bobby Knoop, 1964............3.5
62 Brooks Robinson, 1967......3.5
63 Donie Bush, 1914...............3.5
64 Dick Bartell, 1937...............3.5
65 Neifi Perez, 2000..........3.5
66 Garry Templeton, 1978......3.5
67 Bobby Knoop, 1969............3.4
68 Luis Aparicio, 1969.............3.4
69 Mickey Doolan, 1915..........3.4
70 Billy Shindle, 1892..............3.4
71 Joe Gerhardt, 1890............3.4
72 Horace Clarke, 1968...........3.4
73 Buck Herzog, 1915.............3.4
74 John Farrell, 1902..............3.4
75 Bruno Betzel, 1916.............3.4
76 Graig Nettles, 1973............3.3
77 Arlie Latham, 1884.............3.3
78 Mike Benjamin, 1999..........3.3
79 Clete Boyer, 1962...............3.3
80 Ozzie Smith, 1984..............3.3
81 Vinny Castilla, 1996.....3.3
82 Ski Melillo, 1931.................3.3
83 Ed Brinkman, 1970.............3.3
84 Jack Glasscock, 1889.........3.3
85 Cupid Childs, 1896..............3.3
86 Ron Santo, 1967.................3.3
87 Jack Glasscock, 1887.........3.3
88 Eddie Collins, 1910.............3.3
89 Mike Bordick, 1999......3.3
90 Darrell Evans, 1975............3.3
91 Lave Cross, 1899...............3.2
92 Jim Sundberg, 1977............3.2
93 Alex Gonzalez, 2001.....3.2
94 Dave Cash, 1974................3.2
95 Paul LoDuca, 2003.......3.2
96 Roy Smalley, 1979.............3.2
97 Ozzie Smith, 1978..............3.2
98 Dave Bancroft, 1917..........3.2
99 Art Devlin, 1906..................3.2
100 Bid McPhee, 1889.............3.2

Batter-Fielder Wins

1 Barry Bonds, 2001......12.0
2 Barry Bonds, 2002......11.7
3 Babe Ruth, 1923.............10.1
4 Babe Ruth, 1921.................9.4
Cal Ripken, 1984.................9.4
6 Babe Ruth, 1920.................9.3
Rogers Hornsby, 1924.......9.3
8 Nap Lajoie, 1910.................8.9
Rogers Hornsby, 1922.......8.9
Sammy Sosa, 2001.......8.9
11 Babe Ruth, 1927.................8.8
Barry Bonds, 2003.......8.8
13 Cal Ripken, 1991.................8.6
14 Babe Ruth, 1926.................8.5
Ted Williams, 1941..............8.5
Ted Williams, 1942..............8.5
17 Babe Ruth, 1924.................8.4
Lou Gehrig, 1927..................8.4
19 Craig Biggio, 1997.......8.3
20 Mickey Mantle, 1957..........8.2
21 Nap Lajoie, 1901.................8.1
Nap Lajoie, 1903..................8.1
Babe Ruth, 1931...................8.1
Ted Williams, 1946..............8.1
Mickey Mantle, 1956............8.1
26 Nap Lajoie, 1908.................8.0
Joe Morgan, 1975.................8.0
Barry Bonds, 1992.......8.0
Barry Bonds, 1993.......8.0
30 Rogers Hornsby, 1920.......7.9
George Sisler, 1920.............7.9
Lou Gehrig, 1934..................7.9
33 Rogers Hornsby, 1917.......7.8
Johnny Mostil, 1926.............7.8
Rickey Henderson, 1990.......7.8
Barry Bonds, 1996.......7.8
Mike Piazza, 1997........7.8
38 Rogers Hornsby, 1921.......7.7
Lou Gehrig, 1930..................7.7
Jeff Bagwell, 1994.......7.7
Ken Caminiti, 1996...............7.7
42 Nap Lajoie, 1906.................7.6
Babe Ruth, 1930...................7.6
Norm Cash, 1961..................7.6
Ron Santo, 1967...................7.6
46 Honus Wagner, 1905..........7.5
Lou Boudreau, 1944.............7.5
Rico Petrocelli, 1969............7.5
Joe Morgan, 1973.................7.5
Albert Pujols, 2003.......7.5
51 Nap Lajoie, 1904.................7.4
Ty Cobb, 1917......................7.4
Harlond Clift, 1937................7.4
Al Rosen, 1953.....................7.4
Mickey Mantle, 1961............7.4
Mike Schmidt, 1974..............7.4
57 Tris Speaker, 1914.............7.3
Babe Ruth, 1919...................7.3
Jackie Robinson, 1951.........7.3
Ron Santo, 1966...................7.3
Robin Yount, 1982................7.3
62 Honus Wagner, 1906..........7.2
Tris Speaker, 1912...............7.2
Frankie Frisch, 1927............7.2
Snuffy Stirnweiss, 1945..........7.2
Ted Williams, 1947...............7.2
Stan Musial, 1948.................7.2
Mike Schmidt, 1981..............7.2
69 Fred Dunlap, 1884...............7.1
Joe Jackson, 1912...............7.1
Babe Ruth, 1928...................7.1
Lou Boudreau, 1948.............7.1
Ted Williams, 1957...............7.1
Ron Santo, 1964...................7.1
Cal Ripken, 1983..................7.1
Jeff Bagwell, 1996.......7.1
Mark McGwire, 1998.............7.1
Alex Rodriguez, 2002...7.1
79 Nap Lajoie, 1907.................7.0
Eddie Collins, 1910..............7.0
Eddie Collins, 1913..............7.0
Joe Morgan, 1974.................7.0
Rickey Henderson, 1985.......7.0
Barry Bonds, 2000........7.0
85 Honus Wagner, 1908..........6.9
Eddie Collins, 1914..............6.9
Joe Cronin, 1930..................6.9
Jimmie Foxx, 1933................6.9
Carl Yastrzemski, 1967.........6.9
Rod Carew, 1974..................6.9
Mike Schmidt, 1980..............6.9
Gary Carter, 1982.................6.9
Alex Rodriguez, 2001....6.9
94 Cupid Childs, 1890..............6.8
Dan Brouthers, 1892............6.8
Rogers Hornsby, 1925.........6.8
Rogers Hornsby, 1927.........6.8
Rogers Hornsby, 1929.........6.8
Lou Boudreau, 1943.............6.8
Snuffy Stirnweiss, 1944..........6.8

Batter-Fielder Wins

Willie Mays, 1955................6.8
Hank Aaron, 1959................6.8
Toby Harrah, 1975...............6.8
Barry Bonds, 1998........6.8
Alex Rodriguez, 2000...6.8
106 Hughie Jennings, 1896.......6.7
Honus Wagner, 1907...........6.7
Jimmie Foxx, 1932...............6.7
Rod Carew, 1975..................6.7
Joe Morgan, 1976.................6.7
George Brett, 1985...............6.7
112 Art Devlin, 1906...................6.6
Ty Cobb, 1911.......................6.6
Frank Baker, 1913................6.6
Eddie Collins, 1915...............6.6
Arky Vaughan, 1935.............6.6
Lou Gehrig, 1936..................6.6
Joe DiMaggio, 1941..............6.6
Willie Mays, 1965..................6.6
Willie McCovey, 1969............6.6
Johnny Bench, 1972.............6.6
Rod Carew, 1977..................6.6
George Brett, 1980................6.6
Jeff Kent, 2000.............6.6
125 Joe Jackson, 1911...............6.5
Frank Baker, 1912................6.5
Tris Speaker, 1913...............6.5
Tris Speaker, 1923...............6.5
Babe Ruth, 1932...................6.5
Eddie Lake, 1945..................6.5
Red Schoendienst, 1953.......6.5
Frank Robinson, 1966...........6.5
Willie McCovey, 1970............6.5
Bobby Grich, 1975.................6.5
Mike Schmidt, 1977..............6.5
Mike Schmidt, 1982..............6.5
Mike Schmidt, 1983..............6.5
Ryne Sandberg, 1984............6.5
Wade Boggs, 1987................6.5
Barry Bonds, 1990........6.5
Alex Rodriguez, 2003...6.5
142 Eddie Collins, 1912..............6.4
Mel Ott, 1938........................6.4
Arky Vaughan, 1938..............6.4
Ted Williams, 1949................6.4
Reggie Jackson, 1969...........6.4
Wade Boggs, 1988................6.4
148 Hughie Jennings, 1895........6.3
Cupid Childs, 1896................6.3
Ty Cobb, 1910.......................6.3
George Sisler, 1922..............6.3
Luke Appling, 1943................6.3
Willie Mays, 1958..................6.3
Darrell Evans, 1973..............6.3
Dickie Thon, 1983.................6.3
Barry Bonds, 1997........6.3
Jason Giambi, 2001.......6.3
158 Joe Sewell, 1923..................6.2
Willie Mays, 1954..................6.2
Ernie Banks, 1959.................6.2
Willie Mays, 1962..................6.2
Ron Santo, 1965...................6.2
Carl Yastrzemski, 1968.........6.2
Kevin Mitchell, 1989..............6.2
Barry Larkin, 1991.........6.2
Barry Larkin, 1996.........6.2
167 George Davis, 1899............6.1
Rogers Hornsby, 1928.........6.1
Jimmie Foxx, 1934................6.1
Charlie Gehringer, 1936..........6.1
Dick Bartell, 1937..................6.1
Stan Musial, 1951.................6.1
Eddie Mathews, 1953...........6.1
Nellie Fox, 1957....................6.1
Willie Mays, 1963..................6.1
Bobby Grich, 1974.................6.1
Alan Trammell, 1987..............6.1
Roberto Alomar, 1996..6.1
179 Fred Pfeffer, 1884................6.0
Ty Cobb, 1909.......................6.0
Harry Heilmann, 1923...........6.0
Frankie Frisch, 1924.............6.0
Lou Gehrig, 1931...................6.0
Charlie Gehringer, 1934..........6.0
Joe Medwick, 1937................6.0
Mickey Mantle, 1958.............6.0
Eddie Mathews, 1959............6.0
Ernie Banks, 1960.................6.0
Johnny Bench, 1970.............6.0
Mike Schmidt, 1976..............6.0
Jose Canseco, 1988.............6.0
Gary Sheffield, 1992.....6.0
Jeff Bagwell, 1997.........6.0
Ken Griffey, 1997...........6.0
195 22 players tied....................5.9

Wins

1 Charley Radbourn, 1884.....59
2 John Clarkson, 1885..........53
3 Guy Hecker, 1884..............52
4 John Clarkson, 1889..........49
5 Charley Radbourn, 1883....48
Charlie Buffinton, 1884..........48
7 Al Spalding, 1876..............47
John Ward, 1879..................47
9 Jim Galvin, 1883................46
Jim Galvin, 1884..................46
Matt Kilroy, 1887.................46
12 George Bradley, 1876.........45
Jim McCormick, 1880...........45
Silver King, 1888..................45
15 Mickey Welch, 1885............44
Bill Hutchison, 1891.............44
17 Billy Taylor, 1884...............43
Tommy Bond, 1879...............43
Will White, 1879...................43
Larry Corcoran, 1880............43
Will White, 1883....................43
22 Lady Baldwin, 1886.............42
Tim Keefe, 1886....................42
Bill Hutchison, 1890..............42
25 Charlie Sweeney, 1884........41
Tim Keefe, 1883.....................41
Dave Foutz, 1886...................41
Ed Morris, 1886......................41
Jack Chesbro, 1904................41
30 Jim McCormick, 1884..........40
Tommy Bond, 1877.................40
Tommy Bond, 1878.................40
Will White, 1882......................40
Bill Sweeney, 1884..................40
Bob Caruthers, 1885...............40
Bob Caruthers, 1889...............40
Ed Walsh, 1908.......................40
38 John Ward, 1880...................39
Mickey Welch, 1884................39
Ed Morris, 1885.......................39
41 Toad Ramsey, 1886...............38
John Clarkson, 1887................38
Kid Gleason, 1890....................38
44 Jim Galvin, 1879......................37
Jim Whitney, 1883....................37
Tim Keefe, 1884........................37
Jack Lynch, 1884......................37
Toad Ramsey, 1887..................37
Christy Mathewson, 1908.........37
50 Jim McCormick, 1882..........36
Tony Mullane, 1884.................36
John Clarkson, 1886................36
Sadie McMahon, 1890..............36
Bill Hutchison, 1892.................36
Cy Young, 1892.........................36
Frank Killen, 1893.....................36
Amos Rusie, 1894.....................36
Walter Johnson, 1913...............36
59 Jim Devlin, 1877......................35
Tony Mullane, 1883...................35
Larry Corcoran, 1884................35
Tim Keefe, 1887.........................35
Tim Keefe, 1888.........................35
Ed Seward, 1888........................35
Silver King, 1889........................35
Sadie McMahon, 1891...............35
Kid Nichols, 1892.......................35
Jack Stivetts, 1892.....................35
Cy Young, 1895..........................35
Joe McGinnity, 1904..................35
71 Mickey Welch, 1880.................34
Larry Corcoran, 1883.................34
Ed Morris, 1884..........................34
Will White, 1884.........................34
Elmer Smith, 1887......................34
Scott Stratton, 1890....................34
George Haddock, 1891...............34
Kid Nichols, 1893........................34
Cy Young, 1893...........................34
Joe Wood, 1912..........................34
81 Charley Radbourn, 1882.....33
Dave Foutz, 1885........................33
Henry Porter, 1885.....................33
Mickey Welch, 1886....................33
Tony Mullane, 1886....................33
John Clarkson, 1888...................33
Mark Baldwin, 1890....................33
John Clarkson, 1891...................33
Amos Rusie, 1891.......................33
Jack Stivetts, 1891.....................33
Amos Rusie, 1893.......................33
Jouett Meekin, 1894...................33
Cy Young, 1901...........................33
Christy Mathewson, 1904..........33
Walter Johnson, 1912.................33
Grover Alexander, 1916.............33
97 10 players tied.......................32

Wins by era

1988-2003

1 Bob Welch, 1990.................27
2 Frank Viola, 1988................24
John Smoltz, 1996.........24
4 Orel Hershiser, 1988...........23
Danny Jackson, 1988...........23
Bret Saberhagen, 1989........23
7 Doug Drabek, 1990.............22
Dave Stewart, 1990..............22
John Burkett, 1993........22
Tom Glavine, 1993.........22
Jack McDowell, 1993...........22

1973-1987

1 Catfish Hunter, 1974...........25
Fergie Jenkins, 1974...........25
Ron Guidry, 1978.................25
Steve Stone, 1980................25
5 Ron Bryant, 1973................24
Wilbur Wood, 1973...............24
Steve Carlton, 1980..............24
La Marr Hoyt, 1983...............24
Dwight Gooden, 1985............24
Roger Clemens, 1986....24

1961-1972

1 Denny McLain, 1968............31
2 Sandy Koufax, 1966............27
Steve Carlton, 1972..............27
4 Sandy Koufax, 1965............26
Juan Marichal, 1968..............26
6 Whitey Ford, 1961...............25
Don Drysdale, 1962...............25
Sandy Koufax, 1963..............25
Juan Marichal, 1963..............25
Juan Marichal, 1966..............25
Jim Kaat, 1966......................25
Tom Seaver, 1969..................25
Mickey Lolich, 1971...............25

1943-1960

1 Hal Newhouser, 1944..........29
2 Robin Roberts, 1952............28
3 Dizzy Trout, 1944.................27
Don Newcombe, 1956...........27
5 Hal Newhouser, 1946..........26
Bob Feller, 1946...................26
7 Hal Newhouser, 1945..........25
Dave Ferriss, 1946................25
Mel Parnell, 1949..................25
10 Johnny Sain, 1948..............24
Bobby Shantz, 1952..............24

1921-1942

1 Lefty Grove, 1931................31
2 Dizzy Dean, 1934.................30
3 Dazzy Vance, 1924..............28
Lefty Grove, 1930..................28
Dizzy Dean, 1935...................28
6 Carl Mays, 1921...................27
Urban Shocker, 1921.............27
Eddie Rommel, 1922.............27
Dolf Luque, 1923...................27
George Uhle, 1926.................27
Bucky Walters, 1939..............27
Bob Feller, 1940.....................27

1901-1920

1 Jack Chesbro, 1904.............41
2 Ed Walsh, 1908....................40
3 Christy Mathewson, 1908.........37
4 Walter Johnson, 1913...........36
5 Joe McGinnity, 1904............35
6 Joe Wood, 1912...................34
7 Cy Young, 1901...................33
Christy Mathewson, 1904..........33
Walter Johnson, 1912............33
Grover Alexander, 1916.........33

1893-1900

1 Frank Killen, 1893...............36
Amos Rusie, 1894.................36
3 Cy Young, 1895...................35
4 Kid Nichols, 1893................34
Cy Young, 1893.....................34
6 Amos Rusie, 1893...............33
Jouett Meekin, 1894.............33
8 Kid Nichols, 1894................32
9 Pink Hawley, 1895...............31
Bill Hoffer, 1895....................31
Kid Nichols, 1897..................31
Kid Nichols, 1898..................31

1876-1892

1 Charley Radbourn, 1884.....59
2 John Clarkson, 1885..........53
3 Guy Hecker, 1884...............52
4 John Clarkson, 1889...........49
5 Charley Radbourn, 1883.....48
Charlie Buffinton, 1884..........48
7 Al Spalding, 1876...............47
John Ward, 1879....................47
9 Jim Galvin, 1883..................46
Jim Galvin, 1884....................46
Matt Kilroy, 1887....................46

Losses

1 John Coleman, 1883...........48
2 Will White, 1880..................42
3 Larry McKeon, 1884............41
4 George Bradley, 1879..........40
Jim McCormick, 1879............40
6 Henry Porter, 1888..............37
Kid Carsey, 1891...................37
George Cobb, 1892................37
9 Stump Wiedman, 1886.........36
Bill Hutchison, 1892...............36
11 Jim Devlin, 1876..................35
Jim Galvin, 1880.....................35
Fleury Sullivan, 1884..............35
Adonis Terry, 1884..................35
Hardie Henderson, 1885.........35
Red Donahue, 1897................35
17 Bobby Mathews, 1876.........34
Bob Barr, 1884........................34
Matt Kilroy, 1886.....................34
Al Mays, 1887.........................34
Mark Baldwin, 1889................34
Amos Rusie, 1890..................34
23 Hardie Henderson, 1883.....33
Dupee Shaw, 1884.................33
Harry McCormick, 1879..........33
Jim Whitney, 1881...................33
Lee Richmond, 1882...............33
Frank Mountain, 1883.............33
Jersey Bakely, 1888................33
30 Lee Richmond, 1880............32
John Harkins, 1884.................32
Jim Whitney, 1885...................32
Jim Whitney, 1886...................32
34 Sam Weaver, 1878...............31
Will White, 1879......................31
Charley Radbourn, 1886.........31
Dupee Shaw, 1886..................31
Billy Crowell, 1887..................31
Amos Rusie, 1892..................31
40 Mickey Welch, 1880............30
Jim McCormick, 1881.............30
Jim McCormick, 1882.............30
Jersey Bakely, 1884...............30
Jack Lynch, 1886....................30
Phenomenal Smith, 1887.......30
Toad Ramsey, 1888...............30
John Ewing, 1889...................30
Ed Beatin, 1890......................30
Ted Breitenstein, 1895............30
Jim Hughey, 1899...................30
51 Tommy Bond, 1880..............29
Doc Landis, 1882....................29
Jim Galvin, 1883.....................29
John Healy, 1887....................29
Hank O'Day, 1888...................29
Bert Cunningham, 1888..........29
Red Ehret, 1889......................29
Silver King, 1891....................29
Bill Hart, 1896.........................29
Jack Taylor, 1898...................29
Vic Willis, 1905.......................29
62 Jim McCormick, 1880..........28
Hank O'Day, 1884...................28
Hugh Daily, 1884....................28
Gus Weyhing, 1887................28
Mark Baldwin, 1891................28
Duke Esper, 1893...................28
Bill Hill, 1896..........................28
69 Jim Galvin, 1879..................27
Tim Keefe, 1881......................27
Tim Keefe, 1883......................27
Charlie Buffinton, 1885............27
Al Mays, 1886.........................27
Tony Mullane, 1886................27
Toad Ramsey, 1886...............27
Toad Ramsey, 1887...............27
Park Swartzel, 1889...............27
Phil Knell, 1891.......................27
Mark Baldwin, 1892................27
Pink Hawley, 1894..................27
Chick Fraser, 1896.................27
Bill Hart, 1897.........................27
Willie Sudhoff, 1898...............27
Bill Carrick, 1899....................27
Dummy Taylor, 1901..............27
George Bell, 1910...................27
Paul Derringer, 1933..............27
88 20 players tied......................26

Winning Percentage

1 Roy Face, 1959..................947
2 Johnny Allen, 1937............938
3 Greg Maddux, 1995.....905
4 Randy Johnson, 1995..900
5 Ron Guidry, 1978...............893
6 Freddie Fitzsimmons, 1940....889
7 Lefty Grove, 1931..............886
8 Bob Stanley, 1978..............882
9 Preacher Roe, 1951...........880
10 Fred Goldsmith, 1880.......875
11 Joe Wood, 1912...............872
12 David Cone, 1988........870
Roger Clemens, 2001..870
14 Orel Hershiser, 1985........864
15 Bill Donovan, 1907............862
Whitey Ford, 1961................862
17 Dwight Gooden, 1985........857
Roger Clemens, 1986..857
19 Pedro Martinez, 1999..852
20 Chief Bender, 1914...........850
John Smoltz, 1998.......850
22 Lefty Grove, 1930.............848
23 Mike Hampton, 1999....846
24 Tom Hughes, 1916............842
Emil Yde, 1924.....................842
Schoolboy Rowe, 1940.........842
Sandy Consuegra, 1954.......842
Ralph Terry, 1961.................842
Ron Perranoski, 1963...........842
30 Lefty Gomez, 1934...........839
31 Bill Hoffer, 1895................838
Denny McLain, 1968.............838
33 Walter Johnson, 1913.......837
34 Henry Boyle, 1884............833
King Cole, 1910....................833
Spud Chandler, 1943............833
Hoyt Wilhelm, 1952..............833
Sandy Koufax, 1963..............833
Randy Johnson, 1997..833
Pedro Martinez, 2002..833
41 Charley Radbourn, 1884...831
42 Randy Johnson, 2002..828
43 Ed Reulbach, 1906...........826
Elmer Riddle, 1941...............826
Greg Maddux, 1997.....826
46 Jay Hughes, 1899............824
Jack Chesbro, 1902.............824
Dazzy Vance, 1924..............824
49 Chief Bender, 1910..........821
Bob Purkey, 1962................821
Barry Zito, 2002...........821
52 Sal Maglie, 1950..............818
Bob Welch, 1990..................818
Mark Portugal, 1993.............818
David Wells, 1998........818
56 Joe McGinnity, 1904........814
57 Mordecai Brown, 1906.....813
Russ Ford, 1910...................813
Eddie Plank, 1912................813
Carl Hubbell, 1936................813
61 Dizzy Dean, 1934............811
62 Ed Reulbach, 1907..........810
Doc Crandall, 1910..............810
Johnny Allen, 1932..............810
Ted Wilks, 1944...................810
Phil Niekro, 1982.................810
Jimmy Key, 1994..................810
Paul Abbott, 2001........810
69 Alvin Crowder, 1928........808
Bobo Newsom, 1940...........808
Tiny Bonham, 1942.............808
Larry Jansen, 1947.............808
Dave McNally, 1971............808
Catfish Hunter, 1973...........808
75 Christy Mathewson, 1909......806
Howie Camnitz, 1909...........806
Dave Ferriss, 1946..............806
Juan Marichal, 1966............806
79 Eddie Cicotte, 1919..........806
80 Mickey Welch, 1885.........800
Ed Doheny, 1902.................800
Sam Leever, 1905...............800
Bert Humphries, 1913..........800
Stan Coveleski, 1925...........800
Firpo Marberry, 1931...........800
Robin Roberts, 1952............800
Ed Lopat, 1953....................800
Don Newcombe, 1955.........800
Jim Palmer, 1969.................800
John Candelaria, 1977.........800
Larry Gura, 1978..................800
Tommy Greene, 1993...........800
Denny Neagle, 1997....800
94 Al Spalding, 1876............797
95 Don Newcombe, 1956.....794
96 Jocko Flynn, 1886...........793
Ellis Kinder, 1949................793
Sal Maglie, 1951..................793
Bret Saberhagen, 1989........793
100 4 players tied..................792

Games

1 Mike Marshall, 1974.........106
2 Kent Tekulve, 1979.............94
3 Mike Marshall, 1973...........92
4 Kent Tekulve, 1978.............91
5 Wayne Granger, 1969.........90
Mike Marshall, 1979..............90
Kent Tekulve, 1987................90
8 Mark Eichhorn, 1987...........89
Julian Tavarez, 1997.....89
Steve Kline, 2001..........89
Paul Quantrill, 2003.......89
12 Wilbur Wood, 1968.............88
Mike Myers, 1997..........88
Sean Runyan, 1998...............88
15 Rob Murphy, 1987...............87
16 Paul Quantrill, 2002.......86
Oscar Villarreal, 2003..........86
18 Kent Tekulve, 1982.............85
Frank Williams, 1987.............85
Mitch Williams, 1987..............85
21 Ted Abernathy, 1965...........84
Enrique Romo, 1979...............84
Dick Tidrow, 1980..................84
Dan Quisenberry, 1985...........84
Stan Belinda, 1997.................84
Graeme Lloyd, 2001......84
Billy Koch, 2002............84
28 Ken Sanders, 1971..............83
Craig Lefferts, 1986................83
Eddie Guardado, 1996...83
Mike Myers, 1996...........83
Steve Kline, 2000...........83
Kelly Wunsch, 2000.......83
Octavio Dotel, 2002.......83
35 Eddie Fisher, 1965..............82
Bill Campbell, 1983.................82
Juan Agosto, 1990...................82
Paul Quantrill, 1998.......82
Steve Kline, 1999...........82
Jeff Fassero, 2001.........82
Ray King, 2001..............82
42 John Wyatt, 1964................81
Dale Murray, 1976...................81
Jeff Robinson, 1987................81
Duane Ward, 1991...................81
Joe Boever, 1992....................81
Kenny Rogers, 1992......81
Mike Jackson, 1993.................81
Brad Clontz, 1996....................81
Mike Stanton, 1996.......81
Rod Beck, 1998.............81
Greg Swindell, 1998.................81
J.C. Romero, 2002.........81
54 Mudcat Grant, 1970............80
Pedro Borbon, 1973................80
Willie Hernandez, 1984...........80
Mitch Williams, 1986................80
Doug Jones, 1992....................80
Greg Harris, 1993....................80
Turk Wendell, 1999........80
Felix Rodriguez, 2001.............80
David Weathers, 2001...80
Paul Quantrill, 2001.......80
Tim Worrell, 2002...........80
Ray King, 2003..............80
Tom Martin, 2003...........80
67 Scott Sauerbeck, 2003...........79
Dick Radatz, 1964...................79
Duane Ward, 1992...................79
Bob Patterson, 1996................79
Eddie Guardado, 1998...79
Scott Sullivan, 1999......79
Anthony Telford, 1999.............79
Scott Sullivan, 2000......79
Robb Nen, 2001............79
Scott Sullivan, 2001......79
Todd Jones, 2002..........79
Mike Stanton, 2002.......79
Trever Miller, 2003........79
80 30 players tied.....................78

Games by era

1988-2003

- 1 **Eddie Guardado, 1996...83**
- **Mike Myers, 1996...83**
- 3 Juan Agosto, 1990...82
- 4 Duane Ward, 1991...81
- Joe Boever, 1992...81
- **Kenny Rogers, 1992...81**
- Mike Jackson, 1993...81
- Brad Clontz, 1996...81
- **Mike Stanton, 1996...81**
- 10 Doug Jones, 1992...80
- Greg Harris, 1993...80

1973-1987

- 1 Mike Marshall, 1974...106
- 2 Kent Tekulve, 1979...94
- 3 Mike Marshall, 1973...92
- 4 Kent Tekulve, 1978...91
- 5 Mike Marshall, 1979...90
- Kent Tekulve, 1987...90
- 7 Mark Eichhorn, 1987...89
- 8 Rob Murphy, 1987...87
- 9 Kent Tekulve, 1982...85
- Frank Williams, 1987...85
- Mitch Williams, 1987...85

1961-1972

- 1 Wayne Granger, 1969...90
- 2 Wilbur Wood, 1968...88
- 3 Ted Abernathy, 1965...84
- 4 Ken Sanders, 1971...83
- 5 Eddie Fisher, 1965...82
- 6 John Wyatt, 1964...81
- 7 Mudcat Grant, 1970...80
- 8 Dick Radatz, 1964...79
- 9 Hal Woodeshick, 1965...78
- Ted Abernathy, 1968...78

1943-1960

- 1 Jim Konstanty, 1950...74
- 2 Hoyt Wilhelm, 1952...71
- 3 Ace Adams, 1943...70
- Mike Fornieles, 1960...70
- 5 Ellis Kinder, 1953...69
- Don Elston, 1958...69
- 7 Hoyt Wilhelm, 1953...68
- Roy Face, 1956...68
- Roy Face, 1960...68
- 10 Andy Karl, 1945...67
- Turk Lown, 1957...67
- Gerry Staley, 1959...67

1921-1942

- 1 Firpo Marberry, 1926...64
- 2 Clint Brown, 1939...61
- Ace Adams, 1942...61
- 4 Garland Braxton, 1927...58
- Russ Van Atta, 1935...58
- 6 Eddie Rommel, 1923...56
- Firpo Marberry, 1927...56
- Hugh Mulcahy, 1937...56
- 9 Firpo Marberry, 1925...55
- Bump Hadley, 1931...55
- Jim Walkup, 1935...55

1901-1920

- 1 Ed Walsh, 1908...66
- 2 Ed Walsh, 1912...62
- 3 Dave Davenport, 1916...59
- 4 Ed Walsh, 1907...56
- Christy Mathewson, 1908...56
- Ed Walsh, 1911...56
- Reb Russell, 1916...56
- 8 Joe McGinnity, 1903...55
- Jack Chesbro, 1904...55
- Dave Davenport, 1915...55

1893-1900

- 1 Amos Rusie, 1893...56
- Ted Breitenstein, 1894...56
- Pink Hawley, 1895...56
- 4 Frank Killen, 1893...55
- Ted Breitenstein, 1895...55
- 6 Amos Rusie, 1894...54
- 7 Cy Young, 1893...53
- Pink Hawley, 1894...53
- Jouett Meekin, 1894...53
- 10 Kid Nichols, 1893...52
- Cy Young, 1894...52
- Frank Killen, 1896...52

1876-1892

- 1 Will White, 1879...76
- Jim Galvin, 1883...76
- Charley Radbourn, 1883...76
- 4 Charley Radbourn, 1884...75
- Guy Hecker, 1884...75
- Bill Hutchison, 1892...75
- 7 Jim McCormick, 1880...74
- Lee Richmond, 1880...74
- 9 John Clarkson, 1889...73
- 10 Jim Galvin, 1884...72

Games Started by era

1988-2003

- 1 Dave Stewart, 1988...37
- Tom Browning, 1989...37
- **Greg Maddux, 1991...37**
- 4 Frank Viola, 1989...36
- Tom Browning, 1988...36
- Rick Reuschel, 1988...36
- Bob Welch, 1988...36
- Jose DeLeon, 1989...36
- Mark Gubicza, 1989...36
- Bob Milacki, 1989...36
- Dave Stewart, 1989...36
- Jack Morris, 1990...36
- Dave Stewart, 1990...36
- Tom Browning, 1991...36
- Charlie Leibrandt, 1991...36
- **John Smoltz, 1991...36**
- Mike Moore, 1992...36
- Rick Sutcliffe, 1992...36
- **Tom Glavine, 1993...36**
- **Greg Maddux, 1993...36**
- Jose Rijo, 1993...36
- **Cal Eldred, 1993...36**
- Mike Moore, 1993...36
- **Tom Glavine, 1996...36**
- **Mike Mussina, 1996...36**

1973-1987

- 1 Wilbur Wood, 1973...48
- 2 Phil Niekro, 1979...44
- 3 Wilbur Wood, 1975...43
- Phil Niekro, 1977...43
- 5 Stan Bahnsen, 1973...42
- Mickey Lolich, 1973...42
- Wilbur Wood, 1974...42
- Phil Niekro, 1978...42
- 9 9 players tied...41

1961-1972

- 1 Wilbur Wood, 1972...49
- 2 Mickey Lolich, 1971...45
- 3 Don Drysdale, 1963...42
- Jack Sanford, 1963...42
- Don Drysdale, 1965...42
- Jim Kaat, 1965...42
- Fergie Jenkins, 1969...42
- Wilbur Wood, 1971...42
- 9 14 players tied...41

1943-1960

- 1 Bob Feller, 1946...42
- Bob Friend, 1956...42
- 3 Bill Voiselle, 1944...41
- Robin Roberts, 1953...41
- 5 Dizzy Trout, 1944...40
- 6 Johnny Sain, 1948...39
- Robin Roberts, 1950...39
- Warren Spahn, 1950...39
- Vern Bickford, 1950...39
- Robin Roberts, 1951...39
- Ron Kline, 1956...39
- Lew Burdette, 1959...39

1921-1942

- 1 George Uhle, 1923...44
- 2 Stan Coveleski, 1921...40
- George Uhle, 1922...40
- George Caster, 1938...40
- Bobo Newsom, 1938...40
- Bob Feller, 1941...40
- 7 Red Faber, 1921...39
- Hooks Dauss, 1923...39
- Howard Ehmke, 1923...39
- Watty Clark, 1929...39
- George Earnshaw, 1930...39
- Alvin Crowder, 1932...39
- Kirby Higbe, 1941...39

1901-1920

- 1 Jack Chesbro, 1904...51
- 2 Ed Walsh, 1908...49
- 3 Joe McGinnity, 1903...48
- 4 Vic Willis, 1902...46
- Christy Mathewson, 1904...46
- Rube Waddell, 1904...46
- Ed Walsh, 1907...46
- Dave Davenport, 1915...46
- 9 Jack Powell, 1904...45
- Grover Alexander, 1916...45

1893-1900

- 1 Amos Rusie, 1893...52
- 2 Ted Breitenstein, 1895...51
- 3 Ted Breitenstein, 1894...50
- Amos Rusie, 1894...50
- Pink Hawley, 1895...50
- Frank Killen, 1896...50
- 7 Jouett Meekin, 1894...49
- 8 Frank Killen, 1893...48
- 9 3 players tied...47

1876-1892

- 1 Will White, 1879...75
- Jim Galvin, 1883...75
- 3 Jim McCormick, 1880...74
- 4 Charley Radbourn, 1884...73
- Guy Hecker, 1884...73
- 6 Jim Galvin, 1884...72
- John Clarkson, 1889...72
- 8 John Clarkson, 1885...70
- Bill Hutchison, 1892...70
- 10 Matt Kilroy, 1887...69

Complete Games

- 1 Will White, 1879...75
- 2 Charley Radbourn, 1884...73
- 3 Jim McCormick, 1880...72
- Jim Galvin, 1883...72
- Guy Hecker, 1884...72
- 6 Jim Galvin, 1884...71
- 7 Tim Keefe, 1883...68
- John Clarkson, 1885...68
- John Clarkson, 1889...68
- 10 Bill Hutchison, 1892...67
- 11 Jim Devlin, 1876...66
- Charley Radbourn, 1883...66
- Matt Kilroy, 1886...66
- Toad Ramsey, 1886...66
- Matt Kilroy, 1887...66
- 16 Jim Galvin, 1879...65
- Jim McCormick, 1882...65
- Bill Hutchison, 1890...65
- 19 Mickey Welch, 1880...64
- Will White, 1883...64
- Tony Mullane, 1884...64
- Silver King, 1888...64
- 23 Jim McCormick, 1884...63
- George Bradley, 1876...63
- Charlie Buffinton, 1884...63
- Ed Morris, 1885...63
- Ed Morris, 1886...63
- 28 Mickey Welch, 1884...62
- Tim Keefe, 1886...62
- 30 Jim Devlin, 1877...61
- Toad Ramsey, 1887...61
- 32 Dupee Shaw, 1884...60
- Jersey Bakely, 1888...60
- 34 Billy Taylor, 1884...59
- Tommy Bond, 1879...59
- Jim McCormick, 1879...59
- John Ward, 1880...59
- John Coleman, 1883...59
- Larry McKeon, 1884...59
- Hardie Henderson, 1885...59
- Amos Rusie, 1892...59
- 42 Tommy Bond, 1877...58
- John Ward, 1879...58
- Will White, 1880...58
- Bill Sweeney, 1884...58
- 46 Tommy Bond, 1878...57
- Terry Larkin, 1879...57
- Larry Corcoran, 1880...57
- Lee Richmond, 1880...57
- Jim McCormick, 1881...57
- Jim Whitney, 1881...57
- Frank Mountain, 1883...57
- Larry Corcoran, 1884...57
- Charley Radbourn, 1886...57
- Ed Seward, 1888...57
- 56 Terry Larkin, 1878...56
- Tim Keefe, 1884...56
- Hugh Daily, 1884...56
- Mickey Welch, 1886...56
- John Clarkson, 1887...56
- Amos Rusie, 1890...56
- Bill Hutchison, 1891...56
- 63 Bobby Mathews, 1876...55
- Terry Larkin, 1877...55
- George Derby, 1881...55
- Mickey Welch, 1885...55
- Lady Baldwin, 1886...55
- Dave Foutz, 1886...55
- Tony Mullane, 1886...55
- Matt Kilroy, 1889...55
- Sadie McMahon, 1890...55
- 72 Jim Whitney, 1883...54
- Adonis Terry, 1884...54
- Tim Keefe, 1887...54
- Phenomenal Smith, 1887...54
- Ed Morris, 1888...54
- Mark Baldwin, 1889...54
- Kid Gleason, 1890...54
- 79 Charlie Sweeney, 1884...53
- Al Spalding, 1876...53
- George Bradley, 1879...53
- Jack Lynch, 1884...53
- Bob Caruthers, 1885...53
- Henry Porter, 1885...53
- Gus Weyhing, 1887...53
- John Clarkson, 1888...53
- Henry Porter, 1888...53
- Ed Beatin, 1890...53
- Mark Baldwin, 1890...53
- Sadie McMahon, 1891...53
- 91 Will White, 1878...52
- Will White, 1882...52
- Will White, 1884...52
- Ed Seward, 1887...52
- Bob Barr, 1890...52
- Amos Rusie, 1891...52
- 97 6 players tied...51

Complete Games by era

1988-2003

- 1 Orel Hershiser, 1988...15
- Danny Jackson, 1988...15
- Jack McDowell, 1991...15
- **4 Roger Clemens, 1988...14**
- Dave Stewart, 1988...14
- 6 Eric Show, 1988...13
- Bobby Witt, 1988...13
- **Roger Clemens, 1991...13**
- Jack McDowell, 1992...13
- Chuck Finley, 1993...13

1973-1987

- 1 Catfish Hunter, 1975...30
- 2 Gaylord Perry, 1973...29
- Fergie Jenkins, 1974...29
- 4 Gaylord Perry, 1974...28
- Rick Langford, 1980...28
- 6 Mickey Lolich, 1974...27
- 7 Nolan Ryan, 1973...26
- Nolan Ryan, 1974...26
- 9 Bert Blyleven, 1973...25
- Luis Tiant, 1974...25
- Jim Palmer, 1975...25
- Gaylord Perry, 1975...25
- Randy Jones, 1976...25

1961-1972

- 1 Juan Marichal, 1968...30
- Fergie Jenkins, 1971...30
- Steve Carlton, 1972...30
- 4 Mickey Lolich, 1971...29
- Gaylord Perry, 1972...29
- 6 Bob Gibson, 1968...28
- Denny McLain, 1968...28
- Bob Gibson, 1969...28
- 9 Sandy Koufax, 1965...27
- Sandy Koufax, 1966...27
- Juan Marichal, 1969...27

1943-1960

- 1 Bob Feller, 1946...36
- 2 Dizzy Trout, 1944...33
- Robin Roberts, 1953...33
- 4 Robin Roberts, 1952...30
- 5 Hal Newhouser, 1945...29
- Hal Newhouser, 1946...29
- Robin Roberts, 1954...29
- 8 Jim Tobin, 1944...28
- Johnny Sain, 1948...28
- Bob Lemon, 1952...28

1921-1942

- 1 Burleigh Grimes, 1923...33
- 2 Red Faber, 1921...32
- George Uhle, 1926...32
- 4 Red Faber, 1922...31
- Wes Ferrell, 1935...31
- Bobo Newsom, 1938...31
- Bucky Walters, 1939...31
- Bob Feller, 1940...31
- 9 Burleigh Grimes, 1921...30
- Carl Mays, 1921...30
- Urban Shocker, 1921...30
- Dazzy Vance, 1924...30
- Burleigh Grimes, 1924...30
- Ted Lyons, 1927...30
- Thornton Lee, 1941...30

1901-1920

- 1 Jack Chesbro, 1904...48
- 2 Vic Willis, 1902...45
- 3 Joe McGinnity, 1903...44
- 4 George Mullin, 1904...42
- Ed Walsh, 1908...42
- 6 Noodles Hahn, 1901...41
- Cy Young, 1902...41
- Irv Young, 1905...41
- 9 Cy Young, 1904...40
- 10 Joe McGinnity, 1901...39
- Bill Dinneen, 1902...39
- Vic Willis, 1904...39
- Jack Taylor, 1904...39
- Rube Waddell, 1904...39

1893-1900

- 1 Amos Rusie, 1893...50
- 2 Ted Breitenstein, 1895...47
- 3 Ted Breitenstein, 1894...46
- 4 Amos Rusie, 1894...45
- 5 Cy Young, 1894...44
- Pink Hawley, 1895...44
- Frank Killen, 1896...44
- 8 Kid Nichols, 1893...43
- Kid Nichols, 1895...43
- 10 Cy Young, 1893...42
- Amos Rusie, 1895...42
- Cy Young, 1896...42
- Jack Taylor, 1898...42

1876-1892

- 1 Will White, 1879...75
- 2 Charley Radbourn, 1884...73
- 3 Jim McCormick, 1880...72
- Jim Galvin, 1883...72
- Guy Hecker, 1884...72
- 6 Jim Galvin, 1884...71
- 7 Tim Keefe, 1883...68
- John Clarkson, 1885...68
- John Clarkson, 1889...68
- 10 Bill Hutchison, 1892...67

Shutouts

- 1 George Bradley, 1876...16
- Grover Alexander, 1916...16
- 3 Jack Coombs, 1910...13
- Bob Gibson, 1968...13
- 5 Jim Galvin, 1884...12
- Ed Morris, 1886...12
- Grover Alexander, 1915...12
- 8 Tommy Bond, 1879...11
- Charley Radbourn, 1884...11
- Dave Foutz, 1886...11
- Christy Mathewson, 1908...11
- Ed Walsh, 1908...11
- Walter Johnson, 1913...11
- Sandy Koufax, 1963...11
- Dean Chance, 1964...11
- 16 Jim McCormick, 1884...10
- John Clarkson, 1885...10
- Cy Young, 1904...10
- Ed Walsh, 1906...10
- Joe Wood, 1912...10
- Dave Davenport, 1915...10
- Carl Hubbell, 1933...10
- Mort Cooper, 1942...10
- Bob Feller, 1946...10
- Bob Lemon, 1948...10
- Juan Marichal, 1965...10
- Jim Palmer, 1975...10
- John Tudor, 1985...10
- 29 Tommy Bond, 1878...9
- George Derby, 1881...9
- Cy Young, 1892...9
- Joe McGinnity, 1904...9
- Mordecai Brown, 1906...9
- Addie Joss, 1906...9
- Mordecai Brown, 1908...9
- Addie Joss, 1908...9
- Orval Overall, 1909...9
- Grover Alexander, 1913...9
- Walter Johnson, 1914...9
- Cy Falkenberg, 1914...9
- Babe Ruth, 1916...9
- Stan Coveleski, 1917...9
- Grover Alexander, 1919...9
- Bill Lee, 1938...9
- Bob Porterfield, 1953...9
- Luis Tiant, 1968...9
- Denny McLain, 1969...9
- Don Sutton, 1972...9
- Nolan Ryan, 1972...9
- Bert Blyleven, 1973...9
- Ron Guidry, 1978...9
- 52 Al Spalding, 1876...8
- John Ward, 1880...8
- Will White, 1882...8
- Charlie Buffinton, 1884...8
- Tim Keefe, 1888...8
- Ben Sanders, 1888...8
- John Clarkson, 1889...8
- Jack Taylor, 1902...8
- Christy Mathewson, 1902...8
- Jack Chesbro, 1902...8
- Rube Waddell, 1904...8
- Christy Mathewson, 1905...8
- Ed Killian, 1905...8
- Lefty Leifield, 1906...8
- Rube Waddell, 1906...8
- Orval Overall, 1907...8
- Christy Mathewson, 1907...8
- Eddie Plank, 1907...8
- Mordecai Brown, 1909...8
- Christy Mathewson, 1909...8
- Ed Walsh, 1909...8
- Russ Ford, 1910...8
- Walter Johnson, 1910...8
- Reb Russell, 1913...8
- Jeff Tesreau, 1914...8
- Al Mamaux, 1915...8
- Jeff Tesreau, 1915...8
- Joe Bush, 1916...8
- Grover Alexander, 1917...8
- Jim Bagby, 1917...8
- Walter Johnson, 1917...8
- Hippo Vaughn, 1918...8
- Walter Johnson, 1918...8
- Carl Mays, 1918...8
- Babe Adams, 1920...8
- Hal Newhouser, 1945...8
- Steve Barber, 1961...8
- Camilo Pascual, 1961...8
- Whitey Ford, 1964...8
- Sandy Koufax, 1965...8
- Don Drysdale, 1968...8
- Juan Marichal, 1969...8
- Vida Blue, 1971...8
- Steve Carlton, 1972...8
- Wilbur Wood, 1972...8
- Fernando Valenzuela, 1981...8
- Dwight Gooden, 1985...8
- Orel Hershiser, 1988...8
- **Roger Clemens, 1988...8**
- Tim Belcher, 1989...8

Saves

1 Bobby Thigpen, 1990 ... 57
2 John Smoltz, 2002 ... 55
Eric Gagne, 2003 ... 55
4 Randy Myers, 1993 ... 53
Trevor Hoffman, 1998 ... 53
6 Eric Gagne, 2002 ... 52
7 Dennis Eckersley, 1992 ... 51
Rod Beck, 1998 ... 51
9 Mariano Rivera, 2001 ... 50
10 Dennis Eckersley, 1990 ... 48
Rod Beck, 1993 ... 48
Jeff Shaw, 1998 ... 48
13 Lee Smith, 1991 ... 47
14 Lee Smith, 1993 ... 46
Dave Righetti, 1986 ... 46
Bryan Harvey, 1991 ... 46
Jose Mesa, 1995 ... 46
Tom Gordon, 1998 ... 46
Mike Williams, 2002 ... 46
20 Dan Quisenberry, 1983 ... 45
Bruce Sutter, 1984 ... 45
Dennis Eckersley, 1988 ... 45
Bryan Harvey, 1993 ... 45
Jeff Montgomery, 1993 ... 45
Duane Ward, 1993 ... 45
Randy Myers, 1997 ... 45
Mariano Rivera, 1999 ... 45
Antonio Alfonseca, 2000 ... 45
Robb Nen, 2001 ... 45
Kazuhiro Sasaki, 2001 ... 45
Jose Mesa, 2002 ... 45
Eddie Guardado, 2002 ... 45
John Smoltz, 2003 ... 45
34 Dan Quisenberry, 1984 ... 44
Mark Davis, 1989 ... 44
Jeff Brantley, 1996 ... 44
Todd Worrell, 1996 ... 44
Billy Koch, 2002 ... 44
Billy Wagner, 2003 ... 44
40 Doug Jones, 1990 ... 43
Dennis Eckersley, 1991 ... 43
Lee Smith, 1992 ... 43
John Wetteland, 1993 ... 43
Mitch Williams, 1993 ... 43
John Wetteland, 1996 ... 43
Mariano Rivera, 1997 ... 43
Roberto Hernandez, 1999 ... 43
John Wetteland, 1999 ... 43
Trevor Hoffman, 2000 ... 43
Armando Benitez, 2001 ... 43
Trevor Hoffman, 2001 ... 43
Jeff Shaw, 2001 ... 43
Robb Nen, 2002 ... 43
Keith Foulke, 2003 ... 43
55 Jeff Reardon, 1988 ... 42
Rick Aguilera, 1991 ... 42
Trevor Hoffman, 1996 ... 42
Jeff Shaw, 1997 ... 42
Troy Percival, 1998 ... 42
John Wetteland, 1998 ... 42
Todd Jones, 2000 ... 42
Derek Lowe, 2000 ... 42
Jose Mesa, 2001 ... 42
Keith Foulke, 2001 ... 42
65 Jeff Reardon, 1985 ... 41
Rick Aguilera, 1992 ... 41
Ugueth Urbina, 1999 ... 41
Armando Benitez, 2000 ... 41
Robb Nen, 2000 ... 41
Jose Jimenez, 2002 ... 41
Eddie Guardado, 2003 ... 41
72 Steve Bedrosian, 1987 ... 40
Jeff Reardon, 1991 ... 40
Tom Henke, 1993 ... 40
Robb Nen, 1998 ... 40
Mike Jackson, 1998 ... 40
Trevor Hoffman, 1999 ... 40
Troy Percival, 2002 ... 40
Ugueth Urbina, 2002 ... 40
Mariano Rivera, 2003 ... 40
81 John Franco, 1988 ... 39
Jeff Montgomery, 1992 ... 39
Mark Wohlers, 1996 ... 39
Jose Mesa, 1996 ... 39
Billy Wagner, 1999 ... 39
Mike Jackson, 1999 ... 39
Billy Wagner, 2001 ... 39
Troy Percival, 2001 ... 39
89 John Hiller, 1973 ... 38
Jeff Russell, 1989 ... 38
Randy Myers, 1992 ... 38
Roberto Hernandez, 1993 ... 38
Randy Myers, 1995 ... 38
Roberto Hernandez, 1996 ... 38
John Franco, 1998 ... 38
Rick Aguilera, 1998 ... 38
John Rocker, 1999 ... 38
Trevor Hoffman, 2002 ... 38
Kelvim Escobar, 2002 ... 38
Tim Worrell, 2003 ... 38

Saves by era

1988-2003

1 Bobby Thigpen, 1990 ... 57
2 Randy Myers, 1993 ... 53
3 Dennis Eckersley, 1992 ... 51
4 Dennis Eckersley, 1990 ... 48
Rod Beck, 1993 ... 48
6 Lee Smith, 1991 ... 47
7 Lee Smith, 1993 ... 46
Bryan Harvey, 1991 ... 46
Jose Mesa, 1995 ... 46
10 Dennis Eckersley, 1988 ... 45
Bryan Harvey, 1993 ... 45
Jeff Montgomery, 1993 ... 45
Duane Ward, 1993 ... 45

1973-1987

1 Dave Righetti, 1986 ... 46
2 Dan Quisenberry, 1983 ... 45
Bruce Sutter, 1984 ... 45
4 Dan Quisenberry, 1984 ... 44
5 Jeff Reardon, 1985 ... 41
6 Steve Bedrosian, 1987 ... 40
7 John Hiller, 1973 ... 38
8 Rollie Fingers, 1978 ... 37
Bruce Sutter, 1979 ... 37
Dan Quisenberry, 1985 ... 37

1961-1972

1 Clay Carroll, 1972 ... 37
2 Wayne Granger, 1970 ... 35
Sparky Lyle, 1972 ... 35
4 Ron Perranoski, 1970 ... 34
5 Jack Aker, 1966 ... 32
6 Ted Abernathy, 1965 ... 31
Ron Perranoski, 1969 ... 31
Ken Sanders, 1971 ... 31
9 Dave Giusti, 1971 ... 30
10 Luis Arroyo, 1961 ... 29
Dick Radatz, 1964 ... 29
Ron Kline, 1965 ... 29
Fred Gladding, 1969 ... 29
Lindy McDaniel, 1970 ... 29
Terry Forster, 1972 ... 29

1943-1960

1 Joe Page, 1949 ... 27
Ellis Kinder, 1953 ... 27
3 Lindy McDaniel, 1960 ... 26
4 Jim Hughes, 1954 ... 24
Roy Face, 1960 ... 24
6 Jim Konstanty, 1950 ... 22
Johnny Sain, 1954 ... 22
8 Frank Smith, 1954 ... 20
Roy Face, 1958 ... 20
Ryne Duren, 1958 ... 20

1921-1942

1 Firpo Marberry, 1926 ... 22
2 Johnny Murphy, 1939 ... 19
3 Clint Brown, 1937 ... 18
Clint Brown, 1939 ... 18
5 Al Benton, 1940 ... 17
6 Firpo Marberry, 1924 ... 15
Firpo Marberry, 1925 ... 15
Jack Quinn, 1931 ... 15
Johnny Murphy, 1941 ... 15
10 Wilcy Moore, 1927 ... 13
Garland Braxton, 1927 ... 13
Firpo Marberry, 1932 ... 13
Jack Russell, 1933 ... 13
Hugh Casey, 1942 ... 13

1901-1920

1 Mordecai Brown, 1911 ... 13
Chief Bender, 1913 ... 13
3 Larry Cheney, 1913 ... 11
4 Ed Walsh, 1912 ... 10
Hugh Bedient, 1915 ... 10
6 Tom Hughes, 1915 ... 9
Dave Danforth, 1917 ... 9
8 Frank Arellanes, 1909 ... 8
Red Ames, 1916 ... 8
Bob Shawkey, 1916 ... 8

1893-1900

1 Tony Mullane, 1894 ... 4
Kid Nichols, 1898 ... 4
Frank Kitson, 1900 ... 4
4 Bill Hawke, 1894 ... 3
Win Mercer, 1894 ... 3
Kid Nichols, 1895 ... 3
Tom Parrott, 1895 ... 3
Cy Young, 1896 ... 3
Win Mercer, 1897 ... 3
Kid Nichols, 1897 ... 3
Sam Leever, 1899 ... 3

1876-1892

1 Jack Manning, 1876 ... 5
Tony Mullane, 1889 ... 5
3 Billy Taylor, 1884 ... 4
Herb Goodall, 1890 ... 4
5 Lee Richmond, 1880 ... 3
Tommy Burns, 1885 ... 3
Adonis Terry, 1887 ... 3
Bill Sowders, 1889 ... 3
Hank O'Day, 1890 ... 3
George Hemming, 1890 ... 3
John Clarkson, 1891 ... 3
Kid Nichols, 1891 ... 3
Joe Neale, 1891 ... 3
Gus Weyhing, 1892 ... 3

Save percentage

1 Rod Beck, 1994 ... 100.0
Eric Gagne, 2003 ... 100.0
3 Trevor Hoffman, 1998 ... 98.1
4 Tom Gordon, 1998 ... 97.9
5 Randy Myers, 1997 ... 97.8
6 Willie Hernandez, 1984 ... 97.0
7 Dennis Eckersley, 1990 ... 96.0
8 Jose Mesa, 1995 ... 95.8
9 Ken Tatum, 1969 ... 95.7
10 Billy Wagner, 2001 ... 95.1
11 Tom Henke, 1995 ... 94.7
Doug Jones, 1997 ... 94.7
13 Dennis Eckersley, 1992 ... 94.4
14 Billy Wagner, 2003 ... 93.6
15 Armando Benitez, 2001 ... 93.5
Trevor Hoffman, 2001 ... 93.5
17 Keith Foulke, 2001 ... 93.3
18 John Smoltz, 2002 ... 93.2
19 Doug Jones, 1994 ... 93.1
20 Trevor Hoffman, 1999 ... 93.0
21 John Franco, 1988 ... 92.9
Billy Wagner, 1999 ... 92.9
Troy Percival, 2001 ... 92.9
Eric Gagne, 2002 ... 92.9
25 Trevor Hoffman, 2002 ... 92.7
26 Clay Carroll, 1972 ... 92.5
Kazuhiro Sasaki, 2000 ... 92.5
28 Mudcat Grant, 1970 ... 92.3
Tom Burgmeier, 1980 ... 92.3
Dave Righetti, 1990 ... 92.3
Rod Beck, 1993 ... 92.3
Troy Percival, 1996 ... 92.3
33 Mike Williams, 2002 ... 92.0
34 Tom Henke, 1992 ... 91.9
35 Bryan Harvey, 1993 ... 91.8
Mariano Rivera, 1999 ... 91.8
Antonio Alfonseca, 2000 ... 91.8
John Smoltz, 2003 ... 91.8
39 Rick Camp, 1980 ... 91.7
Dan Quisenberry, 1980 ... 91.7
Mark Davis, 1989 ... 91.7
Matt Anderson, 2001 ... 91.7
43 John Wetteland, 1996 ... 91.5
Roberto Hernandez, 1999 ... 91.5
45 Tom Henke, 1991 ... 91.4
Bob Wickman, 2001 ... 91.4
47 Todd Jones, 2000 ... 91.3
Jose Mesa, 2001 ... 91.3
Dan Kolb, 2003 ... 91.3
50 Eddie Guardado, 2003 ... 91.1

Blown Saves

1 Rollie Fingers, 1976 ... 14
Bruce Sutter, 1978 ... 14
Bob Stanley, 1983 ... 14
Ron Davis, 1984 ... 14
5 John Hiller, 1976 ... 13
Rich Gossage, 1983 ... 13
Jeff Reardon, 1986 ... 13
Dan Plesac, 1987 ... 13
Dave Righetti, 1987 ... 13
10 Mike Marshall, 1973 ... 12
Mike Marshall, 1974 ... 12
Enrique Romo, 1978 ... 12
Bruce Sutter, 1985 ... 12
Dan Quisenberry, 1985 ... 12
Matt Young, 1986 ... 12
Lee Smith, 1987 ... 12
Duane Ward, 1989 ... 12
Mark Leiter, 1998 ... 12
19 Ron Perranoski, 1969 ... 11
Dick Selma, 1970 ... 11
Darold Knowles, 1970 ... 11
Ron Perranoski, 1970 ... 11
Rollie Fingers, 1977 ... 11
Bill Campbell, 1977 ... 11
Bill Campbell, 1978 ... 11
Kent Tekulve, 1980 ... 11
Ed Farmer, 1980 ... 11
Joey McLaughlin, 1983 ... 11
Rich Gossage, 1984 ... 11
Rich Gossage, 1986 ... 11
Greg Harris, 1986 ... 11
Lance McCullers, 1987 ... 11
Tim Burke, 1989 ... 11
Mitch Williams, 1989 ... 11
Jeff Reardon, 1989 ... 11
Greg McMichael, 1997 ... 11
Norm Charlton, 1997 ... 11
Scott Radinsky, 1998 ... 11
Rick Aguilera, 1998 ... 11
40 50 players tied ... 10

Innings Pitched

1 Will White, 1879 ... 680.0
2 Charley Radbourn, 1884 ... 678.2
3 Guy Hecker, 1884 ... 670.2
4 Jim McCormick, 1880 ... 657.2
5 Jim Galvin, 1883 ... 656.1
6 Jim Galvin, 1884 ... 636.1
7 Charley Radbourn, 1883 ... 632.1
8 John Clarkson, 1885 ... 623.0
9 Jim Devlin, 1876 ... 622.0
Bill Hutchison, 1892 ... 622.0
11 John Clarkson, 1889 ... 620.0
12 Tim Keefe, 1883 ... 619.0
13 Bill Hutchison, 1890 ... 603.0
14 Jim McCormick, 1882 ... 595.2
15 John Ward, 1880 ... 595.0
16 Jim Galvin, 1879 ... 593.0
17 Lee Richmond, 1880 ... 590.2
18 Matt Kilroy, 1887 ... 589.1
19 Toad Ramsey, 1886 ... 588.2
20 John Ward, 1879 ... 587.0
Charlie Buffinton, 1884 ... 587.0
22 Silver King, 1888 ... 584.2
23 Matt Kilroy, 1886 ... 583.0
24 Ed Morris, 1885 ... 581.0
25 Will White, 1883 ... 577.0
26 Mickey Welch, 1880 ... 574.0
27 George Bradley, 1876 ... 573.0
28 Jim McCormick, 1884 ... 569.0
29 Tony Mullane, 1884 ... 567.0
30 Toad Ramsey, 1887 ... 561.0
Bill Hutchison, 1891 ... 561.0
32 Jim Devlin, 1877 ... 559.0
33 Mickey Welch, 1884 ... 557.1
34 Tommy Bond, 1879 ... 555.1
Ed Morris, 1886 ... 555.1
36 Jim Whitney, 1881 ... 552.1
37 Amos Rusie, 1890 ... 548.2
38 Jim McCormick, 1879 ... 546.1
39 Dupee Shaw, 1884 ... 543.1
40 Amos Rusie, 1892 ... 541.0
41 Hardie Henderson, 1885 ... 539.1
42 John Coleman, 1883 ... 538.1
43 Bill Sweeney, 1884 ... 538.0
44 Larry Corcoran, 1880 ... 536.1
45 Tim Keefe, 1886 ... 535.0
46 Tommy Bond, 1878 ... 532.2
Jersey Bakely, 1888 ... 532.2
48 Tony Mullane, 1886 ... 529.2
49 Al Spalding, 1876 ... 528.2
50 Jim McCormick, 1881 ... 526.0
51 Billy Taylor, 1884 ... 523.0
John Clarkson, 1887 ... 523.0
53 Tommy Bond, 1877 ... 521.0
54 Ed Seward, 1888 ... 518.2
55 Will White, 1880 ... 517.1
56 Larry Corcoran, 1884 ... 516.2
57 Bobby Mathews, 1876 ... 516.0
58 Jim Whitney, 1883 ... 514.0
59 Mark Baldwin, 1889 ... 513.2
60 Terry Larkin, 1879 ... 513.1
61 Larry McKeon, 1884 ... 512.0
62 Charley Radbourn, 1886 ... 509.1
63 Sadie McMahon, 1890 ... 509.0
64 Terry Larkin, 1878 ... 506.0
Kid Gleason, 1890 ... 506.0
66 Dave Foutz, 1886 ... 504.0
67 Frank Mountain, 1883 ... 503.0
Sadie McMahon, 1891 ... 503.0
69 Terry Larkin, 1877 ... 501.0
70 Hugh Daily, 1884 ... 500.2
71 Amos Rusie, 1891 ... 500.1
72 Mickey Welch, 1886 ... 500.0
73 Jack Lynch, 1884 ... 496.0
74 George Derby, 1881 ... 494.2
75 Bob Barr, 1890 ... 493.1
76 Tommy Bond, 1880 ... 493.0
77 Charlie Sweeney, 1884 ... 492.0
Mickey Welch, 1885 ... 492.0
Mark Baldwin, 1890 ... 492.0
80 Phenomenal Smith, 1887 ... 491.1
81 George Bradley, 1879 ... 487.0
Lady Baldwin, 1886 ... 487.0
83 John Clarkson, 1888 ... 483.1
84 Tim Keefe, 1884 ... 483.0
85 Bob Caruthers, 1885 ... 482.1
86 Amos Rusie, 1893 ... 482.0
87 Henry Porter, 1885 ... 481.2
88 Matt Kilroy, 1889 ... 480.2
89 Will White, 1882 ... 480.0
Guy Hecker, 1885 ... 480.0
Ed Morris, 1888 ... 480.0
92 Tim Keefe, 1887 ... 476.2
93 Adonis Terry, 1884 ... 476.0
94 Ed Beatin, 1890 ... 474.1
95 Jim Galvin, 1881 ... 474.0
Henry Porter, 1888 ... 474.0
97 Larry Corcoran, 1883 ... 473.2
98 Ed Seward, 1887 ... 470.2
99 Gus Weyhing, 1892 ... 469.2
100 Guy Hecker, 1883 ... 469.0

Innings Pitched by era

1988-2003

1 Dave Stewart, 1988 ... 275.2
2 Roger Clemens, 1991 ... 271.1
3 Mark Gubicza, 1988 ... 269.2
4 Greg Maddux, 1992 ... 268.0
5 Orel Hershiser, 1988 ... 267.0
Dave Stewart, 1990 ... 267.0
Greg Maddux, 1993 ... 267.0
8 Kevin Brown, 1992 ... 265.2
Pat Hentgen, 1996 ... 265.2
10 Roger Clemens, 1988 ... 264.0

1973-1987

1 Wilbur Wood, 1973 ... 359.1
2 Gaylord Perry, 1973 ... 344.0
3 Phil Niekro, 1979 ... 342.0
4 Phil Niekro, 1978 ... 334.1
5 Nolan Ryan, 1974 ... 332.2
6 Phil Niekro, 1977 ... 330.1
7 Fergie Jenkins, 1974 ... 328.1
8 Catfish Hunter, 1975 ... 328.0
9 Nolan Ryan, 1973 ... 326.0
10 Bert Blyleven, 1973 ... 325.0

1961-1972

1 Wilbur Wood, 1972 ... 376.2
2 Mickey Lolich, 1971 ... 376.0
3 Steve Carlton, 1972 ... 346.1
4 Gaylord Perry, 1972 ... 342.2
5 Denny McLain, 1968 ... 336.0
6 Sandy Koufax, 1965 ... 335.2
7 Wilbur Wood, 1971 ... 334.0
8 Gaylord Perry, 1970 ... 328.2
9 Mickey Lolich, 1972 ... 327.1
10 Juan Marichal, 1968 ... 326.0

1943-1960

1 Bob Feller, 1946 ... 371.1
2 Dizzy Trout, 1944 ... 352.1
3 Robin Roberts, 1953 ... 346.2
4 Robin Roberts, 1954 ... 336.2
5 Robin Roberts, 1952 ... 330.0
6 Robin Roberts, 1951 ... 315.0
7 Johnny Sain, 1948 ... 314.2
8 Bob Friend, 1956 ... 314.1
9 Hal Newhouser, 1945 ... 313.1
10 Bill Voiselle, 1944 ... 312.2

1921-1942

1 George Uhle, 1923 ... 357.2
2 Red Faber, 1922 ... 352.0
3 Urban Shocker, 1922 ... 348.0
4 Bob Feller, 1941 ... 343.0
5 Carl Mays, 1921 ... 336.2
6 Red Faber, 1921 ... 330.2
Burleigh Grimes, 1928 ... 330.2
8 Bobo Newsom, 1938 ... 329.2
9 Wilbur Cooper, 1921 ... 327.0
Burleigh Grimes, 1923 ... 327.0
Alvin Crowder, 1932 ... 327.0

1901-1920

1 Ed Walsh, 1908 ... 464.0
2 Jack Chesbro, 1904 ... 454.2
3 Joe McGinnity, 1903 ... 434.0
4 Ed Walsh, 1907 ... 422.1
5 Vic Willis, 1902 ... 410.0
6 Joe McGinnity, 1904 ... 408.0
7 Ed Walsh, 1912 ... 393.0
8 Dave Davenport, 1915 ... 392.2
9 Christy Mathewson, 1908 ... 390.2
10 Jack Powell, 1904 ... 390.1

1893-1900

1 Amos Rusie, 1893 ... 482.0
2 Ted Breitenstein, 1894 ... 447.1
3 Pink Hawley, 1895 ... 444.1
4 Amos Rusie, 1894 ... 444.0
5 Ted Breitenstein, 1895 ... 438.2
6 Frank Killen, 1896 ... 432.1
7 Kid Nichols, 1893 ... 425.0
8 Cy Young, 1893 ... 422.2
9 Jouett Meekin, 1894 ... 418.0
10 Frank Killen, 1893 ... 415.0

1876-1892

1 Will White, 1879 ... 680.0
2 Charley Radbourn, 1884 ... 678.2
3 Guy Hecker, 1884 ... 670.2
4 Jim McCormick, 1880 ... 657.2
5 Jim Galvin, 1883 ... 656.1
6 Jim Galvin, 1884 ... 636.1
7 Charley Radbourn, 1883 ... 632.1
8 John Clarkson, 1885 ... 623.0
9 Jim Devlin, 1876 ... 622.0
Bill Hutchison, 1892 ... 622.0

Fewest Hits/Game

1 Nolan Ryan, 1972 ....5.26
2 Luis Tiant, 1968 ....5.30
3 Nolan Ryan, 1991 ....5.31
4 Pedro Martinez, 2000........5.31
5 Ed Reulbach, 1906 ....5.33
6 Dutch Leonard, 1914 ....5.57
7 Carl Lundgren, 1907 ....5.65
8 Sid Fernandez, 1985........5.71
9 Tommy Byrne, 1949 ....5.74
10 Dave McNally, 1968 ....5.77
11 Sandy Koufax, 1965..........5.79
12 Russ Ford, 1910...............5.83
13 Tim Keefe, 1880...............5.83
14 Hideo Nomo, 1995......5.83
15 Al Downing, 1963..............5.84
16 Herb Score, 1956..............5.85
17 Bob Gibson, 1968 ....5.85
18 Sam McDowell, 1965 ....5.87
19 Ed Walsh, 1910.................5.89
20 Pedro Martinez, 1997........5.89
21 Mike Scott, 1986 ....5.95
22 Mario Soto, 1980..............5.96
23 Floyd Youmans, 1986.........5.96
24 Nolan Ryan, 1977 ....5.96
25 Nolan Ryan, 1974 ....5.98
26 Nolan Ryan, 1981 ....5.98
27 Nolan Ryan, 1986 ....6.02
28 Sam McDowell, 1966 ....6.02
29 Vida Blue, 1971................6.03
30 Walter Johnson, 1913 ....6.03
31 Nolan Ryan, 1990 ....6.04
32 Grover Alexander, 1915 ...6.05
33 Sam McDowell, 1968 ....6.06
34 Joe Horlen, 1964..............6.07
35 Andy Messersmith, 1969 .6.08
36 Nolan Ryan, 1989 ....6.09
37 Stan Coveleski, 1917 ....6.09
38 Catfish Hunter, 1972 ....6.09
39 Nolan Ryan, 1976 ....6.11
40 Sid Fernandez, 1988.........6.11
41 Bob Turley, 1957 ....6.12
42 Bob Turley, 1955 ....6.13
43 Don Sutton, 1972...............6.14
44 Nolan Ryan, 1983 ....6.14
45 Ron Guidry, 1978 ....6.15
46 Mordecai Brown, 1908.....6.17
47 Sandy Koufax, 1963..........6.19
48 Randy Johnson, 1997 ....6.21
49 Jack Pfiester, 1906............6.21
50 Sandy Koufax, 1964...........6.22
51 Roger Nelson, 1972 ....6.23
52 Herb Score, 1955..............6.26
53 Cy Morgan, 1909 ....6.26
54 Dean Chance, 1964 ....6.27
55 Christy Mathewson, 1909.....6.28
J.R. Richard, 1978 ....6.28
57 Art Fromme, 1909 ....6.28
58 Greg Maddux, 1995....6.31
59 Walter Johnson, 1912 ......6.32
60 Kerry Wood, 1998.........6.32
61 Jack Coombs, 1910 ....6.32
62 Rube Waddell, 1905 ....6.33
63 Vean Gregg, 1911 ....6.33
64 Jeff Robinson, 1988...........6.33
65 Larry Cheney, 1916............6.33
66 Sonny Siebert, 1968 ....6.33
67 Allie Reynolds, 1943 ....6.34
68 Roger Clemens, 1986........6.34
69 Willie Mitchell, 1913 ....6.35
70 Jose DeLeon, 1989............6.36
71 Pascual Perez, 1988 ....6.37
72 Walter Johnson, 1910 ....6.37
73 Dave Boswell, 1966 ....6.38
74 Harry Krause, 1909............6.38
75 Dutch Leonard, 1915 ....6.38
76 Eddie Cicotte, 1917...........6.39
77 Wayne Simpson, 1970.....6.39
78 Al Leiter, 1996 ....6.39
79 Babe Ruth, 1916...............6.40
80 Spec Shea, 1947 ....6.40
81 Jim Bibby, 1973................6.42
82 Ed Reulbach, 1905 ....6.42
83 Gaylord Perry, 1974 ....6.42
84 Eddie Fisher, 1965 ....6.42
85 Addie Joss, 1908 ....6.42
86 Mordecai Brown, 1906.......6.43
87 Luis Tiant, 1972 ....6.44
88 Frank Smith, 1908.............6.44
89 Dwight Gooden, 1985 ......6.44
90 Orval Overall, 1909...........6.44
91 Sid Fernandez, 1989.........6.44
92 Denny McLain, 1968 ....6.46
93 Mordecai Brown, 1909.....6.46
94 Ray Caldwell, 1914...........6.46
95 Fred Toney, 1915..............6.47
96 Gary Peters, 1967.............6.47
97 Christy Mathewson, 1908.....6.47
98 Bob Turley, 1954 ....6.48
99 Roger Clemens, 1998.......6.48
100 Kerry Wood, 2003.......6.48

Fewest Hits/Game by era

1988-2003

1 Nolan Ryan, 1991 ....5.31
2 Hideo Nomo, 1995......5.83
3 Nolan Ryan, 1990 ....6.04
4 Nolan Ryan, 1989 ....6.09
5 Sid Fernandez, 1988........6.11
6 Greg Maddux, 1995....6.31
7 Jeff Robinson, 1988..........6.33
8 Jose DeLeon, 1989...........6.36
9 Pascual Perez, 1988 ....6.37
10 Al Leiter, 1996 ....6.39

1973-1987

1 Sid Fernandez, 1985........5.71
2 Mike Scott, 1986 ....5.95
3 Mario Soto, 1980..............5.96
4 Floyd Youmans, 1986.......5.96
5 Nolan Ryan, 1977 ....5.96
6 Nolan Ryan, 1974 ....5.98
7 Nolan Ryan, 1981 ....5.98
8 Nolan Ryan, 1986 ....6.02
9 Nolan Ryan, 1976 ....6.11
10 Nolan Ryan, 1983 ....6.14

1961-1972

1 Nolan Ryan, 1972 ....5.26
2 Luis Tiant, 1968 ....5.30
3 Dave McNally, 1968 ....5.77
4 Sandy Koufax, 1965..........5.79
5 Al Downing, 1963..............5.84
6 Bob Gibson, 1968 ....5.85
7 Sam McDowell, 1965 ....5.87
8 Sam McDowell, 1966 ....6.02
9 Vida Blue, 1971................6.03
10 Sam McDowell, 1968 ....6.06

1943-1960

1 Tommy Byrne, 1949.........5.74
2 Herb Score, 1956..............5.85
3 Bob Turley, 1957 ....6.12
4 Bob Turley, 1955 ....6.13
5 Herb Score, 1955..............6.26
6 Allie Reynolds, 1943 ....6.34
7 Spec Shea, 1947 ....6.40
8 Bob Turley, 1954 ....6.48
9 Sam Jones, 1955 ....6.52
10 Bob Turley, 1958 ....6.53

1921-1942

1 Mort Cooper, 1942 ....6.69
2 Hal Newhouser, 1942.......6.71
3 Johnny Vander Meer, 1941...6.84
4 Bob Feller, 1940...............6.88
5 Bob Feller, 1939 ....6.89
6 Hal Schumacher, 1933.....6.92
7 Johnny Vander Meer, 1942...6.93
8 Dazzy Vance, 1924 ....6.95
9 Whit Wyatt, 1941..............6.96
10 Bucky Walters, 1939 ....7.05

1901-1920

1 Ed Reulbach, 1906 ....5.33
2 Dutch Leonard, 1914 ....5.57
3 Carl Lundgren, 1907.........5.65
4 Russ Ford, 1910...............5.83
5 Ed Walsh, 1910................5.89
6 Walter Johnson, 1913 ....6.03
7 Grover Alexander, 1915 ...6.05
8 Stan Coveleski, 1917 ....6.09
9 Mordecai Brown, 1908.....6.17
10 Jack Pfiester, 1906...........6.21

1893-1900

1 Vic Willis, 1899.................7.28
2 Kid Nichols, 1898..............7.33
3 Rube Waddell, 1900 ....7.59
4 Vic Willis, 1898.................7.64
5 Ted Lewis, 1898 ....7.67
6 Jay Hughes, 1899 ....7.71
7 Al Maul, 1898....................7.77
8 Doc McJames, 1898 ....7.87
9 Cy Seymour, 1898.............7.90
10 Jay Hughes, 1898 ....8.02

1876-1892

1 Tim Keefe, 1880...............5.83
2 Guy Hecker, 1882 ....6.49
3 Tim Keefe, 1888 ....6.57
4 Charlie Sweeney, 1884 .....6.59
5 Adonis Terry, 1888 ....6.69
6 Silver King, 1888...............6.70
7 Frank Knauss, 1890 ....6.73
8 Ed Seward, 1888 ....6.73
9 Tim Keefe, 1885 ....6.75
10 Tony Mullane, 1892...........6.77

Fewest HR Allowed/Game by era

1988-2003

1 Greg Maddux, 1994....0.18
2 Joe Magrane, 1989..........0.19
3 Greg Maddux, 1992....0.24
4 Tom Glavine, 1992......0.24
5 Bob Walk, 1988.................0.25
6 Danny Jackson, 1992 ......0.27
7 Roger Clemens, 1990........0.28
8 Bob Ojeda, 1988 ....0.28
9 Dwight Gooden, 1988 ......0.29
10 Juan Guzman, 1992.........0.30

1973-1987

1 Nolan Ryan, 1981 ....0.12
2 Reggie Cleveland, 1976...0.16
3 Bill Gullickson, 1981 ....0.17
4 Ron Reed, 1975................0.18
5 Burt Hooton, 1981 ....0.19
6 Lary Sorensen, 1981 ....0.19
7 Randy Jones, 1978 ....0.21
8 Bruce Berenyi, 1981 ....0.21
9 Ken Brett, 1976.................0.22
10 Al Fitzmorris, 1976...........0.25

1961-1972

1 Bob Veale, 1965...............0.17
2 Bill Singer, 1967 ....0.22
3 Claude Osteen, 1966 ....0.22
4 Dean Chance, 1964 ....0.23
5 Bob Veale, 1964................0.26
6 Tommie Sisk, 1967............0.26
Don Sutton, 1968..............0.26
8 Bob Moose, 1968...............0.26
9 Andy Messersmith, 1972 .....0.27
10 Sam McDowell, 1965.......0.30

1943-1960

1 Ewell Blackwell, 1946 ....0.05
2 Rube Melton, 1944...........0.05
3 Stubby Overmire, 1944 ....0.09
4 Eddie Smith, 1943 ....0.10
5 Jack Kramer, 1944 ....0.11
6 Allie Reynolds, 1944 ....0.11
7 Marino Pieretti, 1945.........0.12
8 Oscar Judd, 1943..............0.12
9 Max Lanier, 1943..............0.13
10 Early Wynn, 1944 ....0.13

1921-1942

1 Allen Sothoron, 1921 ....0.00
2 Slim Harriss, 1926 ....0.00
3 Eppa Rixey, 1921 ....0.03
4 Sam Jones, 1921 ....0.03
5 Stan Coveleski, 1926 ....0.04
6 Babe Adams, 1922 ....0.05
7 Dolf Luque, 1923 ....0.06
8 George Mogridge, 1924 ...0.08
9 Herb Pennock, 1928 ....0.09
10 Eppa Rixey, 1923 ....0.09

1901-1920

1 Walter Johnson, 1916 ......0.00
2 Jack Coombs, 1910 ....0.00
3 Ed Killian, 1904 ....0.00
4 Babe Ruth, 1916...............0.00
5 Vic Willis, 1906.................0.00
6 Rube Vickers, 1908...........0.00
7 Ed Killian, 1905 ....0.00
8 Jake Weimer, 1906...........0.00
9 Frank Smith, 1905.............0.00
10 Cy Morgan, 1910 ....0.00

1893-1900

1 Billy Rhines, 1898 ....0.00
2 Brownie Foreman, 1895...0.00
3 Clark Griffith, 1898............0.03
4 Bill Hoffer, 1896................0.03
5 Chick Fraser, 1899 ....0.03
6 Jerry Nops, 1899 ....0.03
7 Ed Doheny, 1898...............0.04
8 Harry Howell, 1899 ....0.04
9 Ned Garvin, 1899..............0.05
10 Pink Hawley, 1896............0.05

1876-1892

1 Jersey Bakely, 1884 ....0.00
2 Lon Knight, 1876...............0.00
3 Frank Hankinson, 1879 ....0.00
4 Candy Cummings, 1876 ..0.00
5 Denny Driscoll, 1882.........0.00
6 Joe Blong, 1877 ....0.00
7 Ren Deagle, 1883 ....0.00
8 Bobby Mathews, 1877 .....0.00
John Kirby, 1885...............0.00
10 John Fox, 1881 ....0.00

Walks

1 Amos Rusie, 1890.............289
2 Mark Baldwin, 1889 274
3 Amos Rusie, 1892.............270
4 Amos Rusie, 1891.............262
5 Mark Baldwin, 1890 249
6 Jack Stivetts, 1891 232
7 Mark Baldwin, 1891 227
8 Phil Knell, 1891 226
9 Bob Barr, 1890...................219
10 Amos Rusie, 1893.............218
11 Cy Seymour, 1898.............213
12 Gus Weyhing, 1889...........212
13 Ed Crane, 1890.................208
Bob Feller, 1938 208
15 Toad Ramsey, 1886 207
16 Elton Chamberlain, 1891 206
17 Mike Morrison, 1887 205
18 Henry Gruber, 1890 204
Nolan Ryan, 1977 204
20 Ed Crane, 1891 203
John Clarkson, 1889.........203
22 Nolan Ryan, 1974 202
23 Bert Cunningham, 1890....201
24 Amos Rusie, 1894.............200
25 Bill Hutchison, 1890 199
26 Mark Baldwin, 1892 194
Bob Feller, 1941 194
28 Bobo Newsom, 1938 192
29 Ted Breitenstein, 1894 191
30 Bill Hutchison, 1892 190
31 Ed Crane, 1892.................189
Tony Mullane, 1893...........189
33 Tony Mullane, 1891 187
Kid Gleason, 1893 187
35 Ed Beatin, 1890 186
36 Sam Jones, 1955...............185
37 Tom Vickery, 1890.............184
38 Nolan Ryan, 1976 183
39 Matt Kilroy, 1886 182
Frank Killen, 1892 182
Ted Breitenstein, 1895 182
42 Willie McGill, 1893 181
Bob Harmon, 1911 181
Bob Turley, 1954 181
45 Jack Stivetts, 1890 179
Gus Weyhing, 1890...........179
Tommy Byrne, 1949 179
48 Bill Hutchison, 1891 178
49 Bob Turley, 1955 177
50 Phenomenal Smith, 1887 .176
Jouett Meekin, 1894...........176
52 George Hemming, 1893....175
53 Silver King, 1892...............171
Jack Stivetts, 1892 171
Bump Hadley, 1932...........171
56 Elton Chamberlain, 1892 170
Ed Stein, 1894 170
Cy Seymour, 1899.............170
59 Gus Weyhing, 1892...........168
Brickyard Kennedy, 1893.......168
Cy Seymour, 1897.............168
Elmer Myers, 1916.............168
63 Toad Ramsey, 1887 167
Gus Weyhing, 1887...........167
Darby O'Brien, 1889 167
Kid Gleason, 1890 167
Bill Daley, 1890 167
Bobo Newsom, 1937 167
69 Tony Mullane, 1886...........166
Sadie McMahon, 1890......166
Phil Knell, 1890..................166
Chick Fraser, 1896 166
73 Elton Chamberlain, 1889 165
Dan Casey, 1890................165
Kid Gleason, 1891 165
Weldon Wyckoff, 1915 165
77 Earl Moore, 1911 164
Phil Niekro, 1977................164
79 Mickey Welch, 1886 163
Silver King, 1890................163
Willie McGill, 1891 163
George Haddock, 1892......163
83 Johnny Vander Meer, 1943 162
Nolan Ryan, 1973 162
85 Hank O'Day, 1890..............161
John Sowders, 1890 161
Kid Carsey, 1891................161
Gus Weyhing, 1891............161
89 Tommy Byrne, 1950...........160
90 George Hemming, 1894....159
Amos Rusie, 1895..............159
Marty O'Toole, 1912...........159
93 Ed Doheny, 1899...............158
Joe Coleman, 1974............158
95 Matt Kilroy, 1887 157
Bert Cunningham, 1888....157
Pink Hawley, 1896..............157
Grover Lowdermilk, 1915......157
Nolan Ryan, 1972 157
100 4 players tied 156

Strikeouts

1 Matt Kilroy, 1886 513
2 Toad Ramsey, 1886 499
3 Hugh Daily, 1884...............483
4 Dupee Shaw, 1884............451
5 Charley Radbourn, 1884...441
6 Charlie Buffinton, 1884 417
7 Guy Hecker, 1884 385
8 Nolan Ryan, 1973 383
9 Sandy Koufax, 1965..........382
10 Bill Sweeney, 1884 374
11 Randy Johnson, 2001..372
12 Jim Galvin, 1884 369
13 Mark Baldwin, 1889 368
14 Nolan Ryan, 1974 367
15 Randy Johnson, 1999..364
16 Tim Keefe, 1883.................359
17 Toad Ramsey, 1887 355
18 Rube Waddell, 1904 349
19 Bob Feller, 1946 348
20 Randy Johnson, 2000..347
21 Hardie Henderson, 1884...346
22 Jim Whitney, 1883..............345
Mickey Welch, 1884...........345
24 Jim McCormick, 1884 343
25 Amos Rusie, 1890..............341
Nolan Ryan, 1977 341
27 Charlie Sweeney, 1884 337
Amos Rusie, 1891 337
29 Tim Keefe, 1888.................335
30 Tim Keefe, 1884.................334
Randy Johnson, 2002..334
32 Randy Johnson, 1998..329
Nolan Ryan, 1972 329
34 Nolan Ryan, 1976 327
35 Ed Morris, 1886 326
36 Tony Mullane, 1884 325
Sam McDowell, 1965 325
38 Lady Baldwin, 1886............323
39 Curt Schilling, 1997.....319
40 Sandy Koufax, 1966...........317
41 Curt Schilling, 2002.....316
42 Charley Radbourn, 1883...315
43 Bill Hutchison, 1892 314
44 John Clarkson, 1886 313
Walter Johnson, 1910 313
J.R. Richard, 1979 313
Pedro Martinez, 1999 ..313
48 Steve Carlton, 1972 310
49 Larry McKeon, 1884 308
John Clarkson, 1885..........308
Mickey Lolich, 1971 308
Randy Johnson, 1993..308
53 Sandy Koufax, 1963..........306
Mike Scott, 1986 306
55 Pedro Martinez, 1997 ..305
56 Amos Rusie, 1892..............304
Sam McDowell, 1970.........304
58 Walter Johnson, 1912 303
J.R. Richard, 1978 303
60 Ed Morris, 1884 302
Rube Waddell, 1903 302
62 Vida Blue, 1971..................301
Nolan Ryan, 1989 301
64 Curt Schilling, 1998.....300
65 Ed Morris, 1885 298
66 Tim Keefe, 1886.................297
67 Randy Johnson, 1995..294
68 Curt Schilling, 2001.....293
69 Jack Lynch, 1884 292
Roger Clemens, 1997 ..292
71 Sadie McMahon, 1890.......291
Roger Clemens, 1988..291
Randy Johnson, 1997..291
74 Bill Hutchison, 1890 289
Jack Stivetts, 1890 289
Tom Seaver, 1971 289
77 Rube Waddell, 1905 287
78 Bobby Mathews, 1884 286
Bobby Mathews, 1885 286
Steve Carlton, 1980 286
Steve Carlton, 1982 286
82 Billy Taylor, 1884 284
John Clarkson, 1889 284
Pedro Martinez, 2000 ..284
85 Dave Foutz, 1886...............283
Sam McDowell, 1968 283
Tom Seaver, 1970 283
88 Denny McLain, 1968...........280
89 Jim Galvin, 1883.................279
Sam McDowell, 1969 279
91 Bob Veale, 1965 276
Dwight Gooden, 1984 276
John Smoltz, 1996.......276
94 Hal Newhouser, 1946........275
Steve Carlton, 1983 275
96 Bob Gibson, 1970 274
Fergie Jenkins, 1970..........274
Mario Soto, 1982...............274
99 Fergie Jenkins, 1969.........273
100 3 players tied 272

Strikeouts/Game

1 Randy Johnson, 2001 ...... 13.41
2 Pedro Martinez, 1999 ...... 13.20
3 Kerry Wood, 1998 ..... 12.58
4 Randy Johnson, 2000 ...... 12.56
5 Randy Johnson, 1995 ...... 12.35
6 Randy Johnson, 1997 ...... 12.30
7 Randy Johnson, 1998 ...... 12.12
8 Randy Johnson, 1999 ...... 12.06
9 Pedro Martinez, 2000 ...... 11.78
10 Randy Johnson, 2002 ...... 11.56
11 Nolan Ryan, 1987 .... 11.48
12 Dwight Gooden, 1984 .... 11.39
13 Pedro Martinez, 1997 ...... 11.37
14 Kerry Wood, 2003 ..... 11.35
15 Nolan Ryan, 1989 .... 11.32
16 Curt Schilling, 1997 ...... 11.29
17 Kerry Wood, 2001 ..... 11.20
18 Hideo Nomo, 1995 .... 11.10
19 Curt Schilling, 2002 ...... 10.97
20 Randy Johnson, 1993 ...... 10.86
21 Pedro Martinez, 2002 ...... 10.79
22 Sam McDowell, 1965 ..... 10.71
23 Randy Johnson, 1994 ...... 10.67
24 Nolan Ryan, 1973 .... 10.57
25 Nolan Ryan, 1991 .... 10.56
26 Sandy Koufax, 1962 .... 10.55
27 Mark Prior, 2003 .... 10.43
28 Nolan Ryan, 1972 .... 10.43
29 Sam McDowell, 1966 ..... 10.42
30 Roger Clemens, 1998 ...... 10.39
31 Curt Schilling, 2003 .... 10.39
32 Nolan Ryan, 1976 .... 10.35
33 Randy Johnson, 1992 ...... 10.31
34 Curt Schilling, 2001 .... 10.27
35 Nolan Ryan, 1977 .... 10.26
36 David Cone, 1997 ..... 10.25
37 Sandy Koufax, 1965 .... 10.24
38 Nolan Ryan, 1990 .... 10.24
39 Randy Johnson, 1991 ...... 10.19
40 Bartolo Colon, 2000 .... 10.15
41 Sandy Koufax, 1960 .... 10.13
42 Hideo Nomo, 1997 .... 10.11
43 Curt Schilling, 1998 .... 10.05
44 Mike Scott, 1986 .... 10.00
45 Hideo Nomo, 2001 .... 10.00
46 Rick Ankiel, 2000 .... 9.98
47 Nolan Ryan, 1978 .... 9.97
48 Roger Clemens, 1997 .... 9.95
49 Pedro Martinez, 2003 .... 9.93
50 Nolan Ryan, 1974 .... 9.93
51 Roger Clemens, 1988 .... 9.92
52 David Cone, 1990 ...... 9.91
53 J.R. Richard, 1978 .... 9.90
54 Andy Benes, 1994 .... 9.87
55 Nolan Ryan, 1986 .... 9.81
56 John Smoltz, 1996 ...... 9.79
57 Herb Score, 1955 .... 9.70
58 Pedro Martinez, 1998 .... 9.67
59 Nolan Ryan, 1984 .... 9.65
60 J.R. Richard, 1979 .... 9.64
61 Roger Clemens, 2002 .... 9.60
62 Mario Soto, 1982 .... 9.57
63 Tom Griffin, 1969 .... 9.56
64 Roger Clemens, 1996 .... 9.53
65 Jim Maloney, 1963 .... 9.53
66 Jason Schmidt, 2002 .... 9.52
67 Sid Fernandez, 1985 .... 9.51
68 Herb Score, 1956 .... 9.49
69 Sandy Koufax, 1961 .... 9.47
70 Sam McDowell, 1968 .... 9.47
71 Matt Clement, 2002 ..... 9.44
72 David Cone, 1992 .... 9.41
73 Frank Tanana, 1975 .... 9.41
74 Javier Vazquez, 2003 .... 9.40
75 Don Wilson, 1969 .... 9.40
76 Bob Veale, 1965 .... 9.34
77 Nolan Ryan, 1988 .... 9.33
78 David Cone, 1991 .... 9.32
79 John Smoltz, 1998 ...... 9.29
80 Luis Tiant, 1967 .... 9.22
81 Hideo Nomo, 1996 ...... 9.22
82 Pedro Martinez, 1996 .... 9.22
83 Brandon Duckworth, 2002 .. 9.22
84 Mark Langston, 1986 .... 9.21
85 Luis Tiant, 1968 .... 9.20
86 Dave Boswell, 1966 .... 9.19
87 Sam McDowell, 1964 .... 9.19
88 Kerry Wood, 2002 .... 9.14
89 Sonny Siebert, 1965 .... 9.11
90 Sid Fernandez, 1988 .... 9.10
91 Tom Seaver, 1971 .... 9.08
92 Sid Fernandez, 1990 .... 9.08
93 David Cone, 1998 .... 9.06
94 Dennis Eckersley, 1976 .... 9.03
95 John Smoltz, 1995 .... 9.02
96 Jason Schmidt, 2003 .... 9.01
97 Nolan Ryan, 1979 .... 9.01
98 Sandy Koufax, 1964 .... 9.00
Darryl Kile, 1996 .... 9.00
Kevin Brown, 1998 ..... 9.00

Earned Run Average

1 Tim Keefe, 1880 .... 0.86
2 Dutch Leonard, 1914 .... 0.96
3 Mordecai Brown, 1906 ..... 1.04
4 Bob Gibson, 1968 .... 1.12
5 Christy Mathewson, 1909 ..... 1.14
6 Walter Johnson, 1913 ...... 1.14
7 Jack Pfiester, 1907 .... 1.15
8 Addie Joss, 1908 .... 1.16
9 Carl Lundgren, 1907 .... 1.17
10 Denny Driscoll, 1882 .... 1.21
11 Grover Alexander, 1915 ... 1.22
12 George Bradley, 1876 ...... 1.23
13 Cy Young, 1908 .... 1.26
14 Ed Walsh, 1910 .... 1.27
15 Walter Johnson, 1918 ...... 1.27
16 Christy Mathewson, 1905 ..... 1.28
17 Jack Taylor, 1902 .... 1.29
18 Guy Hecker, 1882 .... 1.30
19 Jack Coombs, 1910 .... 1.30
20 Mordecai Brown, 1909 ...... 1.31
21 Walter Johnson, 1910 ...... 1.36
22 George Bradley, 1880 ...... 1.38
23 Charley Radbourn, 1884 .. 1.38
24 Walter Johnson, 1912 ...... 1.39
25 Mordecai Brown, 1907 ..... 1.39
26 Harry Krause, 1909 .... 1.39
27 Ed Walsh, 1909 .... 1.41
28 Ed Walsh, 1908 .... 1.42
29 Ed Reulbach, 1905 .... 1.42
30 Orval Overall, 1909 .... 1.42
31 Christy Mathewson, 1908 ..... 1.43
32 Fred Anderson, 1917 .... 1.44
33 Mordecai Brown, 1908 ...... 1.47
34 Rube Waddell, 1905 .... 1.48
35 Joe Wood, 1915 .... 1.49
36 Walter Johnson, 1919 ...... 1.49
37 Jack Pfiester, 1906 .... 1.51
38 John Ward, 1878 .... 1.51
39 Harry McCormick, 1882 ... 1.52
40 Doc White, 1906 .... 1.52
41 George McQuillan, 1908 .. 1.53
42 Dwight Gooden, 1985 .... 1.53
43 Eddie Cicotte, 1917 .... 1.53
44 Will White, 1882 .... 1.54
45 Cy Morgan, 1910 .... 1.55
46 Grover Alexander, 1916 ... 1.55
47 Walter Johnson, 1915 ...... 1.55
48 Howie Camnitz, 1908 .... 1.56
49 Greg Maddux, 1994 .... 1.56
50 Jim Devlin, 1876 .... 1.56
51 Tim Keefe, 1885 .... 1.58
52 Fred Toney, 1915 .... 1.58
53 Eddie Cicotte, 1913 .... 1.58
54 Rube Marquard, 1916 ...... 1.58
55 Chief Bender, 1910 .... 1.58
56 Barney Pelty, 1906 .... 1.59
57 Addie Joss, 1904 .... 1.59
58 Ed Walsh, 1907 .... 1.60
59 Luis Tiant, 1968 .... 1.60
60 Joe McGinnity, 1904 .... 1.61
61 Ray Collins, 1910 .... 1.62
62 Rube Waddell, 1904 .... 1.62
63 Howie Camnitz, 1909 .... 1.62
64 Cy Young, 1901 .... 1.62
65 Greg Maddux, 1995 .... 1.63
66 Silver King, 1888 .... 1.63
67 Spud Chandler, 1943 .... 1.64
68 Ernie Shore, 1915 .... 1.64
69 Ed Summers, 1908 .... 1.64
70 Dean Chance, 1964 .... 1.65
71 Walter Johnson, 1908 .... 1.65
72 Ed Reulbach, 1906 .... 1.65
73 Russ Ford, 1910 .... 1.65
74 Chief Bender, 1909 .... 1.66
75 Sam Leever, 1907 .... 1.66
76 Carl Hubbell, 1933 .... 1.66
77 Mickey Welch, 1885 .... 1.66
78 Candy Cummings, 1876 .. 1.67
79 Tommy Bond, 1876 .... 1.68
80 Orval Overall, 1907 .... 1.68
81 Ed Reulbach, 1907 .... 1.69
82 Claude Hendrix, 1914 .... 1.69
83 Nolan Ryan, 1981 .... 1.69
84 Jim McCormick, 1878 .... 1.69
85 Joe Wood, 1910 .... 1.69
86 Rube Foster, 1914 .... 1.70
87 Charlie Sweeney, 1884 .... 1.70
Bill Burns, 1908 .... 1.70
89 Addie Joss, 1909 .... 1.71
90 Ed Killian, 1909 .... 1.71
91 Walter Johnson, 1914 .... 1.72
92 Ned Garvin, 1904 .... 1.72
93 Doc White, 1909 .... 1.72
94 Bill Doak, 1914 .... 1.72
95 Addie Joss, 1906 .... 1.72
Grover Alexander, 1919 ... 1.72
97 Sandy Koufax, 1966 .... 1.73
98 Bob Ewing, 1907 .... 1.73
99 Vic Willis, 1906 .... 1.73
100 Sandy Koufax, 1964 .... 1.74

Earned Run Average by era

1988-2003

1 Greg Maddux, 1994 .... 1.56
2 Greg Maddux, 1995 .... 1.63
3 Kevin Brown, 1996 .... 1.89
4 Roger Clemens, 1990 .... 1.93
5 Bill Swift, 1992 .... 2.08
6 Bret Saberhagen, 1989 .... 2.16
7 Bob Tewksbury, 1992 .... 2.16
8 Joe Magrane, 1988 .... 2.18
9 Greg Maddux, 1992 .... 2.18
10 Danny Darwin, 1990 .... 2.21

1973-1987

1 Dwight Gooden, 1985 ...... 1.53
2 Nolan Ryan, 1981 .... 1.69
3 Ron Guidry, 1978 .... 1.74
4 John Tudor, 1985 .... 1.93
5 Orel Hershiser, 1985 .... 2.03
6 Tom Seaver, 1973 .... 2.08
7 Jim Palmer, 1975 .... 2.09
8 Bob Knepper, 1981 .... 2.18
9 Don Sutton, 1980 .... 2.20
10 Mike Scott, 1986 .... 2.22

1961-1972

1 Bob Gibson, 1968 .... 1.12
2 Luis Tiant, 1968 .... 1.60
3 Dean Chance, 1964 .... 1.65
4 Sandy Koufax, 1966 .... 1.73
5 Sandy Koufax, 1964 .... 1.74
6 Tom Seaver, 1971 .... 1.76
7 Sam McDowell, 1968 .... 1.81
8 Vida Blue, 1971 .... 1.82
9 Phil Niekro, 1967 .... 1.87
10 Joe Horlen, 1964 .... 1.88

1943-1960

1 Spud Chandler, 1943 .... 1.64
2 Hal Newhouser, 1945 .... 1.81
3 Max Lanier, 1943 .... 1.90
4 Hal Newhouser, 1946 .... 1.94
5 Billy Pierce, 1955 .... 1.97
6 Whitey Ford, 1958 .... 2.01
7 Al Benton, 1945 .... 2.02
8 Allie Reynolds, 1952 .... 2.06
9 Howie Pollet, 1946 .... 2.10
10 Spud Chandler, 1946 .... 2.10

1921-1942

1 Carl Hubbell, 1933 .... 1.66
2 Mort Cooper, 1942 .... 1.78
3 Dolf Luque, 1923 .... 1.93
4 Lon Warneke, 1933 .... 2.00
5 Lefty Grove, 1931 .... 2.06
6 Dazzy Vance, 1928 .... 2.09
7 Ted Lyons, 1942 .... 2.10
8 Johnny Beazley, 1942 .... 2.13
9 Hal Schumacher, 1933 ..... 2.16
10 Dazzy Vance, 1924 .... 2.16

1901-1920

1 Dutch Leonard, 1914 .... 0.96
2 Mordecai Brown, 1906 ..... 1.04
3 Christy Mathewson, 1909 ..... 1.14
4 Walter Johnson, 1913 .... 1.14
5 Jack Pfiester, 1907 .... 1.15
6 Addie Joss, 1908 .... 1.16
7 Carl Lundgren, 1907 .... 1.17
8 Grover Alexander, 1915 ... 1.22
9 Cy Young, 1908 .... 1.26
10 Ed Walsh, 1910 .... 1.27

1893-1900

1 Clark Griffith, 1898 .... 1.88
2 Al Maul, 1898 .... 2.10
3 Kid Nichols, 1898 .... 2.13
4 Doc McJames, 1898 .... 2.36
5 Rube Waddell, 1900 .... 2.37
6 Ned Garvin, 1900 .... 2.41
7 Al Maul, 1895 .... 2.45
Billy Rhines, 1896 .... 2.45
9 Nixey Callahan, 1898 .... 2.46
10 Vic Willis, 1899 .... 2.50

1876-1892

1 Tim Keefe, 1880 .... 0.86
2 Denny Driscoll, 1882 .... 1.21
3 George Bradley, 1876 .... 1.23
4 Guy Hecker, 1882 .... 1.30
5 George Bradley, 1880 .... 1.38
6 Charley Radbourn, 1884 .. 1.38
7 John Ward, 1878 .... 1.51
8 Harry McCormick, 1882 ... 1.52
9 Will White, 1882 .... 1.54
10 Jim Devlin, 1876 .... 1.56

Adjusted Earned Run Average

1 Tim Keefe, 1880 294
2 Pedro Martinez, 2000 .. 290
3 Dutch Leonard, 1914 280
4 Greg Maddux, 1994 272
5 Greg Maddux, 1995 262
6 Walter Johnson, 1913 258
7 Bob Gibson, 1968 258
8 Mordecai Brown, 1906 254
9 Pedro Martinez, 1999 .. 241
10 Walter Johnson, 1912 240
11 Christy Mathewson, 1905 230
12 Dwight Gooden, 1985 226
13 Grover Alexander, 1915 225
14 Roger Clemens, 1997 .. 225
15 Christy Mathewson, 1909 223
16 Pedro Martinez, 1997 .. 221
17 Lefty Grove, 1931 218
18 Cy Young, 1901 217
19 Jack Pfiester, 1907 216
20 Denny Driscoll, 1882 216
21 Walter Johnson, 1919 216
22 Kevin Brown, 1996 215
23 Walter Johnson, 1918 215
24 Carl Lundgren, 1907 213
25 Roger Clemens, 1990 .. 212
26 Ed Reulbach, 1905 210
27 Jack Taylor, 1902 209
28 Ron Guidry, 1978 209
29 Charley Radbourn, 1884 ... 206
30 Pedro Martinez, 2003 .. 206
31 Addie Joss, 1908 206
32 Billy Pierce, 1955 201
33 Dolf Luque, 1923 200
34 Silver King, 1888 200
35 Pedro Martinez, 2002 .. 199
36 Dean Chance, 1964 199
37 Randy Johnson, 1997 .. 197
38 Spud Chandler, 1943 197
39 Al Maul, 1895 196
40 Nolan Ryan, 1981 195
41 Cy Young, 1908 195
42 Hal Newhouser, 1945 194
43 Tom Seaver, 1971 194
44 Mordecai Brown, 1909 193
45 Carl Hubbell, 1933 193
46 Mort Cooper, 1942 193
47 Randy Johnson, 1995 .. 191
48 Randy Johnson, 2002 .. 191
49 Walter Johnson, 1915 191
50 Monty Stratton, 1937 191
51 Guy Hecker, 1882 191
52 Lefty Gomez, 1937 191
53 Sandy Koufax, 1966 191
54 Greg Maddux, 1997 191
55 Ed Siever, 1902 191
56 Clark Griffith, 1898 191
57 Dazzy Vance, 1928 191
58 Amos Rusie, 1894 189
59 Lefty Grove, 1936 189
60 Vean Gregg, 1911 189
61 Ed Walsh, 1910 189
62 Hal Newhouser, 1946 189
63 Dazzy Vance, 1930 188
64 Billy Rhines, 1896 188
65 Wilbur Wood, 1971 188
66 Jack Stivetts, 1889 188
67 Greg Maddux, 1998 187
68 Joe Wood, 1915 187
69 Warren Spahn, 1953 187
70 Sandy Koufax, 1964 187
71 Lefty Grove, 1939 186
72 Eddie Cicotte, 1913 185
73 Luis Tiant, 1968 185
74 Lefty Grove, 1930 184
75 Hank Aguirre, 1962 184
76 Randy Johnson, 1999 .. 184
77 Randy Johnson, 2001 .. 184
78 Joe Horlen, 1964 184
79 Vida Blue, 1971 184
80 John Tudor, 1985 183
81 Walter Johnson, 1910 183
82 Harry Brecheen, 1948 183
83 Henry Boyle, 1886 183
84 Billy Rhines, 1890 183
85 Jack Coombs, 1910 182
86 Steve Carlton, 1972 182
87 Fred Toney, 1915 182
88 Johnny Allen, 1937 181
89 Rube Waddell, 1905 180
90 Mordecai Brown, 1907 179
91 Kevin Appier, 1993 179
92 Orval Overall, 1909 179
93 Rube Waddell, 1902 179
94 Bret Saberhagen, 1989 178
95 Randy Johnson, 2000 .. 178
96 Joe Wood, 1912 178
97 Phil Niekro, 1967 178
98 Max Lanier, 1943 177
99 Roger Clemens, 1994 .. 177
100 Fred Anderson, 1917 177

Opponent Batting Average

1 Pedro Martinez, 2000 167
2 Luis Tiant, 1968 168
3 Nolan Ryan, 1972 171
4 Nolan Ryan, 1991 172
5 Ed Reulbach, 1906 175
6 Tim Keefe, 1880 178
7 Sandy Koufax, 1965 179
8 Dutch Leonard, 1914 180
9 Sid Fernandez, 1985 181
10 Hideo Nomo, 1995 182
11 Dave McNally, 1968 182
12 Tommy Byrne, 1949 183
13 Pedro Martinez, 1997 .. 184
14 Al Downing, 1963 184
15 Bob Gibson, 1968 184
16 Sam McDowell, 1965 185
17 Carl Lundgren, 1907 185
18 Herb Score, 1956 186
19 Mike Scott, 1986 186
20 Nolan Ryan, 1989 187
21 Ed Walsh, 1910 187
22 Mario Soto, 1980 187
23 Nolan Ryan, 1981 188
24 Russ Ford, 1910 188
25 Nolan Ryan, 1986 188
26 Nolan Ryan, 1990 188
27 Floyd Youmans, 1986 188
28 Sam McDowell, 1966 188
29 Guy Hecker, 1882 188
30 Sandy Koufax, 1963 189
31 Sam McDowell, 1968 189
32 Don Sutton, 1972 189
33 Catfish Hunter, 1972 189
34 Vida Blue, 1971 189
35 Walter Johnson, 1913 190
36 Nolan Ryan, 1974 190
37 Andy Messersmith, 1969 .. 190
38 Joe Horlen, 1964 190
39 Sid Fernandez, 1988 191
40 Grover Alexander, 1915 191
41 Sandy Koufax, 1964 191
42 Bob Turley, 1955 193
43 Nolan Ryan, 1977 193
44 Fred Beebe, 1908 193
45 Charlie Sweeney, 1884 193
46 Ron Guidry, 1978 193
47 Stan Coveleski, 1917 194
48 Bob Turley, 1957 194
49 Randy Johnson, 1997 .. 194
50 Herb Score, 1955 194
51 Jack Pfiester, 1906 194
52 Mordecai Brown, 1908 195
53 Nolan Ryan, 1976 195
54 Nolan Ryan, 1983 195
55 Dean Chance, 1964 195
56 Roger Clemens, 1986 .. 195
57 Tim Keefe, 1888 196
58 Kerry Wood, 1998 196
59 Walter Johnson, 1912 196
60 Roger Nelson, 1972 196
61 J.R. Richard, 1978 196
62 Pascual Perez, 1988 196
63 Greg Maddux, 1995 197
64 Jeff Robinson, 1988 197
65 Lady Baldwin, 1885 197
66 Jose DeLeon, 1989 197
67 Dave Boswell, 1966 197
68 Sandy Koufax, 1962 197
69 Addie Joss, 1908 197
70 Christy Mathewson, 1908 197
71 Roger Clemens, 1998 .. 197
72 Sonny Siebert, 1968 198
73 Sid Fernandez, 1989 198
74 Toad Ramsey, 1886 198
75 Larry Cheney, 1916 198
76 Wayne Simpson, 1970 198
77 Pedro Martinez, 2002 .. 198
78 Orval Overall, 1909 198
79 Gary Peters, 1967 199
80 Larry Corcoran, 1880 199
81 Adonis Terry, 1888 199
82 Nolan Ryan, 1987 199
83 Mordecai Brown, 1904 199
84 Silver King, 1888 200
85 Christy Mathewson, 1909 200
86 Rube Waddell, 1905 200
87 Denny McLain, 1968 200
88 Larry Corcoran, 1882 200
89 Bobby Bolin, 1968 200
Jim Palmer, 1969 200
Sid Fernandez, 1990 200
92 Jason Schmidt, 2003 ... 200
93 Spec Shea, 1947 200
94 Ed Seward, 1888 200
95 Tony Mullane, 1892 201
96 Art Fromme, 1909 201
97 Babe Ruth, 1916 201
98 Randy Johnson, 1995 .. 201
99 Dwight Gooden, 1985 201
100 Cannonball Titcomb, 1888 201

Opponent On-Base Pct.

1	Guy Hecker, 1882	.199
2	Charlie Sweeney, 1884	.211
3	Tim Keefe, 1880	.212
4	**Pedro Martinez, 2000**	**.214**
5	Henry Boyle, 1884	.215
6	George Bradley, 1880	.217
7	Denny Driscoll, 1882	.218
8	Addie Joss, 1908	.218
9	Walter Johnson, 1913	.220
10	Christy Mathewson, 1908	.222
11	Jim Whitney, 1884	.223
12	George Bradley, 1876	.224
13	**Greg Maddux, 1995**	**.225**
14	Guy Hecker, 1884	.226
15	Ed Walsh, 1910	.226
16	Tommy Bond, 1876	.227
17	Lady Baldwin, 1885	.228
18	Sandy Koufax, 1965	.228
19	Christy Mathewson, 1909	.228
20	Sandy Koufax, 1963	.230
21	Juan Marichal, 1966	.230
22	John Ward, 1880	.232
23	Mordecai Brown, 1908	.232
24	Ed Walsh, 1908	.232
25	Luis Tiant, 1968	.233
26	Bob Gibson, 1968	.233
27	Grover Alexander, 1915	.234
28	Dave McNally, 1968	.234
29	Larry Corcoran, 1882	.234
30	Charley Radbourn, 1884	.234
31	Ed Morris, 1884	.234
32	Perry Werden, 1884	.235
33	Jim Devlin, 1876	.235
34	Jack Lynch, 1884	.236
35	Larry Corcoran, 1880	.236
36	Roger Nelson, 1972	.236
37	Silver King, 1888	.237
38	Charlie Getzien, 1884	.237
39	Tim Keefe, 1883	.237
40	Tony Mullane, 1883	.238
41	John Clarkson, 1885	.239
42	Tim Keefe, 1884	.239
43	Mordecai Brown, 1909	.239
44	Fred Corey, 1880	.239
45	Juan Marichal, 1965	.240
46	Cy Young, 1908	.240
47	Don Sutton, 1972	.240
48	Cy Young, 1905	.241
49	Babe Adams, 1919	.241
50	Sandy Koufax, 1964	.241
51	Catfish Hunter, 1972	.242
52	Pete Conway, 1888	.243
53	Harry McCormick, 1882	.243
54	Denny McLain, 1968	.243
55	Tim Keefe, 1888	.243
56	Lady Baldwin, 1886	.243
57	Mike Scott, 1986	.244
58	Charley Radbourn, 1883	.244
59	Will White, 1883	.244
60	Charlie Ferguson, 1886	.244
61	Charlie Buffinton, 1888	.244
62	Will White, 1882	.244
63	Charlie Buffinton, 1884	.244
64	Russ Ford, 1910	.245
65	Grover Alexander, 1919	.245
66	Christy Mathewson, 1905	.245
67	**Greg Maddux, 1994**	**.245**
68	Dutch Leonard, 1914	.246
69	Bobby Mathews, 1882	.246
70	Jim Galvin, 1884	.246
71	Sam Weaver, 1878	.247
72	Charley Radbourn, 1882	.247
73	Charlie Gagus, 1884	.247
74	Christy Mathewson, 1907	.247
75	Warren Hacker, 1952	.247
76	Jim McCormick, 1880	.247
77	Ed Morris, 1885	.247
78	Fred Goldsmith, 1880	.247
79	Dupee Shaw, 1884	.247
80	Eddie Cicotte, 1917	.248
81	Walter Johnson, 1912	.248
82	Doc White, 1906	.249
83	John Clarkson, 1884	.249
84	Jumbo McGinnis, 1883	.249
85	John Tudor, 1985	.249
86	**Pedro Martinez, 1999**	**.249**
87	Henry Gruber, 1888	.249
88	Hugh Daily, 1884	.250
89	Ron Guidry, 1978	.250
90	Joe Horlen, 1964	.250
91	**Pedro Martinez, 1997**	**.250**
92	Terry Larkin, 1879	.250
93	John Ward, 1879	.250
94	John Ward, 1878	.251
95	Billy Taylor, 1884	.251
96	**Jason Schmidt, 2003**	**.251**
97	Candy Cummings, 1876	.251
98	Jim Whitney, 1883	.251
99	Cy Young, 1904	.251
100	Claude Hendrix, 1914	.251

Adjusted Pitching Wins

1	Charley Radbourn, 1884	10.5
2	Amos Rusie, 1894	9.7
3	Guy Hecker, 1884	9.7
4	Silver King, 1888	9.4
5	Walter Johnson, 1912	9.4
6	Walter Johnson, 1913	9.3
7	Lefty Grove, 1931	8.6
8	John Clarkson, 1889	8.5
9	**Pedro Martinez, 2000**	**8.3**
10	**Pedro Martinez, 1999**	**7.9**
11	Cy Young, 1901	7.9
12	**Roger Clemens, 1997**	**7.7**
13	Dolf Luque, 1923	7.3
14	Jim Galvin, 1884	7.3
15	Bob Gibson, 1968	7.3
16	Red Faber, 1921	7.1
17	Toad Ramsey, 1886	7.1
18	Will White, 1883	7.0
19	Lefty Gomez, 1937	7.0
20	Charley Radbourn, 1883	7.0
21	Grover Alexander, 1915	7.0
22	Cy Young, 1892	7.0
23	John Clarkson, 1885	7.0
24	Silver King, 1890	7.0
25	Christy Mathewson, 1905	7.0
26	Scott Stratton, 1890	7.0
27	Sandy Koufax, 1966	7.0
28	Lefty Grove, 1930	6.9
29	Steve Carlton, 1972	6.9
30	Cy Young, 1895	6.9
31	John Clarkson, 1887	6.9
32	Dazzy Vance, 1930	6.9
33	Cy Young, 1893	6.9
34	Hal Newhouser, 1945	6.8
35	Bob Feller, 1940	6.8
36	Lefty Grove, 1936	6.8
37	Dave Foutz, 1886	6.7
38	Dwight Gooden, 1985	6.7
39	Dazzy Vance, 1928	6.7
40	Kid Nichols, 1897	6.7
41	Carl Hubbell, 1933	6.7
42	**Kevin Brown, 1996**	**6.6**
43	Billy Rhines, 1890	6.5
44	Gaylord Perry, 1972	6.5
45	Amos Rusie, 1893	6.5
46	Dean Chance, 1964	6.4
47	Walter Johnson, 1915	6.4
48	Walter Johnson, 1918	6.4
49	Walter Johnson, 1919	6.4
50	Hal Newhouser, 1946	6.4
51	**Greg Maddux, 1994**	**6.3**
52	Kid Nichols, 1898	6.3
53	Grover Alexander, 1920	6.3
54	Bucky Walters, 1939	6.3
55	Robin Roberts, 1953	6.3
56	Warren Spahn, 1953	6.3
57	Dizzy Trout, 1944	6.3
58	Wilbur Wood, 1971	6.3
59	Ron Guidry, 1978	6.2
60	Elmer Smith, 1887	6.2
61	Dazzy Vance, 1924	6.2
62	**Greg Maddux, 1995**	**6.2**
63	Carl Hubbell, 1936	6.2
64	Grover Alexander, 1916	6.1
65	**Derek Lowe, 2002**	**6.1**
66	Tom Seaver, 1971	6.1
67	Cy Young, 1902	6.0
68	Clark Griffith, 1898	6.0
69	Pink Hawley, 1895	6.0
70	Mickey Welch, 1885	6.0
71	Lefty Grove, 1932	6.0
72	Matt Kilroy, 1887	6.0
73	**Roger Clemens, 1990**	**6.0**
74	Ted Breitenstein, 1893	6.0
75	Jouett Meekin, 1894	6.0
76	**Pedro Martinez, 1997**	**6.0**
77	**Randy Johnson, 2002**	**6.0**
78	Lefty Grove, 1935	6.0
79	Lefty Gomez, 1934	5.9
80	Walter Johnson, 1914	5.9
81	Thornton Lee, 1941	5.9
82	Juan Marichal, 1965	5.9
83	Vida Blue, 1971	5.9
84	Dizzy Dean, 1934	5.9
85	Jack Stivetts, 1891	5.9
86	Joe Wood, 1912	5.9
87	Mordecai Brown, 1906	5.8
88	George Bradley, 1876	5.8
89	Kid Nichols, 1893	5.8
90	Kid Nichols, 1890	5.8
91	Jim Devlin, 1876	5.8
92	Jack Coombs, 1910	5.8
93	Carl Hubbell, 1934	5.7
94	Mel Harder, 1934	5.7
95	Bob Caruthers, 1885	5.7
96	Bob Feller, 1946	5.7
97	**Randy Johnson, 2001**	**5.7**
98	Christy Mathewson, 1908	5.7
99	Eddie Cicotte, 1917	5.7
100	Will White, 1882	5.7

Relief Wins

1	Roy Face, 1959	18
2	John Hiller, 1974	17
	Bill Campbell, 1976	17
4	Jim Konstanty, 1950	16
	Ron Perranoski, 1963	16
	Dick Radatz, 1964	16
	Tom Johnson, 1977	16
8	Mace Brown, 1938	15
	Hoyt Wilhelm, 1952	15
	Luis Arroyo, 1961	15
	Dick Radatz, 1963	15
	Eddie Fisher, 1965	15
	Mike Marshall, 1974	15
	Dale Murray, 1975	15
15	Joe Page, 1947	14
	Joe Black, 1952	14
	Hersh Freeman, 1956	14
	Stu Miller, 1961	14
	Stu Miller, 1965	14
	Phil Regan, 1966	14
	Frank Linzy, 1969	14
	Mike Marshall, 1972	14
	Mike Marshall, 1973	14
	Ron Davis, 1979	14
	Mark Clear, 1982	14
	Jim Slaton, 1983	14
	Roger McDowell, 1986	14
	Mark Eichhorn, 1986	14
29	Dick Tidrow, 1979	13
	Wilcy Moore, 1927	13
	Earl Caldwell, 1946	13
	Clyde Shoun, 1943	13
	Joe Page, 1949	13
	Clyde King, 1951	13
	Lindy McDaniel, 1959	13
	Larry Sherry, 1960	13
	Gerry Staley, 1960	13
	Lindy McDaniel, 1963	13
	Al Hrabosky, 1975	13
	Rollie Fingers, 1976	13
	Bill Campbell, 1977	13
	Sparky Lyle, 1977	13
	Gary Lavelle, 1978	13
	Bob Stanley, 1978	13
	Ron Reed, 1979	13
	Jim Kern, 1979	13
	Aurelio Lopez, 1980	13
	Jesse Orosco, 1983	**13**
	Rich Gossage, 1983	13
50	33 players tied	12

Relief Losses

1	Gene Garber, 1979	16
2	Darold Knowles, 1970	14
	John Hiller, 1974	14
	Mike Marshall, 1975	14
	Mike Marshall, 1979	14
6	Wilbur Wood, 1970	13
	Rollie Fingers, 1978	13
	Skip Lockwood, 1978	13
9	Roy Face, 1956	12
	Roy Face, 1961	12
	Ken Sanders, 1971	12
	Mike Marshall, 1974	12
	Gene Garber, 1975	12
	Jim Willoughby, 1976	12
	Charlie Hough, 1977	12
	Mike Marshall, 1978	12
	Kent Tekulve, 1980	12
	Ken Howell, 1986	12
	Roger Mason, 1993	12
20	Nels Potter, 1949	11
	Frank Funk, 1961	11
	Dick Radatz, 1965	11
	Frank Linzy, 1966	11
	Wilbur Wood, 1968	11
	Wilbur Wood, 1969	11
	Mike Marshall, 1973	11
	Rollie Fingers, 1976	11
	Rich Gossage, 1978	11
	Dave Heaverlo, 1979	11
	Mark Clear, 1980	11
	Greg Minton, 1983	11
	Ron Davis, 1984	11
	Mark Davis, 1985	11
	Joe Boever, 1989	11
	Jose Paniagua, 1999	**11**
36	48 players tied	10

Relief Games

1	Mike Marshall, 1974	106
2	Kent Tekulve, 1979	94
3	Mike Marshall, 1973	92
4	Kent Tekulve, 1978	91
5	Wayne Granger, 1969	90
	Kent Tekulve, 1987	90
7	Mike Marshall, 1979	89
	Mark Eichhorn, 1987	89
	Julian Tavarez, 1997	**89**
	Steve Kline, 2001	**89**
	Paul Quantrill, 2003	**89**
12	**Mike Myers, 1997**	**88**
	Sean Runyan, 1998	88
14	Rob Murphy, 1987	87
15	Wilbur Wood, 1968	86
	Paul Quantrill, 2002	**86**
17	Kent Tekulve, 1982	85
	Frank Williams, 1987	85
	Oscar Villarreal, 2003	**85**
20	Ted Abernathy, 1965	84
	Enrique Romo, 1979	84
	Dick Tidrow, 1980	84
	Dan Quisenberry, 1985	84
	Mitch Williams, 1987	84
	Stan Belinda, 1997	84
	Graeme Lloyd, 2001	**84**
	Billy Koch, 2002	**84**
28	Ken Sanders, 1971	83
	Craig Lefferts, 1986	83
	Eddie Guardado, 1996	**83**
	Mike Myers, 1996	**83**
	Steve Kline, 2000	**83**
	Kelly Wunsch, 2000	**83**
	Octavio Dotel, 2002	**83**
35	Eddie Fisher, 1965	82
	Bill Campbell, 1983	82
	Juan Agosto, 1990	82
	Paul Quantrill, 1998	**82**
	Steve Kline, 1999	**82**
	Jeff Fassero, 2001	**82**
	Ray King, 2001	**82**
42	12 players tied	81

Relief Innings Pitched

1	Mike Marshall, 1974	208.1
2	Mike Marshall, 1973	179.0
3	Bob Stanley, 1982	168.1
4	Bill Campbell, 1976	167.2
5	Andy Karl, 1945	166.2
6	Eddie Fisher, 1965	165.1
7	Hoyt Wilhelm, 1952	159.1
8	Dick Radatz, 1964	157.0
	Mark Eichhorn, 1986	157.0
10	Jim Konstanty, 1950	152.0
11	John Hiller, 1974	150.0
12	Tom Johnson, 1977	146.2
13	Garland Braxton, 1927	146.0
14	Bob Stanley, 1983	145.1
15	Hoyt Wilhelm, 1953	145.0
	Wilbur Wood, 1968	145.0
17	Allan Russell, 1923	144.2
	Wayne Granger, 1969	144.2
19	Steve Foucault, 1974	144.1
20	Hoyt Wilhelm, 1965	144.0
21	Jim Kern, 1979	143.0
22	Charlie Hough, 1976	142.2
23	Rich Gossage, 1975	141.2
24	Mike Marshall, 1979	140.2
25	Sammy Stewart, 1983	140.1
	Willie Hernandez, 1984	140.1
27	Bill Campbell, 1977	140.0
28	Jack Lamabe, 1963	139.2
29	Pedro Borbon, 1974	139.0
	Dan Quisenberry, 1983	139.0
31	Lindy McDaniel, 1973	138.1
32	Aurelio Lopez, 1984	137.2
33	Clay Carroll, 1966	137.1
34	Sparky Lyle, 1977	137.0
	Tom Hume, 1980	137.0
36	Dan Quisenberry, 1982	136.2
37	Ted Abernathy, 1965	136.1
	Ken Sanders, 1971	136.1
	Doug Corbett, 1980	136.1
40	Mudcat Grant, 1970	135.1
	Joe Page, 1949	135.1
	Kent Tekulve, 1978	135.1
43	Clay Carroll, 1968	135.0
44	Ted Abernathy, 1968	134.2
	Phil Regan, 1968	134.2
	Rollie Fingers, 1976	134.2
47	Bill Henry, 1959	134.1
	Dick Selma, 1970	134.1
	Rich Gossage, 1978	134.1
	Kent Tekulve, 1979	134.1

Adjusted Relievers' Runs

1	Mark Eichhorn, 1986	44.0
2	Jim Kern, 1979	39.0
3	John Hiller, 1973	35.0
	Doug Corbett, 1980	35.0
	Mariano Rivera, 1996	**35.0**
6	Rich Gossage, 1977	34.0
	Willie Hernandez, 1984	34.0
8	Dan Quisenberry, 1983	33.0
9	Rich Gossage, 1975	31.0
	Bruce Sutter, 1977	31.0
	Keith Foulke, 1999	**31.0**
12	Lindy McDaniel, 1960	29.8
13	Mudcat Grant, 1970	28.0
	Sid Monge, 1979	28.0
	Tim Burke, 1987	28.0
	Derek Lowe, 1999	**28.0**
17	Wilcy Moore, 1927	27.3
18	Ellis Kinder, 1951	27.1
19	Aurelio Lopez, 1979	27.0
	Roberto Hernandez, 1996	**27.0**
	Eric Gagne, 2003	**27.0**
22	Bob Lee, 1964	26.8
23	Mike Marshall, 1979	26.7
24	Dick Radatz, 1962	26.0
	Dick Radatz, 1963	26.0
	Dick Radatz, 1964	26.0
	Ted Abernathy, 1967	26.0
	Sparky Lyle, 1977	26.0
	Bruce Sutter, 1984	26.0
	Jeff Zimmerman, 1999	26.0
	Gabe White, 2000	**26.0**
	Octavio Dotel, 2002	**26.0**
	Guillermo Mota, 2003	**26.0**
	Damaso Marte, 2003	**26.0**
35	Ellis Kinder, 1953	25.0
	Bob James, 1985	25.0
	Jeff Montgomery, 1989	25.0
	Dennis Eckersley, 1990	25.0
	John Wetteland, 1993	25.0
	Jose Mesa, 1995	**25.0**
	Derek Lowe, 2000	**25.0**
	Billy Wagner, 2003	**25.0**
	Shigetoshi Hasegawa, 2003	25.0
44	14 players tied	24.0

Relief Ranking

1	Jim Kern, 1979	62.0
2	John Hiller, 1973	61.5
3	Rich Gossage, 1977	59.6
4	Mark Eichhorn, 1986	55.9
5	**Roberto Hernandez, 1996**	**54.0**
6	Mike Marshall, 1979	53.3
7	Lindy McDaniel, 1960	52.8
8	Sid Monge, 1979	51.5
9	John Wetteland, 1993	50.0
10	Dick Radatz, 1963	48.2
11	Ellis Kinder, 1953	47.8
12	Donnie Moore, 1985	47.6
13	**Keith Foulke, 2003**	**47.3**
14	Dick Radatz, 1964	46.9
15	**Eric Gagne, 2003**	**46.8**
16	Rich Gossage, 1975	46.3
17	**Jesse Orosco, 1983**	**46.1**
18	Doug Jones, 1997	46.0
	Robb Nen, 1998	**46.0**
	Ugueth Urbina, 1998	**46.0**
	Mariano Rivera, 1999	**46.0**
22	Doug Corbett, 1980	45.5
23	Bob James, 1985	44.9
24	Dennis Eckersley, 1990	44.6
25	Bruce Sutter, 1977	44.2
26	Mike Marshall, 1972	44.0
	Jeff Montgomery, 1993	44.0
	Scott Williamson, 1999	**44.0**
29	Tom Murphy, 1974	43.9
30	**Trevor Hoffman, 1998**	**43.9**
31	**Jose Mesa, 1995**	**43.6**
32	Stu Miller, 1965	43.5
33	**Mariano Rivera, 2003**	**43.0**
34	Joe Page, 1949	42.4
35	Bill Campbell, 1977	42.1
36	Luis Arroyo, 1961	42.0
	Bill Caudill, 1982	42.0
	Dave Righetti, 1986	42.0
	Mariano Rivera, 1997	**42.0**
	Robb Nen, 2000	**42.0**
	Keith Foulke, 2001	**42.0**
42	Dan Quisenberry, 1985	41.9
43	Sparky Lyle, 1977	41.8
44	Willie Hernandez, 1984	41.6
45	**Derek Lowe, 2000**	**41.2**
46	Rich Gossage, 1978	40.9
47	Ken Sanders, 1971	40.6
48	Byung-Hyun Kim, 2002	40.5
49	Jim Konstanty, 1950	40.5
50	Rollie Fingers, 1981	40.4

Pitcher Wins

1 Guy Hecker, 1884 ....12.9
2 Walter Johnson, 1913 ....10.9
3 Charley Radbourn, 1884..10.7
4 Walter Johnson, 1912 ....10.6
5 Silver King, 1888 ....10.2
Amos Rusie, 1894 ....10.2
7 John Clarkson, 1889 ....8.9
Scott Stratton, 1890 ....8.9
9 Christy Mathewson, 1905 ....8.5
10 Pedro Martinez, 2000 ...8.4
11 Charley Radbourn, 1883....8.3
12 Lefty Grove, 1931 ....8.2
Bucky Walters, 1939 ....8.2
Dizzy Trout, 1944 ....8.2
15 Pedro Martinez, 1999 ...8.0
16 Cy Young, 1901 ....7.9
Roger Clemens, 1997 ...7.9
18 Dave Foutz, 1886 ....7.6
Joe Wood, 1912 ....7.6
Walter Johnson, 1918 ....7.6
Dolf Luque, 1923 ....7.6
Hal Newhouser, 1945 ....7.6
Bob Gibson, 1968 ....7.6
24 John Clarkson, 1887 ....7.5
Grover Alexander, 1915 ....7.5
Dwight Gooden, 1985 ....7.5
27 Pink Hawley, 1895 ....7.4
Walter Johnson, 1915 ....7.4
29 John Clarkson, 1885 ....7.3
Carl Hubbell, 1933 ....7.3
Steve Carlton, 1972 ....7.3
32 Bob Caruthers, 1886 ....7.2
Matt Kilroy, 1887 ....7.2
Walter Johnson, 1914 ....7.2
Grover Alexander, 1916 ....7.2
Dazzy Vance, 1928 ....7.2
37 Tony Mullane, 1884 ....7.1
38 Warren Spahn, 1953 ....7.0
39 Will White, 1883 ....6.9
Cy Young, 1895 ....6.9
Kid Nichols, 1897 ....6.9
Grover Alexander, 1920 ....6.9
Lefty Grove, 1930 ....6.9
Kevin Brown, 1996 ....6.9
45 Jack Stivetts, 1891 ....6.8
Amos Rusie, 1893 ....6.8
Ed Walsh, 1908 ....6.8
Red Faber, 1921 ....6.8
Wes Ferrell, 1935 ....6.8
Lefty Gomez, 1937 ....6.8
Bob Feller, 1940 ....6.8
Greg Maddux, 1994 ....6.8
53 Will White, 1882 ....6.7
Toad Ramsey, 1886 ....6.7
Walter Johnson, 1919 ....6.7
Tom Seaver, 1971 ....6.7
Gaylord Perry, 1972 ....6.7
John Hiller, 1973 ....6.7
59 Charlie Sweeney, 1884 ....6.6
Silver King, 1890 ....6.6
Christy Mathewson, 1909 ....6.6
Lefty Grove, 1936 ....6.6
Bob Lemon, 1948 ....6.6
64 Charlie Ferguson, 1886 ....6.5
Cy Young, 1893 ....6.5
Christy Mathewson, 1908 ....6.5
Ed Walsh, 1912 ....6.5
Thornton Lee, 1941 ....6.5
69 Cy Young, 1892 ....6.4
Kid Nichols, 1898 ....6.4
Dazzy Vance, 1930 ....6.4
Hal Newhouser, 1946 ....6.4
Robin Roberts, 1953 ....6.4
Rich Gossage, 1977 ....6.4
Ron Guidry, 1978 ....6.4
Greg Maddux, 1995 ....6.4
Greg Maddux, 1998 ....6.4
78 Jim Galvin, 1884 ....6.3
Bob Caruthers, 1885 ....6.3
Elmer Smith, 1887 ....6.3
Ed Walsh, 1910 ....6.3
Bob Gibson, 1969 ....6.3
Jim Kern, 1979 ....6.3
Derek Lowe, 2002 ....6.3
85 George Bradley, 1876 ....6.2
Jim Devlin, 1876 ....6.2
Jouett Meekin, 1894 ....6.2
Carl Hubbell, 1936 ....6.2
Roger Clemens, 1990 ...6.2
90 Jack Taylor, 1902 ....6.1
Jack Chesbro, 1904 ....6.1
Mordecai Brown, 1906 ....6.1
Dizzy Dean, 1934 ....6.1
Hal Newhouser, 1944 ....6.1
Sandy Koufax, 1966 ....6.1
96 8 players tied 6.0

Player Overall Wins alpha

Hank Aaron, 1959 ....6.8
Grover Alexander, 1915 ....7.5
Grover Alexander, 1916 ....7.2
Grover Alexander, 1920 ....6.9
Jeff Bagwell, 1994 ....7.7
Jeff Bagwell, 1996 ....7.1
Frank Baker, 1913 ....6.6
Johnny Bench, 1972 ....6.6
Craig Biggio, 1997 ....8.3
Barry Bonds, 1992 ....8.0
Barry Bonds, 1993 ....8.0
Barry Bonds, 1996 ....7.8
Barry Bonds, 1998 ....6.8
Barry Bonds, 2000 ....7.0
Barry Bonds, 2001 ....12.0
Barry Bonds, 2002 ....11.7
Barry Bonds, 2003 ....8.8
Lou Boudreau, 1943 ....6.8
Lou Boudreau, 1944 ....7.5
Lou Boudreau, 1948 ....7.1
George Brett, 1980 ....6.6
George Brett, 1985 ....6.7
Dan Brouthers, 1892 ....6.8
Kevin Brown, 1996 ....6.9
Ken Caminiti, 1996 ....7.7
Rod Carew, 1974 ....6.9
Rod Carew, 1975 ....6.7
Rod Carew, 1977 ....6.6
Steve Carlton, 1972 ....7.3
Gary Carter, 1982 ....6.9
Bob Caruthers, 1886 ....7.2
Norm Cash, 1961 ....7.6
Cupid Childs, 1890 ....6.8
John Clarkson, 1885 ....7.3
John Clarkson, 1887 ....7.5
John Clarkson, 1889 ....8.9
Roger Clemens, 1997 ...7.9
Harlond Clift, 1937 ....7.4
Ty Cobb, 1911 ....6.6
Ty Cobb, 1917 ....7.4
Eddie Collins, 1910 ....7.0
Eddie Collins, 1913 ....7.0
Eddie Collins, 1914 ....6.9
Eddie Collins, 1915 ....6.6
Joe Cronin, 1930 ....6.9
Art Devlin, 1906 ....6.6
Joe DiMaggio, 1941 ....6.6
Fred Dunlap, 1884 ....7.1
Red Faber, 1921 ....6.8
Bob Feller, 1940 ....6.8
Wes Ferrell, 1935 ....6.8
Dave Foutz, 1886 ....7.6
Jimmie Foxx, 1932 ....6.7
Jimmie Foxx, 1933 ....6.9
Frankie Frisch, 1927 ....7.2
Lou Gehrig, 1927 ....8.4
Lou Gehrig, 1930 ....7.7
Lou Gehrig, 1934 ....7.9
Lou Gehrig, 1936 ....6.6
Bob Gibson, 1968 ....7.6
Lefty Gomez, 1937 ....6.8
Dwight Gooden, 1985 ....7.5
Lefty Grove, 1930 ....6.9
Lefty Grove, 1931 ....8.2
Lefty Grove, 1936 ....6.6
Toby Harrah, 1975 ....6.8
Pink Hawley, 1895 ....7.4
Guy Hecker, 1884 ....12.9
Rickey Henderson, 1985 ....7.0
Rickey Henderson, 1990 ....7.8
John Hiller, 1973 ....6.7
Rogers Hornsby, 1917 ....7.8
Rogers Hornsby, 1920 ....7.9
Rogers Hornsby, 1921 ....7.7
Rogers Hornsby, 1922 ....8.9
Rogers Hornsby, 1924 ....9.3
Rogers Hornsby, 1925 ....6.8
Rogers Hornsby, 1927 ....6.8
Rogers Hornsby, 1929 ....6.8
Carl Hubbell, 1933 ....7.3
Joe Jackson, 1912 ....7.1
Hughie Jennings, 1896 ....6.7
Walter Johnson, 1912 ....10.6
Walter Johnson, 1913 ....10.9
Walter Johnson, 1914 ....7.2
Walter Johnson, 1915 ....7.4
Walter Johnson, 1918 ....7.6
Walter Johnson, 1919 ....6.7
Jeff Kent, 2000 ....6.6
Matt Kilroy, 1887 ....7.2
Silver King, 1888 ....10.2
Silver King, 1890 ....6.6
Nap Lajoie, 1901 ....8.1
Nap Lajoie, 1903 ....8.1
Nap Lajoie, 1904 ....7.4
Nap Lajoie, 1906 ....7.6
Nap Lajoie, 1907 ....7.0
Nap Lajoie, 1908 ....8.0
Nap Lajoie, 1910 ....8.9
Bob Lemon, 1948 ....6.6

Player Overall Wins alpha

Dolf Luque, 1923 ....7.6
Greg Maddux, 1994 ....6.8
Mickey Mantle, 1956 ....8.1
Mickey Mantle, 1957 ....8.2
Mickey Mantle, 1961 ....7.4
Pedro Martinez, 1999 ....8.0
Pedro Martinez, 2000 ....8.4
Christy Mathewson, 1905 ....8.5
Christy Mathewson, 1909 ....6.6
Willie Mays, 1955 ....6.8
Willie Mays, 1965 ....6.6
Willie McCovey, 1969 ....6.6
Mark McGwire, 1998 ....7.1
Joe Morgan, 1973 ....7.5
Joe Morgan, 1974 ....7.0
Joe Morgan, 1975 ....8.0
Joe Morgan, 1976 ....6.7
Johnny Mostil, 1926 ....7.8
Tony Mullane, 1884 ....7.1
Stan Musial, 1948 ....7.2
Hal Newhouser, 1945 ....7.6
Kid Nichols, 1897 ....6.9
Gaylord Perry, 1972 ....6.7
Rico Petrocelli, 1969 ....7.5
Mike Piazza, 1997 ....7.8
Albert Pujols, 2003 ....7.5
Charley Radbourn, 1883 ....8.3
Charley Radbourn, 1884..10.7
Toad Ramsey, 1886 ....6.7
Cal Ripken, 1983 ....7.1
Cal Ripken, 1984 ....9.4
Cal Ripken, 1991 ....8.6
Jackie Robinson, 1951 ....7.3
Alex Rodriguez, 2000 ...6.8
Alex Rodriguez, 2001 ...6.9
Alex Rodriguez, 2002 ...7.1
Al Rosen, 1953 ....7.4
Amos Rusie, 1893 ....6.8
Amos Rusie, 1894 ....10.2
Babe Ruth, 1919 ....7.3
Babe Ruth, 1920 ....9.3
Babe Ruth, 1921 ....9.4
Babe Ruth, 1923 ....10.1
Babe Ruth, 1924 ....8.4
Babe Ruth, 1926 ....8.5
Babe Ruth, 1927 ....8.8
Babe Ruth, 1928 ....7.1
Babe Ruth, 1930 ....7.6
Babe Ruth, 1931 ....8.1
Ron Santo, 1964 ....7.1
Ron Santo, 1966 ....7.3
Ron Santo, 1967 ....7.6
Mike Schmidt, 1974 ....7.4
Mike Schmidt, 1980 ....6.9
Mike Schmidt, 1981 ....7.2
Tom Seaver, 1971 ....6.7
George Sisler, 1920 ....7.9
Sammy Sosa, 2001 ....8.9
Warren Spahn, 1953 ....7.0
Tris Speaker, 1912 ....7.2
Tris Speaker, 1914 ....7.3
Snuffy Stirnweiss, 1944 ....6.8
Snuffy Stirnweiss, 1945 ....7.2
Jack Stivetts, 1891 ....6.8
Scott Stratton, 1890 ....8.9
Charlie Sweeney, 1884 ....6.6
Dizzy Trout, 1944 ....8.2
Dazzy Vance, 1928 ....7.2
Arky Vaughan, 1935 ....6.6
Honus Wagner, 1905 ....7.5
Honus Wagner, 1906 ....7.2
Honus Wagner, 1907 ....6.7
Honus Wagner, 1908 ....6.9
Ed Walsh, 1908 ....6.8
Bucky Walters, 1939 ....8.2
Will White, 1882 ....6.7
Will White, 1883 ....6.9
Ted Williams, 1941 ....8.5
Ted Williams, 1942 ....8.5
Ted Williams, 1946 ....8.1
Ted Williams, 1947 ....7.2
Ted Williams, 1957 ....7.1
Joe Wood, 1912 ....7.6
Carl Yastrzemski, 1967 ....6.9
Cy Young, 1895 ....6.9
Cy Young, 1901 ....7.9
Robin Yount, 1982 ....7.3

Player Overall Wins

1 Guy Hecker, 1884 ....12.9
2 Barry Bonds, 2001 ....12.0
3 Barry Bonds, 2002 ....11.7
4 Walter Johnson, 1913 ....10.9
5 Charley Radbourn, 1884..10.7
6 Walter Johnson, 1912 ....10.6
7 Silver King, 1888 ....10.2
Amos Rusie, 1894 ....10.2
9 Babe Ruth, 1923 ....10.1
10 Babe Ruth, 1921 ....9.4
Cal Ripken, 1984 ....9.4
12 Babe Ruth, 1920 ....9.3
Rogers Hornsby, 1924 ....9.3
14 John Clarkson, 1889 ....8.9
Scott Stratton, 1890 ....8.9
Nap Lajoie, 1910 ....8.9
Rogers Hornsby, 1922 ....8.9
Sammy Sosa, 2001 ....8.9
19 Babe Ruth, 1927 ....8.8
Barry Bonds, 2003 ....8.8
21 Cal Ripken, 1991 ....8.6
22 Christy Mathewson, 1905 ....8.5
Babe Ruth, 1926 ....8.5
Ted Williams, 1941 ....8.5
Ted Williams, 1942 ....8.5
26 Pedro Martinez, 2000 ...8.4
Babe Ruth, 1924 ....8.4
Lou Gehrig, 1927 ....8.4
29 Charley Radbourn, 1883....8.3
Craig Biggio, 1997 ....8.3
31 Lefty Grove, 1931 ....8.2
Bucky Walters, 1939 ....8.2
Dizzy Trout, 1944 ....8.2
Mickey Mantle, 1957 ....8.2
35 Nap Lajoie, 1901 ....8.1
Nap Lajoie, 1903 ....8.1
Babe Ruth, 1931 ....8.1
Ted Williams, 1946 ....8.1
Mickey Mantle, 1956 ....8.1
40 Pedro Martinez, 1999 ...8.0
Nap Lajoie, 1908 ....8.0
Joe Morgan, 1975 ....8.0
Barry Bonds, 1992 ....8.0
Barry Bonds, 1993 ....8.0
45 Cy Young, 1901 ....7.9
Roger Clemens, 1997 ...7.9
Rogers Hornsby, 1920 ....7.9
George Sisler, 1920 ....7.9
Lou Gehrig, 1934 ....7.9
50 Rogers Hornsby, 1917 ....7.8
Johnny Mostil, 1926 ....7.8
Rickey Henderson, 1990 ....7.8
Barry Bonds, 1996 ....7.8
Mike Piazza, 1997 ....7.8
55 Rogers Hornsby, 1921 ....7.7
Lou Gehrig, 1930 ....7.7
Jeff Bagwell, 1994 ....7.7
Ken Caminiti, 1996 ....7.7
59 Dave Foutz, 1886 ....7.6
Joe Wood, 1912 ....7.6
Walter Johnson, 1918 ....7.6
Dolf Luque, 1923 ....7.6
Hal Newhouser, 1945 ....7.6
Bob Gibson, 1968 ....7.6
Nap Lajoie, 1906 ....7.6
Babe Ruth, 1930 ....7.6
Norm Cash, 1961 ....7.6
Ron Santo, 1967 ....7.6
69 John Clarkson, 1887 ....7.5
Grover Alexander, 1915 ....7.5
Dwight Gooden, 1985 ....7.5
Honus Wagner, 1905 ....7.5
Lou Boudreau, 1944 ....7.5
Rico Petrocelli, 1969 ....7.5
Joe Morgan, 1973 ....7.5
Albert Pujols, 2003 ....7.5
77 Pink Hawley, 1895 ....7.4
Walter Johnson, 1915 ....7.4
Nap Lajoie, 1904 ....7.4
Ty Cobb, 1917 ....7.4
Harlond Clift, 1937 ....7.4
Al Rosen, 1953 ....7.4
Mickey Mantle, 1961 ....7.4
Mike Schmidt, 1974 ....7.4
85 John Clarkson, 1885 ....7.3
Carl Hubbell, 1933 ....7.3
Steve Carlton, 1972 ....7.3
Tris Speaker, 1914 ....7.3
Babe Ruth, 1919 ....7.3
Jackie Robinson, 1951 ....7.3
Ron Santo, 1966 ....7.3
Robin Yount, 1982 ....7.3
93 Bob Caruthers, 1886 ....7.2
Matt Kilroy, 1887 ....7.2
Walter Johnson, 1914 ....7.2
Grover Alexander, 1916 ....7.2
Dazzy Vance, 1928 ....7.2
Honus Wagner, 1906 ....7.2
Tris Speaker, 1912 ....7.2
Frankie Frisch, 1927 ....7.2
Snuffy Stirnweiss, 1945 ....7.2
Ted Williams, 1947 ....7.2
Stan Musial, 1948 ....7.2
Mike Schmidt, 1981 ....7.2

Player Overall Wins

105 Tony Mullane, 1884 ....7.1
Fred Dunlap, 1884 ....7.1
Joe Jackson, 1912 ....7.1
Babe Ruth, 1928 ....7.1
Lou Boudreau, 1948 ....7.1
Ted Williams, 1957 ....7.1
Ron Santo, 1964 ....7.1
Cal Ripken, 1983 ....7.1
Jeff Bagwell, 1996 ....7.1
Mark McGwire, 1998 ....7.1
Alex Rodriguez, 2002 ...7.1
116 Warren Spahn, 1953 ....7.0
Nap Lajoie, 1907 ....7.0
Eddie Collins, 1910 ....7.0
Eddie Collins, 1913 ....7.0
Joe Morgan, 1974 ....7.0
Rickey Henderson, 1985 ....7.0
Barry Bonds, 2000 ....7.0
123 Will White, 1883 ....6.9
Cy Young, 1895 ....6.9
Kid Nichols, 1897 ....6.9
Grover Alexander, 1920 ....6.9
Lefty Grove, 1930 ....6.9
Kevin Brown, 1996 ....6.9
Honus Wagner, 1908 ....6.9
Eddie Collins, 1914 ....6.9
Joe Cronin, 1930 ....6.9
Jimmie Foxx, 1933 ....6.9
Carl Yastrzemski, 1967 ....6.9
Rod Carew, 1974 ....6.9
Mike Schmidt, 1980 ....6.9
Gary Carter, 1982 ....6.9
Alex Rodriguez, 2001 ...6.9
138 Jack Stivetts, 1891 ....6.8
Amos Rusie, 1893 ....6.8
Ed Walsh, 1908 ....6.8
Red Faber, 1921 ....6.8
Wes Ferrell, 1935 ....6.8
Lefty Gomez, 1937 ....6.8
Bob Feller, 1940 ....6.8
Greg Maddux, 1994 ....6.8
Cupid Childs, 1890 ....6.8
Dan Brouthers, 1892 ....6.8
Rogers Hornsby, 1925 ....6.8
Rogers Hornsby, 1927 ....6.8
Rogers Hornsby, 1929 ....6.8
Lou Boudreau, 1943 ....6.8
Snuffy Stirnweiss, 1944 ....6.8
Willie Mays, 1955 ....6.8
Hank Aaron, 1959 ....6.8
Toby Harrah, 1975 ....6.8
Barry Bonds, 1998 ....6.8
Alex Rodriguez, 2000 ...6.8
158 Will White, 1882 ....6.7
Toad Ramsey, 1886 ....6.7
Walter Johnson, 1919 ....6.7
Tom Seaver, 1971 ....6.7
Gaylord Perry, 1972 ....6.7
John Hiller, 1973 ....6.7
Hughie Jennings, 1896 ....6.7
Honus Wagner, 1907 ....6.7
Jimmie Foxx, 1932 ....6.7
Rod Carew, 1975 ....6.7
Joe Morgan, 1976 ....6.7
George Brett, 1985 ....6.7
170 Charlie Sweeney, 1884 ....6.6
Silver King, 1890 ....6.6
Christy Mathewson, 1909 ....6.6
Lefty Grove, 1936 ....6.6
Bob Lemon, 1948 ....6.6
Art Devlin, 1906 ....6.6
Ty Cobb, 1911 ....6.6
Frank Baker, 1913 ....6.6
Eddie Collins, 1915 ....6.6
Arky Vaughan, 1935 ....6.6
Lou Gehrig, 1936 ....6.6
Joe DiMaggio, 1941 ....6.6
Willie Mays, 1965 ....6.6
Willie McCovey, 1969 ....6.6
Johnny Bench, 1972 ....6.6
Rod Carew, 1977 ....6.6
George Brett, 1980 ....6.6
Jeff Kent, 2000 ....6.6
188 22 players tied 6.5

THE NATURALS: THE HALL OF FAME

While lesser sports have copied the National Baseball Hall of Fame and Museum, no other athletic Hall of Fame commands nearly so much respect, interest, or passion. In a cynical modern era when very few athletic heroes are idolized, those fortunate few inducted into Cooperstown have achieved a kind of immortality. Many of these bronze demigods were *naturals* in the true sense of the word, whether they triumphed over their demons like Robert Redford in Barry Levinson's 1984 film *The Natural*—or whether they succumbed like Roy Hobbs in Bernard Malamud's classic novella on which the movie was based.

In 1934 in the middle of the Great Depression, Alexander Cleland, a civic leader in Cooperstown, New York, came up with an idea to boost tourism in his small city: He decided that Cooperstown could benefit from building a baseball museum. Cooperstown was (and still is) an out-of-the-way place. However, the town was home to a rich foundation—Cleland's employer, the Clark Foundation—that would support these types of projects, and it was also the supposed birthplace of baseball. Even then, many people realized that Abner Doubleday most certainly did *not* invent baseball in Cooperstown, and that neither the famous general nor the picturesque town had even played a role in the development of baseball. Nonetheless, creation myths are very powerful, and Cooperstown has been able to take great advantage of its part in this fictional tale.

Once Cooperstown officials were convinced of the wisdom of building a baseball museum, they contacted Major League Baseball. Coincidentally, NL President Ford Frick had come up with an idea of his own that would enhance any baseball museum: a Hall of Fame. Frick had recently visited the Hall of Fame for Great Americans at New York University and been inspired to do something similar for baseball's legendary stars.

While the phrase "Hall of Fame" was well known at the time, it was almost always used as a metaphor. Today there are more Halls of Fame in the United States than anyone has the patience to count—there's even a Shuffleboard Hall of Fame in Texas—but the Hall for Great Americans was the first of its kind when it opened in 1900. The Baseball Hall of Fame would be the first such institution devoted to a sport. So Cooperstown leaders and baseball officials reached an agreement to build the National Baseball Hall of Fame and Museum in upstate New York.

Though the museum would not be ready to open until 1939, the process of electing players to the Hall began in 1936. Two groups were formed to elect players—a large group of more than 200 writers from the Baseball Writers Association of America and a 78-member Old-Timers Committee. While the Old-Timers Committee was formed specifically to evaluate long-retired players, the two sets of voters were given almost no further guidance on whom to elect. Several active players received significant support from the BBWAA, while other players received votes from both the writers and the Old Timers. A 75-percent vote of either group was needed to earn induction in the Hall. In the end, the writers selected five of the all-time greats: Ty Cobb, Babe Ruth, Honus Wagner Christy Mathewson, and Walter Johnson. A divided and confused Old-Timers Committee elected no one.

The BBWAA would hold three more elections before the official opening of the Hall of Fame, electing Nap Lajoie, Tris Speaker, and Cy Young in 1937, Grover Cleveland Alexander in 1938, and George Sisler, Eddie Collins, and Willie Keeler in 1939. Afterward, the BBWAA held a vote only once every three years. The organization went back to having an annual election in 1946, then reduced the frequency of their balloting to every two years after 1956. Finally, the BBWAA permanently returned to an annual election in 1966. In 1954, it was decided that all future candidates would not appear on the BBWAA ballot until five years after retirement. After Roberto Clemente's death in 1972, the rules were modified so that any player who died before eligibility could be considered by the writers only six months later.

After the failure of the Old-Timers Committee to elect anyone in 1936, a smaller Centennial Commission was formed to elect executives, managers, and other pioneers. This commission elected Morgan B. Bulkeley, Ban Johnson, Connie Mack, John McGraw, and George Wright in 1937, and added Alexander Cartwright (though not Abner Doubleday) and Henry Chadwick in 1938. The idea of an Old-Timers Committee was revived in 1939, electing various players and officials in 1939, 1944, 1945, 1946, and 1949. The committee's election of 21 players and executives in 1945 and 1946 started a long tradition of questionable choices, which didn't stop the formation of a permanent Veterans Committee in 1953. The Veterans Committee continued to elect managers and executives—as well as players that the writers had passed over—until it was disbanded after 2001.

While the Veterans Committee certainly made some worthy selections, its voting process was politicized from the start: The number of friends or teammates a player under consideration had on the committee was often the best indicator of whether he would be elected. Separate committees for the Negro Leagues and for the nineteenth century did a much better job dealing with leagues and eras of which previous voters showed little knowledge. However, even the Negro Leagues Committee was criticized for relying too much on the opinion of one man, Buck O'Neil.

A new Veterans Committee (which includes all living Hall of Famers and all living recipients of either the Frick or the Spink awards) has now been assembled to consider players every two years; the group also votes on umpires, managers, and executives every four years. No one came remotely close to winning induction into the Hall in the new committee's first vote in 2003. Unless the rules or the composition of the committee is changed, it seems unlikely that it will elect very many candidates, especially any Negro Leaguers or nineteenth-century players. Hall of Famers always want the Hall to be more exclusive after they've been elected, and few realize how much harder it's been for post-World War II players to earn induction when compared to their predecessors. In a group far too big for the kind of personal politicking that was so effective on the old Veterans Committee, it will probably be very hard to reach consensus.

What follows is a listing of every member of the Hall of Fame. Also listed are those not in the Hall of Fame who have received even one vote at some time, plus the leading vote-getters each year. The first and last years of everyone's **Career** is shown, regardless of whether their seasons were consecutive. Voting totals include the candidate's first-year percentage of votes **(1st Yr./Pct.)** and the final year totals **(Last Yr./Pct.)** through 2004, as well as the year the player received his highest vote total and the percentage of that vote he received **(Max. Yr./Pct.)**. The Year-by-Year section includes the totals of all candidates who received at least 25 percent of the BBWAA votes in a given year; also provided are the number of votes (which fluctuate each year) required to gain induction.

Hall of Famers and other candidates are listed by their primary **Position**; non-players are listed as executives (*Exe*), managers (*Mgr*), pioneers (*Pio*), or umpires (*Ump*). Special elections and abbreviations include *1936V* (for Veteran's Election) and *1946N* (for Nominating Ballot, where no one was to be elected). The Negro Leagues Committee is represented by an *N*, while *C* stands for Centennial, *V* for Veterans, and *S* for Special. An *R* after a year indicates a run-off election, held after no one was elected on the regular ballot. A maximum of one player could be elected in the three run-off elections, even if more than one received 75 percent of the run-off vote.

MEMBERS OF THE HALL OF FAME

Member	Career	Position	Elected	Max. Yr.	Pct.	1st Yr.	Pct.	Last Yr.	Pct.
Hank Aaron	1954-1976	RF	1982	1982	97.8				
Grover Alexander	1911-1930	P	1938	1938	80.9	1936	24.3	1938	80.9
Walter Alston	1954-1976	Mgr	1983V						
Sparky Anderson	1970-1995	Mgr	2000V						
Cap Anson	1871-1897	1B	1939O	1936V	51.3				
Luis Aparicio	1956-1973	SS	1984	1984	84.6	1979	27.8	1984	84.6
Luke Appling	1930-1950	SS	1964	1964R	83.6	1953	0.8	1964R	83.6
Richie Ashburn	1948-1962	CF	1995V	1978	41.7	1968	2.1	1982	30.4
Earl Averill	1929-1941	CF	1975V	1958	5.3	1949	0.7	1962	1.9
Frank Baker	1908-1922	3B	1955V	1947	30.4	1936	0.4	1951	3.5
Dave Bancroft	1915-1930	SS	1971V	1958	16.2	1937	1.5	1960	11.2
Ernie Banks	1953-1971	1B	1977	1977	83.8				
Al Barlick	1940-1971	Ump	1989V						
Ed Barrow	1903-1947	Exe	1953V						
Jake Beckley	1888-1907	1B	1971V	1936V	1.3	1936V	1.3	1942	0.4
Cool Papa Bell	1922-1946	CF	1974N						
Johnny Bench	1967-1983	C	1989	1989	96.4				
Chief Bender	1903-1917	P	1953V	1947	44.7	1936	0.9	1953	39.4
Yogi Berra	1946-1965	C	1972	1972	85.6	1971	67.2	1972	85.6
Jim Bottomley	1922-1937	1B	1974V	1960	33.1	1948	3.3	1962	12.5
Lou Boudreau	1938-1952	SS	1970	1970	77.3	1956	1.0	1970	77.3
Roger Bresnahan	1897-1915	C	1945O	1945	53.8	1936	20.8	1945	53.8
George Brett	1973-1993	3B	1999	1999	98.2				
Lou Brock	1961-1979	LF	1985	1985	79.7				
Dan Brouthers	1879-1896	1B	1945O	1936V	2.6				
Mordecai Brown	1903-1916	P	1949O	1946N	27.7	1936	2.7	1946	18.3
Morgan Bulkeley	1876-1876	Exe	1937C						
Jim Bunning	1955-1971	P	1996V	1988	74.2	1977	38.1	1991	63.7
Jesse Burkett	1890-1905	LF	1946O	1942	1.7	1936V	1.3	1946N	1.0
Roy Campanella	1948-1957	C	1969	1969	79.4	1964	57.2	1969	79.4
Rod Carew	1967-1985	1B	1991	1991	90.5				
Max Carey	1910-1929	CF	1961V	1958	51.1	1937	3.0	1958	51.1
Steve Carlton	1965-1988	P	1994	1994	95.8				
Gary Carter	1974-1992	C	2003	2003	78.0	1998	42.3	2003	78.0
Alexander Cartwright	1845-1848	Pio	1938C						
Orlando Cepeda	1958-1974	1B	1999V	1994	73.6	1980	12.5	1994	73.6
Henry Chadwick	1858-1908	Pio	1938C						
Frank Chance	1898-1914	1B	1946O	1945	72.5	1936	2.2	1946	57.0
Happy Chandler	1945-1951	Exe	1982V						
Oscar Charleston	1915-1940	CF	1976N						
Jack Chesbro	1899-1909	P	1946O	1939	2.2	1937	0.5	1946N	0.5
Nestor Chylak	1954-1978	Ump	1999V						
Fred Clarke	1894-1915	LF	1945O	1942	24.9	1936V	11.5	1945	21.5
John Clarkson	1882-1894	P	1963V	1936V	6.4	1936V	6.4	1946N	0.5
Roberto Clemente	1955-1972	RF	1973S						
Ty Cobb	1905-1928	CF	1936	1936	98.2				
Mickey Cochrane	1925-1937	C	1947	1947	79.5	1936	35.4	1947	79.5
Eddie Collins	1906-1930	2B	1939	1939	77.7	1936	26.5	1939	77.7
Jimmy Collins	1895-1908	3B	1945O	1945	49.0	1936V	10.3	1945	49.0
Earle Combs	1924-1935	CF	1970V	1960	16.0	1937	2.0	1962	3.8
Charlie Comiskey	1882-1894	Exe	1939O	1936V	7.7				
Jocko Conlan	1941-1964	Ump	1974V						
Tommy Connolly	1898-1931	Ump	1953V						
Roger Connor	1880-1897	1B	1976V						
Stan Coveleski	1912-1928	P	1969V	1958	12.8	1938	0.4	1958	12.8
Sam Crawford	1899-1917	RF	1957V	1946N	4.5	1936	0.4	1946N	4.5
Joe Cronin	1926-1945	SS	1956	1956	78.8	1947	3.7	1956	78.8
Candy Cummings	1872-1877	Pio	1939O						
Kiki Cuyler	1921-1938	RF	1968V	1958	33.8	1948	2.5	1962	19.4
Ray Dandridge	1933-1949	3B	1987V						
George Davis	1890-1909	SS	1998V						
Leon Day	1934-1950	P	1995V						
Dizzy Dean	1930-1940	P	1953	1953	79.2	1936	0.4	1953	79.2
Ed Delahanty	1888-1903	LF	1945O	1939	52.9	1936V	28.2	1945	44.9
Bill Dickey	1928-1946	C	1954	1954	80.2	1945	6.9	1954	80.2
Martin Dihigo	1923-1945	2B	1977N						
Joe DiMaggio	1936-1951	CF	1955	1955	88.8	1945	0.4	1955	88.8
Larry Doby	1947-1959	CF	1998V	1967	3.4	1966	2.3	1967R	0.3
Bobby Doerr	1937-1951	2B	1986V	1970	25.0	1953	0.8	1971	21.7
Don Drysdale	1956-1969	P	1984	1984	78.4	1975	21.0	1984	78.4
Hugh Duffy	1888-1906	CF	1945O	1942	33.0	1936V	5.1	1945	25.9
Leo Durocher	1939-1973	Mgr	1994V	1958	10.5	1948	0.8	1964R	0.9
Dennis Eckersley	1975-1998	P	2004	2004	83.2				
Billy Evans	1906-1927	Ump	1973V						
Johnny Evers	1902-1929	2B	1946O	1946N	64.4	1936	2.7	1946	41.8
Buck Ewing	1880-1897	C	1939O	1936V	51.3	1936V	51.3	1939	0.7
Red Faber	1914-1933	P	1964V	1960	30.9	1937	1.5	1962	18.8
Bob Feller	1936-1956	P	1962	1962	93.8				
Rick Ferrell	1929-1947	C	1984V	1956	0.5	1956	0.5	1960	0.4
Rollie Fingers	1968-1985	P	1992	1992	81.2	1991	65.7	1992	81.2
Carlton Fisk	1969-1993	C	2000	2000	79.6	1999	66.4	2000	79.6
Elmer Flick	1898-1910	RF	1963V	1938	0.4				
Whitey Ford	1950-1967	P	1974	1974	77.8	1973	67.1	1974	77.8
Bill Foster	1923-1937	P	1996V						
Rube Foster	1902-1926	Mgr	1981V						
Nellie Fox	1947-1965	2B	1997V	1985	74.7	1971	10.8	1985	74.7
Jimmie Foxx	1925-1945	1B	1951	1951	79.2	1936	9.3	1951	79.2
Ford Frick	1934-1965	Exe	1970V						
Frankie Frisch	1919-1937	2B	1947	1947	84.5	1936	6.2	1947	84.5
Jim Galvin	1875-1892	P	1965V						
Lou Gehrig	1923-1939	1B	1939S	1936	22.6				
Charlie Gehringer	1924-1942	2B	1949	1949R	85.0	1936	0.4	1949R	85.0
Josh Gibson	1930-1946	C	1972N						
Bob Gibson	1959-1975	P	1981	1981	84.0				
Warren Giles	1946-1969	Exe	1979V						
Lefty Gomez	1930-1943	P	1972V	1956	46.1	1945	2.8	1962	12.5
Goose Goslin	1921-1938	LF	1968V	1956	13.5	1948	0.8	1962	8.8
Hank Greenberg	1930-1947	1B	1956	1956	85.0	1945	1.2	1956	85.0
Clark Griffith	1891-1907	Exe	1946O	1945	43.7	1937	2.0	1946	31.2
Burleigh Grimes	1916-1934	P	1964V	1960	34.2	1937	0.5	1962	26.9
Lefty Grove	1925-1941	P	1947	1947	76.4	1936	5.3	1947	76.4
Chick Hafey	1924-1937	LF	1971V	1960	10.8	1948	0.8	1962	4.4
Jesse Haines	1918-1937	P	1970V	1958	8.3	1939	0.4	1962	1.9
Billy Hamilton	1888-1901	CF	1961V	1936V	2.6	1936V	2.6	1942	0.4
Ned Hanlon	1889-1907	Mgr	1996V						
Will Harridge	1931-1959	Exe	1972V						
Bucky Harris	1924-1956	Mgr	1975V	1958	16.9	1938	0.4	1960	11.5

Member	Career	Position	Elected	Max. Yr.	Pct.	1st Yr.	Pct.	Last Yr.	Pct.
Gabby Hartnett	1922-1941	C	1955	1955	77.7	1936	0.4	1955	77.7
Harry Heilmann	1914-1932	RF	1952	1952	86.8	1937	5.0	1952	86.8
Billy Herman	1931-1947	2B	1975V	1967	20.2	1948	0.8	1967R	4.6
Harry Hooper	1909-1925	RF	1971V	1937	3.0	1937	3.0	1951	1.3
Rogers Hornsby	1915-1937	2B	1942	1942	78.1	1936	46.5	1942	78.1
Waite Hoyt	1918-1938	P	1969V	1956	19.2	1939	0.4	1962	11.3
Cal Hubbard	1936-1951	Ump	1976V						
Carl Hubbell	1928-1943	P	1947	1947	87.0	1945	9.7	1947	87.0
Miller Huggins	1913-1929	Mgr	1964V	1946N	63.9	1937	2.5	1950	1.2
William Hulbert	1877-1882	Exe	1995V						
Catfish Hunter	1965-1979	P	1987	1987	76.3	1985	53.7	1987	76.3
Monte Irvin	1939-1956	LF	1973N						
Reggie Jackson	1967-1987	LF	1993	1993	93.6				
Travis Jackson	1922-1936	SS	1982V	1956	7.3	1948	4.1	1962	0.6
Fergie Jenkins	1965-1983	P	1991	1991	75.4	1989	52.3	1991	75.4
Hughie Jennings	1891-1903	SS	1945O	1945	37.2	1936V	14.1	1945	37.2
Ban Johnson	1901-1927	Exe	1937C						
Judy Johnson	1921-1938	3B	1975N						
Walter Johnson	1907-1927	P	1936	1936	83.6				
Addie Joss	1902-1910	P	1978V	1942	14.2	1937	5.5	1960	0.4
Al Kaline	1953-1974	RF	1980	1980	88.3				
Tim Keefe	1880-1893	P	1964V	1936V	1.3				
Willie Keeler	1892-1910	RF	1939	1939	75.5	1936V	42.3	1939	75.5
George Kell	1943-1957	3B	1983V	1977	36.8	1964	16.4	1977	36.8
Joe Kelley	1891-1908	LF	1971V	1942	0.4	1939	0.4	1942	0.4
George Kelly	1915-1932	1B	1973V	1960	1.9	1947	0.6	1962	0.6
King Kelly	1878-1893	C	1945O	1936V	19.2				
Harmon Killebrew	1954-1975	1B	1984	1984	83.1	1981	59.6	1984	83.1
Ralph Kiner	1946-1955	LF	1975	1975	75.4	1962	3.1	1975	75.4
Chuck Klein	1928-1944	RF	1980V	1964	27.9	1948	2.5	1964R	8.0
Bill Klem	1905-1941	Ump	1953V						
Sandy Koufax	1955-1966	P	1972	1972	86.9				
Nap Lajoie	1896-1916	2B	1937	1937	83.6	1936V	2.6	1937	83.6
Judge Landis	1920-1944	Exe	1944O						
Tom Lasorda	1976-1996	Mgr	1997V						
Tony Lazzeri	1926-1939	2B	1991V	1956	33.2	1945	0.4	1962	5.0
Bob Lemon	1941-1958	P	1976	1976	78.6	1964	11.9	1976	78.6
Buck Leonard	1933-1950	1B	1972N						
Freddie Lindstrom	1924-1936	3B	1976V	1962	4.4	1949	0.7	1962	4.4
John Henry Lloyd	1905-1931	SS	1977N						
Ernie Lombardi	1931-1947	C	1986V	1964	16.4	1950	1.8	1967R	8.2
Al Lopez	1928-1947	Mgr	1977V	1967	39.0	1949	0.7	1967R	16.3
Ted Lyons	1923-1946	P	1955	1955	86.5	1945	1.6	1955	86.5
Connie Mack	1894-1950	Mgr	1937C	1936	0.4				
Larry MacPhail	1934-1947	Exe	1978V						
Lee MacPhail	1941-1985	Exe	1998V						
Mickey Mantle	1951-1968	CF	1974	1974	88.2				
Heinie Manush	1923-1939	LF	1964V	1962	9.4	1948	0.8	1962	9.4
Rabbit Maranville	1912-1935	SS	1954	1954	82.9	1937	12.4	1954	82.9
Juan Marichal	1960-1975	P	1983	1983	83.7	1981	58.1	1983	83.7
Rube Marquard	1908-1925	P	1971V	1955	13.9	1936	0.4	1955	13.9
Eddie Mathews	1952-1968	3B	1978	1978	79.4	1974	32.3	1978	79.4
Christy Mathewson	1900-1916	P	1936	1936	90.7				
Willie Mays	1951-1973	CF	1979	1979	94.7				
Bill Mazeroski	1956-1972	2B	2001V	1992	42.3	1978	6.1	1992	42.3
Joe McCarthy	1926-1950	Mgr	1957V	1947	1.2	1939	1.1	1958	0.8
Tommy McCarthy	1884-1896	RF	1946O	1936V	1.3				
Willie McCovey	1959-1980	1B	1986	1986	81.4				
Joe McGinnity	1899-1908	P	1946O	1946N	26.2	1937	6.0	1946	17.9
Bill McGowan	1925-1954	Ump	1992V						
John McGraw	1891-1906	Mgr	1937C	1936V	21.8	1936V	21.8	1937	17.4
Bill McKechnie	1922-1946	Mgr	1962V	1951	3.5	1945	0.8	1951	3.5
Bid McPhee	1882-1899	2B	2000V						
Joe Medwick	1932-1948	LF	1968	1968	84.8	1948	0.8	1968	84.8
Johnny Mize	1936-1953	1B	1981V	1971	43.6	1960	16.7	1973	41.3
Paul Molitor	1978-1998	DH	2004	2004	85.2				
Joe Morgan	1963-1984	2B	1990	1990	81.8				
Eddie Murray	1977-1997	1B	2003	2003	85.3				
Stan Musial	1941-1963	LF	1969	1969	93.2				
Hal Newhouser	1939-1955	P	1992V	1975	42.8	1962	2.5	1975	42.8
Kid Nichols	1890-1906	P	1949O	1936V	3.8	1936V	3.8	1946N	0.5
Phil Niekro	1964-1987	P	1997	1997	80.3	1993	65.7	1997	80.3
Jim O'Rourke	1872-1893	LF	1945O						
Mel Ott	1926-1947	RF	1951	1951	87.2	1949	61.4	1951	87.2
Satchel Paige	1927-1953	P	1971N	1951	0.4				
Jim Palmer	1965-1984	P	1990	1990	92.6				
Herb Pennock	1912-1934	P	1948	1948	77.7	1937	7.5	1948	77.7
Tony Perez	1964-1986	1B	2000	2000	77.2	1992	50.0	2000	77.2
Gaylord Perry	1962-1983	P	1991	1991	77.2	1989	68.0	1991	77.2
Eddie Plank	1901-1917	P	1946O	1942	27.0	1937	11.4	1946N	16.8
Kirby Puckett	1984-1995	CF	2001	2001	82.1				
Charley Radbourn	1880-1891	P	1939O	1936V	20.5				
Pee Wee Reese	1940-1958	SS	1984V	1976	47.9	1964	36.3	1978	44.6
Sam Rice	1915-1934	RF	1963V	1960	53.2	1938	0.4	1962	50.6
Branch Rickey	1913-1965	Exe	1967V	1942	1.3	1942	1.3	1945	0.8
Eppa Rixey	1912-1933	P	1963V	1960	52.8	1937	0.5	1962	30.6
Phil Rizzuto	1941-1956	SS	1994V	1976	38.4	1956	0.5	1976	38.4
Robin Roberts	1948-1966	P	1976	1976	86.9	1973	56.1	1976	86.9
Brooks Robinson	1955-1977	3B	1983	1983	92.0				
Frank Robinson	1956-1976	RF	1982	1982	89.2				
Jackie Robinson	1947-1956	2B	1962	1962	77.5				
Wilbert Robinson	1886-1902	Mgr	1945O	1942	38.2	1936V	7.7	1945	32.8
Bullet Joe Rogan	1920-1938	P	1998V						
Edd Roush	1913-1931	CF	1962V	1960	54.3	1936	0.9	1960	54.3
Red Ruffing	1924-1947	P	1967	1967R	86.9	1948	3.3	1967R	86.9
Amos Rusie	1889-1901	P	1977V	1936V	15.4	1936V	15.4	1945	0.4
Babe Ruth	1914-1935	RF	1936	1936	95.1				
Nolan Ryan	1966-1993	P	1999	1999	98.8				
Ray Schalk	1912-1929	C	1955V	1955	45.0	1936	1.8	1955	45.0
Mike Schmidt	1972-1989	3B	1995	1995	96.5				
Red Schoendienst	1945-1963	2B	1989V	1980	42.6	1969	19.1	1983	39.0
Tom Seaver	1967-1986	P	1992	1992	98.8				
Frank Selee	1890-1905	Mgr	1999V						
Joe Sewell	1920-1933	SS	1977V	1960	8.6	1937	0.5	1960	8.6
Al Simmons	1924-1944	LF	1953	1953	75.4	1936	1.8	1953	75.4
George Sisler	1915-1930	1B	1939	1939	85.8	1936	34.1	1939	85.8
Enos Slaughter	1938-1959	RF	1985V	1978	68.9	1966	33.1	1979	68.8
Hilton Smith	1933-1948	P	2001V						
Ozzie Smith	1978-1996	SS	2002	2002	91.7				

Member	Career	Position	Elected	Max. Yr.	Pct.	1st Yr.	Pct.	Last Yr.	Pct.
Duke Snider	1947-1964	CF	1980	1980	86.5	1970	17.0	1980	86.5
Warren Spahn	1942-1965	P	1973	1973	83.2				
Al Spalding	1871-1878	Pio	1939O	1936V	5.1				
Tris Speaker	1907-1928	CF	1937	1937	82.1	1936	58.8	1937	82.1
Willie Stargell	1962-1982	LF	1988	1988	82.4				
Turkey Stearnes	1923-1940	CF	2000V						
Casey Stengel	1934-1965	Mgr	1966V	1953	23.1	1938	0.8	1953	23.1
Don Sutton	1966-1988	P	1998	1998	81.6	1994	56.9	1998	81.6
Bill Terry	1923-1936	1B	1954	1954	77.4	1936	4.0	1954	77.4
Sam Thompson	1885-1898	RF	1974V						
Joe Tinker	1902-1916	SS	1946O	1946N	27.2	1937	7.5	1946	17.1
Pie Traynor	1920-1937	3B	1948	1948	76.9	1936	7.1	1948	76.9
Dazzy Vance	1915-1935	P	1955	1955	81.7	1936	0.4	1955	81.7
Arky Vaughan	1932-1948	SS	1985V	1968	29.0	1953	0.4	1968	29.0
Bill Veeck	1933-1980	Exe	1991V						
Rube Waddell	1897-1910	P	1946O	1939	65.3	1936	14.6	1946	33.1
Honus Wagner	1897-1917	SS	1936	1936	95.1	1936V	6.4	1936	95.1
Bobby Wallace	1894-1918	SS	1953V	1938	2.7	1936V	1.3	1945	1.2
Ed Walsh	1904-1917	P	1946O	1946N	56.9	1936	8.8	1946	40.3
Lloyd Waner	1927-1945	CF	1967V	1964	23.4	1949	2.0	1964R	5.3
Paul Waner	1926-1945	RF	1952	1952	83.3	1946N	2.0	1952	83.3
John Ward	1878-1894	SS	1964V	1936V	3.8				
Earl Weaver	1968-1986	Mgr	1996V						
George Weiss	1932-1971	Exe	1971V						
Mickey Welch	1880-1892	P	1973V						
Willie Wells	1924-1948	SS	1997V						
Zack Wheat	1909-1927	LF	1959V	1947	23.0	1937	2.5	1956	13.5
Hoyt Wilhelm	1952-1972	P	1985	1985	83.8	1978	41.7	1985	83.8
Billy Williams	1959-1976	LF	1987	1987	85.7	1982	23.4	1987	85.7
Joe Williams	1910-1932	P	1999V						
Ted Williams	1939-1960	LF	1966	1966	93.4				
Vic Willis	1898-1910	P	1995V						
Hack Wilson	1923-1934	CF	1979V	1956	38.3	1937	0.5	1962	24.4
Dave Winfield	1973-1995	RF	2001	2001	84.5				
George Wright	1871-1882	Pio	1937C	1936V	7.7				
Harry Wright	1871-1893	Pio	1953V						
Early Wynn	1939-1963	P	1972	1972	76.0	1969	27.9	1972	76.0
Tom Yawkey	1933-1976	Exe	1980V						
Carl Yastrzemski	1961-1983	LF	1989	1989	94.6				
Cy Young	1890-1911	P	1937	1937	76.1	1936V	41.0	1937	76.1
Ross Youngs	1917-1926	RF	1972V	1947	22.4	1936	4.4	1956	9.8
Robin Yount	1974-1993	SS	1999	1999	77.5				

THOSE NOT IN HALL OF FAME WHO HAVE RECEIVED VOTES

Candidate	Career	Position	Max. Yr./Pct.		1st Yr./Pct.		Last Yr./Pct.	
Babe Adams	1906-1926	P	1947	13.7	1937	4.0	1955	9.6
Sparky Adams	1922-1934	2B	1958	0.4	1958	0.4	1960	0.4
Bobby Adams	1946-1959	2B	1966	0.3				
Dick Allen	1963-1977	1B	1996	18.9	1983	3.7	1997	16.7
Johnny Allen	1932-1944	P	1955	0.4				
Doug Allison	1871-1883	C	1936V	1.3				
Felipe Alou	1958-1974	RF	1980	0.8				
Jesus Alou	1963-1979	LF	1985	0.3				
Matty Alou	1960-1974	CF	1980	1.3				
Nick Altrock	1898-1909	P	1958	7.5	1937	1.5	1960	6.7
Jimmy Archer	1904-1918	C	1937	3.0	1937	3.0	1939	1.1
Jimmy Austin	1909-1922	3B	1958	0.4				
Bob Bailey	1962-1978	3B	1984	0.2				
Dusty Baker	1968-1986	LF	1992	0.9				
Sal Bando	1966-1981	3B	1987	0.7				
Ross Barnes	1871-1881	2B	1936V	3.8				
Jack Barry	1908-1919	SS	1938	1.1	1938	1.1	1939	0.4
Dick Bartell	1927-1946	SS	1948	0.8	1948	0.8	1960	0.4
Joe Battin	1871-1890	3B	1936V	1.3				
Don Baylor	1970-1988	DH	1994	2.6	1994	2.6	1995	2.6
Hank Bauer	1948-1961	RF	1967	7.9	1967	7.9	1967R	2.9
Ginger Beaumont	1899-1910	CF	1946N	0.5	1938	0.4	1946N	0.5
Glenn Beckert	1965-1975	2B	1981	0.2				
Steve Bedrosian	1981-1995	P	2001	0.2				
Mark Belanger	1965-1982	SS	1988	3.7				
Buddy Bell	1972-1989	3B	1995	1.7				
George Bell	1981-1993	LF	1999	1.2				
Charlie Bennett	1878-1893	C	1936V	3.8				
Larry Benton	1923-1935	P	1958	0.4				
Moe Berg	1923-1939	C	1960	1.9	1958	1.1	1960	1.9
Marty Bergen	1896-1899	C	1937	1.0	1937	1.0	1939	0.4
Wally Berger	1930-1940	CF	1958	0.8	1956	0.5	1958	0.8
Charlie Berry	1925-1938	C	1958	1.1	1955	0.4	1958	1.1
Jim Bibby	1972-1984	P	1990	0.2				
Carson Bigbee	1916-1926	LF	1948	0.8				
Jack Billingham	1968-1980	P	1986	0.2				
Max Bishop	1924-1935	2B	1960	1.9	1955	0.4	1960	1.9
Ewell Blackwell	1942-1955	P	1970	4.7	1968	1.8	1970	4.7
Ray Blades	1922-1932	LF	1958	0.4	1958	0.4	1960	0.4
Paul Blair	1964-1980	CF	1986	1.9				
Steve Blass	1964-1974	P	1980	0.5				
Lu Blue	1921-1933	1B	1954	0.4				
Vida Blue	1969-1986	P	1993	8.7	1992	5.3	1995	5.7
Ossie Bluege	1922-1939	3B	1948	1.7	1948	1.7	1960	1.1
Bert Blyleven	1970-1992	P	2004	35.4	1998	17.5	2004	35.4
Ping Bodie	1911-1921	CF	1937	1.0	1937	1.0	1949	0.7
Joe Boley	1927-1932	SS	1942	0.4				
Tommy Bond	1874-1884	P	1936V	1.3				
Bobby Bonds	1968-1981	RF	1993	10.6	1987	5.8	1997	4.2
Bob Boone	1972-1990	C	1996	7.7	1996	7.7	2000	4.2
Jim Bouton	1962-1970	P	1984	0.7				
Larry Bowa	1970-1985	SS	1991	2.5				
Clete Boyer	1955-1971	3B	1979	0.7	1978	0.3	1979	0.7
Ken Boyer	1955-1969	3B	1988	25.5	1975	2.5	1994	11.9
Bill Bradley	1899-1915	3B	1937	2.5	1936	0.4	1946N	0.5
Harry Brecheen	1940-1953	P	1960	2.6	1960	2.6	1973	0.8
Ted Breitenstein	1891-1901	P	1937	0.5				
Jim Brewer	1960-1976	P	1982	0.5				
Tommy Bridges	1930-1946	P	1964	7.5	1956	1.6	1966	5.3
Gates Brown	1963-1975	LF	1981	0.2				
Tom Browning	1984-1995	P	2001	0.2				
Bill Bruton	1953-1964	CF	1971	0.3				
Bill Buckner	1969-1990	1B	1996	2.1				
Lew Burdette	1950-1967	P	1984	24.1	1973	3.2	1987	23.2

Candidate	Career	Position	Max. Yr./Pct.		1st Yr./Pct.		Last Yr./Pct.	
Smoky Burgess	1949-1967	C	1974	0.5	1973	0.3	1974	0.5
George J. Burns	1911-1925	LF	1937	1.5	1937	1.5	1950	1.2
Jeff Burroughs	1970-1985	RF	1991	0.2				
Guy Bush	1923-1945	P	1956	1.0				
Joe Bush	1912-1928	P	1958	1.9				
Donie Bush	1908-1923	SS	1946N	1.0	1937	0.5	1953	0.4
Brett Butler	1981-1997	CF	2003	0.4				
Leon Cadore	1915-1924	P	1948	0.8				
Johnny Callison	1958-1973	RF	1979	0.2				
Dolf Camilli	1933-1945	1B	1958	1.5	1948	0.8	1960	1.1
Howie Camnitz	1904-1915	P	1945	0.4				
Bert Campaneris	1964-1983	SS	1989	3.1				
Bill Campbell	1973-1987	P	1993	0.2				
John Candelaria	1975-1993	P	1999	0.2				
Jose Cardenal	1963-1980	CF	1986	0.2				
Leo Cardenas	1960-1975	SS	1981	0.2	1981	0.2	1982	0.2
Chico Carrasquel	1950-1959	SS	1966	0.3				
Bill Carrigan	1913-1929	Mgr	1937	2.5	1937	2.5	1945	1.2
Clay Carroll	1964-1978	P	1984	0.2				
Joe Carter	1983-1998	LF	2004	3.8				
Rico Carty	1963-1979	LF	1985	0.3				
George Case	1937-1947	LF	1964	1.0	1958	0.4	1964	1.0
Dave Cash	1969-1980	2B	1986	0.5				
Norm Cash	1958-1974	1B	1980	1.6				
Phil Cavaretta	1934-1955	1B	1975	35.6	1962	1.3	1975	35.6
Cesar Cedeno	1970-1986	CF	1992	0.5				
Ron Cey	1971-1987	3B	1993	1.9				
Spud Chandler	1937-1947	P	1964	3.0	1950	1.2	1964	3.0
Ben Chapman	1930-1946	CF	1949	0.7	1949	0.7	1952	0.4
Ray Chapman	1912-1920	SS	1938	0.4				
Sam Chapman	1938-1951	CF	1958	0.4				
Hal Chase	1905-1919	1B	1937	9.0	1936	4.9	1937	9.0
Bill Cissell	1938-1938	2B	1937	0.5				
Jack Clark	1975-1992	RF	1998	1.5				
Watty Clark	1924-1937	P	1958	0.4				
Andy Coakley	1902-1911	P	1938	0.4				
Rocky Colavito	1955-1968	RF	1974	0.5	1974	0.5	1975	0.3
Vince Coleman	1985-1997	LF	2003	0.6				
Shano Collins	1910-1925	RF	1937	0.5				
Dave Concepcion	1970-1988	SS	1998	16.9	1994	6.8	2004	11.3
Wid Conroy	1901-1911	3B	1945	0.4				
Jack Coombs	1906-1920	P	1948	1.7	1937	1.0	1951	0.4
Mort Cooper	1938-1949	P	1958	1.1	1956	1.0	1969	0.9
Walker Cooper	1940-1957	C	1976	14.4	1968	2.8	1977	11.7
Wilbur Cooper	1912-1926	P	1955	4.4	1938	0.4	1955	4.4
Clint Courtney	1951-1961	C	1967	0.3				
Billy Cox	1941-1955	3B	1962	0.6				
Doc Cramer	1929-1948	CF	1964	6.0	1956	2.1	1964	6.0
Del Crandall	1949-1966	C	1976	3.9	1976	3.9	1979	2.1
Doc Crandall	1908-1918	P	1938	0.4				
Gavvy Cravath	1908-1920	Exe	1947	1.2	1937	1.0	1947	1.2
Lou Criger	1896-1912	C	1937	8.0	1936V	1.3	1946N	3.0
Hughie Critz	1924-1935	2B	1956	1.0				
Frank Crosetti	1932-1948	SS	1968	5.3	1950	0.6	1968	5.3
Lave Cross	1887-1907	3B	1942	0.4	1939	0.4	1942	0.4
Al Crowder	1926-1936	P	1958	0.4	1958	0.4	1960	0.4
Walt Cruise	1914-1924	LF	1938	0.4				
Jose Cruz	1970-1988	LF	1994	0.4				
Tony Cuccinello	1930-1945	2B	1958	1.1	1956	0.5	1958	1.1
Bill Dahlen	1891-1911	SS	1936V	1.3	1936V	1.3	1938	0.4
Harry Danning	1933-1942	C	1958	0.4	1958	0.4	1960	0.4
Alvin Dark	1946-1960	SS	1979	18.5	1966	5.6	1980	11.2
Ron Darling	1983-1995	P	2001	0.2				
Jake Daubert	1910-1924	1B	1937	1.0	1936	0.4	1955	0.4
Darren Daulton	1983-1997	C	2003	0.2				
Curt Davis	1934-1946	P	1958	0.4				
Harry Davis	1895-1911	1B	1946N	1.0	1945	0.4	1946N	1.0
Mark Davis	1980-1997	P	2003	0.2				
Tommy Davis	1959-1976	LF	1982	1.2				
Spud Davis	1928-1945	C	1948	0.8	1948	0.8	1949	0.7
Andre Dawson	1976-1996	RF	2003	50.0	2002	45.3	2004	50.0
Doug DeCinces	1973-1987	3B	1993	0.5				
Rick Dempsey	1969-1992	C	1998	0.2				
Jerry Denny	1881-1894	3B	1936V	7.7				
Bucky Dent	1973-1984	SS	1990	0.7				
Paul Derringer	1931-1945	P	1956	6.2	1948	0.8	1960	3.0
Jim Deshaies	1984-1995	P	2001	0.2				
Dom DiMaggio	1940-1953	CF	1973	11.3	1960	1.5	1973	11.3
Bill Dinneen	1898-1909	P	1939	2.6	1938	1.5	1946N	0.5
Bill Doak	1912-1929	P	1958	1.1				
Mike Donlin	1899-1914	RF	1937	3.0	1937	3.0	1945	0.4
Bill Donovan	1898-1918	P	1946N	2.0	1937	1.5	1946N	2.0
Red Dooin	1902-1916	C	1937	0.5	1937	0.5	1938	0.4
Brian Downing	1973-1992	LF	1998	0.4				
Jack Doyle	1889-1905	1B	1936V	1.3				
Larry Doyle	1907-1920	2B	1938	1.5	1937	1.0	1939	0.4
Doug Drabek	1986-1998	P	2004	0.4				
Walt Dropo	1949-1961	1B	1967	0.3				
Joe Dugan	1917-1931	3B	1960	3.0	1937	0.5	1960	3.0
Fred Dunlap	1880-1891	2B	1936V	2.6				
Jack Dunn	1907-1928	Exe	1946N	0.5	1942	0.4	1946N	0.5
Eddie Dyer	1946-1950	Mgr	1947	0.6				
Jimmy Dykes	1918-1939	3B	1960	10.0	1948	4.1	1962	3.8
Lenny Dykstra	1985-1996	CF	2002	0.2				
George Earnshaw	1928-1936	P	1948	2.5	1948	2.5	1956	1.6
Hank Edwards	1941-1953	RF	1960	0.7				
Howard Ehmke	1915-1930	P	1960	4.5	1938	0.4	1960	4.5
Jim Eisenreich	1982-1998	RF	2004	0.6				
Kid Elberfeld	1898-1914	SS	1945	0.8	1936	0.4	1945	0.8
Jumbo Elliott	1923-1934	P	1958	0.4				
Bob Elliott	1939-1953	3B	1964	2.0	1960	0.7	1964	2.0
Dock Ellis	1968-1979	P	1985	0.3				
Del Ennis	1946-1959	RF	1966	1.0	1966	1.0	1967	0.7
Jewel Ens	1929-1931	Mgr	1950	0.6				
Carl Erskine	1948-1959	P	1968	3.2	1966	2.0	1974	3.0
Darrell Evans	1969-1989	3B	1995	1.7				
Dwight Evans	1972-1991	RF	1998	10.4	1997	5.9	1999	3.6
Elroy Face	1953-1969	P	1987	18.9	1976	5.9	1990	11.3
Ron Fairly	1959-1978	1B	1985	0.8				

Candidate	Career	Position	Max. Yr./Pct.		1st Yr./Pct.		Last Yr./Pct.	
Cy Falkenberg	1903-1917	P	1937	0.5				
Sid Fernandez	1983-1997	P	2003	0.4				
Wes Ferrell	1927-1941	P	1956	3.6	1948	0.8	1962	0.6
Cecil Fielder	1985-1998	1B	2004	0.2				
Fred Fitzsimmons	1925-1943	P	1958	6.0	1948	1.7	1962	0.6
Mike Flanagan	1975-1992	P	1998	0.4				
Art Fletcher	1909-1922	SS	1948	2.5	1937	1.0	1951	1.8
Curt Flood	1956-1971	CF	1996	15.1	1977	4.2	1996	15.1
Lew Fonseca	1921-1933	1B	1950	1.2	1948	0.8	1960	1.1
Bob Forsch	1974-1989	P	1995	0.4				
Eddie Foster	1910-1923	2B	1938	0.8				
George Foster	1969-1986	LF	1993	6.9	1992	5.6	1995	4.1
Chick Fraser	1896-1909	P	1939	0.4				
Bill Freehan	1961-1976	C	1982	0.5				
Jim Fregosi	1961-1978	SS	1984	1.0				
Carl Furillo	1946-1960	RF	1971	1.4	1966	0.7	1972	0.5
Augie Galan	1934-1949	LF	1970	1.0	1968	0.7	1970	1.0
Phil Garner	1973-1988	2B	1994	0.4				
Ned Garver	1948-1961	P	1967	0.3				
Steve Garvey	1969-1987	1B	1995	42.6	1993	41.6	2004	24.3
Charlie Gelbert	1929-1940	SS	1949	1.3	1947	0.6	1951	0.4
Kirk Gibson	1979-1995	LF	2001	2.5				
Dave Giusti	1962-1977	P	1983	0.3				
Jack Glasscock	1879-1895	SS	1936V	2.6				
Kid Gleason	1888-1912	2B	1937	0.5	1937	0.5	1945	0.4
Mike Gonzales	1912-1932	C	1958	1.1	1950	0.6	1960	0.7
Joe Gordon	1938-1950	2B	1969	28.5	1945	0.4	1970	26.3
Rich Gossage	1972-1994	P	2001	44.3	2000	33.3	2004	40.7
Hank Gowdy	1910-1930	C	1955	35.9	1937	1.0	1960	14.1
Eddie Grant	1905-1915	2B	1942	1.3	1938	0.4	1946N	0.5
George Grantham	1922-1934	2B	1958	0.4				
Mike Greenwell	1985-1996	LF	2002	0.4				
Bobby Grich	1970-1986	2B	1992	2.6				
Ken Griffey Sr.	1973-1991	RF	1997	4.7				
Charlie Grimm	1916-1936	1B	1958	9.8	1939	0.4	1962	1.3
Marv Grissom	1946-1959	P	1966	0.7				
Dick Groat	1952-1967	SS	1973	1.8	1973	1.8	1978	0.8
Heinie Groh	1912-1927	3B	1955	2.0	1937	0.5	1960	0.4
Steve Gromek	1941-1957	P	1964	0.5				
Orval Grove	1940-1949	P	1960	2.6	1958	1.9	1960	2.6
Pedro Guerrero	1978-1992	1B	1998	1.3				
Ron Guidry	1975-1988	P	2000	8.8	1994	5.3	2002	4.9
Bill Gullickson	1979-1994	P	2000	0.2				
Frank Gustine	1939-1950	3B	1958	1.1				
Mule Haas	1925-1938	CF	1956	0.5	1955	0.4	1960	0.4
Stan Hack	1932-1947	3B	1950	4.8	1948	1.7	1960	2.2
Harvey Haddix	1952-1965	P	1985	3.8	1971	2.8	1985	3.8
Noodles Hahn	1899-1906	P	1939	0.4				
Bill Hallahan	1925-1938	P	1948	0.8	1948	0.8	1960	0.7
Mel Harder	1928-1947	P	1964	25.4	1949	2.6	1967R	4.6
Bubbles Hargrave	1913-1930	C	1947	0.6	1947	0.6	1960	0.4
Mike Hargrove	1974-1985	1B	1991	0.2				
Toby Harrah	1969-1986	3B	1992	0.2				
Bud Harrelson	1965-1980	SS	1986	0.2				
Grady Hatton	1946-1960	3B	1966	1.3	1966	1.3	1967	0.3
Jim Hearn	1947-1959	P	1967	0.3	1966	0.3	1967	0.3
Richie Hebner	1968-1985	3B	1991	0.2				
Jim Hegan	1941-1960	C	1966	1.7	1966	1.7	1967	0.7
Tommy Helms	1964-1977	2B	1983	0.3				
Solly Hemus	1949-1959	SS	1966	0.3				
Dave Henderson	1981-1994	CF	2000	0.4				
Tom Henke	1982-1995	P	2001	1.2				
Tommy Henrich	1937-1950	RF	1970	20.7	1952	1.7	1970	20.7
Babe Herman	1926-1937	RF	1956	5.7	1942	0.4	1960	2.6
Keith Hernandez	1974-1990	1B	1998	10.8	1996	5.1	2004	4.3
Willie Hernandez	1977-1989	P	1995	0.4				
Buck Herzog	1908-1920	2B	1938	0.4				
Jim Hickman	1962-1974	CF	1980	0.3				
Mike Higgins	1930-1946	3B	1958	2.3	1950	1.2	1960	1.1
John Hiller	1965-1980	P	1986	2.6				
Bill Hinchman	1905-1920	RF	1937	0.5				
Gil Hodges	1943-1963	1B	1983	63.4	1969	24.1	1983	63.4
Tommy Holmes	1942-1952	RF	1958	0.8	1958	0.8	1960	0.7
Ken Holtzman	1965-1979	P	1986	1.2	1985	1.0	1986	1.2
Rick Honeycutt	1977-1997	P	2003	0.4				
Burt Hooton	1971-1985	P	1991	0.2				
Willie Horton	1963-1980	LF	1986	0.9				
Charlie Hough	1970-1994	P	2000	0.8				
Art Houtteman	1945-1957	P	1964	1.0				
Elston Howard	1955-1968	C	1981	20.7	1974	5.2	1988	12.4
Frank Howard	1958-1973	LF	1979	1.4				
Al Hrabosky	1970-1982	P	1988	0.2				
Kent Hrbek	1981-1994	1B	2000	1.0				
Bruce Hurst	1980-1994	P	2000	0.2				
Fred Hutchinson	1939-1953	P	1964	5.0	1962	0.6	1964	5.0
Charlie Irwin	1893-1902	3B	1938	0.4	1938	0.4	1939	0.4
Joe Jackson	1908-1920	LF	1946N	1.0	1936	0.9	1946N	1.0
Sonny Jackson	1963-1974	SS	1980	0.3				
Jackie Jensen	1950-1961	RF	1968	1.1	1967	1.0	1972	0.3
Tommy John	1963-1989	P	2001	28.3	1995	21.3	2004	21.9
Bob Johnson	1933-1945	LF	1948	0.8	1948	0.8	1956	0.5
Dave Johnson	1965-1978	2B	1984	0.7				
Fielder Jones	1896-1908	CF	1946N	0.5				
Sam P. Jones	1914-1935	P	1956	0.5	1939	0.4	1956	0.5
Tim Jordan	1901-1910	1B	1951	0.4				
Mike Jorgensen	1968-1985	1B	1991	0.2				
Joe Judge	1915-1934	1B	1960	5.6	1937	0.5	1960	5.6
Billy Jurges	1931-1947	SS	1949	1.3	1949	1.3	1958	0.4
Jim Kaat	1959-1983	P	1993	29.6	1989	19.5	2003	26.2
Willie Kamm	1923-1935	3B	1958	1.1	1958	1.1	1960	0.4
Charlie Keller	1939-1952	LF	1972	6.1	1953	0.4	1972	6.1
Ken Keltner	1937-1955	3B	1958	0.4	1958	0.4	1960	0.4
Terry Kennedy	1978-1991	C	1997	0.2				
Dickie Kerr	1919-1925	P	1955	10.0	1937	0.5	1955	10.0
Don Kessinger	1964-1979	SS	1985	0.5				
Jimmy Key	1984-1998	P	2004	0.6				
Daryl Kile	1991-2002	P	2003	1.4				
Bill Killefer	1909-1921	C	1946N	0.5				
Matt Kilroy	1886-1898	P	1936V	1.3				

Candidate	Career	Position	Max. Yr./Pct.		1st Yr./Pct.		Last Yr./Pct.	
Ellis Kinder	1946-1957	P	1964	1.5				
Dave Kingman	1971-1986	LF	1992	0.7				
Johnny Kling	1900-1913	C	1937	10.0	1936	3.5	1953	0.4
Ted Kluszewski	1947-1961	1B	1977	14.4	1967	3.1	1981	14.0
Otto Knabe	1905-1916	2B	1946N	0.5	1939	0.4	1946N	0.5
Ray Knight	1974-1988	3B	1994	0.2				
Jerry Koosman	1967-1985	P	1991	0.9				
Ray Kremer	1924-1933	P	1948	0.8	1948	0.8	1958	0.8
Red Kress	1927-1940	SS	1960	1.1	1958	0.4	1960	1.1
John Kruk	1986-1995	1B	2001	0.2				
Mike Krukow	1976-1989	P	1995	0.2				
Harvey Kuenn	1952-1966	SS	1988	39.3	1977	14.9	1991	22.6
Joe Kuhel	1930-1947	1B	1956	0.5				
Bob Kuzava	1946-1957	P	1964	0.5				
Bill Lange	1893-1899	CF	1936V	7.7	1936V	7.7	1953	0.4
Hal Lanier	1964-1973	SS	1979	0.2				
Carney Lansford	1978-1992	3B	1998	0.6				
Don Larsen	1953-1967	P	1979	12.3	1974	7.9	1988	7.3
Arlie Latham	1880-1899	3B	1936V	1.3	1936V	1.3	1942	0.4
Cookie Lavagetto	1934-1947	3B	1958	1.5	1958	1.5	1960	0.7
Vern Law	1950-1967	P	1973	2.4	1973	2.4	1979	2.1
Fred Leach	1923-1932	LF	1958	0.8	1958	0.8	1960	0.4
Tommy Leach	1898-1918	CF	1937	0.5	1937	0.5	1939	0.4
Bill Lee	1969-1982	P	1988	0.7				
Sam Leever	1898-1910	P	1937	0.5				
Chet Lemon	1975-1990	CF	1996	0.2				
Dennis Leonard	1974-1986	P	1992	0.2				
Emil Leonard	1933-1953	P	1968	1.8	1960	0.7	1973	1.6
Duffy Lewis	1910-1921	LF	1955	13.5	1937	1.5	1955	13.5
Hans Lobert	1903-1917	3B	1937	1.0	1937	1.0	1960	0.4
Whitey Lockman	1945-1960	1B	1966	1.3				
Mickey Lolich	1963-1979	P	1988	25.5	1985	19.7	1999	5.2
Jim Lonborg	1965-1979	P	1985	0.8	1985	0.8	1986	0.7
Herman Long	1889-1904	SS	1936V	20.5	1936V	20.5	1946N	0.5
Ed Lopat	1944-1955	P	1971	1.1	1968	0.7	1972	0.5
Davey Lopes	1972-1987	2B	1993	0.5				
Bobby Lowe	1890-1907	2B	1936V	2.6	1936V	2.6	1945	0.8
John Lowenstein	1970-1985	LF	1991	0.2				
Red Lucas	1923-1938	P	1949	1.3	1949	1.3	1958	0.4
Dolph Luque	1919-1935	P	1958	5.6	1937	0.5	1960	1.5
Greg Luzinski	1970-1984	LF	1990	0.2				
Sparky Lyle	1967-1982	P	1988	13.1	1988	13.1	1991	3.4
Fred Lynn	1974-1990	CF	1996	5.5	1996	5.5	1997	4.7
Bill Madlock	1973-1987	3B	1993	4.5				
Sherry Magee	1904-1919	LF	1937	1.0	1937	1.0	1951	0.9
Sal Maglie	1945-1958	P	1964	6.5	1964	6.5	1968	3.9
Jim Maloney	1960-1971	P	1978	0.5	1978	0.5	1979	0.5
Gus Mancuso	1928-1945	C	1958	0.4				
Firpo Marberry	1923-1936	P	1958	1.9	1938	0.4	1962	1.3
Marty Marion	1940-1953	SS	1970	40.0	1956	0.5	1973	33.4
Roger Maris	1957-1968	RF	1988	43.1	1974	21.4	1988	43.1
Mike Marshall	1967-1981	P	1987	1.5				
Billy Martin	1950-1961	2B	1967	0.3				
Pepper Martin	1928-1944	CF	1958	17.3	1942	0.9	1964R	2.2
Morrie Martin	1949-1959	P	1966	0.7				
Dennis Martinez	1976-1998	P	2004	3.2				
Don Mattingly	1982-1995	1B	2001	28.2	2001	28.2	2004	12.8
Lee May	1965-1982	1B	1988	0.5				
Carl Mays	1915-1929	P	1958	2.3				
Jim McAleer	1889-1902	CF	1936V	1.3				
Tim McCarver	1959-1980	C	1986	3.8				
Frank McCormick	1934-1948	1B	1964	3.0	1956	1.6	1968	1.1
Lindy McDaniel	1955-1975	P	1982	0.7	1981	0.2	1982	0.7
Gil McDougald	1951-1960	2B	1966	1.7	1966	1.7	1974	0.8
Tug McGraw	1965-1984	P	1990	1.4				
Stuffy McInnis	1909-1927	1B	1949	5.2	1937	0.5	1951	1.3
Denny McLain	1963-1972	P	1979	0.7	1978	0.3	1985	0.5
Larry McLean	1901-1915	C	1937	0.5				
Don McMahon	1957-1974	P	1980	0.3				
Marty McManus	1920-1934	2B	1958	0.8	1958	0.8	1960	0.7
Roy McMillan	1951-1966	SS	1972	2.3	1972	2.3	1974	1.1
Dave McNally	1962-1975	P	1986	2.8	1981	1.2	1986	2.8
Cal McVey	1871-1879	1B	1936V	1.3				
Lee Meadows	1915-1929	P	1958	0.8				
Andy Messersmith	1968-1979	P	1985	0.8	1985	0.8	1986	0.7
Bob Meusel	1920-1930	LF	1948	5.0	1937	0.5	1960	3.7
Eddie Miksis	1944-1958	2B	1964	0.5				
Clyde Milan	1907-1922	CF	1955	2.4	1938	0.4	1955	2.4
Felix Millan	1966-1977	2B	1983	0.3				
Bing Miller	1921-1936	RF	1960	2.2	1958	0.4	1960	2.2
Dots Miller	1909-1921	1B	1948	0.8				
Hack Miller	1916-1925	LF	1937	0.5				
Minnie Minoso	1949-1964	LF	1988	21.1	1969	1.8	1999	14.7
Kevin Mitchell	1984-1998	LF	2004	0.4				
Rick Monday	1966-1984	CF	1990	0.5				
Don Money	1968-1983	3B	1989	0.2				
Wally Moon	1954-1965	LF	1971	0.6				
Jo-Jo Moore	1930-1941	LF	1950	0.6				
Terry Moore	1935-1948	CF	1968	11.7	1950	0.6	1968	11.7
Pat Moran	1901-1914	C	1937	0.5	1937	0.5	1945	0.4
Jack Morris	1977-1994	P	2004	26.3	2000	22.2	2004	26.3
Wally Moses	1935-1951	RF	1971	1.9	1958	0.4	1971	1.9
Johnny Mostil	1918-1929	CF	1956	0.5	1956	0.5	1958	0.4
Manny Mota	1962-1982	LF	1988	4.2	1988	4.2	1989	2.0
Hugh Mulcahy	1935-1947	P	1948	0.8				
Van Mungo	1931-1945	P	1948	0.8	1945	0.4	1960	0.7
Thurman Munson	1969-1979	C	1981	15.5	1981	15.5	1995	6.5
Bobby Murcer	1965-1983	RF	1989	0.7				
Dale Murphy	1976-1993	CF	2000	23.2	1999	19.3	2004	8.5
Danny Murphy	1900-1915	2B	1937	0.5	1937	0.5	1945	0.4
Red Murray	1906-1917	RF	1937	0.5	1937	0.5	1938	0.4
Buddy Myer	1925-1941	2B	1949	0.7				
Randy Myers	1985-1998	P	2004	0.2				
Art Nehf	1915-1929	P	1958	4.9	1937	1.5	1958	4.9
Graig Nettles	1967-1988	3B	1994	8.4	1994	8.4	1997	4.7
Don Newcombe	1949-1960	P	1980	15.3	1966	2.3	1980	15.3
Bobo Newsom	1929-1953	P	1969	9.4	1960	2.2	1973	8.7
Bill Nicholson	1936-1953	RF	1960	0.4				
Joe Niekro	1967-1988	P	1994	1.3				

Candidate	Career	Position	Max. Yr./Pct.		1st Yr./Pct.		Last Yr./Pct.	
Ron Northey	1942-1957	RF	1964	0.5				
Jim Northrup	1964-1975	RF	1981	0.2				
Lefty O'Doul	1919-1934	LF	1960	16.7	1948	3.3	1962	8.1
Joe Oeschger	1914-1925	P	1948	0.8				
Bob O'Farrell	1915-1935	C	1950	2.4	1950	2.4	1960	1.1
Charlie O'Leary	1904-1913	SS	1953	0.4	1953	0.4	1960	0.4
Tony Oliva	1962-1976	RF	1988	47.3	1982	15.2	1996	36.2
Al Oliver	1968-1985	CF	1991	4.3				
Steve O'Neill	1911-1928	C	1953	4.9	1948	1.7	1958	3.8
Claude Osteen	1957-1975	P	1981	0.5				
Charlie Pabor	1871-1875	LF	1936V	1.3				
Andy Pafko	1943-1959	CF	1966	0.7	1966	0.7	1967	0.3
Milt Pappas	1957-1973	P	1979	1.2				
Dave Parker	1973-1991	RF	1998	24.5	1997	17.5	2004	10.5
Lance Parrish	1977-1995	C	2001	1.7				
Larry Parrish	1974-1988	3B	1994	0.4				
Camilo Pascual	1954-1971	P	1977	0.8	1977	0.8	1978	0.3
Dode Paskert	1907-1921	CF	1937	0.5				
Monte Pearson	1932-1941	P	1958	0.4				
Roger Peckinpaugh	1910-1927	SS	1937	1.5	1937	1.5	1955	0.4
Heinie Peitz	1893-1906	C	1939	0.4				
Tony Pena	1980-1997	C	2003	0.4				
Terry Pendleton	1984-1998	3B	2004	0.2				
Hub Perdue	1911-1915	P	1938	0.4	1938	0.4	1939	0.4
Cy Perkins	1915-1931	C	1958	0.8				
Ron Perranoski	1961-1973	P	1979	1.4				
Jim Perry	1959-1975	P	1983	1.9	1981	1.5	1983	1.9
Johnny Pesky	1942-1954	SS	1960	0.4				
Rico Petrocelli	1963-1976	SS	1982	0.7				
Deacon Phillippe	1899-1911	P	1945	0.8	1939	0.4	1946N	0.5
Billy Pierce	1945-1964	P	1971	1.9	1970	1.7	1974	1.1
Lip Pike	1871-1881	CF	1936V	1.3				
Lou Piniella	1964-1984	LF	1990	0.5				
Vada Pinson	1958-1975	CF	1988	15.7	1981	4.5	1996	10.9
Wally Pipp	1913-1928	1B	1958	0.4				
Johnny Podres	1953-1969	P	1975	0.8	1975	0.8	1977	0.8
Bob Porterfield	1948-1959	P	1966	0.3				
Boog Powell	1961-1977	1B	1983	1.3				
Vic Power	1954-1965	1B	1972	0.8	1971	0.6	1972	0.8
Herb Pruett	1922-1932	P	1949	0.7	1949	0.7	1953	0.4
Terry Puhl	1977-1991	RF	1997	0.2				
Jack Quinn	1909-1933	P	1958	3.4	1948	1.7	1960	0.7
Dan Quisenberry	1979-1990	P	1996	3.8				
Willie Randolph	1975-1992	2B	1998	1.1				
Vic Raschi	1946-1955	P	1975	10.2	1962	0.6	1975	10.2
Bugs Raymond	1904-1911	P	1937	0.5				
Jeff Reardon	1979-1994	P	2000	4.8				
Pete Reiser	1940-1952	CF	1960	3.0	1958	2.3	1960	3.0
Jack Remsen	1872-1884	CF	1936V	1.3				
Jerry Remy	1975-1984	2B	1990	0.2				
Rick Reuschel	1972-1991	P	1997	0.4				
Jerry Reuss	1969-1990	P	1996	0.4				
Allie Reynolds	1942-1954	P	1968	33.6	1956	0.5	1974	27.7
Del Rice	1945-1961	C	1966	0.7				
Jim Rice	1974-1989	LF	2001	57.9	1995	29.8	2004	54.5
J. R. Richard	1971-1980	P	1986	1.6				
Hardy Richardson	1879-1892	2B	1936V	1.3				
Bobby Richardson	1955-1966	2B	1972	2.0	1972	2.0	1974	1.4
Dave Righetti	1979-1995	P	2001	0.4				
Jose Rijo	1984-1995	P	2001	0.2				
Jimmy Ring	1917-1928	P	1949	0.7				
Claude Ritchey	1897-1909	2B	1945	0.4				
Mickey Rivers	1970-1984	CF	1990	0.5				
Dave Robertson	1912-1922	RF	1953	0.4				
Preacher Roe	1938-1954	P	1971	0.8	1960	0.4	1972	0.5
Red Rolfe	1931-1942	3B	1958	4.9	1950	4.2	1962	0.6
Eddie Rommel	1920-1932	P	1960	4.5	1948	2.5	1960	4.5
Charlie Root	1923-1941	P	1948	2.5	1945	0.4	1960	0.7
Pete Rose	1963-1986	RF	1992	9.5	1992	9.5	2000	3.4
Schoolboy Rowe	1933-1949	P	1969	5.0	1958	4.5	1969	5.0
Nap Rucker	1907-1916	P	1942	6.4	1936	0.4	1946N	6.4
Dick Rudolph	1910-1923	P	1937	0.5	1937	0.5	1951	0.4
Muddy Ruel	1915-1934	C	1956	8.3	1946N	0.5	1960	3.3
Bill Russell	1969-1986	SS	1992	0.7				
Ray Sadecki	1960-1977	P	1983	0.5				
Johnny Sain	1942-1955	P	1975	34.0	1962	0.6	1975	34.0
Juan Samuel	1983-1998	2B	2004	0.4				
Ryne Sandberg	1981-1997	2B	2004	61.1	2003	49.2	2004	61.1
Manny Sanguillen	1967-1980	C	1986	0.5				
Ron Santo	1960-1974	3B	1998	43.1	1980	3.9	1998	43.1
Hank Sauer	1941-1959	LF	1966	1.3				
Steve Sax	1981-1994	2B	2000	0.4				
Al Schacht	1919-1921	P	1951	1.8	1939	0.4	1956	0.5
Germany Schaefer	1901-1918	2B	1942	0.4	1942	0.4	1953	0.4
Wally Schang	1913-1931	C	1960	4.1	1948	0.8	1960	4.1
Ossie Schreck	1897-1908	C	1937	1.0	1937	1.0	1939	0.7
Frank Schulte	1904-1918	RF	1937	0.5				
Hal Schumacher	1931-1946	P	1964	5.0	1948	0.8	1964	5.0
Everett Scott	1914-1926	SS	1955	3.2	1937	1.0	1956	0.5
George Scott	1969-1979	1B	1986	0.2				
Jack Scott	1916-1929	P	1958	0.4				
Mike Scott	1979-1991	P	1997	0.4				
George Selkirk	1934-1942	LF	1951	0.9	1948	0.8	1953	0.4
Hank Severeid	1911-1926	C	1948	0.8				
Luke Sewell	1921-1942	C	1958	1.1	1948	0.8	1962	0.6
Rip Sewell	1932-1949	P	1962	0.6	1958	0.4	1964	0.5
Cy Seymour	1896-1913	CF	1945	0.4				
Bobby Shantz	1949-1964	P	1970	2.3	1970	2.3	1974	0.8
Jim Sheckard	1897-1913	LF	1946N	0.5	1938	0.4	1946N	0.5
Bill Sherdel	1918-1932	P	1948	0.8	1948	0.8	1960	0.7
Urban Shocker	1916-1928	P	1958	1.5	1938	0.4	1958	1.5
Chris Short	1959-1973	P	1979	0.2				
Sonny Siebert	1964-1975	P	1981	0.2				
Roy Sievers	1949-1965	1B	1971	1.1	1971	1.1	1972	0.8
Curt Simmons	1947-1967	P	1973	1.3	1973	1.3	1974	0.8
Ted Simmons	1968-1988	C	1994	3.7				
Sibby Sisti	1939-1954	2B	1960	0.4				
Roy Smalley	1948-1958	SS	1964	0.5				
Earl Smith	1919-1930	C	1948	0.8	1948	0.8	1956	0.5

Candidate	Career	Position	Max. Yr./Pct.		1st Yr./Pct.		Last Yr./Pct.	
Lee Smith	1980-1997	P	2003	42.3	2003	42.3	2004	36.6
Lonnie Smith	1978-1994	LF	2000	0.2				
Reggie Smith	1966-1982	RF	1988	0.7				
Sherry Smith	1911-1927	P	1948	0.8				
Billy Southworth	1940-1951	Mgr	1958	6.8	1945	0.4	1958	6.8
Tully Sparks	1897-1910	P	1946N	0.5				
Chris Speier	1971-1989	SS	1995	0.2				
Jake Stahl	1903-1913	1B	1938	0.4	1938	0.4	1939	0.4
Eddie Stanky	1943-1953	2B	1960	1.1				
Mickey Stanley	1964-1978	CF	1984	0.5				
Rusty Staub	1963-1985	RF	1994	7.9	1991	6.3	1997	3.8
Harry Steinfeldt	1898-1911	3B	1937	0.5	1937	0.5	1942	0.4
Riggs Stephenson	1921-1934	LF	1960	1.5	1956	1.0	1962	0.6
Dave Stewart	1978-1995	P	2001	7.4	2001	7.4	2002	4.9
Dave Stieb	1979-1998	P	2004	1.4				
Mel Stottlemyre	1964-1974	P	1980	0.8				
Harry Stovey	1880-1893	1B	1936V	7.7				
Gabby Street	1904-1912	C	1937	0.5	1937	0.5	1953	0.4
Gus Suhr	1930-1940	1B	1956	0.5	1956	0.5	1960	0.4
Clyde Sukeforth	1926-1934	C	1958	0.4				
Billy Sullivan	1899-1916	C	1937	0.5	1937	0.5	1946N	0.5
Jim Sundberg	1974-1989	C	1995	0.2				
Rick Sutcliffe	1976-1994	P	2000	1.8				
Bruce Sutter	1976-1988	P	2004	59.5	1994	24.0	2004	59.5
Bill Sweeney	1907-1914	2B	1945	0.4				
Jess Tannehill	1894-1911	P	1946N	0.5				
Danny Tartabull	1984-1997	RF	2003	0.2				
Birdie Tebbetts	1936-1952	C	1958	3.0	1958	3.0	1960	0.4
Kent Tekulve	1974-1989	P	1995	1.3				
Gary Templeton	1976-1991	SS	1997	0.4				
Gene Tenace	1969-1983	C	1989	0.2				
Fred Tenney	1894-1911	1B	1938	3.1	1936V	1.3	1946N	0.5
Tommy Thevenow	1924-1938	SS	1950	1.2				
Ira Thomas	1906-1915	C	1938	0.4				
Bobby Thomson	1946-1960	CF	1968	4.6	1966	4.0	1979	2.5
Andre Thornton	1973-1987	DH	1993	0.5				
Luis Tiant	1964-1982	P	1988	30.9	1988	30.9	2002	18.0
Jim Tobin	1914-1927	RF	1956	1.0				
Fred Toney	1911-1923	P	1949	0.7				
Earl Torgeson	1947-1961	1B	1967	0.7				
Joe Torre	1960-1977	C	1997	22.2	1983	5.3	1997	22.2
Mike Torrez	1967-1984	P	1990	0.2				
Alan Trammell	1977-1996	SS	2002	15.7	2002	15.7	2004	13.8
Dizzy Trout	1939-1952	P	1964	0.5				
Virgil Trucks	1941-1958	P	1964	2.0				
John Tudor	1979-1990	P	1996	0.4				
Jim Turner	1937-1945	P	1956	0.5				
Terry Turner	1901-1919	SS	1947	1.2				
George Uhle	1919-1936	P	1958	1.5	1956	0.5	1960	1.5
Ellis Valentine	1975-1985	RF	1991	0.2				
Fernando Valenzuela	1980-1997	P	2003	6.3	2003	6.3	2004	3.8
Elmer Valo	1940-1961	RF	1967	0.7				
Johnny Vander Meer	1937-1951	P	1967	29.8	1945	0.4	1971	27.2
George Van Haltren	1887-1903	CF	1936V	1.3				
Bobby Veach	1912-1925	LF	1937	0.5				
Mickey Vernon	1939-1960	1B	1980	24.9	1966	6.6	1980	24.9
Frank Viola	1982-1996	P	2002	0.4				
Bill Virdon	1955-1968	CF	1974	0.8	1974	0.8	1975	0.3
Rube Walberg	1923-1937	P	1958	0.4	1958	0.4	1960	0.4
Dixie Walker	1931-1949	RF	1964	3.0	1962	0.6	1969	2.6
Harry Walker	1940-1951	CF	1958	0.4				
Tim Wallach	1980-1996	3B	2002	0.2				
Bucky Walters	1931-1950	P	1968	23.7	1950	2.4	1970	9.7
Bill Wambsganss	1914-1926	2B	1955	2.0	1942	0.4	1956	0.5
Lon Warneke	1930-1945	P	1964	6.5	1949	1.3	1964	6.5
Bob Watson	1966-1984	1B	1990	0.7				
Bob Welch	1978-1994	P	2000	0.2				
Billy Werber	1930-1942	3B	1958	1.1	1949	0.7	1958	1.1
Vic Wertz	1947-1963	RF	1975	1.4	1970	0.7	1978	1.1
Sam West	1927-1942	CF	1948	0.8				
Wes Westrum	1947-1957	C	1964	1.0				
Lou Whitaker	1977-1995	2B	2001	2.9				
Deacon White	1871-1890	3B	1936V	1.3				
Frank White	1973-1990	2B	1996	3.8				
Will White	1877-1886	P	1975	1.9	1975	1.9	1977	1.0
Burgess Whitehead	1933-1946	2B	1956	0.5				
Earl Whitehill	1923-1939	P	1960	1.1	1956	0.5	1960	1.1
Fred Williams	1912-1930	CF	1956	5.7	1938	0.4	1960	4.1
Ken Williams	1915-1929	LF	1956	0.5	1956	0.5	1958	0.4
Ned Williamson	1878-1890	3B	1936V	2.6				
Maury Wills	1959-1972	SS	1981	40.6	1978	30.3	1992	25.6
Jimmie Wilson	1923-1940	C	1956	8.8	1948	6.6	1962	2.5
Jim Wilson	1945-1958	P	1964	1.0				
Willie Wilson	1976-1994	CF	2000	2.0				
Whitey Witt	1916-1926	CF	1949	0.7				
Joe Wood	1908-1922	P	1947	18.0	1937	6.5	1951	2.2
Wilbur Wood	1961-1978	P	1988	7.0	1984	3.5	1989	3.1
Glenn Wright	1924-1935	SS	1960	6.7	1948	1.7	1962	0.6
Whit Wyatt	1929-1945	P	1958	0.4				
Steve Yeager	1972-1986	C	1992	0.5				
Steve Yerkes	1909-1916	2B	1945	0.4				
Rudy York	1934-1948	1B	1964	5.0	1962	0.6	1964	5.0
Pep Young	1933-1945	2B	1958	0.4				
Tom Zachary	1918-1936	P	1958	0.4	1958	0.4	1960	0.4
Chief Zimmer	1884-1903	C	1938	0.4				

1936 Veterans
Needed to Elect: 59
Cap Anson 40
Buck Ewing 40
Willie Keeler 33
Cy Young 32
Ed Delahanty 22

1936
Needed to Elect: 170
Ty Cobb 222
Babe Ruth 215
Honus Wagner 215
Christy Mathewson 205
Walter Johnson 189
Nap Lajoie 146
Tris Speaker 133
Cy Young 111
Rogers Hornsby 105
Mickey Cochrane 80
George Sisler 77
Eddie Collins 60
Jimmy Collins 58

1937
Needed to Elect: 151
Nap Lajoie 168
Tris Speaker 165
Cy Young 153
Pete Alexander 125
Eddie Collins 115
Willie Keeler 115
George Sisler 106
Ed Delahanty 70
Rube Waddell 67
Jimmy Collins 66
Ed Walsh 56
Rogers Hornsby 53

1938
Needed to Elect: 197
Pete Alexander 212
George Sisler 179
Willie Keeler 177
Eddie Collins 175
Rube Waddell 148
Frank Chance 133
Ed Delahanty 132
Ed Walsh 110
Johnny Evers 91
Jimmy Collins 79
Rabbit Maranville 73
Roger Bresnahan 67

1939
Needed to Elect: 206
George Sisler 235
Eddie Collins 213
Willie Keeler 207
Rube Waddell 179
Rogers Hornsby 176
Frank Chance 158
Ed Delahanty 145
Ed Walsh 132
Johnny Evers 107
Miller Huggins 97
Rabbit Maranville 82
Jimmy Collins 72

1942
Needed to Elect: 175
Rogers Hornsby 182
Frank Chance 136
Rube Waddell 126
Ed Walsh 113
Miller Huggins 111
Ed Delahanty 104
Johnny Evers 91
Wilbert Robinson 89
Mickey Cochrane 88
Frankie Frisch 84
Hugh Duffy 77
Herb Pennock 72
Clark Griffith 71
Jimmy Collins 68
Rabbit Maranville 66
Hughie Jennings 64
Mordecai Brown 63
Eddie Plank 63
Joe McGinnity 59
Fred Clarke 58

1945
Needed to Elect: 185
Frank Chance 179
Rube Waddell 154
Ed Walsh 137
Johnny Evers 134
Roger Bresnahan 133
Miller Huggins 133
Mickey Cochrane 125
Jimmy Collins 121
Ed Delahanty 111
Clark Griffith 108
Frankie Frisch 101
Hughie Jennings 92
Wilbert Robinson 81
Pie Traynor 81
Hugh Duffy 64

1946 Nominating
Total Voting: 202
Frank Chance 144
Johnny Evers 130
Miller Huggins 129
Rube Waddell 122
Ed Walsh 115
Frankie Frisch 104
Carl Hubbell 101
Mickey Cochrane 80
Clark Griffith 73
Lefty Grove 71
Pie Traynor 65

1946
Needed to Elect: 197
Frank Chance 150
Johnny Evers 110
Miller Huggins 106
Ed Walsh 106
Rube Waddell 87
Clark Griffith 82
Carl Hubbell 75
Frankie Frisch 67

1947
Needed to Elect: 121
Carl Hubbell 140
Frankie Frisch 136
Mickey Cochrane 128
Lefty Grove 123
Pie Traynor 119
Charlie Gehringer 105
Rabbit Maranville 91
Dizzy Dean 88
Herb Pennock 86
Chief Bender 72
Harry Heilmann 65
Ray Schalk 50
Dazzy Vance 50
Frank Baker 49
Bill Terry 46

1948
Needed to Elect: 91
Herb Pennock 94
Pie Traynor 93
Al Simmons 60
Charlie Gehringer 52
Bill Terry 52
Paul Waner 51
Jimmie Foxx 50
Dizzy Dean 40
Harry Heilmann 40
Bill Dickey 39
Rabbit Maranville 38
Gabby Hartnett 33

1949
Needed to Elect: 115
Charlie Gehringer 102
Mel Ott 94
Al Simmons 89
Dizzy Dean 88
Jimmie Foxx 85
Bill Terry 81
Paul Waner 73
Hank Greenberg 67
Bill Dickey 65
Harry Heilmann 59
Rabbit Maranville 58

1949 Run Off
Needed to Elect: 140
One Player Maximum
Charlie Gehringer 159
Mel Ott 128
Jimmie Foxx 89
Dizzy Dean 81
Al Simmons 76
Paul Waner 63
Harry Heilmann 52
Bill Terry 48

1950
Needed to Elect: 125
Mel Ott 115
Bill Terry 105
Jimmie Foxx 103
Paul Waner 95
Al Simmons 90
Harry Heilmann 87
Dizzy Dean 85
Bill Dickey 78
Rabbit Maranville 66
Hank Greenberg 64
Gabby Hartnett 54
Dazzy Vance 52
Ted Lyons 42

1951
Needed to Elect: 170
Mel Ott 197
Jimmie Foxx 179
Paul Waner 162
Harry Heilmann 153
Bill Terry 148
Dizzy Dean 145
Bill Dickey 118
Al Simmons 116
Rabbit Maranville 110
Ted Lyons 71
Dazzy Vance 70
Hank Greenberg 67
Gabby Hartnett 57

1952
Needed to Elect: 176
Harry Heilmann 203
Paul Waner 195
Bill Terry 155
Dizzy Dean 152
Al Simmons 141
Bill Dickey 139
Rabbit Maranville 133
Dazzy Vance 105
Ted Lyons 101
Gabby Hartnett 77
Hank Greenberg 75
Chief Bender 70

1953
Needed to Elect: 198
Dizzy Dean 209
Al Simmons 199
Bill Terry 191
Bill Dickey 179
Rabbit Maranville 164
Dazzy Vance 150
Ted Lyons 139
Joe DiMaggio 117
Chief Bender 104
Gabby Hartnett 104
Hank Greenberg 80
Joe Cronin 69

1954
Needed to Elect: 189
Rabbit Maranville 209
Bill Dickey 202
Bill Terry 195
Joe DiMaggio 175
Ted Lyons 170
Dazzy Vance 158
Gabby Hartnett 151
Hank Greenberg 97
Joe Cronin 85

1955
Needed to Elect: 188
Joe DiMaggio 223
Ted Lyons 217
Dazzy Vance 205
Gabby Hartnett 195
Hank Greenberg 157
Joe Cronin 135
Max Carey 119
Ray Schalk 113
Edd Roush 97
Hank Gowdy 90
Hack Wilson 81
Lefty Gomez 71
Tony Lazzeri 66

1956
Needed to Elect: 145
Hank Greenberg 164
Joe Cronin 152
Red Ruffing 97
Edd Roush 91
Lefty Gomez 89
Hack Wilson 74
Max Carey 65
Tony Lazzeri 64
Kiki Cuyler 55
Hank Gowdy 49

1958
Needed to Elect: 200
Max Carey 136
Edd Roush 112
Red Ruffing 99
Hack Wilson 94
Kiki Cuyler 90
Sam Rice 90
Tony Lazzeri 80
Luke Appling 77
Lefty Gomez 76
Burleigh Grimes 71
Red Faber 68

1960
Needed to Elect: 202
Edd Roush 146
Sam Rice 143
Eppa Rixey 142
Burleigh Grimes 92
Jim Bottomley 89
Red Ruffing 86
Red Faber 83
Luke Appling 72
Kiki Cuyler 72
Hack Wilson 72

1962
Needed to Elect: 120
Bob Feller 150
Jackie Robinson 124
Sam Rice 81
Red Ruffing 72
Eppa Rixey 49
Luke Appling 48
Phil Rizzuto 44
Burleigh Grimes 43

1964
Needed to Elect: 151
Luke Appling 142
Red Ruffing 141
Roy Campanella 115
Joe Medwick 108
Pee Wee Reese 73
Lou Boudreau 68
Al Lopez 57
Chuck Klein 56
Johnny Mize 54
Mel Harder 51
Johnny Vander Meer 51
Marty Marion 50

1964 Run Off
Needed to Elect: 170
One Player Maximum
Luke Appling 189
Red Ruffing 184
Roy Campanella 138
Joe Medwick 130

1966
Needed to Elect: 227
Ted Williams 282
Red Ruffing 208
Roy Campanella 197
Joe Medwick 187
Lou Boudreau 115
Al Lopez 109
Enos Slaughter 100
Pee Wee Reese 95
Marty Marion 86
Johnny Mize 81

1967
Needed to Elect: 219
Joe Medwick 212
Red Ruffing 212
Roy Campanella 204
Lou Boudreau 143
Ralph Kiner 124
Enos Slaughter 123
Al Lopez 114
Marty Marion 90
Johnny Mize 89
Pee Wee Reese 89
Johnny Vander Meer 87
Allie Reynolds 77

1967 Run Off
Needed to Elect: 230
One Player Maximum
Red Ruffing 266
Joe Medwick 248
Roy Campanella 170

1968
Needed to Elect: 212
Joe Medwick 240
Roy Campanella 205
Lou Boudreau 146
Enos Slaughter 129
Ralph Kiner 118
Johnny Mize 103
Allie Reynolds 95
Marty Marion 89
Arky Vaughan 82
Pee Wee Reese 81
Johnny Vander Meer 79
Joe Gordon 77
Phil Rizzuto 74

1969
Needed to Elect: 255
Stan Musial 317
Roy Campanella 270
Lou Boudreau 218
Ralph Kiner 137
Enos Slaughter 128
Johnny Mize 116
Marty Marion 112
Allie Reynolds 98
Joe Gordon 97
Johnny Vander Meer 95
Early Wynn 95
Pee Wee Reese 89

1970
Needed to Elect: 225
Lou Boudreau 232
Ralph Kiner 167
Gil Hodges 145
Early Wynn 140
Enos Slaughter 133
Johnny Mize 126
Marty Marion 120
Pee Wee Reese 97
Red Schoendienst 97
George Kell 90
Allie Reynolds 89
Johnny Vander Meer 88
Hal Newhouser 80
Joe Gordon 79
Phil Rizzuto 79
Bobby Doerr 75

1971
Needed to Elect: 270
Yogi Berra 242
Early Wynn 240
Ralph Kiner 212
Gil Hodges 180
Enos Slaughter 165
Johnny Mize 157
Pee Wee Reese 127
Marty Marion 123
Red Schoendienst 123
Allie Reynolds 110
George Kell 105
Johnny Vander Meer 98
Hal Newhouser 94
Phil Rizzuto 92
Bob Lemon 90

1972
Needed to Elect: 297
Sandy Koufax 344
Yogi Berra 339
Early Wynn 301
Ralph Kiner 235
Gil Hodges 161
Johnny Mize 157
Enos Slaughter 149
Pee Wee Reese 129
Marty Marion 120
Bob Lemon 117
George Kell 115
Allie Reynolds 105
Red Schoendienst 104
Phil Rizzuto 103

1973
Needed to Elect: 285
Warren Spahn 316
Whitey Ford 255
Ralph Kiner 235
Gil Hodges 218
Robin Roberts 213
Bob Lemon 177
Johnny Mize 157
Enos Slaughter 145
Marty Marion 127
Pee Wee Reese 126
George Kell 114
Phil Rizzuto 111
Duke Snider 101
Red Schoendienst 96

1974
Needed to Elect: 274
Mickey Mantle 322
Whitey Ford 284
Robin Roberts 224
Ralph Kiner 215
Gil Hodges 198
Bob Lemon 190
Enos Slaughter 145
Pee Wee Reese 141
Eddie Mathews 118
Phil Rizzuto 111
Duke Snider 111
Red Schoendienst 110
Allie Reynolds 101
George Kell 94

1975
Needed to Elect: 272
Ralph Kiner 273
Robin Roberts 263
Bob Lemon 233
Gil Hodges 188
Enos Slaughter 177
Hal Newhouser 155
Pee Wee Reese 154
Eddie Mathews 148
Phil Cavaretta 129
Duke Snider 129

Johnny Sain 123
Phil Rizzuto 117
George Kell 114
Red Schoendienst...... 94

1976
Needed to Elect: 291
Robin Roberts 337
Bob Lemon 305
Gil Hodges 233
Enos Slaughter 197
Eddie Mathews 189
Pee Wee Reese 186
Nellie Fox 174
Duke Snider 159
Phil Rizzuto 149
George Kell 129
Red Schoendienst......129
Don Drysdale 114

1977
Needed to Elect: 287
Ernie Banks................321
Eddie Mathews 239
Gil Hodges 224
Enos Slaughter 222
Duke Snider 212
Don Drysdale 197
Pee Wee Reese 163
Nellie Fox 152
Jim Bunning 146
George Kell................141
Richie Ashburn 139
Red Schoendienst......105

1978
Needed to Elect: 284
Eddie Mathews 301
Enos Slaughter 261
Duke Snider 254
Gil Hodges 226
Don Drysdale 219
Jim Bunning 181
Pee Wee Reese 169
Richie Ashburn 158
Hoyt Wilhelm..............158
Nellie Fox 149
Red Schoendienst......130
Maury Wills 115

1979
Needed to Elect: 324
Willie Mays 409
Duke Snider 308
Enos Slaughter 297
Gil Hodges 242
Don Drysdale 233
Nellie Fox 174
Hoyt Wilhelm..............168
Maury Wills 166
Red Schoendienst......159
Jim Bunning 147
Richie Ashburn 130
Roger Maris 127
Luis Aparicio 120

1980
Needed to Elect: 289
Al Kaline 340
Duke Snider 333
Don Drysdale 238
Gil Hodges 230
Hoyt Wilhelm..............209
Jim Bunning 177
Red Schoendienst......164
Nellie Fox 161
Maury Wills 146
Richie Ashburn 134
Luis Aparicio 124
Roger Maris 111
Mickey Vernon 96

1981
Needed to Elect: 301
Bob Gibson 337
Don Drysdale 243
Gil Hodges 241
Harmon Killebrew 239
Hoyt Wilhelm..............238
Juan Marichal 233
Nellie Fox 168
Red Schoendienst......166
Jim Bunning 164
Maury Wills 163
Richie Ashburn 142

1982
Needed to Elect: 311
Hank Aaron 406
Frank Robinson..........370
Juan Marichal 305
Harmon Killebrew 246
Hoyt Wilhelm..............236
Don Drysdale 233
Gil Hodges 205
Luis Aparicio 174
Jim Bunning 138
Red Schoendienst......135
Nellie Fox 127
Richie Ashburn 126

1983
Needed to Elect: 281
Brooks Robinson........344
Juan Marichal 313
Harmon Killebrew 269
Luis Aparicio 252
Hoyt Wilhelm..............243
Don Drysdale 242
Gil Hodges 237
Nellie Fox 173
Billy Williams 153
Red Schoendienst......146
Jim Bunning 138

1984
Needed to Elect: 302
Luis Aparicio 341
Harmon Killebrew 335
Don Drysdale 316
Hoyt Wilhelm..............290
Nellie Fox 246
Billy Williams 202
Jim Bunning 201
Orlando Cepeda 124
Tony Oliva 124
Roger Maris 107
Harvey Kuenn 106
Maury Wills 104

1985
Needed to Elect: 296
Hoyt Wilhelm..............331
Lou Brock 315
Nellie Fox 295
Billy Williams 252
Jim Bunning 214
Catfish Hunter 212
Roger Maris 128
Harvey Kuenn 125
Orlando Cepeda 114
Tony Oliva 114

1986
Needed to Elect: 319
Willie McCovey 346
Billy Williams 315
Catfish Hunter............289
Jim Bunning 279
Roger Maris 177
Tony Oliva 154
Orlando Cepeda 152
Harvey Kuenn 144
Maury Wills 124

1987
Needed to Elect: 310
Billy Williams..............354
Catfish Hunter............315
Jim Bunning 289
Orlando Cepeda 179
Roger Maris 176
Tony Oliva 160
Harvey Kuenn 144
Bill Mazeroski 125
Maury Wills 113

1988
Needed to Elect: 320
Willie Stargell 352
Jim Bunning 317
Tony Oliva 202
Orlando Cepeda 199
Roger Maris 184
Harvey Kuenn 168
Bill Mazeroski 143
Luis Tiant....................132
Maury Wills 127
Ken Boyer 109
Mickey Lolich 109
Ron Santo 108

1989
Needed to Elect: 335
Johnny Bench 431
Carl Yastrzemski 423
Gaylord Perry 304
Jim Bunning 283
Fergie Jenkins............234
Orlando Cepeda 176
Tony Oliva 135
Bill Mazeroski 134
Harvey Kuenn 115

1990
Needed to Elect: 333
Jim Palmer 411
Joe Morgan 363
Gaylord Perry 320
Fergie Jenkins............296
Jim Bunning 257
Orlando Cepeda 211
Tony Oliva 142
Bill Mazeroski 131

1991
Needed to Elect: 332
Rod Carew 401
Gaylord Perry 342
Fergie Jenkins............334
Rollie Fingers 291
Jim Bunning 282
Orlando Cepeda 192
Tony Oliva 160
Bill Mazeroski 142
Ron Santo 116

1992
Needed to Elect: 323
Tom Seaver................425
Rollie Fingers 349
Orlando Cepeda 246
Tony Perez 215
Bill Mazeroski 182
Tony Oliva 175
Ron Santo 136
Jim Kaat 114
Maury Wills 110

1993
Needed to Elect: 317
Reggie Jackson 396
Phil Niekro..................278
Orlando Cepeda 252
Tony Perez 233
Steve Garvey 176
Tony Oliva 157
Ron Santo 155
Jim Kaat 125

1994
Needed to Elect: 341
Steve Carlton 436
Orlando Cepeda 335
Phil Niekro..................273
Tony Perez 263
Don Sutton 259
Steve Garvey 166
Tony Oliva 158
Ron Santo 150

1995
Needed to Elect: 345
Mike Schmidt 444
Phil Niekro..................286
Don Sutton 264
Tony Perez 259
Steve Garvey 196
Tony Oliva 149
Ron Santo 139
Jim Rice 137
Bruce Sutter 137

1996
Needed to Elect: 353
Phil Niekro..................321
Tony Perez 309
Don Sutton 300
Steve Garvey 175
Ron Santo 174
Tony Oliva 170
Jim Rice 166
Bruce Sutter 137

1997
Needed to Elect: 355
Phil Niekro..................380
Don Sutton 346
Tony Perez 312
Ron Santo 186
Jim Rice 178
Steve Garvey 167
Bruce Sutter 130

1998
Needed to Elect: 355
Don Sutton 386
Tony Perez 321
Ron Santo 204
Jim Rice 203
Gary Carter 200
Steve Garvey 195
Bruce Sutter 147
Tommy John 129
Jim Kaat 129

1999
Needed to Elect: 373
Nolan Ryan 491
George Brett 488
Robin Yount................385
Carlton Fisk................330
Tony Perez 302
Gary Carter 168
Steve Garvey 150
Jim Rice 146

2000
Needed to Elect: 374
Carlton Fisk................397
Tony Perez 385
Jim Rice 257
Gary Carter 248
Bruce Sutter 192
Goose Gossage 166
Steve Garvey 160
Tommy John 135
Jim Kaat 125

2001
Needed to Elect: 386
Dave Winfield 435
Kirby Puckett..............423
Gary Carter 334
Jim Rice 298
Bruce Sutter 245
Goose Gossage 228
Steve Garvey 176
Tommy John 146
Don Mattingly 145
Jim Kaat 139

2002
Needed to Elect: 354
Ozzie Smith................433
Gary Carter 343
Jim Rice 260
Bruce Sutter 238
Andre Dawson 214
Goose Gossage 203
Steve Garvey 134
Tommy John 127
Bert Blyleven..............124

2003
Needed to Elect: 372
Eddie Murray..............423
Gary Carter 387
Bruce Sutter 266
Jim Rice 259
Andre Dawson 248
Ryne Sandberg..........244
Lee Smith 210
Goose Gossage 209
Bert Blyleven..............145
Steve Garvey 138
Jim Kaat 130

2004
Needed to Elect: 380
Paul Molitor................431
Dennis Eckersley 421
Ryne Sandberg..........309
Bruce Sutter 301
Jim Rice 276
Andre Dawson 253
Rich Gossage 206
Lee Smith 185
Bert Blyleven..............179
Jack Morris 133

THE BOYS OF SUMMER: AWARDS AND OTHER HONORS

Roger Kahn's 1971 masterwork about baseball and life struck a deep chord with Americans. As a result, the term *Boys of Summer* established itself forever in the popular lexicon. Merely playing in the big leagues, even for a moment, is certainly a tremendous accomplishment. However, the boys of our fondest summer memories are typically the stars whose ability, skill, and determination make them rise above the ordinary and place them ahead of their peers. Recognition by others in their field usually follows.

Most of this encyclopedia—indeed, most of any baseball encyclopedia—is filled with statistics. This section, however, is different: It records what the people who have watched baseball for a living thought about the players who produced the statistics. Who was the most valuable player? The *best* player? The best pitcher? The most impressive rookie? Which managers did the best job? Who were the best minor league prospects? Which players were leaders in their communities?

If you look carefully at the players who won the major awards, you'll also see signs of how the game has evolved. Different eras have brought different skills to the forefront, and the weight that the voters have given the various aspects of baseball has changed significantly over time. The major awards shown in this section represent the collective opinions of writers, editors, managers, coaches, and ballplayers over the past century, from the Chalmers Award in 1911 to the Rookie of the Year Award in 2003. Unanimous selections for all awards are indicated by asterisks.

Lists of "Ex Post Facto" awards for Most Valuable Player, Cy Young, and Rookie of the Year, are also presented. Going back in time, we have chosen the players that we think would have won the major awards if they had been given out then (or if the awards had been given out in both leagues). Note that these Ex Post Facto awards do not necessarily represent who we think *should* have won. Instead, we have tried to apply the standards of times past and, based on what the writers historically valued, we have chosen who we think *would have won* had the writers of the time been given the opportunity to vote.

MOST VALUABLE PLAYER AWARD

The most important award in baseball is undoubtedly the Most Valuable Player Award. No other annual sports award generates as much debate as much as the AL and MVPs. Furthermore, no other award in American sports has as long and controversial a history.

The first incarnation of the MVP award was the Chalmers Award, named after Hugh Chalmers, an automobile manufacturer who decided in 1910 that it would be great publicity to give one of his company's automobiles to the player with the highest batting average in each league at the season's end. Unfortunately for the sponsor, the AL batting race that year ended in a white-hot controversy as the St. Louis Browns allowed Nap Lajoie to lay down 7 bunt hits on the last day of the season to give him an edge over the widely disliked Ty Cobb. AL President Ban Johnson ruled that a recalculation showed that Cobb had won the race anyway, and Chalmers ended up awarding cars to both Lajoie and Cobb.

To avoid this type of embarrassment, Chalmers decided in 1911 to change the rules of the contest, constituting a committee of baseball writers to determine—following the season—the "most important and useful player to his club and to the league." This was clearly the first Most Valuable Player Award. However, the Chalmers Award did not prove to be the hoped-for marketing bonanza, and the award was discontinued after 1914.

In 1922 the American League created a new award to honor "the baseball player who is of greatest all-around service to his club." Regrettably, the league saddled the new award with several rules that led to widespread dissatisfaction. Voters were required to select one (and only one) player from each team and were not allowed to vote for player-managers. Moreover, previous award winners were disqualified from consideration. Flawed from its inception, the award was dropped in 1929. The National League, which had in 1924 instituted its own contest (without the controversial restrictions), again followed the AL's lead and eliminated its award in 1930.

After a brief interregnum the Baseball Writers Association of America created the modern MVP award in 1931, adopting the same system that the NL had used for its abandoned MVP award. One writer in each league city was asked to fill out a ten-place ballot; ten points was awarded to the recipient of a first-place vote, nine points for a second-place vote, and so on, with one point awarded for a tenth place vote. In 1938 the BBWAA began polling three writers in each league city and raised the number of points for first-place votes to fourteen. The only significant change in the MVP balloting since then has been the reduction of writers polled to two per league city in 1961.

Despite continuing debate, the BBWAA has never spelled out the definition of the Most Valuable Player. Is the MVP simply the *best* player? Should candidates on pennant winners get special consideration? Must the MVP play on a contending team? Should starting pitchers qualify for the honor despite not participating in the great majority of their team's games? What about relief pitchers? Can any player be "most valuable" if his team finishes last?

While there have never been official answers to these questions, it is clear that the voting patterns of the BBWAA have changed over time. In the 1950s, for example, MVP voting favored "up the middle" players: center fielders, middle infielders, and catchers. Players like Nellie Fox (who won the 1959 AL MVP) and Dick Groat (1960 NL MVP) would not be serious candidates for the award today; in the last twenty-five years, writers have valued sluggers with high RBI totals (e.g., Juan Gonzalez and Jeff Kent) more highly than any other type of player. It is difficult to tell whether these voting patterns will persist; the argument over whether Alex Rodriguez of the last-place Rangers deserved the 2003 AL MVP is a perfect example of the utter lack of definition for the award.

Award voting, especially MVP balloting, frequently seems to stir up more controversy than it used to. Voters in the last twenty years have made some very debatable selections, including some outright mistakes, but it's wise to recall that their counterparts in earlier times were perfectly capable of picking less-than-qualified winners. Glamour statistics, mostly RBIs, have always tended to help players that are having otherwise modest seasons win prestigious trophies. Jackie Jensen, Hank Sauer, Frank McCormick, and Jeff Burroughs—MVP winners all—are good examples. Furthermore, decent but otherwise unspectacular players having that one "career year" (e.g., Zoilo Versalles, Bobby Shantz, and Bob Elliott) have copped awards despite clearly superior competition. Compared to some of the stranger BBWAA decisions of earlier times, the 2003 AL selection of Rodriguez is a piece of cake.

Chalmers Award

American League	National League
1911 Ty Cobb*, Det	1911 Frank Schulte, Chi
1912 Tris Speaker, Bos	1912 Larry Doyle, NY
1913 Walter Johnson, Was	1913 Jake Daubert, Bro
1914 Eddie Collins, Phi	1914 Johnny Evers, Bos

American League Award	National League Award
1922 George Sisler, StL	
1923 Babe Ruth*, NY	
1924 Walter Johnson, Was	1924 Dazzy Vance, Bro
1925 Roger Peckinpaugh, Was	1925 Rogers Hornsby, StL

American League Award	National League Award
1926 George Burns, Cle	1926 Bob O'Farrell, StL
1927 Lou Gehrig, NY	1927 Paul Waner, Pit
1928 Mickey Cochrane, Phi	1928 Jim Bottomley, StL
	1929 Rogers Hornsby, Chi

BBWAA AL & NL MVP Awards

American League		National League	
1931	Lefty Grove, Phi	1931	Frankie Frisch, StL
1932	Jimmie Foxx, Phi	1932	Chuck Klein, Phi
1933	Jimmie Foxx, Phi	1933	Carl Hubbell, NY
1934	Mickey Cochrane, Det	1934	Dizzy Dean, StL
1935	Hank Greenberg*, Det	1935	Gabby Hartnett, Chi
1936	Lou Gehrig, NY	1936	Carl Hubbell*, NY
1937	Charlie Gehringer, Det	1937	Joe Medwick, StL
1938	Jimmie Foxx, Bos	1938	Ernie Lombardi, Cin
1939	Joe DiMaggio, NY	1939	Bucky Walters, Cin
1940	Hank Greenberg, Det	1940	Frank McCormick, Cin
1941	Joe DiMaggio, NY	1941	Dolph Camilli, Bro
1942	Joe Gordon, NY	1942	Mort Cooper, StL
1943	Spud Chandler, NY	1943	Stan Musial, StL
1944	Hal Newhouser, Det	1944	Marty Marion, StL
1945	Hal Newhouser, Det	1945	Phil Cavarretta, Chi
1946	Ted Williams, Bos	1946	Stan Musial, StL
1947	Joe DiMaggio, NY	1947	Bob Elliott, Bos
1948	Lou Boudreau, Cle	1948	Stan Musial, StL
1949	Ted Williams, Bos	1949	Jackie Robinson, Bro
1950	Phil Rizzuto, NY	1950	Jim Konstanty, Phi
1951	Yogi Berra, NY	1951	Roy Campanella, Bro
1952	Bobby Shantz, Phi	1952	Hank Sauer, Chi
1953	Al Rosen*, Cle	1953	Roy Campanella, Bro
1954	Yogi Berra, NY	1954	Willie Mays, NY
1955	Yogi Berra, NY	1955	Roy Campanella, Bro
1956	Mickey Mantle*, NY	1956	Don Newcombe, Bro
1957	Mickey Mantle, NY	1957	Hank Aaron, Mil
1958	Jackie Jensen, Bos	1958	Ernie Banks, Chi
1959	Nellie Fox, Chi	1959	Ernie Banks, Chi
1960	Roger Maris, NY	1960	Dick Groat, Pit
1961	Roger Maris, NY	1961	Frank Robinson*, Cin
1962	Mickey Mantle, NY	1962	Maury Wills, LA
1963	Elston Howard, NY	1963	Sandy Koufax, LA
1964	Brooks Robinson, Bal	1964	Ken Boyer, StL
1965	Zoilo Versalles, Min	1965	Willie Mays, SF
1966	Frank Robinson*, Bal	1966	Roberto Clemente, Pit
1967	Carl Yastrzemski, Bos	1967	Orlando Cepeda*, StL

American League		National League	
1968	Denny McLain*, Det	1968	Bob Gibson, StL
1969	Harmon Killebrew, Min	1969	Willie McCovey, SF
1970	Boog Powell, Bal	1970	Johnny Bench, Cin
1971	Vida Blue, Oak	1971	Joe Torre, StL
1972	Dick Allen, Chi	1972	Johnny Bench, Cin
1973	Reggie Jackson*, Oak	1973	Pete Rose, Cin
1974	Jeff Burroughs, Tex	1974	Steve Garvey, LA
1975	Fred Lynn, Bos	1975	Joe Morgan, Cin
1976	Thurman Munson, NY	1976	Joe Morgan, Cin
1977	Rod Carew, Min	1977	George Foster, Cin
1978	Jim Rice, Bos	1978	Dave Parker, Pit
1979	Don Baylor, Cal	1979	Keith Hernandez, StL
		(tie)	Willie Stargell, Pit
1980	George Brett, KC	1980	Mike Schmidt*, Phi
1981	Rollie Fingers, Mil	1981	Mike Schmidt, Phi
1982	Robin Yount, Mil	1982	Dale Murphy, Atl
1983	Cal Ripken, Bal	1983	Dale Murphy, Atl
1984	Willie Hernandez, Det	1984	Ryne Sandberg, Chi
1985	Don Mattingly, NY	1985	Willie McGee, StL
1986	Roger Clemens, Bos	1986	Mike Schmidt, Phi
1987	George Bell, Tor	1987	Andre Dawson, Chi
1988	Jose Canseco*, Oak	1988	Kirk Gibson, LA
1989	Robin Yount, Mil	1989	Kevin Mitchell, SF
1990	Rickey Henderson, Oak	1990	Barry Bonds, Pit
1991	Cal Ripken, Bal	1991	Terry Pendleton, Atl
1992	Dennis Eckersley, Oak	1992	Barry Bonds, Pit
1993	Frank Thomas*, Chi	1993	Barry Bonds, SF
1994	Frank Thomas, Chi	1994	Jeff Bagwell*, Hou
1995	Mo Vaughn, Bos	1995	Barry Larkin, Cin
1996	Juan Gonzalez, Tex	1996	Ken Caminiti*, SD
1997	Ken Griffey Jr.*, Sea	1997	Larry Walker, Col
1998	Juan Gonzalez, Tex	1998	Sammy Sosa, Chi
1999	Ivan Rodriguez, Tex	1999	Chipper Jones, Atl
2000	Jason Giambi, Oak	2000	Jeff Kent, SF
2001	Ichiro Suzuki, Sea	2001	Barry Bonds, SF
2002	Miguel Tejada, Oak	2002	Barry Bonds, SF
2003	Alex Rodriguez, Tex	2003	Barry Bonds, SF

Ex Post Facto MVP Award

National Association

1871	Levi Meyerle, Ath
1872	Ross Barnes, Bos
1873	Ross Barnes, Bos
1874	Cal McVey, Bos
1875	Cal McVey, Bos

American Association

1882	Hick Carpenter, Cin
1883	Harry Stovey, Phi
1884	Guy Hecker, Lou
1885	Bob Caruthers, StL
1886	Bob Caruthers, StL
1887	Tip O'Neill, StL
1888	Silver King, StL
1889	Harry Stovey, Phi
1890	Jimmy Wolf, Lou
1891	Dan Brouthers, Bos

Union Association

1884	Fred Dunlap, StL

Players League

1890	Hardy Richardson, Bos

Federal League

1914	Benny Kauff, Ind
1915	Ed Konetchy, Pit

National League

1876	Ross Barnes, Chi
1877	Deacon White, Bos
1878	Paul Hines, Pro
1879	Paul Hines, Pro
1880	George Gore, Chi
1881	Cap Anson, Chi
1882	Cap Anson, Chi
1883	Jim Whitney, Bos
1884	Charley Radbourn, Pro
1885	John Clarkson, Chi
1886	King Kelly, Chi
1887	Sam Thompson, Det
1888	Buck Ewing, NY
1889	John Clarkson, Bos
1890	Jack Glasscock, NY
1891	Billy Hamilton, Phi
1892	Dan Brouthers, Bro
1893	Ed Delahanty, Phi
1894	Hugh Duffy, Bos
1895	Hughie Jennings, Bal
1896	Hughie Jennings, Bal
1897	Willie Keeler, Bal
1898	Jimmy Collins, Bos
1899	Ed Delahanty, Phi
1900	Honus Wagner, Pit
1901	Honus Wagner, Pit
1902	Honus Wagner, Pit
1903	Honus Wagner, Pit
1904	Joe McGinnity, NY
1905	Christy Mathewson, NY
1906	Frank Chance, Chi
1907	Honus Wagner, Pit
1908	Christy Mathewson, NY
1909	Honus Wagner, Pit
1910	Sherry Magee, Phi
[1911-14	See Chalmers Awards]
1915	Grover Alexander, Phi
1916	Grover Alexander, Phi
1917	Grover Alexander, Phi
1918	Hippo Vaughn, Chi
1919	Edd Roush, Cin
1920	Rogers Hornsby, StL
1921	Rogers Hornsby, StL
1922	Rogers Hornsby, StL
1923	Dolf Luque, Cin
[1924-29	See NL Awards]
1930	Hack Wilson, Chi

American League

1901	Nap Lajoie, Phi
1902	Cy Young, Bos
1903	Nap Lajoie, Cle
1904	Jack Chesbro, NY
1905	Rube Waddell, Phi
1906	Nap Lajoie, Cle
1907	Ty Cobb, Det
1908	Ed Walsh, Chi
1909	Ty Cobb, Det
1910	Jack Coombs, Phi
[1911-14	See Chalmers Awards]
1915	Ty Cobb, Det
1916	Ty Cobb, Det
1917	Eddie Cicotte, Chi
1918	Babe Ruth, Bos
1919	Eddie Cicotte, Chi
1920	Babe Ruth, NY
1921	Babe Ruth, NY
[1922-28	See AL Awards]
1929	Lew Fonseca, Cle
1930	Joe Cronin, Was

BBWAA CY YOUNG AWARD

In 1956 the BBWAA, prodded by Commissioner Ford Frick, created the Cy Young Award in order to annually honor the best pitcher in the major leagues. The award was named after Cy Young, the all-time leader in pitching wins (and losses), who had died in 1955. The impetus for the award's creation was the lack of support pitchers had been receiving in MVP balloting. Ironically, the creation of the Cy Young would further reduce that support. In 1967 voters began selecting one Cy Young winner in each league. In 1970 a three-place ballot replaced the original one-place ballot.

There's no debating the goal of the Cy Young Award; voters do not give extra credit to pitchers on contenders, and you'll rarely hear talk about a pitcher's leadership skills from the electorate. However, there has been one major change over the last forty years in the voting pattern—the rise in the status of relief pitchers. No relief pitcher had ever appeared in the Cy Young results until Lindy McDaniel in 1960. It would not be until 1974 that a relief pitcher, in this case Mike Marshall, would capture a Cy Young Award. No reliever has yet won one unanimously, though Eric Gagne came within two first-place votes of doing so in 2003. Some baseball writers have argued that it would be more appropriate for relievers to compete against everyday players in the MVP race rather than against starting pitchers for the Cy Young.

Cy Young Award

1956	Don Newcombe, Bro NL
1957	Warren Spahn, Mil NL
1958	Bob Turley, NY AL
1959	Early Wynn, Chi AL
1960	Vern Law, Pit NL
1961	Whitey Ford, NY AL
1962	Don Drysdale, LA NL
1963	Sandy Koufax*, LA NL
1964	Dean Chance, LA AL
1965	Sandy Koufax*, LA NL
1966	Sandy Koufax*, LA NL

AL & NL Cy Young Awards

	AL	NL
1967	Jim Lonborg, Bos	Mike McCormick, SF
1968	Denny McLain*, Det	Bob Gibson*, StL
1969	Mike Cuellar, Bal	Tom Seaver, NY
	(tie) Denny McLain, Det	
1970	Jim Perry, Min	Bob Gibson, StL
1971	Vida Blue, Oak	Fergie Jenkins, Chi
1972	Gaylord Perry, Cle	Steve Carlton*, Phi
1973	Jim Palmer, Bal	Tom Seaver, NY
1974	Catfish Hunter, Oak	Mike Marshall, LA
1975	Jim Palmer, Bal	Tom Seaver, NY
1976	Jim Palmer, Bal	Randy Jones, SD
1977	Sparky Lyle, NY	Steve Carlton, Phi
1978	Ron Guidry*, NY	Gaylord Perry, SD
1979	Mike Flanagan, Bal	Bruce Sutter, Chi
1980	Steve Stone, Bal	Steve Carlton, Phi
1981	Rollie Fingers, Mil	Fernando Valenzuela, LA
1982	Pete Vuckovich, Mil	Steve Carlton, Phi
1983	La Marr Hoyt, Chi	John Denny, Phi
1984	Willie Hernandez, Det	Rick Sutcliffe*, Chi
1985	Bret Saberhagen, KC	Dwight Gooden*, NY
1986	Roger Clemens*, Bos	Mike Scott, Hou
1987	Roger Clemens, Bos	Steve Bedrosian, Phi
1988	Frank Viola, Min	Orel Hershiser*, LA
1989	Bret Saberhagen, KC	Mark Davis, SD
1990	Bob Welch, Oak	Doug Drabek, Pit
1991	Roger Clemens, Bos	Tom Glavine, Atl
1992	Dennis Eckersley, Oak	Greg Maddux, Chi
1993	Jack McDowell, Chi	Greg Maddux, Atl
1994	David Cone, KC	Greg Maddux*, Atl
1995	Randy Johnson, Sea	Greg Maddux*, Atl
1996	Pat Hentgen, Tor	John Smoltz, Atl
1997	Roger Clemens, Tor	Pedro Martinez*, Mon
1998	Roger Clemens*, Tor	Tom Glavine, Atl
1999	Pedro Martinez*, Bos	Randy Johnson, Ari
2000	Pedro Martinez*, Bos	Randy Johnson, Ari
2001	Roger Clemens, NY	Randy Johnson, Ari
2002	Barry Zito, Oak	Randy Johnson*, Ari
2003	Roy Halladay, Tor	Eric Gagne, LA

Ex Post Facto Cy Young Award

National Association

1871	George Zettlein, Chi
1872	Al Spalding, Bos
1873	Al Spalding, Bos
1874	Al Spalding, Bos
1875	Al Spalding, Bos

American Association

1882	Will White, Cin
1883	Will White, Cin
1884	Guy Hecker, Lou
1885	Bob Caruthers, StL
1886	Dave Foutz, StL
1887	Matt Kilroy, Bal
1888	Silver King, StL
1889	Bob Caruthers, Bro
1890	Scott Stratton, Lou
1891	George Haddock, Bos

Union Association

1884	Bill Sweeney, Bal

Players League

1890	Silver King, Chi

Federal League

1914	Claude Hendrix, Chi
1915	George McConnell, Chi

National League

1876	George Bradley, StL
1877	Tommy Bond, Bos
1878	Tommy Bond, Bos
1879	Tommy Bond, Bos
1880	Larry Corcoran, Chi
1881	Larry Corcoran, Chi
1882	Charley Radbourn, Pro
1883	Charley Radbourn, Pro
1884	Charley Radbourn, Pro
1885	John Clarkson, Chi
1886	Lady Baldwin, Det
1887	John Clarkson, Chi
1888	Tim Keefe, NY
1889	John Clarkson, Bos
1890	Bill Hutchison, Chi
1891	Bill Hutchison, Chi
1892	Cy Young, Cle
1893	Amos Rusie, NY
1894	Amos Rusie, NY
1895	Cy Young, Cle
1896	Kid Nichols, Bos
1897	Kid Nichols, Bos
1898	Kid Nichols, Bos
1899	Vic Willis, Bos
1900	Joe McGinnity, Bro
1901	Deacon Phillippe, Pit
1902	Jack Chesbro, Pit
1903	Christy Mathewson, NY
1904	Joe McGinnity, NY
1905	Christy Mathewson, NY
1906	Mordecai Brown, Chi
1907	Orval Overall, Chi
1908	Christy Mathewson, NY
1909	Mordecai Brown, Chi
1910	Christy Mathewson, NY
1911	Christy Mathewson, NY
1912	Rube Marquard, NY
1913	Christy Mathewson, NY
1914	Bill James, Bos
1915	Grover Alexander, Phi
1916	Grover Alexander, Phi
1917	Grover Alexander, Phi
1918	Hippo Vaughn, Chi
1919	Hippo Vaughn, Chi
1920	Pete Alexander, Chi
1921	Burleigh Grimes, Bro
1922	Wilbur Cooper, Pit
1923	Dolf Luque, Cin
1924	Dazzy Vance, Bro
1925	Dazzy Vance, Bro
1926	Ray Kremer, Pit
1927	Charles Root, Chi
1928	Burleigh Grimes, Pit
1929	Burleigh Grimes, Pit
1930	Pat Malone, Chi
1931	Ed Brandt, Bos
1932	Lou Warneke, Chi
1933	Carl Hubbell, NY
1934	Dizzy Dean, StL
1935	Dizzy Dean, StL
1936	Carl Hubbell, NY
1937	Carl Hubbell, NY
1938	Bill Lee, Chi
1939	Bucky Walters, Cin
1940	Bucky Walters, Cin
1941	Whit Wyatt, Bro
1942	Mort Cooper, StL
1943	Mort Cooper, StL
1944	Bucky Walters, Cin
1945	Red Barrett, Bos-StL
1946	Howie Pollet, StL
1947	Ewell Blackwell, Cin
1948	Johnny Sain, Bos
1949	Warren Spahn, Bos
1950	Jim Konstanty, Phi
1951	Sal Maglie, NY
1952	Robin Roberts, Phi
1953	Warren Spahn, Mil
1954	Johnny Antonelli, NY
1955	Robin Roberts, Phi
1958	Warren Spahn, Mil
1959	Sam Jones, SF
1961	Warren Spahn, Mil
1964	Sandy Koufax, LA

American League

1901	Cy Young, Bos
1902	Cy Young, Bos
1903	Cy Young, Bos
1904	Jack Chesbro, NY
1905	Rube Waddell, Phi
1906	Al Orth, NY
1907	Bill Donovan, Det
1908	Ed Walsh, Chi
1909	George Mullin, Det
1910	Jack Coombs, Phi
1911	Walter Johnson, Was
1912	Walter Johnson, Was
1913	Walter Johnson, Was
1914	Walter Johnson, Was
1915	Walter Johnson, Was
1916	Babe Ruth, Bos
1917	Eddie Cicotte, Chi
1918	Walter Johnson, Was
1919	Eddie Cicotte, Chi
1920	Jim Bagby, Cle
1921	Red Faber, Chi
1922	Eddie Rommel, Phi
1923	George Uhle, Cle
1924	Walter Johnson, Was
1925	Stan Coveleski, Was
1926	George Uhle, Cle
1927	Waite Hoyt, NY
1928	Lefty Grove, Phi
1929	Lefty Grove, Phi
1930	Lefty Grove, Phi
1931	Lefty Grove, Phi
1932	Lefty Grove, Phi
1933	Lefty Grove, Phi
1934	Lefty Gomez, NY
1935	Wes Ferrell, Bos
1936	Tommy Bridges, Det
1937	Lefty Gomez, NY
1938	Red Ruffing, NY
1939	Bob Feller, Cle
1940	Bob Feller, Cle
1941	Bob Feller, Cle
1942	Tex Hughson, Bos
1943	Spud Chandler, NY
1944	Hal Newhouser, Det
1945	Hal Newhouser, Det
1946	Hal Newhouser, Det
1947	Bob Feller, Cle
1948	Bob Lemon, Cle
1949	Mel Parnell, Bos
1950	Bob Lemon, Cle
1951	Ed Lopat, NY
1952	Bobby Shantz, Phi
1953	Billy Pierce, Chi
1954	Bob Lemon, Cle
1955	Whitey Ford, NY
1956	Billy Pierce, Chi
1957	Jim Bunning, Det
1960	Chuck Estrada, Bal
1962	Dick Donovan, Cle
1963	Whitey Ford, NY
1965	Mudcat Grant, Min
1966	Jim Kaat, Min

BBWAA Rookie of the Year Award

Inspired by its Chicago branch, which had been honoring top rookies since 1940, the Baseball Writers Association of America took the Rookie of the Year awards national starting in 1947. After honoring only one rookie in 1947 and 1948, the BBWAA started giving the award to a rookie in each league in 1949. In the early days of the award, there was significant confusion over which players qualified as rookies. The first set of standards dealing with this was established in 1957. The current standards, which say that any player who has accumulated more than 130 at bats, 50 innings, or a certain amount of time on the major league roster is no longer a rookie, took effect in 1971. Writers used a one-place ballot for most the award's history until 1980, when voters shifted over to a three-place ballot.

Though there's no longer any debate over which players are technically rookies, there is discussion as to whether certain players should be *considered* rookies. Hideki Matsui lost the 2003 AL Rookie of the Year Award because two voters purposely left him off their ballots as a result of his Japanese pro experience. Ironically, the first BBWAA Rookie of the Year Award winner, Jackie Robinson, and many of the other players who won the award in its first decade of existence, came from the high-level Negro Leagues and thus had a similar baseball background to the Japanese players of today who are competing for MLB's rookie awards.

A more general issue is whether voters should favor younger rookies who show greater potential over older rookies who perform better in their first years but have much lower ceilings. With more Japanese players entering the majors, this issue will remain a hot topic, but it appears unlikely that the rules will be altered anytime soon.

Rookie of the Year Award

1947	Jackie Robinson, Bro NL
1948	Alvin Dark, Bos NL

AL Rookie of the Year Award

1949	Roy Sievers, StL
1950	Walt Dropo, Bos
1951	Gil McDougald, NY
1952	Harry Byrd, Phi
1953	Harvey Kuenn, Det
1954	Bob Grim, NY
1955	Herb Score, Cle
1956	Luis Aparicio, Chi
1957	Tony Kubek*, NY
1958	Albie Pearson, Was
1959	Bob Allison, Was
1960	Ron Hansen, Bal
1961	Don Schwall, Bos
1962	Tom Tresh, NY
1963	Gary Peters, Chi
1964	Tony Oliva, Min
1965	Curt Blefary, Bal
1966	Tommie Agee, Chi
1967	Rod Carew, Min
1968	Stan Bahnsen, NY
1969	Lou Piniella, KC
1970	Thurman Munson, NY
1971	Chris Chambliss, Cle
1972	Carlton Fisk, Bos
1973	Al Bumbry, Bal
1974	Mike Hargrove, Tex
1975	Fred Lynn*, Bos
1976	Mark Fidrych, Det

NL Rookie of the Year Award

1949	Don Newcombe, Bro
1950	Sam Jethroe, Bos
1951	Willie Mays, NY
1952	Joe Black, Bro
1953	Jim Gilliam, Bro
1954	Wally Moon, StL
1955	Bill Virdon, StL
1956	Frank Robinson*, Cin
1957	Jack Sanford, Phi
1958	Orlando Cepeda*, SF
1959	Willie McCovey*, SF
1960	Frank Howard, LA
1961	Billy Williams, Chi
1962	Ken Hubbs, Chi
1963	Pete Rose, Cin
1964	Richie Allen, Phi
1965	Jim Lefebvre, LA
1966	Tommy Helms, Cin
1967	Tom Seaver, NY
1968	Johnny Bench, Cin
1969	Ted Sizemore, LA
1970	Carl Morton, Mon
1971	Earl Williams, Atl
1972	Jon Matlack, NY
1973	Gary Matthews, SF
1974	Bake McBride, StL
1975	John Montefusco, SF
1976	Pat Zachary, Cin (tie) Butch Metzger, SD

AL Rookie of the Year Award

1977	Eddie Murray, Bal
1978	Lou Whitaker, Det
1979	Alfredo Griffin, Tor (tie) John Castino, Min
1980	Joe Charboneau, Cle
1981	Dave Righetti, NY
1982	Cal Ripken, Bal
1983	Ron Kittle, Chi
1984	Alvin Davis, Sea
1985	Ozzie Guillen, Chi
1986	Jose Canseco, Oak
1987	Mark McGwire*, Oak
1988	Walt Weiss, Oak
1989	Gregg Olson, Bal
1990	Sandy Alomar Jr.*, Cle
1991	Chuck Knoblauch, Min
1992	Pat Listach, Mil
1993	Tim Salmon*, Cal
1994	Bob Hamelin, KC
1995	Marty Cordova, Min
1996	Derek Jeter*, NY
1997	Nomar Garciaparra, Bos
1998	Ben Grieve, Oak
1999	Carlos Beltran, KC
2000	Kazuhiro Sasaki, Sea
2001	Ichiro Suzuki, Sea
2002	Eric Hinske, Tor
2003	Angel Berroa, KC

NL Rookie of the Year Award

1977	Andre Dawson, Mon
1978	Bob Horner, Atl
1979	Rick Sutcliffe, LA
1980	Steve Howe, LA
1981	Fernando Valenzuela, LA
1982	Steve Sax, LA
1983	Darryl Strawberry, NY
1984	Dwight Gooden, NY
1985	Vince Coleman*, StL
1986	Todd Worrell, StL
1987	Benito Santiago*, SD
1988	Chris Sabo, Cin
1989	Jerome Walton, Chi
1990	David Justice, Atl
1991	Jeff Bagwell, Hou
1992	Eric Karros, LA
1993	Mike Piazza*, LA
1994	Raul Mondesi*, LA
1995	Hideo Nomo, LA
1996	Todd Hollandsworth, LA
1997	Scott Rolen*, Phi
1998	Kerry Wood, Chi
1999	Scott Williamson, Cin
2000	Rafael Furcal, Atl
2001	Albert Pujols*, StL
2002	Jason Jennings, Col
2003	Dontrelle Willis, Fla

Ex Post Facto Rookie of the Year Award

National Association

1872	Candy Cummings, Mut
1873	Paul Hines, Was
1874	Tommy Bond, Atl
1875	George Bradley, StL

American Association

1882	Pete Browning, Lou
1883	Arlie Latham, StL
1884	Dave Orr, NY
1885	Norm Baker, Lou
1886	Matt Kilroy, Bal
1887	Mike Griffin, Bal
1888	Mickey Hughes, Bro
1889	Jesse Duryea, Cin
1890	Cupid Childs, Syr
1891	Willard Mains, Cin

Union Association

1884	Harry Moore, Was

Players League

1890	Phil Knell, Phi

Federal League

1914	Benny Kauff, Ind
1915	Jim Kelly, Pit

National League

1876	Charley Jones, Cin
1877	Terry Larkin, Har
1878	Abner Dalrymple, Mil
1879	John O'Rourke, Bos
1880	Roger Connor, Tro
1881	Jim Whitney, Bos
1882	Mike Muldoon, Cle
1883	Charlie Buffinton, Bos
1884	John Clarkson, Chi
1885	Ed Daily, Phi
1886	Jocko Flynn, Chi
1887	Mark Baldwin, Chi
1888	Ben Sanders, Phi
1889	Patsy Tebeau, Cle
1890	Billy Rhines, Cin
1891	Bill Dahlen, Chi
1892	Nig Cuppy, Cle
1893	Heinie Reitz, Bal
1894	Win Mercer, Was
1895	Bill Hoffer, Bal
1896	Gene DeMontreville, Was
1897	Chick Stahl, Bos
1898	Elmer Flick, Phi
1899	Jimmy Williams, Pit
1900	Jimmy Barrett, Cin
1901	Christy Mathewson, NY
1902	Homer Smoot, StL
1903	Jake Weimer, Chi
1904	Harry Lumley, Bro
1905	George Stone, StL
1906	Jack Pfiester, Chi
1907	Nap Rucker, Bro
1908	George McQuillan, Phi
1909	Harry Gaspar, Cin
1910	King Cole, Chi
1911	Grover Alexander, Phi
1912	Larry Cheney, Chi
1913	Jim Viox, Pit
1914	Jeff Pfeffer, Bro
1915	Tom Long, StL
1916	Rogers Hornsby, StL
1917	Leon Cadore, Bro
1918	Charlie Hollocher, Chi
1919	Oscar Tuero, StL
1920	Pat Duncan, Cin
1921	Ray Grimes, Chi
1922	Hack Miller, Chi
1923	George Grantham, Chi
1924	Kiki Cuyler, Pit
1925	Jimmy Welsh, Bos
1926	Paul Waner, Pit
1927	Lloyd Waner, Pit
1928	Del Bissonette, Bro
1929	Johnny Frederick, Bro
1930	Wally Berger, Bos
1931	Paul Derringer, StL
1932	Dizzy Dean, StL
1933	Frank Demaree, Chi
1934	Curt Davis, Phi
1935	Cy Blanton, Pit
1936	Johnny Mize, StL
1937	Cliff Melton, NY
1938	Johnny Rizzo, Pit
1939	Bob Bowman, StL
1940	Babe Young, NY
1941	Elmer Riddle, Cin
1942	Johnny Beazley, StL
1943	Lou Klein, StL
1944	Bill Voiselle, NY
1945	Ken Burkhart, StL
1946	Del Ennis, Phi

American League

1901	Socks Seybold, Phi
1902	Addie Joss, Cle
1903	Chief Bender, Phi
1904	Fred Glade, StL
1905	George Stone, StL
1906	Claude Rossman, Cle
1907	Glenn Liebhardt, Cle
1908	Ed Summers, Det
1909	Frank Baker, Phi
1910	Russ Ford, NY
1911	Vean Gregg, Cle
1912	Del Pratt, StL
1913	Reb Russell, Chi
1914	George Burns, Det
1915	Babe Ruth, Bos
1916	Jim Bagby, Cle
1917	Joe Harris, Cle
1918	Scott Perry, Phi
1919	Dickie Kerr, Chi
1920	Bob Meusel, NY
1921	Joe Sewell, Cle
1922	Herman Pillette, Det
1923	Homer Summa, Cle
1924	Ike Boone, Bos
1925	Earle Combs, NY
1926	Tony Lazzeri, NY
1927	Wilcy Moore, NY
1928	Ed Morris, Bos
1929	Dale Alexander, Det
1930	Smead Jolley, Chi
1931	Joe Vosmik, Cle
1932	Johnny Allen, NY
1933	Bob Johnson, Phi
1934	Hal Trosky, Cle
1935	Jake Powell, Was
1936	Joe DiMaggio, NY
1937	Rudy York, Det
1938	Ken Keltner, Cle
1939	Ted Williams, Bos
1940	Walt Judnich, StL
1941	Phil Rizzuto, NY
1942	Johnny Pesky, Bos
1943	Billy Johnson, NY
1944	Joe Berry, Phi
1945	Dave Ferriss, Bos
1946	Hoot Evers, Det
1947	Spec Shea, NY
1948	Gene Bearden, Cle

BBWAA Manager of the Year Award

The Baseball Writers Association of America was a latecomer to honoring the major leagues' best managers, but today the trophy given to the BBWAA's Manager of the Year is the most prestigious of its kind. Voting is done with the same three-place ballot that the BBWAA uses for the Cy Young and Rookie of the Year.

	AL	NL
1983	Tony La Russa, Chi	Tommy Lasorda, LA
1984	Sparky Anderson, Det	Jim Frey, Chi
1985	Bobby Cox, Tor	Whitey Herzog, StL
1986	John McNamara, Bos	Hal Lanier, Hou
1987	Sparky Anderson, Det	Buck Rodgers, Mon
1988	Tony La Russa, Oak	Tommy Lasorda, La
1989	Frank Robinson, Bal	Don Zimmer, Chi
1990	Jeff Torborg, Chi	Jim Leyland, Pit
1991	Tom Kelly, Min	Bobby Cox, Atl
1992	Tony La Russa, Oak	Jim Leyland, Pit
1993	Gene Lamont, Chi	Dusty Baker, SF

	AL	NL
1994	Buck Showalter, NY	Felipe Alou, Mon
1995	Lou Piniella, Sea	Don Baylor, Col
1996	Johnny Oates, Tex (tie) Joe Torre, NY	Bruce Bochy, SD
1997	Davey Johnson, Bal	Dusty Baker, SF
1998	Joe Torre, NY	Larry Dierker, Hou
1999	Jimy Williams, Bos	Jack McKeon, Cin
2000	Jerry Manuel, Chi	Dusty Baker, SF
2001	Lou Piniella, Sea	Larry Bowa, Phi
2002	Mike Scioscia, Ana	Tony La Russa, StL
2003	Tony Pena, KC	Jack McKeon, Fla

The Sporting News Player and Pitcher of the Year Awards

The Sporting News was once known as "Baseball's Bible." (Some especially avid baseball fans referred to the Bible as "*The Sporting News* of religion.") That reputation endowed *The Sporting News*' awards with a great deal of prestige. Many fans held the newspaper's selections in equal or even higher regard than the choices made by the BBWAA. That time is long gone, but *The Sporting News* still gives out more baseball awards than any other organization, and the long tradition of these awards gives them unmatched historical value.

The Sporting News started its tradition of awards in 1929 after the American League abandoned choosing a Most Valuable Player. Over the following twenty years, *The Sporting News* alternated between competing with the BBWAA's MVP awards and endorsing them. In 1948, *The Sporting News* started annually selecting Players and Pitchers of the Year in each league as well as continuing their Major League Player of the Year, which had been selected annually since 1935. In 1992, *The Sporting News* decided to drop its AL and NL Player of the Year Awards in order to focus exclusively on its Major League Player of the Year Award, which would heretofore be selected by big league players. The remaining *Sporting News* awards are still selected by the magazine's editors.

	AL PLAYER	AL PITCHER	NL PLAYER	NL PITCHER	ML PLAYER
1929	Al Simmons, Phi				
1930	Joe Cronin, Was		Bill Terry, NY		
1931	Lou Gehrig, NY		Chuck Klein, Phi		
1932	Jimmie Foxx, Phi		Chuck Klein, Phi		
1933	Jimmie Foxx, Phi			Carl Hubbell, NY	
1934	Lou Gehrig, NY			Dizzy Dean, StL	
1935	Hank Greenberg, Det		Arky Vaughan, Pit		
1936	Lou Gehrig, NY			Carl Hubbell, NY	Carl Hubbell, NY
1937	Charlie Gehringer, Det	Johnny Allen, Cle	Joe Medwick, StL		Johnny Allen, Cle
1938	Jimmie Foxx, Bos		Ernie Lombardi, Cin	Johnny Vander Meer, Cin	Johnny Vander Meer, Cin
1939	Joe DiMaggio, NY			Bucky Walters, Cin	Joe DiMaggio, NY
1940	Hank Greenberg, Det	Bob Feller, Cle	Frank McCormick, Cin		Bob Feller, Cle
1941	Joe DiMaggio, NY		Dolf Camilli, Bro		Ted Williams, Bos
1942	Joe Gordon, NY			Mort Cooper, StL	Ted Williams, Bos
1943		Spud Chandler, NY	Stan Musial, StL		Spud Chandler, NY
1944	Bobby Doerr, Bos	Hal Newhouser, Det	Marty Marion, StL	Bill Voiselle, NY	Marty Marion, StL
1945	Eddie Mayo, Det	Hal Newhouser, Det	Tommy Holmes, Bos	Hank Borowy, Chi	Hal Newhouser, Det
1946			Stan Musial, StL		Stan Musial, StL
1947	Ted Williams, Bos				Ted Williams, Bos
1948	Lou Boudreau, Cle	Bob Lemon, Cle	Stan Musial, StL	Johnny Sain, Bos	Lou Boudreau, Cle
1949	Ted Williams, Bos	Ellis Kinder, Bos	Enos Slaughter, StL	Howie Pollet, StL	Ted Williams, Bos
1950	Phil Rizzuto, NY	Bob Lemon, Cle	Ralph Kiner, Pit	Jim Konstanty, Phi	Phil Rizzuto, NY
1951	Ferris Fain, Phi	Bob Feller, Cle	Stan Musial, StL	Preacher Roe, Bro	Stan Musial, StL
1952	Luke Easter, Cle	Bobby Shantz, Phi	Hank Sauer, Chi	Robin Roberts, Phi	Robin Roberts, Phi
1953	Al Rosen, Cle	Bob Porterfield, Was	Roy Campanella, Bro	Warren Spahn, Mil	Al Rosen, Cle
1954	Bobby Avila, Cle	Bob Lemon, Cle	Willie Mays, NY	John Antonelli, NY	Willie Mays, NY
1955	Al Kaline, Det	Whitey Ford, NY	Duke Snider, Bro	Robin Roberts, Phi	Duke Snider, Bro
1956	Mickey Mantle, NY	Billy Pierce, Chi	Hank Aaron, Mil	Don Newcombe, Bro	Mickey Mantle, NY
1957	Ted Williams, Bos	Billy Pierce, Chi	Stan Musial, StL	Warren Spahn, Mil	Ted Williams, Bos
1958	Jackie Jensen, Bos	Bob Turley, NY	Ernie Banks, Chi	Warren Spahn, Mil	Bob Turley, NY
1959	Nellie Fox, Chi	Early Wynn, Chi	Ernie Banks, Chi	Sam Jones, SF	Early Wynn, Chi
1960	Roger Maris, NY	Chuck Estrada, Bal	Dick Groat, Pit	Vern Law, Pit	Bill Mazeroski, Pit
1961	Roger Maris, NY	Whitey Ford, NY	Frank Robinson, Cin	Warren Spahn, Mil	Roger Maris, NY
1962	Mickey Mantle, NY	Dick Donovan, Cle	Maury Wills, LA	Don Drysdale, LA	Don Drysdale, LA
1963	Al Kaline, Det	Whitey Ford, NY	Hank Aaron, Mil	Sandy Koufax, LA	Sandy Koufax, LA
1964	Brooks Robinson, Bal	Dean Chance, LA	Ken Boyer, StL	Sandy Koufax, LA	Ken Boyer, StL
1965	Tony Oliva, Min	Mudcat Grant, Min	Willie Mays, SF	Sandy Koufax, LA	Sandy Koufax, LA
1966	Frank Robinson, Bal	Jim Kaat, Min	Roberto Clemente, Pit	Sandy Koufax, LA	Frank Robinson, Bal
1967	Carl Yastrzemski, Bos	Jim Lonborg, Bos	Orlando Cepeda, StL	Mike McCormick, SF	Carl Yastrzemski, Bos
1968	Ken Harrelson, Bos	Denny McLain, Det	Pete Rose, Cin	Bob Gibson, StL	Denny McLain, Det
1969	Harmon Killebrew, Min	Denny McLain, Det	Willie McCovey, SF	Tom Seaver, NY	Willie McCovey, SF
1970	Harmon Killebrew, Min	Sam McDowell, Cle	Johnny Bench, Cin	Bob Gibson, StL	Johnny Bench, Cin
1971	Tony Oliva, Min	Vida Blue, Oak	Joe Torre, StL	Fergie Jenkins, Chi	Joe Torre, StL
1972	Dick Allen, Chi	Wilbur Wood, Chi	Billy Williams, Chi	Steve Carlton, Phi	Billy Williams, Chi
1973	Reggie Jackson, Oak	Jim Palmer, Bal	Bobby Bonds, SF	Ron Bryant, SF	Reggie Jackson, Oak
1974	Jeff Burroughs, Tex	Catfish Hunter, Oak	Lou Brock, StL	Mike Marshall, LA	Lou Brock, StL
1975	Fred Lynn, Bos	Jim Palmer, Bal	Joe Morgan, Cin	Tom Seaver, NY	Joe Morgan, Cin
1976	Thurman Munson, NY	Jim Palmer, Bal	George Foster, Cin	Randy Jones, SD	Joe Morgan, Cin
1977	Rod Carew, Min	Nolan Ryan, Cal	George Foster, Cin	Steve Carlton, Phi	Rod Carew, Min
1978	Jim Rice, Bos	Ron Guidry, NY	Dave Parker, Pit	Vida Blue, SF	Ron Guidry, NY
1979	Don Baylor, Cal	Mike Flanagan, Bal	Keith Hernandez, StL	Joe Niekro, Hou	Willie Stargell, Pit
1980	George Brett, KC	Steve Stone, Bal	Mike Schmidt, Phi	Steve Carlton, Phi	George Brett, KC
1981	Tony Armas, Oak	Jack Morris, Det	Andre Dawson, Mon	Fernando Valenzuela, LA	Fernando Valenzuela, LA
1982	Robin Yount, Mil	Dave Stieb, Tor	Dale Murphy, Atl	Steve Carlton, Phi	Robin Yount, Mil
1983	Cal Ripken, Bal	La Marr Hoyt, Chi	Dale Murphy, Atl	John Denny, Phi	Cal Ripken, Bal
1984	Don Mattingly, NY	Willie Hernandez, Det	Ryne Sandberg, Chi	Rick Sutcliffe, Chi	Ryne Sandberg, Chi
1985	Don Mattingly, NY	Bret Saberhagen, KC	Willie McGee, StL	Dwight Gooden, NY	Don Mattingly, NY
1986	Don Mattingly, NY	Roger Clemens, Bos	Mike Schmidt, Phi	Mike Scott, Hou	Roger Clemens, Bos
1987	George Bell, Tor	Jimmy Key, Tor	Andre Dawson, Chi	Rick Sutcliffe, Chi	George Bell, Tor
1988	Jose Canseco, Oak	Frank Viola, Min	Andy Van Slyke, Pit	Orel Hershiser, LA	Orel Hershiser, LA
1989	Ruben Sierra, Tex	Bret Saberhagen, KC	Kevin Mitchell, SF	Mark Davis, SD	Kevin Mitchell, SF
1990	Cecil Fielder, Det	Bob Welch, Oak	Barry Bonds, Pit	Doug Drabek, Pit	Barry Bonds, Pit
1991	Cal Ripken, Bal	Roger Clemens, Bos	Barry Bonds, Pit	Tom Glavine, Atl	Cal Ripken, Bal
1992		Dennis Eckersley, Oak		Greg Maddux, Chi	Gary Sheffield, SD
1993		Jack McDowell, Chi		Greg Maddux, Atl	Frank Thomas, Chi
1994		Jimmy Key, NY		Greg Maddux, Atl	Jeff Bagwell, Hou
1995		Randy Johnson, Sea		Greg Maddux, Atl	Albert Belle, Cle
1996		Pat Hentgen, Tor		John Smoltz, Atl	Alex Rodriguez, Sea
1997		Roger Clemens, Tor		Pedro Martinez, Mon	Ken Griffey Jr., Sea
1998		Roger Clemens, Tor		Kevin Brown, SD	Sammy Sosa, Chi
1999		Pedro Martinez, Bos		Mike Hampton, Hou	Rafael Palmeiro, Tex
2000		Pedro Martinez, Bos		Tom Glavine, Atl	Carlos Delgado, Tor
2001		Roger Clemens, NY		Curt Schilling, Ari	Barry Bonds, SF
2002		Barry Zito, Oak		Curt Schilling, Ari	Alex Rodriguez, Tex
2003		Roy Halladay, Oak		Eric Gagne, LA	Albert Pujols, StL

The Sporting News Rookie Player and Pitcher of the Year Awards

The Sporting News started selecting a Rookie of the Year in 1946, and moved tentatively to selecting one player from each league in 1949. It selected a separate Rookie Pitcher of the Year in 1957, one in each league in 1958 and 1961, and no pitchers at all in 1959, 1960, and 1962. Finally, in 1963, *The Sporting News* settled on annually picking both a Rookie Player of the Year and a Rookie Pitcher of the Year from each league. *The Sporting News* is the only organization today that celebrates rookie pitchers. (The top rookie—if a pitcher—is listed under the pitcher heading until 1957 but, in those cases, the pitcher is simply *The Sporting News* Rookie of the Year for his league.)

	AL PLAYER	AL PITCHER	NL PLAYER	NL PITCHER
1946			Del Ennis, Phi	
1947			Jackie Robinson, Bro	
1948			Richie Ashburn, Phi	
1949	Roy Sievers, StL			Don Newcombe, Bro
1950		Whitey Ford, NY		
1951	Minnie Minoso, Chi		Willie Mays, NY	
1952	Clint Courtney, StL			Joe Black, Bro
1953	Harvey Kuenn, Det		Junior Gilliam, Bro	
1954		Bob Grim, NY	Wally Moon, StL	
1955		Herb Score, Cle	Bill Virdon, StL	
1956	Luis Aparicio, Chi		Frank Robinson, Cin	
1957	Tony Kubek, NY		Ed Bouchee, Phi	Jack Sanford, Phi
1958	Albie Pearson, Was	Ryne Duren, NY	Orlando Cepeda, SF	Carlton Willey, Mil
1959	Bob Allison, Was		Willie McCovey, SF	
1960	Ron Hansen, Bal		Frank Howard, LA	
1961	Dick Howser, KC	Don Schwall, Bos	Billy Williams, Chi	Ken Hunt, Cin
1962	Tom Tresh, NY		Ken Hubbs, Chi	
1963	Pete Ward, Chi	Gary Peters, Chi	Pete Rose, Cin	Ray Culp, Phi
1964	Tony Oliva, Min	Wally Bunker, Bal	Richie Allen, Phi	Billy McCool, Cin
1965	Curt Blefary, Bal	Marcelino Lopez, Cal	Joe Morgan, Hou	Frank Linzy, SF
1966	Tommie Agee, Chi	Jim Nash, KC	Tommy Helms, Cin	Don Sutton, La
1967	Rod Carew, Min	Tom Phoebus, Bal	Lee May, Cin	Dick Hughes, StL
1968	Del Unser, Was	Stan Bahnsen, NY	Johnny Bench, Cin	Jerry Koosman, NY
1969	Carlos May, Chi	Mike Nagy, Bos	Coco Laboy, Mon	Tom Griffin, Hou
1970	Roy Foster, Cle	Bert Blyleven, Min	Bernie Carbo, Cin	Carl Morton, Mon
1971	Chris Chambliss, Cle	Bill Parsons, Mil	Earl Williams, Atl	Reggie Cleveland, StL
1972	Carlton Fisk, Bos	Dick Tidrow, Cle	Dave Rader, SF	Jon Matlack, NY
1973	Al Bumbry, Bal	Steve Busby, KC	Gary Matthews, SF	Steve Rogers, Mon
1974	Mike Hargrove, Tex	Frank Tanana, Cal	Greg Gross, Hou	John D'Acquisto, SF
1975	Fred Lynn, Bos	Dennis Eckersley, Cle	Gary Carter, Mon	John Montefusco, SF
1976	Butch Wynegar, Min	Mark Fidrych, Det	Larry Herndon, SF	Butch Metzger, SD
1977	Mitchell Page, Oak	Dave Rozema, Det	Andre Dawson, Mon	Bob Owchinko, SD
1978	Paul Molitor, Mil	Rich Gale, KC	Bob Horner, Atl	Don Robinson, Pit
1979	Pat Putnam, Tex	Mark Clear, Cal	Jeff Leonard, Hou	Rick Sutcliffe, LA
1980	Joe Charboneau, Cle	Britt Burns, Chi	Lonnie Smith, Phi	Bill Gullickson, Mon
1981	Rich Gedman, Bos	Dave Righetti, NY	Tim Raines, Mon	Fernando Valenzuela, La
1982	Cal Ripken, Bal	Ed Vande Berg, Sea	Johnny Ray, Pit	Steve Bedrosian, Atl
1983	Ron Kittle, Chi	Mike Boddicker, Bal	Darryl Strawberry, NY	Craig McMurtry, Atl
1984	Alvin Davis, Sea	Mark Langston, Sea	Juan Samuel, Phi	Dwight Gooden, NY
1985	Ozzie Guillen, Chi	Ted Higuera, Mil	Vince Coleman, StL	Tom Browning, Cin
1986	Jose Canseco, Oak	Mark Eichhorn, Tor	Robby Thompson, SF	Todd Worrell, StL
1987	Mark McGwire, Oak	Mike Henneman, Det	Benito Santiago, SD	Mike Dunne, Pit
1988	Walt Weiss, Oak	Bryan Harvey, Cal	Mark Grace, Chi	Tim Belcher, LA
1989	Craig Worthington, Bal	Tom Gordon, KC	Jerome Walton, Chi	Andy Benes, SD
1990	Sandy Alomar Jr., Cle	Kevin Appier, KC	Dave Justice, Atl	Mike Harkey, Chi
1991	Chuck Knoblauch, Min	Juan Guzman, Tor	Jeff Bagwell, Hou	Al Osuna, Hou
1992	Pat Listach, Mil	Cal Eldred, Mil	Eric Karros, LA	Tim Wakefield, Pit
1993	Tim Salmon, Cal	Aaron Sele, Bos	Mike Piazza, LA	Kirk Rueter, Mon
1994	Bob Hamelin, KC	Brian Anderson, Cal	Raul Mondesi, LA	Steve Trachsel, Chi
1995	Garret Anderson, Cal	Julian Tavarez, Cle	Chipper Jones, Atl	Hideo Nomo, LA
1996	Derek Jeter, NY	James Baldwin, Chi	Jason Kendall, Pit	Alan Benes, StL
1997	Nomar Garciaparra, Bos	Jason Dickson, Ana	Scott Rolen, Phi	Matt Morris, StL
1998	Ben Grieve, Oak	Rolando Arrojo, TB	Todd Helton, Col	Kerry Wood, Chi
1999	Carlos Beltran, KC	Tim Hudson, Oak	Preston Wilson, Fla	Scott Williamson, Cin
2000	Mark Quinn, KC	Kazuhiro Sasaki, Sea	Rafael Furcal, Atl	Rick Ankiel, StL
2001	Ichiro Suzuki, Sea	C.C. Sabathia, Cle	Albert Pujols, StL	Roy Oswalt, Hou
2002	Eric Hinske, Tor	Rodrigo Lopez, Bal	Brad Wilkerson, Mon	Jason Jennings, Col
2003	Jody Gerut, Cle	Rafael Soriano, Sea	Scott Podsednik, Mil	Dontrelle Willis, Fla

The Sporting News Manager of the Year Award

The Sporting News has honored a Manager of the Year since 1936, forty-six years before the BBWAA first gave a comparable award. In response to the BBWAA's selection of a Manager of the Year for each major league, *The Sporting News* started doing the same in 1986.

1936	Joe McCarthy, NY AL	1949	Casey Stengel, NY AL	1962	Bill Rigney, LA AL	1975	Darrell Johnson, Bos AL
1937	Bill McKechnie, Bos NL	1950	Red Rolfe, Det AL	1963	Walt Alston, LA NL	1976	Danny Ozark, Phi NL
1938	Joe McCarthy, NY AL	1951	Leo Durocher, NY NL	1964	Johnny Keane, StL NL	1977	Earl Weaver, Bal AL
1939	Leo Durocher, Bro NL	1952	Eddie Stanky, StL NL	1965	Sam Mele, Min AL	1978	George Bamberger, Mil AL
1940	Bill McKechnie, Cin NL	1953	Casey Stengel, NY AL	1966	Hank Bauer, Bal AL	1979	Earl Weaver, Bal AL
1941	Billy Southworth, StL NL	1954	Leo Durocher, NY NL	1967	Dick Williams, Bos AL	1980	Bill Virdon, Hou NL
1942	Billy Southworth, StL NL	1955	Walt Alston, Bro NL	1968	Mayo Smith, Det AL	1981	Billy Martin, Oak AL
1943	Joe McCarthy, NY AL	1956	Birdie Tebbetts, Cin NL	1969	Gil Hodges, NY NL	1982	Whitey Herzog, StL NL
1944	Luke Sewell, StL AL	1957	Fred Hutchinson, StL NL	1970	Danny Murtaugh, Pit NL	1983	Tony La Russa, Chi AL
1945	Ossie Bluege, Was AL	1958	Casey Stengel, NY AL	1971	Charlie Fox, SF NL	1984	Jim Frey, Chi NL
1946	Eddie Dyer, StL NL	1959	Walt Alston, LA NL	1972	Chuck Tanner, Chi AL	1985	Bobby Cox, Tor AL
1947	Bucky Harris, NY AL	1960	Danny Murtaugh, Pit NL	1973	Gene Mauch, Mon NL		
1948	Billy Meyer, Pit NL	1961	Ralph Houk, NY AL	1974	Bill Virdon, NY AL		

	AL	NL		AL	NL
1986	John McNamara, Bos	Hal Lanier, Hou	1995	Mike Hargrove, Cle	Don Baylor, Col
1987	Sparky Anderson, Det	Buck Rodgers, Mon	1996	Johnny Oates, Tex	Bruce Bochy, SD
1988	Tony La Russa, Oak	Jim Leyland, Pit	1997	Davey Johnson, Bal	Dusty Baker, SF
1989	Frank Robinson, Bal	Don Zimmer, Chi	1998	Joe Torre, NY	Bruce Bochy, SD
1990	Jeff Torborg, Chi	Jim Leyland, Pit	1999	Jimy Williams, Bos	Bobby Cox, Atl
1991	Tom Kelly, Min	Bobby Cox, Atl	2000	Jerry Manuel, Chi	Dusty Baker, SF
1992	Tony La Russa, Oak	Jim Leyland, Pit	2001	Lou Piniella, Sea	Larry Bowa, Phi
1993	Johnny Oates, Bal	Bobby Cox, Atl	2002	Mike Scioscia, Ana	Bobby Cox, Atl
1994	Buck Showalter, NY	Felipe Alou, Mon	2003	Tony Peña, KC	Bobby Cox, Atl

The Sporting News Comeback Player of the Year Award

Other organizations have selected Comeback Player of the Year awards, but only *The Sporting News* version has stood the test of time. No one has ever really defined a "comeback" for the purposes of this award, but it's safe to say that no other award for on-field achievement in baseball honors players with a higher average age.

	AL	NL		AL	NL
1965	Norm Cash, Det	Vern Law, Pit	1973	John Hiller, Det	Davey Johnson, Atl
1966	Boog Powell, Bal	Phil Regan, LA	1974	Ferguson Jenkins, Tex	Jimmy Wynn, LA
1967	Dean Chance, Min	Mike McCormick, SF	1975	Boog Powell, Cle	Randy Jones, SD
1968	Ken Harrelson, Bos	Alex Johnson, Cin	1976	Dock Ellis, NY	Tommy John, LA
1969	Tony Conigliaro, Bos	Tommie Agee, NY	1977	Eric Soderholm, Chi	Willie McCovey, SF
1970	Clyde Wright, Cal	Jim Hickman, Chi	1978	Mike Caldwell, Mil	Willie Stargell, Pit
1971	Norm Cash, Det	Al Downing, LA	1979	Willie Horton, Sea	Lou Brock, StL
1972	Luis Tiant, Bos	Bobby Tolan, Cin	1980	Matt Keough, Oak	Jerry Reuss, LA

	AL	NL		AL	NL
1981	Richie Zisk, Sea	Bob Knepper, Hou	1993	Bo Jackson, Chi	Andres Galarraga, Col
1982	Andre Thornton, Cle	Joe Morgan, SF	1994	Jose Canseco, Tex	Tim Wallach, LA
1983	Alan Trammell, Det	John Denny, Phi	1995	Tim Wakefield, Bos	Ron Gant, Cin
1984	Dave Kingman, Oak	Joaquin Andujar, StL	1996	Kevin Elster, Tex	Eric Davis, Cin
1985	Gorman Thomas, Sea	Rick Reuschel, Pit	1997	David Justice, Cle	Darren Daulton, Phi-Fla
1986	John Candelaria, Cal	Ray Knight, NY	1998	Bret Saberhagen, Bos	Greg Vaughn, SD
1987	Bret Saberhagen, KC	Rick Sutcliffe, Chi	1999	John Jaha, Oak	Rickey Henderson, NY
1988	Storm Davis, Oak	Tim Leary, LA	2000	Frank Thomas, Chi	Andres Galarraga, Atl
1989	Bert Blyleven, Cal	Lonnie Smith, Atl	2001	Ruben Sierra, Tex	Matt Morris, StL
1990	Dave Winfield, Cal	John Tudor, StL	2002	Tim Salmon, Phi	Mike Lieberthal, Phi
1991	Jose Guzman, Tex	Terry Pendleton, Atl	2003	Gil Meche, Sea	Javy Lopez, Atl
1992	Rick Sutcliffe, Bal	Gary Sheffield, SD			

The Sporting News Fireman/Reliever of the Year Award

No comparison of baseball teams these days is complete without a discussion about relief pitchers, especially closers. Many baseball fans today view closers as one of their team's most valuable commodities, and blown leads by relievers earn the ire of baseball fans unlike any other failure in the game. Contrast that to the first half of the twentieth century, when relief pitchers were an anonymous and unappreciated lot. When *The Sporting News* created their Fireman of the Year award in 1960, no reliever had ever received a Cy Young vote, and only one, Hoyt Wilhelm in 1952, had ever finished in the top ten in MVP voting. The Fireman award winner was originally selected based on a strict statistical formula, devised by Jerome Holtzman, which added relief wins and saves. Today, the award winner (called Reliever of the Year as of 2001) is chosen by the magazine's editors.

	AL	NL
1960	Mike Fornieles, Bos	Lindy McDaniel, StL
1961	Luis Arroyo, NY	Stu Miller, SF
1962	Dick Radatz, Bos	Roy Face, Pit
1963	Stu Miller, Bal	Lindy McDaniel, Chi
1964	Dick Radatz, Bos	Al McBean, Pit
1965	Eddie Fisher, Chi	Ted Abernathy, Chi
1966	Jack Aker, KC	Phil Regan, LA
1967	Minnie Rojas, Cal	Ted Abernathy, Cin
1968	Wilbur Wood, Chi	Phil Regan, Chi
1969	Ron Perranoski, Min	Wayne Granger, Cin
1970	Ron Perranoski, Min	Wayne Granger, Cin
1971	Ken Sanders, Mil	Dave Giusti, Pit
1972	Sparky Lyle, NY	Clay Carroll, Cin
1973	John Hiller, Det	Mike Marshall, Mon
1974	Terry Forster, Chi	Mike Marshall, LA
1975	Rich Gossage, Chi	Al Hrabosky, StL
1976	Bill Campbell, Min	Rawly Eastwick, Cin
1977	Bill Campbell, Bos	Rollie Fingers, SD
1978	Rich Gossage, NY	Rollie Fingers, SD
1979	Jim Kern, Tex	Bruce Sutter, Chi
	(tie) Mike Marshall, Min	
1980	Dan Quisenberry, KC	Rollie Fingers, SD
		(tie) Tom Hume, Cin
1981	Rollie Fingers, Mil	Bruce Sutter, StL
1982	Dan Quisenberry, KC	Bruce Sutter, StL
1983	Dan Quisenberry, KC	Al Holland, Phi
		(tie) Lee Smith, Chi

	AL	NL
1984	Dan Quisenberry, KC	Bruce Sutter, StL
1985	Dan Quisenberry, KC	Jeff Reardon, Mon
1986	Dave Righetti, NY	Todd Worrell, StL
1987	Jeff Reardon, Min	Steve Bedrosian, Phi
	(tie) Dave Righetti, NY	
1988	Dennis Eckersley, Oak	John Franco, Cin
1989	Jeff Russell, Tex	Mark Davis, SD
1990	Bobby Thigpen, Chi	John Franco, NY
1991	Dennis Eckersley, Oak	Lee Smith, StL
	(tie) Bryan Harvey, Cal	
1992	Dennis Eckersley, Oak	Doug Jones, Hou
		(tie) Lee Smith, StL
1993	Jeff Montgomery, KC	Randy Myers, Chi
1994	Lee Smith, Bal	John Franco, NY
1995	Jose Mesa, Cle	Randy Myers, Chi
1996	John Wetteland, NY	Trevor Hoffman, SD
1997	Mariano Rivera, NY	Jeff Shaw, Cin
1998	Tom Gordon, Bos	Trevor Hoffman, SD
1999	Mariano Rivera, NY	Ugueth Urbina, Mon
2000	Todd Jones, Det	Antonio Alfonseca, Fla
2001	Mariano Rivera, NY	Armando Benitez, NY
		(tie) Robb Nen, SF
2002	Billy Koch, Oak	John Smoltz, Atl
2003	Keith Foulke, Oak	Eric Gagne, LA

The Sporting News Major League Executive of the Year Award

Nearly all baseball awards honor on-field performance, but there may be no one more responsible for a team's on-field performance than its top executive. This *Sporting News* award has long honored the men behind the scenes who build baseball teams. While many of today's fans are familiar with their team's top front office personnel, this was not the case when the award was created. The most frequent recipient of this award was George Weiss, selected four times while running the Yankees during their most successful dynasty from the late 1940s to the early 1960s.

1936	Branch Rickey, StL NL	1953	Lou Perini, Mil NL	1970	Harry Dalton, Bal AL	1987	Al Rosen, SF NL
1937	Ed Barrow, NY AL	1954	Horace Stoneham, NY NL	1971	Cedric Tallis, KC AL	1988	Fred Claire, LA NL
1938	Warren Giles, Cin NL	1955	Walter O'Malley, Bro NL	1972	Roland Hemond, Chi AL	1989	Roland Hemond, Bal AL
1939	Larry MacPhail, Bro NL	1956	Gabe Paul, Cin NL	1973	Bob Howsam, Cin NL	1990	Bob Quinn, Cin NL
1940	Walter Briggs Sr., Det AL	1957	Frank Lane, StL NL	1974	Gabe Paul, NY AL	1991	Andy MacPhail, Min AL
1941	Ed Barrow, NY AL	1958	Joe Brown, Pit NL	1975	Dick O'Connell, Bos AL	1992	Dan Duquette, Mon NL
1942	Branch Rickey, StL NL	1959	Buzzie Bavasi, LA NL	1976	Joe Burke, KC AL	1993	Lee Thomas, Phi NL
1943	Calvin Griffith, Was AL	1960	George Weiss, NY AL	1977	Bill Veeck, Chi AL	1994	John Hart, Cle AL
1944	William DeWitt, StL AL	1961	Dan Topping, NY AL	1978	Spec Richardson, SF NL	1995	John Hart, Cle AL
1945	Phil Wrigley, Chi NL	1962	Fred Haney, LA AL	1979	Hank Peters, Bal AL	1996	Doug Melvin, Tex AL
1946	Tom Yawkey, Bos AL	1963	Bing Devine, StL NL	1980	Tal Smith, Hou NL	1997	Cam Bonifay, Pit NL
1947	Branch Rickey, Bro NL	1964	Bing Devine, StL NL	1981	John McHale, Mon NL	1998	Gerry Hunsicker, Hou NL
1948	Bill Veeck, Cle AL	1965	Calvin Griffith, Min AL	1982	Harry Dalton, Mil AL	1999	Billy Beane, Oak AL
1949	Bob Carpenter, Phi NL	1966	Lee MacPhail, MLB	1983	Hank Peters, Bal AL	2000	Walt Jocketty, StL NL
1950	George Weiss, NY AL	1967	Dick O'Connell, Bos AL	1984	Dallas Green, Chi AL	2001	Pat Gillick, Sea AL
1951	George Weiss, NY AL	1968	Jim Campbell, Det AL	1985	John Schuerholz, KC AL	2002	Terry Ryan, Min AL
1952	George Weiss, NY AL	1969	Johnny Murphy, NY NL	1986	Frank Cashen, NY NL	2003	Brian Sabean, SF NL

Rolaids Relief Man of the Year Award

The owners of Rolaids® antacids created this award for relief pitchers in order to impress upon potential customers that Rolaids did indeed "spell relief" for heartburn and indigestion. This marketing effort proved enormously successful, raising the profile of both the antacid and the pitchers. The winners of the award have always been determined by a statistical formula, which originally took into account saves, wins, and losses, and later included blown saves as well as tough saves. Rolaids® has expanded this promotional award throughout the minor leagues.

	AL	NL		AL	NL		AL	NL
1976	Bill Campbell, Min	Rawly Eastwick, Cin	1986	Dave Righetti, NY	Todd Worrell, StL	1996	John Wetteland, NY	Jeff Brantley, Cin
1977	Bill Campbell, Bos	Rollie Fingers, SD	1987	Dave Righetti, NY	Steve Bedrosian, Phi	1997	Randy Myers, Bal	Jeff Shaw, Cin
1978	Rich Gossage, NY	Rollie Fingers, SD	1988	Dennis Eckersley, Oak	John Franco, Cin	1998	Tom Gordon, Bos	Trevor Hoffman, SD
1979	Jim Kern, Tex	Bruce Sutter, Chi	1989	Jeff Russell, Tex	Mark Davis, SD	1999	Mariano Rivera, NY	Billy Wagner, Hou
1980	Dan Quisenberry, KC	Rollie Fingers, SD	1990	Bobby Thigpen, Chi	John Franco, NY	2000	Todd Jones, Det	Antonio Alfonseca, Fla
1981	Rollie Fingers, Mil	Bruce Sutter, StL	1991	Bryan Harvey, Cal	Lee Smith, StL	2001	Mariano Rivera, NY	Armando Benitez, NY
1982	Dan Quisenberry, KC	Bruce Sutter, StL	1992	Dennis Eckersley, Oak	Lee Smith, StL	2002	Billy Koch, Oak	John Smoltz, Atl
1983	Dan Quisenberry, KC	Al Holland, Phi	1993	Jeff Montgomery, KC	Randy Myers, Chi	2003	Keith Foulke, Oak	Eric Gagne, LA
1984	Dan Quisenberry, KC	Bruce Sutter, StL	1994	Lee Smith, Bal	Rod Beck, SF			
1985	Dan Quisenberry, KC	Jeff Reardon, Mon	1995	Jose Mesa, Cle	Tom Henke, StL			

GOLD GLOVE AWARDS

MLB Gold Gloves

Defense is the most difficult skill in baseball to judge by sight alone. The way a player looks when he makes plays is often misleading, because positioning is very important and poor defenders can make easy plays look hard. Defense is also the hardest act in baseball to statistically measure. The Gold Glove Awards were created to systematically use subjective analysis to bring recognition to the best fielders at each position.

Rawlings, the manufacturer of the great majority of big-leaguers' gloves at the time, teamed up in 1957 to present the Gold Gloves to *The Sporting News* All-Fielding Team. The awards were given to one player at each position in the major leagues, as selected by a panel of sportswriters. In 1958 voting was handed over to major league players and gold gloves were awarded for each position in each league. In 1961 voters were told to simply select three outfielders, regardless of whether they were left fielders, center fielders, or right fielders (which remains the practice today). In 1966 major league managers and coaches took over the voting.

Knowledgeable baseball observers are skeptical about the results of Gold Glove voting, largely because so many players win year after year. Many great defensive players earn their first Gold Gloves several years after they have established their defensive prowess, then keep winning Gold Gloves even after their defensive decline has become obvious. Some players seem to be given this defensive award partly for their offense, while weak hitters with great gloves are frequently ignored. The award's most recent controversy occurred when the AL's 1999 first base Gold Glove was awarded to designated hitter Rafael Palmeiro, who played first base in only 28 games.

1957 Gold Gloves

P	Bobby Shantz, NY AL
C	Sherm Lollar, Chi AL
1B	Gil Hodges, Bro NL
2B	Nellie Fox, Chi AL
3B	Frank Malzone, Bos AL
SS	Roy McMillan, Cin NL
LF	Minnie Minoso, Chi AL
CF	Willie Mays, NY NL
RF	Al Kaline, Det AL

AL Gold Gloves / NL Gold Gloves

1958	AL		NL
P	Bobby Shantz, NY	P	Harvey Haddix, Cin
C	Sherm Lollar, Chi	C	Del Crandall, Mil
1B	Vic Power, KC-Cle	1B	Gil Hodges, LA
2B	Frank Bolling, Det	2B	Bill Mazeroski, Pit
3B	Frank Malzone, Bos	3B	Ken Boyer, StL
SS	Luis Aparicio, Chi	SS	Roy McMillan, Cin
LF	Norm Siebern, NY	LF	Frank Robinson, Cin
CF	Jim Piersall, Bos	CF	Willie Mays, SF
RF	Al Kaline, Det	RF	Hank Aaron, Mil

1959	AL		NL
P	Bobby Shantz, NY	P	Harvey Haddix, Pit
C	Sherm Lollar, Chi	C	Del Crandall, Mil
1B	Vic Power, Cle	1B	Gil Hodges, LA
2B	Nellie Fox, Chi	2B	Charlie Neal, LA
3B	Frank Malzone, Bos	3B	Ken Boyer, StL
SS	Luis Aparicio, Chi	SS	Roy McMillan, Cin
LF	Minnie Minoso, Cle	LF	Jackie Brandt, SF
CF	Al Kaline, Det	CF	Willie Mays, SF
RF	Jackie Jensen, Bos	RF	Hank Aaron, Mil

1960	AL		NL
P	Bobby Shantz, NY	P	Harvey Haddix, Pit
C	Earl Battey, Was	C	Del Crandall, Mil
1B	Vic Power, Cle	1B	Bill White, StL
2B	Nellie Fox, Chi	2B	Bill Mazeroski, Pit
3B	Brooks Robinson, Bal	3B	Ken Boyer, StL
SS	Luis Aparicio, Chi	SS	Ernie Banks, Chi
LF	Minnie Minoso, Chi	LF	Wally Moon, LA
CF	Jim Landis, Chi	CF	Willie Mays, SF
RF	Roger Maris, NY	RF	Hank Aaron, Mil

1961	AL		NL
P	Frank Lary, Det	P	Bobby Shantz, Pit
C	Earl Battey, Min	C	Johnny Roseboro, LA
1B	Vic Power, Cle	1B	Bill White, StL
2B	Bobby Richardson, NY	2B	Bill Mazeroski, Pit
3B	Brooks Robinson, Bal	3B	Ken Boyer, StL
SS	Luis Aparicio, Chi	SS	Maury Wills, LA
OF	Jim Piersall, Cle	OF	Willie Mays, SF
OF	Jim Landis, Chi	OF	Roberto Clemente, Pit
OF	Al Kaline, Det	OF	Vada Pinson, Cin

1962	AL		NL
P	Jim Kaat, Min	P	Bobby Shantz, Hou-StL
C	Earl Battey, Min	C	Del Crandall, Mil
1B	Vic Power, Min	1B	Bill White, StL
2B	Bobby Richardson, NY	2B	Ken Hubbs, Chi
3B	Brooks Robinson, Bal	3B	Jim Davenport, SF
SS	Luis Aparicio, Chi	SS	Maury Wills, LA
OF	Mickey Mantle, NY	OF	Willie Mays, SF
OF	Jim Landis, Chi	OF	Roberto Clemente, Pit
OF	Al Kaline, Det	OF	Bill Virdon, Pit

1963	AL		NL
P	Jim Kaat, Min	P	Bobby Shantz, StL
C	Elston Howard, NY	C	Johnny Edwards, Cin
1B	Vic Power, Min	1B	Bill White, StL
2B	Bobby Richardson, NY	2B	Bill Mazeroski, Pit
3B	Brooks Robinson, Bal	3B	Ken Boyer, StL
SS	Zoilo Versalles, Min	SS	Bobby Wine, Phi
OF	Carl Yastrzemski, Bos	OF	Willie Mays, SF
OF	Jim Landis, Chi	OF	Curt Flood, StL
OF	Al Kaline, Det	OF	Roberto Clemente, Pit

1964	AL		NL
P	Jim Kaat, Min	P	Bobby Shantz, StL-Chi-Phi
C	Elston Howard, NY	C	Johnny Edwards, Cin
1B	Vic Power, Min-LA	1B	Bill White, StL
2B	Bobby Richardson, NY	2B	Bill Mazeroski, Pit
3B	Brooks Robinson, Bal	3B	Ron Santo, Chi
SS	Luis Aparicio, Bal	SS	Ruben Amaro, Phi
OF	Vic Davalillo, Cle	OF	Willie Mays, SF
OF	Jim Landis, Chi	OF	Curt Flood, StL
OF	Al Kaline, Det	OF	Roberto Clemente, Pit

1965	AL		NL
P	Jim Kaat, Min	P	Bob Gibson, StL
C	Bill Freehan, Det	C	Joe Torre, Mil
1B	Joe Pepitone, NY	1B	Bill White, StL
2B	Bobby Richardson, NY	2B	Bill Mazeroski, Pit
3B	Brooks Robinson, Bal	3B	Ron Santo, Chi
SS	Zoilo Versalles, Min	SS	Leo Cardenas, Cin
OF	Al Kaline, Det	OF	Roberto Clemente, Pit
OF	Carl Yastrzemski, Bos	OF	Willie Mays, SF
OF	Tom Tresh, NY	OF	Curt Flood, StL

1966	AL		NL
P	Jim Kaat, Min	P	Bob Gibson, StL
C	Bill Freehan, Det	C	John Roseboro, LA
1B	Joe Pepitone, NY	1B	Bill White, Phi
2B	Bobby Knoop, Cal	2B	Bill Mazeroski, Pit
3B	Brooks Robinson, Bal	3B	Ron Santo, Chi
SS	Luis Aparicio, Bal	SS	Gene Alley, Pit
OF	Al Kaline, Det	OF	Curt Flood, StL
OF	Tommie Agee, Chi	OF	Roberto Clemente, Pit
OF	Tony Oliva, Min	OF	Willie Mays, SF

1967	AL		NL
P	Jim Kaat, Min	P	Bob Gibson, StL
C	Bill Freehan, Det	C	Randy Hundley, Chi
1B	George Scott, Bos	1B	Wes Parker, LA
2B	Bobby Knoop, Cal	2B	Bill Mazeroski, Pit
3B	Brooks Robinson, Bal	3B	Ron Santo, Chi
SS	Jim Fregosi, Cal	SS	Gene Alley, Pit
OF	Paul Blair, Bal	OF	Curt Flood, StL
OF	Al Kaline, Det	OF	Roberto Clemente, Pit
OF	Carl Yastrzemski, Bos	OF	Willie Mays, SF

1968	AL		NL
P	Jim Kaat, Min	P	Bob Gibson, StL
C	Bill Freehan, Det	C	Johnny Bench, Cin
1B	George Scott, Bos	1B	Wes Parker, LA
2B	Bobby Knoop, Cal	2B	Glenn Beckert, Chi
3B	Brooks Robinson, Bal	3B	Ron Santo, Chi
SS	Luis Aparicio, Chi	SS	Dal Maxvill, StL
OF	Mickey Stanley, Det	OF	Curt Flood, StL
OF	Reggie Smith, Bos	OF	Roberto Clemente, Pit
OF	Carl Yastrzemski, Bos	OF	Willie Mays, SF

1969	AL		NL
P	Jim Kaat, Min	P	Bob Gibson, StL
C	Bill Freehan, Det	C	Johnny Bench, Cin
1B	Joe Pepitone, NY	1B	Wes Parker, LA
2B	Davey Johnson, Bal	2B	Felix Millan, Atl
3B	Brooks Robinson, Bal	3B	Clete Boyer, Atl
SS	Mark Belanger, Bal	SS	Don Kessinger, Chi
OF	Carl Yastrzemski, Bos	OF	Curt Flood, StL
OF	Paul Blair, Bal	OF	Roberto Clemente, Pit
OF	Mickey Stanley, Det	OF	Pete Rose, Cin

1970	AL		NL
P	Jim Kaat, Min	P	Bob Gibson, StL
C	Ray Fosse, Cle	C	Johnny Bench, Cin
1B	Jim Spencer, Cal	1B	Wes Parker, LA
2B	Davey Johnson, Bal	2B	Tommy Helms, Cin
3B	Brooks Robinson, Bal	3B	Doug Rader, Hou
SS	Luis Aparicio, Chi	SS	Don Kessinger, Chi
OF	Paul Blair, Bal	OF	Tommie Agee, NY
OF	Mickey Stanley, Det	OF	Roberto Clemente, Pit
OF	Ken Berry, Chi	OF	Pete Rose, Cin

1971	AL		NL
P	Jim Kaat, Min	P	Bob Gibson, StL

C	Ray Fosse, Cle	C	Johnny Bench, Cin
1B	George Scott, Bos	1B	Wes Parker, LA
2B	Davey Johnson, Bal	2B	Tommy Helms, Cin
3B	Brooks Robinson, Bal	3B	Doug Rader, Hou
SS	Mark Belanger, Bal	SS	Bud Harrelson, NY
OF	Amos Otis, KC	OF	Roberto Clemente, Pit
OF	Carl Yastrzemski, Bos	OF	Bobby Bonds, SF
OF	Paul Blair, Bal	OF	Willie Davis, LA
1972	**AL**	**NL**	
P	Jim Kaat, Min	P	Bob Gibson, StL
C	Carlton Fisk, Bos	C	Johnny Bench, Cin
1B	George Scott, Mil	1B	Wes Parker, LA
2B	Doug Griffin, Bos	2B	Felix Millan, Atl
3B	Brooks Robinson, Bal	3B	Doug Rader, Hou
SS	Ed Brinkman, Det	SS	Larry Bowa, Phi
OF	Bobby Murcer, NY	OF	Roberto Clemente, Pit
OF	Paul Blair, Bal	OF	Cesar Cedeno, Hou
OF	Ken Berry, Cal	OF	Willie Davis, LA
1973	**AL**	**NL**	
P	Jim Kaat, Min-Chi	P	Bob Gibson, StL
C	Thurman Munson, NY	C	Johnny Bench, Cin
1B	George Scott, Mil	1B	Mike Jorgensen, Mon
2B	Bobby Grich, Bal	2B	Joe Morgan, Cin
3B	Brooks Robinson, Bal	3B	Doug Rader, Hou
SS	Mark Belanger, Bal	SS	Roger Metzger, Hou
OF	Paul Blair, Bal	OF	Willie Davis, LA
OF	Amos Otis, KC	OF	Cesar Cedeno, Hou
OF	Mickey Stanley, Det	OF	Bobby Bonds, SF
1974	**AL**	**NL**	
P	Jim Kaat, Chi	P	Andy Messersmith, LA
C	Thurman Munson, NY	C	Johnny Bench, Cin
1B	George Scott, Mil	1B	Steve Garvey, LA
2B	Bobby Grich, Bal	2B	Joe Morgan, Cin
3B	Brooks Robinson, Bal	3B	Doug Rader, Hou
SS	Mark Belanger, Bal	SS	Dave Concepcion, Cin
OF	Paul Blair, Bal	OF	Cesar Geronimo, Cin
OF	Joe Rudi, Oak	OF	Cesar Cedeno, Hou
OF	Amos Otis, KC	OF	Bobby Bonds, SF
1975	**AL**	**NL**	
P	Jim Kaat, Chi	P	Andy Messersmith, LA
C	Thurman Munson, NY	C	Johnny Bench, Cin
1B	George Scott, Mil	1B	Steve Garvey, LA
2B	Bobby Grich, Bal	2B	Joe Morgan, Cin
3B	Brooks Robinson, Bal	3B	Ken Reitz, StL
SS	Mark Belanger, Bal	SS	Dave Concepcion, Cin
OF	Paul Blair, Bal	OF	Garry Maddox, SF-Phi
OF	Joe Rudi, Oak	OF	Cesar Geronimo, Cin
OF	Fred Lynn, Bos	OF	Cesar Cedeno, Hou
1976	**AL**	**NL**	
P	Jim Palmer, Bal	P	Jim Kaat, Phi
C	Jim Sundberg, Tex	C	Johnny Bench, Cin
1B	George Scott, Mil	1B	Steve Garvey, LA
2B	Bobby Grich, Bal	2B	Joe Morgan, Cin
3B	Aurelio Rodriguez, Det	3B	Mike Schmidt, Phi
SS	Mark Belanger, Bal	SS	Dave Concepcion, Cin
OF	Rick Manning, Cle	OF	Cesar Cedeno, Hou
OF	Dwight Evans, Bos	OF	Garry Maddox, Phi
OF	Joe Rudi, Oak	OF	Cesar Geronimo, Cin
1977	**AL**	**NL**	
P	Jim Palmer, Bal	P	Jim Kaat, Phi
C	Jim Sundberg, Tex	C	Johnny Bench, Cin
1B	Jim Spencer, Chi	1B	Steve Garvey, LA
2B	Frank White, KC	2B	Joe Morgan, Cin
3B	Graig Nettles, NY	3B	Mike Schmidt, Phi
SS	Mark Belanger, Bal	SS	Dave Concepcion, Cin
OF	Al Cowens, KC	OF	Cesar Geronimo, Cin
OF	Carl Yastrzemski, Bos	OF	Dave Parker, Pit
OF	Juan Beniquez, Tex	OF	Garry Maddox, Phi
1978	**AL**	**NL**	
P	Jim Palmer, Bal	P	Phil Niekro, Atl
C	Jim Sundberg, Tex	C	Bob Boone, Phi
1B	Chris Chambliss, NY	1B	Keith Hernandez, StL
2B	Frank White, KC	2B	Davey Lopes, LA
3B	Graig Nettles, NY	3B	Mike Schmidt, Phi
SS	Mark Belanger, Bal	SS	Larry Bowa, Phi
OF	Rick Miller, Cal	OF	Garry Maddox, Phi
OF	Fred Lynn, Bos	OF	Ellis Valentine, Mon
OF	Dwight Evans, Bos	OF	Dave Parker, Pit
1979	**AL**	**NL**	
P	Jim Palmer, Bal	P	Phil Niekro, Atl
C	Jim Sundberg, Tex	C	Bob Boone, Phi
1B	Cecil Cooper, Mil	1B	Keith Hernandez, StL
2B	Frank White, KC	2B	Manny Trillo, Phi
3B	Buddy Bell, Tex	3B	Mike Schmidt, Phi
SS	Rick Burleson, Bos	SS	Dave Concepcion, Cin
OF	Fred Lynn, Bos	OF	Dave Parker, Pit
OF	Sixto Lezcano, Mil	OF	Garry Maddox, Phi
OF	Dwight Evans, Bos	OF	Dave Winfield, SD
1980	**AL**	**NL**	
P	Mike Norris, Oak	P	Phil Niekro, Atl
C	Jim Sundberg, Tex	C	Gary Carter, Mon
1B	Cecil Cooper, Mil	1B	Keith Hernandez, StL
2B	Frank White, KC	2B	Doug Flynn, NY
3B	Buddy Bell, Tex	3B	Mike Schmidt, Phi
SS	Alan Trammell, Det	SS	Ozzie Smith, SD
OF	Dwayne Murphy, Oak	OF	Garry Maddox, Phi
OF	Fred Lynn, Bos	OF	Dave Winfield, SD
OF	Willie Wilson, KC	OF	Andre Dawson, Mon
1981	**AL**	**NL**	
P	Mike Norris, Oak	P	Steve Carlton, Phi
C	Jim Sundberg, Tex	C	Gary Carter, Mon
1B	Mike Squires, Chi	1B	Keith Hernandez, StL
2B	Frank White, KC	2B	Manny Trillo, Phi
3B	Buddy Bell, Tex	3B	Mike Schmidt, Phi
SS	Alan Trammell, Det	SS	Ozzie Smith, SD
OF	Dwayne Murphy, Oak	OF	Dusty Baker, LA
OF	Rickey Henderson, Oak	OF	Garry Maddox, Phi
OF	Dwight Evans, Bos	OF	Andre Dawson, Mon
1982	**AL**	**NL**	
P	Ron Guidry, NY	P	Phil Niekro, Atl
C	Bob Boone, Cal	C	Gary Carter, Mon
1B	Eddie Murray, Bal	1B	Keith Hernandez, StL
2B	Frank White, KC	2B	Manny Trillo, Phi
3B	Buddy Bell, Tex	3B	Mike Schmidt, Phi
SS	Robin Yount, Mil	SS	Ozzie Smith, StL
OF	Dwayne Murphy, Oak	OF	Andre Dawson, Mon
OF	Dwight Evans, Bos	OF	Dale Murphy, Atl
OF	Dave Winfield, NY	OF	Garry Maddox, Phi
1983	**AL**	**NL**	
P	Ron Guidry, NY	P	Phil Niekro, Atl
C	Lance Parrish, Det	C	Tony Peña, Pit
1B	Eddie Murray, Bal	1B	Keith Hernandez, StL-NY
2B	Lou Whitaker, Det	2B	Ryne Sandberg, Chi
3B	Buddy Bell, Tex	3B	Mike Schmidt, Phi
SS	Alan Trammell, Det	SS	Ozzie Smith, StL
OF	Dwayne Murphy, Oak	OF	Dale Murphy, Atl
OF	Dave Winfield, NY	OF	Willie McGee, StL
OF	Dwight Evans, Bos	OF	Andre Dawson, Mon
1984	**AL**	**NL**	
P	Ron Guidry, NY	P	Joaquin Andujar, StL
C	Lance Parrish, Det	C	Tony Peña, Pit
1B	Eddie Murray, Bal	1B	Keith Hernandez, NY
2B	Lou Whitaker, Det	2B	Ryne Sandberg, Chi
3B	Buddy Bell, Tex	3B	Mike Schmidt, Phi
SS	Alan Trammell, Det	SS	Ozzie Smith, StL
OF	Dwight Evans, Bos	OF	Dale Murphy, Atl
OF	Dwayne Murphy, Oak	OF	Bob Dernier, Chi
OF	Dave Winfield, NY	OF	Andre Dawson, Mon
1985	**AL**	**NL**	
P	Ron Guidry, NY	P	Rick Reuschel, Pit
C	Lance Parrish, Det	C	Tony Peña, Pit
1B	Don Mattingly, NY	1B	Keith Hernandez, NY
2B	Lou Whitaker, Det	2B	Ryne Sandberg, Chi
3B	George Brett, KC	3B	Tim Wallach, Mon
SS	Alfredo Griffin, Oak	SS	Ozzie Smith, StL
OF	Dave Winfield, NY	OF	Dale Murphy, Atl
OF	Dwight Evans, Bos	OF	Willie McGee, StL
OF	Gary Pettis, Cal	OF	Andre Dawson, Mon
OF	Dwayne Murphy, Oak		
1986	**AL**	**NL**	
P	Ron Guidry, NY	P	Fernando Valenzuela, LA
C	Bob Boone, Cal	C	Jody Davis, Chi
1B	Don Mattingly, NY	1B	Keith Hernandez, NY
2B	Frank White, KC	2B	Ryne Sandberg, Chi
3B	Gary Gaetti, Min	3B	Mike Schmidt, Phi
SS	Tony Fernandez, Tor	SS	Ozzie Smith, StL
OF	Kirby Puckett, Min	OF	Dale Murphy, Atl
OF	Jesse Barfield, Tor	OF	Willie McGee, StL
OF	Gary Pettis, Cal	OF	Tony Gwynn, SD
1987	**AL**	**NL**	
P	Mark Langston, Sea	P	Rick Reuschel, Pit-SF
C	Bob Boone, Cal	C	Mike LaValliere, Pit
1B	Don Mattingly, NY	1B	Keith Hernandez, NY
2B	Frank White, KC	2B	Ryne Sandberg, Chi
3B	Gary Gaetti, Min	3B	Terry Pendleton, StL
SS	Tony Fernandez, Tor	SS	Ozzie Smith, StL
OF	Dave Winfield, NY	OF	Andre Dawson, Chi
OF	Jesse Barfield, Tor	OF	Eric Davis, Cin
OF	Kirby Puckett, Min	OF	Tony Gwynn, SD
1988	**AL**	**NL**	
P	Mark Langston, Sea	P	Orel Hershiser, LA
C	Bob Boone, Cal	C	Benito Santiago, SD
1B	Don Mattingly, NY	1B	Keith Hernandez, NY
2B	Harold Reynolds, Sea	2B	Ryne Sandberg, Chi
3B	Gary Gaetti, Min	3B	Tim Wallach, Mon
SS	Tony Fernandez, Tor	SS	Ozzie Smith, StL
OF	Gary Pettis, Det	OF	Andre Dawson, Chi
OF	Devon White, Cal	OF	Andy Van Slyke, Pit
OF	Kirby Puckett, Min	OF	Eric Davis, Cin
1989	**AL**	**NL**	
P	Bret Saberhagen, KC	P	Ron Darling, NY
C	Bob Boone, KC	C	Benito Santiago, SD
1B	Don Mattingly, NY	1B	Andres Galarraga, Mon
2B	Harold Reynolds, Sea	2B	Ryne Sandberg, Chi
3B	Gary Gaetti, Min	3B	Terry Pendleton, StL
SS	Tony Fernandez, Tor	SS	Ozzie Smith, StL
OF	Kirby Puckett, Min	OF	Tony Gwynn, SD
OF	Gary Pettis, Det	OF	Andy Van Slyke, Pit
OF	Devon White, Cal	OF	Eric Davis, Cin
1990	**AL**	**NL**	
P	Mike Boddicker, Bos	P	Greg Maddux, Chi
C	Sandy Alomar Jr., Cle	C	Benito Santiago, SD
1B	Mark McGwire, Oak	1B	Andres Galarraga, Mon
2B	Harold Reynolds, Sea	2B	Ryne Sandberg, Chi
3B	Kelly Gruber, Tor	3B	Tim Wallach, Mon
SS	Ozzie Guillen, Chi	SS	Ozzie Smith, StL
OF	Gary Pettis, Tex	OF	Tony Gwynn, SD
OF	Ken Griffey Jr., Sea	OF	Andy Van Slyke, Pit
OF	Ellis Burks. Bos	OF	Barry Bonds, Pit
1991	**AL**	**NL**	
P	Mark Langston, Cal	P	Greg Maddux, Chi
C	Tony Pena, Bos	C	Tom Pagnozzi, StL
1B	Don Mattingly, NY	1B	Will Clark, SF
2B	Roberto Alomar, Tor	2B	Ryne Sandberg, Chi
3B	Robin Ventura, Chi	3B	Matt Williams, SF
SS	Cal Ripken, Bal	SS	Ozzie Smith, StL
OF	Devon White, Tor	OF	Barry Bonds, Pit
OF	Ken Griffey Jr., Sea	OF	Tony Gwynn, SD
OF	Kirby Puckett, Min	OF	Andy Van Slyke, Pit
1992	**AL**	**NL**	
P	Mark Langston, Cal	P	Greg Maddux, Chi
C	Ivan Rodriguez, Tex	C	Tom Pagnozzi, StL
1B	Don Mattingly, NY	1B	Mark Grace, Chi

2B	Roberto Alomar, Tor	2B	Jose Lind, Pit
3B	Robin Ventura, Chi	3B	Terry Pendleton, Atl
SS	Cal Ripken, Bal	SS	Ozzie Smith, StL
OF	Devon White, Tor	OF	Andy Van Slyke, Pit
OF	Ken Griffey Jr., Sea	OF	Barry Bonds, Pit
OF	Kirby Puckett, Min	OF	Larry Walker, Mon
1993	**AL**		**NL**
P	Mark Langston, Cal	P	Greg Maddux, Atl
C	Ivan Rodriguez, Tex	C	Kirt Manwaring, SF
1B	Don Mattingly, NY	1B	Mark Grace, Chi
2B	Roberto Alomar, Tor	2B	Robby Thompson, SF
3B	Robin Ventura, Chi	3B	Matt Williams, SF
SS	Omar Vizquel, Sea	SS	Jay Bell, Pit
OF	Kenny Lofton, Cle	OF	Barry Bonds, SF
OF	Devon White, Tor	OF	Larry Walker, Mon
OF	Ken Griffey Jr., Sea	OF	Marquis Grissom, Mon
1994	**AL**		**NL**
P	Mark Langston, Cal	P	Greg Maddux, Atl
C	Ivan Rodriguez, Tex	C	Tom Pagnozzi, StL
1B	Don Mattingly, NY	1B	Jeff Bagwell, Hou
2B	Roberto Alomar, Tor	2B	Craig Biggio, Hou
3B	Wade Boggs, NY	3B	Matt Williams, SF
SS	Omar Vizquel, Cle	SS	Barry Larkin, Cin
OF	Kenny Lofton, Cle	OF	Marquis Grissom, Mon
OF	Ken Griffey Jr., Sea	OF	Barry Bonds, SF
OF	Devon White, Tor	OF	Darren Lewis, SF
1995	**AL**		**NL**
P	Mark Langston, Cal	P	Greg Maddux, Atl
C	Ivan Rodriguez, Tex	C	Charles Johnson, Fla
1B	J.T. Snow, Cal	1B	Mark Grace, Chi
2B	Roberto Alomar, Tor	2B	Craig Biggio, Hou
3B	Wade Boggs, NY	3B	Ken Caminiti, SD
SS	Omar Vizquel, Cle	SS	Barry Larkin, Cin
OF	Kenny Lofton, Cle	OF	Marquis Grissom, Atl
OF	Ken Griffey Jr., Sea	OF	Steve Finley, SD
OF	Devon White, Tor	OF	Raul Mondesi, LA
1996	**AL**		**NL**
P	Mike Mussina, Bal	P	Greg Maddux, Atl
C	Ivan Rodriguez, Tex	C	Charles Johnson, Fla
1B	J.T. Snow, Cal	1B	Mark Grace, Chi
2B	Roberto Alomar, Bal	2B	Craig Biggio, Hou
3B	Robin Ventura, Chi	3B	Ken Caminiti, SD
SS	Omar Vizquel, Cle	SS	Barry Larkin, Cin
OF	Ken Griffey Jr., Sea	OF	Marquis Grissom, Atl
OF	Jay Buhner, Sea	OF	Steve Finley, SD
OF	Kenny Lofton, Cle	OF	Barry Bonds, SF
1997	**AL**		**NL**
P	Mike Mussina, Bal	P	Greg Maddux, Atl
C	Ivan Rodriguez, Tex	C	Charles Johnson, Fla
1B	Rafael Palmeiro, Bal	1B	J.T. Snow, SF
2B	Chuck Knoblauch, Min	2B	Craig Biggio, Hou
3B	Matt Williams, Cle	3B	Ken Caminiti, SD
SS	Omar Vizquel, Cle	SS	Rey Ordoñez, NY
OF	Ken Griffey Jr., Sea	OF	Raul Mondesi, LA
OF	Bernie Williams, NY	OF	Larry Walker, Col
OF	Jim Edmonds, Ana	OF	Barry Bonds, SF
1998	**AL**		**NL**
P	Mike Mussina, Bal	P	Greg Maddux, Atl
C	Ivan Rodriguez, Tex	C	Charles Johnson, Fla-LA
1B	Rafael Palmeiro, Bal	1B	J.T. Snow, SF
2B	Roberto Alomar, Bal	2B	Bret Boone, Cin
3B	Robin Ventura, Chi	3B	Scott Rolen, Phi
SS	Omar Vizquel, Cle	SS	Rey Ordoñez, NY
OF	Ken Griffey Jr., Sea	OF	Larry Walker, Col
OF	Bernie Williams, NY	OF	Barry Bonds, SF
OF	Jim Edmonds, Ana	OF	Andruw Jones, Atl
1999	**AL**		**NL**
P	Mike Mussina, Bal	P	Greg Maddux, Atl
C	Ivan Rodriguez, Tex	C	Mike Lieberthal, Phi
1B	Rafael Palmeiro, Tex	1B	J.T. Snow, SF
2B	Roberto Alomar, Cle	2B	Pokey Reese, Cin
3B	Scott Brosius, NY	3B	Robin Ventura, NY
SS	Omar Vizquel, Cle	SS	Rey Ordoñez, NY
OF	Ken Griffey Jr., Sea	OF	Larry Walker, Col
OF	Shawn Green, Tor	OF	Andruw Jones, Atl
OF	Bernie Williams, NY	OF	Steve Finley, Ari
2000	**AL**		**NL**
P	Kenny Rogers, Tex	P	Greg Maddux, Atl
C	Ivan Rodriguez, Tex	C	Mike Matheny, StL
1B	John Olerud, Sea	1B	J.T. Snow, SF
2B	Roberto Alomar, Cle	2B	Pokey Reese, Cin
3B	Travis Fryman, Cle	3B	Scott Rolen, Phi
SS	Omar Vizquel, Cle	SS	Neifi Perez, Col
OF	Darin Erstad, Ana	OF	Andruw Jones, Atl
OF	Bernie Williams, NY	OF	Steve Finley, Ari
OF	Jermaine Dye, KC	OF	Jim Edmonds, StL
2001	**AL**		**NL**
P	Mike Mussina, NY	P	Greg Maddux, Atl
C	Ivan Rodriguez, Tex	C	Brad Ausmus, Hou
1B	Doug Mientkiewicz, Min	1B	Todd Helton, Col
2B	Roberto Alomar, Cle	2B	Fernando Viña, StL
3B	Eric Chavez, Oak	3B	Scott Rolen, Phi
SS	Omar Vizquel, Cle	SS	Orlando Cabrera, Mon
OF	Mike Cameron, Sea	OF	Andruw Jones, Atl
OF	Ichiro Suzuki, Sea	OF	Jim Edmonds, StL
OF	Torii Hunter, Min	OF	Larry Walker, Col
2002	**AL**		**NL**
P	Kenny Rogers, Tex	P	Greg Maddux, Atl
C	Bengie Molina, Ana	C	Brad Ausmus, Hou
1B	John Olerud, Sea	1B	Todd Helton, Col
2B	Bret Boone, Sea	2B	Fernando Viña, StL
3B	Eric Chavez, Oak	3B	Scott Rolen, Phi-StL
SS	Alex Rodriguez, Tex	SS	Edgar Renteria, StL
OF	Torii Hunter, Min	OF	Andruw Jones, Atl
OF	Darin Erstad, Ana	OF	Larry Walker, Col
OF	Ichiro Suzuki, Sea	OF	Jim Edmonds, StL
2003	**AL**		**NL**
P	Mike Mussina, NY	P	Mike Hampton, Atl
C	Bengie Molina, Ana	C	Mike Matheny, StL
1B	John Olerud, Sea	1B	Derrek Lee, Fla
2B	Bret Boone, Sea	2B	Luis Castillo, Fla
3B	Eric Chavez, Oak	3B	Scott Rolen, StL
SS	Alex Rodriguez, Tex	SS	Edgar Renteria, StL
OF	Mike Cameron, Sea	OF	Jim Edmonds, StL
OF	Torii Hunter, Min	OF	Andruw Jones, Atl
OF	Ichiro Suzuki, Sea	OF	Jose Cruz Jr., SF

Baseball America Minor League Player of the Year Award

When *The Sporting News* sharply reduced its coverage of baseball—especially minor league baseball—in the early 1980s, a new publication called *Baseball America* stepped into the breach. In its two decades-plus of regular publication, *Baseball America* has emerged as an authority on the minor leagues and on minor league prospects. Each year, this award honors the best performing prospect, ignoring older players who succeed in the minors as a result of many more years of experience.

1981	Mike Marshall, 1B (Dodgers)
1982	Ron Kittle, OF (White Sox)
1983	Dwight Gooden, RHP (Mets)
1984	Mike Bielecki, RHP (Pirates)
1985	Jose Canseco, OF (Athletics)
1986	Gregg Jefferies, SS (Mets)
1987	Gregg Jefferies, SS (Mets)
1988	Tom Gordon, RHP (Royals)
1989	Sandy Alomar Jr., C (Padres)
1990	Frank Thomas, 1B (White Sox)
1991	Derek Bell, of (Blue Jays)
1992	Tim Salmon, OF (Angels)
1993	Manny Ramirez, OF (Indians)
1994	Derek Jeter, SS (Yankees)
1995	Andruw Jones, OF (Braves)
1996	Andruw Jones, OF (Braves)
1997	Paul Konerko, 1B (Dodgers)
1998	Eric Chavez, 3B (Athletics)
1999	Rick Ankiel, LHP (Cardinals)
2000	Jon Rauch, RHP (White Sox)
2001	Josh Beckett, RHP (Marlins)
2002	Rocco Baldelli, OF (Devil Rays)
2003	Joe Mauer, C (Twins)

Baseball America Organization of the Year Award

Baseball America has helped emphasize the importance of building major league teams through their minor league systems by annually awarding this honor to organizations that have assembled a deep talent pool at every level and shown the ability to further develop that talent.

1982	Oakland Athletics	AL
1983	New York Mets	NL
1984	New York Mets	NL
1985	Milwaukee Brewers	AL
1986	Milwaukee Brewers	AL
1987	Milwaukee Brewers	AL
1988	Montreal Expos	NL
1989	Texas Rangers	AL
1990	Montreal Expos	NL
1991	Atlanta Braves	NL
1992	Cleveland Indians	AL
1993	Toronto Blue Jays	AL
1994	Kansas City Royals	AL
1995	New York Mets	NL
1996	Atlanta Braves	NL
1997	Detroit Tigers	AL
1998	New York Yankees	AL
1999	Oakland Athletics	AL
2000	Chicago White Sox	AL
2001	Houston Astros	NL
2002	Minnesota Twins	AL
2003	Florida Marlins	NL

The Roberto Clemente Award

Created in 1971 by Commissioner Bowie Kuhn, this was originally known as the Commissioner's Award. The award was renamed after Roberto Clemente, the much beloved right fielder from Puerto Rico, died in a plane crash while on a humanitarian mission to assist earthquake victims in Nicaragua on New Year's Day, 1973. This trophy is given annually to the player who best combines good play on the field with strong work in his community.

1971	Willie Mays, SF NL
1972	Brooks Robinson, Bal AL
1973	Al Kaline, Det AL
1974	Willie Stargell, Pit NL
1975	Lou Brock, StL NL
1976	Pete Rose, Cin NL
1977	Rod Carew, Min AL
1978	Greg Luzinski, Phi AL
1979	Andy Thornton, Cle AL
1980	Phil Niekro, Atl NL
1981	Steve Garvey, LA NL
1982	Ken Singleton, Bal AL
1983	Cecil Cooper, Mil AL
1984	Ron Guidry, NY AL
1985	Don Baylor, NY AL
1986	Garry Maddox, Phi NL
1987	Rick Sutcliffe, Chi NL
1988	Dale Murphy, Atl NL
1989	Gary Carter, NY NL
1990	Dave Stewart, Oak AL
1991	Harold Reynolds, Sea AL
1992	Cal Ripken, Bal AL
1993	Barry Larkin, Cin NL
1994	Dave Winfield, Min AL
1995	Ozzie Smith, StL NL
1996	Kirby Puckett, Min AL
1997	Eric Davis, Bal AL
1998	Sammy Sosa, Chi NL
1999	Tony Gwynn, SD NL
2000	Al Leiter, NY NL
2001	Curt Schilling, Ari NL
2002	Jim Thome, Cle AL
2003	Jamie Moyer, Sea AL

The Fred Hutchinson Memorial Award

This award was created in 1965 to honor Fred Hutchinson, a highly-respected major league manager and former player who had died the previous year from cancer. Given annually to the major league player with the high character and strong level of competitiveness that Hutchinson was known for, the award honors those who have overcome physical adversity and shown strong commitments to their family and community.

1965	Mickey Mantle, NY AL
1966	Sandy Koufax, LA NL
1967	Carl Yastrzemski, Bos NL
1968	Pete Rose, Cin NL
1969	Al Kaline, Det AL
1970	Tony Conigliaro, Bos AL
1971	Joe Torre, StL NL
1972	Bobby Tolan, Cin NL
1973	John Hiller, Det AL
1974	Danny Thompson, Min AL
1975	Gary Nolan, Cin NL
1976	Tommy John, LA NL
1977	Willie McCovey, SF NL
1978	Willie Stargell, Pit NL
1979	Lou Brock, StL NL
1980	George Brett, KC AL
1981	Johnny Bench, Cin NL
1982	Andre Thornton, Cle AL
1983	Ray Knight, Hou NL
1984	Don Robinson, Pit NL
1985	Rick Reuschel, Chi NL
1986	Dennis Leonard, KC AL
1987	Paul Molitor, Mil AL
1988	Ron Oester, Cin NL
1989	Dave Dravecky, SF NL
1990	Sid Bream, Pit NL
1991	Bill Wegman, Mil AL
1992	Carney Lansford, Oak AL
1993	John Olerud, Tor AL
1994	Andre Dawson, Bos AL
1995	Jim Abbott, Cal AL
1996	Omar Vizquel, Cle AL
1997	Eric Davis, Bal AL
1998	David Cone, NY AL
1999	Sean Casey, Cin NL
2000	Jason Giambi, Oak AL
2001	Curt Schilling, Ari NL
2002	Tim Salmon, Cal AL
2003	Jamie Moyer, Sea AL

The Lou Gehrig Memorial Award

The Lou Gehrig Memorial Award was established in 1955 by Phi Delta Theta, Gehrig's college fraternity. It is given annually to a player who gives back to his community and strongly exemplifies the integrity, spirit, and giving nature that Gehrig possessed. The award is announced each spring for the previous year.

1955	Alvin Dark, NY NL
1956	Pee Wee Reese, Bro NL
1957	Stan Musial, StL NL
1958	Gil McDougald, NY AL
1959	Gil Hodges, LA NL
1960	Dick Groat, Pit NL
1961	Warren Spahn, Mil NL
1962	Robin Roberts, Bal AL
1963	Bobby Richardson, NY NL
1964	Ken Boyer, StL NL
1965	Vern Law, Pit NL
1966	Brooks Robinson, Bal AL
1967	Ernie Banks, Chi NL
1968	Al Kaline, Det AL
1969	Pete Rose, Cin NL
1970	Hank Aaron, Atl NL
1971	Harmon Killebrew, Min AL
1972	Wes Parker, LA NL
1973	Ron Santo, Chi NL
1974	Willie Stargell, Pit NL
1975	Johnny Bench, Cin NL
1976	Don Sutton, LA NL
1977	Lou Brock, StL NL
1978	Don Kessinger, Chi AL
1979	Phil Niekro, Atl NL
1980	Tony Perez, Bos AL
1981	Tommy John, NY AL
1982	Ron Cey, LA NL
1983	Mike Schmidt, Phi NL
1984	Steve Garvey, SD NL
1985	Dale Murphy, Atl NL
1986	George Brett, KC AL
1987	Rick Sutcliffe, Chi NL
1988	Buddy Bell, Cin NL
1989	Ozzie Smith, StL NL
1990	Glenn Davis, Hou NL
1991	Kent Hrbek, Min AL
1992	Cal Ripken, Bal AL
1993	Don Mattingly, NY AL
1994	Barry Larkin, Cin NL
1995	Curt Schilling, Phi NL
1996	Brett Butler, LA NL
1997	Paul Molitor, Min AL
1998	Tony Gwynn, SD NL
1999	Mark McGwire, StL NL
2000	Todd Stottlemyre, Ari NL
2001	John Franco, NY NL
2002	Danny Graves, Cin NL

The J.G. Taylor Spink Award

The J.G. Taylor Spink Award, given annually (and sometimes posthumously) to a sportswriter for "meritorious contributions to baseball writing," is named after the founder and longtime editor of *The Sporting News,* who was the first recipient. Each winner is presented with the award at the annual Hall of Fame induction ceremony (though they are not inducted into the Hall themselves) and is permanently recognized in the "Scribes & Mikemen" exhibit in Cooperstown. In several seasons, more than one writer has been so honored. They are listed along with the city where they worked.

1962	J.G. Taylor Spink, St Louis
1963	Ring Lardner, New York
1964	Hugh Fullerton, New York
1965	Charles Dryden, Chicago
1966	Grantland Rice, New York
1967	Damon Runyon, New York
1968	Harry G. Salsinger, Detroit
1969	Sid Mercer, New York
1970	Heywood C. Broun, New York
1971	Frank Graham, New York
1972	Dan Daniel, New York
	Fred Lieb, New York
	J. Roy Stockton, St Louis
1973	Warren Brown, Chicago
	John Drebinger, New York
	John F. Kieran, New York
1974	John Carmichael, Chicago
	James Isaminger, Philadelphia
1975	Tom Meany, New York
	Shirley Povich, Washington DC
1976	Harold Kaese, Boston
	Red Smith, New York
1977	Gordon Cobbledick, Cleveland
	Edgar Munzel, Chicago
1978	Tim Murnane, Boston
	Dick Young, New York
1979	Bob Broeg, St Louis
	Tommy Holmes, Brooklyn
1980	Joe Reichler, New York
	Milton Richman, New York
1981	Allen Lewis, Philadelphia
	Bob Addie, Washington DC
1982	Si Burick, Dayton
1983	Ken Smith, New York
1984	Joe McGuff, Kansas City
1985	Earl Lawson, Cincinnati
1986	Jack Lang, Brooklyn
1987	Jim Murray, Los Angeles
1988	Bob Hunter, Los Angeles
	Ray Kelly, Philadelphia
1989	Jerome Holtzman, Chicago
1990	Phil Collier, San Diego
1991	Ritter Collett, Dayton, Ohio
1992	Leonard Koppett, New York
	Bus Saidt, Philadelphia
1993	Wendell Smith, Pittsburgh
1994	(no selection)
1995	Joseph Durso, New York
1996	Charley Feeney, New York
1997	Sam Lacy, Washington DC
1998	Bob Stevens, San Francisco
1999	Hal Lebovitz, Cleveland
2000	Ross Newhan, Los Angeles
2001	Joe Falls, Detroit
2002	Hal McCoy, Cincinnati
2003	Murray Chass, New York

The Ford C. Frick Award

This award, named after the former broadcaster and commissioner Ford C. Frick, is presented annually to a baseball voice in recognition of "excellence in baseball broadcasting." The Frick Award, clearly modeled after the Spink Award, was first presented in 1979 to the two best known pioneers of baseball broadcasting, Mel Allen and Red Barber, and has been awarded to one announcer every year since. As in the case of the Spink Award, the winner is honored at the Hall of Fame induction ceremony, and recognized by a permanent exhibit, but is not himself an inductee.

1978	Mel Allen, Red Barber
1979	Bob Elson
1980	Russ Hodges
1981	Ernie Harwell
1982	Vin Scully
1983	Jack Brickhouse
1984	Curt Gowdy
1985	Buck Canel
1986	Bob Prince
1987	Jack Buck
1988	Lindsey Nelson
1989	Harry Caray
1990	By Saam
1991	Joe Garagiola
1992	Milo Hamilton
1993	Chuck Thompson
1994	Bob Murphy
1995	Bob Wolff
1996	Herb Carneal
1997	Jimmy Dudley
1998	Jaime Jarrin
1999	Arch McDonald
2000	Marty Brennaman
2001	Rafael "Felo" Ramirez
2002	Harry Kalas
2003	Bob Uecker

RETIRED UNIFORM NUMBERS

It took a long time for uniform numbers to catch on in baseball after they were first promoted in the 1880s. In 1883 the Cincinnati Red Stockings tried to convince their players to wear numbers on their sleeves, but the players rejected the notion. It wasn't until 1916 that another team, the Cleveland Indians, tried again, but the idea did not stick. However, the pressure on baseball teams to use numbers grew since many football and basketball teams were already using them. In 1929 the Indians tried again, successfully. The New York Yankees soon followed suit and, by 1932, all teams had put numbers on at least their road uniforms. The Philadelphia Athletics were the last team to add numbers to their jerseys.

The first number to be retired was "the luckiest man of the face of the earth," Lou Gehrig, whose No. 4 was retired by the Yankees on July 4, 1939. The second number to be retired was Carl Hubbell's No. 11 by the New York Giants. Babe Ruth's No. 3 was retired in 1948. The Yankees retired No. 8 in honor of two players: Hall of Fame catchers, Bill Dickey and Yogi Berra. Montreal retired No. 10 to honor both Andre Dawson and Rusty Staub.

Retiring numbers has become much more popular during the last two decades, though teams vary widely on what makes a player's number worthy of being retired. The Seattle Mariners, Arizona Diamondbacks, Colorado Rockies, and Toronto Blue Jays have not retired any uniform numbers, and the Marlins have not retired the number of any player. Some teams have now gone so far to "retire" numbers for players or managers who never wore a number on their back.

In 1997 Major League Baseball retired former Brooklyn Dodger Jackie Robinson's No. 42 on behalf of all teams, though players who were wearing the number at that time—most of whom who took the number to honor Robinson in the first place—have been allowed to keep wearing the number until retirement.

TEAM/NAME	Number
Anaheim/California/Los Angeles (AL)	
Jim Fregosi	11
Gene Autry	26
Rod Carew	29
Nolan Ryan	30
Jimmie Reese (Coach)	50
Atlanta/Milwaukee/Boston (NL)	
Dale Murphy	3
Warren Spahn	21
Phil Niekro	35
Eddie Mathews	41
Hank Aaron	44
Baltimore (AL)	
Earl Weaver (Manager)	4
Brooks Robinson	5
Cal Ripken	8
Frank Robinson	20
Jim Palmer	22
Eddie Murray	33
Boston (AL)	
Bobby Doerr	1
Joe Cronin	4
Carl Yastrzemski	8
Ted Williams	9
Carlton Fisk	27
Chicago (AL)	
Nellie Fox	2
Harold Baines	3
Luke Appling	4
Minnie Minoso	9
Luis Aparicio	11
Ted Lyons	16
Billy Pierce	19
Carlton Fisk	72
Chicago (NL)	
Ron Santo	10
Ernie Banks	14
Billy Williams	26
Cincinnati (NL)	
Fred Hutchinson	1
Johnny Bench	5
Joe Morgan	8
Ted Kluszewski	18
Frank Robinson	20
Tony Perez	24
Cleveland (AL)	
Earl Averill	3
Lou Boudreau	5
Larry Doby	14
Mel Harder	18
Bob Feller	19
Bob Lemon	21
Detroit (AL)	
Charlie Gehringer	2
Hank Greenberg	5
Al Kaline	6

TEAM/NAME	Number
Hal Newhouser	16
Willie Horton	23
Ty Cobb	—
Ernie Harwell	—
Florida (NL)	
Carl Barger (Executive)	5
Houston (NL)	
Jose Cruz	25
Jim Umbricht	32
Mike Scott	33
Nolan Ryan	34
Don Wilson	40
Larry Dierker	49
Kansas City (AL)	
George Brett	5
Dick Howser (Manager)	10
Frank White	20
Los Angeles/Brooklyn (NL)	
Pee Wee Reese	1
Tommy Lasorda	2
Duke Snider	4
Jim Gilliam	19
Don Sutton	20
Walt Alston (Manager)	24
Sandy Koufax	32
Roy Campanella	39
Jackie Robinson	42
Don Drysdale	53
Milwaukee (AL-NL)	
Paul Molitor	4
Robin Yount	19
Rollie Fingers	34
Hank Aaron	44
Minnesota/Washington (AL)	
Harmon Killebrew	3
Tony Oliva	6
Kent Hrbek	14
Rod Carew	29
Kirby Puckett	34
Montreal (NL)	
Gary Carter	8
Andre Dawson	10
Rusty Staub	10
New York (AL)	
Billy Martin	1
Babe Ruth	3
Lou Gehrig	4
Joe DiMaggio	5
Mickey Mantle	7
Bill Dickey	8
Yogi Berra	8
Roger Maris	9
Phil Rizzuto	10
Thurman Munson	15
Whitey Ford	16
Don Mattingly	23
Elston Howard	32

TEAM/NAME	Number
Casey Stengel (Manager)	37
Reggie Jackson	44
Ron Guidry	49
New York (NL)	
Gil Hodges (Manager)	14
Casey Stengel (Manager)	37
Tom Seaver	41
Oakland (AL)	
Catfish Hunter	27
Rollie Fingers	34
Philadelphia (NL)	
Richie Ashburn	1
Jim Bunning	14
Mike Schmidt	20
Steve Carlton	32
Robin Roberts	36
Chuck Klein	—
Grover Alexander	—
Pittsburgh (NL)	
Billy Meyer (Manager)	1
Ralph Kiner	4
Willie Stargell	8
Bill Mazeroski	9
Pie Traynor	20
Roberto Clemente	21
Honus Wagner	33
Danny Murtaugh (Manager)	40
San Diego (NL)	
Steve Garvey	6
Tony Gwynn	19
Dave Winfield	31
Randy Jones	35
San Francisco/New York (NL)	
Bill Terry	3
Mel Ott	4
Carl Hubbell	11
Willie Mays	24
Juan Marichal	27
Orlando Cepeda	30
Willie McCovey	44
Christy Mathewson	—
John McGraw (Manager)	—
St. Louis (NL)	
Ozzie Smith	1
Red Schoendienst	2
Stan Musial	6
Enos Slaughter	9
Ken Boyer	14
Dizzy Dean	17
Lou Brock	20
Bob Gibson	45
August Busch (Owner)	85
Rogers Hornsby	—
Tampa Bay (AL)	
Wade Boggs	12
Texas (AL)	
Nolan Ryan	34

GREAT PERFORMANCES

Even a complete statistical register leaves out important information about a player's career. This section details some of the greatest individual performances, including those that don't show up in annual statistical lines or in the single-season and career leader lists.

Joe DiMaggio's 56-game hitting streak is one of the most revered records in baseball; no player has ever come remotely close to breaking it. Since DiMaggio set the record, only three players have accomplished a 36-game hitting streak or better. The late Stephen Jay Gould wrote that DiMaggio's hitting streak is the "most extraordinary thing that ever happened in American sports" because it totally defied the laws of probability.

DiMaggio didn't accomplish the streak without some controversy. There certainly were some questionable calls that enabled the streak to continue, but the streak lasted until DiMaggio was finally shut down on July 17, 1941 in Cleveland. The Yankees won, 4–3, but DiMaggio grounded out in each of his 3 at bats. In his final chance to extend the streak in eighth inning, Indians pitcher Jim Bagby induced DiMaggio to hit into a double play. DiMaggio's record may never be broken, but that hasn't prevented baseball fans from getting excited every time a player makes any kind of run at his record. Even a 20-game hitting streak quickens the pulses of the media and generates detailed coverage.

Most Consecutive Games Batted Safely, Season

Games	Player, Team	Year	Games	Player, Team	Year	Games	Player, Team	Year	Games	Player, Team	Year
56	Joe DiMaggio, NY AL	1941	35	Ty Cobb, Det AL	1917	31	Ed Delahanty, Phi NL	1899	30	Goose Goslin, Det AL	1934
44	Willie Keeler, Bal NL	1897	35	Luis Castillo, Fla NL	2002	31	Nap Lajoie, Cle AL	1906	30	Stan Musial, StL NL	1950
44	Pete Rose, Cin NL	1978	34	George Sisler, StL AL	1925	31	Sam Rice, Was AL	1924	30	Ron LeFlore, Det AL	1976
42	Bill Dahlen, Chi NL	1894	34	George McQuinn, StL AL	1938	31	Willie Davis, LA NL	1969	30	George Brett, KC AL	1980
41	George Sisler, StL AL	1922	34	Dom DiMaggio, Bos AL	1949	31	Rico Carty, Atl NL	1970	30	Jerome Walton, Chi NL	1989
40	Ty Cobb, Det AL	1911	34	Benito Santiago, SD NL	1987	31	Ken Landreaux, Min AL	1980	30	Sandy Alomar Jr., Cle AL	1997
39	Paul Molitor, Mil AL	1987	33	Hal Chase, NY AL	1907	31	Vladimir Guerrero, Mon NL	1999	30	Nomar Garciaparra, Bos AL	1997
37	Tommy Holmes, Bos NL	1945	33	George Davis, NY NL	1893	30	Cal McVey, Chi NL	1876	30	Eric Davis, Bal AL	1998
36	Billy Hamilton, Phi NL	1894	33	Rogers Hornsby, StL NL	1922	30	Elmer Smith, Cin NL	1898	30	Luis Gonzalez, Ari NL	1999
35	Fred Clarke, Lou NL	1895	33	Heinie Manush, Was AL	1933	30	Tris Speaker, Bos AL	1912	30	Albert Pujols, StL NL	2003

DiMaggio's 56-game Hitting Streak

Joltin' Joe's legendary hitting streak caused a national sensation, became a song, made him a celebrity, and overshadowed a superior overall season by Ted Williams. Below (sans melody) is how The Yankee Clipper did it. Numbers in parentheses refer to hits off each pitcher on a given date.

Date	Opposing Pitcher, Team	AB	H	2B	3B	HR
May 15	Eddie Smith, Chi	4	1	0	0	0
May 16	Thornton Lee, Chi	4	2	0	1	1
May 17	Johnny Rigney, Chi	3	1	0	0	0
May 18	Bob Harris (2), Johnny Niggeling (1), StL	3	3	1	0	0
May 19	Denny Galehouse, StL	3	1	1	0	0
May 20	Eldon Auker, StL	5	1	0	0	0
May 21	Schoolboy Rowe (1), Al Benton (1), Det	5	2	0	0	0
May 22	Archie McKain, Det	4	1	0	0	0
May 23	Dick Newsome, Bos	5	1	0	0	0
May 24	Earl Johnson, Bos	4	1	0	0	0
May 25	Lefty Grove, Bos	4	1	0	0	0
May 27	Ken Chase (1), Red Anderson (2), Alex Carrasquel (1), Was	5	4	0	0	1
May 28	Sid Hudson, Was	4	1	0	1	0
May 29	Steve Sundra, Was	3	1	0	0	0
May 30G1	Earl Johnson, Bos	2	1	0	0	0
May 30G2	Mickey Harris, Bos	3	1	1	0	0
June 1G1	Al Milnar, Cle	4	1	0	0	0
June 1G2	Mel Harder, Cle	4	1	0	0	0
June 2	Bob Feller, Cle	4	2	1	0	0
June 3	Dizzy Trout, Det	4	1	0	0	1
June 5	Hal Newhouser, Det	5	1	0	1	0
June 7	Bob Muncrief (1), Johnny Allen (1), George Caster (1), StL	5	3	0	0	0
June 8G1	Elden Auker, StL	4	2	0	0	2
June 8G2	George Caster (1), Jack Kramer (1), StL	4	2	1	0	1
June 10	Johnny Rigney, Chi	5	1	0	0	0
June 12	Thornton Lee, Chi	4	2	0	0	1
June 14	Bob Feller, Cle	2	1	1	0	0
June 15	Jim Bagby Jr., Cle	3	1	0	0	1
June 16	Al Milnar, Cle	5	1	1	0	0
June 17	Johnny Rigney, Chi	4	1	0	0	0
June 18	Thornton Lee, Chi	3	1	0	0	0
June 19	Eddie Smith (1), Buck Ross (1), Chi	3	3	0	0	1
June 20	Bobo Newsom (2), Archie McKain (2), Det	5	4	1	0	0
June 21	Dizzy Trout, Det	4	1	0	0	0
June 22	Hal Newhouser (1), Bobo Newsom (1) Det	5	2	1	0	1
June 24	Bob Muncrief, StL	4	1	0	0	0
June 25	Denny Galehouse, StL	4	1	0	0	1
June 26	Eldon Auker, StL	4	1	1	0	0
June 27	Chubby Dean, Phi	3	2	0	0	1
June 28	Johnny Babich (1), Lum Harris (1), Phi	5	2	1	0	0
June 29G1	Emil "Dutch" Leonard, Was	4	1	1	0	0
June 29G2	Red Anderson, Was	5	1	0	0	0
July 1G1	Mickey Harris (1), Mike Ryba (1), Bos	4	2	0	0	0
July 1G2	Jack Wilson, Bos	3	1	0	0	0
July 2	Dick Newsome, Bos	5	1	0	0	1
July 5	Phil Marchildon, Phi	4	1	0	0	1
July 6G1	Johnny Babich (1), Bump Hadley (3), Phi	5	4	1	0	0
July 6G2	Jack Knott, Phi	4	2	0	1	0
July 10	Johnny Niggeling, StL	2	1	0	0	0
July 11	Bob Harris (3), Jack Kramer (1), StL	5	4	0	0	1
July 12	Eldon Auker (1), Bob Muncrief (1), StL	5	2	1	0	0
July 13G1	Ted Lyons (2), Jack Hallett (1), Chi	4	3	0	0	0
July 13G2	Thornton Lee, Chi	4	1	0	0	0
July 14	Johnny Rigney, Chi	3	1	0	0	0
July 15	Eddie Smith, Chi	4	2	1	0	0
July 16	Al Milnar (2), Joe Krakauskas (1), Cle	4	3	1	0	0
Totals (56 games)		223	91	16	4	15

Consecutive Games On-Base Streak

Even when DiMaggio's great hitting steak was finally stopped by the Indians, he managed to extend another streak with a walk, eventually reaching base in 74 consecutive games that year. At the time, that was a record. Ted Williams, however, broke that mark eight years later when he reached base an incredible 84 games in a row. These records were unknown at the time, but researcher Herman Krabbenhoft has recently documented the history of on-base streaks. In 2003 Barry Bonds tied the NL all-time mark by getting on base in 58 consecutive games. Here is a list of all on-base streaks that have lasted at least 50 games.

Player, Team	Year	Games	Player, Team	Year	Games	Player, Team	Year	Games	Player, Team	Year	Games
Ted Williams, Bos AL	1949	84	Ed Delahanty, Phi NL	1896	56	Shawn Green, LA NL	2000	53	Tris Speaker, Cle AL	1920	52
Joe DiMaggio, NY AL	1941	74	Bill Joyce, WAS NL-NY NL	1896	56	Derek Jeter, NY AL	1999	53	Frank Thomas, Chi AL	1996	52
Ted Williams, Bos AL	1941	69	Ryan Klesko, SD NL	2002	56	Luke Appling, Chi AL	1936	53	Jimmy Wynn, Hou NL	1969	52
Ted Williams, Bos AL	1948	65	Arky Vaughn, Pit NL	1936	56	Mel Amada, StL AL	1938	52	George Brett, KC AL	1980	51
Barry Bonds, SF NL	2003	58	Ty Cobb, Det AL	1915	55	Ty Cobb, Det AL	1914	52	Joe DiMaggio, NY AL	1937	51
Jack Tobin, StL AL	1922	58	Billy Hamilton, Bos NL	1896	55	Lou Gehrig, NY AL	1934	52	Joe Kelley, Bal NL	1896	51
Duke Snider, Bro NL	1954	58	Stan Musial, StL NL	1943	55	Greg Gross, Hou NL	1975	52	Babe Ruth, NY AL	1923	51
Wade Boggs, Bos AL	1985	57	Jim Thome, Cle AL	2002	55	Denny Lyons, Phi AA	1887	52	Ken Williams, StL AL	1923	51
Cupid Childs, Cle NL	1892	57	Ray Blades, StL NL	1925	54	Tony Phillips, Det AL	1993	52	Vince Coleman, StL	1987	50
George Kell, Det AL	1950	57	Bill Joyce, Was NL	1894	54	Gary Sheffield, Atl NL	2002	52	Lou Whitaker, Det	1991	50

Consecutive Games Played

It was only twenty years ago that most people considered Lou Gehrig's consecutive games played record to be unbreakable. Then ironman Cal Ripken came along and eventually surpassed Gehrig's record by a wide margin. Even Ripken's record is breakable, but it will take a unique combination of fortitude and luck to surpass it. Miguel Tejada, another shortstop, holds the longest consecutive games played streak of any active player, with 584 consecutive games at the end of 2003. It will take Tejada two more years of playing everyday to make the all-time top 10 in this category, as seen below.

Games Played Streaks

Cal Ripken	2,632	Joe Sewell	1,103
Lou Gehrig	2,130	Stan Musial	895
Everett Scott	1,307	Eddie Yost	829
Steve Garvey	1,207	Gus Suhr	822
Billy Williams	1,117	Nellie Fox	798

Four-Homer Games

Only fifteen players have hit 4 home runs in a game, and only twelve of those players did it in a regulation nine-inning game. Some great players are on the list, but there are also a few surprises: Mark Whiten, who hit only 105 home runs in his career, and Pat Seerey, who hit only 85 home runs. Carlos Delgado slugged his way onto this short list during the last week of the 2003 season.

Player, Team	Date	Player, Team	Date	Player, Team	Date
Bobby Lowe, Bos NL	May 30, 1894	Gil Hodges, Bro NL	Aug. 31, 1950	Bob Horner, Atl NL	July 6, 1986
Ed Delahanty, Phi	July 13, 1896	Joe Adcock, Mil NL	July 31, 1954	Mark Whiten, StL NL	Sept. 7, 1993 G2
Lou Gehrig, NY AL	June 3, 1932	Rocky Colavito, Cle AL	June 10, 1959	Mike Cameron, Sea AL	May 2, 2002
Chuck Klein, Phi NL	July 10, 1936 (10 inn)	Willie Mays, SF NL	Apr. 30, 1961	Shawn Green, LA NL	May 23, 2002
Pat Seerey, Chi AL	July 18, 1948 G1 (11 inn)	Mike Schmidt, Phi NL	Apr. 17, 1976 (10 inn)	Carlos Delgado, Tor AL	Sept. 25, 2003

The Single-Season Home Run Record

Widespread perception to the contrary, the major league single-season home run record has actually changed quite often over the course of baseball history. Despite all the hoopla over Mark McGwire setting the home run record in 1998, he held the mark for the shortest length of time of any individual since the 1880s.

Year	Player, Team	HR	Year	Player, Team	HR	Year	Player, Team	HR
1876	George Hall, Phi NL	5	1919	Babe Ruth, Bos AL	29	1961	Roger Maris, NY AL	61
1879	Charley Jones, Bos NL	9	1920	Babe Ruth, NY AL	54	1998	Mark McGwire, StL NL	70
1883	Buck Ewing, NY NL	10	1921	Babe Ruth, NY AL	59	2001	Barry Bonds, SF NL	73
1887	Ned Williamson, Chi NY	24	1927	Babe Ruth, NY AL	60			

Bonds' 73-Home Run Season

In Barry Bonds' long and magnificent career, he has only hit 50 or more homers once—when he broke the all-time record by bashing 73 in 2001. Bonds did so while playing in Pacific Bell Park, a notoriously bad home run venue for hitters. Here is an accounting of those record 73 home runs, with those hit at home indicated by an asterisk.

HR#	Date	Off Pitcher, Team	HR#	Date	Off Pitcher, Team	HR#	Date	Off Pitcher, Team
1*	Apr. 2	Woody Williams, SD NL	26*	May 27	Denny Neagle, Col NL	51*	Aug. 14	Ricky Bones, Fla NL
2	Apr. 12	Adam Eaton, SD NL	27*	May 30	Robert Ellis, Ari NL	52*	Aug. 16	A.J. Burnett, Fla NL
3	Apr. 13	Jamey Wright, Mil NL	28*	May 30	Robert Ellis, Ari NL	53*	Aug. 16	Vic Darensbourg, Fla NL
4	Apr. 14	Jimmy Haynes, Mil NL	29	June 1	Shawn Chacon, Col NL	54*	Aug. 18	Jason Marquis, Atl NL
5	Apr. 15	David Weathers, Mil NL	30*	June 4	Bobby J. Jones, SD NL	55	Aug. 23	Graeme Lloyd, Mon NL
6*	Apr. 17	Terry Adams, LA NL	31*	June 5	Wascar Serrano, SD NL	56	Aug. 27	Kevin Appier, NY NL
7*	Apr. 18	Chan Ho Park, LA NL	32*	June 7	Brian Lawrence, SD NL	57*	Aug. 31	John Thomson, Col NL
8*	Apr. 20	Jimmy Haynes, Mil NL	33*	June 12	Pat Rapp, Ana AL	58*	Sept. 3	Jason Jennings, Col NL
9*	Apr. 24	Jim Brower, Cin NL	34*	June 14	Lou Pote, Ana AL	59*	Sept. 4	Miguel Batista, Ari NL
10*	Apr. 26	Scott Sullivan, Cin NL	35*	June 15	Mark Mulder, Oak AL	60*	Sept. 6	Albie Lopez, Ari NL
11*	Apr. 29	Manny Aybar, Chi NL	36*	June 15	Mark Mulder, Oak AL	61	Sept. 9	Scott Elarton, Col NL
12	May 2	Todd Ritchie, Pit NL	37	June 19	Adam Eaton, SD NL	62	Sept. 9	Scott Elarton, Col NL
13	May 3	Jimmy Anderson, Pit NL	38	June 20	Rodney Myers, SD NL	63	Sept. 9	Todd Belitz, Col NL
14	May 4	Bruce Chen, Phi NL	39	June 23	Darryl Kile, StL, NL	64*	Sept. 20	Wade Miller, Hou NL
15*	May 11	Steve Trachsel, NY NL	40	July 12	Paul Abbott, Sea AL	65	Sept. 23	Jason Middlebrook, SD NL
16	May 17	Chuck Smith, Fla NL	41*	July 18	Mike Hampton, Col NL	66	Sept. 23	Jason Middlebrook, SD NL
17	May 18	Mike Remlinger, Atl NL	42*	July 18	Mike Hampton, Col NL	67	Sept. 24	James Baldwin, LA NL
18	May 19	Odalis Perez, Atl NL	43	July 26	Curt Schilling, Ari NL	68*	Sept. 28	Jason Middlebrook, SD NL
19	May 19	Jose Cabrera, Atl NL	44	July 26	Curt Schilling, Ari NL	69*	Sept. 29	Chuck McElroy, SD NL
20	May 19	Jason Marquis, Atl NL	45	July 27	Brian Anderson, Ari NL	70	Oct. 4	Wilfredo Rodriguez, Hou NL
21	May 20	John Burkett, Atl NL	46*	Aug. 1	Joe Beimel, Pit NL	71*	Oct. 5	Chan Ho Park, LA NL
22	May 20	Mike Remlinger, Atl NL	47	Aug. 4	Nelson Figueroa, Phi NL	72*	Oct. 5	Chan Ho Park, LA NL
23	May 21	Curt Schilling, Ari NL	48	Aug. 7	Danny Graves, Cin NL	73*	Oct. 7	Dennis Springer, LA NL
24	May 22	Russ Springer, Ari NL	49	Aug. 9	Scott Winchester, Cin NL			
25*	May 24	John Thomson, Col NL	50	Aug. 11	Joe Borowski, Chi NL			

Most Consecutive Hits

The ability to get 9 or more consecutive hits is not the sign of a great hitter; however, it is the sign of a good hitter who has gotten very lucky. Here is a list of those players who qualified as both skilled and fortunate.

No.	Player, Team	Year(s)	No.	Player, Team	Year(s)	No.	Player, Team	Year(s)	No.	Player, Team	Year(s)
12	Pinky Higgins, Bos AL	1938	10	Buddy Hassett, Bos NL	1940	9	Hal Trosky, Cle AL	1936	9	Andres Galarraga, Col NL	1993
12	Walt Dropo, Det AL	1952	10	Woody Williams, Cin NL	1943	9	Ted Williams, Bos AL	1939	9	Sammy Sosa, Chi NL	1993
11	Tris Speaker, Cle AL	1920	10	Ken Singleton, Bal AL	1981	9	Billy Jurges, NY NL	1941	9	Lance Johnson, Chi AL	1995
11	Johnny Pesky, Bos AL	1946	10	Bip Roberts, Cin NL	1992	9	Terry Moore, StL NL	1947	9	Jose Vizcaino, NY NL	1996
10	Ed Delahanty, Phi NL	1897	10	Frank Thomas, Chi AL	1997	9	Dick Sisler, Phi NL	1950	9	Barry Bonds, SF NL	1998
10	Jake Gettman, Was NL	1897	10	Joe Randa, KC AL	1999	9	Eddie Waitkus, Phi NL	1950	9	John Olerud, NY NL	1998
10	Ed Konetchy, Bro NL	1919	10	Frank Catalanotto, Tex AL	2000	9	Dave Philley, Phi NL	1958–59	9	Todd Walker, Min AL	1998
10	George Sisler, StL AL	1921	9	Joe Kelley, Bal NL	1894	9	Felipe Alou, SF NL	1962	9	Charles Johnson, Bal AL	1999
10	Harry Heilmann, Det AL	1922	9	Doc Johnston, Cle AL	1919	9	Willie Stargell, Pit NL	1966	9	Jim Edmonds, StL NL	2000
10	Kiki Cuyler, Pit NL	1925	9	Rogers Hornsby, StL NL	1924	9	Tony Oliva, Min AL	1967	9	Ben Molina, Ana AL	2001
10	Harry McCurdy, Chi AL	1926	9	Ty Cobb, Det AL	1925	9	Rennie Stennett, Pit NL	1975	9	Dmitri Young, Cin NL	2001
10	Chick Hafey, StL NL	1929	9	Sam Rice, Was AL	1925	9	Ron Cey, LA NL	1977	9	Manny Ramirez, Bos AL	2002
10	Joe Medwick, StL NL	1936	9	Taylor Douthit, StL NL	1926	9	Jorge Orta, Cle AL	1980	9	Marcus Giles, Atl NL	2003
10	Rip Radcliff, Chi AL	1938	9	Babe Herman, Bro NL	1926	9	Mickey Hatcher, Min AL	1985			

Triple Crown Batters

It's been thirty-seven years since some last won the Triple Crown, and an incredible sixty-seven years since a NL player has won one. With today's significantly stronger and larger talent base, it's much harder for an individual player to lead the league in all three glamorous offensive categories in a single year. The Triple Crown's three categories ensure that only a multidimensional hitter can win it, not just a home run hitter or a singles hitter with a very high average. Every twentieth-century Triple Crown winner is in the Hall of Fame.

Player, Team	Year	AVG	HR	RBI
Tip O'Neill, StL AA	1887	.435	14	123
Nap Lajoie, Phi AL	1901	.422	14	125
Ty Cobb, Det AL	1909	.377	9	115
Rogers Hornsby, StL NL	1922	.401	42	152
Rogers Hornsby, StL NL	1925	.403	39	143
Jimmie Foxx, Phi AL	1933	.356	48	163
Chuck Klein, Phi NL	1933	.368	28	120
Lou Gehrig, NY AL	1934	.363	49	165
Joe Medwick, StL NL	1937	.374	31	154
Ted Williams, Bos AL	1942	.356	48	163
Ted Williams, Bos AL	1947	.343	32	114
Mickey Mantle, NY AL	1956	.353	52	130
Frank Robinson, Bal AL	1966	.316	49	122
Carl Yastrzemski, Bos AL	1967	.325	44	121

Triple Crown Pitchers

Pitchers have won their Triple Crown more than twice as often as their batting counterparts, yet it remains an achievement that garners much less attention than its batting counterpart. The pitchers who win have to be dominating hurlers who receive solid run support from their offenses, but the skills required to win all three categories tend to work with each other, not against each other. Twenty-five of the 28 pitching Triple Crowns achieved since 1900 have been won by Hall of Famers or by recent pitchers seemingly assured of future Hall of Fame status.

Year	Player, Team	Wins	ERA	SO
1877	Tommy Bond, Bos NL	40	2.11	170
1884	Guy Hecker, Lou AA	52	1.80	385
1884	Charley Radbourn, Pro NL	59	1.38	441
1888	Tim Keefe, NY NL	35	1.74	335
1889	John Clarkson, Bos NL	49	2.73	284
1894	Amos Rusie, NY NL	36	2.78	195
1901	Cy Young, Bos NL	33	1.62	158
1905	Rube Waddell, Phi, AL	27	1.48	287
1905	Christy Mathewson, NY NL	31	1.28	206
1913	Walter Johnson, Was AL	36	1.14	243
1915	Grover Alexander, Phi NL	31	1.22	241
1916	Grover Alexander, Phi NL	33	1.55	167
1917	Grover Alexander, Phi, NL	30	1.83	200
1918	Hippo Vaughn, Chi NL	22	1.74	148
1918	Walter Johnson, Was AL	23	1.27	162
1920	Grover Alexander, Chi NL	27	1.91	173
1924	Walter Johnson, Was	23	2.72	158
1924	Dazzy Vance, Bro NL	28	2.16	262
1930	Lefty Grove, Phi AL	28	2.54	209
1931	Lefty Grove, Phi AL	31	2.06	175
1934	Lefty Gomez, NY AL	26	2.33	158
1937	Lefty Gomez, NY AL	21	2.33	194
1939	Bucky Walters, Cin AL	27	2.29	137
1940	Bob Feller, Cle AL	27	2.61	261
1945	Hal Newhouser, Det AL	25	1.81	212
1963	Sandy Koufax, LA NL	25	1.88	306
1965	Sandy Koufax, LA NL	26	2.04	382
1966	Sandy Koufax, LA NL	27	1.73	317
1972	Steve Carlton, Phi NL	27	1.97	310
1985	Dwight Gooden, NY NL	24	1.53	268
1997	Roger Clemens, Tor AL	21	2.05	292
1998	Roger Clemens, Tor AL	20	2.65	271
1999	Pedro Martinez Bos AL	23	2.07	313
2002	Randy Johnson, Ari NL	24	2.32	334

Most Strikeouts in a Game

When a pitcher strikes out at least 18 batters in a nine-inning game, he's almost certainly a dominating pitcher. If he's not yet a great pitcher, he probably will be one someday if he can refine his control. Pitching a game of this type is far more rare than a no-hitter, and it may be more of an achievement. Of the pitchers who have fanned 18 or more in a nine-inning game, only Randy Johnson failed to complete the game, pitching 9 of 11 innings in 2001 when he registered 20 K's. Tom Seaver struck out 10 in a row (a record in itself) on the way to his 19-strikeout game in 1970.

Not more than 9 innings pitched

Pitcher, Team	Date	No.
Roger Clemens, Bos AL	Apr. 29, 1986	20
Roger Clemens, Bos AL	Sept. 18, 1996	20
Kerry Wood, Chi NL	May 6, 1998	20
Randy Johnson, Ari NL	May 8, 2001	20
Charlie Sweeney, Pro NL	June 7, 1884	19
Hugh Daily, Chi UA	July 7, 1884	19
Steve Carlton, StL NL	Sept. 15, 1969	19
Tom Seaver, NY NL	Apr. 22, 1970	19
Nolan Ryan, Cal AL	Aug. 12, 1974	19
David Cone, NY NL	Oct. 6, 1991	19
Randy Johnson, Sea AL	June 24, 1997	19
Randy Johnson, Sea AL	Aug. 8, 1997	19
Dupee Shaw, Bos UA	July 19, 1884	18
Henry Porter, Mil UA	Oct. 3, 1884	18
Bob Feller, Cle AL	Oct. 2, 1938 G1	18
Sandy Koufax, LA NL	Aug. 31, 1959	18
Sandy Koufax, LA NL	Apr. 24, 1962	18
Don Wilson, Hou NL	July 14, 1968	18
Nolan Ryan, Cal AL	Sept. 10, 1976	18
Ron Guidry, NY AL	June 17, 1978	18
Bill Gullickson, Mon NL	Sept. 10, 1980	18
Ramon Martinez, LA NL	June 4, 1990	18
Randy Johnson, Sea AL	Sept. 27, 1992	18
Roger Clemens, Tor AL	Aug. 25, 1998	18

More than 9 innings pitched

Pitcher, Team	Date	No.	
Tom Cheney, Was AL	Sept. 12, 1962	21	16 innings
Luis Tiant, Cle AL	July 3, 1968	19	10 innings
Nolan Ryan, Cal AL	June 14, 1974	19	12 innings
Nolan Ryan, Cal AL	Aug. 20, 1974	19	11 innings
Nolan Ryan, Cal AL	June 8, 1977	19	10 innings
Jim Whitney, Bos NL	June 14, 1884	18	15 innings
Jack Coombs, Phi AL	Sept. 1, 1906	18	24 innings
Warren Spahn, Bos NL	June 14, 1952	18	15 innings
Jim Maloney, Cin NL	June 14, 1965	18	11 innings
Chris Short, Cin NL	Oct. 2, 1965	18	15 IP of 18

Consecutive Scoreless Inning Streaks

Orel Hershiser was the biggest baseball story of the year in 1988, even before he earned MVP awards in the NLCS and World Series. He broke Don Drysdale's record of 58.2 consecutive scoreless innings, hurling 10 shutout innings in his final start of the season to do it. It's a feat unlikely to be matched in the near future. Virtually all of the top streaks listed below were achieved in low-scoring environments, quite the opposite of the current state of baseball.

Year	Dates	Pitcher, Team	IP
1988	Aug. 30-Sept. 28	Orel Hershiser, LA NL	59.0
1968	May 14-June 8	Don Drysdale, LA NL	58.2
1913	Apr. 10-May 14	Walter Johnson, Was AL	55.2
1910	Sept. 5-Sept. 25	Jack Coombs, Phi AL	53.0
1968	June 2-June 26	Bob Gibson, StL NL	47.0
1933	July 13-Aug. 1	Carl Hubbell, NY NL	45.1
1950	Aug. 16-Sept. 13	Sal Maglie, SF NL	45.0
1904	Sept. 12-Sept. 30	Doc White, Chi AL	45.0
1904	Apr. 25-May 17	Cy Young, Bos AL	45.0
1908	Sept. 17-Oct. 3	Ed Reulbach, Chi NL	44.0
1905	Aug. 22-Sept. 5	Rube Waddell, Phi AL	43.2
1914	May 1-May 26	Rube Foster, Bos AL	42.0
1902	June 26-July 16	Jack Chesbro, Pit NL	41.0
1911	Sept. 7-Sept. 24	Grover Alexander, Phi NL	41.0
1917	Sept. 13-Oct. 4	Art Nehf, Bos NL	41.0
1968	Apr. 28-May 17	Luis Tiant, Cle AL	41.0
1918	May 7-May 26	Walter Johnson, Was AL	40.0
1967	Aug. 28-Sept. 10	Gaylord Perry, SF NL	40.0
1972	Aug. 19-Sept. 8	Luis Tiant, Bos AL	40.0

Multiple No-Hitters

Lots of mediocre pitchers have pitched a no-hitter, but throwing 2 no-hitters is a different story—that can't happen just by luck. Below is a list of all the pitchers who have thrown at least two no-hitters. Following this distinguished list are lists of perfect games, no-hitters, and unofficial no-hitters.

Some no-hitters came with their own unique twist. Hugh Daily's no-hitter in September 1883 was the first no-hitter ever thrown by a one-handed pitcher; Jim Abbott duplicated the feat 110 years later. Johnny Vander Meer's no-hitter on June 15, 1938 marked the only time a major leaguer has thrown no-hitters in consecutive starts. The only Opening Day no-hitter was thrown by Bob Feller on Apr. 16, 1940. The only postseason no-hitter was a perfect game pitched by Don Larsen during the World Series on October 8, 1956. Mike Scott pitched the only no-hitter to clinch a title—the 1986 NL Western Division championship—on September 25, 1986.

Perhaps the oddest no-hitter ever came on June 23, 1917 when Ernie Shore pitched one in relief. Shore rang up 27 outs by retiring 26 hitters in a row after Babe Ruth walked the first batter and argued himself out of the game; that runner was subsequently thrown out stealing. The most recent no-hitter also deserves notice, because it required a record six pitchers: the starter, Roy Oswalt, had to be pulled after the first inning due to injury, and the Astros ran out five relief pitchers over the next eight innings on June 11, 2003.

Notes. Perfect games are listed separately from no-hitters. Italics indicate that it was the pitcher's first major league start. G1 and G2 denote first and second games of doubleheaders. Extra-inning games are noted in parentheses. CD means game was called on account of darkness. WS indicates World Series game. Finally, Loss means that the pitcher who threw the no-hitter also lost the game.

Pitchers with More Than One No-Hitter

Nolan Ryan	7	Jim Galvin	2	Dutch Leonard	2	Don Wilson	2
Sandy Koufax	4	Al Atkinson	2	Johnny Vander Meer	2	Ken Holtzman	2
Larry Corcoran	3	Adonis Terry	2	Allie Reynolds	2	Bill Stoneman	2
Cy Young	3	Ted Breitenstein	2	Virgil Trucks	2	Steve Busby	2
Bob Feller	3	Frank Smith	2	Carl Erskine	2	Bob Forsch	2
Jim Maloney	3	Addie Joss	2	Warren Spahn	2		
Christy Mathewson	2	Tom L. Hughes	2	Jim Bunning	2		

Perfect Games

Pitcher	Opponents	Score	Date
Lee Richmond	Wor vs. Cle NL	1–0	June 12, 1880
John M. Ward	Pro vs. Buf NL	5–0	June 17, 1880
Cy Young	Bos vs. Phi AL	3–0	May 5, 1904
Addie Joss	Cle vs. Chi AL	1–0	Oct. 2, 1908
Charlie Robertson	Chi at Det AL	2–0	Apr. 30, 1922
Jim Bunning	Phi at NY NL	6–0	June 21, 1964 G1
Don Larsen	NY AL vs. Bro NL	2–0	Oct. 8, 1956 WS
Sandy Koufax	LA vs. Chi NL,	1–0	Sept. 9, 1965
Catfish Hunter	Oak vs. Min AL	4–0	May 8, 1968
Len Barker	Cle vs. Tor AL	3–0	May 15, 1981
Mike Witt	Cal at Tex AL	1–0	Sept. 30, 1984
Tom Browning	Cin vs. LA NL	1–0	Sept. 16, 1988
Dennis Martinez	Mon at LA NL	2–0	July 28, 1991
Kenny Rogers	Tex vs. Cal AL	4–0	July 28, 1994
David Wells	NY vs. Min AL	4–0	May 17, 1998
David Cone	NY AL vs. Mon NL	6–0	July 18, 1999

No-Hit Games, Nine or More Innings

Pitcher	Opponents	Score	Date
Joe Borden	Phi vs. Chi NA	4–0	July 28, 1875
George Bradley	StL vs. Har NL	2–0	July 15, 1876
Larry Corcoran	Chi vs. Bos NL	6–0	Aug. 19, 1880
Jim Galvin	Buf at Wor NL	1–0	Aug. 20, 1880
Tony Mullane	Lou at Cin AA	2–0	Sept. 11, 1882
Guy Hecker	Lou at Pit AA	3–1	Sept. 19, 1882
Larry Corcoran	Chi vs. Wor NL	5–0	Sept. 20, 1882
Charley Radbourn	Pro at Cle NL	8–0	July 25, 1883
Hugh Daily	Cle at Phi NL	1–0	Sept. 13, 1883
Al Atkisson	Phi vs. Pit AA	10–1	May 24, 1884
Ed Morris	Col at Pit AA	5–0	May 29, 1884
Frank Mountain	Col at Was AA	12–0	June 5, 1884
Larry Corcoran	Chi vs. Pro NL	6–0	June 27, 1884
Jim Galvin	Buf at Det NL	18–0	Aug. 4, 1884
Dick Burns	Cin at KC UA	3–1	Aug. 26, 1884
Ed Cushman	Mil vs. Was UA	5–0	Sept. 28, 1884
Sam Kimber	Bro vs. Tol AA	0–0	Oct. 4, 1884 CD (10 inn)
John Clarkson	Chi at Pro NL	4–0	July 27, 1885
Charlie Ferguson	Phi vs. Pro NL	1–0	Aug. 29, 1885
Al Atkisson	Phi vs. NY AA	3–2	May 1, 1886
Adonis Terry	Bro vs. StL AA	1–0	July 24, 1886
Matt Kilroy	Bal at Pit AA	6–0	Oct. 6, 1886
Adonis Terry	Bro vs. Lou AA	4–0	May 27, 1888
Henry Porter	KC at Bal AA	4–0	June 6, 1888
Ed Seward	Phi vs. Cin AA	12–2	July 26, 1888
Gus Weyhing	Phi vs. KC AA	4–0	July 31, 1888
Cannonball Titcomb	Roc vs. Syr AA	7–0	Sept. 15, 1890
Tom Lovett	Bro vs. NY NL	4–0	June 22, 1891
Amos Rusie	NY vs. Bro NL	6–0	July 31, 1891
Ted Breitenstein	StL vs. Lou AA	8–0	Oct. 4, 1891 G1
Jack Stivetts	Bos vs. Bro NL	11–0	Aug. 6, 1892
Ben Sanders	Lou vs. Bal NL	6–2	Aug. 22, 1892
Bumpus Jones	Cin vs. Pit NL	7–1	Oct. 15, 1892
Bill Hawke	Bal vs. Was NL	5–0	Aug. 16, 1893
Cy Young	Cle vs. Cin NL	6–0	Sept. 18, 1897 G1
Ted Breitenstein	Cin vs. Pit NL	11–0	Apr. 22, 1898
Jim Hughes	Bal vs. Bos NL	8–0	Apr. 22, 1898
Red Donahue	Phi vs. Bos NL	5–0	July 8, 1898
Walter Thornton	Chi vs. Bro NL	2–0	Aug. 21, 1898 G2
Deacon Phillippe	Lou vs. NY NL	7–0	May 25, 1899
Noodles Hahn	Cin vs. Phi NL	4–0	July 12, 1900
Christy Mathewson	NY at StL NL	5–0	July 15, 1901
Nixey Callahan	Chi vs. Det AL	3–0	Sept. 20, 1902 G1
Chick Fraser	Phi at Chi NL	10–0	Sept. 18, 1903 G2
Jesse Tannehill	Bos at Chi AL	6–0	Aug. 17, 1904
Christy Mathewson	NY at Chi NL	1–0	June 13, 1905
Weldon Henley	Phi at StL AL	6–0	July 22, 1905 G1
Frank Smith	Chi at Det AL	15–0	Sept. 6, 1905 G2
Bill Dinneen	Bos vs. Chi AL	2–0	Sept. 27 1905 G1
Johnny Lush	Phi at Bro NL	6–0	May 1, 1906
Mal Eason	Bro at StL NL	2–0	July 20, 1906
Frank (Jeff) Pfeffer	Bos vs. Cin NL	6–0	May 8, 1907
Nick Maddox	Pit vs. Bro NL	2–1	Sept. 20, 1907
Cy Young	Bos at NY AL	8–0	June 30, 1908
Hooks Wiltse	NY vs. Phi NL	1–0	July 4, 1908 G1 (10 inn)
Nap Rucker	Bro vs. Bos NL	6–0	Sept. 5, 1908 G2
Dusty Rhoads	Cle vs. Bos AL	2–1	Sept. 18, 1908
Frank Smith	Chi vs. Phi AL	1–0	Sept. 20, 1908
Addie Joss	Cle at Chi AL	1–0	Apr. 20, 1910
Chief Bender	Phi vs. Cle AL	4–0	May 12, 1910
Joe Wood	Bos vs. StL AL	5–0	July 29, 1911 G2
Ed Walsh	Chi vs. Bos AL	5–0	Aug. 27, 1911
George Mullin	Det vs. StL AL	7–0	July 4, 1912 G2
Earl Hamilton	StL at Det AL	5–1	Aug. 30, 1912
Jeff Tesreau	NY at Phi NL	3–0	Sept. 6, 1912 G1
Joe Benz	Chi vs. Cle AL	6–1	May 31, 1914
George Davis	Bos vs. Phi NL	7–0	Sept. 9, 1914 G2
Ed Lafitte	Bro vs. KC FL	6–2	Sept. 19, 1914 G1
Rube Marquard	NY vs. Bro NL	2–0	Apr. 15, 1915
Frank Allen	Pit at StL FL	2–0	Apr. 24, 1915
Claude Hendrix	Chi at Pit FL	10–0	May 15, 1915
Alex Main	KC at Buf FL	5–0	Aug. 16, 1915
Jimmy Lavender	Chi at NY NL	2–0	Aug. 31, 1915 G1
Dave Davenport	StL vs. Chi FL	3–0	Sept. 7, 1915 G1
Tom L. Hughes	Bos vs. Pit NL	2–0	June 16, 1916
Rube Foster	Bos vs. NY AL	2–0	June 21, 1916
Joe Bush	Phi vs. Cle AL	5–0	Aug. 26, 1916
Dutch Leonard	Bos vs. StL AL	4–0	Aug. 30, 1916
Eddie Cicotte	Chi at StL AL	11–0	Apr. 14, 1917
George Mogridge	NY at Bos AL	2–1	Apr. 24, 1917
Fred Toney	Cin at Chi NL	1–0	May 2, 1917 (10 inn)
Ernie Koob	StL vs. Chi AL	1–0	May 5, 1917
Bob Groom	StL vs. Chi AL	3–0	May 6, 1917 G2
Ernie Shore	Bos vs. Was AL	4–0	June 23, 1917 G1
Dutch Leonard	Bos at Det AL	5–0	June 3, 1918
Hod Eller	Cin vs. StL NL	6–0	May 11, 1919
Ray Caldwell	Cle at NY AL	3–0	Sept. 10, 1919 G1
Walter Johnson	Was at Bos AL	1–0	July 1, 1920
Jesse Barnes	NY vs. Phi NL	6–0	May 7, 1922
Sam Jones	NY at Phi AL	2–0	Sept. 4, 1923
Howard Ehmke	Bos at Phi AL	4–0	Sept. 7, 1923
Jesse Haines	StL vs. Bos NL	5–0	July 17, 1924
Dazzy Vance	Bro vs. Phi NL	10–1	Sept. 13, 1925 G1
Ted Lyons	Chi at Bos AL	6–0	Aug. 21, 1926
Carl Hubbell	NY vs. Pit NL	11–0	May 8, 1929
Wes Ferrell	Cle vs. StL AL	9–0	Apr. 29, 1931
Bobby Burke	Was vs. Bos AL	5–0	Aug. 8, 1931
Paul Dean	StL at Bro NL	3–0	Sept. 21, 1934 G2
Vern Kennedy	Chi vs. Cle AL	5–0	Aug. 31, 1935
Bill Dietrich	Chi vs. StL AL	8–0	June 1, 1937
Johnny Vander Meer	Cin vs. Bos NL	3–0	June 11, 1938
Johnny Vander Meer	Cin at Bro NL	6–0	June 15, 1938
Monte Pearson	NY vs. Cle AL	13–0	Aug. 27, 1938 G2
Bob Feller	Cle at Chi AL	1–0	Apr. 16, 1940 OD
Tex Carleton	Bro at Cin NL	3–0	Apr. 30, 1940
Lon Warneke	StL at Cin NL	2–0	Aug. 30, 1941
Jim Tobin	Bos vs. Bro NL	2–0	Apr. 27, 1944
Clyde Shoun	Cin vs. Bos NL	1–0	May 15, 1944
Dick Fowler	Phi vs. StL AL	1–0	Sept. 9, 1945 G2
Ed Head	Bro vs. Bos NL	5–0	Apr. 23, 1946
Bob Feller	Cle at NY AL	1–0	Apr. 30, 1946
Ewell Blackwell	Cin vs. Bos NL	6–0	June 18, 1947
Don Black	Cle vs. Phi AL	3–0	July 10, 1947 G1
Bill McCahan	Phi vs. Was AL	3–0	Sept. 3, 1947

Pitcher	Opponents	Score	Date
Bob Lemon	Cle at Det AL	2–0	June 30, 1948
Rex Barney	Bro at NY NL	2–0	Sept. 9, 1948
Vern Bickford	Bos vs. Bro NL	7–0	Aug. 11, 1950
Cliff Chambers	Pit at Bos NL	3–0	May 6, 1951 G2
Bob Feller	Cle vs. Det AL	2–1	July 1, 1951 G1
Allie Reynolds	NY at Cle AL	1–0	July 12, 1951
Allie Reynolds	NY vs. Bos AL	8–0	Sept. 28, 1951 G1
Virgil Trucks	Det vs. Was AL	1–0	May 15, 1952
Carl Erskine	Bro vs. Chi NL	5–0	June 19, 1952
Virgil Trucks	Det at NY AL	1–0	Aug. 25, 1952
Bobo Holloman	StL vs. Phi AL	6–0	May 6, 1953
Jim Wilson	Mil vs. Phi NL	2–0	June 12, 1954
Sam Jones	Chi vs. Pit NL	4–0	May 12, 1955
Carl Erskine	Bro vs. NY NL	3–0	May 12, 1956
Mel Parnell	Bos vs. Chi AL	4–0	July 14, 1956
Sal Maglie	Bro vs. Phi NL	5–0	Sept. 25, 1956
Bob Keegan	Chi vs. Was AL	6–0	Aug. 20, 1957 G2
Jim Bunning	Det at Bos AL	3–0	July 20, 1958 G1
Hoyt Wilhelm	Bal vs. NY AL	1–0	Sept. 20, 1958
Don Cardwell	Chi vs. StL NL	4–0	May 15, 1960 G2
Lew Burdette	Mil vs. Phi NL	1–0	Aug. 18, 1960
Warren Spahn	Mil vs. Phi NL	4–0	Sept. 16, 1960
Warren Spahn	Mil vs. SF NL	1–0	Apr. 28, 1961
Bo Belinsky	LA vs. Bal AL	2–0	May 5, 1962
Earl Wilson	Bos vs. LA AL	2–0	June 26, 1962
Sandy Koufax	LA vs. NY NL	5–0	June 30, 1962
Bill Monbouquette	Bos at Chi AL	1–0	Aug. 1, 1962
Jack Kralick	Min vs. KC AL	1–0	Aug. 26, 1962
Sandy Koufax	LA vs. SF NL	8–0	May 11, 1963
Don Nottebart	Hou vs. Phi NL	4–1	May 17, 1963
Juan Marichal	SF vs. Hou NL	1–0	June 15, 1963
Ken T. Johnson	Hou vs. Cin NL	0–1	Apr. 23, 1964 Loss
Sandy Koufax	LA at Phi NL	3–0	June 4, 1964
Jim Maloney	Cin at Chi NL	1–0	Aug. 19, 1965 G1 (10 inn)
Dave Morehead	Bos vs. Cle AL	2–0	Sept. 16, 1965
Sonny Siebert	Cle vs. Was AL	2–0	June 10, 1966
Steve D. Barber (8.2 IP) & Stu Miller (0.1 IP)	Bal vs. Det AL	1–2	Apr. 30, 1967 G1 Loss
Don Wilson	Hou vs. Atl NL	2–0	June 18, 1967
Dean Chance	Min at Cle AL	2–1	Aug. 25, 1967 G2
Joe Horlen	Chi vs. Det AL	6–0	Sept. 10, 1967 G1
Tom Phoebus	Bal vs. Bos AL	6–0	Apr. 27, 1968
George Culver	Cin at Phi NL	6–1	July 29, 1968 G2
Gaylord Perry	SF vs. StL NL	1–0	Sept. 17, 1968
Ray Washburn	StL at SF NL	2–0	Sept. 18, 1968
Bill Stoneman	Mon at Phi NL	7–0	Apr. 17, 1969
Jim Maloney	Cin vs. Hou NL	10–0	Apr. 30, 1969
Don Wilson	Hou at Cin NL	4–0	May 1, 1969
Jim Palmer	Bal vs. Oak AL	8–0	Aug. 13, 1969
Ken Holtzman	Chi vs. Atl NL	3–0	Aug. 19, 1969
Bob Moose	Pit at NY NL	4–0	Sept. 20, 1969
Dock Ellis	Pit at SD NL	2–0	June 12, 1970 G1
Clyde Wright	Cal vs. Oak AL	4–0	July 3, 1970
Bill Singer	LA vs. Phi NL	5–0	July 20, 1970
Vida Blue	Oak vs. Min AL	6–0	Sept. 21, 1970
Ken Holtzman	Chi at Cin NL	1–0	June 3, 1971
Rick Wise	Phi at Cin NL	4–0	June 23, 1971
Bob Gibson	StL at Pit NL	11–0	Aug. 14, 1971
Burt Hooton	Chi vs. Phi NL	4–0	Apr. 16, 1972
Milt Pappas	Chi vs. SD NL	8–0	Sept. 2, 1972
Bill Stoneman	Mon vs. NY NL	7–0	Oct. 2, 1972 G1
Steve Busby	KC at Det AL	3–0	Apr. 16, 1973
Nolan Ryan	Cal at KC AL	3–0	May 15, 1973
Nolan Ryan	Cal at Det AL	6–0	July 15, 1973
Jim Bibby	Tex at Oak AL	6–0	July 30, 1973
Phil Niekro	Atl vs. SD NL	9–0	Aug. 5, 1973
Steve Busby	KC at Mil AL	2–0	June 19, 1974
Dick Bosman	Cle vs. Oak AL	4–0	July 19, 1974
Nolan Ryan	Cal vs. Min AL	4–0	Sept. 28, 1974
Nolan Ryan	Cal vs. Bal AL	1–0	June 1, 1975
Ed Halicki	SF vs. NY NL	6–0	Aug. 24, 1975 G2
Vida Blue (5 IP), Glenn Abbott (1 IP), Paul Lindblad (1 IP) & Rollie Fingers (2 IP)	Oak vs. Cal AL	5–0	Sept. 28, 1975
Larry Dierker	Hou vs. Mon NL	6–0	July 9, 1976
Blue Moon Odom (5 IP) & Francisco Barrios (4 IP)	Chi at Oak AL	2–1	July 28, 1976
John Candelaria	Pit vs. LA NL	2–0	Aug. 9, 1976
John Montefusco	SF at Atl NL	9–0	Sept. 29, 1976
Jim Colborn	KC vs. Tex AL	6–0	May 14, 1977
Dennis Eckersley	Cle vs. Cal AL	1–0	May 30, 1977
Bert Blyleven	Tex at Cal AL	6–0	Sept. 22, 1977
Bob Forsch	StL vs. Phi NL	5–0	Apr. 16, 1978
Tom Seaver	Cin vs. StL NL	4–0	June 16, 1978
Ken Forsch	Hou vs. Atl NL	6–0	Apr. 7, 1979
Jerry Reuss	LA at SF NL	8–0	June 27, 1980
Charlie Lea	Mon vs. SF NL	4–0	May 10, 1981 G2
Nolan Ryan	Hou vs. LA NL	5–0	Sept. 26, 1981
Dave Righetti	NY vs. Bos AL	4–0	July 4, 1983
Bob Forsch	StL vs. Mon NL	3–0	Sept. 26, 1983
Mike Warren	Oak vs. Chi AL	3–0	Sept. 29, 1983
Jack Morris	Det at Chi AL	4–0	Apr. 7, 1984
Joe Cowley	Chi at Cal AL	7–1	Sept. 19, 1986
Mike Scott	Hou vs. SF NL	2–0	Sept. 25, 1986
Juan Nieves	Mil at Bal AL	7–0	Apr. 15, 1987
Mark Langston (7 IP) & Mike Witt (2 IP)	Cal vs. Sea AL	1–0	Apr. 11, 1990
Randy Johnson	Sea vs. Det AL	2–0	June 2, 1990
Nolan Ryan	Tex at Oak AL	5–0	June 11, 1990
Dave Stewart	Oak at Tor AL	5–0	June 29, 1990
Fernando Valenzuela	LA vs. StL NL	6–0	June 29, 1990
Terry Mulholland	Phi vs. SF NL	6–0	Aug. 15, 1990
Dave Stieb	Tor at Cle AL	3–0	Sept. 2, 1990
Nolan Ryan	Tex vs. Tor AL	3–0	May 1, 1991
Tommy Greene	Phi at Mon NL	2–0	May 23, 1991
Bob Milacki (6 IP), Mike Flanagan (1 IP), Mark Williamson (1 IP) & Gregg Olson (1 IP)	Bal at Oak AL	2–0	July 13, 1991
Wilson Alvarez	Chi at Bal AL	7–0	Aug. 11, 1991
Bret Saberhagen	KC vs. Chi AL	7–0	Aug. 26, 1991
Kent Mercker (6 IP), Mark Wohlers (2 IP) & Alejandro Pena (1 IP)	Atl at SD NL	1–0	Sept. 11, 1991
Kevin Gross	LA vs. SF NL	2–0	Aug. 17, 1992
Chris Bosio	Sea vs. Bos AL	7–0	Apr. 22, 1993
Jim Abbott	NY vs. Cle AL	4–0	Sept. 4, 1993
Darryl Kile	Hou vs. NY NL	7–1	Sept. 8, 1993
Kent Mercker	Atl at LA NL	6–0	Apr. 8, 1994
Scott Erickson	Min vs. Mil AL	6–0	Apr. 27, 1994
Ramon Martinez	LA vs. Fla NL	7–0	July 14, 1995
Al Leiter	Fla vs. Col NL	11–0	May 11, 1996
Dwight Gooden	NY vs. Sea AL	2–0	May 14, 1996
Hideo Nomo	LA at Col NL	9–0	Sept. 17, 1996
Kevin Brown	Fla at SF NL	9–0	June 10, 1997
Francisco Cordova (9 IP) & Ricardo Rincon (1 IP)	Pit vs. Hou NL	3–0	July 12, 1997
Jose Jimenez	StL at Ari NL	1–0	June 25, 1999
Eric Milton	Min vs. Ana AL	7–0	Sept. 11, 1999
Hideo Nomo	Bos at Bal AL	3–0	Apr. 4, 2001
A.J. Burnett	Fla at SD NL	3–0	May 12, 2001
Bud Smith	StL at SD NL	4–0	Sept. 3, 2001
Derek Lowe	Bos vs. TB AL	10–0	Apr. 27, 2002
Kevin Millwood	Phi vs. SF NL	1–0	Apr. 27, 2003
Roy Oswalt (1 IP), Peter Munro (2.2 IP), Kirk Saarloos (1.1 IP), Brad Lidge (2 IP), Octavio Dotel (1 IP) & Billy Wagner (1 IP)	Hou NL at NY AL	8–0	June 11, 2003

No-Hit Games, Less Than 9 Innings Pitched

Sometimes even the best days end too soon. Many no-hit bids have been spoiled by rain, by darkness, by having to catch a train, or simply by prior agreement. Three times a pitcher has held the home club hitless for 8 innings, only to not pitch the ninth because his team lost and the game was over. Two much luckier pitchers actually allowed hits, but rain conveniently washed those blemishes from the record books. In the 1906 combination no-no, Rube Waddell allowed a hit and 2 runs in the sixth inning, and in 1959 Mike McCormick allowed a hit in the sixth, but in both cases rain caused the game to revert to 5 innings. Both pitchers won. Bold signifies an abbreviated perfect game.

Pitcher	Innings	Reason	Matchup	Score	Date
Larry McKeon	6	rain	Ind at Cin AA	0–0	May 6, 1884
Charlie Gagus	8	darkness	Was vs. Wil UA	12–1	Aug. 21, 1884
Charlie Getzien	6	rain	Det vs. Phi NL	1–0	Oct. 1, 1884
Charlie Sweeney & Henry Boyle	(2 IP) (3 IP) 5	rain	StL vs. StP UA	0–1	Oct. 5, 1884
Dupee Shaw	5	agreement	Pro at Buf NL	4–0	Oct. 7, 1885 G1
George Van Haltren	6	rain	Chi vs. Pit NL	1–0	June 21, 1888
Ed Crane	7	darkness	NY vs. Was NL	3–0	Sept. 27, 1888
Matt Kilroy	7	darkness	Bal vs. StL AA	0–0	July 29, 1888 G2
Silver King	8	road loss	Chi vs. Bro PL	0–1	June 21, 1890 Loss
George Nicol	7	darkness	StL vs. Phi AA	21–2	Sept. 23, 1890
Hank Gastright	8	darkness	Col vs. Tol AA	6–0	Oct. 12, 1890
Jack Stivetts	5	Bos. train	Bos at Was NL	6–0	Oct. 15, 1892 G2
Elton Chamberlain	7	darkness	Cin vs. Bos NL	6–0	Sept. 23, 1893 G2
Ed Stein	6	rain	Bro vs. Chi NL	6–0	June 2, 1894
Red Ames	5	darkness	NY at StL NL	5–0	Sept. 14, 1903 G2
Rube Waddell	5	rain	Phi vs. StL AL	2–0	Aug. 15, 1905
Jake Weimer	7	agreement	Cin vs. Bro NL	1–0	Aug. 24, 1906 G2
Jimmy Dygert & Rube Waddell	(3 IP) (2 IP) 5	rain	Phi vs. Chi AL	4–3	Aug. 29, 1906
Stoney McGlynn	7	agreement	StL at Bro NL	1–1	Sept. 24, 1906 G2
Lefty Leifield	6	darkness	Pit at Phi NL	8–0	Sept. 26, 1906 G2
Ed Walsh	5	rain	Chi vs. NY AL	8–1	May 26, 1907
Ed Karger	7	agreement	StL vs. Bos NL	4–0	Aug. 11, 1907 G2
Howie Camnitz	5	agreement	Pit at NY NL	1–0	Aug. 23, 1907 G2
Rube Vickers	5	darkness	Phi at Was AL	4–0	Oct. 5, 1907 G2
Johnny Lush	6	rain	StL at Bro NL	2–0	Aug. 6, 1908
King Cole	7	Chi. train	Chi at StL NL	4–0	July 31, 1910 G2
Jay Cashion	6	Cle. train	Was vs. Cle AL	2–0	Aug. 20, 1912 G2
Walter Johnson	7	rain	Was vs. StL AL	2–0	Aug. 25, 1924
Fred Frankhouse	7.2	rain	Bro vs. Cin NL	5–0	Aug. 27, 1937
John Whitehead	6	rain	StL vs. Det AL	4–0	Aug. 5, 1940 G2
Jim Tobin	5	darkness	Bos vs. Phi NL	7–0	June 22, 1944 G2
Mike McCormick	5	rain	SF at Phi NL	3–0	June 12, 1959
Sam Jones	7	rain	SF at StL NL	4–0	Sept. 26, 1959
Dean Chance	5	rain	Min vs. Bos AL	2–0	Aug. 6, 1967
David Palmer	5	rain	Mon at StL NL	4–0	Apr. 21, 1984 G2
Pascual Perez	5	rain	Mon at Phi NL	1–0	Sept. 24, 1988
Andy Hawkins	8	road loss	NY at Chi AL	4–0	July 1, 1990 Loss
Melido Perez	6	rain	Chi at NY AL	8–0	July 12, 1990
Matt Young	8	road loss	Bos at Cle AL	1–2	Apr. 12, 1992 G1 Loss

No–Hitters Broken Up in Extra Innings

Sometimes even the best days can be spoiled by bad luck or by a lack of support. Harvey Haddix's famous 1959 perfect game remains the benchmark for magnificent failure, but many other pitchers have had their no-hit efforts torpedoed after the regulation 9 innings.

Pitcher	Opponents	Score	Date	Comment
Earl Moore	Cle vs. Chi AL	2–4	May 9, 1901	Lost on 2 hits in 10th
Bob Wicker	Chi at NY NL	1–0	June 11, 1904	Won in 12 inn. after 1st hit in 10th
Harry McIntyre	Bro vs. Pit NL	0–1	Aug. 1, 1906	Lost on 4 hits in 13 inn. after 1st hit in 11th
Red Ames	NY vs. Bro NL	0–3	Apr. 15, 1909	Lost on 7 hits in 13 inn. after 1st hit in 10th
Tom L. Hughes	NY vs. Cle AL	0–5	Aug. 30, 1910 G2	Lost on 7 hits in 11 inn. after 1st hit in 10th
Jim Scott	Chi at Was AL	0–1	May 14, 1914	Lost on 2 hits in 10th
Hippo Vaughn	Chi vs. Cin NL	0–1	May 2, 1917	Lost on 2 hits in 10th; Fred Toney pitched no-hitter in this game
Bobo Newsom	StL vs. Bos AL	1–2	Sept. 18, 1934	Lost on 1 hit in 10th
Johnny Klippstein (7 IP), Hershell Freeman (1 IP) & Joe Black (3 IP)	Cin at Mil NL	1–2	May 26, 1956	Lost on 3 hits in 11 inn. after 1st hit in 10th
Harvey Haddix	Pit at Mil NL	0–1	May 26, 1959	Lost on hit in 13th after 12 perfect innings
Jim Maloney	Cin vs. NY NL	0–1	June 14, 1965	Lost on 2 hits in 11th
Mark Gardner	Mon at LA NL	0–1	July 26, 1991	9 IP, lost on 2 hits in 10th; relieved by Jeff Fassero, who allowed 1 hit
Pedro J. Martinez (9 IP) & Mel Rojas (1 IP)	Mon at SD NL	1–0	June 3, 1995	Martinez pitched 9 perfect innings but allowed hit in 10th; Rojas finished game

FIELDS OF DREAMS: BIG LEAGUE BALLPARKS

After the success of Phil Alden Robinson's 1989 movie *Field of Dreams*—based upon W.P. Kinsella's terrific novel *Shoeless Joe*— the phrase has become a staple of American vocabulary. Baseball parks are truly fields of dreams, both for those who play there as well as those who root from the stands. They are idiosyncratic, individual, and—when designed and built with care—as much a part of urban life as commercial buildings, or government offices. Other sports have their stadiums, but only *baseball* has *ballparks,* a felicitous marriage of two of the most joyous words in the English language.

Since the 1870s, the parks that baseball has been played in have evolved as much as the game itself. Ballparks have always been constructed using the latest technology available, whether they were the wood parks of the game's early days, the concrete-and-steel edifices of the early 1900s, the enormous superstadiums of the 1960s and 1970s, or today's fashionable steel-and-brick retro designs. Many ballparks have been built on a tight budget, from the quickly constructed skeletons of the 1880s to some of the latest retro parks.

Ballparks didn't start out by simply providing cheap seats for the regular guys. Contrary to what many might think, private boxes—constructed to separate the rich from the rest of the crowd—existed almost from the inception of the first ballpark as the moneyed sat apart from their lower-class brethren. Al Spalding, owner of the Chicago White Stockings, had a private telephone line run into his owner's box at Lakefront Park in the 1880s so he could conduct business during the games. At the same time, St. Louis' American Association ballpark had a special seating pavilion devoted just to high society.

There's no such discrimination in this section of the encyclopedia, where low-grade facilities in out-of-the-way cities like Altoona in 1884 rub shoulders with the splendor of modern Meccas like Oriole Park at Camden Yards in Baltimore. Each facility served, however briefly, as a venue for big league games and qualifies, therefore, as a major league ballpark. Some parks served as home fields for several teams and will, therefore, have two or more entries.

On the following pages you will see an entry with details on every park that has hosted a major league game since 1871. The section is organized by major league city, with each park in a city shown chronologically from 1871 to the present. Ballparks are listed under their current (or their last) name, with any earlier (official) names noted in italics. Common nicknames for ballparks are in quotes. Current major league ballparks are shown in bold.

The **Open** column shows the first and last years that a park was used for major league games. Current parks will have only an opening year. Parks that are no longer used by a major league team but which are still standing (e.g., Tiger Stadium) are indicated with an asterisk.

All clubs that called a park home for even one game are included in the **Tenants** column. Current (or last) team names are used for all entries; so the NL Dodgers are called the Dodgers in all entries, even if they were known as the Robins or Superbas at one time. Short-lived St. Paul in the Union Association never played any home games and therefore, has no listing. League abbreviations are the same as in the player registers.

Capacity lists each park's current or final seating capacity along with it initial seating capacity (when known) in parentheses. There were no recorded capacities or dimensions for most nineteenth century ballparks, and such details for early twentieth century parks are frequently lacking.

The next two columns give details on each ballpark's configuration by showing important dimensions (**Dimensions**). The **Current** or **Final** dimensions for parks are listed in the fifth column. Each park's **Original** dimensions, if known, are listed in the sixth column. From left to right, the dimensions shown are left field foul line (**LF**), left-center field (**LCF**), center field (**CF**), right-center field (**RCF**), and right field foul line (**RF**). LF-LCF and RF-RCF are separated by hyphens; CF is delimited by slashes. If the deepest part of the ballpark was *not* straightaway center field, the deepest dimension (if known) is shown in the **Notes** column. Question marks indicate unknown dimensions.

Despite the painstaking research done by Philip Lowry, Michael Benson, Michael Gershman, Larry Ritter, and others, there is still much that we do not know about the parks of the nineteenth century. This is, in part, because no one kept careful records of such things. However, another reason is that, back in the very "old days," baseball fields often did not even *have* dimensions as such—they were essentially big pastures with the playing diamonds laid out on them.

Some of the earliest parks lacked grandstands as well; those that did have grandstands lacked bleachers until the twentieth century. Overflow crowds were typically accommodated by allowing them to stand in foul territory or in fair territory behind the outfielders—in many pictures from the 1890s, horse-drawn carriages, holding fans, still ringed the outfield.

It is very interesting to note how dimensions have changed over the years. In days of yore, ballparks were built on whatever convenient piece of land could hold them, thus rendering most parks asymmetrical. For instance, New York's Polo Grounds, through its demise in 1962, had foul lines of less than 300 feet and a center field fence more than 200 feet deeper. To mitigate somewhat the effects of extremely short fences, the leagues drew up ground rules to eliminate cheap home runs. Finally, in the 1950s, the major leagues instituted minimum fence distances for newly built parks.

From the mid–1960s through the 1980s, new park design involved symmetrical dimensions designed to accommodate football fields. These uniform venues seemed to reflect clean-lined, suburban spaciousness rather than the intimate urban settings of classic ballparks. The paradigm shift caused by the opening of Camden Yards has convinced teams that fans want odd dimensions and asymmetrical features as well as intimate spaces and comfortable seats and amenities. So these retro ballparks are deliberately asymmetrical, though this is now being done mostly for aesthetic reasons.

The **Notes** column includes miscellaneous information about artificial turf; domes or retractable roofs; and when lights were installed (if the park didn't have lights when it opened). No ballpark that closed before 1935 ever had lights; every ballpark built afterward always had lights. A *p* next to a year indicates the information applied for only part of that year.

Finally, if a team played a "home" game in a park that was not located in its hometown, the location of that park is shown in square brackets. In the 1800s, clubs often played official league games at neutral sites, either to benefit from a larger gate or to squeeze in a game between long road destinations.

City/Park	Open	Tenants	Capacity	Dimensions LF–LCF/CF/RCF–RF Current/Final	Original	Notes
ALTOONA, PA						
Columbia Park	1884	UA Mountain Citys				
ANAHEIM [CALIFORNIA 1966-96]						
Angel Stadium of Anaheim	1966-	AL Angels	45,050 (43,204)	330-387/400/370-330	333-?/406/?-333	*Anaheim Stadium 1966–97; Edison International Field of Anaheim 1998–03 "The Big A"*; rebuilt as EIF 1997–98
ARLINGTON [TEXAS]						
Arlington Stadium	1972-1993	AL Rangers	43,521 (35,185)	330-380/400/380-330		OF configuration different 1974–80
The Ballpark In Arlington	**1994-**	**AL Rangers**	**49,115** (49,292)	**332-390/400/381-325**		
ATLANTA						
Atlanta-Fulton County Stadium	1966-1996	NL Braves	52,769 (50,893)	330-385/402/385-330	325-385/402/385-325	
Turner Field	**1997-**	**NL Braves**	**50,091** (50,528)	**335-380/401/390-330**		Built for 1996 Olympics; rebuilt for MLB
BALTIMORE						
Newington Park	1872-1874	NA Lord Baltimores				
	1873	NA Maryland				
	1882	AA Orioles				
Oriole Park (I)	1883-1889	AA Orioles				
Oriole Park (II)	1890-1891	AA Orioles			300-?/?/?-350	
Belair Lot	1884	UA Monumentals				
Monumental Park	1884	UA Monumentals				Selected dates
Oriole Park (III)	1891	AA Orioles	11,000 (30,000)	300-?/?/?-350		
	1892-1899	NL Orioles				
Oriole Park (IV)	1901-02	AL Orioles				
Terrapin Park	1914-1915	FL Terrapins	16,000	300-?/450/?-335		
Memorial Stadium	1954-1991	AL Orioles	53,371 (47,855)	309-385/405/385-309	309-446/445/446-309	
Oriole Park at Camden Yards	**1992-**	**AL Orioles**	**47,915** (48,041)	**333-410/400/373-318**		
BOSTON						
South End Grounds (I)	1871-1875	NA Red Stockings				Became NL Braves
Hampden Park Race Track	1873	NA Red Stockings				[Springfield MA] 2 games
South End Grounds (I)	1876-1887	NL Braves				
Dartmouth Grounds	1884	UA Unions				
South End Grounds (II)	1888-1894	NL Braves	6,800			
Congress Street Grounds	1890	PL Red Stockings		250-?/?/?-?		
	1891	AA Red Stockings				
	1894	NL Braves				
South End Grounds (III)	1894-1914	NL Braves		250-450/440/?-255		
Huntington Avenue Grounds	1901-1911	AL Red Sox	9,000	350-440/635/?-320	350-440/530/?-280	
Fenway Park	**1912-**	**AL Red Sox**	**34,898** (35,000)	**310-379/390/380-302**	321-?/488/?-314	RCF 420; lights 1947
	1914-1915	NL Braves				28 Sept. games & World Series, 1914
Braves Field	1915-1952	NL Braves	37,106 (40,000)	337-355/370/355-318	402-403/440/402-402	RCF 390 (550); lights 1946
	1915-1916	AL Red Sox				World Series only
	1929-1932	AL Red Sox				Sundays
BROOKLYN						
Capitoline Grounds	1872	NA Atlantics				
Union Grounds	1872	NA Eckfords	1,500	500-500/500/500-350		
	1873-1875	NA Atlantics				
Washington Park (I)	1884-1889	AA Atlantics	2,000			
Ridgewood Park	1886-1889	AA Atlantics				14 Sunday games
	1890	AA Gladiators				29 games
Washington Park (II)	1889	AA Atlantics	3,000			
	1890	NL Dodgers				
Long Island Grounds	1890	AA Gladiators				[Maspeth NY] 2 games
Eastern Park	1890	PL Ward's Wonders				
	1891-1897	NL Dodgers				
Washington Park (III)	1898-1912	NL Dodgers		376-444/425/300-302	335-500/445/300-215	
	1914-1915	FL Tip-Tops	18,800	300-?/400/?-275		Rebuilt 1914 for Federal League
West NY Field Club Grounds	1898	NL Dodgers				[West New York NJ] 3 games
Ebbets Field	1913-1957	NL Dodgers	31,902 (18,000)	348-351/393/352-297	419-?/450/?-301	Lights 1938
Roosevelt Stadium	1956-1957	NL Dodgers	24,500 (24,167)	330-397/411/397-330		[Jersey City NJ] 14 games total
BUFFALO						
Riverside Grounds	1879-1883	NL Bisons			210-420/410/420-210	
Olympic Park (I)	1884-1885	NL Bisons				
Maple Avenue Driving Park	1885	NL Bisons				[Elmira NY] 1 game
Olympic Park (II)	1890	PL Bisons				
Federal Field	1914-1915	FL Blues	20,000	290-?/400/?-300		*aka Federal League Park*
CHICAGO						
Union Base-Ball Grounds	1871	NA White Stockings	7,000			Became NL Cubs; *aka Lake Park*
23rd Street Grounds	1874-1875	NA White Stockings				
	1876-1877	NL Cubs				
Lake Front Park (I)	1878-1882	NL Cubs				
Lake Front Park (II)	1883-1884	NL Cubs	5,000	180-280/300/252-196	186-280/300/252-196	
South Side Park (I)	1884	UA Browns				
Belair Lot	1884	UA Browns				[Baltimore MD] 1 game
West Side Park	1885-1891	NL Cubs			216-?/?/?-216	Mondays/Wednesdays/Fridays 1891
South Side Park (II)	1890	PL Pirates				
	1891-1893	NL Cubs				Tuesdays/Thursdays/Saturdays 1891
West Side Grounds	1893-1915	NL Cubs	16,000 (12,500)	340-441/560/435-316		
South Side Park (III)	1901-1910	AL White Sox	15,000			
Comiskey Park (I)	1910-1990	AL White Sox	43,951 (28,800)	347-382/409/382-347	363-382/420/382-363	Lights 1939; turf IF/grass OF 1969–75 *White Sox Park 1967–75*
Wrigley Field	1914-1915	FL Whales	**39,241** (18,000)	**355-368/400/368-353**	310-?/400/?-350	Lights 1988; *Weeghman Park 1914–18, Cubs Park 1919–25*
	1916-	**NL Cubs**				
Milwaukee County Stadium	1968-1969	AL White Sox	53,192 (35,911)	315-392/402/392-315	320-397/404/397-320	[Milwaukee WI] 20 games total
U.S. Cellular Field	**1991-**	**AL White Sox**	**47,098 (44,702)**	**330-377/400/372-335**	347-383/400/383-347	*Comiskey Park (II) 1991–2002 "New Comiskey"*
Tokyo Dome*	2000	NL Cubs	55,000	318-360/400/360-318		[Japan] Dome; turf; 1 game
CINCINNATI						
Avenue Grounds	1876-1879	NL Reds				
Bank St. Grounds	1880	NL Reds				
	1882-1883	AA Red Stockings				
	1884	UA Outlaw Reds				
League Park (I)	1884-1889	AA Red Stockings				
	1890-1893	NL Reds				
Pendleton Park	1891	AA Kelly's Killers				[Pendleton Park OH]
League Park (II)	1894-1901	NL Reds		253-?/?/?-?		
Palace Of The Fans	1902-1911	NL Reds	6,000	?-?/?/?-450		

City/Park	Open	Tenants	Capacity	Dimensions LF–LCF/CF/RCF–RF Current/Final	Original	Notes
CrosleyÏ Field	1912-1970	NL Reds	29,603 (23,500)	328-380/387/383-366	360-380/420/?-385	Lights 1935; *Redland Field 1912-33;* replica built in Blue Ash OH
Cinergy Field	1970-2002	NL Reds	40,007 (50,000)	325-370/393/374-325	330-375/404/375-330	Turf 1970-2000; *Riverfront Stadium 1970-96* LF-CF seats demolished after 2000
Great American Ball Park	**2003-**	**NL Reds**	**42,263**	**328-379/404/370-325**		
CLEVELAND						
National Association Grounds	1871-1872	NA Forest City				
Lincoln Park Grounds	1871	NA Forest City				[Cincinnati OH] 1 date
National League Park (I)	1879-1884	NL Blues				
National League Park (II)	1887-1888	AA Blues			410/?/420/?-410	
	1889-1890	NL Spiders			410-?/420/?-410	
Geauga Lake Baseball Grounds	1888	AA Blues				[Geauga Lake OH] 3 games
Beyerle's Park	1888	AA Blues				[Newburgh OH] 1 date
Brotherhood Park	1890	PL Infants				
Indianapolis Park	1890	NL Spiders				[Indianapolis IN] a few dates
League Park (I)	1891-1899	NL Spiders	9,000		?-?/?/?-290	
	1901-1909	AL Indians				
Euclid Beach Park	1898	NL Spiders				[Collinwood OH] selected dates
Ontario Beach Grounds	1898	NL Spiders				[Charlotte NY] 1 date
League Park (II)	1910-1946	AL Indians	21,000	375-415/420/400-290	385-505/420/400-290	Selected dates 1932–46
Cleveland Stadium	1932-1993	AL Indians	74,483 (78,000)	320-375/404/370-320	320-435/470/435-320	Lights 1939; selected dates 1932–46; *Lakefront Stadium 1932–37; Cleveland Public Municipal Stadium 1938; Municipal Stadium 1939–64*
Jacobs Field	**1994-**	**AL Indians**	**43,389 (42,865)**	**325-370/405/375-325**		*"The Jake"*
COLUMBUS, OH						
Recreation Park (I)	1883-1884	AA Buckeyes				
Recreation Park (II)	1889-1891	AA Solons			?-?/?/?-400	
DENVER [COLORADO]						
Mile High Stadium	1993-1994	NL Rockies	76,100	333-366/423/400-370	335-375/423/400-370	
Coors Field	**1995-**	**NL Rockies**	**50,449** (50,000)	**347-390/415/375-350**		RCF 424
DETROIT						
Recreation Park	1881-1888	NL Wolverines				
Bennett Park	1901-1911	AL Tigers	14,000 (6,000)			
Burns Park	1901-1902	AL Tigers	8,000 (5,500)			23 Sunday games
Tiger Stadium*	1912-1999	AL Tigers	46,846 (23,000)	340-365/440/370-325	345-?/467/?-370	Lights 1948; *Navin Field 1912–33; Briggs Stadium 1934–60*
Comerica Park	**2000-**	**AL Tigers**	**40,120**	**345-370/420/365-330**	345-395/420/365-330	
ELIZABETH, NJ						
Waverly Fairgrounds	1873	NA Resolutes				[Waverly NJ]
FORT WAYNE, IN						
Hamilton Field	1871	NA Kekiongas				
HARTFORD						
Hartford Ball Club Grounds	1874-1875	NA Dark Blues				
South End Grounds	1874	NA Dark Blues				[Boston MA] 1 date
Hartford Ball Club Grounds	1876	NL Dark Blues				
Union Grounds	1877	NL Dark Blues		?-500/500/500-?		[Brooklyn NY]
HOUSTON						
Colt Stadium	1962-1964	NL Colt .45s	33,010 (32,601)	360-395/420/395-360		RCF & LCF 427; Most of ballpark moved to Torreon, Mexico, in 1969
Astrodome*	1965-1999	NL Astros	54,370 (46,217)	325-375/400/375-325	340-375/406/375-340	Dome; turf (turf IF/grass OF 1966p)
Minute Maid Park	**2000-**	**NL Astros**	**40,950** (42,180)	**315-362/435/373-326**		Retractable roof; RCF 436; *Enron Field 2000–01, Astros Field 2002*
INDIANAPOLIS						
South Street Park	1878	NL Blues				
Seventh St. Park (I)	1884	AA Hoosiers				
Bruce Grounds	1884	AA Hoosiers				11 Sunday games
Seventh St. Park (II)	1887	NL Hoosiers			286-?/?/?-261	
Seventh St. Park (III)	1888-1889	NL Hoosiers				
Hoosier Park	1914	FL Hoosiers	20,000	375-?/400/?-310		*aka Greenlawn Park/Federal League Park*
KANSAS CITY						
Athletic Park	1884	UA Cowboys				
Association Park	1886	NL Cowboys				
	1888	AA Cowboys				
Gordon & Koppel Field	1914-1915	FL Packers	12,000			
Municipal Stadium	1955-1967	AL Athletics	35,561 (30,296)	369-408/421/382-338	312-382/430/382-347	
	1969-1972	AL Royals				
Kauffman Stadium	**1973-**	**AL Royals**	**40,793** (40,613)	**330-375/400/375-330**	330-375/405/375-330	Turf 1973–94; *Royals Stadium 1973–93p*
KEOKUK, IA						
Perry Park	1875	NA Westerns				
LOS ANGELES [incl. CALIFORNIA 1965] (also see Anaheim)						
Memorial Coliseum*	1958-1961	NL Dodgers	94,600 (93,000)	252-417/420/380-300	250-425/425/440-301	
Wrigley Field	1961	AL Angels	20,457	340-345/412/345-339		
Dodger Stadium	**1962-**	**NL Dodgers**	**56,000**	**330-385/395/385-330**	330-380/410/380-330	
	1962-1965	AL Angels				*Chavez Ravine Stadium 1962–65 (Angels games only);* LA Angels changed name to California in 1965 before move to Anaheim
LOUISVILLE						
Louisville Baseball Park	1876-1877	NL Grays				
Eclipse Park (I)	1882-1891	AA Colonels (1885)		360-405/495/360-320		
	1892-1893	NL Colonels				
Eclipse Park (II)	1893-1899	NL Colonels				
MIAMI [FLORIDA]						
Pro Player Stadium	**1993-**	**NL Marlins**	**36,331** (43,909)	**330-385/404/385-345**	335-380/410/380-345	RCF 434; postseason cap. 65,000+; *Joe Robbie Stadium 1993–96*
MIDDLETOWN, CT						
Mansfield Club Grounds	1872	NA Mansfields				
Hartford Trotting Park	1872	NA Mansfields				[Hartford CT] 3 games
MILWAUKEE						
Milwaukee Base-Ball Grounds	1878	NL Grays				
Wright Street Grounds	1884	UA Brewers				

City/Park	Open	Tenants	Capacity	Dimensions LF–LCF/CF/RCF–RF		Notes
				Current/Final	Original	
Borchert Field	1891	AA Brewers	10,000		266-?/395/?-266	
Athletic Park	1891	AA Brewers			275-?/?/?-250	[Minneapolis MN] 1 date
Lloyd Street Grounds	1901	AL Brewers				
Milwaukee County Stadium	1953-1965	NL Braves	53,192 (35,911)	315-392/402/392-315	320-397/404/397-320	
	1968-1969	AL White Sox				20 games total
	1970-1997	AL Brewers				
	1998-2000	NL Brewers				
Miller Park	**2001-**	**NL Brewers**	**41,900** (42,500)	**344-371/400/374-345**		**Retractable roof**
MINNEAPOLIS [MINNESOTA]						
Metropolitan Stadium	1961-81	AL Twins	45,919 (30,022)	343-406/402/410-330	329-402/412/402-329	[Bloomington MN]
Hubert H. Humphrey Metrodome	**1982-**	**AL Twins**	**48,678** (54,711)	**343-385/408/367-327**		Dome; turf; *"The Homerdome"*
MONTREAL						
Parc Jarry (Jarry Park)	1969-1976	NL Expos	28,456 (28,000)	340-368/420/368-340	340-368/415/368-340	
Stade Olympique	**1977-**	**NL Expos**	**46,338** (58,838)	**325-375/404/375-325**		Turf; built for 1976 Olympics; *Olympic Stadium; "The Big O";* Open-air 1977–86; fixed roof 1987–88; retractable roof 1989–91p; fixed roof p1991–98p; no roof 1998p; fixed roof 1999
Estadio Hiram Bithorn	**2003-2004**	**NL Expos**	**20,000**	**315-340/399/340-315**		*Hiram Bithorn Stadium* [San Juan PR] turf; Power alleys listed 360', actually 340'; 22 games each season in 2003–04
NEWARK						
Harrison Park	1915	FL Peppers	21,000	375-?/450/?-375		*aka Peppers Park*
NEW HAVEN, CT						
Howard Avenue Grounds	1875	NA Elm Citys				*aka Brewster Park*
Adelaide Avenue Grounds	1875	NA Elm Citys				[Providence RI] 1 date
NEW YORK						
Union Grounds	1871-1875	NA Mutuals	1,500	500-500/500/500-350		[Brooklyn NY]
	1876	NL Mutuals				
Polo Grounds (I)	1883-1888	NL Giants				
	1884-1885	AA Metropolitans				
Polo Grounds (II)	1883	AA Metropolitans				
Metropolitan Park	1884	AA Metropolitans				33 games
St. George Cricket Grounds	1886-1887	AA Metropolitans	4,100			[St. George NY]
Monitor Park	1887	AA Metropolitans				[Weehawken NJ] 1 date
Polo Grounds (III)	1889-1890	NL Giants		?-?/360/?-?		
Oakdale Park	1889	NL Giants				[Jersey City NJ] 2 games
Polo Grounds (IV)	1890	PL Giants	16,000	277-?/500/?-258	335-?/500/?-335	
	1891-1911	NL Giants				*Brotherhood Park 1890*
West N.Y. Field Club Grounds	1899	NL Giants				[West New York NJ] selected dates
Hilltop Park	1903-1912	AL Yankees	15,000	365-?/542/?-400		
	1911	NL Giants				
Polo Grounds (V)	1911-1957	NL Giants	56,000 (16,000)	279-455/483/449-258	277-?/433/?-257	Lights 1940
	1913-1922	AL Yankees				
	1962-1963	NL Mets				
Yankee Stadium	**1923-**	**AL Yankees**	**57,478** (58,000)	**318-399/408/385-314**	281-395/490/429-295	LCF 411; lights 1946; rebuilt 1974–75 *"The House That Ruth Built"*
Shea Stadium	**1964-**	**NL Mets**	**57,393** (55,000)	**338-378/410/378-338**	341-371/410/371-341	
	1974-75; 1998	AL Yankees				1 game in 1998
Tokyo Dome*	2000	NL Mets	55,000	318-360/400/360-318		[Japan] Dome; turf; 1 game
OAKLAND						
Network Associates Coliseum	**1968-**	**AL Athletics**	**43,662** (50,000)	**330-388/400/388-330**	330-378/410/378-330	Postseason cap. 50,000+; *Oakland-Alameda County Coliseum 1968–98*
Cashman Field*	1996	AL Athletics	9,370	328-364/433/364-328		[Las Vegas NV] 6 games
PHILADELPHIA						
Jefferson Street Grounds	1871-1875	NA Athletics			?-?/500/?-?	First press box installed here
	1873-1875	NA White Stockings				
	1876	NL Athletics				
	1883-1890	AA Athletics				*aka Athletic Park*
Fairview Park Fairgrounds	1875	NA Athletics				[Dover DE] 1 date
Centennial Park	1875	NA Centennials				*aka Centennial Grounds*
Star Baseball Park	1875	NA White Stockings				[Covington KY] 1 date
Ludlow Baseball Park	1875	NA White Stockings				[Ludlow KY] 1 date
Oakdale Park	1882	AA Athletics				
Recreation Park	1883-1886	NL Phillies				
Keystone Park	1884	UA Keystones				
Philadelphia Baseball Grounds	1887-1894	NL Phillies	15,000	500-?/?/?-310		
Gloucester Point Grounds	1888-1890	AA Athletics				[Gloucester City NJ] 30 Sunday games
University of Pennsylvania Athletic Field	1894	NL Phillies			One week	
Forepaugh Park	1890	PL Quakers		345-?/450/?-380		
	1891	AA Athletics				
Columbia Park	1901-1908	AL Athletics	13,600 (9,500)			
	1903	NL Phillies				16 games
Baker Bowl	1895-1938	NL Phillies	18,800 (18,000)	342-359/408/300-281	?-?/408/300-?	
Connie Mack Stadium	1909-1954	AL Athletics	33,608 (20,000)	334-387/410/390-329	360-393/515/393-360	*Shibe Park 1909–52;* lights 1939
	1938-1970	NL Phillies				
Veterans Stadium	1971-2003	NL Phillies	61,831 (56,371)	330-371/408/371-330		Turf
Citizens Bank Park	**2004-**	**NL Phillies**	**43,000**	**329-369/401/369-330**		LCF 409
PHOENIX [ARIZONA]						
Bank One Ballpark	**1998-**	**NL Diamondbacks**	**49,033** (48,500)	**330-376/407/376-334**		"The BOB"; retractable roof; RCF 412
PITTSBURGH						
Exposition Park (I)	1882-1883	AA Alleghenys				
	1884	UA Stogies				
Exposition Park (II)	1883	AA Alleghenys				
Recreation Park	1884-1886	AA Alleghenys	17,000			
	1887-1890	NL Pirates	17,000			
Exposition Park (III)	1890	PL Burghers		400-?/450/?-400		
	1891-1909	NL Pirates				
	1914-1915	FL Rebels	16,000			
Mahaffey Park	1890	NL Pirates		324-?/382/?-302		[Canton OH] 1 date
Island Grounds	1890	NL Pirates				[Wheeling WV] 1 date
Forbes Field	1909-1970	NL Pirates	35,000 (28,000)	365-406/435/408-300	360-419/447/410-376	LCF 457 (462); lights 1940
Three Rivers Stadium	1970-2000	NL Pirates	47,687 (49,023)	335-375/400/375-335	340-385/410/385-340	Turf
PNC Park	**2001-**	**NL Pirates**	**37,898**	**325-389/399/375-320**		LCF 410
PROVIDENCE, RI						
Messer Street Grounds	1878	NL Grays				

City/Park	Open	Tenants	Capacity	Dimensions LF–LCF/CF/RCF–RF Current/Final	Original	Notes
Union Park	1878	NL Grays	2,500			[Pittsburgh PA] selected dates
RICHMOND, VA						
Virginia Baseball Park	1884	AA Virginians				
ROCHESTER, NY						
Culver Field (I)	1890	AA Broncos				
Windsor Beach	1890	AA Broncos				[Irondequoit NY] 6 games
ROCKFORD, IL						
Agricultural Society Fairgrounds	1871	NA Forest City	500			
ST. LOUIS						
Red Stocking Base-Ball Park	1875	NA Red Stockings				
Grand Avenue Park	1875	NA Brown Stockings				
	1876-1877	NL Brown Stockings	3,000			
Union Grounds	1884	UA Maroons	10,000	285-?/?/?-285		
	1885-1886	NL Maroons				
Seventh Street Park (I)	1885	NL Maroons				[Indianapolis IN] selected dates
Sportsman's Park (I)	1882-1891	AA Cardinals	12,000 (6,000)	350-400/460/330-285		
	1892	NL Cardinals				
Robison Field	1893-1920	NL Cardinals	21,000 (10,000)	380-400/435/320-?	470-520/500/330-290	
Athletic Park	1901	NL Cardinals				1 game
Sportsman's Park (II)	1902-1908	AL Browns	18,000			
Busch Stadium (I)	1909-1953	AL Browns	30,500 (17,600)	351-379/420/354-3109	368-379/?/?-335	Lights 1940
	1920-1966	NL Cardinals				*Sportsman's Park (III) 1909–53*
Handlan's Park	1914-1915	FL Terriers	15,000 (12,000)	325-?/375/?-300		*aka Steininger Field*
Busch Stadium (II)	**1966-**	**NL Cardinals**	**50,354** (49,275)	**330-372/402/372-330**	330-386/414/386-330	*Busch Memorial Stadium 1966–83;* turf 1970–95
ST. PETERSBURG [TAMPA BAY]						
Tropicana Field	**1998-**	**AL Devil Rays**	**43,761** (45,200)	**315-370/404/370-322**	315-370/410/370-322	Dome; turf; LCF 410 (417)
SAN DIEGO						
Qualcomm Stadium*	1969-2003	NL Padres	63,890 (50,000)	327-370/405/370-330	330-370/420/370-330	*San Diego Stadium 1969–80; San Diego/ Jack Murphy Stadium 1981–97*
Estadio Monterrey*	1996	NL Padres	25,644	325-?/405/?-325		*Monterrey Stadium* [Mexico] 3 games
	1999	NL Padres				1 game
Aloha Stadium*	1997	NL Padres	50,000	325-375/420/375-325		[Honolulu HI] 3 games; turf
Petco Park	**2004-**	**NL Padres**	**46,000**	**334-367/396/387-322**		RCF 411
SAN FRANCISCO						
Seals Stadium	1958-1959	NL Giants	22,900	361-364/400/397-350	365-375/410/397-355	
3Com Park at Candlestick Point*	1960-1999	NL Giants	63,000 (42,500)	335-365/400/365-328	330-365/410/375-330	*Candlestick Park 1960–95* Turf IF/grass OF 1971; turf 1972–78
SBC Park	**2000-**	**Giants**	**41,503** (40,800)	**339-364/399/421-309**	335-364/404/420-307	*Pacific Bell Park 2000–03*
SEATTLE						
Sick's Stadium	1969	AL Pilots	25,420 (18,000)	305-345/402/345-305		
Kingdome	1977-1999	AL Mariners	59,084 (59,059)	331-389/405/380-312	315-375/405/365-315	Dome; turf
SAFECO Field	**1999-**	**AL Mariners**	**47,447** (47,116)	**331-390/405/387-327**		Retractable roof
SYRACUSE, NY						
Star Park (I)	1879	NL Stars				
Star Park (II)	1890	AA Stars				
Iron Pier	1890	AA Stars				1 game scheduled; forfeited
Three Rivers Park	1890	AA Stars				[Three Rivers, NY] 5 games
TOLEDO, OH						
League Park	1884	AA Blue Stockings				
Tri-State Fair Grounds	1884	AA Blue Stockings				
Speranza Park	1890	AA Maumees				
TORONTO						
Exhibition Stadium	1977-1989	AL Blue Jays	43,737 (38,522)	330-375/400/375-330		Turf
SkyDome	**1989-**	**AL Blue Jays**	**50,516**	**328-375/400/375-328**	330-375/400/375-330	Retractable roof; turf
Estadio Hiram Bithorn*	2001	AL Blue Jays	20,000	315-340/398/340-313		*Hiram Bithorn Stadium;* turf; 1 game Power alleys listed 360', actually 340'
TROY, NY						
Haymakers' Grounds	1871-1872	NA Haymakers				
	1880-1881	NL Trojans				
Hampden Park Race Track	1872	NA Haymakers				[Springfield MA] 1 date
Putnam Grounds	1879	NL Trojans				
Riverside Park	1880-1882	NL Trojans				[Albany NY] selected dates
Troy Ball Club Grounds	1882	NL Trojans				[Watervliet NY]
WASHINGTON, DC						
Olympic Grounds	1871-1872	NA Olympics				
	1873	NA Nationals				
	1875	NA Nationals				
Madison Avenue Grounds	1871	NA Olympics				[Baltimore MD] 1 date
Lincoln Park Grounds	1871	NA Olympics				[Cincinnati OH] 2 games
White Lot	1871-1872	NA Olympics				Selected dates
Maryland Avenue Park	1871-1872	NA Olympics				Selected dates
Nationals Grounds	1872	NA Nationals				
Newington Park	1875	NA Nationals				[Baltimore MD] 2 games
Virginia State Agricultural Society	1875	NA Nationals				[Richmond VA] selected dates
Athletic Park	1884	AA Nationals				
Capitol Grounds	1884	UA Nationals	6,000			
Swampoodle Grounds	1886-1889	NL Senators	6,000			
Boundary Field	1891	AA Statesmen	6,500			
	1892-1899	NL Senators				
American League Park (I)	1901-1903	AL Senators	(6,000)		200-?/?/?-?	
American League Park (II)	1904-1910	AL Senators				
Griffith Stadium	1911-1960	AL Senators (I)	28,669 (12,000)	388-372/408/373-320	407-391/421/378-328	*League Park 1911–19;* LCF 426;
	1961	AL Senators (II)				lights 1941
Robert F. Kennedy Memorial Stadium*	1962-71	AL Senators (II)	45,016 (42,000)	335-381/410/378-335	335-385/410/385-335	*District of Columbia Stadium 1962–68*
WILMINGTON, DE						
Union Street Park	1884	UA Quicksteps				
WORCESTER, MA						
Agricultural County Fair Grounds	1880-1882	NL Brown Stockings				

THE GLOBAL GAME: INTERNATIONAL BASEBALL

While America's national game doesn't have the far-reaching popularity of soccer, baseball is played enthusiastically all around the world. Outside of the United States, baseball remains most popular in the Caribbean and in East Asia, but the game is continuing to spread. Twelve countries participated in the European Baseball Championships in 2003, and Australia, Korean, and Taiwan continue to produce major league prospects.

In 1992 baseball finally became an Olympic sport, although its future as such is currently in question. Major League Baseball is also planning a World Cup for 2005 that would feature an unprecedented international gathering of baseball talent. However, baseball's future growth, especially in the Eastern Hemisphere, is tied to its status in the Olympics.

BASEBALL IN LATIN AMERICA

The passion much of Latin America has for baseball is no secret in the United States. Baseball has a longer tradition in the Caribbean than anywhere else except for the U.S. In the Dominican Republic, Cuba, Venezuela, and Puerto Rico, baseball is still the king of all sports, and it has been so for a very long time.

The first place that the American National Pastime landed in the Caribbean was Cuba, where American sailors and local workers were reportedly playing as early as 1866. Cuba had its first real team two years later and a professional league began competition in 1878, only two years after the National League's debut. Until the political upheavals of the late 1950s, Cuba was a baseball hub, attracting players from many other countries and sending many of its own to the major leagues and Negro Leagues. Cuba was also baseball's ambassador to the rest of the Caribbean. By the end of the nineteenth century, baseball was a fixture in every country in the area. U.S. military activity around the turn of the century helped push baseball further along in many of these places.

In the 1930s and 1940s the Caribbean winter leagues were attracting many major leaguers and Negro Leaguers in need of supplemental incomes. Following World War II, some rich owners in the Mexican League even raided the major leagues by signing more than twenty American players, though the threat from south of the border was short-lived.

After the color line was broken in the majors in 1947 and the crisis over the Mexican League raids had passed, Organized Baseball established official ties with most of the Caribbean leagues. The Caribbean Series began in that period, bringing together the winners of the winter leagues from Cuba, Panama, Puerto Rico, and Venezuela for an annual tournament. Cuba's 1959 revolution disrupted not only the Serie del Caribe, which took a hiatus from 1961–69, but all of baseball. While newly communist Cuba continued to field strong amateur teams, most of the connections between the island and the rest of the baseball world were severed by the revolution. Therefore, the nexus of Latin American baseball moved to the Dominican Republic.

In recent years the importance of the winter leagues has faded. With the astronomical leaps in major league salaries, few ballplayers need to supplement their income. Moreover, big league teams want to keep their investments safe and often discourage veteran players from playing winter ball and risking injury. These days most of the major leaguers who play winter ball are either local heroes or are playing to develop a new skill or increase their marketability as free agents. This trend has not, however, diminished the level of popularity of baseball in these countries or the skill level of their players, as 30 percent of today's major leaguers are Latinos, more than double the percentage of fifteen years ago.

While the winter leagues may no longer attract as many baseball stars or baseball fans, the leagues themselves are still mostly successful (though the 2002–03 Venezuelan season was cancelled as a result of domestic unrest). The Caribbean Series was revived in 1970, with Mexico and the Dominican Republic replacing Panama and Cuba. It has been played every year since then, with the exception of 1981. In 2003–04 Major League Baseball arranged for the Montreal Expos to play part of their home schedule in Puerto Rico, and both San Juan and Monterrey, Mexico are said to be contenders for a future major league franchise. The Mexican League, the only significant summer league in the region, still attracts many former major leaguers, though it continues to struggle for financial security.

Baseball faces many more challenges in the Caribbean than it did a century ago, but it still remains the favorite pastime of many Latin nations.

Caribbean Series (Serie Del Caribe) Results

Year (Series)	Winning Team and Country	Host	Year (Series)	Winning Team and Country	Host	Year (Series)	Winning Team and Country	Host
1949 (I)	Almendares, Cuba	Cuba	1973 (XVI)	Licey, D.R.	Venez.	1989 (XXXI)	Zulia, Venez.	Mex.
1950 (II)	Carta Vieja, Pan.	P.R.	1974 (XVII)	Caguas, P.R.	Mex.	1990 (XXXII)	Escogido, D.R.	U.S.
1951 (III)	Santurce, P.R.	Venez.	1975 (XVIII)	Bayamon, P.R.	P.R.	1991 (XXXIII)	Licey, D.R.	U.S.
1952 (IV)	La Habana, Cuba	Pan.	1976 (XIX)	Hermosillo, Mex.	D.R.	1992 (XXXIV)	Mayaguez, P.R.	Mex.
1953 (V)	Santurce, P.R.	Cuba	1977 (XX)	Licey, D.R.	Venez.	1993 (XXXV)	Mayaguez, P.R.	Mex.
1954 (VI)	Caguas, P.R.	P.R.	1978 (XXI)	Mayaguez, P.R.	Mex.	1994 (XXXVI)	Licey, D.R.	Mex.
1955 (VII)	Santurce, P.R.	Venez.	1979 (XXII)	Magallanes, Venez.	P.R.	1995 (XXXVII)	San Juan, P.R.	P.R.
1956 (VIII)	Cienfuegos, Cuba	Pan.	1980 (XXIII)	Licey, D.R.	D.R.	1996 (XXXVIII)	Culiacan, D.R.	D.R.
1957 (IX)	Marianao, Cuba	Cuba	1982 (XXIV)	Caracas, Venez.	Mex.	1997 (XXXIX)	Aguilas, D.R.	Mex.
1958 (X)	Marianao, Cuba	P.R.	1983 (XXV)	Arecibo, P.R.	Venez.	1998 (XL)	Aguilas, D.R.	Venez.
1959 (XI)	Almendares, Cuba	Venez.	1984 (XXVI)	Zulia, Venez.	P.R.	1999 (XLI)	Licey, D.R.	P.R.
1960 (XII)	Cienfuegos, Cuba	Pan.	1985 (XXVII)	Licey, D.R.	Mex.	2000 (XLII)	Santurce, P.R.	D.R.
1970 (XIII)	Magallanes, Venez.	Venez.	1986 (XXVIII)	Mexicali, Mex.	Venez.	2001 (XLIII)	Aguilas, D.R.	Mex.
1971 (XIV)	Licey, D.R.	P.R.	1987 (XXIX)	Caguas, Venez.	Mex.	2002 (XLIV)	Culiacan, D.R.	Venez.
1972 (XV)	Ponce, P.R.	D.R.	1988 (XXX)	Escogido, D.R.	D.R.	2003 (XLV)	Aguilas, D.R.	P.R.

Cuban Professional Baseball League Champions

Season	Team	Season	Team	Season	Team	Season	Team	Season	Team	Season	Team
1878-79	Habana	1892-93	Matanza	1910	Almendares	1923-24	Santa Clara	1937-38	Santa Clara	1950-51	Habana
1879-80	Habana	1893-94	Almendares	1910-11	Almendares	1924-25	Almendares	1938-39	Santa Clara	1951-52	Habana
1880-81	Habana &	1898-99	Habanista	1912	Habana	1925-26	Almendares	1939-40	Almendares	1952-53	Habana
	Fe (disputed)	1900	San Francisco	1913	Fe	1926-27	Habana	1940-41	Habana	1953-54	Almendares
1882-83	Habana	1901	Habana	1913-14	Almendares	1927-28	Habana	1941-42	Almendares	1954-55	Almendares
1885	Habana	1902	Habana	1914-15	Habana	1928-29	Habana	1942-43	Almendares	1955-56	Cienfuegos
1885-86	Habana	1903	Habana	1915-16	Almendares	1929-30	Cienfuegos	1943-44	Habana	1956-57	Marianao
1886-87	Habana	1904	Habana	1917	Orientals	1931-32	Almendares	1944-45	Almendares	1957-58	Marianao
1887-88	Fe	1905	Almendares	1918-19	Habana	1932–33	Almendares	1945-46	Cienfuegos	1958-59	Almendares
1888-89	Habana	1906	Fe	1919-20	Almendares		& Habana (tie)	1946-47	Almendares	1959-60	Cienfuegos
1889-90	Habana	1907	Almendares	1920-21	Habana	1934-35	Almendares	1947-48	Habana	1960-61	Cienfuegos
1890-91	Fe	1908	Almendares	1921	Habana	1935-36	Santa Clara	1948-49	Almendares		
1891-92	Habana	1908-09	Habana	1922-23	Marianao	1936-37	Marianao	1949-50	Almendares		

Cuban Baseball Federation Champions

Year	Team	Year	Team	Year	Team	Year	Team	Year	Team
1967	Orientales	1970	Henequeneros	1973	Industriales	1976	Ganaderos	1979	Sancti Spiritus
1968	Habana	1971	Azucareros	1974	Habana	1977	Citricultores	1980	Santiago de Cuba
1969	Azucareros	1972	Azucareros	1975	Agricultores	1978	Vegueros	1981	Vegueros

Year	Team
1982	Vegueros
1983	Villa Clara
1984	Citricultores
1985	Vegueros
1986	Industriales
1987	Vegueros
1988	Vegueros
1989	Santiago de Cuba
1990	Henequeneros
1991	Henequeneros
1992	Industriales
1993	Villa Clara
1994	Villa Clara
1995	Villa Clara
1996	Villa Clara
1997	Pinar del Rio
1998	Pinar del Rio
1999	Santiago de Cuba
2000	Santiago de Cuba
2001	Santiago de Cuba
2002	Holguin
2003	Industriales

Latin American Winter Leagues

Season	Puerto Rican	Venezuelan	Dominican Republic	Mexican Pacific
1940-41	Caguas			
1941-42	Ponce			
1942-43	Ponce			
1943-44	Ponce			
1944-45	Ponce			
1945-46	San Juan	Vargas		
1946-47	Ponce	Vargas		
1947-48	Caguas	Caracas		
1948-49	Mayaguez	Caracas		
1949-50	Caguas			
1950-51	Santurce	Magallanes		
1951-52	San Juan	Magallanes	Licey (1951)	
1952-53	Santurce	Caracas	Aguilas (1952)	
1953-54	Caguas	Caracas	Licey (1953)	
1954-55	Santurce	Occidente	Estrellas Orientales (1954)	
1955-56	Caguas	Magallanes	Escogido	
1956-57	Mayaguez	Valencia	Escogido	
1957-58	Caguas	Caracas	Escogido	
1958-59	Santurce	Valencia	Licey	Guaymas
1959-60	Caguas	Valencia	Escogido	Guaymas
1960-61	San Juan	Valencia	Escogido	Hermosillo
1961-62	Santurce	Caracas		Hermosillo
1962-63	Mayaguez	Valencia		Guaymas
1963-64	San Juan	Caracas	Licey	Hermosillo
1964-65	Santurce	La Guaira	Aguilas	Guaymas
1965-66	Mayaguez	La Guaira		Obregon
1966-67	Santurce	Caracas	Aguilas	Culiacan
1967-68	Caguas	Caracas	Estrellas Orientales	Guaymas
1968-69	Ponce	La Guaira	Escogido	Los Mochis
1969-70	Ponce	Magallanes	Licey	Culiacan
1970-71	Santurce		Licey	Hermosillo
1971-72	Ponce	Aragua	Aguilas	Guasave
1972-73	Santurce	Caracas	Licey	Obregon
1973-74	Caguas		Licey	Mazatlan
1974-75	Bayamon	Aragua	Aguilas	Hermosillo
1975-76	Bayamon	Aragua	Aguilas	Hermosillo
1976-77	Caguas	Magallanes	Licey	Mazatlan
1977-78	Mayaguez	Caracas	Aguilas	Culiacan
1978-79	Caguas	Magallanes	Aguilas	Navojoa
1979-80	Bayamon	Caracas	Licey	Hermosillo
1980-81	Caguas	Caracas	Escogido	Obregon
1981-82	Ponce	Caracas	Escogido	Hermosillo
1982-83	Arecibo	La Guaira	Licey	Culiacan
1983-84	Mayaguez	Zulia	Licey	Los Mochis
1984-85	San Juan	La Guaira	Licey	Culiacan
1985-86	Mayaguez	La Guaira	Aguilas	Mexicali
1986-87	Caguas	Caracas	Aguilas	Mazatlan
1987-88	Mayaguez	Caracas	Escogido	Tijuana
1988-89	Mayaguez	Zulia	Licey	Mexicali
1989-90	San Juan	Caracas	Escogido	Hermosillo
1990-91	Santurce	Lara	Licey	Tijuana
1991-92	Mayaguez	Zulia	Escogido	Hermosillo
1992-93	Santurce	Zulia	Aguilas	Mazatlan
1993-94	San Juan	Magallanes	Licey	Hermosillo
1994-95	San Juan	Caracas	Azucueros	Hermosillo
1995-96	Arecibo	Magallanes	Aguilas	Culiacan
1996-97	Mayaguez	Magallanes	Aguilas	Culiacan
1997-98	Mayaguez	Lara	Aguilas	Mazatlan
1998-99	Mayaguez	Lara	Licey	Mexicali
1999-00	Santurce	Zulia	Aguilas	Navojoa
2000-01	Caguas	Lara	Aguilas	Hermosillo
2001-02	Bayamon	Magallanes	Licey	Culiacan
2002-03	Mayaguez		Aguilas	Los Mochis

Mexican League Champions

Year	Team
1925	Puebla 74th Regiment
1926	Jalapa Ocampo
1927	Mexico City Police Station
1928	Mexico City Police
1929	Mexico City Adams Chiclets
1930	Comintra Tigers
1931	Mexico City Traffic
1932	Mexico City Public Works
1933	Comintra Tigers
1934	Mexico City Mercy Hill
1935	Mexico City Agrarians
1936	Mexico City Agrarians
1937	Veracruz Eagle
1938	Veracruz Eagle
1939	Cordoba Coffee Growers
1940	Veracruz Blues
1941	Veracruz Blues
1942	Torreon (Union Laguna) Cotton Dealers
1943	Monterrey Sultans
1944	Veracruz Blues
1945	Tampico Lightermen
1946	Tampico Lightermen
1947	Monterrey Sultans
1948	Monterrey Sultans
1949	Monterrey Sultans
1950	Torreon (Union Laguna) Cotton Dealers
1951	Veracruz Blues
1952	Veracruz Eagle
1953	Nuevo Laredo Owls
1954	Nuevo Laredo Owls
1955	Mexico City Tigers
1956	Mexico City Red Devils
1957	Yucatan Lions
1958	New Laredo Owls
1959	Poza Rica Oilers
1960	Mexico City Tigers
1961	Veracruz Eagles
1962	Monterrey Sultans
1963	Puebla Parrots
1964	Mexico City Red Devils
1965	Mexico City Tigers
1966	Mexico City Tigers
1967	Jalisco Charros
1968	Mexico City Red Devils
1969	Reynosa Broncos
1970	Veracruz Eagle
1971	Jalisco Charros
1972	Cordoba Coffee Growers
1973	Mexico City Red Devils
1974	Mexico City Red Devils
1975	Tampico Lightermen
1976	Mexico City Red Devils
1977	New Laredo Owls
1978	Aguascalientes Railroadmen
1979	Puebla Angels
1980	Puebla Angels
1981	Mexico City Red Devils
1982	Ciudad Juarez Indians
1983	Campeche Pirates
1984	Yucatan Lions
1985	Mexico City Red Devils
1986	Puebla Angels
1987	Mexico City Red Devils
1988	Mexico City Red Devils
1989	Laredo Owls
1990	Leon Braves
1991	Monterrey Sultans
1992	Mexico City Tigers
1993	Tabasco Olmecs
1994	Mexico City Red Devils
1995	Monterrey Sultans
1996	Monterrey Sultans
1997	Mexico City Tigers
1998	Oaxaca Warriors
1999	Mexico City Red Devils
2000	Mexico City Tigers
2001	Mexico City Tigers
2002	Mexico City Red Devils
2003	Mexico City Red Devils

Note: Mexican League championship series were played in 1949–51, 1966, 1970–79, and 1981–present. Prior to 1970, the first-half winner played the second-half winner. Since 1970 the league has been divided into divisions. In 1980, Puebla had the best record in a strike-shortened season.

THE OLYMPICS

Baseball appeared as a demonstration sport in six different Olympics (1912, 1936, 1956, 1964, 1984, and 1988) before being accepted as a medal sport. Its future in the Olympics, however, is not assured. Despite the lifting of the ban on professional players before the 2000 Olympics in Sydney, Australia, Major League Baseball has shown no interest in interrupting its regular season to let the best players in the world participate in Olympic competition. Consequently, the International Olympic Committee's program committee has proposed dropping baseball from the Olympics after the 2008 Olympic Games in Beijing, China.

The International Baseball Federation is working hard to convince the IOC not to approve that recommendation. Nevertheless, USA Baseball's failure to earn its way to the 2004 Olympics—as a result of losing to Mexico in a qualifying tournament—will certainly not help ensure baseball's future as an Olympic sport.

Olympic Medal Winners

	Gold	Silver	Bronze
1992 Barcelona	Cuba	Chinese Taipei	Japan
1996 Atlanta	Cuba	Japan	United States
2000 Sydney	United States	Cuba	South Korea

Note: Japan won the virtual gold medal when baseball was a demonstration sport in 1984; the United States won the demonstration competition in 1988.

BASEBALL IN JAPAN

Japanese baseball and American baseball have moved much closer during the last decade. Stars such as Hideo Nomo, Kazuhiro Sasaki, Ichiro Suzuki, and Hideki Matsui have successfully moved from Japan to America, as have lesser players in non-starring roles. Players with experience in the United States, such as Roberto Petagine, still cross the Pacific in the other direction seeking greater opportunity. American fans who know little about Japanese baseball are now almost forced to pay some attention.

Baseball has been played in Japan since the nineteenth century, first in 1873 at Tokyo University under the tutelage of an American professor. After the turn of the century, baseball became extremely popular in both high school and college. American baseball players started touring Japan after 1910, and the efforts of a man named Herbert Hunter helped school thousands of Japanese boys in the fundamentals of the game. An All-Star tour in 1934, featuring Babe Ruth, Lou Gehrig, Jimmy Foxx, Al Simmons and Lefty Gomez, left the greatest impression. The first professional Japanese team was the group organized to play these All-Stars. That team would become known as the Tokyo Giants, and by 1936 six other teams would join the Giants in the new Japanese Professional Baseball League.

World War II disrupted the new league, but the American occupying force brought the game back in 1946. In 1950 Japanese professional baseball added seven new teams and split into two leagues, the Central and the Pacific. Professional baseball grew in popularity over the next several decades, with television giving it a big boost. The Giants dominated Japanese baseball during this period, winning far more Japan Series (and fans) than any other team. Baseball remains Japan's most popular sport, though there are serious concerns about what the continuing loss of much of its star talent to the United States will mean for the Japanese game in the future.

Japan Professional Baseball League Champions

Year	Team	Year	Team
1937	Spring: Tokyo Giants	1942	Tokyo Giants
	Fall: Osaka Tigers	1943	Tokyo Giants
1938	Spring: Osaka Tigers	1944	Hanshin
	Fall: Tokyo Giants	1946	Kinki Greatring
1939	Tokyo Giants	1947	Osaka Tigers
1940	Tokyo Giants	1948	Nankai Hawks
1941	Tokyo Giants	1949	Yomiuri Giants

Japan Series Champions

Year	Central League Winner	Pacific League Winner	Series Result	Year	Central League Winner	Pacific League Winner	Series Result
1950	Shochiku Robins	Mainichi Orions	Orions, 4–2	1977	Yomiuri Giants	Hankyu Braves	Braves, 4–1
1951	Yomiuri Giants	Nankai Hawks	Giants, 4–1	1978	Yakult Swallows	Hankyu Braves	Swallows, 4–3
1952	Yomiuri Giants	Nankai Hawks	Giants, 4–2	1979	Hiroshima Carp	Kintetsu Buffaloes	Carp, 4–3
1953	Yomiuri Giants	Nankai Hawks	Giants, 4–2–1	1980	Hiroshima Carp	Kintetsu Buffaloes	Carp, 4–3
1954	Chunichi Dragons	Nishitetsu Lions	Dragons, 4–3	1981	Yomiuri Giants	Nippon Ham Fighters	Giants, 4–2
1955	Yomiuri Giants	Nankai Hawks	Giants, 4–3	1982	Chunichi Dragons	Seibu Lions	Lions, 4–2
1956	Yomiuri Giants	Nishitetsu Lions	Lions, 4–2	1983	Yomiuri Giants	Seibu Lions	Lions, 4–3
1957	Yomiuri Giants	Nishitetsu Lions	Lions, 4–0–1	1984	Hiroshima Carp	Hankyu Braves	Carp, 4–3
1958	Yomiuri Giants	Nishitetsu Lions	Lions, 4–3	1985	Hanshin Tigers	Seibu Lions	Tigers, 4–3
1959	Yomiuri Giants	Nankai Hawks	Hawks, 4–0	1986	Hiroshima Carp	Seibu Lions	Lions, 4–3–1
1960	Taiyo Whales	Daimai Orions	Whales, 4–0	1987	Yomiuri Giants	Seibu Lions	Lions, 4–2
1961	Yomiuri Giants	Nankai Hawks	Giants, 4–2	1988	Chunichi Dragons	Seibu Lions	Lions 4–1
1962	Hanshin Tigers	Toei Flyers	Flyers, 4–2–1	1989	Yomiuri Giants	Kintetsu Buffaloes	Giants, 4–3
1963	Yomiuri Giants	Nishitetsu Lions	Giants, 4–3	1990	Yomiuri Giants	Seibu Lions	Lions, 4–3
1964	Hanshin Tigers	Nankai Hawks	Hawks, 4–3	1991	Hiroshima Carp	Seibu Lions	Lions, 4–0
1965	Yomiuri Giants	Nankai Hawks	Giants, 4–1	1992	Yakult Swallows	Seibu Lions	Lions, 4–0
1966	Yomiuri Giants	Nankai Hawks	Giants, 4–2	1993	Yakult Swallows	Seibu Lions	Swallows, 4–3
1967	Yomiuri Giants	Hankyu Braves	Giants, 4–2	1994	Yomiuri Giants	Seibu Lions	Giants, 4–2
1968	Yomiuri Giants	Hankyu Braves	Giants, 4–2	1995	Yakult Swallows	Orix BlueWave	Swallows, 4–1
1969	Yomiuri Giants	Hankyu Braves	Giants, 4–2	1996	Yomiuri Giants	Orix BlueWave	BlueWave, 4–1
1970	Yomiuri Giants	Lotte Orions	Giants, 4–1	1997	Yakult Swallows	Seibu Lions	Swallows, 4–1
1971	Yomiuri Giants	Hankyu Braves	Giants, 4–1	1998	Yokohama BayStars	Seibu Lions	Bay Stars, 4–2
1972	Yomiuri Giants	Hankyu Braves	Giants, 4–1	1999	Chunichi Dragons	Fukuoka Daiei Hawks	Hawks, 4–1
1973	Yomiuri Giants	Nankai Hawks	Giants, 4–1	2000	Yomiuri Giants	Fukuoka Daiei Hawks	Giants, 4–2
1974	Chunichi Dragons	Lotte Orions	Orions, 4–2	2001	Yakult Swallows	Kintetsu Buffaloes	Swallows, 4–1
1975	Hiroshima Carp	Hankyu Braves	Braves, 4–0–2	2002	Yomiuri Giants	Seibu Lions	Giants, 4–0
1976	Yomiuri Giants	Hankyu Braves	Braves, 4–3	2003	Hanshin Tigers	Fukuoka Daiei Hawks	Hawks, 4–3

TAIWAN

Japanese occupying forces introduced baseball to Taiwan in 1905. The Taiwanese picked up the game in the 1920s and even provided Japan with a few professional players before World War II. Baseball grew in Taiwan after the war, though primarily on the amateur level. The nation became a juggernaut in Little League competition and also had significant success in other international competitions.

It wasn't until 1990 that the country's first professional baseball league, the Chinese Professional Baseball League, was organized. The league was successful almost immediately, but a huge gambling operation that was fixing CPBL games came to light in 1996, greatly damaging the loop's credibility. A second baseball league, the Taiwan Major League, emerged in 1997 and further weakened the CPBL. The two leagues finally merged in 2003, and that fall came more good news when the national team upset South Korea to qualify for the Olympics. Baseball is arguably the most popular sport in Taiwan, so the CPBL could have a bright future if it can avoid repeating its past problems.

Chinese Professional Baseball League Champions

Year	Team	Year	Team
1989	Weichuan Dragons	1997	Weichuan Dragons
1990	President Lions	1998	Weichuan Dragons
1991	Brother Elephants	1999	President Lions
1992	Brother Elephants	2000	Sinon Bulls
1993	Brother Elephants	2001	Brother Elephants
1994	President Lions	2002	Brother Elephants
1995	President Lions	2003	Brother Elephants
1996	Weichuan Dragons		

Taiwan Major League Champions

Year	Team
1997	Chia-Nan Braves
1998	Taipei Suns
1999	Taichung Robots
2000	Taipei Suns
2001	Taichung Robots
2002	Taichung Robots

SOUTH KOREA

In 1905 an American missionary introduced baseball to Korea, but it wasn't until 1982 that the government of South Korea decided to instigate the creation of a professional league. The newly formed Korean Baseball Organization proved to be a success, but its progress was halted in the mid-1990s by the country's financial crisis. More recently, Korean baseball has lost a number of talented players to the major leagues. In response the KBO began allowing teams to sign non-Koreans in 1998. The league still faces many challenges, including fallout from the recent failure of the South Korean national team to qualify for the 2004 Olympics.

Korean Series Winners

Year	Team	Year	Team	Year	Team	Year	Team	Year	Team
1982	OB Bears	1987	Haitai Tigers	1992	Lotte Giants	1997	Haitai Tigers	2002	Samsung Lions
1983	Haitai Tigers	1988	Haitai Tigers	1993	Haitai Tigers	1998	Hyundai Unicorns	2003	Hyundai Unicorns
1984	Lotte Giants	1989	Haitai Tigers	1994	LG Twins	1999	Hyundai Unicorns		
1985	Samsung Lions	1990	LG Twins	1995	OB Bears	2000	Hyundai Unicorns		
1986	Haitai Tigers	1991	Haitai Tigers	1996	Haitai Tigers	2001	Doosan Bears		

AUSTRALIA

According to legend, the first baseball game in Australia was played by American visitors in the 1850s. Australians first participated in a baseball game in 1879 when a local cricket team played a visiting minstrel group from the United States. Most Australians remained ignorant about baseball until A.G. Spalding and his Chicago White Stockings team came to Australia in late 1888 to promote the sport throughout the country. Spalding's tour was very successful and planted the game "down under" permanently.

In 1934, three Australian states sent their teams to Adelaide to compete for the first Claxton Shield. All of Australia's mainland states were participating in the competition by 1939 and, following World War II, the Shield competition would be held annually until 1989.

Controversy ended the Claxton Shield and left an opening in the Australia baseball world, which was quickly filled by Australia's first professional league, the Australian Baseball League. Unfortunately, the league proved to have a lot more talent on the field than off it. By 1998 it was clear that the ABL was in terrible financial trouble. Former ABL player (and major league All-Star) David Nilsson purchased the ABL's assets and tried to build a better league, the International Baseball League of Australia, out of the ABL's ashes. The new league was a disaster, though, and barely made it through one season before collapsing.

Australia today continues to do without a national baseball competition. However, baseball is still very popular on the local level and the country continues to produce talent capable of playing at a very high level. It is certainly possible that a new national league will rise again during the next decade, perhaps with the aid of Major League Baseball.

Australian Baseball League Champions

Season	Team
1989-90	Waverly
1990-91	Perth
1991-92	Gold Coast
1992-93	Melbourne
1993-94	Brisbane
1994-95	Waverly
1995-96	Sydney Blues
1996-97	Perth
1997-98	Melbourne Reds
1998-99	Gold Coast
1999-00	Western Heelers

GLOSSARY

At Bats: The definition of at bat has varied over the years, primarily due to the changing definitions of events that constitute plate appearances that are not at bats, such as sacrifice hits and sacrifice flies.

Average Value: Virtually every analytical statistic in this encyclopedia uses league average as a baseline. The use of this baseline, which is set to equal either 0 or 100, depending on the statistic, makes the quality of a player's performance—whether a player is above average, average, or below average—immediately obvious most of the time. Above-average players are needed to win pennants. Average and below-average players who are better than a typical replacement make only minor contributions toward a winning season.

Average is not the only reasonable baseline, of course—there is no "right" baseline, though there are more useful and less useful baselines. Some analysts use "replacement level" as their baseline. That baseline is hard to define, but there are circumstances where it may be more useful than the average baseline. Different tasks require different tools and, thus, different baselines. The primary advantage of an average baseline is that it clearly shows how the performance of players translates into wins and losses on the field. All teams start the season 0–0; only better-than-average players enable a team to rise above .500.

Bases on Balls: Permanently established at the count of 4 balls in 1889. The number had come down one at a time since 1874, when 9 balls were required to reach first base.

Basestealing Runs: The formula for calculating BSR is (.22*SB) – (.38*CS). SB stands for stolen bases, CS is for caught stealing, and * signifies multiplication.

Basestealing Wins: Divide basestealing runs by runs per win, which in this case equals 10 times the square root of runs per inning.

Batter-Fielder Wins: The sum of a player's batting wins, basestealing wins, and fielding wins.

Batting Runs: The formula for calculating batting runs is .33*(BB+HBP) plus .47*H plus .38*2B plus .55*3B plus .93*HR–ABF*(AB–H).

ABF, known as the league batting factor, makes the value of an average batter equal 0. ABF is computed with the following formula (all statistics in the equation are league statistics):

$$\frac{.33*(BB+HBP) + .47*H + .38*2B + .55*3B + .93*HR)}{(AB - LGF*H).}$$

LGF, the league factor, adjusts for the quality of league play, and equals 1 except for the Union Association (1884), for which it equals 0.8, and the Federal League (1914–15), for which it equals 0.9.

Adjusted batting runs, which appear in the batting register, are calculated with the following formula: (BR – (batters' park factor – 1)*RPA*PA/batters' park factor). RPA is the number of runs per plate appearance in the league.

Batting Wins: This is calculated by dividing adjusted batting runs by runs per win. In this case, runs per win equals 10 times the square root of (runs per inning + player adjusted batting runs/games/9).

Blown Saves: Save opportunities not converted because the relief pitcher allowed the tying or go-ahead run to score. Only calculated since 1969.

Caught Stealing: The data is available for 1914, 1915, and from 1920 onward for the AL; and for 1913, 1915, 1920–1925, and from 1951 onward in the NL.

Differential: This measures the difference between the won-lost record a team was *projected* to achieve (based on its batting, pitching, fielding, and basestealing), and the record that the team *actually* attained. If a team was projected to finish 89–73 (that is, +8) but actually concluded the season at 85–77 (that is, +4), the team's differential would be –4.

Earned Run Average: The number of earned runs allowed per 9 innings pitched. It is calculated by multiplying earned runs by 9 and dividing by innings pitched. Adjusted ERA is calculated by dividing league ERA by the pitcher (or team) ERA and then multiplying by the pitchers' park factor. Note that a small number of runs can be earned runs for the pitcher but unearned runs for the team.

ERA has been kept officially since 1912 in the NL and 1913 in the AL. Before then, Information Concepts Inc. researchers calculated earned runs from game accounts. Some earned run data include estimates, although in every case, at least half the earned runs for a team were known from game accounts. This was for 1881–86 (all leagues) and 1887 and 1890 in the American Association. Earned run data in box scores and the official guides in the nineteenth century were not used. Bases on balls were usually considered errors in those years and, in fact, the fielding stats often gave pitchers assists on strikeouts and errors on walks. Such assists and errors have been removed from the fielding averages in this book.

Fielding Runs: Fielding runs are based on the player's fielding statistics at each position compared to the league average for the number of innings played. The number of innings played was obtained from play-by-play data for 1969 onward. For most years before 1969, innings are estimated from defensive and offensive data for all players on the team. Comparing the formulas for estimated defensive innings to actual defensive innings taken from 1969–2003 play-by-play data showed an average difference of 12 for infielders and 19 for outfielders for players with 1,000 or more innings.

The basic formula is:

PFR/(PO – SO for team) – LFR/(PO – SO for league)*Player Innings.

PFR is the player fielding rate, while LFR is the league fielding rate.

The ratings used as fielding rates vary by position as follows:

1B	.2*(2*A – E)
P, 2B, SS, 3B	.2*(PO + 2*A – E + DP)
OF	.2*(PO + 4*A – E + DP)
C	.2*(PO – SO + .4*(A – CS) – E + DP + PB/2).

A stands for assists, PO for putouts, E for errors, SO for strikeouts, DP is for double plays, and PB for passed balls. Strikeouts are subtracted because a team that strikes out a lot of batters will have many fewer chances to create outs from balls put into play. When calculating a pitchers' fielding, his actual strikeout total is used; for other fielders, the team average strikeout total is used.

Two more factors are used to adjust for the amount of left-handed and right-handed pitching on a team and for the number of double play opportunities. Teams with more left-handed pitching tend to face more right-handed batters as a result of platooning, and this effect in turn alters the distribution of balls hit into play. A careful historical study of this factor showed that its effect was non-existent before 1910, then slowly grew until 1970, when it hit a similar level to today.

Right-handed batters shift the distribution of ground balls over from the right side of the infield to the left side while shifting fly-balls and popups from the left side of the field to the right side. Second basemen also gain more putouts with a right-handed hitter at the plate since they are more likely to be covering second base.

To adjust the number of expected league average putouts and assists for each player, the relevant statistic is multiplied by this equation:

(1 + ADJ*YF*DLHP).

ADJ is the adjustment figure appropriate for the position (1B, 2B, 3B, SS, LF, or RF) and statistic (putouts or assists). The chart below supplies the appropriate figure.

ADJ	*PO*	*A*
1B	n/a	–.40
2B	.23	–.27
SS	–.10	.14
3B	–.22	.34
LF	–.16	n/a
RF	.09	n/a

YF is the year factor, necessary because this factor steadily increased in importance from 1910 to 1970. Before 1910 the YF is 0, so no adjustment is necessary. The adjustment can be calculated for each year from 1910 through 1970 by subtracting 1910 from the year in question and then dividing by 60. After 1970 the YF is always 1.

DLHP is the difference in the percentage of left-handed pitching from the league average.

So if a second baseman was on a team with 10 percent more innings by left-handed pitchers than average in 1960, his adjustment is:

Assists = (1 – .27 x (1960-1910)/60 x .10) = .9775
Putouts = (1 + .23 x (1960-1910)/60 x .10) = 1.0192.

If the league average second baseman in 1960 finished the season with 400 assists and 200 putouts, the expected league average would be adjusted to 391 and 204.

Pitchers have a further correction, since left-handed pitchers have fewer putouts as a result of facing fewer left-handed batters. Up until 1910 left- and right-handed pitcher putouts were about equal, declining to about 62 percent for left-handers in 1970 before leveling off. Thus, a separate expected putout rate is calculated for each type of pitcher based on the year and the number of left-handed innings.

Double play opportunities were estimated from hits, bases on balls, hit-by-pitches, and home runs allowed, plus errors committed. (On average, 57.5 percent of errors result in a runner reaching base; the other errors just allow existing baserunners to take extra bases.) Using a multiplier for homers to account for double play opportunities lost did not improve the estimate in years where there are actual data; the average error in these years was around 2 percent. The formula for calculating double play opportunities is:

.662*(H – HR + BB + HB + .575*E).

Individual double plays were divided by the team double play opportunities divided by the league average double play opportunities.

For catchers, there is an additional defensive calculation made to rate them on other defensive aspects. The formula for that calculation is:

(–.22*SB) + (CSF*CS) + .1*APR*IP/TIP.

APR is the catcher's team's adjusted pitching runs; IP is the catcher's innings pitched to; TIP is team innings pitched; and CSF is the caught stealing factor that ensures that the average value of a catcher defensively stays at 0. The formula to calculate CSF is:

22*(LSB – TSB) divided by (LCS – TCS).

Also, since artificial turf results in about a 5 percent higher stolen base success rate, a small adjustment is made to the results of players and teams from the turf era. The size of the adjustment depends on the exact split of games between ballparks with turf in the basepaths and those with dirt basepaths. Most ballparks with turf fields have turf basepaths with dirt only in the sliding cutouts around the bases. However, a few ballparks, especially in the early years of artificial turf, have had all-dirt basepaths with turf fields.

Fielding Wins: Divide fielding runs by runs per win, which in this case equals 10 times the square root of runs per inning.

Games Behind: This is the number of games one team is behind another team in the standing, almost always measured from first place. If a team's record stands at 78–71 and the first-place team's record is 82–68, then the former team is 3½ games behind the first-place team.

Grounded into Double Play: This became an official statistic in 1933 in the NL and in 1939 in the AL.

Hit-by-Pitch: The rule awarding first base to batters hit by a pitch was instituted in 1884 by the American Association and in 1887 by the National League.

Innings Pitched: Fractions of innings pitched in a season have only been officially counted since 1982. Prior to that, both leagues rounded off fractional innings. This encyclopedia has full innings pitched (i.e., not rounded off) for all major league seasons.

Normalizing: Baseball statistics tell us very little without context. A .450 slugging average in Dodger Stadium in 1965 means something very different than a .450 slugging average in Coors Field in 2003—the former is an impressive performance while the latter is sub-par. Many of the statistics in this encyclopedia are normalized using league average as a baseline, enabling readers to see

whether a player is better than or worse than his average peer as well as to what extent he is better or worse. By putting different seasons played in different circumstances on the same scale, normalization makes it much easier to compare seasons. Some statistics in this encyclopedia are further normalized to account for the home parks of players since some ballparks are far more conducive to scoring than others. As a result, both the ease of producing a run and the value of a run can vary significantly from ballpark to ballpark, even in the same season. Normalizing a statistic for ballpark effects ensures that players can be compared on a level playing field.

On-Base Percentage: Declared an official statistic in 1984, OBP is defined as (hits plus bases on balls plus hit-by-pitches) divided by (at bats plus bases on balls plus hit-by-pitches plus sacrifice flies). This encyclopedia uses the current definition back to 1954, when sacrifice fly data became permanently available. Previous to 1954, sacrifice flies were either counted as outs or were included with sacrifice hits (1908–30 and 1939) and, therefore, cannot be used.

On-Base plus Slugging: Often referred to as OPS, this statistic, which was introduced by Pete Palmer and John Thorn in *The Hidden Game of Baseball* in 1984, has exploded in popularity the past few years. This encyclopedia does not feature a separate column for the basic version of OPS in the batter register since it is very easy to calculate—simply adds on-base percentage and slugging average—and the two columns are adjacent. Adjusted OPS (which has its own column) then normalizes OPS for the league and the player's home park(s), then converts it to a scale in which 100 is league average. The exact calculation is ((player OBP/league OBP) plus (player slugging/league slugging) – 1) divided by batters' park factor. When calculating adjusted OPS for non-pitchers, league average statistics do not include pitcher batting. For consistency in historical comparisons, the definition of on-base percentage used in adjusted OPS does not use sacrifice flies in the denominator.

Opponents' Batting Average: Figures are based on estimated at bats from 1901–07 in the AL; from 1889–1902 in the NL; in 1882–83 and 1888–91 in the American Association; in 1884 in the Union Association; and in 1890 in the Player's League.

Opponents' Caught Stealing: Exact totals for 1969 to the present came from play-by-play records. Estimated totals for catchers came from team totals found in league records from 1920–68 for the AL and from 1920–25 and from 1951–68 for the NL. For most other years since 1890, team totals were estimated from other team data and catcher totals were estimated from the team estimates. Some years from 1912–19 have only runner caught stealing data, some have team caught stealing, and some have individual catcher caught stealing.

Opponents' On-Base Percentage: Based on the official definition of OBP since 1954. The definition used in previous years depends on the available data (as with the OBP definition above).

Opponents' Stolen Bases: Exact totals for 1969 to the present came from play-by-play records. Estimated totals for catchers came from team totals found in league records for 1890–1968 (except for the 1890 NL data, which came from box scores).

Park Factor: This measure of how the team's home park affects hitters and pitchers is used to adjust the team's performance in a way that takes into account the context of the team's home park. Separate park factors are used for batting and pitching in order to adjust for the fact that pitchers and hitters never get to face their own teammates.

Pitching Runs: This measure of how many runs a pitcher prevented compared to the average pitcher is calculated with this formula:

$$LERA^* IP/9 - ER + URF.$$

LERA is the league ERA and ER stands for earned runs. URF is the unearned run factor that accounts for the unearned runs the pitcher is responsible for and is calculated by multiplying (0.5) times (ER – R*TER/TR).

Adjusted pitching runs is calculated the same as pitching runs above, except that LERA* PPF is used instead of plain LERA—that is, the league ERA is multiplied by the pitcher park factor. Then the result of the entire calculation is divided by the pitcher park factor. Thus the formula is (PPF*LERA*IP/9 – ER + URF)/PPF.

Pitcher Batting: This measure of a pitcher's offensive performance is calculated the same way as adjusted batting runs; the difference is that a pitcher is compared to the average-hitting pitcher, not the average hitter. If a pitcher spent time at other defensive positions, his offense will be divided proportionately based on how much he played each position; only the appropriate fraction will count for pitcher batting.

Pitcher Wins: The total number of wins a pitcher is worth to his team compared to the average pitcher (including pitching, fielding, batting, and basestealing).

Pitching Wins: The wins a pitcher achieves by his pitching is calculated by dividing adjusted pitcher runs by runs per win, then multiplying by XMULR (see below). In this case, the formula for runs per win is 10 times the square root of (RPI – APR/G/9). Thus, if a pitcher reduces the number of runs scored by the opponent in his games, the value of each run is increased by a reduction in the runs per win figure. Pitchers, especially starting pitchers, have a much stronger effect on runs per win because their effect on scoring is spread out over fewer games.

In order to properly credit relief pitchers for the extra or lesser value of their innings pitched, a factor is used when converting adjusted pitching runs to pitching wins. The formula for that multiplier (XMULR) is:

$$9^*(W + L + SV/XSV)/IP.$$

XSV is calculated by dividing league saves by league wins and multiplying by 10. XSV cannot be less than 4, so any result lower than 4 is set at 4. The multiplier cannot not be less than 0.5 or more than 2, so any result not in that range is considered to be either 0.5 or 2, depending on whether it was above or below the range.

Positional Adjustment: Baseball fans know not to expect a shortstop to hit like a first baseman, exceptions like Alex Rodriguez notwithstanding. Second basemen who slug .370 can usually hold on to their starting spot, but first basemen who slug .370 are likely to be benched or dropped off the roster. That's because it's fairly easy to find an acceptable defensive first baseman that can hit with power, while players who can handle second base defensively and hit with power are usually scarce. In order to account for the ability of players to handle the most valuable positions defensively, the offense of these players is compared to their peers at the same position. This approach accounts for the differing value major league teams place on fielding ability at each position and also makes it simple to adjust for the changing demands of a position. For example, higher defensive expectations for third basemen a century ago made it significantly harder to find a third baseman with a good bat back then than today. Whether that was because teams demanded a higher level of defense from third basemen then, or because there are more good defensive third

basemen these days who can hit is irrelevant. We don't have to know the answer to that question to account for the decreasing scarcity of good-hitting third basemen by using a smaller positional adjustment.

POWR (Player Overall Win Rating): POWR, featured in the All-Time Leaders section, adds the batting wins, fielding wins, basestealing wins, and pitching wins of every player to rate his overall value compared to an average player.

Range: This category is calculated different ways for different positions. For infielders, range is based on assists per inning. For outfielders, range is based on putouts per inning. For catchers, the statistic in the range column is based on stolen bases allowed per inning. Outfielders are rated for their (weighted) play at all outfield positions, while infielders are only rated for their play at their primary position. The data is then adjusted in comparison to the league average, with 100 equaling league average. *Higher is always better.* All statistics are adjusted for context, including the number of balls put into play and the distribution of balls in play. The adjustments for each statistic are detailed in the fielding runs entry. Innings played data are calculated from play-by-play accounts from 1969 onward; it is estimated prior to 1969.

Relative Batting Average: A normalized translation of batting average. The formula is player average divided by league average.

Runs Batted In: RBIs have been recognized as an official statistic since 1920. Runs driven in by a force double play were no longer counted as RBIs after 1938.

Relief Ranking: Generated by multiplying the XMULR factor (described in the pitcher wins entry) by adjusted pitcher runs. Since innings pitched in relief is not historically available, relief pitchers are classified as those pitchers who average less than 3 innings per appearance.

Run Support: Basic run support is calculated by adding up all the runs scored in a pitcher's starts and then dividing that total by his games started. The support figures presented in the pitcher register have been normalized for the context of the offensive level of the league and the player's home park(s), then converted to a scale in which 100 is league average. A run support figure of 90 would indicate that pitcher had 10 percent less runs scored in his starts than average; a figure of 110 would indicated 10 percent above-average. The formula to produce the adjusted run support is (pitcher run support) divided by (league average run support) divided by (batters' park factor) times 100.

Run support stats have been published widely since 1990, usually counting all appearances for a pitcher and normalizing the runs scored by his team while he was in the game to 9 innings pitched. While this stat is useful, it is not calculable pre-1969. Furthermore, it is not a substitute for calculating run support for starting pitchers, since runs scored after a pitcher leaves the game materially affect a pitcher's record. If a starter leaves the game in the seventh inning with his team trailing 5–1, then his team scores 6 times in the eighth to take the lead, he avoids being tagged with the loss and clearly benefits from runs scored after he had left the game.

Runs Per Win: The number of runs needed, on average, to gain an additional win in the standings. Historically, about 10 runs have equaled a win. The value of runs per win is used in several entries in this glossary to translate runs into wins. Individual players, especially starting pitchers, can have a significant effect on the number of runs that it takes to achieve a win in their own games, so the runs per win calculation often takes into account the performance level of the individual or team being evaluated.

Sacrifice Fly: First recognized as a distinct statistical category in 1954. Previous to 1975, only fair fly balls which drove in runners were counted in this category. From 1908–1930 and again in 1939, sacrifice flies were counted as sacrifice hits. In all other seasons before 1954, sacrifice flies are indistinguishable from other at bats.

Save: Recognized as an official statistic in 1969, saves were at first awarded to any relief pitcher that finished pitching a victory and was not credited with the win. In 1973 requirements were significantly tightened so that saves were only awarded if the pitcher either entered the game with the potential tying run on base or at the plate or pitched at least 3 effective innings while preserving the lead. In 1975 the rule was set to where it stands today: In order to earn a save, a reliever must finish off a victory without ever giving up the lead after entering the game with a lead of no more than 3 runs and pitching at least an inning, or he can earn a save by finishing a victory without giving up the lead after entering the game with the tying run on base, at the plate, or on deck. Saves may also be earned by pitching effectively for at least the last 3 innings of a victory, without getting credit for the win. The original 1969 rule has been used in awarding saves prior to 1969.

Stolen Bases: Stolen bases were always a part of the game, but they were not officially tabulated from 1876–85. This statistic is available for all seasons in all leagues from 1886 onward. National Association stolen bases were obtained from box scores, which did not always report them, so 1871–75 data is incomplete.

The exact scoring definition of a stolen base was changed repeatedly before 1955, when most of the current rules regarding stolen bases were put into place. Before 1898, stolen bases were sometimes awarded for taking extra bases on hits and outs, so the data in this earlier period is not strictly comparable to later data.

Strikeouts: Available for batters in all years except for the 1882–88 and 1890 American Association, the 1884 Union Association, from 1897–1909 in the NL, and from 1901–12 in the AL. There is no missing data for pitchers' strikeouts. As in the case of bases on balls and stolen bases, there were some very different rules governing strikeouts in the nineteenth century, making comparisons across time rather tricky.

Throwing: This new category is calculated in different ways for different positions. For infielders, the throwing column shows their double plays per inning. For outfielders, throwing is based on assists per inning. For catchers, throwing is based on caught stealing rates per inning. The data is then adjusted in comparison to league average, with 100 equaling league average. All statistics are adjusted for context by various methods; the adjustments for each statistic are detailed in the fielding runs entry. Innings played data was calculated from play-by-play accounts from 1969 to the present; it is estimated for previous seasons. Outfielders are rated for their play at all outfield positions, while infielders are only rated for their play at their primary position.

Editors and Contributors

Gary Gillette is a baseball author, analyst, researcher, and editor who spoke about the future of baseball at the Society for American Baseball Research's 2003 convention. He is currently working on two books: *Going, Going … Gone?* which will examine the dramatic decline in popularity of the National Pastime since World War II; and a revised and updated *Hidden Game of Baseball,* on which he is collaborating with Pete Palmer. Gillette was a contributor to *Total Baseball* for five editions and to the *Baseball Prospectus 2003*. Among the many baseball books that Gillette has written, co-authored, or edited are the *Baseball Weekly Insider; The Spy: Baseball '98; The Scouting Report;* and *The Great American Baseball Stat Book*.

Gillette was a co-founder and vice president of Total Sports, Inc., and executive editor of *Total Baseball Daily* from 1996–99. From 1992–97, Gillette was the president of The Baseball Workshop which produced and maintained a unique set of databases about the National Pastime. Prior to founding The Baseball Workshop, Gillette was vice president of SportSource, Inc., the publisher of the *Baseball Blue Book*, in 1991, executive director or chairman of Project Scoresheet, Inc., from 1987–92, and a member of the board of directors of Project Scoresheet from its inception.

Gillette has contributed to many periodicals, including *USA Today* and *Baseball Weekly* as well as *Bill Mazeroski's Baseball.* He has been a baseball commentator and analyst for several National Public Radio stations and currently works as a legal expert witness on baseball-related litigation, as a consultant on player insurance, and as an adviser on salary arbitration. He lives in Raleigh, North Carolina, with his wife, Vicki.

Pete Palmer has been one of the foremost chroniclers of the National Pastime for the past four decades. Co-author of the seminal analytical work, *The Hidden Game of Baseball,* and co-editor of the groundbreaking encyclopedia *Total Baseball,* the depth and breadth of Palmer's work is truly remarkable. Palmer served as editor of the original *Barnes Official Encyclopedia of Baseball* and as a consultant to the Sports Information Center, official statisticians for the American League, from 1976–87. While with SIC, he introduced on-base percentage as an official AL statistic in 1979. He is a long-time contributor to *Who's Who in Baseball* as well as *The Sporting News Official MLB Fact Book* and *Record Book.* He has contributed to many books and periodicals, including *USA Today,* the *Baseball Weekly Almanac,* and *SPORT* magazine.

Palmer was a member of the board of directors of Project Scoresheet and is a contributor to Retrosheet. He has been a member of SABR since 1973 and served as chair of its Statistical Analysis Committee for fifteen years. In 1989, he was awarded SABR's highest honor, the Bob Davids Award.

Outside of baseball, Palmer was the co-author of *The Hidden Game of Football,* a contributor to *Total Football,* and the editor of the *Barnes Encyclopedia of Football.* He is married to the former Beth Statz, grand-niece of the legendary Jigger Statz.

Stuart Shea has been involved in baseball writing and research for more than a decade as an author, columnist, reporter, and editor. He contributed to three editions of *The Great American Baseball Stat Book*, two editions of *The Scouting Report*, to the *The Spy: Baseball 1998*, and two editions of *The USA Today Baseball Weekly Insider*. A Chicagoan for most of his life, Shea is the author of the upcoming *Wrigley Field: An Unauthorized Biography*, the first full history of America's most storied ballpark. As a musician and cultural history buff, he has also authored *Rock & Roll's Most Wanted* and *1960's Most Wanted.*

Matthew Silverman has been a professional writer and editor for twenty years. He served as associate publisher at Total Sports Publishing and was principal editor for *Baseball: The Biographical Encyclopedia* as well as managing editor for the sixth and seventh editions of *Total Baseball* and the second edition of *Total Football.* He edited seven offshoots of *Total Football*, including *Total Packers*, *Total Steelers*, *Total Cowboys*, and *Total Super Bowl*. He served as editor for the first edition of Ted Williams' 2001 autobiography, *Ted Williams: My Life in Pictures*. He also co-edited *Total Mets*. He resides in High Falls, New York, with his wife, Debbie, daughter, Jan, and son, Tyler.

Greg Spira is a writer, editor, and researcher who lives in Kingston, New York. He was a co-editor for the seventh edition of *Total Baseball* and served as an editor at Total Sports Publishing. He has contributed to books such as *Baseball: The Biographical Encyclopedia*, *Total Basketball*, and *Baseball Prospectus*. He has been a member of the Society for American Baseball Research for fifteen years. As an Internet denizen for more than a decade, he has contributed to many web sites both editorially and conceptually. BaseballBooks.net, a website he maintains, focuses on sports books. He grew up in Whitestone, New York, and was graduated with a degree in history from Harvard College.

Bill Deane is a freelance baseball researcher and writer based near Cooperstown, New York, where he spent eight years as senior research associate for the National Baseball Library. He has published seven books and hundreds of articles for publications such as *Total Baseball, USA Today Baseball Weekly*, *The Sporting News*, and *Baseball America*. He received the 1989 SABR-Macmillan Baseball Research Award, the 2001 SABR Salute, and the 2003 Cliff Kachline Award. Deane resides in Fly Creek, New York, with his wife, Pam, and daughter, Sarah.

Sean Lahman is a columnist for the *New York Sun* and the author of the annual *Pro Football Prospectus*. He has edited or contributed to a number of sports reference books, including *Total Baseball, Sports Illustrated Sports Almanac, Total Tennis, Total Basketball,* and *Baseball: The Biographical Encyclopedia*. Over the past ten years, he has led the effort to make sports statistics available to the general public, developing or contributing to a number of pioneering web sites. He attended the University of Cincinnati and lives in upstate New York with his wife, Heather, and their three children.

Doug White has been writing about baseball since 1996. He has contributed to many publications, including *The Great American Baseball Stat Book*, *The Scouting Report*, and *The USA Today Baseball Weekly Insider*. A contributing editor to *Total Baseball Daily*, he now covers the Cincinnati Reds as a stringer for MLB.com. He writes for John Benson's annual *Rotisserie League Baseball* scouting book and Benson's *Rotisserie Baseball Annual*. White umpires college and semi-pro baseball. He and his wife, Anita, live in Muncie, Indiana, with their son, Aaron.

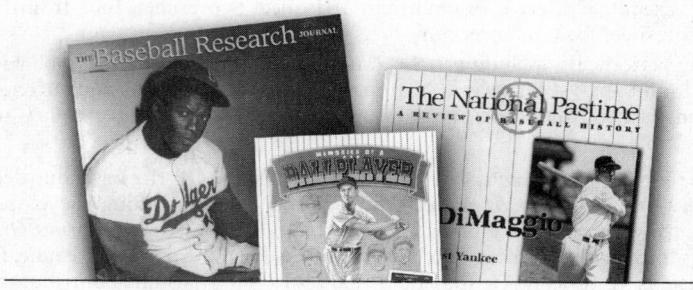